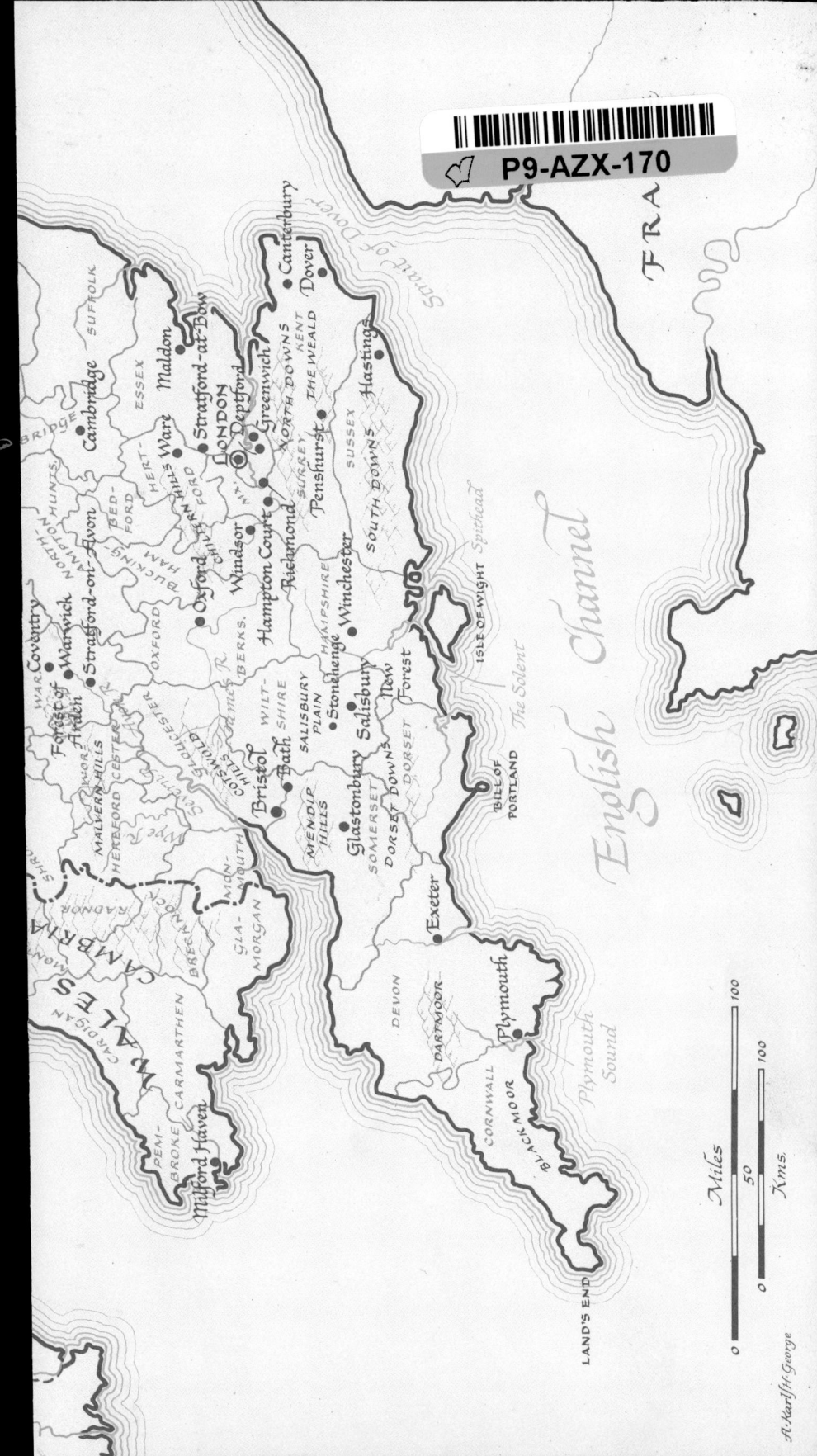

THE MIDDLE AGES
Donaldson / David

THE SIXTEENTH CENTURY
Smith / Lewalski

THE EARLY SEVENTEENTH CENTURY
Adams / Logan

THE RESTORATION AND THE EIGHTEENTH CENTURY
Monk / Lipking

THE ROMANTIC PERIOD
Abrams / Stillinger

THE VICTORIAN AGE
Ford / Christ

THE TWENTIETH CENTURY
Daiches / Stallworthy

The Norton Anthology of English Literature

SIXTH EDITION
THE MAJOR AUTHORS

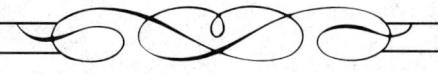

The Norton Anthology
of English Literature

SIXTH EDITION
THE MAJOR AUTHORS

M. H. Abrams, *General Editor*
CLASS OF 1916 PROFESSOR OF ENGLISH EMERITUS,

CORNELL UNIVERSITY

W · W · NORTON & COMPANY · *New York* · *London*

Printed in the United States of America.

The text of this book is composed in Electra, with display set in Bernhard Modern
Composition by Maple-Vail Manufacturing Group
Manufacturing by R. R. Donnelley
Book design by Antonina Krass

Cover painting is *The Bard* (c. 1818) by John Martin. Reproduced by courtesy of the Yale Center for British Art, Paul Mellon Collection.

Library of Congress Cataloging-in-Publication Data

The Norton anthology of English literature. The major authors / M. H.
Abrams, general editor.—6th ed.
        p.   cm.
Includes bibliographical references and index.
        1. English literature.   I. Abrams, M. H. (Meyer Howard), 1912–

PR1109.N6   1996
820.8—dc20   95-4659

ISBN 0-393-96803-0
ISBN 0-393-96808-1 (pbk.)

W. W. Norton & Company, Inc., 500 Fifth Avenue, New York, N.Y. 10110
W. W. Norton & Company Ltd., 10 Coptic Street, London WC1A 1PU

3 4 5 6 7 8 9 0

Contents

The Sixteenth Century (1485–1603)   253

The Early Seventeenth Century (1603–1660)

The Restoration and the Eighteenth Century
(1660–1785)   819

The Twentieth Century   2135

Preface to the Sixth Edition

This volume contains a selection of the best and most characteristic writings, in diverse literary genres, of major English authors. The present edition has been expanded so that it includes not only the thirty-four authors in the preceding edition, but also four additional authors, the medieval drama *Noah's Flood*, and three sections of notable lyric poems by writers of the sixteenth, seventeenth, and eighteenth centuries. The texts and editorial materials are reprinted (with a few exceptions) from the sixth edition of the two-volume *Norton Anthology of English Literature*. There is a biographical and critical headnote for each author, as well as an introduction to each period that sets forth the historical and social contexts of the literature and indicates the relations of individual authors to literary and historical developments in their era.

The anthology had its genesis in a course on English literature devised and taught at Cornell by two of its editors, M. H. Abrams and David Daiches. A continuing source of strength is that each successive edition has been tested in the classroom by the original editors and by a younger group that was added while the fifth edition was being prepared. All the versions have been guided by the principles established for the first edition. These are: (1) that the selections be adequate for a study in depth of major British writers in verse and prose; (2) that so far as feasible the selections be complete, and also abundant enough to allow each instructor to choose the authors and works that he or she prefers to teach; (3) that the student be given the most reliable texts available, edited so as to be readily accessible, in a format that is easy in the hand and inviting to the eye; (4) that the introductions, glosses, and other informative materials suffice to free the student from dependence on reference books, so that the anthology may be read anywhere—in one's room, on a bus, or under a tree; (5) that each editor, within shared guidelines, be allowed to keep his or her distinctive voice; (6) that the anthology be comfortably portable, for if students won't carry the book to class, lectures are hampered and discussions made profitless.

A vital literary culture, however, is always on the move. Our policy accordingly has been to prepare periodic revisions that take advantage of newly recovered or more-accurately edited texts, stay in touch with the altering literary interests of scholars and readers, and keep the anthology within the mainstream of critical and intellectual concerns. The revisions also make it possible to take advantage of the steady flow of suggestions volunteered by both teachers and students, who read the anthology with a loyal but critical eye. And the present revision has provided occasion once again to solicit information about which texts are actually assigned, proposals for deletions and additions, and suggestions for editorial improvements from a large number of teachers who assign the anthology in a course. Like its predecessors, therefore, this volume is the evolving product of a collaboration among editors, teachers, and students. The anthology does not, as is sometimes claimed, simply reproduce a pre-established literary "canon." Instead, it presents writers and writings that have been chosen, then winnowed, by a running consensus of its users; and the continuing appeal of the selections is attested by the number of teachers who request and assign them year after year.

A cardinal innovation in this sixth edition—which has been enthusiastically received in the two-volume version of the anthology—is the use of a larger trim-size that makes for a more readable page with larger margins and allows the volume, even in its middle section, to open out and stay flat. The altered format also makes it possible to add a number of new authors and selections while retaining (and in some instances augmenting) the authors and texts included in the preceding edition. The only exceptions are a scattering of texts that our questionnaires showed to be assigned infrequently or not at all.

In response to suggestions by a number of teachers, we have made the following improvements and additions to the literary contents, editorial procedures, and appended materials for study:

Contents

The list of authors has been augmented by Sir Thomas Malory (selections from *Morte Darthur*), Christina Rossetti (nineteen poems), Bernard Shaw (*Mrs. Warren's Profession*), and Katherine Mansfield (two short stories). There are also added writings by some of the authors carried over from the preceding edition: Marlowe's *Passionate Shepherd*; the Dedication to Shakespeare's sonnets; five of Byron's incomparable letters (mainly on literary matters); substantial selections from Book 2 of Elizabeth Barrett Browning's *Aurora Leigh*; two added texts by Virginia Woolf (*Professions for Women* and her short story *The Legacy*); and Samuel Beckett's major drama *Endgame* (in place of his shorter and slighter *Happy Days*).

A conspicuous innovation in this edition was generated by requests from instructors for classic or historically important poems by writers who might not rank as "major"—poems such as early sonnets by Wyatt, Surrey, and Sidney, Marvell's *To His Coy Mistress*, and Gray's *Elegy Written in a Country Church-yard*. In response, we introduce sections of lyric poets of the sixteenth, seventeenth, and eighteenth centuries, comprising a total of fifty-six poems written by nineteen poets.

In response to the altering interests of many instructors, we have continued to increase the number of female writers, as well as to enlarge the selections by major women who were included in the preceding edition. E. B. Browning, Christina Rossetti, Virginia Woolf, and Katherine Mansfield are now represented at length, and poems by Queen Elizabeth, Aemilia Lanyer, Lady Mary Wroth, Anne Finch, and Lady Mary Wortley Montagu are included in the sections of lyric poets.

The representation of drama has also been substantially strengthened. The inclusion of three new plays makes available (in addition to selections from Shelley's drama *Prometheus Unbound*) five complete works, ranging from the medieval to the contemporary: the Chester play of *Noah's Flood*, Marlowe's *Doctor Faustus*, Shakespeare's *1 Henry IV*, Shaw's *Mrs. Warren's Profession*, and Beckett's *Endgame*.

The greatest challenge for the editors of this anthology has been to represent the major writers of prose fiction. In preceding editions, we reprinted eight works, written by five authors, that represented important developments in narrative forms, techniques, and styles: Swift's *Gulliver's Travels*, Johnson's *Rasselas*, Conrad's *Heart of Darkness*, Joyce's *The Dead* and selections from *Ulysses* and *Finnegans Wake*, and Lawrence's *Odor of Chrysanthemums* and *The Horse-Dealer's Daughter*. To these we now add selections from Sir Thomas Malory's great prose narrative, *Morte Darthur*, as well as three short stories: Virginia Woolf's *The Legacy* and Katherine Mansfield's *The Daughters of the Late Colonel* and *The Garden-Party*. With this sixth edition we also introduce a set of volumes, the Norton Anthology Editions, that make available at a low price the five full-length novels most in demand as supplementary assignments in courses that use *Major Authors*. Our questionnaires identified these novels as Jane Austen's *Pride and Prejudice*, Emily Brontë's *Wuthering Heights*, Charlotte Brontë's *Jane Eyre*, Mary Shelley's *Frankenstein*, and Charles Dickens's *Hard Times*. Each volume, in a format that matches the anthology proper, consists of the text, footnotes, and bibliography of the Norton Critical Edition of the novel, together with a short introduction by one of the editors of *Major Authors*. Information for ordering the Norton Anthology Editions, packaged with this anthology, may be obtained from the publisher.

Editorial Procedures

In each literary period or lyric section, the anthology presents writers in the order of their birth dates, and the works of each writer in the order of first publication. The variety of the included materials, however, makes feasible for teachers not only a chronological approach to major writers, but also generic or topical modes of dealing with literary texts.

In accord with our policy that students, no less than scholars, deserve the most accurate texts available, we continue to introduce improved versions of the works we reprint. We replace the B text (1616) of *Doctor Faustus* with Roma Gill's edition based on the A text of 1604, since this earlier text is less likely to include scenes interpolated by writers other than Marlowe. We also introduce the texts of Byron as printed in Jerome J. McGann's edition of Byron's *Complete Poetic Works* (Oxford, 1980 ff.). To ease a student's access to the contents of the anthology, we have normalized spelling and capitalization according to modern usage, with two large exceptions: (1) We leave unaltered texts in which modernizing would change the meaning or meter, or would occlude distinctive features of the original. Accordingly, the verse of Spenser and the prose of Keats's letters, of James Joyce, and of Bernard Shaw have been reproduced exactly. Only minor changes in the author's erratic punctuation have been made in the texts etched by William Blake. The works of Chaucer have also been reprinted in the original language; each word, however, has been spelled consistently in that form of its scribal variants closest to modern English. (2) We also leave virtually unaltered texts for which we use specially edited versions (identified in a headnote or footnote). These include Wordsworth's *Ruined Cottage* and *Prelude*, Dorothy Wordsworth's *Journals*, and the writings of Byron, Shelley, and Keats.

To take advantage of recent scholarship, the editors have revised all introductions, headnotes, and footnotes, and have totally rewritten some of them. We continue to minimize commentary that is interpretive rather than, in a very limited sense, explanatory. It has, however, seemed unwise to us (as to many instructors) to eliminate all help whatever to students with respect to works or passages that are especially problematic. Typically, teachers assign a number of texts that there is no time to discuss in detail—or sometimes, to discuss at all—in the classroom. We undertake, therefore, in difficult instances to offer a modicum of suggestion, but in a way that invites independent judgment and provides no more than a point of departure for lectures or discussions.

The introductions to periods and authors, although succinct, are sufficiently informative to obviate any immediate need for supplementary books on literary, political, or cultural history or on the lives of individual authors. In most of the introductions, we list at the beginning a few crucial dates to serve as orientation to the student. As an additional aid to placing literary works in context, we introduce in this edition a series of timelines, devised by Alfred David, that set the authors and works included within the anthology in temporal relation to important historical, social, and literary events in Great Britain, Europe, and America. Each of the timelines—there are seven in all—is placed immediately after the corresponding introduction to the literary period.

At the end of each literary text, we cite (when known) the date of composition on the left and that of first publication on the right; in some instances, the latter is followed by the date of a revised reprinting. Texts with a large proportion of archaic, dialectal, or otherwise unfamiliar words are glossed in the margin, so that students need not interrupt the flow of their reading in order to search out the relevant footnote. When parts of a work have had to be omitted, that fact is signaled by the word *From* before the title, and the omissions are indicated within the text by three asterisks. If the omitted section is important for following the plot or argument, a brief summary is provided, either bracketed within the text or else in a footnote. To make it easier to identify the included portions of an excerpted work, the editors also provide, when feasible, invented titles (listed in the table of contents and bracketed in the printed text) that indicate the subject matter of each passage.

Appended Materials

We continue to include, and improve, the diverse appendices that have demonstrated their usefulness to students. "Poems in Process" reproduces from manuscripts and printed texts the genesis and evolution of selected poems; to this section we now add a part of Gray's *Elegy*, the whole of which is newly included in the body of the anthology. All the "Selected Bibliographies" have been revised and brought up to date; the titles have been chosen and annotated to encourage students to read further, as well as to serve as references for assigned essays. Also appended are illustrations of a Shakespearean playhouse and of the Ptolemaic universe, a useful section on "Poetic Forms and Literary Terminology," and brief expositions, written by Robert M. Adams, that deal with the intricacies of the money, the religious sects, and the baronage of England. New to the essay on the baronage is a table of the royal lines of England and Great Britain.

The editors are deeply grateful to the hundreds of teachers, in North America and other continents, who volunteered suggestions that have helped us to improve this anthology; we cannot name them all, but many will recognize changes that they have proposed. A list of "Acknowledgments" identifies the advisors who, on request, prepared detailed critiques of the total anthology or of single periods, or else have advised us about some aspect of the editorial materials.

The publishers in turn would like to express their thanks to Allen Clawson, Marian Johnson, Diane O'Connor, Tara Parmiter, Peter Simon, and Kurt Wildermuth. Once again, the editors wish to acknowledge their debt to George P. Brockway, who as president of W. W. Norton conceived and helped design the early editions of this anthology; to his successor Donald Lamm, who participated vigorously in planning later editions; and to the late John Benedict, the great textbook editor who played an important role in every detail of planning and producing the preceding editions of *Major Authors*. His successor, Julia Reidhead, has been an unfailingly helpful, informed, and tactful mentor in accomplishing this sixth edition. All these friends have helped to mitigate the chronic dilemmas of trying to represent, justly, accurately, and in a single volume, the unparalleled scope and variety of English literature.

M. H. ABRAMS

Acknowledgments

The following instructors were of especial help in telling us what they teach in their major-author courses: I. Robert Adams (Sam Houston State University); Rosemary Allen (Georgetown College); Nathaniel B. Atwater (Southeastern Massachusetts University); Christopher Baker (Lamar University); Michael Becker (Montana State University); R. M. Bedell (Virginia Military Institute); Vereen Bell (Vanderbilt University); Kenneth Bleeth (Connecticut College); Harry Boardmore (University College of Cape Breton); Kristin Brady (University of Western Ontario); Matthew C. Brennan (Indiana State University); M. Brosser (Wilfred Laurier University); Paula Buck (Florida Southern College); Gary Budd (Diablo Valley College); Ursula Carfague (Montgomery County Community College); Janice Carlisle (Washington University); Charles W. Carter (Shepherd College); Robert Christopher (Ramapo College); Howard Cole (University Of Illinois); Richard B. Dircks (St. John's University); Roman Dubinski (University of Waterloo); Ann Fadley (Florida Southern College); Anthony Farrow (St. Bonaventure University); W. Craig Ferguson (Queen's University); Susan Fox (Queens College); John L. Gaunt (West Chester University); Allan J. Gedalof (University of Western Ontario); Thomas B. Gentry (Virginia Military Institute); Marilyn Georgas (Lamar University); R. K. Gilley (Vancouver Community College); Kenneth Graham (University of Guelph); Carolyn Hample (University of Winnipeg); Claudia Harris (Brigham Young University); Matt Hearn (Valdosta State College); Elizabeth Hedrick (University of Texas, Austin); John Mark Heumann (Lamar University); Nelson Hilton (University of Georgia); Claude Hunsberger (West Chester University); Glenn James (Florida Southern College); Ruth Jenkins (California State University, Fresno); Emily Jensen (Lycoming College); Ernest Kalbach (University of Texas, Austin); Wayne R. Kime (Fairmont State College); Elaine Kleiner (Indiana State University); Robert Laird (Carleton University); Frances Lister (Wilfred Laurier University); John Loftis (University of Northern Colorado); Raymond Lott (Florida Southern College); Mark Lucas (Centre College); M. MacDonald (Mount Allison University); H. R. MacGallum (University of Toronto); R. G. MacGregor (Dalhousie University); Richard Matlak (College of the Holy Cross); Murray McArthur (University of Waterloo); Michael McClintok (University of Montana); John McDermott (California State University, Fresno); Philip Milner (St. Francis Xavier University); Anne B. Morgan (Fairmont State University); Louise Murdy (Winthrop College): David Nelson (Bates College); Robert Nichol (Niagara University); Joseph Nordgren (Lamar University); Dermot O'Dwyer (Allen Hancock College); Steven Olson (University of Illinois); Dorothy Parker (University of Toronto); Adam Parks (University of Georgia); Sara Pfaffenroth (County College of Morris); Ken Phillips (Okanagan University); A. H. de Quehen (University of Toronto); Wayne A. Rebhorn (University of Texas, Austin); Stanley

Rich (University of South Carolina at Aiken); Elizabeth Savage (Medaille College); Sue Seyfarth (Valdosta State College); Michael Shea (Southern Connecticut State University); Michael Shelden (Indiana State University); Antony Shuttleworth (University of Georgia); William W. E. Slights (University of Saskatchewan); William Southerland (University of Texas, Austin); Claudia Stein (Florida Southern College); Charles H. Vivian (Bentley College); David Ward (University of Pittsburgh at Johnston); Ruth Warkentin (California State College, Dominguez Hills); Elaine Woodruff (Colorado Christian University); Mallory Young (Tarleton State University); Elizabeth Zaranek (Penn State University); Gwendolyn Ziemann (Florida Southern College).

Among our many critics, advisers, and friends, the following were of especial help in providing critiques of particular periods or of the anthology as a whole, or else assisted in preparing texts and editorial matter: Paul Alpers (University of California, Berkeley); Lisa Miller Barnes (Queen's University); W. J. Barnes (Queen's University); Stephen A. Barney (University of California, Irvine); David Bevington (University of Chicago); Mary Carruthers (New York University); Paul Christianson (Queen's University); Lawrence M. Clopper (Indiana University); R. W. Crump (Louisiana State University); Eugene R. Cunnar (New Mexico State University); Seamus Deane (University College, Dublin); Jennifer Di Toro (Oxford University); Hubert English, Jr. (University of Michigan); Robert Essick (University of California, Riverside); Barbara C. Ewell (Loyola University); W. Craig Ferguson (Queen's University); Robert D. Fulk (Indiana University); Paul Gabriner (University of Amsterdam); Nancy M. Goslee (University of Tennessee); Donald J. Gray (Indiana University); Isobel Grundy (University of Alberta); A. C. Hamilton (Queen's University); Elizabeth Hanson (Queen's University); Richard Haswell (Washington State University); Carolyn G. Heilbrun (Columbia University); Mary Jacobus (Cornell University); Carol Kaske (Cornell University); James R. Kincaid (University of Southern California); Joanna Lipking (Northwestern University); Norman H. MacKenzie (Professor Emeritus, Queen's University); Hugh Maclean (Professor Emeritus, State University of New York at Albany); Phillip L. Marcus (Cornell University); Kevin J. McManus (College of William and Mary); Juliet McMaster (University of Alberta); Janice Haney Peritz (Queens College, City University of New York); Ruth Perry (Massachusetts Institute of Technology); Jonathan Post (University of California, Los Angeles); Stephen Prickett (The Australian National University); John R. Reed (Wayne State University); David G. Riede (Ohio State University); James Rieger (Late of the University of Rochester); Sue Sandera Rummel (State University of New York College of Technology at Canton); Harry Rusche (Emory University); Peter Sabor (Queen's University); Paul Sawyer (Bradley University); Daniel Schwarz (Cornell University); Ronald A. Sharp (Kenyon College); Elaine Showalter (Princeton University); Sandra Siegel (Cornell University); Pincus Silverman (El Centro College); Paul Stevens (Queen's University); Marta Straznicky (Queen's University); Gordon Teskey (Cornell University); John Tinkler (University of Sydney); Joseph Viscomi (University of North Carolina at Chapel Hill); and Gernot Wieland (University of British Columbia).

The Middle Ages

to ca. 1485

43–ca. 420:	Roman invasion and occupation of Britain.
ca. 450:	Anglo-Saxon Conquest.
597:	St. Augustine arrives in Kent; beginning of Anglo-Saxon conversion to Christianity.
871–899:	Reign of King Alfred.
1066:	Norman Conquest.
ca. 1200:	Beginnings of Middle English literature.
1360–1400:	The summit of Middle English literature: Geoffrey Chaucer; *Piers Plowman; Sir Gawain and the Green Knight.*
1485:	William Caxton's printing of Sir Thomas Malory's *Morte Darthur,* one of the first books printed in England.

The Middle Ages, or medieval (from Latin *medium,* "middle," plus *aevum,* "age") period, designates the time span roughly from the collapse of the Roman empire to the Renaissance (so named because it had supposedly brought a "rebirth" of Greek and Latin learning). The very notion of a "middle" age—between the ancient and modern eras—falsely implies a sense of loss and decline in European culture. Thus in the sixteenth century Sir Philip Sidney expresses wonder that Geoffrey Chaucer "in that misty time could see so clearly." In fact, art and literature flourished during the Middle Ages, rooted in the Christian culture that preserved, transmitted, and transformed classical tradition.

For English literature the medieval period extends for more than eight hundred years, from Cædmon's *Hymn* at the end of the seventh century to *Everyman* at the beginning of the sixteenth. The date 1485, with the accession of Henry VII and the beginning of the Tudor dynasty, is an arbitrary but convenient one to mark the "end" of the Middle Ages.

Although the Roman Catholic church provided continuity, the period was one of enormous historical, social, and linguistic change and could easily be subdivided into several shorter units. Two periods, however—the Old English (or Anglo-Saxon) and the Middle English—are sharply distinguished from each other as a result of the Norman Conquest of the island in 1066 and will be discussed separately in this introduction.

Because reading the Old English language requires a great deal of study, Old English texts printed in this anthology are given in translation. The more difficult Middle English texts (*Sir Gawain and the Green Knight*) are also given in translation, but Chaucer and other Middle English works may be read in the original, even by the beginner, with the help of marginal glosses and notes. These texts have been spelled in a way that is intended to aid the reader. Analyses of the sounds and grammar of Middle English and of Old and Middle English prosody are discussed in "Medieval English" (p. 10).

1

THE OLD ENGLISH PERIOD

ENGLAND UP TO THE NORMAN CONQUEST

From the first to the fifth century, England was a province of the Roman empire and was named Britannia after its Celtic-speaking inhabitants, the Britons. The Britons adapted themselves to Roman civilization, of which the ruins survived to impress the poet of *The Wanderer*, who refers to them as "the old works of giants." The withdrawal of the Roman legions during the fifth century in a vain attempt to protect Rome itself from the threat of Germanic conquest left the island vulnerable to seafaring Germanic invaders. These belonged primarily to three related tribes, the Angles, the Saxons, and the Jutes. The name *English* derives from the Angles, and the names of the counties Essex, Sussex, and Wessex refer to the territories occupied by the East, South, and West Saxons.

The Anglo-Saxon occupation was no sudden conquest but extended over decades of fighting against the native Britons. The latter were finally confined to the mountainous region of Wales where the modern form of their language is spoken alongside English to this day. In defeat, the Britons produced a body of stories revolving around a legendary ruler called Arthur who had fought heroically against the Anglo-Saxon invaders, a tradition that the descendants of those invaders would later adopt as their own.

The Britons had become Christians in the fourth century after the conversion of Emperor Constantine along with most of the rest of the Roman empire, but for about 150 years after the beginning of the invasion, Christianity was maintained only in the remoter regions where the Anglo-Saxons failed to penetrate. In the year 597, however, a Benedictine monk (afterward St. Augustine of Canterbury) was sent by Pope Gregory as a missionary to King Ethelbert of Kent, the most southerly of the kingdoms into which England was then divided, and about the same time missionaries from Ireland began to preach Christianity in the north. Within 75 years the island was once more predominantly Christian. Before Christianity there had been no books. The impact of Christianity on literacy is evident from the fact that the first extended written specimen of the Old English (Anglo-Saxon) language is a code of laws promulgated by Ethelbert, the first English Christian king.

In the centuries that followed up to the Norman Conquest, England produced many distinguished churchmen. One of the earliest of these was Bede, whose Latin *Ecclesiastical History of the English People*, which tells the story of the conversion and of the English church, was completed in 731; this remains one of our most important sources of knowledge about the period. In the next generation Alcuin (735–804), a man of wide culture, became the friend and adviser of Frankish Emperor Charlemagne, whom he assisted in making the Frankish court a great center of learning; thus by the year 800 English culture had developed so richly that it overflowed its insular boundaries.

In the ninth century the Christian Anglo-Saxons were themselves subjected to new Germanic invasions by the Danes who in their longboats repeatedly ravaged the coast, sacking Bede's monastery among others. Such a raid in the tenth century inspired *The Battle of Maldon*, the last of the Old English heroic poems. The Danes also occupied the northern part of the island, threatening to overrun the rest. They were stopped by Alfred, king of the West Saxons from 871 to 899, who for a time united all the kingdoms of southern England. This most active king was also an enthusiastic patron of literature. He himself translated various works from Latin, the most important of which was Boethius's *Consolation of Philosophy*, a sixth-century Roman work also translated in the fourteenth century by Chaucer. Alfred probably also instigated a translation of Bede's *History* and the beginning of the *Anglo-Saxon Chronicle*: this year-by-year record in Old English of important events in England was maintained at one monastery until the middle of the twelfth century. Practically all of Old English poetry is preserved in copies made in the West Saxon dialect after the reign of Alfred.

The Anglo-Saxon invaders brought with them a tradition of oral poetry. Because nothing was written down before the conversion to Christianity, we have only circumstantial evidence of what that poetry must have been like. Aside from a few short inscriptions on small artifacts, the earliest records in the English language are in manuscripts produced at monasteries and other religious establishments, beginning in the seventh century. Literacy was mainly restricted to servants of the church, and so it is natural that the bulk of Old English literature deals with religious subjects and is mostly drawn from Latin sources. Manuscripts were costly and time-consuming to produce, because they required the copying of texts word by word onto parchment, a durable material made from the prepared skins of domestic animals (paper would not be used in Europe before the twelfth century). Under these difficult circumstances, few texts were written down that did not pertain directly to the work of the church. Secular literature remained primarily an oral medium. Stories, new and old, were put into alliterative verse (see "Old and Middle English Prosody," p. 14) and, as popular entertainment, were declaimed or sung to the accompaniment of a harp. A relatively small amount of Old English secular verse has survived in manuscripts, confirming other evidence that the interests of Anglo-Saxon monks and nuns were not isolated from those of laypeople and that popular narrative poetry was a diversion even within the walls of religious houses. Although comparatively small, this body of secular poetry, which includes epic poems like *Beowulf* and *The Battle of Maldon*, is of a very high literary interest and quality.

The subject matter of this verse is sometimes of great antiquity, concerning legendary or historical figures who lived before the Anglo-Saxon conquest of England. Thus the major characters in *Beowulf* are pagan Danes and Geats, and the only connection to England is an obscure allusion to the ancestor of one of the kings of the Angles. Germanic heroic society, as represented in Old English poetry, shares many characteristics with the Hellenic heroic world described by Homer. Nations are reckoned as groups of people related by kinship rather than by geographical areas, and kinship is the basis of the heroic code. The tribe is ruled by a chieftain who is called *king*, a word that has "kin" for its root. The *lord* (a word derived from Old English *hlaf*, "loaf," plus *weard*, "protector") surrounds himself with a band of retainers (many of them his blood kindred) who are members of his household. He leads his men in battle and rewards them with the spoils; royal generosity was one of the most important aspects of heroic behavior. In return, the retainers are obligated to fight for their lord to the death, and if he is slain, to avenge him or die in the attempt. Blood vengeance is regarded as a sacred duty, and in poetry, everlasting shame awaits those who fail to observe it.

Of course, the heroic world described in the poetry was already remote from the Christian world of Anglo-Saxon England. Moreover, the heroic code is difficult to reconcile with a religion that teaches that we should "forgive those that trespass against us" and that "all they that take the sword shall perish with the sword." Nevertheless, Christian poets like the *Beowulf* poet were fascinated by the culture of their pagan ancestors, and the Christian heroes of *The Battle of Maldon* still invoke the heroic code as an ideal in fighting to the death against the pagan Vikings.

Much of Anglo-Saxon Christian poetry is also cast in the heroic mode: although the Anglo-Saxons adapted themselves readily to the ideals of Christianity, they did not do so without adapting Christianity to their own heroic ideal. Thus Moses and St. Andrew, Christ and God the Father are represented in the style of heroic verse.

In the *Dream of the Rood*, the Cross speaks of Christ as "the young hero, . . . strong and stouthearted." In Cædmon's *Hymn* the creation of heaven and earth is seen as a mighty deed, an "establishment of wonders." Anglo-Saxon heroines, too, are portrayed in the heroic manner. St. Helena, who leads an expedition to the Holy Land to discover the true Cross, is described as a "battle-queen." Christian and heroic ideals are poignantly blended in *The Wanderer*, which laments the separation from one's lord and kinsmen and the transience of all earthly treasures.

The world of Old English poetry is predominantly harsh. Men are said to be cheerful in the mead hall, but even there they think of struggle in war, of possible triumph but more possible failure. Romantic love—one of the principal topics of later literature—appears hardly at all. There is nothing in Old English that closely resembles those lyrics of the later Middle Ages that portray the playfulness of animals at the return of spring. Even in its most lyrical moments there is an austere dignity to Old English verse, which rarely strays from the themes of the glory of God and His champions and the pain and sorrow of this world.

The style of such poetry inevitably seems strange in a modern prose translation, which does not attempt to convey the rhythms of the alliterative meter, yet must somehow render the poetic diction, formulaic phrases, and the repetition, with variations, of parallel syntactic structures that are to a large extent determined by the versification. Certain features may be anticipated here and studied in the "Last Survivor's Speech" (p. 22).

Poetic language is created out of a special vocabulary that contains a multiplicity of terms for *lord, warrior, spear, shield*, and so on. Synecdoche and metonymy are common figures of speech as when *keel* is used for "ship" or *iron*, for "sword." A particularly striking effect is achieved by the kenning, a compound of two words in place of another as when *sea* becomes "whale-road" or *body* is called "life-house."

Because special vocabulary and compounds are among the chief poetic effects, the verse is constructed in such a way as to show off such terms by creating a series of them in apposition. In the second sentence of Cædmon's *Hymn*, for example, God is referred to five times appositively as "he," "holy Creator," "mankind's Guardian," "eternal Lord," and "Master Almighty." This use of parallel and appositive expressions, known as *variation*, gives the verse, which is highly structured and musical, a peculiarly halting and repetitive quality in prose translation.

The overall effect of the language is to formalize and elevate speech. Instead of being straighforward, it moves at a slow and stately pace with steady indirection. A favorite mode of this indirection is irony. A grim irony pervades heroic poetry even at the level of diction where *fighting* is called "battle-play." A positive statement is often expressed negatively as when the poet, having enumerated the splendid gifts Beowulf receives for killing Grendel, remarks: "He had no need to be ashamed before fighting men of those rich gifts." A favorite device, known by the rhetorical term *litotes*, is ironic understatement. "They cared not for battle," says the author of *The Battle of Maldon* about the cowards who fled from the fight after their lord was killed.

More than a figure of speech, irony is also a mode of perception in Old English poetry. In a famous passage, the Wanderer articulates the theme of *Ubi sunt* (where are they now): "Where has the horse gone? Where the young warrior? Where the giver of treasure? . . ." *Beowulf* is full of ironic balances and contrasts— between the aged Danish king and the youthful Beowulf, and between Beowulf, the high-spirited young warrior at the beginning, and Beowulf, the gray-haired king at the end, facing the dragon and death.

The formal and dignified speech of Old English poetry was always distant from the everyday language of the Anglo-Saxons, and this poetic idiom remained remarkably uniform throughout the roughly three hundred years that separate Cædmon's *Hymn* from *The Battle of Maldon*. This clinging to old forms—grammatical and orthographic as well as literary—by the Anglo-Saxon church and aristocracy conceals from us the enormous changes that were taking place in the English language and the diversity of its dialects. The dramatic changes between Old and Middle English did not happen overnight or over the course of a single century. The Normans displaced the English ruling class with their own barons and clerics, whose native language was a dialect of Old French that we call Anglo-Norman. Without a ruling literate class to preserve English traditions, the custom of transcribing vernacular texts in an earlier form of the West-Saxon dialect was abandoned, and both language and literature were allowed to develop unchecked in new directions.

THE MIDDLE ENGLISH PERIOD

The period of more than four hundred years that followed the Norman Conquest presents a much more diversified picture than the Old English period. Whereas most Old English literature seems to be uttered by a single aristocratic voice, grave, decorous, speaking in terms of high communal aspirations, Middle English literature is uttered by a medley of different voices addressing themselves to different audiences—learned and unlearned, aristocratic and middle class, male and female, and frequently to several of these at the same time. The native English language and culture continued side by side with, and heavily influenced by, the language and culture of the Anglo-Norman ruling class. English literature, of course, continued, as before, in oral tradition, but we do not get much in the way of literary English texts before the beginning of the thirteenth century. Yet, already when written English literature begins to reappear at the end of the twelfth century, it presents an extraordinary diversity, not only of language but of subject matter, styles, and tones. Much of it carries the stamp of popular or semipopular origin. Many more details of everyday life can be seen and more of the accents of everyday speech heard in the varieties of Middle English literature. Although the alliterative meter of Old English verse, in a looser structure, continued into the fifteenth century, rhyme, composed in couplets and different stanzaic patterns, became the dominant poetic form. Laughter is rarely heard in Old English literature: Birhtnoth, the hero of Maldon, laughs with pleasure after killing one of his enemies. In Middle English works a lighter kind of humor is apt to flash anywhere, even in the most solemn and foreboding moralizations. Middle English literature owes its heterogeneity to historical, linguistic, and social crosscurrents that span the course of four centuries.

ANGLO-NORMAN ENGLAND

The Normans, who took possession of England after the decisive Battle of Hastings, were, like the Anglo-Saxons, descendants of Germanic adventurers who at the beginning of the tenth century had seized a wide part of northern France. Their name is actually a form of "Norsemen." A highly adaptable people, they had adopted the French language of the land they had settled in and its Christian religion. They were great builders of castles, with which they enforced their political dominance, and magnificent churches, wielding both spiritual and political authority. Although the dukes of Normandy were technically subjects of the king of France, they were, in effect, independent rulers, a status that was enhanced by their becoming kings of England. The earlier Norman kings were, however, often absentee rulers, less interested in their newly acquired kingdom than in their Continental possessions. The latter were enormously increased in 1152 when Henry II married Eleanor of Aquitaine, the divorced wife of the French king Louis VII, thereby annexing vast provinces in the south of France to his domain. It was not until the fifteenth century that English monarchs finally gave up trying to make good their claims in France.

Although the conquest brought about a long hiatus in written English literature, important works continued to be written in England in Latin and in French. Latin, as it had been for Bede, was the international language of learning, used for theology, science, and history. St. Anselm, who became archbishop of Canterbury in 1093, was one of the great theologians of the Middle Ages. The first medieval drama in the vernacular, *The Play of Adam*, with elaborate stage directions in Latin and realistic dialogue in Anglo-Norman French, may have been produced in England. The greatest woman author of the Middle Ages, Marie de France—who wrote a series of short verse romances, known as lays—was associated with the court of Henry II.

Little was known about the history of the island before the Anglo-Saxon invasion. That gap was filled in about 1136 by a remarkable book in Latin, *The History of the Kings of Britain*, by Geoffrey of Monmouth, a Welsh cleric. According to Geoffrey, a certain Brutus was the founding father of Britain for whom the island was named (*Brut > Brit*ain). This Brutus was a descendant of the Trojan Aeneas, the legendary founder of Rome. He defeated a race of giant inhabitants of the island and established a dynasty of kings that culminated in Arthur, who had conquered Rome but was finally defeated by the treachery of his nephew, Mordred, in alliance with the barbarian Saxon invaders. Geoffrey claimed to have based his "history" on a book in the British tongue (i.e., Welsh), although no one has ever seen such a book. He drew on a few written sources, but the bulk of his history was probably fabricated from Celtic oral tradition and his own fertile imagination. Although denounced by contemporary chroniclers as a fraud, Geoffrey's history caught on and was not finally discredited until the sixteenth century. The Normans could thus think of themselves as reigning over the land that had belonged to one of the greatest kings of ancient times and whose story has lived on ever since in literature, art, and film. Geoffrey's book was quickly translated into French verse as the *Roman de Brut* by the poet Wace, who dedicated the work to Henry II's queen, Eleanor of Aquitaine, a great patron of courtly literature. Next Layamon, an English priest, made over and greatly expanded Wace's poem. Written in a combination of alliterative lines and rhyme, Layamon's *Brut* (ca. 1205) is among the earliest works of Middle English literature. Layamon's battle scenes show that the Old English epic tradition was still very much alive. He also drew independently on Celtic folklore and is the first writer to mention Arthur's round table.

It is doubly ironic, but also indicative of the international character of medieval literature, that not only did the British Arthur become the legendary national hero of the English—whose ancestors he had fought against and often defeated—but also Arthurian legend reached its fullest development in France, carried there by British refugees fleeing from the Anglo-Saxons to the French province of Brittany (often called "Little Britain" during the Middle Ages). The characteristically medieval genre we call romance was first developed in French; indeed, the word initially meant simply "a work written in the 'romance language,'" i.e., the French vernacular; thus Wace's *Roman de Brut* means "the story of Brutus in French." Romance, like epic, often involves a large amount of fighting against men and monsters; it makes liberal use of the improbable, often the supernatural. Unlike epic, however, romance usually deals also with romantic love; indeed, the themes of love and war are often connected, the hero's martial exploits having a direct influence on his love affair. The earliest romance to tell the tragic love story of Tristan and Isolt is the work of an Anglo-Norman poet named Thomas. The twelfth-century French poet Chrétien de Troyes is the principal creator of the romance of chivalry in which knightly adventures are a means of exploring psychological and ethical problems. Chrétien's romances are aristocratic, witty, and extremely sophisticated tales aimed at a court audience. But romance, stripped of the psychological and ethical subtleties it has in Chrétien, also had an immense popular appeal. Romances comprise a large fraction of the secular Middle English literature that has been preserved. Many of these are simplified adaptations of French poems, recounting in a rollicking and rambling style the adventures of heroes like Guy of Warwick, a poor steward who must prove his knightly worth to win the love of Fair Phyllis. The ethos of many romances, aristocratic and popular alike, involves the proving of a knight's worthiness through noble character and deeds rather than through high birth, and in this respect romances reflect the aspirations of a lower order of the nobility to rise in the world, as historically some of them did. William the Marshall, for example, the fourth son of a baron of middle rank, through his talents in war and in tournaments became tutor to the oldest son of Henry II and Eleanor of Aquitaine, married a great heiress, and became the most powerful noble in England and the subject of a verse biography in French, which often reads like a romance.

By far the larger proportion of surviving literature in Middle as in Old English is religious. Medieval Latin writing flourished at new institutions called "universities," which were developing at Paris, Oxford, and Cambridge and at great cathedral schools like that of Chartres. Education was conducted in Latin, and the reason for receiving an education was to become a "clerk," i.e., a cleric. The church offered a path for gifted commoners to make a career, occasionally rising to positions of eminence and power. One such person was Thomas à Becket (1118?–1170) who served Henry II as chancellor and then as archbishop of Canterbury.

Although learned churchmen wrote for one another in Latin, there was also a need for religious books in the vernacular for laypeople and for priests who would preach to the laity. The liturgy of the church was exclusively in Latin and sermons to religious communities were preached in Latin, but preaching in the vernacular was the most common form of religious instruction. Preaching was regarded as an art, and sermons to the laity often included short stories, called exempla, to illustrate biblical texts. Chaucer's *The Pardoner's Tale* is actually a sermon with an exemplum. Vernacular manuals of instruction, homilies, collections of sermons and exempla, saints' lives, penitential tracts on the seven deadly sins, and religious lyrics proliferate during the medieval period.

Among the audiences addressed by these religious works are women, including nuns and anchoresses, i.e., female religious recluses who were not members of religious orders but chose to live secluded in a cell, sometimes built on to a church with a window opening on to the street and one looking into the church. Among the earliest and finest of Middle English works is the *Ancrene Riwle* (Rule for Anchoresses), a book of religious instruction for three sisters, which deals profoundly, compassionately, and sometimes humorously with such topics as temptation, the seven deadly sins, and spiritual love as well as with the details of the anchoresses' daily life.

THE FOURTEENTH CENTURY

War and disease were prevalent throughout the Middle Ages, but never more devastatingly than during the fourteenth century. In 1336 Edward III began the war to enforce his claims to the throne of France that continued intermittently for one hundred years until the English were driven from all of their French territories except for the port of Calais, to which they managed to cling for another century. The gains of two spectacular victories at Crécy in 1346 and Poitiers in 1356 were gradually frittered away in futile campaigns, which ravaged the French countryside without obtaining any clear advantage for the English. In 1348 the first and most virulent epidemic of the bubonic plague—the Black Death—swept Europe, wiping out a quarter to a third of the population. Among the results were high prices, a scarcity of labor, and a sudden expansion of the possibilities of social mobility that fostered considerable discontent. One consequence was a widespread popular uprising in 1381, commonly known as the Peasants' Revolt, although the partici-

pants and leaders were for the most part tenants farming small acreages, day laborers, apprentices, and rural workers not attached to one of the big manorial
households. The movement was quickly suppressed; however, the rebels burned
down the London palace of John of Gaunt, duke of Lancaster, and killed several
eminent personages, among them the archbishop of Canterbury. The church had
become the target of popular resentment because it was among the greatest of the
oppressive landowners and because of the wealth, worldliness, and venality of
many of the higher clergy. The reputation of the church had been further damaged by a split in the papacy. A French pope held court at Avignon, while the
English supported a rival pope at Rome.

　These calamities and upheavals nevertheless bred rising expectations, the principal beneficiaries of which were the increasingly wealthy and influential urban
middle class. Thriving cities like London ran their own affairs under politically
powerful mayors and aldermen. Edward III, chronically in need of money to
finance his wars, was obliged to negotiate for revenues with the commons in the
English Parliament, an institution that became a major political force during this
period. A large part of the king's revenues depended on taxing the highly profitable
export of English wool to the Continent. In the portrait of Chaucer's merchant we
see the budding of capitalism based on credit and interest. The Crown thus
became increasingly involved in the country's economic affairs, and this involvement led to a need for capable administrators. These were no longer drawn mainly
from the church, as they had been in the past, but from a newly educated laity
that occupied a rank somewhere between that of the lesser nobility and the upper
bourgeoisie. The career of Geoffrey Chaucer, who served Edward III and his successor Richard II in a number of civil posts, is typical of this class—with the exception that he was also a great poet.

　The emergence during the second half of the fourteenth century of Chaucer
and two other great poets—William Langland and the anonymous author of *Sir
Gawain and the Green Knight*—is probably not a pure coincidence but has something to do with the fact that all three were responding to an age of crisis and
transition. One very important change is that English finally began to displace
French as the language for conducting business in Parliament and in the law
courts. Although the high nobility continued to speak French by preference, they
were certainly bilingual, whereas some earlier Norman kings had known no
English at all. Chaucer's choice to write in English is significant of a change in
the status of English as a literary language, and his own works were greatly to
enhance its prestige as a vehicle for serious literature. His friend John Gower
(1325?–1408), a prolific and highly moralistic poet, wrote his first long work, *Le
Miroir de l'homme* (The Mirror of Man), in French and a second, the *Vox Cla-
mantis* (The Voice of One Crying Out), in Latin. His third and last major poem,
Confessio Amantis (The Lover's Confession), in spite of its Latin title, is composed
in English; a lover confesses to a priest named Genius, who tells him a series of
entertaining exempla, which illustrate the seven deadly sins. Gower is a very competent poet, although not regarded as highly today as his three major contemporaries, but his works, too, react to the challenge of the times.

　The *Gawain* poet not only produced the best Middle English romance but also
wrote some of its finest religious poetry—two biblical narratives in alliterative
verse, *Cleanness* and *Patience*, and *Pearl*, a moving and beautiful elegy for a child
that deals profoundly with the differences between heaven and earth. Langland in
his dream allegory, *Piers Plowman*, also written in alliterative verse, squarely faced
the major religious and social issues of his day that would become the great issues
leading to the Reformation of which, in the sixteenth century, the author was
regarded as a prophet. Chaucer's familiarity with the Latin classics (especially Virgil and Ovid) and Dante's *Divine Comedy* and the earlier works of Giovanni Boccaccio vastly enlarged the literary horizons of English poetry. The *Gawain* poet's

unique manuscript was not discovered until the nineteenth century, and the difficulty and strangeness both of his and of Langland's dialect and alliterative verse make their works challenging even to specialists reading them in modern annotated editions. The large body of Chaucer's works, composed in language and versification easier and more familiar to future readers and printed and reprinted from 1532 on in large collected editions, led to his establishment as the first English classic—in John Dryden's phrase, "the father of English poetry."

THE FIFTEENTH CENTURY

In 1399 Henry Bolingbroke, the duke of Lancaster, deposed his cousin Richard II, who was murdered in prison. As Henry IV, he successfully defended his crown against several insurrections and passed it on to Henry V, who briefly united the country once more and achieved one last apparently decisive victory over the French at the Battle of Agincourt (1415). The premature death of Henry V, however, left England exposed to the civil wars known as the Wars of the Roses, the red rose being the emblem of the house of Lancaster; the white, of York. These wars did not end until Henry Tudor defeated Richard III at Bosworth Field and acceded to the throne as Henry VII, the event we declared to be a convenient "end" to the Middle Ages in England.

Social, economic, and literary life continued as they had throughout all of the previous wars. The continuing prosperity of the towns was marked by performances of the mystery plays—a sequence or "cycle" of plays based on the Bible and produced by the city guilds, the organizations representing the various trades and crafts. The cycles of several towns are lost, but those of York, Wakefield, and Chester have been preserved. Under the guise of dramatizing biblical history, playwrights such as the Wakefield Master manage to comment satirically on the social ills of the times. The century also saw the development of the morality play, in which personified vices and virtues struggle for the soul of "mankind" or "Everyman." Performed by strolling players, the morality plays were precursors of the professional theater in the reign of Elizabeth I.

While religious works of all kinds continued to be produced, the fourteenth and fifteenth centuries are notable, both in England and on the Continent, for mystical writings in which the authors, many of whom were women, tell of their direct personal experience of God. The anchoress Julian of Norwich spent her life meditating and writing about a series of visions, which she called "showings," that she had received in 1373 when she was thirty years old. Early in the fifteenth century she was still in her cell, attached to a church in Norwich, when she was consulted by Margery Kempe, a housewife, whom a series of visions had directed to lead a spiritual life. Kempe, a controversial figure, made a pilgrimage to the Holy Land and during the 1430s dictated the first autobiography in English. Both Julian of Norwich and Margery Kempe, in highly individual ways, allow us to see the medieval church and its doctrines from female points of view.

The most prolific poet of the fifteenth century was the monk John Lydgate (1370?–1451?) who produced dream visions; a life of the Virgin; translations of French religious allegories; a *Troy Book*; *The Siege of Thebes*, which he framed as a "new" Canterbury tale; and a thirty-six-thousand-line poem called *The Fall of Princes*, a free translation of a French work, itself based on a Latin work by Boccaccio. The last illustrates the late medieval idea of tragedy, namely that emperors, kings, and other famous men enjoy power and fortune only to be cast down in misery. Lydgate shapes these tales as a "mirror" for princes, i.e., as object lessons to the powerful men of his own day, several of whom were his patrons. A self-styled imitator of Chaucer, Lydgate had a reputation almost equal to his master's in the fifteenth century, but his laurels quickly faded. The best of Chaucer's imitators was the "Scottish Chaucerian," Robert Henryson (1425?–1508?), who wrote *The Testament of Cressid*, a continuation of Chaucer's great poem *Troilus and Cri-*

seyde, as well as a sequel to Chaucer's *The Nun's Priest's Tale,* in his *Moral Fables of Aesop.*

The great writer of the century was Sir Thomas Malory, who spent years in prison Englishing a series of Arthurian romances that he translated and abridged chiefly from several enormously long thirteenth-century French prose romances. Malory was a passionate devotee of chivalry, which he personified in his hero Sir Lancelot. In the jealousies and rivalries that finally break up the round table and destroy Arthur's kingdom, Malory saw a distant image of the civil wars of his own time. A manuscript of Malory's works fell into the hands of William Caxton (1422?–1491), who had introduced the new art of printing by movable type to England in 1476. Caxton divided Malory's tales into the chapters and books of a single long work, as though it were a chronicle history, and gave it the title *Morte Darthur,* which has stuck to it ever since. Caxton also printed *The Canterbury Tales* and some of Chaucer's earlier works and Gower's *Confessio Amantis.* Caxton himself translated many of the works he printed for English readers: a history of Troy, a book on chivalry, Aesop's fables, and *The Game and Playe of Chesse.* The new technology put an end to the manuscript age, extended literacy, and made books more easily accessible to new classes of readers. Printing made the production of literature a business and made possible the bitter political and doctrinal disputes that, in the sixteenth century, were waged in print as well as on the field of battle.

MEDIEVAL ENGLISH

The medieval works in this book were composed in two different states of our language: Old English, the language that took shape among the Germanic settlers of England and preserved its integrity until the Norman Conquest radically altered English civilization, and Middle English, the earliest records of which date from the early twelfth century and which gave way to Modern English shortly after the introduction of printing at the end of the fifteenth century. Old English is a very heavily inflected language. (That is, the words change form to indicate changes in usage, such as person, number, tense, case, mood, and so on. Most languages have some inflection—for example, the personal pronouns in Modern English have different forms when used as objects—but a "heavily inflected" language is one in which almost all classes of words undergo elaborate patterns of change.) Its vocabulary is almost entirely Germanic. In Middle English, the inflectional system was weakened, and a large number of words were introduced into it from France, so that many of the older native words disappeared. Because of the difficulty of Old English, all selections from it in this book have been given in translation. So that the reader may see an example of the language, a passage from *Beowulf* has been printed in the original, together with translations. The present discussion, then, is concerned only with Middle English.

The chief difficulty with Middle English for the modern reader is caused not by its inflections so much as by its spelling, which may be described as a rough-and-ready phonetic system, and by the fact that it is not a single standardized language, but consists of a number of regional dialects each with its own peculiarities of sound and its own systems for representing sounds in writing. The Midland dialect—the dialect of London and of Chaucer, which is the ancestor of our own standard speech—differs greatly from the dialect spoken in the west of England, and from that of the northwest (*Sir Gawain and the Green Knight*), and from that of the north, and these dialects differ from one another. In this book, the long texts composed in the more difficult dialects have been translated or modernized, and those that—like Chaucer—appear in the original, have been respelled in a way that it is hoped will aid the reader. The remarks that follow apply chiefly to Chaucer's Midland English, although certain non-Midland dialectal variations are noted if they occur in some of the other selections.

I. THE SOUNDS OF MIDDLE ENGLISH: GENERAL RULES

The following general analysis of the sounds of Middle English will enable the reader who has not time for detailed study to read Middle English aloud so as to preserve some of its most essential characteristics, without, however, giving heed to many important details. The next section, "Detailed Analysis," is designed for the reader who wishes to go more deeply into the pronunciation of Middle English.

Middle English differs from Modern English in three principal respects: (1) the pronunciation of the long vowels *a, e, i* (or *y*), *o*, and *u* (spelled *ou, ow*); (2) the fact that Middle English final *e* is often sounded; and (3) the fact that all Middle English consonants are sounded.

1. Long Vowels

Middle English vowels are long when they are doubled (*aa, ee, oo*) or when they are terminal (*he, to, holy*); *a, e,* and *o* are long when followed by a single consonant plus a vowel (*name, mete, note*). Middle English vowels are short when they are followed by two consonants.

Long *a* is sounded like the *a* in Modern English "father": *maken, maad.*

Long *e* may be sounded like the *a* in Modern English "name" (ignoring the distinction between the close and open vowel): *be, sweete.*

Long *i* (or *y*) is sounded like the *i* in Modern English "machine": *lif, whit; myn, holy.*

Long *o* may be sounded like the *o* in Modern English "note" (again ignoring the distinction between the close and open vowel): *do, soone.*

Long *u* (spelled *ou, ow*) is sounded like the *oo* in Modern English "goose": *hous, flowr.*

Note that in general Middle English long vowels are pronounced like long vowels in modern languages other than English. Short vowels and diphthongs, however, may be pronounced as in Modern English.

2. Final e

In Middle English syllabic verse, final *e* is sounded like the *a* in "sofa" to provide a needed unstressed syllable: *Another Nonnë with hire haddë she.* But (cf. *hire* in the example) final *e* is suppressed when not needed for the meter. It is commonly silent before words beginning with a vowel or *h.*

3. Consonants

Middle English consonants are pronounced separately in all combinations— *gnat: g-nat; knave: k-nave; write: w-rite; folk: fol-k.* In a simplified system of pronunciation the combination *gh* as in *night* or *thought* may be treated as if it were silent.

II. THE SOUNDS OF MIDDLE ENGLISH: DETAILED ANALYSIS

1. Simple Vowels

Sound	Pronunciation	Example
long *a* (spelled *a, aa*)	*a* in "father"	*maken, maad*
short *a*	*o* in "hot"	*cappe*
long *e* close (spelled *e, ee*)	*a* in "name"	*be, sweete*
long *e* open (spelled *e, ee*)	*e* in "there"	*mete, heeth*
short *e*	*e* in "set"	*setten*
final *e*	*a* in "sofa"	*large*
long *i* (spelled *i, y*)	*i* in "machine"	*lif, myn*
short *i*	*i* in "wit"	*wit*
long *o* close (spelled *o, oo*)	*o* in "note"	*do, soone*

long o open (spelled o, oo)	oa in "broad"	go, goon
short o	o in "oft"	pot
long u when spelled ou, ow	oo in "goose"	hous, flowr
long u when spelled u	u in "pure"	vertu
short u (spelled u, o)	u in "full"	ful, love

Doubled vowels and terminal vowels are always long, whereas single vowels before two consonants other than th, ch are always short. The vowels a, e, and o are long before a single consonant followed by a vowel: nāmë, sēkë (sick), hōly. In general, words that have descended into Modern English reflect their original Middle English quantity: līven (to live), but līf (life).

The close and open sounds of long e and long o may often be identified by the Modern English spellings of the words in which they appear. Original long close e is generally represented in Modern English by ee: "sweet," "knee," "teeth," "see" have close e in Middle English, but so does "be"; original long open e is generally represented in Modern English by ea: "meat," "heath," "sea," "great," "breath" have open e in Middle English. Similarly, original long close o is now generally represented by oo: "soon," "food," "good," but also "do," "to"; original long open o is represented either by oa or by o: "coat," "boat," "moan," but also "go," "bone," "foe," "home." Notice that original close o is now almost always pronounced like the oo in "goose," but that original open o is almost never so pronounced; thus it is often possible to identify the Middle English vowels through Modern English sounds.

The nonphonetic Middle English spelling of o for short u has been preserved in a number of Modern English words ("love," "son," "come"), but in others u has been restored: "sun" (sonne), "run" (ronne).

For the treatment of final e, see "General Rules," "Final e."

2. Diphthongs

Sound	Pronunciation	Example
ai, ay, ei, ay	between ai in "aisle" and ay in "day"	saide, day, veine, preye
au, aw	ou in "out"	chaunge, bawdy
eu, ew	ew in "few"	newe
oi, oy	oy in "joy"	joye, point
ou, ow	ou in "thought"	thought, lowe

Note that in words with ou, ow that in Modern English are sounded with the ou of "about," the combination indicates not the diphthong but the simple vowel long u (see "Simple Vowels").

3. Consonants

In general, all consonants except h were always sounded in Middle English, including consonants that have become silent in Modern English, such as the g in gnaw, the k in knight, the l in folk, and the w in write. In noninitial gn, however, the g was silent as in Modern English "sign." Initial h was silent in short common English words and in words borrowed from French and may have been almost silent in all words. The combination gh as in night or thought was sounded like the ch of German ich or nach. Note that Middle English gg represents both the hard sound of "dagger" and the soft sound of "bridge."

III. PARTS OF SPEECH AND GRAMMAR

1. Nouns

The plural and possessive of nouns end in es, formed by adding s or es to the singular: knight, knightes; roote, rootes; a final consonant is frequently doubled before es: bed, beddes. A common irregular plural is yën, from yë, eye.

2. *Pronouns*

The chief differences from Modern English are as follows:

Modern English	Middle English
I	*I, ich* (*ik* is a northern form)
you (singular)	*thou* (subjective); *thee* (objective)
her	*hir(e), her(e)*
its	*his*
you (plural)	*ye* (subjective); *you* (objective)
their	*hir*
them	*hem*

In formal speech, the second person plural is often used for the singular. The possessive adjectives *my, thy* take *n* before a word beginning with a vowel or *h*: *thyn yë, myn host.*

3. *Adjectives*

Adjectives ending in a consonant add final *e* when they stand before the noun they modify and after another modifying word such as *the, this, that,* or nouns or pronouns in the possessive: *a good hors,* but *the (this, my, the kinges) goode hors.* They also generally add *e* when standing before and modifying a plural noun, a noun in the vocative, or any proper noun: *goode men, oh goode man, faire* Venus.

Adjectives are compared by adding *er(e)* for the comparative, *est(e)* for the superlative. Sometimes the stem vowel is shortened or altered in the process: *sweete, swettere, swettest; long, lenger, lengest.*

4. *Adverbs*

Adverbs are formed from adjectives by adding *e, ly,* or *liche;* the adjective *fair* thus yields *faire, fairly, fairliche.*

5. *Verbs*

Middle English verbs, like Modern English verbs, are either "weak" or "strong." Weak verbs form their preterites and past participles with a *t* or *d* suffix and preserve the same stem vowel throughout their systems, although it is sometimes shortened in the preterite and past participle: *love, loved; bend, bent; hear, heard; meet, met.* Strong verbs do not use the *t* or *d* suffix, but vary their stem vowel in the preterite and past participle: *take, took, taken; begin, began, begun; find, found, found.*

The inflectional endings are the same for Middle English strong verbs and weak verbs except in the preterite singular and the imperative singular. In the following paradigms, the weak verbs *loven* (to love) and *heeren* (to hear), and the strong verbs *taken* (to take) and *ginnen* (to begin) serve as models.

	Present Indicative	Preterite Indicative
I	*love, heere*	*loved(e), herde*
	take, ginne	*took, gan*
thou	*lovest, heerest*	*lovedest, herdest*
	takest, ginnest	*tooke, gonne*
he, she, it	*loveth, heereth*	*loved(e), herde*
	taketh, ginneth	*took, gan*
we, ye, they	*love(n) (th), heere(n) (th)*	*loved(e) (en), herde(n)*
	take(n) (th), ginne(n) (th)	*tooke(n), gonne(n)*

The present plural ending *eth* is southern, whereas the *e(n)* ending is Midland and characteristic of Chaucer. In the north, *s* may appear as the ending of all persons of the present. In the weak preterite, when the ending *e* gave a verb three or more syllables, it was frequently dropped. Note that in certain strong verbs like *ginnen* there are two distinct stem vowels in the preterite; even in Chaucer's time, however, one of these had begun to replace the other, and Chaucer occasionally writes *gan* for all persons of the preterite.

	Present Subjunctive	Preterite Subjunctive
Singular	*love, heere*	*lovede, herde*
	take, ginne	*tooke, gonne*
Plural	*love(n), heere(n)*	*lovede(n), herde(n)*
	take(n), ginne(n)	*tooke(n), gonne(n)*

In verbs like *ginnen*, which have two stem vowels in the indicative preterite, it is the vowel of the plural and of the second person singular that is used for the preterite subjunctive.

The imperative singular of most weak verbs is *e: (thou) love*, but of some weak verbs and all strong verbs, the imperative singular is without termination: *(thou) heer, taak, gin*. The imperative plural of all verbs is either *e* or *eth: (ye) love(th), heere(th), take(th), ginne(th)*.

The infinitive of verbs is *e* or *en: love(n), heere(n), take(n), ginne(n)*.

The past participle of weak verbs is the same as the preterite without inflectional ending: *loved, herd*. In strong verbs the ending is either *e* or *en: take(n), gonne(n)*. The prefix *y* often appears on past participles: *yloved, yherd, ytake(n)*.

OLD AND MIDDLE ENGLISH PROSODY

All the poetry of Old English is in the same verse form. The verse unit is the single line, because rhyme was not used to link one line to another, except very occasionally in late Old English. The organizing device of the line is alliteration, the beginning of several words with the same sound ("Foemen fled"). The Old English alliterative line contains, on the average, four principal stresses and is divided into two half-lines of two stresses each by a strong medial caesura, or pause. These two half-lines are linked to each other by the alliteration; at least one of the two stressed words in the first half-line, and often both of them, begin with the same sound as the first stressed word of the second half-line (the second stressed word is generally nonalliterative). The fourth line of *Beowulf* is an example *(sc* has the value of modern *sh;* þ is a runic symbol with the value of modern *th):*

Oft Scyld Scefing   sceaþena þreatum.

For further examples, see the passage from *Beowulf*. It will be noticed that any vowel alliterates with any other vowel. In addition to the alliteration, the length of the unstressed syllables and their number and pattern is governed by a highly complex set of rules. When sung or intoned—as it was—to the rhythmic strumming of a harp, Old English poetry must have been wonderfully impressive in the dignified, highly formalized way that aptly fits both its subject matter and tone.

The majority of Middle English verse is either in alternately stressed rhyming verse, adapted from French after the conquest, or in alliterative verse that is descended from Old English. The latter preserves the caesura of Old English and in its purest form the same alliterative system, the two stressed words of the first half-line (or at least one of them) alliterating with the first stressed word in the second half-line. But most of the alliterative poets allowed themselves a number of deviations from the norm. All four stressed words may alliterate, as in the first line of *Piers Plowman:*

In a summer season   when soft was the sun.

Or the line may contain five, six, or even more stressed words, of which all or only the basic minimum may alliterate:

A *fair f*ield *f*ull of *f*olk   *f*ound I therebetween.

There is no rule determining the number of unstressed syllables, and at times some poets seem to ignore alliteration entirely. As in Old English, any vowel may alliterate with any other vowel; furthermore, since initial *h* was silent or lightly pronounced in Middle English, words beginning with *h* are treated as though they began with the following vowel.

There are two general types of stressed verse with rhyme. In the more common, stressed and unstressed syllables alternate regularly as x X x X x X or, with two unstressed syllables intervening as x x X x x X x x X or a combination of the two as x x X x X x x X (of the reverse patterns, only X x X x X x is common in English). There is also a line that can be defined only as containing a predetermined number of stressed syllables but an irregular number and pattern of unstressed syllables. Much Middle English verse has to be read without expectation of regularity; some of this was evidently composed in the irregular meter, but some was probably originally composed according to a strict metrical system that has been obliterated by scribes careless of fine points. One receives the impression that many of the lyrics were at least composed with regular syllabic alternation. In the ballads, on the other hand, only the number of stresses is predetermined, but not the number or placement of unstressed syllables.

In pre-Chaucerian verse the number of stresses, whether regularly or irregularly alternated, was most often four, although sometimes the number was three and rose in some poems to seven. Rhyme in Middle English as in Modern English may be between either adjacent or alternate lines or may occur in more complex patterns. *The Canterbury Tales* are in rhymed couplets, the line containing five stresses with regular alternation—technically known as iambic pentameter, the standard English poetic line, perhaps introduced into English by Chaucer. In reading Chaucer and much pre-Chaucerian verse one must remember that the final *e*, which is silent in Modern English, could be pronounced at any time to provide a needed unstressed syllable. Evidence seems to indicate that it was also pronounced at the end of the line, even though it thus produced a line with eleven syllables. Although he was a very regular metricist, Chaucer used various conventional devices that are apt to make the reader stumble until he or she understands them. Final *e* is often not pronounced before a word beginning with a vowel or *h*, and may be suppressed whenever metrically convenient. The same medial and terminal syllables that are slurred in Modern English are apt to be suppressed in Chaucer's English: *Canterb'ry* for *Canterbury*; *ev'r* (perhaps *e'er*) for *evere*. The plural in *es* may either be syllabic or reduced to *s* as in Modern English. Despite these seeming irregularities, Chaucer's verse is not difficult to read if one constantly bears in mind the basic pattern of the iambic pentameter line.

TEXTS	CONTEXTS
	43–c. 420 Romans conquer Britons; Brittania a province of the Roman Empire
	c. 450 Withdrawal of Roman legions; Anglo-Saxon conquest of Britons begins
	597 St. Augustine of Canterbury's mission to Kent begins conversion of Anglo-Saxons to Christianity
c. 658–80 *Cædmon's Hymn*, first poem recorded in English	
c. 750 *Beowulf* composed	
	871–99 Reign of King Alfred
c. 1000 Only extant *Beowulf* manuscript written	
	1066 Norman Conquest by William I, duke of Normandy, establishes French-speaking ruling class in England
	1095–1291 Crusades
c. 1138 Geoffrey of Monmouth's Latin *History of the Kings of Britain* gives pseudohistorical status to Arthurian and other legends	
	1152 Future Henry II marries Eleanor of Aquitaine, adding vast French territories to English Crown
c. 1165–80 Marie de France, *Lais*, in Anglo-Norman French from Breton sources	
	1170 Murder of Thomas Becket, archbishop of Canterbury
c. 1200 Layamon's *Brut*; beginnings of Middle English literature	
1304–13 Dante Alighieri, *Divine Comedy*	

Boldface titles indicate works in the anthology.

TEXTS	CONTEXTS
	1337–1453 Hundred Years' War
	1348 Black Death ravages Europe
	1362 English first used in the courts and Parliament
	1372 Chaucer's first journey to Italy
c. 1375–1400 *Sir Gawain and the Green Knight*	
	1376 Earliest record showing performance of drama at York
c. 1387–99 Chaucer working on *The Canterbury Tales* (unfinished)	
	1399 Richard II deposed by his cousin, who succeeds him as Henry IV
	1400 Richard II murdered • Chaucer buried in Westminster Abbey
	1415 Henry V defeats French at Agincourt
	1431 English burn Joan of Arc at Rouen
	1455–85 Wars of the Roses, the red rose of Lancaster versus the white rose of York
c. 1470 Sir Thomas Malory in prison working on *Morte Darthur*	
	1476 William Caxton sets up first printing press in England
	1478 Birth of Thomas More
1485 Malory's *Morte Darthur,* among the first books in English printed by William Caxton	1485 Richard III killed at Bosworth Field; succeeded by Henry VII, founder of the Tudor dynasty
	1575 Last performance of mystery plays at Chester

BEOWULF

Beowulf, the oldest of the great long poems written in English, may have been composed more than twelve hundred years ago, in the first half of the eighth century, although some scholars would place it as late as the tenth century. Its author may have been a native of what was then Mercia, the Midlands of England today, although the late tenth-century manuscript, which alone preserves the poem, originated in the south in the kingdom of the West Saxons. In 1731, before any modern transcription of the text had been made, the manuscript was seriously damaged in the fire that destroyed the building in London that housed the extraordinary collection of medieval English manuscripts made by Sir Robert Bruce Cotton (1571–1631). As a result of the fire and of subsequent deterioration of the manuscript, a number of lines and words have been lost from the poem, but even if the manuscript had not been damaged, the poem would still have been difficult, because the poetic Old English (or Anglo-Saxon) in which it was written is itself hard, the style is allusive, the ideas often seem remote and strange to modern perceptions, and the text was inevitably corrupted during the transcriptions, which must have intervened between the poem's composition and the copying of the extant manuscript. Yet despite its difficulty, the somber grandeur of *Beowulf* is still capable of stirring the hearts of readers, and because of its excellence as well as its antiquity, the poem merits the high position that it is generally assigned in the study of English poetry.

Although the poem itself is English in language and origin, it deals not with native Englishmen but with their Germanic forebears, especially with two south Scandinavian tribes, the Danes and the Geats, who lived on the Danish island of Zealand and in southern Sweden, respectively. Thus the historical period it concerns—insofar as it may be said to refer to history at all—is some centuries before the poem was written; that is, it concerns a time following the initial invasion of England by Germanic tribes in 449, but before the Anglo-Saxon migration was completed, and perhaps before the arrival of the ancestors of the audience to whom the poem was sung. This audience may have considered itself to be of the same Geatish stock as the hero, Beowulf. The one datable fact of history mentioned in the poem is a raid on the Franks made by Hygelac, the king of the Geats at the time Beowulf was a young man, and this raid occurred in the year 520. Yet despite their antiquity, the poet's materials must have been very much alive to his audience, because the elliptical way in which he alludes to events not directly concerned with his plot demands of the listener a wide knowledge of traditional Germanic history. This knowledge was probably kept alive by other heroic poetry, of which little has been preserved in English, although much must once have existed. As it stands, *Beowulf* not only is unique as an example of the Old English epic, but is also the greatest of the surviving epics composed by the Germanic peoples.

It is generally agreed that the poet who put the old materials into their present form was a Christian and that his poem reflects a Christian tradition; the conversion of the Germanic settlers in England had largely been completed during the centuries preceding the one in which the poet wrote. But there is little general agreement as to how clearly *Beowulf* reflects a Christian tradition or, conversely, the actual nature of the Christian tradition that it is held to reflect. Many specifically Christian references occur, especially to the Old Testament. God is said to be the creator of all things and His will seems recognized (sporadically if not systematically) as being identical with Fate (*wyrd*); Grendel is described as a descendant of Cain, and the sword that Beowulf finds in Grendel's mother's lair has engraved on it the story of the race of giants and their destruction by flood; the dead await God's judgment, and hell and the devil are ready to receive the souls of Grendel and his mother, while believers will find the Father's embrace; and Hrothgar's speech of advice to Beowulf (pp. 45–46) seems to reflect patristic doctrine in its emphasis on conscience and the devil's lying in wait for the unwary. Yet there is no reference to the New Testament—to Christ and His Sacrifice, which are the real bases of Christianity in any intelligible sense of the term. Furthermore, readers may well feel that the poem achieves rather little of its emotional power through any direct invocation of Christian values or of values that are consonant with Christian doctrine as we know it. Perhaps the sense of tragic waste that pervades the Finnsburg episode (pp. 37–38) springs from a Christian perception of the insane futility of the primitive Germanic thirst for vengeance; and the facts that Beowulf's chief adversaries are not men but monsters and that before his death he is able to boast that as king of the Geats he did not seek wars with neighboring tribes may reflect a Christian's appreciation for peace among humans. But while admitting such values, the poet also invokes many others of a very different order, values that seem to belong to an ancient, pagan, warrior society of the kind described by the Roman historian Tacitus at the end of the first century. It should be noted that even Hrothgar's speech about conscience is directed more toward making Beowulf a good Germanic leader than a good Christian. One must, indeed, draw the conclusion from the poem itself that although *Christian* is a correct term for the religion of the poet and of his audience, it was a Christianity that had not yet by any means succeeded in obliterating an older pagan tradition, which still called forth powerful responses from the hearts of men and women, despite the fact that many aspects of this tradition must be abhorrent to a sophisticated Christian. In this connection it is well to recall that the missionaries from Rome who initiated the conversion of the English proceeded in a conciliatory manner, not so much uprooting paganism in order to plant Christianity as planting Christianity in the faith that it would ultimately choke out the weeds of paganism. And the English clung long to some of their ancient traditions. For instance, the legal principle of the payment of *wergild* (defined below) remained in force until the Norman Conquest, four centuries after the conversion of the English.

In the warrior society, the values of which the poem constantly invokes, the most important of human relationships was that which existed between the warrior—the thane—and his lord, a relationship based less on subordination of one man's will to another's than on mutual trust and respect. When a warrior vowed loyalty to his lord, he became not so much his servant as his voluntary companion, one who would take pride in defending him and fighting in his wars. In return, the lord was expected to take affectionate care of his thanes and to reward them richly for their valor; a good king, one like Hrothgar or Beowulf, is referred to by such poetic epithets as "protector of warriors" and "dispenser of treasure" or "ring giver," and the failure of bad kings is ascribed to their ill-temper and avarice, both of which alienate them from their retainers. The material benefit of this arrangement between lord and thane is obvious, yet under a good king the relationship seems to have had a significance more spiritual than material. Thus the treasure that an ideal Germanic king seizes from his enemies and rewards his retainers with is regarded as something more than mere wealth that will serve the well-being of its possessor; rather, it is a kind of visible proof that all parties are realizing themselves to the full in a spiritual sense—that the men of this band are congenially and successfully united with one another. The symbolic importance of treasure is illustrated by the poet's remark that the gift Beowulf gave the Danish coast guard brought the latter honor among his companions, and even more by the fact that although Beowulf dies while obtaining a great treasure for his people, such objects as are removed from the dragon's hoard are actually buried with him as a fitting sign of his ultimate achievement.

The relationship between kinsmen was also of deep significance to this society and provides another emotional value for Old English heroic poetry. If one of his kinsmen had been slain, a man had the special duty of either killing the slayer or exacting from him the payment of *wergild* ("manprice"). Each rank of society was evaluated at a definite price, which had to be paid to the dead man's kinsmen by the killer who wished to avoid their vengeance—even if the killing had been accidental. Again, the money itself had less significance as wealth than as a proof that the kinsmen had done what was right. Relatives who failed either to exact *wergild* or to take vengeance could never be happy, having found no practical way of satisfying their grief for their kinsman's death. "It is better for a man to avenge his friend than much mourn," Beowulf says to the old Hrothgar, who is bewailing Aeschere's killing by Grendel's mother. And one of the most poignant passages in the poem describes the sorrow of King Hrethel after one of his sons had accidentally killed another; by the code of kinship Hrethel was forbidden to kill or to exact compensation from a kinsman, yet by the same code he was required to do one or the other to avenge the dead. Caught in this curious dilemma, Hrethel became so disconsolate that he could no longer face life.

It is evident that the need to take vengeance would create never-ending feuds, which the practice of marrying royal princesses to the kings or princes of hostile tribes did little to mitigate, although the purpose of such marriages was to replace hostility by alliance. Hrothgar wishes to make peace with the Heatho-Bards by marrying his daughter to their king, Ingeld, whose father was killed by the Danes, but as Beowulf predicts, sooner or later the Heatho-Bards' desire for vengeance on the Danes will erupt, and there will be more bloodshed. And the Danish princess Hildeburh, married to Finn of the Jutes, will see her son and her brother both killed while fighting on opposite sides in a battle at her own home and, ultimately, will see her husband killed by the Danes in revenge for her brother's death. Beowulf himself is, for a Germanic hero, curiously free of involvement in feuds of this sort, although he does boast that he avenged the death of his king, Heardred, on his slayer, Onela. Yet the potentiality—or inevitability—of sudden attack, sudden change, swift death is omnipresent in *Beowulf*; men seem to be caught in a vast web of reprisals and counterreprisals from which there is little hope of escape. This is the aspect of the poem that is apt to make the most powerful impression on the reader—its strong sense of doom.

Beowulf himself is chiefly concerned not with tribal feuds but with fatal evil both less and more complex. Grendel and the dragon are threats to the security of the lands they infest just as human enemies would be, but they are not part of the social order and presumably have no one to avenge their deaths (that Grendel's mother appeared as an avenger seems to have been a surprise both to Beowulf and to the Danes). On the other hand, because they are outside the normal order of things, they require of their conqueror something greater than normal warfare requires. In each case, it is the clear duty of the king and his companions to put down the evil. But the Danish Hrothgar is old and his companions unenterprising, and excellent though Hrothgar has been in the kingship, he nevertheless lacks the quality that later impels the old Beowulf to fight the dragon that threatens his people. The poem makes no criticism of Hrothgar for this lack; he merely seems not to be the kind of man—one might almost say he was not fated—to develop his human potential to the fullest extent that Fate would permit; that is Beowulf's role. In undertaking to slay Grendel, and later Grendel's mother, Beowulf is testing his relationship with unknowable destiny. At any time, as he is fully aware, his luck may abandon him and he may be killed, as, indeed, he is in the otherwise successful encounter with the dragon. But whether he lives or dies, he will have done all that any man could do to develop his character heroically. It is this consciousness of testing Fate that probably explains the boasting that modern readers of heroic poetry often find offensive. When he boasts, Beowulf not only is demonstrating that he has chosen the heroic way of life but is also choosing it, because when he invokes his former courage as pledge of his future courage, his boast becomes a vow; the hero has put himself in a position from which he cannot withdraw.

Courage is the instrument by which the hero realizes himself. "Fate often saves an undoomed man when his courage is good," says Beowulf in his account of his swimming match; that is, if Fate has not entirely doomed a man in advance, courage is the quality that can perhaps influence Fate against its natural tendency to doom him now. It is this complex statement (in which it is hard to read "the will of God" for *Fate*) that Beowulf's life explores; he will use his great strength in the most courageous way by going alone, even unarmed, against monsters. Doom, of course, ultimately claims him, but not until he has fulfilled to its limits the pagan ideal of a heroic life. And despite the desire he often shows to Christianize pagan virtues, the Christian poet remains true to the older tradition when, at the end of his poem, he leaves us with the impression that Beowulf's chief reward is pagan immortality: the memory in the minds of later generations of a hero's heroic actions. The poem itself is, indeed, a noble expression of that immortality.

TRIBES AND GENEALOGIES

1. *The Danes (Bright-, Half-, Ring-, Spear-, North-, East-, South-, West-Danes; Scyldings, Honor-, Victor-, War-Scyldings; Ing's friends).*

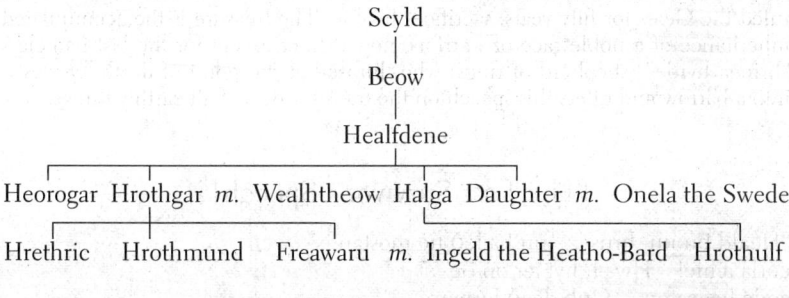

Scyld
|
Beow
|
Healfdene
|
Heorogar Hrothgar *m.* Wealhtheow Halga Daughter *m.* Onela the Swede

Hrethric Hrothmund Freawaru *m.* Ingeld the Heatho-Bard Hrothulf

2. *The Geats (Sea-, War-, Weather-Geats).*

Hrethel
|
Herebeald Haethcyn Hygelae *m.* Hygd Daughter *m.* Ecgtheow

Heardred Daughter* *m.* Eofor Beowulf the Geat

3. *The Swedes.*

Ongentheow
|
Ohthere Onela *m.* Healfdene's Daughter

Eanmund Eadgils

* The daughter of Hygelac who was given to Eofor may have been born to him by a former wife, older than Hygd.

4. *Miscellaneous.*

A. The Half-Danes (also called Scyldings) involved in the fight at Finns-burg may represent a different tribe from the Danes described above. Their king Hoc had a son, Hnaef, who succeeded him, and a daughter Hildeburh, who married Finn, king of the Jutes.

B. The Jutes or Frisians are represented as enemies of the Danes in the fight at Finnsburg and as allies of the Franks or Hugas at the time Hygelac the Geat made the attack in which he lost his life and from which Beowulf swam home. Also allied with the Franks at this time were the Hetware.

C. The Heatho-Bards (i.e., "Battle-Bards") are represented as inveterate enemies of the Danes. Their king, Froda, had been killed in an attack on the Danes, and Hrothgar's attempt to make peace with them by marrying his daughter Freawaru to Froda's son Ingeld failed when the latter attacked Heorot. The attack was repulsed, although Heorot was burned.

The Last Survivor's Speech in Old English with Verse Translation

To give the reader a sample of the language, style, and texture of *Beowulf* we print the following passage in the original followed by a verse translation that attempts to convey the terseness and strong beat of the alliterative measure, although to observe the strict rules of classical Old English alliterative verse is hardly possible in modern idiom. The famous passage comes late in the poem (pp. 52–53). It tells the history of the dragon's hoard for which Beowulf, now an old king who has ruled the Geats for fifty years, sacrifices his life. The treasure is the accumulated inheritance of a noble race of warriors, now extinct except for the last nameless "hringa hyrde" (shepherd of rings) who, himself at the point of death, carries it into a barrow and utters this speech on the transitoriness of all earthly things.

[The Last Survivor's Speech][1]

"Heald þu nu, hruse,   nu hæleð ne mostan,
eorla æhte!   Hwæt, hyt ær on ðe
gode begeaton.   Guþ-deað fornam,
feorh-bealo frecne   fyra gehwylcne   2250
leoda minra,   þara ðe þis lif ofgeaf,
gesawon sele-dreamas.   Nah hwa sweord wege
oððe feormie   fæted wæge,
drync-fæt deore;   duguð ellor scoc.
Sceal se hearda helm   hyrsted golde   2255
fætum befeallen;   feormynd swefað,
þa ðe beado-griman   bywan sceoldon;
ge swylce seo here-pad,   sio æt hilde gebad
ofer borda gebræc   bite irena,
brosnað æfter beorne;   ne mæg byrnan hring   2260
æfter wig-fruman   wide feran
hæleðum be healfe.   Næs hearpan wyn
gomen gleo-beames,   ne god hafoc
geond sæl swingeð,   ne se swifta mearh
burh-stede beateð.   Bealo-cwealm hafað   2265
fela feorh-cynna   forð onsended!"

1. The verse translation is by Alfred David.

"Hold thou now, Earth,   now hand of man cannot,
A great tribe's treasures.   Truly, from thee
Brave men first got them;   battle-death has taken,
Murderous fighting,   the men, one and all,   2250
Peers of my people: they have passed from this life,
Rest from hall-joys.   None remains with me
To bear the sword,   burnish the rich goblet,
Costly drinking-cup;   the company has gone elsewhere.
Now the hard helmet,   hammered with gold,   2255
Must be stripped of its plating;   the polishers sleep
Who once made bright   those grim battle-masks;
Also the armor,   which endured in battle,
Mid breaking of shields,   the bite of swords,
Rots with the warrior.   The ringed-corslet   2260
May not wander far   on the war-chief's path,
At the soldiers' side.   The harp is silent,
No glad music sounds,   nor any good hawk
Sweeps through the hall,   nor swift hoofbeats
Drum in the courtyard.   Death-qualm has sent   2265
Full many a folk   forth on their way."

Beowulf[1]

[Prologue: The Earlier History of the Danes]

Yes, we have heard of the glory of the Spear-Danes' kings in the old days—
how the princes of that people did brave deeds.

Often Scyld Scefing[2] took mead-benches away from enemy bands, from
many tribes, terrified their nobles—after the time that he was first found destitute. He lived to find comfort for that, became great under the skies, prospered
in honors until every one of those who lived about him, across the whale-road,
had to obey him, pay him tribute. That was a good king.

Afterwards a son was born to him, a young boy in his house, whom God
sent to comfort the people: He had seen the sore need they had suffered
during the long time they lacked a king. Therefore the Lord of Life, the Ruler
of Heaven, gave him honor in the world: Beow[3] was famous, the glory of the
son of Scyld spread widely in the Northlands. In this way a young man ought
by his good deeds, by giving splendid gifts while still in his father's house, to
make sure that later in life beloved companions will stand by him, that people
will serve him when war comes. Through deeds that bring praise, a man shall
prosper in every country.

Then at the fated time Scyld the courageous went away into the protection
of the Lord. His dear companions carried him down to the sea-currents, just
as he himself had bidden them do when, as protector of the Scyldings,[4] he

---

1. The translation into modern English, by E. T. Donaldson (1966), is based on F. Klaeber's 3rd ed. of the
poem (1950); in general, the emendations suggested
by J. C. Pope, *The Rhythm of Beowulf*, 2nd ed. (1966),
have been adopted.
2. The meaning is probably "son of Sceaf," although
Scyld's origins are mysterious.
3. Although the manuscript reads "Beowulf," most
scholars now agree it should read "Beow." Beow was
the grandfather of Danish King Hrothgar.
4. I.e., the Danes ("descendants of Scyld").

had ruled them with his words—long had the beloved prince governed the land. There in the harbor stood the ring-prowed ship, ice-covered and ready to sail, a prince's vessel. Then they laid down the ruler they had loved, the ring-giver, in the hollow of the ship, the glorious man beside the mast. There was brought great store of treasure, wealth from lands far away. I have not heard of a ship more splendidly furnished with war-weapons and battle-dress, swords and mail-shirts. On his breast lay a great many treasures that should voyage with him far out into the sea's possession. They provided him with no lesser gifts, treasure of the people, than those had done who at his beginning first sent him forth on the waves, a child alone.[5] Then also they set a golden standard high over his head, let the water take him, gave him to the sea. Sad was their spirit, mournful their mind. Men cannot truthfully say who received that cargo, neither counsellors in the hall nor warriors under the skies.

Then in the cities was Beow of the Scyldings beloved king of the people, long famous among nations (his father had gone elsewhere, the king from his land), until later great Healfdene was born to him. As long as he lived, old and fierce in battle, he upheld the glorious Scyldings. To him all told were four children born into the world, to the leader of the armies: Heorogar and Hrothgar and the good Halga. I have heard tell that [. . . was On]ela's queen,[6] beloved bed-companion of the Battle-Scylfing.

[Beowulf and Grendel]

[THE HALL HEOROT IS ATTACKED BY GRENDEL]

Then Hrothgar was given success in warfare, glory in battle, so that his retainers gladly obeyed him and their company grew into a great band of warriors. It came to his mind that he would command men to construct a hall, a great mead-building that the children of men should hear of forever, and therein he would give to young and old all that God had given him, except for common land and men's bodies.[7] Then I have heard that the work was laid upon many nations, wide through this middle-earth, that they should adorn the folk-hall. In time it came to pass—quickly, as men count it—that it was finished, the largest of hall-dwellings. He gave it the name of Heorot,[8] he who ruled wide with his words. He did not forget his promise: at the feast he gave out rings, treasure. The hall stood tall, high and wide-gabled: it would wait for the fierce flames of vengeful fire;[9] the time was not yet at hand for sword-hate between son-in-law and father-in-law to awaken after murderous rage.

Then the fierce spirit[1] painfully endured hardship for a time, he who dwelt in the darkness, for every day he heard loud mirth in the hall; there was the sound of the harp, the clear song of the scop.[2] There he spoke who could relate the beginning of men far back in time, said that the Almighty made earth, a bright field fair in the water that surrounds it, set up in triumph the

---

5. In view of the fact that Scyld was said to have arrived destitute, this statement should probably be taken as a kind of curious understatement emphasizing the reversal in Scyld's fortunes.
6. The text is faulty, so that the name of Healfdene's daughter has been lost; her husband, Onela, was a Swedish (Scylfing) king.
7. Or "men's lives." Apparently slaves, along with public land, were not in the king's power to give away.

8. I.e., "Hart."
9. The destruction by fire of Heorot occurred at a later time than that of the poem's action, probably during the otherwise unsuccessful attack of the Heatho-Bard Ingeld on his father-in-law, Hrothgar, mentioned in the next clause.
1. I.e., Grendel.
2. The Anglo-Saxon minstrel, who recited poetic stories to the accompaniment of a harp.

lights of the sun and the moon to lighten land-dwellers, and adorned the surfaces of the earth with branches and leaves, created also life for each of the kinds that move and breathe.—Thus these warriors lived in joy, blessed, until one began to do evil deeds, a hellish enemy. The grim spirit was called Grendel, known as a rover of the borders, one who held the moors, fen and fastness. Unhappy creature, he lived for a time in the home of the monsters' race, after God had condemned them as kin of Cain. The Eternal Lord avenged the murder in which he slew Abel. Cain had no pleasure in that feud, but He banished him far from mankind, the Ruler, for that misdeed. From him sprang all bad breeds, trolls and elves and monsters—likewise the giants who for a long time strove with God: He paid them their reward for that.

Then, after night came, Grendel went to survey the tall house—how, after their beer-drinking, the Ring-Danes had disposed themselves in it. Then he found therein a band of nobles asleep after the feast: they felt no sorrow, no misery of men. The creature of evil, grim and fierce, was quickly ready, savage and cruel, and seized from their rest thirty thanes. From there he turned to go back to his home, proud of his plunder, sought his dwelling with that store of slaughter.

Then in the first light of dawning day Grendel's war-strength was revealed to men: then after the feast weeping arose, great cry in the morning. The famous king, hero of old days, sat joyless; the mighty one suffered, felt sorrow for his thanes, when they saw the track of the foe, of the cursed spirit: that hardship was too strong, too loathsome and long-lasting. Nor was there a longer interval, but after one night Grendel again did greater slaughter—and had no remorse for it—vengeful acts and wicked: he was too intent on them. Thereafter it was easy to find the man who sought rest for himself elsewhere, farther away, a bed among the outlying buildings—after it was made clear to him, told by clear proof, the hatred of him who now controlled the hall.[3] Whoever escaped the foe held himself afterwards farther off and more safely. Thus Grendel held sway and fought against right, one against all, until the best of houses stood empty. It was a long time, the length of twelve winters, that the lord of the Scyldings suffered grief, all woes, great sorrows. Therefore, sadly in songs, it became well-known to the children of men that Grendel had fought a long time with Hrothgar, for many half-years maintained mortal spite, feud, and enmity—constant war. He wanted no peace with any of the men of the Danish host, would not withdraw his deadly rancor, or pay compensation: no counselor there had any reason to expect splendid repayment at the hands of the slayer.[4] For the monster was relentless, the dark death-shadow, against warriors old and young, lay in wait and ambushed them. In the perpetual darkness he held to the misty moors: men do not know where hell-demons direct their footsteps.

Thus many crimes the enemy of mankind committed, the terrible walker-alone, cruel injuries one after another. In the dark nights he dwelt in Heorot, the richly adorned hall. He might not approach the throne, [receive] treasure, because of the Lord; He had no love for him.[5]

3. I.e., Grendel.
4. According to old Germanic law, a slayer could achieve peace with his victim's kinsmen only by paying them *wergild*, i.e., compensation for the life of the slain man.

5. Behind this obscure passage seems to lie the idea that Grendel, unlike Hrothgar's thanes, could not approach the throne to receive gifts from the king, having been condemned by God as an outlaw.

This was great misery to the lord of the Scyldings, a breaking of spirit. Many a noble sat often in council, sought a plan, what would be best for strong-hearted men to do against the awful attacks. At times they vowed sacrifices at heathen temples, with their words prayed that the soul-slayer[6] would give help for the distress of the people. Such was their custom, the hope of heathens; in their spirits they thought of Hell, they knew not the Ruler, the Judge of Deeds, they recognized not the Lord God, nor indeed did they know how to praise the Protector of Heaven, the glorious King. Woe is him who in terrible trouble must thrust his soul into the fire's embrace, hope for no comfort, not expect change. Well is the man who after his death-day may seek the Lord and find peace in the embrace of the Father.

[THE COMING OF BEOWULF TO HEOROT]

So in the cares of his times the son of Healfdene constantly brooded, nor might the wise warrior set aside his woe. Too harsh, hateful and long-lasting was the hardship that had come upon the people, distress dire and inexorable, worst of night-horrors.

A thane of Hygelac,[7] a good man among the Geats, heard in his homeland of Grendel's deeds: of mankind he was the strongest of might in the time of this life, noble and great. He bade that a good ship be made ready for him, said he would seek the war-king over the swan's road, the famous prince, since he had need of men. Very little did wise men blame him for that adventure, though he was dear to them; they urged the brave one on, examined the omens. From the folk of the Geats the good man had chosen warriors of the bravest that he could find; one of fifteen he led the way, the warrior sought the wooden ship, the sea-skilled one the land's edge. The time had come: the ship was on the waves, the boat under the cliff. The warriors eagerly climbed on the prow—the sea-currents eddied, sea against sand; men bore bright weapons into the ship's bosom, splendid armor. Men pushed the well-braced ship from shore, warriors on a well-wished voyage. Then over the sea-waves, blown by the wind, the foam-necked boat traveled, most like a bird, until at good time on the second day the curved prow had come to where the seafarers could see land, the sea-cliffs shine, towering hills, great headlands. Then was the sea crossed, the journey at end. Then quickly the men of the Geats climbed upon the shore, moored the wooden ship; mail-shirts rattled, dress for battle. They thanked God that the wave-way had been easy for them.

Then from the wall the Scyldings' guard who should watch over the sea-cliffs saw bright shields borne over the gangway, armor ready for battle; strong desire stirred him in mind to learn what the men were. He went riding on his horse to the shore, thane of Hrothgar, forcefully brandished a great spear in his hands, with formal words questioned them: "What are you, bearers of armor, dressed in mail-coats, who thus have come bringing a tall ship over the sea-road, over the water to this place? Lo, for a long time I have been guard of the coast, held watch by the sea so that no foe with a force of ships might work harm on the Danes' land: never have shieldbearers more openly undertaken to come ashore here; nor did you know for sure of a word of leave from our

---

6. I.e., the devil. It was believed that pagan deities were actually devils. 7. I.e., Beowulf the Geat, whose king was Hygelac.

warriors, consent from my kinsmen. I have never seen a mightier warrior on
earth than is one of you, a man in battle-dress. That is no retainer made to
seem good by his weapons—may his appearance, his unequalled form, never
belie him. Now I must learn your lineage before you go any farther from here,
spies on the Danes' land. Now you far-dwellers, sea-voyagers, hear what I
think: you must straightway say where you have come from."

To him replied the leader, the chief of the band unlocked his word-hoard:
"We are men of the Geatish nation and Hygelac's hearth-companions. My
father was well-known among the tribes, a noble leader named Ecgtheow. He
lived many winters before he went on his way, an old man, from men's dwellings. Every wise man wide over the earth readily remembers him. Through
friendly heart we have come to seek your lord, the son of Healfdene, protector
of the people. Be good to us and tell us what to do: we have a great errand to
the famous one, the king of the Danes. And I too do not think that anything
ought to be kept secret: you know whether it is so, as we have indeed heard,
that among the Scyldings I know not what foe, what dark doer of hateful
deeds in the black nights, shows in terrible manner strange malice, injury and
slaughter. In openness of heart I may teach Hrothgar remedy for that, how he,
wise and good, shall overpower the foe—if change is ever to come to him,
relief from evil's distress—and how his surging cares may be made to cool. Or
else ever after he will suffer tribulations, constraint, while the best of houses
remains there on its high place."

The guard spoke from where he sat on his horse, brave officer: "A sharp-
witted shield-warrior who thinks well must be able to judge each of the two
things, words and works. I understand this: that here is a troop friendly to the
Scyldings' king. Go forward, bearing weapons and war-gear. I will show you
the way; I shall also bid my fellow-thanes honorably to hold your boat against
all enemies, your new-tarred ship on the sand, until again over the sea-streams
it bears its beloved men to the Geatish shore, the wooden vessel with curved
prow. May it be granted by fate that one who behaves so bravely pass whole
through the battle-storm."

Then they set off. The boat lay fixed, rested on the rope, the deep-bosomed
ship, fast at anchor. Boar-images[8] shone over cheek-guards gold-adorned,
gleaming and fire-hardened—the war-minded boar held guard over fierce
men. The warriors hastened, marched together until they might see the tim-
bered hall, stately and shining with gold; for earth-dwellers under the skies
that was the most famous of buildings in which the mighty one waited—its
light gleamed over many lands. The battle-brave guide pointed out to them
the shining house of the brave ones so that they might go straight to it. War-
rior-like he turned his horse, then spoke words: "It is time for me to go back.
The All-Wielding Father in His grace keep you safe in your undertakings. I
shall go back to the sea to keep watch against hostile hosts."

The road was stone-paved, the path showed the way to the men in ranks.
War-corselet shone, hard and hand-wrought, bright iron rings sang on their
armor when they first came walking to the hall in their grim gear. Sea-weary
they set down their broad shields, marvelously strong protections, against the
wall of the building. Then they sat down on the bench—mail-shirts, warrior's

8. Carved images of boars (sometimes represented as clothed like human warriors) were placed on helmets in the
belief that they would protect the wearer in battle.

clothing, rang out. Spears stood together, seamen's weapons, ash steel-gray at the top. The armed band was worthy of its weapons.

Then a proud-spirited man[9] asked the warriors there about their lineage: "Where do you bring those gold-covered shields from, gray mail-shirts and visored helmets, this multitude of battle-shafts? I am Hrothgar's herald and officer. I have not seen strangers—so many men—more bold. I think that it is for daring—not for refuge, but for greatness of heart—that you have sought Hrothgar." The man known for his courage replied to him; the proud man of the Geats, hardy under helmet, spoke words in return: "We are Hygelac's table-companions. Beowulf is my name. I will tell my errand to Healfdene's son, the great prince your lord, if, good as he is, he will grant that we might address him." Wulfgar spoke—he was a man of the Wendels, his bold spirit known to many, his valor and wisdom: "I will ask the lord of the Danes about this, the Scyldings' king, the ring-giver, just as you request—will ask the glorious ruler about your voyage, and will quickly make known to you the answer the good man thinks best to give me."

He returned at once to where Hrothgar sat, old and hoary, with his company of earls. The man known for his valor went forward till he stood squarely before the Danes' king: he knew the custom of tried retainers. Wulfgar spoke to his lord and friend: "Here have journeyed men of the Geats, come far over the sea's expanse. The warriors call their chief Beowulf. They ask that they, my prince, might exchange words with you. Do not refuse them your answer, gracious Hrothgar. From their wargear they seem worthy of earls' esteem. Strong indeed is the chief who has led the warriors here."

Hrothgar spoke, protector of the Scyldings: "I knew him when he was a boy His father was called Ecgtheow: Hrethel of the Geats[1] gave him his only daughter for his home. Now has his hardy offspring come here, sought a fast friend. Then, too, seafarers who took gifts there to please the Geats used to say that he has in his handgrip the strength of thirty men, a man famous in battle. Holy God of His grace has sent him to us West-Danes, as I hope, against the terror of Grendel. I shall offer the good man treasures for his daring. Now make haste, bid them come in together to see my company of kinsmen. In your speech say to them also that they are welcome to the Danish people."

Then Wulfgar went to the hall's door, gave the message from within: "The lord of the East-Danes, my victorious prince, has bidden me say to you that he knows your noble ancestry, and that you brave-hearted men are welcome to him over the sea-swells. Now you may come in your war-dress, under your battle helmets, to see Hrothgar. Let your war-shields, your wooden spears, await here the outcome of the talk."

Then the mighty one rose, many a warrior about him, a company of strong thanes. Some waited there, kept watch over the weapons as the brave one bade them. Together they hastened, as the warrior directed them, under Heorot's roof. The war-leader, hardy under helmet, advanced till he stood on the hearth. Beowulf spoke, his mail-shirt glistened, armor-net woven by the blacksmith's skill: "Hail, Hrothgar! I am kinsman and thane of Hygelac. In my youth I have set about many brave deeds. The affair of Grendel was made known to me on my native soil: sea-travelers say that this hall, best of buildings,

9. Identified below as Wulfgar.
1. Hrethel was the father of Hygelac and Beowulf's grandfather and guardian.

stands empty and useless to all warriors after the evening-light becomes hidden
beneath the cover of the sky. Therefore my people, the best wise earls, advised
me thus, lord Hrothgar, that I should seek you because they know what my
strength can accomplish. They themselves looked on when, bloody from my
foes, I came from the fight where I had bound five, destroyed a family of
giants, and at night in the waves slain water-monsters, suffered great pain,
avenged an affliction of the Weather-Geats on those who had asked for trouble—ground enemies to bits. And now alone I shall settle affairs with Grendel,
the monster, the demon. Therefore, lord of the Bright-Danes, protector of the
Scyldings, I will make a request of you, refuge of warriors, fair friend of
nations, that you refuse me not, now that I have come so far, that alone with
my company of earls, this band of hardy men, I may cleanse Heorot. I have
also heard say that the monster in his recklessness cares not for weapons.
Therefore, so that my liege lord Hygelac may be glad of me in his heart, I
scorn to bear sword or broad shield, yellow wood, to the battle, but with my
grasp I shall grapple with the enemy and fight for life, foe against foe. The one
whom death takes can trust the Lord's judgment. I think that if he may accomplish it, unafraid he will feed on the folk of the Geats in the war-hall as he has
often done on the flower of men. You will not need to hide my head[2] if death
takes me, for he will have me blood-smeared; he will bear away my bloody
flesh meaning to savor it, he will eat ruthlessly, the walker alone, will stain his
retreat in the moor; no longer will you need trouble yourself to take care of
my body. If battle takes me, send to Hygelac the best of war-clothes that protects my breast, finest of mail-shirts. It is a legacy of Hrethel, the work of
Weland.[3] Fate always goes as it must."

   Hrothgar spoke, protector of the Scyldings: "For deeds done, my friend
Beowulf, and for past favors you have sought us. A fight of your father's
brought on the greatest of feuds. With his own hands he became the slayer of
Heatholaf among the Wylfings. After that the country of the Weather-Geats
might not keep him, for fear of war. From there he sought the folk of the
South-Danes, the Honor-Scyldings, over the sea-swell. At that time I was first
ruling the Danish people and, still in my youth, held the wide kingdom,
hoard-city of heroes. Heorogar had died then, gone from life, my older
brother, son of Healfdene—he was better than I. Afterwards I paid blood-
money to end the feud; over the sea's back I sent to the Wylfings old treasures;
he[4] swore oaths to me.

   "It is a sorrow to me in spirit to say to any man what Grendel has brought
me with his hatred—humiliation in Heorot, terrible violence. My hall-troop,
warrior-band, has shrunk; fate has swept them away into Grendel's horror.
(God may easily put an end to the wild ravager's deeds!) Full often over the
ale-cups warriors made bold with beer have boasted that they would await with
grim swords Grendel's attack in the beer-hall. Then in the morning this mead-
hall was a hall shining with blood, when the day lightened, all the bench-floor
blood-wet, a gore-hall. I had fewer faithful men, beloved retainers, for death
had destroyed them. Now sit down to the feast and unbind your thoughts,
your famous victories, as heart inclines."

2. I.e., "bury my body."   4. Ecgtheow, whose feud with the Wylfings Hrothgar
3. The blacksmith of the Norse gods.   had settled.

[THE FEAST AT HEOROT]

Then was a bench cleared in the beer-hall for the men of the Geats all together. Then the stout-hearted ones went to sit down, proud in their might. A thane did his work who bore in his hands an embellished ale-cup, poured the bright drink. At times a scop sang, clear-voiced in Heorot. There was joy of brave men, no little company of Danes and Weather-Geats.

Unferth spoke, son of Ecglaf, who sat at the feet of the king of the Scyldings, unbound words of contention—to him was Beowulf's undertaking, the brave seafarer, a great vexation, for he would not allow that any other man of middle-earth should ever achieve more glory under the heavens than himself: "Are you that Beowulf who contended with Breca, competed in swimming on the broad sea, where for pride you explored the water, and for foolish boast ventured your lives in the deep? Nor might any man, friend nor enemy, keep you from the perilous venture of swimming in the sea. There you embraced the sea-streams with your arms, measured the sea-ways, flung forward your hands, glided over the ocean; the sea boiled with waves, with winter's swell. Seven nights you toiled in the water's power. He overcame you at swimming, had more strength. Then in the morning the sea bore him up among the Heatho-raemas; from there he sought his own home, dear to his people, the land of the Brondings, the fair stronghold, where he had folk, castle, and treasures. All his boast against you the son of Beanstan carried out in deed. Therefore I expect the worse results for you—though you have prevailed everywhere in battles, in grim war—if you dare wait near Grendel a night-long space."

Beowulf spoke, the son of Ecgtheow: "Well, my friend Unferth, drunk with beer you have spoken a great many things about Breca—told about his adventures. I maintain the truth that I had more strength in the sea, hardship on the waves, than any other man. Like boys we agreed together and boasted—we were both in our first youth—that we would risk our lives in the salt sea, and that we did even so. We had naked swords, strong in our hands, when we went swimming; we thought to guard ourselves against whale-fishes. He could not swim at all far from me in the flood-waves, be quicker in the water, nor would I move away from him. Thus we were together on the sea for the time of five nights until the flood drove us apart, the swelling sea, coldest of weathers, darkening night, and the north wind battle-grim turned against us: rough were the waves. The anger of the sea-fishes was roused. Then my body-mail, hard and hand-linked, gave me help against my foes; the woven war-garment, gold-adorned, covered my breast. A fierce cruel attacker dragged me to the bottom, held me grim in his grasp, but it was granted me to reach the monster with my sword-point, my battle-blade. The war-stroke destroyed the mighty sea-beast—through my hand.

"Thus often loathsome assailants pressed me hard. I served them with my good sword, as the right was. They had no joy at all of the feast, the malice-workers, that they should eat me, sit around a banquet near the sea-bottom. But in the morning, sword-wounded they lay on the shore, left behind by the waves, put to sleep by the blade, so that thereafter they would never hinder the passage of sea-voyagers over the deep water. Light came from the east, bright signal of God, the sea became still so that I might see the headlands, the windy walls of the sea. Fate often saves an undoomed man when his courage is good. In any case it befell me that I slew with my sword nine sea-monsters. I have not heard tell of a harder fight by night under heaven's arch, nor of a man more hard-pressed in the sea-streams. Yet I came out of the enemies' grasp alive, weary of my adventure. Then the sea bore me onto the lands of the Finns, the flood with its current, the surging waters.

"I have not heard say of you any such hard matching of might, such sword-terror. Breca never yet in the games of war—neither he nor you—achieved so bold a deed with bright swords (I do not much boast of it), though you became your brothers' slayer, your close kin; for that you will suffer punishment in hell, even though your wit is keen. I tell you truly, son of Ecglaf, that Grendel, awful monster, would never have performed so many terrible deeds against your chief, humiliation in Heorot, if your spirit, your heart, were so fierce in fight as you claim. But he has noticed that he need not much fear the hostility, not much dread the terrible sword-storm of your people, the Victory-Scyld-ings. He exacts forced levy, shows mercy to none of the Danish people; but he is glad, kills, carves for feasting, expects no fight from the Spear-Danes. But I shall show him soon now the strength and courage of the Geats, their war-fare. Afterwards he will walk who may, glad to the mead, when the morning light of another day, the bright-clothed sun, shines from the south on the children of men."

Then was the giver of treasure in gladness, gray-haired and battle-brave. The lord of the Bright-Danes could count on help. The folk's guardian had heard from Beowulf a fast-resolved thought.

There was laughter of warriors, voices rang pleasant, words were cheerful. Wealhtheow came forth, Hrothgar's queen, mindful of customs, gold-adorned, greeted the men in the hall; and the noble woman offered the cup first to the keeper of the land of the East-Danes, bade him be glad at the beer-drinking, beloved of the people. In joy he partook of feast and hall-cup, king famous for victories. Then the woman of the Helmings went about to each one of the retainers, young and old, offered them the costly cup, until the time came that she brought the mead-bowl to Beowulf, the ring-adorned queen, mature of mind. Sure of speech she greeted the man of the Geats, thanked God that her wish was fulfilled, that she might trust in some man for help against deadly deeds. He took the cup, the warrior fierce in battle, from Wealhtheow, and then spoke, one ready for fight—Beowulf spoke, the son of Ecgtheow: "I resolved, when I set out on the sea, sat down in the sea-boat with my band of men, that I should altogether fulfill the will of your people or else fall in slaughter, fast in the foe's grasp. I shall achieve a deed of manly courage or else have lived to see in this mead-hall my ending day." These words were well-pleasing to the woman, the boast of the Geat. Gold-adorned, the noble folk-queen went to sit by her lord.

Then there were again as at first strong words spoken in the hall, the people in gladness, the sound of a victorious folk, until, in a little while, the son of Healfdene wished to seek his evening rest. He knew of the battle in the high hall that had been plotted by the monster, plotted from the time that they might see the light of the sun until the night, growing dark over all things, the shadowy shapes of darkness, should come gliding, black under the clouds. The company all arose. Then they saluted each other, Hrothgar and Beowulf, and Hrothgar wished him good luck, control of the wine-hall, and spoke these words: "Never before, since I could raise hand and shield, have I entrusted to any man the great hall of the Danes, except now to you. Hold now and guard the best of houses: remember your fame, show your great courage, keep watch against the fierce foe. You will not lack what you wish if you survive that deed of valor."

[THE FIGHT WITH GRENDEL]

Then Hrothgar went out of the hall with his company of warriors, the protector of the Scyldings. The war-chief would seek the bed of Wealhtheow the queen. The King of Glory—as men had learned—had appointed a hall-guard against Grendel; he had a special mission to the prince of the Danes: he kept watch against monsters.

And the man of the Geats had sure trust in his great might, the favor of the Ruler. Then he took off his shirt of armor, the helmet from his head, handed his embellished sword, best of irons, to an attendant, bade him keep guard over his war-gear. Then the good warrior spoke some boast-words before he went to his bed, Beowulf of the Geats: "I claim myself no poorer in war-strength, war works, than Grendel claims himself. Therefore I will not put him to sleep with a sword, so take away his life, though surely I might. He knows no good tools with which he might strike against me, cut my shield in pieces, though he is strong in fight. But we shall forgo the sword in the night— if he dare seek war without weapon—and then may wise God, Holy Lord, assign glory on whichever hand seems good to Him."

The battle-brave one laid himself down, the pillow received the earl's head, and about him many a brave seaman lay down to hall rest. None of them thought that he would ever again seek from there his dear home, people or town where he had been brought up; for they knew that bloody death had carried off far too many men in the wine-hall, folk of the Danes. But the Lord granted to weave for them good fortune in war, for the folk of the Weather-Geats, comfort and help that they should quite overcome their foe through the might of one man, through his sole strength: the truth has been made known that mighty God has always ruled mankind.

There came gliding in the black night the walker in darkness. The warriors slept who should hold the horned house—all but one. It was known to men that when the Ruler did not wish it the hostile creature might not drag them away beneath the shadows. But he, lying awake for the fierce foe, with heart swollen in anger awaited the outcome of the fight.

Then from the moor under the mist-hills Grendel came walking, wearing God's anger. The foul ravager thought to catch some one of mankind there in the high hall. Under the clouds he moved until he could see most clearly the wine-hall, treasure-house of men, shining with gold. That was not the first time that he had sought Hrothgar's home. Never before or since in his life-days did he find harder luck, hardier hall-thanes. The creature deprived of joy came walking to the hall. Quickly the door gave way, fastened with fire-forged bands, when he touched it with his hands. Driven by evil desire, swollen with rage, he tore it open, the hall's mouth. After that the foe at once stepped onto the shining floor, advanced angrily. From his eyes came a light not fair, most like a flame. He saw many men in the hall, a band of kinsmen all asleep together, a company of war-men. Then his heart laughed: dreadful monster, he thought that before the day came he would divide the life from the body

of every one of them, for there had come to him a hope of full-feasting. It was
not his fate that when that night was over he should feast on more of mankind.
The kinsman of Hygelac, mighty man, watched how the evil-doer would
make his quick onslaught. Nor did the monster mean to delay it, but, starting
his work, he suddenly seized a sleeping man, tore at him ravenously, bit into
his bone-locks, drank the blood from his veins, swallowed huge morsels;
quickly he had eaten all of the lifeless one, feet and hands. He stepped closer,
then felt with his arm for the brave-hearted man on the bed, reached out
towards him, the foe with his hand; at once in fierce response Beowulf seized
it and sat up, leaning on his own arm. Straightway the fosterer of crimes knew
that he had not encountered on middle-earth, anywhere in this world, a
harder hand-grip from another man. In mind he became frightened, in his
spirit: not for that might he escape the sooner. His heart was eager to get away,
he would flee to his hiding-place, seek his rabble of devils. What he met there
was not such as he had ever before met in the days of his life. Then the
kinsman of Hygelac, the good man, thought of his evening's speech, stood
upright and laid firm hold on him: his fingers cracked. The giant was pulling
away, the earl stepped forward. The notorious one thought to move farther
away, wherever he could, and flee his way from there to his fen-retreat; he
knew his fingers' power to be in a hateful grip. That was a painful journey that
the loathsome despoiler had made to Heorot. The retainers' hall rang with the
noise—terrible drink[5] for all the Danes, the house-dwellers, every brave man,
the earls. Both were enraged, fury-filled, the two who meant to control the
hall. The building resounded. Then was it much wonder that the wine-hall
withstood them joined in fierce fight, that it did not fall to the ground, the fair
earth-dwelling; but it was so firmly made fast with iron bands, both inside and
outside, joined by skillful smith-craft. There started from the floor—as I have
heard say—many a mead-bench, gold-adorned, when the furious ones fought.
No wise men of the Scyldings ever before thought that any men in any manner might break it down, splendid with bright horns, have skill to destroy it,
unless flame should embrace it, swallow it in fire. Noise rose up, sound strange
enough. Horrible fear came upon the North-Danes, upon every one of those
who heard the weeping from the wall, God's enemy sing his terrible song,
song without triumph—the hell-slave bewail his pain. There held him fast he
who of men was strongest of might in the days of this life.
    Not for anything would the protector of warriors let the murderous guest go
off alive: he did not consider his life-days of use to any of the nations. There
more than enough of Beowulf's earls drew swords, old heirlooms, wished to
protect the life of their dear lord, famous prince, however they might. They
did not know when they entered the fight, hardy-spirited warriors, and when
they thought to hew him on every side, to seek his soul, that not any of the
best of irons on earth, no war-sword, would touch the evil-doer: for with a
charm he had made victory-weapons useless, every sword-edge. His departure
to death from the time of this life was to be wretched; and the alien spirit was
to travel far off into the power of fiends. Then he who before had brought
trouble of heart to mankind, committed many crimes—he was at war with

5. The metaphor reflects the idea that the chief purpose of a hall such as Heorot was as a place for men to feast
in.

God—found that his body would do him no good, for the great-hearted kinsman of Hygelac had him by the hand. Each was hateful to the other alive.
The awful monster had lived to feel pain in his body, a huge wound in his
shoulder was exposed, his sinews sprang apart, his bone-locks broke. Glory in
battle was given to Beowulf. Grendel must flee from there, mortally sick, seek
his joyless home in the fen-slopes. He knew the more surely that his life's end
had come, the full number of his days. For all the Danes was their wish
fulfilled after the bloody fight. Thus he who had lately come from far off, wise
and stout-hearted, had purged Heorot, saved Hrothgar's house from affliction.
He rejoiced in his night's work, a deed to make famous his courage. The man
of the Geats had fulfilled his boast to the East-Danes; so too he had remedied
all the grief, the malice-caused sorrow that they had endured before, and had
had to suffer from harsh necessity, no small distress. That was clearly proved
when the battle-brave man set the hand up under the curved roof—the arm
and the shoulder: there all together was Grendel's grasp.

[CELEBRATION AT HEOROT]

   Then in the morning, as I have heard, there was many a warrior about the
gift-hall. Folk-chiefs came from far and near over the wide-stretching ways to
look on the wonder, the footprints of the foe. Nor did his going from life seem
sad to any of the men who saw the tracks of the one without glory—how,
weary-hearted, overcome with injuries, he moved on his way from there to the
mere[6] of the water-monsters with life-failing footsteps, death-doomed and in
flight. There the water was boiling with blood, the horrid surge of waves swirling, all mixed with hot gore, sword-blood. Doomed to die he had hidden,
then, bereft of joys, had laid down his life in his fen-refuge, his heathen soul:
there hell took him.
   From there old retainers—and many a young man, too—turned back in
their glad journey to ride from the mere, high-spirited on horseback, warriors
on steeds. There was Beowulf's fame spoken of; many a man said—and not
only once—that, south nor north, between the seas, over the wide earth, no
other man under the sky's expanse was better of those who bear shields, more
worthy of ruling. Yet they found no fault with their own dear lord, gracious
Hrothgar, for he was a good king. At times battle-famed men let their brown
horses gallop, let them race where the paths seemed fair, known for their
excellence. At times a thane of the king, a man skilled at telling adventures,
songs stored in his memory, who could recall many of the stories of the old
days, wrought a new tale in well-joined words; this man undertook with his art
to recite in turn Beowulf's exploit, and skillfully to tell an apt tale, to lend
words to it.
   He spoke everything that he had heard tell of Sigemund's valorous deeds,
many a strange thing, the strife of Waels's son,[7] his far journeys, feuds and
crimes, of which the children of men knew nothing—except for Fitela with
him, to whom he would tell everything, the uncle to his nephew, for they
were always friends in need in every fight. Many were the tribes of giants that
they had laid low with their swords. For Sigemund there sprang up after his
death-day no little glory—after he, hardy in war, had killed the dragon, keeper

---

6. Lake.   7. Waels was Sigemund's father.

of the treasure-hoard: under the hoary stone the prince's son had ventured alone, a daring deed, nor was Fitela with him. Yet it turned out well for him, so that his sword went through the gleaming worm and stood fixed in the wall, splendid weapon: the dragon lay dead of the murdering stroke. Through his courage the great warrior had brought it about that he might at his own wish enjoy the ring-hoard. He loaded the sea-boat, bore into the ship's bosom the bright treasure, offspring of Waels. The hot dragon melted.

He was adventurer most famous, far and wide through the nations, for deeds of courage—he had prospered from that before, the protector of warriors— after the war-making of Heremod had come to an end, his strength and his courage.[8] Among the Jutes Heremod came into the power of his enemies, was betrayed, quickly dispatched. Surging sorrows had oppressed him too long: he had become a great care to his people, to all his princes; for many a wise man in former times had bewailed the journey of the fierce-hearted one—people who had counted on him as a relief from affliction—that that king's son should prosper, take the rank of his father, keep guard over the folk, the treasure and stronghold, the kingdom of heroes, the home of the Scyldings. The kinsman of Hygelac became dearer to his friends, to all mankind: crime took possession of Heremod.

Sometimes racing their horses they passed over the sand-covered ways. By then the morning light was far advanced, hastening on. Many a stout-hearted warrior went to the high hall to see the strange wonder. The king himself walked forth from the women's apartment, the guardian of the ring-hoards, secure in his fame, known for his excellence, with much company; and his queen with him passed over the path to the mead-hall with a troop of attendant women.

Hrothgar spoke—he had gone to the hall, taken his stand on the steps, looked at the high roof shining with gold, and at Grendel's hand: "For this sight may thanks be made quickly to the Almighty: I endured much from the foe, many griefs from Grendel: God may always work wonder upon wonder, the Guardian of Heaven. It was not long ago that I did not expect ever to live to see relief from any of my woes—when the best of houses stood shining with blood, stained with slaughter, a far-reaching woe for each of my counselors, for every one, since none thought he could ever defend the people's stronghold from its enemies, from demons and evil spirits. Now through the Lord's might a warrior has accomplished the deed that all of us with our skill could not perform. Yes, she may say, whatever woman brought forth this son among mankind—if she still lives—that the God of Old was kind to her in her childbearing. Now, Beowulf, best of men, in my heart I will love you as a son: keep well this new kinship. To you will there be no lack of the good things of the world that I have in my possession. Full often I have made reward for less, done honor with gifts to a lesser warrior, weaker in fighting. With your deeds you yourself have made sure that your glory will be ever alive. May the Almighty reward you with good—as just now he has done."

Beowulf spoke, the son of Ecgtheow: "With much good will we have achieved this work of courage, that fight, have ventured boldly against the strength of the unknown one. I should have wished rather that you might have

---

8. Heremod was an unsuccessful king of the Danes, one who began brilliantly but became cruel and avaricious, ultimately having to take refuge among the Jutes, who put him to death. His reputation was thus overshadowed by that of Sigemund.

seen him, your enemy brought low among your furnishings. I thought quickly to bind him on his deathbed with hard grasp, so that because of my hand-grip he should lie struggling for life—unless his body should escape. I could not stop his going, since the Lord did not wish it, nor did I hold him firmly enough for that, my life-enemy: he was too strong, the foe in his going. Yet to save his life he has left his hand behind to show that he was here—his arm and shoulder; nor by that has the wretched creature bought any comfort; none the longer will the loathsome ravager live, hard-pressed by his crimes, for a wound has clutched him hard in its strong grip, in deadly bonds. There, like a man outlawed for guilt, he shall await the great judgment, how the bright Lord will decree for him."

Then was the warrior more silent in boasting speech of warlike deeds, the son of Ecglaf,[9] after the nobles had looked at the hand, now high on the roof through the strength of a man, the foe's fingers. The end of each one, each of the nail-places, was most like steel; the hand-spurs of the heathen warrior were monstrous spikes. Everyone said that no hard thing would hurt him, no iron good from old times would harm the bloody battle-hand of the monster.

Then it was ordered that Heorot be within quickly adorned by hands. Many there were, both men and women, who made ready the wine-hall, the guest-building. The hangings on the walls shone with gold, many a wondrous sight for each man who looks on such things. That bright building was much damaged, though made fast within by iron bonds, and its door-hinges sprung; the roof alone came through unharmed when the monster, outlawed for his crimes, turned in flight, in despair of his life. That is not easy to flee from— let him try it who will—but driven by need one must seek the place prepared for earth-dwellers, soul-bearers, the sons of men, the place where, after its feasting, one's body will sleep fast in its death-bed.

Then had the proper time come that Healfdene's son should go to the hall; the king himself would share in the feast. I have never heard that a people in a larger company bore themselves better about their treasurer-giver. Men who were known for courage sat at the benches, rejoiced in the feast. Their kinsmen, stout-hearted Hrothgar and Hrothulf, partook fairly of many a mead-cup in the high hall. Heorot within was filled with friends: the Scylding-people had not then known treason's web.[1]

Then the son of Healfdene gave Beowulf a golden standard to reward his victory—a decorated battle-banner—a helmet and mail-shirt: many saw the glorious, costly sword borne before the warrior. Beowulf drank of the cup in the mead-hall. He had no need to be ashamed before fighting men of those rich gifts. I have not heard of many men who gave four precious, gold-adorned things to another on the ale-bench in a more friendly way. The rim around the helmet's crown had a head-protection, wound of wire, so that no battle-hard sharp sword might badly hurt him when the shield-warrior should go against his foe. Then the people's protector commanded eight horses with golden bridles to be led into the hall, within the walls. The saddle of one of them stood shining with hand-ornaments, adorned with jewels: that had been the war-seat of the high king when the son of Healfdene would join sword-

9. I.e., Unferth, who had taunted Beowulf the night before.

1. A reference to the later history of the Danes, when, after Hrothgar's death, his nephew Hrothulf apparently drove his son and successor Hrethric from the throne.

play: never did the warfare of the wide-known one fail when men died in battle. And then the prince of Ing's friends[2] yielded possession of both, horses and weapons, to Beowulf: he bade him use them well. So generously the famous prince, guardian of the hoard, repaid the warrior's battle-deeds with horses and treasure that no man will ever find fault with them—not he that will speak truth according to what is right.

Then further the lord gave treasure to each of the men on the mead-bench who had made the sea-voyage with Beowulf, gave heirlooms; and he commanded that gold be paid for the one whom in his malice Grendel had killed—as he would have killed more if wise God and the man's courage had not forestalled that fate. The Lord guided all the race of men then, as he does now. Yet is discernment everywhere best, fore-thought of mind. Many a thing dear and loath he shall live to see who here in the days of trouble long makes use of the world.

There was song and music together before Healfdene's battle-leader, the wooden harp touched, tale oft told, when Hrothgar's scop should speak hall-pastime among the mead-benches . . . [of] Finn's retainers when the sudden disaster fell upon them.[3] . . .

The hero of the Half-Danes, Hnaef of the Scyldings, was fated to fall on Frisian battlefield. And no need had Hildeburh[4] to praise the good faith of the Jutes: blameless she was deprived of her dear ones at the shield-play, of son and brother; wounded by spears they fell to their fate. That was a mournful woman. Not without cause did Hoc's daughter lament the decree of destiny when morning came and she might see, under the sky, the slaughter of kinsmen—where before she had the greatest of world's joy. The fight took away all Finn's thanes except for only a few, so that he could in no way continue the battle on the field against Hengest, nor protect the survivors by fighting against the prince's thane. But they offered them peace-terms,[5] that they should clear another building for them, hall and high seat, that they might have control of half of it with the sons of the Jutes; and at givings of treasure the son of Folcwalda[6] should honor the Danes each day, should give Hengest's company rings, such gold-plated treasure as that with which he would cheer the Frisians' kin in the high hall. Then on both sides they confirmed the fast peace-compact. Finn declared to Hengest, with oaths deep-sworn, unfeigned, that he would hold those who were left from the battle in honor in accordance with the judgment of his counselors, so that by words or by works no man should break the treaty nor because of malice should ever mention that, princeless, the Danes followed the slayer of their own ring-giver, since neces-

2. Ing was a Germanic deity, and his "friends" are the Danes.
3. The lines introducing the scop's song seem faulty. The story itself is recounted in a highly allusive way and many of its details are obscure, although some help is offered by an independent version of the story given in a fragmentary Old English lay called *The Fight at Finnsburg.*
4. Hildeburh, daughter of the former Danish king Hoc and sister of the ruling Danish king Hnaef, was married to Finn, king of the Jutes (Frisians). Hnaef, with a party of Danes, made what was presumably a friendly visit to Hildeburh and Finn at their home Finnsburg, but during a feast a quarrel broke out be-

tween the Jutes and the Danes (because the scop's sympathies are with the Danes, he ascribes the cause to the bad faith of the Jutes), and in the ensuing fight, Hnaef and his nephew, the son of Finn and Hildeburh, were killed along with many other Danes and Jutes.
5. It is not clear who proposed the peace terms, but in view of the teller's Danish sympathies, it was probably the Jutes that sought the uneasy truce from Hengest, who became the Danes' leader after Hnaef's death. The truce imposed on Hengest and the Danes the intolerable condition of having to dwell in peace with the Jutish king who was responsible for the death of their own king.
6. I.e., Finn.

sity forced them. If with rash speech any of the Frisians should insist upon calling to mind the cause of murderous hate, then the sword's edge should settle it.

The funeral pyre was made ready and gold brought up from the hoard. The best of the warriors of the War-Scyldings[7] was ready on the pyre. At the fire it was easy to see many a blood-stained battle-shirt, boar-image all golden— iron-hard swine—many a noble destroyed by wounds: more than one had died in battle. Then Hildeburh bade give her own son to the flames on Hnaef's pyre, burn his body, put him in the fire at the shoulder of his uncle. The woman mourned, sang her lament. The warrior took his place.[8] The greatest of death-fires wound to the skies, roared before the barrow. Heads melted as blood sprang out—wounds opened wide, hate-bites of the body. Fire swallowed them—greediest of spirits—all of those whom war had taken away from both peoples: their strength had departed.

Then warriors went to seek their dwellings, bereft of friends, to behold Friesland, their homes and high city.[9] Yet Hengest stayed on with Finn for a winter darkened with the thought of slaughter, all desolate. He thought of his land, though he might not drive his ring-prowed ship over the water—the sea boiled with storms, strove with the wind, winter locked the waves in ice-bonds—until another year came to men's dwellings, just as it does still, glorious bright weather always watching for its time. Then winter was gone, earth's lap fair, the exile was eager to go, the guest from the dwelling: [yet] more he thought of revenge for his wrongs than of the sea-journey—if he might bring about a fight where he could take account of the sons of the Jutes with his iron. So he made no refusal of the world's custom when the son of Hunlaf[1] placed on his lap Battle-Bright, best of swords: its edges were known to the Jutes. Thus also to war-minded Finn in his turn cruel sword-evil came in his own home, after Guthlaf and Oslaf complained of the grim attack, the injury after the sea-journey, assigned blame for their lot of woes: breast might not contain the restless heart. Then was the hall reddened from foes' bodies, and thus Finn slain, the king in his company, and the queen taken. The warriors of the Scyldings bore to ship all the hall-furnishings of the land's king, whatever of necklaces, skillfully wrought treasures, they might find at Finn's home. They brought the noble woman on the sea-journey to the Danes, led her to her people.

The lay was sung to the end, the song of the scop. Joy mounted again, bench-noise brightened, cup-bearers poured wine from wonderful vessels. Then Wealhtheow came forth to walk under gold crown to where all good men sat, nephew and uncle: their friendship was then still unbroken, each true to the other.[2] There too Unferth the spokesman sat at the feet of the prince of the Scyldings: each of them trusted his spirit, that he had much courage, though he was not honorable to his kinsmen at sword-play. Then the woman of the Scyldings spoke:

7. I.e., Hnaef.
8. The line is obscure, but it perhaps means that the body of Hildeburh's son was placed on the pyre.
9. This seems to refer to the few survivors on the Jutish side.
1. The text is open to various interpretations. The one adopted here assumes that the Dane Hunlaf, brother of Guthlaf and Oslaf, had been killed in the fight, and that ultimately Hunlaf's son demanded vengeance by

the symbolical act of placing his father's sword in Hengest's lap, while at the same time Guthlaf and Oslaf reminded Hengest of the Jutes' treachery. It is not clear whether the subsequent fight in which Finn was killed was waged by the Danish survivors alone or whether the party first went back to Denmark and then returned to Finnsburg with reinforcements.
2. See n. 1, p. 36.

"Take this cup, my noble lord, giver of treasure. Be glad, gold-friend of warriors, and speak to the Geats with mild words, as a man ought to do. Be gracious to the Geats, mindful of gifts [which][3] you now have from near and far. They have told me that you would have the warrior for your son. Heorot is purged, the bright ring-hall. Enjoy while you may many rewards, and leave to your kinsmen folk and kingdom when you must go forth to look on the Ruler's decree. I know my gracious Hrothulf, that he will hold the young warriors in honor if you, friend of the Scyldings, leave the world before him. I think he will repay our sons with good if he remembers all the favors we did to his pleasure and honor when he was a child."

Then she turned to the bench where her sons were, Hrethric and Hrothmund, and the sons of the warriors, young men together. There sat the good man Beowulf of the Geats beside the two brothers.

The cup was borne to him and welcome offered in friendly words to him, and twisted gold courteously bestowed on him, two arm-ornaments, a mail-shirt and rings, the largest of necklaces of those that I have heard spoken of on earth. I have heard of no better hoard-treasure under the heavens since Hama carried away to his bright city the necklace of the Brosings,[4] chain and rich setting: he fled the treacherous hatred of Eormenric, got eternal favor. This ring Hygelac of the Geats,[5] grandson of Swerting, had on his last venture, when beneath his battle-banner he defended his treasure, protected the spoils of war: fate took him when for pride he sought trouble, feud with the Frisians. Over the cup of the waves the mighty prince wore that treasure, precious stone. He fell beneath his shield; the body of the king came into the grasp of the Franks, his breast-armor and the neck-ring together. Lesser warriors plundered the fallen after the war-harvest: people of the Geats held the place of corpses.

The hall was filled with noise. Wealhtheow spoke, before the company she said to him: "Wear this ring, beloved Beowulf, young man, with good luck, and make use of this mail-shirt from the people's treasure, and prosper well; make yourself known with your might, and be kind of counsel to these boys: I shall remember to reward you for that. You have brought it about that, far and near, for a long time all men shall praise you, as wide as the sea surrounds the shores, home of the winds. While you live, prince, be prosperous. I wish you well of your treasure. Much favored one, be kind of deeds to my son. Here is each earl true to other, mild of heart, loyal to his lord; the thanes are at one, the people obedient, the retainers cheered with drink do as I bid."

Then she walked to her seat. There was the best of feasts, men drank wine. They did not know the fate, the grim decree made long before, as it came to pass to many of the earls after evening had come and Hrothgar had gone to his chambers, the noble one to his rest. A great number of men remained in the hall, just as they had often done before. They cleared the benches from the floor. It was spread over with beds and pillows. One of the beer-drinkers, ripe and fated to die, lay down to his hall-rest. They set at their heads their battle-shields, bright wood; there on the bench it was easy to see above each

3. The text seems corrupt.
4. The Brisings' ("Brosings") necklace had been worn by the goddess Freya. Nothing more is known of this story of Hama, who seems to have stolen the necklace from the famous Gothic king Eormenric.

5. Beowulf is later said to have presented the necklace to Hygelac's queen, Hygd, although here Hygelac is said to have been wearing it on his ill-fated expedition against the Franks and Frisians, into whose hands it fell at his death.

man his helmet that towered in battle, his ringed mail-shirt, his great spear-wood. It was their custom to be always ready for war whether at home or in the field, in any case at any time that need should befall their liege lord: that was a good nation.

[GRENDEL'S MOTHER'S ATTACK]

Then they sank to sleep. One paid sorely for his evening rest, just as had often befallen them when Grendel guarded the gold-hall, wrought wrong until the end came, death after misdeeds. It came to be seen, wide-known to men, that after the bitter battle an avenger still lived for an evil space: Grendel's mother, woman, monster-wife, was mindful of her misery, she who had to dwell in the terrible water, the cold currents, after Cain became sword-slayer of his only brother, his own father's son. Then Cain went as an outlaw to flee the cheerful life of men, marked for his murder, held to the wasteland. From him sprang many a devil sent by fate. Grendel was one of them, hateful out-cast who at Heorot found a waking man waiting his warfare. There the monster had laid hold upon him, but he was mindful of the great strength, the large gift God had given him, and relied on the Almighty for favor, comfort and help. By that he overcame the foe, subdued the hell-spirit. Then he went off wretched, bereft of joy, to seek his dying-place, enemy of mankind. And his mother, still greedy and gallows-grim, would go on a sorrowful venture, avenge her son's death.

Then she came to Heorot where the Ring-Danes slept throughout the hall Then change came quickly to the earls there, when Grendel's mother made her way in. The attack was the less terrible by just so much as is the strength of women, the war-terror of a wife, less than an armed man's when a hard blade, forge-hammered, a sword shining with blood, good of its edges, cuts the stout boar on a helmet opposite. Then in the hall was hard-edged sword raised from the seat, many a broad shield lifted firmly in hand: none thought of helmet, of wide mail-shirt, when the terror seized him. She was in haste, would be gone out from there, protect her life after she was discovered. Swiftly she had taken fast hold on one of the nobles, then she went to the fen. He was one of the men between the seas most beloved of Hrothgar in the rank of retainer, a noble shield-warrior whom she destroyed at his rest, a man of great repute. Beowulf was not there, for earlier, after the treasure-giving, another lodging had been appointed for the renowned Geat. Outcry arose in Heorot: she had taken, in its gore, the famed hand. Care was renewed, come again on the dwelling. That was not a good bargain, that on both sides they had to pay with the lives of friends.

Then was the old king, the hoary warrior, of bitter mind when he learned that his chief thane was lifeless, his dearest man dead. Quickly Beowulf was fetched to the bed-chamber, man happy in victory. At daybreak together with his earls he went, the noble champion himself with his retainers, to where the wise one was, waiting to know whether after tidings of woe the All-Wielder would ever bring about change for him. The worthy warrior walked over the floor with his retainers—hall-wood resounded—that he might address words to the wise prince of Ing's friends, asked if the night had been pleasant according to his desires.

Hrothgar spoke, protector of the Scyldings: "Ask not about pleasure. Sorrow is renewed to the people of the Danes: Aeschere is dead, Yrmen-laf's elder brother, my speaker of wisdom and my bearer of counsel, my shoulder-companion when we used to defend our heads in battle, when troops clashed, beat on boar-images. Whatever an earl should be, a man good from old times, such was Aeschere. Now a wandering murderous spirit has slain him with its hands in Heorot. I do not know by what way the awful creature, glorying in its prey, has made its retreat, gladdened by its feast. She has avenged the feud—that last night you killed Grendel with hard hand-grips, savagely, because too long he had diminished and destroyed my people. He fell in the fight, his life forfeited, and now the other has come, a mighty worker of wrong, would avenge her kinsman, and has carried far her revenge—as many a thane may think who weeps in his spirit for his treasure-giver, bitter sorrow in heart. Now the hand lies lifeless that was strong in support of all your desires.

"I have heard landsmen, my people, hall-counselors, say this, that they have seen two such huge walkers in the wasteland holding to the moors, alien spirits. One of them, so far as they could clearly discern, was the likeness of a woman. The other wretched shape trod the tracks of exile in the form of a man, except that he was bigger than any other man. Land-dwellers in the old days named him Grendel. They know of no father, whether in earlier times any was begotten for them among the dark spirits. They hold to the secret land, the wolf-slopes, the windy headlands, the dangerous fen-paths where the mountain stream goes down under the darkness of the hills, the flood under the earth. It is not far from here, measured in miles, that the mere stands; over it hang frost-covered woods, trees fast of root close over the water. There each night may be seen fire on the flood, a fearful wonder. Of the sons of men there lives none, old of wisdom, who knows the bottom. Though the heath-stalker, the strong-horned hart, harassed by hounds makes for the forest after long flight, rather will he give his life, his being, on the bank than save his head by entering. That is no pleasant place. From it the surging waves rise up black to the heavens when the wind stirs up awful storms, until the air becomes gloomy, the skies weep. Now once again is the cure in you alone. You do not yet know the land, the perilous place, where you might find the seldom-seen creature: seek if you dare. I will give you wealth for the feud, old treasure, as I did before, twisted gold—if you come away."

Beowulf spoke, the son of Ecgtheow: "Sorrow not, wise warrior. It is better for a man to avenge his friend than much mourn. Each of us must await his end of the world's life. Let him who may get glory before death: that is best for the warrior after he has gone from life. Arise, guardian of the kingdom, let us go at once to look on the track of Grendel's kin. I promise you this: she will not be lost under cover, not in the earth's bosom nor in the mountain woods nor at the bottom of the sea, go where she will. This day have patience in every woe—as I expect you to."

Then the old man leapt up, thanked God, the mighty Lord, that the man had so spoken. Then was a horse bridled for Hrothgar, a curly-maned mount. The wise king moved in state; the band of shield-bearers marched on foot. The tracks were seen wide over the wood-paths where she had gone on the ground, made her way forward over the dark moor, borne lifeless the best of retainers of those who watched over their home with Hrothgar. The son of noble forebears[6] moved over the steep rocky slopes, narrow paths where only one could go at a time, an unfamiliar trail, steep hills, many a lair of water-monsters. He went before with a few wise men to spy out the country, until suddenly he found mountain trees leaning out over hoary stone, a joyless wood: water lay beneath, bloody and troubled. It was pain of heart for all the Danes to suffer, for the friends of the Scyldings, for many a thane, grief to each earl when on the cliff over the water they came upon Aeschere's head. The flood boiled with blood—the men looked upon it—with hot gore. Again and again the horn sang its urgent war-song. The whole troop sat down to rest. Then they saw on the water many a snake-shape, strong sea-serpents exploring the mere, and water-monsters lying on the slopes of the shore such as those that in the morning often attend a perilous journey on the paths of the sea, serpents and wild beasts.

These fell away from the shore, fierce and rage-swollen: they had heard the bright sound, the war-horn sing. One of them a man of the Geats with his bow cut off from his life, his water-warring, after the hard war-arrow stuck in his heart: he was weaker in swimming the lake when death took him. Straightway he was hard beset on the waves with barbed boar-spears, strongly surrounded, pulled up on the shore, strange spawn of the waves. The men looked on the terrible alien thing.

Beowulf put on his warrior's dress, had no fear for his life. His war-shirt, hand-fashioned, broad and well-worked, was to explore the mere: it knew how to cover his body-cave so that foe's grip might not harm his heart, or grasp of angry enemy his life. But the bright helmet guarded his head, one which was to stir up the lake-bottom, seek out the troubled water   made rich with gold, surrounded with splendid bands, as the weapon-smith had made it in far-off days, fashioned it wonderfully, set it about with boar-images so that thereafter no sword or battle-blade might bite into it. And of his strong supports that was not the least which Hrothgar's spokesman[7] lent to his need: Hrunting was the name of the hilted sword; it was one of the oldest of ancient treasures; its edge was iron, decorated with poison-stripes, hardened with battle-sweat. Never had it failed in war any man of those who grasped it in their hands, who dared enter on dangerous enterprises, onto the common meeting place of foes: this was not the first time that it should do work of courage. Surely the son of Ecglaf, great of strength, did not have in mind what, drunk with wine, he had spoken, when he lent that weapon to a better swordfighter. He did not himself dare to risk his life under the warring waves, to engage his courage: there he lost his glory, his name for valor. It was not so with the other when he had armed himself for battle.

[BEOWULF ATTACKS GRENDEL'S MOTHER]

Beowulf spoke, the son of Ecgtheow: "Think now, renowned son of Healf-dene, wise king, now that I am ready for the venture, gold-friend of warriors, of what we said before, that, if at your need I should go from life, you would always be in a father's place for me when I am gone: be guardian of my young retainers, my companions, if battle should take me. The treasure you gave me,

6. I.e., Hrothgar.   7. I.e., Unferth.

beloved Hrothgar, send to Hygelac. The lord of the Geats may know from the gold, the son of Hrethel may see when he looks on that wealth, that I found a ring-giver good in his gifts, enjoyed him while I might. And let Unferth have the old heirloom, the wide-known man my splendid-waved sword, hard-edged: with Hrunting I shall get glory, or death will take me."

After these words the man of the Weather-Geats turned away boldly, would wait for no answer: the surging water took the warrior. Then was it a part of a day before he might see the bottom's floor. Straightway that which had held the flood's tract a hundred half-years, ravenous for prey, grim and greedy, saw that some man from above was exploring the dwelling of monsters. Then she groped toward him, took the warrior in her awful grip. Yet not the more for that did she hurt his hale body within: his ring-armor shielded him about on the outside so that she could not pierce the war-dress, the linked body-mail, with hateful fingers. Then as she came to the bottom the sea-wolf bore the ring-prince to her house so that—no matter how brave he was—he might not wield weapons; but many monsters attacked him in the water, many a sea-beast tore at his mail-shirt with war-tusks, strange creatures afflicted him. Then the earl saw that he was in some hostile hall where no water harmed him at all, and the flood's onrush might not touch him because of the hall-roof. He saw firelight, a clear blaze shine bright.

Then the good man saw the accursed dweller in the deep, the mighty mere-woman. He gave a great thrust to his sword—his hand did not withhold the stroke—so that the etched blade sang at her head a fierce war-song. Then the stranger found that the battle-lightning would not bite, harm her life, but the edge failed the prince in his need: many a hand-battle had it endured before, often sheared helmet, war-coat of man fated to die: this was the first time for the rare treasure that its glory had failed.

But still he was resolute, not slow of his courage, mindful of fame, the kinsman of Hygelac. Then, angry warrior, he threw away the sword, wavy-patterned, bound with ornaments, so that it lay on the ground, hard and steel-edged: he trusted in his strength, his mighty hand-grip. So ought a man to do when he thinks to get long-lasting praise in battle: he cares not for his life. Then he seized by the hair Grendel's mother—the man of the War-Geats did not shrink from the fight. Battle-hardened, now swollen with rage, he pulled his deadly foe so that she fell to the floor. Quickly in her turn she repaid him his gift with her grim claws and clutched at him: then weary-hearted, the strongest of warriors, of foot-soldiers, stumbled so that he fell. Then she sat upon the hall-guest and drew her knife, broad and bright-edged. She would avenge her child, her only son. The woven breast-armor lay on his shoulder: that protected his life, withstood entry of point or of edge. Then the son of Ecgtheow would have fared amiss under the wide ground, the champion of the Geats, if the battle-shirt had not brought help, the hard war-net—and holy God brought about victory in war; the wise Lord, Ruler of the Heavens, decided it with right, easily, when Beowulf had stood up again.

Then he saw among the armor a victory-blessed blade, an old sword made by the giants, strong of its edges, glory of warriors: it was the best of weapons, except that it was larger than any other man might bear to war-sport, good and adorned, the work of giants. He seized the linked hilt, he who fought for the Scyldings, savage and slaughter-bent, drew the patterned-blade; desperate of life, he struck angrily so that it bit her hard on the neck, broke the bone-rings. The blade went through all the doomed body. She fell to the floor, the sword was sweating, the man rejoiced in his work.

The blaze brightened, light shone within, just as from the sky heaven's candle shines clear. He looked about the building; then he moved along the wall, raised his weapon hard by the hilt, Hygelac's thane, angry and resolute: the edge was not useless to the warrior, for he would quickly repay Grendel for the many attacks he had made on the West-Danes—many more than the one time when he slew in their sleep fifteen hearth-companions of Hrothgar, devoured men of the Danish people while they slept, and another such number bore away, a hateful prey. He had paid him his reward for that, the fierce champion, for there he saw Grendel, weary of war, lying at rest, lifeless with the wounds he had got in the fight at Heorot. The body bounded wide when it suffered the blow after death, the hard sword-swing; and thus he cut off his head.

At once the wise men who were watching the water with Hrothgar saw that the surging waves were troubled, the lake stained with blood. Gray-haired, old, they spoke together of the good warrior, that they did not again expect of the chief that he would come victorious to seek their great king; for many agreed on it, that the sea-wolf had destroyed him.

Then came the ninth hour of the day. The brave Scyldings left the hill. The gold-friend of warriors went back to his home. The strangers sat sick at heart and stared at the mere. They wished—and did not expect—that they would see their beloved lord himself.

Then the blade began to waste away from the battle-sweat, the war-sword into battle-icicles. That was a wondrous thing, that it should all melt, most like the ice when the Father loosens the frost's fetters, undoes the water-bonds—He Who has power over seasons and times: He is the true Ruler. Beowulf did not take from the dwelling, the man of the Weather-Geats, more treasures—though he saw many there—but only the head and the hilt, bright with jewels. The sword itself had already melted, its patterned blade burned away: the blood was too hot for it, the spirit that had died there too poisonous. Quickly he was swimming, he who had lived to see the fall of his foes; he plunged up through the water. The currents were all cleansed, the great tracts of the water, when the dire spirit left her life-days and this loaned world.

Then the protector of seafarers came toward the land, swimming stout-hearted; he had joy of his sea-booty, the great burden he had with him. They went to meet him, thanked God, the strong band of thanes, rejoiced in their chief that they might see him again sound. Then the helmet and war-shirt of the mighty one were quickly loosened. The lake drowsed, the water beneath the skies, stained with blood. They went forth on the foot-tracks, glad in their hearts, measured the path back, the known ways, men bold as kings. They bore the head from the mere's cliff, toilsomely for each of the great-hearted ones: four of them had trouble in carrying Grendel's head on spear-shafts to the gold-hall—until at last they came striding to the hall, fourteen bold warriors of the Geats; their lord, high-spirited, walked in their company over the fields to the mead-hall.

Then the chief of the thanes, man daring in deeds, enriched by new glory, warrior dear to battle, came in to greet Hrothgar. Then Grendel's head was dragged by the hair over the floor to where men drank, a terrible thing to the earls and the woman with them, an awful sight: the men looked upon it.

[FURTHER CELEBRATION AT HEOROT]

Beowulf spoke, the son of Ecgtheow: "Yes, we have brought you this sea-booty, son of Healfdene, man of the Scyldings, gladly, as evidence of glory—what you look on here. Not easily did I come through it with my life, the war under water, not without trouble carried out the task. The fight would have been ended straightway if God had not guarded me. With Hrunting I might not do anything in the fight, though that is a good weapon. But the Wielder of Men granted me that I should see hanging on the wall a fair, ancient great-sword—most often He has guided the man without friends—that I should wield the weapon. Then in the fight when the time became right for me I hewed the house-guardians. Then that war-sword, wavy-patterned, burnt away as their blood sprang forth, hottest of battle-sweats. I have brought the hilt away from the foes. I have avenged the evil deeds, the slaughter of Danes, as it was right to do. I promise you that you may sleep in Heorot without care with your band of retainers, and that for none of the thanes of your people, old or young, need you have fear, prince of the Scyldings—for no life-injury to your men on that account, as you did before."

Then the golden hilt was given into the hand of the old man, the hoary war-chief—the ancient work of giants. There came into the possession of the prince of the Danes, after the fall of devils, the work of wonder-smiths. And when the hostile-hearted creature, God's enemy, guilty of murder, gave up this world, and his mother too, it passed into the control of the best of worldly kings between the seas, of those who gave treasure in the Northlands.

Hrothgar spoke—he looked on the hilt, the old heirloom, on which was written the origin of ancient strife, when the flood, rushing water, slew the race of giants—they suffered terribly: that was a people alien to the Everlasting Lord. The Ruler made them a last payment through water's welling. On the sword-guard of bright gold there was also rightly marked through rune-staves, set down and told, for whom that sword, best of irons, had first been made, its hilt twisted and ornamented with snakes. Then the wise man spoke, the son of Healfdene—all were silent: "Lo, this may one say who works truth and right for the folk, recalls all things far distant, an old guardian of the land: that this earl was born the better man. Glory is raised up over the far ways—your glory over every people, Beowulf my friend. All of it, all your strength, you govern steadily in the wisdom of your heart. I shall fulfill my friendship to you, just as we spoke before. You shall become a comfort, whole and long-lasting, to your people, a help to warriors.

"So was not Heremod to the sons of Ecgwela, the Honor-Scyldings. He grew great not for their joy, but for their slaughter, for the destruction of Danish people. With swollen heart he killed his table-companions, shoulder-comrades, until he turned away from the joys of men, alone, notorious king, although mighty God had raised him in power, in the joys of strength, had set him up over all men. Yet in his breast his heart's thought grew blood-thirsty: no rings did he give to the Danes for glory. He lived joyless to suffer the pain of that strife, the long-lasting harm of the people. Teach yourself by him, be mindful of munificence. Old of winters, I tell this tale for you.

"It is a wonder to say how in His great spirit mighty God gives wisdom to mankind, land and earlship—He possesses power over all things. At times He lets the thought of a man of high lineage move in delight, gives him joy of earth in his homeland, a stronghold of men to rule over, makes regions of the world so subject to him, wide kingdoms, that in his unwisdom he may not himself have mind of his end. He lives in plenty; illness and age in no way grieve him, neither does dread care darken his heart, nor does enmity bare sword-hate, for the whole world turns to his will—he knows nothing worse— until his portion of pride increases and flourishes within him; then the watcher sleeps, the soul's guardian; that sleep is too sound, bound in its own cares, and the slayer most near whose bow shoots treacherously. Then is he hit in the heart, beneath his armor, with the bitter arrow—he cannot protect himself—with the crooked dark commands of the accursed spirit. What he has long held seems to him too little, angry-hearted he covets, no plated rings does he give in men's honor, and then he forgets and regards not his destiny because of what God, Wielder of Heaven, has given him before, his portion of glories. In the end it happens in turn that the loaned body weakens, falls doomed; another takes the earl's ancient treasure, one who recklessly gives precious gifts, does not fearfully guard them.

"Keep yourself against that wickedness, beloved Beowulf, best of men, and choose better—eternal gains. Have no care for pride, great warrior. Now for a time there is glory in your might: yet soon it shall be that sickness or sword will diminish your strength, or fire's fangs, or flood's surge, or sword's swing, or spear's flight, or appalling age; brightness of eyes will fail and grow dark; then it shall be that death will overcome you, warrior.

"Thus I ruled the Ring-Danes for a hundred half-years under the skies, and protected them in war with spear and sword against many nations over middle-earth, so that I counted no one as my adversary underneath the sky's expanse. Well, disproof of that came to me in my own land, grief after my joys, when Grendel, ancient adversary, came to invade my home. Great sorrow of heart I have always suffered for his persecution. Thanks be to the Ruler, the Eternal Lord, that after old strife I have come to see in my lifetime, with my own eyes, his blood-stained head. Go now to your seat, have joy of the glad feast, made famous in battle. Many of our treasures will be shared when morning comes."

The Geat was glad at heart, went at once to seek his seat as the wise one bade. Then was a feast fairly served again, for a second time, just as before, for those famed for courage, sitting about the hall.

Night's cover lowered, dark over the warriors. The retainers all arose. The gray-haired one would seek his bed, the old Scylding. It pleased the Geat, the brave shield-warrior, immensely that he should have rest. Straightway a hall-thane led the way on for the weary one, come from far country, and showed every courtesy to the thane's need, such as in those days seafarers might expect as their due.

Then the great-hearted one rested; the hall stood high, vaulted and gold-adorned; the guest slept within until the black raven, blithe-hearted, announced heaven's joy. Then the bright light came passing over the shadows. The warriors hastened, the nobles were eager to set out again for their people. Bold of spirit, the visitor would seek his ship far thence.

Then the hardy one bade that Hrunting be brought to the son of Ecglaf,[8] that he take back his sword, precious iron. He spoke thanks for that loan, said that he accounted it a good war-friend, strong in battle; in his words he found no fault at all with the sword's edge; he was a thoughtful man. And then they were eager to depart, the warriors ready in their armor. The prince who had earned honor of the Danes went to the high seat where the other was: the man dear to war greeted Hrothgar.

[Beowulf Returns Home]

Beowulf spoke, the son of Ecgtheow: "Now we sea-travelers come from afar wish to say that we desire to seek Hygelac. Here we have been entertained splendidly according to our desire: you have dealt well with us. If on earth I might in any way earn more of your heart's love, prince of warriors, than I have done before with warlike deeds, I should be ready at once. If beyond the sea's expanse I hear that men dwelling near threaten you with terrors, as those who hated you did before, I shall bring you a thousand thanes, warriors to your aid. I know of Hygelac, lord of the Geats, though he is young as a guardian of the people, that he will further me with words and works so that I may do you honor and bring spears to help you, strong support where you have need of men. If Hrethric, king's son, decides to come to the court of the Geats, he can find many friends there; far countries are well sought by him who is himself strong."

Hrothgar spoke to him in answer: "The All-Knowing Lord sent those words into your mind: I have not heard a man of so young age speak more wisely. You are great of strength, mature of mind, wise of words. I think it likely if the spear, sword-grim war, takes the son of Hrethel, sickness or weapon your prince, the people's ruler, and you have your life, that the Sea-Geats will not have a better to choose as their king, as guardian of their treasure, if you wish to hold the kingdom of your kinsmen. So well your heart's temper has long pleased me, beloved Beowulf. You have brought it about that peace shall be shared by the peoples, the folk of the Geats and the Spear-Danes, and enmity shall sleep, acts of malice which they practiced before; and there shall be, as long as I rule the wide kingdom, sharing of treasures, many a man shall greet his fellow with good gifts over the sea-bird's baths; the ring-prowed ship will bring gifts and tokens of friendship over the sea. I know your people, blameless in every respect, set firm after the old way both as to foe and to friend."

Then the protector of earls, the kinsman of Healfdene, gave him there in the hall twelve precious things; he bade him with these gifts seek his own dear people in safety, quickly come back. Then the king noble of race, the prince of the Scyldings, kissed the best of thanes and took him by his neck: tears fell from the gray-haired one. He had two thoughts of the future, the old and wise man, one more strongly than the other—that they would not see each other again, bold men at council. The man was so dear to him that he might not restrain his breast's welling, for fixed in his heartstrings a deep-felt longing for the beloved man burned in his blood. Away from him Beowulf, warrior glorious with gold, walked over the grassy ground, proud of his treasure. The sea-goer awaited its owner, riding at anchor. Then on the journey the gift of

8. I.e., Unferth.

Hrothgar was oft-praised: that was a king blameless in all things until age took from him the joys of his strength—old age that has often harmed many.

There came to the flood the band of brave-hearted ones, of young men. They wore mail-coats, locked limb-shirts. The guard of the coast saw the coming of the earls, just as he had done before. He did not greet the guests with taunts from the cliff's top, but rode to meet them, said that the return of the warriors in bright armor in their ship would be welcome to the people of the Weather-Geats. There on the sand the broad sea-boat was loaded with armor, the ring-prowed ship with horses and rich things. The mast stood high over Hrothgar's hoard-gifts. He gave the boat-guard a sword wound with gold, so that thereafter on the mead-bench he was held the worthier for the treasure, the heirloom. The boat moved out to furrow the deep water, left the land of the Danes. Then on the mast a sea-cloth, a sail, was made fast by a rope. The boat's beams creaked: wind did not keep the sea-floater from its way over the waves. The sea-goer moved, foamy-necked floated forth over the swell, the ship with bound prow over the sea-currents until they might see the cliffs of the Geats, the well-known headlands. The ship pressed ahead, borne by the wind, stood still at the land. Quickly the harbor-guard was at the sea-side, he who had gazed for a long time far out over the currents, eager to see the beloved men. He[9] moored the deep ship in the sand, fast by its anchor ropes, lest the force of the waves should drive away the fair wooden vessel. Then he bade that the prince's wealth be borne ashore, armor and plated gold. It was not far for them to seek the giver of treasure, Hygelac son of Hrethel, where he dwelt at home near the sea-wall, himself with his retainers.

The building was splendid, its king most valiant, set high in the hall, Hygd[1] most youthful, wise and well-taught, though she had lived within the castle walls few winters, daughter of Haereth. For she was not niggardly, nor too sparing of gifts to the men of the Geats, of treasures. Modthryth,[2] good folk-queen, did dreadful deeds [in her youth]: no bold one among her retainers dared venture—except her great lord—to set his eyes on her in daylight, but [if he did] he should reckon deadly bonds prepared for him, arresting hands: that straightway after his seizure the sword awaited him, that the patterned blade must settle it, make known its death-evil. Such is no queenly custom for a woman to practice, though she is peerless—that one who weaves peace[3] should take away the life of a beloved man after pretended injury. However the kinsman of Hemming stopped that:[4] ale-drinkers gave another account, said that she did less harm to the people, fewer injuries, after she was given, gold-adorned, to the young warrior, the beloved noble, when by her father's teaching she sought Offa's hall in a voyage over the pale sea. There on the throne she was afterwards famous for generosity, while living made use of her life, held high love toward the lord of warriors, [who was] of all mankind the best, as I have heard, between the seas of the races of men. Since Offa was a

9. Beowulf.
1. Hygd is Hygelac's young queen. The suddenness of her introduction here is perhaps due to a faulty text.
2. A transitional passage introducing the contrast between Hygd's good behavior and Modthryth's bad behavior as young women of royal blood seems to have been lost. Modthryth's practice of having those who looked into her face put to death may reflect the folk motif of the princess whose unsuccessful suitors are executed, although the text does not say that

Modthryth's victims were suitors. Modthryth's "great lord" was probably her father.
3. Daughters of kings were frequently given in marriage to the king of a hostile nation to bring about peace, hence Modthryth may be called "one who weaves peace."
4. I.e., Offa I, a legendary king of the Angles and presumably the ancestor of his namesake Offa II, who ruled Mercia (757–796); who Hemming was—besides being Offa's forebear—is not known.

man brave of wars and gifts, wide-honored, he held his native land in wisdom. From him sprang Eomer to the help of warriors, kinsman of Hemming, grandson of Garmund, strong in battle.[5]

Then the hardy one came walking with his troop over the sand on the sea-plain, the wide shores. The world-candle shone, the sun moved quickly from the south. They made their way, strode swiftly to where they heard that the protector of earls, the slayer of Ongentheow,[6] the good young war-king, was dispensing rings in the stronghold. The coming of Beowulf was straightway made known to Hygelac, that there in his home the defender of warriors, his comrade in battle, came walking alive to the court, sound from the battle-play. Quickly the way within was made clear for the foot-guests, as the mighty one bade.

Then he sat down with him, he who had come safe through the fight, kinsman with kinsman, after he had greeted his liege lord with formal speech, loyal, with vigorous words. Haereth's daughter moved through the hall-building with mead-cups, cared lovingly for the people, bore the cup of strong drink to the hands of the warriors. Hygelac began fairly to question his companion in the high hall, curiosity pressed him, what the adventures of the Sea-Geats had been. "How did you fare on your journey, beloved Beowulf, when you suddenly resolved to seek distant combat over the salt water, battle in Heorot? Did you at all help the wide-known woes of Hrothgar, the famous prince? Because of you I burned with seething sorrows, care of heart—had no trust in the venture of my beloved man. I entreated you long that you should in no way approach the murderous spirit, should let the South-Danes themselves settle the war with Grendel. I say thanks to God that I may see you sound."

Beowulf spoke, the son of Ecgtheow: "To many among men it is not hidden, lord Hygelac, the great encounter—what a fight we had, Grendel and I, in the place where he made many sorrows for the Victory-Scyldings, constant misery. All that I avenged, so that none of Grendel's kin over the earth need boast of that clash at night—whoever lives longest of the loathsome kind, wrapped in malice. There I went forth to the ring-hall to greet Hrothgar. At once the famous son of Healfdene, when he knew my purpose, gave me a seat with his own sons. The company was in joy: I have not seen in the time of my life under heaven's arch more mead-mirth of hall-sitters. At times the famous queen, peace-pledge of the people, went through all the hall, cheered the young men; often she would give a man a ring-band before she went to her seat. At times Hrothgar's daughter bore the ale-cup to the retainers, to the earls throughout the hall. I heard hall-sitters name her Freawaru when she offered the studded cup to warriors. Young and gold-adorned, she is promised to the fair son of Froda.[7] That has seemed good to the lord of the Scyldings, the guardian of the kingdom, and he believes of this plan that he may, with this woman, settle their portion of deadly feuds, of quarrels.[8] Yet most often after the fall of a prince in any nation the deadly spear rests but a little while, even though the bride is good.

5. Stories about Offa, who provides the only English connection in this English poem, and the names of his father (Garmund) and son (Eomer) would presumably have been familiar to the poet's audience. The passage has been seen as a compliment to the royal house of Mercia.
6. Ongentheow was a Scylfing (Swedish) king, whose story is fully told below. In fact Hygelac was not his slayer, but is called so because he led the attack on the Scylfings in which Ongentheow was killed.
7. I.e., Ingeld, who succeeded his father as king of the Heatho-Bards.
8. I.e., the feud between the Danes and Heatho-Bards.

"It may displease the lord of the Heatho-Bards and each thane of that people when he goes in the hall with the woman, [that while] the noble sons of the Danes, her retainers, [are] feasted,[9] the heirlooms of their ancestors will be shining on them—the hard and wave-adorned treasure of the Heatho-Bards, [which was theirs] so long as they might wield those weapons, until they led to the shield-play, to destruction, their dear companions and their own lives.[1] Then at the beer he[2] who sees the treasure, an old ash-warrior who remembers it all, the spear-death of warriors—grim is his heart—begins, sad of mind, to tempt a young fighter in the thoughts of his spirit, to awaken war-evil, and speaks this word:

" 'Can you, my friend, recognize that sword, the rare iron-blade, that your father, beloved man, bore to battle his last time in armor, where the Danes slew him, the fierce Scyldings, got possession of the battle-field, when Withergeld[3] lay dead, after the fall of warriors? Now here some son of his murderers walks in the hall, proud of the weapon, boasts of the murder, and wears the treasure that you should rightly possess.' So he will provoke and remind at every chance with wounding words until that moment comes that the woman's thane,[4] forfeiting life, shall lie dead, blood-smeared from the sword-bite, for his father's deeds. The other escapes with his life, knows the land well. Then on both sides the oath of the earls will be broken; then deadly hate will well up in Ingeld, and his wife-love after the surging of sorrows will become cooler. Therefore I do not think the loyalty of the Heatho-Bards, their part in the alliance with the Danes, to be without deceit—do not think their friendship fast.

"I shall speak still more of Grendel, that you may readily know, giver of treasure, what the hand-fight of warriors came to in the end. After heaven's jewel had glided over the earth, the angry spirit came, awful in the evening, to visit us where, unharmed, we watched over the hall. There the fight was fatal to Hondscioh, deadly to one who was doomed. He was dead first of all, armed warrior. Grendel came to devour him, good young retainer, swallowed all the body of the beloved man. Yet not for this would the bloody-toothed slayer, bent on destruction, go from the gold-hall empty-handed; but, strong of might, he made trial of me, grasped me with eager hand. His glove[5] hung huge and wonderful, made fast with cunning clasps: it had been made all with craft; with devil's devices and dragon's skins. The fell doer of evils would put me therein, guiltless, one of many. He might not do so after I had stood up in anger. It is too long to tell how I repaid the people's foe his due for every crime. My prince, there with my deeds I did honor to your people. He slipped away, for a little while had use of life's joy. Yet his right hand remained as his spoor in Heorot, and he went from there abject, mournful of heart sank to the mere's bottom.

"The lord of the Scyldings repaid me for that bloody combat with much plated gold, many treasures, after morning came and we sat down to the feast.

---

9. The text is faulty here.
1. I.e., the weapons and armor that had once belonged to the Heatho-Bards and were captured by the Danes will be worn by the Danish attendants of Hrothgar's daughter Freawaru when she goes to the Heatho-Bards to marry King Ingeld.
2. I.e., some old Heatho-Bard warrior.

3. Apparently a leader of the Heatho-Bards in their unsuccessful war with the Danes.
4. I.e., the Danish attendant of Freawaru who is wearing the sword of his Heatho-Bard attacker's father.
5. Apparently a large glove that could be used as a pouch.

There was song and mirth. The old Scylding, who has learned many things, spoke of times far-off. At times a brave one in battle touched the glad wood, the harp's joy; at times he told tales, true and sad; at times he related strange stories according to right custom; at times, again, the great-hearted king, bound with age, the old warrior, would begin to speak of his youth, his battle-strength. His heart welled within when, old and wise, he thought of his many winters. Thus we took pleasure there the livelong day until another night came to men.

"Then in her turn Grendel's mother swiftly made ready to take revenge for his injuries, made a sorrowful journey. Death had taken her son, war-hate of the Weather-Geats. The direful woman avenged her son, fiercely killed a warrior: there the life of Aeschere departed, a wise old counselor. And when morning came the folk of the Danes might not burn him, death-weary, in the fire, nor place him on the pyre, beloved man: she had borne his body away in fiend's embrace beneath the mountain stream. That was the bitterest of Hrothgar's sorrows, of those that had long come upon the people's prince. Then the king, sore-hearted, implored me by your life[6] that I should do a man's work in the tumult of the waters, venture my life, finish a glorious deed. He promised me reward. Then I found the guardian of the deep pool, the grim horror, as is now known wide. For a time there we were locked hand in hand. Then the flood boiled with blood, and in the war-hall I cut off the head of Grendel's mother with a mighty sword. Not without trouble I came from there with my life. I was not fated to die then, but the protector of earls again gave me many treasures, the son of Healfdene.

"Thus the king of that people lived with good customs. I had lost none of the rewards, the meed of my might, but he gave me treasures, the son of Healfdene, at my own choice. I will bring these to you, great king, show my good will. On your kindnesses all still depends: I have few close kinsmen besides you, Hygelac."

Then he bade bring in the boar-banner—the head-sign—the helmet towering in battle, the gray battle-shirt, the splendid sword—afterwards spoke words: "Hrothgar, wise king, gave me this armor; in his words he bade that I should first tell you about his gift: he said that king Heorogar,[7] lord of the Scyldings, had had it for a long time; not for that would he give it, the breast-armor, to his son, bold Heoroweard, though he was loyal to him. Use it all well!"

I have heard that four horses, swift and alike, followed that treasure, fallow as apples. He gave him the gift of both horses and treasure. So ought kinsmen do, not weave malice-nets for each other with secret craft, prepare death for comrades. To Hygelac his nephew was most true in hard fights, and each one mindful of helping the other. I have heard that he gave Hygd the neck-ring, the wonderfully wrought treasure, that Wealhtheow had given him—gave to the king's daughter as well three horses, supple and saddle-bright. After the gift of the necklace, her breast was adorned with it.

Thus Beowulf showed himself brave, a man known in battles, of good deeds, bore himself according to discretion. Drunk, he slew no hearth-companions. His heart was not savage, but he held the great gift that God had given him, the most strength of all mankind, like one brave in battle. He had long been

6. I.e., "in your name."
7. Hrothgar's elder brother, whom Hrothgar succeeded as king.

despised,[8] so that the sons of the Geats did not reckon him brave, nor would the lord of the Weather-Geats do him much gift-honor on the mead-bench. They strongly suspected that he was slack, a young man unbold. Change came to the famous man for each of his troubles.

Then the protector of earls bade fetch in the heirloom of Hrethel,[9] king famed in battle, adorned with gold. There was not then among the Geats a better treasure in sword's kind. He laid that in Beowulf's lap, and gave him seven thousand [hides of land], a hall and a throne. To both of them alike land had been left in the nation, home and native soil: to the other more especially wide was the realm, to him who was higher in rank.

[Beowulf and the Dragon]

Afterwards it happened, in later days, in the crashes of battle, when Hygelac lay dead and war-swords came to slay Heardred[1] behind the shield-cover, when the Battle-Scylfings, hard fighters, sought him among his victorious nation, attacked bitterly the nephew of Hereric—then the broad kingdom came into Beowulf's hand. He held it well fifty winters—he was a wise king, an old guardian of the land—until in the dark nights a certain one, a dragon, began to hold sway, which on the high heath kept watch over a hoard, a steep stone-barrow. Beneath lay a path unknown to men. By this there went inside a certain man [who made his way near to the heathen hoard; his hand took a cup, large, a shining treasure. The dragon did not afterwards conceal it though in his sleep he was tricked by the craft of the thief. That the people discovered, the neighboring folk—that he was swollen with rage].[2]

Not of his own accord did he who had sorely harmed him[3] break into the worm's hoard, not by his own desire, but for hard constraint; the slave of some son of men fled hostile blows, lacking a shelter, and came there, a man guilty of wrong-doing. As soon as he saw him,[4] great horror arose in the stranger; [yet the wretched fugitive escaped the terrible worm . . . When the sudden shock came upon him, he carried off a precious cup].[5] There were many such ancient treasures in the earth-house, as in the old days some one of mankind had prudently hidden there the huge legacy of a noble race, rare treasures. Death had taken them all in earlier times, and the only one of the nation of people who still survived, who walked there longest, a guardian mourning his friends, supposed the same of himself as of them—that he might little while enjoy the long-got treasure. A barrow stood all ready on the shore near the sea-waves, newly placed on the headland, made fast by having its entrances skill-fully hidden. The keeper of the rings carried in the part of his riches worthy of hoarding, plated gold; he spoke few words:

"Hold now, you earth, now that men may not, the possession of earls. What, from you good men got it first! War-death has taken each man of my people, evil dreadful and deadly, each of those who has given up this life, the hall-joys of men. I have none who wears sword or cleans the plated cup, rich drinking vessel. The company of retainers has gone elsewhere. The hard helmet must

---

8. Beowulf's poor reputation as a young man is mentioned only here.
9. Hygelac's father.
1. Hygelac's son Heardred, who succeeded Hygelac as king, was killed by the Swedes (Battle-Scylfings) in his own land (n. 9, p. 54). His uncle Hereric was perhaps

Hygd's brother.
2. This part of the manuscript is badly damaged, and the text within brackets is highly conjectural.
3. The dragon.
4. The dragon.
5. Several lines of the text have been lost.

be stripped of its fair-wrought gold, of its plating. The polishers are asleep who should make the war-mask shine. And even so the coat of mail, which withstood the bite of swords after the crashing of the shields, decays like its warrior. Nor may the ring-mail travel wide on the war-chief beside his warriors. There is no harp-delight, no mirth of the singing wood, no good hawk flies through the hall, no swift horse stamps in the castle court. Baleful death has sent away many races of men."

So, sad of mind, he spoke his sorrow, alone of them all, moved joyless through day and night until death's flood reached his heart. The ancient night-ravager found the hoard-joy standing open, he who burning seeks barrows, the smooth hateful dragon who flies at night wrapped in flame. Earth-dwellers much dread him. He it is who must seek a hoard in the earth where he will guard heathen gold, wise for his winters: he is none the better for it.

So for three hundred winters the harmer of folk held in the earth one of its treasure-houses, huge and mighty, until one man angered his heart. He bore to his master a plated cup, asked his lord for a compact of peace: thus was the hoard searched, the store of treasures diminished. His requests were granted the wretched man: the lord for the first time looked on the ancient work of men. Then the worm woke; cause of strife was renewed: for then he moved over the stones, hard-hearted beheld his foe's footprints—with secret stealth he had stepped forth too near the dragon's head. (So may an undoomed man who holds favor from the Ruler easily come through his woes and misery.) The hoard-guard sought him eagerly over the ground, would find the man who had done him injury while he slept. Hot and fierce-hearted, often he moved all about the outside of the barrow. No man at all was in the emptiness. Yet he took joy in the thought of war, in the work of fighting. At times he turned back into the barrow, sought his rich cup. Straightway he found that some man had tampered with his gold, his splendid treasure. The hoard-guard waited restless until evening came; then the barrow-keeper was in rage: he would requite that precious drinking cup with vengeful fire. Then the day was gone—to the joy of the worm. He would not wait long on the sea-wall, but set out with fire, ready with flame. The beginning was terrible to the folk on the land, as the ending was soon to be sore to their giver of treasure.

Then the evil spirit began to vomit flames, burn bright dwellings; blaze of fire rose, to the horror of men; there the deadly flying thing would leave nothing alive. The worm's warfare was wide-seen, his cruel malice, near and far— how the destroyer hated and hurt the people of the Geats. He winged back to the hoard, his hidden hall, before the time of day. He had circled the land-dwellers with flame, with fire and burning. He had trust in his barrow, in his war and his wall: his expectation deceived him.

Then the terror was made known to Beowulf, quickly in its truth, that his own home, best of buildings, had melted in surging flames, the throne-seat of the Geats. That was anguish of spirit to the good man, the greatest of heart-sorrows. The wise one supposed that he had bitterly offended the Ruler, the Eternal Lord, against old law. His breast within boiled with dark thoughts—as was not for him customary. The fiery dragon with his flames had destroyed the people's stronghold, the land along the sea, the heart of the country. Because of that the war-king, the lord of the Weather-Geats, devised punishment for him. The protector of fighting men, lord of earls, commanded that a wonderful battle-shield be made all of iron. Well he knew that the wood of the forest might not help him—linden against flame. The prince good from old times was to come to the end of the days that had been lent him, life in the world, and the worm with him, though he had long held the hoarded wealth. Then the ring-prince scorned to seek the far-flier with a troop, a large army. He had no fear for himself of the combat, nor did he think the worm's war-power anything great, his strength and his courage, because he himself had come through many battles before, dared perilous straits, clashes of war, after he had purged Hrothgar's hall, victorious warrior, and in combat crushed to death Grendel's kin, loathsome race.

Nor was that the least of his hand-combats where Hygelac was slain, when the king of the Geats, the noble lord of the people, the son of Hrethel, died of sword-strokes in the war-storm among the Frisians, laid low by the blade. From there Beowulf came away by means of his own strength, performed a feat of swimming; he had on his arm the armor of thirty earls when he turned back to the sea. There was no need for the Hetware[6] to exult in the foot-battle when they bore their shields against him: few came again from that warrior to seek their homes. Then the son of Ecgtheow swam over the water's expanse, forlorn and alone, back to his people. There Hygd offered him hoard and kingdom, rings and a prince's throne. She had no trust in her son, that he could hold his native throne against foreigners now that Hygelac was dead. By no means the sooner might the lordless ones get consent from the noble that he would become lord of Heardred or that he would accept royal power.[7] Yet he held him up among the people by friendly counsel, kindly with honor, until he became older,[8] ruled the Weather-Geats.

Outcasts from over the sea sought him, sons of Ohthere.[9] They had rebelled against the protector of the Scylfings, the best of the sea-kings of those who gave treasure in Sweden, a famous lord. For Heardred that became his life's limit: because of his hospitality there the son of Hygelac got his life's wound from the strokes of a sword. And the son of Ongentheow went back to seek his home after Heardred lay dead, let Beowulf hold the royal throne, rule the Geats: that was a good king.

In later days he was mindful of repaying the prince's fall, became the friend of the destitute Eadgils;[1] with folk he supported the son of Ohthere over the wide sea, with warriors and weapons. Afterwards he got vengeance by forays that brought with them cold care: he took the king's life.

Thus he had survived every combat, every dangerous battle, every deed of courage, the son of Ecgtheow, until that one day when he should fight with the worm. Then, one of twelve, the lord of the Geats, swollen with anger, went to look on the dragon. He had learned then from what the feud arose, the fierce malice to men: the glorious cup had come to his possession from the hand of the finder: he was the thirteenth of that company, the man who had brought on the beginning of the war, the sad-hearted slave—wretched, he must direct them to the place. Against his will he went to where he knew of

6. I.e., a tribe, with whom the Frisians were allied.
7. I.e., Beowulf refused to take the throne from the rightful heir, Heardred.
8. I.e., Beowulf supported the young Heardred.
9. Ohthere succeeded his father, Ongentheow, as king of the Scylfings (Swedes), but after his death his brother, Onela, seized the throne, driving out Ohthere's sons Eanmund and Eadgils. They were given

refuge at the Geatish court by Heardred, whom Onela attacked for this act of hospitality. In the fight, Eanmund and Heardred were killed, and Onela left the kingdom in Beowulf's charge.
1. The surviving son of Ohthere was befriended by Beowulf, who supported him in his successful attempt to gain the Swedish throne and who killed the usurper Onela.

an earth-hall, a barrow beneath the ground close to the sea-surge, to the strug-gling waves: within, it was full of ornaments and gold chains. The terrible guardian, ready for combat, held the gold treasure, old under the earth. It was no easy bargain for any man to obtain. Then the king, hardy in fight, sat down on the headland; there he saluted his hearth-companions, gold-friend of the Geats. His mind was mournful, restless and ripe for death: very close was the fate which should come to the old man, seek his soul's hoard, divide life from his body; not for long then was the life of the noble one wound in his flesh.

Beowulf spoke, the son of Ecgtheow: "In youth I lived through many battle-storms; times of war. I remember all that. I was seven winters old when the lord of treasure, the beloved king of the folk, received me from my father: King Hrethel had me and kept me, gave me treasure and feast, mindful of kinship. During his life I was no more hated by him as a man in his castle than any of his own sons, Herebeald and Haethcyn, or my own Hygelac. For the eldest a murder-bed was wrongfully spread through the deed of a kinsman, when Haethcyn struck him down with an arrow from his horned bow—his friend and his lord—missed the mark and shot his kinsman dead, one brother the other, with the bloody arrowhead. That was a fatal fight, without hope of recompense, a deed wrongly done, baffling to the heart; yet it had happened that a prince had to lose life unavenged.

"So it is sad for an old man to endure that his son should ride young on the gallows. Then he may speak a story, a sorrowful song, when his son hangs for the joy of the raven, and, old in years and knowing, he can find no help for him. Always with every morning he is reminded of his son's journey else-where. He cares not to wait for another heir in his hall, when the first through death's force has come to the end of his deeds. Sorrowful he sees in his son's dwelling the empty wine-hall, the windy resting place without joy—the riders sleep, the warriors in the grave. There is no sound of the harp, no joy in the dwelling, as there was of old. Then he goes to his couch, sings a song of sorrow, one alone for one gone. To him all too wide has seemed the land and the dwelling.

"So the protector of the Weather-Geats bore in his heart swelling sorrow for Herebeald. In no way could he settle his feud with the life-slayer; not the sooner could he wound the warrior with deeds of hatred, though he was not dear to him. Then for the sorrow that had too bitterly befallen him he gave up the joys of men, chose God's light. To his sons he left—as a happy man does—his land and his town when he went from life.

"Then there was battle and strife of Swedes and Geats, over the wide water a quarrel shared, hatred between hardy ones, after Hrethel died. And the sons of Ongentheow[2] were bold and active in war, wanted to have no peace over the seas, but about Hreosnabeorh often devised awful slaughter. That my friends and kinsmen avenged, both the feud and the crime, as is well-known, though one of them bought it with his life, a hard bargain: the war was mortal to Haethcyn, lord of the Geats.[3] Then in the morning, I have heard, one

2. I.e., the Swedes Onela and Ohthere: the reference is, of course, to a time earlier than that referred to in n. 9, p. 54.
3. Haethcyn had succeeded his father, Hrethel, as king of the Geats after his accidental killing of his brother Herebeald. When Haethcyn was killed while attacking the Swedes, he was succeeded by Hygelac, who, as the next sentence relates, avenged Haethcyn's death on Ongentheow. The death of Ongentheow is described below.

kinsman avenged the other on his slayer with the sword's edge, when Ongentheow attacked Eofor: the war-helm split, the old Scylfing fell mortally
wounded: his hand remembered feuds enough, did not withstand the life-
blow.

"I repaid in war the treasures that he[4] gave me—with my bright sword, as
was granted me by fate: he had given me land, a pleasant dwelling. There was
not any need for him, any reason, that he should have to seek among the
Gifthas or the Spear-Danes or in Sweden in order to buy with treasure a worse
warrior. I would always go before him in the troop, alone in the front. And so
all my life I shall wage battle while this sword endures that has served me early
and late ever since I became Daeghrefn's slayer in the press—the warrior of
the Hugas.[5] He could not bring armor to the king of the Frisians, breast ornament, but fell in the fight, keeper of the standard, a noble man. Nor was my
sword's edge his slayer, but my warlike grip broke open his heart-streams, his
bone-house. Now shall the sword's edge, the hand and hard blade, fight for
the hoard."

[BEOWULF ATTACKS THE DRAGON]

Beowulf spoke, for the last time spoke words in boast: "In my youth I
engaged in many wars. Old guardian of the people, I shall still seek battle,
perform a deed of fame, if the evil-doer will come to me out of the earth-hall."

Then he saluted each of the warriors, the bold helmet-bearers, for the last
time—his own dear companions. "I would not bear sword, weapon, to the
worm, if I knew how else according to my boast I might grapple with the
monster, as I did of old with Grendel. But I expect here hot battle-fire, steam
and poison. Therefore I have on me shield and mail-shirt. I will not flee a
foot-step from the barrow-ward, but it shall be with us at the wall as fate allots,
the ruler of every man. I am confident in heart, so I forgo help against the
war-flier. Wait on the barrow, safe in your mail-shirts, men in armor—which
of us two may better bear wounds after our bloody meeting. This is not your
venture, nor is it right for any man except me alone that he should spend his
strength against the monster, do this man's deed. By my courage I shall get
gold, or war will take your king, dire life-evil."

Then the brave warrior arose by his shield; hardy under helmet he went in
his mail-shirt beneath the stone-cliffs, had trust in his strength—that of one
man: such is not the way of the cowardly. Then he saw by the wall—he who
had come through many wars, good in his great-heartedness, many clashes in
battle when troops meet together—a stone arch standing, through it a stream
bursting out of the barrow: there was welling of a current hot with killing fires,
and he might not endure any while unburnt by the dragon's flame the hollow
near the hoard. Then the man of the Weather-Geats, enraged as he was, let a
word break from his breast. Stout-hearted he shouted; his voice went roaring,
clear in battle, in under the gray stone. Hate was stirred up, the hoard's guard
knew the voice of a man. No more time was there to ask for peace. First the
monster's breath came out of the stone, the hot war-steam. The earth
resounded. The man below the barrow, the lord of the Geats, swung his shield

4. Hygelac.
5. I.e., the Franks. The battle is the one in which Hygelac was slain.

against the dreadful visitor. Then the heart of the coiled thing was aroused to seek combat. The good war-king had drawn his sword, the old heirloom, not blunt of edge. To each of them as they threatened destruction there was terror of the other. Firm-hearted he stood with his shield high, the lord of friends, while quickly the worm coiled itself; he waited in his armor. Then, coiling in flames, he came gliding on, hastening to his fate. The good shield protected the life and body of the famous prince, but for a shorter while than his wish was. There for the first time, the first day in his life, he might not prevail, since fate did not assign him such glory in battle. The lord of the Geats raised his hand, struck the shining horror so with his forged blade that the edge failed, bright on the bone, bit less surely than its folk-king had need, hard-pressed in perils. Then because of the battle-stroke the barrow-ward's heart was savage, he exhaled death-fire—the war-flames sprang wide. The gold-friend of the Geats boasted of no great victories: the war blade had failed, naked at need, as it ought not to have done, iron good from old times. That was no pleasant journey, not one on which the famous son of Ecgtheow would wish to leave his land; against his will he must take up a dwelling-place elsewhere—as every man must give up the days that are lent him.

It was not long until they came together again, dreadful foes. The hoard-guard took heart, once more his breast swelled with his breathing. Encircled with flames, he who before had ruled a folk felt harsh pain. Nor did his companions, sons of nobles, take up their stand in a troop about him with the courage of fighting men, but they crept to the wood, protected their lives. In only one of them the heart surged with sorrows: nothing can ever set aside kinship in him who means well.

He was called Wiglaf, son of Weohstan, a rare shield-warrior, a man of the Scylfings,[6] kinsman of Aelfhere. He saw his liege lord under his war-mask suffer the heat. Then he was mindful of the honors he had given him before, the rich dwelling-place of the Waegmundings, every folk-right such as his father possessed. He might not then hold back, his hand seized his shield, the yellow linden-wood; he drew his ancient sword. Among men it was the heirloom of Eanmund, the son of Ohthere:[7] Weohstan had become his slayer in battle with sword's edge—an exile without friends; and he bore off to his kin the bright-shining helmet, the ringed mail-armor, the old sword made by giants that Onela had given him,[8] his kinsman's war-armor, ready battle-gear: he did not speak of the feud, though he had killed his brother's son.[9] He[1] held the armor many half-years, the blade and the battle-dress, until his son might do manly deeds like his old father. Then he gave him among the Geats war-armor of every kind, numberless, when, old, he went forth on the way from life. For the young warrior this was the first time that he should enter the war-

6. Although in the next sentence Wiglaf is said to belong to the family of the Waegmundings, the Geatish family to which Beowulf belonged, he is here called a Scylfing (Swede), and immediately below, his father, Weohstan, is represented as having fought for the Swede Onela in his attack on the Geats. But for a man to change his nation was not unusual, and Weohstan, who may have had both Swedish and Geatish blood, had evidently become a Geat long enough before to have brought up his son Wiglaf as one. The identity of Aelfhere is not known.
7. Weohstan not only supported Onela's attack on Geat King Heardred but actually killed Eanmund,

whom Heardred was supporting, and it is Eanmund's sword that Wiglaf is now wielding (see n. 9, p. 54).
8. The spoils of war belonged to the victorious king, who apportioned them among his fighters; thus Onela gave Weohstan the armor of Eanmund, whom Weohstan had killed.
9. This ironic remark points out that Onela did not claim wergild or seek vengeance from Weohstan, as in other circumstances he ought to have done inasmuch as Weohstan had killed Onela's close kinsman, his nephew Eanmund, but Onela was himself trying to kill Eanmund.
1. Weohstan.

storm with his dear lord. His heart's courage did not slacken, nor did the heirloom of his kinsman fail in the battle. That the worm found when they had come together.

Wiglaf spoke, said many fit words to his companions—his mind was mournful: "I remember that time we drank mead, when we promised our lord in the beer-hall—him who gave us these rings—that we would repay him for the war-arms if a need like this befell him—the helmets and the hard swords. Of his own will he chose us among the host for this venture, thought us worthy of fame—and gave me these treasures—because he counted us good war-makers, brave helm-bearers, though our lord intended to do this work of courage alone, as keeper of the folk, because among men he had performed the greatest deeds of glory, daring actions. Now the day has come that our liege lord has need of the strength of good fighters. Let us go to him, help our war-chief while the grim terrible fire persists. God knows of me that I should rather that the flame enfold my body with my gold-giver. It does not seem right to me for us to bear our shields home again unless we can first fell the foe, defend the life of the prince of the Weather-Geats. I know well that it would be no recompense for past deeds that he alone of the company of the Geats should suffer pain, fall in the fight. For us both shall there be a part in the work of sword and helmet, of battle-shirt and war-clothing."

Then he waded through the deadly smoke, bore his war-helmet to the aid of his king, spoke in few words: "Beloved Beowulf, do all well, for, long since in your youth, you said that you would not let your glory fail while you lived. Now, great-spirited noble, brave of deeds, you must protect your life with all your might. I shall help you."

After these words, the worm came on, angry, the terrible malice-filled foe, shining with surging flames, to seek for the second time his enemies, hated men. Fire advanced in waves; shield burned to the boss; mail-shirt might give no help to the young spear-warrior; but the young man went quickly under his kinsman's shield when his own was consumed with flames. Then the war-king was again mindful of fame, struck with his war-sword with great strength so that it stuck in the head-bone, driven with force: Naegling broke, the sword of Beowulf failed in the fight, old and steel-gray. It was not ordained for him that iron edges might help in the combat. Too strong was the hand that I have heard strained every sword with its stroke, when he bore wound-hardened weapon to battle: he was none the better for it.

Then for the third time the folk-harmer, the fearful fire-dragon, was mindful of feuds, set upon the brave one when the chance came, hot and battle-grim seized all his neck with his sharp fangs: he was smeared with life-blood, gore welled out in waves.

Then, I have heard, at the need of the folk-king the earl at his side made his courage known, his might and his keenness—as was natural to him. He took no heed for that head,[2] but the hand of the brave man was burned as he helped his kinsman, as the man in armor struck the hateful foe a little lower down, so that the sword sank in, shining and engraved; and then the fire began to subside. The king himself then still controlled his senses, drew the battle-knife, biting and war-sharp, that he wore on his mail-shirt: the protector of the Weather-Geats cut the worm through the middle. They felled the foe,

---

2. I.e., the dragon's flame-breathing head.

courage drove his life out, and they had destroyed him together, the two noble
kinsmen. So ought a man be, a thane at need. To the prince that was the last
moment of victory for his own deeds, of work in the world.

Then the wound that the earth-dragon had caused began to burn and to
swell; at once he felt dire evil boil in his breast, poison within him. Then the
prince, wise of thought, went to where he might sit on a seat near the wall.
He looked on the work of giants, how the timeless earth-hall held within it
stone-arches fast on pillars. Then with his hands the thane, good without limit,
washed him with water, blood-besmeared, the famous prince, his beloved lord,
sated with battle; and he unfastened his helmet.

Beowulf spoke—despite his wounds spoke, his mortal hurts. He knew well
he had lived out his days' time, joy on earth; all passed was the number of his
days, death very near. "Now I would wish to give my son my war-clothing, if
any heir after me, part of my flesh, were granted. I held this people fifty winters. There was no folk-king of those dwelling about who dared approach me
with swords, threaten me with fears. In my land I awaited what fate brought
me, held my own well, sought no treacherous quarrels, nor did I swear many
oaths unrightfully. Sick with life-wounds, I may have joy of all this, for the
Ruler of Men need not blame me for the slaughter of kinsmen when life goes
from my body. Now quickly go to look at the hoard under the gray stone,
beloved Wiglaf, now that the worm lies sleeping from sore wounds, bereft of
his treasure. Be quick now, so that I may see the ancient wealth, the golden
things, may clearly look on the bright curious gems, so that for that, because
of the treasure's richness, I may the more easily leave life and nation I have
long held."

Then I have heard that the son of Weohstan straightway obeyed his lord,
sick with battle-wounds, according to the words he had spoken, went wearing
his ring-armor, woven battle-shirt, under the barrow's roof. Then he saw, as he
went by the seat, the brave young retainer, triumphant in heart, many precious
jewels, glittering gold lying on the ground, wonders on the wall, and the
worm's lair, the old night-flier's—cups standing there, vessels of men of old,
with none to polish them, stripped of their ornaments. There was many a
helmet old and rusty, many an arm-ring skillfully twisted. (Easily may treasure,
gold in the ground, betray each one of the race of men, hide it who will.) Also
he saw a standard all gold hang high over the hoard, the greatest of hand-
wonders, linked with fingers' skill. From it came a light so that he might see
the ground, look on the works of craft. There was no trace of the worm, for
the blade had taken him. Then I have heard that one man in the mound
pillaged the hoard, the old work of giants, loaded in his bosom cups and plates
at his own desire. He took also the standard, brightest of banners. The sword
of the old lord—its edge was iron—had already wounded the one who for a
long time had been guardian of the treasure, waged his fire-terror, hot for the
hoard, rising up fiercely at midnight, till he died in the slaughter.

The messenger was in haste, eager to return, urged on by the treasures.
Curiosity tormented him, whether eagerly seeking he should find the lord of
the Weather-Geats, strength gone, alive in the place where he had left him
before. Then with the treasures he found the great prince, his lord, bleeding,
at the end of his life. Again he began to sprinkle him with water until this
word's point broke through his breast-hoard—he spoke, the king, old man in
sorrow, looked on the gold: "I speak with my words thanks to the Lord of All

for these treasures, to the King of Glory, Eternal Prince, for what I gaze on here, that I might get such for my people before my death-day. Now that I have bought the hoard of treasures with my old life, you attend to the people's needs hereafter: I can be here no longer. Bid the battle-renowned make a mound, bright after the funeral fire, on the sea's cape. It shall stand high on Hronesness as a reminder to my people, so that sea-travelers later will call it Beowulf's barrow, when they drive their ships far over the darkness of the seas."

He took off his neck the golden necklace, bold-hearted prince, gave it to the thane, to the young spear-warrior—gold-gleaming helmet, ring, and mail-shirt, bade him use them well. "You are the last left of our race, of the Waeg-mundings. Fate has swept away all my kinsmen, earls in their strength, to destined death. I have to go after." That was the last word of the old man, of the thoughts of his heart, before he should taste the funeral pyre, hot hostile flames. The soul went from his breast to seek the doom of those fast in truth.

[Beowulf's Funeral]

Then sorrow came to the young man that he saw him whom he most loved on the earth, at the end of his life, suffering piteously. His slayer likewise lay dead, the awful earth-dragon bereft of life, overtaken by evil. No longer should the coiled worm rule the ring-hoard, for iron edges had taken him, hard and battle-sharp work of the hammers, so that the wide-flier, stilled by wounds, had fallen on the earth near the treasure-house. He did not go flying through the air at midnight, proud of his property, showing his aspect, but he fell to earth through the work of the chief's hands. Yet I have heard of no man of might on land, though he was bold of every deed, whom it should prosper to rush against the breath of the venomous foe or disturb with hands the ring-hall, if he found the guard awake who lived in the barrow. The share of the rich treasures became Beowulf's, paid for by death: each of the two had jour-neyed to the end of life's loan.

Then it was not long before the battle-slack ones left the woods, ten weak troth-breakers together, who had not dared fight with their spears in their liege lord's great need. But they bore their shields, ashamed, their war-clothes, to where the old man lay, looked on Wiglaf. He sat wearied, the foot-soldier near the shoulders of his lord, would waken him with water: it gained him nothing. He might not, though he much wished it, hold life in his chieftain on earth nor change anything of the Ruler's: the judgment of God would control the deeds of every man, just as it still does now. Then it was easy to get from the young man a grim answer to him who before had lost courage. Wiglaf spoke, the son of Weohstan, a man sad at heart, looked on the unloved ones:

"Yes, he who will speak truth may say that the liege lord who gave you treasure, the war-gear that you stand in there, when he used often to hand out to hall-sitters on the ale-benches, a prince to his thanes, helmets and war-shirts such as he could find mightiest anywhere, both far and near—that he quite threw away the war-gear, to his distress when war came upon him. The folk-king had no need to boast of his war-comrades. Yet God, Ruler of Victories, granted him that he might avenge himself, alone with his sword, when there was need for his courage. I was able to give him little life-protection in the fight, and yet beyond my power I did begin to help my kinsman. The deadly foe was ever the weaker after I struck him with my sword, fire poured less strongly from his head. Too few defenders thronged about the prince when the hard time came upon him. Now there shall cease for your race the receiving of treasure and the giving of swords, all enjoyment of pleasant homes, comfort. Each man of your kindred must go deprived of his land-right when nobles from afar learn of your flight, your inglorious deed. Death is better for any earl than a life of blame."

Then he bade that the battle-deed be announced in the city, up over the cliff-edge, where the band of warriors sat the whole morning of the day, sad-hearted, shield-bearers in doubt whether it was the beloved man's last day or whether he would come again. Little did he fail to speak of new tidings, he who rode up the hill, but spoke to them all truthfully: "Now the joy-giver of the people of the Weathers, the lord of the Geats, is fast on his death-bed, lies on his slaughter-couch through deeds of the worm. Beside him lies his life-enemy, struck down with dagger-wounds—with his sword he might not work wounds of any kind on the monster. Wiglaf son of Weohstan sits over Beowulf, one earl by the lifeless other, in weariness of heart holds death-watch over the loved and the hated.

"Now may the people expect a time of war, when the king's fall becomes wide-known to the Franks and the Frisians. A harsh quarrel was begun with the Hugas when Hygelac came traveling with his sea-army to the land of the Frisians, where the Hetware assailed him in battle, quickly, with stronger forces, made the mailed warrior bow; he fell in the ranks: that chief gave no treasure to his retainers. Ever since then the good will of the Merewioing king has been denied us.

"Nor do I expect any peace or trust from the Swedish people, for it is wide-known that Ongentheow took the life of Haethcyn, Hrethel's son, near Ravenswood when in their over-pride the people of the Geats first went against the War-Scylfings. Straightway the wary father of Ohthere,[3] old and terrible, gave a blow in return, cut down the sea-king,[4] rescued his wife, old woman of times past, bereft of her gold, mother of Onela and Ohthere, and then he followed his life-foes until they escaped, lordless, painfully, to Ravenswood. Then with a great army he besieged those whom the sword had left, weary with wounds, often vowed woes to the wretched band the livelong night, said that in the morning he would cut them apart with sword-blades, [hang] some on gallows-trees as sport for birds. Relief came in turn to the sorry-hearted together with dawn when they heard Hygelac's horn and trumpet, his sound as the good man came on their track with a body of retainers. Wide-seen was the bloody track of Swedes and Geats, the slaughter-strife of men, how the peoples stirred up the feud between them. Then the good man went with his kinsmen, old and much-mourning, to seek his stronghold: the earl Ongentheow moved further away. He had heard of the warring of Hygelac, of the war-power of the proud one. He did not trust in resistance, that he might fight off the sea-men, defend his hoard against the war-sailors, his children and wife. Instead he drew back, the old man behind his earth-wall.

"Then pursuit was offered to the people of the Swedes, the standards of

---

3. I.e., Ongentheow.
4. I.e., Haethcyn, king of the Geats. Haethcyn's brother Hygelac, who succeeded him, was not present at this battle but arrived after the death of Haethcyn with reinforcements to relieve the survivors and to pursue Ongentheow in his retreat to his city.

Hygelac overran the stronghold as Hrethel's people pressed forward to the citadel. There Ongentheow the gray-haired was brought to bay by sword-blades, and the people's king had to submit to the judgment of Eofor alone. Wulf[5] son of Wonred had struck him angrily with his weapon so that for the blow the blood sprang forth in streams beneath his hair. Yet not for that was he afraid, the old Scylfing, but he quickly repaid the assault with worse exchange, the folk-king, when he turned toward him. The strong son of Wonred could not give the old man a return blow, for Ongentheow had first cut through the helmet of his head so that he had to sink down, smeared with blood—fell on the earth: he was not yet doomed, for he recovered, though the wound hurt him. The hardy thane of Hygelac,[6] when his brother lay low, let his broad sword, old blade made by giants, break the great helmet across the shield-wall; then the king bowed, the keeper of the folk was hit to the quick.

"Then there were many who bound up the brother, quickly raised him up after it was granted them to control the battle-field. Then one warrior stripped the other, took from Ongentheow his iron-mail, hard-hilted sword, and his helmet, too; he bore the arms of the hoary one to Hygelac. He accepted that treasure and fairly promised him rewards among the people, and he stood by it thus: the lord of the Geats, the son of Hrethel, when he came home, repaid Wulf and Eofor for their battle-assault with much treasure, gave each of them a hundred thousand [units] of land and linked rings: there was no need for any man on middle-earth to blame him for the rewards, since they had performed great deeds. And then he gave Eofor his only daughter as a pledge of friendship—a fair thing for his home.

"That is the feud and the enmity, the death-hatred of men, for which I expect that the people of the Swedes, bold shield-warriors after the fall of princes, will set upon us after they learn that our prince has gone from life, he who before held hoard and kingdom against our enemies, did good to the people, and further still, did what a man should. Now haste is best, that we look on the people's king there and bring him who gave us rings on his way to the funeral pyre. Nor shall only a small share melt with the great-hearted one, but there is a hoard of treasure, gold uncounted, grimly purchased, and rings bought at the last now with his own life. These shall the fire devour, flames enfold—no earl to wear ornament in remembrance, nor any bright maiden add to her beauty with neck-ring; but mournful-hearted, stripped of gold, they shall walk, often, not once, in strange countries—now that the army-leader has laid aside laughter, his game and his mirth. Therefore many a spear, cold in the morning, shall be grasped with fingers, raised by hands; no sound of harp shall waken the warriors, but the dark raven, low over the doomed, shall tell many tales, say to the eagle how he fared at the feast when with the wolf he spoiled the slain bodies."

Thus the bold man was a speaker of hateful news, nor did he much lie in his words or his prophecies. The company all arose. Without joy they went below Earnaness[7] to look on the wonder with welling tears. Then they found on the sand, soulless, keeping his bed of rest, him who in former times had given them rings. Then the last day of the good man had come, when the war-king,

---

5. The two sons of Wonred, Wulf and Eofor, attacked Ongentheow in turn. Wulf was struck down but not killed by the old Swedish king, who was then slain by Eofor.

6. I.e., Eofor.

7. The headland near where Beowulf had fought the dragon.

prince of the Weather-Geats, died a wonderful death. First they saw the stranger creature, the worm lying loathsome, opposite him in the place. The fire-dragon was grimly terrible with his many colors, burned by the flames; he was fifty feet long in the place where he lay. Once he had joy of the air at night, came back down to seek his den. Then he was made fast by death, had made use of the last of his earth-caves. Beside him stood cups and pitchers, plates and rich swords lay eaten through by rust, just as they had been there in the bosom of the earth for a thousand winters. Then that huge heritage, gold of men of old, was wound in a spell, so that no one of men must touch the ring-hall unless God himself, the True King of Victories—He is men's protection—should grant to whom He wished to open the hoard—whatever man seemed fit to Him.

Then it was seen that the act did not profit him who wrongly kept hidden the handiworks under the wall. The keeper had first slain a man like few others, then the feud had been fiercely avenged. It is a wonder where an earl famed for courage may reach the end of his allotted life—then may dwell no longer in the mead-hall, man with his kin. So it was with Beowulf when he sought quarrels, the barrow's ward: he himself did not then know in what way his parting with the world should come. The great princes who had put it[8] there had laid on it so deep a curse until doomsday that the man who should plunder the place should be guilty of sins, imprisoned in idol-shrines, fixed with hell-bonds, punished with evils—unless the Possessor's favor were first shown the more clearly to him who desired the gold.

Wiglaf spoke, the son of Weohstan: "Often many a man must suffer distress for the will of one man, as has happened to us. We might by no counsel persuade our dear prince, keeper of the kingdom, not to approach the gold-guardian, let him lie where he long was, live in his dwelling to the world's end. He held to his high destiny. The hoard has been made visible, grimly got. What drove the folk-king thither was too powerfully fated. I have been therein and looked at it all, the rare things of the chamber, when it was granted me—not at all friendly was the journey that I was permitted beneath the earth-wall. In haste I seized with my hands a huge burden of hoard-treasures, of great size, bore it out here to my king. He was then still alive, sound-minded and aware. He spoke many things, old man in sorrow, and bade greet you, commanded that for your lord's deeds you make a high barrow in the place of his pyre, large and conspicuous, since he was of men the worthiest warrior through the wide earth, while he might enjoy wealth in his castle.

"Let us now hasten to see and visit for the second time the heap of precious jewels, the wonder under the walls. I shall direct you so that you may look on enough of them from near at hand—rings and broad gold. Let the bier be made ready, speedily prepared, when we come out, and then let us carry our prince, beloved man, where he shall long dwell in the Ruler's protection."

Then the son of Weohstan, man brave in battle, bade command many warriors, men who owned houses, leaders of the people, that they carry wood from afar for the pyre for the good man. "Now shall flame eat the chief of warriors—the fire shall grow dark—who often survived the iron-shower when the storm of arrows driven from bow-strings passed over the shield-wall—the shaft did its task, made eager by feather-gear served the arrowhead."

8. The treasure.

And then the wise son of Weohstan summoned from the host thanes of the king, seven together, the best; one of eight warriors, he went beneath the evil roof. One who walked before bore a torch in his hands. Then there was no lot to decide who should plunder that hoard, since the men could see that every part of it rested in the hall without guardian, lay wasting. Little did any man mourn that hastily they should bear out the rare treasure. Also they pushed the dragon, the worm, over the cliff-wall, let the wave take him, the flood enfold the keeper of the treasure. Then twisted gold was loaded on a wagon, an uncounted number of things, and the prince, hoary warrior, borne to Hronesness.

Then the people of the Geats made ready for him a funeral pyre on the earth, no small one, hung with helmets, battle-shields, bright mail-shirts, just as he had asked. Then in the midst they laid the great prince, lamenting their hero, their beloved lord. Then warriors began to awaken on the barrow the greatest of funeral-fires; the wood-smoke climbed, black over the fire; the roaring flame mixed with weeping—the wind-surge died down—until it had broken the bone-house, hot at its heart. Sad in spirit they lamented their heart-care, the death of their liege lord. [And the Geatish woman, wavy-haired, sang a sorrowful song about Beowulf, said][9] again and again that she sorely feared for herself invasions of armies, many slaughters, terror of troops, humiliation, and captivity. Heaven swallowed the smoke.

Then the people of the Weather-Geats built a mound on the promontory, one that was high and broad, wide-seen by seafarers, and in ten days completed a monument for the bold in battle, surrounded the remains of the fire with a wall, the most splendid that men most skilled might devise. In the barrow they placed rings and jewels, all such ornaments as troubled men had earlier taken from the hoard. They let the earth hold the wealth of earls, gold in the ground, where now it still dwells, as useless to men as it was before. Then the brave in battle rode round the mound, children of nobles, twelve in all, would bewail their sorrow and mourn their king, recite dirges and speak of the man. They praised his great deeds and his acts of courage, judged well of his prowess. So it is fitting that man honor his liege lord with words, love him in heart when he must be led forth from the body. Thus the people of the Geats, his hearth-companions, lamented the death of their lord. They said that he was of world-kings the mildest of men and the gentlest, kindest to his people, and most eager for fame.

---

9. The manuscript is badly damaged and the interpretation conjectural.

Middle English Literature

GEOFFREY CHAUCER
ca. 1343–1400

1372: First Italian journey: contact with Italian literature.
1385: *Troilus and Criseide.*
1386: *Canterbury Tales* begun.

Medieval social theory held that society was made up of three "estates": the nobility, composed of a small hereditary aristocracy, whose mission on earth was to rule over and defend the body politic; the church, whose duty was to look after the spiritual welfare of that body; and everyone else, the large mass of commoners who were supposed to do the work that provided for its physical needs. By the late fourteenth century, however, these basic categories were layered into complex, interrelated, and unstable social strata among which birth, wealth, profession, and personal ability all played a part in determining one's status in a world that was rapidly changing economically, politically, and socially. Chaucer's life and his works, especially *The Canterbury Tales*, were profoundly influenced by these forces. A large and prosperous middle class was beginning to play increasingly important roles in church and state, blurring the traditional class boundaries, and it was into this middle class that Chaucer was born.

Chaucer was the son of a prosperous wine merchant and probably spent his boyhood in the mercantile atmosphere of London's Vintry, where ships docked with wines from France and Spain. Here he would have mixed daily with people of all sorts, heard several languages spoken, become fluent in French, and received schooling in Latin. Instead of apprenticing Chaucer to the family business, however, his father was apparently able to place him, in his early teens, as a page in one of the great aristocratic households of England, that of the countess of Ulster who was married to Prince Lionel, the second son of Edward III. There Chaucer would have acquired the manners and skills required for a career in the service of the ruling class, not only in the role of personal attendant in royal households but in a series of administrative posts.

We can trace Chaucer's official and personal life in a considerable number of surviving historical documents, beginning with a reference, in Elizabeth of Ulster's household accounts, to an outfit he received as a page (1357). He was captured by the French and ransomed in one of Edward III's campaigns during the Hundred Years War (1359). He was a member of King Edward's personal household (1367) and took part in several diplomatic missions to Spain (1366), France (1368), and Italy (1372). As controller of customs on wool, sheepskins, and leather for the port of London (1374–85), Chaucer audited and kept books on the export taxes, which were one of the Crown's main sources of revenue. During this period he was living in a rent-free apartment over one of the gates in the city wall, probably as a perquisite of the customs job. He served as a justice of the peace and knight of the shire (the title given to members of Parliament) for the county of Kent (1385–86) where he moved after giving up the controllership. As clerk of the king's works (1389–91), Chaucer was responsible for the maintenance of numerous royal residences, parks, and other holdings; his duties included supervision of the construction of the nave of Westminster Abbey and of stands and lists for a celebrated tournament staged by Richard II. While the records show Chaucer receiving many grants and annuities in addition to his salary for these services, they also show that at times he was being pressed by creditors and obliged to borrow money.

These activities brought Chaucer into association with the ruling nobility of the kingdom, with Prince Lionel and his younger brother John of Gaunt, duke of Lancaster, England's most powerful baron during much of Chaucer's lifetime; with their father, King Edward; and with Edward's grandson, who succeeded to the throne as Richard II. Near the end of his life Chaucer addressed a comic *Complaint to His Purse* to Henry IV—John of Gaunt's son, who had usurped the crown from his cousin Richard—as a reminder that the treasury owed Chaucer his annuity. Chaucer's wife, Philippa, who, as a knight's daughter, was of higher birth than the poet, served in the households of Edward's queen and of John of Gaunt's second wife, Constance, daughter of the king of Castile. Chaucer's sister-in-law, Katherine Swynford, served in John of Gaunt's household, where she became the duke's mistress and, after the death of Constance, his third duchess. A Thomas Chaucer, who was probably Chaucer's son, was an eminent man in the next generation, and Thomas's daughter Alice was married successively to the earl of Salisbury and the duke of Suffolk. The gap between the commoners and the aristocracy would thus have been bridged by Chaucer's family in the course of three generations.

None of these documents contains any hint that this hardworking civil servant wrote poetry, although poetry would certainly have been among the diversions cultivated at English courts in Chaucer's youth. That poetry, however, would have been in French, which still remained the fashionable language and literature of the English aristocracy, whose culture in many ways had more in common with that of the French nobles with whom they warred than with that of their English subjects. Chaucer's earliest models, works by Guillaume de Machaut (1300?–1377) and Jean Froissart (1333?–1400?), the leading French poets of the day, were lyrics and narratives about courtly love, often cast in the form of a dream in which the poet acted as a protagonist or participant in some aristocratic love affair. The poetry of Machaut and Froissart derives from the thirteenth-century *Romance of the Rose*, a long dream allegory in which the dreamer suffers many agonies and trials for the love of a symbolic rosebud. Chaucer's apprentice work may well have been a partial translation of the twenty-one-thousand-line *Romance*. His first important original poem is *The Book of the Duchess*, an elegy in the form of a dream vision commemorating John of Gaunt's first wife, the young duchess of Lancaster, who died in 1368.

The diplomatic mission that sent Chaucer to Italy in 1372 was in all likelihood a milestone in his literary development. Although he may have acquired some knowledge of the language and literature from Italian merchants and bankers posted in London, this visit and a subsequent one to Florence (1378) brought him into direct contact with the Italian Renaissance. Probably he acquired manuscripts of works by Dante, Petrarch, and Boccaccio—the last two still alive at the time of Chaucer's visit, although he probably did not meet them. These writers presented him with new verse forms, new subject matter, and new modes of representation. *The House of Fame*, still a dream vision, takes the poet on a journey in the talons of a gigantic eagle to the celestial palace of the goddess Fame, a trip that at many points affectionately parodies Dante's journey in the *Divine Comedy*. In his dream vision *The Parliament of Fowls*, all the birds meet on St. Valentine's Day to choose their mates; their "parliament" humorously depicts the ways in which different classes in human society think and talk about love. Boccaccio provided sources for two of Chaucer's finest poems—although Chaucer never mentions his name. *The Knight's Tale*, the first of *The Canterbury Tales*, is based on Boccaccio's romance *Il Teseida* (The Story of Theseus). His longest completed poem, *Troilus and Criseide* (ca. 1385), which tells the story of how Trojan Prince Troilus loved and finally lost Criseide to the Greek warrior Diomede, is an adaptation of Boccaccio's *Il Filostrato* (The Love-Stricken). Chaucer reworked the latter into one of the greatest love poems in any language. Even if he had never written *The Canterbury Tales*, *Troilus* would have secured Chaucer a place among the major English poets.

A final dream vision provides the frame for Chaucer's first experiment with a series of tales, the unfinished *Legend of Good Women*. In the dream, Chaucer is accused of heresy and antifeminism by Cupid, the god of love himself, and ordered to do penance by writing a series of "legends," i.e., saints' lives, of Cupid's martyrs, women who were betrayed by false men and died for love. Perhaps a noble patron, possibly Queen Anne, asked the poet to write something to make up for telling about Criseide's betrayal of Troilus.

Throughout his life Chaucer also wrote moral and religious works, chiefly translations, both in prose and poetry. Besides French, which was a second language for him, and Italian, Chaucer also read Latin. He made a prose translation of the Latin *Consolation of Philosophy*, written by the sixth-century Roman statesman Boethius while he was in prison awaiting execution for crimes for which he had been unjustly condemned. The *Consolation* became a favorite book for the Middle Ages, providing inspiration and comfort through its lesson that worldly fortune is deceitful and ephemeral and through the platonic doctrine that the body itself is only a prison house for the soul that aspires to eternal things. The influence of Boethius is deeply ingrained in *The Knight's Tale* and *Troilus*. The ballade *Truth* compresses the Boethian and Christian teaching into three stanzas of homely moral advice.

Thus long before Chaucer conceived of *The Canterbury Tales*, his writings were many faceted: they embrace prose and poetry; human and divine love; French, Italian, and Latin sources; secular and religious influences; comedy and philosophy. Moreover, different elements are likely to mix in the same work, often making it difficult to extract from Chaucer simple, direct, and certain meanings.

This Chaucerian complexity owes much to the wide range of Chaucer's learning and his exposure to new literary currents on the Continent but perhaps even more to the special social position he occupied as a member of a new class of civil servants. Born into the urban middle class, Chaucer, through his association with the court and service of the Crown, had attained the rank of "esquire," roughly equivalent to what would later be termed a "gentleman." His career brought him into contact with overlapping bourgeois and aristocratic social worlds, without being securely anchored in either. Situated thus, Chaucer was able to view with both sympathy and detached amusement the behavior, beliefs, and pretensions of the diverse people who made up those worlds. Although he was born a commoner and continued to associate with commoners in his official life, he did not live as a commoner; and although his training and service at court, his wife's connections, and probably his poetry brought him into contact with the nobility, he must always have been conscious of the fact that he did not really belong to that society of which birth alone could make one a true member. Chaucer's art of being at once involved in and detached from a given situation is peculiarly his own, but that art would have been appreciated by a small group of friends close to Chaucer's social position—men like Sir Philip de la Vache, to whom Chaucer addressed the humorous envoy to *Truth*. Chaucer belongs to an age when poetry was read aloud. A beautiful frontispiece to a manuscript of *Troilus* pictures the poet's public performance before a magnificently dressed royal audience, and he may well have been invited at times to read his poems at court. But besides addressing a listening audience, to whose allegedly superior taste and sensibility the poet often ironically defers (for example, *The General Prologue*, lines 745–748), Chaucer has in mind a few discriminating readers whom he might expect to share his sense of humor and his complex attitudes toward the company of "sondry folk" who make the pilgrimage to Canterbury.

The text given here is from E. T. Donaldson's *Chaucer's Poetry: An Anthology for the Modern Reader* (1958, 1975) with some modifications. For *The Canterbury Tales* the Hengwrt Manuscript has provided the textual basis. The spelling has been altered to improve consistency and has been modernized in so far as is possible without distorting the phonological values of the Middle English. A discussion of Middle English pronunciation, grammar, and prosody is included in the introduction "The Middle Ages" (pp. 10–15).

The Canterbury Tales   Chaucer's original plan for *The Canterbury Tales* projected about one hundred twenty stories, two for each pilgrim to tell on the way to Canterbury and two more on the way back. Chaucer actually completed only twenty-two, although two more exist in fragments. He did not stick to his original plan, because the Host says to the Parson, who tells the last tale, that everyone except him has told "his tale." Indeed, the pilgrims never even get to Canterbury. The work was probably first conceived in 1386, when Chaucer was living in Greenwich, some miles east of London. From his house he might have been able to see the pilgrim road that led toward the shrine of the famous English saint, Thomas à Becket, the archbishop of Canterbury who was murdered in his cathedral in 1170. Medieval pilgrims were notorious tale tellers, and the sight and sound of the bands riding toward Canterbury may well have suggested to Chaucer the idea of using a fictitious pilgrimage as a framing device for a number of stories. Collections of stories linked by such a device were common in the later Middle Ages. Chaucer's contemporary John Gower had used one in his *Confessio Amantis*. The most famous medieval framing tale besides Chaucer's is Boccaccio's *Decameron*, in which ten different narrators each tell a tale a day for ten days. Chaucer could have known the *Decameron*, which contains tales with plots analogous to plots found also in *The Canterbury Tales*, but these stories were widespread, and there is no proof that Chaucer got them from Boccaccio.

Chaucer's artistic exploitation of the device is, in any case, altogether his own. Whereas in Gower a single speaker relates all the stories, and in Boccaccio the ten speakers—three young gentlemen and seven young ladies—all belong to the same sophisticated social elite, Chaucer's pilgrim narrators represent a wide spectrum of ranks and occupations. The great variety of tales is matched by the diversity of their tellers; tales are assigned to appropriate narrators and juxtaposed to bring out contrasts in genre, style, tone, and values. Thus the Knight's courtly romance about the rivalry of two noble lovers for a lady is followed by the Miller's fabliau of the seduction of an old carpenter's young wife by a student. In several of *The Canterbury Tales* there is a fascinating accord between the narrators and their stories, so that the story takes on rich overtones from what we have learned of its teller in *The General Prologue* and elsewhere, and the character itself grows and is revealed by the story. Chaucer conducts two fictions simultaneously—that of the individual tale and that of the pilgrim to whom he has assigned it. He develops the second fiction not only through *The General Prologue* but also through the "links," the interchanges among pilgrims connecting the stories. These interchanges sometimes lead to quarrels. Thus *The Miller's Tale* offends the Reeve, who takes the figure of the Miller's foolish, cuckolded carpenter as directed personally at himself, and he retaliates with a story satirizing an arrogant miller very much like the pilgrim Miller. The antagonism of the two tellers provides comedy in the links and enhances the comedy of their tales. The links also offer interesting literary commentary on the tales by members of the pilgrim audience, especially the Host, whom the pilgrims have declared "governour" and "juge" of the storytelling. Further dramatic interest is created by the fact that several tales respond to topics taken up by previous tellers. The Wife of Bath's thesis that women should have sovereignty over men in marriage gets a reply from the Clerk, which, in turn, elicits responses from the Merchant and the Franklin. The tales have their own logic and interest quite apart from the framing fiction; no other medieval framing fiction, however, has such varied and lively interaction between the frame and the individual stories.

The composition of none of the tales can be accurately dated; most of them were written during the last fourteen years of Chaucer's life, although a few were probably written earlier and inserted into *The Canterbury Tales*. The popularity of the poem in late medieval England is attested by the number of surviving manuscripts: more than eighty, none from Chaucer's lifetime. It was also twice printed by William Caxton, who introduced printing to England in 1476, and often reprinted by Caxton's early successors. The manuscripts reflect the unfinished state of the poem—the fact that when he died Chaucer had not made up his mind about a number of details and hence left many inconsistencies. The poem appears in the manuscripts as nine or ten "fragments" or blocks of tales; the order of the poems within each fragment is generally the same, but the order of the fragments themselves varies widely. The fragment containing *The General Prologue*; the Knight's, Miller's, and Reeve's tales; and the Cook's unfinished tale, always comes first, and the fragment consisting of *The Parson's Tale* and *The Retraction* always comes last. But the others, such as that containing the Wife of Bath, the Friar, and the Summoner or that consisting of the Physician and Pardoner or the longest fragment, consisting of six tales concluding with the Nun's Priest's, are by no means stable in relation to one another. The order followed here, that of the Ellesmere manuscript, has been adopted as the most nearly satisfactory.

THE GENERAL PROLOGUE

Chaucer did not need to make a pilgrimage himself to meet the types of people that his fictitious pilgrimage includes, because most of them had long inhabited literature as well as life: the ideal Knight, who had taken part in all the major expeditions and battles of the crusades during the last half-century; his fashionably dressed son, the Squire, a typical young lover; the lady Prioress, the hunting Monk, and the flattering Friar, who practice the little vanities and larger vices for which such ecclesiastics were conventionally attacked; the prosperous Franklin; the fraudulent Doctor; the lusty and domineering Wife of Bath; the austere Parson; and so on down through the lower orders to that spellbinding preacher and mercenary, the Pardoner, peddling his paper indulgences and phony relics. One meets all these types throughout medieval literature, but particularly in a genre called estates satire, which sets out to expose and pillory typical examples of corruption at all levels of society. A remarkable number of details in *The General Prologue* could have been taken straight out of books as well as drawn from life. Although it has been argued that some of the pilgrims are portraits of actual people, the impression that they are drawn from life is more likely to be a function of Chaucer's art, which is able to endow types with a reality we generally associate only with people we know. The salient features of each pilgrim leap out randomly at the reader, as they might to an observer concerned only with what meets the eye. This imitation of the way our minds actually perceive reality may make us fail to notice the care with which Chaucer has selected his details to give an integrated sketch of the person being described. Most of these details give something more than mere verisimilitude to the description. The pilgrims' facial features, the clothes they wear, the foods they like to eat, the things they say, the work they do are all clues not only to their social rank but to their moral and spiritual condition and, through the accumulation of detail, to the condition of late-medieval society, of which, collectively, they are representative. What uniquely distinguishes Chaucer's prologue from conventional estates satire, however, is the suppression in all but a few instances of overt moral judgment. The narrator, in fact, seems to be expressing chiefly admiration and praise at the superlative skills and accomplishments of this particular group, even such dubious ones as the Friar's begging techniques or the Manciple's success in cheating the learned lawyers who employ him. It is up to the reader to draw up the moral indictment from the evidence presented with such seeming artlessness, even while falling in with the easygoing mood of "felaweship" that pervades Chaucer's prologue to the pilgrimage.

From THE CANTERBURY TALES

The General Prologue

	Whan that April with his° showres soote°	its/fresh
	The droughte of March hath perced to the roote,	
	And bathed every veine[1] in swich° licour,°	such/liquid
	Of which vertu[2] engendred is the flowr;	
5	Whan Zephyrus eek° with his sweete breeth	also
	Inspired[3] hath in every holt° and heeth°	grove/field
	The tendre croppes,° and the yonge sonne[4]	shoots
	Hath in the Ram his halve cours yronne,	
	And smale fowles° maken melodye	birds
10	That sleepen al the night with open yë°—	eye
	So priketh hem° Nature in hir corages[5]—	them
	Thanne longen folk to goon° on pilgrimages,	go
	And palmeres for to seeken straunge strondes	
	To ferne halwes,[6] couthe° in sondry° londes;	known/various
15	And specially from every shires ende	
	Of Engelond to Canterbury they wende,	
	The holy blisful martyr[7] for to seeke	
	That hem hath holpen° whan that they were seke.°	helped/sick
	Bifel° that in that seson on a day,	It happened
20	In Southwerk[8] at the Tabard as I lay,	
	Redy to wenden on my pilgrimage	
	To Canterbury with ful° devout corage,	very
	At night was come into that hostelrye	
	Wel nine and twenty in a compaignye	
25	Of sondry folk, by aventure° yfalle	chance
	In felaweshipe, and pilgrimes were they alle	
	That toward Canterbury wolden° ride.	would
	The chambres and the stables weren wide,	

1. I.e., in plants.
2. By the power of which.
3. Breathed into. "Zephyrus": the west wind.
4. The sun is young because it has run only halfway through its course in Aries, the Ram—the first sign of the zodiac in the solar year.
5. Their hearts.
6. Far-off shrines. "Palmeres": palmers, wide-ranging pilgrims—especially those who sought out the "straunge strondes" (foreign shores) of the Holy Land.
7. St. Thomas à Becket, murdered in Canterbury Cathedral in 1170.
8. Southwark, site of the Tabard Inn, was then a suburb of London, south of the Thames River.

	And wel we weren esed° at the beste.[9]	accommodated

30 And shortly,° whan the sonne was to reste,[1]   *in brief*
So hadde I spoken with hem everichoon°   *every one*
That I was of hir felaweshipe anoon,°   *at once*
And made forward[2] erly for to rise,
To take oure way ther as[3] I you devise.°   *describe*
35 But nathelees,° whil I have time and space,[4]   *nevertheless*
Er° that I ferther in this tale pace,°   *before/proceed*
Me thinketh it accordant to resoun[5]
To telle you al the condicioun
Of eech of hem, so as it seemed me,
40 And whiche they were, and of what degree,°   *social rank*
And eek° in what array that they were inne: *also*
And at a knight thanne° wol I first biginne.   *then*
   A Knight ther was, and that a worthy man,
That fro the time that he first bigan
45 To riden out, he loved chivalrye,
Trouthe and honour, freedom and curteisye.[6]
Ful worthy was he in his lordes werre,°   *war*
And therto hadde he riden, no man ferre,°   *further*
As wel in Cristendom as hethenesse,°   *heathen lands*
50 And[7] evere honoured for his worthinesse.
   At Alisandre[8] he was whan it was wonne;
Ful ofte time he hadde the boord bigonne[9]
Aboven alle nacions in Pruce;
In Lettou had he reised,° and in Ruce,   *campaigned*
55 No Cristen man so ofte of his degree;
In Gernade° at the sege eek hadde he be   *Granada*
Of Algezir, and riden in Belmarye;
At Lyeis was he, and at Satalye,
Whan they were wonne; and in the Grete See[1]
60 At many a noble arivee° hadde he be.   *military landing*
   At mortal batailes[2] hadde he been fifteene,
And foughten for oure faith at Tramissene
In listes[3] thries,° and ay° slain his fo.   *thrice/always*
   This ilke° worthy Knight hadde been also   *same*
65 Sometime with the lord of Palatye[4]
Again° another hethen in Turkye;   *against*
And everemore he hadde a soverein pris.°   *reputation*
And though that he were worthy, he was wis,[5]
And of his port° as meeke as is a maide.   *demeanor*
70 He nevere yit no vilainye° ne saide   *rudeness*

9. In the best possible way.
1. Had set.
2. I.e., (we) made an agreement.
3. Where.
4. I.e., opportunity.
5. It seems to me according to reason.
6. Courtesy. "Trouthe": integrity. "Freedom": generosity of spirit.
7. I.e., and he was.
8. The Knight has taken part in campaigns fought against three groups who threatened Christian Europe during the 14th century: the Moslems in the Near East, from whom Alexandria was seized after a famous siege; the northern barbarians in Prussia, Lithuania, and Russia; and the Moors in North Africa. The place names in the following lines refer to battlegrounds in these continuing wars.
9. Sat in the seat of honor at military feasts.
1. The Mediterranean.
2. Tournaments fought to the death.
3. Lists, tournament grounds.
4. A Moslem: alliances of convenience were often made during the Crusades between Christians and Moslems.
5. I.e., he was wise as well as bold.

In al his lif unto no manere wight:[6]
He was a verray,° parfit,° gentil° knight.   *true/perfect/noble*
But for to tellen you of his array,
His hors° were goode, but he was nat gay.[7]   *horses*
75   Of fustian° he wered° a gipoun[8]   *thick cloth/wore*
Al bismotered with his haubergeoun,[9]
For he was late° come from his viage,°   *lately/expedition*
And wente for to doon his pilgrimage.
      With him ther was his sone, a yong Squier,[1]
80   A lovere and a lusty bacheler,
With lokkes crulle° as° they were laid in presse.   *curly/as if*
Of twenty yeer of age he was, I gesse.
Of his stature he was of evene° lengthe,   *moderate*
And wonderly delivere,° and of greet° strengthe.   *agile/great*
85   And he hadde been som time in chivachye[2]
In Flandres, in Artois, and Picardye,
And born him wel as of so litel space,[3]
In hope to stonden in his lady° grace.   *lady's*
      Embrouded° was he as it were a mede,[4]   *embroidered*
90   Al ful of fresshe flowres, white and rede;°   *red*
Singing he was, or floiting,° al the day: *whistling*
He was as fressh as is the month of May.
Short was his gowne, with sleeves longe and wide.
Wel coude he sitte on hors, and faire ride;
95   He coude songes make, and wel endite,°   *compose verse*
Juste[5] and eek° daunce, and wel portraye° and write.   *also/sketch*
So hote° he loved that by nightertale[6]   *hotly*
He slepte namore than dooth a nightingale.
Curteis he was, lowely,° and servisable,   *humble*
100   And carf biforn his fader at the table.[7]
      A Yeman hadde he[8] and servants namo°   *no more*
At that time, for him liste[9] ride so;
And he[1] was clad in cote and hood of greene.
A sheef of pecok arwes,° bright and keene,   *arrows*
105   Under his belt he bar° ful thriftily;°   *bore/properly*
Wel coude he dresse° his takel° yemanly:[2]   *tend to/gear*
His arwes drouped nought with fetheres lowe.
And in his hand he bar a mighty bowe.
A not-heed° hadde he with a brown visage.   *close-cut head*
110   Of wodecraft wel coude° he al the usage.   *knew*
Upon his arm he bar a gay bracer,[3]
And by his side a swerd° and a bokeler,[4]   *sword*

6. Any sort of person. In Middle English, negatives are multiplied for emphasis: as in these two lines: "nevere," "no," "ne," "no."
7. I.e., gaily dressed.
8. Tunic worn underneath the coat of mail.
9. All rust-stained from his hauberk (coat of mail).
1. The vague term "Squier" (Squire) here seems to be the equivalent of "bacheler," a young knight still in the service of an older one.
2. On cavalry expeditions. The places in the next line are sites of skirmishes in the constant warfare between the English and the French.
3. I.e., considering the little time he had been in ser-

vice.
4. Mead, meadow.
5. Joust, fight in a tournament.
6. At night.
7. It was a squire's duty to carve his lord's meat.
8. I.e., the Knight. The "Yeman" (Yeoman) is an independent commoner who acts as the Knight's military servant.
9. It pleased him to.
1. I.e., the Yeoman.
2. In a workmanlike way.
3. Wrist guard for archers.
4. Buckler (a small shield).

And on that other side a gay daggere,
Harneised° wel and sharp as point of spere;   *mounted*
115 A Cristophre⁵ on his brest of silver sheene;°   *bright*
An horn he bar, the baudrik⁶ was of greene.
A forster° was he soothly,° as I gesse.   *forester/truly*
   Ther was also a Nonne, a Prioresse,
That of hir smiling was ful simple and coy.⁷
120 Hir gretteste ooth was but by sainte Loy!°   *Eloi*
And she was cleped° Madame Eglantine.   *named*
Ful wel she soong° the service divine,   *sang*
Entuned° in hir nose ful semely;⁸   *chanted*
And Frenssh she spak ful faire and fetisly,°   *elegantly*
125 After the scole° of Stratford at the Bowe⁹—   *school*
For Frenssh of Paris was to hire unknowe.
At mete° wel ytaught was she withalle:°   *meals/besides*
She leet° no morsel from hir lippes falle,   *let*
Ne wette hir fingres in hir sauce deepe;
130 Wel coude she carye a morsel, and wel keepe°   *take care*
That no drope ne fille° upon hir brest.   *should fall*
In curteisye was set ful muchel hir lest.¹
Hir over-lippe° wiped she so clene   *upper lip*
That in hir coppe° ther was no ferthing° seene   *cup/bit*
135 Of grece,° whan she dronken hadde hir draughte;   *grease*
Ful semely after hir mete she raughte.°   *reached*
And sikerly° she was of greet disport,²   *certainly*
And ful plesant, and amiable of port,°   *mien*
And pained hire to countrefete cheere³
140 Of court, and to been statlich° of manere,   *dignified*
And to been holden digne⁴ of reverence.
But, for to speken of hir conscience,
She was so charitable and so pitous°   *merciful*
She wolde weepe if that she saw a mous
145 Caught in a trappe, if it were deed° or bledde.   *dead*
Of⁵ smale houndes hadde she that she fedde
With rosted flessh, or milk and wastelbreed;°   *fine white bread*
But sore wepte she if oon of hem were deed,
Or if men smoot it with a yerde smerte;⁶
150 And al was conscience and tendre herte.
Ful semely hir wimpel° pinched° was,   *headdress/pleated*
Hir nose tretis,° hir yën° greye as glas,   *well-formed/eyes*
Hir mouth ful smal, and therto° softe and reed,°   *moreover/red*
But sikerly° she hadde a fair forheed: *certainly*
155 It was almost a spanne brood,⁷ I trowe,°   *believe*
For hardily,° she was nat undergrowe.   *assuredly*
Ful fetis° was hir cloke, as I was war;°   *becoming/aware*

---

5. St. Christopher medal.
6. Baldric (a supporting strap).
7. Sincere and shy. The Prioress is the mother superior of her nunnery.
8. In a seemly, proper manner.
9. The French learned in a convent school in Stratford-at-the-Bow, a suburb of London, was evidently not up to the Parisian standard.

1. I.e., her chief delight lay in good manners.
2. Of great good cheer.
3. And took pains to imitate the behavior.
4. And to be considered worthy.
5. I.e., some.
6. If someone struck it with a rod sharply.
7. A handsbreadth wide.

	Of smal° coral aboute hir arm she bar	*dainty*
	A paire of bedes, gauded all with greene,[8]	
160	And theron heeng° a brooch of gold ful sheene,°	*hung/bright*
	On which ther was first writen a crowned A,[9]	
	And after, *Amor vincit omnia.*[1]	
	Another Nonne with hire hadde she	
	That was hir chapelaine,° and preestes three.[2]	*secretary*
165	A Monk ther was, a fair for the maistrye,[3]	
	An outridere[4] that loved venerye,°	*hunting*
	A manly man, to been an abbot able.°	*worthy*
	Ful many a daintee° hors hadde he in stable,	*fine*
	And whan he rood,° men mighte his bridel heere	*rode*
170	Ginglen° in a whistling wind as clere	*jingle*
	And eek° as loude as dooth the chapel belle	*also*
	Ther as this lord was kepere of the celle.[5]	
	The rule of Saint Maure or of Saint Beneit,	
	By cause that it was old and somdeel strait[6]—	
175	This ilke° Monk leet olde thinges pace,°	*same/pass away*
	And heeld° after the newe world the space.°	*held/course*
	He yaf° nought of that text a pulled hen[7]	*gave*
	That saith that hunteres been° nought holy men,	*are*
	Ne that a monk, whan he is recchelees,[8]	
180	Is likned til° a fissh that is waterlees—	*to*
	This is to sayn, a monk out of his cloistre;	
	But thilke° text heeld he nat worth an oystre.	*that same*
	And I saide his opinion was good:	
	What° sholde he studye and make himselven wood°	*why/crazy*
185	Upon a book in cloistre alway to poure,°	*pore*
	Or swinke° with his handes and laboure,	*work*
	As Austin bit?[9] How shal the world be served?	
	Lat Austin have his swink to him reserved!	
	Therefore he was a prikasour° aright.	*hard rider*
190	Grehoundes he hadde as swift as fowl in flight.	
	Of priking° and of hunting for the hare	*riding*
	Was al his lust,° for no cost wolde he spare.	*pleasure*
	I sawgh his sleeves purfiled° at the hand	*fur lined*
	With gris,° and that the fineste of a land;	*gray fur*
195	And for to festne his hood under his chin	
	He hadde of gold wrought a ful curious[1] pin:	
	A love-knotte in the grettere° ende ther was.	*greater*
	His heed was balled,° that shoon as any glas,	*bald*
	And eek his face, as he hadde been anoint:	
200	He was a lord ful fat and in good point;[2]	
	His yën steepe,° and rolling in his heed,	*protruding*

8. Provided with green beads to mark certain prayers. "A paire": string (i.e., a rosary).
9. An A with an ornamental crown on it.
1. "Love conquers all."
2. The three get reduced to just one nun's priest.
3. I.e., a superlatively fine one.
4. A monk charged with supervising property distant from the monastery. Monasteries obtained income from large landholdings.

5. Prior of an outlying cell (branch) of the monastery.
6. Somewhat strict. St. Maurus and St. Benedict were authors of monastic rules.
7. He didn't give a plucked hen for that text.
8. Reckless, careless of rule.
9. I.e., as St. Augustine bids. St. Augustine had written that monks should perform manual labor.
1. Of careful workmanship.
2. In good shape, plump.

That stemed as a furnais of a leed,[3]
His bootes souple,° his hors in greet estat°—   *supple/condition*
Now certainly he was a fair prelat.[4]
205 He was nat pale as a forpined° gost: *wasted away*
A fat swan loved he best of any rost.
His palfrey° was as brown as is a berye.   *saddle horse*
   A Frere ther was, a wantoune° and a merye,   *jovial*
A limitour,[5] a ful solempne° man.   *ceremonious*
210 In alle the ordres foure is noon that can°   *knows*
So muche of daliaunce° and fair langage: *sociability*
He hadde maad ful many a mariage
Of yonge wommen at his owene cost;
Unto his ordre he was a noble post.[6]
215 Ful wel biloved and familier was he
With frankelains over al[7] in his contree,
And with worthy wommen of the town—
For he hadde power of confessioun,
As saide himself, more than a curat,°   *parish priest*
220 For of° his ordre he was licenciat.[8]   *by*
Ful swetely herde he confessioun,
And plesant was his absolucioun.
He was an esy man to yive penaunce
Ther as he wiste to have[9] a good pitaunce;°   *donation*
225 For unto a poore ordre for to yive
Is signe that a man is wel yshrive,[1]
For if he yaf, he dorste make avaunt°   *boast*
He wiste° that a man was repentaunt;   *knew*
For many a man so hard is of his herte
230 He may nat weepe though him sore smerte:[2]
Therfore, in stede of weeping and prayeres,
Men mote° yive silver to the poore freres.[3]   *may*
   His tipet° was ay farsed° ful of knives   *hood/stuffed*
And pinnes, for to yiven faire wives;
235 And certainly he hadde a merye note;
Wel coude he singe and playen on a rote;°   *fiddle*
Of yeddinges he bar outrely the pris.[4]
His nekke whit was as the flowr-de-lis;°   *lily*
Therto he strong was as a champioun.
240 He knew the tavernes wel in every town,
And every hostiler° and tappestere,°   *innkeeper/barmaid*
Bet° than a lazar or a beggestere.[5]   *better*
For unto swich a worthy man as he
Accorded nat, as by his facultee,[6]

3. That glowed like a furnace with a pot in it.
4. Prelate (an important churchman).
5. The "Frere" (Friar) is a member of one of the four religious orders whose members live by begging; as a "limitour" he has been granted by his order exclusive begging rights within a certain limited area.
6. I.e., pillar, a staunch supporter.
7. I.e., with franklins everywhere. Franklins were well-to-do country men.
8. I.e., licensed to hear confessions.
9. Where he knew he would have.

1. Shriven, absolved.
2. Although he is sorely grieved.
3. Before granting absolution, the confessor must be sure the sinner is contrite; moreover, the absolution is contingent on the sinner's performance of an act of satisfaction. In the case of Chaucer's Friar, a liberal contribution served both as proof of contrition and as satisfaction.
4. He absolutely took the prize for ballads.
5. "Beggestere": female beggar. "Lazar:" leper.
6. It was not suitable because of his position.

245   To have with sike° lazars aquaintaunce: *sick*
It is nat honeste,° it may nought avaunce,°   *dignified/profit*
For to delen with no swich poraile,[7]
But al with riche, and selleres of vitaile;°   *foodstuffs*
And over al ther as[8] profit sholde arise,
250   Curteis he was, and lowely of servise.
Ther was no man nowher so vertuous:°   *effective*
He was the beste beggere in his hous.°   *friary*
And yaf a certain ferme for the graunt:[9]
Noon of his bretheren cam ther in his haunt.[1]
255   For though a widwe° hadde nought a sho,°   *widow/shoe*
So plesant was his In *principio*[2]
Yit wolde he have a ferthing° er he wente;   *small coin*
His purchas was wel bettre than his rente.[3]
And rage he coude as it were right a whelpe;[4]
260   In love-dayes[5] ther coude he muchel° helpe,   *much*
For ther he was nat lik a cloisterer,
With a thredbare cope, as is a poore scoler,
But he was lik a maister[6] or a pope.
Of double worstede was his semicope,°   *short robe*
265   And rounded as a belle out of the presse.°   *bell mold*
Somwhat he lipsed° for his wantounesse°   *lisped/affectation*
To make his Englissh sweete upon his tonge;
And in his harping, whan he hadde songe,°   *sung*
His yën twinkled in his heed aright
270   As doon the sterres° in the frosty night.   *stars*
This worthy limitour was cleped Huberd.
     A Marchant was ther with a forked beerd,
In motelee,[7] and hye on hors he sat,
Upon his heed a Flandrissh° bevere hat,   *Flemish*
275   His bootes clasped faire and fetisly.°   *elegantly*
His resons° he spak ful solempnely,   *opinions*
Souning° alway th' encrees of his winning.°   *implying/profit*
He wolde the see were kept for any thing[8]
Bitwixen Middelburgh and Orewelle.
280   Wel coude he in eschaunge sheeldes[9] selle.
This worthy man ful wel his wit bisette:°   *employed*
Ther wiste° no wight° that he was in dette,   *knew/person*
So statly° was he of his governaunce,[1]   *dignified*
With his bargaines,° and with his chevissaunce.°   *bargainings/borrowing*
285   Forsoothe° he was a worthy man withalle;   *in truth*

---

7. I.e., poor trash. The oldest order of friars had been founded by St. Francis to administer to the spiritual needs of precisely those classes the Friar avoids.
8. Everywhere.
9. And he paid a certain rent for the privilege of begging.
1. Assigned territory.
2. A friar's usual salutation: "In the beginning [was the Word]" (John 1.1).
3. I.e., the money he got through such activity was more than his proper income.
4. And he could flirt wantonly, as if he were a puppy.

5. Days appointed for the settlement of lawsuits out of court.
6. A man of recognized learning.
7. Motley, a cloth of mixed color.
8. I.e., he wished the sea to be guarded at all costs. The sea route between Middelburgh (in the Netherlands) and Orwell (in Suffolk) was vital to the Merchant's export and import of wool—the basis of England's chief trade at the time.
9. Shields were units of transfer in international credit, which he exchanged at a profit.
1. The management of his affairs.

But, sooth to sayn, I noot° how men him calle.   *don't know*
   A Clerk[2] ther was of Oxenforde also
That unto logik hadde longe ygo.[3]
As lene was his hors as is a rake,
290   And he was nought right fat, I undertake,
But looked holwe,° and therto sobrely.   *hollow*
Ful thredbare was his overeste courtepy,
For he hadde geten him yit no benefice,[4]
Ne was so worldly for to have office.°   *secular employment*
295   For him was levere[5] have at his beddes heed
Twenty bookes, clad in blak or reed,
Of Aristotle and his philosophye,
Than robes riche, or fithele,° or gay sautrye.[6]   *fiddle*
But al be that he was a philosophre[7]
300   Yit hadde he but litel gold in cofre;°   *coffer*
But al that he mighte of his freendes hente,°   *take*
On bookes and on lerning he it spente,
And bisily gan for the soules praye
Of hem that yaf him wherwith to scoleye.°   *study*
305   Of studye took he most cure° and most heede.   *care*
Nought oo° word spak he more than was neede,   *one*
And that was said in forme[8] and reverence,
And short and quik,° and ful of heigh sentence:[9]   *lively*
Souning° in moral vertu was his speeche,   *resounding*
310   And gladly wolde he lerne, and gladly teche.
   A Sergeant of the Lawe, war and wis,[1]
That often hadde been at the Parvis[2]
Ther was also, ful riche of excellence.
Discreet he was, and of greet reverence—
315   He seemed swich, his wordes weren so wise.
Justice he was ful often in assise°   *circuit courts*
By patente[3] and by plein° commissioun.   *full*
For his science° and for his heigh renown   *knowledge*
Of fees and robes hadde he many oon.
320   So greet a purchasour° was nowher noon;   *speculator in land*
Al was fee simple[4] to him in effect—
His purchasing mighte nat been infect.[5]
Nowher so bisy a man as he ther nas;°   *was not*
And yit he seemed bisier than he was.
325   In termes hadde he caas and doomes[6] alle
That from the time of King William[7] were falle.

---

2. The Clerk is a student at Oxford; to become a student, he would have had to signify his intention of becoming a cleric, but he was not bound to proceed to a
position of responsibility in the church.
3. Who had long since matriculated in philosophy.
4. Ecclesiastical living, such as the income a parish
priest receives. "Courtepy": outer cloak.
5. He would rather.
6. Psaltery (a kind of harp).
7. The word may also mean alchemist, someone who
tries to turn base metals into gold. The Clerk's "philosophy" does not pay either way.

8. With decorum.
9. Elevated thought.
1. Wary and wise. The Sergeant is not only a practicing lawyer but one of the high justices of the nation.
2. The Paradise, the porch of St. Paul's Cathedral, a
meeting place for lawyers and their clients.
3. Royal warrant.
4. Owned outright without legal impediments.
5. Invalidated on a legal technicality.
6. Lawcases and decisions. "By termes": i.e., by heart.
7. I.e., the Conqueror (reigned 1066–87).

Therto he coude endite and make a thing,[8]
Ther coude no wight pinchen° at his writing;   *cavil*
And every statut coude° he plein° by rote.[9]   *knew/entire*
330   He rood but hoomly° in a medlee cote,[1]   *unpretentiously*
Girt with a ceint° of silk, with barres[2] smale.   *belt*
Of his array telle I no lenger tale.
    A Frankelain[3] was in his compaignye:
Whit was his beerd as is the dayesye;°   *daisy*
335   Of his complexion he was sanguin.[4]
Wel loved he by the morwe a sop in win.[5]
To liven in delit° was evere his wone,°   *sensual delight/wont*
For he was Epicurus[6] owene sone,
That heeld opinion that plein° delit   *full*
340   Was verray felicitee parfit.
An housholdere and that a greet was he:
Saint Julian[7] he was in his contree.
His breed, his ale, was always after oon;[8]
A bettre envined° man was nevere noon.   *wine-stocked*
345   Withouten bake mete was nevere his hous,
Of fissh and flessh, and that so plentevous°   *plenteous*
It snewed° in his hous of mete° and drinke,   *snowed/food*
Of alle daintees that men coude thinke.
After° the sondry sesons of the yeer   *according to*
350   So chaunged he his mete° and his soper.°   *dinner/supper*
Ful many a fat partrich hadde he in mewe,°   *cage*
And many a breem,[8] and many a luce[9] in stewe.[9]   *carp/pike*
Wo was his cook but if his sauce were
Poinant° and sharp, and redy all his gere.   *pungent*
355   His table dormant in his halle alway
Stood redy covered all the longe day.[1]
At sessions ther was he lord and sire.
Ful ofte time he was Knight of the Shire.[2]
An anlaas° and a gipser° al of silk   *dagger/purse*
360   Heeng at his girdel,[3] whit as morne° milk.   *morning*
A shirreve° hadde he been, and countour.[4]   *sheriff*
Was nowhere swich a worthy vavasour.[5]
    An Haberdasshere and a Carpenter,
A Webbe,° a Dyere, and a Tapicer°—   *weaver/tapestry maker*
365   And they were clothed alle in oo liveree[6]
Of a solempne and greet fraternitee.
Ful fresshe and newe hir gere apiked° was;   *trimmed*

---

8. Compose and draw up a deed.
9. By heart.
1. A coat of mixed color.
2. Transverse stripes.
3. The "Frankelain" (Franklin) is a prosperous country man, whose lower-class ancestry is no impediment to the importance he has attained in his county.
4. A reference to the fact that the Franklin's temperament, "humor," is dominated by blood as well as to his red face (see p. 80, n. 7).
5. I.e., in the morning he was very fond of a piece of bread soaked in wine.
6. The Greek philosopher whose teaching is popularly believed to make pleasure the chief goal of life.

7. The patron saint of hospitality.
8. Always of the same high quality.
9. Fishpond.
1. Tables were usually dismounted when not in use, but the Franklin kept his mounted and set ("covered"), hence "dormant."
2. County representative in Parliament. "Sessions": i.e., sessions of the justices of the peace.
3. Hung at his belt.
4. Auditor of county finances.
5. Feudal landholder of lowest rank; a provincial gentleman.
6. In one livery, i.e., the uniform of their "fraternitee" or guild, a partly religious, partly social organization.

Hir knives were chaped° nought with bras,   *mounted*
But al with silver; wrought ful clene and weel
370   Hir girdles and hir pouches everydeel.°   *altogether*
Wel seemed eech of hem a fair burgeis°   *burgher*
To sitten in a yeldehalle° on a dais.   *guildhall*
Everich, for the wisdom that he can,[7]
Was shaply° for to been an alderman.   *suitable*
375   For catel° hadde they ynough and rente,°   *property/income*
And eek hir wives wolde it wel assente—
And elles certain were they to blame:
It is ful fair to been ycleped° "Madame,"   *called*
And goon to vigilies all bifore,[8]
380   And have a mantel royalliche ybore.[9]
A Cook they hadde with hem for the nones,[1]
To boile the chiknes with the marybones,°   *marrowbones*
And powdre-marchant tart and galingale.[2]
Wel coude he knowe° a draughte of London ale.   *recognize*
385   He coude roste, and seethe,° and broile, and frye,   *boil*
Maken mortreux,° and wel bake a pie.   *stews*
But greet harm was it, as it thoughte° me,   *seemed to*
That on his shine a mormal° hadde he,   *ulcer*
For blankmanger,[3] that made he with the beste.
390   A Shipman was ther, woning° fer by weste—   *dwelling*
For ought I woot,° he was of Dertemouthe.[4]   *know*
He rood upon a rouncy° as he couthe,[5]   *large nag*
In a gowne of falding° to the knee.   *heavy wool*
A daggere hanging on a laas° hadde he   *strap*
395   Aboute his nekke, under his arm adown.
The hote somer hadde maad his hewe° al brown;   *color*
And certainly he was a good felawe.
Ful many a draughte of win hadde he drawe[6]
Fro Burdeuxward, whil that the chapman sleep:[7]
400   Of nice° conscience took he no keep;°   *fastidious/heed*
If that he faught and hadde the hyer° hand,   *upper*
By water he sente hem hoom to every land.[8]
But of his craft, to rekene wel his tides,
His stremes° and his daungers° him bisides,[9]   *currents/hazards*
405   His herberwe° and his moone, his lodemenage,[1]   *anchorage*
There was noon swich from Hulle to Cartage.[2]
Hardy he was and wis to undertake;
With many a tempest hadde his beerd been shake;
He knew alle the havenes° as they were   *harbors*
410   Fro Gotlond to the Cape of Finistere,[3]

---

7. Was capable of.
8. I.e., at the head of the procession. "Vigiles": feasts held on the eve of saints' days.
9. Royally carried.
1. For the occasion.
2. "Powdre-marchant" and "galingale" are flavoring materials.
3. A white stew or mousse.
4. Dartmouth, a port in the southwest of England.
5. As best he could.
6. Drawn, i.e., stolen.

7. Merchant slept. "Fro Burdeauxward": from Bordeaux; i.e., while carrying wine from Bordeaux (the wine center of France).
8. He drowned his prisoners.
9. Around him.
1. Pilotage, art of navigation.
2. From Hull (in northern England) to Cartagena (in Spain).
3. From Gotland (an island in the Baltic) to Finisterre (the westernmost point in Spain).

And every crike° in Britaine° and in Spaine.   *inlet/Brittany*
His barge ycleped was the Maudelaine.°   *Magdalene*
    With us ther was a Doctour of Physik:°   *medicine*
In al this world ne was ther noon him lik
415   To speken of physik and of surgerye.
For° he was grounded in astronomye,°   *because/astrology*
He kepte° his pacient a ful greet deel[4]   *tended to*
In houres by his magik naturel.[5]
Wel coude he fortunen the ascendent
420   Of his images[6] for his pacient.
He knew the cause of every maladye,
Were it of hoot or cold or moiste or drye,
And where engendred and of what humour:[7]
He was a verray parfit praktisour.[8]
425   The cause yknowe,° and of his° harm the roote,   *known/its*
Anoon he yaf the sike man his boote.°   *remedy*
    Ful redy hadde he his apothecaries
To senden him drogges° and his letuaries,°   *drugs/medicines*
For eech of hem made other for to winne:
430   Hir frendshipe was nought newe to biginne.
Wel knew he the olde Esculapius,[9]
And Deiscorides and eek Rufus,
Olde Ipocras, Hali, and Galien,
Serapion, Razis, and Avicen,
435   Averrois, Damascien, and Constantin,
Bernard, and Gatesden, and Gilbertin.
Of his diete mesurable° was he,   *moderate*
For it was of no superfluitee,
But of greet norissing° and digestible.   *nourishment*
440   His studye was but litel on the Bible.
In sanguin° and in pers° he clad was al,   *blood red/blue*
Lined with taffata and with sendal;°   *silk*
And yit he was but esy of dispence;°   *expenditure*
He kepte that he wan in pestilence.[1]
445   For° gold in physik is a cordial,[2]   *because*
Therfore he loved gold in special.
    A good Wif was ther of biside Bathe,
But she was somdeel deef, and that was scathe.°   *a pity*
Of cloth-making she hadde swich an haunt,°   *skill*

---

4. Closely.
5. Natural—as opposed to black—magic. "In houres":
i.e., the astrologically important hours (when conjunctions of the planets might help his recovery).
6. Assign the propitious time, according to the position
of stars, for using talismanic images. Such images, representing either the patient himself or points in the
zodiac, were thought to be influential on the course of
the disease.
7. Diseases were thought to be caused by a disturbance of one or another of the four bodily "humors,"
each of which, like the four elements, was a compound
of two of the elementary qualities mentioned in line
422: the melancholy humor, seated in the black bile,
was cold and dry (like earth); the sanguine, seated in
the blood, hot and moist (like air); the choleric, seated
in the yellow bile, hot and dry (like fire); the phlegma-

tic, seated in the phlegm, cold and moist (like water).
8. True perfect practitioner.
9. The Doctor is familiar with the treatises that the
Middle Ages attributed to the "great names" of medical
history, whom Chaucer names: the purely legendary
Greek demigod Aesculapius; the Greeks Dioscorides,
Rufus, Hippocrates, Galen, and Serapion; the Persians
Hali and Rhazes; the Arabians Avicenna and Averroës;
the early Christians John (?) of Damascus and Constantine Afer; the Scotsman Bernard Gordon; the Englishmen John of Gatesden and Gilbert, the former an
early contemporary of Chaucer.
1. He saved the money he made during the plague
time.
2. A stimulant. Gold was thought to have some medicinal properties.

450 She passed° hem of Ypres and of Gaunt.³   *surpassed*
In al the parissh wif ne was ther noon
That to the offring⁴ bifore hire sholde goon,
And if ther dide, certain so wroth° was she   *angry*
That she was out of alle charitee.
455 Hir coverchiefs ful fine were of ground°—   *texture*
I dorste° swere they weyeden° ten pound   *dare/weighed*
That on a Sonday weren° upon hir heed.   *were*
Hir hosen° weren of fin scarlet reed,°   *leggings/red*
Ful straite yteyd,⁵ and shoes ful moiste° and newe.   *supple*
460 Bold was hir face and fair and reed of hewe.
She was a worthy womman al hir live:
Housbondes at chirche dore⁶ she hadde five,
Withouten° other compaignye in youthe—   *not counting*
But therof needeth nought to speke as nouthe.°   *now*
465 And thries hadde she been at Jerusalem;
She hadde passed many a straunge° streem;   *foreign*
At Rome she hadde been, and at Boloigne,
In Galice at Saint Jame, and at Coloigne:⁷
She coude° muchel of wandring by the waye: *knew*
470 Gat-toothed⁸ was she, soothly for to saye.
Upon an amblere⁹ esily she sat,
Ywimpled° wel, and on hir heed an hat   *veiled*
As brood as is a bokeler or a targe,¹
A foot-mantel° aboute hir hipes large,   *riding skirt*
475 And on hir feet a paire of spores° sharpe.   *spurs*
In felaweshipe wel coude she laughe and carpe:°   *talk*
Of remedies of love she knew parchaunce,°   *as it happened*
For she coude of that art the olde daunce.²
    A good man was ther of religioun,
480 And was a poore Person° of a town,   *parson*
But riche he was of holy thought and werk.
He was also a lerned man, a clerk,
That Cristes gospel trewely° wolde preche;   *faithfully*
His parisshens° devoutly wolde he teche.   *parishioners*
485 Benigne he was, and wonder° diligent,   *wonderfully*
And in adversitee ful pacient,
And swich he was preved° ofte sithes.°   *proved/times*
Ful loth were him to cursen for his tithes,³
But rather wolde he yiven, out of doute,⁴
490 Unto his poore parisshens aboute
Of his offring⁵ and eek of his substaunce:°   *property*
He coude in litel thing have suffisaunce.°   *sufficiency*
Wid was his parissh, and houses fer asonder,

3. Ypres and Ghent ("Gaunt") were Flemish cloth-making centers.
4. The offering in church, when the congregation brought its gifts forward.
5. Tightly laced.
6. In medieval times, weddings were performed at the church door.
7. Rome, Boulogne (in France), St. James (of Compostella) in Galicia (Spain), and Cologne (in Germany) were all sites of shrines much visited by pil-grims.
8. Gap-toothed, thought to be a sign of amorousness.
9. Horse with an easy gait.
1. "Bokeler" and "targe": small shields.
2. I.e., she knew all the tricks of that trade.
3. He would be most reluctant to invoke excommuni-cation in order to collect his tithes.
4. Without doubt.
5. The offering made by the congregation of his church was at the Parson's disposal.

But he ne lafte° nought for rain ne thonder,   neglected
495   In siknesse nor in meschief,° to visite   misfortune
The ferreste° in his parissh, muche and lite,[6]   farthest
Upon his feet, and in his hand a staf.
This noble ensample° to his sheep he yaf   example
That first he wroughte,[7] and afterward he taughte.
500   Out of the Gospel he tho° wordes caughte,°   those/took
And this figure° he added eek therto: metaphor
That if gold ruste, what shal iren do?
For if a preest be foul, on whom we truste,
No wonder is a lewed° man to ruste.   uneducated
505   And shame it is, if a preest take keep,°   heed
A shiten° shepherde and a clene sheep.   befouled
Wel oughte a preest ensample for to yive
By his clennesse how that his sheep sholde live.
He sette nought his benefice[8] to hire
510   And leet° his sheep encombred in the mire   left
And ran to London, unto Sainte Poules,[9]
To seeken him a chaunterye[1] for soules,
Or with a bretherhede to been withholde,[2]
But dwelte at hoom and kepte wel his folde,
515   So that the wolf ne made it nought miscarye:
He was a shepherde and nought a mercenarye.
And though he holy were and vertuous,
He was to sinful men nought despitous,°   scornful
Ne of his speeche daungerous° ne digne,°   disdainful/haughty
520   But in his teching discreet and benigne,
To drawen folk to hevene by fairnesse
By good ensample—this was his bisinesse.
But it° were any persone obstinat,   if there
What so he were, of heigh or lowe estat,
525   Him wolde he snibben° sharply for the nones:[3]   scold
A bettre preest I trowe° ther nowher noon is.   believe
He waited after[4] no pompe and reverence,
Ne maked him a spiced conscience,[5]
But Cristes lore° and his Apostles twelve   teaching
530   He taughte, but first he folwed it himselve.
With him ther was a Plowman, was his brother,
That hadde ylad° of dong° ful many a fother.[6]   carried/dung
A trewe swinkere° and a good was he,   worker
Living in pees° and parfit charitee.   peace
535   God loved he best with al his hoole° herte   whole
At alle times, though him gamed or smerte,[7]
And thanne his neighebor right as himselve.
He wolde thresshe, and therto dike° and delve,°   work hard/dig

6. Great and small.
7. I.e., he practiced what he preached.
8. I.e., his parish. A priest might rent his parish to another and take a more profitable position.
9. St. Paul's Cathedral.
1. Chantry, i.e., a foundation that employed priests for the sole duty of saying masses for the souls of wealthy persons. St. Paul's had many of them.
2. Or to be employed by a brotherhood; i.e., to take a

lucrative and fairly easy position as chaplain with a parish guild (see p. 78, 2nd n. 6).
3. On the spot, promptly.
4. I.e., expected.
5. Nor did he assume an overfastidious conscience, a holier-than-thou attitude.
6. Load.
7. Whether he was pleased or grieved.

For Cristes sake, for every poore wight,
540 Withouten hire, if it laye in his might.
His tithes payed he ful faire and wel,
Bothe of his propre swink[8] and his catel.°   property
In a tabard° he rood upon a mere.°   workman's smock/mare
        Ther was also a Reeve° and a Millere,   estate manager
545 A Somnour, and a Pardoner[9] also,
A Manciple,° and myself—ther were namo.   steward
        The Millere was a stout carl° for the nones.   fellow
Ful big he was of brawn° and eek of bones—   muscle
That preved[1] wel, for overal ther he cam
550 At wrastling he wolde have alway the ram.[2]
He was short-shuldred, brood,° a thikke knarre.[3]   broad
Ther was no dore that he nolde heve of harre,[4]
Or breke it at a renning° with his heed.°   running/head
His beerd as any sowe or fox was reed,°   red
555 And therto brood, as though it were a spade;
Upon the cop right[5] of his nose he hade
A werte,° and theron stood a tuft of heres,   wart
Rede as the bristles of a sowes eres;°   ears
His nosethirles° blake were and wide.   nostrils
560 A swerd and a bokeler° bar° he by his side.   shield/bore
His mouth as greet was as a greet furnais.°   furnace
He was a janglere° and a Goliardais,[6]   chatterer
And that was most of sinne and harlotries.°   obscenities
Wel coude he stelen corn and tollen thries[7]—
565 And yit he hadde a thombe[8] of gold, pardee.°   by heaven
A whit cote and a blew hood wered° he.   wore
A baggepipe wel coude he blowe and soune,°   sound
And therwithal° he broughte us out of towne.   therewith
        A gentil Manciple[9] was ther of a temple,
570 Of which achatours° mighte take exemple   buyers of food
For to been wise in bying of vitaile;°   victuals
For wheither that he paide or took by taile,[1]
Algate he waited so in his achat[2]
That he was ay biforn and in good stat.[3]
575   Now is nat that of God a ful fair grace
That swich a lewed° mannes wit shal pace°   uneducated/surpass
The wisdom of an heep of lerned men?
Of maistres° hadde he mo than thries ten   masters
That weren of lawe expert and curious,°   cunning
580 Of whiche ther were a dozeine in that hous
Worthy to been stiwardes of rente° and lond   income

Of any lord that is in Engelond,
To make him live by his propre good[4]
In honour dettelees but if he were wood,[5]
585   Or live as scarsly° as him list° desire,   *economically/it pleases*
And able for to helpen al a shire
In any caas° that mighte falle° or happe,   *event/befall*
And yit this Manciple sette hir aller cappe![6]
    The Reeve was a sclendre° colerik[7] man;   *slender*
590   His beerd was shave as neigh° as evere he can;   *close*
His heer was by his eres ful round yshorn;
His top was dokked[8] lik a preest biforn;°   *in front*
Ful longe were his legges and ful lene,
Ylik a staf, ther was no calf yseene.°   *visible*
595   Wel coude he keepe° a gerner° and a binne—   *guard/granary*
Ther was noon auditour coude on him winne.[9]
Wel wiste° he by the droughte and by the rain   *knew*
The yeelding of his seed and of his grain.
His lordes sheep, his neet,° his dayerye,°   *cattle/dairy herd*
600   His swin, his hors, his stoor,° and his pultrye   *stock*
Was hoolly° in this Reeves governinge,   *wholly*
And by his covenant yaf[1] the rekeninge,
Sin° that his lord was twenty-yeer of age.   *since*
There coude no man bringe him in arrerage.[2]
605   Ther nas baillif, hierde, nor other hine,
That he ne knew his sleighte and his covine[3]—
They were adrad° of him as of the deeth.°   *afraid/plague*
His woning° was ful faire upon an heeth;°   *dwelling/meadow*
With greene trees shadwed was his place.
610   He coude bettre than his lord purchace.°   *acquire goods*
Ful riche he was astored° prively.°   *stocked/secretly*
His lord wel coude he plesen subtilly,
To yive and lene° him of his owene good,°   *lend/property*
And have a thank, and yit a cote and hood.
615   In youthe he hadde lerned a good mister:°   *occupation*
He was a wel good wrighte, a carpenter.
This Reeve sat upon a ful good stot°   *stallion*
That was a pomely° grey and highte° Scot.   *dapple/was named*
A long surcote° of pers° upon he hade,[4]   *overcoat/blue*
620   And by his side he bar° a rusty blade.   *bore*
Of Northfolk was this Reeve of which I telle,
Biside a town men clepen Baldeswelle.°   *Bawdswell*
Tukked[5] he was as is a frere aboute,
And evere he rood the hindreste of oure route.[6]

4. His own money.
5. Out of debt unless he were crazy.
6. This Manciple made fools of them all.
7. Choleric describes a person whose dominant humor is yellow bile (choler)—i.e., a hot-tempered person. The Reeve is the superintendent of a large farming estate.
8. Cut short; the clergy wore the head partially shaved.
9. I.e., find him in default.

1. And according to his contract he gave.
2. Convict him of being in arrears financially.
3. There was no bailiff (i.e., foreman), shepherd, or other farm laborer whose craftiness and plots he didn't know.
4. He had on.
5. With clothing tucked up like a friar.
6. Hindmost of our group.

625   A Somnour[7] was ther with us in that place
        That hadde a fir-reed° cherubinnes[8] face,   *fire-red*
        For saucefleem° he was, with yën narwe,   *pimply*
        And hoot° he was, and lecherous as a sparwe,°   *hot/sparrow*
        With scaled° browes blake and piled[9] beerd: *scabby*
630   Of his visage children were aferd.°   *afraid*
        Ther nas quiksilver, litarge, ne brimstoon,
        Boras, ceruce, ne oile of tartre noon,[1]
        Ne oinement that wolde clense and bite,
        That him mighte helpen of his whelkes° white,   *pimples*
635   Nor of the knobbes° sitting on his cheekes.   *lumps*
        Wel loved he garlek, oinons, and eek leekes,
        And for to drinke strong win reed as blood.
        Thanne wolde he speke and crye as he were wood;°   *mad*
        And whan that he wel dronken hadde the win,
640   Thanne wolde he speke no word but Latin:
        A fewe termes hadde he, two or three,
        That he hadde lerned out of som decree;
        No wonder is—he herde it al the day,
        And eek ye knowe wel how that a jay°   *parrot*
645   Can clepen "Watte"[2] as wel as can the Pope—
        But whoso coude in other thing him grope,°   *examine*
        Thanne hadde he spent all his philosophye;[3]
        Ay *Questio quid juris*[4] wolde he crye.
          He was a gentil harlot° and a kinde;   *rascal*
650   A bettre felawe sholde men nought finde:
        He wolde suffre,° for a quart of win,   *permit*
        A good felawe to have his concubin
        A twelfmonth, and excusen him at the fulle;[5]
        Ful prively° a finch eek coude he pulle.[6]   *secretly*
655   And if he foond° owher° a good felawe   *found/anywhere*
        He wolde techen him to have noon awe
        In swich caas of the Ercedekenes curs,[7]
        But if[8] a mannes soule were in his purs,
        For in his purs he sholde ypunisshed be.
660   "Purs is the Ercedekenes helle," saide he.
          But wel I woot he lied right in deede:
         Of cursing° oughte eech gilty man him drede,   *excommunication*
        For curs wol slee° right as assoiling° savith—   *slay/absolution*
        And also war him of a *significavit*.[9]

7. The "Somnour" (Summoner) is an employee of the ecclesiastical court, whose duty is to bring to court persons whom the archdeacon—the justice of the court—suspects of offenses against canon law. By this time, however, summoners had generally transformed themselves into corrupt detectives who spied out offenders and blackmailed them by threats of summonses.
8. Cherub's, often depicted in art with a red face.
9. Uneven, partly hairless.
1. These are all ointments for diseases affecting the skin, probably diseases of venereal origin.
2. Call out: "Walter"—like modern parrots' "Polly."
3. I.e., learning.

4. "What point of law does this investigation involve?" A phrase frequently used in ecclesiastical courts.
5. Fully. Ecclesiastical courts had jurisdiction over many offenses that today would come under civil law, including sexual offenses.
6. "To pull a finch" (pluck a bird) is to have sexual relations with a woman.
7. Archdeacon's sentence of excommunication.
8. Unless.
9. And also one should be careful of a *significavit* (the writ that transferred the guilty offender from the ecclesiastical to the civil arm for punishment).

665	In daunger[1] hadde he at his owene gise°	*disposal*
	The yonge girles of the diocise,	
	And knew hir conseil,° and was al hir reed.[2]	*secrets*
	A gerland hadde he set upon his heed	
	As greet as it were for an ale-stake,[3]	
670	A bokeler hadde he maad him of a cake.	
	With him ther rood a gentil Pardoner[4]	
	Of Rouncival, his freend and his compeer,°	*comrade*
	That straight was comen fro the Court of Rome.[5]	
	Ful loude he soong,° "Com hider, love, to me."	*sang*
675	This Somnour bar to him a stif burdoun:[6]	
	Was nevere trompe° of half so greet a soun.	*trumpet*
	This Pardoner hadde heer as yelow as wex,	
	But smoothe it heeng° as dooth a strike° of flex;°	*hung/hank/flax*
	By ounces[7] heenge his lokkes that he hadde,	
680	And therwith he his shuldres overspradde,°	*overspread*
	But thinne it lay, by colpons,° oon by oon;	*strands*
	But hood for jolitee° wered° he noon,	*nonchalance/wore*
	For it was trussed up in his walet:°	*pack*
	Him thoughte he rood al of the newe jet.°	*fashion*
685	Dischevelee° save his cappe he rood al bare.	*with hair down*
	Swiche glaring yën hadde he as an hare.	
	A vernicle[8] hadde he sowed upon his cappe,	
	His walet biforn him in his lappe,	
	Bretful° of pardon, come from Rome al hoot.°	*brimful/hot*
690	A vois he hadde as smal° as hath a goot;°	*fine/goat*
	No beerd hadde he, ne nevere sholde have;	
	As smoothe it was as it were late yshave:	
	I trowe° he were a gelding or a mare.	*believe*
	But of his craft, fro Berwik into Ware,[9]	
695	Ne was ther swich another pardoner;	
	For in his male° he hadde a pilwe-beer°	*bag/pillowcase*
	Which that he saide was Oure Lady veil;	
	He saide he hadde a gobet° of the sail	*piece*
	That Sainte Peter hadde whan that he wente	
700	Upon the see, til Jesu Crist him hente.°	*seized*
	He hadde a crois° of laton,° ful of stones,	*cross/brassy metal*
	And in a glas he hadde pigges bones,	
	But with thise relikes[1] whan that he foond°	*found*
	A poore person° dwelling upon lond,[2]	*parson*
705	Upon° a day he gat° him more moneye	*in/got*
	Than that the person gat in monthes twaye;	
	And thus with feined° flaterye and japes°	*false/tricks*

1. Under his domination.
2. Was their chief source of advice.
3. A tavern was signalized by a pole ("ale-stake"), rather like a modern flagpole, projecting from its front wall; on this hung a garland, or "bush."
4. A Pardoner dispensed papal pardon for sins to those who contributed to the charitable institution that he was licensed to represent; this Pardoner purported to be collecting for the hospital of Roncesvalles ("Rouncival") in Spain, which had a London branch.
5. The papal court.

6. I.e., provided him with a strong bass accompaniment.
7. I.e., thin strands.
8. Portrait of Christ's face as it was said to have been impressed on St. Veronica's handkerchief, i.e., a souvenir reproduction of a famous relic in Rome.
9. I.e., from one end of England to the other.
1. Relics, i.e., the pigs' bones that the Pardoner represented as saints' bones.
2. Upcountry.

He made the person and the peple his apes.°   *dupes*
But trewely to tellen at the laste,
710   He was in chirche a noble ecclesiaste;
Wel coude he rede a lesson and a storye,°   *liturgical narrative*
But alderbest° he soong an offertorye,[3]   *best of all*
For wel he wiste° whan that song was songe,   *knew*
He moste° preche and wel affile° his tonge   *must/sharpen*
715   To winne silver, as he ful wel coude—
Therefore he soong the merierly° and loude.   *more merrily*
   Now have I told you soothly in a clause[4]
Th'estaat, th'array, the nombre, and eek the cause
Why that assembled was this compaignye
720   In Southwerk at this gentil hostelrye
That highte the Tabard, faste° by the Belle;[5]   *close*
But now is time to you for to telle
How that we baren us[6] that ilke° night   *same*
Whan we were in that hostelrye alight;
725   And after wol I telle of oure viage,°   *trip*
And al the remenant of oure pilgrimage.
But first I praye you of youre curteisye
That ye n'arette it nought my vilainye[7]
Though that I plainly speke in this matere
730   To telle you hir wordes and hir cheere,°   *behavior*
Ne though I speke hir wordes proprely;°   *accurately*
For this ye knowen also wel as I:
Who so shal telle a tale after a man
He moot° reherce,° as neigh as evere he can,   *must/repeat*
735   Everich a word, if it be in his charge,°   *responsibility*
Al speke he[8] nevere so rudeliche and large,°   *broadly*
Or elles he moot telle his tale untrewe,
Or feine° thing, or finde° wordes newe;   *falsify/devise*
He may nought spare[9] although he were his brother:
740   He moot as wel saye oo word as another.
Crist spak himself ful brode° in Holy Writ,   *broadly*
And wel ye woot no vilainye° is it;   *rudeness*
Eek Plato saith, who so can him rede,
The wordes mote be cosin to the deede.
745   Also I praye you to foryive it me
Al° have I nat set folk in hir degree   *although*
Here in this tale as that they sholde stonde:
My wit is short, ye may wel understonde.
   Greet cheere made oure Host[1] us everichoon,
750   And to the soper sette he us anoon.°   *at once*
He served us with vitaile° at the beste.   *food*
Strong was the win, and wel to drinke us leste.°   *it pleased*
A semely man oure Hoste was withalle
For to been a marchal[2] in an halle;

---

3. Part of the mass sung before the offering of alms.   8. Although he speak.
4. I.e., in a short space.   9. I.e., spare anyone.
5. Another tavern in Southwark.   1. The landlord of the Tabard Inn.
6. Bore ourselves.   2. Marshal, one who was in charge of feasts.
7. That you do not attribute it to my boorishness.

755 A large man he was, with yën steepe,°   *prominent*
A fairer burgeis° was ther noon in Chepe³—   *burgher*
Bold of his speeche, and wis, and wel ytaught,
And of manhood him lakkede right naught.
Eek therto he was right a merye man,
760 And after soper playen he bigan,
And spak of mirthe amonges othere thinges—
Whan that we hadde maad oure rekeninges⁴—
And saide thus, "Now, lordinges, trewely,
Ye been to me right welcome, hertely.°   *heartily*
765 For by my trouthe, if that I shal nat lie,
I sawgh nat this yeer so merye a compaignye
At ones in this herberwe° as is now.   *inn*
Fain° wolde I doon you mirthe, wiste I⁵ how.   *gladly*
And of a mirthe I am right now bithought,
770 To doon you ese, and it shal coste nought.
"Ye goon to Canterbury—God you speede;
The blisful martyr quite you youre meede.⁶
And wel I woot as ye goon by the waye
Ye shapen you⁷ to talen° and to playe,   *converse*
775 For trewely, confort ne mirthe is noon
To ride by the waye domb as stoon;°   *stone*
And therefore wol I maken you disport
As I saide erst,° and doon you som confort;   *before*
And if you liketh alle, by oon assent,
780 For to stonden at⁸ my juggement,
And for to werken as I shall you saye,
Tomorwe whan ye riden by the waye—
Now by my fader° soule that is deed,   *father's*
But° ye be merye I wol yive you myn heed!°   *unless/head*
785 Holde up youre handes withouten more speeche."
Oure counseil was nat longe for to seeche;°   *seek*
Us thought it was not worth to make it wis,⁹
And graunted him withouten more avis,°   *deliberation*
And bade him saye his voirdit° as him leste.¹   *verdict*
790 "Lordinges," quod he, "now herkneth for the beste;
But taketh it nought, I praye you, in desdain.
This is the point, to speken short and plain,
That eech of you, to shorte° with oure waye   *shorten*
In this viage, shal tellen tales twaye°—   *two*
795 To Canterburyward, I mene it so,
And hoomward he shal tellen othere two,
Of aventures that whilom° have bifalle;   *once upon a time*
And which of you that bereth him best of alle—
That is to sayn, that telleth in this cas
800 Tales of best sentence° and most solas°—   *meaning/delight*
Shal have a soper at oure aller cost,²

---

3. Cheapside, business center of London.
4. Had paid our bills.
5. If I knew.
6. Pay you your reward.
7. Intend.

8. Abide by.
9. We didn't think it worthwhile to make an issue of it.
1. It pleased.
2. At the cost of us all.

Here in this place, sitting by this post,
Whan that we come again fro Canterbury.
And for to make you the more mury°   *merry*
805 I wol myself goodly° with you ride—   *kindly*
Right at myn owene cost—and be youre gide.
And who so wol my juggement withsaye°   *contradict*
Shal paye al that we spende by the waye.
And if ye vouche sauf that it be so,
810 Telle me anoon, withouten wordes mo,°   *more*
And I wol erly shape me³ therefore."
    This thing was graunted and oure othes swore
With ful glad herte, and prayden⁴ him also
That he wolde vouche sauf for to do so,
815 And that he wolde been oure governour,
And of oure tales juge and reportour,°   *accountant*
And sette a soper at a certain pris,°   *price*
And we wol ruled been at his devis,°   *disposal*
In heigh and lowe; and thus by oon assent
820 We been accorded to his juggement.
And therupon the win was fet° anoon;   *fetched*
We dronken and to reste wente eechoon°   *each one*
Withouten any lenger° taryinge.   *longer*
    Amorwe° whan that day bigan to springe   *in the morning*
825 Up roos oure Host and was oure aller cok,⁵
And gadred us togidres in a flok,
And forth we riden, a litel more than pas,°   *walking pace*
Unto the watering of Saint Thomas;⁶
And ther oure Host bigan his hors arreste,°   *halt*
830 And saide, "Lordes, herkneth if you leste:°   *it please*
Ye woot youre forward° and it you recorde:⁷   *agreement*
If evensong and morwesong° accorde,°   *morning song/agree*
Lat see now who shal telle the firste tale.
As evere mote° I drinken win or ale,   *may*
835 Who so be rebel to my juggement
Shal paye for al that by the way is spent.
Now draweth cut er that we ferrer twinne:⁸
He which that hath the shorteste shal biginne.
    "Sire Knight," quod he, "my maister and my lord,
840 Now draweth cut, for that is myn accord.°   *will*
Cometh neer," quod he, "my lady Prioresse,
And ye, sire Clerk, lat be youre shamefastnesse°—   *modesty*
Ne studieth nought. Lay hand to, every man!"
    Anoon to drawen every wight bigan,
845 And shortly for to tellen as it was
Were it by aventure, or sort, or cas,⁹
The soothe° is this, the cut fil° to the Knight;   *truth/fell*
Of which ful blithe and glad was every wight,
And telle he moste° his tale, as was resoun,   *must*

---

3. Prepare myself.
4. I.e., we prayed.
5. Was rooster for us all.
6. A watering place near Southwark.

7. You recall it.
8. Go farther. "Draweth cut": i.e., draw straws.
9. Whether it was luck, fate, or chance.

850 By forward and by composicioun,[1]
     As ye han herd. What needeth wordes mo?
     And whan this goode man sawgh that it was so,
     As he that wis was and obedient
     To keepe his forward by his free assent,
855 He saide, "Sin° I shal biginne the game,   *since*
     What, welcome be the cut, in Goddes name!
     Now lat us ride, and herkneth what I saye."
     And with that word we riden forth oure waye,
     And he bigan with right a merye cheere°   *countenance*
860 His tale anoon, and saide as ye may heere.

The Miller's Prologue and Tale[1]

The Prologue

     Whan that the Knight hadde thus his tale ytold,[2]
     In al the route° nas° ther yong ne old   *group/was not*
     That he ne saide it was a noble storye,
     And worthy for to drawen° to memorye,   *recall*
5   And namely° the gentils everichoon.   *especially*
       Oure Hoste lough° and swoor, "So mote I goon,[3]   *laughed*
     This gooth aright: unbokeled is the male.°   *pouch*
     Lat see now who shal telle another tale.
     For trewely the game is wel bigonne.
10   Now telleth ye, sire Monk, if that ye conne,°   *can*
     Somwhat to quite° with the Knightes tale."   *repay*
       The Millere, that for dronken[4] was al pale,
     So that unnethe° upon his hors he sat,   *with difficulty*
     He nolde° avalen° neither hood ne hat,   *would not/doff*
15   Ne abiden no man for his curteisye,
     But in Pilates vois[5] he gan to crye,
     And swoor, "By armes[6] and by blood and bones,
     I can° a noble tale for the nones,   *know*
     With which I wol now quite the Knightes tale."
20   Oure Hoste sawgh that he was dronke of ale,
     And saide, "Abide, Robin, leve° brother,   *dear*
     Som bettre man shal telle us first another.
     Abide, and lat us werken thriftily."°   *with propriety*
       "By Goddes soule," quod he, "that wol nat I,
25   For I wol speke or elles go my way."
       Oure Host answerde, "Tel on, a devele way![7]
     Thou art a fool; thy wit is overcome."

1. By agreement and compact.
1. *The Miller's Tale* belongs to the literary genre known as the "fabliau," a short story in verse that generally involves bourgeois or lower-class characters in an outrageous, often obscene plot. The fabliau is peculiarly French, and aside from the three or four examples in Chaucer there are few representatives of it in English. Yet Chaucer was supreme in this kind of tale as in many others, and *The Miller's Tale* is generally considered the best-told fabliau in any language.

2. *The Knight's Tale* is actually the first one told on the Canterbury pilgrimage, immediately following *The General Prologue.*
3. So might I walk, an oath
4. I.e., drunkenness.
5. The harsh voice usually associated with the character of Pontius Pilate in the mystery plays.
6. I.e., by God's arms, a blasphemous oath.
7. I.e., in the devil's name.

"Now herkneth," quod the Millere, "alle and some.[8]
But first I make a protestacioun°   *public affirmation*
30   That I am dronke: I knowe it by my soun.°   *tone of voice*
And therfore if that I mis° speke or saye,   *amiss*
Wite it[9] the ale of Southwerk, I you praye;
For I wol telle a legende and a lif
Bothe of a carpenter and of his wif,
35   How that a clerk hath set the wrightes cappe."[1]
     The Reeve answerde and saide, "Stint thy clappe![2]
Lat be thy lewed° dronken harlotrye.°   *ignorant/obscenity*
It is a sinne and eek° a greet folye   *also*
To apairen° any man or him defame,   *injure*
40   And eek to bringen wives in swich fame.°   *reputation*
Thou maist ynough of othere thinges sayn."
     This dronken Millere spak ful soone again,
And saide, "Leve° brother Osewold,   *dear*
Who hath no wif, he is no cokewold.°   *cuckold*
45   But I saye nat therfore that thou art oon.
Ther ben ful goode wives many oon,°   *a one*
And evere a thousand goode ayains oon badde.
That knowestou wel thyself but if thou madde.°   *rave*
Why artou angry with my tale now?
50   I have a wif, pardee,° as wel as thou,   *by God*
Yit nolde° I, for the oxen in my plough,   *would not*
Take upon me more than ynough°   *enough*
As deemen of myself that I were oon:[3]
I wol bileve wel that I am noon.
55   An housbonde shal nought been inquisitif
Of Goddes privetee,° nor of his wif.   *secrets*
So[4] he may finde Goddes foison° there,   *plenty*
Of the remenant° needeth nought enquere."°   *rest/inquire*
     What sholde I more sayn but this Millere
60   He nolde his wordes for no man forbere,
But tolde his cherles tale in his manere.
M'athinketh° that I shal reherce° it here,   *I regret/repeat*
And therefore every gentil wight I praye,
Deemeth nought, for Goddes love, that I saye
65   Of yvel entente, but for ° I moot reherse   *because*
Hir tales alle, be they bet° or werse,   *better*
Or elles falsen° som of my matere.   *falsify*
And therfore, whoso list it nought yheere°   *hear*
Turne over the leef,° and chese° another tale,   *page/choose*
70   For he shal finde ynowe,° grete and smale,   *enough*
Of storial[5] thing that toucheth gentilesse,°   *gentility*
And eek moralitee and holinesse:
Blameth nought me if that ye chese amis.
The Millere is a cherl, ye knowe wel this,
75   So was the Reeve eek, and othere mo,

---

8. Each and every one.   3. To think that I were one (a cuckold).
9. Blame it on.   4. Provided that.
1. I.e., how a clerk made a fool of a carpenter.   5. Historical, i.e., true.
2. Stop your chatter.

And harlotrye° they tolden bothe two.   *ribaldry*
Aviseth you,[6] and putte me out of blame:
And eek men shal nought maken ernest of game.

The Tale

    Whilom° ther was dwelling at Oxenforde   *once upon a time*
80 A riche gnof° that gestes heeld to boorde,[7]   *churl*
And of his craft he was a carpenter.
With him ther was dwelling a poore scoler,
Hadde lerned art,[8] but al his fantasye°   *desire*
Was turned for to lere° astrologye,   *learn*
85 And coude a certain of conclusiouns,
To deemen by interrogaciouns,[9]
If that men axed° him in certain houres   *asked*
Whan that men sholde have droughte or elles showres,
Or if men axed him what shal bifalle
90 Of every thing—I may nat rekene hem alle.
    This clerk was cleped° hende[1] Nicholas.   *called*
Of derne love he coude, and of solas,[2]
And therto he was sly and ful privee,°   *secretive*
And lik a maide meeke for to see.
95 A chambre hadde he in that hostelrye
Allone, withouten any compaignye,
Ful fetisly ydight[3] with herbes swoote,°   *sweet*
And he himself as sweete as is the roote
Of licoris or any setewale.[4]
100 His *Almageste*[5] and bookes grete and smale,
His astrelabye,[6] longing for his art,
His augrim stones,[7] layen faire apart
On shelves couched° at his beddes heed;   *set*
His presse° ycovered with a falding reed;[8]   *storage chest*
105 And al above ther lay a gay sautrye,°   *psaltery (harp)*
On which he made a-nightes melodye
So swetely that al the chambre roong,°   *rang*
And *Angelus ad Virginem*[9] he soong,
And after that he soong the *Kinges Note:*[1]
110 Ful often blessed was his merye throte.
And thus this sweete clerk his time spente
After his freendes finding and his rente.[2]
    This carpenter hadde wedded newe° a wif   *lately*
Which that he loved more than his lif.
115 Of eighteteene yeer she was of age;

---

6. Take heed.
7. I.e., took in boarders.
8. Who had completed the first stage of university education (the trivium).
9. I.e., and he knew a number of propositions on
which to base astrological analyses (which would reveal the matters in the next three lines).
1. Courteous, handy, attractive.
2. I.e., he knew about secret love and pleasurable
practices.
3. Elegantly furnished.

4. Setwall, a spice.
5. The 2nd-century treatise by Ptolemy, still the standard astronomy textbook.
6. Belonging to. "Astrelabye": astrolabe, an astronomical instrument.
7. Counters used in arithmetic.
8. Red coarse woolen cloth.
9. "The Angel's Address to the Virgin," a hymn.
1. Probably a popular song of the time.
2. In accordance with his friends' provision and his
own income.

Jalous he was, and heeld hire narwe in cage,
For she was wilde and yong, and he was old,
And deemed himself been lik a cokewold.[3]
He knew nat Caton,[4] for his wit was rude,
120 That bad men sholde wedde his similitude:[5]
Men sholde wedden after hir estat,[6]
For youthe and elde° is often at debat.   age
But sith that he was fallen in the snare,
He moste endure, as other folk, his care.
125 Fair was this yonge wif, and therwithal
As any wesele° hir body gent and smal.[7]   weasel
A ceint she wered, barred[8] al of silk;
A barmcloth° as whit as morne milk   apron
Upon hir lendes,° ful of many a gore;°   loins/strip of cloth
130 Whit was hir smok,° and broiden° al bifore undergarment/embroidered
And eek bihinde, on hir coler° aboute,   collar
Of° col-blak silk, withinne and eek withoute;   with
The tapes° of hir white voluper°   ribbons/cap
Were of the same suite of[9] hir coler;
135 Hir filet° brood° of silk and set ful hye;   headband/broad
And sikerly° she hadde a likerous° yë;   certainly/wanton
Ful smale ypulled[1] were hir browes two,
And tho were bent,° and blake as any slo.°   arching/sloeberry
She was ful more blisful on to see
140 Than is the newe perejonette° tree,   pear
And softer than the wolle° is of a wether;°   wool/ram
And by hir girdel° heeng° a purs of lether,   belt/hung
Tasseled with silk and perled with latoun.[2]
In al this world, to seeken up and down,
145 Ther nis no man so wis that coude thenche°   imagine
So gay a popelote° or swich° a wenche.   doll/such
Ful brighter was the shining of hir hewe
Than in the Tow[3] the noble° yforged newe.   gold coin
But of hir song, it was as loud and yerne°   lively
150 As any swalwe° sitting on a berne.°   swallow/barn
Therto she coude skippe and make game°   play
As any kide or calf folwing his dame.°   mother
Hir mouth was sweete as bragot or the meeth,[4]
Or hoord of apples laid in hay or heeth.°   heather
155 Winsing° she was as is a joly° colt,   skittish/high-spirited
Long as a mast, and upright° as a bolt.°   straight/arrow
A brooch she bar upon hir lowe coler
As brood as is the boos° of a bokeler;°   boss/shield
Hir shoes were laced on hir legges hye.[5]
160 She was a primerole,° a piggesnye,[5]   primrose
For any lord to leggen° in his bedde,   lay

3. I.e., suspected of himself that he was like a cuckold.   9. The same kind as, i.e., black.
4. Dionysius Cato, the supposed author of a book of   1. Delicately plucked.
maxims used in elementary education.   2. I.e., with brassy spangles on it.
5. Commanded that one should wed his equal.   3. The Tower of London, the Mint.
6. Men should marry according to their condition.   4. "Bragot" and "meeth" are honey drinks.
7. Slender and delicate.   5. A pig's eye, a name for a common flower.
8. A belt she wore, with transverse stripes.

Or yit for any good yeman to wedde.

   Now sire, and eft° sire, so bifel the cas   *again*
That on a day this hende Nicholas
165 Fil° with this yonge wif to rage° and playe,   *happened/flirt*
Whil that hir housbonde was at Oseneye[6]
(As clerkes been ful subtil and ful quainte),°   *clever*
And prively he caughte hire by the queinte,[7]
And saide, "Ywis, but° if ich° have my wille,   *unless/I*
170 For derne° love of thee, lemman, I spille,"°   *secret/die*
And heeld hire harde by the haunche-bones,°   *thighs*
And saide, "Lemman,° love me al atones,[8]   *sweetheart*
Or I wol dien, also° God me save."   *so*
And she sproong° as a colt dooth in a trave,[9]   *sprang*
175 And with hir heed she wried° faste away;   *twisted*
She saide, "I wol nat kisse thee, by my fay.°   *faith*
Why, lat be," quod she, "lat be, Nicholas!
Or I wol crye 'Out, harrow,° and allas!'   *help*
Do way youre handes, for your curteisye!"
180   This Nicholas gan mercy for to crye,
And spak so faire, and profred him so faste,[1]
That she hir love him graunted atte laste,
And swoor hir ooth by Saint Thomas of Kent[2]
That she wolde been at his comandement,
185 Whan that she may hir leiser[3] wel espye.
"Myn housbonde is so ful of jalousye
That but ye waite° wel and been privee   *be on guard*
I woot right wel I nam but deed,"[4] quod she.
"Ye moste been ful derne as in this cas."
190   "Nay, therof care thee nought," quod Nicholas.
"A clerk hadde litherly biset his while,[5]
But if he coude a carpenter bigile."
And thus they been accorded and ysworn
To waite° a time, as I have told biforn.   *watch for*
195 Whan Nicholas hadde doon this everydeel,°   *every bit*
And thakked° hire upon the lendes° weel,   *patted/loins*
He kiste hire sweete, and taketh his sautrye,
And playeth faste, and maketh melodye.
    Thanne fil° it thus, that to the parissh chirche,   *befell*
200 Cristes owene werkes for to wirche,°   *perform*
This goode wif wente on an haliday:°   *holy day*
Hir forheed shoon as bright as any day,
So was it wasshen whan she leet° hir werk.   *left*
    Now was ther of that chirche a parissh clerk,[6]
205 The which that was ycleped° Absolon: *called*
Crul° was his heer, and as the gold it shoon,   *curly*
And strouted° as a fanne[7] large and brode;   *spread out*

6. A town near Oxford.
7. Elegant (thing); a euphemism for the female genitals.
8. Right now.
9. Frame for holding a horse to be shod.
1. I.e., made such vigorous advances.
2. Thomas à Becket.

3. I.e., opportunity.
4. I am no more than dead, I am done for.
5. Poorly employed his time.
6. Assistant to the parish priest, not a cleric or student.
7. Wide-mouthed basket for separating grain from chaff.

Ful straight and evene lay his joly shode.[8]
His rode° was reed, his yën greye as goos.°   *complexion/goose*
210 With Poules window corven[9] on his shoos,
In hoses° rede he wente fetisly.°   *stockings/elegantly*
Yclad he was ful smale° and proprely,   *finely*
Al in a kirtel° of a light waget°—   *tunic/blue*
Ful faire and thikke been the pointes[1] set—
215 And therupon he hadde a gay surplis,°   *surplice*
As whit as is the blosme upon the ris.°   *bough*
A merye child° he was, so God me save.   *lad*
Wel coude he laten blood, and clippe,[2] and shave,
And maken a chartre of land, or acquitaunce;[3]
220 In twenty manere° coude he trippe and daunce   *ways*
After the scole of Oxenforde tho,°   *then*
And with his legges casten° to and fro,   *prance*
And playen songes on a smal rubible;°   *fiddle*
Therto he soong somtime a loud quinible,[4]
225 And as wel coude he playe on a giterne:°   *guitar*
In al the town nas brewhous ne taverne
That he ne visited with his solas,°   *entertainment*
Ther any gailard tappestere[5] was.
But sooth to sayn, he was somdeel squaimous°   *squeamish*
230 Of farting, and of speeche daungerous.°   *fastidious*
      This Absolon, that joly° was and gay,   *pretty, amorous*
Gooth with a cencer° on the haliday,   *incense burner*
Cencing the wives of the parissh faste,
And many a lovely look on hem he caste,
235 And namely° on this carpenteres wif: *especially*
To looke on hire him thoughte a merye lif.
She was so propre° and sweete and likerous,[6]   *neat*
I dar wel sayn, if she hadde been a mous,
And he a cat, he wolde hire hente° anoon.   *pounce on*
240 This parissh clerk, this joly Absolon,
Hath in his herte swich a love-longinge°   *lovesickness*
That of no wif ne took he noon offringe—
For curteisye he saide he wolde noon.
The moone, whan it was night, ful brighte shoon,°   *shone*
245 And Absolon his giterne° hath ytake—   *guitar*
For paramours° he thoughte for to wake—   *love*
And forth he gooth, jolif° and amorous,   *pretty*
Til he cam to the carpenteres hous,
A litel after cokkes hadde ycrowe,
250 And dressed him up by a shot-windowe[7]
That was upon the carpenteres wal.
He singeth in his vois gentil and smal,°   *dainty*
"Now dere lady, if thy wille be,
I praye you that ye wol rewe° on me,"   *have pity*

8. Parting of the hair.
9. Carved with intricate designs, like the tracery in the windows of St. Paul's.
1. Laces for fastening the tunic and holding up the hose.
2. Let blood and give haircuts. Bleeding was a medical treatment performed by barbers.
3. Legal release.
4. Part requiring a very high voice.
5. Gay barmaid.
6. Wanton, appetizing.
7. Took his position by a hinged window.

255 Ful wel accordant to his giterninge.[8]
    This carpenter awook and herde him singe,
    And spak unto his wif, and saide anoon,
    "What, Alison, heerestou nought Absolon
    That chaunteth thus under oure bowres° wal?"   bedroom's
260 And she answerde hir housbonde therwithal,
    "Yis, God woot, John, I heere it everydeel."°   every bit
      This passeth forth. What wol ye bet than weel?[9]
    Fro day to day this joly Absolon
    So woweth° hire that him is wo-bigoon: woos
265 He waketh° al the night and al the day;   stays awake
    He kembed° his lokkes brode[1] and made him gay;   combed
    He woweth hire by menes and brocage,[2]
    And swoor he wolde been hir owene page°   personal servant
    He singeth, brokking° as a nightingale;   trilling
270 He sente hire piment,° meeth,° and spiced ale,   spiced wine/mead
    And wafres° piping hoot out of the gleede;°   pastries/coals
    And for she was of towne,[3] he profred meede°—   money
    For som folk wol be wonnen for richesse,
    And som for strokes,° and som for gentilesse.   blows (force)
275 Somtime to shewe his lightnesse and maistrye,[4]
    He playeth Herodes[5] upon a scaffold° hye.   platform, stage
    But what availeth him as in this cas?
    She loveth so this hende Nicholas
    That Absolon may blowe the bukkes horn;[6]
280 He ne hadde for his labour but a scorn.
    And thus she maketh Absolon hir ape,[7]
    And al his ernest turneth til° a jape.°   to/joke
    Ful sooth is this proverbe, it is no lie;
    Men saith right thus: "Alway the nye slye
285 Maketh the ferre leve to be loth."[8]
    For though that Absolon be wood° or wroth,   furious
    By cause that he fer was from hir sighte,
    This nye° Nicholas stood in his lighte.   nearby
      Now beer° thee wel, thou hende Nicholas,   bear
290 For Absolon may waile and singe allas.
      And so bifel it on a Saterday
    This carpenter was goon til Oseney,
    And hende Nicholas and Alisoun
    Accorded been to this conclusioun,
295 That Nicholas shal shapen° hem a wile°   arrange/trick
    This sely[9] jalous housbonde to bigile,
    And if so be this game wente aright,
    She sholden sleepen in his arm al night—
    For this was his desir and hire° also.   hers
300 And right anoon, withouten wordes mo,

8. In harmony with his guitar playing.   mystery plays.
9. Better than well.   6. Blow the buck's horn, i.e., go whistle.
1. I.e., wide-spreading.   7. I.e., thus she makes a monkey out of Absolon.
2. By go-betweens and agents.   8. Always the sly man at hand makes the distant dear
3. Because she was a town woman.   one hated.
4. Facility and virtuosity.   9. Poor innocent.
5. Herod, a role traditionally played as a bully in the

This Nicholas no lenger wolde tarye,
But dooth ful softe unto his chambre carye
Bothe mete and drinke for a day or twaye,
And to hir housbonde bad hire for to saye,
305   If that he axed after Nicholas,
She sholde saye she niste° wher he was—   *didn't know*
Of al that day she sawgh him nought with yë:
She trowed° that he was in maladye,   *believed*
For for no cry hir maide coude him calle,
310   He nolde answere for no thing that mighte falle.°   *happen*
    This passeth forth al thilke° Saterday   *this*
That Nicholas stille in his chambre lay,
And eet,° and sleep,° or dide what him leste,[1]   *ate/slept*
Til Sonday that the sonne gooth to reste.
315   This sely carpenter hath greet mervaile
Of Nicholas, or what thing mighte him aile,
And saide, "I am adrad,° by Saint Thomas,   *afraid*
It stondeth nat aright with Nicholas.
God shilde° that he deide sodeinly!   *forbid*
320   This world is now ful tikel,° sikerly: *changeable*
I sawgh today a corps yborn to chirche
That now a° Monday last I sawgh him wirche.°   *on/work*
Go up," quod he unto his knave° anoon,   *manservant*
"Clepe° at his dore or knokke with a stoon.°   *call/stone*
325   Looke how it is and tel me boldely."
    This knave gooth him up ful sturdily,
And at the chambre dore whil that he stood
He cride and knokked as that he were wood,°   *mad*
"What? How? What do ye, maister Nicholay?
330   How may ye sleepen al the longe day?"
But al for nought: he herde nat a word.
An hole he foond ful lowe upon a boord,
Ther as the cat was wont in for to creepe,
And at that hole he looked in ful deepe,
335   And atte laste he hadde of him a sighte.
    This Nicholas sat evere caping° uprighte   *gaping*
As he hadde kiked° on the newe moone.   *gazed*
Adown he gooth and tolde his maister soone
In what array° he saw this ilke° man.   *condition/same*
340   This carpenter to blessen him[2] bigan,
And saide, "Help us, Sainte Frideswide!
A man woot litel what him shal bitide.
This man is falle, with his astromye,[3]
In som woodnesse° or in som agonye.   *madness*
345   I thoughte ay° wel how that it sholde be: *always*
Men sholde nought knowe of Goddes privetee.
Ye, blessed be alway a lewed° man   *ignorant*
That nought but only his bileve° can.°   *creed/knows*
So ferde° another clerk with astromye: *fared*
350   He walked in the feeldes for to prye

1. He wanted.   3. Illiterate form of "astronomye."
2. Cross himself.

Upon the sterres,° what ther sholde bifalle,   *stars*
Til he was in a marle-pit[4] yfalle—
He saw nat that. But yit, by Saint Thomas,
Me reweth sore[5] for hende Nicholas.
355   He shal be rated of[6] his studying,
If that I may, by Jesus, hevene king!
Get me a staf that I may underspore,°   *pry up*
Whil that thou, Robin, hevest° up the dore.   *heave*
He shal[7] out of his studying, as I gesse."
360   And to the chambre dore he gan him dresse.[8]
His knave was a strong carl° for the nones,°   *fellow/purpose*
And by the haspe he haaf° it up atones: *heaved*
Into° the floor the dore fil° anoon.   *on/fell*
This Nicholas sat ay as stille as stoon,
365   And evere caped up into the air.
This carpenter wende° he were in despair,   *thought*
And hente° him by the shuldres mightily,   *seized*
And shook him harde, and cride spitously,°   *vehemently*
"What, Nicholay, what, how! What! Looke adown!
370   Awaak and thenk on Cristes passioun![9]
I crouche[1] thee from elves and fro wightes."°   *wicked creatures*
Therwith the nightspel saide he anoonrightes[2]
On foure halves° of the hous aboute,   *sides*
And on the thresshfold° on the dore withoute: *threshold*
375   "Jesu Crist and Sainte Benedight,°   *Benedict*
Blesse this hous from every wikked wight!
For nightes nerye the White Pater Noster.[3]
Where wentestou,° thou Sainte Petres soster?°   *did you go/sister*
And at the laste this hende Nicholas
380   Gan for to sike° sore, and saide, "Allas,   *sigh*
Shal al the world be lost eftsoones° now?"   *again*
    This carpenter answerde, "What saistou?
What, thenk on God as we doon, men that swinke."°   *work*
    This Nicholas answerde, "Fecche me drinke,
385   And after wol I speke in privetee
Of certain thing that toucheth me and thee.
I wol telle it noon other man, certain."
    This carpenter gooth down and comth again,
And broughte of mighty° ale a large quart,   *strong*
390   And when that eech of hem hadde dronke his part,
This Nicholas his dore faste shette,°   *shut*
And down the carpenter by him he sette,
And saide, "John, myn hoste lief° and dere,   *beloved*
Thou shalt upon thy trouthe° swere me here   *word of honor*
395   That to no wight thou shalt this conseil° wraye;°   *secret/disclose*
For it is Cristes conseil that I saye,

---

4. Pit from which a fertilizing clay is dug.   1. Make the sign of the cross on.
5. I sorely pity.   2. The night-charm he said right away (to ward off evil
6. Scolded for.   spirits).
7. I.e., shall come.   3. I.e., the White Lord's Prayer defend (us). This per-
8. Took his stand.   sonification was considered a powerful beneficent
9. I.e., the Crucifixion.   spirit.

	And if thou telle it man,[4] thou art forlore,°	*lost*
	For this vengeance thou shalt have therfore,	
	That if thou wraye me, thou shalt be wood."[5]	
400	"Nay, Crist forbede it, for his holy blood,"	
	Quod tho this sely° man. "I nam no labbe,°	*innocent/blabbermouth*
	And though I saye, I nam nat lief to gabbe.[6]	
	Say what thou wilt, I shal it nevere telle	
	To child ne wif, by him that harwed helle."[7]	
405	"Now John," quod Nicholas, "I wol nought lie.	
	I have yfounde in myn astrologye,	
	As I have looked in the moone bright,	
	That now a Monday next, at quarter night,[8]	
	Shal falle a rain, and that so wilde and wood,°	*furious*
410	That half so greet was nevere Noees° flood.	*Noah's*
	This world," he saide, "in lasse° than an hour	*less*
	Shal al be dreint,° so hidous is the showr.	*drowned*
	Thus shal mankinde drenche° and lese° hir lif."	*drown/lose*
	This carpenter answerde, "Allas, my wif!	
415	And shal she drenche? Allas, myn Alisoun!"	
	For sorwe of this he fil almost[9] adown,	
	And saide, "Is there no remedye in this cas?"	
	"Why yis, for[1] Gode," quod hende Nicholas,	
	"If thou wolt werken after lore and reed[2]—	
420	Thou maist nought werken after thyn owene heed;°	*head*
	For thus saith Salomon that was ful trewe,	
	'Werk al by conseil and thou shalt nought rewe.'°	*be sorry*
	And if thou werken wolt by good conseil,	
	I undertake, withouten mast or sail,	
425	Yit shal I save hire and thee and me.	
	Hastou nat herd how saved was Noee	
	Whan that oure Lord hadde warned him biforn	
	That al the world with water sholde be lorn?"°	*lost*
	"Yis," quod this carpenter, "ful yore° ago."	*long*
430	"Hastou nat herd," quod Nicholas, "also	
	The sorwe of Noee with his felaweshipe?	
	Er° that he mighte gete his wif to shipe,	*before*
	Him hadde levere,[3] I dar wel undertake,	
	At thilke time than alle his wetheres[4] blake	
435	That she hadde had a ship hirself allone.[5]	
	And therfore woostou° what is best to doone?	*do you know*
	This axeth° haste, and of an hastif° thing	*requires/urgent*
	Men may nought preche or maken tarying.	
	Anoon go gete us faste into this in°	*lodging*
440	A kneeding trough or elles a kimelin°	*brewing tub*
	For eech of us, but looke that they be large,°	*wide*

4. To anyone.
5. Go mad.
6. And though I say it myself, I don't like to gossip.
7. By Him that despoiled hell—i.e., Christ.
8. I.e., shortly before dawn.
9. Almost fell.
1. I.e., by.

2. Act according to learning and advice.
3. He had rather.
4. Rams. I.e., he'd have given all the black rams he had.
5. The reluctance of Noah's wife to board the ark is a traditional comic theme in the mystery plays.

In whiche we mowen swimme as in a barge,[6]
And han therinne vitaile suffisaunt[7]
But for a day—fy° on the remenaunt!   *fie*
445 The water shal aslake° and goon away   *diminish*
Aboute prime[8] upon the nexte day.
But Robin may nat wite° of this, thy knave,   *know*
Ne eek thy maide Gille I may nat save.
Axe nought why, for though thou axe me,
450 I wol nought tellen Goddes privetee.°   *secrets*
Suffiseth thee, but if thy wittes madde,°   *go mad*
To han° as greet a grace as Noee hadde.   *have*
Thy wif shal I wel saven, out of doute.
Go now thy way, and speed thee heraboute.
455 But whan thou hast for hire° and thee and me   *her*
Ygeten us thise kneeding-tubbes three,
Thanne shaltou hangen hem in the roof ful hye,
That no man of oure purveyance° espye.   *preparations*
And whan thou thus hast doon as I have said,
460 And hast oure vitaile faire in hem ylaid,
And eek an ax to smite the corde atwo,
Whan that the water comth that we may go,
And broke an hole an heigh[9] upon the gable
Unto the gardinward,[1] over the stable,
465 That we may freely passen forth oure way,
Whan that the grete showr is goon away,
Thanne shaltou swimme as merye, I undertake,
As dooth the white doke° after hir drake.   *duck*
Thanne wol I clepe,° 'How, Alison? How, John?   *call*
470 Be merye, for the flood wol passe anoon.'
And thou wolt sayn, 'Hail, maister Nicholay!
Good morwe, I see thee wel, for it is day!'
And thanne shal we be lordes al oure lif
Of al the world, as Noee and his wif.
475 But of oo thing I warne thee ful right:
Be wel avised° on that ilke night   *warned*
That we been entred into shippes boord
That noon of us ne speke nought a word,
Ne clepe, ne crye, but been in his prayere,
480 For it is Goddes owene heeste dere.[2]
Thy wif and thou mote hange fer atwinne,[3]
For that bitwixe you shal be no sinne—
Namore in looking than ther shal in deede.
This ordinance is said: go, God thee speede.
485 Tomorwe at night whan men been alle asleepe,
Into oure kneeding-tubbes wol we creepe,
And sitten there, abiding Goddes grace.
Go now thy way, I have no lenger space°   *time*
To make of this no lenger sermoning.

6. In which we can float as in a vessel.   1. Toward the garden.
7. Sufficient food.   2. Precious commandment.
8. 9 A.M.   3. Far apart.
9. On high.

490 Men sayn thus: 'Send the wise and say no thing.'
     Thou art so wis it needeth thee nat teche:
     Go save oure lif, and that I thee biseeche."
         This sely carpenter gooth forth his way:
     Ful ofte he saide allas and wailaway,
495 And to his wif he tolde his privetee,
     And she was war,° and knew it bet° than he,   *aware/better*
     What al this quainte cast was for to saye.[4]
     But nathelees she ferde° as she wolde deye,   *acted*
     And saide, "Allas, go forth thy way anoon.
500 Help us to scape,° or we been dede eechoon.   *escape*
     I am thy trewe verray wedded wif:
     Go, dere spouse, and help to save oure lif."
         Lo, which a greet thing is affeccioun!°   *emotion*
     Men may dien of imaginacioun,
505 So deepe° may impression be take.   *deeply*
     This sely carpenter biginneth quake;
     Him thinketh verrailiche° that he may see   *truly*
     Noees flood come walwing° as the see   *rolling*
     To drenchen° Alison, his hony dere.   *drown*
510 He weepeth, waileth, maketh sory cheere;
     He siketh° with ful many a sory swough,°   *sighs/groan*
     And gooth and geteth him a kneeding-trough,
     And after a tubbe and a kimelin,
     And prively he sente hem to his in,°   *dwelling*
515 And heeng° hem in the roof in privetee;   *hung*
     His° owene hand he made laddres three,   *with his*
     To climben by the ronges° and the stalkes°   *rungs/uprights*
     Unto the tubbes hanging in the balkes,°   *rafters*
     And hem vitailed,° bothe trough and tubbe,   *victualed*
520 With breed and cheese and good ale in a jubbe,°   *jug*
     Suffising right ynough as for a day.
     But er° that he hadde maad al this array,   *before*
     He sente his knave, and eek his wenche also,
     Upon his neede[5] to London for to go.
525 And on the Monday whan it drow to[6] nighte,
     He shette° his dore withouten candel-lighte,   *shut*
     And dressed° alle thing as it sholde be,   *arranged*
     And shortly up they clomben° alle three.   *climbed*
     They seten° stille wel a furlong way.[7]   *sat*
530 "Now, Pater Noster, clum,"[8] saide Nicholay,
     And "Clum" quod John, and "Clum" saide Alisoun.
     This carpenter saide his devocioun,
     And stille he sit° and biddeth° his prayere,   *sits/prays*
     Awaiting on the rain, if he it heere.°   *might hear*
535   The dede sleep, for wery bisinesse,
     Fil° on this carpenter right as I gesse   *fell*
     Aboute corfew time,[9] or litel more.

---

4. What all this clever plan meant.
5. On an errand for him.
6. Drew toward.
7. The time it takes to go a furlong (i.e., a few min-

utes).
8. Hush (?). "Pater Noster": Our Father.
9. Probably about 8 P.M.

For travailing of his gost[1] he groneth sore,
And eft° he routeth,° for his heed mislay.[2]　　　　*then/snores*
540　　Down of the laddre stalketh Nicholay,
And Alison ful softe adown she spedde:
Withouten wordes mo they goon to bedde
Ther as the carpenter is wont to lie.
Ther was the revel and the melodye,
545　And thus lith° Alison and Nicholas　　　　*lies*
In bisinesse of mirthe and of solas,°　　　　*pleasure*
Til that the belle of Laudes[3] gan to ringe,
And freres° in the chauncel° gonne singe.　　　　*friars/chancel*
　　This parissh clerk, this amorous Absolon,
550　That is for love alway so wo-bigoon,
Upon the Monday was at Oseneye,
With compaignye him to disporte and playe,
And axed upon caas a cloisterer[4]
Ful prively after John the carpenter;
555　And he drow him apart out of the chirche,
And saide, "I noot:[5] I sawgh him here nought wirche°　　　　*work*
Sith Saterday. I trowe that he be went
For timber ther oure abbot hath him sent.
For he is wont for timber for to go,
560　And dwellen atte grange[6] a day or two.
Or elles he is at his hous, certain.
Where that he be I can nought soothly sayn."
　　This Absolon ful jolif was and light,[7]
And thoughte, "Now is time to wake al night,
565　For sikerly,° I sawgh him nought stiringe　　　　*certainly*
Aboute his dore sin day bigan to springe.
So mote° I thrive, I shal at cokkes crowe　　　　*may*
Ful prively knokken at his windowe
That stant° ful lowe upon his bowres° wal.　　　　*stands/bedroom's*
570　To Alison now wol I tellen al
My love-longing,° for yet I shal nat misse　　　　*lovesickness*
That at the leeste way[8] I shal hire kisse.
Som manere confort shal I have, parfay.°　　　　*in faith*
My mouth hath icched al this longe day:
575　That is a signe of kissing at the leeste.
Al night me mette[9] eek I was at a feeste.
Therfore I wol go sleepe an hour or twaye,
And al the night thanne wol I wake and playe."
　　Whan that the firste cok hath crowe, anoon
580　Up rist° this joly lovere Absolon,　　　　*rises*
And him arrayeth gay at point devis.[1]
But first he cheweth grain[2] and licoris,
To smellen sweete, er he hadde kembd° his heer.　　　　*combed*

1. Affliction of his spirit.
2. Lay in the wrong position.
3. The first church service of the day, before daybreak.
4. Here a member of the religious order of Osney Abbey. "Upon caas": by chance.
5. Don't know.
6. The outlying farm belonging to the abbey.
7. Was very amorous and cheerful.
8. I.e., at least.
9. I dreamed.
1. To perfection.
2. Grain of paradise; a spice.

Under his tonge a trewe-love[3] he beer,°   *bore*
585 For therby wende° he to be gracious.°   *supposed/pleasing*
He rometh° to the carpenteres hous,   *strolls*
And stille he stant° under the shot-windowe—   *stands*
Unto his brest it raughte,° it was so lowe—   *reached*
And ofte he cougheth with a semisoun.°   *small sound*
590 "What do ye, hony-comb, sweete Alisoun,
My faire brid,[4] my sweete cinamome?°   *cinnamon*
Awaketh, lemman° myn, and speketh to me.   *sweetheart*
Wel litel thinken ye upon my wo
That for your love I swete° ther I go.   *sweat*
595 No wonder is though that I swelte° and swete: *melt*
I moorne as doth a lamb after the tete.°   *teat*
Ywis, lemman, I have swich love-longinge,
That lik a turtle° trewe is my moorninge: *dove*
I may nat ete namore than a maide."
600 "Go fro the windowe, Jakke fool," she saide.
"As help me God, it wol nat be com-pa-me.°   *come-kiss-me*
I love another, and elles I were to blame,
Wel bet° than thee, by Jesu, Absolon.   *better*
Go forth thy way or I wol caste a stoon,
605 And lat me sleepe, a twenty devele way."[5]
"Allas," quod Absolon, "and wailaway,
That trewe love was evere so yvele biset.[6]
Thanne kis me, sin that it may be no bet,
For Jesus love and for the love of me."
610 "Woltou thanne go thy way therwith?" quod she.
"Ye, certes, lemman," quod this Absolon.
"Thanne maak thee redy," quod she. "I come anoon."
And unto Nicholas she saide stille,°   *quietly*
"Now hust,° and thou shalt laughen al thy fille."   *hush*
615 This Absolon down sette him on his knees,
And said, "I am a lord at alle degrees,[7]
For after this I hope ther cometh more.
Lemman, thy grace, and sweete brid, thyn ore!"°   *mercy*
The windowe she undooth, and that in haste.
620 "Have do," quod she, "come of and speed thee faste,
Lest that oure neighebores thee espye."
This Absolon gan wipe his mouth ful drye:
Derk was the night as pich or as the cole,
And at the windowe out she putte hir hole,
625 And Absolon, him fil no bet ne wers,[8]
But with his mouth he kiste hir naked ers,
Ful savourly,° er he were war of this.   *with relish*
Abak he sterte,° and thoughte it was amis,   *started*
For wel he wiste a womman hath no beerd.°   *beard*
630 He felte a thing al rough and longe yherd,°   *haired*
And saide, "Fy, allas, what have I do?"

---

3. Sprig of a cloverlike plant.   6. Ill-used.
4. Bird or bride.   7. In every way.
5. In the name of twenty devils.   8. It befell him neither better nor worse.

"Teehee," quod she, and clapte the windowe to.
And Absolon gooth forth a sory pas.[9]
"A beerd, a beerd!"[1] quod hende Nicholas,

635 "By Goddes corpus,° this gooth faire and weel."   *body*
This sely Absolon herde everydeel,°   *every bit*
And on his lippe he gan for anger bite,
And to himself he saide, "I shal thee quite."°   *repay*
Who rubbeth now, who froteth° now his lippes   *wipes*

640 With dust, with sond,° with straw, with cloth, with chippes,   *sand*
But Absolon, that saith ful ofte allas?
"My soule bitake° I unto Satanas,°   *commit/Satan*
But me were levere[2] than all this town," quod he,
"Of this despit° awroken° for to be.   *insult/avenged*

645 Allas," quod he, "allas I ne hadde ybleint!"°   *turned aside*
His hote love was cold and al yqueint,°   *quenched*
For fro that time that he hadde kist hir ers
Of paramours he sette nought a kers,[3]
For he was heled° of his maladye.   *cured*

650 Ful ofte paramours he gan defye,°   *renounce*
And weep° as dooth a child that is ybete.   *wept*
A softe paas[4] he wente over the streete
Until° a smith men clepen daun Gervais,[5]   *to*
That in his forge smithed plough harneis:°   *equipment*

655 He sharpeth shaar and cultour[6] bisily.
This Absolon knokketh al esily,°   *quietly*
And saide, "Undo, Gervais, and that anoon."°   *at once*
"What, who artou?" "It am I, Absolon."
"What, Absolon? What, Cristes sweete tree!°   *cross*

660 Why rise ye so rathe?° Ey, benedicite,°   *early/bless me*
What aileth you? Som gay girl, God it woot,
Hath brought you thus upon the viritoot.[7]
By Sainte Note, ye woot wel what I mene."
This Absolon ne roughte nat a bene[8]

665 Of al his play. No word again he yaf:
He hadde more tow on his distaf[9]
Than Gervais knew, and saide, "Freend so dere,
This hote cultour in the chimenee° here,   *fireplace*
As lene[1] it me: I have therwith to doone.

670 I wol bringe it thee again ful soone."
Gervais answerde, "Certes, were it gold,
Or in a poke nobles alle untold,[2]
Thou sholdest have, as I am trewe smith.
Ey, Cristes fo,[3] what wol ye do therwith?"

675 "Therof," quod Absolon, "be as be may.
I shal wel telle it thee another day."
And caughte the cultour by the colde stele.°   *handle*

---

9. I.e., walking sadly.
1. A trick (slang), but with a play on line 629.
2. I had rather.
3. He didn't care a piece of cress for woman's love.
4. I.e., quiet walk.
5. Master Gervais.
6. He sharpens plowshare and coulter (the turf cutter on a plow).
7. I.e., on the prowl.
8. Didn't care a bean.
9. I.e., more on his mind.
1. I.e., please lend.
2. Or gold coins all uncounted in a bag.
3. Foe, i.e., Satan.

Ful softe out at the dore he gan to stele,
And wente unto the carpenteres wal:
680   He cougheth first and knokketh therwithal
Upon the windowe, right as he dide er.°   *before*
    This Alison answerde, "Who is ther
That knokketh so? I warante[4] it a thief."
    "Why, nay," quod he, "God woot, my sweete lief,°   *dear*
685   I am thyn Absolon, my dereling.°   *darling*
Of gold," quod he, "I have thee brought a ring—
My moder yaf it me, so God me save;
Ful fin it is and therto wel ygrave:°   *engraved*
This wol I yiven thee if thou me kisse."
690   This Nicholas was risen for to pisse,
And thoughte he wolde amenden[5] al the jape:°   *joke*
He sholde kisse his ers er that he scape.
And up the windowe dide he hastily,
And out his ers he putteth prively,
695   Over the buttok to the haunche-boon.
    And therwith spak this clerk, this Absolon,
"Speek, sweete brid, I noot nought wher thou art."
This Nicholas anoon leet flee[6] a fart
As greet as it hadde been a thonder-dent°   *thunderbolt*
700   That with the strook he was almost yblent,°   *blinded*
And he was redy with his iren hoot,°   *hot*
And Nicholas amidde the ers he smoot:°   *smote*
Of° gooth the skin an hande-brede° aboute;   *off/handsbreadth*
The hote cultour brende so his toute°   *buttocks*
705   That for the smert° he wende for to[7] die;   *pain*
As he were wood° for wo he gan to crye,   *crazy*
"Help! Water! Water! Help, for Goddes herte!"
    This carpenter out of his slomber sterte,
And herde oon cryen "Water!" as he were wood,
710   And thoughte, "Allas, now cometh Noweles[8] flood!"
He sette him up[9] withoute wordes mo,
And with his ax he smoot the corde atwo,
And down gooth al: he foond neither to selle
Ne breed ne ale til he cam to the celle,[1]
715   Upon the floor, and ther aswoune° he lay.   *in a faint*
    Up sterte hire[2] Alison and Nicholay,
And criden "Out" and "Harrow" in the streete.
The neighebores, bothe smale and grete,
In ronnen for to gauren° on this man   *gape*
720   That aswoune lay bothe pale and wan,
For with the fal he brosten° hadde his arm;   *broken*
But stonde he moste° unto his owene harm,   *must*
For whan he spak he was anoon bore down[3]
With° hende Nicholas and Alisoun: *by*

4. I.e., wager.   9. Got up.
5. Improve on.   1. He found time to sell neither bread nor ale until he
6. Let fly.   arrived at the foundation, i.e., he did not take time out.
7. Thought he would.   2. Started.
8. The carpenter is confusing Noah and Noel   3. Refuted.
(Christmas).

725 They tolden every man that he was wood—
      He was agast so of Noweles flood,
      Thurgh fantasye, that of his vanitee°   folly
      He hadde ybought him kneeding-tubbes three,
      And hadde hem hanged in the roof above,
730 And that he prayed hem, for Goddes love,
      To sitten in the roof, *par compaignye*.[4]
         The folk gan laughen at his fantasye.
      Into the roof they kiken° and they cape,°   peer/gape
      And turned al his harm unto a jape,°   joke
735 For what so that this carpenter answerde,
      It was for nought: no man his reson° herde;   argument
      With othes grete he was so sworn adown,
      That he was holden° wood in al the town,   considered
      For every clerk anoonright heeld with other:
740 They saide, "The man was wood, my leve brother,"
      And every wight gan laughen at this strif.°   fuss
      Thus swived[5] was the carpenteres wif
      For al his keeping° and his jalousye,   guarding
      And Absolon hath kist hir nether° yë,   lower
745 And Nicholas is scalded in the toute:
      This tale is doon, and God save al the route!°   company

The Wife of Bath's Prologue and Tale

The Prologue[1]

         Experience, though noon auctoritee
      Were in this world, is right ynough for me
      To speke of wo that is in mariage:
      For lordinges,° sith I twelf yeer was of age—   gentlemen
5   Thanked be God that is eterne on live—
      Housbondes at chirche dore[2] I have had five
      (If I so ofte mighte han wedded be),
      And alle were worthy men in hir degree.
      But me was told, certain, nat longe agoon is,
10   That sith that Crist ne wente nevere but ones°   once
      To wedding in the Cane[3] of Galilee,
      That by the same ensample° taughte he me   example
      That I ne sholde wedded be but ones.

<hr>

4. For company's sake.
5. The vulgar verb for having sexual intercourse.
1. The Wife of Bath is the remarkable culmination of many centuries of an antifeminism that was particularly nurtured by the medieval church. In their eagerness to exalt the spiritual ideal of chastity, certain theologians, among whom St. Jerome was perhaps the most extreme, developed an idea of most women as insatiably lecherous and indomitable shrewish. Throughout her prologue, as in the opening lines, the Wife puts her experience as a woman above "auctoritee," the authority of books written by clerics. After defending her five marriages, she launches into a lesson on how to tame husbands and drifts gradually into fond reminiscences of her fifth. Although her life seems to confirm many of the accusations of the antifeminist writers, and she is herself a comic figure, the Wife of Bath's humor, honesty, and vitality have the effect of satirizing antifeminist literature and exposing the shallowness of the stereotype it seeks to impose on her.
2. The actual wedding ceremony was celebrated at the church door, not in the chancel.
3. Cana (see John 2.1).

Herke eek,° lo, which° a sharp word for the nones,[4]   *also/what*
15   Biside a welle, Jesus, God and man,
Spak in repreve° of the Samaritan: *reproof*
"Thou hast yhad five housbondes," quod he,
"And that ilke° man that now hath thee   *same*
Is nat thyn housbonde." Thus saide he certain.
20   What that he mente therby I can nat sayn,
But that I axe° why the fifthe man   *ask*
Was noon housbonde to the Samaritan?[5]
How manye mighte she han in mariage?
Yit herde I nevere tellen in myn age
25   Upon this nombre diffinicioun.°   *definition*
Men may divine° and glosen° up and down,   *guess/interpret*
But wel I woot,° expres,° withouten lie,   *know/expressly*
God bad us for to wexe[6] and multiplye:
That gentil text can I wel understonde.
30   Eek wel I woot° he saide that myn housbonde   *know*
Sholde lete° fader and moder and take to me,[7]   *leave*
But of no nombre mencion made he—
Of bigamye or of octogamye:[8]
Why sholde men thanne speke of it vilainye?
35   Lo, here the wise king daun° Salomon: *master*
I trowe° he hadde wives many oon,[9]   *believe*
As wolde God it leveful° were to me   *permissible*
To be refresshed half so ofte as he.
Which yifte[1] of God hadde he for alle his wives!
40   No man hath swich that in this world alive is.
God woot this noble king, as to my wit,°   *knowledge*
The firste night hadde many a merye fit°   *bout*
With eech of hem, so wel was him on live.[2]
Blessed be God that I have wedded five,
45   Of whiche I have piked out the beste,[3]
Bothe of hir nether° purs and of hir cheste.°   *lower/money box*
Diverse scoles maken parfit° clerkes,   *perfect*
And diverse practikes[4] in sondry werkes
Maken the werkman parfit sikerly:°   *certainly*
50   Of five housbondes scoleying° am I.   *schooling*
Welcome the sixte whan that evere he shal![5]
For sith I wol nat kepe me chast in al,
Whan my housbonde is fro the world agoon,
Som Cristen man shal wedde me anoon.°   *right away*
55   For thanne th'Apostle[6] saith that I am free
To wedde, a Goddes half, where it liketh me.[7]
He saide that to be wedded is no sinne:
Bet° is to be wedded than to brinne.°   *better/burn*

---

4. To the purpose.
5. Christ was actually referring to a sixth man who was not married to the Samaritan woman (cf. John 4.6 ff.).
6. I.e., increase (see Genesis 1.28).
7. See Matthew 19.5.
8. I.e., of two or even eight marriages. The Wife of Bath is referring to successive, rather than simultaneous marriages.
9. Solomon had seven hundred wives and three hundred concubines (1 Kings 11.3).
1. What a gift.
2. I.e., so pleasant a life he had.
3. Whom I have cleaned out of everything worthwhile.
4. Practical experiences.
5. I.e., shall come along.
6. St. Paul.
7. I please. "A Goddes half": on God's behalf.

What rekketh me[8] though folk saye vilainye
60 Of shrewed° Lamech[9] and his bigamye?   *cursed*
I woot wel Abraham was an holy man,
And Jacob eek, as fer as evere I can,°   *know*
And eech of hem hadde wives mo than two,
And many another holy man also.
65   Where can ye saye in any manere age
That hye God defended° mariage   *prohibited*
By expres word? I praye you, telleth me.
Or where comanded he virginitee?
I woot as wel as ye, it is no drede,°   *doubt*
70 Th'Apostle, whan he speketh of maidenhede,°   *virginity*
He saide that precept therof hadde he noon:
Men may conseile a womman to be oon,°   *single*
But conseiling nis° no comandement.   *is not*
He putte it in oure owene juggement.
75 For hadde God comanded maidenhede,
Thanne hadde he dampned° wedding with the deede;[1]   *condemned*
And certes, if there were no seed ysowe,
Virginitee, thanne wherof sholde it growe?
Paul dorste nat comanden at the leeste
80 A thing of which his maister yaf° no heeste.°   *gave/command*
The dart[2] is set up for virginitee:
Cacche whoso may, who renneth° best lat see.   *runs*
But this word is nought take of[3] every wight,°   *person*
But ther as[4] God list° yive it of his might.   *it pleases*
85 I woot wel that th'Apostle was a maide,°   *virgin*
But nathelees, though that he wroot and saide
He wolde that every wight were swich° as he,   *such*
Al nis but conseil to virginitee;
And for to been a wif he yaf me leve
90 Of indulgence; so nis it no repreve°   *disgrace*
To wedde me[5] if that my make° die,   *mate*
Withouten excepcion of bigamye[6]—
Al° were it good no womman for to touche   *although*
(He mente as in his bed or in his couche,
95 For peril is bothe fir° and tow° t'assemble—   *fire/flax*
Ye knowe what this ensample may resemble).[7]
This al and som,[8] he heeld virginitee
More parfit than wedding in freletee.°   *frailty*
(Freletee clepe I but if[9] that he and she
100 Wolde leden al hir lif in chastitee.)
I graunte it wel, I have noon envye
Though maidenhede preferre° bigamye:°   *excel/remarriage*
It liketh hem to be clene in body and gost.°   *spirit*
Of myn estaat ne wol I make no boost;

---

8. What do I care.
9. The first man whom the Bible mentions as having two wives (Genesis 4.19–24).
1. I.e., at the same time.
2. I.e., prize in a race.
3. Understood for, i.e., applicable to.
4. Where.

5. For me to marry.
6. I.e., without there being any legal objection on the score of remarriage.
7. I.e., what this metaphor may apply to.
8. This is all there is to it.
9. Frailty I call it unless.

105 For wel ye knowe, a lord in his houshold
    Ne hath nat every vessel al of gold:
    Some been of tree,° and doon hir lord servise.   *wood*
    God clepeth° folk to him in sondry wise,   *calls*
    And everich hath of God a propre[1] yifte,
110 Som this, som that, as him liketh shifte.°   *ordain*
    Virginitee is greet perfeccioun,
    And continence eek with devocioun,
    But Crist, that of perfeccion is welle,°   *source*
    Bad nat every wight he sholde go selle
115 Al that he hadde and yive it to the poore,
    And in swich wise folwe him and his fore:°[2]   *footsteps*
    He spak to hem that wolde live parfitly°—   *perfectly*
    And lordinges, by youre leve, that am nat I.
    I wol bistowe the flour of al myn age
120 In th'actes and in fruit of mariage.
        Telle me also, to what conclusioun°   *end*
    Were membres maad of generacioun
    And of so parfit wis a wrighte ywrought?[3]
    Trusteth right wel, they were nat maad for nought.
125 Glose° whoso wol, and saye bothe up and down   *interpret*
    That they were maked for purgacioun
    Of urine, and oure bothe thinges smale
    Was eek° to knowe a femele from a male,   *also*
    And for noon other cause—saye ye no?
130 Th'experience woot it is nought so.
    So that the clerkes be nat with me wrothe,
    I saye this, that they been maad for bothe—
    That is to sayn, for office° and for ese°   *excretion/pleasure*
    Of engendrure,° ther we nat God displese.   *procreation*
135 Why sholde men elles in hir bookes sette
    That man shal yeelde[4] to his wif hir dette?°   *(marital) debt*
    Now wherwith sholde he make his payement
    If he ne used his sely° instrument?   *innocent*
    Thanne were they maad upon a creature
140 To purge urine, and eek for engendrure.
        But I saye nought that every wight is holde,°   *bound*
    That hath swich harneis° as I to you tolde,   *equipment*
    To goon and usen hem in engendrure:
    Thanne sholde men take of chastitee no cure.°   *heed*
145 Crist was a maide° and shapen as a man,   *virgin*
    And many a saint sith that the world bigan,
    Yit lived they evere in parfit chastitee.
    I nil° envye no virginitee: *will not*
    Lat hem be breed° of pured° whete seed,   *bread/refined*
150 And lat us wives hote° barly breed—   *be called*
    And yit with barly breed, Mark telle can,
    Oure Lord Jesu refresshed many a man.[5]

1. I.e., his own.
2. Matthew 19.21.
3. And wrought by so perfectly wise a maker.
4. I.e., pay.

5. In the descriptions of the miracle of the loaves and fishes, it is actually John, not Mark, who mentions barley bread (6.9).

In swich estaat as God hath cleped us
I wol persevere: I nam nat precious.°   *fastidious*
155   In wifhood wol I use myn instrument
As freely° as my Makere hath it sent.   *generously*
If I be daungerous,° God yive me sorwe: *hard to get*
Myn housbonde shal it han both eve and morwe,°   *morning*
Whan that him list[6] come forth and paye his dette.
160   An housbonde wol I have, I wol nat lette,[7]
Which shal be bothe my dettour° and my thral,°   *debtor/slave*
And have his tribulacion withal°   *as well*
Upon his flessh whil that I am his wif.
I have the power during al my lif
165   Upon his propre° body, and nat he: *own*
Right thus th'Apostle tolde it unto me,
And bad oure housbondes for to love us weel.
Al this sentence° me liketh everydeel.°   *sense/entirely*

[AN INTERLUDE]

Up sterte° the Pardoner and that anoon: *started*
170   "Now dame," quod he, "by God and by Saint John,
Ye been a noble prechour in this cas.
I was aboute to wedde a wif: allas,
What° sholde I bye° it on my flessh so dere?   *why/purchase*
Yit hadde I levere° wedde no wif toyere."°   *rather/this year*
175   "Abid," quod she, "my tale is nat bigonne.
Nay, thou shalt drinken of another tonne,°   *tun*
Er° that I go, shal savoure wors than ale.   *before*
And whan that I have told thee forth my tale
Of tribulacion in mariage,
180   Of which I am expert in al myn age —
This is to saye, myself hath been the whippe —
Thanne maistou chese° wheither thou wolt sippe   *choose*
Of thilke° tonne that I shal abroche;°   *this same/open*
Be war of it, er thou too neigh approche,
185   For I shal telle ensamples mo than ten.
'Whoso that nil° be war by othere men,   *will not*
By him shal othere men corrected be.'
Thise same wordes writeth Ptolomee:
Rede in his *Almageste* and take it there."[8]
190   "Dame, I wolde praye you if youre wil it were,"
Saide this Pardoner, "as ye bigan,
Telle forth youre tale; spareth for no man,
And teche us yonge men of youre practike."°   *mode of operation*
"Gladly," quod she, "sith it may you like;°   *please*
195   But that I praye to al this compaignye,
If that I speke after my fantasye,[9]

6. When he wishes to.
7. I will not leave off, desist.
8. "He who will not be warned by the example of others shall become an example to others." The *Almagest*,

an astronomical work by the Greek astronomer and mathematician Ptolemy (2nd century A.D.), contains no such aphorism.
9. If I speak according to my whim.

As taketh nat agrief° of that I saye,   *amiss*
For myn entente nis but for to playe."

[THE WIFE CONTINUES]

Now sire, thanne wol I telle you forth my tale.
200   As evere mote I drinke win or ale,
I shal saye sooth: tho° housbondes that I hadde,   *those*
As three of hem were goode, and two were badde.
The three men were goode, and riche, and olde;
Unnethe° mighte they the statut holde   *with difficulty*
205   In which they were bounden unto me—
Ye woot wel what I mene of this, pardee.
As help me God, I laughe whan I thinke
How pitously anight I made hem swinke;°   *work*
And by my fay,° I tolde of it no stoor:[1]   *faith*
210   They hadde me yiven hir land and hir tresor;
Me needed nat do lenger diligence
To winne hir love or doon hem reverence.
They loved me so wel, by God above,
That I ne tolde no daintee of[2] hir love.
215   A wis womman wol bisye hire evere in oon[3]
To gete hire love, ye, ther as she hath noon.
But sith I hadde hem hoolly in myn hand,
And sith that they hadde yiven me al hir land,
What° sholde I take keep° hem for to plese,   *why/care*
220   But it were for my profit and myn ese?
I sette hem so awerke,° by my fay,   *awork*
That many a night they songen° wailaway.   *sang*
The bacon was nat fet° for hem, I trowe,   *brought back*
That some men han in Essexe at Dunmowe.[4]
225   I governed hem so wel after° my lawe   *according to*
That eech of hem ful blisful was and fawe°   *glad*
To bringe me gaye thinges fro the faire;
They were ful glade whan I spak hem faire,
For God it woot, I chidde° hem spitously.°   *chided/cruelly*
230   Now herkneth how I bar me[5] proprely:
Ye wise wives, that conne understonde,
Thus sholde ye speke and bere him wrong on honde[6]—
For half so boldely can ther no man
Swere and lie as a woman can.
235   I saye nat this by wives that been wise,
But if it be whan they hem misavise.[7]
A wis wif, if that she can hir good,[8]
Shal bere him on hande the cow is wood,[9]

1. I set no store by it.
2. Set no value on.
3. Busy herself constantly.
4. At Dunmow, a side of bacon was awarded to the couple who after a year of marriage could claim no quarrels, no regrets, and the desire, if freed, to remarry one another.
5. Bore myself, behaved.
6. Accuse him falsely.
7. Unless it happens that they make a mistake.
8. If she knows what's good for her.
9. Shall persuade him the chough has gone crazy. The chough, a talking bird, was popularly supposed to tell husbands of their wives' infidelity.

And take witnesse of hir owene maide
240 Of hir assent.[1] But herkneth how I saide:
  "Sire olde cainard,° is this thyn array?[2]   *sluggard*
Why is my neighebores wif so gay?
She is honoured overal° ther she gooth: *wherever*
I sitte at hoom; I have no thrifty° cloth.   *decent*
245 What doostou at my neighebores hous?
Is she so fair? Artou so amorous?
What roune° ye with oure maide, benedicite?[3]   *whisper*
Sire olde lechour, lat thy japes° be.   *tricks, intrigues*
And if I have a gossib° or a freend,   *confidant*
250 Withouten gilt ye chiden as a feend,
If that I walke or playe unto his hous.
Thou comest hoom as dronken as a mous,
And prechest on thy bench, with yvel preef.[4]
Thou saist to me, it is a greet meschief°   *misfortune*
255 To wedde a poore womman for costage.[5]
And if that she be riche, of heigh parage,°   *descent*
Thanne saistou that it is a tormentrye
To suffre hir pride and hir malencolye.°   *bad humor*
And if that she be fair, thou verray knave,
260 Thou saist that every holour° wol hire have: *whoremonger*
She may no while in chastitee abide
That is assailed upon eech a side.
  "Thou saist som folk desiren us for richesse,
Som[6] for oure shap, and som for oure fairnesse,
265 And som for she can outher° singe or daunce,   *either*
And som for gentilesse and daliaunce,°   *flirtatiousness*
Som for hir handes and hir armes smale°—   *slender*
Thus gooth al to the devel by thy tale![7]
Thou saist men may nat keepe[8] a castel wal,
270 It may so longe assailed been overal.°   *everywhere*
And if that she be foul,° thou saist that she   *ugly*
Coveiteth° every man that she may see;   *desires*
For as a spaniel she wol on him lepe,
Til that she finde som man hire to chepe.°   *buy, take*
275 Ne noon so grey goos gooth ther in the lake,
As, saistou, wol be withoute make;°   *mate*
And saist it is an hard thing for to weelde°   *possess*
A thing that no man wol, his thankes, heelde.[9]
Thus saistou, lorel,° whan thou goost to bedde,   *wretch*
280 And that no wis man needeth for to wedde,
Ne no man that entendeth° unto hevene—   *aims*
With wilde thonder-dint° and firy levene°   *thunderbolt/lightning*
Mote thy welked nekke be tobroke![1]
Thou saist that dropping° houses and eek smoke   *leaking*
285 And chiding wives maken men to flee

1. And call as a witness her maid, who is on her side.
2. I.e., is this how you behave?
3. Bless me.
4. I.e., (may you have) bad luck.
5. Because of the expense.
6. "Som," in this and the following lines, means "one."
7. I.e., according to your story.
8. I.e., keep safe.
9. No man would willingly hold.
1. May thy withered neck be broken!

Out of hir owene hous: a, benedicite,
What aileth swich an old man for to chide?
Thou saist we wives wil oure vices hide
Til we be fast,[2] and thanne we wol hem shewe—
290 Wel may that be a proverbe of a shrewe!°   *rascal*
Thou saist that oxen, asses, hors,° and houndes,   *horses*
They been assayed° at diverse stoundes;°   *tried out/times*
Bacins, lavours,° er that men hem bye,°   *washbowls/buy*
Spoones, stooles, and al swich housbondrye,°   *household goods*
295 And so be° pottes, clothes, and array°—   *are/clothing*
But folk of wives maken noon assay
Til they be wedded—olde dotard shrewe!
And thanne, saistou, we wil oure vices shewe.
Thou saist also that it displeseth me
300 But if° that thou wolt praise my beautee,   *unless*
And but thou poure° alway upon my face,   *gaze*
And clepe me 'Faire Dame' in every place,
And but thou make a feeste on thilke day
That I was born, and make me fressh and gay,
305 And but thou do to my norice° honour,   *nurse*
And to my chamberere within my bowr,[3]
And to my fadres folk, and his allies[4]—
Thus saistou, olde barel-ful of lies.
And yit of our apprentice Janekin,
310 For his crispe° heer, shining as gold so fin,   *curly*
And for° he squiereth me bothe up and down,   *because*
Yit hastou caught a fals suspecioun;
I wil° him nat though thou were deed° tomorwe.   *want/dead*
 "But tel me this, why hidestou with sorwe[5]
315 The keyes of thy cheste° away fro me?   *money box*
It is my good° as wel as thyn, pardee.   *property*
What, weenestou° make an idiot of oure dame?[6]   *do you think to*
Now by that lord that called is Saint Jame,
Thou shalt nought bothe, though thou were wood,°   *furious*
320 Be maister of my body and of my good:
That oon thou shalt forgo, maugree thine yën.[7]
 "What helpeth it of me enquere° and spyen?   *inquire*
I trowe thou woldest loke° me in thy cheste.   *lock*
Thou sholdest saye, 'Wif, go wher thee leste.°   *it may please*
325 Taak youre disport. I nil leve° no tales: *believe*
I knowe you for a trewe wif, dame Alis.'
We love no man that taketh keep or charge[8]
Wher that we goon: we wol been at oure large.[9]
Of alle men yblessed mote he be
330 The wise astrologen° daun Ptolomee,   *astronomer*
That saith this proverbe in his *Almageste*:
'Of alle men his wisdom is the hyeste
That rekketh° nat who hath the world in honde.'   *cares*

2. I.e., married.
3. And to my chambermaid within my bedroom.
4. Relatives by marriage.
5. I.e., with sorrow to you.
6. I.e., me, the mistress of the house.
7. Despite your eyes, i.e., despite anything you can do about it.
8. Notice or interest.
9. I.e., liberty.

By this proverbe thou shalt understonde,
335　Have thou[1] ynough, what thar° thee rekke or care　　　　　*need*
How merily that othere folkes fare?
For certes, olde dotard, by youre leve,
Ye shal han queinte[2] right ynough at eve:
He is too greet a nigard that wil werne°　　　　　*refuse*
340　A man to lighte a candle at his lanterne;
He shal han nevere the lasse° lighte, pardee.　　　　　*less*
Have thou ynough, thee thar nat plaine thee.[3]
　　　"Thou saist also that if we make us gay
With clothing and with precious array,
345　That it is peril of oure chastitee,
And yit, with sorwe, thou moste enforce thee,[4]
And saye thise wordes in th' Apostles[5] name:
'In habit° maad with chastitee and shame　　　　　*clothing*
Ye wommen shal apparaile you,' quod he,
350　'And nat in tressed heer[6] and gay perree,°　　　　　*jewelry*
As perles, ne with gold ne clothes riche.'[7]
After thy text, ne after thy rubriche,[8]
I wol nat werke as muchel as a gnat.
Thou saidest this, that I was lik a cat:
355　For whoso wolde senge° a cattes skin,　　　　　*singe*
Thanne wolde the cat wel dwellen in his in;°　　　　　*lodging*
And if the cattes skin be slik° and gay,　　　　　*sleek*
She wol nat dwelle in house half a day,
But forth she wol, er any day be dawed,°
360　To shewe her skin and goon a-caterwawed.°　　　　　*caterwauling*
This is to saye, if I be gay, sire shrewe,
I wol renne° out, my borel° for to shewe.　　　　　*run/clothing*
Sir olde fool, what helpeth[1] thee t'espyen?
Though thou praye Argus with his hundred yën
365　To be my wardecors,° as he can best,　　　　　*bodyguard*
In faith, he shal nat keepe° me but me lest:[2]　　　　　*guard*
Yit coude I make his beerd,[3] so mote I thee.°　　　　　*prosper*
　　　"Thou saidest eek that ther been thinges three,
The whiche thinges troublen al this erthe,
370　And that no wight may endure the ferthe.°　　　　　*fourth*
O leve° sire shrewe, Jesu shorte° thy lif!　　　　　*dear/shorten*
Yit prechestou and saist an hateful wif
Yrekened is for oon of thise meschaunces.
Been ther nat none othere resemblaunces
375　That ye may likne youre parables to,[4]
But if° a sely° wif be oon of tho?　　　　　*unless/innocent*
　　　"Thou liknest eek wommanes love to helle,
To bareine° land ther water may nat dwelle;　　　　　*barren*

---

1. If you have.
2. Elegant, pleasing thing; a euphemism for sexual enjoyment.
3. I.e., you need not complain.
4. Strengthen your position.
5. I.e., St. Paul's.
6. I.e., elaborate hairdo.
7. See 1 Timothy 2.9.

8. Rubric, i.e., direction.
9. Has dawned.
1. What does it help.
2. Unless I please.
3. I.e., deceive him.
4. Isn't there something else appropriate to which you can apply your metaphors?

      Thou liknest it also to wilde fir—

380 The more it brenneth,° the more it hath desir   *burns*

      To consumen every thing that brent° wol be;   *burned*

      Thou saist right° as wormes shende° a tree,   *just/destroy*

      Right so a wif destroyeth hir housbonde—

      This knowen they that been to wives bonde."°   *bound*

385   Lordinges, right thus, as ye han understonde,

      Bar I stifly mine olde housbondes on honde[5]

      That thus they saiden in hir dronkenesse—

      And al was fals, but that I took witnesse

      On Janekin and on my nece also.

390 O Lord, the paine I dide hem and the wo,

      Ful giltelees, by Goddes sweete pine!°   *suffering*

      For as an hors I coude bite and whine;°   *whinny*

      I coude plaine° and° I was in the gilt,   *complain/if*

      Or elles often time I hadde been spilt.°   *ruined*

395 Whoso that first to mille comth first grint.°   *grinds*

      I plained first: so was oure werre stint.[6]

      They were ful glade to excusen hem ful blive°   *quickly*

      Of thing of which they nevere agilte hir live.[7]

      Of wenches wolde I beren hem on honde,[8]

400 Whan that for sik[9] they mighte unnethe° stonde,   *scarcely*

      Yit tikled I his herte for that he

      Wende° I hadde had of him so greet cheertee.°   *thought/affection*

      I swoor that al my walking out by nighte

      Was for to espye wenches that he dighte.[1]

405 Under that colour[2] hadde I many a mirthe.

      For al swich wit is yiven us in oure birthe:

      Deceite, weeping, spinning God hath yive

      To wommen kindely° whil they may live.   *naturally*

      And thus of oo thing I avaunte me:[3]

410 At ende I hadde the bet° in eech degree,   *better*

      By sleighte or force, or by som manere thing,

      As by continuel murmur° or grucching;°   *complaint/grumbling*

      Namely° abedde hadden they meschaunce: *especially*

      Ther wolde I chide and do hem no plesaunce;[4]

415 I wolde no lenger in the bed abide

      If that I felte his arm over my side,

      Til he hadde maad his raunson° unto me;   *ransom*

      Thanne wolde I suffre him do his nicetee.°   *foolishness (sex)*

      And therfore every man this tale I telle:

420 Winne whoso may, for al is for to selle;

      With empty hand men may no hawkes lure.

      For winning° wolde I al his lust endure,   *profit*

      And make me a feined° appetit—   *pretended*

      And yit in bacon[5] hadde I nevere delit.

425 That made me that evere I wolde hem chide;

---

5. I rigorously accused my old husbands.
6. Our war brought to an end.
7. Of which they were never guilty in their lives.
8. Falsely accuse them.
9. I.e., sickness.

1. Had intercourse with.
2. I.e., pretense.
3. Boast.
4. Show them no affection.
5. I.e., old meat.

For though the Pope hadde seten° hem biside,   *sat*
I wolde nought spare hem at hir owene boord.°   *table*
For by my trouthe, I quitte° hem word for word.   *repaid*
As help me verray God omnipotent,
430   Though I right now sholde make my testament,
I ne owe hem nat a word that it nis quit.
I broughte it so aboute by my wit
That they moste yive it up as for the beste,
Or elles hadde we nevere been in reste;
435   For though he looked as a wood° leoun,   *furious*
Yit sholde he faile of his conclusioun.°   *object*
          Thanne wolde I saye, "Goodelief, taak keep,[6]
How mekely looketh Wilekin,[7] oure sheep!
Com neer my spouse, lat me ba° thy cheeke—   *kiss*
440   Ye sholden be al pacient and meeke,
And han a sweete-spiced[8] conscience,
Sith ye so preche of Jobes pacience;
Suffreth alway, sin ye so wel can preche;
And but ye do, certain, we shal you teche
445   That it is fair to han a wif in pees.
Oon of us two moste bowen, doutelees,
And sith a man is more resonable
Than womman is, ye mosten been suffrable.°   *patient*
What aileth you to grucche° thus and grone?   *grumble*
450   Is it for ye wolde have my queinte° allone?   *sexual organ*
Why, taak it al—lo, have it everydeel.°   *altogether*
Peter,[9] I shrewe° you but ye love it weel.   *curse*
For if I wolde selle my bele chose,[1]
I coude walke as fressh as is a rose;
455   But I wol keepe it for youre owene tooth.°   *taste*
Ye be to blame. By God, I saye you sooth!"°   *the truth*
Swiche manere° wordes hadde we on honde.   *kind of*
Now wol I speke of my ferthe° housbonde.   *fourth*
          My ferthe housbonde was a revelour°—   *reveler*
460   This is to sayn, he hadde a paramour°—   *mistress*
And I was yong and ful of ragerye,°   *passion*
Stibourne° and strong and joly as a pie:°   *untamable/magpie*
How coude I daunce to an harpe smale,°   *gracefully*
And singe, ywis,° as any nightingale,   *indeed*
465   Whan I hadde dronke a draughte of sweete win.
Metellius, the foule cherl, the swin,
That with a staf birafte° his wif hir lif   *deprived*
For° she drank win, though I hadde been his wif,   *because*
Ne sholde nat han daunted° me fro drinke;   *frightened*
470   And after win on Venus moste° I thinke,   *must*
For also siker° as cold engendreth hail,   *sure*
A likerous° mouth moste han a likerous° tail: *greedy/lecherous*
In womman vinolent° is no defence—   *who drinks*
This knowen lechours by experience.

6. Good friend, take notice.   9. By St. Peter.
7. I.e., Willie.   1. French for "beautiful thing"; a euphemism for sex-
8. I.e., delicate.   ual organs.

475   But Lord Crist, whan that it remembreth me[2]
     Upon my youthe and on my jolitee,
     It tikleth me aboute myn herte roote—
     Unto this day it dooth myn herte boote°   *good*
     That I have had my world as in my time.
480   But age, allas, that al wol envenime,°   *poison*
     Hath me biraft[3] my beautee and my pith°—   *vigor*
     Lat go, farewel, the devel go therwith!
     The flour is goon, ther is namore to telle:
     The bren° as I best can now moste I selle;   *bran*
485   But yit to be right merye wol I fonde.°   *strive*
     Now wol I tellen of my ferthe housbonde.
        I saye I hadde in herte greet despit
     That he of any other hadde delit,
     But he was quit,° by God and by Saint Joce: *paid back*
490   I made him of the same wode a croce[4]—
     Nat of my body in no foul manere—
     But, certainly, I made folk swich cheere[5]
     That in his owene grece I made him frye,
     For angre and for verray jalousye.
495   By God, in erthe I was his purgatorye,
     For which I hope his soule be in glorye.
     For God it woot, he sat ful ofte and soong°   *sang*
     Whan that his sho ful bitterly him wroong.°   *pinched*
     Ther was no wight save God and he that wiste°   *knew*
500   In many wise how sore I him twiste.
     He deide whan I cam fro Jerusalem,
     And lith ygrave under the roode-beem,[6]
     Al° is his tombe nought so curious[7]   *although*
     As was the sepulcre of him Darius,
505   Which that Apelles wroughte subtilly:[8]
     It nis but wast to burye him preciously.°   *expensively*
     Lat him fare wel, God yive his soule reste;
     He is now in his grave and in his cheste.°   *coffin*
        Now of my fifthe housbonde wol I telle—
510   God lete his soule nevere come in helle—
     And yit he was to me the moste shrewe:[9]
     That feele I on my ribbes al by rewe,[1]
     And evere shal unto myn ending day.
     But in oure bed he was so fressh and gay,
515   And therwithal so wel coulde he me glose°   *wheedle*
     Whan that he wolde han my bele chose,
     That though he hadde me bet° on every boon,° *beaten/bone*
     He coude winne again my love anoon.°   *immediately*
     I trowe I loved him best for that he
520   Was of his love daungerous[2] to me.

---

2. When I look back.
3. Has taken away from me.
4. I made him a cross of the same wood. The proverb has much the same sense as the one quoted in line 493.
5. Pretended to be in love with others.
6. And lies buried under the rood beam (the crucifix beam running between nave and chancel).
7. Carefully wrought.
8. Accordingly to medieval legend, the artist Apelles decorated the tomb of Darius, king of the Persians.
9. Worst rascal.
1. In a row.
2. I.e., he played hard to get.

We wommen han, if that I shal nat lie,
In this matere a quainte fantasye:
Waite what³ thing we may nat lightly° have,   *easily*
Therafter wol we crye al day and crave;
525 Forbede us thing, and that desiren we;
Preesse on us faste, and thanne wol we flee.
With daunger oute we al oure chaffare:⁴
Greet prees° at market maketh dere° ware,   *crowd/expensive*
And too greet chepe is holden at litel pris.⁵
530 This knoweth every womman that is wis.
     My fifthe housbonde—God his soule blesse!—
Which that I took for love and no richesse,
He somtime was a clerk at Oxenforde,
And hadde laft° scole and wente at hoom to boorde   *left*
535 With my gossib,° dwelling in oure town—   *confidante*
God have hir soule!—hir name was Alisoun;
She knew myn herte and eek my privetee°   *secrets*
Bet° than oure parissh preest, as mote I thee.°   *better/prosper*
To hire biwrayed° I my conseil° al,   *disclosed/secrets*
540 For hadde myn housbonde pissed on a wal,
Or doon a thing that sholde han cost his lif,
To hire,° and to another worthy wif,   *her*
And to my nece which I loved weel,
I wolde han told his conseil everydeel;°   *entirely*
545 And so I dide ful often, God it woot,
That made his face often reed° and hoot°   *red/hot*
For verray shame, and blamed himself for he
Hadde told to me so greet a privetee.
     And so bifel that ones° in a Lente—   *once*
550 So often times I to my gossib wente,
For evere yit I loved to be gay,
And for to walke in March, Averil, and May,
From hous to hous, to heere sondry tales—
That Janekin clerk and my gossib dame Alis
555 And I myself into the feeldes wente.
Myn housbonde was at London al that Lente:
I hadde the better leiser for to playe,
And for to see, and eek for to be seye°   *seen*
Of lusty folk—what wiste I wher my grace°   *luck*
560 Was shapen° for to be, or in what place?   *destined*
Therfore I made my visitaciouns
To vigilies⁶ and to processiouns,
To preching eek, and to thise pilgrimages,
To playes of miracles and to mariages,
565 And wered upon⁷ my gaye scarlet gites°—   *gowns*
Thise wormes ne thise motthes ne thise mites,
Upon my peril,⁸ frete° hem neveradeel: *ate*
And woostou why? For they were used weel.
     Now wol I tellen forth what happed me.

3. Whatever.   6. Feasts preceding a saint's day.
4. With coyness, we spread out our merchandise.   7. Wore.
5. Too good a bargain is held at little value.   8. On peril (to my soul), an oath.

570 I saye that in the feeldes walked we,
Til trewely we hadde swich daliaunce,°   *flirtation*
This clerk and I, that of my purveyaunce°   *foresight*
I spak to him and saide him how that he,
If I were widwe, sholde wedde me.
575 For certainly, I saye for no bobaunce,°   *boast*
Yit was I nevere withouten purveyaunce
Of mariage n'of othere thinges eek:
I holde a mouses herte nought worth a leek
That hath but oon hole for to sterte° to,   *run*
580 And if that faile thanne is al ydo.[9]
I bar him on hand[1] he hadde enchaunted me
(My dame° taughte me that subtiltee);   *mother*
And eek I saide I mette° of him al night: *dreamed*
He wolde han slain me as I lay upright,°   *on my back*
585 And al my bed was ful of verray blood—
"But yit I hope that ye shul do me good;
For blood bitokeneth° gold, as me was taught."   *signifies*
And al was fals, I dremed of it right naught,
But as I folwed ay my dames° lore°   *mother's/teaching*
590 As wel of that as othere thinges more.
But now sire—lat me see, what shal I sayn?
Aha, by God, I have my tale again.
    Whan that my ferthe housbonde was on beere,°   *bier*
I weep,° algate,° and made sory cheere,   *wept/anyhow*
595 As wives moten,° for it is usage,°   *must/custom*
And with my coverchief covered my visage;
But for I was purveyed° of a make.°   *provided/mate*
I wepte but smale, and that I undertake.°   *guarantee*
    To chirche was myn housbonde born amorwe[2]
600 With neighebores that for him maden sorwe,
And Janekin oure clerk was oon of tho.
As help me God, whan that I saw him go
After the beere, me thoughte he hadde a paire
Of legges and of feet so clene[3] and faire,
605 That al myn herte I yaf unto his hold.°   *possession*
He was, I trowe,° twenty winter old,   *believe*
And I was fourty, if I shal saye sooth—
But yit I hadde alway a coltes tooth:[4]
Gat-toothed[5] was I, and that bicam me weel;
610 I hadde the prente[6] of Sainte Venus seel.°   *seal*
As help me God, I was a lusty oon,
And fair and riche and yong and wel-bigoon,°   *well-situated*
And trewely, as mine housbondes tolde me,
I hadde the beste quoniam[7] mighte be.
615 For certes I am al Venerien
In feeling, and myn herte is Marcien:[8]

9. I.e., the game is up.
1. I pretended to him.
2. In the morning.
3. I.e., neat.
4. I.e., youthful appetites.
5. Gap-toothed women were considered to be amorous.
6. Print, i.e., a birthmark.
7. Latin for "because"; another euphemism for a sexual organ.
8. Influenced by Mars. "Venerien": astrologically influenced by Venus.

Venus me yaf my lust, my likerousnesse,°   *amorousness*
And Mars yaf me my sturdy hardinesse.
Myn ascendent was Taur[9] and Mars therinne—
620   Allas, allas, that evere love was sinne!
I folwed ay° my inclinacioun   *ever*
By vertu of my constellacioun;[1]
That made me I coude nought withdrawe
My chambre of Venus from a good felawe.
625   Yit have I Martes° merk upon my face,   *Mars's*
And also in another privee place.
For God so wis° be my savacioun,°   *surely/salvation*
I loved nevere by no discrecioun,
But evere folwede myn appetit,
630   Al were he short or long or blak or whit;
I took no keep,° so that he liked° me,   *heed/pleased*
How poore he was, ne eek of what degree.
      What sholde I saye but at the monthes ende
This joly clerk Janekin that was so hende°   *courteous, nice*
635   Hath wedded me with greet solempnitee,°   *splendor*
And to him yaf I al the land and fee°   *property*
That evere was me yiven therbifore—
But afterward repented me ful sore:
He nolde suffre no thing of my list.°   *wish*
640   By God, he smoot° me ones on the list°   *struck/ear*
For that I rente° out of his book a leef,   *tore*
That of the strook° myn ere weex° al deef.   *blow/grew*
Stibourne° I was as is a leonesse,   *stubborn*
And of my tonge a verray jangleresse,°   *chatterbox*
645   And walke I wolde, as I hadde doon biforn,
From hous to hous, although he hadde it[2] sworn;
For which he often times wolde preche,
And me of olde Romain geestes° teche,   *stories*
How he Simplicius Gallus lafte° his wif,   *left*
650   And hire forsook for terme of al his lif,
Nought but for open-heveded he hire sey[3]
Looking out at his dore upon a day.
      Another Romain tolde he me by name
That, for his wif was at a someres° game   *summer's*
655   Withouten his witing,° he forsook hire eke;   *knowledge*
And thanne wolde he upon his Bible seke
That ilke proverbe of Ecclesiaste[4]
Where he comandeth and forbedeth faste°   *strictly*
Man shal nat suffre his wif go roule° aboute;   *roam*
660   Thanne wolde he saye right thus withouten doute:
"Whoso that buildeth his hous al of salwes,°   *willow sticks*
And priketh° his blinde hors over the falwes,[5]   *rides*
And suffreth his wif to go seeken halwes,°   *shrines*
Is worthy to be hanged on the galwes."°   *gallows*

9. My birth sign was the constellation Taurus, a sign   3. Just because he saw her bareheaded.
in which Venus is dominant.   4. Ecclesiasticus (25.25).
1. I.e., horoscope.   5. Plowed land.
2. I.e., the contrary.

665 But al for nought—I sette nought an hawe[6]
    Of his proverbes n'of his olde sawe;
    N' I wolde nat of him corrected be:
    I hate him that my vices telleth me,
    And so doon mo, God woot, of us than I.
670 This made him with me wood al outrely:°   *entirely*
    I nolde nought forbere° him in no cas.   *submit to*
        Now wol I saye you sooth, by Saint Thomas,
    Why that I rente° out of his book a leef,   *tore*
    For which he smoot me so that I was deef.
675 He hadde a book that gladly night and day
    For his disport he wolde rede alway.
    He cleped it *Valerie*[7] *and Theofraste*,
    At which book he lough° alway ful faste;   *laughed*
    And eek ther was somtime a clerk at Rome,
680 A cardinal, that highte Saint Jerome,
    That made a book[8] again° Jovinian;   *against*
    In which book eek ther was Tertulan,
    Crysippus, Trotula, and Helouis,[9]
    That was abbesse nat fer fro Paris;
685 And eek the Parables of Salomon,
    Ovides *Art*,[1] and bookes many oon—
    And alle thise were bounden in oo volume.
    And every night and day was his custume,
    Whan he hadde leiser and vacacioun°   *free time*
690 From other worldly occupacioun,
    To reden in this book of wikked wives.
    He knew of hem mo legendes and lives
    Than been of goode wives in the Bible.
    For trusteth wel, it is an impossible°   *impossibility*
695 That any clerk wol speke good of wives,
    But if it be of holy saintes lives,
    N'of noon other womman nevere the mo—
    Who painted the leon, tel me who?[2]
    By God, if wommen hadden writen stories,
700 As clerkes han within hir oratories,°   *chapels*
    They wolde han writen of men more wikkednesse
    Than al the merk[3] of Adam may redresse.
    The children of Mercurye and Venus[4]
    Been in hir werking° ful contrarious:°   *operation/opposed*
705 Mercurye loveth wisdom and science,
    And Venus loveth riot° and dispence;°   *parties/expenditures*
    And for hir diverse disposicioun

6. I did not rate at the value of a hawthorn berry.
7. "*Valerie*": i.e., the *Letter of Valerius Concerning Not Marrying*, by Walter Map; "*Theofraste*": Theophrastus's *Book Concerning Marriage*. Medieval manuscripts often contained a number of different works, sometimes, as here, dealing with the same subject.
8. St. Jerome's antifeminist *Reply to Jovinian*.
9. "Tertulan": i.e., Tertullian, author of treatises on sexual modesty. "Crysippus": i.e., Crysippus, mentioned by Jerome as an antifeminist. "Trotula": a female doctor whose presence here is unexplained.

"Helouis": i.e., Eloise, whose love affair with the great scholar Abelard was a medieval scandal.
1. Ovid's *Art of Love*. "Parables of Salomon": the biblical Book of Proverbs.
2. In one of Aesop's fables, the lion, shown a picture of a man killing a lion, asked who painted the picture. Had a lion been the artist, of course, the roles would have been reversed.
3. Mark, sex.
4. I.e., clerks and women, astrologically ruled by Mercury and Venus, respectively.

Each falleth in otheres exaltacioun,[5]
And thus, God woot, Mercurye is desolat
710 In Pisces wher Venus is exaltat,[6]
And Venus falleth ther Mercurye is raised:
Therfore no womman of no clerk is praised.
The clerk, whan he is old and may nought do
Of Venus werkes worth his olde sho,°   *shoe*
715 Thanne sit° he down and writ° in his dotage   *sits/writes*
That wommen can nat keepe hir mariage.
     But now to purpose why I tolde thee
That I was beten for a book, pardee:
Upon a night Janekin, that was our sire,[7]
720 Redde on his book as he sat by the fire
Of Eva first, that for hir wikkednesse
Was al mankinde brought to wrecchednesse,
For which that Jesu Crist himself was slain
That boughte° us with his herte blood again—   *redeemed*
725 Lo, heer expres of wommen may ye finde
That womman was the los° of al mankinde.[8]   *ruin*
     Tho° redde he me how Sampson loste his heres: *then*
Sleeping his lemman° kitte° it with hir sheres,   *lover/cut*
Thurgh which treson loste he both his yën.
730   Tho redde he me, if that I shal nat lien,
Of Ercules and of his Dianire,[9]
That caused him to sette himself afire.
     No thing forgat he the sorwe and wo
That Socrates hadde with his wives two—
735 How Xantippa caste pisse upon his heed:
This sely° man sat stille as he were deed;   *poor, hapless*
He wiped his heed, namore dorste° he sayn   *dared*
But "Er that thonder stinte,° comth a rain."   *stops*
     Of Pasipha[1] that was the queene of Crete—
740 For shrewednesse° him thoughte the tale sweete—   *malice*
Fy, speek namore, it is a grisly thing
Of hir horrible lust and hir liking.°   *pleasure*
     Of Clytermistra[2] for hir lecherye
That falsly made hir housbonde for to die,
745 He redde it with ful good devocioun.
     He tolde me eek for what occasioun
Amphiorax[3] at Thebes loste his lif:
Myn housbonde hadde a legende of his wif
Eriphylem, that for an ouche° of gold   *trinket*
750 Hath prively unto the Greekes told
Wher that hir housbonde hidde him in a place,
For which he hadde at Thebes sory grace.

5. Because of their contrary positions (as planets),
each one descends (in the belt of the zodiac) as the
other rises, hence one loses its power as the other becomes dominant.
6. I.e., Mercury is deprived of power in Pisces (the
sign of the Fish), where Venus is most powerful.
7. My husband.
8. The stories of wicked women Chaucer drew mainly
from St. Jerome and Walter Map.

9. Dejanira unwittingly gave Hercules a poisoned
shirt, which hurt him so much that he committed suicide by fire.
1. Pasiphaë, who fell in love with a bull.
2. Clytemnestra, who, with her lover, Aegisthus, slew
her husband, Agamemnon.
3. Amphiaraus, betrayed by his wife, Eriphyle, and
forced to go to the war against Thebes.

Of Livia tolde he me and of Lucie:[4]
They bothe made hir housbondes for to die,
755 That oon for love, that other was for hate;
Livia hir housbonde on an even late
Empoisoned hath for that she was his fo;
Lucia likerous° loved hir housbonde so   *lecherous*
That for° he sholde alway upon hire thinke,   *in order that*
760 She yaf him swich a manere love-drinke
That he was deed er it were by the morwe.[5]
And thus algates° housbondes han sorwe.   *constantly*
  Thanne tolde he me how oon Latumius
Complained unto his felawe Arrius
765 That in his garden growed swich a tree,
On which he saide how that his wives three
Hanged hemself for herte despitous.[6]
  "O leve° brother," quod this Arrius,   *dear*
"Yif me a plante of thilke blessed tree,
770 And in my gardin planted shal it be."
  Of latter date of wives hath he red
That some han slain hir housbondes in hir bed
And lete hir lechour dighte[7] hire al the night,
Whan that the cors° lay in the floor upright;° *corpse/on his back*
775 And some han driven nailes in hir brain
Whil that they sleepe, and thus they han hem slain;
Some han hem yiven poison in hir drinke.
He spak more harm than herte may bithinke,°   *imagine*
And therwithal he knew of mo proverbes
780 Than in this world ther growen gras or herbes:
"Bet° is," quod he, "thyn habitacioun   *better*
Be with a leon or a foul dragoun
Than with a womman using° for to chide."   *accustomed*
"Bet is," quod he, "hye in the roof abide
785 Than with an angry wif down in the hous:
They been so wikked° and contrarious,   *perverse*
They haten that hir housbondes loveth ay."
He saide, "A womman cast° hir shame away   *casts*
When she cast of° hir smok,"[8] and ferthermo,   *off*
790 "A fair womman, but she be chast also,
Is like a gold ring in a sowes nose."
Who wolde weene,° or who wolde suppose   *think*
The wo that in myn herte was and pine?°   *suffering*
  And whan I sawgh he wolde nevere fine°   *end*
795 To reden on this cursed book al night,
Al sodeinly three leves have I plight°   *snatched*
Out of his book right as he redde, and eke
I with my fist so took[9] him on the cheeke
That in oure fir he fil° bakward adown.   *fell*

---

4. Livia murdered her husband in behalf of her lover, Sejanus. "Lucie": i.e., Lucilla, who was said to have poisoned her husband, the poet Lucretius, with a potion designed to keep him faithful.
5. He was dead before it was near morning.
6. For malice of heart.
7. Have intercourse with.
8. Undergarment.
9. I.e., hit.

800 And up he sterte as dooth a wood° leoun,   *raging*
    And with his fist he smoot me on the heed°   *head*
    That in the floor I lay as I were deed.°   *dead.*
    And whan he sawgh how stille that I lay,
    He was agast, and wolde have fled his way,
805 Til atte laste out of my swough° I braide:°   *swoon/started*
    "O hastou slain me, false thief?" I saide,
    "And for my land thus hastou mordred° me?   *murdered*
    Er I be deed yit wol I kisse thee."
    And neer he cam and kneeled faire adown,
810 And saide, "Dere suster Alisoun,
    As help me God, I shal thee nevere smite.
    That I have doon, it is thyself to wite.°   *blame*
    Foryif it me, and that I thee biseeke."°   *beseech*
    And yit eftsoones° I hitte him on the cheeke,   *again*
815 And saide, "Thief, thus muchel am I wreke.°   *avenged*
    Now wol I die: I may no lenger speke."
      But at the laste with muchel care and wo
    We fille¹ accorded by us selven two.
    He yaf me al the bridel° in myn hand,   *bridle*
820 To han the governance of hous and land,
    And of his tonge and his hand also;
    And made² him brenne° his book anoonright tho.   *burn*
    And whan that I hadde geten unto me
    By maistrye° al the sovereinetee,°   *skill/dominion*
825 And that he saide, "Myn owene trewe wif,
    Do as thee lust° the terme of al thy lif;   *it pleases*
    Keep thyn honour, and keep eek myn estat,"
    After that day we hadde nevere debat.
    God help me so, I was to him as kinde
830 As any wif from Denmark unto Inde,°   *India*
    And also trewe, and so was he to me.
    I praye to God that sit° in majestee,   *sits*
    So blesse his soule for his mercy dere.
    Now wol I saye my tale if ye wol heere.

                    [ANOTHER INTERRUPTION]

835   The Frere lough° whan he hadde herd all this: *laughed*
    "Now dame," quod he, "so have I joye or blis,
    This is a long preamble of a tale."
    And whan the Somnour herde the Frere gale,°   *exclaim*
    "Lo," quod the Somnour, "Goddes armes two,
840 A frere wol entremette him³ everemo!
    Lo, goode men, a flye and eek a frere
    Wol falle in every dissh and eek matere.
    What spekestou of preambulacioun?
    What, amble or trotte or pisse or go sitte down!
845 Thou lettest° oure disport in this manere."   *hinder*
      "Ye, woltou so, sire Somnour?" quod the Frere.

1. I.e., became.   3. Intrude himself.
2. I.e., I made.

"Now by my faith, I shal er that I go
Telle of a somnour swich a tale or two
That al the folk shal laughen in this place."
850   "Now elles, Frere, I wol bishrewe° thy face,"   *curse*
Quod this Somnour, "and I bishrewe me,
But if I telle tales two or three
Of freres, er I come to Sidingborne,[4]
That I shal make thyn herte for to moorne°—   *mourn*
855 For wel I woot thy pacience is goon."
   Oure Hoste cride, "Pees, and that anoon!"
And saide, "Lat the womman telle hir tale:
Ye fare as folk that dronken been of ale.
Do, dame, tel forth youre tale, and that is best."
860   "Al redy, sire," quod she, "right as you lest°—   *it pleases*
If I have licence of this worthy Frere."
"Yis, dame," quod he, "tel forth and I wol heere."

The Tale[5]

In th'olde dayes of the King Arthour,
Of which that Britouns° speken greet honour,   *Bretons*
865 Al was this land fulfild of faïrye:[6]
The elf-queene° with hir joly compaignye   *queen of the fairies*
Daunced ful ofte in many a greene mede°—   *meadow*
This was the olde opinion as I rede;
I speke of many hundred yeres ago.
870 But now can no man see none elves mo,
For now the grete charitee and prayeres
Of limitours,[7] and othere holy freres,
That serchen every land and every streem,
As thikke as motes° in the sonne-beem,   *dust particles*
875 Blessing halles, chambres, kichenes, bowres,
Citees, burghes,° castels, hye towres,   *townships*
Thropes, bernes, shipnes,[8] dayeries—
This maketh that ther been no faïries.
For ther as wont to walken was an elf
880 Ther walketh now the limitour himself,
In undermeles° and in morweninges,°   *afternoons/mornings*
And saith his Matins and his holy thinges,
As he gooth in his limitacioun.[9]
Wommen may go saufly° up and down: *safely*
885 In every bussh or under every tree
Ther is noon other incubus[1] but he,
And he ne wol doon hem but[2] dishonour.
   And so bifel it that this King Arthour

---

4. Sittingbourne (a town forty miles from London).
5. The story of a mortal who marries a fairy bride was popular in Chaucer's time. In two other versions, the hero is Sir Gawain, whose exemplary courtesy contrasts sharply with the behavior of the knight in the Wife of Bath's tale. Chaucer has transformed the story so as to reflect the opinions, the style, and the character of the Wife.

6. I.e., filled full of supernatural creatures.
7. Friars licensed to beg in a certain territory.
8. Thorps (villages), barns, stables.
9. I.e., the friar's assigned area. His "holy thinges" are prayers.
1. An evil spirit that seduces mortal women.
2. "Ne . . . but": only.

Hadde in his hous a lusty bacheler,°   *young knight*
890 That on a day cam riding fro river,[3]
And happed° that, allone as he was born,   *it happened*
He sawgh a maide walking him biforn;
Of which maide anoon, maugree hir heed,[4]
By verray force he rafte° hir maidenheed;   *deprived her of*
895 For which oppression° was swich clamour,   *rape*
And swich pursuite° unto the King Arthour,   *petitioning*
That dampned was this knight for to be deed[5]
By cours of lawe, and sholde han lost his heed—
Paraventure° swich was the statut tho—   *perchance*
900 But that the queene and othere ladies mo
So longe prayeden the king of grace,
Til he his lif him graunted in the place,
And yaf him to the queene, al at hir wille,
To chese° wheither she wolde him save or spille.[6]   *choose*
905 The queene thanked the king with al hir might,
And after this thus spak she to the knight,
Whan that she saw hir time upon a day:
"Thou standest yit," quod she, "in swich array°   *condition*
That of thy lif yit hastou no suretee.°   *guarantee*
910 I graunte thee lif if thou canst tellen me
What thing it is that wommen most desiren:
Be war and keep thy nekke boon° from iren.   *bone*
And if thou canst nat tellen me anoon,°   *right away*
Yit wol I yive thee leve for to goon
915 A twelfmonth and a day to seeche° and lere°   *search/learn*
An answere suffisant° in this matere,   *satisfactory*
And suretee wol I han er that thou pace,°   *pass*
Thy body for to yeelden in this place."
Wo was this knight, and sorwefully he siketh.°   *sighs*
920 But what, he may nat doon al as him liketh,
And atte laste he chees° him for to wende,   *chose*
And come again right at the yeres ende,
With swich answere as God wolde him purveye,°   *provide*
And taketh his leve and wendeth forth his waye.
925 He seeketh every hous and every place
Wher as he hopeth for to finde grace,
To lerne what thing wommen love most.
But he ne coude arriven in no coost[7]
Wher as he mighte finde in this matere
930 Two creatures according in fere.[8]
Some saiden wommen loven best richesse;
Some saide honour, some saide jolinesse;°   *pleasure*
Some riche array, some saiden lust abedde,
And ofte time to be widwe and wedde.
935 Some saide that oure herte is most esed
Whan that we been yflatered and yplesed—

3. Hawking, usually carried out on the banks of a stream.
4. Despite her head, i.e., despite anything she could do.
5. This knight was condemned to death.
6. Put to death.
7. I.e., country.
8. Agreeing together.

He gooth ful neigh the soothe, I wol nat lie:
A man shal winne us best with flaterye,
And with attendance° and with bisinesse°   *attention/solicitude*
940   Been we ylimed,° bothe more and lesse.   *ensnared*
      And some sayen that we loven best
For to be free, and do right as us lest,°   *it pleases*
And that no man repreve° us of oure vice,   *reprove*
But saye that we be wise and no thing nice.°   *foolish*
945   For trewely, ther is noon of us alle,
If any wight wol clawe° us on the galle,°   *rub/sore spot*
That we nil kike° for° he saith us sooth: *kick/because*
Assaye° and he shal finde it that so dooth.   *try*
For be we nevere so vicious withinne,
950   We wol be holden° wise and clene of sinne.   *considered*
      And some sayn that greet delit han we
For to be holden stable and eek secree,[9]
And in oo° purpos stedefastly to dwelle,   *one*
And nat biwraye° thing that men us telle—   *disclose*
955   But that tale is nat worth a rake-stele.°   *rake handle*
Pardee,° we wommen conne no thing hele:°   *by God/conceal*
Witnesse on Mida.° Wol ye heere the tale?   *Midas*
      Ovide, amonges othere thinges smale,
Saide Mida hadde under his longe heres,
960   Growing upon his heed, two asses eres,
The whiche vice° he hidde as he best mighte   *defect*
Ful subtilly from every mannes sighte,
That save his wif ther wiste° of it namo.   *knew*
He loved hire most and trusted hire also.
965   He prayed hire that to no creature
She sholde tellen of his disfigure.°   *deformity*
      She swoor him nay, for al this world to winne,
She nolde do that vilainye or sinne
To make hir housbonde han so foul a name:
970   She nolde nat telle it for hir owene shame.
But nathelees, hir thoughte that she dyde°   *would die*
That she so longe sholde a conseil° hide;   *secret*
Hire thoughte it swal° so sore about hir herte   *swelled*
That nedely som word hire moste asterte,[1]
975   And sith she dorste nat telle it to no man,
Down to a mareis° faste° by she ran—   *marsh/close*
Til she cam there hir herte was afire—
And as a bitore bombleth[2] in the mire,
She laide hir mouth unto the water down:
980   "Biwray° me nat, thou water, with thy soun,"°   *betray/sound*
Quod she. "To thee I telle it and namo:°   *to no one else*
Myn housbonde hath longe asses eres two.
Now is myn herte al hool,[3] now is it oute.
I mighte no lenger keep it, out of doute."
985   Here may ye see, though we a time abide,
Yit oute it moot:° we can no conseil hide.   *must*

---

9. Reliable and also closemouthed.   2. Makes a booming noise. "Bittore": bittern, a heron.
1. Of necessity some word must escape her.   3. I.e., sound.

The remenant of the tale if ye wol heere,
Redeth Ovide, and ther ye may it lere.[4]
   This knight of which my tale is specially,
990   Whan that he sawgh he mighte nat come thereby—
This is to saye what wommen loven most—
Within his brest ful sorweful was his gost,°   *spirit*
But hoom he gooth, he mighte nat sojourne:°   *delay*
The day was come that hoomward moste° he turne.   *must*
995   And in his way it happed him to ride
In al this care under° a forest side,   *by*
Wher as he sawgh upon a daunce go
Of ladies foure and twenty and yit mo;
Toward the whiche daunce he drow ful yerne,[5]
1000   In hope that som wisdom sholde he lerne.
But certainly, er he cam fully there,
Vanisshed was this daunce, he niste° where.   *knew not*
No creature sawgh he that bar° lif,   *bore*
Save on the greene he sawgh sitting a wif°—   *woman*
1005   A fouler wight ther may no man devise.°   *imagine*
Again[6] the knight this olde wif gan rise,
And saide, "Sire knight, heer forth lith° no way.°   *lies/road*
Telle me what ye seeken, by youre fay.°   *faith*
Paraventure it may the better be:
1010   Thise olde folk conne° muchel thing," quod she.   *know*
   "My leve moder,"° quod this knight, "certain,   *mother*
I nam but deed but if that I can sayn
What thing it is that wommen most desire.
Coude ye me wisse,° I wolde wel quite youre hire."[7]   *teach*
1015   "Plight° me thy trouthe here in myn hand," quod she,   *pledge*
"The nexte thing that I requere° thee,   *require of*
Thou shalt it do, if it lie in thy might,
And I wol telle it you er it be night."
   "Have heer my trouthe," quod the knight. "I graunte."
1020   "Thanne," quod she, "I dar me wel avaunte°   *boast*
Thy lif is sauf,° for I wol stande therby.   *safe*
Upon my lif the queene wol saye as I.
Lat see which is the pruddeste° of hem alle   *proudest*
That wereth on[8] a coverchief or a calle°   *headdress*
1025   That dar saye nay of that I shal thee teche.
Lat us go forth withouten lenger speeche."
Tho rouned° she a pistel° in his ere,   *whispered/message*
And bad him to be glad and have no fere.
   Whan they be comen to the court, this knight
1030   Saide he hadde holde his day as he hadde hight,°   *promised*
And redy was his answere, as he saide.
Ful many a noble wif, and many a maide,
And many a widwe—for that they been wise—
The queene hirself sitting as justise,
1035   Assembled been this answere for to heere,

---

4. Learn. The reeds disclosed the secret by whispering   6. I.e., to meet.
"aures aselli" (ass's ears).   7. Repay your trouble.
5. Drew very quickly.   8. That wears.

And afterward this knight was bode° appere.   *bidden to*
To every wight comanded was silence,
And that the knight sholde telle in audience°   *open hearing*
What thing that worldly wommen loven best.
1040 This knight ne stood nat stille as dooth a best,°   *beast*
But to his question anoon answerde
With manly vois that al the court it herde.
   "My lige° lady, generally," quod he,   *liege*
"Wommen desire to have sovereinetee°   *dominion*
1045 As wel over hir housbonde as hir love,
And for to been in maistrye him above.
This is youre moste desir though ye me kille.
Dooth as you list:° I am here at youre wille."   *please*
   In al the court ne was ther wif ne maide
1050 Ne widwe that contraried° that he saide,   *contradicted*
But saiden he was worthy han° his lif.   *to have*
   And with that word up sterte° that olde wif,   *started*
Which that the knight sawgh sitting on the greene;
"Mercy," quod she, "my soverein lady queene,
1055 Er that youre court departe, do me right.
I taughte this answere unto the knight,
For which he plighte me his trouthe there
The firste thing I wolde him requere°   *require*
He wolde it do, if it laye in his might.
1060 Bifore the court thanne praye I thee, sire knight,"
Quod she, "that thou me take unto thy wif,
For wel thou woost that I have kept° thy lif.   *saved*
If I saye fals, say nay, upon thy fay."
   This knight answerde, "Allas and wailaway,
1065 I woot right wel that swich was my biheeste.°   *promise*
For Goddes love, as chees° a newe requeste: *choose*
Taak al my good and lat my body go."
   "Nay thanne," quod she, "I shrewe° us bothe two.   *curse*
For though that I be foul and old and poore,
1070 I nolde for al the metal ne for ore
That under erthe is grave° or lith° above,   *buried/lies*
But if thy wif I were and eek thy love."
   "My love," quod he. "Nay, my dampnacioun!°   *damnation*
Allas, that any of my nacioun[9]
1075 Sholde evere so foule disparaged° be."   *degraded*
But al for nought, th'ende is this, that he
Constrained was: he needes moste hire wedde,
And taketh his olde wif and gooth to bedde.
   Now wolden some men saye, paraventure,
1080 That for my necligence I do no cure[1]
To tellen you the joye and al th'array
That at the feeste was that ilke day.
To which thing shortly answere I shal:
I saye ther nas no joye ne feeste at al;
1085 Ther nas but hevinesse and muche sorwe.

9. I.e., family.   1. I do not take the trouble.

For prively he wedded hire on morwe,[2]
And al day after hidde him as an owle,
So wo was him, his wif looked so foule.
    Greet was the wo the knight hadde in his thought:
1090 Whan he was with his wif abedde brought,
He walweth° and he turneth to and fro.   *tosses*
His olde wif lay smiling everemo,
And saide, "O dere housbonde, benedicite,°   *bless me*
Fareth° every knight thus with his wif as ye?   *behaves*
1095 Is this the lawe of King Arthures hous?
Is every knight of his thus daungerous?°   *standoffish*
I am youre owene love and youre wif;
I am she which that saved hath youre lif;
And certes yit ne dide I you nevere unright.
1100 Why fare ye thus with me this firste night?
Ye faren like a man hadde lost his wit.
What is my gilt? For Goddes love, telle it,
And it shal been amended if I may."
    "Amended!" quod this knight. "Allas, nay, nay,
1105 It wol nat been amended neveremo.
Thou art so lothly° and so old also,   *loathsome*
And therto comen of so lowe a kinde,°   *lineage*
That litel wonder is though I walwe and winde.°   *turn*
So wolde God myn herte wolde breste!"°   *break*
1110 "Is this," quod she, "the cause of youre unreste?"
"Ye, certainly," quod he. "No wonder is."
    "Now sire," quod she, "I coude amende al this,
If that me liste, er it were dayes three,
So° wel ye mighte bere you[3] unto me.   *provided that*
1115 "But for ye speken of swich gentilesse°   *nobility*
As is descended out of old richesse—
That therfore sholden ye be gentilmen—
Swich arrogance is nat worth an hen.
Looke who that is most vertuous alway,
1120 Privee and apert,[4] and most entendeth° ay°   *tries/always*
To do the gentil deedes that he can,
Taak him for the gretteste° gentilman.   *greatest*
Crist wol° we claime of him oure gentilesse,   *desires that*
Nat of oure eldres for hir 'old richesse.'
1125 For though they yive us al hir heritage,
For which we claime to been of heigh parage,°   *descent*
Yit may they nat biquethe for no thing
To noon of us hir vertuous living,
That made hem gentilmen ycalled be,
1130 And bad[5] us folwen hem in swich degree.
    "Wel can the wise poete of Florence,
That highte Dant,[6] speken in this sentence;°   *topic*
Lo, in swich manere rym is Dantes tale:

---

2. In the morning.   5. I.e., they bade.
3. Behave.   6. Dante (see his *Convivio*).
4. Privately and publicly.

     'Ful selde° up riseth by his braunches[7] smale   *seldom*
1135 Prowesse° of man, for God of his prowesse   *excellence*
     Wol that of him we claime oure gentilesse.'
     For of oure eldres may we no thing claime
     But temporel thing that man may hurte and maime.
     Eek every wight woot this as wel as I,
1140 If gentilesse were planted natureely
     Unto a certain linage down the line,
     Privee and apert, thanne wolde they nevere fine°   *cease*
     To doon of gentilesse the faire office°—   *function*
     They mighte do no vilainye or vice.
1145   "Taak fir and beer° it in the derkeste hous   *bear*
     Bitwixe this and the Mount of Caucasus,
     And lat men shette° the dores and go thenne,°   *shut/thence*
     Yit wol the fir as faire lye° and brenne°   *blaze/burn*
     As twenty thousand men mighte it biholde:
1150 His° office natureel ay wol it holde,   *its*
     Up° peril of my lif, til that it die.   *upon*
     Heer may ye see wel how that genterye°   *gentility*
     Is nat annexed° to possessioun,[8]   *related*
     Sith folk ne doon hir operacioun
1155 Alway, as dooth the fir, lo, in his kinde.°   *nature*
     For God it woot, men may wel often finde
     A lordes sone do shame and vilainye;
     And he that wol han pris of his gentrye,[9]
     For he was boren° of a gentil hous,   *born*
1160 And hadde his eldres noble and vertuous,
     And nil himselven do no gentil deedes,
     Ne folwen his gentil auncestre that deed° is,   *dead*
     He nis nat gentil, be he duc or erl—
     For vilaines sinful deedes maken a cherl.
1165 Thy gentilesse[1] nis but renomee°   *renown*
     Of thine auncestres for hir heigh bountee,°   *magnanimity*
     Which is a straunge° thing for thy persone.   *alien*
     For gentilesse[2] cometh fro God allone.
     Thanne comth oure verray gentilesse of grace:
1170 It was no thing biquethe us with oure place.
     Thenketh how noble, as saith Valerius,[3]
     Was thilke Tullius Hostilius
     That out of poverte° roos to heigh noblesse.   *poverty*
     Redeth Senek° and redeth eek Boece:°   *Seneca/Boethius*
1175 Ther shul ye seen expres that no drede° is   *doubt*
     That he is gentil that dooth gentil deedes.
     And therfore, leve housbonde, I thus conclude:
     Al° were it that mine auncestres weren rude,[4]   *although*
     Yit may the hye God—and so hope I—
1180 Graunte me grace to liven vertuously.

---

7. I.e., by the branches of a man's family tree.
8. I.e., inheritable property.
9. Have credit for his noble birth.
1. I.e., the gentility you claim.

2. I.e., true gentility.
3. A Roman historian.
4. I.e., low born.

Thanne am I gentil whan that I biginne
To liven vertuously and waive° sinne.   *avoid*
    "And ther as ye of poverte me repreve,°   *reprove*
The hye God, on whom that we bileve,
1185 In wilful° poverte chees° to live his lif;   *voluntary/chose*
And certes every man, maiden, or wif
May understonde that Jesus, hevene king,
Ne wolde nat chese° a vicious living.   *choose*
Glad poverte is an honeste° thing, certain;   *honorable*
1190 This wol Senek and othere clerkes sayn.
Whoso that halt him paid of⁵ his poverte,
I holde him riche al hadde he nat a sherte.°   *shirt*
He that coveiteth⁶ is a poore wight,
For he wolde han that is nat in his might;
1195 But he that nought hath, ne coveiteth° have,   *desires to*
Is riche, although we holde him but a knave.
Verray° poverte it singeth proprely.°   *true/appropriately*
Juvenal saith of poverte, 'Merily
The poore man, whan he gooth by the waye,
1200 Biforn the theves he may singe and playe.'
Poverte is hateful good, and as I gesse,
A ful greet bringere out of bisinesse;⁷
A greet amendere eek of sapience°   *wisdom*
To him that taketh it in pacience;
1205 Poverte is thing, although it seeme elenge,°   *wretched*
Possession that no wight wol chalenge;⁸
Poverte ful often, whan a man is lowe,
Maketh⁹ his God and eek himself to knowe;
Poverte a spectacle° is, as thinketh me,   *pair of spectacles*
1210 Thurgh which he may his verray° freendes see.   *true*
And therfore, sire, sin that I nought you greve,
Of my poverte namore ye me repreve.°   *reproach*
    "Now sire, of elde° ye repreve me: *old age*
And certes sire, though noon auctoritee
1215 Were in no book, ye gentils of honour
Sayn that men sholde an old wight doon favour,
And clepe him fader for youre gentilesse—
And auctours¹ shal I finde, as I gesse.
    "Now ther ye saye that I am foul and old:
1220 Thanne drede you nought to been a cokewold,°   *cuckold*
For filthe and elde, also mote I thee,²
Been grete wardeins° upon chastitee.   *guardians*
But nathelees, sin I knowe your delit,
I shal fulfille youre worldly appetit.
1225   "Chees now," quod she, "oon of thise thinges twaye:
To han me foul and old til that I deye
And be to you a trewe humble wif,

5. Considers himself satisfied with.   9. I.e., makes him.
6. I.e., suffers desires.   1. I.e., authorities.
7. I.e., cares.   2. So may I prosper.
8. Claim as his property.

And nevere you displese in al my lif,
Or elles ye wol han me yong and fair,
1230 And take youre aventure° of the repair³   *chance*
That shal be to youre hous by cause of me—
Or in some other place, wel may be.
Now chees youreselven wheither° that you liketh."   *whichever*
This knight aviseth him⁴ and sore siketh;°   *sighs*
1235 But atte laste he saide in this manere:
"My lady and my love, and wif so dere,
I putte me in youre wise governaunce:
Cheseth° yourself which may be most plesaunce°   *choose/pleasure*
And most honour to you and me also.
1240 I do no fors the wheither⁵ of the two,
For as you liketh it suffiseth° me."   *satisfies*
"Thanne have I gete° of you maistrye," quod she,   *got*
"Sin I may chese and governe as me lest?"°   *it pleases*
"Ye, certes, wif," quod he. "I holde it best."
1245 "Kisse me," quod she. "We be no lenger wrothe.
For by my trouthe, I wol be to you bothe—
This is to sayn, ye, bothe fair and good.
I praye to God that I mote sterven wood,⁶
But° I to you be al so good and trewe   *unless*
1250 As evere was wif sin that the world was newe.
And but I be tomorn° as fair to seene   *tomorrow morning*
As any lady, emperisse, or queene,
That is bitwixe the eest and eek the west,
Do with my lif and deeth right as you lest:
1255 Caste up the curtin,⁷ looke how that it is."
And whan the knight sawgh verraily al this,
That she so fair was and so yong therto,
For joye he hente° hire in his armes two;   *took*
His herte bathed in a bath of blisse;
1260 A thousand time arewe° he gan hire kisse,   *in a row*
And she obeyed him in every thing
That mighte do him plesance or liking.°   *pleasure*
And thus they live unto hir lives ende
In parfit° joye. And Jesu Crist us sende   *perfect*
1265 Housbondes meeke, yonge, and fresshe abedde—
And grace t'overbide° hem that we wedde.   *outlive*
And eek I praye Jesu shorte° hir lives   *shorten*
That nought wol be governed by hir wives,
And olde and angry nigardes of dispence°—   *expenditure*
1270 God sende hem soone a verray° pestilence!   *veritable*

3. I.e., visits.
4. Considers.
5. I do not care whichever.
6. Die mad.
7. The curtain around the bed.

The Pardoner's Prologue and Tale[1]

The Introduction

Oure Hoste gan to swere as he were wood;°   *insane*
"Harrow,"° quod he, "by nailes and by blood,[2]   *help*
This was a fals cherl and a fals justise.[3]
As shameful deeth as herte may devise
5 Come to thise juges and hir advocats.
Algate° this sely° maide is slain, allas!   *at any rate/innocent*
Allas, too dere boughte she beautee!
Wherfore I saye alday° that men may see   *always*
The yiftes of Fortune and of Nature
10 Been cause of deeth to many a creature.
As bothe yiftes that I speke of now,
Men han ful ofte more for harm than prow.°   *benefit*
   "But trewely, myn owene maister dere,
This is a pitous tale for to heere.
15 But nathelees, passe over, is no fors:[4]
I praye to God to save thy gentil cors,°   *body*
And eek thine urinals and thy jurdones,[5]
Thyn ipocras and eek thy galiones,[6]
And every boiste° ful of thy letuarye°—   *box/medicine*
20 God blesse hem, and oure lady Sainte Marye.
So mote I theen,[7] thou art a propre man,
And lik a prelat, by Saint Ronian![8]
Saide I nat wel? I can nat speke in terme.[9]
But wel I woot, thou doost° myn herte to erme°   *make/grieve*
25 That I almost have caught a cardinacle.[1]
By corpus bones,[2] but if° have triacle,°   *unless/medicine*
Or elles a draughte of moiste° and corny° ale,   *fresh/malty*

	Or but I here anoon° a merye tale,	at once
	Myn herte is lost for pitee of this maide.	
30	"Thou bel ami,[3] thou Pardoner," he saide,	
	"Tel us som mirthe or japes° right anoon."	jokes
	"It shal be doon," quod he, "by Saint Ronion.	
	But first," quod he, "here at this ale-stake[4]	
	I wol bothe drinke and eten of a cake."	
35	And right anoon thise gentils gan to crye,	
	"Nay, lat him telle us of no ribaudye.°	ribaldry
	Tel us som moral thing that we may lere,°	learn
	Som wit,[5] and thanne wol we gladly heere."	
	"I graunte, ywis,"° quod he, "but I moot thinke	certainly
40	Upon som honeste° thing whil that I drinke."	decent

The Prologue

	Lordinges—quod he—in chirches whan I preche,	
	I paine me[6] to han° an hautein° speeche,	have/loud
	And ringe it out as round as gooth a belle,	
	For I can al by rote[7] that I telle.	
45	My theme is alway oon,[8] and evere was:	
	Radix malorum est cupiditas.[9]	
	First I pronounce whennes° that I come,	whence
	And thanne my bulles shewe I alle and some:[1]	
	Oure lige lordes seel on my patente,[2]	
50	That shewe I first, my body to warente,°	keep safe
	That no man be so bold, ne preest ne clerk,	
	Me to destourbe of Cristes holy werk.	
	And after that thanne telle I forth my tales[3] —	
	Bulles of popes and of cardinales,	
55	Of patriarkes and bisshopes I shewe,	
	And in Latin I speke a wordes fewe,	
	To saffron with[4] my predicacioun,°	preaching
	And for to stire hem to devocioun.	
	Thanne shewe I forth my longe crystal stones,°	jars
60	Ycrammed ful of cloutes° and of bones—	rags
	Relikes been they, as weenen° they eechoon.	suppose
	Thanne have I in laton° a shulder-boon	brass
	Which that was of an holy Jewes sheep.	
	"Goode men," I saye, "take of my wordes keep:°	notice
65	If that this boon be wasshe in any welle,	
	If cow, or calf, or sheep, or oxe swelle,	
	That any worm hath ete or worm ystonge,[5]	
	Take water of that welle and wassh his tonge,	
	And it is hool[6] anoon. And ferthermoor,	

3. Fair friend.
4. Sign of a tavern.
5. I.e., something with significance.
6. Take pains.
7. I know all by heart.
8. I.e., the same. "Theme": biblical text on which the sermon is based.
9. Avarice is the root of evil (1 Timothy 6.10).

1. Each and every one. "Bulles": papal bulls, official documents.
2. I.e., the pope's seal on my papal license.
3. I go on with my yarn.
4. To add spice to.
5. That has eaten any worm or been bitten by any snake.
6. I.e., sound.

70 Of pokkes° and of scabbe and every soor°   *pox/sore*
    Shal every sheep be hool that of this welle
    Drinketh a draughte. Take keep eek° that I telle: *also*
    If that the goode man that the beestes oweth°   *owns*
    Wol every wike,° er° that the cok him croweth,   *week/before*
75 Fasting drinken of this welle a draughte—
    As thilke° holy Jew oure eldres taughte—   *that same*
    His beestes and his stoor° shal multiplye.   *stock*
        "And sire, also it heleth jalousye:
    For though a man be falle in jalous rage,
80 Lat maken with this water his potage,°   *soup*
    And nevere shal he more his wif mistriste,°   *mistrust*
    Though he the soothe of hir defaute wiste,[7]
    Al hadde she[8] taken preestes two or three.
        "Here is a mitein° eek that ye may see: *mitten*
85 He that his hand wol putte in this mitein
    He shal have multiplying of his grain,
    Whan he hath sowen, be it whete or otes—
    So that he offre pens or elles grotes.[9]
        "Goode men and wommen, oo thing warne I you:
90 If any wight be in this chirche now
    That hath doon sinne horrible, that he
    Dar nat for shame of it yshriven° be,   *absolved*
    Or any womman, be she yong or old,
    That hath ymaked hir housbonde cokewold,°   *cuckold*
95 Swich folk shal have no power ne no grace
    To offren to[1] my relikes in this place;
    And whoso findeth him out of swich blame,
    He wol come up and offre in Goddes name,
    And I assoile° him by the auctoritee   *absolve*
100 Which that by bulle ygraunted was to me."
        By this gaude° have I wonne, yeer by yeer,   *trick*
    An hundred mark[2] sith° I was pardoner.   *since*
    I stonde lik a clerk in my pulpet,
    And whan the lewed° peple is down yset,   *ignorant*
105 I preche so as ye han herd bifore,
    And telle an hundred false japes° more.   *tricks*
    Thanne paine I me[3] to strecche forth the nekke,
    And eest and west upon the peple I bekke°   *nod*
    As dooth a douve,° sitting on a berne;°   *dove/barn*
110 Mine handes and my tonge goon so yerne°   *fast*
    That it is joye to see my bisinesse.
    Of avarice and of swich cursednesse°   *sin*
    Is al my preching, for to make hem free°   *generous*
    To yiven hir pens, and namely° unto me,   *especially*
115 For myn entente is nat but for to winne,[4]
    And no thing for correccion of sinne:
    I rekke° nevere whan that they been beried°   *care/buried*

---

7. Knew the truth of her infidelity.   2. Marks (pecuniary units).
8. Even if she had.   3. I take pains.
9. Pennies, groats, coins.   4. My intent is only to make money.
1. To make gifts in reverence of.

Though that hir soules goon a-blakeberied.[5]
For certes, many a predicacioun°   *sermon*
120 Comth ofte time of yvel entencioun:
Som for plesance of folk and flaterye,
To been avaunced° by ypocrisye,   *promoted*
And som for vaine glorye, and som for hate;
For whan I dar noon otherways debate,°   *fight*
125 Thanne wol I stinge him with my tonge smerte
In preching, so that he shal nat asterte°   *escape*
To been defamed falsly, if that he
Hath trespassed to my bretheren[6] or to me.
For though I telle nought his propre name,
130 Men shal wel knowe that it is the same
By signes and by othere circumstaunces.
Thus quite° I folk that doon us displesaunces;[7]   *pay back*
Thus spete° I out my venim under hewe°   *spit/false colors*
Of holinesse, to seeme holy and trewe.
135 But shortly myn entente I wol devise:°   *explain*
I preche of no thing but for coveitise;
Therfore my theme is yit and evere was
Radix malorum est cupiditas.
        Thus can I preche again that same vice
140 Which that I use, and that is avarice.
But though myself be gilty in that sinne,
Yit can I make other folk to twinne°   *separate*
From avarice, and sore to repente—
But that is nat my principal entente:
145 I preche no thing but for coveitise.
Of this matere it oughte ynough suffise.
        Thanne telle I hem ensamples[8] many oon
Of olde stories longe time agoon,
For lewed° peple loven tales olde—   *ignorant*
150 Swiche° things can they wel reporte and holde.[9]   *such*
What, trowe° ye that whiles I may preche,   *believe*
And winne gold and silver for° I teche,   *because*
That I wol live in poverte wilfully?°   *voluntarily*
Nay, nay, I thoughte° it nevere, trewely,   *intended*
155 For I wol preche and begge in sondry landes;
I wol nat do no labour with mine handes,
Ne make baskettes and live therby,
By cause I wol nat beggen idelly.[1]
I wol none of the Apostles countrefete:°   *imitate*
160 I wol have moneye, wolle,° cheese, and whete,   *wool*
Al were it[2] yiven of the pooreste page,
Or of the pooreste widwe in a village—
Al sholde hir children sterve[3] for famine.
Nay, I wol drinke licour of the vine
165 And have a joly wenche in every town.

---

5. Go blackberrying, i.e., go to hell.
6. Injured my fellow pardoners.
7. Make trouble for us.
8. Exempla (stories illustrating moral principles).

9. Repeat and remember.
1. I.e., without profit.
2. Even though it were.
3. Even though her children should die.

But herkneth, lordinges, in conclusioun,
Youre liking° is that I shal telle a tale: *pleasure*
Now have I dronke a draughte of corny ale,
By God, I hope I shal you telle a thing
170 That shal by reson been at youre liking;
For though myself be a ful vicious man,
A moral tale yit I you telle can,
Which I am wont to preche for to winne.
Now holde youre pees, my tale I wol biginne.

The Tale

175   In Flandres whilom° was a compaignye   *once*
Of yonge folk that haunteden° folye—   *practiced*
As riot, hasard, stewes,[4] and tavernes,
Wher as with harpes, lutes, and giternes°   *guitars*
They daunce and playen at dees° bothe day and night,   *dice*
180 And ete also and drinke over hir might,[5]
Thurgh which they doon the devel sacrifise
Within that develes temple in cursed wise
By superfluitee° abhominable.   *overindulgence*
Hir othes been so grete and so dampnable
185 That it is grisly for to heere hem swere:
Oure blessed Lordes body they totere[6]—
Hem thoughte that Jewes rente° him nought ynough.   *tore*
And eech of hem at otheres sinne lough.°   *laughed*
And right anoon thanne comen tombesteres,°   *dancing girls*
190 Fetis° and smale,° and yonge frutesteres,[7]   *shapely/neat*
Singeres with harpes, bawdes,° wafereres[8]—   *pimps*
Whiche been the verray develes officeres,
To kindle and blowe the fir of lecherye
That is annexed unto glotonye:[9]
195 The Holy Writ take I to my witnesse
That luxure° is in win and dronkenesse.   *lechery*
Lo, how that dronken Lot[1] unkindely°   *unnaturally*
Lay by his doughtres two unwitingly:
So dronke he was he niste° what he wroughte.   *didn't know*
200 Herodes, who so wel the stories soughte,[2]
Whan he of win was repleet° at his feeste,   *filled*
Right at his owene table he yaf his heeste°   *command*
To sleen° the Baptist John, ful giltelees.   *slay*
     Senek[3] saith a good word doutelees:
205 He saith he can no difference finde
Bitwixe a man that is out of his minde
And a man which that is dronkelewe,°   *drunken*
But that woodnesse, yfallen in a shrewe,[4]

4. Wild parties, gambling, brothels.
5. Beyond their capacity.
6. Tear apart (a reference to oaths sworn by parts of His body, such as "God's bones!" or "God's teeth!").
7. Fruit-selling girls.
8. Girl cake vendors.
9. I.e., closely related to gluttony.

1. See Genesis 19.30–36.
2. For the story of Herod and St. John the Baptist, see Mark 6.17–29. "Who so . . . soughte": i.e., whoever looked it up in the Gospel would find.
3. Seneca, the Roman Stoic philosopher.
4. But that madness, occurring in a wicked man.

Persevereth lenger than dooth dronkenesse.
210 O glotonye, ful of cursednesse!°   *wickedness*
O cause first of oure confusioun!°   *downfall*
O original of oure dampnacioun,°   *damnation*
Til Crist hadde bought° us with his blood again!   *redeemed*
Lo, how dere, shortly for to sayn,
215 Abought° was thilke° cursed vilainye;   *paid for/that same*
Corrupt was al this world for glotonye:
Adam oure fader and his wif also
Fro Paradis to labour and to wo
Were driven for that vice, it is no drede.°   *doubt*
220 For whil that Adam fasted, as I rede,
He was in Paradis; and whan that he
Eet° of the fruit defended° on a tree,   *ate/forbidden*
Anoon he was out cast to wo and paine.
O glotonye, on thee wel oughte us plaine!°   *complain*
225   O, wiste a man⁵ how manye maladies
Folwen of excesse and of glotonies,
He wolde been the more mesurable°   *moderate*
Of his diete, sitting at his table.
Allas, the shorte throte, the tendre mouth,
230 Maketh that eest and west and north and south,
In erthe, in air, in water, men to swinke,°   *work*
To gete a gloton daintee mete and drinke.
Of this matere, O Paul, wel canstou trete:
"Mete unto wombe,° and wombe eek unto mete,   *belly*
235 Shal God destroyen bothe," as Paulus saith.⁶
Allas, a foul thing is it, by my faith,
To saye this word, and fouler is the deede
Whan man so drinketh of the white and rede⁷
That of his throte he maketh his privee°   *privy*
240 Thurgh thilke cursed superfluitee.°   *overindulgence*
    The Apostle⁸ weeping saith ful pitously,
"Ther walken manye of which you told have I—
I saye it now weeping with pitous vois—
They been enemies of Cristes crois,°   *cross*
245 Of whiche the ende is deeth—wombe is hir god!"⁹
O wombe, O bely, O stinking cod,°   *bag*
Fulfilled° of dong° and of corrupcioun!   *filled full/dung*
At either ende of thee foul is the soun.°   *sound*
How greet labour and cost is thee to finde!°   *provide for*
250 Thise cookes, how they stampe° and straine and grinde,   *pound*
And turnen substance into accident¹
To fulfillen al thy likerous° talent!°   *greedy/appetite*
Out of the harde bones knokke they
The mary,° for they caste nought away   *marrow*
255 That may go thurgh the golet² softe and soote.°   *sweetly*

---

5. If a man knew.
6. See 1 Corinthians 6.13.
7. I.e., white and red wines.
8. I.e., St. Paul.
9. See Philippians 3.18.

1. A philosophic joke, depending on the distinction between inner reality (substance) and outward appearance (accident).
2. Through the gullet.

Of spicerye° of leef and bark and roote   *spices*
Shal been his sauce ymaked by delit,
To make him yit a newer appetit.
But certes, he that haunteth swiche delices°   *pleasures*
260   Is deed° whil that he liveth in tho° vices.   *dead/those*
    A lecherous thing is win, and dronkenesse
Is ful of striving° and of wrecchednesse.   *quarreling*
O dronke man, disfigured is thy face!
Sour is thy breeth, foul artou to embrace!
265   And thurgh thy dronke nose seemeth the soun
As though thou saidest ay,° "Sampsoun, Sampsoun."   *always*
And yit, God woot,° Sampson drank nevere win.[3]   *knows*
Thou fallest as it were a stiked swin;°   *stuck pig*
Thy tonge is lost, and al thyn honeste cure,[4]
270   For dronkenesse is verray sepulture°   *burial*
Of mannes wit° and his discrecioun.   *intelligence*
In whom that drinke hath dominacioun
He can no conseil° keepe, it is no drede.°   *secrets/doubt*
Now keepe you fro the white and fro the rede—
275   And namely° fro the white win of Lepe[5]   *particularly*
That is to selle in Fisshstreete or in Chepe:[6]
The win of Spaine creepeth subtilly
In othere wines growing faste° by,   *close*
Of which ther riseth swich fumositee°   *heady fumes*
280   That whan a man hath dronken draughtes three
And weeneth° that he be at hoom in Chepe,   *supposes*
He is in Spaine, right at the town of Lepe,
Nat at The Rochele ne at Burdeux town;[7]
And thanne wol he sayn, "Sampsoun, Sampsoun."
285   But herkneth, lordinges, oo° word I you praye,   *one*
That alle the soverein actes,[8] dar I saye,
Of victories in the Olde Testament,
Thurgh verray God that is omnipotent,
Were doon in abstinence and in prayere:
290   Looketh° the Bible and ther ye may it lere.°   *behold/learn*
    Looke Attila, the grete conquerour,[9]
Deide° in his sleep with shame and dishonour,   *died*
Bleeding at his nose in dronkenesse:
A capitain sholde live in sobrenesse.
295   And overal this, aviseth you[1] right wel
What was comanded unto Lamuel[2]—
Nat Samuel, but Lamuel, saye I—
Redeth the Bible and finde it expresly,
Of win-yiving° to hem that han[3] justise: *wine-serving*
300   Namore of this, for it may wel suffise.

---

3. Before Samson's birth an angel told his mother that
he would be a Nazarite throughout his life; members
of this sect took no strong drink.
4. Care for self-respect.
5. A town in Spain.
6. Fishstreet and Cheapside in the London market district.
7. The Pardoner is joking about the illegal custom of
adulterating fine wines of Bordeaux and La Rochelle

with strong Spanish wine.
8. Distinguished deeds.
9. Attila was the leader of the Huns who captured
Rome in the 5th century.
1. Consider.
2. Lemuel's mother told him that kings should not
drink (Proverbs 31.4–5).
3. I.e., administer.

And now that I have spoken of glotonye,
Now wol I you defende° hasardrye:°   *prohibit/gambling*
Hasard is verray moder° of lesinges,°   *mother/lies*
And of deceite and cursed forsweringes,°   *perjuries*
305   Blaspheme of Crist, manslaughtre, and wast° also   *waste*
Of catel° and of time; and ferthermo,   *property*
It is repreve° and contrarye of honour   *disgrace*
For to been holden a commune hasardour,°   *gambler*
And evere the hyer he is of estat
310   The more is he holden desolat.[4]
If that a prince useth hasardrye,
In alle governance and policye
He is, as by commune opinioun,
Yholde the lasse° in reputacioun.   *less*
315   Stilbon, that was a wis embassadour,
Was sent to Corinthe in ful greet honour
Fro Lacedomye° to make hir alliaunce,   *Sparta*
And whan he cam him happede° parchaunce   *it happened*
That alle the gretteste° that were of that lond   *greatest*
320   Playing at the hasard he hem foond,°   *found*
For which as soone as it mighte be
He stal him[5] hoom again to his contree,
And saide, "Ther wol I nat lese° my name,   *lose*
N'I wol nat take on me so greet defame°   *dishonor*
325   You to allye unto none hasardours:
Sendeth othere wise embassadours,
For by my trouthe, me were levere[6] die
Than I you sholde to hasardours allye.
For ye that been so glorious in honours
330   Shal nat allye you with hasardours
As by my wil, ne as by my tretee."°   *treaty*
This wise philosophre, thus saide he.
      Looke eek that to the king Demetrius
The King of Parthes,° as the book[7] saith us,   *Parthians*
335   Sente him a paire of dees° of gold in scorn,   *dice*
For he hadde used hasard therbiforn,
For which he heeld his glorye or his renown
At no value or reputacioun.
Lordes may finden other manere play
340   Honeste° ynough to drive the day away.   *honorable*
      Now wol I speke of othes false and grete
A word or two, as olde bookes trete:
      Greet swering is a thing abhominable,
And fals swering is yit more reprevable.°   *reprehensible*
345   The hye God forbad swering at al—
Witnesse on Mathew.[8] But in special
Of swering saith the holy Jeremie,[9]
"Thou shalt swere sooth thine othes and nat lie,

---

4. I.e. dissolute.
5. He stole away.
6. I had rather.
7. The book that relates this and the previous incident is the *Policraticus* of the 12th-century Latin writer John

of Salisbury.
8. "But I say unto you, Swear not at all" (Matthew 5.34).
9. Jeremiah 4.2.

And swere in doom° and eek in rightwisnesse,°   *equity/righteousness*
350   But idel swering is a cursednesse."°   *wickedness*
      Biholde and see that in the firste Table[1]
      Of hye Goddes heestes° honorable   *commandments*
      How that the seconde heeste of him is this:
      "Take nat my name in idel or amis."
355   Lo, rather° he forbedeth swich swering   *sooner*
      Than homicide, or many a cursed thing.
      I saye that as by ordre thus it stondeth—
      This knoweth that[2] his heestes understondeth
      How that the seconde heeste of God is that.
360   And fertherover,° I wol thee telle al plat°   *moreover/plain*
      That vengeance shal nat parten° from his hous   *depart*
      That of his othes is too outrageous.
      "By Goddes precious herte!" and "By his nailes!"°   *fingernails*
      And "By the blood of Crist that is in Hailes,[3]
365   Sevene is my chaunce,° and thyn is cink and traye!"[4]   *winning number*
      "By Goddes armes, if thou falsly playe
      This daggere shal thurghout thyn herte go!"
      This fruit cometh of the bicche bones[5] two—
      Forswering, ire, falsnesse, homicide.
370   Now for the love of Crist that for us dyde,°   *died*
      Lete° youre othes bothe grete and smale.   *leave*
      But sires, now wol I telle forth my tale.
            Thise riotoures° three of whiche I telle,   *revelers*
      Longe erst er prime[6] ronge of any belle,
375   Were set hem in a taverne to drinke,
      And as they sat they herde a belle clinke
      Biforn a cors° was caried to his grave.   *corpse*
      That oon of hem gan callen to his knave:°   *servant*
      Go bet,"[7] quod he, "and axe° redily°   *ask/promptly*
380   What cors is this that passeth heer forby,
      And looke° that thou reporte his name weel."°   *be sure/well*
            "Sire," quod this boy, "it needeth neveradeel:[8]
      It was me told er ye cam heer two houres.
      He was, pardee,° an old felawe of youres,   *by God*
385   And sodeinly he was yslain tonight,°   *last night*
      Fordronke° as he sat on his bench upright;   *very drunk*
      Ther cam a privee° thief men clepeth° Deeth,   *stealthy/call*
      That in this contree al the peple sleeth,°   *slays*
      And with his spere he smoot his herte atwo,
390   And wente his way withouten wordes mo.
      He hath a thousand slain this° pestilence.   *during this*
      And maister, er ye come in his presence,
      Me thinketh that it were necessarye
      For to be war of swich an adversarye;
395   Beeth redy for to meete him everemore:

---

1. I.e., the first three of the Ten Commandments.   5. I.e., damned dice.
2. I.e., he that.   6. Long before 9 A.M.
3. An abbey in Gloucestershire supposed to possess   7. Better, i.e., quick.
some of Christ's blood.   8. It isn't a bit necessary.
4. Five and three.

Thus taughte me my dame.° I saye namore."   *mother*
   "By Sainte Marye," saide this taverner,
"The child saith sooth, for he hath slain this yeer,
Henne° over a mile, within a greet village,   *hence*
400 Bothe man and womman, child and hine⁹ and page.
I trowe° his habitacion be there.   *believe*
To been avised° greet wisdom it were   *wary*
Er that he dide a man a dishonour."
   "Ye, Goddes armes," quod this riotour,
405 "Is it swich peril with him for to meete?
I shal him seeke by way and eek by streete,¹
I make avow to Goddes digne° bones.   *worthy*
Herkneth, felawes, we three been alle ones:°   *of one mind*
Lat eech of us holde up his hand to other
410 And eech of us bicome otheres brother,
And we wol sleen this false traitour Deeth.
He shal be slain, he that so manye sleeth,
By Goddes dignitee, er it be night."
   Togidres han thise three hir trouthes plight²
415 To live and dien eech of hem with other,
As though he were his owene ybore° brother.   *born*
And up they sterte,° al dronken in this rage,   *started*
And forth they goon towardes that village
Of which the taverner hadde spoke biforn,.
420 And many a grisly ooth thanne han they sworn,
And Cristes blessed body they torente:°   *tore apart*
Deeth shal be deed° if that they may him hente.°   *dead/catch*
   Whan they han goon nat fully half a mile,
Right as they wolde han treden° over a stile,   *stepped*
425 An old man and a poore with hem mette;
This olde man ful mekely hem grette,°   *greeted*
And saide thus, "Now lordes, God you see."³
   The pruddeste° of thise riotoures three   *proudest*
Answerde again, "What, carl° with sory grace,   *churl*
430 Why artou al forwrapped° save thy face?   *muffled up*
Why livestou so longe in so greet age?"
   This olde man gan looke in his visage,
And saide thus, "For° I ne can nat finde   *because*
A man, though that I walked into Inde,°   *India*
435 Neither in citee ne in no village,
That wolde chaunge his youthe for myn age;
And therefore moot° I han myn age stille,   *must*
As longe time as it is Goddes wille.
   "Ne Deeth, allas, ne wol nat have my lif.
440 Thus walke I lik a restelees caitif,°   *wretch*
And on the ground which is my modres° gate   *mother's*
I knokke with my staf bothe erly and late,
And saye, 'Leve° moder, leet me in: *dear*
Lo, how I vanisshe, flessh and blood and skin.
445 Allas, whan shal my bones been at reste?

---

9. Farm laborer.   2. Pledged their words of honor.
1. By highway and byway.   3. May God protect you.

Moder, with you wolde I chaunge° my cheste[4]   *exchange*
That in my chambre longe time hath be,
Ye, for an haire-clout[5] to wrappe me.'
But yit to me she wol nat do that grace,
450   For which ful pale and welked° is my face.   *withered*
But sires, to you it is no curteisye
To speken to an old man vilainye,°   *rudeness*
But° he trespasse° in word or elles in deede.   *unless/offend*
In Holy Writ ye may yourself wel rede,
455   'Agains[6] an old man, hoor° upon his heed,   *hoar*
Ye shall arise.'[7] Wherfore I yive you reed,°   *advice*
Ne dooth unto an old man noon harm now,
Namore than that ye wolde men dide to you
In age, if that ye so longe abide.[8]
460   And God be with you wher ye go° or ride: *walk*
I moot go thider as I have to go."
        "Nay, olde cherl, by God thou shalt nat so,"
Saide this other hasardour anoon.
"Thou partest nat so lightly,° by Saint John!   *easily*
465   Thou speke° right now of thilke traitour Deeth,   *spoke*
That in this contree alle oure freendes sleeth:
Have here my trouthe, as thou art his espye,°   *spy*
Tel wher he is, or thou shalt it abye,°   *pay for*
By God and by the holy sacrament!
470   For soothly thou art oon of his assent[9]
To sleen us yonge folk, thou false thief."
        "Now sires," quod he, "if that ye be so lief°   *anxious*
To finde Deeth, turne up this crooked way,
For in that grove I lafte° him, by my fay,°   *left/faith*
475   Under a tree, and ther he wol abide:
Nat for youre boost° he wol him no thing hide.   *boast*
See ye that ook?° Right ther ye shal him finde.   *oak*
God save you, that boughte again[1] mankinde,
And you amende." Thus saide this olde man.
480   And everich of thise riotoures ran
Til he cam to that tree, and ther they founde
Of florins° fine of gold ycoined rounde   *coins*
Wel neigh an eighte busshels as hem thoughte—
Ne lenger thanne after Deeth they soughte,
485   But eech of hem so glad was of the sighte,
For that the florins been so faire and brighte,
That down they sette hem by this precious hoord.
The worste of hem he spak the firste word:
        "Bretheren," quod he, "take keep° what that I saye: *heed*
490   My wit is greet though that I bourde° and playe.   *joke*
This tresor hath Fortune unto us yiven
In mirthe and jolitee oure lif to liven,
And lightly° as it cometh so wol we spende.   *easily*

4. Chest for one's belongings, used here as the symbol   7. Cf. Leviticus 19.32.
for life—or perhaps a coffin.   8. I.e., if you live so long.
5. Haircloth, for a winding sheet.   9. I.e., one of his party.
6. In the presence of.   1. Redeemed.

Ey, Goddes precious dignitee, who wende[2]
495   Today that we sholde han so fair a grace?
But mighte this gold be caried fro this place
Hoom to myn hous—or elles unto youres—
For wel ye woot that al this gold is oures—
Thanne were we in heigh felicitee.
500   But trewely, by daye it mighte nat be:
Men wolde sayn that we were theves stronge,°   *flagrant*
And for oure owene tresor doon us honge.[3]
This tresor moste ycaried be by nighte,
As wisely and as slyly as it mighte.
505   Therefore I rede° that cut° amonges us alle   *advise/straws*
Be drawe, and lat see wher the cut wol falle;
And he that hath the cut with herte blithe
Shal renne° to the town, and that ful swithe,°   *run/quickly*
And bringe us breed and win ful prively;
510   And two of us shal keepen° subtilly   *guard*
This tresor wel, and if he wol nat tarye,
Whan it is night we wol this tresor carye
By oon assent wher as us thinketh best."
That oon of hem the cut broughte in his fest°   *fist*
515   And bad hem drawe and looke wher it wol falle;
And it fil° on the yongeste of hem alle,   *fell*
And forth toward the town he wente anoon.
And also° soone as that he was agoon,°   *as/gone away*
That oon of hem spak thus unto that other:
520   "Thou knowest wel thou art my sworen brother;
Thy profit wol I telle thee anoon:
Thou woost wel that oure felawe is agoon,
And here is gold, and that ful greet plentee,
That shall departed° been among us three.   *divided*
525   But nathelees, if I can shape° it so   *arrange*
That it departed were among us two,
Hadde I nat doon a freendes turn to thee?"
   That other answerde, "I noot[4] how that may be:
He woot that the gold is with us twaye.
530   What shal we doon? What shal we to him saye?"
   "Shal it be conseil?"[5] saide the firste shrewe.°   *villain*
"And I shal telle in a wordes fewe
What we shul doon, and bringe it wel aboute."
   "I graunte," quod that other, "out of doute,
535   That by my trouthe I wol thee nat biwraye."°   *expose*
   "Now," quod the firste, "thou woost wel we be twaye,
And two of us shal strenger° be than oon: *stronger*
Looke whan that he is set that right anoon
Aris as though thou woldest with him playe,
540   And I shal rive° him thurgh the sides twaye,   *pierce*
Whil that thou strugelest with him as in game,
And with thy daggere looke thou do the same;
And thanne shal al this gold departed be,

---

2. Who would have supposed.   4. Don't know.
3. Have us hanged.   5. A secret.

My dere freend, bitwixe thee and me.
545   Thanne we may bothe oure lustes° al fulfille,   desires
And playe at dees° right at oure owene wille."   dice
And thus accorded been thise shrewes twaye
To sleen the thridde, as ye han herd me saye.
        This yongeste, which that wente to the town,
550   Ful ofte in herte he rolleth up and down
The beautee of thise florins newe and brighte.
"O Lord," quod he, "if so were that I mighte
Have al this tresor to myself allone,
Ther is no man that liveth under the trone°   throne
555   Of God that sholde live so merye as I."
And at the laste the feend oure enemy
Putte in his thought that he sholde poison beye,°   buy
With which he mighte sleen his felawes twaye—
Forwhy° the feend° foond him in swich livinge   because/devil
560   That he hadde leve° him to sorwe bringe:⁶   permission
For this was outrely° his fulle entente,   plainly
To sleen hem bothe, and nevere to repente.
        And forth he gooth—no lenger wolde he tarye—
Into the town unto a pothecarye,°   apothecary
565   And prayed him that he him wolde selle
Som poison that he mighte his rattes quelle,°   kill
And eek ther was a polcat⁷ in his hawe°   yard
That, as he saide, his capons hadde yslawe,°   slain
And fain he wolde wreke him⁸ if he mighte
570   On vermin that destroyed him⁹ by nighte.
        The pothecarye answerde, "And thou shalt have
A thing that, also° God my soule save,   as
In al this world there is no creature
That ete or dronke hath of this confiture°—   mixture
575   Nat but the mountance° of a corn° of whete—   amount/grain
That he ne shal his lif anoon forlete.°   lose
Ye, sterve° he shal, and that in lasse° while   die/less
Than thou wolt goon a paas¹ nat but a mile,
The poison is so strong and violent."
580   This cursed man hath in his hand yhent°   taken
This poison in a box and sith° he ran   then
Into the nexte streete unto a man
And borwed of him large botels three,
And in the two his poison poured he—
585   The thridde he kepte clene for his drinke,
For al the night he shoop him² for to swinke°   work
In carying of the gold out of that place.
And whan this riotour with sory grace
Hadde filled with win his grete botels three,
590   To his felawes again repaireth he.

6. Christian doctrine teaches that the devil may not   9. I.e., were ruining his farming.
tempt people except with God's permission.   1. Take a walk.
7. A weasellike animal.   2. He was preparing.
8. He would gladly avenge himself.

    What needeth it to sermone of it more?
    For right as they had cast° his deeth bifore,   *plotted*
    Right so they han him slain, and that anoon.
    And whan that this was doon, thus spak that oon:
595   "Now lat us sitte and drinke and make us merye,
    And afterward we wol his body berye."°   *bury*
    And with that word it happed him par cas[3]
    To take the botel ther the poison was,
    And drank, and yaf his felawe drinke also,
600   For which anoon they storven° bothe two.   *died*
      But certes I suppose that Avicen
    Wroot nevere in no canon ne in no *fen*[4]
    Mo wonder signes[5] of empoisoning
    Than hadde thise wrecches two er hir ending:
605   Thus ended been thise homicides two,
    And eek the false empoisonere also.
      O cursed sinne of alle cursednesse!
    O traitours homicide, O wikkednesse!
    O glotonye, luxure,° and hasardrye!   *lechery*
610   Thou blasphemour of Crist with vilainye
    And othes grete of usage° and of pride!   *habit*
    Allas, mankinde, how may it bitide
    That to thy Creatour which that thee wroughte,
    And with his precious herte blood thee boughte,°   *redeemed*
615   Thou art so fals and so unkinde,° allas?   *unnatural*
      Now goode men, God foryive you youre trespas,
    And ware° you fro the sinne of avarice: *guard*
    Myn holy pardon may you alle warice°—   *save*
    So that ye offre nobles or sterlinges,[6]
620   Or elles silver brooches, spoones, ringes.
    Boweth your heed under this holy bulle!
    Cometh up, ye wives, offreth of youre wolle!°   *wool*
    Youre name I entre here in my rolle: anoon
    Into the blisse of hevene shul ye goon.
625   I you assoile° by myn heigh power—   *absolve*
    Ye that wol offre—as clene and eek as cleer
    As ye were born.—And lo, sires, thus I preche.
    And Jesu Crist that is oure soules leeche°   *physician*
    So graunte you his pardon to receive,
630   For that is best—I wol you nat deceive.

The Epilogue

    "But sires, oo word forgat I in my tale:
    I have relikes and pardon in my male°   *bag*
    As faire as any man in Engelond,
    Whiche were me yiven by the Popes hond.
635   If any of you wol of devocioun

---

3. By chance.   called "fens."
4. The *Canon of Medicine*, by Avicenna, an 11th-   5. More wonderful symptoms.
century Arabic philosopher, was divided into sections   6. "Nobles" and "sterlinges" were valuable coins.

Offren and han myn absolucioun,
Come forth anoon, and kneeleth here adown,
And mekely receiveth my pardoun,
Or elles taketh pardon as ye wende,°   ride along
640   Al newe and fressh at every miles ende—
So that ye offre alway newe and newe[7]
Nobles or pens whiche that be goode and trewe.
It is an honour to everich° that is heer   everyone
That ye have a suffisant° pardoner   competent
645   T'assoile you in contrees as ye ride,
For aventures° whiche that may bitide: accidents
Paraventure ther may falle oon or two
Down of his hors and breke his nekke atwo;
Looke which a suretee° is it to you alle   safeguard
650   That I am in youre felaweshipe yfalle
That may assoile you, bothe more and lasse,[8]
Whan that the soule shal fro the body passe.
I rede° that oure Hoste shal biginne,   advise
For he is most envoluped° in sinne.   involved
655   Com forth, sire Host, and offre first anoon,
And thou shalt kisse the relikes everichoon,°   each one
Ye, for a grote: unbokele° anoon thy purs."   unbuckle
      "Nay, nay," quod he, "thanne have I Cristes curs!
Lat be," quod he, "it shal nat be, so theech!°   may I prosper
660   Thou woldest make me kisse thyn olde breech°   breeches
And swere it were a relik of a saint,
Though it were with thy fundament° depeint.°   anus/stained
But, by the crois which that Sainte Elaine foond,[9]
I wolde I hadde thy coilons° in myn hond,   testicles
665   In stede of relikes or of saintuarye.°   relic-box
Lat cutte hem of: I wol thee helpe hem carye.
They shal be shrined in an hogges tord."°   turd
      This Pardoner answerde nat a word:
So wroth he was no word ne wolde he saye.
670   "Now," quod oure Host, "I wol no lenger playe
With thee, ne with noon other angry man."
      But right anoon the worthy Knight bigan,
When that he sawgh that al the peple lough,°   laughed
"Namore of this, for it is right ynough.
675   Sire Pardoner, be glad and merye of cheere,
And ye, sire Host that been to me so dere,
I praye you that ye kisse the Pardoner,
And Pardoner, I praye thee, draw thee neer,
And as we diden lat us laughe and playe."
680   Anoon they kiste and riden forth hir waye.

---

7. Over and over.   mother of Constantine the Great, was reputed to have
8. Both high and low (i.e., everybody).   found the True Cross.
9. I.e., by the cross that St. Helena found. Helena,

The Nun's Priest's Tale[1]

	A poore widwe somdeel stape° in age	advanced
	Was whilom° dwelling in a narwe[2] cotage,	once upon a time
	Biside a grove, stonding in a dale:	
	This widwe of which I telle you my tale,	
5	Sin thilke° day that she was last a wif,	that same
	In pacience ladde° a ful simple lif.	led
	For litel was hir catel° and hir rente,°	property/income
	By housbondrye° of swich as God hire sente	economy
	She foond° hirself and eek hir doughtren two.	provided for
10	Three large sowes hadde she and namo,	
	Three kin,° and eek a sheep that highte° Malle.	cows/was called
	Ful sooty was hir bowr° and eek hir halle.	bedroom
	In which she eet ful many a sclendre° meel;	scanty
	Of poinant° sauce hire needed neveradeel:°	pungent/not a bit
15	No daintee morsel passed thurgh hir throte—	
	Hir diete was accordant to hir cote.°	cottage
	Repleccioun° ne made hire nevere sik:	overeating
	Attempre° diete was al hir physik,°	moderate/medicine
	And exercise and hertes suffisaunce.°	contentment
20	The goute lette hire nothing for to daunce,[3]	
	N'apoplexye shente° nat hir heed.°	hurt/head
	No win ne drank she, neither whit ne reed:°	red
	Hir boord° was served most with whit and blak,[4]	table
	Milk and brown breed, in which she foond no lak;[5]	
25	Seind bacon, and somtime an ey° or twaye,	egg
	For she was as it were a manere daye.[6]	
	A yeerd° she hadde, enclosed al withoute	yard
	With stikkes, and a drye dich aboute,	
	In which she hadde a cok heet° Chauntecleer:	named
30	In al the land of crowing nas° his peer.	was not
	His vois was merier than the merye orgon	
	On massedayes that in the chirche goon;[7]	
	Wel sikerer[8] was his crowing in his logge°	dwelling
	Than is a clok or an abbeye orlogge;°	timepiece
35	By nature he knew eech ascensioun	
	Of th'equinoxial[9] in thilke town:	
	For whan degrees fifteene were ascended,	

1. *The Nun's Priest's Tale* is an example of the literary genre known as the "beast fable," familiar from the fables of Aesop, in which animals behave like human beings. This story derives from an episode in the French *Roman de Renard*, a popular mock-heroic work that revolves around the exploits of Reynard the Fox, who constantly makes trouble in the feudal animal kingdom ruled over by Noble the Lion. Fables satirize human nature by attributing human vanities and follies to animals. They are also told to teach morals and were thought suitable for the education of children. In *The Nun's Priest's Tale*, morals proliferate; both the priest and his hero, Chauntecleer the rooster, spout examples, learned allusions, proverbs, and sententious generalizations, often in highly inflated rhetoric. The simple beast fable is thus blown up into a delightful satire of learning and moralizing and of the pompous rhetoric by which some medieval writers sought to elevate their works.
2. I.e., small.
3. The gout didn't hinder her at all from dancing.
4. I.e., milk and bread.
5. Found no fault.
6. I.e., a kind of dairymaid. "Seind": scorched (i.e., broiled).
7. I.e., is played.
8. More reliable.
9. I.e., he knew by instinct each step in the progression of the celestial equator. The celestial equator was thought to make a 360° rotation around the earth every twenty-four hours; therefore, a progression of 15° would be equal to the passage of an hour (line 37).

Thanne crew° he that it mighte nat been amended.°   *crowed/improved*
His comb was redder than the fin coral,
40   And batailed° as it were a castel wal;   *battlemented*
His bile° was blak, and as the jeet° it shoon;   *bill/jet*
Like asure¹ were his legges and his toon;°   *toes*
His nailes whitter° than the lilye flowr,   *whiter*
And lik the burned° gold was his colour.   *burnished*
45   This gentil° cok hadde in his governaunce   *noble*
Sevene hennes for to doon al his plesaunce,°   *pleasure*
Whiche were his sustres and his paramours,²
And wonder like to him as of colours;
Of whiche the faireste hewed° on hir throte   *colored*
50   Was cleped° faire damoisele Pertelote: *called*
Curteis she was, discreet, and debonaire,°   *meek*
And compaignable,° and bar° hirself so faire,   *companionable/bore*
Sin thilke day that she was seven night old,
That trewely she hath the herte in hold
55   Of Chauntecleer, loken° in every lith.°   *locked/limb*
He loved hire so that wel was him therwith.³
But swich a joye was it to heere hem singe,
Whan that the brighte sonne gan to springe,
In sweete accord *My Lief is Faren in Londe*⁴—
60   For thilke time, as I have understonde,
Beestes and briddes couden speke and singe.
     And so bifel that in a daweninge,
As Chauntecleer among his wives alle
Sat on his perche that was in the halle,
65   And next him sat this faire Pertelote,
This Chauntecleer gan gronen in his throte,
As man that in his dreem is drecched° sore.   *troubled*
     And whan that Pertelote thus herde him rore,°   *roar*
She was agast, and saide, "Herte dere,
70   What aileth you to grone in this manere?
Ye been a verray slepere,⁵ fy, for shame!"
     And he answerde and saide thus, "Madame,
I praye you that ye take it nat agrief.°   *amiss*
By God, me mette I was in swich meschief⁶
75   Right now, that yit myn herte is sore afright.
Now God," quod he, "my swevene recche aright,⁷
And keepe my body out of foul prisoun!
Me mette° how that I romed up and down   *dreamed*
Within oure yeerd, wher as I sawgh a beest,
80   Was lik an hound and wolde han maad arrest⁸
Upon my body, and han had me deed.⁹
His colour was bitwixe yelow and reed,
And tipped was his tail and bothe his eres
With blak, unlik the remenant° of his heres;°   *rest/hairs*

1. Blue (lapis lazuli).
2. His sisters and his mistresses.
3. That he was well contented.
4. "My Love Has Gone Away," a popular song of the time.
5. Sound sleeper.
6. I dreamed that I was in such misfortune.
7. Interpret my dream correctly (i.e., in an auspicious manner).
8. Would have laid hold.
9. I.e., killed me.

85 His snoute smal, with glowing yën twaye.
    Yit of his look for fere almost I deye:°   *die*
    This caused me my groning, doutelees."
        "Avoi,"° quod she, "fy on you, hertelees!°   *fie/coward*
    Allas," quod she, "for by that God above,
90 Now han ye lost myn herte and al my love!
    I can nat love a coward, by my faith.
    For certes, what so any womman saith,
    We alle desiren, if it mighte be,
    To han housbondes hardy, wise, and free,°   *generous*
95 And secree,° and no nigard, ne no fool,   *discreet*
    Ne him that is agast of every tool,°   *weapon*
    Ne noon avauntour.° By that God above,   *boaster*
    How dorste° ye sayn for shame unto youre love   *dare*
    That any thing mighte make you aferd?
100 Have ye no mannes herte and han a beerd?°   *beard*
    Allas, and conne° ye been agast of swevenes?°   *can/dreams*
    No thing, God woot, but vanitee[1] in swevene is!
    Swevenes engendren of replexiouns,[2]
    And ofte of fume° and of complexiouns,°   *gas/bodily humors*
105 Whan humours been too habundant in a wight.[3]
    Certes, this dreem which ye han met° tonight   *dreamed*
    Comth of the grete superfluitee
    Of youre rede colera,[4] pardee,
    Which causeth folk to dreden° in hir dremes   *fear*
110 Of arwes,° and of fir with rede lemes,°   *arrows/flames*
    Of rede beestes, that they wol hem bite,
    Of contek,° and of whelpes grete and lite[5] —   *strife*
    Right° as the humour of malencolye[6]   *just*
    Causeth ful many a man in sleep to crye
115 For fere of blake beres° or boles° blake,   *bears/bulls*
    Or elles blake develes wol hem take.
    Of othere humours coude I tell also
    That werken many a man in sleep ful wo,
    But I wol passe as lightly° as I can.   *quickly*
120 Lo, Caton,[7] which that was so wis a man,
    Saide he nat thus? 'Ne do no fors of[8] dremes.'
    Now, sire," quod she, "whan we flee fro the bemes,[9]
    For Goddes love, as take som laxatif.
    Up° peril of my soule and of my lif,   *upon*
125 I conseile you the beste, I wol nat lie,
    That bothe of colere and of malencolye
    Ye purge you; and for° ye shal nat tarye,   *in order that*
    Though in this town is noon apothecarye,
    I shal myself to herbes techen you,
130 That shal been for youre hele° and for youre prow,°   *health/benefit*

---

1. I.e., empty illusion.
2. Dreams have their origin in overeating.
3. I.e., when humors are too abundant in a person. Pertelote's diagnosis is based on the familiar concept that an overabundance of one of the bodily humors in a person affected his or her temperament (see p. 80, n.7).
4. Red bile.
5. And of big and little dogs.
6. I.e., black bile.
7. Dionysius Cato, supposed author of a book of maxims used in elementary education.
8. Pay no attention to.
9. Fly down from the rafters.

And in oure yeerd tho° herbes shal I finde,   *those*
The whiche han of hir propretee by kinde°   *nature*
To purge you binethe and eek above.
Foryet° nat this, for Goddes owene love.   *forget*
135 Ye been ful colerik° of complexioun;   *bilious*
Ware° the sonne in his ascencioun   *beware that*
Ne finde you nat repleet° of humours hote;°   *filled/hot*
And if it do, I dar wel laye° a grote   *bet*
That ye shul have a fevere terciane,[1]
140 Or an agu° that may be youre bane.°   *ague/death*
A day or two ye shul han digestives
Of wormes, er° ye take youre laxatives   *before*
Of lauriol, centaure, and fumetere,[2]
Or elles of ellebor° that groweth there,   *hellebore*
145 Of catapuce, or of gaitres beries,[3]
Of herb-ive° growing in oure yeerd ther merye is[4]   *herb ivy*
Pekke hem right up as they growe and ete hem in.
Be merye, housbonde, for youre fader° kin!   *father's*
Dredeth no dreem: I can saye you namore."
150   "Madame," quod he, "graunt mercy of youre lore,[5]
But nathelees, as touching daun° Catoun,   *master*
That hath of wisdom swich a greet renown,
Though that he bad no dremes for to drede,
By God, men may in olde bookes rede
155 Of many a man more of auctoritee°   *authority*
Than evere Catoun was, so mote I thee,°   *prosper*
That al the revers sayn of his sentence,°   *opinion*
And han wel founden by experience
That dremes been significaciouns
160 As wel of joye as tribulaciouns
That folk enduren in this lif present.
Ther needeth make of this noon argument:
The verray preve[6] sheweth it in deede.
    "Oon of the gretteste auctour[7] that men rede
165 Saith thus, that whilom two felawes wente
On pilgrimage in a ful good entente,
And happed so they comen in a town,
Wher as ther was swich congregacioun
Of peple, and eek so strait of herbergage,[8]
170 That they ne founde as muche as oo cotage
In which they bothe mighte ylogged° be;   *lodged*
Wherfore they mosten° of necessitee   *must*
As for that night departe° compaignye.   *part*
And eech of hem gooth to his hostelrye,
175 And took his logging as it wolde falle.°   *befall*
That oon of hem was logged in a stalle,
Fer° in a yeerd, with oxen of the plough;   *far away*

1. Tertian (recurring every other day).
2. Of laureole, centaury, and fumitory. These, and the
herbs mentioned in the next lines, were all common
medieval medicines used as cathartics.
3. Of caper berry or of gaiter berry.
4. Where it is pleasant.

5. Many thanks for your instruction.
6. Actual experience.
7. I.e., one of the greatest authors (perhaps Cicero or
Valerius Maximus).
8. And also such a shortage of lodging.

That other man was logged wel ynough,
As was his aventure° or his fortune,   *lot*
180 That us governeth alle as in commune.
And so bifel that longe er it were day,
This man mette° in his bed, ther as he lay,   *dreamed*
How that his felawe gan upon him calle,
And saide, 'Allas, for in an oxes stalle
185 This night I shal be mordred° ther I lie!   *murdered*
Now help me, dere brother, or I die!
In alle haste com to me,' he saide.
     "This man out of his sleep for fere abraide,°   *started up*
But whan that he was wakened of his sleep,
190 He turned him and took of this no keep:°   *heed*
Him thoughte his dreem nas but a vanitee.
Thus twies in his sleeping dremed he,
And atte thridde time yit his felawe
Cam, as him thoughte, and saide, 'I am now slawe:°   *slain*
195 Bihold my bloody woundes deepe and wide.
Aris up erly in the morwe tide[9]
And atte west gate of the town,' quod he,
'A carte ful of dong° ther shaltou see,   *dung*
In which my body is hid ful prively:
200 Do thilke carte arresten boldely.[1]
My gold caused my mordre, sooth to sayn'
—And tolde him every point how he was slain,
With a ful pitous face, pale of hewe.
And truste wel, his dreem he foond° ful trewe,   *found*
205 For on the morwe° as soone as it was day,   *morning*
To his felawes in° he took the way,   *lodging*
And whan that he cam to this oxes stalle,
After his felawe he bigan to calle.
     "The hostiler° answerde him anoon,   *innkeeper*
210 And saide, 'Sire, youre felawe is agoon:°   *gone away*
As soone as day he wente out of the town.'
     "This man gan fallen in suspecioun,
Remembring on his dremes that he mette;°   *dreamed*
And forth he gooth, no lenger wolde he lette,°   *tarry*
215 Unto the west gate of the town, and foond
A dong carte, wente as it were to donge° lond,   *put manure on*
That was arrayed in that same wise
As ye han herd the dede° man devise;   *dead*
And with an hardy herte he gan to crye,
220 'Vengeance and justice of this felonye!
My felawe mordred is this same night,
And in this carte he lith° gaping upright!°   *lies/on his back*
I crye out on the ministres,' quod he,
'That sholde keepe and rulen this citee.
225 Harrow,° allas, here lith my felawe slain!'   *help*
What sholde I more unto this tale sayn?
The peple up sterte° and caste the carte to grounde,   *started*

9. In the morning.   1. Boldly have this same cart seized.

And in the middel of the dong they founde
The dede man that mordred was al newe.[2]

230   "O blisful God that art so just and trewe,
Lo, how that thou biwrayest° mordre alway!   *disclose*
Mordre wol out, that see we day by day:
Mordre is so wlatsom° and abhominable   *loathsome*
To God that is so just and resonable,

235   That he ne wol nat suffre it heled° be,   *concealed*
Though it abide a yeer or two or three.
Mordre wol out: this my conclusioun.
And right anoon ministres of that town
Han hent° the cartere and so sore him pined,[3]   *seized*

240   And eek the hostiler so sore engined,°   *racked*
That they biknewe° hir wikkednesse anoon,   *confessed*
And were anhanged° by the nekke boon.   *hanged*
Here may men seen that dremes been to drede.[4]

        "And certes, in the same book I rede—
245   Right in the nexte chapitre after this—
I gabbe° nat, so have I joye or blis—   *lie*
Two men that wolde han passed over see
For certain cause into a fer contree,
If that the wind ne hadde been contrarye

250   That made hem in a citee for to tarye,
That stood ful merye upon an haven° side—   *harbor's*
But on a day again° the even-tide   *toward*
The wind gan chaunge, and blewe right as hem leste:[5]
Jolif° and glad they wenten unto reste,   *merry*

255   And casten° hem ful erly for to saile.   *determined*
        "But to that oo man fil° a greet mervaile; *befell*
That oon of hem, in sleeping as he lay,
Him mette[6] a wonder dreem again the day:
Him thoughte a man stood by his beddes side,

260   And him comanded that he sholde abide,
And saide him thus, 'If thou tomorwe wende,
Thou shalt be dreint:° my tale is at an ende.'   *drowned*
        "He wook and tolde his felawe what he mette,
And prayed him his viage° to lette;°   *voyage/delay*

265   As for that day he prayed him to bide.
        "His felawe that lay by his beddes side
Gan for to laughe, and scorned him ful faste.°   *hard*
'No dreem,' quod he, 'may so myn herte agaste°   *terrify*
That I wol lette° for to do my thinges.°   *delay/business*

270   I sette nat a straw by thy dreminges,[7]
For swevenes been but vanitees and japes:[8]
Men dreme alday° of owles or of apes,[9]   *constantly*
And of many a maze° therwithal—   *delusion*
Men dreme of thing that nevere was ne shal.[1]

275   But sith I see that thou wolt here abide,

2. Recently.
3. Tortured.   7. I don't care a straw for your dreamings.
4. Worthy of being feared.   8. Dreams are but illusions and frauds.
5. Just as they wished.   9. I.e., of absurdities.
6. He dreamed.   1. I.e., shall be.

And thus forsleuthen° wilfully thy tide,°   *waste/time*
God woot, it reweth me;[2] and have good day.'
And thus he took his leve and wente his way.
But er that he hadde half his cours ysailed—
280   Noot I nat why ne what meschaunce it ailed—
But casuelly the shippes botme rente,[3]
And ship and man under the water wente,
In sighte of othere shippes it biside,
That with hem sailed at the same tide.
285   And therfore, faire Pertelote so dere,
By swiche ensamples olde maistou lere°   *learn*
That no man sholde been too recchelees°   *careless*
Of dremes, for I saye thee doutelees
That many a dreem ful sore is for to drede.
290   "Lo, in the lif of Saint Kenelm[4] I rede—
That was Kenulphus sone, the noble king
Or Mercenrike°—how Kenelm mette a thing   *Mercia*
A lite° er he was mordred on a day.   *little*
His mordre in his avision° he sey.°   *dream/saw*
295   His norice° him expounded everydeel°   *nurse/every bit*
His swevene, and bad him for to keepe him[5] weel
For traison, but he nas but seven yeer old,
And therfore litel tale hath he told
Of any dreem,[6] so holy was his herte.
300   By God, I hadde levere than my sherte[7]
That ye hadde rad° his legende as have I.   *read*
     "Dame Pertelote, I saye you trewely,
Macrobeus,[8] that writ the *Avisioun*
In Affrike of the worthy Scipioun,
305   Affermeth° dremes, and saith that they been   *confirms*
Warning of thinges that men after seen.
     "And ferthermore, I praye you looketh wel
In the Olde Testament of Daniel,
If he heeld° dremes any vanitee.[9]   *considered*
310   "Rede eek of Joseph[1] and ther shul ye see
Wher° dremes be sometime—I saye nat alle—   *whether*
Warning of thinges that shul after falle.
     "Looke of Egypte the king daun Pharao,
His bakere and his botelere° also,   *butler*
315   Wher they ne felte noon effect in dremes.[2]
Whoso wol seeke actes of sondry remes°   *realms*
May rede of dremes many a wonder thing.
     "Lo Cresus, which that was of Lyde° king,   *Lydia*
Mette° he nat that he sat upon a tree,   *dreamed*
320   Which signified he sholde anhanged° be?   *hanged*
     "Lo here Andromacha, Ectores° wif,   *Hector's*

2. I'm sorry.
3. I don't know why nor what was the trouble with it— but accidentally the ship's bottom split.
4. Kenelm succeeded his father as king of Mercia at the age of seven, but was slain by his aunt (in 821).
5. Guard himself.
6. Therefore he has set little store by any dream.
7. I.e., I'd give my shirt.

8. Macrobius wrote a famous commentary on Cicero's account in *De Republica* of the dream of Scipio Africanus Minor; the commentary came to be regarded as a standard authority on dream lore.
9. See Daniel 7.
1. See Genesis 37.
2. See Genesis 39–41.

That day that Ector sholde lese° his lif,   *lose*
She dremed on the same night biforn
How that the lif of Ector sholde be lorn,°   *lost*
325   If thilke° day he wente into bataile;   *that same*
She warned him, but it mighte nat availe:°   *do any good*
He wente for to fighte nathelees,
But he was slain anoon° of Achilles.   *right away*
But thilke tale is al too long to telle,
330   And eek it is neigh day, I may nat dwelle.
Shortly I saye, as for conclusioun,
That I shal han of this avisioun[3]
Adversitee, and I saye ferthermoor
That I ne telle of[4] laxatives no stoor,
335   For they been venimes,° I woot it weel: *poisons*
I hem defye, I love hem neveradeel.°   *not a bit*
     "Now lat us speke of mirthe and stinte° al this.   *stop*
Madame Pertelote, so have I blis,
Of oo thing God hath sente me large grace:
340   For whan I see the beautee of youre face—
Ye been so scarlet reed° aboute youre yën—   *red*
It maketh al my drede for to dien.
For also siker° as *In principio*,[5]   *certain*
Mulier est hominis confusio.[6]
345   Madame, the sentence° of this Latin is,   *meaning*
'Womman is mannes joye and al his blis.'
For whan I feele anight youre softe side—
Al be it that I may nat on you ride,
For that oure perche is maad so narwe, allas—
350   I am so ful of joye and of solas°   *delight*
That I defye bothe swevene and dreem."
And with that word he fleigh° down fro the beem,   *flew*
For it was day, and eek his hennes alle,
And with a "chuk" he gan hem for to calle,
355   For he hadde founde a corn lay in the yeerd.
Real° he was, he was namore aferd:°   *regal/afraid*
He fethered[7] Pertelote twenty time,
And trad hire as ofte er it was prime.[8]
He looketh as it were a grim leoun,
360   And on his toes he rometh up and down:
Him deined[9] nat to sette his foot to grounde.
He chukketh whan he hath a corn yfounde,
And to him rennen° thanne his wives alle.   *run*
Thus royal, as a prince is in his halle,
365   Leve I this Chauntecleer in his pasture,
And after wol I telle his aventure.
     Whan that the month in which the world bigan,
That highte° March, whan God first maked man,   *is called*

---

3. Divinely inspired dream (as opposed to the more   was the Word."
ordinary "swevene" or "dreem").   6. Woman is man's ruination.
4. Set by.   7. I.e., embraced.
5. A tag from the Gospel of St. John that gives the   8. 9 A.M. "Trad": trod, copulated with.
essential premises of Christianity: "In the beginning   9. He deigned.

Was compleet, and passed were also,

370 Sin March biran,° thritty days and two,[1]   *passed by*
Bifel that Chauntecleer in al his pride,
His sevene wives walking him biside,
Caste up his yën to the brighte sonne,
That in the signe of Taurus hadde yronne

375 Twenty degrees and oon and somwhat more,
And knew by kinde,° and by noon other lore,   *nature*
That it was prime, and crew with blisful stevene.°   *voice*
"The sonne," he saide, "is clomben[2] up on hevene
Fourty degrees and oon and more, ywis.°   *indeed*

380 Madame Pertelote, my worldes blis,
Herkneth thise blisful briddes° how they singe,   *birds*
And see the fresshe flowers how they springe:
Ful is myn herte of revel and solas."
But sodeinly him fil° a sorweful cas,°   *befell/chance*

385 For evere the latter ende of joye is wo —
God woot that worldly joye is soone ago,
And if a rethor° coude faire endite,   *rhetorician*
He in a cronicle saufly° mighte it write,   *safely*
As for a soverein notabilitee.[3]

390 Now every wis man lat him herkne me:
This storye is also° trewe, I undertake,   *as*
As is the book of *Launcelot de Lake*,[4]
That wommen holde in ful greet reverence.
Now wol I turne again to my sentence.°   *main point*

395   A colfox[5] ful of sly iniquitee,
That in the grove hadde woned° yeres three,   *dwelled*
By heigh imaginacion forncast,[6]
The same night thurghout the hegges° brast°   *hedges/burst*
Into the yeerd ther Chauntecleer the faire

400 Was wont, and eek his wives, to repaire;
And in a bed of wortes° stille he lay   *cabbages*
Til it was passed undren° of the day,   *midmorning*
Waiting his time on Chauntecleer to falle,
As gladly doon thise homicides alle,

405 That in await liggen to mordre[7] men.
O false mordrour, lurking in thy den!
O newe Scariot! Newe Geniloun![8]
False dissimilour!° O Greek Sinoun,[9]   *dissembler*
That broughtest Troye al outrely° to sorwe!   *utterly*

410 O Chauntecleer, accursed be that morwe°   *morning*
That thou into the yeerd flaugh° fro the bemes!   *flew*
Thou were ful wel ywarned by thy dremes
That thilke day was perilous to thee;
But what that God forwoot° moot° needes be,   *foreknows/must*

---

1. The rhetorical time telling yields the date May 3.
2. Has climbed.
3. Indisputable fact.
4. Romances of the courteous knight Lancelot of the Lake were very popular.
5. Fox with black markings.
6. Predestined by divine planning.

7. That lie in ambush to murder.
8. I.e., Ganelon, who betrayed Roland to the Saracens (in the medieval French epic *The Song of Roland*). "Scariot": Judas Iscariot.
9. Sinon, who persuaded the Trojans to take the Greeks' wooden horse into their city—with, of course, the result that the city was destroyed.

415	After° the opinion of certain clerkes:	*according to*
	Witnesse on him that any parfit° clerk is	*perfect*
	That in scole is greet altercacioun	
	In this matere, and greet disputisoun,°	*disputation*
	And hath been of an hundred thousand men.	
420	But I ne can nat bulte it to the bren,[1]	
	As can the holy doctour Augustin,	
	Or Boece, or the bisshop Bradwardin[2]—	
	Wheither that Goddes worthy forwiting°	*foreknowledge*
	Straineth me nedely[3] for to doon a thing	
425	("Nedely" clepe I simple necessitee),	
	Or elles if free chois be graunted me	
	To do that same thing or do it naught,	
	Though God forwoot° it er that I was wrought;	*foreknew*
	Or if his witing° straineth neveradeel,	*knowledge*
430	But by necessitee condicionel[4]—	
	I wol nat han to do of swich matere:	
	My tale is of a cok, as ye may heere,	
	That took his conseil of his wif with sorwe,	
	To walken in the yeerd upon that morwe	
435	That he hadde met° the dreem that I you tolde.	*dreamed*
	Wommenes conseils been ful ofte colde,[5]	
	Wommanes conseil broughte us first to wo,	
	And made Adam fro Paradis to go,	
	Ther as he was ful merye and wel at ese.	
440	But for I noot° to whom it mighte displese	*don't know*
	If I conseil of wommen wolde blame,	
	Passe over, for I saide it in my game°—	*sport*
	Rede auctours where they trete of swich matere,	
	And what they sayn of wommen ye may heere—	
445	Thise been the cokkes wordes and nat mine:	
	I can noon harm of no womman divine.°	*guess*
	Faire in the sond° to bathe hire merily	*sand*
	Lith° Pertelote, and alle hir sustres by,	*lies*
	Again° the sonne, and Chauntecleer so free°	*in/noble*
450	Soong° merier than the mermaide in the see—	*sang*
	For Physiologus[6] saith sikerly	
	How that they singen wel and merily.	
	And so bifel that as he caste his yë	
	Among the wortes on a boterflye,°	*butterfly*
455	He was war of this fox that lay ful lowe.	
	No thing ne liste him[7] thanne for to crowe,	
	But cride anoon "Cok cok!" and up he sterte,°	*started*
	As man that[8] was affrayed in his herte—	
	For naturelly a beest desireth flee	

---

1. Sift it to the bran, i.e., get to the bottom of it.
2. St. Augustine, Boethius (6th-century Roman philosopher, whose *Consolation of Philosophy* was translated by Chaucer), and Thomas Bradwardine (archbishop of Canterbury, d. 1349) were all concerned with the interrelationship between people's free will and God's foreknowledge.
3. Constrains me necessarily.
4. Boethius's "conditional necessity" permitted a large measure of free will.
5. I.e., baneful.
6. Supposed author of a bestiary, a book of moralized zoology describing both natural and supernatural animals (including mermaids).
7. He wished.
8. Like one who.

460   Fro his contrarye[9] if he may it see,
      Though he nevere erst° hadde seen it with his yë.   *before*
      This Chauntecleer, whan he gan him espye,
      He wolde han fled, but that the fox anoon
      Saide, "Gentil sire, allas, wher wol ye goon?
465   Be ye afraid of me that am youre freend?
      Now certes, I were worse than a feend
      If I to you wolde° harm or vilainye.   *meant*
      I am nat come youre conseil° for t'espye,   *secrets*
      But trewely the cause of my cominge
470   Was only for to herkne how ye singe:
      For trewely, ye han as merye a stevene°   *voice*
      As any angel hath that is in hevene.
      Therwith ye han in musik more feelinge
      Than hadde Boece,[1] or any that can singe.
475   My lord your fader—God his soule blesse!—
      And eek youre moder, of hir gentilesse,°   *gentility*
      Han in myn hous ybeen, to my grete ese.
      And certes sire, ful fain° wolde I you plese.   *gladly*
         "But for men speke of singing, I wol saye,
480   So mote I brouke[2] wel mine yën twaye,
      Save ye, I herde nevere man to singe
      As dide youre fader in the morweninge.
      Certes, it was of herte° al that he soong.°   *heartfelt/sang*
      And for to make his vois the more strong,
485   He wolde so paine him[3] that with bothe his yën
      He moste winke,[4] so loude wolde he cryen;
      And stonden on his tiptoon therwithal,
      And strecche forth his nekke long and smal;
      And eek he was of swich discrecioun
490   That ther nas no man in no regioun
      That him in song or wisdom mighte passe.
      I have wel rad° in *Daun Burnel the Asse*[5]   *read*
      Among his vers how that ther was a cok,
      For a preestes sone yaf him a knok[6]
495   Upon his leg whil he was yong and nice,°   *foolish*
      He made him for to lese° his benefice.[7]   *lose*
      But certain, ther nis no comparisoun
      Bitwixe the wisdom and discrecioun
      Of youre fader and of his subtiltee.[8]
500   Now singeth, sire, for sainte° charitee!   *holy*
      Lat see, conne° ye youre fader countrefete?"°   *can/imitate*
         This Chauntecleer his winges gan to bete,
      As man that coude his traison nat espye,
      So was he ravisshed with his flaterye.
505   Allas, ye lordes, many a fals flatour°   *flatterer*
      Is in youre court, and many a losengeour°   *deceiver*

---

9. I.e., his natural enemy.
1. Boethius also wrote a treatise on music.
2. So might I enjoy the use of.
3. Take pains.
4. He had to shut his eyes.
5. Master Brunellus, a discontented donkey, was the

hero of a 12th-century satirical poem by Nigel Wireker.
6. Because a priest's son gave him a knock.
7. The offended cock neglected to crow so that his master, now grown to manhood, overslept, missing his ordination and losing his benefice.
8. His (the cock in the story) cleverness.

That plesen you wel more, by my faith,
Than he that soothfastnesse° unto you saith!   *truth*
Redeth Ecclesiaste[9] of flaterye.
510 Beeth war, ye lordes, of hir trecherye.
        This Chauntecleer stood hye upon his toos,
Strecching his nekke, and heeld his yën cloos,
And gan to crowe loude for the nones;°   *occasion*
And daun Russel the fox sterte° up atones,   *jumped*
515 And by the gargat° hente° Chauntecleer,   *throat/seized*
And on his bak toward the wode him beer,°   *bore*
For yit ne was ther no man that him sued.°   *followed*
        O destinee that maist nat been eschued!°   *eschewed*
Allas that Chauntecleer fleigh° fro the bemes!   *flew*
520 Allas his wif ne roughte nat of[1] dremes!
And on a Friday fil° al this meschaunce!   *befell*
        O Venus that art goddesse of plesaunce,
Sin that thy servant was this Chauntecleer,
And in thy service dide al his power—
525 More for delit than world[2] to multiplye—
Why woldestou suffre him on thy day[3] to die?
        O Gaufred,[4] dere maister soverein,
That, whan thy worthy king Richard was slain
With shot,[5] complainedest his deeth so sore,
530 Why ne hadde I now thy sentence and thy lore,[6]
The Friday for to chide as diden ye?
For on a Friday soothly slain was he.
Thanne wolde I shewe you how that I coude plaine°   *lament*
For Chauntecleres drede and for his paine.
535   Certes, swich cry ne lamentacioun
Was nevere of ladies maad when Ilioun°   *Ilium, Troy*
Was wonne, and Pyrrus[7] with his straite° swerd,   *drawn*
Whan he hadde hent° King Priam by the beerd   *seized*
And slain him, as saith us *Eneidos*,[8]
540 As maden alle the hennes in the cloos,°   *yard*
Whan they hadde seen of Chauntecleer the sighte.
But sovereinly° Dame Pertelote shrighte°   *supremely/shrieked*
Ful louder than dide Hasdrubales[9] wif
Whan that hir housbonde hadde lost his lif,
545 And that the Romains hadden brend° Cartage: *burned*
She was so ful of torment and of rage°   *madness*
That wilfully unto the fir she sterte,°   *jumped*
And brende hirselven with a stedefast herte.
        O woful hennes, right so criden ye
550 As, whan that Nero brende the citee
Of Rome, criden senatoures wives
For that hir housbondes losten alle hir lives:[1]

9. The Book of Ecclesiasticus, in the Apocrypha.
1. Didn't care for.
2. I.e., population.
3. Friday is Venus's day.
4. Geoffrey of Vinsauf, a famous medieval rhetorician, who wrote a lament on the death of Richard I in which he scolded Friday, the day on which the king died.
5. I.e., a missile.
6. Thy wisdom and thy learning.
7. Pyrrhus was the Greek who slew Priam, king of Troy.
8. As the *Aeneid* tells us.
9. Hasdrubal was king of Carthage when it was destroyed by the Romans.
1. According to the legend, Nero not only set fire to Rome (in A.D. 64) but also put many senators to death.

Withouten gilt this Nero hath hem slain.
Now wol I turne to my tale again.

555   The sely° widwe and eek hir doughtres two   *innocent*
Herden thise hennes crye and maken wo,
And out at dores sterten° they anoon,   *leapt*
And sien° the fox toward the grove goon,   *saw*
And bar upon his bak the cok away,
560   And criden, "Out, harrow,° and wailaway,   *help*
Ha, ha, the fox," and after him they ran,
And eek with staves many another man;
Ran Colle oure dogge, and Talbot and Gerland,[2]
And Malkin with a distaf in hir hand,
565   Ran cow and calf, and eek the verray hogges,
Sore aferd° for berking of the dogges   *frightened*
And shouting of the men and wommen eke.
They ronne° so hem thoughte hir herte breke;[3]   *ran*
They yelleden as feendes doon in helle;
570   The dokes° criden as men wolde hem quelle;°   *ducks/kill*
The gees for fere flowen° over the trees;   *flew*
Out of the hive cam the swarm of bees;
So hidous was the noise, a, benedicite,°   *bless me*
Certes, he Jakke Straw[4] and his meinee°   *company*
575   Ne made nevere shoutes half so shrille
Whan that they wolden any Fleming kille,
As thilke day was maad upon the fox:
Of bras they broughten bemes° and of box,°   *trumpets/boxwood*
Of horn, of boon,° in whiche they blewe and pouped,°   *bone/tooted*
580   And therwithal they skriked° and they houped°—   *shrieked/whooped*
It seemed as that hevene sholde falle.
        Now goode men, I praye you herkneth alle:
Lo, how Fortune turneth° sodeinly   *reverses, overturns*
The hope and pride eek of hir enemy.
585   This cok that lay upon the foxes bak,
In al his drede unto the fox he spak,
And saide, "Sire, if that I were as ye,
Yit sholde I sayn, as wis° God helpe me,   *surely*
'Turneth ayain, ye proude cherles alle!
590   A verray pestilence upon you falle!
Now am I come unto this wodes side,
Maugree your heed,[5] the cok shal here abide.
I wol him ete, in faith, and that anoon.'"
        The fox answerde, "In faith, it shal be doon."
595   And as he spak that word, al sodeinly
The cok brak from his mouth deliverly,°   *nimbly*
And hye upon a tree he fleigh° anoon.   *flew*
        And whan the fox sawgh that he was agoon,
"Allas," quod he, "O Chauntecleer, allas!
600   I have to you," quod he, "ydoon trespas,

2. Two other dogs.
3. Would break.
4. One of the leaders of the Peasants' Revolt in 1381, which was partially directed against the Flemings liv-

ing in London.
5. Despite your head—i.e., despite anything you can do.

In as muche as I maked you aferd
Whan I you hente° and broughte out of the yeerd.   *seized*
But sire, I dide it in no wikke° entente: *wicked*
Come down, and I shal telle you what I mente.
605   I shal saye sooth to you, God help me so."
      "Nay thanne," quod he, "I shrewe° us bothe two: *curse*
But first I shrewe myself, bothe blood and bones,
If thou bigile me ofter than ones;
Thou shalt namore thurgh thy flaterye
610   Do° me to singe and winken with myn yë.   *cause*
For he that winketh whan he sholde see,
Al wilfully, God lat him nevere thee."°   *prosper*
      "Nay," quod the fox, "but God yive him meschaunce
That is so undiscreet of governaunce°   *self-control*
615   That jangleth° whan he sholde holde his pees."   *chatters*
      Lo, swich it is for to be reccheless°   *careless*
And necligent and truste on flaterye.
But ye that holden this tale a folye
As of a fox, or of a cok and hen,
620   Taketh the moralitee, goode men.
For Saint Paul saith that al that writen is
To oure doctrine it is ywrit, ywis:[6]
Taketh the fruit, and lat the chaf be stille.[7]
Now goode God, if that it be thy wille,
625   As saith my lord, so make us alle goode men,
And bringe us to his hye blisse. Amen.

Close of Canterbury Tales

At the end of *The Canterbury Tales*, Chaucer invokes a common allegorical theme, that life on earth is a pilgrimage. As Chaucer puts it in his moral ballade *Truth*, "Here in noon home . . . / Forth, pilgrim, forth!" In the final fragment, he makes explicit a metaphor that has been implicit all along in the journey to Canterbury. The pilgrims never arrive at the shrine of St. Thomas, but in *The Parson's Tale*, and in its short introduction and in the "Retraction" that follows it, Chaucer seems to be making an end for two pilgrimages that had become one, that of his fiction and that of his life.

In the introduction to the tale we find the twenty-nine pilgrims moving through a nameless little village as the sun sinks to within twenty-nine degrees of the horizon. The atmosphere contains something of both the chill and the urgency of a late autumn afternoon, and we are surprised to find that the pilgrimage is almost over, that there is need for haste to make that "good end" that every medieval Christian hoped for. This delicately suggestive passage, rich with allegorical overtones, introduces an extremely long sermon on penitence and the deadly sins, probably translated by Chaucer from French or Latin some years earlier, before he had begun *The Canterbury Tales*.

The Retraction that follows and concludes *The Parson's Tale* offers Chaucer's apology for having written all the works on which his reputation as a great poet depends, not only such stories as *The Miller's Tale* but also his loveliest and seemingly most harmless poems. Yet a readiness to deny his own reality before the

6. See Romans 15.4.
7. The "fruit" refers to the kernel of moral or doctrinal meaning; the "chaf," or husk, is the narrative containing that meaning. The metaphor was commonly applied to scriptural interpretation.

reality of his God is implicit in many of Chaucer's works, and the placement of the "Retraction" within the artistic structure of *The Canterbury Tales* suggests that although Chaucer denied his art, he seems to have recognized that he and it were inseparable.

From The Parson's Tale

The Introduction

By that[1] the Manciple hadde his tale al ended,
The sonne fro the south line[2] was descended
So lowe, that he has nat to my sighte
Degrees nine and twenty as in highte.
5 Four of the clokke it was, so as I gesse,
For elevene foot, or litel more or lesse,
My shadwe was at thilke time as there,
Of swich feet as° my lengthe parted° were   *as if/divided*
In sixe feet equal of proporcioun.[3]
10 Therwith the moones exaltacioun[4]—
I mene Libra—always gan ascende,
As we were entring at a thropes° ende.   *village's*
For which oure Host, as he was wont to gie°   *lead*
As in this caas oure joly compaignye,
15 Saide in this wise, "Lordinges everichoon,
Now lakketh us no tales mo than oon:
Fulfild is my sentence° and my decree;   *purpose*
I trowe° that we han herd of ech degree;   *believe*
Almost fulfild is al myn ordinaunce.
20 I praye to God, so yive him right good chaunce
That telleth this tale to us lustily.
Sire preest," quod he, "artou a vicary,°   *vicar*
Or arte a Person? Say sooth, by thy fay.°   *faith*
Be what thou be, ne breek° thou nat oure play,   *break*
25 For every man save thou hath told his tale.
Unbokele and shew us what is in thy male!°   *bag*
For trewely, me thinketh by thy cheere°   *expression*
Thou sholdest knitte up wel a greet matere.
Tel us a fable anoon, for cokkes bones!"[5]
30   This Person answerde al atones,°   *immediately*
"Thou getest fable noon ytold for me,
For Paul, that writeth unto Timothee,
Repreveth° hem that waiven soothfastnesse,[6]   *reproves*
And tellen fables and swich wrecchednesse.
35 Why sholde I sowen draf° out of my fest,°   *chaff/fist*
Whan I may sowen whete if that me lest?[7]
For which I saye that if you list to heere
Moralitee and vertuous matere,

1. By the time that.
2. I.e., the line that runs some 28° to the south of the celestial equator and parallel to it.
3. This detailed analysis merely says that the shadows are lengthening.
4. I.e., the astrological sign in which the moon's influence was dominant.
5. Cock's bones, a euphemism for God's bones.
6. Depart from truth (see 1 Timothy 1.4).
7. It pleases me.

And thanne that ye wol yive me audience,
40 I wol ful fain,° at Cristes reverence,   *gladly*
    Do you plesance leveful° as I can.   *lawful*
    But trusteth wel, I am a southren man:
    I can nat geeste Rum-Ram-Ruf by lettre[8]—
    Ne, God woot, rym holde° I but litel bettre.   *consider*
45 And therfore, if you list, I wol nat glose;[9]
    I wol you telle a merye tale in prose,
    To knitte up al this feeste and make an ende.
    And Jesu for his grace wit me sende
    To shewe you the way in this viage°   *journey*
50 Of thilke parfit glorious pilgrimage
    That highte° Jerusalem celestial.   *is called*
    And if ye vouche sauf, anoon I shal
    Biginne upon my tale, for which I praye
    Telle youre avis:° I can no bettre saye.   *opinion*
55 But nathelees, this meditacioun
    I putte it ay under correccioun
    Of clerkes, for I am nat textuel:[1]
    I take but the sentence,° trusteth wel.   *meaning*
    Therefore I make protestacioun°   *public acknowledgment*
60 That I wol stonde to correccioun."
        Upon this word we han assented soone,
    For, as it seemed, it was for to doone
    To enden in som vertuous sentence,°   *doctrine*
    And for to yive him space° and audience;   *time*
65 And bede[2] oure Host he sholde to him saye
    That alle we to telle his tale him praye.
        Oure Hoste hadde the wordes for us alle:
    "Sire preest," quod he, "now faire you bifalle:
    Telleth," quod he, "youre meditacioun.
70 But hasteth you; the sonne wol adown.
    Beeth fructuous,° and that in litel space,°   *fruitful/time*
    And to do wel God sende you his grace.
    Saye what you list, and we wol gladly heere."
    And with that word he saide in this manere.

Chaucer's Retraction

Now praye I to hem alle that herkne this litel tretis[3] or rede, that if ther be
any thing in it that liketh[4] hem, that therof they thanken oure Lord Jesu Crist,
of whom proceedeth al wit[5] and al goodnesse. And if ther be any thing that
displese hem, I praye hem also that they arrette it to the defaute of myn uncon-
ning,[6] and nat to my wil, that wolde ful fain have said bettre if I hadde had
conning. For oure book saith, "Al that is writen is writen for oure doctrine,"[7]
and that is myn entente. Wherfore I biseeke[8] you mekely, for the mercy of

---

8. I.e., I cannot tell stories in the alliterative measure   3. Hear this little treatise, i.e., *The Parson's Tale*.
(without rhyme): this form of poetry was not common   4. Pleases.
in southeastern England.   5. Understanding.
9. I.e., speak in order to please.   6. Ascribe it to the defect of my lack of skill.
1. Literal, faithful to the letter.   7. Romans 15.4.
2. I.e., we bade.   8. Beseech.

God, that ye praye for me that Crist have mercy on me and foryive me my giltes, and namely of my translacions and enditinges[9] of worldly vanitees, the whiche I revoke in my retraccions: as is the *Book of Troilus*; the Book also of *Fame*; the *Book of the Five and Twenty Ladies*;[1] the *Book of the Duchesse*; the *Book of Saint Valentines Day of the Parlement of Briddes*; the *Tales of Canterbury*, thilke that sounen into[2] sinne; the *Book of the Leon*;[3] and many another book, if they were in my remembrance, and many a song and many a leccherous lay: that Crist for his grete mercy foryive me the sinne. But of the translacion of Boece[4] *De Consolatione*, and othere bookes of legendes of saintes, and omelies,[5] and moralitee, and devocion, that thanke I oure Lord Jesu Crist and his blisful Moder and alle the saintes of hevene, biseeking hem that they from hennes[6] forth unto my lives ende sende me grace to biwaile my giltes and to studye to the salvacion of my soule, and graunte me grace of verray penitence, confession, and satisfaccion to doon in this present lif, thurgh the benigne grace of him that is king of kinges and preest over alle preestes, that boughte[7] us with the precious blood of his herte, so that I may been oon of hem at the day of doom that shulle be saved. *Qui cum patre et Spiritu Sancto vivis et regnas Deus per omnia saecula.*[8] *Amen.*

1386–1400

9. Compositions. "Namely": especially.
1. I.e., the *Legend of Good Women*.
2. Those that tend toward.
3. The *Book of the Lion* has not been preserved.
4. Boethius.

5. Homilies.
6. Hence.
7. Redeemed.
8. Who with the Father and the Holy Spirit livest and reignest God forever.

SIR GAWAIN AND THE GREEN KNIGHT
ca. 1375–1400

Nothing is known about the author of *Sir Gawain and the Green Knight* except that he probably wrote the three religious poems—*Pearl*, *Patience*, and *Purity*—that are preserved in the same manuscript as *Sir Gawain* (no other copies of any of the poems have come to light), and he may also have written a fifth poem that, like the others, is alliterative but is preserved in a different manuscript—a charming legend of St. Erkenwald. The dialect of *Sir Gawain* points to an origin in provincial England, about one hundred fifty miles northwest of the capital: thus of the three great poets of late medieval England, two—the authors of *Sir Gawain* and *Piers Plowman*—were representatives of cultural centers remote from the royal court at London where Geoffrey Chaucer spent his life. We know almost nothing about these provincial centers, but the works that emanated from them demonstrate a high level of culture. The poet of *Sir Gawain*, indeed, was a most sophisticated and urbane writer, and even though his language (a dialect most difficult for us today and probably difficult for Londoners in his own time) and his alliterative measure would have been considered barbaric by Chaucer's London audience, the subtlety of his perceptions and the delicacy with which he handles his narrative is worthy of Chaucer himself. And although it is impossible to date the poem with any accuracy, its author must have been an almost exact contemporary of Chaucer.

Sir Gawain ingeniously combines two plots, common in folklore and romance, although not found together elsewhere: the beheading contest, in which two parties agree to an exchange of blows with a sword or ax, and the temptation, an attempted seduction of the hero by a lady. The motif of the green man's decapitation originates in very ancient folklore, probably in a vegetation myth in which the beheading would have been a ritual death that ensured the return of spring to the earth and the regrowth of the crops. But this primitive theme has been entirely rationalized by the late medieval poet, who sees in his inherited plot an opportunity to study how successfully Gawain, as a man wholly dedicated to Christian ideals, maintains those ideals when he is subjected to unusual pressures. The poem is a rare combination: at once a comedy—even a satire—of manners and a profoundly Christian view of character and its destiny. The court of King Arthur is presented, in the most grandiose and laudatory of language, as the place where the ideal of chivalry has reached its zenith, where all is courtesy and martial prowess in defense of the right. The praise bestowed by the poet on this court may seem excessive, and indeed the sequel suggests that the author made it so intentionally. For when the court is invaded by the Green Knight, arrogant, monstrous, and yet exasperatingly reasonable, it suddenly seems to become slightly unreal, as if, the Green Knight insultingly implies, its reputation were founded more on fiction than on fact—as if the poets that celebrated it had been working harder to enhance its glory than the knights themselves. In any case, the court is to receive a testing, which is naturally entrusted to the most courteous and valiant knight of the Round Table (in this most English of Arthurian romances Gawain has not been replaced as the best of knights by the Continental-born Lancelot).

Sir Gawain's coat of arms, displayed on his shield, is the five-pointed star called the pentangle, which the poet tells us is a symbol of truth—the first of the chivalric virtues also loved by Chaucer's Knight. Truth is the quality, even more than martial courage, that is put to the test in Gawain's quest to seek out the Green Chapel where he will presumably die under the Green Knight's return blow. It is also tested, however, in the bedroom of a magical castle in the wilderness in ways that are by no means obvious to the hero—or to the reader—until the final encounter with the Green Knight.

Sir Gawain is one of the latest and certainly the best of the Middle English romances; yet its greatness lies in the fact that, without ever ceasing to be a romance, a fiction full of the most exquisite comic touches, it is something much larger, one of the really significant literary achievements of the Middle Ages.

Sir Gawain belongs to the so-called Alliterative Revival, a sudden emergence of a body of poems in the alliterative meter of Old English verse. Actually the alliterative tradition must have continued almost without interruption, but only a handful of alliterative poems survives to testify to it from the eleventh century until the revival in the latter half of the fourteenth. Although the Middle English alliterative line preserves the essential feature of Old English verse—the binding of the two halves of the line together through alliteration—it is longer and does not observe all the rules governing alliteration and stress in Old English. For details, see "Old and Middle English Prosody," (pp. 14–15). Sir Gawain is written in a unique stanza combining alliteration and rhyme. A group of long alliterative lines (the number of lines varies) concludes with a word or phrase of two syllables—the "bob"—followed by a quatrain—the "wheel"—rhyming *ababa* with the bob. The opening stanza is given below in Middle English with a literal interlinear translation. The alliterating sounds, which should be stressed in reading, have been italicized.

Sithen the *s*ege and the *a*ssaut was *s*esed at Troye,
After the siege and the assault was ceased at Troy,

The *b*orgh *b*rittened and *b*rent to *b*rondes and askes,
The city crumbled and burned to brands and ashes,

The *t*ulk that the *t*rammes of *t*resoun ther wroght
The man who the plots of treason there wrought

Was *t*ried for his *t*richerie, the *t*rewest on erthe.
Was tried for his treachery, the truest on earth.

Hit was Ennias the *a*thel and his highe kynde,
It was Aeneas the noble and his high race,

That sithen de*p*reced *p*rovinces, and *p*atrounes bicome
Who after subjugated provinces, and lords became

Welneghe of al the *w*ele in the *w*est iles.
Wellnigh of all the wealth in the west isles.

Fro *r*iche Romulus to Rome *r*icchis hym swythe,
Then noble Romulus to Rome proceeds quickly,

With gret *b*obbaunce that *b*urghe he *b*iges upon fyrst
With great pride that city he builds at first

And *n*evenes hit his aune *n*ome, as hit *n*ow hat;
And names it his own name, as it now is called;

Ticius to Tuskan and *t*eldes bigynnes,
Ticius (goes) to Tuscany and houses begins,

Langaberde in Lumbardie *l*yftes up homes,
Longbeard in Lombardy raises up homes,

And *f*er over the French *f*lod, Felix Brutus
And far over the English Channel, Felix Brutus

On mony *b*onkkes ful *b*rode Bretayn he settes
On many banks very broad Brittain he sets

> Wyth wynne,
> With joy,

Where *w*erre and *w*rake and *w*onder
Where war and revenge and wondrous happenings

Bi sythes has wont therinne,
On occasions have dwelled therein

And oft *b*othe *b*lysse and *b*lunder
And often both joy and strife

Ful skete has skyfted synne.
Very swiftly have alternated since.

Sir Gawain and the Green Knight[1]

Part 1

Since the siege and the assault was ceased at Troy,
The walls breached and burnt down to brands and ashes,
The knight that had knotted the nets of deceit

---

1. The Modern English translation is by Marie Borroff (1967), who has reproduced the alliterative meter of the original as well as the "bob" and "wheel," the five- line rhyming group that concludes each of the long irregular stanzas.

Was impeached for his perfidy, proven most true,[2]
It was high-born Aeneas and his haughty race   5
That since prevailed over provinces, and proudly reigned
Over well-nigh all the wealth of the West Isles.[3]
Great Romulus[4] to Rome repairs in haste;
With boast and with bravery builds he that city
And names it with his own name, that it now bears.   10
Ticius to Tuscany, and towers raises,
Langobard[5] in Lombardy lays out homes,
And far over the French Sea, Felix Brutus[6]
On many broad hills and high Britain he sets,
                    most fair.   15
        Where war and wrack and wonder
        By shifts have sojourned there,
        And bliss by turns with blunder
        In that land's lot had share.

And since this Britain was built by this baron great,   20
Bold boys bred there, in broils delighting,
That did in their day many a deed most dire.
More marvels have happened in this merry land
Than in any other I know, since that olden time,
But of those that here built, of British kings,   25
King Arthur was counted most courteous of all,
Wherefore an adventure I aim to unfold,
That a marvel of might some men think it,
And one unmatched among Arthur's wonders.
If you will listen to my lay but a little while,   30
As I heard it in hall, I shall hasten to tell
                    anew.
        As it was fashioned featly
        In tale of derring-do,
        And linked in measures meetly   35
        By letters tried and true.

This king lay at Camelot[7] at Christmastide;
Many good knights and gay his guests were there,
Arrayed of the Round Table[8] rightful brothers,
With feasting and fellowship and carefree mirth.   40
There true men contended in tournaments many,
Joined there in jousting these gentle knights,
Then came to the court for carol-dancing,
For the feast was in force full fifteen days,
With all the meat and the mirth that men could devise,   45
Such gaiety and glee, glorious to hear,

---

2. The treacherous knight is Aeneas, who was a traitor
to his city, Troy, according to medieval tradition, but
Aeneas was actually tried ("impeached") by the Greeks
for his refusal to hand over to them his sister Polyxena.
3. Perhaps Western Europe.
4. The legendary founder of Rome is here given Trojan ancestry, like Aeneas.
5. The reputed founder of Lombardy. "Ticius": not
otherwise known.
6. Great-grandson of Aeneas and legendary founder of
Britain; not elsewhere given the name Felix (Latin
"happy").
7. Capital of Arthur's kingdom, presumably located in
southwest England or southern Wales.
8. According to legend, Merlin made the Round Table after a dispute broke out among Arthur's knights
about precedence: it seated one hundred knights. The
table described in the poem is not round.

Brave din by day, dancing by night.
High were their hearts in halls and chambers,
These lords and these ladies, for life was sweet.
In peerless pleasures passed they their days,   50
The most noble knights known under Christ,
And the loveliest ladies that lived on earth ever,
And he the comeliest king, that that court holds,
For all this fair folk in their first age
                    were still.   55
          Happiest of mortal kind,
          King noblest famed of will;
          You would now go far to find
          So hardy a host on hill.

While the New Year was new, but yesternight come,   60
This fair folk at feast two-fold was served,
When the king and his company were come in together,
The chanting in chapel achieved and ended.
Clerics and all the court acclaimed the glad season,
Cried Noel anew, good news to men;   65
Then gallants gather gaily, hand-gifts to make,
Called them out clearly, claimed them by hand,
Bickered long and busily about those gifts.
Ladies laughed aloud, though losers they were,
And he that won was not angered, as well you will know.[9]   70
All this mirth they made until meat was served;
When they had washed them worthily, they went to their seats,
The best seated above, as best it beseemed,
Guenevere the goodly queen gay in the midst
On a dais well-decked and duly arrayed   75
With costly silk curtains, a canopy over,
Of Toulouse and Turkestan tapestries rich,
All broidered and bordered with the best gems
Ever brought into Britain, with bright pennies
                    to pay.   80
          Fair queen, without a flaw,
          She glanced with eyes of grey.
          A seemlier that once he saw,
          In truth, no man could say.

But Arthur would not eat till all were served;   85
So light was his lordly heart, and a little boyish;
His life he liked lively—the less he cared
To be lying for long, or long to sit,
So busy his young blood, his brain so wild.
And also a point of pride pricked him in heart,   90
For he nobly had willed, he would never eat
On so high a holiday, till he had heard first
Of some fair feat or fray some far-borne tale,
Of some marvel of might, that he might trust,

9. The dispensing of New Year's gifts seems to have involved kissing.

By champions of chivalry achieved in arms,   95
Or some suppliant came seeking some single knight
To join with him in jousting, in jeopardy each
To lay life for life, and leave it to fortune
To afford him on field fair hap or other.
Such is the king's custom, when his court he holds   100
At each far-famed feast amid his fair host
                             so dear.
                 The stout king stands in state
                 Till a wonder shall appear;
                 He leads, with heart elate,   105
                 High mirth in the New Year.

So he stands there in state, the stout young king,
Talking before the high table of trifles fair.
There Gawain the good knight by Guenevere sits,
With Agravain à la dure main on her other side,   110
Both knights of renown, and nephews of the king.
Bishop Baldwin above begins the table,
And Yvain, son of Urien, ate with him there.
These few with the fair queen were fittingly served;
At the side-tables[1] sat many stalwart knights.   115
Then the first course comes, with clamor of trumpets
That were bravely bedecked with bannerets bright,
With noise of new drums and the noble pipes.
Wild were the warbles that wakened that day
In strains that stirred many strong men's hearts.   120
There dainties were dealt out, dishes rare,
Choice fare to choose, on chargers so many
That scarce was there space to set before the people
The service of silver, with sundry meats,
                             on cloth.   125
                 Each fair guest freely there
                 Partakes, and nothing loth;
                 Twelve dishes before each pair;
                 Good beer and bright wine both.

Of the service itself I need say no more,   130
For well you will know no tittle was wanting.
Another noise and a new was well-nigh at hand,
That the lord might have leave his life to nourish;
For scarce were the sweet strains still in the hall,
And the first course come to that company fair,   135
There hurtles in at the hall-door an unknown rider,
One the greatest on ground in growth of his frame:
From broad neck to buttocks so bulky and thick,
And his loins and his legs so long and so great,
Half a giant on earth I hold him to be,   140
But believe him no less than the largest of men,
And that the seemliest in his stature to see, as he rides,

---

1. The side tables are on the main floor and run along the walls at a right angle with the high table, which is on a dais.

For in back and in breast though his body was grim,
His waist in its width was worthily small,
And formed with every feature in fair accord   145
                was he.
          Great wonder grew in hall
          At his hue most strange to see,
          For man and gear and all
          Were green as green could be.   150

And in guise all of green, the gear and the man:
A coat cut close, that clung to his sides,
And a mantle to match, made with a lining
Of furs cut and fitted—the fabric was noble,
Embellished all with ermine, and his hood beside,   155
That was loosed from his locks, and laid on his shoulders.
With trim hose and tight, the same tint of green,
His great calves were girt, and gold spurs under
He bore on silk bands that embellished his heels,
And footgear well-fashioned, for riding most fit.   160
And all his vesture verily was verdant green;
Both the bosses on his belt and other bright gems
That were richly ranged on his raiment noble
About himself and his saddle, set upon silk,
That to tell half the trifles would tax my wits,   165
The butterflies and birds embroidered thereon
In green of the gayest, with many a gold thread.
The pendants of the breast-band, the princely crupper,
And the bars of the bit were brightly enameled;
The stout stirrups were green, that steadied his feet,   170
And the bows of the saddle and the side-panels both,
That gleamed all and glinted with green gems about.
The steed he bestrides of that same green
               so bright.
          A green horse great and thick;   175
          A headstrong steed of might;
          In broidered bridle quick,
          Mount matched man aright.

Gay was this goodly man in guise all of green,
And the hair of his head to his horse suited;   180
Fair flowing tresses enfold his shoulders;
A beard big as a bush on his breast hangs,
That with his heavy hair, that from his head falls,
Was evened all about above both his elbows,
That half his arms thereunder were hid in the fashion   185
Of a king's cap-à-dos,[2] that covers his throat.
The mane of that mighty horse much to it like,
Well curled and becombed, and cunningly knotted
With filaments of fine gold amid the fair green,

2. The word *capados* occurs in this form in Middle English only in *Gawain*, here and in line 572. The translator has interpreted it, as the poet apparently did also, as *cap-à-dos*, i.e., a garment covering its wearer "from head to back," on the model of *cap-à-pie*, "from head to foot," referring to armor.

Here a strand of the hair, here one of gold;   190
His tail and his foretop twin in their hue,
And bound both with a band of a bright green
That was decked adown the dock with dazzling stones
And tied tight at the top with a triple knot
Where many bells well burnished rang bright and clear.   195
Such a mount in his might, nor man on him riding,
None had seen, I dare swear, with sight in that hall
                    so grand.
                    As lightning quick and light
                    He looked to all at hand;   200
                    It seemed that no man might
                    His deadly dints withstand.

Yet had he no helm, nor hauberk neither,
Nor plate, nor appurtenance appending to arms,
Nor shaft pointed sharp, nor shield for defense,   205
But in his one hand he had a holly bob
That is goodliest in green when groves are bare,
And an ax in his other, a huge and immense,
A wicked piece of work in words to expound:
The head on its haft was an ell long;   210
The spike of green steel, resplendent with gold;
The blade burnished bright, with a broad edge,
As well shaped to shear as a sharp razor;
Stout was the stave in the strong man's gripe,
That was wound all with iron to the weapon's end,   215
With engravings in green of goodliest work.
A lace lightly about, that led to a knot,
Was looped in by lengths along the fair haft,
And tassels thereto attached in a row,
With buttons of bright green, brave to behold.   220
This horseman hurtles in, and the hall enters;
Riding to the high dais, recked he no danger;
Not a greeting he gave as the guests he o'erlooked,
Nor wasted his words, but "Where is," he said,
"The captain of this crowd? Keenly I wish   225
To see that sire with sight, and to himself say
                    my say."
                    He swaggered all about
                    To scan the host so gay;
                    He halted, as if in doubt   230
                    Who in that hall held sway.

There were stares on all sides as the stranger spoke,
For much did they marvel what it might mean
That a horseman and a horse should have such a hue,
Grow green as the grass, and greener, it seemed,   235
Than green fused on gold more glorious by far.
All the onlookers eyed him, and edged nearer,
And awaited in wonder what he would do,
For many sights had they seen, but such a one never,

So that phantom and faerie the folk there deemed it,   240
Therefore chary of answer was many a champion bold,
And stunned at his strong words stone-still they sat
In a swooning silence in the stately hall.
As all were slipped into sleep, so slackened their speech
                    apace.   245
              Not all, I think, for dread,
              But some of courteous grace
              Let him who was their head
              Be spokesman in that place.

Then Arthur before the high dais that entrance beholds,   250
And hailed him, as behooved, for he had no fear,
And said "Fellow, in faith you have found fair welcome;
The head of this hostelry Arthur am I;
Leap lightly down, and linger, I pray,
And the tale of your intent you shall tell us after."   255
"Nay, so help me," said the other, "He that on high sits,
To tarry here any time, 'twas not mine errand;
But as the praise of you, prince, is puffed up so high,
And your court and your company are counted the best,
Stoutest under steel-gear on steeds to ride,   260
Worthiest of their works the wide world over,
And peerless to prove in passages of arms,
And courtesy here is carried to its height,
And so at this season I have sought you out.
You may be certain by the branch that I bear in hand   265
That I pass here in peace, and would part friends,
For had I come to this court on combat bent,
I have a hauberk at home, and a helm beside,
A shield and a sharp spear, shining bright,
And other weapons to wield, I ween well, to boot,   270
But as I willed no war, I wore no metal.
But if you be so bold as all men believe,
You will graciously grant the game that I ask
                    by right."
              Arthur answer gave   275
              And said, "Sir courteous knight,
              If contest bare you crave,
              You shall not fail to fight."

"Nay, to fight, in good faith, is far from my thought;
There are about on these benches but beardless children,   280
Were I here in full arms on a haughty steed,
For measured against mine, their might is puny.
And so I call in this court for a Christmas game,
For 'tis Yule and New Year, and many young bloods about;
If any in this house such hardihood claims,   285
Be so bold in his blood, his brain so wild,
As stoutly to strike one stroke for another,
I shall give him as my gift this gisarme noble,
This ax, that is heavy enough, to handle as he likes,

And I shall bide the first blow, as bare as I sit.   290
If there be one so wilful my words to assay,
Let him leap hither lightly, lay hold of this weapon;
I quitclaim it forever, keep it as his own,
And I shall stand him a stroke, steady on this floor,
So you grant me the guerdon to give him another,   295
     sans blame.
    In a twelvemonth and a day
    He shall have of me the same;
    Now be it seen straightway
    Who dares take up the game."   300

If he astonished them at first, stiller were then
All that household in hall, the high and the low;
The stranger on his green steed stirred in the saddle,
And roisterously his red eyes he rolled all about,
Bent his bristling brows, that were bright green,   305
Wagged his beard as he watched who would arise.
When the court kept its counsel he coughed aloud,
And cleared his throat coolly, the clearer to speak:
"What, is this Arthur's house," said that horseman then,
"Whose fame is so fair in far realms and wide?   310
Where is now your arrogance and your awesome deeds,
Your valor and your victories and your vaunting words?
Now are the revel and renown of the Round Table
Overwhelmed with a word of one man's speech,
For all cower and quake, and no cut felt!"   315
With this he laughs so loud that the lord grieved;
The blood for sheer shame shot to his face,
     and pride.
    With rage his face flushed red,
    And so did all beside.
    Then the king as bold man bred   320
    Toward the stranger took a stride.

And said "Sir, now we see you will say but folly,
Which whoso has sought, it suits that he find.
No guest here is aghast of your great words.   325
Give to me your gisarme, in God's own name,
And the boon you have begged shall straight be granted."
He leaps to him lightly, lays hold of his weapon;
The green fellow on foot fiercely alights.
Now has Arthur his ax, and the haft grips,   330
And sternly stirs it about, on striking bent.
The stranger before him stood there erect,
Higher than any in the house by a head and more;
With stern look as he stood, he stroked his beard,
And with undaunted countenance drew down his coat,   335
No more moved nor dismayed for his mighty dints
Than any bold man on bench had brought him a drink
     of wine.

Gawain by Guenevere
Toward the king doth now incline: 340
"I beseech, before all here,
That this melee may be mine."

"Would you grant me the grace," said Gawain to the king,
"To be gone from this bench and stand by you there,
If I without discourtesy might quit this board,   345
And if my liege lady misliked it not,
I would come to your counsel before your court noble.
For I find it not fit, as in faith it is known,
When such a boon is begged before all these knights,
Though you be tempted thereto, to take it on yourself   350
While so bold men about upon benches sit,
That no host under heaven is hardier of will,
Nor better brothers-in-arms where battle is joined;
I am the weakest, well I know, and of wit feeblest;
And the loss of my life would be least of any;   355
That I have you for uncle is my only praise;
My body, but for your blood, is barren of worth;
And for that this folly befits not a king,
And 'tis I that have asked it, it ought to be mine,
And if my claim be not comely let all this court judge,   360
                      in sight."
            The court assays the claim,
            And in counsel all unite
            To give Gawain the game
            And release the king outright.   365

Then the king called the knight to come to his side,
And he rose up readily, and reached him with speed,
Bows low to his lord, lays hold of the weapon,
And he releases it lightly, and lifts up his hand,
And gives him God's blessing, and graciously prays   370
That his heart and his hand may be hardy both.
"Keep, cousin," said the king, "what you cut with this day,
And if you rule it aright, then readily, I know,
You shall stand the stroke it will strike after."
Gawain goes to the guest with gisarme in hand,   375
And boldly he bides there, abashed not a whit.
Then hails he Sir Gawain, the horseman in green:
"Recount we our contract, ere you come further.
First I ask and adjure you, how you are called
That you tell me true, so that trust it I may."   380
"In good faith," said the good knight, "Gawain am I
Whose buffet befalls you, what'er betide after,
And at this time twelvemonth take from you another
With what weapon you will, and with no man else
                      alive."   385
            The other nods assent:
            "Sir Gawain, as I may thrive,

I am wondrous well content
That you this dint shall drive."

"Sir Gawain," said the Green Knight, "By God, I rejoice   390
That your fist shall fetch this favor I seek,
And you have readily rehearsed, and in right terms,
Each clause of my covenant with the king your lord,
Save that you shall assure me, sir, upon oath,
That you shall seek me yourself, wheresoever you deem   395
My lodgings may lie, and look for such wages
As you have offered me here before all this host."
"What is the way there?" said Gawain. "Where do you dwell?
I heard never of your house, by him that made me,
Nor I know you not, knight, your name nor your court.   400
But tell me truly thereof, and teach me your name,
And I shall fare forth to find you, so far as I may,
And this I say in good certain, and swear upon oath."
"That is enough in New Year, you need say no more,"
Said the knight in the green to Gawain the noble,   405
"If I tell you true, when I have taken your knock,
And if you handily have hit, you shall hear straightway
Of my house and my home and my own name;
Then follow in my footsteps by faithful accord.
And if I spend no speech, you shall speed the better: 410
You can feast with your friends, nor further trace
                              my tracks.
                    Now hold your grim tool steady
                    And show us how it hacks."
                    "Gladly, sir; all ready,"   415
                    Says Gawain; he strokes the ax.

The Green Knight upon ground girds him with care:
Bows a bit with his head, and bares his flesh:
His long lovely locks he laid over his crown,
Let the naked nape for the need be shown.   420
Gawain grips to his ax and gathers it aloft—
The left foot on the floor before him he set—
Brought it down deftly upon the bare neck,
That the shock of the sharp blow shivered the bones
And cut the flesh cleanly and clove it in twain,   425
That the blade of bright steel bit into the ground.
The head was hewn off and fell to the floor;
Many found it at their feet, as forth it rolled;
The blood gushed from the body, bright on the green,
Yet fell not the fellow, nor faltered a whit,   430
But stoutly he starts forth upon stiff shanks,
And as all stood staring he stretched forth his hand,
Laid hold of his head and heaved it aloft,
Then goes to the green steed, grasps the bridle,
Steps into the stirrup, bestrides his mount,   435
And his head by the hair in his hand holds,

And as steady he sits in the stately saddle
As he had met with no mishap, nor missing were
                         his head.
              His bulk about he haled,   440
              That fearsome body that bled;
              There were many in the court that quailed
              Before all his say was said.

For the head in his hand he holds right up;
Toward the first on the dais directs he the face,   445
And it lifted up its lids, and looked with wide eyes,
And said as much with its mouth as now you may hear:
"Sir Gawain, forget not to go as agreed,
And cease not to seek till me, sir, you find,
As you promised in the presence of these proud knights.   450
To the Green Chapel come, I charge you, to take
Such a dint as you have dealt—you have well deserved
That your neck should have a knock on New Year's morn.
The Knight of the Green Chapel I am well-known to many,
Wherefore you cannot fail to find me at last;   455
Therefore come, or be counted a recreant knight."
With a roisterous rush he flings round the reins,
Hurtles out at the hall-door, his head in his hand,
That the flint-fire flew from the flashing hooves.
Which way he went, not one of them knew   460
Nor whence he was come in the wide world
                         so fair.
              The king and Gawain gay
              Make game of the Green Knight there,
              Yet all who saw it say   465
              'Twas a wonder past compare.

Though high-born Arthur at heart had wonder,
He let no sign be seen, but said aloud
To the comely queen, with courteous speech,
"Dear dame, on this day dismay you no whit;   470
Such crafts are becoming at Christmastide,
Laughing at interludes, light songs and mirth,
Amid dancing of damsels with doughty knights.
Nevertheless of my meat now let me partake,
For I have met with a marvel, I may not deny."   475
He glanced at Sir Gawain, and gaily he said,
"Now, sir, hang up your ax,[3] that has hewn enough,"
And over the high dais it was hung on the wall
That men in amazement might on it look,
And tell in true terms the tale of the wonder.   480
Then they turned toward the table, these two together,
The good king and Gawain, and made great feast,
With all dainties double, dishes rare,

---

3. A colloquial expression equivalent to "bury the hatchet," but here with an appropriate literal sense also.

With all manner of meat and minstrelsy both,
Such happiness wholly had they that day   485
                         in hold.
                    Now take care, Sir Gawain,
                    That your courage wax not cold
                    When you must turn again
                    To your enterprise foretold.   490

Part 2

This adventure had Arthur of handsels[4] first
When young was the year, for he yearned to hear tales;
Though they wanted for words when they went to sup,
Now are fierce deeds to follow, their fists stuffed full.
Gawain was glad to begin those games in hall,   495
But if the end be harsher, hold it no wonder,
For though men are merry in mind after much drink,
A year passes apace, and proves ever new:
First things and final conform but seldom.
And so this Yule to the young year yielded place,   500
And each season ensued at its set time;
After Christmas there came the cold cheer of Lent,
When with fish and plainer fare our flesh we reprove;
But then the world's weather with winter contends:
The keen cold lessens, the low clouds lift;   505
Fresh falls the rain in fostering showers
On the face of the fields; flowers appear.
The ground and the groves wear gowns of green;
Birds build their nests, and blithely sing
That solace of all sorrow with summer comes   510
                         ere long.
                    And blossoms day by day
                    Bloom rich and rife in throng;
                    Then every grove so gay
                    Of the greenwood rings with song.   515

And then the season of summer with the soft winds,
When Zephyr sighs low over seeds and shoots;
Glad is the green plant growing abroad,
When the dew at dawn drops from the leaves,
To get a gracious glance from the golden sun.   520
But harvest with harsher winds follows hard after,
Warns him to ripen well ere winter comes;
Drives forth the dust in the droughty season,
From the face of the fields to fly high in air.
Wroth winds in the welkin wrestle with the sun,   525
The leaves launch from the linden and light on the ground,
And the grass turns to gray, that once grew green.
Then all ripens and rots that rose up at first,

---

4. New Year's presents.

And so the year moves on in yesterdays many,
And winter once more, by the world's law,   530
     draws nigh.
    At Michaelmas[5] the moon
    Hangs wintry pale in sky;
    Sir Gawain girds him soon
    For travails yet to try.   535

Till All-Hallows' Day[6] with Arthur he dwells,
And he held a high feast to honor that knight
With great revels and rich, of the Round Table.
Then ladies lovely and lords debonair
With sorrow for Sir Gawain were sore at heart;   540
Yet they covered their care with countenance glad:
Many a mournful man made mirth for his sake.
So after supper soberly he speaks to his uncle
Of the hard hour at hand, and openly says,
"Now, liege lord of my life, my leave I take;   545
The terms of this task too well you know—
To count the cost over concerns me nothing.
But I am bound forth betimes to bear a stroke
From the grim man in green, as God may direct."
Then the first and foremost came forth in throng: 550
Yvain and Eric and others of note,
Sir Dodinal le Sauvage, the Duke of Clarence,
Lionel and Lancelot and Lucan the good,
Sir Bors and Sir Bedivere, big men both,
And many manly knights more, with Mador de la Porte.   555
All this courtly company comes to the king
To counsel their comrade, with care in their hearts;
There was much secret sorrow suffered that day
That one so good as Gawain must go in such wise
To bear a bitter blow, and his bright sword   560
     lay by.
    He said, "Why should I tarry?"
    And smiled with tranquil eye;
    "In destinies sad or merry,
    True men can but try."   565

He dwelt there all that day, and dressed in the morning;
Asked early for his arms, and all were brought.
First a carpet of rare cost was cast on the floor
Where much goodly gear gleamed golden bright;
He takes his place promptly and picks up the steel,   570
Attired in a tight coat of Turkestan silk
And a kingly cap-à-dos, closed at the throat,
That was lavishly lined with a lustrous fur.
Then they set the steel shoes on his sturdy feet
And clad his calves about with comely greaves,   575

---

5. September 29.   6. All Saints' Day, November 1.

And plate well-polished protected his knees,
Affixed with fastenings of the finest gold.
Fair cuisses enclosed, that were cunningly wrought,
His thick-thewed thighs, with thongs bound fast,
And massy chain-mail of many a steel ring   580
He bore on his body, above the best cloth,
With brace burnished bright upon both his arms,
Good couters and gay, and gloves of plate,
And all the goodly gear to grace him well
                              that tide.   585
              His surcoat blazoned bold;
              Sharp spurs to prick with pride;
              And a brave silk band to hold
              The broadsword at his side.

When he had on his arms, his harness was rich,   590
The least latchet or loop laden with gold;
So armored as he was, he heard a mass,
Honored God humbly at the high altar.
Then he comes to the king and his comrades-in-arms,
Takes his leave at last of lords and ladies,   595
And they clasped and kissed him, commending him to Christ.
By then Gringolet was girt with a great saddle
That was gaily agleam with fine gilt fringe,
New-furbished for the need with nail-heads bright;
The bridle and the bars bedecked all with gold;   600
The breast-plate, the saddlebow, the side-panels both,
The caparison and the crupper accorded in hue,
And all ranged on the red the resplendent studs
That glittered and glowed like the glorious sun.
His helm now he holds up and hastily kisses,   605
Well-closed with iron clinches, and cushioned within;
It was high on his head, with a hasp behind,
And a covering of cloth to encase the visor,
All bound and embroidered with the best gems
On broad bands of silk, and bordered with birds,   610
Parrots and popinjays preening their wings,
Lovebirds and love-knots as lavishly wrought
As many women had worked seven winters thereon,
                              entire.
              The diadem costlier yet   615
              That crowned that comely sire,
              With diamonds richly set,
              That flashed as if on fire.

Then they showed forth the shield, that shone all red,
With the pentangle[7] portrayed in purest gold.   620
About his broad neck by the baldric he casts it,
That was meet for the man, and matched him well.
And why the pentangle is proper to that peerless prince

7. A five-pointed star, formed by five lines that are drawn without lifting the pencil from the paper, supposed to
have mystical significance; as Solomon's sign (line 625) it was enclosed in a circle.

I intend now to tell, though detain me it must.
It is a sign by Solomon sagely devised   625
To be a token of truth, by its title of old,
For it is a figure formed of five points,
And each line is linked and locked with the next
For ever and ever, and hence it is called
In all England, as I hear, the endless knot.   630
And well may he wear it on his worthy arms,
For ever faithful five-fold in five-fold fashion
Was Gawain in good works, as gold unalloyed,
Devoid of all villainy, with virtues adorned
                              in sight.   635
          On shield and coat in view
          He bore that emblem bright,
          As to his word most true
          And in speech most courteous knight.

And first, he was faultless in his five senses,   640
Nor found ever to fail in his five fingers,
And all his fealty was fixed upon the five wounds
That Christ got on the cross, as the creed tells;
And wherever this man in melee took part,
His one thought was of this, past all things else,   645
That all his force was founded on the five joys[8]
That the high Queen of heaven had in her child.
And therefore, as I find, he fittingly had
On the inner part of his shield her image portrayed,
That when his look on it lighted, he never lost heart.   650
The fifth of the five fives followed by this knight
Were beneficence boundless and brotherly love
And pure mind and manners, that none might impeach,
And compassion most precious—these peerless five
Were forged and made fast in him, foremost of men.   655
Now all these five fives were confirmed in this knight,
And each linked in other, that end there was none,
And fixed to five points, whose force never failed,
Nor assembled all on a side, nor asunder either,
Nor anywhere at an end, but whole and entire   660
However the pattern proceeded or played out its course.
And so on his shining shield shaped was the knot
Royally in red gold against red gules,
That is the peerless pentangle, prized of old
                              in lore.   665
               Now armed is Gawain gay,
               And bears his lance before,
               And soberly said good day,
               He thought forevermore.

He struck his steed with the spurs and sped on his way   670
So fast that the flint-fire flashed from the stones.

8. The Annunciation, Nativity, Resurrection, Ascension, and Assumption.

When they saw him set forth they were sore aggrieved,
And all sighed softly, and said to each other,
Fearing for their fellow, "Ill fortune it is
That you, man, must be marred, that most are worthy!   675
His equal on this earth can hardly be found;
To have dealt more discreetly had done less harm,
And have dubbed him a duke, with all due honor.
A great leader of lords he was like to become,
And better so to have been than battered to bits,   680
Beheaded by an elf-man,[9] for empty pride!
Who would credit that a king could be counseled so,
And caught in a cavil in a Christmas game?"
Many were the warm tears they wept from their eyes
When goodly Sir Gawain was gone from the court   685
          that day.
     No longer he abode,
     But speedily went his way
     Over many a wandering road,
     As I heard my author say.   690

Now he rides in his array through the realm of Logres,[1]
Sir Gawain, God knows, though it gave him small joy!
All alone must he lodge through many a long night
Where the food that he fancied was far from his plate;
He had no mate but his mount, over mountain and plain,   695
Nor man to say his mind to but almighty God,
Till he had wandered well-nigh into North Wales.
All the islands of Anglesey he holds on his left,
And follows, as he fares, the fords by the coast,
Comes over at Holy Head, and enters next   700
The Wilderness of Wirral[2]—few were within
That had great good will toward God or man.
And earnestly he asked of each mortal he met
If he had ever heard aught of a knight all green,
Or of a Green Chapel, on ground thereabouts,   705
And all said the same, and solemnly swore
They saw no such knight all solely green
          in hue.
     Over country wild and strange
     The knight sets off anew;   710
     Often his course must change
     Ere the Chapel comes in view.

Many a cliff must he climb in country wild;
Far off from all his friends, forlorn must he ride;
At each strand or stream where the stalwart passed   715
'Twere a marvel if he met not some monstrous foe,
And that so fierce and forbidding that fight he must.

9. Supernatural being.
1. One of the names for Arthur's kingdom.
2. Gawain went from Camelot north to the northern
coast of Wales, opposite the islands of Anglesey; there
he turned east across the Dee to the forest of Wirral in
Cheshire.

So many were the wonders he wandered among
That to tell but the tenth part would tax my wits.
Now with serpents he wars, now with savage wolves,   720
Now with wild men of the woods, that watched from the rocks,
Both with bulls and with bears, and with boars besides,
And giants that came gibbering from the jagged steeps.
Had he not borne himself bravely, and been on God's side,
He had met with many mishaps and mortal harms.   725
And if the wars were unwelcome, the winter was worse,
When the cold clear rains rushed from the clouds
And froze before they could fall to the frosty earth.
Near slain by the sleet he sleeps in his irons
More nights than enough, among naked rocks,   730
Where clattering from the crest the cold stream ran
And hung in hard icicles high overhead.
Thus in peril and pain and predicaments dire
He rides across country till Christmas Eve,
                    our knight.   735
            And at that holy tide
            He prays with all his might
            That Mary may be his guide
            Till a dwelling comes in sight.

By a mountain next morning he makes his way   740
Into a forest fastness, fearsome and wild;
High hills on either hand, with hoar woods below,
Oaks old and huge by the hundred together.
The hazel and the hawthorn were all intertwined
With rough raveled moss, that raggedly hung,   745
With many birds unblithe upon bare twigs
That peeped most piteously for pain of the cold.
The good knight on Gringolet glides thereunder
Through many a marsh and mire, a man all alone;
He feared for his default, should he fail to see   750
The service of that Sire that on that same night
Was born of a bright maid, to bring us his peace.
And therefore sighing he said, "I beseech of Thee, Lord,
And Mary, thou mildest mother so dear,
Some harborage where haply I might hear mass   755
And Thy matins tomorrow—meekly I ask it,
And thereto proffer and pray my pater and ave
                    and creed."
            He said his prayer with sighs,
            Lamenting his misdeed;   760
            He crosses himself, and cries
            On Christ in his great need.

No sooner had Sir Gawain signed himself thrice
Than he was ware, in the wood, of a wondrous dwelling,
Within a moat, on a mound, bright amid boughs   765
Of many a tree great of girth that grew by the water—

A castle as comely as a knight could own,
On grounds fair and green, in a goodly park
With a palisade of palings planted about
For two miles and more, round many a fair tree.   770
The stout knight stared at that stronghold great
As it shimmered and shone amid shining leaves,
Then with helmet in hand he offers his thanks
To Jesus and Saint Julian,[3] that are gentle both,
That in courteous accord had inclined to his prayer;   775
"Now fair harbor," said he, "I humbly beseech!"
Then he pricks his proud steed with the plated spurs,
And by chance he has chosen the chief path
That brought the bold knight to the bridge's end
                   in haste.   780
         The bridge hung high in air;
         The gates were bolted fast;
         The walls well-framed to bear
         The fury of the blast.

The man on his mount remained on the bank   785
Of the deep double moat that defended the place.
The wall went in the water wondrous deep,
And a long way aloft it loomed overhead.
It was built of stone blocks to the battlements' height,
With corbels under cornices in comeliest style;   790
Watch-towers trusty protected the gate,
With many a lean loophole, to look from within:
A better-made barbican the knight beheld never.
And behind it there hoved a great hall and fair:
Turrets rising in tiers, with tines[4] at their tops,   795
Spires set beside them, splendidly long,
With finials[5] well-fashioned, as filigree fine.
Chalk-white chimneys over chambers high
Gleamed in gay array upon gables and roofs;
The pinnacles in panoply, pointing in air,   800
So vied there for his view that verily it seemed
A castle cut of paper for a king's feast.[6]
The good knight on Gringolet thought it great luck
If he could but contrive to come there within
To keep the Christmas feast in that castle fair   805
                 and bright.
         There answered to his call
         A porter most polite;
         From his station on the wall
         He greets the errant knight.   810

"Good sir," said Gawain, "Wouldst go to inquire
If your lord would allow me to lodge here a space?"
"Peter!" said the porter, "For my part, I think

---

3. Patron saint of hospitality.   5. Gable ornaments.
4. Spikes.   6. A common table decoration at feasts.

So noble a knight will not want for a welcome!"
Then he bustles off briskly, and comes back straight,   815
And many servants beside, to receive him the better.
They let down the drawbridge and duly went forth
And kneeled down on their knees on the naked earth
To welcome this warrior as best they were able.
They proffered him passage—the portals stood wide—   820
And he beckoned them to rise, and rode over the bridge.
Men steadied his saddle as he stepped to the ground,
And there stabled his steed many stalwart folk.
Now come the knights and the noble squires
To bring him with bliss into the bright hall.   825
When his high helm was off, there hied forth a throng
Of attendants to take it, and see to its care;
They bore away his brand[7] and his blazoned shield;
Then graciously he greeted those gallants each one,
And many a noble drew near, to do the knight honor.   830
All in his armor into hall he was led,
Where fire on a fair hearth fiercely blazed.
And soon the lord himself descends from his chamber
To meet with good manners the man on his floor.
He said, "To this house you are heartily welcome: 835
What is here is wholly yours, to have in your power
                    and sway."
            "Many thanks," said Sir Gawain;
            "May Christ your pains repay!"
            The two embrace amain   840
            As men well met that day.

Gawain gazed on the host that greeted him there,
And a lusty fellow he looked, the lord of that place:
A man of massive mold, and of middle age;
Broad, bright was his beard, of a beaver's hue,   845
Strong, steady his stance, upon stalwart shanks,
His face fierce as fire, fair-spoken withal,
And well-suited he seemed in Sir Gawain's sight
To be a master of men in a mighty keep.
They pass into a parlor, where promptly the host   850
Has a servant assigned him to see to his needs,
And there came upon his call many courteous folk
That brought him to a bower where bedding was noble,
With heavy silk hangings hemmed all in gold,
Coverlets and counterpanes curiously wrought,   855
A canopy over the couch, clad all with fur,
Curtains running on cords, caught to gold rings,
Woven rugs on the walls of eastern work,
And the floor, under foot, well-furnished with the same.
Amid light talk and laughter they loosed from him then   860
His war-dress of weight and his worthy clothes.
Robes richly wrought they brought him right soon,
To change there in chamber and choose what he would.

7. Sword.

When he had found one he fancied, and flung it about,
Well-fashioned for his frame, with flowing skirts,   865
His face fair and fresh as the flowers of spring,
All the good folk agreed, that gazed on him then,
His limbs arrayed royally in radiant hues,
That so comely a mortal never Christ made
                    as he.   870
            Whatever his place of birth,
            It seemed he well might be
            Without a peer on earth
            In martial rivalry.

A couch before the fire, where fresh coals burned,   875
They spread for Sir Gawain splendidly now
With quilts quaintly stitched, and cushions beside,
And then a costly cloak they cast on his shoulders
Of bright silk, embroidered on borders and hems,
With furs of the finest well-furnished within,   880
And bound about with ermine, both mantle and hood;
And he sat at that fireside in sumptuous estate
And warmed himself well, and soon he waxed merry.
Then attendants set a table upon trestles broad,
And lustrous white linen they laid thereupon,   885
A saltcellar of silver, spoons of the same.
He washed himself well and went to his place,
Men set his fare before him in fashion most fit.
There were soups of all sorts, seasoned with skill,
Double-sized servings, and sundry fish,   890
Some baked, some breaded, some broiled on the coals,
Some simmered, some in stews, steaming with spice,
And with sauces to sup that suited his taste.
He confesses it a feast with free words and fair;
They requite him as kindly with courteous jests,   895
                    well-sped.
            "Tonight you fast[8] and pray;
            Tomorrow we'll see you fed."
            The knight grows wondrous gay
            As the wine goes to his head.   900

Then at times and by turns, as at table he sat,
They questioned him quietly, with queries discreet,
And he courteously confessed that he comes from the court,
And owns him of the brotherhood of high-famed Arthur,
The right royal ruler of the Round Table,   905
And the guest by their fireside is Gawain himself,
Who has happened on their house at that holy feast.
When the name of the knight was made known to the lord,
Then loudly he laughed, so elated he was,
And the men in that household made haste with joy   910
To appear in his presence promptly that day,

8. Gawain is said to be "fasting" because the meal, although elaborate, consisted only of fish dishes, appropriate
to a fasting day.

That of courage ever-constant, and customs pure,
Is pattern and paragon, and praised without end:
Of all knights on earth most honored is he.
Each said solemnly aside to his brother,   915
"Now displays of deportment shall dazzle our eyes
And the polished pearls of impeccable speech;
The high art of eloquence is ours to pursue
Since the father of fine manners is found in our midst.
Great is God's grace, and goodly indeed,   920
That a guest such as Gawain he guides to us here
When men sit and sing of their Savior's birth
                          in view.
          With command of manners pure
          He shall each heart imbue;   925
          Who shares his converse, sure,
          Shall learn love's language true."

When the knight had done dining and duly arose,
The dark was drawing on; the day nigh ended.
Chaplains in chapels and churches about   930
Rang the bells aright, reminding all men
Of the holy evensong of the high feast.
The lord attends alone: his fair lady sits
In a comely closet, secluded from sight.
Gawain in gay attire goes thither soon;   935
The lord catches his coat, and calls him by name,
And has him sit beside him, and says in good faith
No guest on God's earth would he gladlier greet.
For that Gawain thanked him; the two then embraced
And sat together soberly the service through.   940
Then the lady, that longed to look on the knight,
Came forth from her closet with her comely maids.
The fair hues of her flesh, her face and her hair
And her body and her bearing were beyond praise,
And excelled the queen herself, as Sir Gawain thought.   945
He goes forth to greet her with gracious intent;
Another lady led her by the left hand
That was older than she—an ancient, it seemed,
And held in high honor by all men about.
But unlike to look upon, those ladies were,   950
For if the one was fresh, the other was faded:
Bedecked in bright red was the body of one;
Flesh hung in folds on the face of the other;
On one a high headdress, hung all with pearls;
Her bright throat and bosom fair to behold,   955
Fresh as the first snow fallen upon hills;
A wimple the other one wore round her throat;
Her swart chin well swaddled, swathed all in white;
Her forehead enfolded in flounces of silk
That framed a fair fillet, of fashion ornate,   960
And nothing bare beneath save the black brows,
The two eyes and the nose, the naked lips,

And they unsightly to see, and sorrily bleared.
A beldame, by God, she may well be deemed,
                              of pride!   965
          She was short and thick of waist,
          Her buttocks round and wide;
          More toothsome, to his taste,
          Was the beauty by her side.

When Gawain had gazed on that gay lady,   970
With leave of her lord, he politely approached;
To the elder in homage he humbly bows;
The lovelier he salutes with a light embrace.
He claims a comely kiss, and courteously he speaks;
They welcome him warmly, and straightway he asks   975
To be received as their servant, if they so desire.
They take him between them; with talking they bring him
Beside a bright fire; bade then that spices
Be freely fetched forth, to refresh them the better,
And the good wine therewith, to warm their hearts.   980
The lord leaps about in light-hearted mood;
Contrives entertainments and timely sports;
Takes his hood from his head and hangs it on a spear,
And offers him openly the honor thereof
Who should promote the most mirth at that Christmas feast;   985
"And I shall try for it, trust me—contend with the best,
Ere I go without my headgear by grace of my friends!"
Thus with light talk and laughter the lord makes merry
To gladden the guest he had greeted in hall
                              that day.   990
          At the last he called for light
          The company to convey;
          Gawain says goodnight
          And retires to bed straightway.

On the morn when each man is mindful in heart   995
That God's son was sent down to suffer our death,
No household but is blithe for his blessed sake;
So was it there on that day, with many delights.
Both at larger meals and less they were lavishly served
By doughty lads on dais, with delicate fare;   1000
The old ancient lady, highest she sits;
The lord at her left hand leaned, as I hear;
Sir Gawain in the center, beside the gay lady,
Where the food was brought first to that festive board,
And thence throughout the hall, as they held most fit,   1005
To each man was offered in order of rank.
There was meat, there was mirth, there was much joy,
That to tell all the tale would tax my wits,
Though I pained me, perchance, to paint it with care;
But yet I know that our knight and the noble lady   1010
Were accorded so closely in company there,
With the seemly solace of their secret words,

With speeches well-sped, spotless and pure,
That each prince's pastime their pleasures far
                      outshone.   1015
          Sweet pipes beguile their cares,
          And the trumpet of martial tone;
          Each tends his affairs
          And those two tend their own.

That day and all the next, their disport was noble,   1020
And the third day, I think, pleased them no less;
The joys of St. John's Day[9] were justly praised,
And were the last of their like for those lords and ladies;
Then guests were to go in the gray morning,
Wherefore they whiled the night away with wine and with mirth,   1025
Moved to the measures of many a blithe carol;
At last, when it was late, took leave of each other,
Each one of those worthies, to wend his way.
Gawain bids goodbye to his goodly host
Who brings him to his chamber, the chimney beside,   1030
And detains him in talk, and tenders his thanks
And holds it an honor to him and his people
That he has harbored in his house at that holy time
And embellished his abode with his inborn grace.
"As long as I may live, my luck is the better   1035
That Gawain was my guest at God's own feast!"
"Noble sir," said the knight, "I cannot but think
All the honor is your own—may heaven requite it!
And your man to command I account myself here
As I am bound and beholden, and shall be, come   1040
              what may."
          The lord with all his might
          Entreats his guest to stay;
          Brief answer makes the knight:
          Next morning he must away.   1045

Then the lord of that land politely inquired
What dire affair had forced him, at that festive time,
So far from the king's court to fare forth alone
Ere the holidays wholly had ended in hall.
"In good faith," said Gawain, "you have guessed the truth: 1050
On a high errand and urgent I hastened away,
For I am summoned by myself to seek for a place—
I would I knew whither, or where it might be!
Far rather would I find it before the New Year
Than own the land of Logres, so help me our Lord!   1055
Wherefore, sir, in friendship this favor I ask,
That you say in sober earnest, if something you know
Of the Green Chapel, on ground far or near,
Or the lone knight that lives there, of like hue of green.
A certain day was set by assent of us both

9. December 27.

To meet at that landmark, if I might last,
And from now to the New Year is nothing too long,
And I would greet the Green Knight there, would God but allow,
More gladly, by God's Son, than gain the world's wealth!
And I must set forth to search, as soon as I may;   1065
To be about the business I have but three days
And would as soon sink down dead as desist from my errand."
Then smiling said the lord, "Your search, sir, is done,
For we shall see you to that site by the set time.
Let Gawain grieve no more over the Green Chapel;   1070
You shall be in your own bed, in blissful ease,
All the forenoon, and fare forth the first of the year,
And make the goal by midmorn, to mind your affairs,
                              no fear!
            Tarry till the fourth day   1075
            And ride on the first of the year.
            We shall set you on your way;
            It is not two miles from here."

Then Gawain was glad, and gleefully he laughed:
"Now I thank you for this, past all things else!   1080
Now my goal is here at hand! With a glad heart I shall
Both tarry, and undertake any task you devise."
Then the host seized his arm and seated him there;
Let the ladies be brought, to delight them the better,
And in fellowship fair by the fireside they sit;   1085
So gay waxed the good host, so giddy his words,
All waited in wonder what next he would say.
Then he stares on the stout knight, and sternly he speaks:
"You have bound yourself boldly my bidding to do—
Will you stand by that boast, and obey me this once?"   1090
"I shall do so indeed," said the doughty knight;
"While I lie in your lodging, your laws will I follow."
"As you have had," said the host, "many hardships abroad
And little sleep of late, you are lacking, I judge,
Both in nourishment needful and nightly rest;   1095
You shall lie abed late in your lofty chamber
Tomorrow until mass, and meet then to dine
When you will, with my wife, who will sit by your side
And talk with you at table, the better to cheer
                              our guest.   1100
            A-hunting I will go
            While you lie late and rest."
            The knight, inclining low,
            Assents to each behest.

"And Gawain," said the good host, "agree now to this: 1105
Whatever I win in the woods I will give you at eve,
And all you have earned you must offer to me;
Swear now, sweet friend, to swap as I say,
Whether hands, in the end, be empty or better."

"By God," said Sir Gawain, "I grant it forthwith!   1110
If you find the game good, I shall gladly take part."
"Let the bright wine be brought, and our bargain is done,"
Said the lord of that land—the two laughed together.
Then they drank and they dallied and doffed all constraint,
These lords and these ladies, as late as they chose,   1115
And then with gaiety and gallantries and graceful adieux
They talked in low tones, and tarried at parting.
With compliments comely they kiss at the last;
There were brisk lads about with blazing torches
To see them safe to bed, for soft repose   1120
     long due.
    Their covenants, yet awhile,
    They repeat, and pledge anew;
    That lord could well beguile
    Men's hearts, with mirth in view.   1125

Part 3

Long before daylight they left their beds;
Guests that wished to go gave word to their grooms,
And they set about briskly to bind on saddles,
Tend to their tackle, tie up trunks.
The proud lords appear, appareled to ride,   1130
Leap lightly astride, lay hold of their bridles,
Each one on his way to his worthy house.
The liege lord of the land was not the last
Arrayed there to ride, with retainers many;
He had a bite to eat when he had heard mass;   1135
With horn to the hills he hastens amain.
By the dawn of that day over the dim earth,
Master and men were mounted and ready.
Then they harnessed in couples the keen-scented hounds,
Cast wide the kennel-door and called them forth,   1140
Blew upon their bugles bold blasts three;
The dogs began to bay with a deafening din,
And they quieted them quickly and called them to heel,
A hundred brave huntsmen, as I have heard tell,
     together.   1145
    Men at stations meet;
    From the hounds they slip the tether;
    The echoing horns repeat,
    Clear in the merry weather.

At the clamor of the quest, the quarry trembled;   1150
Deer dashed through the dale, dazed with dread;
Hastened to the high ground, only to be
Turned back by the beaters, who boldly shouted.
They harmed not the harts, with their high heads,
Let the bucks go by, with their broad antlers,   1155
For it was counted a crime, in the close season,

If a man of that demesne should molest the male deer.
The hinds were headed up, with "Hey!" and "Ware!"
The does with great din were driven to the valleys.
Then you were ware, as they went, of the whistling of arrows;   1160
At each bend under boughs the bright shafts flew
That tore the tawny hide with their tapered heads.
Ah! they bray and they bleed, on banks they die,
And ever the pack pell-mell comes panting behind;
Hunters with shrill horns hot on their heels—   1165
Like the cracking of cliffs their cries resounded.
What game got away from the gallant archers
Was promptly picked off at the posts below
When they were harried on the heights and herded to the streams:
The watchers were so wary at the waiting-stations,   1170
And the greyhounds so huge, that eagerly snatched,
And finished them off as fast as folk could see
                         with sight.
            The lord, now here, now there,
            Spurs forth in sheer delight.   1175
            And drives, with pleasures rare,
            The day to the dark night.

So the lord in the linden-wood leads the hunt
And Gawain the good knight in gay bed lies,
Lingered late alone, till daylight gleamed   1180
Under coverlet costly, curtained about.
And as he slips into slumber, slyly there comes
A little din at his door, and the latch lifted,
And he holds up his heavy head out of the clothes;
A corner of the curtain he caught back a little   1185
And waited there warily, to see what befell.
Lo! it was the lady, loveliest to behold,
That drew the door behind her deftly and still
And was bound for his bed—abashed was the knight,
And laid his head low again in likeness of sleep;   1190
And she stepped stealthily, and stole to his bed,
Cast aside the curtain and came within,
And set herself softly on the bedside there,
And lingered at her leisure, to look on his waking.
The fair knight lay feigning for a long while,   1195
Conning in his conscience what his case might
Mean or amount to—a marvel he thought it.
But yet he said within himself, "More seemly it were
To try her intent by talking a little."
So he started and stretched, as startled from sleep,   1200
Lifts wide his lids in likeness of wonder,
And signs himself swiftly, as safer to be,
                         with art.
            Sweetly does she speak
            And kindling glances dart,   1205
            Blent white and red on cheek
            And laughing lips apart.

"Good morning, Sir Gawain," said that gay lady,
"A slack sleeper you are, to let one slip in!
Now you are taken in a trice—a truce we must make,   1210
Or I shall bind you in your bed, of that be assured."
Thus laughing lightly that lady jested.
"Good morning, good lady," said Gawain the blithe,
"Be it with me as you will; I am well content!
For I surrender myself, and sue for your grace,   1215
And that is best, I believe, and behooves me now."
Thus jested in answer that gentle knight.
"But if, lovely lady, you misliked it not,
And were pleased to permit your prisoner to rise,
I should quit this couch and accoutre me better,   1220
And be clad in more comfort for converse here."
"Nay, not so, sweet sir," said the smiling lady;
"You shall not rise from your bed; I direct you better:
I shall hem and hold you on either hand,
And keep company awhile with my captive knight.   1225
For as certain as I sit here, Sir Gawain you are,
Whom all the world worships, whereso you ride;
Your honor, your courtesy are highest acclaimed
By lords and by ladies, by all living men;
And lo! we are alone here, and left to ourselves: 1230
My lord and his liegemen are long departed,
The household asleep, my handmaids too,
The door drawn, and held by a well-driven bolt,
And since I have in this house him whom all love,
I shall while the time away with mirthful speech   1235
                    at will.
          My body is here at hand,
          Your each wish to fulfill;
          Your servant to command
          I am, and shall be still."   1240

"In good faith," said Gawain, "my gain is the greater,
Though I am not he of whom you have heard;
To arrive at such reverence as you recount here
I am one all unworthy, and well do I know it.
By heaven, I would hold me the happiest of men   1245
If by word or by work I once might aspire
To the prize of your praise—'twere a pure joy!"
"In good faith, Sir Gawain," said that gay lady,
"The well-proven prowess that pleases all others,
Did I scant or scout it, 'twere scarce becoming.   1250
But there are ladies, believe me, that had liefer far
Have thee here in their hold, as I have today,
To pass an hour in pastime with pleasant words,
Assuage all their sorrows and solace their hearts,
Than much of the goodly gems and gold they possess.   1255
But laud be to the Lord of the lofty skies,
For here in my hands all hearts' desire
                    doth lie."

Great welcome got he there
From the lady who sat him by;   1260
With fitting speech and fair
The good knight makes reply.

"Madame," said the merry man, "Mary reward you!
For in good faith, I find your beneficence noble.
And the fame of fair deeds runs far and wide,   1265
But the praise you report pertains not to me,
But comes of your courtesy and kindness of heart."
"By the high Queen of heaven" (said she) "I count it not so,
For were I worth all the women in this world alive,
And all wealth and all worship were in my hands,   1270
And I should hunt high and low, a husband to take,
For the nurture I have noted in thee, knight, here,
The comeliness and courtesies and courtly mirth—
And so I had ever heard, and now hold it true—
No other on this earth should have me for wife."   1275
"You are bound to a better man," the bold knight said,
"Yet I prize the praise you have proffered me here,
And soberly your servant, my sovereign I hold you,
And acknowledge me your knight, in the name of Christ."
So they talked of this and that until 'twas nigh noon,   1280
And ever the lady languishing in likeness of love.
With feat words and fair he framed his defense,
For were she never so winsome, the warrior had
The less will to woo, for the wound that his bane
                              must be.   1285
        He must bear the blinding blow,
        For such is fate's decree:
        The lady asks leave to go;
        He grants it full and free.

Then she gaily said goodbye, and glanced at him, laughing,   1290
And as she stood, she astonished him with a stern speech:
"Now may the Giver of all good words these glad hours repay!
But our guest is not Gawain—forgot is that thought."
"How so?" said the other, and asks in some haste,
For he feared he had been at fault in the forms of his speech.   1295
But she held up her hand, and made answer thus:
"So good a knight as Gawain is given out to be,
And the model of fair demeanor and manners pure,
Had he lain so long at a lady's side,
Would have claimed a kiss, by his courtesy,   1300
Through some touch or trick of phrase at some tale's end."
Said Gawain, "Good lady, I grant it at once!
I shall kiss at your command, as becomes a knight,
And more, lest you mislike, so let be, I pray."
With that she turns toward him, takes him in her arms,   1305
Leans down her lovely head, and lo! he is kissed.
They commend each other to Christ with comely words,
He sees her forth safely, in silence they part,

And then he lies no later in his lofty bed,
But calls to his chamberlain, chooses his clothes,   1310
Goes in those garments gladly to mass,
Then takes his way to table, where attendants wait,
And made merry all day, till the moon rose
                              in view
                    Was never knight beset   1315
                    'Twixt worthier ladies two:
                    The crone and the coquette;
                    Fair pastimes they pursue.

And the lord of the land rides late and long,
Hunting the barren hind over the broad heath.   1320
He had slain such a sum, when the sun sank low,
Of does and other deer, as would dizzy one's wits.
Then they trooped in together in triumph at last,
And the count of the quarry quickly they take.
The lords lent a hand with their liegemen many,   1325
Picked out the plumpest and put them together
And duly dressed the deer, as the deed requires.
Some were assigned the assay of the fat:
Two fingers' width fully they found on the leanest.
Then they slit the slot open and searched out the paunch,   1330
Trimmed it with trencher-knives and tied it up tight.
They flayed the fair hide from the legs and trunk,
Then broke open the belly and laid bare the bowels,
Deftly detaching and drawing them forth.
And next at the neck they neatly parted   1335
The weasand[1] from the windpipe, and cast away the guts.
At the shoulders with sharp blades they showed their skill,
Boning them from beneath, lest the sides be marred;
They breached the broad breast and broke it in twain,
And again at the gullet they begin with their knives,   1340
Cleave down the carcass clear to the breach;
Two tender morsels they take from the throat,
Then round the inner ribs they rid off a layer
And carve out the kidney-fat, close to the spine,
Hewing down to the haunch, that all hung together,   1345
And held it up whole, and hacked it free,
And this they named the numbles,[2] that knew such terms
                              of art.
                    They divide the crotch in two,
                    And straightway then they start   1350
                    To cut the backbone through
                    And cleave the trunk apart.

With hard strokes they hewed off the head and the neck,
Then swiftly from the sides they severed the chine,
And the corbie's bone[3] they cast on a branch.   1355

---

1. Esophagus.   3. A bit of gristle assigned to the ravens ("corbies").
2. The other internal organs.

Then they pierced the plump sides, impaled either one
With the hock of the hind foot, and hung it aloft,
To each person his portion most proper and fit.
On a hide of a hind the hounds they fed
With the liver and the lights,[4] the leathery paunches,   1360
And bread soaked in blood well blended therewith.
High horns and shrill set hounds a-baying,
Then merrily with their meat they make their way home,
Blowing on their bugles many a brave blast.
Ere dark had descended, that doughty band   1365
Was come within the walls where Gawain waits
                              at leisure.
              Bliss and hearth-fire bright
              Await the master's pleasure;
              When the two men met that night,   1370
              Joy surpassed all measure.

Then the host in the hall his household assembles,
With the dames of high degree and their damsels fair.
In the presence of the people, a party he sends
To convey him his venison in view of the knight.   1375
And in high good-humor he hails him then,
Counts over the kill, the cuts on the tallies,
Holds high the hewn ribs, heavy with fat.
"What think you, sir, of this? Have I thriven well?
Have I won with my woodcraft a worthy prize?"   1380
"In good earnest," said Gawain, "this game is the finest
I have seen in seven years in the season of winter."
"And I give it to you, Gawain," said the goodly host,
"For according to our convenant, you claim it as your own."
"That is so," said Sir Gawain, "the same say I: 1385
What I worthily have won within these fair walls,
Herewith I as willingly award it to you."
He embraces his broad neck with both his arms,
And confers on him a kiss in the comeliest style.
"Have here my profit, it proved no better;   1390
Ungrudging do I grant it, were it greater far."
"Such a gift," said the good host, "I gladly accept—
Yet it might be all the better, would you but say
Where you won this same award, by your wits alone."
"That was no part of the pact; press me no further,   1395
For you have had what behooves; all other claims
                              forbear."
              With jest and compliment
              They conversed, and cast off care;
              To the table soon they went;   1400
              Fresh dainties wait them there.

And then by the chimney-side they chat at their ease;
The best wine was brought them, and bounteously served;

4. Lungs.

And after in their jesting they jointly accord
To do on the second day the deeds of the first: 1405
That the two men should trade, betide as it may,
What each had taken in, at eve when they met.
They seal the pact solemnly in sight of the court;
Their cups were filled afresh to confirm the jest;
Then at last they took their leave, for late was the hour,   1410
Each to his own bed hastening away.
Before the barnyard cock had crowed but thrice
The lord had leapt from his rest, his liegemen as well.
Both of mass and their meal they made short work:
By the dim light of dawn they were deep in the woods   1415
                     away.
          With huntsmen and with horns
          Over plains they pass that day;
          They release, amid the thorns,
          Swift hounds that run and bay.   1420

Soon some were on a scent by the side of a marsh;
When the hounds opened cry, the head of the hunt
Rallied them with rough words, raised a great noise.
The hounds that had heard it came hurrying straight
And followed along with their fellows, forty together.   1425
Then such a clamor and cry of coursing hounds
Arose, that the rocks resounded again.
Hunters exhorted them with horn and with voice;
Then all in a body bore off together
Between a mere in the marsh and a menacing crag,   1430
To a rise where the rock stood rugged and steep,
And boulders lay about, that blocked their approach.
Then the company in consort closed on their prey:
They surrounded the rise and the rocks both,
For well they were aware that it waited within,   1435
The beast that the bloodhounds boldly proclaimed.
Then they beat on the bushes and bade him appear,
And he made a murderous rush in the midst of them all;
The best of all boars broke from his cover,
That had ranged long unrivaled, a renegade old,   1440
For of tough-brawned boars he was biggest far,
Most grim when he grunted—then grieved were many,
For three at the first thrust he threw to the earth,
And dashed away at once without more damage.
With "Hi!" "Hi!" and "Hey!" "Hey!" the others followed,   1445
Had horns at their lips, blew high and clear.
Merry was the music of men and of hounds
That were bound after this boar, his bloodthirsty heart
                   to quell.
          Often he stands at bay,   1450
          Then scatters the pack pell-mell;
          He hurts the hounds, and they
          Most dolefully yowl and yell.

Men then with mighty bows moved in to shoot,
Aimed at him with their arrows and often hit,   1455
But the points had no power to pierce through his hide,
And the barbs were brushed aside by his bristly brow;
Though the shank of the shaft shivered in pieces,
The head hopped away, wheresoever it struck.
But when their stubborn strokes had stung him at last,   1460
Then, foaming in his frenzy, fiercely he charges,
Hies at them headlong that hindered his flight,
And many feared for their lives, and fell back a little.
But the lord on a lively horse leads the chase;
As a high-mettled huntsman his horn he blows;   1465
He sounds the assembly and sweeps through the brush,
Pursuing this wild swine till the sunlight slanted.
All day with this deed they drive forth the time
While our lone knight so lovesome lies in his bed,
Sir Gawain safe at home, in silken bower   1470
                    so gay.
          The lady, with guile in heart,
          Came early where he lay;
          She was at him with all her art
          To turn his mind her way.   1475

She comes to the curtain and coyly peeps in;
Gawain thought it good to greet her at once,
And she richly repays him with her ready words,
Settles softly at his side, and suddenly she laughs,
And with a gracious glance, she begins on him thus: 1480
"Sir, if you be Gawain, it seems a great wonder—
A man so well-meaning, and mannerly disposed,
And cannot act in company as courtesy bids,
And if one takes the trouble to teach him, 'tis all in vain.
That lesson learned lately is lightly forgot,   1485
Though I painted it as plain as my poor wit allowed."
"What lesson, dear lady?" he asked all alarmed;
"I have been much to blame, if your story be true."
"Yet my counsel was of kissing," came her answer then,
"Where favor has been found, freely to claim   1490
As accords with the conduct of courteous knights."
"My dear," said the doughty man, "dismiss that thought;
Such freedom, I fear, might offend you much;
It were rude to request if the right were denied."
"But none can deny you," said the noble dame,   1495
"You are stout enough to constrain with strength, if you choose,
Were any so ungracious as to grudge you aught."
"By heaven," said he, "you have answered well,
But threats never throve among those of my land,
Nor any gift not freely given, good though it be.   1500
I am yours to command, to kiss when you please;
You may lay on as you like, and leave off at will."
                    With this,
          The lady lightly bends

And graciously gives him a kiss;   1505
The two converse as friends
Of true love's trials and bliss.

"I should like, by your leave," said the lovely lady,
"If it did not annoy you, to know for what cause
So brisk and so bold a young blood as you,   1510
And acclaimed for all courtesies becoming a knight—
And name what knight you will, they are noblest esteemed
For loyal faith in love, in life as in story;
For to tell the tribulations of these true hearts,
Why, 'tis the very title and text of their deeds,   1515
How bold knights for beauty have braved many a foe,
Suffered heavy sorrows out of secret love,
And then valorously avenged them on villainous churls
And made happy ever after the hearts of their ladies.
And you are the noblest knight known in your time;   1520
No household under heaven but has heard of your fame,
And here by your side I have sat for two days
Yet never has a fair phrase fallen from your lips
Of the language of love, not one little word!
And you, that with sweet vows sway women's hearts,   1525
Should show your winsome ways, and woo a young thing,
And teach by some tokens the craft of true love.
How! are you artless, whom all men praise?
Or do you deem me so dull, or deaf to such words?
                    Fie! Fie!   1530
          In hope of pastimes new
          I have come where none can spy;
          Instruct me a little, do,
          While my husband is not nearby."

"God love you, gracious lady!" said Gawain then;   1535
"It is a pleasure surpassing, and a peerless joy,
That one so worthy as you would willingly come
And take the time and trouble to talk with your knight
And content you with his company—it comforts my heart.
But to take to myself the task of telling of love,   1540
And touch upon its texts, and treat of its themes
To one that, I know well, wields more power
In that art, by a half, than a hundred such
As I am where I live, or am like to become,
It were folly, fair dame, in the first degree!   1545
In all that I am able, my aim is to please,
As in honor behooves me, and am evermore
Your servant heart and soul, so save me our Lord!"
Thus she tested his temper and tried many a time,
Whatever her true intent, to entice him to sin,   1550
But so fair was his defense that no fault appeared,
Nor evil on either hand, but only bliss
                    they knew.
          They linger and laugh awhile;

She kisses the knight so true,   1555
Takes leave in comeliest style
And departs without more ado.

Then he rose from his rest and made ready for mass,
And then a meal was set and served, in sumptuous style;
He dallied at home all day with the dear ladies,   1560
But the lord lingered late at his lusty sport;
Pursued his sorry swine, that swerved as he fled,
And bit asunder the backs of the best of his hounds
When they brought him to bay, till the bowmen appeared
And soon forced him forth, though he fought for dear life,   1565
So sharp were the shafts they shot at him there.
But yet the boldest drew back from his battering head,
Till at last he was so tired he could travel no more,
But in as much haste as he might, he makes his retreat
To a rise on rocky ground, by a rushing stream.   1570
With the bank at his back he scrapes the bare earth,
The froth foams at his jaws, frightful to see.
He whets his white tusks—then weary were all
Those hunters so hardy that hoved round about
Of aiming from afar, but ever they mistrust   1575
          his mood.
     He had hurt so many by then
     That none had hardihood
     To be torn by his tusks again,
     That was brainsick, and out for blood.   1580

Till the lord came at last on his lofty steed,
Beheld him there at bay before all his folk;
Lightly he leaps down, leaves his courser,
Bares his bright sword, and boldly advances;
Straight into the stream he strides towards his foe.   1585
The wild thing was wary of weapon and man;
His hackles rose high; so hotly he snorts
That many watched with alarm, lest the worst befall.
The boar makes for the man with a mighty bound
So that he and his hunter came headlong together   1590
Where the water ran wildest—the worse for the beast,
For the man, when they first met, marked him with care,
Sights well the slot, slips in the blade,
Shoves it home to the hilt, and the heart shattered,
And he falls in his fury and floats down the water,   1595
          ill-sped.
     Hounds hasten by the score
     To maul him, hide and head;
     Men drag him in to shore
     And dogs pronounce him dead.   1600

With many a brave blast they boast of their prize,
All hallooed in high glee, that had their wind;

The hounds bayed their best, as the bold men bade
That were charged with chief rank in that chase of renown.
Then one wise in woodcraft, and worthily skilled,   1605
Began to dress the boar in becoming style:
He severs the savage head and sets it aloft,
Then rends the body roughly right down the spine;
Takes the bowels from the belly, broils them on coals,
Blends them well with bread to bestow on the hounds.   1610
Then he breaks out the brawn in fair broad flitches,
And the innards to be eaten in order he takes.
The two sides, attached to each other all whole,
He suspended from a spar that was springy and tough;
And so with this swine they set out for home;   1615
The boar's head was borne before the same man
That had stabbed him in the stream with his strong arm,
                    right through.
              He thought it long indeed
              Till he had the knight in view;   1620
              At his call, he comes with speed
              To claim his payment due.

The lord laughed aloud, with many a light word,
When he greeted Sir Gawain—with good cheer he speaks.
They fetch the fair dames and the folk of the house;   1625
He brings forth the brawn, and begins the tale
Of the great length and girth, the grim rage as well,
Of the battle of the boar they beset in the wood.
The other man meetly commended his deeds
And praised well the prize of his princely sport,   1630
For the brawn of that boar, the bold knight said,
And the sides of that swine surpassed all others.
Then they handled the huge head; he owns it a wonder,
And eyes it with abhorrence, to heighten his praise.
"Now, Gawain," said the good man, "this game becomes yours 1635
By those fair terms we fixed, as you know full well."
"That is true," returned the knight, "and trust me, fair friend,
All my gains, as agreed, I shall give you forthwith."
He clasps him and kisses him in courteous style,
Then serves him with the same fare a second time.   1640
"Now we are even," said he, "at this evening feast,
And clear is every claim incurred here to date,
                    and debt."
              "By Saint Giles!" the host replies,
              "You're the best I ever met!   1645
              If your profits are all this size,
              We'll see you wealthy yet!"

Then attendants set tables on trestles about,
And laid them with linen; light shone forth,
Wakened along the walls in waxen torches.   1650
The service was set and the supper brought;

Royal were the revels that rose then in hall
At that feast by the fire, with many fair sports:
Amid the meal and after, melody sweet,
Carol-dances comely and Christmas songs,   1655
With all the mannerly mirth my tongue may describe.
And ever our gallant knight beside the gay lady;
So uncommonly kind and complaisant was she,
With sweet stolen glances, that stirred his stout heart,
That he was at his wits' end, and wondrous vexed;   1660
But he could not rebuff her, for courtesy forbade,
Yet took pains to please her, though the plan might
                              go wrong.
              When they to heart's delight
              Had reveled there in throng,   1665
              To his chamber he calls the knight,
              And thither they go along.

And there they dallied and drank, and deemed it good sport
To enact their play anew on New Year's Eve,
But Gawain asked again to go on the morrow,   1670
For the time until his tryst was not two days.
The host hindered that, and urged him to stay,
And said, "On my honor, my oath here I take
That you shall get to the Green Chapel to begin your chores
By dawn on New Year's Day, if you so desire.   1675
Wherefore lie at your leisure in your lofty bed,
And I shall hunt hereabouts, and hold to our terms,
And we shall trade winnings when once more we meet,
For I have tested you twice, and true have I found you;
Now think this tomorrow: the third pays for all;   1680
Be we merry while we may, and mindful of joy,
For heaviness of heart can be had for the asking."
This is gravely agreed on and Gawain will stay.
They drink a last draught and with torches depart
                              to rest.   1685
              To bed Sir Gawain went:
              His sleep was of the best;
              The lord, on his craft intent,
              Was early up and dressed.

After mass, with his men, a morsel he takes;   1690
Clear and crisp the morning; he calls for his mount;
The folk that were to follow him afield that day
Were high astride their horses before the hall gates.
Wondrous fair were the fields, for the frost was light;
The sun rises red amid radiant clouds,   1695
Sails into the sky, and sends forth his beams.
They let loose the hounds by a leafy wood;
The rocks all around re-echo to their horns;
Soon some have set off in pursuit of the fox,
Cast about with craft for a clearer scent;   1700

A young dog yaps, and is yelled at in turn;
His fellows fall to sniffing, and follow his lead,
Running in a rabble on the right track,
And he scampers all before; they discover him soon,
And when they see him with sight they pursue him the faster,   1705
Railing at him rudely with a wrathful din.
Often he reverses over rough terrain,
Or loops back to listen in the lee of a hedge;
At last, by a little ditch, he leaps over the brush,
Comes into a clearing at a cautious pace,   1710
Then he thought through his wiles to have thrown off the hounds
Till he was ware, as he went, of a waiting-station
Where three athwart his path threatened him at once,
                    all gray.
    Quick as a flash he wheels   1715
    And darts off in dismay;
    With hard luck at his heels
    He is off to the wood away.

Then it was heaven on earth to hark to the hounds
When they had come on their quarry, coursing together!   1720
Such harsh cries and howls they hurled at his head
As all the cliffs with a crash had come down at once.
Here he was hailed, when huntsmen met him;
Yonder they yelled at him, yapping and snarling;
There they cried "Thief!" and threatened his life,   1725
And ever the harriers at his heels, that he had no rest.
Often he was menaced when he made for the open,
And often rushed in again, for Reynard was wily;
And so he leads them a merry chase, the lord and his men,
In this manner on the mountains, till midday or near,   1730
While our hero lies at home in wholesome sleep
Within the comely curtains on the cold morning.
But the lady, as love would allow her no rest,
And pursuing ever the purpose that pricked her heart,
Was awake with the dawn, and went to his chamber   1735
In a fair flowing mantle that fell to the earth,
All edged and embellished with ermines fine;
No hood on her head, but heavy with gems
Were her fillet and the fret[5] that confined her tresses;
Her face and her fair throat freely displayed;   1740
Her bosom all but bare, and her back as well.
She comes in at the chamber-door, and closes it with care,
Throws wide a window—then waits no longer,
But hails him thus airily with her artful words,
      with cheer: 1745
    "Ah, man, how can you sleep?
    The morning is so clear!"
    Though dreams have drowned him deep,
    He cannot choose but hear.

5. Ornamental net.

Deep in his dreams he darkly mutters   1750
As a man may that mourns, with many grim thoughts
Of that day when destiny shall deal him his doom
When he greets his grim host at the Green Chapel
And must bow to his buffet, bating all strife.
But when he sees her at his side he summons his wits,   1755
Breaks from the black dreams, and blithely answers.
That lovely lady comes laughing sweet,
Sinks down at his side, and salutes him with a kiss.
He accords her fair welcome in courtliest style;
He sees her so glorious, so gaily attired,   1760
So faultless her features, so fair and so bright,
His heart swelled swiftly with surging joys.
They melt into mirth with many a fond smile,
Nor was fair language lacking, to further that hour's
                        delight.   1765
            Good were their words of greeting;
            Each joyed in other's sight;
            Great peril attends that meeting
            Should Mary forget her knight.

For that high-born beauty so hemmed him about,   1770
Made so plain her meaning, the man must needs
Either take her tendered love or distastefully refuse.
His courtesy concerned him, lest crass he appear,
But more his soul's mischief, should he commit sin
And belie his loyal oath to the lord of that house.   1775
"God forbid!" said the bold knight, "That shall not befall!"
With a little fond laughter he lightly let pass
All the words of special weight that were sped his way;
"I find you much at fault," the fair one said,
"Who can be cold toward a creature so close by your side,   1780
Of all women in this world most wounded in heart,
Unless you have a sweetheart, one you hold dearer,
And allegiance to that lady so loyally knit
That you will never love another, as now I believe.
And, sir, if it be so, then say it, I beg you;   1785
By all your heart holds dear, hide it no longer
                        with guile."
            "Lady, by Saint John,"
            He answers with a smile,
            "Lover have I none,   1790
            Nor will have, yet awhile."

"Those words," said the woman, "are the worst of all,
But I have had my answer, and hard do I find it!
Kiss me now kindly: I can but go hence
To lament my life long like a maid lovelorn."   1795
She inclines her head quickly and kisses the knight,
Then straightens with a sigh, and says as she stands,
"Now, dear, ere I depart, do me this pleasure:
Give me some little gift, your glove or the like,

That I may think on you, man, and mourn the less."   1800
"Now by heavens," said he, "I wish I had here
My most precious possession, to put it in your hands,
For your deeds, beyond doubt, have often deserved
A repayment far passing my power to bestow.
But a love-token, lady, were of little avail;   1805
It is not to your honor to have at this time
A glove as a guerdon from Gawain's hand,
And I am here on an errand in unknown realms
And have no bearers with baggage with becoming gifts,
Which distresses me, madame, for your dear sake.   1810
A man must keep within his compass: account it neither grief
                    nor slight."
               "Nay, noblest knight alive,"
               Said that beauty of body white,
               "Though you be loath to give,   1815
               Yet you shall take, by right."

She reached out a rich ring, wrought all of gold,
With a splendid stone displayed on the band
That flashed before his eyes like a fiery sun;
It was worth a king's wealth, you may well believe.   1820
But he waved it away with these ready words:
"Before God, good lady, I forgo all gifts;
None have I to offer, nor any will I take."
And she urged it on him eagerly, and ever he refused,
And vowed in very earnest, prevail she would not.   1825
And she sad to find it so, and said to him then,
"If my ring is refused for its rich cost—
You would not be my debtor for so dear a thing—
I shall give you my girdle; you gain less thereby."
She released a knot lightly, and loosened a belt   1830
That was caught about her kirtle, the bright cloak beneath,
Of a gay green silk, with gold overwrought,
And the borders all bound with embroidery fine,
And this she presses upon him, and pleads with a smile,
Unworthy though it were, that it would not be scorned.   1835
But the man still maintains that he means to accept
Neither gold nor any gift, till by God's grace
The fate that lay before him was fully achieved.
"And be not offended, fair lady, I beg,
And give over your offer, for ever I must   1840
                    decline.
               I am grateful for favor shown
               Past all deserts of mine,
               And ever shall be your own
               True servant, rain or shine."   1845

"Now does my present displease you," she promptly inquired,
"Because it seems in your sight so simple a thing?
And belike, as it is little, it is less to praise,

But if the virtue that invests it were verily known,
It would be held, I hope, in higher esteem.   1850
For the man that possesses this piece of silk,
If he bore it on his body, belted about,
There is no hand under heaven that could hew him down,
For he could not be killed by any craft on earth."
Then the man began to muse, and mainly he thought   1855
It was a pearl for his plight, the peril to come
When he gains the Green Chapel to get his reward:
Could he escape unscathed, the scheme were noble!
Then he bore with her words and withstood them no more,
And she repeated her petition and pleaded anew,   1860
And he granted it, and gladly she gave him the belt,
And besought him for her sake to conceal it well,
Lest the noble lord should know—and, the knight agrees
That not a soul save themselves shall see it thenceforth
                              with sight.   1865
              He thanked her with fervent heart,
              As often as ever he might;
              Three times, before they part,
              She has kissed the stalwart knight.

Then the lady took her leave, and left him there,   1870
For more mirth with that man she might not have.
When she was gone, Sir Gawain got from his bed,
Arose and arrayed him in his rich attire;
Tucked away the token the temptress had left,
Laid it reliably where he looked for it after.   1875
And then with good cheer to the chapel he goes,
Approached a priest in private, and prayed to be taught
To lead a better life and lift up his mind,
Lest he be among the lost when he must leave this world.
And shamefaced at shrift he showed his misdeeds   1880
From the largest to the least, and asked the Lord's mercy,
And called on his confessor to cleanse his soul,
And he absolved him of his sins as safe and as clean
As if the dread Day of Doom were to dawn on the morrow.
And then he made merry amid the fine ladies   1885
With deft-footed dances and dalliance light,
As never until now, while the afternoon wore
                              away.
              He delighted all around him,
              And all agreed, that day,   1890
              They never before had found him
              So gracious and so gay.

Now peaceful be his pasture, and love play him fair!
The host is on horseback, hunting afield;
He has finished off this fox that he followed so long: 1895
As he leapt a low hedge to look for the villain
Where he heard all the hounds in hot pursuit,

Reynard comes racing out of a rough thicket,
And all the rabble in a rush, right at his heels.
The man beholds the beast, and bides his time,   1900
And bares his bright sword, and brings it down hard,
And he blenches from the blade, and backward he starts;
A hound hurries up and hinders that move,
And before the horse's feet they fell on him at once
And ripped the rascal's throat with a wrathful din.   1905
The lord soon alighted and lifted him free,
Swiftly snatched him up from the snapping jaws,
Holds him over his head, halloos with a will,
And the dogs bayed the dirge, that had done him to death.
Hunters hastened thither with horns at their lips,   1910
Sounding the assembly till they saw him at last.
When that comely company was come in together,
All that bore bugles blew them at once,
And the others all hallooed, that had no horns.
It was the merriest medley that ever a man heard,   1915
The racket that they raised for Sir Reynard's soul
      that died.
    Their hounds they praised and fed,
    Fondling their heads with pride,
    And they took Reynard the Red   1920
    And stripped away his hide.

And then they headed homeward, for evening had come,
Blowing many a blast on their bugles bright.
The lord at long last alights at his house,
Finds fire on the hearth where the fair knight waits,   1925
Sir Gawain the good, that was glad in heart.
With the ladies, that loved him, he lingered at ease;
He wore a rich robe of blue, that reached to the earth
And a surcoat lined softly with sumptuous furs;
A hood of the same hue hung on his shoulders;   1930
With bands of bright ermine embellished were both.
He comes to meet the man amid all the folk,
And greets him good-humoredly, and gaily he says,
"I shall follow forthwith the form of our pledge
That we framed to good effect amid fresh-filled cups."   1935
He clasps him accordingly and kisses him thrice,
As amiably and as earnestly as ever he could.
"By heaven," said the host, "you have had some luck
Since you took up this trade, if the terms were good."
"Never trouble about the terms," he returned at once,   1940
"Since all that I owe here is openly paid."
"Marry!" said the other man, "mine is much less,
For I have hunted all day, and nought have I got
But this foul fox pelt, the fiend take the goods!
Which but poorly repays such precious things   1945
That you have cordially conferred, such kisses three
      so good."
    "Enough!" said Sir Gawain;

"I thank you, by the rood!"
And how the fox was slain   1950
He told him, as they stood.

With minstrelsy and mirth, with all manner of meats,
They made as much merriment as any men might
(Amid laughing of ladies and light hearted girls;
So gay grew Sir Gawain and the goodly host)   1955
Unless they had been besotted, or brainless fools.
The knight joined in jesting with that joyous folk,
Until at last it was late; ere long they must part,
And be off to their beds, as behooved them each one.
Then politely his leave of the lord of the house   1960
Our noble knight takes, and renews his thanks:
"The courtesies countless accorded me here,
Your kindness at this Christmas, may heaven's King repay!
Henceforth, if you will have me, I hold you my liege,
And so, as I have said, I must set forth tomorrow,   1965
If I may take some trusty man to teach, as you promised,
The way to the Green Chapel, that as God allows
I shall see my fate fulfilled on the first of the year."
"In good faith," said the good man, "with a good will
Every promise on my part shall be fully performed."   1970
He assigns him a servant to set him on the path,
To see him safe and sound over the snowy hills,
To follow the fastest way through forest green
                         and grove.
            Gawain thanks him again,   1975
            So kind his favors prove,
            And of the ladies then
            He takes his leave, with love.

Courteously he kissed them, with care in his heart,
And often wished them well, with warmest thanks,   1980
Which they for their part were prompt to repay.
They commend him to Christ with disconsolate sighs;
And then in that hall with the household he parts—
Each man that he met, he remembered to thank
For his deeds of devotion and diligent pains,   1985
And the trouble he had taken to tend to his needs;
And each one as woeful, that watched him depart,
As he had lived with him loyally all his life long.
By lads bearing lights he was led to his chamber
And blithely brought to his bed, to be at his rest.   1990
How soundly he slept, I presume not to say,
For there were matters of moment his thoughts might well
                         pursue.
            Let him lie and wait;
            He has little more to do,   1995
            Then listen, while I relate
            How they kept their rendezvous.

Part 4

Now the New Year draws near, and the night passes,
The day dispels the dark, by the Lord's decree;
But wild weather awoke in the world without: 2000
The clouds in the cold sky cast down their snow
With great gusts from the north, grievous to bear.
Sleet showered aslant upon shivering beasts;
The wind warbled wild as it whipped from aloft,
And drove the drifts deep in the dales below.   2005
Long and well he listens, that lies in his bed;
Though he lifts not his eyelids, little he sleeps;
Each crow of the cock he counts without fail.
Readily from his rest he rose before dawn,
For a lamp had been left him, that lighted his chamber.   2010
He called to his chamberlain, who quickly appeared,
And bade him get him his gear, and gird his good steed,
And he sets about briskly to bring in his arms,
And makes ready his master in manner most fit.
First he clad him in his clothes, to keep out the cold,   2015
And then his other harness, made handsome anew,
His plate-armor of proof, polished with pains,
The rings of his rich mail rid of their rust,
And all was fresh as at first, and for this he gave thanks
        indeed.   2020
      With pride he wears each piece,
      New-furbished for his need:
      No gayer from here to Greece;
      He bids them bring his steed.

In his richest raiment he robed himself then: 2025
His crested coat-armor, close-stitched with craft,
With stones of strange virtue on silk velvet set;
All bound with embroidery on borders and seams
And lined warmly and well with furs of the best.
Yet he left not his love-gift, the lady's girdle;   2030
Gawain, for his own good, forgot not that:
When the bright sword was belted and bound on his haunches,
Then twice with that token he twined him about.
Sweetly did he swathe him in that swatch of silk,
That girdle of green so goodly to see,   2035
That against the gay red showed gorgeous bright.
Yet he wore not for its wealth that wondrous girdle,
Nor pride in its pendants, though polished they were,
Though glittering gold gleamed at the tips,
But to keep himself safe when consent he must   2040
To endure a deadly dint, and all defense
        denied.
      And now the bold knight came
      Into the courtyard wide;
      That folk of worthy fame   2045
      He thanks on every side.

Then was Gringolet girt, that was great and huge,
And had sojourned safe and sound, and savored his fare;
He pawed the earth in his pride, that princely steed.
The good knight draws near him and notes well his look,   2050
And says sagely to himself, and soberly swears,
"Here is a household in hall that upholds the right!
The man that maintains it, may happiness be his!
Likewise the dear lady, may love betide her!
If thus they in charity cherish a guest   2055
That are honored here on earth, may they have his reward
That reigns high in heaven—and also you all;
And might I live in this land but a little while,
I should willingly reward you, and well, if I might."
Then he steps into the stirrup and bestrides his mount;   2060
His shield is shown forth; on his shoulder he casts it;
Strikes the side of his steed with his steel spurs,
And he starts across the stones, nor stands any longer
                                to prance.
                    On horseback was the swain   2065
                    That bore his spear and lance;
                    "May Christ this house maintain
                    And guard it from mischance!"

The bridge was brought down, and the road gates
Unbarred and carried back upon both sides;   2070
He commended him to Christ, and crossed over the planks;
Praised the noble porter, who prayed on his knees
That God save Sir Gawain, and bade him good day,
And went on his way alone with the man
That was to lead him ere long to that luckless place   2075
Where the dolorous dint must be dealt him at last.
Under bare boughs they ride, where steep banks rise,
Over high cliffs they climb, where cold snow clings;
The heavens held aloof, but heavy thereunder
Mist mantled the moors, moved on the slopes.   2080
Each hill had a hat, a huge cape of cloud;
Brooks bubbled and broke over broken rocks,
Flashing in freshets that waterfalls fed.
Roundabout was the road that ran through the wood
Till the sun at that season was soon to rise,   2085
                                that day.
                    They were on a hilltop high;
                    The white snow round them lay;
                    The man that rode nearby
                    Now bade his master stay.   2090

"For I have seen you here safe at the set time,
And now you are not far from that notable place
That you have sought for so long with such special pains.
But this I say for certain, since I know you, sir knight,
And have your good at heart, and hold you dear—   2095
Would you heed well my words, it were worth your while—

You are rushing into risks that you reck not of:
There is a villain in yon valley, the veriest on earth,
For he is rugged and rude, and ready with his fists,
And most immense in his mold of mortals alive,   2100
And his body bigger than the best four
That are in Arthur's house, Hector[6] or any.
He gets his grim way at the Green Chapel;
None passes by that place so proud in his arms
That he does not dash him down with his deadly blows,   2105
For he is heartless wholly, and heedless of right,
For be it chaplain or churl that by the Chapel rides,
Monk or mass-priest or any man else,
He would as soon strike him dead as stand on two feet.
Wherefore I say, just as certain as you sit there astride,   2110
You cannot but be killed, if his counsel holds,
For he would trounce you in a trice, had you twenty lives
                           for sale.
            He has lived long in this land
            And dealt out deadly bale;   2115
            Against his heavy hand
            Your power cannot prevail.

"And so, good Sir Gawain, let the grim man be;
Go off by some other road, in God's own name!
Leave by some other land, for the love of Christ,   2120
And I shall get me home again, and give you my word
That I shall swear by God's self and the saints above,
By heaven and by my halidom[7] and other oaths more,
To conceal this day's deed, nor say to a soul
That ever you fled for fear from any that I knew."   2125
"Many thanks!" said the other man—and demurring he speaks—
"Fair fortune befall you for your friendly words!
And conceal this day's deed I doubt not you would,
But though you never told the tale, if I turned back now,
Forsook this place for fear, and fled, as you say,   2130
I were a caitiff coward; I could not be excused.
But I must to the Chapel to chance my luck
And say to that same man such words as I please,
Befall what may befall through Fortune's will
                           or whim.   2135
            Though he be a quarrelsome knave
            With a cudgel great and grim,
            The Lord is strong to save:
            His servants trust in him."

"Marry," said the man, "since you tell me so much,   2140
And I see you are set to seek your own harm,
If you crave a quick death, let me keep you no longer!
Put your helm on your head, your hand on your lance,
And ride the narrow road down yon rocky slope

6. Either the Trojan hero or one of Arthur's knights.   7. Holiness or, more likely, patron saints.

Till it brings you to the bottom of the broad valley.   2145
Then look a little ahead, on your left hand,
And you will soon see before you that self-same Chapel,
And the man of great might that is master there.
Now goodbye in God's name, Gawain the noble!
For all the world's wealth I would not stay here,   2150
Or go with you in this wood one footstep further!"
He tarried no more to talk, but turned his bridle,
Hit his horse with his heels as hard as he might,
Leaves the knight alone, and off like the wind
       goes leaping.   2155
    "By God," said Gawain then,
    "I shall not give way to weeping;
    God's will be done, amen!
    I commend me to his keeping."

He puts his heels to his horse, and picks up the path;   2160
Goes in beside a grove where the ground is steep,
Rides down the rough slope right to the valley.
And then he looked a little about him—the landscape was wild,
And not a soul to be seen, nor sign of a dwelling,
But high banks on either hand hemmed it about,   2165
With many a ragged rock and rough-hewn crag;
The skies seemed scored by the scowling peaks.
Then he halted his horse, and hoved there a space,
And sought on every side for a sight of the Chapel,
But no such place appeared, which puzzled him sore,   2170
Yet he saw some way off what seemed like a mound,
A hillock high and broad, hard by the water,
Where the stream fell in foam down the face of the steep
And bubbled as if it boiled on its bed below.
The knight urges his horse, and heads for the knoll;   2175
Leaps lightly to earth; loops well the rein
Of his steed to a stout branch, and stations him there.
He strides straight to the mound, and strolls all about,
Much wondering what it was, but no whit the wiser;
It had a hole at one end, and on either side,   2180
And was covered with coarse grass in clumps all without,
And hollow all within, like some old cave,
Or a crevice of an old crag—he could not discern
      aright.
    "Can this be the Chapel Green?   2185
    Alack!" said the man, "here might
    The devil himself be seen
    Saying matins at black midnight!"

"Now by heaven," said he, "it is bleak hereabouts;
This prayer-house is hideous, half-covered with grass!   2190
Well may the grim man mantled in green
Hold here his orisons, in hell's own style!
Now I feel it is the Fiend, in my five wits,

That has tempted me to this tryst, to take my life;
This is a Chapel of mischance, may the mischief take it!   2195
As accursed a country church as I came upon ever!"
With his helm on his head, his lance in his hand,
He stalks toward the steep wall of that strange house.
Then he heard, on the hill, behind a hard rock,
Beyond the brook, from the bank, a most barbarous din: 2200
Lord! it clattered in the cliff fit to cleave it in two,
As one upon a grindstone ground a great scythe!
Lord! it whirred like a mill-wheel whirling about!
Lord! it echoed loud and long, lamentable to hear!
Then "By heaven," said the bold knight, "that business
        up there   2205
Is arranged for my arrival, or else I am much
                    misled.
            Let God work! Ah me!
            All hope of help has fled!
            Forfeit my life may be   2210
            But noise I do not dread."

Then he listened no longer, but loudly he called,
"Who has power in this place, high parley to hold?
For none greets Sir Gawain, or gives him good day;
If any would a word with him, let him walk forth   2215
And speak now or never, to speed his affairs."
"Abide," said one on the bank above over his head,
"And what I promised you once shall straightway be given."
Yet he stayed not his grindstone, nor stinted its noise,
But worked awhile at his whetting before he would rest,   2220
And then he comes around a crag, from a cave in the rocks,
Hurtling out of hiding with a hateful weapon,
A Danish[8] ax devised for that day's deed,
With a broad blade and bright, bent in a curve,
Filed to a fine edge—four feet it measured   2225
By the length of the lace that was looped round the haft.
And in form as at first, the fellow all green,
His lordly face and his legs, his locks and his beard,
Save that firm upon two feet forward he strides,
Sets a hand on the ax-head, the haft to the earth;   2230
When he came to the cold stream, and cared not to wade,
He vaults over on his ax, and advances amain
On a broad bank of snow, overbearing and brisk
                    of mood.
            Little did the knight incline   2235
            When face to face they stood;
            Said the other man, "Friend mine,
            It seems your word holds good!"

"God love you, Sir Gawain!" said the Green Knight then,
"And well met this morning, man, at my place!   2240

8. I.e., long-bladed.

And you have followed me faithfully and found me betimes,
And on the business between us we both are agreed:
Twelve months ago today you took what was yours,
And you at this New Year must yield me the same.
And we have met in these mountains, remote from all eyes: 2245
There is none here to halt us or hinder our sport;
Unhasp your high helm, and have here your wages;
Make no more demur than I did myself
When you hacked off my head with one hard blow."
"No, by God," said Sir Gawain, "that granted me life,   2250
I shall grudge not the guerdon, grim though it prove;
Bestow but one stroke, and I shall stand still,
And you may lay on as you like till the last of my part
                    be paid."
              He proffered, with good grace,   2255
              His bare neck to the blade,
              And feigned a cheerful face:
              He scorned to seem afraid.

Then the grim man in green gathers his strength,
Heaves high the heavy ax to hit him the blow.   2260
With all the force in his frame he fetches it aloft,
With a grimace as grim as he would grind him to bits;
Had the blow he bestowed been as big as he threatened,
A good knight and gallant had gone to his grave.
But Gawain at the great ax glanced up aside,   2265
As down it descended with death-dealing force,
And his shoulders shrank a little from the sharp iron.
Abruptly the brawny man breaks off the stroke,
And then reproved with proud words that prince among knights.
"You are not Gawain the glorious," the green man said,   2270
"That never fell back on field in the face of the foe,
And now you flee for fear, and have felt no harm:
Such news of that knight I never heard yet!
I moved not a muscle when you made to strike,
Nor caviled at the cut in King Arthur's house;   2275
My head fell to my feet, yet steadfast I stood,
And you, all unharmed, are wholly dismayed—
Wherefore the better man I, by all odds,
                    must be."
              Said Gawain, "Strike once more;   2280
              I shall neither flinch nor flee;
              But if my head falls to the floor
              There is no mending me!"

"But go on, man, in God's name, and get to the point!
Deliver me my destiny, and do it out of hand,   2285
For I shall stand to the stroke and stir not an inch
Till your ax has hit home—on my honor I swear it!"
"Have at thee then!" said the other, and heaves it aloft,
And glares down as grimly as he had gone mad.
He made a mighty feint, but marred not his hide;   2290

Withdrew the ax adroitly before it did damage.
Gawain gave no ground, nor glanced up aside,
But stood still as a stone, or else a stout stump
That is held in hard earth by a hundred roots.
Then merrily does he mock him, the man all in green: 2295
"So now you have your nerve again, I needs must strike;
Uphold the high knighthood that Arthur bestowed,
And keep your neck-bone clear, if this cut allows!"
Then was Gawain gripped with rage, and grimly he said,
"Why, thrash away, tyrant, I tire of your threats;   2300
You make such a scene, you must frighten yourself."
Said the green fellow, "In faith, so fiercely you speak
That I shall finish this affair, nor further grace
                    allow."
                He stands prepared to strike   2305
                And scowls with both lip and brow;
                No marvel if the man mislike
                Who can hope no rescue now.

He gathered up the grim ax and guided it well:
Let the barb at the blade's end brush the bare throat;   2310
He hammered down hard, yet harmed him no whit
Save a scratch on one side, that severed the skin;
The end of the hooked edge entered the flesh,
And a little blood lightly leapt to the earth.
And when the man beheld his own blood bright on the snow,   2315
He sprang a spear's length with feet spread wide,
Seized his high helm, and set it on his head,
Shoved before his shoulders the shield at his back,
Bares his trusty blade, and boldly he speaks—
Not since he was a babe born of his mother   2320
Was he once in this world one-half so blithe—
"Have done with your hacking—harry me no more!
I have borne, as behooved, one blow in this place;
If you make another move I shall meet it midway
And promptly, I promise you, pay back each blow   2325
                with brand.
                One stroke acquits me here;
                So did our covenant stand
                In Arthur's court last year—
                Wherefore, sir, hold your hand!"   2330

He lowers the long ax and leans on it there,
Sets his arms on the head, the haft on the earth,
And beholds the bold knight that bides there afoot,
How he faces him fearless, fierce in full arms,
And plies him with proud words—it pleases him well.   2335
Then once again gaily to Gawain he calls,
And in a loud voice and lusty, delivers these words:
"Bold fellow, on this field your anger forbear!
No man has made demands here in manner uncouth,
Nor done, save as duly determined at court.   2340

I owed you a hit and you have it; be happy therewith!
The rest of my rights here I freely resign.
Had I been a bit busier, a buffet, perhaps,
I could have dealt more directly, and done you some harm.
First I flourished with a feint, in frolicsome mood,   2345
And left your hide unhurt—and here I did well
By the fair terms we fixed on the first night;
And fully and faithfully you followed accord:
Gave over all your gains as a good man should.
A second feint, sir, I assigned for the morning   2350
You kissed my comely wife—each kiss you restored.
For both of these there behooved two feigned blows
                    by right.
            True men pay what they owe;
            No danger then in sight.   2355
            You failed at the third throw,
            So take my tap, sir knight.

"For that is my belt about you, that same braided girdle,
My wife it was that wore it; I know well the tale,
And the count of your kisses and your conduct too,   2360
And the wooing of my wife—it was all my scheme!
She made trial of a man most faultless by far
Of all that ever walked over the wide earth;
As pearls to white peas, more precious and prized,
So is Gawain, in good faith, to other gay knights.   2365
Yet you lacked, sir, a little in loyalty there,
But the cause was not cunning, nor courtship either,
But that you loved your own life; the less, then, to blame."
The other stout knight in a study stood a long while,
So gripped with grim rage that his great heart shook.   2370
All the blood of his body burned in his face
As he shrank back in shame from the man's sharp speech.
The first words that fell from the fair knight's lips:
"Accursed be a cowardly and covetous heart!
In you is villainy and vice, and virtue laid low!"   2375
Then he grasps the green girdle and lets go the knot,
Hands it over in haste, and hotly he says:
"Behold there my falsehood, ill hap betide it!
Your cut taught me cowardice, care for my life,
And coveting came after, contrary both   2380
To largesse and loyalty belonging to knights.
Now am I faulty and false, that fearful was ever
Of disloyalty and lies, bad luck to them both!
                    and greed.
            I confess, knight, in this place,   2385
            Most dire is my misdeed;
            Let me gain back your good grace,
            And thereafter I shall take heed."

Then the other laughed aloud, and lightly he said,
"Such harm as I have had, I hold it quite healed.   2390

You are so fully confessed, your failings made known,
And bear the plain penance of the point of my blade,
I hold you polished as a pearl, as pure and as bright
As you had lived free of fault since first you were born.
And I give you, sir, this girdle that is gold-hemmed   2395
And green as my garments, that, Gawain, you may
Be mindful of this meeting when you mingle in throng
With nobles of renown—and known by this token
How it chanced at the Green Chapel, to chivalrous knights.
And you shall in this New Year come yet again   2400
And we shall finish out our feast in my fair hall,
                    with cheer."
          He urged the knight to stay,
          And said, "With my wife so dear
          We shall see you friends this day,   2405
          Whose enmity touched you near."

"Indeed," said the doughty knight, and doffed his high helm,
And held it in his hands as he offered his thanks,
"I have lingered long enough—may good luck be yours,
And he reward you well that all worship bestows!   2410
And commend me to that comely one, your courteous wife,
Both herself and that other, my honoured ladies,
That have trapped their true knight in their trammels so quaint.
But if a dullard should dote, deem it no wonder,
And through the wiles of a woman be wooed into sorrow,   2415
For so was Adam by one, when the world began,
And Solomon by many more, and Samson the mighty—
Delilah was his doom, and David thereafter
Was beguiled by Bathsheba, and bore much distress;
Now these were vexed by their devices—'twere a very joy   2420
Could one but learn to love, and believe them not.
For these were proud princes, most prosperous of old,
Past all lovers lucky, that languished under heaven,
                    bemused.
          And one and all fell prey   2425
          To women that they had used;
          If I be led astray,
          Methinks I may be excused.

"But your girdle, God love you! I gladly shall take
And be pleased to possess, not for the pure gold,   2430
Nor the bright belt itself, nor the beauteous pendants,
Nor for wealth, nor worldly state, nor workmanship fine,
But a sign of excess it shall seem oftentimes
When I ride in renown, and remember with shame
The faults and the frailty of the flesh perverse,   2435
How its tenderness entices the foul taint of sin;
And so when praise and high prowess have pleased my heart,
A look at this love-lace will lower my pride.
But one thing would I learn, if you were not loath,
Since you are lord of yonder land where I have long sojourned   2440

With honor in your house—may you have His reward
That upholds all the heavens, highest on throne!
How runs your right name?—and let the rest go."
"That shall I give you gladly," said the Green Knight then;
"Bercilak de Hautdesert this barony I hold,   2445
Through the might of Morgan le Faye,[9] that lodges at my house,
By subtleties of science and sorcerers' arts,
The mistress of Merlin,[1] she has caught many a man,
For sweet love in secret she shared sometime
With that wizard, that knows well each one of your knights   2450
                    and you.
              Morgan the Goddess, she,
              So styled by title true;
              None holds so high degree
              That her arts cannot subdue.   2455

"She guided me in this guise to your glorious hall,
To assay, if such it were, the surfeit of pride
That is rumored of the retinue of the Round Table.
She put this shape upon me to puzzle your wits,
To afflict the fair queen, and frighten her to death   2460
With awe of that elvish man that eerily spoke
With his head in his hand before the high table.
She was with my wife at home, that old withered lady,
Your own aunt[2] is she, Arthur's half-sister,
The Duchess' daughter of Tintagel, that dear King Uther   2465
Got Arthur on after, that honored is now.
And therefore, good friend, come feast with your aunt;
Make merry in my house; my men hold you dear,
And I wish you as well, sir, with all my heart,
As any man God ever made, for your great good faith."   2470
But the knight said him nay, that he might by no means.
They clasped then and kissed, and commended each other
To the Prince of Paradise, and parted with one
                    assent.
              Gawain sets out anew;   2475
              Toward the court his course is bent;
              And the knight all green in hue,
              Wheresoever he wished, he went.

Wild ways in the world our worthy knight rides
On Gringolet, that by grace had been granted his life.   2480
He harbored often in houses, and often abroad,
And with many valiant adventures verily he met
That I shall not take time to tell in this story.
The hurt was whole that he had had in his neck,
And the bright green belt on his body he bore,   2485
Oblique, like a baldric, bound at his side,

9. Arthur's half-sister, an enchantress who sometimes
abetted him, sometimes made trouble for him.
1. The wise magician who had helped Arthur become
king.

2. Morgan was the daughter of Igraine, duchess of
Tintagel, and her husband the duke; Igraine conceived
Arthur when his father, Uther, lay with her through
one of Merlin's trickeries.

Below his left shoulder, laced in a knot,
In betokening of the blame he had borne for his fault;
And so to court in due course he comes safe and sound.
Bliss abounded in hall when the high-born heard   2490
That good Gawain was come; glad tidings they thought it.
The king kisses the knight, and the queen as well,
And many a comrade came to clasp him in arms,
And eagerly they asked, and awesomely he told,
Confessed all his cares and discomfitures many,   2495
How it chanced at the Chapel, what cheer made the knight,
The love of the lady, the green lace at last.
The nick on his neck he naked displayed
That he got in his disgrace at the Green Knight's hands,
                alone.   2500
        With rage in heart he speaks,
        And grieves with many a groan;
        The blood burns in his cheeks
        For shame at what must be shown.

"Behold, sir," said he, and handles the belt,   2505
"This is the blazon of the blemish that I bear on my neck;
This is the sign of sore loss that I have suffered there
For the cowardice and coveting that I came to there;
This is the badge of false faith that I was found in there,
And I must bear it on my body till I breathe my last.   2510
For one may keep a deed dark, but undo it no whit,
For where a fault is made fast, it is fixed evermore."
The king comforts the knight, and the court all together
Agree with gay laughter and gracious intent
That the lords and the ladies belonging to the Table,   2515
Each brother of that band, a baldric should have,
A belt borne oblique, of a bright green,
To be worn with one accord for that worthy's sake.
So that was taken as a token by the Table Round,
And he honored that had it, evermore after,   2520
As the best book of knighthood bids it be known.
In the old days of Arthur this happening befell;
The books of Brutus' deeds bear witness thereto
Since Brutus, the bold knight, embarked for this land
After the siege ceased at Troy and the city fared   2525
                amiss.
        Many such, ere we were born,
        Have befallen here, ere this.
        May He that was crowned with thorn
        Bring all men to His bliss! Amen.   2530

Hony Soyt Qui Mal Pense[3]

---

3. "Shame be to the man who has evil in his mind."
This is the motto of the Order of the Garter, founded

ca. 1350: apparently a copyist of the poem associated
this order with the one founded to honor Gawain.

220

MYSTERY PLAYS

ca. 1475:   Wakefield Master active.
1575:   Last performance of the Chester Cycle.

The word *mystery*, as applied to medieval drama, refers to the spiritual mystery of Christ's redemption of humankind, and mystery plays are dramatizations of incidents of the Old Testament, which foretells that redemption, and of the New, which recounts it. In England the mysteries were generally composed in cycles containing as many as forty-eight individual plays: a typical cycle would begin with the Creation, continue with the Fall of Man, and proceed through the most significant events of the Old Testament, such as the Flood, to the New Testament, which provided plays on the Nativity, the chief events of Christ's life, the Crucifixion, the Harrowing of Hell (based on sources now deemed apocryphal), and the Last Judgment.

The church had its own drama in Latin, dating back to the tenth century, which developed through the dramatization and elaboration of the liturgy—the regular service—for certain holidays, the Easter morning service in particular. The vernacular drama was once thought to have evolved from the liturgical, passing by stages from the church into the streets of the town. However, even though the vernacular plays at times echo their Latin counterparts and although their authors may have been clerics, the mysteries represent an old and largely independent tradition of vernacular religious drama. As early as the twelfth century a *Play of Adam* in Anglo-Norman French was performed in England, a dramatization of the Fall with highly sophisticated dialogue, characterization, and stagecraft. During the late fourteenth and the fifteenth centuries the great English mystery cycles, four of which have survived complete, were formed in the towns that, in spite of war and plague, became increasingly prosperous and independent. Most of our knowledge of the plays, apart from the texts themselves, comes through municipal records pertaining to their production by the guilds.

Every trade in urban society had its guild, an organization combining the functions of a modern club, trade union, and religious society, and each of these guilds had its traditional play to perform on the days when the cycles were presented. In certain of the towns each company had a wagon that served as a stage. The wagon would proceed from one strategic point in the town to another, and the play would be performed a number of times on the same day: the spectators gathered at any one strategic point would never be without a play before them, and might see the whole cycle without moving. In other towns, however, the plays were probably acted out in sequence on a platform erected at a single location such as the main city square.

The plays were performed every year at the time of one of two great early summer festivals—Whitsuntide, the week following the seventh Sunday after Easter, or Corpus Christi, a week later. They served as both religious instruction and entertainment for a wide audience, including unlearned folk like the Carpenter in *The Miller's Tale* (pp. 99–100, lines 405–474), who recalls from them the trouble Noah had getting his wife aboard the ark, but also educated laypeople and clerics, who besides enjoying the sometimes boisterous comedy would find the plays acting out traditional interpretations of Scripture such as the ark as a type, or prefiguration, of the church.

The Chester Play of Noah's Flood   The most durable of the four surviving English mystery cycles was that of Chester, which was still occasionally performed when Shakespeare was a boy and was produced for the last time in 1575. The plays, however, remained of great interest to antiquarians and were a source of municipal pride. The five surviving manuscripts are all later than the final performance. Because the cycle had been extensively revised during the sixteenth century, we cannot know what it was like during the medieval period. The text we have is certainly very late. God's lengthy instructions to Noah concerning "clean" and "unclean" beasts reflect a new, probably Protestant, interest in Jewish law, also seen in other plays of the Chester cycle. But the revisers were also concerned to preserve what they felt to be traditional medieval features and, in the case of *Noah's Flood*, to introduce such a feature when it was missing. Thus the entertaining scene in which Noah and his wife quarrel and she gives him a box on the ear is an interpolation based on an old comic tradition that is well attested in the other cycle plays and in Chaucer's *The Miller's Tale*. The Chester play is a typical example of the composite authorship so characteristic of many medieval works, by which a text, passing through many hands and generations, carries with it traces of its past that blend in a rich, although not always smooth mixture. An interesting feature of the play is its stage directions, which show how such business as the animals on the ark was managed. A few additional stage directions are provided in braces.

Noah's Flood[1]

The Waterleaders and Drawers of Dee[2]

CAST OF CHARACTERS

GOD	NOAH'S WIFE
NOAH	SHEM'S WIFE
SHEM	HAM'S WIFE
HAM	JAPHET'S WIFE
JAPHETH	GOSSIPS

And first in some high place—or in the clouds, if it may be—God speaketh to Noah, standing without the ark[3] with all his family.

GOD. I, God, that[4] all this world hath wrought,
    Heaven and earth, and all of nought,
    I see my people in deed and thought
        Are set foully[5] in sin.
5   My ghost shall not leng in mon,
    That through flesh-liking is my fon,

---

1. The text is based on that of R. M. Lumiansky and David Mills in *The Chester Mystery Cycle* (1974), but has been freely edited. Spelling has been normalized except in some cases for the sake of rhyme and meter. Stage directions are original except for a few added in braces.
2. The guild responsible for the production of the play, the Waterleaders and Drawers, carted and sold water, a trade appropriate for the producers of Noah's flood.
3. Outside the ark. Evidently the ark is already on stage, although Noah and his family will simulate its building.
4. Who. *That* is used throughout as the relative pronoun.
5. Are mired.

But till six score years be comen and gone,
  To look if they will blin.[6]

10 Man that I made will I destroy,
   Beast, worm, and fowl to fly;[7]
   For on earth they do me noy,°   *harm*
    The folk that are thereon.
   It harmes me so hurtfully,°   *grievously*
   The malice that doth now multiply,
15   That sore it grieves me inwardly
    That ever I made mon.

  Therefore Noah, my servant free,°   *noble*
  That righteous man art as I see,
  A ship soon thou shalt make thee
20   Of trees dry and light.
  Little chambers therein thou make
  And binding slitch also thou take;
  Within and without thou ne slake
  To annoint it through all thy might.[8]

25 Three hundred cubits it shall be long
  And fifty broad to make it strong;
  Of height sixty. The meet thou fong;[9]
   Thus measure thou it about.
  One window work through thy wit;
30 A cubit of length and breadth make it.
  Upon the side a door shall shut,
   For to come in and out.

  Eating-places thou make also,
  Three roofed chambers on a row,[1]
35 For with water I think to flow°   *drown*
   Man that I can° make.   *did*
  Destroyed all the world shall be—
  Save thou, thy wife, thy sonnes three,
  And their wives also with thee—
40   Shall saved be for thy sake.

NOAH. A, Lord, I thank thee loud and still[2]
  That to me art in such will

---

6. My spirit shall remain with mankind, who through fleshly lust are my foes, only till six score [120] years be come and gone, to see if they will stop [sinning]. I.e., God allows the human race a probationary period to reform (cf. lines 149–150), probably a misunderstanding of Genesis 6.3, where God limits the human life span to 120 years. "Mon": man. In the West-Midland dialect, *a* is rounded before a nasal and rhymes with the vowel of *gone* and *on*. Both spellings *mon* and *man* occur in the manuscripts.
7. Animal, reptile, and bird flying.
8. Do not slacken to smear it [to make it watertight], inside and out, with all your might. "Slitch": mud (for caulking).
9. Take thou the measurement.
1. May refer to three decks, but the text is obscure.
2. Aloud and silent, i.e., at all times.

And spares me and my household to spill.[3]
   As now I soothly° find.   *truly*
45 Thy bidding, Lord, I shall fulfill
   Nor never more Thee grieve ne grill,°   *offend*
   That such grace has sent me till°   *to me*
    Amonges all mankind.

Have done, you men and women all,
50 Hie° you, lest this water fall,   *haste*
   To work this ship, chamber and hall,
    As God hath bidden us do.
SHEM. Father, I am already boun:°   *prepared*
   An ax I have, by my crown,[4]
55 As sharp as any in all this town,
    For to go thereto.

HAM. I have a hatchet wonder keen
   To bite well, as may be seen;
   A better ground,° as I ween,°   *sharpened/think*
60   Is not in all this town.
JAPHETH. And I can well make a pin°   *peg*
   And with this hammer knock in it.
   Go we work but° more din,°   *without/fuss*
    And I am ready boun.

65 NOAH'S WIFE. And we shall bring timber to,°   *thereto*
   For we mun° nothing else do—   *may*
   Woman been weak to underfo°   *undertake*
    Any great travail.°   *labor*
SHEM'S WIFE. Here is a good hackestock;°   *chopping block*
70   On this you may hewe and knock,
   Shall none be idle in this flock,
    Ne now may no man fail.

HAM'S WIFE. And I will go gather slitch,°   *pitch*
   The ship for to cleam° and pitch.   *caulk*
75 Annoint° it must be every stitch—   *smeared*
    Board, tree,° and pin.   *mast*
JAPHETH'S WIFE. And I will gather chippes here
   To make a fire for you in fere,°   *together*
   And for to dighte° your dinner   *prepare*
80   Against° you come in.   *before*

[*Then they make signs as if they were working with different tools.*]

---

3. Who are so minded toward me and refrain from   4. By my head (an oath).
destroying me and my household.

NOAH. Now in the name of God I begin
    To make the ship that we shall in,°   *go in*
    That we may be ready for to swim°   *float*
        At the coming of the flood.
85 These boards I pin here together
    To bear us safe from the weather
    That we may row both hither and thither
        And safe be from this flood.

    Of this tree will I make a mast
90 Tied with cables that will last,
    With a sail-yard° for each blast,   *spar*
        And each thing in their kind.
    With topcastle[5] and bowsprit,
    Both cords and ropes I have all meet°   *suitable*
95 To sail forth at the nexte wet;°   *rain*
        This ship is at an end.

    ⟨Wife, in this vessel we shall be kept;
    My children and thou, I would in ye leapt.[6]
NOAH'S WIFE. In faith, Noah, I had as lief thou slept.
100   For all thy frankish fare,
    I will not do after thy rede.[7]
NOAH. Good wife, do now as I thee bid.
NOAH'S WIFE. By Christ, not ere I see more need,
      Though thou stand all day and stare.

105 NOAH. Lord, that° women been crabbed ay,°   *how/always*
    And none are meek, I dare well say.
    That is well seen by me today
      In witness of you each one.[8]
    Good wife, let be all this bear°   *behavior*
110 That thou makest in this place here,
    For all they ween° that thou art master—   *think*
      And so thou art, by Saint John.⟩

    GOD. Noah, take thou thy meinie,°   *household*
    And in the ship hie° that ye be;   *hasten*
115 For none so righteous man to me
      Is now on earth living.
    Of clean beasts with thee thou take

---

5. An armed platform at the masthead. "And each thing in their kind": and each kind of thing (required).
6. I would like you to jump aboard. The behavior of Noah's Wife in the next two stanzas and in lines 193–252, both enclosed in angle brackets, is inconsistent with her cooperation and meek words in lines 65–68 and elsewhere. Nor does it make sense that Noah orders her to board the ark before God tells him to take his family inside. Stylistic evidence strongly suggests that these comic exchanges were added, probably in the early 16th century, to bring the Chester play in line with the tradition of the shrewish and recalcitrant Wife of the other mystery cycles.
7. I'd just as soon have you go to bed. In spite of your polite ("Frenchified") manner, I won't follow your direction.
8. As each one of you (i.e., in the audience) witnesses.

Seven and seven ere then thou slake;[9]
He and she, make to make,°   *mate with mate*
120   Belive in that thou bring.[1]

Of beasts unclean two and two,
Male and female, but mo;°   *no more*
Of clean fowls seven also
      The he and she together;
125 Of fowls unclean, twain and no more,
As I of beasts said before,
That shall be saved through my lore,°   *teaching*
      Against° I send this weather.   *before*

Of meats° that may be eaten,   *foods*
130 Into the ship look they be gotten,
For that may be no way forgotten.
      And do this al bedene.°   *at once*
To sustain man and beasts therein.
Ay till the water cease and blin.°   *stop*
135 This world is filled full of sin,
      And that is now well seen.

Seven days been yet coming;°   *are yet to come*
You shall have space° them in to bring.   *time*
After that it is my liking
140   Mankind to annoy.°   *afflict*
Forty days and forty nights
Rain shall fall for their unrights,°   *sins*
And that I have made through mights[2]
      Now think I to destroy.

145 NOAH. Lord, at Your bidding I am bain.°   *ready*
Sithen° no other grace will gain,°   *since/avail*
It will I fulfill fain,°   *gladly*
      For gracious I Thee find.
An hundred winters and twenty
150 This ship-making tarried° have I,   *delayed*
If through amendment Thy mercy
      Would fall to mankind.[3]

Have done, ye men and women all;
Hie you lest this water fall,
155 That each beast were in his stall
      And into the ship brought.

<hr/>

9. I.e., seven by seven before you leave off. See Genesis 7.2–4, where God's instructions follow Jewish dietary laws. According to Genesis 6.19–21, Noah is to take only one pair of each.

1. [See] that you bring in quickly.
2. That [which] I have made through [my] power.
3. If through reform mankind would obtain Thy mercy (cf. lines 7–8).

Of clean beastes seven shall be,
Of unclean two; thus God bade me.
The flood is nigh, you may well see;
160   Therefore tarry you nought.

[*Then* NOAH *shall go into the ark with all his family, his wife except,
and the ark must be boarded*[4] *round about. And on the boards all the
beasts and fowls hereafter rehearsed must be painted, that their words
may agree with the pictures.*]

SHEM. Sir, here are lions, leopards in;
Horses, mares, oxen, and swine,
Goats, calves, sheep, and kine
Here sitten thou may see.
165 HAM. Camels, asses, man may find,
Buck and doe, hart and hind.
All beasts of all manner kind
Here been, as thinketh me.

JAPHETH. Take here cattes, dogges too,
170   Otters and foxes, fulmarts° also;   *polecats*
Hares hopping gaily can go
Here have cole° for to eat.   *cabbage*
NOAH'E WIFE And here are bears, wolves set,
Apes, owls, marmoset,
175   Weasels, squirrels, and ferret;
Here they eat their meat.°   *food*

SHEM'S WIFE. Here are beasts in this house;
Here cats maken it crouse;[5]
Here a raton,° here a mouse   *rat*
180   That standen near together.
HAM'S WIFE. And here are fowles less and more—
Herons, cranes, and bittor,°   *bittern*
Swanes, peacocks—and them before,
Meat for this weather.

185 JAPHETH'S WIFE. Here are cockes, kites, crowes,
Rookes, ravens, many rowes,
Duckes, curlews, whoever knowes,
Each one in this kind.
And here are doves, digges,° drakes,   *ducks*
190   Redshanks running through the lakes;
And each fowl that leden° makes   *song*
In this ship man may find.

---

4. Supplied with boards.   5. Have a merry time.

⟨NOAH. Wife, come in. Why stands thou there?
    Thou art ever froward;[6] that dare I swear.
195 Come, in God's name! Time it were,
    For fear lest that we drown!
NOAH'S WIFE. Yea, sir, set up your sail
    And row forth with evil hail;°   *ill luck*
    For withouten any fail°   *doubt*
200 I will not out of this town.

    But° I have my gossips° every one,   *unless/friends*
    One foot further I will not gone.°   *go*
    They shall not drown, by Saint John,
    And° I may save their life.   *if*
205 They loved me full well, by Christ.
    But thou wilt let them into thy chist,°   *ark (chest)*
    Else row forth, Noah, when thee list°   *you please*
    And get thee a new wife.

NOAH. Shem, son, lo thy mother is wrow;°   *angry*
210 By God, such another I do not know.
SHEM. Father, I shall fetch her in, I trow,°   *trust*
    Withouten any fail.
    Mother, my father after thee send
    And bids thee into yonder ship wend.°   *go*
215 Look up and see the wind,
    For we been ready to sail.

NOAH'S WIFE. Son, go again to him and say
    I will not come therein today.
NOAH. Come in, Wife, in twenty devils way,[7]
220 Or else stand there without.°   *outside*
HAM. Shall we all fetch her in?
NOAH. Yea, son, in Christ's blessing and mine,
    I would ye hied you betime,
    For of this flood I stand in doubt.[8]

Song

225 THE GOOD GOSSIPS. The flood comes fleeting in full fast,[9]
    On every side that spreadeth full far.
    For fear of drowning I am aghast;
    Good gossip, let us draw near.

    And let us drink ere we depart,
230 For oftentimes we have done so.

---

6. Bold, presumptuous.   afraid of the flood.
7. In the name of twenty devils.   9. The flood comes flowing in very fast.
8. I want you to hurry before it's too late because I'm

For at one draught thou drink a quart,
And so will I do ere I go.

NOAH'S WIFE. Here is a pottle of Malmsey[1] good and strong;
It will rejoice both heart and tongue.
235   Though Noah think us never so long,
Yet we will drink atyte.°   *at once*

JAPHETH. Mother, we pray you all together—
For we are here, your own childer°—   *children*
Come into the ship for fear of the weather,
240   For his love that you bought![2]
NOAH'S WIFE. That will I not for all your call
But° I have my gossips all.   *unless*
SHEM. I° faith, mother, yet thou shall,   *in*
Whether thou will or nought.   {*Drags her aboard.*}

245 NOAH. Welcome, wife, into this boat.
NOAH'S WIFE. {*slaps him*} Have thou that for thy note!°   *trouble*
NOAH. Aha, Mary,[3] this is hot!
It is good for to be still.
Ah, children, methinks my boat remeves.°   *moves off*
250   Our tarrying here me highly grieves.
Over the land the water spreads,
God do as He will.)

[*Then they sing and* NOAH *shall speak again.*[4]]

NOAH. Ah, great God that art so good,
That° workes not thy will is wood.°   *whoever/crazy*
255 Now all this world is on a flood.
As we see well in sight.
The windows I will shut anon,
And into my chamber I will gone.
Till this water, so great one,
260   Is slaked° through Thy might.   *diminished*

[*Then shall* NOAH *shut the window of the ark, and for a little space within the boards he shall be silent; and afterward opening the window and looking round about saying:*]

Now forty days are fully gone.
Send a raven I will anon,
If aughtwhere° earth, tree, or stone   *anywhere*

---

1. A sweet wine. "Pottle": two-quart measure.
2. For the love of him who redeemed you (i.e., Christ).
3. [By] Mary (an oath).

4. The manuscripts do not indicate what song Noah and his family sing. A song might originally have followed after line 192.

Be dry in any place.
265   And if this fowl come not again,
It is a sign, sooth to sayn,°   *truth to say*
That dry it is on hill or plain,
    And God hath done some grace.

[Then he shall send forth a raven, and taking a dove in his hands, let him say:]

Ah, Lord, wherever this raven be,
270   Somewhere is dry, well I see;
But yet a dove, by my lewty,°   *faith*
    After I will send.
Thou wilt turn again to me,
For of all fowls that may fle°   *fly*
275   Thou art most meek and hend.°   *gentle*

[Then he shall send forth the dove; and there shall be another dove in the ship, bearing an olive branch in its mouth, which someone shall let down from the mast into NOAH's *hands with a rope; and then let* NOAH *say:]*

Ah, Lord, blessed be thou ay,
That me hast comfort° thus today.   *comforted*
By this sight I may well say
    This flood begins to cease.
280   My sweet dove to me brought has
A branch of olive from some place,
This betokeneth God has done us some grace,
    And is a sign of peace.

Ah, Lord, honored must Thou be;
285   All earth dries now I see.
But yet till thou command me,
    Hence I will not hie.
All this water is away;
Therefore, as soon as I may,
290   Sacrifice I shall do in fay°   *faith*
    To Thee devoutly.

GOD. Noah, take thy wife anon,
And thy children every one;
Out of the ship thou shalt gone,
295   And they all with thee.
Beasts and all that can fly,
Out anon they shall hie.
On earth to grow and multiply.
    I will that it so be.

³⁰⁰ NOAH. Lord, I thank Thee through Thy might;
       Thy bidding shall be done in hight,°   *haste*
       And, as fast as I may dight,°   *get ready*
          I will do Thee honor.
       And to Thee offer sacrifice
³⁰⁵ Therefore comes in all wise,[5]
       For of these beasts that been His,
          Offer I will this store.°   *great number*

[*Then, going out of the ark with his whole family he shall take his ani-*
mals and birds and offer and sacrifice them.]

       Lord God in majesty,
       That such grace has granted me,
³¹⁰ Where all was lorn,° safe to be,   *lost*
          Therefore now am I boun,°   *ready*
       My wife, my children, and my meinie,°   *household*
       With sacrifice to honor Thee
       Of beasts, fowls, as Thou mayst see,
³¹⁵   And full devotioun.

       GOD. Noah, to me thou art full able°   *very worthy*
       And thy sacrifice acceptable,
       For I have found thee true and stable,
          On thee now must I min.[6]
³²⁰ Wary° earth I will no more   *curse*
       For man's sins that grieve me sore;
       For of youth man full yore
          Has been inclined to sin.[7]

       Ye shall now grow and multiply
³²⁵ And earth again to edify.°   *replenish*
       Each beast, and fowl that may fly,
          Shall be feared° of you;   *afraid*
       And fish in sea, all that may flete,°   *swim*
       Shall sustain you, I thee beheet;°   *promise*
³³⁰ To eat of them ye ne let
          That clean been you may know.[8]

       Thereas° ye have eaten before   *whereas*
       Trees and roots since ye were bore,°   *born*
       Of clean beasts now, less and more,
³³⁵   I give you leave to eat—
       Save blood and flesh both in fere.[9]

---

5. Is, therefore, becoming in every way.
6. I must now be mindful of you.
7. Because for a very long time man, from his youth,
has been inclined to sin.
8. Do not abstain from eating those you know to be
clean (Genesis 9.1–3). The eating of meat will henceforth be permissible so long as the dietary laws are observed. "Ye": God speaks not just to Noah but to all the
human race.
9. Except for blood and flesh both together (Genesis
9.4).

Of wrong dead carrion that is here,
Eat ye not of that in no manner,
   For that ay ye shall let.[1]

340 Manslaughter also ay ye shall flee,
For that is not pleasant unto me.
They that shed blood, he or she,
   Aughtwhere° amongst mankin,°   *anywhere/mankind*
That blood foully shed shall be
345 And vengeance have, that men shall see.
Therefore beware now all ye,
   Ye fall not into that sin.

A forward,° Noah, with thee I make   *covenant*
And all thy seed for thy sake,
350 Of such vengeance for to slake,[2]
   For now I have my will.
Here I beheet thee an hest[3]
That man, woman, fowl, ne beast,
With water while this world shall last
355   I will no more spill.°   *destroy*

My bow° between you and me   *rainbow*
In the firmament shall be
By very° tokening that you may see   *true*
   That such vengeance shall cease.
360 That man ne woman shall never more
Be wasted by water as hath before;[4]
But for sin that grieveth me sore,
   Therefore this vengeance was.

Where cloudes in the welkin° been,   *sky*
365 That ilke° bow shall be seen,   *same*
In tokening that my wrath and teen°   *anger*
   Shall never thus wroken° be.   *avenged*
The string is turned towards you,
And towards me is bent the bow,[5]
370 That such weather shall never show;[6]
   And this beheet° I thee.   *promise*

My blessing now I give thee here,
To thee, Noah, my servant dear,
For vengeance shall no more appear;
375 And now farewell, my darling dear.

---

1. Of wrongly dead carrion (i.e., meat not killed according to dietary law), which is here, of that do not eat at all, for you must always leave that alone.
2. To give over such vengeance (as the flood).
3. Here I make you a promise.

4. Be destroyed by water as has happened.
5. The rainbow is visualized as a bow aimed away from the earth at the sky.
6. [A sign] that such a flood shall never appear.

SIR THOMAS MALORY

ca. 1405–1471

1451:	First of a long series of arrests and imprisonments.
ca. 1469–70:	*Morte Darthur* completed in prison.
1485:	*Morte Darthur* printed by William Caxton.

The little that we know of Malory (and that the Malory discussed here was indeed the Malory who wrote the *Morte Darthur* is an assumption that has been challenged severely although by no means fatally) suggests a man of violent temperament much given to lawless action. He seems to have been a respectable enough person in his youth, but in 1451 he got into difficulties with the law that lasted the rest of his life. In that year he was arrested to prevent his doing injury—presumably further injury—to a priory in Lincolnshire, and shortly thereafter he was accused of a number of criminal acts. These included escaping from prison after his first arrest, twice breaking into and plundering the Abbey of Coombe, extorting money from various persons, and committing rape. Malory pleaded innocent of all charges, and it is indeed possible that he was less guilty of (or had more provocation for) the crimes than the records make it appear. The years of the Wars of the Roses were violent ones, when a supporter of the party out of power was apt to be subjected to much persecution by the ruling group; such a man might at times feel himself justified in taking the law into his own hands to recover what had wrongfully been taken from him. But one suspects that Malory took the law into his own hands with unnecessary enthusiasm.

How much time Malory passed in prison is not known, but he was surely a prisoner in 1468 after he had supported an unsuccessful Lancastrian revolt against the Yorkist king, Edward IV, who specifically excluded Malory from two amnesties granted to the Lancastrians. It was probably in prison that he became engaged on the *Morte Darthur*; he was still in prison when he completed it, and may have died there. The book was printed (and edited) in 1485 by William Caxton, the first English printer. A manuscript of it discovered in 1934 helps us to a better text than Caxton's.

Arthurian romance, of which Malory's book is a compilation, is a body of highly diverse narrative materials that originated at various times among various peoples and that only gradually became associated with the name of Arthur. Arthur himself was probably a British or Roman-British leader who resisted the Anglo-Saxon invasions of England in the sixth century, but his historical reality is less important than the legendary role he played as the great figure around whom the medieval ideal of chivalry flourished. At its simplest, chivalry is the code that governs the actions of the knight-adventurer who rides out in search of wrongs that he may right—typically in search of ladies whom he may rescue from monsters, churls, and wicked knights. The ideal was invented and given a local habitation in the brilliantly imaginative and idealistic twelfth century. History had, of course, never witnessed such knights, such ladies, or such a landscape as that on which their adventures took place, and when chivalry was first invented it was already placed in the past. The human urge to devise an idealized past seems to be recurrent, for the Camelot of Arthur has its counterpart in the Sherwood Forest of Robin Hood and in the American West. All three of these fictions have the same ideal: that of maintaining order in an essentially lawless land by the efforts of the individual,

who fights for the right against seemingly overwhelming odds. Naive as the practice of this ideal may seem in the Arthurian fiction, the ideal itself has made
an important contribution to civilization—although if one imitates literally the
Arthurian practice of enforcing the right by violence, as Malory's life suggests that
he did, one will find oneself not maintaining order, but disrupting it.

The Arthurian milieu attracted to itself all sorts of diverse motifs, such as the
remnants of primitive pagan religious rites, heavily moralized Christianity, an elaborate and in general flagrantly immoral code of romantic love, and others equally
miscellaneous. In thirteenth-century France the amorphous Arthurian material
was given a kind of order in a series of prose narratives. Long and often rather
vaguely told, these formed the chief material that Malory further edited and
ordered while translating it into English.

His book is attractive, however, not only because it is the best and most complete
treatment of the story of Arthur and his knights but also because it is one of the
greatest pieces of prose in English. Malory was the first English writer to make
prose as sensitive an instrument of narrative as English poetry had always been.
Indeed, Malory achieves in his prose that wonderful impression of simplicity that
Chaucer achieves only in his poetry. No matter how extravagant the adventure
Malory is recounting, he always manages to give it a hard base of realism. He is in
particular a master of naturalistic dialogue, with which he keeps his narrative close
to earth. And both he and the majority of his characters are masters of understatement who express themselves, in moments of great emotional tension, with a bare
minimum of words. The result is highly provocative to the reader's imagination,
which is made, in a sense, to do the writer's work for him. This appeal to the
reader's creative imagination probably explains why the *Morte Darthur* brings forth
such widely differing responses from its readers, who agree, perhaps, only in their
affection for the work.

Although Malory considerably abridged the immensely long French romances
he was adapting, the *Morte Darthur* remains a work of imposing length. Its title,
the "Death of Arthur" (which was given to it by its first editor, Caxton), although
it rightly emphasizes the tragic nature of the ending, is misleading; for the bulk of
the work is taken up with the separate adventures of the knights of the Round
Table. Preeminent among these is Sir Lancelot, the "head of all Christian
knights," as he is called in a great eulogy by his brother, Sir Ector. But Lancelot
is compromised by his fatal liaison with Arthur's queen and torn between the
incompatible loyalties that bind him as an honorable knight, on the one hand, to
his lord Arthur and, on the other, to his lady Guinevere. Malory loves his character
Lancelot even to the point of indulging in the fleeting speculation, after Lancelot
has been admitted to the queen's chamber, that their activities might have been
innocent, "for love that time was not as love is nowadays." But when the jealousy
and malice of two wicked knights forces the affair into the open, nothing can avert
the breaking up of the fellowship of the Round Table and the death of Arthur
himself, which Malory relates with somber magnificence in one of his finest passages, the one on which Tennyson based a famous *Idyll*. This catastrophic chain
of events is the subject of the last of eight romances into which the unique manuscript of Malory's work is divided (a division suppressed in Caxton's edition). All
the selections, starting with the opening, are taken from this final one of Malory's
tales.

From Morte Darthur[1]

[*The Conspiracy against Lancelot and Guinevere*]

In May, when every lusty[2] heart flourisheth and burgeoneth, for as the season is lusty to behold and comfortable,[3] so man and woman rejoiceth and gladdeth of summer coming with his fresh flowers, for winter with his rough winds and blasts causeth lusty men and women to cower and to sit fast by the fire—so this season it befell in the month of May a great anger and unhap that stinted not[4] till the flower of chivalry of all the world was destroyed and slain. And all was long upon two unhappy[5] knights which were named Sir Agravain and Sir Mordred that were brethren unto Sir Gawain.[6] For this Sir Agravain and Sir Mordred had ever a privy[7] hate unto the Queen, Dame Guinevere, and to Sir Lancelot, and daily and nightly they ever watched upon Sir Lancelot.

So it misfortuned Sir Gawain and all his brethren were in King Arthur's chamber, and then Sir Agravain said thus openly, and not in no counsel,[8] that many knights might hear: "I marvel that we all be not ashamed both to see and to know how Sir Lancelot lieth daily and nightly by the Queen. And all we know well that it is so, and it is shamefully suffered of us all[9] that we should suffer so noble a king as King Arthur is to be shamed."

Then spoke Sir Gawain and said, "Brother, Sir Agravain, I pray you and charge you, move no such matters no more afore[1] me, for wit you well, I will not be of your counsel."[2]

"So God me help," said Sir Gaheris and Sir Gareth,[3] "we will not be known of your deeds."[4]

"Then will I!" said Sir Mordred.

"I lieve[5] you well," said Sir Gawain, "for ever unto all unhappiness, sir, ye will grant.[6] And I would that ye left all this and make you not so busy, for I know," said Sir Gawain, "what will fall of it."[7]

"Fall whatsoever fall may," said Sir Agravain, "I will disclose it to the King."

"Not by my counsel," said Sir Gawain, "for and[8] there arise war and wrack betwixt[9] Sir Lancelot and us, wit you well, brother, there will many kings and great lords hold with Sir Lancelot. Also, brother, Sir Agravain," said Sir Gawain, "ye must remember how often times Sir Lancelot hath rescued the King and the Queen. And the best of us all had been full cold at the heart-root[1] had not Sir Lancelot been better than we, and that has he proved himself full oft. And as for my part," said Sir Gawain, "I will never be against Sir

---

1. The selections given here are from the section that Caxton called book 20, chaps. 1–4, 8–10, and book 21, chaps. 3–7, 10–12, with omissions. In the Winchester manuscript this section is titled "The Most Piteous Tale of the Morte Arthur Saunz Guerdon" (i.e., the death of Arthur without reward or compensation). The text has been based on Winchester, with some readings introduced from the Caxton edition; spelling has been modernized and modern punctuation added.
2. Merry.
3. Pleasant.
4. Misfortune that ceased not.
5. On account of two ill-fated.
6. Gawain and Agravain are sons of King Lot of Orkney and his wife, Arthur's half-sister Morgause. Mor-

dred is the illegitimate son of Arthur and Morgause.
7. Secret.
8. Secret manner.
9. Put up with by all of us.
1. Before. "Move": propose.
2. On your side. "Wit you well": know well, i.e., give you to understand.
3. Sons of King Lot and Gawain's brothers.
4. A party to your doings.
5. Believe.
6. You will consent to all mischief.
7. Come of it.
8. If.
9. Strife between.
1. Would have been dead.

Lancelot for[2] one day's deed, when he rescued me from King Carados of the Dolorous Tower and slew him and saved my life. Also, brother, Sir Agravain and Sir Mordred, in like wise Sir Lancelot rescued you both and three score and two[3] from Sir Tarquin. And therefore, brother, methinks such noble deeds and kindness should be remembered."

"Do as ye list,"[4] said Sir Agravain, "for I will layne[5] it no longer."

So with these words came in Sir Arthur.

"Now, brother," said Sir Gawain, "stint your noise."[6]

"That will I not," said Sir Agravain and Sir Mordred.

"Well, will ye so?" said Sir Gawain. "Then God speed you, for I will not hear of your tales, neither be of your counsel."

"No more will I," said Sir Gaheris.

"Neither I," said Sir Gareth, "for I shall never say evil by[7] that man that made me knight." And therewithal they three departed making great dole.[8]

"Alas!" said Sir Gawain and Sir Gareth, "now is this realm wholly destroyed and mischieved,[9] and the noble fellowship of the Round Table shall be disparbeled."[1]

So they departed, and then King Arthur asked them what noise they made. "My lord," said Sir Agravain, "I shall tell you, for I may keep[2] it no longer. Here is I and my brother Sir Mordred broke[3] unto my brother Sir Gawain, Sir Gaheris, and to Sir Gareth—for this is all, to make it short—how that we know all that Sir Lancelot holdeth your queen, and hath done long; and we be your sister[4] sons, we may suffer it no longer. And all we woot[5] that ye should be above Sir Lancelot, and ye are the king that made him knight, and therefore we will prove it that he is a traitor to your person."

"If it be so," said the King, "wit[6] you well, he is none other. But I would be loath to begin such a thing but[7] I might have proofs of it, for Sir Lancelot is an hardy knight, and all ye know that he is the best knight among us all. And but if he be taken with the deed,[8] he will fight with him that bringeth up the noise, and I know no knight that is able to match him. Therefore, and[9] it be sooth as ye say, I would that he were taken with the deed."

For, as the French book saith, the King was full loath that such a noise should be upon Sir Lancelot and his queen. For the King had a deeming[1] of it, but he would not hear of it, for Sir Lancelot had done so much for him and for the Queen so many times that, wit you well, the King loved him passingly[2] well.

"My lord," said Sir Agravain, "ye shall ride tomorn[3] on hunting, and doubt ye not, Sir Lancelot will not go with you. And so when it draweth toward night, ye may send the Queen word that ye will lie out all that night, and so may ye send for your cooks. And then, upon pain of death, that night we

---

2. On account of.
3. I.e., sixty-two.
4. You please.
5. Conceal.
6. Stop making scandal.
7. About.
8. Lamentation.
9. Put to shame.
1. Dispersed.
2. Conceal.

3. Revealed.
4. Sister's.
5. Know.
6. Know.
7. Unless.
8. Unless he is caught in the act.
9. If.
1. Suspicion.
2. Exceedingly.
3. Tomorrow.

shall take him with the Queen, and we shall bring him unto you, quick[4] or dead."

"I will well,"[5] said the King. "Then I counsel you to take with you sure fellowship."

"Sir," said Sir Agravain, "my brother, Sir Mordred, and I will take with us twelve knights of the Round Table."

"Beware," said King Arthur, "for I warn you, ye shall find him wight."[6]

"Let us deal!"[7] said Sir Agravain and Sir Mordred.

So on the morn King Arthur rode on hunting and sent word to the Queen that he would be out all that night. Then Sir Agravain and Sir Mordred got to them[8] twelve knights and hid themself in a chamber in the castle of Carlisle. And these were their names: Sir Colgrevance, Sir Mador de la Porte, Sir Guingalen, Sir Meliot de Logres, Sir Petipace of Winchelsea, Sir Galeron of Galway, Sir Melion de la Mountain, Sir Ascamore, Sir Gromore Somyr Jour, Sir Curselayne, Sir Florence, and Sir Lovell. So these twelve knights were with Sir Mordred and Sir Agravain, and all they were of Scotland, or else of Sir Gawain's kin, or well-willers[9] to his brother.

So when the night came, Sir Lancelot told Sir Bors[1] how he would go that night and speak with the Queen.

"Sir," said Sir Bors, "ye shall not go this night by my counsel."

"Why?" said Sir Lancelot.

"Sir," said Sir Bors, "I dread me[2] ever of Sir Agravain that waiteth upon[3] you daily to do you shame and us all. And never gave my heart against no going that ever ye went[4] to the queen so much as now, for I mistrust[5] that the King is out this night from the Queen because peradventure he hath lain[6] some watch for you and the Queen. Therefore, I dread me sore of some treason."

"Have ye no dread," said Sir Lancelot, "for I shall go and come again and make no tarrying."

"Sir," said Sir Bors, "that me repents,[7] for I dread me sore that your going this night shall wrath[8] us all."

"Fair nephew," said Sir Lancelot, "I marvel me much why ye say thus, sithen[9] the Queen hath sent for me. And wit you well, I will not be so much a coward, but she shall understand I will[1] see her good grace."

"God speed you well," said Sir Bors, "and send you sound and safe again!"

So Sir Lancelot departed and took his sword under his arm, and so he walked in his mantel,[2] that noble knight, and put himself in great jeopardy. And so he passed on till he came to the Queen's chamber, and so lightly he was had[3] into the chamber. And then, as the French book saith, the Queen and Sir Lancelot were together. And whether they were abed or at other manner of disports, me list[4] not thereof make no mention, for love that time[5] was not as love is nowadays.

---

4. Alive.
5. Readily agree.
6. Strong.
7. Leave it to us.
8. Gathered to themselves.
9. Partisans.
1. Nephew and confidant of Sir Lancelot.
2. I am afraid.
3. Lies in wait.
4. Never misgave my heart against any visit you made.

5. Suspect.
6. Perhaps he has set.
7. I regret.
8. Cause injury to.
9. Since.
1. Wish to.
2. Cloak. Lancelot goes unarmed.
3. Quickly he was received.
4. I care. "Disports": pastimes.
5. At that time.

But thus as they were together there came Sir Agravain and Sir Mordred with twelve knights with them of the Round Table, and they said with great crying and scaring[6] voice: "Thou traitor, Sir Lancelot, now are thou taken!" And thus they cried with a loud voice that all the court might hear it. And these fourteen knights all were armed at all points, as[7] they should fight in a battle.

"Alas!" said Queen Guinevere, "now are we mischieved[8] both!"

"Madam," said Sir Lancelot, "is there here any armor within your chamber that I might cover my body withal? And if there be any, give it me, and I shall soon stint[9] their malice, by the grace of God!"

"Now, truly," said the Queen, "I have none armor neither helm, shield, sword, neither spear, wherefore I dread me sore our long love is come to a mischievous end. For I hear by their noise there be many noble knights, and well I woot they be surely[1] armed, and against them ye may make no resistance. Wherefore ye are likely to be slain, and then shall I be burned! For and[2] ye might escape them," said the Queen, "I would not doubt but that ye would rescue me in what danger that ever I stood in."

"Alas!" said Sir Lancelot, "in all my life thus was I never bestead[3] that I should be thus shamefully slain for lack of mine armor."

But ever in one[4] Sir Agravain and Sir Mordred cried: "Traitor knight, come out of the Queen's chamber! For wit thou well thou art beset so that thou shalt not escape."

"Ah, Jesu mercy!" said Sir Lancelot, "this shameful cry and noise I may not suffer, for better were death at once than thus to endure this pain." Then he took the Queen in his arms and kissed her and said, "Most noblest Christian queen, I beseech you, as ye have been ever my special good lady, and I at all times your poor knight and true unto[5] my power, and as I never failed you in right nor in wrong sithen the first day King Arthur made me knight, that ye will pray for my soul if that I be slain. For well I am assured that Sir Bors, my nephew, and all the remnant of my kin, with Sir Lavain and Sir Urry,[6] that they will not fail you to rescue you from the fire. And therefore, mine own lady, recomfort yourself,[7] whatsoever come of me, that ye go with Sir Bors, my nephew, and Sir Urry and they all will do you all the pleasure that they may, and ye shall live like a queen upon my lands."

"Nay, Sir Lancelot, nay!" said the Queen. "Wit thou well that I will not live long after thy days. But and[8] ye be slain I will take my death as meekly as ever did martyr take his death for Jesu Christ's sake."

"Well, Madam," said Sir Lancelot, "sith it is so that the day is come that our love must depart,[9] wit you well I shall sell my life as dear as I may. And a thousandfold," said Sir Lancelot, "I am more heavier[1] for you than for myself! And now I had liefer[2] than to be lord of all Christendom that I had sure armor upon me, that men might speak of my deeds ere ever I were slain."

---

6. Terrifying.
7. Completely, as if.
8. Come to grief.
9. Stop.
1. Securely.
2. If.
3. Beset.
4. In unison.
5. To the utmost of.

6. The brother of Elaine, the Fair Maid of Astolat, and a knight miraculously healed of his wound by Sir Lancelot. "Remnant": rest.
7. Take heart again.
8. If.
9. Come to an end.
1. More grieved.
2. Rather.

"Truly," said the Queen, "and[3] it might please God, I would that they would take me and slay me and suffer[4] you to escape."

"That shall never be," said Sir Lancelot. "God defend me from such a shame! But, Jesu Christ, be Thou my shield and mine armor!" And therewith Sir Lancelot wrapped his mantel about his arm well and surely; and by then they had gotten a great form[5] out of the hall, and therewith they all rushed at the door. "Now, fair lords," said Sir Lancelot, "leave[6] your noise and your rushing, and I shall set open this door, and then may ye do with me what it liketh you."[7]

"Come off,[8] then," said they all, "and do it, for it availeth thee not to strive against us all. And therefore let us into this chamber, and we shall save thy life until thou come to King Arthur."

Then Sir Lancelot unbarred the door, and with his left hand he held it open a little, that but one man might come in at once. And so there came striding a good knight, a much[9] man and a large, and his name was called Sir Colgrevance of Gore. And he with a sword struck at Sir Lancelot mightily. And he put aside[1] the stroke and gave him such a buffet[2] upon the helmet that he fell groveling dead within the chamber door. Then Sir Lancelot with great might drew the knight within[3] the chamber door. And then Sir Lancelot, with help of the Queen and her ladies, he was lightly[4] armed in Colgrevance's armor. And ever stood Sir Agravain and Sir Mordred, crying, "Traitor knight! Come forth out of the Queen's chamber!"

"Sirs, leave[5] your noise," said Sir Lancelot, "for wit you well, Sir Agravain, ye shall not prison me this night. And therefore, and [6] ye do by my counsel, go ye all from this chamber door and make you no such crying and such manner of slander as ye do. For I promise you by my knighthood, and ye will depart and make no more noise, I shall as tomorn appear afore you all and before the King, and then let it be seen which of you all, other else ye all,[7] that will deprove[8] me of treason. And there shall I answer you, as a knight should, that hither I came to the Queen for no manner of mal engine,[9] and that will I prove and make it good upon you with my hands."

"Fie upon thee, traitor," said Sir Agravain and Sir Mordred, "for we will have thee malgré thine head[1] and slay thee, and we list. For we let thee wit we have the choice of [2] King Arthur to save thee other slay thee."

"Ah, sirs," said Sir Lancelot, "is there none other grace with you? Then keep[3] yourself!" And then Sir Lancelot set all open the chamber door and mightily and knightly he strode in among them. And anon[4] at the first stroke he slew Sir Agravain, and after twelve of his fellows. Within a little while he had laid them down cold to the earth, for there was none of the twelve knights might stand Sir Lancelot one buffet.[5] And also he wounded Sir Mordred, and therewithal he fled with all his might.

---

3. If.
4. Allow.
5. Bench.
6. Stop.
7. Pleases you.
8. Go ahead.
9. Big.
1. Fended off.
2. Blow.
3. Inside.
4. Quickly.

5. Stop.
6. If.
7. Or else all of you.
8. Accuse.
9. Evil design.
1. In spite of you.
2. From.
3. Defend.
4. Right away.
5. Withstand Sir Lancelot one blow.

And then Sir Lancelot returned again unto the Queen and said, "Madam, now wit you well, all our true love is brought to an end, for now will King Arthur ever be my foe. And therefore, Madam, and it like you[6] that I may have you with me, I shall save you from all manner adventurous[7] dangers."

"Sir, that is not best," said the Queen, "me seemeth, for[8] now ye have done so much harm, it will be best that ye hold you still with this. And if ye see that as tomorn they will put me unto death, then may ye rescue me as ye think best."

"I will well,"[9] said Sir Lancelot, "for have ye no doubt, while I am a man living I shall rescue you." And then he kissed her, and either of them gave other a ring, and so there he left the Queen and went until[1] his lodging.

[War Breaks Out between Arthur and Lancelot][2]

Then said King Arthur unto Sir Gawain, "Dear nephew, I pray you make ready in your best armor with your brethren, Sir Gaheris and Sir Gareth, to bring my Queen to the fire, there to have her judgment and receive the death."

"Nay, my most noble king," said Sir Gawain, "that will I never do, for wit you well I will never be in that place where so noble a queen as is my lady Dame Guinevere shall take such a shameful end. For wit you well," said Sir Gawain, "my heart will not serve me for to see her die, and it shall never be said that ever I was of your counsel for her death."

"Then," said the King unto Sir Gawain, "suffer[3] your brethren Sir Gaheris and Sir Gareth to be there."

"My lord," said Sir Gawain, "wit you well they will be loath to be there present because of many adventures[4] that is like to fall, but they are young and full unable to say you nay."

Then spake Sir Gaheris and the good knight Sir Gareth unto King Arthur: "Sir, ye may well command us to be there, but wit you well it shall be sore against our will. But and[5] we be there by your straight commandment, ye shall plainly[6] hold us there excused—we will be there in peaceable wise and bear none harness of war upon us."

"In the name of God," said the King, "then make you ready, for she shall have soon[7] her judgment."

"Alas," said Sir Gawain, "that ever I should endure[8] to see this woeful day." So Sir Gawain turned him and wept heartily, and so he went into his chamber.

And then the Queen was led forth without[9] Carlisle, and anon she was dispoiled into[1] her smock. And then her ghostly father[2] was brought to her to be shriven of her misdeeds.[3] Then was there weeping and wailing and wring-

---

6. If it please you.
7. Perilous.
8. Because.
9. Agree.
1. To.
2. Lancelot and Sir Bors mobilize their friends for the rescue of Guinevere. In the morning Mordred reports the events of the night to Arthur who, against Gawain's strong opposition, condemns the queen to be burned, for "the law was such in those days that whatsoever they were, of what estate or degree, if they were found guilty of treason there should be none other remedy but death."

3. Allow.
4. Chance occurrences.
5. If.
6. Openly. "Straight": strict.
7. Right away.
8. Live.
9. Outside.
1. Undressed down to.
2. Spiritual father, i.e., her priest.
3. For her to be confessed of her sins.

ing of hands of many lords and ladies, but there were but few in comparison that would bear any armor for to strengthen[4] the death of the Queen.

Then was there one that Sir Lancelot had sent unto that place, which went to espy what time the Queen should go unto her death. And anon as[5] he saw the Queen dispoiled into her smock and shriven, then he gave Sir Lancelot warning. Then was there but spurring and plucking up[6] of horses, and right so they came unto the fire. And who[7] that stood against them, there were they slain—there might none withstand Sir Lancelot. So all that bore arms and withstood them, there were they slain, full many a noble knight. * * * And so in this rushing and hurling, as Sir Lancelot thrang[8] here and there, it misfortuned him[9] to slay Sir Gaheris and Sir Gareth, the noble knight, for they were unarmed and unwares.[1] As the French book saith, Sir Lancelot smote Sir Gaheris and Sir Gareth upon the brain-pans, wherethrough[2] that they were slain in the field, howbeit[3] Sir Lancelot saw them not. And so were they found dead among the thickest of the press.

Then when Sir Lancelot had thus done, and slain and put to flight all that would withstand him, then he rode straight unto Queen Guinevere and made a kirtle[4] and a gown to be cast upon her, and then he made her to be set behind him and prayed her to be of good cheer. Now wit you well the Queen was glad that she was escaped from death, and then she thanked God and Sir Lancelot.

And so he rode his way with the Queen, as the French book saith, unto Joyous Garde,[5] and there he kept her as a noble knight should. And many great lords and many good knights were sent him, and many full noble knights drew unto him. When they heard that King Arthur and Sir Lancelot were at debate,[6] many knights were glad, and many were sorry of their debate.

Now turn we again unto King Arthur, that when it was told him how and in what manner the Queen was taken away from the fire, and when he heard of the death of his noble knights, and in especial Sir Gaheris and Sir Gareth, then he swooned for very pure[7] sorrow. And when he awoke of his swoon, then he said: "Alas, that ever I bore crown upon my head! For now have I lost the fairest fellowship of noble knights that ever held Christian king[8] together. Alas, my good knights be slain and gone away from me. Now within these two days I have lost nigh forty knights and also the noble fellowship of Sir Lancelot and his blood,[9] for now I may nevermore hold them together with my worship.[1] Alas, that ever this war began!

"Now, fair fellows," said the King, "I charge you that no man tell Sir Gawain of the death of his two brethren, for I am sure," said the King, "when he heareth tell that Sir Gareth is dead, he will go nigh out of his mind. Mercy Jesu," said the King, "why slew he Sir Gaheris and Sir Gareth? For I dare say, as for Sir Gareth, he loved Sir Lancelot above all men earthly."[2]

"That is truth," said some knights, "but they were slain in the hurling,[3] as Sir Lancelot thrang in the thickest of the press. And as they were unarmed, he

4. Secure.
5. As soon as.
6. Urging forward.
7. Whoever.
8. Pressed. "Hurling": turmoil.
9. He had the misfortune.
1. Unaware.
2. Through which.
3. Although.

4. Petticoat.
5. Lancelot's castle in England.
6. Strife.
7. Sheer.
8. That Christian king ever held.
9. Kin.
1. Glory.
2. Earthly men.
3. Turmoil.

smote them and wist[4] not whom that he smote, and so unhappily[5] they were slain."

"Well," said Arthur, "the death of them will cause the greatest mortal war that ever was, for I am sure that when Sir Gawain knoweth hereof that Sir Gareth is slain, I shall never have rest of him[6] till I have destroyed Sir Lancelot's kin and himself both, other else he to destroy me. And therefore," said the King, "wit you well, my heart was never so heavy as it is now. And much more I am sorrier for my good knights' loss[7] than for the loss of my fair queen; for queens I might have enough, but such a fellowship of good knights shall never be together in no company. And now I dare say," said King Arthur, "there was never Christian king that ever held such a fellowship together. And alas, that ever Sir Lancelot and I should be at debate. Ah, Agravain, Agravain!" said the King, "Jesu forgive it thy soul, for thine evil will that thou and thy brother Sir Mordred haddest unto Sir Lancelot hath caused all this sorrow." And ever among these complaints the King wept and swooned.

Then came there one to Sir Gawain and told him how the Queen was led away with[8] Sir Lancelot, and nigh a four-and-twenty knights slain. "Ah, Jesu, save me my two brethren!" said Sir Gawain. "For full well wist I," said Sir Gawain, "that Sir Lancelot would rescue her, other else he would die in that field. And to say the truth he were not of worship but if he had[9] rescued the Queen, insomuch as she should have been burned for his sake. And as in that," said Sir Gawain, "he hath done but knightly, and as I would have done myself and I had stood in like case. But where are my brethren?" said Sir Gawain. "I marvel that I hear not of them."

Then said that man, "Truly, Sir Gaheris and Sir Gareth be slain."

"Jesu defend!"[1] said Sir Gawain. "For all this world I would not that they were slain, and in especial my good brother Sir Gareth."

"Sir," said the man, "he is slain, and that is great pity."

"Who slew him?" said Sir Gawain.

"Sir Lancelot," said the man, "slew them both."

"That may I not believe," said Sir Gawain, "that ever he slew my good brother Sir Gareth, for I dare say my brother loved him better than me and all his brethren and the King both. Also I dare say, an[2] Sir Lancelot had desired my brother Sir Gareth with him, he would have been with him against the King and us all. And therefore I may never believe that Sir Lancelot slew my brethren."

"Verily, sir," said the man, "it is noised[3] that he slew him."

"Alas," said Sir Gawain, "now is my joy gone." And then he fell down and swooned, and long he lay there as he had been dead. And when he arose out of his swoon, he cried out sorrowfully and said, "Alas!" And forthwith he ran unto the King, crying and weeping, and said, "Ah, mine uncle King Arthur! My good brother Sir Gareth is slain, and so is my brother Sir Gaheris, which were two noble knights."

Then the King wept and he both, and so they fell on swooning. And when they were revived, then spake Sir Gawain and said, "Sir, I will go and see my brother Sir Gareth."

---

4. Knew.
5. Unluckily.
6. He will never give me any peace.
7. The loss of my good knights.
8. By.

9. Of honor if he had not.
1. Forbid.
2. If.
3. Reported.

"Sir, ye may not see him," said the King, "for I caused him to be interred and Sir Gaheris both, for I well understood that ye would make overmuch sorrow, and the sight of Sir Gareth should have caused your double sorrow."

"Alas, my lord," said Sir Gawain, "how slew he my brother Sir Gareth? Mine own good lord, I pray you tell me."

"Truly," said the King, "I shall tell you as it hath been told me—Sir Lancelot slew him and Sir Gaheris both."

"Alas," said Sir Gawain, "they bore none arms against him, neither of them both."

"I woot not how it was," said the King, "but as it is said, Sir Lancelot slew them in the thickest of the press and knew them not. And therefore let us shape a remedy for to revenge their deaths."

"My king, my lord, and mine uncle," said Sir Gawain, "wit you well, now I shall make you a promise which I shall hold by my knighthood, that from this day forward I shall never fail[4] Sir Lancelot until that one of us have slain the other. And therefore I require you, my lord and king, dress[5] you unto the wars, for wit you well, I will be revenged upon Sir Lancelot; and therefore, as ye will have my service and my love, now haste you thereto and assay[6] your friends. For I promise unto God," said Sir Gawain, "for the death of my brother Sir Gareth I shall seek Sir Lancelot throughout seven kings' realms, but I shall slay him, other else he shall slay me."

"Sir, ye shall not need to seek him so far," said the King, "for as I hear say, Sir Lancelot will abide me and us all within the castle of Joyous Garde. And much people draweth unto him, as I hear say."

"That may I right well believe," said Sir Gawain, "but my lord," he said, "assay your friends and I will assay mine."

"It shall be done," said the King, "and as I suppose I shall be big[7] enough to drive him out of the biggest tower of his castle."

So then the King sent letters and writs throughout all England, both the length and the breadth, for to summon all his knights. And so unto King Arthur drew many knights, dukes, and earls, that he had a great host, and when they were assembled the King informed them how Sir Lancelot had bereft him his Queen. Then the King and all his host made them ready to lay siege about Sir Lancelot where he lay within Joyous Garde.

[The Death of Arthur][8]

So upon Trinity Sunday at night King Arthur dreamed a wonderful dream, and in his dream him seemed that he saw upon a chafflet[9] a chair, and the chair was fast to a wheel, and thereupon sat King Arthur in the richest cloth of gold that might be made. And the King thought there was under him, far from him, an hideous deep black water, and therein was all manner of serpents, and worms, and wild beasts, foul and horrible. And suddenly the King

4. Give up the pursuit of.
5. Prepare.
6. Appeal to.
7. Strong.
8. The pope arranges a truce, Guinevere is returned to Arthur, and Lancelot and his kin leave England to become rulers of France. At Gawain's instigation Arthur invades France to resume the war against

Lancelot. Word comes to the king that Mordred has seized the kingdom, and Arthur leads his forces back to England. Mordred attacks them upon their landing, and Gawain is mortally wounded and dies, although not before he has repented for having insisted that Arthur fight Lancelot and has written Lancelot to come to the aid of his former lord.
9. Scaffold. "Him seemed": it seemed to him.

thought that the wheel turned upside down, and he fell among the serpents, and every beast took him by a limb. And then the King cried as he lay in his bed, "Help, help!"

And then knights, squires, and yeomen awaked the King, and then he was so amazed that he wist[1] not where he was. And then so he awaked[2] until it was nigh day, and then he fell on slumbering again, not sleeping nor thoroughly waking. So the King seemed[3] verily that there came Sir Gawain unto him with a number of fair ladies with him. So when King Arthur saw him, he said, "Welcome, my sister's son. I weened ye had been dead. And now I see thee on-live, much am I beholden unto Almighty Jesu. Ah, fair nephew and my sister's son, what been these ladies that hither be come with you?"

"Sir," said Sir Gawain, "all these be ladies for whom I have foughten for when I was man living. And all these are tho[4] that I did battle for in righteous quarrels, and God hath given them that grace, at their great prayer, because I did battle for them for their right, that they should bring me hither unto you. Thus much hath given me leave God, for to warn you of your death. For and ye fight as tomorn[5] with Sir Mordred, as ye both have assigned,[6] doubt ye not ye must be slain, and the most party of your people on both parties. And for the great grace and goodness that Almighty Jesu hath unto you, and for pity of you and many mo other good men there[7] shall be slain, God hath sent me to you of his special grace to give you warning that in no wise ye do battle as tomorn, but that ye take a treatise for a month-day.[8] And proffer you largely,[9] so that tomorn ye put in a delay. For within a month shall come Sir Lancelot with all his noble knights and rescue you worshipfully and slay Sir Mordred and all that ever will hold with him."

Then Sir Gawain and all the ladies vanished. And anon the King called upon his knights, squires, and yeomen, and charged them wightly[1] to fetch his noble lords and wise bishops unto him. And when they were come the King told them of his avision,[2] that Sir Gawain had told him and warned him that, and he fought on the morn, he should be slain. Then the King commanded Sir Lucan the Butler[3] and his brother Sir Bedivere the Bold, with two bishops with them, and charged them in any wise to take a treatise for a month-day with Sir Mordred. "And spare not: proffer him lands and goods as much as ye think reasonable."

So then they departed and came to Sir Mordred where he had a grim host of an hundred thousand, and there they entreated[4] Sir Mordred long time. And at the last Sir Mordred was agreed for to have Cornwall and Kent by King Arthur's days,[5] and after that, all England, after the days of King Arthur.

Then were they condescended[6] that King Arthur and Sir Mordred should meet betwixt both their hosts, and everich[7] of them should bring fourteen persons. And so they came with this word unto Arthur. Then said he, "I am glad that this is done," and so he went into the field.

And when King Arthur should depart, he warned all his host that, and they

---

1. Knew.
2. Lay awake.
3. It seemed to the king.
4. Those.
5. If you fight tomorrow.
6. Decided.
7. I.e., who there. "Mo": more.
8. For a month from today. "Treatise": treaty, truce.
9. Make generous offers.

1. Quickly.
2. Dream.
3. "Butler" here is probably only a title of high rank, although it was originally used to designate the officer who had charge of wine for the king's table.
4. Dealt with.
5. During King Arthur's lifetime.
6. Agreed.
7. Each.

see any sword drawn, "Look ye come on fiercely and slay that traitor Sir Mordred, for I in no wise trust him." In like wise Sir Mordred warned his host that
"And ye see any manner of sword drawn, look that ye come on fiercely, and
so slay all that ever before you standeth, for in no wise I will not trust for this
treatise." And in the same wise said Sir Mordred unto his host, "For I know
well my father will be avenged upon me."

   And so they met as their pointment[8] was and were agreed and accorded
thoroughly. And wine was fetched and they drank together. Right so came an
adder out of a little heath-bush, and it stung a knight in the foot. And so when
the knight felt him so stung, he looked down and saw the adder. And anon he
drew his sword to slay the adder, and thought[9] none other harm. And when
the host on both parties saw that sword drawn, then they blew beams,[1] trumpets, and horns, and shouted grimly. And so both hosts dressed them[2] together.
And King Arthur took his horse and said, "Alas, this unhappy day!" and so
rode to his party, and Sir Mordred in like wise.

   And never since was there never seen a more dolefuller battle in no Christian land, for there was but rushing and riding, foining[3] and striking; and
many a grim word was there spoken of either to other, and many a deadly
stroke. But ever King Arthur rode throughout the battle[4] of Sir Mordred many
times and did full nobly, as a noble king should do, and at all times he fainted
never. And Sir Mordred did his devoir[5] that day and put himself in great peril.

   And thus they fought all the long day, and never stinted[6] till the noble
knights were laid to the cold earth. And ever they fought still till it was near
night, and by then was there an hundred thousand laid dead upon the down.
Then was King Arthur wood-wroth[7] out of measure when he saw his people
so slain from him. And so he looked about him and could see no mo[8] of all
his host, and good knights left no mo on-live, but two knights: the t'one[9] was
Sir Lucan the Butler and [the other] his brother Sir Bedivere. And yet they
were full sore wounded.

   "Jesu, mercy," said the King, "where are all my noble knights become?[1]
Alas that ever I should see this doleful day! For now," said King Arthur, "I am
come to mine end. But would to God," said he, "that I wist[2] now where were
that traitor Sir Mordred that has caused all this mischief."

   Then King Arthur looked about and was ware where stood Sir Mordred
leaning upon his sword among a great heap of dead men.

   "Now give me my spear," said King Arthur unto Sir Lucan, "for yonder I
have espied the traitor that all this woe hath wrought."

   "Sir, let him be," said Sir Lucan, "for he is unhappy.[3] And if ye pass this
unhappy day ye shall be right well revenged upon him. And, good lord,
remember ye of your night's dream, and what the spirit of Sir Gawain told
you tonight, and yet God of his great goodness hath preserved you hitherto.
And for God's sake, my lord, leave off by this,[4] for, blessed be God, ye have
won the field: for yet we been here three on-live, and with Sir Mordred is not

8. Arrangement.   7. Mad with rage.
9. Meant.   8. Others.
1. A kind of trumpet.   9. That one, i.e., the first.
2. Prepared to come.   1. What has become of all my noble knights?
3. Lunging.   2. Knew.
4. Battalion.   3. I.e., unlucky for you.
5. Knightly duty.   4. I.e., with this much accomplished.
6. Stopped.

one on-live. And therefore if ye leave off now, this wicked day of destiny is past."

"Now, tide[5] me death, tide me life," said the King, "now I see him yonder alone, he shall never escape mine hands. For at a better avail[6] shall I never have him."

"God speed you well!" said Sir Bedivere.

Then the King got his spear in both his hands and ran toward Sir Mordred, crying and saying, "Traitor, now is thy deathday come!"

And when Sir Mordred saw King Arthur he ran until him with his sword drawn in his hand, and there King Arthur smote Sir Mordred under the shield, with a foin[7] of his spear, throughout the body more than a fathom.[8] And when Sir Mordred felt that he had his death's wound, he thrust himself with the might that he had up to the burr[9] of King Arthur's spear, and right so he smote his father King Arthur with his sword holden in both his hands, upon the side of the head, that the sword pierced the helmet and the tay[1] of the brain. And therewith Sir Mordred dashed down stark dead to the earth.

And noble King Arthur fell in a swough[2] to the earth, and there he swooned oftentimes, and Sir Lucan and Sir Bedivere ofttimes heaved him up. And so, weakly betwixt them, they led him to a little chapel not far from the seaside, and when the King was there, him thought him reasonably eased. Then heard they people cry in the field. "Now go thou, Sir Lucan," said the King, "and do me to wit[3] what betokens that noise in the field."

So Sir Lucan departed, for he was grievously wounded in many places. And so as he yede[4] he saw and harkened by the moonlight how that pillers[5] and robbers were come into the field to pill and to rob many a full noble knight of brooches and bees[6] and of many a good ring and many a rich jewel. And who that were not dead all out there they slew them for their harness[7] and their riches. When Sir Lucan understood this work, he came to the King as soon as he might and told him all what he had heard and seen. "Therefore by my read,"[8] said Sir Lucan, "it is best that we bring you to some town."

"I would it were so," said the King, "but I may not stand, my head works[9] so. Ah, Sir Lancelot," said King Arthur, "this day have I sore missed thee. And alas that ever I was against thee, for now have I my death, whereof Sir Gawain me warned in my dream."

Then Sir Lucan took up the King the t'one party[1] and Sir Bedivere the other party; and in the lifting up the King swooned and in the lifting Sir Lucan fell in a swoon that part of his guts fell out of his body, and therewith the noble knight's heart burst. And when the King awoke he beheld Sir Lucan how he lay foaming at the mouth and part of his guts lay at his feet.

"Alas," said the King, "this is to me a full heavy[2] sight to see this noble duke so die for my sake, for he would have holpen[3] me that had more need of help than I. Alas that he would not complain him for[4] his heart was so set to help me. Now Jesu have mercy upon his soul."

---

5. Betide.
6. Advantage.
7. Thrust.
8. I.e., six feet.
9. Hand guard.
1. Edge.
2. Swoon.
3. Let me know.
4. Walked.

5. Plunderers.
6. Bracelets.
7. Armor. "All out": entirely.
8. Advice.
9. Aches.
1. On one side.
2. Sorrowful.
3. Helped.
4. Because.

Then Sir Bedivere wept for the death of his brother.

"Now leave this mourning and weeping, gentle knight," said the King, "for all this will not avail me. For wit thou well, and[5] I might live myself, the death of Sir Lucan would grieve me evermore. But my time passeth on fast," said the King. "Therefore," said King Arthur unto Sir Bedivere, "take thou here Excalibur[6] my good sword and go with it to yonder water's side; and when thou comest there I charge thee throw my sword in that water and come again and tell me what thou sawest there."

"My lord," said Sir Bedivere, "your commandment shall be done, and [I shall] lightly[7] bring you word again."

So Sir Bedivere departed. And by the way he beheld that noble sword, that the pommel and the haft[8] was all precious stones. And then he said to himself, "If I throw this rich sword in the water, thereof shall never come good, but harm and loss." And then Sir Bedivere hid Excalibur under a tree. And so, as soon as he might, he came again unto the King and said he had been at the water and had thrown the sword into the water.

"What saw thou there?" said the King.

"Sir," he said, "I saw nothing but waves and winds."

"That is untruly said of thee," said the King. "And therefore go thou lightly again and do my commandment; as thou art to me lief[9] and dear, spare not, but throw it in."

Then Sir Bedivere returned again and took the sword in his hand. And yet him thought[1] sin and shame to throw away that noble sword. And so eft[2] he hid the sword and returned again and told the King that he had been at the water and done his commandment.

"What sawest thou there?" said the King.

"Sir," he said, "I saw nothing but waters wap and waves wan."[3]

"Ah, traitor unto me and untrue," said King Arthur, "now hast thou betrayed me twice. Who would have weened that thou that has been to me so lief and dear, and thou art named a noble knight, and would betray me for the riches of this sword. But now go again lightly, for thy long tarrying putteth me in great jeopardy of my life, for I have taken cold. And but if thou do now as I bid thee, if ever I may see thee I shall slay thee mine[4] own hands, for thou wouldest for my rich sword see me dead."

Then Sir Bedivere departed and went to the sword and lightly took it up, and so he went to the water's side; and there he bound the girdle[5] about the hilts, and threw the sword as far into the water as he might. And there came an arm and an hand above the water and took it and clutched it, and shook it thrice and brandished; and then vanished away the hand with the sword into the water. So Sir Bedivere came again to the King and told him what he saw.

"Alas," said the King, "help me hence, for I dread me I have tarried overlong."

Then Sir Bedivere took the King upon his back and so went with him to

---

5. If.
6. The sword that Arthur had received as a young man from the Lady of the Lake; it is presumably she who catches it when Bedivere finally throws it into the water.
7. Quickly.
8. Handle. "Pommel": rounded knob on the hilt.

9. Beloved.
1. It seemed to him.
2. Again.
3. The phrase seems to mean "waters wash the shore and waves grow dark."
4. I.e., with mine.
5. Sword belt.

that water's side. And when they were at the water's side, even fast[6] by the bank hoved[7] a little barge with many fair ladies in it; and among them all was a queen; and all they had black hoods, and all they wept and shrieked when they saw King Arthur.

"Now put me into that barge," said the King; and so he did softly. And there received him three ladies with great mourning, and so they set them[8] down. And in one of their laps King Arthur laid his head, and then the queen said, "Ah, my dear brother, why have ye tarried so long from me? Alas, this wound on your head hath caught overmuch cold." And anon they rowed fromward the land, and Sir Bedivere beheld all tho ladies go froward him.

Then Sir Bedivere cried and said, "Ah, my lord Arthur, what shall become of me, now ye go from me and leave me here alone among mine enemies?"

"Comfort thyself," said the King, "and do as well as thou mayest, for in me is no trust for to trust in. For I must into the vale of Avilion[9] to heal me of my grievous wound. And if thou hear nevermore of me, pray for my soul."

But ever the queen and ladies wept and shrieked that it was pity to hear. And as soon as Sir Bedivere had lost the sight of the barge he wept and wailed and so took the forest, and went[1] all that night. And in the morning he was ware betwixt two holts hoar[2] of a chapel and an hermitage.[3]

* * *

Thus of Arthur I find no more written in books that been authorized,[4] neither more of the very certainty of his death heard I never read,[5] but thus was he led away in a ship wherein were three queens: that one was King Arthur's sister, Queen Morgan la Fée, the t'other[6] was the Queen of North Wales, and the third was the Queen of the Waste Lands. * * *

Now more of the death of King Arthur could I never find but that these ladies brought him to his burials,[7] and such one was buried there that the hermit bore witness that sometime was Bishop of Canterbury.[8] But yet the hermit knew not in certain that he was verily the body of King Arthur, for this tale Sir Bedivere, a Knight of the Table Round, made it to be written. Yet some men say in many parts of England that King Arthur is not dead, but had by the will of our Lord Jesu into another place. And men say that he shall come again and he shall win the Holy Cross. Yet I will not say that it shall be so, but rather I will say, Here in this world he changed his life. And many men say that there is written upon his tomb this verse: *Hic iacet Arthurus, rex quondam, rexque futurus.*[9]

---

6. Close.
7. Waited.
8. I.e., they sat.
9. A legendary island, sometimes identified with the earthly paradise.
1. Walked. "Took": took to.
2. Ancient copses.
3. In the passage here omitted, Sir Bedivere meets the former bishop of Canterbury, now a hermit, who describes how on the previous night a company of ladies had brought to the chapel a dead body, asking that it

be buried. Sir Bedivere exclaims that the dead man must have been King Arthur and vows to spend the rest of his life there in the chapel as a hermit.
4. That have authority.
5. Tell.
6. The second.
7. Grave.
8. Of whom the hermit, who was formerly bishop of Canterbury, bore witness.
9. "Here lies Arthur, who was once king and king will be again."

[The Deaths of Lancelot and Guinevere][1]

And thus upon a night there came a vision to Sir Lancelot and charged him, in remission[2] of his sins, to haste him unto Amesbury: "And by then[3] thou come there, thou shalt find Queen Guinevere dead. And therefore take thy fellows with thee, and purvey them of an horse-bier,[4] and fetch thou the corse[5] of her, and bury her by her husband, the noble King Arthur. So this avision[6] came to Lancelot thrice in one night. Then Sir Lancelot rose up ere day and told the hermit.

"It were well done," said the hermit, "that ye made you ready and that ye disobey not the avision."

Then Sir Lancelot took his eight fellows with him, and on foot they yede[7] from Glastonbury to Amesbury, the which is little more than thirty mile, and thither they came within two days, for they were weak and feeble to go. And when Sir Lancelot was come to Amesbury within the nunnery, Queen Guinevere died but half an hour afore. And the ladies told Sir Lancelot that Queen Guinevere told them all ere she passed that Sir Lancelot had been priest near a twelve-month:[8] "and hither he cometh as fast as he may to fetch my corse, and beside my lord King Arthur he shall bury me." Wherefore the Queen said in hearing of them all, "I beseech Almighty God that I may never have power to see Sir Lancelot with my worldly eyes."

"And thus," said all the ladies, "was ever her prayer these two days till she was dead."

Then Sir Lancelot saw her visage, but he wept not greatly, but sighed. And so he did all the observance of the service himself, both the *dirige*[9] and on the morn he sang mass. And there was ordained[1] an horse-bier, and so with an hundred torches ever burning about the corse of the Queen, and ever Sir Lancelot with his eight fellows went about[2] the horse-bier, singing and reading many an holy orison,[3] and frankincense upon the corse incensed.[4]

Thus Sir Lancelot and his eight fellows went on foot from Amesbury unto Glastonbury, and when they were come to the chapel and the hermitage, there she had a *dirige* with great devotion.[5] And on the morn the hermit that sometime[6] was Bishop of Canterbury sang the mass of requiem with great devotion, and Sir Lancelot was the first that offered, and then als[7] his eight fellows. And then she was wrapped in cered cloth of Rennes, from the top[8] to the toe, in thirtyfold, and after she was put in a web[9] of lead, and then in a coffin of marble.

And when she was put in the earth Sir Lancelot swooned and lay long still, while[1] the hermit came and awaked him, and said, "Ye be to blame, for ye displease God with such manner of sorrow-making."

1. Guinevere enters a convent at Amesbury where Lancelot, returned with his companions to England, visits her, but she commands him never to see her again. Emulating her example, Lancelot joins the bishop of Canterbury and Bedivere in their hermitage where he takes holy orders and is joined in turn by seven of his fellow knights.
2. For the remission.
3. By the time.
4. Provide them with a horse-drawn hearse.
5. Body.
6. Dream.
7. Went.

8. Nearly twelve months.
9. Funeral service.
1. Prepared.
2. Around.
3. Reciting many a prayer.
4. Burned frankincense over the body.
5. Solemnity.
6. Once.
7. Also. "Offered": made his donation.
8. Head. "Cloth of Rennes": A shroud made of fine linen smeared with wax, produced at Rennes.
9. Afterward she was put in a sheet.
1. Until.

"Truly," said Sir Lancelot, "I trust I do not displease God, for He knoweth mine intent—for my sorrow was not, nor is not, for any rejoicing of sin, but my sorrow may never have end. For when I remember of her beaulté and of her noblesse[2] that was both with her king and with her,[3] so when I saw his corse and her corse so lie together, truly mine heart would not serve to sustain my careful[4] body. Also when I remember me how by my defaute and mine orgule[5] and my pride that they were both laid full low, that were peerless that ever was living of Christian people, wit you well," said Sir Lancelot, "this remembered, of their kindness and mine unkindness, sank so to mine heart that I might not sustain myself." So the French book maketh mention.

Then Sir Lancelot never after ate but little meat,[6] nor drank, till he was dead, for then he sickened more and more and dried and dwined[7] away. For the Bishop nor none of his fellows might not make him to eat, and little he drank, that he was waxen by a kibbet[8] shorter than he was, that the people could not know him. For evermore, day and night, he prayed, but sometime he slumbered a broken sleep. Ever he was lying groveling on the tomb of King Arthur and Queen Guinevere, and there was no comfort that the Bishop nor Sir Bors, nor none of his fellows could make him—it availed not.

So within six weeks after, Sir Lancelot fell sick and lay in his bed. And then he sent for the Bishop that there was hermit, and all his true fellows. Then Sir Lancelot said with dreary steven,[9] "Sir Bishop, I pray you give to me all my rights that longeth[1] to a Christian man."

"It shall not need you,"[2] said the hermit and all his fellows. "It is but heaviness of your blood. Ye shall be well mended by the grace of God tomorn."

"My fair lords," said Sir Lancelot, "wit you well my careful body will into the earth; I have warning more than now I will say. Therefore give me my rights."

So when he was houseled and annealed[3] and had all that a Christian man ought to have, he prayed the Bishop that his fellows might bear his body to Joyous Garde. (Some men say it was Alnwick, and some men say it was Bamborough.) "Howbeit," said Sir Lancelot, "me repenteth[4] sore, but I made mine avow sometime that in Joyous Garde I would be buried. And because of breaking[5] of mine avow, I pray you all, lead me thither." Then there was weeping and wringing of hands among his fellows.

So at a season of the night they all went to their beds, for they all lay in one chamber. And so after midnight, against[6] day, the Bishop that was hermit, as he lay in his bed asleep, he fell upon a great laughter. And therewith all the fellowship awoke and came to the Bishop and asked him what he ailed.[7]

"Ah, Jesu mercy," said the Bishop, "why did ye awake me? I was never in all my life so merry and so well at ease."

"Wherefore?" said Sir Bors.

"Truly," said the Bishop, "here was Sir Lancelot with me, with mo[8] angels

---

2. Her beauty and nobility.
3. That she and her king both had.
4. Sorrowful.
5. My fault and my haughtiness.
6. Food.
7. Wasted.
8. Grown by a cubit.
9. Sad voice.

1. Pertains. "Rights": last sacrament.
2. You shall not need it.
3. Given communion and extreme unction.
4. I am sorry.
5. In order not to break.
6. Toward.
7. Ailed him.
8. More.

than ever I saw men in one day. And I saw the angels heave[9] up Sir Lancelot unto heaven, and the gates of heaven opened against him."

"It is but dretching of swevens,"[1] said Sir Bors, "for I doubt not Sir Lancelot aileth nothing but good."[2]

"It may well be," said the Bishop. "Go ye to his bed and then shall ye prove the sooth."

So when Sir Bors and his fellows came to his bed, they found him stark dead. And he lay as he had smiled, and the sweetest savor[3] about him that ever they felt. Then was there weeping and wringing of hands, and the greatest dole they made that ever made men. And on the morn the Bishop did his mass of Requiem, and after the Bishop and all the nine knights put Sir Lancelot in the same horse-bier that Queen Guinevere was laid in tofore that she was buried. And so the Bishop and they all together went with the body of Sir Lancelot daily, till they came to Joyous Garde. And ever they had an hundred torches burning about him.

And so within fifteen days they came to Joyous Garde. And there they laid his corse in the body of the choir,[4] and sang and read many psalters[5] and prayers over him and about him. And ever his visage was laid open and naked, that all folks might behold him; for such was the custom in tho[6] days that all men of worship should so lie with open visage till that they were buried.

And right thus as they were at their service, there came Sir Ector de Maris that had seven year sought all England, Scotland, and Wales, seeking his brother, Sir Lancelot. And when Sir Ector heard such noise and light in the choir of Joyous Garde, he alight and put his horse from him and came into the choir. And there he saw men sing and weep, and all they knew Sir Ector, but he knew not them. Then went Sir Bors unto Sir Ector and told him how there lay his brother, Sir Lancelot, dead. And then Sir Ector threw his shield, sword, and helm from him, and when he beheld Sir Lancelot's visage, he fell down in a swoon. And when he waked, it were hard any tongue to tell the doleful complaints that he made for his brother.

"Ah, Lancelot!" he said, "thou were head of all Christian knights. And now I dare say," said Sir Ector, "thou Sir Lancelot, there thou liest, that thou were never matched of earthly knight's hand. And thou were the courteoust[7] knight that ever bore shield. And thou were the truest friend to thy lover that ever bestrode horse, and thou were the truest lover, of a sinful man,[8] that ever loved woman, and thou were the kindest man that ever struck with sword. And thou were the goodliest person that ever came among press of knights, and thou was the meekest man and the gentlest that ever ate in hall among ladies, and thou were the sternest knight to thy mortal foe that ever put spear in the rest."[9]

Then there was weeping and dolor out of measure.

Thus they kept Sir Lancelot's corse aloft fifteen days, and then they buried it with great devotion. And then at leisure they went all with the Bishop of Canterbury to his hermitage, and there they were together more than a month.

Then Sir Constantine that was Sir Cador's son of Cornwall was chosen king

---

9. Lift.
1. Illusion of dreams.
2. Has nothing wrong with him.
3. Odor. A sweet scent is a conventional sign in saints' lives of a sanctified death.
4. The center of the chancel, the place of honor.

5. Psalms.
6. Those.
7. Most courteous.
8. Of any man born in original sin.
9. Support for the butt of the lance.

of England, and he was a full noble knight, and worshipfully he ruled this realm. And then this King Constantine sent for the Bishop of Canterbury, for he heard say where he was. And so he was restored unto his bishopric and left that hermitage, and Sir Bedivere was there ever still hermit to his life's end.

Then Sir Bors de Ganis, Sir Ector de Maris, Sir Gahalantine, Sir Galihud, Sir Galihodin, Sir Blamour, Sir Bleoberis, Sir Villiars le Valiant, Sir Clarrus of Clermount, all these knights drew them to their countries. Howbeit[1] King Constantine would have had them with him, but they would not abide in this realm. And there they all lived in their countries as holy men.

And some English books make mention that they went never out of England after the death of Sir Lancelot—but that was but favor of makers.[2] For the French book maketh mention—and is authorized—that Sir Bors, Sir Ector, Sir Blamour, and Sir Bleoberis went into the Holy Land, thereas Jesu Christ was quick[3] and dead, and anon as they had stablished their lands;[4] for the book saith so Sir Lancelot commanded them for to do ere ever he passed out of this world. There these four knights did many battles upon the miscreaunts,[5] or Turks, and there they died upon a Good Friday for God's sake.

Here is the end of the whole book of King Arthur and of his noble knights of the Round Table, that when they were whole together there was ever an hundred and forty. And here is the end of *The Death of Arthur*.[6]

I pray you all gentlemen and gentlewomen that readeth this book of Arthur and his knights from the beginning to the ending, pray for me while I am alive that God send me good deliverance. And when I am dead, I pray you all pray for my soul.

For this book was ended the ninth year of the reign of King Edward the Fourth, by Sir Thomas Malory, knight, as Jesu help him for His great might, as he is the servant of Jesu both day and night.

1469–70   1485

---

1. However.
2. The authors' bias.
3. Living. "Thereas": where.
4. As soon as they had put their lands in order.
5. Infidels.

6. By the "whole book" Malory refers to the entire work; the *Death of Arthur*, which Caxton made the title of the entire work, refers to the last part of Malory's book.

The Sixteenth Century
1485-1603

1485: Accession of Henry VII inaugurates age of the Tudor sovereigns.
1509: Accession of Henry VIII.
1517: Martin Luther's Wittenberg Theses; beginning of the Reformation.
1534: Henry VIII acknowledged "Supreme Head on Earth" of the English church.
1557: Publication of *Tottel's Miscellany*, containing poems by Sir Thomas Wyatt; Henry Howard, earl of Surrey; and others.
1558: Accession of Queen Elizabeth I.
1576: Building of The Theatre, the first permanent structure in England for the presentation of plays.
1588: Defeat of the Spanish Armada.
1603: Death of Elizabeth I; accession of James I, the first of the Stuart kings.

ENGLAND UNDER HENRY VII

The sixteenth century in England is the age of the Tudor sovereigns. Three generations of Tudors ruled England from 1485 to 1603. The earl of Richmond became Henry VII, the first Tudor monarch: he won his crown by defeating Richard III at Bosworth field, ending the dynastic strife that had raged for more than thirty years between the noble houses of York and Lancaster. Henry VII was Lancastrian, but he married Elizabeth of the house of York, niece of the Yorkist king Richard III. The barons, impoverished and divided by the dynastic wars, could not effectively oppose the power of the Crown, and the church also generally supported the royal power. So Henry VII was able to counter the multiple and competing power structures characteristic of feudal society and to impose a much stronger central authority and order on the nation.

Seven years after Henry VII became king, Christopher Columbus sailed to America, and a few years later Vasco da Gama reached India by sailing around the Cape of Good Hope. The English were not pioneers in the exploration of the Western Hemisphere, but these explorations affected their place in the world profoundly, for in the next century they became great colonizers and merchant adventurers.

Significant changes in trade and in the arts of war also marked the early years of the Tudor regime. Henry VII made commercial treaties with European countries; England, which had always been a sheep-raising country, was by now manufacturing and exporting significant amounts of cloth. As lands were enclosed to permit grazing on a larger scale, people were driven off the land to the cities, and London grew into a metropolitan market with sophisticated commercial institutions. At the same time the feudal order continued its decline, partly because the introduction of firearms made armored knights on horseback obsolete, as well as the English bowmen who had won famous victories in France under King Henry V. The "new

253

men" who supported the Tudors and profited from their favor could adapt themselves more easily to a changed society than could the descendants of the great families of the feudal fifteenth century.

About a decade before Henry VII won his throne, the art of printing from movable type, a German invention, was introduced into England by William Caxton (ca. 1422–1491), who had learned and practiced it in the Low Countries. Literacy increased during the fifteenth century, so that many more people could read than in Geoffrey Chaucer's time; estimates suggest that about 30 percent of the people could read English in the early fifteenth century and about 60 percent by 1530. Printing made books cheaper and more plentiful, providing more opportunity to read and more incentive to learn.

Yet it would be a mistake to imagine these changes as sudden and dramatic. Although Caxton introduced printed books and was an author and translator as well as a printer, his publications consisted of long prose romances translated from the French, collections of moral sayings, and other works—such as Thomas Malory's *Morte Darthur*—that were medieval rather than modern. Also, jousts and tournaments continued at court for a century, and the approved code of behavior was the traditional code of chivalry. As often in an age of spectacular novelty, many people looked back to an idealized past. The best writers of the time of Henry VII were imitators of Chaucer, who had died about a century before. They were Scottish rather than English: William Dunbar (ca. 1460–1530), Gavin Douglas (1475–1522), and Sir David Lindsay (1485–1555). English writers also looked back, for example, Stephen Hawes (1474–1523), who imitated not Chaucer but John Lydgate, a monk of Bury.

HUMANISM

During the fifteenth century a few English clerics and government officials had journeyed to Italy and had seen something of the extraordinary cultural and intellectual movement flourishing in the city-states there. That movement, generally known as the Renaissance, involved a rebirth of letters and arts stimulated by the recovery and study of texts from classical antiquity and the development of new aesthetic norms based on classical models. It also unleashed new ideas and new social, political, and economic forces that displaced the otherworldly and communal values of the Middle Ages, emphasizing instead the dignity and potential of the individual and the worth of life in this world. These Renaissance ideals were variously reflected in the poetry of Petrarch, the philosophy of Pico della Mirandola, the art of Leonardo da Vinci, and the statecraft of Lorenzo di Medici. But it was not until Henry VII's reign brought some measure of political stability to England that the Renaissance could take root there, and it was not until the accession of Henry VIII that it began to flower.

Humanism was a fundamental intellectual current in the Renaissance, the first major exponents of which in England were Sir Thomas More and Desiderius Erasmus of Rotterdam. More rose to become lord chancellor to Henry VIII: his masterpiece, *Utopia*, written in Latin, was a critique of European social, political, and religious institutions and practices from the vantage point of an imaginary society based on reason. In English he chiefly wrote controversial tracts against Martin Luther and the Protestants and also a vivid and impressive history of Richard III. More's friend Erasmus spent some time in England, and his influence was widely diffused there through his scripture translations and commentaries and his writings on rhetoric and education.

Education—of the Christian prince, of the courtier, of the Christian gentleman—was a prime concern of the English humanists. John Colet (founder of St. Paul's School), Roger Ascham (tutor to Princess Elizabeth), and Sir Thomas Elyot, among others, wrote treatises on education to promote the kind of learning they regarded as the most suitable preparation for public service. That education—

conducted by tutors in the great families or in grammar schools—was ordered according to the subjects of the medieval *trivium* (grammar, logic, and rhetoric) and the *quadrivium* (arithmetic, geometry, astronomy, and music) but with new emphasis on rhetoric and classical texts. The grammar studied was Latin grammar, and the rhetoric was a rigorous discipline in all the stylistic devices used by classical authors. The purpose was to train the sons of the nobility and gentry to speak and write good Latin, the language of diplomacy, of the professions, and of all higher learning. Their sisters were always educated at home or in other noble houses. They chiefly learned modern languages, religion, music, and art, but they very seldom received the firm grounding in Latin and classical literature so central to Renaissance culture. Elizabethan schoolmasters might use the system of double translation, from English into Latin and then from Latin back into English, to develop facility and rhetorical elegance. But the books read and studied rhetorically were not considered mere exhibitions of literary style: from the *Sententiae Pueriles* (Childish Maxims) for beginners on up through the dramatist Terence, the poets Virgil and Horace, and the orator Cicero, the classics were also studied for the moral, political, and philosophical truth they contained and as a means to inculcate moral values.

From the outset, English humanism was vitally concerned with Christianity as well as with classical learning. The second generation of humanists—men like Ascham (1515–1568); Sir John Cheke (1514–1557), professor of Greek at Cambridge; and Thomas Wilson (1525–1581), rhetorician and translator—combined an earnest Protestantism with their classical learning, and Ascham vigorously opposed the more secular, pagan humanism coming out of Italy. These men had a profound influence on the University of Cambridge, and Cambridge, in turn, educated many of the greatest writers of the age—including Edmund Spenser and John Milton.

For humanists committed to classical learning, the question of whether to write one's own works in Latin or in English became an issue of great seriousness. Sir Thomas More turned naturally to Latin in writing his *Utopia*. And to many other learned men, influenced both by the humanist exaltation of the classical languages and by the characteristic Renaissance desire for eternal fame, the vernacular languages seemed relatively new and unstable. But at the same time, a revolt was being mounted in Italy, France, and England against the slavish imitation, in Latin, of Cicero and other classical writers. In his *Défense et Illustration de la Langue Française* (1549), Joachim Du Bellay argued that the value of a language depends on the great works written in it and urged scholars and poets to refine and improve the native tongue by writing ambitious works in it, thereby promoting a sense of national identity. In his book on archery, *Toxophilus*, dedicated to Henry VIII, Ascham defended the vernacular, although he said he found it easier to write in Latin or Greek. Later, Richard Mulcaster (ca. 1530–1611), principal of the Merchant Taylors' School and teacher of Spenser, waxed eloquent in praise of English:

> Is it not indeed a marvelous bondage, to become servants to one tongue for learning's sake the most of our time, with loss of most time, whereas we may have the very same treasure in our own tongue, with the gain of more time? our own bearing the joyful title of our liberty and freedom, the Latin tongue remembering us of our thralldom and bondage? I love Rome, but London better; I favor Italy, but England more; I honor the Latin, but I worship the English.

These two impulses—humanist reverence for the classics and English pride in the vernacular language—gave rise to many distinguished translations throughout the century: Virgil's *Aeneid* by the earl of Surrey, Homer's *Iliad* and *Odyssey* by

George Chapman, Plutarch's *Lives of the Noble Grecians and Romans* by Sir Thomas North, and Ovid's *Metamorphoses* by Arthur Golding. Translators also sought to make available in English the most notable literary works in the modern languages: Castiglione's *Il Cortegiano* ("The Courtier") by Sir Thomas Hoby, Ariosto's *Orlando Furioso* ("Orlando Mad") by Sir John Harington, and Tasso's *Gerusalemme Liberata* ("Jerusalem Delivered") by Edward Fairfax. At the midcentury, Ralph Robynson put into English the Latin *Utopia* of that notable English humanist, Sir Thomas More.

THE REFORMATION

Humanists like Erasmus advocated and engaged in a scholarly and critical study of the Scriptures; humanists like More satirized the corrupt and ignorant clergy and such abuses as the sale of papal indulgences and pardons. But neither Erasmus nor More followed the course that led to the Protestant Reformation: for both, the unity of Christendom was an overriding value. Nor did Luther at first intend schism: when he nailed his famous ninety-five theses to the church door in Wittenberg on the first of November 1517, he was simply proposing some topics for academic discussion. But his ideas soon sparked a mass revolution.

What was the Reformation? To those who supported it, it was a return to pure Christianity—cleansing the church of all the corruption and idolatry that had accumulated over the centuries. To the Roman Catholic church it was, of course, damnable heresy. From the perspective of later ages, it can be recognized as a major factor in the breakup of Western Christendom, the secularization of society, the establishment of princely ascendancy over the church, and consequently, the identification of religion and nationalism.

For medieval people, the Roman Catholic church was a universal, infallible, omnicompetent guide to the conduct of life from cradle to grave. They were instructed by its teachings, corrected by its discipline, sustained by its sacraments, and comforted by its promises. A vast system of confession, pardons, penance, absolution, indulgences, sacred relics, and ceremonies gave the hierarchy great power over their largely illiterate flock. The Bible, the order of the Mass, and most of the theological discussions were in Latin, which laypeople could not understand; however, religious doctrine and spirituality were mediated to them by priests and hierarchy, by church art and music, and by the liturgical ceremonies of daily life—festivals, holy days, baptisms, marriages, and funerals.

When Luther revolted against the ancient church, was cast out by it, and founded his own church, he did so in the name of private conscience enlightened by a personal reading of the Scriptures. The common watchwords of the Reformation were these: only the Scriptures (not the church or tradition) have authority in matters of religion, only God's grace and personal faith (not good works or religious practices) can effect a Christian's salvation, and only the enlightened private conscience (not priests or ministers or hierarchies) can determine what an individual must believe and do. Despite differences in many matters of doctrine and church order, these principles were common to Lutherans in Germany, Calvinists in Geneva, and other Protestant groups throughout Europe.

In England, however, the Reformation did not begin with ideological controversy. In the time of Chaucer, John Wycliffe and the Lollard movement had mounted a grass-roots challenge to some practices and doctrines of the church, elements of which lasted into the sixteenth century. But the split with the Church of Rome was caused by a man who considered himself a Catholic champion against Luther and his opinions: Henry VIII, who received from Pope Leo X the title "Defender of the Faith" for writing a book against Luther. Henry's motives for the break with Rome were dynastic, not religious: he needed a legitimate son and his queen, Catherine of Aragon, could not give him one. He was unable after long negotiations to obtain permission from Rome to divorce her. He then declared himself Supreme Head of the English church and required oaths of allegiance affirming his right to that role. His lord chancellor, Sir Thomas More, resigned and was at length executed for refusing to sign that oath. Thomas Cromwell, Henry's powerful secretary of state, dissolved the monasteries, and Henry distributed their property to his courtiers, thereby binding them firmly to his cause. In his earlier role as Defender of the (Roman Catholic) Faith, Henry persecuted, drove out of England, and in 1536 executed the great English translator of the Bible, William Tyndale. But after his break with Rome, Henry authorized a vernacular translation (The Great Bible), making the Bible available in English to anyone who could read.

Henry's son (by his third wife, Lady Jane Seymour) was the boy king Edward VI (1537–1553). In his brief reign (1547–53) the English Reformation acquired a strong doctrinal basis and spiritual energy, as Lutheran and Calvinist theologians from the Continent swarmed into England. The Book of Common Prayer was published in 1549 and 1552, and by 1553 the beliefs of the English church were officially defined in forty-two articles, thoroughly Protestant in formulation.

The successor to the short-lived Protestant king was his older sister, Mary Tudor, the half-Spanish and devoutly Catholic daughter of Henry and Catherine of Aragon, who married her cousin Philip II of Spain. In her reign, the leading Protestants either fled to the Continent or were burned at the stake as heretics. Mary tried to reverse the doctrinal changes of the Reformation, but some of its practical consequences, like the distribution of monastery lands, were irreversible. A Spaniard on the throne of England was greatly resented, and Mary dared not press her people too far: her accession had been opposed by the Privy Council, which proclaimed Lady Jane Grey queen, and she was also challenged by a rebellion led by Sir Thomas Wyatt the Younger, son of the poet. Mary maintained her Roman allegiance, she burned many Protestants at the stake, but she could not undo the work of her father and half-brother. Had she been able to produce an heir she might have done so, but failing that, her death in 1558 brought the Protestants back to power. The Protestant exiles returned from the Continent to become a potent force in English society during the long reign of Mary's half-sister, Elizabeth Tudor, daughter of Henry's second wife, Anne Boleyn.

Queen Elizabeth established the English church in terms acceptable to the vast majority of her subjects. She imposed a form of service (retaining much of the old Roman ritual), and although she compelled her subjects to attend it, she left their consciences to themselves. The Elizabethan manifesto of faith, the Thirty-Nine Articles, formulated the chief matters of doctrinal controversy in somewhat ambiguous terms, and Elizabeth made every effort to eliminate controversial preaching from the pulpits. That compromise satisfied neither the Roman Catholics, who sought to return to Rome, nor the Puritans, who pressed for more radical reform. But it accommodated most of the populace, who now looked neither to Rome nor to Geneva as the prime source of authority in religion, but to their own sovereign.

NATIONALISM — ELIZABETH I

Queen Elizabeth I, who ascended the throne in 1558 and ruled until 1603, was one of the most remarkable political geniuses England has ever produced. Vain and headstrong, she nevertheless had a very shrewd sense of her country's strengths and weaknesses, and she identified herself with England as no previous ruler had done. Although she invited the flattery of courtiers and favorites, she entrusted the power of state to solid men such as William Cecil (Lord Burleigh) and Francis Walsingham. Cecil (1520–1598) was her chief and most trusted secretary. With unswerving loyalty he devoted his great talents to the service of the queen in domestic affairs as well as in complex relations with the governments of Europe. He sought also, with limited success, to raise money from Parliament to pay for the increasing cost of government. Walsingham (ca. 1530–1590) was a radical

Protestant who tried to promote a more ideologically committed foreign policy than the queen and Cecil were prepared to support.

England's strength lay in its ability to sway the balance of power in Europe: it could throw its weight either way in the ongoing power struggle between Spain and France, and it could support or fail to support the Protestant uprisings against Spain in the Low Countries. Moreover, Elizabeth made adroit use of her situation as an unmarried monarch who was expected to marry so as to provide a legitimate heir to the throne. She kept all Europe guessing as to her intentions, skillfully playing her several suitors off against one another—and at length insisted that England alone was her spouse. By the time it was too late for her to marry and bear children, England was strong and united.

Ironically, the papal bull (decree) of 1570, excommunicating Elizabeth and relieving her subjects of their loyalty to her, contributed greatly to that unity. This bull was intended to bring to the throne Mary Stuart, Queen of Scots, who was Catholic by faith and French by culture. The English rallied to their queen, and she became a symbol of Englishness and nationalism. The adulation of her, in the face of trouble on the Scottish border, near-chaos in Ireland, and continued threats from the Continent, took on religious intensity. Her reputation for beauty (which was exaggerated) and for wisdom (which was not) became articles of faith. In 1588 God Himself seemed to testify to her divine mission to guide England: Philip II of Spain sent out the mightiest invasion fleet ever mounted against England, but the Spanish Armada was almost wholly destroyed by a violent storm, which the English saw as an act of God.

Despite the Elizabethan settlement of the English church, Elizabeth's reign continued to be plagued by political and religious unrest. Catholics who adhered to the pro-Spanish faction of the previous reign continued their plots to put Mary Stuart on the throne (leading Elizabeth at length to concur in her execution). And the Protestant exiles whose sojourn on the Continent had sharpened their zeal for more radical reforms coalesced into a strong and vocal Puritan movement. But most English people, remembering the civil conflicts of the previous century, placed a high value on order in church and state, and for them Elizabeth became, in her person and her policy, a symbol of national unity.

The desire for commercial profit also strengthened nationalistic feelings. In 1493 the Pope had divided the New World between the Spanish and the Portuguese by drawing a line from pole to pole (hence Brazil speaks Portuguese today, and the rest of Latin America speaks Spanish): the English were not in the picture. But by the end of Edward VI's reign the Company of Merchant Adventurers was founded, and Englishmen began to explore Asia and North America. Some of these adventurers turned to piracy, preying on Spanish ships that were returning laden with wealth from the New World. These activities soon became a private undeclared war, with the queen and her courtiers investing in these raids privately but accepting no responsibility for them. The greatest of many dazzling exploits was the voyage of Francis Drake (1577–80): he sailed through the Strait of Magellan, pillaged Spanish towns on the Pacific, reached as far north as San Francisco, crossed to the Philippines, and returned around the Cape of Good Hope; he came back with £1 million in treasure, and his investors earned a dividend of 5,000 percent. Queen Elizabeth knighted him on the deck of his ship, *The Golden Hind*.

The excitement but also the darker side of this nationalist, expansionist endeavor is reflected in the burgeoning travel literature, propaganda for colonization, and reports on the New World and its inhabitants. But the chief focus of English colonization during Elizabeth's reign was Ireland: here the combined impulses of nationalism, religion, and colonialism gave rise to brutal measures to eradicate the Roman Catholic religion and Celtic culture and to seize land. At the end of Elizabeth's reign, a series of bloody rebellions and massacres culminated in open war; the English victory led to the impoverishment and entire subjugation of the Irish populace. The Irish situation figures importantly and ambiguously in the major English epic of the era—also a glorification of Elizabeth—Spenser's *Faerie Queene.*

The mere survival of Elizabeth for so long provided the opportunity for nationalistic consciousness to become firmly established. When she came to the throne in 1558 she was only twenty-five years old, and she remained queen for almost forty-five years. It is wholly appropriate, therefore, that the second half of the sixteenth century bear her name, the Elizabethan Age.

PATRONS, WRITERS, AND PUBLISHERS

During Elizabeth's reign patronage was a social institution of the first importance, a major force in transforming the great nobles and gentry from independently powerful local magnates into courtiers dependent on the monarch. The queen's chief ministers and favorites (Cecil, Leicester, and Essex) were the primary channels through which patronage was dispensed to courtiers who wanted offices in the court, the government bureaucracies, the royal household, the army, the church, or the universities or who sought titles, grants of land, leases, or similar favors. In their turn, successful courtiers could dispense benefits to their petitioners. Men like Sir Christopher Hatton and Sir Walter Ralegh leapt from obscurity to great power and prominence as a result of their success as courtiers, which owed as much to their gallantry and their dancing as to their more solid abilities. And some noble women also wielded considerable power and influence as patrons, notably Mary Herbert, countess of Pembroke; Margaret Clifford, countess of Cumberland; Anne Dudley, countess of Warwick; and Lucy (Harington) Russell, countess of Bedford.

The great guide and conduct book for the courtier was Castiglione's *Il Cortegiano* (1528, translated into English by Hoby in 1561). This book emphasized the importance to the courtier of displaying *sprezzatura*, or easy grace, in all he says or does, underscoring the importance of role-playing and pleasing his prince. That book also declared (admitting the conflict) that the chief function of the courtier is to give good and honest advice to the prince. Courtiers who followed that honorable course were very likely to provoke a monarch's resentment, as Sir Philip Sidney found out when he tried to advise Queen Elizabeth against a proposed French marriage.

Literary patronage was part of the interlocking patronage system whereby grants, offices, and honors were exchanged for service and praise. We must recognize that the career of a professional man or woman of letters did not exist: literature was regarded as an adjunct activity, not a primary occupation, and there were comparatively few readers, purchasers, and publishers of books. Elizabethan writers of higher rank, like Sidney, thought of themselves as courtiers, statesmen, and landowners; they considered poetry a social grace and a courtly pastime. Writers of lower rank, such as Samuel Daniel and Michael Drayton, sought careers as civil servants, secretaries, tutors, and divines; they might take up more or less permanent residence in a noble household, or more casually, they might offer their literary work to actual or prospective patrons, amid lavish praises, in the hope of support, career advancement, or financial reward. Even Ben Jonson, who more than most of his contemporaries claimed the role of poet and managed to live tolerably well by it, summed up the situation in these words:

> Poetry in this latter age hath proved but a mean mistress to such as have wholly addicted themselves to her, or given their names up to her family. Those who have but saluted her on the way, and now and then tendered their visits, she hath done much for, and advanced in the way of their own professions (both the law and the gospel) beyond all they could have hoped or done for themselves without her favor.

Literary men of lower rank who were not in a position to be courtiers might still look to the court for livelihood, notice, and encouragement, but that prospect was often discouraging. "A thousand hopes, but all nothing," wailed John Lyly, alluding to his long wait for the office of Master of the Revels, "a hundred promises, but yet nothing." Spenser's bitter disappointment in failing to win court patronage (reflected in *Mother Hubberds Tale* and *Colin Clouts Come Home Againe*) was dispelled only toward the end of his life when Queen Elizabeth awarded him a pension of fifty pounds. Indeed, a pervasive sense of court life as precarious, superficial, and hypocritical gave rise to works in the vein of the poems of Horace, praising the retired country life far from corruptions of the court: early examples are Wyatt's verse epistles to Sir Francis Bryan and John Poins, and the motif remained prominent to the time of Ralegh.

Financial rewards for writing prose or poetry came mostly in the form of gifts from patrons, who sought to enhance their status and flatter their vanity through the service and lavish praises of many clients. Some Elizabethan patrons were well-educated humanists motivated by genuine literary interests, and with them, patronage extended beyond financial support to the creation of literary and intellectual circles. Several writers (among them Daniel, Fulke Greville, and Spenser) enjoyed long- or short-term hospitality and stimulation as members of the circles of the Sidneys at Penshurst or the Pembrokes at Wilton. And Shakespeare's relations with his patron, the earl of Southampton, little as we know about them, were apparently satisfactory, as the dedication to *The Rape of Lucrece* (1594) attests. But we hear constant complaints about patrons who do not reward authors for dedications (the usual reward was two or three pounds for a pamphlet or small volume of verse). The experience of Robert Greene is perhaps typical: the fact that he had sixteen different patrons for seventeen books suggests that he did not find much favor or support from any one of them. Indeed, a practice grew up of printing off several dedications to be inserted into particular copies of a book, so that an impecunious author could deceive each of several patrons into thinking that he or she was the one to be honored by the volume.

The ambiguities and anxieties of being a courtier or a client in such a society are often inscribed in the literary texts Elizabethan writers produce. Even sonnet sequences and pastoral poetry may reflect these tensions as they praise the queen in the guise of Eliza, queen of Shepherds (poets), or analyze a sonnet lady's arbitrary power over her courtly servant.

In addition to the court and the great families as dispensers of patronage, the two universities and the city of London were also major influences on the literary production of this period. Before Elizabeth's time, the universities were mainly devoted to educating the clergy, and that remained an important part of their function. But in the second half of the century the sons of the gentry and the aristocracy were going in increasing numbers to the universities and the Inns of Court (law schools), though often they did not take degrees or practice as lawyers. Their residence in these places was simply an educational preparation for public service or managing their estates. A group of graduates, the so-called university wits, associated themselves with the literary scene in London; these men (among them Thomas Nashe, Christopher Marlowe, Greene, and George Peele) gave to the Elizabethan drama some elements of classical form and contributed to the great outpouring of literature in the 1590s. But their lives testify to the difficulties they found trying to sustain themselves by writing. The diary of Philip Henslowe, a leading theatrical manager, has entry after entry showing university graduates in prison or in debt or at best eking out a miserable existence patching plays.

The city of London itself had a major impact on the literature of Elizabeth's reign. In Chaucer's time London's population was about 50,000, in 1563 it was around 93,000, and it was nearly 225,000 in 1605. It was by far the most important city in the realm, and the political history of the seventeenth century is incomprehensible unless one recognizes the great power the City had, even as against the Crown. The printing presses were located in London, the printers and booksellers were in London, and the mass of the middle-class population that set the style for literature written for ordinary people was also in London. And although Nashe scornfully rejected the claim of the bourgeoisie to have any literary taste at all or any ability to produce literature, that class had its own writers, for example, Thomas Deloney, and it knew what it liked—books of instruction, romances, religious tracts, conduct books, and sensational ballads. The London populace also found among the university men some writers who catered to them: Thomas Heywood is a good example. Whether the aristocrats admitted it or not, the standards and tastes of the middle class affected all publishing and literary success. The customers who frequented the stalls of St. Paul's churchyard—the center of the book trade—were more often members of the middle class than of the court circle. Louis B. Wright has shown (in his *Middle-Class Culture in Elizabethan England*) how extensive and profound was the influence of the citizenry on the writing and publication of books and how bourgeois standards of edification and utility dictated to many authors of the time.

The sixteenth century was the first century of the printed book, and the Elizabethan Age was an extremely prolific one in writing and publishing. The *Short Title Catalogue* of the Bibliographical Society, which lists works and editions published in England between 1475 and 1640, includes more than 26,000 items, and that is an incomplete list. But the rewards for having books published were nothing like they are today. There was no such thing as copyright and no such thing, in the ordinary way, as royalties paid to an author according to the sale of the book. Authors sold their manuscripts to the printer or bookseller outright, for what now seems like a ridiculously low price—for a pamphlet or small book of poetry, usually forty shillings.

Nor did the author's troubles end with that sale. Writers as well as their publishers had to abide by stringent regulations governing the publication of books and might be punished for failure to do so by several political and ecclesiastical authorities. The regulations provided that the number of printers (not booksellers) be strictly limited, that nothing could be printed except in the city of London and at the universities of Oxford and Cambridge, that everything printed must receive the imprimatur of the archbishop of Canterbury and the bishop of London or their representatives, and that everything published in London must be entered on the registers of the Stationers' Company—a regulation that protected the property rights of the publisher and printer rather than the author. The enforcing authorities included the Privy Council, the highest political authority in the realm below the queen; the Court of Star Chamber, which punished breaches of censorship; the Court of High Commission, the supreme ecclesiastical authority; and the Stationers' Company.

An extreme example of the dangers besetting authors is provided by the history of John Stubbs, who protested against Elizabeth's projected French marriage in a pamphlet called *The Discovery of a Gaping Gulf* (1579). For writing this pamphlet, Stubbs had his right hand cut off with one stroke of a butcher's cleaver—after which he took up his hat with his left hand and cried, "God save the queen." Many writers of the period got into some sort of trouble for publishing a book: it might be prison, it might be merely a reprimand, it might be an investigation by the Star Chamber. Not surprisingly, therefore, literary texts sometimes reveal signs of inner censorship and sometimes inscribe strategies of covert allusion to mislead the censor. It was dangerous to put pen to paper and so unprofitable that it is a wonder any original writing was published at all.

However, to suppose that poetry, or even prose, circulated only in printed form would be a mistake. The older way of passing works around in manuscript lingered on into the seventeenth century and was especially the practice of poets of gentle or noble rank. Sidney is the most prominent example. Sir John Harington, in his translation of Ariosto's *Orlando Furioso* in 1591, mentions a sonnet of Sidney's "which many I am sure have read"; but that sonnet was not published until seven years later. This was certainly the practice of some noble women: we have a few manuscript poems by Queen Elizabeth and the countess of Pembroke, but those of certain other women reputed to have written poetry have been lost. Many people kept commonplace books in which they copied down poems from borrowed manuscripts—often enough confusing or failing to record the writer's name. Professional scribes made a living by copying manuscripts for authors and for readers. There are even complaints by printers that literary manuscripts are being hoarded by "their grand possessors." Difference of anticipated audience affected the kinds of literature produced—on the one hand by professional writers intending to publish and, on the other, by gentle or noble poets who passed their work about among their coteries of cultivated friends.

Such conditions of patronage, censorship, manuscript transmission, and collaboration—as well as the acceptability of borrowing plots, characters, and language from other authors, classical and contemporary—meant that the Elizabethans had a very different sense of what it means to be a writer than we have. Dramatists especially felt themselves engaged in a collaborative enterprise, because texts for particular performances were shaped and altered by the actors available and other local circumstances, and the plays were understood to belong to the company. Indeed, the notion of authorship as entailing a writer's proprietary rights over a literary text was only beginning to be asserted at the turn of the century—most forcefully by Ben Jonson, who caused much comment by setting forth a magnificent Folio edition of his poems and plays under the title *Works* (1616).

ART AND NATURE: ELIZABETHAN AESTHETICS

We can read Elizabethan literature with more comprehension if we recognize the differences between the aesthetic principles of the sixteenth century and those of our own day. At the root of the matter is a different conception of art and of the relation between art and nature. The Romantic movement (which still profoundly affects our aesthetics) glorified nature and valued art that seems "natural," personal, sincere, and uncontrived; it also valued the artist for originality and often ascribed that quality to a special, mysterious inspiration. Such views would have seemed strange indeed to the Elizabethans. They recognized that nature is the basis of art but had no uneasiness about a possible conflict between art and nature. The term *artificial* had for them good rather than dubious meanings, referring to the proper use of human ingenuity to enhance nature, to enable it to outdo itself. The point is underscored in Shakespeare's *Winter's Tale*, in an amusing exchange about horticulture. Perdita exclaims that she will have no streaked carnations or gillyflowers in her garden because the art that produces them seems to challenge "great creating nature," but Polixenes replies that such art is itself a part of nature:

> Yet Nature is made better by no mean
> But Nature makes that mean; so over that art
> Which you say adds to Nature, is an art
> That Nature makes. You see, sweet maid, we marry
> A gentler scion to the wildest stock,
> And make conceive a bark of baser kind
> By bud of nobler race. This is an art
> Which does mend Nature—change it rather; but
> The art itself is Nature.

Such concern with the improvement of something naturally beautiful—by device, by arrangement, by human ingenuity, or by art—extended to all aspects of life, so that there was no great gulf between the art or craft of writing and the techniques of other crafts: hawking, archery, building, cookery, managing a great horse in a tournament, sailing, or planting a garden. Intricacy of design and elaborateness of pattern were especially valued. The Elizabethan garden was designed as a square, filled with elaborate and intricate, but perfectly regular, design. Some Elizabethans had their houses built in the shape of an *E*, out of honor to the queen, and one man, John Thorpe, designed his house in the form of his own initials. The several Elizabethan dances—pavans, galliards, almains, and sarabands—also presented elaborate, highly patterned designs. Contrapuntal music (composed of several independent melodies joined together) was very intricate, with its elaborate patterns and complex harmonies. The composer Thomas Morley (ca. 1557–1603) praises the madrigal for displaying just such qualities:

> As for the music it is, next unto the motet, the most artificial and to men of understanding most delightful. If therefore you will compose in this kind . . . you must in your music be wavering like the wind, sometime wanton, sometime grave and staid, otherwise effeminate; you may maintain points and revert them, use triplaes [triplets] and show the very uttermost of your variety, and the more variety you show the better shall you please.

But a rigid form was to control all of this extravagance, and the fusion of such complexity with such order was often seen, as in Sir John Davies's poem *Orchestra, or A Poem of Dancing*, as an emblem of concord and harmony in the universe.

Another vital principle of Elizabethan aesthetics was the concern with models, with conventions, with the literary tradition as the very vehicle for artistic expression. Renaissance writers were in their own way profoundly original, but they did not think of originality as involving opposition to or revolt against literary traditions or artistic conventions. These were not, however, slavish imitators. Rather, they looked to classical (and Continental) works as models to learn from, emulate, transform, and if possible surpass. The chief models were Homer and Virgil for epic, Theocritus and Virgil for pastoral, Cicero for rhetoric and prose style, Plautus and Terence for comedy, Seneca for tragedy, Petrarch for the sonnet, Ariosto and Tasso for the romantic epic, and Ovid for love poetry and erotic mythological narratives.

Sidney's *The Defence of Poesy* is the only major work of literary criticism in sixteenth-century England, a period during which Italy and France produced large numbers of critical treatises, heavily influenced by Aristotle's *Poetics*. By contrast, Sidney's engaging tract is highly eclectic, drawing together aesthetic precepts from several traditions and underscoring those that are of primary importance to the Elizabethans: ideal imitation, moral teaching, and decorum. Looking back to Aristotle, Sidney defines poetry as an imitation of nature, but links that imitation to his view of the poet as maker, whose activity reflects that of the Divine Creator. The poet imitates not the real, fallen nature we see, but "lifted up with the vigor of his own invention," he imitates an ideal nature: "her world is brazen, the Poets only deliver a golden." Sidney also makes large claims for the didactic role of poetry: he invokes Horace's formula that poetry teaches by delighting, but (staunch Protestant that he is) he emphasizes even more its rhetorical power to move us to be virtuous. He also highlights the importance of suiting subject to genre and style—the idea of literary decorum that Milton was later to term "the grand masterpiece to observe."

From Sidney, from George Puttenham's *Art of English Poesy*, and from numerous Elizabethan treatises on rhetoric that define and illustrate literally hundreds of rhetorical and poetic figures of speech, we can identify some other aesthetic principles: the delight in *copia* or "abundance" of words, poetic figures, and ornament; the close relation of poetry and rhetoric; the concern with levels of style (high, middle, and low); and the continuing importance of allegory as a means to teach moral truths as well as to suggest the mysterious analogies and symbolic relationships that permeate and order God's universe. Among such symbolic relationships are those suggested by the pervasive macrocosm-microcosm analogy, according to which everything in the vast universe may be found, replicated in little, in the human body, and also those suggested by the image of the Great Chain of Being, according to which all orders of being, from speck of dust to highest angel, are ranged hierarchically in their divinely ordered stations.

POETIC CONVENTIONS, MODES, AND GENRES

Literary conventions are patterns that have become habitual and arouse certain expectations in the reader. We all recognize the conventions in a patriotic song or a religious hymn pertaining to subject, topics, tone, and expected responses. Literary conventions challenged Elizabethan poets to find fit forms for their experiences, to show their learning and virtuosity by the ingenious elaboration of these well-known patterns, and to create from these patterns something fresh and new. Because such conventions are shared cultural codes, they enable poets to elicit particular responses from readers and to relate both poets and readers to other times, other languages, and other cultures.

Clusters of such literary conventions—pertaining to subject matter, attitude, tone, values, and some set topics—identify several important literary modes (or "kinds" as Sidney terms them) in the period, including pastoral, heroic, lyric, satiric, elegiac, tragic, and comic. Other conventions—pertaining not only to subject matter and attitude but also to formal structure, meter, style, size, occasion, and the like—identify such important Elizabethan genres as epic, tragedy, sonnet, verse epistle, epigram, hymn, masque, funeral elegy, and many more. Although Aristotle considered tragedy the noblest form, Elizabethans commonly placed epic at the pinnacle of their genre system and pastoral poems at the base. Accordingly, Renaissance poets of lofty ambition, like Spenser and Milton, consciously followed the course of poetic development set by Virgil, beginning with pastoral and rising to epic. It is important to remember, however, that such genres and modes are not simply a cluster of conventions and patterns: they carry with them a whole range of culturally defined assumptions and values relating to man and woman, nature, language, heroism, virtue, pleasure, work, and love.

The conventions of the pastoral mode (or kind) present a simple and idealized world inhabited by shepherds and shepherdesses who are chiefly concerned to tend their flocks, fall in love, and engage in friendly poetry contests. The values of this mode are defined by *otium* (leisure and humble contentment)—which is at the opposite pole from pride, ambition, and the pursuit of fame and fortune. Pastoral exalts the simple country life over the city and its business, the military camp and its warfare, the court and its burdens of rule. The conventions of the pastoral mode could be assimilated to several different genres. Pastoral songs commonly expressed the joys of the shepherd's life or disappointment in love. Pastoral eclogues were dialogues between shepherds, which might stage a simple poetry contest or might conceal serious, satiric comment on abuses in the great world under the guise of homely, local concerns. There were also pastoral funeral elegies, pastoral dramas, pastoral romances (prose fiction), and even pastoral episodes within epics.

Poems in the satirical mode were also placed among the "low" kinds, plain in matter and style. The genres for satire were less well fixed in the sixteenth century than they were later, but there is a good deal of satirical verse. Some early examples belong to a medieval tradition coming down from *Piers Plowman*, while others, notably Wyatt's epistolary satires, are related to the classical satirists Horace and Juvenal. In the 1590s verse satires, chiefly in rhymed iambic pentameter couplets and closely modeled on Horace, Juvenal, and Persius, were published by Joseph

Hall and John Marston; at the same time, the young John Donne was circulating satires in manuscript that were published only after his death (in 1631). These satires hold up to ridicule and scorn a society (usually a city society) peopled by fops and fools, venal lawyers, toadying courtiers, money-grubbing merchants, self-deluded lovers, and all their ilk. The brief, pointed epigram in the tradition of Martial (often with a surprise ending or "sting" in the tail) was probably the most important of the Elizabethan satiric genres, but throughout the sixteenth and seventeenth centuries epigrams were still often written in Latin. The most notable English achievement in this kind is Jonson's *Epigrams*, first published in 1616. It is worth noting, however, that some epigrams were lyric in mode, sometimes in the form of words for a madrigal: *The Silver Swan* is an example.

Poems in the lyric mode were comparatively brief and usually concerned with praises of various kinds; with love in its various moods; or with celebrations of nature, the good life, or other such matters. The noblest lyric genres were thought to be hymns (praises of God or the gods) and odes (celebrating worthy men and women and notable occasions); such poems were conventionally exalted in tone, elevated in language, and charged with feeling; they often had complex stanzaic patterns and frequent apostrophes. An important variety of ode in the sixteenth century was the epithalamium, a poem in praise of marriage, conventionally following the course of the wedding day—and night. The most famous example is Spenser's *Epithalamion*, whose long stanzas (varying from seventeen to nineteen lines) display an astonishing metrical complexity, fairly illustrating the height of Elizabethan craft in verse. Notable classical models were Horace, Catullus, Pindar, and Callimachus, and notable biblical models were the Book of Psalms and the Song of Songs.

Often, Elizabethan lyrics retained something of the original association of this mode with song (the lyre). There were dance songs with their definite rhythms and refrains, and many well-known tunes provided the formula by which poet after poet composed new words. There were also many varieties of song, written to fixed formal specifications: the popular ballad with its simple four-line stanza of anonymous or perhaps composite authorship; the polyphonic madrigal for two or more voices in counterpoint, which had to be short and simple both in language and ideas; and the stanzaic air for single voice and lute, its more complex thought carried by the recurrent melody.

A most important lyric genre in the sixteenth century was the sonnet, which reached the height of its vogue in the 1590s. Its conventions were established by Petrarch (1304–1374), carried on by his numerous imitators in Italy and France, and introduced into England by Wyatt and Surrey in the reign of Henry VIII. The Petrarchan sonnet sequence is a series of fourteen-line sonnets (with songs interspersed) exploring the contrary states of feeling a lover experiences as he desires and idolizes an unattainable lady: some conventional themes concern the lady's great beauty, her power over him, her cruelty to him, his sleeplessness, the fire of his love and the ice of her chastity, the pain of absence, the renunciation of love, and the eternity and originality of his poems. One late sequence by Lady Mary Wroth (*Pamphilia to Amphilanthus*) reverses the conventional situation, presenting a female speaker who explores her various emotions, conflicts, and experiences in love. These sequences, whatever their purposes, utilized the elaborate rhetorical and stylistic devices available in the Petrarchan tradition.

All love sonnets were not Petrarchan, nor were all sonnets, or sonnet sequences, devoted to love: some sequences treated religious devotion, and occasional sonnets might address a wide variety of topics. More than most genres, the sonnet has come to be identified by its formal structure, a fourteen-line poem in iambic pentameter, in three principal rhyming patterns. The most common Italian form, which Wyatt, Sidney, and others imitated, was divided structurally into an octave (first eight lines, rhymed *abba abba*) and a sestet (last six, typically rhymed *cdecde* or some variant thereof). The so-called English sonnet, introduced by Surrey and practiced by Shakespeare, is divided structurally into three quatrains and a couplet, rhymed *abab cdcd efef gg*. Spenser, the most experimental prosodist of the century, preferred a form that is harder to write and richer in rhymes: *abab bcbc cdcd ee*. Yet sonnets were not so rigidly defined in the sixteenth century: Elizabethans often called them *quatorzains* and frequently used the term *sonnet* quite loosely, to refer to any short poem.

There were also poems (as well as dramas) in the tragic mode. A principal genre was the complaint, developed especially by the Italian Boccaccio and his English imitators, Lydgate and the authors of *The Mirror for Magistrates*. The chief convention of the complaint is that the ghost of someone who fell from high place bemoans his fate and warns others; the warning carries a moral lesson. A female ghost like Daniel's Rosamond often ascribes her fall to the frailty of her sex. A related kind of poem is the heroical epistle, in which the complaint is written as a letter, usually by a wronged woman to the man who abandoned or betrayed her. Drayton was the chief Elizabethan writer in this kind, which harks back to Ovid.

Another set of conventions defined a mythological-erotic mode, derived mainly from the *Metamorphoses* of Ovid but influenced also by his Italian imitators. The medieval disposition to allegorize and moralize Ovid's poetry continued into the seventeenth century (as did the habit of allegorizing the erotic love songs in the Song of Solomon in the Old Testament). But in the late sixteenth century the Ovidian erotic mode was revived: its values and conventions of lush and elaborate descriptions of physical beauty, of delight in the pleasures of the senses, and of frank eroticism appealed to a courtly taste. In this vein were several poems in the genre of the epyllion, or short mythological narrative, among them Shakespeare's *Venus and Adonis* and Marlowe's *Hero and Leander*.

Finally of course, there was the heroic mode, with its values of honor, battle courage, loyalty, leadership, endurance, and glorification of nation or people. The chief genre was the epic, conventionally a long, exalted poem in the high style, based on a heroic story from the nation's distant history and imitating Homer and Virgil in structure and specific topics. Renaissance poets throughout Europe undertook to honor their nations and their vernacular languages by writing this highest kind of poetry. In sixteenth-century England the only real success in epic is Spenser's *Faerie Queene*, which is, properly speaking, a romantic epic, in that it draws more heavily on the conventions of the romantic Italian epics of Ariosto and Tasso—with their interwoven plots, their exotic adventures and marvels, and their fundamental concern with love as well as war—than on the classical epics. Spenser points to that genre explicitly when he declares, "Fierce warres and faithfull loves shall moralize my song." By convention, epics had to achieve an elevated, high style, and Spenser devised an elaborate nine-line stanza (called after him the "Spenserian stanza") to serve his special narrative and descriptive needs. It consisted of eight lines of iambic pentameter (rhymed *ababbcbc*), concluding with a line of twelve syllables, an Alexandrine, which rhymes with the preceding line and provides firm closure for each stanza.

We should remember that genres and modes were often mixed in Renaissance England and that long poems like *The Faerie Queene* contained elements of many kinds. Some new, mixed kinds—like tragicomedy—attracted considerable criticism but flourished nonetheless. Some others, like Sidney's *Arcadia*, are obviously experimental—a prose romance incorporating both pastoral and heroic elements. The Elizabethans did not approach genre with the rigidity and purism of the Italian or French neoclassicists but in the spirit of Sidney's inclusivism: "if severed they be good, the conjunction cannot be hurtful."

Also worth noting are some distinctive verse patterns that came to be associated, conventionally, with certain kinds of poems. Henry Howard, earl of Surrey, introduced blank verse (unrhymed iambic pentameter) into England, in his translation of Virgil; this became the conventional meter for Elizabethan tragedy (and later for Milton's epics). The most common verse form in the 1560s and 1570s was an iambic couplet in which the first line had twelve syllables and the second fourteen; it was called "poulter's measure" (because a poultryman typically gave twelve eggs in the first dozen and fourteen in the second). An example is

> The young man eke that feels his bones with pains oppressed,
> How he would be a rich old man, to live and lie at rest.

The dreary monotony of this meter is matched only by the "fourteener" couplet of fourteen syllables to a line. But both were taken into the Elizabethan hymnbooks and survive there: when each line of poulter's measure is printed as two lines it is called "short meter"; when fourteeners are so divided it is called "common meter." Also, some Chaucerian verse forms survive, to be used by Shakespeare in his narrative poems: the six-line pentameter stanza (a quatrain and a couplet, rhymed *ababcc*) in *Venus and Adonis*, and the rhyme royal stanza (seven iambic pentameter lines, rhymed *ababbcc*) in *The Rape of Lucrece*.

DRAMATIC LITERATURE AND THE THEATER

If the morality play *Everyman* at the end of the fifteenth century marks the end of medieval drama, some new beginnings are in evidence at the same time in the household of John Morton, archbishop of Canterbury and chancellor of England under Henry VII, where young Thomas More served as a page. There at Christmastime, plays or revels were put on, and the story goes that young More would sometimes improvise a part and step in with the players. Cardinal Morton even maintained a chaplain on his staff, Henry Medwall, to write plays for his entertainment; two of them survive, called *Nature* and *Fulgens and Lucrece*. These short plays were given in the great hall at Lambeth Palace and were called "interludes." Some interludes, especially those by John Heywood, depend heavily on French farce.

Interludes and morality plays continued to be popular down to Shakespeare's lifetime, but the development of drama into a sophisticated art form required another influence, the classics. In the middle of the century a schoolmaster, Nicholas Udall, wrote a classical comedy in English, based on the Latin comedies his students had been reading; he called it *Ralph Roister Doister*. At about the same time another comedy, putting vivid, native English material into classical form, was amusing the students at Cambridge. It was called *Gammar Gurton's Needle*. In the development of comedy as a genre the great classical models were the Latin comic playwrights Plautus and Terence, from whom English dramatists derived some elements of structure and content: plots based on intrigue, division into acts and scenes, and type characters such as the rascally servant and the *miles gloriosus* (cowardly braggart soldier). The latter type appears in *Ralph Roister Doister* and is a remote ancestor of Shakespeare's Sir John Falstaff in *1 Henry IV*. Comedy was generally taken to be a lower genre than tragedy, and the style often mixes prose and verse: middle- and lower-class characters tend to speak prose.

Many varieties of comedy developed during the Elizabethan and Jacobean age, influenced by classical models and also by Italian and French examples. The conventions of romantic comedy call for noble characters and a central love plot (as in Shakespeare's *As You Like It* and *Twelfth Night*). Domestic comedy, as the name implies, has a domestic situation at the center of the plot (as in Thomas Dekker's *Shoemaker's Holiday*). City comedy typically has bourgeois characters, a London setting, and much satire (as in Thomas Middleton's *A Chaste Maid in Cheapside*). Humor comedy (such as Ben Jonson's *Every Man in His Humor*) has type characters created on the theory that the predominance of a particular fluid, or humor, in the body creates a specific temperament (melancholic, choleric, splenetic, and phlegmatic). Jonson also wrote classical intrigue comedy in *The Alchemist* and *Volpone*, with their complex, fast-paced plots and discoveries, their characters based on classical types, and their witty dialogue. Tragicomedy was a mixed kind, in which evils and problems that seem destined to end tragically are brought to sudden, happy resolution (as in Shakespeare's *Measure for Measure* and, in a different mood, *The Winter's Tale*).

Elizabethan tragedy also began with a fusion of medieval and classical elements. The precarious position of men in high estate formed the basis for medieval notions of tragedy; it owed much to the Latin tragedies of Seneca (known throughout the Middle Ages) that portray the Roman goddess Fortuna turning her wheel, and thereby bringing low those that were high. This is the tragic vision of the narrative tales in Giovanni Boccaccio's *Falls of Illustrious Men*, in Chaucer's *Monk's Tale*, and Lydgate's *Falls of Princes*; it is also the conception of tragedy in the collection of tales and complaints about the falls of princes called *The Mirror for Magistrates*, first published in 1559 and reprinted with additions in 1563, 1587, and 1610. A "mirror" in this sense is a warning, something to see oneself in and learn from; a "magistrate" is anyone in a position of power or authority.

When tragedies began to be dramatized, they took over very different elements from Seneca: violent and bloody plots, resounding rhetorical speeches, the frequent use of ghosts among the cast of characters, and sometimes the five-act structure. The first regular English tragedy using some of these elements was called *Gorboduc, or Ferrex and Porrex*; it was written by two lawyers, Thomas Sackville and Thomas Norton, was first produced at the Inner Temple (a law school) in 1561, and was later acted before the queen. Significantly, *Gorboduc* was written in blank verse rather than in one of the awkward verse forms characteristic of much midcentury writing; its use here begins the establishment of blank verse as the accepted medium for English tragedy. In due course it evolved into "Marlowe's mighty line" and Shakespeare's wonderfully flexible and expressive poetry.

While Aristotle's *Poetics* did not provide rigid norms for tragedy in England as it did on the Continent, it did influence the conception of the genre. Particularly important were the Aristotelian principles that the tragic fall should be caused by some error or moral weakness in the protagonist; that the plot should involve a fall from eminent success into misery, marked by reversals and discoveries; that the characters should be persons of high estate, "better than we"; and that the tragedy should evoke pity and fear in the viewers, working at last to achieve a purgation (catharsis) of those emotions. Some of Shakespeare's great tragedies (e.g., *Othello* and *King Lear*) can be analyzed in such terms, although, like most other Elizabethan tragedies, they are far from classical in their use of subplots and comic relief, their violations of the unities of time and place, and their sheer expansiveness.

Several distinct varieties of tragedy developed during the Elizabethan period. The Senecan influence remained pervasive, giving rise to a subgenre of revenge tragedy, in which a wronged protagonist plots and executes revenge, destroying himself (or herself) in the process. An early, highly influential example is Thomas Kyd's *Spanish Tragedy* (1592), and for all its psychological complexity Shakespeare's *Hamlet* is also of this kind. A related but distinct kind (which Aristotle considered untragic) is the villain tragedy in which the protagonist is blatantly evil, as in Shakespeare's *Richard III* and *Macbeth*. Still another sort is the heroic tragedy, in which the hero is larger than life, continually challenging the limits of human possibility: Marlowe's "overreaching" heroes (Tamberlaine and Dr. Faustus) are of this kind, as are the two protagonists of Shakespeare's *Antony and Cleopatra*.

This era also gave rise to dramatic kinds that fall quite outside the generic boundaries of comedy and tragedy. The festival beginnings of drama in entertainments presented by the servants of a lord in the hall of his castle (often at winter and midsummer holidays and festivals) find some continuity in the several dramatic entertainments provided for Queen Elizabeth when she made progresses through her realm, visiting her nobles in their great houses. Another offshoot was the masque, an entertainment at court combining dance, song, dialogue, and spectacle; there were masques at the courts of Henry VIII and Queen Elizabeth, but the form was especially fostered by the Stuart monarchs in the next century—at which time it took on its characteristic qualities of extravagant display in costume and scenery. Yet another Elizabethan kind is the history play: taking its subjects from English history, it was especially suited to reflect the nationalistic sentiment, the sense of epic destiny, and the moral complexities of gaining and holding on to sovereign power. Shakespeare offers the prime example in his two cycles of history plays; *1 Henry IV* is perhaps his supreme achievement in that kind.

This flowering of English drama depended centrally on professional actors, a theater, and an audience. The earliest English drama had been acted by members of the clergy in the church, and medieval miracle and mystery plays had been acted by amateurs—members of the local trade guilds—ordinarily on wagons in the streets of the towns. Moralities and interludes were produced by the servants of a lord in the hall of his castle, or by semiprofessional groups who traveled about, giving their performances wherever they could. Such actors did not have respectable status; they tended to be classified with jugglers, acrobats, mountebanks, and other persons of dubious character. In 1545 they were classified by statute as idle rogues and vagabonds and as such were subject to arrest.

Some noblemen, however, maintained a company of actors as personal servants; because they wore the livery and badge of their master they were exempt from the statute and could travel when not needed by their master and practice their craft where they would. This practice explains why the professional acting companies of Shakespeare's time, including Shakespeare's own, attached themselves to a nobleman and were technically his servants (the Lord Chamberlain's Men, the Lord Admiral's Men), even though virtually all their time was devoted to, and their income came from, the public. The rise in social status of actors during Shakespeare's lifetime is illustrated by the fact that he and his fellows were attached to the royal household when James came to the throne and became known as the King's Men. However, the earliest successful acting companies, if success is measured by acceptance at court, were companies of boys. Richard Edwards, master of the children of the Chapel Royal in the 1560s, wrote plays for them, and for almost twenty years the rival company, the Children of Paul's (the choir school of St. Paul's cathedral) regularly presented plays at court.

At first, the adult companies played in various places—great houses, the hall of an Inn of Court, on makeshift stages, or in London inn yards. In 1576 James Burbage, one of the earl of Leicester's players, built a structure to house their performances and called it The Theatre. It was in Shoreditch, outside the limits of the city of London and, accordingly, beyond the jurisdiction of the city authorities who were generally hostile to dramatic spectacles. Soon, other public theaters were erected, which could accommodate some 2,000 spectators: they were usually oval in shape, with an unroofed yard in the center where the groundlings (apprentices, servants, and men of the lower classes) stood, and covered seats in three rising tiers around the yard for the spectators of higher social status. A large platform stage jutted out into the yard, surrounded on three sides by spectators—who sometimes also sat on the stage (see the drawing of a typical London playhouse on p. 2626).

Plays were acted at high speed, without the act and scene breaks we are used to; there was no scenery and few props, but costumes were usually sumptuous and elaborate. Performances were given in the afternoon and were subject to cancelation by bad weather or by epidemics of plague that periodically ravaged the city. Before long there were also enclosed private theaters, secured under conditions that would also allow them freedom from municipal control; they were indoors, artificially lighted, and patronized by a more select audience. After 1608 Shakespeare's company had its regular public theater, the Globe, and a private theater, the Blackfriars.

The companies of players were what would now be called "repertory companies"—that is, they filled the roles of each play from members of their own group, not employing outsiders. They performed a number of different plays on consecutive days, and the principal actors were shareholders in the profits of the company. Boys were apprenticed to actors just as they had been apprenticed to master craftsmen in the guilds; they took the women's parts in plays until their voices changed. The plays might be bought for the company from hack writers, or as in Shakespeare's company, the group might include an actor-playwright who could supply it with some (but by no means all) of its plays. The text remained the property of the company, but a popular play was eagerly sought by the printers, and the company sometimes had trouble achieving effective control over its rights to the play. The editors of the first collected edition of Shakespeare's plays, the First Folio (1623) alluded to the prior publication of "divers stolen and surreptitious copies" of his plays, "maimed and deformed by the frauds and stealths of injurious imposters."

Elizabethan culture was itself notably theatrical—executions were staged as public spectacles, the queen displayed herself to her people in elaborate progresses, and civic pageants and religious ceremonies were splendid performances. Such public enactments served to evoke awe and to reinforce the power of monarch and magistrates. The public theater stood in uneasy relaton to these displays: set up in the "Liberties" where they escaped control by the City, the playhouses put monarchs and magistrates on their stages, showing them sometimes weak and evil and sometimes subject to rebellion, overthrow, and execution. The players also unleashed on their stages the force of the carnavalesque and the licensed fool who mocks all authority. How far Elizabethan plays reinforce established authority by serving as a kind of steam valve for discontent, and how far they challenge it, is a complex issue. That plays could be read as direct political challenges is evident from Queen Elizabeth's reaction to a performance of *Richard II* just at the time the earl of Essex mounted a rebellion against her: "I am Richard II, know ye not that."

ATTITUDES, ANXIETIES, AND AMBIGUITIES

The sixteenth century made no sharp break with the past. George Gascoigne, the leading poet of the 1570s, has in many ways a medieval point of view, as well as a notably plain style, and the flamboyant and "modern" Elizabethan Sir Walter Ralegh also dwells on the vanity and transitoriness of all earthly ambitions and achievements. The Dance of Death and related images were still living symbols to the Elizabethans, as Shakespeare's *Richard II* (3.2.155–162) indicates:

> For God's sake let us sit upon the ground
> And tell sad stories of the death of kings:
> How some have been depos'd; some slain in war,
> Some haunted by the ghosts they have deposed,
> Some poisoned by their wives, some sleeping killed,
> All murthered—for within the hollow crown
> That rounds the mortal temples of a king
> Keeps Death his court.

Yet Elizabethans could at the same time indulge a spirit of joy and gaiety, of lighthearted pastoral delight, as in Marlowe's playful pastoral seduction lyric *The Passionate Shepherd to His Love* and several of the songs from Shakespeare's comedies. In a very different vein, Marlowe's several heroes express the burning desire for conquest, for achievement, and for surmounting all obstacles: Barrabas and his lust for gold ("Infinite riches in a little room"), Tamburlaine and his pursuit of power ("Is it not passing brave to be a king / And ride in triumph through Persepolis?"), and Faustus and his search for knowledge ("His dominion that excels in this / Stretches as far as doth the mind of man").

There were other paradoxes as well. The Elizabethan spirit has been described as sensuous, comprehensive, extravagant, disorderly, thirsty for beauty, abounding in the zest for life. But Jonson, who shared some of these qualities, also emphasized classical principles of structure and decorum, an ideal of the centered self and the balanced moral life, the primacy of learning, and the reconciliation of classical and native English elements in his poetry and drama. Sidney is perhaps the most striking exemplar of the Elizabethan Renaissance man in all his paradoxical comprehensiveness—courtier, statesman, soldier, humanist scholar, Petrarchan sonneteer, romance writer, literary critic, and earnest supporter of Protestant reform at home and abroad.

If optimism and exuberance are characteristics of the Elizabethan Age, so also are anxiety, ambivalence, and conflict. On the one hand, the dual impact of humanism and the Reformation promoted self-consciousness and the emergence of individualism. On the other hand, the comprehensive social structures—family, church, patronage systems, and government—constrained men and women to define themselves through and by their several social roles. So even a "personal" lyric form like the sonnet may become a site for the playing out of many roles. On the one hand, patriarchal ideology firmly instated gender hierarchy and the subordination of woman to man, defining the feminine ideal as "chaste, silent, and obedient." On the other hand, that ideology had to confront the unsettling spectacle of a woman on top—on the throne—as well as powerful patronesses, a few female intellectuals and classical scholars, cross-dressed viragoes, and ordinary wives who sometimes ruled their husbands. Literary representations of gender throughout this period reflect the resulting anxieties, giving us heroines who challenge the patriarchal ideal by their power, wickedness, wit, courage, or independence of spirit but who are often brought to conform to it. On the one hand, Elizabethans exalted order and degree, natural and social hierarchy, and the Great Chain of Being. On the other hand, they confronted radical social tensions brought on by the impoverishment of the aristocracy, the growing power of the city merchants and traders, and the increasingly unruly lower orders and vagabonds ("masterless men") who had lost or escaped their assigned place in the scheme of things. These social tensions are also played out in Elizabethan literature, especially the drama.

If the beginning of the Tudor era showed more links with the past than with the future, the end of Elizabeth's reign prefigured conflicts and uncertainties to come. In 1599, the year of Spenser's death, the headstrong earl of Essex returned from Ireland and at length mounted a rebellion at home that led to his execution in 1601. Elizabeth was old, a peaceful succession was by no means assured, and the rifts (religious, social, and political) that were to lead to the civil wars in the midseventeenth century were already in evidence. An outbreak of satire and epigrams in the 1590s was thought to be dangerous and was repressed by the authorities. And some of the cynical undercurrents in Shakespeare's *Hamlet* and *Troilus and Cressida* reflect the general disenchantment and disillusionment. In 1603, Elizabeth, the last of the Tudors, died, and to the immense relief of anxious Englishmen, the succession that brought in the Stuart kings took place peacefully. The new monarch was the Protestant James VI of Scotland, who became James I of England.

TEXTS	CONTEXTS
	1485 Accession of Henry VII inaugurates Tudor dynasty
	1509–47 Reign of Henry VIII
1516 Sir Thomas More, *Utopia*	
	1517 Martin Luther's Ninety-five Theses; beginning of Reformation in Germany
	1519–21 Hernando Cortés conquers Mexico
	1521 Pope bestows title "Defender of the Faith" on Henry VIII for anti-Lutheran tract
1523 William Tyndale begins English translation of Bible	
	1529–32 More is Lord Chancellor
1532 Niccolò Machiavelli, *The Prince*	
	1533–34 Henry VIII divorces Catherine of Aragon to marry Ann Boleyn; declares himself head of the Church of England
	1535 Execution of More
	1543 Nicolaus Copernicus, *Revolution of the Celestial Spheres,* proposes heliocentric theory of the universe
	1547–53 Reign of Edward VI
1549 *Book of Common Prayer* establishes liturgy for Church of England	
	1553–58 Reign of Mary Tudor; attempt to restore Catholic Church; persecution of Protestants
	1555–56 Archbishop Cranmer and former bishops Latimer and Ridley burned at the stake
1557 *Tottel's Miscellany (Songs and Sonnets)* publishes poems by the earl of Surrey, Sir Thomas Wyatt, and others	

TEXTS	CONTEXTS
	1558–1603 Reign of Elizabeth I
	1576 Building of The Theatre, first permanent structure in England for the presentation of plays
	1577–80 Francis Drake circumnavigates the globe
c. 1582 Sir Philip Sidney, *Astrophil and Stella* (published 1591)	
	1584–87 Sir Walter Ralegh's earliest attempts to explore and colonize Virginia
	1586 Sidney killed fighting for freedom of the Netherlands from Catholic Spain
c. 1587 Christopher Marlowe's *Tamburlaine* introduces blank verse to the stage	**1587** Execution of Mary Stuart, Queen of Scots
	1588 Defeat of the Spanish Armada
1590 Spenser, *The Faerie Queene,* Books 1–3 published; Books 4–6 published 1596	
c. 1592–93 Marlowe, *Dr. Faustus*	
c. 1592–98 John Donne's erotic poems (not published until 1633) • Shakespeare's history plays, early comedies, sonnets	**1593** Marlowe killed in a tavern brawl
1598 Quarto edition of Shakespeare's *1 Henry IV* • Ben Jonson's first play, *Every Man in His Humor*	
	1599 Globe Theater opens
	1603 Death of Elizabeth; accession of James I, son of Mary, Queen of Scots

Boldface titles indicate works in the anthology.

EDMUND SPENSER
1552–1599

1579: Publication of *The Shepheardes Calender.*
1590: Publication of *The Faerie Queene,* books 1 to 3; 1596, books 1 to 6.

The greatest nondramatic poet of the Elizabethan era, Edmund Spenser, was born in London, probably in 1552, and attended the Merchant Taylors' School under its famous headmaster Richard Mulcaster. In 1569 he went to Cambridge as a "sizar," or poor scholar. In the Puritan environment of Cambridge, where the popular preacher Thomas Cartwright was beginning to make the authorities uneasy, Spenser began as a poet by translating some poems for a volume of anti-Catholic propaganda. He also began his friendship with Gabriel Harvey, an eccentric Cambridge don, humanist, and pamphleteer. Their correspondence shows that both men were interested in theories of poetry and in experiments in quantitative versification in English; it also shows that Spenser had ambitious plans as a poet.

After receiving the A.B. degree in 1573 and the A.M. in 1576, Spenser served as personal secretary and aide to several prominent men, including Dr. John Young, bishop of Rochester, and the earl of Leicester, the queen's favorite. During his employment in Leicester's household he came to know Sir Philip Sidney and his friend Sir Edward Dyer, courtiers who sought to promote a new English poetry. Spenser's contribution to the movement is *The Shepheardes Calender,* published in 1579 and dedicated to Sidney.

There are thirteen different meters in *The Shepheardes Calender.* Some of these Spenser invented, some he adapted, but most of them were novel; only three or four were at all common in 1579. Spenser was a prolific experimenter who went on to make further innovations in his later poems: the special rhyme scheme of the Spenserian sonnet, the remarkably beautiful adaptation of the Italian *canzone* forms for the *Epithalamion* and *Prothalamion,* and the nine-line stanza of *The Faerie Queene,* with its extraordinary six-foot line at the end, are the best known. Spenser is sometimes called the "poet's poet" because so many later English poets learned the art of versification from him. In the nineteenth century alone his influence may be seen in Shelley's *Revolt of Islam,* Byron's *Childe Harold's Pilgrimage,* Keats's *Eve of St. Agnes,* and Tennyson's *The Lotos-Eaters.*

The year after the publication of *The Shepheardes Calender,* Spenser went to Ireland as secretary and aide to Lord Grey of Wilton, lord deputy of Ireland. Although he tried continually to obtain appointments in England, he spent the rest of his life in Ireland, holding various minor government posts and obtaining grants of sequestered lands; in 1596 or thereabouts he wrote a vigorous apology for the brutally repressive English colonialist regime, *A View of the Present State of Ireland.* He was at work on his great romantic epic when Sir Walter Ralegh visited him at Kilcolman Castle; the result was a trip to England and the publication, in 1590, of the first three books of *The Faerie Queene,* which made a strong bid for the queen's favor and patronage. Soon after, he published a volume of poems called *Complaints;* a pastoral called *Colin Clouts Come Home Againe* (1595), commenting on the courtiers and ladies at the center of English court life at the time of his 1590 visit; the sonnet cycle *Amoretti;* and two marriage poems, *Epithalamion* and *Prothalamion.* The six-book *Faerie Queene* was published in 1596, with some revisions in the first part and a changed ending to book 3, to provide a bridge to the added books; the so-called Mutability cantos and two stanzas of a third—perhaps part of an intended seventh book—appeared first in the edition of 1609.

In the second half of the decade, Ireland was torn by revolt and civil war; Spenser's castle was destroyed, and the poet was sent to England with messages from the besieged English garrison. He died in Westminster on January 13, 1599, and was buried near his beloved Chaucer in what is now called the Poets' Corner of Westminster Abbey.

Spenser cannot be put into neatly labeled categories. He was strongly influenced by Renaissance neoplatonism, but was also earthy and practical. He is a lover and celebrator of physical beauty, yet also a profound analyst of good and evil in all their perplexing shapes and complexities. He was strongly influenced by Puritanism in his early days, remained a thoroughgoing Protestant all his life, and portrayed the Roman Catholic church as a villain in *The Faerie Queene*; yet his understanding of faith and of sin owes much to Catholic thinkers. He is a poet of sensuous images yet also something of an iconoclast, deeply suspicious of the power of images (material and verbal) to turn into idols. He is an idealist, yet also a celebrant of English nationalism, empire, and martial power. He is in some ways a backward-looking poet who paid homage to Chaucer, used archaic language, and compared his own age unfavorably with the antique world. Yet as British epic poet and poet-prophet, he points forward to the poetry of the Romantics and especially Milton—who himself paid homage to Spenser as "a better teacher than Scotus or Aquinas."

Because it was a deliberate choice on Spenser's part that his language should seem antique, Spenser's poetry is here printed in the original spelling and punctuation; a few of the most confusing punctuation marks have, however, been altered in the present text. Spenser also spells words in such a way as to suggest rhymes to the eye, or to suggest etymologies (often incorrect ones). This inconsistency in his spelling is typical of his time; in the sixteenth century people even varied the spelling of their own names.

The Faerie Queene

Spenser's exuberant, multifaceted poem is peculiarly characteristic of its age. In some respects it is a "courtesy book," like Castiglione's *Courtier*, intended to "fashion a gentleman or noble person" by exhibiting the qualities such a person should have. The six books that Spenser completed exhibit the virtues of Holiness, Temperance, Chastity, Friendship, Justice, and Courtesy. We also have a fragment of another book, the cantos on Mutability (the principle of constant change in nature).

In other respects *The Faerie Queene* is a romantic epic, like Ariosto's *Orlando Furioso* (*Orlando Mad*, 1516), full of adventures and marvels, dragons, witches, enchanted trees, giants, jousting knights, and castles. As such it fulfills the expectation that a romance will produce wonder, that it will enthrall us with its intricate plots, amazing episodes, heroic characters, elaborate descriptions. It also fulfills the common Elizabethan expectation that poetry should teach by delighting.

The poem is also a national epic: as Tasso's *Gerusalemme Liberata* (*Jerusalem Delivered*, 1575) celebrates an Italian ruling family, so Spenser's poem celebrates the Tudors, Queen Elizabeth, and the English nation. Spenser's letter to Sir Walter Ralegh, appended to the 1590 edition, terms the poem an allegory, and invites us to interpret the characters and adventures in the several books in terms of particular virtues and vices. The Redcrosse Knight in book 1 is the knight of Holiness (and also St. George, the patron saint of England). Sir Guyon in book 2 is the knight of Temperance. The female knight Britomart in book 3 is the knight of Chastity (in her, chaste love leading to marriage), and also alludes to Queen Elizabeth. However, far from being a static embodiment of the named virtue, each knight advances in the understanding and practice of that virtue in the course of his or her adventures. Accordingly, the meaning of the various characters, episodes, and places is dense and complex, revealed to us only by degrees as we read and interpret the poem. In addition, persistent allusion to personages, events, and issues in Spenser's England and Ireland—e.g., the queen, the English Reformation, the Continental religious wars, the iconoclastic controversies, and colonialism—lead us to recognize that the poem incorporates historical allegory. Spenser's poem may be enjoyed as a fascinating story with multiple meanings, which works on several levels at once. Although helpful, the letter to Ralegh is at times (and perhaps deliberately) misleading in its simplified account of Spenser's allegorical scheme.

The introductory lines of the poem are intended to remind the reader of Virgil, who began his poetic career with pastoral poetry and moved on to the epic, as Spenser did in moving from *The Shepheardes Calender* to *The Faerie Queene*. The organization of each book into twelve cantos also imitates the twelve books of Virgil's *Aeneid*. But Spenser replaces Virgil's theme of epic heroism, "Arms and the man," with something more romantic—"Fierce warres and faithfull loves." The scenery too is romantic: plains and forests and caves and castles and magical trees and springs, where one meets dwarfs and giants and lions and pilgrims and magicians and Saracens or "paynims" (with French names). In Spenser's Faerie Land, if you are going somewhere you just start out, and after many adventures you may (or may not) get there. A clear, pleasant stream may be dangerous to drink because it produces loss of strength. Any stranger you meet may well be a villain and may be in disguise. Houses, castles, and gardens are often places of education or of especially dense allegorical significance, affording special keys to the meaning of the books in which they appear.

The *Faerie Queene's* subjects in Faerie Land are called Faeries or elves. They are human beings, and undergo the trials and tribulations people undergo in the ordinary world. But Faerie Land is also inhabited by knights and ladies who are not Faeries but Britons—Redcrosse, Britomart, and Prince Arthur (who loves and seeks the Faerie Queene throughout the poem). The bad creatures, people and monsters, represent various vices, evils, and temptations. Spenser's characters, both good and evil, may be initially identified to the reader by their names or by the short verse summaries at the beginning of each canto, but their natures are revealed progressively, in the course of the narrative. Some of Spenser's characters are identified by conventional symbols and attributes that would be obvious to every reader of his time. For example, such a reader would know immediately that a woman who wears a miter and scarlet clothes and who dwells near the river Tiber represents (in one sense at least) the Roman Catholic church, which had often been identified by Protestant preachers with the Whore of Babylon in the Book of Revelation.

The various books are composed on different structural principles. Book 1 is almost entirely self-contained; it has been called a miniature epic in itself, centering on the adventures of one principal hero, Redcrosse, who at length achieves the quest he undertakes at Una's behest—killing the dragon who has imprisoned her parents; and winning her as his bride. The spiritual allegory is similarly self-contained; it presents the Christian struggling heroically against many evils—error, hypocrisy, the seven deadly sins, and despair—but succumbing to some of them. It shows him separated from the one true faith and, aided by many interventions of divine grace, at length reunited with it once more. Then it treats his purgation from sin, his education in the House of Holiness, and his final salvation. By contrast, the structure of book 3 is romancelike, with its many heroines and heroes (who present, allegorically, several varieties of chaste and unchaste love), its interwoven stories (Amoret and Scudamore, Belphoebe and Timias, Florimell and

Marinell, Britomart and Arthegall), and its lack of closure—for the adventures of all these characters extend into books 4 and 5.

The Faerie Queene draws constantly on literary and pictorial traditions. Entire episodes are adapted from the Italian romantic epics of Ariosto and Tasso and, either through them or independently, from Homer, Virgil, or Ovid. (In the Renaissance, borrowing from and reworking older materials was praiseworthy in a poet.) Places such as Lucifera's castle or the garden of Adonis, individual attributes such as Una's lamb or Speranza's anchor or Britomart's spear, and even certain names or colors come to Spenser from the classics, from theologians, from liturgical tradition, from folk tales and pageants, from tapestries, and paintings, and from emblem books. Our notes point to some of these sources—but more important is the understanding that these were living traditions for Spenser and his readers. They flow together, separate, and recombine to produce the unique delights of The Faerie Queene.

From THE FAERIE QUEENE

A Letter of the Authors

EXPOUNDING HIS WHOLE INTENTION IN THE COURSE OF THIS WORKE: WHICH FOR THAT IT GIVETH GREAT LIGHT TO THE READER, FOR THE BETTER UNDERSTANDING IS HEREUNTO ANNEXED

To the Right noble, and Valorous, Sir Walter Raleigh knight, Lo. Wardein of the Stanneryes, and her Majesties liefetenaunt of the County of Cornewayll

Sir knowing how doubtfully all Allegories may be construed, and this booke of mine, which I have entituled the *Faery Queene*, being a continued Allegory, or darke conceit,[1] I have thought good as well for avoyding of gealous opinions and misconstructions, as also for your better light in reading thereof, (being so by you commanded,) to discover unto you the general intention and meaning, which in the whole course thereof I have fashioned, without expressing of any particular purposes or by-accidents[2] therein occasioned. The generall end therefore of all the booke is to fashion a gentleman or noble person in vertuous and gentle[3] discipline: Which for that I conceived shoulde be most plausible and pleasing, being coloured with an historicall fiction, the which the most part of men delight to read, rather for variety of matter, then for profite of the ensample:[4] I chose the historye of King Arthure, as most fitte for the excellency of his person, being made famous by many mens former workes, and also furthest from the daunger of envy, and suspition of present time.[5] In which I have followed all the antique Poets historicall, first Homere, who in the Persons of Agamemnon and Ulysses hath ensampled a good governour and a vertuous man, the one in his *Ilias*, the other in his *Odysseis*: then Virgil, whose like intention was to doe in the person of Aeneas: after him Ariosto comprised them both in his Orlando: and lately Tasso dissevered them againe, and formed both parts in two persons, namely that part which they in Philosophy call Ethice, or vertues of a private man, coloured in his Rinaldo:

1. Obscure or difficult poetic figure.
2. Secondary matters.
3. Pertaining to a gentleman. "Fashion": (1) to repre-

sent; (2) to educate.
4. Example.
5. I.e., free from current political controversy.

The other named Politice in his Godfredo.[6] By ensample of which excellente
Poets, I labour to pourtraict in Arthure, before he was king, the image of a
brave knight, perfected in the twelve private morall vertues, as Aristotle hath
devised,[7] the which is the purpose of these first twelve bookes: which if I finde
to be well accepted, I may be perhaps encouraged, to frame the other part of
polliticke vertues in his person, after that hee came to be king. To some I know
this Methode will seeme displeasaunt, which had rather have good discipline
delivered plainly in way of precepts, or sermoned at large, as they use, then
thus clowdily enwrapped in Allegoricall devises. But such, me seeme, should
be satisfide with the use of these dayes, seeing all things accounted by their
showes, and nothing esteemed of, that is not delightfull and pleasing to commune sence.[8] For this cause is Xenophon preferred before Plato, for that the
one in the exquisite depth of his judgment, formed a Commune welth[9] such
as it should be, but the other in the person of Cyrus and the Persians fashioned
a governement such as might best be: So much more profitable and gratious
is doctrine by ensample, then by rule. So have I laboured to doe in the person
of Arthure: whome I conceive after his long education by Timon, to whom he
was by Merlin delivered to be brought up, so soone as he was borne of the
Lady Igrayne, to have seene in a dream or vision the Faery Queen, with whose
excellent beauty ravished, he awaking resolved to seeke her out, and so being
by Merlin armed, and by Timon throughly instructed, he went to seeke her
forth in Faerye land. In that Faery Queene I meane glory in my generall
intention, but in my particular I conceive the most excellent and glorious
person of our soveraine the Queene, and her kingdome in Faery land. And
yet in some places els, I doe otherwise shadow[1] her. For considering she
beareth two persons, the one of a most royall Queene or Empresse, the other
of a most vertuous and beautifull Lady, this latter part in some places I doe
express in Belphoebe, fashioning her name according to your owne excellent
conceipt of Cynthia,[2] (Phoebe and Cynthia being both names of Diana.) So
in the person of Prince Arthure I sette forth magnificence in particular, which
vertue for that (according to Aristotle and the rest) it is the perfection of all
the rest, and conteineth in it them all, therefore in the whole course I mention
the deedes of Arthure applyable to that vertue, which I write of in that booke.
But of the xii. other vertues, I make xii. other knights the patrones, for the
more variety of the history. Of which these three bookes contayn three, The
first of the knight of the Redcrosse, in whome I expresse Holynes: The seconde
of Sir Guyon, in whome I sette forth Temperaunce: The third of Britomartis
a Lady knight, in whome I picture Chastity. But because the beginning of the
whole worke seemeth abrupte and as depending upon other antecedents, it
needs that ye know the occasion of these three knights severall adventures.
For the Methode of a Poet historical is not such, as of an Historiographer.[3]
For an Historiographer discourseth of affayres orderly as they were donne,
accounting as well the times as the actions, but a Poet thrusteth into the

6. Lodovico Ariosto (1474–1533) was author of the
epic romance *Orlando Furioso*, first published in complete form in 1532. Torquato Tasso (1544–1595) published his chivalric romance *Rinaldo* in 1562 and the
epic *Gerusalemme Liberata* (centered on the heroic
figure of Count Godfredo) in 1581.
7. Aristotle did not devise twelve private moral virtues:
Spenser was in fact relying on more modern philosophers—his friend Lodowick Bryskett and the Italian

Piccolomini. That Spenser may have planned a poem
four times as long as the six books we now have rather
staggers the imagination.
8. The notions of the many. "Showes": appearances.
9. The allusion is to Plato's *Republic* and Xenophon's
Cyropaedia.
1. Picture, portray.
2. Ralegh's poem *Cynthia* praised Queen Elizabeth.
3. Historian.

middest, even where it most concerneth him, and there recoursing to the thinges forepaste,[4] and divining of thinges to come, maketh a pleasing Analysis of all. The beginning therefore of my history, if it were to be told by an Historiographer, should be the twelfth booke, which is the last, where I devise that the Faery Queene kept her Annuall feaste xii. dayes, uppon which xii. severall dayes, the occasions of the xii. severall adventures hapned, which being undertaken by xii. severall knights, are in these xii books severally handled and discoursed. The first was this. In the beginning of the feaste, there presented him selfe a tall clownishe[5] younge man, who falling before the Queen of Faeries desired a boone (as the manner then was) which during that feast she might not refuse: which was that hee might have the atchievement of any adventure, which during that feaste should happen, that being graunted, he rested him on the floore, unfitte through his rusticity for a better place. Soone after entred a faire Ladye in mourning weedes, riding on a white Asse, with a dwarfe behind her leading a warlike steed, that bore the Armes of a knight, and his speare in the dwarfes hand. Shee falling before the Queene of Faeries, complayned that her father and mother an ancient King and Queene, had bene by an huge dragon many years shut up in a brasen Castle, who thence suffred them not to yssew:[6] and therefore besought the Faery Queene to assygne her some one of her knights to take on him that exployt. Presently that clownish person upstarting, desired that adventure: whereat the Queene much wondering, and the Lady much gainesaying, yet he earnestly importuned his desire. In the end the Lady told him that unlesse that armour which she brought, would serve him (that is the armour of a Christian man specified by Saint Paul v. Ephes.[7]) that he could not succeed in that enterprise, which being forthwith put upon him with dewe furnitures[8] thereunto, he seemed the goodliest man in al that company, and was well liked of the Lady. And eftesoones taking on him knighthood, and mounting on that straunge Courser, he went forth with her on that adventure: where beginneth the first booke, vz.

A gentle knight was pricking on the playne. &c.

The second day ther came in a Palmer bearing an Infant with bloody hands, whose Parents he complained to have bene slayn by an Enchaunteresse called Acrasia: and therfore craved of the Faery Queene, to appoint him some knight, to performe that adventure, which being assigned to Sir Guyon, he presently went forth with that same Palmer: which is the beginning of the second booke and the whole subject thereof. The third day there came in, a Groome who complained before the Faery Queene, that a vile Enchaunter called Busirane had in hand a most faire Lady called Amoretta, whom he kept in most grievous torment, because she would not yield him the pleasure of her body. Whereupon Sir Scudamour the lover of that Lady presently tooke on him that adventure. But being unable to performe it by reason of the hard Enchauntments, after long sorrow, in the end met with Britomartis, who succoured him, and reskewed his love.

---

4. Past.
5. Rustic-looking.
6. Come forth.
7. Ephesians 6.11, "Put on the whole armor of God, that ye may be able to stand against the wiles of the devil." The parts (verses 14 to 17) are loins girt about with truth, breastplate of righteousness; feet shod with the gospel of peace, shield of faith "wherewith ye shall be able to quench all the fiery darts of the wicked," helmet of salvation, and "sword of the Spirit, which is the word of God."
8. Suitable equipment.

But by occasion hereof, many other adventures are intermedled, but rather as Accidents, then intendments.[9] As the love of Britomart, the overthrow of Marinell, the misery of Florimell, the vertuousnes of Belphoebe, the lasciviousnes of Hellenora, and many the like.

Thus much Sir, I have briefly overronne to direct your understanding to the wel-head of the History, that from thence gathering the whole intention of the conceit,[1] ye may as in a handfull gripe al the discourse, which otherwise may happily[2] seeme tedious and confused. So humbly craving the continuaunce of your honorable favour towards me, and th' eternall establishment of your happines, I humbly take leave.

23. January, 1589[1590][3]

Yours most humbly affectionate.

ED. SPENSER.

The First Booke of the Faerie Queene

Contayning
The Legende of the
Knight of the Red Crosse,
or
Of Holinesse

1

Lo I the man, whose Muse whilome did maske,
  As time her taught, in lowly Shepheards weeds,°[1]   *garb*
  Am now enforst a far unfitter taske,
  For trumpets sterne to chaunge mine Oaten reeds,[2]
5 And sing of Knights and Ladies gentle° deeds;   *noble*
  Whose prayses having slept in silence long,[3]
  Me, all too meane, the sacred Muse areeds°   *appoints*
  To blazon° broad emongst her learned throng: *proclaim*
Fierce warres and faithfull loves shall moralize my song.

2

10 Helpe then, O holy Virgin chiefe of nine,[4]
  Thy weaker° Novice to performe thy will,   *too weak*
  Lay forth out of thine everlasting scryne[5]
  The antique rolles, which there lye hidden still,
  Of Faerie knights and fairest Tanaquill,[6]
15 Whom that most noble Briton Prince[7] so long
  Sought through the world, and suffered so much ill,
  That I must rue his undeservèd wrong:
O helpe thou my weake wit, and sharpen my dull tong.

9. I.e., there are episodes that are not part of these principal stories.
1. Conception.
2. By chance.
3. The date is actually 1590, because until England adopted the Gregorian calendar in 1752, the new year began on March 25.
1. The poet appeared before ("whilome") as a writer of humble pastoral (i.e., *The Shepheardes Calender*). These lines are imitated from the verses prefixed to

Renaissance editions of Virgil's *Aeneid*.
2. To write heroic poetry, of which the trumpet is a symbol, instead of pastoral poetry symbolized by the humble shepherd's pipe ("Oaten reeds").
3. Lines 5 and 6 are imitated from the opening lines of Ariosto's *Orlando Furioso*.
4. Clio, the muse of history.
5. A chest for papers.
6. I.e., Gloriana.
7. I.e., Arthur, named in 1.9.50.

3

And thou most dreaded impe[8] of highest Jove,
20   Faire Venus sonne, that with thy cruell dart
      At that good knight so cunningly didst rove,°   shoot
      That glorious fire it kindled in his hart,
      Lay now thy deadly Heben° bow apart,   ebony
      And with thy mother milde come to mine ayde:
25   Come both, and with you bring triumphant Mart,[9]
      In loves and gentle jollities arrayd,
After his murdrous spoiles and bloudy rage allayd.

4

And with them eke,° O Goddesse heavenly bright,   also
      Mirrour of grace and Majestie divine,
30   Great Lady of the greatest Isle, whose light
      Like Phoebus lampe throughout the world doth shine,
      Shed thy faire beames into my feeble eyne,
      And raise my thoughts too humble and too vile,°   lowly
      To thinke of that true glorious type[1] of thine,
35   The argument of mine afflicted stile:
The which to heare, vouchsafe, O dearest dred[2] a-while.

Canto 1

The Patron of true Holinesse,
    Foule Errour doth defeate:
Hypocrisie him to entrappe,
    Doth to his home entreate.

1

A Gentle Knight was pricking° on the plaine,   cantering
      Ycladd in mightie armes and silver shielde,
      Wherein old dints of deepe wounds did remaine,
      The cruell markes of many a bloudy fielde;
5   Yet armes till that time did he never wield:[3]
      His angry steede did chide his foming bitt,
      As much disdayning to the curbe to yield:
      Full jolly° knight he seemd, and faire did sitt,   gallant
As one for knightly giusts° and fierce encounters   tourneys, jousts
      fitt.

2

10   But on his brest a bloudie Crosse he bore,
      The deare remembrance of his dying Lord,
      For whose sweete sake that glorious badge he wore,
      And dead as living ever him adored:
      Upon his shield the like was also scored,
15   For soveraine[4] hope, which in his helpe he had:
      Right faithfull true[5] he was in deede and word,

8. Child, i.e., Cupid.
9. Mars, god of war and lover of Venus.
1. I.e., Gloriana is the "type" (foreshadowing) of
Queen Elizabeth.
2. Object of awe.
3. Redcrosse wears the armor of the Christian man, as
Spenser explained in the letter to Ralegh. It bears the

dents of every Christian's fight against evil.
4. Having greatest power (often applied to medical
remedies).
5. An echo of Revelation 19.11: "And I saw heaven
opened; and behold a white horse; and he that sat
upon him was called Faithful and True."

But of his cheere[6] did seeme too solemne sad;°   *grave*
Yet nothing did he dread, but ever was ydrad.°   *dreaded, feared*

3

Upon a great adventure he was bond,
20   That greatest Gloriana to him gave,
That greatest Glorious Queene of Faerie Lond,
To winne him worship,° and her grace to have,   *honor*
Which of all earthly things he most did crave;
And ever as he rode, his hart did earne°   *yearn*
25   To prove his puissance in battell brave
Upon his foe, and his new force to learne;
Upon his foe, a Dragon horrible and stearne.

4

A lovely Ladie rode him faire beside,
Upon a lowly Asse more white then snow,
30   Yet she much whiter, but the same did hide
Under a vele, that wimpled° was full low,   *lying in folds*
And over all a blacke stole she did throw,
As one that inly mournd: so was she sad,
And heavie sat upon her palfrey slow:
35   Seemèd in heart some hidden care she had,
And by her in a line a milke white lambe she lad.

5

So pure an innocent, as that same lambe,
She was in life and every vertuous lore,
And by descent from Royall lynage came
40   Of ancient Kings and Queenes, that had of yore
Their scepters stretcht from East to Westerne shore,
And all the world in their subjection held;
Till that infernall feend with foule uprore
Forwasted° all their land, and them expeld: *laid waste*
45   Whom to avenge, she had this Knight from far compeld.° *summoned*

6

Behind her farre away a Dwarfe did lag,
That lasie seemd in being ever last,
Or wearied with bearing of her bag
Of needments at his backe. Thus as they past,
50   The day with cloudes was suddeine overcast,
And angry Jove an hideous storme of raine
Did poure into his Lemans[7] lap so fast,
That every wight° to shrowd° it did constrain,   *creature/cover*
And this faire couple eke° to shroud themselves were fain.° *also/content*

7

55   Enforst to seeke some covert nigh at hand,
A shadie grove not far away they spide,
That promist ayde the tempest to withstand:
Whose loftie trees yclad with sommers pride,
Did spred so broad, that heavens light did hide,
60   Not perceable° with power of any starre: *penetrable*
And all within were pathes and alleies wide,

---

6. Facial expression, mood.   7. His lover, i.e., the earth.

With footing worne, and leading inward farre:
Faire harbour that them seemes; so in they entred arre.

8

65 And foorth they passe, with pleasure forward led,
  Joying to heare the birdes sweete harmony,
  Which therein shrouded from the tempest dred,°   *fearful*
  Seemd in their song to scorne the cruell sky.
  Much can° they prayse the trees, so straight and hy,   *did*
70   The sayling Pine, the Cedar proud and tall,
  The vine-prop Elme, the Poplar never dry,
  The builder Oake, sole king of forrests all,
The Aspine good for staves, the Cypresse funerall.

9

  The Laurell, meed° of mightie Conquerours   *reward*
  And Poets sage, the Firre that weepeth still,
75   The Willow worne of forlorne Paramours,
  The Eugh° obedient to the benders will,   *yew*
  The Birch for shaftes, the Sallow° for the mill,   *willow*
  The Mirrhe sweete bleeding in the bitter wound,
  The warlike Beech, the Ash for nothing ill,
80   The fruitfull Olive, and the Platane° round,   *plane-tree*
The carver Holme, the Maple seeldom inward sound.[8]

10

  Led with delight, they thus beguile the way,
  Untill the blustring storme is overblowne;
  When weening° to returne, whence they did stray,   *supposing*
85   They cannot finde that path, which first was showne,
  But wander too and fro in wayes unknowne,
  Furthest from end then, when they neerest weene,
  That makes them doubt, their wits be not their owne:
  So many pathes, so many turnings seene,
90 That which of them to take, in diverse doubt they been.

11

  At last resolving forward still to fare,
  Till that some end they finde or° in or out,   *either*
  That path they take, that beaten seemed most bare,
  And like to lead the labyrinth about;°   *out of*
95   Which when by tract[9] they hunted had throughout,
  At length it brought them to a hollow cave,
  Amid the thickest woods. The Champion stout
  Eftsoones° dismounted from his courser brave,   *forthwith*
And to the Dwarfe a while his needlesse spere[1] he gave.

12

100 "Be well aware,"° quoth then that Ladie milde,   *watchful*
  "Least suddaine mischiefe° ye too rash provoke: *misfortune*
  The danger hid, the place unknowne and wilde,
  Breedes dreadfull doubts: Oft fire is without smoke,
  And perill without show: therefore your stroke

---

8. Spenser here imitates Chaucer's catalog of trees in the *Parliament of Fowls*; the convention goes back to Ovid. The oak is used in building, the cypress is used to dress graves, and the holly ("holm") is suitable for carving.
9. By following the track.
1. "Needlesse" because the spear is used only on horseback.

105   Sir knight with-hold, till further triall made."
       "Ah Ladie," said he, "shame were to revoke°   *draw back*
       The forward footing for° an hidden shade: *because of*
       Vertue gives her selfe light, through darkenesse for to wade."

                              13
       "Yea but," quoth she, "the perill of this place
110   I better wot then² you, though now too late
       To wish you backe returne with foule disgrace,
       Yet wisedome warnes, whilest foot is in the gate,
       To stay the stepe, ere forcèd to retrate.
       This is the wandring wood, this Errours den,
115   A monster vile, whom God and man does hate:
       Therefore I read° beware." "Fly fly," quoth then   *advise*
       The fearefull Dwarfe: "this is no place for living men."

                              14
       But full of fire and greedy hardiment,°   *boldness*
       The youthfull knight could not for ought° be staide,   *anything*
120   But forth unto the darksome hole he went,
       And lookèd in: his glistring° armor made   *shining*
       A litle glooming light, much like a shade,
       By which he saw the ugly monster plaine,
       Halfe like a serpent horribly displaide,³
125   But th' other halfe did womans shape retaine,
       Most lothsom, filthie, foule, and full of vile
              disdaine.°   *loathsomeness*

                              15
       And as she lay upon the durtie ground,
       Her huge long taile her den all overspred,
       Yet was in knots and many boughtes° upwound,   *coils*
130   Pointed with mortall sting. Of her there bred
       A thousand yong ones, which she dayly fed,
       Sucking upon her poisonous dugs, eachone
       Of sundry shapes, yet all ill favorèd:
       Soone as that uncouth° light upon them shone,   *unfamiliar*
135   Into her mouth they crept, and suddain all were gone.

                              16
       Their dam upstart, out of her den effraide,°   *alarmed*
       And rushèd forth, hurling her hideous taile
       About her cursèd head, whose folds displaid°   *extended*
       Were stretcht now forth at length without entraile.°   *coiling*
140   She lookt about, and seeing one in mayle
       Armèd to point,⁴ sought backe to turne againe;
       For light she hated as the deadly bale,°   *evil*
       Ay wont in desert darknesse to remain,
       Where plaine none might her see, nor she see any plaine.

                              17
145   Which when the valiant Elfe⁵ perceived, he lept
       As Lyon fierce upon the flying pray;

---

2. Know than.   (cf. Revelation 9.7–10).
3. That Errour is half serpent reminds us of the primal   4. I.e., completely.
error in Eden, which the serpent instigated. The   5. Knight of Faerie Land.
description echoes both classical and biblical monsters

And with his trenchand° blade her boldly kept   *cutting*
From turning backe, and forcèd her to stay:
Therewith enraged she loudly gan to bray,
150   And turning fierce, her speckled taile advaunst,
Threatning her angry sting, him to dismay:°   *defeat*
Who nough° aghast, his mightie hand enhaunst:°   *now/lifted up*
The stroke down from her head unto her shoulder glaunst.

18

Much daunted with that dint,° her sence was dazd,   *blow*
155   Yet kindling rage, her selfe she gathered round,
And all attonce her beastly body raizd
With doubled forces high above the ground:
Tho° wrapping up her wrethèd sterne arownd,   *then*
Lept fierce upon his shield, and her huge traine°   *tail*
160   All suddenly about his body wound,
That hand or foot to stirre he strove in vaine:
God helpe the man so wrapt in Errours endlesse traine.

19

His Lady sad to see his sore constraint,°   *fettered state*
Cride out, "Now now Sir knight, shew what ye bee,
165   Add faith unto your force, and be not faint:
Strangle her, else she sure will strangle thee."
That when he heard, in great perplexitie,°   *entangled state*
His gall did grate for griefe° and high disdaine,   *wrath*
And knitting all his force got one hand free,
170   Wherewith he grypt her gorge° with so great paine,   *neck*
That soone to loose her wicked bands did her constraine.

20

Therewith she spewd out of her filthy maw
A floud of poyson horrible and blacke,
Full of great lumpes of flesh and gobbets raw,
175   Which stunck so vildly, that it forst him slacke
His grasping hold, and from her turne him backe:
Her vomit full of bookes and papers was,[6]
With loathly frogs and toades, which eyes did lacke,
And creeping sought way in the weedy gras:
180   Her filthy parbreake° all the place defilèd has.[7]   *vomit*

21

As when old father Nilus gins to swell
With timely° pride above the Aegyptian vale,   *in season*
His fattie° waves do fertile slime outwell,   *rich*
And overflow each plaine and lowly dale:
185   But when his later spring gins to avale,°   *subside*
Huge heapes of mudd he leaves, wherein there breed
Ten thousand kindes of creatures, partly male
And partly female of his fruitfull seed;
Such ugly monstrous shapes elswhere may no man reed.°   *see*

6. Alluding (at one level) to books and pamphlets of Catholic propaganda, notably attacks on Queen Elizabeth in 1588.
7. Revelation 16.13: "And I saw three unclean spirits like frogs come out of the mouth of the dragon, and out of the mouth of the beast, and out of the mouth of the false prophet."

22

190 The same so sore annoyèd has the knight,
        That welnigh chokèd with the deadly stinke,
        His forces faile, ne can no longer fight.
        Whose corage when the feend perceived to shrinke,
        She pourèd forth out of her hellish sinke
195   Her fruitfull cursèd spawne of serpents small,
        Deformèd monsters, fowle, and blacke as inke,
        Which swarming all about his legs did crall,
    And him encombred sore, but could not hurt at all.

23

    As gentle Shepheard in sweete even-tide,
200   When ruddy Phoebus gins to welke° in west,   sink
        High on an hill, his flocke to vewen wide,
        Markes° which do byte their hasty supper best;   observes
        A cloud of combrous° gnattes do him molest,   encumbering
        All striving to infixe their feeble stings,
205   That from their noyance he no where can rest,
        But with his clownish° hands their tender wings   rustic
    He brusheth oft, and oft doth mar their murmurings.

24

    Thus ill bestedd,° and fearful more of shame,   situated
        Then of the certaine perill he stood in,
210   Halfe furious unto his foe he came,
        Resolved in minde all suddenly to win,
        Or soone to lose, before he once would lin;°   cease, stop
        And strooke at her with more then manly force,
        That from her body full of filthie sin
215   He raft° her hatefull head without remorse;   cut away
    A streame of cole black bloud forth gushèd from her corse.

25

    Her scattred brood, soone as their Parent deare
        They saw so rudely° falling to the ground,   with great force
        Groning full deadly, all with troublous feare,
220   Gathred themselves about her body round,
        Weening° their wonted entrance to have found   thinking
        At her wide mouth: but being there withstood
        They flockèd all about her bleeding wound,
        And suckèd up their dying mothers blood,
225 Making her death their life, and eke° her hurt their good.   also

26

    That detestable sight him much amazde,°   stunned
        To see th' unkindly Impes[8] of heaven accurst,
        Devoure their dam; on whom while so he gazd,
        Having all satisfide their bloudy thurst,
230   Their bellies swolne he saw with fulnesse burst,
        And bowels gushing forth: well worthy end
        Of such as drunke her life, the which them nurst;
        Now needeth him no lenger labour spend,
    His foes have slaine themselves, with whom he should contend.

---

8. Unnatural offspring.

27

235 His Ladie seeing all, that chaunst, from farre
     Approcht in hast to greet° his victorie,   *congratulate*
     And said, "Faire knight, borne under happy starre,
     Who see your vanquisht foes before you lye;
     Well worthy be you of that Armorie,⁹
240 Wherein ye have great glory wonne this day,
     And prooved your strength on a strong enimie,
     Your first adventure: many such I pray,
And henceforth ever wish, that like succeed it may."

28

     Then mounted he upon his Steede againe,
245 And with the Lady backward sought to wend;°   *go*
     That path he kept, which beaten was most plaine,
     Ne ever would to any by-way bend,
     But still did follow one unto the end,
     The which at last out of the wood them brought.
250 So forward on his way (with God to frend¹)
     He passèd forth, and new adventure sought;
Long way he travelèd, before he heard of ought.

29

     At length they chaunst to meet upon the way
     An aged Sire, in long blacke weedes yclad,²
255 His feete all bare, his beard all hoarie gray,
     And by his belt his booke he hanging had;
     Sober he seemde, and very sagely sad,°   *grave*
     And to the ground his eyes were lowly bent,
     Simple in shew, and voyde of malice bad,
260 And all the way he prayèd, as he went,
And often knockt his brest, as one that did repent.

30

     He faire the knight saluted, louting° low,   *bowing*
     Who faire him quited,° as that courteous was: *answered*
     And after askèd him, if he did know
265 Of straunge adventures, which abroad did pas.
     "Ah my deare Sonne," quoth he, "how should, alas,
     Silly° old man, that lives in hidden cell,   *simple*
     Bidding° his beades all day for his trespas,   *telling*
     Tydings of warre and worldly trouble tell?
270 With holy father sits not with such things to mell.³

31

     "But if of daunger which hereby doth dwell,
     And homebred evill ye desire to heare,
     Of a straunge man I can you tidings tell,
     That wasteth all this countrey farre and neare."
275 "Of such," said he, "I chiefly do inquere,
     And shall you well reward to shew the place,
     In which that wicked wight his dayes doth weare.°   *spend*

9. I.e., Christian armor.   3. I.e., it is not fitting for a holy hermit to meddle
1. With God as friend.   ("mell") with such things.
2. Dressed in long black garments.

                 For to all knighthood it is foule disgrace,
              That such a cursed creature lives so long a space."
                                       32
₂₈₀   "Far hence," quoth he, "in wastfull° wildernesse   *desolate*
                 His dwelling is, by which no living wight
                 May ever passe, but thorough great distresse."
                 "Now," sayd the Lady, "draweth toward night,
                 And well I wote, that of your later° fight   *recent*
₂₈₅   Ye all forwearied be: for what so strong,
                 But wanting rest will also want of might?
                 The Sunne that measures heaven all day long,
              At night doth baite° his steedes the Ocean waves emong.   *feed, refresh*
                                       33
              "Then with the Sunne take Sir, your timely rest,
₂₉₀   And with new day new worke at once begin:
                 Untroubled night they say gives counsell best."
                 "Right well Sir knight ye have advisèd bin,"
                 Quoth then that aged man; "the way to win
                 Is wisely to advise:° now day is spent;   *take thought*
₂₉₅   Therefore with me ye may take up your In°   *lodging*
                 For this same night." The knight was well content.
              So with that godly father to his home they went.
                                       34
              A little lowly Hermitage it was,
                 Downe in a dale, hard by a forests side,
₃₀₀   Far from resort of people, that did pas
                 In travell to and froe: a little wyde°   *apart*
                 There was an holy Chappell edifyde,°   *built*
                 Wherein the Hermite dewly wont° to say   *was wont*
                 His holy things° each morne and eventyde: *prayers*
₃₀₅   Thereby a Christall streame did gently play,
              Which from a sacred fountaine wellèd forth alway.
                                       35
              Arrivèd there, the little house they fill,
                 Ne looke for entertainement, where none was:
                 Rest is their feast, and all things at their will;
₃₁₀   The noblest mind the best contentment has.
                 With faire discourse the evening so they pas:
                 For that old man of pleasing wordes had store,
                 And well could file° his tongue as smooth as glas;   *polish*
                 He told of Saintes and Popes, and evermore
₃₁₅   He strowd an *Ave-Mary* after and before.
                                       36
              The drouping Night thus creepeth on them fast,
                 And the sad humour⁴ loading their eye liddes,
                 As messenger of Morpheus⁵ on them cast
                 Sweet slombring deaw, the which to sleepe them biddes.
₃₂₀   Unto their lodgings then his guestes he riddes:°   *leads*
                 Where when all drownd in deadly sleepe⁶ he findes,
                 He to his study goes, and there amiddes

───

4. Heavy moisture.   6. Sleep like death.
5. The god of sleep.

His Magick bookes and artes of sundry kindes,
He seekes out mighty charmes, to trouble sleepy mindes.
37

325 Then choosing out few wordes most horrible
    (Let none them read), thereof did verses frame,
    With which and other spelles like terrible,
    He bade awake blacke Plutoes griesly Dame,[7]
    And cursèd heaven, and spake reprochfull shame
330 Of highest God, the Lord of life and light;
    A bold bad man, that dared to call by name
    Great Gorgon,[8] Prince of darknesse and dead night,
At which Cocytus quakes, and Styx is put to flight.
38

And forth he cald out of deepe darknesse dred
335 Legions of Sprights, the which like little flyes[9]
    Fluttring about his ever damnèd hed,
    A-waite whereto their service he applyes,
    To aide his friends, or fray° his enimies: *frighten*
    Of those he chose out two, the falsest twoo,
340 And fittest for to forge true-seeming lyes;
    The one of them he gave a message too,
The other by him selfe staide other worke to doo.
39

He making speedy way through spersèd° ayre,   *dispersed*
    And through the world of waters wide and deepe,
345 To Morpheus house doth hastily repaire.
    Amid the bowels of the earth full steepe,
    And low, where dawning day doth never peepe,
    His dwelling is; there Tethys[1] his wet bed
    Doth ever wash, and Cynthia[2] still° doth steepe   *continually*
350 In silver deaw his ever-drouping hed,
Whiles sad° Night over him her mantle black doth spred.   *sober*
40

Whose double gates he findeth lockèd fast,
    The one faire framed of burnisht Yvory,
    The other all with silver overcast;
355 And wakefull dogges before them farre do lye,
    Watching to banish Care their enimy,
    Who oft is wont° to trouble gentle Sleepe.   *accustomed to*
    By them the Sprite doth passe in quietly,
    And unto Morpheus comes, whom drownèd deepe
360 In drowsie fit he findes: of nothing he takes keepe.°   *notice*
41

And more, to lulle him in his slumber soft,
    A trickling streame from high rocke tumbling downe
    And ever-drizling raine upon the loft,
    Mixt with a murmuring winde, much like the sowne°   *sound*
365 Of swarming Bees, did cast him in a swowne:°   *faint*

7. Proserpine, as patron of witchcraft.
8. Demogorgon, in some myths the progenitor of all the gods, so powerful that the mention of his name causes hell's rivers (Styx and Cocytus) to tremble.
9. The simile associates him with Beelzebub (Lord of Flies).
1. The wife of Ocean.
2. Diana, the goddess of the moon.

No other noyse, nor peoples troublous cryes,
As still° are wont t'annoy the wallèd towne,   *always*
Might there be heard: but carelesse° Quiet lyes,   *free from care*
Wrapt in eternall silence farre from enemyes.[3]

42

370   The messenger approching to him spake,
    But his wast° wordes returnd to him in vaine: *wasted*
    So sound he slept, that nought mought° him awake.   *might*
    Then rudely he him thrust, and pusht with paine,°   *effort*
    Whereat he gan to stretch: but he againe
375   Shooke him so hard, that forced him to speake.
    As one then in a dreame, whose dryer braine[4]
    Is tost with troubled sights and fancies° weake,   *fantasies*
He mumbled soft, but would not all his silence breake.

43

  The Sprite then gan more boldly him to wake,
380   And threatned unto him the dreaded name
    Of Hecate:[5] whereat he gan to quake,
    And lifting up his lumpish head, with blame
    Halfe angry askèd him, for what° he came.   *why*
    "Hither," quoth he, "me Archimago[6] sent,
385   He that the stubborne Sprites can wisely tame,
    He bids thee to him send for his intent
A fit false dreame, that can delude the sleepers sent."°   *senses*

44

  The God obayde, and calling forth straight way
    A diverse° dreame out of his prison darke,   *misleading*
390   Delivered it to him, and downe did lay
    His heavie head, devoide of carefull carke,[7]
    Whose sences all were straight benumbd and starke.
    He backe returning by the Yvorie dore,[8]
    Remounted up as light as chearefull Larke,
395   And on his litle winges the dreame he bore
In hast unto his Lord, where he him left afore.

45

  Who all this while with charmes and hidden artes,
    Had made a Lady of that other Spright,
    And framed of liquid ayre her tender partes
400   So lively,° and so like in all mens sight,   *lifelike*
    That weaker° sence it could have ravisht quight   *too weak*
    The maker selfe for all his wondrous witt,
    Was nigh beguilèd with so goodly sight:
    Her all in white he clad, and over it
405   Cast a blacke stole, most like to seeme for Una[9] fit.

---

3. Spenser is imitating descriptions of the house of Morpheus in Chaucer, Ovid, and other ancient writers.
4. According to the old physiology, old people and other light sleepers had too little moisture in the brain.
5. Queen of Hades.
6. Archmagician, architect of images.

7. Anxious concerns.
8. False dreams came through the ivory door; true dreams, through the gate of horn (Homer, *Odyssey* 19.562–567; Virgil, *Aeneid* 6.893–896).
9. Her name means "one, unity." Elizabethan readers would know the Latin *Una Vera Fides* ("one true faith") and also the proverb, "Truth is one."

46

Now when that ydle dreame was to him brought
  Unto that Elfin knight he bad him fly,
  Where he slept soundly void of evill thought
  And with false shewes abuse his fantasy,°   *imagination*
410 In sort as[1] he him schoolèd privily:
  And that new creature borne without her dew[2]
  Full of the makers guile, with usage sly
  He taught to imitate that Lady trew,
Whose semblance she did carrie under feignèd hew.°   *form*

47

415 Thus well instructed, to their worke they hast
  And comming where the knight in slomber lay
  The one upon his hardy head him plast,°   *placed*
  And made him dreame of loves and lustfull play
  That nigh his manly hart did melt away,
420 Bathèd in wanton blis and wicked joy:
  Then seemèd him his Lady by him lay,
  And to him playnd,° how that false wingèd boy[3]   *complained*
Her chast hart had subdewd, to learne Dame pleasures toy.

48

And she her selfe of beautie soveraigne Queene
425 Faire Venus seemde unto his bed to bring
  Her, whom he waking evermore did weene°   *think*
  To be the chastest flowre, that ay° did spring   *ever*
  On earthly braunch, the daughter of a king,
  Now a loose Leman° to vile service bound: *paramour*
430 And eke° the Graces seemèd all to sing,   *also*
  Hymen iô Hymen, dauncing all around,
Whilst freshest Flora her with Yvie girlond crownd.[4]

49

In this great passion of unwonted° lust,   *unaccustomed*
  Or wonted feare of doing ought amis,
435 He started up, as seeming to mistrust°   *suspect*
  Some secret ill, or hidden foe of his:
  Lo there before his face his Lady is,
  Under blake stole hyding her bayted hooke,
  And as halfe blushing offred him to kis,
440 With gentle blandishment and lovely° looke,   *loving*
Most like that virgin true, which for her knight him took.

50

All cleane dismayd to see so uncouth° sight,   *unseemly*
  And halfe enragèd at her shamelesse guise,
  He thought have slaine her in his fierce despight:°   *indignation*
445 But hasty heat tempring with sufferance wise,
  He stayde his hand, and gan himselfe advise
  To prove his sense, and tempt° her faignèd truth.   *test*

1. In that way.
2. Unnaturally.
3. Cupid.
4. The three graces of classical mythology were personifications of grace and beauty; here they sing a call to the pleasures of the marriage bed (Hymen was god of marriage). In the March eclogue, E. K. glossed Flora as "the Goddesse of flowres, but indede (as saith Tacitus) a famous harlot."

Wringing her hands in wemens pitteous wise,
Tho can she[5] weepe, to stirre up gentle ruth,°   *pity*
450 Both for her noble bloud, and for her tender youth.

51

And said, "Ah Sir, my liege Lord and my love,
Shall I accuse the hidden cruell fate,
And mightie causes wrought in heaven above,
Or the blind God, that doth me thus amate,°   *dismay*
455 For° hopèd love to winne me certaine hate?   *instead of*
Yet thus perforce° he bids me do, or die.   *forcibly*
Die is my dew:[6] yet rew my wretched state
You, whom my hard avenging destinie
Hath made judge of my life or death indifferently.

52

460 "Your owne deare sake forst me at first to leave
My Fathers kingdome," There she stopt with teares;
Her swollen hart her speach seemd to bereave,
And then againe begun, "My weaker yeares
Captived to fortune and frayle worldly feares,
465 Fly to your faith for succour and sure ayde:
Let me not dye in languor° and long teares.   *sorrow*
"Why Dame," quoth he, "what hath ye thus dismayd?
What frayes° ye, that were wont to comfort me affrayd?"   *frightens*

53

"Love of your selfe," she said, "and deare° constraint   *dire*
470 Lets me not sleepe, but wast the wearie night
In secret anguish and unpittied plaint,
Whiles you in carelesse sleepe are drownèd quight."
Her doubtfull words made that redoubted[7] knight
Suspect her truth: yet since no untruth he knew,
475 Her fawning love with foule disdainefull spight
He would not shend,° but said, "Deare dame I rew,°   *reject/pity*
That for my sake unknowne such griefe unto you grew.

54

"Assure your selfe, it fell not all to ground;
For all so deare as life is to my hart,
480 I deeme your love, and hold me to you bound;
Ne let vaine feares procure your needlesse smart,
Where cause is none, but to your rest depart."
Not all content, yet seemd she to appease°   *cease*
Her mournefull plaintes, beguiléd° of her art,   *foiled*
485 And fed with words, that could not chuse but please,
So slyding softly forth, she turnd° as to her ease.   *returned*

55

Long after lay he musing at her mood,
Much grieved to thinke that gentle Dame so light,
For whose defence he was to shed his blood.
490 At last dull wearinesse of former fight
Having yrockt a sleepe his irkesome spright,°   *spirit*
That troublous dreame gan freshly tosse his braine,

5. Then she began to.   7. Dreaded, also doubting again. "Doubtfull": fearful,
6. I.e., I deserve to die.   also questionable.

With bowres and beds, and Ladies deare delight:
But when he[8] saw his labour all was vaine,
495 With that misformèd spright he backe returnd againe.

Canto 2

*The guilefull great Enchaunter parts
The Redcrosse Knight from Truth:
Into whose stead faire falshood steps,
And workes him wofull ruth.*

1

By this the Northerne wagoner had set
  His seven fold teame behind the stedfast starre,[9]
  That was in Ocean waves yet never wet,
  But firme is fixt, and sendeth light from farre
5 To all, that in the wide deepe wandring arre.
  And chearefull Chaunticlere with his note shrill
  Had warnèd once, that Phoebus fiery carre[1]
  In hast was climbing up the Easterne hill,
Full envious that night so long his roome did fill.

2

10 When those accursèd messengers of hell,
  That feigning dreame, and that faire-forgèd Spright
  Came to their wicked maister, and gan tell
  Their bootelesse° paines, and ill succeeding night: *useless*
  Who all in rage to see his skilfull might
15 Deluded so, gan threaten hellish paine
  And sad Prosèrpines wrath, them to affright.
  But when he saw his threatning was but vaine,
He cast about, and searcht his balefull° of bookes againe.   *deadly*

3

Eftsoones° he tooke that miscreated faire,   *soon after*
20 And that false other Spright, on whom he spred
  A seeming body of the subtile° aire,   *rarefied*
  Like a young Squire, in loves and lusty-hed
  His wanton dayes that ever loosely led,
  Without regard of armes and dreaded fight:
25 Those two he tooke, and in a secret bed,
  Covered with darknesse and misdeeming° night,   *misleading*
Them both together laid, to joy in vaine delight.

4

Forthwith he runnes with feignèd faithfull hast
  Unto his guest, who after troublous sights
30 And dreames, gan now to take more sound repast,°   *rest*
  Whom suddenly he wakes with fearefull frights,
  As one aghast with feends or damnèd sprights,
  And to him cals, "Rise rise unhappy Swaine,
  That here wex° old in sleepe, whiles wicked wights   *grows*
35 Have knit themselves in Venus shamefull chaine;
Come see, where your false Lady doth her honour staine."

8. I.e., Archimago.   North Star.
9. I.e., by this time the Big Dipper had set behind the   1. The chariot of the sun.

5

All in amaze he suddenly up start
   With sword in hand, and with the old man went;
   Who soone him brought into a secret part,
40   Where that false couple were full closely ment°   *mingled*
   In wanton lust and lewd embracèment:
   Which when he saw, he burnt with gealous fire,
   The eye of reason was with rage yblent,°   *blinded*
   And would have slaine them in his furious ire,
45 But hardly° was restreinèd of that aged sire.   *with difficulty*

6

Returning to his bed in torment great,
   And bitter anguish of his guiltie sight,
   He could not rest, but did his stout heart eat,
   And wast his inward gall with deepe despight,°   *malice*
50 Yrkesome° of life, and too long lingring night.   *tired*
   At last faire Hesperus[2] in highest skie
   Had spent his lampe, and brought forth dawning light
   Then up he rose, and clad him hastily;
The Dwarfe him brought his steed: so both away do fly.

7

55 Now when the rosy-fingred Morning faire,
   Weary of aged Tithones[3] saffron bed,
   Had spred her purple robe through deawy aire,
   And the high hils Titan° discoverèd,°   *the sun/revealed*
   The royall virgin shooke off drowsy-hed,
60 And rising forth out of her baser° bowre,   *humbler*
   Lookt for her knight, who far away was fled,
   And for her Dwarfe, that wont to wait each houre:
Then gan she waile and weepe, to see that woefull stowre.° *affliction*

8

And after him she rode with so much speede
65 As her slow beast could make; but all in vaine:
   For him so far had borne his light-foot steede,
   Prickèd with wrath and fiery fierce disdaine,°   *indignation*
   That him to follow was but fruitlesse paine;
   Yet she her weary limbes would never rest,
70 But every hill and dale, each wood and plaine
   Did search, sore grievèd in her gentle brest,
He so ungently left her, whom she lovèd best.

9

But subtill° Archimago, when his guests   *cunning*
   He saw divided into double parts,
75 And Una wandring in woods and forrests,
   Th' end of his drift,° he praisd his divelish arts   *plot*
   That had such might over true meaning harts;
   Yet rests not so, but other meanes doth make,
   How he may worke unto her further smarts:
80 For her he hated as the hissing snake,
And in her many troubles did most pleasure take.

2. The evening star.   3. The husband of Aurora, goddess of the dawn.

10

He then devisde himselfe how to disguise;
  For by his mightie science° he could take   *knowledge*
  As many formes and shapes in seeming wise,°   *in appearance*
85 As ever Proteus to himselfe could make:
  Sometime a fowle, sometime a fish in lake,
  Now like a foxe, now like a dragon fell,°   *fierce*
  That of himselfe he oft for feare would quake,
  And oft would flie away. O who can tell
90 The hidden power of herbes, and might of Magicke spell?

11

But now seemde best, the person to put on
  Of that good knight, his late beguilèd guest:
  In mighty armes he was yclad anon,
  And silver shield: upon his coward brest
95 A bloudy crosse, and on his craven crest
  A bounch of haires discolourd diversly:°   *variously colored*
  Full jolly° knight he seemde, and well addrest,°   *gallant/armed*
  And when he sate upon his courser free,
Saint George himself ye would have deemèd him to be.

12

100 But he the knight, whose semblaunt° he did beare,   *likeness*
  The true Saint George was wandred far away,
  Still flying from° his thoughts and gealous feare;   *because of*
  Will was his guide,[4] and griefe led him astray.
  At last him chaunst to meete upon the way
105 A faithlesse Sarazin° all armed to point,   *Saracen*
  In whose great shield was writ with letters gay
  Sans foy:[5] full large of limbe and every joint
He was, and carèd not for God or man a point.°   *at all*

13

He had a faire companion of his way,
110 A goodly Lady clad in scarlot red,
  Purfled° with gold and pearle of rich assay,[6]   *decorated*
  And like a Persian mitre on her hed
  She wore, with crownes and owches° garnishèd,   *brooches*
  The which her lavish lovers to her gave;[7]
115 Her wanton° palfrey all was overspred   *unruly*
  With tinsell trappings, woven like a wave,
Whose bridle rung with golden bels and bosses brave.[8]

14

With faire disport° and courting dalliaunce   *diversion*
  She intertainde her lover all the way:
120 But when she saw the knight his speare advaunce,
  She soone left off her mirth and wanton play,
  And bad her knight addresse him to the fray:

4. Will should itself be under the guidance of reason or truth.
5. Literally, without faith, faithless.
6. Proven valuable by analysis.
7. The lady's garb associates her with the Whore of Babylon (Revelation 17.3–4): "And I saw a woman sit upon a scarlet colored beast, full of names of blas-phemy, having seven heads and ten horns. And the woman was arrayed in purple and scarlet color, and decked with gold and precious stones and pearls, having a golden cup in her hand full of abominations and filthiness of her fornication."
8. Handsome metal knobs.

His foe was nigh at hand. He prickt° with pride   *pranced*
And hope to winne his Ladies heart that day,
125   Forth spurrèd fast: adowne his coursers side
The red bloud trickling staind the way, as he did ride.

15

The knight of the Redcrosse when him he spide,
Spurring so hote with rage dispiteous,°   *cruel*
Gan fairely couch° his speare, and towards ride: *lower*
130   Soone meete they both, both fell and furious,
That daunted with their forces hideous,
Their steeds do stagger, and amazèd stand,
And eke° themselves too rudely rigorous,°   *also/violent*
Astonied° with the stroke of their owne hand,   *stunned*
135   Do backe rebut,° and each to other yeeldeth land.   *recoil*

16

As when two rams stird with ambitious pride,
Fight for the rule of the rich fleecèd flocke,
Their hornèd fronts so fierce on either side
Do meete, that with the terrour of the shocke
140   Astonied both, stand sencelesse as a blocke,°   *inanimate object*
Forgetfull of the hanging[9] victory:
So stood these twaine, unmovèd as a rocke,
Both staring fierce, and holding idely
The broken reliques of their former cruelty.

17

145   The Sarazin sore daunted with the buffe
Snatcheth his sword, and fiercely to him flies;
Who well it wards, and quyteth° cuff with cuff: *requites*
Each others equall puissaunce envies,
And through their iron sides with cruell spies°   *looks*
150   Does seeke to perce: repining courage yields
No foote to foe. The flashing fier flies
As from a forge out of their burning shields,
And streames of purple bloud new dies the verdant fields.

18

"Curse on that Crosse," quoth then the Sarazin,
155   "That keepes thy body from the bitter fit;°   *stroke*
Dead long ygoe I wote° thou haddest bin,   *thought*
Had not that charme from thee forwarnéd° it: *prevented*
But yet I warne thee now assurèd° sitt,   *securely*
And hide thy head." Therewith upon his crest
160   With rigour° so outrageous he smitt,   *violence*
That a large share it hewd out of the rest,
And glauncing downe his shield, from blame him fairely blest.[1]

19

Who thereat wondrous wroth, the sleeping spark
Of native vertue° gan eftsoones revive,   *strength*
165   And at his haughtie helmet making mark,
So hugely° stroke, that it the steele did rive,   *mightily*
And cleft his head. He tumbling downe alive,

---

9. In the balance.   1. Preserved him from harm.

With bloudy mouth his mother earth did kis
 Greeting his grave: his grudging° ghost did strive   *complaining*
170 With the fraile flesh; at last it flitted is,
Whither the soules do fly of men, that live amis.

20

The Lady when she saw her champion fall,
 Like the old ruines of a broken towre,
 Staid not to waile his woefull funerall,°   *death*
175 But from him fled away with all her powre;
 Who after her as hastily gan scowre,°   *scurry*
 Bidding the Dwarfe with him to bring away
 The Sarazins shield, signe of the conqueroure.
 Her soone he overtooke, and bad to stay,
180 For present cause was none of dread her to dismay.

21

She turning backe with ruefull countenaunce,
 Cride, "Mercy mercy Sir vouchsafe to show
 On silly° Dame, subject to hard mischaunce,   *helpless*
 And to your mighty will." Her humblesse low
185 In so ritch weedes and seeming glorious show,
 Did much emmove his stout heroicke heart,
 And said, "Deare dame, your suddein overthrow
 Much rueth° me; but now put feare apart,   *grieves*
And tell, both who ye be, and who that tooke your part."

22

190 Melting in teares, then gan she thus lament;
 "The wretched woman, whom unhappy howre
 Hath now made thrall° to your commandèment, *slave*
 Before that angry heavens list to lowre,°   *frown*
 And fortune false betraide me to your powre
195 Was (O what now availeth that I was!)
 Borne the sole daughter of an Emperour,
 He that the wide West under his rule has,
And high hath set his throne, where Tiberis doth pas.[2]

23

"He in the first flowre of my freshest age,
200 Betrothèd me unto the onely haire°   *heir*
 Of a most mighty king, most rich and sage;
 Was never Prince so faithfull and so faire,
 Was never Prince so meeke and debonaire;°   *gracious*
 But ere my hopèd day of spousall shone,
205 My dearest Lord fell from high honours staire,
 Into the hands of his accursed fone,°   *foes*
And cruelly was slaine, that shall I ever mone.[3]

24

'His blessed body spoild of lively breath,
 Was afterward, I know not how, convaid°   *carried away*
210 And fro me hid: of whose most innocent death

---

2. The Tiber River runs through Rome. The lady is hence associated with the Roman Catholic church. Her father, she says, is ruler of the west—but Una's father had the rule of both east *and* west (1.1.41); his- torically, the true church once embraced east and west. 3. The lady claims to be betrothed to Christ, bride- groom of the church.

When tidings came to me unhappy maid,
O how great sorrow my sad soule assaid.°   *afflicted*
Then forth I went his woefull corse to find,
And many yeares throughout the world I straid,
215   A virgin widow, whose deepe wounded mind
With love, long time did languish as the striken hind.°   *deer*

25

"At last it chauncèd this proud Sarazin
To meete me wandring, who perforce° me led   *by violence*
With him away, but yet could never win
220   The fort, that Ladies hold in soveraigne dread.
There lies he now with foule dishonour dead,
Who whiles he livde, was callèd proud Sans foy,
The eldest of three brethren, all three bred
Of one bad sire, whose youngest is Sans joy,
225   And twixt them both was borne the bloudy bold Sans loy.[4]

26

"In this sad plight, friendlesse, unfortunate,
Now miserable I Fidessa[5] dwell,
Craving of you in pitty of my state,
To do none° ill, if please ye not do well."   *no*
230   He in great passion all this while did dwell,°   *continue*
More busying his quicke eyes, her face to view,
Then his dull eares, to heare what she did tell;
And said, "Faire Lady hart of flint would rew
The undeservèd woes and sorrowes, which ye shew.

27

235   "Henceforth in safe assauraunce may ye rest,
Having both found a new friend you to aid,
And lost an old foe, that did you molest:
Better new friend than an old foe is[6] said."
With chaunge of cheare the seeming simple maid
240   Let fall her eyen, as shamefast[7] to the earth,
And yeelding soft, in that she nought gain-said,
So forth they rode, he feining° seemely merth,   *simulating*
And she coy lookes: so dainty they say maketh derth.[8]

28

Long time they thus together traveilèd,
245   Till weary of their way, they came at last,
Where grew two goodly trees, that faire did spred
Their armes abroad, with gray mosse overcast,
And their greene leaves trembling with every blast,°   *breeze*
Made a calme shadow far in compasse round:
250   The fearefull Shepheard often there aghast
Under them never sat, ne wont[9] there sound
His mery oaten pipe, but shund th' unlucky ground.

---

4. Literally, without law. *Sans joy* means "without joy,
darkness of spirit."
5. Faith.
6. I.e., it is.

7. As if modestly.
8. Proverbial: what's dear is rare; here, coyness creates
unsatisfied desire.
9. Nor was accustomed to.

29

But this good knight soone as he them can° spie,   *did*
   For the coole shade him thither hastly got:
255   For golden Phoebus now ymounted hie,
   From fiery wheeles of his faire chariot
   Hurlèd his beame so scorching cruell hot,
   That living creature mote° it not abide;   *might*
   And his new Lady it endurèd not.
260   There they alight, in hope themselves to hide
From the fierce heat, and rest their weary limbs a tide.°   *time*

30

Faire seemely pleasaunce° each to other makes,   *courtesy*
   With goodly purposes there as they sit:
   And in his falsèd° fancy he her takes   *deceived*
265   To be the fairest wight that livèd yit;
   Which to expresse, he bends his gentle wit,
   And thinking of those braunches greene to frame
   A girlond for her dainty forehead fit,
   He pluckt a bough; out of whose rift there came
270   Small drops of gory bloud, that trickled downe the same.

31

Therewith a piteous yelling voyce was heard,
   Crying, "O spare with guilty hands to teare
   My tender sides in this rough rynd embard,°   *imprisoned*
   But fly, ah fly far hence away, for feare
275   Least to you hap, that happened to me heare,
   And to this wretched Lady, my deare love,
   O too deare love, love bought with death too deare."
   Astond he stood, and up his haire did hove°   *heave, raise*
And with that suddein horror could no member move.

32

280 At last whenas the dreadfull passion
   Was overpast, and manhood well awake,
   Yet musing at the straunge occasion,
   And doubting much his sence, he thus bespake;
   "What voyce of damnèd Ghost from Limbo[1] lake,
285   Or guilefull spright wandring in empty aire,
   Both which fraile men do oftentimes mistake,°   *mislead*
   Sends to my doubtfull eares these speaches rare,
And ruefull plaints, me bidding guiltlesse bloud to spare?"

33

Then groning deepe, "Nor damned Ghost," quoth he,
290   "Nor guilefull sprite to thee these wordes doth speake,
   But once a man Fradubio,[2] now a tree,
   Wretched man, wretched tree; whose nature weake,
   A cruell witch her cursèd will to wreake,
   Hath thus transformed, and plast in open plaines,
295   Where Boreas° doth blow full bitter bleake,   *the north wind*

1. A region of hell, traditionally the abode of the unbaptized.
2. *Fra* (Italian "in" or "brother") + *dubbio* ("doubt").

The motif of a man imprisoned in a tree derives from Virgil (*Aeneid* 3.27–42) and is used by Ariosto (*Orlando Furioso* 6.26–53).

And scorching Sunne does dry my secret vaines:
For though a tree I seeme, yet cold and heat me paines."

34

"Say on Fradubio then, or° man, or tree,"   *whether*
  Quoth then the knight, "by whose mischievous arts
300   Art thou misshapèd thus, as now I see?
  He oft finds med'cine, who his griefe imparts;
  But double griefs afflict concealing harts,
  As raging flames who striveth to suppresse."
  "The author then," said he, "of all my smarts,
305   Is one Duessa[3] a false sorceresse,
That many errant° knights hath brought to wretchednesse.   *wandering*

35

"In prime of youthly yeares, when corage hot
  The fire of love and joy of chevalree
  First kindled in my brest, it was my lot
310   To love this gentle Lady, whom ye see,
  Now not a Lady, but a seeming tree;
  With whom as once I rode accompanyde,
  Me chauncèd of a knight encountred bee,
  That had a like faire Lady by his syde,
315 Like a faire Lady, but did fowle Duessa hyde.

36

"Whose forgèd beauty he did take in hand,[4]
  All other Dames to have exceeded farre,
  I in defence of mine did likewise stand,
  Mine, that did then shine as the Morning starre:
320   So both to battell fierce arraungèd arre,
  In which his harder fortune was to fall
  Under my speare: such is the dye° of warre: *hazard*
  His Lady left as a prise martiall,[5]
Did yield her comely person, to be at my call.

37

325 "So doubly loved of Ladies unlike° faire,   *diversely*
  Th' one seeming such, the other such indeede,
  One day in doubt I cast° for to compare,   *determined*
  Whether° in beauties glorie did exceede;   *which one (of two)*
  A Rosy girlond was the victors meede:°   *reward*
330   Both seemde to win, and both seemde won to bee,
  So hard the discord was to be agreede.
  Fraelissa[6] was as faire, as faire mote bee,
And ever false Duessa seemde as faire as shee.

38

"The wicked witch now seeing all this while
335   The doubtfull ballaunce equally to sway,
  What not by right, she cast to win by guile,
  And by her hellish science° raisd streight way   *magic*
  A foggy mist, that overcast the day,
  And a dull blast, that breathing on her face,

---

3. *Duessa* means "double being." *Due* (Italian "two")   5. Spoil of battle.
+ *esse* (Latin "being").   6. Frailty (Italian *Fralezza*).
4. He maintained.

340   Dimmed her former beauties shining ray,
       And with foule ugly forme did her disgrace:
Then was she[7] faire alone, when none was faire in place.

39

"Then cride she out, 'Fye, fye, deformèd wight,
    Whose borrowed beautie now appeareth plaine
345   To have before bewitchèd all mens sight;
    O leave her soone, or let her soone be slaine.'
    Her lothly visage viewing with disdaine,
    Eftsoones° I thought her such, as she me told,   *before*
    And would have kild her; but with faignèd paine,
350   The false witch did my wrathfull hand withhold;
So left her, where she now is turnd to trëen mould.[8]

40

"Thens forth I tooke Duessa for my Dame,
    And in the witch unweeting° joyd long time,   *unknowingly*
    Ne ever wist, but that she was the same,
355   Till on a day (that day is every Prime,[9]
    When Witches wont do penance for their crime)
    I chaunst to see her in her proper hew,[1]
    Bathing her selfe in origane and thyme:[2]
    A filthy foule old woman I did vew,
360 That ever to have toucht her, I did deadly rew.°   *regret*

41

"Her neather partes misshapen, monstruous,
    Were hidd in water, that I could not see,
    But they did seeme more foule and hideous,
    Then womans shape man would beleeve to bee.
365   Thens forth from her most beastly companie
    I gan refraine, in minde to slip away,
    Soone as appeard safe opportunitie:
    For danger great, if not assured decay°   *destruction*
I saw before mine eyes, if I were knowne to stray.

42

370 "The divelish hag by chaunges of my cheare°   *countenance*
    Perceived my thought, and drownd in sleepie night,
    With wicked herbes and ointments did besmeare
    My bodie all, through charmes and magicke might,
    That all my senses were bereavèd quight:°   *quite*
375   Then brought she me into this desert waste,
    And by my wretched lovers side me pight,°   *planted*
    Where now enclosd in wooden wals full faste,[3]
Banisht from living wights,° our wearie dayes we waste."   *persons*

43

"But how long time," said then the Elfin knight,
380   "Are you in this misformèd house to dwell?"
    "We may not chaunge," quoth he, "this evil plight,
    Till we be bathèd in a living well;[4]

7. When nobody else was fair. "She": Duessa.
8. The form of a tree.
9. The first appearance of the new moon.
1. In her own shape.
2. Oregano and thyme were used to cure scabs and itching.
3. I.e., imprisoned within the trees.
4. With allusion to 1 John 4.14, the "well of water, springing up into eternal life."

That is the terme prescribèd by the spell."
"O how," said he, "mote° I that well out find,   *might*
385   That may restore you to your wonted well?"°   *well-being*
"Time and suffisèd fates to former kynd
Shall us restore,[5] none else from hence may us unbynd."

44

The false Duessa, now Fidessa hight,°   *called*
Heard how in vaine Fradubio did lament,
390   And knew well all was true. But the good knight
Full of sad feare and ghastly dreriment,°   *gloom*
When all this speech the living tree had spent,
The bleeding bough did thrust into the ground,
That from the bloud he might be innocent,
395   And with fresh clay did close the wooden wound:
Then turning to his Lady, dead with feare her found.

45

Her seeming dead he found with feignèd feare,
As all unweeting of that well she knew,[6]
And paynd himselfe with busie care to reare
400   Her out of carelesse° swowne. Her eylids blew   *unconscious*
And dimmèd sight with pale and deadly hew[7]
At last she up gan lift: with trembling cheare°   *demeanor*
Her up he tooke, too simple and too trew,
And oft her kist. At length all passèd feare,[8]
405   He set her on her steede, and forward forth did beare.

Canto 3

Forsaken Truth long seekes her love,
And makes the Lyon mylde,
Marres° blind Devotions mart,° and fals   *spoils/business*
In hand of leachour° vylde.   *lecher*

1

Nought is there under heav'ns wide hollownesse,°   *concavity*
That moves more deare compassion of mind,
Then beautie brought t' unworthy° wretchednesse   *undeserved*
Through envies snares or fortunes freakes° unkind: *sudden changes*
5   I, whether lately through her brightnesse blind,
Or through alleageance and fast fealtie,
Which I do owe unto all woman kind,
Feele my heart perst° with so great agonie,   *pierced*
When such I see, that all for pittie I could die.

2

10   And now it is empassionèd° so deepe,   *moved*
For fairest Unas sake, of whom I sing,
That my fraile eyes these lines with teares do steepe,
To thinke how she through guilefull handeling,°   *treatment*
Though true as touch,° though daughter of a king,   *touchstone*
15   Though faire as ever living wight was faire,

---

5. I.e., time and the satisfaction of the fates alone can   7. Deathlike appearance.
restore us to our former human nature.   8. I.e., having overcome all fear.
6. I.e., pretending ignorance of what she knew well.

Though nor in word nor deede ill meriting,
   Is from her knight divorcèd° in despaire   *separated*
And her due loves derived° to that vile witches share.   *diverted*

3

Yet she most faithfull Ladie all this while
20   Forsaken, wofull, solitarie mayd
   Farre from all peoples prease,° as in exile,   *press, crowd*
   In wildernesse and wastfull° deserts strayd,   *desolate*
   To seeke her knight; who subtilly betrayd
   Through that late vision, which th' Enchaunter wrought,
25   Had her abandond. She of nought affrayd,
   Through woods and wastnesse° wide him daily sought;   *wilderness*
Yet wishèd tydings more of him unto her brought.

4

One day nigh wearie of the yrkesome way,
   From her unhastie° beast she did alight,   *slow*
30   And on the grasse her daintie limbes did lay
   In secret shadow,° farre from all mens sight: *shade*
   From her faire head her fillet she undight,[9]
   And laid her stole aside. Her angels face
   As the great eye of heaven shynèd bright,
35   And made a sunshine in the shadie place;
Did never mortall eye behold such a heavenly grace.

5

It fortunèd° out of the thickest wood   *chanced*
   A ramping° Lyon rushèd suddainly,   *raging*
   Hunting full greedie after salvage blood;[1]
40   Soone as the royall virgin he did spy,
   With gaping mouth at her ran greedily,
   To have attonce devoured her tender corse;°   *body*
   But to the pray when as he drew more ny,
   His bloudie rage asswagèd with remorse,
45   And with the sight amazd, forgat his furious forse.

6

In stead thereof he kist her wearie feet,
   And lickt her lilly hands with fawning tong,
   As he her wrongèd innocence did weet.°   *understand*
   O how can beautie maister the most strong,
50   And simple truth subdue avenging wrong?
   Whose yeelded pride and proud submission,
   Still dreading death, when she had markèd long,
   Her hart gan melt in great compassion,
And drizling teares did shed for pure affection.

7

55   "The Lyon Lord of everie beast in field,"[2]
   Quoth she, "his princely puissance° doth abate   *power*
   And mightie proud to humble weake does yield,
   Forgetfull of the hungry rage, which late
   Him prickt, in pittie of my sad estate:°   *condition*
60   But he my Lyon, and my noble Lord,

9. She took off her headband.   2. Lions are an emblem of the British Crown.
1. Wild game.

How does he find in cruell hart to hate
Her that him loved, and ever most adord,
As the God of my life? why hath he me abhord?"
8

Redounding° teares did choke th' end of her plaint,   *overflowing*
65   Which softly ecchoed from the neighbour wood;
And sad to see her sorrowfull constraint°   *affliction*
The kingly beast upon her gazing stood;
With pittie calmd, downe fell his angry mood.
At last in close hart shutting up her paine,
70   Arose the virgin borne of heavenly brood,°   *parentage*
And to her snowy Palfrey got againe,
To seeke her strayèd Champion, if she might attaine.°   *overtake*
9

The Lyon would not leave her desolate,
But with her went along, as a strong gard
75   Of her chast person, and a faithfull mate
Of her sad troubles and misfortunes hard:
Still° when she slept, he kept both watch and ward,   *always*
And when she wakt, he waited diligent,
With humble service to her will prepard:
80   From her faire eyes he tooke commaundement,
And ever by her lookes conceivèd her intent.
10

Long she thus traveilèd through deserts wyde,
By which she thought her wandring knight shold pas,
Yet never shew of living wight espyde;
85   Till that at length she found the troden gras,
In which the tract° of peoples footing was,   *track*
Under the steepe foot of a mountaine hore;°   *gray*
The same she followes, till at last she has
A damzell spyde slow footing her before,[3]
90   That on her shoulders sad° a pot of water bore.   *heavy*
11

To whom approching she to her gan call,
To weet, if dwelling place were nigh at hand;
But the rude° wench her answered nought at all,   *ignorant*
She could not heare, nor speake, nor understand;[4]
95   Till seeing by her side the Lyon stand,
With suddaine feare her pitcher downe she threw,
And fled away: for never in that land
Face of faire Ladie she before did vew,
And that dread Lyons looke her cast in deadly° hew.   *deathlike*
12

100 Full fast she fled, ne ever lookt behynd,
As if her life upon the wager lay,[5]
And home she came, whereas her mother blynd
Sate in eternall night: nought could she say,
But suddaine catching hold, did her dismay

---

3. I.e., walking slowly in front of her.
4. Cf. Mark 4.11–12: "unto them that are without, all
these things are done in parables: / That seeing they

may see, and not perceive; and hearing they may hear,
and not understand."
5. Were at stake.

105   With quaking hands, and other signes of feare:
        Who full of ghastly fright and cold affray,°   *terror*
        Gan shut the dore. By this arrivèd there
    Dame Una, wearie Dame, and entrance did requere.°   *request*

13

    Which when none yeelded, her unruly Page
110   With his rude° clawes the wicket° open rent,   *rough/door*
        And let her in; where of his cruell rage
        Nigh dead with feare, and faint astonishment,[6]
        She found them both in darkesome corner pent;°   *huddled*
        Where that old woman day and night did pray
115   Upon her beades° devoutly penitent;   *rosary*
        Nine hundred *Pater nosters* every day,
  And thrise nine hundred *Aves* she was wont to say.[7]

14

    And to augment her painefull pennance more,
        Thrise every weeke in ashes she did sit,
120   And next her wrinkled skin rough sackcloth wore,[8]
        And thrise three times did fast from any bit:°   *food*
        But now for feare her beads she did forget.
        Whose needlesse dread for to remove away,
        Faire Una framèd words and count'nance fit:
125   Which hardly° doen, at length she gan them pray,   *with difficulty*
  That in their cotage small, that night she rest her may.[9]

15

    The day is spent, and commeth drowsie night,
        When every creature shrowded is in sleepe;
        Sad Una downe her laies in wearie plight,
130   And at her feet the Lyon watch doth keepe:
        In stead of rest, she does lament, and weepe
        For the late° losse of her deare lovèd knight,   *recent*
        And sighes, and grones, and evermore does steepe
        Her tender brest in bitter teares all night,
135   All night she thinks too long, and often lookes for light.

16

    Now when Aldeboran was mounted hie
        Above the shynie Cassiopeias chaire,[1]
        And all in deadly sleepe did drownèd lie,
        One knockèd at the dore, and in would fare;°   *come*
140   He knockèd fast,° and often curst, and sware,   *insistently*
        That readie entrance was not at his call:
        For on his backe a heavy load he bare
        Of nightly stelths and pillage severall,[2]
  Which he had got abroad by purchase° criminall.   *acquisition*

17

145   He was to weete° a stout and sturdie thiefe,   *in fact*
        Wont to robbe Churches of their ornaments,
        And poore mens boxes[3] of their due reliefe,

6. I.e., fainting with amazement.
7. Her prayers are the Lord's Prayer ("Our Father") and the Hail Mary.
8. Sackcloth and ashes are symbols of penitence.
9. I.e., that she might rest herself.

1. The star Aldebaran, in the constellation Taurus, mounts over the constellation Cassiopeia.
2. I.e., he carried the booty gained from nightly thefts and various kinds of pillage.
3. A box for alms for the poor.

Which given was to them for good intents;
The holy Saints of their rich vestiments
150   He did disrobe, when all men carelesse slept,
And spoild the Priests of their habiliments,°   *vestments*
Whiles none the holy things in safety kept;
Then he by cunning sleights in at the window crept.

18

And all that he by right or wrong could find,
155   Unto this house he brought, and did bestow
Upon the daughter of this woman blind,
Abessa daughter of Corceca[4] slow,
With whom he whoredome usd, that few did know,
And fed her fat with feast of offerings,
160   And plentie, which in all the land did grow;
Ne sparèd he to give her gold and rings:
And now he to her brought part of his stolen things.

19

Thus long the dore with rage and threats he bet,°   *beat*
Yet of those fearefull women none durst rize,
165   The Lyon frayèd them, him in to let:[5]
He would no longer stay him to advize,°   *consider*
But open breakes the dore in furious wize,
And entring is; when that disdainfull° beast   *indignant*
Encountring fierce, him suddaine doth surprize,
170   And seizing° cruell clawes on trembling brest,   *fastening*
Under his Lordly foot him proudly hath supprest.

20

Him booteth not resist,[6] nor succour call,
His bleeding hart is in the vengers hand,
Who streight him rent in thousand peeces small,
175   And quite dismembred hath: the thirstie land
Drunke up his life; his corse left on the strand.°   *ground*
His fearefull friends weare out the wofull night,
Ne dare to weepe, nor seeme to understand
The heavie hap,° which on them is alight,°   *lot/fallen*
180   Affraid, least to themselves the like mishappen might.[7]

21

Now when broad day the world discovered° has,   *revealed*
Up Una rose, up rose the Lyon eke,
And on their former journey forward pas,
In wayes unknowne, her wandring knight to seeke,
185   With paines farre passing that long wandring Greeke,
That for his love refusèd deitie;[8]
Such were the labours of this Lady meeke,
Still seeking him, that from her still did flie,
Then furthest from her hope, when most she weenèd nie.[9]

---

4. *Corceca* means "blind heart." Abessa's name comes from "abbess," also *ab* + *esse* (Latin): "from being," e.g., without substance.
5. I.e., neither of the women dared rise to let him in because the lion terrified ("frayed") them.
6. It does him no good to resist.

7. I.e., lest the same thing might happen amiss ("mishappen") to them.
8. Odysseus, who renounced immortality and the love of the nymph Calypso for his wife, Penelope.
9. Believed near.

22

190 Soone as she parted thence, the fearefull twaine,
That blind old woman and her daughter deare
Came forth, and finding Kirkrapine° there slaine,   *church robber*
For anguish great they gan to rend their heare,
And beat their brests, and naked flesh to teare.
195 And when they both had wept and wayld their fill,
Then forth they ranne like two amazèd deare,
Halfe mad through malice, and revenging will,[1]
To follow her, that was the causer of their ill.

23

Whom overtaking, they gan loudly bray,
200 With hollow howling, and lamenting cry,
Shamefully at her rayling all the way,
And her accusing of dishonesty,°   *unchastity*
That was the flowre of faith and chastity;
And still amidst her rayling, she[2] did pray,
205 That plagues, and mischiefs, and long misery
Might fall on her, and follow all the way,
And that in endlesse error° she might ever stray.   *wandering*

24

But when she saw her prayers nought prevaile,
She backe returnèd with some labour lost;
210 And in the way as she did weepe and waile
A knight her met in mighty armes embost,°   *encased*
Yet knight was not for all his bragging bost,°   *boast*
But subtill Archimag, that Una sought
By traynes° into new troubles to have tost: *tricks*
215 Of that old woman tydings he besought,
If that of such a Ladie she could tellen ought.[3]

25

Therewith she gan her passion to renew,
And cry, and curse, and raile, and rend her heare,°   *hair*
Saying, that harlot she too lately knew,
220 That causd her shed so many a bitter teare,
And so forth told the story of her feare:
Much seemèd he to mone her haplesse chaunce,
And after for that Ladie did inquere;
Which being taught, he forward gan advaunce
225 His fair enchaunted steed, and eke° his charmèd launce.   *also*

26

Ere long he came, where Una traveild slow,
And that wilde Champion wayting° her besyde: *attending*
Whom seeing such, for dread he durst not show
Himselfe too nigh at hand, but turnèd wyde
230 Unto an hill; from whence when she him spyde,
By his like seeming shield, her knight by name
She weend it was, and towards him gan ryde:
Approching nigh, she wist° it was the same,

---

1. Desire of revenge.
2. Corceca.

3. I.e., if she could tell anything ("ought") about such
a lady.

believed

And with faire fearefull humblesse° towards him shee   *humility*
  came.
27

235 And weeping said, "Ah my long lackèd Lord,
  Where have ye bene thus long out of my sight?
  Much fearèd I to have bene quite abhord,
  Or ought° have done, that ye displeasen might,   *aught*
  That should as death unto my deare hart light:[4]
240 For since mine eye your joyous sight did mis,
  My chearefull day is turnd to chearelesse night,
  And eke my night of death the shadow is;
But welcome now my light, and shining lampe of blis."
28

He thereto meeting[5] said, "My dearest Dame,
245 Farre be it from your thought, and fro my will,
  To thinke that knighthood I so much should shame,
  As you to leave, that have me lovèd still.
  And chose in Faery court of meere° goodwill,   *pure*
  Where noblest knights were to be found on earth:
250 The earth shall sooner leave her kindly° skill   *natural*
  To bring forth fruit, and make eternall derth,°   *desert*
Then I leave you, my liefe,° yborne of heavenly berth.   *beloved*
29

"And sooth to say, why I left you so long,
  Was for to seeke adventure in strange place,
255 Where Archimago said a felon strong
  To many knights did daily worke disgrace;
  But knight he now shall never more deface:°   *discredit*
  Good cause of mine excuse; that mote° ye please   *may*
  Well to accept, and evermore embrace
260 My faithfull service, that by land and seas
Have vowd you to defend, now then your plaint appease."°   *cease*
30

His lovely° words her seemd due recompence   *loving*
  Of all her passèd paines: one loving howre
  For many yeares of sorrow can dispence:°   *make amends*
265 A dram of sweet is worth a pound of sowre:
  She has forgot, how many a wofull stowre°   *trouble*
  For him she late endured; she speakes no more
  Of past: true is, that true love hath no powre
  To looken backe; his eyes be fixt before.
270 Before her stands her knight, for whom she toyld so sore.
31

Much like, as when the beaten marinere,
  That long hath wandred in the Ocean wide,
  Oft soust° in swelling Tethys[6] saltish teare,   *soaked*
  And long time having tand his tawney hide
275 With blustring breath of heaven, that none can bide,
  And scorching flames of fierce Orions hound,[7]

---

4. I.e., be as a death blow to my sad heart. 7. Sirius, the dog star, symbolizing hot weather (the
5. Answering in like manner. dog days).
6. The wife of Ocean; here, the Ocean.

Soone as the port from farre he has espide,
His chearefull whistle merrily doth sound,
And Nereus crownes with cups;[8] his mates him pledg° around.   *toast*

32

280 Such joy made Una, when her knight she found;
And eke° th' enchaunter joyous seemd no lesse,   *also*
Then the glad marchant, that does vew from ground
His ship farre come from watrie wildernesse,
He hurles out vowes, and Neptune oft doth blesse:
285 So forth they past, and all the way they spent
Discoursing of her dreadfull late distresse,
In which he askt her, what the Lyon ment:
Who told her all that fell° in journey as she went.[9]   *befell*

33

They had not ridden farre, when they might see
290 One pricking° towards them with hastie heat,   *riding*
Full strongly armd, and on a courser free,
That through his fiercenesse fomed all with sweat,
And the sharpe yron° did for anger eat,   *bit*
When his hot ryder spurd his chauffèd° side;   *heated*
295 His looke was sterne, and seemèd still to threat
Cruell revenge, which he in hart did hyde,
And on his shield Sans loy in bloudie lines was dyde.

34

When nigh he drew unto this gentle payre
And saw the Red-crosse, which the knight did beare,
300 He burnt in fire, and gan eftsoones prepare
Himselfe to battell with his couchèd speare.
Loth was that other, and did faint through feare,
To taste th' untryed dint° of deadly steele;   *blow*
But yet his Lady did so well him cheare,
305 That hope of new good hap he gan to feele;
So bent° his speare, and spurnd his horse with yron heele.   *lowered*

35

But that proud Paynim° forward came so fierce,   *pagan*
And full of wrath, that with his sharp-head speare
Through vainely crossèd shield[1] he quite did pierce,
310 And had his staggering steede not shrunke for feare,
Through shield and bodie eke° he should him beare:°   *also/thrust*
Yet so great was the puissance of his push,
That from his saddle quite he did him beare:
He tombling rudely° downe to ground did rush,   *violently*
315 And from his gorèd wound a well of bloud did gush.

36

Dismounting lightly from his loftie steed,
He to him lept, in mind to reave° his life,   *take*
And proudly said, "Lo there the worthie meed°   *recompense*
Of him, that slew Sans foy with bloudie knife;
320 Henceforth his ghost freed from repining strife,

8. Nereus is god of the Mediterranean, to whom the
mariner in gratitude makes libations.
9. I.e., she told all that befell her.

1. The cross on Archimago's shield was false and did
not give him the protection the Redcrosse knight
received in his fight with Sans Foy (see 1.2, stanza 18).

In peace may passen over Lethe[2] lake,
When mourning altars purgd° with enemies life,   *cleansed*
The blacke infernall Furies[3] doen aslake:°   *appease*
Life from Sans foy thou tookst, Sans loy shall from thee take."

37

325   Therewith in haste his helmet gan unlace,
Till Una cride, "O hold that heavie hand,
Deare Sir, what ever that thou be in place:[4]
Enough is, that thy foe doth vanquisht stand
Now at thy mercy: Mercie not withstand:
330   For he is one the truest knight alive,[5]
Though conquered now he lie on lowly land,[6]
And whilest him fortune favourd, faire did thrive
In bloudie field: therefore of life him not deprive."

38

Her piteous words might not abate his rage,
335   But rudely rending up his helmet, would
Have slaine him straight: but when he sees his age,
And hoarie head of Archimago old,
His hastie hand he doth amazèd hold,
And halfe ashamèd, wondred at the sight:
340   For the old man well knew he, though untold,
In charmes and magicke to have wondrous might,
Ne ever wont in field, ne in round lists[7] to fight.

39

And said, "Why Archimago, lucklesse syre,
What doe I see? what hard mishap is this,
345   That hath thee hither brought to taste mine yre?
Or thine the fault, or mine the error is,
In stead of foe to wound my friend amis?"
He answered nought, but in a traunce still lay,
And on those guilefull dazèd eyes of his
350   The cloud of death did sit. Which doen away,[8]
He left him lying so, ne would no lenger stay.

40

But to the virgin comes, who all this while
Amasèd stands, her selfe so mockt° to see   *deceived*
By him, who has the guerdon° of his guile,   *reward*
355   For so misfeigning her true knight to bee:
Yet is she now in more perplexitie,°   *trouble*
Left in the hand of that same Paynim bold,
From whom her booteth not[9] at all to flie;
Who by her cleanly° garment catching hold,   *pure*
360   Her from her Palfrey pluckt, her visage to behold.

41

But her fierce servant full of kingly awe
And high disdaine,° whenas his soveraine Dame   *indignation*
So rudely handled by her foe he sawe,

---

2. The river of forgetfulness in Hades.
3. Spirits of discord and revenge.
4. Whoever you are.
5. I.e., do not withhold mercy, for he is the one truest knight.

6. I.e., low on the ground.
7. Enclosures for fighting tournaments.
8. When the swoon passed.
9. Is of no use.

With gaping jawes full greedy at him came,
365 And ramping on his shield, did weene° the same   *intend*
Have reft away with his sharpe rending clawes
But he was stout, and lust did now inflame
His corage more, that from his griping pawes
He hath his shield redeemed,° and foorth his swerd he   *recovered*
   drawes.

42

370 O then too weake and feeble was the forse
Of salvage beast, his puissance to withstand:
For he was strong, and of so mightie corse,
As ever wielded speare in warlike hand,
And feates of armes did wisely° understand.   *skilfully*
375 Eftsoones he percèd through his chaufèd chest
With thrilling point of deadly yron brand,[1]
And launcht° his Lordly hart: with death opprest   *pierced*
He roared aloud, whiles life forsooke his stubborne brest.

43

Who now is left to keepe the forlorne maid
380 From raging spoile of lawlesse victors will?
Her faithfull gard removed, her hope dismaid,
Her selfe a yeelded pray to save or spill.°   *destroy*
He now Lord of the field, his pride to fill,
With foule reproches, and disdainfull spight
385 Her vildly entertaines, and will or nill,
Beares her away upon his courser light:[2]
Her prayers nought prevaile; his rage is more of might.

44

And all the way, with great lamenting paine,
And piteous plaints she filleth his dull° eares,   *deaf*
390 That stony hart could riven have in twaine,
And all the way she wets with flowing teares:
But he enraged with rancor, nothing heares.
Her servile beast yet would not leave her so,
But followes her farre off, ne ought he feares,
395 To be partaker of her wandring woe,
More mild in beastly kind,° then that her beastly foe.   *nature*

Canto 4

To sinfull house of Pride, Duessa
   guides the faithfull knight,
Where brothers death to wreak° Sansjoy   *avenge*
   doth chalenge him to fight.

1

Young knight, what ever that dost armes professe,
And through long labours huntest after fame,
Beware of fraud, beware of ficklenesse,
In choice, and change of thy deare lovèd Dame,

1. I.e., afterwards he pierced through the lion's angry ("chaufèd") chest with the penetrating ("thrilling") point of his sword.

2. I.e., he treats her basely ("vildly") and willingly or not bears her away quickly ("light") on his horse.

5   Least thou of her beleeve too lightly blame,
   And rash misweening° doe thy hart remove: *misjudgment*
   For unto knight there is no greater shame,
   Then lightnesse and inconstancie in love;
That doth this Redcrosse knights ensample° plainly prove.   *example*

2

10 Who after that he had faire Una lorne,°   *forsaken*
   Through light misdeeming° of her loialtie,   *misjudging*
   And false Duessa in her sted had borne,[3]
   Called Fidess', and so supposd to bee;
   Long with her traveild, till at last they see
15 A goodly building, bravely garnishèd,°   *adorned*
   The house of mightie Prince it seemd to bee:
   And towards it a broad high way[4] that led,
All bare through peoples feet, which thither traveilèd.

3

Great troupes of people traveild thitherward
20 Both day and night, of each degree and place,°   *rank*
   But few returnèd, having scapèd hard,°   *with difficulty*
   With balefull° beggerie, or foule disgrace,   *wretched*
   Which ever after in most wretched case,
   Like loathsome lazars,° by the hedges lay.   *lepers*
25 Thither Duessa bad him bend his pace:[5]
   For she is wearie of the toilesome way,
And also nigh consumèd is the lingring day.

4

A stately Pallace built of squarèd bricke,
   Which cunningly was without morter laid,
30 Whose wals were high, but nothing strong, nor thick,
   And golden foile[6] all over them displaid,
   That purest skye with brightnesse they dismaid:°   *outdid*
   High lifted up were many loftie towres,
   And goodly galleries farre over laid,[7]
35 Full of faire windowes, and delightfull bowres;
And on the top a Diall told the timely howres.[8]

5

It was a goodly heape° for to behould,   *building*
   And spake the praises of the workmans wit;°   *skill*
   But full great pittie, that so faire a mould°   *structure*
40 Did on so weake foundation ever sit:
   For on a sandie hill,[9] that still did flit,°   *shift*
   And fall away, it mounted was full hie,
   That every breath of heaven shakèd it:
   And all the hinder parts, that few could spie,
45 Were ruinous and old, but painted cunningly.

---

3. Taken as companion.
4. "Broad is the way that leadeth to destruction" (Matthew 7.13).
5. Direct his steps.
6. Thin layer of gold.
7. Placed above.

8. A sundial measured the hours of the day.
9. Matthew 7.26–27: "A foolish man . . . built his house upon the sand: / And the rain descended, and the floods came, and the winds blew, and beat upon that house; and it fell; and great was the fall of it."

6

Arrivèd there they passèd in forth right;
    For still to all the gates stood open wide,
    Yet charge of them was to a Porter hight°   *committed*
    Cald Malvenù,[1] who entrance none denide:
50   Thence to the hall, which was on every side
    With rich array and costly arras dight:[2]
    Infinite sorts of people did abide
    There waiting long, to win the wishèd sight
Of her, that was the Lady of that Pallace bright.

7

55 By them they passe, all gazing on them round,
    And to the Presence[3] mount; whose glorious vew
    Their frayle amazèd senses did confound:
    In living Princes court none ever knew
    Such endlesse richesse, and so sumptuous shew;
60   Ne Persia selfe, the nourse of pompous pride
    Like ever saw. And there a noble crew
    Of Lordes and Ladies stood on every side,
Which with their presence faire, the place much beautifide.

8

High above all a cloth of State° was spred,   *canopy*
65   And a rich throne, as bright as sunny day,
    On which there sate most brave embellishèd[4]
    With royall robes and gorgeous array,
    A mayden Queene, that shone as Titans° ray,   *the sun's*
    In glistring gold, and peerelesse pretious stone:
70   Yet her bright blazing beautie did assay°   *attempt*
    To dim the brightnesse of her glorious throne,
As envying her selfe, that too exceeding shone.

9

Exceeding shone, like Phoebus fairest childe,
    That did presume his fathers firie wayne,°   *chariot*
75   And flaming mouthes of steedes unwonted° wilde   *unusually*
    Through highest heaven with weaker° hand to rayne;   *too weak*
    Proud of such glory and advancement vaine,
    While flashing beames do daze his feeble eyen,
    He leaves the welkin° way most beaten plaine,   *skyey*
80   And rapt° with whirling wheeles, inflames the skyen, *carried away*
With fire not made to burne, but fairely for to shyne.[5]

10

So proud she shynèd in her Princely state,°   *throne*
    Looking to heaven; for earth she did disdayne,
    And sitting high; for lowly° she did hate: *lowliness*
85   Lo underneath her scornefull feete, was layne
    A dreadfull Dragon with an hideous trayne,°

1. The name means unwelcome. In courtly love allegories, the porter is often called Bienvenu or Bel-
accueil ("welcome").
2. Decorated with costly wall hangings.
3. Presence chamber, where a sovereign receives
guests.
4. Handsomely clad.
5. Phaëthon tried to drive the chariot of Phoebus, his
father, but set the skies on fire and fell.

tail

And in her hand she held a mirrhour bright,[6]
Wherein her face she often vewèd fayne,°   *with pleasure*
And in her selfe-loved semblance tooke delight;
90   For she was wondrous faire, as any living wight.

11

Of griesly° Pluto she the daughter was,   *horrid*
And sad Proserpina the Queene of hell;
Yet did she thinke her pearelesse worth to pas°   *surpass*
That parentage, with pride so did she swell,
95   And thundring Jove, that high in heaven doth dwell,
And wield° the world, she claymèd for her syre,   *govern*
Or if that any else did Jove excell:
For to the highest she did still aspyre,
Or if ought° higher were then that, did it desyre.   *anything*

12

100   And proud Lucifera men did her call,
That made her selfe a Queene, and crownd to be,
Yet rightfull kingdome she had none at all,
Ne heritage of native soveraintie,
But did usurpe with wrong and tyrannie
105   Upon the scepter, which she now did hold:
Ne ruld her Realmes with lawes, but pollicie,°   *political cunning*
And strong advizement of six wisards old,
That with their counsels bad her kingdome did uphold.

13

Soone as the Elfin knight in presence came,
110   And false Duessa seeming Lady faire,
A gentle Husher,° Vanitie by name   *usher*
Made rowme, and passage for them did prepaire:
So goodly° brought them to the lowest staire   *graciously*
Of her high throne, where they on humble knee
115   Making obeyssance,° did the cause declare,   *submission*
Why they were come, her royall state to see,
To prove° the wide report of her great Majestee.   *verify*

14

With loftie eyes, halfe loth to looke so low,
She thankèd them in her disdainefull wise,
120   Ne other grace vouchsafèd them to show
Of Princesse worthy, scarse them bad arise.
Her Lordes and Ladies all this while devise°   *make ready*
Themselves to setten forth to straungers sight:
Some frounce° their curlèd haire in courtly guise,   *frizzle*
125   Some prancke° their ruffes, and others trimly dight°   *pleat/arrange*
Their gay attire: each others greater pride does spight.

15

Goodly they all that knight do entertaine,
Right glad with him to have increast their crew:
But to Duess' each one himselfe did paine
130   All kindnesse and faire courtesie to shew;

---

6. Pride and figures associated with her in Renaissance literature and art often hold a mirror, emblematic of self-love.

For in that court whylome° her well they knew: *formerly*
Yet the stout Faerie mongst the middest° crowd   *thickest*
Thought all their glorie vaine in knightly vew,
And that great Princesse too exceeding prowd,
135   That to strange° knight no better countenance° allowd.   *stranger/favor*

16

Suddein upriseth from her stately place
The royall Dame, and for her coche doth call:
All hurtlen° forth and she with Princely pace,   *rush*
As faire Aurora in her purple pall,[7]
140   Out of the East the dawning day doth call:
So forth she comes: her brightnesse brode° doth blaze;   *abroad*
The heapes of people thronging in the hall,
Do ride° each other, upon her to gaze: *climb up*
Her glorious glitterand° light doth all mens eyes amaze.   *glittering*

17

145   So forth she comes, and to her coche does clyme,
Adornèd all with gold, and girlonds gay,
That seemd as fresh as Flora in her prime,
And strove to match, in royall rich array,
Great Junos golden chaire,° the which they say   *chariot*
150   The Gods stand gazing on, when she does ride
To Joves high house through heavens bras-pavèd way
Drawne of by faire Pecocks, that excell in pride,
And full of Argus eyes their tailes dispredden wide.[8]

18

But this was drawne of six unequall beasts,
155   On which her six sage Counsellours did ryde,
Taught to obay their bestiall beheasts,
With like conditions to their kinds applyde:[9]
Of which the first, that all the rest did guyde,
Was sluggish Idlenesse the nourse of sin;
160   Upon a slouthfull Asse he chose to ryde,
Arayd in habit blacke, and amis thin,[1]
Like to an holy Monck, the service to begin.

19

And in his hand his Portesse° still he bare,   *breviary*
That much was worne, but therein little red,
165   For of devotion he had little care,
Still drownd in sleepe, and most of his dayes ded;
Scarse could he once uphold his heavie hed,
To looken, whether it were night or day:
May seeme the wayne° was very evill led,   *chariot*
170   When such an one had guiding of the way,
That knew not, whether right he went, or else astray.

7. Goddess of dawn, in her crimson robe ("purple pall").
8. Peacocks, with their tails outspread ("dispredden wide") are a symbol of pride. The hundred-eyed monster Argus was set by Juno to watch Io, Jupiter's love. When Mercury killed Argus, his eyes were put in the peacock's tail feathers.
9. Because riders and their mounts are alike bestial, the same conditions pertain (are "applyde") to both natures ("kinds"). This procession of the seven deadly sins—of which Pride is queen—had a long tradition in medieval art and literature (see also Marlowe, *Dr. Faustus* 5.276–322, pp. 446–447).
1. Idleness wears the gown ("habit") and hood or amice ("amis") of a monk. Traditionally, Idleness led the procession of the deadly sins.

20

From worldly cares himselfe he did esloyne,°   *withdraw*
    And greatly shunnèd manly exercise,
    From every worke he chalengèd essoyne,[2]
175 For contemplation sake: yet otherwise,
    His life he led in lawlesse riotise;°   *riotous conduct*
    By which he grew to grievous malady;
    For in his lustlesse° limbs through evill guise°   *feeble/living*
    A shaking fever raignd continually:
180 Such one was Idlenesse, first of this company
                              21
And by his side rode loathsome Gluttony,
    Deformèd creature, on a filthie swyne,
    His belly was up-blowne with luxury.°   *indulgence*
    And eke with fatnesse swollen were his eyne,
185 And like a Crane his necke was long and fyne,[3]
    With which he swallowd up excessive feast,
    For want whereof poore people oft did pyne;°   *starve*
    And all the way, most like a brutish beast,
He spuèd up his gorge,[4] that all did him deteast.
                              22
190 In greene vine leaves he was right fitly clad;
    For other clothes he could not weare for heat,
    And on his head an yvie girland had,[5]
    From under which fast trickled downe the sweat:
    Still as he rode, he somewhat° still did eat,   *something*
195 And in his hand did beare a bouzing° can,   *drinking*
    Of which he supt so oft, that on his seat
    His dronken corse° he scarse upholden can,   *body*
In shape and life more like a monster, then a man.
                              23
Unfit he was for any worldly thing,
200 And eke unhable once° to stirre or go,°   *at all/walk*
    Not meet to be of counsell to a king,
    Whose mind in meat and drinke was drownèd so,
    That from his friend he seldome knew his fo:
    Full of diseases was his carcas blew,
205 And a dry dropsie through his flesh did flow:
    Which by misdiet daily greater grew:
Such one was Gluttony, the second of that crew.
                              24
And next° to him rode lustfull Lechery,   *just after*
    Upon a bearded Goat,[6] whose rugged haire,
210 And whally° eyes (the signe of gelosy,)   *glaring*
    Was like the person selfe, whom he did beare:
    Who rough, and blacke, and filthy did appeare,
    Unseemely man to please faire Ladies eye;
    Yet he of Ladies oft was lovèd deare,

2. Claimed exemption.
3. The crane is a common symbol of gluttony because
its long and thin ("fyne") neck allows more pleasure in
swallowing.
4. Vomited.

5. He resembles the drunken satyr Silenus, foster
father of Bacchus, god of wine; ivy is sacred to Bacchus.
6. Traditional symbol of Lust.

215   When fairer faces were bid standen by:°   *away*
       O who does know the bent of womens fantasy?

25

       In a greene gowne he clothèd was full faire,
         Which underneath did hide his filthinesse,
         And in his hand a burning hart he bare,
220   Full of vaine follies, and new fangleness:°   *fickleness*
         For he was false, and fraught with ficklenesse,
         And learnèd had to love with secret lookes,
         And well could daunce, and sing with ruefulnesse,°   *pity*
         And fortunes tell, and read in loving° bookes,   *erotic*
225   And thousand other wayes, to bait his fleshly hookes.

26

       Inconstant man, that lovèd all he saw,
         And lusted after all, that he did love,
         Ne would his looser life be tide to law,
         But joyd weake wemens hearts to tempt and prove°   *try*
230   If from their loyall loves he might them move;
         Which lewdnesse fild him with reprochfull paine
         Of that fowle evill, which all men reprove,
         That rots the marrow, and consumes the braine:[7]
       Such one was Lecherie, the third of all this traine.

27

235   And greedy Avarice by him did ride,
         Upon a Camell loaden all with gold;[8]
         Two iron coffers hong on either side,
         With precious mettall full, as they might hold,
         And in his lap an heape of coine he told;°   *counted*
240   For of his wicked pelfe° his God he made,   *money*
         And unto hell him selfe for money sold;
         Accursèd usurie was all his trade,
       And right and wrong ylike in equall ballaunce waide.[9]

28

       His life was nigh unto deaths doore yplast,
245   And thread-bare cote, and cobled shoes he ware,
         Ne scarse good morsell all his life did tast,
         But both from backe and belly still did spare,
         To fill his bags, and richesse to compare;°   *acquire*
         Yet chylde ne kinsman living had he none
250   To leave them to; but thorough daily care
         To get, and nightly feare to lose his owne,
       He led a wretched life unto him selfe unknowne.

29

       Most wretched wight, whom nothing might suffise,
         Whose greedy lust did lacke in greatest store,°   *plenty*
255   Whose need had end, but no end covetise,
         Whose wealth was want, whose plenty made him pore,
         Who had enough, yet wishèd ever more;

7. Syphilis.
8. The camel as a symbol of avarice is based on Matthew 19.24: "It is easier for a camel to go through the eye of a needle, than for a rich man to enter into the kingdom of God."
9. I.e., he made no distinction between right and wrong.

A vile disease, and eke in foote and hand
A grievous gout tormented him full sore,
260   That well he could not touch, not go,° nor stand: *walk*
Such one was Avarice, the fourth of this faire band.

                                30
And next to him malicious Envie rode,
Upon a ravenous wolfe,[1] and still° did chaw   *continually*
Betweene his cankred° teeth a venemous tode,   *ulcerated*
265   That all the poison ran about his chaw;°   *jaw*
But inwardly he chawèd his owne maw°   *entrails*
At neighbours wealth, that made him ever sad;
For death it was, when any good he saw,
And wept, that cause of weeping none he had,
270   But when he heard of harme, he wexèd wondrous glad.

                                31
All in a kirtle of discolourd say[2]
He clothèd was, ypainted full of eyes;
And in his bosome secretly there lay
An hatefull Snake,[3] the which his taile uptyes
275   In many folds, and mortall sting implyes.°   *enfolds*
Still as he rode, he gnasht his teeth, to see
Those heapes of gold with griple° Covetyse,   *grasping*
And grudgèd at the great felicitie
Of proud Lucifera, and his owne companie.

                                32
280   He hated all good workes and vertuous deeds,
And him no lesse, that any like did use,°   *perform*
And who with gracious bread the hungry feeds,
His almes for want of faith he doth accuse;
So every good to bad he doth abuse:°   *twist*
285   And eke° the verse of famous Poets witt   *also*
He does backebite, and spightfull poison spues
From leprous mouth on all, that ever writt:
Such one vile Envie was, that fifte in row did sitt.

                                33
And him beside rides fierce revenging Wrath,
290   Upon a Lion,[4] loth for to be led;
And in his hand a burning brond° he hath,   *sword*
The which he brandisheth about his hed;
His eyes did hurle forth sparkles fiery red,
And starèd sterne on all, that him beheld,
295   As ashes pale of hew and seeming ded;
And on his dagger still his hand he held,
Trembling through hasty rage, when choler° in him sweld.   *anger*
                                34
His ruffin° raiment all was staind with blood,   *disorderly*
Which he had spilt, and all to rags yrent,°   *torn*
300   Through unadvisèd rashnesse woxen wood,[5]
For of his hands he had no governement,°   *control*

1. Traditional symbol of Envy.   4. The symbol of Wrath.
2. Jacket of many-colored wool.   5. Grown insane.
3. Traditional attribute of Envy.

He cared for bloud in his avengement:
But when the furious fit was overpast,
His cruell facts° he often would repent;   actions
305 Yet wilfull man he never would forecast,
How many mischieves should ensue his heedlesse hast.[6]

35

Full many mischiefes follow cruell Wrath;
Abhorrèd bloudshed, and tumultuous strife,
Unmanly murder, and unthrifty scath,[7]
310 Bitter despight,° with rancours rusty knife,   malice
And fretting griefe the enemy of life;
All these, and many evils moe° haunt ire,°   more/anger
The swelling Splene,[8] and Frenzy raging rife,
The shaking Palsey, and Saint Fraunces fire:[9]
315 Such one was Wrath, the last of this ungoldly tire.°   train

36

And after all, upon the wagon beame
Rode Sathan, with a smarting whip in hand,
With which he forward lasht the laesie teme,
So oft as Slowth[1] still in the mire did stand.
320 Huge routs° of people did about them band,   crowds
Showting for joy, and still before their way
A foggy mist had covered all the land;
And underneath their feet, all scattered lay
Dead sculs and bones of men, whose life had gone astray.

37

325 So forth they marchen in this goodly sort,
To take the solace° of the open aire,   recreation
And in fresh flowring fields themselves to sport;
Emongst the rest rode that false Lady faire,
The fowle Duessa, next unto the chaire
330 Of proud Lucifera, as one of the traine:
But that good knight would not so nigh repaire,°   approach
Him selfe estraunging from their joyaunce° vaine,   festivity
Whose fellowship seemd far unfit for warlike swaine.

38

So having solacèd themselves a space
335 With pleasaunce of the breathing° fields yfed,   emitting fragrance
They backe returnèd to the Princely Place;
Whereas an errant knight in armes ycled,°   clad
And heathnish shield, wherein with letters red
Was writ Sans joy, they new arrivèd find:
340 Enflamed with fury and fiers hardy-hed,°   boldness
He seemd in hart to harbour thoughts unkind,
And nourish bloudy vengeaunce in his bitter mind.

39

Who when the shamèd shield[2] of slaine Sans foy
He spied with that same Faery champions page,

6. I.e., he never would foresee ("forecast") the calamities his "heedless haste" caused.
7. I.e., inhuman murder and destructive harm.
8. Organ associated with anger in Renaissance physiology.

9. St. Anthony's fire, erysipelas, or the flaming itch;
appropriate to Wrath.
1. Idleness (stanzas 18–20).
2. Carrying a shield upside down, with the heraldic
arms reversed, was a great insult (see line 369).

345 Bewraying° him, that did of late destroy   *revealing*
  His eldest brother, burning all with rage
  He to him leapt, and that same envious gage[3]
  Of victors glory from him snatcht away:
  But th 'Elfin knight, which ought that warlike wage,[4]
350 Disdaind to loose the meed he wonne in fray,°   *battle*
And him rencountring fierce, reskewd the noble pray.

        40

Therewith they gan to hurtlen° greedily,   *rush together*
  Redoubted battaile ready to darrayne,°   *contest*
  And clash their shields, and shake their swords on hy,
355 That with their sturre° they troubled all the traine; *tumult*
  Till that great Queene upon eternall paine
  Of high displeasure, that ensewen° might,   *ensue*
  Commaunded them their fury to refraine,
  And if that either to that shield had right,
360 In equall lists[5] they should the morrow next it fight.

        41

"Ah dearest Dame," quoth then the Paynim bold,
  "Pardon the errour of enragèd wight,
  Whom great griefe made forget the raines to hold
  Of reasons rule, to see this recreant° knight,   *cowardly*
365 No knight, but treachour° full of false despight° *deceiver/disdain*
  And shamefull treason, who through guile hath slayn
  The prowest° knight, that ever field did fight,   *bravest*
  Even stout Sans foy (O who can then refrayn?)
Whose shield he beares renverst, the more to heape disdayn.

        42

370 "And to augment the glorie of his guile,
  His[6] dearest love the faire Fidessa loe
  Is there possessed of° the traytour vile,   *by*
  Who reapes the harvest sowen by his foe,
  Sowen in bloudy field, and bought with woe:
375 That[7] brothers hand shall dearely well requight
  So be, O Queene, you equall favour showe."[8]
  Him litle answerd th 'angry Elfin knight:
He never meant with words, but swords to plead his right.

        43

But threw his gauntlet as a sacred pledge,
380 His cause in combat the next day to try:
  So been they parted both, with harts on edge,
  To be avenged each on his enimy.
  That night they pas in joy and jollity,
  Feasting and courting both in bowre and hall;
385 For Steward was excessive Gluttonie,
  That of his plenty pourèd forth to all;
Which doen,° the Chamberlain[9] Slowth did to rest them call. *done*

---

3. Envied prize.
4. The knight (Redcrosse) who owned ("ought") that spoil of war ("warlike wage").
5. Impartial formal combat.
6. I.e., Sans Foy's.
7. I.e., that act.
8. I.e., if, O Queen, you show impartiality ("equall favour").
9. The court attendant in charge of the bedchambers.

44

Now whenas darkesome night had all displayd
　　Her coleblacke curtein over brightest skye,
390　The warlike youthes on dayntie° couches layd,　　　　　　　　*fine*
　　Did chace away sweet sleepe from sluggish eye,
　　To muse on meanes of hopèd victory.
　　But whenas Morpheus[1] had with leaden mace
　　Arrested all that courtly company,
395　Up-rose Duessa from her resting place,
And to the Paynims° lodging comes with silent pace.　　　　*pagan*

45

Whom broad awake she finds, in troublous fit,[2]
　　Forecasting, how his foe he might annoy,°　　　　　　　　*injure*
　　And him amoves° with speaches seeming fit:　　　　　　　*arouses*
400　"Ah deare Sans joy, next dearest to Sans foy,
　　Cause of my new griefe, cause of my new joy,
　　Joyous, to see his ymage in mine eye,
　　And greeved, to thinke how foe did him destroy,
　　That was the flowre of grace and chevalrye;
405　Lo his Fidessa to thy secret faith I flye."

46

With gentle wordes he can° her fairely° greet,　　　　*did/courteously*
　　And bad say on the secret of her hart.
　　Then sighing soft, "I learne that litle sweet
　　Oft tempred is," quoth she, "with muchell° smart:　　　　*much*
410　For since my brest was launcht with lovely dart[3]
　　Of deare Sans foy, I never joyèd howre,
　　But in eternall woes my weaker hart
　　Have wasted, loving him with all my powre,
And for his sake have felt full many an heavie stowre.°　　*grief*

47

415　"At last when perils all I weenèd past,
　　And hoped to reape the crop of all my care,
　　Into new woes unweeting° I was cast,　　　　　　　　*unknowing*
　　By this false faytor,° who unworthy ware°　　　　*deceiver/wore*
　　His worthy shield, whom he with guilefull snare
420　Entrappèd slew, and brought to shamefull grave.
　　Me silly° maid away with him he bare,　　　　　　　　*helpless*
　　And ever since hath kept in darksome cave,
For that I would not yeeld, that° to Sans foy I gave.　　*what*

48

"But since faire Sunne hath sperst° that lowring clowd,　　*dispersed*
425　And to my loathèd life now shewes some light,
　　Under your beames I will me safely shroud,°　　　　*take shelter*
　　From dreaded storme of his disdainfull spight:
　　To you th' inheritance belongs by right
　　Of brothers prayse, to you eke longs° his love.　　　　*belongs*
430　Let not his love, let not his restlesse spright°　　　　*ghost*

---

1. The god of sleep.　　　　　　　　3. I.e., since my breast was pierced with the dart of
2. Troubled mood.　　　　　　　　　love.

Be unrevenged, that calles to you above
From wandring Stygian[4] shores, where it doth endlesse move."

49

Thereto said he, "Faire Dame be nought dismaid
For sorrowes past; their griefe is with them gone:
Ne yet of present perill be affraid;
For needlesse feare did never vantage° none,   *aid*
And helplesse hap it booteth not to mone.[5]
Dead is Sans-foy, his vitall° paines are past,   *living*
Though greevèd ghost for vengeance deepe do grone:
He lives, that shall him pay his dewties° last,   *rites*
And guiltie Elfin bloud shall sacrifice in hast."

50

"O but I feare the fickle freakes,"[6] quoth shee,
"Of fortune false, and oddes of armes[7] in field."
"Why dame," quoth he, "what oddes can ever bee,
Where both do fight alike, to win or yield?"
"Yea but," quoth she, "he beares a charmèd shield,
And eke enchaunted armes, that none can perce,
Ne none can wound the man, that does them wield."
"Charmd or enchaunted," answerd he then ferce,°   *fiercely*
"I no whit reck,[8] ne you the like need to reherce.°   *recount*

51

"But faire Fidessa, sithens° fortunes guile,   *since*
Or enimies powre hath now captivèd you,
Returne from whence ye came, and rest a while
Till morrow next, that I the Elfe subdew,
And with Sans foyes dead dowry you endew."[9]
"Ay me, that is a double death," she said,
"With proud foes sight my sorrow to renew:
Where ever yet I be, my secrete aid
Shall follow you." So passing forth she him obaid.

Canto 5

*The faithfull knight in equall field
subdewes his faithlesse foe,
Whom false Duessa saves, and for
his cure to hell does goe.*

1

The noble hart, that harbours vertuous thought,
And is with child of glorious great intent,
Can never rest, untill it forth have brought
Th 'eternall brood of glorie excellent:[1]
Such restlesse passion did all night torment
The flaming corage of that Faery knight,
Devizing, how that doughtie° turnament   *worthy*

---

4. I.e., from wandering on the banks of the river Styx, in Hades.
5. I.e., it does not help to moan over that which is beyond help ("helplesse hap").
6. Unpredictable tricks.
7. Advantage of superior arms.

8. I do not care at all.
9. I.e., endow you with the legacy of the dead Sans Joy.
1. That good is manifested only in action, not in mere intent, is an important Renaissance commonplace.

With greatest honour he atchieven might;
Still did he wake, and still did watch for dawning light.

2

10   At last the golden Orientall gate
       Of greatest heaven gan to open faire,
       And Phoebus[2] fresh, as bridegrome to his mate,
       Came dauncing forth, shaking his deawie haire:
       And hurld his glistring beames through gloomy aire.
15   Which when the wakeful Elfe perceived, streight way
       He started up, and did him selfe prepaire,
       In sun-bright armes, and battailous° array: *warlike*
And for with that Pagan proud he combat will that day.

3

And forth he comes into the commune hall,
20   Where earely waite him many a gazing eye,
       To weet what end to straunger knights may fall.
       There many Minstrales maken melody,
       To drive away the dull melancholy,
       And many Bardes, that to the trembling chord
25   Can tune their timely° voyces cunningly,   *measured*
       And many Chroniclers, that can record
Old loves, and warres for ladies doen° by many a Lord.[3]   *done*

4

Soone after comes the cruell Sarazin,
       In woven maile all armèd warily,
30   And sternly lookes at him, who not a pin
       Does care for looke of living creatures eye.
       They bring them wines of Greece and Araby,
       And daintie spices fetcht from furthest Ynd,°   *India*
       To kindle heat of courage privily:°   *within*
35   And in the wine a solemne oth they bynd
T'observe the sacred lawes of armes, that are assynd.

5

At last forth comes that far renowmèd Queene,
       With royall pomp and Princely majestie;
       She is ybrought unto a palèd° greene,   *fenced*
40   And placèd under stately canapee,°   *canopy*
       The warlike feates of both those knights to see.
       On th' other side in all mens open vew
       Duessa placèd is, and on a tree
       Sans-foy his shield is hangd with bloudy hew:
45   Both those the lawrell girlonds[4] to the victor dew.

6

A shrilling trompet sownded from on hye,
       And unto battaill bad them selves addresse:
       Their shining shieldes about their wrestes° they tye,   *wrists*
       And burning blades about their heads do blesse,°   *brandish*
50   The instruments of wrath and heavinesse:°   *rage*

---

2. The sun. Cf. Psalm 19.4–5: "In them hath he set
a Tabernacle for the sun, / Which is as a bridegroom
coming out of his chamber."
3. Minstrels play the music on their instruments,
Bards sing the words, Chroniclers—historians, epic
poets—write of love and war.
4. Laurel wreaths were awarded to the victor of a joust.

With greedy force each other doth assayle,
And strike so fiercely, that they do impresse
Deepe dinted furrowes in the battred mayle;
The yron walles to ward their blowes are weake and fraile.⁵

7

55 The Sarazin was stout,° and wondrous strong,   *fierce*
And heapèd blowes like yron hammers great:
For after bloud and vengeance he did long.
The knight was fiers,° and full of youthly heat: *high spirited*
And doubled strokes, like dreaded thunders threat:
60 For all for prayse and honour he did fight.
Both stricken strike, and beaten both do beat,
That from their shields forth flyeth firie light,
And helmets hewen deepe, shew marks of eithers might.

8

So th' one for wrong, the other strives for right:
65 As when a Gryfon⁶ seizèd° of his pray,   *in possession*
A Dragon fiers encountreth in his flight,
Through widest ayre making his ydle° way,   *casual*
That would his rightfull ravine° rend away;   *plunder*
With hideous horrour both together smight,
70 And souce° so sore, that they the heavens affray: *strike*
The wise Southsayer° seeing so sad sight,   *soothsayer*
Th' amazèd vulgar tels of warres and mortall fight.

9

So th' one for wrong, the other strives for right,
And each to deadly shame would drive his foe:
75 The cruell steele so greedily doth bight
In tender flesh, that streames of bloud down flow,
With which the armes, that earst so bright did show,
Into a pure vermillion now are dyde:
Great ruth° in all the gazers harts did grow,   *pity*
80 Seeing the gorèd woundes to gape so wyde,
That victory they dare not wish to either side.

10

At last the Paynim chaunst to cast his eye,
His suddein° eye, flaming with wrathfull fyre,   *darting*
Upon his brothers shield, which hong thereby:
85 Therewith redoubled was his raging yre,°   *anger*
And said, "Ah wretched sonne of wofull syre,
Doest thou sit wayling by black Stygian lake
Whilest here thy shield is hangd for victors hyre,°   *reward*
And sluggish german⁷ doest thy forces slake,°   *slacken*
90 To after-send his foe, that him may overtake?

11

"Goe caytive° Elfe, him quickly overtake,   *miserable*
And soone redeeme from his long wandring woe;
Goe guiltie ghost, to him my message make,
That I his shield have quit° from dying foe."   *rescued*
95 Therewith upon his crest he stroke him so,

---

5. I.e., their armor is too frail to withstand such blows.   7. Kinsman, here, brother.
6. A legendary monster, half-eagle, half-lion.

That twise he reelèd, readie twise to fall;
End of the doubtfull battell deemèd tho
The lookers on,[8] and lowd to him gan call
The false Duessa, "Thine the shield, and I, and all."

12

100 Soone as the Faerie heard his Ladie speake,
     Out of his swowning dreame he gan awake,
     And quickning° faith, that earst was woxen weake,   *life-restoring*
     The creeping deadly cold away did shake:
     Tho moved with wrath, and shame, and Ladies sake,°   *cause*
105 Of all attonce he cast° avengd to bee,   *determined*
     And with so'exceeding furie at him strake,
     That forcèd him to stoupe upon his knee;
     Had he not stoupèd so, he should have cloven bee,

13

     And to him said, "Goe now proud Miscreant,°   *misbeliever*
110 Thy selfe thy message doe° to german deare,   *give*
     Alone he wandring thee too long doth want:
     Goe say, his foe thy shield with his doth beare."
     Therewith his heavie hand he high gan reare,
     Him to have slaine; when loe a darkesome clowd
115 Upon him fell: he no where doth appeare,
     But vanisht is. The Elfe him cals alowd,
     But answer none receives: the darknes him does shrowd.[9]

14

     In haste Duessa from her place arose,
     And to him running said, "O prowest° knight,   *bravest*
120 That ever Ladie to her love did chose,
     Let now abate the terror of your might,
     And quench the flame of furious despight,°   *anger*
     And bloudie vengeance; lo th' infernall powres
     Covering your foe with cloud of deadly night,
125 Have borne him hence to Plutoes balefull bowres.[1]
     The conquest yours, I yours, the shield, and glory yours."

15

     Not all so satisfide, with greedie eye
     He sought all round about, his thirstie blade
     To bath in bloud of faithlesse enemy;
130 Who all that while lay hid in secret shade:
     He standes amazèd, how he thence should fade.
     At last the trumpets Triumph sound on hie,
     And running Heralds humble homage made,
     Greeting him goodly with new victorie,
135 And to him brought the shield, the cause of enmitie.

16

     Wherewith he goeth to that soveraine Queene,
     And falling her before on lowly knee,
     To her makes present of his service seene;°   *proved*

8. I.e., the onlookers then ("tho") thought this would   *Aeneid* 5.810–812, and *Gerusalemme Liberata* 7.44–
end the battle, heretofore in doubt ("doubtfull").   45.
9. The device of a god rescuing a hero in danger by   1. Hades.
hiding him in a cloud has parallels in *Iliad* 3.380,

Which she accepts, with thankes, and goodly gree,°   *favor*
140 Greatly advauncing° his gay chevalree.   *extolling*
So marcheth home, and by her takes the knight,
Whom all the people follow with great glee,
Shouting, and clapping all their hands on hight,°   *aloud*
That all the aire it fils, and flyes to heaven bright.

17

145 Home is he brought, and laid in sumptuous bed:
Where many skilfull leaches° him abide,°   *doctors/attend*
To salve° his hurts, that yet still freshly bled.   *annoint*
In wine and oyle they wash his woundes wide,
And softly can embalme[2] on every side.
150 And all the while, most heavenly melody
About the bed sweet musicke did divide,[3]
Him to beguile of griefe and agony:
And all the while Duessa wept full bitterly.

18

As when a wearie traveller that strayes
155 By muddy shore of broad seven-mouthèd Nile,
Unweeting of the perillous wandring wayes,
Doth meet a cruell craftie Crocodile,
Which in false griefe hyding his harmefull guile,
Doth weepe full sore, and sheddeth tender teares:
160 The foolish man, that pitties all this while
His mournefull plight, is swallowed up unwares,°   *unexpectedly*
Forgettull of his owne, that mindes anothers cares.

19

So wept Duessa untill eventide,
That shyning lampes in Joves high house were light:[4]
165 Then forth she rose, ne lenger would abide,
But comes unto the place, where th' Hethen knight
In slombring swownd nigh voyd of vitall spright,[5]
Lay covered with inchaunted cloud all day:
Whom when she found, as she him left in plight,[6]
170 To wayle his woefull case she would not stay,
But to the easterne coast of heaven makes speedy way.

20

Where griesly° Night, with visage deadly sad,   *grim, horrible*
That Phoebus chearefull face durst never vew,
And in a foule blacke pitchie mantle clad,
175 She findes forth comming from her darkesome mew,°   *den*
Where she all day did hide her hated hew.°   *shape, color*
Before the dore her yron charet stood,
Alreadie harnessèd for journey new;
And cole blacke steedes yborne of hellish brood,
180 That on their rustie bits did champ, as they were wood.°   *mad*

21

Who when she saw Duessa sunny bright,
Adorned with gold and jewels shining cleare,°   *brightly*

---

2. Carefully did anoint.
3. Played variations.
4. I.e., when ("that") the stars came out.
5. Nearly ("nigh") devoid of life.
6. I.e., in the same desperate state she left him.

She greatly grew amazèd at the sight,
And th' unacquainted° light began to feare: *unfamiliar*
185   For never did such brightnesse there appeare,
And would have backe retyred to her cave,
Untill the witches speech she gan to heare,
Saying, "Yet O thou dreaded Dame, I crave
Abide,° till I have told the message, which I have."   *stay*

                    22
190   She stayd, and foorth Duessa gan proceede,
"O thou most auncient Grandmother of all,[7]
More old then Jove, whom thou at first didst breede,
Or that great house of Gods caelestiall,
Which wast begot in Daemogorgons hall,
195   And sawst the secrets of the world unmade,[8]
Why suffredst thou thy Nephewes° deare to rall   *grandsons*
With Elfin sword, most shamefully betrade?
Lo where the stout Sans joy doth sleepe in deadly shade.

                    23
"And him before, I saw with bitter eyes
200   The bold Sans foy shrinke underneath his speare;
And now the pray of fowles in field he lyes,
Nor wayld of friends, nor laid on groning beare,[9]
That whylome was to me too dearely deare.
O what of Gods then boots it[1] to be borne,
205   If old Aveugles sonnes so evill heare?[2]
Or who shall not great Nightes children scorne,
When two of three her Nephews are so fowle forlorne.[3]

                    24
"Up then, up dreary Dame, of darknesse Queene,
Go gather up the reliques of thy race,
210   Or else goe them avenge, and let be seene,
That dreaded Night in brightest day hath place,
And can the children of faire light deface."°   *destroy*
Her feeling speeches some compassion moved
In hart, and chaunge in that great mothers face:
215   Yet pittie in her hart was never proved°   *known*
Till then: for evermore she hated, never loved.

                    25
And said, "Deare daughter rightly may I rew
The fall of famous children borne of mee,
And good successes, which their foes ensew:°   *attend*
220   But who can turne the streame of destinee,
Or breake the chayne° of strong necessitee,
Which fast is tyde to Joves eternall seat?[4]
The sonnes of Day he favoureth, I see,
And by my ruines thinkes to make them great:
225   To make one great by others losse, is bad excheat.°   *exchange*

7. By tradition Night was eldest of the gods, existing before the world was formed and the Olympian gods were begotten in the hall of Demogorgon (Chaos).
8. Before it was made.
9. Bier attended by mourners ("groning").
1. What is it worth ("boots it").

2. I.e., are so badly thought of. "Aveugle": "blind." He is the son of Night and father of Sans Foy, Sans Joy, and Sans Loy.
3. Wretchedly lost.
4. The golden chain that binds the entire universe; the image goes back as far as Homer (*Iliad* 8.18–27).

26

"Yet shall they not escape so freely all;
   For some shall pay the price of others guilt:
   And he the man that made Sans foy to fall,
   Shall with his owne bloud price° that he hath spilt.   *pay for*
230 But what art thou, that telst of Nephews kilt?"
   "I that do seeme not I, Duessa am,"
   Quoth she, "how ever now in garments gilt,
   And gorgeous gold arayd I to thee came:
Duessa I, the daughter of Deceipt and Shame."

27

235 Then bowing downe her agèd backe, she kist
   The wicked witch, saying; "In that faire face
   The false resemblance of Deceipt, I wist
   Did closely° lurke; yet so true-seeming grace   *secretly*
   It carried, that I scarse in darkesome place
240 Could it discerne, though I the mother bee
   Of falshood, and root of Duessaes race.
   O welcome child, whom I have longd to see,
And now have seene unwares.° Lo now I go with thee."   *unexpectedly*

28

Then to her yron wagon she betakes,
245 And with her beares the fowle welfavour'd witch:
   Through mirkesome° aire her readie way she makes.   *murky, dense*
   Her twyfold° Teme, of which two blacke as pitch,   *twofold*
   And two were browne, yet each to each unlich,°   *unlike*
   Did softly swim away, ne ever stampe,
250 Unlesse she chaunst their stubborne mouths to twitch;
   Then forming tarre,[5] their bridles they would champe,
And trampling the fine element,[6] would fiercely rampe.°   *rear up*

29

So well they sped, that they be come at length
   Unto the place, whereas the Paynim lay,
255 Devoid of outward sense, and native strength,
   Coverd with charmèd cloud from vew of day,
   And sight of men, since his late luckelesse fray.
   His cruell wounds with cruddy° bloud congealed,   *clotted*
   They binden up so wisely,° as they may,   *skillfully*
260 And handle softly, till they can be healed:
So lay him in her charet, close in night concealed.

30

And all the while she stood upon the ground,
   The wakefull dogs did never cease to bay,
   As giving warning of th' unwonted° sound,   *unusual*
265 With which her yron wheeles did them affray,
   And her darke griesly° looke them much dismay;   *horrid*
   The messenger of death, the ghastly Owle
   With drearie shriekes did also her bewray;°   *reveal*
   And hungry Wolves continually did howle,
270 At her abhorrèd face, so filthy and so fowle.

---

5. Black froth.   6. The air.

31

Thence turning backe in silence soft they stole,
　And brought the heavie corse with easie pace
　To yawning gulfe of deepe Avernus hole.[7]
　By that same hole an entrance darke and bace
275　With smoake and sulphure hiding all the place,
　Descends to hell: there creature never past,
　That backe returnèd without heavenly grace;
　But dreadfull Furies, which their chaines have brast,°　　　burst
And damnèd sprights sent forth to make ill° men aghast.　　　evil

32

280　By that same way the direfull dames doe drive
　Their mournefull charet, fild° with rusty blood,　　　defiled
　And downe to Plutoes house are come bilive:°　　　quickly, alive
　Which passing through, on every side them stood
　The trembling ghosts with sad amazèd mood,
285　Chattring their yron teeth, and staring wide
　With stonie eyes; and all the hellish brood
　Of feends infernall flockt on every side,
To gaze on earthly wight, that with the Night durst ride.

33

They pas the bitter waves of Acheron,
290　Where many soules sit wailing woefully,
　And come to fiery flood of Phlegeton,[8]
　Whereas the damnèd ghosts in torments fry,
　And with sharpe shrilling shriekes doe bootlesse° cry,　　　without avail
　Cursing high Jove, the which them thither sent.
295　The house of endlesse paine is built thereby,
　In which ten thousand sorts of punishment
The cursèd creatures doe eternally torment.

34

Before the threshold dreadfull Cerberus[9]
　His three deformèd heads did lay along,°　　　at full length
300　Curled with thousands adders venemous,
　And lillèd° forth his bloudie flaming tong:　　　lolled
　At them he gan to reare his bristles strong,
　And felly gnarre,[1] untill dayes enemy
　Did him appease; then downe his taile he hong
305　And suffered them to passen quietly:
For she in hell and heaven had power equally.

35

There was Ixion turnèd on a wheele,
　For daring tempt the Queene of heaven to sin;
　And Sisyphus an huge round stone did reele°　　　roll
310　Against an hill, ne° might from labour lin;°　　　nor/cease
　There thirstie Tantalus hong by the chin;
　And Tityus fed a vulture on his maw;°　　　liver
　Typhoeus joynts were stretchèd on a gin,°　　　rack

7. In classical mythology Avernus is hell, where Pluto
(line 282) reigns.
8. Acheron and Phlegeton are rivers in hell.
9. The three-headed dog that guards hell. Stanzas 31–

35 recall Aeneas's descent into hell (Virgil, Aeneid
6.200, 239–240).
1. Savagely snarl.

Theseus condemned to endlesse slouth° by law,   *sloth*
315 And fifty sisters water in leake vessels draw.²

36

They all beholding worldly° wights in place,°   *mortal/there*
    Leave off their worke, unmindfull of their smart,
    To gaze on them; who forth by them doe pace,
    Till they be come unto the furthest part:
320   Where was a Cave ywrought by wondrous art,
    Deepe, darke, uneasie,° dolefull, comfortlesse,   *lacking ease*
    In which sad Aesculapius³ farre a part
    Emprisond was in chaines remedilesse,°   *beyond any remedy*
For that Hippolytus rent corse he did redresse.°   *cure*

37

325 Hippolytus a jolly° huntsman was,   *gallant*
    That wont° in charet chace the foming Bore;   *used to*
    He all his Peeres in beautie did surpas,
    But Ladies love as losse of time forbore:
    His wanton stepdame⁴ lovèd him the more,
330   But when she saw her offred sweets refused
    Her love she turnd to hate, and him before
    His father fierce of treason false accused,
And with her gealous° termes his open eares abused.   *arousing jealousy*

38

Who all in rage his Sea-god syre⁵ besought,
335   Some cursèd vengeance on his sonne to cast:
    From surging gulf two monsters straight were brought,
    With dread whereof his chasing steedes aghast,
    Both charet swift and huntsman overcast.
    His goodly corps on ragged cliffs yrent,
340   Was quite dismembred, and his members chast
    Scattered on every mountaine, as he went,
That of Hippolytus was left no moniment.⁶

39

His cruell stepdame seeing what was donne,
    Her wicked dayes with wretched knife did end,
345   In death avowing th' innocence of her sonne.
    Which hearing his rash Syre, began to rend
    His haire, and hastie tongue, that did offend:
    Tho° gathering up the relicks of his smart⁷   *then*
    By Dianes meanes, who was Hippolyts frend,
350   Them brought to Aesculape, that by his art
Did heale them all againe, and joynèd every part.

40

Such wondrous science in mans wit to raine
    When Jove avizd,° that could the dead revive,   *discovered*

---

2. Ixion was being punished for attempting to seduce Juno; Sisyphus, for refusing to pray to the gods; Tantalus, for stealing the gods' nectar; Tityus, for having tried to seduce Apollo's mother; the monster Typhoeus, for creating destructive winds; Theseus, for stealing Persephone from Hades; and the daughters of King Danaus, for having killed their husbands on their wedding night. Tantalus stood chin-deep in water that receded whenever he tried to drink—hence he is "thirstie." Ovid, Virgil, and Homer are Spenser's sources here.
3. God of medicine.
4. Phaedra, the wife of his father, Theseus.
5. Poseidon (Neptune).
6. I.e., no trace of identity.
7. I.e., his son's remains, that caused his grief.

And fates expirèd[8] could renew againe,
355   Of endlesse life he might him not deprive,
But unto hell did thrust him downe alive,
With flashing thunderbolt ywounded sore:
Where long remaining, he did alwaies strive
Himselfe with salves to health for to restore,
360 And slake the heavenly fire, that raged evermore.

41

There auncient Night arriving, did alight
From her nigh wearie waine,[9] and in her armes
To Aesculapius brought the wounded knight:
Whom having softly disarayd of armes,
365   Tho gan to him discover all his harmes,
Beseeching him with prayer, and with praise,
If either salves, or oyles, or herbes, or charmes
A fordonne° wight from dore of death mote raise,   *undone*
He would at her request prolong her nephews daies.

42

370 "Ah Dame," quoth he, "thou temptest me in vaine,
To dare the thing, which daily yet I rew,
And the old cause of my continued paine
With like attempt to like end to renew.
Is not enough, that thrust from heaven dew[1]
375   Here endlesse penance for one fault I pay,
But that redoubled crime with vengeance new
Thou biddest me to eeke?° Can Night defray°   *increase/appease*
The wrath of thundring Jove, that rules both night and day?"

43

"Not so," quoth she; "but sith that heavens king
380   From hope of heaven hath thee excluded quight,
Why fearest thou, that canst not hope for thing,°   *anything*
And fearest not, that more thee hurten might,
Now in the powre of everlasting Night?
Goe to them, O thou farre renowmèd sonne
385   Of great Apollo, shew thy famous might
In medicine, that else° hath to thee wonne   *already*
Great paines, and greater praise, both never to be donne."°   *ended*

44

Her words prevaild: And then the learnèd leach°   *doctor*
His cunning hand gan to his wounds to lay,
390   And all things else, the which his art did teach:
Which having seene, from thence arose away
The mother of dread darknesse, and let stay
Aveugles sonne there in the leaches cure,°   *care*
And backe returning tooke her wonted way,
395   To runne her timely race,[2] whilst Phoebus pure
In westerne waves his wearie wagon did recure.°   *refresh*

---

8. The completed term of life as fixed by the Fates.
9. I.e., the horses of Night's chariot are nearly exhausted.
1. The proper ("dew") place for a god.
2. Her nightly journey.

45

The false Duessa leaving noyous° Night,   *harmful*
   Returnd to stately pallace of dame Pride;
   Where when she came, she found the Faery knight
400 Departed thence, albe° his woundes wide   *although*
   Not throughly heald, unreadie were to ride.
   Good cause he had to hasten thence away;
   For on a day his wary Dwarfe had spide,
   Where in a dongeon deepe huge numbers lay
405 Of caytive° wretched thrals,° that waylèd night   *captive/slaves*
   and day.

46

A ruefull sight, as could be seene with eie;
   Of whom he learnèd had in secret wise
   The hidden cause of their captivitie,
   How mortgaging their lives to Covetise,
410 Through wastfull° Pride, and wanton Riotise,   *causing desolation*
   They were by law of that proud Tyrannesse[3]
   Provokt with Wrath, and Envies false surmise,
   Condemnèd to that Dongeon mercilesse,
Where they should live in woe, and die in wretchednesse.

47

415 There was that great proud king of Babylon[4]
   That would compell all nations to adore,
   And him as onely God to call upon,
   Till through celestiall doome° throwne out of dore,   *judgment*
   Into an Oxe he was transformed of yore:
420 There also was king Croesus,[5] that enhaunst°   *exalted*
   His heart too high through his great riches store;
   And proud Antiochus,[6] the which advaunst
His cursèd hand gainst God, and on his altars daunst.°   *danced*

48

And them long time before, great Nimrod[7] was,
425 That first the world with sword and fire warrayd;°   *ravaged*
   And after him old Ninus farre did pas°   *surpass*
   In princely pompe, of all the world obayd;
   There also was that mightie Monarch layd
   Low under all, yet above all in pride,
430 That name of native° syre did fowle upbrayd,   *natural*
   And would as Ammons sonne[8] be magnifide,
Till scornd of God and man a shamefull death he dide.

49

All these together in one heape were throwne,
   Like carkases of beasts in butchers stall.
435 And in another corner wide were strowne
   The antique ruines of the Romaines fall:

3. Lucifera. The noble sinners named in stanzas 47–
50 exemplify a theme common in Renaissance morality, the fall of princes.
4. Nebuchadnezzar (Daniel 3–4).
5. King of Lydia, famous for his riches.
6. King of Syria, who desecrated the Jewish temple of
Jerusalem (1 Maccabees 1.20–24).

7. Nimrod, identified as the first tyrant, caused the
Tower of Babel to be built in defiance of God (Genesis
10.9). Ninus was founder of Ninevah, archetype of the
wicked city (see the Book of Jonah).
8. Alexander the Great, occasionally worshiped as the
son of Jupiter Ammon.

Great Romulus the Grandsyre of them all,
Proud Tarquin, and too lordly Lentulus,
Stout Scipio, and stubborne Hanniball,
440   Ambitious Sylla, and sterne Marius,
High Caesar, great Pompey, and fierce Antonius.[9]

50

Amongst these mighty men were wemen mixt,
    Proud wemen, vaine, forgetfull of their yoke:°   *duty*
    The bold Semiramis,[1] whose sides transfixt
445   With sonnes owne blade, her fowle reproches spoke;
    Faire Sthenoboea,[2] that her selfe did choke
    With wilfull cord, for wanting° of her will;   *lacking*
    High minded Cleopatra, that with stroke
    Of Aspes sting her selfe did stoutly kill:
450   And thousands moe the like, that did that dongeon fill.

51

Besides the endlesse routs° of wretched thralles,   *crowds*
    Which thither were assembled day by day,
    From all the world after their wofull falles,
    Through wicked pride, and wasted wealthes decay.
455   But most of all, which in that Dongeon lay
    Fell from high Princes courts, or Ladies bowres,
    Where they in idle pompe, or wanton play,
    Consumèd had their goods, and thriftlesse howres,
And lastly throwne themselves into these heavy stowres.°   *disasters*

52

460   Whose case wheneas the carefull° Dwarfe had tould,   *anxious*
    And made ensample of their mournefull sight
    Unto his maister, he no lenger would
    There dwell in perill of like painefull plight,
    But early rose, and ere that dawning light
465   Discovered had the world to heaven wyde,
    He by a privie Posterne° tooke his flight,   *gate*
    That of no envious eyes he mote be spyde:
For doubtlesse death ensewd, if any him descryde.

53

Scarse could he footing find in that fowle way,
470   For many corses, like a great Lay-stall°   *rubbish heap*
    Of murdred men which therein strowèd lay,
    Without remorse, or decent funerall:
    Which all through that great Princesse pride did fall
    And came to shamefull end. And them beside
475   Forth ryding underneath the castell wall,
    A donghill of dead carkases he spide,
The dreadfull spectacle° of that sad house of Pride.[3]   *example*

---

9. Romulus was the founder of Rome; Tarquin, a roman tyrant; Lentulus, a conspirator with Catiline; Scipio, a Roman general, conqueror of Carthage; Hannibal, a Carthaginian general; Sulla, a Roman civil war general; Marius, Sulla's rival; Julius Caesar; Pompey the Great; and Mark Anthony. All are memorialized in Plutarch's *Lives*.

1. Wife of Ninus.

2. Queen of King Proteus of Argos, who lusted after her brother-in-law Bellerophon.

3. Named now, after we have been shown what the name means.

Canto 6

From lawlesse lust by wondrous grace
fayre Una is releast:
Whom salvage° nation does adore,   wild, of the woods
and learnes her wise beheast.°   bidding

1

As when a ship, that flyes faire under saile,
    An hidden rocke escapèd hath unwares,°   unexpectedly
    That lay in waite her wrack for to bewaile,[4]
    The Marriner yet halfe amazèd stares
5   At perill past, and yet in doubt ne dares
    To joy at his foole-happie oversight:[5]
    So doubly is distrest twixt joy and cares
    The dreadlesse° courage of this Elfin knight,   fearless
Having escapt so sad ensamples in his sight.

2

10 Yet sad he was that his too hastie speed
    The faire Duess' had forst him leave behind;
    And yet more sad, that Una his deare dreed°   object of reverence
    Her truth had staind with treason so unkind;
    Yet crime in her could never creature find,
15   But for his love, and for her owne selfe sake,
    She wandred had from one to other Ynd,[6]
    Him for to seeke, ne ever would forsake,
Till her unwares the fierce Sansloy did overtake.

3

Who after Archimagoes fowle defeat,
20   Led her away into a forrest wilde,
    And turning wrathfull fire to lustfull heat,
    With beastly sin thought her to have defilde,
    And made the vassall of his pleasures vilde.°   vile
    Yet first he cast by treatie,° and by traynes,°   persuasion/tricks
25   Her to perswade, that stubborne fort to yilde:
    For greater conquest of hard love he gaynes,
That workes it to his will, then he that it constraines.°   forces

4

With fawning wordes he courted her a while,
    And looking lovely,° and oft sighing sore,   lovingly
30   Her constant hart did tempt with diverse guile:
    But wordes, and lookes, and sighes she did abhore,
    As rocke of Diamond stedfast evermore.[7]
    Yet for to feed his fyrie lustfull eye,
    He snatcht the vele, that hong her face before;
35   Then gan her beautie shine, as brightest skye,
And burnt his beastly hart t' efforce° her chastitye.   violate

---

4. I.e., cause the shipwreck and thereby cause it to be
bewailed.
5. Lucky ignorance.
6. I.e., she would have wandered from the East to the
West Indies.
7. The diamond, because of its hardness, was an
emblem of fidelity.

5

So when he saw his flatt'ring arts to fayle,
  And subtile engines bet from batteree,[8]
  With greedy force he gan the fort assayle,
40 Whereof he weend° possessèd soone to bee,   *thought*
  And win rich spoile of ransackt chastetee.
  Ah heavens, that do this hideous act behold,
  And heavenly virgin thus outragèd see,
  How can ye vengeance just so long withhold,
45 And hurle not flashing flames upon that Paynim bold?

6

The pitteous maden carefull° comfortlesse,   *full of cares*
  Does throw out thrilling° shriekes, and shrieking cryes, *piercing*
  The last vaine helpe of womens great distresse,
  And with loud plaints importuneth the skyes,
50 That molten starres do drop like weeping eyes;
  And Phoebus flying so most shamefull sight,
  His blushing face in foggy cloud[9] implyes,°   *buries*
  And hides for shame. What wit of mortall wight
Can now devise to quit a thrall[1] from such a plight?

7

55 Eternall providence exceeding° thought,   *transcending*
  Where none appeares can make her selfe a way:
  A wondrous way it for this Lady wrought,
  From Lyons clawes to pluck the gripèd pray.
  Her shrill outcryes and shriekes so loud did bray,
60 That all the woodes and forestes did resownd;
  A troupe of Faunes and Satyres[2] far away
  Within the wood were dauncing in a rownd,
Whiles old Sylvanus slept in shady arber sownd.

8

Who when they heard that pitteous strainèd voice,
65 In hast forsooke their rurall meriment,
  And ran towards the far rebownded° noyce,   *re-echoed*
  To weet, what wight so loudly did lament.
  Unto the place they come incontinent:°   *immediately*
  Whom when the raging Sarazin espide,
70 A rude, misshapen, monstrous rablement,
  Whose like he never saw, he durst not bide,
But got his ready steed, and fast away gan ride.

9

The wyld woodgods arrivèd in the place,
  There find the virgin dolefull desolate,
75 With ruffled rayments, and faire blubbred° face, *flooded with tears*
  As her outrageous foe had left her late,
  And trembling yet through feare of former hate;
  All stand amazèd at so uncouth° sight,   *strange*

8. I.e., beaten ("bet") from their fruitless assault ("batteree") on her unmovable virtue.
9. The sun is overcast by clouds.
1. Release a victim.

2. Woodland deities with men's bodies above the waist
and goats' bodies below, noted for their sensuality. Sylvanus, Roman god of the woods, is traditionally associated with fauns.

And gin to pittie her unhappie state,

80 All stand astonied° at her beautie bright, *stupified*

In their rude° eyes unworthie° of so wofull plight. *rustic/undeserving*

10

She more amazed, in double dread doth dwell;

And every tender part for feare does shake:

As when a greedie Wolfe through hunger fell

85 A seely° Lambe farre from the flocke does take, *innocent*

Of whom he meanes his bloudie feast to make,

A Lyon spyes fast running towards him,

The innocent pray in hast he does forsake,

Which quit from death yet quakes in every lim

90 With chaunge of feare, to see the Lyon looke so grim.° *savage*

11

Such fearefull fit assaid° her trembling hart, *assailed*

Ne word to speake, ne joynt to move she had:

The salvage nation feele her secret smart,

And read her sorrow in her count'nance sad;

95 Their frowning forheads with rough hornes yclad,

And rusticke horror° all a side doe lay, *roughness*

And gently grenning, shew a semblance glad

To comfort her, and feare to put away,

Their backward bent knees teach her humbly to obay.[3]

12

100 The doubtfull Damzell dare not yet commit

Her single person to their barbarous truth,[4]

But still twixt feare and hope amazd does sit,

Late learnd° what harme to hastie trust ensu'th, *taught*

They in compassion of her tender youth,

105 And wonder of her beautie soveraine,

Are wonne with pitty and unwonted ruth,° *pity*

And all prostrate upon the lowly plaine,

Do kisse her feete, and fawne on her with count'nance faine.° *glad*

13

Their harts she ghesseth by their humble guise,° *appearance*

110 And yieldes her to extremitie of time;[5]

So from the ground she fearelesse doth arise,

And walketh forth without suspect° of crime: *suspicion*

They all as glad, as birdes of joyous Prime,° *springtime*

Thence lead her forth, about her dauncing round,

115 Shouting, and singing all a shepheards ryme,

And with greene braunches strowing all the ground,

Do worship her, as Queene, with olive girlond cround.

14

And all the way their merry pipes they sound,

That all the woods with doubled Eccho ring,

120 And with their hornèd feet do weare the ground,

Leaping like wanton kids in pleasant Spring.

So towards old Sylvanus they her bring;

---

3. I.e., teach their knees, bent backward like a goat's, to obey her.
4. I.e., her solitary self to their wild allegiance ("barbarous truth").
5. I.e., necessity of the time.

Who with the noyse awakèd, commeth out,
   To weet° the cause, his weake steps governing   *learn*
125 And agèd limbs on Cypresse stadle° stout,   *staff*
And with an yvie twyne his wast is girt about.

15

Far off he wonders, what them makes so glad,
   Or Bacchus merry fruit they did invent,[6]
   Or Cybeles franticke rites[7] have made them mad;
130 They drawing nigh, unto their God present
That flowre of faith and beautie excellent.
   The God himselfe vewing that mirrhour rare,
   Stood long amazd, and burnt in his intent;[8]
His owne faire Dryope now he thinkes not faire,
135 And Pholoe fowle, when her to this he doth compaire.[9]

16

The woodborne people fall before her flat,
   And worship her as Goddesse of the wood;
   And old Sylvanus selfe bethinkes not,[1] what
To thinke of wight so faire, but gazing stood,
140 In doubt to deeme her borne of earthly brood;
   Sometimes Dame Venus selfe he seemes to see,
   But Venus never had so sober mood;
   Sometimes Diana he her takes to bee,
But misseth bow, and shaftes, and buskins° to her knee.   *soft boots*

17

145 By vew of her he ginneth to revive
   His ancient love, and dearest Cyparisse,[2]
   And calles to mind his pourtraiture alive,[3]
   How faire he was, and yet not faire to this,
And how he slew with glauncing dart amisse
150 A gentle Hynd, the which the lovely boy
   Did love as life, above all worldly blisse;
   For griefe whereof the lad n'ould° after joy,   *would not*
But pynd away in anguish and selfe-wild annoy.°   *suffering*

18

The wooddy Nymphes, faire Hamadryades[4]
155 Her to behold do thither runne apace,
   And all the troupe of light-foot Naiades,[5]
   Flocke all about to see her lovely face:
But when they vewèd have her heavenly grace,
   They envie her in their malitious mind,
160 And fly away for feare of fowle disgrace:
   But all the Satyres scorne their woody kind,[6]
And henceforth nothing faire, but her on earth they find.

---

6. I.e., whether ("or") they did find ("invent") wine
grapes.
7. Orgiastic dances in worship of Cybele, goddess of
the powers of Nature.
8. Glowed with intense concentration. Una is a "mirrhour rare" in that she reflects heavenly beauty.
9. Dryope and Pholoe were nymphs loved by Faunus
and Pan; for Spenser, the names *Faunus, Pan,* and *Sylvanus* were apparently interchangeable.

1. Cannot decide.
2. A fair youth, beloved of Sylvanus, turned into a
cypress tree.
3. I.e., his appearance when alive.
4. Spirits of trees whose lives ended when the tree they
inhabited died.
5. Water nymphs.
6. Forest inhabitants.

19

Glad of such lucke, the luckelesse lucky maid,
    Did her content to please their feeble eyes,
165   And long time with that salvage people staid,
    To gather breath in many miseries.
    During which time her gentle wit she plyes,
    To teach them truth, which worshipt her in vaine,
    And made her th' Image of Idolatryes;[7]
170   But when their bootlesse zeale she did restraine
From her own worship, they her Asse would worship fayn.°   *willingly*

20

It fortunèd a noble warlike knight
    By just occasion to that forrest came,
    To seeke his kindred, and the lignage right,°   *true*
175   From whence he tooke his well deservèd name:
    He had in armes abroad wonne muchell° fame,   *great*
    And fild far landes with glorie of his might,
    Plaine, faithfull, true, and enimy of shame,
    And ever loved to fight for Ladies right,
180   But in vaine glorious frayes he litle did delight.

21

A Satyres sonne yborne in forrest wyld,
    By straunge adventure as it did betyde,°   *happen*
    And there begotten of a Lady myld,
    Faire Thyamis the daughter of Labryde,
185   That was in sacred bands of wedlocke tyde
    To Therion,[8] a loose unruly swayne;
    Who had more joy to raunge the forrest wyde,
    And chase the salvage beast with busie payne,°   *painstaking care*
Then serve his Ladies love, and wast° in pleasures vayne.   *live idly*

22

190   The forlorne mayd did with loves longing burne,
    And could not lacke° her lovers company,   *be without*
    But to the wood she goes, to serve her turne,
    And seeke her spouse, that from her still does fly,
    And followes other game and venery:[9]
195   A Satyre chaunst her wandring for to find,
    And kindling coles of lust in brutish eye,
    The loyall links of wedlocke did unbind,
And made her person thrall unto his beastly kind.

23

So long in secret cabin there he held
200   Her captive to his sensuall desire,
    Till that with timely fruit her belly sweld,
    And bore a boy unto that salvage sire:
    Then home he suffred her for to retire,°   *return*
    For ransome leaving him the late borne childe;
205   Whom till to ryper yeares he gan aspire,°   *grow up*
    He noursled° up in life and manners wilde,   *reared*
Emongst wild beasts and woods, from lawes of men exilde.

---

7. The idol of their idolatries.
8. Wild beast. "Thyamis": passion. "Labryde": turbu-   lence.
9. The word means both hunting and sexual play.

24

For all he taught the tender ymp,° was but   child
　　To banish cowardize and bastard° feare;   base
210　His trembling hand he would him force to put
　　Upon the Lyon and the rugged Beare,
　　And from the she Beares teats her whelps to teare;
　　And eke wyld roring Buls he would him make
　　To tame, and ryde their backes not made to beare;
215　And the Robuckes[1] in flight to overtake,
That every beast for feare of him did fly and quake.

25

Thereby so fearelesse, and so fell° he grew,   fierce
　　That his owne sire and maister of his guise[2]
　　Did often tremble at his horrid vew,[3]
220　And oft for dread of hurt would him advise,
　　The angry beasts not rashly to despise,
　　Nor too much to provoke; for he would learne°   teach
　　The Lyon stoup to him in lowly wise,
　　(A lesson hard) and make the Libbard° sterne   leopard
225　Leave roaring, when in rage he for revenge did earne.°   yearn

26

And for to make his powre approvèd° more,   demonstrated
　　Wyld beasts in yron yokes he would compell;
　　The spotted Panther, and the tuskèd Bore,
　　The Pardale° swift, and the Tigre cruell;   female leopard
230　The Antelope, and Wolfe both fierce and fell;°   savage
　　And them constraine in equall teme[4] to draw.
　　Such joy he had, their stubborne harts to quell,
　　And sturdie courage tame with dreadfull aw,
That his beheast they fearèd, as a tyrans law.

27

235　His loving mother came upon a day
　　Unto the woods, to see her little sonne;
　　And chaunst unwares° to meet him in the way,   unexpectedly
　　After his sportes, and cruell pastime donne,
　　When after him a Lyonesse did runne,
240　That roaring all with rage, did lowd requere°   demand
　　Her children deare, whom he away had wonne:°   seized
　　The Lyon whelpes she saw how he did beare,
And lull in rugged armes, withouten childish feare.

28

The fearefull Dame all quakèd at the sight,
245　And turning backe, gan fast to fly away,
　　Untill with love revokt° from vaine affright,   recalled
　　She hardly° yet perswaded was to stay,   with difficulty
　　And then to him these womanish words gan say;
　　"Ah Satyrane, my dearling, and my joy,
250　For love of me leave off this dreadfull play;
　　To dally thus with death, is no fit toy,
Go find some other play-fellowes, mine own sweet boy."

1. Deer, especially noted for their speed.   3. Of rough appearance.
2. Teacher of his behavior.   4. Side by side, yoked together in a team.

29

In these and like delights of bloudy game
    He traynèd was, till ryper yeares he raught,°   *reached*
255   And there abode, whilst any beast of name
    Walkt in that forest, whom he had not taught
    To feare his force: and then his courage haught°   *high*
    Desird of forreine foemen to be knowne;
    And far abroad for straunge adventures sought:
260   In which his might was never overthrowne,
But through all Faery lond his famous worth was blown.°   *spread*

30

Yet evermore it was his manner faire,
    After long labours and adventures spent,
    Unto those native woods for to repaire,°   *return*
265   To see his sire and ofspring° auncient.   *origin*
    And now he thither came for like intent;
    Where he unwares the fairest Una found,
    Straunge Lady, in so straunge habiliment,°   *attire*
    Teaching the Satyres, which her sat around,
270   Trew sacred lore, which from her sweet lips did redound.°   *flow*

31

He wondred at her wisedome heavenly rare,
    Whose like in womens wit he never knew;
    And when her curteous deeds he did compare,
    Gan her admire, and her sad sorrowes rew,°   *pity*
275   Blaming of Fortune, which such troubles threw,
    And joyd to make proofe of her crueltie
    On gentle Dame, so hurtlesse,° and so trew: *harmless*
    Thenceforth he kept her goodly company,
And learnd her discipline° of faith and veritie.   *teachings*

32

280   But she all vowd[5] unto the Redcrosse knight,
    His wandring perill closely° did lament,   *secretly*
    Ne in this new acquaintaunce could delight,
    But her deare° heart with anguish did torment,   *loving*
    And all her wit in secret counsels spent,
285   How to escape. At last in privie wise°   *privately*
    To Satyrane she shewèd her intent;
    Who glad to gain such favour, gan devise,
How with that pensive Maid he best might thence arise.°   *depart*

33

So on a day when Satyres all were gone,
290   To do their service to Sylvanus old,
    The gentle virgin left behind alone
    He led away with courage stout and bold.
    Too late it was, to Satyres to be told,
    Or ever hope recover her againe:
295   In vaine he seekes that having cannot hold.
    So fast he carried her with carefull paine,°   *painstaking care*
That they the woods are past, and come now to the plaine.

---

5. Entirely promised.

34

The better part now of the lingring day,
    They traveild had, when as they farre espide
300   A wearie wight forwandring° by the way,   *wandering far and wide*
    And towards him they gan in hast to ride,
    To weet of newes, that did abroad betide,
    Or tydings of her knight of the Redcrosse.
    But he them spying, gan to turne aside,
305   For feare as seemid, or for some feignèd losse;[6]
More greedy they of newes, fast towards him do crosse.

35

A silly° man, in simple weedes forworne,°   *simple/worn out*
    And soild with dust of the long dried way;
    His sandales were with toilesome travell torne,
310   And face all tand with scorching sunny ray,
    As he had traveild many a sommers day,
    Through boyling sands of Arabie and Ynde;°   *India*
    And in his hand a Jacobs staffe,[7] to stay
    His wearie limbes upon: and eke behind,
315   His scrip° did hang, in which his needments he did bind.   *bag*

36

The knight approching nigh, of him inquerd
    Tydings of warre, and of adventures new;
    But warres, nor new adventures none he herd.
    Then Una gan to aske, if ought he knew,
320   Or heard abroad of that her champion trew,
    That in his armour bare a croslet° red.   *small cross*
    "Aye me, Deare dame," quoth he, "well may I rew
    To tell the sad sight, which mine eies have red:°   *beheld*
These eyes did see that knight both living and eke ded."

37

325   That cruell word her tender hart so thrild,°   *pierced*
    That suddein cold did runne through every vaine,
    And stony horrour all her sences fild
    With dying fit,[8] that downe she fell for paine.
    The knight her lightly° rearèd up againe,   *quickly*
330   And comforted with curteous kind reliefe:
    Then wonne from death, she bad him tellen plaine
    The further processe° of her hidden griefe;   *account*
The lesser pangs can beare, who hath endured the chiefe.

38

Then gan the Pilgrim thus, "I chaunst this day,
335   This fatall day, that shall I ever rew,
    To see two knights in travell on my way
    (A sory° sight) arraunged in battell new,   *grievous*
    Both breathing vengeaunce, both of wrathfull hew:
    My fearefull flesh did tremble at their strife,
340   To see their blades so greedily imbrew,[9]
    That drunke with bloud, yet thristed after life:
What more? the Redcrosse knight was slaine with Paynim knife."

6. Pretended harm.
7. I.e., pilgrim's staff.
8. Deathlike swoon.
9. Soak themselves in blood.

39

"Ah dearest Lord," quoth she, "how might that bee,
   And he the stoutest knight, that ever wonne?"°   *lived*
345 "Ah dearest dame," quoth he, "how might I see
   The thing, that might not be, and yet was donne?"
   "Where is," said Satyrane, "that Paynims sonne,
   That him of life, and us of joy hath reft?"
   "Not far away," quoth he, "he hence doth wonne°   *stay*
350 Foreby° a fountaine, where I late him left   *close by*
Washing his bloudy wounds, that through° the steele were cleft."   *by*

40

Therewith the knight thence marchèd forth in hast,
   Whiles Una with huge heavinesse° opprest,   *grief*
   Could not for sorrow follow him so fast;
355 And soone he came, as he the place had ghest,
   Whereas that Pagan proud him selfe did rest,
   In secret shadow by a fountaine side:
   Even he it was, that earst would have supprest°   *violated*
   Faire Una: whom when Satyrane espide,
360 With fowle reprochfull words he boldly him defide.

41

And said, "Arise thou cursèd Miscreaunt,°   *infidel*
   That hast with knightlesse° guile and trecherous   *unknightly*
     train°   *deceit*
   Faire knighthood fowly shamed, and doest vaunt
   That good knight of the Redcrosse to have slain:
365 Arise, and with like treason now maintain°   *defend*
   Thy guilty wrong, or else thee guilty yield."
   The Sarazin this hearing, rose amain,°   *at once*
   And catching up in hast his three square° shield,   *triangular*
And shining helmet, soone him buckled to the field.

42

370 And drawing nigh him said, "Ah misborne Elfe,[1]
   In evill houre thy foes thee hither sent,
   Anothers wrongs to wreake upon thy selfe:
   Yet ill thou blamest me, for having blent°   *stained*
   My name with guile and traiterous intent;
375 That Redcrosse knight, perdie, I never slew,
   But had he beene, where earst° his armes were lent,   *before*
   Th' enchaunter vaine his errour should not rew:
But thou his errour shalt, I hope now proven trew."[2]

43

Therewith they gan, both furious and fell,°   *fierce*
380 To thunder blowes, and fiersly to assaile
   Each other bent° his enimy to quell,°   *determined/kill*
   That with their force they perst° both plate and maile,   *pierced*
   And made wide furrowes in their fleshes fraile,
   That it would pitty° any living eie.   *bring pity to*
385 Large floods of bloud adowne their sides did raile:°   *flow*

---

1. Base-born knight of Faerie Land ("Elfe").
2. I.e., had Redcrosse been wearing his arms the enchanter Archimago would not have to regret his error in fighting me. But you will now repeat that error and that regret.

But floods of bloud could not them satisfie:
Both hungred after death: both chose to win, or die.

44

So long they fight, and fell revenge pursue,
    That fainting each, themselves to breathen let,
390   And oft refreshèd, battell oft renue:
    As when two Bores with rancling malice met,
    Their gory sides fresh bleeding fiercely fret,°   *tear*
    Til breathlesse both them selves aside retire,
    Where foming wrath, their cruell tuskes they whet,
395   And trample th' earth, the whiles they may respire
Then backe to fight againe, new breathèd and entire.°   *fresh*

45

So fiersly, when these knights had breathèd once,
    They gan to fight returne, increasing more
    Their puissant force, and cruell rage attonce,
400   With heapèd strokes more hugely, then before,
    That with their drerie° wounds and bloudy gore   *gory*
    They both deformèd,° scarsely could be known.   *disfigured*
    By this sad Una fraught with anguish sore,
    Led with their noise, which through the aire was thrown,
405 Arrived, where they in erth their fruitles bloud had sown.

46

Whom all so soone as that proud Sarazin
    Espide, he gan revive the memory
    Of his lewd lusts, and late attempted sin,
    And left the doubtfull° battell hastily,   *undecided*
410   To catch her, newly offred to his eie:
    But Satyrane with strokes him turning, staid,
    And sternely bad him other businesse plie,
    Then hunt the steps of pure unspotted Maid:
Wherewith he all enraged, these bitter speaches said.

47

415 "O foolish faeries sonne, what furie mad
    Hath thee incenst, to hast thy dolefull fate?
    Were it not better, I that Lady had,
    Then that thou hadst repented it too late?
    Most sencelesse man he, that himselfe doth hate,
420   To love another. Lo then for thine ayd
    Here take thy lovers token on thy pate."
    So they to fight; the whiles the royall Mayd
Fled farre away, of that proud Paynim sore afrayd.

48

But that false Pilgrim, which that leasing° told,   *lie*
425   Being in deed old Archimage, did stay
    In secret shadow, all this to behold,
    And much rejoycèd in their bloudy fray:
    But when he saw the Damsell passe away
    He left his stond,° and her pursewd apace,   *place*
430   In hope to bring her to her last decay.°   *death*
    But for to tell her lamentable cace,
And eke° this battels end, will need another place.   *also*

Canto 7

The Redcrosse knight is captive made
By Gyaunt proud opprest,°   *overwhelmed*
Prince Arthur meets with Una great-
ly with those newes distrest.

1

What man so wise, what earthly wit so ware,°   *wary*
As to descry° the crafty cunning traine,°   *perceive/guile*
By which deceipt doth maske in visour° faire,   *a mask*
And cast her colours dyèd deepe in graine,³
5   To seeme like Truth, whose shape she well can faine,
And fitting gestures to her purpose frame,
The guiltlesse man with guile to entertaine?°   *receive*
Great maistresse of her art was that false Dame,
The false Duessa, clokèd with Fidessaes name.

2

10 Who when returning from the drery° Night,   *dismal*
She fownd not in that perilous house of Pryde,
Where she had left, the noble Redcrosse knight,
Her hopèd pray, she would no lenger bide,
But forth she went, to seeke him far and wide.
15 Ere long she fownd, whereas° he wearie sate,   *where*
To rest him selfe, foreby° a fountaine side,   *beside*
Disarmèd all of yron-coted Plate,
And by his side his steed the grassy forage ate.

3

He feedes upon⁴ the cooling shade, and bayes°   *bathes*
20 His sweatie forehead in the breathing wind,
Which through the trembling leaves full gently playes
Wherein the cherefull birds of sundry kind
Do chaunt sweet musick, to delight his mind:
The Witch approaching gan him fairely° greet,   *courteously*
25 And with reproch of carelesnesse unkind
Upbrayd, for leaving her in place unmeet,°   *unfitting*
With fowle words tempring faire, soure gall with hony sweet.

4

Unkindnesse past, they gan of solace treat,°   *speak*
And bathe in pleasaunce of the joyous shade,
30 Which shielded them against the boyling heat,
And with greene boughes decking a gloomy glade,
About the fountaine like a girlond made;
Whose bubbling wave did ever freshly well,
Ne ever would through fervent° sommer fade:°   *hot/dry up*
35 The sacred Nymph, which therein wont to dwell,
Was out of Dianes favour, as it then befell.

5

The cause was this: one day when Phoebe⁵ fayre
With all her band was following the chace,
This Nymph, quite tyred with heat of scorching ayre

---

3. I.e., Deceit disposes her colors, thoroughly dyed, so   4. I.e., enjoys.
as to seem like Truth.   5. I.e., Diana, goddess of the moon and of chastity.

40 Sat downe to rest in middest of the race:
    The goddesse wroth gan fowly her disgrace,
    And bad the waters, which from her did flow,
    Be such as she her selfe was then in place.[6]
    Thenceforth her waters waxèd dull and slow,
45 And all that drunke thereof, did faint and feeble grow.

                            6
    Hereof this gentle knight unweeting° was,   *ignorant*
        And lying downe upon the sandie graile,°   *gravel*
        Drunke of the streame, as cleare as cristall glas;
        Eftsoones his manly forces gan to faile,
50   And mightie strong was turnd to feeble fraile.
        His chaunged powres at first themselves not felt,
        Till crudled° cold his corage° gan assaile,   *congealing/vigor*
        And chearefull° bloud in faintnesse chill did melt,   *lively*
    Which like a fever fit through all his body swelt.°   *raged*

                            7
55 Yet goodly court he made still to his Dame,
        Pourd out in loosnesse[7] on the grassy grownd,
        Both carelesse of his health, and of his fame:
        Till at the last he heard a dreadfull sownd,
        Which through the wood loud bellowing, did rebownd,
60   That all the earth for terrour seemed to shake,
        And trees did tremble. Th' Elfe therewith astownd,°   *amazed*
        Upstarted lightly° from his looser make,[8]   *quickly*
    And his unready weapons gan in hand to take.

                            8
    But ere he could his armour on him dight,
65   Or get his shield, his monstrous enimy
        With sturdie steps came stalking in his sight,
        An hideous Geant horrible and hye,
        That with his talnesse seemd to threat the skye,
        The ground eke° groned under him for dreed;   *also*
70   His living like saw never living eye,
        Ne durst behold: his stature did exceed
    The hight of three the tallest sonnes of mortall seed.

                            9
    The greatest Earth his uncouth mother was,
        And blustring Aeolus his boasted sire,[9]
75   Who with his breath, which through the world doth pas,
        Her hollow womb did secretly inspire,°   *breathe into*
        And fild her hidden caves with stormie yre,
        That she conceived; and trebling the dew time,
        In which the wombes of women do expire,°   *bring forth*
80   Brought forth this monstrous masse of earthly slime,
    Puft up with emptie wind, and fild with sinfull crime.

                            10
    So growen great through arrogant delight
        Of th' high descent, whereof he was yborne,

6. I.e., in that place.   8. More licentious ("looser") companion.
7. Stretched out and indulging in amorous play   9. Aeolus was keeper of the winds. The giant's descent
("loosnesse").   from Earth and Wind links him to earthquakes.

And through presumption of his matchlesse might,
85   All other powres and knighthood he did scorne.
        Such now he marcheth to this man forlorne,°   *abandoned*
        And left to losse:° his stalking steps are stayde   *destruction*
        Upon a snaggy Oke,[1] which he had torne
        Out of his mothers bowelles, and it made
90   His mortall° mace, wherewith his foemen he dismayde.[2]   *death-dealing*

                                11
        That when the knight he spide, he gan advance
            With huge force and insupportable mayne,[3]
            And towardes him with dreadfull fury praunce;
            Who haplesse, and eke hopelesse, all in vaine
95   Did to him pace, sad battaile to darrayne,°   *engage*
            Disarmd, disgrast, and inwardly dismayde,
            And eke° so faint in every joynt and vaine,   *also*
            Through that fraile° fountaine, which him feeble made,   *enfeebling*
        That scarsely could he weeld his bootlesse° single blade.   *useless*

                                12
100   The Geaunt strooke so maynly° mercilesse,   *mightily*
            That could have overthrowne a stony towre,
            And were not heavenly grace, that him did blesse,
            He had beene pouldred° all, as thin as flowre: *powdered*
            But he was wary of that deadly stowre,°   *peril*
105   And lightly° lept from underneath the blow: *quickly*
            Yet so exceeding was the villeins powre,
            That with the wind it did him overthrow,
        And all his sences stound,° that still he lay full low.   *stunned*

                                13
        As when that divelish yron Engin[4] wrought
110   In deepest Hell, and framd by Furies skill,
            With windy Nitre and quick Sulphur fraught,[5]
            And ramd with bullet round, ordaind to kill,
            Conceiveth fire, the heavens it doth fill
            With thundring noyse, and all the ayre doth choke,
115   That none can breath, nor see, nor heare at will,
            Through smouldry cloud of duskish stincking smoke,
        That th' onely breath him daunts,[6] who hath escapt the stroke.

                                14
        So daunted when the Geaunt saw the knight,
            His heavie hand he heavèd up on hye,
120   And him to dust thought to have battred quight,
            Untill Duessa loud to him gan crye;
            "O great Orgoglio,[7] greatest under skye,
            O hold thy mortall hand for Ladies sake,
            Hold for my sake, and do him not to dye,[8]
125   But vanquisht thine eternall bondslave make,
        And me thy worthy meed unto thy Leman take."[9]

---

1. I.e., he uses as walking stick a knotty ("snaggy") oak   "Sulphur").
tree.   6. I.e., the blast or smell alone ("onely") overcomes
2. Dis-made, dissolved (also in line 96).   him.
3. Irresistible power.   7. "Orgoglio": Italian for "pride, haughtiness, disdain."
4. I.e., cannon.   8. Do not cause him to die.
5. Filled ("fraught") with gunpowder ("Nitre" and   9. I.e., take me, your worthy reward, as your mistress.

15

He hearkned, and did stay° from further harmes,   refrain
   To gayne so goodly guerdon,° as she spake: reward
   So willingly she came into his armes,
130 Who her as willingly to grace° did take,   favor
   And was possessèd of his new found make.°   mate
   Then up he tooke the slombred° sencelesse corse,   unconscious
   And ere he could out of his swowne awake,
   Him to his castle brought with hastie forse,
135 And in a Dongeon deepe him threw without remorse.

16

From that day forth Duessa was his deare,
   And highly honourd in his haughtie eye,
   He gave her gold and purple pall[1] to weare,
   And triple crowne set on her head full hye,[2]
140 And her endowd with royall majestye:
   Then for to make her dreaded more of men,
   And peoples harts with awfull terrour tye,°   enthrall
   A monstrous beast ybred in filthy fen
He chose, which he had kept long time in darksome den.

17

145 Such one it was, as that renowmèd Snake
   Which great Alcides in Stremona slew,
   Long fostred in the filth of Lerna lake,[3]
   Whose many heads out budding ever new,
   Did breed° him endlesse labour to subdew: cause
150 But this same Monster much more ugly was;
   For seven great heads out of his body grew,
   An yron brest, and backe of scaly bras,
And all embrewd° in bloud, his eyes did shine as glas.   stained

18

His tayle was stretchèd out in wondrous length,
155 That to the house of heavenly gods it raught,°   reached
   And with extorted powre, and borrowed strength,
   The ever-burning lamps° from thence it brought,   stars
   And prowdly threw to ground, as things of nought;
   And underneath his filthy feet did tread
160 The sacred things, and holy heasts foretaught.[4]
   Upon this dreadfull Beast with sevenfold head
He set the false Duessa, for more aw and dread.

19

The wofull Dwarfe, which saw his maisters fall,
   Whiles he had keeping of his grasing steed,
165 And valiant knight become a caytive° thrall,   captive
   When all was past, tooke up his forlorne weed,[5]

---

1. Crimson robe of royalty.
2. Duessa is attired like the Whore of Babylon in Revelation 17.3–4; the triple crown is that of the papacy
(see 1.2, stanza 13 and nn. 6–8; also stanza 22 and n.
2).
3. The nine-headed Lernean hydra slain by Hercules
(Alcides). The seven-headed monster recalls the red
dragon of Revelation: "behold a great red dragon, having seven heads and ten horns, and seven crowns upon
his heads . . . [whose] tail drew the third part of the
stars of heaven, and did cast them to the earth . . . [he
is] that old serpent, called the Devil, and Satan, which
deceiveth the whole world" (12.3–14.9). Many Protestants associated the Beast with the Roman church.
4. Doctrines ("holy heasts") previously taught.
5. Abandoned garment.

His mightie armour, missing most at need;
  His silver shield, now idle maisterlesse;
  His poynant° speare, that many made to bleed,   *sharp*
170   The ruefull moniments° of heavinesse,°   *memorials/grief*
And with them all departes, to tell his great distresse.

20

He had not travaild long, when on the way
  He wofull Ladie, wofull Una met,
  Fast flying from the Paynims greedy pray,°   *clutch*
175   Whilest Satyrane him from pursuit did let:°   *prevent*
  Who when her eyes she on the Dwarfe had set,
  And saw the signes, that deadly tydings spake,
  She fell to ground for sorrowfull regret,°   *grief*
  And lively breath her sad brest did forsake,
180 Yet might her pitteous hart be seene to pant and quake.

21

The messenger of so unhappie newes
  Would faine have dyde: dead was his hart within,
  Yet outwardly some little comfort shewes:
  At last recovering hart, he does begin
185   To rub her temples, and to chaufe her chin,
  And every tender part does tosse and turne:
  So hardly he the flitted life does win,
  Unto her native prison to retourne:[6]
Then gins her grievèd ghost° thus to lament and mourne.   *spirit*

22

190 "Ye dreary instruments of dolefull sight,
  That doe this deadly spectacle behold,
  Why do ye lenger feed on loathèd light,
  Or liking find to gaze on earthly mould,[7]
  Sith cruell fates the carefull° threeds unfould,   *intricate*
195   The which my life and love together tyde?
  Now let the stony dart of senselesse cold[8]
  Perce to my hart, and pas through every side,
And let eternall night so sad sight fro me hide.

23

"O lightsome day, the lampe of highest Jove,
200   First made by him,[9] mens wandring wayes to guyde,
  When darknesse he in deepest dongeon drove,
  Henceforth thy hated face for ever hyde,
  And shut up heavens windowes shyning wyde:
  For earthly sight can nought but sorrow breed,
205   And late° repentance, which shall long abyde.   *too late*
  Mine eyes no more on vanitie shall feed,
But seelèd up with death, shall have their deadly meed."[1]

24

Then downe againe she fell unto the ground;
  But he her quickly rearèd up againe:

---

6. I.e., with such difficulty ("so hardly") he persuades ("does win") the life back to her body ("native prison").
7. I.e., or find it pleasure to gaze on earthly forms ("mould").

8. I.e., death.
9. An allusion to Genesis 1.3: "And God said, Let there be light: and there was light."
1. Reward of death.

210 Thrise did she sinke adowne in deadly swownd,
     And thrise he her revived with busie paine:°   *care*
     At last when life recovered had the raine,°   *rein*
     And over-wrestled his strong enemie,
     With foltring° tong, and trembling every vaine,   *faltering*
215 "Tell on," quoth she, "the wofull Tragedie,
     The which these reliques sad present unto mine eie.

                              25
     "Tempestuous fortune hath spent all her spight,
     And thrilling° sorrow throwne his utmost dart;   *piercing*
     Thy sad tongue cannot tell more heavy plight,
220 Then that I feele, and harbour in mine hart:
     Who hath endured the whole, can beare each part.
     If death it be, it is not the first wound,
     That launchèd° hath my brest with bleeding smart.   *pierced*
     Begin, and end the bitter balefull stound;°   *blow*
225 If lesse, then that I feare, more favour I have found."

                              26
     Then gan the Dwarfe the whole discourse° declare,   *story*
     The subtill traines° of Archimago old;   *wiles*
     The wanton loves of false Fidessa faire,
     Bought with the bloud of vanquisht Paynim bold:
230 The wretched payre transformed to treen mould;[2]
     The house of Pride, and perils round about;
     The combat, which he with Sans joy did hould;
     The lucklesse conflict with the Gyant stout,
     Wherein captived, of life or death he stood in doubt.

                              27
235 She heard with patience all unto the end,
     And strove to maister sorrowfull assay,°   *affliction*
     Which greater grew, the more she did contend,
     And almost rent her tender hart in tway°   *two*
     And love fresh coles unto her fire did lay:
240 For greater love, the greater is the losse.
     Was never Ladie lovèd dearer day,[3]
     Then she did love the knight of the Redcrosse;
     For whose deare sake so many troubles her did tosse.

                              28
     At last when fervent sorrow slakèd was,
245 She up arose, resolving him to find
     Alive or dead: and forward forth doth pas,
     All° as the Dwarfe the way to her assynd:°   *just/showed*
     And evermore in constant carefull mind
     She fed her wound with fresh renewèd bale;°   *anguish*
250 Long tost with stormes, and bet° with bitter wind,   *beaten*
     High over hils, and low adowne the dale,
     She wandred many a wood, and measurd many a vale.

                              29
     At last she chauncèd by good hap to meet
     A goodly knight, faire marching by the way

2. Shape of a tree.   more dearly than she loved Redcrosse.
3. I.e., there was never a lady who loved life ("day")

255   Together with his Squire, arayèd meet:°   *properly*
      His glitterand° armour shinéd farre away,   *glittering*
      Like glauncing° light of Phoebus brightest ray;   *flashing*
      From top to toe no place appearèd bare,
      That deadly dint° of steele endanger may: *stroke*
260   Athwart his brest a bauldrick[4] brave he ware,
    That shynd, like twinkling stars, with stons most pretious rare.

                   30

    And in the midst thereof one pretious stone
      Of wondrous worth, and eke° of wondrous mights,°   *also/powers*
      Shapt like a Ladies head, exceeding shone,
265   Like Hesperus° emongst the lesser lights,°   *evening star/stars*
      And strove for to amaze the weaker sights;
      Thereby his mortall blade full comely hong
      In yvory sheath, ycarved with curious slights;°   *designs*
      Whose hilts were burnisht gold, and handle strong
270   Of mother pearle, and buckled with a golden tong.°   *pin*

                   31

    His haughtie helmet, horrid° all with gold,   *bristling*
      Both glorious brightnesse, and great terrour bred;
      For all the crest a Dragon did enfold
      With greedie pawes, and over all did spred
275   His golden wings: his dreadfull hideous hed
      Close couchèd on the bever,° seemed to throw   *visor*
      From flaming mouth bright sparkles fierie red,
      That suddeine horror to faint harts did show;
    And scaly tayle was stretcht adowne his backe full low

                   32

280   Upon the top of all his loftie crest,°   *top of helmet*
      A bunch of haires discolourd° diversly,   *dyed*
      With sprincled pearle, and gold full richly drest,
      Did shake, and seemed to daunce for jollity,
      Like to an Almond tree ymounted hye
285   On top of greene Selinis[5] all alone,
      With blossomes brave bedeckèd daintily;
      Whose tender locks do tremble every one
    At every little breath, that under heaven is blowne.

                   33

    His warlike shield all closely covered was,
290   Ne might of mortall eye be ever seene;
      Not made of steele, nor of enduring bras,
      Such earthly mettals soone consumèd bene:
      But all of Diamond perfect pure and cleene°   *clear*
      It framèd was, one massie entire mould,[6]
295   Hewen out of Adamant rocke with engines keene,
      That point of speare it never percen could,
    Ne dint of direfull sword divide the substance would.

---

4. Sash worn over the shoulder to support the sword.
5. Town associated with the palm awarded to victors (Virgil, *Aeneid* 3.705).
6. The shield was made of one solid piece of diamond, whose qualities—unflawed, unpierceable, translucent—point to this knight's significance and role.

34

The same to wight° he never wont disclose,   *creature*
  But° when as monsters huge he would dismay,   *except*
300 Or daunt unequall armies of his foes,
Or when the flying heavens he would affray;[7]
For so exceeding shone his glistring ray,
That Phoebus golden face it did attaint,°   *make dim*
As when a cloud his beames doth over-lay;
305 And silver Cynthia° wexèd pale and faint,   *the moon*
As when her face is staynd with magicke arts constraint.[8]

35

No magicke arts hereof had any might,
  Nor bloudie wordes of bold Enchaunters call,
But all that was not such, as seemd in sight,
310 Before that shield did fade, and suddeine fall:
And when him list the raskall routes[9] appall,
Men into stones therewith he could transmew,°   *change*
And stones to dust, and dust to nought at all;
And when him list the prouder lookes subdew,
315 He would them gazing blind, or turne to other hew.°   *form*

36

Ne let it seeme, that credence this exceedes,
  For he that made the same, was knowne right well
To have done much more admirable° deedes.   *marvelous*
It Merlin was, which whylome° did excell   *formerly*
320 All living wightes in might of magicke spell:
Both shield, and sword, and armour all he wrought
For this young Prince, when first to armes he fell;°   *came*
But when he dyde, the Faerie Queene it brought
To Faerie lond, where yet it may be seene, if sought.[1]

37

325 A gentle youth, his dearely lovèd Squire
  His speare of heben° wood behind him bare,   *ebony*
Whose harmefull head, thrice heated in the fire,
Had riven many a brest with pikehead square;
A goodly person, and could menage° faire   *control*
330 His stubborne steed with curbèd canon bit,[2]
Who under him did trample as the aire,
And chauft,° that any on his backe should sit;   *fretted*
The yron rowels° into frothy fome he bit.   *ends of the bit*

38

When as this knight nigh to the Ladie drew,
335 With lovely° court he gan her entertaine;   *kind*
But when he heard her answers loth, he knew
Some secret sorrow did her heart distraine:°   *afflict*
Which to allay, and calme her storming paine,

7. I.e., when he would frighten ("affray") the revolving constellations.
8. Magicians were believed to be able to cause an eclipse of the moon.
9. Unruly mobs.
1. I.e., Arthur's virtues may be seen still in Queen Eliz-

abeth's England. By the references to Merlin and the Faerie Queene, we now know that this knight is Arthur, identified in the *Letter to Ralegh* with "magnificence," understood as the perfection of all the virtues and containing them all.
2. "Cannon bit": a smooth, round bit.

Faire feeling words he wisely gan display,°   *pour forth*
340   And for her humour fitting purpose faine,[3]
Τo tempt the cause it selfe for to bewray;°   *reveal*
Wherewith emmoved, these bleeding words she gan to say.
                              39
"What worlds delight, or joy of living speach
Can heart, so plungèd in sea of sorrowes deepe,
345   And heapèd with so huge misfortunes, reach?
The carefull° cold beginneth for to creepe,   *afflicting*
And in my heart his yron arrow steepe,
Soone as I thinke upon my bitter bale:°   *grief*
Such helplesse harmes yts better hidden keepe,
350   Then rip up griefe, where it may not availe,
My last left comfort is, my woes to weepe and waile."
                              40
"Ah Ladie deare," quoth then the gentle knight,
"Well may I weene, your griefe is wondrous great;
For wondrous great griefe groneth in my spright,°   *spirit*
355   Whiles thus I heare you of your sorrowes treat.
But wofull Ladie let me you intrete,
For to unfold the anguish of your hart:
Mishaps are maistred by advice discrete,
And counsell mittigates the greatest smart;
360   Found never helpe, who never would his hurts impart."[4]
                              41
"O but," quoth she "great griefe will not be tould,
And can more easily be thought, then said."
"Right so"; quoth he, "but he, that never would,
Could never: will to might gives greatest aid."[5]
365   "But grief," quoth she, "does greater grow displaid,
If then it find not helpe, and breedes despaire."
"Despaire breedes not," quoth he, "where faith is staid."°   *firm*
"No faith so fast," quoth she, "but flesh does paire."°   *impair*
"Flesh may empaire," quoth he, "but reason can repaire."
                              42
370   His goodly reason, and well guided speach
So deepe did settle in her gratious thought,
That her perswaded to disclose the breach,
Which love and fortune in her heart had wrought,
And said; "Faire Sir, I hope good hap hath brought
375   You to inquire the secrets of my griefe,
Or° that your wisedome will direct my thought,   *either*
Or that your prowesse can me yield reliefe:
Then heare the storie sad, which I shall tell you briefe.
                              43
"The forlorne° Maiden, whom your eyes have seene   *forsaken*
380   The laughing stocke of fortunes mockeries,
Am th' only daughter of a King and Queene,
Whose parents deare, whilest equall destinies

---

3. I.e., suited his manner to her mood.   5. I.e., he that fails to will something cannot do it:
4. I.e., he never found help who would not tell his   willing gives the greatest help to one's power ("might").
sorrows.

Did runne about,[6] and their felicities
The favourable heavens did not envy,
385   Did spread their rule through all the territories,
Which Phison and Euphrates floweth by,
And Gehons golden waves doe wash continually.[7]

                    44

"Till that their cruell cursèd enemy,
An huge great Dragon horrible in sight,
390   Bred in the loathly lakes of Tartary,°   *Tartarus (hell)*
With murdrous ravine,° and devouring might   *destruction*
Their kingdome spoild, and countrey wasted quight:
Themselves, for feare into his jawes to fall,
He forst to castle strong to take their flight,
395   Where fast embard° in mightie brasen wall,   *imprisoned*
He has them now foure yeres besiegd to make them thrall.

                    45

"Full many knights adventurous and stout
Have enterprizd that Monster to subdew;
From every coast° that heaven walks about,   *land*
400   Have thither come the noble Martiall crew,
That famous hard atchievements still pursew,
Yet never any could that girlond win,
But all still shronke,° and still he greater grew: *quailed*
All they for want of faith, or guilt of sin,
405   The pitteous pray of his fierce crueltie have bin.

                    46

"At last yledd° with farre reported praise,   *led*
Which flying fame throughout the world had spread,
Of doughtie° knights, whom Faery land did raise,   *brave*
That noble order hight° of Maidenhed,[8]   *called*
410   Forthwith to court of Gloriane I sped,
Of Gloriane great Queene of glory bright,
Whose kingdomes seat Cleopolis[9] is red,°   *named*
There to obtaine some such redoubted knight,
That Parents deare from tyrants powre deliver might.

                    47

415   "It was my chance (my chance was faire and good)
There for to find a fresh unprovèd° knight,   *untried*
Whose manly hands imbrewed in guiltie blood
Had never bene,[1] ne ever by his might
Had throwne to ground the unregarded° right: *unrespected*
420   Yet of his prowesse proofe he since hath made
(I witnesse am) in many a cruell fight;
The groning ghosts of many one dismaide°   *defeated*
Have felt the bitter dint of his avenging blade.

                    48

"And ye the forlorne reliques of his powre,
425   His byting sword, and his devouring speare,

---

6. I.e., while the impartial fates ran their course.
7. Because these three rivers flow in the Garden of Eden (Genesis 2.11–14), we know that Eden is the country of Una's parents.
8. The type or analogue of the Order of the Garter. Its

emblem shows St. George killing the dragon and its star is the Red Cross.
9. *Cleopolis* means "famous city."
1. I.e., his strong hands had never been guiltily stained ("imbrewed") with blood.

Which have endurèd many a dreadfull stowre,°   *conflict*
Can speake his prowesse, that did earst° you beare,   *before*
And well could rule: now he hath left you heare,
To be the record of his ruefull losse,
430   And of my dolefull disaventurous deare:[2]
O heavie record of the good Redcrosse,
Where have you left your Lord, that could so well you tosse?°   *handle*
49
"Well hopèd I, and faire beginnings had,
That he my captive langour should redeeme,[3]
435   Till all unweeting,° an Enchaunter bad   *unknowing*
His sence abusd, and made him to misdeeme°   *misjudge*
My loyalty, not such as it did seeme;
That rather death desire, then such despight.[4]
Be judge ye heavens, that all things right esteeme,
440   How I him loved, and love with all my might,
So thought I eke° of him, and thinke I thought aright.   *also*
50
"Thenceforth me desolate he quite forsooke,
To wander, where wilde fortune would me lead,
And other bywaies he himselfe betooke,
445   Where never foot of living wight did tread,
That brought not backe the balefull body dead;[5]
In which him chauncèd false Duessa meete,
Mine onely foe, mine onely deadly dread,[6]
Who with her witchcraft and misseeming° sweete,   *false appearance*
450   Inveigled him to follow her desires unmeete.°   *improper*
51
"At last by subtill sleights she him betraid
Unto his foe, a Gyant huge and tall,
Who him disarmèd, dissolute,° dismaid,   *enfeebled*
Unwares surprisèd and with mightie mall°   *club*
455   The monster mercilesse him made to fall,
Whose fall did never foe before behold;
And now in darkesome dungeon, wretched thrall,
Remedilesse, for aie[7] he doth him hold;
This is my cause of griefe, more great, then may be told."
52
460   Ere she had ended all, she gan to faint:
But he her comforted and faire bespake,
"Certes, Madame, ye have great cause of plaint,
That stoutest heart, I weene, could cause to quake.
But be of cheare, and comfort to you take:
465   For till I have acquit° your captive knight,   *freed*
Assure your selfe, I will you not forsake."
His chearefull words revived her chearelesse spright,
So forth they went, the Dwarfe them guiding ever right.

2. Sad unfortunate dear one.   5. I.e., who returned alive.
3. I.e., relieve my state, captive to sadness. 6. I.e., the only object of my mortal fear.
4. I.e., I, who prefer death to such treachery ("des-   7. I.e., forever ("for aie") without hope of rescue
pight").   ("remedilesse").

Canto 8

Faire virgin to redeeme her deare
    brings Arthur to the fight:
Who slayes the Gyant, wounds the beast,
    and strips Duessa quight.

1

Ay me, how many perils doe enfold
    The righteous man, to make him daily fall?
    Were not, that heavenly grace doth him uphold,
    And stedfast truth acquite° him out of all.   deliver
5   Her love is firme, her care continuall,
    So oft as he through his owne foolish pride,
    Or weaknesse is to sinfull bands° made thrall: bonds
    Else should this Redcrosse knight in bands have dyde,
For whose deliverance she this Prince doth thither guide.

2

10 They sadly traveild thus, untill they came
    Nigh to a castle builded strong and hie:
    Then cryde the Dwarfe, "lo yonder is the same;
    In which my Lord my liege doth lucklesse lie,
    Thrall to that Gyants hatefull tyrannie:
15   Therefore, deare Sir, your mightie powres assay."°   put to trial
    The noble knight alighted by and by[8]
    From loftie steede, and bad the Ladie stay,
To see what end of fight should him befall that day.

3

So with the Squire, th' admirer of his might,
20   He marchèd forth towards that castle wall;
    Whose gates he found fast shut, ne living wight
    To ward° the same, nor answere commers call.   guard
    Then tooke that Squire an horne of bugle[9] small,
    Which hong adowne his side in twisted gold,
25   And tassels gay. Wyde wonders over all[1]
    Of that same hornes great vertues weren told,
Which had approvèd° bene in uses manifold.   demonstrated

4

Was never wight, that heard that shrilling sound,
    But trembling feare did feele in every vaine;°   vein
30   Three miles it might be easie heard around,
    And Ecchoes three answered it selfe againe:
    No false enchauntment, nor deceiptfull traine°   snare
    Might once abide the terror of that blast,
    But presently° was voide and wholly vaine: at once
35   No gate so strong, no locke so firme and fast,
But with that percing noise flew open quite, or brast.°   burst

5

The same before the Geants gate he blew,
    That all the castle quakèd from the ground,

---

8. Immediately.
9. A wild ox.
1. Everywhere. "Wide wonders": (marvelous tales) told of the horn connect it with the horn of Roland and the ram's horn of Joshua, with which he razed the walls of Jericho (Joshua 6.5); see also Romans 10.18, referring to the word of God as the horn of salvation.

And every dore of freewill open flew.
40   The Gyant selfe dismaièd with that sownd,
  Where he with his Duessa dalliance° fownd,   *amorous play*
  In hast came rushing forth from inner bowre,
  With staring° countenance sterne, as one astownd,   *glaring*
  And staggering steps, to weet, what suddein stowre°   *disturbance*
45 Had wrought that horror strange, and dared his dreaded powre.

6

And after him the proud Duessa came,
  High mounted on her manyheaded beast,
  And every head with fyrie tongue did flame,
  And every head was crownèd on his creast,
50   And bloudie mouthèd with late cruell feast.
  That when the knight beheld, his mightie shild
  Upon his manly arme he soone addrest,°   *made ready*
  And at him fiercely flew, with courage fild,
And eger greedinesse[2] through every member thrild.

7

55 Therewith the Gyant buckled him to fight,
  Inflamed with scornefull wrath and high disdaine,°   *indignation*
  And lifting up his dreadfull club on hight,
  All armed with ragged snubbes° and knottie graine,   *snags*
  Him thought at first encounter to have slaine.
60   But wise and warie was that noble Pere,°   *peer*
  And lightly leaping from so monstrous maine,°   *force*
  Did faire° avoide the violence him nere;   *quite*
It booted nought, to thinke, such thunderbolts to beare.[3]

8

Ne shame he thought to shunne so hideous might:
65   The idle° stroke, enforcing furious way,   *useless*
  Missing the marke of his misaymèd sight
  Did fall to ground, and with his° heavie sway°   *its/force*
  So deepely dinted in the driven clay,
  That three yardes deepe a furrow up did throw:
70   The sad earth wounded with so sore assay,°   *assault*
  Did grone full grievous underneath the blow,
And trembling with strange feare, did like an earthquake show.

9

As when almightie Jove in wrathfull mood,
  To wreake° the guilt of mortall sins is bent,   *punish*
75   Hurles forth his thundring dart with deadly food,[4]
  Enrold in flames, and smouldring dreriment,°   *horror*
  Through riven cloudes and molten firmament;
  The fierce threeforkèd engin° making way,   *weapon*
  Both loftie towres and highest trees hath rent,
80   And all that might his angrie passage stay,
And shooting in the earth, casts up a mount of clay.

10

His boystrous° club, so buried in the ground,   *massive*
  He could not rearen up againe so light,°   *easily*

---

2. Intense eagerness for battle.   4. Hatred (feud).
3. I.e., it is useless to think to withstand such blows.

But that the knight him at avantage found,
85   And whiles he strove his combred° clubbe to   *encumbered*
          quight°   *release*
      Out of the earth, with blade all burning bright
      He smote off his left arme, which like a blocke
      Did fall to ground, deprived of native might;
      Large streames of bloud out of the truncked stocke
90   Forth gushèd, like fresh water streame from riven rocke.[5]

                              11

      Dismaièd with so desperate deadly wound,
          And eke° impatient of unwonted paine,[6]   *also*
      He loudly brayd with beastly yelling sound,
      That all the fields rebellowèd againe;
95   As great a noyse, as when in Cymbrian[7] plaine
      An heard of Bulles, whom kindly° rage doth sting,   *natural*
      Do for the milkie mothers want complaine,[8]
      And fill the fields with troublous bellowing,
      The neighbour woods around with hollow murmur ring.

                              12

100   That when his deare Duessa heard, and saw
      The evill stownd, that daungerd her estate,[9]
      Unto his aide she hastily did draw
      Her dreadfull beast, who swolne with bloud of late
      Came ramping° forth with proud presumpteous gate,°   *rearing/gait*
105   And threatned all his heads like flaming brands.°   *torches*
      But him the Squire made quickly to retrate,
      Encountring fierce with single° sword in hand,   *only*
      And twixt him and his Lord did like a bulwarke stand,

                              13

      The proud Duessa full of wrathfull spight,
110   And fierce disdaine, to be affronted so,
      Enforst her purple beast with all her might
      That stop° out of the way to overthroe,   *obstacle*
      Scorning the let° of so unequall foe: *hindrance*
      But nathemore° would that courageous swayne   *never the more*
115   To her yeeld passage, gainst his Lord to goe,
      But with outrageous° strokes did him restraine,   *exceedingly fierce*
      And with his bodie bard the way atwixt them twaine.

                              14

      Then tooke the angrie witch her golden cup,
          Which still she bore, replete with magick artes;[1]
120   Death and despeyre did many thereof sup,
      And secret poyson through their inner parts,
      Th' eternall bale° of heavie wounded harts;   *woe*
      Which after charmes and some enchauntments said,
      She lightly sprinkled on his weaker° parts;   *too weak*

---

5. Cf. Exodus 17.6, where Moses smites the rock and
water flows forth.
6. I.e., unable to bear ("impatient of") this unfamiliar
("unwonted") pain.
7. Probably Wales.
8. I.e., mourn the cows' absence.

9. I.e., the peril ("stownd") that endangered her state.
1. Alludes to the golden cup of the woman in Revelation, which is "full of abominations and filthiness of
her fornications" (17.4); the chalice of the Roman
church; and the cup of Circe, the sorceress who turned
men into beasts (in *Odyssey* 10).

125   Therewith his sturdie courage soone was quayd,°   *quelled*
            And all his senses were with suddeine dread dismayd.
                                    15
            So downe he fell before the cruell beast,
                Who on his necke his bloudie clawes did seize,
                That life nigh crusht out of his panting brest:
130   No powre he had to stirre, nor will to rize.
                That when the carefull° knight gan well avise,°   *watchful/observe*
                He lightly° left the foe, with whom he fought,   *quickly*
                And to the beast gan turne his enterprise;
                For wondrous anguish in his hart it wrought,
135   To see his lovèd Squire into such thraldome° brought.   *slavery*
                                    16
            And high advauncing° his bloud-thirstie blade,   *lifting up*
                Stroke one of those deformèd heads so sore,[2]
                That of his puissance proud ensample made;
                His monstrous scalpe° downe to his teeth it tore   *skull*
140   And that misformèd shape mis-shapèd more:
                A sea of bloud gusht from the gaping wound,
                That her gay garments staynd with filthy gore,
                And overflowèd all the field around;
            That over shoes in bloud he waded on the ground.
                                    17
145   Thereat he roarèd for exceeding paine,
                That to have heard, great horror would have bred,°   *produced*
                And scourging th' emptie ayre with his long traine,°   *tail*
                Through great impatience of his grievèd hed[3]
                His gorgeous ryder from her loftie sted°   *place*
150   Would have cast downe, and trod in durtie myre,
                Had not the Gyant soone her succourèd;
                Who all enraged with smart° and franticke yre,°   *pain/anger*
            Came hurtling in full fierce, and forst the knight retyre.
                                    18
            The force, which wont in two to be disperst,
155   In one alone left hand[4] he now unites,
                Which is through rage more strong then both were erst;°   *before*
                With which his hideous club aloft he dites,°   *raises*
                And at his foe with furious rigour° smites,   *violence*
                That strongest Oake might seeme to overthrow:
160   The stroke upon his shield so heavie lites,
                That to the ground it doubleth him full low:
            What mortall wight could ever beare so monstrous blow?
                                    19
            And in his fall his shield, that covered was,
                Did loose his vele[5] by chaunce, and open flew:
165   The light whereof, that heavens light did pas,°   *surpass*
                Such blazing brightnesse through the aier threw,
                That eye mote not the same endure to vew.
                Which when the Gyaunt spyde with staring° eye,   *awed*

2. "I saw one of [the beast's] heads as it were wounded   afflicted ("grieved") head.
to death" (Revelation 13.3).   4. I.e., in the one hand left to him.
3. I.e., through inability to endure ("impatience") his   5. Its covering.

He downe let fall his arme, and soft withdrew
170   His weapon huge, that heavèd was on hye
For to have slaine the man, that on the ground did lye.

20

And eke the fruitfull-headed° beast, amazed   *many-headed*
    At flashing beames of that sunshiny shield,
    Became starke blind, and all his senses dazed,
175   That downe he tumbled on the durtie field,
    And seemed himselfe as conquerèd to yield.
    Whom when his maistresse proud perceived to fall,
    Whiles yet his feeble feet for faintnesse reeld,
    Unto the Gyant loudly she gan call,
180 "O helpe Orgoglio, helpe, or else we perish all."

21

At her so pitteous cry was much amooved
    Her champion stout, and for to ayde his frend,°   *lover*
    Againe his wonted angry weapon prooved:°   *tried*
    But all in vaine: for he has read his end
185   In that bright shield, and all their forces spend
    Themselves in vaine: for since that glauncing° sight,   *flashing*
    He hath no powre to hurt, nor to defend;
    As where th' Almighties lightning brond does light,
It dimmes the dazèd eyen, and daunts the senses quight.

22

190 Whom when the Prince, to battell new addrest,
    And threatning high his dreadfull stroke did see,
    His sparkling blade about his head he blest,°   *brandished*
    And smote off quite his right leg by the knee,
    That downe he tombled; as an aged tree,
195   High growing on the top of rocky clift,
    Whose hartstrings with keene steele nigh hewen be,
    The mightie trunck halfe rent, with ragged rift°   *split*
Doth roll adowne the rocks, and fall with fearefull drift.°   *impact*

23

Or as a Castle rearèd high and round,
200   By subtile engins and malitious slight[6]
    Is underminèd from the lowest ground,
    And her foundation forst,° and feebled quight,   *shattered*
    At last downe falles, and with her heapèd hight
    Her hastie ruine does more heavie make,
205   And yields it selfe unto the victours might;
    Such was this Gyaunts fall, that seemed to shake
The stedfast globe of earth, as it for feare did quake.

24

The knight then lightly° leaping to the pray,   *quickly*
    With mortall steele him smot againe so sore,
210   That headlesse his unweldy bodie lay,
    All wallowd in his owne fowle bloudy gore,
    Which flowèd from his wounds in wondrous store.
    But soone as breath out of his breast did pas,

---

6. Clever machines of war ("engins") and evil strategy.

That huge great body, which the Gyaunt bore,
215   Was vanisht quite, and of that monstrous mas
Was nothing left, but like an emptie bladder was.

25

Whose grievous fall, when false Duessa spide,
  Her golden cup she cast unto the ground,
  And crownèd mitre[7] rudely° threw aside;   *violently*
220   Such percing griefe her stubborne hart did wound,
  That she could not endure that dolefull stound,°   *sorrow*
  But leaving all behind her, fled away:
  The light-foot Squire her quickly turned around,
  And by hard meanes enforcing her to stay,
225 So brought unto his Lord, as his deservèd pray.

26

The royall Virgin, which beheld from farre,
  In pensive° plight, and sad perplexitie,   *anxious*
  The whole atchievement of this doubtfull warre,[8]
  Came running fast to greet his victorie,
230   With sober gladnesse, and myld modestie,
  And with sweet joyous cheare him thus bespake;
  "Faire braunch of noblesse, flowre of chevalrie,
  That with your worth the world amazèd make,
How shall I quite° the paines, ye suffer for my sake?   *requite*

27

235 "And you[9] fresh bud of vertue springing fast,
  Whom these sad eyes saw nigh unto deaths dore,
  What hath poore Virgin for such perill past,
  Wherewith you to reward? Accept therefore
  My simple selfe, and service evermore;
240   And he that high does sit, and all things see
  With equall° eyes, their merites to restore,°   *impartial/reward*
  Behold what ye this day have done for mee,
And what I cannot quite, requite with usuree.°   *interest*

28

"But sith the heavens, and your faire handeling°   *conduct*
245   Have made you maister of the field this day,
  Your fortune maister eke with governing,[1]
  And well begun end all so well, I pray,
  Ne let that wicked woman scape away;
  For she it is, that did my Lord bethrall,
250   My dearest Lord, and deepe in dongeon lay,
  Where he his better dayes hath wasted all.[2]
O heare, how piteous he to you for ayd does call."

29

Forthwith he gave in charge unto his Squire,
  That scarlot whore to keepen carefully;
255   Whiles he himselfe with greedie° great desire   *eager*
  Into the Castle entred forcibly,

---

7. An allusion to the pope's triple tiara.
8. I.e., the final outcome, long in doubt ("doubtfull")
of this battle.
9. I.e., the Squire.

1. Secure your good fortune also by prudent management.
2. I.e., he has consumed ("wasted") here his best days.

Where living creature none he did espye;
Then gan he lowdly through the house to call:
But no man cared to answere to his crye.
260   There raignd a solemne silence over all,
Nor voice was heard, nor wight was seene in bowre or hall.

30

At last with creeping crooked pace forth came
An old old man, with beard as white as snow,
That on a staffe his feeble steps did frame,°   support
265   And guide his wearie gate° both too and fro: gait
For his eye sight him failèd long ygo,
And on his arme a bounch of keyes he bore,
The which unusèd rust did overgrow:
Those were the keyes of every inner dore,
270   But he could not them use, but kept them still in store.

31

But very uncouth° sight was to behold,   strange
How he did fashion his untoward° pace,   awkward
For as he forward mooved his footing old,
So backward still was turned his wrincled face,
275   Unlike to men, who ever as they trace,°   walk
Both feet and face one way are wont to lead.
This was the auncient keeper of that place,
And foster father of the Gyant dead;
His name Ignaro did his nature right aread.[3]

32

280   His reverend haires and holy gravitie
The knight much honord, as beseemèd well,[4]
And gently askt, where all the people bee,
Which in that stately building wont to dwell.
Who answerd him full soft, he could not tell.
285   Againe he askt, where that same knight was layd,
Whom great Orgoglio with his puissaunce fell
Had made his caytive° thrall; againe he sayde,   captive
He could not tell: ne ever other answere made.

33

Then askèd he, which way he in might pas:
290   He could not tell, againe he answerèd.
Thereat the curteous knight displeasèd was,
And said, "Old sire, it seemes thou hast not red°   recognized
How ill it sits with° that same silver hed   suits
In vaine to mocke, or mockt in vaine to bee:
295   But if thou be, as thou art pourtrahèd
With natures pen, in ages grave degree,[5]
Aread° in graver wise, what I demaund of thee."   answer

34

His answere likewise was, he could not tell.
Whose sencelesse speach, and doted° ignorance   foolish
300   When as the noble Prince had markèd well,
He ghest his nature by his countenance,

---

3. His name Ignaro makes clear ("did aread") that his
nature is Ignorance.

4. Seemed proper.

5. I.e., dignity.

  And calmd his wrath with goodly temperance.
  Then to him stepping, from his arme did reach
  Those keyes, and made himselfe free enterance.
305 Each dore he openèd without any breach;°   *forcing*
  There was no barre to stop, nor foe him to empeach.° *hinder*

         35
  There all within full rich arayd he found,
  With royal arras° and resplendent gold.   *tapestry*
  And did with store of every thing abound,
310 That greatest Princes presence° might behold.   *person*
  But all the floore (too filthy to be told)
  With bloud of guiltlesse babes, and innocents trew,[6]
  Which there were slaine, as sheepe out of the fold,
  Defilèd was, that dreadfull was to vew,
315 And sacred ashes over it was strowèd new.

         36
  And there beside of marble stone was built
  An Altare, carved with cunning imagery,°   *images*
  On which true Christians bloud was often spilt,
  And holy Martyrs often doen to dye,[7]
320 With cruell malice and strong tyranny:
  Whose blessed sprites from underneath the stone
  To God for vengeance cryde continually,[8]
  And with great griefe were often heard to grone,
  That hardest heart would bleede, to heare their piteous mone.

         37
325 Through every rowme he sought, and every bowr,
  But no where could he find that wofull thrall:
  At last he came unto an yron doore,
  That fast was lockt, but key found not at all
  Emongst that bounch, to open it withall;
330 But in the same a little grate was pight,°   *placed*
  Through which he sent his voyce, and lowd did call
  With all his powre, to weet, if living wight
  Were housèd therewithin, whom he enlargen° might. *set free*

         38
  Therewith an hollow, dreary, murmuring voyce
335 These piteous plaints and dolours° did resound; *laments*
  "O who is that, which brings me happy choyce° *chance*
  Of death, that here lye dying every stound,°   *moment*
  Yet live perforce in balefull° darkenesse bound? *evil*
  For now three Moones have changèd thrice their hew,° *shape*
340 And have beene thrice hid underneath the ground,
  Since I the heavens chearefull face did vew,
  O welcome thou, that doest of death bring tydings trew."

---

6. Probably a reference to Herod's massacre of the Innocents (Matthew 2.16), traditionally viewed as the first martyrs for Christ.
7. Put to death.
8. "And when he had opened the fifth seal, I saw under the altar the souls of them that were slain for the word of God, and for the testimony which they held: / And they cried with a loud voice, saying, How long, O Lord, holy and true, dost thou not judge and avenge our blood on them that dwell on the earth?" (Revelation 6.9–10).

39

Which when that Champion heard, with percing point
  Of pitty deare° his hart was thrillèd sore,   *extreme*
345 And trembling horrour ran through every joynt,
  For ruth of gentle knight so fowle forlore:[9]
  Which shaking off, he rent that yron dore,
  With furious force, and indignation fell;°   *fierce*
  Where entred in, his foot could find no flore,
350 But all a deepe descent, as darke as hell,
That breathèd ever forth a filthie banefull smell.

40

But neither darkenesse fowle, nor filthy bands,
  Nor noyous° smell his purpose could withhold,   *noxious*
  (Entire affection hateth nicer° hands)   *too fastidious*
355 But that with constant zeale, and courage bold,
  After long paines and labours manifold,
  He found the meanes that Prisoner up to reare;
  Whose feeble thighes, unhable to uphold
  His pinèd° corse, him scarse to light could beare,   *wasted*
360 A ruefull spectacle of deathe and ghastly drere.°   *wretchedness*

41

His sad dull eyes deepe sunck in hollow pits,
  Could not endure th' unwonted sunne to view;
  His bare thin cheekes for want of better bits,°   *food*
  And empty sides deceivèd° of their dew,   *cheated*
365 Could make a stony hart his hap to rew;
  His rawbone armes, whose mighty brawnèd bowrs[1]
  Were wont to rive steele plates, and helmets hew,
  Were cleane consumed, and all his vitall powres
Decayd, and all his flesh shronk up like withered flowres.

42

370 Whom when his Lady saw, to him she ran
  With hasty joy: to see him made her glad,
  And sad to view his visage pale and wan,
  Who earst in flowres of freshest youth was clad.
  Tho when her well of teares she wasted had,
375 She said, "Ah dearest Lord, what evill starre
  On you hath frownd, and pourd his influence bad,
  That of your selfe ye thus berobbèd arre,
And this misseeming hew[2] your manly looks doth marre?

43

"But welcome now my Lord, in wele or woe,
380 Whose presence I have lackt to long a day;
  And fie on Fortune mine avowèd foe,
  Whose wrathfull wreakes° them selves do now alay.   *punishments*
  And for these wrongs shall treble penaunce pay
  Of treble good: good growes of evils priefe."[3]
385 The chearelesse man, whom sorrow did dismay,°   *unnerve*

9. Foully forsaken.
1. Brawny muscles.
2. Unseemly shape.

3. I.e., Fortune will now make amends for his wrongs
with triple benefits, as good comes from evils endured
("priefe").

Had no delight to treaten° of his griefe;   *speak*
His long endurèd famine needed more reliefe.

                    44
"Faire Lady," then said that victorious knight,[4]
    "The things, that grievous were to do, or beare,
390   Them to renew,° I wote,° breeds no delight;   *recall/know*
    Best musicke breeds delight in loathing eare
    But th' onely good, that growes of passèd feare,
    Is to be wise, and ware° of like agein.   *wary*
    This dayes ensample hath this lesson deare
395   Deepe written in my heart with yron pen,
That blisse may not abide in state of mortall men.

                    45
"Henceforth sir knight, take to you wonted strength,
    And maister these mishaps with patient might;
    Loe where your foe lyes stretcht in monstrous length,
400   And loe that wicked woman in your sight,
    The roote of all your care, and wretched plight,
    Now in your powre, to let her live, or dye."
    "To do her dye," quoth Una, "were despight,[5]
    And shame t' avenge so weake an enimy;
405 But spoile° her of her scarlot robe, and let her fly."   *despoil*

                    46
So as she bad, that witch they disaraid,
    And robd of royall robes, and purple pall,°   *cloak*
    And ornaments that richly were displaid;
    Ne sparèd they to strip her naked all.
410   Then when they had despoild her tire° and call,°   *robe/headdress*
    Such as she was, their eyes might her behold,
    That her misshapèd parts did them appall,
    A loathly, wrinckled hag, ill favoured, old,
Whose secret filth good manners biddeth not be told.

                    47
415 Her craftie head was altogether bald,
    And as in hate of honorable eld,°   *age*
    Was overgrowne with scurfe° and filthy scald;[6]   *scabs*
    Her teeth out of her rotten gummes were feld,°   *fallen*
    And her sowre breath abhominably smeld;
420   Her dried dugs, like bladders lacking wind,
    Hong downe, and filthy matter from them weld;°   *welled*
    Her wrizled° skin as rough, as maple rind,   *wrinkled*
So scabby was, that would have loathd all womankind.

                    48
Her neather parts, the shame of all her kind,[7]
425   My chaster Muse for shame doth blush to write;
    But at her rompe she growing had behind
    A foxes taile, with dong all fowly dight;°   *covered*
    And eke her feete most monstrous were in sight;
    For one of them was like an Eagles claw,
430   With griping talaunts armd to greedy fight,

---

4. Arthur.   6. A scabby disease of the scalp.
5. I.e., to cause her to die would be despicable.   7. I.e., womankind.

The other like a Beares uneven° paw: *rough*
More ugly shape yet never living creature saw.[8]

49

Which when the knights beheld, amazd they were,
And wondred at so fowle deformèd wight.
435 "Such their," said Una, "as she seemeth here,
Such is the face of falshood, such the sight
Of fowle Duessa, when her borrowed light
Is laid away, and counterfesaunce° knowne."   *deceit*
Thus when they had the witch disrobèd quight,
440 And all her filthy feature° open showne,   *form*
They let her goe at will, and wander wayes unknowne.

50

She flying fast from heavens hated face,
And from the world that her discovered wide,
Fled to the wastfull° wildernesse apace,   *desolate*
445 From living eyes her open shame to hide,
And lurkt in rocks and caves long unespide.
But that faire crew° of knights, and Una faire   *company*
Did in that castle afterwards abide,
To rest them selves, and weary powres repaire,
450 Where store they found of all, that dainty° was and rare. *precious*

Canto 9

His loves and lignage Arthur tells:
 The knights knit friendly bands:°   *bonds*
Sir Trevisan flies from Despayre,
 Whom Redcrosse knight withstands.

1

O goodly golden chaine,[9] wherewith yfere°   *together*
The vertues linkèd are in lovely wize:
And noble minds of yore allyèd were,
In brave poursuit of chevalrous emprize,°   *adventure*
5 That none did others safety despize,°   *disregard*
Nor aid envy° to him, in need that stands,   *begrudge*
But friendly each did others prayse devize
How to advaunce with favourable hands,
As this good Prince redeemd the Redcrosse knight from bands.

2

10 Who when their powres, empaird through labour long,
With dew repast they had recurèd° well,   *restored*
And that weake captive wight now wexèd strong,
Them list no lenger there at leasure dwell,
But forward fare, as their adventures fell,
15 But ere they parted, Una faire besought
That straunger knight his name and nation tell;

---

8. An allusion to Revelation 17.16: "these shall hate the whore, and shall make her desolate and naked." Foxes were emblems of cunning; eagles and bears, of rapacity, cruelty, and brutality.

9. The golden chain of love or concord that binds the world and the human race together (cf. 1.5.25 and n. 4).

   Least so great good, as he for her had wrought,
  Should die unknown, and buried be in thanklesse thought.

3

   "Faire virgin," said the Prince, "ye me require
20 A thing without the compas[1] of my wit:
  For both the lignage and the certain Sire,
  From which I sprong, from me are hidden yit.
  For all so soone as life did me admit
  Into this world, and shewèd heavens light,
25 From mothers pap I taken was unfit:[2]
  And streight delivered to a Faery knight,
  To be upbrought in gentle thewes° and martiall might.   *manners*

4

   "Unto old Timon[3] he me brought bylive,°   *immediately*
  Old Timon, who in youthly yeares hath beene
30 In warlike feates th' expertest man alive,
  And is the wisest now on earth I weene;
  His dwelling is low in a valley greene,
  Under the foot of Rauran mossy hore,°   *gray*
  From whence the river Dee as silver cleene°   *pure*
35 His tombling billowes rolls with gentle rore:[4]
  There all my dayes he traind me up in vertuous lore.

5

   "Thither the great Magicien Merlin came,
  As was his use, ofttimes to visit me:
  For he had charge my disciplne° to frame,   *education*
40 And Tutours nouriture° to oversee.   *upbringing*
  Him oft and oft I askt in privitie,
  Of what loines and what lignage I did spring:
  Whose aunswere bad me still assurèd bee,
  That I was sonne and heire unto a king,
45 As time in her just terme[5] the truth to light should bring."

6

   "Well worthy impe,"° said then the Lady gent,°   *offspring/gentle*
  "And Pupill fit for such a Tutours hand.
  But what adventure, or what high intent
  Hath brought you hither into Faery land,
50 Aread° Prince Arthur,[6] crowne of Martiall band?"   *declare*
  "Full hard it is," quoth he, "to read° aright   *discern*
  The course of heavenly cause, or understand
  The secret meaning of th' eternall might,
  That rules mens wayes, and rules the thoughts of living wight.

7

55 "For whither he through fatall deepe foresight[7]
  Me hither sent, for cause to me unghest,
  Or that fresh bleeding wound, which day and night
  Whilome° doth rancle in my riven brest,   *all the while*

---

1. I.e., beyond the reach of.
2. I.e., not yet weaned.
3. The name means "honor."
4. The hill Rauran is in Wales; the river Dee also flows in, and forms part of, the boundary of Wales. The Tudors (Queen Elizabeth's family) were originally

Welsh, and the legends of Arthur had their beginnings in the Celtic mythology of early Wales.
5. Due course.
6. Arthur is named here for the first time.
7. I.e., whether he (God, "eternal might") sent me here through foresight ordained by fate ("fatall").

With forcèd fury following his° behest,   *its*
60   Me hither brought by wayes yet never found,
You to have helpt I hold my selfe yet blest."
"Ah curteous knight," quoth she, "what secret wound
Could ever find,° to grieve the gentlest hart on ground?"   *succeed*

8

"Deare Dame," quoth he, "you sleeping sparkes awake,
65   Which trubled once, into huge flames will grow,
Ne ever will their fervent fury slake
Till living moysture into smoke do flow,
And wasted° life do lye in ashes low.   *consumed*
Yet sithens° silence lesseneth not my fire,   *since*
70   But told it flames, and hidden it does glow,
I will revele, what ye so much desire:
Ah Love, lay downe thy bow, the whiles I may respire.°   *breathe*

9

"It was in freshest flowre of youthly yeares,
When courage first does creepe in manly chest,
75   Then first the coale of kindly° heat appeares   *natural*
To kindle love in every living brest;
But me had warnd old Timons wise behest,
Those creeping flames by reason to subdew,
Before their rage grew to so great unrest,
80   As miserable lovers use to rew,
Which still wex° old in woe, whiles woe still wexeth new.   *grow*

10

"That idle name of love, and lovers life,
As losse of time, and vertues enimy
I ever scornd, and joyd to stirre up strife,
85   In middest of their mournfull Tragedy,
Ay wont to laugh, when them I heard to cry,
And blow the fire, which them to ashes brent:°   *burned*
Their God himselfe, grieved at my libertie,
Shot many a dart at me with fiers intent,
90   But I them warded all with wary government.[8]

11

"But all in vaine: no fort can be so strong,
Ne fleshly brest can armèd be so sound,
But will at last be wonne with battrie° long,   *siege*
Or unawares at disavantage found;
95   Nothing is sure, that growes on earthly ground:
And who most trustes in arme of fleshly might,
And boasts, in beauties chaine not to be bound,
Doth soonest fall in disaventrous° fight.   *disastrous*
And yeeldes his caytive neck to victours most° despight.   *greatest*

12

100   "Ensample make of him your haplesse joy,
And of my selfe now mated,° as ye see;   *overcome*
Whose prouder° vaunt that proud avenging boy   *too proud*
Did soone pluck downe, and curbd my libertie.

8. I.e., self-control. The descriptions here of Cupid's archery and of the siege of the castle of chastity (in the next stanza) have many echoes from the courtly love traditions.

    For on a day prickt° forth with jollitie   *spurred*
105   Of looser life, and heat of hardiment,°   *boldness*
    Raunging the forest wide on courser free,
    The fields, the floods, the heavens with one consent
Did seeme to laugh° on me, and favour mine intent.   *smile*

13

    "For-wearied° with my sports, I did alight   *utterly wearied*
110   From loftie steed, and downe to sleepe me layd;
    The verdant° gras my couch did goodly dight,°   *green/make*
    And pillow was my helmet faire displayd:
    Whiles every sence the humour sweet embayd,[9]
    And slombring soft my hart did steale away,
115   Me seemèd, by my side a royall Mayd
    Her daintie limbes full softly down did lay:
So faire a creature yet saw never sunny day.

14

    "Most goodly glee° and lovely blandishment°   *entertainment/compliment*
    She to me made, and bad me love here deare,
120   For dearely sure her love was to me bent,
    As when just time expirèd[1] should appeare.
    But whether dreames delude, or true it were,
    Was never hart so ravisht with delight,
    Ne living man like words did ever heare,
125   As she to me delivered all that night;
And at her parting said, She Queene of Faeries hight.°[2]   *was called*

15

    "When I awoke, and found her place devoyd,°   *empty*
    And nought but pressèd gras, where she had lyen,
    I sorrowed all so much, as earst I joyd,
130   And washèd all her place with watry eyen.
    From that day forth I loved that face divine;
    From that day forth I cast in carefull° mind,   *care-filled*
    To seeke her out with labour, and long tyne,°   *hardship*
    And never vow to rest, till her I find,
135   Nine monethes I seeke in vaine yet ni'll° that vow unbind."   *will not*

16

    Thus as he spake, his visage wexèd pale,
    And chaunge of hew great passion did bewray;°   *reveal*
    Yet still he strove to cloke his inward bale,°   *grief*
    And hide the smoke, that did his fire display,
140   Till gentle Una thus to him gan say;
    "Oh happy Queene of Faeries, that hast found
    Mongst many, one that with his prowesse may
    Defend thine honour, and thy foes confound:
True Loves are often sown, but seldom grow on ground."

17

145   "Thine, O then," said the gentle Redcrosse knight,
    "Next to that Ladies love, shalbe the place,

9. I.e., while the dew of sleep ("humour") pervaded ("embayd") every sense.
1. A fitting length of time having passed.
2. In the background are many folktales and ballads of a hero bewitched by the Queen of Faerie Land. Spenser's *Letter to Ralegh* identifies Gloriana allegorically with glory and with Queen Elizabeth.

  O fairest virgin, full of heavenly light,
  Whose wondrous faith, exceeding earthly race,
  Was firmest fixt in mine extremest case.°   *plight*
150 And you, my Lord, the Patrone° of my life,   *protector*
  Of that great Queene may well gaine worthy grace:
  For onely worthy you through prowes priefe³
Yf living man mote° worthy be, to be her liefe."°   *may/love*
        18
  So diversly discoursing of their loves,
155 The golden Sunne his glistring head gan shew,
  And sad remembraunce now the Prince amoves,
  With fresh desire his voyage to pursew:
  Als° Una earnd° her traveill to renew.   *so/yearned*
  Then those two knights, fast friendship for to bynd,
160 And love establish each to other trew,
  Gave goodly gifts, the signes of gratefull mynd,
And eke as pledges firme, right hands together joynd.
        19
  Prince Arthur gave a boxe of Diamond sure,°   *true*
  Embowd° with gold and gorgeous ornament,   *bound*
165 Wherein were closd few drops of liquor pure,
  Of wondrous worth, and vertue excellent,
  That any wound could heale incontinent:°   *immediately*
  Which to requite, the Redcrosse knight him gave
  A booke, wherein his Saveours testament
170 Was writ with golden letters rich and brave;° *splendid*
A worke of wondrous grace, and able soules to save.⁴
        20
  Thus beene they parted, Arthur on his way
  To seeke his love, and th' other for to fight
  With Unas foe, that all her realme did pray.°   *prey on*
175 But she now weighing the decayèd plight,
  And shrunken synewes of her chosen knight,
  Would not a while her forward course pursew,
  Ne bring him forth in face of dreadfull fight,
  Till he recovered had his former hew:°   *appearance*
180 For him to be yet weake and wearie well she knew.
        21
  So as they traveild, lo they gan espy
  An armèd knight towards them gallop fast,
  That seemèd from some fearèd foe to fly,
  Or other griesly thing, that him agast.°   *terrified*
185 Still as he fled, his eye was backward cast,
  As if his feare still followed him behind;
  Als flew his steed, as he his bands had brast,° *broken*
  And with his wingèd heeles did tread the wind,
As he had beene a fole of Pegasus his kind.⁵

---

3. Demonstration of prowess.
4. Medieval romances mention such healing balms, but here the "drops of liquor pure" represent grace, perhaps in the Eucharist; Redcrosse gives Arthur the

New Testament.
5. I.e., as if he had been a foal of a horse like Pegasus (a flying horse).

22

190   Nigh as he drew, they might perceive his head
     To be unarmd, and curld uncombèd heares
     Upstaring° stiffe, dismayd with uncouth° dread;   *bristling/unknown*
     Nor drop of bloud in all his face appeares
     Nor life in limbe: and to increase his feares,
195   In fowle reproch° of knighthoods faire degree,°   *disgrace/condition*
     About his neck an hempen rope he weares,
     That with his glistring armes does ill agree;
But he of rope or armes has now no memoree.

23

   The Redcrosse knight toward him crossèd fast,
200   To weet, what mister° wight was so dismayd: *kind of*
     There him he finds all sencelesse and aghast,
     That of him selfe he seemd to be afrayd;
     Whom hardly he from flying forward stayd,
     Till he these wordes to him deliver might;
205   "Sir knight, aread° who hath ye thus arayd,   *declare*
     And eke° from whom make ye this hasty flight: *also*
For never knight I saw in such misseeming° plight."   *unseemly*

24

   He answerd nought at all, but adding new
     Feare to his first amazment, staring wide
210   With stony eyes, and hartlesse hollow hew,[6]
     Astonisht stood, as one that had aspide
     Infernall furies, with their chaines untido.
     Him yet againe, and yet againe bespake
     The gentle knight; who nought to him replide,
215   But trembling every joynt did inly quake,
And foltring tongue at last these words seemd forth to shake.

25

   "For Gods deare love, Sir knight, do me not stay;
     For loe he comes, he comes fast after mee."
     Eft° looking backe would faine have runne away;   *again*
220   But he him forst to stay, and tellen free
     The secret cause of his perplexitie:°   *distress*
     Yet nathemore° by his bold hartie speach,   *not at all*
     Could his bloud-frosen hart emboldned bee,
     But through his boldnesse rather feare did reach,
225   Yet forst, at last he made through silence suddein breach.

26

   "And am I now in safetie sure," quoth he,
     "From him, that would have forcèd me to dye?
     And is the point of death now turnd fro mee,
     That I may tell this haplesse history?"
230   "Feare nought:" quoth he, "no daunger now is nye."
     "Then shall I you recount a ruefull cace,"°   *event*
     Said he, "the which with this unlucky eye
     I late beheld, and had not greater grace
Me reft° from it, had bene partaker of the place.[7]   *carried*

---

6. I.e., with blanched, bloodless countenance.   7. I.e., shared the same fate.

27

235 "I lately chaunst (Would I had never chaunst)
        With a faire knight to keepen companee,
        Sir Terwin hight, that well himselfe advaunst
        In all affaires, and was both bold and free,
        But not so happie as mote happie bee:
240   He loved, as was his lot, a Ladie gent,°   *noble*
        That him againe° loved in the least degree: *in return*
        For she was proud, and of too high intent,°   *spirit*
    And joyd to see her lover languish and lament.

28

    "From whom returning sad and comfortlesse,°   *desolate*
245   As on the way together we did fare,
        We met that villen (God from him me blesse°)   *defend*
        That cursèd wight, from whom I scapt why leare,[8]
        A man of hell, that cals himselfe Despaire;[9]
        Who first us greets, and after faire areedes°   *tells*
250   Of tydings strange, and of adventures rare:
    So creeping close, as Snake in hidden weedes,
    Inquireth of our states, and of our knightly deedes.

29

    "Which when he knew, and felt our feeble harts
        Embost° with bale,° and bitter byting griefe,   *exhausted/sorrow*
255   Which love had launchèd° with his deadly darts,   *pierced*
        With wounding words and termes of foule repriefe°   *insult*
        He pluckt from us all hope of due reliefe,
        That earst us held in love of lingring life;
        Then hopelesse hartlesse, gan the cunning thiefe
260   Perswade us die, to stint° all further strife: *end*
    To me he lent this rope, to him a rustie knife.

30

    "With which sad instrument of hastie death,
        That wofull lover, loathing lenger° light,   *longer*
        A wide way made to let forth living breath.
265   But I more fearefull, or more luckie wight,
        Dismayd with that deformèd dismall sight,
        Fled fast away, halfe dead with dying feare:[1]
        Ne yet assured of life by you, Sir knight,
        Whose like infirmitie like chaunce may beare:
270   But God you never let his charmèd speeches heare."[2]

31

    "How may a man," said he, "with idle speach
        Be wonne, to spoyle° the Castle of his health?"   *destroy*
        "I wote," quoth he, "whom triall° late did teach,   *experience*
        That like would not[3] for all this worldes wealth:
275   His subtill tongue, like dropping honny, mealt'th°   *melts*
        Into the hart, and searcheth every vaine,
        That ere one be aware, by secret stealth

8. A while before.
9. Despair is the ultimate Christian sin, denying the
possibility of Divine mercy and grace. Dr. Faustus at
the end of Marlowe's play is in a state of despair (pp.
463–464).

1. Fear of death.
2. I.e., may God never let you hear his mesmerizing
("charmed") speeches.
3. I.e., would not do the like again.

His powre is reft, and weaknesse doth remaine.
O never Sir desire to try° his guilefull traine."°   *test/treachery*

32

280 "Certes,"° said he, "hence shall I never rest,   *surely*
    Till I that treachours art have heard and tride;
    And you Sir knight, whose name mote° I request,   *might*
    Of grace° do me unto his cabin° guide."   *favor/cave*
    "I that hight° Trevisan,"[4] quoth he, "will ride   *am called*
285 Against my liking backe, to doe you grace:
    But nor for gold nor glee[5] will I abide
    By you, when ye arrive in that same place;
For lever° had I die, then see his deadly face."   *rather*

33

Ere long they come, where that same wicked wight
290 His dwelling has, low in an hollow cave,
    Farre underneath a craggie clift ypight,°   *placed*
    Darke, dolefull, drearie, like a greedie grave,
    That still for carrion carcases doth crave:
    On top whereof aye dwelt the ghastly Owle,[6]
295 Shrieking his balefull note, which ever drave
    Farre from that haunt all other chearefull fowle;
And all about it wandring ghostes did waile and howle.

34

And all about old stockes° and stubs of trees,   *stumps*
    Whereon nor fruit, nor leafe was ever seene,
300 Did hang upon the ragged rocky knees,°   *crags*
    On which had many wretches hangèd beene,
    Whose carcases were scattered on the greene,
    And throwne about the cliffs. Arrivèd there,
    That bare-head knight for dread and dolefull teene,°   *grief*
305 Would faine° have fled, ne durst approachen neare,   *gladly*
But th' other forst him stay, and comforted in feare.

35

That darkesome cave they enter, where they find
    That cursèd man, low sitting on the ground,
    Musing full sadly in his sullein° mind;   *morose*
310 His griesie° lockes, long growen, and unbound,   *gray*
    Disordred hong about his shoulders round,
    And hid his face; through which his hollow eyne
    Lookt deadly dull, and starèd as astound;
    His raw-bone cheekes through penurie and pine,°   *starvation*
315 Were shronke into his jawes, as° he did never dine.   *as if*

36

His garment nought but many ragged clouts,°   *rags*
    With thornes together pind and patchèd was,
    The which his naked sides he wrapt abouts;
    And him beside there lay upon the gras
320 A drearie° corse, whose life away did pas,   *bloody*
    All wallowd in his owne yet luke-warme blood,
    That from his wound yet wellèd fresh alas;

---

4. His name may connote weariness or fatigue ("terwyn").   5. Song; i.e., anything you can say to me.
6. Traditionally a messenger of death.

In which a rustie° knife fast fixèd stood,   *bloodstained*
And made an open passage for the gushing flood.

37

325 Which piteous spectacle, approving° trew   *confirming*
        The wofull tale that Trevisan had told,
        When as the gentle Redcrosse knight did vew,
        With firie zeale he burnt in courage bold,
        Him to avenge, before his bloud were cold,
330   And to the villein said, "Thou damnèd wight,
        The author of this fact,° we here behold,   *deed*
        What justice can but judge against thee right,
With thine owne bloud to price° his bloud, here shed in sight?" *pay for*

38

"What franticke fit," quoth he,[7] "hath thus distraught
335   Thee, foolish man, so rash a doome° to give?   *judgment*
        What justice ever other judgement taught,
        But he should die, who merites not to live?
        None else to death this man despayring drive,°   *drove*
        But his owne guiltie mind deserving death.
340   Is then unjust to each his due to give?
        Or let him die, that loatheth living breath?
Or let him die at ease, that liveth here uneath?°   *in unease*

39

"Who travels by the wearie wandring way,
        To come unto his wishèd home in haste,
345   And meetes a flood, that doth his passage stay,
        Is not great grace to helpe him over past,
        Or free his feet, that in the myre sticke fast?
        Most envious man, that grieves at neighbours good,
        And fond,° that joyest in the woe thou hast,   *foolish*
350   Why wilt not let him passe, that long hath stood
Upon the banke, yet wilt thy selfe not passe the flood?

40

"He there does now enjoy eternall rest
        And happie ease, which thou doest want and crave,
        And further from it daily wanderest:
355   What if some litle paine the passage have,
        That makes fraile flesh to feare the bitter wave?
        Is not short paine well borne, that brings long ease,
        And layes the soule to sleepe in quiet grave?
        Sleepe after toyle, port after stormie seas,
360   Ease after warre, death after life does greatly please."[8]

41

The knight much wondred at his suddeine wit,[9]
        And said, "The terme of life is limited,
        Ne may a man prolong, nor shorten it;
        The souldier may not move from watchfull sted,[1]
365   Nor leave his stand, untill his Captaine bed."°   *commands*

7. I.e., Despaire.
8. Despaire's arguments on behalf of suicide as against a painful life are derived, like those of Hamlet in his third soliloquy (*Hamlet* 3.1.56–88), principally from Seneca, Marcus Aurelius, other ancient Stoics, and Old Testament statements on divine justice. His speech is devised according to classical rules of rhetoric.
9. Quick intelligence.
1. The sentry post assigned him.

"Who life did limit by almightie doome,"
Quoth he,[2] "knowes best the termes establishèd;
And he, that points the Centonell his roome,°   *station*
Doth license him depart at sound of morning droome.[3]

42

370   "Is not his deed, what ever thing is donne,
In heaven and earth? did not he all create
To die againe? all ends that was begonne.
Their times in his eternall booke of fate
Are written sure, and have their certaine° date.   *fixed*
375   Who then can strive with strong necessitie,
That holds the world in his still chaunging state,
Or shunne the death ordaynd by destinie?
When houre of death is come, let none aske whence, nor why.

43

"The lenger life, I wote° the greater sin,   *know*
380   The greater sin, the greater punishment:
All those great battels, which thou boasts to win,
Through strife, and bloud-shed, and avengement,
Now praysd, hereafter deare° thou shalt repent: *bitterly*
For life must life, and bloud must bloud repay.[4]
385   Is not enough thy evill life forespent?
For he, that once hath missèd the right way,
The further he doth goe, the further he doth stray.

44

"Then do no further goe, no further stray,
But here lie downe, and to thy rest betake,
390   Th' ill to prevent, that life ensewen may.[5]
For what hath life, that may it lovèd make,
And gives not rather cause it to forsake?
Feare, sicknesse, age, losse, labour, sorrow, strife,
Paine, hunger, cold, that makes the hart to quake;
395   And ever fickle fortune rageth rife,
All which, and thousands mo° do make a loathsome life.   *more*

45

"Thou wretched man, of death hast greatest need,
If in true ballance thou wilt weigh thy state:
For never knight, that darèd warlike deede,
400   More lucklesse disaventures° did amate:°   *misfortunes/appall*
Witnesse the dongeon deepe, wherein of late
Thy life shut up, for death so oft did call;
And though good lucke prolongèd hath thy date,°   *span of life*
Yet death then, would the like mishaps forestall,
405   Into the which hereafter thou maiest happen fall.[6]

46

"Why then doest thou, O man of sin, desire
To draw thy dayes forth to their last degree?
Is not the measure of thy sinfull hire[7]

2. Despaire.
3. Drum, with a pun on *doom.*
4. An echo of Genesis 9.6: "Whoso sheddeth man's blood, by man shall his blood be shed."

5. I.e., to prevent the evil that will ensue in the rest of your life.
6. Happen to fall.
7. Service to sin.

  High heapèd up with huge iniquitie,
410 Against the day of wrath,[8] to burden thee?
  Is not enough that to this Ladie milde
   Thou falsèd° hast thy faith with perjurie,   *betrayed*
   And sold thy selfe to serve Duessa vilde,°   *vile*
  With whom in all abuse thou hast thy selfe defilde?

47

415 "Is not he just, that all this doth behold
  From highest heaven, and beares an equall° eye?   *impartial*
  Shall he thy sins up in his knowledge fold,
  And guiltie be of thine impietie?
  Is not his law, Let every sinner die:[9]
420 Die shall all flesh? what then must needs be donne,
  Is it not better to doe willinglie,
   Then linger, till the glasse° be all out ronne?   *hourglass*
  Death is the end of woes: die soone, O faeries sonne."

48

  The knight was much enmovèd with his speach,
425 That as a swords point through his hart did perse,
  And in his conscience made a secret breach,
   Well knowing true all, that he did reherse°   *recount*
   And to his fresh remembrance did reverse°   *bring back*
  The ugly vew of his deformèd crimes,
430 That all his manly powres it did disperse,
  As he were charmèd with inchaunted rimes,
  That oftentimes he quakt, and fainted oftentimes.

49

  In which amazement, when the Miscreant°   *wretch*
  Perceivèd him to waver weake and fraile,
435 Whiles trembling horror did his conscience dant,° *daunt*
  And hellish anguish[1] did his soule assaile,
  To drive him to despaire, and quite to quaile,° *be dismayed*
   He shewed him painted in a table° plaine,   *picture*
   The damnèd ghosts, that doe in torments waile,
440 And thousand feends that doe them endlesse paine
  With fire and brimstone, which for ever shall remaine.

50

  The sight whereof so throughly him dismaid,
  That nought but death before his eyes he saw,
  And ever burning wrath before him laid,
445 By righteous sentence of th' Almighties law:
  Then gan the villein him to overcraw,°   *exult over*
  And brought unto him swords, ropes, poison, fire,
  And all that might him to perdition draw;
  And bad him choose, what death he would desire:
450 For death was due to him, that had provokt Gods ire.

51

  But when as none of them he saw him take,
  He to him raught° a dagger sharpe and keene,   *reached*

8. Judgment Day.
9. Despaire cites only half of the scripture verse: "The
wages of sin is death; but the gift of God is eternal life
through Jesus Christ our Lord" (Romans 6.23).
1. I.e., fear of hell.

And gave it him in hand: his hand did quake,
And tremble like a leafe of Aspin greene,
455   And troubled bloud through his pale face was seene
To come, and goe with tydings from the hart,
As it a running messenger had beene.
At last resolved to worke his finall smart,
He lifted up his hand, that backe againe did start.

52

460   Which when as Una saw, through every vaine
The crudled° cold ran to her well of life,°   *congealing/heart*
As in a swowne: but soone relived° againe,   *revived*
Out of his hand she snatcht the cursèd knife,
And threw it to the ground, enragèd rife,°   *deeply*
465   And to him said, "Fie, fie, faint harted knight,
What meanest thou by this reprochfull° strife?   *deserving reproach*
Is this the battell, which thou vauntst to fight
With the fire-mouthèd Dragon, horrible and bright?

53

"Come, come away, fraile, feeble, fleshly wight,
470   Ne let vaine words bewitch thy manly hart,
Ne divelish thoughts dismay thy constant spright.
In heavenly mercies hast thou not a part?
Why shouldst thou then despeire, that chosen art?
Where justice growes, there grows eke° greater grace,   *also*
475   The which doth quench the brond of hellish smart,
And that accurst hand-writing[2] doth deface.°   *blot out*
Arise, Sir knight arise, and leave this cursèd place."

54

So up he rose, and thence amounted[3] streight.
Which when the carle° beheld, and saw his guest   *churl*
480   Would safe depart, for° all his subtill sleight,   *in spite of*
He chose an halter from among the rest,
And with it hung himselfe, unbid° unblest.   *unprayed for*
But death he could not worke himselfe thereby;
For thousand times he so himselfe had drest,°   *made ready*
485   Yet nathelesse it could not doe him die,
Till he should die his last, that is eternally.

Canto 10

Her faithfull knight faire Una brings
to house of Holinesse,
Where he is taught repentance, and
the way to heavenly blesse.°   *bliss*

1

What man is he, that boasts of fleshly might,
And vaine assurance of mortality,°   *mortal life*
Which all so soone, as it doth come to fight,
Against spirituall foes, yeelds by and by,[4]

2. An echo of Colossians 2.14: "Blotting out the hand-   nailing it to his cross."
writing that was against us, which was contrary to us   3. Mounted his horse.
[The Old Testament Law], and took it out of the way,   4. Immediately.

5   Or from the field most cowardly doth fly?
     Ne let the man ascribe it to his skill,
     That thorough grace hath gainèd victory.
     If any strength we have, it is to ill,
     But all the good is Gods, both power and eke° will.[5]   *also*

                              2
10   By that, which lately hapned, Una saw,
     That this her knight was feeble, and too faint;
     And all his sinews woxen weake and raw,°   *unready*
     Through long enprisonment, and hard constraint,°   *affliction*
     Which he endurèd in his late restraint,
15   That yet he was unfit for bloudie fight:
     Therefore to cherish him with diets daint,°   *choice*
     She cast to bring him, where he chearen° might,   *be cheered*
     Till he recovered had his[6] late decayèd plight.

                              3
     There was an auntient house not farre away,
20   Renowmd throughout the world for sacred lore,
     And pure unspotted life: so well they say
     It governd was, and guided evermore,
     Through wisedome of a matrone grave and hore;°   *venerable*
     Whose onely joy was to relieve the needes
25   Of wretched soules, and helpe the helpelesse pore:
     All night she spent in bidding of her bedes,[7]
     And all the day in doing good and godly deedes.

                              4
     Dame Caelia[8] men did her call, as thought
     From heaven to come, or thither to arise,
30   The mother of three daughters, well upbrought
     In goodly thewes,° and godly exercise: *habits*
     The eldest two most sober, chast, and wise,
     Fidelia and Speranza virgins were,
     Though spousd,° yet wanting wedlocks solemnize;   *bethrothed*
35   But faire Charissa to a lovely fere[9]
     Was linckèd, and by him had many pledges dere.[1]

                              5
     Arrivèd there, the dore they find fast lockt;
     For it was warely watchèd night and day,
     For feare of many foes: but when they knockt,
40   The Porter opened unto them streight way:
     He was an agèd syre, all hory gray,
     With lookes full lowly cast, and gate full slow,
     Wont on a staffe his feeble steps to stay,
     Hight° Humilta.° They passe in stouping low;   *called/humility*
45   For streight and narrow was the way, which he did show.[2]

5. "For by grace are ye saved through faith; and that not of yourselves: it is the gift of God: Not of works, lest any men should boast" (Ephesians 2.8–9).
6. I.e., from his.
7. Saying prayers.
8. The name means "heavenly."
9. Loving mate.
1. I.e., many children. The daughters' names mean "faith," "hope," and "charity"; cf. the three Saracens: Sans Foy, Sans Joy, and Sans Loy. This canto draws heavily on scriptural references, especially 1 Corinthians 13.13. "And now abideth faith, hope, charity, these three; but the greatest of these is charity." Many aspects of the House of Holiness oppose their counterparts in the House of Pride (1.4).
2. See p. 378, stanza 10 and p. 379, n. 6.

6

Each goodly thing is hardest to begin,
　　But entred in a spacious court they see,
　　Both plaine, and pleasant to be walkèd in,
　　Where them does meete a francklin° faire and free,　　*freeholder*
50　　And entertaines with comely courteous glee,
　　His name was Zele,° that him right well became,　　*zeal*
　　For in his speeches and behaviour hee
　　Did labour lively to expresse the same,
And gladly did them guide, till to the Hall they came.

7

55　There fairely them receives a gentle Squire,
　　Of milde demeanure, and rare courtesie,
　　Right cleanly clad in comely sad° attire;　　*sober*
　　In word and deede that shewed great modestie,
　　And knew his good° to all of each degree,　　*proper respect*
60　　Hight Reverence. He them with speeches meet
　　Does faire entreat; no courting nicetie,[3]
　　But simple true, and eke° unfainèd sweet,　　*also*
As might become a Squire so great persons to greet.

8

And afterwards them to his Dame he leades,
65　　That agèd Dame, the Ladie of the place:
　　Who all this while was busie at her beades:
　　Which doen, she up arose with seemely grace,
　　And toward them full matronely[4] did pace.
　　Where when that farest Una she beheld,
70　　Whom well she knew to spring from heavenly race,
　　Her hart with joy unwonted inly sweld,°　　*swelled*
As feeling wondrous comfort in her weaker eld.°　　*older age*

9

And her embracing said, "O happie earth,
　　Whereon thy innocent feet doe ever tread,
75　　Most vertuous virgin borne of heavenly berth,
　　That to redeeme thy woefull parents head,
　　From tyrans rage, and ever-dying dread,
　　Hast wandred through the world now long a day;[5]
　　Yet ceasest not thy wearie soles to lead,
80　　What grace hath thee now hither brought this way?
Or doen thy feeble feet unweeting° hither stray?　　*unknowing*

10

"Strange thing it is an errant° knight to see　　*wandering*
　　Here in this place, or any other wight,
　　That hither turnes his steps. So few there bee,
85　　That chose the narrow path, or seeke the right:
　　All keepe the broad high way, and take delight
　　With many rather for to go astray,
　　And be partakers of their evill plight,

---

3. He treats them courteously ("faire"); no courtly
affectation ("nicetie").
4. Like a matron, i.e., a woman in charge of an establishment.
5. Many a long day. "Every-dying dread": continuing
fear of death.

Then with a few to walke the rightest way;[6]
90 O foolish men, why haste ye to your owne decay?"
11
"Thy selfe to see, and tyred limbs to rest,
    O matrone sage," quoth she, "I hither came,
    And this good knight his way with me addrest,°   directed
    Led with thy prayses and broad-blazèd fame,
95 That up to heaven is blowne."[7] The aunciant Dame
    Him goodly greeted in her modest guise,
    And entertaynd them both, as best became,
    With all the court'sies,° that she could devise,   courtesies
Ne wanted ought, to shew her bounteous or wise.
12
100 Thus as they gan of sundry things devise,°   talk
    Loe two most goodly virgins came in place,
    Ylinkèd arme in arme in lovely° wise,   loving
    With countenance demure, and modest grace,
    They numbred even steps and equall pace:
105 Of which the eldest, that Fidelia hight,
    Like sunny beames threw from her Christall face,
    That could have dazd° the rash beholders sight,   dazzled
And round about her head did shine like heavens light.
13
    She was araièd° all in lilly white,   arrayed
110 And in her right hand bore a cup of gold,
    With wine and water fild up to the hight,
    In which a Serpent[8] did himselfe enfold,
    That horrour made to all, that did behold;
    But she no whit did chaunge her constant mood:°   expression
115 And in her other hand she fast did hold
    A booke, that was both signd and seald with blood,
Wherein darke things were writ, hard to be understood.[9]
14
    Her younger sister, that Speranza hight,
    Was clad in blew, that her beseemèd well;
120 Not all so chearefull seemèd she of sight,[1]
    As was her sister; whether dread° did dwell,   fear
    Or anguish in her hart, is hard to tell:
    Upon her arme a silver anchor[2] lay,
    Whereon she leanèd ever, as befell:
125 And ever up to heaven, as she did pray,
Her stedfast eyes were bent, ne swarvèd other way.
15
    They seeing Una, towards her gan wend,°   walk
    Who them encounters° with like courtesie;   meets

6. An echo of Matthew 7.13–14: "Broad is the way that leadeth to destruction, and many there be which go in thereat: / . . . strait is the gate and narrow is the way, which leadeth unto life, and few there be that find it."
7. I.e., your praises and fame are widely celebrated ("blazed"), reaching ("blowne") up to heaven.
8. The cup of wine and water signifies the sacrament

of Communion: the serpent is a symbol of the crucified Christ (of whom the serpent lifted up by Moses, Numbers 21.9, is a recognized type).
9. The New Testament. See 2 Peter 3.16: "in which are some things hard to be understood."
1. In appearance.
2. The iconographic symbol of hope.

Many kind speeches they betwene them spend,

130   And greatly joy each other well to see:

Then to the knight with shamefast° modestie   *humble*

They turne themselves, at Unas meeke request,

And him salute with well beseeming glee;[3]

Who faire them quites,° as him beseeméd best,   *returns the salute*

135 And goodly gan discourse of many a noble gest.°   *deed*

16

Then Una thus; "But she your sister deare;

The deare Charissa where is she become?°   *gone to*

Or wants she health, or busie is elsewhere?"

"Ah no," said they, "but forth she may not come:

140 For she of late is lightned of her wombe,

And hath encreast the world with one sonne more,[4]

That her to see should be but troublesome."

"Indeede," quoth she, "that should her trouble sore,

But thankt be God, that her encrease so evermore."[5]

17

145 Then said the aged Caelia, "Deare dame,

And you good Sir, I wote that of your toyle,

And labours long, through which ye hither came,

Ye both forwearied° be: therefore a whyle   *utterly weary*

I read° you rest, and to your bowres recoyle."[6]   *counsel*

150 Then callèd she a Groome, that forth him led

Into a goodly lodge, and gan despoile°   *disrobe*

Of puissant armes, and laid in easio bed;

His name was meeke Obedience rightfully aréd.°   *understood*

18

Now when their wearie limbes with kindly° rest,   *natural*

155 And bodies were refresht with due repast,

Faire Una gan Fidelia faire request,

To have her knight into her schoolehouse plaste,

That of her heavenly learning he might taste,

And heare the wisedome of her words divine.

160 She graunted, and that knight so much agraste,°   *favored*

That she him taught celestiall discipline,

And opened his dull eyes, that light mote in them shine.

19

And that her sacred Booke, with bloud[7] ywrit,

That none could read, except she did them teach,

165 She unto him disclosèd every whit,

And heavenly documents° thereout did preach,   *doctrines*

That weaker wit of man could never reach,

Of God, of grace, of justice, of free will,

That wonder was to heare her goodly speach:

170 For she was able, with her words to kill,

And raise againe to life the hart, that she did thrill.°   *pierce*

---

3. Appropriate joy.

4. Charity, the fruitful virtue, is often depicted pictorially as a mother with many children.

5. I.e., God be thanked, who continually increases her

thus.

6. Retire to your rooms.

7. I.e., the blood of Christ.

20

And when she list poure out her larger spright,[8]
 She would commaund the hastie Sunne to stay,
 Or backward turne his course from heavens hight;
175 Sometimes great hostes of men she could dismay,
 Dry-shod to passe, she parts the flouds in tway;
 And eke huge mountaines from their native seat
 She would commaund, themselves to beare away,
 And throw in raging sea with roaring threat.
180 Almightie God her gave such powre, and puissance great.[9]

21

The faithfull knight now grew in litle space,°   *time*
 By hearing her, and by her sisters lore,
 To such perfection of all heavenly grace,
 That wretched world he gan for to abhore,[1]
185 And mortall life gan loath, as thing forelore,°   *doomed*
 Greeved with remembrance of his wicked wayes,
 And prickt with anguish of his sinnes so sore,
 That he desirde to end his wretched dayes:
So much the dart of sinfull guilt the soule dismayes.

22

190 But wise Speranza gave him comfort sweet,
 And taught him how to take assurèd hold
 Upon her silver anchor, as was meet;
 Else had his sinnes so great, and manifold
 Made him forget all that Fidelia told.
195 In this distressèd doubtfull° agonie,   *fearful*
 When him his dearest Una did behold,
 Disdeining life, desiring leave to die,
She found her selfe assayld with great perplexitie.° *distress*

23

And came to Caelia to declare her smart,
200 Who well acquainted with that commune° plight, *common*
 Which sinfull horror[2] workes in wounded hart,
 Her wisely comforted all that she might,
 With goodly counsell and advisement right;
 And streightway sent with carefull diligence,
205 To fetch a Leach,° the which had great insight *doctor*
 In that disease of grievèd° conscience,   *distressed*
And well could cure the same; His name was Patience.

24

Who comming to that soule-diseasèd knight,
 Could hardly° him intreat, to tell his griefe: *with difficulty*
210 Which knowne, and all that noyd° his heavie spright *troubled*
 Well searcht,° eftsoones° he gan apply reliefe *probed/soon after*
 Of salves and med'cines, which had passing priefe,[3]

8. Full spiritual power.
9. Joshua made the sun stand still (Joshua 10.12); Hezekiah made it turn backward (2 Kings 20.10); Gideon was victorious over the Midianite hosts (Judges 7.7); Moses led the Israelites through the parted waters of the Red Sea (Exodus 14.21–31); faith, said Christ, can move mountains (Matthew 21.21). All these are miracles of faith.
1. I.e., he began to abhor the world.
2. Horror of sin.
3. Which had extraordinary power.

And thereto added words of wondrous might:
By which to ease he him recurèd briefe,[4]
215   And much asswaged the passion° of his plight,   *suffering*
That he his paine endured, as seeming now more light.

25

But yet the cause and root of all his ill,
Inward corruption, and infected sin,[5]
Not purged nor heald, behind remainéd still,
220   And festring sore did rankle yet within,
Close° creeping twixt the marrow and the skin.   *secretly*
Which to extirpe,° he laid him privily   *extirpate*
Downe in a darkesome lowly place farre in,
Whereas he meant his corrosives to apply,
225   And with streight° diet tame his stubborne malady.   *strict*

26

In ashes and sackcloth he did array
His daintie corse, proud humors[6] to abate,
And dieted with fasting every day,
The swelling of his wounds to mitigate,
230   And made him pray both earely and eke° late: *also*
And ever as superfluous flesh did rot
Amendment readie still at hand did wayt,
To pluck it out with pincers firie whot,°   *hot*
That soone in him was left no one corrupted jot.

27

235   And bitter Penance with an yron whip,
Was wont him once to disple° every day: *discipline*
And sharpe Remorse his hart did pricke and nip,
That drops of bloud thence like a well did play;
And sad Repentance usèd to embay°   *bathe*
240   His bodie in salt water smarting sore,
The filthy blots of sinne to wash away.[7]
So in short space they did to health restore
The man that would not live, but earst° lay at deathes dore.   *formerly*

28

In which his torment often was so great,
245   That like a Lyon he would cry and rore,
And rend his flesh, and his owne synewes eat.
His own deare Una hearing evermore
His ruefull shriekes and gronings, often tore
Her guiltlesse garments, and her golden heare,
250   For pitty of his paine and anguish sore;
Yet all with patience wisely she did beare;
For well she wist, his crime could else be never cleare.°   *cleansed*

29

Whom thus recovered by wise Patience,
And trew Repentance they to Una brought:
255   Who joyous of his curèd conscience,
Him dearely kist, and fairely° eke° besought   *courteously/also*

---

4. I.e., he spoke words of spiritual consolation to ease
the knight he had quickly cured of sin.
5. I.e., the effects of original sin.

6. Whatever is conducive to pride.
7. "Wash me throughly from mine iniquity, and
cleanse me from my sin" (Psalms 51.2).

Himselfe to chearish,° and consuming thought   *cheer, cherish*
   To put away out of his carefull° brest.   *care-full*
   By this[8] Charissa, late in child-bed brought,
260   Was woxen strong, and left her fruitfull nest;
To her faire Una brought this unacquainted guest.

30

She was a woman in her freshest age,
   Of wondrous beauty, and of bountie° rare,   *goodness*
   With goodly grace and comely personage,°   *appearance*
265   That was on earth not easie to compare;°   *rival*
   Full of great love, but Cupids wanton snare
   As hell she hated, chast in worke and will;
   Her necke and breasts were ever open bare,
   That ay thereof her babes might sucke their fill;
270 The rest was all in yellow robes arayèd still.[9]

31

A multitude of babes about her hong,
   Playing their sports, that joyd her to behold,
   Whom still she fed, whiles they were weake and young,
   But thrust them forth still, as they wexèd old:
275   And on her head she wore a tyre° of gold,   *headdress*
   Adornd with gemmes and owches° wondrous faire,   *jewels*
   Whose passing° price uneath° was to be told;   *surpassing/scarcely*
   And by her side there sate a gentle paire
Of turtle doves,[1] she sitting in an yvorie chaire.

32

280 The knight and Una entring, faire her greet,
   And bid her joy of that her happie brood;
   Who them requites with court'sies seeming meet,°   *appropriate*
   And entertaines with friendly chearefull mood.
   Then Una her besought, to be so good,
285   As in her vertuous rules to schoole her knight,
   Now after all his torment well withstood,
   In that sad° house of Penaunce, where his spright   *solemn*
Had past° the paines of hell, and long enduring night. *passed through*

33

She was right joyous of her just request,
290   And taking by the hand that Faeries sonne,
   Gan him instruct in every good behest,°   *command*
   Of love, and righteousness, and well to donne,[2]
   And wrath, and hatred warely° to shonne,   *warily*
   That drew on men Gods hatred, and his wrath,
295   And many soules in dolours° had fordonne:° *misery/destroyed*
   In which when him she well instructed hath,
From thence to heaven she teacheth him the ready° path.   *direct*

34

Wherein his weaker° wandring steps to guide,   *too weak*
   An auncient matrone she to her does call,

---

8. By this time.
9. Her yellow (saffron) robe is the color of marriage, fertility, and maternity. Her chaste, fruitful love (Christian *agape*) is opposed to "Cupid's wanton snare" (*eros*).
1. Emblem of true love and faithful marriage.
2. I.e., right action.

300   Whose sober lookes her wisedome well describe:°   *made known*
      Her name was Mercie, well knowne over all,
      To be both gratious, and eke° liberall: *also*
      To whom the carefull charge of him she gave,
      To lead aright, that he should never fall
305   In all his wayes through this wide worldès wave,°   *expanse*
      That Mercy in the end his righteous soule might save.

                              35

      The godly Matrone by the hand him beares°   *leads*
      Forth from her[3] presence, by a narrow way,
      Scattred with bushy thornes, and ragged breares,°   *briers*
310   Which still before him she removed away,
      That nothing might his ready passage stay:
      And ever when his feet encombred were,
      Or gan to shrinke, or from the right to stray,
      She held him fast, and firmely did upbeare,
315   As carefull Nourse her child from falling oft does reare.

                              36

      Eftsoones unto an holy Hospitall,[4]
      That was fore° by the way, she did him bring,   *close*
      In which seven Bead-men[5] that had vowèd all
      Their life to service of high heavens king
320   Did spend their dayes in doing godly thing:
      Their gates to all were open evermore,
      That by the wearie way were traveiling,
      And one sate wayting ever them before,
      To call in commers-by, that needy were and pore.[6]

                              37

325   The first of them that eldest was, and best,°   *chief*
      Of all the house had charge and governement,
      As Guardian and Steward of the rest:
      His office was to give entertainement
      And lodging, unto all that came, and went:
330   Not unto such, as could him feast againe,°   *in return*
      And double quite,° for that he on them spent,   *repay*
      But such, as want of harbour° did constraine:°   *shelter/afflict*
      Those for Gods sake his dewty was to entertaine.

                              38

      The second was as Almner[7] of the place,
335   His office was, the hungry for to feed,
      And thristy give to drinke, a worke of grace:
      He feard not once him selfe to be in need,
      Ne cared to hoord for those, whom he did breede:[8]
      The grace of God he layd up still in store,
340   Which as a stocke° he left unto his seede;°   *resource/children*
      He had enough, what need him care for more?
      And had he lesse, yet some he would give to the pore.

---

3. I.e., Charissa's.
4. House of rest for pilgrims and travelers.
5. Men of prayer.
6. I.e., one beadsman sat in front of the gates, to call in needy wayfarers.
7. An almoner distributed charity to the poor.
8. I.e., his children.

39

The third had of their wardrobe custodie,
  In which were not rich tyres,° nor garments gay,   *robes*
345 The plumes of pride, and wings of vanitie,
  But clothes meet to keepe keene could° away,   *cold*
  And naked nature seemely° to aray;   *decently*
  With which bare wretched wights he dayly clad,
  The images of God in earthly clay;
350 And if that no spare clothes to give he had,
His owne coate he would cut, and it distribute glad.

40

The fourth appointed by his office was,
  Poore prisoners to relieve with gratious ayd,
  And captives to redeeme with price of bras,⁹
355 From Turkes and Sarazins, which them had stayd;°   *held captive*
  And though they faultie were, yet well he wayd,
  That God to us forgiveth every howre
  Much more then that, why° they in bands were layd,   *for which*
  And he that harrowd hell¹ with heavie stowre,°   *assault*
360 The faultie° soules from thence brought to his heavenly bowre. *sinful*

41

The fift had charge sicke persons to attend,
  And comfort those, in point of death which lay;
  For them most needeth comfort in the end,
  When sin, and hell, and death do most dismay
365 The feeble soule departing hence away.
  All is but lost, that living we bestow,°   *store up*
  If not well ended at our dying day.
  O man have mind of that last bitter throw;°   *throes of death*
For as the tree does fall, so lyes it ever low.

42

370 The sixt had charge of them now being dead,
  In seemely sort their courses to engrave,²
  And deck with dainty flowres their bridall bed,
  That to their heavenly spouse both sweet and brave°   *fair*
  They might appeare, when he their soules shall save.
375 The wondrous workemanship of Gods owne mould,³
  Whose face he made, all beasts to feare, and gave
  All in his hand, even dead we honour should.
Ah dearest God me graunt, I dead be not defould.°   *defiled*

43

The seventh now after death and buriall done,
380 Had charge the tender Orphans of the dead
  And widowes ayd, least they should be undone:
  In face of judgement⁴ he their right would plead,
  Ne ought⁵ the powre of mighty men did dread

9. Payment of money.
1. Christ, who journeyed to hell to deliver those good people who lived before his time, according to a popular story in the Middle Ages. It originated in the apocryphal gospel of Nicodemus.
2. Bodies ("courses," i.e., corpses) to bury.
3. The human body is God's own image ("mould") and a "mould" of God's making (see Genesis 1.26–30, 2.7).
4. I.e., in court.
5. Neither at all.

In their defence, nor would for gold or fee°   *bribe*
385   Be wonne their rightfull causes downe to tread:
And when they stood in most necessitee,
He did supply their want, and gave them ever free.[6]

44

There when the Elfin knight arrivèd was,
The first and chiefest of the seven, whose care
390   Was guests to welcome, towardes him did pas:
Where seeing Mercie, that his steps up bare,[7]
And alwayes led, to her with reverence rare
He humbly louted° in meeke lowlinesse,   *bowed*
And seemely welcome for her did prepare:
395   For of their order she was Patronesse,
Albe° Charissa were their chiefest founderesse.   *although*

45

There she awhile him stayes, him selfe to rest,
That to the rest more able he might bee:
During which time, in every good behest°   *command*
400   And godly worke of Almes and charitee
She him instructed with great industree;
Shortly therein so perfect he became,
That from the first unto the last degree,
His mortall life he learnèd had to frame
405   In holy righteousnesse, without rebuke or blame.

46

Thence forward by that painfull way they pas,
Forth to an hill, that was both steepe and hy;
On top whereof a sacred chappell was,
And eke° a litle Hermitage thereby,   *also*
410   Wherein an agèd holy man did lye,°   *live*
That day and night said his devotion,
Ne other worldly busines did apply;[8]
His name was heavenly Contemplation;
Of God and goodnesse was his meditation.

47

415   Great grace that old man to him given had;
For God he often saw from heavens hight,
All° were his earthly eyen both blunt° and bad,   *although/dim*
And through great age had lost their kindly° sight,   *natural*
Yet wondrous quick and persant° was his spright,°   *piercing/spirit*
420   As Eagles eye, that can behold the Sunne:
That hill they scale with all their powre and might,
That his frayle thighes nigh wearie and fordonne°   *exhausted*
Gan faile, but by her helpe the top at last he wonne.

48

There they do finde that godly agèd Sire,
425   With snowy lockes adowne his shoulders shed,
As hoarie frost with spangles doth attire

---

6. Always freely. The seven beadsmen here correspond to, and perform, the seven works of charity, or
corporal mercy: lodging the homeless, feeding the
hungry, clothing the naked, redeeming the captive,
comforting the sick, burying the dead, and succoring
the orphan.
7. Supported.
8. I.e., he did not attend to any worldly activities.

The mossy braunches of an Oke halfe ded.
Each bone might through his body well be red,°   *observed*
And every sinew seene through° his long fast: *because of*
430   For nought he cared his carcas long unfed;
He mind was full of spirituall repast,
And pyned° his flesh, to keepe his body low° and chast.   *starved/thin*

49

Who when these two approching he aspide,
At their first presence grew agrievèd sore,[9]
435   That forst him lay his heavenly thoughts aside;
And had he not that Dame respected more,°   *greatly*
Whom highly he did reverence and adore,
He would not once have movèd for the knight.
They him saluted standing far afore;°   *away*
440   Who well them greeting, humbly did requight,°   *respond*
And asked, to what end they clomb° that tedious height.   *had climbed*

50

"What end," quoth she, "should cause us take such paine,
But that same end, which every living wight
Should make his marke,° high heaven to attaine?   *goal*
445   Is not from hence the way, that leadeth right
To that most glorious house, that glistreth bright
With burning starres, and everliving fire,
Whereof the keyes are to thy hand behight°   *entrusted*
By wise Fidelia? she doth thee require,
450   To shew it to this knight, according his desire."

51

"Thrise happy man," said then the father grave,
"Whose staggering steps thy[1] steady hand doth lead,
And shewes the way, his sinfull soule to save.
Who better can the way to heaven aread°   *direct*
455   Then thou thy selfe, that was both borne and bred
In heavenly throne, where thousand Angels shine?
Thou doest the prayers of the righteous sead°   *seed*
Present before the majestie divine,
And his avenging wrath to clemencie incline.

52

460   "Yet since thou bidst, thy pleasure shalbe donne.
Then come thou man of earth,[2] and see the way,
That never yet was seene of Faeries sonne,
That never leads the traveiler astray,
But after labours long, and sad delay,
465   Brings them to joyous rest and endlesse blis.
But first thou must a season fast and pray,
Till from her bands the spright assoilèd° is,   *released*
And have her strength recured° from fraile infirmitis."   *recovered*

53

That done, he leads him to the highest Mount;
470   Such one, as that same mighty man of God,

9. I.e., he was at first sorely grieved at their arrival.
1. I.e., Mercy's.
2. An allusion to humankind's formation from the

dust of the earth (Genesis 2.7) and also to the knight's
name (p. 390, 10.66 and n. 5).

That bloud-red billowes like a wallèd front
On either side disparted° with his rod,   *parted asunder*
Till that his army dry-foot through them yod,°   *went*
Dwelt fortie dayes upon; where writ in stone
475   With bloudy letters by the hand of God,
The bitter doome of death and balefull mone[3]
He did receive, whiles flashing fire about him shone.

                                   54

Or like that sacred hill, whose head full hie,
Adornd with fruitfull Olives all arownd,
480   Is, as it were for endlesse memory
Of that deare Lord, who oft thereon was fownd,
For ever with a flowring girlond crownd:
Or like that pleasaunt Mount, that is for ay
Through famous Poets verse each where° renownd,   *everywhere*
485   On which the thrise three learned Ladies play
Their heavenly notes, and make full many a lovely lay.°[4]   *song*

                                   55

From thence, far off he unto him did shew
A litle path, that was both steepe and long,
Which to a goodly Citie led his vew;
490   Whose wals and towres were builded high and strong
Of perle and precious stone, that earthly tong
Cannot describe, nor wit of man can tell;
Too high a ditty° for my simple song;   *subject*
The Citie of the great king hight it well,
495   Wherein eternall peace and happinesse doth dwell.

                                   56

As he thereon stood gazing, he might see
The blessed Angels to and fro descend
From highest heaven, in gladsome companee,
And with great joy into that Citie wend,
500   As commonly° as friend does with his frend.[5]   *familiarly*
Whereat he wondred much, and gan enquere,
What stately building durst so high extend
Her loftie towres unto the starry sphere,
And what unknowen nation there empeopled were.

                                   57

505   "Faire knight," quoth he, "Hierusalem that is,
The new Hierusalem, that God has built
For those to dwell in, that are chosen his,
His chosen people purged from sinfull guilt,
With pretious bloud, which cruelly was spilt
510   On cursèd tree, of that unspotted lam,[6]
That for the sinnes of all the world was kilt:

---

3. I.e., the Ten Commandments ("bloudy letters")
carried with them the judgment ("doome") of death
and pain (causing sorrowful moans—"balefull mone").
4. The mountain is successively compared with Mt.
Sinai, where Moses, after parting the "bloud-red billowes" of the Red Sea, received the tablets of the Ten
Commandments; to the Mount of Olives, associated
with Christ; and to Mt. Parnassus, where the Nine
Muses of art and poetry dwelt.
5. Cf. Jacob's ladder, which "reached to heaven; and
behold the angels of God ascending and descending
on it" (Genesis 28.12).
6. Lamb; a reference to Christ (the lamb of God),
whose death on the cross ("cursèd tree") purged the
guilt of sin from those "chosen his."

Now are they Saints all in that Citie sam,°   together
More deare unto their God, then younglings to their dam."[7]

58

"Till now," said then the knight, "I weenèd well,
515   That great Cleopolis,[8] where I have beene,
In which that fairest Faerie Queene doth dwell,
The fairest Citie was, that might be seene;
And that bright towre all built of christall cleene,°   clear
Panthea,[9] seemd the brightest thing, that was:
520   But now by proofe all otherwise I weene;
For this great Citie that[1] does far surpas,
And this bright Angels towre quite dims that towre of glas."

59

"Most trew," then said the holy aged man;
"Yet is Cleopolis for earthly frame,°   structure
525   The fairest peece,° that eye beholden can: masterpiece
And well beseemes° all knights of noble name,   becomes
That covet in th' immortall booke of fame
To be eternizèd, that same to haunt,°   frequent
And doen their service to that soveraigne Dame,
530   That glorie does to them for guerdon° graunt: reward
For she is heavenly borne, and heaven may justly vaunt.°   claim

60

"And thou faire ymp,° sprong out from English race,   youth
How ever now accompted° Elfins sonne,   accounted
Well worthy doest thy service for her grace,°   favor
535   To aide a virgin desolate foredonne.°   undone
But when thou famous victorie hast wonne,
And high emongst all knights has hong thy shield,
Thenceforth the suit° of earthly conquest shonne,   pursuit
And wash thy hands from guilt of bloudy field:
540   For bloud can nought but sin, and wars but sorrowes yield.

61

"Then seeke this path, that I to thee presage,°   point out prophetically
Which after all to heaven shall thee send;
Then peaceably thy painefull° pilgrimage   laborious
To yonder same Hierusalem do bend,
545   Where is for thee ordaind a blessed end:
For thou emongst those Saints, whom thou doest see,
Shalt be a Saint, and thine owne nations frend
And Patrone: thou Saint George shalt callèd bee,
Saint George of mery England, the signe of victoree."[2]

62

550   "Unworthy wretch," quoth he, "of so great grace,
How dare I thinke such glory to attaine?"
"These that have it attaind, were in like cace,"

7. The New Jerusalem is described in Revelation 21–22; "the nations of them which are saved shall walk in the light of it" (21.24).
8. London, Camelot—the earthly counterpart of the Heavenly Kingdom.
9. Reminiscent of the temple of glass in Chaucer's *Hous of Fame*; perhaps intended to allude to Richmond Palace or Westminster Abbey.
1. I.e., The New Jerusalem far surpasses Cleopolis ("that").
2. Spenser's conception of St. George, patron saint of England, draws on the *Legenda Aurea* (translated by Caxton in 1487) and on pictures, tapestries, pageants, and folklore.

Quoth he, "as wretched, and lived in like paine."

"But deeds of armes must I at last be faine,°   *content to leave*

555   And Ladies love to leave so dearely bought?"

"What need of armes, where peace doth ay remaine,"

Said he, "and battailes none are to be fought?

As for loose loves are³ vaine, and vanish into nought."

63

"O let me not," quoth he, "then turne againe

560   Backe to the world, whose joyes so fruitlesse are;

But let me here for aye in peace remaine,

Or streight way on that last long voyage fare,

That nothing may my present hope empare."°   *impair*

"That may not be," said he, "ne maist thou yit

565   Forgo that royall maides bequeathèd care,°   *charge*

Who did her cause into thy hand commit,

Till from her cursèd foe thou have her freely quit."°   *released*

64

"Then shall I soone," quoth he, "so God me grace,

Abet° that virgins cause disconsolate,   *maintain*

570   And shortly backe returne unto this place

To walke this way in Pilgrims poore estate.

But now aread,° old father, why of late   *declare*

Didst thou behight° me borne of English blood,   *call*

Whom all a Faeries sonne doen nominate?"°   *name*

575   "That word shall I," said he, "avouchen° good,   *prove*

Sith to thee is unknowne the cradle of thy brood.

65

"For well I wote,° thou springst from ancient race   *know*

Of Saxon kings, that have with mightie hand

And many bloudie battailes fought in place°   *there*

580   High reard their royall throne in Britane land,

And vanquisht them, unable to withstand:

From thence a Faerie thee unweeting reft,⁴

There as thou slepst in tender swadling band,

And her base Elfin brood there for thee left.

585   Such men do Chaungelings call, so chaungd by Faeries theft.

66

"Thence she thee brought into this Faerie lond,

And in an heapèd furrow did thee hyde,

Where thee a Ploughman all unweeting° fond,   *unknowing*

As he his toylesome teme° that way did guyde,   *team of oxen*

590   And brought thee up in ploughmans state to byde,

Whereof Georgos he thee gave to name;⁵

Till prickt° with courage, and thy forces pryde,   *spurred*

To Faery court thou cam'st to seeke for fame,

And prove thy puissaunt armes, as seemes thee best became."⁶

67

595   "O holy Sire," quoth he, "how shall I quight°   *repay*

The many favours I with thee have found,

---

3. I.e., they are.
4. Secretly stole.
5. I.e., as a name. *Georgos* is Greek for "farmer" (cf.

Virgil's *Georgics*, on farming).
6. As best suited you.

That has my name and nation red aright,
And taught the way that does to heaven bound?"°   go
This said, adowne he lookèd to the ground,
600   To have returnd, but dazèd° were his eyne,   dazzled
Through passing° brightnesse, which did quite confound   surpassing
His feeble sence, and too exceeding shyne.
So darke are earthly things compard to things divine.

68

At last whenas himselfe he gan to find,°   recover
605   To Una back he cast him to retire;
Who him awaited still with pensive° mind.   anxious
Great thankes and goodly meed° to that good syre,   gift
He thence departing gave for his paines hyre.°   reward
So came to Una, who him joyd to see,
610   And after litle rest, gan him desire,
Of her adventure mindfull for to bee.
So leave they take of Caelia, and her daughters three.

Canto 11

The knight with that old Dragon fights
two dayes incessantly:
The third him overthrowes, and gayns
most glorious victory.

1

High time now gan it wex° for Una faire,   grow
To thinke of those her captive Parents deare,
And their forwasted kingdome to repaire:[7]
Whereto whenas they now approachèd neare,
5   With hartie° words her knight she gan to cheare,   bold
And in her modest manner thus bespake;
"Deare knight, as deare, as ever knight was deare,
That all these sorrowes suffer for my sake,
High heaven behold the tedious toyle, ye for me take.

2

10   "Now are we come unto my native soyle,
And to the place, where all our perils dwell;
Here haunts that feend, and does his dayly spoyle,
Therefore henceforth be at your keeping well,[8]
And ever ready for your foeman fell.
15   The sparke of noble courage now awake,
And strive your excellent selfe to excell;
That shall ye evermore renowmèd make,
Above all knights on earth, that batteill undertake."

3

And pointing forth, "lo yonder is," said she,
20   "The brasen towre in which my parents deare
For dread of that huge feend emprisond be,
Whom I from far see on the walles appeare,
Whose sight my feeble° soule doth greatly cheare: doleful

7. I.e., to restore their kingdom, laid waste (by the   8. I.e., be well on your guard.
dragon).

And on the top of all I do espye
25   The watchman wayting tydings glad to heare,
That O my parents might I happily
Unto you bring, to ease you of your misery."

4

With that they heard a roaring hideous sound,
That all the ayre with terrour fillèd wide,
30   And seemd uneath° to shake the stedfast ground.   *almost*
Eftsoones° that dreadfull Dragon they espide,   *soon after*
Where stretcht he lay upon the sunny side
Of a great hill, himselfe like a great hill.
But all so soone, as he from far descride
35   Those glistring armes, that heaven with light díd fill,
He rousd himselfe full blith,° and hastned them untill.°   *joyfully/toward*

5

Then bad the knight his Lady yede° aloofe,   *step*
And to an hill her selfe withdraw aside,
From whence she might behold that battailles proof°   *outcome*
40   And eke be safe from daunger far descryde:
She him obayd, and turnd a little wyde.°   *aside*
Now O thou sacred Muse,[9] most learned Dame,
Faire ympe° of Phoebus, and his aged bride,[1]   *child*
The Nourse of time, and everlasting fame,
45   That warlike hands ennoblest with immortall name;

6

O gently come into my feeble brest,
Come gently, but not with that mighty rage,
Wherewith the martiall troupes thou doest infest,°   *arouse*
And harts of great Heroës doest enrage,
50   That nought their kindled courage may aswage,
Soone as thy dreadfull trompe° begins to sownd;   *trumpet*
The God of warre with his fiers equipage
Thou doest awake, sleepe never he so sownd,°   *sound*
And scarèd nations doest with horrour sterne astown.°   *appall*

7

55   Faire Goddesse lay that furious fit° aside,   *strain*
Till I of warres and bloudy Mars do sing[2]
And Briton fields with Sarazin bloud bedyde,
Twixt that great faery Queene and Paynim king,
That with their horrour heaven and earth did ring,
60   A worke of labour long, and endlesse prayse:
But now a while let downe that haughtie string,
And to my tunes thy second tenor rayse,[3]
That I this man of God his godly armes may blaze.°   *describe*

8

By this the dreadfull Beast drew nigh to hand,
65   Halfe flying, and halfe footing° in his hast,   *walking*
That with his largenesse measurèd much land,

9. Calliope, muse of epic poetry, or Clio, muse of history.
1. I.e., Mnemosyne (memory).
2. Perhaps a reference to a projected but unwritten book of *The Faerie Queene*.
3. The "haughtie" (high-pitched) mode would be appropriate to a large-scale epic war; the "second tenor" (lower in pitch) to this present battle.

And made wide shadow under his huge wast;°   *girth*
   As mountaine doth the valley overcast.
   Approching nigh, he rearèd high afore
70   His body monstrous, horrible, and vast,
   Which to increase his wondrous greatnesse more,
Was swolne with wrath, and poyson, and with bloudy gore.

9

And over, all with brasen scales was armd,
   Like plated coate of steele, so couchèd neare,[4]
75   That nought mote perce,[5] ne might his corse° be harmd   *body*
   With dint of sword, nor push of pointed speare;
   Which as an Eagle, seeing pray appeare,
   His acry Plumes doth rouze,° full rudely dight,[6]   *shake*
   So shakèd he, that horrour was to heare,
80   For as the clashing of an Armour bright,
Such noyse his rouzèd scales did send unto the knight.

10

His flaggy° wings when forth he did display,   *drooping*
   Were like two sayles, in which the hollow wynd
   Is gathered full, and worketh speedy way:
85   And eke° the pennes,° that did his pineons bynd,   *also/quills*
   Were like mayne-yards, with flying canvas lynd,
   With which whenas him list the ayre to beat,
   And there by force unwonted° passage find,   *unaccustomed*
   The cloudes before him fled for terrour great,
90   And all the heavens stood still amazèd with his threat.

11

His huge long tayle wound up in hundred foldes,
   Does overspred his long bras-scaly backe,
   Whose wreathèd boughts° when ever he unfoldes,   *coils*
   And thicke entangled knots adown does slacke,
95   Bespotted as with shields° of red and blacke,   *scales*
   It sweepeth all the land behind him farre,
   And of three furlongs does but litle lacke;
   And at the point two stings in-fixèd arre,
Both deadly sharpe, that sharpest steele exceeden farre.

12

100   But stings and sharpest steele did far exceed[7]
   The sharpnesse of his cruell rending clawes;
   Dead was it sure, as sure as death in deed,[8]
   What ever thing does touch his ravenous pawes,
   Or what within his reach he ever drawes.
105   But his most hideous head my toung to tell
   Does tremble: for his deepe devouring jawes
   Wide gapèd, like the griesly° mouth of hell,   *horrid*
Through which into his darke abisse all ravin° fell.   *prey, booty*

13

And that° more wondrous was, in either jaw   *what*
110   Threeranckes of yron teeth enraungèd were,

---

4. Closely overlaid.   7. I.e., were far exceeded by.
5. Nothing might pierce ("perce").   8. In its effect.
6. Ruggedly arrayed.

In which yet trickling bloud and gobbets raw[9]
   Of late devourèd bodies did appeare,
   That sight thereof bred cold congealèd feare:
   Which to increase, and all at once to kill,
115   A cloud of smoothering smoke and sulphur seare°   *burning*
   Out of his stinking gorge° forth steemèd still,   *maw*
That all the ayre about with smoke and stench did fill.

14

His blazing eyes, like two bright shining shields,
   Did burne with wrath, and sparkled living fyre;
120   As two broad Beacons, set in open fields,
   Send forth their flames farre off to every shyre,°   *shire*
   And warning give, that enemies conspyre,
   With fire and sword the region to invade;
   So flamed his eyne° with rage and rancorous yre:°   *eyes/anger*
125   But farre within, as in a hollow glade,
Those glaring lampes were set, that made a dreadfull shade.

15

So dreadfully he towards him did pas,
   Forelifting up aloft his speckled brest,
   And often bounding on the brusèd gras,
130   As for great joyance of his newcome guest.
   Eftsoones he gan advance his haughtie crest,
   As chauffèd° Bore his bristles doth upreare,   *vexed*
   And shoke his scales to battell readie drest;°   *prepared*
   That made the Redcrosse knight nigh quake for feare,
135   As bidding bold defiance to his foeman neare.

16

The knight gan fairely couch° his steadie speare,   *rest, aim*
   And fiercely ran at him with rigorous° might: *violent*
   The pointed steele arriving rudely° theare,   *roughly*
   His harder hide would neither perce, nor bight,
140   But glauncing by forth passèd forward right;
   Yet sore amovèd with so puissant push,
   The wrathfull beast about him turnèd light,°   *quickly*
   And him so rudely passing by, did brush
With his long tayle, that horse and man to ground did rush.

17

145 Both horse and man up lightly rose againe,
   And fresh encounter towards him addrest:
   But th' idle stroke yet backe recoyld in vaine,
   And found no place his° deadly point to rest.   *its*
   Exceeding rage enflamed the furious beast,
150   To be avengèd of so great despight;°   *outrage*
   For never felt his imperceable brest
   So wondrous force, from hand of living wight;
Yet had he proved° the powre of many a puissant knight.   *tested*

18

Then with his waving wings displayèd wyde,
155   Himselfe up high he lifted from the ground,

---

9. Chunks of undigested food.

And with strong flight did forcibly divide
    The yielding aire, which nigh too feeble found
    Her flitting° partes, and element unsound,°   *moving/weak*
    To beare so great a weight: he cutting way
160   With his broad sayles, about him soarèd round:
    At last low stouping with unweldie sway,[1]
Snatcht up both horse and man, to beare them quite away.

19

Long he them bore above the subject plaine,[2]
    So farre as Ewghen[3] bow a shaft may send,
165   Till struggling strong did him at last constraine,
    To let them downe before his flightès end:
    As hagard° hauke presuming to contend   *untamed*
    With hardie fowle, above his hable might,[4]
    His wearie pounces° all in vaine doth spend,   *claws*
170   To trusse° the pray too heavie for his flight;   *seize*
Which comming downe to ground, does free it selfe by fight.

20

He so disseizèd of his gryping grosse,[5]
    The knight his thrilant° speare againe assayd   *piercing*
    In his bras-plated body to embosse,°   *plunge*
175   And three mens strength unto the stroke he layd;
    Wherewith the stiffe beame quakèd, as affrayd,
    And glauncing from his scaly necke, did glyde
    Close under his left wing, then broad displayd.
    The percing steele there wrought a wound full wyde,
180 That with the uncouth° smart the Monster lowdly cryde.   *unusual*

21

He cryde, as raging seas are wont to rore,
    When wintry storme his wrathfull wreck does threat,
    The rolling billowes beat the ragged shore,
    As they the earth would shoulder from her seat,
185   And greedie gulfe[6] does gape, as he would eat
    His neighbour element[7] in his revenge:
    Then gin the blustring brethren[8] boldly threat,
    To move the world from off his stedfast henge,°   *axis*
And boystrous battell make, each other to avenge.

22

190 The steely head stucke fast still in his flesh,
    Till with his cruell clawes he snatcht the wood,
    And quite a sunder broke. Forth flowèd fresh
    A gushing river of blacke goarie° blood,   *clotted*
    That drownèd all the land, whereon he stood;
195   The stream thereof would drive a water-mill.
    Trebly augmented was his furious mood
    With bitter sense of his deepe rooted ill,°   *injury*
That flames of fire he threw forth from his large noséthrill.

---

1. Ponderous force.
2. I.e., the ground below.
3. Yewen, of yew.
4. Able power.

5. Freed from his formidable grip.
6. I.e., the sea.
7. I.e., earth.
8. I.e., the winds.

23

His hideous tayle then hurlèd he about,
    And therewith all enwrapt the nimble thyes°   *thighs*
    Of his froth-fomy steed, whose courage stout
    Striving to loose the knot, that fast him tyes,
    Himselfe in streighter° bandes too rash implyes,[9]   *tighter*
    That to the ground he is perforce constraynd
    To throw his rider: who can° quickly ryse   *began to*
    From off the earth, with durty bloud distaynd,°   *defiled*
For that reprochfull fall right fowly he disdaynd.

24

And fiercely tooke his trenchand° blade in hand,   *sharp*
    With which he stroke so furious and so fell,
    That nothing seemd the puissance could withstand:
    Upon his crest the hardned yron fell,
    But his more hardned crest was armd so well,
    That deeper dint therein it would not make;[1]
    Yet so extremely did the buffe° him quell,°   *blow/dismay*
    That from thenceforth he shund the like to take,
But when he saw them come, he did them still forsake.°   *avoid*

25

The knight was wrath to see his stroke beguyld,°   *foiled*
    And smote againe with more outrageous might;
    But backe againe the sparckling steele recoyld,
    And left not any marke, where it did light;
    As if in Adamant rocke it had bene pight.°   *struck against*
    The beast impatient of his smarting wound,
    And of so fierce and forcible despight,[2]
    Thought with his wings to stye° above the ground;   *mount*
But his late wounded wing unserviceable found.

26

Then full of griefe and anguish vehement,
    He lowdly brayd, that like was never heard,
    And from his wide devouring oven sent
    A flake° of fire, that flashing in his beard,   *flash*
    Him all amazd, and almost made affeard;
    The scorching flame sore swingèd° all his face,   *singed*
    And through his armour all his bodie seard,
    That he could not endure so cruell cace,°   *plight*
But thought his armes to leave, and helmet to unlace.

27

Not that great Champion of the antique world,
    Whom famous Poetes verse so much doth vaunt,
    And hath for twelve huge labours high extold,
    So many furies and sharpe fits did haunt,
    When him the poysoned garment did enchaunt
    With Centaures bloud, and bloudie verses charmed,
    As did this knight twelve thousand dolours° daunt,   *sufferings*

---

9. I.e., too suddenly entangles.   2. Powerful injury.
1. I.e., it could not make a deep gash there.

Whom fyrie steele now burnt, that earst° him armed,   *formerly*
That erst him goodly armed, now most of all him harmed.[3]

28

Faint, wearie, sore, emboylèd, grievèd, brent°   *burned*
245   With heat, toyle, wounds, armes, smart, and inward fire
That never man such mischiefes° did torment;   *misfortunes*
Death better were, death did he oft desire,
But death will never come, when needes require.
Whom so dismayd when that his foe beheld,
250   He cast to suffer him no more respire,°   *rest*
But gan his sturdie sterne° about to weld,°   *tail/lash*
And him so strongly stroke, that to the ground him feld.

29

It fortunèd (as faire it then befell)
Behind his backe unweeting,° where he stood,   *unnoticed*
255   Of auncient time there was a springing well,
From which fast trickled forth a silver flood,
Full of great vertues, and for med'cine good.
Whylome,° before that cursèd Dragon got   *formerly*
That happie land, and all with innocent blood
260   Defyld those sacred waves, it rightly hot°   *was called*
The Well of Life,[4] ne yet his vertues had forgot.

30

For unto life the dead it could restore,
And guilt of sinfull crimes cleane wash away,
Those that with sicknesse were infected sore,
265   It could recure, and aged long decay
Renew, as one were borne that very day.
Both Silo this, and Jordan did excell,
And th' English Bath, and eke° the german Spau,   *also*
Ne can Cephise, nor Hebrus match this well:
270   Into the same the knight backe overthrowen, fell.[5]

31

Now gan the golden Phoebus for to steepe
His fierie face in billowes of the west,
And his faint steedes watred in Ocean deepe,
Whiles from their journall° labours they did rest,   *daily*
275   When that infernall Monster, having kest°   *cast*
His wearie foe into that living well,
Can° high advaunce his broad discoloured brest,   *did*
Above his wonted pitch,° with countenance fell,°   *height/sinister*
And clapt his yron wings, as victor he did dwell.°   *remain*

---

3. Redcrosse's fire baptism is compared with the burning shirt of Nessus, which killed Hercules, "that great Champion of the antique world" (line 235). His "twelve huge labours" are replicated in the knight's "twelve thousand dolours."

4. An allusion to Revelation 22.1–2: "And he showed me a pure river of water of life, clear as crystal, proceeding out of the throne of God, and of the Lamb. In the midst of the street of it, and on either side of the river, was the tree of life which bore twelve manner of fruits and gave fruit every month, and the leaves of the tree served to heal the nation with."

5. The Well of Life, with its powers of renewal, is successively compared with waters of the Bible, of England and Europe, and of classical antiquity. In Siloam ("Silo") a blind man was cured by Christ (John 9.7); the crossing of the river Jordan saved the Jews (Deuteronomy 27.2–9), and Christ was baptized therein (Matthew 3.16). "Bath" and "Spau" (Spa) were famed for their medicinal waters. "Cephise" and "Hebrus" in Greece were noted for purifying and healing powers.

32

280 Which when his pensive Ladie saw from farre,
  Great woe and sorrow did her soule assay,°   *attack*
  As weening that the sad end of the warre,
  And gan to highest God entirely° pray,   *earnestly*
  That fearèd chaunce° from her to turne away;   *fate*
285 With folded hands and knees full lowly bent
  All night she watcht, ne once adowne would lay
  Her daintie limbs in her sad dreriment,[6]
But praying still did wake, and waking did lament.

33

The morrow next gan early to appeare,
290 That° Titan[7] rose to runne his daily race;   *when*
  But early ere the morrow next gan reare
  Out of the sea faire Titans deawy face,
  Up rose the gentle virgin from her place,
  And lookèd all about, if she might spy
295 Her loved knight to move his manly pace:
  For she had great doubt of his safety,
Since late she saw him fall before his enemy.

34

At last she saw, where he upstarted brave
  Out of the well, wherein he drenchèd lay;
300 As Eagle fresh out of the Ocean wave,
  Where he hath left his plumes all hoary gray,
  And deckt himselfe with feathers youthly gay,
  Like Eyas° hauke up mounts unto the skies,   *young*
  His newly budded pineons to assay,
305 And marveiles at himselfe, still as he flies:
So new this new-borne knight to battell new did rise.[8]

35

Whom when the damnèd feend so fresh did spy,
  No wonder if he wondred at the sight,
  And doubted, whether his late enemy
310 It were, or other new supplièd knight.
  He, now to prove his late renewèd might,
  High brandishing his bright deaw-burning blade,
  Upon his crested scalpe so sore did smite,
  That to the scull a yawning wound it made:
315 The deadly dint° his dullèd senses all dismaid.   *blow*

36

I wote° not, whether the revenging steele   *know*
  Were hardnèd with that holy water dew,
  Wherein he fell, or sharper edge did feele,
  Or his baptizèd hands now greater° grew;   *stronger*
320 Or other secret vertue did ensew;
  Else never could the force of fleshly arme,
  Ne molten mettall in his bloud embrew:°   *plunge*

---

6. Dismal condition.   8. Legend had it that the eagle could renew its youth
7. The sun god.   by bathing in a spring.

For till that stownd° could never wight him harme,   *stunning blow*
By subtilty, nor slight,° nor might, nor mighty charme.   *trickery*

37

325   The cruell wound enragèd him so sore,
     That loud he yellèd for exceeding paine;
     As hundred ramping Lyons seemed to rore,
     Whom ravenous hunger did there to constraine:
     Then gan he tosse aloft his stretchèd traine,°   *tail*
330   And therewith scourge the buxome° aire so sore,   *yielding*
     That to his force to yeelden it was faine;°   *obliged*
     Ne ought his sturdie strokes might stand afore,[9]
That high trees overthrew, and rocks in peeces tore.

38

The same advauncing high above his head,
335   With sharpe intended° sting so rude° him smot,   *extended/roughly*
     That to the earth him drove, as stricken dead,
     Ne living wight would have him life behot:°[1]   *called*
     The mortall sting his angry needle shot
     Quite through his shield, and in his shoulder seasd,
340   Where fast it stucke, ne would there out be got:
     The griefe° thereof him wondrous sore diseasd,°   *pain/afflicted*
Ne might his ranckling paine with patience be appeasd.

39

But yet more mindfull of his honour deare,
     Then of the grievous smart, which him did wring,°   *torment*
345   From loathèd soile he can° him lightly reare,   *began to*
     And strove to loose the farre infixèd sting:
     Which when in vaine he tryde with struggeling,
     Inflamed with wrath, his raging blade he heft,°   *heaved*
     And strooke so strongly, that the knotty string
350   Of his huge taile he quite a sunder cleft,
Five joynts thereof he hewd, and but the stump him left.

40

Hart cannot thinke, what outrage,° and what cryes,   *violent clamor*
     With foule enfouldred[2] smoake and flashing fire,
     The hell-bred beast threw forth unto the skyes,
355   That all was coverèd with darknesse dire:
     Then fraught with rancour, and engorgèd° ire,   *choking*
     He cast at once him to avenge for all,
     And gathering up himselfe out of the mire,
     With his uneven wings did fiercely fall
360   Upon his sunne-bright shield, and gript it fast withall.

41

Much was the man encombred with his hold,
     In feare to lose his weapon in his paw,
     Ne wist yet, how his talents° to unfold;   *talons*
     Nor harder was from Cerberus[3] greedie jaw
365   To plucke a bone, then from his cruell claw

---

9. I.e., neither could anything ("ought") stand before
his violent ("sturdie") strokes.
1. I.e., no one would have thought him alive.

2. Black as a thunderbolt.
3. The dog that guards the mouth of hell.

To reave° by strength the gripéd gage° away: *seize/prize*
     Thrise he assayd it from his foot to draw,
     And thrise in vaine to draw it did assay,
It booted nought to thinke, to robbe him of his pray.

42

370 Tho° when he saw no power might prevaile,   *then*
     His trustie sword he cald to his last aid,
     Wherewith he fiercely did his foe assaile,
     And double blowes about him stoutly laid,
     That glauncing fire out of the yron plaid;
375 As sparckles from the Andvile° use to fly,   *anvil*
     When heavie hammers on the wedge are swaid;°   *struck*
     Therewith at last he forst him to unty°   *loosen*
One of his grasping feete, him to defend thereby.

43

The other foot, fast fixèd on his shield,
380 Whenas no strength, nor stroks mote° him constraine   *might*
     To loose, ne yet the warlike pledge to yield,
     He smot thereat with all his might and maine,
     That nought so wondrous puissance might sustaine;
     Upon the joynt the lucky steele did light,
385 And made such way, that hewd it quite in twaine;
     The paw yet missèd not his minisht° might,   *lessened*
But hong still on the shield, as it at first was pight.°   *placed*

44

For griefe thereof, and divelish despight,
     From his infernall fournace forth he threw
390 Huge flames, that dimmèd all the heavens light,
     Enrold in duskish smoke and brimstone blew;
     As burning Aetna from his boyling stew°   *cauldron*
     Doth belch out flames, and rockes in peeces broke,
     And ragged ribs of mountaines molten new
395 Enwrapt in coleblacke clouds and filthy smoke,
That all the land with stench, and heaven with horror choke.

45

The heate whereof, and harmefull pestilence
     So sore him noyd,° that forst him to retire   *troubled*
     A little backward for his best defence,
400 To save his bodie from the scorching fire,
     Which he from hellish entrailes did expire.°   *breathe out*
     It chaunst (eternall God that chaunce did guide)
     As he recoylèd backward, in the mire
     His nigh forwearied feeble feet did slide,
405 And downe he fell, with dread of shame sore terrifide.

46

There grew a goodly tree him faire beside,
     Loaden with fruit and apples rosie red,
     As they in pure vermilion had beene dide,
     Whereof great vertues over all were red:°   *declared*
410 For happie life to all, which thereon fed,
     And life eke° everlasting did befall: *also*
     Great God it planted in that blessed sted°   *place*

With his almightie hand, and did it call
The Tree of Life, the crime of our first fathers fall.[4]

47

415 In all the world like was not to be found,
Save in that soile, where all good things did grow,
And freely sprong out of the fruitfull ground,
As incorrupted Nature did them sow,
Till that dread Dragon all did overthrow.
420 Another like faire tree eke° grew thereby,   *also*
Whereof who so did eat, eftsoones did know
Both good and ill: O mornefull memory:
That tree through one mans fault hath doen us all to dy.[5]

48

From that first tree forth flowd, as from a well,
425 A trickling streame of Balme, most soveraine°   *powerful for cures*
And daintie deare,[6] which on the ground still fell,
And overflowèd all the fertill plaine,
As it had deawèd bene with timely° raine: *seasonable*
Life and long health that gratious° ointment gave,   *full of grace*
430 And deadly woundes could heale, and reare° againe   *raise*
The senselesse corse appointed° for the grave.   *made ready*
Into that same he fell: which did from death him save.[7]

49

For nigh thereto the ever damnèd beast
Durst not approch, for he was deadly made,[8]
435 And all that life preservèd, did detest:
Yet he it oft adventured° to invade.   *attempted*
By this the drouping day-light gan to fade,
And yeeld his roome to sad succeeding night,
Who with her sable mantle gan to shade
440 The face of earth, and wayes of living wight,
And high her burning torch set up in heaven bright.

50

When gentle Una saw the second fall
Of her deare knight, who wearie of long fight,
And faint through losse of bloud, moved not at all,
445 But lay as in a dreame of deepe delight,
Besmeard with pretious Balme, whose vertuous might
Did heale his wounds, and scorching heat alay,[9]
Againe she stricken was with sore affright,
And for his safetie gan devoutly pray;
450 And watch the noyous° night, and wait for joyous day.   *afflicting*

51

The joyous day gan early to appeare,
And faire Aurora from the deawy bed

---

4. Genesis 2.9 describes the Tree of Life and also the Tree of Knowledge of Good and Evil, both of which God planted in the Garden of Eden. The "crime of our first fathers fall" is that Adam, in eating of the second and being banished from Eden, separated himself—and us—from the first. The Tree of Life appears again in the New Jerusalem (Revelation 22.2).
5. I.e., killed us.

6. Precious.
7. The healing balm flowing from the Tree of Life is understood to be Christ's blood, shed to redeem humankind from eternal damnation.
8. I.e., a child of death.
9. Cf. Revelation 2.7,11: "To him that overcometh will I give to eat of the tree of life" and "He that overcometh shall not be hurt of the second death."

Of aged Tithone gan her selfe to reare,[1]
With rosie cheekes, for shame as blushing red;
455　Her golden lockes for haste were loosely shed
About her eares, when Una her did marke
Clymbe to her charet, all with flowers spred,
From heaven high to chase the chearelesse darke;
With merry note her loud salutes the mounting larke.

52

460　Then freshly up arose the doughtie knight,
All healèd of his hurts and woundès wide,
And did himselfe to battell readie dight;°   *prepare*
Whose early foe awaiting him beside
To have devourd, so soone as day he spyde,
465　When now he saw himselfe so freshly reare,
As if late fight had nought him damnifyde,°   *injured*
He woxe° dismayd, and garr his fate to feare;   *grew*
Nathlesse° with wonted rage he him advauncèd neare.   *nevertheless*

53

And in his first encounter, gaping wide,
470　He thought attonce him to have swallowed quight,
And rusht upon him with outragious pride;
Who him r'encountring fierce, as hauke in flight,
Perforce rebutted° backe. The weapon bright   *drove*
Taking advantage of his open jaw,
475　Ran through his mouth with so importune° might,   *violent*
That deepe emperst his darksome hollow maw,
And back retyrd,[2] his life bloud forth with all did draw.

54

So downe he fell, and forth his life did breath,
That vanisht into smoke and cloudès swift;
480　So downe he fell, that th' earth him underneath
Did grone, as feeble so great load to lift;
So downe he fell, as an huge rockie clift,
Whose false° foundation waves have washt away,   *insecure*
With dreadfull poyse° is from the mayneland rift,° *falling weight/split*
485　And rolling downe, great Neptune doth dismay;
So downe he fell, and like an heapèd mountaine lay.

55

The knight himselfe even trembled at his fall,
So huge and horrible a masse it seemed;
And his deare Ladie, that beheld it all,
490　Durst not approch for dread, which she misdeemed,°   *misjudged*
But yet at last, when as the direfull feend
She saw not stirre, off-shaking vaine affright,
She nigher drew, and saw that joyous end:
Then God she praysd, and thankt her faithfull knight,
495　That had atchieved so great a conquest by his might.

---

1. Aurora is goddess of the dawn, Tithones her husband ("aged" because he was granted everlasting life
without everlasting youth).
2. On being drawn back.

Canto 12

Faire Una to the Redcrosse knight
betrouthéd is with joy:
Though false Duessa it to barre
her false sleights doe imploy.

1

Behold I see the haven nigh at hand,
　　To which I meane my wearie course to bend;
　　Vere the maine shete, and beare up with the land,[3]
　　The which afore is fairely to be kend,°   *recognized*
5　　And seemeth safe from stormes, that may offend;
　　There this faire virgin wearie of her way
　　Must landed be, now at her journeyes end:
　　There eke my feeble barke° a while may stay,   *ship*
Till merry° wind and weather call her thence away.   *favorable*

2

10　Scarsely had Phoebus in the glooming East[4]
　　Yet harnessèd his firie-footed teeme,
　　Ne reard above the earth his flaming creast,°   *crest*
　　When the last deadly smoke aloft did steeme,
　　That signe of last outbreathèd life did seeme
15　　Unto the watchman on the castle wall;
　　Who thereby dead that balefull° Beast did deeme,   *evil*
　　And to his Lord and Ladie lowd gan call,
To tell, how he had seene the Dragons fatall fall.

3

Uprose with hastie joy, and feeble speed
20　　That aged Sire, the Lord of all that land,
　　And lookèd forth, to weet, if true indeede
　　Those tydings were, as he did understand,
　　Which whenas true by tryall he out fond,
　　He bad to open wyde his brazen gate,
25　　Which long time had bene shut, and out of hond°   *straightway*
　　Proclaymèd joy and peace through all his state;
For dead now was their foe, which them forrayèd late.[5]

4

Then gan triumphant Trompets sound on hie,
　　That sent to heaven the ecchoèd report
30　　Of their new joy, and happie victorie
　　Gainst him, that had them long opprest with tort,°   *wrong*
　　And fast imprisonèd in siegèd fort.
　　Then all the people, as in solemne feast,
　　To him assembled with one full consort,[6]
35　　Rejoycing at the fall of that great beast,
From whose eternall bondage now they were releast.

5

Forth came that auncient Lord and aged Queene,
　　Arayd in antique robes downe to the ground,

---

3. Release the mainsail line and sail toward the land.　　4. I.e., dawn.
The nautical metaphor echoes many classical authors　　5. Had recently ravaged.
and Chaucer's *Troilus and Criseyde* (2.1–7).　　6. All together.

And sad habiliments right well beseene;[7]
40   A noble crew about them waited round
     Of sage and sober Peres,° all gravely gownd;   *peers*
     Whom farre before did march a goodly band
     Of tall young men, all hable armes to sownd,[8]
     But now they laurell braunches bore in hand;
45   Glad signe of victorie and peace in all their land.

6

Unto that doughtie Conquerour they came,
     And him before themselves prostrating low,
     Their Lord and Patrone° loud did him proclaime,   *defender*
     And at his feet their laurell boughes did throw.
50   Soone after them all dauncing on a row
     The comely virgins came, with girlands dight,°   *adorned*
     As fresh as flowres in medow greene do grow,
     When morning deaw upon their leaves doth light:
And in their hands sweet Timbrels° all upheld on hight.   *tambourines*

7

55   And them before, the fry° of children young   *crowd*
     Their wanton° sports and childish mirth did play,   *playful*
     And to the Maydens sounding tymbrels sung
     In well attunèd notes, a joyous lay,
     And made delightfull musicke all the way,
60   Untill they came, where that faire virgin stood;
     As faire Diana[9] in fresh sommers day
     Beholds her Nymphes, enraunged° in shadie wood,   *ranged*
Some wrestle, some do run, some bathe in christall flood.

8

So she beheld those maydens meriment
65   With chearefull vew; who when to her they came,
     Themselves to ground with gratious humblesse° bent,   *humility*
     And her adored by honorable name,[1]
     Lifting to heaven her everlasting fame:
     Then on her head they set a girland greene,
70   And crownèd her twixt earnest and twixt game:[2]
     Who in her selfe-resemblance well beseene,[3]
Did seeme such, as she was, a goodly maiden Queene.

9

And after all, the raskall many° ran,   *rabble throng*
     Heapèd together in rude rablement,[4]
75   To see the face of that victorious man:
     Whom all admired,° as from heaven sent,   *wondered at*
     And gazd upon with gaping wonderment.
     But when they came, where that dead Dragon lay,
     Stretcht on the ground in monstrous large extent,
80   The sight with idle° feare did them dismay,   *baseless*
Ne durst approch him nigh, to touch, or once assay.

---

7. I.e., their sober, appropriate ("right well beseene")
attire.
8. Able to fight with weapons.
9. Goddess of the hunt.

1. With titles of honor.
2. I.e., half in fun.
3. I.e., looking appropriately like herself.
4. Discordant confusion.

10

Some feard, and fled; some feard and well it faynd;°　　　*concealed*
One that would wiser seeme, then all the rest,
Warnd him not touch, for yet perhaps remaynd
Some lingring life within his hollow brest,
Or in his wombe might lurke some hidden nest
Of many Dragonets,° his fruitfull seed;　　　*young dragons*
Another said, that in his eyes did rest
Yet sparckling fire, and bad thereof take heed;
Another said, he saw him move his eyes indeed.

11

One mother, when as her foolehardie chyld
Did come too neare, and with his talants° play,　　　*talons*
Halfe dead through feare, her litle babe revyld,°　　　*scolded*
And to her gossips° gan in counsell° say;　　*women friends/private*
"How can I tell, but that his talants may
Yet scratch my sonne, or rend his tender hand?"
So diversly themselves in vaine they fray;°　　　*scare*
Whiles some more bold, to measure him nigh stand,
To prove° how many acres he did spread of land.　　　*determine*

12

Thus flockèd all the folke him round about,
The whiles that hoarie° king, with all his traine,　　　*gray-haired*
Being arrivèd, where that champion stout
After his foes defeasance° did remaine,　　　*defeat*
Him goodly greetes, and faire does entertaine,
With princely gifts of yvorie and gold,
And thousand thankes him yeelds for all his paine.
Then when his daughter deare he does behold,
Her dearely doth imbrace, and kisseth manifold.°　　　*many times*

13

And after to his Pallace he them brings,
With shaumes,[5] and trompets, and with Clarions sweet;
And all the way the joyous people sings,
And with their garments strowes the pavèd street:
Whence mounting up, they find purveyance° meet　　　*provisions*
Of all, that royall Princes court became,°　　　*suited*
And all the floore was underneath their feet
Bespred with costly scarlot of great name,[6]
On which they lowly sit, and fitting purpose frame.

14

What needs me tell their feast and goodly guize,°　　　*behavior*
In which was nothing riotous nor vaine?
What needs of daintie dishes to devize,°　　　*talk*
Of comely services, or courtly trayne?
My narrow leaves cannot in them containe
The large discourse[7] of royall Princes state.
Yet was their manner then but bare and plaine:

5. Ancient wind instrument like an oboe.　　7. I.e., full description.
6. I.e., famous scarlet cloth.

125   For th' antique world excesse and pride did hate,
Such proud luxurious pompe is swollen up but late.[8]

15

Then when with meates and drinkes of every kinde
     Their fervent appetites they quenchèd had,
     That auncient Lord gan fit occasion finde,
130   Of straunge adventures, and of perils sad,°   *grave*
     Which in his travell him befallen had,
     For to demaund of his renowmèd guest:
     Who then with utt'rance grave, and count'nance sad,
     From point to point, as is before exprest,
135 Discourst his voyage long, according° his request.   *granting*

16

Great pleasure mixt with pittifull° regard,   *sympathetic*
     That godly King and Queene did passionate,[9]
     Whiles they his pittifull° adventures heard,   *deserving pity*
     That oft they did lament his lucklesse state,
140   And often blame the too importune° fate,   *severe*
     That heapd on him so many wrathfull wreakes:[1]
     For never gentle knight, as he of late,
     So tossèd was in fortunes cruell freakes,°   *whims*
And all the while salt teares bedeawd the hearers cheaks.

17

145 Then said that royall Pere in sober wise:
     "Deare Sonne, great beene the evils, which ye bore
     From first to last In your late enterprise,
     That I note,° whether prayse, or pitty more: *know not*
     For never living man, I weene, so sore
150   In sea of deadly daungers was distrest;
     But since now safe ye seisèd° have the shore,   *reached*
     And well arrivèd are (high God be blest),
Let us devize° of ease and everlasting rest."   *think*

18

"Ah dearest Lord," said then that doughty knight,
155   "Of ease or rest I may not yet devize;
     For by the faith, which I to armes have plight,°   *pledged*
     I bounden am streight after this emprize,°   *enterprise*
     As that your daughter can ye well advize,
     Backe to returne to that great Faerie Queene,
160   And her to serve six yeares in warlike wize,
     Gainst that proud Paynim king, that workes her teene:°   *sorrow*
Therefore I ought° crave pardon, till I there have beene."[2]   *must*

19

"Unhappie falles that hard necessitie,"
     Quoth he, "the troubler of my happie peace,
165   And vowèd foe of my felicitie;
     Ne° I against the same can justly preace:°   *neither/press*
     But since that band° ye cannot now release,   *obligation*

---

8. Just recently.
9. I.e., did feel and express.
1. Vengeful injuries.
2. The final Christian triumph, the marriage of Christ and the true church, will be achieved only at the end of time. Meanwhile, the struggle against evil (and the Roman church) continues.

Nor doen undo (for vowes may not be vaine),[3]
  Soone as the terme of those six yeares shall cease,
170 Ye then shall hither backe returne againe,
The marriage to accomplish vowd betwixt you twain.

20

"Which for my part I covet to performe,
  In sort as through the world I did proclame,
  That who so kild that monster most deforme,
175 And him in hardy battaile overcame,
  Should have mine onely daughter to his Dame,°   *wife*
  And of my kingdome heire apparaunt bee:
  Therefore since now to thee perteines° the same,   *belongs*
  By dew desert of noble chevalree,
180 Both daughter and eke° kingdome, lo I yield to thee."   *also*

21

Then forth he callèd that his daughter faire,
  The fairest Un' his onely daughter deare,
  His onely daughter, and his onely heyre;
  Who forth proceeding with sad° sober cheare,°   *grave/countenance*
185 As bright as doth the morning starre appeare
  Out of the East, with flaming lockes bedight,°   *bedecked*
  To tell that dawning day is drawing neare,
  And to the world does bring long wishèd light;
So faire and fresh that Lady shewd her selfe in sight.

22

190 So faire and fresh, as freshest flowre in May;
  For she had layd her mournefull stole aside,
  And widow-like sad wimple° throwne away,   *veil*
  Wherewith her heavenly beautie she did hide,
  Whiles on her wearie journey she did ride;
195 And on her now a garment she did weare,
  All lilly white, withoutten spot, or pride,°   *ornament*
  That seemed like silke and silver woven neare,°   *tightly*
But neither silke nor silver therein did appeare.[4]

23

The blazing brightnesse of her beauties beame,
200 And glorious light of her sunshyny face[5]
  To tell, were as to strive against the streame.
  My ragged rimes are all too rude and bace,
  Her heavenly lineaments for to enchace.°   *adorn*
  Ne wonder; for her owne deare lovèd knight,
205 All° were she dayly with himselfe in place,   *although*
  Did wonder much at her celestiall sight:
Oft had he seene her faire, but never so faire dight.

24

So fairely dight, when she in presence came,
  She to her Sire made humble reverence,

3. I.e., you cannot undo what is done ("doen"), for vows may not be (made) vain.
4. "The marriage of the Lamb is come, and his wife hath made herself ready. And to her was granted that she should be arrayed in fine linen, clean and white: for the fine linen is the righteousness of saints" (Revelation 19.7–8).
5. Revelation 21.9,11 describes the New Jerusalem as "the bride, the Lamb's wife . . . her light was like unto a stone most precious."

210   And bowèd low, that her right well became,
           And added grace unto her excellence:
           Who with great wisdome, and grave eloquence
           Thus gan to say. But eare° he thus had said,   *ere*
           With flying speede, and seeming great pretence,°   *purpose*
215   Came running in, much like a man dismaid,
           A Messenger with letters, which his message said.

                               25
       All in the open hall amazèd stood,
           At suddeinnesse of that unwarie° sight,   *unexpected*
           And wondred at his breathlesse hastie mood.
220   But he for nought would stay his passage right°   *direct*
           Till fast° before the king he did alight;   *close*
           Where falling flat, great humblesse he did make,
           And kist the ground, whereon his foot was pight;°   *placed*
           Then to his hands that writ° he did betake,°   *document/deliver*
225   Which he disclosing, red thus, as the paper spake.

                               26
       "To thee, most mighty king of Eden faire,
           Her greeting sends in these sad lines addrest,
           The wofull daughter, and forsaken heire
           Of that great Emperour of all the West;
230   And bids thee be advizèd for the best,
           Ere thou thy daughter linck in holy band
           Of wedlocke to that new unknowen guest:
           For he already plighted his right hand
       Unto another love, and to another land.

                               27
235   "To me sad mayd, or rather widow sad,
           He was affiauncèd long time before,
           And sacred pledges he both gave, and had,
           False erraunt knight, infamous, and forswore:
           Witnesse the burning Altars, which° he swore,   *by which*
240   And guiltie heavens of[6] his bold perjury,
           Which though he hath polluted oft of yore,
           Yet I to them for judgement just do fly,
       And them conjure° t' avenge this shamefull injury.   *implore*

                               28
       "Therefore since mine he is, or° free or bond,°   *whether/bound*
245   Or false or trew, or living or else dead,
           Withhold, O soveraine Prince, your hasty hond
           From knitting league with him, I you aread;°   *advise*
           Ne wene° my right with strength adowne to tread,   *think*
           Through weakenesse of my widowhed, or woe:
250   For truth is strong, her rightfull cause to plead,
           And shall find friends, if need requireth soe,
       So bids thee well to fare, Thy neither friend, nor foe, Fidessa."

                               29
       When he these bitter byting words had red,
           The tydings straunge did him abashèd make,

---

6. I.e., and heavens polluted by.

255   That still he sate long time astonishèd
      As in great muse,° ne word to creature spake.   *amazement*
      At last his solemne silence thus he brake,
      With doubtfull eyes fast fixèd on his guest:
      "Redoubted° knight, that for mine onely sake[7]   *honored*
260   Thy life and honour late adventurest,
  Let nought be hid from me, that ought to be exprest.

30

  "What meane these bloudy vowes, and idle threats,
      Throwne out from womanish impatient mind?
      What heavens? what altars? what enragèd heates
265   Here heapèd up with termes of love unkind,°   *unnatural*
      My conscience cleare with guilty bands[8] would bind?
      High God be witnesse, that I guiltlesse ame.
      But if your selfe, Sir knight, ye faultie° find,   *guilty*
      Or wrappèd be in loves of former Dame,
270 With crime do not it cover, but disclose the same."

31

  To whom the Redcrosse knight this answere sent,
      "My Lord, my King, be nought hereat dismayd,
      Till well ye wote by grave intendiment,[9]
      What woman, and wherefore doth me upbrayd
275   With breach of love, and loyalty betrayd.
      It was in my mishaps, as hitherward
      I lately traveild, that unwares I strayd
      Out of my way, through perils straunge and hard;
  That day should faile me, ere I had them all declard.

32

280 "There did I find, or rather I was found
      Of this false woman, that Fidessa hight,
      Fidessa hight the falsest Dame on ground,
      Most false Duessa, royall richly dight,
      That easie was t' invegle° weaker sight: *deceive*
285   Who by her wicked arts, and wylie skill,
      Too false and strong for earthly skill or might,
      Unwares me wrought unto her wicked will,
  And to my foe betrayd, when least I fearèd ill."

33

  Then steppèd forth the goodly royall Mayd,
290   And on the ground her selfe prostrating low,
      With sober countenaunce thus to him sayd:
      "O pardon me, my soveraigne Lord, to show
      The secret treasons, which of late I know
      To have bene wroght by that false sorceresse.
295   She onely she it is, that earst did throw
      This gentle knight into so great distresse,
  That death him did awaite in dayly wretchednesse.

34

  "And now it seemes, that she subornèd hath
      This craftie messenger with letters vaine,

7. For my sake alone.
8. I.e., bonds of guilt.
9. I.e., serious investigation.

300 To worke new woe and improvided scath,[1]
By breaking of the band betwixt us twaine;
Wherein she usèd hath the practicke paine[2]
Of this false footman, clokt with simplenesse,
Whom if ye please for to discover plaine,
305 Ye shall him Archimago find, I ghesse,
The falsest man alive; who tries shall find no lesse."

35

The king was greatly movèd at her speach,
And all with suddein indignation fraight,°   filled
Bad° on that Messenger rude hands to reach.   bade
310 Eftsoones° the Gard, which on his state did wait,   forthwith
Attacht that faitor° false, and bound him strait: impostor
Who seeming sorely chauffèd° at his band,   angered
As chainèd Beare, whom cruell dogs do bait,
With idle force did faine them to withstand,
315 And often semblaunce made to scape out of their hand.

36

But they him layd full low in dungeon deepe,
And bound him hand and foote with yron chains.
And with continuall watch did warely° keepe;   vigilantly
Who then would thinke, that by his subtile trains
320 He could escape fowle death or deadly paines?[3]
Thus when that Princes wrath was pacifide,
He gan renew the late forbidden banes,[4]
And to the knight his daughter deare he tyde,
With sacred rites and vowes for ever to abyde.

37

325 His owne two hands the holy knots did knit,
That none but death for ever can devide;
His owne two hands, for such a turne° most fit,   act
The housling° fire did kindle and provide,   sacramental
And holy water thereon sprinckled wide;[5]
330 At which the bushy Teade° a groome did light,   marriage torch
And sacred lampe in secret chamber hide,
Where it should not be quenchèd day nor night,
For feare of evill fates, but burnen ever bright.

38

Then gan they sprinckle all the posts with wine,
335 And made great feast to solemnize that day;
They all perfumde with frankencense divine,
And precious odours fetcht from far away,
That all the house did sweat with great aray:
And all the while sweete Musicke did apply
340 Her curious° skill, the warbling notes to play,   intricate

1. Unexpected harm.
2. Treacherous skill.
3. "And he laid hold on the dragon, that old serpent, which is the Devil, and Satan, and bound him a thousand years, And cast him into the bottomless pit, and shut him up, and set a seal upon him, that he should deceive the nations no more, till the thousand years should be fulfilled: and after that he must be loosed a little season" (Revelation 20.2–3).
4. Banns, i.e., announcements of marriage.
5. Marriages in ancient times were solemnized with sacramental fire and water.

To drive away the dull Melancholy;
The whiles one sung a song of love and jollity.

39

During the which there was an heavenly noise
    Heard sound through all the Pallace pleasantly,
345   Like as it had bene many an Angels voice,
    Singing before th' eternall majesty,
    In their trinall triplicities[6] on hye;
    Yet wist no creature, whence that heavenly sweet°   *delight*
    Proceeded, yet each one felt secretly°   *inwardly*
350   Himselfe thereby reft of his sences meet,°   *proper*
And ravishèd with rare impression in his sprite.°[7]   *spirit*

40

Great joy was made that day of young and old,
    And solemne feast proclaimd throughout the land,
    That their exceeding merth may not be told:
355   Suffice it heare by signes to understand
    The usuall joyes at knitting of loves band.
    Thrise happy man the knight himselfe did hold,
    Possessèd of his Ladies hart and hand,
    And ever, when his eye did her behold,
360   His heart did seeme to melt in pleasures manifold.

41

Her joyous presence and sweet company
    In full content he there did long enjoy,
    Ne wicked envie, ne vile gealosy
    His deare delights were able to annoy:
365   Yet swimming in that sea of blisfull joy,
    He nought forgot, how he whilome had sworne,
    In case he could that monstrous beast destroy,
    Unto his Faerie Queene backe to returne:
The which he shortly did, and Una left to mourne.

42

370 Now strike your sailes ye jolly Mariners,
    For we be come unto a quiet rode,°   *harbor*
    Where we must land some of our passengers,
    And light this wearie vessell of her lode.
    Here she a while may make her safe abode,
375   Till she repairèd have her tackles spent,°   *worn out*
    And wants supplide. And then againe abroad
    On the long voyage whereto she is bent:
Well may she speede and fairely finish her intent.

---

6. The "trinall triplicities" are the nine angelic orders, divided into three groups of three, the whole hierarchy corresponding to the nine spheres of the universe. The music heard in this stanza is the music of the spheres, not audible on earth since the Fall.

7. "Let us be glad and rejoice, and give honor to him: for the marriage of the Lamb is come" (Revelation 9.6). In Revelation, the marriage of Christ and the New Jerusalem signals the general redemption.

From Amoretti[1]

Sonnet 1

Happy ye leaves when as those lilly hands,
Which hold my life in their dead doing[2] might,
Shall handle you and hold in loves soft bands,
Lyke captives trembling at the victors sight.
5 And happy lines, on which with starry light,
Those lamping° eyes will deigne sometimes to look   *flashing*
And reade the sorrowes of my dying spright,°   *spirit*
Written with teares in harts close° bleeding book.   *secret*
And happy rymes bathed in the sacred brooke,
10 Of Helicon[3] whence she derivèd is,
When ye behold that Angels blessed looke,
My soules long lackèd foode, my heavens blis.
Leaves, lines, and rymes, seeke her to please alone,
Whom if ye please, I care for other none.

Sonnet 34

Lyke as a ship that through the ocean wyde,
By conduct of some star doth make her way,
Whenas a storme hath dimd her trusty guyde,
Out of her course doth wander far astray.
5 So I whose star, that wont with her bright ray,
Me to direct, with cloudes is overcast,
Doe wander now in darknesse and dismay,
Through hidden perils round about me plast.°   *placed*
Yet hope I well, that when this storme is past
10 My Helice[4] the lodestar of my lyfe
Will shine again, and looke on me at last,
With lovely light to cleare my cloudy grief.
Till then I wander carefull° comfortlesse,   *full of cares*
In secret sorow and sad pensivenesse.

Sonnet 37

What guyle is this, that those her golden tresses,
She doth attyre under a net of gold:
And with sly° skill so cunningly them dresses,   *clever*
That which is gold or heare,° may scarse be told?   *hair*
5 Is it that mens frayle eyes, which gaze too bold,
She may entangle in that golden snare:
And being caught may craftily enfold,
Theyr weaker harts, which are not wel aware?

1. "Little loves" or "little love poems." They are sonnets to a woman named Elizabeth—probably Elizabeth Boyle, who became Spenser's second wife. The sequence, or cycle, tells of a courtship; *Epithalamion*, with which these sonnets were published, is a song for a wedding. The *Amoretti* draws, like other sonnet cycles, on characteristic and conventional themes and conceits; what is characteristically Spenserian about them is his yoking of the spirit and the flesh. The rhyme scheme is *abab bcbc cdcd ee*, a difficult pattern requiring four words for two of the rhymes.
2. I.e., killing.
3. The "sacred brooke" is the Hippocrene, which flows from Mt. Helicon, the mountain sacred to the Muses.
4. The Big Dipper or North Star.

Take heed therefore, myne eyes, how ye doe stare
10 Henceforth too rashly on that guilefull net,
In which if ever ye entrappèd are,
Out of her bands ye by no means shall get.
Fondnesse° it were for any being free,   *foolishness*
To covet fetters, though they golden bee.

Sonnet 54

Of this worlds theatre in which we stay,
My love like the spectator ydly sits
Beholding me that all the pageants° play,   *roles*
Disguysing diversly my troubled wits.
5 Sometimes I joy when glad occasion fits,
And mask in myrth lyke to a comedy:
Soone after when my joy to sorrow flits,
I waile and make my woes a tragedy.
Yet she, beholding me with constant eye,
10 Delights not in my merth nor rues my smart:
But when I laugh she mocks, and when I cry
She laughs and hardens evermore her heart.
What then can move her? if nor merth nor mone,°   *moan*
She is no woman, but a sencelesse stone.

Sonnet 64[5]

Comming to kisse her lyps (such grace I found)
Me seemd I smelt a gardin of sweet flowres
That dainty odours from them threw around
For damzels fit to decke their lovers bowres.
5 Her lips did smell lyke unto gillyflowers,°   *carnations*
Her ruddy cheeks like unto roses red;
Her snowy browes lyke budded bellamoures,°   *bellflowers*
Her lovely eyes like pincks but newly spred,
Her goodly bosome lyke a strawberry bed,
10 Her neck lyke to a bounch of cullambynes;
Her brest lyke lillyes ere theyr leaves be shed,
Her nipples lyke yong blossomd jessemynes.°   *jasmines*
Such fragrant flowres doe give most odorous smell,
But her sweet odour did them all excell.

Sonnet 65

The doubt which ye misdeeme, fayre love, is vaine,
That fondly feare to loose your liberty,
When loosing one, two liberties ye gayne,
And make him bond that bondage earst° dyd fly.   *formerly*
5 Sweet be the bands, the which true love doth tye,
Without constraynt or dread of any ill:
The gentle birde feels no captivity

---

5. Much of the imagery of this sonnet is imitated from the Song of Solomon 4.10–16.

Within her cage, but singes and feeds her fill.
There pride dare not approch, nor discord spill°   *destroy*
10   The league twixt them, that loyal love hath bound;
But simple truth and mutuall good will,
Seekes with sweet peace to salve each others wound.
There fayth doth fearlesse dwell in brasen towre,
And spotlesse pleasure builds her sacred bowre.

Sonnet 67[6]

Lyke as a huntsman after weary chace,
Seeing the game from him escapt away,
Sits downe to rest him in some shady place,
With panting hounds beguiled of their pray,
5   So after long pursuit and vaine assay,
When I all weary had the chace forsooke,
The gentle deare returnd the selfe-same way,
Thinking to quench her thirst at the next brooke.
There she beholding me with mylder looke,
10   Sought not to fly, but fearelesse still did bide,
Till I in hand her yet halfe trembling tooke,
And with her owne goodwill hir fyrmely tyde.
Strange thing me seemd to see a beast so wyld,
So goodly wonne with her owne will beguyld.°   *entangled*

Sonnet 68

Most glorious Lord of lyfe, that on this day,[7]
Didst make thy triumph over death and sin:
And having harrowed hell,[8] didst bring away
Captivity thence captive us to win:
5   This joyous day, deare Lord, with joy begin,
And grant that we for whom thou diddest dye
Being with thy deare blood clene washt from sin,
May live for ever in felicity.
And that thy love we weighing worthily,
10   May likewise love thee for the same againe:
And for thy sake that all lyke deare didst buy,
With love may one another entertayne.
So let us love, deare love, lyke as we ought,
Love is the lesson which the Lord us taught.[9]

Sonnet 74

Most happy letters framed by skilfull trade,°   *practice*
With which that happy name was first desynd:
The which three times thrise happy hath me made,

---

6. An imitation of Petrarch's *Rime* 190, *Una candida cerva*, but with a very different ending.
7. Easter day.
8. In the apocryphal gospels, Christ descended into hell and led out those who had lived before his time that deserved to be saved. "Captivity thence captive" is a biblical phrase, as in Judges 5.12 and Ephesians 4.8.
9. Cf. John 15.12: "This is my commandment, That ye love one another, as I have loved you."

With guifts of body, fortune and of mind.
5   The first my being to me gave by kind,°   *nature*
     From mothers womb derived by dew descent,
     The second is my sovereigne Queene most kind,
     That honour and large richesse to me lent.
     The third my love, my lives last ornament,
10   By whom my spirit out of dust was raysed:
     To speake her prayse and glory excellent,
     Of all alive most worthy to be praysed.
     Ye three Elizabeths for ever live,
     That three such graces did unto me give.

Sonnet 75

     One day I wrote her name upon the strand,°   *beach*
     But came the waves and washèd it away:
     Agayne I wrote it with a second hand,
     But came the tyde, and made my paynes his pray.°   *prey*
5   "Vayne man," sayd she, "that doest in vaine assay,°   *attempt*
     A mortall thing so to immortalize,
     For I my selve shall lyke to this decay,
     And eek° my name bee wypèd out lykewize."   *also*
     "Not so," quod° I, "let baser things devize,°   *quoth/contrive*
10   To dy in dust, but you shall live by fame:
     My verse your vertues rare shall eternize,
     And in the heavens wryte your glorious name.
     Where whenas death shall all the world subdew,
     Our love shall live, and later life renew."

Sonnet 79

     Men call you fayre, and you doe credit° it,   *believe*
     For that your selfe ye dayly such doe see:
     But the trew fayre,° that is the gentle wit,   *beauty*
     And vertuous mind, is much more praysd of me.
5   For all the rest, how ever fayre it be,
     Shall turne to nought and loose that glorious hew:°   *form*
     But onely that is permanent and free
     From frayle corruption, that doth flesh ensew.°   *outlast*
     That is true beautie: that doth argue you
10   To be divine and borne of heavenly seed:
     Derived from that fayre Spirit,[1] from whom al true
     And perfect beauty did at first proceed.
     He onely fayre, and what he fayre hath made:
     All other fayre, lyke flowres, untymely fade.

1595

Epithalamion   An epithalamion is a wedding song or poem; its Greek name
conveys that it was sung on the threshold of the bridal chamber. The genre was

1. I.e., God.

widely practiced by the Latin poets, particularly Catullus. Common elements are the invocation to the Muses, the bringing home of the bride, the singing and dancing at the wedding party, and the preparations for the wedding night. The poem's merit is not in its originality but in its evocative commingling of the conventions, with which Spenser blends his own Irish setting and native folklore.

The *Epithalamion* has a complex structure. First there is an introductory stanza, then two ten-stanza sections on each side of the two central stanzas about the church ceremony itself. Each of the ten-stanza sections is divided into units of three-four-three. As A. Kent Hieatt has pointed out in *Short Time's Endless Monument* (1960), the poem also has a numerical structure that reinforces the motif of the passage of time. For example, the poem has exactly 365 long lines (composed of five or more metrical feet) matching the number of days in the year. There are twenty-four stanzas, counting the envoy, matching the hours of one full day. Of these stanzas, the first sixteen describe the course of the day, in which the woods echo the various sounds; the last eight describe the night, a time of silence in which the woods no longer echo. At the summer solstice (cf. line 266 and note 6) in the latitude of Ireland, night falls after sixteen hours of daylight.

The subtle time structure serves to emphasize the endless cycle of time, measured by the passing of the hours and the years. But this marriage—and this celebratory poem—will endure, linking time with eternity.

Epithalamion

    Ye learned sisters which have oftentimes
    Beene to me ayding, others to adorne:[1]
    Whom ye thought worthy of your gracefull rymes,
    That even the greatest did not greatly scorne
5   To heare theyr names sung in your simple layes,
    But joyèd in theyr prayse.
    And when ye list your owne mishaps to mourne,
    Which death, or love, or fortunes wreck did rayse,
    Your string could soone to sadder tenor° turne,   *mood*
10   And teach the woods and waters to lament
    Your dolefull dreriment.°   *sorrow*
    Now lay those sorrowfull complaints aside,
    And having all your heads with girland crownd,
    Helpe me mine owne loves prayses to resound,
15   Ne let the same of° any be envide: *by*
    So Orpheus did for his owne bride,[2]
    So I unto my selfe alone will sing,
    The woods shall to me answer and my Eccho ring.

    Early before the worlds light giving lampe,
20   His golden beame upon the hils doth spred,
    Having disperst the nights unchearefull dampe,
    Doe ye awake, and with fresh lustyhed°   *vigor*
    Go to the bowre° of my belovèd love,   *bedchamber*
    My truest turtle dove,
25   Bid her awake; for Hymen[3] is awake,

1. To write poems in praise of others. The "learned sisters" are the Muses.
2. Orpheus, archetype of the poet in classical antiqui-

ty, was famous for his love for his wife, Eurydice.
3. The god of marriage, who leads a "maske" or procession at weddings.

And long since ready forth his maske to move,
With his bright Tead[4] that flames with many a flake,°   *spark*
And many a bachelor to waite on him,
In theyr fresh garments trim.
30   Bid her awake therefore and soone her dight,°   *dress*
For lo the wishèd day is come at last,
That shall for al the paynes and sorrowes past,
Pay to her usury° of long delight: *interest*
And whylest she doth her dight,
35   Doe ye to her of joy and solace sing,
That all the woods may answer and your Eccho ring.

Bring with you all the Nymphes that you can heare[5]
Both of the rivers and the forrests greene:
And of the sea that neighbours to her neare,
40   Al with gay girlands goodly wel beseene.[6]
And let them also with them bring in hand,
Another gay girland
For my fayre love of lillyes and of roses,
Bound truelove wize[7] with a blew silke riband.
45   And let them make great store of bridale poses,°   *posies*
And let them eeke° bring store of other flowers   *also*
To deck the bridale bowers.
And let the ground whereas her foot shall tread,
For feare the stones her tender foot should wrong
50   Be strewed with fragrant flowers all along,
And diapred lyke the discolored mead.[8]
Which done, doe at her chamber dore awayt,
For she will waken strayt,°   *straightway*
The whiles doe ye this song unto her sing,
55   The woods shall to you answer and your Eccho ring.

Ye Nymphes of Mulla[9] which with careful heed,
The silver scaly trouts doe tend full well,
And greedy pikes which use therein to feed,
(Those trouts and pikes all others doo excell)
60   And ye likewise, which keepe the rushy lake,
Where none doo fishes take,
Bynd up the locks the which hang scatterd light,
And in his waters which your mirror make,
Behold your faces as the christall bright,
65   That when you come whereas° my love doth lie,   *where*
No blemish she may spie.
And eke° ye lightfoot mayds which keepe the deere,   *also*
That on the hoary mountayne use to towre,[1]
And the wylde wolves which seeke them to devoure,
70   With your steele darts doo chace from comming neer
Be also present heere,

4. A ceremonial torch, associated with marriages since classical times.
5. That can hear you.
6. Beautified.
7. In a love knot.
8. Ornamented like the many-colored meadow.
9. The vale of Mulla, near Spenser's home in Ireland.
1. A falconry term meaning to occupy heights. "The deere": all wild animals, kept by the forest nymphs.

To helpe to decke her and to help to sing,
That all the woods may answer and your Eccho ring.

Wake, now my love, awake; for it is time,
75 The Rosy Morne long since left Tithones bed,[2]
All ready to her silver coche° to clyme,   *coach*
And Phoebus gins to shew his glorious hed.
Hark how the cheerefull birds do chaunt theyr laies
And carroll of loves praise.
80 The merry Larke hir mattins° sings aloft,   *morning prayers*
The thrush replyes, the Mavis descant playes,
The Ouzell shrills, the Ruddock warbles soft,[3]
So goodly all agree with sweet consent,
To this dayes merriment.
85 Ah my deere love why doe ye sleepe thus long,
When meeter° were that ye should now awake,   *more fitting*
T' awayt the comming of your joyous make,°   *mate*
And hearken to the birds lovelearnèd song,
The deawy leaves among.
90 For they of joy and pleasance to you sing,
That all the woods them answer and theyr Eccho ring.

My love is now awake out of her dreame,
And her fayre eyes like stars that dimmèd were
With darksome cloud, now shew theyr goodly beams
95 More bright then Hesperus° his head doth rere.   *evening star*
Come now ye damzels, daughters of delight,
Helpe quickly her to dight,°   *adorn*
But first come ye fayre houres which were begot
In Joves sweet paradice, of Day and Night,
100 Which doe the seasons of the yeare allot,
And al that ever in this world is fayre
Doe make and still repayre.°   *continuously*
And ye three handmayds of the Cyprian Queene,[4]
The which doe still adorne her beauties pride,
105 Helpe to addorne my beautifullest bride:
And as ye her array, still throw betweene°   *now and then*
Some graces to be seene,
And as ye use to Venus, to her sing,
The whiles the woods shal answer and your Eccho ring.

110 Now is my love all ready forth to come,
Let all the virgins therefore well awayt,
And ye fresh boyes that tend upon her groome
Prepare your selves; for he is comming strayt.
Set all your things in seemely good aray°   *order*

2. See Song of Songs 2.10–13: "Rise up, my love, my fair one, and come away. For, lo, the winter is past, the rain is over and gone; the flowers appear on the earth; the time of the singing of birds is come." In myth, Tithones is the aged husband of Aurora, the dawn.
3. "Descant": a melody or counterpoint written above a musical theme—a soprano obbligato. The "Mavis" is the thrush; the "Ouzell," the blackbird (which sings in England); and the "Ruddock," the European robin. The birds' concert is a convention of medieval love poetry.
4. The Graces attending on Venus ("Cyprian Queene"), representing brightness, joy, and bloom.

115 Fit for so joyfull day,
    The joyfulst day that ever sunne did see.
    Faire Sun, shew forth thy favourable ray,
    And let thy lifull° heat not fervent be   *life-giving*
    For feare of burning her sunshyny face,
120 Her beauty to disgrace.
    O fayrest Phoebus, father of the Muse,[5]
    If ever I did honour thee aright,
    Or sing the thing, that mote° thy mind delight,   *might*
    Doe not thy servants simple boone° refuse,   *request*
125 But let this day let this one day be myne,
    Let all the rest be thine.
    Then I thy soverayne prayses loud wil sing,
    That all the woods shal answer and theyr Eccho ring.

    Harke how the Minstrels gin° to shrill aloud   *begin*
130 Their merry Musick that resounds from far,
    The pipe, the tabor,° and the trembling Croud,[6]   *small drum*
    That well agree withouten breach or jar.°   *discord*
    But most of all the Damzels doe delite,
    When they their tymbrels° smyte,   *tambourines*
135 And thereunto doe daunce and carrol sweet,
    That all the sences they doe ravish quite,
    The whyles the boyes run up and downe the street,
    Crying aloud with strong confusèd noyce,
    As if it were one voyce.
140 *Hymen iô Hymen, Hymen*[7] they do shout,
    That even to the heavens theyr shouting shrill
    Doth reach, and all the firmament doth fill,
    To which the people standing all about,
    As in approvance doe thereto applaud
145 And loud advaunce her laud,°   *praise*
    And evermore they *Hymen Hymen* sing,
    That all the woods them answer and theyr Eccho ring.

    Loe where she comes along with portly° pace   *stately*
    Lyke Phoebe from her chamber of the East,
150 Arysing forth to run her mighty race,[8]
    Clad all in white, that seemes° a virgin best.   *suits*
    So well it her beseems that ye would weene
    Some angell she had beene.
    Her long loose yellow locks lyke golden wyre,
155 Sprinckled with perle, and perling° flowres a tweene,   *winding*
    Doe lyke a golden mantle her attyre,
    And being crownèd with a girland greene,
    Seeme lyke some mayden Queene.
    Her modest eyes abashèd to behold

---

5. Phoebus (Apollo), god of the sun, was also father of
the Nine Muses.
6. Primitive fiddle. Spenser here designates Irish, not
classical, instruments and music for the classical
masque or ballet.

7. The name of the god of marriage, used as a conventional exclamation at weddings.
8. Phoebe is the moon, a virgin like the bride; the reference to her anticipates the night.

160 So many gazers, as on her do stare,
Upon the lowly ground affixèd are.
Ne dare lift up her countenance too bold,
But blush to heare her prayses sung so loud,
So farre from being proud.
165 Nathlesse doe ye still loud her prayses sing.
That all the woods may answer and your Eccho ring.

Tell me ye merchants daughters did ye see
So fayre a creature in your towne before,
So sweet, so lovely, and so mild as she,
170 Adornd with beautyes grace and vertues store,
Her goodly eyes lyke Saphyres shining bright,
Her forehead yvory white,
Her cheekes lyke apples which the sun hath rudded,°   *made red*
Her lips lyke cherryes charming men to byte,
175 Her brest like to a bowle of creame uncrudded,°   *uncurdled*
Her paps lyke lyllies budded,
Her snowie necke lyke to a marble towre,
And all her body like a pallace fayre,
Ascending uppe with many a stately stayre,
180 To honors seat and chastities sweet bowre.[9]
Why stand ye still ye virgins in amaze,
Upon her so to gaze,
Whiles ye forget your former lay to sing,
To which the woods did answer and your Eccho ring.

185 But if ye saw that which no eyes can see,
The inward beauty of her lively spright,°   *soul*
Garnisht with heavenly guifts of high degree,
Much more then would ye wonder at that sight,
And stand astonisht lyke to those which red°   *saw*
190 Medusaes mazeful hed.[1]
There dwels sweet love and constant chastity,
Unspotted fayth and comely womanhood,
Regard of honour and mild modesty,
There vertue raynes as Queene in royal throne,
195 And giveth lawes alone.
The which the base° affections doe obay,   *lower*
And yeeld theyr services unto her will,
Ne thought of thing uncomely ever may
Thereto approch to tempt her mind to ill.
200 Had ye once seene these her celestial threasures,
And unrevealèd pleasures,
Then would ye wonder and her prayses sing,
That all the woods should answer and your Eccho ring.

---

9. The head, where the higher faculties are. The catalog of qualities is a convention in love poetry (cf. Song of Solomon 4–8).

1. Medusa, one of the Gorgons, had serpents instead of hair (hence a "mazeful hed"): the effect on a beholder was to turn him to stone.

Open the temple gates unto my love,
205   Open them wide that she may enter in,[2]
And all the postes adorne as doth behove,[3]
And all the pillours deck with girlands trim,
For to recyve this Saynt with honour dew,
That commeth in to you.
210   With trembling steps and humble reverence,
She commeth in, before th' almighties vew,
Of her ye virgins learne obedience,
When so ye come into those holy places,
To humble your proud faces:
215   Bring her up to th' high altar, that she may
The sacred ceremonies there partake,
The which do endless matrimony make,
And let the roring Organs loudly play
The praises of the Lord in lively notes,
220   The whiles with hollow throates
The Choristers the joyous Antheme sing,
That all the woods may answere and theyr Eccho ring.

Behold whiles she before the altar stands
Hearing the holy priest that to her speakes
225   And blesseth her with his two happy hands,
How the red roses flush up in her cheekes,
And the pure snow with goodly vermill° stayne,   *vermilion*
Like crimsin dyde in grayne,°   *fast color*
That even th' Angels which continually,
230   About the sacred Altare doe remaine,
Forget their service and about her fly,
Ofte peeping in her face that seemes more fayre,
The more they on it stare.
But her sad° eyes still fastened on the ground,   *modest*
235   Are governèd with goodly modesty,
That suffers not one looke to glaunce awry,
Which may let in a little thought unsownd.
Why blush ye love to give to me your hand,
The pledge of all our band?°   *bond, tie*
240   Sing ye sweet Angels, Alleluya sing,
That all the woods may answere and your Eccho ring.

Now al is done; bring home the bride againe,
Bring home the triumph of our victory,
Bring home with you the glory of her gaine,[4]
245   With joyance bring her and with jollity.
Never had man more joyfull day then this,
Whom heaven would heape with blis.
Make feast therefore now all this live long day,

---

2. Cf. Psalm 24.7: "Lift up your heads, O ye gates; and   dings in classical times, and the custom was often re-
be ye lift up, ye everlasting doors; and the King of glory   ferred to in classical and medieval love poetry.
shall come in."   4. I.e., the glory of gaining her.
3. As is proper. The doorposts were trimmed for wed-

This day for ever to me holy is,
250   Poure out the wine without restraint or stay,
Poure not by cups, but by the belly full,
Poure out to all that wull,°   *want it*
And sprinkle all the postes and wals with wine,
That they may sweat, and drunken be withall.
255   Crowne ye God Bacchus[5] with a coronall,°   *flower garland*
And Hymen also crowne with wreathes of vine,
And let the Graces daunce unto the rest;
For they can doo it best:
The whiles the maydens doe theyr carroll sing,
260   To which the woods shall answer and theyr Eccho ring.

Ring ye the bels, ye young men of the towne,
And leave your wonted° labors for this day: *usual*
This day is holy; doe ye write it downe,
That ye for ever it remember may.
265   This day the sunne is in his chiefest hight,
With Barnaby the bright,[6]
From whence declining daily by degrees,
He somewhat loseth of his heat and light,
When once the Crab[7] behind his back he sees.
270   But for this time it ill ordainèd was,
To chose the longest day in all the yeare,
And shortest night, when longest fitter weare;
Yet never day so long, but late° would passe.   *at last*
Ring ye the bels, to make it weare away,
275   And bonefiers make all day,
And daunce about them, and about them sing:
That all the woods may answer, and your Eccho ring.

Ah when will this long weary day have end,
And lende me leave to come unto my love?
280   How slowly do the houres theyr numbers spend?
How slowly does sad Time his feathers move?
Hast thee O fayrest Planet to thy home
Within the Westerne fome:
Thy tyred steedes long since have need of rest.[8]
285   Long though it be, at last I see it gloome,
And the bright evening star[9] with golden creast
Appeare out of the East.
Fayre childe of beauty, glorious lampe of love
That all the host of heaven in rankes doost lead,
290   And guydest lovers through the nightès dread,
How chearefully thou lookest from above,
And seemst to laugh atweene thy twinkling light
As joying in the sight

5. God of wine.
6. St. Barnabas's Day, at the time of the summer solstice.
7. The constellation Cancer between Gemini and
Leo. The sun, passing through the zodiac, leaves the
Crab behind toward the end of July.
8. The sun's chariot completes its daily course in the
western sea.
9. Hesperus

Of these glad many which for joy doe sing,
295 That all the woods them answer and theyr Eccho ring.

Now ceasse ye damsels your delights forepast;
Enough is it, that all the day was youres:
Now day is doen, and night is nighing fast:
Now bring the Bryde into the brydall boures.
300 Now night is come, now soone her disaray,
And in her bed her lay;
Lay her in lillies and in violets,
And silken courteins over her display,°   *spread*
And odourd sheetes, and Arras° coverlets.   *tapestry*
305 Behold how goodly my faire love does ly
In proud humility;
Like unto Maia,[1] when as Jove her tooke,
In Tempe, lying on the flowry gras,
Twixt sleepe and wake, after she weary was,
310 With bathing in the Acidalian brooke.
Now it is night, ye damsels may be gon,
And leave my love alone,
And leave likewise your former lay to sing:
The woods no more shall answere, nor your Eccho ring.

315 Now welcome night, thou night so long expected,
That long daies labour doest at last defray,°   *pay*
And all my cares, which cruell love collected,
Hast sumd in one, and cancellèd for aye:
Spread thy broad wing over my love and me,
320 That no man may us see,
And in thy sable mantle us enwrap,
From feare of perrill and foule horror free.
Let no false treason seeke us to entrap,
Nor any dread disquiet once annoy
325 The safety of our joy:
But let the night be calme and quietsome,
Without tempestuous storms or sad afray:
Lyke as when Jove with fayre Alcmena[2] lay,
When he begot the great Tirynthian groome:
330 Or lyke as when he with thy selfe[3] did lie,
And begot Majesty.
And let the mayds and yongmen cease to sing:
Ne let the woods them answer, nor theyr Eccho ring.

Let no lamenting cryes, nor dolefull teares,
335 Be heard all night within nor yet without:
Ne let false whispers, breeding hidden feares,
Breake gentle sleepe with misconceivèd dout.°   *fear*
Let no deluding dreames, nor dreadful sights
Make sudden sad affrights;

1. The eldest and most beautiful of the Pleiades.   three.
2. The mother of Hercules ("the great Tirynthian   3. Night. This is Spenser's own myth.
groome"). Jove made that first night last as long as

340 Ne let housefyres, nor lightnings helpelesse harmes,
    Ne let the Pouke,[4] nor other evill sprights,
    Ne let mischivous witches with theyr charmes,
    Ne let hob Goblins, names whose sence we see not,
    Fray° us with things that be not.   *terrify*
345 Let not the shriech Oule, nor the Storke be heard:
    Nor the night Raven that still° deadly yels,[5]   *continuously*
    Nor damnèd ghosts cald up with mighty spels,
    Nor griesly° vultures make us once affeard: *horrid*
    Ne let th' unpleasant Quyre of Frogs still croking
350 Make us to wish theyr choking.
    Let none of these theyr drery accents sing;
    Ne let the woods them answer, nor theyr Eccho ring.

    But let stil Silence trew night watches keepe,
    That sacred peace may in assurance rayne,
355 And tymely sleep, when it is tyme to sleepe,
    May poure his limbs forth on your pleasant playne,
    The whiles an hundred little wingèd loves,[6]
    Like divers fethered doves,
    Shall fly and flutter round about your bed,
360 And in the secret darke, that none reproves,
    Their prety stealthes shal worke, and snares shal spread
    To filch away sweet snatches of delight,
    Conceald through covert night.
    Ye sonnes of Venus, play your sports at will,
365 For greedy pleasure, carelesse of your toyes,°   *amorous dallying*
    Thinks more upon her paradise of joyes,
    Then what ye do, albe it good or ill.
    All night therefore attend your merry play,
    For it will soone be day:
370 Now none doth hinder you, that say or sing,
    Ne will the woods now answer, nor your Eccho ring.

    Who is the same, which at my window peepes?
    Or whose is that faire face, that shines so bright,
    Is it not Cinthia,[7] she that never sleepes,
375 But walkes about high heaven al the night?
    O fayrest goddesse, do thou not envy
    My love with me to spy:
    For thou likewise didst love, though now unthought,°   *unsuspected*
    And for a fleece of woll,° which privily,   *wool*
380 The Latmian shephard[8] once unto thee brought,
    His pleasures with thee wrought,
    Therefore to us be favorable now;
    And sith of wemens labours thou hast charge,[9]
    And generation goodly dost enlarge,

4. Puck, Robin Goodfellow—here more powerful and evil than Shakespeare made him.
5. The owl and the night raven were birds of ill omen; the stork, in Chaucer's *Parliament of Fowls*, is called an avenger of adultery.
6. Cupids (or amoretti).
7. The moon.
8. Endymion, beloved by the moon. The "fleece of woll," however, comes from another story—that of Pan's enticement of the moon.
9. Diana (or Cinthia) is, as Lucina, patroness of births. The "labours" are, of course, those of childbirth.

385   Encline thy will t' effect our wishfull vow,
And the chast wombe informe° with timely seed,   *give life to*
That may our comfort breed:
Till which we cease our hopefull hap[1] to sing,
Ne let the woods us answer, nor our Eccho ring.

390   And thou great Juno, which with awful might
The lawes of wedlock still dost patronize,
And the religion° of the faith first plight   *sanctity*
With sacred rites hast taught to solemnize:
And eeke° for comfort often callèd art   *also*
395   Of women in their smart,°   *labor*
Eternally bind thou this lovely band,
And all thy blessings unto us impart.
And thou glad Genius,[2] in whose gentle hand,
The bridale bowre and geniall bed remaine,
400   Without blemish or staine,
And the sweet pleasures of theyr loves delight
With secret ayde doest succour and supply,
Till they bring forth the fruitfull progeny,
Send us the timely fruit of this same night.
405   And thou fayre Hebe,[3] and thou Hymen free,
Grant that it may so be.
Til which we cease your further prayse to sing,
Ne any woods shall answer, nor your Eccho ring.

And ye high heavens, the temple of the gods,
410   In which a thousand torches flaming bright
Doe burne, that to us wretched earthly clods,
In dreadful darknesse lend desirèd light;
And all ye powers which in the same remayne,
More than we men can fayne,°   *imagine*
415   Poure out your blessing on us plentiously,
And happy influence upon us raine,
That we may raise a large posterity,
Which from the earth, which they may long possesse,
With lasting happinesse,
420   Up to your haughty pallaces may mount,
And for the guerdon° of theyr glorious merit   *reward*
May heavenly tabernacles there inherit,
Of blessed Saints for to increase the count.
So let us rest, sweet love, in hope of this,
425   And cease till then our tymely joyes to sing,
The woods no more us answer, nor our Eccho ring.

Song made in lieu of many ornaments,
With which my love should duly have bene dect,°   *adorned*
Which cutting off through hasty accidents,
430   Ye would not stay your dew time to expect,°   *await*

---

1. The fortune we hope for.   3. Patron of youth and freedom.
2. Patron of sex, pregnancy, and reproduction.

> But promist both to recompens,
> Be unto her a goodly ornament,
> And for short time an endlesse moniment.[4]

1595

4. The envoy is traditionally apologetic in tone: the poem is offered as a substitute for wedding presents ("ornaments") that did not arrive in time for the wed- ding. But this elaborate poem is itself a "goodly orna- ment," for it stands as a timeless monument of art to the passing day that it celebrates.

CHRISTOPHER MARLOWE
1564–1593

ca. 1587:   *Tamburlaine* produced, introducing blank verse,
               "Marlowe's mighty line," to the stage.
ca. 1592–93:   *Dr. Faustus, Hero and Leander.*

Christopher Marlowe was born two months before William Shakespeare. He was the son of a Canterbury shoemaker; in 1580 he went to Corpus Christi College, Cambridge, on a scholarship that was ordinarily awarded to students preparing for the ministry. He held the scholarship for the maximum time, six years, but did not take holy orders. Instead, he began to write plays. When he came to supplicate for his master of arts degree in 1587, the university was about to deny it to him on the grounds that he intended to go abroad to Reims, the center of Catholic intrigue and propaganda against Elizabeth, and remain there. But the Privy Council intervened and requested that, because Marlowe had done the queen good service as some kind of secret agent, he be granted his degree at the next commencement "because it is not Her Majesty's pleasure that anyone employed as he had been in matters touching the benefit of his country should be defamed by those that are ignorant in the affairs he went about." Although much sensational information about Marlowe has been discovered in modern times, we are still "ignorant in the affairs he went about."

Before he left Cambridge, he had certainly written his tremendously successful play *Tamburlaine* and perhaps also, in collaboration with his younger Cambridge contemporary Thomas Nashe, the tragedy of *Dido, Queen of Carthage. Tamburlaine,* which soon was followed by a sequel (*Tamburlaine,* part 2), dramatizes the exploits of a fourteenth-century Mongol chieftain who conquered much of the known world, as Alexander had before him. In some sixteenth-century narratives Tamburlaine is represented as the type of modern (i.e., Renaissance) man, and in others he is portrayed as God's scourge. In Marlowe's play he is the vehicle for the expression of boundless energy and ambition, the impulse to strive constantly for absolute power. When one of his victims accuses him of bloody cruelty, Tamburlaine answers that ambition to rule is embedded in the laws of nature and in basic human psychology:

> Nature, that framed us of four elements
> Warring within our breasts for regiment,
> Doth teach us all to have aspiring minds;
> Our souls, whose faculties can comprehend
> The wondrous architecture of the world
> And measure every planet's wandering course,

Still climbing after knowledge infinite,
And always moving as the restless spheres,
Wills us to wear ourselves and never rest
Until we reach the ripest fruit of all,
That perfect bliss and sole felicity,
The sweet fruition of an earthly crown.

The English theater had heard nothing like this before. Here is a resonant, rhetorical blank verse, eminently suited to projection from the stage, and appropriate also, as it turned out, for the robust talents of the actor Edward Alleyn, who happily appeared in time to portray Marlowe's heroes.

From the time of his first great success, when he was twenty-three, Marlowe had only six years to live. They were not calm years. In 1589 he was involved in a brawl with one William Bradley, in which the poet Thomas Watson intervened and killed Bradley. Both poets were jailed, but Watson got off on a plea of self-defense and Marlowe was released. In 1591 Marlowe was living in London with the playwright Thomas Kyd, who later gave information to the Privy Council accusing Marlowe of atheism and treason. On May 30, 1593, at the inn of the Widow Bull in Deptford, Marlowe was killed by a dagger thrust in an argument over the bill. In these six violent years, Marlowe composed five more plays: his sequel to *Tamburlaine*; *The Massacre at Paris*; two major tragedies, *The Jew of Malta* and *Dr. Faustus*; and a chronicle history play, *Edward II*.

The Passionate Shepherd to His Love[1]

Come live with me and be my love,
And we will all the pleasures prove[2]
That valleys, groves, hills, and fields,
Woods, or steepy mountain yields.

And we will sit upon the rocks,   5
Seeing the shepherds feed their flocks,
By shallow rivers to whose falls
Melodious birds sing madrigals.

And I will make thee beds of roses
And a thousand fragrant posies,   10
A cap of flowers, and a kirtle
Embroidered all with leaves of myrtle;

A gown made of the finest wool
Which from our pretty lambs we pull;
Fair lined slippers for the cold,   15
With buckles of the purest gold;

A belt of straw and ivy buds,
With coral clasps and amber studs:
And if these pleasures may thee move,
Come live with me, and be my love.   20

---

1. This pastoral lyric of invitation is one of the most famous of Elizabethan songs, and a few lines from it are sung in Shakespeare's *Merry Wives of Windsor*. Many poets have written replies to it, the finest of which is by Sir Walter Ralegh (p. 556). 2. Test, experience.

The shepherds' swains shall dance and sing
For thy delight each May morning:
If these delights thy mind may move,
Then live with me and be my love.

                                                          1599, 1600

Dr. Faustus   Marlowe's major tragedies, *Tamburlaine, The Jew of Malta,* and
Dr. Faustus, all portray heroes who passionately seek power—the power of rule,
the power of money, and the power of knowledge, respectively. Each of the heroes
is an overreacher, striving beyond the bounds of human capacity.

   Unlike Tamburlaine, whose aim and goal is "the sweet fruition of an earthly
crown," and Barabas, the Jew of Malta, who lusts for "infinite riches in a little
room," Faustus seeks the power that comes from knowledge, no matter at what
cost. To get this power Faustus must make (or chooses to make) a bargain with
the devil. This is an old folklore motif, but it would have been taken seriously in a
time when everyone believed in the reality of devils. Faustus for his part desires
the power that comes from black magic, but the devil on his side exacts a fearful
price in exchange—the eternal damnation of Faustus's soul. This would also have
been taken literally by an Elizabethan audience. Faustus aspires to be more than
a man—a demigod, a deity. His fall is caused by the same pride and ambition that
caused the fall of the angels in heaven, and of humanity in the Garden of Eden.
But it is characteristic of Marlowe that he makes those aspirations nonetheless
magnificent.

   The immediate source of the play is a German narrative called, in its English
translation, *The History of the Damnable Life and Deserved Death of Doctor John
Faustus.* That source supplies Marlowe's drama with the scenes of horseplay and
low practical joking that contrast so markedly with the passages of grand aspiration.
It is quite possible that these scenes of low comedy are the work of a collaborator;
but no other Elizabethan could have written the first scene (which projects the
insatiable aspiring mind of the hero), the famous address to Helen of Troy, or the
final scene of Faustus's last hour.

   Marlowe's play exists in two very different forms: the A text (1604) and the much
longer B text (1616), which according to theatrical records contains yet more
scenes of other hands and that has also been revised to conform to the severe
censorship statutes of 1606. We use Roma Gill's edition, based on the A text.

The Tragical History
of Doctor Faustus

DRAMATIS PERSONAE

CHORUS
DR. JOHN FAUSTUS
WAGNER, *his servant, a student*
VALDES   } *his friends, magicians*
CORNELIUS
THREE SCHOLARS
THE GOOD ANGEL
THE EVIL ANGEL
MEPHASTOPHILIS
LUCIFER

BELZEBUB
OLD MAN
THE CLOWN
ROBIN } ostlers at an inn
RAFE
VINTNER
HORSE-COURSER
THE POPE
THE CARDINAL OF LORRAINE
THE EMPEROR CHARLES V
A KNIGHT *at the* EMPEROR'S *court*
DUKE OF VANHOLT
DUCHESS OF VANHOLT

Spirits presenting
THE SEVEN DEADLY SINS
   PRIDE
   COVETOUSNESS
   WRATH
   ENVY
   GLUTTONY
   SLOTH
   LECHERY
ALEXANDER THE GREAT *and his* PARAMOUR
HELEN OF TROY
ATTENDANTS, FRIARS, *and* DEVILS

Prologue

[*Enter* CHORUS.[1]]
CHORUS. Not marching now in fields of Thrasimene,
   Where Mars[2] did mate° the Carthaginians,   *join with*
   Nor sporting in the dalliance of love,
   In courts of kings where state° is overturned,   *political power*
5   Nor in the pomp of proud audacious deeds,
   Intends our Muse to vaunt his heavenly verse:
   Only this (Gentlemen) we must perform,
   The form of Faustus' fortunes good or bad.
   To patient judgments we appeal our plaud,
10   And speak for Faustus in his infancy:
   Now is he born, his parents base of stock,
   In Germany, within a town called Rhodes;
   Of riper years to Wittenberg[3] he went,
   Whereas° his kinsmen chiefly brought him up.   *where*
15   So soon he profits in divinity,
   The fruitfull plot of scholarism graced,[4]

1. A single actor who recited a prologue to an act or a whole play, and occasionally delivered an epilogue.
2. God of war. The battle of Lake Trasimene (217 B.C.) was one of the Carthaginian leader Hannibal's great victories.
3. The famous university where Martin Luther studied, as did Shakespeare's Hamlet and Horatio. "Rhodes": Roda, or Stadtroda, in Germany.
4. Grazed. In line 17 "graced" means permission to proceed to a degree.

That shortly he was graced with doctor's name,
Excelling all, whose sweet delight disputes[5]
In heavenly matters of theology.

20   Till, swollen with cunning,° of a self conceit,   *knowledge*
His waxen wings did mount above his reach,
And melting heavens conspired his overthrow.[6]
For falling to a devilish exercise,
And glutted more with learning's golden gifts,

25   He surfeits upon cursed necromancy:°   *black magic*
Nothing so sweet as magic is to him,
Which he prefers before his chiefest bliss.[7]
And this the man[8] that in his study sits.   [*Exit.*]

                              SCENE 1

[*Enter* FAUSTUS *in his study.*]

FAUSTUS. Settle thy studies, Faustus, and begin
To sound the depth of that thou wilt profess:
Having commenced, be a divine in show,[9]
Yet level° at the end of every art,   *aim*

5   And live and die in Aristotle's works.
Sweet *Analytics*, 'tis thou hast ravished me:
Bene disserere est finis logices.[1]
Is, to dispute well, logic's chiefest end?
Affords this art no greater miracle?

10   Then read no more, thou hast attained the end;
A greater subject fitteth Faustus' wit.
Bid *on kai me on* farewell; Galen[2] come:
Seeing, *ubi desinit philosophus, ibi incipit medicus.*[3]
Be a physician, Faustus, heap up gold,

15   And be eternized for some wondrous cure.
Summum bonum medicinae sanitas:[4]
The end of physic° is our body's health.   *medicine*
Why Faustus, hast thou not attained that end?
Is not thy common talk found aphorisms?[5]

20   Are not thy bills° hung up as monuments,   *prescriptions*
Whereby whole cities have escaped the plague,
And thousand desperate maladies been eased?
Yet art thou still but Faustus, and a man.
Couldst thou make men to live eternally,

---

5. Disputations, academic exercises that took the place of examinations.
6. In Greek myth, Icarus flew too near the sun on wings of feathers and wax made by his father, Daedalus; the wax melted, and he fell into the sea and was drowned.
7. The salvation of his soul.
8. Apparently a cue for the Prologue to draw aside the curtain to the enclosed space at the rear of the stage.
9. In external appearance. "Commenced": graduated, i.e., received the doctor's degree.

1. To carry on a disputation well is the end or purpose of logic. "Analytics": the title of two treatises on logic by Aristotle.
2. The ancient authority on medicine (2nd century A.D.). The Greek means, "Being and not being," i.e., philosophy.
3. Where the philosopher leaves off the physician begins.
4. The Latin is translated in the line below.
5. I.e., generally accepted wisdom.

25   Or, being dead, raise them to life again,
      Then this profession were to be esteemed.
      Physic farewell! Where is Justinian?[6]
      Si una eademque res legatur duobus,
      Alter rem alter valorem rei, etc.[7]
30   A pretty case of paltry legacies:
      Exhereditare filium non potest pater nisi . . .[8]
      Such is the subject of the Institute,
      And universal body of the law:
      This study fits a mercenary drudge
35   Who aims at nothing but external trash!
      Too servile and illiberal for me.
      When all is done, divinity is best:
      Jerome's Bible,[9] Faustus, view it well:
      Stipendium peccati mors est: ha! *Stipendium, etc.*[1]
40   The reward of sin is death? That's hard.
      Si pecasse negamus, fallimur, et nulla est in nobis veritas.[2]
      If we say that we have no sin,
      We deceive ourselves, and there's no truth in us.
      Why then belike we must sin,
45   And so consequently die.
      Ay, we must die an everlasting death.
      What doctrine call you this? *Che sara, sara:*[3]
      What will be, shall be! Divinity, adieu!
      These metaphysics° of magicians,   basic principles
50   And necromantic books are heavenly!
      Lines, circles, schemes, letters and characters!
      Ay, these are those that Faustus most desires.
      O what a world of profit and delight,
      Of power, of honour, of omnipotence
55   Is promised to the studious artisan![4]
      All things that move between the quiet° poles   unmoving
      Shall be at my command: emperors and kings
      Are but obeyed in their several provinces,
      Nor can they raise the wind, or rend the clouds;
60   But his dominion that exceeds in this
      Stretcheth as far as doth the mind of man:
      A sound magician is a mighty god.
      Here Faustus, try thy brains to gain a deity.
           [*Enter* WAGNER.]
      Wagner, commend me to my dearest friends,
65   The German Valdes, and Cornelius,
      Request them earnestly to visit me.

6. Roman emperor and authority on law (483–565
A.D.), author of the *Institutes*.
7. If something is bequeathed to two persons, one shall
have the thing itself, the other something of equal
value.
8. A father cannot disinherit his son unless . . .

9. The Latin translation, or "Vulgate," of St. Jerome
(ca. 340–420 A.D.).
1. Romans 6.23, translated in the line below.
2. 1 John 1.8, translated in the next two lines.
3. Translated in the first half of the next line.
4. A master of the occult arts, such as necromancy.

WAGNER. I will sir.   [*Exit.*]
FAUSTUS. Their conference will be a greater help to me,
    Than all my labors, plod I ne'er so fast.
      [*Enter the* GOOD ANGEL *and the* EVIL ANGEL.]
70 GOOD ANGEL. O Faustus, lay that damned book aside,
    And gaze not on it, lest it tempt thy soul,
    And heap God's heavy wrath upon thy head:
    Read, read the Scriptures; that is blasphemy.
    EVIL ANGEL. Go forward, Faustus, in that famous art,
75   Wherein all nature's treasury is contained:
    Be thou on earth as Jove[5] is in the sky,
    Lord and commander of these elements.   [*Exeunt.*]
    FAUSTUS. How am I glutted with conceit[6] of this!
    Shall I make spirits fetch me what I please,
80   Resolve me of all ambiguities,
    Perform what desperate enterprise I will?
    I'll have them fly to India[7] for gold,
    Ransack the ocean for orient pearl,
    And search all corners of the new found world
85   For pleasant fruits and princely delicates,
    I'll have them read me strange philosophy,
    And tell the secrets of all foreign kings;
    I'll have them wall all Germany with brass,
    And make swift Rhine circle fair Wittenberg;[8]
90   I'll have them fill the public schools[9] with silk,
    Wherewith the students shall be bravely clad.
    I'll levy soldiers with the coin they bring,
    And chase the Prince of Parma[1] from our land,
    And reign sole king of all our provinces.
95   Yea, stranger engines for the brunt of war,
    Than was the fiery keel at Antwerp's bridge,[2]
    I'll make my servile spirits to invent.
    Come German Valdes and Cornelius,
    And make me blest with your sage conference.
      [*Enter* VALDES *and* CORNELIUS.]
100 Valdes, sweet Valdes, and Cornelius,
    Know that your words have won me at the last
    To practise magic and concealed arts;
    Yet not your words only, but mine own fantasy,
    That will receive no object[3] for my head,
105   But ruminates on necromantic skill.
    Philosophy is odious and obscure,
    Both law and physic are for petty wits;

5. God, a common substitution in Elizabethan drama.
6. Filled with the idea.
7. "India" could refer to the West Indies, America, or Ophir (in the east).
8. Wittenberg is in fact on the Elbe River.
9. The university lecture rooms.
1. The duke of Parma was the Spanish governor-gen-

eral of the Low Countries, 1579–92.
2. A reference to the burning ship sent by The Netherlanders in 1585 against the barrier on the river Scheldt that Parma had built as a part of the blockade of Antwerp.
3. That will pay no attention to physical reality.

Divinity is basest of the three,
Unpleasant, harsh, contemptible and vile.
110   'Tis magic, magic that hath ravished me.
Then, gentle friends, aid me in this attempt,
And I, that have with concise syllogisms
Gravelled° the pastors of the German church,   confounded
And made the flowering pride of Wittenberg
115   Swarm to my problems,[4] as the infernal spirits
On sweet Musaeus when he came to hell,
Will be as cunning as Agrippa was,
Whose shadows made all Europe honor him.[5]

VALDES. Faustus, these books, thy wit, and our experience
120   Shall make all nations to canonize us.
As Indian Moors[6] obey their Spanish lords,
So shall the spirits of every element
Be always serviceable to us three.
Like lions shall they guard us when we please,
125   Like Almaine rutters° with their horsemen's   German horsemen
    staves,
Or Lapland giants trotting by our sides;
Sometimes like women, or unwedded maids,
Shadowing° more beauty in their airy brows   harboring
Than in the white breasts of the Queen of Love.
130   From Venice shall they drag huge argosies,
And from America the golden fleece
That yearly stuffs old Philip's[7] treasury,
If learned Faustus will be resolute.

FAUSTUS. Valdes, as resolute am I in this
135   As thou to live, therefore object it not.[8]

CORNELIUS. The miracles that magic will perform
Will make thee vow to study nothing else.
He that is grounded in astrology,
Enriched with tongues, well seen° in minerals,   expert
140   Hath all the principles magic doth require:
Then doubt not, Faustus, but to be renowned
And more frequented for this mystery,°   craft
Than heretofore the Delphian oracle.[9]
The spirits tell me they can dry the sea,
145   And fetch the treasure of all foreign wrecks,
Ay, all the wealth that our forefathers hid
Within the massy° entrails of the earth.   massive
Then tell me, Faustus, what shall we three want?

FAUSTUS. Nothing Cornelius. O this cheers my soul!

---

4. Lectures in logic and mathematics.
5. Musaeus was a mythical singer, son of Orpheus; it was, however, Orpheus who charmed the denizens of hell with his music. Cornelius Agrippa, German author of *The Vanity and Uncertainty of Arts and Sciences* (1530), popularly supposed to have the power of calling up the "shadows" or shades of the dead.
6. Dark-skinned native Americans.
7. Philip II, king of Spain.
8. Do not make it a condition.
9. The oracle of Apollo.

150   Come, show me some demonstrations magical,
       That I may conjure in some lusty° grove,   *flourishing, beautiful*
       And have these joys in full possession.
       VALDES. Then haste thee to some solitary grove,
       And bear wise Bacon's and Abanus'[1] works,
155   The Hebrew Psalter, and New Testament;
       And whatsoever else is requisite
       We will inform thee ere our conference cease.
       CORNELIUS. Valdes, first let him know the words of art,
       And then, all other ceremonies learned,
160   Faustus may try his cunning by himself.
       VALDES. First, I'll instruct thee in the rudiments,
       And then wilt thou be perfecter than I.
       FAUSTUS. Then come and dine with me, and after meat
       We'll canvass every quiddity° thereof: *essential feature*
165   For ere I sleep, I'll try what I can do.
       This night I'll conjure,° though I die therefore.   *call up spirits*

                                                                  [*Exeunt.*]

                              SCENE 2

       [*Enter two* SCHOLARS.]
       1 SCHOLAR. I wonder what's become of Faustus, that was wont to
       make our schools ring with *sic probo*.[2]
       2 SCHOLAR. That shall we know; for see, here comes his boy.[3]
                   [*Enter* WAGNER.]
       1 SCHOLAR. How now sirra, where's thy master?
5   WAGNER. God in heaven knows.
       2 SCHOLAR. Why, dost not thou know?
       WAGNER. Yes I know, but that follows not.
       1 SCHOLAR. Go to sirra, leave your jesting, and tell us where he is.
       WAGNER. That follows not necessary by force of argument, that you,
10   being licentiates,[4] should stand upon't; therefore acknowledge your
       error, and be attentive.
       2 SCHOLAR. Why, didst thou not say thou knew'st?
       WAGNER. Have you any witness on't?
       1 SCHOLAR. Yes sirra, I heard you.
15   WAGNER. Ask my fellow if I be a thief.
       2 SCHOLAR. Well, you will not tell us.
       WAGNER. Yes sir, I will tell you; yet if you were not dunces you would
       never ask me such a question. For is not he *corpus naturale*? And
       is not that *mobile*?[5] Then wherefore should you ask me such a
20   question? But that I am by nature phlegmatic,[6] slow to wrath, and

---

1. Roger Bacon, the medieval friar and scientist popularly thought to be a magician, and Pietro d'Abano,
13th-century alchemist.
2. Thus I prove; a phrase in scholastic disputation.
3. Poor student acting as servant to earn his living.
4. Graduate students.

5. *Corpus naturale et mobile* ("matter natural and
movable") was a scholastic definition of the subject
matter of physics. Wagner is here parodying the language of learning at the university.
6. Dominated by the phlegm, one of the four humors
of medieval medicine and psychology.

prone to lechery—to love I would say—it were not for you to come within forty foot of the place of execution,[7] although I do not doubt to see you both hanged the next sessions. Thus having triumphed over you, I will set my countenance like a precisian,[8] and begin to speak thus: Truly my dear brethren, my master is within at dinner with Valdes and Cornelius, as this wine, if it could speak, it would inform your worships. And so the Lord bless you, preserve you, and keep you, my dear brethren, my dear brethren.   [*Exit.*]

25

1 SCHOLAR. Nay then, I fear he is fallen into that damned art, for which they two are infamous through the world.

30

2 SCHOLAR. Were he a stranger, and not allied to me, yet should I grieve for him. But come, let us go and inform the Rector,[9] and see if he by his grave counsel can reclaim him.

1 SCHOLAR. Ay, but I fear me nothing can reclaim him.

35

2 SCHOLAR. Yet let us try what we can do.   [*Exeunt.*]

SCENE 3

[*Enter* FAUSTUS *to conjure.*]

FAUSTUS. Now that the gloomy shadow of the earth,
Longing to view Orion's drizzling look,[1]
Leaps from th'antarctic world unto the sky,
And dims the welkin° with her pitchy breath: sky
Faustus, begin thine incantations,

5

And try if devils will obey thy hest,
Seeing thou hast prayed and sacrificed to them.
Within this circle[2] is Jehovah's name,
Forward and backward anagrammatized;
Th'abbreviated names of holy saints,

10

Figures of every adjunct to the heavens,
And characters of signs and erring stars,[3]
By which the spirits are enforced to rise.
Then fear not Faustus, but be resolute,
And try the uttermost magic can perform.

15

Sint mihi dei acherontis propitii. Valeat numen triplex Jehovae!
Ignei, aerii, terreni, aquatici spiritus salvete! Orientis princeps, Bel-
zebub inferni ardentis monarcha, et Demogorgon, propitiamus vos,
ut appareat et surgat Mephastophilis. Quid tu moraris? Per Jeho-

20

vam, Gehennam, et consecratam aquam quam nunc spargo, sig-
numque crucis quod nunc facio; et per vota nostra, ipse nunc surgat
nobis dicatus Mephastophilis.[4]

---

7. The dining room.
8. Puritan. The rest of his speech is in the style of the Puritans.
9. The head of a German university.
1. Orion appears at the beginning of winter. The phrase is a reminiscence of Virgil.
2. The magic circle drawn on the ground, within which the spirits rise.
3. The moving planets. "Adjunct": heavenly body, thought to be joined to the solid firmament. "Charac-

ters of signs": signs of the zodiac and the planets.
4. May the gods of the lower regions favor me! Farewell to the Trinity! Hail, spirits of fire, air, water, and earth! Prince of the East, Belzebub, monarch of burning hell, and Demogorgon, we pray to you that Mephastophilis may appear and rise. What are you waiting for? By Jehovah, Gehenna, and the holy water that I now sprinkle, and the sign of the cross that I now make, and by our vows, may Mephastophilis himself now rise to serve us.

[*Enter a* DEVIL.]
I charge thee to return and change thy shape,
Thou art too ugly to attend on me;
25   Go and return an old Franciscan friar,
That holy shape becomes a devil best.   [*Exit* DEVIL.]
I see there's virtue in my heavenly words!
Who would not be proficient in this art?
How pliant is this Mephastophilis,
30   Full of obedience and humility,
Such is the force of magic and my spells.
Now Faustus, thou art conjurer laureate
That canst command great Mephastophilis.
Quin redis, Mephastophilis, fratris imagine![5]
[*Enter* MEPHASTOPHILIS.]
35 MEPHASTOPHILIS. Now Faustus, what would'st thou have me do?
FAUSTUS. I charge thee wait upon me whilst I live,
To do what ever Faustus shall command,
Be it to make the moon drop from her sphere,
Or the ocean to overwhelm the world.
40   MEPHASTOPHILIS. I am a servant to great Lucifer,
And may not follow thee without his leave;
No more than he commands must we perform.
FAUSTUS. Did not he charge thee to appear to me?
MEPHASTOPHILIS No, I came now hither of mine own accord.
45 FAUSTUS. Did not my conjuring speeches raise thee? Speak!
MEPHASTOPHILIS. That was the cause, but yet *per accidens,*[6]
For when we hear one rack[7] the name of God,
Abjure the Scriptures, and his saviour Christ,
We fly in hope to get his glorious soul,
50   Nor will we come, unless he use such means
Whereby he is in danger to be damned:
Therefore the shortest cut for conjuring
Is stoutly to abjure the Trinity,
And pray devoutly to the prince of hell.
55 FAUSTUS. So Faustus hath already done, and hold this principle:
There is no chief but only Belzebub,
To whom Faustus doth dedicate himself.
This word damnation terrifies not him,
For he confounds hell in Elysium:
60   His ghost be with the old philosophers.[8]
But leaving these vain trifles of men's souls,
Tell me, what is that Lucifer thy lord?
MEPHASTOPHILIS. Arch-regent and commander of all spirits.
FAUSTUS. Was not that Lucifer an angel once?

---

5. Return, Mephastophilis, in the shape of a friar.
6. The immediate, not ultimate, cause.
7. Torture (by anagrammatizing).

8. Faustus considers hell to be the Elysium of the classical philosophers, not the Christian hell of torment.

65 MEPHASTOPHILIS. Yes Faustus, and most dearly loved of God.
 FAUSTUS. How comes it then that he is prince of devils?
 MEPHASTOPHILIS. O, by aspiring pride and insolence,
   For which God threw him from the face of heaven.
 FAUSTUS. And what are you that live with Lucifer?
70 MEPHASTOPHILIS. Unhappy spirits that fell with Lucifer,
   Conspired against our God with Lucifer,
   And are for ever damned with Lucifer.
 FAUSTUS. Where are you damned?
 MEPHASTOPHILIS. In hell.
75 FAUSTUS. How comes it then that thou art out of hell?
 MEPHASTOPHILIS. Why this is hell, nor am I out of it.
   Think'st thou that I, who saw the face of God,
   And tasted the eternal joys of heaven,
   Am not tormented with ten thousand hells
80   In being deprived of everlasting bliss![9]
   O Faustus, leave these frivolous demands,
   Which strike a terror to my fainting soul.
 FAUSTUS. What, is great Mephastophilis so passionate
   For being deprived of the joys of heaven?
85   Learn thou of Faustus manly fortitude,
   And scorn those joys thou never shalt possess.
   Go bear these tidings to great Lucifer,
   Seeing Faustus hath incurred eternal death
   By desperate thoughts against Jove's deity:
90   Say, he surrenders up to him his soul
   So he will spare him four and twenty years,
   Letting him live in all voluptuousness,
   Having thee ever to attend on me,
   To give me whatsoever I shall ask,
95   To tell me whatsoever I demand,
   To slay mine enemies, and aid my friends,
   And always be obedient to my will.
   Go, and return to mighty Lucifer,
   And meet me in my study at midnight
100   And then resolve me of thy master's mind.[1]
 MEPHASTOPHILIS. I will Faustus.   [*Exit.*]
 FAUSTUS. Had I as many souls as there be stars
   I'd give them all for Mephastophilis.
   By him I'll be great emperor of the world,
105   And make a bridge through the moving air
   To pass the ocean with a band of men;
   I'll join the hills that bind the Afric shore,
   And make that land continent to Spain,

9. This is the punishment of loss of God's presence,   1. Give me his decision.
which is supposed to be the greatest torment of hell.

And both contributory to my crown.
110 The emperor[2] shall not live but by my leave,
Nor any potentate of Germany.
Now that I have obtained what I desire
I'll live in speculation° of this art   *contemplation*
Till Mephastophilis return again.   [*Exit.*]

SCENE 4

[*Enter* WAGNER *and the* CLOWN.[3]]

WAGNER. Sirra boy, come hither.

CLOWN. How, boy? Zounds, boy! I hope you have seen many boys
with such pickadevants as I have. Boy, quotha![4]

WAGNER. Tell me sirra, hast thou any comings in?[5]

5 CLOWN. Ay, and goings out too; you may see else.

WAGNER. Alas poor slave, see how poverty jesteth in his nakedness!
The villain is bare, and out of service,[6] and so hungry, that I know
he would give his soul to the devil for a shoulder of mutton, though
it were blood raw.

10 CLOWN. How, my soul to the devil for a shoulder of mutton though
'twere blood raw? Not so good friend; by'rlady,[7] I had need have it
well roasted, and good sauce to it, if I pay so dear.

WAGNER. Well, wilt thou serve me, and I'll make thee go like *qui mihi
discipulus*?[8]

15 CLOWN. How, in verse?

WAGNER. No sirra; in beaten silk and stavesacre.[9]

CLOWN. How, how, knavesacre?[1] Ay I thought that was all the land
his father left him! Do ye hear, I would be sorry to rob you of your
living.

20 WAGNER. Sirra, I say in stavesacre.

CLOWN. Oho, oho, stavesacre! Why then belike, if I were your man, I
should be full of vermin.

WAGNER. So thou shalt, whether thou be'st with me or no. But sirra,
leave your jesting, and bind your self presently unto me for seven
25 years, or I'll turn all the lice about thee into familiars,[2] and they
shall tear thee in pieces.

CLOWN. Do you hear sir? You may save that labour: they are too familiar with me already—zounds, they are as bold with my flesh as if
they had paid for my meat and drink.

30 WAGNER. Well, do you hear sirra? Hold, take these guilders.[3]

CLOWN. Gridirons; what be they?

2. The holy Roman emperor.
3. Not a court jester (as in some of Shakespeare's plays) but an older stock character, a rustic buffoon.
4. The point of the clown's retort is that he is a man and wears a beard. "Zounds": an oath, meaning "God's wounds." "Pickadevants": small, pointed beards.
5. Income, but the clown then puns on the literal meaning.
6. Out of a job.
7. An oath, meaning "by Our Lady."
8. You who are my pupil (the opening phrase of a poem on how students should behave, from Lily's *Latin Grammar*, ca. 1509). Wagner means "like a proper servant of a learned man."
9. A kind of delphinium used for killing vermin.
1. Wordplay, here and below.
2. Familiar spirits, demons.
3. Coins.

WAGNER. Why, French crowns.[4]

CLOWN. 'Mass, but for the name of French crowns a man were as good have as many English counters![5] And what should I do with
35   these?

WAGNER. Why, now, sirra, thou art at an hour's warning whensoever or wheresoever the devil shall fetch thee.

CLOWN. No, no, here take your gridirons again.

WAGNER. Truly I'll none of them.

40   CLOWN. Truly but you shall.

WAGNER. Bear witness I gave them him.

CLOWN. Bear witness I give them you again.

WAGNER. Well, I will cause two devils presently to fetch thee away. Baliol[6] and Belcher!

45   CLOWN. Let your Baliol and your Belcher come here, and I'll knock[7] them, they were never so knocked since they were devils! Say I should kill one of them, what would folks say? Do ye see yonder tall fellow in the round slop,[8] he has killed the devil! So I should be called "Killdevil" all the parish over.

        [*Enter two* DEVILS, *and the* CLOWN *runs up and down crying.*]

50   WAGNER. Baliol and Belcher, spirits, away!   [*Exeunt* DEVILS.]

CLOWN. What, are they gone? A vengeance on them! They have vile long nails. There was a he devil and a she devil. I'll tell you how you shall know them: all he devils has horns, and all she devils has clefts[9] and cloven feet.

55   WAGNER. Well sirra, follow me.

CLOWN. But do you hear? If I should serve you, would you teach me to raise up Banios and Belcheos?

WAGNER. I will teach thee to turn thy self to anything, to a dog, or a cat, or a mouse, or a rat, or any thing.

60   CLOWN. How! A Christian fellow to a dog, or a cat, a mouse, or a rat? No, no sir, if you turn me into anything, let it be in the likeness of a little pretty frisking flea, that I may be here, and there, and everywhere. O I'll tickle the pretty wenches' plackets! I'll be amongst them i'faith.

65   WAGNER. Well sirra, come.

CLOWN. But, do you hear Wagner . . . ?

WAGNER. Baliol and Belcher!

CLOWN. O Lord I pray sir, let Banio and Belcher go sleep.

WAGNER. Villain, call me Master Wagner; and let thy left eye be
70   diametarily fixed upon my right heel, with *quasi vestigias nostras insistere.*[1]   [*Exit.*]

CLOWN. God forgive me, he speaks Dutch fustian![2] Well, I'll follow him, I'll serve him; that's flat.   [*Exit.*]

4. French crowns, legal tender in England at this period, were easily counterfeited.
5. Worthless tokens.
6. Probably a corruption of Belial.
7. Beat.
8. Baggy pants. "Tall": fine.
9. Allusion to the female genitalia.
1. A pedantic way of saying "Follow my footsteps." "Diametarily": diametrically.
2. Gibberish.

SCENE 5

[*Enter* FAUSTUS *in his study.*]
FAUSTUS. Now Faustus, must thou needs be damned,
    And canst thou not be saved.
    What boots° it then to think of God or heaven?   *avails*
    Away with such vain fancies and despair,
5   Despair in God, and trust in Belzebub.
    Now go not backward: no, Faustus, be resolute;
    Why waverest thou? O, something soundeth in mine ears:
    "Abjure this magic, turn to God again."
    Ay, and Faustus will turn to God again.
10 To God? He loves thee not:
    The god thou servest is thine own appetite
    Wherein is fixed the love of Belzebub.
    To him I'll build an altar and a church,
    And offer luke-warm blood of new-born babes.
          [*Enter* GOOD ANGEL *and* EVIL (ANGEL).]
15 GOOD ANGEL. Sweet Faustus, leave that execrable art.
    FAUSTUS. Contrition, prayer, repentance: what of them?
    GOOD ANGEL. O they are means to bring thee unto heaven.
    EVIL ANGEL. Rather illusions, fruits of lunacy,
    That makes men foolish that do trust them most.
20 GOOD ANGEL. Sweet Faustus, think of heaven, and heavenly things.
    EVIL ANGEL. No Faustus, think of honor and of wealth
          [*Exeunt* (ANGELS).]
    FAUSTUS. Of wealth!
    Why, the signory of Emden³ shall be mine
    When Mephastophilis shall stand by me.
25 What god can hurt thee, Faustus? Thou art safe,
    Cast no more doubts. Come, Mephastophilis,
    And bring glad tidings from great Lucifer.
    Is't not midnight? Come, Mephastophilis:
    *Veni, veni, Mephastophile.*⁴
          [*Enter* MEPHASTOPHILIS.]
30 Now tell me, what says Lucifer thy lord?
    MEPHASTOPHILIS. That I shall wait on Faustus whilst he lives,
    So he will buy my service with his soul.
    FAUSTUS. Already Faustus hath hazarded that for thee.
    MEPHASTOPHILIS. But Faustus, thou must bequeath it solemnly,
35 And write a deed of gift with thine own blood,
    For that security craves great Lucifer.
    If thou deny it, I will back to hell.
    FAUSTUS. Stay Mephastophilis, and tell me,
    What good will my soul do thy lord?
40 MEPHASTOPHILIS. Enlarge his kingdom.

---

3. A wealthy German trade center.   4. Come, come, Mephastophilis!

FAUSTUS. Is that the reason he tempts us thus?
MEPHASTOPHILIS. *Solamen miseris socios habuisse doloris.*[5]
FAUSTUS. Have you any pain that tortures others?
MEPHASTOPHILIS. As great as have the human souls of men.
45   But tell me Faustus, shall I have thy soul?
     And I will be thy slave and wait on thee,
     And give thee more than thou hast wit to ask.
FAUSTUS. Ay Mephastophilis, I give it thee.
MEPHASTOPHILIS. Then stab thine arm courageously,
50   And bind thy soul, that at some certain day
     Great Lucifer may claim it as his own,
     And then be thou as great as Lucifer.
FAUSTUS. Lo Mephastophilis, for love of thee,
     I cut my arm, and with my proper° blood   own
55   Assure my soul to be great Lucifer's,
     Chief lord and regent of perpetual night.
     View here the blood that trickles from mine arm,
     And let it be propitious for my wish.
MEPHASTOPHILIS. But Faustus, thou must write it
60   In manner of a deed of gift.
FAUSTUS. Ay, so I will; but, Mephastophilis,
     My blood congeals and I can write no more.
MEPHASTOPHILIS. I'll fetch thee fire to dissolve it straight.   [*Exit.*]
FAUSTUS. What might the staying of my blood portend?
65   Is it unwilling I should write this bill?°   contract
     Why streams it not, that I may write afresh:
     "Faustus gives to thee his soul": ah, there it stayed!
     Why should'st thou not? Is not thy soul thine own?
     Then write again: "Faustus gives to thee his soul."
     [*Enter* MEPHASTOPHILIS *with a chafer*[6] *of coals.*]
70   MEPHASTOPHILIS. Here's fire, come Faustus, set it on.
FAUSTUS. So, now the blood begins to clear again.
     Now will I make an end immediately.
MEPHASTOPHILIS. Oh what will not I do to obtain his soul!
FAUSTUS. *Consummatum est,*[7] this bill is ended,
75   And Faustus hath bequeathed his soul to Lucifer.
     But what is this inscription on mine arm?
     Homo fuge.[8] Whither should I fly?
     If unto God, he'll throw me down to hell;
     My senses are deceived, here's nothing writ;
80   I see it plain, here in this place is writ,
     Homo fuge! Yet shall not Faustus fly.
MEPHASTOPHILIS. I'll fetch him somewhat to delight his mind. [*Exit.*]
     [*Enter (again) with* DEVILS, *giving crowns and rich apparel to*

5. Misery loves company.   words of Christ on the cross (John 19.30).
6. A portable grate.   8. O man, fly.
7. It is finished; a blasphemy, because these are the

FAUSTUS; *they dance, and then depart.*]
FAUSTUS. Speak Mephastophilis, what means this show?
MEPHASTOPHILIS. Nothing Faustus, but to delight thy mind withal,
85   And to show thee what magic can perform.
FAUSTUS. But may I raise up spirits when I please?
MEPHASTOPHILIS. Ay Faustus, and do greater things than these.
FAUSTUS. Then there's enough for a thousand souls!
         Here Mephastophilis, receive this scroll,
90   A deed of gift of body and of soul:
         But yet conditionally, that thou perform
         All articles prescribed between us both.
MEPHASTOPHILIS. Faustus, I swear by hell and Lucifer
         To effect all promises between us made.
95   FAUSTUS. Then hear me read them. On these conditions following:
         First, that Faustus may be a spirit[9] *in form and substance.*
         Secondly, that Mephastophilis shall be his servant, and at his com-
         mand.
         Thirdly, that Mephastophilis shall do for him, and bring him
100   *whatsoever.*
         Fourthly, that he shall be in his chamber or house invisible.
         Lastly, that he shall appear to the said John Faustus at all times, in
         what form or shape soever he please.
         I, John Faustus of Wittenberg, doctor, by these presents,[1] *do give*
105   *both body and soul to Lucifer, Prince of the East, and his minister*
         Mephastophilis; and furthermore grant unto them that, four and
         twenty years being expired, the articles above written inviolate, full
         power to fetch or carry the said John Faustus, body and soul, flesh,
         blood, or goods, into their habitation wheresoever.
110   *By me John Faustus.*
MEPHASTOPHILIS. Speak Faustus, do you deliver this as your deed?
FAUSTUS. Ay, take it; and the devil give thee good on't.
MEPHASTOPHILIS. Now Faustus, ask what thou wilt.
FAUSTUS. First will I question with thee about hell:
115   Tell me, where is the place that men call hell?
MEPHASTOPHILIS. Under the heavens.
FAUSTUS. Ay, but whereabouts?
MEPHASTOPHILIS. Within the bowels of these elements,
         Where we are tortured and remain for ever.
120   Hell hath no limits, nor is circumscribed
         In one self place; for where we are is hell,
         And where hell is, there must we ever be.
         And to conclude, when all the world dissolves,
         And every creature shall be purified,
125   All places shall be hell that is not heaven.
FAUSTUS. Come, I think hell's a fable.
MEPHASTOPHILIS. Ay, think so still, till experience change thy mind.

___

9. I.e., have the supernatural powers of a spirit.   1. The legal articles.

FAUSTUS. Why? think'st thou then that Faustus shall be damned?

MEPHASTOPHILIS. Ay, of necessity, for here's the scroll

130   Wherein thou hast given thy soul to Lucifer.

FAUSTUS. Ay, and body too; but what of that?

    Thinkest thou that Faustus is so fond° to imagine   *foolish*

    That after this life there is any pain?

    Tush, these are trifles and mere old wives' tales.

135   MEPHASTOPHILIS. But Faustus, I am an instance to prove the contrary;

    For I am damned, and am now in hell.

FAUSTUS. How, now in hell? Nay, and this be hell, I'll willingly be

    damned here! What, walking, disputing, etc. . . . But leaving off

    this, let me have a wife, the fairest maid in Germany, for I am

140   wanton and lascivious, and cannot live without a wife.

MEPHASTOPHILIS. How, a wife? I prithee Faustus, talk not of a wife.[2]

FAUSTUS. Nay sweet Mephastophilis, fetch me one, for I will have

    one.

MEPHASTOPHILIS. Well, thou wilt have one; sit there till I come.

145   I'll fetch thee a wife in the devil's name.   [*Exit.*]

    [*Enter (again) with a* DEVIL *dressed like a woman, with fire-*
    works.]

MEPHASTOPHILIS. Tell Faustus, how dost thou like thy wife?

FAUSTUS. A plague on her for a hot whore!

MEPHASTOPHILIS. Tut Faustus, marriage is but a ceremonial toy;

    If thou lovest me, think no more of it.

150   I'll cull thee out the fairest courtesans,

    And bring them every morning to thy bed:

    She whom thine eye shall like, thy heart shall have,

    Be she as chaste as was Penelope,

    As wise as Saba,[3] or as beautiful

155   As was bright Lucifer before his fall.

    Hold, take this book, peruse it thoroughly:

    The iterating° of these lines brings gold;   *repeating*

    The framing° of this circle on the ground   *drawing*

    Brings whirlwinds, tempests, thunder, and lightning.

160   Pronounce this thrice devoutly to thy self,

    And men in armor shall appear to thee,

    Ready to execute what thou desirest.

FAUSTUS. Thanks Mephastophilis, yet fain would I have a book

    wherein I might behold all spells and incantations, that I might

165   raise up spirits when I please.

MEPHASTOPHILIS. Here they are in this book.   [*There turn to them.*]

FAUSTUS. Now would I have a book where I might see all characters

    and planets of the heavens, that I might know their motions and

    dispositions.

170   MEPHASTOPHILIS. Here they are too.   [*Turn to them.*]

FAUSTUS. Nay, let me have one book more, and then I have done,

---

2. Mephastophilis cannot produce a wife for Faustus because marriage is a sacrament.   3. The queen of Sheba. "Penelope": the wife of Ulysses, famed for chastity and fidelity.

wherein I might see all plants, herbs and trees that grow upon the
earth.

MEPHASTOPHILIS. Here they be.

175 FAUSTUS. O thou art deceived!

MEPHASTOPHILIS. Tut, I warrant thee.   [*Turn to them.*]

FAUSTUS. When I behold the heavens, then I repent,
    And curse thee, wicked Mephastophilis,
    Because thou hast deprived me of those joys.

180 MEPHASTOPHILIS. Why Faustus,
    Think'st thou that heaven is such a glorious thing?
    I tell thee 'tis not half so fair as thou,
    Or any man that breathes on earth.

FAUSTUS. How prov'st thou that?

185 MEPHASTOPHILIS. It was made for man, therefore is man more excellent.

FAUSTUS. If it were made for man, 'twas made for me:
    I will renounce this magic, and repent.

        [*Enter* GOOD ANGEL *and* EVIL ANGEL.]

GOOD ANGEL. Faustus repent, yet God will pity thee.

190 EVIL ANGEL. Thou art a spirit,° God cannot pity thee.   *evil spirit, devil*

FAUSTUS. Who buzzeth in mine ears I am a spirit?
    Be I a devil, yet God may pity me.
    Ay, God will pity me if I repent.

EVIL ANGEL. Ay, but Faustus never shall repent.   [*Exeunt* (ANGELS).]

195 FAUSTUS. My heart's so hardened[4] I cannot repent!
    Scarce can I name salvation, faith, or heaven,
    But fearful echoes thunders in mine ears,
    "Faustus, thou are damned"; then swords and knives,
    Poison, guns, halters,[5] and envenomed steel,

200   Are laid before me to dispatch myself:
    And long ere this I should have slain myself,
    Had not sweet pleasure conquered deep despair.
    Have I not made blind Homer sing to me
    Of Alexander's[6] love, and Oenon's death?

205   And hath not he that built the walls of Thebes
    With ravishing sound of his melodious harp,[7]
    Made music with my Mephastophilis?
    Why should I die then, or basely despair?
    I am resolved! Faustus shall ne'er repent.

210   Come Mephastophilis, let us dispute again,
    And argue of divine astrology.
    Tell me, are there many heavens above the moon?

---

4. Hardness of heart is the desperate spiritual state of
the reprobate who will suffer eternal damnation.
5. Ropes for hanging.
6. Alexander is another name for Paris, the lover of
Oenone; later he deserted her and abducted Helen,
causing the Trojan War. Oenone refused to heal the
wounds Paris received in battle, and when he died of
them, she killed herself in remorse.
7. The legendary musician Amphion, whose harp
caused stones, of themselves, to form the walls of
Thebes.

Are all celestial bodies but one globe,
As is the substance of this centric earth?[8]
215 MEPHASTOPHILIS. As are the elements, such are the spheres,
Mutually folded in each other's orb.
And, Faustus, all jointly move upon one axletree
Whose termine° is termed the world's wide pole,   *end*
Nor are the names of Saturn, Mars, or Jupiter
220 Feigned, but are erring stars.[9]
FAUSTUS. But tell me, have they all one motion, both *situ et tempore?*[1]
MEPHASTOPHILIS. All jointly move from east to west in four-and-
twenty hours upon the poles of the world, but differ in their motion
upon the poles of the zodiac.[2]
225 FAUSTUS. Tush, these slender trifles Wagner can decide!
Hath Mephastophilis no greater skill?
Who knows not the double motion of the planets?
The first is finished in a natural day, the second thus: as Saturn in
thirty years; Jupiter in twelve; Mars in four; the Sun, Venus, and
230 Mercury in a year; the Moon in twenty-eight days. Tush, these are
freshmen's suppositions. But tell me, hath every sphere a dominion
or *intelligentia?*[3]
MEPHASTOPHILIS. Ay.
FAUSTUS. How many heavens or spheres are there?
235 MEPHASTOPHILIS. Nine: the seven planets, the firmament, and the
empyreal heaven.[4]
FAUSTUS. Well, resolve me then in this question: why have we not
conjunctions, oppositions,[5] aspects, eclipses, all at one time, but in
some years we have more, in some less?
240 MEPHASTOPHILIS. *Per inaequalem motum respectu totius.*[6]
FAUSTUS. Well, I am answered. Tell me who made the world?
MEPHASTOPHILIS. I will not.
FAUSTUS. Sweet Mephastophilis, tell me.
MEPHASTOPHILIS. Move° me not, for I will not tell thee.   *anger*
245 FAUSTUS. Villain, have I not bound thee to tell me anything?
MEPHASTOPHILIS. Ay, that is not against our kingdom; but this is.
Think thou on hell Faustus, for thou art damned.
FAUSTUS. Think, Faustus, upon God, that made the world.
MEPHASTOPHILIS. Remember this.   [*Exit.*]
250 FAUSTUS. Ay, go accursed spirit, to ugly hell,
'Tis thou hast damned distressed Faustus' soul:
Is't not too late?

8. Faustus asks whether all the apparently different heavenly bodies form really "one globe" like the earth. Mephastophilis answers that like the elements, which are separate but combined, the heavenly bodies are separate but their spheres are infolded and they move on one axletree.
9. It is appropriate to give individual names to Saturn, Mars, Jupiter, and the other planets—which are called wandering, or "erring" stars. The fixed stars were in the eighth sphere (the firmament, or crystalline sphere).

1. In position and time.
2. The common axletree on which all the spheres revolve.
3. An angel, or intelligence, thought to be the source of motion in each sphere.
4. The ninth sphere was the immovable empyrean.
5. "Conjunctions": the apparent joinings of two planets. "Oppositions": when two planets are most remote.
6. Because of their unequal velocities within the system.

[*Enter* GOOD ANGEL *and* EVIL (ANGEL).]

EVIL ANGEL. Too late.

GOOD ANGEL. Never too late, if Faustus will repent.

255   EVIL ANGEL. If thou repent, devils shall tear thee in pieces.

GOOD ANGEL. Repent, and they shall never rase° thy skin.   *tear*

     [*Exeunt* (ANGELS).]

FAUSTUS. Ah Christ my Savior! seek to save

  Distressed Faustus' soul.

     [*Enter* LUCIFER, BELZEBUB, *and* MEPHASTOPHILIS.]

LUCIFER. Christ cannot save thy soul, for he is just.

260   There's none but I have interest in the same.

FAUSTUS. O who art thou that look'st so terrible?

LUCIFER. I am Lucifer, and this is my companion prince in hell.

FAUSTUS. O Faustus, they are come to fetch away thy soul!

LUCIFER. We come to tell thee thou dost injure us.

265   Thou talk'st of Christ, contrary to thy promise.

  Thou should'st not think of God; think of the devil,

  And his dam⁷ too.

FAUSTUS. Nor will I henceforth: pardon me in this,

  And Faustus vows never to look to heaven,

270   Never to name God, or to pray to him,

  To burn his Scriptures, slay his ministers,

  And make my spirits pull his churches down.

LUCIFER. Do so, and we will highly gratify thee. Faustus, we are come

  from hell to show thee some pastime; sit down, and thou shalt see

275   all the Seven Deadly Sins⁸ appear in their proper shapes.

FAUSTUS. That sight will be as pleasing unto me, as Paradise was to

  Adam, the first day of his creation.

LUCIFER. Talk not of Paradise, nor creation, but mark this show; talk

  of the devil and nothing else. Come away.

     [*Enter the* SEVEN DEADLY SINS.]

280   Now Faustus, examine them of their several names and disposi-

  tions.

FAUSTUS. What art thou, the first?

PRIDE. I am Pride: I disdain to have any parents. I am like to Ovid's

  flea,⁹ I can creep into every corner of a wench: sometimes like a

285   periwig, I sit upon her brow; or like a fan of feathers, I kiss her lips.

  Indeed I do—what do I not! But fie, what a scent is here? I'll not

  speak another word, except the ground were perfumed and covered

  with cloth of arras.¹

FAUSTUS. What art thou, the second?

290   COVETOUSNESS. I am Covetousness, begotten of an old churl in an

  old leathern bag; and might I have my wish, I would desire that

---

7. Mother. "The devil and his dam" was a common colloquial expression.

8. Pride, avarice, lust, anger, gluttony, envy, and sloth, called deadly because all other sins grow out of them (cf. the procession of the seven deadly sins in Spenser's

The Faerie Queene 1.4, stanzas 16–37, pp. 315–319).

9. A salacious medieval poem *Carmen de Pulice* ("Song of the Flea") was attributed to Ovid.

1. Arras in Flanders exported fine cloth used for tapestry hangings.

this house, and all the people in it, were turned to gold, that I might lock you up in my good chest. O my sweet gold!

FAUSTUS. What art thou, the third?

295 WRATH. I am Wrath. I had neither father nor mother: I leaped out of a lion's mouth when I was scarce half an hour old, and ever since I have run up and down the world, with this case of rapiers, wounding myself when I had nobody to fight withal. I was born in hell—and look to it, for some of you shall be my father.

300 FAUSTUS. What art thou, the fourth?

ENVY. I am Envy, begotten of a chimney-sweeper, and an oyster-wife. I cannot read, and therefore wish all books were burnt; I am lean with seeing others eat—O that there would come a famine through all the world, that all might die, and I live alone; then thou
305 should'st see how fat I would be! But must thou sit and I stand? Come down, with a vengeance.

FAUSTUS. Away, envious rascal! What art thou, the fifth?

GLUTTONY. Who, I sir? I am Gluttony. My parents are all dead, and the devil a penny they have left me but a bare pension, and that is
310 thirty meals a day and ten bevers[2]—a small trifle to suffice nature. O, I come of a royal parentage: my grandfather was a gammon[3] of bacon, my grandmother a hogshead of claret wine; my godfathers were these: Peter Pickled-Herring, and Martin Martlemas-Beef.[4] O, but my godmother! She was a jolly gentlewoman, and well-
315 beloved in every good town and city; her name was Mistress Margery March-Beer.[5] Now, Faustus, thou hast heard all my progeny;[6] wilt thou bid me to supper?

FAUSTUS. No, I'll see thee hanged; thou wilt eat up all my victuals.

GLUTTONY. Then the devil choke thee!

320 FAUSTUS. Choke thyself, Glutton. What art thou, the sixth?

SLOTH. I am Sloth; I was begotten on a sunny bank, where I have lain ever since—and you have done me great injury to bring me from thence. Let me be carried thither again by Gluttony and Lechery. I'll not speak another word for a king's ransom.

325 FAUSTUS. What are you Mistress Minx, the seventh and last?

LECHERY. Who, I, sir? I am one that loves an inch of raw mutton better than an ell of fried stockfish;[7] and the first letter of my name begins with Lechery.

LUCIFER. Away! To hell, to hell! [*Exeunt the* (SEVEN DEADLY) SINS.]
330 Now Faustus, how dost thou like this?

FAUSTUS. O this feeds my soul.

LUCIFER. Tut Faustus, in hell is all manner of delight.

FAUSTUS. O might I see hell, and return again, how happy were I then!

2. Snacks.
3. The lower side of pork, including the leg.
4. Meat, salted to preserve it during the winter, was prepared around Martinmas (November 11).
5. A rich ale, made in March.

6. Ancestry, lineage.
7. Dried cod. "Mutton": frequently a bawdy term in Elizabethan English, here, the penis. "Ell": forty-five inches.

335 LUCIFER. Thou shalt; I will send for thee at midnight. In meantime, take this book, peruse it thoroughly, and thou shalt turn thyself into what shape thou wilt.

FAUSTUS. Great thanks, mighty Lucifer; this will I keep as chary[8] as my life.

340 LUCIFER. Farewell, Faustus; and think on the devil.

FAUSTUS. Farewell, great Lucifer; come, Mephastophilis.

[*Exeunt* OMNES.]

SCENE 6

[*Enter* ROBIN *the ostler with a book in his hand.*]

ROBIN. O this is admirable! here I ha' stolen one of Doctor Faustus' conjuring books, and i'faith I mean to search some circles[9] for my own use: now will I make all the maidens in our parish dance at my pleasure stark naked before me, and so by that means I shall
5   see more than ere I felt, or saw yet.

[*Enter* RAFE *calling* ROBIN.]

RAFE. Robin, prithee come away, there's a gentleman tarries to have his horse, and he would have his things rubbed and made clean. He keeps such a chafing[1] with my mistress about it, and she has sent me to look thee out. Prithee, come away.

10   ROBIN. Keep out, keep out; or else you are blown up, you are dismembered, Rafe. Keep out, for I am about a roaring[2] piece of work.

RAFE. Come, what dost thou with that same book? Thou canst not read!

ROBIN. Yes, my master and mistress shall find that I can read—he for
15   his forehead, she for her private study. She's born to bear with me, or else my art fails.

RAFE. Why Robin, what book is that?

ROBIN. What book? Why the most intolerable[3] book for conjuring that ere was invented by any brimstone devil.

20   RAFE. Canst thou conjure with it?

ROBIN. I can do all these things easily with it: first, I can make thee drunk with 'ipocrase[4] at any tavern in Europe for nothing, that's one of my conjuring works.

RAFE. Our master parson says that's nothing.

25   ROBIN. True Rafe! And more, Rafe, if thou hast any mind to Nan Spit, our kitchen-maid, then turn her and wind her to thy own use, as often as thou wilt, and at midnight.

RAFE. O brave Robin! Shall I have Nan Spit, and to mine own use? On that condition I'll feed thy devil with horsebread as long as he
30   lives, of free cost.[5]

ROBIN. No more, sweet Rafe; let's go and make clean our boots which

8. Carefully.
9. Magicians' circles, but with an obvious sexual pun.
1. Scolding.
2. Dangerous.

3. Incomparable (probably).
4. Robin's pronunciation of *hippocras*, a spiced wine.
5. Free of charge. "Horsebread": fodder.

lie foul upon our hands, and then to our conjuring in the devil's
name.

[*Exeunt.*]

CHORUS 2

[*Enter* WAGNER *solus.*]
WAGNER. Learned Faustus,
   To know the secrets of astronomy
   Graven in the book of Jove's high firmament,
   Did mount himself to scale Olympus'[6] top.
5 Being seated in a chariot burning bright,
   Drawn by the strength of yoked dragons' necks.
   He now is gone to prove cosmography,[7]
   And, as I guess, will first arrive at Rome,
   To see the pope, and manner of his court,
10 And take some part of holy Peter's feast,[8]
   That to this day is highly solemnized.   [*Exit* WAGNER.]

SCENE 7

[*Enter* FAUSTUS *and* MEPHASTOPHILIS.]   *grand tour*
FAUSTUS. Having now, my good Mephastophilis,
   Passed with delight the stately town of Trier,[9]
   Environed round with airy mountain tops,
   With walls of flint, and deep entrenched lakes,°   moats
5 Not to be won by any conquering prince;
   From Paris next, coasting the realm of France,
   We saw the river Main fall into Rhine,
   Whose banks are set with groves of fruitful vines;
   Then up to Naples, rich Campania,
10 With buildings fair and gorgeous to the eye,
   The streets straight forth, and paved with finest brick,
   Quarters the town in four equivalents;
   There saw we learned Maro's[1] golden tomb,
   The way° he cut, an English mile in length,   tunnel
15 Thorough a rock of stone in one night's space.
   From thence to Venice, Padua, and the rest,
   In midst of which a sumptuous temple[2] stands,
   That threats the stars with her aspiring top.
   Thus hitherto hath Faustus spent his time.
20 But tell me now, what resting place is this?
   Hast thou, as erst° I did command,   earlier
   Conducted me within the walls of Rome?

6. The home of the gods in Greek mythology.
7. To test the accuracy of maps.
8. St. Peter's feast is June 29.
9. Treves (in Prussia).
1. Virgil's. In medieval legend the Roman poet Virgil
was considered a magician whose powers produced a
tunnel on the promontory of Posilippo at Naples, near
his tomb.
2. St. Mark's in Venice.

MEPHASTOPHILIS. Faustus, I have; and because we will not be unprovided, I have taken up his holiness' privy chamber for our use.

25   FAUSTUS. I hope his holiness will bid us welcome.

MEPHASTOPHILIS. Tut, 'tis no matter man, we'll be bold with his good
cheer.
And now, my Faustus, that thou may'st perceive
What Rome containeth to delight thee with,

30   Know that this city stands upon seven hills
That underprop the groundwork of the same;
Just through the midst runs flowing Tiber's stream,
With winding banks, that cut it in two parts;
Over the which four stately bridges lean,

35   That makes safe passage to each part of Rome.
Upon the bridge called Ponte Angelo
Erected is a castle passing strong,
Within whose walls such store of ordinance are,
And double cannons, framed of carved brass,

40   As match the days within one complete year;
Besides the gates, and high pyramides°   obelisks
Which Julius Caesar brought from Africa.

FAUSTUS. Now by the kingdoms of infernal rule,
Of Styx, Acheron, and the fiery lake

45   Of ever-burning Phlegethon,[3] I swear
That I do long to see the monuments
And situation of bright-splendent Rome.
Come therefore, let's away.

MEPHASTOPHILIS. Nay Faustus stay, I know you'd fain see the pope,

50   And take some part of holy Peter's feast,
Where thou shalt see a troup of bald-pate friars,
Whose summum bonum[4] is in belly-cheer.

FAUSTUS. Well, I am content to compass° then some sport,   take part in
And by their folly make us merriment.

55   Then charm me that I may be invisible, to do what I please
Unseen of any whilst I stay in Rome.

MEPHASTOPHILIS. [casts a spell on him] So Faustus, now do what thou
wilt, thou shall not be discerned.
        [Sound a sennet;[5] enter the POPE and the CARDINAL OF LOR-
        RAINE to the banquet, with FRIARS attending.]

POPE. My lord of Lorraine, will't please you draw near.

60   FAUSTUS. Fall to; and the devil choke you and[6] you spare.

POPE. How now, who's that which spake? Friars, look about.

1 FRIAR. Here's nobody, if it like[7] your holiness.

POPE. My lord, here is a dainty dish was sent to me from the bishop
of Milan.

---

3. Classical names for rivers of the underworld.   6. If. "Fall to": get on with it.
4. The greatest good; often refers to God.   7. Please.
5. A set of notes on the trumpet or cornet.

65 FAUSTUS. I thank you, sir.   [*snatch it*]

POPE. How now, who's that which snatched the meat from me? Will no man look? My lord, this dish was sent me from the cardinal of Florence.

FAUSTUS. You say true? I'll have't.   [*snatch it*]

70 POPE. What, again! My lord, I'll drink to your grace.

FAUSTUS. I'll pledge[8] your grace.   [*snatch the cup*]

LORRAINE. My lord, it may be some ghost newly crept out of purgatory come to beg a pardon of your holiness.

POPE. It may be so; friars; prepare a dirge[9] to lay the fury of this ghost.

75 Once again my lord, fall to.   [*the POPE crosseth himself*]

FAUSTUS. What, are you crossing of your self? Well, use that trick no more, I would advise you.
[*Cross again.*]

FAUSTUS. Well, there's the second time; aware the third! I give you fair warning.
[*Cross again, and FAUSTUS hits him a box of the ear, and they all run away.*]

80 FAUSTUS. Come Mephastophilis, what shall we do?

MEPHASTOPHILIS. Nay, I know not; we shall be cursed with bell, book, and candle.[1]

FAUSTUS. How! Bell, book, and candle; candle, book, and bell, Forward and backward, to curse Faustus to hell.

85 Anon you shall hear a hog grunt, a calf bleat, and an ass bray, Because it is St. Peter's holy day.
[*Enter all the FRIARS to sing the Dirge.*]

1 FRIAR. Come brethren, let's about our business with good devotion.
[*Sing this.*]
Cursed be he that stole away his holiness' meat from the table.
Maledicat Dominus.[2]

90 Cursed be he that struck his holiness a blow on the face.
Maledicat Dominus.
Cursed be he that took Friar Sandelo a blow on the pate.
Maledicat Dominus.
Cursed be he that disturbeth our holy dirge.

95 Maledicat Dominus.
Cursed be he that took away his holiness' wine.
Maledicat dominus.
Et omnes sancti.[3] Amen.
[*Beat the FRIARS, and fling fireworks among them, and so Exeunt.*]

8. Toast.
9. Here, a formal curse.
1. The traditional paraphernalia for cursing and ex-   communication.
2. May the Lord curse him.
3. And all the saints [also curse him].

SCENE 8

[*Enter* ROBIN *and* RAFE *with a silver goblet.*]

ROBIN. Come Rafe, did not I tell thee we were for ever made by this
Doctor Faustus' book? *Ecce signum!*[4] Here's a simple purchase for
horse-keepers: our horses shall eat no hay as long as this lasts.

[*Enter the* VINTNER.]

RAFE. But Robin, here comes the vintner.

5 ROBIN. Hush, I'll gull[5] him supernaturally! Drawer, I hope all is paid;
God be with you. Come, Rafe.

VINTNER. Soft sir, a word with you. I must yet have a goblet paid from
you ere you go.

ROBIN. I a goblet, Rafe! I a goblet? I scorn you: and you are but a
10 &c.[6] . . . I a goblet? Search me.

VINTNER. I mean so, sir, with your favor.   [*searches* ROBIN]

ROBIN. How say you now?

VINTNER. I must say somewhat to your fellow; you sir!

RAFE. Me sir! Me sir? Search your fill. Now sir, you may be ashamed
15 to burden honest men with a matter of truth.

VINTNER. [*searches* RAFE] Well, t'one of you hath this goblet about
you.

ROBIN. You lie, drawer; 'tis afore me. Sirra you, I'll teach ye to
impeach honest men: [*to* RAFE] stand by. [*to the* VINTNER] I'll scour
20 you for a goblet—stand aside, you were best—I charge you in the
name of Belzebub—look to the goblet, Rafe!

VINTNER. What mean you, sirra?

ROBIN. I'll tell you what I mean: [*he reads*] *Sanctobulorum Periphrasti-
con*—nay, I'll tickle you, vintner—look to the goblet, Rafe—
25 *Polypragmos Belseborams framanto pacostiphos tostis Mephastophilis, &c. . . .*[7]

[*Enter* MEPHASTOPHILIS: *sets squibs at their backs: they run about.*]

VINTNER. O *nomine Domine!*[8] What mean'st thou Robin? Thou hast
no goblet.

RAFE. *Peccatum peccatorum!*[9] Here's thy goblet, good Vintner.

30 ROBIN. *Misericordia pro nobis!*[1] What shall I do? Good devil, forgive
me now, and I'll never rob thy library more.

[*Enter to them* (again) MEPHASTOPHILIS.]

MEPHASTOPHILIS. Vanish villains, th'one like an ape, an other like a
bear, the third an ass, for doing this enterprise.   [*Exit* VINTNER.]
Monarch of hell, under those black survey
35 Great potentates do kneel with awful fear;
Upon whose altars thousand souls do lie;
How am I vexed with these villains' charms!
From Constantinople am I hither come,

4. Behold the proof.
5. Trick.
6. The actor might ad lib abuse at this point.
7. Dog-Latin, as Robin attempts to conjure from Faustus's book.

8. In the name of the Lord; the Latin invocations are
used in swearing.
9. Sins of sins!
1. Have mercy on us!

Only for pleasure of these damned slaves.

40   ROBIN. How, from Constantinople? You have had a great journey!
Will you take sixpence in your purse to pay for your supper, and be
gone?

MEPHASTOPHILIS. Well villains, for your presumption, I transform
thee into an ape, and thee into a dog; and so begone!   [*Exit.*]

45   ROBIN. How, into an ape? That's brave: I'll have fine sport with the
boys; I'll get nuts and apples enow.

RAFE. And I must be a dog.

ROBIN. I'faith, thy head will never be out of the potage² pot. [*Exeunt.*]

CHORUS 3

[*Enter* CHORUS (WAGNER).]

CHORUS. When Faustus had with pleasure ta'en the view
Of rarest things, and royal courts of kings,
He stayed his course, and so returnèd home;
Where such as bare his absence but with grief—

5   I mean his friends and nearest companions—
Did gratulate his safety with kind words.
And in their conference of what befell,
Touching his journey through the world and air,
They put forth questions of astrology,

10   Which Faustus answered with such learned skill,
As they admired and wondered at his wit.
Now is his fame spread forth in every land:
Amongst the rest the emperor is one,
Carolus the fifth,³ at whose palace now

15   Faustus is feasted 'mongst his noblemen.
What there he did in trial of his art
I leave untold: your eyes shall see performed.   [*Exeunt.*]

SCENE 9

[*Enter* EMPEROR, FAUSTUS, *and a* KNIGHT, *with Attendants.*]

EMPEROR. Master Doctor Faustus, I have heard strange report of thy
knowledge in the black art, how that none in my empire, nor in
the whole world, can compare with thee for the rare effects of
magic. They say thou hast a familiar spirit, by whom thou canst

5   accomplish what thou list! This therefore is my request: that thou
let me see some proof of thy skill, that mine eyes may be witnesses
to confirm what mine ears have heard reported. And here I swear
to thee, by the honor of mine imperial crown, that whatever thou
dost, thou shalt be in no ways prejudiced or endamaged.

10   KNIGHT. [*aside*] I'faith, he looks much like a conjuror.

FAUSTUS. My gracious sovereign, though I must confess myself far

---

2. Porridge.   3. The Holy Roman Emperor Charles V (1519–1556).

inferior to the report men have published, and nothing answerable
to the honor of your imperial majesty, yet for that love and duty
binds me thereunto, I am content to do whatsoever your majesty
15   shall command me.
EMPEROR. Then Doctor Faustus, mark what I shall say. As I was sometime solitary set within my closet, sundry thoughts arose about the
honor of mine ancestors—how they had won by prowess such
exploits, got such riches, subdued so many kingdoms, as we that do
20   succeed, or they that shall hereafter possess our throne, shall (I fear
me) never attain to that degree of high renown and great authority.
Amongst which kings is Alexander the Great,[4] chief spectacle of
the world's pre-eminence:
The bright shining of whose glorious acts
25   Lightens the world with his reflecting beams;
As when I hear but motion° made of him,   mention
It grieves my soul I never saw the man.
If therefore thou, by cunning of thine art,
Canst raise this man from hollow vaults below,
30   Where lies entombed this famous conqueror,
And bring with him his beauteous paramour,[5]
Both in their right shapes, gesture, and attire
They used to wear during their time of life,
Thou shalt both satisfy my just desire,
35   And give me cause to praise thee whilst I live.
FAUSTUS. My gracious lord, I am ready to accomplish your request, so
far forth as by art and power of my spirit I am able to perform.
KNIGHT. [aside] I'faith, that's just nothing at all.
FAUSTUS. But, if it like your grace, it is not in my ability to present
40   before your eyes the true substantial bodies of those two deceased
princes which long since are consumed to dust.
KNIGHT. [aside] Ay, marry, master doctor, now there's a sign of grace
in you, when you will confess the truth.
FAUSTUS. But such spirits as can lively resemble Alexander and his
45   paramour shall appear before your grace, in that manner that they
best lived in, in their most flourishing estate: which I doubt not
shall sufficiently content your imperial majesty.
EMPEROR. Go to, master doctor, let me see them presently.[6]
KNIGHT. Do you hear, master doctor? You bring Alexander and his
50   paramour before the emperor!
FAUSTUS. How then, sir?
KNIGHT. I'faith, that's as true as Diana turned me to a stag.
FAUSTUS. No sir; but when Actaeon died, he left the horns[7] for you!
Mephastophilis, begone!   [Exit MEPHASTOPHILIS.]

4. The great world conqueror (356–323 B.C.).
5. Probably Roxana, Alexander's wife.
6. Immediately.
7. Horns were traditionally a sign of the cuckolded

husband. "Actaeon": the hunter of classical legend
who happened to see the goddess Diana bathing. For
punishment he was changed into a stag; he was then
chased and killed by his own hounds.

55 KNIGHT. Nay, and[8] you go to conjuring I'll be gone.   [*Exit* KNIGHT.]
    FAUSTUS. I'll meet with you anon for interrupting me so. Here they
        are, my gracious lord.
            [*Enter* MEPHASTOPHILIS *with* ALEXANDER *and his* PARAMOUR.]
    EMPEROR. Master doctor, I heard this lady, while she lived, had a wart
        or mole in her neck; how shall I know whether it be so or no?
60 FAUSTUS. Your highness may boldly go and see.
            [*The* EMPEROR *examines the lady's neck.*]
    EMPEROR. Sure, these are no spirits, but the true substantial bodies of
        those two deceased princes.
            [*Exit* ALEXANDER (*and his* PARAMOUR).]
    FAUSTUS. Will't please your highness now to send for the knight that
        was so pleasant with me here of late?
65 EMPEROR. One of you call him forth.
            [*Enter the* KNIGHT *with a pair of horns on his head.*]
    EMPEROR. How now sir knight? Why, I had thought thou hadst beena
        bachelor, but now I see thou hast a wife that not only gives thee
        horns but makes thee wear them! Feel on thy head.
    KNIGHT. Thou damned wretch and exercrable dog,
70   Bred in the concave of some monstrous rock,
        How dar'st thou thus abuse a gentleman?
        Villain I say, undo what thou hast done.
    FAUSTUS. O not so fast sir, there's no haste but good. Are you
        remembered[9] how you crossed me in my conference with the
75   emperor? I think I have met with you for it.
    EMPEROR. Good master doctor, at my entreaty release him; he hath
        done penance sufficient.
    FAUSTUS. My gracious lord, not so much for the injury he offered me
        here in your presence, as to delight you with some mirth, hath
80   Faustus worthily requited this injurious knight; which being all I
        desire, I am content to release him of his horns. And, sir knight,
        hereafter speak well of scholars: Mephastophilis, transform him
        straight. Now my good lord, having done my duty, I humbly take
        my leave.
85 EMPEROR. Farewell master doctor; yet ere you go, expect from me a
        bounteous reward.
            [*Exit* EMPEROR (*and his* ATTENDANTS).]
    FAUSTUS. Now Mephastophilis, the restless course
        That time doth run with calm and silent foot,
        Shortening my days and thread of vital life,
90   Calls for the payment of my latest years;
        Therefore, sweet Mephastophilis, let us make haste to Wittenberg.
    MEPHASTOPHILIS. What, will you go on horseback, or on foot?
    FAUSTUS. Nay, till I am past this fair and pleasant green, I'll walk on
        foot.

8. If.   9. Have you forgotten.

SCENE 10

[*Enter (to them)* a HORSE-COURSER.]¹

HORSE-COURSER. I have been all this day seeking one Master Fustian:²
'mass, see where he is! God save you, master doctor.

FAUSTUS. What, horse-courser: you are well met.

HORSE-COURSER. Do you hear, sir; I have brought you forty dollars³
5   for your horse.

FAUSTUS. I cannot sell him so: if thou lik'st him for fifty, take him.

HORSE-COURSER. Alas sir, I have no more. I pray you speak for me.

MEPHASTOPHILIS. I pray you let him have him; he is an honest fellow,
and he has a great charge—neither wife nor child.

10   FAUSTUS. Well; come, give me your money; my boy will deliver him
to you. But I must tell you one thing before you have him: ride
him not into the water at any hand.

HORSE-COURSER. Why sir, will he not drink of all waters?

FAUSTUS. O yes, he will drink of all waters, but ride him not into the
15   water. Ride him over hedge or ditch, or where thou wilt, but not
into the water.

HORSE-COURSER. Well sir. Now am I made man for ever: I'll not leave
my horse for forty! If he had but the quality of hey ding ding, hey
ding ding,⁴ I'd make a brave living on him! He has a buttock as
20   slick as an eel. Well, God b'y sir; your boy will deliver him me. But
hark ye sir, if my horse be sick, or ill at ease, if I bring his water⁵ to
you, you'll tell me what it is?

[*Exit* HORSE-COURSER.]

FAUSTUS. Away you villain! What, dost think I am a horse-doctor?
What art thou, Faustus, but a man condemned to die?
25   Thy fatal time doth draw to final end.
Despair doth drive distrust unto my thoughts:
Confound these passions with a quiet sleep.
Tush, Christ did call the thief upon the cross;⁶
Then rest thee, Faustus, quiet in conceit.°   *in mind*

[*Sleep in his chair.*]

[*Enter* HORSE-COURSER *all wet, crying.*]

30   HORSE-COURSER. Alas, alas, Doctor Fustian, quoth 'a: 'mass, Doctor
Lopus⁷ was never such a doctor! H'as given me a purgation, h'as
purged me of forty dollars! I shall never see them more. But yet, like
an ass as I was, I would not be ruled by him; for he bade me I should
ride him into no water. Now I, thinking my horse had had some rare
35   quality that he would not have had me known of, I, like a vent'rous

1. Horse trader, traditionally a sharp bargainer or
cheat.
2. The horse-courser's mispronunciation of Faustus's
name.
3. Common German coins.
4. He wishes his horse were a stallion, not a gelding,
so he could put him to stud.

5. Urine.
6. In Luke 23.39–43 one of the two thieves crucified
with Jesus is promised paradise.
7. In February 1594, Roderigo Lopez, the queen's personal physician, was executed for plotting to poison the
queen.

youth, rid him into the deep pond at the town's end. I was no sooner in the middle of the pond, but my horse vanished away, and I sat upon a bottle[8] of hay, never so near drowning in my life! But I'll seek out my doctor, and have my forty dollars again, or I'll make it the dearest horse. O, yonder is his snipper-snapper! Do you hear, you hey-pass,[9] where's your master?

MEPHASTOPHILIS. Why, sir, what would you? You cannot speak with him.

HORSE-COURSER. But I will speak with him.

MEPHASTOPHILIS. Why, he's fast asleep; come some other time.

HORSE-COURSER. I'll speak with him now, or I'll break his glass-windows[1] about his ears.

MEPHASTOPHILIS. I tell thee, he has not slept this eight nights.

HORSE-COURSER. And he has not slept this eight weeks I'll speak with him.

MEPHASTOPHILIS. See where he is, fast asleep.

HORSE-COURSER. Ay, this is he; God save ye master doctor, master doctor, master Doctor Fustian, forty dollars, forty dollars for a bottle of hay.

MEPHASTOPHILIS. Why, thou seest he hears thee not.

HORSE-COURSER. So ho ho; so ho ho.[2] [halloo in his ear] No, will you not wake? I'll make you wake ere I go. [pull him by the leg, and pull it away.] Alas, I am undone! What shall I do?

FAUSTUS. O my leg, my leg! Help, Mephastophilis! Call the officers! My leg, my leg!

MEPHASTOPHILIS. Come villain, to the constable.

HORSE-COURSER. O Lord, sir! Let me go, and I'll give you forty dollars more.

MEPHASTOPHILIS. Where be they?

HORSE-COURSER. I have none about me: come to my ostry[3] and I'll give them you.

MEPHASTOPHILIS. Begone quickly!

[HORSE-COURSER runs away.]

FAUSTUS. What, is he gone? Farewell he: Faustus has his leg again, and the horse-courser—I take it—a bottle of hay for his labor! Well, this trick shall cost him forty dollars more.

[Enter WAGNER.]

How now Wagner, what's the news with thee?

WAGNER. Sir, the Duke of Vanholt doth earnestly entreat your company.

FAUSTUS. The Duke of Vanholt! An honorable gentleman, to whom I must be no niggard of my cunning. Come Mephastophilis, let's away to him.   [Exeunt.]

8. Bundle.
9. A conjurer's phrase.
1. Spectacles.

2. The huntsman's cry, when he sights the quarry.
3. Inn.

SCENE 11

[FAUSTUS *and* MEPHASTOPHILIS *return to the stage. Enter to them the* DUKE *and the* DUCHESS; *the* DUKE *speaks.*]

DUKE. Believe me, master doctor, this merriment hath much pleased me.

FAUSTUS. My gracious Lord, I am glad it contents you so well: but it may be, madam, you take no delight in this; I have heard that great-
5 bellied women do long for some dainties or other—what is it, madam? Tell me, and you shall have it.

DUCHESS. Thanks, good master doctor; and for I see your courteous intent to pleasure me, I will not hide from you the thing my heart desires. And were it now summer, as it is January and the dead of
10 winter, I would desire no better meat than a dish of ripe grapes.

FAUSTUS. Alas madam, that's nothing! Mephastophilis, begone! [*Exit* MEPHASTOPHILIS.] Were it a greater thing than this, so it would content you, you should have it. [*Enter* MEPHASTOPHILIS *with the grapes.*] Here they be, madam; will't please you taste on them?

15 DUKE. Believe me, master doctor, this makes me wonder above the rest: that being in the dead time of winter, and in the month of January, how you should come by these grapes?

FAUSTUS. If it like your grace, the year is divided into two circles over the whole world, that when it is here winter with us, in the contrary
20 circle it is summer with them, as in India, Saba,[4] and farther coun- tries in the east; and by means of a swift spirit that I have, I had them brought hither, as ye see. How do you like them, madam; be they good?

DUCHESS. Believe me, master doctor, they be the best grapes that ere
25 I tasted in my life before.

FAUSTUS. I am glad they content you so, madam.

DUKE. Come madam, let us in, where you must well reward this learned man for the great kindness he hath showed to you.

DUCHESS. And so I will my lord; and whilst I live, rest beholding for
30 this courtesy.

FAUSTUS. I humbly thank your grace.

DUKE. Come, master doctor, follow us, and receive your reward.

[*Exeunt.*]

CHORUS 4

[*Enter* WAGNER *solus.*]

WAGNER. I think my master means to die shortly,
For he hath given to me all his goods!
And yet methinks, if that death were near,
He would not banquet, and carouse, and swill,
5 Amongst the students, as even now he doth,
Who are at supper with such belly-cheer,

4. Sheba, Yemen.

As Wagner ne'er beheld in all his life.
See where they come: belike the feast is ended.   [*Exit.*]

SCENE 12

[*Enter* FAUSTUS (*and* MEPHASTOPHILIS), *with two or three* SCHOLARS.]

1 SCHOLAR. Master Doctor Faustus, since our conference about fair
ladies, which was the beautifullest in all the world, we have determined with ourselves that Helen of Greece was the admirablest lady
that ever lived. Therefore, master doctor, if you will do us that favor
5   as to let us see that peerless dame of Greece, whom all the world
admires for majesty, we should think ourselves much beholding
unto you.
FAUSTUS. Gentlemen, for that I know your friendship is unfeigned,
   And Faustus' custom is not to deny
10 The just requests of those that wish him well,
   You shall behold that peerless dame of Greece,
   No otherways for pomp and majesty
   Than when Sir Paris crossed the seas with her,
   And brought the spoils to rich Dardania.[5]
15 Be silent then, for danger is in words.
          [*Music sounds, and* HELEN *passeth over the stage.*]
2 SCHOLAR. Too simple is my wit to tell her praise,
   Whom all the world admires for majesty.
3 SCHOLAR. No marvel though the angry Greeks pursued
   With ten years' war the rape of such a queen,
20 Whose heavenly beauty passeth all compare.
1 SCHOLAR. Since we have seen the pride of Nature's works,
   And only paragon of excellence,
   Let us depart; and for this glorious deed
   Happy and blest be Faustus evermore.
25 FAUSTUS. Gentlemen farewell; the same I wish to you.
                                      [*Exeunt* SCHOLARS.]
          [*Enter an* OLD MAN.]
OLD MAN. Ah Doctor Faustus, that I might prevail
   To guide thy steps unto the way of life,
   By which sweet path thou may'st attain the goal
   That shall conduct thee to celestial rest.
30 Break heart, drop blood, and mingle it with tears,
   Tears falling from repentant heaviness
   Of thy most vile and loathsome filthiness,
   The stench whereof corrupts the inward soul
   With such flagitious crimes of heinous sins,
35 As no commiseration may expel;
   But mercy, Faustus, of thy savior sweet,
   Whose blood alone must wash away thy guilt.

5. Troy.

FAUSTUS. Where art thou Faustus? Wretch, what hast thou done!
    Damned art thou Faustus, damned; despair and die!
        [MEPHASTOPHILIS *gives him a dagger.*]
40   Hell calls for right, and with a roaring voice
    Says, "Faustus, come: thine hour is come"!
    And Faustus will come to do thee right.
OLD MAN. Ah stay, good Faustus, stay thy desperate steps!
    I see an angel hovers o'er thy head,
45   And with a vial full of precious grace
    Offers to pour the same into thy soul!
    Then call for mercy, and avoid despair.
FAUSTUS. Ah my sweet friend, I feel thy words
    To comfort my distressed soul;
50   Leave me awhile to ponder on my sins.
OLD MAN. I go, sweet Faustus; but with heavy cheer,
    Fearing the ruin of thy hopeless soul.   [*Exit.*]
FAUSTUS. Accursèd Faustus, where is mercy now?
    I do repent, and yet I do despair:
55   Hell strives with grace for conquest in my breast!
    What shall I do to shun the snares of death?
MEPHASTOPHILIS. Thou traitor, Faustus: I arrest thy soul
    For disobedience to my sovereign lord.
    Revolt,[6] or I'll in piecemeal tear thy flesh.
60   FAUSTUS. Sweet Mephastophilis, entreat thy lord
    To pardon my unjust presumption;
    And with my blood again I will confirm
    My former vow I made to Lucifer.
MEPHASTOPHILIS. Do it then quickly, with unfeigned heart,
65   Lest greater danger do attend thy drift.
FAUSTUS. Torment, sweet friend, that base and crooked age
    That durst dissuade me from thy Lucifer,
    With greatest torments that our hell affords.
MEPHASTOPHILIS. His faith is great, I cannot touch his soul,
70   But what I may afflict his body with,
    I will attempt—which is but little worth.
FAUSTUS. One thing, good servant, let me crave of thee,
    To glut the longing of my heart's desire:
    That I might have unto my paramour
75   That heavenly Helen which I saw of late,
    Whose sweet embracings may extinguish clean
    These thoughts that do dissuade me from my vow:
    And keep mine oath I made to Lucifer.
MEPHASTOPHILIS. Faustus, this, or what else thou shalt desire,
80   Shall be performed in twinkling of an eye.
        [*Enter* HELEN.]

---

6. Turn back to your allegiance [to Lucifer].

FAUSTUS. Was this the face that launched a thousand ships,
And burnt the topless[7] towers of Ilium?°   *Troy*
Sweet Helen, make me immortal with a kiss:
Her lips sucks forth my soul, see where it flies!
85   Come Helen, come, give me my soul again.
Here will I dwell, for heaven be in these lips,
And all is dross that is not Helena!
    [*Enter* OLD MAN.]
I will be Paris, and for love of thee,
Instead of Troy shall Wittenberg be sacked;
90   And I will combat with weak Menelaus,
And wear thy colors on my plumed crest:
Yea, I will wound Achilles in the heel,[8]
And then return to Helen for a kiss.
O thou art fairer than the evening air,
95   Clad in the beauty of a thousand stars,
Brighter art thou than flaming Jupiter
When he appeared to hapless Semele;[9]
More lovely than the monarch of the sky
In wanton Arethusa's azured arms;[1]
100   And none but thou shalt be my paramour.
    [*Exeunt* (FAUSTUS *and* HELEN).]
OLD MAN. Accursed Faustus, miserable man,
That from thy soul exclud'st the grace of heaven,
And fliest the throne of His tribunal seat!
    [*Enter the* DEVILS.]
Satan begins to sift me with his pride,[2]
105   As in this furnace God shall try my faith.
My faith, vile hell, shall triumph over thee!
Ambitious fiends, see how the heavens smiles
At your repulse, and laughs your state to scorn.
Hence hell, for hence I fly unto my God.   [*Exeunt.*]

SCENE 13

    [*Enter* FAUSTUS *with the* SCHOLARS.]
FAUSTUS. Ah, gentlemen!
1 SCHOLAR. What ails Faustus?
FAUSTUS. Ah, my sweet chamber-fellow, had I lived with thee, then
    had I lived still; but now I die eternally. Look, comes he not, comes
5   he not?
2 SCHOLAR. What means Faustus?

---

7. So high they seemed to have no tops.
8. Achilles could be wounded only in his heel—where he was shot by Paris.
9. A Theban girl, loved by Jupiter and destroyed by the fire of his lightning when he appeared to her in his full splendor.

1. Arethusa was the nymph of a fountain, as well as the fountain itself; she excited the passion of the river god Alphaeus, who was by some accounts related to the sun.
2. To test me with his strength.

3 SCHOLAR. Belike he is grown into some sickness, by being oversoli-
tary.

1 SCHOLAR. If it be so, we'll have physicians to cure him; 'tis but a
10   surfeit: never fear, man.

FAUSTUS. A surfeit[3] of deadly sin, that hath damned both body and
soul.

2 SCHOLAR. Yet Faustus, look up to heaven; remember God's mercies
are infinite.

15 FAUSTUS. But Faustus' offence can ne'er be pardoned! The serpent
that tempted Eve may be saved, but not Faustus. Ah gentlemen,
hear me with patience, and tremble not at my speeches, though
my heart pants and quivers to remember that I have been a student
here these thirty years—O would I had never seen Wittenberg,
20   never read book—and what wonders I have done, all Wittenberg
can witness—yea, all the world; for which Faustus hath lost both
Germany and the world—yea, heaven itself—heaven, the seat of
God, the throne of the blessed, the kingdom of joy; and must
remain in hell for ever—hell, ah, hell for ever! Sweet friends, what
25   shall become of Faustus, being in hell for ever?

3 SCHOLAR. Yet Faustus, call on God.

FAUSTUS. On God, whom Faustus hath abjured? On God, whom Faustus hath blasphemed? Ah my God—I would weep, but the devil
draws in my tears! gush forth blood, instead of tears—yea, life and
30   soul! O, he stays my tongue! I would lift up my hands, but see, they
hold them, they hold them!

ALL. Who, Faustus?

FAUSTUS. Lucifer and Mephastophilis! Ah gentlemen, I gave them my
soul for my cunning.

35 ALL. God forbid!

FAUSTUS. God forbade it indeed, but Faustus hath done it: for the
vain pleasure of four-and-twenty years hath Faustus lost eternal joy
and felicity. I writ them a bill with mine own blood, the date is
expired, the time will come, and he will fetch me.

40 1 SCHOLAR. Why did not Faustus tell us of this before, that divines
might have prayed for thee?

FAUSTUS. Oft have I thought to have done so, but the devil threatened
to tear me in pieces if I named God, to fetch both body and soul,
if I once gave ear to divinity; and now 'tis too late. Gentlemen
45   away, lest you perish with me!

2 SCHOLAR. O what shall we do to save Faustus?

3 SCHOLAR. God will strengthen me. I will stay with Faustus.

1 SCHOLAR. Tempt not God, sweet friend, but let us into the next
room, and there pray for him.

50 FAUSTUS. Ay, pray for me, pray for me; and what noise soever ye hear,
come not unto me, for nothing can rescue me.

---

3. Indigestion caused by overeating.

2 SCHOLAR. Pray thou, and we will pray, that God may have mercy
    upon thee.
FAUSTUS. Gentlemen, farewell. If I live till morning, I'll visit you; if
55   not, Faustus is gone to hell.
ALL. Faustus, farewell.   [*Exeunt* SCHOLARS.]
    [*The clock strikes eleven.*]
FAUSTUS. Ah Faustus,
    Now hast thou but one bare hour to live,
    And then thou must be damned perpetually.
60   Stand still, you ever-moving spheres of heaven,
    That time may cease, and midnight never come.
    Fair Nature's eye, rise, rise again, and make
    Perpetual day, or let this hour be but
    A year, a month, a week, a natural day,
65   That Faustus may repent and save his soul.
    O lente, lente currite noctis equi![4]
    The stars move still, time runs, the clock will strike,
    The devil will come, and Faustus must be damned.
    O, I'll leap up to my God! Who pulls me down?
70   See, see where Christ's blood streams in the firmament!
    One drop would save my soul, half a drop: ah my Christ—
    Ah, rend not my heart for naming of my Christ;
    Yet will I call on him—O spare me, Lucifer!
    Where is it now? 'Tis gone: and see where God
75   Stretcheth out his arm, and bends his ireful brows!
    Mountains and hills, come, come and fall on me,
    And hide me from the heavy wrath of God.
    No, no?
    Then will I headlong run into the earth:
80   Earth, gape! O no, it will not harbor me.
    You stars that reigned at my nativity,
    Whose influence hath allotted death and hell,
    Now draw up Faustus like a foggy mist
    Into the entails of yon laboring cloud,
85   That when you vomit forth into the air,
    My limbs may issue from your smoky mouths,
    So that my soul may but ascend to heaven.[5]
    [*The watch strikes.*]
    Ah, half the hour is past: 'twill all be past anon.
    O God, if thou wilt not have mercy on my soul,
90   Yet for Christ's sake, whose blood hath ransomed me,
    Impose some end to my incessant pain:
    Let Faustus live in hell a thousand years,

4. Slowly, slowly run, O horses of the night; adapted from a line in Ovid's *Amores*.
5. Faustus wants to be drawn up into a cloud, which would compact his body into a thunderstone so that his soul, thus purified, might ascend to heaven.

A hundred thousand, and at last be saved.
O, no end is limited to damned souls!
95   Why wert thou not a creature wanting soul?
Or why is this immortal that thou hast?
Ah, Pythagoras' *metempsychosis*[6]—were that true,
This soul should fly from me, and I be changed
Unto some brutish beast:
100   All beasts are happy, for when they die,
Their souls are soon dissolved in elements;
But mine must live still° to be plagued in hell.   *always*
Cursed be the parents that engendered me:
No, Faustus, curse thy self, curse Lucifer,
105   That hath deprived thee of the joys of heaven.
          [*The clock strikes twelve.*]
O it strikes, it strikes! Now body, turn to air,
Or Lucifer will bear thee quick° to hell.   *alive*
          [*Thunder and lightning.*]
O soul, be changed into little water drops,
And fall into the ocean, ne'er be found.
110   My God, my God, look not so fierce on me!
          [*Enter* DEVILS.]
Adders and serpents, let me breathe awhile!
Ugly hell gape not! Come not, Lucifer!
I'll burn my books—ah, Mephastophilis!
          [*Exeunt with him.*]

Epilogue

[*Enter* CHORUS.]
Cut is the branch that might have grown full straight,
And burnèd is Apollo's laurel bough,[7]
That sometime grew within this learnèd man.
Faustus is gone! Regard his hellish fall,
5   Whose fiendful fortune° may exhort the wise   *devilish fate*
Only to wonder at[8] unlawful things:
Whose deepness doth entice such forward wits,
To practise more than heavenly power permits.   [*Exit.*]

Terminat hora diem, terminat author opus.[9]

1604, 1616

---

6. Pythagoras's doctrine of the transmigration of souls.
7. Laurel is a symbol of wisdom and learning. Apollo is the god of divination, whose oracle was at Delphi. The image, although it sounds classical, is Marlowe's.

8. Be content simply to observe with awe.
9. The hour ends the day, the author ends his work; this motto, together with the final emblem, was probably added by the printer.

WILLIAM SHAKESPEARE
1564–1616

ca. 1588–92:   In London as actor and playwright.
ca. 1592–98:   Devotes himself mainly to chronicle histories and comedies.
ca. 1601–9:   Period of the great tragedies and romantic comedies.
ca. 1610:   Retires to Stratford.

William Shakespeare was born in Stratford-on-Avon in April (probably April 23), 1564. His father was a citizen of some prominence who became an alderman and bailiff, but who later suffered financial reverses. Shakespeare presumably attended the Stratford grammar school, where he could have acquired a respectable knowledge of Latin, but he did not proceed to Oxford or Cambridge. There are legends about Shakespeare's youth but no documented facts. The first record we have of his life after his christening is that of his marriage in 1582 to Anne Hathaway. A daughter was born to the young Shakespeares in 1583 and twins, a boy and a girl, in 1585. We possess no information about his activities for the next seven years, but by 1592 he was in London as an actor and apparently well known as a playwright, for Robert Greene refers to him resentfully in *A Groatsworth of Wit* as "an upstart crow, beautified with our feathers," who, "being an absolute *Johannes Factotum*, is in his own conceit the only Shake-scene in a country."

At this time, there were several companies of actors in London and in the provinces. What connection Shakespeare had with one or more of them before 1592 is conjectural, but we do know of his long and fruitful connection with the most successful troupe, the Lord Chamberlain's Men, who later, when James I came to the throne, became the King's Men. Shakespeare not only acted with this company but eventually became a leading shareholder and the principal playwright. The company included some of the most famous actors of the day, such as Richard Burbage, who no doubt created the roles of Hamlet, Lear, and Othello, and Will Kempe and Robert Armin, who acted Shakespeare's clowns and fools. In 1599 the Chamberlain's Men built and occupied that best known of Elizabethan theaters, the Globe.

Shakespeare did not, in his early years, confine himself to the theater. In 1593 he published a mythological-erotic poem, *Venus and Adonis*, dedicated to the earl of Southampton; in the next year he dedicated a "graver labor," *The Rape of Lucrece*, to the same noble patron. By 1597 Shakespeare had so prospered that he was able to purchase New Place, a handsome house in Stratford; he could now call himself a gentleman, as his father had been granted a coat of arms in the previous year.

Our first record of the playwright's actual work occurs in Francis Meres's *Palladis Tamia: Wit's Treasury* (1598), in which Meres compared English poets with the ancients; of Shakespeare he says, "As Plautus and Seneca are accounted the best for Comedy and Tragedy among the Latins, so Shakespeare among the English is the most excellent in both kinds for the stage." He goes on to list *Richard II*, *Richard III*, *Henry IV*, *King John*, *Titus Andronicus*, and *Romeo and Juliet* for tragedy and *Two Gentlemen of Verona*, *The Comedy of Errors*, *A Midsummer Night's Dream*, *The Merchant of Venice*, *Love's Labor's Lost*, and the unknown (or perhaps retitled) *Love's Labor's Won* as comedy. All of the plays Meres lists as tragedy (except for *Romeo and Juliet* and the very early *Titus Andronicus*) we would call chronicle history plays, a popular kind of drama based on historical accounts like Raphael Holinshed's *Chronicle* and presenting dramatically the events in the reigns of various English kings. About the turn of the century Shakespeare wrote his great romantic comedies, *As You Like It, Twelfth Night,* and *Much Ado About Nothing.* The next decade was the period of the great tragedies: *Hamlet, Macbeth, Othello, King Lear,* and *Antony and Cleopatra.* About 1610 Shakespeare apparently retired to Stratford, although he continued to write, both by himself (*The Tempest*) and in collaboration (*Henry VIII*). This is the period of the romances, or tragicomedies, which include *The Tempest, Cymbeline,* and *The Winter's Tale.*

Although Shakespeare devoted his genius primarily to the stage, he was as well the foremost lyric poet of his age. Aside from his two early nondramatic poems, he was according to Meres (1598) known for "his sugared sonnets among private friends"; the sonnets were published in 1609. His cycle is quite unlike the other sonnet sequences of his day, notably in its idealization of a young man (rather than a sonnet lady) as the object of praise, love, and devotion and in its portrait of a dark, sensuous, and sexually promiscuous mistress (rather than the usual chaste and aloof blond beauty). Nor are the moods confined to what the Renaissance thought were those of the despairing Petrarchan lover: they include delight, pride, melancholy, shame, disgust, and fear. Shakespeare's sequence suggests a story, although the details are vague, and there is even doubt whether the sonnets as published are in the correct order. Certain motifs are evident: an introductory series (*1* to *17*) celebrates the beauty of a young man and urges him to marry so as to propagate and preserve that beauty. The subsequent long sequence (*18* to *126*) focuses on (probably) the same ideal young man, developing as a dominant motif the transience and destructive power of time, countered only by the force of love and friendship and the permanence of poetry. The remaining sonnets chiefly focus on the so-called Dark Lady as a tempting but degrading object of desire. Some sonnets (like *144*) intimate a love triangle involving the speaker, the male friend, and the woman; others take note of a rival poet (sometimes identified as George Chapman or Christopher Marlowe). The biographical background of the sonnets has aroused much speculation but very little of it has any factual support.

Although the vocabulary of the sonnets is usually simple the metaphorical style is very rich. "Shall I compare thee to a summer's day" is a question that might lead to a very ordinary comparison, but instead it introduces a profound meditation on time, change, and beauty. The structure of a given sonnet frequently reinforces the power of the metaphors: for example, each quatrain in 73 develops an image of lateness, of approaching extinction—of a season, of a day, and of a fire—but they also apply to a life. In structural terms, the three quatrains may work equally and successively to prepare for a conclusion in the couplet (the so-called Shakespearean sonnet pattern), or the first eight lines may set forth a situation and the last six turn in quite a different direction (the usual Petrarchan structure). The rhetorical strategy of the sonnets is also worth careful attention. Some begin with a reminiscence, some are imperative, others make an almost proverbial statement and then elaborate it. The imagery is drawn from a wide variety of sources: gardening, navigation, law, farming, business, pictorial art, astrology, and domestic affairs.

Some of the finest songs ever written are contained in Shakespeare's plays. They are of various types: the aubade, or morning song, the pastoral invitation to love; several kinds of love songs; the ballad sung by wandering minstrels; and the funeral dirge. They illustrate many sides of Shakespeare's genius—his incomparable lyric gift, his ready humor, and his keen sensitivity to the sights and sounds of English life.

When Shakespeare died, in Stratford in 1616, no collected edition of his plays had been published. Some of them had appeared in separate editions ("quartos") without editorial supervision, sometimes taken from his manuscripts, sometimes from playhouse prompt books, sometimes from pirated texts based on shorthand reports of a performance or on reconstruction from memory by an actor or specta-tor. In 1623, two members of Shakespeare's company, John Heminges and Henry Condell, published the great collection of all the plays they considered authentic: it is called the First Folio. They printed the best texts they had, according to their lights; modern editors consider the claims of the Folio and of any quartos that may exist in establishing the text of each play.

One preliminary document in the First Folio is by Shakespeare's great rival, critic, and opposite, Ben Jonson. In it he asserts the superiority of Shakespeare not only to other English playwrights but to the Greek and Latin masters:

> Triumph, my Britain, thou hast one to show
> To whom all scenes of Europe homage owe.
> He was not of an age, but for all time!

That tribute is the first formulation of a judgment often reiterated in later periods, explaining Shakespeare's place at the very center of the English literary canon. Many earlier critics found Shakespearean "universality" displayed in the human truth of his characters and his enduringly relevant themes. Many contemporary critics are concerned instead to show that Shakespeare was indeed of his age, manifesting in complex ways its theatricality; its politics; its ideology relating to gender, religion, and social hierarchy; and its discourses about sexuality, the body, medicine, law, the family, and more. What seems incontrovertible is that succes-sive generations of critics, of all persuasions, have found a primary locus for their very diverse interests and questions in Shakespeare's rich and multifarious texts.

SONGS FROM THE PLAYS

Under the Greenwood Tree[1]

Under the greenwood tree
Who loves to lie with me,
And turn his merry note
Unto the sweet bird's throat,[2]
Come hither, come hither, come hither: 5
   Here shall he see
   No enemy
But winter and rough weather.

Who doth ambition shun
And loves to live i' th' sun,   10
Seeking the food he eats,
And pleased with what he gets,
Come hither, come hither, come hither!
   Here shall he see
   No enemy   15
But winter and rough weather.

---

1. *As You Like It* (1599–1600) 2.5.1ff.; this song pro-vides a comment on the happy existence of the ban-ished duke and his followers in the Forest of Arden, where life is "more sweet / Than that of painted pomp."
2. I.e., improvise his song in harmony with the bird's.

Blow, Blow, Thou Winter Wind[1]

Blow, blow, thou winter wind,
Thou art not so unkind
   As man's ingratitude;
Thy tooth is not so keen,
Because thou art not seen,   5
   Although thy breath be rude.
Heigh-ho! sing, heigh-ho! unto the green holly:
Most friendship is feigning, most loving mere folly:
   Then, heigh-ho, the holly!
      This life is most jolly.   10

Freeze, freeze, thou bitter sky,
That dost not bite so nigh
   As benefits forgot:
Though thou the waters warp,[2]
Thy sting is not so sharp   15
   As friend remembered not.
Heigh-ho! sing, etc.

It Was a Lover and His Lass[1]

It was a lover and his lass,
   With a hey, and a ho, and a hey nonino,
That o'er the green corn-field[2] did pass,
   In spring time, the only pretty ring time,[3]
When birds do sing, hey ding a ding, ding,   5
Sweet lovers love the spring.

Between the acres of the rye,[4]
   With a hey, and a ho, and a hey nonino,
These pretty country folks would lie,
   In spring time, etc.   10

This carol they began that hour,
   With a hey, and a ho, and a hey nonino,
How that a life was but a flower,
   In spring time, etc.

And therefore take[5] the present time,   15
   With a hey, and a ho, and a hey nonino,
For love is crownèd with the prime,[6]
   In spring time, etc.

1. From *As You Like It* 2.7.174ff. The contrast here between nature and people's willful behavior is one of the continuing themes of the play.
2. I.e., roughen by freezing.
1. Sung by two pages to the clown Touchstone and his "country wench," Audrey, in *As You Like It* 5.3.16ff. This *carpe diem* ("seize the time") song anticipates the happy marriages that will conclude the play.
2. Wheat field.
3. Marriage season.
4. On unplowed ground separating the planted fields.
5. Seize.
6. Springtime.

Oh Mistress Mine[1]

Oh mistress mine! where are you roaming?
O, stay and hear; your true love's coming,
    That can sing both high and low.
Trip no further, pretty sweeting;
Journeys end in lovers meeting,   5
    Every wise man's son doth know.

What is love? 'tis not hereafter;
Present mirth hath present laughter;
    What's to come is still unsure:
In delay there lies no plenty;   10
Then come kiss me, sweet and twenty,
    Youth's a stuff will not endure.

Where the Bee Sucks, There Suck I[1]

Where the bee sucks, there suck I:
In a cowslip's bell I lie;
There I couch when owls do cry.
On the bat's back I do fly
After summer merrily.   5
Merrily, merrily shall I live now
Under the blossom that hangs on the bough.

SONNETS

To the Only Begetter of
These Ensuing Sonnets
MR. W. H. All Happiness
and That Eternity
Promised
By
Our Ever-Living Poet
Wisheth
the Well-Wishing
Adventurer in
Setting Forth
T.T.[1]

1. *Twelfth Night* (1601–02) 2.3.40ff.
1. *The Tempest*, (1611–12) 5.1.88ff.: Ariel, the airy spirit of the enchanted isle, is happily anticipating the freedom of his future life.
1. This odd dedication bears the initials of the publisher, Thomas Thorpe. The W. H. addressed here may or may not be the male friend addressed in sonnets 1 to 126. Leading candidates for that role are Henry Wriothesley, earl of Southampton, the dedicatee of *Venus and Adonis* (1593) and *Lucrece* (1594), and William Herbert, earl of Pembroke, a dedicatee of the First Folio. But there is no hard evidence to support these or other suggested identifications of the male friend or of the so-called Dark Lady; these sonnet personages may or may not have had real-life counterparts.

3

Look in thy glass and tell the face thou viewest
Now is the time that face should form another,
Whose fresh repair if now thou not renewest,
Thou dost beguile the world, unbless some mother.
For where is she so fair whose uneared[1] womb   5
Disdains the tillage of thy husbandry?
Or who is he so fond[2] will be the tomb
Of his self-love, to stop posterity?
Thou art thy mother's glass,[3] and she in thee
Calls back the lovely April of her prime;   10
So thou through windows of thine age shalt see,
Despite of wrinkles, this thy golden time.
    But if thou live rememb'red not to be,
    Die single, and thine image dies with thee.

                                   1609

12

When I do count the clock that tells the time
And see the brave[1] day sunk in hideous night,
When I behold the violet past prime
And sable curls all silvered o'er with white,
When lofty trees I see barren of leaves,   5
Which erst[2] from heat did canopy the herd
And summer's green all girded up in sheaves
Borne on the bier with white and bristly beard:
Then of thy beauty do I question make
That thou among the wastes of time must go,   10
Since sweets and beauties do themselves forsake,
And die as fast as they see others grow,
    And nothing 'gainst Time's scythe can make defense
    Save breed, to brave[3] him when he takes thee hence.

                                   1609

15

When I consider every thing that grows
Holds[1] in perfection but a little moment;
That this huge stage presenteth naught but shows
Whereon the stars in secret influence comment;[2]
When I perceive that men as plants increase,   5
Cheerèd and checked[3] even by the selfsame sky,

---

1. Unplowed.
2. Foolish.
3. Mirror.
1. Splendid.
2. Formerly.

3. To defy. "Breed": offspring.
1. Remains.
2. The stars secretly affect human actions. "Shows":
(1) appearances, (2) performances.
3. Encouraged and reproached or stopped.

Vaunt[4] in their youthful sap, at height decrease,
And wear their brave state out of memory;[5]
Then the conceit[6] of this inconstant stay
Sets you most rich in youth before my sight,   10
Where wasteful Time debateth[7] with Decay
To change your day of youth to sullied[8] night,
    And all in war with Time for love of you,
    As he takes from you, I ingraft[9] you new.

                                        1609

18

Shall I compare thee to a summer's day?
Thou art more lovely and more temperate:
Rough winds do shake the darling buds of May,
And summer's lease hath all too short a date:
Sometime too hot the eye of heaven shines   5
And often is his gold complexion dimmed;
And every fair from fair sometimes declines,
By chance or nature's changing course untrimmed;[1]
But thy eternal summer shall not fade,
Nor lose possession of that fair thou ow'st;[2]   10
Nor shall death brag thou wander'st in his shade,
When in eternal lines to time thou grow'st:[3]
    So long as men can breathe, or eyes can see,
    So long lives this, and this gives life to thee.[4]

                                        1609

19

Devouring Time, blunt thou the lion's paws,
And make the earth devour her own sweet brood;
Pluck the keen teeth from the fierce tiger's jaws,
And burn the long-lived phoenix in her blood;[1]
Make glad and sorry seasons as thou fleet'st,   5
And do what e'er thou wilt, swift-footed Time,
To the wide world and all her fading sweets:
But I forbid thee one most heinous crime,
O carve not with thy hours my love's fair brow,
Nor draw no lines there with thine antique[2] pen;   10
Him in thy course untainted[3] do allow,

---

4. Exult, display themselves.
5. Wear their showy splendor out and are forgotten.
6. Conception.
7. Discusses.
8. Soiled, blackened.
9. Renew by grafting, implant beauty again (by my verse).
1. Stripped of gay apparel.
2. Ownest.
3. When in [this] immortal poetry you become even with time.

4. The boast of immortality for one's verse was a Renaissance convention and goes back to the classics. It implies, not egotism on the part of the poet, but faith in the permanence of poetry.
1. In full vigor of life (a hunting term). The phoenix was a mythical bird that lived five hundred years, then died in flames, to rise again from its ashes.
2. (1) Old, (2) fantastic.
3. (1) Undefiled, (2) untouched by a weapon (a term from tilting).

For beauty's pattern to succeeding men.
  Yet do thy worst, old Time: despite thy wrong,
  My love shall in my verse ever live young.

1609

20

A woman's face with Nature's own hand painted[1]
Hast thou, the master mistress of my passion;[2]
A woman's gentle heart but not acquainted
With shifting change as is false women's fashion;
An eye more bright than theirs, less false in rolling,[3]
Gilding the object whereupon it gazeth;
A man in hue all hues in his controlling,
Which steals men's eyes and women's souls amazeth.
And for a woman wert thou first created,
Till Nature as she wrought thee fell a-doting,[4]
And by addition me of thee defeated,
By adding one thing to my purpose nothing.
  But since she pricked[5] thee out for women's pleasure,
  Mine be thy love, and thy love's use their treasure.[6]

5

10

1609

29

When, in disgrace[1] with Fortune and men's eyes,
I all alone beweep my outcast state,
And trouble deaf heaven with my bootless[2] cries,
And look upon myself and curse my fate,
Wishing me like to one more rich in hope,
Featured like him, like him with friends possessed,
Desiring this man's art and that man's scope,
With what I most enjoy contented least;
Yet in these thoughts myself almost despising,
Haply I think on thee, and then my state[3]
(Like to the lark at break of day arising
From sullen earth) sings hymns at heaven's gate;
  For thy sweet love remembered such wealth brings
  That then I scorn to change my state with kings.

5

10

1609

30

When to the sessions of sweet silent thought
I summon up[1] remembrance of things past,

1. I.e., not made up with cosmetics.
2. (1) Strong feeling, (2) poem.
3. Roving.
4. (1) Crazy, (2) infatuated.
5. Marked, with obvious sexual pun.
6. (1) Sexual enjoyment, (2) interest (as in usury).

1. Out of favor.
2. Futile.
3. Condition, state of mind; but in line 14 there is a pun on *state* meaning chair of state, throne.
1. "Sessions": sittings of court. "Summon up" continues the metaphor.

I sigh the lack of many a thing I sought,
And with old woes new wail[2] my dear time's waste:
Then can I drown an eye (unused to flow)   5
For precious friends hid in death's dateless[3] night,
And weep afresh love's long since canceled woe,
And moan th' expense[4] of many a vanished sight:
Then can I grieve at grievances foregone,
And heavily from woe to woe tell[5] o'er   10
The sad account of fore-bemoanèd moan,
Which I new pay as if not paid before.
     But if the while I think on thee, dear friend,
     All losses are restored and sorrows end.

                                                                  1609

35

No more be grieved at that which thou hast done:
Roses have thorns, and silver fountains mud.
Clouds and eclipses stain[1] both moon and sun,
And loathsome canker[2] lives in sweetest bud.
All men make faults, and even I in this,   5
Authorizing thy trespass with compare,
Myself corrupting, salving thy amiss,
Excusing thy sins more than thy sins are;
For to thy sensual fault I bring in sense[3] —
Thy adverse party is thy advocate —   10
And 'gainst myself a lawful plea commence.
Such civil war is in my love and hate,
     That I an accessary needs must be
     To that sweet thief which sourly robs from me.

                                                                  1609

55

Not marble, nor the gilded monuments
Of princes, shall outlive this powerful rhyme;
But you shall shine more bright in these contents
Than unswept stone, besmeared with sluttish time.[1]
When wasteful war shall statues overturn,   5
And broils root out the work of masonry,
Nor Mars his[2] sword nor war's quick fire shall burn
The living record of your memory.
'Gainst death and all-oblivious enmity[3]

2. Bewail anew.
3. Endless.
4. Loss.
5. Count. "Grievances foregone": old subjects for grief.
1. Dim.

2. Rose worm.
3. Reason.
1. I.e., than in a stone tomb or effigy that time wears away and covers with dust.
2. Mars'.
3. The enmity of oblivion, of being forgotten.

Shall you pace forth; your praise shall still find room   10
Even in the eyes of all posterity
That wear this world out to the ending doom.[4]
    So, till the judgment that yourself arise,[5]
    You live in this, and dwell in lovers' eyes.

1609

60

Like as the waves make towards the pibbled[1] shore,
So do our minutes hasten to their end;
Each changing place with that which goes before,
In sequent toil all forwards do contend.[2]
Nativity, once in the main[3] of light,   5
Crawls to maturity, wherewith being crowned,
Crooked eclipses 'gainst his glory fight,
And Time that gave doth now his gift confound.
Time doth transfix the flourish set on youth
And delves the parallels[4] in beauty's brow,   10
Feeds on the rarities of nature's truth,
And nothing stands but for his scythe to mow.
    And yet to times in hope[5] my verse shall stand,
    Praising thy worth, despite his cruel hand.

1609

65

Since[1] brass, nor stone, nor earth, nor boundless sea,
But sad mortality o'ersways their power,
How with this rage[2] shall beauty hold a plea,
Whose action is no stronger than a flower?
O how shall summer's honey breath hold out   5
Against the wrackful[3] siege of batt'ring days,
When rocks impregnable are not so stout,
Nor gates of steel so strong, but Time decays?
O fearful meditation! where, alack,
Shall Time's best jewel from Time's chest lie hid?[4]   10
Or what strong hand can hold his swift foot back?
Or who his spoil[5] of beauty can forbid?
    O none, unless this miracle have might,
    That in black ink my love may still shine bright.

1609

4. Judgment Day.
5. Until you rise from the dead on Judgment Day.
1. Pebbled.
2. Toiling and following each other, the waves struggle to press forward.
3. Broad expanse.
4. Digs the parallel furrows (wrinkles). "Transfix the flourish": remove the embellishment. To "flourish" is also to blossom.

5. Future times.
1. I.e., because there is neither.
2. Destructive power.
3. Destructive.
4. Time, like any wealthy person, keeps his jewels in a chest. Once it is taken out, where can his best jewel be hidden from destructive forces?
5. Ravaging.

71

No longer mourn for me when I am dead
Than you shall hear the surly sullen bell[1]
Give warning to the world that I am fled
From this vile world, with vilest worms to dwell:
Nay, if you read this line, remember not   5
The hand that writ it; for I love you so,
That I in your sweet thoughts would be forgot,
If thinking on me then should make you woe.
Oh, if, (I say,) you look upon this verse
When I (perhaps) compounded am with clay,   10
Do not so much as my poor name rehearse,
But let your love even with my life decay;
 Lest the wise world should look into your moan,
 And mock you with me after I am gone.

1609

73

That time of year thou mayst in me behold
When yellow leaves, or none, or few, do hang
Upon those boughs which shake against the cold,
Bare ruined choirs, where late the sweet birds sang.
In me thou seest the twilight of such day   5
As after sunset fadeth in the west;
Which by and by black night doth take away,
Death's second self that seals up all in rest.
In me thou seest the glowing of such fire,
That on the ashes of his youth doth lie,   10
As the deathbed whereon it must expire,
Consumed with that which it was nourished by.[1]
 This thou perceiv'st, which makes thy love more strong,
 To love that well, which thou must leave ere long.

1609

87

Farewell: thou art too dear[1] for my possessing,
And like enough thou know'st thy estimate.[2]
The charter[3] of thy worth gives thee releasing;
My bonds in thee are all determinate.[4]
For how do I hold thee but by thy granting,   5
And for that riches where is my deserving?
The cause of this fair gift in me is wanting,

1. The bell was tolled to announce the death of a member of the parish—one stroke for each year of his life.
1. Choked by the ashes of that which once nourished its flame.

1. Expensive, beloved.
2. Value.
3. Deed, contract for property.
4. Expired.

And so my patent[5] back again is swerving.
Thy self thou gav'st, thy own worth then not knowing,
Or me, to whom thou gav'st it, else mistaking;   10
So thy great gift, upon misprision[6] growing,
Comes home again, on better judgment making.
    Thus have I had thee as a dream doth flatter,
    In sleep a king, but waking no such matter.

1609

94

They that have power to hurt and will do none,
That do not do the thing they most do show,[1]
Who, moving others, are themselves as stone,
Unmovèd, cold, and to temptation slow;
They rightly do inherit heaven's graces   5
And husband nature's riches from expense;[2]
They are the lords and owners of their faces,
Others but stewards of their excellence.
The summer's flower is to the summer sweet,
Though to itself it only live and die,   10
But if that flower with base infection meet,
The basest weed outbraves[3] his dignity:
    For sweetest things turn sourest by their deeds;
    Lilies that fester smell far worse than weeds.[4]

1609

97

How like a winter hath my absence been
From thee, the pleasure of the fleeting year!
What freezings have I felt, what dark days seen!
What old December's bareness everywhere!
And yet this time removed was summer's time,   5
The teeming autumn, big with rich increase,
Bearing the wanton burthen of the prime,[1]
Like widowed wombs after their lords' decease;
Yet this abundant issue seemed to me
But hope of orphans and unfathered fruit;   10
For summer and his pleasures wait on thee,
And, thou away, the very birds are mute;
    Or, if they sing, 'tis with so dull a cheer
    That leaves look pale, dreading the winter's near.

1609

5. Title.
6. Mistake, oversight.
1. Seem to do.
2. I.e., they do not squander nature's gifts.
3. Surpasses. Gerard's *Herbal* (1597) says "the lilies of the field outbraved him."

4. This line appears in *Edward III* (2.1.451), an apocryphal Shakespearean play licensed December 1, 1595.
1. Spring, which has engendered the lavish crop ("wanton burthen") that autumn is now left to bear.
2. Disposition.

106

When in the chronicle of wasted[1] time
I see descriptions of the fairest wights,[2]
And beauty making beautiful old rhyme
In praise of ladies dead and lovely knights,
Then, in the blazon[3] of sweet beauty's best,   5
Of hand, of foot, of lip, of eye, of brow,
I see their antique pen would have expressed
Even such a beauty as you master now.
So all their praises are but prophecies
Of this our time, all you prefiguring;   10
And, for they looked but with divining eyes,[4]
They had not still enough your worth to sing:
    For we, which now behold these present days,
    Have eyes to wonder, but lack tongues to praise.

1609

107

Not mine own fears, nor the prophetic soul
Of the wide world dreaming on things to come,[1]
Can yet the lease of my true love control,
Supposed as forfeit to a confinèd doom.[2]
The mortal moon hath her eclipse endured,   5
And the sad augurs mock their own presage;[3]
Incertainties now crown themselves assured,
And peace[4] proclaims olives of endless age.
Now with the drops of this most balmy time
My love looks fresh, and death to me subscribes,[5]   10
Since, spite of him, I'll live in this poor rhyme,
While he insults o'er dull and speechless tribes:
    And thou in this shalt find thy monument,
    When tyrants' crests and tombs of brass are spent.[6]

1609

116

Let me not to the marriage of true minds
Admit impediments;[1] love is not love

1. Past.
2. Persons.
3. Display.
4. Because ("for") they were able only ("but") to fore-see prophetically.
1. This sonnet refers to contemporary events and the prophecies, common in Elizabethan almanacs, of disaster.
2. I.e., can yet put an end to my love, which I thought doomed to early forfeiture.
3. The "mortal moon" is Queen Elizabeth; her "eclipse" is probably her climacteric year, her sixty-

third (thought meaningful because the product of two "significant" numbers, 7 and 9), which ended in September 1596. The sober astrologers ("sad augurs") now ridicule their own predictions ("presage") of catastrophe, because they turned out to be false.
4. Probably the agreement between Henry IV of France and Elizabeth.
5. Submits.
6. Wasted away.
1. From the marriage service: "If any of you know cause or just impediment why these persons should not be joined together . . ."

Which alters when it alteration finds,
Or bends with the remover to remove:
O, no, it is an ever-fixèd mark,[2]   5
That looks on tempests and is never shaken;
It is the star to every wand'ring bark,
Whose worth's unknown, although his highth[3] be taken.
Love's not Time's fool,[4] though rosy lips and cheeks
Within his[5] bending sickle's compass come;   10
Love alters not with his brief hours and weeks,
But bears it out even to the edge of doom.[6]
   If this be error and upon me proved,
   I never writ, nor no man ever loved.

                                                       1609

126

O thou, my lovely boy, who in thy power
Dost hold Time's fickle glass,[1] his sickle, hour;
Who hast by waning grown and therein show'st
Thy lovers withering as thy sweet self grow'st;
If Nature (sovereign mistress over wrack[2])   5
As thou goest onwards still will pluck thee back,
She keeps thee to this purpose, that her skill
May Time disgrace and wretched minutes kill.
Yet fear her, O thou minion[3] of her pleasure,
She may detain, but not still[4] keep, her treasure!   10
   Her audit[5] (though delayed) answered must be,
   And her quietus is to render[6] thee.

                                                       1609

128

How oft when thou, my music, music play'st
Upon that blessèd wood[1] whose motion sounds
With thy sweet fingers when thou gently sway'st[2]
The wiry concord that mine ear confounds,[3]
Do I envy those jacks[4] that nimble leap   5
To kiss the tender inward of thy hand,
Whilst my poor lips, which should that harvest reap,
At the wood's boldness by thee blushing stand.
To be so tickled they would change their state

2. Seamark (cf. *landmark*).
3. The star's value is incalculable, although the star's
"highth" (altitude) may be known and used for practical purposes.
4. Slave or victim.
5. Time's (as also in line 11).
6. Brink of Judgment Day.
1. (1) Mirror, fickle because as the subject ages the
mirror reflects a changed image, (2) an hourglass.
2. Destruction, ruin.

3. Darling.
4. Always, forever.
5. Accounting.
6. Surrender. "Quietus": settlement.
1. Keys of the spinet or virginal.
2. Governest.
3. The harmony from the strings that overcomes my
ear with delight.
4. The keys (actually, "jacks" are the plectra that pluck
the strings when activated by the keys).

And situation[5] with those dancing chips,   10
O'er whom thy fingers walk with gentle gait,
Making dead wood more blessed than living lips.
  Since saucy jacks[6] so happy are in this,
  Give them thy fingers, me thy lips to kiss.

1609

129

Th' expense of spirit in a waste of shame
Is lust in action;[1] and till action, lust
Is perjured, murd'rous, bloody, full of blame,
Savage, extreme, rude, cruel, not to trust;
Enjoyed no sooner but despisèd straight: 5
Past reason hunted; and no sooner had,
Past reason hated, as a swallowed bait,
On purpose laid to make the taker mad:
Mad in pursuit, and in possession so;
Had, having, and in quest to have, extreme;   10
A bliss in proof[2] and proved, a very woe;
Before, a joy proposed; behind, a dream.
  All this the world well knows; yet none knows well
  To shun the heaven that leads men to this hell.

1609

130

My mistress' eyes are nothing like the sun;[1]
Coral is far more red than her lips' red;
If snow be white, why then her breasts are dun;
If hairs be wires, black wires grow on her head.
I have seen roses damasked,[2] red and white,   5
But no such roses see I in her cheeks;
And in some perfumes is there more delight
Than in the breath that from my mistress reeks.
I love to hear her speak, yet well I know
That music hath a far more pleasing sound;   10
I grant I never saw a goddess go;[3]
My mistress, when she walks, treads on the ground.
  And yet, by heaven, I think my love as rare[4]
  As any she belied[5] with false compare.

1609

5. Physical location. "State": place in the order of things.
6. With a quibble on the sense "impertinent fellows."
1. The word order here is inverted and slightly obscures the meaning. Lust, when put into action, expends "spirit" (life, vitality) in a "waste" (desert, with a possible pun on *waist*) of shame.
2. A bliss during the experience.

1. An anti-Petrarchan sonnet. All of the details commonly attributed by other Elizabethan sonneteers to their ladies are here denied to the poet's mistress.
2. Variegated. The damask rose (supposedly from Damascus, originally) is pink.
3. Walk.
4. Admirable, extraordinary.
5. Misrepresented.

135

Whoever hath her wish, thou hast thy Will,[1]
And Will to boot, and Will in overplus;
More than enough am I that vex thee still,
To thy sweet will making addition thus.
Wilt thou, whose will is large and spacious,   5
Not once vouchsafe to hide my will in thine?
Shall will in others seem right gracious,
And in my will no fair acceptance shine?
The sea, all water, yet receives rain still,
And in abundance addeth to his store,[2]   10
So thou being rich in Will add to thy Will
One will of mine to make thy large Will more.
    Let no unkind, no fair beseechers kill;[3]
    Think all but one, and me in that one Will.

                                                        1609

138

When my love swears that she is made of truth,
I do believe her, though I know she lies,
That she might think me some untutored youth,
Unlearnèd in the world's false subtleties.
Thus vainly thinking that she thinks me young,   5
Although she knows my days are past the best,[1]
Simply[2] I credit her false-speaking tongue:
On both sides thus is simple truth suppressed.
But wherefore says she not she is unjust?[3]
And wherefore say not I that I am old?   10
Oh, love's best habit[4] is in seeming trust,
And age in love loves not to have years told.
    Therefore I lie with her and she with me,
    And in our faults by lies we flattered be.

                                                    1599, 1609

144

Two loves I have of comfort and despair,
Which like two spirits do suggest me still:[1]
The better angel is a man right fair,
The worser spirit a woman, colored ill.[2]
To win me soon to hell, my female evil   5

---

1. (1) Wishes, (2) carnal desire, (3) the male and female sexual organs, (4) a lover—Shakespeare?—
named Will. This is one of three, possibly four, sonnets
punning on the word.
2. Plenty.
3. I.e., do not kill with unkindness any of your wooers.
1. Shakespeare was thirty-five or younger when he
wrote this sonnet (it first appeared in *The Passionate
Pilgrim*, 1599).
2. Like a simpleton.
3. Unfaithful.
4. Appearance, deportment.
1. Tempt me constantly.
2. Dark.

Tempteth my better angel from my side,
And would corrupt my saint to be a devil,
Wooing his purity with her foul pride.
And whether that my angel be turned fiend
Suspect I may, yet not directly tell;   10
But being both from me, both to each[3] friend,
I guess one angel in another's hell.
   Yet this shall I ne'er know, but live in doubt,
   Till my bad angel fire[4] my good one out.

                                  1599, 1609

146

Poor soul, the center of my sinful earth,
Lord of[1] these rebel powers that thee array,[2]
Why dost thou pine within and suffer dearth,
Painting thy outward walls so costly gay?
Why so large cost, having so short a lease,   5
Dost thou upon thy fading mansion spend?
Shall worms, inheritors of this excess,
Eat up thy charge? Is this thy body's end?
Then, soul, live thou upon thy servant's loss,
And let that pine to aggravate thy store;[3]   10
Buy terms divine in selling hours of dross;[4]
Within be fed, without be rich no more.
   So shalt thou feed on death, that feeds on men,
   And death once dead, there's no more dying then.

                                              1609

147

My love is as a fever, longing still[1]
For that which longer nurseth[2] the disease,
Feeding on that which doth preserve the ill,[3]
Th' uncertain sickly appetite[4] to please.
My reason, the physician to my love,   5
Angry that his prescriptions are not kept,
Hath left me, and I desperate now approve
Desire is death, which physic did except.[5]
Past cure I am, now reason is past care,[6]
And frantic mad with evermore unrest;   10
My thoughts and my discourse as madmen's are,

---

3. Each other. "From": away from.
4. Drive out by fire.
1. An emendation. The quarto repeats the last three words of line 1. Other suggestions are "Thrall to," "Starved by," "Pressed by," and leaving the repetition but dropping "that thee" in line 2.
2. Dress out, often used in a military sense.
3. Let "that" (i.e., the body) deteriorate to increase ("aggravate") the soul's riches ("thy store").

4. Refuse, rubbish. "Terms": long periods.
1. Continually.
2. (1) Nourishes, (2) takes care of.
3. Maintain the illness.
4. (1) Desire for food, (2) lust.
5. I.e., I learn by experience, that desire, which medicine forbade, is death.
6. I.e., medical care (of me). The line is a version of the proverb "past cure, past care."

At random from the truth vainly expressed;[7]
For I have sworn thee fair, and thought thee bright,
Who art as black as hell, as dark as night.

1609

1 Henry IV   The title page of the first quarto edition of Shakespeare's *1 Henry IV*, published in 1598, reads: "THE HISTORY OF HENRIE THE FOURTH; With the battell at Shrewsburie, *betweene the King and Lord* Henry Percy, surnamed Henrie Hotspur of the North. *With the humorous conceits of Sir* John Falstalffe." It had been performed on the stage and at court before publication, and from that time to this it has remained one of Shakespeare's most popular plays.

Shakespeare had already inaugurated a new dramatic type by writing four plays dealing with fairly recent English history, and had then gone back to a period two centuries earlier to portray, in *Richard II*, the downfall of the weak, effeminate, and poetic young King Richard ("that sweet lovely rose," as he is called in this play) at the hands of the strong, efficient Bullingbrook, who came to the throne as Henry IV. Before this seizure of the crown there had been a prophecy, put by Shakespeare into the mouth of the bishop of Carlisle in *Richard II* (4.1.136–144), of the dire consequences to follow:

> And if you crown him, let me prophesy,
> The blood of English shall manure the ground
> And future ages groan for this foul act;
> Peace shall go sleep with Turks and infidels,
> And in this seat of peace tumultuous wars
> Shall kin with kin and kind with kind confound;
> Disorder, horror, fear, and mutiny
> Shall here inhabit, and this land be called
> The field of Golgotha and dead men's skulls.

The ominous civil wars and rebellions of Carlisle's prophecy are central to *1 Henry IV* and its sequel, *2 Henry IV*. *Henry V* (the final play in what is often termed Shakespeare's Second Tetralogy) focuses on that king's glittering military triumphs, culminating in the reconquest of France at the Battle of Agincourt. These plays trace the struggles of the Lancastrian usurper (Henry IV) to secure his hold on the throne and the transformation of his son, Prince Hal, from madcap roisterer to English national hero and idealized monarch.

Some background in fifteenth-century English history, as Shakespeare understood it, is needed if we are to respond readily to the play. Henry Hereford, called Bullingbrook, was in exile in France when his father, John of Gaunt, died in 1399. He returned to England to claim his inheritance and profited from the aid of the Percy family, powerful nobles in the north. The two brothers, Henry Percy, earl of Northumberland, and Thomas Percy, earl of Worcester, together with Northumberland's son Henry (called Hotspur) received Bullingbrook's oath at Doncaster (see 5.1.41–46) to seize only his inheritance. But King Richard II was in Ireland fighting, having named Edmund Mortimer, earl of March, his successor if he did not return. In the confused situation in England, Bullingbrook was able to collect enough power so that on Richard's return he could force him to abdicate and then have him killed in prison. Various troubles on the borders made the throne of the new king (Henry IV) insecure. Hotspur managed to defeat the Scots under Doug-

---

7. Wide of the mark and senselessly uttered.

las at Holmedon (see 1.1.62–75) and took many important prisoners. But Mortimer, fighting against Glendower in Wales, was taken captive and married
Glendower's daughter. Henry IV refused to ransom Mortimer, and the indignation
of Mortimer's brother-in-law, Hotspur, led him to refuse to turn over his prisoners
to the king. So came the conspiracy into being—and such a formidable opposition
as that of the Percies, Douglas, Glendower, and certain disaffected churchmen
like the archbishop of York meant a critical danger to Henry's throne. The Battle
of Shrewsbury (1403), the climax of this play, decides the conflict.

Shakespeare drew his historical material from the prose chronicle histories, specifically Raphael Holinshed's *Chronicle of England, Scotland, and Ireland*, as well
as Samuel Daniel's historical poem *The Civil Wars*, and an earlier play about
Henry V. Besides the narrative of events, these sources gave him the portrait of
Prince Hal as a wild youth cavorting with a disorderly crew of wastrels, chief
among them a fat knight, Sir John Oldcastle. Shakespeare at first used that name,
but because of protests from the descendants of that Protestant martyr he changed
the name to Sir John Falstaff—and made of him one of the greatest comic creations in all literature. Shakespeare notably altered his sources in portraying Hotspur: in the *Chronicle* he is older than Hal's father, but Shakespeare makes him
Hal's foil, coeval, and rival—valorous and chivalrous as Hal finally proves to be,
but also (unlike Hal) fiery and impatient, driven by ambition for honor and fame,
scornful of the soft, civilized arts of music and poetry. He also creates another foil
to the English prince in the portrait of the wild Welshman Glendower—an egoist,
a believer in and practitioner of magic, an accomplished poet, and a valiant
although superstitious warrior. In reworking his sources Shakespeare highlights
psychological conflicts: Hal's need to define himself in relation to two very different fathers—Henry IV and his disreputable surrogate father, Falstaff—and against
his siblinglike rival, Hotspur.

1 Henry IV is centrally concerned with political power—its sources, uses, manifestations, theatrical displays, ambiguities, and subversions. Recent criticism has
focused attention on several political issues: how far does this play (and the tetralogy) serve to reinforce the "Tudor myth" of providential kingship? And to what
extent does it undermine that myth by exposing the basis of kingship as Machiavel-
lian force and fraud? How far does Prince Hal's prodigal son transformation make
him into an ideal monarch who assumes and fulfills his filial and regal responsibilities? And to what extent is that image seriously undercut by the representation of
Hal as self-proclaimed hypocrite and playactor (and in *2 Henry IV* by his cold-
hearted repudiation of Falstaff and his former cronies)? How far does the play
reaffirm the traditional values of order and degree and the evils of rebellion, civil
strife, and rampant disorder? And to what extent does Falstaff's wild super-
abundance, his cynical critique of knightly honor and warfare, his parody of paternal and regal authority serve to undermine those values and the ideology that
supports them?

In structure, this play melds history and comedy, moving back and forth
between court and tavern, and setting the affairs of state in counterpoint to the
affairs of bawds, thieves, and drunkards. The fulcrum in this precarious balance is
Falstaff, by all odds the most fascinating figure in the play for generations of readers and critics. His splendid uniqueness is constructed, surprisingly enough, from
a number of literary components: the braggart soldier *(miles gloriosus)* of Roman
comedy, the Vice figure in medieval morality plays, the folk festival lord of Misrule, the martyred ballad-hero Sir John Oldcastle, the figure of Gluttony from the
pageant of the seven deadly sins, and the picaresque rogue or highwayman. Even
more remarkable is the stunning variety and sheer comic excess that Shakespeare
has built into this figure: he is liar, glutton, knave, coward, thief, lecher, drunkard,
wit, skilled rhetorician, master of the arts of language, the very embodiment of
carnavalesque misrule. Shakespeare continued to exploit his inexhaustible exuber-

ance in 2 *Henry IV* and also (reportedly by Queen Elizabeth's express command) in a comedy of middle-class life, *The Merry Wives of Windsor*.

The First Part of King Henry the Fourth

DRAMATIS PERSONAE

KING HENRY THE FOURTH
HENRY, *Prince of Wales*
PRINCE JOHN OF LANCASTER } *Sons to the* KING
EARL OF WESTMORELAND
SIR WALTER BLUNT
THOMAS PERCY, *Earl of Worcester*
HENRY PERCY, *Earl of Northumberland*
HENRY PERCY, *surnamed* HOTSPUR, *his son*
EDMUND MORTIMER, *Earl of March*
RICHARD SCROOP, *Archbishop of York*
ARCHIBALD, *Earl of Douglas*
OWEN GLENDOWER
SIR RICHARD VERNON
SIR MICHAEL, *a friend to the* ARCHBISHOP OF YORK
SIR JOHN FALSTAFF
POINS
GADSHILL } *Companions of* FALSTAFF
PETO
BARDOLPH
LADY PERCY, *wife to* HOTSPUR, *and sister to* MORTIMER
LADY MORTIMER, *daughter to* GLENDOWER, *and wife to* MORTIMER
MISTRESS QUICKLY, *hostess of a tavern in Eastcheap*
LORDS, OFFICERS, SHERIFF, VINTNER, CHAMBERLAIN, DRAWERS, *two* CARRIERS, TRAVELERS, *and* ATTENDANTS

England and Wales

Act 1

SCENE 1

[*Enter the* KING, PRINCE JOHN OF LANCASTER, THE EARL OF WESTMORELAND, SIR WALTER BLUNT, *with others.*]
KING. So shaken as we are, so wan with care,
Find we a time for frighted peace to pant,[1]
And breathe short-winded accents of new broils[2]
To be commenced in stronds° afar remote.   strands, regions
5   No more the thirsty entrance[3] of this soil
Shall daub her lips with her own children's blood;
No more shall trenching war channel her fields,

---

1. I.e., let us allow peace to catch her breath.
2. I.e., news of new wars.
3. Parched mouth.

Nor bruise her flow'rets with the armèd hoofs
Of hostile paces.[4] Those opposèd eyes,
10   Which, like the meteors of a troubled heaven,
All of one nature, of one substance bred,
Did lately meet in the intestine shock[5]
And furious close° of civil butchery,   *encounter*
Shall now, in mutual well-beseeming ranks,
15   March all one way and be no more opposed
Against acquaintance, kindred, and allies.
The edge of war, like an ill-sheathèd knife,
No more shall cut his master. Therefore, friends,
As far as to the sepulchre of Christ,—
20   Whose soldier now, under whose blessed cross
We are impressèd° and engaged to fight,   *enlisted*
Forthwith a power[6] of English shall we levy,
Whose arms were molded in their mother's womb
To chase these pagans in those holy fields
25   Over whose acres walked those blessed feet
Which fourteen hundred years ago were nailed
For our advantage on the bitter cross.
But this our purpose now is twelve month old,
And bootless° 'tis to tell you we will go.   *useless*
30   Therefore we meet not now.[7] Then let me hear
Of you, my gentle cousin° Westmoreland,   *kinsman*
What yesternight our Council did decree
In forwarding this dear expedience.[8]
WESTMORELAND. My liege, this haste was hot in question,
35   And many limits of the charge[9] set down
But yesternight, when all athwart[1] there came
A post° from Wales loaden with heavy news,   *messenger*
Whose worst was that the noble Mortimer,
Leading the men of Herefordshire to fight
40   Against the irregular° and wild Glendower,   *guerilla*
Was by the rude hands of that Welshman taken,
A thousand of his people butcherèd,
Upon whose dead corpse° there was such misuse,   *corpses*
Such beastly shameless transformatiòn,
45   By those Welshwomen done as may not be
Without much shame retold or spoken of.
KING. It seems then that the tidings of this broil
Brake off our business for the Holy Land.
WESTMORELAND. This matched with other did, my gracious lord,
50   For more uneven and unwelcome news
Came from the north, and thus it did import:
On Holyrood Day[2] the gallant Hotspur there,
Young Harry Percy, and brave Archibald,

---

4. The tread of war-horses.
5. Internal violence, civil war.
6. Army. He is planning a crusade, in expiation of his guilt for the death of Richard II.
7. I.e., that is not the reason for our present meeting.
8. Important, urgent matter.
9. Assignment of military responsibilities. "Hot in question": actively discussed.
1. Interrupting, crossing our purpose.
2. Holy Cross Day (September 14).

That ever-valiant and approvèd Scot,
55   At Holmedon met,
Where they did spend a sad and bloody hour,
As by discharge of their artillery,
And shape of likelihood,[3] the news was told;
For he that brought them[4] in the very heat
60   And pride° of their contention did take horse,   *height*
Uncertain of the issue any way.
    KING. Here is a dear, a true industrious friend,
Sir Walter Blunt, new lighted from his horse,
Stained with the variation of each soil
65   Betwixt that Holmedon and this seat of ours;
And he hath brought us smooth and welcome news.
The Earl of Douglas is discomfited;
Ten thousand bold Scots, two and twenty knights
Balked° in their own blood did Sir Walter see   *heaped*
70   On Holmedon's plains. Of prisoners Hotspur took
Mordake Earl of Fife, and eldest son
To beaten Douglas, and the Earl of Athol,
Of Murray, Angus, and Menteith;
And is not this an honorable spoil,
75   A gallant prize? Ha, cousin, is it not?
    WESTMORELAND. In faith,
It is a conquest for a prince to boast of.
    KING. Yea, there thou mak'st me sad and mak'st me sin
In envy that my Lord Northumberland
80   Should be the father to so blest a son,
A son who is the theme of honor's tongue,
Amongst a grove the very straightest plant,
Who is sweet Fortune's minion° and her pride;   *favorite*
Whilst I, by looking on the praise of him,
85   See riot and dishonor stain the brow
Of my young Harry. O that it could be proved
That some night-tripping fairy had exchanged
In cradle-clothes our children where they lay,
And called mine Percy, his Plantagenet![5]
90   Then would I have his Harry, and he mine.
But let him from my thoughts. What think you, coz,
Of this young Percy's pride? The prisoners
Which he in this adventure hath surprised
To his own use he keeps, and sends me word
95   I shall have none but Mordake Earl of Fife.
    WESTMORELAND. This is his uncle's teaching, this is Worcester,
Malevolent to you in all aspects,[6]
Which makes him prune himself,[7] and bristle up
The crest of youth against your dignity.
100   KING. But I have sent for him to answer this;
And for this cause awhile we must neglect

---

3. Probable inference.
4. I.e., the news (usually a plural in Shakespeare).
5. The family name of the English royal family.

6. Hostile in every way. The figure is from astrology.
7. Plume himself. "Bristle up" and "crest" continue the image, which is that of a fighting cock.

Our holy purpose to Jerusalem.
Cousin, on Wednesday next our council we
Will hold at Windsor, so inform the lords;
105   But come yourself with speed to us again,
For more is to be said and to be done
Than out of anger can be utterèd.
WESTMORELAND. I will, my liege.   [*Exeunt.*]

SCENE 2

[*Enter* HENRY, PRINCE OF WALES, *and* SIR JOHN FALSTAFF.]
FALSTAFF. Now Hal, what time of day is it, lad?
PRINCE. Thou art so fat-witted with drinking of old sack,[8] and unbuttoning
thee after supper, and sleeping upon benches after noon, that thou
hast forgotten to demand that truly which thou wouldst truly know.
5   What a devil hast thou to do with the time of the day? Unless hours
were cups of sack, and minutes capons, and clocks the tongues of
bawds, and dials the signs of leaping-houses,[9] and the blessed sun himself a fair hot wench in flame-colored taffeta, I see no reason why thou
shouldst be so superfluous to demand the time of the day.
10   FALSTAFF. Indeed you come near me now, Hal, for we that take purses
go by the moon and the seven stars, and not by Phoebus,[1] he, "that
wandering knight so fair." And I prithee, sweet wag, when thou art
king, as, God save thy grace—majesty I should say, for grace[2] thou wilt
have none—
15   PRINCE. What, none?
FALSTAFF. No, by my troth, not so much as will serve to be prologue to
an egg and butter.
PRINCE. Well, how then? come, roundly, roundly.[3]
FALSTAFF. Marry then, sweet wag, when thou art king, let not us that
20   are squires of the night's body be called thieves of the day's beauty;[4] let
us be Diana's foresters, gentlemen of the shade, minions of the moon;
and let men say we be men of good government, being governed as
the sea is, by our noble and chaste mistress the moon, under whose
countenance we steal.
25   PRINCE. Thou sayest well, and it holds well too, for the fortune of us that
are the moon's men doth ebb and flow like the sea, being governed as
the sea is by the moon. As for proof now: a purse of gold most resolutely
snatched on Monday night and most dissolutely spent on Tuesday
morning, got with swearing "Lay by" and spent with crying "Bring in,"
30   now in as low an ebb as the foot of the ladder and by and by in as high
a flow as the ridge of the gallows.[5]

---

8. Dry Spanish wine.
9. Whorehouses.
1. The sun. Falstaff then quotes from a popular ballad.
2. A triple pun: (1) "your Grace," the correct manner
of addressing a prince or duke; (2) the divine influence
that produces sanctity; and (3) a short prayer before a
meal—hence Falstaff's allusion to "egg and butter," a
common hasty breakfast.
3. Plainly.

4. Two puns: (1) a "squire of the body" was an attendant on a knight and (2) "body" would be pronounced
bawdy. "Beauty" also puns with *booty*, which thieves
take. Diana is the moon goddess.
5. The "foot of the ladder" is at the bottom of the gallows (robbery was a hanging offense); the "ridge" is the
crosspiece at the top. "Lay by": hand over (a robber's
command to the victim). "Bring in": a customer's command for more drink at a tavern.

FALSTAFF. By the Lord thou sayest true, lad. And is not my hostess of the
tavern a most sweet wench?

PRINCE. As the honey of Hybla, my old lad of the castle.[6] And is not a
35   buff jerkin a most sweet robe of durance?[7]

FALSTAFF. How now, how now, mad wag! what, in thy quips and thy
quiddities?[8] what a plague have I to do with a buff jerkin?

PRINCE. Why, what a pox[9] have I to do with my hostess of the tavern?

FALSTAFF. Well, thou hast called her to a reckoning[1] many a time and
40   oft.

PRINCE. Did I ever call for thee to pay thy part?

FALSTAFF. No, I'll give thee thy due, thou hast paid all there.

PRINCE. Yea, and elsewhere, so far as my coin would stretch, and where
it would not I have used my credit.

45   FALSTAFF. Yea, and so used it that were it not here apparent that thou
art heir apparent[2]—but I prithee, sweet wag, shall there be gallows
standing in England when thou art king? and resolution thus fobbed
as it is with the rusty curb of old father antic[3] the law? Do not thou,
when thou art king, hang a thief.

50   PRINCE. No, thou shalt.

FALSTAFF. Shall I? O rare! By the Lord, I'll be a brave judge.

PRINCE. Thou judgest false already; I mean thou shalt have the hanging
of the thieves and so become a rare hangman.

FALSTAFF. Well, Hal, well; and in some sort it jumps with my humor[4]
55   as well as waiting in the court, I can tell you.

PRINCE. For obtaining of suits?[5]

FALSTAFF. Yea, for obtaining of suits, whereof the hangman hath no lean
wardrobe. 'Sblood, I am as melancholy as a gib cat or a lugged[6] bear.

PRINCE. Or an old lion, or a lover's lute.

60   FALSTAFF. Yea, or the drone of a Lincolnshire bagpipe.

PRINCE. What sayest thou to a hare, or the melancholy of Moorditch?[7]

FALSTAFF. Thou hast the most unsavory similes and art indeed the most
comparative,[8] rascalliest, sweet young prince. But Hal, I prithee, trouble me no more with vanity. I would to God thou and I knew where a
65   commodity of good names were to be bought. An old lord of the council rated[9] me the other day in the street about you, sir, but I marked
him not; and yet he talked very wisely, but I regarded him not; and yet
he talked wisely, and in the street too.

PRINCE. Thou didst well, for wisdom cries out in the streets and no
70   man regards it.[1]

FALSTAFF. O, thou hast damnable iteration[2] and art indeed able to corrupt
a saint. Thou hast done much harm upon me, Hal, God forgive thee

---

6. A reference to Falstaff's original name, Oldcastle.
Hybla is a town in Sicily, famous for honey.
7. A pun: (1) lasting quality, (2) imprisonment. "Buff
jerkin": the leather jacket worn by a sheriff's sergeant.
8. Quibbles.
9. Common oath, alluding to venereal disease.
1. The bill; also (here) sexual intercourse.
2. "Here" and "heir" would pun in Elizabethan pronunciation.
3. A clown. "Resolution": bravery. "Fobbed": cheated.
4. I.e., agrees with my disposition.
5. Special favors, but "clothing" in the next line. The

hangman was given the clothes of his victims.
6. Baited (in the bearbaiting pits a bear was attacked
by dogs as a public amusement). "'Sblood": God's
blood, a common oath. "Gib cat": tomcat.
7. A foul-smelling ditch on the outskirts of London.
The "hare" was traditionally associated with melancholy.
8. Given to (insulting) comparisons.
9. Scolded, berated.
1. Prince Hal is quoting Proverbs 1.20 and 24.
2. Repetition, especially of sacred texts.

for it! Before I knew thee, Hal, I knew nothing, and now am I, if a
man should speak truly, little better than one of the wicked. I must
75   give over this life, and I will give it over; by the Lord, an[3] I do not, I
am a villain; I'll be damned for never a king's son in Christendom.

PRINCE. Where shall we take a purse tomorrow, Jack?

FALSTAFF. Zounds, where thou wilt, lad; I'll make one; an I do not, call
me villain and baffle[4] me.

80   PRINCE. I see a good amendment of life in thee—from praying to
purse-taking.

FALSTAFF. Why, Hal, 'tis my vocation,[5] Hal; 'tis no sin for a man to labor
in his vocation.

        [*Enter* POINS.]

Poins! Now shall we know if Gadshill[6] have set a match. O, if men
85   were to be saved by merit, what hole in hell were hot enough for
him? This is the most omnipotent villain that ever cried "stand" to a
true man.

PRINCE. Good morrow, Ned.

POINS. Good morrow, sweet Hal. What says Monsieur Remorse? what
90   says Sir John Sack and Sugar? Jack! how agrees the devil and thee
about thy soul, that thou soldest him on Good Friday last for a cup of
Madeira and a cold capon's leg?

PRINCE. Sir John stands to his word; the devil shall have his bargain, for
he was never yet a breaker of proverbs; he will give the devil his due.

95   POINS. Then art thou damned for keeping thy word with the devil.

PRINCE. Else he had been damned for cozening[7] the devil.

POINS. But my lads, my lads, tomorrow morning by four o'clock, early at
Gadshill, there are pilgrims going to Canterbury with rich offerings,
and traders riding to London with fat purses. I have vizards
100   for you all, you have horses for yourselves; Gadshill lies[8] tonight in
Rochester; I have bespoke supper tomorrow night in Eastcheap;[9] we
may do it as secure as sleep. If you will go, I will stuff your purses full
of crowns; if you will not, tarry at home and be hanged.

FALSTAFF. Hear ye, Yedward[1] if I tarry at home and go not, I'll hang
105   you for going.

POINS. You will, chops?[2]

FALSTAFF. Hal, wilt thou make one?

PRINCE. Who, I rob? I a thief? not I, by my faith.

FALSTAFF. There's neither honesty, manhood, nor good fellowship in
110   thee, nor thou camest not of the blood royal, if thou darest not
stand for[3] ten shillings.

PRINCE. Well then, once in my days I'll be a madcap.

---

3. If.
4. A knight in the days of chivalry was "baffled" or
disgraced by having his shield hung upside down, sig-
naling his loss of rank."Zounds": a common oath, a
contraction of "by God's wounds" (i.e., Jesus's wounds
on the Cross).
5. Falstaff is here making fun of the Puritan doctrine
of "calling" or vocation, based on the parable of the
talents (Matthew 25.25ff.).
6. Gadshill is both a man and a place: the place is a
hill twenty-seven miles from London on the road to
Rochester; it was notorious for robberies. The man, so

called from the place, is the thieves' "setter," who arranges when and where the robbery will occur.
7. Cheating.
8. Lodges. "Vizards": masks.
9. A thoroughfare in London, site of Mistress Quickly's tavern.
1. Dialect for Edward.
2. Fat face.
3. A pun: "stand for" means both "represent" and
"fight for." "Royal" is also a pun: the coin called *royal*
was worth ten shillings.

FALSTAFF. Why, that's well said.

PRINCE. Well, come what will, I'll tarry at home.

115　FALSTAFF. By the Lord, I'll be a traitor then, when thou art king.

PRINCE. I care not.

POINS. Sir John, I prithee leave the prince and me alone; I will lay him down such reasons for this adventure that he shall go.

FALSTAFF. Well, God give thee the spirit of persuasion and him the

120　ears of profiting, that what thou speakest may move and what he hears may be believed, that the true prince may (for recreation sake) prove a false thief; for the poor abuses of the time want countenance.[4] Farewell; you shall find me in Eastcheap.

PRINCE. Farewell, thou latter spring, farewell, Allhallown summer![5]

　　　[⟨*Exit* FALSTAFF.⟩][6]

125　POINS. Now, my good sweet honey lord, ride with us tomorrow; I have a jest to execute that I cannot manage alone. Falstaff, Bardolph, Peto, and Gadshill shall rob those men that we have already waylaid;[7] yourself and I will not be there, and when they have the booty, if you and I do not rob them, cut this head off from my shoulders.

130　PRINCE. How shall we part with them in setting forth?

POINS. Why, we will set forth before or after them, and appoint them a place of meeting, wherein it is at our pleasure to fail, and then will they adventure upon the exploit themselves, which they shall have no sooner achieved but we'll set upon them.

135　PRINCE. Yea, but 'tis like that they will know us by our horses, by our habits,[8] and by every other appointment to be ourselves.

POINS. Tut, our horses they shall not see—I'll tie them in the wood; our vizards we will change after we leave them: and, sirrah, I have cases of buckram for the nonce,[9] to immask our noted outward garments.

140　PRINCE. Yea, but I doubt they will be too hard[1] for us.

POINS. Well, for two of them, I know them to be as true-bred cowards as ever turned back; and for the third, if he fight longer than he sees reason, I'll forswear arms. The virtue of this jest will be the incomprehensible lies that this same fat rogue will tell us when we meet at

145　supper: how thirty at least he fought with; what wards,[2] what blows, what extremities he endured; and in the reproof[3] of this lies the jest.

PRINCE. Well, I'll go with thee. Provide us all things necessary and meet me tomorrow night[4] in Eastcheap; there I'll sup. Farewell.

POINS. Farewell, my lord.　　　　　　　　　　　　　　　[*Exit* POINS.]

150　PRINCE. I know you all, and will awhile uphold

　　　The unyoked humor° of your idleness;　　　　*undisciplined whim*

4. A satirical reference to the common complaint that the nobility did not properly give "countenance" to (i.e., encourage) good causes and to the Puritan habit of attacking the "abuses of the time." This entire speech parodies the language of the Puritans.

5. I.e., Indian summer; All Hallows' Day (All Saints' Day) is November 1. The two epithets are intended to suggest how unseasonable it is for Falstaff, an old man, to be engaged in youthful, hoodlum exploits.

6. This stage direction, like some others in the play, does not appear in the earliest editions; it was added by a later editor. All such interpolated directions are indicated in our text by the special double brackets

used here.

7. Set an ambush for.

8. Clothes.

9. I.e., outer clothes (of a coarse, stiff cloth) for the occasion.

1. I.e., too many. "Doubt": suspect.

2. Defensive postures.

3. Disproof.

4. Either the text should read "tonight" (before the robbery) or else Shakespeare intends to show Prince Hal's mind intent, not on the robbery, but on its aftermath. The soliloquy of the Prince that follows has provoked much critical discussion.

Yet herein will I imitate the sun,
Who doth permit the base contagious° clouds   *pestilence-breeding*
To smother up his beauty from the world,
155 That, when he please again to be himself,
Being wanted, he may be more wondered at
By breaking through the foul and ugly mists
Of vapors that did seem to strangle him.
If all the year were playing holidays,
160 To sport would be as tedious as to work;
But when they seldom come, they wished-for come,
And nothing pleaseth but rare accidents.
So, when this loose behavior I throw off
And pay the debt I never promisèd,
165 By how much better than my word I am,
By so much shall I falsify men's hopes,
And like bright metal on a sullen ground,°   *dull background*
My reformation, glitt'ring o'er my fault,
Shall show more goodly and attract more eyes
170 Than that which hath no foil° to set it off.   *contrast*
I'll so offend to make offense a skill,
Redeeming time⁵ when men think least I will.   [*Exit.*]

SCENE 3

[*Enter the* KING, NORTHUMBERLAND, WORCESTER, HOTSPUR,
SIR WALTER BLUNT, *with others.*]
KING. My blood hath been too cold and temperate,
Unapt to stir at these indignities,
And you have found me,⁶ for accordingly
You tread upon my patience; but be sure
5 I will from henceforth rather be myself,
Mighty and to be feared, than my condition,°   *disposition*
Which hath been smooth as oil, soft as young down,
And therefore lost that title of respect
Which the proud soul ne'er pays but to the proud.
10 WORCESTER. Our house, my sovereign liege, little deserves
The scourge of greatness to be used on it,
And that same greatness too which our own hands
Have holp° to make so portly°.   *helped/stately*
NORTHUMBERLAND. My lord—
15 KING. Worcester, get thee gone, for I do see
Danger and disobedience in thine eye;
O, sir, your presence is too bold and peremptory,
And majesty might never yet endure
The moody frontier of a servant brow.⁷
20 You have good leave to leave us; when we need

5. Making good use of time, following the advice given to Christians in a non-Christian world (see Ephesians 5.16). "Skill": piece of good policy.
6. Discovered this to be true.
7. I.e., a servant's brow showing defiance, like a fortification ("frontier").

Your use and counsel we shall send for you.   [*Exit* WORCESTER.]
You were about to speak.   [⟨*to* NORTHUMBERLAND.⟩]
NORTHUMBERLAND.   Yea, my good lord.
Those prisoners in your highness' name demanded,
Which Harry Percy here at Holmedon took,
25   Were, as he says, not with such strength denied
As is delivered to your majesty.
Either envy° therefore or misprisiòn°   malice/mistake
Is guilty of this fault, and not my son.
HOTSPUR. My liege, I did deny no prisoners.
30   But I remember, when the fight was done,
When I was dry with rage and extreme toil,
Breathless and faint, leaning upon my sword,
Came there a certain lord, neat and trimly dressed,
Fresh as a bridegroom, and his chin new reaped
35   Showed like a stubble-land at harvest-home.
He was perfumèd like a milliner,[8]
And 'twixt his finger and his thumb he held
A pouncet box,° which ever and anon   perfume box
He gave his nose and took 't away again;
40   Who therewith angry, when it next came there,
Took it in snuff;[9] and still he smiled and talked,
And as the soldiers bore dead bodies by,
He called them untaught knaves, unmannerly,
To bring a slovenly° unhandsome corse°   disgusting/corpse
45   Betwixt the wind and his nobility.
With many holiday and lady terms[1]
He questioned me; amongst the rest, demanded
My prisoners in your majesty's behalf.
I then, all smarting with my wounds being cold,
50   To be so pestered with a popinjay,°   parrot
Out of my grief and my impatience
Answered neglectingly I know not what,
He should, or he should not—for he made me mad
To see him shine so brisk and smell so sweet
55   And talk so like a waiting-gentlewoman
Of guns and drums and wounds, God save the mark!
And telling me the sovereign'st° thing on earth   most curative
Was parmaceti[2] for an inward bruise,
And that it was great pity, so it was,
60   This villanous saltpeter[3] should be digged
Out of the bowels of the harmless earth,
Which many a good tall° fellow had destroyed   brave
So cowardly, and but for these vile guns
He would himself have been a soldier.
65   This bald° unjointed chat of his, my lord,   trivial
I answered indirectly as I said,
And I beseech you, let not his report

---

8. Not a maker of hats, but a dealer in perfumes, wom-
en's gloves, etc.
9. I.e., was annoyed at it, with a pun on *snuffing it up.*

1. Affected and effeminate language.
2. Spermaceti, whale oil used as an ointment.
3. Used in gunpowder.

Come current[4] for an accusation
Betwixt my love and your high majesty.

70 BLUNT. The circumstance considered, good my lord,
Whate'er Lord Harry Percy then had said
To such a person and in such a place,
At such a time, with all the rest retold,
May reasonably die and never rise
75 To do him wrong or any way impeach
What then he said, so he unsay it now.

KING. Why, yet° he doth deny his prisoners,   *still*
But° with proviso and exceptiòn,   *except*
That we at our own charge shall ransom straight°   *immediately*
80 His brother-in-law, the foolish Mortimer,
Who, on my soul, hath willfully betrayed
The lives of those that he did lead to fight
Against that great magician, damned Glendower,
Whose daughter, as we hear, the Earl of March
85 Hath lately married. Shall our coffers then
Be emptied to redeem a traitor home?
Shall we buy treason? and indent with fears,[5]
When they have lost and forfeited themselves?
No, on the barren mountains let him starve;
90 For I shall never hold that man my friend
Whose tongue shall ask me for one penny cost
To ransom home revolted Mortimer.

HOTSPUR. Revolted Mortimer!
He never did fall off, my sovereign liege,
95 But by the chance of war. To prove that true
Needs no more but one tongue for all those wounds,
Those mouthèd wounds which valiantly he took
When on the gentle Severn's sedgy[6] bank
In single opposition, hand to hand,
100 He did confound° the best part of an hour   *spend*
In changing hardiment[7] with great Glendower;
Three times they breathed° and three times did   *paused for breath*
    they drink
Upon agreement of swift Severn's flood,
Who then, affrighted with their bloody looks,
105 Ran fearfully among the trembling reeds,
And hid his crisp[8] head in the hollow bank
Bloodstainèd with these valiant combatants.
Never did bare and rotten policy°   *craftiness, conspiracy*
Color° her working with such deadly wounds,   *disguise*
110 Nor never could the noble Mortimer
Receive so many, and all willingly;
Then let not him be slandered with revolt.

KING. Thou dost belie him, Percy, thou dost belie him;

---

4. Be considered valid.
5. Enter into a contract with cowards.
6. A river on the England-Wales border. Wounds are often likened to mouths in Shakespeare. The image may derive from their appearance and from the idea

that they could speak as witnesses to what caused them (cf. *Julius Caesar* 3.2.229–231 and *Richard III* 1.2.55–56).
7. Testing prowess and exchanging blows.
8. I.e., curly (because of the waves).

He never did encounter with Glendower.
115   I tell thee,
He durst as well have met the devil alone
As Owen Glendower for an enemy.
Art thou not ashamed? But, sirrah,[9] henceforth
Let me not hear you speak of° Mortimer;   *mention*
120   Send me your prisoners with the speediest means,
Or you shall hear in such a kind from me
As will displease you. My Lord Northumberland,
We license your departure with your son.
Send us your prisoners, or you will hear of it.
      [Exeunt KING, ⟨BLUNT, *and train.*⟩]
125 HOTSPUR. An if the devil come and roar for them
I will not send them; I will after straight
And tell him so, for I will ease my heart
Albeit I make a hazard of my head.
NORTHUMBERLAND. What, drunk with choler?° stay and pause   *anger*
    awhile.
Here comes your uncle.
      [Enter WORCESTER.]
130 HOTSPUR.   Speak of Mortimer!
Zounds, I will speak of him, and let my soul
Want mercy if I do not join with him;
Yea, on his part° I'll empty all these veins,   *behalf*
And shed my dear blood drop by drop in the dust,
135   But I will lift the downtrod Mortimer
As high in the air as this unthankful king,
As this ingrate° and cankered° Bullingbrook.   *ungrateful/malignant*
NORTHUMBERLAND. Brother, the king hath made your nephew mad.
WORCESTER. Who struck this heat up after I was gone?
140 HOTSPUR. He will, forsooth, have all my prisoners;
And when I urged the ransom once again
Of my wife's brother, then his cheek looked pale,
And on my face he turned an eye of death,
Trembling even at the name of Mortimer.
145 WORCESTER. I cannot blame him; was not he proclaimed
By Richard, that dead is, the next of blood?
NORTHUMBERLAND. He was—I heard the proclamatìon;
And then it was when the unhappy king
(Whose wrongs in us God pardon![1]) did set forth
150   Upon his Irish expeditìon;
From whence he intercepted did return
To be deposed and shortly murderèd.
WORCESTER. And for whose death we in the world's wide mouth
Live scandalized and foully spoken of.
155 HOTSPUR. But soft, I pray you; did King Richard then
Proclaim my brother[2] Edmund Mortimer
Heir to the crown?

---

9. A form of "sir," but used familiarly, and sometimes, as here, with a tone of contempt.

1. I.e., God pardon in us the wrongs we did to him.
2. Brother-in-law.

NORTHUMBERLAND.   He did; myself did hear it.

HOTSPUR. Nay, then I cannot blame his cousin king

That wished him on the barren mountains starve.

160 But shall it be that you, that set the crown

Upon the head of this forgetful man

And for his sake wear the detested blot

Of murderous subornation³—shall it be

That you a world of curses undergo,

165 Being the agents, or base second means,°   *tools, helpers*

The cords, the ladder, or the hangman rather?

O pardon me that I descend so low

To show the line and the predicament

Wherein you range⁴ under this subtle king!

170 Shall it for shame be spoken in these days,

Or fill up chronicles in time to come,

That men of your nobility and power

Did gage° them both in an unjust behalf,°   *pledge/cause*

As both of you—God pardon it!—have done,

175 To put down Richard, that sweet lovely rose,

And plant this thorn, this canker,⁵ Bullingbrook?

And shall it in more shame be further spoken,

That you are fooled, discarded, and shook off

By him for whom these shames ye underwent?

180 No; yet time serves wherein you may redeem

Your banished honors and restore yourselves

Into the good thoughts of the world again,

Revenge the jeering and disdained° contempt   *disdainful*

Of this proud king, who studies day and night

185 To answer all the debt he owes to you

Even with the bloody payment of your deaths:

Therefore, I say—

WORCESTER.   Peace, cousin, say no more;

And now I will unclasp a secret book,

And to your quick-conceiving discontents

190 I'll read you matter deep and dangerous,

As full of peril and adventurous spirit

As to o'er-walk a current roaring loud

On the unsteadfast footing of a spear.⁶

HOTSPUR. If he fall in, good night, or sink or swim.

195 Send danger from the east unto the west,

So° honor cross it from the north to south,   *provided that*

And let them grapple. O, the blood more stirs

To rouse a lion than to start⁷ a hare!

NORTHUMBERLAND. Imagination of some great exploit

200 Drives him beyond the bounds of patience.

HOTSPUR. By heaven, methinks it were an easy leap

To pluck bright honor from the pale-faced moon,

---

3. I.e., the stain of aiding and abetting murder.
4. I.e., to show the position and the category (or class) in which you are placed.

5. A wild rose, also a diseased spot in a nose.
6. A spear laid down as a footbridge.
7. Arouse, in hunting.

Or dive into the bottom of the deep,
Where fathom line could never touch the ground,
205   And pluck up drownèd honor by the locks,
So he that doth redeem her thence might wear
Without corrival° all her dignities;   *rival*
But out upon this half-faced fellowship![8]
WORCESTER. He apprehends a world of figures[9] here,
210   But not the form of what he should attend.
Good cousin, give me audience for a while.
HOTSPUR. I cry you mercy.[1]
WORCESTER.   Those same noble Scots
That are your prisoners—
HOTSPUR.   I'll keep them all;
By God, he shall not have a Scot of them;
215   No, if a Scot would save his soul he shall not.
I'll keep them, by his hand.
WORCESTER.   You start away
And lend no ear unto my purposes.
Those prisoners you shall keep.
HOTSPUR.   Nay, I will; that's flat.
He said he would not ransom Mortimer,
220   Forbade my tongue to speak of Mortimer,
But I will find him when he lies asleep,
And in his ear I'll holla "Mortimer!"
Nay,
I'll have a starling shall be taught to speak[2]
225   Nothing but "Mortimer," and give it him
To keep his anger still in motion.
WORCESTER. Hear you, cousin, a word.
HOTSPUR. All studies here I solemnly defy,
Save how to gall° and pinch this Bullingbrook,   *irritate*
230   And that same sword-and-buckler[3] Prince of Wales,
But that I think his father loves him not
And would be glad he met with some mischance,
I would have him poisoned with a pot of ale.[4]
WORCESTER. Farewell, kinsman; I'll talk to you
235   When you are better tempered to attend.
NORTHUMBERLAND. Why, what a wasp-stung and impatient fool
Art thou to break into this woman's mood,
Tying thine ear to no tongue but thine own!
HOTSPUR. Why, look you, I am whipped and scourged with rods,
240   Nettled and stung with pismires,° when I hear   *ants*
Of this vile politician Bullingbrook.
In Richard's time—what do you call the place?—
A plague upon it, it is in Gloucestershire—
'Twas where the madcap duke his uncle kept,°   *lived*

---

8. Miserable sharing (of honor) with someone else.
9. Rhetorical figures of speech.
1. Beg your pardon.
2. Starlings used to be taught to speak, as parrots are

now.
3. Weapons used by the lowest class of soldiers and servants. Gentlemen used rapiers.
4. The drink of the lower classes.

245 His uncle York, where I first bow'd my knee
     Unto this king of smiles, this Bullingbrook
     'Sblood! —
     When you and he came back from Ravenspurgh.
     NORTHUMBERLAND. At Berkeley castle.
250 HOTSPUR. You say true.
     Why, what a candy deal of courtesy
     This fawning greyhound[5] then did proffer me!
     "Look when his infant fortune came to age,"
     And "gentle Harry Percy," and "kind cousin";
255 O, the devil take such cozeners![6] God forgive me!
     Good uncle, tell your tale; I have done.
     WORCESTER. Nay, if you have not, to it again;
     We will stay your leisure.
     HOTSPUR.   I have done, i' faith.
     WORCESTER. Then once more to your Scottish prisoners.
260 Deliver them up without their ransom straight,
     And make the Douglas' son your only mean
     For powers in Scotland, which, for divers reasons
     Which I shall send you written, be assured
     Will easily be granted. You, my lord, [⟨to NORTHUMBERLAND⟩]
265 Your son in Scotland being thus employed,
     Shall secretly into the bosom creep
     Of that same noble prelate well beloved,
     The archbishop.
     HOTSPUR. Of York, is it not?
270 WORCESTER. True; who bears hard
     His brother's death at Bristol, the Lord Scroop.
     I speak not this in estimation,°   *by conjecture*
     As what I think might be, but what I know
     Is ruminated, plotted, and set down,
275 And only stays but to behold the face
     Of that occasion that shall bring it on.
     HOTSPUR. I smell it; upon my life, it will do well.
     NORTHUMBERLAND. Before the game is afoot, thou still let'st slip.[7]
     HOTSPUR. Why, it cannot choose but be a noble plot;
280 And then the power of Scotland and of York
     To join with Mortimer, ha?
     WORCESTER.   And so they shall.
     HOTSPUR. In faith, it is exceedingly well aimed.
     WORCESTER. And 'tis no little reason bids us speed,
     To save our heads by raising of a head;[8]
285 For, bear ourselves as even as we can,
     The king will always think him in our debt,
     And think we think ourselves unsatisfied,
     Till he hath found a time to pay us home;

5. A complex image that occurs in Shakespeare several times (cf. *Hamlet* 3.2.50–52 and *Antony and Cleopatra* 4.12.20–23). The idea of fawning or flattery called up to Shakespeare's mind the image of a dog begging for sweetmeats ("candy").

6. Cheaters, with, of course, a pun on *cousin*.
7. An image from hunting. The meaning is "You always ('still') release the dogs before we are ready to pursue the game."
8. Raising an army.

And see already how he doth begin
290   To make us strangers to his looks of love.
HOTSPUR. He does, he does; we'll be revenged on him.
WORCESTER. Cousin, farewell. No further go in this
        Than I by letters shall direct your course.
        When time is ripe, which will be suddenly,
295   I'll steal to Glendower and Lord Mortimer,
        Where you and Douglas and our powers at once,
        As I will fashion it, shall happily meet,
        To bear our fortunes in our own strong arms,
        Which now we hold at much uncertainty.
300 NORTHUMBERLAND. Farewell, good brother; we shall thrive, I trust.
HOTSPUR. Uncle, adieu; O, let the hours be short
        Till fields and blows and groans applaud our sport!   [*Exeunt.*]

Act 2

SCENE 1

[*Enter a* CARRIER *with a lantern in his hand.*]
FIRST CARRIER. Heigh-ho! an it be not four by the day, I'll be hanged;
        Charles' wain[9] is over the new chimney, and yet our horse not packed.
        What, ostler!
OSTLER. [*within*] Anon, anon.
5 FIRST CARRIER. I prithee, Tom, beat Cut's saddle,[1] put a few flocks in the
        point;[2] poor jade, is wrung in the withers out of all cess.[3]
                [*Enter another* CARRIER.]
SECOND CARRIER. Peas and beans are as dank here as a dog, and that is
        the next way to give poor jades the bots;[4] this house is turned upside
        down since Robin Ostler died.
10 FIRST CARRIER. Poor fellow, never joyed since the price of oats rose; it was
        the death of him.
SECOND CARRIER. I think this be the most villainous house in all London
        road for fleas; I am stung like a tench.[5]
FIRST CARRIER. Like a tench! by the mass, there is ne'er a king chris-
15   ten[6] could be better bit than I have been since the first cock.
SECOND CARRIER. Why, they will allow us ne'er a jordan, and then we
        leak in your chimney, and your chamber-lye breeds fleas like a loach.[7]
FIRST CARRIER. What, ostler! come away and be hanged, come away!
SECOND CARRIER. I have a gammon of bacon and two razes[8] of ginger,
20   to be delivered as far as Charing Cross.
FIRST CARRIER. God's body! the turkeys in my pannier[9] are quite starved.
        What, ostler! A plague on thee, hast thou never an eye in thy head?

---

9. The constellation of the Great Bear, or Big Dipper.
1. A saddle was beaten to make it soft. "Cut" is a name
for a horse with a docked tail.
2. Pieces of wool under the point of the saddle.
3. I.e., is sore excessively in the shoulders.
4. I.e., that is the easiest way to give poor nags worms
in the stomach.

5. A fish covered with red spots, like fleabites.
6. Christian king.
7. A fish that breeds prolifically. "Jordan": chamber
pot. "Chamber-lye": urine.
8. Roots. "Gammon": haunch.
9. Basket.

canst not hear? An 'twere not as good deed as drink to break the pate
on thee, I am a very villain. Come and be hanged!
25   hast no faith in thee?
            [*Enter* GADSHILL.]
GADSHILL. Good morrow, carriers. What's o'clock?
FIRST CARRIER. I think it be two o'clock.
GADSHILL. I prithee lend me thy lantern to see my gelding in the stable.
FIRST CARRIER. Nay, by God, soft; I know a trick worth two of that, i'
30   faith.
GADSHILL. I pray thee lend me thine.
SECOND CARRIER. Aye, when? canst tell?[1] Lend me thy lantern, quoth he?
marry, I'll see thee hanged first.
GADSHILL. Sirrah carrier, what time do you mean to come to London?
35   SECOND CARRIER. Time enough to go to bed with a candle, I warrant
thee. Come, neighbor Mugs, we'll call up the gentlemen; they will
along with company, for they have great charge.[2]
            [*Exeunt* ⟨CARRIERS.⟩]
GADSHILL. What ho! chamberlain!
            [*Enter* CHAMBERLAIN.]
CHAMBERLAIN. At hand, quoth pickpurse.
40   GADSHILL. That's even as fair as At hand, quoth the chamberlain, for thou
variest no more from picking of purses than giving direction doth from
laboring; thou layest the plot how.[3]
CHAMBERLAIN. Good morrow, Master Gadshill. It holds current[4] that I
told you yesternight; there's a franklin in the weald of Kent[5] hath
45   brought three hundred marks with him in gold—I heard him tell it to
one of his company last night at supper—a kind of auditor, one that
hath abundance of charge[6] too, God knows what. They are up already
and call for eggs and butter; they will away presently.[7]
GADSHILL. Sirrah, if they meet not with Saint Nicholas' clerks,[8] I'll
50   give thee this neck.
CHAMBERLAIN. No, I'll none of it; I pray thee, keep that for the hangman,
for I know thou worshipest Saint Nicholas as truly as a man of falsehood may.
GADSHILL. What talkest thou to me of the hangman? if I hang, I'll make
55   a fat pair of gallows; for if I hang, old Sir John hangs with me, and thou
knowest he is no starveling. Tut! there are other Trojans[9] that thou
dream'st not of, the which for sport sake are content to do the profession some grace, that would, if matters should be looked into, for
their own credit sake make all whole. I am joined with no foot land-
60   rakers, no long-staff sixpenny strikers,[1] none of these mad mustachio
purple-hued maltworms, but with nobility and tranquility, burgomas-
ters and great oneyers, such as can hold in,[2] such as will strike sooner

---

1. A colloquial expression of contemptuous refusal.
2. Valuable cargo.
3. A pun: "giving direction" means supervising, as contrasted with "laboring," but it was also the name for informing thieves about the journeys of prospective victims (laying "the plot how").
4. Remains true.
5. A section of that county, formerly wooded. "Frank-

lin": a freeholder, just below a gentleman in rank.
6. Considerable property. "Auditor": revenue officer.
7. At once.
8. Highwaymen.
9. Roisterers, good fellows.
1. "Land-rakers": footpads. Small-time thieves.
2. Keep secret. "Purple-hued maltworms": flushed, swaggering barflies. "Oneyers": dignitaries.

than speak, and speak sooner than drink, and drink sooner than pray;
and yet, zounds, I lie, for they pray continually to their saint, the com-
65   monwealth, or rather, not pray to her but prey on her, for they ride
up and down on her and make her their boots.[3]

CHAMBERLAIN. What, the commonwealth their boots? will she hold out
water in foul way?[4]

GADSHILL. She will, she will; justice hath liquored her.[5] We steal as in a
70   castle, cocksure; we have the receipt of fern seed,[6] we walk invisible.

CHAMBERLAIN. Nay, by my faith, I think you are more beholding to the
night than to fern seed for your walking invisible.

GADSHILL. Give me thy hand; thou shalt have a share in our purchase,[7]
as I am a true man.

75 CHAMBERLAIN. Nay, rather let me have it, as you are a false thief.

GADSHILL. Go to; *homo* is a common name to all men. Bid the ostler
bring my gelding out of the stable. Farewell, you muddy[8] knave.

                                                  [*Exeunt.*]

SCENE 2

[*Enter* PRINCE *and* POINS.]

POINS. Come shelter, shelter; I have removed Falstaff's horse, and he frets
like a gummed velvet.

PRINCE. Stand close.[9]

        [*Enter* FALSTAFF.]

FALSTAFF. Poins! Poins, and be hanged! Poins!

5 PRINCE. Peace, ye fat kidneyed rascal! what a brawling dost thou keep!

FALSTAFF. Where's Poins, Hal?

PRINCE. He is walked up to the top of the hill; I'll go seek him.

        [⟨*He pretends to go, but hides onstage with* POINS.⟩]

FALSTAFF. I am accursed to rob in that thief's company; the rascal hath
removed my horse, and tied him I know not where. If I travel but four
10   foot by the squier[1] further afoot, I shall break my wind. Well, I doubt
not but to die a fair death for all this, if I 'scape hanging for killing that
rogue. I have forsworn his company hourly any time this two and twenty
years, and yet I am bewitched with the rogue's company. If the rascal
have not given me medicines to make me love him, I'll be hanged; it
15   could not be else; I have drunk medicines. Poins! Hal! a plague upon
you both! Bardolph! Peto! I'll starve ere I'll rob a foot further. An 'twere
not as good a deed as drink to turn true man and to leave these rogues,
I am the veriest varlet that ever chewed with a tooth. Eight yards of
uneven ground is threescore and ten miles afoot with me, and the
20   stony-hearted villains know it well enough; a plague upon it when
thieves cannot be true one to another! [*They whistle.*] Whew! A plague
upon you all! Give me my horse, you rogues; give me my horse, and be
hanged!

---

3. Booty.
4. Keep one dry in muddy roads, i.e., give protection.
5. I.e., those who control the laws have greased (or bribed) her.
6. I.e., we have the recipe for fern seed (supposed to make one invisible).

7. Takings.
8. Muddleheaded.
9. Hide. "Gummed velvet": cheap velvet was treated with gum to make the pile stiff; as a result it soon fretted or wore away.
1. Ruler, yardstick.

PRINCE. Peace, ye fat-guts! lie down; lay thine ear close to the ground
25   and list if thou canst hear the tread of travelers.

FALSTAFF. Have you any levers to lift me up again, being down? 'Sblood,
    I'll not bear my own flesh so far afoot again for all the coin in thy
    father's exchequer. What a plague mean ye to colt me thus?

PRINCE. Thou liest; thou art not colted, thou art uncolted.[2]

30   FALSTAFF. I prithee, good Prince, Hal, help me to my horse, good king's
    son.

PRINCE. Out, ye rogue! shall I be your ostler?

FALSTAFF. Go hang thyself in thine own heir-apparent garters![3] If I be
    ta'en, I'll peach for this. An I have not ballads made on you all and
35   sung to filthy tunes, let a cup of sack be my poison; when a jest is so
    forward, and afoot too! I hate it.

        [Enter GADSHILL.]

GADSHILL. Stand.

FALSTAFF. So I do, against my will.

POINS. [Coming forward with BARDOLPH and PETO] O, 'tis our setter;
40   I know his voice. Bardolph, what news?

BARDOLPH. Case[4] ye, case ye, on with your vizards; there's money of the
    king's coming down the hill; 'tis going to the king's exchequer.

FALSTAFF. You lie, you rogue; 'tis going to the king's tavern.

GADSHILL. There's enough to make us all.

45   FALSTAFF. To be hanged.

PRINCE. Sirs, you four shall front them in the narrow lane; Ned Poins
    and I will walk lower; if they 'scape from your encounter, then they
    light on us.

PETO. How many be there of them?

50   GADSHILL. Some eight or ten.

FALSTAFF. Zounds, will they not rob us?

PRINCE. What, a coward, Sir John Paunch?

FALSTAFF. Indeed, I am not John of Gaunt, your grandfather, but yet no
    coward, Hal.

55   PRINCE. Well, we leave that to the proof.

POINS. Sirrah Jack, thy horse stands behind the hedge; when thou need'st
    him, there thou shalt find him. Farewell, and stand fast.

FALSTAFF. Now cannot I strike him, if I should be hanged.

PRINCE. [⟨aside to POINS⟩] Ned, where are our disguises?

60   POINS. [⟨aside⟩] Here, hard by; stand close.

        [⟨Exeunt PRINCE and POINS.⟩]

FALSTAFF. Now, my masters, happy man be his dole,[5] say I; every man to
    his business.

        [Enter the TRAVELERS.]

FIRST TRAVELER. Come, neighbor, the boy shall lead our horses down the
    hill; we'll walk afoot awhile, and ease our legs.

65   THIEVES. Stand!

TRAVELERS. Jesus bless us!

FALSTAFF. Strike; down with them; cut the villains' throats. Ah, whoreson

---

2. You have had your horse stolen. "To colt": trick.   4. Mask.
3. As heir apparent to the throne, Hal would be a   5. I.e., good luck!
knight of the Order of the Garter.

caterpillars,[6] bacon-fed knaves, they hate us youth! Down with them, fleece them.

70   TRAVELERS. O, we are undone, both we and ours forever!

FALSTAFF. Hang ye, gorbellied knaves, are ye undone? No, ye fat chuffs,[7] I would your store were here! On, bacons, on! What, ye knaves, young men must live! You are grand jurors, are ye? we'll jure ye, faith.

[*Here they rob them and bind them. Exeunt.*]
[*Enter the* PRINCE *and* POINS *in buckram.*]

PRINCE. The thieves have bound the true men. Now could thou and I
75   rob the thieves and go merrily to London; it would be argument[8] for a week, laughter for a month, and a good jest forever.

POINS. Stand close; I hear them coming.

[*Enter the* THIEVES *again.*]

FALSTAFF. Come, my masters, let us share, and then to horse before day. An the Prince and Poins be not two arrant cowards, there's no
80   equity stirring;[9] there's no more valor in that Poins than in a wild duck.

PRINCE. Your money!

POINS. Villains!

[*As they are sharing, the* PRINCE *and* POINS *set upon them; they all run away; and* FALSTAFF, *after a blow or two, runs away too, leaving the booty behind them.*]

PRINCE. Got with much ease. Now merrily to horse;
The thieves are all scattered and possessed with fear
85   So strongly that they dare not meet each other;
Each takes his fellow for an officer.
Away, good Ned. Falstaff sweats to death,
And lards the lean earth as he walks along;
Were't not for laughing, I should pity him.

90   POINS. How the fat rogue roared!   [*Exeunt.*]

SCENE 3

[*Enter* HOTSPUR, *alone, reading a letter.*]

HOTSPUR. "But for mine own part, my lord, I could be well contented to be there, in respect of the love I bear your house." He could be contented; why is he not, then? In respect of the love he bears our house, he shows in this, he loves his own barn better than he loves our house.
5   Let me see some more. "The purpose you undertake is dangerous." Why, that's certain. 'Tis dangerous to take a cold, to sleep, to drink; but I tell you, my lord fool, out of this nettle, danger, we pluck this flower, safety.[1] "The purpose you undertake is dangerous, the friends you have named uncertain, the time itself unsorted,[2] and your whole
10   plot too light for the counterpoise of so great an opposition." Say you so, say you so? I say unto you again, you are a shallow cowardly hind,[3] and you lie. What a lackbrain is this! By the Lord, our plot is a good

---

6. "Caterpillars of the commonwealth" was a common phrase, referring to rogues. Falstaff here applies ridiculously inappropriate terms to the travelers and to himself (e.g., "youth").
7. Misers. "Gorbellied": fat.
8. Subject of stories.

9. There's no justice.
1. The nettle if touched tenderly will sting; if grasped firmly, will not.
2. Unsuitable.
3. Peasant.

plot as ever was laid, our friends true and constant; a good plot, good
friends, and full of expectation; an excellent plot, very good friends.
15   What a frosty-spirited rogue is this! Why, my lord of York⁴ commends
the plot and the general course of the action. Zounds, an I were now
by this rascal I could brain him with his lady's fan. Is there not my
father, my uncle, and myself? Lord Edmund Mortimer, my lord of
York, and Owen Glendower? is there not besides the Douglas? have I
20   not all their letters to meet me in arms by the ninth of the next month,
and are they not some of them set forward already? What a pagan rascal
is this, an infidel! Ha! you shall see now in very sincerity of fear and
cold heart, will he to the king and lay open all our proceedings. O, I
could divide myself and go to buffets,⁵ for moving⁶ such a dish of skim
25   milk with so honorable an action! Hang him! let him tell the king.
We are prepared; I will set forward tonight.

       [*Enter his* LADY.]

How now, Kate! I must leave you within these two hours.

LADY. O, my good lord, why are you thus alone?
   For what offense have I this fortnight been
30   A banished woman from my Harry's bed?
   Tell me, sweet lord, what is 't that takes from thee
   Thy stomach,° pleasure, and thy golden sleep?   *appetite*
   Why dost thou bend thine eyes upon the earth,
   And start so often when thou sit'st alone?
35   Why hast thou lost the fresh blood in thy cheeks,
   And given my treasures and my rights of thee
   To thick-eyed musing and cursed melancholy?
   In thy faint slumbers I by thee have watched
   And heard thee murmur tales of iron wars,
40   Speak terms of manage° to thy bounding steed,   *horsemanship*
   Cry "Courage! to the field!" And thou hast talked
   Of sallies and retires, of trenches, tents,
   Of palisadoes, frontiers, parapets,
   Of basilisks, of cannon, culverin,⁷
45   Of prisoners' ransom and of soldiers slain,
   And all the currents of a heady fight.
   Thy spirit within thee hath been so at war
   And thus hath so bestirred thee in thy sleep
   That beads of sweat have stood upon thy brow
50   Like bubbles in a late-disturbèd stream,
   And in thy face strange motions have appeared
   Such as we see when men restrain their breath
   On some great sudden hest.° O, what portents are these?   *command*
   Some heavy business hath my lord in hand
55   And I must know it, else he loves me not.

HOTSPUR. What, ho!

       [⟨*Enter* SERVANT.⟩]

       Is Gilliams with the packet gone?

---

4. The archbishop of York.   7. Three kinds of artillery (named here in decreasing
5. Split myself in two and let the parts fight each other.   order of weight).
6. Urging.

SERVANT. He is, my lord, an hour ago.
HOTSPUR. Hath Butler brought those horses from the sheriff?
SERVANT. One horse, my lord, he brought even now.
60   HOTSPUR. What horse? a roan, a crop-ear, is it not?
SERVANT. It is, my lord.
HOTSPUR.   That roan shall be my throne.
Well, I will back° him straight; O Esperance!⁸   mount
Bid Butler lead him forth into the park.   [⟨*Exit* SERVANT.⟩]
LADY. But hear you, my lord.
65   HOTSPUR. What say'st thou, my lady?
LADY. What is it carries you away?
HOTSPUR. Why, my horse, my love, my horse.
LADY. Out, you mad-headed ape!
A weasel hath not such a deal of spleen⁹
70   As you are tossed with. In faith
I'll know your business, Harry, that I will.
I fear my brother Mortimer doth stir
About his title, and hath sent for you
To line° his enterprise; but if you go¹ —   support
75   HOTSPUR. So far afoot, I shall be weary, love.
LADY. Come, come, you paraquito,° answer me   parrot
Directly unto this question that I ask.
In faith, I'll break thy little finger, Harry,
An if thou wilt not tell me all things true.
80   HOTSPUR. Away,
Away, you trifler! Love! I love thee not,
I care not for thee, Kate; this is no world
To play with mammets° and to tilt with lips;   dolls
We must have bloody noses and cracked crowns,²
85   And pass them current too. God's me, my horse!
What say'st thou, Kate? what wouldst thou have with me?
LADY. Do you not love me? do you not, indeed?
Well, do not then, for since you love me not
I will not love myself. Do you not love me?
90   Nay, tell me if you speak in jest or no.
HOTSPUR. Come, wilt thou see me ride?
And when I am o' horseback, I will swear
I love thee infinitely. But hark you, Kate,
I must not have you henceforth question me
95   Whither I go, nor reason whereabout;
Whither I must, I must; and, to conclude,
This evening must I leave you, gentle Kate.
I know you wise, but yet no farther wise
Than Harry Percy's wife; constant you are,
100 But yet a woman, and for secrecy
No lady closer; for I well believe

8. The battle cry of the Percies: "Hope!"
9. The spleen was supposed to be the source of sudden and violent emotions. The weasel was considered a very impetuous animal.
1. Besides its ordinary sense, which Lady Percy uses,

"go" also meant "walk," the sense in which Hotspur takes it.
2. Broken heads, with a pun on *crowns* as coins and with allusion to the overthrow of kings.

Thou wilt not utter what thou dost not know,
And so far will I trust thee, gentle Kate.
LADY. How! so far?
105 HOTSPUR. Not an inch further. But hark you, Kate,
Whither I go, thither shall you go too;
Today will I set forth, tomorrow you.
Will this content you, Kate?
LADY.   It must of force.³   [*Exeunt.*]

SCENE 4

[*Enter the* PRINCE *and* POINS.]
PRINCE. Ned, prithee come out of that fat⁴ room, and lend me thy hand
to laugh a little.
POINS. Where hast been, Hal?
PRINCE. With three or four loggerheads⁵ amongst three or four-score hogs-
5   heads. I have sounded the very bass string of humility. Sirrah, I am
sworn brother to a leash of drawers,⁶ and can call them all by their
christen names, as Tom, Dick, and Francis. They take it already upon
their salvation, that though I be but Prince of Wales, yet I am the king
of courtesy, and tell me flatly I am no proud Jack, like Falstaff, but a
10   Corinthian,⁷ a lad of mettle, a good boy—by the Lord, so they call me—
and when I am king of England I shall command all the good lads in
Eastcheap. They call drinking deep, dyeing scarlet, and when you
breathe in your watering⁸ they cry "hem!" and bid you play it off. To
conclude, I am so good a proficient in one quarter of an hour that
15   I can drink with any tinker in his own language during my life. I tell
thee, Ned, thou hast lost much honor, that thou wert not with me in
this action. But, sweet Ned—to sweeten which name of Ned, I give thee
this pennyworth of sugar, clapped even now into my hand by an under-
skinker,⁹ one that never spake other English in his life than "Eight
20   shillings and sixpence," and "You are welcome," with this shrill addition, "Anon, anon, sir! Score a pint of bastard in the Half-Moon,"¹ or so.
But, Ned, to drive away the time till Falstaff come, I prithee do thou
stand in some by-room, while I question my puny drawer to what end
he gave me the sugar, and do thou never leave calling "Francis,"
25   that his tale to me may be nothing but "Anon." Step aside, and I'll show
thee a precedent.²
POINS. Francis!
PRINCE. Thou art perfect.
POINS. Francis!   [⟨*Exit* POINS.⟩]
[*Enter* DRAWER.]
30   FRANCIS. Anon, anon, sir. Look down into the Pomgarnet,³ Ralph.
PRINCE. Come hither, Francis.

---

3. Of necessity.
4. Vat. This establishes that the scene is a tavern.
5. Blockheads.
6. Group of tapsters, waiters.
7. Good fellow.
8. Drink.
9. Assistant waiter.

1. I.e., charge a pint of "bastard" (a sweet Spanish wine) to a customer in the room called "Half-Moon." "Anon": immediately (the reply of a servant when called, equivalent to "Coming!").
2. Example.
3. Pomegranate (another room in the tavern).

FRANCIS. My lord?

PRINCE. How long hast thou to serve,[4] Francis?

FRANCIS. Forsooth, five years, and as much as to—

35 POINS. [*within*] Francis!

FRANCIS. Anon, anon, sir.

PRINCE. Five year! by 'r Lady, a long lease for the clinking of pewter. But, Francis, darest thou be so valiant as to play the coward with thy indenture and show it a fair pair of heels and run from it?

40 FRANCIS. O Lord, sir, I'll be sworn upon all the books[5] in England, I could find in my heart—

POINS. [*within*] Francis!

FRANCIS. Anon, sir.

PRINCE. How old art thou, Francis?

45 FRANCIS. Let me see— about Michaelmas[6] next I shall be—

POINS. [*within*] Francis!

FRANCIS. Anon, sir. Pray stay a little, my lord.

PRINCE. Nay, but hark you, Francis: for the sugar thou gavest me, 'twas a pennyworth, was't not?

50 FRANCIS. O Lord, I would it had been two!

PRINCE. I will give thee for it a thousand pound; ask me when thou wilt, and thou shalt have it.

POINS. [*within*] Francis!

FRANCIS. Anon, anon.

55 PRINCE. Anon, Francis? No, Francis, but tomorrow, Francis; or Francis, o' Thursday, or indeed, Francis, when thou wilt. But, Francis!

FRANCIS. My lord?

PRINCE. Wilt thou rob this leathern-jerkin, crystal-button, not-pated, agate-ring, puke-stocking, caddis-garter,[7] smooth-tongue, Spanish-pouch—

60 FRANCIS. O Lord, sir, who do you mean?

PRINCE. Why, then, your brown bastard is your only drink, for look you, Francis, your white canvas doublet will sully. In Barbary, sir, it cannot come to so much.[8]

FRANCIS. What, sir?

65 POINS. [*within*] Francis!

PRINCE. Away, you rogue, dost thou not hear them call?

[*Here they both call him; the drawer stands amazed, not knowing which way to go.*]

[*Enter* VINTNER.]

VINTNER. What, stand'st thou still, and hear'st such a calling? Look to the guests within. [*Exit* FRANCIS.] My lord, old Sir John with half-a-dozen more are at the door; shall I let them in?

70 PRINCE. Let them alone awhile, and then open the door. [*Exit* VINTNER.] Poins!

[*Enter* POINS.]

POINS. Anon, anon, sir.

PRINCE. Sirrah, Falstaff and the rest of the thieves are at the door; shall we be merry?

4. I.e., to finish out his apprenticeship, usually a seven-year period under an "indenture" or agreement.
5. I.e., Bibles.
6. September 29.
7. Worsted tape garter. "Leathern-jerken": leather-jacketed. "Not-pated": with short hair. "Puke": dark gray.
8. Deliberate nonsense to confuse Francis, and one of the first instances of double-talk in English literature.

75   POINS. As merry as crickets, my lad. But hark ye, what cunning match
        have you made with this jest of the drawer? come, what's the issue?
     PRINCE. I am now of all humors[9] that have showed themselves humors
        since the old days of goodman Adam to the pupil[1] age of this present
        twelve o'clock at midnight.
            [⟨Enter FRANCIS.⟩]
80   What's o'clock, Francis?
     FRANCIS. Anon, anon, sir.   [⟨Exit.⟩]
     PRINCE. That ever this fellow should have fewer words than a parrot, and
        yet the son of a woman! His industry is upstairs and downstairs, his
        eloquence the parcel[2] of a reckoning. I am not yet of Percy's mind, the
85   Hotspur of the north, he that kills me some six or seven dozen of Scots
        at a breakfast, washes his hands, and says to his wife "Fie upon this
        quiet life! I want work." "O my sweet Harry," says she, "how many hast
        thou killed today?" "Give my roan horse a drench," says he, and
        answers "Some fourteen," an hour after, "a trifle, a trifle." I prithee,
90   call in Falstaff; I'll play Percy, and that damned brawn shall play Dame
        Mortimer his wife. "Rivo!"[3] says the drunkard. Call in ribs, call in
        tallow.
            [Enter FALSTAFF, ⟨GADSHILL, BARDOLPH, and PETO, FRANCIS fol-
            lowing with wine.⟩]
     POINS. Welcome, Jack; where hast thou been?
     FALSTAFF. A plague of all cowards, I say, and a vengeance too, marry
95   and amen! Give me a cup of sack, boy. Ere I lead this life long, I'll sew
        nether stocks[4] and mend them and foot them too. A plague of all cow-
        ards! Give me a cup of sack, rogue. Is there no virtue extant?
                                                              [He drinks.]
     PRINCE. Didst thou ever see Titan[5] kiss a dish of butter, pitiful-hearted
        butter that melted at the sweet tale of the sun's? If thou didst, then
100   behold that compound.
     FALSTAFF. You rogue, here's lime in this sack too;[6] there is nothing but
        roguery to be found in villainous man, yet a coward is worse than a
        cup of sack with lime in it. A villainous coward! Go thy ways, old Jack,
        die when thou wilt; if manhood, good manhood, be not forgot upon
105   the face of the earth, then am I a shotten herring.[7] There lives not
        three good men unhanged in England, and one of them is fat and
        grows old. God help the while; a bad world, I say. I would I were a
        weaver; I could sing psalms[8] or anything. A plague of all cowards, I say
        still.
110 PRINCE. How now, woolsack, what mutter you?
     FALSTAFF. A king's son! If I do not beat thee out of thy kingdom with a
        dagger of lath,[9] and drive all thy subjects afore thee like a flock of
        wild geese, I'll never wear hair on my face more. You Prince of Wales!
     PRINCE. Why, you whoreson round man, what's the matter?
115 FALSTAFF. Are not you a coward? answer me to that; and Poins there?
     POINS. Zounds, ye fat paunch, an ye call me coward, by the Lord I'll stab
        thee.

---

9. Temperaments, dispositions, i.e., as a result of teas-   5. The sun.
ing the servant, I am now in the mood for anything.   6. Lime was used to make wine sparkle.
1. Youthful.   7. A herring that has cast its spawn and is lean.
2. Item.   8. Protestant weavers from Flanders were notorious for
3. Drink up!   singing psalms.
4. Stockings.   9. A stick used by Vice in the old morality plays.

FALSTAFF. I call thee coward! I'll see thee damned ere I call thee but I
would give a thousand pound I could run as fast as thou canst.
120   You are straight enough in the shoulders, you care not who sees your
back; call you that backing of your friends? A plague upon such backing! give me them that will face me. Give me a cup of sack; I am a
rogue if I drunk today.

PRINCE. O villain! thy lips are scarce wiped since thou drunk'st last.

125   FALSTAFF. All's one for that. [*He drinks.*] A plague of all cowards, still say
I.

PRINCE. What's the matter?

FALSTAFF. What's the matter! there be four of us here have ta'en a
thousand pound this day morning.

130   PRINCE. Where is it, Jack? where is it?

FALSTAFF. Where is it? taken from us it is—a hundred upon poor four of
us.

PRINCE. What, a hundred, man?

FALSTAFF. I am a rogue if I were not at half-sword[1] with a dozen of them
135   two hours together. I have 'scaped by miracle. I am eight times thrust
through the doublet, four through the hose,[2] my buckler cut through
and through, my sword hacked like a handsaw—*ecce signum!*[3] I never
dealt better since I was a man; all would not do. A plague of all cowards! Let them speak; if they speak more or less than truth, they are
140   villains and the sons of darkness.

PRINCE. Speak, sirs; how was it?

GADSHILL. We four set upon some dozen—

FALSTAFF. Sixteen at least, my lord.

GADSHILL. And bound them.

145   PETO. No, no, they were not bound.

FALSTAFF. You rogue, they were bound, every man of them, or I am a
Jew else, an Ebrew Jew.

GADSHILL. As we were sharing, some six or seven fresh men set upon us—

FALSTAFF. And unbound the rest, and then come in the other.

150   PRINCE. What, fought you with them all?

FALSTAFF. All! I know not what you call all, but if I fought not with fifty
of them, I am a bunch of radish; if there were not two or three and
fifty upon poor old Jack, then am I no two-legged creature.

PRINCE. Pray God you have not murdered some of them.

155   FALSTAFF. Nay, that's past praying for; I have peppered two of them. Two
I am sure I have paid, two rogues in buckram suits. I tell thee what,
Hal, if I tell thee a lie, spit in my face, call me horse. Thou knowest
my old ward; here I lay,[4] and thus I bore my point. Four rogues inbuck-
ram let drive at me—

160   PRINCE. What, four? thou saidst but two even now.

FALSTAFF. Four, Hal; I told thee four.

POINS. Aye, aye, he said four.

FALSTAFF. These four came all a-front, and mainly[5] thrust at me. I made
me no more ado but took all their seven points in my target,[6] thus.

---

1. At half a sword's length.   4. This was my stance. "Ward": defense.
2. Breeches.   5. Strongly.
3. Here's the proof!   6. Shield.

165 PRINCE. Seven? why, there were but four even now.

  FALSTAFF. In buckram?

  POINS. Aye, four, in buckram suits.

  FALSTAFF. Seven, by these hilts, or I am a villain else.

  PRINCE. Prithee, let him alone; we shall have more anon.

170 FALSTAFF. Dost thou hear me, Hal?

  PRINCE. Aye, and mark thee too, Jack.

  FALSTAFF. Do so, for it is worth the listening to. These nine in buckram
   that I told thee of—

  PRINCE. So, two more already.

175 FALSTAFF. Their points being broken—

  POINS. Down fell their hose.[7]

  FALSTAFF. Began to give me ground; but I followed me close, came in
   foot and hand, and with a thought[8] seven of the eleven I paid.

  PRINCE. O monstrous! eleven buckram men grown out of two!

180 FALSTAFF. But, as the devil would have it, three misbegotten knaves in
   Kendal green[9] came at my back and let drive at me, for it was so dark,
   Hal, that thou couldst not see thy hand.

  PRINCE. These lies are like their father that begets them—gross as a mountain, open, palpable. Why, thou clay-brained guts, thou knotty-pated
185 fool, thou whoreson, obscene, greasy tallow-catch[1]—

  FALSTAFF. What, art thou mad? art thou mad? is not the truth the truth?

  PRINCE. Why, how couldst thou know these men in Kendal green, when
   it was so dark thou couldst not see thy hand? come, tell us your reason.
   What sayest thou to this?

190 POINS. Come, your reason, Jack, your reason.

  FALSTAFF. What, upon compulsion? Zounds, an I were at the strappado,
   or all the racks[2] in the world, I would not tell you on compulsion. Give
   you a reason on compulsion! if reasons[3] were as plentiful as blackberries, I would give no man a reason upon compulsion, I.

195 PRINCE. I'll be no longer guilty of this sin; this sanguine coward, this bed-
   presser, this horseback-breaker, this huge hill of flesh—

  FALSTAFF. 'Sblood, you starveling, you eelskin, you dried neat's tongue,
   you bull's pizzle, you stockfish![4] O for breath to utter what is like thee!
   you tailor's yard, you sheath, you bow case, you vile standing-tuck[5]—

200 PRINCE. Well, breathe awhile, and then to it again; and when thou hast
   tired thyself in base comparisons, hear me speak but this.

  POINS. Mark, Jack.

  PRINCE. We two saw you four set on four and bound them, and were
   masters of their wealth. Mark now, how a plain tale shall put you down.
205 Then did we two set on you four; and, with a word, outfaced you from
   your prize, and have it, yea, and can show it you here in the house;
   and, Falstaff, you carried your guts away as nimbly, with as quick dexterity, and roared for mercy and still run and roared, as ever I heard
   bullcalf. What a slave art thou, to hack thy sword as thou hast

---

7. Poins puns on the other meaning of *points:* the laces used to tie up trousers ("hose").
8. As quick as thought.
9. A coarse cloth.
1. Piece of tallow from which chandlers made candles.

2. "Strappado" and "racks" are methods of torture.
3. A pun on the word *raisin,* which was spelled and pronounced like *reason* in Elizabethan England.
4. I.e., you ox tongue, you bull's penis, you dried cod!
5. Stiff rapier.

210 done, and then say it was in fight! What trick, what device, what starting-hole,[6] canst thou now find out to hide thee from this open and apparent shame?

POINS. Come, let's hear, Jack; what trick hast thou now?

FALSTAFF. By the Lord, I knew ye as well as he that made ye. Why, hear
215 you, my masters: was it for me to kill the heir apparent? should I turn upon the true prince? why, thou knowest I am as valiant as Hercules; but beware instinct; the lion will not touch the true prince.[7] Instinct is a great matter; I was now a coward on instinct. I shall think the better of myself and thee during my life; I for a valiant lion, and thou for a
220 true prince. But, by the Lord, lads, I am glad you have the money. Hostess, clap to the doors; watch[8] tonight, pray tomorrow. Gallants, lads, boys, hearts of gold, all the titles of good fellowship come to you! What, shall we be merry? shall we have a play extempore?

PRINCE. Content; and the argument[9] shall be thy running away.
225 FALSTAFF. Ah, no more of that, Hal, an thou lovest me!

[Enter HOSTESS.]

HOSTESS. O Jesu, my lord the prince!

PRINCE. How now, my lady the hostess! what sayest thou to me?

HOSTESS. Marry, my lord, there is a nobleman of the court at door would speak with you; he says he comes from your father.
230 PRINCE. Give him as much as will make him a royal[1] man, and send him back again to my mother.

FALSTAFF. What manner of man is he?

HOSTESS. An old man.

FALSTAFF. What doth gravity out of his bed at midnight? Shall I give
235 him his answer?

PRINCE. Prithee, do, Jack.

FALSTAFF. Faith, and I'll send him packing.   [Exit.]

PRINCE. Now, sirs. By 'r Lady, you fought fair; so did you, Peto; so did you, Bardolph; you are lions too, you ran away upon instinct, you will
240 not touch the true prince; no, fie!

BARDOLPH. Faith, I ran when I saw others run.

PRINCE. Faith, tell me now in earnest, how came Falstaff's sword so hacked?

PETO. Why, he hacked it with his dagger, and said he would swear truth out of England but he would make you believe it was done in fight,
245 and persuaded us to do the like.

BARDOLPH. Yea, and to tickle our noses with speargrass to make them bleed, and then to beslubber our garments with it and swear it was the blood of true men. I did that I did not this seven year before, I blushed to hear his monstrous devices.
250 PRINCE. O villain, thou stolest a cup of sack eighteen years ago, and wert taken with the manner,[2] and ever since thou hast blushed extempore. Thou hadst fire and sword on thy side, and yet thou ran'st away; what instinct hadst thou for it?

6. Evasion.
7. In many medieval romances the lion, as king of beasts, shows respect for royalty.
8. Stay up.
9. Plot or story.
1. A "royal" was half of a pound sterling, a "noble" was a third.
2. In the act.

BARDOLPH. My lord, do you see these meteors? do you behold these
255   exhalations?[3]

PRINCE. I do.

BARDOLPH. What think you they portend?

PRINCE. Hot livers and cold purses.[4]

BARDOLPH. Choler, my lord, if rightly taken.

260   PRINCE. No, if rightly taken, halter.[5]

[*Enter* FALSTAFF.]

Here comes lean Jack, here comes bare-bone. How now, my sweet
creature of bombast,[6] how long is 't ago, Jack, since thou sawest thine
own knee?

FALSTAFF. My own knee! when I was about thy years, Hal, I was not an
265   eagle's talon in the waist; I could have crept into any alderman's thumb
ring. A plague of sighing and grief—it blows a man up like a bladder.
There's villainous news abroad; here was Sir John Bracy from your
father; you must to the court in the morning. That same mad fellow of
the north, Percy, and he of Wales, that gave Amamon the bastinado[7]
270   and made Lucifer cuckold and swore the devil his true liegeman upon
the cross of a Welsh hook[8]—what a plague call you him?

POINS. O, Glendower.

FALSTAFF. Owen, Owen, the same; and his son-in-law Mortimer, and old
Northumberland, and that sprightly Scot of Scots, Douglas, that runs
275   o' horseback up a hill perpendicular—

PRINCE. He that rides at high speed and with his pistol kills a sparrow
flying.

FALSTAFF. You have hit it.

PRINCE. So did he never the sparrow.

280   FALSTAFF. Well, that rascal hath good mettle in him; he will not run.

PRINCE. Why, what a rascal art thou then, to praise him so for running!

FALSTAFF. O' horseback, ye cuckoo; but afoot he will not budge a foot.

PRINCE. Yes, Jack, upon instinct.

FALSTAFF. I grant ye, upon instinct. Well, he is there too, and one Mor-
285   dake, and a thousand blue-caps[9] more. Worcester is stolen away
tonight; thy father's beard is turned white with the news; you may buy
land now as cheap as stinking mackerel.

PRINCE. Why then, it is like, if there come a hot June, and this civil
buffeting hold, we shall buy maidenheads as they buy hobnails, by the
290   hundreds.

FALSTAFF. By the mass, lad, thou sayest true; it is like we shall have good
trading that way. But tell me, Hal, art not thou horrible afeard? thou
being heir apparent, could the world pick thee out three such enemies
again as that fiend Douglas, that spirit Percy, and that devil Glen-
295   dower? Art thou not horribly afraid? doth not thy blood thrill at it?

PRINCE. Not a whit, i' faith; I lack some of thy instinct.

FALSTAFF. Well, thou wilt be horribly chid tomorrow when thou comest
to thy father; if thou love me, practice an answer.

---

3. "Fire" and the allusions to "meteors" and "exhalations" (shooting stars) refer to Bardolph's red nose.
4. I.e., drunkenness and poverty.
5. Hangman's noose, with a pun on *collar*. "Choler":
fiery complexion, indicating a choleric (angry) temperament.
6. Padding, stuffing.
7. A beating, cudgeling. "Amamon": a devil.
8. A long spear with a hook on it.
9. Scots.

PRINCE. Do thou stand for[1] my father and examine me upon the particu-
300   lars of my life.

FALSTAFF. Shall I? Content. This chair shall be my state,[2] this dagger my
      scepter, and this cushion my crown.

PRINCE. Thy state is taken for a joint-stool,[3] thy golden scepter for a
      leaden dagger, and thy precious rich crown for a pitiful bald crown!

305   FALSTAFF. Well, an the fire of grace be not quite out of thee, now shalt
      thou be moved. Give me a cup of sack to make my eyes look red, that
      it may be thought I have wept, for I must speak in passion, and I will
      do it in King Cambyses'[4] vein.

PRINCE. Well, here is my leg.[5]

310   FALSTAFF. And here is my speech. Stand aside, nobility.

HOSTESS. O Jesu, this is excellent sport, i' faith!

FALSTAFF. Weep not, sweet queen, for trickling tears are vain.

HOSTESS. O, the father, how he holds his countenance!

FALSTAFF. For God's sake, lords, convey my tristful queen,

315   For tears do stop the floodgates of her eyes.[6]

HOSTESS. O Jesu, he doth it as like one of these harlotry players as ever I
      see!

FALSTAFF. Peace, good pint pot, peace, good ticklebrain. Harry, I do not
      only marvel where thou spendest thy time, but also how thou art
320   accompanied, for though the camomile,[7] the more it is trodden on the
      faster it grows, so youth, the more it is wasted the sooner it wears. That
      thou art my son, I have partly thy mother's word, partly my own opin-
      ion, but chiefly a villainous trick of thine eye and a foolish hanging of
      thy nether lip that doth warrant[8] me. If then thou be son to me, here
325   lies the point; why, being son to me, art thou so pointed at? Shall the
      blessed sun of heaven prove a micher[9] and eat blackberries? a question
      not to be asked. Shall the son of England prove a thief and take purses?
      a question to be asked. There is a thing, Harry, which thou hast often
      heard of and it is known to many in our land by the name of pitch.
330   This pitch, as ancient writers do report, doth defile; so doth the com-
      pany thou keepest: for, Harry, now I do not speak to thee in drink but
      in tears, not in pleasure but in passion, not in words only, but in woes
      also: and yet there is a virtuous man whom I have often noted in thy
      company, but I know not his name.

335   PRINCE. What manner of man, an it like[1] your majesty?

FALSTAFF. A goodly portly man, i' faith, and a corpulent; of a cheerful
      look, a pleasing eye and a most noble carriage, and, as I think, his age
      some fifty, or, by 'r Lady, inclining to threescore; and now I remember
      me, his name is Falstaff. If that man should be lewdly given, he deceiv-
340   eth me, for, Harry, I see virtue in his looks. If then the tree may be
      known by the fruit, as the fruit by the tree, then, peremptorily I speak
      it, there is virtue in that Falstaff; him keep with, the rest banish. And

1. Represent.
2. Throne.
3. An ordinary stool, made by a joiner (cabinetmaker).
4. Like the bombastic hero of the old play *Cambyses*.
5. I.e., he bows, makes an obeisance.
6. Falstaff's blank verse lines parody the old-fashioned tragedies of the 1570s and 1580s.

7. An aromatic herb. The style in this speech is a parody of Euphuism, the ornate, elaborate, balanced style made popular by Lyly's *Euphues*.
8. Assure.
9. Truant.
1. If it please.

tell me now, thou naughty varlet, tell me, where hast thou been this month?

345 PRINCE. Dost thou speak like a king? Do thou stand for me, and I'll play my father.

FALSTAFF. Depose me? if thou dost it half so gravely, so majestically, both in word and matter, hang me up by the heels for a rabbit-sucker[2] or a poulter's hare.

350 PRINCE. Well, here I am set.[3]

FALSTAFF. And here I stand; judge, my masters.

PRINCE. Now, Harry, whence come you?

FALSTAFF. My noble lord, from Eastcheap.

PRINCE. The complaints I hear of thee are grievous.

355 FALSTAFF. 'Sblood, my lord, they are false: nay, I'll tickle ye for a young prince, i' faith.

PRINCE. Swearest thou, ungracious boy? Henceforth ne'er look on me. Thou art violently carried away from grace; there is a devil haunts thee in the likeness of an old fat man; a tun[4] of man is thy companion. Why
360 dost thou converse with that trunk of humors, that bolting-hutch of beastliness, that swollen parcel of dropsies, that huge bombard[5] of sack, that stuffed cloak-bag of guts, that roasted Manningtree ox with the pudding in his belly, that reverend vice,[6] that gray iniquity, that father ruffian, that vanity in years? Wherein is he good, but to taste sack and
365 drink it? wherein neat and cleanly, but to carve a capon and eat it? wherein cunning, but in craft? wherein crafty, but in villainy? wherein villainous, but in all things? wherein worthy, but in nothing?

FALSTAFF. I would your grace would take me with you; whom means your grace?

370 PRINCE. That villainous abominable misleader of youth, Falstaff, that old white-bearded Satan.

FALSTAFF. My lord, the man I know.

PRINCE. I know thou dost.

FALSTAFF. But to say I know more harm in him than in myself were to
375 say more than I know. That he is old the more the pity, his white hairs do witness it; but that he is, saving your reverence, a whoremaster, that I utterly deny. If sack and sugar be a fault, God help the wicked! if to be old and merry be a sin, then many an old host that I know is damned; if to be fat be to be hated, then Pharaoh's lean kine[7] are to be loved.
380 No, my good lord, banish Peto, banish Bardolph, banish Poins, but for sweet Jack Falstaff, kind Jack Falstaff, true Jack Falstaff, valiant Jack Falstaff, and therefore more valiant, being as he is old Jack Falstaff, banish not him thy Harry's company, banish not him thy Harry's company; banish plump Jack, and banish all the world.

385 PRINCE. I do, I will.   [⟨A knocking heard.⟩]
                                              [⟨Exeunt HOSTESS and BARDOLPH.⟩]
        [Enter BARDOLPH, running.]

2. Suckling rabbit.
3. Seated.
4. Large barrel.
5. Leather wine vessel. "Bolting-hutch": trough.
6. The Vice was a comic character in the old morality

plays. Falstaff is in some respects a descendant of this type character. "Manningtree": a town in Essex, noted for barbecues. "Pudding": sausage.
7. In the dream Joseph interpreted (Genesis 41.19–21).

BARDOLPH. O, my lord, my lord, the sheriff with a most monstrous watch
   is at the door.
FALSTAFF. Out, ye rogue! Play out the play; I have much to say in the
   behalf of that Falstaff.
   [*Enter the* HOSTESS.]
390   HOSTESS. O Jesu, my lord, my lord!
FALSTAFF. Heigh, heigh! the devil rides upon a fiddlestick;[8] what's the
   matter?
HOSTESS. The sheriff and all the watch are at the door; they are come to
   search the house. Shall I let them in?
395   FALSTAFF. Dost thou hear, Hal? never call a true piece of gold a counterfeit; thou art essentially mad, without seeming so.[9]
PRINCE. And thou a natural coward, without instinct.
FALSTAFF. I deny your major;[1] if you will deny the sheriff, so; if not, let
   him enter. If I become not a cart as well as another man, a plague on
400   my bringing up! I hope I shall as soon be strangled with a halter as
   another.[2]
PRINCE. Go hide thee behind the arras; the rest walk up above.[3] Now my
   masters, for a true face and good conscience.
FALSTAFF. Both which I have had; but their date is out,[4] and therefore I'll
405   hide me.
PRINCE. Call in the sheriff.
                      [*Exeunt ⟨all except the* PRINCE *and* POINS.⟩]
         [*Enter* SHERIFF *and the* CARRIER.]
   Now, master sheriff, what is your will with me?
SHERIFF. First pardon me, my lord. A hue and cry
   Hath followed certain men unto this house.
410   PRINCE. What men?
SHERIFF. One of them is well known, my gracious lord,
   A gross fat man.
CAR.   As fat as butter.
PRINCE. The man, I do assure you, is not here,
   For I myself at this time have employed him,
415   And, sheriff, I will engage my word to thee
   That I will by tomorrow dinnertime
   Send him to answer thee or any man
   For anything he shall be charged withal;
   And so let me entreat you leave the house.
420   SHERIFF. I will, my lord. There are two gentlemen
   Have in this robbery lost three hundred marks.
PRINCE. It may be so; if he have robbed these men
   He shall be answerable; and so farewell.
SHERIFF. Good night, my noble lord.
425   PRINCE. I think it is good morrow, is it not?
SHERIFF. Indeed, my lord, I think it be two o'clock.
         [*Exeunt ⟨*SHERIFF *and* CARRIER.⟩]

---

8. I.e., there's a commotion.
9. I.e., don't give a true man (me, Falstaff) away as a
thief. He goes on to accuse the prince, in his reversal
of values in the play scene, of being out of his mind,
though he appears rational.
1. Your major premise (that I, Falstaff, am a coward).
2. I.e., I hope my fat neck will not make the process

of strangling on the gallows longer for me than for the
rest of you. The "cart" is the wagon on which criminals
were taken to be hanged.
3. On the balcony. "Arras": the hangings or draperies
that covered the walls.
4. Lease has expired.

PRINCE. This oily rascal is known as well as Paul's.[5] Go call him forth.

POINS. Falstaff!—Fast asleep behind the arras, and snorting like a horse.

PRINCE. Hark, how hard he fetches breath. Search his pockets. [*He sear-*
430   *cheth his pockets, and findeth certain papers.*] What hast thou found?

POINS. Nothing but papers, my lord.

PRINCE. Let's see what they be: read them.

POINS. [*reads*] "Item, a capon .   .   .   .   .   2s. 2d.
                        Item, sauce.   .   .   .   .   .   4d.
435   Item, sack, two gallons . . 5s. 8d.
                        Item, anchovies and sack
                              after supper .   .   .   .   2s. 6d.
                        Item, bread .   .   .   .   .   .   ob."[6]

PRINCE. O monstrous! but one halfpennyworth of bread to this intolerable
440   deal of sack! What there is else, keep close; we'll read it at more advan-
         tage; there let him sleep till day. I'll to the court in the morning. We
         must all to the wars, and thy place shall be honorable. I'll procure this
         fat rogue a charge of foot,[7] and I know his death will be a march of
         twelvescore. The money shall be paid back again with advantage. Be
445   with me betimes[8] in the morning, and so good morrow, Poins.

POINS. Good morrow, good my lord.   [*Exeunt.*]

Act 3

SCENE 1

[*Enter* HOTSPUR, WORCESTER, LORD MORTIMER, *and* OWEN GLEN-
DOWER.]

MORTIMER. These promises are fair, the parties sure,
         And our induction° full of prosperous hope.   *initial step*

HOTSPUR. Lord Mortimer, and cousin Glendower,
         Will you sit down?
5   And uncle Worcester; a plague upon it,
         I have forgot the map.

GLENDOWER.   No, here it is.
         Sit, cousin Percy, sit, good cousin Hotspur,
         For by that name as oft as Lancaster[9]
         Doth speak of you, his cheek looks pale and with
10   A rising sigh he wisheth you in heaven.

HOTSPUR. And you in hell as often as he hears Owen Glendower spoke
         of.

GLENDOWER. I cannot blame him; at my nativity
         The front° of heaven was full of fiery shapes,   *forehead*
15   Of burning cressets,° and at my birth   *lamps*
         The frame and huge foundation of the earth
         Shaked like a coward.

HOTSPUR. Why, so it would have done at the same season if your mother's
         cat had but kittened, though yourself had never been born.
20   GLENDOWER. I say the earth did shake when I was born.

---

5. St. Paul's Cathedral.
6. Oble, a halfpenny.
7. Company of infantry.

8. Early. "Twelvescore": i.e., 240 yards.
9. I.e., King Henry IV. To call him by his lesser title
is insulting.

HOTSPUR. And I say the earth was not of my mind,
    If you suppose as fearing you it shook.
GLENDOWER. The heavens were all on fire, the earth did tremble.
HOTSPUR. O then the earth shook to see the heavens on fire,
25   And not in fear of your nativity.
    Diseasèd nature oftentimes breaks forth
    In strange eruptions; oft the teeming earth
    Is with a kind of colic pinched and vexed
    By the imprisoning of unruly wind
30   Within her womb, which for enlargement striving
    Shakes the old beldam° earth and topples down   *old woman*
    Steeples and moss-grown towers. At your birth
    Our grandam earth, having this distemperature,°   *ailment*
    In passion shook.
GLENDOWER.   Cousin, of many men
35   I do not bear these crossings. Give me leave
    To tell you once again that at my birth
    The front of heaven was full of fiery shapes,
    The goats ran from the mountains, and the herds
    Were strangely clamorous to the frighted fields.
40   These signs have marked me extraordinary,
    And all the courses of my life do show
    I am not in the roll of common men.
    Where is he living, clipped in with[1] the sea
    That chides the banks of England, Scotland, Wales,
45   Which calls me pupil or hath read to me?
    And bring him out that is but woman's son
    Can trace me in the tedious ways of art[2]
    And hold me pace in deep experiments.
HOTSPUR. I think there's no man speaks better Welsh. I'll to dinner.
50 MORTIMER. Peace, cousin Percy; you will make him mad.
GLENDOWER. I can call spirits from the vasty deep.
HOTSPUR. Why, so can I, or so can any man;
    But will they come when you do call for them?
GLENDOWER. Why, I can teach you, cousin, to command
    the devil.
55 HOTSPUR. And I can teach thee, coz, to shame the devil
    By telling truth; tell truth and shame the devil.[3]
    If thou have power to raise him, bring him hither,
    And I'll be sworn I have power to shame him hence.
    O, while you live, tell truth and shame the devil!
60 MORTIMER. Come, come, no more of this unprofitable chat.
GLENDOWER. Three times hath Henry Bullingbrook made head
    Against my power, thrice from the banks of Wye
    And sandy-bottomed Severn have I sent him
    Bootless[4] home and weather-beaten back.
65 HOTSPUR. Home without boots, and in foul weather too!

---

1. Within the limits of.
2. Follow me in practicing difficult magic.
3. A proverb.

4. Unsuccessful; but Hotspur takes it in the other sense.

How 'scapes he agues,° in the devil's name?   *fevers and chills*
GLENDOWER. Come, here is the map; shall we divide our right
    According to our threefold order ta'en?⁵
MORTIMER. The archdeacon hath divided it
70   Into three limits very equally:
    England, from Trent and Severn hitherto,
    By south and east is to my part assigned;
    All westward, Wales beyond the Severn shore,
    And all the fertile land within that bound,
75   To Owen Glendower; and, dear coz, to you
    The remnant northward lying off from Trent.
    And our indentures tripartite are drawn,
    Which being sealèd interchangeably,
    A business that this night may execute,
80   Tomorrow, cousin Percy, you and I
    And my good Lord of Worcester will set forth
    To meet your father and the Scottish power,
    As is appointed us, at Shrewsbury.
    My father⁶ Glendower is not ready yet,
85   Nor shall we need his help these fourteen days.
    Within that space you may have drawn together
    Your tenants, friends, and neighboring gentlemen.
GLENDOWER. A shorter time shall send me to you, lords,
    And in my conduct shall your ladies come,
90   From whom you now must steal and take no leave,
    For there will be a world of water shed
    Upon the parting of your wives and you.
HOTSPUR. Methinks my moiety,° north from Burton here,   *share*
    In quantity equals not one of yours;
95   See how this river comes me cranking° in,   *curving*
    And cuts me from the best of all my land
    A huge half-moon, a monstrous cantle° out.   *corner*
    I'll have the current in this place dammed up;
    And here the smug° and silver Trent shall run   *smooth*
100   In a new channel, fair and evenly;
    It shall not wind with such a deep indent
    To rob me of so rich a bottom° here.   *valley*
GLENDOWER. Not wind? it shall, it must; you see it doth.
MORTIMER. Yea, but
105   Mark how he bears his course, and runs me up
    With like advantage on the other side;
    Gelding the opposèd continent⁷ as much
    As on the other side it takes from you.
WORCESTER. Yea, but a little charge will trench him here
110   And on this north side win this cape of land,
    And then he runs straight and even.
HOTSPUR. I'll have it so; a little charge will do it.
GLENDOWER. I'll not have it altered.

---

5. Divide our property according to the arrangement   6. Father-in-law.
for division into three parts.   7. I.e., cutting off from the opposite side.

HOTSPUR.   Will not you?
GLENDOWER. No, nor you shall not.
HOTSPUR.   Who shall say me nay?
115   GLENDOWER. Why, that will I.
HOTSPUR. Let me not understand you then; speak it in Welsh.
GLENDOWER. I can speak English, lord, as well as you,
   For I was trained up in the English court,
   Where, being but young, I framèd to the harp
120   Many an English ditty lovely well
   And gave the tongue a helpful ornament,
   A virtue that was never seen in you.
HOTSPUR. Marry,
   And I am glad of it with all my heart;
125   I had rather be a kitten and cry mew
   Than one of these same meter ballad-mongers;
   I had rather hear a brazen canstick turned,[8]
   Or a dry wheel grate on the axletree,
   And that would set my teeth nothing on edge,
130   Nothing so much as mincing° poetry;   *affected*
   'Tis like the forced gait of a shuffling° nag.   *hobbled*
GLENDOWER. Come, you shall have Trent turned.
HOTSPUR. I do not care; I'll give thrice so much land
   To any well-deserving friend;
135   But in the way of bargain, mark ye me,
   I'll cavil° on the ninth part of a hair.   *quibble*
   Are the indentures drawn? shall we be gone?
GLENDOWER. The moon shines fair; you may be away by night.
   I'll haste the writer, and withal
140   Break with° your wives of your departure hence.   *inform*
   I am afraid my daughter will run mad,
   So much she doteth on her Mortimer.   [*Exit.*]
MORTIMER. Fie, cousin Percy, how you cross my father!
HOTSPUR. I cannot choose; sometime he angers me
145   With telling me of the moldwarp[9] and the ant,
   Of the dreamer Merlin and his prophecies,
   And of a dragon and a finless fish,
   A clip-winged griffin and a molten raven,
   A couching lion and a ramping[1] cat,
150   And such a deal of skimble-skamble stuff
   As puts me from my faith. I tell you what;
   He held me last night at least nine hours
   In reckoning up the several devils' names
   That were his lackeys. I cried "hum" and "well, go to,"
155   But marked him not a word. O, he is as tedious
   As a tired horse, a railing° wife,   *nagging*
   Worse than a smoky house. I had rather live
   With cheese and garlic in a windmill,[2] far,

---

8. A brass candlestick turned on a lathe.
9. Mole. According to the chronicler Holinshed there
were prophecies in which Henry IV was referred to as
"a moldwarp, cursed of God." Merlin was the famous
prophet of King Arthur's court; many later prophecies
were attributed to him.

1. "Couching" and "ramping" are Hotspur's versions
of the heraldic terms "couchant" (lying down) and
"rampant" (erect, on hind feet).
2. Cheese and garlic would be smelly, and the living
quarters in a mill would be noisy.

Than feed on cates° and have him talk to me   *delicacies*
160   In any summer house in Christendom.
        MORTIMER. In faith, he is a worthy gentleman,
        Exceedingly well read, and profited
        In strange concealments,³ valiant as a lion
        And wondrous affable and as bountiful
165   As mines of India. Shall I tell you, cousin?
        He holds your temper° in a high respect   *character*
        And curbs himself even of his natural scope
        When you come 'cross his humor; faith, he does.
        I warrant you that man is not alive
170   Might so have tempted him as you have done
        Without the taste of danger and reproof;
        But do not use it oft, let me entreat you.
        WORCESTER. In faith, my lord, you are too willful-blame,
        And since your coming hither have done enough
175   To put him quite beside his patience.
        You must needs learn, lord, to amend this fault.
        Though sometimes it show greatness, courage, blood°—   *breeding,*
        And that's the dearest grace it renders you—   *bloodlines*
        Yet oftentimes it doth present harsh rage,
180   Defect of manners, want of government,°   *self-control*
        Pride, haughtiness, opinion,° and disdain;   *arrogance*
        The least of which haunting a nobleman
        Loseth men's hearts and leaves behind a stain
        Upon the beauty of all parts besides,
185   Beguiling them of commendation.
        HOTSPUR. Well, I am schooled; good manners be your speed!
        Here come our wives, and let us take our leave.
                [*Enter* GLENDOWER *with the ladies.*]
        MORTIMER. This is the deadly spite that angers me;
        My wife can speak no English, I no Welsh.
190   GLENDOWER. My daughter weeps; she will not part with you,
        She'll be a soldier too, she'll to the wars.
        MORTIMER. Good father, tell her that she and my aunt Percy
        Shall follow in your conduct speedily.
                [GLENDOWER *speaks to her in Welsh, and she answers him in the*
                same.]
        GLENDOWER. She is desperate here; a peevish self-willed harlotry,⁴ one
195   that no persuasion can do good upon.
                [*The lady speaks in Welsh.*]
        MORTIMER. I understand thy looks; that pretty Welsh
        Which thou pour'st down from these swelling heavens⁵
        I am too perfect in; and, but for shame,
        In such a parley should I answer thee.⁶
                [*The lady speaks again in Welsh.*]
200   I understand thy kisses and thou mine,
        And that's a feeling disputation,
        But I will never be a truant, love,

3. Experienced in secret mysteries.   5. I.e., tears from her eyes.
4. Wench; used affectionately, not seriously.   6. Cry likewise.

Till I have learned thy language, for thy tongue
Makes Welsh as sweet as ditties highly penned,
205   Sung by a fair queen in a summer's bower,
With ravishing division,° to her lute.   *musical variation*
GLENDOWER. Nay, if you melt, then will she run mad.
     [*The lady speaks again in Welsh.*]
MORTIMER. O, I am ignorance itself in this!
GLENDOWER. She bids you on the wanton rushes⁷ lay you down
210   And rest your gentle head upon her lap,
And she will sing the song that pleaseth you
And on your eyelids crown the god of sleep,
Charming your blood with pleasing heaviness,°   *drowsiness*
Making such difference 'twixt wake and sleep
215   As is the difference betwixt day and night
The hour before the heavenly-harnessed team⁸
Begins his golden progress in the east.
MORTIMER. With all my heart I'll sit and hear her sing;
By that time will our book,⁹ think, be drawn.
220 GLENDOWER. Do so:
And those musicians that shall play to you
Hang in the air a thousand leagues from hence,
And straight they shall be here; sit, and attend.
HOTSPUR. Come, Kate, thou art perfect in lying down; come, quick,
225   quick, that I may lay my head in thy lap.
LADY PERCY. Go, ye giddy goose.
     [*The music plays.*]
HOTSPUR. Now I perceive the devil understands Welsh,
And 'tis no marvel, he is so humorous.¹
By 'r Lady, he is a good musician.
230 LADY PERCY. Then should you be nothing but musical, for you are alto-
gether governed by humors. Lie still, ye thief, and hear the lady sing
in Welsh.
HOTSPUR. I had rather hear Lady, my brach,² howl in Irish.
LADY PERCY. Wouldst thou have thy head broken?
235 HOTSPUR. No.
LADY PERCY. Then be still.
HOTSPUR. Neither; 'tis a woman's fault.³
LADY PERCY. Now God help thee.
HOTSPUR. To the Welsh lady's bed.
240 LADY PERCY. What's that?
HOTSPUR. Peace! she sings.
     [*Here the lady sings a Welsh song.*]
HOTSPUR. Come, Kate, I'll have your song too.
LADY PERCY. Not mine, in good sooth.°   *truth*
HOTSPUR. Not yours, in good sooth! Heart! you swear like a comfitmaker's⁴
245   wife. "Not you, in good sooth," and "as true as I live," and "as God
shall mend me," and "as sure as day,"

---

7. The dry reeds used as a floor covering in Elizabe-   2. My bitch hound, Lady.
than England.   3. Hotspur sarcastically reverses the usual saying about
8. The horses of the sun.   women and talkativeness.
9. The indenture.   4. Confectioner's.
1. Capricious, governed by humors.

And givest such sarcenet° surety for thy oaths   *thin silk*
As if thou never walk'st further than Finsbury.[5]
Swear me, Kate, like a lady as thou art,
250   A good mouth-filling oath, and leave "in sooth,"
And such protest of pepper-gingerbread,
To velvet-guards and Sunday citizens.[6]
Come, sing.
LADY PERCY. I will not sing.
255   HOTSPUR. 'Tis the next way to turn tailor, or be redbreast teacher.[7] An the
indentures be drawn, I'll away within these two hours; and so, come in
when ye will.   [*Exit.*]
GLENDOWER. Come, come, Lord Mortimer, you are as slow
As hot Lord Percy is on fire to go.
260   By this our book is drawn; we will but seal,
And then to horse immediately.
MORTIMER.   With all my heart.   [*Exeunt.*]

SCENE 2

[*Enter the* KING, PRINCE OF WALES, *and others.*]
KING. Lords, give us leave; the Prince of Wales and I
Must have some private conference; but be near at hand,
For we shall presently have need of you.   [*Exeunt* LORDS.]
I know not whether God will have it so
5   For some displeasing service I have done,
That, in his secret doom, out of my blood[8]
He'll breed revengement and a scourge for me;
But thou dost in thy passages° of life   *actions*
Make me believe that thou art only marked
10   For the hot vengeance and the rod of heaven
To punish my mistreadings.° Tell me else,   *misdeeds*
Could such inordinate and low desires,
Such poor, such bare, such lewd,° such mean attempts,   *low*
Such barren pleasures, rude society
15   As thou art matched withal and grafted to
Accompany the greatness of thy blood
And hold their level with thy princely heart?
PRINCE. So please your majesty, I would I could
Quit[9] all offenses with as clear excuse
20   As well as I am doubtless° I can purge   *sure*
Myself of many I am charged withal;
Yet such extenuation let me beg,
As, in reproof of many tales devised
(Which oft the ear of greatness needs must hear)
25   By smiling pickthanks° and base newsmongers,°   *flatters/tattletales*
I may, for some things true, wherein my youth

---

5. A recreation ground outside London, frequented by
citizens and their wives on Sundays, but not by ladies
of Lady Percy's class.
6. "Pepper-gingerbread": i.e., such tame oaths, as
crumbly and unsubstantial as gingerbread. "Velvet-
guards": respectable people of the middle class, who
wore velvet stripes on their clothes. City folk out for a
stroll on Sunday.
7. I.e., it is the easiest way to become a tailor (supposedly tailors sang at their work) or a person who teaches
birds to sing. Hotspur is equally scornful of music and
of people who work for a living.
8. Unknown judgment, through my son.
9. Acquit myself of.

Hath faulty wandered and irregular,
Find pardon on my true submissiòn.
KING. God pardon thee; yet let me wonder, Harry,
30   At thy affections, which doth hold a wing
Quite from the flight of all thy ancestors.
Thy place in council thou hast rudely lost,
Which by thy younger brother is supplied,
And art almost an alien to the hearts
35   Of all the court and princes of my blood.
The hope and expectation of thy time[1]
Is ruined, and the soul of every man
Prophetically do forethink thy fall.
Had I so lavish of my presence been,
40   So common-hackneyed[2] in the eyes of men,
So stale and cheap to vulgar company,
Opinion,[3] that did help me to the crown,
Had still kept loyal to possessiòn
And left me in reputeless banishment,
45   A fellow of no mark nor likelihood.
By being seldom seen, I could not stir
But like a comet I was wondered at,
That men would tell their children "This is he";
Others would say "Where, which is Bullingbrook?"
50   And then I stole all courtesy from heaven,
And dressed myself in such humility.
That I did pluck allegiance from men's hearts,
Loud shouts and salutations from their mouths,
Even in the presence of the crownèd king.
55   Thus did I keep my person fresh and new,
My presence like a robe pontifical,
Ne'er seen but wondered at; and so my state,[4]
Seldom but sumptuous, showed like a feast
And wan° by rareness such solemnity.[5]   *won*
60   The skipping king, he ambled up and down
With shallow jesters and rash° bavin[6] wits,   *quick*
Soon kindled and soon burnt, carded his state,[7]
Mingled his royalty with cap'ring fools,
Had his great name profanèd with their scorns
65   And gave his countenance° against his name[8]   *authority*
To laugh at gibing boys and stand the push
Of every beardless vain comparative,[9]
Grew a companion to the common streets,
Enfeoffed himself to popularity,[1]
70   That, being daily swallowed by men's eyes,

---

1. Lifetime.
2. Cheapened, vulgarized.
3. Popularity, public opinion.
4. Public ceremonial appearances.
5. "Such solemnity": i.e., the greatest possible majestic effect.
6. Brushwood; the image is explained in the next line.
7. Degraded his royal dignity; "card" also means "to adulterate wine."
8. Reputation.
9. Tolerate the impertinent witticisms of every beardless youth.
1. Made himself the common property of the public.

They surfeited with honey and began
To loathe the taste of sweetness, whereof a little
More than a little is by much too much.
So when he had occasion to be seen
75 He was but as the cuckoo is in June,[2]
Heard, not regarded, seen, but with such eyes
As, sick and blunted with community,°   *commonness*
Afford no extraordinary gaze
Such as is bent on sunlike majesty
80 When it shines seldom in admiring eyes,
But rather drowsed and hung their eyelids down,
Slept in his face[3] and rendered such aspèct°   *looks*
As cloudy° men use to their adversaries,   *sullen*
Being with his presence glutted, gorged, and full.
85 And in that very line, Harry, standest thou,
For thou hast lost thy princely privilege
With vile participation.[4] Not an eye
But is a-weary of thy common sight,
Save mine, which hath desired to see thee more,
90 Which now doth that I would not have it do,
Make blind itself with foolish tenderness.
PRINCE. I shall hereafter, my thrice gracious lord,
Be more myself.
KING.   For all the world
As thou art to this hour was Richard then
95 When I from France set foot at Ravenspurgh,
And even as I was then is Percy now.
Now, by my scepter and my soul to boot,
He hath more worthy interest to the state
Than thou the shadow of succession;[5]
100 For of no right, nor color[6] like to right,
He doth fill fields with harness° in the realm,   *armor*
Turns head against the lion's armèd jaws,[7]
And, being no more in debt to years than thou,
Leads ancient lords and reverend bishops on
105 To bloody battles and to bruising arms.
What never-dying honor hath he got
Against renownèd Douglas! whose high deeds,
Whose hot incursions° and great name in arms   *raids*
Holds from all soldiers chief majority°   *superiority*
110 And military title capital[8]
Through all the kingdoms that acknowledge Christ.
Thrice hath this Hotspur, Mars in swaddling clothes,
This infant warrior, in his enterprises
Discomfited great Douglas, ta'en him once,
115 Enlargèd° him and made a friend of him,   *freed*

2. The cuckoo is noticed in April, when its song is first heard; by June it is commonplace.
3. I.e., yawned in his face.
4. Association with vile companions.
5. I.e., Hotspur's claim to the throne is more solid, because of his achievements, than is Hal's, which rests only on shadowy rights of succession by birth.
6. False pretense.
7. I.e., takes military action against the king's army.
8. Has the greatest reputation among soldiers.

To fill the mouth of deep defiance up[9]
And shake the peace and safety of our throne.
And what say you to this? Percy, Northumberland,
The Archbishop's grace of York, Douglas, Mortimer,
120   Capitulate[1] against us and are up.
But wherefore do I tell these news to thee?
Why, Harry, do I tell thee of my foes,
Which art my nearest and dearest enemy?
Thou that art like enough through vassal fear,
125   Base inclinatìon and the start of spleen,[2]
To fight against me under Percy's pay,
To dog his heels and curtsy at his frowns,
To show how much thou art degenerate.
    PRINCE. Do not think so; you shall not find it so;
130   And God forgive them that so much have swayed
Your majesty's good thoughts away from me.
I will redeem all this on Percy's head
And in the closing of some glorious day
Be bold to tell you that I am your son,
135   When I will wear a garment all of blood
And stain my favors° in a bloody mask,   features
Which, washed away, shall scour my shame with it;
And that shall be the day, whene'er it lights,
That this same child of honor and renown,
140   This gallant Hotspur, this all-praisèd knight,
And your unthought of Harry chance to meet
For every honor sitting on his helm—
Would they were multitudes, and on my head
My shames redoubled!—for the time will come
145   That I shall make this northern youth exchange
His glorious deeds for my indignities.
Percy is but my factor,° good my lord,   agent
To engross up° glorious deeds on my behalf,   collect, acquire
And I will call him to so strict account,
150   That he shall render every glory up,
Yea, even the slightest worship° of his time,   honor
Or I will tear the reckoning from his heart.
This in the name of God I promise here,
The which if He be pleased I shall perform,
155   I do beseech your majesty, may salve
The long-grown wounds of my intemperance;
If not, the end of life cancels all bands,°   bonds, debts
And I will die a hundred thousand deaths
Ere break the smallest parcel of this vow.
160   KING. A hundred thousand rebels die in this;
Thou shalt have charge and sovereign trust herein.
        [Enter BLUNT.]
How now, good Blunt? thy looks are full of speed.

9. I.e., to swell the chorus of defiance.   2. Unreasoning impulse.
1. Raise a head, revolt.

BLUNT. So hath the business that I come to speak of.
Lord Mortimer of Scotland hath sent word
165   That Douglas and the English rebels met
The eleventh of this month at Shrewsbury;
A mighty and a fearful head° they are,   *power*
If promises be kept on every hand,
As ever offered foul play in a state.
170   KING. The Earl of Westmoreland set forth today,
With him my son, Lord John of Lancaster,
For this advertisement° is five days old.   *news*
On Wednesday next, Harry, you shall set forward;
On Thursday we ourselves will march. Our meeting
175   Is Bridgenorth and, Harry, you shall march
Through Gloucestershire, by which account,°   *method*
Our business valued,³ some twelve days hence
Our general forces at Bridgenorth shall meet.
Our hands are full of business: let's away;
180   Advantage feeds him fat while men delay.⁴   [*Exeunt.*]

SCENE 3

[*Enter* FALSTAFF *and* BARDOLPH.]

FALSTAFF. Bardolph, am I not fall'n away vilely⁵ since this last action? do
I not bate? do I not dwindle? Why, my skin hangs about me like an old
lady's loose gown; I am withered like an old applejohn. Well, I'll repent,
and that suddenly, while I am in some liking;⁶ I shall be out of heart
5   shortly, and then I shall have no strength to repent. An I have not
forgotten what the inside of a church is made of, I am a peppercorn, a
brewer's horse. The inside of a church! Company, villainous company,
hath been the spoil of me.
BARDOLPH. Sir John, you are so fretful you cannot live long.
10   FALSTAFF. Why, there is it; come sing me a bawdy song, make me merry.
I was as virtuously given as a gentleman need to be: virtuous enough:
swore little; diced not above seven times a week; went to a bawdyhouse
not above once in a quarter—of an hour; paid money that I borrowed
three or four times; lived well and in good compass; and now I live out
15   of all order, out of all compass.
BARDOLPH. Why, you are so fat, Sir John, that you must needs be out of
all compass, out of all reasonable compass, Sir John.
FALSTAFF. Do thou amend thy face, and I'll amend my life; thou art our
admiral,⁷ thou bearest the lantern in the poop, but 'tis in the nose of
20   thee; thou art the Knight of the Burning Lamp.
BARDOLPH. Why, Sir John, my face does you no harm.
FALSTAFF. No, I'll be sworn; I make as good use of it as many a man doth
of a death's-head or a *memento mori.*⁸ I never see thy face but I think
upon hell-fire and Dives⁹ that lived in purple, for there he is in his

---

3. According to estimates.
4. I.e., the rebels' "advantage" (opportunity) grows as
the king's men delay.
5. Lose weight. "Last action": i.e., the Gadshill robbery.
6. In good condition, in the mood. "Applejohn": an

apple with a wrinkled skin.
7. Flagship.
8. I.e., a skull or some other reminder of death.
9. The rich man who would not give food to Lazarus
and was punished in hell for it (Luke 16.19–31).

25 robes, burning, burning. If thou wert any way given to virtue, I would
swear by thy face; my oath should be "By this fire, that's God's angel";
but thou art altogether given over, and wert indeed, but for the light in
thy face, the son of utter darkness. When thou ran'st up Gadshill in
the night to catch my horse, if I did not think thou hadst been an *ignis*
30 *fatuus* or a ball of wildfire,[1] there's no purchase in money. O, thou art
a perpetual triumph, an everlasting bonfire light![2] Thou hast saved me
a thousand marks in links[3] and torches, walking with thee in the night
betwixt tavern and tavern, but the sack that thou hast drunk me would
have bought me lights as good cheap at the dearest chandler's in
35 Europe. I have maintained that salamander[4] of yours with fire any time
this two and thirty years, God reward me for it.

BARDOLPH. 'Sblood, I would my face were in your belly!

FALSTAFF. God-a-mercy! so should I be sure to be heartburnt.

[*Enter* HOSTESS.]

How now, Dame Partlet[5] the hen! have you inquired yet who picked
40 my pocket?

HOSTESS. Why, Sir John, what do you think, Sir John? do you think I
keep thieves in my house? I have searched, I have inquired, so has my
husband, man by man, boy by boy, servant by servant; the tithe[6] of a
hair was never lost in my house before.

45 FALSTAFF. Ye lie, hostess; Bardolph was shaved and lost many a hair, and
I'll be sworn my pocket was picked. Go to, you are a woman, go.

HOSTESS. Who, I? no, I defy thee; God's light, I was never called so in
mine own house before.

FALSTAFF. Go to, I know you well enough.

50 HOSTESS. No, Sir John; you do not know me, Sir John. I know you, Sir
John; you owe me money, Sir John, and now you pick a quarrel to
beguile me of it; I bought you a dozen of shirts to your back.

FALSTAFF. Dowlas, filthy dowlas; I have given them away to bakers' wives,
and they have made bolters[7] of them.

55 HOSTESS. Now, as I am a true woman, holland of eight shillings an ell.[8]
You owe money here besides, Sir John, for your diet and by-drinkings,[9]
and money lent you, four and twenty pound.

FALSTAFF. He had his part of it; let him pay.

HOSTESS. He? alas, he is poor; he hath nothing.

60 FALSTAFF. How! poor? look upon his face; what call you rich? let them
coin his nose, let them coin his cheeks; I'll not pay a denier. What,
will you make a younker[1] of me? shall I not take mine ease in mine
inn but I shall have my pocket picked? I have lost a seal ring of my
grandfather's worth forty mark.[2]

65 HOSTESS. O Jesu, I have heard the prince tell him I know not how oft
that that ring was copper.

FALSTAFF. How! the prince is a Jack, a sneak-up;[3] 'sblood, an he were
here, I would cudgel him like a dog if he would say so.

---

1. A firework used for military purposes. "*Ignis fatuus*":
will-o'-the-wisp.
2. Illumination at a public festival.
3. Small torches carried at night.
4. Lizards that supposedly lived in fire and ate it.
"Chandler's": candlemaker's.
5. A nickname from the hen in Chaucer's *The Nun's
Priest's Tale*; in Shakespeare's time a conventional
name for a scolding woman.

6. Tenth part.
7. Sieves for flour. "Dowlas": a coarse cloth.
8. Forty-five inches. "Holland": fine linen.
9. Drinks between meals.
1. Youngster, novice. "Denier": French penny, worth
a tenth of an English penny.
2. A mark was worth two-thirds of a pound.
3. A sneak. "Jack": rascal.

[*Enter the* PRINCE ⟨*and* POINS⟩, *marching, and* FALSTAFF *meets them playing upon his truncheon like a fife.*]

How now, lad, is the wind in that door, i' faith? must we all march?

70 BARDOLPH. Yea, two and two, Newgate fashion.[4]

HOSTESS. My lord, I pray you hear me.

PRINCE. What say'st thou, Mistress Quickly? How doth thy husband? I love him well; he is an honest man.

HOSTESS. Good my lord, hear me.

75 FALSTAFF. Prithee let her alone, and list to me.

PRINCE. What say'st thou, Jack?

FALSTAFF. The other night I fell asleep here behind the arras and had my pocket picked; this house is turned bawdyhouse, they pick pockets.

PRINCE. What didst thou lose, Jack?

80 FALSTAFF. Wilt thou believe me, Hal? three or four bonds of forty pound apiece, and a seal ring of my grandfather's.

PRINCE. A trifle, some eightpenny matter.

HOSTESS. So I told him, my lord, and I said I heard your grace say so; and, my lord, he speaks most vilely of you, like a foulmouthed man as

85 he is, and said he would cudgel you.

PRINCE. What, he did not?

HOSTESS. There's neither faith, truth, nor womanhood in me else.

FALSTAFF. There's no more faith in thee than in a stewed prune, nor no more truth in thee than in a drawn[5] fox, and for womanhood Maid

90 Marian may be the deputy's wife of the ward[6] to thee. Go, you thing, go.

HOSTESS. Say, what thing, what thing?

FALSTAFF. What thing! why, a thing to thank God on.

HOSTESS. I am no thing to thank God on, I would thou shouldst know it;

95 I am an honest man's wife, and, setting thy knighthood aside,[7] thou art a knave to call me so.

FALSTAFF. Setting thy womanhood aside, thou art a beast to say otherwise.

HOSTESS. Say, what beast, thou knave, thou?

FALSTAFF. What beast? why, an otter.

100 PRINCE. An otter, Sir John, why an otter?

FALSTAFF. Why, she's neither fish nor flesh, a man knows not where to have her.[8]

HOSTESS. Thou art an unjust man in saying so; thou or any man knows where to have me, thou knave, thou!

105 PRINCE. Thou sayest true, hostess, and he slanders thee most grossly.

HOSTESS. So he doth you, my lord, and said this other day you ought[9] him a thousand pound.

PRINCE. Sirrah, do I owe you a thousand pound?

FALSTAFF. A thousand pound, Hal! A million. Thy love is worth a mil-

110 lion; thou owest me thy love.

HOSTESS. Nay, my lord, he called you Jack, and said he would cudgel you.

---

4. Chained together, like prisoners at Newgate.
5. Hunted. Stewed prunes were commonly served in bawdyhouses, as a supposed protection against venereal disease.
6. "Maid Marian" was a female character of low morals in the popular Robin Hood plays; a "deputy's wife of the ward" would be a respectable woman.

7. I.e., ignoring, or intending no disrespect to, the rank of knighthood. Falstaff intentionally misunderstands the phrase.
8. I.e., how to understand her. But the Hostess's retort is, unconsciously, equivalent to saying that she is completely promiscuous.
9. Owed.

FALSTAFF. Did I, Bardolph?

BARDOLPH. Indeed, Sir John, you said so.

115 FALSTAFF. Yea, if he said my ring was copper.

PRINCE. I say 'tis copper; darest thou be as good as thy word now?

FALSTAFF. Why, Hal, thou knowest, as thou art but man, I dare; but as thou art prince, I fear thee as I fear the roaring of the lion's whelp.

PRINCE. And why not as the lion?

120 FALSTAFF. The king himself is to be feared as the lion; dost thou think I'll fear thee as I fear thy father? Nay, an I do, I pray God my girdle[1] break.

PRINCE. O, if it should, how would thy guts fall about thy knees! But, sirrah, there's no room for faith, truth, nor honesty in this bosom of thine; it is all filled up with guts and midriff. Charge an honest woman

125 with picking thy pocket! Why, thou whoreson, impudent, embossed rascal[2] if there were anything in thy pocket but tavern-reckonings, memorandums of bawdyhouses, and one poor pennyworth of sugar candy to make thee long-winded, if thy pocket were enriched with any other injuries[3] but these, I am a villain. And yet you will stand to it,

130 you will not pocket up wrong; art thou not ashamed?

FALSTAFF. Dost thou hear, Hal? thou knowest in the state of innocency Adam fell, and what should poor Jack Falstaff do in the days of villainy? Thou seest I have more flesh than another man, and therefore more frailty.[4] You confess then, you picked my pocket?

135 PRINCE. It appears so by the story.

FALSTAFF. Hostess, I forgive thee; go make ready breakfast, love thy husband, look to thy servants, cherish thy guests; thou shalt find me tractable to any honest reason; thou seest I am pacified still.[5] Nay, prithee begone. [*Exit* HOSTESS.] Now, Hal, to the news at court; for the rob-

140 bery, lad, how is that answered?

PRINCE. O, my sweet beef, I must still be good angel to thee; the money is paid back again.

FALSTAFF. O, I do not like that paying back; 'tis a double labor.

PRINCE. I am good friends with my father and may do anything.

145 FALSTAFF. Rob me the exchequer the first thing thou doest, and do it with unwashed hands[6] too.

BARDOLPH. Do, my lord.

PRINCE. I have procured thee, Jack, a charge of foot.

FALSTAFF. I would it had been of horse.[7] Where shall I find one that can

150 steal well? O for a fine thief, of the age of two and twenty or there-abouts! I am heinously unprovided. Well, God be thanked for these rebels, they offend none but the virtuous; I laud them, I praise them.

PRINCE. Bardolph!

BARDOLPH. My lord?

155 PRINCE. Go bear this letter to Lord John of Lancaster, to my brother John; this to my Lord of Westmoreland. [*Exit* BARDOLPH.] Go, Poins, to horse, to horse; for thou and I have thirty miles to ride yet ere dinnertime. [*Exit* POINS.] Jack, meet me tomorrow in the Temple Hall at two o'clock in the afternoon.

---

1. Belt.
2. Swollen rascal.
3. Things, the loss of which you claim as injuries.
4. "The flesh is frail is proverbial" (cf. Matthew 26.41), meaning the flesh is weak.

5. Always easily pacified.
6. I.e., hastily.
7. Cavalry. "A charge of foot": command of a company of foot soldiers.

160 There shalt thou know thy charge, and there receive
Money and order for their furniture.⁸
The land is burning, Percy stands on high,
And either we or they must lower lie.   [⟨Exit.⟩]
FALSTAFF. Rare words, brave world! Hostess, my breakfast, come.
165 O, I could wish this tavern were my drum!⁹   [Exit.]

Act 4

SCENE 1

[*Enter* HOTSPUR, WORCESTER, *and* DOUGLAS.]
HOTSPUR. Well said, my noble Scot. If speaking truth
In this fine age were not thought flattery,
Such attribution° should the Douglas have   *praise*
As not a soldier of this season's stamp
5 Should go so general current¹ through the world.
By God, I cannot flatter; I do defy
The tongues of soothers,° but a braver² place   *flatterers*
In my heart's love hath no man than yourself;
Nay, task me to my word,³ approve° me, lord.   *prove, test*
10 DOUGLAS. Thou art the king of honor;
No man so potent breathes upon the ground
But I will beard him.⁴
HOTSPUR.   Do so, and 'tis well.
      [*Enter a* MESSENGER *with letters.*]
What letters hast thou there?—I can but thank you.
MESSENGER. These letters come from your father.
15 HOTSPUR. Letters from him! why comes he not himself?
MESSENGER. He cannot come, my lord; he is grievous sick.
HOTSPUR. Zounds! how has he the leisure to be sick
In such a justling° time? Who leads his power?   *turbulent*
Under whose government come they along?
20 MESSENGER. His letters bears his mind, not I, my lord.
WORCESTER. I prithee tell me, doth he keep his bed?
MESSENGER. He did, my lord, four days ere I set forth,
And at the time of my departure thence
He was much feared by his physicians.
25 WORCESTER. I would the state of time⁵ had first been whole
Ere he by sickness had been visited;
His health was never better worth than now.
HOTSPUR. Sick now! droop now! this sickness doth infect
The very lifeblood of our enterprise;
30 'Tis catching hither, even to our camp.
He writes me here that inward sickness—
And that his friends by deputation could not
So soon be drawn,⁶ nor did he think it meet

8. Furnishings, equipment.   3. Compare my actions with my speech.
9. Headquarters.   4. I.e., I will take on anybody, however powerful.
1. I.e., that not a soldier of this age's coinage should 5. Public affairs. "Feared by": feared for by.
achieve such currency.   6. Could not quickly be organized under a deputy.
2. More distinguished.

To lay so dangerous and dear a trust
35   On any soul removed[7] but on his own.
Yet doth he give us bold advertisement
That with our small conjunction[8] we should on
To see how fortune is disposed to us;
For, as he writes, there is no quailing now,
40   Because the king is certainly possessed°   *informed*
Of all our purposes. What say you to it?
WORCESTER. Your father's sickness is a maim to us.
HOTSPUR. A perilous gash, a very limb lopped off;
And yet in faith it is not; his present want[9]
45   Seems more than we shall find it. Were it good
To set the exact wealth of all our states
All at one cast, to set so rich a main
On the nice hazard[1] of one doubtful hour?
It were not good, for therein should we read
50   The very bottom and the soul of hope,[2]
The very list,° the very utmost bound   *limit*
Of all our fortunes.
DOUGLAS.   Faith, and so we should,
Where now remains a sweet reversiòn.[3]
We may boldly spend upon the hope of what
55   Is to come in;
A comfort of retirement[4] lives in this.
HOTSPUR. A rendezvous, a home to fly unto,
If that the devil and mischance look big
Upon the maidenhead of our affairs.[5]
60 WORCESTER. But yet I would your father had been here.
The quality and hair° of our attempt   *character*
Brooks° no division; it will be thought   *allows*
By some that know not why he is away
That wisdom, loyalty, and mere dislike
65   Of our proceedings kept the earl from hence.
And think how such an apprehensiòn
May turn the tide of fearful factiòn°   *conspiracy*
And breed a kind of question in our cause,
For well you know we of the off'ring° side   *challenging*
70   Must keep aloof from strict arbitrement,°   *investigation*
And stop all sight-holes, every loop° from whence   *loophole*
The eye of reason may pry in upon us.
This absence of your father's draws a curtain,
That shows the ignorant a kind of fear
Before not dreamt of.
75 HOTSPUR.   You strain too far.
I rather of his absence make this use:
It lends a luster and more great opinion,
A larger dare to our great enterprise,

---

7. Other person.
8. Unified forces.
9. Our present awareness of his absence.
1. Risky chance. "Main": stake, in betting.

2. Foundation and essence of our expectations.
3. A fund to be inherited in the future.
4. Sustaining place to fall back on.
5. I.e., threaten the beginning of our affairs.

Than if the earl were here, for men must think,
80   If we without his help can make a head
To push against a kingdom, with his help
We shall o'erturn it topsy-turvy down.
Yet all goes well, yet all our joints are whole.
DOUGLAS. As heart can think; there is not such a word
85   Spoke of in Scotland as this term of fear.
        [*Enter* SIR RICHARD VERNON.]
HOTSPUR. My cousin Vernon, welcome, by my soul!
VERNON. Pray God my news be worth a welcome, lord.
The Earl of Westmoreland, seven thousand strong,
Is marching hitherwards; with him Prince John.
HOTSPUR. No harm; what more?
90 VERNON.   And further I have learned
The king himself in person is set forth,
Or hitherwards intended speedily,
With strong and mighty preparatiòn.
HOTSPUR. He shall be welcome too. Where is his son,
95   The nimble-footed madcap Prince of Wales,
And his comrades that daft° the world aside   push
And bid it pass?
VERNON.   All furnished, all in arms,
All plumed like estridges° that with the wind   ostriches
Bated, like eagles having lately bathed,[6]
100   Glittering in golden coats like images,
As full of spirit as the month of May,
And gorgeous as the sun at midsummer,
Wanton as youthful goats, wild as young bulls.
I saw young Harry, with his beaver° on,   helmet
105   His cushes[7] on his thighs, gallantly armed,
Rise from the ground like feathered Mercury,
And vaulted with such ease into his seat,
As if an angel dropped down from the clouds,
To turn and wind° a fiery Pegasus[8]   direct
110   And witch the world with noble horsemanship.
HOTSPUR. No more, no more. Worse than the sun in March
This praise doth nourish agues.[9] Let them come;
They come like sacrifices in their trim,
And to the fire-eyed maid of smoky war[1]
115   All hot and bleeding will we offer them;
The mailèd Mars shall on his altar sit
Up to the ears in blood. I am on fire
To hear this rich reprisal° is so nigh   prise
And yet not ours. Come, let me taste my horse,
120   Who is to bear me like a thunderbolt
Against the bosom of the Prince of Wales;
Harry to Harry shall, hot horse to horse,

---

6. Eagles were supposed to renew their youth by bathing in the ocean. "Bated": fluttering their wings.
7. Cuisses, armor for the thighs.
8. A winged horse.

9. Fevers. Malaria was thought to be caused by vapors
from the marshes, drawn up by the sun in spring.
1. Bellona, goddess of war.

Meet and ne'er part till one drop down a corse.
O that Glendower were come!
VERNON.   There is more news;
125   I learned in Worcester, as I rode along,
He cannot draw his power² this fourteen days.
DOUGLAS. That's the worst tidings that I hear of yet.
WORCESTER. Aye, by my faith, that bears a frosty sound.
HOTSPUR. What may the king's whole battle° reach unto?   *army*
VERNON. To thirty thousand.
130   HOTSPUR.   Forty let it be;
My father and Glendower being both away,
The powers of us may serve so great a day.
Come, let us take a muster speedily;
Doomsday is near; die all, die merrily.
135   DOUGLAS. Talk not of dying; I am out of fear
Of death or death's hand for this one-half year.   [*Exeunt.*]

SCENE 2

[*Enter* FALSTAFF *and* BARDOLPH.]
FALSTAFF. Bardolph, get thee before to Coventry; fill me a bottle of sack,
our soldiers shall march through. We'll to Sutton Co'fil'³ tonight.
BARDOLPH. Will you give me money, captain?
FALSTAFF. Lay out, lay out.
5   BARDOLPH. This bottle makes an angel.⁴
FALSTAFF. An if it do, take it for thy labor; and if it make twenty, take
them all; I'll answer the coinage. Bid my lieutenant Peto meet me at
town's end.
BARDOLPH. I will, captain; farewell.   [*Exit.*]
10   FALSTAFF. If I be not ashamed of my soldiers, I am a soused gurnet. I have
misused the king's press⁵ damnably. I have got in exchange of a hundred and fifty soldiers three hundred and odd pounds. I press me none
but good householders, yeomen's sons, inquire me out contracted
bachelors, such as had been asked twice on the banns,⁶ such a
15   commodity of warm slaves as had as lieve hear the devil as a drum,
such as fear the report of a caliver⁷ worse than a struck fowl or a hurt
wild duck. I pressed me none but such toasts-and-butter⁸ with hearts in
their bellies no bigger than pins' heads, and they have bought out their
services, and now my whole charge consists of ancients,⁹ corporals,
20   lieutenants, gentlemen of companies, slaves as ragged as Lazarus in the
painted cloth where the glutton's dogs licked his sores, and such as
indeed were never soldiers, but discarded unjust serving-men, younger
sons to younger brothers, revolted tapsters and ostlers trade-fall'n,¹ the
cankers² of a calm world and a long peace, ten times more dishonor-
25   able ragged than an old-fac'd ancient,³ and such have I to fill up the

---

2. Assemble his forces.
3. Sutton Coldfield, about twenty-five miles from Coventry.
4. Ten shillings' worth.
5. The draft or impressment of soldiers into service.
"Soused gurnet": pickled anchovy.
6. Notice of approaching marriage, announced three
times publicly in church before the marriage could

take place.
7. Musket. "Commodity": collection. "Warm": well-
to-do.
8. Sissies.
9. Ensigns.
1. Hostlers out of work.
2. Canker worms.
3. Frayed flag.

rooms of them that have bought out their services, that you would
think that I had a hundred and fifty tattered prodigals lately come from
swine-keeping, from eating draff[4] and husks. A mad fellow met me on
the way and told me I had unloaded all the gibbets and pressed the
30   dead bodies. No eye hath seen such scarecrows. I'll not march through
Coventry with them, that's flat; nay, and the villains march wide betwixt
the legs, as if they had gyves[5] on, for indeed I had the most of them out
of prison. There's but a shirt and a half in all my company, and the half
shirt is two napkins tacked together and thrown over the shoul-
35   ders like a herald's coat without sleeves, and the shirt, to say the truth,
stolen from my host at Saint Alban's, or the red-nose innkeeper of
Daventry. But that's all one; they'll find linen enough on every hedge.[6]
      [*Enter the* PRINCE *and the* LORD OF WESTMORELAND.]
PRINCE. How now, blown Jack! how now, quilt![7]
FALSTAFF. What, Hal, how now, mad wag! what a devil dost thou in
40   Warwickshire? My good Lord of Westmoreland, I cry you mercy; I
thought your honor had already been at Shrewsbury.
WESTMORELAND. Faith, Sir John, 'tis more than time that I were there,
and you too; but my powers are there already. The king, I can tell you,
looks for us all; we must away all night.
45   FALSTAFF. Tut, never fear me; I am as vigilant as a cat to steal cream.
PRINCE. I think, to steal cream indeed, for thy theft hath already made
thee butter. But tell me, Jack, whose fellows are these that come after?
FALSTAFF. Mine, Hal, mine.
PRINCE. I did never see such pitiful rascals.
50   FALSTAFF. Tut, tut, good enough to toss,[8] food for powder, food for powder; they'll fill a pit as well as better; tush, man, mortal men, mortal
men.
WESTMORELAND. Aye, but, Sir John, methinks they are exceeding poor
and bare, too beggarly.
55   FALSTAFF. Faith, for their poverty I know not where they had that, and
for their bareness I am sure they never learned that of me.
PRINCE. No, I'll be sworn, unless you call three fingers[9] on the ribs bare.
But, sirrah, make haste; Percy is already in the field.
FALSTAFF. What, is the king encamped?
60   WESTMORELAND. He is, Sir John; I fear we shall stay too long.
FALSTAFF. Well,
      To the latter end of a fray and the beginning of a feast
      Fits a dull fighter and a keen guest.   [*Exeunt.*]

SCENE 3

      [*Enter* HOTSPUR, WORCESTER, DOUGLAS, *and* VERNON.]
HOTSPUR. We'll fight with him tonight.
WORCESTER.   It may not be.
DOUGLAS. You give him then advantage.
VERNON.   Not a whit.
HOTSPUR. Why say you so? looks he not for supply?

---

4. Garbage. The prodigal son, in the Bible, fed on   7. Padded material, a substitute for armor.
husks before returning to the paternal board.   8. I.e., on a pike, or long spear.
5. Leg-irons.   9. Layers of fat. A finger was three-quarters of an inch.
6. Laundry was customarily hung on hedges to dry.

VERNON. So do we.

HOTSPUR.   His is certain, ours is doubtful.

5 WORCESTER. Good cousin, be advised; stir not tonight.

VERNON. Do not, my lord.

DOUGLAS.   You do not counsel well;
You speak it out of fear and cold heart.

VERNON. Do me no slander, Douglas; by my life,
And I dare well maintain it with my life,

10   If well-respected honor[1] bid me on,
I hold as little counsel with weak fear
As you, my lord, or any Scot that this day lives.
Let it be seen tomorrow in the battle
Which of us fears.

DOUGLAS.   Yea, or tonight.

VERNON.   Content.

15 HOTSPUR. Tonight, say I.

VERNON. Come, come, it may not be. I wonder much,
Being men of such great leading as you are,
That you foresee not what impediments
Drag back our expedition;[2] certain horse

20   Of my cousin Vernon's are not yet come up,
Your uncle Worcester's horse came but today,
And now their pride and mettle is asleep,
Their courage with hard labor tame and dull,
That not a horse is half the half of himself.

25 HOTSPUR. So are the horses of the enemy
In general, journey-bated[3] and brought low;
The better part of ours are full of rest.

WORCESTER. The number of the king exceedeth ours;
For God's sake, cousin, stay till all come in.

     [*The trumpet sounds a parley. Enter* SIR WALTER BLUNT.]

30 BLUNT. I come with gracious offers from the king,
If you vouchsafe me hearing and respect.

HOTSPUR. Welcome, Sir Walter Blunt; and would to God
You were of our determination!
Some of us love you well, and even those some

35   Envy your great deservings and good name
Because you are not of our quality,[4]
But stand against us like an enemy.

BLUNT. And God defend° but still° I should stand so,   *forbid/always*
So long as out of limit and true rule

40   You stand against anointed majesty.
But to my charge. The king hath sent to know
The nature of your griefs, and whereupon
You conjure from the breast of civil peace
Such bold hostility, teaching his duteous land

45   Audacious cruelty. If that the king
Have any way your good deserts forgot,

---

1. Well-considered (not rash, like Hotspur's).
2. Retard our speed.

3. Tired from travel.
4. Fellowship, party.

Which he confesseth to be manifold,
He bids you name your griefs, and with all speed
You shall have your desires with interest
50   And pardon absolute for yourself and these
Herein misled by your suggestiòn.°   *temptation*
HOTSPUR. The king is kind, and well we know the king
Knows at what time to promise, when to pay.
My father and my uncle and myself
55   Did give him that same royalty he wears;
And when he was not six and twenty strong,
Sick in the world's regard, wretched and low,
A poor unminded outlaw sneaking home,
My father gave him welcome to the shore;
60   And when he heard him swear and vow to God
He came but to be Duke of Lancaster,
To sue his livery[5] and beg his peace,
With tears of innocency and terms of zeal,
My father, in kind heart and pity moved,
65   Swore him assistance and performed it too.
Now when the lords and barons of the realm
Perceived Northumberland did lean to him,
The more and less came in with cap and knee,[6]
Met him in boroughs, cities, villages,
70   Attended him on bridges, stood in lanes,
Laid gifts before him, proffered him their oaths,
Gave him their heirs as pages, followed him
Even at the heels in golden multitudes.
He presently, as greatness knows itself,
75   Steps me a little higher than his vow,
Made to my father while his blood was poor
Upon the naked shore at Ravenspurgh,
And now, forsooth, takes on him to reform
Some certain edicts and some strait° decrees   *strict*
80   That lie too heavy on the commonwealth,
Cries out upon abuses, seems to weep
Over his country's wrongs, and by this face,°   *pretense*
This seeming brow of justice, did he win
The hearts of all that he did angle for;
85   Proceeded further, cut me off the heads
Of all the favorites that the absent king
In deputation left behind him here,
When he was personal[7] in the Irish war.
BLUNT. Tut, I came not to hear this.
HOTSPUR.   Then to the point.
90   In short time after he deposed the king,
Soon after that deprived him of his life,
And in the neck of that tasked[8] the whole state;
To make that worse, suffered his kinsman March

---

5. I.e., claim title to his late father's lands (held by
King Richard II).
6. Cap in hand and on bended knee; i.e., offering
homage.
7. Actively participating in person.
8. I.e., immediately after that, (he) taxed.

(Who is, if every owner were well placed,
95   Indeed his king) to be engaged[9] in Wales,
There without ransom to lie forfeited;
Disgraced[1] me in my happy victories,
Sought to entrap me by intelligence,°   *spying*
Rated[2] mine uncle from the council board,
100   In rage dismissed my father from the court,
Broke oath on oath, committed wrong on wrong,
And in conclusion drove us to seek out
This head of safety,[3] and withal to pry
Into his title, the which we find
105   Too indirect for long continuance.
BLUNT. Shall I return this answer to the king?
HOTSPUR. Not so, Sir Walter; we'll withdraw awhile.
Go to the king, and let there be impawned°   *pledged*
Some surety° for a safe return again,   *guarantee*
110   And in the morning early shall mine uncle
Bring him our purposes; and so farewell.
BLUNT. I would you would accept of grace and love.
HOTSPUR. And may be so we shall.
BLUNT.   Pray God you do.   [*Exeunt.*]

SCENE 4

[*Enter the* ARCHBISHOP OF YORK *and* SIR MICHAEL.]
ARCHBISHOP. Hie, good Sir Michael; bear this sealèd brief°   *letter*
With wingèd haste to the lord marshal,
This to my cousin Scroop, and all the rest
To whom they are directed. If you knew
5   How much they do import you would make haste.
SIR MICHAEL. My good lord,
I guess their tenor.
ARCHBISHOP.   Like enough you do.
Tomorrow, good Sir Michael, is a day
Wherein the fortune of ten thousand men
10   Must bide the touch;[4] for, sir, at Shrewsbury,
As I am truly given to understand,
The king with mighty and quick-raisèd power
Meets with Lord Harry; and I fear, Sir Michael,
What with the sickness of Northumberland,
15   Whose power was in the first proportiòn,[5]
And what with Owen Glendower's absence thence,
Who with them was a rated[6] sinew too
And comes not in, o'er-ruled by prophecies—
I fear the power of Percy is too weak
20   To wage an instant trial with the king.
SIR MICHAEL. Why, my good lord, you need not fear;
There is Douglas and Lord Mortimer.

9. Pawned as a hostage.
1. I.e., did not favor.
2. Angrily dismissed.
3. Army for our safety.

4. Stand the test.
5. The largest part.
6. Highly regarded.

ARCHBISHOP. No, Mortimer is not there.

SIR MICHAEL. But there is Mordake, Vernon, Lord Harry Percy,

25   And there is my Lord of Worcester and a head
      Of gallant warriors, noble gentlemen.

ARCHBISHOP. And so there is; but yet the king hath drawn
      The special head⁷ of all the land together:
      The Prince of Wales, Lord John of Lancaster,

30   The noble Westmoreland, and warlike Blunt,
      And many more corrivals° and dear° men   *associates/noble*
      Of estimation and command in arms.

SIR MICHAEL. Doubt not, my lord, they shall be well opposed.

ARCHBISHOP. I hope no less, yet needful 'tis to fear,

35   And to prevent° the worst, Sir Michael, speed;   *forestall*
      For if Lord Percy thrive not, ere the king
      Dismiss his power, he means to visit° us,   *attack*
      For he hath heard of our confederacy,
      And 'tis but wisdom to make strong against him;

40   Therefore make haste. I must go write again
      To other friends; and so farewell, Sir Michael.   [*Exeunt.*]

Act 5

SCENE 1

[*Enter the* KING, PRINCE OF WALES, PRINCE JOHN OF LANCASTER,
SIR WALTER BLUNT, *and* FALSTAFF.]

KING. How bloodily the sun begins to peer
      Above yon busky° hill! The day looks pale   *wooded*
      At his distemp'rature.⁸

PRINCE.   The southern wind
      Doth play the trumpet to his purposes,⁹

5   And by his hollow whistling in the leaves
      Foretells a tempest and a blustering day.

KING. Then with the losers let it sympathize,
      For nothing can seem foul to those that win.

      [*The trumpet sounds. Enter* WORCESTER ⟨*and* VERNON.⟩]
      How now, my lord of Worcester! 'Tis not well

10   That you and I should meet upon such terms
      As now we meet. You have deceived our trust
      And made us doff our easy robes of peace,
      To crush° our old limbs in ungentle steel;   *enfold, cramp*
      This is not well, my lord, this is not well.

15   What say you to it? will you again unknit
      This churlish knot of all-abhorrèd war
      And move in that obedient orb¹ again
      Where you did give a fair and natural light,
      And be no more an exhaled meteor,²

20   A prodigy of fear and a portent

---

7. Principal army.
8. I.e., the sun's illness or malevolence.
9. I.e., the sun's intentions; the southern wind supports them.

1. Regular orbit, as of a planet.
2. Meteors were thought to be made of gas exhaled by a planet and were commonly associated with civil commotion.

        Of brochèd mischief to the unborn times?[3]
WORCESTER. Hear me, my liege:
        For mine own part I could be well content
        To entertain the lag end of my life
25   With quiet hours, for I do protest
        I have not sought the day of this dislike.
KING. You have not sought it! how comes it then?
FALSTAFF. Rebellion lay in his way, and he found it.
PRINCE. Peace, chewet,[4] peace!
30 WORCESTER. It pleased your majesty to turn your looks
        Of favor from myself and all our house,
        And yet I must remember° you, my lord,   *remind*
        We were the first and dearest of your friends.
        For you my staff of office did I break
35   In Richard's time, and posted day and night
        To meet you on the way and kiss your hand
        When yet you were in place and in account
        Nothing so strong and fortunate as I.
        It was myself, my brother, and his son
40   That brought you home and boldly did outdare
        The dangers of the time. You swore to us,
        And you did swear that oath at Doncaster,
        That you did nothing purpose 'gainst the state
        Nor claim no further than your new-fall'n[5] right,
45   The seat of Gaunt, dukedom of Lancaster.
        To this we swore our aid. But in short space
        It rained down fortune showering on your head
        And such a flood of greatness fell on you,
        What with our help, what with the absent king,
50   What with the injuries of a wanton time,
        The seeming sufferances° that you had borne,   *sufferings*
        And the contrarious winds that held the king
        So long in his unlucky Irish wars
        That all in England did repute him dead;
55   And from this swarm of fair advantages
        You took occasion to be quickly wooed
        To gripe the general sway[6] into your hand,
        Forgot your oath to us at Doncaster,
        And being fed by us you used us so
60   As that ungentle gull[7] the cuckoo's bird
        Useth the sparrow, did oppress our nest,
        Grew by our feeding to so great a bulk
        That even our love durst not come near your sight
        For fear of swallowing;[8] but with nimble wing
65   We were enforced for safety sake to fly
        Out of your sight and raise this present head,
        Whereby we stand opposèd by such means

---

3. I.e., of harm or disaster opened up ("broached") to plague the future. "Mischief" conveyed a stronger meaning to Shakespeare than it does to us.
4. Chattering bird.
5. Recently inherited.

6. Seize power over the whole state.
7. Rude nestling; the cuckoo hatches its young in other birds' nests.
8. Being swallowed.

As you yourself have forged against yourself
By unkind usage, dangerous countenance,[9]
70   And violation of all faith and troth
Sworn to us in your younger enterprise.
KING. These things indeed you have articulate,[1]
Proclaimed at market crosses, read in churches,
To face° the garment of rebellìon   *decorate*
75   With some fine color that may please the eye
Of fickle changelings and poor discontents,
Which gape and rub the elbow at the news
Of hurlyburly innovatìon;
And never yet did insurrection want
80   Such water colors to impaint his cause,
Nor moody beggars starving for a time
Of pellmell havoc and confusìon.
PRINCE. In both our armies there is many a soul
Shall pay full dearly for this encounter,
85   If once they join in trial. Tell your nephew
The Prince of Wales doth join with all the world
In praise of Henry Percy; by my hopes,
This present enterprise set off his head,[2]
I do not think a braver gentleman,
90   More active-valiant or more valiant-young,
More daring or more bold, is now alive
To grace this latter age with noble deeds.
For my part, I may speak it to my shame,
I have a truant been to chivalry—
95   And so I hear he doth account me too—
Yet this before my father's majesty:
I am content that he shall take the odds
Of his great name and estimatìon,
And will, to save the blood on either side,
100   Try fortune with him in a single fight.
KING. And, Prince of Wales, so dare we venture thee,
Albeit considerations infinite
Do make° against it. No, good Worcester, no,   *weigh*
We love our people well; even those we love
105   That are misled upon your cousin's part;
And, will they take the offer of our grace,
Both he and they and you, yea, every man
Shall be my friend again and I'll be his.
So tell your cousin, and bring me word
110   What he will do; but if he will not yield,
Rebuke and dread correction wait on° us   *accompany*
And they shall do their office. So, be gone;
We will not now be troubled with reply.
We offer fair; take it advisedly.
        [*Exit* WORCESTER ⟨*and* VERNON.⟩]
115   PRINCE. It will not be accepted, on my life;

9. Threatening looks.   2. Deducted from his account.
1. Drawn up in detail.

The Douglas and the Hotspur both together
Are confident against the world in arms.
KING. Hence, therefore, every leader to his charge,
For on their answer will we set on them,
120 And God befriend us, as our cause is just!
        [*Exeunt all but the* PRINCE *and* FALSTAFF.]
FALSTAFF. Hal, if thou see me down in the battle and bestride me, so; 'tis
    a point of friendship.
PRINCE. Nothing but a colossus can do thee that friendship. Say thy pray-
    ers, and farewell.
125 FALSTAFF. I would 'twere bedtime, Hal, and all well.
PRINCE. Why, thou owest God a death.   [⟨*Exit.*⟩]
FALSTAFF. 'Tis not due yet; I would be loath to pay him before his day.
    What need I be so forward with him that calls not on me? Well, 'tis no
    matter; honor pricks me on. Yea, but how if honor prick me off when
130 I come on? How then? can honor set to a leg? No. Or an arm? No. Or
    take away the grief³ of a wound? No. Honor hath no skill in surgery,
    then? No. What is honor? A word. What is in that word honor? what
    is that honor? Air. A trim reckoning!⁴ Who hath it? He that died o'
    Wednesday. Doth he feel it? No. Doth he hear it? No. 'Tis insensible,⁵
135 then? Yea, to the dead. But will it not live with the living? No. Why?
    Detraction will not suffer it. Therefore I'll none of it; Honor is a mere
    scutcheon.⁶ And so ends my catechism.   [*Exit.*]

SCENE 2

[*Enter* WORCESTER *and* SIR RICHARD VERNON.]
WORCESTER. O no, my nephew must not know, Sir Richard,
    The liberal and kind offer of the king.
VERNON. 'Twere best he did.
WORCESTER.   Then are we all undone.
    It is not possible, it cannot be,
5   The king should keep his word in loving us;
    He will suspect us still and find a time
    To punish this offense in other faults.
    Suspicion all our lives shall be stuck full of eyes,
    For treason is but trusted like the fox
10 Who, ne'er so tame, so cherished and locked up,
    Will have a wild trick of his ancestors;
    Look how we can, or sad or merrily,
    Interpretation will misquote° our looks,   misinterpret
    And we shall feed like oxen at a stall,
15 The better cherished, still the nearer death.
    My nephew's trespass may be well forgot;
    It hath the excuse of youth and heat of blood
    And an adopted name of privilege,⁷
    A harebrained Hotspur, governed by a spleen.⁸
20 All his offenses live upon my head

---

3. Pain.   6. A coat of arms, often put on a tombstone.
4. A fine totaling of the bill.   7. A nickname that gives him privileges.
5. Not capable of being felt.   8. Impetuous temperament.

And on his father's; we did train° him on,   *entice*
And, his corruption being ta'en from us,[9]
We, as the spring of all, shall pay for all.
Therefore, good cousin, let not Harry know
25   In any case the offer of the king.
VERNON. Deliver what you will; I'll say 'tis so.
    Here comes your cousin.
        [*Enter* HOTSPUR ⟨*and* DOUGLAS.⟩]
HOTSPUR. My uncle is returned;
    Deliver up my Lord of Westmoreland.
30   Uncle, what news?
WORCESTER. The king will bid you battle presently.°   *immediately*
DOUGLAS. Defy him by the Lord of Westmoreland.
HOTSPUR. Lord Douglas, go you and tell him so.
DOUGLAS. Marry, and shall, and very willingly.   [*Exit.*]
35 WORCESTER. There is no seeming mercy in the king.
HOTSPUR. Did you beg any? God forbid!
WORCESTER. I told him gently of our grievances,
    Of his oath-breaking, which he mended thus,
    By now forswearing[1] that he is forsworn;
40   He calls us rebels, traitors, and will scourge
    With haughty arms this hateful name in us.
        [*Enter* DOUGLAS.]
DOUGLAS. Arm, gentlemen, to arms! for I have thrown
    A brave defiance in King Henry's teeth,
    And Westmoreland, that was engaged,[2] did hear it,
45   Which cannot choose but bring him quickly on.
WORCESTER. The Prince of Wales stepped forth before the king,
    And, nephew, challenged you to single fight.
HOTSPUR. O, would the quarrel lay upon our heads,
    And that no man might draw short breath today
50   But I and Harry Monmouth! Tell me, tell me,
    How showed his tasking?° seemed it in contempt?   *challenge*
VERNON. No, by my soul; I never in my life
    Did hear a challenge urged more modestly,
    Unless a brother should a brother dare
55   To gentle exercise and proof of arms.
    He gave you all the duties[3] of a man,
    Trimmed up your praises with a princely tongue,
    Spoke your deservings like a chronicle,
    Making you ever better than his praise
60   By still dispraising praise valued° with you;   *compared*
    And, which became him like a prince indeed,
    He made a blushing cital[4] of himself,
    And chid his truant youth with such a grace
    As if he mastered there a double spirit
65   Of teaching and of learning instantly.
    There did he pause; but let me tell the world,

9. Being attributed to.   3. Good qualities.
1. Swearing falsely.   4. Mention, recital.
2. Held as a hostage.

If he outlive the envy° of this day,   *malice*
England did never owe° so sweet a hope,   *own*
So much miscònstrued in his wantonness.°   *frivolity*

70   HOTSPUR. Cousin, I think thou art enamoured
On his follies; never did I hear
Of any prince so wild a liberty.[5]
But be he as he will, yet once ere night
I will embrace him with a soldier's arm,
75   That he shall shrink under my courtesy.
Arm, arm with speed; and, fellows, soldiers, friends,
Better consider what you have to do
Than I, that have not well the gift of tongue,
Can lift your blood up with persuasiòn.
        [*Enter a* MESSENGER.]
80   MESSENGER. My lord, here are letters for you.
HOTSPUR. I cannot read them now.
O gentlemen, the time of life is short!
To spend that shortness basely were too long,
If life did ride upon a dial's point,
85   Still° ending at the arrival of an hour;[6]   *always*
And if we live, we live to tread on kings,
If die, brave death when princes die with us!
Now, for our consciences, the arms are fair,
When the intent of bearing them is just.
        [*Enter another* MESSENGER.]
90   MESSENGER. My lord, prepare, the king comes on apace.
HOTSPUR. I thank him that he cuts me from my tale,
For I profess not talking; only this—
Let each man do his best; and here draw I
A sword whose temper I intend to stain
95   With the best blood that I can meet withal
In the adventure of this perilous day.
Now, *Esperance! Percy!*[7] and set on.
Sound all the lofty instruments of war,
And by that music let us all embrace;
100   For, heaven to earth,[8] some of us never shall
A second time do such a courtesy.
        [*The trumpets sound. They embrace and exeunt.*]

SCENE 3

[*The* KING *enters with his power. Alarum*[9] *to the battle.
Then enter* DOUGLAS *and* SIR WALTER BLUNT.]
BLUNT. What is thy name, that in the battle thus
Thou crossest me? what honor dost thou seek
Upon my head?
DOUGLAS.   Know then, my name is Douglas,
And I do haunt thee in the battle thus

---

5. Reckless dissipation.   7. Hope, Percy! (the family motto).
6. Hotspur's meaning is that a base life would be too   8. I.e., the odds are heaven to earth that.
long even if it lasted only one hour. "Dial's point":   9. Trumpet signal.
hands of a clock.

5   Because some tell me that thou art a king.[1]

BLUNT. They tell thee true.

DOUGLAS. The Lord of Stafford dear° today hath bought   *expensively*
    Thy likeness, for instead of thee, King Harry,
    This sword hath ended him; so shall it thee,
10   Unless thou yield thee as my prisoner.

BLUNT. I was not born a yielder, thou proud Scot,
    And thou shalt find a king that will revenge
    Lord Stafford's death.   *[They fight. DOUGLAS kills BLUNT.]*
     [Enter HOTSPUR.]

HOTSPUR. O Douglas, hadst thou fought at Holmedon thus,
15   I never had triumphed upon a Scot.

DOUGLAS. All's done, all's won; here breathless lies the king.

HOTSPUR. Where?

DOUGLAS. Here.

HOTSPUR. This, Douglas? No, I know this face full well;
20   A gallant knight he was, his name was Blunt;
    Semblably furnished like the king himself.

DOUGLAS. Ah fool, go with thy soul whither it goes!
    A borrowed title hast thou bought too dear;
    Why didst thou tell me that thou wert a king?

25 HOTSPUR. The king hath many marching in his coats.

DOUGLAS. Now, by my sword, I will kill all his coats;
    I'll murder all his wardrobe, piece by piece,
    Until I meet the king.

HOTSPUR.   Up and away!
    Our soldiers stand full fairly for the day.   *[Exeunt.]*
     [Alarum. Enter FALSTAFF alone.]

30 FALSTAFF. Though I could 'scape shot-free[2] at London, I fear the shot
here; here's no scoring but upon the pate. Soft, who are you? Sir Walter
Blunt; there's honor for you, here's no vanity! I am as hot as molten
lead, and as heavy too; God keep lead out of me! I need no more weight
than mine own bowels. I have led my ragamuffins where they are pep-
35 pered; there's not three of my hundred and fifty left alive, and they are
for the town's end, to beg during life. But who comes here?
     [Enter the PRINCE.]

PRINCE. What, stand'st thou idle here? lend me thy sword;
    Many a nobleman lies stark and stiff
    Under the hoofs of vaunting enemies,
40   Whose deaths are yet unrevenged; I prithee, lend me thy sword.

FALSTAFF. O Hal, I prithee give me leave to breathe awhile. Turk Gregory[3] never did such deeds in arms as I have done this day. I have paid
Percy, I have made him sure.

PRINCE. He is indeed, and living to kill thee. I prithee, lend me thy sword.

45 FALSTAFF. Nay, before God, Hal, if Percy be alive, thou get'st not my
sword; but take my pistol if thou wilt.

PRINCE. Give it me; what, is it in the case?

---

1. Blunt and others are dressed to look like the king.
2. Scot-free, without paying the bill at a tavern. "Scor-ing" continues the pun; it means (1) marking up a charge, (2) cutting with a sword.

3. Falstaff combines Pope Gregory VII, of whom fantastic stories were told, with "Turk" (the Turks were noted for ferocity).

FALSTAFF. Aye, Hal; 'tis hot, 'tis hot; there's that will sack a city.
   [*The* PRINCE *draws it out, and finds it to be a bottle of sack.*]
PRINCE. What, is it a time to jest and dally now?
   [*He throws the bottle at him. Exit.*]
50 FALSTAFF. Well, if Percy be alive, I'll pierce him. If he do come in my
   way, so; if he do not, if I come in his willingly, let him make a car-
   bonado[4] of me. I like not such grinning honor as Sir Walter hath; give
   me life, which if I can save, so; if not, honor comes unlooked for, and
   there's an end.   [*Exit.*]

                                 SCENE 4

      [*Alarum. Excursions.*[5] *Enter the* KING, *the* PRINCE, PRINCE JOHN
         OF LANCASTER, *and* EARL OF WESTMORELAND.]
   KING. I prithee,
      Harry, withdraw thyself; thou bleed'st too much.
      Lord John of Lancaster, go you with him.
   LANCASTER. Not I, my lord, unless I did bleed too.
5   PRINCE. I beseech your majesty, make up,°   advance
      Lest your retirement do amaze° your friends.   dismay
   KING. I will do so.
      My Lord of Westmoreland, lead him to his tent.
   WESTMORELAND. Come, my lord, I'll lead you to your tent.
10 PRINCE. Lead me, my lord? I do not need your help,
      And God forbid a shallow scratch should drive
      The Prince of Wales from such a field as this,
      Where stained nobility lies trodden on,
      And rebels' arms triumph in massacres!
15 LANCASTER. We breathe too long; come, cousin Westmoreland,
      Our duty this way lies; for God's sake, come.
         [⟨*Exeunt* PRINCE JOHN *and* WESTMORELAND.⟩]
   PRINCE. By God, thou hast deceived me, Lancaster;
      I did not think thee lord of such a spirit.
      Before, I loved thee as a brother, John,
20   But now I do respect thee as my soul.
   KING. I saw him hold Lord Percy at the point
      With lustier maintenance than I did look for
      Of such an ungrown warrior.
   PRINCE.   O, this boy
      Lends mettle to us all!   [*Exit.*]
         [*Enter* DOUGLAS.]
25 DOUGLAS. Another king! they grow like Hydra's heads.[6]
      I am the Douglas, fatal to all those
      That wear those colors on them; what art thou,
      That counterfeit'st the person of a king?
   KING. The king himself, who, Douglas, grieves at heart
30   So many of his shadows° thou hast met   likenesses
      And not the very king. I have two boys
      Seek Percy and thyself about the field,

---

4. A cubed steak.   6. The heads of this fabulous monster grew back as
5. Brief appearances and exits of soldiers fighting.   fast as they could be cut off.

But seeing thou fall'st on me so luckily
I will assay thee; so defend thyself.
35 DOUGLAS. I fear thou art another counterfeit,
And yet, in faith, thou bearest thee like a king;
But mine I am sure thou art, whoe'er thou be.
And thus I win thee.
  [*They fight; the* KING *being in danger, enter* PRINCE OF WALES.]
PRINCE. Hold up thy head, vile Scot, or thou art like
40 Never to hold it up again! the spirits
Of valiant Shirley, Stafford, Blunt, are in my arms;
It is the Prince of Wales that threatens thee,
Who never promiseth but he means to pay.
  [*They fight;* DOUGLAS *flieth.*]
Cheerly, my lord; how fares your grace?
45 Sir Nicholas Gawsey hath for succor sent,
And so hath Clifton; I'll to Clifton straight.
KING. Stay, and breathe awhile.
Thou hast redeemed thy lost opinion,°   reputation
And showed thou makest some tender of⁷ my life
50 His fair rescue thou hast brought to me.
PRINCE. O God, they did me too much injury
That ever said I hearkened for your death.
If it were so, I might have let alone
The insulting hand of Douglas over you,
55 Which would have been as speedy in your end
As all the poisonous potions in the world
And saved the treacherous labor of your son.
KING. Make up to Clifton; I'll to Sir Nicholas Gawsey.   [*Exit.*]
  [*Enter* HOTSPUR.]
HOTSPUR. If I mistake not, thou art Harry Monmouth.
60 PRINCE. Thou speak'st as if I would deny my name.
HOTSPUR. My name is Harry Percy.
PRINCE.   Why then I see
A very valiant rebel of the name.
I am the Prince of Wales, and think not, Percy,
To share with me in glory any more:
65 Two stars keep not their motion in one sphere,°   orbit
Nor can one England brook° a double reign   endure
Of Harry Percy and the Prince of Wales.
HOTSPUR. Nor shall it, Harry, for the hour is come
To end the one of us; and would to God
70 Thy name in arms were now as great as mine!
PRINCE. I'll make it greater ere I part from thee,
And all the budding honors on thy crest
I'll crop to make a garland for my head.
HOTSPUR. I can no longer brook thy vanities.   [*They fight.*]
  [*Enter* FALSTAFF.]
75 FALSTAFF. Well said, Hal, to it, Hal! Nay, you shall find no boy's play
here, I can tell you.

7. I.e., you have some concern for.

[*Enter* DOUGLAS; *he fighteth with* FALSTAFF, *who falls down as if he were dead.* ⟨*Exit* DOUGLAS.⟩ *The* PRINCE *killeth* PERCY.]

HOTSPUR. O Harry, thou hast robbed me of my youth!
　　I better brook the loss of brittle life
　　Than those proud titles thou hast won of me;
80　　They wound my thoughts worse than thy sword my flesh;
　　But thought's the slave of life, and life time's fool,
　　And time, that takes survey of all the world,
　　Must have a stop. O, I could prophesy,
　　But that the earthy and cold hand of death
85　　Lies on my tongue; no, Percy, thou art dust,
　　And food for—　　　　　　　　　　　　　　　　　　[⟨*Dies.*⟩]
PRINCE. For worms, brave Percy; fare thee well, great heart!
　　Ill-weaved ambition, how much art thou shrunk!
　　When that this body did contain a spirit
90　　A kingdom for it was too small a bound,
　　But now two paces of the vilest earth
　　Is room enough; this earth that bears thee dead
　　Bears not alive so stout° gentleman.　　　　　　　　　　*valiant*
　　If thou wert sensible of courtesy,
95　　I should not make so dear° show of zeal;　　　　　　　　*open*
　　But let my favors hide thy mangled face[8]
　　And, even in thy behalf, I'll thank myself
　　For doing these fair rites of tenderness.
　　Adieu, and take thy praise with thee to heaven;
100　　Thy ignominy sleep with thee in the grave,
　　But not remembered in thy epitaph!
　　　　[*He spieth* FALSTAFF *on the ground.*]
　　What, old acquaintance, could not all this flesh
　　Keep in a little life? Poor Jack, farewell;
　　I could have better spared a better man.
105　　O, I should have a heavy miss of thee,
　　If I were much in love with vanity!°　　　　　　　　　　*frivolty*
　　Death hath not struck so fat a deer today,
　　Though many dearer,° in this bloody fray.　　　　　　　*nobler*
　　Emboweled° will I see thee by and by;　　　　　　　　*embalmed*
110　　Till then in blood by noble Percy lie.　　　　　　　　　[*Exit.*]
FALSTAFF. [*rising up*] Emboweled! if thou embowel me today, I'll give
　　you leave to powder[9] me and eat me tomorrow. 'Sblood, 'twas time to
　　counterfeit, or that hot termagant Scot had paid me scot and lot[1] too.
　　Counterfeit? I lie, I am no counterfeit; to die is to be a counterfeit, for
115　　he is but the counterfeit of a man who hath not the life of a man; but
　　to counterfeit dying when a man thereby liveth is to be no counterfeit,
　　but the true and perfect image of life indeed. The better part[2] of valor
　　is discretion, in the which better part I have saved my life. Zounds, I
　　am afraid of this gunpowder Percy, though he be dead; how if he should
120　　counterfeit too and rise? By my faith, I am afraid he would prove the
　　better counterfeit. Therefore I'll make him sure; yea, and I'll swear I
　　killed him. Why may not he rise as well as I? Nothing confutes me but

---

8. Prince Hal here covers Hotspur's face with a scarf.　　1. Completely. "Termagant": violent.
9. Pickle.　　　　　　　　　　　　　　　　　　　　2. Quality, not "portion."

eyes, and nobody sees me. Therefore, sirrah [*stabbing him*], with a new
wound in your thigh, come you along with me.

> [*He takes up* HOTSPUR *on his back.*]
> [*Enter the* PRINCE *and* JOHN OF LANCASTER.]

125 PRINCE. Come, brother John, full bravely hast thou fleshed°   initiated
Thy maiden sword.

LANCASTER.   But soft, whom have we here?
Did you not tell me this fat man was dead?

PRINCE. I did; I saw him dead,
Breathless and bleeding on the ground. Art thou alive?

130 Or is it fantasy° that plays upon our eyesight?   illusion
I prithee speak; we will not trust our eyes
Without our ears; thou art not what thou seem'st.

FALSTAFF. No, that's certain, I am not a double man; but if I be not Jack
Falstaff, then am I a Jack.³ There is Percy [*throwing the body down*]; if

135 your father will do me any honor, so; if not, let him kill the next Percy
himself. I look to be either earl or duke, I can assure you.

PRINCE. Why, Percy I killed myself and saw thee dead.

FALSTAFF. Didst thou? Lord, Lord, how this world is given to lying! I grant
you I was down and out of breath, and so was he; but we rose both at

140 an instant and fought a long hour by Shrewsbury clock. If I may be
believed, so; if not, let them that should reward valor bear the sin upon
their own heads. I'll take it upon my death, I gave him this wound in
the thigh; if the man were alive and would deny it, zounds, I would
make him eat a piece of my sword.

145 LANCASTER. This is the strangest tale that ever I heard.

PRINCE. This is the strangest fellow, brother John.
Come, bring your luggage nobly on your back;
For my part, if a lie may do thee grace,
I'll gild it with the happiest terms I have.

> [*A retreat is sounded.*]

150 The trumpet sounds retreat;⁴ the day is ours.
Come, brother, let us to the highest⁵ of the field,
To see what friends are living, who are dead.

> [*Exeunt ⟨*PRINCE OF WALES *and* LANCASTER.⟩]

FALSTAFF. I'll follow, as they say, for reward. He that rewards me, God
reward him! If I do grow great, I'll grow less, for I'll purge⁶ and leave

155 sack, and live cleanly as a nobleman should do.   [*Exit.*]

SCENE 5

> [*The trumpets sound. Enter the* KING, PRINCE OF WALES, PRINCE
> JOHN OF LANCASTER, EARL OF WESTMORELAND, *with* WORCESTER
> *and* VERNON *prisoners.*]

KING. Thus ever did rebellion find rebuke.
Ill-spirited Worcester, did not we send grace,
Pardon, and terms of love to all of you?
And wouldst thou turn our offers contrary,

5 Misuse the tenor of thy kinsman's trust?

---

3. I.e., a worthless fellow.
4. The signal to stop pursuit of the defeated enemy.
5. Highest part.

6. Take laxatives, also repent. "Grow great": i.e., become either earl or duke.

    Three knights upon our party slain today,
    A noble earl and many a creature else
    Had been alive this hour,
    If like a Christian thou hadst truly borne
10   Betwixt our armies true intelligence.
WORCESTER. What I have done my safety urged me to,
    And I embrace this fortune patiently,
    Since not to be avoided it falls on me.
KING. Bear Worcester to the death and Vernon too;
15   Other offenders we will pause upon.
        [*Exeunt* WORCESTER *and* VERNON ⟨*guarded.*⟩]
    How goes the field?
PRINCE. The noble Scot, Lord Douglas, when he saw
    The fortune of the day quite turned from him,
    The noble Percy slain, and all his men
20   Upon the foot of fear,[7] fled with the rest,
    And falling from a hill he was so bruised
    That the pursuers took him. At my tent
    The Douglas is, and I beseech your grace
    I may dispose of him.
    KING.   With all my heart.
25 PRINCE. Then, brother John of Lancaster, to you
    This honorable bounty shall belong;
    Go to the Douglas and deliver him
    Up to his pleasure, ransomless and free;
    His valor shown upon our crests today
30   Hath taught us how to cherish such high deeds
    Even in the bosom of our adversaries.
LANCASTER. I thank your grace for this high courtesy,
    Which I shall give away immediately.
KING. Then this remains, that we divide our power.
35   You, son John and my cousin Westmoreland,
    Towards York shall bend you with your dearest° speed   *greatest*
    To meet Northumberland and the prelate Scroop,
    Who, as we hear, are busily in arms;
    Myself and you, son Harry, will towards Wales
40   To fight with Glendower and the Earl of March.
    Rebellion in this land shall lose his sway,
    Meeting the check[8] of such another day;
    And since this business so fair is done,
    Let us not leave till all our own be won.   [*Exeunt.*]
                                        1598

---

7. Fleeing in panic.   8. (1) Hindrance, (2) rebuke.

Lyric Poets of the Sixteenth Century

The sixteenth century was a great age for poetry of all kinds, on every subject: amorous, religious, heroic, pastoral, didactic. Besides romantic epics like Spenser's *The Faerie Queene* and Ovidian narratives like Marlowe's *Hero and Leander*, there were also historical epics and philosophical poems, collections of pastoral eclogues and songs like Spenser's *The Shepheardes Calender*, and many lovely lyrics—ballads, madrigals, lute songs—intended to be set to music and sung. Songs were often incorporated in plays, sung by such characters as Shakespeare's Feste in *Twelfth Night*, Amiens in *As You Like It*, and Ariel in *The Tempest*. Poems on that most conventional topic, love, might take various conventional forms: invitations to love (like Marlowe's famous "Come live with me and be my love"), valedictions, complaints and laments, and palinodes (renunciations of love).

The last decade of the sixteenth century saw the publication of a dozen or so sonnet sequences imitating Petrarch and his French imitators; the most notable are by Sidney, Spenser, and Shakespeare. Such sequences have a loose plot framework marking the stages of a love relationship, from its starting point in the lover's attraction to the lady's beauty, through various trials, sufferings, conflicts, and occasional encouragements, to a conclusion in which nothing is resolved. The poet undertook to display all the conflicting feelings of a lover—hope and despair, tenderness and bitterness, exultation and anguish—by the use of "conceits" (ingenious comparisons): for example, in love he both burns and freezes, his sighs are as winds, he tosses on a stormy sea. In addition, the Elizabethan sequences reflect the anxieties and tensions of courtiership, in which the poet-client's relation to his patron or to the great queen is an analogue of the lover's service to the high-born lady who rejects him.

Making verse was among the expected accomplishments of cultivated Elizabethans—courtiers, statesmen, explorers, clergymen, soldiers, lawyers, noblemen and noblewomen, and queens. Aristocrats and courtiers usually did not publish their verse, as that would have been beneath them; such poems circulated in manuscript and were copied into manuscript books, often without much care for identifying authorship. By far the largest number of poems—in manuscript or in print— were occasional, often written to attract or please patrons: an example is Aemilia Lanyer's *The Description of Cooke-ham*, celebrating the sometime residence of the countess of Cumberland.

SIR THOMAS WYATT THE ELDER
1503–1542

Thomas Wyatt was born in Kent, was educated at St. John's College, Cambridge, and spent most of his life as a courtier and diplomat. He served King Henry VIII as clerk of the king's jewels, as ambassador to Spain and to Emperor Charles V, and as a member of various missions to France and Italy. His extensive experience abroad stimulated his interest in foreign literature, leading him to translate and imitate Petrarch and other Italian sonneteers. In 1541 he was charged with treason, lodged in the Tower of London, and stripped of his property, but was granted a pardon and regained the king's favor. Several of his poems reflect his experience with court intrigue.

Wyatt introduced the sonnet into English literature. Several of his sonnets ("The Long Love" is an example) are versions of sonnets by Petrarch, and many employ Petrarchan subject matter and topics: the abject, despairing lover; the cold, aloof lady; the lover's doleful complaints; elaborate conceits or comparisons rendering the lover's torments and passions. However, his most common sonnet rhyme scheme—*abba abba cddc ee*—shows a tendency to overlay the Italian structure of octave and sestet with what will become the typical English form of three quatrains and a couplet. Wyatt also wrote many delightful lyrics with short stanzas and refrains in the manner of the native English "ballet" or dance song. Stylistically, his verse often displays a rough vigor rather than regularity of accent and smoothness of rhythm. A large number of Wyatt's poems were published, fifteen years after his death, in the most important midcentury collection of poetry: *Tottel's Miscellany* (1557) contained 271 poems, of which 91 were attributed to Wyatt and the rest to assorted named and unnamed authors.

The Long Love That in My Thought Doth Harbor[1]

The long love that in my thought doth harbor,
And in mine heart doth keep his residence,
Into my face presseth with bold pretense
And therein campeth, spreading his banner.[2]
She that me learneth to love and suffer   5
And will that my trust and lust's negligence[3]
Be reined by reason, shame,[4] and reverence
With his hardiness taketh displeasure.
Wherewithal unto the heart's forest he fleeth,
Leaving his enterprise with pain and cry,   10
And there him hideth, and not appeareth.
What may I do, when my master feareth,
But in the field with him to live and die?
For good is the life ending faithfully.

                                                                E. MS.

Whoso List to Hunt[1]

Whoso list[2] to hunt, I know where is an hind,
But as for me, alas, I may no more.

1. Wyatt's version of Petrarch's *Rime* 140; his younger friend, the earl of Surrey, also translated it (p. 553).
2. I.e., the poet's blush. The first four lines of this sonnet introduce the "conceit" (or elaborately sustained metaphor) of love as a kind of warrior who, "with bold pretense" (i.e., making bold claim), flaunts his warlike presence by means of the "banner." Elaborate metaphors of this kind are found often in Elizabethan love poetry and sometimes, as in this instance, an entire sonnet will turn on a single conceit.
3. I.e., my open and careless revelation of my love.

"Learneth": teaches.
4. Modesty, shamefastness.
1. An adaptation of Petrarch's *Rime* 190, perhaps influenced by commentators on Petrarch, who said that *Noli me tangere quia Caesaris sum* ("Touch me not, for I am Caesar's") was inscribed on the collars of Caesar's hinds, which were then set free and were presumably safe from hunters. Wyatt's sonnet is usually supposed to refer to Anne Boleyn, in whom Henry VIII became interested in 1526.
2. Cares.

The vain travail hath wearied me so sore
I am of them that farthest cometh behind.
Yet may I, by no means, my wearied mind   5
Draw from the deer, but as she fleeth afore,
Fainting I follow. I leave off therefore,
Since in a net I seek to hold the wind.
Who list her hunt, I put him out of doubt,
As well as I, may spend his time in vain.   10
And graven with diamonds in letters plain
There is written, her fair neck round about,
"*Noli me tangere*, for Caesar's I am,
And wild for to hold, though I seem tame."

E. MS.

My Lute, Awake!

My lute, awake! Perform the last
Labor that thou and I shall waste,
And end that I have now begun;
For when this song is sung and past,
My lute, be still, for I have done.   5

As to be heard where ear is none,
As lead to grave in marble stone[1]
My song may pierce her heart as soon.
Should we then sigh or sing or moan?
No, no, my lute, for I have done.   10

The rocks do not so cruelly
Repulse the waves continually
As she my suit and affection.
So that I am past remedy,
Whereby my lute and I have done.   15

Proud of the spoil that thou hast got
Of simple hearts, thorough love's shot;
By whom, unkind, thou hast them won,
Think not he hath his bow forgot,
Although my lute and I have done.   20

Vengeance shall fall on thy disdain
That makest but game on earnest pain.
Think not alone under the sun
Unquit to cause thy lovers plain,[2]
Although my lute and I have done.   25

Perchance thee lie withered and old
The winter nights that are so cold,

---

1. I.e., when sound may be heard with no ear to hear
it or when soft lead is able to carve ("grave") hard
marble.
2. To complain. "Unquit": unrevenged.

Plaining in vain unto the moon.
Thy wishes then dare not be told.
Care then who list,[3] for I have done.   30

And then may chance thee to repent
The time that thou hast lost and spent
To cause thy lovers sigh and swoon.
Then shalt thou know beauty but lent,
And wish and want as I have done.   35

Now cease, my lute. This is the last
Labor that thou and I shall waste,
And ended is that we begun.
Now is this song both sung and past;
My lute, be still, for I have done.   40

                                                        E. MS.

They Flee from Me

They flee from me, that sometime did me seek,
With naked foot stalking in my chamber.
I have seen them, gentle, tame, and meek,
That now are wild, and do not remember
That sometime they put themselves in danger   5
To take bread at my hand, and now they range,
Busily seeking with a continual change.

Thankèd be fortune it hath been otherwise,
Twenty times better; but once in special,
In thin array, after a pleasant guise,   10
When her loose gown from her shoulders did fall,
And she me caught in her arms long and small,[1]
Therewithall sweetly did me kiss
And softly said, "Dear heart, how like you this?"

It was no dream, I lay broad waking.   15
But all is turned, thorough my gentleness,
Into a strange fashion of forsaking;
And I have leave to go, of her goodness,
And she also to use newfangleness.[2]
But since that I so kindely[3] am servèd,   20
I fain would know what she hath deservèd.

                                                        E. MS.

3. Likes.
1. Slender.
2. Fickleness.

3. Naturally, but with an ironic suggestion of the modern meaning of "kindly."

HENRY HOWARD, EARL OF SURREY
1517–1547

Surrey was the oldest son of the duke of Norfolk, who was the chief bulwark of the old aristocracy against the rising tide of "new men" and the reformed religion. Surrey was descended from kings on both sides of his family, and was raised with Henry VIII's illegitimate son, the duke of Richmond, who married Surrey's sister. Like his father and grandfather he was an able soldier, but the fortunes of the Howard family at court depended on Henry's queens. The Howards were in high favor when Surrey's cousin Catherine Howard was queen, but they were low on Fortune's wheel when Jane Seymour ascended the throne. The poet was condemned on a frivolous charge of treason and beheaded when he was barely thirty years old.

Surrey continued the practice of the sonnet begun by Wyatt, establishing the "English" form used by Shakespeare and many others: three quatrains and a couplet, rhyming *abab cdcd efef gg*. His verse maintains a more regular accent than Wyatt's and is generally more fluent and musical, but the language often seems less vivid and vigorous. Surrey was the first English poet to publish blank verse— unrhymed iambic pentameter—a form that became exceedingly popular throughout the next four centuries. He used it for translations of Virgil's *Aeneid*, Books 4 (in 1554) and 2 (in 1557). His poems circulated in manuscript during his lifetime, and the bulk of them (some forty) were published in *Tottel's Miscellany*, ten years after his death.

Love, That Doth Reign and Live Within My Thought[1]

Love, that doth reign and live within my thought,
And built his seat within my captive breast,
Clad in the arms wherein with me he fought,
Oft in my face he doth his banner rest.
But she that taught me love and suffer pain,   5
My doubtful hope and eke my hot desire
With shamefast[2] look to shadow and refrain,
Her smiling grace converteth straight to ire.
And coward Love, then, to the heart apace
Taketh his flight, where he doth lurk and plain,[3]   10
His purpose lost, and dare not show his face.
For my lord's guilt thus faultless bide I pain,
Yet from my lord shall not my foot remove:
Sweet is the death that taketh end by love.

1557

1. Cf. Surrey's version of Petrarch's *Rime* 140 with   2. Modest. "Eke": also.
Wyatt's adaptation of the same original (p. 550).   3. Complain.

QUEEN ELIZABETH
1533–1603

Besides exercising her remarkable political skills as a ruler, Queen Elizabeth was also the dominant cultural presence of the brilliant era named for her, the inspiration and subject of countless poems, dedications, and works of art. She was also a well-educated woman who took pride in displaying her considerable knowledge of the Latin and Greek languages and her wide reading in the classics, begun under the tutelage of Roger Ascham and other humanist scholars. Her own writing includes speeches on several state occasions; poetic translations of selections from the Psalms, Petrarch, Seneca, and Horace; prose translations from Boethius, Plutarch, and the French Protestant Queen Margaret of Navarre; and a few original poems. The original poems known to be hers deal with actual events in her life. They are chiefly in octosyllabics or poulter's measure (rhyming couplets in which the first line has twelve and the second line fourteen syllables) and are rough-hewn, vigorous, and moralistic.

The Doubt of Future Foes[1]

The doubt of future foes exiles my present joy,
And wit me warns to shun such snares as threaten mine annoy.[2]
For falsehood now doth flow, and subject faith doth ebb,[3]
Which would not be, if reason ruled or wisdom weaved the web.
But clouds of toys untried do cloak aspiring minds,   5
Which turn to rain of late repent, by course of changèd winds.[4]
The top of hope supposed, the root of ruth will be,
And fruitless all their graffèd guiles, as shortly ye shall see.[5]
The dazzled eyes with pride, which great ambition blinds,
Shall be unsealed by worthy wights whose foresight falsehood finds.   10
The daughter of debate, that eke[6] discord doth sow
Shall reap no gain where former rule hath taught still[7] peace to grow.
No foreign banished wight[8] shall anchor in this port,
Our realm it brooks no stranger's force, let them elsewhere resort.
Our rusty sword with rest,[9] shall first his edge employ   15
To poll[1] their tops that seek such change and gape for joy.
ca. 1568

---

1. The poem concerns Elizabeth's Roman Catholic cousin Mary Stuart, queen of Scotland, who in 1568 sought refuge in England from her rebellious subjects. Mary was the focus of several Roman Catholic conspiracies to place her on the English throne in place of Elizabeth. "Doubt": fear.
2. I.e., threaten to harm ("annoy") me. "Wit": intelligence.
3. I.e., the tide of faith (loyalty) is ebbing, because it is now subject to the rising tide of falsehood.
4. Clouds of tricks ("toys") not yet tested and detected ("untried") hide the "aspiring minds" of ambitious foes, but those clouds will turn at last into rains of repentance.
5. The deceptions ("guiles") grafted ("graffed") into them will not bear fruit. "Ruth": sorrow.
6. Also. Mary Stuart also was sometimes called "Mother of Debate," because she was constantly the focus of conspiracies and plots.
7. Stable. "Former rule": either the reign of Henry VIII or Edward VI, which established the Reformation in England.
8. Person.
9. Sword rusty from disuse.
1. Strike off their heads.

On Monsieur's Departure[1]

I grieve and dare not show my discontent,
I love and yet am forced to seem to hate,
I do, yet dare not say I ever meant,
I seem stark mute but inwardly do prate.[2]
    I am and not, I freeze and yet am burned,   5
    Since from myself another self I turned.

My care is like my shadow in the sun,
Follows me flying, flies when I pursue it,
Stands and lies by me, doth what I have done.[3]
His too familiar care[4] doth make me rue[5] it.   10
    No means I find to rid him from my breast,
    Till by the end of things it be suppressed.

Some gentler passion slide into my mind,
For I am soft and made of melting snow;
Or be more cruel, love, and so be kind.   15
Let me or float or sink, be high or low.
    Or let me live with some more sweet content,
    Or die and so forget what love ere meant.

ca. 1582

---

1. The heading, present in two manuscripts, identifies the occasion of this poem as the breaking off of marriage negotiations between Queen Elizabeth and the French duke of Anjou in 1582. A third manuscript implies instead an association with Elizabeth's favorite, the earl of Essex, who led an abortive rebellion and was executed for treason in 1601.
2. Chatter.
3. Does everything I do.
4. I.e., my own care (i.e., sorrow) that he caused.
5. Regret.

SIR WALTER RALEGH
1552-1618

The brilliant and versatile Sir Walter Ralegh was a soldier, courtier, philosopher, explorer and colonist, student of science, historian, and poet. He fought in Ireland and Cádiz, directed the colonization of Virginia, introduced the potato to Ireland and tobacco to Europe, brought Spenser from Ireland to the English court, conducted scientific experiments, led expeditions to Guiana in an unsuccessful effort to find gold, and wrote several reports urging England to challenge Spanish dominance in the New World. He was known for his violent temper, his dramatic sense of life, his extravagant dress, his skepticism in religious matters, his bitter hatred of Spain, and his great favor with Queen Elizabeth, interrupted in 1592 when he seduced, and then married, one of her ladies-in-waiting. His long poem to the queen, *The Ocean to Cynthia*, remains in fragments of manuscript, one containing more than five hundred lines. His best-known shorter poems include the reply to Marlowe's *Passionate Shepherd*, and *The Lie*, an attack on social classes and institutions that provoked many answers.

    King James suspected Ralegh of opposing his succession and threw him into the Tower of London on trumped-up charges of treason; there he remained for the rest of his life save for an ill-fated last voyage to Guiana in 1617, which again failed to discover gold. In prison he wrote his long, unfinished *History of the World*, which begins with the Creation, emphasizes the providential punishment of evil princes, and projects a treatment of English history—although not of recent events because, he declared, he who follows truth too closely at the heels might get kicked in the teeth. The work was to have been dedicated to Henry, Prince of Wales, Ralegh's most powerful friend and supporter. But Henry died in 1612, and Ralegh broke off his narrative at 168 B.C. Six years later James, bowing to Spanish pressure, had Ralegh executed on the old treason charge.

The Nymph's Reply to the Shepherd

If all the world and love were young,
And truth in every shepherd's tongue,
These pretty pleasures might me move
To live with thee and be thy love.

Time drives the flocks from field to fold   5
When rivers rage and rocks grow cold,
And Philomel[1] becometh dumb;
The rest complains of cares to come.

The flowers do fade, and wanton fields
To wayward winter reckoning yields;   10
A honey tongue, a heart of gall,
Is fancy's spring, but sorrow's fall.

Thy gowns, thy shoes, thy beds of roses,
Thy cap, thy kirtle,[2] and thy posies
Soon break, soon wither, soon forgotten—   15
In folly ripe, in reason rotten.

Thy belt of straw and ivy buds,
Thy coral clasps and amber studs,
All these in me no means can move
To come to thee and be thy love.   20

But could youth last and love still breed,
Had joys no date[3] nor age no need,
Then these delights my mind might move
To live with thee and be thy love.

         1600

---

1. The nightingale.   3. Ending.
2. Skirt, outer petticoat.

SIR PHILIP SIDNEY
1554–1586

Sir Philip Sidney—courtier, soldier, poet, and patron of poets (including Spenser)—seemed to the Elizabethans to be Castiglione's perfect courtier come to life. His lifelong devotion to the cause of Protestantism at home and abroad was shaped initially by family connections: his father was Sir Henry Sidney, thrice lord deputy (governor) of Ireland, and his mother was a sister of Robert Dudley, earl of Leicester, the most spectacular and powerful of all the queen's subjects. His religious commitment was strengthened by extensive travels and contacts on the continent, where he witnessed the massacre of French Protestants in Paris on St. Bartholomew's Day (August 24, 1572). In 1580 he incurred the queen's displeasure by opposing her proposed marriage to the Catholic duke of Anjou, and was briefly banished from the court. In 1585 he went to the Low Countries to support their war against Spain, and was badly wounded at Zutphen. A famous story records that despite his own parching thirst he offered his bottle of water to a dying man with the words "thy necessity is yet greater than mine." He died at the age of thirty-two after lingering for twenty-six days, and all England mourned.

He spent his brief banishment from court at the estate of his beloved sister Mary Herbert, countess of Pembroke, where he wrote for her entertainment a long pastoral romance, *Arcadia*, which exists complete in an unpublished original version and in a much revised but incomplete later version (published posthumously in 1593; a hybrid of the two versions also was published in 1593). Sidney composed, at some uncertain date, the major work of literary criticism produced during the English Renaissance, *The Defence of Poesy* (1595), also titled *An Apology for Poetry*. In it he defends imaginative literature against its attackers and greatly exalts the role of the poet and the moral value of poetry. *Astrophil and Stella* ("Starlover and Star") is the first of the great Elizabethan sonnet sequences. Some of the 108 sonnets and eleven songs allude to Sidney's ambiguous relationship with Penelope Devereaux through the use of puns on her married name, Rich. English sonnet sequences often contain autobiographical elements that are, as here, subsumed into the created fiction and its Petrarchan conventions.

Astrophil and Stella

Sidney's sonnet sequence, like most of the Elizabethan sequences, imitates Petrarch and his French imitators, and employs well-understood conventions. Sonnet cycles have a loose framework of plot, marking the stages of a love relationship from its starting point in the lover's attraction to the lady's beauty, through various trials, sufferings, conflicts, and occasional encouragements, to a conclusion in which nothing is resolved. The poet undertook to display all the conflicting feelings of a lover—hope and despair, tenderness and bitterness, exultation and modesty—by the use of "conceits" or ingenious comparisons. Many of these became traditional and, eventually, stale: the poet who complained that in love he both burned and froze or that his sighs were the winds driving his ship on a tossing sea was echoing many an earlier poet. So Sidney protests, in the role of Astrophil, that he uses no standard conventional phrases, that his verse is original and comes from the heart—though this pretense is itself conventional. But what gives Sidney's sonnets their extraordinary vigor and freshness is his ability to dramatize Astrophil's state of mind through the use of dialogue, colloquial speech, and probing self-analysis. Stella's voice is heard in dialogic exchange with Astrophil in some of the songs—including the two presented here. In addition, the Elizabethan sequences reflect the anxieties and tensions of courtiership, in which the poet-client's relation to his patron or to the great queen is an analogue of the lover's service to the virtuous high-born lady who rejects him.

From Astrophil and Stella

1[1]

Loving in truth, and fain[2] in verse my love to show,
That the dear she might take some pleasure of my pain,
Pleasure might cause her read, reading might make her know,
Knowledge might pity win, and pity grace obtain,
    I sought fit words to paint the blackest face of woe: 5
Studying inventions fine, her wits to entertain,
Oft turning others' leaves, to see if thence would flow
Some fresh and fruitful showers upon my sunburned brain.
    But words came halting forth, wanting Invention's stay;[3]
Invention, Nature's child, fled step-dame Study's blows,   10
And others' feet still seemed but strangers in my way.
Thus great with child to speak, and helpless in my throes,
    Biting my trewand[4] pen, beating myself for spite,
    "Fool," said my Muse to me, "look in thy heart and write."

2

Not at first sight, nor with a dribbèd[5] shot
    Love gave the wound, which while I breathe will bleed,
    But known worth did in mine[6] of time proceed,
Till by degrees it had full conquest got.
I saw and liked, I liked but lovèd not,   5
    I loved, but straight did not what *Love* decreed;
    At length to Love's decrees, I, forced, agreed,
Yet with repining at so partial[7] lot.
    Now even that footstep of lost liberty
Is gone, and now like slave-borne Muscovite,[8]   10
I call it praise to suffer tyranny;
And now employ the remnant of my wit,[9]
    To make myself believe, that all is well,
    While with a feeling skill I paint my hell.

6

Some lovers speak, when they their muses entertain,
Of hopes begot by fear, of wot[1] not what desires,

---

1. One of six sonnets in the sequence written in hexameters.
2. Desirous.
3. Prop.
4. Truant.
5. Ineffectual or at random.
6. Tunnel dug to undermine a beseiged fortress.

7. Unfair.
8. Inhabitant of Muscovy, an important Russian principality ruled from Moscow; 16th-century travel books describe Muscovites as contented slaves.
9. Intelligence.
1. Know.

Of force of heavenly beams, infusing hellish pain,
Of living deaths, dear wounds, fair storms and freezing fires;[2]
   Someone his song in Jove, and Jove's strange tales attires,
Broidered with bulls and swans, powdered with golden rain;[3]
Another humbler wit to shepherd's pipe retires,
Yet hiding royal blood full oft in rural vein.[4]
To some a sweetest plaint a sweetest style affords,[5]
   While tears pour out his ink, and sighs breathe out his words,
His paper pale dispair, and pain his pen doth move.
   I can speak what I feel, and feel as much as they,
   But think that all the map of my state I display,
When trembling voice brings forth that I do Stella love.

7

When Nature made her chief work, Stella's eyes,
   In colour black, why wrapped she beams so bright?
Would she in beamy[6] black, like painter wise,
Frame daintiest lustre, mixed of shades and light?
   Or did she else that sober hue devise,
In object best to knit and strength[7] our sight,
Least if no veil those brave gleams did disguise,
They sun-like should more dazzle than delight?
   Or would she her miraculous power show,
That whereas black seems beauty's contrary,
She even in black doth make all beauties flow?
Both so and thus, she, minding[8] Love should be
   Placed ever there, gave him this mourning weed,[9]
   To honor all their deaths, who for her bleed.

31

With how sad steps, O Moon, thou climb'st the skies,
   How silently, and with how wan a face!
   What, may it be that even in heavenly place
That busy archer[1] his sharp arrows tries?
Sure, if that long-with-love-acquainted eyes
   Can judge of Love, thou feel'st a Lover's case;
   I read it in thy looks: thy languished grace,
To me that feel the like, thy state descries.
   Then even of fellowship, O Moon, tell me
Is constant *love* deemed there but want of wit?
Are beauties there as proud as here they be?
Do they above love to be loved, and yet

2. Conventional Petrarchan oxymorons (see "Figurative Language," p. 2645).
3. I.e., embroidered with mythological figures. Jove courted Europa in the shape of a bull; Leda, as a swan; and Danae, as a golden shower.
4. Pastoral allegory. By convention, a pastoral poet pipes his songs on an oaten or reed pipe.
5. Overuse of the word *sweet* in love complaints, with allusion to the very musical *dolce stil nuovo* (sweet new style) associated with Dante and his Italian contemporaries.
6. Radiant.
7. Strengthen.
8. Remembering.
9. Funeral garb.
1. Cupid.

Those lovers scorn whom that *love* doth possess?
Do they call *virtue* there ungratefulness?[2]

39

Come sleep! O sleep the certain knot of peace,
The baiting place[3] of wit, the balm of woe,
The poor man's wealth, the prisoner's release,
Th' indifferent[4] judge between the high and low;
    With shield of proof shield me from out the prease[5]   5
Of those fierce darts, Despair at me doth throw;
O make in me those civil wars to cease;
I will good tribute pay if thou do so.
    Take thou of me smooth pillows, sweetest bed,
A chamber deaf to noise and blind to light,   10
A rosy garland, and a weary head;[6]
And if these things, as being thine by right,
    Move not thy heavy grace, thou shalt in me,
    Livelier then elsewhere, Stella's image see.

61

Oft with true sighs, oft with uncallèd tears,
Now with slow words, now with dumb eloquence
I Stella's eyes assail, invade her ears;
But this at last is her sweet-breathed defence:
    That who indeed infelt affection bears,   5
So captives to his saint both soul and sense,
That, wholly hers, all selfness[7] he forbears;
Thence his desires he learns, his life's course thence.
    Now since her chaste mind hates this love in me,
    With chastened mind I straight must shew that she   10
Shall quickly me from what she hates remove.
    O Doctor[8] Cupid, thou for me reply,
    Driven else to grant by angel's sophistry,
That I love not, without I leave to love.[9]

71

Who will in fairest book of Nature know
    How Virtue may best lodged in beauty be,
    Let him but learn of *Love* to read in thee,
Stella, those fair lines, which true goodness show.
There shall he find all vices' overthrow,   5
    Not by rude force, but sweetest sovereignty
    Of reason, from whose light those night-birds[1] fly;

---

2. I.e., is the lady's ingratitude considered virtue in heaven (as here)? Also, is the lover's virtue (fidelity) considered distasteful in heaven (as here)?
3. Resting place on a journey.
4. Impartial.
5. Throng. "Proof": proven strength.
6. The offer of gifts to Morpheus, god of sleep, is a poetic convention. A likely source is Chaucer's *Book of the Duchess*, lines 240–269.
7. Concern with self.
8. Eminently learned scholar.
9. Unless I stop loving.
1. The owl, for example, was an emblem of various vices.

That inward sun in thine eyes shineth so.
   And not content to be Perfection's heir
Thyself, dost strive all minds that way to move,   10
Who mark in thee what is in thee most fair.
So while thy beauty draws the heart to love,
   As fast thy Virtue bends that love to good;
   "But, ah," Desire still cries, "give me some food."

72

Desire, though thou my old companion art
   And oft so clings to my pure love, that I
   One from the other scarcely can descry,[2]
While each doth blow the fire of my heart,
Now from thy fellowship I needs must part.   5
   Venus is taught with Dian's wings to fly;[3]
   I must no more in thy sweet passions lie;
Virtue's gold now must head my Cupid's dart.
   Service and honor, wonder with delight,
Fear to offend, will worthy to appear,   10
Care shining in mine eyes, faith in my sprite:[4]
These things are left me by my only dear;
   But thou, Desire, because thou wouldst have all,
   Now banished art, but yet alas how shall?

74

I never drank of Aganippe well,
Nor ever did in shade of Tempe[5] sit;
And Muses scorn with vulgar brains to dwell;
Poor layman I, for sacred rites unfit.
   Some do I hear of Poets' fury[6] tell,   5
But God wot,[7] wot not what they mean by it;
And this I swear by blackest brook of hell,[8]
I am no pick-purse of another's wit.
   How falls it then that with so smooth an ease
My thoughts I speak, and what I speak doth flow   10
In verse, and that my verse best wits doth please?
Guess we the cause. "What, is it thus?" Fie no.
   "Or so?" Much less. "How then?" Sure thus it is:
   My lips are sweet, inspired with Stella's kiss.

108[9]

When Sorrow (using mine own fire's might)
   Melts down his lead into my boiling breast,

---

2. Distinguish.
3. Diana, goddess of the moon and patron of chastity. Venus, goddess of beauty and love, mother of Cupid.
4. Spirit.
5. Valley beside Mt. Olympus, sacred to Apollo, the god of song. "Aganippe": well at the foot of Mt. Helicon in Greece, sacred to the Muses.
6. Inspiration.
7. Knows.
8. The most binding of all oaths were those sworn by the river Styx.
9. In many sequences, as here, the final sonnet brings no resolution.

Through that dark furnace to my heart oppressed
There shines a joy from thee, my only light;
But soon as thought of thee breeds my delight,   5
    And my young soul flutters to thee, his nest,
    Most rude Despair, my daily unbidden guest,
Clips straight my wings, straight wraps me in his night,
    And makes me then bow down my head, and say,
"Ah, what doth Phoebus'[1] gold that wretch avail,   10
Whom iron doors do keep from use of day?"
So strangely (alas) thy works in me prevail
    That in my woes for thee thou art my joy,
    And in my joys for thee my only annoy.

1582   1591, 1598

Leave Me, O Love

Leave me, O Love which reachest but to dust,
And thou my mind aspire to higher things;
Grow rich in that which never taketh rust;
Whatever fades but fading pleasure brings.

Draw in thy beams, and humble all thy might   5
To that sweet yoke where lasting freedoms be;
Which breaks the clouds and opens forth the light,
That doth both shine and give us sight to see.

O take fast hold; let that light be thy guide
In this small course which birth draws out to death,   10
And think how evil becometh him to slide,
Who seeketh heaven, and comes of heavenly breath.[1]
    Then farewell world; thy uttermost I see;
    Eternal Love, maintain thy life in me.

1581   1598

1. God of the sun.
1. I.e., it ill becomes one who has a soul and seeks heaven to "slide" to earthly things.

MICHAEL DRAYTON
1563–1631

Michael Drayton was born about a year before Shakespeare and in the same county, Warwickshire. He had a long career as poet, extending from the early 1590s until well into the seventeenth century. He collaborated on plays, wrote sonnets, pastorals, odes, poetic epistles, and a historical "epic" called *The Barons' Wars.* His self-styled masterpiece, however, is *Poly-Olbion,* a thirty-thousand-line historical-geographical poem celebrating all the counties of England and Wales. His lifelong devotion to Anne Goodyere, Lady Rainsford (in the manner of a courtly lover), is memorialized in his sonnets addressed to "Idea," e.g., the embodiment of the Platonic idea of virtue and beauty. He revised and added to his sonnets and poems as they were republished, so one can trace his development from an Elizabethan to a Jacobean poet.

From Idea

61

Since there's no help, come let us kiss and part;
Nay, I have done, you get no more of me,
And I am glad, yea glad with all my heart
That thus so cleanly I myself can free;
Shake hands forever, cancel all our vows,   5
And when we meet at any time again,
Be it not seen in either of our brows
That we one jot of former love retain.
Now at the last gasp of love's latest breath,
When, his pulse failing, passion speechless lies,   10
When faith is kneeling by his bed of death,
And innocence is closing up his eyes;
Now if thou wouldst, when all have given him over,
From death to life thou mightst him yet recover.

1619

THOMAS NASHE
1567–1601

Thomas Nashe, a Cambridge graduate, was a versatile writer of controversial pamphlets, satire, plays, a novel, and lyric verse. He was one of the university wits who came to London and wrote for the stage and the press. They lived short and precarious lives: Nashe was about thirty-three when he died; his friend Christopher Marlowe died at twenty-nine; George Peele, at thirty; and Robert Greene, at thirty-two. Nashe's personal enemy was an older man, Gabriel Harvey, Spenser's friend; Nashe exchanged a series of vituperative and slanderous pamphlets with Harvey in which Nashe's talent for invective was exploited to the fullest. In June 1599, the ecclesiastical authorities ordered that "all Nashe's books and Doctor Harvey's books be taken wheresoever they may be found and that none of their books be ever printed hereafter."

Nashe's picaresque narrative *The Unfortunate Traveler, or the Life of Jack Wilton* is a rambling account of escapades all over Europe, including some fictional exploits attributed to the poet Surrey. He wrote a festive comedy, *Summer's Last Will and Testament;* an attack on women called *The Anatomy of Absurdity;* an attack on social abuses of every kind titled *Pierce Penniless, His Supplication to the Devil;* and a strident comparison called *Christ's Tears Over Jerusalem* between the sins of the Jews that led to the destruction of Jerusalem and the current morals and manners of London. His prose style sometimes sounds quite modern: it is headlong, impatient, colloquial, and vivid. This poem shows his elegant, sometimes haunting, lyric gift.

A Litany in Time of Plague[1]

Adieu, farewell, earth's bliss;
This world uncertain is;
Fond[2] are life's lustful joys;
Death proves them all but toys;[3]
None from his darts can fly;   5
I am sick, I must die.
　　Lord, have mercy on us!

Rich men, trust not in wealth,
Gold cannot buy you health;
Physic himself must fade.   10
All things to end are made,
The plague full swift goes by;
I am sick, I must die.
　　Lord, have mercy on us!

Beauty is but a flower   15
Which wrinkles will devour;
Brightness falls from the air;
Queens have died young and fair;
Dust hath closèd Helen's eye.
I am sick, I must die.   20
　　Lord, have mercy on us!

Strength stoops unto the grave,
Worms feed on Hector brave;
Swords may not fight with fate,
Earth still holds ope her gate.   25
"Come, come!" the bells do cry.
I am sick, I must die.
　　Lord, have mercy on us.

Wit with his wantonness
Tasteth death's bitterness;   30
Hell's executioner
Hath no ears for to hear
What vain art can reply.
I am sick, I must die.
　　Lord, have mercy on us.   35

Haste, therefore, each degree,
To welcome destiny;
Heaven is our heritage,

1. This lyric is from *A Pleasant Comedy Called Summer's Last Will and Testament*, acted before the archbishop of Canterbury in his palace at Croydon in 1592 and published in 1600.   2. Foolish.   3. Trifles.

Earth but a player's stage;
Mount we unto the sky.   40
I am sick, I must die.
Lord, have mercy on us.

1592   1600

AEMILIA LANYER
1569–1645

Aemilia Lanyer, one of the very few published women poets of the Renaissance,
was the daughter of and wife of gentlemen musicians attached to the courts of
Elizabeth I and James I. Her single volume of poems, *Salve Deus Rex Judaeorum*
(1611), has a decided feminist thrust. A series of dedicatory poems to patronesses
praises them as a community of contemporary good women; the title poem on
Christ's Passion contrasts the good women associated with the Passion story with
the weak and evil men and incorporates a defense of Eve and all women; the
final poem, *The Description of Cooke-ham*, celebrates the estate occupied by her
patronness, Margaret, countess of Cumberland, as an Edenic paradie of women,
now lost. The defence of Eve and the prose epistle *To the Virtuous Reader* are
spirited and forceful contributions to the so-called *querelle des femmes*, a massive
body of writings that argue the issue of women's worthiness or faultiness, beginning
in the Middle Ages and extending over several centuries. Such writings—both
serious and satiric and in several languages—included sermonds, tracts, manuals
of domestic advice, poems, and plays. Some notable examples are *The Wife of
Bath's Prologue and Tale*; John Knox's denunciation of Mary Queen of Scots,
and Shakespeare's *The Taming of the Shrew*. The final poem in the volume, *The
Description of Cooke-ham*, celebrates the estate occupied by Lanyer's patroness,
Margaret, countess of Cumberland, as an Edenic paradise of women, now lost.

The Description of Cooke-ham[1]

Farewell (sweet *Cooke-ham*) where I first obtained
Grace[2] from that grace where perfect grace remained;
And where the muses gave their full consent,
I should have power the virtuous to content;
Where princely palace[3] willed me to indite,   5
The sacred story of the soul's delight.
Farewell (sweet place) where virtue then did rest,

1. The poem was written in honor of Margaret Clifford, countess of Cumberland, and celebrates a royal
estate leased to her brother, at which the countess occasionally resided. The poem may predate, and should
be compared with, Jonson's *To Penshurst* (p. 625), usually taken to be the first poem in the English country-
house genre. It is based on a familiar classical topic,
the "Farewell to a Place," which had its most famous
development in Virgil's *Eclogue* 1. Lanyer's poem
makes extensive use of the common pastoral motif of
nature's active sympathy with and response to human

emotion—which later came to be called the "pathetic
fallacy."
2. Here, both God's grace and the favor of her grace,
the countess of Cumberland. Lanyer attributes both
her religious conversion and her vocation as poet to
a period of residence at Cookeham in the countess's
household. We do not know how long or under what
circumstances Lanyer resided there.
3. Apparently a reference to the countess as her patron, commissioning her Passion poem.

And all delights did harbor in her breast;
Never shall my sad eyes again behold
Those pleasures which my thoughts did then unfold.   10
Yet you (great Lady) Mistress of that place,
From whose desires did spring this work of grace;
Vouchsafe to think upon those pleasures past,
As fleeting worldly joys that could not last,
Or, as dim shadows of celestial pleasures,   15
Which are desired above all earthly treasures.
Oh how (methought) against[4] you thither came,
Each part did seem some new delight to frame!
The house received all ornaments to grace it,
And would endure no foulness to deface it.   20
And walks put on their summer liveries,[5]
And all things else did hold like similes:[6]
The trees with leaves, with fruits, with flowers clad,
Embraced each other, seeming to be glad,
Turning themselves to beauteous Canopies,   25
To shade the bright sun from your brighter eyes;
The crystal streams with silver spangles graced,
While by the glorious sun they were embraced;
The little birds in chirping notes did sing,
To entertain both you and that sweet spring.   30
And _Philomela_[7] with her sundry lays,
Both you and that delightful place did praise.
Oh how me thought each plant, each flower, each tree
Set forth their beauties then to welcome thee!
The very hills right humbly did descend,   35
When you to tread on them did intend.
And as you set your feet, they still did rise,
Glad that they could receive so rich a prize.
The gentle winds did take delight to be
Among those woods that were so graced by thee,   40
And in sad murmur uttered pleasing sound,
That pleasure in that place might more abound.
The swelling banks delivered all their pride
When such a _Phoenix_[8] once they had espied.
Each arbor, bank, each seat, each stately tree,   45
Thought themselves honored in supporting thee.
The pretty birds would oft come to attend thee,
Yet fly away for fear they should offend thee;
The little creatures in the burrough by
Would come abroad to sport them in your eye,   50
Yet fearful of the bow in your fair hand,
Would run away when you did make a stand.

---

4. In preparation for your coming.
5. Distinctive garments worn by persons in the service of great families, to indicate whose servants they were.
6. Behaved in similar fashion.
7. In myth, Philomela was raped by her brother-in-law Tereus, who also tore out her tongue; the gods transformed her into a nightingale. Here the bird's song is joyous but later mournful (line 189), associat-ing her own woes with those of Cookeham at the women's departure.
8. Mythical bird that lived alone of its kind for five hundred years, then was consumed in flame and re-born from its own ashes; metaphorically, a person of rare excellence. "All their pride": fish (cf. _To Penshurst_, lines 31–36, p. 625).

Now let me come unto that stately tree,
Wherein such goodly prospects you did see;
That oak that did in height his fellows pass,   55
As much as lofty trees, low growing grass,
Much like a comely cedar straight and tall,
Whose beauteous stature far exceeded all.
How often did you visit this fair tree,
Which seeming joyful in receiving thee,   60
Would like a palm tree spread his arms abroad,
Desirous that you there should make abode;
Whose fair green leaves much like a comely veil,
Defended[9] *Phoebus* when he would assail;
Whose pleasing boughs did yield a cool fresh air,   65
Joying[1] his happiness when you were there.
Where being seated, you might plainly see
Hills, vales, and woods, as if on bended knee
They had appeared, your honor to salute,
Or to prefer some strange unlooked-for suit;[2]   70
All interlaced with brooks and crystal springs,
A prospect fit to please the eyes of kings.
And thirteen shires appeared all in your sight,
Europe could not afford much more delight.
What was there then but gave you all content,   75
While you the time in meditation spent
Of their Creator's power, which there you saw,
In all his creatures held a perfect law;
And in their beauties did you plain descry[3]
His beauty, wisdom, grace, love, majesty.   80
In these sweet woods how often did you walk,
With Christ and his Apostles there to talk;
Placing his holy Writ in some fair tree
To meditate what you therein did see.
With *Moses* you did mount his holy hill   85
To know his pleasure, and perform his will.[4]
With lowly *David* you did often sing
His holy hymns to Heaven's eternal King.[5]
And in sweet music did your soul delight
To sound his praises, morning, noon, and night.   90
With blessed *Joseph* you did often feed
Your pined brethren, when they stood in need.[6]
And that sweet Lady sprung from *Clifford's* race,
Of noble *Bedford's* blood, fair stem of grace,[7]
To honorable *Dorset* now espoused,[8]   95
In whose fair breast true virtue then was housed,
Oh what delight did my weak spirits find

9. Defended against, resisted.
1. Enjoying.
2. To urge some unexpected petition, as to a monarch.
3. Perceive.
4. You sought out and followed God's law, like Moses who received the Ten Commandments on Mt. Sinai.
5. You often sang David's psalms.
6. Like Joseph, who fed the starving Israelites in Egypt, you fed the hungry.

7. Main line of the family tree. Anne Clifford, only surviving child of the seaman-adventurer George Clifford, third earl of Cumberland, and the countess, a Russell (of "Bedford's blood"). She was tutored by Samuel Daniel and her *Diary* offers interesting insights into this period.
8. Anne Clifford was married to Richard Sackville, third earl of Dorset, on February 25, 1609; the reference helps date Lanyer's poem.

In those pure parts of her well framéd mind.
And yet it grieves me that I cannot be
Near unto her, whose virtues did agree   100
With those fair ornaments of outward beauty,
Which did enforce from all both love and duty.
Unconstant Fortune, thou art most to blame,
Who casts us down into so low a frame
Where our great friends we cannot daily see,   105
So great a difference is there in degree.[9]
Many are placed in those orbs of state,
Parters[1] in honor, so ordained by Fate,
Nearer in show, yet farther off in love,
In which, the lowest always are above.[2]   110
But whither am I carried in conceit,
My wit too weak to conster[3] of the great.
Why not? although we are but born of earth,
We may behold the heavens, despising death;
And loving heaven that is so far above,   115
May in the end vouchsafe us entire love.[4]
Therefore sweet memory do thou retain
Those pleasures past, which will not turn again:
Remember beauteous *Dorset's* former sports,[5]
So far from being touched by ill reports,   120
Wherein myself did always bear a part,
While reverend love presented my true heart.
Those recreations let me bear in mind,
Which her sweet youth and noble thoughts did find,
Whereof deprived, I evermore must grieve,   125
Hating blind Fortune, careless to relieve.
And you sweet Cooke-ham, whom these ladies leave,
I now must tell the grief you did conceive
At their departure, when they went away,
How everything retained a sad dismay.   130
Nay long before, when once an inkling came,
Methought each thing did unto sorrow frame:
The trees that were so glorious in our view,
Forsook both flowers and fruit, when once they knew
Of your depart, their very leaves did wither,   135
Changing their colors as they grew together.
But when they saw this had no power to stay you,
They often wept, though, speechless, could not pray you,
 Letting their tears in your fair bosoms fall,
As if they said, Why will ye leave us all?   140
This being vain, they cast their leaves away
Hoping that pity would have made you stay:
Their frozen tops, like age's hoary hairs,
Shows their disasters, languishing in fears.

9. These lines probably exaggerate Lanyer's former familiarity with Anne Clifford.
1. Separators, i.e., the various honorific ranks "orbs of state" act to separate person from person.
2. An egalitarian sentiment playing on the Christian notion that in spiritual things—love and charity—the poor and lowly surpass the great ones.
3. Construe, analyze.
4. I.e., we (lowly) may also love God and enjoy God's love, and hence are equal to anyone.
5. As was common enough, Anne Clifford is here referred to by her husband's title.

A swarthy riveled rind[6] all over spread, 145
Their dying bodies half alive, half dead.
But your occasions[7] called you so away
That nothing there had power to make you stay.
Yet did I see a noble grateful mind
Requiting each according to their kind, 150
Forgetting not to turn and take your leave
Of these sad creatures, powerless to receive
Your favor, when with grief you did depart,
Placing their former pleasures in your heart,
Giving great charge to noble memory 155
There to preserve their love continually.
But specially the love of that fair tree,
That first and last you did vouchsafe to see,
In which it pleased you oft to take the air
With noble *Dorset*, then a virgin fair, 160
Where many a learned book was read and scanned,
To this fair tree, taking me by the hand,
You did repeat the pleasures which had passed,
Seeming to grieve they could no longer last.
And with a chaste, yet loving kiss took leave, 165
Of which sweet kiss I did it soon bereave,[8]
Scorning a senseless creature should possess
So rare a favor, so great happiness.
No other kiss it could receive from me,
For fear to give back what it took of thee, 170
So I ungrateful creature did deceive it
Of that which you in love vouchsafed to leave it.
And though it oft had given me much content,
Yet this great wrong I never could repent;
But of the happiest made it most forlorn, 175
To show that nothing's free from Fortune's scorne,
While all the rest with this most beauteous tree
Made their sad comfort sorrow's harmony.
The flowers that on the banks and walks did grow,
Crept in the ground, the grass did weep for woe. 180
The winds and waters seemed to chide together
Because you went away they knew not whither;
And those sweet brooks that ran so fair and clear,
With grief and trouble wrinkled did appear.
Those pretty birds that wonted were to sing, 185
Now neither sing, nor chirp, nor use their wing,
But with their tender feet on some bare spray,
Warble forth sorrow, and their own dismay.
Fair *Philomela* leaves her mournful ditty,
Drowned in deep sleep, yet can procure no pity. 190
Each arbor, bank, each seat, each stately tree
Looks bare and desolate now for want of thee,
Turning green tresses into frosty gray,

---

6. Bark.
7. After her husband's death (1605) Margaret Clifford
chiefly resided in her dower properties in the north;

Anne Clifford was married in 1609.
8. Take from it.

While in cold grief they wither all away.
The sun grew weak, his beams no comfort gave,   195
While all green things did make the earth their grave.
Each brier, each bramble, when you went away
Caught fast your clothes, thinking to make you stay;
Delightful Echo wonted[9] to reply
To our last words, did now for sorrow die;   200
The house cast off each garment that might grace it,
Putting on dust and cobwebs to deface it.
All desolation then there did appear,
When you were going whom they held so dear.
This last farewell to *Cooke-ham* here I give,   205
When I am dead thy name in this may live,
Wherein I have performed her noble hest[1]
Whose virtues lodge in my unworthy breast,
And ever shall, so long as life remains,
Tying my life to her by those rich chains.[2]   210

                                                                  1611

9. Was accustomed.   2. Her virtues.
1. Commission, charge.

The Early Seventeenth Century

1603-1660

According to the usual division of English literary history by periods, the "early seventeenth century" extends from the accession of the first Stuart king (James I) in 1603 to the coronation of the third (Charles II) in 1660. But the events, literary and otherwise, that occurred between these boundaries make much more sense if they are seen in a larger pattern extending from 1588 to 1688. Between these two dates massive political and social events took place that, in their cumulative effect, bridge the gap between the Tudor "tyranny by consent" of the sixteenth century and the equally ill-defined but equally functional constitutional monarchy of the eighteenth century.

Accompanying that vast political change, and intimately related to it, are parallel changes that have as common denominator a growing skepticism of dogmas old and new, and an increasing tolerance of divergency. In religion, politics, literature, commercial practices, and social observances, the traditional codes and hierarchies of English life gave way to new (and often bitterly resented) diversities. At the heart of this century of rapid change lies the Puritan Revolt of 1640–60. The quarrels and controversies that culminated in this upheaval began to reach an inflammatory stage shortly after 1588; its tremors and aftershocks largely subsided after 1688. In more senses than one, the revolt and its civil wars were the pivotal events of the century.

Armada year, 1588, changed dramatically the tone of Elizabeth's reign. Like most of her subjects, she had reason to expect that the island nation's triumph over a long-awaited, much-hated invader would release a tide of patriotic good feeling. Nothing of the sort happened: quite the contrary. Deep fault lines crisscrossed the structure of Elizabethan society, both before and after Armada year; the deepest of them pitted those who wanted to preserve the established privileges and monopo-

571

lies of class and religious authority against those increasingly vociferous and organized groups who were discontented with them. Because of the Spanish threat,
these interior tensions had been largely muted in the interests of national unity;
once the nation was safe from Spain, they surfaced again, in the form of bitter and
divisive quarrels. These were fought out most conspicuously between the aging
queen, aided by her council, and headstrong individuals (later groups) in her
successive Houses of Commons. But the same issues also emerged in local
encounters throughout the land. Wherever a stiff-necked parson encountered a
strong-willed bishop, a grumbling consumer confronted an unjust monopoly, or a
truculent House of Commons man complained that his freedom of speech was
being abridged, the frictions of society built up. Individually, perhaps, many of the
grievances were minor, but being neglected or irritated over the years, they festered
and tended to reinforce one another. The queen's traditional measures of cajolery
and grandiose rhetoric failed to placate the malcontents, and throwing the ringleaders into jail simply infuriated them. The peaceful accession of Elizabeth's
Scottish cousin James did nothing to diminish the growing list of grievances. By
pleas and remonstrations, and by voting to withhold taxes from the royal administration, the Commons sought redress, but to little avail. Agitation against the
authoritarian episcopal church continued, mostly subsurface, but flaring up occasionally in acts of fierce despair, as when a little band of Puritans left their native
land forever rather than submit to episcopal rule. (They went to Amsterdam in
1608, and then in 1620 to the wilderness of Plymouth, Massachusetts, where, for
subsequent Americans, they became the Pilgrims.) Under the increasingly strict
rule of James's son Charles, discontent spread more widely, if less openly; the
complaints became secular as well as religious. From Puritan preachers and their
relatively small congregations, agitation spread through the merchant classes, the
lawyers, the Parliament-men, and the gentry to the mercantile towns, through
the cloth-making countryside of East Anglia. By the late 1630s tempers were
strained, and an attempt to introduce Anglican forms of worship into the presbyte-
rian-minded Church of Scotland led, in 1639, to the first of two half-hearted wars
between England and Scotland. But domestic peace was an ingrained habit in
most of the island, and it was not until 1642, after five years of muted struggle and
negotiation, that open conflict broke out within England itself.

In the wars that followed, the forces of insurrection (the parliamentary, Puritan,
or Roundhead armies) were successful in one of their aims. They rendered King
Charles powerless, brought him to trial, and executed him (1649). But they failed
to set up a stable government of their own, free from the faults of the one they had
destroyed, and they failed to set up a new national church to replace the epis-
copacy that they had long criticized. The Long Parliament, convened by Charles
in 1640 and variously purged after that of its royalist and other opposition groups,
lingered on until 1649, when Cromwell sent it packing and set up a military
government of his own, which was declared a Commonwealth and then, in 1653,
a Protectorate. After Cromwell's death in 1658, his son Richard tried to succeed
him as Protector. But without Cromwell's iron force of character, the Protectorate—which was in any case no more than a makeshift effort to contain a political
instability that had got out of hand—could not survive. When Charles II was
recalled from exile (1660) and put back on his father's throne (but without the
most troublesome of his father's powers), it became clear that England was bound
to have, in politics as well as religion, some sort of organization looser than anyone
had anticipated, looser than most people wanted. But its exact form was subject to
constant pulling and hauling among the parties, and no solid settlement was
reached until Charles's brother and successor, James II, was ejected from the
throne and sent into exile. (He was a Roman Catholic, as, to be sure, his predecessor Charles had been, but Charles kept quiet about his beliefs and James did not.
Besides, the persecution of Protestants in France after 1685 inflamed traditional

English hatred of Catholicism.) Replacing the now permanently dismissed Stuarts were the Dutch Protestant William of Orange and his wife, Mary, daughter of James II. Neither was properly in the line of royal succession, but there was little complaint. After 1688, its social problems compromised if not solved to universal satisfaction, the country settled down to a long constitutional nap under a series of monarchs who made little trouble for their parliaments and therefore had little trouble sticking on their thrones. The crisis was over.

Though infinitely complex in details, the main social problems that exercised the seventeenth century can be broadly stated, with their solutions, in two sentences. In the religious sphere, the basic issue was, "How far should the reformation of the Protestant church be carried?" and the solution accomplished in 1688 was, "As far as each individual self-defined religious group wants." In the sphere of constitutional politics, the basic issue was, "How much authority should the monarch have independent of Parliament?" and the solution accomplished in 1688 was, "Almost none."

BEFORE AND AFTER THE PURITAN REVOLT

To gain a clearer sense of the immense changes wrought by the Puritan Revolt and its many reverberations, it may be useful to anatomize roughly the value structure of English society before and after the event. Under Elizabeth Tudor the court was the undisputed center of national authority, influence, power, reward, and intellectual inspiration. Careers were made and fortunes established through court connections. London was the center of the kingdom, and the court was the unchallenged center of London. This was particularly true in matters of the intellect, of literature and the arts. The characteristic forms of literature under Elizabeth were courtly, and court life, whether praised or criticized, was a principal focus of literary attention. Courtiers patronized the theater by attending plays (of which the middle class generally disapproved) and by lending the prestige of their names to different acting companies. The sonnet sequence, the pastoral romance (Sidney's *Arcadia*), the chivalric allegory (Spenser's *Faerie Queene*), the learned sermon, the erotic idyll (Marlowe's *Hero and Leander* or Shakespeare's *Venus and Adonis*), the masque, the epic—all these were courtly forms, implying courtly readers and writers who were either courtiers themselves or concerned with pleasing courtiers. For patronage flowed, when it flowed at all, from courtly donors, and apart from the precarious rewards of the theater, patronage was almost the only way for the writer to live by writing.

The same pattern continued under the first two Stuarts, James I and Charles I. Whether in his poems or in his sermons, a man like John Donne wrote primarily for courtiers and for the sharp-witted lawyers who clustered around the court. Versatile and various as he was, Ben Jonson channeled almost all his energies into writing for court and courtiers. Carew, Suckling, Lovelace, and a host of lesser writers were themselves courtiers, full- or part-time. The poet George Herbert was much remarked because he could have been a courtier and chose not to be. There were exceptions, of course: country doctors, soldiers, university dons, tutors to the gentry. But the court influence was predominant, and so far as a literary society existed, it took its tone from the court. Because court circles were narrow, a poet did not have to wait for publication to be well-known to those readers who mattered most. Manuscript collections of poems by one author, or by several, circulated through the court; a poem could become popular, be set to music several times over, yet never appear in print. The books that were printed appeared, as a rule, in small editions and, being destined for an audience trained in the classics and the court literature of the European Renaissance, could take for granted a good deal of specialized information. A court preacher like Lancelot Andrewes assumed in his hearers acquaintance with at least the rudiments of three ancient languages: Latin, Greek, and Hebrew. Courtly romances imitated from Sir Philip

Sidney and the Continental authors whom he imitated continued to attract readers, as in the case of Lady Mary Wroth's *Urania* (1621) and Francis Quarles's *Argalus and Parthenia* (1629); better known than either was the Latin romance *Argenis* (1621) of John Barclay, a Scotsman resident in France. All these artificial, elegant, long-winded romances assume familiarity not only with the codes of romantic pastoralism but with the conventions of genteel courtly behavior. For court society had many characteristic and distinctive values. It implied a belief in hierarchical order within a strict framework of social uniformity, involving obedience to the established church, loyalty to the anointed monarch, and deference to one's social superiors. Within that framework, it tended to produce intricate, allusive, and highly decorative writing. Courtiers generally valued the heroic passions—love (but not necessarily marriage), warfare (largely free of a political context), and devotional piety (quite separate from practical morality). The controlling principle behind all these distinctions was an emphasis on honor as the supreme principle in life, not to be estimated in any way by criteria of mere prudence. Literature written within this framework—rarely taking it with complete solemnity and sometimes questioning its assumptions—was prevalent, though not universal, under the old regime.

After 1660, and even more strikingly after 1688, the pattern of values was quite different. The court, largely dissolved during the twenty years of the Puritan Interregnum, could not, after the Restoration, any longer pretend to be an unchallenged center of intellectual and literary influence. It did not have the power, social or financial, to be anything of the sort. For now money and influence no longer flowed exclusively from the court. London City (a network of bankers and merchants, financiers, jobbers, brokers, tradesmen, and credit managers) was one rival source of power and influence. Another was Parliament itself, which had executed one Stuart king and in 1688 would throw out another, appointing a Dutchman to be his successor. Instead of purporting to stand above interest as the sole fountain of honor, the court thus clearly became one of several competing interests. The relatively conservative "landed interest" tended toward the court, as the more innovative "money interest" found its chief support in the City. Members of Parliament, ranking themselves under the deliberately meaningless nicknames of "Tory" and "Whig," sided with either interest as they chose, or alternately with both. One's connection with an interest was not through the inflexible principle of honor but through the infinitely fluent one of . . . interest itself.

In the same way, the established church, which had once claimed to be sole guardian of the spiritual welfare of the English people and, therefore, of their worldly behavior—the authoritative voice disciplining every individual's private interests—became after 1660 simply one of many religious communities. (It was the most powerful, the most acceptable socially, and for the moment the largest one; but it was not, and could not be made, the only one.) The Puritan sects, originally factions within the English church, had been freed to multiply their numbers and expand their independence during the Interregnum; after the Restoration, they could not be got back into the episcopal (Anglican) church by force or persuasion. When several sects exist side by side in open competition, they are all voluntary. Each interprets Scripture after its own fashion; all agree (at least in public) in not trying to exterminate one another. But that creates problems of discipline: a member of a particular sect who does not like its social code simply transfers to a more understanding sect (or out of them all). Thus alongside the established Anglican church there appeared in villages all across England the Nonconformist chapel, an alternative approach to God.

Anglicans could drive Puritans from their posts in the church, forcing them to preach in the chapel, but to stop their preaching was impossible. Many dispossessed parsons opened independent academies for the young; some were so good that they attracted, and thus influenced, the children even of the Anglican gentry.

Censorship of books and plays did not disappear overnight, but it became much less strict. What could an episcopal censor hope to accomplish when Thomas Hobbes (considered the most subversive thinker of the Restoration era) enjoyed the special indulgence of Charles II and when the merry monarch could be found almost every evening guffawing with his mistress (or mistresses) at the bawdiest plays his playwrights could devise? In the publication of books, something like a "literary marketplace" sprang up. Booksellers began specializing in books of a certain sort—Anglican, Nonconformist, whatever. Before long, they were hiring writers to turn out titles on order. The booksellers thus began to supplant the once-unchallenged courtly patrons as makers of public taste.

Around the broad social changes sketched above took place a set of intellectual and spiritual changes no less striking. The Elizabethan court, like the Elizabethan church, had been hierarchical in organization. Queen, courtiers, and clergy united in declaring that this was in accord with the inevitable, God-given structure of things. Every creature, according to this conservative myth, had its place in the great order of divine appointments, and the different families of being were bound together by a chain of universal analogy or correspondence. The monarch was to his or her subjects as the lion was to other beasts, as the eagle was to other birds, as gold was to other metals—as the bishop was to his pastors and the pastors to their parishioners. Throughout, the higher power ruled the lower. The head ruled the other parts of the body because, as the seat of reason, it was the noblest part. Reason, which (supposedly) ruled in man, made him the natural ruler of the family because passion was supposed to rule in woman. And the greater part of all this ruling was necessary because of Adam and Eve's fall, as a result of which not only human psychology but the whole structure of the once-harmonious universe had been disordered. Though they differed over the form of rule and the name of the ruler, almost all the contestants in the civil wars agreed that the people needed strict discipline of some sort, because in themselves they were radically imperfect—tainted by the original sin and then by lots of other, subsequent ones. But while the various leaders were disputing over forms of discipline, the people, simply as a result of slow experience (by living under an "illegitimate" secular authority and without much religious conformity at all), demonstrated that they were less imperfect and needed less rigid discipline than had been supposed.

One universal truth emerged from the revolt and civil wars—that no one universal truth was to be had, whether by sword, prayer, or study. Nor was it really needed. Individuals, it seemed, could hold differing views about foreign policy, the nature of Christ's presence in the sacrament, or the lawfulness of infant baptism without necessarily precipitating social chaos. A single true belief in these matters, and in many others, was unnecessary. And thus the whole notion of human beings as radically fallen creatures, who needed a special saving truth and a dose of stiff preacherly discipline to redeem their faults, slowly began fading toward obsolescence. A reasonable person (one who behaved sensibly and didn't bother the neighbors) seemed to be almost as good as need be. In a long list of controversies over which people had once been willing to slit throats, it turned out that nobody was right and nobody was wrong. And thus the English community changed from one founded on the concepts of hierarchy, uniformity, and personal loyalty to one founded on the concepts of difference (verging sometimes on indifference) and mutual toleration. In less than a hundred years, the nation had passed through a stage of blood, hatred, and profound anxiety to a renewed sensation of relative calm. On the surface, it may have looked as if relatively little had changed. But subsurface, the whole character of the society had shifted, from a strict authoritarian regime legitimated (in its own eyes) by eternal divine constitutions—to a vigorous, materialistic, pragmatic community of competing pressure groups. Differences within the community were to be contained and managed, not eradicated. Slowly, the notion that a critic of the government must be a heretic and a traitor gave way to a gentler formula, which in the nineteenth century achieved classic expression: one could be "a member of His Majesty's loyal opposition."

With the obvious and important exceptions of Milton and Marvell, plus a scattering of minor poets like Francis Quarles and George Wither, very little of the enduring literature of the early seventeenth century was the work of Puritans or Puritan sympathizers. The great Puritan art forms of the age were the sermon and the religious tract. This is not just the joke it may seem. Puritan sermons, of which there were many thousands, explored in intimate detail the psychology of the Christian groping for evidence of salvation, and Puritan tracts developed forceful ways of exciting the zeal of their readers. Yet on the whole, the Puritans mistrusted the adornments of literary art on the same principle that they suspected graven idols (statues, stained-glass windows, and paintings), music, and religious rituals. These were all allurements and enticements of the sensual world; they threatened to contaminate and diffuse the pure spiritual energy of divinely infused faith. Though the Puritans did not directly compete with the old forms of courtly literature, they subjected those who did follow the old forms to heavy moral and social pressure. And on another level entirely, philosophers like Bacon and Hobbes campaigned unrelentingly against the use of insignificant words and merely decorative language. Like the Puritans, but from another angle, they insisted on a plain, direct manner of unequivocal prose. Though doubtless not put forward with this intent, one effect of the new plain language (sometimes summarized as "one-word-one-thing") was to undermine the whole intricate structure of the correspondent universe.

A sense of deep disquiet, of traditions under challenge, is felt everywhere in the literary culture of the early seventeenth century. Long before the term was applied to our own time, the era of Donne and Robert Burton (the obsessive anatomist of melancholy) deserved to be called the Age of Anxiety. One may well think of the "Metaphysical" poets who followed Donne (such as Herbert, Crashaw, Vaughan, and Cowley) as trying to reinforce the traditional lyric forms of love and devotion by stretching them to comprehend new and extreme intellectual energies. In the other direction, Jonson and his "sons" the so-called Cavalier poets (such as Herrick, Suckling, Lovelace, Waller, and Denham) generally tried to compress and limit their poems, giving them a high polish and a sense of easy domination at the expense (sometimes) of their intellectual content. Though these alternate "schools" do not by any means represent watertight compartments (Donne wrote some poems that sound like Jonson, Jonson some in the manner of Donne), the common contrast of Cavalier with Metaphysical does describe two poetic alternatives of the early century. Yet both styles were wholly inadequate containers for the sort of gigantic energy that Milton was trying to express.

For Milton, with his deep sense of moral imperative, his heroic ambitions for poetry, and his proud English Protestantism, the fashionable verses of his contemporaries must have seemed unbearably constricting. Like any great artist, Milton was capable of profiting from the study of craftsmen with temperaments and styles very different from his own; and he did profit by a study of Donne and Jonson, no doubt about it. But for his central inspiration Milton reached back beyond Metaphysicals and Jonsonians to a potent predecessor—Edmund Spenser. In youth, particularly, his mind ran to Spenserian projects, including epics of Arthurian and pre-Arthurian heroes, semiallegorical narratives, biblical pastorals, and similar fanciful schemes. Milton's style was fully formed by the late 1630s—it is usual to say that he found his voice in *Lycidas* (1637), and he might well have proceeded to complete one or more of these visionary projects. But it is not altogether a loss that the civil wars intervened and prevented him for twenty years from engaging his mind full-time with poetry.

Agonizing as they were, the wars did not involve constant bloodshed; rather, they were intervals of fighting separated by periods of negotiation and argument and accompanied by a constant, deep-seated turmoil of popular agitation. Especially on the parliamentary side, enthusiasts for a wide array of causes—political, social, and religious—began appealing for public support in the only way available to them, through the printing press. Most of their pamphlets, broadsheets, and newsletters made no pretensions to literary art; but some achieved a direct and forceful prose style, and a few attained not only eloquence but distinction of thought. The pamphlet wars, in which over twenty thousand verbal shots were fired off, wrought a mighty change in English public life. They accustomed thousands of English men and women, whose thinking had previously been fenced by strict censorship, to free reading and open argumentation; they created something close to what we now call public opinion. And the experience of Puritanism gave to English life a strong, steady moral tone, never so widely or deeply established before.

Thus when Milton returned to his epic ambitions after 1660, neither he nor his potential audience was anything like what it had been before the wars. Chivalric romance was out of the question; the issue on Milton's mind, and the nation's, was whether God maintained, behind the chaotic reversals of history, a sustaining plan for his favored people. That theme could not be approached through the favorite metaphors of Spenser, jousting knights, lovely ladies, dark enchanters, and hospitals for sick souls. It had to be approached through the central and very simple biblical narrative of creation, fall, and redemption. As the work of Milton's fifties, *Paradise Lost* was deeper, larger, more evangelical than anything he might have written in his thirties; it was well suited to a nation that had just passed through a massive spiritual crisis. Its author could never have dramatized so vividly the twin temptations of pride and despair had he himself not experienced both in full measure.

But *Paradise Lost* was also, inevitably, the product of Milton's surpassingly thorough classical education. It is thus a major monument—one of the last, one of the most admired—of the Renaissance tradition of Christian humanism. This is the assurance, shared by many writers of the period, that classical learning and the classical virtues (such as justice, magnanimity, and temperance), when joined in the service of Christian faith, strengthen both it and themselves. Gathering together in a grasp of unparalleled amplitude these major strands of European culture and forging them into a poised and balanced structure of epic dimensions, Milton created a poem that would be regarded for centuries as a supreme literary achievement.

Under the first two Stuarts, stage tragedy took on a particularly dark coloration. The oppressive mood is almost unbroken in the work of writers like Webster, Ford, Tourneur, and Middleton. But alongside this somber, sometimes morbid, tragedy, and serving as a relief from it, flourished a great variety of tragicomic spectacles, romantic comedies, and pastoral entertainments. Very often these plays were influenced by the masques so popular at court—that is, they included a great deal in the way of display, pageant, music, and sometimes fantasy. Though Shakespeare died in 1616, though Jonson—the great comic dramatist of the early century— gradually lost much of his creative power, and though none of the successors to these two men quite met their measure, the stage continued vigorously active right up to the onset of civil war. But then a Puritan edict shut the theaters, abruptly and apparently forever. By the time they reopened in 1660, most of the playwrights of the early century were dead, and the players had to rely at first on a backlog of old plays. The revival of drama depended very largely on the work of one man, Sir William Davenant, and on the example of the French stage, then at its height. Gradually the theaters built up a repertoire of new comedies (generally bawdy) and tragedies in the rhetorical, declamatory manner that gave them, and the couplets in which they were cast, the name "heroic." Both these fashions, like so much else in the Restoration, were extreme and temporary. Dryden, who practiced both modes, lived to see them both at an end—heroic tragedies under the weight of their own pomposity, bawdy comedies under the onslaught of an infuriated clergyman, Jeremy Collier.

Beyond, and perhaps outside, literature as such, but influencing it strongly, lies a change in the intellectual tone of the century, which was basically a shift in the relative importance of the intellectual disciplines. The great minds of the early century were mostly lawyers and theologians. Coke, Bacon, Selden, and Spelman among the lawyers and Laud, Andrewes, Cudworth, Ussher, and Chillingworth among the theologians were men famous in their generation. Of the lawyers, some are still consulted as authorities to this day—Coke is a name to conjure with in English law, and Selden's treatise *Titles of Honor* (1614) is obsolete only because the subject itself is. As for the theologians, their work too has lost its topicality; but a brief browsing expedition through the *Library of Anglo-Catholic Theology* cannot fail to convince the student that they were men who worked, in their chosen trade, to very high standards of precise and authoritative scholarship. And yet, as the century's intellectual weather changed, these disciplines ceased to be at the center of things. There were great lawyers after 1660, but they were not the makers and shakers of society; there were famous clergymen, but they did not determine society's central codes of belief. Starting about midcentury, the great names belong to other disciplines—they are physicists like Boyle, Hooke, and Newton; John Wallis the mathematician; Edmund Halley the astronomer; and William Harvey the anatomist—not to mention Hobbes and Locke, who as philosophers had particular influence on the assumptions of psychology and the exercise of precision in language. Few of these powerful figures set out deliberately to reconstruct an entire view of the cosmos; and Newton, who did so most successfully, retained to the end shreds and patches of the old beliefs. (He wrote a commentary on the Book of Revelation that has rather baffled those who admire his scientific works.) But a secular, materialist world view was in fact what emerged from the cumulative work of the scientists; even while some Puritans still clung to their dream of a community of saints, others of their own party were finding biblical texts to show that the kingdom of heaven might be brought closer by a dedicated pursuit of earthly knowledge.

BIRTH AND DEATH OF LITERARY FORMS

The stress and strain of a revolutionary age can thus be read at large in the century's literature, from the somber, sluggish melancholy prevalent in the early decades, through the hoarse, incoherent warfare of the middle years, to the slow firming up of new standards of correctness and decorum after 1660. Still another mark of violent change is provided by the number of literary forms that perished or dropped from favor in the course of the century, even as others were being born.

Sonnets, for example, were all the rage in the last years of Elizabeth and the first years of James. Almost always they dealt with erotic themes, often they were linked together in sequences to suggest, if not to tell, a story. Donne turned the sonnet entirely to religious themes; Milton's sonnets are mostly on religion and politics, though a few are personal. And many seventeenth-century poets had no use at all for sonnets: the form simply faded from the poetic repertory, not to revive again until the Romantic era. Allegory suffered an even more curious fate. It was the essential method of Spenser's *Faerie Queene*, and the figures of Sin and Death in the midst of *Paradise Lost* testify to its survival. But when Dryden used allegory (exceptionally, as in *The Hind and the Panther* [1687]), a kind of grotesque comedy clung to it, as if the form were fundamentally a joke. Serious allegory had slid far down the social scale; it was now the natural mode for an inspired primitive like John Bunyan, who wrote *The Pilgrim's Progress* (1678) and *The Life and Death of Mr. Badman* (1680).

Blighted by the frosts of Puritan disapproval, the masque and the madrigal both perished. The one was a courtly and the other a popular form, but both were suspect as vain, sensual, and worldly. Madrigals, as a blend of folk and art songs, were particularly to be regretted. For many years they had been sung in the yeoman's home or the merchant's parlor, to the accompaniment of lutes, viols, or recorders. Many made use of complex polyphonic harmonies; distinguished musicians devoted their talents to madrigals. But they faded away, and beside them faded all sorts of folk arts and folk customs—rounds and carols and morris dancing, maypoles, rural pageants, and country games—to make way for psalm singing and sermon listening. For the gentry after the Restoration, indigenous music was replaced by oratorios and operas, many of them imported from Italy, Germany, or France.

Alongside perishing forms, new ones developed. As had the Spenserians, the Metaphysical poets often preferred intricate stanzaic forms. When these lost favor, rhymed couplets—of which Jonson was an early and Waller a later exponent— came to the fore. Couplets are a superb meter for verse argumentation because they can combine the stinging effect of epigrams with the impetus of cumulative rhythms that build into splendid verse paragraphs. Whether coincidentally or as a consequence, the rise of regular couplets and discursive argument accompanied a perceptible decline of the lyric impulse. Elizabethan and Jacobean lyrics make up (to imitate the memorable title of an older collection) a "paradise of dainty devices." Restoration lyrics, though occasionally elegant and sometimes magnificently indecent, are far less numerous as well as less expressive.

The growing regularity of most Restoration metrics contrasted with a brief and not very widespread vogue for vehement and irregular verses fashioned after what Abraham Cowley understood by the Great Odes of Pindar. Modern opinion generally holds Cowley to have misunderstood his Greek models and finds a more accurate conception of Pindar in Jonson's *Ode on Cary and Morison*. Most of Cowley's *Pindaric Odes* (1656) were in fact not only extravagant but clumsy. His influence, however, was better than his examples, and modified Pindarics continued to be used occasionally through the eighteenth and nineteenth centuries to express lofty and dignified sentiments. These latter-day Pindarics (as by Dryden, and subsequently Gray and Wordsworth) don't sound much like Cowley, but Cowley's precedent did something to free them from the stiffness that is the besetting fault of the Great Ode in English.

Formal verse satire, which had been a self-conscious novelty at the beginning of the century, was a well-established mode of poetry by its end. Under the molding of many hands, satire grew subtler and more various; satirists recognized their responsibility to divert their readers as well as to insult their antagonists. Indeed a whole new mode of sharp gentlemanly discourse grew up after the Restoration; it went sometimes by the name of "raillery," sometimes "banter," and amounted to nothing more than light irony. But serious things could be said in it, about which nonetheless a gentleman might not want to show himself too earnest. Below satire, burlesque was another literary mode that the seventeenth century nurtured, with the aid of France. After the unrelieved earnestness of the Puritans, derision and buffoonery delighted the popular taste, and with the advent of burlesque, we find ourselves on the very threshold of the modern novel, one vein of which reaches as far back as *Don Quixote*.

The advent of the novel was also prepared for by major changes in the character of English prose, which took place especially in consequence of the pamphlet wars and the twenty-year hegemony of Puritan taste from 1640 to 1660. Prose as an art form flourished under the first Stuarts, not always without a flavor of self-display. Donne, preaching before King James or the societies of learned lawyers at the Inns of Court, put on pyrotechnical exhibitions of wit, ingenuity, and visionary eloquence. Not that he was insincere; his mind worked that way, and so did the minds of his auditory. Similarly with the infinitely erudite, infinitely patient Lancelot Andrewes, and so with dozens of less renowned clerics, who saw that the path to preferment lay through a special sort of witty eloquence. Like these witty preachers, Sir Thomas Browne wrote in response to his own private impulses and turns of feeling, but for inward, meditative, and very learned readers. A kind of embryonic fiction flourished quite widely in the form of "characters"—detailed, static, humorous accounts, generally of social types, on whom the writer exercised his wit. Most character writers tipped their pens with a touch of satire; all implied, sooner or later, a moral attitude. Witty moralists like Owen Felltham and Dr. Thomas Fuller (the latter notable also as a church historian and annalist) contribute to our sense of prose in the age of Donne and Browne as a flourishing and various art form.

Milton as a prose writer represents a specially instructive case. His learned and often intricate style was formed well before the revolt, in the privacy of his library, to the taste of an imagined aristocracy of learning. But then it was first brought forth into the turmoil and rough confusion of the civil wars to jostle for public favor with productions of the butcher, the baker, and the unlearned candlestick maker. For all his flights of soaring eloquence (to which posterity has paid ample respect), Milton was not in his own time an effective controversialist. His ideas were too complex and erudite; their expression was too allusive. How could a pamphlet called *Areopagitica* hope for popular success when most potential purchasers could not pronounce (far less understand) the title?

The lesson taught by the pamphlet wars on the advantage of a simple style was reinforced by the teachings of the philosophers Bacon, Hobbes, and Locke and by the example of the scientists who began quietly meeting during the Protectorate as a "Philosophical College" and became after the Restoration the Royal Society. Plain speech became, first, a technique to be learned and then a natural formula for "transparent," apparently artless prose. Dorothy Osborne tells a fine story about an old uncle of hers who despised metaphorical speech. Trying to communicate with a friend, he told his secretary to say he would have written himself, but had the gout in his hand. What the fellow wrote was that the gout in his hand would not allow his master to put pen to paper—a piece of fancying-up that so enraged the old gentleman that he flung the inkwell at his servant's head.

Whether untutored and "natural" or carefully practiced, the plain style (which inevitably developed into a thousand different degrees and sorts of plainness) proved immensely useful. In Locke's philosophical writings it became the vehicle of a commonsense British empiricism; in Dryden's prefaces it adapted to careful critical balances; and in politicians it served to express graceful, unemphatic innuendos. Genteel comment on occasional, and sometimes on learned, topics was voiced by Abraham Cowley and later by Sir William Temple. For better or worse, the first English newsletters, and then newspapers, sprang up during the civil wars. Political commentators started to make themselves heard, and Izaak Walton completed his series of reverential biographies of English divines. As the century passed, preachers found that they could no longer entertain audiences with intricate similitudes and microscopic, word-by-word explication of texts; ranting and raving (known more politely as "zeal") were also out of fashion. Instead, they turned increasingly to plainly phrased, commonsense discussions of practical morality and found that such discourses pleased their audiences about as well as anything.

All these developments presupposed a reading audience responsive, alert, and eager to be informed—not necessarily instructed in classical culture or trained in courtly conventions, but ready to follow a sustained discourse in unrhetorical, commonsense English. Such an audience, so tuned and so motivated, not expecting too much from its reading, but responsive to acute arguments or vivid touches of the imagination, is a first premise of modern literature. We are apt to consider it as normal and natural a phenomenon as the air we breathe, but it is not. It had to be created slowly, hesitantly, without much conscious direction on anyone's part, by a process of gradual accretion and expansion. Its existence is the foundation of the new literary age and the culminating achievement of the early seventeenth century.

Being diverse out of harsh necessity and tolerant only reluctantly, the century was often halting and unsteady in its taste. It was forging new standards, not accepting the guidance of old ones. Women did important work on both sides during the civil wars; their letters and diaries provide vivid pictures of a rapidly changing social landscape. But their contributions to the traditional genres of *belles-lettres*, while increasingly numerous, often lack the sureness of purpose of their informal prose and the formal polish of the works of their male counterparts. For centuries, the most elementary learning had been begrudged to most women. Even the humanists who urged most strongly education for women often did so only on the score that education would make them more devout and docile Christians. Erotic love, which was the major theme of Renaissance versifying, was not acceptable as a theme for a woman to write about. Katherine Philips, whose sobriquet "the matchless Orinda" indicates her status as the most renowned female poet of the midcentury, made a specialty of celebrating her platonic relationships with friends of both sexes. Naturally, a woman of great wealth and social prestige, like the duchess of Newcastle, was less inhibited from writing and publishing; but Lady Mary Wroth, after one rash act of publication, was silenced for the rest of her life. Though the women struggled (and with only partial success) to find voices of their own, the age to come would speak more assuredly because of them.

Science also advanced gropingly through a series of corrected errors and inspired guesses. The same age saw Sir Kenelm Digby's solemn proposal that one could cure wounds by medicating the sword that caused them, and William Harvey's proclamation of the circulation of the blood. Though much of Inigo Jones's work in architecture was destroyed, some of his actual structures and more of his important translations of Italian books on architecture survived, to provide a lead for neoclassical building in England and North America during the eighteenth century. Though the Puritan commonwealth went to smash as a political organization, many of the ideas expressed during those hectic midcentury years maintained an underground existence and blossomed at the time of the American Revolution, more than a century later.

Thus the early seventeenth century brought to its culmination much that had been characteristic from the beginning of the English Renaissance and at the same time advanced boldly across the threshold of the next age, whatever one prefers to call it. Although its elapsed time is relatively brief, the period changed not only the tone of literature but the very definition of what literature could be. Like all great cultural shifts, this one was too complex to be captured in a single phrase or attributed to a single cause. It had neither a fixed beginning nor a precise end. But in the seamless web of history we can hardly fail to notice new colors and textures that, over the short course of the early seventeenth century, enter into the warp and woof of the nation's literary as of its social life, to make it look and feel like a whole new piece of cloth.

TEXTS	CONTEXTS
c. 1603–07 Shakespeare, *Othello, King Lear, Macbeth*	1603–25 Reign of James I
1605 Sir Francis Bacon, *Advancement of Learning* • Cervantes, first part of *Don Quixote*	1605 Gunpowder Plot, a failed effort by Catholic extremists to blow up Parliament and the king
	1607 Founding of Jamestown colony in Virginia
	1608 French explorer Samuel de Champlain founds Quebec
1611 "King James" version of the Bible	
	1615 Donne ordained as priest in the Church of England
1616 Folio edition of Jonson's *Works*	1616 Death of Shakespeare
	1619 First African slaves in North America exchanged by Dutch frigate for food and supplies at Jamestown
	1620 Pilgrims land at Plymouth
1621 Lady Mary Wroth, *Urania*	1621 Donne appointed dean of St. Paul's Cathedral
1623 Shakespeare Folio, first collected edition of his works	
	1625–49 Reign of Charles I
	1629 Charles I dissolves Parliament
1633 Donne's collected poems and George Herbert's *The Temple*, both published posthumously	1633 The Inquisition forces Galileo Galilei to recant the Copernican theory
1637 John Milton, **Lycidas**	
	1640 Long Parliament called • William Laud, archbishop of Canterbury, is impeached
	1642 Outbreak of civil war • Parliament closes the theaters

Boldface titles indicate works in the anthology.

TEXTS	CONTEXTS
	1643–1715 Reign of Louis XIV of France
1644 Milton's *Areopagitica,* opposing censorship law by Parliament	
	1645 Archbishop Laud executed • Parliamentary army decisively defeats Royalists at the Battle of Naseby
1648 Robert Herrick, evicted from his parish by the Puritans, publishes *Hesperides*	
	1649 Charles I tried and executed • Milton defends the regicide and is appointed Latin secretary to the Council of State
	1651 Milton becomes blind but continues work as Latin secretary
	1653 Oliver Cromwell made Lord Protector
	1658 Death of Cromwell; he is succeeded by his son Richard
	1660 Return of Charles II from exile in France and restoration of the monarchy
1667 Milton, *Paradise Lost*	
	1674 Death of Milton
1681 Andrew Marvell, *Miscellaneous Poems,* published posthumously	

JOHN DONNE
1572–1631

1601:   Secret marriage to Ann More.
1615:   Becomes an Anglican priest.
1621:   Appointed dean of St. Paul's Cathedral.
1633:   First publication of *Poems*.

Donne himself originated an observation about his life and character that, though only partly accurate, has become commonplace. In a private letter, he distinguished Jack Donne, an adventurous young spark who wrote bawdy and cynical verses to an assortment of mistresses, from the grave and eloquent divine, Dr. Donne, the dean of St. Paul's. The contrast is striking, but the key to both characters is the same: it is a restless, searching energy that scorns the easy platitude and the smooth, vacant phrase; that is vivid, immediate, troubling. Whether he is flaunting his pleasure at chasing every woman in sight (as in *The Indifferent*) or voicing total repentance and devotion to God (as in the *Holy Sonnets*), Donne's poetry demands imaginative effort of the reader, whom it absorbs in a tense, complex experience.

Donne was born into an old Roman Catholic family, at a time when anti-Catholic feeling in England was near its height and Catholics were subject to constant harassment by the Elizabethan secret police. His faith barred him from many of the usual avenues of success, and his point of view was always that of an insecure outsider. Though he attended both Oxford and Cambridge universities, as well as Lincoln's Inn (where lawyers got their training), he never took any academic degrees and never practiced law. After quietly abandoning Catholicism some time during the 1590s, he had scruples about becoming an Anglican. He had no gift for commerce, and though he inherited money from his father (who died when Donne was only four), it was far from enough to render him independent. Hence he had to make his way in the world indirectly—by wit, charm, learning, valor, and above all, favor. Partly from sheer intellectual curiosity, he read enormously in divinity, medicine, law, and the classics; he wrote to display his learning and wit. He traveled on the Continent, especially, it would seem, to Spain; even in later years, he did a good deal of moving around. With Ralegh and Essex he took part in two hit-and-run expeditions against Cádiz and the Azores. He put himself in the way of court employment, danced attendance on great court ladies, and generally lived the life of a brilliant young man hopeful of preferment.

When in 1598 Donne was appointed private secretary to Sir Thomas Egerton, one of the highest officials in the queen's court, his prospects for worldly advancement seemed good. He sat in Elizabeth's last Parliament; he cultivated those who wielded power and had patronage to dispense. But in 1601, he secretly married Lady Egerton's niece, seventeen-year-old Ann More, and thereby ruined his own worldly hopes. The marriage turned out happily, but Donne's bad faith to his employer was neither forgotten nor forgiven. Sir George More had Donne imprisoned and dismissed from his post, and for the next dozen years the poet had to struggle at a series of makeshift employments to support his growing family. In his midthirties, Donne was far from the brilliant young gallant of the 1590s; sick, poor, and unhappy, he wrote, but dared not publish, a treatise of the lawfulness of suicide (*Biathanatos*). As he approached forty, he published two anti-Catholic polemics (*Pseudo-Martyr*, 1610; *Ignatius his Conclave*, 1611); they sealed publicly his renunciation of the Catholic faith. In return for patronage from Sir Robert Drury, he wrote in 1611 and 1612 a pair of long poems, the *Anniversaries*, on the death of Sir Robert's daughter Elizabeth. None of these activities represented a full employment of Donne's pent-up intellectual energy. To be sure, his social position should not be painted too blackly. He still had friends among courtiers, politicians, poets, and the great ladies around court, like Lucy, countess of Bedford, and Magdalen Herbert with her two poet sons, George and Edward. Donne was never quite without resources; yet, broadly speaking, the middle years of his life were a period of uncertainty and discontent.

Though Donne had flatly refused in 1607 to take Anglican orders, King James was certain that he would some day make a great Anglican preacher. Hence he declared that Donne could have no preferment or employment from him, except in the church. Finally, in 1615, Donne overcame his scruples, not the least of which was the fear of seeming ambitious, and entered the ministry. He was in due course appointed Reader in Divinity at Lincoln's Inn. In the seventeenth century, among court circles and at the Inns of Court where lawyers congregated, preaching was at once a form of spiritual devotion, an intellectual exercise, and a dramatic entertainment. Donne's metaphorical style, bold erudition, and dramatic wit at once established him as a great preacher in an age of great preachers. Fully 160 of his sermons survive. In 1621 he was made dean of St. Paul's, where he preached to great congregations of "City" lawyers, courtiers, merchants, and tradesmen. In addition, his private devotions were published in 1624, and he continued to write sacred poetry into his late years. Obsessed with the idea of death, Donne preached what was called his own funeral sermon, just a few weeks before he died. It is a terrifyingly personal meditation on dissolution, as befits a man who arranged for a final portrait of himself to be painted, dressed in his shroud.

The poetry of Donne represents a sharp break with that written by his predecessors and most of his contemporaries. Much Elizabethan verse is decorative and flowery. Its images adorn, its rhythm is mellifluous. Its frequent "conceits" (elaborately sustained metaphors) are often variations on comparisons passed down through generations of poets in a line from Petrarch in the fourteenth century. But Donne, taking his cue from recent Continental poets who had freshened the Petrarchan tradition by developing a more intellectualized form of conceit, created highly concentrated images that involve a major element of dramatic contrast or of intellectual strain. The clichés of earlier love poetry—bleeding hearts, cheeks like roses, lips like cherries, Cupid shooting the arrows of love—appear in Donne's poetry only to be mocked or in some ingenious transmutation. The tears that flow in *A Valediction: Of Weeping* are different from, and more complex than, the ordinary saline fluid of unhappy lovers; they are ciphers, naughts, symbols of the world's emptiness without the beloved; or else, suddenly reflecting her image, they are globes, worlds, they contain the sum of things. By using such conceits, the poet not only displays his own ingenuity but may express a deep vision of the world and the strands of analogy that seem to hold it together. Donne's conceits leap continually in a restless orbit from the personal to the cosmic and back again.

Donne likes to twist and distort not only images and ideas but traditional rhythmic and stanzaic patterns. His speech patterns are colloquial and various. Ben Jonson expressed the shock of some contemporaries by saying that "Donne, for not keeping of accent [i.e., metrical uniformity], deserved hanging"—though he also said that Donne was "the first poet in the world in some things." While Donne sometimes uses traditional verse forms, and indeed very simple ones, he is also fond of inventing elaborate and intricate stanzas. His penchant for compressed and elliptical expression often produces difficulty for the reader. In the satires, which Renaissance writers understood to be "harsh" and "crabbed" as a genre, Donne's distortions often threaten to choke off the stream of expression entirely. But in the lyrics (both those that are worldly and those that are religious in theme), as in the elegies and sonnets, the verse repeatedly achieves a complex and memorable melody.

Donne and his followers are known to literary history as the "Metaphysical school" of poets. Strictly speaking, this is a misnomer. There was no organized group of poets who imitated Donne, and if there had been, they would not have called themselves Metaphysical poets. That term was invented by John Dryden and Samuel Johnson. But the influence of Donne's poetic style was widely felt, especially by writers whose taste was formed before 1660. George Herbert, Richard Crashaw, Henry Vaughan, Andrew Marvell, and Abraham Cowley are only the best known of those in whom this influence is recognizable. The great change of taste that took place around 1660 threw Donne and the "conceited" style out of fashion; during the eighteenth and nineteenth centuries both he and his followers were rarely read and still more rarely appreciated. Finally, in the late nineteenth and early twentieth centuries, three new editions of Donne appeared, of which Sir H. J. C. Grierson's, published in 1912, was quickly accepted as standard. By clarifying and purifying the often-garbled text, Grierson did a great deal to make Donne's poetry more available to the modern reader. Almost at once it started to exert an influence on modern poetic practice, the modern poets being hungry for a "tough" style that would free them from the worn-out rhetoric of late-nineteenth-century Romanticism. And Donne's status among the English poets quickly climbed from that of a curiosity to that of an acknowledged master.

No more than a couple of the poems on which Donne's modern reputation is built were published during his lifetime, though most of them were widely circulated through court and literary circles in handwritten copies. There were practical reasons for this halfway state of affairs. Many of the poems would have constituted black marks on Donne's reputation as an earnest and godly divine, and because they were difficult and allusive, only a few people wanted to read them. Thus Donne was known, outside the relatively limited circles that had access to manuscript collections, primarily as a preacher and devotional writer. His collected poems were first published in 1633; in the second edition (1635) the poems were divided into nine generic groups (one of which includes only a single long poem, *The Progress of the Soul*). The *Songs and Sonnets*, which open the volume, are generally amorous in theme; the *Divine Poems*, which close it, treat religious themes. In between fall groups of epigrams, love elegies, epithalamia (wedding songs), satires, verse letters, and funeral elegies. For convenience, our selections from the poetry, like those of most other editors, generally follow the order of the 1635 edition, though this is distinctly *not* the order in which Donne wrote the poems. Indeed, a detailed chronology is impossible to construct. The basic text for most of the poems, though, is that of the first, 1633, edition, sometimes supplemented and corrected by reference to other early editions and to manuscript materials. Recent editions, especially those by Helen Gardner and W. Milgate, have also been consulted.

The Good-Morrow[1]

I wonder, by my troth, what thou and I
Did, till we loved? Were we not weaned till then,
But sucked on country pleasures, childishly?

1. Like many other modern editors, we follow H. J. C. Grierson in making *The Good-Morrow* the first poem in the *Songs and Sonnets* group—by declining to follow, in this one instance, the order of the second (1635) edition of Donne's *Poems*, where pride of place is given to *The Flea*. Confusingly, the *Songs and Sonnets* do not include any sonnets in our sense: in Donne's time, the term often meant simply "love lyric." Though precise dating is impossible, it is safe to suppose that Donne wrote all, or almost all, of the fifty-three poems in the last decade of the 16th and first decade of the 17th centuries.

Or snorted we in the seven sleepers' den?[2]
'Twas so; but[3] this, all pleasures fancies be.   5
If ever any beauty I did see,
Which I desired, and got, 'twas but a dream of thee.

And now good morrow to our waking souls,
Which watch not one another out of fear;
For love all love of other sights controls,   10
And makes one little room an everywhere.
Let sea-discoverers to new worlds have gone,
Let maps to others, worlds on worlds have shown:[4]
Let us possess one world;[5] each hath one, and is one.

My face in thine eye, thine in mine appears,   15
And true plain hearts do in the faces rest;
Where can we find two better hemispheres,
Without sharp North, without declining West?
Whatever dies was not mixed equally;[6]
If our two loves be one, or thou and I   20
Love so alike that none do slacken, none can die.

                                                            1633

Song

Go and catch a falling star,
    Get with child a mandrake root,[1]
Tell me where all past years are,
    Or who cleft the Devil's foot,
Teach me to hear mermaids[2] singing,   5
Or to keep off envy's stinging,
        And find
        What wind
Serves to advance an honest mind.

If thou beest born to strange sights,   10
    Things invisible to see,
Ride ten thousand days and nights,
    Till age snow white hairs on thee,
Thou, when thou return'st, wilt tell me
All strange wonders that befell thee,   15
        And swear
        No where
Lives a woman true, and fair.

2. Many ancient authors recite the legend of seven youths of Ephesus who hid in a cave from their pagan persecutors and slept there for 187 years, awakening to find, amazedly, that the world had become Christian while they slept.
3. Except for.
4. I.e., let us concede that maps (or charts of the heavens) have shown to other investigators, etc.
5. An alternative reading is "Let us possess our world."

6. Scholastic philosophy taught that when the elements were imperfectly ("not equally") mixed, matter was mutable and mortal, but when they were perfectly mixed, it was unchanging and undying.
1. The mandrake root, or mandragora, is forked like the lower part of the human body. Getting such a vegetable root with child presents obvious difficulties.
2. Identified with the sirens, whose song only the wily Odysseus survived.

If thou find'st one, let me know,
    Such a pilgrimage were sweet;   20
Yet do not, I would not go,
    Though at next door we might meet;
Though she were true when you met her,
And last till you write your letter,
      Yet she   25
      Will be
False, ere I come, to two, or three.

1633

The Undertaking

I have done one braver thing
    Than all the Worthies[1] did,
And yet a braver thence doth spring,
    Which is, to keep that hid.

It were but madness now t' impart   5
    The skill of specular stone,[2]
When he which can have learned the art
    To cut it, can find none.

So, if I now should utter this,
    Others (because no more   10
Such stuff to work upon, there is)
    Would love but as before.

But he who loveliness within
    Hath found, all outward loathes,
For he who color loves, and skin,   15
    Loves but their[3] oldest clothes.

If, as I have, you also do
    Virtue attired in woman see,
And dare love that, and say so too,
    And forget the He and She;   20

And if this love, though placèd so,
    From profane men you hide,
Which will no faith on this bestow,
    Or, if they do, deride;

Then you have done a braver thing   25
    Than all the Worthies did;

1. According to medieval legend, the Nine Worthies, or supreme heroes of history, included three Jews (Joshua, David, Judas Maccabeus), three pagans (Hector, Alexander, Julius Caesar), and three Christians (Arthur, Charlemagne, Godfrey of Bouillon).
2. A transparent or translucent material, reputed to have been used in antiquity for windows, but no longer known.
3. I.e., women's.

And a braver thence will spring,
    Which is, to keep that hid.

1633

The Sun Rising

Busy old fool, unruly sun,
    Why dost thou thus
Through windows and through curtains call on us?
Must to thy motions lovers' seasons run?
        Saucy pedantic wretch, go chide   5
        Late schoolboys and sour prentices,
    Go tell court huntsmen that the King will ride,[1]
    Call country ants to harvest offices;[2]
Love, all alike, no season knows nor clime,
Nor hours, days, months, which are the rags of time.   10

        Thy beams, so reverend and strong
        Why shouldst thou think?
I could eclipse and cloud them with a wink,
But that I would not lose her sight so long;
        If her eyes have not blinded thine,   15
        Look, and tomorrow late, tell me,
    Whether both th' Indias of spice and mine[3]
    Be where thou leftst them, or lie here with me.
Ask for those kings whom thou saw'st yesterday,
And thou shalt hear, All here in one bed lay.   20

        She is all states,[4] and all princes I,
        Nothing else is.
Princes do but play us; compared to this,
All honor's mimic, all wealth alchemy.[5]
        Thou, sun, art half as happy as we,   25
        In that the world's contracted thus;
    Thine age asks ease, and since thy duties be
    To warm the world, that's done in warming us.
Shine here to us, and thou art everywhere;
This bed thy center is,[6] these walls thy sphere.   30

1633

The Indifferent

I can love both fair and brown,[1]
Her whom abundance melts, and her whom want betrays,

1. King James was addicted to hunting.
2. Autumn chores. The "country ants" may imply an allusion to the old fable of the ant and the grasshopper.
3. The India of "spice" is East India, that of "mine" (gold) the West Indies.
4. All the nations of the world.

5. I.e., fraudulent.
6. As the earth was the center of the sun's orbit (according to the old Ptolemaic astronomy), so the bed will be the new center of the sun's activities and the walls of the bedroom will outline its motion.
1. Both blond and brunet.

Her who loves loneness best, and her who masks and plays,
Her whom the country formed, and whom the town,
Her who believes, and her who tries,[2]   5
Her who still weeps with spongy eyes,
And her who is dry cork, and never cries;
I can love her, and her, and you, and you,
I can love any, so she be not true.

Will no other vice content you?   10
Will it not serve your turn to do as did your mothers?
Or have you all old vices spent, and now would find out others?
Or doth a fear that men are true torment you?
O we are not, be not you so;
Let me, and do you, twenty know.   15
Rob me, but bind me not, and let me go.
Must I, who came to travail thorough[3] you,
Grow your fixed subject, because you are true?

Venus heard me sigh this song,
And by love's sweetest part, variety, she swore,   20
She heard not this till now; and that it should be so no more.
She went, examined, and returned ere long,
And said, Alas, some two or three
Poor heretics in love there be,
Which think to 'stablish dangerous constancy.   25
But I have told them, Since you will be true,
You shall be true to them who are false to you.

                                                                    1633

The Canonization

For God's sake hold your tongue, and let me love,
     Or chide my palsy, or my gout,
My five gray hairs, or ruined fortune, flout,
     With wealth your state, your mind with arts improve,
          Take you a course, get you a place,[1]   5
          Observe His Honor, or His Grace,
Or the King's real, or his stampèd face[2]
     Contemplate; what you will, approve,[3]
          So you will let me love.

     Alas, alas, who's injured by my love?   10
          What merchant's ships have my sighs drowned?
     Who says my tears have overflowed his ground?
          When did my colds a forward spring remove?[4]
               When did the heats which my veins fill

2. Tests.
3. Through. "Travail": grief, sorrow, but also journey, travel.
1. A "place" is an appointment, at court or elsewhere. "Take you a course": in the general sense of "settle yourself in life."

2. On coins.
3. Put to proof, find by experience.
4. Petrarchan lovers traditionally sigh, weep, and are frozen by their mistresses' neglect. "Forward": early or well-advanced.

Add one man to the plaguy bill?[5]   15
Soldiers find wars, and lawyers find out still
    Litigious men, which quarrels move,
    Though she and I do love.

Call us what you will, we are made such by love;
    Call her one, me another fly,   20
We're tapers too, and at our own cost die,[6]
And we in us find the eagle and the dove.[7]
        The phoenix riddle hath more wit
        By us:[8] we two being one, are it.
So, to one neutral thing both sexes fit.   25
    We die and rise the same, and prove
    Mysterious by this love.

We can die by it, if not live by love,
    And if unfit for tombs and hearse
Our legend be, it will be fit for verse;   30
    And if no piece of chronicle we prove,
        We'll build in sonnets pretty rooms;
        As well a well-wrought urn becomes[9]
The greatest ashes, as half-acre tombs,
    And by these hymns,[1] all shall approve   35
    Us canonized for love:

And thus invoke us: You whom reverend love
    Made one another's hermitage;
You, to whom love was peace, that now is rage;
    Who did the whole world's soul contract,[2] and drove   40
        Into the glasses of your eyes
        (So made such mirrors, and such spies,
    That they did all to you epitomize)
    Countries, towns, courts: Beg from above
    A pattern of your love![3]   45

                                                              1633

5. Deaths from the hot weather plague were recorded, by parish, in weekly bills.
6. We're both fly (the ephemeral moth) and the self-consuming candle that attracts it. Donne hints here at the old superstition that intercourse shortens life. (To "die," in the punning terminology of the 17th century, was to experience orgasm.)
7. The eagle signifies such qualities as strength and vision; the dove, meekness and mercy. The phoenix was a fabulous Arabian bird, only one of which existed at any one time. After living five hundred years, it lit its nest of spices, jumped in, and sang its funeral song as it was consumed—then rose triumphantly from its ashes, a new bird. Thus it was a symbol of immortality and was sometimes associated with Christ. "Eagle" and "dove" are also alchemical terms for processes leading to the rise of "phoenix," a stage in the transmutation of metals.
8. I.e., the story of the phoenix seems more plausible, now that we've shown how male and female can fuse.
9. Befits. The "rooms" (punning on the Italian meaning of "stanza") will hold the ashes—i.e., record their exploits—as prose history records great deeds in other spheres.
1. The lover's own poems, which become hymns for a new love religion. "All" (posterity) shall "approve" (confirm) us as love's saints.
2. An alternative reading is "extract."
3. The poet and his mistress, turned to saints, are implored by the rest of the population to get from heaven ("above") a pattern of their love for general distribution. "Countries, towns, courts" are objects of the verb "drove": the notion that eyes both see and reflect the outside world, and so "contain" it doubly, was very delightful to Donne.

Air and Angels

Twice or thrice had I loved thee,
Before I knew thy face or name;
So in a voice, so in a shapeless flame,
Angels affect us oft, and worshipped be;
      Still when, to where thou wert, I came,   5
Some lovely glorious nothing I did see.
      But since my soul, whose child love is,
Takes limbs of flesh, and else could nothing do,[1]
      More subtle than the parent is
Love must not be, but take a body too;   10
      And therefore what thou wert, and who,
        I bid love ask, and now
That it assume thy body I allow,
And fix itself in thy lip, eye, and brow.

Whilst thus to ballast love I thought,   15
And so more steadily to have gone,
With wares which would sink admiration,
I saw I had love's pinnace overfraught;[2]
      Every thy hair for love to work upon
Is much too much, some fitter must be sought;   20
      For, nor in nothing, nor in things
Extreme and scatt'ring[3] bright, can love inhere.
      Then as an angel, face and wings
Of air, not pure as it, yet pure doth wear,
      So thy love may be my love's sphere;   25
        Just such disparity
As is 'twixt air and angels' purity,
'Twixt women's love and men's will ever be.[4]

1633

Break of Day[1]

'Tis true, 'tis day; what though it be?
O wilt thou therefore rise from me?
Why should we rise because 'tis light?
Did we lie down because 'twas night?
Love, which in spite of darkness brought us hither,   5
Should in despite of light keep us together.

Light hath no tongue, but is all eye;
If it could speak as well as spy,

1. As my soul could not function unless it were in a body, so love, which is the soul's child, must also be corporeal.
2. Her physical beauty (his "wares") would sink admiration—i.e., overwhelm wonder itself. This is too much ballast for love's "pinnace" (a small boat).
3. Diffused, dazzling.
4. Some Scholastic philosophers held that angels, when they appeared to humans, assumed a body of air.

Such a body, though pure, was less so than the angel's spiritual being. Similarly, women's love, which Donne assumes to be less pure than that of men, may serve as the "sphere" within which the love of men moves as a governing angel.
1. Recalling the Provençal aubade or song of the lovers' parting at dawn, this poem is unusual for Donne in that it assumes a feminine point of view.

This were the worst that it could say,
That being well, I fain would stay,   10
And that I loved my heart and honor so
That I would not from him, that had them, go.

Must business thee from hence remove?
O, that's the worst disease of love.
The poor, the foul, the false, love can   15
Admit, but not the busied man.
He which hath business, and makes love, doth do
Such wrong, as when a married man doth woo.

1633

A Valediction: Of Weeping

Let me pour forth
My tears before thy face whilst I stay here,
For thy face coins them,[1] and thy stamp they bear,
And by this mintage they are something worth,
For thus they be   5
Pregnant of thee;
Fruits of much grief they are, emblems of more—
When a tear falls, that Thou falls which it bore,
So thou and I are nothing then, when on a diverse shore.[2]

On a round ball   10
A workman that hath copies by can lay
An Europe, Afric, and an Asia,
And quickly make that, which was nothing, all;[3]
So doth each tear
Which thee doth wear,[4]   15
A globe, yea world, by that impression grow,
Till thy tears mixed with mine do overflow
This world; by waters sent from thee, my heaven dissolvèd so.

O more than moon,
Draw not up seas to drown me in thy sphere;   20
Weep me not dead in thine arms, but forbear
To teach the sea what it may do too soon.
Let not the wind
Example find
To do me more harm than it purposeth;   25
Since thou and I sigh one another's breath,
Whoe'er sighs most is cruelest, and hastes the other's death.

1633

---

1. I.e., they reflect her face.
2. The extinction of the lovers in their separation is prefigured in the fall of a tear that contains the image of the mistress.
3. I.e., on a blank globe an artist can paste maps of the continents and so convert a cipher, the image of nothingness, to the whole world.
4. Bears your image.

Love's Alchemy

Some that have deeper digged love's mine than I,
Say where his centric happiness doth lie:
   I have loved, and got, and told,[1]
But should I love, get, tell, till I were old,
I should not find that hidden mystery;   5
     O, 'tis imposture all:
And as no chemic yet the elixir[2] got,
    But glorifies his pregnant pot[3]
    If by the way to him befall
Some odoriferous thing, or medicinal;   10
   So lovers dream a rich and long delight,
   But get a winter-seeming summer's night.[4]

Our ease, our thrift, our honor, and our day,
Shall we for this vain bubble's shadow pay?
    Ends love in this, that my man   15
Can be as happy as I can, if he can
Endure the short scorn of a bridegroom's play?
    That loving wretch that swears
'Tis not the bodies marry, but the minds,
    Which he in her angelic finds,   20
    Would swear as justly that he hears,
In that day's rude hoarse minstrelsy, the spheres.[5]
   Hope not for mind in women; at their best
Sweetness and wit they are but mummy possessed.[6]

                                   1633

The Flea

Mark but this flea, and mark in this,
How little that which thou deniest me is;
Me it sucked first, and now sucks thee,
And in this flea our two bloods mingled be;
Thou know'st that this cannot be said   5
A sin, or shame, or loss of maidenhead,
   Yet this enjoys before it woo,
   And pampered swells with one blood made of two,
   And this, alas, is more than we would do.[1]

Oh stay, three lives in one flea spare,   10
Where we almost, nay more than married are.

1. Counted, calculated.
2. A magic medicine sought by alchemists and reputed to heal all ills. "Chemic": alchemist.
3. Praises his fertile (and womb-shaped) retort.
4. A night cold as in winter and short as in summer.
5. The perfect harmony of the planets, moving in concentric crystalline spheres, is contrasted with the charivari, a boisterous serenade for pots, pans, and trumpets, performed on the wedding night.
6. The syntax of the last two lines is very dark; the last line in particular may be read with a comma after "wit," after "are," or after "mummy." The final word may modify "mummy," to signify "mummy with a demon in it," or "they," to signify "women who when you have possessed them." A comma after "best" would change the whole balance of the ending. Some sort of misogyny is almost certainly expressed.
1. I.e., we, alas, don't dare hope for this consummation of our love, which the flea freely accepts. The idea of swelling suggests pregnancy.

This flea is you and I, and this
Our marriage bed and marriage temple is;
Though parents grudge, and you, we are met,
And cloistered in these living walls of jet.   15
     Though use[2] make you apt to kill me,
     Let not to that, self-murder added be,
     And sacrilege, three sins in killing three.

Cruel and sudden, hast thou since
Purpled thy nail in blood of innocence?[3]   20
Wherein could this flea guilty be,
Except in that drop which it sucked from thee?
Yet thou triumph'st, and say'st that thou
Find'st not thy self nor me the weaker now;
     'Tis true; then learn how false fears be: 25
     Just so much honor, when thou yield'st to me,
     Will waste, as this flea's death took life from thee.

                                                                              1633

A Nocturnal upon Saint Lucy's Day, Being the Shortest Day[1]

'Tis the year's midnight and it is the day's,
Lucy's, who scarce seven hours herself unmasks;
     The sun is spent, and now his flasks
     Send forth light squibs,[2] no constant rays.
          The world's whole sap is sunk;   5
The general balm th' hydroptic[3] earth hath drunk,
Whither, as to the bed's feet, life is shrunk,
Dead and interred; yet all these seem to laugh,
Compared with me, who am their epitaph.

Study me, then, you who shall lovers be   10
At the next world, that is, at the next spring;
     For I am every dead thing
     In whom love wrought new alchemy.
          For his art did express[4]
A quintessence even from nothingness,   15
From dull privations and lean emptiness.
He ruined me, and I am re-begot
Of absence, darkness, death: things which are not.

2. Habit.
3. Like Herod, Donne's mistress has slaughtered the
innocents and is now clothed in imperial purple.
1. A "nocturnal" seems to suggest a dreamy, meditative poem about dark thoughts, but the more common
17th-century usage alluded to a kind of astrolabe for
finding one's latitude or telling the time at night.
Donne probably wanted both meanings. St. Lucy's
Day falls on December 13, which under the old calendar was very close to the winter solstice (December 21

under our modern calendar). At this time of year the
sun rises after eight o'clock in the latitude of London,
and sets well before four o'clock.
2. The sun is compared to a gun shooting powder
from powder flasks, but in small "squibs" like fire-
crackers.
3. Dropsical, thus insatiably thirsty. "General balm":
the supposed life-preserving essence of all things.
4. Squeeze out.

All others from all things draw all that's good,
Life, soul, form, spirit, whence they being have;
   I, by love's limbeck,[5] am the grave
   Of all that's nothing. Oft a flood
      Have we two wept, and so
Drowned the whole world, us two; oft did we grow
To be two chaoses when we did show
Care to aught else; and often absences
Withdrew our souls, and made us carcasses.

But I am by her death (which word wrongs her)[6]
Of the first nothing the elixir grown;[7]
   Were I a man, that I were one
   I needs must know; I should prefer,
      If I were any beast,
Some ends, some means; yea plants, yea stones detest
And love.[8] All, all some properties invest.
If I an ordinary nothing were,
As shadow, a light and body must be here.

But I am none; nor will my sun renew.
You lovers, for whose sake the lesser sun
   At this time to the Goat[9] is run
   To fetch new lust and give it you,
      Enjoy your summer all.
Since she enjoys her long night's festival,
Let me prepare towards her, and let me call
This hour her vigil and her eve, since this
Both the year's and the day's deep midnight is.

                                 1633

(line numbers: 20, 25, 30, 35, 40, 45)

The Apparition

When by thy scorn, O murderess, I am dead,
   And that thou thinkst thee free
   From all solicitation from me,
Then shall my ghost come to thy bed,
And thee, feigned vestal,[1] in worse arms shall see;
Then thy sick taper will begin to wink,[2]
And he whose thou art then, being tired before,
Will, if thou stir, or pinch to wake him, think
      Thou call'st for more,
   And in false sleep will from thee shrink,
   And then, poor aspen wretch,[3] neglected thou

(line numbers: 5, 10)

5. Alembic, retort; a vessel used in distilling.
6. To speak of her death "wrongs" her by implying that she is not now among the immortals, a saint.
7. He is now "grown" (become) the "elixir of the first nothing," i.e., the quintessence of that absolute nothingness that existed before the creation.
8. Beasts have intentions; plants, tropisms; even stones (like lodestones), attractions and antipathies.

9. The sign of Capricorn, which the sun enters at the winter solstice; the goat is an emblem of sexual vigor. The "lesser sun" is the real, everyday sun; "my sun" is the dead mistress.
1. In Roman history the "vestals" were sacred virgins.
2. Flicker (from the presence of a ghost).
3. Aspen leaves flutter in the slightest breeze.

Bathed in a cold quicksilver sweat[4] wilt lie
　　A verier ghost than I;
What I will say, I will not tell thee now,
Lest that preserve thee; and since my love is spent,   15
I had rather thou shouldst painfully repent,
Than by my threatenings rest still innocent.

1633

A Valediction: Forbidding Mourning[1]

As virtuous men pass mildly away,
　　And whisper to their souls to go,
Whilst some of their sad friends do say
　　The breath goes now, and some say, No;

So let us melt, and make no noise,   5
　　No tear-floods, nor sigh-tempests move;
'Twere profanation of our joys
　　To tell the laity our love.

Moving of th' earth brings harms and fears,
　　Men reckon what it did and meant;   10
But trepidation of the spheres,
　　Though greater far, is innocent.[2]

Dull sublunary[3] lovers' love
　　(Whose soul[4] is sense) cannot admit
Absence, because it doth remove   15
　　Those things which elemented[5] it.

But we, by a love so much refined
　　That our selves know not what it is,
Inter-assurèd of the mind,
　　Care less, eyes, lips, and hands to miss.   20

Our two souls therefore, which are one,
　　Though I must go, endure not yet
A breach, but an expansion,
　　Like gold to airy thinness beat.

If they be two, they are two so   25
　　As stiff twin compasses[6] are two;

4. Sweating in terror; quicksilver (mercury) was a stock prescription for venereal disease, and sweating was part of the cure.
1. The particularly serious and steady tone of this poem may be due to the circumstances of its composition. Izaak Walton tells us it was addressed to Donne's wife on the occasion of his trip to the Continent in 1611. Donne had many forebodings of misfortune, which were verified when his wife gave birth to a still-born child during his absence. Still, Walton's linkage of these events with this poem is only a speculation.
2. Earthquakes cause damage and were thought portentous. "Trepidation" (in the Ptolemaic cosmology, an oscillation of the ninth or "crystalline" sphere, imparted to all the inner spheres), though a vastly greater motion than an earthquake, is neither destructive nor sinister.
3. Beneath the moon, therefore mundane and subject to change.
4. Essence.
5. Composed.
6. I.e., drawing compasses—an emblem of constancy in change, as the circle they produce signifies perfection. This simile is the most famous example of the "metaphysical conceit" (see "Figurative Language," p. 2645).

Thy soul, the fixed foot, makes no show
    To move, but doth, if th' other do.

And though it in the center sit,
    Yet when the other far doth roam,   30
It leans and hearkens after it,
    And grows erect, as that comes home.

Such wilt thou be to me, who must,
    Like th' other foot, obliquely run;
Thy firmness makes my circle just,   35
    And makes me end where I begun.

                                                            1633

The Ecstasy[1]

Where, like a pillow on a bed,
    A pregnant bank swelled up to rest
The violet's reclining head,
    Sat we two, one another's best.

Our hands were firmly cemented   5
    With a fast balm[2] which thence did spring,
Our eye-beams twisted, and did thread
    Our eyes upon one double string;

So to intergraft our hands, as yet
    Was all our means to make us one,[3]   10
And pictures in our eyes to get[4]
    Was all our propagation.

As 'twixt two equal armies Fate
    Suspends uncertain victory,
Our souls (which to advance their state   15
    Were gone out) hung 'twixt her and me;

And whilst our souls negotiate there,
    We like sepulchral statues lay;
All day the same our postures were,
    And we said nothing all the day.   20

If any, so by love refined
    That he soul's language understood,
And by good love were grown all mind,
    Within convenient distance stood,

---

1. For Donne's readers the word *ecstasy* implied, not wild delight, as it commonly does nowadays, but a standing apart, a movement of the soul outside of the body.
2. I.e., perspiration. "Fast": strong.
3. Joining hands and eyes is the only intercourse of the lovers: "eye-beams" are invisible shafts of light, thought of as going out of the eyes and so enabling one to see things.
4. Beget. "Pictures in our eyes": reflections of each other, often called "babies."

He (though he know not which soul spake,   25
    Because both meant, both spake the same)
Might thence a new concoction[5] take,
    And part far purer than he came.

This ecstasy doth unperplex,
    We said, and tell us what we love;   30
We see by this it was not sex;
    We see we saw not what did move;[6]

But as all several souls contain
    Mixture of things, they know not what,
Love these mixed souls doth mix again,   35
    And makes both one, each this and that.

A single violet transplant,
    The strength, the color, and the size
(All which before was poor and scant)
    Redoubles still, and multiplies.   40

When love with one another so
    Interinanimates two souls,
That abler soul, which thence doth flow,
    Defects of loneliness controls.[7]

We then, who are this new soul, know   45
    Of what we are composed and made,
For th' atomies[8] of which we grow
    Are souls, whom no change can invade.

But O alas, so long, so far
    Our bodies why do we forbear?   50
They are ours, though they are not we; we are
    The intelligences, they the sphere.[9]

We owe them thanks because they thus
    Did us to us at first convey,
Yielded their forces, sense, to us,   55
    Nor are dross to us, but allay.[1]

On man heaven's influence works not so
    But that it first imprints the air:[2]
So soul into the soul may flow,
    Though it to body first repair.   60

---

5. Literally, ingredients "cooked together"; the word
has alchemical overtones.
6. I.e., we see that we did not understand before what
motivated ("did move") us. "Several" (line 33): separate.
7. The "abler soul" that derives from the union of two
lesser ones can eliminate the defects with which each
of the component souls is afflicted.
8. Units.
9. In Ptolemaic astronomy, each planet, set in a trans-

parent globe ("sphere") that revolved and so carried it
round the earth, was inhabited by a controlling angelic
"intelligence." Similarly, Donne says, our bodies are
guided and controlled by our souls.
1. "Dross" is an impurity that weakens metal; "allay"
(alloy), an impurity that strengthens it. Our bodies contribute sensation ("sense") to the soul, and therefore
reinforce it.
2. Astrological influences were thought to work on
people through the surrounding air.

As our blood labors to beget
   Spirits as like souls as it can,
Because such fingers need³ to knit
   That subtle knot which makes us man,

So must pure lovers' souls descend   65
   T' affections, and to faculties
Which sense may reach and apprehend;
   Else a great prince in prison lies.

To our bodies turn we then, that so
   Weak men on love revealed may look;   70
Love's mysteries in souls do grow,
   But yet the body is his book.⁴

And if some lover, such as we,
   Have heard this dialogue of one,⁵
Let him still mark⁶ us; he shall see   75
   Small change when we are to bodies gone.

                        1633

The Funeral

Whoever comes to shroud me, do not harm
   Nor question much
That subtle wreath of hair which crowns my arm;
The mystery, the sign you must not touch,
   For 'tis my outward soul,   5
Viceroy to that, which then to heaven being gone,
   Will leave this to control,
And keep these limbs, her¹ provinces, from dissolution.

For if the sinewy thread² my brain lets fall
   Through every part   10
Can tie those parts and make me one of all,
These hairs which upward grew, and strength and art
   Have from a better brain,
Can better do it; except³ she meant that I
   By this should know my pain,   15
As prisoners then are manacled, when they're condemned to die.

Whate'er she meant by it, bury it with me,
   For since I am
Love's martyr, it might breed idolatry,
   If into others' hands these relics came: 20

3. Are needed. "Spirits" were subtle substances thought to be begotten by the blood to serve as intermediaries between body and soul.
4. I.e., Love puts forth in the body a book where his mysteries may be read (as God's mysteries may be read in the book of Nature and the book of Scripture).
5. "Dialogue of one" because "both meant, both spake the same" (line 26).
6. Regard.
1. The soul's, but also the mistress's (cf. "she," line 14).
2. The spinal cord and nervous system.
3. Unless.

As 'twas humility[4]
To afford to it all that a soul can do,
    So 'tis some bravery,
That since you would save none of me, I bury some of you.

                                                        1633

The Blossom

Little think'st thou, poor flower,
    Whom I have watched six or seven days,
And seen thy birth, and seen what every hour
Gave to thy growth, thee to this height to raise,
And now dost laugh and triumph on this bough,   5
    Little think'st thou
That it will freeze anon, and that I shall
Tomorrow find thee fall'n, or not at all.

Little think'st thou, poor heart,
    That labor'st yet to nestle thee,   10
And think'st by hovering here to get a part
In a forbidden or forbidding tree,[1]
And hop'st her stiffness by long siege to bow,
    Little think'st thou
That thou tomorrow, ere that sun[2] doth wake,   15
Must with this sun and me a journey take.

But thou, which lov'st to be
    Subtle to plague thyself, wilt say,
Alas, if you must go, what's that to me?
Here lies my business, and here I will stay: 20
You go to friends whose love and means present
    Various content
To your eyes, ears, and tongue, and every part.
If then your body go, what need you a heart?

Well, then, stay here; but know,   25
    When thou hast stayed and done thy most,
A naked thinking heart that makes no show
Is to a woman but a kind of ghost.
How shall she know my heart; or, having none,
    Know thee for one?   30
Practice may make her know some other part,
But take my word, she doth not know a heart.

Meet me at London, then,
    Twenty days hence, and thou shalt see

---

4. It was humility to grant, in the first part of the poem, that her hair could act as a soul; it is also "bravery" (defiance) to bury a part of the mistress in revenge for her cruelty. In the last line, all the early printed texts read "have" instead of "save," which is the reading of several manuscripts.

1. The fruit of this tree is "forbidden" (presumably because the woman is married) or "forbidding" (because she is unwilling).

2. I.e., the woman.

Me fresher and more fat by being with men[3]   35
Than if I had stayed still with her and thee.
For God's sake, if you can, be you so too:
        I would give you
There to another friend, whom we shall find
As glad to have my body as my mind.   40

1633

The Relic

When my grave is broke up again
Some second guest to entertain
(For graves have learned that woman-head[1]
To be to more than one a bed),
        And he that digs it spies   5
A bracelet of bright hair about the bone,
        Will he not let us alone,
And think that there a loving couple lies,
Who thought that this device might be some way
To make their souls, at the last busy day,[2]   10
Meet at this grave, and make a little stay?

If this fall in a time, or land,
Where mis-devotion[3] doth command,
Then he that digs us up will bring
Us to the Bishop and the King,   15
        To make us relics; then
Thou shalt be a Mary Magdalen, and I
        A something else[4] thereby;
All women shall adore us, and some men;
And since at such times, miracles are sought,   20
I would have that age by this paper taught
What miracles we harmless lovers wrought.

First, we loved well and faithfully,
Yet knew not what we loved, nor why,
Difference of sex no more we knew,   25
        Than our guardian angels do;
        Coming and going, we
Perchance might kiss, but not between those meals;[5]
        Our hands ne'er touched the seals
Which nature, injured by late law, sets free:[6]   30
These miracles we did: but now, alas,

---

3. I.e., with people (not necessarily just males).
1. Feminine trait. Graves were often used to inter successive corpses, the bones of previous occupants being deposited in charnel houses.
2. Judgment Day.
3. False devotion, superstition. Donne seems to have in mind Roman Catholicism.

4. What the indefinite subterfuge "something else" stands for, Donne leaves deliberately unclear; the reader may—and indeed, must—speculate.
5. The kiss of salutation and parting was, in the 17th century, a peculiarly English custom.
6. Human law forbids the free love permitted by nature. "Late": recent (comparatively speaking).

All measure and all language I should pass,
Should I tell what a miracle she was.

1633

A Lecture upon the Shadow

Stand still, and I will read to thee
A lecture, Love, in love's philosophy.
  These three hours that we have spent
  Walking here, two shadows went
Along with us, which we ourselves produced;   5
But, now the sun is just above our head,
  We do those shadows tread
  And to brave clearness all things are reduced.
So, whilst our infant loves did grow,
Disguises did and shadows flow   10
From us and our care;[1] but now, 'tis not so.

That love hath not attained the high'st degree
Which is still diligent lest others see.

Except[2] our loves at this noon stay,
We shall new shadows make the other way.   15
  As the first were made to blind
  Others, these which come behind
Will work upon ourselves, and blind our eyes.
If our loves faint and westwardly decline,
  To me thou falsely thine   20
  And I to thee mine actions shall disguise.
The morning shadows wear away,
But these grow longer all the day,
But, oh, love's day is short if love decay.

Love is a growing or full constant light,   25
And his first minute after noon is night.

1635

Elegy 16.[1] On His Mistress

By our first strange and fatal interview,
By all desires which thereof did ensue,

---

1. Metaphorically, morning shadows were the disguises with which they anxiously concealed their love from outsiders.
2. Unless.
1. In Latin poetry, an elegy is not necessarily a funeral lament but may be simply a discursive or reflective poem written in "elegiacs" (unrhymed couplets of alternating dactylic hexameters and pentameters). In fact the subject matter primarily associated with this meter

was not death but sex, the most famous collection of elegies being Ovid's *Amores*. Donne's elegies—some fifteen poems, almost all written in the 1590s—take Ovid as their principal model, and resemble him in ingenious wit and, for the most part, in frank and unapologetic eroticism. Elegy 16 is uncharacteristically tender. (We retain Grierson's numbering, though he included among the elegies some poems that are probably not Donne's.)

By our long starving hopes, by that remorse
Which my words' masculine persuasive force
Begot in thee, and by the memory   5
Of hurts which spies and rivals threatened me,
I calmly beg; but by thy father's wrath,
By all pains which want and divorcement hath,
I conjure thee; and all the oaths which I
And thou have sworn to seal joint constancy   10
Here I unswear and overswear them thus:
Thou shalt not love by ways so dangerous.
Temper, oh fair love, love's impetuous rage;
Be my true mistress still, not my feigned page.[2]
I'll go, and, by thy kind leave, leave behind   15
Thee, only worthy to nurse in my mind
Thirst to come back. Oh, if thou die before,
My soul from other lands to thee shall soar.
Thy (else almighty) beauty cannot move
Rage from the seas, nor thy love teach them love,   20
Nor tame wild Boreas' harshness.[3] Thou hast read
How roughly he in pieces shiverèd
Fair Orithea, whom he swore he loved.
Fall ill or good, 'tis madness to have proved[4]
Dangers unurged; feed on this flattery,   25
That absent lovers one in th' other be.
Dissemble nothing, not a boy, nor change
Thy body's habit, nor mind's; be not strange
To thyself only; all will spy in thy face
A blushing womanly discovering grace.   30
Richly clothed apes are called apes, and as soon
Eclipsed as bright we call the moon the moon.[5]
Men of France, changeable chameleons,
Spitals[6] of diseases, shops of fashions,
Love's fuellers and the rightest company   35
Of players which upon the world's stage be,
Will quickly know thee, and know thee; and alas!
Th' indifferent Italian, as we pass
His warm land, well content to think thee page,
Will hunt[7] thee with such lust and hideous rage   40
As Lot's fair guests were vexed.[8] But none of these
Nor spongy, hydroptic[9] Dutch shall thee displease
If thou stay here. O stay here, for, for thee,
England is only a worthy gallery
To walk in expectation, till from thence   45
Our greatest king call thee to his presence.[1]

---

2. Evidently Donne's mistress wanted to accompany him abroad, disguised as a page boy. Such escapades occasionally took place in real life; in 1605, Elizabeth Southwell, disguised as a page, went abroad with the scapegrace Sir Robert Dudley.
3. Boreas is god of the north wind; Ovid in *Metamorphoses* 6 describes his boisterous abduction of Orithea.
4. Sought out.
5. I.e., we recognize the moon as easily when it's in eclipse as when it's not.

6. Hospitals.
7. An alternative reading is "haunt."
8. The inhabitants of Sodom brought destruction on themselves when they tried to rape two angels who visited Lot (Genesis 19.1–11).
9. Dropsical, thus insatiably thirsty ("spongy").
1. Throne rooms commonly had antechambers (galleries) where visitors waited until the monarch was ready to see them. The world itself is such a gallery for the greatest king of all, God.

When I am gone, dream me some happiness,
Nor let thy looks our long-hid love confess;
Nor praise nor dispraise me, bless nor curse
Openly love's force, nor in bed fright thy nurse   50
With midnight's startings, crying out "Oh, oh!
Nurse, oh my love is slain, I saw him go
O'er the white Alps alone; I saw him, I,
Assailed, fight, taken, stabbed, bleed, fall, and die."
Augur me better chance, except dread Jove   55
Think it enough for me t' have had thy love.

1635

Elegy 19. To His Mistress Going to Bed

Come, Madam, come, all rest my powers defy,
Until I labor, I in labor lie.[1]
The foe oft-times, having the foe in sight,
Is tired with standing though he never fight.
Off with that girdle, like heaven's zone[2] glistering,   5
But a far fairer world encompassing.
Unpin that spangled breastplate which you wear
That th' eyes of busy fools may be stopped there.
Unlace yourself, for that harmonious chime
Tells me from you that now it is bed-time.   10
Off with that happy busk,[3] which I envy,
That still can be and still can stand so nigh.
Your gown going off, such beauteous state reveals
As when from flowery meads th' hill's shadow steals.
Off with that wiry coronet and show   15
The hairy diadem which on you doth grow;
Now off with those shoes, and then safely tread
In this love's hallowed temple, this soft bed.
In such white robes, heaven's angels used to be
Received by men; thou, angel, bring'st with thee   20
A heaven like Mahomet's paradise;[4] and though
Ill spirits walk in white, we easily know
By this these angels from an evil sprite,
Those set our hairs, but these our flesh upright.
        License my roving hands, and let them go   25
Before, behind, between, above, below.
O my America! my new-found-land,
My kingdom, safeliest when with one man manned,
My mine of precious stones, my empery,
How blest am I in this discovering thee!   30
To enter in these bonds is to be free;
There where my hand is set, my seal shall be.[5]

---

1. Labor in the senses of "get to work" and "distress."
2. The zodiac.
3. Bodice.
4. Populated by seductive houris, for the delectation

of the faithful.
5. The jokes mingle law with sex: having signed the document with his hand, he will now seal it, and in the bonds of her arms he will find freedom.

Full nakedness! All joys are due to thee.
As souls unbodied, bodies unclothed must be,
To taste whole joys. Gems which you women use   35
Are like Atalanta's balls,[6] cast in men's views,
That when a fool's eye lighteth on a gem,
His earthly soul may covet theirs, not them.
Like pictures, or like books' gay coverings, made
For laymen, are all women thus arrayed;   40
Themselves are mystic books, which only we
(Whom their imputed grace will dignify)
Must see revealed.[7] Then since that I may know,
As liberally as to a midwife show
Thyself: cast all, yea, this white linen hence,   45
There is no penance due to innocence.[8]
  To teach thee, I am naked first; why then
What need'st thou have more covering than a man?

                                                                 1669

Satire 3   Like his elegies, Donne's five satires were written in his twenties and
follow, though remotely, in classical footsteps. The essence of satire is an attitude:
the author holds a subject up to laughter or scorn. Elements of such an attitude
appear in many works of prose and poetry that are not, as a whole, satiric—in
Chaucer, in England, as early as the figure of Thersites in Homer's *Iliad*. But the
great examples of formal satiric writing in classical times were the Roman poets
Horace and Juvenal, models respectively of the urbanely jocose and the indignant
satire. During the sixteenth century, their satires were imitated on the Continent
by the Italian poet Ariosto and some of his contemporaries. Even in England, Sir
Thomas Wyatt felt through an Italian intermediary the influence of Juvenal. Yet
satiric poems as such remained rare in English until the 1590s; their sudden
appearance at that time seems to have grown out of moods of skepticism, discontent, and melancholy that marked the last years of the sixteenth and the first years
of the seventeenth century.

   Donne's third satire is not conventional, in terms of the genre, because it does
not assume a position of derisive superiority to its victim—indeed, it does not have
a proper victim. It is a strenuous, inconclusive discussion of an acute theological
problem: How may a seeker recognize the true Christian church among the many
competing sects? Its theme was of paramount importance to Donne as an ex-
Catholic, and to many others in his age for whom religious polemic was a passion.
The poem offers no easy answer to the problem it raises; the point it makes most
forcefully is the folly of not thinking about the matter. Its language and meter are
harsh and rough, as was traditional in the genre, and its concentration is complete;
it is a powerful piece of wrought-iron work in poetry.

6. Atalanta, running a race against her suitor Hippomenes, was beaten when he dropped golden balls
(apples) for her to pick up. Donne reverses the story.
7. By granting favors to their lovers, women impute to
them grace that they don't deserve, as God imputes

grace to undeserving sinners. Laymen can only look at
the covers of mystic books (women), but "we" who
have saving grace can read them.
8. An alternative reading is "Here is no penance,
much less innocence."

Satire 3

Kind pity chokes my spleen;[1] brave scorn forbids
Those tears to issue which swell my eyelids;
I must not laugh, nor weep[2] sins, and be wise:
Can railing then cure these worn maladies?
Is not our mistress, fair Religion,   5
As worthy of all our souls' devotion
As virtue was to the first blinded age?[3]
Are not heaven's joys as valiant to assuage
Lusts, as earth's honor was to them?[4] Alas,
As we do them in means, shall they surpass   10
Us in the end, and shall thy father's spirit
Meet blind philosophers in heaven, whose merit
Of strict life may be imputed faith,[5] and hear
Thee, whom he taught so easy ways and near
To follow, damned? O, if thou dar'st, fear this;   15
This fear great courage and high valor is.
Dar'st thou aid mutinous Dutch,[6] and dar'st thou lay
Thee in ships, wooden sepulchers, a prey
To leaders' rage, to storms, to shot, to dearth?
Dar'st thou dive seas and dungeons of the earth?   20
Hast thou courageous fire to thaw the ice
Of frozen North discoveries? and thrice
Colder than salamanders, like divine
Children in the oven,[7] fires of Spain, and the line,
Whose countries limbecks to our bodies be,   25
Canst thou for gain bear?[8] And must every he
Which cries not "Goddess!" to thy mistress, draw,[9]
Or eat thy poisonous words? Courage of straw!
O desperate coward, wilt thou seem bold, and
To thy foes and his[1] (who made thee to stand   30
Sentinel in his world's garrison) thus yield,
And for forbidden wars leave th' appointed field?
Know thy foes: The foul Devil (whom thou
Strivest to please) for hate, not love, would allow
Thee fain his whole realm to be quit;[2] and as   35
The world's all parts wither away and pass,[3]
So the world's self, thy other loved foe, is
In her decrepit wane, and thou, loving this,

---

1. The seat of bile, hence scorn and ridicule.
2. Lament. "Laugh": mock.
3. The age of paganism, blind to Christianity but capable of natural morality ("virtue").
4. I.e., hope of heaven should be as strong ("valiant") against our lusts as earthly honor was against theirs, the pagans'.
5. Specially virtuous pagans, it was felt, might achieve heaven by behavior so good that it virtually constituted faith.
6. English volunteers took frequent part with the Dutch in their wars against Spain. Donne himself had sailed in two raiding expeditions against the Spanish.
7. The "divine children in the oven" are Shadrach,

Meshach, and Abednego, rescued from the fiery furnace in Daniel 3. The salamander was traditionally so cold-blooded that it could live even in a fire.
8. The object of "bear" is "fires of Spain, and the line"—Inquisitorial and equatorial heats, which roast people as chemists heat materials in "limbecks" (alembics, or retorts for distilling).
9. I.e., fight a duel.
1. God's.
2. I.e., the devil would gladly give you a free hand with his whole kingdom.
3. It was a common belief in the 17th century that the world was getting old and decrepit.

Dost love a withered and worn strumpet; last,
Flesh (itself's death) and joys which flesh can taste   40
Thou lovest; and thy fair goodly soul, which doth
Give this flesh power to taste joy, thou dost loathe.
Seek true religion. O, where? Mirreus,[4]
Thinking her unhoused here, and fled from us,
Seeks her at Rome; there, because he doth know   45
That she was there a thousand years ago.
He loves her rags so, as we here obey
The statecloth[5] where the Prince sat yesterday.
Crantz to such brave loves will not be enthralled,
But loves her only, who at Geneva is called   50
Religion—plain, simple, sullen, young,
Contemptuous, yet unhandsome; as among
Lecherous humors,[6] there is one that judges
No wenches wholesome but coarse country drudges.
Graius stays still at home here, and because   55
Some preachers, vile ambitious bawds, and laws
Still new, like fashions, bid him think that she
Which dwells with us is only perfect, he
Embraceth her whom his godfathers will
Tender to him, being tender, as wards still   60
Take such wives as their guardians offer, or
Pay values.[7] Careless Phrygius doth abhor
All, because all cannot be good, as one
Knowing some women whores, dares marry none.
Graccus loves all as one, and thinks that so   65
As women do in divers countries go
In divers habits, yet are still one kind,
So doth, so is religion; and this blind-
ness too much light breeds; but unmoved thou
Of force must one, and forced but one allow;   70
And the right;[8] ask thy father which is she,
Let him ask his; though truth and falsehood be
Near twins, yet truth a little elder is;[9]
Be busy to seek her, believe me this,
He's not of none, nor worst, that seeks the best.[1]   75
To adore, or scorn an image, or protest,
May all be bad; doubt wisely; in strange way
To stand inquiring right, is not to stray;
To sleep, or run wrong, is. On a huge hill,
Cragged and steep, Truth stands, and he that will   80
Reach her, about must, and about must go,
And what the hill's suddenness resists, win so;

---

4. The imaginary characters in this passage represent different creeds. "Mirreus" is a Roman Catholic; "Crantz," a Geneva Presbyterian; "Graius," an Erastian (i.e., believing in any religion sponsored by the state); "Phrygius," a skeptic; and "Graccus," a Universalist.
5. The royal canopy, a symbol of kingly power.
6. Tempers, temperaments.
7. Young men (of "tender" years) might reject the wives offered ("tendered") them by their guardians but, if they did so, had to pay "values," i.e., fines.

8. I.e., being blind to the differences between religions, Graccus has too much light to see anything (lines 68–69). But the poet insists that without being swayed by human pressures, we must find just one religion, "the right" true religion.
9. I.e., the true church is the one most like the primitive church.
1. The person who seeks the best church is neither an unbeliever nor the worst sort of believer.

Yet strive so, that before age, death's twilight,
Thy soul rest, for none can work in that night.
To will[2] implies delay, therefore now do.   85
Hard deeds, the body's pains; hard knowledge too
The mind's endeavors reach,[3] and mysteries
Are like the sun, dazzling, yet plain to all eyes.
Keep the truth which thou hast found; men do not stand
In so ill case here, that God hath with his hand   90
Signed kings' blank charters to kill whom they hate,
Nor are they vicars, but hangmen to fate.[4]
Fool and wretch, wilt thou let thy soul be tied
To man's laws, by which she shall not be tried
At the last day? O, will it then boot thee   95
To say a Philip, or a Gregory,
A Harry, or a Martin taught thee this?[5]
Is not this excuse for mere[6] contraries
Equally strong? Cannot both sides say so?
That thou mayest rightly obey power, her bounds know;   100
Those passed, her nature and name is changed; to be
Then humble to her is idolatry.
As streams are, power is; those blest flowers that dwell
At the rough stream's calm head, thrive and prove well,
But having left their roots, and themselves given   105
To the stream's tyrannous rage, alas, are driven
Through mills, and rocks, and woods, and at last, almost
Consumed in going, in the sea are lost:
So perish souls, which more choose men's unjust
Power from God claimed, than God himself to trust.   110

                                                                    1633

From Holy Sonnets[1]

1

Thou hast made me, and shall thy work decay?
Repair me now, for now mine end doth haste;
I run to death, and death meets me as fast,
And all my pleasures are like yesterday.
I dare not move my dim eyes any way,   5
Despair behind, and death before doth cast

---

2. To intend a future action.
3. I.e., the body's pains achieve ("reach") hard deeds;
the mind's endeavors will reach hard knowledge.
4. Human authority does not represent divine justice
on earth; rulers are not God's vicars on earth (the hit
here is at both the pope and the secular monarch),
but His hangmen at best—agents through whom His
justice is fulfilled without *carte blanche* ("blank charters") to use their own judgments.
5. "Philip" is Philip II of Spain, and "Gregory" any
one of several Pope Gregorys (VII, XIII, XIV). "Harry"
is England's Henry VIII, and "Martin" is Martin Luther. Laymen and clergy, Protestants and Catholics, all
are covered. "Boot": profit.

6. Absolute, complete.
1. Donne's religious poetry is collectively known as
the *Divine Poems.* Among these, the largest group is
that of the nineteen *Holy Sonnets.* Like others of
Donne's poems, these sonnets reflect his interest in the
formal meditative exercises of the Jesuits—though
Donne began writing them around 1609, at least a decade after leaving the Catholic church.
    Our selections are numbered as in Sir Herbert
Grierson's influential edition (1912), since it is his
numbers that the sonnets usually go by. But there is no
reason to suppose that this is the order Donne intended.

Such terror, and my feeble flesh doth waste
By sin in it, which it towards hell doth weigh.
Only thou art above, and when towards thee
By thy leave I can look, I rise again;   10
But our old subtle foe so tempteth me
That not one hour myself I can sustain.
Thy grace may wing me to prevent[2] his art,
And thou like adamant[3] draw mine iron heart.

                                   1635

5

I am a little world made cunningly
Of elements, and an angelic sprite;[1]
But black sin hath betrayed to endless night
My world's both parts, and O, both parts must die.
You which beyond that heaven which was most high   5
Have found new spheres, and of new lands can write,[2]
Pour new seas in mine eyes, that so I might
Drown my world with my weeping earnestly,
Or wash it if it must be drowned no more.[3]
But O, it must be burnt! Alas, the fire   10
Of lust and envy have burnt it heretofore,
And made it fouler; let their flames retire,
And burn me, O Lord, with a fiery zeal
Of thee and thy house, which doth in eating heal.[4]

                                   1635

7

At the round earth's imagined corners,[1] blow
Your trumpets, angels; and arise, arise
From death, you numberless infinities
Of souls, and to your scattered bodies go:
All whom the flood did, and fire shall, o'erthrow,   5
All whom war, dearth, age, agues, tyrannies,
Despair, law, chance hath slain, and you whose eyes
Shall behold God, and never taste death's woe.[2]
But let them sleep, Lord, and me mourn a space;
For, if above all these, my sins abound,   10
'Tis late to ask abundance of thy grace
When we are there. Here on this lowly ground,
Teach me how to repent; for that's as good
As if thou hadst sealed my pardon with thy blood.

                                   1633

2. Forestall. "Wing": give wings to.
3. Lodestone.
1. I.e., I am both body and soul—the former made of elements, the latter an "angelic sprite" (spirit).
2. Astronomers and explorers are to find new oceans for tears to weep or waters to wash away the poet's sins.
3. After Noah's experience, God promised (Genesis 9.11) never to flood the earth again.

4. See Psalm 69.9: "For the zeal of thine house hath eaten me up." The passage involves three sorts of flame—those of the Last Judgment, those of lust and envy, and those of zeal, which alone save.
1. Cf. Revelation 7.1: "I saw four angels standing on the four corners of the earth."
2. I.e., those who will be alive at the Second Coming.

9

If poisonous minerals, and if that tree
Whose fruit threw death on else-immortal us,
If lecherous goats, if serpents envious
Cannot be damned, alas! why should I be?
Why should intent or reason, born in me,   5
Make sins, else equal, in me more heinous?
And, mercy being easy and glorious
To God, in his stern wrath why threatens he?
But who am I that dare dispute with thee
O God? Oh,[1] of thine only worthy blood   10
And my tears, make a heavenly Lethean[2] flood,
And drown in it my sin's black memory.
That thou remember them some claim as debt;
I think it mercy if thou wilt forget.

                                                                        1633

10

Death, be not proud, though some have callèd thee
Mighty and dreadful, for thou art not so;
For those whom thou think'st thou dost overthrow
Die not, poor Death, nor yet canst thou kill me.
From rest and sleep, which but thy pictures be,   5
Much pleasure; then from thee much more must flow,
And soonest our best men with thee do go,
Rest of their bones, and soul's delivery.[1]
Thou art slave to fate, chance, kings, and desperate men,
And dost with poison, war, and sickness dwell,   10
And poppy[2] or charms can make us sleep as well
And better than thy stroke; why swell'st thou then?[3]
One short sleep past, we wake eternally
And death shall be no more; Death, thou shalt die.

                                                                        1633

13

What if this present were the world's last night?
Mark in my heart, O soul, where thou dost dwell,
The picture of Christ crucified, and tell
Whether that countenance can thee affright.
Tears in his eyes quench the amazing light,   5
Blood fills his frowns, which from his pierced head fell;
And can that tongue adjudge thee unto hell
Which prayed forgiveness for his foes' fierce spite?
No, no; but as in my idolatry
I said to all my profane[1] mistresses,   10

1. The first edition punctuates as follows: "thee? / O
God, oh!"
2. In classical mythology, the waters of the river Lethe
in the underworld caused total forgetfulness.
1. I.e., to find rest for their bones and freedom ("delivery") for their souls.
2. Opium.
3. Why do you puff with pride?
1. Worldly.

Beauty of pity, foulness only is
A sign of rigor:[2] so I say to thee,
To wicked spirits are horrid shapes assigned,
This beauteous form assures a piteous mind.

1633

14

Batter my heart, three-personed God; for you
As yet but knock, breathe, shine, and seek to mend;
That I may rise and stand, o'erthrow me, and bend
Your force to break, blow, burn, and make me new.
I, like an usurped town, to another due,   5
Labor to admit you, but O, to no end;
Reason, your viceroy in me, me should defend,
But is captived, and proves weak or untrue.
Yet dearly I love you, and would be loved fain,
But am betrothed unto your enemy.   10
Divorce me, untie or break that knot again;
Take me to you, imprison me, for I,
Except you enthrall me, never shall be free,
Nor ever chaste, except you ravish me.

1633

17

Since she whom I loved hath paid her last debt
To Nature, and to hers, and my good is dead,[1]
And her soul early into heaven ravishèd,
Wholly on heavenly things my mind is set.
Here the admiring her my mind did whet   5
To seek thee, God; so streams do show the head;
But though I have found thee, and thou my thirst hast fed,
A holy thirsty dropsy melts me yet.
But why should I beg more love, whenas thou
Dost woo my soul, for hers offering all thine: 10
And dost not only fear lest I allow
My love to saints and angels, things divine,
But in thy tender jealousy dost doubt
Lest the world, flesh, yea, devil put thee out.[2]

1894

18

Show me, dear Christ, thy spouse so bright and clear.[1]
What! is it she which on the other shore

---

2. Beautiful features are a sign of a gentle disposition, ugliness of the contrary.
1. Donne's wife died in 1617 at the age of thirty-three, having just borne her twelfth child. This rough and very personal sonnet, and the following one, survive in a single manuscript, which came to light only in 1892.
2. Donne seems to imply that God took away Ann More to have a monopoly of John Donne's love. The last lines even suggest that the bereaved husband saw his wife as having been a temptation to deadly sin.
1. This sonnet embodies Donne's lifelong distress at the fragmentation of the church ("the bride of Christ"). Whether it also embodies doubts as to the superiority of the Anglican church has been a subject of dispute.

Goes richly painted? or which, robbed and tore,
Laments and mourns in Germany and here?[2]
Sleeps she a thousand, then peeps up one year? 5
Is she self-truth, and errs? now new, now outwore?
Doth she, and did she, and shall she evermore
On one, on seven, or on no hill appear?[3]
Dwells she with us, or like adventuring knights
First travel we to seek, and then make love? 10
Betray, kind husband, thy spouse to our sights,
And let mine amorous soul court thy mild dove,
Who is most true and pleasing to thee then
When she is embraced and open to most men.[4]

1899

Good Friday, 1613. Riding Westward

Let man's soul be a sphere, and then, in this,
The intelligence that moves, devotion is,[1]
And as the other spheres, by being grown
Subject to foreign motions, lose their own,
And being by others hurried every day, 5
Scarce in a year their natural form[2] obey;
Pleasure or business, so, our souls admit
For their first mover, and are whirled by it.[3]
Hence is 't, that I am carried towards the West
This day, when my soul's form bends toward the East. 10
There I should see a Sun[4] by rising, set,
And by that setting endless day beget:
But that Christ on this cross did rise and fall,
Sin had eternally benighted all.
Yet dare I almost be glad I do not see 15
That spectacle, of too much weight for me.
Who sees God's face, that is self-life, must die;[5]
What a death were it then to see God die?
It made his own lieutenant, Nature, shrink;
It made his footstool crack, and the sun wink.[6] 20
Could I behold those hands which span the poles,

---

2. I.e., neither the painted woman (the Church of Rome) nor the ravished virgin (the Protestant churches) seems very like a bride. "Robbed and tore" may allude to a military defeat suffered by German Protestants in 1620.
3. The church on seven hills is, inescapably, that of Rome; that "on no hill" could be either the presbyterian church of Geneva or the episcopal Church of England, with its head at Canterbury. But what then is the church on one hill that could conceivably be the bride of Christ? It is a crux, not easy of solution.
4. The final lines echo the Song of Solomon (5.2), which was often interpreted as the song of love between Christ and the church: "Open to me, my sister, my love, my dove, my undefiled."

1. As angelic intelligences guide the celestial spheres, so devotion is or should be the guiding principle of human life.
2. Moving principle.
3. I.e., spheres are deflected from their true orbits by outside influences; so our souls are deflected by business or pleasure.
4. The sun-Son pun was an ancient one. Christ, the Son of God, set when He rose on the Cross, and His setting (death) gave rise to the Christian era, with the hope of ultimate immortality.
5. God told Moses, "Thou canst not see my face: for there shall no man see me, and live" (Exodus 33.20).
6. An earthquake and eclipse supposedly accompanied the Crucifixion.

And tune[7] all spheres at once, pierced with those holes?
Could I behold that endless height which is
Zenith to us, and t'our antipodes,[8]
Humbled below us? Or that blood which is   25
The seat[9] of all our souls, if not of his,
Make dirt of dust, or that flesh which was worn
By God for his apparel, ragg'd and torn?
If on these things I durst not look, durst I
Upon his miserable mother cast mine eye,   30
Who was God's partner here, and furnished thus
Half of that sacrifice which ransomed us?
Though these things, as I ride, be from mine eye,
They are present yet unto my memory,
For that looks towards them; and thou look'st towards me,   35
O Savior, as thou hang'st upon the tree.
I turn my back to thee but to receive
Corrections, till thy mercies bid thee leave.[1]
O think me worth thine anger; punish me;
Burn off my rusts and my deformity;   40
Restore thine image so much, by thy grace,
That thou may'st know me, and I'll turn my face.

                                                                      1633

A Hymn to Christ, at the Author's Last Going into Germany[1]

In what torn ship soever I embark,
That ship shall be my emblem of thy ark;
What sea soever swallow me, that flood
Shall be to me an emblem of thy blood;
Though thou with clouds of anger do disguise   5
Thy face, yet through that mask I know those eyes,
    Which, though they turn away sometimes, they never will despise.[2]

I sacrifice this island unto thee,
And all whom I loved there, and who loved me;
When I have put our seas twixt them and me,   10
Put thou thy sea[3] betwixt my sins and thee.
As the tree's sap doth seek the root below
In winter, in my winter now I go
    Where none but thee, th' eternal root of true love, I may know.

Nor thou nor thy religion dost control   15
    The amorousness of an harmonious soul,

7. Some manuscripts read "turn."
8. "Zenith" is the highest reach of heaven; the "antipodes" are the opposite side of the earth.
9. Center (as of magnetic attraction).
1. Cease.
1. Donne went to Germany in 1619 as chaplain to the earl of Doncaster. The mission was a diplomatic one, to the king and queen of Bohemia, King James's son-in-law and daughter, who at that time were mainstays

of the Protestant cause on the Continent.
2. The early printed texts break in two parts (an unrhymed tetrameter and a trimeter) the long last line of each stanza. Unrhymed lines would be unique in Donne's poetry, and the manuscripts are unanimous for the "fourteeners" as we print them.
3. An alternate reading is "blood," reemphasizing the metaphor of lines 3 and 4.

But thou wouldst have that love thyself; as thou
Art jealous, Lord, so I am jealous now.
Thou lov'st not, till from loving more[4] thou free
My soul; whoever gives, takes liberty;   20
   Oh, if thou car'st not whom I love, alas, thou lov'st not me.

Seal then this bill of my divorce to all
On whom those fainter beams of love did fall;
Marry those loves which in youth scattered be
On fame, wit, hopes (false mistresses) to thee.   25
Churches are best for prayer that have least light:
To see God only, I go out of sight,
   And to 'scape stormy days, I choose an everlasting night.

1633

Hymn to God My God, in My Sickness[1]

Since I am coming to that holy room
   Where, with thy choir of saints for evermore,
I shall be made thy music; as I come
   I tune the instrument here at the door,
   And what I must do then, think now before.   5

Whilst my physicians by their love are grown
   Cosmographers, and I their map, who lie
Flat on this bed, that by them may be shown
   That this is my southwest discovery[2]
   Per fretum febris,[3] by these straits to die,   10

I joy, that in these straits, I see my West;[4]
   For, though their currents yield return to none,
What shall my West hurt me? As West and East
   In all flat maps (and I am one) are one,
   So death doth touch the resurrection.   15

Is the Pacific Sea my home? Or are
   The Eastern riches? Is Jerusalem?
Anyan,[5] and Magellan, and Gibraltar,
   All straits, and none but straits, are ways to them,
   Whether where Japhet dwelt, or Cham, or Shem.[6]   20

We think that Paradise and Calvary,
   Christ's cross and Adam's tree, stood in one place;
Look, Lord and find both Adams[7] met in me;

4. From loving elsewhere. The idea is, "To give me true love, you must take away my freedom to love anyone else."
1. Though Izaak Walton, Donne's pious biographer, assigns this poem to the last days of his life, it was probably written in December 1623.
2. The Strait of Magellan, or something spiritual that is analogous to it.
3. I.e., through the strait of fever.
4. Where the sun sets, hence where life ends.
5. The Bering Strait. Behind these anxious questions lie many ancient speculations about the location of Paradise—which is analogous to heaven, as the various straits are to death.
6. Japhet, Cham (Ham), and Shem were the three sons of Noah by whom the world was repopulated after the Flood (Genesis 10). The descendants of Japhet were thought to inhabit Europe; those of Ham, Africa; and those of Shem, Asia.
7. I.e., Adam and Christ. "In one place": in the same region.

As the first Adam's sweat surrounds my face,
May the last Adam's blood my soul embrace.   25

So, in his purple wrapped,[8] receive me, Lord;
By these his thorns give me his other crown;
And, as to others' souls I preached thy word,
Be this my text, my sermon to mine own:
Therefore that he may raise the Lord throws down.   30

                                                        1635

A Hymn to God the Father[1]

Wilt thou forgive that sin where I begun,
    Which is my sin, though it were done before?[2]
Wilt thou forgive that sin through which I run,
    And do run still, though still I do deplore?
        When thou hast done, thou hast not done,   5
        For I have more.

Wilt thou forgive that sin by which I have won
    Others to sin? and made my sin their door?
Wilt thou forgive that sin which I did shun
    A year or two, but wallowed in a score?   10
        When thou hast done, thou hast not done,
        For I have more.

I have a sin of fear, that when I have spun
    My last thread, I shall perish on the shore;
Swear by thy self, that at my death thy Son   15
    Shall shine as he shines now and heretofore;
        And, having done that, thou hast done,
        I fear[3] no more.

                                                        1633

From Devotions upon Emergent Occasions[1]

Meditation 17

Nunc lento sonitu dicunt, morieris.
Now this bell tolling softly for another, says to me, Thou must die.

Perchance he for whom this bell[2] tolls may be so ill as that he knows not it
tolls for him; and perchance I may think myself so much better than I am, as

8. The purple of Christ is his blood.
1. Izaak Walton tells us that this hymn was written
during Donne's illness of 1623. Donne had it set to
music and frequently performed by the choir and organist of St. Paul's Cathedral.
2. I.e., through his parents he inherits the original sin
of Adam and Eve.
3. An alternative reading is "have."
1. Donne's Devotions were composed in the aftermath
of a serious illness in the winter of 1623—though
Donne characteristically writes as if the events of the
illness were happening at the moment he describes
them. The Devotions recount the stages of his disease

and recovery; each stage comprises a "meditation upon
our human condition," an "expostulation and de-
batement with God," and a prayer to Him. The book
was published almost immediately after it was written
and to great effect—the blend of private feeling and
public moralizing rendering it particularly accessible
to 17th-century readers. And its eloquent, richly metaphorical sentences have provided a title for at least one
major modern novel.
    "Emergent" occasions are those that arise casually
or unexpectedly.
2. The "passing bell" for the dying.

that they who are about me and see my state may have caused it to toll for me, and I know not that. The church is catholic, universal, so are all her actions; all that she does belongs to all. When she baptizes a child, that action concerns me; for that child is thereby connected to that head which is my head too, and ingrafted into that body[3] whereof I am a member. And when she buries a man, that action concerns me: all mankind is of one author and is one volume; when one man dies, one chapter is not torn out of the book, but translated[4] into a better language; and every chapter must be so translated. God employs several translators; some pieces are translated by age, some by sickness, some by war, some by justice; but God's hand is in every translation, and his hand shall bind up all our scattered leaves again for that library where every book shall lie open to one another. As therefore the bell that rings to a sermon calls not upon the preacher only, but upon the congregation to come, so this bell calls us all; but how much more me, who am brought so near the door by this sickness. There was a contention as far as a suit (in which piety and dignity, religion and estimation,[5] were mingled) which of the religious orders should ring to prayers first in the morning; and it was determined that they should ring first that rose earliest. If we understand aright the dignity of this bell that tolls for our evening prayer, we would be glad to make it ours by rising early, in that application, that it might be ours as well as his whose indeed it is. The bell doth toll for him that thinks it doth; and though it intermit again, yet from that minute that that occasion wrought upon him, he is united to God. Who casts not up his eye to the sun when it rises? but who takes off his eye from a comet when that breaks out? Who bends not his ear to any bell which upon any occasion rings? but who can remove it from that bell which is passing a piece of himself out of this world? No man is an island, entire of itself; every man is a piece of the continent, a part of the main.[6] If a clod be washed away by the sea, Europe is the less, as well as if a promontory were, as well as if a manor of thy friend's or of thine own were. Any man's death diminishes me, because I am involved in mankind; and therefore never send to know for whom the bell tolls; it tolls for thee. Neither can we call this a begging of misery or a borrowing of misery, as though we were not miserable enough of ourselves but must fetch in more from the next house, in taking upon us the misery of our neighbors. Truly it were an excusable covetousness if we did; for affliction is a treasure, and scarce any man hath enough of it. No man hath affliction enough that is not matured and ripened by it, and made fit for God by that affliction. If a man carry treasure in bullion, or in a wedge of gold, and have none coined into current moneys, his treasure will not defray him as he travels. Tribulation is treasure in the nature of it, but it is not current money in the use of it, except we get nearer and nearer our home, heaven, by it. Another man may be sick too, and sick to death, and this affliction may lie in his bowels as gold in a mine and be of no use to him; but this bell that tells me of his affliction digs out and applies that gold to me, if by this consideration of another's danger I take mine own into contemplation and so secure myself by making my recourse to my God, who is our only security.

3. The church.
4. Punning on the literal sense, "carried across."
5. Self-esteem. "Contention as far as a suit": controversy that went as far as a lawsuit.
6. Mainland.

BEN JONSON

1572–1637

1598:   *Every Man in His Humor*, Jonson's first published play.
1606:   *Volpone*.
1616:   Jonson appointed poet laureate; publishes his *Works*.
1629:   Decisive failure of *The New Inn*.

Ben Jonson did so many different things in the literary world of the early seventeenth century, and made use of so many different styles to do them, that he is difficult to see as a whole person. Actor, playwright, poet and poet laureate, scholar, critic, translator, man of letters, and head, for the first time in English, of a literary "school," the so-called Sons of Ben, he was a giant of a man. Yet we cannot easily take a perspective of him.

Jonson's life was tough and turbulent. The posthumous child of a clergyman, he was stepson to a master bricklayer of Westminster. He was educated at Westminster School by the great classical scholar and antiquarian William Camden, worked briefly at his stepfather's trade, and then entered the army. In Flanders, where the Dutch with English help were warring against the Spaniards, he fought single-handed with one of the enemy before the massed armies and killed his man. Returning to England about 1594, he began to work as an actor and playwright but was drawn from one storm center to another. He killed a fellow actor in a duel and escaped the gallows only by pleading "benefit of clergy" (i.e., by proving he could read and write, which entitled him to plead before a more lenient ecclesiastical court). He was jailed for insulting the Scottish nation at a time when King James was newly arrived from Scotland. He took furious part in an intricate set of literary wars with his fellow playwrights. Having converted to Catholicism, he was the object of deep suspicion after the Gunpowder Plot of Guy Fawkes (1605), when the phobia against his religion reached its height. Yet he rode out all these troubles, growing mellower as he grew older (and reconverting to Anglicanism); in his latter years he became the unofficial literary dictator of London, the king's pensioned poet, a favorite around the court, and the good friend of men like Shakespeare, Donne, Francis Beaumont, John Selden, and Francis Bacon as well as of dukes, diplomats, and distinguished folk generally. In addition, he engaged the affection of younger men (poets like Robert Herrick, Thomas Carew, and Sir John Suckling and speculative thinkers like Lord Falkland and Sir Kenelm Digby), who delighted to christen themselves his "sons." Sons of Ben provided the nucleus of the entire "Cavalier school" of English poets.

The first of Jonson's great plays was *Every Man in His Humor*, in which Shakespeare acted a leading role. It was also the first of the so-called comedies of humors, in which the prevailing eccentricities and ruling passions of men (i.e., their "humors") were exposed to satiric deflation. Though Jonson's classical tragedy *Sejanus* (1603) has not been much liked (it is gloomy in mood, static in action, and weighty with antiquarian lore), *Volpone* (1606) and *The Alchemist* (1610) are two supreme satiric comedies of the English stage. Both have been repeatedly "adapted" and "modernized," but even now the original texts are likely to seem more lively and vital than the doctored versions. Meanwhile, starting in 1605, Jonson began writing for the court a series of masques—elaborate semitheatrical displays involving spectacle, allegory, and compliment to the king or queen. Thus he became closely involved with the life of the court, a connection that was formalized in 1616, when he was appointed poet laureate with a substantial pension. In the same year, he published in a splendid volume his collected *Works*, a body of plays and poetry to which he kept adding in the years before his death. Though his later plays were not very successful, he turned out many occasional poems, verse letters, translations, complimentary verses before other poets' volumes— finding in all these different forms a grave, incisive pattern of formal speech through which the reverberations of his immense classical learning make them- selves heard.

The bulk of Jonson's poetry falls, without undue strain, into five groups, based mostly on stylistic qualities. He wrote a number of poems of festive ceremony, poems celebrating those qualities of ordered richness and dignified delight that represent his image of the good life. A poem like *To Penshurst* turns a physical building and its surrounding countryside into an emblem of modest yet noble opulence; the poem *Inviting a Friend to Supper* is an imitation of Horace, yet its tonality is thoroughly English, and the "modest little supper" to which he invites his friend would scandalize a modern weight watcher. Quite a different side of Jonson's talent is represented by his elegies and epitaphs; they are brief, full, simple poems, such as one could imagine being carved on a marble slab—direct, imper- sonal, inevitable. Allied to these are his compliments and tributes; often prefixed to his friends' books but sometimes simple tributes of friendship and admiration, they summarize warmly yet judiciously an author's or a patron's character and achievement. Jonson the pure poet finds expression in his songs, sometimes occurring in the plays and masques but sometimes standing alone, often intended for musical accompaniment, but generally beautifully melodic even without it. Finally, Jonson wrote (in imitation of the Roman poet Martial) a great number of epigrams, on a wide variety of subjects.

Jonson took his calling as a poet with the greatest seriousness, asserting the dignity of the profession with (sometimes) a kind of pedantry and emphasis that contrasts with Shakespeare's inconspicuous anonymity. When Jonson published in 1616 his collected works—*The Works of Benjamin Jonson*—it was the first time an English author had been so presumptuous. Yet he succeeded in making the fact of professional authorship somehow respectable; an author like John Dryden, who owed so much to Jonson on stylistic grounds, owed him a social debt as well. His career stood on foundations that Ben, with his pedantry and his pugnacity, was the first to lay down.

To My Book[1]

It will be looked for, book, when some but see
    Thy title, *Epigrams*, and named of me,
Thou should'st be bold, licentious, full of gall,
    Wormwood and sulphur, sharp and toothed[2] withal,
Become a petulant thing, hurl ink and wit   5
    As madmen stones, not caring whom they hit.
Deceive their malice who could wish it so,
    And by thy wiser temper let men know

1. Epigrams are commonly thought of as short, inci- sive poems of personal invective; but when Jonson included in his collected *Works* of 1616 a separate sec- tion headed "Epigrams (Book 1)," he was using the word in a more liberal sense. His "epigrams" included (besides some sharp and sarcastic verses) several poems of compliment and courtesy, some memorial epitaphs, and a verse letter, *Inviting a Friend to Supper*. In our anthology, *To My Book* and the next several poems (through *Epitaph on Elizabeth, L. H.*) come from this section. The "Book 1" of Jonson's title implied at least the promise of a "Book 2," and there are, scattered through his later poetry, a number of verses that might have entered into such a book. But, for whatever rea- son, Jonson never assembled them under any such title.
2. The distinction between toothed (biting) and tooth- less (general) satires—originally made by Joseph Hall (1574–1656), who claimed to be the first English sati- rist—was a commonplace of Jonson's age.

Thou art not covetous of least self-fame
    Made from the hazard of another's shame—   10
Much less with lewd, profane, and beastly phrase
    To catch the world's loose laughter or vain gaze.
He that departs[3] with his own honesty
    For vulgar praise, doth it too dearly buy.

                                                    1616

On Something, That Walks Somewhere

At court I met it, in clothes brave[1] enough
    To be a courtier, and looks grave enough
To seem a statesman: as I near it came,
    It made me a great face. I asked the name.
"A lord," it cried, "buried in flesh and blood,   5
    And such from whom let no man hope least good,
For I will do none; and as little ill,
    For I will dare none." Good lord, walk dead still.

                                                    1616

To William Camden[1]

Camden, most reverend head, to whom I owe
    All that I am in arts, all that I know
(How nothing's that!), to whom my country owes
    The great renown and name wherewith she goes;[2]
Than thee the age sees not that thing more grave,   5
    More high, more holy, that she more would crave.
What name, what skill, what faith hast thou in things!
    What sight in searching the most antique springs!
What weight and what authority in thy speech!
    Man scarce can make that doubt, but thou canst teach.[3]   10
Pardon free truth and let thy modesty,
    Which conquers all, be once o'ercome by thee.
Many of thine[4] this better could than I;
    But for their powers, accept my piety.

                                                    1616

On My First Daughter

Here lies, to each her parents' ruth,[1]
    Mary, the daughter of their youth;
    Yet all heaven's gifts being heaven's due,

---

3. I.e., parts.
1. Fine.
1. Camden, a distinguished scholar, had been Jonson's teacher at Westminster School.
2. Camden's antiquarian studies of his native land in *Britannia* (1586) and *Remains of a Greater Work Concerning Britain* (1605) ran into several editions and were translated abroad.
3. I.e., man can scarcely ask a question to which you don't know the answer.
4. I.e., your pupils. "But for" (line 14): but in lieu of.
1. Grief. There is no positive date of composition for this poem.

It makes the father less to rue.
At six months' end she parted hence   5
With safety of her innocence;
Whose soul heaven's queen, whose name she bears,
In comfort of her mother's tears,
Hath placed amongst her virgin-train:
Where, while that severed doth remain,   10
This grave partakes the fleshly birth;
Which cover lightly, gentle earth!

1616

To John Donne

Donne, the delight of Phoebus and each Muse,
Who, to thy one, all other brains refuse;[1]
Whose every work, of thy most early wit,
Came forth example and remains so yet;
Longer a-knowing than most wits do live,   5
And which no affection praise enough can give.
To it[2] thy language, letters, arts, best life,
Which might with half mankind maintain a strife.
All which I meant to praise, and yet I would,
But leave, because I cannot as I should.   10

1616

On Giles and Joan

Who says that Giles and Joan at discord be?
    Th' observing neighbors no such mood can see.
Indeed, poor Giles repents he married ever,
    But that his Joan doth too. And Giles would never
By his free will be in Joan's company;   5
    No more would Joan he should. Giles riseth early,
And having got him out of doors is glad;
    The like is Joan. But turning home is sad,
And so is Joan. Ofttimes, when Giles doth find
    Harsh sights at home, Giles wisheth he were blind: 10
All this doth Joan. Or that his long-yearned[1] life
    Were quite outspun. The like wish hath his wife.
The children that he keeps Giles swears are none
    Of his begetting; and so swears his Joan.
In all affections she concurreth still.   15
    If now, with man and wife, to will and nill[2]
The self-same things a note of concord be,
    I know no couple better can agree.

1616

1. I.e., the muses shower their favors exclusively on you.
2. The verb *add* is understood.

1. Spun from long skeins of yarn, but with the extra implication of long and futile yearning.
2. To desire and reject; cf. modern "willy-nilly."

On My First Son

Farewell, thou child of my right hand,[1] and joy;
My sin was too much hope of thee, loved boy:
Seven years thou wert lent to me, and I thee pay,
Exacted by thy fate, on the just day.
O could I lose all father[2] now! For why   5
Will man lament the state he should envy,
To have so soon 'scaped world's and flesh's rage,
And, if no other misery, yet age?
Rest in soft peace, and asked, say, "Here doth lie
Ben Jonson his best piece of poetry."   10
For whose sake henceforth all his vows be such
As what he loves may never like too much.[3]

                                          1616

To Lucy, Countess of Bedford, with Mr. Donne's Satires[1]

Lucy, you brightness of our sphere, who are
    Life of the Muses' day, their morning star!
If works, not th' authors, their own grace should look,
    Whose poems would not wish to be your book?
But these, desired by you, the maker's ends   5
    Crown with their own. Rare poems ask rare friends.
Yet satires, since the most of mankind be
    Their unavoided subject, fewest see:
For none e'er took that pleasure in sin's sense,
    But, when they heard it taxed, took more offense. 10
They then that, living where the matter is bred,
    Dare for these poems yet both ask and read
And like them too, must needfully, though few,
    Be of the best: and 'mongst those, best are you;
Lucy, you brightness of our sphere, who are   15
    The Muses' evening, as their morning star.

                                          1616

Inviting a Friend to Supper

Tonight, grave sir, both my poor house and I
    Do equally desire your company:
Not that we think us worthy such a guest,

---

1. "Child of the right hand" is a literal translation of the Hebrew name "Benjamin," which implies the meaning "dexterous" or "fortunate." The boy was born in 1596 and died on his birthday in 1603.
2. Relinquish all fatherly thoughts.
3. The obscure grammar of the last lines seems to recapitulate the feeling in line 2, that too much affection is fatal to the loved one. "Whose sake" is the boy's;

"like" may carry the sense of "please."
1. The countess of Bedford was a famous patroness of the age, to whom both Jonson and Donne addressed poems of compliment. With this poem, Jonson was not offering a printed volume of Donne's *Satires*, but simply a manuscript collection, such as commonly passed from hand to hand in court circles.

But that your worth will dignify our feast
With those that come; whose grace may make that seem   5
   Something, which else could hope for no esteem.
It is the fair acceptance, Sir, creates
   The entertainment perfect: not the cates.[1]
Yet shall you have, to rectify your palate,
   An olive, capers, or some better salad   10
Ushering the mutton; with a short-legged hen,
   If we can get her, full of eggs, and then
Lemons and wine for sauce; to these, a coney[2]
   Is not to be despaired of for our money;
And though fowl now be scarce, yet there are clerks,[3]   15
   The sky not falling, think we may have larks.
I'll tell you of more, and lie, so you will come:
   Of partridge, pheasant, woodcock, of which some
May yet be there; and godwit if we can,
   Knot, rail, and ruff, too.[4] Howsoe'er, my man   20
Shall read a piece of Virgil, Tacitus,
   Livy, or of some better book to us,
Of which we'll speak our minds amidst our meat;
   And I'll profess[5] no verses to repeat:
To this, if aught appear which I not know of,   25
   That will the pastry, not my paper, show of.[6]
Digestive cheese and fruit there sure will be;
   But that which most doth take my muse and me
Is a pure cup of rich Canary wine,
   Which is the Mermaid's now, but shall be mine;   30
Of which, had Horace or Anacreon[7] tasted,
   Their lives, as do their lines, till now had lasted.
Tobacco, Nectar, or the Thespian spring[8]
   Are all but Luther's beer to this I sing.
Of this we will sup free but moderately,   35
   And we will have no Pooly or Parrot[9] by;
Nor shall our cups make any guilty men,
   But at our parting we will be as when
We innocently met. No simple word
   That shall be uttered at our mirthful board   40
Shall make us sad next morning, or affright
   The liberty that we'll enjoy tonight.

                                               1616

1. Dishes.
2. Rabbit.
3. Scholars (pronounced "clarks").
4. The treat of the feast will be these various game birds.
5. Promise.
6. I.e., papers may appear, but they will be under pies (to keep them from sticking to the pan), not for declamation. "To this": add to this.
7. Horace and Anacreon (one in Latin, the other in Greek) wrote many poems in praise of wine. The Mermaid tavern was a favorite haunt of the poets; sweet wine from the Canary Islands was popular in England.
8. One of two springs on Mt. Helicon near the village of Thespiae, both reputed to be sources of poetic inspiration. Compared to Canary, all these other intoxicants are no better than "Luther's beer" (line 34), i.e., weak stuff.
9. Pooly and Parrot were government spies, though their conjunction also suggests a talkative bird, Poll Parrot. While a Roman Catholic and even after he formally left that communion, Jonson had reason to be wary of undercover agents.

Epitaph on S. P., a Child of Queen Elizabeth's Chapel[1]

Weep with me, all you that read
    This little story;
And know for whom a tear you shed,
    Death's self is sorry.
'Twas a child that so did thrive   5
    In grace and feature,
As Heaven and Nature seemed to strive
    Which owned the creature.
Years he numbered scarce thirteen
    When Fates turned cruel,   10
Yet three filled zodiacs had he been
    The stage's jewel;[2]
And did act (what now we moan)
    Old men so duly,
As, sooth, the Parcae[3] thought him one,   15
    He played so truly.
So, by error, to his fate
    They all consented;
But, viewing him since (alas, too late),
    They have repented,   20
And have sought (to give new birth)
    In baths[4] to steep him;
But, being so much too good for earth,
    Heaven vows to keep him.

                                        1616

Epitaph on Elizabeth, L. H.[1]

Wouldst thou hear what man can say
    In a little? Reader, stay.
Underneath this stone doth lie
    As much beauty as could die;
Which in life did harbor give   5
    To more virtue than doth live.
If at all she had a fault,
    Leave it buried in this vault.
One name was Elizabeth;
    Th' other, let it sleep with death: 10
Fitter, where it died, to tell,
    Than that it lived at all. Farewell!

                                        1616

---

1. "S. P." was Salomon Pavy, a boy actor in the troupe known as the Children of Queen Elizabeth's Chapel, who had appeared in several of Jonson's plays; he died in 1602.
2. I.e., he had been on the stage for three seasons.
3. The Fates, one of whose functions was to determine the length of lives.

4. Jonson may have had in mind such magic baths as that of Medea, which restored old Aeson, Jason's father, to his first youth (Ovid, *Metamorphoses* 7).
1. The subject of this epitaph has not been identified; her full name (though we can guess that the "L." probably stood for "Lady") has slept with death.

To Penshurst[1]

Thou art not, Penshurst, built to envious show,
    Of touch[2] or marble; nor canst boast a row
Of polished pillars, or a roof of gold;
    Thou hast no lantern[3] whereof tales are told,
Or stair, or courts; but stand'st an ancient pile,   5
    And, these grudged at,[4] art reverenced the while.
Thou joy'st in better marks, of soil, of air,
    Of wood, of water; therein thou art fair.
Thou hast thy walks for health, as well as sport;
    Thy mount, to which the dryads[5] do resort,   10
Where Pan and Bacchus their high feasts have made,
    Beneath the broad beech and the chestnut shade;
That taller tree, which of a nut was set
    At his great birth where all the Muses met.[6]
There in the writhèd bark are cut the names   15
    Of many a sylvan, taken with his flames;[7]
And thence the ruddy satyrs oft provoke
    The lighter fauns to reach thy Lady's Oak.[8]
Thy copse too, named of Gamage,[9] thou hast there,
    That never fails to serve thee seasoned deer   20
When thou wouldst feast or exercise thy friends.
    The lower land, that to the river bends,
Thy sheep, thy bullocks, kine, and calves do feed;
    The middle grounds thy mares and horses breed.
Each bank doth yield thee conies;[1] and the tops,   25
    Fertile of wood, Ashore and Sidney's copse,[2]
To crown thy open table, doth provide
    The purpled pheasant with the speckled side;
The painted partridge lies in every field,
    And for thy mess is willing to be killed.   30
And if the high-swollen Medway[3] fail thy dish,
    Thou hast thy ponds, that pay thee tribute fish:
Fat agèd carps that run into thy net,
    And pikes, now weary their own kind to eat,
As loath the second draught or cast to stay,   35
    Officiously at first themselves betray;
Bright eels that emulate them, and leap on land
    Before the fisher, or into his hand.
Then hath thy orchard fruit, thy garden flowers,

1. The country seat of the Sidney family (famous for Sir Philip) in Kent. Jonson's is one of the first English poems celebrating a specific place. Later examples are *Cooper's Hill* by Sir John Denham and *Windsor Forest* (1713) by Alexander Pope.
    In the 1616 *Works*, Jonson grouped some of his non-epigrammatic poems under the heading *The Forest*. This was a translation of the term *Silvae*, used by the late Latin poet Statius to designate a poetical miscellany. *To Penshurst* and the two following poems are from that grouping.
2. Touchstone, a fine black (and expensive) variety of basalt.
3. Cupola.
4. More pretentious houses attract envy.

5. Wood nymphs.
6. Sir Philip Sidney was born at Penshurst; an oak tree, planted the day of his birth, is still shown as "Sidney's oak."
7. Woodsman, in love because of reading Sidney's poems. "His flames" are the fires of love.
8. Lady Leicester's oak, named after a lady of the house who once entered into labor under its branches. "Provoke": challenge to a race.
9. Lady Barbara Gamage gave her name to a grove near the park entrance.
1. Rabbits.
2. Little woods and thickets of the estate, still surviving under their ancient names.
3. The local river.

Fresh as the air, and new as are the hours.   40
The early cherry, with the later plum,
  Fig, grape, and quince, each in his time doth come;
The blushing apricot and woolly peach
  Hang on thy walls, that every child may reach.
And though thy walls be of the country stone,   45
  They're reared with no man's ruin, no man's groan;
There's none that dwell about them wish them down;
  But all come in, the farmer and the clown,[4]
And no one empty-handed, to salute
  Thy lord and lady, though they have no suit.   50
Some bring a capon, some a rural cake,
  Some nuts, some apples; some that think they make
The better cheeses bring them, or else send
  By their ripe daughters, whom they would commend
This way to husbands, and whose baskets bear   55
  An emblem of themselves in plum or pear.
But what can this (more than express their love)
  Add to thy free provisions, far above
The need of such? whose liberal board doth flow
  With all that hospitality doth know;   60
Where comes no guest but is allowed to eat,
  Without his fear, and of thy lord's own meat;
Where the same beer and bread, and selfsame wine,
  That is his lordship's shall be also mine,
And I not fain to sit (as some this day   65
  At great men's tables), and yet dine away.[5]
Here no man tells[6] my cups; nor, standing by,
  A waiter doth my gluttony envy,
But gives me what I call, and lets me eat;
  He knows below he shall find plenty of meat.   70
Thy tables hoard not up for the next day;
  Nor, when I take my lodging, need I pray
For fire, or lights, or livery;[7] all is there,
  As if thou then wert mine, or I reigned here:
There's nothing I can wish, for which I stay.[8]   75
  That found King James when, hunting late this way
With his brave son, the Prince, they saw thy fires
  Shine bright on every hearth, as the desires
Of thy Penates[9] had been set on flame
  To entertain them; or the country came   80
With all their zeal to warm their welcome here.
  What (great I will not say, but) sudden cheer
Didst thou then make 'em! and what praise was heaped
  On thy good lady then, who therein reaped
The just reward of her high housewifery;   85
  To have her linen, plate, and all things nigh,
When she was far; and not a room but dressed

4. Yokel.
5. When tables were large, different courses might be served at the two ends; hence one could sit at a person's table and dine away, eating different food entirely.
6. Counts.
7. In the old sense, provisions, food.
8. Wait.
9. Roman household gods. A room in the house is still known as "King James's room."

As if it had expected such a guest!
These, Penshurst, are thy praise, and yet not all.
   Thy lady's noble, fruitful, chaste withal.   90
His children thy great lord may call his own,
   A fortune in this age but rarely known.
They are, and have been, taught religion; thence
   Their gentler spirits have sucked innocence.
Each morn and even they are taught to pray,   95
   With the whole household, and may, every day,
Read in their virtuous parents' noble parts
   The mysteries of manners, arms, and arts.
Now, Penshurst, they that will proportion[1] thee
   With other edifices, when they see   100
Those proud, ambitious heaps, and nothing else,
   May say, their lords have built, but thy lord dwells.

                        1616

Song: To Celia[1]

Drink to me only with thine eyes,
   And I will pledge with mine;
Or leave a kiss but in the cup,
   And I'll not look for wine.
The thirst that from the soul doth rise   5
   Doth ask a drink divine:
But might I of Jove's nectar sup,
   I would not change for thine.

I sent thee late a rosy wreath,
   Not so much honoring thee,   10
As giving it a hope that there
   It could not withered be.
But thou thereon didst only breathe,
   And sent'st it back to me;
Since when it grows and smells, I swear,   15
   Not of itself, but thee.

                        1616

To Heaven

Good and great God, can I not think of thee
   But it must straight my melancholy be?
Is it interpreted in me disease
   That, laden with my sins, I seek for ease?
Oh, be thou witness, that the reins[1] dost know   5

1. Compare.
1. These famous lines are a patchwork of five separate prose passages by Philostratus, a Greek sophist (3rd century A.D.). Jonson very carefully reworded the phrases (there are several manuscript versions of the poem) into this classic lyric. The music that has made it a barroom favorite is by an anonymous 18th-century composer.
1. Literally, kidneys, but also the seat of the affections, with a further glance at Psalm 7.9: "the righteous God trieth the hearts and reins."

And hearts of all, if I be sad for show,
And judge me after, if I dare pretend
   To aught but grace, or aim at other end.
As thou art all, so be thou all to me,
   First, midst, and last, converted[2] one and three,   10
My faith, my hope, my love; and in this state,
   My judge, my witness, and my advocate.
Where have I been this while exiled from thee,
   And whither rapt, now thou but stoop'st[3] to me?
Dwell, dwell here still: Oh, being everywhere,   15
   How can I doubt to find thee ever here?
I know my state, both full of shame and scorn,
   Conceived in sin and unto labor born,
Standing with fear, and must with horror fall,
   And destined unto judgment after all.   20
I feel my griefs too, and there scarce is ground
   Upon my flesh to inflict another wound.
Yet dare I not complain or wish for death
   With holy Paul,[4] lest it be thought the breath
Of discontent; or that these prayers be   25
   For weariness of life, not love of thee.

                                        1616

In the Person of Womankind
(In Defense of their Inconstancy)

Hang up those dull and envious fools
   That talk abroad of woman's change;
We were not bred to sit on stools,
   Our proper virtue is to range:
      Take that away, you take our lives,   5
      We are no women then, but wives.

Such as in valor would excel
   Do change, though man, and often fight,
Which we in love must do as well
   If ever we will love aright.   10
      The frequent varying of the deed
      Is that which doth perfection breed.

Nor is 't inconstancy to change
   For what is better, or to make
(By searching) what before was strange   15
   Familiar for the use's sake.
      The good from bad is not descried
      But as 'tis often vexed[1] and tried.

---

2. Interchanging.
3. Falcons stoop (i.e., dive from the heavens) to snatch their quarry.

4. In Romans 7.24, Paul cries out despairingly, "Who shall deliver me from the body of this death?"
1. Examined severely.

And this profession of a store
   In love doth not alone help forth[2]   20
Our pleasure, but preserves us more
   From being forsaken than doth worth:
      For were the worthiest woman cursed
      To love one man, he'd leave her first.

                                 1640–41

My Picture Left in Scotland[1]

I now think Love is rather deaf than blind,
   For else it could not be
      That she
Whom I adore so much should so slight me
   And cast my love behind;   5
I'm sure my language to her was as sweet,
   And every close did meet
      In sentence of as subtle feet,
      As hath the youngest he
That sits in shadow of Apollo's tree.[2]   10

O, but my conscious fears
   That fly my thoughts between,
   Tell me that she hath seen
My hundreds of gray hairs,
   Told seven and forty years,   15
Read so much waste[3] as she cannot embrace
My mountain belly and my rocky face;
And all these through her eyes have stopped her ears.

1619   1640–41

Slow, Slow, Fresh Fount[1]

Slow, slow, fresh fount, keep time with my salt tears;
Yet slower, yet, O faintly, gentle springs!
List to the heavy part the music bears:
Woe weeps out her division,[2] when she sings.
   Droop herbs and flowers;   5
   Fall grief in showers;
   Our beauties are not ours.
     O, I could still,

2. Not only contribue to. "Store": abundance.
1. After his walking tour of Scotland in 1618–19, Jonson sent a manuscript version of this poem to William Drummond, with whom he had stayed. No one knows who the woman of the poem was, or if she existed at all.
2. Jonson claims his words to the lady were as eloquent and profound as any younger poet's. "Close": cadence. "Sentence": judgment or opinion.

3. "Waist" is understood behind "waste" and may have been the primary meaning.
1. From the satiric comedy *Cynthia's Revels.* The play deals with the sin of self-love, and this lyric is a lament sung by Echo for Narcissus, who was entranced by his own reflection and ultimately transformed into a flower.
2. Grief at parting, but also a rapid melodic passage of music.

Like melting snow upon some craggy hill,
    Drop, drop, drop, drop,   10
Since nature's pride is now a withered daffodil.

                                                 1600

Queen and Huntress[1]

Queen and huntress, chaste and fair,
Now the sun is laid to sleep,
Seated in thy silver chair,
State in wonted manner keep;
Hesperus entreats thy light,   5
Goddess excellently bright.

Earth, let not thy envious shade
Dare itself to interpose;
Cynthia's shining orb was made
Heaven to clear, when day did close.   10
Bless us then with wishèd sight,
Goddess excellently bright.

Lay thy bow of pearl apart,
And thy crystal-shining quiver;
Give unto the flying hart   15
Space to breathe, how short soever.
Thou that mak'st a day of night,
Goddess excellently bright.

                                                 1600

Still to Be Neat[1]

Still to be neat, still to be dressed
As you were going to a feast,
Still to be powdered, still perfumed;
Lady, it is to be presumed,
Though art's hid causes are not found,   5
All is not sweet, all is not sound.

Give me a look, give me a face
That makes simplicity a grace;
Robes loosely flowing, hair as free—
Such sweet neglect more taketh me   10
Than all the adulteries of art.
They strike mine eyes, but not my heart.

                                               1609

1. Also from *Cynthia's Revels*, this song is sung by Hesperus, the evening star, to Cynthia or Diana, goddess of chastity and the moon—with whom Queen Elizabeth was, almost automatically, equated.

1. This song is sung in the play *Epicoene* at the request of Clerimont, supposed to be its composer; he is irked at the Lady Haughty, who, he says, overdoes the art of makeup.

Though I Am Young[1]

Though I am young and cannot tell
  Either what Death or Love is well,
Yet I have heard they both bear darts,
  And both do aim at human hearts.
And then again, I have been told   5
  Love wounds with heat, as Death with cold;
So that I fear they do but bring
  Extremes to touch, and mean one thing.

As in a ruin we it call
  One thing to be blown up or fall;   10
Or to our end like way may have
  By a flash of lightning or a wave;
So Love's inflamèd shaft or brand
  May kill as soon as Death's cold hand;
Except[2] Love's fires the virtue have   15
  To fright the frost out of the grave.

1640–41

To the Memory of My Beloved, The Author, Mr. William Shakespeare, and What He Hath Left Us[1]

To draw no envy, Shakespeare, on thy name,
  Am I thus ample to thy book and fame,
While I confess thy writings to be such
  As neither man nor Muse can praise too much.
'Tis true, and all men's suffrage.[2] But these ways   5
  Were not the paths I meant unto thy praise;
For silliest[3] ignorance on these may light,
  Which, when it sounds at best, but echoes right;
Or blind affection,[4] which doth ne'er advance
  The truth, but gropes, and urgeth all by chance;   10
Or crafty malice might pretend this praise,
  And think to ruin where it seemed to raise.
These are as some infamous bawd or whore
  Should praise a matron. What could hurt her more?
But thou art proof against them, and, indeed,   15
  Above th' ill fortune of them, or the need.
I therefore will begin. Soul of the age!
  The applause! delight! the wonder of our stage!
My Shakespeare, rise; I will not lodge thee by
  Chaucer or Spenser, or bid Beaumont lie   20
A little further to make thee a room:[5]

1. This song is sung in *The Sad Shepherd*, by Karolin; the pastoral simplicity of his character is caught in the naive monosyllables of the poem.
2. Unless.
1. This poem was prefixed to the first Folio of Shakespeare's plays, published in 1623.
2. Consent.
3. Emptiest.
4. Prejudice.
5. Chaucer, Spenser, and Francis Beaumont were buried in Westminster Abbey; Shakespeare, of course, in Stratford. Jonson endorses the separation: Shakespeare should not be crowded.

Thou art a monument without a tomb,
And art alive still while thy book doth live,
　　And we have wits to read and praise to give.
That I not mix thee so, my brain excuses,　　　　　　　　　　25
　　I mean with great, but disproportioned[6] Muses;
For, if I thought my judgment were of years,
　　I should commit thee surely with thy peers,
And tell how far thou didst our Lyly outshine,
　　Or sporting Kyd, or Marlowe's mighty line.[7]　　　　　　30
And though thou hadst small Latin and less Greek,
　　From thence to honor thee I would not seek[8]
For names, but call forth thund'ring Aeschylus,
　　Euripides, and Sophocles to us,
Pacuvius, Accius, him of Cordova dead,[9]　　　　　　　　　35
　　To life again, to hear thy buskin[1] tread
And shake a stage; or, when thy socks were on,
　　Leave thee alone for the comparison
Of all that insolent Greece or haughty Rome
　　Sent forth, or since did from their ashes come.　　　　　40
Triumph, my Britain; thou hast one to show
　　To whom all scenes[2] of Europe homage owe.
He was not of an age, but for all time!
　　And all the Muses still were in their prime
When like Apollo he came forth to warm　　　　　　　　　45
　　Our ears, or like a Mercury to charm.
Nature herself was proud of his designs,
　　And joyed to wear the dressing of his lines,
Which were so richly spun, and woven so fit,
　　As, since, she will vouchsafe no other wit:　　　　　　　50
The merry Greek, tart Aristophanes,
　　Neat Terence, witty Plautus[3] now not please,
But antiquated and deserted lie,
　　As they were not of Nature's family.
Yet must I not give Nature all; thy Art,　　　　　　　　　55
　　My gentle Shakespeare, must enjoy a part.
For though the poet's matter Nature be,
　　His Art doth give the fashion; and that he
Who casts[4] to write a living line must sweat
　　(Such as thine are) and strike the second heat　　　　60
Upon the Muses' anvil; turn the same,
　　And himself with it, that he thinks to frame,
Or for the laurel he may gain a scorn;

---

6. Not comparable.
7. John Lyly, Thomas Kyd, and Christopher Marlowe, Elizabethan dramatists put in the shade by Shakespeare.
8. Be short of, lacking in. Shakespeare had, by modern standards, a very adequate command of Latin; Jonson is speaking from the lofty height of his own remarkable scholarship. Shakespeare's French and Italian (he was competent in both tongues) Jonson does not think worthy of mention.
9. Marcus Pacuvius and Lucius Accius (2nd century B.C.) and "him of Cordova," Seneca the Younger (1st

century A.D.), the greatest of the Latin tragedians. Only fragments survive of the plays of Pacuvius and Accius; Jonson's comparisons are more pedantic, in these instances, than relevant.
1. The symbol of tragedy, as contrasted with "socks" (in the next line), symbols of comedy.
2. Stages.
3. Aristophanes, the Greek satirist and comic writer; Terence and Plautus (2nd and 3rd centuries B.C.), Roman writers of comedy.
4. Undertakes. "Fashion": form, style.

For a good poet's made as well as born.
And such wert thou! Look how the father's face   65
   Lives in his issue; even so the race
Of Shakespeare's mind and manners brightly shines
   In his well-turnèd and true-filèd lines,
In each of which he seems to shake a lance,[5]
   As brandished at the eyes of ignorance.   70
Sweet swan of Avon, what a sight it were
   To see thee in our waters yet appear,
And make those flights upon the banks of Thames
   That so did take Eliza and our James![6]
But stay; I see thee in the hemisphere   75
   Advanced and made a constellation there![7]
Shine forth, thou star of poets, and with rage
   Or influence[8] chide or cheer the drooping stage,
Which, since thy flight from hence, hath mourned like night,
   And despairs day, but for thy volume's light.   80

                                                                  1623

Ode to Himself[1]

   Come, leave the loathèd stage,
      And the more loathsome age,
   Where pride and impudence, in faction knit,
            Usurp the chair of wit,
   Indicting and arraigning every day   5
            Something they call a play.
      Let their fastidious, vain
      Commission of the brain
   Run on and rage, sweat, censure, and condemn:
   They were not made for thee, less thou for them.   10

   Say that thou pour'st them wheat,
      And they will acorns eat;
   'Twere simple fury still thyself to waste
            On such as have no taste!
   To offer them a surfeit of pure bread,   15
            Whose appetites are dead!
      No, give them grains their fill,
      Husks, draff to drink, and swill:[2]
   If they love lees, and leave the lusty wine,
   Envy them not; their palate's with the swine.   20

      No doubt some moldy tale
      Like *Pericles*,[3] and stale

---

5. Pun on Shake-speare.
6. Queen Elizabeth and King James.
7. Heroes and demigods were typically exalted after death to a place among the stars.
8. "Rage" and "influence" describe the supposed effects of the planets on earthly affairs. "Rage" also implies poetic inspiration.

1. The failure of Jonson's *The New Inn* (1629) inspired this assault on criticism and the public taste.
2. Jonson gets into one line three words suggestive of pig food.
3. Shakespeare's play, at least in part (printed 1609). "Shrieve" (line 23): sheriff. The basket outside the jail to receive food for the poor was called the sheriff's tub.

As the shrieve's crusts, and nasty as his fish —
   Scraps, out of every dish
Thrown forth and raked into the common tub,   25
   May keep up the play club:
   There, sweepings do as well
   As the best-ordered meal;
For who the relish of these guests will fit
Needs set them but the alms basket of wit.   30

   And much good do 't you then:
   Brave plush and velvet men
Can feed on orts;[4] and, safe in your stage clothes,
   Dare quit,[5] upon your oaths,
The stagers and the stage-wrights[6] too, your peers,   35
   Of larding your large ears
   With their foul comic socks,[7]
   Wrought upon twenty blocks;
Which, if they're torn, and turned, and patched enough,
The gamesters share your guilt, and you their stuff.   40

   Leave things so prostitute
   And take th' Alcaic lute;[8]
Or thine own Horace, or Anacreon's lyre;
   Warm thee by Pindar's fire:
And though thy nerves be shrunk, and blood be cold,   45
   Ere years have made thee old,
   Strike that disdainful heat
   Throughout, to their defeat,
As curious fools, and envious of thy strain,
May, blushing, swear no palsy's in thy brain.   50

   But when they hear thee sing
   The glories of thy king,
His zeal to God and his just awe o'er men,
   They may, blood-shaken then,
Feel such a flesh-quake to possess their powers   55
   As they shall cry, "Like ours,
   In sound of peace or wars,
   No harp e'er hit the stars
In tuning forth the acts of his sweet reign,
And raising Charles his chariot 'bove his Wain."[9]   60

1629   1631, 1640–41

---

4. Scraps. Actors often wore on the stage clothes cast
off by the gentry; these parasites, Jonson seems to be
saying, wear clothes cast off by actors (cf. line 40, "you
[share] their stuff").
5. Acquit.
6. Playwrights. "Stagers": actors (also "gamesters,"
below).
7. Symbols of comedy, as buskins (high boots) were of

tragedy (cf. p. 632, n. 1).
8. That of Alcaeus, who lived ca. 600 B.C., and became
famous, along with Horace, Anacreon, and Pindar,
among the greatest lyric poets.
9. Jonson's poetry will elevate the chariot of Charles
I (symbol of his royal power) above Charles's Wain
(Wagon) — the seven bright stars of Ursa Major.

JOHN MILTON
1608–1674

1637:	*Lycidas.*
1640–1660:	The pamphlet wars.
1651:	Blindness.
1667:	*Paradise Lost.*

The life of John Milton falls conveniently into three divisions. There is a period of youthful education and apprenticeship, which culminates in the writing of *Lycidas* (1637) and Milton's foreign travels (1638–39). There is a period of prose and controversy (1640–60), when almost all his verse was the by-product of events public or private, and when his major preoccupations were political and social; and finally, there are the last fourteen years of his life, when he returned to literature, a mature and somewhat embittered figure, to publish his three major poems, *Paradise Lost* (1667), *Paradise Regained* (1671), and *Samson Agonistes* (1671).

Milton was born in Bread Street, Cheapside, the elder son of a self-made businessman, who, under the title of scrivener, drew up contracts, lent money at interest, and dealt in real estate. From the beginning, young Milton showed prodigious gifts as a student of languages. At St. Paul's School he mastered Latin and Greek, and before long he was adept in most modern European tongues, as well as Hebrew. Sent to Christ's College, Cambridge, he graduated B.A. in 1629 and M.A. in 1632, meanwhile continuing to read voraciously and writing (too infrequently for his own satisfaction) an occasional poem. In the normal course of events, an education like this would have culminated in ordination to the ministry and a career in the church. But after his M.A., Milton, who disliked the trend of religious and civil affairs in England, did not take orders; leaving the university, first for London, then for his father's country house at Horton in Buckinghamshire, he read, day and night, under his own direction, for six more years. It seems likely that Milton in his time read just about everything of importance written in English, Latin, Greek, and Italian. (Of course, he had the Bible by heart.) In 1634 he wrote, at the invitation of a noble family in Shropshire, the masque known as *Comus*; and in 1637 he contributed to a volume memorializing a college classmate the elegy *Lycidas.* Finally, in 1638, his most indulgent father sent this most avid of students abroad, to put the finishing touches on an already splendid education. For a little over a year Milton traveled on the Continent, visiting famous literary figures and scenes; then, hearing rumors of impending troubles in England, he returned home.

Of Milton's complex and troubled career in controversy, we need not say much. It too is divided into three major phases. He began by publishing antiprelatical tracts, against government of the church by bishops. These are rough, knockabout, name-calling pamphlets in the style of the times, which take a popular position on a relatively popular issue. In 1644, responding to a book by a German exile in England named Samuel Hartlib, he wrote a short essay, *Of Education*; later in the same year, responding to a severe if ineffectual parliamentary ordinance to regulate printing, he published his defense of a free press, *Areopagitica.* But in the meanwhile his personal circumstances had led to a second series of pamphlets that earned Milton a reputation as a radical. In May or June 1642, he had married Mary Powell, daughter of a royalist country squire. The bride was just seventeen years old, half her husband's age. Within a few weeks she left him, to return to her parents' house; and from 1643 to 1645, Milton published a series of pamphlets arguing that divorce should be granted on grounds of incompatibility. Respectable Englishmen, already disturbed by the social troubles of the time, took a dim view of what they called "divorce at pleasure"; it looked like the end of all social order. In fact, Milton's position appears moderate today and is accepted practice in many modern societies; but it was scandalous in his time, and Milton was much embittered by ridicule of his ideas. After the execution of Charles I in 1649, he published a third set of pamphlets; they were Latin disputations against Continental critics of the Cromwell regime, and they explicitly defended the execution of Charles. In the middle of this work he went blind, as a result of eyestrain continued over many years. With the help of assistants, however, he was able to fulfill his duties as Latin secretary to Cromwell's Council of State and to contribute very substantially to the diplomatic dignity of the new government.

Meanwhile, his wife had returned to him in 1645, and having borne him three daughters, died in 1652. In 1656 Milton married Katherine Woodcock, who died in childbirth in 1658. Finally, in 1660, the whole political movement for which Milton had sacrificed so much went to smash. Though Milton boldly published pamphlets in its support to the very last minute, the Good Old Cause was defeated, and Charles II recalled from his travels. For a time under the Restoration, Milton was imprisoned and in danger of his life; but friends intervened (among them, Andrew Marvell), and he escaped with a fine and the loss of most of his property.

In 1663 Milton married his third wife, Elizabeth Minshull, and in blindness, poverty, defeat, and relative isolation, he set about completing a poem "justifying the ways of God to men," which he had first envisaged many years before. It was published in 1667, as *Paradise Lost*; and despite the many difficulties that it presented, despite its unfamiliar meter (blank verse was rare outside drama), despite the unpopularity of its attitudes and Milton's reputation as a dangerous man, it was recognized at once as a supreme epic achievement. In 1671 Milton published *Paradise Regained*, an epic poem in four books describing Christ's temptation in the wilderness, and *Samson Agonistes*, a "closet" tragedy (i.e., not intended for the stage). He died, of complications arising from gout, in 1674.

In the writings of Milton, the work of two tremendous intellectual and social movements comes to a head. The Renaissance is responsible for the rich and complex texture of Milton's style, the multiplicity of its classical references, its wealth of ornament and decoration. *Paradise Lost*, being an epic, not only challenges comparison with Homer and Virgil but undertakes to encompass the whole life of humankind—war, love, religion, hell, heaven, the cosmos. It is a poem vastly capacious of worldly experience. On the other hand, the Reformation speaks with equal, if not greater, authority in Milton's earnest and individually minded Christianity. The great epic, which resounds with the grandeur and multiplicity of the world, is also a poem of which the central actions take place inwardly, at the core of the human conscience. Adam is Milton's epic hero, but unlike his classical predecessors', his fate culminates in an act of passive suffering, not of active heroism. He does not kill Hector or Turnus, much less Satan; with Eve, he picks up the burden of worldly existence and triumphs over his guilt by admitting it and repenting of it.

These two contrasting aspects of Milton's life and thought place him within the long tradition of Renaissance Christian humanism. His literary art places him in the small circle of great epic writers.

On Shakespeare[1]

What needs my Shakespeare for his honored bones
The labor of an age in pilèd stones,
Or that his hallowed relics should be hid
Under a star-ypointing pyramid?
Dear son of memory,[2] great heir of fame,   5
What need'st thou such weak witness of thy name?
Thou in our wonder and astonishment
Hast built thyself a livelong monument.
For whilst to th' shame of slow-endeavoring art
Thy easy numbers flow, and that each heart   10
Hath from the leaves of thy unvalued[3] book
Those Delphic lines with deep impression took,
Then thou, our fancy of itself bereaving,
Dost make us marble with too much conceiving;[4]
And so sepùlchered in such pomp dost lie,   15
That kings for such a tomb would wish to die.

1630   1632

L'Allegro[1]

Hence loathèd Melancholy,
    Of Cerberus[2] and blackest midnight born,
In Stygian[3] cave forlorn
    'Mongst horrid shapes, and shrieks, and sights unholy,
Find out some uncouth cell,   5
    Where brooding Darkness spreads his jealous wings,
And the night-raven sings;
    There under ebon shades and low-browed rocks,
As ragged as thy locks,
    In dark Cimmerian[4] desert ever dwell.   10
But come thou goddess fair and free,
In heaven yclept Euphrosyne,[5]

1. Milton's tribute to Shakespeare appeared in the Second Folio of the plays. The poem answers the common complaint of the day, that Shakespeare should have been buried in some place more splendid than Stratford.
2. Shakespeare is described as the "son of memory" because that makes him a brother of the Muses, daughters of Mnemosyne (four syllables; the word means "memory") by Zeus.
3. Beyond all value, invaluable.
4. The monuments of Shakespeare's tomb are all the enchanted and motionless readers of his book.
1. L'Allegro and Il Penseroso are companion poems, written in those dancing tetrameter couplets that are so hard to keep from sinking into singsong, so delightful when controlled. Milton's handling of this difficult meter may be compared with other virtuoso performances like Marvell's To His Coy Mistress and Housman's Terence, This Is Stupid Stuff.
    The titles of Milton's poems are almost untranslatable. Within the framework of two contrasted yet parallel days we see the cheerful, social man and the

melancholy, contemplative man in their typical postures. Milton's interest in the typical accounts for the striking generality of the pictures; they are in effect "characters" in verse. Melancholy has been much analyzed; in addition to Burton's famous Anatomy, it is discussed in Erwin Panofsky's Albrecht Dürer (1945), where it arises in connection with Dürer's magnificent engraving Melencolia, as well as in the immense study by Saxl, Panofsky, and Klibansky, Saturn and Melancholy (1964). There is a history of literary cheerfulness, too—The Happy Man, by Maren Sofie Røstvig (1954).
2. The three-headed hellhound of classical mythology.
3. I.e., near the river Styx, in the underworld.
4. The Cimmerians, who gave their name to Crimea, were supposed to live on the outer edge of the world, in perpetual twilight.
5. Euphrosyne (four syllables), Aglaia, and Thalia were the Graces, goddesses of beauty and delight; antiquity assigned them a variety of parents, though they were most often regarded as products of Zeus' leisure hours.

And by men, heart-easing Mirth,
Whom lovely Venus at a birth
With two sister Graces more   15
To ivy-crownèd Bacchus bore;[6]
Or whether (as some sager sing)[7]
The frolic wind that breathes the spring,
Zephyr with Aurora playing,
As he met her once a-Maying,   20
There on beds of violets blue,
And fresh-blown[8] roses washed in dew,
Filled her with thee a daughter fair,
So buxom,[9] blithe, and debonair.
Haste thee nymph, and bring with thee   25
Jest and youthful Jollity,
Quips and Cranks,[1] and wanton Wiles,
Nods, and Becks, and wreathèd Smiles,
Such as hang on Hebe's[2] cheek,
And love to live in dimple sleek;   30
Sport that wrinkled Care derides,
And Laughter holding both his sides.
Come, and trip it as ye go
On the light fantastic toe,
And in thy right hand lead with thee   35
The mountain nymph, sweet Liberty;
And if I give thee honor due,
Mirth, admit me of thy crew
To live with her and live with thee,
In unreprovèd pleasures free;   40
To hear the lark begin his flight,
And, singing, startle the dull night,
From his watch-tower in the skies,
Till the dappled dawn doth rise;
Then to come in spite of[3] sorrow,   45
And at my window bid good morrow,
Through the sweetbriar or the vine,
Or the twisted eglantine.
While the cock with lively din
Scatters the rear of darkness thin,   50
And to the stack or the barn door,
Stoutly struts his dames before;
Oft listening how the hounds and horn
Cheerly rouse the slumbering morn,
From the side of some hoar hill,   55
Through the high wood echoing shrill.
Sometime walking not unseen
By hedgerow elms, on hillocks green,
Right against the eastern gate,

6. Bacchus is god of wine.
7. The "sager" poets who describe the Graces as born
of Zephyr (the west wind) and Aurora (the dawn) are
in fact Milton himself; the story is his invention.
8. Newly opened.
9. Lively.

1. Jokes.
2. Goddess of youth and cupbearer to the other gods.
Pronounced *Hee-bee*.
3. In defiance of. "Then to come": i.e., then admit me
to come.

Where the great sun begins his state,[4]   60
Robed in flames and amber light,
The clouds in thousand liveries dight;[5]
While the plowman near at hand
Whistles o'er the furrowed land,
And the milkmaid singeth blithe,   65
And the mower whets his scythe,
And every shepherd tells his tale
Under the hawthorn in the dale.
Straight mine eye hath caught new pleasures
Whilst the landscape round it measures,   70
Russet lawns and fallows gray,
Where the nibbling flocks do stray,
Mountains on whose barren breast
The laboring clouds do often rest;
Meadows trim with daisies pied,[6]   75
Shallow brooks, and rivers wide.
Towers and battlements it sees
Bosomed high in tufted trees,
Where perhaps some beauty lies,
The cynosure[7] of neighboring eyes.   80
Hard by, a cottage chimney smokes
From betwixt two agèd oaks,
Where Corydon and Thyrsis met
Are at their savory dinner set
Of herbs and other country messes,   85
Which the neat-handed Phyllis dresses;
And then in haste her bower she leaves,
With Thestylis[8] to bind the sheaves;
Or if the earlier season lead
To the tanned haycock in the mead.   90
Sometimes with secure delight
The upland hamlets will invite,
When the merry bells ring round
And the jocund rebecks[9] sound
To many a youth and many a maid,   95
Dancing in the checkered shade;
And young and old come forth to play
On a sunshine holiday,
Till the livelong daylight fail;
Then to the spicy nut-brown ale,   100
With stories told of many a feat,
How fairy Mab the junkets[1] eat;
She was pinched and pulled, she said,
And he, by friar's lantern led,
Tells how the drudging goblin[2] sweat   105

4. Procession.
5. Dressed.
6. Dappled.
7. Literally, the bright polestar, by which mariners steer; here, a splendid, eminent object, much gazed at.
8. Since the days of Theocritus, "Corydon," "Thyrsis," "Phyllis," and "Thestylis" have been traditional shepherds' names.

9. A rebeck is a small three-stringed fiddle; "jocund" implies a festive occasion.
1. Sweetmeats, especially with cream. Queen Mab is the consort of Oberon, the fairy king. "She" and "he" in the next two lines are country folk, telling of their experiences with the fairies.
2. Robin Goodfellow, alias Puck, Pook, or Hobgoblin. "Friar's lantern": will-o'-the-wisp.

To earn his cream-bowl duly set,
When in one night, ere glimpse of morn,
His shadowy flail hath threshed the corn
That ten day-laborers could not end;
Then lies him down the lubber fiend,[3]   110
And stretched out all the chimney's length,
Basks at the fire his hairy strength;
And crop-full out of doors he flings
Ere the first cock his matin rings.
Thus done the tales, to bed they creep,   115
By whispering winds soon lulled asleep.
Towered cities please us then,
And the busy hum of men,
Where throngs of knights and barons bold
In weeds of peace high triumphs[4] hold,   120
With store of ladies, whose bright eyes
Rain influence,[5] and judge the prize
Of wit or arms, while both contend
To win her grace, whom all commend.
There let Hymen[6] oft appear   125
In saffron robe, with taper clear,
And pomp and feast and revelry,
With masque and antique pageantry;
Such sights as youthful poets dream
On summer eves by haunted stream.   130
Then to the well-trod stage anon,
If Jonson's learned sock be on,
Or sweetest Shakespeare, fancy's child,
Warble his native wood-notes wild.[7]
And ever against eating cares[8]   135
Lap me in soft Lydian airs,[9]
Married to immortal verse
Such as the meeting soul may pierce
In notes with many a winding bout[1]
Of linkèd sweetness long drawn out,   140
With wanton heed and giddy cunning,
The melting voice through mazes running,
Untwisting all the chains that tie
The hidden soul of harmony;
That Orpheus' self may heave his head   145
From golden slumber on a bed
Of heaped Elysian flowers, and hear
Such strains as would have won the ear
Of Pluto, to have quite set free

3. Drudging spirit.
4. Festive ceremonies. "Weeds": garments.
5. The ladies' eyes are stars, and so have astrological influence over the men.
6. Roman god of marriage, wearing an orange-yellow ("saffron") robe.
7. The contrast of Jonson as a "learned" poet with Shakespeare as a "natural" one was conventional. "Sock": a low-heeled slipper, worn by actors in classical

comedy and often contrasted with the buskin (high-heeled boot) appropriate to tragedy.
8. "Eating cares" is but one of many classical phrases in the poem; it is from Horace, Odes 2.11.18 (curas edaces).
9. "Lydian airs" in music would be soft, languishing, sensual—unlike those in the chaste Dorian and brisk Ionian modes.
1. Turn, involution.

His half-regained Eurydice.[2]   150
These delights if thou canst give,
Mirth, with thee I mean to live.

ca. 1631   1645

Il Penseroso

Hence vain deluding Joys,
    The brood of Folly without father bred,
How little you bestead,[1]
    Or fill the fixèd mind with all your toys;[2]
Dwell in some idle brain,   5
    And fancies fond[3] with gaudy shapes possess,
As thick and numberless
    As the gay motes that people the sunbeams,
Or likest hovering dreams,
    The fickle pensioners of Morpheus'[4] train.   10
But hail thou Goddess sage and holy,
Hail, divinest Melancholy,
Whose saintly visage is too bright
To hit[5] the sense of human sight,
And therefore to our weaker view   15
O'erlaid with black, staid Wisdom's hue;
Black, but such as in esteem,
Prince Memnon's sister[6] might beseem,
Or that starred Ethiope queen[7] that strove
To set her beauty's praise above   20
The sea nymphs, and their powers offended.
Yet thou art higher far descended;
Thee bright-haired Vesta long of yore
To solitary Saturn bore;[8]
His daughter she (in Saturn's reign   25
Such mixture was not held a stain).
Oft in glimmering bowers and glades
He met her, and in secret shades
Of woody Ida's inmost grove,
While yet there was no fear of Jove.   30
Come pensive nun, devout and pure,

2. Orpheus went to the underworld to regain his wife Eurydice (four syllables, accent on the second) and by his music dissolved the guardians of Hades in tears. But as they left, he violated the condition of her release by looking back at her and so lost her again. Milton uses the Orpheus story again in *Il Penseroso, Lycidas,* and *Paradise Lost* 7.32ff.
1. Avail, help.
2. Trifles.
3. Foolish.
4. Morpheus is the god of sleep; the melancholy man feels the cheerful man lives in a dream. "Pensioners": followers.
5. Suit, agree with.
6. Memnon in *Odyssey* 11 was a handsome Ethiopian prince who fought for Troy; his sister, not mentioned by Homer but by later commentators, was Himera.
7. Cassiopeia was turned into a constellation ("starred") for bragging that her daughter Andromeda or she herself (Milton follows this second version) was more beautiful than the sea nymphs.
8. Vesta was goddess of the household, and virgin, as were her priestesses; Milton invented the story of her connection with Saturn on Mt. Ida in Crete, and of her giving birth to Melancholy. But Saturn helps out the poem because he was a primitive deity (hence melancholy is "natural") and because a saturnine complexion is said to evidence a dark and melancholy disposition.

Sober, steadfast, and demure,
All in a robe of darkest grain,[9]
Flowing with majestic train,
And sable stole of cypress lawn   35
Over thy decent[1] shoulders drawn.
Come, but keep thy wonted state,
With even step and musing gait,
And looks commercing with the skies,
Thy rapt soul sitting in thine eyes: 40
There held in holy passion still,
Forget thyself to marble, till
With a sad leaden downward cast
Thou fix them on the earth as fast.
And join with thee calm Peace and Quiet,   45
Spare Fast, that oft with gods doth diet,
And hears the Muses in a ring
Aye round about Jove's altar sing.
And add to these retired Leisure,
That in trim gardens takes his pleasure;   50
But first, and chiefest, with thee bring
Him that yon soars on golden wing,
Guiding the fiery-wheelèd throne,
The cherub Contemplatiòn;[2]
And the mute Silence hist[3] along,   55
'Less Philomel[4] will deign a song,
In her sweetest, saddest plight,
Smoothing the rugged brow of night,
While Cynthia[5] checks her dragon yoke
Gently o'er th' accustomed oak;   60
Sweet bird that shunn'st the noise of folly,
Most musical, most melancholy!
Thee chantress oft the woods among
I woo to hear thy evensong;
And missing thee, I walk unseen   65
On the dry smooth-shaven green,
To behold the wandering moon,
Riding near her highest noon,
Like one that had been led astray
Through the heaven's wide pathless way;   70
And oft as if her head she bowed,
Stooping through a fleecy cloud.
Oft on a plat[6] of rising ground,
I hear the far-off curfew sound
Over some wide-watered shore,   75
Swinging slow with sullen roar;
Or if the air will not permit,

---

9. Color.
1. Comely, proper. "Cypress lawn": a delicate cloth (originally Cyprus, from the island; but the cypress is also the tree of death).
2. The special function of cherubim is contemplation; the fiery-wheeled throne recalls the biblical vision of Ezekiel.

3. Summon.
4. The nightingale, whose song is traditionally one of grief.
5. Goddess of the moon and of the underworld as well, she drives a pair of sleepless dragons.
6. Plot, open space.

Some still removèd place will fit,
Where glowing embers through the room
Teach light to counterfeit a gloom,   80
Far from all resort of mirth,
Save the cricket on the hearth,
Or the bellman's[7] drowsy charm,
To bless the doors from nightly harm;
Or let my lamp at midnight hour   85
Be seen in some high lonely tower,
Where I may oft outwatch the Bear,[8]
With thrice-great Hermes,[9] or unsphere
The spirit of Plato to unfold
What words or what vast regions hold   90
The immortal mind that hath forsook
Her mansion in this fleshly nook;
And of those demons[1] that are found
In fire, air, flood, or under ground,
Whose power hath a true consent[2]   95
With planet, or with element.
Sometime let gorgeous Tragedy
In sceptered pall[3] come sweeping by,
Presenting Thebes, or Pelops' line,
Or the tale of Troy divine,[4]   100
Or what (though rare) of later age
Ennobled hath the buskined[5] stage.
But, O sad virgin, that thy power
Might raise Musaeus[6] from his bower,
Or bid the soul of Orpheus[7] sing   105
Such notes as, warbled to the string,
Drew iron tears down Pluto's cheek,
And made Hell grant what Love did seek.
Or call up him[8] that left half told
The story of Cambuscan bold,   110
Of Camball and of Algarsife,
And who had Canacee to wife,
That owned the virtuous[9] ring and glass,
And of the wondrous horse of brass,
On which the Tartar king did ride;   115
And if aught else great bards beside
In sage and solemn tunes have sung,

7. The night watchman in towns rang a bell to mark the hours.
8. Since the Great Bear never sets in northern skies, outwatching it is a major task.
9. The Egyptian god Thoth or Hermes, to whom were attributed various esoteric books of the 3rd and 4th centuries; under the name Hermes Trismegistus ("thrice-great"), he later became a patron of magicians and alchemists. To "unsphere" Plato is to bring him magically back to earth from the sphere he now inhabits.
1. Not devils but halfway beings, between gods and men. There were four sorts of demons (or "daemons"), corresponding with the four elements.
2. Sympathetic agreement.

3. Royal robe (from Latin *palla*, the robe of tragic actors).
4. Tragedies about Thebes would include Sophocles' Oedipus cycle; those about the line of Pelops, Aeschylus' *Oresteia*; and those about Troy, Euripides' *Trojan Women*.
5. The buskin of tragedy, contrasted with the sock of comedy.
6. A mythical poet-priest of the pre-Homeric age, supposedly son or pupil of the equally mythical Orpheus.
7. For the story of Orpheus, see *L'Allegro*, line 145 (p. 640; also p. 641, first n. 2).
8. I.e., Chaucer, who in *The Squire's Tale* left the story of Cambuscan unfinished.
9. Having special power.

Of tourneys and of trophies hung,
Of forests and enchantments drear,
Where more is meant than meets the ear.[1]   120
Thus, Night, oft see me in thy pale career,
Till civil-suited Morn[2] appear,
Not tricked and frounced as she was wont
With the Attic boy to hunt,
But kerchiefed in a comely cloud,   125
While rocking winds are piping loud,
Or ushered with a shower still,
When the gust hath blown his fill,
Ending on the rustling leaves,
With minute drops from off the eaves.   130
And when the sun begins to fling
His flaring beams, me, Goddess, bring
To archèd walks of twilight groves,
And shadows brown that Sylvan[3] loves
Of pine or monumental oak,   135
Where the rude ax with heavèd stroke
Was never heard the nymphs to daunt,
Or fright them from their hallowed haunt.
There in close covert by some brook,
Where no profaner eye may look,   140
Hide me from day's garish eye,
While the bee with honeyed thigh,
That at her flowery work doth sing,
And the waters murmuring
With such consort[4] as they keep,   145
Entice the dewy-feathered sleep;
And let some strange mysterious dream
Wave at his wings in airy stream
Of lively portraiture displayed
Softly on my eyelids laid.[5]   150
And as I wake, sweet music breathe
Above, about, or underneath,
Sent by some spirit to mortals good,
Or th' unseen genius[6] of the wood.
But let my due feet never fail   155
To walk the studious cloister's pale,[7]
And love the high embowèd roof,
With antic pillars massy proof,[8]
And storied windows richly dight,[9]
Casting a dim religious light.   160

1. A capsule description of allegory.
2. The goddess Aurora, who once fell in love with Cephalus ("the Attic boy,") and used to go hunting with him. "Tricked and frounced": adorned and frizzled.
3. Roman god of the woodlands.
4. Accompaniment.
5. Milton's syntax gets loose and dreamy too, here. He means, "Let some strange dream wave at the wings of sleep, while a stream of vivid pictures passes softly over my eyelids."
6. Guardian deity.
7. Enclosure.
8. Massive and strong. "Antic": i.e., covered with quaint, grotesque, or antic carvings; but "antique," which derives from the same Latin root, was not excluded from the sense.
9. Dressed. "Storied windows": i.e., with stories told by stained-glass images.

There let the pealing organ blow
To the full-voiced choir below,
In service high and anthems clear,
As may with sweetness, through mine ear,
Dissolve me into ecstasies, 165
And bring all heaven before mine eyes.
And may at last my weary age
Find out the peaceful hermitage,
The hairy gown and mossy cell,
Where I may sit and rightly spell[1] 170
Of every star that heaven doth shew,
And every herb that sips the dew,
Till old experience do attain
To something like prophetic strain.
These pleasures, Melancholy, give, 175
And I with thee will choose to live.

ca. 1631   1645

Lycidas This poem is a pastoral elegy; that is, it uses the sometimes artificial imagery supplied by an idyllic shepherd's existence to bewail the loss of a friend. Among its many predecessors in the Renaissance and in classical antiquity are poems by Spenser, Ronsard, Castiglione, Mantuan, Petrarch, Virgil, Theocritus, Moschus, and Bion; its successors include poems like *Adonais* by Shelley and *Thyrsis* by Matthew Arnold

All pastoral poems enjoy the privilege of saying something about the world as a whole while seeming to talk simply of an artificial play-society; they are irresistibly allegorical. They have certain conventions—the swain (i.e., the shepherd) is ignorant but unspoiled, naturally virtuous, inherently poetic; life is pleasant and easy, yet just for this reason the basic human preoccupations stand out. The pastoral elegy has a further list of conventions—a history of past friendship, a questioning of destiny, a procession of mourners, a laying-on of flowers, a consolation, and usually a refrain. Milton adapted all but the last of these to *Lycidas*.

Edward King, who was the occasion of the poem if not its subject, was a junior contemporary of Milton's at Cambridge. He had written a few short Latin poems, and intended to enter the ministry. On his way to visit family in his native Ireland, he was drowned, in 1637; and Milton joined with his schoolfellows the following year to produce a little memorial volume. *Justa Edouardo King* ("For Edward King") includes thirty-six poems, twenty in Latin, three in Greek, the rest in English; only *Lycidas* is of literary consequence.

It is written in a flowing, extended manner, with many run-on lines and great impetus, predominantly in pentameter but with a number of trimeter lines mixed in, and an irregular rhyme scheme, including ten unrhymed lines and two perfectly formed stanzas of ottava rima. Many of these technical qualities are reminiscent of the Italian *canzone* or song, already domesticated in English by poems like Spenser's *Epithalamion*.

There are usually taken to be three explicit climaxes in *Lycidas*, each having to do with an aspect of the shepherd's life and with a problem that Milton wished to pose regarding the meaning of existence. Apollo answers his first question about the reward of poetry; St. Peter answers a second question, about the spiritual shep-

1. Study. The melancholy man wants to think his way into the cosmos until he becomes a prophet.

herd who betrays his flock; and finally Lycidas is translated into the Christian Paradise, to be at one with the Lamb of God, the Good Shepherd, the supreme giver of poetic fame and the proper subject of all song.

For some of the author's revisions while composing *Lycidas*, see "Poems in Process" (p. 2572).

Lycidas

IN THIS MONODY[1] THE AUTHOR BEWAILS A LEARNED FRIEND, UNFORTUNATELY DROWNED IN HIS PASSAGE FROM CHESTER ON THE IRISH SEAS, 1637. AND BY OCCASION FORETELLS THE RUIN OF OUR CORRUPTED CLERGY, THEN IN THEIR HEIGHT.

```
    Yet once more, O ye laurels, and once more
Ye myrtles brown, with ivy never sere,[2]
I come to pluck your berries harsh and crude,[3]
And with forced fingers rude,
Shatter your leaves before the mellowing year.              5
Bitter constraint, and sad occasion dear,[4]
Compels me to disturb your season due;
For Lycidas is dead, dead ere his prime,
Young Lycidas, and hath not left his peer.
Who would not sing for Lycidas? He knew                    10
Himself to sing, and build the lofty rhyme.
He must not float upon his watery bier
Unwept, and welter to the parching wind,
Without the meed[5] of some melodious tear.
    Begin then, sisters of the sacred well[6]               15
That from beneath the seat of Jove doth spring,
Begin, and somewhat loudly sweep the string.
Hence with denial vain, and coy excuse;
So may some gentle Muse
With lucky words favor my destined urn,[7]                  20
And as he passes turn,
And bid fair peace be to my sable shroud.
For we were nursed upon the selfsame hill,
Fed the same flock, by fountain, shade, and rill.
    Together both, ere the high lawns[8] appeared           25
Under the opening eyelids of the morn,
We drove afield, and both together heard
What time the grayfly winds her sultry horn,[9]
Battening our flocks with the fresh dews of night,
Oft till the star that rose at evening bright              30
```

1. A dirge sung by a single voice. This Miltonic headnote was added in the edition of 1645.
2. "Laurels" for the crown of poetry given by Apollo; "myrtles" for the undying love granted by Venus; "ivy," the plant of Bacchus, also the reward of learning. All three plants are evergreens associated with poetic inspiration.
3. Unripe.
4. Heartfelt, profoundly moving; but also, in the 17th century, with overtones of "dire."
5. Reward.
6. The Nine (sister) Muses were reported to dwell by various springs or "wells"; most likely Milton had in mind that of Aganippe near Mt. Helicon.
7. The speaker suggests that if he sings for Lycidas, "some gentle Muse" (i.e., poet) may someday sing for him.
8. Upland pastures.
9. I.e., heard the grayfly when she buzzes. "Battening" (next line): feeding.

Toward heaven's descent had sloped his westering wheel.
Meanwhile the rural ditties were not mute,
Tempered to th' oaten flute,[1]
Rough satyrs danced, and fauns with cloven heel
From the glad sound would not be absent long,   35
And old Damoetas[2] loved to hear our song.
    But O the heavy change, now thou art gone,
Now thou art gone, and never must return!
Thee, shepherd, thee the woods and desert caves,
With wild thyme and the gadding[3] vine o'ergrown,   40
And all their echoes mourn.
The willows and the hazel copses green
Shall now no more be seen,
Fanning their joyous leaves to thy soft lays.
As killing as the canker[4] to the rose,   45
Or taint-worm to the weanling herds that graze,
Or frost to flowers that their gay wardrobe wear
When first the white-thorn blows;[5]
Such, Lycidas, thy loss to shepherd's ear.
    Where were ye, nymphs,[6] when the remorseless deep   50
Closed o'er the head of your loved Lycidas?
For neither were ye playing on the steep
Where your old bards, the famous Druids,[7] lie,
Nor on the shaggy top of Mona high,
Nor yet where Deva spreads her wizard stream:[8]   55
Ay me! I fondly dream—
Had ye been there—for what could that have done?
What could the Muse[9] herself that Orpheus bore,
The Muse herself, for her inchanting[1] son
Whom universal Nature did lament,   60
When by the rout[2] that made the hideous roar
His gory visage down the stream was sent,
Down the swift Hebrus to the Lesbian shore?
    Alas! What boots[3] it with incessant care
To tend the homely slighted shepherd's trade,   65
And strictly meditate the thankless Muse?[4]
Were it not better done as others use,
To sport with Amaryllis in the shade,
Or with the tangles of Neaera's hair?[5]

---

1. Traditional panpipes, played by shepherds.
2. A type name from pastoral poetry, possibly referring to some specific tutor at Cambridge.
3. Straggling.
4. Cankerworm.
5. Blossoms (as in the surviving expression, "full-blown").
6. Nature deities.
7. The Druids, priestly poet-kings of Celtic Britain, worshiped the forces of nature. They lie dead in their burying ground on the mountain ("steep") Kerig-y-Druidion in Wales.
8. "Deva" is the river Dee in Cheshire; it was magic ("wizard") because the size and position of its shifting stream foretold prosperity or dearth for the land. "Mona" is the island of Anglesey. All the places mentioned in lines 52–55 are in the West Country, near

where King drowned.
9. Calliope, Muse of epic poetry, was the mother of Orpheus.
1. Implies both song and magic; the root word survives as "incantation."
2. Orpheus was torn to pieces by a mob ("rout") of screaming Thracian women (Bacchantes), who threw his gory head into the river Hebrus, down which it floated, still singing, and out to Lesbos in the Aegean. The fate of Orpheus and the Druids suggests that nature everywhere is indifferent to the destruction of the priest-poet.
3. Profits.
4. I.e., study to write poetry (the phrase is Virgil's).
5. "Amaryllis" and "Neaera" (Nee-eye-ra), conventional names for pretty shepherdesses, a passing hour's diversion for idle shepherds.

Fame is the spur that the clear spirit doth raise   70
(That last infirmity of noble mind)
To scorn delights, and live laborious days;
But the fair guerdon[6] when we hope to find,
And think to burst out into sudden blaze,
Comes the blind Fury[7] with th' abhorrèd shears,   75
And slits the thin-spun life. "But not the praise,"
Phoebus replied, and touched my trembling ears;[8]
"Fame is no plant that grows on mortal soil,
Nor in the glistering foil[9]
Set off to th' world, nor in broad rumor lies,   80
But lives and spreads aloft by those pure eyes,
And perfect witness of all-judging Jove;
As he pronounces lastly on each deed,
Of so much fame in heaven expect thy meed."
   O fountain Arethuse, and thou honored flood,   85
Smooth-sliding Mincius, crowned with vocal reeds,
That strain I heard was of a higher mood.[1]
But now my oat[2] proceeds,
And listens to the herald of the sea[3]
That came in Neptune's plea.   90
He asked the waves, and asked the felon winds,
"What hard mishap hath doomed this gentle swain?"
And questioned every gust of rugged wings
That blows from off each beakèd promontory;
They knew not of his story,   95
And sage Hippotades[4] their answer brings,
That not a blast was from his dungeon strayed;
The air was calm, and on the level brine,
Sleek Panope[5] with all her sisters played.
It was that fatal and perfidious bark,   100
Built in th' eclipse,[6] and rigged with curses dark,
That sunk so low that sacred head of thine.
   Next Camus,[7] reverend sire, went footing slow,
His mantle hairy, and his bonnet sedge,
Inwrought with figures dim, and on the edge   105
Like to that sanguine flower inscribed with woe.[8]
"Ah! who hath reft," quoth he, "my dearest pledge?"

6. Reward.
7. Atropos, one of the three Fates, bearing scissors with which she cuts the thread of human life. Milton, to suggest the bitterness of death, makes her an avenging Fury.
8. Phoebus Apollo, god of poetic inspiration. Touching the ears of one's hearers was a traditional Roman way of asking them to remember something that had been said.
9. Flashy metal, used to add glitter to gems.
1. Arethusa was a fountain in Sicily, Mincius a river in Lombardy, the former associated with the pastorals of Theocritus, the latter with those of Virgil. Arethusa was originally a nymph who went bathing in the river Alpheus, in Arcadian Greece. The river god grew enamored and gave chase; she dove into the ocean and fled undersea to Sicily, where she came up as a foun-

tain. Milton plays here with the idea of his pastoral going underground while the "strain of a higher mood" is heard.
2. Pipe, hence song.
3. Neptune's "herald" is Triton, pleading his master's innocence in the death of Lycidas.
4. Aeolus, god of winds, and son of Hippotas.
5. The chief Nereid or sea nymph.
6. I.e., time of the worst possible luck.
7. God of the river Cam (properly, Granta), representing the ancient University of Cambridge, but slow and shaggy like the stream.
8. The bonnet and mantle of Camus have marks of woe on the edge like the AI AI supposedly found on the hyacinth, a "sanguine flower" sprung from the blood of a youth killed accidentally by Apollo.

Last came and last did go
The pilot of the Galilean lake;[9]
Two massy keys he bore of metals twain   110
(The golden opes, the iron shuts amain).[1]
He shook his mitered locks,[2] and stern bespake:
"How well could I have spared for thee, young swain,
Enow[3] of such as for their bellies' sake
Creep and intrude and climb into the fold!   115
Of other care they little reckoning make,
Than how to scramble at the shearers' feast,
And shove away the worthy bidden guest.
Blind mouths![4] that scarce themselves know how to hold
A sheep-hook,[5] or have learned aught else the least   120
That to the faithful herdsman's art belongs!
What recks it them? What need they? They are sped;[6]
And when they list,[7] their lean and flashy songs
Grate on their scrannel[8] pipes of wretched straw.
The hungry sheep look up, and are not fed,   125
But swoln with wind, and the rank mist they draw,
Rot inwardly, and foul contagion spread,
Besides what the grim wolf with privy paw[9]
Daily devours apace, and nothing said.
But that two-handed engine at the door[1]   130
Stands ready to smite once, and smite no more."
    Return, Alpheus,[2] the dread voice is past,
That shrunk thy streams; return, Sicilian muse,
And call the vales, and bid them hither cast
Their bells and flowerets of a thousand hues.   135
Ye valleys low where the mild whispers use,[3]
Of shades and wanton winds, and gushing brooks,
On whose fresh lap the swart star sparely looks,[4]
Throw hither all your quaint enameled eyes,
That on the green turf suck the honeyed showers,   140
And purple all the ground with vernal flowers.
Bring the rathe[5] primrose that forsaken dies,

9. St. Peter, originally a fisherman on Lake Tiberias (the Sea of Galilee), was first founder and bishop of the Christian church; his keys open and shut the gates of heaven.
1. Literally, "in full force," "exceedingly"; in this context, "for good," "once and for all."
2. He wears the bishop's miter.
3. An old plural form of "enough," used here with contemptuous intensification, as if to say, "enough and more than enough."
4. This audacious metaphor, as of tapeworms, takes on new depth when one notes that the word *episcopus* (bishop) originally meant "overseer" and that a "pastor" is properly one who feeds his flock.
5. The bishop's staff, or crozier, is made in the form of a shepherd's crook.
6. I.e., they have prospered in a worldly sense; but also, "their doom is sealed." "What recks it them?": what do they care?
7. Choose (that is, choose to play on their pipes, as shepherds should); but with the secondary meaning of

"listen."
8. Harsh, meager. Milton's is the first recorded literary use of the word in English; it existed previously only in a North Country dialect.
9. I.e., Roman Catholicism, whose agents operated in secret ("privy").
1. Many guesses as to the specific meaning of the "two-handed engine" are on record; it may be St. Peter's keys, the two houses of Parliament, or a big sword; but there is no harm in letting it remain an indistinct, apocalyptic instrument of revenge.
2. With the return of Alpheus, the pastoral mode of the poem revives (see lines 85–87), and a catalog of flowers serves, as in Castiglione's *Alcon*, to "interpose a little ease."
3. I.e., are used or accustomed to be heard.
4. The Dog Star, Sirius, associated with the heats of late summer, looks but "sparely" (gently) on the shady valleys. It may not be irrelevant that Edward King drowned on August 10.
5. Early.

The tufted crow-toe, and pale jessamine,
The white pink, and the pansy freaked[6] with jet,
The glowing violet,   145
The musk-rose, and the well-attired woodbine,
With cowslips wan that hang the pensive head,
And every flower that sad embroidery wears:
Bid amaranthus[7] all his beauty shed,
And daffadillies fill their cups with tears,   150
To strew the laureate hearse[8] where Lycid lies.
For so to interpose a little ease,
Let our frail thoughts dally with false surmise.[9]
Ay me! whilst thee the shores and sounding seas
Wash far away, where'er thy bones are hurled,   155
Whether beyond the stormy Hebrides,[1]
Where thou perhaps under the whelming tide
Visit'st the bottom of the monstrous world;
Or whether thou, to our moist vows denied,
Sleep'st by the fable of Bellerus old,[2]   160
Where the great vision of the guarded mount
Looks toward Namancos and Bayona's hold;[3]
Look homeward angel now, and melt with ruth:[4]
And, O ye dolphins,[5] waft the hapless youth.
     Weep no more, woeful shepherds, weep no more,   165
For Lycidas your sorrow is not dead,
Sunk though he be beneath the wat'ry floor;
So sinks the day-star[6] in the ocean bed,
And yet anon repairs his drooping head,
And tricks[7] his beams, and with new-spangled ore   170
Flames in the forehead of the morning sky:
So Lycidas sunk low, but mounted high,
Through the dear might of him that walked the waves,
Where, other groves and other streams along,
With nectar pure his oozy locks he laves,   175
And hears the unexpressive nuptial song,[8]
In the blest kingdoms meek of joy and love.
There entertain him all the saints above,
In solemn troops and sweet societies
That sing, and singing in their glory move,   180
And wipe the tears forever from his eyes.
Now, Lycidas, the shepherds weep no more;

6. Flecked (the verb survives in our word *freckle*).
7. The amaranth is an imaginary flower that never fades; but for Lycidas it will.
8. Bier decked with laurels (see line 1).
9. The "false surmise" is that the body of Lycidas has been recovered and can receive Christian burial.
1. Islands off the coast of Scotland, representing the northern terminus of the Irish Sea.
2. The fabulous giant Bellerus is supposed to lie buried on Land's End in Cornwall.
3. St. Michael's Mount, in Cornwall, from which the archangel is envisioned as looking south, over miles of open Atlantic, across the Bay of Biscay, to Bayona (not far from Vigo) and the district of Nemancos, near Cape Finisterre in northern Spain, where the historical Catholic enemy of Protestant England lay entrenched.
4. Michael is implored to look homeward, relaxing his stern guard for a moment of grief and pity ("ruth").
5. Dolphins, admirable sea beasts, brought the Greek poet Arion safely ashore for love of his verses, and also wafted the dead body of Melicertes to land, where he was promptly transformed to a sea god, Palaemon.
6. The sun.
7. Dresses.
8. Inexpressible hymn of joy, sung at "the marriage supper of the Lamb" (Revelation 19).

Henceforth thou art the genius[9] of the shore,
In thy large recompense, and shalt be good
To all that wander in that perilous flood.   185
    Thus sang the uncouth swain[1] to th' oaks and rills,
While the still morn went out with sandals gray;
He touched the tender stops of various quills,[2]
With eager thought warbling his Doric[3] lay:
And now the sun had stretched out all the hills,   190
And now was dropped into the western bay;
At last he rose, and twitched his mantle blue:
Tomorrow to fresh woods, and pastures new.

November 1637   1638

Areopagitica   This pamphlet appeared on November 24, 1644. The title, which Milton took from a famous oration delivered by Isocrates in 355 B.C., means "things to be said before the Areopagus." The Areopagus was an ancient, powerful, and much-respected tribunal in Athens, and Milton's title thus implies a comparison between the Greek institution and the English Parliament, and between Isocrates' role and his own. These comparisons may be thought to validate the florid, oratorical tone of the tract—which was, in fact, subtitled "A Speech," and is structured in accordance with the precepts of classical rhetoric.

Areopagitica is a plea for the liberty of unlicensed printing; its occasion was a severe ordinance for the control of printing that had been passed by Parliament on June 14, 1643. This ordinance, however disagreeable at the moment, was no striking novelty in English history. On the contrary, control of the press had been actively exercised by all the Tudors and both the early Stuarts. The aim of this government regulation was traditionally defined as the preservation of order and uniformity in church and state, but it also had an economic motive. Unlicensed printers threatened a monopoly enjoyed by the twenty licensed printers of London. Thus the censorship laws familiar to Englishmen had generally been strictly defined and had bristled with penalties. But to enforce them was another matter entirely. Tudor and Stuart police forces being what they were, few printers or authors had to worry about the consequences of going to print without a license. As a matter of fact, Areopagitica was itself unlicensed, Milton's third unlicensed pamphlet since the passage of the Ordinance for Printing only seventeen months before.

Thus the practical effects of the Ordinance for Printing were less important (particularly, we may be sure, in Milton's eyes) than the principle involved. Having taken the lead in destroying the licensing system of the Stuarts, Parliament was now setting up a censorship of its own. Milton's first effort was to show, through a condensed history of censorship, that the institution was only fit for, and only used by, degenerate cultures. His next argument is still more general, that censorship is evil and un-Christian in itself. As God left human beings free to choose among the many physical foods of this world, urging only temperance, so (Milton argues) He left them free to pick and choose for themselves among ideas.

---

9. Protective deity.
1. Unknown, unlettered shepherd (a stock convention of this supremely literary form).

2. The oaten stalks of panpipes.
3. Rustic, simple.

From Areopagitica

* * * Good and evil we know in the field of this world grow up together almost inseparably; and the knowledge of good is so involved and interwoven with the knowledge of evil, and in so many cunning resemblances hardly to be discerned, that those confused seeds which were imposed on Psyche as an incessant labor to cull out and sort asunder[1] were not more intermixed. It was from out the rind of one apple tasted, that the knowledge of good and evil, as two twins cleaving together, leaped forth into the world. And perhaps this is that doom which Adam fell into of knowing good and evil, that is to say of knowing good by evil.

As therefore the state of man now is, what wisdom can there be to choose, what continence to forbear, without the knowledge of evil? He that can apprehend and consider vice with all her baits and seeming pleasures, and yet abstain, and yet distinguish, and yet prefer that which is truly better, he is the true wayfaring[2] Christian. I cannot praise a fugitive and cloistered virtue, unexercised and unbreathed, that never sallies out and sees her adversary, but slinks out of the race where that immortal garland[3] is to be run for, not without dust and heat. Assuredly we bring not innocence into the world, we bring impurity much rather; that which purifies us is trial, and trial is by what is contrary. That virtue therefore which is but a youngling in the contemplation of evil, and knows not the utmost that vice promises to her followers, and rejects it, is but a blank virtue, not a pure; her whiteness is but an excremental[4] whiteness; which was the reason why our sage and serious poet Spenser (whom I dare be known to think a better teacher than Scotus or Aquinas[5]), describing true temperance under the person of Guyon, brings him in with his palmer through the cave of Mammon and the bower of earthly bliss, that he might see and know, and yet abstain.

Since therefore the knowledge and survey of vice is in this world so necessary to the constituting of human virtue, and the scanning of error to the confirmation of truth, how can we more safely, and with less danger, scout into the regions of sin and falsity than by reading all manner of tractates and hearing all manner of reason? And this is the benefit which may be had of books promiscuously read.

But of the harm that may result hence, three kinds are usually reckoned. First is feared the infection that may spread; but then all human learning and controversy in religious points must remove out of the world, yea, the Bible itself; for that ofttimes relates blasphemy not nicely,[6] it describes the carnal sense of wicked men not unelegantly, it brings in holiest men passionately murmuring against providence through all the arguments of Epicurus;[7] in other great disputes it answers dubiously and darkly to the common reader; and ask a Talmudist what ails the modesty of his marginal Keri, that Moses

---

1. Angry at her son Cupid's love for Psyche, Venus set Psyche to sorting out a vast mound of mixed seeds; but the ants took pity on her and did the work (see Apuleius, *The Golden Ass*).
2. There has been debate whether this word should be "wayfaring" or "warfaring," but in the image of Christian life as a pilgrimage, a crusade, the two ideas are united.
3. The crown of righteousness, the garland of virtue.
4. Exterior (like a whited sepulcher, covering corruption within).
5. Duns Scotus and Thomas Aquinas, taken as types of the Scholastic theologian. The Cave of Mammon (below) is described in *The Faerie Queene* 2.7, the Bower of Bliss in 2.12.
6. Daintily.
7. See the Book of Ecclesiastes.

and all the prophets cannot persuade him to pronounce the textual Chetiv.[8] For these causes we all know the Bible itself put by the papist into the first rank of prohibited books. The ancientest Fathers must be next removed, as Clement of Alexandria, and that Eusebian book of evangelic preparation, transmitting our ears through a hoard of heathenish obscenities to receive the Gospel. Who finds not that Irenaeus, Epiphanius, Jerome,[9] and others discover[1] more heresies than they well confute, and that oft for heresy which is the truer opinion?[2]

* * *

Impunity and remissness, for certain, are the bane of a commonwealth; but here the great art lies, to discern in what the law is to bid restraint and punishment, and in what things persuasion only is to work. If every action which is good or evil in man at ripe years were to be under pittance[3] and prescription and compulsion, what were virtue but a name, what praise could be then due to well-doing, what gramercy[4] to be sober, just, or continent?

Many there be that complain of divine providence for suffering Adam to transgress; foolish tongues! when God gave him reason, he gave him freedom to choose, for reason is but choosing; he had been else a mere artificial Adam, such an Adam as he is in the motions.[5] We ourselves esteem not of that obedience, or love, or gift, which is of force: God therefore left him free, set before him a provoking object, ever almost in his eyes; herein consisted his merit, herein the right of his reward, the praise of his abstinence. Wherefore did he create passions within us, pleasures round about us, but that these rightly tempered are the very ingredients of virtue? They are not skillful considerers of human things, who imagine to remove sin by removing the matter of sin; for, besides that it is a huge heap increasing under the very act of diminishing, though some part of it may for a time be withdrawn from some persons, it cannot from all, in such a universal thing as books are; and when this is done, yet the sin remains entire. Though ye take from a covetous man all his treasure, he has yet one jewel left: ye cannot bereave him of his covetousness. Banish all objects of lust, shut up all youth into the severest discipline that can be exercised in any hermitage, ye cannot make them chaste that came not thither so: such great care and wisdom is required to the right managing of this point.

Suppose we could expel sin by this means; look how much we thus expel of sin, so much we expel of virtue: for the matter of them both is the same; remove that, and ye remove them both alike. This justifies the high providence of God, who, though he commands us temperance, justice, continence, yet pours out before us, even to a profuseness, all desirable things, and gives

---

8. "Keri" are the marginal comments of rabbinical scholars on the "Chetiv" of the Bible, the text itself. When the text was too free-spoken for later commentators, Keri was sometimes read in place of Chetiv.
9. Eusebius's *Preparatio Evangelica*, like many early Christian books of polemic, describes heathen wickedness in fascinating detail, as an encouragement to Christian faith. St. Irenaeus, St. Jerome, and even that ancient and edifying convert, Clement of Alexandria, are all subject to this charge.
1. Describe (and so preserve, report).
2. Milton now argues that books cannot pervert people

unless they are given force and vitality by a teacher, who, if a good teacher, needs no books. A fool, he urges, can find material for folly in the best books, and a wise person material for wisdom in the worst. Plato, indeed, recommended censorship in his *Laws*; but in real life one cannot censor books without censoring ballads, fiddlers, clothing, conversation, and social life as a whole.
3. Rationing.
4. Reward, thanks.
5. Puppet shows.

us minds that can wander beyond all limit and satiety. Why should we then affect a rigor contrary to the manner of God and of nature, by abridging or scanting those means, which books freely permitted are, both to the trial of virtue and the exercise of truth?[6]

*   *   *

Well knows he who uses to consider, that our faith and knowledge thrives by exercise, as well as our limbs and complexion.[7] Truth is compared in Scripture to a streaming fountain;[8] if her waters flow not in a perpetual progression, they sicken into a muddy pool of conformity and tradition. A man may be a heretic in the truth; and if he believe things only because his pastor says so, or the Assembly[9] so determines, without knowing other reason, though his belief be true, yet the very truth he holds becomes his heresy. There is not any burden that some would gladlier post off to another than the charge and care of their religion. There be, who knows not that there be, of Protestants and professors who live and die in as arrant an implicit faith as any lay papist of Loreto.[1] A wealthy man, addicted to his pleasure and to his profits, finds religion to be a traffic so entangled, and of so many piddling accounts, that of all mysteries he cannot skill[2] to keep a stock going upon that trade. What should he do? Fain he would have the name to be religious, fain he would bear up with his neighbors in that. What does he therefore, but resolves to give over toiling, and to find himself out some factor,[3] to whose care and credit he may commit the whole managing of his religious affairs; some divine of note and estimation that must be. To him he adheres, resigns the whole warehouse of his religion, with all the locks and keys, into his custody; and indeed makes the very person of that man his religion; esteems his associating with him a sufficient evidence and commendatory of his own piety. So that a man may say his religion is now no more within himself, but is become a dividual[4] movable, and goes and comes near him, according as that good man frequents the house. He entertains him, gives him gifts, feasts him, lodges him; his religion comes home at night, prays, is liberally supped, and sumptuously laid to sleep, rises, is saluted, and after the malmsey, or some well-spiced brewage, and better breakfasted than He whose morning appetite would have gladly fed on green figs between Bethany and Jerusalem,[5] his religion walks abroad at eight, and leaves his kind entertainer in the shop trading all day without his religion.

Another sort there be who, when they hear that all things shall be ordered, all things regulated and settled, nothing written but what passes through the custom-house of certain publicans that have the tonnaging and poundaging[6]

---

6. Censorship, Milton urges, is a vulgar, mechanical job; no person of intelligence will undertake it, and a dunderhead will make serious blunders. Besides, putting stupid people in authority over intelligent ones will discourage the pursuit of learning on every hand, except so far as censorship, by giving authority to banned books, will encourage people to seek out and cling to perverse opinions.
7. Constitution, regarded as the proper mingling of certain qualities in one's body.
8. In Psalms 85.11.
9. The Westminster Assembly—convened by Parliament in 1643 for the purpose of reorganizing the English church along Presbyterian lines.

1. Featured at the Catholic shrine of Loreto in Italy is a house supposed to have been angelically transported from the Holy Land. "Professors" in this context are people professing the Protestant faith.
2. In no way can he manage.
3. Agent.
4. I.e., separate or separable. Milton is describing the common institution of the household chaplain.
5. Mark 11.12–13. Jesus, hungry, found nothing but leaves on the fig tree, for the time of the figs was not yet.
6. Tonnage and poundage were excise taxes levied illegally by the king before 1641 and, therefore, specially odious to Milton's readers. "Publicans": tax collectors.

of all free-spoken truth, will straight give themselves up into your hands, make 'em and cut 'em out what religion ye please: there be delights, there be recreations and jolly pastimes that will fetch the day about from sun to sun, and rock the tedious year as in a delightful dream. What need they torture their heads with that which others have taken so strictly and so unalterably into their own purveying? These are the fruits which a dull ease and cessation of our knowledge will bring forth among the people. How goodly and how to be wished were such an obedient unanimity as this, what a fine conformity would it starch us all into! Doubtless a staunch and solid piece of framework, as any January could freeze together.[7]

*   *   *

    Truth indeed came once into the world with her Divine Master, and was a perfect shape most glorious to look on: but when he ascended, and his apostles after him were laid asleep, then straight arose a wicked race of deceivers, who, as that story goes of the Egyptian Typhon with his conspirators, how they dealt with the good Osiris,[8] took the virgin Truth, hewed her lovely form into a thousand pieces, and scattered them to the four winds. From that time ever since, the sad friends of Truth, such as durst appear, imitating the careful search that Isis made for the mangled body of Osiris, went up and down gathering up limb by limb, still as they could find them. We have not yet found them all, Lords and Commons, nor ever shall do, till her Master's second coming; he shall bring together every joint and member, and shall mold them into an immortal feature of loveliness and perfection. Suffer not these licensing prohibitions to stand at every place of opportunity, forbidding and disturbing them that continue seeking, that continue to do our obsequies to the torn body of our martyred saint.

    We boast our light; but if we look not wisely on the sun itself, it smites us into darkness. Who can discern those planets that are oft combust,[9] and those stars of brightest magnitude that rise and set with the sun, until the opposite motion of their orbs bring them to such a place in the firmament where they may be seen evening or morning? The light which we have gained was given us, not to be ever staring on, but by it to discover onward things more remote from our knowledge. It is not the unfrocking of a priest, the unmitering of a bishop, and the removing him from off the Presbyterian shoulders, that will make us a happy nation. No, if other things as great in the church, and in the rule of life both economical and political, be not looked into and reformed, we have looked so long upon the blaze that Zwinglius and Calvin[1] hath beaconed up to us, that we are stark blind.

    There be who perpetually complain of schisms and sects, and make it such a calamity that any man dissents from their maxims. 'Tis their own pride and ignorance which causes the disturbing, who neither will hear with meekness, nor can convince; yet all must be suppressed which is not found in their

---

7. To set barriers in the way of fresh truths implies that a nation has all the truth it needs; but this, Milton argues, is far from the case. England has no grounds for smugness; the nation needs every bit of truth it can discover.
8. Plutarch tells, in his *Isis and Osiris*, of Typhon's scattering the fragments of his brother Osiris and of

Isis' efforts to recover them.
9. Literally, burned up; in astrology, so close to the sun as not to be visible.
1. Zwingli and Calvin, both radical Swiss reformers, were mainstays of the Presbyterian cause, which Milton was already feeling to be a little narrow. "Economical": domestic.

syntagma.[2] They are the troublers, they are the dividers of unity, who neglect and permit not others to unite those disseuered pieces which are yet wanting to the body of Truth. To be still searching what we know not by what we know, still closing up truth to truth as we find it (for all her body is homogeneal and proportional), this is the golden rule in theology as well as in arithmetic, and makes up the best harmony in a church; not the forced and outward union of cold and neutral and inwardly divided minds.

Lords and Commons of England, consider what nation it is whereof ye are, and whereof ye are the governors: a nation not slow and dull, but of a quick, ingenious, and piercing spirit, acute to invent, subtle and sinewy to discourse, not beneath the reach of any point the highest that human capacity can soar to. Therefore the studies of learning in her deepest sciences have been so ancient and so eminent among us, that writers of good antiquity and ablest judgment have been persuaded that even the school of Pythagoras and the Persian wisdom took beginning from the old philosophy of this island.[3] And that wise and civil Roman, Julius Agricola, who governed once here for Caesar, preferred the natural wits of Britain before the labored studies of the French. Nor is it for nothing that the grave and frugal Transylvanian sends out yearly from as far as the mountainous borders of Russia, and beyond the Hercynian wilderness, not their youth, but their staid men, to learn our language and our theologic arts.

Yet that which is above all this, the favor and the love of heaven we have great argument to think in a peculiar manner propitious and propending[4] towards us. Why else was this nation chosen before any other, that out of her, as out of Zion,[5] should be proclaimed and sounded forth the first tidings and trumpet of Reformation to all Europe? And had it not been the obstinate perverseness of our prelates against the divine and admirable spirit of Wycliffe to suppress him as a schismatic and innovator, perhaps neither the Bohemian Huss and Jerome,[6] no, nor the name of Luther or of Calvin, had been ever known: the glory of reforming all our neighbors had been completely ours. But now, as our obdurate clergy have with violence demeaned the matter, we are become hitherto the latest and the backwardest scholars of whom[7] God offered to have made us the teachers.

Now once again by all concurrence of signs, and by the general instinct of holy and devout men, as they daily and solemnly express their thoughts, God is decreeing to begin some new and great period in his church, even to the reforming of Reformation itself; what does he then but reveal himself to his servants, and as his manner is, first to his Englishmen? I say, as his manner is, first to us, though we mark not the method of his counsels, and are unworthy. Behold now this vast city: a city of refuge, the mansion house of liberty, encompassed and surrounded with his protection; the shop of war hath not there more anvils and hammers waking, to fashion out the plates[8] and instru-

2. Compilation of beliefs, creed.
3. So far as it concerns Pythagoras and the Persians, this sentence is better patriotism than it is intellectual history. Agricola's opinion of the British intellect (referred to next) is found in Tacitus's *Life of Agricola*; "civil" means "cultured, civilized." The Transylvanians, being Protestants, did sometimes come to England from "beyond the Hercynian wilderness" (the Harz mountains) to study.
4. Inclining, favorable. "Argument": reason.

5. Mt. Zion, in Jerusalem, the site of the temple, the holy of holies.
6. John Wycliffe was a 14th-century English reformer, whose books were forbidden by Pope Alexander V in 1409. John Huss spread Wycliffe's doctrines on the Continent. He was burned at the stake in 1415, as was (the next year) his follower Jerome of Prague.
7. Of those whom. "Demeaned": conducted.
8. Plate mail, armor plate.

ments of armed justice in defense of beleaguered truth, than there be pens and heads there, sitting by their studious lamps, musing, searching, revolving new notions and ideas wherewith to present, as with their homage and their fealty, the approaching Reformation: others as fast reading, trying all things, assenting to the force of reason and convincement.

What could a man require more from a nation so pliant and so prone to seek after knowledge? What wants there to such a towardly[9] and pregnant soil, but wise and faithful laborers, to make a knowing people, a nation of prophets, of sages, and of worthies? We reckon more than five months yet to harvest; there need not be five weeks; had we but eyes to lift up, the fields are white already.[1] Where there is much desire to learn, there of necessity will be much arguing, much writing, many opinions; for opinion in good men is but knowledge in the making. Under these fantastic terrors of sect and schism we wrong the earnest and zealous thirst after knowledge and understanding which God hath stirred up in this city.

What some lament of, we rather should rejoice at, should rather praise this pious forwardness among men, to reassume the ill-deputed care of their religion into their own hands again. A little generous prudence, a little forbearance of one another, and some grain of charity might win all these diligences to join, and unite into one general and brotherly search after truth; could we but forego this prelatical tradition of crowding free consciences and Christian liberties into canons and precepts of men. I doubt not, if some great and worthy stranger should come among us, wise to discern the mold and temper of a people, and how to govern it, observing the high hopes and aims, the diligent alacrity of our extended thoughts and reasonings in the pursuance of truth and freedom, but that he would cry out as Pyrrhus did, admiring the Roman docility and courage: "If such were my Epirots, I would not despair the greatest design that could be attempted, to make a church or kingdom happy."[2] Yet these are the men cried out against for schismatics and sectaries;[3] as if, while the temple of the Lord was building, some cutting, some squaring the marble, others hewing the cedars, there should be a sort of irrational men, who could not consider there must be many schisms and many dissections[4] made in the quarry and in the timber, ere the house of God can be built. And when every stone is laid artfully together, it cannot be united into a continuity, it can but be contiguous in this world; neither can every piece of the building be of one form; nay rather the perfection consists in this, that out of many moderate varieties and brotherly dissimilitudes that are not vastly disproportional, arises the goodly and the graceful symmetry that commends the whole pile and structure. Let us therefore be more considerate builders, more wise in spiritual architecture, when great reformation is expected. For now the time seems come, wherein Moses the great prophet may sit in heaven rejoicing to see that memorable and glorious wish of his fulfilled, when not only our seventy elders, but all the Lord's people, are become prophets.[5]

* * *

9. Favorable.
1. Milton is paraphrasing Christ's words to the disciples (John 4.35).
2. Though King Pyrrhus of Epirus beat the Roman armies at Heraclea in 280 B.C., he was much impressed by their discipline.
3. Sectarians, dividers of the church.
4. Literally, cuttings-up; figuratively, dissensions and divisions.
5. In Numbers 11.29 Moses expresses the wish that not only the Sanhedrin, or council of seventy, but the whole people of Israel should be prophets.

Methinks I see in my mind a noble and puissant nation rousing herself like a strong man after sleep, and shaking her invincible locks: methinks I see her as an eagle mewing[6] her mighty youth, and kindling her undazzled eyes at the full midday beam; purging and unscaling her long-abused sight at the fountain itself of heavenly radiance; while the whole noise of timorous and flocking birds, with those also that love the twilight, flutter about, amazed at what she means, and in their envious gabble would prognosticate a year of sects and schisms.

What should ye do then, should ye suppress all this flowery crop of knowledge and new light sprung up and yet springing daily in this city? Should ye set an oligarchy of twenty engrossers[7] over it, to bring a famine upon our minds again, when we shall know nothing but what is measured to us by their bushel? Believe it, Lords and Commons, they who counsel ye to such a suppressing do as good as bid ye suppress yourselves; and I will soon show how.[8]

* * *

And now the time in special is by privilege to write and speak what may help to the further discussing of matters in agitation. The temple of Janus with his two controversial faces might now not unsignificantly be set open.[9] And though all the winds of doctrine were let loose to play upon the earth, so Truth be in the field, we do injuriously by licensing and prohibiting to misdoubt her strength. Let her and Falsehood grapple; who ever knew Truth put to the worse in a free and open encounter? Her confuting is the best and surest suppressing. He who hears what praying there is for light and clearer knowledge to be sent down among us would think of other matters to be constituted beyond the discipline of Geneva framed and fabricked already to our hands.[1]

Yet when the new light which we beg for shines in upon us, there be who envy and oppose if it come not first in at their casements. What a collusion is this, whenas we are exhorted by the wise man to use diligence, to seek for wisdom as for hidden treasures early and late,[2] that another order shall enjoin us to know nothing but by statute. When a man hath been laboring the hardest labor in the deep mines of knowledge, hath furnished out his findings in all their equipage, drawn forth his reasons as it were a battle[3] ranged, scattered and defeated all objections in his way, calls out his adversary into the plain, offers him the advantage of wind and sun if he please, only that he may try the matter by dint of argument; for his opponents then to skulk, to lay ambushments, to keep a narrow bridge of licensing where the challenger should pass, though it be valor enough in soldiership, is but weakness and cowardice in the wars of Truth.

6. Molting, shaking off. Or the word may be "newing," i.e., renewing.
7. Engrossers, much hated in the English countryside, bought great quantities of grain and held it for times of famine and consequent high prices.
8. By its liberal and enlightened policies, Milton argues, Parliament has actually created the vigorous and enquiring minds that censorship seeks to suppress. For Parliament to destroy its own creation would be like a father killing his own children.
9. Janus, who gives us our month of January, had two faces looking in opposite directions, because he was god of beginnings and endings. A special door in

Rome, dedicated to him, was kept open in times of war, closed in times of peace.
1. Milton's Calvinism, a major ingredient of which was hostility to English bishops, was fading fast in 1644, because bishops had been abolished; within a year or so he would be writing his sonnet On the New Forcers of Conscience, meaning by them the Presbyterians. "Fabricked": fabricated.
2. Solomon was the wise man; the allusion is to Proverbs 8.11.
3. Line of battle, array. Wind and sun (below) were significant advantages in a fight with swords.

For who knows not that Truth is strong, next to the Almighty? She needs no policies nor stratagems nor licensings to make her victorious—those are the shifts and the defenses that error uses against her power. Give her but room, and do not bind her when she sleeps, for then she speaks not true, as the old Proteus[4] did, who spake oracles only when he was caught and bound, but then rather she turns herself into all shapes except her own, and perhaps tunes her voice according to the time, as Micaiah did before Ahab,[5] until she be adjured into her own likeness.

Yet it is not impossible that she may have more shapes than one. What else is all that rank of things indifferent, wherein Truth may be on this side or on the other without being unlike herself? What but a vain shadow else is the abolition of those ordinances, that handwriting nailed to the cross?[6] what great purchase is this Christian liberty which Paul so often boasts of? His doctrine is that he who eats or eats not, regards a day or regards it not, may do either to the Lord.[7] How many other things might be tolerated in peace and left to conscience, had we but charity, and were it not the chief stronghold of our hypocrisy to be ever judging one another? I fear yet this iron yoke of outward conformity hath left a slavish print upon our necks; the ghost of a linen decency[8] yet haunts us. We stumble and are impatient at the least dividing of one visible congregation from another, though it be not in fundamentals; and through our forwardness to suppress and our backwardness to recover any enthralled piece of truth out of the gripe of custom, we care not[9] to keep truth separated from truth, which is the fiercest rent and disunion of all. We do not see that while we still affect by all means a rigid and external formality, we may as soon fall again into a gross conforming stupidity, a stark and dead congealment of "wood and hay and stubble," forced and frozen together, which is more to the sudden degenerating of a church than many sub-dichotomies of petty schisms.

Not that I can think well of every light separation, or that all in a church is to be expected "gold and silver and precious stones."[1] It is not possible for man to sever the wheat from the tares, the good fish from the other fry; that must be the angels' ministry at the end of mortal things.[2] Yet if all cannot be of one mind—as who looks they should be?—this doubtless is more wholesome, more prudent, and more Christian, that many be tolerated rather than all compelled. I mean not tolerated popery and open superstition, which, as it extirpates all religions and civil supremacies, so itself should be extirpate, provided first that all charitable and compassionate means be used to win and regain the weak and the misled; that also which is impious or evil absolutely, either against faith or manners,[3] no law can possibly permit that intends not to unlaw itself; but those neighboring differences or rather indifferences are what I speak of, whether in some point of doctrine or of discipline, which

---

4. The old man of the sea, who tried to escape capture by changing shapes, in *Odyssey* 4.
5. The story of Micaiah, who tried to disguise an unpleasant prophecy from King Ahab, is in 1 Kings 22.
6. The locution, from Colossians 2.14, implies that the crucifixion canceled out all the rules and penalties of Mosaic law. Paul's doctrine is expressed in Galatians 5.
7. In the Lord's service.
8. Strips of white linen at neck and wrist were worn by many men in the 17th century, especially (under the name of "bands") by clergymen. Milton uses them as emblems of formal purity.
9. Scruple not. "Gripe": grip.
1. The contrast between "wood, hay, stubble" and "gold, silver, precious stones" is from 1 Corinthians 3.12.
2. This is the parable of the wheat and the tares (weeds) in Matthew 13.24–30, 36–43.
3. Morals.

though they may be many yet need not interrupt "the unity of spirit," if we could but find among us the "bond of peace."[4]

In the meanwhile, if anyone would write and bring his helpful hand to the slow-moving reformation which we labor under, if truth have spoken to him before others, or but seemed at least to speak, who hath so bejesuited us that we should trouble that man with asking license to do so worthy a deed? And not consider this, that if it come to prohibiting, there is not aught more likely to be prohibited than truth itself; whose first appearance to our eyes bleared and dimmed with prejudice and custom is more unsightly and unplausible than many errors, even as the person is of many a great man slight and contemptible to see to. And what do they tell us vainly of new opinions, when this very opinion of theirs, that none must be heard but whom they like, is the worst and newest opinion of all others, and is the chief cause why sects and schisms do so much abound, and true knowledge is kept at distance from us; besides yet a greater danger which is in it. For when God shakes a kingdom with strong and healthful commotions to a general reforming, it is not untrue that many sectaries and false teachers are then busiest in seducing; but yet more true it is that God then raises to his own work men of rare abilities and more than common industry, not only to look back and revise what hath been taught heretofore, but to gain further and go on some new enlightened steps in the discovery of truth.[5]

*   *   *

1644

Sonnets   Between 1630 and 1658 Milton wrote twenty-four sonnets. Five he wrote in Italian, no doubt partly as linguistic exercises, the rest in English, on a variety of occasions, both public and private. Unlike the sonnets of Sidney, Spenser, and Shakespeare, those of Milton do not form any sort of sequence, and they lay very little emphasis on erotic themes. Neither are they devotional like the *Holy Sonnets* of Donne. They are more often public and political than simply personal. Yet, whatever their theme, they speak with a massive and authoritative voice like none other in English.

The form of the sonnets is Petrarchan rather than Shakespearean (see "Poetic Forms and Literary Terminology," p. 2644). A special feature of Milton's later sonnets is the way he runs on the sense from line to line, deliberately avoiding end-stopped lines (see particularly *On the Late Massacre in Piedmont*). In this as in other respects, Milton was following the example of an Italian sonneteer, Giovanni Della Casa, who broke sharply with the Petrarchan tradition of metrical regularity. Milton's break with his English predecessors was just as sharp.

4. The phrases are from Paul's letter to the Ephesians.
5. After a few final thoughts, *Areopagitica* ends with an exhortation to Parliament. In practical terms, the argument was unsuccessful; the ordinance against which Milton protested was not repealed, though it was never effectively enforced. In time, Milton himself became for a while a licenser of news sheets under Cromwell, commissioned to give editorial supervision to a small, progovernment paper. But this biographical fact need not be taken as a retraction of the position assumed in *Areopagitica*, which moves throughout on a lofty plane of policy far above mundane details of politics.

SONNETS

How Soon Hath Time

How soon hath Time, the subtle thief of youth,
  Stol'n on his wing my three and twentieth year!
  My hasting days fly on with full career,
  But my late spring no bud or blossom shew'th.
Perhaps my semblance[1] might deceive the truth,   5
  That I to manhood am arrived so near,
  And inward ripeness doth much less appear,
  That some more timely-happy spirits endu'th.[2]
Yet be it less or more, or soon or slow,
  It shall be still in strictest measure even[3]   10
  To that same lot, however mean or high,
Toward which Time leads me, and the will of Heaven;
  All is, if I have grace to use it so,
  As ever in my great Taskmaster's eye.[4]

1632?   1645

When I Consider How My Light Is Spent[1]

When I consider how my light is spent,
  Ere half my days, in this dark world and wide,
  And that one talent which is death to hide[2]
  Lodged with me useless, though my soul more bent
To serve therewith my Maker, and present   5
  My true account, lest he returning chide;
  "Doth God exact day-labor, light denied?"
  I fondly ask; but Patience to prevent[3]
That murmur, soon replies, "God doth not need
  Either man's work or his own gifts; who best   10
  Bear his mild yoke, they serve him best. His state
Is kingly. Thousands at his bidding speed
  And post o'er land and ocean without rest:
  They also serve who only stand and wait."

1652?   1673

1. Appearance.
2. Endoweth.
3. Equal, adequate. Whenever it appears and however much it amounts to, Milton's inner growth will be adequate to the destiny that time and heaven are preparing.
4. I.e., nothing has been lost in God's eyes—if only I can see ("use") it that way.
1. Milton's sonnet on his blindness is close in theme to *How Soon Hath Time*; but his affliction (fresh at the time of writing) represents a far more severe test.
2. The parable of the talents (Matthew 25) loomed large in Puritan minds, and particularly in Milton's. The servants who put their master's money (talents of gold and silver) out to earn interest while he was away were called "good and faithful"; the one who simply returned what he had been given was deprived of everything and cast into outer darkness. Usury, which under Catholic theology had been a deadly sin, changed its meaning for the Puritans; it became a metaphor, and sometimes more than a metaphor, for "working out one's salvation."
3. Forestall. "Fondly": foolishly.

On the Late Massacre in Piedmont[1]

Avenge, O Lord, thy slaughtered saints, whose bones
  Lie scattered on the Alpine mountains cold;
  Even them who kept thy truth so pure of old
  When all our fathers worshiped stocks and stones,
Forget not: in thy book record their groans   5
  Who were thy sheep and in their ancient fold
  Slain by the bloody Piemontese that rolled
  Mother with infant down the rocks. Their moans
The vales redoubled to the hills, and they
  To heaven. Their martyred blood and ashes sow   10
  O'er all th' Italian fields, where still doth sway
The triple tyrant:[2] that from these may grow
  A hundredfold, who having learnt thy way
  Early may fly the Babylonian woe.[3]

1655   1673

Methought I Saw My Late Espousèd Saint

Methought I saw my late espousèd saint
  Brought to me like Alcestis[1] from the grave,
  Whom Jove's great son to her glad husband gave,
  Rescued from death by force though pale and faint.
Mine, as whom washed from spot of childbed taint,   5
  Purification in the old law did save,[2]
  And such, as yet once more I trust to have
  Full sight of her in heaven without restraint,
Came vested all in white, pure as her mind.
  Her face was veiled, yet to my fancied sight   10
  Love, sweetness, goodness, in her person shined
So clear, as in no face with more delight.
  But O, as to embrace me she inclined,
  I waked, she fled, and day brought back my night.

1658   1673

Paradise Lost   Milton's epic begins with a rush. Carried along by the impetus of Satan's tremendous adventures, readers are apt to forget there is any other part to the poem. Indeed, while we are getting acclimated to the Miltonic world, there

---

1. The Waldenses were a heretical sect, probably of Eastern origin by way of Venice. They lived in the valleys of northern Italy ("the Piedmont") and southern France, professing a creed that was particularly akin to Protestantism in its avoidance of graven images ("stocks and stones"). The understanding that had allowed them freedom of worship was terminated in 1655, and the massacre that ensued was widely protested by the Protestant powers of Europe. Milton, as Secretary for Foreign Tongues to Cromwell's Council of State, wrote several indignant letters.
2. I.e., the pope, wearing his tiara with three crowns.

3. Protestants in Milton's day frequently identified the Roman Church with the "whore of Babylon" (Revelation 17–18).
1. Alcestis, wife of Admetus, was rescued from the underworld by Hercules ("Jove's great son").
2. The Mosaic law prescribing periods for the purification of women after childbirth is found in Leviticus 12. Line 5 is very compressed; expanded, it would read, "My wife, like the woman whom, when washed from spot of childbed taint," etc. Milton's second wife died after childbirth.

is no reason to hold back our sympathy with Satan, our admiration for his heroic energy. It is energy in a bad cause, clearly; but it is energy, it is heroically exercised, and there is as yet no source of virtuous power to oppose or offset it. With the appearance of Christ the Son, at the opening of Book 3, we begin to see in heavenly Love the counterpoise of Satan's hellish Hate; and in Book 4, as we are introduced not only to Adam and Eve but to Paradise, our sympathies gradually shift. Satan is no longer a glamorous underdog, fighting his adventurous way through the universe against enormous odds; he is a menacing vulture, a cormorant, a toad, a snake. He is not only dangerous, he is dull; whatever richness and variety he discovers in the universe serve only to produce in him envious hatred and destructiveness. His sin is incestuous, as the allegory of Sin and Death points out; it breeds out of itself ever fresh occasions of sin. Adam and Eve, who are weaker, less active, and less spectacular in every way, finally outweigh Satan in our interest and sympathy simply because they can respond to life, and to the terrifying experience of guilt, more vigorously than Satan can.

Seen overall—from above, as it were—*Paradise Lost* is a vast but delicately balanced structure. Its first half rises from Hell through Chaos to Heaven, and takes place mostly in these cosmic locales; its second half opens with the word *Descend*, and is largely confined to earth, ending with Adam and Eve's descent from the Mount of Paradise to the "subjected plain" of our world. The adventure of the fallen Satan in the opening books balances the history of fallen mankind in the closing ones. Book 4, the entry of Satan (and the reader) into Paradise, balances Book 9, describing the loss of Paradise. Books 5 and 10 provide contrasting views of life in Eden before and after the Fall. At the center of the poem, balanced as on a fulcrum, are the account of the destructive war in Heaven (Book 6), and that of the Creation (Book 7).

Within the poem's larger structure, there are all sorts of secondary balances that readers will recognize for themselves. The consult in Hell (Book 2) is paralleled by a consult in Heaven (Book 3); Eve is generated from Adam as Sin is generated from Satan; Satan's fall parallels Adam's fall, and the parallel is prolonged into that extended series of falls and recoveries that is human history. Moloch contrasts with Mammon; the Son's mercy with the Father's justice; Raphael's affability with Michael's severity; and so on, almost without limit.

The structure of the poem is at once massive and delicate; its language is also both rich and strong. Milton's range of classical reference and gift for epithet are undoubtedly staggering at first view, and his long, complexly subordinated sentences are sometimes hard to follow. Footnotes, alas, provide the only proper solution to this problem. But one need not equal, or even follow, all Milton's learning in order to appreciate his poem, especially at a first reading. The poem progresses as through a garden of metaphor and reference that stretches away on either side of one, as far as the eye can see; on a first tour, it is enough to get the general prospect clear, without learning the name of each particular blossom. Ultimately, the reader who is experienced in the poem comes to appreciate its details—epic similes like Leviathan the sea beast (1.201), no less than the one-eyed Arimaspians and the gryphon (2.943); its epithets and circumlocutions like Mulciber (1.740), who is Vulcan, and Amram's son (1.339), who is Moses—without sense of strain or strangeness. Milton himself moved securely through the literatures of half a dozen languages and as many cultures; it is one of the supreme rewards of literary study to be able to follow him with an equivalent security.

Paradise Lost is at once a deeply traditional and a boldly original poem. Milton takes pains to fulfill the traditional prescriptions of the epic form; he gives us love, war, supernatural characters, a descent into hell, a catalog of warriors, all the conventional items of epic machinery. Yet no poem in which the climax of the central action is a woman eating a piece of fruit can be a conventional epic. Similarly, Milton himself defined his moral purpose as being to "justify the ways of God to men." This seems no more than conventionally meek. Yet we cannot even think of equating the message of Milton's poem with Pope's injunction to "submit" because "whatever is is right." The way of life that Adam and Eve take up as the poem ends is that of the Christian pilgrimage through this world. Expelled from Eden, our first "grand parents" pick up the burdens of humanity as we know them, sustained by a faith that we also know, and go forth to seek a blessing that we do not know yet. They are to become wayfaring, warfaring Christians, like John Milton; and in this condition, with its weaknesses and strivings and inevitable defeats, there is a glory that no devil can ever understand. Thus Milton strikes, humanly as well as artistically, a grand resolving chord. It is the careful, triumphant balancing and tempering of this conclusion that completes the noble architecture of his poem, and that makes of the end a richer, if not a more exciting, experience than the beginning.

From PARADISE LOST

Book 1

The Argument[1]

   This first book proposes, first in brief, the whole subject, man's disobedience, and the loss thereupon of Paradise, wherein he was placed: then touches the prime cause of his fall, the serpent, or rather Satan in the serpent; who, revolting from God, and drawing to his side many legions of angels, was, by the command of God, driven out of Heaven with all his crew, into the great deep. Which action passed over, the poem hastes into the midst of things;[2] presenting Satan, with his angels, now fallen into Hell—described here not in the center (for heaven and earth may be supposed as yet not made, certainly not yet accursed), but in a place of utter darkness, fitliest called Chaos. Here Satan with his angels lying on the burning lake, thunderstruck and astonished, after a certain space recovers, as from confusion; calls up him who, next in order and dignity, lay by him; they confer of their miserable fall. Satan awakens all his legions, who lay till then in the same manner confounded. They rise: their numbers; array of battle; their chief leaders named, according to the idols known afterwards in Canaan and the countries adjoining. To these Satan directs his speech; comforts them with hope yet of regaining Heaven; but tells them, lastly, of a new world and new kind of creature to be created, according to an ancient prophecy or report in Heaven; for that angels were long before this visible creation was the opinion of many ancient fathers.[3] To find out the truth of this prophecy, and what to determine[4] thereon, he refers to a full council. What his associates thence attempt. Pandemonium, the palace of Satan, rises, suddenly built out of the deep: the infernal peers there sit in council.

1. *Paradise Lost* appeared originally without any sort of prose aid to the reader, but since many readers found the poem hard going, the printer asked Milton for some "Arguments," or summary explanations of the action in the various books, and prefixed them to later issues of the poem. We reprint those for the first two books and the ninth.
2. Adapted from Horace's prescription that the epic poet should start "in medias res."
3. I.e., Church Fathers, the Christian writers of the first few centuries of the church.
4. I.e., what action to take upon their information.

Of man's first disobedience, and the fruit[5]
Of that forbidden tree whose mortal[6] taste
Brought death into the world, and all our woe,
With loss of Eden, till one greater Man[7]
Restore us, and regain the blissful seat,   5
Sing, Heavenly Muse,[8] that on the secret top
Of Oreb, or of Sinai, didst inspire
That shepherd who first taught the chosen seed
In the beginning how the heavens and earth
Rose out of Chaos: or, if Sion hill[9]   10
Delight thee more, and Siloa's brook that flowed
Fast[1] by the oracle of God, I thence
Invoke thy aid to my adventurous song,
That with no middle flight intends to soar
Above th' Aonian mount, while it pursues   15
Things unattempted yet in prose or rhyme.[2]
And chiefly thou, O Spirit,[3] that dost prefer
Before all temples th' upright heart and pure,
Instruct me, for thou know'st; thou from the first
Wast present, and with mighty wings outspread   20
Dovelike sat'st brooding[4] on the vast abyss,
And mad'st it pregnant: what in me is dark
Illumine; what is low, raise and support;
That to the height of this great argument
I may assert Eternal Providence,   25
And justify[5] the ways of God to men.
    Say first (for Heaven hides nothing from thy view,
Nor the deep tract of Hell), say first what cause
Moved our grand[6] parents, in that happy state,
Favored of Heaven so highly, to fall off   30
From their Creator, and transgress his will
For[7] one restraint, lords of the world besides?[8]
Who first seduced them to that foul revolt?
    Th' infernal serpent; he it was, whose guile,
Stirred up with envy and revenge, deceived   35

---

5. Eve's apple, of course, but also all the consequences of eating it.
6. Deadly, but also "to mortals" (i.e., human beings).
7. Christ, the second Adam.
8. In Greek mythology, Urania, Muse of astronomy; but here identified, by references to Oreb and Sinai, with the Holy Spirit of the Bible, which inspired Moses ("that shepherd") to write Genesis and the other four books of the Pentateuch for the instruction of the Jews ("the chosen seed").
9. The Temple Mount ("Sion hill") and the brook of Siloa nearby are two features of the landscape around Jerusalem likely to appeal to a Muse, whose natural haunts are springs and mountains (see *Lycidas*, line 15, p. 646). Milton's aim is to show that poetry is everywhere recognized as an inspiration close to that of religion.
1. Close.
2. "Th' Aonian mount": Helicon, home of the classical Muses; Milton is deliberately courting comparison with Homer and Virgil. In the very line ("Things unat-

tempted yet in prose or rhyme") where he vaunts his originality, Milton is translating a line in the invocation of Ariosto's *Orlando Furioso*—thus acknowledging, and challenging, another of his predecessors.
3. The Spirit is an impulse or voice of God, by which the Hebrew prophets were directly inspired.
4. A composite of phrases and ideas from Genesis 1.2 ("And the earth was without form, and void; and darkness was upon the face of the deep. And the Spirit of God moved upon the face of the waters"); Matthew 3.16 ("and he saw the Spirit of God descending like a dove, and lighting upon him"); and Luke 3.22 ("and the Holy Ghost descended in a bodily shape like a dove upon him"). Milton's mind as he wrote was impregnated with expressions from the King James Bible, only a small proportion of which can be indicated in the notes.
5. Show the justice of. "Argument": theme.
6. First in importance; by implication, in time also.
7. Because of.
8. In every other respect.

The mother of mankind, what time[9] his pride
Had cast him out from Heaven, with all his host
Of rebel angels, by whose aid aspiring
To set himself in glory above his peers,[1]
He trusted to have equaled the Most High,   40
If he opposed; and with ambitious aim
Against the throne and monarchy of God
Raised impious war in Heaven and battle proud,
With vain attempt. Him the Almighty Power
Hurled headlong flaming from th' ethereal sky   45
With hideous ruin and combustion down
To bottomless perdition, there to dwell
In adamantine chains and penal fire,
Who durst defy th' Omnipotent to arms.
    Nine times the space that measures day and night   50
To mortal men, he with his horrid crew
Lay vanquished, rolling in the fiery gulf
Confounded though immortal. But his doom
Reserved him to more wrath; for now the thought
Both of lost happiness and lasting pain   55
Torments him; round he throws his baleful[2] eyes,
That witnessed huge affliction and dismay,
Mixed with obdùrate pride and steadfast hate.
At once, as far as angels ken,[3] he views
The dismal situation waste and wild: 60
A dungeon horrible, on all sides round
As one great furnace flamed; yet from those flames
No light,[4] but rather darkness visible
Served only to discover sights of woe,
Regions of sorrow, doleful shades, where peace   65
And rest can never dwell, hope never comes
That comes to all,[5] but torture without end
Still urges,[6] and a fiery deluge, fed
With ever-burning sulphur unconsumed:
Such place Eternal Justice had prepared   70
For those rebellious; here their prison ordained
In utter[7] darkness and their portion set
As far removed from God and light of Heaven
As from the center thrice to th' utmost pole.[8]
O how unlike the place from whence they fell!   75

---

9. I.e., at the time when.
1. His equals. The sentence mimics Satan's action, piling clause loosely upon clause and building ever higher, until "with vain attempt" (line 44) brings the whole structure crashing down. It is a dramatic entry into "the midst of things," where epics begin. Book 6 will recount more largely the war in Heaven, in the full narrative form which Aeneas used to tell Dido of the last days of Troy (*Aeneid* 2).
2. Malignant, as well as suffering.
3. As far as angels can see.
4. Omitting the verb conveys abruptly the paradox: fire without light.
5. The phrase echoes an expression in Dante ("All hope abandon, ye who enter here"), but Milton

couches it as a logical absurdity. Hope comes to "all" but not to Hell-dwellers; they are not included in "all."
6. Afflicts.
7. Complete, but also outer.
8. The earth. Milton makes use in *Paradise Lost* of two images of the cosmos: (1) the earth is the center of the *created* (Ptolemaic) cosmos of ten concentric spheres; but (2) the earth and the whole created cosmos are a mere appendage, hanging from Heaven by a golden chain, in the larger, aboriginal, and less shapely cosmos. In the present passage, the fall from Heaven to Hell (through the aboriginal universe) is described as thrice as far as the distance (in the created universe) from the center (earth) to the outermost sphere.

There the companions of his fall, o'erwhelmed
With floods and whirlwinds of tempestuous fire,
He soon discerns; and, weltering by his side,
One next himself in power, and next in crime,
Long after known in Palestine, and named   80
Beëlzebub.[9] To whom th' arch-enemy,
And thence in Heaven called Satan,[1] with bold words
Breaking the horrid silence thus began:
     "If thou beëst he—but O how fallen! how changed
From him who in the happy realms of light   85
Clothed with transcendent brightness didst outshine
Myriads, though bright! if he whom mutual league,
United thoughts and counsels, equal hope
And hazard in the glorious enterprise,
Joined with me once, now misery hath joined   90
In equal ruin; into what pit thou seest[2]
From what height fallen, so much the stronger proved
He with his thunder:[3] and till then who knew
The force of those dire arms? Yet not for those,
Nor what the potent Victor in his rage   95
Can else inflict, do I repent or change,
Though changed in outward luster, that fixed mind
And high disdain, from sense of injured merit,
That with the Mightiest raised me to contend,
And to the fierce contention brought along   100
Innumerable force of spirits armed,
That durst dislike his reign, and me preferring,
His utmost power with adverse power opposed
In dubious battle on the plains of Heaven,
And shook his throne. What though the field be lost?   105
All is not lost: the unconquerable will,
And study[4] of revenge, immortal hate,
And courage never to submit or yield:
And what is else not to be overcome?
That glory[5] never shall his wrath or might   110
Extort from me. To bow and sue for grace
With suppliant knee, and deify his power[6]
Who from the terror of this arm so late
Doubted[7] his empire—that were low indeed;
That were an ignominy and shame beneath   115
This downfall; since, by fate, the strength of gods
And this empyreal substance cannot fail;[8]

9. A Phoenician deity, or Baal (the name means "Lord
of Flies"); traditionally, a prince of devils and enemy
of Jehovah. The Phoenician Baal, a sun god, had many
aspects and therefore many names; most Baals were
nature deities. But in the poem's time scheme all this
lies in the future; Beelzebub's angelic name, whatever
it was, has been erased from the Book of Life, and as
he has not yet got another one, he must be called by
the name he will have later on.
1. In Hebrew, the name means "Adversary."
2. Satan's syntax, like that of a man recovering from a
stunning blow, is not of the clearest.
3. God with his thunderbolts.

4. Pursuit.
5. I.e., the glory of hearing Satan confess himself overcome. "What is else not to be overcome?": What else
does it mean not to be beaten?
6. I.e., deify the power of him who. Milton sometimes
writes English as if it were an inflected language.
7. Feared for. In the next line, "ignominy" is pronounced "ignomy."
8. Cease to exist. When used by the Father (3.341),
"gods" is simply another term for "angels." But to Satan
and his followers, it obviously means something more:
the essence of Satan's fault is his claim to the position
of a god, subject to fate but to nothing else. His sub-

Since, through experience of this great event,
In arms not worse, in foresight much advanced,
We may with more successful hope resolve   120
To wage by force or guile eternal war,
Irreconcilable to our grand Foe,
Who now triùmphs, and in th' excess of joy
Sole reigning holds the tyranny[9] of Heaven."
    So spake th' apostate angel, though in pain,   125
Vaunting aloud, but racked with deep despair;
And him thus answered soon his bold compeer:[1]
    "O prince, O chief of many thronèd powers,
That led th' embattled seraphim[2] to war
Under thy conduct, and in dreadful deeds   130
Fearless, endangered Heaven's perpetual King,
And put to proof his high supremacy,
Whether upheld by strength, or chance, or fate![3]
Too well I see and rue the dire event[4]
That with sad overthrow and foul defeat   135
Hath lost us Heaven, and all this mighty host
In horrible destruction laid thus low,
As far as gods and heavenly essences
Can perish: for the mind and spirit remains
Invincible, and vigor soon returns,   140
Though all our glory extinct, and happy state
Here swallowed up in endless misery,
But what if he our Conqueror (whom I now
Of force[5] believe almighty, since no less
Than such could have o'erpowered such force as ours)   145
Have left us this our spirit and strength entire,
Strongly to suffer and support our pains,
That we may so suffice[6] his vengeful ire,
Or do him mightier service as his thralls
By right of war, whate'er his business be,   150
Here in the heart of Hell to work in fire,
Or do his errands in the gloomy deep?
What can it then avail though yet we feel
Strength undiminished, or eternal being
To undergo eternal punishment?"   155
    Whereto with speedy words th' arch-fiend[7] replied:
"Fallen cherub, to be weak is miserable,
Doing or suffering:[8] but of this be sure,
To do aught good never will be our task,
But ever to do ill our sole delight,   160

---

stance is "empyreal" (heavenly, from the empyrean) and cannot be destroyed, but as he learns in the poem, it can be confounded by God's greater power and weakened by its own corruption and self-contradictions.
9. The accusation is bold, but one of the aims of the poem is to show that Satan is a tyrant and God is not.
1. Comrade and equal.
2. According to tradition, there were nine orders of angels—seraphim, cherubim, thrones, dominions, virtues, powers, principalities, archangels, and angels; but

Milton does not use these systematic categories systematically.
3. The devils can conceive of any reason for God's continuing rule, except goodness and justice.
4. Outcome.
5. Perforce, necessarily.
6. Satisfy.
7. A fiend is an enemy, one who hates; the word is an antonym of "friend."
8. Whether one is active or passive.

As being the contrary to his high will
Whom we resist. If then his providence
Out of our evil seek to bring forth good,
Our labor must be to pervert that end,
And out of good still to find means of evil;   165
Which ofttimes may succeed, so as perhaps
Shall grieve him, if I fail not,[9] and disturb
His inmost counsels from their destined aim.
But see! the angry Victor hath recalled
His ministers of vengeance and pursuit   170
Back to the gates of Heaven; the sulphurous hail,
Shot after us in storm, o'erblown hath laid
The fiery surge that from the precipice
Of Heaven received us falling; and the thunder,
Winged with red lightning and impetuous rage,   175
Perhaps hath spent his shafts, and ceases now
To bellow through the vast and boundless deep.
Let us not slip[1] th' occasion, whether scorn
Or satiate fury yield it from our Foe.
Seest thou yon dreary plain, forlorn and wild,   180
The seat of desolation, void of light,
Save what the glimmering of these livid flames
Casts pale and dreadful? Thither let us tend
From off the tossing of these fiery waves;
There rest, if any rest can harbor there;   185
And reassembling our afflicted powers,[2]
Consult how we may henceforth most offend
Our enemy, our own loss how repair,
How overcome this dire calamity,
What reinforcement we may gain from hope,   190
If not, what resolution from despair."[3]
    Thus Satan talking to his nearest mate
With head uplift above the wave, and eyes
That sparkling blazed; his other parts besides
Prone on the flood, extended long and large   195
Lay floating many a rood,[4] in bulk as huge
As whom[5] the fables name of monstrous size,
Titanian or Earth-born, that warred on Jove,
Briareos or Typhon,[6] whom the den
By ancient Tarsus held, or that sea beast   200
Leviathan,[7] which God of all his works
Created hugest that swim th' ocean-stream.
Him, haply, slumbering on the Norway foam,

9. "Unless I'm mistaken" (paralleling the Latin, *nisi fallor*).
1. I.e., let slip.
2. Stricken armies.
3. Of the last nine lines of Satan's speech, no fewer than five rhyme. Milton may have felt the need for something like the couplet with which blank-verse dramatists cut off their scenes.
4. An old unit of measure, between six and eight yards.
5. I.e., as those whom.
6. Both the Titans, led by Briareos, and the earth-born

Giants, represented by Typhon (who lived in Cilicia near Tarsus), fought with Jove. Briareos was said to have a hundred hands and Typhon, a hundred heads; and both were said, by different authors, to have been punished for their rebellion (like Satan for his) by being thrown into the underworld. Briareos and Typhon are still heard grumbling from time to time under Mt. Etna.
7. The great sea monster of Isaiah 27.1 or Job 41; for Milton and us, simply a whale, but scaly (line 206).

The pilot of some small night-foundered[8] skiff,
Deeming some island, oft, as seamen tell,   205
With fixèd anchor in his scaly rind
Moors by his side under the lee, while night
Invests[9] the sea, and wishèd morn delays:
So stretched out huge in length the arch-fiend lay,
Chained on the burning lake; nor ever thence   210
Had risen or heaved his head, but that the will
And high permission of all-ruling Heaven
Left him at large to his own dark designs,
That with reiterated crimes he might
Heap on himself damnation, while he sought   215
Evil to others, and enraged might see
How all his malice served but to bring forth
Infinite goodness, grace, and mercy shown
On man by him seduced, but on himself
Treble confusion, wrath, and vengeance poured.   220
     Forthwith upright he rears from off the pool
His mighty stature; on each hand the flames
Driven backward slope their pointing spires,[1] and rolled
In billows, leave i' th' midst a horrid[2] vale.
Then with expanded wings he steers his flight   225
Aloft, incumbent on[3] the dusky air,
That felt unusual weight; till on dry land
He lights, if it were land that ever burned
With solid, as the lake with liquid fire,
And such appeared in hue; as when the force   230
Of subterranean wind transports a hill
Torn from Pelorus or the shattered side
Of thundering Etna,[4] whose combustible
And fuelèd entrails thence conceiving fire,
Sublimed with mineral fury, aid the winds,   235
And leave a singèd bottom all involved[5]
With stench and smoke: such resting found the sole
Of unblest feet. Him followed his next mate,
Both glorying to have 'scaped the Stygian[6] flood
As gods, and by their own recovered strength,   240
Not by the sufferance[7] of supernal power.
     "Is this the region, this the soil, the clime,"
Said then the lost archangel, "this the seat
That we must change for Heaven? this mournful gloom
For that celestial light? Be it so, since he   245
Who now is sovereign can dispose and bid
What shall be right: farthest from him is best,
Whom reason hath equaled, force hath made supreme

8. Overtaken by darkness.
9. Wraps, covers. The story of sailors mooring to
whales was an old one, but the reference to Norway
suggests that Milton was thinking of a 16th-century version by Olaus Magnus, a Swedish historian.
1. Points of flame.
2. Not simply "ghastly," but in the Latin sense, "bristling."

3. Resting upon.
4. Pelorus and Etna are volcanic mountains in Sicily,
which Milton pictures as exploding under pressure of
underground winds.
5. Wrapped. "Sublimed": vaporized.
6. Of the river Styx, i.e., demonic, hellish.
7. Permission.

Above his equals.[8] Farewell, happy fields,
Where joy forever dwells! Hail, horrors! hail,   250
Infernal world! and thou, profoundest Hell,
Receive thy new possessor, one who brings
A mind not to be changed by place or time.
The mind is its own place, and in itself
Can make a Heaven of Hell, a Hell of Heaven.[9]   255
What matter where, if I be still the same,
And what I should be, all but less[1] than he
Whom thunder hath made greater? Here at least
We shall be free; th' Almighty hath not built
Here for his envy, will not drive us hence.   260
Here we may reign secure; and in my choice
To reign is worth ambition, though in Hell:
Better to reign in Hell than serve in Heaven.[2]
But wherefore let we then our faithful friends,
Th' associates and copartners of our loss,   265
Lie thus astonished on th' oblivious pool,[3]
And call them not to share with us their part
In this unhappy mansion, or once more
With rallied arms to try what may be yet
Regained in Heaven, or what more lost in Hell?"   270
    So Satan spake: and him Beëlzebub
Thus answered: "Leader of those armies bright,
Which but th' Omnipotent none could have foiled!
If once they hear that voice, their liveliest pledge
Of hope in fears and dangers, heard so oft   275
In worst extremes, and on the perilous edge[4]
Of battle when it raged, in all assaults
Their surest signal, they will soon resume
New courage and revive, though now they lie
Groveling and prostrate on yon lake of fire,   280
As we erewhile, astounded and amazed;
No wonder, fallen such a pernicious height!"
    He scarce had ceased when the superior fiend
Was moving toward the shore; his ponderous shield,
Ethereal temper,[5] massy, large, and round,   285
Behind him cast; the broad circumference
Hung on his shoulders like the moon, whose orb
Through optic glass the Tuscan artist[6] views
At evening, from the top of Fesolè,
Or in Valdarno, to descry new lands,   290

8. Satan likes to think that by "reason" he is God's equal; this only shows how far he is from "right reason," that is, reason directed and corrected by a proper sense of religious values.
9. Satan's heroic resolution takes another turn when at the beginning of Book 4 we find him bringing the Hell of his own mind into Paradise.
1. Second only to. The expression "all but less than" telescopes "all but equal to" and "only less than."
2. An ironic echo of *Odyssey* 11.489–491, where the shade of Achilles tells Odysseus emphatically that it is better to be a farmhand on earth than king among the

dead.
3. The epithet "oblivious" is transferred from the fallen angels to the pool in which they have fallen. "Astonished": stunned.
4. Not the fringe of battle but the front line (Latin *acies*).
5. Tempered in celestial fire.
6. Galileo, who looked through a telescope ("optic glass") from the hill town of Fiesole outside Florence in the Val d'Arno, is the only contemporary mentioned by Milton in *Paradise Lost*.

Rivers, or mountains in her spotty globe.
His spear, to equal which the tallest pine
Hewn on Norwegian hills, to be the mast
Of some great admiral,[7] were but a wand,
He walked with, to support uneasy steps   295
Over the burning marl,[8] not like those steps
On Heaven's azure; and the torrid clime
Smote on him sore besides, vaulted with fire.
Nathless[9] he so endured, till on the beach
Of that inflamèd[1] sea he stood, and called   300
His legions, angel forms, who lay entranced,
Thick as autumnal leaves that strow the brooks
In Vallombrosa,[2] where th' Etrurian shades
High over-arched embower;[3] or scattered sedge
Afloat, when with fierce winds Orion armed   305
Hath vexed the Red Sea coast, whose waves o'erthrew
Busiris and his Memphian chivalry,
While with perfidious hatred they pursued
The sojourners of Goshen, who beheld
From the safe shore their floating carcasses   310
And broken chariot wheels;[4] so thick bestrown,
Abject and lost, lay these, covering the flood,
Under amazement of their hideous change.
He called so loud that all the hollow deep
Of Hell resounded: "Princes, potentates,   315
Warriors, the flower of Heaven, once yours, now lost,
If such astonishment as this can seize
Eternal spirits! or have ye chosen this place
After the toil of battle to repose
Your wearied virtue,[5] for the ease you find   320
To slumber here, as in the vales of Heaven?
Or in this abject posture have ye sworn
To adore the Conqueror, who now beholds
Cherub and seraph rolling in the flood
With scattered arms and ensigns,[6] till anon   325
His swift pursuers from Heaven-gates discern
Th' advantage, and descending tread us down
Thus drooping, or with linkèd thunderbolts
Transfix us to the bottom of this gulf?
Awake, arise, or be forever fallen!"   330
     They heard, and were abashed, and up they sprung
Upon the wing, as when men wont to watch
On duty, sleeping found by whom they dread,

---

7. Not the naval commander, but his flagship, usually the biggest of the fleet.
8. Soil.
9. A compressed, archaic form of "nevertheless."
1. Flaming, of course, but also fevered.
2. "Vallombrosa": "Shady Valley," high in the Apennines about twenty miles from Florence. "Etruria" is Etruscan land, i.e., Tuscany.
3. I.e., form bowers by enclosing space.
4. Orion is a constellation, whose rising near sunset in late summer and autumn was associated with storms;

in the Red Sea, where sedge grows thick, these storms result in much floating seaweed. This reminds Milton of how the sea must have looked after the Israelites ("sojourners of Goshen") passed through it while escaping from Egypt, when it was covered with the littered corpses of Pharaoh ("Busiris") and his pursuing horsemen ("Memphian chivalry").
5. Strength, but Satan's sarcasm makes use of the other meaning too.
6. Standards, battle flags.

Rouse and bestir themselves ere well awake.
Nor did they not perceive[7] the evil plight   335
In which they were, or the fierce pains not feel;
Yet to their general's voice they soon obeyed
Innumerable. As when the potent rod
Of Amram's son[8] in Egypt's evil day
Waved round the coast, up called a pitchy cloud   340
Of locusts, warping[9] on the eastern wind,
That o'er the realm of impious Pharaoh hung
Like night, and darkened all the land of Nile;
So numberless were those bad angels seen
Hovering on wing under the cope[1] of Hell   345
'Twixt upper, nether, and surrounding fires;
Till, as a signal given, th' uplifted spear
Of their great sultan[2] waving to direct
Their course, in even balance down they light
On the firm brimstone, and fill all the plain;   350
A multitude like which the populous North
Poured never from her frozen loins to pass
Rhene or the Danaw, when her barbarous sons
Came like a deluge on the South, and spread
Beneath Gibraltar to the Libyan sands.[3]   355
    Forthwith from every squadron and each band
The heads and leaders thither haste where stood
Their great commander; godlike shapes and forms
Excelling human; princely dignities,
And powers that erst in Heaven sat on thrones,   360
Though of their names in Heavenly records now
Be no memorial, blotted out and rased[4]
By their rebellion from the Books of Life.
Nor had they yet among the sons of Eve
Got them new names, till, wandering o'er the earth,   365
Through God's high sufferance for the trial of man,
By falsities and lies the greatest part
Of mankind they corrupted to forsake
God their Creator, and th' invisible
Glory of him that made them to transform   370
Oft to the image of a brute, adorned
With gay religions[5] full of pomp and gold,
And devils to adore for deities:
Then were they known to men by various names,
And various idols through the heathen world.   375
    Say, Muse, their names then known, who first, who last,[6]

7. The double negatives make a positive: they did indeed perceive both plight and pains. (Latin, *neque non*,
"nor . . . not," "and.")
8. Moses, who drew down a plague of locusts on Egypt
(Exodus 10.12–15). Milton's learned locution is designed to keep Moses out of Hell, as well as from appearing too often in the poem (cf. lines 307–311).
9. Floating.
1. Roof.
2. A first use of the image, which will be reinforced
later, of Satan as an Oriental despot.

3. The barbarian invasions of falling Rome began with
crossings of the Rhine ("Rhene") and Danube ("Danaw") Rivers and spread across Spain, via Gibraltar, to
North Africa.
4. Erased (see lines 80–81). Though reluctant to state
the view strongly, Milton believed all the pagan deities
had been devils in disguise.
5. Ceremonies.
6. The catalog of gods here is an epic convention:
Homer catalogs ships; Virgil, warriors.

Roused from the slumber on that fiery couch,
At their great emperor's call, as next in worth
Came singly[7] where he stood on the bare strand,
While the promiscuous crowd stood yet aloof.   380
    The chief were those who, from the pit of Hell
Roaming to seek their prey on Earth, durst fix
Their seats, long after, next the seat of God,[8]
Their altars by his altar, gods adored
Among the nations round, and durst abide   385
Jehovah thundering out of Sion, throned
Between the cherubim; yea, often placed
Within his sanctuary itself their shrines,
Abominations; and with cursèd things
His holy rites and solemn feasts profaned,   390
And with their darkness durst affront his light.
First Moloch, horrid king, besmeared with blood
Of human sacrifice, and parents' tears;
Though, for the noise of drums and timbrels[9] loud,
Their children's cries unheard, that passed through fire   395
To his grim idol. Him the Ammonite[1]
Worshiped in Rabba and her watery plain,
In Argob and in Basan, to the stream
Of utmost Arnon. Nor content with such
Audacious neighborhood, the wisest heart   400
Of Solomon he led by fraud to build
His temple right against the temple of God
On that opprobrious hill, and made his grove
The pleasant valley of Hinnom, Tophet thence
And black Gehenna called, the type of Hell.[2]   405
Next Chemos,[3] th' obscene dread of Moab's sons,
From Aroar to Nebo and the wild
Of southmost Abarim; in Hesebon
And Horonaim, Seon's realm, beyond
The flowery dale of Sibma clad with vines,   410
And Elealè to th' asphaltic pool:
Peor[4] his other name, when he enticed
Israel in Sittim, on their march from Nile,
To do him wanton rites, which cost them woe.
Yet thence his lustful orgies he enlarged   415
Even to that hill of scandal, by the grove

7. One at a time. The diabolical aristocrats rally round Satan, while the "promiscuous crowd" (line 380), the vulgar devils, stand apart.
8. The first group of devils come from the Near East, close neighbors and intimate enemies of Jehovah at Jerusalem.
9. Tambourines. Moloch was a sun god, sometimes represented as a roaring bull or with a calf's head, within whose brazen image living children might be burned as sacrifices (for a lurid fictional account, see Flaubert's *Salammbô*).
1. The Ammonites lived east of the Jordan, and Milton uses uncouth place names ("Rabba," "Argob," "Basan," "utmost Arnon") to suggest wildness.

2. The rites of Moloch on "that opprobrious hill" (the Mount of Olives) right opposite the Jewish temple, and in the valley of Hinnom, so polluted these places that they were turned into the refuse dump of Jerusalem. Under the names "Tophet" and "Gehenna," Hinnom became a "type" (analogue) of hell.
3. Chemos or Chemosh was another name for Moloch, used in Moab, a nation lying south and east of the Dead Sea ("th' asphaltic pool"). Many of the geographical names clustered here come from Isaiah 15–16.
4. For the story of how Peor seduced "Israel in Sittim," see Numbers 25.

Of Moloch homicide,[5] lust hard by hate,
Till good Josiah drove them thence to Hell.
With these came they who, from the bordering flood
Of old Euphrates to the brook that parts   420
Egypt from Syrian ground,[6] had general names
Of Baalim and Ashtaroth, those male,
These feminine.[7] For spirits when they please
Can either sex assume, or both; so soft
And uncompounded is their essence pure,   425
Not tied or manacled with joint or limb,
Nor founded on the brittle strength of bones,
Like cumbrous flesh; but in what shape they choose,
Dilated or condensed, bright or obscure,
Can execute their airy purposes,   430
And works of love or enmity fulfill.
For those the race of Israel oft forsook
Their Living Strength,[8] and unfrequented left
His righteous altar, bowing lowly down
To bestial gods; for which their heads as low   435
Bowed down in battle, sunk before the spear
Of despicable foes. With these in troop
Came Astoreth, whom the Phoenicians called
Astartè, queen of heaven, with crescent horns;
To whose bright image nightly by the moon   440
Sidonian virgins[9] paid their vows and songs;
In Sion also not unsung, where stood
Her temple on th' offensive mountain,[1] built
By that uxorious king[2] whose heart, though large,
Beguiled by fair idolatresses, fell   445
To idols foul. Thammuz[3] came next behind,
Whose annual wound in Lebanon allured
The Syrian damsels to lament his fate
In amorous ditties all a summer's day,
While smooth Adonis[4] from his native rock   450
Ran purple to the sea, supposed with blood
Of Thammuz yearly wounded: the love-tale
Infected Sion's daughters with like heat,
Whose wanton passions in the sacred porch
Ezekiel[5] saw, when, by the vision led,   455
His eye surveyed the dark idolatries

5. An epithet was often joined to a god's name as a surname (e.g., *Jupiter Tonans*, Jove the Thunderer); Milton's epithet involves almost a parody, Moloch the Mankiller. The story of "good Josiah" (next line) and his campaign against pagan gods is told in 2 Kings 23 and in 2 Chronicles 34.
6. Palestine lies between the Euphrates and "the brook Besor" (1 Samuel 30.10).
7. I.e., plural forms, masculine and feminine respectively, for Baal and Astarte. As Baals were aspects of the sun god, Astartes (Ishtars) were manifestations of the moon goddess.
8. The Jews lost battles, Milton says, when they neglected Jehovah.

9. Sidon and Tyre were the chief cities of Phoenicia.
1. The Mount of Olives again (see lines 403 and 416).
2. Solomon, who "loved many strange women" (2 Kings 11.1–8).
3. A Syrian god, who was supposed to have been killed by a boar in Lebanon; annual festivals mourned his death and celebrated his revival, imitating the cycle of vegetable life. In his Greek form he was Adonis, god of the solar year.
4. A Lebanese river, named after the deity because every spring it turned blood-red with sedimentary mud.
5. Ezekiel complained that the Jewish women of his day were worshiping Thammuz (Ezekiel 8.14).

Of alienated Judah. Next came one
Who mourned in earnest, when the captive ark
Maimed his brute image, head and hands lopped off
In his own temple, on the grunsel-edge,[6]   460
Where he fell flat, and shamed his worshipers:
Dagon his name, sea monster, upward man
And downward fish; yet had his temple high
Reared in Azotus, dreaded through the coast
Of Palestine, in Gath and Ascalon,   465
And Accaron and Gaza's frontier bounds.[7]
Him followed Rimmon, whose delightful seat
Was fair Damascus, on the fertile banks
Of Abbana and Pharphar, lucid streams.
He also 'gainst the house of God was bold: 470
A leper once he lost, and gained a king,
Ahaz,[8] his sottish conqueror, whom he drew
God's altar to disparage and displace
For one of Syrian mode, whereon to burn
His odious offerings, and adore the gods   475
Whom he had vanquished. After these appeared
A crew who, under names of old renown,
Osiris, Isis, Orus,[9] and their train,
With monstrous shapes[1] and sorceries abused
Fanatic Egypt and her priests to seek   480
Their wandering gods disguised in brutish forms
Rather than human. Nor did Israël 'scape
Th' infection, when their borrowed gold composed
The calf in Oreb;[2] and the rebel king
Doubled that sin in Bethel and in Dan,   485
Likening his Maker to the grazèd ox[3]—
Jehovah, who in one night when he passed
From Egypt marching, equaled with one stroke
Both her first-born and all her bleating gods.[4]
Belial came last;[5] than whom a spirit more lewd   490
Fell not from Heaven, or more gross to love
Vice for itself. To him no temple stood
Or altar smoked; yet who more oft than he
In temples and at altars, when the priest
Turns atheist, as did Eli's sons,[6] who filled   495

---

6. When the Philistines stole the ark of God, they tried to store it in the temple of their sea god, Dagon; but in the morning the mutilated statue of Dagon was found on the threshold ("grunsel-edge") (see 1 Samuel 5.1–5).
7. Milton names the five chief cities of the Philistines as places where Dagon was worshiped.
8. A Syrian general, Naaman, was cured of leprosy and converted from worship of Rimmon by the waters of the Jordan (2 Kings 5). King Ahaz, on the other hand, an Israelite monarch who conquered Damascus, was converted there to worship of Rimmon (2 Kings 16).
9. The second group of devils includes those from Egypt, driven in terror from heaven by the revolt of the giants (so Ovid tells us in *Metamorphoses* 5) and forced to wander through Egypt in animal disguises.
1. Monstrous, because often represented with animals' heads.

2. Aaron made a golden calf in the wilderness (Exodus 32); Milton thought it an idol of the Egyptian god Apis because the gold of which it was made had been borrowed from the Egyptians.
3. Jeroboam, "the rebel king," doubled Aaron's sin by making *two* golden calves (1 Kings 12.28–30).
4. See Exodus 12.12 for Jehovah's vengeance on the firstborn of Egypt and their gods. "Equaled": leveled.
5. Belial was never worshiped as a god; his name was originally an abstract noun meaning "wickedness"; hence used mainly in set phrases like "sons of Belial." He comes last, because weak and slothful.
6. The misdeeds of Eli's sons, and the epithet "sons of Belial" applied to them, will be found in 1 Samuel 2.12–17.

With lust and violence the house of God?
In courts and palaces he also reigns,
And in luxurious cities, where the noise
Of riot ascends above their loftiest towers,
And injury and outrage; and when night   500
Darkens the streets, then wander forth the sons
Of Belial, flown[7] with insolence and wine.
Witness the streets of Sodom, and that night
In Gibeah,[8] when the hospitable door
Exposed a matron, to avoid worse rape.   505
    These were the prime in order and in might;
The rest were long to tell, though far renowned,
Th' Ionian gods, of Javan's issue held
Gods, yet confessed later than Heaven and Earth,
Their boasted parents;[9] Titan, Heaven's first-born,   510
With his enormous brood, and birthright seized
By younger Saturn; he from mightier Jove,
His own and Rhea's son, like measure found;
So Jove usurping reigned.[1] These, first in Crete
And Ida known, thence on the snowy top   515
Of cold Olympus ruled the middle air,
Their highest heaven; or on the Delphian cliff,
Or in Dodona, and through all the bounds
Of Doric land; or who with Saturn old
Fled over Adria to th' Hesperian fields,   520
And o'er the Celtic roamed the utmost isles.
    All these and more came flocking; but with looks
Downcast and damp,[2] yet such wherein appeared
Obscure some glimpse of joy, to have found their chief
Not in despair, to have found themselves not lost   525
In loss itself; which on his countenance cast
Like doubtful hue.[3] But he, his wonted pride
Soon recollecting, with high words that bore
Semblance of worth, not substance, gently raised
Their fainting courage, and dispelled their fears: 530
Then straight commands that at the warlike sound
Of trumpets loud and clarions[4] be upreared
His mighty standard. That proud honor claimed
Azazel[5] as his right, a cherub tall:
Who forthwith from the glittering staff unfurled   535

---

7. Flushed. Puritans liked to call their enemies sons of Belial; this passage, with its present-tense verbs, may reflect Milton's view of Restoration London.

8. In Sodom and Gibeah ancient outrages befell, described in Genesis 19 and Judges 19.

9. The Titans were regarded as gods by the Greeks ("Javan's issue," i.e., offspring of Javan, son of Japhet, son of Noah), but were admittedly created later than Heaven and Earth (Uranus and Ge), whose children they were said to be. Milton's Christian humanism naturally led him, wherever possible, to use classic myths as analogues (parallels or reflections) of Christian history.

1. Cronos or Saturn, one of the Titans, deposed his elder brother, married his sister Rhea, and ruled until Zeus, who had been reared in secret on Mt. Ida in

Crete, overthrew his own father and came to rule on Mt. Olympus. The Olympic gods, headed by Zeus, were also worshiped in Delphi, Dodona, and throughout the "Doric (Grecian) land." Meanwhile Saturn (lines 519–521), after his downfall, fled across the Adriatic Sea ("Adria") to Italy ("th' Hesperian fields"), crossed "the Celtic" (fields) of France, and finally reached Britain ("the utmost isles").

2. Depressed.

3. Their comfort is the chilly one of finding themselves not completely annihilated, and at first it is reflected in Satan's face.

4. Small, shrill, treble trumpets.

5. Among the historians of angels and devils, a traditional diabolic leader.

Th' imperial ensign; which, full high advanced,
Shone like a meteor streaming to the wind,
With gems and golden luster rich emblazed,
Seraphic arms and trophies; all the while
Sonorous metal[6] blowing martial sounds: 540
At which the universal host up sent
A shout that tore Hell's concave,[7] and beyond
Frighted the reign of Chaos and old Night.[8]
All in a moment through the gloom were seen
Ten thousand banners rise into the air,   545
With orient[9] colors waving: with them rose
A forest huge of spears; and thronging helms
Appeared, and serried[1] shields in thick array
Of depth immeasurable. Anon they move
In perfect phalanx to the Dorian[2] mood   550
Of flutes and soft recorders; such as raised
To height of noblest temper heroes old
Arming to battle, and instead of rage
Deliberate valor breathed, firm and unmoved
With dread of death to flight or foul retreat;   555
Nor wanting power to mitigate and swage[3]
With solemn touches troubled thoughts, and chase
Anguish and doubt and fear and sorrow and pain
From mortal or immortal minds. Thus they,
Breathing united force with fixèd thought,   560
Moved on in silence to soft pipes that charmed
Their painful steps o'er the burnt soil. And now
Advanced in view they stand, a horrid[4] front
Of dreadful length and dazzling arms, in guise
Of warriors old with ordered spear and shield,   565
Awaiting what command their mighty chief
Had to impose. He through the armèd files
Darts his experienced eye, and soon traverse[5]
The whole battalion views, their order due,
Their visages and stature as of gods;   570
Their number last he sums. And now his heart
Distends with pride, and hardening in his strength
Glories: for never, since created man,[6]
Met such embodied force as named with these
Could merit more than that small infantry   575
Warred on by cranes:[7] though all the giant brood
Of Phlegra with th' heroic race were joined
That fought at Thebes and Ilium, on each side

---

6. Reverberant trumpets.
7. Vault.
8. Disorder and darkness, the first materials of the cosmos, still maintain a kingdom between Heaven and Hell.
9. Lustrous, like the colors of a pearl.
1. Locked together.
2. Severe, simple. The shrill trumpet, which first roused the courage of the devils, now gives way to firm, martial tones, played on instruments of softer timbre, in the Spartan manner.

3. Assuage.
4. Bristling.
5. Across. Satan glances, like a reviewing officer, down the files and columns.
6. I.e., since the creation of man.
7. The pygmies had periodic fights with the cranes, which (according to Pliny) they won by riding to battle on pigs and goats. This would make them cavalry, but Milton wanted the pun on *infants*. His idea is that, compared with the devils, all other armies that ever were would look puny.

Mixed with auxiliar[8] gods; and what resounds
In fable or romance of Uther's son, 580
Begirt with British and Armoric knights;
And all who since, baptized or infidel,
Jousted in Aspramont or Montalban,
Damasco, or Marocco, or Trebisond;
Or whom Biserta sent from Afric shore 585
When Charlemagne with all his peerage fell
By Fontarabbia.[9] Thus far these beyond
Compare of mortal prowess, yet observed[1]
Their dread commander. He above the rest
In shape and gesture proudly eminent 590
Stood like a tower. His form had yet not lost
All her[2] original brightness, nor appeared
Less than archangel ruined, and th' excess
Of glory obscured: as when the sun new-risen
Looks through the horizontal[3] misty air 595
Shorn of his beams, or from behind the moon
In dim eclipse[4] disastrous twilight sheds
On half the nations, and with fear of change
Perplexes monarchs. Darkened so, yet shone
Above them all th' archangel; but his face 600
Deep scars of thunder had intrenched, and care
Sat on his faded cheek, but under brows
Of dauntless courage, and considerate[5] pride
Waiting revenge. Cruel his eye, but cast
Signs of remorse and passion[6] to behold 605
The fellows of his crime, the followers rather
(Far other once beheld in bliss), condemned
Forever now to have their lot in pain;
Millions of spirits for his fault amerced[7]
Of Heaven, and from eternal splendors flung 610
For his revolt; yet faithful how they stood,
Their glory withered; as when heaven's fire
Hath scathed the forest oaks or mountain pines,
With singèd top their stately growth, though bare,
Stands on the blasted heath. He now prepared 615
To speak; whereat their doubled ranks they bend
From wing to wing, and half enclose him round
With all his peers: attention held them mute.
Thrice he essayed, and thrice, in spite of scorn,
Tears such as angels weep burst forth; at last 620
Words interwove with sighs found out their way:

8. Allied.
9. The Giants of Greek mythology were born at Phlegra (line 577); Milton imagines them joined with the Seven who fought against Thebes and the whole Greek host that besieged Troy ("Ilium"), plus the various gods who helped on both sides. He even adds the knights "British or Armoric" (from Brittany) who fought with King Arthur ("Uther's son") and includes a list of proper names taken from the cycles of romance and suggesting vast, remote armies. Fontarabbia, the best known, was reputed to be the scene of Roland's last

stand in the *Chanson de Roland*; Milton thus mingles the fall of Charlemagne with that of his best-known knight.
1. Obeyed.
2. *Forma*, in Latin, is feminine; hence "her."
3. The rays of the sun as it first rises are almost horizontal.
4. Time of ill omen. "Disastrous": threatening disaster.
5. Thoughtful, conscious.
6. Compassion.
7. Deprived.

"O myriads of immortal spirits! O powers
Matchless, but with th' Almighty!—and that strife
Was not inglorious, though th' event[8] was dire,
As this place testifies, and this dire change,   625
Hateful to utter. But what power of mind,
Foreseeing or presaging, from the depth
Of knowledge past or present, could have feared
How such united force of gods, how such
As stood like these, could ever know repulse?   630
For who can yet believe, though after loss,
That all these puissant[9] legions, whose exile
Hath emptied Heaven, shall fail to reascend,
Self-raised, and repossess their native seat?
For me, be witness all the host of Heaven,   635
If counsels different,[1] or danger shunned
By me, have lost our hopes. But he who reigns
Monarch in Heaven, till then as one secure
Sat on his throne, upheld by old repute,
Consent or custom, and his regal state   640
Put forth at full, but still his strength concealed,
Which tempted our attempt,[2] and wrought our fall.
Henceforth his might we know, and know our own,
So as not either to provoke or dread
New war provoked: our better part remains   645
To work in close design,[3] by fraud or guile,
What force effected not; that he no less
At length from us may find, who overcomes
By force hath overcome but half his foe.
Space may produce new worlds; whereof so rife   650
There went a fame[4] in Heaven that he ere long
Intended to create, and therein plant
A generation whom his choice regard
Should favor equal to the sons of Heaven.
Thither, if but to pry, shall be perhaps   655
Our first eruption—thither, or elsewhere;
For this infernal pit shall never hold
Celestial spirits in bondage, nor th' abyss
Long under darkness cover. But these thoughts
Full counsel must mature. Peace is despaired,   660
For who can think submission? War, then, war
Open or understood,[5] must be resolved."
    He spake; and, to confirm his words, out flew
Millions of flaming swords, drawn from the thighs
Of mighty cherubim; the sudden blaze   665
Far round illumined Hell. Highly they raged
Against the Highest, and fierce with graspèd arms,
Clashed on their sounding shields the din of war,[6]
Hurling defiance toward the vault of Heaven.

8. Outcome, result.
9. Potent, powerful.
1. Contradictory or even selfish, but also, in an obsolete sense, delaying.
2. Satan is an inveterate punster and player on words.

3. I.e., our best choice is to achieve by secret schemes.
4. Rumor. "Rife": common.
5. Agreed-upon, tacit, hence secret.
6. Like Roman legionaries, the fallen angels applaud
by beating swords on shields.

There stood a hill not far, whose grisly[7] top   670
Belched fire and rolling smoke; the rest entire
Shone with a glossy scurf,[8] undoubted sign
That in his womb was hid metallic ore,
The work of sulphur.[9] Thither, winged with speed,
A numerous brìgade hastened: as when bands   675
Of pioneers[1] with spade and pickax armed
Forerun the royal camp, to trench a field
Or cast a rampart. Mammon led them on,
Mammon, the least erected[2] spirit that fell
From Heaven; for even in Heaven his looks and thoughts   680
Were always downward bent, admiring more
The riches of Heaven's pavement, trodden gold,
Than aught divine or holy else enjoyed
In vision beatific. By him first
Men also, and by his suggestion taught,   685
Ransacked the center, and with impious hands
Rifled the bowels of their mother earth
For treasures better hid. Soon had his crew
Opened into the hill a spacious wound
And digged out ribs of gold. Let none admire   690
That riches grow in Hell; that soil may best
Deserve the precious bane.[3] And here let those
Who boast in mortal things, and wondering tell
Of Babel, and the works of Memphian kings,
Learn how their greatest monuments of fame   695
And strength and art are easily outdone
By spirits reprobate,[4] and in an hour
What in an age they with incessant toil
And hands innumerable scarce perform.
Nigh on the plain, in many cells prepared,   700
That underneath had veins of liquid fire
Sluiced from the lake, a second multitude
With wondrous art founded the massy ore,
Severing each kind, and scummed the bullion-dross.
A third as soon had formed within the ground   705
A various mold, and from the boiling cells
By strange conveyance filled each hollow nook:[5]
As in an organ, from one blast of wind
To many a row of pipes the soundboard breathes.
Anon out of the earth a fabric huge   710
Rose like an exhalation, with the sound
Of dulcet symphonies and voices sweet,
Built like a temple, where pilasters[6] round
Were set, and Doric pillars[7] overlaid

7. Horrible.
8. Crust.
9. Sulfur and mercury were considered the basic substances of all metals.
1. Sappers, engineers.
2. Elevated. Mammon is not a god but an abstract word meaning "wealth"; cf. Belial.
3. "Ribs": bars, of course, but also suggesting golden-haired Eve, who was a "precious bane" (sweet poison)

dug out of Adam's side. "Admire": wonder.
4. The Tower of Babel and the Pyramids of Egypt ("works of Memphian kings") are easily outdone by the devils ("spirits reprobate").
5. After melting the gold with fire from the lake and pouring it into molds, the devils cause their building to rise by a sort of spiritual-musical magic.
6. Columns set in a wall.
7. Doric pillars are severe and plain.

With golden architrave; nor did there want   715
Cornice or frieze, with bossy[8] sculptures graven;
The roof was fretted[9] gold. Not Babylon
Nor great Alcairo such magnificence
Equaled in all their glories, to enshrine
Belus or Serapis[1] their gods, or seat   720
Their kings, when Egypt with Assyria strove
In wealth and luxury. Th' ascending pile
Stood fixed her stately height; and straight[2] the doors
Opening their brazen folds discover, wide
Within, her ample spaces o'er the smooth   725
And level pavement: from the archèd roof,
Pendent by subtle magic, many a row
Of starry lamps and blazing cressets[3] fed
With naphtha and asphaltus yielded light
As from a sky. The hasty multitude   730
Admiring entered; and the work some praise,
And some the architect. His hand was known
In Heaven by many a towered structure high,
Where sceptered angels held their residence,
And sat as princes, whom the sùpreme King   735
Exalted to such power, and gave to rule,
Each in his hierarchy, the orders bright.
Nor was his name unheard or unadored
In ancient Greece; and in Ausonian land
Men called him Mulciber;[4] and how he fell   740
From Heaven they fabled, thrown by angry Jove
Sheer o'er the crystal battlements: from morn
To noon he fell, from noon to dewy eve,
A summer's day, and with the setting sun
Dropped from the zenith like a falling star,   745
On Lemnos th' Aegean isle. Thus they relate,
Erring;[5] for he with this rebellious rout
Fell long before; nor aught availed him now
To have built in Heaven high towers; nor did he 'scape
By all his engines, but was headlong sent   750
With his industrious crew to build in Hell.
    Meanwhile the wingèd heralds, by command
Of sovereign power, with awful ceremony
And trumpet's sound, throughout the host proclaim
A solemn council forthwith to be held   755
At Pandemonium,[6] the high capital
Of Satan and his peers.[7] Their summons called

8. Embossed.
9. Patterned.
1. At Babylon in Assyria there were temples to "Belus" or Baal; at Alcairo (modern Cairo, ancient Memphis) in Egypt, they were to Osiris, one of whose names was Serapis (here, but not ordinarily, accented on the first syllable).
2. Straightway. "Fixed": complete.
3. Basketlike lamps, hung from the ceiling.
4. Hephaestus, or Vulcan, was sometimes known in "Ausonian land" (Italy) by the secondary epithet of

"Mulciber." The story of Jove's tossing him out of heaven is told, to the accompaniment of much Homeric laughter, in *Iliad* 1.
5. Milton tells the story, and gives it six lines of splendid poetry, but in the end condemns it as a corrupt version of the biblical truth.
6. "Pandemonium" (a Miltonic coinage) means literally "All-Demons"; an inversion of Pantheon, "All-Gods."
7. Nobility.

From every band and squarèd regiment
By place or choice the worthiest; they anon
With hundreds and with thousands trooping came   760
Attended.[8] All access was thronged, the gates
And porches wide, but chief the spacious hall
(Though like a covered field, where champions bold
Wont ride in armed, and at the soldan's chair
Defied the best of paynim[9] chivalry   765
To mortal combat, or career with lance)
Thick swarmed, both on the ground and in the air,
Brushed with the hiss of rustling wings. As bees
In springtime, when the sun with Taurus[1] rides,
Pour forth their populous youth about the hive   770
In clusters; they among fresh dews and flowers
Fly to and fro, or on the smoothèd plank,
The suburb of their straw-built citadel,
New rubbed with balm, expatiate, and confer[2]
Their state-affairs: so thick the airy crowd   775
Swarmed and were straitened; till, the signal given,
Behold a wonder! They but now who seemed
In bigness to surpass Earth's giant sons,
Now less than smallest dwarfs, in narrow room
Throng numberless—like that pygmean race   780
Beyond the Indian mount;[3] or fairy elves,
Whose midnight revels by a forest side
Or fountain some belated peasant sees,
Or dreams he sees, while overhead the moon
Sits arbitress,[4] and nearer to the earth   785
Wheels her pale course; they, on their mirth and dance
Intent, with jocund music charm his ear;[5]
At once with joy and fear his heart rebounds.
Thus incorporeal spirits to smallest forms
Reduced their shapes immense, and were at large,   790
Though without number still, amidst the hall
Of that infernal court. But far within,
And in their own dimensions like themselves,
The great seraphic lords and cherubim
In close recess and secret conclave sat,   795
A thousand demigods on golden seats,
Frequent and full.[6] After short silence then,
And summons read, the great consult began.

8. I.e., each with his bodyguards.
9. Pagan. "Soldan's": sultan's.
1. The sun is in the Zodiacal sign of Taurus from
about April 19 to May 20.
2. Spread out and discuss, bring together. The simile
of bees prepares for the sudden contraction of the devils' size; they can shrink or dilate at will.

3. The pygmies were supposed to live beyond the Himalayas, "the Indian mount."
4. Witness.
5. "His" ear is the belated peasant's. "Jocund": merry.
6. Crowded ("frequent") and in full complement
("full"); all present and accounted for.

Book 2

The Argument

The consultation begun, Satan debates whether another battle be to be hazarded for the recovery of Heaven: some advise it, others dissuade. A third proposal is preferred, mentioned before by Satan—to search the truth of that prophecy or tradition in Heaven concerning another world, and another kind of creature, equal or not much inferior to themselves, about this time to be created. Their doubt who shall be sent on this difficult search; Satan, their chief, undertakes alone the voyage; is honored and applauded. The council thus ended, the rest betake them several ways and to several employments, as their inclinations lead them, to entertain[7] the time till Satan return. He passes on his journey to Hell-gates; finds them shut, and who sat there to guard them; by whom at length they are opened, and discover[8] to him the great gulf between Hell and Heaven; with what difficulty he passes through, directed by Chaos, the power of that place, to the sight of this new world which he sought.

High on a throne of royal state, which far
Outshone the wealth of Ormus and of Ind,[9]
Or where the gorgeous East with richest hand
Showers on her kings barbaric pearl and gold,
Satan exalted sat, by merit raised   5
To that bad eminence; and from despair
Thus high uplifted beyond hope, aspires
Beyond thus high, insatiate to pursue
Vain war with Heaven; and by success[1] untaught,
His proud imaginations thus displayed: 10
   "Powers and dominions, deities of Heaven!
For since no deep within her gulf can hold
Immortal vigor, though oppressed and fallen,
I give not Heaven for lost: from this descent
Celestial virtues rising will appear   15
More glorious and more dread than from no fall,
And trust themselves to fear no second fate.
Me though just right and the fixed laws of Heaven
Did first create your leader, next, free choice,
With what besides, in council or in fight,   20
Hath been achieved of merit, yet this loss
Thus far at least recovered, hath much more
Established in a safe unenvied throne
Yielded with full consent.[2] The happier state
In Heaven, which follows dignity, might draw   25
Envy from each inferior; but who here
Will envy whom the highest place exposes
Foremost to stand against the Thunderer's aim,
Your bulwark, and condemns to greatest share
Of endless pain? Where there is then no good   30

7. Pass.
8. Disclose.
9. India. "Ormus": an island in the Persian Gulf, modern Hormuz, famous for pearls.
1. Outcome, result: experience of either sort, good or bad.
2. He lays claim to the throne by just right, fixed laws, free choice—and the fact that no one else will want such a dangerous job.

For which to strive, no strife can grow up there
From faction; for none sure will claim in Hell
Precèdence, none, whose portion is so small
Of present pain, that with ambitious mind
Will covet more. With this advantage then   35
To union and firm faith and firm accord,
More than can be in Heaven, we now return
To claim our just inheritance of old,
Surer to prosper than prosperity
Could have assured us;[3] and by what best way,   40
Whether of open war or covert guile,
We now debate; who can advise, may speak."
    He ceased, and next him Moloch, sceptered king,
Stood up, the strongest and the fiercest spirit
That fought in Heaven, now fiercer by despair.   45
His trust was with th' Eternal to be deemed
Equal in strength, and rather than be less
Cared not to be at all; with that care lost
Went all his fear: of God, or Hell, or worse
He recked[4] not, and these words thereafter spake: 50
    "My sentence[5] is for open war: of wiles,
More unexpert,[6] I boast not: them let those
Contrive who need, or when they need, not now.
For while they sit contriving, shall the rest,
Millions that stand in arms and longing wait   55
The signal to ascend, sit lingering here
Heaven's fugitives, and for their dwelling place
Accept this dark opprobrious den of shame,
The prison of his tyranny who reigns
By our delay? No! let us rather choose,   60
Armed with Hell-flames and fury, all at once
O'er Heaven's high towers to force resistless way,
Turning our tortures into horrid arms
Against the Torturer; when to meet the noise
Of his almighty engine[7] he shall hear   65
Infernal thunder, and for lightning see
Black fire and horror shot with equal rage
Among his angels, and his throne itself
Mixed with Tartarean[8] sulphur and strange fire,
His own invented torments. But perhaps   70
The way seems difficult and steep to scale
With upright wing against a higher foe.
Let such bethink them, if the sleepy drench[9]
Of that forgetful lake benumb not still,
That in our proper motion[1] we ascend   75
Up to our native seat; descent and fall

---

3. Note the play on "sure—prosper—prosperity—
assured." An Elizabethan critic famous for his picturesque terminology, George Puttenham, calls this figure *"epanalepsis,* or the echo sound, otherwise the slow
return." It is a favorite device of Milton's.
4. Cared.
5. Judgment.

6. Inexperienced. Moloch never had to be clever, and
is proud of it.
7. The thunderbolt.
8. Tartarus is a classical name for hell.
9. A draught of physic, as for animals, hence used contemptuously here.
1. Natural impulse.

To us is adverse. Who but felt of late,
When the fierce foe hung on our broken rear
Insulting,[2] and pursued us through the deep,
With what compulsion and laborious flight   80
We sunk thus low? Th' ascent is easy then;
Th' event[3] is feared: should we again provoke
Our stronger,[4] some worse way his wrath may find
To our destruction; if there be in Hell
Fear to be worse destroyed! What can be worse   85
Than to dwell here, driven out from bliss, condemned
In this abhorrèd deep to utter woe;
Where pain of unextinguishable fire
Must exercise us without hope of end,
The vassals[5] of his anger, when the scourge   90
Inexorably, and the torturing hour,
Calls us to penance? More destroyed than thus,
We should be quite abolished, and expire.
What fear we then? What[6] doubt we to incense
His utmost ire? Which, to the height enraged,   95
Will either quite consume us, and reduce
To nothing this essential,[7] happier far
Than miserable to have eternal being!
Or if our substance be indeed divine,
And cannot cease to be, we are at worst   100
On this side nothing;[8] and by proof we feel
Our power sufficient to disturb his Heaven,
And with perpetual inroads to alarm,
Though inaccessible, his fatal throne:
Which, if not victory, is yet revenge."   105
    He ended frowning, and his look denounced
Desperate revenge, and battle dangerous
To less than gods.[9] On th' other side up rose
Belial, in act more graceful and humane;
A fairer person lost not Heaven; he seemed   110
For dignity composed, and high exploit.
But all was false and hollow; though his tongue
Dropped manna, and could make the worse appear
The better reason, to perplex and dash[1]
Maturest counsels: for his thoughts were low,   115
To vice industrious, but to nobler deeds
Timorous and slothful: yet he pleased the ear,
And with persuasive accent thus began:
    "I should be much for open war, O peers,
As not behind in hate, if what was urged   120
Main reason to persuade immediate war
Did not dissuade me most, and seem to cast

2. With the Latin sense of stamping or dancing on.
3. Outcome.
4. The word *enemy* is understood.
5. Servants, underlings; but perhaps also — or alterna-
tively — "vessels."
6. Why.
7. Essence.

8. I.e., we are now as badly off as we can be without
being nothing, and so need have no fear.
9. Only gods could have withstood Moloch.
1. Confuse. "His tongue / Dropped manna": his
tongue was honeyed. To "make the worse appear / The
better reason" was characteristic of Sophists — mercenary logic-choppers of ancient Greece.

Ominous conjecture on the whole success;
When he who most excels in fact[2] of arms,
In what he counsels and in what excels   125
Mistrustful, grounds his courage on despair
And utter dissolution, as the scope
Of all his aim, after some dire revenge.
First, what revenge? The towers of Heaven are filled
With armèd watch, that render all access   130
Impregnable; oft on the bordering deep
Encamp their legions, or with òbscure wing
Scout far and wide into the realm of Night,
Scorning surprise. Or could we break our way
By force, and at our heels all Hell should rise   135
With blackest insurrection, to confound
Heaven's purest light, yet our great enemy
All incorruptible would on his throne
Sit unpolluted, and th' ethereal mold[3]
Incapable of stain would soon expel   140
Her mischief, and purge off the baser fire,
Victorious. Thus repulsed, our final hope
Is flat despair: we must exasperate
Th' almighty Victor to spend all his rage,
And that must end us, that must be our cure,   145
To be no more. Sad cure! for who would lose,
Though full of pain, this intellectual being,
Those thoughts that wander through eternity,
To perish rather, swallowed up and lost
In the wide womb of uncreated Night,   150
Devoid of sense and motion? And who knows,
Let this be good,[4] whether our angry Foe
Can give it, or will ever? How he can
Is doubtful; that he never will is sure.
Will he, so wise, let loose at once his ire,   155
Belike[5] through impotence, or unaware,
To give his enemies their wish, and end
Them in his anger, whom his anger saves
To punish endless? 'Wherefore cease we then?'
Say they who counsel war, 'we are decreed,   160
Reserved and destined to eternal woe;
Whatever doing, what can we suffer more,
What can we suffer worse?' Is this then worst,
Thus sitting, thus consulting, thus in arms?
What when we fled amain, pursued and strook[6]   165
With Heaven's afflicting thunder, and besought
The deep to shelter us? this Hell then seemed
A refuge from those wounds. Or when we lay
Chained on the burning lake? that sure was worse.
What if the breath that kindled those grim fires,   170

2. Feat. "Success": as in line 9, outcome.
3. Substance. "Ethereal" substance, derived from
"ether," the fifth and purest element, was thought to
be incorruptible.
4. I.e., suppose it is good to be destroyed.
5. Ironically, in the sense of "I dare say."
6. Struck. "Amain": headlong.

Awaked, should blow them into sevenfold rage
And plunge us in the flames? or from above
Should intermitted[7] vengeance arm again
His red right hand to plague us? What if all
Her[8] stores were opened, and this firmament   175
Of Hell should spout her cataracts of fire,
Impendent[9] horrors, threatening hideous fall
One day upon our heads; while we perhaps
Designing or exhorting glorious war,
Caught in a fiery tempest shall be hurled,   180
Each on his rock transfixed, the sport and prey
Of racking whirlwinds, or forever sunk
Under yon boiling ocean, wrapped in chains;
There to converse with everlasting groans,
Unrespited, unpitied, unreprieved,   185
Ages of hopeless end! This would be worse.
War therefore, open or concealed, alike
My voice dissuades; for what can force or guile[1]
With him, or who deceive his mind, whose eye
Views all things at one view? He from Heaven's height   190
All these our motions[2] vain sees and derides,
Not more almighty to resist our might
Than wise to frustrate all our plots and wiles.
Shall we then live thus vile, the race of Heaven
Thus trampled, thus expelled to suffer here   195
Chains and these torments? Better these than worse,
By my advice; since fate inevitable
Subdues us, and omnipotent decree,
The Victor's will. To suffer, as to do,
Our strength is equal,[3] nor the law unjust   200
That so ordains: this was at first resolved,
If we were wise, against so great a foe
Contending, and so doubtful what might fall.
I laugh when those who at the spear are bold
And venturous, if that fail them, shrink and fear   205
What yet they know must follow, to endure
Exile, or ignominy, or bonds, or pain,
The sentence of their Conqueror. This is now
Our doom; which if we can sustain and bear,
Our sùpreme Foe in time may much remit   210
His anger, and perhaps, thus far removed,
Not mind us not offending, satisfied
With what is punished;[4] whence these raging fires
Will slacken, if his breath stir not their flames.
Our purer essence then will overcome   215
Their noxious vapor, or inured[5] not feel,
Or changed at length, and to the place conformed

7. Momentarily suspended.
8. Those of Hell.
9. In the Latin sense, hanging down, threatening.
1. The verb *accomplish* or *achieve* is understood.
2. Proposals, plots.
3. I.e., passive endurance and active energy are both

in the devils' power. Belial points out that they must
have known from the beginning that they might have
to exercise both (lines 201–203).
4. A Latinism, *quod punitum est*; God will be satisfied
with the punishment that has been inflicted.
5. Accustomed.

In temper and in nature, will receive
Familiar the fierce heat, and void of pain;
This horror will grow mild, this darkness light;   220
Besides what hope the never-ending flight
Of future days may bring, what chance, what change
Worth waiting, since our present lot appears
For happy though but ill, for ill not worst,[6]
If we procure not to ourselves more woe."   225
    Thus Belial, with words clothed in reason's garb,
Counseled ignoble ease and peaceful sloth,
Not peace; and after him thus Mammon spake:
    "Either to disenthrone the King of Heaven
We war, if war be best, or to regain   230
Our own right lost: him to unthrone we then
May hope, when everlasting Fate shall yield
To fickle Chance, and Chaos judge the strife.
The former, vain to hope, argues[7] as vain
The latter: for what place can be for us   235
Within Heaven's bound, unless Heaven's Lord supreme
We overpower? Suppose he should relent
And publish grace to all, on promise made
Of new subjection; with what eyes could we
Stand in his presence humble, and receive   240
Strict laws imposed, to celebrate his throne
With warbled hymns, and to his Godhead sing
Forced Halleluiahs; while he lordly sits
Our envied Sovereign, and his altar breathes
Ambrosial odors and ambrosial flowers,   245
Our servile offerings? This must be our task
In Heaven, this our delight; how wearisome
Eternity so spent in worship paid
To whom we hate! Let us not then pursue,
By force impossible, by leave obtained   250
Unàcceptable, though in Heaven, our state
Of spendid vassalage;[8] but rather seek
Our own good from ourselves, and from our own
Live to ourselves, though in this vast recess,
Free, and to none accountable, preferring   255
Hard liberty before the easy yoke
Of servile pomp. Our greatness will appear
Then most conspicuous, when great things of small,
Useful of hurtful, prosperous of adverse,
We can create, and in what place soe'er   260
Thrive under evil, and work ease out of pain
Through labor and endurance. This deep world
Of darkness do we dread? How oft amidst
Thick clouds and dark doth Heaven's all-ruling Sire
Choose to reside, his glory unobscured,   265
And with the majesty of darkness round

6. I.e., from the point of view of happiness, the devils   7. Proves.
are but ill off; from the point of view of evil, they could   8. Servitude.
be worse. This is diabolic relativism.

Covers his throne; from whence deep thunders roar,
Mustering their rage, and Heaven resembles Hell!
As he our darkness, cannot we his light
Imitate when we please? This desert soil   270
Wants[9] not her hidden luster, gems and gold;
Nor want we skill or art, from whence to raise
Magnificence; and what can Heaven show more?
Our torments also may in length of time
Become our elements, these piercing fires   275
As soft as now severe, our temper changed
Into their temper; which must needs remove
The sensible of pain.[1] All things invite
To peaceful counsels, and the settled state
Of order, how in safety best we may   280
Compose our present evils, with regard
Of what we are and where, dismissing quite
All thoughts of war. Ye have what I advise."
    He scarce had finished, when such murmur filled
Th' assembly, as when hollow rocks retain   285
The sound of blustering winds, which all night long
Had roused the sea, now with hoarse cadence lull
Seafaring men o'erwatched,[2] whose bark by chance,
Or pinnace, anchors in a craggy bay
After the tempest: such applause was heard   290
As Mammon ended, and his sentence pleased,
Advising peace; for such another field
They dreaded worse than Hell; so much the fear
Of thunder and the sword of Michaël[3]
Wrought still within them; and no less desire   295
To found this nether empire, which might rise
By policy, and long process of time,
In emulation opposite to Heaven.
Which when Beëlzebub perceived, than whom,
Satan except, none higher sat, with grave   300
Aspect he rose, and in his rising seemed
A pillar of state; deep on his front[4] engraven
Deliberation sat and public care;
And princely counsel in his face yet shone,
Majestic though in ruin. Sage he stood   305
With Atlantean[5] shoulders fit to bear
The weight of mightiest monarchies; his look
Drew audience and attention still as night
Or summer's noontide air, while thus he spake:
    "Thrones and imperial powers, offspring of Heaven,   310
Ethereal virtues; or these titles now
Must we renounce, and, changing style, be called
Princes of Hell? For so the popular vote

9. Lacks. Mammon proposes a tawdry imitation Heaven in Hell; this is the ultimate in diabolic degradation.
1. The aspect of pain that is apprehended by the senses; physical pain.
2. Tired out with watching.

3. The warrior angel, chief stay of the angelic armies.
4. Forehead, brow.
5. Worthy of Atlas, one of the Titans, who as a punishment for rebellion was condemned to stand in North Africa and hold up the heavens.

Inclines, here to continue, and build up here
A growing empire—Doubtless! while we dream,   315
And know not that the King of Heaven hath doomed
This place our dungeon, not our safe retreat
Beyond his potent arm, to live exempt
From Heaven's high jurisdiction, in new league
Banded against his throne, but to remain   320
In strictest bondage, though thus far removed,
Under th' inevitable curb, reserved
His captive multitude. For he, be sure,
In height or depth, still first and last will reign
Sole King, and of his kingdom lose no part   325
By our revolt, but over Hell extend
His empire, and with iron scepter rule
Us here, as with his golden those in Heaven.
What[6] sit we then projecting peace and war?
War hath determined us,[7] and foiled with loss   330
Irreparable; terms of peace yet none
Vouchsafed or sought; for what peace will be given
To us enslaved, but custody severe,
And stripes, and arbitrary punishment
Inflicted? and what peace can we return,   335
But, to our power,[8] hostility and hate,
Untamed reluctance,[9] and revenge, though slow,
Yet ever plotting how the Conqueror least
May reap his conquest, and may least rejoice
In doing what we most in suffering feel?[1]   340
Nor will occasion want, nor shall we need
With dangerous expedition to invade
Heaven, whose high walls fear no assault or siege,
Or ambush from the deep. What if we find
Some easier enterprise? There is a place   345
(If ancient and prophetic fame[2] in Heaven
Err not), another world, the happy seat
Of some new race called *Man*, about this time
To be created like to us,[3] though less
In power and excellence, but favored more   350
Of him who rules above; so was his will
Pronounced among the gods, and by an oath,
That shook Heaven's whole circumference, confirmed.
Thither let us bend all our thoughts, to learn
What creatures there inhabit, of what mold   355
Or substance, how endued,[4] and what their power,
And where their weakness, how attempted[5] best,
By force or subtlety. Though Heaven be shut,
And Heaven's high Arbitrator sit secure

6. Why.
7. I.e., war has decided the question for (but also, limited) us.
8. I.e., to the best of our power.
9. Resistance (in the Latin sense, struggling back).
1. How God may get least pleasure from our pain—a devil's view of the deity.

2. Report, rumor.
3. The created (Ptolemaic) cosmos came into existence only after the fall of Satan, and the fallen angels, being otherwise occupied, could not know of it.
4. Endowed.
5. Attacked, but also tempted.

In his own strength, this place may lie exposed,   360
The utmost border of his kingdom, left
To their defense who hold it;[6] here perhaps
Some advantageous act may be achieved
By sudden onset: either with Hell-fire
To waste[7] his whole creation, or possess   365
All as our own, and drive, as we were driven,
The puny habitants; or if not drive,
Seduce them to our party, that their God
May prove their foe, and with repenting hand
Abolish his own works. This would surpass   370
Common revenge, and interrupt his joy
In our confusion, and our joy upraise
In his disturbance; when his darling sons,
Hurled headlong to partake with us, shall curse
Their frail original,[8] and faded bliss,   375
Faded so soon! Advise if this be worth
Attempting, or to sit in darkness here
Hatching vain empires." Thus Beëlzebub
Pleaded his devilish counsel, first devised
By Satan, and in part proposed; for whence   380
But from the author of all ill could spring
So deep a malice, to confound the race
Of mankind in one root,[9] and Earth with Hell
To mingle and involve, done all to spite
The great Creator? But their spite still serves   385
His glory to augment. The bold design
Pleased highly those infernal states,[1] and joy
Sparkled in all their eyes; with full assent
They vote: whereat his speech he thus renews:
    "Well have ye judged, well ended long debate,   390
Synod of gods, and, like to what ye are,
Great things resolved; which from the lowest deep
Will once more lift us up, in spite of Fate,
Nearer our ancient seat; perhaps in view
Of those bright confines, whence with neighboring arms   395
And opportune excursion we may chance
Re-enter Heaven; or else in some mild zone
Dwell not unvisited of Heaven's fair light,
Secure, and at the brightening orient beam
Purge off this gloom; the soft delicious air,   400
To heal the scar of these corrosive fires,
Shall breathe her balm. But first, whom shall we send
In search of this new world? whom shall we find
Sufficient? who shall tempt[2] with wandering feet
The dark unbottomed infinite abyss,   405
And through the palpable obscure find out
His uncouth[3] way, or spread his airy flight

6. To be defended by the occupants.   "Confound": destroy, ruin.
7. Lay waste.   1. Estates, territorial dignitaries of Hell.
8. Originator, parent; or, perhaps, "their original con-   2. Attempt, venture on (from Latin *temptare*).
dition."   3. Unknown. The "palpable obscure" is darkness so
9. Adam, the first man, is the "root" of mankind.   thick it can be felt.

Upborne with indefatigable wings
Over the vast abrupt,[4] ere he arrive
The happy isle?[5] What strength, what art, can then   410
Suffice, or what evasion bear him safe
Through the strict senteries[6] and stations thick
Of angels watching round? Here he had need
All circumspection, and we now no less
Choice in our suffrage;[7] for on whom we send   415
The weight of all, and our last hope, relies."
     This said, he sat; and expectation held
His look suspense,[8] awaiting who appeared
To second, or oppose, or undertake
The perilous attempt; but all sat mute,   420
Pondering the danger with deep thoughts; and each
In others' countenance read his own dismay,
Astonished. None among the choice and prime
Of those Heaven-warring champions could be found
So hardy as to proffer or accept   425
Alone the dreadful voyage; till at last
Satan, whom now transcendent glory raised
Above his fellows, with monarchal pride
Conscious of highest worth, unmoved thus spake:
     "O progeny of Heaven, empyreal thrones!   430
With reason hath deep silence and demur[9]
Seized us, though undismayed. Long is the way
And hard, that out of Hell leads up to light;
Our prison strong, this huge convex[1] of fire,
Outrageous to devour, immures us round   435
Ninefold,[2] and gates of burning adamant
Barred over us prohibit all egress.
These passed, if any pass, the void profound
Of unessential[3] Night receives him next,
Wide gaping, and with utter loss of being   440
Threatens him, plunged in that abortive gulf.
If thence he 'scape into whatever world,
Or unknown region, what remains him less[4]
Than unknown dangers and as hard escape?
But I should ill become this throne, O peers,   445
And this imperial sovereignty, adorned
With splendor, armed with power, if aught proposed
And judged of public moment,[5] in the shape
Of difficulty or danger, could deter
Me from attempting. Wherefore do I assume   450
These royalties, and not refuse to reign,
Refusing[6] to accept as great a share

---

4. Chaos; a striking example of sound imitating sense.
5. Wherever man is (for the fallen angels do not yet know of Earth).
6. Old spelling of *sentries*, necessary here for the meter.
7. Care in our voting.
8. I.e., everyone sat waiting in suspense.
9. Delay.
1. Vault.

2. Walls us in with nine thicknesses (see lines 645ff.).
3. Without real being, darkness being merely the absence of light. The "abortive gulf" (line 441) expresses again this completely negative quality of Chaos and Night.
4. I.e., what awaits him except.
5. Importance.
6. I.e., if I refuse. "Royalties": insignia of royalty.

Of hazard as of honor, due alike
To him who reigns, and so much to him due
Of hazard more, as he above the rest   455
High honored sits?[7] Go therefore, mighty powers,
Terror of Heaven, though fallen; intend[8] at home,
While here shall be our home, what best may ease
The present misery, and render Hell
More tolerable, if there be cure or charm   460
To respite or deceive or slack the pain
Of this ill mansion; intermit no watch
Against a wakeful foe, while I abroad
Through all the coasts of dark destruction seek
Deliverance for us all: this enterprise   465
None shall partake with me." Thus saying rose
The monarch, and prevented[9] all reply;
Prudent, lest, from his resolution raised,[1]
Others among the chief might offer now
(Certain to be refused) what erst they feared,   470
And so refused might in opinion stand
His rivals, winning cheap the high repute
Which he through hazard huge must earn. But they
Dreaded not more th' adventure than his voice
Forbidding; and at once with him they rose;   475
Their rising all at once was as the sound
Of thunder heard remote. Towards him they bend
With awful[2] reverence prone; and as a god
Extol him equal to the highest in Heaven.
Nor failed they to express how much they praised,   480
That for the general safety he despised
His own: for neither do the spirits damned
Lose all their virtue; lest bad men should boast
Their specious deeds on earth, which glory excites,
Or close ambition varnished o'er with zeal.[3]   485
    Thus they their doubtful consultations dark
Ended, rejoicing in their matchless chief:
As when from mountain tops the dusky clouds
Ascending, while the north wind sleeps, o'erspread
Heaven's cheerful face, the lowering element   490
Scowls o'er the darkened landscape snow or shower;
If chance the radiant sun with farewell sweet
Extend his evening beam, the fields revive,
The birds their notes renew, and bleating herds
Attest their joy, that hill and valley rings.   495
O shame to men! Devil with devil damned
Firm concord holds, men only disagree
Of creatures rational, though under hope

7. Satan's argument, simple though entangled in rhetoric, is that rulers must share in the dangers as well as the rewards of an enterprise.
8. Consider.
9. Forestalled, anticipated.
1. After their courage had been raised by his resolution.

2. Full of respect and awe.
3. The sense is that damned spirits still retain some virtues; lest bad men boast of good deeds they have done out of glory and ambition, Milton has shown us that devils do just as much. "Specious": pretending virtue. "Close": secret.

Of heavenly grace; and, God proclaiming peace,[4]
Yet live in hatred, enmity, and strife   500
Among themselves, and levy cruel wars,
Wasting the earth, each other to destroy:
As if (which might induce us to accord)
Man had not hellish foes enow[5] besides,
That day and night for his destruction wait!   505
    The Stygian council thus dissolved; and forth
In order came the grand infernal peers.
Midst came their mighty paramount,[6] and seemed
Alone th' antagonist of Heaven, nor less
Than Hell's dread emperor, with pomp supreme   510
And godlike imitated state; him round
A globe[7] of fiery seraphim enclosed
With bright emblazonry and horrent[8] arms.
Then of their session ended they bid cry
With trumpets' regal sound the great result: 515
Toward the four winds four speedy cherubim
Put to their mouths the sounding alchemy[9]
By herald's voice explained; the hollow abyss
Heard far and wide, and all the host of Hell
With deafening shout returned them loud acclaim.   520
Thence more at ease their minds and somewhat raised
By false presumptuous hope, the rangèd[1] powers
Disband; and wandering, each his several way
Pursues, as inclination or sad choice
Leads him perplexed where he may likeliest find   525
Truce to his restless thoughts, and entertain
The irksome hours, till his great chief return.
Part on the plain, or in the air sublime[2]
Upon the wing, or in swift race contend,
As at th' Olympian games or Pythian fields;[3]   530
Part curb their fiery steeds, or shun the goal
With rapid wheels, or fronted brìgades form.
As when to warn proud cities war appears
Waged in the troubled sky, and armies rush
To battle in the clouds;[4] before each van   535
Prick forth the airy knights, and couch their spears
Till thickest legions close; with feats of arms
From either end of Heaven the welkin[5] burns.
Others with vast Typhoean[6] rage more fell
Rend up both rocks and hills, and ride the air   540
In whirlwind; Hell scarce holds the wild uproar;
As when Alcides, from Oechalia crowned

---

4. I.e., though God proclaims peace.
5. I.e., enough; the old plural emphatic form.
6. Champion, chief.
7. Band or crowd.
8. Bristling. "Emblazonry": decorated shields.
9. I.e., resonant trumpets (made of the alloy brass by a marriage of metals that Milton associates with alchemy).
1. Arrayed in ranks.
2. Aloft, uplifted (the adjective modifies the flyer, not the air).
3. The Olympic games were held at Olympia, the Pythian games at Delphi. To "shun the goal" (next line) is to drive a chariot as close as possible around a column without hitting it.
4. Warfare in the skies, portending trouble on earth. "Van": vanguard. "Prick" (line 536): spur.
5. Sky.
6. Like that of Typhon, the hundred-headed Titan (see 1.199).

With conquest, felt th' envenomed robe, and tore
Through pain up by the roots Thessalian pines,
And Lichas from the top of Oeta threw   545
Into th' Euboic sea.[7] Others more mild,
Retreated in a silent valley, sing
With notes angelical to many a harp
Their own heroic deeds and hapless fall
By doom of battle; and complain that Fate   550
Free Virtue should enthrall to Force or Chance.
Their song was partial,[8] but the harmony
(What could it less when spirits immortal sing?)
Suspended[9] Hell, and took with ravishment
The thronging audience. In discourse more sweet   555
(For eloquence the soul, song charms the sense)
Others apart sat on a hill retired,
In thoughts more elevate, and reasoned high
Of providence, foreknowledge, will, and fate,
Fixed fate, free will, foreknowledge absolute,   560
And found no end, in wandering mazes lost.
Of good and evil much they argued then,
Of happiness and final misery,
Passion and apathy,[1] and glory and shame,
Vain wisdom all, and false philosophy![2]   565
Yet with a pleasing sorcery could charm
Pain for a while or anguish, and excite
Fallacious hope, or arm th' obdured[3] breast
With stubborn patience as with triple steel.
Another part, in squadrons and gross[4] bands,   570
On bold adventure to discover wide
That dismal world, if any clime perhaps
Might yield them easier habitation, bend
Four ways their flying march, along the banks
Of four infernal rivers that disgorge   575
Into the burning lake their baleful streams:[5]
Abhorrèd Styx, the flood of deadly hate;
Sad Acheron of sorrow, black and deep;
Cocytus, named of lamentation loud
Heard on the rueful stream; fierce Phlegethon   580
Whose waves of torrent fire inflame with rage.
Far off from these a slow and silent stream,
Lethe, the river of oblivion, rolls
Her watery labyrinth, whereof who drinks
Forthwith his former state and being forgets,   585
Forgets both joy and grief, pleasure and pain.

---

7. Poisoned by the malicious centaur Nessus, Hercules in his dying agonies threw his beloved companion Lichas, along with a good part of Mt. Oeta, into the sea of Euboea, near Thermopylae.
8. Prejudiced.
9. Held in suspense.
1. Feeling and lack of feeling; the angels are dabbling in Stoicism.
2. Milton means, not that the subjects themselves are vain (he himself, in the present poem, has a good deal

to say on these topics), but that the very premises with which devils start are bound to land them in error.
3. Hardened.
4. Solid, dense.
5. The four rivers are traditional in hellish geography; Milton takes pains to distinguish them by the original meanings of their Greek names (Styx means "hateful," Acheron "woeful," etc.). Lethe is "far off" and very different from the others, oblivion being relatively a blessed state in hell.

Beyond this flood a frozen continent
Lies dark and wild, beat with perpetual storms
Of whirlwind and dire hail, which on firm land
Thaws not, but gathers heap,[6] and ruin seems   590
Of ancient pile; all else deep snow and ice,
A gulf profound as that Serbonian bog[7]
Betwixt Damiata and Mount Casius old,
Where armies whole have sunk: the parching air
Burns frore,[8] and cold performs th' effect of fire.   595
Thither by harpy-footed[9] Furies haled,
At certain revolutions[1] all the damned
Are brought; and feel by turns the bitter change
Of fierce extremes, extremes by change more fierce,
From beds of raging fire to starve[2] in ice   600
Their soft ethereal warmth, and there to pine
Immovable, infixed, and frozen round,
Periods of time; thence hurried back to fire.
They ferry over this Lethean sound
Both to and fro, their sorrow to augment,   605
And wish and struggle, as they pass, to reach
The tempting stream, with one small drop to lose
In sweet forgetfulness all pain and woe,
All in one moment, and so near the brink;
But Fate withstands, and to oppose th' attempt   610
Medusa[3] with Gorgonian terror guards
The ford, and of itself the water flies
All taste of living wight, as once it fled
The lips of Tantalus.[4] Thus roving on
In cònfused march forlorn, th' adventurous bands   615
With shuddering horror pale, and eyes aghast,
Viewed first their lamentable lot, and found
No rest. Through many a dark and dreary vale
They passed, and many a region dolorous,
O'er many a frozen, many a fiery alp,[5]   620
Rocks, caves, lakes, fens, bogs, dens, and shades of death,
A universe of death, which God by curse
Created evil, for evil only good,
Where all life dies, death lives, and Nature breeds,
Perverse, all monstrous, all prodigious things,   625
Abominable, unutterable, and worse
Than fables yet have feigned, or fear conceived,
Gorgons, and Hydras, and Chimeras[6] dire.
    Meanwhile the adversary of God and man,
Satan with thoughts inflamed of highest design,   630

6. In a heap, so that it looks like the ruin of an old
building ("ancient pile").
7. Lake Serbonis, once famous for its quicksands but
today dried up, used to lie on the coast of Egypt, just
east of the Nile.
8. Frosty.
9. With hooked claws.
1. I.e., of time.
2. Benumb.
3. One of the three Gorgons, women with snaky hair,

scaly bodies, and boar's tusks, the very sight of whose
faces changed men to stone.
4. Tantalus, afflicted with a raging thirst, stood in the
middle of a lake, the water of which always receded
when he tried to drink it (hence, "tantalize").
5. A "fiery alp" is a volcano.
6. The Hydra was a serpent with nine heads, slain by
Hercules; the Chimera was a fire-breathing creature,
part lion, part dragon, part goat. They exemplify abominations of nature.

Puts on swift wings,[7] and toward the gates of Hell
Explores his solitary flight; sometimes
He scours the right-hand coast, sometimes the left;
Now shaves with level wing the deep, then soars
Up to the fiery concave[8] towering high.   635
As when far off at sea a fleet descried
Hangs in the clouds, by equinoctial winds
Close sailing from Bengala,[9] or the isles
Of Ternate and Tidore,[1] whence merchants bring
Their spicy drugs; they on the trading flood   640
Through the wide Ethiopian to the Cape
Ply stemming nightly toward the pole:[2] so seemed
Far off the flying fiend. At last appear
Hell bounds, high reaching to the horrid roof,
And thrice threefold the gates; three folds were brass,   645
Three iron, three of adamantine rock,
Impenetrable, impaled with circling fire,
Yet unconsumed. Before the gates there sat
On either side a formidable shape;[3]
The one seemed woman to the waist, and fair,   650
But ended foul in many a scaly fold
Voluminous and vast, a serpent armed
With mortal sting. About her middle round
A cry[4] of Hellhounds never ceasing barked
With wide Cerberean[5] mouths full loud, and rung   655
A hideous peal; yet, when they list, would creep,
If aught disturbed their noise, into her womb,
And kennel there, yet there still barked and howled
Within unseen. Far less abhorred than these
Vexed Scylla,[6] bathing in the sea that parts   660
Calabria from the hoarse Trinacrian shore;
Nor uglier follow the night-hag,[7] when called
In secret, riding through the air she comes,
Lured with the smell of infant blood, to dance
With Lapland witches, while the laboring moon   665
Eclipses at their charms.[8] The other shape,
If shape it might be called that shape had none
Distinguishable in member, joint, or limb,
Or substance might be called that shadow seemed,
For each seemed either; black it stood as night,   670
Fierce as ten Furies, terrible as Hell,

---

7. Satan does not fasten on his wings; he takes swiftly to wing.
8. Vault.
9. An old form of "Bengal."
1. Two of the Molucca or "Spice" Islands, modern Indonesia.
2. The South Pole. "Ethiopian": the Indian Ocean, east of Africa. "The Cape" is the Cape of Good Hope.
3. The allegorical figures of Sin and Death are founded on James 1.15: "Then when lust hath conceived, it bringeth forth sin: and sin, when it is finished, bringeth forth death." But the incestuous relations of Sin and Death are Milton's own invention. Physically, Sin is modeled on Virgil's or Ovid's Scylla, with some touches adopted from Spenser's Errour; Death is a traditional figure, vague and vast.
4. Pack.
5. Like Cerberus, the traditional hound of hell.
6. Circe out of jealousy threw poison into the water where Scylla bathed, in the straits between Calabria and Sicily ("Trinacria"); as a result of the poison, Scylla developed a ring of barking, snapping dogs around her waist.
7. Hecate (three syllables), goddess of sorcery. She attends the orgies of witches in the home of all witchcraft, Lapland, whither she is drawn by the blood of babies sacrificed for the occasion.
8. Magic formulas, not allurements.

And shook a dreadful dart; what seemed his head
The likeness of a kingly crown had on.
Satan was now at hand, and from his seat
The monster moving onward came as fast,   675
With horrid strides; Hell trembled as he strode.
Th' undaunted fiend what this might be admired,[9]
Admired, not feared; God and his Son except,
Created thing naught valued he nor shunned;
And with disdainful look thus first began: 680
    "Whence and what art thou, execrable shape,
That dar'st, though grim and terrible, advance
Thy miscreated front[1] athwart my way
To yonder gates? Through them I mean to pass,
That be assured, without leave asked of thee.   685
Retire, or taste thy folly, and learn by proof,
Hell-born, not to contend with spirits of Heaven."
    To whom the goblin full of wrath replied:
"Art thou that traitor angel, art thou he,
Who first broke peace in Heaven, and faith, till then   690
Unbroken, and in proud rebellious arms
Drew after him the third part of Heaven's sons
Conjured[2] against the Highest, for which both thou
And they, outcast from God, are here condemned
To waste eternal days in woe and pain?   695
And reckon'st thou thyself with spirits of Heaven,
Hell-doomed, and breath'st defiance here and scorn,
Where I reign king, and, to enrage thee more,
Thy king and lord? Back to thy punishment,
False fugitive, and to thy speed add wings,   700
Lest with a whip of scorpions I pursue
Thy ling'ring, or with one stroke of this dart
Strange horror seize thee, and pangs unfelt before."
    So spake the grisly terror, and in shape,
So speaking and so threatening, grew tenfold   705
More dreadful and deform. On th' other side,
Incensed with indignation Satan stood
Unterrified, and like a comet burned
That fires the length of Ophiuchus[3] huge
In th' arctic sky, and from his horrid hair   710
Shakes pestilence and war. Each at the head
Leveled his deadly aim; their fatal hands
No second stroke intend;[4] and such a frown
Each cast at th' other, as when two black clouds,
With Heaven's artillery fraught,[5] come rattling on   715
Over the Caspian,[6] then stand front to front
Hovering a space, till winds the signal blow
To join their dark encounter in mid-air:

---

9. Wondered.
1. Misshapen forehead, or face.
2. Sworn together by an oath.
3. A vast northern constellation, "The Serpent-Holder" (also called "Serpentarius"). Satan will soon

appear as a snake, and like a comet, he portends "pestilence and war."
4. I.e., the first stroke will do the business.
5. Loaded with thunderbolts.
6. The Caspian is a particularly stormy area.

So frowned the mighty combatants, that Hell
Grew darker at their frown; so matched they stood;   720
For never but once more was either like
To meet so great a foe.[7] And now great deeds
Had been achieved, whereof all Hell had rung,
Had not the snaky sorceress that sat
Fast by Hell-gate, and kept the fatal key,   725
Ris'n, and with hideous outcry rushed between.
    "O father, what intends thy hand," she cried,
"Against thy only son?[8] What fury, O son,
Possesses thee to bend that mortal dart
Against thy father's head? and know'st for whom?   730
For Him who sits above and laughs the while
At thee ordained his drudge, to execute
Whate'er his wrath, which he calls Justice, bids;
His wrath which one day will destroy ye both!"
    She spake, and at her words the hellish pest   735
Forbore; then these to her Satan returned:
    "So strange thy outcry, and thy words so strange
Thou interposest, that my sudden hand
Prevented[9] spares to tell thee yet by deeds
What it intends, till first I know of thee,   740
What thing thou art, thus double-formed, and why,
In this infernal vale first met, thou call'st
Me father, and that phantasm call'st my son?
I know thee not, nor ever saw till now
Sight more detestable than him and thee."   745
    T' whom thus the portress of Hell-gate replied:
"Hast thou forgot me then, and do I seem
Now in thine eye so foul? once deemed so fair
In Heaven, when at th' assembly, and in sight
Of all the seraphim with thee combined   750
In bold conspiracy against Heaven's King,
All on a sudden miserable pain
Surprised thee; dim thine eyes, and dizzy swum
In darkness, while thy head flames thick and fast
Threw forth, till on the left side opening wide,   755
Likest to thee in shape and countenance bright,
Then shining heavenly fair, a goddess armed
Out of thy head I sprung.[1] Amazement seized
All th' host of Heaven; back they recoiled afraid
At first, and called me Sin, and for a sign   760
Portentous held me; but, familiar grown,
I pleased, and with attractive graces won
The most averse, thee chiefly, who full oft
Thyself in me thy perfect image viewing
Becam'st enamored;[2] and such joy thou took'st   765

---

7. I.e., the Son of God.
8. Sin, Death, and Satan, in their various interrela-
tions, parody obscenely the relations between God and
the Son, Adam and Eve.
9. Forestalled.

1. As Athena sprang full-grown from the head of Zeus.
2. Sin looks attractive at first, being a lovely woman at
the top of her body; but she is a serpent below, and
ends in a "mortal sting," i.e., death.

With me in secret, that my womb conceived
A growing burden. Meanwhile war arose,
And fields were fought in Heaven; wherein remained
(For what could else?) to our almighty foe
Clear victory, to our part loss and rout   770
Through all the empyrean. Down they fell,
Driven headlong from the pitch³ of Heaven, down
Into this deep, and in the general fall
I also; at which time this powerful key
Into my hand was given, with charge to keep   775
These gates forever shut, which none can pass
Without my opening. Pensive here I sat
Alone, but long I sat not, till my womb
Pregnant by thee, and now excessive grown,
Prodigious motion felt and rueful throes.   780
At last this odious offspring whom thou seest,
Thine own begotten, breaking violent way
Tore through my entrails, that with fear and pain
Distorted, all my nether shape thus grew
Transformed; but he, my inbred enemy,   785
Forth issued, brandishing his fatal dart,
Made to destroy. I fled, and cried out *Death!*
Hell trembled at the hideous name, and sighed
From all her caves, and back resounded *Death!*
I fled; but he pursued (though more, it seems,   790
Inflamed with lust than rage) and swifter far,
Me overtook, his mother, all dismayed,
And in embraces forcible and foul
Engendering with me, of that rape begot
These yelling monsters that with ceaseless cry   795
Surround me, as thou sawest, hourly conceived
And hourly born, with sorrow infinite
To me; for when they list, into the womb
That bred them they return, and howl and gnaw
My bowels, their repast; then bursting forth   800
Afresh, with conscious terrors vex me round,
That rest or intermission none I find.
Before mine eyes in opposition sits
Grim Death, my son and foe, who sets them on,
And me his parent would full soon devour   805
For want of other prey, but that he knows
His end with mine involved; and knows that I
Should prove a bitter morsel, and his bane,
Whenever that shall be; so Fate pronounced.
But thou, O father, I forewarn thee, shun   810
His deadly arrow; neither vainly hope
To be invulnerable in those bright arms,
Though tempered heavenly; for that mortal dint,
Save he who reigns above, none can resist."⁴
    She finished, and the subtle fiend his lore   815

---

3. Height.   4. I.e., only God is immune to death.

Soon learned, now milder, and thus answered smooth:
"Dear daughter, since thou claimest me for thy sire,
And my fair son here show'st me, the dear pledge
Of dalliance had with thee in Heaven, and joys
Then sweet, now sad to mention, through dire change   820
Befallen us unforeseen, unthought of; know
I come no enemy, but to set free
From out this dark and dismal house of pain
Both him and thee, and all the heavenly host
Of spirits that, in our just pretenses[5] armed,   825
Fell with us from on high. From them I go
This uncouth errand sole,[6] and one for all
Myself expose, with lonely steps to tread
Th' unfounded[7] deep, and through the void immense
To search with wandering quest a place foretold   830
Should be, and, by concurring signs, ere now
Created vast and round, a place of bliss
In the purlieus[8] of Heaven, and therein placed
A race of upstart creatures, to supply
Perhaps our vacant room, though more removed,   835
Lest Heaven surcharged with potent multitude
Might hap to move new broils.[9] Be this or aught
Than this more secret now designed, I haste
To know; and this once known, shall soon return,
And bring ye to the place where thou and Death   840
Shall dwell at ease, and up and down unseen
Wing silently the buxom air, embalmed[1]
With odors: there ye shall be fed and filled
Immeasurably; all things shall be your prey."
He ceased, for both seemed highly pleased, and Death   845
Grinned horrible a ghastly smile, to hear
His famine[2] should be filled, and blessed his maw
Destined to that good hour. No less rejoiced
His mother bad, and thus bespake her sire:
    "The key of this infernal pit by due   850
And by command of Heaven's all-powerful King
I keep, by him forbidden to unlock
These adamantine gates; against all force
Death ready stands to interpose his dart,
Fearless to be o'ermatched by living might.   855
But what owe I to his commands above
Who hates me, and hath hither thrust me down
Into this gloom of Tartarus profound,
To sit in hateful office here confined,
Inhabitant of Heaven and heavenly-born,   860
Here in perpetual agony and pain,
With terrors and with clamors compassed round
Of mine own brood that on my bowels feed?

5. Pretensions, claims.
6. Alone on a desolate journey.
7. Bottomless.
8. Outskirts, suburbs.

9. Controversies. "Surcharged": too full.
1. Made fragrant, but also with a thought of the process associated with death. "Buxom": yielding.
2. Hunger, belly.

Thou art my father, thou my author, thou
My being gav'st me; whom should I obey   865
But thee? whom follow? Thou wilt bring me soon
To that new world of light and bliss, among
The gods who live at ease, where I shall reign
At thy right hand voluptuous,[3] as beseems
Thy daughter and thy darling, without end."   870
  Thus saying, from her side the fatal key,
Sad instrument of all our woe, she took;
And towards the gate rolling her bestial train,[4]
Forthwith the huge portcullis high up-drew,
Which but herself not all the Stygian powers[5]   875
Could once have moved; then in the keyhole turns
Th' intricate wards, and every bolt and bar
Of massy iron or solid rock with ease
Unfastens: on a sudden open fly
With impetuous recoil and jarring sound   880
Th' infernal doors, and on their hinges grate
Harsh thunder, that the lowest bottom shook
Of Erebus.[6] She opened, but to shut
Excelled[7] her power; the gates wide open stood,
That with extended wings a bannered host,   885
Under spread ensigns[8] marching, might pass through
With horse and chariots ranked in loose array;
So wide they stood, and like a furnace-mouth
Cast forth redounding[9] smoke and ruddy flame.
Before their eyes in sudden view appear   890
The secrets of the hoary deep, a dark
Illimitable ocean without bound,
Without dimension; where length, breadth, and height,
And time and place are lost; where eldest Night
And Chaos, ancestors of Nature, hold   895
Eternal anarchy, amidst the noise
Of endless wars, and by confusion stand.
For Hot, Cold, Moist, and Dry, four champions fierce,
Strive here for mastery, and to battle bring
Their embryon atoms;[1] they around the flag   900
Of each his faction, in their several clans,
Light-armed or heavy, sharp, smooth, swift, or slow,
Swarm populous, unnumbered as the sands
Of Barca or Cyrene's torrid soil,[2]
Levied to side with warring winds, and poise[3]   905
Their lighter wings. To whom these most adhere,
He rules a moment; Chaos[4] umpire sits,
And by decision more embroils the fray

3. As the Son sits at God's right hand, Sin will at Satan's: a blasphemous parody of the Creed.
4. I.e., accompanied by her yelping offspring.
5. The powers of Hell.
6. Another classical name for hell.
7. Exceeded.
8. Standards, flags.
9. Billowing.

1. The four elements, fire, earth, water, and air, struggle endlessly in Chaos. "Embryon": embryo, unformed.
2. Barca and Cyrene were cities built on the shifting sands of North Africa.
3. Give weight to. "Levied": both enlisted and raised.
4. Chaos is both the place where confusion reigns and personified confusion itself.

By which he reigns: next him, high arbiter,
Chance governs all. Into this wild abyss—   910
The womb of Nature and perhaps her grave,
Of neither sea, nor shore, nor air, nor fire,
But all these in their pregnant causes[5] mixed
Confusedly, and which thus must ever fight,
Unless th' Almighty Maker them ordain   915
His dark materials to create more worlds[6]—
Into this wild abyss the wary fiend
Stood on the brink of Hell and looked awhile,
Pondering his voyage; for no narrow frith[7]
He had to cross. Nor was his ear less pealed[8]   920
With noises loud and ruinous (to compare
Great things with small) than when Bellona[9] storms,
With all her battering engines bent to raze
Some capital city; or less than if this frame
Of heaven were falling, and these elements   925
In mutiny had from her axle torn
The steadfast earth. At last his sail-broad vans[1]
He spreads for flight, and in the surging smoke
Uplifted spurns the ground; thence many a league,
As in a cloudy chair ascending, rides   930
Audacious; but that seat soon failing, meets
A vast vacuity: all unawares,
Fluttering his pennons[2] vain, plumb down he drops
Ten thousand fathom deep, and to this hour
Down had been falling, had not by ill chance   935
The strong rebuff[3] of some tumultuous cloud
Instinct with fire and niter[4] hurried him
As many miles aloft; that fury stayed,
Quenched in a boggy Syrtis,[5] neither sea,
Nor good dry land, nigh foundered on he fares,   940
Treading the crude consistence, half on foot,
Half flying; behoves[6] him now both oar and sail.
As when a gryphon through the wilderness
With wingèd course o'er hill or moory dale
Pursues the Arimaspian, who by stealth   945
Had from his wakeful custody purloined
The guarded gold:[7] so eagerly the fiend
O'er bog or steep, through strait, rough, dense, or rare,
With head, hands, wings, or feet pursues his way,
And swims, or sinks, or wades, or creeps, or flies.   950
At length a universal hubbub wild

5. Chaos is not organized to the point of being matter;
it is the seeds of all forms of matter.
6. God must impose order on Chaos to create worlds
from it.
7. Channel, firth.
8. Rung.
9. Goddess of war.
1. Wings.
2. Pinions, from Latin *pennae*, "wings."
3. Puff or blast.
4. Saltpeter. "Instinct": filled.

5. Quicksand, from the North African gulfs, famous
for their shifting sandbars.
6. Befits.
7. Gryphons, fabulous creatures, half eagle, half lion,
lived in Northern Europe and were said to hoard gold.
When it was stolen from them by the one-eyed Arimaspians, they pursued these curious malefactors, hopping, flapping, and squawking. The story is a piece of
moralized natural history, directed against the love of
money.

Of stunning sounds and voices all confused
Borne through the hollow dark assaults his ear
With loudest vehemence. Thither he plies
Undaunted, to meet there whatever power   955
Or spirit of the nethermost abyss
Might in that noise reside, of whom to ask
Which way the nearest coast of darkness lies
Bordering on light; when straight behold the throne
Of Chaos, and his dark pavilion spread   960
Wide on the wasteful deep! With him enthroned
Sat sable-vested Night, eldest of things,
The consort of his reign; and by them stood
Orcus and Ades,[8] and the dreaded name
Of Demogorgon;[9] Rumor next and Chance,   965
And Tumult and Confusion all embroiled,
And Discord with a thousand various mouths.
     T' whom Satan turning boldly, thus: "Ye powers
And spirits of this nethermost abyss,
Chaos and ancient Night, I come no spy,   970
With purpose to explore or to disturb
The secrets of your realm; but by constraint
Wandering this darksome desert, as my way
Lies through your spacious empire up to light,
Alone and without guide, half lost, I seek   975
What readiest path leads where your gloomy bounds
Confine with[1] Heaven; or if some other place
From your dominion won, th' Ethereal King
Possesses lately, thither to arrive
I travel this profound.[2] Direct my course: 980
Directed, no mean recompense it brings
To your behoof,[3] if I that region lost,
All usurpation thence expelled, reduce
To her original darkness and your sway
(Which is my present journey),[4] and once more   985
Erect the standard there of ancient Night.
Yours be th' advantage all, mine the revenge!"
     Thus Satan; and him thus the anarch[5] old,
With faltering speech and visage incomposed,[6]
Answered: "I know thee, stranger, who thou art,   990
That mighty leading angel, who of late
Made head against Heaven's King, though overthrown.
I saw and heard; for such a numerous host
Fled not in silence through the frighted deep
With ruin upon ruin, rout on rout,   995
Confusion worse confounded; and Heaven-gates
Poured out by millions her victorious bands
Pursuing. I upon my frontiers here

8. Latin and Greek names of Pluto, god of hell.   3. On your behalf.
9. A mysterious subdeity, stronger than Fate itself,   4. I.e., the purpose of my present journey.
publicized by Boccaccio.   5. Chaos is not "monarch" of his realm, but "anarch,"
1. Border on.   i.e., nonruler.
2. Deep pit.   6. Disturbed.

Keep residence; if all I can will serve
That little which is left so to defend,   1000
Encroached on still through our intestine broils[7]
Weakening the scepter of old Night: first Hell,
Your dungeon, stretching far and wide beneath;
Now lately heaven and earth,[8] another world
Hung o'er my realm, linked in a golden chain   1005
To that side Heaven from whence your legions fell.
If that way be your walk, you have not far;
So much the nearer danger. Go, and speed!
Havoc and spoil and ruin are my gain."
   He ceased; and Satan stayed not to reply,   1010
But glad that now his sea should find a shore,
With fresh alacrity and force renewed
Springs upward like a pyramid of fire
Into the wild expanse, and through the shock
Of fighting elements, on all sides round   1015
Environed, wins his way; harder beset
And more endangered than when Argo passed
Through Bosporus betwixt the jostling rocks;
Or when Ulysses on the larboard shunned
Charybdis, and by th' other whirlpool steered:[9]   1020
So he with difficulty and labor hard
Moved on, with difficulty and labor he;
But, he once past, soon after when man fell,
Strange alteration! Sin and Death amain,[1]
Following his track (such was the will of Heaven),   1025
Paved after him a broad and beaten way
Over the dark abyss, whose boiling gulf
Tamely endured a bridge of wondrous length
From Hell continued reaching th' utmost orb[2]
Of this frail world; by which the spirits perverse   1030
With easy intercourse pass to and fro
To tempt or punish mortals, except whom
God and good angels guard by special grace.
But now at last the sacred influence
Of light appears, and from the walls of Heaven   1035
Shoots far into the bosom of dim Night
A glimmering dawn. Here Nature first begins
Her farthest verge,[3] and Chaos to retire,
As from her outmost works a broken foe
With tumult less and with less hostile din;   1040

7. I.e., the territory of Chaos is continually shrinking because of our civil wars ("intestine broils"). Without textual authority, but with a certain logical force, some scholars have proposed to amend "our" to "your."
8. Our human cosmos, recently carved out of Chaos, and having a little heaven of its own, as distinguished from "Heaven," as used in line 1006 to mean the eternal empyrean, the abode of the deity and His angels.
9. Jason and his fifty Argonauts, sailing through the Bosporus to the Black Sea in pursuit of the Golden Fleece, had to pass through the Symplegades, or clashing rocks. Ulysses also had a tight squeeze to pass be-

tween Scylla and Charybdis, where Italy almost touches Sicily. Charybdis was a whirlpool, but Scylla, the dog monster who ate alive six of Ulysses' best men, is called by Milton "th' other whirlpool."
1. At full speed, vigorously.
2. The world is surrounded by ten spheres, the whole concentric construction making up the created universe. The bridge built by Sin and Death ends on the outermost of these spheres.
3. Threshold. The end of Chaos is the beginning of (created) Nature.

That[4] Satan with less toil, and now with ease,
Wafts on the calmer wave by dubious light,
And like a weather-beaten vessel holds[5]
Gladly the port, though shrouds and tackle torn;
Or in the emptier waste, resembling air,   1045
Weighs his spread wings, at leisure to behold
Far off th' empyreal Heaven, extended wide
In circuit, undetermined[6] square or round,
With opal towers and battlements adorned
Of living sapphire, once his native seat;   1050
And fast by, hanging in a golden chain,
This pendant world,[7] in bigness as a star
Of smallest magnitude close by the moon.
Thither, full fraught with mischievous revenge,
Accursed, and in a cursèd hour, he hies.   1055

From Book 3

[The Invocation, the Council in Heaven, and the Conclusion of Satan's Journey]

Hail, holy Light, offspring of Heaven first-born!
Or of th' Eternal coeternal beam,
May I express thee unblamed?[8] since God is light,
And never but in unapproachèd light
Dwelt from eternity, dwelt then in thee,   5
Bright effluence of bright essence increate![9]
Or hear'st thou rather[1] pure ethereal stream,
Whose fountain who shall tell? Before the sun,
Before the heavens, thou wert, and at the voice
Of God, as with a mantle didst invest[2]   10
The rising world of waters dark and deep,
Won from the void and formless infinite.
Thee I revisit now with bolder wing,
Escaped the Stygian pool, though long detained
In that obscure sojourn, while in my flight,   15
Through utter and through middle darkness[3] borne,
With other notes than to th' Orphean lyre[4]
I sung of Chaos and eternal Night;
Taught by the Heavenly Muse[5] to venture down
The dark descent, and up to reascend,   20

4. So that.
5. Makes for.
6. Heaven is so vast that simply by looking at it one cannot tell its shape.
7. Homer first imagined the world as hanging from Heaven by a golden chain (*Iliad* 8). As Milton uses the image, it has a symbolic meaning as well: earth is dependent on Heaven. The world that hangs from Heaven is not just our earth, but earth and all its ten spheres.
8. Milton feels some hesitation at calling Light coeternal with God himself; his reasons for doing so follow.

9. Uncreated, i.e., eternal.
1. I.e., would you rather be called. The construction is a Latinism.
2. Cover, wrap.
3. Hell and Chaos.
4. One of the so-called Orphic Hymns is *To Night*, and Orpheus himself visited the underworld. But Milton's song, being Christian, is of a different kind.
5. Urania. The following lines echo *Aeneid* 6.126–129, where the Sybil tells Aeneas that the descent to hell is easy; getting back is the hard part.

Though hard and rare. Thee I revisit safe,
And feel thy sovereign vital lamp; but thou
Revisit'st not these eyes, that roll in vain
To find thy piercing ray, and find no dawn;
So thick a drop serene hath quenched their orbs,   25
Or dim suffusion[6] veiled. Yet not the more
Cease I to wander where the Muses haunt
Clear spring, or shady grove, or sunny hill,
Smit with the love of sacred song;[7] but chief
Thee, Sion,[8] and the flowery brooks beneath,   30
That wash thy hallowed feet, and warbling flow,
Nightly I visit: nor sometimes forget[9]
Those other two equaled with me in fate,[1]
So were I equaled with them in renown,
Blind Thamyris and blind Maeonides,   35
And Tiresias and Phineus, prophets old:[2]
Then feed on thoughts that voluntary move
Harmonious numbers; as the wakeful bird
Sings darkling,[3] and in shadiest covert hid
Tunes her nocturnal note. Thus with the year   40
Seasons return; but not to me returns
Day, or the sweet approach of even or morn,
Or sight of vernal bloom, or summer's rose,
Or flocks, or herds, or human face divine;
But cloud instead and ever-during dark   45
Surrounds me, from the cheerful ways of men
Cut off, and for the book of knowledge fair
Presented with a universal blank
Of Nature's works to me expunged and rased,[4]
And wisdom at one entrance quite shut out.   50
So much the rather thou, Celestial Light,
Shine inward, and the mind through all her powers
Irradiate; there plant eyes; all mist from thence
Purge and disperse, that I may see and tell
Of things invisible to mortal sight.   55
     Now had th' Almighty Father from above,
From the pure empyrean where he sits
High throned above all height, bent down his eye,
His own works and their works at once to view:
About him all the sanctities of Heaven   60
Stood thick as stars, and from his sight[5] received
Beatitude past utterance; on his right
The radiant image of his glory sat,

---

6. Cataract—*suffusio nigra*. "Drop serene": *gutta se-*
rena was the medical term for the kind of blindness
from which Milton suffered.
7. Again the phrase is Virgilian, "[Musarum] ingenti
percussus amore" (*Georgics* 2.476); but the adjective
"sacred" is Milton's own reservation.
8. The mountain of scriptural inspiration, with its
brooks Siloa and Kidron.
9. I.e., and never forget; therefore, always remember.
1. Blind like me.
2. Thamyris was a blind Thracian poet, who lived be-

fore Homer. "Maeonides" is an epithet of Homer, either as a son of Maeon or as a native of Maeonia.
Tiresias was the blind prophet of Thebes. Phineus was
a blind king and seer (*Aeneid* 3). For Milton, poetry
and prophecy were intimately joined; blindness of the
outer eye rendered more acute the sight of the inner
eye.
3. In the dark. "Wakeful bird": the nightingale.
4. Shaved off (like a Roman tablet), erased.
5. From sight of him.

His only Son. On Earth he first beheld
Our two first parents, yet the only two   65
Of mankind, in the happy garden placed,
Reaping immortal fruits of joy and love,
Uninterrupted joy, unrivaled love,
In blissful solitude. He then surveyed
Hell and the gulf between, and Satan there   70
Coasting the wall of Heaven on this side Night,
In the dun air sublime,[6] and ready now
To stoop, with wearied wings and willing feet,
On the bare outside of this world, that seemed
Firm land embosomed without firmament,   75
Uncertain which, in ocean or in air.
Him God beholding from his prospect high,
Wherein past, present, future he beholds,
Thus to his only Son foreseeing spake:
    "Only begotten Son, seest thou what rage   80
Transports our adversary? whom no bounds
Prescribed, no bars of Hell, nor all the chains
Heaped on him there, nor yet the main abyss
Wide interrupt,[7] can hold; so bent he seems
On desperate revenge, that shall redound   85
Upon his own rebellious head. And now
Through all restraint broke loose he wings his way
Not far off Heaven, in the precincts of light,
Directly towards the new-created world,
And man there placed, with purpose to essay   90
If him by force he can destroy, or worse,
By some false guile pervert: and shall pervert;
For man will hearken to his glozing[8] lies,
And easily transgress the sole command,
Sole pledge of his obedience; so will fall   95
He and his faithless progeny. Whose fault?
Whose but his own? Ingrate, he had of me
All he could have; I made him just and right,
Sufficient to have stood, though free to fall.
Such I created all th' ethereal powers   100
And spirits, both them who stood and them who failed:
Freely they stood who stood, and fell who fell.
Not free, what proof could they have given sincere[9]
Of true allegiance, constant faith, or love,
Where only what they needs must do appeared,   105
Not what they would? What praise could they receive,
What pleasure I, from such obedience paid,
When Will and Reason (Reason also is Choice),
Useless and vain, of freedom both despoiled,
Made passive both, had served Necessity,   110

---

6. From the aspect of God's radiance the air is "dun," i.e., dusky; Satan is literally "sublime" in it, i.e., lifted up, aloft. But from where Satan hangs, outside the world's outer shell, he cannot be sure the world and its ten concentric spheres are not a single solid (line 75). The points of view are precisely distinguished.
7. Dividing, in between.
8. Flattering.
9. The delayed modifier is a favorite stylistic device of Milton's. "Sincere" goes with "proof."

Not me? They therefore as to right belonged,
So were created, nor can justly accuse
Their Maker or their making or their fate,
As if predestination overruled
Their will, disposed by absolute decree   115
Or high foreknowledge. They themselves decreed
Their own revolt, not I. If I foreknew,
Foreknowledge had no influence on their fault,
Which had no less proved certain unforeknown.[1]
So without least impulse or shadow of fate,   120
Or aught by me immutably foreseen,
They trespass, authors to themselves in all,
Both what they judge and what they choose; for so
I formed them free, and free they must remain
Till they enthrall themselves: I else must change   125
Their nature, and revoke the high decree
Unchangeable, eternal, which ordained
Their freedom; they themselves ordained their fall.
The first sort[2] by their own suggestion fell,
Self-tempted, self-depraved; man falls, deceived   130
By the other first: man therefore shall find grace;
The other, none. In mercy and justice both,[3]
Through Heaven and Earth, so shall my glory excel;
But mercy, first and last, shall brightest shine."
Thus while God spake ambrosial fragrance filled   135
All Heaven, and in the blessèd spirits elect
Sense of new joy ineffable diffused.
Beyond compare the Son of God was seen
Most glorious; in him all his Father shone
Substantially expressed; and in his face   140
Divine compassion visibly appeared,
Love without end, and without measure grace;
Which uttering, thus he to his Father spake:
    "O Father, gracious was that word which closed
Thy sovereign sentence, that man should find grace;   145
For which both Heaven and Earth shall high extol
Thy praises, with th' innumerable sound
Of hymns and sacred songs, wherewith thy throne
Encompassed shall resound thee ever blest.
For should man finally be lost, should man   150
Thy creature late so loved, thy youngest son,
Fall circumvented thus by fraud, though joined
With his own folly? That be from thee far,
That far be from thee, Father, who art judge
Of all things made, and judgest only right!   155
Or shall the adversary[4] thus obtain
His end, and frustrate thine? Shall he fulfill
His malice, and thy goodness bring to naught,

1. I.e., if I had not foreknown it.
2. The bad angels, Satan and his crew.
3. Mercy and justice are key terms in the poem. Their personifications here are separate: God is justice (He claims to be merciful, but His speech does not have this tone at all), the Son is mercy; but by book 12 Milton intends to show their identity.
4. *Satan* in Hebrew means "adversary."

Or proud return, though to his heavier doom,
Yet with revenge accomplished, and to Hell   160
Draw after him the whole race of mankind,
By him corrupted? Or wilt thou thyself
Abolish thy creation, and unmake
For him, what for thy glory thou hast made?
So should thy goodness and thy greatness both   165
Be questioned and blasphemed without defense."[5]
     To whom the great Creator thus replied:
"O Son, in whom my soul hath chief delight,
Son of my bosom, Son who art alone
My word, my wisdom, and effectual might,   170
All hast thou spoken as my thoughts are, all
As my eternal purpose hath decreed.[6]
Man shall not quite be lost, but saved who will;
Yet not of will in him, but grace in me
Freely vouchsafed. Once more I will renew   175
His lapsèd powers, though forfeit, and enthralled
By sin to foul exorbitant desires:
Upheld by me, yet once more he shall stand
On even ground against his mortal foe,
By me upheld,[7] that he may know how frail   180
His fallen condition is, and to me owe
All his deliverance, and to none but me.
Some I have chosen of peculiar grace,
Elect above the rest; so is my will:
The rest shall hear me call, and oft be warned   185
Their sinful state,[8] and to appease betimes
Th' incensèd Deity, while offered grace
Invites; for I will clear their senses dark
What may suffice,[9] and soften stony hearts
To pray, repent, and bring obedience due.   190
To prayer, repentance, and obedience due,
Though but endeavored with sincere intent,
Mine ear shall not be slow, mine eye not shut.
And I will place within them as a guide
My umpire Conscience; whom if they will hear,   195
Light after light well used they shall attain,[1]
And to the end persisting, safe arrive.
This my long sufferance and my day of grace
They who neglect and scorn shall never taste;
But hard be hardened, blind be blinded more,   200
That they may stumble on, and deeper fall;
And none but such from mercy I exclude.
     But yet all is not done. Man, disobeying,
Disloyal breaks his fealty, and sins
Against the high supremacy of Heaven,   205

5. The Son correctly intuits the motives expressed by
Beëlzebub in the great consult (2.362–376).
6. The Lord's speech is notably rhythmic, even rhymed.
7. Note the ambiguity: the second "by me upheld"
(line 180) may modify either "he" (line 178) or "his
mortal foe" (line 179). Both divine and hellish energy
are ultimately divine.
8. I.e., warned about their sinful state.
9. I.e., as much as need be.
1. By using light well, they will reach even more light
and, in the end, salvation.

Affecting godhead, and so losing all,
To expiate his treason hath naught left,
But to destruction sacred and devote,[2]
He with his whole posterity must die;
Die he or Justice must; unless for him   210
Some other, able and as willing,[3] pay
The rigid satisfaction, death for death.
Say, heavenly powers, where shall we find such love?
Which of ye will be mortal to redeem
Man's mortal crime,[4] and just th' unjust to save?   215
Dwells in all Heaven charity so dear?"
      He asked, but all the heavenly choir stood mute,[5]
And silence was in Heaven: on man's behalf
Patron or intercessor none appeared,
Much less that durst upon his own head draw   220
The deadly forfeiture and ransom set.
And now without redemption all mankind
Must have been lost, adjudged to Death and Hell
By doom severe, had not the Son of God,
In whom the fullness dwells of love divine,   225
His dearest mediation[6] thus renewed:
      "Father, thy word is passed, man shall find grace;
And shall Grace not find means, that finds her way,
The speediest of thy wingèd messengers,
To visit all thy creatures, and to all   230
Comes unprevented,[7] unimplored, unsought?
Happy for man, so coming! He her aid
Can never seek, once dead in sins and lost;
Atonement for himself, or offering meet,
Indebted and undone, hath none to bring.   235
Behold me, then: me for him, life for life,
I offer; on me let thine anger fall;
Account me man: I for his sake will leave
Thy bosom, and this glory next to thee
Freely put off, and for him lastly die   240
Well pleased; on me let Death wreak all his rage;
Under his gloomy power I shall not long
Lie vanquished. Thou hast given me to possess
Life in myself forever; by thee I live;
Though now to Death I yield, and am his due,   245
All that of me can die, yet that debt paid,
Thou wilt not leave me in the loathsome grave
His prey, nor suffer my unspotted soul
Forever with corruption there to dwell;
But I shall rise victorious, and subdue   250
My vanquisher, spoiled of his vaunted spoil.
Death his death's wound shall then receive, and stoop[8]

2. Dedicated, given up to. "Affecting": pretending to.
3. I.e., able to pay, and as willing as he is able.
4. Note that "mortal" means "human" in line 214 but "deadly" in line 215.
5. The silence of the good angels in face of a difficult

task parallels that of the devils in the great consult (2.420–426).
6. Intercession.
7. Unanticipated.
8. Be humbled, fall.

Inglorious, of his mortal sting disarmed;
I through the ample air in triumph high
Shall lead Hell captive maugre[9] Hell, and show   255
The powers of darkness bound. Thou at the sight
Pleased, out of Heaven shalt look down and smile,
While, by thee raised, I ruin[1] all my foes,
Death last, and with his carcass glut the grave;
Then with the multitude of my redeemed   260
Shall enter Heaven, long absent, and return,
Father, to see thy face, wherein no cloud
Of anger shall remain, but peace assured
And reconcilement: wrath shall be no more
Thenceforth, but in thy presence joy entire."   265
    His words here ended, but his meek aspèct
Silent yet spake, and breathed immortal love
To mortal men, above which only shone
Filial obedience: as a sacrifice
Glad to be offered, he attends the will   270
Of his great Father. Admiration[2] seized
All Heaven, what this might mean, and whither tend,
Wondering; but soon th' Almighty thus replied:
    "O thou in Heaven and Earth the only peace
Found out for mankind under wrath,[3] O thou   275
My sole complacence![4] well thou know'st how dear
To me are all my works; nor man the least,
Though last created, that for him I spare
Thee from my bosom and right hand, to save,
By losing thee a while, the whole race lost!   280
Thou, therefore, whom thou only canst redeem,
Their nature also to thy nature join,
And be thyself man among men on Earth,[5]
Made flesh, when time shall be, of virgin seed
By wondrous birth; be thou in Adam's room[6]   285
The head of all mankind, though Adam's son.[7]
As in him perish all men, so in thee,
As from a second root, shall be restored
As many as are restored; without thee, none.
His crime makes guilty all his sons; thy merit   290
Imputed shall absolve them who renounce
Their own both righteous and unrighteous deeds,[8]
And live in thee transplanted, and from thee
Receive new life. So man, as is most just,

---

9. In spite of (French *malgré*). The Son's triumph is represented in a series of extreme paradoxes—a vanquisher vanquished, a spoiler spoiled, death dead, Hell captured in all Hell's despite.
1. In the Latin sense, throw down.
2. Wonder, curiosity.
3. The Lord is looking to the future, when mankind will be under His wrath.
4. Contentment.
5. I.e., join the nature of those people (humankind), whom you alone can save, to your own nature; in other words, "Become a man and suffer the pains of mortality." The antecedent of "whom" is, loosely construed,

the "their" that follows it.
6. Place.
7. Adam is, properly, the "Old Adam." Christ is the Second Adam (there was a tradition that the Forbidden Tree and the Cross of Christ stood on the same spot). The Son of God, who long antedates the creation of Adam and who is actually the first created being (3.383), is historical Jesus Christ in one sense, an eternal spiritual principle in another.
8. I.e., the merit of Christ, imputed to human beings, frees from original sin those who renounce their own deeds both good and bad and hope to be saved by faith.

Shall satisfy for man, be judged and die,   295
And dying rise, and rising with him raise
His brethren, ransomed with his own dear life.
So heavenly love shall outdo hellish hate,
Giving to death, and dying to redeem,
So dearly to redeem, what hellish hate   300
So easily destroyed, and still destroys
In those who, when they may, accept not grace.
Nor shalt thou, by descending to assume
Man's nature, lessen or degrade thine own.
Because thou hast, though throned in highest bliss   305
Equal to God, and equally enjoying
Godlike fruition,⁹ quitted all to save
A world from utter loss, and hast been found
By merit more than birthright Son of God,¹
Found worthiest to be so by being good,   310
Far more than great or high; because in thee
Love hath abounded more than glory abounds;
Therefore thy humiliation shall exalt
With thee thy manhood also to this throne:
Here shalt thou sit incarnate, here shalt reign   315
Both God and man, Son both of God and man,
Anointed² universal King. All power
I give thee; reign forever, and assume
Thy merits; under thee, as Head Supreme,
Thrones, princedoms, powers, dominions, I reduce: 320
All knees to thee shall bow of them that bide
In Heaven, or Earth, or under Earth in Hell.
When thou, attended gloriously from Heaven,
Shalt in the sky appear, and from thee send
The summoning archangels to proclaim   325
Thy dread tribunal, forthwith from all winds
The living, and forthwith the cited³ dead
Of all past ages, to the general doom
Shall hasten; such a peal shall rouse their sleep.
Then, all thy saints assembled, thou shalt judge   330
Bad men and angels; they arraigned shall sink
Beneath thy sentence; Hell, her numbers full,
Thenceforth shall be forever shut. Meanwhile
The world shall burn, and from her ashes spring
New Heaven and Earth, wherein the just shall dwell,⁴   335
And after all their tribulations long
See golden days, fruitful of golden deeds,
With Joy and Love triùmphing, and fair Truth.
Then thou thy regal scepter shalt lay by;
For regal scepter then no more shall need;⁵   340
God shall be all in all. But all ye gods,⁶

9. Godlike pleasures, rewards.
1. An audacious doctrine, that Christ was Son of God by merit. Satan, one notes, was sultan of Hell on the same principle (see 2.5).
2. "The Anointed," in Hebrew, is the Messiah.
3. Summoned. "From all winds": from all directions.

4. The burning of Earth is based on 2 Peter 3.12–13.
5. Be needed.
6. In addressing the angels as gods, the Lord is merely indicating their share in His divinity; the word is not literal.

Adore him who, to compass all this, dies;
Adore the Son, and honor him as me."
  No sooner had th' Almighty ceased, but all
The multitude of angels with a shout   345
Loud as from numbers without number, sweet
As from blest voices, uttering joy, Heaven rung[7]
With jubilee, and loud hosannas filled
Th' eternal regions. Lowly reverent
Towards either throne[8] they bow, and to the ground   350
With solemn adoration down they cast
Their crowns inwove with amarant[9] and gold;
Immortal amarant, a flower which once
In Paradise, fast by the Tree of Life,
Began to bloom, but soon for man's offense   355
To Heaven removed, where first it grew, there grows
And flowers aloft, shading the Fount of Life,
And where the River of Bliss through midst of Heaven
Rolls o'er Elysian flowers her amber stream.[1]
With these, that never fade, the spirits elect   360
Bind their resplendent locks enwreathed with beams;
Now in loose garlands thick thrown off, the bright
Pavement, that like a sea of jasper shone,
Empurpled with celestial roses smiled.
Then, crowned again, their golden harps they took,   365
Harps ever tuned, that glittering by their side
Like quivers hung; and with preamble sweet
Of charming symphony they introduce
Their sacred song, and waken raptures high:
No voice exempt,[2] no voice but well could join   370
Melodious part; such concord is in Heaven.
  Thee, Father, first they sung, Omnipotent,
Immutable, Immortal, Infinite,[3]
Eternal King; thee, Author of all being,
Fountain of light, thyself invisible   375
Amidst the glorious brightness where thou sitt'st
Throned inaccessible, but when thou shad'st
The full blaze of thy beams, and through a cloud
Drawn round about thee like a radiant shrine,
Dark with excessive bright thy skirts appear,[4]   380
Yet dazzle Heaven, that brightest seraphim
Approach not, but with both wings veil their eyes.
Thee next they sang, of all creation first,
Begotten Son, divine similitude,
In whose conspicuous countenance, without cloud   385

7. "Multitude" (line 345) is the subject of the sentence, "rung" the verb, and "Heaven" the object.
8. Those of God and the Son.
9. Or "amaranth"; in Greek, "unwithering"—an unfading flower and hence a type of immortality, which could not continue on earth after humans became subject to death.
1. Milton draws freely, and with no sense of incongruity, on pagan properties for his Christian Heaven. "Amber": not yellow, but clear. Milton's epithets are

not always visually strong.
2. Abstaining.
3. Joshua Sylvester, in translating the long, pedestrian poem of Du Bartas on the creation, makes use of this line. It is the only example, and not a very striking one, of Milton's paralleling an English predecessor for ten consecutive syllables.
4. In this hymn, Milton's literary strategy, which hitherto has dictated a legal treatment of God, shifts to one more tinged with awe.

Made visible, th' Almighty Father shines,
Whom else[5] no creature can behold: on thee
Impressed th' effulgence of his glory abides;
Transfused on thee his ample spirit rests.
He Heaven of Heavens, and all the powers therein,   390
By thee created; and by thee threw down
Th' aspiring dominations.[6] Thou that day
Thy Father's dreadful thunder didst not spare,
Nor stop thy flaming chariot wheels that shook
Heaven's everlasting frame, while o'er the necks   395
Thou drov'st of warring angels disarrayed.
Back from pursuit, thy powers with loud acclaim
Thee only extolled, Son of thy Father's might,
To execute fierce vengeance on his foes.
Not so on man: him through their malice fallen,   400
Father of mercy and grace, thou didst not doom
So strictly, but much more to pity incline.
No sooner did thy dear and only Son
Perceive thee purposed not to doom frail man
So strictly, but much more to pity inclined,[7]   405
He, to appease thy wrath, and end the strife
Of mercy and justice in thy face discerned,
Regardless of the bliss wherein he sat
Second to thee, offered himself to die
For man's offense, O unexampled love!   410
Love nowhere to be found less than divine!
Hail, Son of God, Savior of men! Thy name
Shall be the copious matter of my[8] song
Henceforth, and never shall my harp thy praise
Forget, nor from thy Father's praise disjoin!   415
     Thus they in Heaven, above the starry sphere,
Their happy hours in joy and hymning spent.
Meanwhile, upon the firm opacous globe
Of this round world, whose first convex divides
The luminous inferior orbs, enclosed   420
From Chaos and th' inroad of Darkness old,
Satan alighted walks.[9] A globe far off
It seemed; now seems a boundless continent,
Dark, waste, and wild, under the frown of night
Starless exposed, and ever-threatening storms   425
Of Chaos blustering round, inclement sky,
Save on that side which from the wall of Heaven,
Though distant far, some small reflection gains
Of glimmering air less vexed with tempest loud.
Here walked the fiend at large in spacious field.   430
As when a vulture on Imaus bred,

5. Except for whom (if it were not for the Son, no
creature could see God).
6. I.e., the rebel angels.
7. A "than" or "but" is understood at the end of line
405. The repetition (lines 402, 405) suggests the choral
nature of the psalm. Note in lines 406–407 the reem-
phasis on a conflict of mercy and justice.
8. Either the angels are singing as a single chorus, or

Milton wishes to associate himself with them; possibly
both. The change of pronoun is deliberate and striking.
9. Satan is not on the earth's surface but on the outermost of the ten concentric spheres that make up the
created cosmos. This sphere is "opacous" (opaque) by
contrast with the inner nine (containing the planets
and the fixed stars), which are crystalline and transparent.

Whose snowy ridge the roving Tartar bounds,[1]
Dislodging from a region scarce of prey
To gorge the flesh of lambs or yeanling[2] kids
On hills where flocks are fed, flies toward the springs   435
Of Ganges or Hydaspes, Indian streams,[3]
But in his way lights on the barren plains
Of Sericana, where Chineses drive
With sails and wind their cany wagons light;
So, on this windy sea of land, the fiend   440
Walked up and down alone, bent on his prey:
Alone, for other creature in this place,
Living or lifeless, to be found was none—
None yet; but store hereafter from the earth
Up hither like aërial vapors flew   445
Of all things transitory and vain, when sin
With vanity had filled the works of men:
Both all things vain, and all who in vain things
Built their fond hopes of glory or lasting fame,
Or happiness in this or th' other life.[4]   450
All who have their reward on earth, the fruits
Of painful superstition and blind zeal,
Naught seeking but the praise of men, here find
Fit retribution, empty as their deeds;
All th' unaccomplished works of nature's hand,   455
Abortive, monstrous, or unkindly[5] mixed,
Dissolved on earth, fleet hither, and in vain,
Till final dissolution, wander here—
Not in the neighboring moon, as some have dreamed:
Those argent[6] fields more likely habitants,   460
Translated saints, or middle spirits hold,
Betwixt th' angelical and human kind.
Hither, of ill-joined sons and daughters born,
First from the ancient world those giants came,
With many a vain exploit, though then renowned:[7]   465
The builders next of Babel on the plain
Of Sennaar,[8] and still with vain design
New Babels, had they wherewithal, would build;
Others came single; he who, to be deemed
A god, leaped fondly into Etna flames,   470
Empedocles, and he who, to enjoy
Plato's Elysium, leaped into the sea,

1. Imaus, a ridge of mountains beyond the modern Himalayas, is described by Pliny (*Natural History* 6.17), and shown in Mercator's *Atlas*, as running north through Asia from modern Afghanistan to the Arctic Circle.
2. Newborn.
3. Both the Ganges and Hydaspes (a tributary of the Indus) rise from the mountains of northern India. Sericana (line 438) is an area in what is now Sinkiang province, in China.
4. Milton's Paradise of Fools (named in line 496) was probably inspired by Ariosto's equivalent valley on the moon (*Orlando Furioso*, canto 34; see line 459); it serves much the same function as Dante's Limbo, to dispose of those who deserve neither salvation nor

damnation. But, instead of indifferents, Milton's region is reserved for deluded victims of misplaced devotion, chiefly Roman Catholics.
5. Against "kind," against their own natures.
6. Silver. The moon Milton imagines, though only briefly, as a kind of middle Paradise.
7. The "giants in the earth," born of unnatural marriages between the "sons of God" and the daughters of men, are creatures "unkindly mixed" and therefore sent to the Paradise of Fools, "though then renowned," as Genesis 6.4 tells us.
8. Shinär, the plain of Babel, as in Genesis 11.2–9. Babel for Milton is an emblem of human pride and folly.

Cleombrotus; and many more, too long,[9]
Embryos and idiots, eremites and friars,
White, black, and gray, with all their trumpery.[1]   475
Here pilgrims roam, that strayed so far to seek
In Golgotha him dead who lives in Heaven;
And they who to be sure of paradise,
Dying put on the weeds of Dominic,
Or in Franciscan think to pass disguised.[2]   480
They pass the planets seven, and pass the fixed,
And that crystàlline sphere whose balance weighs
The trepidation talked, and that first moved;[3]
And now Saint Peter at Heaven's wicket seems
To wait them with his keys, and now at foot   485
Of Heaven's ascent they lift their feet, when, lo!
A violent cross wind from either coast
Blows them transverse ten thousand leagues awry
Into the devious air. Then might ye see
Cowls, hoods, and habits, with their wearers, tossed   490
And fluttered into rags; then relics, beads,
Indulgences, dispenses, pardons, bulls,
The sport of winds: all these upwhirled aloft
Fly o'er the backside[4] of the world far off
Into a limbo large and broad, since called   495
The Paradise of Fools; to few unknown
Long after, now unpeopled and untrod.
    All this dark globe the fiend found as he passed;
And long he wandered, till at last a gleam
Of dawning light turned thitherward in haste   500
His traveled steps. Far distant he descries,
Ascending by degrees magnificent
Up to the wall of Heaven, a structure high;
At top whereof, but far more rich, appeared
The work as of a kingly palace gate,   505
With frontispiece[5] of diamond and gold
Embellished; thick with sparkling orient gems
The portal shone, inimitable on earth
By model, or by shading pencil drawn.
The stairs were such as whereon Jacob saw   510
Angels ascending and descending, bands
Of guardians bright, when he from Esau fled

---

9. I.e., it would take too long to name them. Both Empedocles and Cleombrotus carried piety to the point of folly and suicide. Hell is reserved for the wilfully malicious; the Paradise of Fools, for the merely misguided.
1. Unnatural mixtures produce embryos and idiots; Milton adds to them hermits and friars (the white are Carmelites; the black, Dominicans; and the gray, Franciscans); he thinks they exemplify unnatural piety, frustrated by its very nature.
2. Pilgrims also are unnatural in their piety, because they worship the relic and forget the spirit. So are those who try to trick God into granting them salvation by wearing religious garb on their deathbeds. The traveler Thomas Coryat reported (1619), with severe Protestant disapproval, that Venetians often buried sinners in the cowls of Franciscan friars, hoping thus to slip them into heaven.
3. Milton follows their souls through the spheres of the moon and sun and the five then-known planets, that of the fixed stars, and the sphere responsible for what astronomers call "the trepidation," a periodic corrective shudder of the cosmos. This brings them to the outermost sphere, the prime mover, or *primum mobile*—the next step seems to be the empyrean itself.
4. Milton certainly means "backside" to have its vulgar connotation. All that Milton considered the "trumpery"—that is, the exterior and legal manifestations—of ecclesiasticism, is here cast aside as vanity.
5. Portico.

To Padan-Aram, in the field of Luz
Dreaming by night under the open sky,
And waking cried, *This is the gate of Heaven.*   515
Each stair mysteriously was meant, nor stood
There always, but drawn up to Heaven sometimes
Viewless;[6] and underneath a bright sea flowed
Of jasper, or of liquid pearl, whereon
Who after came from Earth sailing arrived   520
Wafted by angels, or flew o'er the lake
Rapt in a chariot drawn by fiery steeds.
The stairs were then let down, whether to dare
The fiend by easy ascent, or aggravate
His sad exclusion from the doors of bliss.[7]   525
Direct against which opened from beneath,
Just o'er the blissful seat of Paradise,
A passage down to th' Earth—a passage wide,
Wider by far than that of after-times
Over Mount Sion, and, though that were large,   530
Over the Promised Land to God so dear,
By which, to visit oft those happy tribes,
On high behests his angels to and fro
Passed frequent,[8] and his eye with choice regard
From Paneas, the fount of Jordan's flood,   535
To Beërsaba, where the Holy Land
Borders on Egypt and the Arabian shore.[9]
So wide the opening seemed, where bounds were set
To darkness, such as bound the ocean wave.
Satan from hence, now on the lower stair   540
That scaled by steps of gold to Heaven-gate,
Looks down with wonder at the sudden view
Of all this world at once. As when a scout,
Through dark and desert ways with peril gone
All night, at last by break of cheerful dawn   545
Obtains the brow of some high-climbing hill,
Which to his eye discovers unaware
The goodly prospect of some foreign land
First seen, or some renowned metropolis
With glistering spires and pinnacles adorned,   550
Which now the rising sun gilds with his beams;
Such wonder seized, though after Heaven seen,
The spirit malign, but much more envy seized,
At sight of all this world beheld so fair.
Round he surveys (and well might, where he stood   555
So high above the circling canopy
Of Night's extended shade), from eastern point
Of Libra to the fleecy star that bears

---

6. Invisible. The story of Jacob's vision is summarized from Genesis 28.1–19. The stairs of the ladder were meant "mysteriously"—each represented a stage of spiritual growth.
7. In either case, Milton implies, heavenly authorities were aware of Satan's approach.
8. The crystalline spheres would be impenetrable if there weren't passages, or holes, in them, through which heavenly—and, alas, diabolic—spirits could make their way. The visiting angels (act as) his eye (in maintaining) a choice regard over the chosen people.
9. From Paneas (or Dan) in northern Palestine to Beersaba, or Beersheba, near the Egyptian border—the whole land.

Andromeda far off Atlantic seas[1]
Beyond th' horizon; then from pole to pole   560
He views in breadth—and without longer pause
Down right into the world's first region throws
His flight precipitant, and winds with ease
Through the pure marble air his oblique way[2]
Amongst innumerable stars, that shone   565
Stars distant, but nigh-hand seemed other worlds.
Or other worlds they seemed, or happy isles,
Like those Hesperian gardens famed of old,
Fortunate fields, and groves, and flowery vales;[3]
Thrice happy isles! But who dwelt happy there   570
He stayed not to inquire: above them all
The golden sun, in splendor likest Heaven,
Allured his eye. Thither his course he bends,
Through the calm firmament (but up or down,
By center or eccentric, hard to tell,   575
Or longitude),[4] where the great luminary,
Aloof the vulgar constellations thick,
That from his lordly eye keep distance due,
Dispenses light from far; they, as they move
Their starry dance in numbers that compute   580
Days, months, and years, towards his all-cheering lamp
Turn swift their various motions, or are turned
By his magnetic beam, that gently warms
The universe, and to each inward part
With gentle penetration, though unseen,   585
Shoots invisible virtue even to the deep;[5]
So wondrously was set his station bright.

Summary   Landing on the bright orb of the sun, Satan disguises himself as a youthful cherub and approaches the solar guardian, the archangel Uriel. Pretending interest in the new great works of God, he gets directions to Earth and Adam's bower, then spirals down and lands on Mount Niphates (in modern Iran), overlooking the site of Paradise.

From Book 4

[Satan's Entry into Paradise; Adam and Eve in their Bower]

O for that warning voice which he who saw
Th' Apocalypse heard cry in Heaven aloud,
Then when the dragon, put to second rout,
Came furious down to be revenged on men,

1. In the Zodiac, Libra is diametrically opposite Aries, or the Ram ("the fleecy star"), which seems to carry the constellation Andromeda on its back.
2. "Marble" derives from the Greek word for "shining," but there's also a sense of solidity in the adjective to contrast with Satan's "oblique" approach.
3. The gardens of the Hesperides and the "fortunate isles" of Greek mythology lay far out in the Atlantic, almost like separate miniature worlds.
4. Milton is cautious about saying whether the sun or the earth is at the center of the created cosmos.
5. "Virtue" in the sense of influence or strength. For example, gold was thought to grow in the depths of the earth as a result of solar influence.

Woe to the inhabitants on Earth![6] that now,   5
While time was, our first parents had been warned
The coming of their secret foe, and scaped,
Haply so scaped, his mortal[7] snare! For now
Satan, now first inflamed with rage, came down,
The tempter ere th' accuser of mankind,   10
To wreak on innocent frail man his loss
Of that first battle, and his flight to Hell.
Yet not rejoicing in his speed though bold
Far off and fearless, nor with cause to boast,
Begins his dire attempt; which nigh the birth   15
Now rolling, boils in his tumultuous breast,
And like a devilish engine back recoils
Upon himself. Horror and doubt distract
His troubled thoughts, and from the bottom stir
The Hell within him; for within him Hell   20
He brings, and round about him, nor from Hell
One step no more than from himself can fly
By change of place.[8] Now conscience wakes despair
That slumbered, wakes the bitter memory
Of what he was, what is, and what must be   25
Worse; of worse deeds worse sufferings must ensue.
Sometimes towards Eden, which now in his view
Lay pleasant, his grieved look he fixes sad;
Sometimes towards heaven and the full-blazing sun,
Which now sat high in his meridian tower;[9]   30
Then, much revolving, thus in sighs began:
  "O thou that with surpassing glory crowned
Look'st from thy sole dominion like the god
Of this new world—at whose sight all the stars
Hide their diminished heads—to thee I call,   35
But with no friendly voice, and add thy name,
O sun, to tell thee how I hate thy beams,
That bring to my remembrance from what state
I fell, how glorious once above thy sphere,
Till pride and worse ambition threw me down,   40
Warring in Heaven against Heaven's matchless King!
Ah, wherefore? He deserved no such return
From me, whom he created what I was
In that bright eminence, and with his good
Upbraided none;[1] nor was his service hard.   45
What could be less than to afford him praise,
The easiest recompense, and pay him thanks,
How due! Yet all his good proved ill in me,
And wrought but malice. Lifted up so high,

6. John of Patmos, in Revelation 12, describes a war in heaven between dragon and angels, in the course of which a voice cries from heaven, "Woe to the inhabitants of the earth and of the sea!"
7. Deadly. "Haply": by good luck, happily. The reiterated "first" 's in lines 6, 9, and 12 refer back to "second" in line 3; Milton wants us to remember that his story was the first of all the Bible stories and is, as it were, their root.
8. Satan's proud statement that "the mind is its own place" (1.254) finds here its bitter ironic echo.
9. Midday, the height of noon. Milton's nephew Edward Phillips tells us that the speech that follows was the first part of the poem to be written, when Milton still thought of making it into a drama to be called *Adam Unparadised.*
1. Demanded no return for his benefits; the phrase echoes James 1.5.

I 'sdained subjection, and thought one step higher   50
Would set me highest, and in a moment quit[2]
The debt immense of endless gratitude,
So burdensome, still paying, still to owe,
Forgetful what from him I still received;
And understood not that a grateful mind   55
By owing owes not, but still pays, at once
Indebted and discharged—what burden then?
O had his powerful destiny ordained
Me some inferior angel, I had stood
Then happy; no unbounded hope had raised   60
Ambition. Yet why not? Some other power
As great might have aspired, and me, though mean,
Drawn to his part. But other powers as great
Fell not, but stand unshaken, from within
Or from without to all temptations armed!   65
Hadst thou[3] the same free will and power to stand?
Thou hadst. Whom hast thou then, or what, to accuse,
But Heaven's free love dealt equally to all?
Be then his love accursed, since, love or hate,
To me alike it deals eternal woe.   70
Nay, cursed be thou; since against his thy will
Chose freely what it now so justly rues.
Me miserable![4] which way shall I fly
Infinite wrath and infinite despair?
Which way I fly is Hell; myself am Hell;   75
And in the lowest deep a lower deep
Still threatening to devour me opens wide,
To which the Hell I suffer seems a Heaven.
O then at last relent! Is there no place
Left for repentance, none for pardon left?   80
None left but by submission; and that word
Disdain forbids me, and my dread of shame
Among the spirits beneath, whom I seduced
With other promises and other vaunts
Than to submit, boasting I could subdue   85
Th' omnipotent. Ay me! they little know
How dearly I abide that boast so vain,
Under what torments inwardly I groan.
While they adore me on the throne of Hell,
With diadem and scepter high advanced,   90
The lower still I fall, only supreme
In misery: such joy ambition finds!
But say I could repent and could obtain
By act of grace[5] my former state, how soon
Would height recall high thoughts, how soon unsay   95
What feigned submission swore! Ease would recant
Vows made in pain, as violent and void.
For never can true reconcilement grow

---

2. Acquit, pay off. " 'Sdained": disdained.   4. An exact Latinism, "me miserum!"
3. Satan addresses himself directly, as Adam will do   5. The correct technical term for a formal pardon is
under parallel circumstances in 10.758ff.   an "act of grace."

Where wounds of deadly hate have pierced so deep;
Which would but lead me to a worse relapse   100
And heavier fall: so should I purchase dear
Short intermission, bought with double smart.
This knows my punisher; therefore as far
From granting he, as I from begging, peace.
All hope excluded thus, behold, instead   105
Of us outcast, exiled, his new delight,
Mankind created, and for him this world!
So farewell hope, and with hope farewell fear,
Farewell remorse! All good to me is lost;
Evil, be thou my good: by thee at least   110
Divided empire with Heaven's king I hold,
By thee, and more than half perhaps will reign;
As man ere long, and this new world, shall know."
     Thus while he spake, each passion dimmed his face,
Thrice changed with pale—ire, envy, and despair;   115
Which marred his borrowed visage, and betrayed
Him counterfeit, if any eye beheld:
For heavenly minds from such distempers foul
Are ever clear. Whereof he soon aware
Each perturbation smoothed with outward calm,   120
Artificer of fraud; and was the first
That practiced falsehood under saintly show,
Deep malice to conceal, couched with revenge:
Yet not enough had practiced to deceive
Uriel, once warned; whose eye pursued him down   125
The way he went, and on th' Assyrian mount
Saw him disfigured, more than could befall
Spirit of happy sort: his gestures fierce
He marked and mad demeanor, then alone,
As he supposed, all unobserved, unseen.   130
     So on he fares, and to the border comes
Of Eden, where delicious Paradise,
Now nearer, crowns with her enclosure green
As with a rural mound the champaign[6] head
Of a steep wilderness, whose hairy sides   135
With thicket overgrown, grotesque[7] and wild,
Access denied; and overhead up grew
Insuperable height of loftiest shade,
Cedar, and pine, and fir, and branching palm,
A sylvan scene, and as the ranks ascend   140
Shade above shade, a woody theater[8]
Of stateliest view. Yet higher than their tops
The verdurous wall of Paradise up sprung;
Which to our general sire[9] gave prospect large
Into his nether empire neighboring round.   145
And higher than that wall a circling row

6. From French *champs*, open countryside. Paradise   mean romantic or picturesque.
is an open garden on top of a hill straddling a river in   8. As if in a Greek amphitheater, the trees are set row
the east of Eden.   on row.
7. One of the earliest uses of the word in English to   9. Adam.

Of goodliest trees loaden with fairest fruit,
Blossoms and fruits at once of golden hue,
Appeared, with gay enameled colors mixed;
On which the sun more glad impressed his beams   150
Than in fair evening cloud, or humid bow,[1]
When God hath showered the earth: so lovely seemed
That landscape. And of pure now purer air[2]
Meets his approach, and to the heart inspires
Vernal delight and joy, able to drive[3]   155
All sadness but despair. Now gentle gales,
Fanning their odoriferous wings, dispense
Native perfumes, and whisper whence they stole
Those balmy spoils. As when to them who sail
Beyond the Cape of Hope, and now are past   160
Mozambic, off at sea northeast winds blow
Sabean odors from the spicy shore
Of Araby the Blest,[4] with such delay
Well pleased they slack their course, and many a league
Cheered with the grateful smell old Ocean smiles;   165
So entertained those odorous sweets the fiend
Who came their bane, though with them better pleased
Than Asmodëus with the fishy fume
That drove him, though enamored, from the spouse
Of Tobit's son,[5] and with a vengeance sent   170
From Media post to Egypt, there fast bound.
    Now to th' ascent of that steep savage[6] hill
Satan had journeyed on, pensive and slow;
But further way found none; so thick entwined,
As one continued brake, the undergrowth   175
Of shrubs and tangling bushes had perplexed
All path of man or beast that passed that way.
One gate there only was, and that looked east
On th' other side; which when th' arch-felon saw,
Due entrance he disdained, and in contempt   180
At one slight bound high overleaped all bound[7]
Of hill or highest wall, and sheer within
Lights on his feet. As when a prowling wolf,
Whom hunger drives to seek new haunt for prey,
Watching where shepherds pen their flocks at eve   185
In hurdled cotes[8] amid the field secure,
Leaps o'er the fence with ease into the fold;
Or as a thief, bent to unhoard the cash

1. The rainbow. There is a thick wall of trees around Paradise, which "access denied"; then above them, the shaggy sides of Paradise itself ("the verdurous wall"), and above it the garden of fruit trees.
2. After breathing pure air, Satan now breathes even purer.
3. Drive out.
4. Coasting up East Africa after doubling the Cape of Good Hope, off "Mozambic" (Mozambique) one might, Milton supposes, meet "Sabean" (i.e., as from Sheba) odors coming from "Araby the Blest" (Arabia Felix). This is the fantasy of a man who learned his geography from medieval atlases and Diodorus Sicu-

lus, for the distance between Mozambique and Arabia is close to two thousand miles.
5. Milton retells briefly here the story of Tobias, Tobit's son, who married Sara and was saved from the fate of her seven previous husbands by the advice of Raphael, who showed him how to make a fishy smell that would drive away the devil Asmodeus. See the Book of Tobit among the Apocrypha.
6. Wooded, entangled (from Latin silvaticus, through Italian selvaggio and French sauvage).
7. Satan enters Paradise not only illegally but with a contemptuous pun.
8. Pens made of woven reeds.

Of some rich burgher, whose substantial doors,
Cross-barred and bolted fast, fear no assault,
In at the window climbs, or o'er the tiles; 190
So clomb[9] this first grand thief into God's fold:
So since into his church lewd hirelings[1] climb.
Thence up he flew, and on the Tree of Life,
The middle tree and highest there that grew, 195
Sat like a cormorant; yet not true life
Thereby regained, but sat devising death
To them who lived; nor on the virtue thought
Of that life-giving plant, but only used
For prospect,[2] what, well used, had been the pledge 200
Of immortality. So little knows
Any, but God alone, to value right
The good before him, but perverts best things
To worst abuse, or to their meanest use.
    Beneath him with new wonder now he views 205
To all delight of human sense exposed
In narrow room Nature's whole wealth; yea more,
A Heaven on Earth; for blissful Paradise
Of God the garden was, by him in the east
Of Eden planted. Eden stretched her line 210
From Auran eastward to the royal towers
Of great Seleucia, built by Grecian kings,
Or where the sons of Eden long before
Dwelt in Telassar.[3] In this pleasant soil
His far more pleasant garden God ordained. 215
Out of the fertile ground he caused to grow
All trees of noblest kind for sight, smell, taste;
And all amid them stood the Tree of Life,
High eminent, blooming ambrosial fruit
Of vegetable gold; and next to life, 220
Our death, the Tree of Knowledge, grew fast by—
Knowledge of good bought dear by knowing ill.
Southward through Eden went a river large,
Nor changed his course, but through the shaggy hill
Passed underneath engulfed; for God had thrown 225
That mountain, as his garden-mold,[4] high raised
Upon the rapid current, which, through veins
Of porous earth with kindly[5] thirst up drawn,
Rose a fresh fountain, and with many a rill
Watered the garden; thence united fell 230
Down the steep glade, and met the nether flood,

9. Old past tense of "climb," but used with a special feeling of ungainly energy. The whole metaphor, of God as a rich citizen hoarding Adam and Eve from Satan the second-story man, is instinct with comic feeling. On the devil as a thief, see John 10.1.
1. Base men interested only in money; Milton felt strongly that churchmen should be unsalaried to ensure the purity of their motives.
2. Perspective, lookout.
3. The "line" that Eden stretches is genealogical as well as geographical; the "children of Eden" are re-

ferred to several times in the Bible. "Auran" is an area in Syria, to the south of Damascus; "Seleucia," a powerful city founded by one of Alexander's generals (hence, "built by Grecian kings"), lies near modern Baghdad; and "Telassar" is another Near Eastern kingdom, this one probably on the east bank of the Euphrates.
4. The mountain is God's topsoil, out of which grows Paradise. The river (identified as the Tigris in 9.71) flowed under the hill.
5. Natural.

Which from his darksome passage now appears,
And now, divided into four main streams,
Runs diverse, wandering many a famous realm
And country, whereof here needs no account;[6]   235
But rather to tell how, if art could tell,
How from that sapphire fount the crispèd[7] brooks,
Rolling on orient pearl and sands of gold,
With mazy error[8] under pendant shades
Ran nectar, visiting each plant, and fed   240
Flowers worthy of Paradise; which not nice[9] art
In beds and curious knots, but Nature boon[1]
Poured forth profuse on hill and dale and plain,
Both where the morning sun first warmly smote
The open field, and where the unpierced shade   245
Embrowned[2] the noontide bowers. Thus was this place,
A happy rural seat of various view:[3]
Groves whose rich trees wept odorous gums and balm;
Others whose fruit, burnished with golden rind,
Hung amiable[4]—Hesperian fables true,   250
If true, here only—and of delicious taste.
Betwixt them lawns, or level downs, and flocks
Grazing the tender herb, were interposed,
Or palmy hillock; or the flowery lap
Of some irriguous[5] valley spread her store,   255
Flowers of all hue, and without thorn the rose.[6]
Another side, umbrageous[7] grots and caves
Of cool recess, o'er which the mantling vine
Lays forth her purple grape, and gently creeps
Luxuriant; meanwhile murmuring waters fall   260
Down the slope hills dispersed, or in a lake,
That to the fringèd bank with myrtle crowned
Her crystal mirror holds, unite their streams.
The birds their choir apply; airs,[8] vernal airs,
Breathing the smell of field and grove, attune   265
The trembling leaves, while universal Pan,[9]
Knit with the Graces and the Hours in dance,
Led on th' eternal spring.[1] Not that fair field
Of Enna, where Proserpin gathering flowers,
Herself a fairer flower, by gloomy Dis   270
Was gathered, which cost Ceres all that pain
To seek her through the world; nor that sweet grove
Of Daphne, by Orontes and th' inspired

---

6. Milton has in mind Genesis 2.10, but the expression "whereof here needs no account" dodges many questions about the correct translation of this passage.
7. Wavy, ruffled.
8. From Latin *errare*, "wandering."
9. Particular, careful.
1. Liberal, bounteous.
2. Darkened.
3. Aspect.
4. Lovely. These were real golden apples like those said to have existed in the Hesperides, fabulous islands of the Western Ocean; Paradise was the only place

where the fable of the Hesperides was literally true.
5. Well-watered.
6. Figuratively and literally, there was no need for thorns in Paradise.
7. Shady.
8. Either breezes or melodies, probably both. "Their choir apply": practice their song.
9. The god of all nature. "Pan" in Greek means "all," but it is also the name of the goat-legged nature god.
1. The god of nature dances with the Graces and Hours, an image of perfect harmony.

Castalian spring,[2] might with this Paradise
Of Eden strive; nor that Nyseian isle,   275
Girt with the river Triton, where old Cham,
Whom Gentiles Ammon call and Libyan Jove,
Hid Amalthea and her florid son
Young Bacchus from his stepdame Rhea's eye;[3]
Nor where Abassin kings their issue guard,   280
Mount Amara[4] (though this by some supposed
True Paradise), under the Ethiop line
By Nilus' head, enclosed with shining rock,
A whole day's journey high, but wide remote
From this Assyrian garden, where the fiend   285
Saw undelighted all delight, all kind
Of living creatures, new to sight and strange.
Two of far nobler shape, erect and tall,
Godlike erect,[5] with native honor clad
In naked majesty, seemed lords of all,   290
And worthy seemed; for in their looks divine
The image of their glorious Maker shone,
Truth, wisdom, sanctitude severe and pure—
Severe, but in true filial freedom[6] placed,
Whence true authority in men; though both   295
Not equal, as their sex not equal seemed;
For contemplation he and valor formed,
For softness she and sweet attractive grace;
He for God only, she for God in him.[7]
His fair large front[8] and eye sublime declared   300
Absolute rule; and hyacinthine[9] locks
Round from his parted forelock manly hung
Clustering, but not beneath his shoulders broad:
She, as a veil down to the slender waist,
Her unadornèd golden tresses wore   305
Disheveled, but in wanton ringlets waved
As the vine curls her tendrils,[1] which implied
Subjection, but required with gentle sway,
And by her yielded, by him best received,

2. Milton is comparing Paradise with the famous
beauty spots of antiquity. Enna in Sicily was a lovely
meadow from which "Proserpin" was kidnapped by
"gloomy Dis" (i.e., Pluto); her mother Ceres sought
her throughout the world. The grove of Daphne, near
Antioch and the Orontes River in the Near East, had
a spring called "Castalia" in imitation of the Muses'
fountain near Delphi.
3. The isle of Nysa in the river Triton in Tunisia was
where Ammon hid Bacchus, his child by Amalthea,
from the eye of his wife, Rhea. "Florid" (wine-flushed)
Bacchus, when he grew up, received the name of Dionysus in honor of his birthplace. The identification of
the Egyptian god Ammon or Hammon with Cham or
Ham, the son of Noah, is a piece of comparative anthropology like that in 10.580ff.
4. Finally, Paradise ("this Assyrian garden," line 285)
is finer than the royal residences atop Mt. Amara,
where the "Abassin" (Abyssinian) kings had a splendid
palace. Milton's authority for this exotic scene was Peter Heylyn (Cosmographie 4.64), from whom he took

several phrases direct. His passage then had an influence on the names and phrasings of Coleridge's Kubla
Khan.
5. By emphasizing the word "erect," Milton means to
distinguish humans from the beasts of the field, who
went "prone."
6. Though almost a paradox, the phrase suggests Milton's idea that true freedom always involves respect for
authority and hierarchy. Cf. Eve's foolish question,
"For inferior who is free?" (9.825).
7. Milton's ideas on the relations between the sexes
were the strict ones of his time and of Christian tradition: "The head of every man is Christ; and the head
of the woman is the man" (1 Corinthians 11.3).
8. Forehead.
9. A classical metaphor, often applied to hair, and implying "dark" or perhaps "flowing," but actually not
very definite in its import.
1. Eve's hair is curly, abundant, uncontrolled; like the
vegetation in Paradise, it clings seductively about a severe and masculine virtue.

Yielded with coy[2] submission, modest pride,   310
And sweet, reluctant, amorous delay.
Nor those mysterious parts were then concealed;
Then was not guilty shame. Dishonest shame
Of Nature's works, honor dishonorable,
Sin-bred, how have ye troubled all mankind   315
With shows instead, mere shows of seeming pure,
And banished from man's life his happiest life,
Simplicity and spotless innocence!
So passed they naked on, nor shunned the sight
Of God or angel, for they thought no ill;   320
So hand in hand they passed, the loveliest pair
That ever since in love's embraces met:
Adam the goodliest man of men since born
His sons; the fairest of her daughters Eve.[3]
Under a tuft of shade that on a green   325
Stood whispering soft, by a fresh fountain-side,
They sat them down; and after no more toil
Of their sweet gardening labor than sufficed
To recommend cool Zephyr,[4] and made ease
More easy, wholesome thirst and appetite   330
More grateful, to their supper fruits they fell,
Nectarine fruits which the compliant boughs
Yielded them, sidelong as they sat recline
On the soft downy bank damasked with flowers.
The savory pulp they chew, and in the rind   335
Still as they thirsted scoop the brimming stream;
Nor gentle purpose, nor endearing smiles
Wanted,[5] nor youthful dalliance, as beseems
Fair couple linked in happy nuptial league,
Alone as they. About them frisking played   340
All beasts of th' earth, since wild, and of all chase[6]
In wood or wilderness, forest or den.
Sporting the lion ramped,[7] and in his paw
Dandled the kid; bears, tigers, ounces, pards,[8]
Gamboled before them; th' unwieldy elephant   345
To make them mirth used all his might, and wreathed
His lithe proboscis; close the serpent sly,
Insinuating,[9] wove with Gordian twine
His braided train,[1] and of his fatal guile
Gave proof unheeded. Others on the grass   350
Couched, and now filled with pasture gazing sat,
Or bedward ruminating;[2] for the sun,
Declined, was hasting now with prone career
To th' ocean isles,[3] and in th' ascending scale

2. Shy.
3. Logically these constructions are absurd; Adam was
not born since his day, Eve was not one of her own
daughters. Milton combines comparative with superlative forms for emphatic effect.
4. I.e., to make a cool breeze welcome.
5. Lacked. "Purpose": conversation.
6. Who lurk in every sort of cover.
7. Reared up.

8. Lynxes and leopards.
9. Writhing and twisting, but with a glance at the
Tempter's rhetorical techniques.
1. Checkered body. "Gordian twine": knots, like the
Gordian knot cut by Alexander the Great.
2. The animals are chewing their cuds before bed-
time; in Paradise, where the animal kingdom is not yet
subject to death, they are perforce vegetarians.
3. The Azores.

Of heaven the stars that usher evening rose: 355
When Satan, still in gaze as first he stood,
Scarce thus at length failed speech recovered sad:[4]
    "O Hell! what do mine eyes with grief behold?
Into our room of bliss thus high advanced
Creatures of other mold, Earth-born perhaps,   360
Not spirits, yet to heavenly spirits bright
Little inferior; whom my thoughts pursue
With wonder, and could love; so lively shines
In them divine resemblance, and such grace
The hand that formed them on their shape hath poured.[5]   365
Ah! gentle pair, ye little think how nigh
Your change approaches, when all these delights
Will vanish, and deliver ye to woe,
More woe, the more your taste is now of joy:
Happy, but for so happy[6] ill secured   370
Long to continue, and this high seat, your Heaven,
Ill fenced for Heaven to keep out such a foe
As now is entered; yet no purposed foe
To you, whom I could pity thus forlorn,
Though I unpitied. League with you I seek,   375
And mutual amity so strait, so close,
That I with you must dwell, or you with me,
Henceforth.[7] My dwelling, haply, may not please,
Like this fair Paradise, your sense; yet such
Accept your Maker's work; he gave it me,   380
Which I as freely give. Hell shall unfold,
To entertain you two, her widest gates,
And send forth all her kings; there will be room,
Not like these narrow limits, to receive
Your numerous offspring; if no better place,   385
Thank him who puts me, loath, to this revenge
On you, who wrong me not, for him who wronged.[8]
And should I at your harmless innocence
Melt, as I do, yet public reason just—
Honor and empire with revenge enlarged   390
By conquering this new world—compels me now
To do what else, though damned, I should abhor."[9]
    So spake the fiend, and with necessity,
The tyrant's plea, excused his devilish deeds.
Then from his lofty stand on that high tree   395
Down he alights among the sportful herd
Of those four-footed kinds, himself now one,
Now other, as their shape served best his end
Nearer to view his prey, and unespied
To mark what of their state he more might learn   400

---

4. The choked, laborious line mirrors Satan's heavy, congested mind.
5. Though Satan's moral values are topsy-turvy ("Evil, be thou my good," he has said in the first part of book 4), his aesthetic values are strictly orthodox.
6. Such happiness.
7. Though it starts in simple admiration, Satan's friendship for humankind is, at the end, grisly and sardonic. The turning point seems to be "though I unpitied."
8. I.e., it's not my fault; Satan's favorite evasion.
9. Satan's final reason for destroying Adam and Eve is thoroughly Satanic; it is *ragione di stato*, reason of state, the public interest.

By word or action marked. About them round
A lion now he stalks with fiery glare;
Then as a tiger, who by chance hath spied
In some purlieu[1] two gentle fawns at play,
Straight couches close; then, rising, changes oft   405
His couchant watch, as one who chose his ground,
Whence rushing he might surest seize them both
Gripped in each paw; when Adam first of men
To first of women Eve thus moving speech,
Turned him all ear to hear new utterance flow.   410
     "Sole partner and sole part of all these joys,[2]
Dearer thyself than all; needs must the power
That made us, and for us this ample world,
Be infinitely good, and of his good
As liberal and free as infinite,   415
That raised us from the dust and placed us here
In all this happiness, who at his hand
Have nothing merited, nor can perform
Aught of which he hath need; he who requires
From us no other service than to keep   420
This one, this easy charge, of all the trees
In Paradise that bear delicious fruit
So various, not to taste that only Tree
Of Knowledge, planted by the Tree of Life,
So near grows death to life, whate'er death is,   425
Some dreadful thing, no doubt; for well thou know'st
God hath pronounced it death to taste that tree,
The only sign of our obedience left
Among so many signs of power and rule
Conferred upon us, and dominion given   430
Over all other creatures that possess
Earth, air, and sea. Then let us not think hard
One easy prohibition, who enjoy
Free leave so large to all things else, and choice
Unlimited of manifold delights;   435
But let us ever praise him, and extol
His bounty, following our delightful task
To prune these growing plants and tend these flowers,
Which were it toilsome, yet with thee were sweet."
     To whom thus Eve replied: "O thou for whom   440
And from whom I was formed flesh of thy flesh,
And without whom am to no end, my guide
And head, what thou hast said is just and right.
For we to him indeed all praises owe
And daily thanks, I chiefly who enjoy   445
So far the happier lot, enjoying thee
Preeminent by so much odds, while thou
Like consort to thyself canst nowhere find.

---

1. The outskirt of a forest. Note that Satan can and
does enter any animal he wants; it is only for the
special purposes of the temptation that he finds the
serpent specially convenient.

2. Eve shares Adam's joys, and is herself the principal
part of them. The speeches of the happy couple turn
him (Satan) all ear.

That day I oft remember, when from sleep
I first awaked, and found myself reposed   450
Under a shade on flowers, much wondering where
And what I was, whence thither brought, and how.
Not distant far from thence a murmuring sound
Of waters issued from a cave and spread
Into a liquid plain, then stood unmoved,   455
Pure as th' expanse of heaven; I thither went
With unexperienced thought, and laid me down
On the green bank, to look into the clear
Smooth lake that to me seemed another sky.
As I bent down to look, just opposite,   460
A shape within the wat'ry gleam appeared,
Bending to look on me. I started back,
It started back; but pleased I soon returned,
Pleased it returned as soon with answering looks
Of sympathy and love. There I had fixed   465
Mine eyes till now, and pined with vain desire,[3]
Had not a voice thus warned me: 'What thou seest,
What there thou seest, fair creature, is thyself;
With thee it came and goes. But follow me,
And I will bring thee where no shadow stays   470
Thy coming, and thy soft embraces, he
Whose image thou art, him thou shalt enjoy
Inseparably thine, to him shalt bear
Multitudes like thyself, and thence be called
Mother of human race.' What could I do   475
But follow straight, invisibly thus led?
Till I espied thee, fair indeed and tall
Under a platan,[4] yet methought less fair,
Less winning soft, less amiably mild
Than that smooth wat'ry image. Back I turned;   480
Thou following cried'st aloud, 'Return, fair Eve,
Whom fli'st thou? whom thou fli'st, of him thou art,
His flesh, his bone; to give thee being I lent
Out of my side to thee, nearest my heart,
Substantial life, to have thee by my side   485
Henceforth an individual solace dear.
Part of my soul I seek thee, and thee claim
My other half.' With that, thy gentle hand
Seized mine, I yielded, and from that time see
How beauty is excelled by manly grace   490
And wisdom, which alone is truly fair."
   So spake our general mother, and with eyes
Of conjugal attraction unreproved
And meek surrender, half embracing leaned
On our first father; half her swelling breast   495
Naked met his under the flowing gold

3. The fate of Narcissus, who fell in love with his own
reflection, is hinted at. Like most men of his day, Milton followed the apostle Peter in thinking woman "the
weaker vessel," and the attitude pervades his treatment
of Eve.

4. Plane tree, with broad leaves and spreading
branches.

Of her loose tresses hid. He in delight
Both of her beauty and submissive charms
Smiled with superior love, as Jupiter
On Juno smiles, when he impregns the clouds   500
That shed May flowers, and pressed her matron lip
With kisses pure. Aside the Devil turned
For envy, yet with jealous leer malign
Eyed them askance, and to himself thus plained:[5]
     "Sight hateful, sight tormenting! thus these two   505
Imparadised in one another's arms,
The happier Eden, shall enjoy their fill
Of bliss on bliss, while I to Hell am thrust,
Where neither joy nor love, but fierce desire,
Among our other torments not the least,   510
Still unfulfilled with pain of longing pines.
Yet let me not forget what I have gained
From their own mouths: all is not theirs, it seems.
One fatal tree there stands, of knowledge called,
Forbidden them to taste. Knowledge forbidden?   515
Suspicious, reasonless. Why should their lord
Envy them that? Can it be sin to know,
Can it be death? and do they only stand
By ignorance, is that their happy state,
The proof of their obedience and their faith?   520
O fair foundation laid whereon to build
Their ruin! Hence I will excite their minds
With more desire to know, and to reject
Envious commands, invented with design
To keep them low whom knowledge might exalt   525
Equal with gods. Aspiring to be such,
They taste and die; what likelier can ensue?
But first with narrow search I must walk round
This garden, and no corner leave unspied;
A chance but chance[6] may lead where I may meet   530
Some wandering spirit of Heaven, by fountain side
Or in thick shade retired, from him to draw
What further would be learnt. Live while ye may,
Yet happy pair; enjoy, till I return,
Short pleasures, for long woes are to succeed."   535
     So saying, his proud step he scornful turned,
But with sly circumspection, and began
Through wood, through waste, o'er hill, o'er dale his roam.
Meanwhile, in utmost longitude, where heaven
With earth and ocean meets, the setting sun   540
Slowly descended, and with right aspèct
Against the eastern gate of Paradise
Leveled his evening rays.[7] It was a rock
Of alabaster piled up to the clouds,
Conspicuous far, winding with one ascent   545

5. Complained.   7. Setting in the west, the sun can strike the eastern
6. An opportunity, even if only an accident.   gate only from the inside. "Right aspèct": direct view.

Accessible from earth, one entrance high;
The rest was craggy cliff that overhung
Still as it rose, impossible to climb.
Betwixt these rocky pillars Gabriel sat,
Chief of th' angelic guards, awaiting night;   550
About him exercised heroic games
Th' unarmèd youth of Heaven, but nigh at hand
Celestial armory, shields, helms, and spears,
Hung high with diamond flaming and with gold.
Thither came Uriel, gliding through the even   555
On a sunbeam, swift as a shooting star
In autumn thwarts the night when vapors fired[8]
Impress the air, and shows the mariner
From what point of his compass to beware
Impetuous winds.[9] He thus began in haste: 560
    "Gabriel, to thee thy course by lot hath given
Charge and strict watch that to this happy place
No evil thing approach or enter in.
This day at height of noon came to my sphere
A spirit, zealous (as he seemed) to know   565
More of th' Almighty's works and chiefly man,
God's latest image. I described his way
Bent all on speed, and marked his airy gait;[1]
But in the mount that lies from Eden north,
Where he first lighted, soon discerned his looks   570
Alien from Heaven, with passions foul obscured.
Mine eye pursued him still, but under shade
Lost sight of him. One of the banished crew
I fear hath ventured from the deep to raise
New troubles; him thy care must be to find."   575
    To whom the wingèd warrior thus returned:
"Uriel, no wonder if thy perfect sight
Amid the sun's bright circle where thou sit'st
See far and wide. In at this gate none pass
The vigilance here placed, but such as come   580
Well known from Heaven; and since meridian hour[2]
No creature thence. If spirit of other sort
So minded have o'erleaped these earthy bounds
On purpose, hard thou know'st it to exclude
Spiritual substance with corporeal bar.   585
But if within the circuit of these walks
In whatsoever shape he lurk of whom
Thou tell'st, by morrow dawning I shall know."
    So promised he, and Uriel to his charge
Returned on that bright beam, whose point now raised   590
Bore him slope downward to the sun now fallen
Beneath th' Azores, whether the prime orb,
Incredible how swift, had thither rolled
Diurnal, or this less volùble earth

---

8. Heat lightning. "Thwarts": flies across.   1. Course. "Described": descried.
9. Meteors were thought to indicate by the direction   2. Noon.
of their fall the source of oncoming storms.

By shorter flight to th' east[3] had left him there   595
Arraying with reflected purple and gold
The clouds that on his western throne attend.
Now came still evening on, and twilight gray
Had in her sober livery all things clad.
Silence accompanied, for beast and bird,   600
They to their grassy couch, these to their nests,
Were slunk, all but the wakeful nightingale;
She all night long her amorous descant sung.
Silence was pleased; now glowed the firmament
With living sapphires; Hesperus[4] that led   605
The starry host rode brightest, till the moon,
Rising in clouded majesty, at length
Apparent queen unveiled her peerless light
And o'er the dark her silver mantle threw.
     When Adam thus to Eve: "Fair consort, th' hour   610
Of night and all things now retired to rest
Mind us of like repose, since God hath set
Labor and rest as day and night to men
Successive, and the timely dew of sleep
Now falling with soft slumbrous weight inclines   615
Our eyelids. Other creatures all day long
Rove idle unemployed, and less need rest;
Man hath his daily work of body or mind
Appointed, which declares his dignity
And the regard of Heaven on all his ways,   620
While other animals unactive range,
And of their doings God takes no account.
Tomorrow ere fresh morning streak the east
With first approach of light, we must be risen
And at our pleasant labor, to reform   625
Yon flow'ry arbors, yonder alleys green,
Our walk at noon, with branches overgrown
That mock our scant manuring,[5] and require
More hands than ours to lop their wanton growth.
Those blossoms also and those dropping gums   630
That lie bestrown unsightly and unsmooth
Ask riddance, if we mean to tread with ease;
Meanwhile, as nature wills, night bids us rest."
     To whom thus Eve with perfect beauty adorned:
"My author and disposer, what thou bidd'st   635
Unargued I obey; so God ordains.
God is thy law, thou mine; to know no more
Is woman's happiest knowledge and her praise.
With thee conversing I forget all time,
All seasons and their change, all please alike.[6]   640

3. Again Milton avoids the question whether sun
moves around earth or vice versa; he clearly enjoys Uriel's trick of sliding down a sunbeam to reach the earth
and then (relative positions having changed) down the
same beam back to his sunny post. "Volùble": swift-
turning.
4. The evening star, Venus. "Descant": melody. (Des-

cant has more technical meanings as well, but not
here.)
5. Cultivating.
6. As there are no seasons in Paradise, Eve must mean
the times of day. Her incantatory repetitions echo similar effects in the Song of Solomon.

Sweet is the breath of morn, her rising sweet,
With charm of earliest birds; pleasant the sun
When first on this delightful land he spreads
His orient beams on herb, tree, fruit, and flower
Glistering with dew; fragrant the fertile earth   645
After soft showers; and sweet the coming on
Of grateful evening mild, then silent night
With this her solemn bird and this fair moon
And these the gems of heaven, her starry train:
But neither breath of morn when she ascends   650
With charm of earliest birds, nor rising sun
On this delightful land, nor herb, fruit, flower
Glistering with dew, nor fragrance after showers,
Nor grateful evening mild, nor silent night
With this her solemn bird, nor walk by moon   655
Or glittering starlight without thee is sweet.
But wherefore all night long shine these, for whom
This glorious sight, when sleep hath shut all eyes?"
      To whom our general ancestor replied:
"Daughter of God and Man, accomplished Eve,   660
Those have their course to finish round the earth
By morrow evening, and from land to land
In order, though to nations yet unborn,
Minist'ring light prepared, they set and rise,
Lest total darkness should by night regain   665
Her old possession, and extinguish life
In nature and all things, which these soft fires
Not only enlighten, but with kindly heat
Of various influence foment[7] and warm,
Temper or nourish, or in part shed down   670
Their stellar virtue on all kinds that grow
On earth, made hereby apter to receive
Perfection from the sun's more potent ray.[8]
These, then, though unbeheld in deep of night,
Shine not in vain; nor think, though men were none,   675
That heaven would want spectators, God want praise.
Millions of spiritual creatures walk the earth
Unseen, both when we wake and when we sleep;
All these with ceaseless praise his works behold
Both day and night. How often from the steep   680
Of echoing hill or thicket have we heard
Celestial voices to the midnight air
Sole or responsive each to other's note,
Singing their great Creator: oft in bands
While they keep watch or nightly rounding walk,   685
With heavenly touch of instrumental sounds
In full harmonic number joined, their songs
Divide the night and lift our thoughts to Heaven."
      Thus talking, hand in hand alone they passed
On to their blissful bower. It was a place   690

7. Cherish, nurture.   influence and also to modulate that of the sun. Before
8. The stars were thought to have their own occult   the Fall, all these influences were "kindly" (benign).

Chos'n by the sovereign planter when he framed
All things to man's delightful use; the roof
Of thickest covert was inwoven shade,
Laurel and myrtle, and what higher grew
Of firm and fragrant leaf; on either side,   695
Acanthus and each odorous bushy shrub
Fenced up the verdant wall. Each beauteous flower,
Iris all hues, roses, and jessamine
Reared high their flourished heads between, and wrought
Mosaic; underfoot the violet,   700
Crocus, and hyacinth with rich inlay
Broidered the ground, more colored than with stone
Of costliest emblem.[9] Other creature here,
Beast, bird, insect, or worm durst enter none,
Such was their awe of man. In shadier bower,   705
More sacred and sequestered, though but feigned,
Pan or Silvanus never slept, nor Nymph
Nor Faunus[1] haunted. Here in close recess
With flowers, garlands, and sweet-smelling herbs
Espousèd Eve decked first her nuptial bed,   710
And heavenly choirs the hymenean[2] sung,
What day the genial angel to our sire
Brought her in naked beauty more adorned,
More lovely than Pandora, whom the gods
Endowed with all their gifts, and O too like   715
In sad event, when to th' unwiser son
Of Japhet brought by Hermes, she ensnared
Mankind with her fair looks, to be avenged
On him who had stole Jove's authentic fire.[3]
    Thus at their shady lodge arrived, both stood,   720
Both turned, and under open sky adored
The God that made both sky, air, earth, and heaven
Which they beheld, the moon's resplendent globe
And starry pole: "Thou also mad'st the night,
Maker omnipotent, and thou the day,   725
Which we in our appointed work employed
Have finished happy in our mutual help
And mutual love, the crown of all our bliss
Ordained by thee, and this delicious place
For us too large, where thy abundance wants   730
Partakers, and uncropped falls to the ground.
But thou hast promised from us two a race
To fill the earth, who shall with us extol
Thy goodness infinite, both when we wake
And when we seek, as now, thy gift of sleep."   735
    This said unanimous, and other rites

---

9. Inlaid work.
1. Forest and field divinities of classical mythology.
2. Marriage hymn.
3. Pandora was an artificial woman, molded of clay, bestowed by the gods on Epimetheus, brother of Prometheus. ("Epimetheus" means "hind-sighted"; "Prometheus," "fore-sighted"; "Pandora," "all gifts.") The

brothers were sons of Iapetos, whom Milton identifies with Japhet, Noah's third son. Pandora's dowry consisted of a closed box, which foolish Epimetheus opened; all the ills of the human race flew out, leaving only hope behind. The Eve-Pandora parallel was often used by learned misogynists.

Observing none, but adoration pure
Which God likes best,[4] into their inmost bower
Handed they went; and, eased the putting off
Those troublesome disguises which we wear,   740
Straight side by side were laid. Nor turned, I ween,
Adam from his fair spouse, nor Eve the rites
Mysterious of connubial love refused —
Whatever hypocrites austerely talk
Of purity and place and innocence,   745
Defaming as impure what God declares
Pure and commands to some, leaves free to all.
Our Maker bids increase,[5] who bids abstain
But our destroyer, foe to God and man?
Hail wedded love, mysterious law, true source   750
Of human offspring, sole propriety[6]
In Paradise of all things common else.
By thee adulterous lust was driven from men
Among the bestial herds to range, by thee
Founded in reason, loyal, just, and pure,   755
Relations dear and all the charities[7]
Of father, son, and brother first were known.
Far be 't that I should write thee sin or blame,
Or think thee unbefitting holiest place,
Perpetual fountain of domestic sweets,   760
Whose bed is undefiled and chaste pronounced,
Present or past, as saints and patriarchs used.[8]
Here Love his golden shafts employs, here lights
His constant lamp and waves his purple wings,
Reigns here and revels; not in the bought smile   765
Of harlots, loveless, joyless, unindeared,
Casual fruition, nor in court amours,
Mixed dance or wanton masque or midnight ball
Or serenade, which the starved lover sings
To his proud fair, best quitted with disdain.   770
These, lulled by nightingales, embracing slept,
And on their naked limbs the flowery roof
Showered roses, which the morn repaired.[9] Sleep on,
Blest pair; and O yet happiest if ye seek
No happier state, and know to know no more.[1]   775

Summary   Fulfilling his promise to Uriel, Gabriel divides his night watch into search parties, assigning Ithuriel and Zephon to guard closely the bower of Adam and Eve. They find Satan in the bower, whispering in the ear of the sleeping Eve,

4. Like many Puritans, Milton hated set forms of prayer. Adam and Eve pray spontaneously, hence (we are to think) sincerely. "Handed" (line 739): hand in hand; "eased": spared. (As they wore no clothes, they did not have to undress.)
5. Genesis 1.28.
6. Property, specifically private property.

7. Affections.
8. Throughout history ("present or past"), Milton says, matrimony has been an honorable estate. The "golden shafts" (arrows) of Cupid produce true love.
9. Replaced.
1. I.e., know enough to be content with what you know.

and bring him before Gabriel. A battle impends, but is averted by a heavenly
signal, and Satan flees out of Paradise.

From Book 5

[*Eve's Dream: Trouble in Paradise*]

Now Morn her rosy steps in th' eastern clime
Advancing, sowed the earth with orient pearl,
When Adam waked, so customed, for his sleep
Was airy light, from pure digestion bred
And temperate vapors bland, which the only sound   5
Of leaves and fuming rills, Aurora's fan,
Lightly dispersed, and the shrill matin[2] song
Of birds on every bough; so much the more
His wonder was to find unwakened Eve
With tresses discomposed and glowing cheek   10
As through unquiet rest; he on his side
Leaning half-raised with looks of cordial love
Hung over her enamored, and beheld
Beauty which whether waking or asleep
Shot forth peculiar graces; then with voice   15
Mild as when Zephyrus on Flora[3] breathes,
Her soft hand touching, whispered thus. "Awake,
My fairest, my espoused, my latest found,
Heaven's last best gift, my ever new delight,
Awake, the morning shines, and the fresh field   20
Calls us: we lose the prime, to mark how spring
Our tended plants, how blows the citron grove,
What drops the myrrh and what the balmy reed,
How nature paints her colors, how the bee
Sits on the bloom extracting liquid sweet."[4]   25
    Such whispering waked her, but with startled eye
On Adam, whom embracing, thus she spake:
    "O sole in whom my thoughts find all repose,
My glory, my perfection, glad I see
Thy face, and morn returned, for I this night—   30
Such night till this I never passed—have dreamed,
If dreamed, not as I oft am wont, of thee,
Works of day past or morrow's next design,
But of offense and trouble, which my mind
Knew never till this irksome night. Methought   35
Close at mine ear one called me forth to walk
With gentle voice; I thought it thine; it said,
'Why sleepest thou, Eve? Now is the pleasant time,
The cool, the silent, save where silence yields
To the night-warbling bird, that now awake   40

---

2. Morning. The fan of Aurora (goddess of dawn) is
the rustling leaves, as the "orient pearl" of line 2 is
dewdrops.
3. Zephyrus is god of the gentle west wind, Flora god-

dess of flowers. "Peculiar": distinctive.
4. Adam's good morning to Eve is phrased after the
Song of Solomon.

Tunes sweetest his love-labored song; now reigns
Full-orbed the moon, and with more pleasing light
Shadowy sets off the face of things—in vain
If none regard. Heaven wakes with all his eyes,[5]
Whom to behold but thee, nature's desire,   45
In whose sight all things joy with ravishment
Attracted by thy beauty still to gaze.'
I rose as at thy call, but found thee not;
To find thee I directed then my walk;
And on, methought, alone I passed through ways   50
That brought me on a sudden to the tree
Of interdicted knowledge: fair it seemed,
Much fairer to my fancy than by day;
And as I wondering looked, beside it stood
One shaped and winged like one of those from Heaven   55
By us oft seen. His dewy locks distilled
Ambrosia;[6] on that tree he also gazed:
And 'O fair plant,' said he, 'with fruit surcharged,
Deigns none to ease thy load and taste thy sweet,
Nor god nor man? is knowledge so despised?   60
Or envy or what reserve forbids to taste?[7]
Forbid who will, none shall from me withhold
Longer thy offered good, why else set here?'
This said, he paused not, but with venturous arm
He plucked, he tasted; me damp horror chilled   65
At such bold words vouched with a deed so bold.
But he thus overjoyed: 'O fruit divine,
Sweet of thyself, but much more sweet thus cropped,
Forbidden here, it seems, as only fit
For gods, yet able to make gods of men: 70
And why not gods of men, since good, the more
Communicated, more abundant grows,
The author not impaired, but honored more?
Here, happy creature, fair angelic Eve,
Partake thou also; happy though thou art,   75
Happier thou may'st be, worthier canst not be.
Taste this, and be henceforth among the gods
Thyself a goddess, not to earth confined,
But sometimes in the air, as we, sometimes
Ascend to Heaven, by merit thine, and see   80
What life the gods live there, and such live thou.'
So saying, he drew nigh, and to me held,
Even to my mouth of that same fruit held part
Which he had plucked; the pleasant savory smell
So quickened appetite that I, methought,   85
Could not but taste. Forthwith up to the clouds
With him I flew, and underneath beheld
The earth outstretched immense, a prospect wide
And various: wondering at my flight and change

5. The stars.   7. I.e., does either envy or some other barrier ("re-
6. Technically, the food of the gods; used here of per-   serve") forbid to taste?
fume.

To this high exaltation, suddenly
My guide was gone, and I, methought, sunk down
And fell asleep. But O how glad I waked
To find this but a dream!" Thus Eve her night
Related, and thus Adam answered sad:[8]
    "Best image of myself and dearer half,   95
The trouble of thy thoughts this night in sleep
Affects me equally; nor can I like
This uncouth[9] dream, of evil sprung, I fear;
Yet evil whence? In thee can harbor none,
Created pure. But know that in the soul   100
Are many lesser faculties that serve
Reason as chief; among these fancy next
Her office holds. Of all external things
Which the five watchful senses represent,
She forms imaginations, airy shapes   105
Which reason, joining or disjoining, frames
All what we affirm or what deny, and call
Our knowledge or opinion; then retires
Into her private cell when nature rests.
Oft in her absence mimic fancy wakes   110
To imitate her; but, misjoining shapes,
Wild work produces oft, and most in dreams,
Ill matching words and deeds long past or late.
Some such resemblances methinks I find
Of our last evening's talk in this thy dream,[1]   115
But with addition strange. Yet be not sad,
Evil into the mind of god[2] or man
May come and go, so unapproved, and leave
No spot or blame behind; which gives me hope
That what in sleep thou didst abhor to dream,   120
Waking thou never wilt consent to do.
Be not disheartened then, nor cloud those looks
That wont to be more cheerful and serene
Than when fair morning first smiles on the world;
And let us to our fresh employments rise   125
Among the groves, the fountains, and the flowers
That open now their choicest bosomed smells
Reserved from night, and kept for thee in store."
    So cheered he his fair spouse, and she was cheered,
But silently a gentle tear let fall   130
From either eye, and wiped them with her hair;
Two other precious drops that ready stood,
Each in their crystal sluice, he ere they fell
Kissed as the gracious signs of sweet remorse
And pious awe that feared to have offended.   135

---

8. Grave, serious.
9. Strange; unpleasant. Adam's explanation of the
dream (lines 100–113) summarizes the orthodox psychology of Milton's time—one of many kinds of knowledge with which unfallen man was endued.

1. Adam recalls his own words in 4.411–439.
2. Probably "angel," as elsewhere; but perhaps also
"God," whose omniscience must encompass evil as
well as good.

Summary   Before going to work at their rural tasks, Adam and Eve recite their spontaneous morning prayers. God, seeing and pitying their unprotected innocence, dispatches Raphael to warn them of approaching dangers. The affable archangel enters the bower just about noontime and is promptly invited to join the midday meal, an invitation that he gladly accepts.

[A Visit with the Angel: The Scale of Nature]

        * * * So to the sylvan lodge
They came, that like Pomona's arbor[3] smiled
With flowerets decked and fragrant smells; but Eve,
Undecked save with herself, more lovely fair   380
Than wood nymph or the fairest goddess feigned
Of three that on Mount Ida naked strove,[4]
Stood t' entertain her guest from Heaven; no veil
She needed, virtue-proof, no thought infirm
Altered her cheek. On whom the Angel "Hail"   385
Bestowed, the holy salutation used
Long after to blessed Mary, second Eve:
   "Hail mother of mankind, whose fruitful womb
Shall fill the world more numerous with thy sons
Than with these various fruits the trees of God   390
Have heaped this table." Raised of grassy turf
Their table was, and mossy seats had round,
And on her ample square from side to side
All autumn piled, though spring and autumn here
Danced hand in hand. A while discourse they hold—   395
No fear lest dinner cool—when thus began
Our author.[5] "Heavenly stranger, please to taste
These bounties which our nourisher, from whom
All perfect good, unmeasured-out, descends,
To us for food and for delight hath caused   400
The earth to yield;[6] unsavory food perhaps
To spiritual natures; only this I know,
That one celestial Father gives to all."
   To whom the Angel: "Therefore what he gives
(Whose praise be ever sung) to man in part   405
Spiritual, may of purest spirits be found
No ungrateful food;[7] and food alike those pure
Intelligential substances require
As doth your rational; and both contain
Within them every lower faculty   410
Of sense, whereby they hear, see, smell, touch, taste,
Tasting concoct,[8] digest, assimilate,
And corporeal to incorporeal turn.

3. Pomona, Roman goddess of fruit trees and gardens, dwelt in an orchard.
4. Aphrodite, Hera, and Athena were judged for their beauty on Mt. Ida by Paris, son of Priam. Milton reminds us that the goddesses were only "feigned," i.e., not true in the sense that the Christian god is true.
5. Our creator (i.e., Adam).
6. I.e., please to taste these bounties that God ("our nourisher") has caused the earth to yield to us for food and for delight.
7. I.e., food that is proper for humans, who are partly spiritual, will be proper also for the very purest spirits. The idea that within the hierarchical universe higher powers include and comprehend lower powers is the key to the entire passage that follows.
8. Make ready by heat, warm up.

For know, whatever was created needs
To be sustained and fed; of elements   415
The grosser feeds the purer, earth the sea,
Earth and the sea feed air, the air those fires
Ethereal, and as lowest first the moon—
Whence in her visage round those spots, unpurged
Vapors not yet into her substance turned.[9]   420
Nor doth the moon no nourishment exhale
From her moist continent to higher orbs.
The sun, that light imparts to all, receives
From all his alimental recompense
In humid exhalations, and at even   425
Sups with the ocean.[1] Though in Heaven the trees
Of life ambrosial fruitage bear, and vines
Yield nectar, though from off the boughs each morn
We brush mellifluous dews, and find the ground
Covered with pearly grain, yet God hath here   430
Varied his bounty so with new delights
As may compare with Heaven; and to taste
Think not I shall be nice."[2] So down they sat,
And to their viands fell, nor seemingly
The Angel, nor in mist (the common gloss   435
Of theologians),[3] but with keen dispatch
Of real hunger and concoctive heat
To transubstantiate;[4] what redounds, transpires
Through spirits with ease· nor wonder: if by fire
Of sooty coal the empiric alchemist   440
Can turn, or holds it possible to turn,
Metals of drossiest ore to perfect gold
As from the mine. Meanwhile at table Eve
Ministered naked, and their flowing cups
With pleasant liquors crowned. O innocence   445
Deserving Paradise! if ever, then,
Then had the sons of God excuse t' have been
Enamored at that sight; but in those hearts
Love unlibidinous reigned, nor jealousy
Was understood, the injured lover's hell.   450
   Thus when with meats and drinks they had sufficed,
Not burdened nature, sudden mind arose
In Adam, not to let th' occasion pass
Giv'n him by this great conference to know
Of things above his world, and of their being   455

9. Raphael voices an archaic theory of lunar spots as still-undigested vapors, drawn up as food from the inferior planet, earth. This theory fits with Raphael's exposition of the universal hierarchy, but Milton knew better: he had referred to Galileo's correct explanation of the spots—as landscape features—in 1.287–291.
1. The phenomenon of evaporation Milton interprets as the sun dining off the moisture exhaled from oceans.
2. Scrupulous, finicky.
3. Theologians intent on maintaining the pure spirituality of angels say they experience only the likeness of eating or loving—seemingly, or in a mist; Milton will

have none of this evasion: the angel ate with real hunger.
4. In common theological use, transubstantiation is the Roman Catholic doctrine that the bread and wine of the eucharist really become the body and blood of Christ; Milton would vigorously have denied that doctrine as it applied to the sacrament, but says that here, by transforming material food to spiritual substance, the angel performed an act of true transubstantiation. The excess ("what redounds") is exhaled through spiritual pores.

Who dwell in Heaven, whose excellence he saw
Transcend his own so far, whose radiant forms
Divine effulgence,[5] whose high power so far
Exceeded human, and his wary speech
Thus to th' empyreal[6] minister he framed: 460
   "Inhabitant with God, now know I well
Thy favor in this honor done to man,
Under whose lowly roof thou hast vouchsafed
To enter and these earthly fruits to taste,
Food not of angels, yet accepted so   465
As that more willingly thou couldst not seem
At Heav'n's high feasts t' have fed: yet what compare?"
   To whom the wingèd hierarch replied:
"O Adam, one Almighty is, from whom
All things proceed and up to him return,   470
If not depraved from good, created all
Such to perfection, one first matter all,
Endued with various forms, various degrees
Of substance, and in things that live, of life;[7]
But more refined, more spiritous, and pure,   475
As nearer to him placed or nearer tending,
Each in their several active spheres assigned,
Till body up to spirit work, in bounds
Proportioned to each kind. So from the root
Springs lighter the green stalk, from thence the leaves   480
More airy, last the bright consummate flower
Spirits odorous breathes:[8] flowers and their fruit,
Man's nourishment, by gradual scale sublimed,[9]
To vital spirits aspire, to animal,
To intellectual[1]—give both life and sense,   485
Fancy[2] and understanding, whence the soul
Reason receives, and reason is her being,
Discursive or intuitive;[3] discourse
Is oftest yours, the latter most is ours,
Differing but in degree, of kind the same.   490
Wonder not then, what God for you saw good
If I refuse not,[4] but convert, as you,
To proper substance; time may come when men
With angels may participate, and find
No inconvenient diet, nor too light fare;   495
And from these corporal nutriments perhaps
Your bodies may at last turn all to spirit,

5. A verb to the general effect of "diffused" or "radi-ated" is omitted.
6. A minister from the empyrean, the highest or fiery level of heaven; with a perhaps accidental touch on "imperial," as well.
7. Behind Raphael's speech lies the traditional division of natural things into inanimate objects, vegetable, animal, human, and angelic natures; they all derive from one matter, created by God, but are differentiated by Him into distinct levels of purity.
8. As the flower is the consummation of a plant's existence, its odors are efflorescences analogous to hu-

mans' spiritual life, the consummation of *their* existence.
9. Purified.
1. Humans were thought to have three "souls"—vegetative, sensitive, and rational—each of which worked through subtle fluids called spirits.
2. Imagination.
3. For Milton, discursive reason, which must be learned by rules and study, is quite different from the intuitive reason that especially characterizes angels.
4. I.e., don't be surprised if I accept ("refuse not") what God knew would be good for you.

Improved by tract of time, and winged ascend
Ethereal as we,[5] or may at choice
Here or in heavenly paradises dwell;   500
If ye be found obedient, and retain
Unalterably firm his love entire
Whose progeny you are. Meanwhile, enjoy
Your fill what happiness this happy state
Can comprehend, incapable of more."   505
　　To whom the patriarch of mankind replied:
"O favorable spirit, propitious guest,
Well hast thou taught the way that might direct
Our knowledge, and the scale of nature set
From center to circumference, whereon   510
In contemplation of created things
By steps we may ascend to God. * * *"

Summary　　After this mingled explanation and warning, Raphael, by way of
emphasizing the danger that threatens Adam and Eve, enters upon the story of
Satan's revolt and fall. Satan, pretending that God's exaltation of the Son was an
offense to angelic dignity, persuaded the angels under his command—a third of
the heavenly host—to go off and set up a camp in the north of Heaven. When he
revealed his rebellious purpose, however, one of these angels refused to embrace
it. The seraph Abdiel, though scorned by Satan and all his legions, denounced the
rebellion and returned, heroically alone, to the ranks of God's followers.

Book 6. Summary　　Continuing the story of the war in Heaven, Raphael
describes the assembling of the armies and a first skirmish in which Satan is both
insulted and wounded by Abdiel. After the first day's battle, the evil angels retire
discomfited; but overnight Satan invents cannon, with which, on the second day,
the good angels are put to some disorder. In the fury of the fight, however, they
pull up mountains by the roots and bury the cannon beneath them; thus the issue
remains inconclusive. On the third day, God withdraws all His armies and sends
the Son alone into battle; the Son drives His enemies irresistibly over the wall of
Heaven, and after falling nine days through Chaos they are swallowed up in Hell.

From Book 7

[*The Invocation*]

　　Descend from Heaven, Urania,[6] by that name
If rightly thou art called,[7] whose voice divine
Following, above th' Olympian hill I soar,

5. Raphael is talking to unfallen man, who might in time very well turn all spirit; Milton's view of fallen man, strongly idealistic in an early poem like *Comus*, darkened with time and experience.
6. To start the second half of his poem, Milton must counterbalance the destruction of the war in Heaven with the creation by God of a new universe, centering on the earth. Book 7 is devoted to this topic; and to approach so vast a subject, Milton once more invokes his Muse.
7. Milton has only the names of classical Muses with which to invoke the spiritual principles of Christian theology. Properly the Muse of astronomy, Urania is also the symbol of heavenly love and of divine wisdom.

Above the flight of Pegasean wing![8]
The meaning, not the name I call: for thou   5
Nor of the Muses nine, nor on the top
Of old Olympus dwell'st, but heavenly born,
Before the hills appeared, or fountain flowed,
Thou with eternal Wisdom didst converse,
Wisdom thy sister, and with her didst play   10
In presence of th' Almighty Father,[9] pleased
With thy celestial song. Up led by thee
Into the Heaven of Heavens I have presumed,
An earthly guest, and drawn empyreal air,
Thy tempering;[1] with like safety guided down,   15
Return me to my native element:
Lest from this flying steed unreined (as once
Bellerophon,[2] though from a lower clime),
Dismounted, on th' Aleian field I fall,
Erroneous[3] there to wander and forlorn.   20
Half yet remains unsung, but narrower bound
Within the visible diurnal sphere;
Standing on earth, not rapt above the pole,
More safe I sing with mortal voice, unchanged
To hoarse or mute, though fall'n on evil days,   25
On evil days though fall'n, and evil tongues,
In darkness, and with dangers compassed round,
And solitude; yet not alone, while thou
Visit'st my slumbers nightly, or when morn
Purples the east:[4] still govern thou my song,   30
Urania, and fit audience find, though few.
But drive far off the barbarous dissonance
Of Bacchus and his revelers, the race
Of that wild rout that tore the Thracian bard
In Rhodope,[5] where woods and rocks had ears   35
To rapture, till the savage clamor drowned
Both harp and voice; nor could the Muse defend
Her son. So fail not thou, who thee implores:
For thou art heavenly, she an empty dream.

Summary   At Adam's request, Raphael continues his narration and describes how God, to replace the fallen angels, created the world, its creatures, and finally man, in the course of six days; the story of the creation concludes, on the seventh day, with a chorus of thanksgiving by the angels.

8. Pegasus, the flying horse of poetry, suggests (in connection with Bellerophon, line 18) Milton's sense of his own perilous audacity in writing so vast a poem.
9. In Proverbs 8.30, Wisdom is made to speak of "playing always before God," previous even to the Creation. Milton makes his Muse coeval with divine wisdom.
1. Tempered (i.e., mixed and softened) by thee.
2. Bellerophon tried to explore the stars astride Pegasus; but Zeus sent a gadfly to sting Pegasus, and his rider, after falling onto the Aleian plain in Lycia, wandered there till he died.

3. From Latin *errare*, "to wander," as well as "to be mistaken."
4. Milton composed mostly at night or very early in the morning.
5. The Thracian Bacchantes, female worshipers of Bacchus, tore Orpheus to pieces in Rhodope (a mountain range), though even the rocks and trees were so impressed with his music that they refused to be used against the poet (see *Lycidas*, lines 58–63, p. 647). Orpheus was a son of Calliope, the epic Muse.

From Book 8

Summary   Adam, to prolong his visit with Raphael, asks why so many and such splendid stars seem to be at the service of the earth, which appears smaller and less noble than they. At this point Eve discreetly takes her leave. Replying to Adam's question, Raphael proposes various astronomical possibilities, but gives no conclusive answer, advising Adam to concern himself with matters closer to home. The angel, on the other hand, is much interested to hear the story, which Adam proposes to tell, of his own creation.

[*Adam Describes His Own Creation and that of Eve; Having Repeated His Warning, the Angel Departs*]

So spake the godlike power, and thus our sire:
"For man to tell how human life began   250
Is hard; for who himself beginning knew?
Desire with thee still longer to converse
Induced me. As new waked from soundest sleep,
Soft on the flowery herb I found me laid
In balmy sweat, which with his beams the sun   255
Soon dried, and on the reeking moisture fed.
Straight toward heaven my wondering eyes I turned,
And gazed a while the ample sky, till raised
By quick instinctive motion up I sprung
As thitherward endeavoring, and upright   260
Stood on my feet; about me round I saw
Hill, dale, and shady woods, and sunny plains
And liquid lapse of murmuring streams; by these,
Creatures that lived and moved, and walked or flew,
Birds on the branches warbling. All things smiled;   265
With fragrance and with joy my heart o'erflowed.
Myself I then perused, and limb by limb
Surveyed, and sometimes went[6] and sometimes ran
With supple joints as lively vigor led:
But who I was, or where, or from what cause,   270
Knew not. To speak I tried, and forthwith spake,
My tongue obeyed, and readily could name
Whate'er I saw. 'Thou sun,' said I, 'fair light,
And thou enlightened earth, so fresh and gay,
Ye hills and dales, ye rivers, woods, and plains,   275
And ye that live and move, fair creatures, tell,
Tell, if ye saw, how came I thus, how here?
Not of myself; by some great maker, then,
In goodness and in power preëminent.
Tell me how may I know him, how adore,   280
From whom I have that thus I move and live,
And feel that I am happier than I know.'
    "While thus I called, and strayed I knew not whither
From where I first drew air and first beheld
This happy light, when answer none returned,   285
On a green shady bank profuse of flowers

_____
6. Walked. "Perused": inspected.

Pensive I sat me down; there gentle sleep
First found me and with soft oppression seized
My drowsèd sense—untroubled, though I thought
I then was passing to my former state   290
Insensible, and forthwith to dissolve;
When suddenly stood at my head a dream,
Whose inward apparition gently moved
My fancy to believe I yet had being
And lived. One came, methought, of shape divine,   295
And said, 'Thy mansion[7] wants thee, Adam, rise,
First man, of men innumerable ordained
First father; called by thee I come thy guide
To the garden of bliss, thy seat prepared.'
So saying, by the hand he took me raised,   300
And over fields and waters, as in air
Smooth sliding without step, last led me up
A woody mountain whose high top was plain,
A circuit wide, enclosed, with goodliest trees
Planted, with walks and bowers, that what I saw   305
Of earth before scarce pleasant seemed. Each tree
Loaden with fairest fruit that hung to the eye
Tempting, stirred in me sudden appetite
To pluck and eat; whereat I waked, and found
Before mine eyes all real, as the dream   310
Had lively shadowed. Here had new begun
My wandering, had not he who was my guide
Up hither, from among the trees appeared,
Presence divine. Rejoicing, but with awe,
In adoration at his feet I fell   315
Submiss: he reared me, and, 'Whom thou soughtest I am,'
Said mildly, 'author of all this thou seest
Above or round about thee or beneath.
This Paradise I give thee, count it thine
To till and keep, and of the fruit to eat.   320
Of every tree that in the garden grows
Eat freely with glad heart; fear here no dearth.
But of the tree whose operation brings
Knowledge of good and ill, which I have set
The pledge of thy obedience and thy faith   325
Amid the garden by the Tree of Life,
Remember what I warn thee, shun to taste
And shun the bitter consequence: for know
The day thou eat'st thereof, my sole command
Transgressed, inevitably thou shalt die,   330
From that day mortal, and this happy state
Shalt lose, expelled from hence into a world
Of woe and sorrow.' Sternly he pronounced
The rigid interdiction, which resounds
Yet dreadful in mine ear, though in my choice   335
Not to incur; but soon his clear aspèct

7. Habitation.

Returned, and gracious purpose[8] thus renewed:
'Not only these fair bounds, but all the Earth
To thee and to thy race I give; as lords
Possess it, and all things that therein live,   340
Or live in sea or air, beast, fish, and fowl.
In sign whereof each bird and beast behold
After their kinds; I bring them to receive
From thee their names, and pay thee fealty
With low subjection; understand the same   345
Of fish within their watery residence,
Not hither summoned, since they cannot change
Their element to draw the thinner air.'
As thus he spake, each bird and beast behold
Approaching two and two, these[9] cowering low   350
With blandishment, each bird stooped on his wing.
I named them as they passed, and understood
Their nature, with such knowledge God endued
My sudden apprehension. But in these
I found not what methought I wanted still,   355
And to the heavenly vision thus presumed:
    " 'O by what name, for thou above all these,
Above mankind, or aught than mankind higher,
Surpassest far my naming, how may I
Adore thee, author of this universe   360
And all this good to man, for whose well-being
So amply and with hands so liberal
Thou hast provided all things? But with me
I see not who partakes. In solitude
What happiness? Who can enjoy alone,   365
Or all enjoying, what contentment find?'
Thus I presumptuous; and the vision bright,
As with a smile more brightened, thus replied:
    " 'What callest thou solitude? Is not the earth
With various living creatures, and the air,   370
Replenished, and all these at thy command
To come and play before thee? Knowest thou not
Their language and their ways?[1] They also know
And reason not contemptibly; with these
Find pastime and bear rule; thy realm is large.'   375
So spake the universal Lord, and seemed
So ordering. I with leave of speech implored
And humble deprecation, thus replied:
    " 'Let not my words offend thee, heavenly power,
My maker; be propitious while I speak.   380
Hast thou not made me here thy substitute,
And these inferior far beneath me set?
Among unequals what society
Can sort,[2] what harmony or true delight?

---

8. Speech.
9. I.e., the beasts.
1. Adam in the state of innocence knows instinctively
not only the earliest language (for Milton and his age,

that was Hebrew) but also the languages of all the
creatures.
2. Agree.

Which must be mutual, in proportion due   385
Given and received. But in disparity,
The one intense, the other still remiss,[3]
Cannot well suit with either, but soon prove
Tedious alike. Of fellowship I speak
Such as I seek, fit to participate   390
All rational delight, wherein the brute
Cannot be human consort. They rejoice
Each with their kind, lion with lioness,
So fitly them in pairs thou hast combined;
Much less can bird with beast, or fish with fowl   395
So well converse, nor with the ox the ape;
Worse then can man with beast, and least of all.'
    "Whereto the Almighty answered, not displeased:
'A nice[4] and subtle happiness I see
Thou to thyself proposest, in the choice   400
Of thy associates, Adam, and wilt taste
No pleasure, though in pleasure, solitary.
What thinkest thou then of me and this my state?
Seem I to thee sufficiently possessed
Of happiness or not? who am alone   405
From all eternity, for none I know
Second to me or like, equal much less.
How have I then with whom to hold converse
Save with the creatures which I made, and those
To me inferior, infinite descents   410
Beneath what other creatures are to thee?'
    "He ceased, I lowly answered: 'To attain
The height and depth of thy eternal ways
All human thoughts come short, supreme of things.
Thou in thyself art perfect, and in thee   415
Is no deficience found; not so is man,
But in degree, the cause of his desire[5]
By conversation with his like to help
Or solace his defects. No need that thou
Shouldst propagate, already infinite,   420
And through all numbers absolute, though one.[6]
But man by number is to manifest
His single imperfection,[7] and beget
Like of his like, his image multiplied,
In unity defective, which requires   425
Collateral love and dearest amity.
Thou in thy secrecy although alone,
Best with thyself accompanied, seekest not
Social communication; yet, so pleased,
Canst raise thy creature to what height thou wilt   430
Of union or communion, deified;

3. "Intense . . . remiss": taut . . . slack, continuing the musical metaphor begun with "harmony" (line 384).
4. Delicate, discriminating—with perhaps an overtone of the sense "finicky."
5. Though perfect "in degree" (i.e., for his sort of crea-

ture), man is far from God's perfection, (which is) the cause of his desire, etc.
6. God, as infinity, contains all numbers, though He is also and especially one.
7. Imperfection in being single.

I by conversing cannot these erect
From prone, nor in their ways complacence[8] find.'
Thus I emboldened spake, and freedom used
Permissive, and acceptance found, which gained   435
This answer from the gracious voice divine:
  " 'Thus far to try thee, Adam, I was pleased,
And find thee knowing, not of beasts alone
Which thou hast rightly named, but of thyself,
Expressing well the spirit within thee free,   440
My image, not imparted to the brute,
Whose fellowship, therefore unmeet for thee,
Good reason was thou freely shouldst dislike;
And be so minded still. I, ere thou spak'st,
Knew it not good for man to be alone,   445
And no such company as then thou sawest
Intended thee, for trial only brought,
To see how thou couldst judge of fit and meet.
What next I bring shall please thee, be assured:
Thy likeness, thy fit help, thy other self,   450
Thy wish exactly to thy heart's desire.'
  "He ended, or I heard no more, for now,
My earthly[9] by his heavenly overpowered
Which it had long stood under, strained to the height
In that celestial colloquy sublime,   455
As with an object that excels[1] the sense
Dazzled and spent, sunk down and sought repair
Of sleep, which instantly fell on me, called
By nature as in aid, and closed mine eyes.
Mine eyes he closed, but open left the cell   460
Of fancy, my internal sight, by which
Abstract as in a trance methought I saw,
Though sleeping, where I lay, and saw the shape
Still glorious before whom awake I stood;
Who stooping opened my left side, and took   465
From thence a rib, with cordial[2] spirits warm
And life-blood streaming fresh. Wide was the wound,
But suddenly with flesh filled up and healed.
The rib he formed and fashioned with his hands;
Under his forming hands a creature grew,   470
Manlike, but different sex, so lovely fair
That what seemed fair in all the world seemed now
Mean, or in her summed up, in her contained,
And in her looks, which from that time infused
Sweetness into my heart, unfelt before,   475
And into all things from her air inspired
The spirit of love and amorous delight.
She disappeared, and left me dark; I waked
To find her or forever to deplore
Her loss, and other pleasures all abjure;   480
When out of hope, behold her, not far off,

8. Satisfaction.   1. Exceeds.
9. "Nature" is understood.   2. From the heart.

Such as I saw her in my dream, adorned
With what all Earth or Heaven could bestow
To make her amiable. On she came,
Led by her heavenly maker, though unseen,   485
And guided by his voice, nor uninformed
Of nuptial sanctity and marriage rites.
Grace was in all her steps, heaven in her eye,
In every gesture dignity and love.
I overjoyed could not forbear aloud: 490
    "This turn hath made amends; thou hast fulfilled
Thy words, Creator bounteous and benign,
Giver of all things fair, but fairest this
Of all thy gifts; nor enviest.[3] I now see
Bone of my bone, flesh of my flesh, my self   495
Before me; woman is her name, of man
Extracted; for this cause he shall forego
Father and mother, and to his wife adhere,
And they shall be one flesh, one heart, one soul.'[4]
    "She heard me thus, and though divinely brought,   500
Yet innocence and virgin modesty,
Her virtue and the conscience[5] of her worth
That would be wooed and not unsought be won,
Not obvious, not obtrusive, but retired,
The more desirable—or, to say all,   505
Nature herself, though pure of sinful thought,
Wrought in her so that, seeing me, she turned.
I followed her; she what was honor knew,
And with obsequious[6] majesty approved
My pleaded reason. To the nuptial bower   510
I led her blushing like the morn. All heaven
And happy constellations on that hour
Shed their selectest influence; the earth
Gave sign of gratulation, and each hill;
Joyous the birds; fresh gales and gentle airs   515
Whispered it to the woods, and from their wings
Flung rose, flung odors from the spicy shrub,
Disporting, till the amorous bird of night[7]
Sung spousal, and bid haste the evening star
On his hill-top, to light the bridal lamp.   520
    "Thus have I told thee all my state, and brought
My story to the sum of earthly bliss
Which I enjoy, and must confess to find
In all things else delight indeed, but such
As, used or not, works in the mind no change,   525
Nor vehement desire—these delicacies
I mean of taste, sight, smell, herbs, fruits, and flowers,
Walks and the melody of birds. But here,

3. Unlike some other gods (Jove, for example), Milton's deity does not lust after the females He bestows on men.
4. Adam's speech is largely an expansion of Genesis 2.23–24.
5. Consciousness. Note that Adam cannot find a verb for what Eve does in consequence of her innocence and virgin modesty.
6. Compliant.
7. The nightingale, present on this auspicious occasion, as he was in the more doubtful scene of Eve's tempting dream (5.40).

Far otherwise, transported I behold,
Transported touch; here passion first I felt,   530
Commotion strange, in all enjoyments else
Superior and unmoved, here only weak
Against the charm of beauty's powerful glance.
Or[8] nature failed in me and left some part
Not proof enough such object to sustain,   535
Or from my side subducting[9] took perhaps
More than enough; at least on her bestowed
Too much of ornament, in outward show
Elaborate, of inward less exact.
For well I understand in the prime end   540
Of nature her th' inferior, in the mind
And inward faculties which most excel,
In outward also her resembling less
His image who made both, and less expressing
The character of that dominion given   545
O'er other creatures. Yet when I approach
Her loveliness, so absolute she seems
And in herself complete, so well to know
Her own, that what she wills to do or say
Seems wisest, virtuousest, discreetest, best.   550
All higher knowledge in her presence falls
Degraded; wisdom in discourse with her
Loses discountenanced, and like folly shows;
Authority and reason on her wait
As one intended first, not after made   555
Occasionally;[1] and to consùmmate all,
Greatness of mind and nobleness their seat
Build in her loveliest, and create an awe
About her as a guard angelic placed."
    To whom the Angel with contracted brow: 560
"Accuse not nature, she hath done her part;
Do thou but thine, and be not diffident[2]
Of wisdom; she deserts thee not if thou
Dismiss not her when most thou need'st her nigh
By àttributing overmuch to things   565
Less excellent, as thou thyself perceiv'st.
For what admir'st thou, what transports thee so?
An outside? Fair no doubt, and worthy well
Thy cherishing, thy honoring, and thy love;
Not thy subjection. Weigh her with thyself,   570
Then value. Ofttimes nothing profits more
Then self-esteem, grounded on just and right
Well managed. Of that skill the more thou know'st,
The more she will acknowledge thee her head,
And to realities yield all her shows—   575
Made so adorn for thy delight the more,
So aweful[3] that with honor thou may'st love

8. Either.   2. Mistrustful, without faith.
9. Subtracting.   3. Awe-inspiring.
1. Incidentally.

Thy mate, who sees when thou art seen least wise.
But if the sense of touch whereby mankind
Is propagated seem such dear delight   580
Beyond all other, think the same vouchsafed
To cattle and each beast; which would not be
To them made common and divulged if aught
Therein enjoyed were worthy to subdue
The soul of man, or passion in him move.   585
What higher in her society thou find'st
Attractive, human, rational—love still;
In loving thou dost well, in passion not,
Wherein true love consists not. Love refines
The thoughts, and heart enlarges, hath his seat   590
In reason, and is judicious, is the scale[4]
By which to heavenly love thou may'st ascend,
Not sunk in carnal pleasure, for which cause
Among the beasts no mate for thee was found."
    To whom thus half abashed Adam replied: 595
"Neither her outside formed so fair, nor aught
In procreation common to all kinds
(Though higher of the genial[5] bed by far
And with mysterious reverence I deem)
So much delights me as those graceful acts,   600
Those thousand decencies that daily flow
From all her words and actions, mixed with love
And sweet compliance, which declare unfeigned
Union of mind, or in us both one soul,
Harmony to behold in wedded pair   605
More grateful than harmonious sound to the ear.
Yet these subject not; I to thee disclose
What inward thence I feel, not therefore foiled,
Who meet with various objects from the sense
Variously representing; yet still free   610
Approve the best, and follow what I approve.[6]
    "To love thou blam'st me not, for love thou say'st
Leads up to Heaven, is both the way and guide;
Bear with me then, if lawful what I ask:
Love not the heavenly spirits, and how their love   615
Express they, by looks only, or do they mix
Irradiance, virtual or immediate touch?"
    To whom the Angel with a smile that glowed
Celestial rosy red, love's proper hue,
Answered: "Let it suffice thee that thou know'st   620
Us happy, and without love no happiness.
Whatever pure thou in the body enjoy'st
(And pure thou wert created), we enjoy
In eminence, and obstacle find none

---

4. The scale of nature, as in 5.509, but with an important overtone from Latin or Italian *scala*, meaning "ladder." The ladder of love was a Neoplatonic metaphor, ardently described by Cardinal Bembo in Baldasarre Castiglione's highly influential dialogue of 1528, *Il Cortegiano (The Courtier)*.

5. Procreative, progenitive.

6. The sense of these last few lines is not quite clear. Milton seems to be miming Adam's embarrassment, from which he escapes with an acute question for the angel.

Of membrane, joint, or limb, exclusive bars.   625
Easier than air with air, if spirits embrace,
Total they mix, union of pure with pure
Desiring; nor restrained conveyance need
As flesh to mix with flesh, or soul with soul.
But I can now no more; the parting sun   630
Beyond the earth's green cape and verdant isles[7]
Hesperian sets, my signal to depart.
Be strong, live happy, and love, but first of all
Him whom to love is to obey, and keep
His great command; take heed lest passion sway   635
Thy judgment to do aught which else free will
Would not admit; thine and of all thy sons
The weal or woe in thee is placed: beware.
I in thy persevering shall rejoice,
And all the blest. Stand fast; to stand or fall   640
Free in thine own arbitrement it lies.
Perfect within, no outward aid require;
And all temptation to transgress repel."[8]
    So saying, he arose; whom Adam thus
Followed with benediction: "Since to part,   645
Go, heavenly guest, ethereal messenger,
Sent from whose[9] sovereign goodness I adore.
Gentle to me and affable hath been
Thy condescension, and shall be honored ever
With grateful memory. Thou to mankind   650
Be good and friendly still, and oft return."
    So parted they, the Angel up to Heaven
From the thick shade, and Adam to his bower.

Book 9

The Argument

    Satan, having compassed the Earth, with meditated guile returns as a mist
by night into Paradise; enters into the serpent sleeping. Adam and Eve in the
morning go forth to their labors, which Eve proposes to divide in several
places, each laboring apart: Adam consents not, alleging the danger lest that
enemy of whom they were forewarned should attempt her found alone. Eve,
loath to be thought not circumspect or firm enough, urges her going apart,
the rather desirous to make trial of her strength; Adam at last yields. The
serpent finds her alone: his subtle approach, first gazing, then speaking, with
much flattery extolling Eve above all other creatures. Eve, wondering to hear
the serpent speak, asks how he attained to human speech and such understanding not till now; the serpent answers that by tasting of a certain tree in

---

7. Cape Verde near Dakar and the Islas Verdes off that
coast are the westernmost ("Hesperian") points of Africa, and so of the Old World as a whole.
8. "Require" (i.e., look for, depend on) and "repel" are
the two strong imperative verbs with which the angel
concludes his mission. Don't look for help from outsid-

ers; do repel temptation on your own. It is a curious
touch that Eve, though she overhears, at least in part,
this most forceful of divine warnings (9.276), is not
present to be addressed directly by the admonitory
angel.
9. I.e., from Him whose.

the garden he attained both to speech and reason, till then void of both. Eve requires him to bring her to that tree, and finds it to be the Tree of Knowledge forbidden: the serpent, now grown bolder, with many wiles and arguments induces her at length to eat. She, pleased with the taste, deliberates a while whether to impart thereof to Adam or not; at last brings him of the fruit; relates what persuaded her to eat thereof. Adam, at first amazed, but perceiving her lost, resolves, through vehemence of love, to perish with her, and, extenuating[1] the trespass, eats also of the fruit. The effects thereof in them both; they seek to cover their nakedness; then fall to variance and accusation of one another.

No more of talk where God[2] or angel guest
With man, as with his friend, familiar used
To sit indulgent, and with him partake
Rural repast, permitting him the while
Venial[3] discourse unblamed. I now must change   5
Those notes to tragic; foul distrust and breach
Disloyal on the part of man, revolt
And disobedience; on the part of Heaven
Now alienated, distance and distaste,
Anger and just rebuke, and judgment given,   10
That brought into this world a world of woe,
Sin and her shadow Death, and Misery,
Death's harbinger. Sad task! yet argument
Not less but more heroic than the wrath
Of stern Achilles on his foe pursued   15
Thrice fugitive about Troy wall; or rage
Of Turnus for Lavinia disespoused;
Or Neptune's ire, or Juno's, that so long
Perplexed the Greek and Cytherea's son:[4]
If answerable style I can obtain   20
Of my celestial Patroness,[5] who deigns
Her nightly visitation unimplored,
And dictates to me slumbering, or inspires
Easy my unpremeditated verse,[6]
Since first this subject for heroic song   25
Pleased me, long choosing and beginning late,
Not sedulous[7] by nature to indite
Wars, hitherto the only argument
Heroic deemed, chief mastery to dissect[8]
With long and tedious havoc fabled knights   30
In battles feigned (the better fortitude

1. Not "diminishing" or "excusing" as in customary English usage, but carrying further, drawing out.
2. God, of course, has not been lunching with Adam; but since the Fall is about to occur, the age is now over when such an occasion could be contemplated.
3. Permissible.
4. In the *Iliad* (22), Achilles pursues Hector three times around Troy wall before catching him. In the *Aeneid*, Aeneas must fight with Turnus for the hand of Lavinia. Neptune (or Poseidon) was unfriendly to Odysseus (the Greek); Juno (or Hera) to Aeneas, who was Cytherea's, i.e., Aphrodite's, son by Anchises.
5. The Muse, Urania, here invoked a final time, at

the beginning of the poem's climactic action.
6. Milton, we are told by his nephew Edward Phillips, used to wake up in the morning with lines of poetry fully formed in his head; he would then dictate them to an amanuensis.
7. Eager. Milton's early plans for epics, preserved in manuscript, did center on national heroes; his choice of a sacred subject, though not wholly without precedent, was a relative novelty.
8. I.e., in describing wars one's chief task is to dissect; dissect in its strict Latin sense of "cut apart," but perhaps also with a comic overtone from the anatomy table.

Of patience and heroic martyrdom
Unsung), or to describe races and games,
Or tilting furniture, emblazoned shields,
Impresses quaint, caparisons and steeds,   35
Bases[9] and tinsel trappings, gorgeous knights
At joust and tournament; then marshaled feast
Served up in hall with sewers and seneschals:[1]
The skill of artifice or office mean;
Not that which justly gives heroic name   40
To person or to poem. Me of these
Nor skilled nor studious, higher argument
Remains,[2] sufficient of itself to raise
That name, unless an age too late, or cold
Climate, or years, damp[3] my intended wing   45
Depressed; and much they may if all be mine,
Not hers who brings it nightly to my ear.
   The sun was sunk, and after him the star
Of Hesperus, whose office is to bring
Twilight upon the Earth, short arbiter   50
'Twixt day and night, and now from end to end
Night's hemisphere had veiled the horizon round,
When Satan, who late fled before the threats
Of Gabriel out of Eden,[4] now improved
In meditated fraud and malice, bent   55
On man's destruction, maugre what might hap
Of heavier on himself,[5] fearless returned.
By night he fled, and at midnight returned
From compassing the Earth—cautious of day
Since Uriel, regent of the sun, descried   60
His entrance, and forewarned the cherubim
That kept their watch.[6] Thence, full of anguish, driven,
The space of seven continued nights he rode
With darkness; thrice the equinoctial line
He circled, four times crossed the car of Night   65
From pole to pole, traversing each colure;[7]
On the eighth returned, and on the coast averse
From entrance or cherubic watch by stealth
Found unsuspected way. There was a place
(Now not, though sin, not time, first wrought the change)   70
Where Tigris at the foot of Paradise
Into a gulf shot under ground, till part
Rose up a fountain by the Tree of Life.
In with the river sunk and with it rose

---

9. Trappings for horses. "Tilting furniture": the equipment of tournaments. "Impresses quaint": elaborate
devices on shields.
1. Waiters and stewards, who also dissect.
2. I.e., for me, when these things are set aside, which
I neither can nor want to do, there remains a higher
theme.
3. Stupefy, benumb. "That name": i.e., the name of
heroic poet. "Age too late": not Milton's age, but the
age of the world. Milton felt a "cold climate" was inim-
ical to epic poetry.

4. At the end of book 4.
5. Despite the peril of heavier (punishments).
6. In 4.564–575. These connections with book 4 not
only bridge the intervening narration but emphasize a
balancing of the whole epic (see the headnote).
7. The colures are the two great circles of the celestial
sphere which intersect at the poles. By circling the
globe, either from east to west or over the north and
south poles, Satan can remain continually hidden in
darkness. "Equinoctial line": the equator.

Satan, involved in rising mist; then sought   75
Where to lie hid. Sea he had searched and land
From Eden over Pontus, and the pool
Maeotis, up beyond the river Ob;[8]
Downward as far antarctic; and, in length,
West from Orontes to the ocean barred   80
At Darien, thence to the land where flows
Ganges and Indus.[9] Thus the orb he roamed
With narrow search, and with inspection deep
Considered every creature, which of all
Most opportune might serve his wiles, and found   85
The serpent subtlest beast of all the field.[1]
Him, after long debate, irresolute
Of thoughts revolved,[2] his final sentence chose
Fit vessel, fittest imp[3] of fraud, in whom
To enter, and his dark suggestions hide   90
From sharpest sight; for in the wily snake
Whatever sleights none would suspicious mark,
As from his wit and native subtlety
Proceeding, which, in other beasts observed,
Doubt[4] might beget of diabolic power   95
Active within beyond the sense of brute.
Thus he resolved, but first from inward grief
His bursting passion into plaints thus poured:
    "O Earth, how like to Heaven, if not preferred
More justly, seat worthier of gods, as built   100
With second thoughts, reforming what was old!
For what god, after better, worse would build?
Terrestrial heaven, danced round by other heavens
That shine, yet bear their bright officious lamps,
Light above light, for thee alone, as seems,   105
In thee concent'ring all their precious beams
Of sacred influence![5] As God in Heaven
Is center, yet extends to all, so thou
Cent'ring receiv'st from all those orbs; in thee,
Not in themselves, all their known virtue appears,   110
Productive in herb, plant, and nobler birth
Of creatures animate with gradual life
Of growth, sense, reason,[6] all summed up in man.
With what delight could I have walked thee round,
If I could joy in aught; sweet interchange   115
Of hill and valley, rivers, woods, and plains,
Now land, now sea, and shores with forest crowned,
Rocks, dens, and caves! But I in none of these
Find place or refuge; and the more I see

8. Pontus is the Black Sea, the pool Maeotis the
swamps of the Sea of Azov; the river Ob flows north
through Siberia into the Arctic Ocean.
9. Flying west from Orontes in Syria, Satan crossed
the Atlantic to the Isthmus of Panama (Darien), then
the Pacific and Southeast Asia to India.
1. Genesis 3.1 so describes the serpent.
2. I.e., unable to decide among his revolving thoughts.
"Sentence": decision.

3. Graft, offshoot.
4. Suspicion.
5. Satan, like Adam in book 8, is impressed that so
many heavenly bodies center on (and "serve") the
earth—as the old Ptolemaic astronomy taught that they
did. "Officious": dutiful.
6. Life on earth is gradual, or graduated, from the herb
that merely grows, to the animal that grows and feels,
to the human being, who grows, feels, and thinks.

Pleasures about me, so much more I feel   120
Torment within me, as from the hateful siege[7]
Of contraries; all good to me becomes
Bane,[8] and in Heaven much worse would be my state.
But neither here seek I, no, nor in Heaven,
To dwell, unless by mastering Heaven's Supreme;   125
Nor hope to be myself less miserable
By what I seek, but others to make such
As I, though thereby worse to me redound.
For only in destroying I find ease
To my relentless thoughts, and him[9] destroyed,   130
Or won to what may work his utter loss,
For whom all this was made, all this[1] will soon
Follow, as to him linked in weal or woe:
In woe then, that destruction wide may range!
To me shall be the glory sole among   135
The infernal powers, in one day to have marred
What he, Almighty styled, six nights and days
Continued making, and who knows how long
Before had been contriving? though perhaps
Not longer than since I in one night freed   140
From servitude inglorious well-nigh half
Th' angelic name, and thinner left the throng
Of his adorers. He to be avenged,
And to repair his numbers thus impaired,
Whether such virtue,[2] spent of old, now failed   145
More angels to create (if they at least
Are his created),[3] or to spite us more,
Determined to advance into our room
A creature formed of earth, and him endow,
Exalted from so base original,   150
With heavenly spoils, our spoils. What he decreed
He effected; man he made, and for him built
Magnificent this world, and Earth his seat,
Him lord pronounced, and, O indignity!
Subjected to his service angel-wings   155
And flaming ministers, to watch and tend
Their earthy charge. Of these the vigilance
I dread, and to elude, thus wrapped in mist
Of midnight vapor glide obscure, and pry
In every bush and brake, where hap may find   160
The serpent sleeping in whose mazy folds
To hide me, and the dark intent I bring.
O foul descent! that I, who erst contended
With gods to sit the highest, am now constrained
Into a beast, and mixed with bestial slime,   165
This essence to incarnate and imbrute,[4]

---

7. Conflict.
8. Poison. This is exactly what he willed in 4.110, just reversed.
9. I.e., man.
1. I.e., the created cosmos.
2. Strength, energy.

3. Satan never likes to admit that the angels were created by God: he faces the fact squarely only once, in his soliloquy at the beginning of book 4 (line 43).
4. Satan's incarnation in a snake is a grotesque parody of the Son of God's incarnation in Christ.

That to the height of deity aspired!
But what will not ambition and revenge
Descend to? Who aspires must down as low
As high he soared, obnoxious[5] first or last   170
To basest things. Revenge, at first though sweet,
Bitter ere long back on itself recoils.
Let it; I reck not, so it light well aimed,
Since higher I fall short, on him who next
Provokes my envy, this new favorite   175
Of Heaven, this man of clay, son of despite,
Whom, us the more to spite,[6] his Maker raised
From dust: spite then with spite is best repaid."
    So saying, through each thicket dank or dry,
Like a black mist low-creeping, he held on   180
His midnight search, where soonest he might find
The serpent. Him fast sleeping soon he found
In labyrinth of many a round self-rolled,
His head the midst, well stored with subtle wiles:
Not yet in horrid shade or dismal den,   185
Nor nocent[7] yet, but on the grassy herb,
Fearless, unfeared, he slept. In at his mouth
The devil entered, and his brutal sense,
In heart or head possessing, soon inspired
With act intelligential; but his sleep   190
Disturbed not, waiting close[8] th' approach of morn.
    Now whenas sacred light began to dawn
In Eden on the humid flowers, that breathed
Their morning incense, when all things that breathe
From th' Earth's great altar send up silent praise   195
To the Creator, and his nostrils fill
With grateful smell, forth came the human pair
And joined their vocal worship to the choir
Of creatures wanting voice; that done, partake
The season, prime[9] for sweetest scents and airs;   200
Then còmmune how that day they best may ply
Their growing work; for much their work outgrew
The hands' dispatch of two gardening so wide;
And Eve first to her husband thus began:
    "Adam, well may we labor still[1] to dress   205
This garden, still to tend plant, herb, and flower,
Our pleasant task enjoined; but till more hands
Aid us, the work under our labor grows,
Luxurious by restraint: what we by day
Lop overgrown, or prune, or prop, or bind,   210
One night or two with wanton growth derides,
Tending to wild. Thou, therefore, now advise,
Or hear what to my mind first thoughts present.
Let us divide our labors; thou where choice

---

5. Subject.
6. Satan sees God in his own image, as a spiteful creature.
7. Harmful.

8. In secret.
9. The best. "Partake the season": i.e., go forth into the
morning air.
1. Continually.

Leads thee, or where most needs, whether to wind   215
The woodbine round this arbor, or direct
The clasping ivy where to climb; while I
In yonder spring[2] of roses intermixed
With myrtle find what to redress till noon.
For while so near each other thus all day   220
Our task we choose, what wonder if so near
Looks intervene and smiles, or object new
Casual discourse draw on, which intermits
Our day's work, brought to little, though begun
Early, and th' hour of supper comes unearned!"   225
    To whom mild answer Adam thus returned:
"Sole Eve, associate sole, to me beyond
Compare above all living creatures dear!
Well hast thou motioned,[3] well thy thoughts employed
How we might best fulfill the work which here   230
God hath assigned us, nor of me shalt pass
Unpraised; for nothing lovelier can be found
In woman than to study household good,
And good works in her husband to promote.[4]
Yet not so strictly hath our Lord imposed   235
Labor as to debar us when we need
Refreshment, whether food or talk between,
Food of the mind, or this sweet intercourse
Of looks and smiles; for smiles from reason flow,
To brute denied, and are of love the food,   240
Love, not the lowest end of human life.
For not to irksome toil, but to delight
He made us, and delight to reason joined.
These paths and bowers doubt not but our joint hands
Will keep from wilderness with ease, as wide   245
As we need walk, till younger hands ere long
Assist us. But if much convèrse perhaps
Thee satiate, to short absence I could yield;
For solitude sometimes is best society,
And short retirement urges sweet return.   250
But other doubt possesses me, lest harm
Befall thee, severed from me; for thou know'st
What hath been warned us, what malicious foe,
Envying our happiness, and of his own
Despairing, seeks to work us woe and shame   255
By sly assault; and somewhere nigh at hand
Watches, no doubt, with greedy hope to find
His wish and best advantage, us asunder,[5]
Hopeless to circumvent us joined, where each
To other speedy aid might lend at need.   260
Whether his first design be to withdraw
Our fealty from God, or to disturb
Conjugal love, than which perhaps no bliss

2. Growth.   and Milton doubtless had it in mind here.
3. Suggested.   5. I.e., to find us apart, which will answer his wishes
4. Proverbs 31 is devoted to the praise of a good wife,   and serve his advantage.

Enjoyed by us excites his envy more;
Or this, or worse,[6] leave not the faithful side   265
That gave thee being, still shades thee and protects.
The wife, where danger or dishonor lurks,
Safest and seemliest by her husband stays,
Who guards her, or with her the worst endures."
    To whom the virgin[7] majesty of Eve,   270
As one who loves, and some unkindness meets,
With sweet austere composure thus replied:
    "Offspring of Heaven and Earth, and all Earth's lord!
That such an enemy we have, who seeks
Our ruin, both by thee informed I learn,   275
And from the parting angel overheard
As in a shady nook I stood behind,
Just then returned at shut of evening flowers.
But that thou shouldst my firmness therefore doubt
To God or thee, because we have a foe   280
May tempt it, I expected not to hear.
His violence thou fear'st not, being such
As we, not capable of death or pain,
Can either not receive, or can repel.
His fraud is, then, thy fear; which plain infers   285
Thy equal fear that my firm faith and love
Can by his fraud be shaken or seduced:
Thoughts, which how found they harbor in thy breast,
Adam, misthought of her to thee so dear?"[8]
    To whom with healing words Adam replied: 290
"Daughter of God and man, immortal Eve,
For such thou art, from sin and blame entire;
Not diffident[9] of thee do I dissuade
Thy absence from my sight, but to avoid
Th' attempt itself, intended by our foe.   295
For he who tempts, though in vain, at least asperses[1]
The tempted with dishonor foul, supposed
Not incorruptible of faith, not proof
Against temptation. Thou thyself with scorn
And anger wouldst resent the offered wrong   300
Though ineffectual found; misdeem not, then,
If such affront I labor to avert
From thee alone, which on us both at once
The enemy, though bold, will hardly dare;
Or, daring, first on me th' assault shall light.   305
Nor thou his malice and false guile contemn—
Subtle he needs must be who could seduce
Angels—nor think superfluous others' aid.
I from the influence of thy looks receive
Access[2] in every virtue; in thy sight   310

---

6. I.e., whether this or something worse be his intent.
7. Unspotted.
8. I.e., these thoughts were misthought of (misapplied to) her to thee so dear (me).
9. The usual English meaning is shy or timid; Milton emphasizes the Latin roots, *dis* + *fides* = mistrustful.

"Entire" is from Latin *integer,* "whole" or "intact."
1. The word is from Latin *spargere,* to sprinkle, with overtones from English "aspersion," an ugly insinuation.
2. Extra strength.

More wise, more watchful, stronger, if need were
Of outward strength; while shame, thou looking on,
Shame to be overcome or overreached,[3]
Would utmost vigor raise, and raised unite.
Why shouldst not thou like sense within thee feel   315
When I am present, and thy trial choose
With me, best witness of thy virtue tried?"
   So spake domestic Adam in his care
And matrimonial love; but Eve, who thought
Less[4] àttributed to her faith sincere,   320
Thus her reply with accent sweet renewed:
   "If this be our condition, thus to dwell
In narrow circuit straitened by a foe,
Subtle or violent, we not endued
Single with like defense wherever met,   325
How are we happy, still in fear of harm?
But harm precedes not sin: only our foe
Tempting affronts us with his foul esteem
Of our integrity: his foul esteem
Sticks no dishonor on our front,[5] but turns   330
Foul on himself; then wherefore shunned or feared
By us, who rather double honor gain
From his surmise proved false, find peace within,
Favor from Heaven, our witness, from th' event?
And what is faith, love, virtue, unassayed   335
Alone, without exterior help sustained?
Let us not then suspect our happy state
Left so imperfect by the Maker wise
As not secure to single or combined.
Frail is our happiness, if this be so;   340
And Eden were no Eden, thus exposed."
   To whom thus Adam fervently replied:
"O woman, best are all things as the will
Of God ordained them; his creating hand
Nothing imperfect or deficient left   345
Of all that he created, much less man,
Or aught that might his happy state secure,
Secure from outward force. Within himself
The danger lies, yet lies within his power;
Against his will he can receive no harm.   350
But God left free the will; for what obeys
Reason is free; and reason he made right,[6]
But bid her well beware, and still erect,
Lest by some fair appearing good surprised,
She dictate false, and misinform the will   355
To do what God expressly hath forbid.
Not then mistrust, but tender love, enjoins
That I should mind[7] thee oft; and mind thou me.

3. Overpowered or outwitted.
4. Too little.
5. Forehead.
6. "Right reason" (a classical concept and term—Latin *recta ratio*—inherited by Christian thought) is the
God-given power to apprehend truth and moral law. "Erect" (next line): alert.
7. Remind; in the next phrase, "mind" means "pay heed to."

Firm we subsist, yet possible to swerve,
Since reason not impossibly may meet   360
Some specious object by the foe suborned,
And fall into deception unaware,
Not keeping strictest watch, as she was warned.
Seek not temptation, then, which to avoid
Were better, and most likely if from me   365
Thou sever not: trial will come unsought.
Wouldst thou approve thy constancy, approve[8]
First thy obedience; th' other who can know,
Not seeing thee attempted, who attest?
But if thou think trial unsought may find   370
Us both securer[9] than thus warned thou seem'st,
Go; for thy stay, not free, absents thee more.
Go in thy native innocence; rely
On what thou hast of virtue; summon all;
For God towards thee hath done his part: do thine."   375
    So spake the patriarch of mankind; but Eve
Persisted; yet submiss, though last, replied:
    "With thy permission,[1] then, and thus forewarned,
Chiefly by what thy own last reasoning words
Touched only, that our trial, when least sought,   380
May find us both perhaps far less prepared,
The willinger I go, nor much expect
A foe so proud will first the weaker seek;
So bent, the more shall shame him his repulse."
Thus saying, from her husband's hand her hand   385
Soft she withdrew, and like a wood nymph light,
Oread or dryad, or of Delia's train,[2]
Betook her to the groves, but Delia's self
In gait surpassed and goddess-like deport,
Though not as she with bow and quiver armed,   390
But with such gardening tools as art yet rude,
Guiltless of fire[3] had formed, or angels brought.
To Pales, or Pomona, thus adorned,
Likest she seemed, Pomona when she fled
Vertumnus, or to Ceres in her prime,   395
Yet virgin of Proserpina from Jove.[4]
Her long with ardent look his eye pursued
Delighted, but desiring more her stay.
Oft he to her his charge of quick return
Repeated; she to him as oft engaged   400
To be returned by noon amid the bower,
And all things in best order to invite

---

8. Prove, give evidence of.
9. The Latin word *securus* can mean either "free from care" or "careless." Adam's warning is at once reassuring and ominous.
1. Eve takes a reluctant and extorted permission as free leave to do what she wants.
2. An "oread" is a nymph of the mountain; a "dryad," one of the wood. "Delia" is Diana or Artemis, goddess of the chase, who when she hunted was accompanied by a train of nymphs.

3. There was no need of fire in Paradise; but that fire is a possession that renders one "guilty" suggests an overtone of the Prometheus myth.
4. Pales is a Roman goddess of flocks; Pomona, a Roman divinity of fruits and orchards. Pomona was wooed by Vertumnus, god of the turning year, who assumed all sorts of shapes to win her. Ceres, the Mother Nature of the ancients (hence, the word "cereal"), bore Proserpina to Jupiter. All three goddesses are patronesses of agriculture, like Eve.

Noontide repast, or afternoon's repose.
O much deceived, much failing, hapless Eve,
Of thy presumed return![5] Event perverse!   405
Thou never from that hour in Paradise
Found'st either sweet repast, or sound repose;
Such ambush hid among sweet flowers and shades
Waited with hellish rancor imminent[6]
To intercept thy way, or send thee back   410
Despoiled of innocence, of faith, of bliss.
For now, and since first break of dawn, the fiend,
Mere serpent in appearance, forth was come,
And on his quest, where likeliest he might find
The only two of mankind, but in them   415
The whole included race, his purposed prey.
In bower and field he sought, where any tuft
Of grove or garden-plot more pleasant lay,
Their tendance[7] or plantation for delight;
By fountain or by shady rivulet   420
He sought them both, but wished his hap might find
Eve separate; he wished, but not with hope
Of what so seldom chanced; when to his wish,
Beyond his hope, Eve separate he spies,
Veiled in a cloud of fragrance, where she stood,   425
Half spied, so thick the roses bushing round
About her glowed, oft stooping to support
Each flower of slender stalk, whose head though gay
Carnation, purple, azure, or specked with gold,
Hung drooping unsustained; them she upstays   430
Gently with myrtle band, mindless[8] the while
Herself, though fairest unsupported flower,
From her best prop so far, and storm so nigh.
Nearer he drew, and many a walk traversed
Of stateliest covert, cedar, pine, or palm;   435
Then voluble[9] and bold, now hid, now seen
Among thick-woven arborets and flowers
Embordered on each bank, the hand[1] of Eve:
Spot more delicious than those gardens feigned
Or of revived Adonis, or renowned   440
Alcinous, host of old Laertes' son,[2]
Or that, not mystic, where the sapient king[3]
Held dalliance with his fair Egyptian spouse.
Much he the place admired, the person more.
As one who long in populous city pent,   445

5. "Much deceived" carries over: Eve was "much deceived of" (about) her "presumed return."
6. Threatening.
7. Object of their tending.
8. Heedless. The conceit of the flower gatherer who is herself gathered is repeated here from 4.269–271, where it was applied to Proserpina.
9. Rolling; with a hint from the second sense of "glib," fluent."
1. Handiwork. "Arborets": bushes.
2. The garden of Adonis was a heavenly bower where

Venus's lover was supposed still to lie in secret, recovering from his wound received on earth. (Venus would not allow him to die.) Alcinous was king of the Phaeacians. His garden, visited by Odysseus ("old Laertes' son"), is described in Odyssey 7.
3. Solomon; his "fair Egyptian spouse" is Pharaoh's daughter: Milton is referring to the Song of Solomon 6.2. The fact that it is "not mystic" (i.e., not mythical) distinguishes the Scriptural garden from the "feigned" (line 439) ones of classical legend.

Where houses thick and sewers annoy[4] the air,
Forth issuing on a summer's morn to breathe
Among the pleasant villages and farms
Adjoined, from each thing met conceives delight,
The smell of grain, or tedded grass, or kine,[5]   450
Or dairy, each rural sight, each rural sound:
If chance with nymphlike step fair virgin pass,[6]
What pleasing seemed, for her now pleases more,
She most, and in her look sums all delight.[7]
Such pleasure took the serpent to behold   455
This flowery plat,[8] the sweet recess of Eve
Thus early, thus alone; her heavenly form
Angelic, but more soft and feminine,
Her graceful innocence, her every air
Of gesture or least action overawed   460
His malice, and with rapine[9] sweet bereaved
His fierceness of the fierce intent it brought:
That space the evil one abstracted stood
From his own evil, and for the time remained
Stupidly good,[1] of enmity disarmed,   465
Of guile, of hate, of envy, of revenge.
But the hot Hell that always in him burns,
Though in mid Heaven, soon ended his delight,
And tortures him now more, the more he sees
Of pleasure not for him ordained: then soon   470
Fierce hate he recollects, and all his thoughts
Of mischief, gratulating,[2] thus excites:
    "Thoughts, whither have ye led me? with what sweet
Compulsion thus transported to forget
What hither brought us? hate, not love, nor hope   475
Of Paradise for Hell, hope here to taste[3]
Of pleasure, but all pleasure to destroy,
Save what is in destroying; other joy
To me is lost. Then let me not let pass
Occasion which now smiles: behold alone   480
The woman, opportune to all attempts,
Her husband, for I view far round, not nigh,
Whose higher intellectual more I shun,
And strength, of courage haughty, and of limb
Heroic built, though of terrestrial mold;[4]   485
Foe not informidable, exempt from wound,[5]
I not; so much hath Hell debased and pain
Enfeebled me to what I was in Heaven.
She fair, divinely fair, fit love for gods,
Not terrible, though terror be in love   490

---

4. Make noisome, befoul.
5. Cows. "Tedded": tossed and drying in the sun.
6. I.e., if by chance with nymphlike step a fair virgin
should pass.
7. I.e., in her look epitomizes all delight.
8. Meadow.
9. It is a deliberate paradox that her sweetness can ravish his malice; the word "rapine" is deliberately overvi-

olent.
1. I.e., he is momentarily stunned into a kind of vacant
goodness.
2. Exulting.
3. A "nor" is understood before "hope," carried over
from the negatives of the previous line.
4. Made of earth.
5. Adam in the state of innocence is invulnerable.

And beauty, not approached by stronger hate,
Hate stronger, under show of love well feigned,
The way which to her ruin now I tend."[6]
  So spake the enemy of mankind, enclosed
In serpent, inmate bad, and toward Eve 495
Addressed his way, not with indented wave,
Prone on the ground, as since, but on his rear,
Circular base of rising folds, that towered
Fold above fold a surging maze; his head
Crested aloft, and carbuncle[7] his eyes; 500
With burnished neck of verdant gold, erect
Amidst his circling spires, that on the grass
Floated redundant.[8] Pleasing was his shape,
And lovely; never since of serpent kind
Lovelier, not those that in Illyria changed 505
Hermione and Cadmus,[9] or the god
In Epidaurus;[1] nor to which transformed
Ammonian Jove, or Capitoline was seen,
He with Olympias, this with her who bore
Scipio, the height of Rome.[2] With tract oblique 510
At first, as one who sought accèss, but feared
To interrupt, sidelong he works his way.
As when a ship by skillful steersman wrought
Nigh river's mouth or foreland, where the wind
Veers oft, as oft so steers and shifts her sail: 515
So varied he, and of his tortuous train
Curled many a wanton wreath in sight of Eve,
To lure her eye: she busied heard the sound
Of rustling leaves, but minded not, as used
To such disport before her through the field, 520
From every beast, more duteous at her call
Than at Circean call the herd disguised.[3]
He bolder now, uncalled before her stood:
But as in gaze admiring; oft he bowed
His turret crest, and sleek enameled neck, 525
Fawning, and licked the ground whereon she trod.
His gentle dumb expression turned at length
The eye of Eve to mark his play: he, glad
Of her attention gained, with serpent tongue
Organic, or impulse of vocal air,[4] 530
His fraudulent temptation thus began:
  "Wonder not, sovereign mistress, if perhaps

6. I.e., love and beauty are terrible unless counteracted by hate—as they are being counteracted in Satan, to the ruin of Eve.
7. Deep red, inflamed.
8. Abundantly, to excess. "Spires": coils.
9. Ovid tells how Cadmus and Harmonia (Milton's
"Hermione") were changed to serpents after they retired (in despair at the misfortunes of their children) to
Illyria.
1. Aesculapius, god of medicine, had a temple at Epidaurus, from which he sometimes emerged in the form
of a serpent.
2. Jupiter Ammon ("Ammonian Jove"), in the form of
a snake, was said to have consorted with Olympias to
beget Alexander the Great; and in the same way, the
Jupiter of the Roman capitol (Jove "Capitoline") was
thought to have begotten Scipio Africanus, the savior
and greatest leader ("height") of Rome.
3. Circe, who enchanted men into the shape of beasts,
was attended by an obedient herd in the Odyssey.
4. I.e., Satan either used the actual tongue of the serpent or himself impressed the air with speech.

Thou canst, who art sole wonder; much less arm
Thy looks, the heaven of mildness, with disdain,
Displeased that I approach thee thus, and gaze   535
Insatiate, I thus single, nor have feared
Thy awful brow, more awful thus retired.
Fairest resemblance of thy Maker fair,
Thee all things living gaze on, all things thine
By gift, and thy celestial beauty adore   540
With ravishment beheld, there best beheld
Where universally admired: but here
In this enclosure wild, these beasts among,
Beholders rude and shallow to discern
Half what in thee is fair, one man except,   545
Who sees thee?[5] (and what is one?) who shouldst be seen
A goddess among gods, adored and served
By angels numberless, thy daily train."
    So glozed the tempter, and his proem[6] tuned;
Into the heart of Eve his words made way,   550
Though at the voice much marveling: at length,
Not unamazed, she thus in answer spake:
"What may this mean? Language of man pronounced
By tongue of brute, and human sense expressed?
The first at least of these I thought denied   555
To beasts, whom God on their creation-day
Created mute to all articulate sound;
The latter I demur,[7] for in their looks
Much reason, and in their actions oft appears.
Thee, serpent, subtlest beast of all the field   560
I knew, but not with human voice endued:[8]
Redouble then this miracle, and say,
How cam'st thou speakable of mute,[9] and how
To me so friendly grown above the rest
Of brutal kind, that daily are in sight?   565
Say, for such wonder claims attention due."
    To whom the guileful tempter thus replied:
"Empress of this fair world, resplendent Eve!
Easy to me it is to tell thee all
What thou command'st, and right thou shouldst be obeyed.   570
I was at first as other beasts that graze
The trodden herb, of abject thoughts and low,
As was my food, nor aught but food discerned
Or sex, and apprehended nothing high:
Till on a day, roving the field, I chanced   575
A goodly tree far distant to behold
Loaden with fruit of fairest colors mixed,
Ruddy and gold; I nearer drew to gaze;
When from the boughs a savory odor blown,

5. The beasts cannot see the beauty of Eve's soul, only
Adam can. Satan's entire speech is couched in the extravagant phrases of the Petrarchan love convention.
6. Introduction. "Glozed": flattered.

7. I.e., as to whether rational sense was denied to
brutes, I am doubtful.
8. Endowed.
9. To have speech after being dumb.

Grateful to appetite, more pleased my sense   580
Than smell of sweetest fennel,[1] or the teats
Of ewe or goat dropping with milk at even,
Unsucked of lamb or kid, that tend their play.
To satisfy the sharp desire I had
Of tasting those fair apples, I resolved   585
Not to defer: hunger and thirst at once,
Powerful persuaders, quickened at the scent
Of that alluring fruit, urged me so keen.
About the mossy trunk I wound me soon,
For, high from ground, the branches would require   590
Thy utmost reach, or Adam's: round the tree
All other beasts that saw, with like desire
Longing and envying stood, but could not reach.
Amid the tree now got, where plenty hung
Tempting so nigh, to pluck and eat my fill   595
I spared not;[2] for such pleasure till that hour
At feed or fountain never had I found.
Sated at length, ere long I might perceive
Strange alteration in me, to degree
Of reason in my inward powers, and speech   600
Wanted not long, though to this shape retained.[3]
Thenceforth to speculations high or deep
I turned my thoughts, and with capacious mind
Considered all things visible in Heaven,
Or Earth, or middle, all things fair and good: 605
But all that fair and good in thy divine
Semblance, and in thy beauty's heavenly ray
United I beheld: no fair[4] to thine
Equivalent or second, which compelled
Me thus, though importune perhaps, to come   610
And gaze, and worship thee of right declared
Sovereign of creatures, universal dame."
    So talked the spirited[5] sly snake: and Eve
Yet more amazed, unwary thus replied:
    "Serpent, thy overpraising leaves in doubt   615
The virtue of that fruit, in thee first proved.
But say, where grows the tree, from hence how far?
For many are the trees of God that grow
In Paradise, and various, yet unknown
To us; in such abundance lies our choice,   620
As leaves a greater store of fruit untouched,
Still hanging incorruptible, till men
Grow up to their provision, and more hands
Help to disburden Nature of her bearth."[6]
    To whom the wily adder, blithe and glad: 625
"Empress, the way is ready, and not long,

---

1. Milton learned, probably from Pliny, the natural historian, that serpents were fond of fennel; popular superstition had it that they drank the milk of sheep and goats.
2. Refrained not.
3. His inward powers, his mental constitution and gift of speech, were changed, but he retained his exterior shape as before.
4. Beauty.
5. Possessed by a spirit, inspired. "Dame": mistress.
6. So spelled to pun on the idea of trees bearing fruit and thus in a way giving birth to young.

Beyond a row of myrtles, on a flat,
Fast by a fountain, one small thicket past
Of blowing myrrh and balm: if thou accept
My conduct,[7] I can bring thee thither soon."   630
   "Lead then," said Eve. He leading swiftly rolled
In tangles, and made intricate seem straight,
To mischief swift.[8] Hope elevates, and joy
Brightens his crest; as when a wandering fire
Compact of unctuous vapor,[9] which the night   635
Condenses, and the cold environs round,
Kindled through agitation to a flame
(Which oft, they say, some evil spirit attends),
Hovering and blazing with delusive light,
Misleads th' amazed night-wanderer from his way   640
To bogs and mires, and oft through pond or pool,
There swallowed up and lost, from succor far:
So glistered the dire snake, and into fraud
Led Eve our credulous mother, to the tree
Of prohibition,[1] root of all our woe: 645
Which when she saw, thus to her guide she spake:
   "Serpent, we might have spared our coming hither,
Fruitless to me, though fruit be here to excess,
The credit of whose virtue rest with thee;[2]
Wondrous indeed, if cause of such effects!   650
But of this tree we may not taste nor touch:
God so commanded, and left that command
Sole daughter of his voice; the rest,[3] we live
Law to ourselves; our reason is our law."
   To whom the tempter guilefully replied: 655
"Indeed? Hath God then said that of the fruit
Of all these garden trees ye shall not eat,
Yet lords declared of all in earth or air?"
   To whom thus Eve, yet sinless: "Of the fruit
Of each tree in the garden we may eat,   660
But of the fruit of this fair tree amidst
The garden, God hath said, 'Ye shall not eat
Thereof, nor shall ye touch it, lest ye die.'"
   She scarce had said, though brief, when now more bold
The tempter, but with show of zeal and love   665
To man, and indignation at his wrong,
New part puts on, and as to passion moved,
Fluctuates disturbed, yet comely, and in act
Raised,[4] as of some great matter to begin.
As when of old some orator renowned   670
In Athens or free Rome, where eloquence
Flourished, since mute, to some great cause addressed,
Stood in himself collected, while each part,

7. Guidance. "Blowing": blooming.
8. Milton's physical descriptions of the serpent often
have distinct moral overtones, as here.
9. Composed of oily vapor; Milton's theory of the *ignis
fatuus*, or will-o'-the-wisp, is strikingly material and
"scientific."

1. Prohibited tree (a Hebraism).
2. I.e., you must remain the only evidence of the
fruit's power.
3. In everything else. "Sole daughter of his voice": his
one injunction (a Hebraism).
4. Poised in posture.

Motion, each act, won audience ere the tongue,
Sometimes in height began, as no delay   675
Of preface brooking,[5] through his zeal of right.
So standing, moving, or to height upgrown
The tempter all impassioned thus began:
    "O sacred, wise, and wisdom-giving plant,
Mother of science![6] now I feel thy power   680
Within me clear, not only to discern
Things in their causes, but to trace the ways
Of highest agents, deemed however wise.
Queen of this universe! do not believe
Those rigid threats of death. Ye shall not die;   685
How should ye? by the fruit? it gives you life
To knowledge;[7] by the Threatener? look on me,
Me who have touched and tasted, yet both live,
And life more perfect have attained than Fate
Meant me, by venturing higher than my lot.   690
Shall that be shut to man, which to the beast
Is open? Or will God incense his ire
For such a petty trespass, and not praise
Rather your dauntless virtue, whom the pain
Of death denounced, whatever thing death be,   695
Deterred not from achieving what might lead
To happier life, knowledge of good and evil?
Of good, how just![8] Of evil, if what is evil
Be real, why not known, since easier shunned?
God therefore cannot hurt ye, and be just;   700
Not just, not God; not feared then, nor obeyed:
Your fear itself of death removes the fear.[9]
Why then was this forbid? Why but to awe,
Why but to keep ye low and ignorant,
His worshipers? He knows that in the day   705
Ye eat thereof, your eyes that seem so clear,
Yet are but dim, shall perfectly be then
Opened and cleared, and ye shall be as gods,
Knowing both good and evil, as they know.
That ye should be as gods, since I as man,   710
Internal man,[1] is but proportion meet,
I, of brute, human; ye, of human, gods.
So ye shall die perhaps, by putting off
Human, to put on gods:[2] death to be wished,
Though threatened, which no worse than this can bring.   715
And what are gods that man may not become
As they, participating godlike food?
The gods are first, and that advantage use
On our belief, that all from them proceeds.

5. The orator, as if too much moved to be bothered
with a preface, bursts into the middle of his speech.
6. Knowledge.
7. Life in addition to knowledge, or life with which to
enlarge your knowledge.
8. I.e., how just to have knowledge of good!
9. I.e., your fear of death removes your fear of God,
since if God inflicts death, He will not be just and
hence not God. The serpent's sophism is visible.
1. Man in intellectual powers.
2. The devil can quote Scripture to his purpose, and
here he is perverting St. Paul, who told the Colossians
(3.9–10) to put off the old man and put on the new.
"Participating" (line 717): sharing.

I question it; for this fair Earth I see,   720
Warmed by the sun, producing every kind,
Them nothing: if they all things,³ who enclosed
Knowledge of good and evil in this tree,
That whoso eats thereof forthwith attains
Wisdom without their leave? And wherein lies   725
Th' offense, that man should thus attain to know?
What can your knowledge hurt him, or this tree
Impart against his will, if all be his?
Or is it envy, and can envy dwell
In heavenly breasts?⁴ These, these, and many more   730
Causes import your need of this fair fruit.
Goddess humane,⁵ reach then, and freely taste!"
    He ended, and his words, replete with guile,
Into her heart too easy entrance won:
Fixed on the fruit she gazed, which to behold   735
Might tempt alone, and in her ears the sound
Yet rung of his persuasive words, impregned⁶
With reason, to her seeming, and with truth;
Meanwhile the hour of noon drew on, and waked
An eager appetite, raised by the smell   740
So savory of that fruit, which with desire,
Inclinable now grown to touch or taste,
Solicited her longing eye;⁷ yet first
Pausing a while, thus to herself she mused:
    "Great are thy virtues, doubtless, best of fruits,   745
Though kept from man, and worthy to be admired,
Whose taste, too long forborne, at first essay
Gave elocution to the mute, and taught
The tongue not made for speech to speak thy praise:
Thy praise he also who forbids thy use   750
Conceals not from us,⁸ naming thee the Tree
Of Knowledge, knowledge both of good and evil;
Forbids us then to taste; but his forbidding
Commends thee more, while it infers the good
By thee communicated, and our want: 755
For good unknown, sure is not had, or had
And yet unknown, is as not had at all.⁹
In plain then, what forbids he but to know?
Forbids us good, forbids us to be wise!
Such prohibitions bind not. But if death   760
Bind us with after-bands, what profits then
Our inward freedom? In the day we eat
Of this fair fruit, our doom is, we shall die.
How dies the serpent? He hath eaten and lives,
And knows, and speaks, and reasons, and discerns,   765

---

3. The verb *produced* is understood. Satan is talking now not about "God" but "the gods."
4. Adapted from Virgil (*Aeneid* 1.15). "Import" (next line): imply, suggest.
5. Not so much "human goddess" (a Satanic paradox) as "kindly," "gracious" goddess.
6. Impregnated.

7. Eve's five senses—sight, hearing, smell, taste, and touch—are all solicited by the fruit.
8. God himself, by naming it, has called attention to the tree's magic powers.
9. An unknown good is like no good at all. "In plain" (next line): i.e., in plain language.

Irrational till then. For us alone
Was death invented? Or to us denied
This intellectual food, for beasts reserved?
For beasts it seems: yet that one beast which first
Hath tasted, envies not, but brings with joy   770
The good befallen him, author unsuspect,[1]
Friendly to man, far from deceit or guile.
What fear I then, rather what know to fear[2]
Under this ignorance of good and evil,
Of God or death, of law or penalty?   775
Here grows the cure of all, this fruit divine,
Fair to the eye, inviting to the taste,
Of virtue[3] to make wise: what hinders then
To reach and feed at once both body and mind?"
    So saying, her rash hand in evil hour   780
Forth reaching to the fruit, she plucked, she eat.[4]
Earth felt the wound, and nature from her seat[5]
Sighing through all her works gave signs of woe,
That all was lost. Back to the thicket slunk
The guilty serpent, and well might, for Eve,   785
Intent now wholly on her taste, naught else
Regarded; such delight till then, as seemed,
In fruit she never tasted, whether true
Or fancied so, through expectation high
Of knowledge; nor was godhead from her thought.[6]   790
Greedily she engorged without restraint,
And knew not eating death:[7] satiate at length,
And heightened as with wine, jocund and boon,[8]
Thus to herself she pleasingly began:
    "O sovereign, virtuous, precious of all trees   795
In Paradise! of operation blest
To sapience, hitherto obscured, infamed,[9]
And thy fair fruit let hang, as to no end
Created; but henceforth my early care,
Not without song each morning, and due praise   800
Shall tend thee, and the fertile burden ease
Of thy full branches offered free to all;
Till dieted by thee I grow mature
In knowledge, as the gods who all things know;
Though others[1] envy what they cannot give: 805
For had the gift been theirs, it had not here
Thus grown. Experience, next to thee I owe,
Best guide; not following thee I had remained
In ignorance; thou open'st Wisdom's way,
And giv'st accèss, though secret she retire.   810

1. A witness beyond suspicion.
2. In her ignorance, Eve does not really know what to fear and what not to fear—at least, so she says.
3. Power.
4. In the 17th century, an accepted past tense of *eat*.
5. Wherever Nature is hidden, in the heart of things, she sighs.
6. I.e., she expected to achieve godhead immediately.
7. A grim pun. She is eating death and does not know

it, but death is eating her too. Compare "eating cares" (*L'Allegro*, line 135, p. 640).
8. Joyous and liberal.
9. Defamed, i.e., maligned. "To sapience": to wisdom, for the wise and those of good taste. (Latin *sapere*, "to be wise," has its root in the verb "to taste.")
1. The gods, i.e., other gods. In saying that God did not give the tree, Eve is merely echoing a lesson learned from the serpent.

And I perhaps am secret; Heaven is high,
High and remote to see from thence distinct
Each thing on Earth; and other care perhaps
May have diverted from continual watch
Our great Forbidder,[2] safe with all his spies   815
About him. But to Adam in what sort[3]
Shall I appear? Shall I to him make known
As yet my change, and give him to partake
Full happiness with me, or rather not,
But keep the odds[4] of knowledge in my power   820
Without copartner? so to add what wants
In female sex, the more to draw his love,
And render me more equal, and perhaps,
A thing not undesirable, sometime
Superior: for inferior who is free?[5]   825
This may be well: but what if God have seen
And death ensue? Then I shall be no more,
And Adam, wedded to another Eve,
Shall live with her enjoying, I extinct;
A death to think. Confirmed then I resolve,   830
Adam shall share with me in bliss or woe:
So dear I love him, that with him all deaths
I could endure, without him live no life."[6]
    So saying, from the tree her step she turned,
But first low reverence done,[7] as to the power   835
That dwelt within, whose presence had infused
Into the plant sciential[8] sap, derived
From nectar, drink of gods. Adam the while
Waiting desirous her return, had wove
Of choicest flowers a garland to adorn   840
Her tresses, and her rural labors crown,
As reapers oft are wont their harvest queen.
Great joy he promised to his thoughts, and new
Solace in her return, so long delayed:
Yet oft his heart, divine[9] of something ill,   845
Misgave him; he the faltering measure[1] felt;
And forth to meet her went, the way she took
That morn when first they parted. By the Tree
Of Knowledge he must pass; there he her met,
Scarce from the tree returning; in her hand   850
A bough of fairest fruit that downy smiled,
New gathered, and ambrosial smell diffused.
To him she hasted, in her face excuse
Came prologue, and apology to prompt,[2]
Which with bland words at will she thus addressed: 855
    "Hast thou not wondered, Adam, at my stay?

2. Now that Eve has fallen, God is a "great Forbidder,"
and all His gifts in Paradise are forgotten.
3. Guise.
4. Balance.
5. Eve's fatal foolishness implies that the only person
in the world who can ever be free is an absolute tyrant.
6. Her affection is not unlike Satan's (4.374–385) in
its destructiveness. In reality, there is no chance of her

living "without him," because she is already under sentence of death.
7. Eve's first physical act after falling is idolatry.
8. Knowledge-giving.
9. Foreboding, suspicious.
1. I.e., of his pulse.
2. Her face had an excuse in it, as prologue to an apology that followed after.

Thee I have missed, and thought it long, deprived
Thy presence, agony of love till now
Not felt, nor shall be twice; for never more
Mean I to try what rash untried I sought,   860
The pain of absence from thy sight. But strange
Hath been the cause, and wonderful to hear:
This tree is not as we are told, a tree
Of danger tasted,[3] nor to evil unknown
Opening the way, but of divine effect   865
To open eyes, and make them gods who taste;
And hath been tasted such. The serpent wise,
Or not restrained as we, or not obeying,
Hath eaten of the fruit, and is become,
Not dead, as we are threatened, but thenceforth   870
Endued with human voice and human sense,
Reasoning to admiration, and with me
Persuasively[4] hath so prevailed, that I
Have also tasted, and have also found
Th' effects to correspond, opener mine eyes,   875
Dim erst, dilated spirits, ampler heart,
And growing up to godhead;[5] which for thee
Chiefly I sought, without thee can despise.
For bliss, as thou hast part, to me is bliss;
Tedious, unshared with thee, and odious soon.   880
Thou therefore also taste, that equal lot
May join us, equal joy, as equal love;
Lest, thou not tasting, different degree[6]
Disjoin us, and I then too late renounce
Deity for thee, when Fate will not permit."[7]   885
    Thus Eve with countenance blithe her story told;
But in her cheek distemper[8] flushing glowed.
On th' other side, Adam, soon as he heard
The fatal trespass done by Eve, amazed,
Astonied stood and blank,[9] while horror chill   890
Ran through his veins, and all his joints relaxed;
From his slack hand the garland wreathed for Eve
Down dropped, and all the faded roses shed.
Speechless he stood and pale, till thus at length
First to himself he inward silence broke: 895
    "O fairest of creation, last and best
Of all God's works, creature in whom excelled
Whatever can to sight or thought be formed,
Holy, divine, good, amiable, or sweet!
How art thou lost, how on a sudden lost,   900
Defaced, deflowered, and now to death devote![1]
Rather how hast thou yielded to transgress
The strict forbiddance, how to violate

---

3. If tasted.
4. By persuasion. "Admiration": admirably.
5. Everything that Eve says she feels is what Satan has told her she will feel.
6. Differing rank in the hierarchy of creatures.
7. Contrast Eve's logic when she is alone (lines

817–831).
8. The proportion of Eve's humors—which, in the state of innocence, gave her perfect health—has been disturbed, and she is running a fever.
9. Empty of mind. "Astonied": astonished, "petrified."
1. Doomed.

The sacred fruit forbidden! Some cursèd fraud
Of enemy hath beguiled thee, yet unknown,[2]   905
And me with thee hath ruined, for with thee
Certain my resolution is to die.
How can I live without thee, how forego
Thy sweet converse and love so dearly joined,
To live again in these wild woods forlorn?[3]   910
Should God create another Eve, and I
Another rib afford, yet loss of thee
Would never from my heart; no, no! I feel
The link of nature draw me: flesh of flesh,
Bone of my bone thou art, and from thy state   915
Mine never shall be parted, bliss or woe."
    So having said, as one from sad dismay
Recomforted, and after thoughts disturbed
Submitting to what seemed remediless,
Thus in calm mood his words to Eve he turned: 920
    "Bold deed thou hast presumed, adventurous Eve,
And peril great provoked, who thus hath dared
Had it been only coveting to eye
That sacred fruit, sacred[4] to abstinence,
Much more to taste it, under ban to touch.   925
But past who can recall, or done undo?
Not God omnipotent, nor Fate! Yet so
Perhaps thou shalt not die, perhaps the fact[5]
Is not so heinous now, foretasted fruit,
Profaned first by the serpent, by him first   930
Made common and unhallowed ere our taste,
Nor yet on him found deadly; he yet lives,
Lives, as thou saidst, and gains to live as man
Higher degree of life: inducement strong
To us, as likely tasting to attain   935
Proportional ascent, which cannot be
But to be gods, or angels, demigods.[6]
Nor can I think that God, Creator wise,
Though threatening, will in earnest so destroy
Us his prime creatures, dignified so high,   940
Set over all his works, which in our fall,
For us created, needs with us must fail,
Dependent made; so God shall uncreate,
Be frustrate, do, undo, and labor lose;
Not well conceived of God,[7] who, though his power   945
Creation could repeat, yet would be loath
Us to abolish, lest the adversary
Triùmph and say: 'Fickle their state whom God
Most favors; who can please him long? Me first
He ruined, now mankind; whom will he next?'   950
Matter of scorn, not to be given the foe.

2. "Yet unknown" modifies "enemy."
3. Without Eve, Adam foresees, Paradise will be again what it was before her coming, forlorn.
4. Devoted.
5. Act.
6. Note how Adam agrees first in Eve's harmless errors about the serpent, then in her sinful ambition to achieve a higher form of life.
7. I.e., not a proper conception of God (as making His actions dependent on those of an inferior).

However, I with thee have fixed my lot,
Certain to undergo like doom: if death
Consort with thee, death is to me as life;
So forcible within my heart I feel   955
The bond of nature draw me to my own,
My own in thee, for what thou art is mine;
Our state cannot be severed; we are one,
One flesh; to lose thee were to lose myself."
   So Adam, and thus Eve to him replied: 960
"O glorious trial of exceeding love,
Illustrious evidence, example high!
Engaging me to emulate; but short
Of thy perfection, how shall I attain,
Adam? from whose dear side I boast me sprung,   965
And gladly of our union hear thee speak,
One heart, one soul in both; whereof good proof
This day affords, declaring thee resolved,
Rather than death or aught than death more dread
Shall separate us, linked in love so dear,   970
To undergo with me one guilt, one crime,
If any be, of tasting this fair fruit;
Whose virtue (for of good still good proceeds,
Direct, or by occasion)⁸ hath presented
This happy trial of thy love, which else   975
So eminently never had been known.
Were it I thought death menaced would ensue⁹
This my attempt, I would sustain alone
The worst, and not persuade thee, rather die
Deserted, than oblige¹ thee with a fact   980
Pernicious to thy peace, chiefly assured
Remarkably so late of thy so true,
So faithful love unequaled;² but I feel
Far otherwise th' event;³ not death, but life
Augmented, opened eyes, new hopes, new joys,   985
Taste so divine, that what of sweet before
Hath touched my sense, flat seems to this, and harsh.
On my experience, Adam, freely taste,
And fear of death deliver to the winds."
   So saying, she embraced him, and for joy   990
Tenderly wept, much won that he his love
Had so ennobled, as of choice to incur
Divine displeasure for her sake, or death.
In recompense (for such compliance bad
Such recompense best merits), from the bough   995
She gave him of that fair enticing fruit
With liberal hand; he scrupled not to eat,
Against his better knowledge, not deceived,
But fondly overcome with female charm.⁴

8. Indirectly.
9. Result from.
1. Render liable, involve.
2. Touched by Adam's devotion, Eve feels a little belated remorse at the damage she may have inflicted on

him.
3. Result (of eating the apple).
4. See 1 Timothy 2.14: "And Adam was not deceived,
but the woman being deceived was in the transgression."

Earth trembled from her entrails, as again   1000
In pangs, and Nature gave a second groan,
Sky lowered, and muttering thunder, some sad drops
Wept at completing of the mortal sin
Original; while Adam took no thought,
Eating his fill, nor Eve to iterate   1005
Her former trespass feared, the more to soothe
Him with her loved society; that now
As with new wine intoxicated both,
They swim in mirth, and fancy that they feel
Divinity within them breeding wings   1010
Wherewith to scorn the earth. But that false fruit
Far other operation first displayed,
Carnal desire inflaming; he on Eve
Began to cast lascivious eyes, she him
As wantonly repaid; in lust they burn,   1015
Till Adam thus 'gan Eve to dalliance move:
    "Eve, now I see thou art exact of taste,
And elegant, of sapience[5] no small part,
Since to each meaning savor we apply,
And palate call judicious. I the praise   1020
Yield thee, so well this day thou hast purveyed.[6]
Much pleasure we have lost while we abstained
From this delightful fruit, nor known till now
True relish, tasting; if such pleasure be
In things to us forbidden, it might be wished   1025
For this one tree had been forbidden ten.
But come; so well refreshed, now let us play,
As meet is, after such delicious fare;
For never did thy beauty since the day
I saw thee first and wedded thee, adorned   1030
With all perfections, so enflame my sense
With ardor to enjoy thee, fairer now
Than ever, bounty of this virtuous tree."
    So said he, and forbore not glance or toy[7]
Of amorous intent, well understood   1035
Of[8] Eve, whose eye darted contagious fire.
Her hand he seized, and to a shady bank,
Thick overhead with verdant roof embowered,
He led her, nothing loath; flowers were the couch,
Pansies, and violets, and asphodel,   1040
And hyacinth, Earth's freshest, softest lap.
There they their fill of love and love's disport
Took largely, of their mutual guilt the seal,
The solace of their sin, till dewy sleep
Oppressed them, wearied with their amorous play.   1045
    Soon as the force of that fallacious fruit,
That with exhilarating vapor bland

---

5. "Sapience" means wisdom, but the word comes   "Exact": exacting, demanding.
from Latin *sapere*, "to taste," which gives rise, via an-   6. Provided for us, provisioned us.
other etymology, to the word *savor*. Adam's sentence   7. Caress.
plays rather heavily on these two meanings of *sapere*.   8. By.

About their spirits had played, and inmost powers
Made err, was now exhaled, and grosser sleep
Bred of unkindly fumes,[9] with conscious dreams   1050
Encumbered, now had left them, up they rose
As from unrest, and each the other viewing,
Soon found their eyes how opened, and their minds
How darkened. Innocence, that as a veil
Had shadowed them from knowing ill, was gone;   1055
Just confidence, and native righteousness,
And honor from about them, naked left
To guilty Shame; he covered, but his robe
Uncovered more.[1] So rose the Danite strong,
Herculean Samson, from the harlot-lap   1060
Of Philistean Dalilah, and waked
Shorn of his strength;[2] they destitute and bare
Of all their virtue. Silent, and in face
Confounded, long they sat, as strucken mute;
Till Adam, though not less than Eve abashed,   1065
At length gave utterance to these words constrained:
     "O Eve, in evil hour[3] thou didst give ear
To that false worm, of[4] whomsoever taught
To counterfeit man's voice, true in our fall,
False in our promised rising; since our eyes   1070
Opened we find indeed, and find we know
Both good and evil, good lost and evil got:
Bad fruit of knowledge, if this be to know,
Which leaves us naked thus, of honor void,
Of innocence, of faith, of purity,   1075
Our wonted ornaments now soiled and stained,
And in our faces evident the signs
Of foul concupiscence; whence evil store,[5]
Even shame, the last of evils; of the first
Be sure then.[6] How shall I behold the face   1080
Henceforth of God or angel, erst with joy
And rapture so oft beheld? Those heavenly shapes
Will dazzle now this earthly[7] with their blaze
Insufferably bright. O might I here
In solitude live savage, in some glade   1085
Obscured, where highest woods, impenetrable
To star or sunlight, spread their umbrage broad,
And brown[8] as evening! Cover me, ye pines,
Ye cedars, with innumerable boughs
Hide me, where I may never see them more![9]   1090
But let us now, as in bad plight, devise
What best may for the present serve to hide

---

9. Unnatural vapors.
1. They were covered with shame, which made them
conscious of their nakedness as they had never been
before.
2. See the story of Samson and Delilah, Judges
16.4–20.
3. Even in his misery, Adam cannot resist the word
play on Eve-evil.
4. By. "Worm": serpent, with a connotation of disgust.

5. A store of evil.
6. I.e., since we now feel shame, the last of evils, we
shall soon experience the first ones.
7. A noun such as *vision* is understood.
8. Dark.
9. Cf. Revelation 6.16: "And said to the mountains
and rocks, Fall on us, and hide us from the face of him
that sitteth on the throne, and from the wrath of the
Lamb."

The parts of each from other that seem most
To shame obnoxious,[1] and unseemliest seen;
Some tree whose broad smooth leaves together sewed,   1095
And girded on our loins, may cover round
Those middle parts, that this newcomer, Shame,
There sit not, and reproach us as unclean."
      So counseled he, and both together went
Into the thickest wood; there soon they chose   1100
The fig-tree,[2] not that kind for fruit renowned,
But such as at this day, to Indians known,
In Malabar or Deccan[3] spreads her arms
Branching so broad and long, that in the ground
The bended twigs take root, and daughters grow   1105
About the mother tree, a pillared shade
High overarched, and echoing walks between;
There oft the Indian herdsman, shunning heat,
Shelters in cool, and tends his pasturing herds
At loopholes cut through thickest shade. Those leaves   1110
They gathered, broad as Amazonian targe,[4]
And with what skill they had, together sewed,
To gird their waist; vain covering, if to hide
Their guilt and dreaded shame! O how unlike
To that first naked glory! Such of late   1115
Columbus found th' American so girt
With feathered cincture,[5] naked else and wild
Among the trees on isles and woody shores.
Thus fenced, and, as they thought, their shame in part
Covered, but not at rest or ease of mind,   1120
They sat them down to weep; nor only tears
Rained at their eyes, but high winds worse within
Began to rise, high passions, anger, hate,
Mistrust, suspicion, discord, and shook sore
Their inward state of mind, calm region once   1125
And full of peace, now tossed and turbulent:
For Understanding ruled not, and the Will
Heard not her lore, both in subjection now
To sensual Appetite, who from beneath
Usurping over sovereign Reason claimed   1130
Superior sway.[6] From thus distempered breast,
Adam, estranged in look and altered style,
Speech intermitted thus to Eve renewed:
      "Would thou hadst hearkened to my words, and stayed
With me, as I besought thee, when that strange   1135
Desire of wandering, this unhappy morn,
I know not whence possessed thee! we had then
Remained still happy, not as now, despoiled

1. Vulnerable, liable.
2. The banyan, or Indian fig. It has small leaves, but Milton's knowledge of it came from Gerard's *Herbal* (1597), where all the details of lines 1104–11 may be found.
3. Sections of southern India.
4. Shield. The Amazons, mythical female warriors, carried large crescent-shaped shields.
5. Belt.
6. The psychology of the Fall is made explicit here. The higher faculties of reason are in subjection to the lower faculties of appetite. Moreover, Adam has lost his superiority over Eve.

Of all our good, shamed, naked, miserable.
Let none henceforth seek needless cause to approve   1140
The faith they owe;[7] when earnestly they seek
Such proof, conclude they then begin to fail."
    To whom, soon moved with touch of blame, thus Eve:
"What words have passed thy lips, Adam severe?
Imput'st thou that to my default or will   1145
Of wandering, as thou call'st it, which who knows
But might as ill have happened, thou being by,
Or to thyself perhaps? Hadst thou been there,
Or here th' attempt, thou couldst not have discerned
Fraud in the serpent, speaking as he spake;   1150
No ground of enmity between us known,
Why he should mean me ill, or seek to harm?
Was I to have never parted from thy side?
As good have grown there still, a lifeless rib.
Being as I am, why didst not thou, the head,[8]   1155
Command me absolutely not to go,
Going into such danger, as thou saidst?
Too facile[9] then, thou didst not much gainsay,
Nay, didst permit, approve, and fair dismiss.
Hadst thou been firm and fixed in thy dissent,   1160
Neither had I transgressed, nor thou with me."
    To whom, then first incensed, Adam replied:
"Is this the love, is this the recompense
Of mine to thee, ingrateful Eve, expressed
Immutable[1] when thou were lost, not I,   1165
Who might have lived and joyed immortal bliss,
Yet willingly chose rather death with thee?
And am I now upbraided as the cause
Of thy transgressing? not enough severe,
It seems, in thy restraint? What could I more?   1170
I warned thee, I admonished thee, foretold
The danger, and the lurking enemy
That lay in wait; beyond this had been force,
And force upon free will hath here no place.
But confidence then bore thee on, secure   1175
Either to meet no danger, or to find
Matter of glorious trial; and perhaps
I also erred in overmuch admiring
What seemed in thee so perfect, that I thought
No evil durst attempt thee! but I rue   1180
That error now, which is become my crime,
And thou th' accuser. Thus it shall befall
Him who, to worth in women overtrusting,
Lets her will rule; restraint she will not brook,[2]
And, left to herself, if evil thence ensue,   1185
She first his weak indulgence will accuse."

7. Own. "Approve": test, prove.   9. Easy, permissive.
8. Head of the family, but also the rational director, as   1. Shown to be unchangeable.
the head is to the rest of the body. Cf. 1 Corinthians   2. Accept.
11.3, "the head of the woman is the man."

Thus they in mutual accusation spent
The fruitless hours, but neither self-condemning;[3]
And of their vain contèst appeared no end.

From Book 10

Summary When it is known in Heaven that man has fallen, God sends his
Son to pass judgment on the sinners. Having found them in the garden, he hears
their confession and passes instant sentence, cursing the serpent, condemning Eve
to the pains of childbirth and Adam to those of daily toil; but in mercy, he clothes
the human couple both outwardly with the skins of beasts and inwardly with his
righteousness. Meanwhile Sin and Death, sitting by Hell-gate, feel new strength,
and pass across Chaos, leaving a great bridge behind them. On their way they
meet with their parent, Satan, learn of his success on Earth, and press eagerly
forward in hopes of destroying humankind altogether. Satan, on the other hand,
continues his flight back toward Hell, where he is to report to his constituents.

[Consequences of the Fall]

* * * Th' other way Satan went down	
The causey[4] to Hell-gate; on either side	415
Disparted Chaos overbuilt exclaimed,	
And with rebounding surge the bars assailed,	
That scorned his indignation.[5] Through the gate,	
Wide open and unguarded, Satan passed,	
And all about found desolate; for those	420
Appointed to sit there[6] had left their charge,	
Flown to the upper world; the rest were all	
Far to the inland retired, about the walls	
Of Pandemonium, city and proud seat	
Of Lucifer, so by allusion called	425
Of that bright star to Satan paragoned.	
There kept their watch the legions, while the Grand[7]	
In council sat, solicitous what chance	
Might intercept their emperor sent; so he	
Departing gave command, and they observed.	430
As when the Tartar from his Russian foe,	
By Astracan, over the snowy plains	
Retires, or Bactrian Sophi, from the horns	
Of Turkish crescent, leaves all waste beyond	
The realm of Aladule, in his retreat	435
To Tauris or Casbeen;[8] so these, the late	
Heaven-banished host, left desert utmost Hell	
Many a dark league, reduced in careful watch	
Round their metropolis, and now expecting	

3. Sterile recrimination is a first fruit of the forbidden tree.
4. Causeway.
5. Chaos, as the instinctive enemy of order, is hostile to the bridge built across its gulf by Sin and Death.
6. I.e., Sin and Death.
7. The Grand are the superior devils, Hell's aristocracy. Satan is called Lucifer, the light-bringer, because he was bright as the morning star (before he fell).
8. The comparison is with Tartars retreating before attacking Russians, and Persians before predatory Turks. "Bactrian": Persian. "Tauris": Tabriz. "Casbeen": Kazvin. Milton wants his simile to convey a mingled sense of barbaric Oriental splendor, cruelty, and desolation in Hell.

Each hour their great adventurer from the search   440
Of foreign worlds. He through the midst unmarked,
In show plebeian angel militant[9]
Of lowest order, passed, and from the door
Of that Plutonian hall, invisible
Ascended his high throne, which, under state[1]   445
Of richest texture spread, at th' upper end
Was placed in regal luster. Down a while
He sat, and round about him saw, unseen.
At last, as from a cloud, his fulgent[2] head
And shape star-bright appeared, or brighter, clad   450
With what permissive glory since his fall
Was left him, or false glitter. All amazed
At that so sudden blaze, the Stygian throng
Bent their aspèct, and whom they wished beheld,
Their mighty chief returned: loud was th' acclaim.   455
Forth rushed in haste the great consulting peers,
Raised from their dark divan,[3] and with like joy
Congratulant approached him, who with hand
Silence, and with these words attention, won:
    "Thrones, Dominations, Princedoms, Virtues, Powers!   460
For in possession such, not only of right,
I call ye and declare ye now, returned[4]
Successful beyond hope, to lead ye forth
Triumphant out of this infernal pit
Abominable, accursed, the house of woe,   465
And dungeon of our tyrant! Now possess,
As lords, a spacious world, to our native Heaven
Little inferior, by my adventure hard
With peril great achieved. Long were to tell
What I have done, what suffered, with what pain   470
Voyaged th' unreal, vast, unbounded deep
Of horrible confusion, over which
By Sin and Death a broad way now is paved
To expedite your glorious march; but I
Toiled out my uncouth passage, forced to ride   475
Th' untractable abyss, plunged in the womb
Of unoriginal[5] Night and Chaos wild,
That, jealous of their secrets, fiercely opposed
My journey strange, with clamorous uproar
Protesting Fate supreme; thence how I found   480
The new-created world, which fame in Heaven
Long had foretold, a fabric wonderful
Of absolute perfection; therein man
Placed in a paradise, by our exile
Made happy. Him by fraud I have seduced   485

---

9. Literally, an angelic foot soldier or private, but with
an ironic overtone from the phrase "church militant."
"Unmarked": unnoticed.
1. Canopy.
2. Glittering, refulgent.
3. The Turkish council of state; the Oriental theme
continues.

4. "Returned" modifies "I" at the beginning of the
line: "now that I have returned." Satan makes a distinction much in people's minds since the days of Cromwell and Charles I: a kingdom could be claimed either
by right (in law, de jure) or in act (by possession, de
facto). The devils now have both claims to their titles.
5. Without source or origin, primeval.

From his creator, and, the more to increase
Your wonder, with an apple! He[6] thereat
Offended—worth your laughter!—hath given up
Both his belovèd man and all his world
To Sin and Death a prey, and so to us,   490
Without our hazard, labor, or alarm,
To range in, and to dwell, and over man
To rule, as over all he should have ruled.
True is, me also he hath judged; or rather
Me not, but the brute serpent in whose shape   495
Man I deceived. That which to me belongs
Is enmity, which he will put between
Me and mankind: I am to bruise his heel;
His seed (when, is not set) shall bruise my head.[7]
A world who would not purchase with a bruise,   500
Or much more grievous pain? Ye have th' account
Of my performance; what remains, ye gods,
But up and enter now into full bliss?"
    So having said, a while he stood, expecting
Their universal shout and high applause   505
To fill his ear; when, contrary, he hears,
On all sides from innumerable tongues
A dismal universal hiss, the sound
Of public scorn. He wondered, but not long
Had leisure, wondering at himself now more.   510
His visage drawn he felt to sharp and spare,
His arms clung to his ribs, his legs entwining
Each other, till, supplanted,[8] down he fell
A monstrous serpent on his belly prone,
Reluctant,[9] but in vain; a greater power   515
Now ruled him, punished in the shape he sinned,
According to his doom. He would have spoke,
But hiss for hiss returned with forkèd tongue
To forkèd tongue; for now were all transformed
Alike, to serpents all, as accessories   520
To his bold riot. Dreadful was the din
Of hissing through the hall, thick-swarming now
With complicated[1] monsters, head and tail—
Scorpion, and asp, and amphisbaena dire,
Cerastes horned, hydrus, and ellops drear,   525
And dipsas (not so thick swarmed once the soil
Bedropped with blood of Gorgon, or the isle
Ophiusa);[2] but still greatest he the midst,

6. God.
7. Satan seems to have overheard or understood the curse pronounced by God on the serpent, even though he was not present at the time.
8. The word is used with its Latin force of "tripped up by the heels." Ovid (Metamorphoses 4.576ff.) and Dante (Inferno 25) had made set pieces about people being transformed into serpents. Whether Milton's editorial hand does not intervene against Satan too directly in this scene has been the subject of considerable critical debate.
9. The Latin sense is felt again, "struggling against the change."

1. Again a Latinism, meaning "twined together." "Riot": revolt.
2. Snake Island, in the Balearics. The "amphisbaena" was alleged to have a head at each end of its body. "Cerastes" was a horned snake; "hydrus," a water-snake; "ellops," perhaps the swordfish; and "dipsas," a snake whose bite was supposed to create outrageous thirst. When Perseus flew over Libya with the head of the snaky-haired Gorgon, the drops of her blood fell to the ground and became serpents.

Now dragon grown, larger than whom the sun
Engendered in the Pythian vale on slime,   530
Huge Python;[3] and his power no less he seemed
Above the rest still to retain. They all
Him followed, issuing forth to th' open field,
Where all yet left of that revolted rout,
Heaven-fallen, in station or just array,   535
Sublime[4] with expectation when to see
In triumph issuing forth their glorious chief.
They saw, but other sight instead, a crowd
Of ugly serpents. Horror on them fell,
And horrid sympathy; for what they saw   540
They felt themselves now changing. Down their arms,
Down fell both spear and shield; down they as fast,
And the dire hiss renewed, and the dire form
Catched by contagion, like in punishment
As in their crime. Thus was th' applause they meant   545
Turned to exploding hiss, triumph to shame
Cast on themselves from their own mouths. There stood
A grove hard by, sprung up with this their change,
His will who reigns above,[5] to aggravate
Their penance, laden with fair fruit, like that   550
Which grew in Paradise, the bait of Eve
Used by the tempter. On that prospect strange
Their earnest eyes they fixed, imagining
For one forbidden tree a multitude
Now risen, to work them further woe or shame;[6]   555
Yet, parched with scalding thirst and hunger fierce,
Though to delude them sent, could not abstain,
But on they rolled in heaps, and up the trees
Climbing, sat thicker than the snaky locks
That curled Megaera.[7] Greedily they plucked   560
The fruitage fair to sight, like that which grew
Near that bituminous lake where Sodom flamed;[8]
This more delusive, not the touch, but taste
Deceived; they fondly thinking to allay
Their appetite with gust,[9] instead of fruit   565
Chewed bitter ashes, which th' offended taste
With spattering noise rejected. Oft they assayed,
Hunger and thirst constraining: drugged as oft,
With hatefulest disrelish writhed their jaws
With soot and cinders filled: so oft they fell   570
Into the same illusion, not as man
Whom they triumphed once lapsed.[1] Thus were they plagued,
And worn with famine long and ceaseless hiss,

---

3. A gigantic mythological serpent engendered by Apollo, the sun god, from the slime left by Deucalion's flood; it was slain by Apollo in a great contest.
4. On tiptoes. The ordinary devils are standing in ranks outside Pandemonium, trying to catch a glimpse of Satan.
5. "By the will of him who reigns above."
6. The punishment of the devils not only fits the crime, it *is* the crime (the eating of forbidden fruit),

repeated again and again, in disgust and loathing.
7. Megaera, like her sister Furies, had snakes instead of hair on her head.
8. Sodom apples grew (legend had it) on the spot where that accursed city once stood; though good to look at, they dissolved into ashes when plucked.
9. Taste. "Fondly": foolishly.
1. They fell again and again into delusion, though they had felt superior to man, who fell just once.

Till their lost shape, permitted, they resumed—
Yearly enjoined, some say, to undergo   575
This annual humbling certain numbered days,
To dash their pride, and joy for man seduced.[2]
However, some tradition they dispersed
Among the heathen of their purchase got,
And fabled how the serpent, whom they called   580
Ophion, with Eurynome (the wide-
Encroaching Eve perhaps),[3] had first the rule
Of high Olympus, thence by Saturn driven
And Ops, ere yet Dictaean[4] Jove was born.

Summary   Sin and Death proceed without further interruption to Earth, and enter into possession of it. God sees their arrival and declines to interfere, but prophesies that their triumph will be only temporary; in due course they will be forced back to Hell again, and forever. Meanwhile, the angels are ordered to twist the Earth on its axis, disorder the planets so their influence will in future be bad as well as good, and rearrange the cosmos generally. In consequence, the temperate climate of Paradise at once gives way to extremes of heat and cold, and furious winds begin to blow across the ruined planet.

[Adam, Eve, and the First Steps to Redemption]

* * * Thus began
Outrage from lifeless things; but Discord first,
Daughter of Sin, among th' irrational
Death introduced through fierce antipathy:[5]
Beast now with beast 'gan war, and fowl with fowl,   710
And fish with fish: to graze the herb[6] all leaving,
Devoured each other; nor stood much in awe
Of man, but fled him, or with countenance grim
Glared on him passing. These were from without
The growing miseries, which Adam saw   715
Already in part, though hid in gloomiest shade,
To sorrow abandoned, but worse felt within,
And in a troubled sea of passion tossed,
Thus to disburden sought with sad complaint:
    "O miserable of happy![7] Is this the end   720
Of this new glorious world, and me so late
The glory of that glory? who now, become
Accursed of blessèd, hide me from the face
Of God, whom to behold was then my height
Of happiness! Yet well, if here would end   725

2. There are many folktales about fairies, devils, incubi, and the like being forced periodically to take on the shape of some loathsome creature.
3. There is a mythological story about the Titan Ophion (the name means "snake") and his wife Eurynome ("the wide-reacher"), who ruled Olympus until Saturn and his wife Rhea (or Ops) drove them away. Milton feels this story may be a vague, pagan reminiscence of the real truth, the fall of Satan. But there is an unresolved suggestion here that Eve fell with Satan, becoming a kind of Proserpina to his role as Pluto, king of hell.
4. Zeus was raised in a cave on Mt. Dicte, in Crete; hence, "Dictaean Jove."
5. "Discord" is the subject of the sentence, "Death" the object. "Th' irrational" are the beasts.
6. Grass.
7. I.e., change, to misery from happiness.

The misery; I deserved it, and would bear
My own deservings; but this will not serve.
All that I eat or drink, or shall beget,
Is propagated curse.[8] O voice, once heard
Delightfully, 'Increase and multiply,'   730
Now death to hear! for what can I increase
Or multiply, but curses on my head?
Who of all ages to succeed, but, feeling
The evil on him brought by me, will curse
My head: 'Ill fare our ancestor impure!   735
For this we may thank Adam!' but his thanks
Shall be the execration;[9] so besides
Mine own that bide upon me, all from me
Shall with a fierce reflux on me redound,
On me, as on their natural center, light   740
Heavy, though in their place.[1] O fleeting joys
Of Paradise, dear bought with lasting woes!
Did I request thee, Maker, from my clay
To mold me man? Did I solicit thee
From darkness to promote me, or here place   745
In this delicious garden? As my will
Concurred not to my being, it were but right
And equal[2] to reduce me to my dust,
Desirous to resign and render back
All I received, unable to perform   750
Thy terms too hard, by which I was to hold
The good I sought not. To the loss of that,
Sufficient penalty, why hast thou added
The sense of endless woes? Inexplicable
Thy justice seems; yet to say truth, too late   755
I thus contèst; then should have been refused
Those terms whatever, when they were proposed.
Thou[3] didst accept them; wilt thou enjoy the good,
Then cavil the conditions? And though God
Made thee without thy leave, what if thy son   760
Prove disobedient, and reproved, retort,
'Wherefore didst thou beget me? I sought it not.'
Wouldst thou admit for his contempt of thee
That proud excuse? Yet him not thy election,[4]
But natural necessity begot.   765
God made thee of choice his own, and of his own
To serve him; thy reward was of his grace;
Thy punishment then justly is at his will.
Be it so, for I submit; his doom is fair,
That dust I am and shall to dust return.   770
O welcome hour whenever! Why delays
His hand to execute what his decree

---

8. Whatever prolongs life extends the curse.
9. The only thanks for Adam will be humankind's curses.
1. Adam plays with the notion that natural objects have weight only as long as they are above their "natural" positions; so all curses will flow naturally to him,
but they will still be heavy when they have lighted.
2. Just.
3. "Thou," which referred to God in lines 753 and 755 ("Thy"), here shifts as Adam suddenly addresses himself.
4. Choice.

Fixed on this day? Why do I overlive?
Why am I mocked with death, and lengthened out
To deathless pain? How gladly would I meet   775
Mortality, my sentence, and be earth
Insensible! how glad would lay me down
As in my mother's lap![5] There I should rest
And sleep secure; his dreadful voice no more
Would thunder in my ears; no fear of worse   780
To me and to my offspring would torment me
With cruel expectation. Yet one doubt
Pursues me still, lest all I cannot die;[6]
Lest that pure breath of life, the spirit of man
Which God inspired, cannot together perish   785
With this corporeal clod; then in the grave,
Or in some other dismal place, who knows
But I shall die a living death? O thought
Horrid, if true! Yet why? It was but breath
Of life that sinned; what dies but what had life   790
And sin? the body properly hath neither.
All of me then shall die: let this appease
The doubt, since human reach no further knows.[7]
For though the Lord of all be infinite,
Is his wrath also? Be it, man is not so,   795
But mortal doomed. How can he exercise
Wrath without end on man whom death must end?
Can he make deathless death? That were to make
Strange contradiction, which to God himself
Impossible is held, as argument   800
Of weakness, not of power.[8] Will he draw out,
For anger's sake, finite to infinite
In punished man, to satisfy his rigor
Satisfied never? That were to extend
His sentence beyond dust and nature's law,   805
By which all causes else according still
To the reception of their matter act,
Not to th' extent of their own sphere.[9] But say
That death be not one stroke, as I supposed,
Bereaving[1] sense, but endless misery   810
From this day onward, which I feel begun
Both in me and without me, and so last
To perpetuity—Ay me! that fear
Comes thundering back with dreadful revolution
On my defenseless head! Both death and I   815
Am found eternal, and incorporate[2] both:
Nor I on my part single; in me all

---

5. Adam's lamentations owe a good deal to Job 3.
6. Direct from Horace, *Odes* 3.30.6: "non omnis moriar."
7. Adam convinces himself, as Milton was convinced, that both soul and body die at death; the corollary is that they are resurrected together.
8. For a man in a state of nature, Adam displays a fine command of theological argument. He holds that if

God contradicts himself, it is a sign of weakness.
9. An axiom of traditional philosophy: all agents act according to the capacity of the object, not to the extent of their inherent powers.
1. Taking away.
2. In the same body. Adam is appalled to find that he has become death incarnate; the grammar ("both death and I / *Am*") displays his shock.

Posterity stands cursed. Fair patrimony
That I must leave ye, sons! O, were I able
To waste it all myself, and leave ye none!   820
So disinherited, how would ye bless
Me, now your curse! Ah, why should all mankind
For one man's fault thus guiltless be condemned,
If guiltless? But from me what can proceed,
But all corrupt, both mind and will depraved,   825
Not to do only, but to will the same
With me?³ How can they then acquitted stand
In sight of God? Him, after all disputes,
Forced⁴ I absolve. All my evasions vain
And reasonings, though through mazes, lead me still   830
But to my own conviction: first and last
On me, me only, as the source and spring
Of all corruption, all the blame lights due;⁵
So might the wrath! Fond⁶ wish! Couldst thou support
That burden, heavier than the Earth to bear;   835
Than all the world much heavier, though divided
With that bad woman? Thus, what thou desir'st,
And what thou fear'st, alike destroys all hope
Of refuge, and concludes thee miserable⁷
Beyond all past example and future;   840
To Satan only like, both crime and doom.
O Conscience! into what abyss of fears
And horrors hast thou driven me; out of which
I find no way, from deep to deeper plunged!"
    Thus Adam to himself lamented loud   845
Through the still night, not now, as ere man fell,
Wholesome and cool and mild, but with black air
Accompanied, with damps and dreadful gloom;
Which to his evil conscience represented
All things with double terror. On the ground   850
Outstretched he lay, on the cold ground, and oft
Cursed his creation; Death as oft accused
Of tardy execution, since denounced
The day of his offense. "Why comes not Death,"
Said he, "with one thrice-acceptable stroke   855
To end me? Shall Truth fail to keep her word,
Justice divine not hasten to be just?
But Death comes not at call; Justice divine
Mends not her slowest pace for prayers or cries.
O woods, O fountains, hillocks, dales, and bowers!   860
With other echo late I taught your shades
To answer, and resound far other song."
Whom thus afflicted when sad Eve beheld,
Desolate where she sat, approaching nigh,

3. Not only will subsequent human beings repeat Adam's sin; their will is corrupted and they will *want* to be fallen like Adam.
4. Perforce.
5. In this discovery that he alone must accept the guilt of humankind, Adam has chosen crucially to be like Christ and unlike Satan—at the very moment when he feels exactly the opposite.
6. Foolish.
7. Shows thee to be miserable.

Soft words to his fierce passion she essayed;   865
But her with stern regard he thus repelled:
    "Out of my sight, thou serpent! that name best
Befits thee, with him leagued, thyself as false
And hateful: nothing wants, but that thy shape,
Like his, and color serpentine, may show   870
Thy inward fraud, to warn all creatures from thee
Henceforth; lest that too heavenly form, pretended[8]
To hellish falsehood, snare them. But for thee
I had persisted happy, had not thy pride
And wandering vanity, when least was safe,   875
Rejected my forewarning, and disdained
Not to be trusted, longing to be seen
Though by the devil himself, him overweening[9]
To overreach, but, with the serpent meeting,
Fooled and beguiled; by him thou, I by thee,   880
To trust thee from my side, imagined wise,
Constant, mature, proof against all assaults;
And understood not all was but a show
Rather than solid virtue, all but a rib
Crooked by nature—bent, as now appears,   885
More to the part sinìster[1]—from me drawn;
Well if thrown out, as supernumerary
To my just number found![2] O why did God,
Creator wise, that peopled highest Heaven
With spirits masculine, create at last   890
This novelty on Earth, this fair defect
Of nature, and not fill the world at once
With men, as angels, without feminine;
Or find some other way to generate
Mankind?[3] This mischief had not then befallen,   895
And more that shall befall—innumerable
Disturbances on Earth through female snares,
And strait conjunction[4] with this sex. For either
He never shall find out fit mate, but such
As some misfortune brings him, or mistake;   900
Or whom he wishes most shall seldom gain,
Through her perverseness, but shall see her gained
By a far worse, or, if she love, withheld
By parents, or his happiest choice too late
Shall meet, already linked and wedlock-bound   905
To a fell[5] adversary, his hate or shame:
Which infinite calamity shall cause
To human life, and household peace confound."
    He added not, and from her turned; but Eve,
Not so repulsed, with tears that ceased not flowing,   910
And tresses all disordered, at his feet

---

8. Serving as a mask; literally, "held out before."
9. Overconfident.
1. "On the left hand," as in Latin; also "unlucky."
2. Since men visibly have twelve ribs on both sides, it
was supposed that Adam originally had thirteen ribs on
his left side, so that he could give up one and still have

twelve, the proper ("just") number.
3. Ancient traditions of antifeminist thought lie behind these ungenerous questions.
4. Close connections, i.e., matrimony.
5. Bitter.

Fell humble, and embracing them besought
His peace, and thus proceeded in her plaint:
    "Forsake me not thus, Adam! witness Heaven
What love sincere and reverence in my heart   915
I bear thee, and unweeting[6] have offended,
Unhappily deceived! Thy suppliant[7]
I beg, and clasp thy knees; bereave me not,
Whereon I live, thy gentle looks, thy aid,
Thy counsel in this uttermost distress,   920
My only strength and stay: forlorn of thee,
Whither shall I betake me, where subsist?
While yet we live, scarce one short hour perhaps,
Between us two let there be peace; both joining,
As joined in injuries, one enmity   925
Against a foe by doom express assigned us,
That cruel serpent. On me exercise not
Thy hatred for this misery befallen;
On me already lost, me than thyself
More miserable. Both have sinned, but thou   930
Against God only; I against God and thee,
And to the place of judgment will return,
There with my cries importune Heaven, that all
The sentence, from thy head removed, may light
On me, sole cause to thee of all this woe,   935
Me, me only, just object of his ire."[8]
    She ended weeping; and her lowly plight,
Immovable till peace obtained from fault
Acknowledged and deplored,[9] in Adam wrought
Commiseration. Soon his heart relented   940
Towards her, his life so late and sole delight,
Now at his feet submissive in distress,
Creature so fair his reconcilement seeking,
His counsel, whom she had displeased, his aid;
As one disarmed, his anger all he lost,   945
And thus with peaceful words upraised her soon:
    "Unwary, and too desirous, as before,
So now, of what thou know'st not,[1] who desir'st
The punishment all on thyself! Alas!
Bear thine own first, ill able to sustain   950
His full wrath, whose thou feel'st as yet least part,[2]
And my displeasure bear'st so ill. If prayers
Could alter high decrees, I to that place
Would speed before thee, and be louder heard,
That on my head all might be visited,   955
Thy frailty and infirmer sex forgiven,
To me committed, and by me exposed.

---

6. Unintentionally.
7. As a suppliant to thee.
8. Eve too now offers to accept the blame for the Fall, and the moral regeneration of humankind is hence-forth possible.
9. Her suppliant posture ("lowly plight") would not be changed until she obtained forgiveness ("peace") from

her admission of her fault and repentance for it.
1. Adam's remark is rueful but affectionate; Eve is still looking for more trouble than she knows how to handle.
2. I.e., ill able to sustain the full wrath of God—of whose wrath, so far, you have felt only the least part.

But rise; let us no more contend, nor blame
Each other, blamed enough elsewhere, but strive
In offices of love, how we may lighten   960
Each other's burden in our share of woe;
Since this day's death denounced, if aught I see,
Will prove no sudden, but a slow-paced evil,
A long day's dying to augment our pain,
And to our seed (O hapless seed!) derived."[3]   965
    To whom thus Eve, recovering heart, replied:
"Adam, by sad experiment I know
How little weight my words with thee can find,
Found so erroneous, thence by just event
Found so unfortunate; nevertheless,   970
Restored by thee, vile as I am, to place
Of new acceptance, hopeful to regain
Thy love, the sole contentment of my heart
Living or dying, from thee I will not hide
What thoughts in my unquiet breast are risen,   975
Tending to some relief of our extremes,
Or end, though sharp and sad, yet tolerable,
As in our evils,[4] and of easier choice.
If care of our descent perplex us most,
Which must be born to certain woe, devoured   980
By Death at last—and miserable it is
To be to others cause of misery,
Our own begotten, and of our loins to bring
Into this cursèd world a woeful race
That after wretched life must be at last   985
Food for so foul a monster—in thy power
It lies yet ere conception to prevent[5]
The race unblessed, to being yet unbegot.
Childless thou art, childless remain: so Death
Shall be deceived his glut, and with us two   990
Be forced to satisfy his ravenous maw.
But if thou judge it hard and difficult,
Conversing, looking, loving, to abstain
From love's due rites, nuptial embraces sweet,
And with desire to languish without hope   995
Before the present object[6] languishing
With like desire, which would be misery
And torment less than none of what we dread,
Then both our selves and seed at once to free
From what we fear for both, let us make short;   1000
Let us seek Death, or he not found, supply
With our own hands his office on ourselves.
Why stand we longer shivering under fears
That show no end but Death, and[7] have the power,
Of many ways to die the shortest choosing,   1005

3. Handed down.
4. A Latinism. The English meaning is something like "given the evil plight in which we find ourselves."
5. Literally, in the Latin root, come before, forestall.
6. The present object is of course Eve herself, referring to herself in this oblique fashion apparently because she is shy of admitting that she would pine for Adam as much as he for her.
7. I.e., when we.

Destruction with destruction to destroy?"
    She ended here, or vehement despair
Broke off the rest; so much of death her thoughts
Had entertained as dyed her cheeks with pale.
But Adam, with such counsel nothing swayed,   1010
To better hopes his more attentive mind
Laboring had raised, and thus to Eve replied:
    "Eve, thy contempt of life and pleasure seems
To argue in thee something more sublime
And excellent than what thy mind contemns;[8]   1015
But self-destruction therefore[9] sought refutes
That excellence thought in thee, and implies,
Not thy contempt, but anguish and regret
For loss of life and pleasure overloved.
Or if thou covet death as utmost end   1020
Of misery, so thinking to evade
The penalty pronounced, doubt not but God
Hath wiselier armed his vengeful ire than so
To be forestalled; much more I fear lest death
So snatched will not exempt us from the pain   1025
We are by doom to pay; rather such acts
Of contumacy[1] will provoke the Highest
To make death in us live. Then let us seek
Some safer resolution, which methinks
I have in view, calling to mind with heed   1030
Part of our sentence, that thy seed shall bruise
The serpent's head; piteous amends, unless
Be meant, whom I conjecture, our grand foe
Satan, who in the serpent hath contrived
Against us this deceit. To crush his head   1035
Would be revenge indeed, which will be lost
By death brought on ourselves or childless days
Resolved, as thou proposest; so our foe
Shall 'scape his punishment ordained, and we
Instead shall double ours upon our heads.   1040
No more be mentioned then of violence
Against ourselves and willful barrenness
That cuts us off from hope, and savors only
Rancor and pride, impatience and despite,
Reluctance[2] against God and his just yoke   1045
Laid on our necks. Remember with what mild
And gracious temper he both heard and judged,
Without wrath or reviling; we expected
Immediate dissolution, which we thought
Was meant by death that day, when lo, to thee   1050
Pains only in childbearing were foretold,
And bringing forth, soon recompensed with joy,
Fruit of thy womb. On me the curse aslope

8. Despises.   2. From Latin *luctare*, to struggle; here, to oppose (the
9. For this motive.   will of God).
1. Contempt.

Glanced on the ground:[3] with labor I must earn
My bread. What harm? Idleness had been worse.   1055
My labor will sustain me; and lest cold
Or heat should injure us, his timely care
Hath unbesought provided, and his hands
Clothed us unworthy, pitying while he judged.
How much more, if we pray him, will his ear   1060
Be open and his heart to pity incline,
And teach us further by what means to shun
Th' inclement seasons, rain, ice, hail, and snow,
Which now the sky with various face begins
To show us in this mountain, while the winds   1065
Blow moist and keen, shattering the graceful locks
Of these fair spreading trees—which bids us seek
Some better shroud, some better warmth to cherish
Our limbs benumbed, ere this diurnal star[4]
Leave cold the night, how we his gathered beams,   1070
Reflected, may with matter sere foment,
Or by collision of two bodies grind
The air attrite to fire,[5] as late the clouds,
Justling or pushed with winds rude in their shock,
Tine[6] the slant lightning, whose thwart flame driven down   1075
Kindles the gummy bark of fir or pine,
And sends a comfortable heat from far,
Which might supply[7] the sun. Such fire to use,
And what may else be remedy or cure
To evils which our own misdeeds have wrought,   1080
He will instruct us praying, and of grace
Beseeching him, so as we need not fear
To pass commodiously this life, sustained
By him with many comforts, till we end
In dust, our final rest and native home.   1085
        "What better can we do than to the place
Repairing where he judged us, prostrate fall
Before him reverent, and there confess
Humbly our faults, and pardon beg, with tears
Watering the ground, and with our sighs the air   1090
Frequenting,[8] sent from hearts contrite, in sign
Of sorrow unfeigned, and humiliation meek?
Undoubtedly he will relent and turn
From his displeasure; in whose look serene,
When angry most he seemed and most severe,   1095
What else but favor, grace, and mercy shone?"
        So spake our father penitent, nor Eve
Felt less remorse: they forthwith to the place
Repairing where he judged them, prostrate fell
Before him reverent, and both confessed   1100

3. The curse, like a spear that almost missed its target, glanced aside and stuck in the ground.
4. The sun. "Shroud": shelter.
5. Adam is inventing the burning glass ("matter sere" is dry leaves, twigs, etc.) and the use of flint and steel to start fires. "Attrite": rubbed or worn down; in this sense, the word is more Latin than English.
6. Kindle, light.
7. Take the place of.
8. Filling.

Humbly their faults, and pardon begged, with tears
Watering the ground, and with their sighs the air
Frequenting, sent from hearts contrite, in sign
Of sorrow unfeigned, and humiliation meek.[9]

Book 11. Summary   The prayers of Adam and Eve prove acceptable to God.
But while humankind may now hope for ultimate redemption, they may no longer
dwell in Paradise; and Michael, the warrior archangel, is dispatched to explain the
sentence, offer some hope for the future, and dismiss Adam and Eve from the
happy garden. Adam is at first overcome with grief; but the angel encourages him,
and while Eve is put in a trance, Adam is raised to the peak of a high hill and
shown in a vision the future of the human race as far as the flood of Noah.

From Book 12

Summary   Continuing his instruction of Adam, Michael relates the history of
the world from the time of Noah through the coming of Christ, whose ascent into
Heaven and triumph over Death after the Crucifixion he describes.

[*The Departure from Eden*]

So spake th' archangel Michaël; then paused,
As at the world's great period;[1] and our sire,
Replete with joy and wonder, thus replied:
"O goodness infinite, goodness immense!
That all this good of evil shall produce,   470
And evil turn to good; more wonderful
Than that which by creation first brought forth
Light out of darkness! Full of doubt I stand,
Whether I should repent me now of sin
By me done and occasioned, or rejoice   475
Much more that much more good thereof shall spring;
To God more glory, more good will to men
From God, and over wrath grace shall abound.
But say, if our Deliverer up to Heaven
Must reascend, what will betide the few,   480
His faithful, left among th' unfaithful herd,
The enemies of truth? Who then shall guide
His people, who defend? Will they not deal
Worse with his followers than with him they dealt?"
     "Be sure they will," said th' angel; "but from Heaven   485
He to his own a Comforter will send,
The promise of the Father, who shall dwell,
His Spirit, within them, and the law of faith,
Working through love, upon their hearts shall write,

---

9. The deliberate repetition of six consecutive lines,
almost word for word, with only six lines in between,
is a very strong mark of closure. Adam and Eve have
reached most of the major decisions that will separate
their fate from that of Satan.
1. Conclusion. Michael has just given a brief prophetic glimpse of the Second Coming and the Last
Judgment.

To guide them in all truth, and also arm   490
With spiritual armor, able to resist
Satan's assaults, and quench his fiery darts,
What[2] man can do against them, not afraid,
Though to the death; against such cruelties
With inward consolations recompensed,   495
And oft supported so as shall amaze
Their proudest persecutors.[3] For the Spirit,
Poured first on his Apostles, whom he sends
To evangelize the nations, then on all
Baptized, shall them with wondrous gifts endue[4]   500
To speak all tongues, and do all miracles,
As did their Lord before them. Thus they win
Great numbers of each nation to receive
With joy the tidings brought from Heaven: at length,
Their ministry performed, and race well run,   505
Their doctrine and their story written left,
They die; but in their room, as they forewarn,
Wolves shall succeed for teachers, grievous wolves,[5]
Who all the sacred mysteries of Heaven
To their own vile advantages shall turn   510
Of lucre and ambition, and the truth
With superstitions and traditions taint,
Left only in those written records pure,
Though not but by the Spirit understood.
Then shall they seek to avail themselves of names,   515
Places, and titles,[6] and with these to join
Secular power, though feigning still to act
By spiritual; to themselves appropriating
The Spirit of God, promised alike and given
To all believers; and, from that pretense,   520
Spiritual laws by carnal[7] power shall force
On every conscience, laws which none shall find
Left them enrolled, or what the Spirit within
Shall on the heart engrave.[8] What will they then,
But force the Spirit of Grace itself, and bind   525
His consort, Liberty? what but unbuild
His living temples,[9] built by faith to stand,
Their own faith, not another's? for, on Earth,
Who against faith and conscience can be heard
Infallible? Yet many will presume: 530
Whence heavy persecution shall arise
On all who in the worship persevere
Of Spirit and Truth; the rest, far greater part,
Will deem in outward rites and specious[1] forms

2. As much as.
3. Milton briefly summarizes here the story of the Christian martyrs.
4. Endow.
5. To profit by religion was for Milton the lowest of crimes. In addition, he regularly uses the wolf as an emblem of the papacy (see *Lycidas*, line 128, p. 649).
6. The name "Catholic," the place of court preacher,

and the title of "bishop," for example.
7. Fleshly, i.e., secular, of this world.
8. I.e., the wolves will enforce laws that have no ancient authority or appeal to the conscience.
9. Individual believers. Milton's strict Protestant individualism speaks throughout this passage of protest against persecution.
1. Fair-seeming.

Religion satisfied; Truth shall retire   535
Bestuck with slanderous darts, and works of faith
Rarely be found. So shall the world go on,
To good malignant, to bad men benign,
Under her own weight groaning, till the day
Appear of respiration[2] to the just   540
And vengeance to the wicked, at return
Of Him so lately promised to thy aid,
The Woman's Seed,[3] obscurely then foretold,
Now amplier known thy Savior and thy Lord;
Last in the clouds from Heaven to be revealed   545
In glory of the Father, to dissolve
Satan with his perverted world; then raise
From the conflagrant mass,[4] purged and refined,
New Heavens, new Earth, ages of endless date
Founded in righteousness and peace and love,   550
To bring forth fruits, joy and eternal bliss."
    He ended, and thus Adam last replied:
"How soon hath thy prediction, seer blest,
Measured this transient world, the race of Time,
Till Time stand fixed! Beyond is all abyss,   555
Eternity, whose end no eye can reach.
Greatly instructed I shall hence depart,
Greatly in peace of thought, and have my fill
Of knowledge, what[5] this vessel can contain,
Beyond which was my folly to aspire.   560
Henceforth I learn that to obey is best,
And love with fear the only God, to walk
As in his presence, ever to observe
His providence, and on him sole depend,
Merciful over all his works, with good   565
Still overcoming evil, and by small
Accomplishing great things, by things deemed weak
Subverting worldly-strong, and worldly-wise
By simply meek; that suffering for truth's sake
Is fortitude to highest victory,   570
And to the faithful, death the gate of life;
Taught this by his example whom I now
Acknowledge my Redeemer ever blest."
    To whom thus also th' angel last replied:
"This having learned, thou hast attained the sum   575
Of wisdom; hope no higher, though all the stars
Thou knew'st by name,[6] and all th' ethereal powers,
All secrets of the deep, all Nature's works,
Or works of God in heaven, air, earth, or sea,
And all the riches of this world enjoy'dst,   580
And all the rule, one empire. Only add
Deeds to thy knowledge answerable;[7] add faith,

---

2. Relief, refreshment.
3. Christ, whose Second Coming is here foreseen.
4. The burning world.
5. As much as.

6. Michael glances back at Raphael's cool warning (in book 8) that Adam should concern himself with matters closer to home than the stars.
7. Corresponding.

Add virtue, patience, temperance; add love,
By name to come called charity, the soul
Of all the rest: then wilt thou not be loath   585
To leave this Paradise, but shalt possess
A Paradise within thee, happier far.
Let us descend now, therefore, from this top
Of speculation;[8] for the hour precise
Exacts[9] our parting hence; and, see! the guards,   590
By me encamped on yonder hill, expect
Their motion, at whose front[1] a flaming sword,
In signal of remove, waves fiercely round.
We may no longer stay. Go, waken Eve;
Her also I with gentle dreams have calmed,   595
Portending good, and all her spirits composed
To meek submission: thou, at season fit,
Let her with thee partake what thou hast heard;
Chiefly what may concern her faith to know,
The great deliverance by her seed to come   600
(For by the Woman's Seed)[2] on all mankind;
That ye may live, which will be many days,[3]
Both in one faith unanimous; though sad
With cause for evils past, yet much more cheered
With meditation on the happy end."   605
     He ended, and they both descend the hill;
Descended, Adam to the bower where Eve
Lay sleeping ran before, but found her waked;
And thus with words not sad she him received:
     "Whence thou return'st and whither went'st, I know;   610
For God is also in sleep, and dreams advise,
Which he hath sent propitious, some great good
Presaging, since with sorrow and heart's distress
Wearied I fell asleep. But now lead on;
In me is no delay; with thee to go   615
Is to stay here; without thee here to stay
Is to go hence unwilling; thou to me
Art all things under heaven, all places thou,[4]
Who for my willful crime art banished hence.
This further consolation yet secure   620
I carry hence: though all by me is lost,
Such favor I unworthy am vouchsafed,
By me the Promised Seed shall all restore."
     So spake our mother Eve; and Adam heard
Well pleased, but answered not; for now too nigh   625
Th' archangel stood, and from the other hill
To their fixed station, all in bright array
The cherubim descended; on the ground
Gliding meteorous, as evening mist

---

8. Hill of vision.
9. Requires.
1. Before whom. "Expect / Their motion": await their order to move.
2. The parenthesis seems incomplete; perhaps some-

thing like "deliverance was foretold" is understood.
3. Adam lived to be 930 (Genesis 5.5).
4. Once more, "The mind is its own place . . ." (1.254). Eve's resolution may also owe something to the Book of Ruth 1.16.

Risen from a river o'er the marish[5] glides,   630
And gathers ground fast at the laborer's heel
Homeward returning. High in front advanced,
The brandished sword of God before them blazed
Fierce as a comet; which with torrid heat,
And vapor as the Libyan air adust,[6]   635
Began to parch that temperate clime; whereat
In either hand the hastening angel caught
Our lingering parents, and to th' eastern gate
Led them direct, and down the cliff as fast
To the subjected[7] plain; then disappeared.   640
They, looking back, all th' eastern side beheld
Of Paradise, so late their happy seat,[8]
Waved over by that flaming brand;[9] the gate
With dreadful faces thronged and fiery arms.
Some natural tears they dropped, but wiped them soon;   645
The world was all before them, where to choose
Their place of rest, and Providence their guide.
They, hand in hand, with wandering steps and slow,
Through Eden took their solitary way.

                                                                    1667, 1674

5. Marsh (an old form).   7. Low-lying.
6. The scorched climate of Libya, in North Africa, was   8. Home.
proverbial.   9. Sword, with the extra overtone of "burning."

Lyric Poets of the
Early Seventeenth Century

Like the Elizabethan period, the first half of the seventeenth century was particularly rich in lyric poets. Apart from a few (such as Lady Mary Wroth) who continued to write on the model of Sidney or Spenser or Shakespeare, these poets have traditionally been divided into "Metaphysicals" and "Cavaliers." (The first term derived, via Samuel Johnson's Life of Abraham Cowley [see below, p. 1229], from John Dryden's deprecating observation that Donne "affects the metaphysics" in his poetry, while the second stemmed from the royalist—Cavalier—affiliation of the poets in this group.) An alternative way of labeling the same two groups—one more directly suggestive of the poetic qualities of each—is to call them, respectively, the school of Donne and the school of Jonson. To be sure, no dichotomizing labels can wholly fit the case, because some of these poets—Andrew Marvell, for example—regularly combine Donneian "Metaphysical" ingenuity with Jonsonian polish. Still, the identification of two dominant poetic traditions in the period is of value as a rough approximation to the truth of a complex literary situation.

If one regards them for the moment as alternatives, Jonson was an easier model to follow than Donne. A few powerful talents like George Herbert, Richard Crashaw, and Henry Vaughan found the Metaphysical vein really congenial; lesser writers often made only heavy weather of it. By the end of the century the tradition was (as Dryden's criticism suggests) little esteemed. On the other hand, Jonson's manner of poised, polished, yet "easy" statement developed naturally toward the graceful lyrics of poets like Robert Herrick, Sir John Suckling, and Richard Lovelace, while in Edmund Waller and Sir John Denham the Jonsonian manner moved toward the formal and "correct" style that dominated the neoclassical poetics of the Restoration and eighteenth century.

LADY MARY WROTH
1587?–1651?

Lady Mary Wroth grew up surrounded by writers. Her uncle was Sir Philip Sidney, and her aunt was Mary Sidney Herbert, countess of Pembroke, an important patron of writers and herself a poet and translator. Lady Mary's father, Sir Robert Sidney, also wrote poetry, as did her first cousin and lover, William Herbert, earl of Pembroke (to whom she bore two children after her husband's death in 1614). Her home was the Sidney estate, celebrated in Ben Jonson's *To Penshurst*. She danced in some of Jonson's court masques, and he addressed several poems to her and her husband, Sir Robert Wroth, and dedicated to her one of his finest plays, *The Alchemist*.

It is therefore not surprising that Lady Mary herself took up writing, or that she became one of the most accomplished and prolific female writers of the English Renaissance. Her long but unfinished romance, *The Countess of Montgomery's Urania* (1621), is the first substantial work of prose fiction by an Englishwoman. Modeled on Sidney's *Arcadia*, it also covertly alludes to various personages and scandals of the Jacobean court—a fact that provoked a storm of criticism when it was published. Appended to *Urania* is a sonnet sequence (the only one by an Englishwoman of her time), *Pamphilia to Amphilanthus*, consisting of 103 sonnets and songs; because the speaker in the sequence is a woman, the conventional sonnet roles of male lover and female beloved are interestingly reversed in it.

Until the scandal of her illegitimate children, and the increasing financial difficulties of her widowhood, Lady Mary played a conspicuous part at court. Yet, though her poetry contains a few reminiscences of Donne, her writing is on the whole almost untouched by the literary fashions prevalent in Jacobean courtly circles, reaching back instead to styles and forms of the late Elizabethan era and echoing especially the work of her uncle and her father.

Our texts are based on the original edition of *Urania*, though we follow Josephine A. Roberts's excellent modern edition of Wroth's poetry in adopting some readings from the manuscript version of *Pamphilia to Amphilanthus*.

From The Countess of Montgomery's Urania

SONG[1]

Love what art thou? A vain thought
In our minds by fant'sy wrought.
Idle smiles did thee beget,
While fond wishes made the net
Which so many fools have caught.   5

Love what art thou? Light and fair,
Fresh as morning, clear as th' air.
But too soon thy evening change
Makes thy worth with coldness range;
Still thy joy is mixt with care.   10

Love what art thou? A sweet flower
Once full blown,[2] dead in an hour.
Dust in wind as staid remains
As thy pleasure or our gains,
If thy humor[3] change, to lour.   15

Love what art thou? Childish, vain,
Firm as bubbles made by rain,
Wantonness thy greatest pride.
These foul faults thy virtues hide—
But babes can no staidness gain.   20

---

1. This song, one of a group of eclogues that marks the conclusion of book 1 of *Urania*, is sung by a shepherdess, "being, as it seemed, fallen out with Love." "Love" here is the mischievous boy Cupid.

Since all our Wroth selections were published in 1621, we do not give the date for each one.
2. In full bloom.
3. Whim.

Love what art thou? Causeless cursed,
   Yet alas these not the worst:
   Much more of thee may be said.
   But thy law I once obeyed,
   Therefore say no more at first.   25

From Pamphilia to Amphilanthus[1]

1

When night's black mantle could most darkness prove,
   And sleep, death's image, did my senses hire
From knowledge of myself, then thoughts did move
Swifter than those most swiftness need require.
In sleep, a chariot drawn by winged desire   5
   I saw, where sat bright Venus, Queen of Love,
   And at her feet, her son,[2] still adding fire
To burning hearts, which she did hold above.
But one heart flaming more than all the rest
   The goddess held, and put it to my breast.   10
"Dear son, now shut,"[3] said she: "thus must we win."
He her obeyed, and martyred my poor heart.
   I, waking, hoped as dreams it would depart:
   Yet since, O me, a lover I have been.

16

Am I thus conquered? Have I lost the powers
   That to withstand, which joys to ruin me?[1]
Must I be still while it my strength devours,
   And captive leads me prisoner, bound, unfree?
Love first shall leave men's fant'sies to them free,[2]   5
   Desire shall quench Love's flames, spring hate sweet showers,
   Love shall loose all his darts, have sight, and see
His shame, and wishings hinder happy hours.
Why should we not Love's purblind charms resist?
   Must we be servile, doing what he list?[3]   10
   No, seek some host to harbor thee: I fly
Thy babish tricks, and freedom do profess.
   But O my hurt makes my lost heart confess
   I love, and must: So farewell liberty.

---

1. Pamphilia ("All-loving") is the protagonist of *Urania*. Her unfaithful beloved's name means "Lover of Two." These characters are first cousins, like Mary Wroth and William Herbert; their names adumbrate the main theme of both the romance and the appended sonnet sequence, constancy in the face of unfaithfulness.

   Pamphilia to Amphilanthus is broken into several separately numbered series (the first of which includes forty-eight sonnets, with songs inserted after every sixth sonnet except the last). In Roberts's edition, the poems are also numbered consecutively throughout the work as a whole; we have adopted this convenient renumbering.
2. Cupid.
3. I.e., shut the burning heart into Pamphilia's breast.
1. I.e., have I lost the power to withstand love ("That"), which takes pleasure in ruining me?
2. I.e., this and the other impossibilities that follow will occur before I surrender to love. Cf. Donne, *Song* (p. 587).
3. What pleases him. "Purblind": completely blind.

40

False hope which feeds but to destroy, and spill[1]
  What it first breeds; unnatural to the birth
  Of thine own womb; conceiving but to kill,
  And plenty gives to make the greater dearth,[2]
So tyrants do who falsely ruling earth   5
  Outwardly grace them,[3] and with profits fill,
  Advance those who appointed are to death,
  To make their greater fall to please their will.
Thus shadow[4] they their wicked vile intent,
  Coloring evil with a show of good   10
  While in fair shows their malice so is spent;[5]
  Hope kills the heart, and tyrants shed the blood.
For hope deluding brings us to the pride
Of our desires the farther down to slide.

From *A Crown of Sonnets Dedicated to Love*[1]

77

In this strange labyrinth how shall I turn?
  Ways[2] are on all sides, while the way I miss:
  If to the right hand, there in love I burn;
  Let me go forward, therein danger is;
If to the left, suspicion hinders bliss,   5
  Let me[3] turn back, Shame cries I ought return,
  Nor faint though crosses[4] with my fortunes kiss;
  Stand still is harder, although sure to mourn.[5]
Then let me take the right- or left-hand way;
  Go forward, or stand still, or back retire;   10
  I must these doubts endure without allay
  Or help, but travail find for my best hire.[6]
Yet that which most my troubled sense doth move
Is to leave all, and take the thread of love.[7]

---

1. Kill. The image is of miscarriage or infanticide.
2. I.e., gives abundance only to make scarcity more painful afterward.
3. I.e., those whom they mean to destroy (see the next line).
4. Keep dark, conceal.
5. Expended, employed. "Shows": appearances.
1. The "crown" is a difficult poetic form (originally Italian and usually known by its Italian name, *corona*) in which the last line of each poem serves as the first line of the next, until a circle is completed by the last line of the final poem, which is the same as the first line of the first one. The number of poems varies from seven to (as in Wroth's *corona*) fourteen.
  In contrast to the errant-child Cupid of the preceding part of the sequence, Love in this series is a mature and just monarch, whose true service ennobles lovers. The crown is thus, in part, a recantation of the harsh judgment of love earlier in the sequence. (But Pamphilia relapses into melancholy cynicism afterward.)
2. Paths.
3. If I.
4. Troubles, adversity. "Faint": lose heart.
5. I.e., certain to make me mourn.
6. I.e., I find travail (with a pun on "travel," the spelling in the 1621 edition) is my only reward. "Allay": abatement.
7. The line alludes to the thread that Ariadne gave Theseus to unwind behind him in the Labyrinth at Crete. Having killed the Minotaur at its center, Theseus was able to find his way out by retracing the thread.

ROBERT HERRICK
1591–1674

The son of a prosperous London goldsmith, Robert Herrick was late in starting university—he spent seven years as an apprentice in his father's trade—and, after taking B.A. and M.A. degrees at Cambridge, was long in settling into a career. Clearly he would have liked nothing better than a life of leisured study in London, talking literature and drinking sack with his hero Ben Jonson, while polishing his verses. But eventually he took clerical orders and, in 1630, moved to a parish at Dean Prior, in Devonshire.

As a Londoner, he did not much like the rough West Country or its people, but he gradually adapted to both, settling into his bachelor quarters and accumulating poems, one after another, without making any effort to publish them. For purely poetic purposes, he invented for himself dozens of imaginary mistresses—hectic, bewitching creatures with exotic names; but the maid who kept house for him was prophetically named Prudence. At the top of his poetic bent, in *Corinna's Going A-Maying*, Herrick produced a truly major lyric on the central theme of his life, the happy reconciliation of nature and nature's god. But much of his poetic work seems casual, though one can easily be misled by his apparent offhandedness into overlooking a serious strain that lies subsurface.

When the Puritans came to power, they dispossessed him of his living, and Herrick came back to London with the fruits of his exile. They were published in 1648, in a fat little octavo volume with two titles, *Hesperides* for the secular poems, and *Noble Numbers* for those with religious subjects. Altogether, there were over fourteen hundred poems—some as brief as two lines—in this one volume, the only publication of Herrick's life. But the time was not right for playful lyrics; few readers noticed *Hesperides*, and Herrick disappeared in silence and oblivion, not to be restored to English literature until the nineteenth century. He did manage to survive the harsh weather of Puritanism until the Restoration brought him back to Dean Prior, where he lived out his last years quietly, dying at the ripe age of eighty-three.

For all his indebtedness to Jonson and the classical authors whom Jonson also idolized, Herrick's playfulness is his own, as is his light, quiet poetic touch. Though he took life and art as sacraments, he did not take them, or himself, solemnly. And his poems often achieve both the lightness of snowflakes and the snowflake's perfection of design.

Delight in Disorder

A sweet disorder in the dress
Kindles in clothes a wantonness.[1]
A lawn[2] about the shoulders thrown
Into a fine distraction;
An erring[3] lace, which here and there   5

1. Most of the terms the poem uses to describe women's clothing have an ethical or social overtone. Compare Jonson's *Still to Be Neat*, p. 630.
   Since all of Herrick's poems were published in
1648, we do not repeat the date for each one.
2. A scarf of fine linen.
3. Wandering, floating.

Enthralls the crimson stomacher;[4]
A cuff neglectful, and thereby
Ribbons to flow confusedly;
A winning wave, deserving note,
In the tempestuous petticoat;   10
A careless shoestring, in whose tie
I see a wild civility:
Do more bewitch me than when art
Is too precise[5] in every part.

Corinna's Going A-Maying

Get up! get up for shame! the blooming morn
Upon her wings presents the god unshorn.[1]
  See how Aurora throws her fair
  Fresh-quilted colors through the air:[2]
  Get up, sweet slug-a-bed, and see   5
  The dew bespangling herb and tree.
Each flower has wept and bowed toward the east
Above an hour since, yet you not dressed;
  Nay, not so much as out of bed?
  When all the birds have matins[3] said,   10
  And sung their thankful hymns, 'tis sin,
  Nay, profanation to keep in,
Whenas a thousand virgins on this day
Spring, sooner than the lark, to fetch in May.[4]

Rise, and put on your foliage, and be seen   15
To come forth, like the springtime, fresh and green,
  And sweet as Flora.[5] Take no care
  For jewels for your gown or hair;
  Fear not; the leaves will strew
  Gems in abundance upon you;   20
Besides, the childhood of the day has kept,
Against you come, some orient[6] pearls unwept;
  Come and receive them while the light
  Hangs on the dew-locks of the night,
  And Titan[7] on the eastern hill   25
  Retires himself, or else stands still
Till you come forth. Wash, dress, be brief in praying:
Few beads[8] are best when once we go a-Maying.

---

4. The lower part of the bodice.
5. "Precise" and "precision" were terms used freely of Puritans; Herrick, in praising feminine disarray, defines the "sprezzatura," or careless grace, of his own Cavalier art.
1. Apollo, the sun god, whose hair (the rays of the sun) is never cut.
2. Aurora, goddess of the dawn, is both tossing her blankets aside, like one anxious to be up, and spreading over the earth a freshly composed coverlet of light.
3. Morning prayers, in the Catholic and Anglican liturgies.

4. On May Day morning, it was the custom to gather whitethorn blossoms and trim the house with them (see lines 30–35).
5. Flora, Italian goddess of flowers, had her festival in the spring.
6. Eastern, as pearls come from the Orient, but also rosy and glowing like the rising sun. "Against": until.
7. The sun.
8. A casual term for prayers, but with overtones of the old (Catholic) religion, which in the next stanza is playfully converted into, and identified with, the worship of nature.

Come, my Corinna, come; and, coming, mark
How each field turns a street,[9] each street a park   30
    Made green and trimmed with trees; see how
    Devotion gives each house a bough
    Or branch: each porch, each door ere this,
    An ark, a tabernacle is,[1]
Made up of whitethorn neatly interwove,   35
As if here were those cooler shades of love.
    Can such delights be in the street
    And open fields, and we not see 't?
    Come, we'll abroad; and let's obey
    The proclamation made for May,   40
And sin no more, as we have done, by staying;
But, my Corinna, come, let's go a-Maying.

There's not a budding boy or girl this day
But is got up and gone to bring in May;
    A deal of youth, ere this, is come   45
    Back, and with whitethorn laden, home.
    Some have dispatched their cakes and cream
    Before that we have left to dream;
And some have wept, and wooed, and plighted troth,
And chose their priest, ere we can cast off sloth.   50
    Many a green-gown[2] has been given,
    Many a kiss, both odd and even;[3]
    Many a glance, too, has been sent
    From out the eye, love's firmament;
Many a jest told of the keys betraying   55
This night, and locks picked; yet we're not a-Maying.

Come, let us go while we are in our prime,
And take the harmless folly of the time.
    We shall grow old apace, and die
    Before we know our liberty.   60
    Our life is short, and our days run
    As fast away as does the sun;
And, as a vapor or a drop of rain,
Once lost, can ne'er be found again,
    So when or you or I are made   65
    A fable, song, or fleeting shade,
    All love, all liking, all delight
    Lies drowned with us in endless night.
Then while time serves, and we are but decaying,
Come, my Corinna, come, let's go a-Maying.   70

9. Turns into a street.
1. The doorways, ornamented with whitethorn, are like the Hebrew Ark of the Covenant, or the sanctuary that housed it; May sprigs are the central mystery of the religion of nature.
2. Got by rolling in the grass.
3. Kisses are odd and even in some kissing games.

To the Virgins, to Make Much of Time

Gather ye rosebuds while ye may,
　Old time is still a-flying;
And this same flower that smiles today,
　Tomorrow will be dying.

The glorious lamp of heaven, the sun,   5
　The higher he's a-getting,
The sooner will his race be run,
　And nearer he's to setting.

That age is best which is the first,
　When youth and blood are warmer;   10
But being spent, the worse, and worst
　Times still succeed the former.

Then be not coy, but use your time,
　And while ye may, go marry;
For having lost but once your prime,   15
　You may forever tarry.

Upon Julia's Clothes

Whenas in silks my Julia goes,
Then, then, methinks, how sweetly flows
That liquefaction of her clothes.

Next, when I cast mine eyes and see
That brave[1] vibration each way free,   5
Oh, how that glittering taketh me!

1. Glorious, splendid.

GEORGE HERBERT
1593–1633

Born into an eminent Welsh family, George Herbert was brought up by his mother, Magdalen Herbert, a lady notable for her piety and for her patronage of literary men like Donne. After taking his degrees at Cambridge, Herbert was elected Public Orator of the university, a post that required its incumbent to express in Latin the sentiments of the university on public occasions. Other men had used the position as a stepping-stone to high political office, and this idea surely tantalized Herbert, who also served twice, during the early 1620s, as a member of Parliament. But the death of his influential patrons and the bent of his own

temper drew him in another direction. In 1626 he took a minor office in the
Anglican church, and in 1630 he accepted the living of Bemerton near Salisbury
and was ordained a priest.

Herbert had only three years at Bemerton before he died of consumption, but
in that short time his pious works earned him the reputation of an ideal cleric.
And during these same years, he completed the volume of poems known as *The
Temple*, which was published in 1633, shortly after his death. His enduring fame
rests on this volume, and all our selections are taken from it.

Like Donne, though in a much quieter way, Herbert is a poet of both intense
religious feeling and virtuosic craftsmanship. Though not all the poems of *The
Temple* bear analogy to the specific parts or occasions of a church structure,
enough do so to intimate a recurrent and complex parallelism. Herbert enjoys
complicated stanzas, and titles that imply a figurative relation to the poems themselves. At the same time, he likes to apply homely images—from commerce, law,
or a game of cards—to spiritual matters, and he is a master of the unexpected,
climactic, quiet simplicity. Strikingly among English authors, Herbert is a poet of
silence and humility; yet he also sometimes depicts the awful experience of spiritual barrenness or rebellion.

Because Herbert's poetry is both religious and ecclesiastical, one might not
expect it to have much appeal to an age as secular as our own. But all sorts of
readers not otherwise noticeably devout have responded to Herbert's quiet intensity; and for many of them, he rivals or surpasses Donne as the supreme Metaphysical poet.

The Altar[1]

A broken A L T A R, Lord, thy servant rears,
Made of a heart, and cemented with tears:
   Whose parts are as thy hand did frame;
   No workman's tool hath touched the same.[2]
       A H E A R T alone   5
       Is such a stone,
       As nothing but
       Thy power doth cut.
       Wherefore each part
       Of my hard heart   10
       Meets in this frame,
       To praise thy Name:
   That, if I chance to hold my peace,
   These stones to praise thee may not cease.[3]
Oh let thy blessed S A C R I F I C E be mine,   15
And sanctify this A L T A R to be thine.

1. This poem and *Easter Wings* (below) are "shaped
verses," which represent, by the typographical shape of
the poem on the page, some part of the subject.
Though sometimes condemned as "false wit," this sort
of poem has appealed to an occasional author from
Hellenistic times to the present. Among recent examples are *Vision and Prayer* by Dylan Thomas and *Un
Coup de Dés* by Stéphane Mallarmé.

Because all of Herbert's poems have the same publication date (1633), we do not repeat it for each poem.

2. A reference to Exodus 20.25, in which the Lord enjoins Moses to build an altar without using cut stone
or any tools.

3. Herbert wants his poem to praise God whether or
not it is being read or spoken. There is also a reference
to Luke 19.40: "I tell you that, if these should hold
their peace, the stones would immediately cry out."
Herbert's poetry, like Milton's, is rich to overflowing in
scriptural echoes.

Redemption[1]

Having been tenant long to a rich lord,
   Not thriving, I resolvèd to be bold,
And make a suit unto him, to afford
   A new small-rented lease, and cancel th' old.[2]

In heaven at his manor I him sought: 5
   They told me there that he was lately gone
About some land which he had dearly bought
   Long since on earth, to take possession.

I straight returned, and knowing his great birth,
   Sought him accordingly in great resorts—   10
   In cities, theaters, gardens, parks, and courts:
At length I heard a ragged noise and mirth

   Of thieves and murderers; there I him espied,
   Who straight, "Your suit is granted," said, and died.

Easter Wings[1]

Lord, who createdst man in wealth and store,[2]
   Though foolishly he lost the same,
      Decaying more and more
         Till he became
           Most poor: 5
           With thee
         O let me rise
       As larks, harmoniously,
     And sing this day thy victories:
Then shall the fall further the flight in me.   10

My tender age in sorrow did begin:
   And still with sicknesses and shame
      Thou didst so punish sin,
         That I became
           Most thin.   15
           With thee
         Let me combine,
       And feel this day thy victory;
     For, if I imp[3] my wing on thine,
Affliction shall advance the flight in me.   20

---

1. "Redemption" means literally "buying back." In this sonnet, Herbert figures God as a landlord, himself as a discontented tenant.
2. I.e., to ask him for a new lease, involving a smaller rent, and to cancel the old lease.

1. Early editions of Herbert print *Easter Wings* with the lines running vertically—i.e., each stanza is rotated ninety degrees, so the wing shape is more apparent.
2. Abundance.
3. Graft (a technical term from falconry).

Jordan (1)[1]

Who says that fictions only and false hair
Become a verse? Is there in truth no beauty?
Is all good structure in a winding stair?
May no lines pass, except they do their duty
    Not to a true, but painted chair?[2]   5

Is it no verse, except enchanted groves
And sudden arbors shadow coarse-spun lines?[3]
Must purling streams refresh a lover's loves?
Must all be veiled, while he that reads, divines,
    Catching the sense at two removes?   10

Shepherds are honest people: let them sing;
Riddle who list, for me, and pull for prime:[4]
I envy no man's nightingale or spring;
Nor let them punish me with loss of rhyme,
    Who plainly say, *My God, My King*.   15

The Collar

I struck the board[1] and cried, "No more;
            I will abroad!
What? shall I ever sigh and pine?
My lines and life are free, free as the road,
    Loose as the wind, as large as store.   5
        Shall I be still in suit?[2]
Have I no harvest but a thorn
To let me blood, and not restore
What I have lost with cordial[3] fruit?
            Sure there was wine   10
Before my sighs did dry it; there was corn
        Before my tears did drown it.
Is the year only lost to me?
        Have I no bays[4] to crown it,
No flowers, no garlands gay? all blasted?   15
        All wasted?

1. "Crossing Jordan" is a symbol for entering into the Promised Land, and it seems likely that Herbert means to indicate by his title that for a poet who has crossed the river (i.e., come into God's country), the complexities (and the clichés) of worldly poetry cease to be necessary or desirable.
2. May no poems ("lines") pass as good unless they make a reverence ("do their duty") to a false throne? It has often been the custom for men to bow before a throne, whether it was occupied or not (see Donne, *Satire* 3, lines 47–48), but to require bowing to a throne in a painting would be excessive. Herbert implies that earthly love is a mere painted imitation of divine love.
3. "Sudden": i.e., that appear unexpectedly (an artificial effect much sought after in landscape gardening).

"Shadow": shade, but also overshadow, cause to be overlooked. Herbert is suggesting that flashy dramatic effects and inherited images ("enchanted groves," "purling streams," and so on) obscure poor craftsmanship.
4. To draw a lucky card in the game of primero. Herbert implies that anyone who understands one of the complex poems he is describing (and parodying) has made a wild and lucky guess. "For me": as far as I'm concerned.
1. Table.
2. In attendance, waiting on someone for a favor. "Store": abundance.
3. Giving heart's ease, restorative.
4. The poet's laurel wreath, here used as a general symbol of festivity.

Not so, my heart; but there is fruit,
　　　　And thou hast hands.
Recover all thy sigh-blown age
On double pleasures: leave thy cold dispute　　　　　　　　　20
Of what is fit and not. Forsake thy cage,
　　　　Thy rope of sands,[5]
Which petty thoughts have made, and made to thee
Good cable, to enforce and draw,
　　　　And be thy law,　　　　　　　　　25
While thou didst wink[6] and wouldst not see.
　　　　Away! take heed;
　　　　I will abroad.
Call in thy death's-head[7] there; tie up thy fears.
　　　　He that forbears　　　　　　　　　30
To suit and serve his need,
　　　　Deserves his load."
But as I raved and grew more fierce and wild
　　　　At every word,
Methoughts I heard one calling, *Child!*　　　　　　　　　35
　　　　And I replied, *My Lord.*

The Pulley

When God at first made man,
Having a glass of blessings standing by,
"Let us," said he, "pour on him all we can:
Let the world's riches, which dispersèd lie,
　　　　Contract into a span."　　　　　　　　　5

So strength first made a way;
Then beauty flowed, then wisdom, honor, pleasure.
When almost all was out, God made a stay,
Perceiving that, alone of all his treasure,
　　　　Rest in the bottom lay.[1]　　　　　　　　　10

"For if I should," said he,
"Bestow this jewel also on my creature,
He would adore my gifts instead of me,
And rest in Nature, not the God of Nature;
　　　　So both should losers be.　　　　　　　　　15

"Yet let him keep the rest,
But keep them with repining restlessness:
Let him be rich and weary, that at least,
If goodness lead him not, yet weariness
　　　　May toss him to my breast."　　　　　　　　　20

5. Christian restrictions on behavior, which the "petty thoughts" of the docile believer have made "good cable," i.e., strong.
6. Shut your eyes (to the real weakness of the church's injunctions).
7. The skull that reminds the penitent of approaching death.
1. "Rest" in the poem has two senses ("remainder" and "repose"); Herbert works them against one another. This balance of forces suggests the pulley, which can draw us to God one way or the other.

The Flower

How fresh, O Lord, how sweet and clean
Are thy returns! even as the flowers in spring,
   To which, besides their own demesne,[1]
The late-past frosts tributes of pleasure bring.
        Grief melts away   5
        Like snow in May,
   As if there were no such cold thing.

   Who would have thought my shriveled heart
Could have recovered greenness? It was gone
   Quite underground; as flowers depart   10
To see their mother-root, when they have blown,[2]
        Where they together
        All the hard weather,
   Dead to the world, keep house unknown.

   These are thy wonders, Lord of power,   15
Killing and quickening, bringing down to hell
   And up to heaven in an hour,
Making a chiming of a passing-bell.[3]
        We say amiss
        This or that is: 20
   Thy word is all, if we could spell.

   O that I once past changing were,
Fast in thy Paradise, where no flower can wither!
   Many a spring I shoot up fair,
Offering[4] at heaven, growing and groaning thither;   25
        Nor doth my flower
        Want a spring shower,[5]
   My sins and I joining together.

   But while I grow in a straight line,
Still upwards bent, as if heaven were mine own,   30
   Thy anger comes, and I decline:
What frost to that? what pole is not the zone
        Where all things burn,
        When thou dost turn,
   And the least frown of thine is shown?[6]   35

   And now in age I bud again,
After so many deaths I live and write;
   I once more smell the dew and rain,
And relish versing. O my only light,

---

1. Estate of one's own (here, beauty or pleasure). The word, spelled *demean* in the original text, may also be a short form of "demeanor," i.e., bearing.
2. Bloomed.
3. The "passing-bell," intended to mark the death of a parishioner, is tolled in a monotone; a chiming offers pleasant variety.
4. Aiming.
5. The tears of contrition produced by the "joining together" of the poet's conscience and his sins.
6. Lines 32–35 may be paraphrased: "What cold compares to God's anger? Compared with God's wrath, what polar chill would not seem like the heat of the equator?"

It cannot be   40
That I am he
On whom thy tempests fell all night.

These are thy wonders, Lord of love,
To make us see we are but flowers that glide;[7]
Which when we once can find and prove,[8]   45
Thou hast a garden for us where to bide;
Who would be more,
Swelling through store,
Forfeit their Paradise by their pride.

Love (3)[1]

Love bade me welcome: yet my soul drew back,
Guilty of dust and sin.
But quick-eyed Love, observing me grow slack[2]
From my first entrance in,
Drew nearer to me, sweetly questioning   5
If I lacked anything.[3]

"A guest," I answered, "worthy to be here":
Love said, "You shall be he."
"I, the unkind, ungrateful? Ah, my dear,
I cannot look on thee."   10
Love took my hand, and smiling did reply,
"Who made the eyes but I?"

"Truth, Lord; but I have marred them; let my shame
Go where it doth deserve."
"And know you not," says Love, "who bore the blame?" 15
"My dear, then I will serve."
"You must sit down," says Love, "and taste my meat."
So I did sit and eat.[4]

7. Pass silently away.
8. Experience.
1. This is the final lyric in *The Temple*.
2. Hesitant, as one feeling misgivings.
3. The first question of shopkeepers and tavern waiters to an entering customer would be "What d'ye lack?" (i.e., want).
4. In addition to the sacrament of Communion, the reference is also and ultimately to the final communion in heaven, when God "shall gird himself, and make them to sit down to meat, and will come forth and serve them" (Luke 12.37).

RICHARD LOVELACE
1618–1657

Along with Sir John Suckling, Richard Lovelace has traditionally been regarded as the quintessential Cavalier poet. Lovelace was born of an old and wealthy Kentish family and educated at Oxford; he was a handsome, witty, charming young man, the very model of a courtier, conspicuously marked by royal favor. But the civil wars were hard on him; he fought in King Charles's disastrous Scottish campaigns, was imprisoned by Parliament, went into exile for a time, was wounded while serving as a soldier of fortune abroad, was imprisoned again in England, and, by the time of his release in 1649, was financially ruined. Of the remaining eight or so years of his life, very little is known. He published *Lucasta*—from which our selections are taken—in 1649; a posthumous volume, which contained his remaining writings, appeared in 1659.

To Lucasta, Going to the Wars

Tell me not, sweet, I am unkind,
    That from the nunnery
Of thy chaste breast and quiet mind
    To war and arms I fly.

True, a new mistress now I chase,   5
    The first foe in the field;
And with a stronger faith embrace
    A sword, a horse, a shield.

Yet this inconstancy is such
    As you too shall adore;   10
I could not love thee, dear, so much,
    Loved I not honor more.

To Althea, from Prison

When Love with unconfinèd wings
    Hovers within my gates,
And my divine Althea brings
    To whisper at the grates;
When I lie tangled in her hair   5
    And fettered to her eye,
The gods[1] that wanton in the air
    Know no such liberty.

When flowing cups run swiftly round,
    With no allaying Thames,[2]   10
Our careless heads with roses bound,
    Our hearts with loyal flames;
When thirsty grief in wine we steep,
    When healths and draughts go free,
Fishes that tipple in the deep   15
    Know no such liberty.

1. Some versions read "birds" instead of "gods." Since both of our Lovelace selections were pub-

lished in 1649, we do not repeat the date for each.
2. No mixture of water in the wine.

When, like committed linnets,[3] I
    With shriller throat shall sing
The sweetness, mercy, majesty,
    And glories of my king;   20
When I shall voice aloud how good
    He is, how great should be,
Enlargèd winds, that curl the flood,
    Know no such liberty.

Stone walls do not a prison make,   25
    Nor iron bars a cage;
Minds innocent and quiet take
    That for an hermitage.
If I have freedom in my love,
    And in my soul am free,   30
Angels alone, that soar above,
    Enjoy such liberty.

3. Caged finches.

ANDREW MARVELL
1621–1678

Andrew Marvell is an elusive, enigmatic figure, as a man and as a poet. He
attended Cambridge, graduated B.A. in 1638, and remained for a couple of years
more in residence; after traveling abroad for some years, he disappears from the
biographer's view, turning up around 1650 as tutor to the daughter of Sir Thomas
Fairfax, lord general of the parliamentary forces in the civil wars. At the Yorkshire
seat of this family, Nun Appleton House, Marvell seems to have written, over a
period of about three years, most of his lyric poems.

In 1657 Marvell was appointed assistant to the blind Latin secretary for the
Cromwellian Commonwealth, John Milton; and he seems to have been helpful
after the Restoration in saving Milton from an extended jail term and possible
execution. In 1659 Marvell was elected Member of Parliament for his hometown
of Hull, which he continued to represent until his death. He was a good committee man and devoted to the interests of his riding. His letters to his constituents,
regular as clockwork, are useful historical documents; but one would never guess
from reading them that their author was an accomplished poet.

And, in fact, when Marvell died he was known as the author only of some
rough-and-ready satires in verse and prose that had been printed during the Restoration. The lyric poetry for which he is now primarily known was published three
years after his death, by a woman who gave herself out as his widow but had
probably been his housekeeper. The reputation of these poems has made its way
slowly but steadily, so that it has never stood higher than in our own time. Playful,
casual, and witty in tone, always light on its metrical feet and exact in its diction,
Marvell's verse discloses, beneath its graceful surface, unexpected depth and intellectual hardness; its texture is extraordinarily rich.

To His Coy Mistress

Had we but world enough, and time,
This coyness, lady, were no crime.
We would sit down, and think which way
To walk, and pass our long love's day.
Thou by the Indian Ganges' side   5
Shouldst rubies find; I by the tide
Of Humber would complain.[1] I would
Love you ten years before the Flood,
And you should, if you please, refuse
Till the conversion of the Jews.[2]   10
My vegetable love should grow
Vaster than empires, and more slow;
An hundred years should go to praise
Thine eyes, and on thy forehead gaze;
Two hundred to adore each breast,   15
But thirty thousand to the rest:
An age at least to every part,
And the last age should show your heart.
For, lady, you deserve this state,[3]
Nor would I love at lower rate.   20
     But at my back I always hear
Time's wingèd chariot hurrying near;
And yonder all before us lie
Deserts of vast eternity.
Thy beauty shall no more be found,   25
Nor, in thy marble vault, shall sound
My echoing song; then worms shall try
That long-preserved virginity,
And your quaint honor turn to dust,
And into ashes all my lust: 30
The grave's a fine and private place,
But none, I think, do there embrace.
     Now therefore, while the youthful hue
Sits on thy skin like morning dew,[4]
And while thy willing soul transpires   35
At every pore with instant fires,[5]
Now let us sport us while we may,
And now, like amorous birds of prey,
Rather at once our time devour
Than languish in his slow-chapped[6] power.   40
Let us roll all our strength and all

1. Compared to the gorgeous Oriental Ganges, the Humber (which flows past Marvell's hometown of Hull) is a muddy estuary, where one is more likely to encounter herring boats and coal scows than rubies. "Complain" implies ditties of plaintive, unavailing love.
   Since all of our Marvell selections were published in 1681, we do not repeat the date for each.
2. According to popular chronology, the Jews were to be converted just before the Last Judgment.
3. Dignity.
4. The text reads "glew," a sticky point for interpreters and textual critics alike; the emendation "dew" is very common. In an extended study of *Marvell and Alchemy* (1990), Lyndy Abraham offers an ingenious and erudite reading that aims to reinstate "glew" as a defensible, intricate locution.
5. Immediate, present enthusiasm. "Transpires": breathes forth.
6. Slow-jawed. Time is envisaged as slowly chewing up the world and its people.

Our sweetness up into one ball,
And tear our pleasures with rough strife
Thorough the iron gates of life:
Thus, though we cannot make our sun   45
Stand still, yet we will make him run.[7]

The Definition of Love

My Love is of a birth as rare
As 'tis, for object, strange and high;
It was begotten by Despair
Upon Impossibility.

Magnanimous Despair alone   5
Could show me so divine a thing,
Where feeble Hope could ne'er have flown
But vainly flapped its tinsel wing.

And yet I quickly might arrive
Where my extended soul is fixed;[1]   10
But Fate does iron wedges drive,
And always crowds itself betwixt.

For Fate with jealous eye does see
Two perfect loves, nor lets them close;[2]
Their union would her ruin be,   15
And her tyrannic power depose.[3]

And therefore her decrees of steel
Us as the distant poles have placed
(Though Love's whole world on us doth wheel),
Not by themselves to be embraced,   20

Unless the giddy heaven fall,
And earth some new convulsion tear,
And, us to join, the world should all
Be cramped into a planisphere.[4]

As lines, so loves oblique may well   25
Themselves in every angle greet;[5]
But ours, so truly parallel,
Though infinite, can never meet.

---

7. In the final lines, lover and mistress triumphantly reverse the field, eating time avidly instead of being eaten by it, forcing the sun to race them instead of vainly imploring it to stand still.
1. Marvell thinks of his soul as having gone out of his body ("extended") and attached ("fixed") itself to his mistress.
2. Unite.
3. Fate, and its agents Time and Change, would none of them have any power against a perfect mixture of the elements.
4. A flat sphere, literally absurd, but describing a kind of cartographic projection in which the world was represented in two dimensions and the poles were united.
5. "Oblique" includes the meaning of "deviating from right conduct or thought"; oblique loves, like oblique lines, touch in angles (corners), but Marvell's love and the lady's, being parallel and perfect, can never touch.

Therefore the love which us doth bind,
But Fate so enviously debars,   30
Is the conjunction of the mind,
And opposition of the stars.[6]

The Garden

How vainly men themselves amaze
To win the palm, the oak, or bays,[1]
And their uncessant labors see
Crowned from some single herb or tree,
Whose short and narrow-vergèd shade   5
Does prudently their toils upbraid;
While all flowers and all trees do close[2]
To weave the garlands of repose!

Fair Quiet, have I found thee here,
And Innocence, thy sister dear?   10
Mistaken long, I sought you then
In busy companies of men.
Your sacred plants, if here below,
Only among the plants will grow;
Society is all but rude,   15
To[3] this delicious solitude.

No white nor red[4] was ever seen
So amorous as this lovely green.
Fond lovers, cruel as their flame,
Cut in these trees their mistress' name: 20
Little, alas, they know or heed
How far these beauties hers exceed!
Fair trees, wheresoe'er your barks I wound,
No name shall but your own be found.[5]

When we have run our passion's heat,
Love hither makes his best retreat.   25
The gods, that mortal beauty chase,
Still[6] in a tree did end their race:
Apollo hunted Daphne so,
Only that she might laurel grow;   30
And Pan did after Syrinx speed,
Not as a nymph, but for a reed.[7]

---

6. "Conjunction" and "opposition" are technical terms from astrology, here yoked to Marvell's "definition."
1. Honors, respectively, for military, civic, and poetic achievement.
2. Unite, agree.
3. Compared to.
4. Colors traditionally associated with female beauty.

5. The speaker proposes to carve in the bark of trees, not *Sylvia* or *Laura*, but *Beech* and *Oak*.
6. Always.
7. Apollo chased Daphne until she turned into a laurel, and Pan pursued Syrinx until she became a reed, out of which he made panpipes. The gods' motives were, of course, sexual, not horticultural.

What wondrous life in this I lead!
Ripe apples drop about my head;
The luscious clusters of the vine   35
Upon my mouth do crush their wine;
The nectarine and curious peach
Into my hands themselves do reach;
Stumbling on melons[8] as I pass,
Insnared with flowers, I fall on grass.   40

Meanwhile the mind, from pleasure less,[9]
Withdraws into its happiness;
The mind, that ocean where each kind
Does straight its own resemblance find;[1]
Yet it creates, transcending these,   45
Far other worlds and other seas,
Annihilating all that's made
To a green thought in a green shade.

Here at the fountain's sliding foot,
Or at some fruit tree's mossy root,   50
Casting the body's vest[2] aside,
My soul into the boughs does glide:
There like a bird it sits and sings,
Then whets[3] and combs its silver wings,
And, till prepared for longer flight,   55
Waves in its plumes the various light.[4]

Such was that happy garden-state,
While man there walked without a mate:
After a place so pure and sweet,
What other help could yet be meet![5]   60
But 'twas beyond a mortal's share
To wander solitary there:
Two paradises 'twere in one
To live in paradise alone.

How well the skillful gardener drew   65
Of flowers and herbs this dial new,[6]
Where from above the milder sun
Does through a fragrant zodiac run;
And as it works, th' industrious bee
Computes its time as well as we!   70
How could such sweet and wholesome hours
Be reckoned but with herbs and flowers?

8. "Melons," which have their etymological roots in the Greek word for *apple*, may be intended to recall a particularly remote apple over which all humankind once stumbled. "Curious": exquisite. (The nectarine *is* a curious variety of peach.)
9. "Less" may modify either pleasure or mind. In the latter sense ("drawn in on itself") it chimes on "withdraws" and "annihilating," later in the stanza.
1. As the ocean supposedly contained a counterpart of every creature on land, so also the ocean of the mind.
2. Garment.
3. Preens.
4. The many-colored light of this world, contrasted with the white radiance of eternity.
5. Genesis 2.18 records the Lord's decision to make a "help meet" for Adam, i.e., Eve.
6. The garden itself, enlarged metaphorically to a sundial. While the sun keeps time on it, the bee (line 69) is busy with the thyme in it.

The Restoration and the Eighteenth Century

1660-1785

1660:   Charles II restored to the English throne.
1688–89:   The Glorious Revolution: deposition of James II and accession of William of Orange.
1700:   Death of John Dryden.
1707:   Act of Union unites Scotland and England, which thus become "Great Britain."
1714:   Rule by house of Hanover begins with accession of George I.
1744–45:   Deaths of Alexander Pope and Jonathan Swift.
1784:   Death of Samuel Johnson.

The England to which Charles Stuart returned in 1660 was a nation divided against itself, exhausted by twenty years of civil wars and revolution. Early in Charles's reign, the people were visited by two frightful calamities that seemed to the superstitious to be the work of a divine Providence outraged by rebellion and regicide: the plague of 1665, ravaging the country, carried off over seventy thousand souls in London alone, and in September 1666, a fire that raged for four days destroyed a large part of the City (more than thirteen thousand houses), leaving about two-thirds of the population homeless. Yet the nation rose from its ashes, in the century that followed, to become an empire. Within two decades of the king's return, the Royal Navy had defeated the navy of Holland, England's greatest maritime and commercial rival, and in a series of wars fought between 1689 and 1763 against France, the British acquired dominions that stretched around the world, from Canada in the west to India in the east. Internally, moreover, the nation became whole again. The Glorious Revolution of 1688–89 established a rule of law, and the Act of Union of 1707, a political alliance, under which England was transformed into Great Britain in fact as well as name—a larger country to which people of widely differing backgrounds and origins felt they owed allegiance. Many of the great British writers of the eighteenth century, like Jonathan Swift, Edmund Burke, Richard Sheridan, and Oliver Goldsmith, came from Ireland; many, like James Thomson, James Boswell, and David Hume, came from Scotland. Strengthened from without and from within, Great Britain was able to endure the loss of her thirteen American colonies and to enter the final struggle with Revolutionary and Napoleonic France as a world power.

RELIGION AND POLITICS

Charles came home to the almost universal satisfaction of his subjects, for after the abdication of Richard Cromwell in 1659 the country had seemed at the brink

819

of chaos, and Britons were eager to believe that the king would bring order, peace, freedom under law, and a spirit of mildness back into the national life. But no political settlement could be stable until the religious issues of the age had been resolved. The restoration of the monarchy meant, inevitably, the restoration of the established church, and though Charles had promised mildness toward all but a few of his late father's enemies, the bishops and Anglican clergy felt anything but Christian charity toward their Dissenting brothers. In 1662 Parliament reimposed the Book of Common Prayer on all ministers and congregations, and in 1664 religious meetings in which the forms of the established church were not followed were declared illegal. Thousands of clergymen resigned their livings, and the jails were filled with Nonconformist preachers who, like John Bunyan, refused to be silenced. In 1673 the triumph of the Establishment was completed by the Test Act, which required all holders of civil and military offices to receive the sacrament according to the Anglican rite and to declare their disbelief in transubstantiation. Thus the two adversaries of the Anglican church, Protestant Dissenters and Roman Catholics, were alike excluded from public life, though the practice of occasional conformity (i.e., receiving the sacrament in an Anglican church at rare intervals) enabled many Dissenters to comply with the law. Throughout the closing decades of the seventeenth century, Anglicans associated Nonconformity with revolution, regicide, republicanism, and the rule of the Puritan Saints—hence, with subversion—and with excessive zeal, "enthusiasm" (i.e., belief in private revelation), and irrationality—hence, with absurdity. The scorn and detestation in which Dissenters were held may be measured by the delight that readers took in Samuel Butler's caricature of Presbyterians and Independents in *Hudibras* (1663), an attitude that persisted unchanged for the rest of the century, as Swift's *Tale of a Tub*, written about 1697, makes clear. As for the English Catholics, they appeared always as potential traitors of whom anything evil could be believed. Few doubted, for example, that the Great Fire of 1666 had been set by Catholics.

Although ecclesiastical problems seemed to have been quickly and effectively solved, the constitutional issues that had divided Charles I and Parliament were not so readily settled. Charles II had promised to govern through Parliament, but like other members of his family he held strong views on the power and prerogatives of the Crown. Nevertheless, he was content to avoid crises whenever he could, and because he was an astute politician, he frequently could. He concealed from his subjects his Catholic sympathies (on his deathbed he received the last rites of the Roman church), for he had no wish "to go on his travels" again. The one great religious and constitutional crisis of his reign was the Popish Plot and its political consequences (1678–81)—the unsuccessful attempt of a faction in Parliament to force Charles to accept a bill excluding his Catholic brother, James, duke of York, from the succession. Except in this instance, where he was successful because of his courage, duplicity, and political skill, Charles allowed no opportunity for a test of strength between Crown and Parliament.

One important result of the political and religious turmoils of the decade following the Popish Plot was the emergence of two clearly defined political parties: Whig and Tory. The party of the court, which supported the king in 1681, came to be called Tories; the king's opponents, Whigs. By the end of the century the two parties had developed opposed attitudes on other important issues. The Tories drew their strength largely from the landed gentry and the country clergy. They were the conservatives of the period: strong supporters of the Crown and of the established church as the two great sources of political and social stability, they bitterly (though futilely) opposed toleration of Dissenters and successfully supported the Test Act. They were hostile to the new moneyed interests, whether among the newer nobility or the increasingly well-to-do middle class, for they held that landed wealth is the only responsible wealth. The Whigs were a less homogeneous group: many powerful nobles who were jealous of the powers of the

Crown; the merchants and financiers of London; a number of bishops and low church clergymen; and the Dissenters. These varied groups were united by their policies of toleration and support of commerce.

After James II came to the throne in 1685, determined to advance the cause of the Roman church in England, an atmosphere of crisis rapidly developed. Claiming the right to set aside laws and to overrule Parliament, he issued in 1687 a Declaration of Indulgence, suspending the Tests and penal laws against both Catholics and Dissenters, and he began to fill the army and government—not to mention the universities—with his coreligionists. Matters came to a crisis in the summer of 1688, when a son was born to the queen and the prospect of a succession of Catholic monarchs confronted the nation. Secret negotiations paved the way for the arrival in England of the Dutchman William of Orange at the head of a small armed force. He was the leading champion of Protestantism on the Continent and the husband of James's Protestant daughter Mary. Finding resistance to his hostile subjects impossible, James, after sending his wife and the infant prince out of the country, fled to France on December 11. There he was cordially received by Louis XIV, granted a subsidy, and established with his court at St. Germain. For over half a century the possibility of invasion and the forcible restoration first of James, later of his son "the Old Pretender," and finally of his grandson Prince Charles Edward, was a source of anxiety to the English government. Many of the English and a great many more Scots remained loyal to the house of Stuart until there was nothing left of their cause (called Jacobite from the Latin *Jacobus*, James) but a pleasant sentiment. Two serious Jacobite rebellions actually occurred: in 1715, when the Old Pretender arrived in Scotland to support an uprising against the newly crowned Hanoverian, George I, and more threateningly in 1745, when Prince Charles Edward (the "Bonnie Prince Charlie" of romantic story) came dangerously close to success in his invasion of England, an event that affects the fortunes of the hero in Henry Fielding's novel *Tom Jones* (1749).

It was only with the flight of James that England could begin to bury the past and to turn toward its destiny in the next age. The coming in of William and Mary and the settlement achieved in 1689 were known as the Glorious, or Bloodless, Revolution, all the more glorious for being bloodless. A more tolerant era was opening, as was made apparent in important acts passed by Parliament in the first year of the new reign. In 1689 the Bill of Rights limited the powers of the Crown, reaffirmed the supremacy of Parliament, and guaranteed important legal rights to individuals. Moreover, the Toleration Act, although it did not repeal the Test Act, did grant freedom of worship to Dissenters. A number of the conflicting elements in the national life were thus reconciled through what proved to be a workable compromise, and with the passage of the Act of Settlement in 1701, settling the succession to the throne upon Sophia, Electress of Hanover, and her descendants (as the granddaughter of James I, she was the closest Protestant relative of the Princess Anne, James II's younger daughter, whose sole surviving child died in that year), the difficult problems that had so long divided England seemed resolved. The principles established in 1689 endured unaltered in essentials until the Reform Bill of 1832.

During the reign of Anne, the last Stuart monarch (1702–14), a renewal of tension embittered the political atmosphere. On the Continent England led her allies, Holland, Austria, and Bavaria, to victory in the War of the Spanish Succession against France and Spain (1702–13). The hero of the war was the brilliant Captain-General John Churchill, duke of Marlborough, who, with his duchess, dominated the queen until 1710. The war was a Whig war, supported by powerful Whig lords and the Whig merchants of London, who grew increasingly rich on war profits and who stood to gain by any weakening of the power of France and Spain. The Whigs were anxious to reward the Dissenters for their loyalty by removing the Test. Unfortunately for them, Anne was especially devoted to the church, and when, in 1710, they were made to appear to threaten the health of the Establishment, she dismissed her Whig ministers and called in Robert Harley as lord treasurer and the brilliant young Henry St. John as secretary of state (in charge of foreign relations) to form the Tory ministry, which governed England during the last four years of her reign. The Marlboroughs were dismissed, the duke even losing his command in 1711, but not before the royal favor and a grateful nation had made him immensely rich and had given him the land on which he built his famous palace, Blenheim (pronounced *Blen'm*), in memory of the most brilliant victory (pronounced *Blén-hime*) of the war.

It was these Tory ministers whom Daniel Defoe and Swift served in their different ways; it was for them that Matthew Prior negotiated the Peace of Utrecht, ratified in 1713. To Swift's despair, a bitter rivalry developed between Harley (then earl of Oxford) and St. John (then Viscount Bolingbroke) during 1713–14. And as the queen's life faded in the summer of 1714, Bolingbroke succeeded in ousting Oxford, only to have his own ambitions thwarted by the death of Anne and the return to power of the vindictive Whigs with the accession of George I, son of the late Sophia, electress of Hanover. For a moment it seemed as if this event might not occur without bloodshed, but the crisis quickly passed, the Protestant succession was not immediately opposed by Jacobites, and the Whigs turned happily to investigating the conduct of the former ministers. Harley was imprisoned in the Tower of London (where he remained until 1717), and Bolingbroke, charged with treasonable correspondence with the Pretender, fled to France, where he actually became, for a while, secretary of state to the Jacobite court. Pardoned in 1723, but denied his seat in the House of Lords, he returned to England and directed the opposition to Robert Walpole, while seeing much of Alexander Pope and playing the gentleman-farmer-philosopher at Dawley Farm.

The three Georges who occupied the throne during the rest of the century presided over a nation that grew increasingly prosperous through war, trade, and the beginnings of industrialism. George I (reigned 1714–27) and George II (reigned 1727–60) spoke broken English and had little interest in the affairs of the country. In their hearts they remained petty German princelings even when they were kings of Great Britain, spending as much time as possible in Hanover. Under such circumstances it was inevitable that ministers should become more important and more independent of the Crown than they had been under stronger and more intelligent monarchs. Through the indifference of two kings and the ambition and great abilities of the Whig prime minister Walpole, the modern system of ministerial government began to develop. This was the last important contribution of the age to British political institutions. Walpole's long ascendency (1721–42) brought a period of peace and prosperity and of capable government based, paradoxically, on flagrant political corruption. Although Walpole strengthened the importance of the House of Commons in British politics, he nonetheless continued, if he did not increase, the corruption of its members through bribery. He was a practical man and cared little for literature, preferring to spend money on useful journalists and voting Members of Parliament rather than on poets. Thus with two kings who knew nothing of literature and a prime minister who was indifferent to it, English writers could not expect the shower of offices and government sinecures that had made the age of Anne the great age of patronage: William Congreve, Sir Richard Steele, Joseph Addison, Prior, and Swift had expected and obtained such rewards both for their literary eminence and for their service to party. But after 1715, as patronage declined, authors found that they must turn to the publishers, who could pay them well because of the growing reading public. Indeed, Samuel Johnson was accustomed to declare that the booksellers of the midcentury had become the patrons of literature.

The long reign of George III (1760–1820) was dominated by two great concerns: the emergence of Britain as a colonial power and the cry for a new social order based on liberty and radical reform. In 1763 the Peace of Paris consolidated British rule over Canada and India, and not even the loss of the American colonies could stem the rise of the empire. Great Britain was no longer an isolated island but a nation with interests and responsibilities around the world. At home, however, there was discontent. The wealth brought to England by industrialism and foreign trade did not spread to the working classes. In 1780 the Gordon Riots temporarily put London under mob rule. The king, the first Hanoverian monarch born in England, was popular with his subjects and tried to take government into his own hands. Meanwhile reformers such as John Wilkes and Richard Price called for a new political democracy. Fear of their radicalism would contribute to the British reaction against the French Revolution after 1789. In the last decades of the century, British authors would be torn between two opposing attitudes: loyalty to the old traditions of subordination and local self-sufficiency, and yearning for a new dispensation on principles of liberty, the rule of reason, and human rights.

INTELLECTUAL BACKGROUND

The political turbulence of the seventeenth century subsided only gradually during the last decades of the century, and during the Restoration period (1660–1700) literature also reflected a conflict of values. John Milton's major poems, a culmination of Renaissance art, appeared at the same time that John Dryden was establishing himself as the laureate of a new age of elegance. Bunyan's *Pilgrim's Progress* expressed the Nonconformist conscience at the same time that such court wits as the earl of Rochester and Sir Charles Sedley expressed a libertine creed. The town and the country followed different ideas about art and the conduct of life. The Restoration is best known as a period dominated by a fun-loving, dissolute court, whose style of life was reflected in rakish comedies. But the ordinary life of the nation did not radically change. Rural manners remained conservative and old-fashioned. The London citizens, middle class and respectable, cherishing much of the independence and piety of Dissent, were scandalized by the behavior of upper-class rakes who regarded them with contempt and considered their wives and daughters fair game. Even good Royalists like John Evelyn and Samuel Pepys often speak anxiously in their diaries of the moral laxity of the court and the danger to the country of the king's example.

Charles himself was easygoing, pleasure-loving, and amorous, more fond of the society of boon companions—and mistresses—than he was of state business. But he also had serious intellectual interests and was a patron of the arts. He dabbled in chemistry and was interested in the progress of science. A characteristic act was his chartering in 1662 the Royal Society of London for the Improving of Natural Knowledge, thus giving official approval to the scientific movement that Sir Francis Bacon had initiated early in the century and that was just then coming to maturity. The king's love of music and painting led him to import from the Continent composers, musicians, new musical instruments, the French and Italian opera, and painting and painters largely from the Low Countries. His interest in the theater was demonstrated by the chartering of two companies of actors in 1660, both under royal patronage, the King's Players, and the Duke's—the duke being James, duke of York.

It is natural, therefore, that the most characteristic art of the period reflected the interests and tastes of those who supported it. Artists addressed themselves to court and "town," the western suburbs that were the center of fashion. The middle-class tradespeople, who lodged over their shops in the City (i.e., that part of greater London that was once within the city walls and that was then thickly populated), were scorned as tasteless barbarians. Except in the theater, literature was not in itself a gainful profession (as it was to become in the eighteenth century), and writers looked for patronage from the court and the great nobles. Milton, for example, received only £10 for the first edition of *Paradise Lost*. By the end of the century, however, thanks to the enterprise of the bookseller Jacob Tonson and the new device of publishing books through subscription (i.e., soliciting payment in advance for deluxe copies of a work, in addition to publishing a regular trade edition), Dryden was able to earn between £1,000 and £1,200 for his translation of the works of Virgil (1697). And Pope's Homer, similarly published between 1715 and 1726, was to prove even more profitable.

Perhaps the most important aspect of the Restoration period is the increasing challenge of various forms of secular thought to the old religious orthodoxies that had been matters of life and death since the Reformation. As the contentious voices of Roman, Anglican, and Dissenter grew more and more subdued, other interests attracted adventurous minds. Thomas Hobbes, in *Leviathan* (1651), had taught a philosophic materialism and advocated an absolute government as the most efficacious check to human nature, which he described as wholly driven by egoistic and predatory passions. Detested by the church and attacked on all sides, these ideas nonetheless played their role in the lives and writings of some of the more advanced young people, and they provoked by way of reaction in the next century an optimistic insistence on the natural goodness of humanity. A soberer and more ancient tradition was philosophic skepticism. Originating in ancient Greece, skepticism had found its most persuasive recent statement in the essays of the Frenchman Michel de Montaigne (1533–1592), whose influence was widespread throughout seventeenth-century Europe. The skeptic argued that all our knowledge is derived from our senses, but that our senses do not report the world around us accurately, and that, therefore, reliable knowledge is an impossibility. The safest course is to affirm nothing as absolutely true, to remember that most beliefs are mere opinions, and where possible, to be guided by the traditional in matters intellectual, political, and ethical. Butler, Dryden, and Rochester, among others, more or less adhered to this doctrine. But though skeptics remained in doubt about the results of human reasoning, they were not precluded from religious beliefs, for they could assert (as did Dryden after his conversion to Catholicism) that faith alone is necessary for accepting the mysteries of the Christian religion.

The new science, advanced by members of the Royal Society, was rapidly altering views of nature. Science in the seventeenth century was principally concerned with the physical sciences—with astronomy, physics, and to a lesser degree, chemistry; and the discoveries in these sciences were reassuring in their evidence of universal and immutable law and order, clear proof of the wisdom and goodness of God in His creation. Such laws of nature as Boyle's law of the behavior of gases under pressure or Newton's law of gravitation seemed obviously to support the idea that a beneficent, divine intelligence created and directs the universe. The truest truths proved to be the clearest, the simplest, the most general. Such truths seemed to promise a time, not remote, when mystery would be banished entirely from religion as well as from nature. Indeed, Deism, or natural religion, which had an increasingly wide appeal to "enlightened" minds, deduced its simple rationalistic creed from the Book of Nature, God's first and, to many in the eighteenth century, only valid revelation. The Deists deduced the existence of a supreme being or First Cause from the existence of the universe: a creature presupposes a creator. The laws of nature sufficiently proved the reasonableness, goodness, and wisdom of this creator. Him we can and must revere, but good though He is, it is demonstrable that He does not punish vice and reward virtue in this life; therefore, being good and just, He must do so in some future life: hence, we must believe in immortality. Meanwhile, here on earth, it is our duty to cooperate with Nature and the Deity, cultivating as best we can wisdom, virtue, and benevolence. This creed is as simple and as rational as one of Newton's laws, but its omission of the "second revelation" of the Scriptures, the scheme of salvation in which Christ died to redeem our sins, made it unacceptable to many Christians, although many others found it possible to accept both natural religion and revealed Christianity.

As the seventeenth century drew to a close, its temper became more secular, tolerant, and moderate. The new age was willing to settle for the possible within the limits of human intelligence and of the material world. Its temper was expressed by its most influential philosopher, John Locke (1632–1704), in his *Essay Concerning Human Understanding* (1690):

> If by this inquiry into the nature of the understanding, I can discover the powers thereof; how far they reach; to what things they are in any degree proportionate; and where they fail us, I suppose it may be of use to prevail with the busy mind of man to be more cautious in meddling with things exceeding its comprehension; to stop when it is at the utmost extent of its tether; and to sit down in a quiet ignorance of those things which, upon examination, are found to be beyond the reach of our capacities. . . . Our business here is not to know all things, but those which concern our conduct.

These words might be taken as the creed of eighteenth-century England. Such a position is Swift's, when he inveighs against metaphysics, abstract logical deductions, and theoretical science; it is similar to Pope's in *An Essay on Man*; it prompts Johnson to talk of "the business of living"; it helps to account for the emphasis that the Anglican clergy put on good works, rather than faith, as the way to salvation and for their dislike of emotion and "enthusiasm" in religion.

But if the eighteenth century brought a recognition of human limitations, it also took an optimistic view of human nature. Rejecting Hobbes, some eighteenth-century philosophers asserted that human beings are naturally good and find their highest happiness in the exercise of virtue and benevolence. Such a view of human nature we describe as "sentimental." It found the source of virtue in instinctive and social impulses rather than in a code of conduct sanctioned by divine law. And people began to feel—or to fancy that they felt—exquisite pleasure in the exercise of benevolent impulses. Sentimentalism fostered a benevolence that led to social reforms seldom envisioned in earlier times—to the improvement of jails, to the relief of imprisoned debtors, to the establishment of foundling hospitals and of homes for penitent prostitutes, and ultimately to the abolition of the slave trade—and it also encouraged a ready flow of feeling and tears and a capacity to respond to the joys and sorrows of others. The doctrine of natural goodness seemed to many to suggest that it is civilization that corrupts us and that "noble savages," those who live in a state of nature, might be models of innocence and virtue. Such notions encouraged an interest in primitive societies and even helped to prepare, late in the century, for the warm reception given the peasant poet Robert Burns, an "original genius," as well as for William Wordsworth's interest in children and in simple, rural people.

As the wave of sentimentalism mounted, a parallel rise of religious feeling occurred after about 1740. The great religious revival known as Methodism was led by John Wesley (1703–1791), his brother Charles (1707–1788), and George Whitefield (1714–1770), all Oxford graduates. The Methodists took their gospel to the common people, preaching the necessity of a conviction of sin and of conversion and the joy of the "blessed assurance" of being saved. Often denied the privilege of preaching in village churches, they preached to thousands in the open fields and in barns. The somnolent Anglican church and the self-assured upper classes were repelled by the emotionalism aroused by Methodist preachers among the lower orders. It seemed as if the irrationality, zeal, and enthusiasm of the Puritan sects were being revived. But the religious awakening persisted and affected many clergymen and laymen within the Establishment, who, as "Evangelicals," reanimated the church and promoted unworldliness and piety. And yet the insistence of Methodists on faith over works as the way to salvation did not prevent them or their Anglican counterparts from playing important roles in many of the social reforms of the time, especially in helping to abolish slavery and the slave trade.

The literature of the period between 1660 and 1785 can conveniently, though perhaps too schematically, be considered as falling into three lesser periods of about forty years each: the first, extending to the death of Dryden in 1700, may be thought of as the period in which English "neoclassical" literature came into being and its critical principles were formulated; the second, ending with the death of Pope in 1744 and of Swift in 1745, brought to its culmination the literary movement initiated by Dryden and his generation; the third, concluding with the death of Johnson in 1784 and the publication of William Cowper's *The Task* in 1785, was a period in which the old principles were confronted by new ideas that contained within themselves the origins of the romantic movement of the late eighteenth and early nineteenth centuries.

Apparently, a sudden change of taste took place about 1660, but the change was not so sudden as it appears. Like the English Renaissance, it was part of a general movement in European culture, seen perhaps at its most impressive in seventeenth-century France. Described most simply, it was a reaction against the intricacy and occasional obscurity, boldness, and extravagance of European literature of the late Renaissance, in favor of greater simplicity, clarity, restraint, regularity, and good sense. This tendency is most readily to be observed in the preference of Dryden and his contemporaries for "easy, natural" wit, which aims to surprise rather than to shock. It accompanied, though it was not necessarily caused by, the development of certain rationalistic philosophies and the rise of experimental science, as well as a desire for peace and order after an era of violent extremism.

This movement produced in France the impressive body of classical literature that distinguished the age of Louis XIV. In England it produced a literature often termed "neoclassical," or "Augustan," because it was strongly influenced by the writers of the reign of the first Roman emperor, Augustus Caesar, just before the beginning of the Christian era. Rome's Augustan Age was a period of stability and peace after the civil war that followed the death of Julius Caesar. Its chief poets, Virgil, Horace, and Ovid, addressed their polished works to a sophisticated aristocracy, among whom they found generous patrons. Dryden's generation was aware of an analogy between the situations of post–civil war England and Augustan Rome. Later generations would be suspicious of that analogy; after 1700 most writers stressed that Augustus had been a tyrant who thought himself greater than the law. But in 1660 there was hope that Charles would be a better Augustus, bringing to England the civilized virtues of an Augustan age without its vices.

Charles and his followers inevitably brought back from France an admiration of contemporary French literature as well as of French fashions and elegance. The theories of such writers as Pierre Corneille, René Rapin, and Nicolas Boileau also came into vogue. But English literature remained stubbornly English: English writers took what they required from France, but used it for their own ends. It was not Dryden's aim merely to imitate the French poets or for that matter the Latin, but to produce in England works that would be worthy to stand beside theirs. He knew that this could be done only if English literature remained true to its living tradition: Geoffrey Chaucer, Edmund Spenser, William Shakespeare, Ben Jonson, and John Donne entered into his literary consciousness as well as Virgil, Horace, Longinus, or Corneille.

It is likely that, had Charles never lived abroad, English literature would still have turned toward an ideal of simplicity and elegance. Jonson's poems and criticism had brought the classicizing tendencies of the English Renaissance to a focus. His closed heroic couplets are the model for those of Edmund Waller and Sir John Denham, whom Dryden considered the principal "refiners" of English metrics. One of the lesser "sons of Ben," Sir John Beaumont, at least as early as 1625—and incidentally in couplets that might have been the very pattern of those of Dryden and Pope—proposed critical standards that became dominant after 1660:

> Pure phrase, fit epithets, a sober care
> Of metaphors, descriptions clear, yet rare,
> Similitudes contracted, smooth and round,
> Not vexed by learning, but with Nature crowned:
> Strong figures drawn from deep inventions, springs,
> Consisting less in words, and more in things:
> A language not affecting ancient times,
> Nor Latin shreds, by which the pedant climbs.
> [*To His Late Majesty, Concerning the True Form*
> *of English Poetry*]

Such standards, alien to the poetry of Donne, Richard Crashaw, or Milton, prefigure the poetry of the Augustans and suggest that a native "classicism" existed side by side with metaphysical poetry. The emphasis on the correct ("pure"), the appropriate ("fit"), restraint and discipline ("sober care"), clarity, the fresh and surprising ("rare"), nature, strength, freedom from pedantry—these indicate exactly the direction English literature was to take after the Restoration.

Above all, the new simplicity of style aimed to give pleasure to the common reader—to write about passions that everyone could recognize in language that everyone could understand. From Dryden to Johnson, English critics value poetry according to its power to affect an audience. Readers, in turn, were supposed to cooperate with authors through the exercise of their own imaginations, creating pictures in the mind. Much poetry of the period comes alive only when it is visualized. A phrase from Horace's *Art of Poetry*, *ut pictura poesis* (as in painting, so in poetry), was interpreted to mean that poetry ought to be a visual as well as a verbal art. Eighteenth-century readers tended to be extremely skilled at translating words into pictures, and a modern reader who wants to appreciate eighteenth-century poems as more than dead words on a page must learn to *see* their images in the mind's eye.

What poets tried to see and represent was *Nature*—a word of many meanings. The Augustans were especially conscious of one meaning: Nature as the universal, permanent, and representative elements in human experience. External nature—the landscape—both as a source of aesthetic pleasure and as an object of scientific inquiry or religious contemplation attracted attention throughout the eighteenth century. But Pope's injunction to the critic, "First follow Nature," has primarily *human* nature and *human* experience in view. Nature is truth in the sense that it includes the enduring, general truths that have been, are, and will be true for everyone in all times, everywhere. Johnson, in chapter 10 of *Rasselas*, says that the poet is to examine "not the individual, but the species; to remark general properties and large appearances . . . to exhibit in his portraits of nature such prominent and striking features as recall the original to every mind." Historians during this period studied the particulars of history to observe the universal human nature that those particulars reveal, and scientists formulated, after experiment and observation of particulars, universal and permanent laws of nature. Indeed, Sir Isaac Newton's *Principia* (1687) did much to reinforce scientifically the idea of Nature as order, which underlies such a typical eighteenth-century work as Pope's *Essay on Man*.

But it would be wrong to assume that this emphasis on the general and the representative excluded the particular from the arts. If human nature was held to be uniform, human beings were known to be infinitely varied, and the task of the artist was so to treat the particular as to render it representative. Thus Pope, after praising the characters of Shakespeare because they are "Nature herself," continued: "But every single character in Shakespeare is as much an individual as those in life itself; it is . . . impossible to find any two alike." And Johnson praised the poet Thomson because he looked on external nature "with a mind that at once comprehends the vast, and attends to the minute."

To study Nature was also to study the ancients—the great artists and thinkers of Greece and imperial Rome. They had expressed the perennial forms of life. Homer and Nature, according to Pope, were the same, and both Pope and his readers found Horace's satires on Roman society thoroughly applicable to their own world, for Horace had followed Nature, "one clear, unchanged, and universal light." Moreover, modern poets could also learn from the ancients how to practice their craft. If a poem is an object to be made, the *poet* (a word derived from a Greek word meaning "maker") must follow sound principles or botch the job. The ancients—for instance, Aristotle in his *Poetics* and Horace in his *Art of Poetry*—had deduced such principles from the practice of early masters like Homer and Sophocles, and during the sixteenth and seventeenth centuries Italian and French critics codified those "rules" and invented new rules of their own. The rules directed poets to plan their works in one of the literary "kinds" or genres—epic, tragedy, comedy, pastoral, satire, or ode—to choose a language appropriate to that genre, and to select the right style and tone and rhetorical figures. Such rules could serve as a shortcut to Nature, for as Pope said, they "are Nature methodized."

In England, however, the rules were followed in rather a casual way. Almost everyone acknowledged that Shakespeare had written the greatest body of drama in modern literature without obeying the formulas of ancients or moderns. He had followed Nature directly, impelled by his wit. Wit, like *nature*, is a complicated word of many meanings. Here it implies quickness and liveliness of mind, inventiveness, a readiness to perceive resemblances between things apparently unlike and so to enliven literary discourse with appropriate images, similes, and metaphors. This faculty was often identified with "fancy" or "imagination" and was thought to be irregular, wayward, or extravagant, unless curbed and disciplined by another and soberer faculty, "judgment." Many poets sought to tame what seemed the wildness of metaphysical wit into a sense of "decorum," or the appropriate. Hence Dryden defined wit as "a propriety of thoughts and words; or, in other terms, thoughts and words elegantly adapted to the subject." Similarly, Pope insists in *An Essay on Criticism* on the necessity of a harmonious union of judgment and fancy (which he calls "wit") in a work of literature. Though judgment was to tame, it was not to suppress passion, energy, and originality but to make them more effective through discipline: "The winged courser, like a generous horse, / Shows most true mettle when you check his course."

The test of mettle in a poet is language. When Wordsworth, in the preface to *Lyrical Ballads* (1800), declared that the poems were written "in a selection of the language really used by men," he went on to attack eighteenth-century poets for their use of an artificial and stock "poetic diction." Many poets did employ a special language. It is characterized by personification, representing a thing or abstraction in a human form, as when an "Ace of Hearts steps forth" or "Melancholy frowns"; by periphrasis (a roundabout and elegant way of avoiding homely words: "finny tribe" for "fish," or "household feathery people" for "chickens"); by frequently used stock phrases, such as "shining sword," "verdant mead," "bounding main," and "checkered shade"; by words used in their original Latin sense, such as "genial," "gelid," and "horrid"; and by a fondness for adjectives ending in *y*. This language originated in the attempt of Renaissance poets all over Europe to rival the elegant and golden diction of Virgil and other Roman writers. Milton depended on it to help him obtain "answerable style" for the lofty theme of *Paradise Lost*. Used with discretion it could be both subtle and expressive, but when it became a mannerism, or a dead and conventional language used mechanically, as it did with scores of mere versifiers, it properly became an object of contempt. "Hay and straw were burned in the fields of Thessaly," for instance, was translated into poetic diction:

> There at his words devouring Vulcan feasts
> On all the tribute which Thessalian meads
> Yield to the scythe, and riots on the heaps
> Of Ceres, emptied of the ripened grain.
> [Glover's *Leonidas*, 1737]

But such extremes of mannerism are seldom to be found in the works of the good poets of the century.

Versification also tests the poet's skill. The prevailing form was the "closed" heroic couplet—i.e., a pentameter couplet that more often than not contains within itself a complete statement and so is closed by a semicolon, period, question mark, or exclamation point. Within these two lines it was possible to attain certain rhetorical or witty effects by the use of parallelism, balance, or antithesis within the couplet as a whole or the individual line. The second line of the couplet might be made closely parallel in structure and meaning to the first or the two could be played off against each other in antithesis; taking advantage of the fact that normally a pentameter line of English verse contains at some point a slight pause called a "caesura," one part of a line so divided can be made parallel with or antithetical to the other or even to one of the two parts of the following line. This can be illustrated by a passage from Sir John Denham's *Cooper Hill* (1642), which was quoted and parodied for many years. The poem addresses the Thames and builds up a witty comparison between the flow of a river and the flow of verse (italics are ours, to illustrate the rhetorical effects):

> O could I flow like thee, ‖ and make thy stream
> Parallelism: *My great example,* ‖ as it is *my theme!*
> Double balance: Though *deep*, yet *clear*, ‖ though *gentle*, yet not *dull*,
> Double balance: *Strong* without *rage*, ‖ without *o'erflowing full*.

It only remained for Dryden and Pope to bind such passages more tightly together with alliteration and assonance, and the typical metrical-rhetorical wit of the new age had been perfected.

Shortly after the beginning of the eighteenth century began the vogue of blank verse—the other metrical form most favored by the age. Philosophical poems, descriptive poems, meditative poems, and original or translated epics employed blank verse of one sort or another from Thomson's *Seasons* (1726–30) to Cowper's *The Task* (1785), and the tradition determined Wordsworth's use of the form in *Tintern Abbey* and *The Prelude*. The two chief patterns of blank verse available to the age were the blank verse of Milton in *Paradise Lost* and the dramatic blank verse of Dryden and other Restoration tragic poets. The influence of Milton is easily detected, not by the success with which his manner was imitated but by the amateur performance of most of those who try to play on his instrument. The dramatic blank verse of the Restoration too often led in eighteenth-century poetry to mannerism or bombast. But gradually a more lyrical blank verse developed, of which Cowper is the master, and this more plastic metrical line had a formative influence on the blank verse of Wordsworth.

RESTORATION LITERATURE, 1660–1700

The period between 1660 and 1700 was remarkably varied and vigorous. Dryden was the dominant figure, writing in all the important contemporary forms—occasional verse, comedy, tragedy, heroic play, ode, satire, translation, and critical essay—and both his example and his precepts had great influence. He gave to the England of his day a *modern* literature, cosmopolitan but possessing the richness and variety that he admired in the Elizabethans, the "God's plenty" that he praised in Chaucer's *Canterbury Tales*.

The prose of the Restoration is a clear indication of the direction in which literature was moving. The styles of Donne's sermons, of Milton's pamphlets, or of Browne's writings had come to seem too elaborate, too involved, too insistently musical, or too wittily rhetorical and pointed for mere exposition or social intercourse. The Royal Society decreed that its members must employ only a plain, concise, and utilitarian prose style suitable to the clear communication of scientific truths. Metaphors, similes, and rhetorical flourishes were disapproved because they engaged the emotions, not the reason, and though they were tolerable in poetry, they had no place in rational discourse. In polite literature, thanks to the example of such writers as Cowley, Dryden, and Sir William Temple, the ideal of good prose came to be a clear, simple, and natural style that has the ease and poise of well-bred urbane conversation. This is a social prose, designed for a social age. Later, it was available to the writers of periodical essays, such as Addison or Steele, to the novelists of the eighteenth century, and to the many practitioners of the delightful art of letter writing, one of the minor literary achievements of the eighteenth century; the brilliant but intimate letters of Lady Mary Wortley Montagu, Horace Walpole, Thomas Gray, and Cowper have never been surpassed. This movement toward clarity and simplicity in prose accompanied a similar movement away from the intricacies of metaphysical wit in verse, which found an early statement in Dryden's *An Essay of Dramatic Poesy*.

But if prose was simplified and wit was tamed, the Restoration did not break wholly with the immediate past. It retained the Renaissance admiration for the typically aristocratic heroic ideal. Most Restoration readers associated the "heroic poem" or epic with "fierce wars and faithful loves" and expected it to offer patterns of ideal virtue for the emulation of princes and generals. But the romantic idealism of the heroic mode was most characteristically expressed during the Restoration not in the heroic poem but in the heroic play, which Dryden, its foremost practitioner, defined as "a heroic poem in little." The theme of these plays (their vogue lasted from about 1664 to about 1675) was the conflict between love and honor in the hearts of impossibly valorous heroes and impossibly high-minded and attractive heroines.

Dryden's one undoubted masterpiece in serious drama is his blank verse tragedy *All for Love* (produced 1677), based on the story of Antony and Cleopatra. Instead of Shakespeare's worldwide panorama, his rapid shifts of scene and complex characters, we have the last hours of the tragic lovers presented according to the unities of action, place, and time, in a neatly symmetrical plot. The two other eminent tragic poets of the period were Nathaniel Lee (ca. 1649–1692), known for violent plots, the wild emotions of his characters, and the extravagance of his rhetoric, and Thomas Otway (1652–1685), who excelled in pathos. Not one enduring tragedy was written during the eighteenth century. Addison's *Cato* (produced in 1713) is a museum piece, illustrating the frigidity of "correct" and rule-bound tragedy. George Lillo's *London Merchant* (produced in 1731), dealing with commonplace characters in mercantile life, took a feeble step in the direction of the sort of realistic, middle-class drama with which we are familiar today.

The real distinction of Restoration drama was comedy. The best plays of Sir George Etherege (ca. 1635–1691), William Wycherley (ca. 1640–1716), Aphra

Behn (ca. 1640–1689), William Congreve (1670–1729), and the less-accomplished but witty Sir John Vanbrugh (pronounced *Vánbroo* or *Vanbróok*, 1664–1726) and George Farquhar (ca. 1677–1707) still hold the stage today. These writers excelled in representing—and critically evaluating—the social behavior of the fashionable upper classes of the town. This sort of comedy—brilliantly witty, cynical in its view of human nature, which it shows to be sensual, egoistic, and predatory—is known as "the comedy of manners," because its concern is to bring the moral and social behavior of its characters to the test of comic laughter. The male hero lives not for military glory but for pleasure and the conquests that he can achieve in his amorous campaigns. The object of his very practical game of sexual intrigue is a beautiful, witty, pleasure-loving, and emancipated lady, every bit his equal in the strategies of love. The two are distinguished not for virtue but for the true wit and well-bred grace with which they conduct the often complicated intrigue that makes up the plot. The best examples of the comedy of manners before Congreve's *The Way of the World* (produced in 1700) are Etherege's *The Man of Mode* (produced in 1676), Wycherley's *The Country Wife* (produced ca. 1672–74), and Congreve's earlier *Love for Love* (produced in 1695).

During the 1690s a considerable demand arose for moral reform in both literature and daily life, partly because of the nature of Restoration comedy. "Societies for the Reformation of Manners" were founded with the support of the soberer Anglicans and the resurgent Nonconformists. Their members served not only as propagandists of moral respectability but also as spies and informers who brought offenders to trial for blasphemy, obscenity, and sexual immorality. The most effective attack on the indecencies of language and situation in comedy was made by the Anglican clergyman Jeremy Collier, whose *Short View of the Immorality and Profaneness of the English Stage* (1698) bore hard on Dryden and Congreve, among others. Collier spoke for the outraged moral sense of the godly middle classes as well as for the church, and his attack helped to discredit "wit" and the wits as subversive of religion and morals. One of the tasks that Steele and Addison undertook in the *Tatler* and *Spectator* and Pope in *An Essay on Criticism*, early in the next century, was to rehabilitate "wit" by making it the servant of social and moral decorum. When Dryden died, a more respectable (if not actually more virtuous) society was coming into being.

Decorum was also enforced by the clubs where literary people tended to gather. From 1652 and increasingly during the first half of the eighteenth century, the coffeehouses of London served as informal meeting places. There men could smoke, drink chocolate or coffee, read the newspapers, write and receive letters, exchange news, gossip, and opinions, and observe the oddities of character that the English have always been happy to cultivate. Eventually clubs not unlike Addison's imaginary Spectator Club came to preside over literary life. The groups who frequented them helped to determine the tone of literature, the critical reputation of writers, the success or failure of plays, and the character of such periodicals as the *Tatler* and the *Spectator*. At first women were excluded. Around 1750, however, some intellectual women known as bluestockings because of their informal dress (not black silk hose but blue worsted) established clubs of their own under the leadership of the wealthy Elizabeth Montague, and gradually men began to join them for literary conversation.

EIGHTEENTH-CENTURY LITERATURE, 1700–45

During the forty-five years between the deaths of Dryden and Swift, the literature that Dryden and his contemporaries had created attained full maturity. A new and brilliant group of writers took the stage: Swift, with *A Tale of a Tub* (1704–10); Addison, with his popular poetic celebration of Marlborough's victory at Blenheim, *The Campaign* (1705); Prior, with *Poems on Several Occasions* (1707); Steele, with the *Tatler* (1709); and the youthful Pope, in the same year, with his

Pastorals. On the whole, the literature of this period is chiefly a literature of wit, concerned with civilization and social relationships, and consequently, it is critical and in some degree moral or satiric. It preserves the earlier period's interest in the heroic, but apart from Pope's translations of Homer, no writer succeeded in heroic poetry. On the other hand some of the finest works of the period are mock heroic (individual passages in Swift's *Battle of the Books* and *A Description of a City Shower* and Pope's *Rape of the Lock* and *The Dunciad*) or humorous burlesques of serious classic or modern modes (John Gay's delightful town mock-Georgic *Trivia, or the Art of Walking the Streets of London* [1716], or his burlesque of the heroics of Italian opera, *The Beggar's Opera*, produced in 1728). Such literature is addressed to highly sophisticated and cultivated readers, and it reminds us that earlier eighteenth-century literature retained the aristocratic bias that had marked the literature of the seventeenth century.

Nevertheless, a body of writing that reached a wider audience was coming into being. The reading public expanded steadily throughout the eighteenth century, and its new recruits were upper-class women and the increasingly numerous rich and leisured people of both sexes in the trading middle class. The popular press flourished, producing a succession of newspapers, literary periodicals in the manner of the *Tatler*, miscellanies of various sorts, and finally, in 1731, the first magazine in the modern sense, the *Gentleman's Magazine*, which was to be followed not only by imitations but also by the appearance of such successful literary reviews as the *Monthly Review* (1749) and the *Critical Review* (1756). The new journalism satisfied a hunger for all sorts of information about politics, science, philosophy, and literature as well as for scandal and gossip. It also created a demand for writers—not necessarily for geniuses—who began to subsist, often on harsh terms, as hacks and compilers in a milieu that came to be called Grub Street, from the name of an actual street. To such authors as Pope and Swift, Grub Street with all its denizens (it was to gain the services of both Johnson and Goldsmith) represented a serious threat to humanistic learning, urbane enlightenment, and good taste. But literature became in this period of expanding publication and increasingly numerous readers a gainful profession. The novel as we know it—a long prose narrative concerned with the actual world and the men and women who inhabit it—very probably could not have come into existence had not these new readers existed. The eighteenth-century novel supplied the place in the life of the common reader that the heroic poem had occupied in the life of the courtly reader of the past.

During this period new literary kinds took the place of the old. The lyric, one of the glories of the Elizabethan age and the first half of the seventeenth century, had become in the Restoration a minor and graceful mode, appropriate to a song or a "paper of verses" addressed to a mistress. The wits of Charles II's court could turn out accomplished, conventional poems of this sort that do not lack distinction; and Prior was their counterpart in the time of William of Orange and Queen Anne. But between 1700 and 1740 lyric poetry declined and comedy too lost its edge. The moral reform of the 1690s, together with the increasingly optimistic and flattering view of human nature, made the rakes of Restoration comedy seem distasteful libels on humanity. The old comedy of manners was replaced by a new kind, called "sentimental" not only because of its faith in the triumph of a good heart over vice but also because its dialogue deals in high moral sentiments rather than wit and because its virtuous heroines and virtuous (or penitent) heroes suffer misfortunes that move the audience not to laughter but to tears. One of the pleasures invented in eighteenth-century Europe was the delicious pleasure of weeping, and sentimental comedy (or, as the French phrased it, *la comédie larmoyante*, "weeping comedy") brought that pleasure to playgoers through many decades. As tragedy froze into rhetoric, comedy dissolved in tears. And the successes enjoyed by *The Beggar's Opera* and the laughing comedies of Goldsmith and Sheridan later in the century could not eradicate the taste for sentimentality. Although during the eighteenth century the *theater* prospered and the stage was adorned by a succession of great actors and actresses (such as David Garrick and Sarah Siddons) the authors of *drama* lapsed into obscurity.

On the other hand, satire flourished, its most distinguished practitioners being Pope and Swift, though they are only two among many effective writers. Satirists are usually conservative, using their weapons against those deviations from norms of conduct that threaten to undermine traditional and socially approved behavior. Both Pope and Swift wrote their major satires as Tories, at a time when Britain was dominated by the Whig party. The Tories resisted, but resisted futilely, the social and economic changes that were taking place as England grew from an island kingdom into a world power and transformed its agrarian into a mercantile economy. They looked with gloomy forebodings on the rising tide of popular taste, on what they considered the invasion and debasement of the polite world by the barbarians from the middle classes and the idle rich and on the increase of corruption in public life. The satire of both Swift and Pope is animated by moral urgency and heightened by a tragic sense of doom. Pope saw the issue as a struggle between Darkness and Light, Chaos and Order, Barbarism and Civilization: a vision that he expressed in his greatest work, *The Dunciad*. For Swift the conflict was between "right reason" and "madness"—not clinical insanity, of course, but a blindness to anything but one's own private illusions, which is an abandonment of practical reality.

But the great age of satire also produced a wholly different sort of poetry from that which Pope was writing in the 1730s. After 1726, when Thomson published the first of his nature poems, *Winter*, the poetry of natural description flourished and the characteristic eighteenth-century English taste for natural and picturesque beauty found expression—not only in poetry but also in that typical Georgian art, landscape gardening, and finally in the beginning of the art of landscape in water color or oils, which has been England's principal achievement in painting. A love of external nature inspired many eighteenth-century poets, and Wordsworth was their heir. *Tintern Abbey* not only was written *within* the century but, in most respects, is very much a poem *of* the century.

In the course of the century, Britons not only admired tamed and ordered nature, in large landscape gardens or cultivated fields, but also early learned to enjoy the more thrilling, emotional pleasure that they began to feel in the presence of what they called "the sublime" in nature: vast spaces, mountainous country, and wild and untamed landscape. Whether enthusiasts of nature went to landscape for evidence of the presence of the deity or merely to enjoy natural beauty, they inevitably learned to feel emotions in the presence of external nature and to examine the quality of their feelings. Before the deaths of Pope and Swift, in the poetry of Thomson and others, a literature of feeling had come into existence alongside the dominant literature of wit. The development of such a literature of sentiment is perhaps the crucial fact in the literary history of the century after the era of Pope and Swift.

THE EMERGENCE OF NEW LITERARY THEMES AND MODES, 1740–85

When Arnold, speaking for Victorian taste, called the eighteenth century an "age of prose," he meant to cast doubt on its poetry, but the later part of the century might indeed be honored as an age of prose. Never before or since have so many great writers of prose flourished at once, or so many kinds of intellectual prose been perfected: literary criticism, with Johnson; biography, Boswell; philosophy, Hume; politics, Burke; history, Edward Gibbon; aesthetics, Sir Joshua Reynolds; economics, Adam Smith; and natural history, Gilbert White. Each of these authors is a master stylist, whose effort to express himself clearly and fully creates an art as difficult to achieve, and as precise, as poetry. Indeed, the prose style of the period often seems to build on the principles of neoclassical verse: its elaborately balanced use of parallels and antitheses; its elegant allusions to a classical literature; its public, rhetorical manner; and its craving for generality. At its best, however, such prose depends less on formal virtues than on its weight of thought. Unlike the earlier masters of simplicity in prose—Addison, Swift, and Defoe—the authors of the age of Johnson have little confidence in plain speaking. Readers will not be convinced of the truth, they suspect, merely by having the facts laid before them; they must be offered scientific demonstration or passionate eloquence. Some comments by Johnson on the prose of Swift make the point by example as well as precept:

> His style was well suited to his thoughts, which are never subtilized by nice disquisitions, decorated by sparkling conceit, elevated by ambitious sentences, or variegated by far-sought learning. He pays no court to the passions, he excites neither surprise nor admiration; he always understands himself, and his readers always understand him. . . . This easy and safe conveyance of meaning it was Swift's desire to attain, and for having attained he deserves praise, though perhaps not the highest praise. For purposes merely didactic, when something is to be told that was not known before, it is the best mode; but against that inattention by which known truths are suffered to lie neglected, it makes no provision; it instructs, but does not persuade.

Johnson's prose bristles with long words, qualifications of thought, and "ambitious sentences" that are the very opposite of the style he describes; he attempts not merely to be understood, not merely to instruct, but to persuade. And similar ambitions motivate many of the authors of his time. An unprecedented effort to formulate the first principles of philosophy, history, psychology, and art required a whole new language of persuasion, more subtle, logical, and accurate than English had ever been before.

An age of great prose, however, can put a burden on its poets. Many of the generation of talented young poets who emerged about the time of Pope's death, a group that includes William Collins, Thomas Gray, Mark Akenside, and the brothers Joseph and Thomas Warton, are haunted by the fear that the spirit of poetry may have passed away—driven out by the spirit of prose, by an ideal of mere "correctness," by the end of superstitions that had once peopled the landscape with fairies and demons, the stuff of poetry. In an age barren of magic, they ask, where is poetry to be found? That question becomes obsessive in many poems of the period, suffusing them with melancholy. Indeed, more and more poetry itself was associated with melancholy, a sweet sadness, a yearning for another time and place. The prototype of the mid-eighteenth-century melancholy poet was Milton's Il Penseroso, a night-loving solitary, who sucks pensive sadness from the "far-off curfew" or the swelling organ in the twilight of a Gothic church. Such a figure is most unlike the Augustan poet, a social being, living in a crowded world and little given to the impropriety of the public confession of private feelings. The idea of the poet was changing from that of a maker to that of an introspective, brooding confessor; the materials of poetry were becoming rather the inner life and private vision of the poet than public, social affairs.

Poets who brood in silence are never far from thoughts of death, and an often morbid fascination with death, suicide, and the grave preoccupies the poets of midcentury. The clergyman Edward Young (1683–1765) wrote an immensely long and popular poem in blank verse, The Complaint: or Night Thoughts on Life, Death, and Immortality (1742–46), to supplement the Christian optimism of Pope's An Essay on Man with a darker view of Christianity based on fear of the life to come. But the "graveyard school" is less concerned with religion than with horror and decay. Within an elaborate stage setting of medieval ruins and fleshless bodies, the soul of the graveyard poet self-consciously acts out its secret fears. The revival of Gothic architectural styles, most famously Horace Walpole's tiny and precious pseudo-Gothic castle, Strawberry Hill, helped influence literary styles as well. The Gothic vogue, like a similar vogue for Chinese decor, seemed to suggest that old-fashioned canons of taste—proportion, balance, simplicity, and harmony—might count for less in art than the pleasures of fancy and extravagance— intricacy, asymmetry, and a willful excess. Poets began to cultivate archaic language and antique literary forms, especially, after Thomas Percy's edition of *Reliques of Ancient English Poetry* (1765), the ballad. Thus Thomas Chatterton (1752–1770), whom the Romantics later idolized for his precocious genius and tragic early death, composed sham medieval ballads he pretended to have found in an old manuscript. The most remarkable literary consequence of such medi- evalizing, however, was the invention of the Gothic romance. Walpole's *Castle of Otranto* (1765), a dreamlike tale of terror inspired by the physical appearance of Strawberry Hill, created a mode of fiction that retains its popularity to the present day. In the typical Gothic romance, set amid the glooms and intricacies of a medi- eval castle, the laws of nightmare replace the laws of probability. Forbidden themes—incest, murder, necrophilia, atheism, and the torments of sexual desire— are allowed free play; repressed feelings, morbid fears rise to the surface of the narrative. Although most such romances, like William Beckford's *Vathek* (1786) and Matthew Lewis's *The Monk* (1796), depend on sensationalism and the gro- tesque, Gothicism also resulted in works, like Ann Radcliffe's, that temper romance with reality, as well as in serious novels of social purpose, like William Godwin's *Caleb Williams* (1794); and Mary Shelley, Godwin's daughter, eventu- ally composed a romantic nightmare, *Frankenstein* (1816), that continues to haunt our dreams.

Ultimately, it was not to a medieval revival that poets looked for a renewal of poetry but to their own imaginations and feelings. In his *Ode to Fancy* (1746), Joseph Warton associated "fancy" with the natural, the wild and spontaneous, with solitude, and with enthusiasm and the passions. Such a concept of the fancy or imagination emphasizes not rules and crafts of the maker but original genius, the poet as the seer or nature's priest. True poets, Warton suggests, should not be conversationalists or orators but singers. "The public has seen all that art can do," William Shenstone wrote in 1761, welcoming James Macpherson's bardic *Ossian*, "and they want the more striking efforts of wild, original, enthusiastic genius." But genius is easier to call for than to recognize; when it does come, people are apt to call it madness. Many of the best poets of the period—Collins, Christopher Smart, and later, Cowper—suffered from mental illness, and others, like Chatterton, were scorned by society. Nor did many readers so much as notice the extraordinary work of Smart or, later, of William Blake. The apocalyptic strain of poetry, bursting the bonds of logical transition, of grammar, and even of the natural world, proved difficult to approach. Meanwhile a different sort of poetry flourished: humorous, personal, and down to earth. As the reading public expanded, so did the number of people who wrote verse, and they wrote about whatever interested them, however mundane. Women as well as men described the details of their lives in homely images and graphic language. For much of the public, poetry offered the pleasures of self-expression and companionship. Cowper, the most popular poet of the latter part of the century, won his readers with a modest, intimate kind of verse, never departing far from the accents of friendly conversation. The end of the century also witnessed a revival of the lyric. Amid revolutions in society and thought, poets were asked to teach their readers how to feel. The next generation would try to answer that call.

THE BEGINNING OF THE NOVEL

To say that the modern novel came into existence in the eighteenth century is not to say that there was no prose fiction before 1700. There were the ancient Greek romances and their modern European imitators; the courtly *Arcadia* of Sir Philip Sidney and the humbler fiction of Thomas Deloney and Thomas Nashe and other Elizabethans; the interminable French romances of the seventeenth century and their English translations and imitations, loosely constructed, blending aristocratic refinement, chivalric adventure, and courtly love; the tales of the careers of famous criminals and rogues; scandalous stories loosely based on current events; and, in a world apart, Bunyan's vivid allegories of the spiritual adventures of wayfaring and militant Christians and their adversaries. Nor were clear distinctions drawn between history and fiction; Behn's *Oroonoko* is both. But it remains true that, if we except Defoe, the creator of the modern novel was Samuel Richardson (1689–1761). Both Defoe and Richardson belonged to the middle class and expressed in their works middle-class interests and attitudes. They also wrote about and for women. To a large extent, the development of the novel is identical with the attempt to interest the growing number of female readers by shaping their lives into literature. Defoe simply ignored the sentimental and aristocratic refinements of the earlier romances and was content to show his readers not a world as it might be, a heroic world, but their world as it was, populated with believable people who were motivated by the practical concerns that dominate our daily lives. He did not seek—and except through *Robinson Crusoe* (1719) did not often find—readers among the upper classes. He was content to interest shopkeepers, apprentices, and servants, who were already avid readers of tales of crime and adventure, usually heavily laced with pious moral observations.

Richardson, however, caught the attention of all literate Europe, and once and for all established the novel as we know it, a solid and enduring object in the literary landscape. His three novels were strikingly new in their minute and subtle analysis of emotions and states of mind. It was while he was compiling a little book of model letters that he conceived the idea of *Pamela, or Virtue Rewarded* (1740), a story told in a series of letters, in which a virtuous servant girl who resists her master's base designs on her virtue eventually wins him as her husband. Richardson's masterpiece, *Clarissa* (1747–48), carries the same epistolary method, moral instruction, and sexual titillation to new heights. In the conflict between the libertine Lovelace, an attractive and diabolical aristocrat, and the angelic Clarissa, the perfection of middle-class values, Richardson created a fiction that embodied the ideals and the tensions of his society. No earlier author had involved readers so fully in the thoughts and emotions of the characters, nor had any author paid such close attention to the pressures on women. Such later novelists as Fanny Burney (1752–1840) and Jane Austen (1775–1817) would profit from his example. Richardson's final novel, *Sir Charles Grandison* (1753–54), turns to a model of male perfection with less success.

Henry Fielding (1707–1754), who loved virtue as much as Richardson did, but to whom goodness was a matter of spontaneity and fellow feeling, not of conformity to a code, considered *Pamela* a misleading image of virtue; therefore, in 1742, he published *Joseph Andrews*, which begins as an hilarious burlesque of *Pamela* by describing the staunch resistance offered to the lewd advances of Lady Booby by her servant, the virtuous Joseph, brother of Pamela. Expelled for his chastity from Lady Booby's household, he takes to the road, joining the guileless Parson Adams, who is walking to London to try to sell a bundle of his sermons to a publisher. Their adventures make up what Fielding called "a comic epic in prose." His great novel is *The History of Tom Jones, A Foundling* (1749). The protagonist became the pattern of the good-natured hero of the age: a young man of manly virtues, generous, high spirited, loyal, and courageous, but impulsive, wanting prudence, and full of animal spirits and sensuality. The novel is crowded with incident and with varied types of men and women, and critics have agreed with Coleridge's praise of its brilliantly constructed plot. Fielding's other important novel, *Amelia* (1751), having as its heroine a long-suffering woman, almost wholly passive, is an example of pathos rather than of Fielding's comic vigor and gusto.

The picaresque tradition was continued by Tobias Smollett (1721–1771) in *Roderick Random* (1748), *Peregrine Pickle* (1751), and *Ferdinand, Count Fathom* (1753). Smollett delighted to depict the grotesque side of eighteenth-century life, its brutality, coarse practical jokes, and strong odors. His masterpiece is *Humphry Clinker* (1771), which recounts, through letters written by several members of a traveling party, the comic incidents of a journey through England and Scotland. But the most original novelist of the period was Laurence Sterne (1713–1768), an unclerical clergyman, a humorist, a sentimentalist, and an author who reminds us that one of the roots of the novel is the word *novelty*. *The Life and Opinions of Tristram Shandy*, produced between 1760 and 1767, deliberately frustrated all the stock expectations of its readers. The plot has not the logical order of a beginning, a middle, and an end; instead it abandons clock time for psychological time, interrupts scenes to digress or to recount past or future events, follows whimsically any apparently chance association, digresses for several chapters — in fact, it is designed as an elaborate joke at the reader's expense. And yet the method gets us inside the consciousness of the narrator and the other characters and into a world peopled by the most engaging of comic characters.

Fielding, Smollett, and Sterne gave to English literature not only vivid scenes from the life of their times but a gallery of eccentric and original characters that illustrate the interest of the age not only in the ideal and the general but also in the individual and the unique. The novels of Charles Dickens and of William Makepeace Thackeray in the nineteenth century owe much to their forerunners in the eighteenth.

THE CONTINUITY OF THE AUGUSTAN TRADITION

Despite the emergence of new literary forms, materials, and methods after the death of Pope and Swift, the Augustan line continued vigorously throughout the last half of the eighteenth and even into the nineteenth century. If the years between 1745 and 1784 were years of change and experiment, they were also the period of Johnson's greatest achievement and influence. A conservative in literature as in politics and religion, Johnson defended in conversation and in his critical writings the principles that he had inherited from the older generation. His two major poems, *London* (1738) and *The Vanity of Human Wishes* (1749), are satirical and ethical and show little influence of the new sensibility of the midcentury. He was loyal to the heroic couplet and to the use of generalized diction. His *Dictionary* (1755) was designed not to fix our language permanently but certainly to retard the process of change and to censure words that he considered superfluous. His critical writings sufficiently reveal his devotion to the standards of Dryden and Pope. But his conservatism was saved from pedantry by the empirical bent of his mind and his broad and humanistic learning.

If Johnson speaks for his age, the reason is partly that he shares a faith, with many of his contemporaries, in common sense and the common reader. "By the common sense of readers uncorrupted with literary prejudices," he wrote in the last of his great *Lives of the Poets* (1780), "must be finally decided all claim to poetical honors." A similar respect for common sense and for standards of taste and behavior based on responses that all of us share marks many of the grandest achievements of the century; for instance, the political writings of Burke, the great Whig statesman and orator, or the *Discourses on Art* (1769–90) of Reynolds, who drew the best aesthetic theory of his day into an elegant whole. Moreover, the poets whom everyone read relied less on apocalyptic visions than on a verse that could do justice to the ordinary feelings of ordinary people. Gray's *Elegy*, Gold-smith's *The Deserted Village*, Crabbe's *The Village*, and the lyrics of Burns are only a few of the poems that strive to make poetry from and for the lives of the common man and woman. Nor did Goldsmith, Crabbe, and Burns, for all their attachment to the growing wave of sentimentalism, desert the verse forms—the careful craftsmanship, the rhyming couplets—developed by the earlier Augustan masters. Even Cowper's *The Task* (1785), which brings us to the threshold of the Romantic movement, belongs most definitely in the eighteenth century. Indeed, the Augustan age did not die on that day in 1798 when a small and unsuccessful volume of poems, *Lyrical Ballads*, was published by Wordsworth and Samuel Taylor Coleridge. We hear the accents of that age from time to time in the poems of both Wordsworth and Coleridge, in many of the poems of Lord Byron, and in Byron's ardent defense of Pope and Dryden, when the new age finally brought those masters to judgment. And we hear its old verities expressed in its own vocabulary in the criticism of that archenemy of the Romantic movement, Francis Jeffrey, editor of the *Edinburgh Review*, as when, for example, in a review (1808) of a volume of poems by Crabbe, he paused to rebuke the (as he believed) affectedly eccentric poet Wordsworth for having written *The Thorn* and one of the Lucy poems:

> Now we leave it to any reader of common candor and discernment to say whether these representations of character and sentiment are drawn from the eternal and universal standard of truth and nature, which every one is knowing enough to recognize, and no one great enough to depart from with impunity; or whether they are not formed . . . upon certain fantastic and affected peculiarities in the mind or fancy of the author, into which it is most improbable that many of his readers will enter, and which cannot, in some cases, be comprehended without much effort and explanation.

THE RESTORATION AND THE EIGHTEENTH CENTURY

TEXTS	CONTEXTS
	1660 Charles II restored to the throne • Reopening of the theaters
	1662 Restoration of the Church of England • Chartering of the Royal Society
1664–1700 Restoration comedy, plays of George Etheredge, William Wycherley, and William Congreve	1666 The Great Fire destroys the City of London
	1678 The "Popish Plot" inflames anti-Catholic feeling
	1679–81 The earl of Shaftesbury schemes to have the duke of Monmouth, the king's bastard son and a Protestant, placed first in line of succession
1681 John Dryden, **Absalom and Achitophel**	1681 The king dissolves Parliament
	1685 Death of Charles II, succeeded by his Catholic brother as James II
	1687 Sir Isaac Newton's *Principia Mathematica* formulates the laws of gravitation
	1688–89 The Glorious Revolution; James II exiled and succeeded by the Dutch William of Orange and his wife, Mary, Protestant daughter of James II
	1702 Death of William III; succession of Anne (Protestant daughter of James II), last Stuart sovereign
	1710 Fall of Whig ministry brings Tories to power • Jonathan Swift serves new government as political journalist

Boldface titles indicate works in the anthology.

TEXTS	CONTEXTS
1711 Alexander Pope, *An Essay on Criticism*	
	1714 Death of Queen Anne; succession of the German George I of the House of Hanover, great-grandson of James I; return to power of the Whig party
1717 Pope, final version of *The Rape of the Lock*	
1726 Swift, *Gulliver's Travels*	
	1727–60 Reign of George II
1729 Swift, *A Modest Proposal*	
1733 Pope, *An Essay on Man*	
1743 Pope, final version of *The Dunciad*	
1751 Thomas Gray, *Elegy in a Country Churchyard*	
1755 Johnson's *Dictionary*	
	1757 Robert Clive begins conquest of India
1759 Johnson, *Rasselas*	1759 James Wolfe's capture of Quebec from French assures British control of Canada
	1760–1820 Reign of George III
1765 Johnson's edition of Shakespeare (*Preface*)	
	1775–81 American Revolution
1779–81 Johnson, *Lives of the Poets*	
1791 James Boswell, *Life of Samuel Johnson*	

JOHN DRYDEN
1631–1700

1668:	Made poet laureate.
1681:	*Absalom and Achitophel.*
ca. 1686:	Conversion to Catholicism.
1689:	Loss of court offices upon accession of William and Mary.
1697:	Translation of Virgil.

Although John Dryden's parents seem to have sided with Parliament against the king, there is no evidence that the poet grew up in a strict Puritan family. His father, a country gentleman of moderate fortune, gave his son a gentleman's education at Westminster School, under the renowned Dr. Richard Busby, who used the rod as a pedagogical aid in imparting a sound knowledge of the learned languages and literatures to his charges (among others John Locke and Matthew Prior). From Westminster, Dryden went to Trinity College, Cambridge, where he took his A.B. in 1654. His first important and impressive poem, *Heroic Stanzas* (1659), was written to commemorate the death of Cromwell. The next year, however, in *Astraea Redux*, Dryden joined his countrymen in celebrating the return of Charles II to his throne. During the rest of his life Dryden was to remain entirely loyal to Charles and to his successor, James II.

Dryden is the commanding literary figure of the last four decades of the seventeenth century. He is that rare phenomenon, the author in whose work the image of an age can be discerned. Every important aspect of the life of his times—political, religious, philosophical, artistic—finds expression somewhere in his writings. Dryden is the least personal of our poets. He is not at all the solitary, subjective poet listening to the murmur of his own voice and preoccupied with his own personal view of experience, but rather a citizen of the world commenting publicly on matters of public concern.

From the beginning to the end of his literary career, Dryden's original non-dramatic poems are most typically occasional poems, which celebrate particular events of a public character—a coronation, a military victory, a death, or a political crisis. Such poems are social and ceremonial, written not for the self but for the nation. Dryden's principal achievements in this form are the two poems on the king's return and his coronation; *Annus Mirabilis* (1667), which celebrates the English naval victory over the Dutch and the fortitude of the people of London and the king during the Great Fire, both events of that "wonderful year," 1666; the political poems; the lines on the death of Oldham (1684); the odes; and *The Secular Masque.*

Between 1664 and 1681, however, Dryden was mainly a playwright. The newly chartered theaters needed a modern repertory, and he set out to supply the need. Dryden wrote his plays, as he frankly confessed, to please his audiences, which were not heterogeneous like Shakespeare's but were largely drawn from the court and from people of fashion. In the style of the time, he produced rhymed heroic plays, in which incredibly noble heroes and heroines face incredibly difficult choices between love and honor; comedies, in which male and female rakes engage in intrigue and bright repartee; and later, libretti for the newly introduced dramatic form, the opera. His one great tragedy, *All for Love* (1677), in blank verse, adapts Shakespeare's *Antony and Cleopatra* to the unities of time, place, and action. As his *An Essay of Dramatic Poesy* (1668) shows, Dryden had studied the works of the great playwrights of Greece and Rome, of the English Renaissance, and of contemporary France, seeking sound theoretical principles on which to construct the new drama that the age demanded. Indeed his fine critical intelligence always supported his creative powers, and because he took literature seriously and enjoyed discussing it, he became, it appears almost casually, what Samuel Johnson called him: "the father of English criticism." His abilities as both poet and dramatist brought him to the attention of the king, who in 1668 made him poet laureate. Two years later the post of historiographer royal was added to the laureateship at a combined stipend of £200, enough money to live on.

Between 1678 and 1681, when he was nearing fifty, Dryden discovered his great gift for writing formal verse satire. A quarrel with Thomas Shadwell, a playwright of some talent, prompted the mock-heroic episode *Mac Flecknoe*, which was probably written in 1678 or 1679 but which was not published until 1682. Out of the stresses occasioned by the Popish Plot (1678) and its political aftermath came his major political satires, *Absalom and Achitophel* (1681), and *The Medal* (1682), his final attack on the villain of *Absalom and Achitophel*, the earl of Shaftesbury. Twenty years' experience as poet and playwright had prepared him technically for the triumph of *Absalom and Achitophel*. He had mastered the heroic couplet, having fashioned it into an instrument suitable in his hands for every sort of discourse from the thrust and parry of quick logical argument, to lyric feeling, rapid narrative, or forensic declamation. Thanks to this long discipline, he was able in one stride to assume his proper place beside the masters of verse satire: Horace, Juvenal, Persius, in ancient Rome, and Boileau, his French contemporary.

The consideration of religious and political questions that the events of 1678–1681 forced on Dryden brought a new seriousness to his mind and works. In 1682 he published *Religio Laici*, a poem in which he examined the grounds of his religious faith and defended the middle way of the Anglican church against the rationalism of Deism on the one hand and the authoritarianism of Rome on the other. But he had moved closer to Rome than he perhaps realized when he wrote the poem. Charles II died in 1685 and was succeeded by his Catholic brother, James II. Within less than a year Dryden and his two sons were converted to Catholicism. Though his enemies accused him of opportunism, he proved his sincerity by his steadfast loyalty to the Roman church after James abdicated and the Protestant William and Mary came in; as a result he was to lose his offices and their much-needed stipends. From his new position as a Roman Catholic, Dryden wrote in 1687 *The Hind and the Panther*, in which a milk-white Hind (the Roman church) and a spotted Panther (the Anglican church) eloquently debate theology. The Hind has the better of the argument, but Dryden already knew that James's policies were failing, and with them the Catholic cause in England.

Dryden was now nearing sixty, with a family to support on a much-diminished income. To earn a living, he resumed writing plays and turned to translations. In 1693 appeared his versions of Juvenal and Persius, with the long dedicatory epistle on satire; and in 1697, his greatest achievement in this mode, the works of Virgil. At the very end, two months before his death, came the *Fables Ancient and Modern*, prefaced by one of the finest of his critical essays and made up of translations from Ovid, Boccaccio, and Chaucer.

What was the nature of Dryden's achievement? His drama, by and large, belongs entirely to his age, though its influence persisted into the next century. His critical writings established canons of taste and theoretical principles that determined the character of neoclassic literature in the next century. He helped establish a new sort of prose—easy, lucid, plain, and shaped to the cadences of natural speech. This is the prose that we like to think of as "modern." Johnson praised it for its informality and apparent artlessness: "every word seems to drop by chance, though it falls into its proper place. Nothing is cold or languid; the whole is airy, animated, and vigorous ... though all is easy, nothing is feeble; though all seems careless, there is nothing harsh." His satire, still vital today, exerted a fruitful influence on the most brilliant verse satirist of the next century, Alexander Pope. The vigor and variety of his metrics made inevitable the long-enduring vogue of the heroic couplet among his successors. At the same time, he created a poetic language that remained the basic language of poetry until the early nineteenth century and that even the romantic movement did not wholly destroy. His poems represent the superbly civilized language of the Augustan style at its best: dignified, unaffected, precise, and always musical—a noble instrument of public speech. Johnson's final estimate remains valid: "By him we were taught *sapere et fari*, to think naturally and express forcibly. . . . What was said of Rome, adorned by Augustus, may be applied by an easy metaphor to English poetry embellished by Dryden, *lateritiam invenit, marmoream reliquit*, he found it brick, and he left it marble."

Song from *Marriage à la Mode*

1

Why should a foolish marriage vow,
    Which long ago was made,
Oblige us to each other now,
    When passion is decayed?
We loved, and we loved, as long as we could,   5
    Till our love was loved out in us both;
But our marriage is dead when the pleasure is fled:
    'Twas pleasure first made it an oath.

2

If I have pleasures for a friend,
    And farther love in store,   10
What wrong has he whose joys did end,
    And who could give no more?
'Tis a madness that he should be jealous of me,
    Or that I should bar him of another:
For all we can gain is to give ourselves pain,   15
    When neither can hinder the other.

ca. 1672   1673

Absalom and Achitophel   In 1678 a dangerous crisis, both religious and political, threatened to undo the Restoration settlement and to precipitate England once again into civil war. The Popish Plot and its aftermath not only whipped up extreme anti-Catholic passions, but led between 1679 and 1681 to a bitter political struggle between Charles II (whose adherents came to be called Tories) and the earl of Shaftesbury (whose followers were termed Whigs). The issues were nothing less than the prerogatives of the crown and the possible exclusion of the king's Catholic brother, James, duke of York, from his rightful position as heir-presumptive to the throne. Charles's cool courage and brilliant, if unscrupulous, political genius saved the throne for his brother and gave at least temporary peace to his people.

    Charles was a Catholic at heart—he received the last rites of that church on his deathbed—and was eager to do what he could do discreetly for the relief of his Catholic subjects, who suffered severe civil and religious disabilities imposed by their numerically superior Protestant compatriots. James openly professed the Catholic religion, an awkward fact politically, for he was next in line of succession because Charles had no legitimate children. The household of the duke, as well as that of Charles's neglected queen, Catherine of Braganza, inevitably became the center of Catholic life and intrigue at court and consequently of Protestant prejudice and suspicion.

No one understood, however, that the situation was explosive until 1678, when Titus Oates (a renegade Catholic convert and a man of the most infamous character) offered sworn testimony of the existence of a Jesuit plot to assassinate the king, burn London, massacre Protestants, and reestablish the Roman church.

The country might have kept its head and come to realize (what no historian has doubted) that Oates and his confederates were perjured rascals, as Charles himself quickly perceived. But panic was created by the discovery of the murdered body of a prominent London justice of the peace, Sir Edmund Berry Godfrey, who a few days before had received for safekeeping a copy of Oates's testimony. The crime, immediately ascribed to the Catholics, has never been solved. Fear and indignation reached a hysterical pitch when the seizure of the papers of the duke of York's secretary revealed that he had been in correspondence with the confessor of Louis XIV regarding the reestablishment of the Roman church in England. Before the terror subsided many innocent men were executed on the increasingly bold and always false evidence of Oates and his accomplices.

The earl of Shaftesbury, the duke of Buckingham, and others quickly took advantage of the situation. With the support of the Commons and the City of London, they moved to exclude the duke of York from the succession. Between 1679 and 1681 Charles and Shaftesbury were engaged in a mighty struggle. The Whigs found a candidate of their own in the king's favorite illegitimate son, the handsome and engaging duke of Monmouth, whom they advanced as a proper successor to his father. They urged Charles to legitimize him, and when he refused, they whispered that there was proof that the king had secretly married Monmouth's mother. The young man allowed himself to be used against his father. He was sent on a triumphant progress through western England, where he was enthusiastically received. Twice an Exclusion Bill nearly passed both houses. But by early 1681 Charles had secured his own position by secretly accepting from Louis XIV a three-year subsidy that made him independent of Parliament, which had tried to force his hand by refusing to vote him funds. He summoned Parliament to meet at Oxford in the spring of 1681, and a few moments after the Commons had passed the Exclusion Bill, in a bold stroke he abruptly dissolved Parliament, which never met again during his reign. Already, as Charles was aware, a reaction had set in against the violence of the Whigs. In midsummer, when he felt it safe to move against his enemies, Shaftesbury was sent to the Tower of London, charged with high treason. In November, the grand jury, packed with Whigs, threw out the indictment, and the earl was free, but his power was broken, and he lived only two more years.

Shortly before the grand jury acted, Dryden published anonymously the first part of *Absalom and Achitophel*, apparently hoping to influence their verdict. It is worthy of the occasion that produced it. The issues in question were grave; the chief actors, the most important men in the realm. Dryden, therefore, could not use burlesque and caricature as had Butler, or the mock heroic as he himself had done in *Mac Flecknoe*. Only a heroic style and manner were appropriate to his weighty material, and the poem is most original in its blending of the heroic and the satiric. Dryden's task called for all his tact and literary skill; he had to mention, but to gloss over, the king's faults: his indolence and love of pleasure; his neglect of his wife, and his devotion to his mistresses—conduct that had left him with many children, but no heir except his Catholic brother. He had to deal gently with Monmouth, whom Charles still loved. And he had to present, or appear to present, the king's case objectively.

The remarkable parallels between the rebellion of Absalom against his father King David (2 Samuel 13–18) had already been remarked in sermons, satires, and pamphlets. Dryden took the hint and gave contemporary events a due distance and additional dignity by approaching them indirectly through their biblical analogues. The poem is famous for its brilliant portraits of the king's enemies and friends, but equally admirable are the temptation scene (which, like other passages, is indebted to *Paradise Lost*) and the remarkably astute analysis of the Popish Plot itself.

A second part of *Absalom and Achitophel* appeared in 1682. Most of it is the work of Nahum Tate, but lines 310–509, which include the devastating portraits of Doeg and Og (two Whig poets, Elkanah Settle and Thomas Shadwell), are certainly by Dryden.

Absalom and Achitophel: A Poem

In pious times, ere priestcraft did begin,
Before polygamy was made a sin;
When man on many multiplied his kind,
Ere one to one was cursedly confined;
When nature prompted and no law denied   5
Promiscuous use of concubine and bride;
Then Israel's monarch after Heaven's own heart,[1]
His vigorous warmth did variously impart
To wives and slaves; and, wide as his command,
Scattered his Maker's image through the land.   10
Michal,[2] of royal blood, the crown did wear,
A soil ungrateful to the tiller's care:
Not so the rest; for several mothers bore
To godlike David several sons before.
But since like slaves his bed they did ascend,   15
No true succession could their seed attend.
Of all this numerous progeny was none
So beautiful, so brave, as Absalom:[3]
Whether, inspired by some diviner lust,
His father got him with a greater gust,[4]   20
Or that his conscious destiny made way,
By manly beauty, to imperial sway.
Early in foreign fields he won renown,
With kings and states allied to Israel's crown:[5]
In peace the thoughts of war he could remove,   25
And seemed as he were only born for love.
Whate'er he did, was done with so much ease,
In him alone 'twas natural to please;
His motions all accompanied with grace;
And paradise was opened in his face.   30
With secret joy indulgent David viewed
His youthful image in his son renewed:
To all his wishes nothing he denied;

1. David ("a man after [God's] own heart," according to 1 Samuel 13.14) represents Charles II.
2. One of David's wives, who represents the childless queen, Catherine of Braganza.
3. James Scott, duke of Monmouth (1649–1685).
4. Relish, pleasure.
5. Monmouth had won repute as a soldier fighting for France against Holland and for Holland against France.

And made the charming Annabel[6] his bride.
What faults he had (for who from faults is free?) 35
His father could not, or he would not see.
Some warm excesses which the law forbore,
Were cònstrued youth that purged by boiling o'er:
And Amnon's murther,[7] by a specious name,
Was called a just revenge for injured fame. 40
Thus praised and loved the noble youth remained,
While David, undisturbed, in Sion[8] reigned.
But life can never be sincerely[9] blest;
Heaven punishes the bad, and proves[1] the best.
The Jews,[2] a headstrong, moody, murmuring race, 45
As ever tried the extent and stretch of grace;
God's pampered people, whom, debauched with ease,
No king could govern, nor no God could please
(Gods they had tried of every shape and size
That god-smiths could produce, or priests devise);[3] 50
These Adam-wits, too fortunately free,
Began to dream they wanted liberty;[4]
And when no rule, no precedent was found,
Of men by laws less circumscribed and bound,
They led their wild desires to woods and caves, 55
And thought that all but savages were slaves.
They who, when Saul was dead, without a blow,
Made foolish Ishbosheth[5] the crown forgo;
Who banished David did from Hebron[6] bring,
And with a general shout proclaimed him king: 60
Those very Jews, who, at their very best,
Their humor[7] more than loyalty expressed,
Now wondered why so long they had obeyed
An idol monarch, which their hands had made;
Thought they might ruin him they could create, 65
Or melt him to that golden calf, a state.[8]
But these were random bolts;[9] no formed design
Nor interest made the factious crowd to join:
The sober part of Israel, free from stain,
Well knew the value of a peaceful reign; 70
And, looking backward with a wise affright,
Saw seams of wounds, dishonest[1] to the sight:

---

6. Anne Scott, duchess of Buccleuch (pronounced *Bue-cloo*), a beauty and a great heiress.
7. Absalom killed his half-brother Amnon, who had raped Absalom's sister Tamar (2 Samuel 13.28–29). The parallel with Monmouth is vague. He is known to have committed acts of violence in his youth, but certainly not fratricide.
8. London.
9. Wholly.
1. Tests.
2. The English.
3. Dryden recalls the political and religious controversies that, since the Reformation, had divided England and finally caused civil wars.
4. Adam rebelled because he felt that he lacked

("wanted") liberty, because he was forbidden to eat the fruit of one tree.
5. Saul's son; he stands for Richard Cromwell, who succeeded his father as lord protector. "Saul": Oliver Cromwell.
6. Where David reigned over Judah after the death of Saul and before he became king of Israel (2 Samuel 1–5). Charles had been crowned in Scotland in 1651.
7. Caprice.
8. A republic. "Golden calf": the image worshiped by the children of Israel during the period that Moses spent on Mt. Sinai, receiving the law from God.
9. Shots.
1. Disgraceful.

In contemplation of whose ugly scars
They cursed the memory of civil wars.
The moderate sort of men, thus qualified,[2]   75
Inclined the balance to the better side;
And David's mildness managed it so well,
The bad found no occasion to rebel.
But when to sin our biased[3] nature leans,
The careful Devil is still at hand with means;   80
And providently pimps for ill desires:
The Good Old Cause[4] revived, a plot requires.
Plots, true or false, are necessary things,
To raise up commonwealths and ruin kings.
    The inhabitants of old Jerusalem   85
Were Jebusites;[5] the town so called from them;
And theirs the native right.
But when the chosen people[6] grew more strong,
The rightful cause at length became the wrong;
And every loss the men of Jebus bore,   90
They still were thought God's enemies the more.
Thus worn and weakened, well or ill content,
Submit they must to David's government:
Impoverished and deprived of all command,
Their taxes doubled as they lost their land;   95
And, what was harder yet to flesh and blood,
Their gods disgraced, and burnt like common wood.[7]
This set the heathen priesthood[8] in a flame,
For priests of all religions are the same:
Of whatsoe'er descent their godhead be,   100
Stock, stone, or other homely pedigree,
In his defense his servants are as bold,
As if he had been born of beaten gold.
The Jewish rabbins,[9] though their enemies,
In this conclude them honest men and wise: 105
For 'twas their duty, all the learned think,
To espouse his cause, by whom they eat and drink.
From hence began that Plot, the nation's curse,
Bad in itself, but represented worse;
Raised in extremes, and in extremes decried;   110
With oaths affirmed, with dying vows denied;
Not weighed or winnowed by the multitude;
But swallowed in the mass, unchewed and crude.
Some truth there was, but dashed[1] and brewed with lies,
To please the fools, and puzzle all the wise.   115
Succeeding times did equal folly call,
Believing nothing, or believing all.
The Egyptian rites the Jebusites embraced,

2. Assuaged.
3. Inclined (cf. *Mac Flecknoe*, line 189 and n. 1, p. 874).
4. The Commonwealth. Dryden stigmatizes the Whigs by associating them with subversion.
5. Roman Catholics. The original name of Jerusalem (here, London) was Jebus.

6. Protestants.
7. Such oppressive laws against Roman Catholics date from the time of Elizabeth I.
8. Roman Catholic clergy.
9. Anglican clergy.
1. Adulterated.

Where gods were recommended by their taste.[2]
Such savory deities must needs be good,   120
As served at once for worship and for food.
By force they could not introduce these gods,
For ten to one in former days was odds;
So fraud was used (the sacrificer's trade):
Fools are more hard to conquer than persuade.   125
Their busy teachers mingled with the Jews,
And raked for converts even the court and stews:[3]
Which Hebrew priests the more unkindly took,
Because the fleece accompanies the flock.[4]
Some thought they God's anointed[5] meant to slay   130
By guns, invented since full many a day:
Our author swears it not; but who can know
How far the Devil and Jebusites may go?
This Plot, which failed for want of common sense,
Had yet a deep and dangerous consequence: 135
For, as when raging fevers boil the blood,
The standing lake soon floats into a flood,
And every hostile humor, which before
Slept quiet in its channels, bubbles o'er;
So several factions from this first ferment   140
Work up to foam, and threat the government.
Some by their friends, more by themselves thought wise,
Opposed the power to which they could not rise.
Some had in courts been great, and thrown from thence,
Like fiends were hardened in impenitence;   145
Some, by their monarch's fatal mercy, grown
From pardoned rebels kinsmen to the throne,
Were raised in power and public office high;
Strong bands, if bands ungrateful men could tie.
    Of these the false Achitophel[6] was first;   150
A name to all succeeding ages cursed:
For close designs, and crooked counsels fit;
Sagacious, bold, and turbulent of wit;[7]
Restless, unfixed in principles and place;
In power unpleased, impatient of disgrace: 155
A fiery soul, which, working out its way,
Fretted the pygmy body to decay,
And o'er-informed the tenement of clay.[8]
A daring pilot in extremity;
Pleased with the danger, when the waves went high,   160
He sought the storms; but, for a calm unfit,

2. Here Dryden sneers at the doctrine of transubstantiation. "Egyptian": French, therefore Catholic.
3. Brothels.
4. Dryden charges that the Anglican clergy ("Hebrew priests") resented proselytizing by Catholics chiefly because they stood to lose their tithes ("fleece").
5. The king.
6. Anthony Ashley Cooper, first earl of Shaftesbury (1621–1683). He had served in the parliamentary army and been a member of Cromwell's council of state. He later helped bring back Charles and, in 1670, was made a member of the notorious Cabal Ministry, which formed an alliance with Louis XIV in which England betrayed her ally, Holland, and joined France in war against that country. In 1672 he became lord chancellor, but with the dissolution of the cabal in 1673, he was removed from office. Lines 146–149 apply perfectly to him.
7. Unruly imagination.
8. The soul is thought of as the animating principle, the force that puts the body in motion. Shaftesbury's body seemed too small to house his fiery, energetic soul.

Would steer too nigh the sands, to boast his wit.
Great wits are sure to madness near allied,[9]
And thin partitions do their bounds divide;
Else why should he, with wealth and honor blest,   165
Refuse his age the needful hours of rest?
Punish a body which he could not please;
Bankrupt of life, yet prodigal of ease?
And all to leave what with his toil he won,
To that unfeathered two-legged thing,[1] a son;   170
Got, while his soul did huddled[2] notions try;
And born a shapeless lump, like anarchy.
In friendship false, implacable in hate,
Resolved to ruin or to rule the state.
To compass this the triple bond[3] he broke,   175
The pillars of the public safety shook,
And fitted Israel for a foreign yoke;
Then seized with fear, yet still affecting fame,
Usurped a patriot's all-atoning name.
So easy still it proves in factious times,   180
With public zeal to cancel private crimes.
How safe is treason, and how sacred ill,
Where none can sin against the people's will!
Where crowds can wink, and no offense be known,
Since in another's guilt they find their own!   185
Yet fame deserved, no enemy can grudge;
The statesman we abhor, but praise the judge.
In Israel's courts ne'er sat an Abbethdin[4]
With more discerning eyes, or hands more clean;
Unbribed, unsought, the wretched to redress;   190
Swift of dispatch, and easy of access.
Oh, had he been content to serve the crown,
With virtues only proper to the gown;
Or had the rankness of the soil been freed
From cockle, that oppressed the noble seed;   195
David for him his tuneful harp had strung,
And Heaven had wanted one immortal song.[5]
But wild Ambition loves to slide, not stand,
And Fortune's ice prefers to Virtue's land.
Achitophel, grown weary to possess   200
A lawful fame, and lazy happiness,
Disdained the golden fruit to gather free,
And lent the crowd his arm to shake the tree.
Now, manifest of[6] crimes contrived long since,
He stood at bold defiance with his prince;   205
Held up the buckler of the people's cause

9. "Great wits": men of genius. That genius and madness are akin is a very old idea.
1. Cf. Plato's definition of man: "a featherless biped."
2. Confused, hurried.
3. The triple alliance of England, Sweden, and Holland against France, 1668. Shaftesbury helped to bring about the war against Holland in 1672.
4. The chief of the seventy elders who composed the Jewish supreme court. The allusion is to Shaftesbury's

serving as lord chancellor from 1672 to 1673. Dryden's praise of Shaftesbury's integrity in this office, by suggesting a balanced judgment, makes his condemnation of the statesman more effective than it might otherwise have been.
5. I.e., David would have had occasion to write one less song of praise to heaven. The reference may be to 2 Samuel 22 or to Psalm 4.
6. Detected in.

Against the crown, and skulked behind the laws.
The wished occasion of the Plot he takes;
Some circumstances finds, but more he makes.
By buzzing emissaries fills the ears   210
Of listening crowds with jealousies[7] and fears
Of arbitrary counsels brought to light,
And proves the king himself a Jebusite.
Weak arguments! which yet he knew full well
Were strong with people easy to rebel.   215
For, governed by the moon, the giddy Jews
Tread the same track when she the prime renews;
And once in twenty years, their scribes record,[8]
By natural instinct they change their lord.
Achitophel still wants a chief, and none   220
Was found so fit as warlike Absalom:
Not that he wished his greatness to create
(For politicians neither love nor hate),
But, for he knew his title not allowed,
Would keep him still depending on the crowd,   225
That kingly power, thus ebbing out, might be
Drawn to the dregs of a democracy.[9]
Him he attempts with studied arts to please,
And sheds his venom in such words as these:
    "Auspicious prince, at whose nativity   230
Some royal planet[1] ruled the southern sky;
Thy longing country's darling and desire;
Their cloudy pillar and their guardian fire:
Their second Moses, whose extended wand
Divides the seas, and shows the promised land;[2]   235
Whose dawning day in every distant age
Has exercised the sacred prophet's rage:
The people's prayer, the glad diviners' theme,
The young men's vision, and the old men's dream![3]
Thee, savior, thee, the nation's vows[4] confess,   240
And, never satisfied with seeing, bless:
Swift unbespoken pomps thy steps proclaim,
And stammering babes are taught to lisp thy name.
How long wilt thou the general joy detain,
Starve and defraud the people of thy reign?   245
Content ingloriously to pass thy days
Like one of Virtue's fools that feeds on praise;
Till thy fresh glories, which now shine so bright,
Grow stale and tarnish with our daily sight.
Believe me, royal youth, thy fruit must be   250

7. Suspicions.
8. The moon "renews her prime" when its several
phases recur on the same day of the solar calendar—
i.e., complete a cycle—as happens approximately every
twenty years. The crisis between Charles I and Parliament began to grow acute about 1640; Charles II returned in 1660; it is now 1680 and a full cycle has been
completed.
9. To Dryden, "democracy" meant popular government. The "dregs of a democracy" would be mob rule.

1. A planet whose influence destines him to kingship.
2. After their exodus from Egypt under the leadership
of Moses, whose "extended wand" separated the waters
of the Red Sea so that they crossed over on dry land,
the Israelites were led in their forty-year wandering in
the wilderness by a pillar of cloud by day and a pillar
of fire by night (Exodus 13–14).
3. Cf. Joel 2.28.
4. Solemn promises of fidelity.

Or gathered ripe, or rot upon the tree.
Heaven has to all allotted, soon or late,
Some lucky revolution of their fate;
Whose motions if we watch and guide with skill
(For human good depends on human will),   255
Our Fortune rolls as from a smooth descent,
And from the first impression takes the bent;
But, if unseized, she glides away like wind,
And leaves repenting Folly far behind.
Now, now she meets you with a glorious prize,   260
And spreads her locks before her as she flies.[5]
Had thus old David, from whose loins you spring,
Not dared, when Fortune called him, to be king,
At Gath[6] an exile he might still remain,
And heaven's anointing[7] oil had been in vain.   265
Let his successful youth your hopes engage;
But shun the example of declining age;
Behold him setting in his western skies,
The shadows lengthening as the vapors rise.
He is not now, as when on Jordan's sand[8]   270
The joyful people thronged to see him land,
Covering the beach, and blackening all the strand;
But, like the Prince of Angels, from his height
Comes tumbling downward with diminished light;[9]
Betrayed by one poor plot to public scorn   275
(Our only blessing since his cursed return),
Those heaps of people which one sheaf did bind,
Blown off and scattered by a puff of wind.
What strength can he to your designs oppose,
Naked of friends, and round beset with foes?   280
If Pharaoh's[1] doubtful succor he should use,
A foreign aid would more incense the Jews:
Proud Egypt would dissembled friendship bring;
Foment the war, but not support the king:
Nor would the royal party e'er unite   285
With Pharaoh's arms to assist the Jebusite;
Or if they should, their interest soon would break,
And with such odious aid make David weak.
All sorts of men by my successful arts,
Abhorring kings, estrange their altered hearts   290
From David's rule: and 'tis the general cry,
'Religion, commonwealth, and liberty.'[2]
If you, as champion of the public good,
Add to their arms a chief of royal blood,
What may not Israel hope, and what applause   295

5. Achitophel gives to Fortune the traditional attributes of the allegorical personification of Opportunity: bald except for a forelock, she can be seized only as she approaches.
6. Brussels, where Charles spent his last years in exile. David took refuge from Saul in Gath (1 Samuel 27.4).
7. After God rejected Saul, He sent Samuel to anoint the boy David, as a token that he should finally come

to the throne (1 Samuel 16.1–13).
8. The seashore at Dover, where Charles landed (May 25, 1660).
9. Cf. the fall of Satan in *Paradise Lost* (pp. 666–67), which dims the brightness of the archangel. The choice of the undignified word *tumbling* is deliberate.
1. Louis XIV of France.
2. Cf. line 82 and n. 4.

Might such a general gain by such a cause?
Not barren praise alone, that gaudy flower
Fair only to the sight, but solid power;
And nobler is a limited command,
Given by the love of all your native land,   300
Than a successive title,[3] long and dark,
Drawn from the moldy rolls of Noah's ark."
   What cannot praise effect in mighty minds,
When flattery soothes, and when ambition blinds!
Desire of power, on earth a vicious weed,   305
Yet, sprung from high, is of celestial seed:
In God 'tis glory; and when men aspire,
'Tis but a spark too much of heavenly fire.
The ambitious youth, too covetous of fame,
Too full of angels' metal[4] in his frame,   310
Unwarily was led from virtue's ways,
Made drunk with honor, and debauched with praise.
Half loath, and half consenting to the ill
(For loyal blood within him struggled still),
He thus replied: "And what pretense have I   315
To take up arms for public liberty?
My father governs with unquestioned right;
The faith's defender, and mankind's delight,
Good, gracious, just, observant of the laws:
And heaven by wonders has espoused his cause.   320
Whom has he wronged in all his peaceful reign?
Who sues for justice to his throne in vain?
What millions has he pardoned of his foes,
Whom just revenge did to his wrath expose?
Mild, easy, humble, studious of our good,   325
Inclined to mercy, and averse from blood;
If mildness ill with stubborn Israel suit,
His crime is God's beloved attribute.
What could he gain, his people to betray,
Or change his right for arbitrary sway?   330
Let haughty Pharaoh curse with such a reign
His fruitful Nile, and yoke a servile train.
If David's rule Jerusalem displease,
The Dog Star[5] heats their brains to this disease.
Why then should I, encouraging the bad,   335
Turn rebel and run popularly mad?
Were he a tyrant, who, by lawless might
Oppressed the Jews, and raised the Jebusite,
Well might I mourn; but nature's holy bands
Would curb my spirits and restrain my hands: 340
The people might assert[6] their liberty,
But what was right in them were crime in me.

3. A title to the crown based on succession.
4. An alternative spelling of *mettle* (i.e., spirit). But a pun on "metal" is intended, as is obvious from the pun "angel" (a purely intellectual being and a coin). Ambition caused the revolt of the angels in heaven.

5. Sirius, which in midsummer rises and sets with the sun and is thus associated with the maddening heat of the "dog days."
6. Claim.

His favor leaves me nothing to require,
Prevents my wishes, and outruns desire.
What more can I expect while David lives?   345
All but his kingly diadem he gives:
And that"—But there he paused; then sighing, said—
"Is justly destined for a worthier head.
For when my father from his toils shall rest
And late augment the number of the blest,   350
His lawful issue shall the throne ascend,
Or the collateral line,[7] where that shall end.
His brother, though oppressed with vulgar spite,
Yet dauntless, and secure of native right,
Of every royal virtue stands possessed;   355
Still dear to all the bravest and the best.
His courage foes, his friends his truth proclaim;
His loyalty the king, the world his fame.
His mercy even the offending crowd will find,
For sure he comes of a forgiving kind.[8]   360
Why should I then repine at heaven's decree,
Which gives me no pretense to royalty?
Yet O that fate, propitiously inclined,
Had raised my birth, or had debased my mind;
To my large soul not all her treasure lent,   365
And then betrayed it to a mean descent!
I find, I find my mounting spirits bold,
And David's part disdains my mother's mold.
Why am I scanted by a niggard birth?[9]
My soul disclaims the kindred of her earth;   370
And, made for empire, whispers me within,
'Desire of greatness is a godlike sin.' "
     Him staggering so when hell's dire agent found,[1]
While fainting Virtue scarce maintained her ground,
He pours fresh forces in, and thus replies: 375
     "The eternal god, supremely good and wise,
Imparts not these prodigious gifts in vain:
What wonders are reserved to bless your reign!
Against your will, your arguments have shown,
Such virtue's only given to guide a throne.   380
Not that your father's mildness I contemn,
But manly force becomes the diadem.
'Tis true he grants the people all they crave;
And more, perhaps, than subjects ought to have:
For lavish grants suppose a monarch tame,   385
And more his goodness than his wit[2] proclaim.
But when should people strive their bonds to break,
If not when kings are negligent or weak?
Let him give on till he can give no more,

---

7. In the event of Charles's dying without legitimate issue, the throne would constitutionally pass to his brother, James, or his descendants, the "collateral line."
8. Race, in the sense of family.

9. I.e., why am I limited by a sordid birth?
1. Observe the Miltonic inversion, which helps to maintain the epic tone.
2. Intelligence.

The thrifty Sanhedrin[3] shall keep him poor;   390
And every shekel which he can receive,
Shall cost a limb of his prerogative.[4]
To ply him with new plots shall be my care;
Or plunge him deep in some expensive war;
Which when his treasure can no more supply,   395
He must, with the remains of kingship, buy.
His faithful friends our jealousies and fears
Call Jebusites, and Pharaoh's pensioners;
Whom when our fury from his aid has torn,
He shall be naked left to public scorn.   400
The next successor, whom I fear and hate,
My arts have made obnoxious to the state;
Turned all his virtues to his overthrow,
And gained our elders[5] to pronounce a foe.
His right, for sums of necessary gold,   405
Shall first be pawned, and afterward be sold;
Till time shall ever-wanting David draw,
To pass your doubtful title into law:
If not, the people have a right supreme
To make their kings; for kings are made for them.   410
All empire is no more than power in trust,
Which, when resumed, can be no longer just.
Succession, for the general good designed,
In its own wrong a nation cannot bind;
If altering that the people can relieve,   415
Better one suffer than a nation grieve.
The Jews well know their power: ere Saul they chose,[6]
God was their king, and God they durst depose.
Urge now your piety,[7] your filial name,
A father's right and fear of future fame;   420
The public good, that universal call,
To which even heaven submitted, answers all.
Nor let his love enchant your generous mind;
'Tis Nature's trick to propagate her kind.
Our fond begetters, who would never die,   425
Love but themselves in their posterity.
Or let his kindness by the effects be tried,
Or let him lay his vain pretense aside.
God said he loved your father; could he bring
A better proof than to anoint him king?   430
It surely showed he loved the shepherd well,
Who gave so fair a flock as Israel.
Would David have you thought his darling son?
What means he then, to alienate[8] the crown?

3. The highest judicial counsel of the Jews, here, Parliament.
4. The Whigs hoped to limit the special privileges of
the crown (the royal "prerogative") by refusing to vote
money to Charles. He circumvented them by living on
French subsidies and refusing to summon Parliament.
5. The chief magistrates and rulers of the Jews.
Shaftesbury had won over ("gained") country gentlemen and nobles to his hostile view of James.

6. Before Saul, the first king of Israel, came to the
throne, the Jews were governed by judges. Similarly
Oliver Cromwell ("Saul") as lord protector took over
the reins of government, after he had dissolved the
Rump Parliament in 1653.
7. Dutifulness to a parent.
8. In law, to convey the title to property to another
person.

The name of godly he may blush to bear: 435
'Tis after God's own heart[9] to cheat his heir.
He to his brother gives supreme command;
To you a legacy of barren land,[1]
Perhaps the old harp, on which he thrums his lays,
Or some dull Hebrew ballad in your praise.   440
Then the next heir, a prince severe and wise,
Already looks on you with jealous eyes;
Sees through the thin disguises of your arts,
And marks your progress in the people's hearts.
Though now his mighty soul its grief contains,   445
He meditates revenge who least complains;
And, like a lion, slumbering in the way,
Or sleep dissembling, while he waits his prey,
His fearless foes within his distance draws,
Constrains his roaring, and contracts his paws;   450
Till at the last, his time for fury found,
He shoots with sudden vengeance from the ground;
The prostrate vulgar[2] passes o'er and spares,
But with a lordly rage his hunters tears.
Your case no tame expedients will afford: 455
Resolve on death, or conquest by the sword,
Which for no less a stake than life you draw;
And self-defense is nature's eldest law.
Leave the warm people no considering time;
For then rebellion may be thought a crime.   460
Prevail yourself of what occasion gives,
But try your title while your father lives;
And that your arms may have a fair pretense,[3]
Proclaim you take them in the king's defense;
Whose sacred life each minute would expose   465
To plots, from seeming friends, and secret foes.
And who can sound the depth of David's soul?
Perhaps his fear his kindness may control.
He fears his brother, though he loves his son,
For plighted vows too late to be undone.   470
If so, by force he wishes to be gained,
Like women's lechery, to seem constrained.[4]
Doubt not; but when he most affects the frown,
Commit a pleasing rape upon the crown.
Secure his person to secure your cause: 475
They who possess the prince, possess the laws."
     He said, and this advice above the rest
With Absalom's mild nature suited best:
Unblamed of life (ambition set aside),
Not stained with cruelty, nor puffed with pride,   480
How happy had he been, if destiny
Had higher placed his birth, or not so high!

---

9. An irony (cf. line 7, n. 1).   2. Common people.
1. James was given the title of generalissimo in 1678.   3. Pretext.
In 1679 Monmouth was banished and withdrew to   4. Forced.
Holland.

His kingly virtues might have claimed a throne,
And blest all other countries but his own.
But charming greatness since so few refuse,   485
'Tis juster to lament him than accuse.
Strong were his hopes a rival to remove,
With blandishments to gain the public love;
To head the faction while their zeal was hot,
And popularly prosecute the Plot.   490
To further this, Achitophel unites
The malcontents of all the Israelites;
Whose differing parties he could wisely join,
For several ends, to serve the same design:
The best (and of the princes some were such),   495
Who thought the power of monarchy too much;
Mistaken men, and patriots in their hearts;
Not wicked, but seduced by impious arts.
By these the springs of property were bent,
And wound so high, they cracked the government.   500
The next for interest sought to embroil the state,
To sell their duty at a dearer rate;
And make their Jewish markets of the throne,
Pretending public good, to serve their own.
Others thought kings an useless heavy load,   505
Who cost too much, and did too little good.
These were for laying honest David by,
On principles of pure good husbandry.[5]
With them joined all the haranguers of the throng,
That thought to get preferment by the tongue.   510
Who follow next, a double danger bring,
Not only hating David, but the king:
The Solymaean rout,[6] well-versed of old
In godly faction, and in treason bold;
Cowering and quaking at a conqueror's sword,   515
But lofty to a lawful prince restored;
Saw with disdain an ethnic[7] plot begun,
And scorned by Jebusites to be outdone.
Hot Levites[8] headed these; who, pulled before
From the ark, which in the Judges' days they bore,   520
Resumed their cant, and with a zealous cry
Pursued their old beloved theocracy:
Where Sanhedrin and priest enslaved the nation,
And justified their spoils by inspiration:[9]
For who so fit for reign as Aaron's race,[1]   525

5. Economy.
6. I.e., London rabble. Solyma was a name for Jerusalem.
7. Gentile; here, Roman Catholic.
8. I.e., Presbyterian clergymen. The tribe of Levi, assigned to duties in the tabernacle, carried the ark of the covenant during the forty-year sojourn in the wilderness (Numbers 4). Under the Commonwealth ("in the Judges' days") Presbyterianism became the state religion, and its clergy, therefore, "bore the ark." The Act of Uniformity (1662) forced the Presbyterian clergy out

of their livings: in short, before the Popish Plot, they had been "pulled from the ark." They are represented here as joining the Whigs in the hope of restoring the commonwealth, "their old beloved theocracy."
9. Observe in these lines the cluster of disparaging words: "cant," "zealous," "inspiration." Dryden shared Samuel Butler's contempt for the irrationality of Dissenters.
1. Priests had to be descendants of Aaron (Exodus 28.1, Numbers 18.7).

If once dominion they could found in grace?
These led the pack; though not of surest scent,
Yet deepest-mouthed[2] against the government.
A numerous host of dreaming saints succeed,
Of the true old enthusiastic breed:[3]　　　　　　　　　　530
'Gainst form and order they their power employ,
Nothing to build, and all things to destroy.
But far more numerous was the herd of such,
Who think too little, and who talk too much.
These out of mere instinct, they knew not why,　　　535
Adored their fathers' God and property;
And, by the same blind benefit of fate,
The Devil and the Jebusite did hate:
Born to be saved, even in their own despite,
Because they could not help believing right.　　　　540
Such were the tools; but a whole Hydra more
Remains, of sprouting heads too long to score.
Some of their chiefs were princes of the land:
In the first rank of these did Zimri[4] stand;
A man so various, that he seemed to be　　　　　　545
Not one, but all mankind's epitome:
Stiff in opinions, always in the wrong;
Was everything by starts, and nothing long;
But, in the course of one revolving moon,
Was chymist,[5] fiddler, statesman, and buffoon:　　550
Then all for women, painting, rhyming, drinking,
Besides ten thousand freaks that died in thinking.
Blest madman, who could every hour employ,
With something new to wish, or to enjoy!
Railing[6] and praising were his usual themes;　　　555
And both (to show his judgment) in extremes:
So over-violent, or over-civil,
That every man, with him, was God or Devil.
In squandering wealth was his peculiar art:
Nothing went unrewarded but desert.　　　　　　560
Beggared by fools, whom still he found[7] too late,
He had his jest, and they had his estate.
He laughed himself from court; then sought relief
By forming parties, but could ne'er be chief;
For, spite of him, the weight of business fell　　　565
On Absalom and wise Achitophel:

2. Loudest. The phrase is applied to hunting dogs. "Pack" and "scent" sustain the image.
3. "Dreaming saints": a term used by certain Dissenters for those elected to salvation. The extreme fanaticism of the "saints" and their claims to inspiration are characterized as a form of religious madness ("enthusiastic").
4. George Villiers, second duke of Buckingham (1628–1687), wealthy, brilliant, dissolute, and unstable. He had been an influential member of the cabal, but after 1673 had joined Shaftesbury in opposition to the court party. This is the least political of the satirical portraits in the poem. Buckingham had been the chief author of *The Rehearsal* (1671), the play that satirized the heroic play and ridiculed Dryden in the character of Mr. Bayes. Politics gave Dryden an opportunity to retaliate. He comments on this portrait in his *A Discourse Concerning the Original and Progress of Satire.* Dryden had two biblical Zimris in mind: the Zimri destroyed for his lustfulness and blasphemy (Numbers 25) and the conspirator and regicide of 1 Kings 16.8–20 and 2 Kings 9.31.
5. Chemist.
6. Reviling, abusing.
7. Found out. "Still": constantly.

Thus, wicked but in will, of means bereft,
He left not faction, but of that was left.
   Titles and names 'twere tedious to rehearse
Of lords, below the dignity of verse. 570
Wits, warriors, Commonwealth's men, were the best;
Kind husbands, and mere nobles, all the rest.
And therefore, in the name of dullness, be
The well-hung Balaam and cold Caleb, free;
And canting Nadab let oblivion damn, 575
Who made new porridge for the paschal lamb.[8]
Let friendship's holy band some names assure;
Some their own worth, and some let scorn secure.
Nor shall the rascal rabble here have place,
Whom kings no titles gave, and God no grace: 580
Not bull-faced Jonas,[9] who could statutes draw
To mean rebellion, and make treason law.
But he, though bad, is followed by a worse,
The wretch who heaven's anointed dared to curse:
Shimei,[1] whose youth did early promise bring 585
Of zeal to God and hatred to his king,
Did wisely from expensive sins refrain,
And never broke the Sabbath, but for gain;
Nor ever was he known an oath to vent,
Or curse, unless against the government. 590
Thus heaping wealth, by the most ready way
Among the Jews, which was to cheat and pray,
The city, to reward his pious hate
Against his master, chose him magistrate.
His hand a vare[2] of justice did uphold; 595
His neck was loaded with a chain of gold.
During his office, treason was no crime;
The sons of Belial[3] had a glorious time;
For Shimei, though not prodigal of pelf,
Yet loved his wicked neighbor as himself. 600
When two or three were gathered to declaim
Against the monarch of Jerusalem,
Shimei was always in the midst of them;
And if they cursed the king when he was by,
Would rather curse than break good company. 605
If any durst his factious friends accuse,
He packed a jury of dissenting Jews;

8. The lamb slain during Passover; here, Christ. The identities of Balaam, Caleb, and Nadab have not been certainly established, although various Whig nobles have been suggested. For Balaam see Numbers 22–24; for Caleb, Numbers 13–14; and for Nadab, Leviticus 10.1–2. "Well-hung": fluent of speech or sexually potent or both. "Cold" would contrast with the second meaning of well-hung. "Canting" points to a Nonconformist, as does "new porridge," for Dissenters referred to the Book of Common Prayer contemptuously as "porridge," a hodgepodge, unsubstantial stuff.
9. Sir William Jones, attorney general, had been largely responsible for the passage of the first Exclusion Bill by the House of Commons. He prosecuted the accused in the Popish Plot.
1. Shimei cursed and stoned David when he fled into the wilderness during Absalom's revolt (2 Samuel 16.5–14). His name is used here for one of the two sheriffs of London: Slingsby Bethel, a Whig, former republican, and virulent enemy of Charles. He packed juries with Whigs and so secured the acquittal of enemies of the court, among them Shaftesbury himself.
2. Staff.
3. Sons of wickedness (cf. Milton, *Paradise Lost* 1.490–505, pp. 676–77). Dryden probably intended a pun on Balliol, the Oxford college in which leading Whigs stayed during the brief and fateful meeting of Parliament at Oxford in 1681.

Whose fellow-feeling in the godly cause
Would free the suffering saint from human laws.
For laws are only made to punish those   610
Who serve the king, and to protect his foes.
If any leisure time he had from power
(Because 'tis sin to misemploy an hour),
His business was, by writing, to persuade
That kings were useless, and a clog to trade;   615
And, that his noble style he might refine,
No Rechabite[4] more shunned the fumes of wine.
Chaste were his cellars, and his shrieval board[5]
The grossness of a city feast abhorred:
His cooks, with long disuse, their trade forgot;   620
Cool was his kitchen, though his brains were hot,
Such frugal virtue malice may accuse,
But sure 'twas necessary to the Jews:
For towns once burnt[6] such magistrates require
As dare not tempt God's providence by fire.   625
With spiritual food he fed his servants well,
But free from flesh that made the Jews rebel;
And Moses' laws he held in more account,
For forty days of fasting in the mount.[7]
To speak the rest, who better are forgot,   630
Would tire a well-breathed witness of the Plot.
Yet, Corah,[8] thou shalt from oblivion pass:
Erect thyself, thou monumental brass,
High as the serpent of thy metal made,[9]
While nations stand secure beneath thy shade.   635
What though his birth were base, yet comets rise
From earthy vapors, ere they shine in skies.
Prodigious actions may as well be done
By weaver's issue,[1] as by prince's son.
This arch-attestor for the public good   640
By that one deed ennobles all his blood.
Who ever asked the witnesses' high race
Whose oath with martyrdom did Stephen grace?[2]
Ours was a Levite, and as times went then,
His tribe were God Almighty's gentlemen.   645
Sunk were his eyes, his voice was harsh and loud,
Sure signs he neither choleric[3] was nor proud:
His long chin proved his wit; his saintlike grace
A church vermilion, and a Moses' face.[4]
His memory, miraculously great,   650

---

4. An austere Jewish sect that drank no wine (Jeremiah 35.2–19).
5. Sheriff's dinner table.
6. London burned in 1666.
7. Mt. Sinai, where, during a fast of forty days, Moses received the law (Exodus 34.28).
8. Or Korah, a rebellious Levite, swallowed up by the earth because of his crimes (Numbers 16). Corah is Titus Oates, the self-appointed, perjured, and "well-breathed" (long-winded) witness of the plot.
9. Moses erected a brazen serpent to heal the Jews bit-

ten by fiery serpents (Numbers 21.4–9). "Brass" also means impudence or shamelessness.
1. Oates's father, a clergyman, belonged to an obscure family of ribbon weavers.
2. The first Christian martyr, accused by false witnesses (Acts 6–7).
3. Prone to anger.
4. Moses's face shone when he came down from Mt. Sinai with the tables of the law (Exodus 34.29–30). Oates's face suggests high living, not spiritual illumination.

Could plots, exceeding man's belief, repeat;
Which therefore cannot be accounted lies,
For human wit could never such devise.
Some future truths are mingled in his book;
But where the witness failed, the prophet spoke: 655
Some things like visionary flights appear;
The spirit caught him up, the Lord knows where,
And gave him his rabbinical degree,
Unknown to foreign university.[5]
His judgment yet his memory did excel;   660
Which pieced his wondrous evidence so well,
And suited to the temper of the times,
Then groaning under Jebusitic crimes.
Let Israel's foes suspect his heavenly call,
And rashly judge his writ apocryphal;[6]   665
Our laws for such affronts have forfeits made:
He takes his life, who takes away his trade.
Were I myself in witness Corah's place,
The wretch who did me such a dire disgrace
Should whet my memory, though once forgot,   670
To make him an appendix of my plot.
His zeal to heaven made him his prince despise,
And load his person with indignities;
But zeal peculiar privilege affords,
Indulging latitude to deeds and words;   675
And Corah might for Agag's murder[7] call,
In terms as coarse as Samuel used to Saul.
What others in his evidence did join
(The best that could be had for love or coin),
In Corah's own predicament will fall;   680
For *witness* is a common name to all.
    Surrounded thus with friends of every sort,
Deluded Absalom forsakes the court:
Impatient of high hopes, urged with renown,
And fired with near possession of a crown.   685
The admiring crowd are dazzled with surprise,
And on his goodly person feed their eyes:
His joy concealed, he sets himself to show,
On each side bowing popularly[8] low;
His looks, his gestures, and his words he frames,   690
And with familiar ease repeats their names.
Thus formed by nature, furnished out with arts,
He glides unfelt into their secret hearts.
Then, with a kind compassionating look,
And sighs, bespeaking pity ere he spoke,   695
Few words he said; but easy those and fit,
More slow than Hybla-drops,[9] and far more sweet.

5. Oates falsely claimed to be a doctor of divinity in the University of Salamanca.
6. Not inspired and hence excluded from Holy Writ.
7. Agag is probably one of the five Catholic peers executed for the Popish Plot in 1680, most likely Lord Stafford, against whom Oates fabricated testimony; he is almost certainly not, as is usually suggested, Sir Edmund Berry Godfrey (cf. headnote "Absalom and Achitophel," pp. 844–46). "Agag's murder" and Samuel's coarse terms to Saul are in 1 Samuel 15.
8. "So as to please the crowd" (Johnson's *Dictionary*).
9. The famous honey of Hybla in Sicily.

"I mourn, my countrymen, your lost estate;
Though far unable to prevent your fate:
Behold a banished man, for your dear cause   700
Exposed a prey to arbitrary laws!
Yet oh! that I alone could be undone,
Cut off from empire, and no more a son!
Now all your liberties a spoil are made; ⎤
Egypt and Tyrus[1] intercept your trade, ⎬   705
And Jebusites your sacred rites invade. ⎦
My father, whom with reverence yet I name,
Charmed into ease, is careless of his fame;
And, bribed with petty sums of foreign gold,
Is grown in Bathsheba's[2] embraces old;   710
Exalts his enemies, his friends destroys;
And all his power against himself employs.
He gives, and let him give, my right away;
But why should he his own, and yours betray?
He only, he can make the nation bleed,   715
And he alone from my revenge is freed.
Take then my tears (with that he wiped his eyes),
'Tis all the aid my present power supplies:
No court-informer can these arms accuse;
These arms may sons against their fathers use: 720
And 'tis my wish, the next successor's reign
May make no other Israelite complain."
      Youth, beauty, graceful action seldom fail;
But common interest always will prevail;
And pity never ceases to be shown   725
To him who makes the people's wrongs his own.
The crowd (that still believe their kings oppress)
With lifted hands their young Messiah bless:
Who now begins his progress to ordain
With chariots, horsemen, and a numerous train;   730
From east to west his glories he displays,[3]
And, like the sun, the promised land surveys.
Fame runs before him as the morning star,
And shouts of joy salute him from afar:
Each house receives him as a guardian god,   735
And consecrates the place of his abode:
But hospitable treats did most commend
Wise Issachar,[4] his wealthy western friend.
This moving court, that caught the people's eyes,
And seemed but pomp, did other ends disguise: 740
Achitophel had formed it, with intent
To sound the depths, and fathom, where it went,
The people's hearts; distinguish friends from foes,
And try their strength, before they came to blows.

---

1. France and Holland.
2. With whom David committed adultery (2 Samuel 11); here, Charles II's French mistress, Louise de Keroualle, duchess of Portsmouth.
3. In 1680 Monmouth made a progress through the west of England, seeking popular support for his cause.
4. Thomas Thynne of Longleat. He entertained Monmouth on his journey in the west. "Wise" is, of course, ironic.

Yet all was colored with a smooth pretense   745
Of specious love, and duty to their prince.
Religion, and redress of grievances,
Two names that always cheat and always please,
Are often urged; and good King David's life
Endangered by a brother and a wife.[5]   750
Thus, in a pageant show, a plot is made,
And peace itself is war in masquerade.
O foolish Israel! never warned by ill,
Still the same bait, and circumvented still!
Did ever men forsake their present ease,   755
In midst of health imagine a disease;
Take pains contingent mischiefs to foresee,
Make heirs for monarchs, and for God decree?
What shall we think![6] Can people give away
Both for themselves and sons, their native sway?   760
Then they are left defenseless to the sword
Of each unbounded, arbitrary lord:
And laws are vain, by which we right enjoy,
If kings unquestioned can those laws destroy.
Yet if the crowd be judge of fit and just,   765
And kings are only officers in trust,
Then this resuming covenant was declared
When kings were made, or is forever barred.
If those who gave the scepter could not tie
By their own deed their own posterity,   770
How then could Adam bind his future race?
How could his forfeit on mankind take place?
Or how could heavenly justice damn us all,
Who ne'er consented to our father's fall?
Then kings are slaves to those whom they command,   775
And tenants to their people's pleasure stand.
Add, that the power for property allowed
Is mischievously seated in the crowd;
For who can be secure of private right,
If sovereign sway may be dissolved by might?   780
Nor is the people's judgment always true:
The most may err as grossly as the few;
And faultless kings run down, by common cry,
For vice, oppression, and for tyranny.
What standard is there in a fickle rout,   785
Which, flowing to the mark, runs faster out?
Nor only crowds, but Sanhedrins may be
Infected with this public lunacy,[7]
And share the madness of rebellious times,
To murder monarchs for imagined crimes.[8]   790
If they may give and take whene'er they please,

5. Titus Oates had sworn that both James, duke of York, and the queen were involved in a similar plot to poison Charles II.
6. In the passage that follows, Dryden states his political philosophy. He bases the royal authority on a covenant entered into by the governor and the governed.
7. The fickle crowd flows and ebbs like the tide, which is pulled back and forth by the moon (hence *lunacy* after Latin "luna" or moon). "The mark": highwater mark.
8. An allusion to the execution of Charles I.

Not kings alone (the Godhead's images),
But government itself at length must fall
To nature's state, where all have right to all.
Yet, grant our lords the people kings can make,   795
What prudent men a settled throne would shake?
For whatsoe'er their sufferings were before,
That change they covet makes them suffer more.
All other errors but disturb a state,
But innovation is the blow of fate.   800
If ancient fabrics nod, and threat to fall,
To patch the flaws, and buttress up the wall,
Thus far 'tis duty; but here fix the mark;
For all beyond it is to touch our ark.[9]
To change foundations, cast the frame anew,   805
Is work for rebels, who base ends pursue,
At once divine and human laws control,
And mend the parts by ruin of the whole.
The tampering world is subject to this curse,
To physic their disease into a worse.   810
    Now what relief can righteous David bring?
How fatal 'tis to be too good a king!
Friends he has few, so high the madness grows:
Who dare be such, must be the people's foes:
Yet some there were, even in the worst of days;   815
Some let me name, and naming is to praise.
    In this short file Barzillai[1] first appears;
Barzillai, crowned with honor and with years:
Long since, the rising rebels he withstood
In regions waste, beyond the Jordan's flood: 820
Unfortunately brave to buoy the State;
But sinking underneath his master's fate:
In exile with his godlike prince he mourned;
For him he suffered, and with him returned.
The court he practiced, not the courtier's art: 825
Large was his wealth, but larger was his heart:
Which well the noblest objects knew to choose,
The fighting warrior, and recording Muse.
His bed could once a fruitful issue boast;
Now more than half a father's name is lost.   830
His eldest hope,[2] with every grace adorned,
By me (so Heaven will have it) always mourned,
And always honored, snatched in manhood's prime
By unequal fates, and Providence's crime:
Yet not before the goal of honor won,   835
All parts fulfilled of subject and of son;
Swift was the race, but short the time to run.
O narrow circle, but of power divine,

9. Uzzah was struck dead because he sacrilegiously touched the Ark of the Covenant (2 Samuel 6. 6–7).
1. James Butler, duke of Ormond (1610–1688). He was famous for his loyalty to the Stuart cause. He fought for Charles I in Ireland, and when that cause was hopeless, he joined Charles II in his exile abroad. He spent a large fortune in behalf of the king and continued to serve him loyally after the Restoration.
2. Ormond's son, Thomas, earl of Ossory (1634–1680), a famous soldier and like his father devoted to Charles II.

Scanted in space, but perfect in thy line!
By sea, by land, thy matchless worth was known,   840
Arms thy delight, and war was all thy own:
Thy force, infused, the fainting Tyrians[3] propped;
And haughty Pharaoh found his fortune stopped.
Oh ancient honor! Oh unconquered hand,
Whom foes unpunished never could withstand!   845
But Israel was unworthy of thy name:
Short is the date of all immoderate fame.
It looks as Heaven our ruin had designed,
And durst not trust thy fortune and thy mind.
Now, free from earth, thy disencumbered soul   850
Mounts up, and leaves behind the clouds and starry pole:
From thence thy kindred legions mayst thou bring,
To aid the guardian angel of thy king.
Here stop my Muse, here cease thy painful flight;
No pinions can pursue immortal height: 855
Tell good Barzillai thou canst sing no more,
And tell thy soul she should have fled before:
Or fled she with his life, and left this verse
To hang on her departed patron's hearse?
Now take thy steepy flight from heaven, and see   860
If thou canst find on earth another *he*:
Another *he* would be too hard to find;
See then whom thou canst see not far behind.
Zadoc the priest,[4] whom, shunning power and place,
His lowly mind advanced to David's grace: 865
With him the Sagan of Jerusalem,
Of hospitable soul, and noble stem;
Him of the western dome, whose weighty sense
Flows in fit words and heavenly eloquence.
The prophets' sons, by such example led,   870
To learning and to loyalty were bred:
For colleges on bounteous kinds depend,
And never rebel was to arts a friend.
To these succeed the pillars of the laws,
Who best could plead, and best can judge a cause.   875
Next them a train of loyal peers ascend;
Sharp-judging Adriel, the Muses' friend,
Himself a Muse—in Sanhedrin's debate
True to his prince, but not a slave of state:
Whom David's love with honors did adorn,   880
That from his disobedient son were torn.
Jotham of piercing wit, and pregnant thought,
Indued by nature, and by learning taught
To move assemblies, who but only tried
The worse a while, then chose the better side;   885
Nor chose alone, but turned the balance too;

3. The Dutch.
4. "Zadoc": William Sancroft, archbishop of Canterbury. "Sagan": Henry Compton, bishop of London.
"Him of the western dome": John Dolben, dean of
Westminster. "The prophets' sons": the boys of Westminster School, which Dryden had attended. "Adriel":
John Sheffield, earl of Mulgrave. "Jotham": George
Savile, marquis of Halifax. "Hushai": Laurence Hyde,
earl of Rochester. "Amiel": Edward Seymour, speaker
of the House of Commons.

So much the weight of one brave man can do.
Hushai, the friend of David in distress,
In public storms, of manly steadfastness:
By foreign treaties he informed his youth,   890
And joined experience to his native truth.
His frugal care supplied the wanting throne,
Frugal for that, but bounteous of his own:
'Tis easy conduct when exchequers flow,
But hard the task to manage well the low;   895
For sovereign power is too depressed or high,
When kings are forced to sell, or crowds to buy.
Indulge one labor more, my weary Muse,
For Amiel: who can Amiel's praise refuse?
Of ancient race by birth, but nobler yet   900
In his own worth, and without title great:
The Sanhedrin long time as chief he ruled,
Their reason guided, and their passion cooled:
So dexterous was he in the crown's defense,
So formed to speak a loyal nation's sense,   905
That, as their band was Israel's tribes in small,
So fit was he to represent them all.
Now rasher charioteers the seat ascend,
Whose loose careers his steady skill commend:
They like the unequal ruler of the day,   910
Misguide the seasons, and mistake the way;
While he withdrawn at their mad labor smiles,
And safe enjoys the sabbath of his toils.
　　These were the chief, a small but faithful band ⎞
Of worthies, in the breach who dared to stand, ⎬   915
And tempt the united fury of the land. ⎠
With grief they viewed such powerful engines bent,
To batter down the lawful government:
A numerous faction, with pretended frights,
In Sanhedrins to plume the regal rights;   920
The true successor from the court removed:[5]
The Plot, by hireling witnesses, improved.
These ills they saw, and, as their duty bound,
They showed the king the danger of the wound:
That no concessions from the throne would please,   925
But lenitives[6] fomented the disease;
That Absalom, ambitious of the crown,
Was made the lure to draw the people down;
That false Achitophel's pernicious hate
Had turned the Plot to ruin Church and State: 930
The council violent, the rabble worse;
That Shimei taught Jerusalem to curse.
　　With all these loads of injuries oppressed,
And long revolving, in his careful breast,
The event of things, at last, his patience tired,   935
Thus from his royal throne, by Heaven inspired,

---

5. The duke of York had been banished from England.　　6. Any medicine that relieves pain.

The godlike David spoke: with awful fear
His train their Maker in their master hear.
   "Thus long have I, by native mercy swayed,
My wrongs dissembled, my revenge delayed: 940
So willing to forgive the offending age,
So much the father did the king assuage.
But now so far my clemency they slight,
The offenders question my forgiving right.
That one was made for many, they contend;   945
But 'tis to rule; for that's a monarch's end.
They call my tenderness of blood, my fear;
Though manly tempers can the longest bear.
Yet, since they will divert my native course,
'Tis time to show I am not good by force.   950
Those heaped affronts that haughty subjects bring,
Are burdens for a camel, not a king:
Kings are the public pillars of the State,
Born to sustain and prop the nation's weight:
If my young Samson will pretend a call   955
To shake the column, let him share the fall:[7]
But, oh, that yet he would repent and live!
How easy 'tis for parents to forgive!
With how few tears a pardon might be won
From nature, pleading for a darling son!   960
Poor pitied youth, by my paternal care
Raised up to all the height his frame could bear:
Had God ordained his fate for empire born,
He would have given his soul another turn:
Gulled[8] with a patriot's name, whose modern sense   965
Is one that would by law supplant his prince:
The people's brave, the politician's tool;
Never was patriot yet, but was a fool.
Whence comes it that religion and the laws
Should more be Absalom's than David's cause?   970
His old instructor, ere he lost his place,
Was never thought indued with so much grace.[9]
Good heavens, how faction can a patriot paint!
My rebel ever proves my people's saint:
Would *they* impose an heir upon the throne?   975
Let Sanhedrins be taught to give their own.
A king's at least a part of government,
And mine as requisite as their consent;
Without my leave a future king to choose,
Infers a right the present to depose: 980
True, they petition me to approve their choice;
But Esau's hands suit ill with Jacob's voice.[1]
My pious subjects for my safety pray,
Which to secure, they take my power away.
From plots and treasons Heaven preserve my years,   985
But save me most from my petitioners.

---

7. Judges 16.   9. The earl of Shaftesbury.
8. Deceived.   1. Genesis 27.22.

Unsatiate as the barren womb or grave;
God cannot grant so much as they can crave.
What then is left but with a jealous eye
To guard the small remains of royalty?   990
The law shall still direct my peaceful sway,
And the same law teach rebels to obey:
Votes shall no more established power control—
Such votes as make a part exceed the whole:
No groundless clamors shall my friends remove,   995
Nor crowds have power to punish ere they prove:
For gods and godlike kings, their care express,
Still to defend their servants in distress.
O that my power to saving were confined:
Why am I forced, like Heaven, against my mind,   1000
To make examples of another kind?
Must I at length the sword of justice draw?
O curst effects of necessary law!
How ill my fear they by my mercy scan!
Beware the fury of a patient man.   1005
Law they require, let Law then show her face;
They could not be content to look on Grace,
Her hinder parts, but with a daring eye
To tempt the terror of her front and die.[2]
By their own arts, 'tis righteously decreed,   1010
Those dire artificers of death shall bleed.
Against themselves their witnesses will swear,
Till viper-like their mother Plot they tear:
And suck for nutriment that bloody gore,
Which was their principle of life before.   1015
Their Belial with their Belzebub[3] will fight;
Thus on my foes, my foes shall do me right:
Nor doubt the event; for factious crowds engage,
In their first onset, all their brutal rage.
Then let 'em take an unresisted course,   1020
Retire and traverse, and delude their force:
But when they stand all breathless, urge the fight,
And rise upon 'em with redoubled might:
For lawful power is still superior found,
When long driven back, at length it stands the ground."   1025
    He said. The Almighty, nodding, gave consent;
And peals of thunder shook the firmament.
Henceforth a series of new time began,
The mighty years in long procession ran:
Once more the godlike David was restored,   1030
And willing nations knew their lawful lord.

                                                                         1681

---

2. Moses was not allowed to see the countenance of   3. A god of the Philistines. "Belial": the incarnation of
Jehovah (Exodus 33. 20–23).   all evil.

Mac Flecknoe   The victim of this superb satire, which is cast in the form of
a mock-heroic episode, is Thomas Shadwell (1640–1692), the playwright, with
whom Dryden had been on good terms for a number of years, certainly as late as
March 1678. Shadwell considered himself the successor of Ben Jonson and the
champion of the type of comedy that Jonson had written, the "comedy of humors,"
in which each character is presented under the domination of a single psychological trait or eccentricity, his humor. His plays are not without merit, but they are
often clumsy and prolix and certainly much inferior to Jonson's. For many years
he had conducted a public argument with Dryden on the merits of Jonson's comedies, which he thought Dryden undervalued. Exactly what moved Dryden to
attack him is a matter of conjecture: he may simply have grown progressively bored
and irritated by Shadwell and his tedious argument. The poem seems to have been
written in late 1678 or 1679 and to have circulated only in manuscript until it was
printed in 1682 in a pirated edition by an obscure publisher. By that time, the two
playwrights were alienated by politics as well as by literary quarrels. Shadwell was
a violent Whig and the reputed author of a sharp attack on Dryden as the Tory
author of *Absalom and Achitophel* and *The Medal*. It was probably for this reason
that the printer added the subtitle referring to Shadwell's Whiggism in the phrase
"true-blue-Protestant poet." Political passions were running high and sales would
be helped if the poem seemed to refer to the events of the day.
     Whereas Butler had debased and degraded his victims by using burlesque,
caricature, and the grotesque, Dryden exposed Shadwell to ridicule by using the
devices of mock epic, which treats the low, mean, or absurd in the grand language,
lofty style, and solemn tone of epic poetry. The obvious disparity between subject
and style makes the satiric point. In 1678, a prolific, untalented writer, Richard
Flecknoe, died. Dryden conceived the idea of presenting Shadwell (the self-
proclaimed heir of Ben Jonson, the laureate) as the son and successor of
Flecknoe—hence *Mac* (i.e., son of) *Flecknoe*—from whom he inherits the throne
of dullness. Flecknoe in the triple role of king, priest, and poet hails his successor,
pronounces a panegyric on his perfect fitness for the throne, anoints and crowns
him, foretells his glorious reign, and as he sinks (leaden dullness cannot soar),
leaves his mantle to fall symbolically on Shadwell's shoulders. The poem abounds
in literary allusions—to Roman legend and history and to the *Aeneid*, to Cowley's
fragmentary epic *The Davideis*, to *Paradise Lost*, and to Shadwell's own plays.
Biblical allusions add an unexpected dimension of incongruous dignity to the low
scene. The coronation takes place in the City, to the plaudits of the citizens, who
are fit to admire only what is dull. In 217 lines, Dryden created an image of
Shadwell that has fixed his reputation to this day.

Mac Flecknoe

OR A SATIRE UPON THE TRUE-BLUE-PROTESTANT POET, T. S.

        All human things are subject to decay,
        And when fate summons, monarchs must obey.
        This Flecknoe found, who, like Augustus,[1] young
        Was called to empire, and had governed long;
        In prose and verse, was owned, without dispute,   5
        Through all the realms of Nonsense, absolute.

---

1. In 31 B.C. Octavian became the first Roman emperor at the age of thirty-two. He assumed the title Augustus in
27 B.C.

This aged prince, now flourishing in peace,
And blest with issue of a large increase,
Worn out with business, did at length debate
To settle the succession of the state;   10
And, pondering which of all his sons was fit
To reign, and wage immortal war with wit,
Cried: " 'Tis resolved; for nature pleads that he
Should only rule, who most resembles me.
Sh——[2] alone my perfect image bears,   15
Mature in dullness from his tender years:
Sh—— alone, of all my sons, is he
Who stands confirmed in full stupidity.
The rest to some faint meaning make pretense,
But Sh—— never deviates into sense.   20
Some beams of wit on other souls may fall,
Strike through, and make a lucid interval;
But Sh——'s genuine night admits no ray,
His rising fogs prevail upon the day.
Besides, his goodly fabric[3] fills the eye,   25
And seems designed for thoughtless majesty:
Thoughtless as monarch oaks that shade the plain,
And, spread in solemn state, supinely reign.
Heywood and Shirley were but types of thee,[4]
Thou last great prophet of tautology.[5]   30
Even I, a dunce of more renown than they,
Was sent before but to prepare thy way;
And, coarsely clad in Norwich drugget,[6] came
To teach the nations in thy greater name.[7]
My warbling lute, the lute I whilom strung,   35
When to King John of Portugal I sung,[8]
Was but the prelude to that glorious day,
When thou on silver Thames didst cut thy way,
With well-timed oars before the royal barge,
Swelled with the pride of thy celestial charge;   40
And big with hymn, commander of a host,
The like was ne'er in Epsom blankets tossed.[9]
Methinks I see the new Arion[1] sail,
The lute still trembling underneath thy nail.
At thy well-sharpened thumb from shore to shore   45

2. Thomas Shadwell. The initial and second letter of
the name followed by a dash give the appearance, but
only the appearance, of protecting Dryden's victim by
concealing his name. A common device in the satire
of the period.
3. His body. Shadwell was a corpulent man.
4. Thomas Heywood (ca. 1570–1641) and James Shirley (1596–1666), playwrights popular before the closing of the theaters in 1642 but now out of fashion.
They are introduced here as "types" (i.e., prefigurings)
of Shadwell, in the sense that Solomon was regarded
as an Old Testament prefiguring of Christ, the "last
[final] great prophet."
5. Unnecessary repetition of meaning in different
words.

6. A coarse woolen cloth. Flecknoe was a Catholic
priest.
7. The parallel between Flecknoe, as forerunner of
Shadwell, and John the Baptist, as forerunner of Jesus,
is made plain in lines 32–34 by the use of details and
even words taken from Matthew 3.3–4 and John 1.23.
8. Flecknoe boasted of the patronage of the Portuguese king. "Whilom": formerly.
9. A reference to Shadwell's comedy Epsom Wells and
to the farcical scene in his Virtuoso, in which Sir Samuel Hearty is tossed in a blanket.
1. A legendary Greek poet. Returning home by sea, he
was robbed and thrown overboard by the sailors, but
was saved by a dolphin that had been charmed by his
music.

The treble squeaks for fear, the basses roar;
Echoes from Pissing Alley Sh—— call,
And Sh—— they resound from Aston Hall.
About thy boat the little fishes throng,
As at the morning toast[2] that floats along.   50
Sometimes, as prince of thy harmonious band,
Thou wield'st thy papers in thy threshing hand,
St. André's feet ne'er kept more equal time,
Not ev'n the feet of thy own *Psyche's* rhyme;[3]
Though they in number as in sense excel: 55
So just, so like tautology, they fell,
That, pale with envy, Singleton[4] forswore
The lute and sword, which he in triumph bore,
And vowed he ne'er would act Villerius[5] more."
Here stopped the good old sire, and wept for joy   60
In silent raptures of the hopeful boy.
All arguments, but most his plays, persuade,
That for anointed dullness[6] he was made.
      Close to the walls which fair Augusta bind
(The fair Augusta much to fears inclined),[7]   65
An ancient fabric,[8] raised to inform the sight,
There stood of yore, and Barbican it hight:
A watchtower once; but now, so fate ordains,
Of all the pile an empty name remains.
From its old ruins brothel houses rise,   70
Scenes of lewd loves, and of polluted joys,
Where their vast courts the mother-strumpets keep,
And, undisturbed by watch, in silence sleep.
Near these a Nursery[9] erects its head,
Where queens are formed, and future heroes bred;   75
Where unfledged actors learn to laugh and cry,
Where infant punks[1] their tender voices try,
And little Maximins[2] the gods defy.
Great Fletcher never treads in buskins here,
Nor greater Jonson dares in socks[3] appear;   80
But gentle Simkin[4] just reception finds
Amidst this monument of vanished minds:
Pure clinches[5] the suburbian Muse affords,
And Panton[6] waging harmless war with words.
Here Flecknoe, as a place to fame well known,   85
Ambitiously design'd his Sh——'s throne;

2. Sewage.
3. "St. André": a French dancer who designed the choreography of Shadwell's opera *Psyche* (1675). Dryden's sneer at the mechanical metrics of the songs in *Psyche* is justified.
4. John Singleton (d. 1686), a musician at the Theatre Royal.
5. A character in Sir William Davenant's *Siege of Rhodes* (1656), the first English opera.
6. The anticipated phrase is "anointed *majesty*." English kings are anointed with oil at their coronations.
7. This line alludes to the fears excited by the Popish Plot (cf. *Absalom and Achitophel*, p. 846). "Augusta":

London.
8. Building.
9. The name of a training school for young actors.
1. Prostitutes.
2. Maximin is the cruel emperor in Dryden's *Tyrannic Love* (1669), notorious for his bombast.
3. "Buskins" and "socks" were the symbols of tragedy and comedy. John Fletcher (1579–1625), the playwright and collaborator with Francis Beaumont (ca. 1584–1616).
4. A popular character in low farces.
5. Puns.
6. Said to have been a celebrated punster.

For ancient Dekker[7] prophesied long since, ⎤
That in this pile would reign a mighty prince, ⎬
Born for a scourge of wit, and flail of sense; ⎦
To whom true dullness should some *Psyches* owe,   90
But worlds of *Misers* from his pen should flow;
Humorists and *Hypocrites* it should produce,[8]
Whole *Raymond* families, and tribes of *Bruce.*
    Now Empress Fame had published the renown
Of Sh——'s coronation through the town.   95
Roused by report of Fame, the nations meet,
From near Bunhill, and distant Watling Street.[9]
No Persian carpets spread the imperial way,
But scattered limbs of mangled poets lay;
From dusty shops neglected authors come,   100
Martyrs of pies, and relics of the bum.[1]
Much Heywood, Shirley, Ogilby[2] there lay,
But loads of Sh—— almost choked the way.
Bilked stationers for yeomen stood prepared,
And Herringman was captain of the guard.[3]   105
The hoary prince in majesty appeared,
High on a throne of his own labors reared.
At his right hand our young Ascanius sate,
Rome's other hope, and pillar of the state.
His brows thick fogs, instead of glories, grace,   110
And lambent dullness played around his face,[4]
As Hannibal did to the altars come,
Sworn by his sire a mortal foe to Rome,[5]
So Sh—— swore, nor should his vow be vain,
That he till death true dullness would maintain;   115
And, in his father's right, and realm's defense,
Ne'er to have peace with wit, nor truce with sense.
The king himself the sacred unction[6] made,
As king by office, and as priest by trade.
In his siníster hand, instead of ball,   120
He placed a mighty mug of potent ale;
Love's Kingdom to his right he did convey,
At once his scepter, and his rule of sway;
Whose righteous lore the prince had practiced young,
And from whose loins recorded *Psyche* sprung.   125
His temples, last, with poppies were o'erspread,

7. Thomas Dekker (ca. 1572–1632), the playwright, whom Jonson had satirized in *The Poetaster.*
8. Three of Shadwell's plays; *The Hypocrite*, a failure, was not published. Below, "Raymond" and "Bruce" are characters in *The Humorists* and *The Virtuoso*, respectively.
9. Because Bunhill is about a quarter of a mile and Watling Street little more than half a mile from the site of the Nursery, where the coronation is held, Shadwell's fame is narrowly circumscribed. Moreover, his subjects live in the heart of the City, regarded by men of wit and fashion as the abode of bad taste and middle-class vulgarity.
1. Unsold books eventually went to bakers's shops and privies.
2. John Ogilby, a translator of Homer and Virgil, ridiculed by both Dryden and Pope as a bad poet.
3. "Bilked stationers": cheated publishers, who acted as "yeomen" of the guard, led by Henry Herringman, who until 1679 was the publisher of both Shadwell and Dryden.
4. "Ascanius": or Iulus, son of Aeneas. Virgil referred to him as *"spes altera Romae"* ("Rome's other hope," *Aeneid* 12.168). As Troy fell, he was marked as favored by the gods when a flickering ("lambent") flame played round his head (*Aeneid* 2.680–684).
5. Hannibal, who almost conquered Rome in 216 B.C., during the 2nd Punic War, took this oath at the age of nine (Livy 21.1).
6. The sacramental oil, used in the coronation. "Sinís-ter" (line 120): left.

That nodding seemed to consecrate his head.[7]
Just at that point of time, if fame not lie,
On his left hand twelve reverend owls did fly.[8]
So Romulus, 'tis sung, by Tiber's brook,   130
Presage of sway from twice six vultures took.
The admiring throng loud acclamations make,
And omens of his future empire take.
The sire then shook the honors[9] of his head,
And from his brows damps of oblivion shed   135
Full on the filial dullness: long he stood,   ⎫
Repelling from his breast the raging god;   ⎬
At length burst out in this prophetic mood: ⎭
    "Heavens bless my son, from Ireland let him reign
To far Barbadoes on the western main;[1]   140
Of his dominion may no end be known,
And greater than his father's be his throne;
Beyond *Love's Kingdom* let him stretch his pen!"
He paused, and all the people cried, "Amen."
Then thus continued he: "My son, advance   145
Still in new impudence, new ignorance.
Success let others teach, learn thou from me
Pangs without birth, and fruitless industry.
Let *Virtuosos* in five years be writ;
Yet not one thought accuse thy toil of wit.   150
Let gentle George[2] in triumph tread the stage,
Make Dorimant betray, and Loveit rage;
Let Cully, Cockwood, Fopling, charm the pit,
And in their folly show the writer's wit.
Yet still thy fools shall stand in thy defense,   155
And justify their author's want of sense.
Let 'em be all by thy own model made
Of dullness, and desire no foreign aid;
That they to future ages may be known,
Not copies drawn, but issue of thy own.   160
Nay, let thy men of wit too be the same,
All full of thee, and differing but in name.
But let no alien S—dl—y[3] interpose,
To lard with wit[4] thy hungry *Epsom* prose.
And when false flowers of rhetoric thou wouldst cull,   165
Trust nature, do not labor to be dull;
But write thy best, and top; and, in each line,
Sir Formal's[5] oratory will be thine:
Sir Formal, though unsought, attends thy quill,

7. During the coronation a British monarch holds two
symbols of the throne: a globe ("ball") representing the
world in the left hand and a scepter in the right. Shadwell's symbols of monarchy are a mug of ale,
Flecknoe's dreary play *Love's Kingdom*, and a crown of
poppies—which together suggest heaviness, dullness,
and drowsiness. The poppies also refer obliquely to
Shadwell's addiction to opium.
8. Birds of night, appropriate substitutes for the twelve
vultures whose flight confirmed to Romulus the destined site of Rome, of which he was founder and king.
9. Ornaments, hence locks.

1. Shadwell's empire is vast but empty.
2. Sir George Etherege (ca. 1635–1691), a writer of
brilliant comedies. In the next couplet Dryden names
characters from his plays.
3. Sir Charles Sedley (1638–1701), wit, rake, poet,
and playwright. Dryden hints that he contributed more
than the prologue to Shadwell's *Epsom Wells*.
4. This phrase recalls a sentence in Burton's *Anatomy
of Melancholy:* "They lard their lean books with the fat
of others' works."
5. Sir Formal Trifle, the ridiculous and vapid orator
in *The Virtuoso*.

And does thy northern dedications[6] fill.   170
Nor let false friends seduce thy mind to fame,
By arrogating Jonson's hostile name.
Let father Flecknoe fire thy mind with praise,
And uncle Ogilby thy envy raise.
Thou art my blood, where Jonson has no part: 175
What share have we in nature, or in art?
Where did his wit on learning fix a brand,
And rail at arts he did not understand?
Where made he love in Prince Nicander's vein,[7]
Or swept the dust in *Psyche's* humble strain?   180
Where sold he bargains, 'whip-stitch, kiss my arse,'[8]
Promised a play and dwindled to a farce?[9]
When did his Muse from Fletcher scenes purloin,
As thou whole Eth'rege dost transfuse to thine?
But so transfused, as oil on water's flow,   185
His always floats above, thine sinks below.
This is thy province, this thy wondrous way,
New humors to invent for each new play:
This is that boasted bias[1] of thy mind,
By which one way, to dullness, 'tis inclined;   190
Which makes thy writings lean on one side still,
And, in all changes, that way bends thy will.
Nor let thy mountain-belly make pretense
Of likeness; thine's a tympany[2] of sense.
A tun of man in thy large bulk is writ,   195
But sure thou'rt but a kilderkin[3] of wit.
Like mine, thy gentle numbers feebly creep;
Thy tragic Muse gives smiles, thy comic sleep.
With whate'er gall thou sett'st thyself to write,
Thy inoffensive satires never bite.   200
In thy felonious heart though venom lies,
It does but touch thy Irish pen,[4] and dies.
Thy genius calls thee not to purchase fame
In keen iambics,[5] but mild anagram.
Leave writing plays, and choose for thy command   205
Some peaceful province in acrostic land.
There thou may'st wings display and altars raise,
And torture one poor word ten thousand ways.[6]
Or, if thou wouldst thy different talent suit,
Set thy own songs, and sing them to thy lute."   210

6. Shadwell frequently dedicated his works to the duke of Newcastle and members of his family.
7. In *Psyche.*
8. To "sell bargains" is to answer an innocent question with a coarse or indecent phrase as in this line. "Whipstitch" is a nonsense word frequently used by Sir Samuel Hearty in *The Virtuoso.*
9. Low comedy that depends largely on situation rather than wit, consistently condemned by Dryden and other serious playwrights.
1. In bowling, the spin given to the bowl that causes it to swerve. Dryden closely parodies a passage in Shadwell's epilogue to *The Humorists.*
2. A swelling in some part of the body caused by wind.

3. A very small cask. "Tun": a large wine cask.
4. Dryden accuses Flecknoe and his "son" of being Irish. Ireland suggested only poverty, superstition, and barbarity to 17th-century Londoners.
5. Sharp satire.
6. "Wings" and "altars" refer to poems in the shape of these objects as in George Herbert's *Easter Wings* (p. 808) and *The Altar* (p. 807). "Anagram": the transposition of letters in a word so as to make a new one. "Acrostic": a poem in which the first letter of each line, read downward, makes up the name of the person or thing that is the subject of the poem. Dryden is citing instances of triviality and overingenuity in literature.

> He said: but his last words were scarcely heard ⎫
> For Bruce and Longville had a trap prepared, ⎬
> And down they sent the yet declaiming bard.[7] ⎭
> Sinking he left his drugget robe behind,
> Borne upwards by a subterranean wind.   215
> The mantle fell to the young prophet's part,[8]
> With double portion of his father's art.

ca. 1679   1682

To the Memory of Mr. Oldham[1]

Farewell, too little, and too lately known,
Whom I began to think and call my own:
For sure our souls were near allied, and thine
Cast in the same poetic mold with mine.
One common note on either lyre did strike,   5
And knaves and fools[2] we both abhorred alike.
To the same goal did both our studies drive;
The last set out the soonest did arrive.
Thus Nisus fell upon the slippery place,
While his young friend[3] performed and won the race.   10
O early ripe! to thy abundant store
What could advancing age have added more?
It might (what nature never gives the young)
Have taught the numbers[4] of thy native tongue.
But satire needs not those, and wit will shine   15
Through the harsh cadence of a rugged line.[5]
A noble error, and but seldom made,
When poets are by too much force betrayed.
Thy generous fruits, though gathered ere their prime, ⎫
Still showed a quickness;[6] and maturing time   ⎬   20
But mellows what we write to the dull sweets of rhyme. ⎭
Once more, hail and farewell;[7] farewell, thou young,
But ah too short, Marcellus[8] of our tongue;
Thy brows with ivy, and with laurels bound;[9]
But fate and gloomy night encompass thee around.   25

1684

---

7. In *The Virtuoso*, Bruce and Longville play this trick on Sir Formal Trifle while he makes a speech.
8. When the prophet Elijah was carried to heaven in a chariot of fire borne on a whirlwind, his mantle fell on his successor, the younger prophet Elisha (2 Kings 2.8–14). Flecknoe, prophet of dullness, naturally cannot ascend, but must sink.
1. John Oldham (1653–1683), the young poet whose *Satires upon the Jesuits* (1681) won Dryden's admiration. This elegy was published in Oldham's *Remains in Verse and Prose* (1684).
2. The objects of satire.
3. Nisus, on the point of winning a footrace, slipped in a pool of blood. His "young friend" was Euryalus (Virgil, *Aeneid* 5.315–339).
4. Metrics, verse.

5. Dryden repeats the Renaissance idea that the satirist should avoid smoothness and affect rough meters ("harsh cadence").
6. Sharpness of flavor.
7. Dryden echoes the famous words that conclude Catullus's elegy to his brother: "*Atque in perpetuum, frater, ave atque vale*" ("And forever, brother, hail and farewell!").
8. The nephew of Augustus, adopted by him as his successor. After winning military fame as a youth, he died at the age of twenty. Virgil celebrated him in the *Aeneid* 6.854–886. The last line of Dryden's poem is a reminiscence of *Aeneid* 6.866.
9. The poet's wreath (cf. Milton's *Lycidas*, lines 1–2, p. 646).

A Song for St. Cecilia's Day[1]

1

From harmony, from heavenly harmony
   This universal frame began:
   When Nature underneath a heap
     Of jarring atoms lay,
     And could not heave her head,   5
The tuneful voice was heard from high:
     "Arise, ye more than dead."
Then cold, and hot, and moist, and dry,[2]
   In order to their stations leap,
     And Music's power obey.   10
From harmony, from heavenly harmony
   This universal frame began:
     From harmony to harmony
Through all the compass of the notes it ran,
The diapason[3] closing full in man.   15

2

What passion cannot Music raise and quell![4]
   When Jubal struck the corded shell,[5]
   His listening brethren stood around,
   And, wondering, on their faces fell
   To worship that celestial sound.   20
Less than a god they thought there could not dwell
    Within the hollow of that shell
    That spoke so sweetly and so well.
What passion cannot Music raise and quell!

3

   The trumpet's loud clangor   25
    Excites us to arms,
  With shrill notes of anger,
    And mortal alarms.
The double double double beat
   Of the thundering drum   30

1. St. Cecilia, a Roman lady, was an early Christian martyr. She has long been regarded as the patroness of music and the supposed inventor of the organ. Celebrations of her festival day (November 22) in England were usually devoted to music and the praise of music, and from about 1683 to 1703 the "Musical Society" in London annually commemorated it with a religious service and a public concert. This concert always included an ode written and set to music for the occasion, of which the two by Dryden (A Song for St. Cecilia's Day, 1687, and Alexander's Feast, 1697) are the most distinguished. G. B. Draghi, an Italian brought to England by Charles II, set this ode to music, but Handel's fine score, composed in 1739, has completely obscured the original setting. Like the ode to Mrs. Killigrew, this is an irregular ode in the manner of Cowley. In stanzas 3–6, Dryden boldly attempted to suggest in the sounds of his words the characteristic tones of the instruments mentioned.
2. "Nature": Created nature, ordered by the Divine Wisdom out of chaos, which Dryden, adopting the physics of the Greek philosopher Epicurus, describes as composed of the warring and discordant ("jarring") atoms of the four elements: earth, fire, water, and air ("cold," "hot," "moist," and "dry").
3. The entire compass of tones in the scale. Dryden is thinking of the Chain of Being, the ordered creation from inanimate nature up to man, God's latest and final work. The just gradations of notes in a scale are analogous to the equally just gradations in the ascending scale of created beings. Both are the result of harmony.
4. The power of music to describe, evoke, or subdue emotion ("passion") is a frequent theme in 17th-century literature. In stanzas 2–6, the poet considers music as awakening religious awe, warlike courage, sorrow for unrequited love, jealousy and fury, and the impulse to worship God.
5. According to Genesis 4.21, Jubal was the inventor of the lyre and the pipe. Dryden imagines Jubal's lyre to have been made of a tortoise shell ("corded shell").

Cries: "Hark! the foes come;
Charge, charge, 'tis too late to retreat."

4

    The soft complaining flute
    In dying notes discovers
    The woes of hopeless lovers,   35
Whose dirge is whispered by the warbling lute.

5

    Sharp violins[6] proclaim
Their jealous pangs, and desperation,
Fury, frantic indignation,
Depth of pains, and height of passion,   40
    For the fair, disdainful dame.

6

    But O! what art can teach,
    What human voice can reach,
The sacred organ's praise?
    Notes inspiring holy love,   45
Notes that wing their heavenly ways
    To mend the choirs above.

7

Orpheus could lead the savage race;
And trees unrooted left their place,
    Sequacious of[7] the lyre;   50
But bright Cecilia raised the wonder higher:
When to her organ vocal breath was given,
An angel heard, and straight appeared,[8]
    Mistaking earth for heaven.

GRAND CHORUS

    As from the power of sacred lays   55
      The spheres began to move,
    And sung the great Creator's praise[9]
      To all the blest above;
    So, when the last and dreadful hour
    This crumbling pageant[1] *shall devour,*   60
    The trumpet shall be heard on high,
    The dead shall live, the living die,
    And Music shall untune the sky.[2]

1687

---

6. A reference to the bright tone of the modern violin, introduced into England at the Restoration. The tone of the old-fashioned viol is much duller.

7. Following. Orpheus was a legendary poet, son of one of the Muses, who played so wonderfully on the lyre that wild beasts ("the savage race") grew tame and followed him, as did even rocks and trees.

8. According to the legend, it was Cecilia's piety, not her music, that brought an angel to visit her.

9. As it was harmony that ordered the universe, so it was angelic song ("sacred lays") that put the celestial bodies ("spheres") in motion. The harmonious chord that results from the traditional "music of the spheres" is a hymn of "praise" sung by created nature to its "Creator."

1. The universe: the stage on which the drama of human salvation has been acted out.

2. The "last trump" of 1 Corinthians 15.52, which will announce the Resurrection and the Last Judgment. Dryden develops his theme of harmony as order in such a way as to give full emphasis of the splendid paradox ("Music shall *untune*") in the final line of the ode.

Epigram on Milton[1]

Three poets,[2] in three distant ages born,
Greece, Italy, and England did adorn.
The first in loftiness of thought surpassed,
The next in majesty, in both the last:
The force of Nature could no farther go;   5
To make a third, she joined the former two.

1688

Criticism   Because Dryden liked to talk about literature, he became a critic, indeed the first comprehensive critic in England. The Elizabethans, largely impelled by the example of Italian humanists, had produced an interesting and unsystematic body of critical writings. Dryden could look back to such pioneer works as George Puttenham's *Art of English Poesy* (1589), Sir Philip Sidney's *Defence of Poesy* (1595), Samuel Daniel's *Defense of Rhyme* (ca. 1603), and Ben Jonson's *Timber, or Discoveries* (1641). These and later writings Dryden knew, as he knew the ancients and the important contemporary French critics, notably Pierre Corneille, Fr. René Rapin, and Nicolas Boileau. Taken as a whole, his critical prefaces and dedications, which appeared between 1664 and 1700, are the work of a man of independent mind who has made his own synthesis of critical canons from wide reading, a great deal of thinking, and the constant practice of the art of writing. As a critic he is no one's disciple, and he has the saving grace of being always willing to change his mind.

All but a very few of Dryden's critical works (most notably *An Essay of Dramatic Poesy*) grew out of the works to which they served as prefaces: comedies, heroic plays, tragedies, translations, and poems of various sorts. Each work posed problems that Dryden was eager to discuss with his readers, and the topics that he treated proved to be important in the development of the new literature of which he was the principal apologist. He dealt with the processes of literary creation, the poet's relation to tradition, the forms of modern drama, the craft of poetry, and above all the genius of earlier poets: Shakespeare, Jonson, Chaucer, Juvenal, Horace, Homer, and Virgil. For nearly forty years this voice was heard in the land, and when it was finally silenced, a set of critical standards had come into existence and a new age had been given its direction.

From An Essay of Dramatic Poesy[1]

[*Shakespeare and Ben Jonson Compared*]

"To begin, then, with Shakespeare. He was the man who of all modern, and perhaps ancient poets, had the largest and most comprehensive soul. All

1. Engraved beneath the portrait of Milton in Jacob Tonson's edition of *Paradise Lost* (1688).
2. I.e., Homer, Virgil, and Milton.
1. With the reopening of the theaters in 1660, older plays were revived, but despite their power and charm, they seemed old-fashioned. Although new playwrights, ambitious to create a modern English drama, soon appeared, they were uncertain of their direction. What, if anything, useful could they learn from the dramatic

practice of the ancients? Should they ignore the English dramatists of the late 16th and early 17th centuries? Should they make their example the vigorous contemporary drama of France? Dryden addresses himself to these and other problems in this essay, his first extended piece of criticism. Its purpose, he tells us, was "chiefly to vindicate the honor of our English writers from the censure of those who unjustly prefer the French before them." Its method is skeptical: Dry-

the images of Nature were still present to him, and he drew them, not laboriously, but luckily; when he describes anything, you more than see it, you feel
it too. Those who accuse him to have wanted learning, give him the greater
commendation: he was naturally learned; he needed not the spectacles of
books to read Nature; he looked inwards, and found her there. I cannot say he
is everywhere alike; were he so, I should do him injury to compare him with
the greatest of mankind. He is many times flat, insipid; his comic wit degenerating into clenches, his serious swelling into bombast. But he is always great
when some great occasion is presented to him; no man can say he ever had a
fit subject for his wit and did not then raise himself as high above the rest of
poets,

Quantum lenta solent inter viburna cupressi[2]

The consideration of this made Mr. Hales of Eton[3] say that there was no
subject of which any poet ever writ, but he would produce it much better
treated of in Shakespeare; and however others are now generally preferred
before him, yet the age wherein he lived, which had contemporaries with him
Fletcher and Jonson, never equaled them to him in their esteem: and in the
last king's[4] court, when Ben's reputation was at highest, Sir John Suckling,[5]
and with him the greater part of the courtiers, set our Shakespeare far above
him. . . .

   "As for Jonson, to whose character I am now arrived, if we look upon him
while he was himself (for his last plays were but his dotages), I think him the
most learned and judicious writer which any theater ever had. He was a most
severe judge of himself, as well as others. One cannot say he wanted wit, but
rather that he was frugal of it. In his works you find little to retrench[6] or alter.
Wit, and language, and humor also in some measure, we had before him; but
something of art[7] was wanting to the drama till he came. He managed his
strength to more advantage than any who preceded him. You seldom find him
making love in any of his scenes or endeavoring to move the passions; his
genius was too sullen and saturnine[8] to do it gracefully, especially when he
knew he came after those who had performed both to such an height. Humor
was his proper sphere:[9] and in that he delighted most to represent mechanic
people.[1] He was deeply conversant in the ancients, both Greek and Latin, and
he borrowed boldly from them: there is scarce a poet or historian among the
Roman authors of those times whom he has not translated in *Sejanus* and
Catiline.[2] But he has done his robberies so openly, that one may see he fears

den presents several points of view, but imposes none.
The form is a dialogue among friends, like the *Tusculan Disputations* or the *Brutus* of Cicero. Crites praises
the drama of the ancients; Eugenius protests against
their authority and argues for the idea of progress in
the arts; Lisideius urges the excellence of French plays;
and Neander, speaking in the climactic position, defends the native tradition and the greatness of Shakespeare, Fletcher, and Jonson. The dialogue takes place
on June 3, 1665, in a boat on the Thames. The four
friends are rowed downstream to listen to the cannon-
ading of the English and Dutch fleets, engaged in battle off the Suffolk coast. As the gunfire recedes they are
assured of victory and order their boatman to return to
London, and naturally enough they fall to discussing
the number of bad poems that the victory will evoke.
2. "As do cypresses among the bending shrubs" (Vir-

gil, *Eclogues* 1.25).
3. The learned John Hales (1584–1656), provost of
Eton. He is reputed to have said this to Jonson himself.
4. Charles I.
5. Courtier, poet, playwright, much admired in Dryden's time for his wit and the easy naturalness of his
style.
6. Delete.
7. Craftsmanship.
8. Heavy.
9. In Jonson's comedies the characters are seen under
the domination of some psychological trait, ruling passion, or affectation—i.e., some "humor"—which
makes them unique and ridiculous.
1. I.e., artisans.
2. Jonson's two Roman plays, dated 1605 and 1611,
respectively.

not to be taxed by any law. He invades authors like a monarch; and what would be theft in other poets is only victory in him. With the spoils of these writers he so represents old Rome to us, in its rites, ceremonies, and customs, that if one of their poets had written either of his tragedies, we had seen less of it than in him. If there was any fault in his language, 'twas that he weaved it too closely and laboriously, in his serious plays:[3] perhaps, too, he did a little too much Romanize our tongue, leaving the words which he translated almost as much Latin as he found them: wherein, though he learnedly followed the idiom of their language, he did not enough comply with the idiom of ours. If I would compare him with Shakespeare, I must acknowledge him the more correct poet, but Shakespeare the greater wit.[4] Shakespeare was the Homer, or father of our dramatic poets; Jonson was the Virgil, the pattern of elaborate writing; I admire him, but I love Shakespeare. To conclude of him; as he has given us the most correct plays, so in the precepts which he has laid down in his *Discoveries,* we have as many and profitable rules for perfecting the stage, as any wherewith the French can furnish us."

1668

From A Discourse Concerning the Original and Progress of Satire[1]

[*The Art of Satire*]

* * * How easy is it to call rogue and villain, and that wittily! But how hard to make a man appear a fool, a blockhead, or a knave without using any of those opprobrious terms! To spare the grossness of the names, and to do the thing yet more severely, is to draw a full face, and to make the nose and cheeks stand out, and yet not to employ any depth of shadowing.[2] This is the mystery of that noble trade, which yet no master can teach to his apprentice; he may give the rules, but the scholar is never the nearer in his practice. Neither is it true that this fineness of raillery[3] is offensive. A witty man is tickled while he is hurt in this manner, and a fool feels it not. The occasion of an offense may possibly be given, but he cannot take it. If it be granted that in effect this way does more mischief; that a man is secretly wounded, and though he be not sensible himself, yet the malicious world will find it out for him; yet there is still a vast difference betwixt the slovenly butchering of a man, and the fineness of a stroke that separates the head from the body, and leaves it standing in its place. A man may be capable, as Jack Ketch's[4] wife said of his servant,

3. This is the reading of the first edition. Curiously enough, in the second edition Dryden altered the phrase to "in his comedies especially."
4. Genius.
1. This passage is an excerpt from the long and rambling preface that served as the dedication of a translation of the satires of the Roman satirists Juvenal and Persius to Charles Sackville, sixth earl of Dorset. The translations were made by Dryden and other writers, among them William Congreve. Dryden traces the origin and development of verse satire in Rome and in a very fine passage contrasts Horace and Juvenal as satiric poets. It is plain that he prefers the "tragic" satire

of Juvenal to the urbane and laughing satire of Horace. But in the passage printed here, he praises his own satiric character of Zimri (the duke of Buckingham) in *Absalom and Achitophel* for the very reason that it is modeled on Horatian "raillery," not Juvenalian invective.
2. Early English miniaturists prided themselves on the art of giving roundness to the full face without painting in shadows.
3. Satirical mirth, good-natured satire.
4. A notorious public executioner of Dryden's time (d. 1686). His name later became a generic term for all members of his profession.

of a plain piece of work, a bare hanging; but to make a malefactor die sweetly was only belonging to her husband. I wish I could apply it to myself, if the reader would be kind enough to think it belongs to me. The character of Zimri in my *Absalom*[5] is, in my opinion, worth the whole poem: it is not bloody, but it is ridiculous enough; and he, for whom it was intended, was too witty to resent it as an injury. If I had railed,[6] I might have suffered for it justly; but I managed my own work more happily, perhaps more dexterously. I avoided the mention of great crimes, and applied myself to the representing of blindsides, and little extravagancies; to which, the wittier a man is, he is generally the more obnoxious.[7] It succeeded as I wished; the jest went round, and he was laughed at in his turn who began the frolic. * * *

1693

From The Preface to *Fables Ancient and Modern*[1]

[*In Praise of Chaucer*]

In the first place, as he is the father of English poetry, I hold him in the same degree of veneration as the Grecians held Homer, or the Romans Virgil. He is a perpetual fountain of good sense; learned in all sciences;[2] and, therefore, speaks properly on all subjects. As he knew what to say, so he knows also when to leave off; a continence which is practiced by few writers, and scarcely by any of the ancients, excepting Virgil and Horace. * * *

Chaucer followed Nature everywhere, but was never so bold to go beyond her; and there is a great difference of being *poeta* and *nimis poeta*,[3] if we may believe Catullus, as much as betwixt a modest behavior and affectation. The verse of Chaucer, I confess, is not harmonious to us; but 'tis like the eloquence of one whom Tacitus commends, it was *auribus istius temporis accommodata:*[4] they who lived with him, and some time after him, thought it musical; and it continues so, even in our judgment, if compared with the numbers of Lydgate and Gower,[5] his contemporaries; there is the rude sweetness of a Scotch tune in it, which is natural and pleasing, though not perfect. 'Tis true I cannot go so far as he who published the last edition of him;[6] for he would make us believe the fault is in our ears, and that there were really ten syllables in a verse where we find but nine; but this opinion is not worth confuting; 'tis so gross and obvious an error that common sense (which is a rule in everything but matters of faith and revelation) must convince the reader that equality of

5. *Absalom and Achitophel*, lines 544–568 (pp. 858–59).
6. Reviled, abused. Observe that the verb differed in meaning from its noun, defined above.
7. Liable.
1. Dryden's final work, published in the year of his death, was a collection of translations from Homer, Ovid, Boccaccio, and Chaucer, and one or two other pieces. The Preface, in many ways, is Dryden's ripest and finest critical essay. In it, he is not concerned with critical theory or with a formalistic approach to literature; he is simply a man, grown old in the reading and writing of poetry, who is eager to talk informally with his readers about some of his favorite authors. His praise of Chaucer (unusually sympathetic and perceptive for 1700) is animated by that love of great literature

that is manifest in everything that Dryden wrote.
2. Branches of learning.
3. A poet (*"poeta"*) and too much of a poet (*"nimis poeta"*). The phrase is not from Catullus but from Martial (*Epigrams* 3.44).
4. "Suitable to the ears of that time." Tacitus was a Roman historian and writer on oratory (A.D. ca. 55–ca. 117).
5. John Gower (d. 1408) was a poet and friend of Chaucer. John Lydgate (ca. 1370–ca. 1449) wrote poetry that shows the influence of Chaucer. "Numbers": versification.
6. Thomas Speght's Chaucer, which Dryden used, was first published in 1598; the second edition, published in 1602, was reprinted in 1687.

numbers in every verse which we call heroic[7] was either not known, or not always practiced in Chaucer's age. It were an easy matter to produce some thousands of his verses which are lame for want of half a foot, and sometimes a whole one, and which no pronunciation can make otherwise. We can only say that he lived in the infancy of our poetry, and that nothing is brought to perfection at the first. * * *

He must have been a man of a most wonderful comprehensive nature, because, as it has been truly observed of him, he has taken into the compass of his *Canterbury Tales* the various manners and humors (as we now call them) of the whole English nation in his age. Not a single character has escaped him. All his pilgrims are severally distinguished from each other; and not only in their inclinations but in their very physiognomies and persons. Baptista Porta[8] could not have described their natures better than by the marks which the poet gives them. The matter and manner of their tales, and of their telling, are so suited to their different educations, humors, and callings that each of them would be improper in any other mouth. Even the grave and serious characters are distinguished by their several sorts of gravity: their discourses are such as belong to their age, their calling, and their breeding; such as are becoming of them, and of them only. Some of his persons are vicious, and some virtuous; some are unlearned, or (as Chaucer calls them) lewd, and some are learned. Even the ribaldry of the low characters is different: the Reeve, the Miller, and the Cook are several[9] men, and distinguished from each other as much as the mincing Lady Prioress and the broad-speaking, gaptoothed Wife of Bath. But enough of this; there is such a variety of game springing up before me that I am distracted in my choice, and know not which to follow. 'Tis sufficient to say, according to the proverb, that here is God's plenty. * * *

                                                                              1700

---

7. The pentameter line. In Dryden's time few readers knew how to pronounce Middle English, especially the syllabic *e*. Moreover, Chaucer's works were known only in corrupt printed texts. As a consequence Chau-

cer's verse seemed rough and irregular.
8. Giambattista della Porta (ca. 1535–1615), author of a Latin treatise on physiognomy.
9. Different.

JONATHAN SWIFT
1667–1745

1704:   *A Tale of a Tub* and *The Battle of the Books*.
1710–14:   Alignment with Tories; political writings in defense of the Tory ministry.
1713:   Made dean of St. Patrick's Cathedral, Dublin.
1726:   Publication of *Gulliver's Travels*.

Jonathan Swift—a posthumous child—was born of English parents in Dublin. Through the generosity of an uncle he was educated at Kilkenny School and Trinity College, Dublin, but before he could fix on a career, the troubles that followed upon James II's abdication and his subsequent invasion of Ireland drove him along with other Anglo-Irish to England. Between 1689 and 1699 he was more or less continuously a member of the household of his kinsman Sir William Temple, an urbane, civilized man, a retired diplomat, and a friend of King William. During these years Swift read widely, rather reluctantly decided on the church as a career and so took orders, and discovered his astonishing gifts as a satirist. About 1696–97 he wrote his powerful satires on corruptions in religion and learning, A *Tale of a Tub* and *The Battle of the Books*, which were published in 1704 and reached their final form only in the fifth edition of 1710. These were the years in which he slowly came to maturity. When, at the age of thirty-two, he returned to Ireland as chaplain to the lord justice, the earl of Berkeley, he had a clear sense of his genius.

For the rest of his life, Swift devoted his talents to politics and religion—not clearly separated at the time—and most of his works in prose were written to further a specific cause. As a clergyman, a spirited controversialist, and a devoted supporter of the Anglican church as an institution no less important than the Crown itself, he was hostile to all who seemed to threaten his church—Deists, freethinkers, Roman Catholics, Nonconformists, or merely Whig politicians. In 1710 he abandoned his old party, the Whig, because he disapproved of its indifference to the welfare of the Anglican church in Ireland and of its desire to repeal the Test Act, which required all holders of offices of state to take the Sacrament according to the Anglican rites, thus excluding Roman Catholics and Dissenters. Welcomed by the Tories, he became the most brilliant political journalist of the day, serving the government of Oxford and Bolingbroke as editor of the party organ, the *Examiner*, and as author of its most powerful articles, as well as writing longer pamphlets in support of important policies, such as that favoring the Peace of Utrecht (1713). He was greatly valued by the two ministers, who admitted him to social intimacy, though never to their counsels. The reward of his services was not the English bishopric that he had a right to expect, but the deanship of St. Patrick's Cathedral in Dublin, which came to him in 1713, a year before the death of Queen Anne and the fall of the Tories put an end to all his hopes of preferment in England.

In Ireland, where he lived unwillingly, he became not only an efficient ecclesiastical administrator but also, in 1724, the leader of Irish resistance to English oppression. Under the pseudonym "M. B. Drapier," he published the famous series of public letters that aroused the country to refuse to accept £100,000 in new copper coins (minted in England by William Wood, who had obtained his patent through court corruption), which, it was feared, would further debase the coinage of the already poverty-stricken kingdom. Although his authorship of the letters was known to all Dublin, no one could be found to earn the £300 offered by the government for information as to the identity of the drapier. Swift is still venerated in Ireland as a national hero. He earned the right to refer to himself in the epitaph that he wrote for his tomb as a vigorous defender of liberty.

His last years were less happy. Swift had suffered most of his adult life from what we now recognize as Ménière's disease, which affects the inner ear, causing dizziness, nausea, and deafness. After 1739, when he was seventy-two years old, his infirmities cut him off from his duties as dean, and from then on his social life dwindled. In 1742 guardians were appointed to administer his affairs, and his last three years were spent in gloom and lethargy. But this dark ending should not put his earlier life, so full of energy and humor, into a shadow. The writer of the satires was a man in full control of great intellectual powers.

He also had a gift for friendship. Swift was admired and loved by many of the distinguished men of his time. His friendships with Joseph Addison, Alexander Pope, John Arbuthnot, John Gay, Matthew Prior, Lord Oxford, and Lord Bolingbroke, not to mention those in his less brilliant but amiable Irish circle, bear witness to his moral integrity and social charm. Nor was he, despite some of his writings, indifferent to women. Esther Johnson (Swift's "Stella") was the daughter of Temple's steward, and when Swift first knew her, she was little more than a child. He educated her, formed her character, and came to love her as he was to love no other person. After Temple's death she moved to Dublin, where she and Swift met constantly, but never alone. To her he wrote the famous journal letters, later published (1766) as *The Journal to Stella*, during his four-year residence in London when he was working with the Tories, and to her he wrote charming poems. Whether they were secretly married or whether they never married—and in either case why—has been often debated. A marriage of any sort seems most unlikely, and however perplexing their relationship was to others, it was obviously satisfying to each of them. Not even the violent passion that Swift awakened, no doubt unwittingly, in the much younger woman Hester Vanhomrigh (pronounced Van-úm-mer-y)—with her pleadings and reproaches and early death—could unsettle his devotion to Stella. An enigmatic account of his relations with "Vanessa," as he called Vanhomrigh, is given in his poem *Cadenus and Vanessa*.

For all his involvement in public affairs, Swift seems to stand apart from his contemporaries—a striking figure even among the statesmen of the time, a man who towered above other writers by reason of his imagination, mordant wit, and emotional intensity. He has been called a misanthrope, a hater of humanity, and *Gulliver's Travels* has been considered an expression of savage misanthropy. It is true that Swift proclaimed himself a misanthrope in a letter to Pope, declaring that though he loved individuals, he hated "that animal called man" in general and offering a new definition of the species as not *animal rationale* ("a rational animal") but as merely *animal rationis capax* ("an animal *capable* of reason"). This, he declared, is the "great foundation" on which his "misanthropy" was erected. Swift was stating not his hatred of his fellow creatures but his antagonism to the current optimistic view that human nature is essentially good. To the "philanthropic" flattery that sentimentalism and Deistic rationalism were paying to human nature, Swift opposed a more ancient and plausible view: that human nature is deeply and permanently flawed and that we can do nothing with or for the human race until we recognize its moral and intellectual limitations. In his epitaph he spoke of the "fierce indignation" that had torn his heart, an indignation that found superb expression in his greatest satires. It was provoked by the constant spectacle of creatures capable of reason, and therefore of reasonable conduct, steadfastly refusing to live up to their capabilities.

Swift is one of our greatest writers of prose. He defined a good style as "proper words in proper places," a more complex and difficult saying than at first appears. Clear, simple, concrete diction, uncomplicated syntax, economy and conciseness of language mark all of his writings. His is a style that shuns ornaments and singularity of all kinds, a style that grows more tense and controlled the more fierce the indignation that it is called on to express. The virtues of his prose are those of his poetry, which shocks us with its hard look at the facts of life and the body. It is unpoetic poetry, devoid of, indeed as often as not mocking at, inspiration, romantic love, cosmetic beauty, easily assumed literary attitudes, and conventional poetic language. Like the prose, it is predominantly satiric in purpose, but not without its moments of comedy and light-heartedness, though written most often not so much to divert as to reform the reader.

A Description of a City Shower

Careful observers may foretell the hour
(By sure prognostics) when to dread a shower:
While rain depends,[1] the pensive cat gives o'er

1. Impends, is imminent. An example of elevated diction used frequently throughout the poem to gain a mock dignity, comically inappropriate to the homely and realistic subject.

Her frolics, and pursues her tail no more.
Returning home at night, you'll find the sink[2]   5
Strike your offended sense with double stink.
If you be wise, then go not far to dine;
You'll spend in coach hire more than save in wine.
A coming shower your shooting corns presage,
Old achés throb, your hollow tooth will rage.   10
Sauntering in coffeehouse is Dulman seen;
He damns the climate and complains of spleen.[3]
      Meanwhile the South, rising with dabbled wings,
A sable cloud athwart the welkin flings,
That swilled more liquor than it could contain,   15
And, like a drunkard, gives it up again.
Brisk Susan whips her linen from the rope,
While the first drizzling shower is borne aslope:
Such is that sprinkling which some careless quean[4]
Flirts on you from her mop, but not so clean: 20
You fly, invoke the gods; then turning, stop
To rail; she singing, still whirls on her mop.
Not yet the dust had shunned the unequal strife,
But, aided by the wind, fought still for life,
And wafted with its foe by violent gust,   25
'Twas doubtful which was rain and which was dust.
Ah! where must needy poet seek for aid,
When dust and rain at once his coat invade?
Sole coat, where dust cemented by the rain
Erects the nap, and leaves a mingled stain.   30
      Now in contiguous drops the flood comes down,
Threatening with deluge this devoted town.
To shops in crowds the daggled females fly,
Pretend to cheapen[5] goods, but nothing buy.
The Templar spruce, while every spout's abroach,[6]   35
Stays till 'tis fair, yet seems to call a coach.
The tucked-up sempstress walks with hasty strides,
While streams run down her oiled umbrella's sides.
Here various kinds, by various fortunes led,
Commence acquaintance underneath a shed.   40
Triumphant Tories and desponding Whigs
Forget their feuds,[7] and join to save their wigs.
Boxed in a chair[8] the beau impatient sits,
While spouts run clattering o'er the roof by fits,
And ever and anon with frightful din   45
The leather sounds;[9] he trembles from within.
So when Troy chairmen bore the wooden steed,

2. Sewer.
3. It was commonly believed at this time that the English-man's tendency to melancholy ("the spleen") was attributable to the rainy climate. "Dulman": a type name (from "dull man"), like Congreve's "Petulant" or "Witwoud".
4. Wench, slut.
5. Bargain for. "Daggled": spattered with mud.
6. Pouring out water. "The Templar": a young man engaged in studying law. In the literature of the period the Templar is usually depicted as neglecting his professional studies for the sake of dissipation and the pursuit of literature.
7. The Whig ministry had just fallen and the Tories, led by Harley and St. John, were forming the government with which Swift was to be closely associated until the death of the queen in 1714.
8. Sedan chair.
9. The roof of the sedan chair was made of leather.

Pregnant with Greeks impatient to be freed
(Those bully Greeks, who, as the moderns do,
Instead of paying chairmen, run them through),[1]   50
Laocoön struck the outside with his spear,
And each imprisoned hero quaked for fear.[2]
    Now from all parts the swelling kennels[3] flow,
And bear their trophies with them as they go:
Filth of all hues and odors seem to tell   55
What street they sailed from, by their sight and smell.
They, as each torrent drives with rapid force,
From Smithfield or St. Pulchre's shape their course,
And in huge confluence joined at Snow Hill ridge,
Fall from the conduit prone to Holborn Bridge.[4]   60
Sweepings from butchers' stalls, dung, guts, and blood,   ⎫
Drowned puppies, stinking sprats,[5] all drenched in mud, ⎬
Dead cats, and turnip tops, come tumbling down the flood.[6] ⎭

                           1710

Verses on the Death of Dr. Swift

Occasioned by Reading a Maxim in Rochefoucauld[1]

*Dans l'adversité de nos meilleurs amis nous trouvons toujours quelque chose,
qui ne nous déplaît pas.*[2]

    As Rochefoucauld his maxims drew
From nature, I believe 'em true:
They argue no corrupted mind
In him; the fault is in mankind.
    This maxim more than all the rest   5
Is thought too base for human breast:
"In all distresses of our friends
We first consult our private ends,
While Nature, kindly bent to ease us,
Points out some circumstance to please us."   10
    If this perhaps your patience move,[3]
Let reason and experience prove.
    We all behold with envious eyes
Our equal raised above our size.
Who would not at a crowded show   15

---

1. Run them through with their swords. The bully, always prone to violence, was a familiar figure in London streets and places of amusement.
2. *Aeneid* 2.40–53.
3. The open gutters in the middle of the street.
4. An accurate description of the drainage system of this part of London—the eastern edge of Holborn and West Smithfield, which lie outside the old walls west and east of Newgate. The great cattle and sheep markets were in Smithfield. The church of St. Sepulchre ("St. Pulchre's") stood opposite Newgate Prison. Holborn Conduit was at the foot of Snow Hill. It drained into Fleet Ditch, an evil-smelling open sewer, at Holborn Bridge.
5. Small herrings.

6. In Falkner's edition of Swift's *Works* (Dublin, 1735) a note almost certainly suggested by Swift points to the concluding triplet, with its resonant final alexandrine, as a burlesque of a mannerism of Dryden and other Restoration poets and claims that Swift's ridicule banished the triplet from contemporary poetry.
1. François de la Rochefoucauld (1613–1680), writer of witty, cynical maxims. Writing to Pope (November 26, 1725), Swift, opposing the optimistic philosophy that Pope and Bolingbroke were at that time developing, professed to have founded his whole character on these maxims.
2. "In the misfortune of our best friends we always find something that does not displease us."
3. Should agitate.

Stand high himself, keep others low?
I love my friend as well as you,
But why should he obstruct my view?
Then let me have the higher post;
I ask but for an inch at most.   20
    If in a battle you should find
One, whom you love of all mankind,
Had some heroic action done,
A champion killed, or trophy won;
Rather than thus be overtopped,   25
Would you not wish his laurels cropped?
    Dear honest Ned is in the gout,
Lies racked with pain, and you without:
How patiently you hear him groan!
How glad the case is not your own!   30
    What poet would not grieve to see
His brethren write as well as he?
But rather than they should excel,
He'd wish his rivals all in hell.
    Her end when Emulation misses,   35
She turns to envy, stings, and hisses:
The strongest friendship yields to pride,
Unless the odds be on our side.
    Vain humankind! fantastic race!
Thy various follies who can trace?   40
Self-love, ambition, envy, pride,
Their empire in our hearts divide.
Give others riches, power, and station;
'Tis all on me an usurpation;
I have no title to aspire,   45
Yet, when you sink, I seem the higher.
In Pope I cannot read a line,
But with a sigh I wish it mine:
When he can in one couplet fix
More sense than I can do in six,   50
It gives me such a jealous fit,
I cry, "Pox take him and his wit!"
    I grieve to be outdone by Gay
In my own humorous biting way.
Arbuthnot[4] is no more my friend,   55
Who dares to irony pretend,
Which I was born to introduce,
Refined it first, and showed its use.
St. John, as well as Pulteney,[5] knows
That I had some repute for prose;   60

4. Gay, author of the famous *Beggar's Opera* (1728), intimate friend of Swift and Pope. His *Trivia, or the Art of Walking the Streets of London* (1716) owes something to Swift's *City Shower*. Arbuthnot, physician and wit, friend of Swift and Pope (see Pope's *Epistle to Dr. Arbuthnot*, pp. 1111–22).
5. Henry St. John, Lord Bolingbroke (see headnote "An Essay on Man," p. 1096), though debarred from the House of Lords and from public office, had become the center of a group of Tories and discontented young Whigs (of whom William Pulteney was one) who united in opposing Sir Robert Walpole, the chief minister. They published a political periodical, the *Craftsman*, thus rivaling Swift in his role of political pamphleteer and enemy of Sir Robert.

And, till they drove me out of date,
Could maul a minister of state.
If they have mortified my pride,
And made me throw my pen aside;
If with such talents Heaven hath blessed 'em,   65
Have I not reason to detest 'em?
    To all my foes, dear Fortune, send
Thy gifts, but never to my friend:
I tamely can endure the first,
But this with envy makes me burst.   70
    Thus much may serve by way of proem;
Proceed we therefore to our poem.
    The time is not remote, when I
Must by the course of nature die;
When, I foresee, my special friends   75
Will try to find their private ends:
Though it is hardly understood
Which way my death can do them good;
Yet thus, methinks, I hear 'em speak:
"See how the Dean begins to break!   80
Poor gentleman! he droops apace!
You plainly find it in his face.
That old vertigo[6] in his head
Will never leave him till he's dead.
Besides, his memory decays;   85
He recollects not what he says;
He cannot call his friends to mind;
Forgets the place where last he dined;
Plies you with stories o'er and o'er;
He told them fifty times before.   90
How does he fancy we can sit
To hear his out-of-fashion'd wit?
But he takes up with younger folks,
Who for his wine will bear his jokes.
Faith, he must make his stories shorter,   95
Or change his comrades once a quarter;
In half the time, he talks them round;
There must another set be found.
    "For poetry, he's past his prime;
He takes an hour to find a rhyme;   100
His fire is out, his wit decayed,
His fancy sunk, his Muse a jade.[7]
I'd have him throw away his pen—
But there's no talking to some men."
    And then their tenderness appears   105
By adding largely to my years:
"He's older than he would be reckoned,
And well remembers Charles the Second.
He hardly drinks a pint of wine;

---

6. Johnson in his *Dictionary* authorizes Swift's pro-
nounciation: *ver-ti-go.*
7. A worn-out horse, in contrast to Pegasus, the winged
horse of Greek mythology, emblem of poetic inspiration.

And that, I doubt, is no good sign.   110
His stomach, too, begins to fail;
Last year we thought him strong and hale;
But now he's quite another thing;
I wish he may hold out till spring."
Then hug themselves, and reason thus: 115
"It is not yet so bad with us."
    In such a case they talk in tropes,[8]
And by their fears express their hopes.
Some great misfortune to portend
No enemy can match a friend.   120
With all the kindness they profess,
The merit of a lucky guess
(When daily how-d'ye's come of course,
And servants answer, "Worse and worse!")
Would please 'em better, than to tell   125
That God be praised! the Dean is well.
Then he who prophesied the best,
Approves his foresight to the rest:
"You know I always feared the worst,
And often told you so at first."   130
He'd rather choose that I should die,
Than his prediction prove a lie.
Not one foretells I shall recover,
But all agree to give me over.
    Yet, should some neighbor feel a pain   135
Just in the parts where I complain,
How many a message would he send?
What hearty prayers that I should mend?
Inquire what regimen I kept;
What gave me ease, and how I slept,   140
And more lament, when I was dead,
Than all the snivelers round my bed.
    My good companions, never fear;
For though you may mistake a year,
Though your prognostics run too fast,   145
They must be verified at last.
    Behold the fatal day arrive!
"How is the Dean?"—"He's just alive."
Now the departing prayer is read.
"He hardly breathes"—"The Dean is dead."   150
Before the passing bell begun,
The news through half the town has run.
"Oh! may we all for death prepare!
What has he left? and who's his heir?"
"I know no more than what the news is;   155
'Tis all bequeathed to public uses."
"To public use! a perfect whim!
What had the public done for him?
Mere envy, avarice, and pride:
He gave it all—but first he died.   160

8. Figures of speech.

And had the Dean in all the nation
No worthy friend, no poor relation?
So ready to do strangers good,
Forgetting his own flesh and blood?"
Now Grub Street[9] wits are all employed;   165
With elegies the town is cloyed;
Some paragraph in every paper
To curse the Dean, or bless the Drapier.[1]
   The doctors, tender of their fame,
Wisely on me lay all the blame.   170
"We must confess his case was nice;[2]
But he would never take advice.
Had he been ruled, for aught appears,
He might have lived these twenty years:
For, when we opened him, we found,   175
That all his vital parts were sound."
   From Dublin soon to London spread,
'Tis told at court, "The Dean is dead."
Kind Lady Suffolk, in the spleen,[3]
Runs laughing up to tell the Queen.   180
The Queen, so gracious, mild and good,
Cries, "Is he gone? 'tis time he should.
He's dead, you say; why, let him rot:
I'm glad the medals were forgot.[4]
I promised him, I own; but when?   185
I only was the Princess then;
But now, as consort of the King,
You know, 'tis quite a different thing."
   Now Chartres, at Sir Robert's[5] levee,
Tells with a sneer the tidings heavy: 190
"Why, is he dead without his shoes?"
Cries Bob, "I'm sorry for the news:
Oh, were the wretch but living still,
And in his place my good friend Will![6]
Or had a miter on his head,   195
Provided Bolingbroke were dead!"
   Now Curll his shop from rubbish drains:[7]
Three genuine tomes of Swift's remains.
And then, to make them pass the glibber,
Revised by Tibbalds, Moore, and Cibber.[8]   200

---

9. Originally a street in London largely inhabited by hack writers; later, a generic term applied to all such writers.
1. It was in the character of M. B., a Dublin drapier, that Swift aroused the Irish people to resistance against the importation of Wood's halfpence (see headnote "Jonathan Swift," p. 882).
2. Delicate; hence demanding careful diagnosis and treatment.
3. In low spirits. The phrase is ironic, as "laughing" makes clear. "Lady Suffolk": George II's mistress, with whom Swift became friendly during his visit to Pope in 1726.
4. Queen Caroline had promised Swift some medals when she was princess of Wales during the same year.

5. Walpole. Colonel Francis Chartres was a debauchee, often satirized by Pope.
6. William Pulteney (see n. 5, p. 887).
7. Edmund Curll, shrewd and disreputable bookseller, published pirated works, scandalous biographies, and works falsely ascribed to notable writers of the time.
8. Lewis Theobald (1688–1744), Shakespeare scholar and editor, already enthroned as king of the Dunces in Pope's The Dunciad (1728). Like Pope, Swift spells the name phonetically. James Moore-Smyth, poetaster and playwright, an enemy of Pope. Colley Cibber (1671–1757), comic actor, playwright, and supremely untalented poet laureate. He succeeded Theobald as king of the Dunces in the The Dunciad of 1743.

He'll treat me as he does my betters,
Publish my will, my life, my letters;
Revive the libels born to die,
Which Pope must bear, as well as I.
　Here shift the scene, to represent 205
How those I love, my death lament.
Poor Pope will grieve a month, and Gay
A week, and Arbuthnot a day.
　St. John himself will scarce forbear
To bite his pen, and drop a tear. 210
The rest will give a shrug, and cry,
"I'm sorry—but we all must die."
　Indifference clad in wisdom's guise
All fortitude of mind supplies:
For how can stony bowels melt 215
In those who never pity felt?
When *we* are lashed, *they* kiss the rod,
Resigning to the will of God.
　The fools, my juniors by a year,
Are tortured with suspense and fear; 220
Who wisely thought my age a screen,
When death approached, to stand between:
The screen removed, their hearts are trembling;
They mourn for me without dissembling.
　My female friends, whose tender hearts 225
Have better learned to act their parts,
Receive the news in doleful dumps:
"The Dean is dead (and what is trumps?)
Then, Lord have mercy on his soul!
(Ladies, I'll venture for the vole.)[9] 230
Six deans, they say, must bear the pall.
(I wish I knew what king to call.)
Madam, your husband will attend
The funeral of so good a friend?"
"No, madam, 'tis a shocking sight; 235
And he's engaged tomorrow night:
My Lady Club would take it ill,
If he should fail her at quadrille.
He loved the Dean—(I lead a heart)
But dearest friends, they say, must part. 240
His time was come; he ran his race;
We hope he's in a better place."
　Why do we grieve that friends should die?
No loss more easy to supply.
One year is past; a different scene; 245
No further mention of the Dean,
Who now, alas! no more is missed,
Than if he never did exist.
Where's now this favorite of Apollo?
Departed—and his works must follow, 250

9. The equivalent in the card game quadrille of bidding a grand slam in bridge.

Must undergo the common fate;
His kind of wit is out of date.
   Some country squire to Lintot[1] goes,
Inquires for *Swift* in verse and prose.
Says Lintot, "I have heard the name;   255
He died a year ago."—"The same."
He searches all his shop in vain.
"Sir, you may find them in Duck Lane:[2]
I sent them, with a load of books,
Last Monday to the pastry-cook's.[3]   260
To fancy they could live a year!
I find you're but a stranger here.
The Dean was famous in his time,
And had a kind of knack at rhyme.
His way of writing now is past: 265
The town has got a better taste.
I keep no antiquated stuff;
But spick and span I have enough.
Pray do but give me leave to show 'em:
Here's Colley Cibber's birthday poem.   270
This ode you never yet have seen
By Stephen Duck[4] upon the Queen.
Then here's a letter finely penned.
Against the *Craftsman*[5] and his friend;
It clearly shows that all reflection   275
On ministers is disaffection.
Next, here's Sir Robert's vindication,[6]
And Mr. Henley's last oration.[7]
The hawkers have not got 'em yet:
Your honor please to buy a set?   280
   "Here's Woolston's[8] tracts, the twelfth edition;
'Tis read by every politician:
The country members, when in town,
To all their boroughs send them down;
You never met a thing so smart;   285
The courtiers have them all by heart;
Those maids of honor (who can read)
Are taught to use them for their creed.
The reverend author's good intention
Has been rewarded with a pension.   290
He does an honor to his gown,
By bravely running priestcraft down;
He shows, as sure as God's in Gloucester,[9]
That Jesus was a grand impostor;

1. Bernard Lintot, a bookseller and the publisher of Pope's Homer and some of his early poems.
2. London street where secondhand books and publishers's remainders were sold.
3. To be used as waste paper for lining baking dishes and wrapping parcels.
4. Stephen Duck, "the thresher poet," an agricultural laborer, whose mild poetic gifts brought him to the notice and patronage of Queen Caroline.
5. See n. 5, p. 887.
6. Walpole hires a string of party scribblers who do nothing else but write in his defense [Swift's note].
7. "Orator" John Henley, an Independent preacher, who dazzled unlearned audiences with his oratory and who wrote treatises on elocution.
8. Thomas Woolston (1670–1733), a freethinker, whose Discourses on the Miracles of Our Saviour had recently earned him notoriety.
9. Proverbially, Gloucestershire was full of monks.

That all his miracles were cheats,   295
Performed as jugglers do their feats:
The Church had never such a writer;
A shame he hath not got a miter!"
   Suppose me dead; and then suppose
A club assembled at the Rose;[1]   300
Where, from discourse of this and that,
I grow the subject of their chat:
And while they toss my name about,
With favor some, and some without,
One, quite indifferent in the cause,   305
My character impartial draws:
   "The Dean, if we believe report,
Was never ill received at court.
As for his works in verse and prose,
I own myself no judge of those;   310
Nor can I tell what critics thought 'em:
But this I know, all people bought 'em,
As with a moral view designed
To cure the vices of mankind.
   "His vein, ironically grave,   315
Exposed the fool and lashed the knave;
To steal a hint was never known,
But what he writ was all his own.
   "He never thought an honor done him,
Because a duke was proud to own him;   320
Would rather slip aside and choose
To talk with wits in dirty shoes;
Despised the fools with stars and garters,
So often seen caressing Chartres.
He never courted men in station,   325
Nor persons held in admiration;
Of no man's greatness was afraid,
Because he sought for no man's aid.
Though trusted long in great affairs,
He gave himself no haughty airs;   330
Without regarding private ends,
Spent all his credit for his friends;
And only chose the wise and good;
No flatterers, no allies in blood;
But succored virtue in distress,   335
And seldom failed of good success;
As numbers in their hearts must own,
Who, but for him, had been unknown.
   "With princes kept a due decorum,
But never stood in awe before 'em.   340
He followed David's lesson just;
In princes never put thy trust:[2]
And would you make him truly sour,
Provoke him with a slave in power.

1. A fashionable tavern in Covent Garden.   2. Psalm 146.3.

The Irish senate if you named,   345
With what impatience he declaimed!
Fair Liberty was all his cry,
For her he stood prepared to die;
For her he boldly stood alone;
For her he oft exposed his own.   350
Two kingdoms, just as faction led,
Had set a price upon his head,
But not a traitor could be found,
To sell him for six hundred pound.[3]
    "Had he but spared his tongue and pen,   355
He might have rose like other men;
But power was never in his thought,
And wealth he valued not a groat:
Ingratitude he often found,
And pitied those who meant the wound;   360
But kept the tenor of his mind,
To merit well of human kind:
Nor made a sacrifice of those
Who still were true, to please his foes.
He labored many a fruitless hour,   365
To reconcile his friends in power;
Saw mischief by a faction brewing,
While they pursued each other's ruin.
But, finding vain was all his care,
He left the court in mere despair.[4]   370
    "And, oh! how short are human schemes!
Here ended all our golden dreams.
What St. John's skill in state affairs,
What Ormonde's[5] valor, Oxford's cares,
To save their sinking country lent,   375
Was all destroyed by one event.[6]
Too soon that precious life was ended,
On which alone our weal depended.
When up a dangerous faction starts,[7]
With wrath and vengeance in their hearts;   380
By solemn League and Covenant bound,
To ruin, slaughter, and confound;
To turn religion to a fable,
And make the government a Babel;
Pervert the laws, disgrace the gown,   385
Corrupt the senate, rob the crown;

3. In 1714 the government offered £300 for the discovery of the author of Swift's *Public Spirit of the Whigs*, and in 1724 the Irish government offered a similar amount for the discovery of the author of the fourth of Swift's *Drapier's Letters*.
4. The antagonism between the two chief ministers (his dear friends), Robert Harley, earl of Oxford, and Bolingbroke paralyzed the Tory ministry in the crucial last months of Queen Anne's life and drove Swift to retirement in Ireland, whence he returned in 1714 to make a final effort to heal the breach and save the government. He failed and retired to the country in despair. There he received the news of Anne's death on August 1. The Hanoverian succession brought the Whigs back in triumph, ruined Swift's friends, and brought Swift's public life to a close.
5. James Butler, duke of Ormonde, who succeeded to the command of the English armies on the Continent, when, in 1711, the duke of Marlborough was stripped of his offices by Anne. He went into exile in 1714 and was active in Jacobite intrigue.
6. The death of Queen Anne.
7. Swift's view of the policies of the "dangerous faction" (the Whig party) is hardly impartial. He feared it especially because of its toleration of Dissenters, and so as an enemy of the Church of England.

To sacrifice old England's glory,
And make her infamous in story:
When such a tempest shook the land,
How could unguarded Virtue stand?   390
With horror, grief, despair, the Dean
Beheld the dire destructive scene:
His friends in exile, or the Tower,[8]
Himself within the frown of power,
Pursued by base envenomed pens,   395
Far to the land of slaves and fens;[9]
A servile race in folly nursed,
Who truckle most, when treated worst.
    "By innocence and resolution,
He bore continual persecution;   400
While numbers to preferment rose,
Whose merits were to be his foes;
When even his own familiar friends,
Intent upon their private ends,
Like renegadoes now he feels,   405
Against him lifting up their heels.
    "The Dean did, by his pen, defeat
An infamous destructive cheat;[1]
Taught fools their interest how to know,
And gave them arms to ward the blow.   410
Envy has owned it was his doing,
To save that hapless land from ruin;
While they who at the steerage[2] stood,
And reaped the profit, sought his blood.
    "To save them from their evil fate,   415
In him was held a crime of state.
A wicked monster on the bench,[3]
Whose fury blood could never quench;
As vile and profligate a villain,
As modern Scroggs, or old Tresilian;[4]   420
Who long all justice had discarded,
Nor feared he God, nor man regarded;
Vowed on the Dean his rage to vent,
And make him of his zeal repent:
But Heaven his innocence defends,   425
The grateful people stand his friends;
Not strains of law, nor judge's frown,
Nor topics brought to please the crown,

8. Bolingbroke was in exile; Oxford was sent to the Tower of London by the Whigs.
9. Ireland.
1. The scheme to introduce Wood's copper halfpence into Ireland in 1723–24.
2. Literally the steering of a ship. Here the direction and management of public affairs in Ireland.
3. William Whitshed, lord chief justice of the King's Bench of Ireland. In 1720, when the jury refused to find Swift's anonymous pamphlet *Proposal for the Universal Use of Irish Manufacture* wicked and seditious, Whitshed sent them back nine times, hoping to force

them to another verdict. In 1724 he presided over the trial of Harding, the printer of Swift's fourth *Drapier's Letter*, but again was unable, despite bullying, to force a verdict of guilty.
4. Sir William Scroggs, lord chief justice of England at the time of the Popish Plot, 1678 (see Dryden's *Absalom and Achitophel*, p. 844), was impeached for his misdemeanors in office in 1680. In 1381, Sir Robert Tresilian punished with great severity men who had participated in the Peasants' Revolt; he was impeached and in 1387 was hanged.

Nor witness hired, nor jury picked,
Prevail to bring him in convict.   430
    "In exile, with a steady heart,
He spent his life's declining part;
Where folly, pride, and faction sway,
Remote from St. John, Pope, and Gay.
    "His friendships there, to few confined,   435
Were always of the middling kind;
No fools of rank, a mongrel breed,
Who fain would pass for lords indeed:
Where titles give no right or power,
And peerage is a withered flower;   440
He would have held it a disgrace,
If such a wretch had known his face.
On rural squires, that kingdom's bane,
He vented oft his wrath in vain;
Biennial squires[5] to market brought: 445
Who sell their souls and votes for naught;
The nation stripped, go joyful back,
To rob the church, their tenants rack,
Go snacks with rogues and rapparees;[6]
And keep the peace to pick up fees;   450
In every job to have a share,
A jail or barrack to repair;
And turn the tax for public roads
Commodious to their own abodes.
    "Perhaps I may allow the Dean   455
Had too much satire in his vein;
And seemed determined not to starve it,
Because no age could more deserve it.
Yet malice never was his aim;
He lashed the vice, but spared the name;   460
No individual could resent,
Where thousands equally were meant;
His satire points at no defect,
But what all mortals may correct;
For he abhorred that senseless tribe   465
Who call it humor when they gibe:
He spared a hump, or crooked nose,
Whose owners set not up for beaux.
True genuine dullness moved his pity,
Unless it offered to be witty.   470
Those who their ignorance confessed,
He ne'er offended with a jest;
But laughed to hear an idiot quote
A verse from Horace learned by rote.
    "He knew an hundred pleasant stories,   475
With all the turns of Whigs and Tories:
Was cheerful to his dying day;
And friends would let him have his way.

---

5. Members of the Irish Parliament.   6. Highwaymen.

"He gave the little wealth he had
To build a house for fools and mad;[7]   480
And showed by one satiric touch,
No nation wanted it so much.
That kingdom he hath left his debtor,
I wish it soon may have a better."

1731   1739

From A Tale of a Tub

A Digression Concerning the Original, the Use, and Improvement of Madness in a Commonwealth[1]

Nor shall it any ways detract from the just reputation of this famous sect,[2] that its rise and institution are owing to such an author as I have described Jack to be, a person whose intellectuals were overturned, and his brain shaken out of its natural position; which we commonly suppose to be a distemper, and call by the name of madness or frenzy. For, if we take a survey of the greatest actions that have been performed in the world, under the influence of single men, which are the establishment of new empires by conquest, the advance and progress of new schemes in philosophy, and the contriving, as well as the propagating, of new religions, we shall find the authors of them all to have been persons whose natural reason had admitted great revolutions from their diet, their education, the prevalency of some certain temper, together with the particular influence of air and climate. Besides, there is something individual in human minds, that easily kindles at the accidental approach and collision of certain circumstances, which, though of paltry and mean appearance, do often flame out into the greatest emergencies of life. For great turns are not always given by strong hands, but by lucky adaption, and at proper seasons; and it is of no import where the fire was kindled, if the vapor has once got up into the brain. For the upper region of man is furnished like the middle region of the air; the materials are formed from causes of the widest difference, yet produce at last the same substance and effect. Mists arise from the earth, steams from dunghills, exhalations from the sea, and smoke from fire; yet all clouds are the same in composition as well as consequences, and the fumes issuing from a jakes[3] will furnish as comely and useful a vapor as incense from an altar. Thus far, I suppose, will easily be granted me; and then it will follow, that as the face of nature never produces rain but when it is overcast and disturbed, so human understanding, seated in the brain, must be troubled and overspread by vapors, ascending from the lower faculties to

---

7. Swift left funds to endow a hospital for the insane.
1. A Tale of a Tub, Swift's first major work, recounts the adventures of three brothers: Peter (Roman Catholicism), Martin (Luther, here regarded as inspiring the Church of England), and Jack (Calvin, the spirit of Protestant dissent). But the most memorable character of the book is its narrator, who interrupts the story with numerous digressions (including even "A Digression in Praise of Digressions") and whose pride in learning and lack of common sense represent the zealous modern insanity that Swift takes as his target for satire. "A Digression Concerning Madness," this narrator's mas-

terpiece, is based on Swift's ironical doctrine of "the mechanical operation of the spirit": the notion that all spiritual and mental states derive from physical causes—in this case, the ascent of "vapors" to the brain. Beneath his whimsy, however, the author raises a fearful question: what right has any human being to trust that he or she is sane?
2. The Aeolists, who "maintain the original cause of all things to be wind," are equated by Swift with religious dissenters who believe themselves to be inspired.
3. Latrine.

water the invention and render it fruitful. Now, although these vapors (as it hath been already said) are of as various original as those of the skies, yet the crop they produce differs both in kind and degree, merely according to the soil. I will produce two instances to prove and explain what I am now advancing.

A certain great prince[4] raised a mighty army, filled his coffers with infinite treasures, provided an invincible fleet, and all this without giving the least part of his design to his greatest ministers or his nearest favorites. Immediately the whole world was alarmed; the neighboring crowns in trembling expectation towards what point the storm would burst; the small politicians everywhere forming profound conjectures. Some believed he had laid a scheme for universal monarchy; others, after much insight, determined the matter to be a project for pulling down the Pope, and setting up the reformed religion, which had once been his own. Some again, of a deeper sagacity, sent him into Asia to subdue the Turk, and recover Palestine. In the midst of all these projects and preparations, a certain state-surgeon,[5] gathering the nature of the disease by these symptoms, attempted the cure, at one blow performed the operation, broke the bag, and out flew the vapor; nor did anything want to render it a complete remedy, only that the prince unfortunately happened to die in the performance. Now, is the reader exceeding curious to learn whence this vapor took its rise, which had so long set the nations at a gaze? What secret wheel, what hidden spring, could put into motion so wonderful an engine? It was afterwards discovered that the movement of this whole machine had been directed by an absent female, whose eyes had raised a protuberancy, and before emission, she was removed into an enemy's country. What should an unhappy prince do in such ticklish circumstances as these? He tried in vain the poet's never-failing receipt of *corpora quaeque*;[6] for,

Idque petit corpus mens unde est saucia amore:
Unde feritur, eo tendit, gestitque coire. —LUCRETIUS[7]

Having to no purpose used all peaceable endeavors, the collected part of the semen, raised and inflamed, became adust,[8] converted to choler, turned head upon the spinal duct, and ascended to the brain. The very same principle that influences a bully to break the windows of a whore who has jilted him, naturally stirs up a great prince to raise mighty armies, and dream of nothing but sieges, battles, and victories.

——*Teterrima belli*
Causa——[9]

The other instance is what I have read somewhere in a very ancient author, of a mighty king,[1] who, for the space of above thirty years, amused himself to take and lose towns, beat armies, and be beaten, drive princes out of their dominions; fright children from their bread and butter; burn, lay waste, plunder, dragoon, massacre subject and stranger, friend and foe, male and female. 'Tis recorded, that the philosophers of each country were in grave dispute upon causes natural, moral, and political, to find out where they should assign an original solution of this phenomenon. At last the vapor or spirit, which animated the hero's brain, being in perpetual circulation, seized upon that region of the human body, so renowned for furnishing the *zibeta occidentalis*,[2] and gathering there into a tumor, left the rest of the world for that time in peace. Of such mighty consequence it is where those exhalations fix, and of so little from whence they proceed. The same spirits which, in their superior progress, would conquer a kingdom, descending upon the anus, conclude in a fistula.[3]

Let us next examine the great introducers of new schemes in philosophy, and search till we can find from what faculty of the soul the disposition arises in mortal man, of taking it into his head to advance new systems with such an eager zeal, in things agreed on all hands impossible to be known; from what seeds this disposition springs, and to what quality of human nature these grand innovators have been indebted for their number of disciples. Because it is plain, that several of the chief among them, both ancient and modern, were usually mistaken by their adversaries, and indeed by all except their own followers, to have been persons crazed, or out of their wits; having generally proceeded, in the common course of their words and actions, by a method very different from the vulgar dictates of unrefined reason; agreeing for the most part in their several models, with their present undoubted successors in the academy of modern Bedlam[4] (whose merits and principles I shall farther examine in due place). Of this kind were *Epicurus, Diogenes, Apollonius, Lucretius, Paracelsus, Descartes*,[5] and others, who, if they were now in the world, tied fast, and separate from their followers, would, in this our undistinguishing age, incur manifest danger of phlebotomy,[6] and whips, and chains, and dark chambers, and straw. For what man, in the natural state or course of thinking, did ever conceive it in his power to reduce the notions of all mankind exactly to the same length, and breadth, and height of his own? Yet this is the first humble and civil design of all innovators in the empire of reason. Epicurus modestly hoped, that one time or other a certain fortuitous concourse of all men's opinions, after perpetual justlings, the sharp with the smooth, the light and the heavy, the round and the square, would by certain *clinamina*[7] unite in the notions of atoms and void, as these did in the originals of all things. Cartesius reckoned to see, before he died, the sentiments of all philosophers, like so many lesser stars in his romantic system, wrapped and drawn within his own vortex.[8] Now, I would gladly be informed, how it is possible to account for such imaginations as these in particular men without recourse to my phenomenon of vapors, ascending from the lower faculties to overshadow the brain, and there distilling into conceptions for which the narrowness of our mother-tongue has not yet assigned any other name beside

2. Paracelsus, who was so famous for chemistry, tried an experiment upon human excrement, to make a perfume of it, which when he had brought to perfection, he called *zibeta occidentalis*, or western-civet, the back parts of man . . . being the west [Swift's note].
3. Ulcer shaped like a pipe.
4. Bethlehem hospital, London's lunatic asylum.
5. Each of these famous speculative thinkers was known as a materialist, hence suspected by Swift of

encouraging atheism.
6. Medical bloodletting.
7. Swerves. The Greek philosopher Epicurus held that the universe was formed by atoms swerving together; Swift implies that a similar miracle would be required for people to join in agreement with Epicurus.
8. The physics of René Descartes (1596–1650) is based on a theory of vortices; Swift considered the theory pure romance.

that of madness or frenzy. Let us therefore now conjecture how it comes to pass, that none of these great prescribers do ever fail providing themselves and their notions with a number of implicit disciples. And, I think, the reason is easy to be assigned: for there is a peculiar string in the harmony of human understanding, which in several individuals is exactly of the same tuning. This, if you can dexterously screw up to its right key, and then strike gently upon it, whenever you have the good fortune to light among those of the same pitch, they will, by a secret necessary sympathy, strike exactly at the same time. And in this one circumstance lies all the skill or luck of the matter; for if you chance to jar the string among those who are either above or below your own height, instead of subscribing to your doctrine, they will tie you fast, call you mad, and feed you with bread and water. It is therefore a point of the nicest conduct to distinguish and adapt this noble talent, with respect to the differences of persons and of times. Cicero understood this very well, when writing to a friend in England, with a caution, among other matters, to beware of being cheated by our hackney-coachmen (who, it seems, in those days were as arrant rascals as they are now), has these remarkable words: *Est quod gaudeas te in ista loca venisse, ubi aliquid sapere viderere.*[9] For, to speak a bold truth, it is a fatal miscarriage so ill to order affairs, as to pass for a fool in one company, when in another you might be treated as a philosopher. Which I desire some certain gentlemen of my acquaintance to lay up in their hearts, as a very seasonable *innuendo*.

This, indeed, was the fatal mistake of that worthy gentleman, my most ingenious friend, Mr. W—tt—n,[1] a person, in appearance, ordained for great designs, as well as performances; whether you will consider his notions or his looks. Surely no man ever advanced into the public with fitter qualifications of body and mind, for the propagation of a new religion. Oh, had those happy talents, misapplied to vain philosophy, been turned into their proper channels of dreams and visions, where distortion of mind and countenance are of such sovereign use, the base detracting world would not then have dared to report that something is amiss, that his brain has undergone an unlucky shake; which even his brother modernists themselves, like ungrates, do whisper so loud, that it reaches up to the very garret I am now writing in.

Lastly, whosoever pleases to look into the fountains of enthusiasm,[2] from whence, in all ages, have eternally proceeded such fattening streams, will find the springhead to have been as troubled and muddy as the current. Of such great emolument is a tincture of this vapor, which the world calls madness, that without its help, the world would not only be deprived of those two great blessings, conquests and systems, but even all mankind would unhappily be reduced to the same belief in things invisible. Now, the former *postulatum* being held, that it is of no import from what originals this vapor proceeds, but either in what angles it strikes and spreads over the understanding, or upon what species of brain it ascends; it will be a very delicate point to cut the feather, and divide the several reasons to a nice and curious reader, how this numerical difference in the brain can produce effects of so vast a difference

9. It is ground for rejoicing that you have come to such places, where anyone can seem wise (Cicero, *Familiar Epistles* 7.10).
1. William Wotton (who had championed modern authors against Swift's patron, Sir William Temple, a spokesman for the ancients) is ridiculed in Swift's *The*

Battle of the Books, published in the same volume as *A Tale of a Tub* (1704).
2. For much of the 18th century the word *enthusiasm* (literally, "possessed by a god") signified a deluded belief in personal revelation.

from the same vapor, as to be the sole point of individuation between Alexander the Great, Jack of Leyden[3] and Monsieur Descartes. The present argument is the most abstracted that ever I engaged in; it strains my faculties to their highest stretch; and I desire the reader to attend with utmost perpensity;[4] for I now proceed to unravel this knotty point.

There is in mankind a certain[5]   •   •   •   •   •

•   •   •   •   •   •   •   •   •

Hic multa   •   •   •   •   •
desiderantur.   •   •   •   •   •

•   •   •   •   •   • And this I take to be a clear solution of the matter.

Having therefore so narrowly passed through this intricate difficulty, the reader will, I am sure, agree with me in the conclusion, that if the moderns mean by madness, only a disturbance or transposition of the brain, by force of certain vapors issuing up from the lower faculties, then has this madness been the parent of all those mighty revolutions that have happened in empire, in philosophy, and in religion. For the brain, in its natural position and state of serenity, disposeth its owner to pass his life in the common forms, without any thought of subduing multitudes to his own power, his reasons, or his visions; and the more he shapes his understanding by the pattern of human learning, the less he is inclined to form parties after his particular notions, because that instructs him in his private infirmities, as well as in the stubborn ignorance of the people. But when a man's fancy gets astride on his reason, when imagination is at cuffs with the senses, and common understanding, as well as common sense, is kicked out of doors, the first proselyte he makes is himself; and when that is once compassed, the difficulty is not so great in bringing over others; a strong delusion always operating from without as vigorously as from within. For cant[6] and vision are to the ear and the eye, the same that tickling is to the touch. Those entertainments and pleasures we most value in life, are such as dupe and play the wag with the senses. For, if we take an examination of what is generally understood by happiness, as it has respect either to the understanding or the senses, we shall find all its properties and adjuncts will herd under this short definition, that it is a perpetual possession of being well deceived. And first, with relation to the mind or understanding, 'tis manifest what mighty advantages fiction has over truth; and the reason is just at our elbow, because imagination can build nobler scenes, and produce more wonderful revolutions, than fortune or nature will be at expense to furnish. Nor is mankind so much to blame in his choice thus determining him, if we consider that the debate merely lies between things past and things conceived; and so the question is only this: whether things that have place in the imagination, may not as properly be said to exist, as those that are seated in the memory; which may be justly held in the affirmative, and very much to the advantage of the former, since this is acknowledged to be the womb of things,

---

3. John of Leyden, a tailor and prophet, briefly established a revolutionary Anabaptist community, the "New Jerusalem," in the city of Münster early in the 16th century.
4. Consideration.
5. "Here is another defect in the manuscript, but I think the author did wisely, and that the matter which thus strained his faculties, was not worth a solution; and it were well if all metaphysical cobweb problems were no otherwise answered" [Swift's note]. The Latin phrase ("Much is missing here") indicates a gap in the text Swift pretends to be "editing."
6. "Sudden exclamations, whining, unusual tones, and in fine all praying and preaching like the unlearned of the Presbyterians" (*Spectator* 147).

and the other allowed to be no more than the grave. Again, if we take this definition of happiness, and examine it with reference to the senses, it will be acknowledged wonderfully adapt. How fading and insipid do all objects accost us, that are not conveyed in the vehicle of delusion! How shrunk is everything, as it appears in the glass of nature! So that if it were not for the assistance of artificial mediums, false lights, refracted angles, varnish, and tinsel, there would be a mighty level in the felicity and enjoyments of mortal men. If this were seriously considered by the world, as I have a certain reason to suspect it hardly will, men would no longer reckon among their high points of wisdom, the art of exposing weak sides, and publishing infirmities; an employment, in my opinion, neither better nor worse than that of unmasking, which, I think, has never been allowed[7] fair usage, either in the world, or the playhouse.

In the proportion that credulity is a more peaceful possession of the mind than curiosity, so far preferable is that wisdom, which converses about the surface, to that pretended philosophy which enters into the depth of things, and then comes gravely back with informations and discoveries, that in the inside they are good for nothing. The two senses, to which all objects first address themselves, are the sight and the touch; these never examine farther than the color, the shape, the size, and whatever other qualities dwell, or are drawn by art upon the outward of bodies; and then comes reason officiously with tools for cutting, and opening, and mangling, and piercing, offering to demonstrate, that they are not of the same consistence quite through. Now I take all this to be the last degree of perverting nature; one of whose eternal laws it is, to put her best furniture forward. And therefore, in order to save the charges of all such expensive anatomy for the time to come, I do here think fit to inform the reader, that in such conclusions as these, reason is certainly in the right, and that in most corporeal beings, which have fallen under my cognizance, the outside has been infinitely preferable to the in; whereof I have been farther convinced from some late experiments. Last week I saw a woman flayed, and you will hardly believe how much it altered her person for the worse. Yesterday I ordered the carcass of a beau to be stripped in my presence; when we were all amazed to find so many unsuspected faults under one suit of clothes. Then I laid open his brain, his heart, and his spleen; but I plainly perceived at every operation, that the farther we proceeded, we found the defects increase upon us in number and bulk; from all which, I justly formed this conclusion to myself: that whatever philosopher or projector[8] can find out an art to solder and patch up the flaws and imperfections of nature, will deserve much better of mankind, and teach us a more useful science, than that so much in present esteem, of widening and exposing them (like him who held anatomy to be the ultimate end of physic).[9] And he, whose fortunes and dispositions have placed him in a convenient station to enjoy the fruits of this noble art; he that can with Epicurus content his ideas with the films and images that fly off upon his senses from the superficies[1] of things; such a man, truly wise, creams off nature, leaving the sour and the dregs for philosophy and reason to lap up. This is the sublime and refined point of felicity, called the possession of being well deceived; the serene peaceful state of being a fool among knaves.

7. Admitted to be.
8. Someone given to speculative experiments.
9. Medical practice.

1. Surfaces. Epicurus considered the senses, directly affected by objects, more trustworthy than reason.

But to return to madness. It is certain, that according to the system I have above deduced, every species thereof proceeds from a redundancy of vapors; therefore, as some kinds of frenzy give double strength to the sinews, so there are of other species, which add vigor, and life, and spirit to the brain. Now, it usually happens, that these active spirits, getting possession of the brain, resemble those that haunt other waste and empty dwellings, which for want of business, either vanish, and carry away a piece of the house, or else stay at home and fling it all out of the windows. By which are mystically displayed the two principal branches of madness, and which some philosophers, not considering so well as I, have mistaken to be different in their causes, over-hastily assigning the first to deficiency, and the other to redundance.

I think it therefore manifest, from what I have here advanced, that the main point of skill and address is to furnish employment for this redundancy of vapor, and prudently to adjust the season of it; by which means it may certainly become of cardinal and catholic emolument, in a commonwealth. Thus one man, choosing a proper juncture, leaps into a gulf, from thence proceeds a hero, and is called the saver of his country; another achieves the same enterprise, but unluckily timing it, has left the brand of madness fixed as a reproach upon his memory; upon so nice a distinction, are we taught to repeat the name of Curtius with reverence and love, that of Empedocles[2] with hatred and contempt. Thus also it is usually conceived, that the elder Brutus only personated the fool and madman for the good of the public; but this was nothing else than a redundancy of the same vapor long misapplied, called by the Latins, *ingenium par negotiis*;[3] or (to translate it as nearly as I can) a sort of frenzy, never in its right element, till you take it up in business of the state.

Upon all which, and many other reasons of equal weight, though not equally curious, I do here gladly embrace an opportunity I have long sought for, of recommending it as a very noble undertaking to Sir Edward Seymour, Sir Christopher Musgrave, Sir John Bowls, John How, Esq.,[4] and other patriots concerned, that they would move for leave to bring in a bill for appointing commissioners to inspect into Bedlam, and the parts adjacent; who shall be empowered to send for persons, papers, and records, to examine into the merits and qualifications of every student and professor, to observe with utmost exactness their several dispositions and behavior, by which means, duly distinguishing and adapting their talents, they might produce admirable instruments for the several offices in a state, . . . ,[5] civil, and military, proceeding in such methods as I shall here humbly propose. And I hope the gentle reader will give some allowance to my great solicitudes in this important affair, upon account of the high esteem I have borne that honorable society, whereof I had some time the happiness to be an unworthy member.

Is any student tearing his straw in piece-meal, swearing and blaspheming, biting his grate, foaming at the mouth, and emptying his piss-pot in the spectators' faces? Let the right worshipful the commissioners of inspection give him a regiment of dragoons, and send him into Flanders among the rest. Is another eternally talking, sputtering, gaping, bawling in a sound without period or

2. The Roman hero Marcus Curtius appeased the gods by hurling himself into an ominous crack in the earth of the Forum; Empedocles committed suicide by leaping into the crater of Mt. Etna.
3. A talent for business. Lucius Junius Brutus, like Hamlet, pretended madness to deceive his murderous uncle, Tarquin the Proud.
4. Members of Parliament.
5. Swift omits the third office, ecclesiastical. "Instruments": useful persons.

article? What wonderful talents are here mislaid! Let him be furnished immediately with a green bag and papers, and threepence in his pocket,[6] and away
with him to Westminster Hall. You will find a third gravely taking the dimensions of his kennel, a person of foresight and insight, though kept quite in the
dark; for why, like Moses, *ecce cornuta erat ejus facies.*[7] He walks duly in one
pace, entreats your penny with due gravity and ceremony, talks much of hard
times, and taxes, and the whore of Babylon, bars up the wooden window of
his cell constantly at eight o'clock, dreams of fire, and shoplifters, and court-
customers, and privileged places. Now, what a figure would all these acquirements amount to, if the owner were sent into the city[8] among his brethren!
Behold a fourth, in much and deep conversation with himself, biting his
thumbs at proper junctures, his countenance checkered with business and
design, sometimes walking very fast, with his eyes nailed to a paper that he
holds in his hands; a great saver of time, somewhat thick of hearing, very short
of sight, but more of memory; a man ever in haste, a great hatcher and breeder
of business, and excellent at the famous art of whispering nothing; a huge
idolator of monosyllables and procrastination, so ready to give his word to
everybody, that he never keeps it; one that has forgot the common meaning
of words, but an admirable retainer of the sound; extremely subject to the
looseness,[9] for his occasions are perpetually calling him away. If you approach
his grate in his familiar intervals, "Sir," says he, "give me a penny, and I'll sing
you a song; but give me the penny first." (Hence comes the common saying,
and commoner practice, of parting with money for a song.) What a complete
system of court skill is here described in every branch of it, and all utterly lost
with wrong application! Accost the hole of another kennel, first stopping your
nose, you will behold a surly, gloomy, nasty, slovenly mortal, raking in his own
dung, and dabbling in his urine. The best part of his diet is the reversion of
his own ordure, which expiring into steams, whirls perpetually about, and at
last re-infunds.[1] His complexion is of a dirty yellow, with a thin scattered
beard, exactly agreeable to that of his diet upon its first declination, like other
insects, who having their birth and education in an excrement, from thence
borrow their color and their smell. The student of this apartment is very sparing of his words, but somewhat over-liberal of his breath; he holds his hand
out ready to receive your penny, and immediately upon receipt withdraws to
his former occupations. Now, is it not amazing to think, the society of War-
wick-lane[2] should have no more concern for the recovery of so useful a member, who, if one may judge from these appearances, would become the
greatest ornament to that illustrious body? Another student struts up fiercely
to your teeth, puffing with his lips, half squeezing out his eyes, and very graciously holds you out his hand to kiss. The keeper desires you not to be afraid
of this professor, for he will do you no hurt; to him alone is allowed the liberty
of the antechamber, and the orator of the place gives you to understand, that
this solemn person is a tailor run mad with pride. This considerable student is
adorned with many other qualities, upon which at present I shall not farther

6. "A lawyer's coach-hire" [Swift's note] from the Inns
of Court to Westminster. Most lawyers carried green
bags.
7. "Cornutus is either horned or shining, and by this
term, Moses is described in the vulgar Latin of the Bible" [Swift's note]. Swift puns on the Latin phrase
("Behold his face was shining") by suggesting someone

kept in the dark through being "horned," i.e., a
cuckold.
8. The commercial center of London.
9. Diarrhea.
1. Pours in again.
2. Royal College of Physicians.

enlarge.------*Hark in your ear*[3]------I am strangely mistaken, if all his address, his motions, and his airs, would not then be very natural, and in their proper element.

I shall not descend so minutely, as to insist upon the vast number of beaux, fiddlers, poets, and politicians, that the world might recover by such a reformation; but what is more material, besides the clear gain redounding to the commonwealth, by so large an acquisition of persons to employ, whose talents and acquirements, if I may be so bold as to affirm it, are now buried, or at least misapplied; it would be a mighty advantage accruing to the public from this inquiry, that all these would very much excel, and arrive at great perfection in their several kinds; which, I think, is manifest from what I have already shown, and shall enforce by this one plain instance: that even I myself, the author of these momentous truths, am a person, whose imaginations are hard-mouthed,[4] and exceedingly disposed to run away with his reason, which I have observed from long experience to be a very light rider, and easily shook off; upon which account, my friends will never trust me alone, without a solemn promise to vent my speculations in this, or the like manner, for the universal benefit of human kind; which perhaps the gentle, courteous, and candid reader, brimful of that modern charity and tenderness usually annexed to his office, will be very hardly persuaded to believe.

1704

Gulliver's Travels

Gulliver's Travels is Swift's most enduring satire. Although it is full of allusions to recent and contemporary historical events, it is as valid today as it was in 1726, for its objects are human failings and the defective political, economic, and social institutions that they call into being. Swift adopts an ancient satirical device: the imaginary voyage. Lemuel Gulliver, the narrator, is a ship's surgeon, a reasonably well educated man, kindly, resourceful, cheerful, inquiring, patriotic, truthful, and rather unimaginative. He is, in short, a reasonably decent example of humanity, with whom a reader can readily identify. He undertakes four voyages, all of which end disastrously among "several remote nations of the world." In the first, Gulliver is shipwrecked in the empire of Lilliput, where he finds himself a giant among a diminutive people, charmed by their miniature city and amused by their toylike prettiness. But in the end they prove to be treacherous, malicious, ambitious, vengeful, and cruel. As we read we grow disenchanted with the inhabitants of this fanciful kingdom, and then gradually we begin to recognize our likeness to them, especially in the disproportion between our natural pettiness and our boundless and destructive passions. In the second voyage, Gulliver is abandoned by his shipmates in Brobdingnag, a land of giants, creatures ten times as large as Europeans. Though he fears that such monsters must be brutes, the reverse proves to be the case. Brobdingnag is something of a utopia, governed by a humane and enlightened prince who is the embodiment of moral and political wisdom. In the long interview in which Gulliver pridefully enlarges on the glories of England and its political institutions, the king reduces him to resentful silence by asking questions that reveal the difference between what is and what ought to be in human, especially British, institutions. In Brobdingnag, Gulliver finds himself a Lilliputian, his pride humbled by his helpless state and his human vanity diminished by the realization that his body must have seemed as disgusting to the Lilliputians as do the bodies of the Brobdingnagians to him.

3. I cannot conjecture what the author means here, or how this chasm could be filled, though it is capable of more than one interpretation [Swift's note].
4. (Of a horse) apt to reject control by the bit.

In the third voyage, to Laputa, Swift is chiefly concerned with attacking extremes of theoretical and speculative reasoning, whether in science, politics, or economics. Much of this voyage is an allegory of political life under the administration of the Whig minister, Sir Robert Walpole. The final voyage sets Gulliver between a race of horses, Houyhnhnms (prounced *Hwín-ims*), who live entirely by reason except for a few well-controlled and muted social affections, and their slaves, the Yahoos, whose bodies are obscene caricatures of the human body and who have no glimmer of reason, but are mere creatures of appetite and passion.

When *Gulliver's Travels* first appeared, everyone read it—children for the story and politicians for the satire of current affairs—and ever since it has retained a hold on readers of every kind. Almost unique in world literature, it is simple enough for children, complex enough to carry adults beyond their depth. Swift's art works on many levels. First of all, there is the sheer playfulness of the narrative. Through Gulliver's eyes, we gaze on marvel after marvel: a tiny girl who threads an invisible needle with invisible silk, or a white mare who threads a needle between pastern and hoof. The travels, like a fairy story, transport us to imaginary worlds that function with a perfect, fantastic logic different from our own; Swift exercises our sense of vision. But beyond that, he exercises our perceptions of meaning. In *Gulliver's Travels*, things are seldom what they seem; irony, probing or corrosive, underlies almost every word. In the last chapter, Gulliver insists that the example of the Houyhnhnms has made him incapable of telling a lie—but the oath he swears is quoted from Sinon, whose lies to the Trojans persuaded them to accept the Trojan *horse*. Swift trains us to read alertly, to look beneath the surface. Yet on its deepest level, the book does not offer final meanings, but a question: What is a human being? Voyaging through imaginary worlds, we try to find ourselves. Are we prideful insects or lords of creation? brutes or reasonable beings? In the last voyage, Swift pushes such questions, and Gulliver himself, almost beyond endurance; hating his own humanity, Gulliver forgets who he is. For the reader, however, the outcome cannot be so clear. Swift does not set out to satisfy our minds but to vex and unsettle them. And he leaves us at the moment when the mixed face of humanity—the pettiness of the Lilliputians, the savagery of the Yahoos, the innocence of Gulliver himself—begins to look strangely familiar, like our own faces in a mirror.

Swift's full title for this work was *Travels into Several Remote Nations of the World. In Four Parts. By Lemuel Gulliver, First a Surgeon, and then a Captain of several Ships.* In the first edition (1726), either the bookseller or Swift's friends Charles Ford, Pope, and others, who were concerned in getting the book anonymously into print, altered and omitted so much of the original manuscript (because of its dangerous political implications) that Swift was seriously annoyed. When, in 1735, the Dublin bookseller George Faulkner brought out an edition of Swift's works, the dean seems to have taken pains, surreptitiously, to see that a more authentic version of the work was published. This text is the basis of modern editions.

From Gulliver's Travels

A Letter from Captain Gulliver to His Cousin Sympson[1]

I hope you will be ready to own publicly, whenever you shall be called to it, that by your great and frequent urgency you prevailed on me to publish a

1. In this letter, first published in 1735, Swift complains, among other matters, of the alterations in his original text made by the publisher, Benjamin Motte, in the interest of what he considered political discretion.

very loose and uncorrect account of my travels; with direction to hire some young gentlemen of either University to put them in order, and correct the style, as my Cousin Dampier[2] did by my advice, in his book called A Voyage round the World. But I do not remember I gave you power to consent that anything should be omitted, and much less that anything should be inserted: therefore, as to the latter, I do here renounce everything of that kind; particularly a paragraph about her Majesty the late Queen Anne, of most pious and glorious memory; although I did reverence and esteem her more than any of human species. But you, or your interpolator, ought to have considered that as it was not my inclination, so was it not decent to praise any animal of our composition before my master Houyhnhnm; and besides, the fact was altogether false; for to my knowledge, being in England during some part of her Majesty's reign, she did govern by a chief Minister; nay, even by two successively; the first whereof was the Lord of Godolphin, and the second the Lord of Oxford; so that you have made me *say the thing that was not*. Likewise, in the account of the Academy of Projectors, and several passages of my discourse to my master Houyhnhnm, you have either omitted some material circumstances, or minced or changed them in such a manner, that I do hardly know mine own work. When I formerly hinted to you something of this in a letter, you were pleased to answer that you were afraid of giving offense; that people in power were very watchful over the press; and apt not only to interpret, but to punish everything which looked like an *innuendo* (as I think you called it). But pray, how could that which I spoke so many years ago, and at above five thousand leagues distance, in another reign, be applied to any of the Yahoos, who now are said to govern the herd; especially, at a time when I little thought on or feared the unhappiness of living under them. Have not I the most reason to complain, when I see these very Yahoos carried by Houyhnhnms in a vehicle, as if these were brutes, and those the rational creatures? And, indeed, to avoid so monstrous and detestable a sight was one principal motive of my retirement hither.[3]

Thus much I thought proper to tell you in relation to yourself, and to the trust I reposed in you.

I do in the next place complain of my own great want of judgment, in being prevailed upon by the intreaties and false reasonings of you and some others, very much against mine own opinion, to suffer my travels to be published. Pray bring to your mind how often I desired you to consider, when you insisted on the motive of public good, that the Yahoos were a species of animals utterly incapable of amendment by precepts or examples; and so it hath proved; for instead of seeing a full stop put to all abuses and corruptions, at least in this little island, as I had reason to expect, behold, after above six months warning, I cannot learn that my book hath produced one single effect according to mine intentions; I desired you would let me know by a letter, when party and faction were extinguished; judges learned and upright; pleaders honest and modest, with some tincture of common sense; and Smithfield[4] blazing with pyramids of law books; the young nobility's education entirely changed; the physicians banished; the female Yahoos abounding in virtue, honor, truth, and good sense; courts and levees of great ministers thoroughly weeded and

2. William Dampier (1652–1715), the explorer, whose account of his circumnavigation of the globe Swift had read.
3. To Nottinghamshire.
4. A part of London containing many bookshops.

swept; wit, merit, and learning rewarded; all disgracers of the press in prose
and verse, condemned to eat nothing but their own cotton,[5] and quench their
thirst with their own ink. These, and a thousand other reformations, I firmly
counted upon by your encouragement; as indeed they were plainly deducible
from the precepts delivered in my book. And, it must be owned that seven
months were a sufficient time to correct every vice and folly to which Yahoos
are subject; if their natures had been capable of the least disposition to virtue
or wisdom; yet so far have you been from answering mine expectation in any
of your letters, that on the contrary, you are loading our carrier every week
with libels, and keys, and reflections, and memoirs, and second parts; wherein
I see myself accused of reflecting upon great statesfolk; of degrading human
nature (for so they have still the confidence to style it) and of abusing the
female sex. I find likewise, that the writers of those bundles are not agreed
among themselves; for some of them will not allow me to be author of mine
own travels; and others make me author of books to which I am wholly a
stranger.

I find likewise that your printer hath been so careless as to confound the
times, and mistake the dates of my several voyages and returns; neither
assigning the true year, or the true month, or day of the month; and I hear the
original manuscript is all destroyed, since the publication of my book. Neither
have I any copy left; however, I have sent you some corrections, which you
may insert, if ever there should be a second edition; and yet I cannot stand to
them, but shall leave that matter to my judicious and candid readers, to adjust
it as they please.

I hear some of our sea Yahoos find fault with my sea language, as not proper
in many parts, nor now in use. I cannot help it. In my first voyages, while I
was young, I was instructed by the oldest mariners, and learned to speak as
they did. But I have since found that the sea Yahoos are apt, like the land
ones, to become new fangled in their words; which the latter change every
year; insomuch, as I remember upon each return to mine own country, their
old dialect was so altered, that I could hardly understand the new. And I
observe, when any Yahoo comes from London out of curiosity to visit me at
mine own house, we neither of us are able to deliver our conceptions in a
manner intelligible to the other.[6]

If the censure of Yahoos could any way affect me, I should have great reason
to complain that some of them are so bold as to think my book of travels a
mere fiction out of mine own brain; and have gone so far as to drop hints that
the Houyhnhnms, and Yahoos have no more existence than the inhabitants
of Utopia.

Indeed I must confess that as to the people of Lilliput, Brobdingrag (for so
the word should have been spelled, and not erroneously Brobdingnag) and
Laputa, I have never yet heard of any Yahoo so presumptuous as to dispute
their being, or the facts I have related concerning them; because the truth
immediately strikes every reader with conviction. And, is there less probability
in my account of the Houyhnhnms or Yahoos, when it is manifest as to the
latter, there are so many thousands even in this city, who only differ from their
brother brutes in Houyhnhnmland, because they use a sort of a jabber, and
do not go naked. I wrote for their amendment, and not their approbation. The

---

5. Presumably their paper.   6. Swift was the inveterate enemy of slang.

united praise of the whole race would be of less consequence to me, than the neighing of those two degenerate Houyhnhnms I keep in my stable; because, from these, degenerate as they are, I still improve in some virtues, without any mixture of vice.

Do these miserable animals presume to think that I am so far degenerated as to defend my veracity; Yahoo as I am, it is well known through all Houyhnhnmland, that by the instructions and example of my illustrious master, I was able in the compass of two years (although I confess with the utmost difficulty) to remove that infernal habit of lying, shuffling, deceiving, and equivocating, so deeply rooted in the very souls of all my species; especially the Europeans.

I have other complaints to make upon this vexatious occasion; but I forbear troubling myself or you any further. I must freely confess that since my last return, some corruptions of my Yahoo nature have revived in me by conversing with a few of your species, and particularly those of mine own family, by an unavoidable necessity; else I should never have attempted so absurd a project as that of reforming the Yahoo race in this kingdom; but I have now done with all such visionary schemes for ever.

1727?   1735

The Publisher to the Reader

The author of these travels, Mr. Lemuel Gulliver, is my ancient and intimate friend; there is likewise some relation between us by the mother's side. About three years ago Mr. Gulliver, growing weary of the concourse of curious people coming to him at his house in Redriff,[7] made a small purchase of land, with a convenient house, near Newark, in Nottinghamshire, his native country; where he now lives retired, yet in good esteem among his neighbors.

Although Mr. Gulliver were born in Nottinghamshire, where his father dwelt, yet I have heard him say his family came from Oxfordshire; to confirm which, I have observed in the churchyard at Banbury, in that county, several tombs and monuments of the Gullivers.

Before he quitted Redriff, he left the custody of the following papers in my hands, with the liberty to dispose of them as I should think fit. I have carefully perused them three times; the style is very plain and simple; and the only fault I find is that the author, after the manner of travelers, is a little too circumstantial. There is an air of truth apparent through the whole; and indeed the author was so distinguished for his veracity, that it became a sort of proverb among his neighbors at Redriff, when anyone affirmed a thing, to say, it was as true as if Mr. Gulliver had spoke it.

By the advice of several worthy persons, to whom, with the author's permission, I communicated these papers, I now venture to send them into the world; hoping they may be, at least for some time, a better entertainment to our young noblemen, than the common scribbles of politics and party.

This volume would have been at least twice as large, if I had not made bold to strike out innumerable passages relating to the winds and tides, as well as to the variations and bearings in the several voyages; together with the minute descriptions of the management of the ship in storms, in the style of sailors;

7. Rotherhithe, a district in southern London, below Tower Bridge, then frequented by sailors.

likewise the account of the longitudes and latitudes, wherein I have reason to apprehend that Mr. Gulliver may be a little dissatisfied; but I was resolved to fit the work as much as possible to the general capacity of readers. However, if my own ignorance in sea affairs shall have led me to commit some mistakes, I alone am answerable for them; and if any traveler hath a curiosity to see the whole work at large, as it came from the hand of the author, I will be ready to gratify him.

As for any further particulars relating to the author, the reader will receive satisfaction from the first pages of the book.

RICHARD SYMPSON

Part 1. A Voyage to Lilliput

CHAPTER 1. *The author gives some account of himself and family; his first inducements to travel. He is shipwrecked, and swims for his life; gets safe on shore in the country of Lilliput; is made a prisoner, and carried up the country.*

My father had a small estate in Nottinghamshire; I was the third of five sons. He sent me to Emanuel College in Cambridge, at fourteen years old, where I resided three years, and applied myself close to my studies: but the charge of maintaining me (although I had a very scanty allowance) being too great for a narrow fortune, I was bound apprentice to Mr. James Bates, an eminent surgeon in London, with whom I continued four years; and my father now and then sending me small sums of money, I laid them out in learning navigation, and other parts of the mathematics, useful to those who intend to travel, as I always believed it would be some time or other my fortune to do. When I left Mr. Bates, I went down to my father; where, by the assistance of him and my uncle John, and some other relations, I got forty pounds, and a promise of thirty pounds a year to maintain me at Leyden:[8] there I studied physic two years and seven months, knowing it would be useful in long voyages.

Soon after my return from Leyden, I was recommended by my good master Mr. Bates, to be surgeon to the *Swallow*, Captain Abraham Pannell commander; with whom I continued three years and a half, making a voyage or two into the Levant[9] and some other parts. When I came back, I resolved to settle in London, to which Mr. Bates, my master, encouraged me; and by him I was recommended to several patients. I took part of a small house in the Old Jury; and being advised to alter my condition, I married Mrs.[1] Mary Burton, second daughter to Mr. Edmond Burton, hosier, in Newgate Street, with whom I received four hundred pounds for a portion.

But, my good master Bates dying in two years after, and I having few friends, my business began to fail; for my conscience would not suffer me to imitate the bad practice of too many among my brethren. Having therefore consulted with my wife, and some of my acquaintance, I determined to go again to sea. I was surgeon successively in two ships, and made several voyages, for six years, to the East and West Indies; by which I got some addition to my fortune. My hours of leisure I spent in reading the best authors, ancient and modern, being always provided with a good number of books; and when I was ashore, in

---

8. The University of Leyden, in Holland, a center for the study of "physic" (medicine).
9. The eastern Mediterranean.

1. "Mrs." (pronounced "Mistress") designated any woman, married or unmarried. "Old Jury": a street (once "Old Jewry") in London City.

observing the manners and dispositions of the people, as well as learning their language; wherein I had a great facility by the strength of my memory.

The last of these voyages not proving very fortunate, I grew weary of the sea, and intended to stay at home with my wife and family. I removed from the Old Jury to Fetter Lane, and from thence to Wapping, hoping to get business among the sailors; but it would not turn to account. After three years' expectation that things would mend, I accepted an advantageous offer from Captain William Prichard, master of the *Antelope*, who was making a voyage to the South Sea. We set sail from Bristol, May 4th, 1699, and our voyage at first was very prosperous.

It would not be proper, for some reasons, to trouble the reader with the particulars of our adventures in those seas: let it suffice to inform him, that in our passage from thence to the East Indies we were driven by a violent storm to the northwest of Van Diemen's Land.[2] By an observation, we found ourselves in the latitude of 30 degrees 2 minutes south. Twelve of our crew were dead by immoderate labor, and ill food, the rest were in a very weak condition. On the fifth of November, which was the beginning of summer in those parts, the weather being very hazy, the seamen spied a rock, within half a cable's length of the ship; but the wind was so strong, that we were driven directly upon it, and immediately split. Six of the crew, of whom I was one, having let down the boat into the sea, made a shift to get clear of the ship, and the rock. We rowed by my computation about three leagues, till we were able to work no longer, being already spent with labor while we were in the ship. We therefore trusted ourselves to the mercy of the waves; and in about half an hour the boat was overset by a sudden flurry from the north. What became of my companions in the boat, as well as of those who escaped on the rock, or were left in the vessel, I cannot tell; but conclude they were all lost. For my own part, I swam as fortune directed me, and was pushed forward by wind and tide. I often let my legs drop, and could feel no bottom; but when I was almost gone, and able to struggle no longer, I found myself within my depth; and by this time the storm was much abated. The declivity was so small, that I walked near a mile before I got to the shore, which I conjectured was about eight o'clock in the evening. I then advanced forward near half a mile, but could not discover any sign of houses or inhabitants; at least I was in so weak a condition, that I did not observe them. I was extremely tired, and with that, and the heat of the weather, and about half a pint of brandy that I drank as I left the ship, I found myself much inclined to sleep. I lay down on the grass, which was very short and soft, where I slept sounder than ever I remember to have done in my life, and as I reckoned, above nine hours; for when I awaked, it was just daylight. I attempted to rise, but was not able to stir: for as I happened to lie on my back, I found my arms and legs were strongly fastened on each side to the ground; and my hair, which was long and thick, tied down in the same manner. I likewise felt several slender ligatures across my body, from my armpits to my thighs. I could only look upwards; the sun began to grow hot, and the light offended my eyes. I heard a confused noise about me, but in the posture I lay, could see nothing except the sky. In a little time I felt something alive moving on my left leg, which advancing gently forward over my breast, came almost up to my chin; when bending my eyes downwards as

2. Tasmania.

much as I could, I perceived it to be a human creature not six inches high,[3] with a bow and arrow in his hands, and a quiver at his back. In the meantime, I felt at least forty more of the same kind (as I conjectured) following the first. I was in the utmost astonishment, and roared so loud, that they all ran back in a fright; and some of them, as I was afterwards told, were hurt with the falls they got by leaping from my sides upon the ground. However, they soon returned; and one of them, who ventured so far as to get a full sight of my face, lifting up his hands and eyes by way of admiration,[4] cried out in a shrill, but distinct voice, *Hekinah Degul*: the others repeated the same words several times, but I then knew not what they meant. I lay all this while, as the reader may believe, in great uneasiness; at length, struggling to get loose, I had the fortune to break the strings, and wrench out the pegs that fastened my left arm to the ground; for, by lifting it up to my face, I discovered the methods they had taken to bind me; and, at the same time, with a violent pull, which gave me excessive pain, I a little loosened the strings that tied down my hair on the left side; so that I was just able to turn my head about two inches. But the creatures ran off a second time, before I could seize them; whereupon there was a great shout in a very shrill accent; and after it ceased, I heard one of them cry aloud, *Tolgo phonac*; when in an instant I felt above an hundred arrows discharged on my left hand, which pricked me like so many needles; and besides they shot another flight into the air, as we do bombs in Europe, whereof many, I suppose, fell on my body (though I felt them not) and some on my face, which I immediately covered with my left hand. When this shower of arrows was over, I fell a groaning with grief and pain; and then striving again to get loose, they discharged another volley larger than the first, and some of them attempted with spears to stick me in the sides; but, by good luck, I had on me a buff jerkin,[5] which they could not pierce. I thought it the most prudent method to lie still; and my design was to continue so till night, when, my left hand being already loose, I could easily free myself: and as for the inhabitants, I had reason to believe I might be a match for the greatest armies they could bring against me, if they were all of the same size with him that I saw. But fortune disposed otherwise of me. When the people observed I was quiet, they discharged no more arrows: but by the noise increasing, I knew their numbers were greater; and about four yards from me, over-against my right ear, I heard a knocking for above an hour, like people at work; when turning my head that way, as well as the pegs and strings would permit me, I saw a stage erected about a foot and a half from the ground, capable of holding four of the inhabitatnts, with two or three ladders to mount it: from whence one of them, who seemed to be a person of quality, made me a long speech, whereof I understood not one syllable. But I should have mentioned, that before the principal person began his oration, he cried out three times, *Langro Dehul san:* (these words and the former were afterwards repeated and explained to me). Whereupon immediately about fifty of the inhabitants came, and cut the strings that fastened the left side of my head, which gave me the liberty of turning it to the right, and of observing the person and gesture of him who was to speak. He appeared to be of a middle age, and taller than any of the other three who attended him; whereof one was a page

---

3. Lilliput is scaled, fairly consistently, at one-twelfth   4. Wonderment.
of Gulliver's world.   5. Leather jacket.

who held up his train, and seemed to be somewhat longer than my middle finger; the other two stood one on each side to support him. He acted every part of an orator, and I could observe many periods[6] of threatenings, and others of promises, pity and kindness. I answered in a few words, but in the most submissive manner, lifting up my left hand and both my eyes to the sun, as calling him for a witness; and being almost famished with hunger, having not eaten a morsel for some hours before I left the ship, I found the demands of nature so strong upon me, that I could not forbear showing my impatience (perhaps against the strict rules of decency) by putting my finger frequently on my mouth, to signify that I wanted food. The Hurgo (for so they call a great lord, as I afterwards learned) understood me very well. He descended from the stage, and commanded that several ladders should be applied to my sides, on which above an hundred of the inhabitants mounted, and walked towards my mouth, laden with baskets full of meat, which had been provided and sent thither by the King's orders upon the first intelligence he received of me. I observed there was the flesh of several animals, but could not distinguish them by the taste. There were shoulders, legs, and loins shaped like those of mutton, and very well dressed, but smaller than the wings of a lark. I eat them by two or three at a mouthful, and took three loaves at a time, about the bigness of musket bullets. They supplied me as fast as they could, showing a thousand marks of wonder and astonishment at my bulk and appetite. I then made another sign that I wanted drink. They found by my eating that a small quantity would not suffice me; and being a most ingenious people, they slung up with great dexterity one of their largest hogsheads; then rolled it towards my hand, and beat out the top; I drank it off at a draught, which I might well do, for it hardly held half a pint, and tasted like a small wine of Burgundy, but much more delicious. They brought me a second hogshead, which I drank in the same manner, and made signs for more, but they had none to give me. When I had performed these wonders, they shouted for joy, and danced upon my breast, repeating several times as they did at first, *Hekinah Degul*. They made me a sign that I should throw down the two hogsheads, but first warned the people below to stand out of the way, crying aloud, *Borach Mivola*, and when they saw the vessels in the air, there was an universal shout of *Hekinah Degul*. I confess I was often tempted, while they were passing backwards and forwards on my body, to seize forty or fifty of the first that came in my reach, and dash them against the ground. But the remembrance of what I had felt, which probably might not be the worst they could do; and the promise of honor I made them, for so I interpreted my submissive behavior, soon drove out those imaginations. Besides, I now considered myself as bound by the laws of hospitality to a people who had treated me with so much expense and magnificence. However, in my thoughts I could not sufficiently wonder at the intrepidity of these diminutive mortals, who durst venture to mount and walk on my body, while one of my hands was at liberty, without trembling at the very sight of so prodigious a creature as I must appear to them. After some time, when they observed that I made no more demands for meat, there appeared before me a person of high rank from his Imperial Majesty. His Excellency, having mounted on the small of my right leg, advanced forwards up to my face, with about a dozen of his retinue. And producing his creden-

6. In rhetoric, complete, well-constructed sentences.

tials under the Signet Royal, which he applied[7] close to my eyes, spoke about ten minutes, without any signs of anger, but with a kind of determinate resolution; often pointing forwards, which, as I afterwards found, was towards the capital city, about half a mile distant, whither it was agreed by his Majesty in council that I must be conveyed. I answered in a few words, but to no purpose, and made a sign with my hand that was loose, putting it to the other (but over his Excellency's head, for fear of hurting him or his train) and then to my own head and body, to signify that I desired my liberty. It appeared that he understood me well enough; for he shook his head by way of disapprobation, and held his hand in a posture to show that I must be carried as a prisoner. However, he made other signs to let me understand that I should have meat and drink enough, and very good treatment. Whereupon I once more thought of attempting to break my bonds; but again, when I felt the smart of their arrows upon my face and hands, which were all in blisters, and many of the darts still sticking in them; and observing likewise that the number of my enemies increased; I gave tokens to let them know that they might do with me what they pleased. Upon this the *Hurgo* and his train withdrew, with much civility and cheerful countenances. Soon after I heard a general shout, with frequent repetitions of the words, *Peplom Selan*, and I felt great numbers of the people on my left side relaxing the cords to such a degree, that I was able to turn upon my right, and to ease myself with making water; which I very plentifully did, to the great astonishment of the people, who conjecturing by my motions what I was going to do, immediately opened to the right and left on that side, to avoid the torrent which fell with such noise and violence from me. But before this, they had daubed my face and both my hands with a sort of ointment very pleasant to the smell, which in a few minutes removed all the smart of their arrows. These circumstances, added to the refreshment I had received by their victuals and drink, which were very nourishing, disposed me to sleep. I slept about eight hours, as I was afterwards assured; and it was no wonder; for the physicians, by the Emperor's order, had mingled a sleeping potion in the hogsheads of wine.

It seems that upon the first moment I was discovered sleeping on the ground after my landing, the Emperor had early notice of it by an express; and determined in council that I should be tied in the manner I have related (which was done in the night while I slept), that plenty of meat and drink should be sent me, and a machine prepared to carry me to the capital city.

This resolution perhaps may appear very bold and dangerous, and I am confident would not be imitated by any prince in Europe on the like occasion; however, in my opinion it was extremely prudent as well as generous. For supposing these people had endeavored to kill me with their spears and arrows while I was asleep; I should certainly have awaked with the first sense of smart, which might so far have roused my rage and strength, as to enable me to break the strings wherewith I was tied; after which, as they were not able to make resistance, so they could expect no mercy.

These people are most excellent mathematicians, and arrived to a great perfection in mechanics by the countenance and encouragement of the Emperor, who is a renowned patron of learning. This prince hath several machines fixed on wheels, for the carriage of trees and other great weights. He

---

7. Brought.

often builds his largest men of war, whereof some are nine foot long, in the woods where the timber grows, and has them carried on these engines[8] three or four hundred yards to the sea. Five hundred carpenters and engineers were immediately set at work to prepare the greatest engine they had. It was a frame of wood raised three inches from the ground, about seven foot long and four wide, moving upon twenty-two wheels. The shout I heard was upon the arrival of this engine, which it seems set out in four hours after my landing. It was brought parallel to me as I lay. But the principal difficulty was to raise and place me in this vehicle. Eighty poles, each of one foot high, were erected for this purpose, and very strong cords of the bigness of packthread were fastened by hooks to many bandages, which the workmen had girt round my neck, my hands, my body, and my legs. Nine hundred of the strongest men were employed to draw up these cords by many pulleys fastened on the poles; and thus, in less than three hours, I was raised and slung into the engine, and there tied fast. All this I was told, for while the whole operation was performing, I lay in a profound sleep, by the force of that soporiferous[9] medicine infused into my liquor. Fifteen hundred of the Emperor's largest horses, each about four inches and a half high, were employed to draw me towards the metropolis, which, as I said, was half a mile distant.

About four hours after we began our journey, I awaked by a very ridiculous accident; for, the carriage being stopped a while to adjust something that was out of order, two or three of the young natives had the curiosity to see how I looked when I was asleep; they climbed up into the engine, and advancing very softly to my face, one of them, an officer in the guards, put the sharp end of his half-pike a good way up into my left nostril, which tickled my nose like a straw, and made me sneeze violently: whereupon they stole off unperceived, and it was three weeks before I knew the cause of my awaking so suddenly. We made a long march the remaining part of the day, and rested at night with five hundred guards on each side of me half with torches, and half with bows and arrows, ready to shoot me if I should offer to stir. The next morning at sunrise we continued our march, and arrived within two hundred yards of the city gates about noon. The Emperor and all his court came out to meet us, but his great officers would by no means suffer his Majesty to endanger his person by mounting on my body.

At the place where the carriage stopped, there stood an ancient temple, esteemed to be the largest in the whole kingdom, which having been polluted some years before by an unnatural murder,[1] was, according to the zeal of those people, looked on as profane, and therefore had been applied to common use, and all the ornaments and furniture carried away. In this edifice it was determined I should lodge. The great gate fronting to the north was about four foot high, and almost two foot wide, through which I could easily creep. On each side of the gate was a small window not above six inches from the ground: into that on the left side, the King's smiths conveyed fourscore and eleven chains, like those that hang to a lady's watch in Europe, and almost as large, which were locked to my left leg with six and thirty padlocks. Over against this temple, on the other side of the great highway, at twenty foot distance, there was a turret at least five foot high. Here the Emperor ascended

8. Contrivances.
9. Inducing unnatural sleep.

1. Presumably a reference to the execution of Charles I, who was sentenced in Westminster Hall.

with many principal lords of his court, to have an opportunity of viewing me,
as I was told, for I could not see them. It was reckoned that above an hundred
thousand inhabitants came out of the town upon the same errand; and in spite
of my guards, I believe there could not be fewer than ten thousand, at several
times, who mounted upon my body by the help of ladders. But a proclamation
was soon issued to forbid it upon pain of death. When the workmen found it
was impossible for me to break loose, they cut all the strings that bound me;
whereupon I rose up with as melancholy a disposition as ever I had in my life.
But the noise and astonishment of the people at seeing me rise and walk are
not to be expressed. The chains that held my left leg were about two yards
long, and gave me not only the liberty of walking backwards and forwards in
a semicircle; but, being fixed within four inches of the gate, allowed me to
creep in, and lie at my full length in the temple.

CHAPTER 2. *The Emperor of Lilliput, attended by several of the nobility, comes
to see the author in his confinement. The Emperor's person and habit described.
Learned men appointed to teach the author their language. He gains favor by
his mild disposition. His pockets are searched, and his sword and pistols taken
from him.*

When I found myself on my feet, I looked about me, and must confess I
never beheld a more entertaining prospect. The country round appeared like
a continued garden, and the inclosed fields, which were generally forty foot
square, resembled so many beds of flowers. These fields were intermingled
with woods of half a stang,[2] and the tallest trees, as I could judge, appeared to
be seven foot high. I viewed the town on my left hand, which looked like the
painted scene of a city in a theater.

I had been for some hours extremely pressed by the necessities of nature;
which was no wonder, it being almost two days since I had last disburthened
myself. I was under great difficulties between urgency and shame. The best
expedient I could think on, was to creep into my house, which I accordingly
did; and shutting the gate after me, I went as far as the length of my chain
would suffer; and discharged my body of that uneasy load. But this was the
only time I was ever guilty of so uncleanly an action; for which I cannot but
hope the candid reader will give some allowance, after he hath maturely and
impartially considered my case, and the distress I was in. From this time my
constant practice was, as soon as I rose, to perform that business in open air,
at the full extent of my chain, and due care was taken every morning before
company came, that the offensive matter should be carried off in wheelbar-
rows by two servants appointed for that purpose. I would not have dwelt so
long upon a circumstance, that perhaps at first sight may appear not very
momentous, if I had not thought it necessary to justify my character in point
of cleanliness to the world; which I am told some of my maligners have been
pleased, upon this and other occasions, to call in question.

When this adventure was at an end, I came back out of my house, having
occasion for fresh air. The Emperor was already descended from the tower,
and advancing on horseback towards me, which had like to have cost him
dear; for the beast, although very well trained, yet wholly unused to such a

2. A quarter of an acre.

sight, which appeared as if a mountain moved before him, reared up on his
hinder feet: but that prince, who is an excellent horseman, kept his seat, until
his attendants ran in, and held the bridle, while his Majesty had time to dis-
mount. When he alighted, he surveyed me round with great admiration, but
kept beyond the length of my chains. He ordered his cooks and butlers, who
were already prepared, to give me victuals and drink, which they pushed forward in a sort of vehicles upon wheels until I could reach them. I took these
vehicles, and soon emptied them all; twenty of them were filled with meat,
and ten with liquor; each of the former afforded me two or three good mouth-
fuls, and I emptied the liquor of ten vessels, which was contained in earthen
vials, into one vehicle, drinking it off at a draught; and so I did with the rest.
The Empress, and young princes of the blood, of both sexes, attended by many
ladies, sat at some distance in their chairs; but upon the accident that happened to the Emperor's horse, they alighted, and came near his person; which
I am now going to describe. He is taller, by almost the breadth of my nail, than
any of his court, which alone is enough to strike an awe into the beholders. His
features are strong and masculine, with an Austrian lip, and arched nose, his
complexion olive, his countenance[3] erect, his body and limbs well proportioned, all his motions graceful, and his deportment majestic. He was then
past his prime, being twenty-eight years and three quarters old, of which he
had reigned about seven, in great felicity, and generally victorious. For the
better convenience of beholding him, I lay on my side, so that my face was
parallel to his, and he stood but three yards off: however, I have had him since
many times in my hand, and therefore cannot be deceived in the description.
His dress was very plain and simple, the fashion of it between the Asiatic and
the European; but he had on his head a light helmet of gold, adorned with
jewels, and a plume on the crest. He held his sword drawn in his hand, to
defend himself, if I should happen to break loose; it was almost three inches
long, the hilt and scabbard were gold enriched with diamonds. His voice was
shrill, but very clear and articulate, and I could distinctly hear it when I stood
up. The ladies and courtiers were all most magnificently clad, so that the
spot they stood upon seemed to resemble a petticoat spread on the ground,
embroidered with figures of gold and silver. His Imperial Majesty spoke often
to me, and I returned answers, but neither of us could understand a syllable.
There were several of his priests and lawyers present (as I conjectured by their
habits) who were commanded to address themselves to me, and I spoke to
them in as many languages as I had the least smattering of, which were High
and Low Dutch, Latin, French, Spanish, Italian, and Lingua Franca;[4] but all
to no purpose. After about two hours the court retired, and I was left with a
strong guard, to prevent the impertinence, and probably the malice of the
rabble, who were very impatient to crowd about me as near as they durst; and
some of them had the impudence to shoot their arrows at me as I sat on the
ground by the door of my house, whereof one very narrowly missed my left
eye. But the colonel ordered six of the ringleaders to be seized, and thought
no punishment so proper as to deliver them bound into my hands, which
some of his soldiers accordingly did, pushing them forwards with the butt-
ends of their pikes into my reach; I took them all in my right hand, put five of

---

3. Bearing, appearance. Swift may be satirically ideal-
izing George I, whom most of the British thought
gross.

4. A jargon, based on Italian, used by traders in the
Mediterranean. "High and Low Dutch": German and
Dutch.

them into my coat-pocket; and as to the sixth, I made a countenance as if I would eat him alive. The poor man squalled terribly, and the colonel and his officer were in much pain, especially when they saw me take out my penknife: but I soon put them out of fear; for, looking mildly, and immediately cutting the strings he was bound with, I set him gently on the ground, and away he ran. I treated the rest in the same manner, taking them one by one out of my pocket, and I observed both the soldiers and people were highly obliged at this mark of my clemency, which was represented very much to my advantage at court.

Towards night I got with some difficulty into my house, where I lay on the ground, and continued to do so about a fortnight; during which time the Emperor gave orders to have a bed prepared for me. Six hundred beds of the common measure were brought in carriages, and worked up in my house; an hundred and fifty of their beds sewn together made up the breadth and length, and these were four double, which however kept me but very indifferently from the hardness of the floor, that was of smooth stone. By the same computation they provided me with sheets, blankets, and coverlets, tolerable enough for one who had been so long enured to hardships as I.

As the news of my arrival spread through the kingdom, it brought prodigious numbers of rich, idle, and curious people to see me; so that the villages were almost emptied, and great neglect of tillage and household affairs must have ensued, if his Imperial Majesty had not provided by several proclamations and orders of state against this inconveniency. He directed that those who had already beheld me should return home, and not presume to come within fifty yards of my house without license from court; whereby the secretaries of state got considerable fees.

In the mean time, the Emperor held frequent councils to debate what course should be taken with me; and I was afterwards assured by a particular friend, a person of great quality, who was as much in the secret as any, that the court was under many difficulties concerning me. They apprehended[5] my breaking loose, that my diet would be very expensive, and might cause a famine. Sometimes they determined to starve me, or at least to shoot me in the face and hands with poisoned arrows, which would soon dispatch me: but again they considered, that the stench of so large a carcass might produce a plague in the metropolis, and probably spread through the whole kingdom. In the midst of these consultations, several officers of the army went to the door of the great council chamber; and two of them being admitted, gave an account of my behavior to the six criminals above-mentioned; which made so favorable an impression in the breast of his Majesty, and the whole board, in my behalf, that an imperial commission was issued out, obliging all the villages nine hundred yards round the city to deliver in every morning six beeves, forty sheep, and other victuals for my sustenance; together with a proportionable quantity of bread and wine, and other liquors: for the due payment of which his Majesty gave assignments[6] upon his treasury. For this prince lives chiefly upon his own demesnes; seldom except upon great occasions raising any subsidies upon his subjects, who are bound to attend him in his wars at their own expense. An establishment was also made of six hundred persons to be my domestics, who had board-wages allowed for their maintenance, and

5. Anticipated with fear.   6. Formal mandates of revenue.

tents built for them very conveniently on each side of my door. It was likewise ordered, that three hundred tailors should make me a suit of clothes after the fashion of the country: that six of his Majesty's greatest scholars should be employed to instruct me in their language: and, lastly, that the Emperor's horses, and those of the nobility, and troops of guards, should be exercised in my sight, to accustom themselves to me. All these orders were duly put in execution; and in about three weeks I made a great progress in learning their language; during which time the Emperor frequently honored me with his visits, and was pleased to assist my masters in teaching me. We began already to converse together in some sort; and the first words I learned, were to express my desire that he would please to give me my liberty; which I every day repeated on my knees.[7] His answer, as I could apprehend, was, that this must be a work of time, not to be thought on without the advice of his council; and that first I must *Lumos kelmin pesso desmar lon emposo*; that is, swear a peace with him and his kingdom. However, that I should be used with all kindness; and he advised me to acquire by my patience and discreet behavior, the good opinion of himself and his subjects. He desired I would not take it ill, if he gave orders to certain proper officers to search me; for probably I might carry about me several weapons, which must needs be dangerous things, if they answered the bulk of so prodigious a person.[8] I said, his Majesty should be satisfied, for I was ready to strip myself, and turn up my pockets before him. This I delivered part in words, and part in signs. He replied, that by the laws of the kingdom, I must be searched by two of his officers; that he knew this could not be done without my consent and assistance; that he had so good an opinion of my generosity and justice, as to trust their persons in my hands; that whatever they took from me should be returned when I left the country, or paid for at the rate which I would set upon them. I took up the two officers in my hands, put them first into my coat-pockets, and then into every other pocket about me, except my two fobs, and another secret pocket which I had no mind should be searched, wherein I had some little necessaries of no consequence to any but myself. In one of my fobs there was a silver watch, and in the other a small quantity of gold in a purse. These gentlemen, having pen, ink, and paper about them, made an exact inventory of everything they saw; and when they had done, desired I would set them down, that they might deliver it to the Emperor. This inventory I afterwards translated into English, and is word for word as follows.

Imprimis, In the right coat-pocket of the Great Man-Mountain (for so I interpret the words *Quinbus Flestrin*) after the strictest search, we found only one great piece of coarse cloth, large enough to be a foot-cloth for your Majesty's chief room of state. In the left pocket, we saw a huge silver chest, with a cover of the same metal, which we the searchers were not able to lift. We desired it should be opened; and one of us, stepping into it, found himself up to the mid leg in a sort of dust, some part whereof flying up to our faces, set us both a sneezing for several times together. In his right waistcoat-pocket, we found a prodigious bundle of white thin

---

7. Gulliver's plea for liberty, and the threat of starvation or rebellion he represents to his captors, suggest the situation of Ireland with respect to England.
8. When the Whigs came into power in 1715, the leading Tories, who included Swift's friends Oxford and Bolingbroke (Robert Harley and Henry St. John) as well as Swift himself, were investigated by a committee of secrecy.

substances, folded one over another, about the bigness of three men, tied
with a strong cable, and marked with black figures; which we humbly
conceive to be writings; every letter almost half as large as the palm of
our hands. In the left there was a sort of engine, from the back of which
were extended twenty long poles, resembling the palisados[9] before your
Majesty's court; wherewith we conjecture the Man-Mountain combs his
head; for we did not always trouble him with questions, because we
found it a great difficulty to make him understand us. In the large pocket
on the right side of his middle cover (so I translate the word *ranfu-lo,* by
which they meant my breeches) we saw a hollow pillar of iron, about the
length of a man, fastened to a strong piece of timber, larger than the
pillar; and upon one side of the pillar were huge pieces of iron sticking
out, cut into strange figures; which we know not what to make of. In the
left pocket, another engine of the same kind. In the smaller pocket on
the right side, were several round flat pieces of white and red metal, of
different bulk; some of the white, which seemed to be silver, were so
large and heavy, that my comrade and I could hardly lift them. In the left
pocket were two black pillars irregularly shaped: we could not, without
difficulty, reach the top of them as we stood at the bottom of his pocket.
One of them was covered, and seemed all of a piece; but at the upper
end of the other, there appeared a white round substance, about twice
the bigness of our heads. Within each of these was inclosed a prodigious
plate of steel; which, by our orders, we obliged him to show us, because
we apprehended they might be dangerous engines. He took them out of
their cases, and told us, that in his own country his practice was to shave
his beard with one of these, and to cut his meat with the other. There
were two pockets which we could not enter: these he called his fobs; they
were two large slits cut into the top of his middle cover, but squeezed
close by the pressure of his belly. Out of the right fob hung a great silver
chain, with a wonderful kind of engine at the bottom. We directed him
to draw out whatever was at the end of the chain, which appeared to be
a globe, half silver, and half of some transparent metal: for on the transparent side we saw certain strange figures circularly drawn, and thought
we could touch them, until we found our fingers stopped with that lucid
substance. He put this engine to our ears, which made an incessant noise
like that of a watermill. And we conjecture it is either some unknown
animal, or the god that he worships: but we are more inclined to the
latter opinion, because he assured us (if we understood him right, for he
expressed himself very imperfectly), that he seldom did any thing without
consulting it. He called it his oracle, and said it pointed out the time for
every action of his life. From the left fob he took out a net almost large
enough for a fisherman, but contrived to open and shut like a purse, and
served him for the same use: we found therein several massy pieces of
yellow metal, which if they be of real gold, must be of immense value.

    Having thus, in obedience to your Majesty's commands, diligently
searched all his pockets, we observed a girdle[1] about his waist made of
the hide of some prodigious animal; from which, on the left side, hung a
sword of the length of five men; and on the right, a bag or pouch divided

---

9. Fences of stakes.   1. Belt.

into cells; each cell capable of holding three of your Majesty's subjects. In one of these cells were several globes or balls of a most ponderous metal, about the bigness of our heads, and required a strong hand to lift them: the other cell contained a heap of certain black grains, but of no great bulk or weight, for we could hold above fifty of them in the palms of our hands.

This is an exact inventory of what we found about the body of the Man-Mountain; who used us with great civility, and due respect to your Majesty's commission. Signed and sealed on the fourth day of the eighty-ninth moon of your Majesty's auspicious reign.

CLEFREN FRELOCK, MARSI FRELOCK.

When this inventory was read over to the Emperor, he directed me to deliver up the several particulars. He first called for my scimitar, which I took out, scabbard and all. In the meantime he ordered three thousand of his choicest troops (who then attended him) to surround me at a distance, with their bows and arrows just ready to discharge: but I did not observe it; for my eyes were wholly fixed upon his Majesty. He then desired me to draw my scimitar, which, although it had got some rust by the sea water, was in most parts exceeding bright. I did so, and immediately all the troops gave a shout between terror and surprise; for the sun shone clear, and the reflection dazzled their eyes, as I waved the scimitar to and fro in my hand. His Majesty, who is a most magnanimous[2] prince, was less daunted than I could expect; he ordered me to return it into the scabbard, and cast it on the ground as gently as I could, about six foot from the end of my chain. The next thing he demanded was one of the hollow iron pillars, by which he meant my pocket-pistols. I drew it out, and at his desire, as well as I could, expressed to him the use of it, and charging it only with powder, which by the closeness of my pouch happened to escape wetting in the sea (an inconvenience that all prudent mariners take special care to provide against), I first cautioned the Emperor not to be afraid; and then I let it off in the air. The astonishment here was much greater than at the sight of my scimitar. Hundreds fell down as if they had been struck dead; and even the Emperor, although he stood his ground, could not recover himself in some time. I delivered up both my pistols in the same manner as I had done my scimitar, and then my pouch of powder and bullets; begging him that the former might be kept from fire; for it would kindle with the smallest spark, and blow up his imperial palace into the air. I likewise delivered up my watch, which the Emperor was very curious to see; and commanded two of his tallest yeomen of the guards to bear it on a pole upon their shoulders, as draymen in England do a barrel of ale. He was amazed at the continual noise it made, and the motion of the minute-hand, which he could easily discern; for their sight is much more acute than ours: he asked the opinions of his learned men about him, which were various and remote, as the reader may well imagine without my repeating; although indeed I could not very perfectly understand them. I then gave up my silver and copper money, my purse with nine large pieces of gold, and some smaller ones; my knife and razor, my comb and silver snuffbox, my handkerchief and

---

2. Courageous, great-spirited. Magnanimity, the relation (direct or inverse) between the size of the body and the soul, is a central concern of the first two parts of the *Travels.*

journal book. My scimitar, pistols, and pouch, were conveyed in carriages to his Majesty's stores; but the rest of my goods were returned me.

I had, as I before observed, one private pocket which escaped their search, wherein there was a pair of spectacles (which I sometimes use for the weakness of my eyes), a pocket perspective,[3] and several other little conveniences; which, being of no consequence to the Emperor, I did not think myself bound in honor to discover, and I apprehended they might be lost or spoiled if I ventured them out of my possession.

CHAPTER 3. *The author diverts the Emperor and his nobility of both sexes in a very uncommon manner. The diversions of the court of Lilliput described. The author hath his liberty granted him upon certain conditions.*

My gentleness and good behavior had gained so far on the Emperor and his court, and indeed upon the army and people in general, that I began to conceive hopes of getting my liberty in a short time. I took all possible methods to cultivate this favorable disposition. The natives came by degrees to be less apprehensive of any danger from me. I would sometimes lie down, and let five or six of them dance on my hand. And at last the boys and girls would venture to come and play at hide-and-seek in my hair. I had now made a good progress in understanding and speaking their language. The Emperor had a mind one day to entertain me with several of the country shows; wherein they exceed all nations I have known, both for dexterity and magnificence. I was diverted with none so much as that of the rope-dancers, performed upon a slender white thread, extended about two foot, and twelve inches from the ground. Upon which I shall desire liberty, with the reader's patience, to enlarge a little.

This diversion is only practiced by those persons who are candidates for great employments, and high favor, at court. They are trained in this art from their youth, and are not always of noble birth, or liberal education. When a great office is vacant either by death or disgrace (which often happens) five or six of those candidates petition the Emperor to entertain his Majesty and the court with a dance on the rope; and whoever jumps the highest without falling, succeeds in the office. Very often the chief ministers themselves are commanded to show their skill, and to convince the Emperor that they have not lost their faculty. Flimnap,[4] the Treasurer, is allowed to cut a caper on the strait rope, at least an inch higher than any other lord in the whole empire. I have seen him do the summerset several times together upon a trencher[5] fixed on the rope, which is no thicker than a common packthread in England. My friend Reldresal, Principal Secretary for Private Affairs, is, in my opinion, if I am not partial, the second after the Treasurer; the rest of the great officers are much upon a par.

These diversions are often attended with fatal accidents, whereof great numbers are on record. I myself have seen two or three candidates break a limb. But the danger is much greater when the ministers themselves are commanded to show their dexterity; for, by contending to excel themselves and their fellows, they strain so far, that there is hardly one of them who hath not

3. Telescope.
4. Sir Robert Walpole, the Whig head of the government, was notorious in Swift's circle for his political

acrobatics.
5. Plate. "Summerset": somersault.

received a fall; and some of them two or three. I was assured, that a year or two before my arrival, Flimnap would have infallibly broke his neck, if one of the King's cushions,[6] that accidentally lay on the ground, had not weakened the force of his fall.

There is likewise another diversion, which is only shown before the Emperor and Empress, and first minister, upon particular occasions. The Emperor lays on a table three fine silken threads of six inches long. One is blue, the other red, and the third green.[7] These threads are proposed as prizes for those persons whom the Emperor hath a mind to distinguish by a peculiar mark of his favor. The ceremony is performed in his Majesty's great chamber of state; where the candidates are to undergo a trial of dexterity very different from the former, and such as I have not observed the least resemblance of in any other country of the old or the new world. The Emperor holds a stick in his hands, both ends parallel to the horizon, while the candidates, advancing one by one, sometimes leap over the stick, sometimes creep under it back- wards and forwards several times, according as the stick is advanced or depressed. Sometimes the Emperor holds one end of the stick, and his first minister the other; sometimes the minister has it entirely to himself. Whoever performs his part with most agility, and holds out the longest in *leaping* and *creeping*, is rewarded with the blue-colored silk; the red is given to the next, and the green to the third, which they all wear girt twice round about the middle; and you see few great persons about this court who are not adorned with one of these girdles.

The horses of the army, and those of the royal stables, having been daily led before me, were no longer shy, but would come up to my very feet, without starting. The riders would leap them over my hand as I held it on the ground; and one of the Emperor's huntsmen, upon a large courser, took[8] my foot, shoe and all; which was indeed a prodigious leap. I had the good fortune to divert the Emperor one day after a very extraordinary manner. I desired he would order several sticks of two foot high, and the thickness of an ordinary cane, to be brought me; whereupon his Majesty commanded the master of his woods to give directions accordingly; and the next morning six woodmen arrived with as many carriages, drawn by eight horses to each. I took nine of these sticks, and fixing them firmly in the ground in a quadrangular figure, two foot and a half square, I took four other sticks, and tied them parallel at each corner, about two foot from the ground; then I fastened my handkerchief to the nine sticks that stood erect, and extended it on all sides till it was as tight as the top of a drum; and the four parallel sticks, rising about five inches higher than the handkerchief, served as ledges on each side. When I had finished my work, I desired the Emperor to let a troop of his best horse, twenty- four in number, come and exercise upon this plain. His Majesty approved of the proposal, and I took them up one by one in my hands, ready mounted and armed, with the proper officers to exercise them. As soon as they got into order, they divided into two parties, performed mock skirmishes, discharged blunt arrows, drew their swords, fled and pursued, attacked and retired; and in short discovered the best military discipline I ever beheld. The parallel sticks secured them and their horses from falling over the stage; and the

6. A mistress of George I was supposed to have helped restore Walpole to office in 1721.
7. The Orders of the Garter, the Bath, and the Thistle, conferred for services to the king.
8. Jumped over.

Emperor was so much delighted, that he ordered this entertainment to be repeated several days; and once was pleased to be lifted up, and give the word of command; and, with great difficulty, persuaded even the Empress herself to let me hold her in her close chair[9] within two yards of the stage, from whence she was able to take a full view of the whole performance. It was my good fortune that no ill accident happened in these entertainments, only once a fiery horse that belonged to one of the captains pawing with his hoof struck a hole in my handkerchief, and his foot slipping, he overthrew his rider and himself; but I immediately relieved them both; for covering the hole with one hand, I set down the troop with the other, in the same manner as I took them up. The horse that fell was strained in the left shoulder, but the rider got no hurt, and I repaired my handkerchief as well as I could; however, I would not trust to the strength of it any more in such dangerous enterprises.

About two or three days before I was set at liberty, as I was entertaining the court with these kinds of feats, there arrived an express to inform his Majesty that some of his subjects, riding near the place where I was first taken up, had seen a great black substance lying on the ground, very oddly shaped, extending its edges round as wide as his Majesty's bedchamber, and rising up in the middle as high as a man; that it was no living creature, as they at first apprehended, for it lay on the grass without motion, and some of them had walked round it several times; that by mounting upon each other's shoulders, they had got to the top, which was flat and even; and stamping upon it they found it was hollow within; that they humbly conceived it might be something belonging to the Man-Mountain, and if his Majesty pleased, they would undertake to bring it with only five horses. I presently[1] knew what they meant; and was glad at heart to receive this intelligence. It seems upon my first reaching the shore after our shipwreck, I was in such confusion, that before I came to the place where I went to sleep, my hat, which I had fastened with a string to my head while I was rowing, and had stuck on all the time I was swimming, fell off after I came to land; the string, as I conjecture, breaking by some accident which I never observed, but thought my hat had been lost at sea. I intreated his Imperial Majesty to give orders it might be brought to me as soon as possible, describing to him the use and the nature of it: and the next day the wagoners arrived with it, but not in a very good condition; they had bored two holes in the brim, within an inch and half of the edge, and fastened two hooks in the holes; these hooks were tied by a long cord to the harness, and thus my hat was dragged along for above half an English mile: but the ground in that country being extremely smooth and level, it received less damage than I expected.

Two days after this adventure, the Emperor, having ordered that part of his army which quarters in and about his metropolis to be in a readiness, took a fancy of diverting himself in a very singular manner. He desired I would stand like a colossus, with my legs as far asunder as I conveniently could. He then commanded his general (who was an old experienced leader, and a great patron of mine) to draw up the troops in close order, and march them under me; the foot[2] by twenty-four in a breast, and the horse by sixteen, with drums beating, colors flying, and pikes advanced. This body consisted of three thou-

9. An enclosed or sedan chair.
1. Immediately.

2. Foot soldiers or infantry.

sand foot, and a thousand horse. His Majesty gave orders, upon pain of death, that every soldier in his march should observe the strictest decency with regard to my person; which, however, could not prevent some of the younger officers from turning up their eyes as they passed under me. And, to confess the truth, my breeches were at that time in so ill a condition, that they afforded some opportunities for laughter and admiration.

I had sent so many memorials and petitions for my liberty, that his Majesty at length mentioned the matter first in the cabinet, and then in a full council; where it was opposed by none, except Skyresh Bolgolam,[3] who was pleased, without any provocation, to be my mortal enemy. But it was carried against him by the whole board, and confirmed by the Emperor. That minister was *Galbet*, or Admiral of the Realm; very much in his master's confidence, and a person well versed in affairs, but of a morose and sour complexion.[4] However, he was at length persuaded to comply; but prevailed that the articles and conditions upon which I should be set free, and to which I must swear, should be drawn up by himself. These articles were brought to me by Skyresh Bolgo-lam in person, attended by two under-secretaries, and several persons of dis-tinction. After they were read, I was demanded to swear to the performance of them; first in the manner of my own country, and afterwards in the method prescribed by their laws; which was to hold my right foot in my left hand, to place the middle finger of my right hand on the crown of my head, and my thumb on the tip of my right ear. But because the reader may perhaps be curious to have some idea of the style and manner of expression peculiar to that people, as well as to know the articles upon which I recovered my liberty, I have made a translation of the whole instrument,[5] word for word, as near as I was able; which I here offer to the public.

GOLBASTO MOMAREN EVLAME GURDILO SHEFIN MULLY ULLY GUE, most mighty Emperor of Lilliput, delight and terror of the universe, whose dominions extend five thousand blustrugs (about twelve miles in circumference) to the extremities of the globe; Monarch of all Monarchs; taller than the sons of men; whose feet press down to the center, and whose head strikes against the sun; at whose nod the princes of the earth shake their knees; pleasant as the spring, comfortable as the summer, fruitful as autumn, dreadful as winter. His most sublime Majesty pro-poseth to the Man-Mountain, lately arrived at our celestial dominions, the following articles, which by a solemn oath he shall be obliged to perform.

First, The Man-Mountain shall not depart from our dominions, with-out our license under our great seal.

Secondly, He shall not presume to come into our metropolis, without our express order; at which time the inhabitants shall have two hours warning, to keep within their doors.

Thirdly, The said Man-Mountain shall confine his walks to our princi-pal high roads; and not offer to walk or lie down in a meadow, or field of corn.

---

3. The earl of Nottingham, an enemy of Swift.   5. A formal legal document.
4. Disposition.

Fourthly, As he walks the said roads, he shall take the utmost care not to trample upon the bodies of any of our loving subjects, their horses, or carriages, nor take any of our said subjects into his hands, without their own consent.

Fifthly, If an express require extraordinary dispatch, the Man-Mountain shall be obliged to carry in his pocket the messenger and horse, a six days' journey once in every moon, and return the said messenger back (if so required) safe to our Imperial Presence.

Sixthly, He shall be our ally against our enemies in the island of Blefuscu, and do his utmost to destroy their fleet, which is now preparing to invade us.

Seventhly, That the said Man-Mountain shall, at his times of leisure, be aiding and assisting to our workmen, in helping to raise certain great stones, towards covering the wall of the principal park, and other our royal buildings.

Eighthly, That the said Man-Mountain shall, in two moons' time, deliver in an exact survey of the circumference of our dominions by a computation of his own paces round the coast.

Lastly, That upon his solemn oath to observe all the above articles, the said Man-Mountain shall have a daily allowance of meat and drink sufficient for the support of 1,728 of our subjects; with free access to our Royal Person, and other marks of our favor. Given at our palace at Belfaborac the twelfth day of the ninety-first moon of our reign.

I swore and subscribed to these articles with great cheerfulness and content, although some of them were not so honorable as I could have wished; which proceeded wholly from the malice of Skyresh Bolgolam the High Admiral: whereupon my chains were immediately unlocked, and I was at full liberty: the Emperor himself in person did me the honor to be by at the whole ceremony. I made my acknowledgements by prostrating myself at his Majesty's feet: but he commanded me to rise; and after many gracious expressions, which, to avoid the censure of vanity, I shall not repeat, he added, that he hoped I should prove a useful servant, and well deserve all the favors he had already conferred upon me, or might do for the future.

The reader may please to observe, that in the last article for the recovery of my liberty, the Emperor stipulates to allow me a quantity of meat and drink, sufficient for the support of 1,728 Lilliputians. Some time after, asking a friend at court how they came to fix on that determinate number, he told me, that his Majesty's mathematicians, having taken the height of my body by the help of a quadrant, and finding it to exceed theirs in the proportion of twelve to one, they concluded from the similarity of their bodies, that mine must contain at least 1,728 of theirs, and consequently would require as much food as was necessary to support that number of Lilliputians. By which, the reader may conceive an idea of the ingenuity of that people, as well as the prudent and exact economy of so great a prince.

Chapter 4. *Mildendo, the metropolis of Lilliput, described, together with the Emperor's palace. A conversation between the author and a principal secretary, concerning the affairs of that empire; the author's offers to serve the Emperor in his wars.*

The first request I made after I had obtained my liberty, was, that I might have license to see Mildendo, the metropolis; which the Emperor easily granted me, but with a special charge to do no hurt, either to the inhabitants, or their houses. The people had notice by proclamation of my design to visit the town. The wall which encompassed it is two foot and an half high, and at least eleven inches broad, so that a coach and horses may be driven very safely round it; and it is flanked with strong towers at ten foot distance. I stepped over the great western gate, and passed very gently, and sideling[6] through the two principal streets, only in my short waistcoat, for fear of damaging the roofs and eaves of the houses with the skirts of my coat. I walked with the utmost circumspection, to avoid treading on any stragglers, who might remain in the streets, although the orders were very strict, that all people should keep in their houses, at their own peril. The garret windows and tops of houses were so crowded with spectators, that I thought in all my travels I had not seen a more populous place. The city is an exact square, each side of the wall being five hundred foot long. The two great streets, which run cross and divide it into four quarters, are five foot wide. The lanes and alleys, which I could not enter, but only viewed them as I passed, are from twelve to eighteen inches. The town is capable of holding five hundred thousand souls. The houses are from three to five stories. The shops and markets well provided.

The Emperor's palace is in the center of the city, where the two great streets meet. It is enclosed by a wall of two foot high, and twenty foot distant from the buildings. I had his Majesty's permission to step over this wall; and the space being so wide between that and the palace, I could easily view it on every side. The outward court is a square of forty foot, and includes two other courts: in the inmost are the royal apartments, which I was very desirous to see, but found it extremely difficult; for the great gates, from one square into another, were but eighteen inches high, and seven inches wide. Now the buildings of the outer court were at least five foot high; and it was impossible for me to stride over them, without infinite damage to the pile, although the walls were strongly built of hewn stone, and four inches thick. At the same time the Emperor had a great desire that I should see the magnificence of his palace; but this I was not able to do till three days after, which I spent in cutting down with my knife some of the largest trees in the royal park, about an hundred yards distance from the city. Of these trees I made two stools, each about three foot high, and strong enough to bear my weight. The people having received notice a second time, I went again through the city to the palace, with my two stools in my hands. When I came to the side of the outer court, I stood upon one stool, and took the other in my hand: this I lifted over the roof, and gently set it down on the space between the first and second court, which was eight foot wide. I then stepped over the buildings very conveniently from one stool to the other, and drew up the first after me with a hooked stick. By this contrivance I got into the inmost court; and lying down upon my side, I applied my face to the windows of the middle stories, which were left open on purpose, and discovered the most splendid apartments that can be imagined. There I saw the Empress, and the young princes in their several lodgings, with their chief attendants about them. Her Imperial Majesty

6. Sideways.

was pleased to smile very graciously upon me and gave me out of the window her hand to kiss.

But I shall not anticipate the reader with farther descriptions of this kind, because I reserve them for a greater work, which is now almost ready for the press; containing a general description of this empire, from its first erection, through a long series of princes, with a particular account of their wars and politics, laws, learning, and religion; their plants and animals, their peculiar manners and customs, with other matters very curious and useful; my chief design at present being only to relate such events and transactions as happened to the public, or to myself, during a residence of about nine months in that empire.

One morning, about a fortnight after I had obtained my liberty, Reldresal, Principal Secretary (as they style him) of Private Affairs, came to my house, attended only by one servant. He ordered his coach to wait at a distance, and desired I would give him an hour's audience; which I readily consented to, on account of his quality, and personal merits, as well as of the many good offices he had done me during my solicitations at court. I offered to lie down, that he might the more conveniently reach my ear; but he chose rather to let me hold him in my hand during our conversation. He began with compliments on my liberty, said he might pretend to some merit in it; but, however, added, that if it had not been for the present situation of things at court, perhaps I might not have obtained it so soon. For, said he, as flourishing a condition as we appear to be in to foreigners, we labor under two mighty evils; a violent faction at home, and the danger of an invasion by a most potent enemy from abroad. As to the first, you are to understand, that for above seventy moons past, there have been two struggling parties in the empire, under the names of *Tramecksan*, and *Slamecksan*,[7] from the high and low heels on their shoes, by which they distinguish themselves.

It is alleged indeed, that the high heels are most agreeable to our ancient constitution: but however this be, his Majesty hath determined to make use of only low heels in the administration of the government and all offices in the gift of the crown; as you cannot but observe; and particularly, that his Majesty's imperial heels are lower at least by a *drurr* than any of his court; (*drurr* is a measure about the fourteenth part of an inch). The animosities between these two parties run so high, that they will neither eat nor drink, nor talk with each other. We compute the *Tramecksan*, or High-Heels, to exceed us in number; but the power is wholly on our side. We apprehend his Imperial Highness, the heir to the crown, to have some tendency towards the High-Heels; at least we can plainly discover one of his heels higher than the other, which gives him a hobble in his gait.[8] Now, in the midst of these intestine disquiets, we are threatened with an invasion from the island of Blefuscu,[9] which is the other great empire of the universe, almost as large and powerful as this of his Majesty. For as to what we have heard you affirm, that there are other kingdoms and states in the world, inhabited by human creatures as large as yourself, our philosophers are in much doubt; and would rather conjecture that you dropped from the moon, or one of the stars; because it is certain, that an hundred mortals of your bulk would, in a short time, destroy all the fruits and

7. Tory (High Church) and Whig (Low Church).   in both parties.
8. The prince of Wales (later George II) had friends   9. France.

cattle of his Majesty's dominions. Besides, our histories of six thousand moons make no mention of any other regions, than the two great empires of Lilliput and Blefuscu. Which two mighty powers have, as I was going to tell you, been engaged in a most obstinate war for six and thirty moons past. It began upon the following occasion. It is allowed on all hands, that the primitive way of breaking eggs before we eat them, was upon the larger end: but his present Majesty's grandfather, while he was a boy, going to eat an egg, and breaking it according to the ancient practice, happened to cut one of his fingers. Where-upon the Emperor his father published an edict, commanding all his subjects, upon great penalties, to break the smaller end of their eggs. The people so highly resented this law, that our histories tell us there have been six rebellions raised on that account; wherein one emperor lost his life, and another his crown.[1] These civil commotions were constantly fomented by the monarchs of Blefuscu; and when they were quelled, the exiles always fled for refuge to that empire. It is computed, that eleven thousand persons have, at several times, suffered death, rather than submit to break their eggs at the smaller end. Many hundred large volumes have been published upon this controversy: but the books of the Big-Endians have been long forbidden, and the whole party rendered incapable by law of holding employments.[2] During the course of these troubles, the emperors of Blefuscu did frequently expostulate by their ambassadors, accusing us of making a schism in religion, by offending against a fundamental doctrine of our great prophet Lustrog, in the fifty-fourth chapter of the *Brundecral* (which is their Alcoran[3]). This, however, is thought to be a mere strain upon the text: for the words are these; *That all true believers shall break their eggs at the convenient end:* and which is the convenient end, seems, in my humble opinion, to be left to every man's conscience, or at least in the power of the chief magistrate[4] to determine. Now the Big-Endian exiles have found so much credit in the Emperor of Blefuscu's court, and so much private assistance and encouragement from their party here at home, that a bloody war hath been carried on between the two empires for six and thirty moons with various success;[5] during which time we have lost forty capital ships, and a much greater number of smaller vessels, together with thirty thousand of our best seamen and soldiers; and the damage received by the enemy is reckoned to be somewhat greater than ours. However, they have now equipped a numerous fleet, and are just preparing to make a descent upon us; and his Imperial Majesty, placing great confidence in your valor and strength, hath commanded me to lay this account of his affairs before you.

I desired the Secretary to present my humble duty to the Emperor, and to let him know, that I thought it would not become me, who was a foreigner, to interfere with parties; but I was ready, with the hazard of my life, to defend his person and state against all invaders.

CHAPTER 5. *The author by an extraordinary stratagem prevents an invasion. A high title of honor is conferred upon him. Ambassadors arrive from the Emperor*

1. Swift's satirical allegory of the strife between Catholics (Big-Endians) and Protestants (Little-Endians) touches on Henry VIII (who "broke" with the Pope), Charles I (who lost his life), and James II (who lost his crown).
2. The Test Act (1673) prevented Catholics and Nonconformists from holding office unless they accepted the Anglican Sacrament.
3. Koran.
4. Ruler, sovereign. Swift himself accepted the right of the king to determine religious observances.
5. Reminiscent of the War of the Spanish Succession (1701–13).

of Blefuscu, and sue for peace. The Empress's apartment on fire by an accident;
the author instrumental in saving the rest of the palace.

The empire of Blefuscu is an island situated to the north north-east side of
Lilliput, from whence it is parted only by a channel of eight hundred yards
wide. I had not yet seen it, and upon this notice of an intended invasion, I
avoided appearing on that side of the coast, for fear of being discovered by
some of the enemy's ships, who had received no intelligence of me; all intercourse between the two empires having been strictly forbidden during the
war, upon pain of death; and an embargo laid by our Emperor upon all vessels
whatsoever. I communicated to his Majesty a project I had formed of seizing
the enemy's whole fleet; which, as our scouts assured us, lay at anchor in the
harbor ready to sail with the first fair wind. I consulted the most experienced
seamen upon the depth of the channel, which they had often plumbed; who
told me, that in the middle at high water it was seventy *glumgluffs* deep, which
is about six foot of European measure; and the rest of it fifty *glumgluffs* at
most. I walked to the northeast coast over against Blefuscu; where, lying down
behind a hillock, I took out my small pocket perspective glass, and viewed the
enemy's fleet at anchor, consisting of about fifty men of war, and a great number of transports: I then came back to my house, and gave order (for which I
had a warrant) for a great quantity of the strongest cable and bars of iron. The
cable was about as thick as packthread, and the bars of the length and size of
a knitting-needle. I trebled the cable to make it stronger, and for the same
reason I twisted three of the iron bars together, bending the extremities into a
hook. Having thus fixed fifty hooks to as many cables, I went back to the
northeast coast, and putting off my coat, shoes, and stockings, walked into the
sea in my leathern jerkin, about half an hour before high water. I waded with
what haste I could, and swam in the middle about thirty yards until I felt the
ground; I arrived at the fleet in less than half an hour. The enemy was so
frighted when they saw me, that they leaped out of their ships, and swam to
shore, where there could not be fewer than thirty thousand souls. I then took
my tackling, and fastening a hook to the hole at the prow of each, I tied all
the cords together at the end. While I was thus employed, the enemy discharged several thousand arrows, many of which stuck in my hands and face;
and besides the excessive smart, gave me much disturbance in my work. My
greatest apprehension was for my eyes, which I should have infallibly lost, if I
had not suddenly thought of an expedient. I kept, among other little necessaries, a pair of spectacles in a private pocket, which, as I observed before, had
escaped the Emperor's searchers. These I took out, and fastened as strongly as
I could upon my nose; and thus armed went on boldly with my work in spite
of the enemy's arrows; many of which struck against the glasses of my spectacles, but without any other effect, further than a little to discompose them. I
had now fastened all the hooks, and taking the knot in my hand, began to
pull; but not a ship would stir, for they were all too fast by their anchors, so
that the boldest part of my enterprise remained. I therefore let go the cord,
and leaving the hooks fixed to the ships, I resolutely cut with my knife the
cables that fastened the anchors, receiving about two hundred shots in my
face and hands; then I took up the knotted end of the cables to which my
hooks were tied; and with great ease drew fifty of the enemy's largest men-of-
war after me.

The Blefuscudians, who had not the least imagination of what I intended, were at first confounded with astonishment. They had seen me cut the cables, and thought my design was only to let the ships run adrift, or fall foul on each other: but when they perceived the whole fleet moving in order, and saw me pulling at the end, they set up such a scream of grief and despair, that it is almost impossible to describe or conceive. When I had got out of danger, I stopped a while to pick out the arrows that stuck in my hands and face, and rubbed on some of the same ointment that was given me at my first arrival, as I have formerly mentioned. I then took off my spectacles, and waiting about an hour until the tide was a little fallen, I waded through the middle with my cargo, and arrived safe at the royal port of Lilliput.

The Emperor and his whole court stood on the shore, expecting the issue of this great adventure. They saw the ships move forward in a large half-moon, but could not discern me, who was up to my breast in water. When I advanced to the middle of the channel, they were yet more in pain, because I was under water to my neck. The Emperor concluded me to be drowned, and that the enemy's fleet was approaching in a hostile manner: but he was soon eased of his fears, for the channel growing shallower every step I made, I came in a short time within hearing; and holding up the end of the cable by which the fleet was fastened, I cried in a loud voice, Long live the most puissant Emperor of Lilliput! This great prince received me at my landing with all possible encomiums, and created me a *Nardac* upon the spot, which is the highest title of honor among them.

His Majesty desired I would take some other opportunity of bringing all the rest of his enemy's ships into his ports. And so unmeasurable is the ambition of princes, that he seemed to think of nothing less than reducing the whole empire of Blefuscu into a province, and governing it by a viceroy; of destroying the Big-Endian exiles, and compelling that people to break the smaller end of their eggs, by which he would remain sole monarch of the whole world. But I endeavored to divert him from this design, by many arguments drawn from the topics of policy as well as justice: and I plainly protested, that I would never be an instrument of bringing a free and brave people into slavery. And when the matter was debated in council, the wisest part of the ministry were of my opinion.

This open bold declaration of mine was so opposite to the schemes and politics of his Imperial Majesty, that he could never forgive me; he mentioned it in a very artful manner at council, where I was told that some of the wisest appeared, at least by their silence, to be of my opinion; but others, who were my secret enemies, could not forbear some expressions, which by a side-wind[6] reflected on me. And from this time began an intrigue between his Majesty and a junta of ministers maliciously bent against me, which broke out in less than two months, and had like to have ended in my utter destruction. Of so little weight are the greatest services to princes, when put into the balance with a refusal to gratify their passions.[7]

About three weeks after this exploit, there arrived a solemn embassy from Blefuscu, with humble offers of a peace; which was soon concluded upon conditions very advantageous to our Emperor; wherewith I shall not trouble

---

6. Indirectly.
7. After a series of British naval victories, the Treaty of Utrecht (1713) had ended the war with France, but the Tory ministers who engineered the peace were subsequently accused of having sold out to the enemy.

the reader. There were six ambassadors, with a train of about five hundred persons; and their entry was very magnificent, suitable to the grandeur of their master, and the importance of their business. When their treaty was finished, wherein I did them several good offices by the credit I now had, or at least appeared to have at court, their Excellencies, who were privately told how much I had been their friend, made me a visit in form. They began with many compliments upon my valor and generosity; invited me to that kingdom in the Emperor their master's name; and desired me to show them some proofs of my prodigious strength, of which they had heard so many wonders; wherein I readily obliged them, but shall not interrupt the reader with the particulars.

When I had for some time entertained their Excellencies to their infinite satisfaction and surprise, I desired they would do me the honor to present my most humble respects to the Emperor their master, the renown of whose virtues had so justly filled the whole world with admiration, and whose royal person I resolved to attend before I returned to my own country. Accordingly, the next time I had the honor to see our Emperor, I desired his general license to wait on the Blefuscudian monarch, which he was pleased to grant me, as I could plainly perceive, in a very cold manner; but could not guess the reason, till I had a whisper from a certain person, that Flimnap and Bolgolam had represented my intercourse with those ambassadors as a mark of disaffection, from which I am sure my heart was wholly free. And this was the first time I began to conceive some imperfect idea of courts and ministers.

It is to be observed, that these ambassadors spoke to me by an interpreter; the languages of both empires differing as much from each other as any two in Europe, and each nation priding itself upon the antiquity, beauty, and energy of their own tongues, with an avowed contempt for that of their neighbor; yet our Emperor, standing upon the advantage he had got by the seizure of their fleet, obliged them to deliver their credentials, and make their speech, in the Lilliputian tongue. And it must be confessed, that from the great intercourse of trade and commerce between both realms, from the continual reception of exiles, which is mutual among them, and from the custom in each empire to send their young nobility and richer gentry to the other, in order to polish themselves, by seeing the world, and understanding men and manners, there are few persons of distinction, or merchants, or seamen, who dwell in the maritime parts, but what can hold conversation in both tongues; as I found some weeks after, when I went to pay my respects to the Emperor of Blefuscu, which in the midst of great misfortunes, through the malice of my enemies, proved a very happy adventure to me, as I shall relate in its proper place.

The reader may remember, that when I signed those articles upon which I recovered my liberty, there were some which I disliked upon account of their being too servile, neither could any thing but an extreme necessity have forced me to submit. But being now a *Nardac*, of the highest rank in that empire, such offices[8] were looked upon as below my dignity, and the Emperor (to do him justice) never once mentioned them to me. However, it was not long before I had an opportunity of doing his Majesty, at least as I then thought, a most signal service. I was alarmed at midnight with the cries of many hundred people at my door; by which being suddenly awaked, I was in some kind of

---

8. Duties.

terror. I heard the word *burglum* repeated incessantly; several of the Emperor's court, making their way through the crowd, intreated me to come immediately to the palace, where her Imperial Majesty's apartment was on fire, by the carelessness of a maid of honor, who fell asleep while she was reading a romance. I got up in an instant; and orders being given to clear the way before me, and it being likewise a moonshine night, I made a shift to get to the palace without trampling on any of the people. I found they had already applied ladders to the walls of the apartment, and were well provided with buckets, but the water was at some distance. These buckets were about the size of a large thimble, and the poor people supplied me with them as fast as they could; but the flame was so violent, that they did little good. I might easily have stifled it with my coat, which I unfortunately left behind me for haste, and came away only in my leathern jerkin. The case seemed wholly desperate and deplorable; and this magnificent palace would have infallibly been burnt down to the ground, if, by a presence of mind, unusual to me, I had not suddenly thought of an expedient. I had the evening before drank plentifully of a most delicious wine, called *glimigrim* (the Blefuscudians call it *flunec*, but ours is esteemed the better sort), which is very diuretic. By the luckiest chance in the world, I had not discharged myself of any part of it. The heat I had contracted by coming very near the flames, and by my laboring to quench them, made the wine begin to operate by urine; which I voided in such a quantity, and applied so well to the proper places, that in three minutes the fire was wholly extinguished; and the rest of that noble pile, which had cost so many ages in erecting, preserved from destruction.

It was now daylight, and I returned to my house, without waiting to congratulate with the Emperor; because, although I had done a very eminent piece of service, yet I could not tell how his Majesty might resent the manner by which I had performed it: for, by the fundamental laws of the realm, it is capital[9] in any person, of what quality soever, to make water within the precincts of the palace. But I was a little comforted by a message from his Majesty, that he would give orders to the Grand Justiciary for passing my pardon in form; which, however, I could not obtain. And I was privately assured, that the Empress, conceiving the greatest abhorrence of what I had done,[1] removed to the most distant side of the court, firmly resolved that those buildings should never be repaired for her use; and, in the presence of her chief confidents, could not forbear vowing revenge.

CHAPTER 6. *Of the inhabitants of Lilliput; their learning, laws, and customs, the manner of educating their children. The author's way of living in that country. His vindication of a great lady.*

Although I intend to leave the description of this empire to a particular treatise, yet in the mean time I am content to gratify the curious reader with some general ideas. As the common size of the natives is somewhat under six inches, so there is an exact proportion in all other animals, as well as plants and trees: for instance, the tallest horses and oxen are between four and five inches in height, the sheep an inch and a half, more or less; their geese about

9. Punishable by death.   strongly objected to the coarseness of *A Tale of a Tub.*
1. Queen Anne, whom Swift called "a royal prude,"

the bigness of a sparrow; and so the several gradations downwards, till you come to the smallest, which, to my sight, were almost invisible; but nature hath adapted the eyes of the Lilliputians to all objects proper for their view: they see with great exactness, but at no great distance. And to show the sharpness of their sight towards objects that are near, I have been much pleased with observing a cook pulling[2] a lark, which was not so large as a common fly; and a young girl threading an invisible needle with invisible silk. Their tallest trees are about seven foot high; I mean some of those in the great royal park, the tops whereof I could but just reach with my fist clinched. The other vegetables[3] are in the same proportion; but this I leave to the reader's imagination.

I shall say but little at present of their learning, which for many ages hath flourished in all its branches among them: but their manner of writing is very peculiar; being neither from the left to the right, like the Europeans; nor from the right to the left, like the Arabians; nor from up to down, like the Chinese; nor from down to up, like the Cascagians;[4] but aslant from one corner of the paper to the other, like ladies in England.

They bury their dead with their heads directly downwards; because they hold an opinion that in eleven thousand moons they are all to rise again; in which period, the earth (which they conceive to be flat) will turn upside down, and by this means they shall, at their resurrection, be found ready standing on their feet. The learned among them confess the absurdity of this doctrine; but the practice still continues, in compliance to the vulgar.

There are some laws and customs in this empire very peculiar; and if they were not so directly contrary to those of my own dear country, I should be tempted to say a little in their justification. It is only to be wished, that they were as well executed. The first I shall mention relateth to informers. All crimes against the state are punished here with the utmost severity; but if the person accused make his innocence plainly to appear upon his trial, the accuser is immediately put to an ignominious death; and out of his goods or lands, the innocent person is quadruply recompensed for the loss of his time, for the danger he underwent, for the hardship of his imprisonment, and for all the charges he hath been at in making his defense. Or, if that fund be deficient, it is largely[5] supplied by the crown. The Emperor doth also confer on him some public mark of his favor; and proclamation is made of his innocence through the whole city.

They look upon fraud as a greater crime than theft, and therefore seldom fail to punish it with death; for they allege, that care and vigilance, with a very common understanding, may preserve a man's goods from thieves; but honesty hath no fence against superior cunning: and since it is necessary that there should be a perpetual intercourse of buying and selling, and dealing upon credit, where fraud is permitted or connived at, or hath no law to punish it, the honest dealer is always undone, and the knave gets the advantage. I remember when I was once interceding with the King for a criminal who had wronged his master of a great sum of money, which he had received by order, and ran away with; and happening to tell his Majesty, by way of extenuation, that it was only a breach of trust, the Emperor thought it monstrous in me to offer, as a defense, the greatest aggravation of the crime: and truly, I had little

2. Plucking.
3. Plants.

4. Swift's invention.
5. Fully.

to say in return, farther than the common answer, that different nations had different customs; for, I confess, I was heartily ashamed.

Although we usually call reward and punishment the two hinges upon which all government turns, yet I could never observe this maxim to be put in practice by any nation, except that of Lilliput. Whoever can there bring sufficient proof that he hath strictly observed the laws of his country for seventy-three moons, hath a claim to certain privileges, according to his quality[6] and condition of life, with a proportionable sum of money out of a fund appropriated for that use: he likewise acquires the title of *Snilpall*, or *Legal*, which is added to his name, but doth not descend to his posterity. And these people thought it a prodigious defect of policy among us, when I told them that our laws were enforced only by penalties, without any mention of reward. It is upon this account that the image of Justice, in their courts of judicature, is formed with six eyes, two before, as many behind, and on each side one, to signify circumspection; with a bag of gold open in her right hand, and a sword sheathed in her left, to show she is more disposed to reward than to punish.

In choosing persons for all employments, they have more regard to good morals than to great abilities; for, since government is necessary to mankind, they believe that the common size of human understandings is fitted to some station or other; and that Providence never intended to make the management of public affairs a mystery, to be comprehended only by a few persons of sublime genius, of which there seldom are three born in an age: but they suppose truth, justice, temperance, and the like, to be in every man's power; the practice of which virtues, assisted by experience and a good intention, would qualify any man for the service of his country, except where a course of study is required. But they thought the want of moral virtues was so far from being supplied by superior endowments of the mind, that employments could never be put into such dangerous hands as those of persons so qualified; and at least, that the mistakes committed by ignorance in a virtuous disposition would never be of such fatal consequence to the public weal, as the practices of a man whose inclinations led him to be corrupt, and had great abilities to manage, to multiply, and defend his corruptions.

In like manner, the disbelief of a divine Providence renders a man uncapable of holding any public station; for since kings avow themselves to be the deputies of Providence, the Lilliputians think nothing can be more absurd than for a prince to employ such men as disown the authority under which he acteth.

In relating these and the following laws, I would only be understood to mean the original institutions, and not the most scandalous corruptions into which these people are fallen by the degenerate nature of man. For as to that infamous practice of acquiring great employments by dancing on the ropes, or badges of favor and distinction by leaping over sticks, and creeping under them, the reader is to observe, that they were first introduced by the grandfather of the Emperor now reigning; and grew to the present height by the gradual increase of party and faction.

Ingratitude is among them a capital crime, as we read it to have been in some other countries; for they reason thus, that whoever makes ill returns to his benefactor, must needs be a common enemy to the rest of mankind, from

6. Social position.

whom he hath received no obligation; and therefore such a man is not fit to
live.

Their notions relating to the duties of parents and children differ extremely
from ours. For, since the conjunction of male and female is founded upon
the great law of nature, in order to propagate and continue the species, the
Lilliputians will needs have it, that men and women are joined together like
other animals, by the motives of concupiscence; and that their tenderness
towards their young proceedeth from the like natural principle: for which
reason they will never allow, that a child is under any obligation to his father
for begetting him, or to his mother for bringing him into the world; which,
considering the miseries of human life, was neither a benefit in itself, nor
intended so by his parents, whose thoughts in their love-encounters were otherwise employed. Upon these, and the like reasonings, their opinion is, that
parents are the last of all others to be trusted with the education of their own
children: and therefore they have in every town public nurseries, where all
parents, except cottagers[7] and laborers, are obliged to send their infants of
both sexes to be reared and educated when they come to the age of twenty
moons; at which time they are supposed to have some rudiments of docility.
These schools are of several kinds, suited to different qualities, and to both
sexes. They have certain professors[8] well skilled in preparing children for such
a condition of life as befits the rank of their parents, and their own capacities
as well as inclinations. I shall first say something of the male nurseries, and
then of the female.

The nurseries for males of noble or eminent birth are provided with grave
and learned professors, and their several deputies. The clothes and food of the
children are plain and simple. They are bred up in the principles of honor,
justice, courage, modesty, clemency, religion, and love of their country; they
are always employed in some business, except in the times of eating and sleeping, which are very short, and two hours for diversions, consisting of bodily
exercises. They are dressed by men until four years of age, and then are
obliged to dress themselves, although their quality be ever so great; and the
women attendants, who are aged proportionably to ours at fifty, perform only
the most menial offices. They are never suffered to converse with servants, but
go together in small or greater numbers to take their diversions, and always in
the presence of a professor, or one of his deputies; whereby they avoid those
early bad impressions of folly and vice to which our children are subject.
Their parents are suffered to see them only twice a year; the visit is not to last
above an hour; they are allowed to kiss the child at meeting and parting; but
a professor, who always standeth by on those occasions, will not suffer them to
whisper, or use any fondling expressions, or bring any presents of toys, sweetmeats, and the like.

The pension from each family for the education and entertainment[9] of a
child, upon failure of due payment, is levied by the Emperor's officers.

The nurseries for children of ordinary gentlemen, merchants, traders, and
handicrafts, are managed proportionably after the same manner; only those
designed for trades are put out apprentices at seven years old; whereas those
of persons of quality continue in their exercises until fifteen, which answers to

7. Agricultural workers, peasants.   9. Sustenance.
8. Professional teachers.

one and twenty with us: but the confinement is gradually lessened for the last three years.

In the female nurseries, the young girls of quality are educated much like the males, only they are dressed by orderly servants of their own sex, but always in the presence of a professor or deputy, until they come to dress themselves, which is at five years old. And if it be found that these nurses ever presume to entertain the girls with frightful or foolish stories, or the common follies practiced by chambermaids among us, they are publicly whipped thrice about the city, imprisoned for a year, and banished for life to the most desolate parts of the country. Thus the young ladies there are as much ashamed of being cowards and fools as the men; and despise all personal ornaments beyond decency and cleanliness: neither did I perceive any difference in their education, made by their difference of sex, only that the exercises of the females were not altogether so robust; and that some rules were given them relating to domestic life, and a smaller compass of learning was enjoined them: for their maxim is, that among people of quality, a wife should be always a reasonable and agreeable companion, because she cannot always be young. When the girls are twelve years old, which among them is the marriageable age, their parents or guardians take them home, with great expressions of gratitude to the professors, and seldom without tears of the young lady and her companions.

In the nurseries of females of the meaner sort, the children are instructed in all kinds of works proper for their sex, and their several degrees:[1] those intended for apprentices are dismissed at seven years old, the rest are kept to eleven.

The meaner families who have children at these nurseries are obliged, besides their annual pension, which is as low as possible, to return to the steward of the nursery a small monthly share of their gettings, to be a portion for the child; and therefore all parents are limited in their expenses by the law. For the Lilliputians think nothing can be more unjust, than that people, in subservience to their own appetites, should bring children into the world, and leave the burthen of supporting them on the public. As to persons of quality, they give security to appropriate a certain sum for each child, suitable to their condition; and these funds are always managed with good husbandry, and the most exact justice.

The cottagers and laborers keep their children at home, their business being only to till and cultivate the earth; and therefore their education is of little consequence to the public; but the old and diseased among them are supported by hospitals: for begging is a trade unknown in this empire.

And here it may perhaps divert the curious reader, to give some account of my domestic,[2] and my manner of living in this country, during a residence of nine months and thirteen days. Having a head mechanically turned, and being likewise forced by necessity, I had made for myself a table and chair convenient enough, out of the largest trees in the royal park. Two hundred sempstresses were employed to make me shirts, and linen for my bed and table, all of the strongest and coarsest kind they could get; which, however, they were forced to quilt together in several folds; for the thickest was some degrees finer than lawn. Their linen is usually three inches wide, and three foot make a piece. The sempstresses took my measure as I lay on the ground,

1. Various social ranks.   2. Household.

one standing at my neck, and another at my mid-leg, with a strong cord extended, that each held by the end, while the third measured the length of the cord with a rule of an inch long. Then they measured my right thumb, and desired no more; for by a mathematical computation, that twice round the thumb is one round the wrist, and so on to the neck and the waist; and by the help of my old shirt, which I displayed on the ground before them for a pattern, they fitted me exactly. Three hundred tailors were employed in the same manner to make me clothes; but they had another contrivance for taking my measure. I kneeled down, and they raised a ladder from the ground to my neck; upon this ladder one of them mounted, and let fall a plumb-line from my collar to the floor, which just answered the length of my coat; but my waist and arms I measured myself. When my clothes were finished, which was done in my house (for the largest of theirs would not have been able to hold them), they looked like the patchwork made by the ladies in England, only that mine were all of a color.

I had three hundred cooks to dress my victuals, in little convenient huts built about my house, where they and their families lived, and prepared me two dishes apiece. I took up twenty waiters in my hand, and placed them on the table; an hundred more attended below on the ground, some with dishes of meat, and some with barrels of wine, and other liquors, slung on their shoulders; all which the waiters above drew up as I wanted, in a very ingenious manner, by certain cords, as we draw the bucket up a well in Europe. A dish of their meat was a good mouthful, and a barrel of their liquor a reasonable draught. Their mutton yields to ours, but their beef is excellent. I have had a sirloin so large, that I have been forced to make three bites of it; but this is rare. My servants were astonished to see me eat it bones and all, as in our country we do the leg of a lark. Their geese and turkeys I usually eat at a mouthful, and I must confess they far exceed ours. Of their smaller fowl I could take up twenty or thirty at the end of my knife.

One day his Imperial Majesty, being informed of my way of living, desired that himself and his royal consort, with the young princes of the blood of both sexes, might have the happiness (as he was pleased to call it) of dining with me. They came accordingly, and I placed them upon chairs of state on my table, just over against me, with their guards about them. Flimnap the Lord High Treasurer attended there likewise, with his white staff; and I observed he often looked on me with a sour countenance, which I would not seem to regard, but eat more than usual, in honor to my dear country, as well as to fill the court with admiration. I have some private reasons to believe, that this visit from his Majesty gave Flimnap an opportunity of doing me ill offices to his master. That minister had always been my secret enemy, although he outwardly caressed me more than was usual to the moroseness of his nature. He represented to the Emperor the low condition of his treasury; that he was forced to take up money at great discount; that exchequer bills[3] would not circulate under nine per cent below par; that I had cost his Majesty above a million and a half of *sprugs* (their greatest gold coin, about the bigness of a spangle); and upon the whole, that it would be advisable in the Emperor to take the first fair occasion of dismissing me.

I am here obliged to vindicate the reputation of an excellent lady, who was

3. Government bills of credit. Walpole was noted as a canny financier.

an innocent sufferer upon my account. The Treasurer took a fancy to be jealous of his wife, from the malice of some evil tongues, who informed him that her Grace had taken a violent affection for my person; and the court-scandal ran for some time that she once came privately to my lodging. This I solemnly declare to be a most infamous falsehood, without any grounds, farther than that her Grace was pleased to treat me with all innocent marks of freedom and friendship. I own she came often to my house, but always publicly, nor ever without three more in the coach, who were usually her sister and young daughter, and some particular acquaintance; but this was common to many other ladies of the court. And I still appeal to my servants round, whether they at any time saw a coach at my door without knowing what persons were in it. On those occasions, when a servant had given me notice, my custom was to go immediately to the door; and, after paying my respects, to take up the coach and two horses very carefully in my hands (for if there were six horses, the postillion always unharnessed four) and place them on a table, where I had fixed a moveable rim quite round, of five inches high, to prevent accidents. And I have often had four coaches and horses at once on my table full of company, while I sat in my chair leaning my face towards them; and when I was engaged with one set, the coachmen would gently drive the others round my table. I have passed many an afternoon very agreeably in these conversations. But I defy the Treasurer, or his two informers (I will name them, and let them make their best of it) Clustril and Drunlo, to prove that any person ever came to me *incognito*, except the Secretary Reldresal, who was sent by express command of his Imperial Majesty, as I have before related. I should not have dwelt so long upon this particular, if it had not been a point wherein the reputation of a great lady is so nearly concerned, to say nothing of my own; although I had the honor to be a *Nardac*, which the Treasurer himself is not; for all the world knows he is only a *Clumglum*, a title inferior by one degree, as that of a marquis is to a duke in England; yet I allow he preceded me in right of his post. These false informations, which I afterwards came to the knowledge of, by an accident not proper to mention, made the Treasurer show his lady for some time an ill countenance, and me a worse; for although he was at last undeceived and reconciled to her, yet I lost all credit with him; and found my interest decline very fast with the Emperor himself, who was indeed too much governed by that favorite.

CHAPTER 7. *The author, being informed of a design to accuse him of high treason, makes his escape to Blefuscu. His reception there.*

Before I proceed to give an account of my leaving this kingdom, it may be proper to inform the reader of a private intrigue which had been for two months forming against me.

I had been hitherto all my life a stranger to courts, for which I was unqualified by the meanness of my condition. I had indeed heard and read enough of the dispositions of great princes and ministers; but never expected to have found such terrible effects of them in so remote a country, governed, as I thought, by very different maxims from those in Europe.

When I was just preparing to pay my attendance on the Emperor of Blefuscu, a considerable person at court (to whom I had been very serviceable at a time when he lay under the highest displeasure of his Imperial Majesty) came to my house very privately at night in a close chair, and without sending his name, desired admittance. The chairmen were dismissed; I put the chair, with his Lordship in it, into my coat-pocket; and giving orders to a trusty servant to say I was indisposed and gone to sleep, I fastened the door of my house, placed the chair on the table, according to my usual custom, and sat down by it. After the common salutations were over, observing his Lordship's countenance full of concern, and enquiring into the reason, he desired I would hear him with patience, in a matter that highly concerned my honor and my life. His speech was to the following effect, for I took notes of it as soon as he left me.

You are to know, said he, that several committees of council have been lately called in the most private manner on your account: and it is but two days since his Majesty came to a full resolution.

You are very sensible that Skyresh Bolgolam (*Galbet*, or High Admiral) hath been your mortal enemy almost ever since your arrival. His original reasons I know not; but his hatred is much increased since your great success against Blefuscu, by which his glory, as Admiral, is obscured. This lord, in conjunction with Flimnap the High Treasurer, whose enmity against you is notorious on account of his lady, Limtoc the General, Lalcon the Chamberlain, and Balmuff the Grand Justiciary, have prepared articles of impeachment against you, for treason, and other capital crimes.[4]

This preface made me so impatient, being conscious of my own merits and innocence, that I was going to interrupt; when he entreated me to be silent, and thus proceeded.

Out of gratitude for the favors you have done me, I procured information of the whole proceedings, and a copy of the articles, wherein I venture my head for your service.

Articles of Impeachment against Quinbus Flestrin
(*the* Man-Mountain).

ARTICLE 1

Whereas, by a statute made in the reign of his Imperial Majesty Calin Deffar Plune, it is enacted, that whoever shall make water within the precincts of the royal palace shall be liable to the pains and penalties of high treason: notwithstanding, the said Quinbus Flestrin, in open breach of the said law, under color of extinguishing the fire kindled in the apartment of his Majesty's most dear imperial consort, did maliciously, traitorously, and devilishly, by discharge of his urine, put out the said fire kindled in the said apartment, lying and being within the precincts of the said royal palace; against the statute in that case provided, etc., against the duty, etc.

ARTICLE 2

That the said Quinbus Flestrin, having brought the imperial fleet of Blefuscu into the royal port, and being afterwards commanded by his

---

4. After the Whigs had investigated Oxford and Bolingbroke, both were impeached for high treason, on charges of being sympathetic to the Jacobites and the French.

Imperial Majesty to seize all the other ships of the said empire of Blefuscu, and reduce that empire to a province, to be governed by a viceroy from hence; and to destroy and put to death not only all the Big-Endian exiles, but likewise all the people of that empire who would not immediately forsake the Big-Endian heresy: he, the said Flestrin, like a false traitor against his most auspicious, serene, Imperial Majesty, did petition to be excused from the said service, upon pretense of unwillingness to force the consciences, or destroy the liberties and lives of an innocent people.

ARTICLE 3

That, whereas certain ambassadors arrived from the court of Blefuscu to sue for peace in his Majesty's court: he the said Flestrin did, like a false traitor, aid, abet, comfort, and divert the said ambassadors; although he knew them to be servants to a prince who was lately an open enemy to his Imperial Majesty, and in open war against his said Majesty.

ARTICLE 4

That the said Quinbus Flestrin, contrary to the duty of a faithful subject, is now preparing to make a voyage to the court and empire of Blefuscu, for which he hath received only verbal license from his Imperial Majesty; and under color of the said license, doth falsely and traitorously intend to take the said voyage, and thereby to aid, comfort, and abet the Emperor of Blefuscu, so late an enemy, and in open war with his Imperial Majesty aforesaid.

There are some other articles, but these are the most important, of which I have read you an abstract.

In the several debates upon this impeachment, it must be confessed that his Majesty gave many marks of his great *lenity*; often urging the services you had done him, and endeavoring to extenuate your crimes. The Treasurer and Admiral insisted that you should be put to the most painful and ignominious death, by setting fire on your house at night; and the General was to attend with twenty thousand men armed with poisoned arrows, to shoot you on the face and hands. Some of your servants were to have private orders to strew a poisonous juice on your shirts and sheets, which would soon make you tear your own flesh, and die in the utmost torture. The General came into the same opinion; so that for a long time there was a majority against you. But his Majesty resolving, if possible, to spare your life, at last brought off[5] the Chamberlain.

Upon this incident, Reldresal, Principal Secretary for Private Affairs, who always approved[6] himself your true friend, was commanded by the Emperor to deliver his opinion, which he accordingly did; and therein justified the good thoughts you have of him. He allowed your crimes to be great; but that still there was room for mercy, the most commendable virtue in a prince, and for which his Majesty was so justly celebrated. He said, the friendship between

---

5. Won over.   6. Proved.

you and him was so well known to the world, that perhaps the most honorable board might think him partial: however, in obedience to the command he had received, he would freely offer his sentiments. That if his Majesty, in consideration of your services, and pursuant to his own merciful disposition, would please to spare your life, and only give order to put out both your eyes, he humbly conceived, that by this expedient justice might in some measure be satisfied, and all the world would applaud the *lenity* of the Emperor, as well as the fair and generous proceedings of those who have the honor to be his counselors. That the loss of your eyes would be no impediment to your bodily strength, by which you might still be useful to his Majesty. That blindness is an addition to courage, by concealing dangers from us; that the fear you had for your eyes was the greatest difficulty in bringing over the enemy's fleet; and it would be sufficient for you to see by the eyes of the ministers, since the greatest princes do no more.

This proposal was received with the utmost disapprobation by the whole board. Bolgolam, the Admiral, could not preserve his temper; but rising up in fury, said, he wondered how the Secretary durst presume to give his opinion for preserving the life of a traitor: that the services you had performed were, by all true reasons of state, the great aggravation of your crimes; that you, who were able to extinguish the fire by discharge of urine in her Majesty's apartment (which he mentioned with horror), might, at another time, raise an inundation by the same means, to drown the whole palace; and the same strength which enabled you to bring over the enemy's fleet might serve, upon the first discontent, to carry it back: that he had good reasons to think you were a Big-Endian in your heart; and as treason begins in the heart before it appears in overt acts, so he accused you as a traitor on that account, and therefore insisted you should be put to death.

The Treasurer was of the same opinion; he showed to what straits his Majesty's revenue was reduced by the charge of maintaining you, which would soon grow insupportable: that the Secretary's expedient of putting out your eyes was so far from being a remedy against this evil, that it would probably increase it; as it is manifest from the common practice of blinding some kind of fowl, after which they fed the faster, and grew sooner fat: that his sacred Majesty, and the council, who are your judges, were in their own consciences fully convinced of your guilt; which was a sufficient argument to condemn you to death, without the formal proofs required by the strict letter of the law.

But his Imperial Majesty, fully determined against capital punishment, was graciously pleased to say, that since the council thought the loss of your eyes too easy a censure, some other may be inflicted hereafter. And your friend the Secretary humbly desiring to be heard again, in answer to what the Treasurer had objected concerning the great charge his Majesty was at in maintaining you, said, that his Excellency, who had the sole disposal of the Emperor's revenue, might easily provide against this evil, by gradually lessening your establishment; by which, for want of sufficient food, you would grow weak and faint, and lose your appetite, and consequently decay and consume in a few months; neither would the stench of your carcass be then so dangerous, when it should become more than half diminished; and immediately upon your death, five or six thousand of his Majesty's subjects might, in two or three days, cut your flesh from your bones, take it away by cart-loads, and bury it in distant parts to prevent infection; leaving the skeleton as a monument of admiration to posterity.

Thus by the great friendship of the Secretary, the whole affair was compromised. It was strictly enjoined, that the project of starving you by degrees should be kept a secret; but the sentence of putting out your eyes was entered on the books; none dissenting except Bolgolam the Admiral, who being a creature of the Empress, was perpetually instigated by her Majesty to insist upon your death; she having borne perpetual malice against you, on account of that infamous and illegal method you took to extinguish the fire in her apartment.

In three days your friend the Secretary will be directed to come to your house, and read before you the articles of impeachment; and then to signify the great lenity and favor of his Majesty and council; whereby you are only condemned to the loss of your eyes, which his Majesty doth not question you will gratefully and humbly submit to; and twenty of his Majesty's surgeons will attend, in order to see the operation well performed, by discharging very sharp-pointed arrows into the balls of your eyes, as you lie on the ground.

I leave to your prudence what measures you will take; and to avoid suspicion, I must immediately return in as private a manner as I came.

His Lordship did so, and I remained alone, under many doubts and perplexities of mind.

It was a custom introduced by this prince and his ministry (very different, as I have been assured, from the practices of former times), that after the court had decreed any cruel execution, either to gratify the monarch's resentment, or the malice of a favorite, the Emperor always made a speech to his whole council, expressing his great lenity and tenderness, as qualities known and confessed by all the world. This speech was immediately published through the kingdom; nor did any thing terrify the people so much as those encomiums on his Majesty's mercy; because it was observed, that the more these praises were enlarged and insisted on, the more inhuman was the punishment, and the sufferer more innocent. Yet as to myself, I must confess, having never been designed for a courtier, either by my birth or education, I was so ill a judge of things, that I could not discover the lenity and favor of this sentence, but conceived it (perhaps erroneously) rather to be rigorous than gentle. I sometimes thought of standing my trial; for although I could not deny the facts alleged in the several articles, yet I hoped they would admit of some extenuations. But having in my life perused many state trials, which I ever observed to terminate as the judges thought fit to direct, I durst not rely on so dangerous a decision, in so critical a juncture, and against such powerful enemies. Once I was strongly bent upon resistance: for while I had liberty, the whole strength of that empire could hardly subdue me, and I might easily with stones pelt the metropolis to pieces; but I soon rejected that project with horror, by remembering the oath I had made to the Emperor, the favors I received from him, and the high title of *Nardac* he conferred upon me. Neither had I so soon learned the gratitude of courtiers, to persuade myself that his Majesty's present severities acquitted me of all past obligations.

At last I fixed upon a resolution, for which it is probable I may incur some censure, and not unjustly; for I confess I owe the preserving my eyes, and consequently my liberty, to my own great rashness and want of experience:

because if I had then known the nature of princes and ministers, which I have since observed in many other courts, and their methods of treating criminals less obnoxious than myself, I should with great alacrity and readiness have submitted to so *easy* a punishment. But hurried on by the precipitancy of youth, and having his Imperial Majesty's license to pay my attendance upon the Emperor of Blefuscu, I took this opportunity, before the three days were elapsed, to send a letter to my friend the Secretary, signifying my resolution of setting out that morning for Blefuscu,[7] pursuant to the leave I had got; and without waiting for an answer, I went to that side of the island where our fleet lay. I seized a large man of war, tied a cable to the prow, and lifting up the anchors, I stripped myself, put my clothes (together with my coverlet, which I carried under my arm) into the vessel; and drawing it after me, between wading and swimming, arrived at the royal port of Blefuscu, where the people had long expected me. They lent me two guides to direct me to the capital city, which is of the same name; I held them in my hands until I came within two hundred yards of the gate; and desired them to signify my arrival to one of the secretaries, and let him know, I there waited his Majesty's commands. I had an answer in about an hour, that his Majesty, attended by the royal family, and great officers of the court, was coming out to receive me. I advanced a hundred yards; the Emperor, and his train, alighted from their horses, the Empress and ladies from their coaches; and I did not perceive they were in any fright or concern. I lay on the ground to kiss his Majesty's and the Empress's hand. I told his Majesty that I was come according to my promise, and with the license of the Emperor my master, to have the honor of seeing so mighty a monarch, and to offer him any service in my power, consistent with my duty to my own prince; not mentioning a word of my disgrace, because I had hitherto no regular information of it, and might suppose myself wholly ignorant of any such design; neither could I reasonably conceive that the Emperor would discover the secret while I was out of his power: wherein, however, it soon appeared I was deceived.

I shall not trouble the reader with the particular account of my reception at this court, which was suitable to the generosity of so great a prince; nor of the difficulties I was in for want of a house and bed, being forced to lie on the ground, wrapped up in my coverlet.

CHAPTER 8. *The author, by a lucky accident, finds means to leave Blefuscu; and, after some difficulties, returns safe to his native country.*

Three days after my arrival, walking out of curiosity to the northeast coast of the island, I observed, about half a league off, in the sea, somewhat that looked like a boat overturned. I pulled off my shoes and stockings, and wading two or three hundred yards, I found the object to approach nearer by force of the tide; and then plainly saw it to be a real boat, which I supposed might, by some tempest, have been driven from a ship. Whereupon I returned immediately towards the city, and desired his Imperial Majesty to lend me twenty of the tallest vessels he had left after the loss of his fleet, and three thousand seamen under the command of his Vice Admiral. This fleet sailed round,

7. Before his trial for treason could be held, Bolingbroke had escaped to France.

while I went back the shortest way to the coast where I first discovered the boat; I found the tide had driven it still nearer; the seamen were all provided with cordage, which I had beforehand twisted to a sufficient strength. When the ships came up, I stripped myself, and waded till I came within an hundred yards of the boat; after which I was forced to swim till I got up to it. The seamen threw me the end of the cord, which I fastened to a hole in the fore-part of the boat, and the other end to a man of war: but I found all my labor to little purpose; for being out of my depth, I was not able to work. In this necessity, I was forced to swim behind, and push the boat forwards as often as I could, with one of my hands; and the tide favoring me, I advanced so far, that I could just hold up my chin and feel the ground. I rested two or three minutes, and then gave the boat another shove, and so on till the sea was no higher than my armpits. And now the most laborious part being over, I took out my other cables which were stowed in one of the ships, and fastening them first to the boat, and then to nine of the vessels which attended me, the wind being favorable, the seamen towed, and I shoved till we arrived within forty yards of the shore; and waiting till the tide was out, I got dry to the boat, and by the assistance of two thousand men, with ropes and engines, I made a shift to turn it on its bottom, and found it was but little damaged.

I shall not trouble the reader with the difficulties I was under by the help of certain paddles, which cost me ten days making, to get my boat to the royal port of Blefuscu; where a mighty concourse of people appeared upon my arrival, full of wonder at the sight of so prodigious a vessel. I told the Emperor that my good fortune had thrown this boat in my way, to carry me to some place from whence I might return into my native country; and begged his Majesty's orders for getting materials to fit it up, together with license to depart; which, after some kind expostulations, he was pleased to grant.

I did very much wonder, in all this time, not to have heard of any express relating to me from our Emperor to the court of Blefuscu. But I was afterwards given privately to understand, that his Imperial Majesty, never imagining I had the least notice of his designs, believed I was only gone to Blefuscu in performance of my promise, according to the license he had given me, which was well known at our court; and would return in a few days when that cere-mony was ended. But he was at last in pain at my long absence; and, after consulting with the Treasurer, and the rest of that cabal, a person of quality was dispatched with the copy of the articles against me. This envoy had instructions to represent to the monarch of Blefuscu the great lenity of his master, who was content to punish me no further than with the loss of my eyes; that I had fled from justice, and if I did not return in two hours, I should be deprived of my title of *Nardac*, and declared a traitor. The envoy further added, that in order to maintain the peace and amity between both empires, his master expected, that his brother of Blefuscu would give orders to have me sent back to Lilliput, bound hand and foot, to be punished as a traitor.

The Emperor of Blefuscu, having taken three days to consult, returned an answer consisting of many civilities and excuses. He said, that as for sending me bound, his brother knew it was impossible; that although I had deprived him of his fleet, yet he owed great obligations to me for many good offices I had done him in making the peace. That however, both their Majesties would soon be made easy; for I had found a prodigious vessel on the shore, able to carry me on the sea, which he had given order to fit up with my own assistance and direction; and he hoped in a few weeks both empires would be freed from so insupportable an incumbrance.

With this answer the envoy returned to Lilliput, and the monarch of Blefuscu related to me all that had passed, offering me at the same time (but under the strictest confidence) his gracious protection, if I would continue in his service; wherein although I believed him sincere, yet I resolved never more to put any confidence in princes or ministers, where I could possibly avoid it; and therefore, with all due acknowledgements for his favorable intentions, I humbly begged to be excused. I told him, that since fortune, whether good or evil, had thrown a vessel in my way, I was resolved to venture myself in the ocean, rather than be an occasion of difference between two such mighty monarchs. Neither did I find the Emperor at all displeased; and I discovered by a certain accident, that he was very glad of my resolution, and so were most of his ministers.

These considerations moved me to hasten my departure somewhat sooner than I intended; to which the court, impatient to have me gone, very readily contributed. Five hundred workmen were employed to make two sails to my boat, according to my directions, by quilting thirteen fold of their strongest linen together. I was at the pains of making ropes and cables, by twisting ten, twenty or thirty of the thickest and strongest of theirs. A great stone that I happened to find, after a long search by the seashore, served me for an anchor. I had the tallow of three hundred cows for greasing my boat, and other uses. I was at incredible pains in cutting down some of the largest timber trees for oars and masts, wherein I was, however, much assisted by his Majesty's ship-carpenters, who helped me in smoothing them, after I had done the rough work.

In about a month, when all was prepared, I sent to receive his Majesty's commands, and to take my leave. The Emperor and royal family came out of the palace; I lay down on my face to kiss his hand, which he very graciously gave me: so did the Empress, and young princes of the blood. His Majesty presented me with fifty purses of two hundred *sprugs* apiece, together with his picture at full length, which I put immediately into one of my gloves, to keep it from being hurt. The ceremonies at my departure were too many to trouble the reader with at this time.

I stored the boat with the carcasses of an hundred oxen, and three hundred sheep, with bread and drink proportionable, and as much meat ready dressed as four hundred cooks could provide. I took with me six cows and two bulls alive, with as many ewes and rams, intending to carry them into my own country, and propagate the breed. And to feed them on board, I had a good bundle of hay, and a bag of corn.[8] I would gladly have taken a dozen of the natives; but this was a thing the Emperor would by no means permit; and besides a diligent search into my pockets, his Majesty engaged my honor not to carry away any of his subjects, although with their own consent and desire.

Having thus prepared all things as well as I was able, I set sail on the twenty-fourth day of September, 1701, at six in the morning; and when I had gone about four leagues to the northward, the wind being at southeast, at six in the evening, I descried a small island about half a league to the northwest. I

8. Wheat, not maize.

advanced forward, and cast anchor on the lee-side of the island, which seemed to be uninhabited. I then took some refreshment, and went to my rest. I slept well, and as I conjecture at least six hours; for I found the day broke in two hours after I awaked. It was a clear night; I eat my breakfast before the sun was up; and heaving anchor, the wind being favorable, I steered the same course that I had done the day before, wherein I was directed by my pocket compass. My intention was to reach, if possible, one of those islands which I had reason to believe lay to the northeast of Van Diemen's Land. I discovered nothing all that day; but upon the next, about three in the afternoon, when I had by my computation made twenty-four leagues from Blefuscu, I descried a sail steering to the southeast; my course was due east. I hailed her, but could get no answer; yet I found I gained upon her, for the wind slackened. I made all the sail I could, and in half an hour she spied me, then hung out her ancient,[9] and discharged a gun. It is not easy to express the joy I was in upon the unexpected hope of once more seeing my beloved country, and the dear pledges[1] I had left in it. The ship slackened her sails, and I came up with her between five and six in the evening, September 26; but my heart leapt within me to see her English colors. I put my cows and sheep into my coat-pockets and got on board with all my little cargo of provisions. The vessel was an English merchantman, returning from Japan by the North and South Seas;[2] the captain, Mr. John Biddel of Deptford, a very civil man, and an excellent sailor. We were now in the latitude of 30 degrees south; there were about fifty men in the ship; and here I met an old comrade of mine, one Peter Williams, who gave me a good character to the captain. This gentleman treated me with kindness, and desired I would let him know what place I came from last, and whither I was bound; which I did in few words; but he thought I was raving, and that the dangers I underwent had disturbed my head; whereupon I took my black cattle and sheep out of my pocket, which, after great astonishment, clearly convinced him of my veracity. I then showed him the gold given me by the Emperor of Blefuscu, together with his Majesty's picture at full length, and some other rarities of that country. I gave him two purses of two hundred *sprugs* each, and promised, when we arrived in England, to make him a present of a cow and a sheep big with young.

I shall not trouble the reader with a particular account of this voyage; which was very prosperous for the most part. We arrived in the Downs[3] on the 13th of April, 1702. I had only one misfortune, that the rats on board carried away one of my sheep; I found her bones in a hole, picked clean from the flesh. The rest of my cattle I got safe on shore, and set them a grazing in a bowling-green at Greenwich, where the fineness of the grass made them feed very heartily, though I had always feared the contrary; neither could I possibly have preserved them in so long a voyage, if the captain had not allowed me some of his best biscuit, which rubbed to powder, and mingled with water, was their constant food. The short time I continued in England, I made a considerable profit by showing my cattle to many persons of quality, and others: and before I began my second voyage, I sold them for six hundred pounds. Since my last return, I find the breed is considerably increased, especially the sheep; which

---

9. Flag.
1. Hostages (i.e., his family).
2. North and South Pacific.

3. A rendezvous for ships off the southeast coast of England.

I hope will prove much to the advantage of the woolen manufacture, by the fineness of the fleeces.

I stayed but two months with my wife and family; for my insatiable desire of seeing foreign countries would suffer me to continue no longer. I left fifteen hundred pounds with my wife, and fixed her in a good house at Redriff. My remaining stock I carried with me, part in money, and part in goods, in hopes to improve my fortunes. My eldest uncle, John, had left me an estate in land, near Epping, of about thirty pounds a year; and I had a long lease of the Black Bull in Fetter Lane, which yielded me as much more: so that I was not in any danger of leaving my family upon the parish.[4] My son Johnny, named so after his uncle, was at the grammar school, and a towardly[5] child. My daughter Betty (who is now well married, and has children) was then at her needlework. I took leave of my wife, and boy and girl, with tears on both sides; and went on board the *Adventure*, a merchant-ship of three hundred tons, bound for Surat, Captain John Nicholas of Liverpool, Commander. But my account of this voyage must be referred to the second part of my *Travels*.

Part 2. A Voyage to Brobdingnag

CHAPTER 1. *A great storm described. The longboat sent to fetch water; the Author goes with it to discover the country. He is left on shore, is seized by one of the natives, and carried to a farmer's house. His reception there, with several accidents that happened there. A description of the inhabitants.*

Having been condemned by nature and fortune to an active and restless life, in ten months after my return I again left my native country, and took shipping in the Downs on the 20th day of June, 1702, in the *Adventure*, Captain John Nicholas, a Cornish man, Commander, bound for Surat.[6] We had a very prosperous gale till we arrived at the Cape of Good Hope, where we landed for fresh water, but discovering a leak we unshipped our goods and wintered there; for the Captain falling sick of an ague, we could not leave the Cape till the end of March. We then set sail, and had a good voyage till we passed the Straits of Madagascar; but having got northward of that island, and to about five degrees south latitude, the winds, which in those seas are observed to blow a constant equal gale between the north and west from the beginning of December to the beginning of May, on the 19th of April began to blow with much greater violence and more westerly than usual, continuing so far twenty days together, during which time we were driven a little to the east of the Molucca Islands and about three degrees northward of the Line, as our Captain found by an observation he took the 2nd of May, at which time the wind ceased, and it was a perfect calm, whereat I was not a little rejoiced. But he, being a man well experienced in the navigation of those seas, bid us all prepare against a storm, which accordingly happened the day following: for a southern wind, called the southern monsoon, began to set in.

4. On welfare (living on charity given by the parish).
5. Promising.
6. In India. The geography of the voyage (described next) is simple: The *Adventure*, after sailing up the east coast of Africa to about five degrees south of the equator (the "Line"), is blown past India into the Malay

Archipelago, north of the islands of Buru and Ceram. The storm then drives the ship northward and eastward, away from the coast of Siberia ("Great Tartary") into the northeast Pacific, at that time unexplored. Brobdingnag lies somewhere in the vicinity of Alaska.

Finding it was likely to overblow,[7] we took in our spritsail, and stood by to hand the foresail; but making foul weather, we looked the guns were all fast, and handed the mizzen. The ship lay very broad off, so we thought it better spooning before the sea, than trying or hulling. We reefed the foresail and set him, we hauled aft the foresheet; the helm was hard aweather. The ship wore bravely. We belayed the fore-downhaul; but the sail was split, and we hauled down the yard and got the sail into the ship, and unbound all the things clear of it. It was a very fierce storm; the sea broke strange and dangerous. We hauled off upon the lanyard of the whipstaff, and helped the man at helm. We would not get down our topmast, but let all stand, because she scudded before the sea very well, and we knew that the topmast being aloft, the ship was the wholesomer, and made better way through the sea, seeing we had searoom. When the storm was over, we set foresail and mainsail, and brought the ship to. Then we set the mizzen, main topsail and the fore topsail. Our course was east-northeast, the wind was at southwest. We got the starboard tacks aboard, we cast off our weather braces and lifts; we set in the lee braces, and hauled forward by the weather bowlings, and hauled them tight, and belayed them, and hauled over the mizzen tack to windward, and kept her full and by as near as she would lie.

During this storm, which was followed by a strong wind west-southwest, we were carried by my computation about five hundred leagues to the east, so that the oldest sailor on board could not tell in what part of the world we were. Our provisions held out well, our ship was staunch, and our crew all in good health; but we lay in the utmost distress for water. We thought it best to hold on the same course rather than turn more northerly, which might have brought us to the northwest parts of Great Tartary, and into the frozen sea.

On the 16th day of June, 1703, a boy on the topmast discovered land. On the 17th we came in full view of a great island or continent (for we knew not whether) on the south side whereof was a small neck of land jutting out into the sea, and a creek[8] too shallow to hold a ship of above one hundred tons. We cast anchor within a league of this creek, and our Captain sent a dozen of his men well armed in the longboat, with vessels for water if any could be found. I desired his leave to go with them that I might see the country and make what discoveries I could. When we came to land we saw no river or spring, nor any sign of inhabitants. Our men therefore wandered on the shore to find out some fresh water near the sea, and I walked alone about a mile on the other side, where I observed the country all barren and rocky. I now began to be weary, and seeing nothing to entertain my curiosity, I returned gently down towards the creek; and the sea being full in my view, I saw our men already got into the boat, and rowing for life to the ship. I was going to hollow after them, although it had been to little purpose, when I observed a huge creature walking after them in the sea as fast as he could; he waded not much deeper than his knees and took prodigious strides, but our men had the start of him half a league, and the sea thereabouts being full of sharp-pointed rocks, the monster was not able to overtake the boat. This I was afterwards told, for I durst not stay to see the issue of that adventure, but ran as fast as I could the way I first went, and then climbed up a steep hill, which gave me some pros-

---

7. This paragraph is taken almost literally from Samuel Sturmy's *Mariner's Magazine* (1669). Swift is ridiculing the use of technical terms by writers of popular voyages.

8. A small bay or cove, affording anchorage.

pect of the country. I found it fully cultivated; but that which first surprised me was the length of the grass, which, in those grounds that seemed to be kept for hay, was about twenty foot high.[9]

I fell into a highroad, for so I took it to be, although it served to the inhabitants only as a footpath through a field of barley. Here I walked on for some time, but could see little on either side, it being now near harvest, and the corn[1] rising at least forty foot. I was an hour walking to the end of this field, which was fenced in with a hedge of at least one hundred and twenty foot high, and the trees so lofty that I could make no computation of their altitude. There was a stile to pass from this field into the next: it had four steps, and a stone to cross over when you came to the utmost. It was impossible for me to climb this stile, because every step was six foot high, and the upper stone above twenty. I was endeavoring to find some gap in the hedge when I discovered one of the inhabitants in the next field advancing towards the stile, of the same size with him whom I saw in the sea pursuing our boat. He appeared as tall as an ordinary spire-steeple, and took about ten yards at every stride, as near as I could guess. I was struck with the utmost fear and astonishment, and ran to hide myself in the corn, from whence I saw him at the top of the stile, looking back into the next field on the right hand; and heard him call in a voice many degrees louder than a speaking trumpet; but the noise was so high in the air that at first I certainly thought it was thunder. Whereupon seven monsters like himself came towards him with reaping hooks in their hands, each hook about the largeness of six scythes. These people were not so well clad as the first, whose servants or laborers they seemed to be. For, upon some words he spoke, they went to reap the corn in the field where I lay. I kept from them at as great a distance as I could, but was forced to move with extreme difficulty, for the stalks of the corn were sometimes not above a foot distant, so that I could hardly squeeze my body betwixt them. However, I made a shift to go forward till I came to a part of the field where the corn had been laid by the rain and wind; here it was impossible for me to advance a step, for the stalks were so interwoven that I could not creep through, and the beards of the fallen ears so strong and pointed that they pierced through my clothes into my flesh. At the same time I heard the reapers not above an hundred yards behind me. Being quite dispirited with toil, and wholly overcome by grief and despair, I lay down between two ridges and heartily wished I might there end my days. I bemoaned my desolate widow and fatherless children; I lamented my own folly and willfulness in attempting a second voyage against the advice of all my friends and relations. In this terrible agitation of mind, I could not forbear thinking of Lilliput, whose inhabitants looked upon me as the greatest prodigy that ever appeared in the world; where I was able to draw an imperial fleet in my hand, and perform those other actions which will be recorded forever in the chronicles of that empire, while posterity shall hardly believe them, although attested by millions. I reflected what a mortification it must prove to me to appear as inconsiderable in this nation as one single Lilliputian would be among us. But this I conceived was to be the least of my misfortunes; for as human creatures are observed to be more savage and cruel in proportion to their bulk, what could I expect but to be a morsel in the mouth of the first

9. Swift's intention, not always carried out accurately, is that everything in Brobdingnag should be, in rela- tion to our familiar world, on a scale of ten to one.
1. Wheat.

among these enormous barbarians who should happen to seize me? Undoubtedly philosophers are in the right when they tell us that nothing is great or
little otherwise than by comparison. It might have pleased fortune to let the
Lilliputians find some nation where the people were as diminutive with
respect to them as they were to me. And who knows but that even this prodigious race of mortals might be equally overmatched in some distant part of
the world, whereof we have yet no discovery?

Scared and confounded as I was, I could not forbear going on with these
reflections; when one of the reapers approaching within ten yards of the ridge
where I lay, made me apprehend that with the next step I should be squashed
to death under his foot, or cut in two with his reaping hook. And therefore
when he was again about to move, I screamed as loud as fear could make me.
Whereupon the huge creature trod short, and looking round about under him
for some time, at last espied me as I lay on the ground. He considered a while
with the caution of one who endeavors to lay hold on a small dangerous animal in such a manner that it shall not be able either to scratch or to bite him,
as I myself have sometimes done with a weasel in England. At length he
ventured to take me up behind by the middle between his forefinger and
thumb, and brought me within three yards of his eyes, that he might behold
my shape more perfectly. I guessed his meaning, and my good fortune gave
me so much presence of mind that I resolved not to struggle in the least as he
held me in the air about sixty foot from the ground, although he grievously
pinched my sides, for fear I should slip through his fingers. All I ventured was
to raise mine eyes towards the sun, and place my hands together in a supplicating posture, and to speak some words in an humble melancholy tone, suitable
to the condition I then was in. For I apprehended every moment that he
would dash me against the ground, as we usually do any little hateful animal
which we have a mind to destroy. But my good star would have it that he
appeared pleased with my voice and gestures, and began to look upon me as
a curiosity, much wondering to hear me pronounce articulate words, although
he could not understand them. In the meantime I was not able to forbear
groaning and shedding tears and turning my head towards my sides, letting
him know, as well as I could, how cruelly I was hurt by the pressure of his
thumb and finger. He seemed to apprehend my meaning; for, lifting up the
lappet[2] of his coat, he put me gently into it, and immediately ran along with
me to his master, who was a substantial farmer, and the same person I had
first seen in the field.

The farmer having (as I supposed by their talk) received such an account of
me as his servant could give him, took a piece of a small straw about the size
of a walking staff, and therewith lifted up the lappets of my coat, which it
seems he thought to be some kind of covering that nature had given me. He
blew my hairs aside to take a better view of my face. He called his hinds[3]
about him, and asked them (as I afterwards learned) whether they had ever
seen in the fields any little creature that resembled me. He then placed me
softly on the ground upon all four; but I got immediately up, and walked
slowly backwards and forwards, to let those people see I had no intent to run
away. They all sat down in a circle about me, the better to observe my
motions. I pulled off my hat, and made a low bow towards the farmer; I fell

2. Flap or fold.   3. Farm servants.

on my knees, and lifted up my hands and eyes, and spoke several words as loud as I could; I took a purse of gold out of my pocket, and humbly presented it to him. He received it on the palm of his hand, then applied it close to his eye to see what it was, and afterwards turned it several times with the point of a pin (which he took out of his sleeve), but could make nothing of it. Whereupon I made a sign that he should place his hand on the ground; I then took the purse, and opening it, poured all the gold into his palm. There were six Spanish pieces of four pistoles each, beside twenty or thirty smaller coins. I saw him wet the tip of his little finger upon his tongue, and take up one of my largest pieces, and then another; but he seemed to be wholly ignorant what they were. He made me a sign to put them again into my purse, and the purse again into my pocket, which after offering to him several times, I thought it best to do.

The farmer by this time was convinced I must be a rational creature. He spoke often to me, but the sound of his voice pierced my ears like that of a water mill, yet his words were articulate enough. I answered as loud as I could in several languages, and he often laid his ear within two yards of me, but all in vain, for we were wholly unintelligible to each other. He then sent his servants to their work, and taking his handkerchief out of his pocket, he doubled and spread it on his hand, which he placed flat on the ground with the palm upwards, making me a sign to step into it, as I could easily do, for it was not above a foot in thickness. I thought it my part to obey, and for fear of falling, laid myself at full length upon the handkerchief, with the remainder of which he lapped me up to the head for further security, and in this manner carried me home to his house. There he called his wife, and showed me to her; but she screamed and ran back as women in England do at the sight of a toad or a spider. However, when she had a while seen my behavior, and how well I observed the signs her husband made, she was soon reconciled, and by degrees grew extremely tender of me.

It was about twelve at noon, and a servant brought in dinner. It was only one substantial dish of meat (fit for the plain condition of an husbandman) in a dish of about four-and-twenty foot diameter. The company were the farmer and his wife, three children, and an old grandmother. When they were sat down, the farmer placed me at some distance from him on the table, which was thirty foot high from the floor. I was in a terrible fright, and kept as far as I could from the edge, for fear of falling. The wife minced a bit of meat, then crumbled some bread on a trencher, and placed it before me. I made her a low bow, took out my knife and fork, and fell to eat; which gave them exceeding delight. The mistress sent her maid for a small dram cup, which held about two gallons, and filled it with drink; I took up the vessel with much difficulty in both hands, and in a most respectful manner drank to her ladyship's health, expressing the words as loud as I could in English; which made the company laugh so heartily that I was almost deafened with the noise. This liquor tasted like a small cider,[4] and was not unpleasant. Then the master made me a sign to come to his trencher side; but as I walked on the table, being in great surprise all the time, as the indulgent reader will easily conceive and excuse, I happened to stumble against a crust, and fell flat on my face, but received no hurt. I got up immediately, and observing the good people to

4. I.e., weak cider.

be in much concern, I took my hat (which I held under my arm out of good manners) and waving it over my head, made three huzzas to show I had got no mischief by my fall. But advancing forwards toward my master (as I shall henceforth call him), his youngest son who sat next him, an arch boy of about ten years old, took me up by the legs, and held me so high in the air that I trembled every limb; but his father snatched me from him, and at the same time gave him such a box on the left ear as would have felled an European troop of horse to the earth, ordering him to be taken from the table. But being afraid the boy might owe me a spite, and well remembering how mischievous all children among us naturally are to sparrows, rabbits, young kittens, and puppy dogs, I fell on my knees, and pointing to the boy, made my master to understand, as well as I could, that I desired his son might be pardoned. The father complied, and the lad took his seat again; whereupon I went to him and kissed his hand, which my master took, and made him stroke me gently with it.

In the midst of dinner, my mistress's favorite cat leaped into her lap. I heard a noise behind me like that of a dozen stocking weavers at work; and turning my head, I found it proceeded from the purring of this animal, who seemed to be three times larger than an ox, as I computed by the view of her head and one of her paws, while her mistress was feeding and stroking her. The fierceness of this creature's countenance altogether discomposed me, although I stood at the farther end of the table, about fifty foot off, and although my mistress held her fast for fear she might give a spring and seize me in her talons. But it happened there was no danger, for the cat took not the least notice of me when my master placed me within three yards of her. And as I have been always told, and found true by experience in my travels, that flying or discovering[5] fear before a fierce animal is a certain way to make it pursue or attack you, so I resolved in this dangerous juncture to show no manner of concern. I walked with intrepidity five or six times before the very head of the cat, and came within half a yard of her; whereupon she drew herself back, as if she were more afraid of me. I had less apprehension concerning the dogs, whereof three or four came into the room, as it is usual in farmers' houses; one of which was a mastiff, equal in bulk to four elephants, and a greyhound, somewhat taller than the mastiff, but not so large.

When dinner was almost done, the nurse came in with a child of a year old in her arms, who immediately spied me, and began a squall that you might have heard from London Bridge to Chelsea, after the usual oratory of infants, to get me for a plaything. The mother out of pure indulgence took me up, and put me towards the child, who presently seized me by the middle, and got my head in his mouth, where I roared so loud that the urchin was frighted and let me drop; and I should infallibly have broke my neck if the mother had not held her apron under me. The nurse to quiet her babe made use of a rattle, which was a kind of hollow vessel filled with great stones, and fastened by a cable to the child's waist: but all in vain, so that she was forced to apply the last remedy by giving it suck. I must confess no object ever disgusted me so much as the sight of her monstrous breast, which I cannot tell what to compare with so as to give the curious reader an idea of its bulk, shape, and color. It stood prominent six foot, and could not be less than sixteen in circum-

5. Revealing.

ference. The nipple was about half the bigness of my head, and the hue both of that and the dug so varified with spots, pimples, and freckles that nothing could appear more nauseous: for I had a near sight of her, she sitting down the more conveniently to give suck, and I standing on the table. This made me reflect upon the fair skins of our English ladies, who appear so beautiful to us, only because they are of our own size, and their defects not to be seen but through a magnifying glass, where we find by experiment that the smoothest and whitest skins look rough and coarse and ill colored.

I remember when I was at Lilliput, the complexion of those diminutive people appeared to me the fairest in the world; and talking upon this subject with a person of learning there, who was an intimate friend of mine, he said that my face appeared much fairer and smoother when he looked on me from the ground than it did upon a nearer view when I took him up in my hand and brought him close, which he confessed was at first a very shocking sight. He said he could discover great holes in my skin; that the stumps of my beard were ten times stronger than the bristles of a boar, and my complexion made up of several colors altogether disagreeable: although I must beg leave to say for myself that I am as fair as most of my sex and country and very little sunburnt by all my travels. On the other side, discoursing of the ladies in that Emperor's court, he used to tell me one had freckles, another too wide a mouth, a third too large a nose; nothing of which I was able to distinguish. I confess this reflection was obvious enough; which however I could not forbear, lest the reader might think those vast creatures were actually deformed: for I must do them justice to say they are a comely race of people; and particularly the features of my master's countenance, although he were but a farmer, when I beheld him from the height of sixty foot, appeared very well proportioned.

When dinner was done, my master went out to his laborers; and as I could discover by his voice and gesture, gave his wife a strict charge to take care of me. I was very much tired and disposed to sleep, which my mistress perceiving, she put me on her own bed, and covered me with a clean white handkerchief, but larger and coarser than the mainsail of a man-of-war.

I slept about two hours, and dreamed I was at home with my wife and children, which aggravated my sorrows when I awaked and found myself alone in a vast room, between two and three hundred foot wide, and above two hundred high, lying in a bed twenty yards wide. My mistress was gone about her household affairs, and had locked me in. The bed was eight yards from the floor. Some natural necessities required me to get down; I durst not presume to call, and if I had, it would have been in vain with such a voice as mine at so great a distance from the room where I lay to the kitchen where the family kept. While I was under these circumstances, two rats crept up the curtains, and ran smelling backwards and forwards on the bed. One of them came up almost to my face; whereupon I rose in a fright, and drew out my hanger[6] to defend myself. These horrible animals had the boldness to attack me on both sides, and one of them held his forefeet at my collar; but I had the good fortune to rip up his belly before he could do me any mischief. He fell down at my feet; and the other seeing the fate of his comrade, made his escape, but not without one good wound on the back, which I gave him as he

6. A short, broad sword.

fled, and made the blood run trickling from him. After this exploit I walked gently to and fro on the bed, to recover my breath and loss of spirits. These creatures were of the size of a large mastiff, but infinitely more nimble and fierce; so that if I had taken off my belt before I went to sleep, I must have infallibly been torn to pieces and devoured. I measured the tail of the dead rat, and found it to be two yards long, wanting an inch; but it went against my stomach to drag the carcass off the bed, where it lay still bleeding; I observed it had yet some life, but with a strong slash cross the neck, I thoroughly dispatched it.

Soon after, my mistress came into the room, who seeing me all bloody, ran and took me up in her hand. I pointed to the dead rat, smiling and making other signs to show I was not hurt, whereat she was extremely rejoiced, calling the maid to take up the dead rat with a pair of tongs, and throw it out of the window. Then she set me on a table, where I showed her my hanger all bloody, and wiping it on the lappet of my coat, returned it to the scabbard. I was pressed to do more than one thing, which another could not do for me, and therefore endeavored to make my mistress understand that I desired to be set down on the floor; which after she had done, my bashfulness would not suffer me to express myself farther than by pointing to the door, and bowing several times. The good woman with much difficulty at last perceived what I would be at, and taking me up again in her hand, walked into the garden, where she set me down. I went on one side about two hundred yards; and beckoning to her not to look or to follow me, I hid myself between two leaves of sorrel, and there discharged the necessities of nature.

I hope the gentle reader will excuse me for dwelling on these and the like particulars, which however insignificant they may appear to groveling vulgar minds, yet will certainly help a philosopher[7] to enlarge his thoughts and imagination, and apply them to the benefit of public as well as private life, which was my sole design in presenting this and other accounts of my travels to the world; wherein I have been chiefly studious of truth, without affecting any ornaments of learning or of style. But the whole scene of this voyage made so strong an impression on my mind, and is so deeply fixed in my memory, that in committing it to paper I did not omit one material circumstance; however, upon a strict review, I blotted out several passages of less moment which were in my first copy, for fear of being censured as tedious and trifling, whereof travelers are often, perhaps not without justice, accused.

Chapter 2. *A description of the farmer's daughter. The Author carried to a market town, and then to the metropolis. The particulars of his journey.*

My mistress had a daughter of nine years old, a child of towardly parts for her age, very dexterous at her needle, and skillful in dressing her baby.[8] Her mother and she contrived to fit up the baby's cradle for me against night: the cradle was put into a small drawer of a cabinet, and the drawer placed upon a hanging shelf for fear of the rats. This was my bed all the time I stayed with those people, although made more convenient by degrees as I began to learn their language, and make my wants known. This young girl was so handy, that

7. "Vulgar": commonplace, uncultivated, in contrast   8. Doll. "Towardly parts": promising abilities.
to the scientist ("philosopher"); an irony.

after I had once or twice pulled off my clothes before her, she was able to dress and undress me, although I never gave her that trouble when she would let me do either myself. She made me seven shirts, and some other linen of as fine cloth as could be got, which indeed was coarser than sackcloth, and these she constantly washed for me with her own hands. She was likewise my schoolmistress to teach me the language: when I pointed to anything, she told me the name of it in her own tongue, so that in a few days I was able to call for whatever I had a mind to. She was very good-natured, and not above forty foot high, being little for her age. She gave me the name of *Grildrig*, which the family took up, and afterwards the whole kingdom. The word imports what the Latins call *nanunculus*, the Italian *homunceletino*,[9] and the English *mannikin*. To her I chiefly owe my preservation in that country: we never parted while I was there; I called her my *Glumdalclitch*, or little nurse: and I should be guilty of great ingratitude if I omitted this honorable mention of her care and affection towards me, which I heartily wish it lay in my power to requite as she deserves, instead of being the innocent but unhappy instrument of her disgrace, as I have too much reason to fear.

It now began to be known and talked of in the neighborhood that my master had found a strange animal in the field, about the bigness of a *splacknuck*, but exactly shaped in every part like a human creature, which it likewise imitated in all its actions: seemed to speak in a little language of its own, had already learned several words of theirs, went erect upon two legs, was tame and gentle, would come when it was called, do whatever it was bid, had the finest limbs in the world, and a complexion fairer than a nobleman's daughter of three years old. Another farmer who lived hard by, and was a particular friend of my master, came on a visit on purpose to inquire into the truth of this story. I was immediately produced, and placed upon a table, where I walked as I was commanded, drew my hanger, put it up again, made my reverence to my master's guest, asked him in his own language how he did, and told him he was welcome, just as my little nurse had instructed me. This man, who was old and dimsighted, put on his spectacles to behold me better, at which I could not forbear laughing very heartily, for his eyes appeared like the full moon shining into a chamber at two windows. Our people, who discovered the cause of my mirth, bore me company in laughing, at which the old fellow was fool enough to be angry and out of countenance. He had the character of a great miser, and to my misfortune he well deserved it by the cursed advice he gave my master to show me as a sight upon a market day in the next town, which was half an hour's riding, about two and twenty miles from our house. I guessed there was some mischief contriving when I observed my master and his friend whispering long together, sometimes pointing at me; and my fears made me fancy that I overheard and understood some of their words. But the next morning Glumdalclitch, my little nurse, told me the whole matter, which she had cunningly picked out from her mother. The poor girl laid me on her bosom, and fell a weeping with shame and grief. She apprehended some mischief would happen to me from rude vulgar folks, who might squeeze me to death, or break one of my limbs by taking me in their hands. She had also observed how modest I was in my nature, how nicely I regarded

---

9. The Latin and Italian words are Swift's own coinages, as, of course, are the various words from the Brobdingnagian language.

my honor, and what an indignity I should conceive it to be exposed for money as a public spectacle to the meanest of the people. She said her papa and mamma had promised that Grildrig should be hers; but now she found they meant to serve her as they did last year, when they pretended to give her a lamb, and yet, as soon as it was fat, sold it to a butcher. For my own part, I may truly affirm that I was less concerned than my nurse. I had a strong hope, which never left me, that I should one day recover my liberty; and as to the ignominy of being carried about for a monster, I considered myself to be a perfect stranger in the country, and that such a misfortune could never be charged upon me as a reproach, if ever I should return to England; since the King of Great Britain himself, in my condition, must have undergone the same distress.

My master, pursuant to the advice of his friend, carried me in a box the next market day to the neighboring town, and took along with him his little daughter, my nurse, upon a pillion[1] behind him. The box was close on every side, with a little door for me to go in and out, and a few gimlet holes to let in air. The girl had been so careful to put the quilt of her baby's bed into it, for me to lie down on. However, I was terribly shaken and discomposed in this journey, although it were but of half an hour. For the horse went about forty foot at every step, and trotted so high that the agitation was equal to the rising and falling of a ship in a great storm, but much more frequent. Our journey was somewhat further than from London to St. Albans. My master alighted at an inn which he used to frequent; and after consulting a while with the inn-keeper, and making some necessary preparations, he hired the *Grultrud*, or crier, to give notice through the town of a strange creature to be seen at the Sign of the Green Eagle, not so big as a *splacknuck* (an animal in that country very finely shaped, about six foot long), and in every part of the body resembling an human creature; could speak several words and perform an hundred diverting tricks.

I was placed upon a table in the largest room of the inn, which might be near three hundred foot square. My little nurse stood on a low stool close to the table, to take care of me, and direct what I should do. My master, to avoid a crowd, would suffer only thirty people at a time to see me. I walked about on the table as the girl commanded; she asked me questions as far as she knew my understanding of the language reached, and I answered them as loud as I could. I turned about several times to the company, paid my humble respects, said they were welcome, and used some other speeches I had been taught. I took up a thimble filled with liquor, which Glumdalclitch had given me for a cup, and drank their health. I drew out my hanger, and flourished with it after the manner of fencers in England. My nurse gave me part of a straw, which I exercised as pike, having learned the art in my youth. I was that day shown to twelve sets of company, and as often forced to go over again with the same fopperies, till I was half dead with weariness and vexation. For those who had seen me made such wonderful reports that the people were ready to break down the doors to come in. My master for his own interest would not suffer anyone to touch me except my nurse; and, to prevent danger, benches were set round the table at such a distance as put me out of everybody's reach. However, an unlucky schoolboy aimed a hazelnut directly at my head, which

---

1. A pad attached to the hinder part of a saddle, on which a second person, usually a woman, could ride.

very narrowly missed me; otherwise, it came with so much violence that it would have infallibly knocked out my brains, for it was almost as large as a small pumpion:[2] but I had the satisfaction to see the young rogue well beaten, and turned out of the room.

My master gave public notice that he would show me again the next market day, and in the meantime he prepared a more convenient vehicle for me, which he had reason enough to do; for I was so tired with my first journey, and with entertaining company for eight hours together, that I could hardly stand upon my legs or speak a word. It was at least three days before I recovered my strength; and that I might have no rest at home, all the neighboring gentlemen from an hundred miles round, hearing of my fame, came to see me at my master's own house. There could not be fewer than thirty persons with their wives and children (for the country is very populous); and my master demanded the rate of a full room whenever he showed me at home, although it were only to a single family. So that for some time I had but little ease every day of the week (except Wednesday, which is their Sabbath) although I were not carried to the town.

My master finding how profitable I was like to be, resolved to carry me to the most considerable cities of the kingdom. Having therefore provided himself with all things necessary for a long journey, and settled his affairs at home, he took leave of his wife; and upon the 17th of August, 1703, about two months after my arrival, we set out for the metropolis, situated near the middle of that empire, and about three thousand miles distance from our house. My master made his daughter Glumdalclitch ride behind him. She carried me on her lap in a box tied about her waist. The girl had lined it on all sides with the softest cloth she could get, well quilted underneath, furnished it with her baby's bed, provided me with linen and other necessaries, and made everything as convenient as she could. We had no other company but a boy of the house, who rode after us with the luggage.

My master's design was to show me in all the towns by the way, and to step out of the road for fifty or an hundred miles to any village or person of quality's house where he might expect custom. We made easy journeys of not above seven or eight score miles a day: for Glumdalclitch, on purpose to spare me, complained she was tired with the trotting of the horse. She often took me out of my box at my own desire, to give me air and show me the country, but always held me fast by leading strings. We passed over five or six rivers many degrees broader and deeper than the Nile or the Ganges; and there was hardly a rivulet so small as the Thames at London Bridge. We were ten weeks in our journey, and I was shown in eighteen large towns, besides many large villages and private families.

On the 26th day of October, we arrived at the metropolis, called in their language *Lorbrulgrud*, or Pride of the Universe. My master took a lodging in the principal street of the city, not far from the royal palace, and put out bills in the usual form, containing an exact description of my person and parts. He hired a large room between three and four hundred foot wide. He provided a table sixty foot in diameter, upon which I was to act my part, and palisadoed it round three foot from the edge, and as many high, to prevent my falling over. I was shown ten times a day to the wonder and satisfaction of all people.

2. Pumpkin.

I could now speak the language tolerably well, and perfectly understood every word that was spoken to me. Besides, I had learned their alphabet, and could make a shift to explain a sentence here and there; for Glumdalclitch had been my instructor while we were at home, and at leisure hours during our journey. She carried a little book in her pocket, not much larger than a Sanson's *Atlas;*[3] it was a common treatise for the use of young girls, giving a short account of their religion: out of this she taught me my letters, and interpreted the words.

CHAPTER 3. *The Author sent for to Court. The Queen buys him of his master, the farmer, and presents him to the King. He disputes with his Majesty's great scholars. An apartment at Court provided for the Author. He is in high favor with the Queen. He stands up for the honor of his own country. His quarrels with the Queen's dwarf.*

The frequent labors I underwent every day made in a few weeks a very considerable change in my health: the more my master got by me, the more unsatiable he grew. I had quite lost my stomach, and was almost reduced to a skeleton. The farmer observed it, and concluding I soon must die, resolved to make as good a hand of me as he could. While he was thus reasoning and resolving with himself, a *Slardral,* or Gentleman Usher, came from Court, commanding my master to carry me immediately thither for the diversion of the Queen and her ladies. Some of the latter had already been to see me and reported strange things of my beauty, behavior, and good sense. Her Majesty and those who attended her were beyond measure delighted with my demeanor. I fell on my knees and begged the honor of kissing her Imperial foot; but this gracious princess held out her little finger towards me (after I was set on a table), which I embraced in both my arms, and put the tip of it, with the utmost respect, to my lip. She made me some general questions about my country and my travels, which I answered as distinctly and in as few words as I could. She asked whether I would be content to live at Court. I bowed down to the board of the table, and humbly answered that I was my master's slave, but if I were at my own disposal, I should be proud to devote my life to her Majesty's service. She then asked my master whether he were willing to sell me at a good price. He, who apprehended I could not live a month, was ready enough to part with me, and demanded a thousand pieces of gold, which were ordered him on the spot, each piece being about the bigness of eight hundred moidores;[4] but, allowing for the proportion of all things between that country and Europe, and the high price of gold among them, was hardly so great a sum as a thousand guineas would be in England. I then said to the Queen, since I was now her Majesty's most humble creature and vassal, I must beg the favor that Glumdalclitch, who had always tended me with so much care and kindness, and understood to do it so well, might be admitted into her service, and continue to be my nurse and instructor. Her Majesty agreed to my petition, and easily got the farmer's consent, who was glad enough to have his daughter preferred at Court; and the poor girl herself was not able to hide her joy. My late master withdrew, bidding me farewell, and saying he had left me in a good service; to which I replied not a word, only making him a slight bow.

---

3. I.e., over two feet long and about two feet wide.   4. Portuguese coins.

The Queen observed my coldness, and when the farmer was gone out of the apartment, asked me the reason. I made bold to tell her Majesty that I owed no other obligation to my late master than his not dashing out the brains of a poor harmless creature found by chance in his field; which obligation was amply recompensed by the gain he had made in showing me through half the kingdom, and the price he had now sold me for. That the life I had since led was laborious enough to kill an animal of ten times my strength. That my health was much impaired by the continual drudgery of entertaining the rabble every hour of the day; and that if my master had not thought my life in danger, her Majesty perhaps would not have got so cheap a bargain. But as I was out of all fear of being ill treated under the protection of so great and good an Empress, the Ornament of Nature, the Darling of the World, the Delight of her Subjects, the Phoenix of the Creation; so I hoped my late master's apprehensions would appear to be groundless, for I already found my spirits to revive by the influence of her most august presence.

This was the sum of my speech, delivered with great improprieties and hesitation; the latter part was altogether framed in the style peculiar to that people, whereof I learned some phrases from Glumdalclitch, while she was carrying me to Court.

The Queen, giving great allowance for my defectiveness in speaking, was however surprised at so much wit and good sense in so diminutive an animal. She took me in her own hand, and carried me to the King, who was then retired to his cabinet.[5] His Majesty, a prince of much gravity, and austere countenance, not well observing my shape at first view, asked the Queen after a cold manner how long it was since she grew fond of a *splacknuck*; for such it seems he took me to be, as I lay upon my breast in her Majesty's right hand. But this princess, who hath an infinite deal of wit and humor, set me gently on my feet upon the scrutore,[6] and commanded me to give his Majesty an account of myself, which I did in a very few words; and Glumdalclitch, who attended at the cabinet door, and could not endure I should be out of her sight, being admitted, confirmed all that had passed from my arrival at her father's house.

The King, although he be as learned a person as any in his dominions, had been educated in the study of philosophy and particularly mathematics; yet when he observed my shape exactly, and saw me walk erect, before I began to speak, conceived I might be a piece of clockwork (which is in that country arrived to a very great perfection) contrived by some ingenious artist. But when he heard my voice, and found what I delivered to be regular and rational, he could not conceal his astonishment. He was by no means satisfied with the relation I gave him of the manner I came into his kingdom, but thought it a story concerted between Glumdalclitch and her father, who had taught me a set of words to make me sell at a higher price. Upon this imagination he put several other questions to me, and still received rational answers, no otherwise defective than by a foreign accent, and an imperfect knowledge in the language, with some rustic phrases which I had learned at the farmer's house, and did not suit the polite style of a court.

His Majesty sent for three great scholars who were then in their weekly waiting (according to the custom in that country). These gentlemen, after they

5. Private apartment.   6. Writing desk.

had a while examined my shape with much nicety, were of different opinions concerning me. They all agreed that I could not be produced according to the regular laws of nature, because I was not framed with a capacity of preserving my life, either by swiftness, or climbing of trees, or digging holes in the earth. They observed by my teeth, which they viewed with great exactness, that I was a carnivorous animal; yet most quadrupeds being an overmatch for me, and field mice, with some others, too nimble, they could not imagine how I should be able to support myself, unless I fed upon snails and other insects; which they offered, by many learned arguments, to evince that I could not possibly do. One of them seemed to think that I might be an embryo, or abortive birth. But this opinion was rejected by the other two, who observed my limbs to be perfect and finished, and that I had lived several years, as it was manifested from my beard, the stumps whereof they plainly discovered through a magnifying glass. They would not allow me to be a dwarf, because my littleness was beyond all degrees of comparison; for the Queen's favorite dwarf, the smallest ever known in that kingdom, was nearly thirty foot high. After much debate, they concluded unanimously that I was only *relplum scalcath*, which is interpreted literally, *lusus naturae*; a determination exactly agreeable to the modern philosophy of Europe, whose professors, disdaining the old evasion of *occult causes*, whereby the followers of Aristotle endeavor in vain to disguise their ignorance, have invented this wonderful solution of all difficulties, to the unspeakable advancement of human knowledge.[7]

After this decisive conclusion, I entreated to be heard a word or two. I applied myself to the King, and assured his Majesty that I came from a country which abounded with several millions of both sexes, and of my own stature, where the animals, trees, and houses were all in proportion, and where by consequence I might be as able to defend myself, and to find sustenance, as any of his Majesty's subjects could do here; which I took for a full answer to those gentlemen's arguments. To this they only replied with a smile of contempt, saying that the farmer had instructed me very well in my lesson. The King, who had a much better understanding, dismissing his learned men, sent for the farmer, who by good fortune was not yet gone out of town; having therefore first examined him privately, and then confronted him with me and the young girl, his Majesty began to think that what we told him might possibly be true. He desired the Queen to order that a particular care should be taken of me, and was of opinion that Glumdalclitch should still continue in her office of tending me, because he observed we had a great affection for each other. A convenient apartment was provided for her at Court; she had a sort of governess appointed to take care of her education, a maid to dress her, and two other servants for menial offices; but the care of me was wholly appropriated to herself. The Queen commanded her own cabinetmaker to contrive a box that might serve me for a bedchamber, after the model that Glumdalclitch and I should agree upon. This man was a most ingenious artist, and according to my directions, in three weeks finished for me a wooden chamber of sixteen foot square and twelve high, with sash windows, a door, and two closets, like a London bedchamber. The board that made the ceiling was to be lifted up and down by two hinges, to put in a bed ready furnished

---

7. Swift had contempt for both the medieval Schoolmen, who discussed "occult causes," the unknown causes of observable effects, and modern scientists, who, he believed, often concealed their ignorance by using equally meaningless terms. "*Lusus naturae*": one of nature's sports, or roughly, freaks.

by her Majesty's upholsterer, which Glumdalclitch took out every day to air, made it with her own hands, and letting it down at night, locked up the roof over me. A nice[8] workman, who was famous for little curiosities, undertook to make me two chairs, with backs and frames, of a substance not unlike ivory, and two tables, with a cabinet to put my things in. The room was quilted on all sides, as well as the floor and the ceiling, to prevent any accident from the carelessness of those who carried me, and to break the force of a jolt when I went in a coach. I desired a lock for my door to prevent rats and mice from coming in: the smith, after several attempts, made the smallest that ever was seen among them, for I have known a larger at the gate of a gentleman's house in England. I made a shift[9] to keep the key in a pocket of my own, fearing Glumdalclitch might lose it. The Queen likewise ordered the thinnest silks that could be gotten, to make me clothes, not much thicker than an English blanket, very cumbersome till I was accustomed to them. They were after the fashion of the kingdom, partly resembling the Persian, and partly the Chinese, and are a very grave, decent habit.

The Queen became so fond of my company that she could not dine without me. I had a table placed upon the same at which her Majesty ate, just at her left elbow, and a chair to sit on. Glumdalclitch stood upon a stool on the floor, near my table, to assist and take care of me. I had an entire set of silver dishes and plates, and other necessaries, which, in proportion to those of the Queen, were not much bigger than what I have seen of the same kind in a London toyshop,[1] for the furniture of a baby-house: these my little nurse kept in her pocket in a silver box and gave me at meals as I wanted them, always cleaning them herself. No person dined with the Queen but the two Princesses Royal, the elder sixteen years old, and the younger at that time thirteen and a month. Her Majesty used to put a bit of meat upon one of my dishes, out of which I carved for myself; and her diversion was to see me eat in miniature. For the Queen (who had indeed but a weak stomach) took up at one mouthful as much as a dozen English farmers could eat at a meal, which to me was for some time a very nauseous sight. She would craunch the wing of a lark, bones and all, between her teeth, although it were nine times as large as that of a full-grown turkey; and put a bit of bread into her mouth as big as two twelve-penny loaves. She drank out of a golden cup, above a hogshead at a draught. Her knives were twice as long as a scythe set straight upon the handle. The spoons, forks, and other instruments were all in the same proportion. I remember when Glumdalclitch carried me out of curiosity to see some of the tables at Court, where ten or a dozen of these enormous knives and forks were lifted up together, I thought I had never till then beheld so terrible a sight.

It is the custom that every Wednesday (which, as I have before observed, was their Sabbath) the King and Queen, with the royal issue of both sexes, dine together in the apartment of his Majesty, to whom I was now become a favorite; and at these times my little chair and table were placed at his left hand, before one of the salt-cellars. This prince took a pleasure in conversing with me, inquiring into the manners, religion, laws, government, and learning of Europe; wherein I gave him the best account I was able. His apprehension

---

8. Exact.   1. A shop for selling knickknacks.
9. Contrived.

was so clear, and his judgment so exact, that he made very wise reflections and observations upon all I said. But I confess that after I had been a little too copious in talking of my own beloved country, of our trade and wars by sea and land, of our schisms in religion and parties in the state, the prejudices of his education prevailed so far that he could not forbear taking me up in his right hand, and stroking me gently with the other, after an hearty fit of laughing, asked me whether I were a Whig or a Tory. Then turning to his first minister, who waited behind him with a white staff, near as tall as the mainmast of the *Royal Sovereign*,[2] he observed how contemptible a thing was human grandeur, which could be mimicked by such diminutive insects as I: "and yet," said he, "I dare engage, these creatures have their titles and distinctions of honor; they contrive little nests and burrows, that they call houses and cities; they make a figure in dress and equipage; they love, they fight, they dispute, they cheat, they betray." And thus he continued on, while my color came and went several times with indignation to hear our noble country, the mistress of arts and arms, the scourge of France, the arbitress of Europe, the seat of virtue, piety, honor, and truth, the pride and envy of the world, so contemptuously treated.

But as I was not in a condition to resent injuries, so, upon mature thoughts, I began to doubt whether I were injured or no. For, after having been accustomed several months to the sight and converse of this people, and observed every object upon which I cast my eyes to be of proportionable magnitude, the horror I had first conceived from their bulk and aspect was so far worn off that if I had then beheld a company of English lords and ladies in their finery and birthday clothes,[3] acting their several parts in the most courtly manner of strutting and bowing and prating, to say the truth, I should have been strongly tempted to laugh as much at them as this King and his grandees did at me. Neither indeed could I forbear smiling at myself when the Queen used to place me upon her hand towards a looking glass, by which both our persons appeared before me in full view together; and there could be nothing more ridiculous than the comparison; so that I really began to imagine myself dwindled many degrees below my usual size.

Nothing angered and mortified me so much as the Queen's dwarf, who being of the lowest stature that was ever in that country (for I verily think he was not full thirty foot high) became so insolent at seeing a creature so much beneath him that he would always affect to swagger and look big as he passed by me in the Queen's antechamber, while I was standing on some table talking with the lords or ladies of the court; and he seldom failed of a smart word or two upon my littleness, against which I could only revenge myself by calling him brother, challenging him to wrestle, and such repartees as are usual in the mouths of Court pages. One day at dinner this malicious little cub was so nettled with something I had said to him that, raising himself upon the frame of Her Majesty's chair, he took me up by the middle, as I was sitting down, not thinking any harm, and let me drop into a large silver bowl of cream, and then ran away as fast as he could. I fell over head and ears, and if I had not been a good swimmer, it might have gone very hard with me; for Glumdal-

2. One of the largest ships in the Royal Navy. At the English court the lord treasurer bore a white staff as the symbol of his office.

3. Courtiers dressed with special splendor on the monarch's birthday.

clitch in that instant happened to be at the other end of the room, and the Queen was in such a fright that she wanted presence of mind to assist me. But my little nurse ran to my relief, and took me out, after I had swallowed above a quart of cream. I was put to bed; however, I received no other damage than the loss of a suit of clothes, which was utterly spoiled. The dwarf was soundly whipped, and as further punishment, forced to drink up the bowl of cream into which he had thrown me; neither was he ever restored to favor: for soon after the Queen bestowed him to a lady of high quality, so that I saw him no more, to my very great satisfaction; for I could not tell to what extremity such a malicious urchin might have carried his resentment.

He had before served me a scurvy trick, which set the Queen a laughing, although at the same time she were heartily vexed, and would have immediately cashiered him, if I had not been so generous as to intercede. Her Majesty had taken a marrow bone upon her plate, and after knocking out the marrow, placed the bone again in the dish, erect as it stood before; the dwarf watching his opportunity, while Glumdalclitch was gone to the sideboard, mounted upon the stool she stood on to take care of me at meals, took me up in both hands, and squeezing my legs together, wedged them into the marrow bone above my waist, where I stuck for some time, and made a very ridiculous figure. I believe it was near a minute before anyone knew what was become of me, for I thought it below me to cry out. But, as princes seldom get their meat hot, my legs were not scalded, only my stockings and breeches in a sad condition. The dwarf at my entreaty had no other punishment than a sound whipping.

I was frequently rallied by the Queen upon account of my fearfulness, and she used to ask me whether the people of my country were as great cowards as myself. The occasion was this. The kingdom is much pestered with flies in summer, and these odious insects, each of them as big as a Dunstable lark, hardly gave me any rest while I sat at dinner, with their continual humming and buzzing about my ears. They would sometimes alight upon my victuals, and leave their loathsome excrement or spawn behind, which to me was very visible, although not to the natives of that country, whose large optics were not so acute as mine in viewing smaller objects. Sometimes they would fix upon my nose or forehead, where they stung me to the quick, smelling very offensively; and I could easily trace that viscous matter, which our naturalists tell us enables those creatures to walk with their feet upwards upon a ceiling. I had much ado to defend myself against these detestable animals, and could not forbear starting when they came on my face. It was the common practice of the dwarf to catch a number of these insects in his hand, as schoolboys do among us, and let them out suddenly under my nose, on purpose to frighten me, and divert the Queen. My remedy was to cut them in pieces with my knife as they flew in the air, wherein my dexterity was much admired.

I remember one morning when Glumdalclitch had set me in my box upon a window, as she usually did in fair days to give me air (for I durst not venture to let the box be hung on a nail out of the window, as we do with cages in England), after I had lifted up one of my sashes, and sat down at my table to eat a piece of sweet cake for my breakfast, above twenty wasps, allured by the smell, came flying into the room, humming louder than the drones of as many bagpipes. Some of them seized my cake, and carried it piecemeal away; others flew about my head and face, confounding me with the noise, and putting me in the utmost terror of their stings. However, I had the courage to rise and draw my hanger, and attack them in the air. I dispatched four of them, but the rest got away, and I presently shut my window. These insects were as large as partridges; I took out their stings, found them an inch and a half long, and as sharp as needles. I carefully preserved them all, and having since shown them with some other curiosities in several parts of Europe, upon my return to England I gave three of them to Gresham College,[4] and kept the fourth for myself.

CHAPTER 4. *The country described. A proposal for correcting modern maps. The King's palace, and some account of the metropolis. The Author's way of traveling. The chief temple described.*

I now intend to give the reader a short description of this country, as far as I had traveled in it, which was not above two thousand miles round Lorbrulgrud the metropolis. For the Queen, whom I always attended, never went further when she accompanied the King in his progresses, and there stayed till his Majesty returned from viewing his frontiers. The whole extent of this prince's dominions reacheth about six thousand miles in length, and from three to five in breadth. From whence I cannot but conclude that our geographers of Europe are in a great error by supposing nothing but sea between Japan and California: for it was ever my opinion that there must be a balance of earth to counterpoise the great continent of Tartary; and therefore they ought to correct their maps and charts by joining this vast tract of land to the northwest parts of America, wherein I shall be ready to lend them my assistance.

The kingdom is a peninsula, terminated to the northeast by a ridge of mountains thirty miles high, which are altogether impassable by reason of the volcanoes upon the tops. Neither do the most learned know what sort of mortals inhabit beyond those mountains, or whether they be inhabited at all. On the three other sides it is bounded by the ocean. There is not one seaport in the whole kingdom; and those parts of the coasts into which the rivers issue are so full of pointed rocks, and the sea generally so rough, that there is no venturing with the smallest of their boats; so that these people are wholly excluded from any commerce with the rest of the world. But the large rivers are full of vessels, and abound with excellent fish, for they seldom get any from the sea, because the sea fish are of the same size with those in Europe, and consequently not worth catching; whereby it is manifest that nature, in the production of plants and animals of so extraordinary a bulk, is wholly confined to this continent, of which I leave the reasons to be determined by philosophers. However, now and then they take a whale that happens to be dashed against the rocks, which the common people feed on heartily. These whales I have known so large that a man could hardly carry one upon his shoulders; and sometimes for curiosity they are brought in hampers to Lorbrulgrud: I saw one of them in a dish at the King's table, which passed for a rarity, but I did not observe he was fond of it; for I think indeed the bigness disgusted him, although I have seen one somewhat larger in Greenland.

The country is well inhabited, for it contains fifty-one cities, near an hundred

4. The Royal Society, in its earliest years, met in Gresham College.

walled towns, and a great number of villages. To satisfy my curious reader, it may be sufficient to describe Lorbrulgrud. This city stands upon almost two equal parts on each side the river that passes through. It contains above eight thousand houses, and about six hundred thousand inhabitants. It is in length three *glonglungs* (which make about fifty-four English miles) and two and a half in breadth, as I measured it myself in the royal map made by the King's order, which was laid on the ground on purpose for me, and extended an hundred feet; I paced the diameter and circumference several times barefoot, and computing by the scale, measured it pretty exactly.

The King's palace is no regular edifice, but an heap of buildings about seven miles round: the chief rooms are generally two hundred and forty foot high, and broad and long in proportion. A coach was allowed to Glumdalclitch and me, wherein her governess frequently took her out to see the town, or go among the shops; and I was always of the party, carried in my box, although the girl at my own desire would often take me out, and hold me in her hand, that I might more conveniently view the houses and the people as we passed along the streets. I reckoned our coach to be about a square of Westminster Hall,[5] but not altogether so high; however, I cannot be very exact. One day the governess ordered our coachman to stop at several shops, where the beggars, watching their opportunity, crowded to the sides of the coach, and gave me the most horrible spectacles that ever an English eye beheld. There was a woman with a cancer in her breast, swelled to a monstrous size, full of holes, in two or three of which I could have easily crept, and covered my whole body. There was a fellow with a wen in his neck, larger than five woolpacks, and another with a couple of wooden legs, each about twenty foot high. But the most hateful sight of all was the lice crawling on their clothes. I could see distinctly the limbs of these vermin with my naked eye, much better than those of an European louse through a microscope, and their snouts with which they rooted like swine. They were the first I had ever beheld; and I should have been curious enough to dissect one of them if I had proper instruments (which I unluckily left behind me in the ship), although indeed the sight was so nauseous that it perfectly turned my stomach.

Besides the large box in which I was usually carried, the Queen ordered a smaller one to be made for me, of about twelve foot square and ten high, for the convenience of traveling, because the other was somewhat too large for Glumdalclitch's lap, and cumbersome in the coach; it was made by the same artist, whom I directed in the whole contrivance. This traveling closet was an exact square with a window in the middle of three of the squares, and each window was latticed with iron wire on the outside, to prevent accidents in long journeys. On the fourth side, which had no windows, two strong staples were fixed, through which the person that carried me, when I had a mind to be on horseback, put in a leathern belt, and buckled it about his waist. This was always the office of some grave trusty servant in whom I could confide, whether I attended the King and Queen in their progresses, or were disposed to see the gardens, or pay a visit to some great lady or minister of state in the court, when Glumdalclitch happened to be out of order: for I soon began to be known and esteemed among the greatest officers, I suppose more upon

---

5. The ancient hall, now incorporated into the Houses of Parliament, where the law courts then sat. Swift presumably means the square of its breadth (just under sixty-eight feet).

account of their Majesties' favor than any merit of my own. In journeys, when I was weary of the coach, a servant on horseback would buckle my box, and place it on a cushion before him; and there I had a full prospect of the country on three sides from my three windows. I had in this closet a field bed and a hammock hung from the ceiling, two chairs and a table, neatly screwed to the floor to prevent being tossed about by the agitation of the horse or the coach. And having been long used to sea voyages, those motions, although sometimes very violent, did not much discompose me.

When I had a mind to see the town, it was always in my traveling closet, which Glumdalclitch held in her lap in a kind of open sedan, after the fashion of the country, borne by four men, and attended by two others in the Queen's livery. The people, who had often heard of me, were very curious to crowd about the sedan; and the girl was complaisant enough to make the bearers stop, and to take me in her hand that I might be more conveniently seen.

I was very desirous to see the chief temple, and particularly the tower belonging to it, which is reckoned the highest in the kingdom. Accordingly one day my nurse carried me thither, but I may truly say I came back disappointed; for the height is not above three thousand foot, reckoning from the ground to the highest pinnacle top; which, allowing for the difference between the size of those people and us in Europe, is no great matter for admiration, nor at all equal in proportion (if I rightly remember) to Salisbury steeple.[6] But, not to detract from a nation to which during my life I shall acknowledge myself extremely obliged, it must be allowed that whatever this famous tower wants in height is amply made up in beauty and strength. For the walls are near an hundred foot thick, built of hewn stone, whereof each is about forty foot square, and adorned on all sides with statues of gods and emperors cut in marble larger than the life, placed in their several niches. I measured a little finger which had fallen down from one of these statues, and lay unperceived among some rubbish, and found it exactly four foot and an inch in length. Glumdalclitch wrapped it up in a handkerchief, and carried it home in her pocket to keep among other trinkets, of which the girl was very fond, as children at her age usually are.

The King's kitchen is indeed a noble building, vaulted at top, and about six hundred foot high. The great oven is not so wide by ten paces as the cupola at St. Paul's:[7] for I measured the latter on purpose after my return. But if I should describe the kitchen grate, the prodigious pots and kettles, the joints of meat turning on the spits, with many other particulars, perhaps I should be hardly believed; at least a severe critic would be apt to think I enlarged a little, as travelers are often suspected to do. To avoid which censure, I fear I have run too much into the other extreme, and that if this treatise should happen to be translated into the language of Brobdingnag (which is the general name of that kingdom) and transmitted thither, the King and his people would have reason to complain that I had done them an injury by a false and diminutive representation.

His Majesty seldom keeps above six hundred horses in his stables: they are generally from fifty-four to sixty foot high. But when he goes abroad on solemn days, he is attended for state by a militia guard of five hundred horse, which

6. One of the most beautiful Gothic steeples in England is that of Salisbury Cathedral, 404 feet high.   7. The cupola of St. Paul's Cathedral in London is 108 feet in diameter.

indeed I thought was the most splendid sight that could be ever beheld, till I saw part of his army in battalia,[8] whereof I shall find another occasion to speak.

CHAPTER 5. *Several adventures that happened to the Author. The execution of a criminal. The Author shows his skill in navigation.*

I should have lived happy enough in that country if my littleness had not exposed me to several ridiculous and troublesome accidents, some of which I shall venture to relate. Glumdalclitch often carried me into the gardens of the court in my smaller box, and would sometimes take me out of it and hold me in her hand, or set me down to walk. I remember, before the dwarf left the Queen, he followed us one day into those gardens; and my nurse having set me down, he and I being close together near some dwarf apple trees, I must needs show my wit by a silly allusion between him and the trees, which happens to hold in their language as it doth in ours. Whereupon, the malicious rogue watching his opportunity, when I was walking under one of them, shook it directly over my head, by which a dozen apples, each of them near as large as a Bristol barrel, came tumbling about my ears; one of them hit me on the back as I chanced to stoop, and knocked me down flat on my face, but I received no other hurt; and the dwarf was pardoned at my desire, because I had given the provocation.

Another day Glumdalclitch left me on a smooth grassplot to divert myself while she walked at some distance with her governess. In the meantime there suddenly fell such a violent shower of hail that I was immediately by the force of it struck to the ground: and when I was down, the hailstones gave me such cruel bangs all over the body as if I had been pelted with tennis balls;[9] however I made a shift to creep on all four, and shelter myself by lying on my face on the lee side of a border of lemon thyme, but so bruised from head to foot that I could not go abroad in ten days. Neither is this at all to be wondered at, because nature in that country observing the same proportion through all her operations, a hailstone is near eighteen hundred times as large as one in Europe; which I can assert upon experience, having been so curious to weigh and measure them.

But a more dangerous accident happened to me in the same garden when my little nurse, believing she had put me in a secure place, which I often entreated her to do that I might enjoy my own thoughts, and having left my box at home to avoid the trouble of carrying it, went to another part of the garden with her governess and some ladies of her acquaintance. While she was absent and out of hearing, a small white spaniel belonging to one of the chief gardeners, having got by accident into the garden, happened to range near the place where I lay. The dog following the scent, came directly up, and taking me in his mouth, ran straight to his master, wagging his tail, and set me gently on the ground. By good fortune he had been so well taught that I was carried between his teeth without the least hurt, or even tearing my clothes. But the poor gardener, who knew me well, and had a great kindness for me, was in a terrible fright. He gently took me up in both his hands, and asked me

8. Battle array.
9. Eighteenth-century tennis balls, unlike the modern, were very hard.

how I did; but I was so amazed and out of breath that I could not speak a word. In a few minutes I came to myself, and he carried me safe to my little nurse, who by this time had returned to the place where she left me, and was in cruel agonies when I did not appear nor answer when she called; she severely reprimanded the gardener on account of his dog. But the thing was hushed up and never known at court; for the girl was afraid of the Queen's anger; and truly, as to myself, I thought it would not be for my reputation that such a story should go about.

This accident absolutely determined Glumdalclitch never to trust me abroad for the future out of her sight. I had been long afraid of this resolution, and therefore concealed from her some little unlucky adventures that happened in those times when I was left by myself. Once a kite[1] hovering over the garden made a swoop at me, and if I had not resolutely drawn my hanger, and run under a thick espalier, he would have certainly carried me away in his talons. Another time walking to the top of a fresh molehill, I fell to my neck in the hole through which that animal had cast up the earth, and coined some lie, not worth remembering, to excuse myself for spoiling my clothes. I likewise broke my right shin against the shell of a snail, which I happened to stumble over, as I was walking alone, and thinking on poor England.

I cannot tell whether I were more pleased or mortified to observe in those solitary walks that the smaller birds did not appear to be at all afraid of me; but would hop about within a yard distance, looking for worms and other food with as much indifference and security as if no creature at all were near them. I remember a thrush had the confidence to snatch out of my hand with his bill a piece of cake that Glumdalclitch had just given me for my breakfast. When I attempted to catch any of these birds, they would boldly turn against me, endeavoring to pick my fingers, which I durst not venture within their reach; and then they would hop back unconcerned to hunt for worms or snails, as they did before. But one day I took a thick cudgel, and threw it with all my strength so luckily at a linnet that I knocked him down, and seizing him by the neck with both my hands, ran with him in triumph to my nurse. However, the bird, who had only been stunned, recovering himself, gave me so many boxes with his wings on both sides of my head and body, though I held him at arm's length, and was out of the reach of his claws, that I was twenty times thinking to let him go. But I was soon relieved by one of our servants, who wrung off the bird's neck, and I had him next day for dinner, by the Queen's command. This linnet, as near as I can remember, seemed to be somewhat larger than an English swan.

The Maids of Honor often invited Glumdalclitch to their apartments, and desired she would bring me along with her, on purpose to have the pleasure of seeing and touching me. They would often strip me naked from top to toe and lay me at full length in their bosoms; wherewith I was much disgusted, because, to say the truth, a very offensive smell came from their skins, which I do not mention or intend to the disadvantage of those excellent ladies, for whom I have all manner of respect; but I conceive that my sense was more acute in proportion to my littleness, and that those illustrious persons were no more disagreeable to their lovers, or to each other, than people of the same quality are with us in England. And, after all, I found

---

1. A bird of prey.

their natural smell was much more supportable than when they used perfumes, under which I immediately swooned away. I cannot forget that an
intimate friend of mine in Lilliput took the freedom in a warm day, when I
had used a good deal of exercise, to complain of a strong smell about me,
although I am as little faulty that way as most of my sex: but I suppose his faculty of smelling was as nice with regard to me as mine was to that of this
people. Upon this point, I cannot forbear doing justice to the Queen, my mistress, and Glumdalclitch, my nurse, whose persons were as sweet as those
of any lady in England.

That which gave me most uneasiness among these Maids of Honor, when
my nurse carried me to visit them, was to see them use me without any manner of ceremony, like a creature who had no sort of consequence. For they
would strip themselves to the skin and put on their smocks in my presence,
while I was placed on their toilet[2] directly before their naked bodies; which, I
am sure, to me was very far from being a tempting sight, or from giving me
any other emotions than those of horror and disgust. Their skins appeared so
coarse and uneven, so variously colored, when I saw them near, with a mole
here and there as broad as a trencher, and hairs hanging from it thicker than
pack-threads, to say nothing further concerning the rest of their persons. Neither did they at all scruple, while I was by, to discharge what they had drunk,
to the quantity of at least two hogsheads, in a vessel that held above three tuns.
The handsomest among these Maids of Honor, a pleasant frolicsome girl of
sixteen, would sometimes set me astride upon one of her nipples, with many
other tricks, wherein the reader will excuse me for not being over particular.
But I was so much displeased that I entreated Glumdalclitch to contrive some
excuse for not seeing that young lady any more.

One day a young gentleman, who was nephew to my nurse's governess,
came and pressed them both to see an execution. It was of a man who had
murdered one of that gentleman's intimate acquaintance. Glumdalclitch was
prevailed on to be of the company, very much against her inclination, for she
was naturally tender-hearted: and as for myself, although I abhorred such kind
of spectacles, yet my curiosity tempted me to see something that I thought
must be extraordinary. The malefactor was fixed in a chair upon a scaffold
erected for the purpose, and his head cut off at a blow with a sword of about
forty foot long. The veins and arteries spouted up such a prodigious quantity
of blood, and so high in the air, that the great *jet d'eau* at Versailles was not
equal for the time it lasted; and the head, when it fell on the scaffold floor,
gave such a bounce,[3] as made me start, although I were at least half an English
mile distant.

The Queen, who often used to hear me talk of my sea voyages, and took all
occasions to divert me when I was melancholy, asked me whether I understood how to handle a sail or an oar, and whether a little exercise of rowing
might not be convenient for my health. I answered that I understood both
very well. For although my proper employment had been to be surgeon or
doctor to the ship, yet often, upon a pinch, I was forced to work like a common
mariner. But I could not see how this could be done in their country, where
the smallest wherry was equal to a first-rate man-of-war among us, and such a

2. Toilet table.
3. A sudden noise. "*Jet d'eau* at Versailles": this fountain rose over forty feet in the air.

boat as I could manage would never live in any of their rivers. Her Majesty said, if I would contrive a boat, her own joiner should make it, and she would provide a place for me to sail in. The fellow was an ingenious workman and, by my instructions, in ten days finished a pleasure boat with all its tackling, able conveniently to hold eight Europeans. When it was finished, the Queen was so delighted that she ran with it in her lap to the King, who ordered it to be put in a cistern full of water, with me in it, by way of trial; where I could not manage my two sculls, or little oars, for want of room. But the Queen had before contrived another project. She ordered the joiner to make a wooden trough of three hundred foot long, fifty broad, and eight deep; which being well pitched to prevent leaking, was placed on the floor along the wall in an outer room of the palace. It had a cock near the bottom to let out the water when it began to grow stale, and two servants could easily fill it in half an hour. Here I often used to row for my own diversion, as well as that of the Queen and her ladies, who thought themselves well entertained with my skill and agility. Sometimes I would put up my sail, and then my business was only to steer, while the ladies gave me a gale with their fans; and when they were weary, some of the pages would blow my sail forward with their breath, while I showed my art by steering starboard or larboard as I pleased. When I had done, Glumdalclitch always carried my boat into her closet, and hung it on a nail to dry.

In this exercise I once met an accident which had like to have cost me my life. For one of the pages having put my boat into the trough, the governess who attended Glumdalclitch very officiously[4] lifted me up to place me in the boat; but I happened to slip through her fingers, and should have infallibly fallen down forty foot upon the floor, if by the luckiest chance in the world I had not been stopped by a corking-pin that stuck in the good gentlewoman's stomacher;[5] the head of the pin passed between my shirt and the waistband of my breeches, and thus I was held by the middle in the air until Glumdalclitch ran to my relief.

Another time, one of the servants, whose office it was to fill my trough every third day with fresh water, was so careless to let a huge frog (not perceiving it) slip out of his pail. The frog lay concealed till I was put into my boat, but then seeing a resting place, climbed up, and made it lean so much on one side that I was forced to balance it with all my weight on the other, to prevent overturning. When the frog was got in, it hopped at once half the length of the boat, and then over my head, backwards and forwards, daubing my face and clothes with its odious slime. The largeness of its features made it appear the most deformed animal that can be conceived. However, I desired Glumdalclitch to let me deal with it alone. I banged it a good while with one of my sculls, and at last forced it to leap out of the boat.

But the greatest danger I ever underwent in that kingdom was from a monkey, who belonged to one of the clerks of the kitchen. Glumdalclitch had locked me up in her closet, while she went somewhere upon business or a visit. The weather being very warm, the closet window was left open, as well as the windows in the door of my bigger box, in which I usually lived, because of its largeness and conveniency. As I sat quietly meditating at my table, I

---

4. Kindly, dutifully.
5. An ornamental covering for the front and upper part of the body. "Corking-pin": a pin of the largest size.

heard something bounce in at the closet window, and skip about from one side to the other, whereat, although I was much alarmed, yet I ventured to look out, but stirred not from my seat; and then I saw this frolicsome animal, frisking and leaping up and down, till at last he came to my box, which he seemed to view with great pleasure and curiosity, peeping in at the door and every window. I retreated to the farther corner of my room, or box, but the monkey looking in at every side, put me into such a fright that I wanted presence of mind to conceal myself under the bed, as I might easily have done. After some time spent in peeping, grinning, and chattering, he at last espied me, and reaching one of his paws in at the door, as a cat does when she plays with a mouse, although I often shifted place to avoid him, he at length seized the lappet of my coat (which, being made of that country cloth, was very thick and strong) and dragged me out. He took me up in his right forefoot, and held me as a nurse does a child she is going to suckle, just as I have seen the same sort of creature do with a kitten in Europe: and when I offered to struggle, he squeezed me so hard that I thought it more prudent to submit. I have good reason to believe that he took me for a young one of his own species, by his often stroking my face very gently with his other paw. In these diversions he was interrupted by a noise at the closet door, as if somebody were opening it, whereupon he suddenly leaped up to the window at which he had come in, and thence upon the leads and gutters, walking upon three legs, and holding me in the fourth, till he clambered up to a roof that was next to ours. I heard Glumdalclitch give a shriek at the moment he was carrying me out. The poor girl was almost distracted: that quarter of the palace was all in an uproar; the servants ran for ladders; the monkey was seen by hundreds in the court, sitting upon the ridge of a building, holding me like a baby in one of his forepaws and feeding me with the other, by cramming into my mouth some victuals he had squeezed out of the bag on one side of his chaps, and patting me when I would not eat; whereat many of the rabble below could not forebear laughing; neither do I think they justly ought to be blamed, for without question the sight was ridiculous enough to everybody but myself. Some of the people threw up stones, hoping to drive the monkey down; but this was strictly forbidden, or else very probably my brains had been dashed out.

The ladders were now applied, and mounted by several men; which the monkey observing, and finding himself almost encompassed, not being able to make speed enough with his three legs, let me drop on a ridge tile, and made his escape. Here I sat for some time three hundred yards from the ground, expecting every moment to be blown down by the wind, or to fall by my own giddiness, and come tumbling over and over from the ridge to the eaves. But an honest lad, one of my nurse's footmen, climbed up, and putting me into his breeches pocket, brought me down safe.

I was almost choked with the filthy stuff the monkey had crammed down my throat; but my dear little nurse picked it out of my mouth with a small needle, and then I fell a vomiting, which gave me great relief. Yet I was so weak and bruised in the sides with the squeezes given me by this odious animal that I was forced to keep my bed a fortnight. The King, Queen, and all the Court sent every day to inquire after my health, and her Majesty made me several visits during my sickness. The monkey was killed, and an order made that no such animal should be kept about the palace.

When I attended the King after my recovery, to return him thanks for his favors, he was pleased to rally me a good deal upon this adventure. He asked me what my thoughts and speculations were while I lay in the monkey's paw, how I liked the victuals he gave me, his manner of feeding, and whether the fresh air on the roof had sharpened my stomach. He desired to know what I would have done upon such an occasion in my own country. I told his Majesty that in Europe we had no monkeys, except such as were brought for curiosities from other places, and so small that I could deal with a dozen of them together, if they presumed to attack me. And as for that monstrous animal with whom I was so lately engaged (it was indeed as large as an elephant), if my fears had suffered me to think so far as to make use of my hanger (looking fiercely and clapping my hand upon the hilt as I spoke) when he poked his paw into my chamber, perhaps I should have given him such a wound as would have made him glad to withdraw it with more haste than he put it in. This I delivered in a firm tone, like a person who was jealous lest his courage should be called in question. However, my speech produced nothing else besides a loud laughter, which all the respect due to his Majesty from those about him could not make them contain. This made me reflect how vain an attempt it is for a man to endeavor doing himself honor among those who are out of all degree of equality or comparison with him. And yet I have seen the moral of my own behavior very frequent in England since my return, where a little contemptible varlet, without the least title to birth, person, wit, or common sense, shall presume to look with importance, and put himself upon a foot with the greatest persons of the kingdom.

I was every day furnishing the court with some ridiculous story; and Glumdalclitch, although she loved me to excess, yet was arch enough to inform the Queen whenever I committed any folly that she thought would be diverting to her Majesty. The girl, who had been out of order, was carried by her governess to take the air about an hour's distance, or thirty miles from town. They alighted out of the coach near a small footpath in a field, and Glumdalclitch setting down my traveling box, I went out of it to walk. There was a cow dung in the patch, and I must needs try my activity by attempting to leap over it. I took a run, but unfortunately jumped short, and found myself just in the middle up to my knees. I waded through with some difficulty, and one of the footmen wiped me as clean as he could with his handkerchief; for I was filthily bemired, and my nurse confined me to my box till we returned home, where the Queen was soon informed of what had passed and the footmen spread it about the Court, so that all the mirth, for some days, was at my expense.

CHAPTER 6. *Several contrivances of the Author to please the King and Queen. He shows his skill in music. The King inquires into the state of Europe, which the Author relates to him. The King's observations thereon.*

I used to attend the King's levee once or twice a week, and had often seen him under the barber's hand, which indeed was at first very terrible to behold. For the razor was almost twice as long as an ordinary scythe. His Majesty, according to the custom of the country, was only shaved twice a week. I once prevailed on the barber to give me some of the suds or lather, out of which I picked forty or fifty of the strongest stumps of hair. I then took a piece of fine wood, and cut it like the back of a comb, making several holes in it at equal

distance with as small a needle as I could get from Glumdalclitch. I fixed in
the stumps so artificially,[6] scraping and sloping them with my knife towards
the points, that I made a very tolerable comb; which was a seasonable supply,
my own being so much broken in the teeth that it was almost useless; neither
did I know any artist in that country so nice and exact as would undertake to
make me another.

And this puts me in mind of an amusement wherein I spent many of my
leisure hours. I desired the Queen's woman to save for me the combings of
her Majesty's hair, whereof in time I got a good quantity; and consulting with
my friend the cabinetmaker, who had received general orders to do little jobs
for me, I directed him to make two chair frames, no larger than those I had in
my box, and then to bore little holes with a fine awl round those parts where
I designed the backs and seats; through these holes I wove the strongest hairs
I could pick out, just after the manner of cane chairs in England. When they
were finished, I made a present of them to her Majesty, who kept them in her
cabinet, and used to show them for curiosities, as indeed they were the wonder
of every one that beheld them. The Queen would have made me sit upon one
of these chairs, but I absolutely refused to obey her, protesting I would rather
die a thousand deaths than place a dishonorable part of my body on those
precious hairs that once adorned her Majesty's head. Of these hairs (as I had
always a mechanical genius) I likewise made a neat little purse above five foot
long, with her Majesty's name deciphered in gold letters, which I gave to
Glumdalclitch by the Queen's consent. To say the truth, it was more for show
than use, being not of strength to bear the weight of the larger coins; and
therefore she kept nothing in it but some little toys[7] that girls are fond of.

The King, who delighted in music, had frequent consorts[8] at court, to
which I was sometimes carried, and set in my box on a table to hear them;
but the noise was so great that I could hardly distinguish the tunes. I am
confident that all the drums and trumpets of a royal army, beating and sounding together just at your ears, could not equal it. My practice was to have my
box removed from the places where the performers sat, as far as I could, then
to shut the doors and windows of it, and draw the window curtains, after which
I found their music not disagreeable.

I had learned in my youth to play a little upon the spinet. Glumdalclitch
kept one in her chamber, and a master attended twice a week to teach her: I
call it a spinet, because it somewhat resembled that instrument, and was
played upon in the same manner. A fancy came into my head that I would
entertain the King and Queen with an English tune upon this instrument.
But this appeared extremely difficult: for the spinet was near sixty foot long,
each key being almost a foot wide; so that, with my arms extended, I could
not reach to above five keys, and to press them down required a good smart
stroke with my fist, which would be too great a labor and to no purpose. The
method I contrived was this: I prepared two round sticks about the bigness of
common cudgels; they were thicker at one end than the other, and I covered
the thicker ends with a piece of a mouse's skin, that by rapping on them I
might neither damage the tops of the keys, nor interrupt the sound. Before the
spinet a bench was placed, about four foot below the keys, and I was put upon

6. Skillfully.   8. Concerts.
7. Trifles.

the bench. I ran sideling upon it that way and this, as fast as I could, banging the proper keys with my two sticks; and made a shift to play a jig, to the great satisfaction of both their Majesties: but it was the most violent exercise I ever underwent, and yet I could not strike above sixteen keys, nor, consequently, play the bass and treble together, as other artists do; which was a great disadvantage to my performance.

The King, who, as I before observed, was a prince of excellent understanding, would frequently order that I should be brought in my box and set upon the table in his closet. He would then command me to bring one of my chairs out of the box, and sit down within three yards distance upon the top of the cabinet, which brought me almost to a level with his face. In this manner I had several conversations with him. I one day took the freedom to tell his Majesty that the contempt he discovered towards Europe, and the rest of the world, did not seem answerable to those excellent qualities of mind that he was master of. That reason did not extend itself with the bulk of the body: on the contrary, we observed in our country that the tallest persons were usually least provided with it. That among other animals, bees and ants had the reputation of more industry, art, and sagacity than many of the larger kinds; and that, as inconsiderable as he took me to be, I hoped I might live to do his Majesty some signal service. The King heard me with attention, and began to conceive a much better opinion of me than he had before. He desired I would give him as exact an account of the government of England as I possibly could; because, as fond as princes commonly are of their own customs (for so he conjectured of other monarchs, by my former discourses), he should be glad to hear of anything that might deserve imitation.

Imagine with thyself, courteous reader, how often I then wished for the tongue of Demosthenes or Cicero, that might have enabled me to celebrate the praise of my own dear native country in a style equal to its merits and felicity.

I began my discourse by informing his Majesty that our dominions consisted of two islands, which composed three mighty kingdoms under one sovereign, beside our plantations in America. I dwelt long upon the fertility of our soil, and the temperature[9] of our climate. I then spoke at large upon the constitution of an English Parliament, partly made up of an illustrious body called the House of Peers, persons of the noblest blood, and of the most ancient and ample patrimonies. I described that extraordinary care always taken of their education in arts and arms, to qualify them for being counselors born to the king and kingdom; to have a share in the legislature, to be members of the highest Court of Judicature, from whence there could be no appeal; and to be champions always ready for the defense of their prince and country, by their valor, conduct, and fidelity. That these were the ornament and bulwark of the kingdom, worthy followers of their most renowned ancestors, whose honor had been the reward of their virtue, from which their posterity were never once known to degenerate. To these were joined several holy persons, as part of that assembly, under the title of Bishops, whose peculiar business it is to take care of religion, and of those who instruct the people therein. These were searched and sought out through the whole nation, by the prince and his wisest counselors, among such of the priesthood as were

9. Temperateness.

most deservedly distinguished by the sanctity of their lives and the depth of
their erudition, who were indeed the spiritual fathers of the clergy and the
people.

That the other part of the Parliament consisted of an assembly called the
House of Commons, who were all principal gentlemen, freely picked and
culled out by the people themselves, for their great abilities and love of their
country, to represent the wisdom of the whole nation. And these two bodies
make up the most august assembly in Europe, to whom, in conjunction with
the prince, the whole legislature is committed.

I then descended to the Courts of Justice, over which the Judges, those
venerable sages and interpreters of the law, presided, for determining the disputed rights and properties of men, as well as for the punishment of vice, and
protection of innocence. I mentioned the prudent management of our treasury, the valor and achievements of our forces by sea and land. I computed
the number of our people, by reckoning how many millions there might be
of each religious sect, or political party among us. I did not omit even our
sports and pastimes, or any other particular which I thought might redound to
the honor of my country. And I finished all with a brief historical account of
affairs and events in England for about an hundred years past.

This conversation was not ended under five audiences, each of several
hours, and the King heard the whole with great attention, frequently taking
notes of what I spoke, as well as memorandums of several questions he
intended to ask me.

When I had put an end to these long discourses, his Majesty in a sixth
audience consulting his notes, proposed many doubts, queries, and objections,
upon every article. He asked what methods were used to cultivate the minds
and bodies of our young nobility, and in what kind of business they commonly
spent the first and teachable part of their lives. What course was taken to
supply that assembly when any noble family became extinct. What qualifications were necessary in those who were to be created new lords. Whether the
humor[1] of the prince, a sum of money to a Court lady or a prime minister, or
a design of strengthening a party opposite to the public interest, ever happened
to be motives in those advancements. What share of knowledge these lords
had in the laws of their country, and how they came by it, so as to enable them
to decide the properties of their fellow subjects in the last resort. Whether they
were always so free from avarice, partialities, or want that a bribe or some
other sinister view could have no place among them. Whether those holy
lords I spoke of were constantly promoted to that rank upon account of their
knowledge in religious matters, and the sanctity of their lives; had never been
compliers with the times while they were common priests, or slavish prostitute
chaplains to some nobleman, whose opinions they continued servilely to follow after they were admitted into that assembly.

He then desired to know what arts were practiced in electing those whom I
called Commoners. Whether a stranger with a strong purse might not influence the vulgar voters to choose him before their own landlord or the most
considerable gentleman in the neighborhood. How it came to pass that people
were so violently bent upon getting into this assembly, which I allowed to be
a great trouble and expense, often to the ruin of their families, without any

1. Whim.

salary or pension: because this appeared such an exalted strain of virtue and public spirit that his Majesty seemed to doubt it might possibly not be always sincere; and he desired to know whether such zealous gentlemen could have any views of refunding themselves for the charges and trouble they were at, by sacrificing the public good to the designs of a weak and vicious prince in conjunction with a corrupted ministry. He multiplied his questions, and sifted me thoroughly upon every part of this head, proposing numberless inquiries and objections, which I think it not prudent or convenient to repeat.

Upon what I said in relation to our Courts of Justice, his Majesty desired to be satisfied in several points: and this I was the better able to do, having been formerly almost ruined by a long suit in chancery, which was decreed for me with costs. He asked what time was usually spent in determining between right and wrong, and what degree of expense. Whether advocates and orators had liberty to plead in causes manifestly known to be unjust, vexatious, or oppressive. Whether party in religion or politics were observed to be of any weight in the scale of justice. Whether those pleading orators were persons educated in the general knowledge of equity, or only in provincial, national, and other local customs. Whether they or their judges had any part in penning those laws which they assumed the liberty of interpreting and glossing upon at their pleasure. Whether they had ever at different times pleaded for and against the same cause, and cited precedents to prove contrary opinions. Whether they were a rich or a poor corporation. Whether they received any pecuniary reward for pleading or delivering their opinions. And particularly whether they were ever admitted as members in the lower senate.

He fell next upon the management of our treasury, and said he thought my memory had failed me, because I computed our taxes at about five or six millions a year, and when I came to mention the issues,[2] he found they sometimes amounted to more than double, for the notes he had taken were very particular in this point; because he hoped, as he told me, that the knowledge of our conduct might be useful to him, and he could not be deceived in his calculations. But if what I told him were true, he was still at a loss how a kingdom could run out of its estate like a private person. He asked me, who were our creditors? and where we should find money to pay them? He wondered to hear me talk of such chargeable and extensive wars; that certainly we must be a quarrelsome people, or live among very bad neighbors, and that our generals must needs be richer than our kings.[3] He asked what business we had out of our own islands, unless upon the score of trade or treaty or to defend the coasts with our fleet. Above all, he was amazed to hear me talk of a mercenary standing army[4] in the midst of peace, and among a free people. He said if we were governed by our own consent in the persons of our representatives, he could not imagine of whom we were afraid, or against whom we were to fight; and would hear my opinion whether a private man's house might not better be defended by himself, his children, and family, than by half a dozen rascals picked up at a venture[5] in the streets for small wages, who might get an hundred times more by cutting their throats.

2. Expenditures.
3. An allusion to the enormous fortune gained by the duke of Marlborough, formerly captain-general of the army, whom Swift detested.
4. Since the declaration of the Bill of Rights (1689), a standing army without authorization by Parliament had been illegal. Swift and the Tories in general were vigilant in their opposition to such an army.
5. By chance.

He laughed at my odd kind of arithmetic (as he was pleased to call it) in reckoning the numbers of our people by a computation drawn from the several sects among us in religion and politics. He said he knew no reason why those who entertain opinions prejudicial to the public should be obliged to change, or should not be obliged to conceal them. And as it was tyranny in any government to require the first, so it was weakness not to enforce the second: for a man may be allowed to keep poisons in his closet, but not to vend them about for cordials.[6]

He observed that among the diversions of our nobility and gentry I had mentioned gaming. He desired to know at what age this entertainment was usually taken up, and when it was laid down; how much of their time it employed; whether it ever went so high as to affect their fortunes; whether mean, vicious people, by their dexterity in that art, might not arrive at great riches, and sometimes keep our very nobles in dependence, as well as habituate them to vile companions, wholly take them from the improvement of their minds, and force them, by the losses they received, to learn and practice that infamous dexterity upon others.

He was perfectly astonished with the historical account I gave him of our affairs during the last century, protesting it was only an heap of conspiracies, rebellions, murders, massacres, revolutions, banishments, the very worst effects that avarice, faction, hypocrisy, perfidiousness, cruelty, rage, madness, hatred, envy, lust, malice, or ambition could produce.

His Majesty in another audience was at the pains to recapitulate the sum of all I had spoken; compared the questions he made with the answers I had given; then taking me into his hands, and stroking me gently, delivered himself in these words, which I shall never forget, nor the manner he spoke them in. "My little friend Grildrig, you have made a most admirable panegyric upon your country. You have clearly proved that ignorance, idleness, and vice are the proper ingredients for qualifying a legislator. That laws are best explained, interpreted, and applied by those whose interests and abilities lie in perverting, confounding, and eluding them. I observe among you some lines of an institution which in its original might have been tolerable; but these half erased, and the rest wholly blurred and blotted by corruptions. It doth not appear from all you have said how any one virtue is required towards the procurement of any one station among you; much less that men are ennobled on account of their virtue, that priests are advanced for their piety or learning, soldiers for their conduct or valor, judges for their integrity, senators for the love of their country, or counselors for their wisdom. As for yourself," continued the King, "who have spent the greatest part of your life in traveling, I am well disposed to hope you may hitherto have escaped many vices of your country. But by what I have gathered from your own relation, and the answers I have with much pains wringed and extorted from you, I cannot but conclude the bulk of your natives to be the most pernicious race of little odious vermin that nature ever suffered to crawl upon the surface of the earth."

CHAPTER 7. *The Author's love of his country. He makes a proposal of much advantage to the King; which is rejected. The King's great ignorance in politics.*

---

6. Medicines to stimulate the heart, or, equally commonly, liqueurs.

The learning of that country very imperfect and confined. Their laws, and military affairs, and parties in the State.

Nothing but an extreme love of truth could have hindered me from concealing this part of my story. It was in vain to discover my resentments, which were always turned into ridicule: and I was forced to rest with patience while my noble and most beloved country was so injuriously treated. I am heartily sorry as any of my readers can possibly be that such an occasion was given, but this prince happened to be so curious and inquisitive upon every particular that it could not consist either with gratitude or good manners to refuse giving him what satisfaction I was able. Yet thus much I may be allowed to say in my own vindication: that I artfully eluded many of his questions, and gave to every point a more favorable turn by many degrees than the strictness of truth would allow. For I have always borne that laudable partiality to my own country, which Dionysius Halicarnassensis[7] with so much justice recommends to an historian. I would hide the frailties and deformities of my political mother, and place her virtues and beauties in the most advantageous light. This was my sincere endeavor in those many discourses I had with that mighty monarch, although it unfortunately failed of success.

But great allowances should be given to a King who lives wholly secluded from the rest of the world, and must therefore be altogether unacquainted with the manners and customs that most prevail in other nations: the want of which knowledge will ever produce many *prejudices*, and a certain *narrowness of thinking*, from which we and the politer countries of Europe are wholly exempted. And it would be hard indeed if so remote a prince's notions of virtue and vice were to be offered as a standard for all mankind.

To confirm what I have now said, and further to show the miserable effects of a *confined education*, I shall here insert a passage which will hardly obtain belief. In hopes to ingratiate myself farther into his Majesty's favor, I told him of an invention discovered between three and four hundred years ago, to make a certain powder, into an heap of which the smallest spark of fire falling would kindle the whole in a moment, although it were as big as a mountain, and make it all fly up in the air together, with a noise and agitation greater than thunder. That a proper quantity of this powder rammed into an hollow tube of brass or iron, according to its bigness, would drive a ball of iron or lead with such violence and speed as nothing was able to sustain its force. That the largest balls thus discharged would not only destroy whole ranks of an army at once, but batter the strongest walls to the ground; sink down ships with a thousand men in each, to the bottom of the sea; and, when linked together by a chain, would cut through masts and rigging; divide hundreds of bodies in the middle, and lay all waste before them. That we often put this powder into large hollow balls of iron, and discharged them by an engine into some city we were besieging; which would rip up the pavements, tear the houses to pieces, burst and throw splinters on every side, dashing out the brains of all who came near. That I knew the ingredients very well, which were cheap and common; I understood the manner of compounding them, and could direct

7. A Greek rhetorician and historian, who flourished ca. 25 B.C. His history of Rome was written to reconcile the Greeks to their Roman masters.

his workmen how to make those tubes of a size proportionable to all other things in his Majesty's kingdom, and the largest need not be above two hundred foot long; twenty or thirty of which tubes, charged with the proper quantity of powder and balls, would batter down the walls of the strongest town in his dominions in a few hours; or destroy the whole metropolis, if ever it should pretend to dispute his absolute commands. This I humbly offered to his Majesty as a small tribute of acknowledgement in return of so many marks that I had received of his royal favor and protection.

The King was struck with horror at the description I had given of those terrible engines and the proposal I had made. He was amazed how so impotent and groveling an insect as I (these were his expressions) could entertain such inhuman ideas, and in so familiar a manner as to appear wholly unmoved at all the scenes of blood and desolation which I had painted as the common effects of those destructive machines; whereof he said some evil genius, enemy to mankind, must have been the first contriver. As for himself, he protested that although few things delighted him so much as new discoveries in art or in nature, yet he would rather lose half his kingdom than be privy to such a secret, which he commanded me, as I valued my life, never to mention any more.

A strange effect of *narrow principles* and *short views!* that a prince possessed of every quality which procures veneration, love, and esteem; of strong parts, great wisdom, and profound learning; endued with admirable talents for government, and almost adored by his subjects; should from a *nice, unnecessary scruple,* whereof in Europe we can have no conception, let slip an opportunity put into his hands that would have made him absolute master of the lives, the liberties, and the fortunes of his people. Neither do I say this with the least intention to detract from the many virtues of that excellent King, whose character I am sensible will on this account be very much lessened in the opinion of an English reader: but I take this defect among them to have risen from their ignorance; they not having hitherto reduced politics into a science, as the more acute wits of Europe have done. For I remember very well, in a discourse one day with the King, when I happened to say there were several thousand books among us written upon the art of government, it gave him (directly contrary to my intention) a very mean opinion of our understandings. He professed both to abominate and despise all *mystery, refinement,* and *intrigue,* either in a prince or a minister. He could not tell what I meant by *secrets of state,* where an enemy or some rival nation were not in the case. He confined the knowledge of governing within very *narrow bounds:* to common sense and reason, to justice and lenity, to the speedy determination of civil and criminal causes, with some other obvious topics which are not worth considering. And he gave it for his opinion that whoever could make two ears of corn or two blades of grass to grow upon a spot of ground where only one grew before would deserve better of mankind and do more essential service to his country than the whole race of politicians[8] put together.

The learning of this people is very defective, consisting only in morality, history, poetry, and mathematics; wherein they must be allowed to excel. But the last of these is wholly applied to what may be useful in life, to the improvement of agriculture and all mechanical arts; so that among us it would be little

---

8. By *politicians,* Swift means something like our modern political scientists, or theorists.

esteemed. And as to ideas, entities, abstractions, and transcendentals,[9] I could never drive the least conception into their heads.

No law of that country must exceed in words the number of letters in their alphabet, which consists only in two and twenty. But indeed few of them extend even to that length. They are expressed in the most plain and simple terms, wherein those people are not mercurial enough to discover above one interpretation. And to write a comment upon any law is a capital crime. As to the decision of civil causes, or proceedings against criminals, their precedents are so few that they have little reason to boast of any extraordinary skill in either.

They have had the art of printing as well as the Chinese, time out of mind. But their libraries are not very large; for that of the King's, which is reckoned the biggest, doth not amount to above a thousand volumes, placed in a gallery of twelve hundred foot long, from whence I had liberty to borrow what books I pleased. The Queen's joiner had contrived in one of the Glumdalclitch's rooms a kind of wooden machine five and twenty foot high, formed like a standing ladder; the steps were each fifty foot long. It was indeed a movable pair of stairs, the lowest end placed at ten foot distance from the wall of the chamber. The book I had a mind to read was put up leaning against the wall. I first mounted to the upper step of the ladder, and turning my face towards the book began at the top of the page, and so walking to the right and left about eight or ten paces according to the length of the lines, till I had gotten a little below the level of mine eyes, and then descending gradually till I came to the bottom: after which I mounted again, and began the other page in the same manner, and so turned over the leaf, which I could easily do with both my hands, for it was as thick and stiff as a pasteboard, and in the largest folios not above eighteen or twenty foot long.

Their style is clear, masculine, and smooth, but not florid; for they avoid nothing more than multiplying unnecessary words or using various expressions. I have perused many of their books, especially those in history and morality. Among the rest, I was much diverted with a little old treatise, which always lay in Glumdalclitch's bedchamber, and belonged to her governess, a grave elderly gentlewoman, who dealt in writings of morality and devotion. The book treats of the weakness of human kind, and is in little esteem, except among the women and the vulgar. However, I was curious to see what an author of that country could say upon such a subject. This writer went through all the usual topics of European moralists: showing how diminutive, contemptible, and helpless an animal was man in his own nature; how unable to defend himself from the inclemencies of the air, or the fury of wild beasts; how much he was excelled by one creature in strength, by another in speed, by a third in foresight, by a fourth in industry. He added that nature was degenerated in these latter declining ages of the world, and could now produce only small abortive births in comparison of those in ancient times. He said it was very reasonable to think, not only that the species of men were originally much larger, but also that there must have been giants in former ages; which, as it is asserted by history and tradition, so it hath been confirmed by huge bones and skulls casually dug up in several parts of the kingdom, far exceeding the common dwindled race of man in our days. He argued that the

---

9. In Swift's time, *transcendental* was practically synonymous with *metaphysical*.

very laws of nature absolutely required we should have been made in the beginning of a size more large and robust, not so liable to destruction from every little accident of a tile falling from a house, or a stone cast from the hand of a boy, or of being drowned in a little brook. From this way of reasoning, the author drew several moral applications useful in the conduct of life, but needless here to repeat. For my own part, I could not avoid reflecting how universally this talent was spread, of drawing lectures in morality, or indeed rather matter of discontent and repining, from the quarrels we raise with nature. And I believe, upon a strict inquiry, those quarrels might be shown as ill grounded among us as they are among that people.

As to their military affairs, they boast that the King's army consists of an hundred and seventy-six thousand foot and thirty-two thousand horse: if that may be called an army which is made up of tradesmen in the several cities, and farmers in the country, whose commanders are only the nobility and gentry, without pay or reward. They are indeed perfect enough in their exercises, and under very good discipline, wherein I saw no great merit; for how should it be otherwise, where every farmer is under the command of his own landlord, and every citizen under that of the principal men in his own city, chosen after the manner of Venice by ballot?

I have often seen the militia of Lorbrulgrud drawn out to exercise in a great field near the city, of twenty miles square. They were in all not above twenty-five thousand foot, and six thousand horse; but it was impossible for me to compute their number, considering the space of ground they took up. A cavalier mounted on a large steed might be about an hundred foot high. I have seen this whole body of horse, upon a word of command, draw their swords at once, and brandish them in the air. Imagination can figure nothing so grand, so surprising, and so astonishing. It looked as if ten thousand flashes of lightning were darting at the same time from every quarter of the sky.

I was curious to know how this prince, to whose dominions there is no access from any other country, came to think of armies, or to teach his people the practice of military discipline. But I was soon informed, both by conversation and reading their histories. For in the course of many ages they have been troubled with the same disease to which the whole race of mankind is subject: the nobility often contending for power, the people for liberty, and the King for absolute dominion. All which, however happily tempered by the laws of the kingdom, have been sometimes violated by each of the three parties, and have more than once occasioned civil wars, the last whereof was happily put an end to by this prince's grandfather in a general composition;[1] and the militia, then settled with common consent, hath been ever since kept in the strictest duty.

CHAPTER 8. *The King and Queen make a progress to the frontiers. The Author attends them. The manner in which he leaves the country very particularly related. He returns to England.*

I had always a strong impulse that I should some time recover my liberty, though it were impossible to conjecture by what means, or to form any project with the least hope of succeeding. The ship in which I sailed was the first ever

---

1. A political settlement based on general agreement of all parties.

known to be driven within sight of that coast; and the King had given strict orders that if at any time another appeared, it should be taken ashore, and with all its crew and passengers brought in a tumbrel[2] to Lorbrulgrud. He was strongly bent to get me a woman of my own size, by whom I might propagate the breed: but I think I should rather have died than undergone the disgrace of leaving a posterity to be kept in cages like tame canary birds, and perhaps in time sold about the kingdom to persons of quality for curiosities. I was indeed treated with much kindness: I was the favorite of a great King and Queen, and the delight of the whole Court, but it was upon such a foot as ill became the dignity of human kind. I could never forget those domestic pledges I had left behind me. I wanted to be among people with whom I could converse upon even terms, and walk about the streets and fields without fear of being trod to death like a frog or a young puppy. But my deliverance came sooner than I expected, and in a manner not very common; the whole story and circumstances of which I shall faithfully relate.

I had now been two years in this country; and about the beginning of the third, Glumdalclitch and I attended the King and Queen in progress to the south coast of the kingdom. I was carried as usual in my traveling box, which, as I have already described, was a very convenient closet of twelve foot wide. I had ordered a hammock to be fixed by silken ropes from the four corners at the top, to break the jolts when a servant carried me before him on horseback, as I sometimes desired; and would often sleep in my hammock while we were upon the road. On the roof of my closet, set not directly over the middle of the hammock, I ordered the joiner to cut out a hole of a foot square to give me air in hot weather as I slept, which hole I shut at pleasure with a board that drew backwards and forwards through a groove.

When we came to our journey's end, the King thought proper to pass a few days at a palace he hath near Flanflasnic, a city within eighteen English miles of the seaside. Glumdalclitch and I were much fatigued; I had gotten a small cold, but the poor girl was so ill as to be confined to her chamber. I longed to see the ocean, which must be the only scene of my escape, if ever it should happen. I pretended to be worse than I really was, and desired leave to take the fresh air of the sea with a page whom I was very fond of, and who had sometimes been trusted with me. I shall never forget with what unwillingness Glumdalclitch consented, nor the strict charge she gave the page to be careful of me, bursting at the same time into a flood of tears, as if she had some foreboding of what was to happen. The boy took me out in my box about half an hour's walk from the palace, towards the rocks on the seashore. I ordered him to set me down, and lifting up one of my sashes, cast many a wistful melancholy look towards the sea. I found myself not very well, and told the page that I had a mind to take a nap in my hammock, which I hoped would do me good. I got in, and the boy shut the window close down, to keep out the cold. I soon fell asleep: and all I can conjecture is that while I slept, the page, thinking no danger could happen, went among the rocks to look for birds' eggs; having before observed him from my window searching about, and picking up one or two in the clefts. Be that as it will, I found myself suddenly awaked with a violent pull upon the ring which was fastened at the top of my box for the conveniency of carriage. I felt my box raised very high in the air,

2. A farm wagon.

and then borne forward with prodigious speed. The first jolt had like to have shaken me out of my hammock, but afterwards the motion was easy enough. I called out several times as loud as I could raise my voice, but all to no purpose. I looked towards my windows, and could see nothing but the clouds and sky. I heard a noise just over my head like the clapping of wings, and then began to perceive the woeful condition I was in; that some eagle had got the ring of my box in his beak, with an intent to let it fall on a rock, like a tortoise in a shell, and then pick out my body and devour it. For the sagacity and smell of this bird enable him to discover his quarry at a great distance, although better concealed than I could be within a two-inch board.

In a little time I observed the noise and flutter of wings to increase very fast, and my box was tossed up and down like a signpost in a windy day. I heard several bangs or buffets, as I thought, given to the eagle (for such I am certain it must have been that held the ring of my box in his beak), and then all on a sudden felt myself falling perpendicularly down for above a minute, but with such incredible swiftness that I almost lost my breath. My fall was topped by a terrible squash, that sounded louder to mine ears than the cataract of Niagara; after which I was quite in the dark for another minute, and then my box began to rise so high that I could see light from the tops of my windows. I now perceived that I was fallen into the sea. My box, by the weight of my body, the goods that were in, and the broad plates of iron fixed for strength at the four corners of the top and bottom, floated above five foot deep in water. I did then and do now suppose that the eagle which flew away with my box was pursued by two or three others, and forced to let me drop while he was defending himself against the rest, who hoped to share in the prey. The plates of iron fastened at the bottom of the box (for those were the strongest) preserved the balance while it fell, and hindered it from being broken on the surface of the water. Every joint of it was well grooved, and the door did not move on hinges, but up and down like a sash; which kept my closet so tight that very little water came in. I got with much difficulty out of my hammock, having first ventured to draw back the slip-board on the roof already mentioned, contrived on purpose to let in air, for want of which I found myself almost stifled.

How often did I then wish myself with my dear Glumdalclitch, from whom one single hour had so far divided me! And I may say with truth that in the midst of my own misfortune, I could not forbear lamenting my poor nurse, the grief she would suffer for my loss, the displeasure of the Queen, and the ruin of her fortune. Perhaps many travelers have not been under greater difficulties and distress than I was at this juncture, expecting every moment to see my box dashed in pieces, or at least overset by the first violent blast or a rising wave. A breach in one single pane of glass would have been immediate death, nor could anything have preserved the windows but the strong lattice wires placed on the outside against accidents in traveling. I saw the water ooze in at several crannies, although the leaks were not considerable, and I endeavored to stop them as well as I could. I was not able to lift up the roof of my closet, which otherwise I certainly should have done, and sat on the top of it, where I might at least preserve myself from being shut up, as I may call it, in the hold. Or, if I escaped these dangers for a day or two, what could I expect but a miserable death of cold and hunger! I was four hours under these circumstances, expecting and indeed wishing every moment to be my last.

I have already told the reader that there were two strong staples fixed upon that side of my box which had no window and into which the servant, who used to carry me on horseback, would put a leathern belt, and buckle it about his waist. Being in this disconsolate state, I heard, or at least thought I heard, some kind of grating noise on that side of my box where the staples were fixed; and soon after I began to fancy that the box was pulled or towed along in the sea; for I now and then felt a sort of tugging, which made the waves rise near the tops of my windows, leaving me almost in the dark. This gave me some faint hopes of relief, although I was not able to imagine how it could be brought about. I ventured to unscrew one of my chairs, which were always fastened to the floor; and having made a hard shift to screw it down again directly under the slipping-board that I had lately opened, I mounted on the chair, and putting my mouth as near as I could to the hole, I called for help in a loud voice, and in all the languages I understood. I then fastened my handkerchief to a stick I usually carried, and thrusting it up the hole, waved it several times in the air, that if any boat or ship were near, the seamen might conjecture some unhappy mortal to be shut up in the box.

I found no effect from all I could do, but plainly perceived my closet to be moved along; and in the space of an hour or better, that side of the box where the staples were, and had no window, struck against something that was hard. I apprehended it to be a rock, and found myself tossed more than ever. I plainly heard a noise upon the cover of my closet, like that of a cable, and the grating of it as it passed through the ring. I then found myself hoisted up by degrees at least three foot higher than I was before. Whereupon I again thrust up my stick and handkerchief, calling for help till I was almost hoarse. In return to which, I heard a great shout repeated three times, giving me such transports of joy as are not to be conceived but by those who feel them. I now heard a trampling over my head, and somebody calling through the hole with a loud voice in the English tongue: "If there be anybody below, let them speak." I answered, I was an Englishman, drawn by ill fortune into the greatest calamity that ever any creature underwent, and begged, by all that was moving, to be delivered out of the dungeon I was in. The voice replied, I was safe, for my box was fastened to their ship; and the carpenter should immediately come and saw an hole in the cover, large enough to pull me out. I answered, that was needless and would take up too much time, for there was no more to be done but let one of the crew put his finger into the ring, and take the box out of the sea into the ship, and so into the captain's cabin. Some of them, upon hearing me talk so wildly, thought I was mad; others laughed; for indeed it never came into my head that I was now got among people of my own stature and strength. The carpenter came, and in a few minutes sawed a passage about four foot square; then let down a small ladder, upon which I mounted, and from thence was taken into the ship in a very weak condition.

The sailors were all in amazement, and asked me a thousand questions, which I had no inclination to answer. I was equally confounded at the sight of so many pygmies, for such I took them to be, after having so long accustomed my eyes to the monstrous objects I had left. But the Captain, Mr. Thomas Wilcocks, an honest, worthy Shropshire man, observing I was ready to faint, took me into his cabin, gave me a cordial to comfort me, and made me turn in upon his own bed, advising me to take a little rest, of which I had great need. Before I went to sleep I gave him to understand that I had some valuable furniture in my box, too good to be lost, a fine hammock, an hand-

some field bed, two chairs, a table, and a cabinet; that my closet was hung on
all sides, or rather quilted with silk and cotton; that if he would let one of the
crew bring my closet into his cabin, I would open it before him and show him
my goods. The Captain, hearing me utter these absurdities, concluded I was
raving; however (I suppose to pacify me), he promised to give order as I
desired, and going upon deck, sent some of his men down into my closet,
from whence (as I afterwards found) they drew up all my goods and stripped
off the quilting; but the chairs, cabinet, and bedstead, being screwed to the
floor, were much damaged by the ignorance of the seamen, who tore them
up by force. Then they knocked off some of the boards for the use of the ship;
and when they had got all they had a mind for, let the hulk drop into the sea,
which, by reason of many breaches made in the bottom and sides, sunk to
rights.[3] And indeed I was glad not to have been a spectator of the havoc they
made, because I am confident it would have sensibly touched me, by bringing
former passages into my mind, which I had rather forget.

I slept some hours, but perpetually disturbed with dreams of the place I had
left, and the dangers I had escaped. However, upon waking, I found myself
much recovered. It was now about eight o'clock at night, and the Captain
ordered supper immediately, thinking I had already fasted too long. He entertained me with great kindness, observing me not to look wildly, or talk incon-
sistently; and when we were left alone, desired I would give him a relation of
my travels, and by what accident I came to be set adrift in that monstrous
wooden chest. He said that about twelve o'clock at noon, as he was looking
through his glass, he spied it at a distance, and thought it was a sail, which he
had a mind to make,[4] being not much out of his course, in hopes of buying
some biscuit, his own beginning to fall short. That, upon coming nearer, and
finding his error, he sent out his longboat to discover what I was; that his men
came back in a fright, swearing they had seen a swimming house. That he
laughed at their folly, and went himself in the boat, ordering his men to take
a strong cable along with them. That the weather being calm, he rowed round
me several times, observed my windows, and the wire lattices that defended
them. That he discovered two staples upon one side, which was all of boards,
without any passage for light. He then commanded his men to row up to that
side, and fastening a cable to one of the staples, ordered his men to tow my
chest (as he called it) towards the ship. When it was there, he gave directions
to fasten another cable to the ring fixed in the cover, and to raise up my chest
with pulleys, which all the sailors were not able to do above two or three foot.
He said they saw my stick and handkerchief thrust out of the hole, and concluded that some unhappy man must be shut up in the cavity. I asked whether
he or the crew had seen any prodigious birds in the air about the time he first
discovered me. To which he answered that, discoursing this matter with the
sailors while I was asleep, one of them said he had observed three eagles flying
towards the north, but remarked nothing of their being larger than the usual
size (which I suppose must be imputed to the great height they were at), and
he could not guess the reason of my question. I then asked the Captain how
far he reckoned we might be from land; he said, by the best computation he
could make, we were at least an hundred leagues. I assured him that he must
be mistaken by almost half; for I had not left the country from whence I came

3. At once; altogether.   4. Overtake.

above two hours before I dropped into the sea. Whereupon he began again to think that my brain was disturbed, of which he gave me a hint, and advised me to go to bed in a cabin he had provided. I assured him I was well refreshed with his good entertainment and company, and as much in my senses as ever I was in my life. He then grew serious and desired to ask me freely whether I were not troubled in mind by the consciousness of some enormous crime, for which I was punished at the command of some prince, by exposing me in that chest, as great criminals in other countries have been forced to sea in a leaky vessel without provisions; for although he should be sorry to have taken so ill[5] a man into his ship, yet he would engage his word to set me safe on shore in the first port where we arrived. He added that his suspicions were much increased by some very absurd speeches I had delivered at first to the sailors, and afterwards to himself, in relation to my closet or chest, as well as by my odd looks and behavior while I was at supper.

I begged his patience to hear me tell my story, which I faithfully did from the last time I left England to the moment he first discovered me. And as truth always forceth its way into rational minds, so this honest, worthy gentleman, who had some tincture of learning, and very good sense, was immediately convinced of my candor and veracity. But further to confirm all I had said, I entreated him to give order that my cabinet should be brought, of which I kept the key in my pocket (for he had already informed me how the seamen disposed of my closet). I opened it in his presence and showed him the small collection of rarities I made in the country from whence I had been so strangely delivered. There was the comb I had contrived out of the stumps of the King's beard, and another of the same materials, but fixed into a paring of her Majesty's thumbnail, which served for the back. There was a collection of needles and pins from a foot to half a yard long; four wasp-stings, like joiners' tacks; some combings of the Queen's hair; a gold ring which one day she made me a present of in a most obliging manner, taking it from her little finger, and throwing it over my head like a collar. I desired the Captain would please to accept this ring in return for his civilities, which he absolutely refused. I showed him a corn that I had cut off with my own hand from a Maid of Honor's toe; it was about the bigness of a Kentish pippin, and grown so hard that, when I returned to England, I got it hollowed into a cup and set in silver. Lastly, I desired him to see the breeches I had then on, which were made of a mouse's skin.

I could force nothing on him but a footman's tooth, which I observed him to examine with great curiosity, and found he had a fancy for it. He received it with abundance of thanks, more than such a trifle could deserve. It was drawn by an unskillful surgeon in a mistake from one of Glumdalclitch's men, who was afflicted with the toothache; but it was as sound as any in his head. I got it cleaned, and put it into my cabinet. It was about a foot long, and four inches in diameter.

The Captain was very well satisfied with this plain relation I had given him, and said he hoped when we returned to England I would oblige the world by putting it in paper and making it public. My answer was that I thought we were already overstocked with books of travels; that nothing could now pass which was not extraordinary; wherein I doubted some authors less consulted

5. Evil.

truth than their own vanity or interest, or the diversion of ignorant readers. That my story could contain little besides common events, without those ornamental descriptions of strange plants, trees, birds, and other animals, or the barbarous customs and idolatry of savage people, with which most writers abound. However, I thanked him for his good opinion, and promised to take the matter into my thoughts.

He said he wondered at one thing very much, which was to hear me speak so loud, asking me whether the King or Queen of that country were thick of hearing. I told him it was what I had been used to for above two years past, and that I admired[6] as much at the voices of him and his men, who seemed to me only to whisper, and yet I could hear them well enough. But, when I spoke in that country, it was like a man talking in the street to another looking out from the top of a steeple, unless when I was placed on a table, or held in any person's hand. I told him I had likewise observed another thing: that when I first got into the ship, and the sailors stood all about me, I thought they were the most little contemptible creatures I had ever beheld. For indeed while I was in that prince's country, I could never endure to look in a glass after my eyes had been accustomed to such prodigious objects, because the comparison gave me so despicable a conceit[7] of myself. The Captain said that while we were at supper he observed me to look at everything with a sort of wonder, and that I often seemed hardly able to contain my laughter; which he knew not well how to take, but imputed it to some disorder in my brain. I answered, it was very true; and I wondered how I could forbear, when I saw his dishes of the size of a silver threepence, a leg of pork hardly a mouthful, a cup not so big as a nutshell; and so I went on, describing the rest of his household stuff and provisions after the same manner. For, although the Queen had ordered a little equipage of all things necessary for me while I was in her service, yet my ideas were wholly taken up with what I saw on every side of me, and I winked at my own littleness, as people do at their own faults. The Captain understood my raillery very well, and merrily replied with the old English proverb, that he doubted[8] my eyes were bigger than my belly, for he did not observe my stomach so good, although I had fasted all day; and continuing in his mirth, protested he would have gladly given an hundred pounds to have seen my closet in the eagle's bill, and afterwards in its fall from so great an height into the sea; which would certainly have been a most astonishing object, worthy to have the description of it transmitted to future ages: and the comparison of Phaeton[9] was so obvious, that he could not forbear applying it, although I did not much admire the conceit.

The Captain having been at Tonquin,[1] was in his return to England driven northeastward to the latitude of 44 degrees, and of longitude 143. But meeting a trade wind two days after I came on board him, we sailed southward a long time, and coasting New Holland[2] kept our course west-southwest, and then south-southwest till we doubled the Cape of Good Hope. Our voyage was very prosperous, but I shall not trouble the reader with a journal of it. The Captain called in at one or two ports, and sent in his longboat for provisions and fresh

6. Wondered.
7. Notion.
8. Feared.
9. Son of Helios, the sun god, whose unsuccessful attempt to drive his father's chariot led to his death,
when he lost control and was hurled by Zeus from the sky, falling into the river Eridanus, where he drowned.
1. Tonkin, now in Vietnam.
2. Australia.

water; but I never went out of the ship till we came into the Downs, which was on the third day of June, 1706, about nine months after my escape. I offered to leave my goods in security for payment of my freight; but the Captain protested he would not receive one farthing. We took kind leave of each other, and I made him promise he would come to see me at my house in Redriff. I hired a horse and guide for five shillings, which I borrowed of the Captain.

As I was on the road, observing the littleness of the houses, the trees, the cattle, and the people, I began to think myself in Lilliput. I was afraid of trampling on every traveler I met, and often called aloud to have them stand out of the way, so that I had like to have gotten one or two broken heads for my impertinence.

When I came to my own house, for which I was forced to inquire, one of the servants opening the door, I bent down to go in (like a goose under a gate) for fear of striking my head. My wife ran out to embrace me, but I stooped lower than her knees, thinking she could otherwise never be able to reach my mouth. My daughter kneeled to ask my blessing, but I could not see her till she arose, having been so long used to stand with my head and eyes erect to above sixty foot; and then I went to take her up with one hand by the waist. I looked down upon the servants and one or two friends who were in the house, as if they had been pygmies and I a giant. I told my wife she had been too thrifty; for I found she had starved herself and her daughter to nothing. In short, I behaved myself so unaccountably that they were all of the Captain's opinion when he first saw me, and concluded I had lost my wits. This I mention as an instance of the great power of habit and prejudice.

In a little time I and my family and friends came to a right understanding; but my wife protested I should never go to sea any more, although my evil destiny so ordered that she had not power to hinder me; as the reader may know hereafter. In the meantime I here conclude the second part of my unfortunate voyages.

From *Part* 3. A *Voyage to Laputa, Balnibarbi, Glubbdubdrib, Luggnagg, and Japan*

[*The Flying Island of Laputa*][3]

CHAPTER 2. *The humors and dispositions of the Laputans described. An account of their learning. Of the King and his court. The author's reception there. The inhabitants subject to fears and disquietudes. An account of the women.*

At my alighting I was surrounded by a crowd of people, but those who stood nearest seemed to be of better quality. They beheld me with all the marks and circumstances of wonder; neither indeed was I much in their debt, having never till then seen a race of mortals so singular in their shapes, habits, and countenances. Their heads were all reclined to the right, or the left; one of their eyes turned inward, and the other directly up to the zenith. Their out-

3. In the first chapter of part 3 Gulliver starts on his third voyage, but is captured by pirates and set adrift. Just as he is about to despair, a vast flying island appears in the sky, and the inhabitants draw him up with pulleys.

ward garments were adorned with the figures of suns, moons, and stars, inter-woven with those of fiddles, flutes, harps, trumpets, guitars, harpsichords, and many more instruments of music, unknown to us in Europe.[4] I observed here and there many in the habits of servants, with a blown bladder fastened like a flail to the end of a short stick, which they carried in their hands. In each bladder was a small quantity of dried pease or little pebbles (as I was afterwards informed). With these bladders they now and then flapped the mouths and ears of those who stood near them, of which practice I could not then con-ceive the meaning. It seems, the minds of these people are so taken up with intense speculations, that they neither can speak, or attend to the discourses of others, without being roused by some external taction[5] upon the organs of speech and hearing; for which reason those persons who are able to afford it always keep a flapper (the original is *climenole*) in their family, as one of their domestics; nor ever walk abroad or make visits without him. And the business of this officer is, when two or more persons are in company, gently to strike with his bladder the mouth of him who is to speak, and the right ear of him or them to whom the speaker addresseth himself. This flapper is likewise employed diligently to attend his master in his walks, and upon occasion to give him a soft flap on his eyes, because he is always so wrapped up in cogita-tion, that he is in manifest danger of falling down every precipice, and bounc-ing his head against every post; and in the streets, of jostling others, or being jostled himself into the kennel.[6]

It was necessary to give the reader this information, without which he would be at the same loss with me, to understand the proceedings of these people, as they conducted me up the stairs to the top of the island, and from thence to the royal palace. While we were ascending, they forgot several times what they were about, and left me to myself, till their memories were again roused by their flappers; for they appeared altogether unmoved by the sight of my foreign habit and countenance, and by the shouts of the vulgar, whose thoughts and minds were more disengaged.

At last we entered the palace, and proceeded into the chamber of presence; where I saw the King seated on his throne, attended on each side by persons of prime quality. Before the throne was a large table filled with globes and spheres, and mathematical instruments of all kinds. His Majesty took not the least notice of us, although our entrance was not without sufficient noise, by the concourse of all persons belonging to the court. But he was then deep in a problem, and we attended at least an hour before he could solve it. There stood by him on each side a young page, with flaps in their hands, and when they saw he was at leisure, one of them gently struck his mouth, and the other his right ear; at which he started like one awaked on the sudden, and looking towards me, and the company I was in, recollected the occasion of our com-ing, whereof he had been informed before. He spoke some words, whereupon immediately a young man with a flap came up to my side, and flapped me gently on the right ear; but I made signs as well as I could, that I had no occasion for such an instrument; which as I afterwards found gave his Majesty and the whole court a very mean opinion of my understanding. The King, as

4. The Laputans represent contemporary speculation, deplored by Swift, about abstract theories of science, mathematics, and music. Both the Royal Society and Sir Isaac Newton took an interest in the mathematical basis of music.
5. Touch.
6. Gutter.

far as I could conjecture, asked me several questions, and I addressed myself
to him in all the languages I had. When it was found that I could neither
understand nor be understood, I was conducted by his order to an apartment
in his palace (this prince being distinguished above all his predecessors for his
hospitality to strangers),[7] where two servants were appointed to attend me. My
dinner was brought, and four persons of quality, whom I remembered to have
seen very near the King's person, did me the honor to dine with me. We had
two courses, of three dishes each. In the first course there was a shoulder of
mutton, cut into an equilateral triangle; a piece of beef into a rhomboid; and
a pudding into a cycloid. The second course was two ducks, trussed up into
the form of fiddles; sausages and pudding resembling flutes and hautboys,[8]
and a breast of veal in the shape of a harp. The servants cut our bread into
cones, cylinders, parallelograms, and several other mathematical figures.

While we were at dinner, I made bold to ask the names of several things in
their language, and those noble persons, by the assistance of their flappers,
delighted to give me answers, hoping to raise my admiration of their great
abilities, if I could be brought to converse with them. I was soon able to call
for bread and drink, or whatever else I wanted.

After dinner my company withdrew, and a person was sent to me by the
King's order, attended by a flapper. He brought with him pen, ink, and paper,
and three or four books; giving me to understand by signs, that he was sent to
teach me the language. We sat together four hours, in which time I wrote
down a great number of words in columns, with the translations over against
them. I likewise made a shift to learn several short sentences. For my tutor
would order one of my servants to fetch something, to turn about, to make a
bow, to sit, or stand, or walk, and the like. Then I took down the sentence in
writing. He showed me also in one of his books the figures of the sun, moon,
and stars, the zodiac, the tropics and polar circles, together with the denominations of many figures of planes and solids. He gave me the names and
descriptions of all the musical instruments, and the general terms of art in
playing on each of them. After he had left me, I placed all my words with
their interpretations in alphabetical order. And thus in a few days, by the help
of a very faithful memory, I got some insight into their language.

The word, which I interpret the *Flying* or *Floating Island,* is in the original
Laputa; whereof I could never learn the true etymology. *Lap* in the old obsolete language signifieth *high,* and *untuh* a *governor*; from which they say by
corruption was derived *Laputa*, from *Lapuntuh*. But I do not approve of this
derivation, which seems to be a little strained. I ventured to offer to the learned
among them a conjecture of my own, that *Laputa* was *quasi Lap outed; Lap*
signifying properly the dancing of the sunbeams in the sea, and *outed* a wing,
which however I shall not obtrude, but submit to the judicious reader.[9]

Those to whom the King had entrusted me, observing how ill I was clad,
ordered a tailor to come next morning, and take my measure for a suit of
clothes. This operator did his office after a different manner from those of his
trade in Europe. He first took my altitude by a quadrant, and then, with rule
and compasses, described the dimensions and outlines of my whole body; all
which he entered upon paper, and in six days brought my clothes very ill

7. George I, a patron of music and science, had filled
his court with Hanoverians when he came to England
in 1714.

8. Oboes.

9. Gulliver overlooks a likelier etymology: Spanish *la
puta*, "the whore."

made, and quite out of shape, by happening to mistake a figure in the calculation. But my comfort was, that I observed such accidents very frequent, and
little regarded.

During my confinement for want of clothes, and by an indisposition that
held me some days longer, I much enlarged my dictionary; and when I went
next to court, was able to understand many things the King spoke, and to
return him some kind of answers. His Majesty had given orders that the island
should move northeast and by east, to the vertical point over Lagado, the
metropolis of the whole kingdom, below upon the firm earth. It was about
ninety leagues distant, and our voyage lasted four days and a half. I was not in
the least sensible of the progressive motion made in the air by the island. On
the second morning, about eleven o'clock, the King himself in person,
attended by his nobility, courtiers, and officers, having prepared all their musical instruments, played on them for three hours without intermission, so that
I was quite stunned with the noise; neither could I possibly guess the meaning,
till my tutor informed me. He said, that the people of their island had their
ears adapted to hear the music of the spheres, which always played at certain
periods; and the court was now prepared to bear their part in whatever instrument they most excelled.

In our journey towards Lagado, the capital city, his Majesty ordered that
the island should stop over certain towns and villages, from whence he might
receive the petitions of his subjects. And to this purpose, several packthreads
were let down with small weights at the bottom. On these packthreads the
people strung their petitions, which mounted up directly like the scraps of
paper fastened by schoolboys at the end of the string that holds their kite.[1]
Sometimes we received wine and victuals from below, which were drawn up
by pulleys.

The knowledge I had in mathematics gave me great assistance in acquiring
their phraseology, which depended much upon that science and music; and
in the latter I was not unskilled. Their ideas are perpetually conversant in lines
and figures. If they would, for example, praise the beauty of a woman, or any
other animal, they describe it by rhombs, circles, parallelograms, ellipses, and
other geometrical terms; or else by words of art drawn from music, needless
here to repeat. I observed in the King's kitchen all sorts of mathematical and
musical instruments, after the figures of which they cut up the joints that were
served to his Majesty's table.

Their houses are very ill built, the walls bevil, without one right angle in any
apartment; and this defect ariseth from the contempt they bear for practical
geometry; which they despise as vulgar and mechanic, those instructions they
give being too refined for the intellectuals of their workmen; which occasions
perpetual mistakes. And although they are dextrous enough upon a piece of
paper, in the management of the rule, the pencil, and the divider, yet in the
common actions and behavior of life I have not seen a more clumsy, awkward,
and unhandy people, nor so slow and perplexed in their conceptions upon all
other subjects, except those of mathematics and music. They are very bad
reasoners, and vehemently given to opposition, unless when they happen to

---

1. Petitioners, that is, might as well go fly a kite. Throughout this section Swift satirizes the "distance" of George
I (who spent much of his time in Hanover) from his British subjects.

be of the right opinion, which is seldom their case. Imagination, fancy, and invention, they are wholly strangers to, nor have any words in their language by which those ideas can be expressed; the whole compass of their thoughts and mind being shut up within the two forementioned sciences.

Most of them, and especially those who deal in the astronomical part, have great faith in judicial astrology, although they are ashamed to own it publicly. But what I chiefly admired,[2] and thought altogether unaccountable, was the strong disposition I observed in them towards news and politics; perpetually enquiring into public affairs, giving their judgments in matters of state; and passionately disputing every inch of a party opinion. I have indeed observed the same disposition among most of the mathematicians I have known in Europe; although I could never discover the least analogy between the two sciences; unless those people suppose, that because the smallest circle hath as many degrees as the largest, therefore the regulation and management of the world require no more abilities than the handling and turning of a globe. But I rather take this quality to spring from a very common infirmity of human nature, inclining us to be more curious and conceited in matters where we have least concern, and for which we are least adapted either by study or nature.

These people are under continual disquietudes, never enjoying a minute's peace of mind; and their disturbances proceed from causes which very little affect the rest of mortals. Their apprehensions arise from several changes they dread in the celestial bodies. For instance; that the earth, by the continual approaches of the sun towards it, must in course of time be absorbed or swallowed up. That the face of the sun will by degrees be encrusted with its own effluvia,[3] and give no more light to the world. That the earth very narrowly escaped a brush from the tail of the last comet, which would have infallibly reduced it to ashes; and that the next, which they have calculated for one and thirty years hence, will probably destroy us.[4] For, if in its perihelion it should approach within a certain degree of the sun (as by their calculations they have reason to dread), it will conceive a degree of heat ten thousand times more intense than that of red-hot glowing iron; and in its absence from the sun, carry a blazing tail ten hundred thousand and fourteen miles long; through which if the earth should pass at the distance of one hundred thousand miles from the nucleus, or main body of the comet, it must in its passage be set on fire, and reduced to ashes. That the sun daily spending its rays without any nutriment to supply them, will at last be wholly consumed and annihilated; which must be attended with the destruction of this earth, and of all the planets that receive their light from it.

They are so perpetually alarmed with the apprehensions of these and the like impending dangers, that they can neither sleep quietly in their beds, nor have any relish for the common pleasures or amusements of life. When they meet an acquaintance in the morning, the first question is about the sun's health, how he looked at his setting and rising, and what hopes they have to avoid the stroke of the approaching comet. This conversation they are apt to

2. Wondered at.
3. Sunspots.
4. Halley's comet, some astronomers had feared, might strike the earth on its next appearance (1758).

All the disasters that disquiet the Laputans had occurred to English scientists as possible implications of Newtonian theory.

run into with the same temper that boys discover in delighting to hear terrible stories of sprites and hobgoblins, which they greedily listen to, and dare not go to bed for fear.

The women of the island have abundance of vivacity; they contemn their husbands, and are exceedingly fond of strangers, whereof there is always a considerable number from the continent below, attending at court, either upon affairs of the several towns and corporations, or their own particular occasions; but are much despised, because they want the same endowments. Among these the ladies choose their gallants: but the vexation is, that they act with too much ease and security; for the husband is always so rapt in speculation, that the mistress and lover may proceed to the greatest familiarities before his face, if he be but provided with paper and implements, and without his flapper at his side.

The wives and daughters lament their confinement to the island, although I think it the most delicious spot of ground in the world; and although they live here in the greatest plenty and magnificence, and are allowed to do whatever they please, they long to see the world, and take the diversions of the metropolis, which they are not allowed to do without a particular license from the King; and this is not easy to be obtained, because the people of quality have found by frequent experience, how hard it is to persuade their women to return from below. I was told that a great court lady, who had several children, is married to the prime minister, the richest subject in the kingdom, a very graceful person, extremely fond of her, and lives in the finest palace of the island, went down to Lagado, on the pretense of health, there hid herself for several months, till the King sent a warrant to search for her, and she was found in an obscure eating-house all in rags, having pawned her clothes to maintain an old deformed footman, who beat her every day, and in whose company she was taken much against her will. And although her husband received her with all possible kindness, and without the least reproach, she soon after contrived to steal down again with all her jewels, to the same gallant, and hath not been heard of since.

This may perhaps pass with the reader rather for an European or English story, than for one of a country so remote. But he may please to consider, that the caprices of womankind are not limited by any climate or nation; and that they are much more uniform than can be easily imagined.

In about a month's time I had made a tolerable proficiency in their language, and was able to answer most of the King's questions, when I had the honor to attend him. His Majesty discovered not the least curiosity to enquire into the laws, government, history, religion, or manners of the countries where I had been; but confined his questions to the state of mathematics, and received the account I gave him with great contempt and indifference, though often roused by his flapper on each side.[5]

5. In the omitted chapters, Gulliver visits countries that show the consequences of modern learning. After an account of the Flying Island, whose power of motion (derived from a giant magnet or lodestone) allows it to dominate the regions below, he descends to Balnibarbi, a once fertile land now ruined by the fanciful projects of impractical scientists. In the Grand Academy of Lagado he meets many professors who are contriving such perverse "improvements" as making clothes from cobwebs or breeding naked sheep. Then he visits the part of the academy devoted to speculative learning.

[The Academy of Lagado][6]

The first professor I saw was in a very large room, with forty pupils about him. After salutation, observing me to look earnestly upon a frame, which took up the greatest part of both the length and breadth of the room, he said, perhaps I might wonder to see him employed in a project for improving speculative knowledge by practical and mechanical operations. But the world would soon be sensible[7] of its usefulness, and he flattered himself that a more noble, exalted thought never sprang in any other man's head. Everyone knew how laborious the usual method is of attaining to arts and sciences; whereas by his contrivance the most ignorant person at a reasonable charge, and with a little bodily labor, may write books in philosophy, poetry, politics, law, mathematics, and theology, without the least assistance from genius or study. He then led me to the frame, about the sides whereof all his pupils stood in ranks. It was twenty foot square, placed in the middle of the room. The superficies[8] was composed of several bits of wood, about the bigness of a die, but some larger than others. They were all linked together by slender wires. These bits of wood were covered on every square with papers pasted on them; and on these papers were written all the words of their language in their several moods, tenses, and declensions, but without any order. The professor then desired me to observe, for he was going to set his engine at work. The pupils at his command took each of them hold of an iron handle, whereof there were forty fixed round the edges of the frame; and giving them a sudden turn, the whole disposition[9] of the words was entirely changed. He then commanded six and thirty of the lads to read the several lines softly as they appeared upon the frame; and where they found three or four words together that might make part of a sentence, they dictated to the four remaining boys who were scribes. This work was repeated three or four times, and at every turn the engine was so contrived that the words shifted into new places, as the square bits of wood moved upside down.

Six hours a day the young students were employed in this labor; and the professor showed me several volumes in large folio already collected, of broken sentences, which he intended to piece together, and out of those rich materials to give the world a complete body of all arts and sciences; which however might be still improved, and much expedited, if the public would raise a fund for making and employing five hundred such frames in Lagado, and oblige the managers to contribute in common their several[1] collections.

He assured me, that this invention had employed all his thoughts from his youth, that he had emptied the whole vocabulary into his frame, and made the strictest computation of the general proportion there is in books between the numbers of particles, nouns, and verbs, and other parts of speech.

I made my humblest acknowledgments to this illustrious person for his great communicativeness, and promised if ever I had the good fortune to return to my native country, that I would do him justice, as the sole inventor of this wonderful machine; the form and contrivance of which I desired leave to

6. From chapter 5. The Grand Academy of Lagado satirizes the Royal Society of London, an organization founded in 1662 to encourage the pursuit of scientific knowledge. Some of the projects described by Swift resemble the experiments or speculations of British scientists at the time.
7. Aware.
8. Surface.
9. Arrangement.
1. Separate.

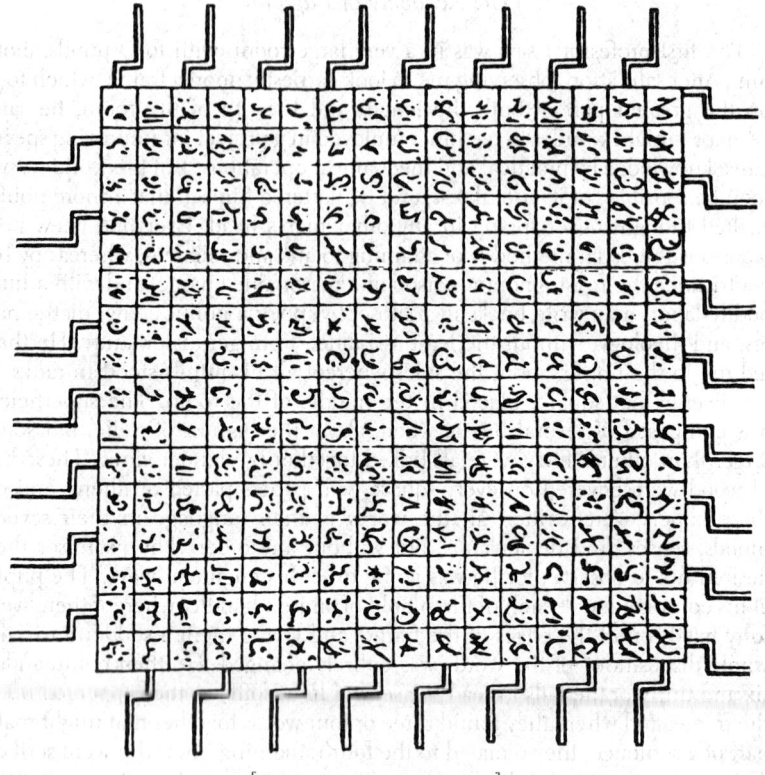

[A PRIMITIVE COMPUTER]

delineate upon paper as in the figure here annexed. I told him, although it were the custom of our learned in Europe to steal inventions from each other, who had thereby at least this advantage, that it became a controversy which was the right owner, yet I would take such caution, that he should have the honor entire without a rival.

We next went to the school of languages, where three professors sat in consultation upon improving that of their own country.[2]

The first project was to shorten discourse by cutting polysyllables into one, and leaving out verbs and participles, because in reality all things imaginable are but nouns.

The other was a scheme for entirely abolishing all words whatsoever; and this was urged as a great advantage in point of health as well as brevity. For it is plain, that every word we speak is in some degree a diminution of our lungs by corrosion, and consequently contributes to the shortening of our lives. An expedient was therefore offered, that since words are only names for *things*, it would be more convenient for all men to carry about them such *things* as were necessary to express the particular business they are to discourse on. And this invention would certainly have taken place, to the great ease as well as

---

2. Many contemporary scientists had proposed a philosophical language that would eliminate the treacherous disparity between words and things and thus allow accurate scientific discourse.

health of the subject, if the women in conjunction with the vulgar and illiterate had not threatened to raise a rebellion, unless they might be allowed the
liberty to speak with their tongues, after the manner of their forefathers. Such
constant irreconcilable enemies to science[3] are the common people. However, many of the most learned and wise adhere to the new scheme of expressing themselves by *things*, which hath only this inconvenience attending it,
that if a man's business be very great, and of various kinds, he must be obliged
in proportion to carry a greater bundle of *things* upon his back, unless he can
afford one or two strong servants to attend him. I have often beheld two of
those sages almost sinking under the weight of their packs, like pedlars among
us, who when they met in the streets would lay down their loads, open their
sacks, and hold conversation for an hour together, then put up their implements, help each other to resume their burdens, and take their leave.

But for short conversations a man may carry implements in his pockets and
under his arms, enough to supply him, and in his house he cannot be at a
loss; therefore the room where company meet who practice this art is full of
all *things* ready at hand, requisite to furnish matter for this kind of artificial
converse.[4]

Another great advantage proposed by this invention was that it would serve
as an universal language to be understood in all civilized nations, whose goods
and utensils are generally of the same kind, or nearly resembling, so that their
uses might easily be comprehended. And thus, ambassadors would be qualified to treat with foreign princes or ministers of state to whose tongues they
were utter strangers.

I was at the mathematical school, where the master taught his pupils after a
method scarce imaginable to us in Europe. The proposition and demonstration were fairly written on a thin wafer, with ink composed of a cephalic
tincture.[5] This the student was to swallow upon a fasting stomach, and for
three days following eat nothing but bread and water. As the wafer digested,
the tincture mounted to his brain, bearing the proposition along with it. But
the success hath not hitherto been answerable, partly by some error in the
quantum or composition, and partly by the perverseness of lads, to whom this
bolus[6] is so nauseous that they generally steal aside, and discharge it upwards
before it can operate; neither have they been yet persuaded to use so long an
abstinence as the prescription requires.[7]

[The Struldbruggs]

CHAPTER 10. *The Luggnaggians commended. A particular description of the
struldbruggs, with many conversations between the author and some eminent
persons upon that subject.*

The Luggnaggians are a polite[8] and generous people, and although they
are not without some share of that pride which is peculiar to all eastern coun-

---

3. Knowledge.
4. The Royal Society had sponsored a collection intended to contain one specimen of every thing in the
world.
5. A solution or dye directed toward the head.
6. A large pill. "*Quantum*": amount.
7. In the omitted chapters Gulliver hears projects for

improving politics and offers some of his own. He sails
to Glubbdubdrib, the Island of Sorcerers, where he
talks with the spirits of the dead; he learns that history
is a pack of lies and that humanity has degenerated
since ancient times. He is then received by the king of
Luggnagg.
8. Refined, cultivated.

tries, yet they show themselves courteous to strangers, especially such who are countenanced by the court. I had many acquaintance among persons of the best fashion, and being always attended by my interpreter, the conversation we had was not disagreeable.

One day in much good company, I was asked by a person of quality, whether I had seen any of their *struldbruggs* or *immortals*. I said I had not; and desired he would explain to me what he meant by such an appellation, applied to a mortal creature. He told me, that sometimes, although very rarely, a child happened to be born in a family with a red circular spot in the forehead, directly over the left eyebrow, which was an infallible mark that it should never die. The spot, as he described it, was about the compass of a silver threepence, but in the course of time grew larger, and changed its color; for at twelve years old it became green, so continued till five and twenty, then turned to a deep blue; at five and forty it grew coal black, and as large as an English shilling; but never admitted any farther alteration. He said these births were so rare, that he did not believe there could be above eleven hundred *struldbruggs* of both sexes in the whole kingdom, of which he computed about fifty in the metropolis, and among the rest a young girl born about three years ago. That these productions were not peculiar to any family, but a mere effect of chance; and the children of the *struldbruggs* themselves were equally mortal with the rest of the people.

I freely own myself to have been struck with inexpressible delight upon hearing this account: and the person who gave it me happening to understand the Balnibarbian language, which I spoke very well, I could not forbear breaking out into expressions perhaps a little too extravagant. I cried out as in a rapture: Happy nation, where every child hath at least a chance for being immortal! Happy people who enjoy so many living examples of ancient virtue, and have masters ready to instruct them in the wisdom of all former ages! But happiest beyond all comparison are those excellent *struldbruggs*, who being born exempt from that universal calamity of human nature, have their minds free and disengaged, without the weight and depression of spirits caused by the continual apprehension of death. I discovered my admiration that I had not observed any of these illustrious persons at court; the black spot on the forehead being so remarkable a distinction, that I could not have easily overlooked it; and it was impossible that his Majesty, a most judicious prince, should not provide himself with a good number of such wise and able counselors. Yet perhaps the virtue of those reverend sages was too strict for the corrupt and libertine manners of a court. And we often find by experience that young men are too opinionative[9] and volatile to be guided by the sober dictates of their seniors. However, since the King was pleased to allow me access to his royal person, I was resolved upon the very first occasion to deliver my opinion to him on this matter freely, and at large by the help of my interpreter; and whether he would please to take my advice or no, yet in one thing I was determined, that his Majesty having frequently offered me an establishment in this country, I would with great thankfulness accept the favor, and pass my life here in the conversation of those superior beings the *struldbruggs*, if they would please to admit me.

The gentleman to whom I addressed my discourse, because (as I have

9. Speculative, impractical.

already observed) he spoke the language of Balnibarbi, said to me with a sort of a smile, which usually ariseth from pity to the ignorant, that he was glad of any occasion to keep me among them, and desired my permission to explain to the company what I had spoke. He did so; and they talked together for some time in their own language, whereof I understood not a syllable, neither could I observe by their countenances what impression my discourse had made on them. After a short silence the same person told me, that his friends and mine (so he thought fit to express himself) were very much pleased with the judicious remarks I had made on the great happiness and advantages of immortal life; and they were desirous to know in a particular manner, what scheme of living I should have formed to myself, if it had fallen to my lot to have been born a *struldbrugg*.

I answered, it was easy to be eloquent on so copious and delightful a subject, especially to me who have been often apt to amuse myself with visions of what I should do if I were a king, a general, or a great lord; and upon this very case I had frequently run over the whole system how I should employ myself, and pass the time if I were sure to live forever.

That, if it had been my good fortune to come into the world a *struldbrugg*, as soon as I could discover my own happiness by understanding the difference between life and death, I would first resolve by all arts and methods whatsoever to procure myself riches: in the pursuit of which, by thrift and management, I might reasonably expect in about two hundred years to be the wealthiest man in the kingdom. In the second place, I would from my earliest youth apply myself to the study of arts and sciences, by which I should arrive in time to excel all others in learning. Lastly, I would carefully record every action and event of consequence that happened in the public, impartially draw the characters of the several successions of princes, and great ministers of state; with my own observations on every point. I would exactly set down the several changes in customs, languages, fashions of dress, diet and diversions. By all which acquirements, I should be a living treasury of knowledge and wisdom, and certainly become the oracle of the nation.

I would never marry after threescore, but live in an hospitable manner, yet still on the saving side. I would entertain myself in forming and directing the minds of hopeful young men, by convincing them from my own remembrance, experience and observation, fortified by numerous examples, of the usefulness of virtue in public and private life. But my choice and constant companions should be a set of my own immortal brotherhood, among whom I would elect a dozen from the most ancient down to my own contemporaries. Where any of these wanted fortunes, I would provide them with convenient lodges round my own estate, and have some of them always at my table, only mingling a few of the most valuable among you mortals, whom length of time would harden me to lose with little or no reluctance, and treat your posterity after the same manner; just as a man diverts himself with the annual succession of pinks and tulips in his garden, without regretting the loss of those which withered the preceding year.

These *struldbruggs* and I would mutually communicate our observations and memorials[1] through the course of time; remark the several gradations by which corruption steals into the world, and oppose it in every step, by giving

1. Memories.

perpetual warning and instruction to mankind; which, added to the strong influence of our own example, would probably prevent that continual degeneracy of human nature, so justly complained of in all ages.

Add to all this, the pleasure of seeing the various revolutions of states and empires; the changes in the lower and upper world;[2] ancient cities in ruins; and obscure villages become the seats of kings. Famous rivers lessening into shallow brooks; the ocean leaving one coast dry, and overwhelming another; the discovery of many countries yet unknown. Barbarity overrunning the politest nations, and the most barbarous becoming civilized. I should then see the discovery of the longitude, the perpetual motion, the universal medicine,[3] and many other great inventions brought to the utmost perfection.

What wonderful discoveries should we make in astronomy, by outliving and confirming our own predictions, by observing the progress and returns of comets, with the changes of motion in the sun, moon and stars.

I enlarged upon many other topics, which the natural desire of endless life and sublunary happiness could easily furnish me with. When I had ended, and the sum of my discourse had been interpreted as before to the rest of the company, there was a good deal of talk among them in the language of the country, not without some laughter at my expense. At last the same gentleman who had been my interpreter said, he was desired by the rest to set me right in a few mistakes, which I had fallen into through the common imbecility[4] of human nature, and upon that allowance was less answerable for them. That this breed of *struldbruggs* was peculiar to their country, for there were no such people either in Balnibarbi or Japan, where he had the honor to be ambassador from his Majesty, and found the natives in both those kingdoms very hard to believe that the fact was possible; and it appeared from my astonishment when he first mentioned the matter to me, that I received it as a thing wholly new, and scarcely to be credited. That in the two kingdoms above mentioned, where during his residence he had conversed very much, he observed long life to be the universal desire and wish of mankind. That whoever had one foot in the grave was sure to hold back the other as strongly as he could. That the oldest had still hopes of living one day longer, and looked on death as the greatest evil, from which nature always prompted him to retreat; only in this island of Luggnagg the appetite for living was not so eager, from the continual example of the *struldbruggs* before their eyes.

That the system of living contrived by me was unreasonable and unjust, because it supposed a perpetuity of youth, health, and vigor, which no man could be so foolish to hope, however extravagant he might be in his wishes. That the question therefore was not whether a man would choose to be always in the prime of youth, attended with prosperity and health; but how he would pass a perpetual life under all the usual disadvantages which old age brings along with it. For although few men will avow their desires of being immortal upon such hard conditions, yet in the two kingdoms before mentioned of Balnibarbi and Japan, he observed that every man desired to put off death for some time longer, let it approach ever so late; and he rarely heard of any man who died willingly, except he were incited by the extremity of grief or torture.

2. Earth and heaven; figuratively, common people and the ruling class. "Revolutions": cycles.
3. The *elixir vitae*, an alchemical formula to preserve life forever, was considered by Swift an impossible dream, like a method for calculating longitude at sea, or a perpetual motion machine.
4. Weakness.

And he appealed to me whether in those countries I had traveled, as well as my own, I had not observed the same general disposition.

After this preface he gave me a particular account of the *struldbruggs* among them. He said they commonly acted like mortals, till about thirty years old, after which by degrees they grew melancholy and dejected, increasing in both till they came to fourscore. This he learned from their own confession; for otherwise there not being above two or three of that species born in an age, they were too few to form a general observation by. When they came to four-score years, which is reckoned the extremity of living in this country, they had not only all the follies and infirmities of other old men, but many more which arose from the dreadful prospect of never dying. They were not only opinion-ative, peevish, covetous, morose, vain, talkative; but uncapable of friendship, and dead to all natural affection, which never descended below their grand-children. Envy and impotent desires are their prevailing passions. But those objects against which their envy seems principally directed, are the vices of the younger sort, and the deaths of the old. By reflecting on the former, they find themselves cut off from all possibility of pleasure; and whenever they see a funeral, they lament and repine that others are gone to an harbor of rest, to which they themselves never can hope to arrive. They have no remembrance of anything but what they learned and observed in their youth and middle age, and even that is very imperfect. And for the truth or particulars of any fact, it is safer to depend on common traditions than upon their best recollec-tions. The least miserable among them appear to be those who turn to dotage, and entirely lose their memories; these meet with more pity and assistance, because they want[5] many bad qualities which abound in others.

If a *struldbrugg* happen to marry one of his own kind, the marriage is dis-solved of course by the courtesy of the kingdom, as soon as the younger of the two comes to be fourscore. For the law thinks it a reasonable indulgence, that those who are condemned without any fault of their own to a perpetual continuance in the world, should not have their misery doubled by the load of a wife.

As soon as they have completed the term of eighty years, they are looked on as dead in law; their heirs immediately succeed to their estates, only a small pittance is reserved for their support; and the poor ones are maintained at the public charge. After that period they are held incapable of any employment of trust or profit; they cannot purchase land, or take leases, neither are they allowed to be witnesses in any cause, either civil or criminal, not even for the decision of meers[6] and bounds.

At ninety they lose their teeth and hair; they have at that age no distinction of taste, but eat and drink whatever they can get, without relish or appetite. The diseases they were subject to still continue without increasing or dimin-ishing. In talking they forget the common appellation of things, and the names of persons, even of those who are their nearest friends and relations. For the same reason they never can amuse themselves with reading, because their memory will not serve to carry them from the beginning of a sentence to the end, and by this defect they are deprived of the only entertainment whereof they might otherwise be capable.

The language of this country being always upon the flux, the *struldbruggs*

5. Lack.   6. Boundaries.

of one age do not understand those of another; neither are they able after two hundred years to hold any conversation (farther than by a few general words) with their neighbors the mortals; and thus they lie under the disadvantage of living like foreigners in their own country.

This was the account given me of the *struldbruggs*, as near as I can remember. I afterwards saw five or six of different ages, the youngest not above two hundred years old, who were brought to me at several times by some of my friends; but although they were told that I was a great traveler, and had seen all the world, they had not the least curiosity to ask me a question; only desired I would give them *slumskudask*, or a token of remembrance; which is a modest way of begging, to avoid the law that strictly forbids it, because they are provided for by the public, although indeed with a very scanty allowance.

They are despised and hated by all sorts of people; when one of them is born, it is reckoned ominous, and their birth is recorded very particularly; so that you may know their age by consulting the registry, which however hath not been kept above a thousand years past, or at least hath been destroyed by time or public disturbances. But the usual way of computing how old they are, is by asking them what kings or great persons they can remember, and then consulting history; for infallibly the last prince in their mind did not begin his reign after they were fourscore years old.

They were the most mortifying sight I ever beheld; and the women more horrible than the men. Besides the usual deformities in extreme old age, they acquired an additional ghastliness in proportion to their number of years, which is not to be described; and among half a dozen I soon distinguished which was the oldest, although there were not above a century or two between them.

The reader will easily believe, that from what I had heard and seen, my keen appetite for perpetuity of life was much abated. I grew heartily ashamed of the pleasing visions I had formed; and thought no tyrant could invent a death into which I would not run with pleasure from such a life. The King heard of all that had passed between me and my friends upon this occasion, and rallied[7] me very pleasantly; wishing I would send a couple of *struldbruggs* to my own country, to arm our people against the fear of death; but this it seems is forbidden by the fundamental laws of the kingdom; or else I should have been well content with the trouble and expense of transporting them.

I could not but agree, that the laws of this kingdom relating to the *struldbruggs*, were founded upon the strongest reasons, and such as any other country would be under the necessity of enacting in the like circumstances. Otherwise, as avarice is the necessary consequent of old age, those immortals would in time become proprietors of the whole nation, and engross[8] the civil power; which, for want of abilities to manage, must end in the ruin of the public.[9]

Part 4. A Voyage to the Country of the Houyhnhnms[1]

CHAPTER 1. *The Author sets out as Captain of a ship. His men conspire against him, confine him a long time to his cabin, set him on shore in an unknown*

---

7. Ridiculed.
8. Absorb, monopolize.
9. In the omitted chapter, Gulliver sails to Japan, where a Dutch ship provides him passage back to Eu-

rope.
1. Pronounced *hwin-ims*. The word suggests the neigh characteristic of a horse.

*land. He travels up into the country. The Yahoos, a strange sort of animal,
described. The Author meets two Houyhnhnms.*

I continued at home with my wife and children about five months in a very
happy condition, if I could have learned the lesson of knowing when I was
well. I left my poor wife big with child, and accepted an advantageous offer
made me to be Captain of the *Adventure*, a stout merchantman of 350 tons;
for I understood navigation well, and being grown weary of a surgeon's
employment at sea, which however I could exercise upon occasion, I took a
skillful young man of that calling, one Robert Purefoy, into my ship. We set
sail from Portsmouth upon the 7th day of September, 1710; on the 14th we
met with Captain Pocock of Bristol, at Tenariff,[2] who was going to the Bay of
Campeachy[3] to cut logwood. On the 16th he was parted from us by a storm; I
heard since my return that his ship foundered and none escaped, but one
cabin boy. He was an honest man and a good sailor, but a little too positive in
his own opinions, which was the cause of his destruction, as it hath been of
several others. For if he had followed my advice, he might at this time have
been safe at home with his family as well as myself.

I had several men died in my ship of calentures,[4] so that I was forced to get
recruits out of Barbadoes and the Leeward Islands, where I touched by the
direction of the merchants who employed me; which I had soon too much
cause to repent, for I found afterwards that most of them had been buccaneers.
I had fifty hands on board; and my orders were that I should trade with the
Indians in the South Sea, and make what discoveries I could. These rogues
whom I had picked up debauched my other men, and they all formed a conspiracy to seize the ship and secure me; which they did one morning, rushing
into my cabin, and binding me hand and foot, threatening to throw me overboard, if I offered to stir. I told them I was their prisoner, and would submit.
This they made me swear to do, and then unbound me, only fastening one of
my legs with a chain near my bed, and placed a sentry at my door with his
piece charged, who was commanded to shoot me dead if I attempted my
liberty. They sent me down victuals and drink, and took the government of
the ship to themselves. Their design was to turn pirates and plunder the Spaniards, which they could not do, till they got more men. But first they resolved
to sell the goods in the ship, and then go to Madagascar for recruits, several
among them having died since my confinement. They sailed many weeks,
and traded with the Indians; but I knew not what course they took, being kept
close prisoner in my cabin, and expecting nothing less than to be murdered,
as they often threatened me.

Upon the 9th day of May, 1711, one James Welch came down to my cabin;
and said he had orders from the Captain to set me ashore. I expostulated with
him, but in vain; neither would he so much as tell me who their new Captain
was. They forced me into the longboat, letting me put on my best suit of
clothes, which were as good as new, and a small bundle of linen, but no arms
except my hanger; and they were so civil as not to search my pockets, into
which I conveyed what money I had, with some other little necessaries. They
rowed about a league, and then set me down on a strand. I desired them to

2. Teneriffe, one of the Canary Islands.
3. Campeche, in the Gulf of Mexico.
4. "A distemper peculiar to sailors, in hot climates; wherein they imagine the sea to be green fields, and will throw themselves into it, if not restrained" (Johnson's *Dictionary*).

tell me what country it was; they all swore, they knew no more than myself, but said that the Captain (as they called him) was resolved, after they had sold the lading, to get rid of me in the first place where they discovered land. They pushed off immediately, advising me to make haste, for fear of being overtaken by the tide, and bade me farewell.

In this desolate condition I advanced forward, and soon got upon firm ground, where I sat down on a bank to rest myself, and consider what I had best to do. When I was a little refreshed, I went up into the country, resolving to deliver myself to the first savages I should meet, and purchase my life from them by some bracelets, glass rings, and other toys, which sailors usually provide themselves with in those voyages, and whereof I had some about me. The land was divided by long rows of trees, not regularly planted, but naturally growing; there was great plenty of grass, and several fields of oats. I walked very circumspectly for fear of being surprised, or suddenly shot with an arrow from behind, or on either side. I fell into a beaten road, where I saw many tracks of human feet, and some of cows, but most of horses. At last I beheld several animals in a field, and one or two of the same kind sitting in trees. Their shape was very singular, and deformed, which a little discomposed me, so that I lay down behind a thicket to observe them better. Some of them coming forward near the place where I lay, gave me an opportunity of distinctly marking their form. Their heads and breasts were covered with a thick hair, some frizzled and others lank; they had beards like goats, and a long ridge of hair down their backs, and the fore parts of their legs and feet; but the rest of their bodies were bare, so that I might see their skins, which were of a brown buff color. They had no tails, nor any hair at all on their buttocks, except about the anus; which, I presume Nature had placed there to defend them as they sat on the ground; for this posture they used, as well as lying down, and often stood on their hind feet. They climbed high trees, as nimbly as a squirrel, for they had strong extended claws before and behind, terminating in sharp points, and hooked. They would often spring, and bound, and leap with prodigious agility. The females were not so large as the males; they had long lank hair on their heads, and only a sort of down on the rest of their bodies, except about the anus, and pudenda. Their dugs hung between their forefeet, and often reached almost to the ground as they walked. The hair of both sexes was of several colors, brown, red, black, and yellow. Upon the whole, I never beheld in all my travels so disagreeable an animal, or one against which I naturally conceived so strong an antipathy. So that thinking I had seen enough, full of contempt and aversion, I got up and pursued the beaten road, hoping it might direct me to the cabin of some Indian. I had not gone far when I met one of these creatures full in my way, and coming up directly to me. The ugly monster, when he saw me, distorted several ways every feature of his visage, and stared as at an object he had never seen before; then approaching nearer, lifted up his forepaw, whether out of curiosity or mischief, I could not tell; but I drew my hanger, and gave him a good blow with the flat side of it; for I durst not strike him with the edge, fearing the inhabitants might be provoked against me, if they should come to know that I had killed or maimed any of their cattle. When the beast felt the smart, he drew back, and roared so loud, that a herd of at least forty came flocking about me from the near field, howling and making odious faces; but I ran to the body of a tree, and leaning my back against it, kept them off, by waving my hanger. Several of this cursed brood getting hold of the branches behind, leaped up into the tree, from whence they began to discharge their excrements on my head; however, I escaped pretty well, by sticking close to the stem of the tree, but was almost stifled with the filth, which fell about me on every side.

In the midst of this distress, I observed them all to run away on a sudden as fast as they could; at which I ventured to leave the tree, and pursue the road, wondering what it was that could put them into this fright. But looking on my left hand, I saw a horse walking softly in the field; which my persecutors having sooner discovered, was the cause of their flight. The horse started a little when he came near me, but soon recovering himself, looked full in my face with manifest tokens of wonder; he viewed my hands and feet, walking round me several times. I would have pursued my journey, but he placed himself directly in the way, yet looking with a very mild aspect, never offering the least violence. We stood gazing at each other for some time; at last I took the boldness, to reach my hand towards his neck, with a design to stroke it; using the common style and whistle of jockies when they are going to handle a strange horse. But this animal, seeming to receive my civilities with disdain, shook his head, and bent his brows, softly raising up his left forefoot to remove my hand. Then he neighed three or four times, but in so different a cadence, that I almost began to think he was speaking to himself in some language of his own.

While he and I were thus employed, another horse came up; who applying himself to the first in a very formal manner, they gently struck each other's right hoof before, neighing several times by turns, and varying the sound, which seemed to be almost articulate. They went some paces off, as if it were to confer together, walking side by side, backward and forward, like persons deliberating upon some affair of weight; but often turning their eyes towards me, as it were to watch that I might not escape. I was amazed to see such actions and behavior in brute beasts; and concluded with myself that if the inhabitants of this country were endued with a proportionable degree of reason, they must needs be the wisest people upon earth. This thought gave me so much comfort, that I resolved to go forward until I could discover some house or village, or meet with any of the natives, leaving the two horses to discourse together as they pleased. But the first, who was a dapple grey, observing me to steal off, neighed after me in so expressive a tone that I fancied myself to understand what he meant; whereupon I turned back, and came near him, to expect his farther commands; but concealing my fear as much as I could; for I began to be in some pain, how this adventure might terminate; and the reader will easily believe I did not much like my present situation.

The two horses came up close to me, looking with great earnestness upon my face and hands. The grey steed rubbed my hat all round with his right fore hoof, and discomposed it so much that I was forced to adjust it better, by taking it off, and settling it again; whereat both he and his companion (who was a brown bay) appeared to be much surprised; the latter felt the lappet of my coat, and finding it to hang loose about me, they both looked with new signs of wonder. He stroked my right hand, seeming to admire the softness, and color; but he squeezed it so hard between his hoof and his pastern, that I was forced to roar; after which they both touched me with all possible tenderness. They were under great perplexity about my shoes and stockings, which they felt very often, neighing to each other, and using various gestures, not unlike those of a philosopher, when he would attempt to solve some new and difficult phenomenon.

Upon the whole, the behavior of these animals was so orderly and rational, so acute and judicious, that I at last concluded, they must needs be magicians, who had thus metamorphosed themselves upon some design; and seeing a stranger in the way, were resolved to divert themselves with him; or perhaps were really amazed at the sight of a man so very different in habit, feature, and complexion from those who might probably live in so remote a climate. Upon the strength of this reasoning, I ventured to address them in the following manner: "Gentlemen, if you be conjurers, as I have good cause to believe, you can understand any language; therefore I make bold to let your worships know that I am a poor distressed Englishman, driven by his misfortunes upon your coast; and I entreat one of you, to let me ride upon his back, as if he were a real horse, to some house or village, where I can be relieved. In return of which favor, I will make you a present of this knife and bracelet" (taking them out of my pocket). The two creatures stood silent while I spoke, seeming to listen with great attention; and when I had ended, they neighed frequently towards each other, as if they were engaged in serious conversation. I plainly observed, that their language expressed the passions very well, and the words might with little pains be resolved into an alphabet more easily than the Chinese.

I could frequently distinguish the word *Yahoo*,[5] which was repeated by each of them several times; and although it were impossible for me to conjecture what it meant, yet while the two horses were busy in conversation, I endeavored to practice this word upon my tongue; and as soon as they were silent, I boldly pronounced "Yahoo" in a loud voice, imitating, at the same time, as near as I could, the neighing of a horse; at which they were both visibly surprised, and the grey repeated the same word twice, as if he meant to teach me the right accent, wherein I spoke after him as well as I could, and found myself perceivably to improve every time, although very far from any degree of perfection. Then the bay tried me with a second word, much harder to be pronounced; but reducing it to the English orthography, may be spelt thus, *Houyhnhnm*. I did not succeed in this so well as the former, but after two or three farther trials, I had better fortune; and they both appeared amazed at my capacity.

After some farther discourse, which I then conjectured might relate to me, the two friends took their leaves, with the same compliment of striking each other's hoof; and the grey made me signs that I should walk before him; wherein I thought it prudent to comply, till I could find a better director. When I offered to slacken my pace, he would cry, "Hhuun, Hhuun"; I guessed his meaning, and gave him to understand, as well as I could that I was weary, and not able to walk faster; upon which, he would stand a while to let me rest.

CHAPTER 2. *The Author conducted by a Houyhnhnm to his house. The house described. The Author's reception. The food of the Houyhnhnms. The Author in distress for want of meat is at last relieved. His manner of feeding in that country.*

5. Perhaps compounded from two expressions of disgust, *yah* and *ugh* (or *hoo*), common in the 18th century.

Having traveled about three miles, we came to a long kind of building, made of timber, stuck in the ground, and wattled across; the roof was low, and covered with straw. I now began to be a little comforted, and took out some toys, which travelers usually carry for presents to the savage Indians of America and other parts, in hopes the people of the house would be thereby encouraged to receive me kindly. The horse made me a sign to go in first; it was a large room with a smooth clay floor, and a rack and manger extending the whole length on one side. There were three nags, and two mares, not eating, but some of them sitting down upon their hams, which I very much wondered at; but wondered more to see the rest employed in domestic business. The last seemed but ordinary cattle; however this confirmed my first opinion, that a people who could so far civilize brute animals must needs excel in wisdom all the nations of the world. The grey came in just after, and thereby prevented any ill treatment, which the others might have given me. He neighed to them several times in a style of authority, and received answers.

Beyond this room there were three others, reaching the length of the house, to which you passed through three doors, opposite to each other, in the manner of a vista; we went through the second room towards the third; here the grey walked in first, beckoning me to attend.[6] I waited in the second room, and got ready my presents, for the master and mistress of the house; they were two knives, three bracelets of false pearl, a small looking glass and a bead necklace. The horse neighed three or four times, and I waited to hear some answers in a human voice, but I heard no other returns than in the same dialect, only one or two a little shriller than his. I began to think that this house must belong to some person of great note among them, because there appeared so much ceremony before I could gain admittance. But, that a man of quality should be served all by horses, was beyond my comprehension. I feared my brain was disturbed by my sufferings and misfortunes; I roused myself, and looked about me in the room where I was left alone; this was furnished as the first, only after a more elegant manner. I rubbed my eyes often, but the same objects still occurred. I pinched my arms and sides, to awaken myself, hoping I might be in a dream. I then absolutely concluded that all these appearances could be nothing else but necromancy and magic. But I had no time to pursue these reflections; for the grey horse came to the door, and made me a sign to follow him into the third room; where I saw a very comely mare, together with a colt and foal, sitting on their haunches, upon mats of straw, not unartfully made, and perfectly neat and clean.

The mare soon after my entrance, rose from her mat, and coming up close, after having nicely observed my hands and face, gave me a most contemptuous look; then turning to the horse, I heard the word Yahoo often repeated betwixt them; the meaning of which word I could not then comprehend, although it were the first I had learned to pronounce; but I was soon better informed, to my everlasting mortification: for the horse beckoning to me with his head, and repeating the word, "Hhuun, Hhuun," as he did upon the road, which I understood was to attend him, led me out into a kind of court, where was another building at some distance from the house. Here we entered, and I saw three of those detestable creatures, which I first met after my landing, feeding upon roots, and the flesh of some animals, which I afterwards found

6. To wait.

to be that of asses and dogs, and now and then a cow dead by accident or disease. They were all tied by the neck with strong withes, fastened to a beam; they held their food between the claws of their forefeet, and tore it with their teeth.

The master horse ordered a sorrel nag, one of his servants, to untie the largest of these animals, and take him into a yard. The beast and I were brought close together; and our countenances diligently compared, both by master and servant, who thereupon repeated several times the word "Yahoo." My horror and astonishment are not to be described, when I observed, in this abominable animal, a perfect human figure; the face of it indeed was flat and broad, the nose depressed, the lips large, and the mouth wide; but these differences are common to all savage nations, where the lineaments of the countenance are distorted by the natives suffering their infants to lie groveling on the earth, or by carrying them on their backs, nuzzling with their face against the mother's shoulders. The forefeet of the Yahoo differed from my hands in nothing else but the length of the nails, the coarseness and brownness of the palms, and the hairiness on the backs. There was the same resemblance between our feet, with the same differences, which I knew very well, although the horses did not, because of my shoes and stockings; the same in every part of our bodies, except as to hairiness and color, which I have already described.

The great difficulty that seemed to stick with the two horses was to see the rest of my body so very different from that of a Yahoo, for which I was obliged to my clothes, whereof they had no conception; the sorrel nag offered me a root, which he held (after their manner, as we shall describe in its proper place) between his hoof and pastern; I took it in my hand, and having smelled it, returned it to him again as civilly as I could. He brought out of the Yahoo's kennel a piece of ass's flesh, but it smelled so offensively that I turned from it with loathing; he then threw it to the Yahoo, by whom it was greedily devoured. He afterwards showed me a wisp of hay, and a fetlock full of oats; but I shook my head, to signify that neither of these were food for me. And indeed, I now apprehended that I must absolutely starve, if I did not get to some of my own species; for as to those filthy Yahoos, although there were few greater lovers of mankind, at that time, than myself, yet I confess I never saw any sensitive being so detestable on all accounts; and the more I came near them, the more hateful they grew, while I stayed in that country. This the master horse observed by my behavior, and therefore sent the Yahoo back to his kennel. He then put his forehoof to his mouth, at which I was much surprised, although he did it with ease, and with a motion that appeared perfectly natural; and made other signs to know what I would eat; but I could not return him such an answer as he was able to apprehend; and if he had understood me, I did not see how it was possible to contrive any way for finding myself nourishment. While we were thus engaged, I observed a cow passing by; whereupon I pointed to her, and expressed a desire to let me go and milk her. This had its effect; for he led me back into the house, and ordered a mare-servant to open a room, where a good store of milk lay in earthen and wooden vessels, after a very orderly and cleanly manner. She gave me a large bowl full, of which I drank very heartily, and found myself well refreshed.

About noon I saw coming towards the house a kind of vehicle, drawn like a sledge by four Yahoos. There was in it an old steed, who seemed to be of quality; he alighted with his hind feet forward, having by accident got a hurt in his left forefoot. He came to dine with our horse, who received him with great civility. They dined in the best room, and had oats boiled in milk for the second course, which the old horse eat warm, but the rest cold. Their mangers were placed circular in the middle of the room, and divided into several partitions, round which they sat on their haunches upon bosses of straw. In the middle was a large rack with angles answering to every partition of the manger. So that each horse and mare eat their own hay, and their own mash of oats and milk, with much decency and regularity. The behavior of the young colt and foal appeared very modest; and that of the master and mistress extremely cheerful and complaisant to their guest. The grey ordered me to stand by him; and much discourse passed between him and his friend concerning me, as I found by the stranger's often looking on me, and the frequent repetition of the word Yahoo.

I happened to wear my gloves; which the master grey observing, seemed perplexed; discovering signs of wonder what I had done to my forefeet; he put his hoof three or four times to them, as if he would signify, that I should reduce them to their former shape, which I presently did, pulling off both my gloves, and putting them into my pocket. This occasioned farther talk, and I saw the company was pleased with my behavior, whereof I soon found the good effects. I was ordered to speak the few words I understood; and while they were at dinner, the master taught me the names for oats, milk, fire, water, and some others which I could readily pronounce after him, having from my youth a great facility in learning languages.

When dinner was done, the master horse took me aside, and by signs and words made me understand the concern he was in that I had nothing to eat. Oats in their tongue are called *hlunnh*. This word I pronounced two or three times; for although I had refused them at first, yet upon second thoughts, I considered that I could contrive to make a kind of bread, which might be sufficient with milk to keep me alive, till I could make my escape to some other country, and to creatures of my own species. The horse immediately ordered a white mare-servant of his family to bring me a good quantity of oats in a sort of wooden tray. These I heated before the fire as well as I could, and rubbed them till the husks came off, which I made a shift to winnow from the grain; I ground and beat them between two stones, then took water, and made them into a paste or cake, which I toasted at the fire, and eat warm with milk. It was at first a very insipid diet, although common enough in many parts of Europe, but grew tolerable by time; and having been often reduced to hard fare in my life, this was not the first experiment I had made how easily nature is satisfied. And I cannot but observe that I never had one hour's sickness, while I staid in this island. It is true, I sometimes made a shift to catch a rabbit, or bird, by springes[7] made of Yahoos' hairs; and I often gathered wholesome herbs, which I boiled, or eat as salads with my bread; and now and then, for a rarity, I made a little butter, and drank the whey. I was at first at a great loss for salt; but custom soon reconciled the want of it; and I am confident that the frequent use of salt among us is an effect of luxury, and was first introduced only as a provocative to drink; except where it is necessary for preserving of flesh in long voyages, or in places remote from great markets. For we observe

7. Snares.

no animal to be fond of it but man;[8] and as to myself, when I left this country, it was a great while before I could endure the taste of it in anything that I eat.

This is enough to say upon the subject of my diet, wherewith other travelers fill their books, as if the readers were personally concerned whether we fare well or ill. However, it was necessary to mention this matter, lest the world should think it impossible that I could find sustenance for three years in such a country, and among such inhabitants.

When it grew towards evening, the master horse ordered a place for me to lodge in; it was but six yards from the house, and separated from the stable of the Yahoos. Here I got some straw, and covering myself with my own clothes, slept very sound. But I was in a short time better accommodated, as the reader shall know hereafter, when I come to treat more particularly about my way of living.

CHAPTER 3. *The Author studious to learn the language, the Houyhnhnm his master assists in teaching him. The language described. Several Houyhnhnms of quality come out of curiosity to see the Author. He gives his master a short account of his voyage.*

My principal endeavor was to learn the language, which my master (for so I shall henceforth call him) and his children, and every servant of his house were desirous to teach me. For they looked upon it as a prodigy, that a brute animal should discover such marks of a rational creature. I pointed to everything, and enquired the name of it, which I wrote down in my journal book when I was alone, and corrected my bad accent, by desiring those of the family to pronounce it often. In this employment, a sorrel nag, one of the under servants, was very ready to assist me.

In speaking, they pronounce through the nose and throat, and their language approaches nearest to the High Dutch or German, of any I know in Europe; but is much more graceful and significant. The Emperor Charles V made almost the same observation, when he said, that if he were to speak to his horse, it should be in High Dutch.[9]

The curiosity and impatience of my master were so great, that he spent many hours of his leisure to instruct me. He was convinced (as he afterwards told me) that I must be a Yahoo, but my teachableness, civility, and cleanliness astonished him; which were qualities altogether so opposite to those animals. He was most perplexed about my clothes, reasoning sometimes with himself whether they were a part of my body; for I never pulled them off till the family were asleep, and got them on before they waked in the morning. My master was eager to learn from whence I came; how I acquired those appearances of reason, which I discovered in all my actions; and to know my story from my own mouth, which he hoped he should soon do by the great proficiency I made in learning and pronouncing their words and sentences. To help my memory, I formed all I learned into the English alphabet, and writ the words down with the translations. This last, after some time, I ventured to do in my master's presence. It cost me much trouble to explain to him what I was doing; for the inhabitants have not the least idea of books or literature.

---

8. Gulliver is, of course, in error; many animals require salt.
9. The emperor is supposed to have said that he would speak to his God in Spanish, to his mistress in Italian, and to his horse in German.

In about ten weeks time I was able to understand most of his questions; and in three months could give him some tolerable answers. He was extremely curious to know from what part of the country I came, and how I was taught to imitate a rational creature; because the Yahoos (whom he saw I exactly resembled in my head, hands, and face, that were only visible) with some appearance of cunning, and the strongest disposition to mischief, were observed to be the most unteachable of all brutes. I answered that I came over the sea, from a far place, with many others of my own kind, in a great hollow vessel made of the bodies of trees; that my companions forced me to land on this coast, and then left me to shift for myself. It was with some difficulty, and by the help of many signs, that I brought him to understand me. He replied that I must needs be mistaken, or that I *said the thing which was not*. (For they have no word in their language to express lying or falsehood.) He knew it was impossible that there could be a country beyond the sea, or that a parcel of brutes could move a wooden vessel whither they pleased upon water. He was sure no Houyhnhnm alive could make such a vessel, or would trust Yahoos to manage it.

The word Houyhnhnm, in their tongue, signifies a Horse; and in its etymology, the Perfection of Nature. I told my master that I was at a loss for expression, but would improve as fast as I could; and hoped in a short time I should be able to tell him wonders. He was pleased to direct his own mare, his colt, and foal, and the servants of the family to take all opportunities of instructing me; and every day for two or three hours, he was at the same pains himself. Several horses and mares of quality in the neighborhood came often to our house, upon the report spread of a wonderful Yahoo, that could speak like a Houyhnhnm, and seemed in his words and actions to discover some glimmerings of reason. These delighted to converse with me; they put many questions, and received such answers as I was able to return. By all which advantages, I made so great a progress, that in five months from my arrival, I understood whatever was spoke, and could express myself tolerably well.

The Houyhnhnms who came to visit my master, out of a design of seeing and talking with me, could hardly believe me to be a right Yahoo, because my body had a different covering from others of my kind. They were astonished to observe me without the usual hair or skin, except on my head, face, and hands; but I discovered that secret to my master, upon an accident, which happened about a fortnight before.

I have already told the reader, that every night when the family were gone to bed, it was my custom to strip and cover myself with my clothes; it happened one morning early, that my master sent for me, by the sorrel nag, who was his valet; when he came, I was fast asleep, my clothes fallen off on one side, and my shirt above my waist. I awaked at the noise he made, and observed him to deliver his message in some disorder; after which he went to my master, and in a great fright gave him a very confused account of what he had seen. This I presently discovered; for going as soon as I was dressed, to pay my attendance upon his honor, he asked me the meaning of what his servant had reported; that I was not the same thing when I slept as I appeared to be at other times; that his valet assured him, some part of me was white, some yellow, at least not so white, and some brown.

I had hitherto concealed the secret of my dress, in order to distinguish myself as much as possible, from that cursed race of Yahoos; but now I found it in vain to do so any longer. Besides, I considered that my clothes and shoes would soon wear out, which already were in a declining condition, and must be supplied by some contrivance from the hides of Yahoos, or other brutes; whereby the whole secret would be known. I therefore told my master, that in the country from whence I came, those of my kind always covered their bodies with the hairs of certain animals prepared by art, as well for decency, as to avoid inclemencies of air both hot and cold; of which, as to my own person I would give him immediate conviction, if he pleased to command me; only desiring his excuse, if I did not expose those parts that Nature taught us to conceal. He said, my discourse was all very strange, but especially the last part; for he could not understand why Nature should teach us to conceal what Nature had given. That neither himself nor family were ashamed of any parts of their bodies; but however I might do as I pleased. Whereupon, I first unbuttoned my coat, and pulled it off. I did the same with my waistcoat; I drew off my shoes, stockings, and breeches. I let my shirt down to my waist, and drew up the bottom, fastening it like a girdle about my middle to hide my nakedness.

My master observed the whole performance with great signs of curiosity and admiration. He took up all my clothes in his pastern, one piece after another, and examined them diligently; he then stroked my body very gently, and looked round me several times; after which he said, it was plain I must be a perfect Yahoo; but that I differed very much from the rest of my species, in the whiteness and smoothness of my skin, my want of hair in several parts of my body, the shape and shortness of my claws behind and before, and my affectation of walking continually on my two hinder feet. He desired to see no more; and gave me leave to put on my clothes again, for I was shuddering with cold.

I expressed my uneasiness at his giving me so often the appellation of Yahoo, an odious animal, for which I had so utter an hatred and contempt. I begged he would forbear applying that word to me, and take the same order in his family, and among his friends whom he suffered to see me. I requested likewise, that the secret of my having a false covering to my body might be known to none but himself, at least as long as my present clothing should last; for as to what the sorrel nag his valet had observed, his honor might command him to conceal it.

All this my master very graciously consented to; and thus the secret was kept till my clothes began to wear out, which I was forced to supply by several contrivances, that shall hereafter be mentioned. In the meantime, he desired I would go on with my utmost diligence to learn their language, because he was more astonished at my capacity for speech and reason, than at the figure of my body, whether it were covered or no; adding that he waited with some impatience to hear the wonders which I promised to tell him.

From thenceforward he doubled the pains he had been at to instruct me; he brought me into all company, and made them treat me with civility, because, as he told them privately, this would put me into good humor, and make me more diverting.

Every day when I waited on him, beside the trouble he was at in teaching, he would ask me several questions concerning myself, which I answered as well as I could; and by those means he had already received some general ideas, although very imperfect. It would be tedious to relate the several steps, by which I advanced to a more regular conversation, but the first account I gave of myself in any order and length was to this purpose:

That, I came from a very far country, as I already had attempted to tell him, with about fifty more of my own species; that we traveled upon the seas, in a great hollow vessel made of wood, and larger than his honor's house. I described the ship to him in the best terms I could; and explained by the help of my handkerchief displayed, how it was driven forward by the wind. That, upon a quarrel among us, I was set on shore on this coast, where I walked forward without knowing whither, till he delivered me from the persecution of those execrable Yahoos. He asked me who made the ship, and how it was possible that the Houyhnhnms of my country would leave it to the management of brutes? My answer was that I durst proceed no farther in my relation, unless he would give me his word and honor that he would not be offended; and then I would tell him the wonders I had so often promised. He agreed; and I went on by assuring him, that the ship was made by creatures like myself, who in all the countries I had traveled, as well as in my own, were the only governing, rational animals; and that upon my arrival hither, I was as much astonished to see the Houyhnhnms act like rational beings, as he or his friends could be in finding some marks of reason in a creature he was pleased to call a Yahoo; to which I owned my resemblance in every part, but could not account for their degenerate and brutal nature. I said farther, that if good fortune ever restored me to my native country, to relate my travels hither, as I resolved to do, everybody would believe that I *said the thing which was not,* that I invented the story out of my own head; and with all possible respect to himself, his family, and friends, and under his promise of not being offended, our countrymen would hardly think it probable, that a Houyhnhnm should be the presiding creature of a nation, and a Yahoo the brute.

CHAPTER 4. *The Houyhnhnms' notion of truth and falsehood. The Author's discourse disapproved by his master. The Author gives a more particular account of himself, and the accidents of his voyage.*

My master heard me with great appearances of uneasiness in his countenance; because *doubting* or *not believing* are so little known in this country, that the inhabitants cannot tell how to behave themselves under such circumstances. And I remember in frequent discourses with my master concerning the nature of manhood, in other parts of the world, having occasion to talk of *lying* and *false representation,* it was with much difficulty that he comprehended what I meant; although he had otherwise a most acute judgment. For he argued thus: that the use of speech was to make us understand one another, and to receive information of facts; now if anyone *said the thing which was not,* these ends were defeated; because I cannot properly be said to understand him; and I am so far from receiving information, that he leaves me worse than in ignorance; for I am led to believe a thing *black* when it is *white,* and *short* when it is *long.* And these were all the notions he had concerning the faculty of *lying,* so perfectly well understood, and so universally practiced among human creatures.

To return from this digression; when I asserted that the Yahoos were the only governing animals in my country, which my master said was altogether past his conception, he desired to know, whether we had Houyhnhnms among us, and what was their employment. I told him we had great numbers; that in summer they grazed in the fields, and in winter were kept in houses, with hay and oats, where Yahoo servants were employed to rub their skins smooth, comb their manes, pick their feet, serve them with food, and make their beds. "I understand you well," said my master; "it is now very plain from all you have spoken, that whatever share of reason the Yahoos pretend to, the Houyhnhnms are your masters; I heartily wish our Yahoos would be so tractable." I begged his honor would please to excuse me from proceeding any farther, because I was very certain that the account he expected from me would be highly displeasing. But he insisted in commanding me to let him know the best and the worst; I told him he should be obeyed. I owned that the Houyhnhnms among us, whom we called Horses, were the most generous[1] and comely animal we had; that they excelled in strength and swiftness; and when they belonged to persons of quality, employed in traveling, racing, and drawing chariots, they were treated with much kindness and care, till they fell into diseases, or became foundered in the feet; but then they were sold, and used to all kind of drudgery till they died; after which their skins were stripped and sold for what they were worth, and their bodies left to be devoured by dogs and birds of prey. But the common race of horses had not so good fortune, being kept by farmers and carriers, and other mean people, who put them to greater labor, and feed them worse. I described as well as I could, our way of riding; the shape and use of a bridle, a saddle, a spur, and a whip; of harness and wheels. I added, that we fastened plates of a certain hard substance called iron at the bottom of their feet, to preserve their hoofs from being broken by the stony ways on which we often traveled.

My master, after some expressions of great indignation, wondered how we dared to venture upon a Houyhnhnm's back; for he was sure, that the weakest servant in his house would be able to shake off the strongest Yahoo; or by lying down, and rolling upon his back, squeeze the brute to death. I answered that our horses were trained up from three or four years old to the several uses we intended them for; that if any of them proved intolerably vicious, they were employed for carriages; that they were severely beaten while they were young for any mischievous tricks; that the males, designed for the common use of riding or draught, were generally castrated about two years after their birth, to take down their spirits, and make them more tame and gentle; that they were indeed sensible of rewards and punishments; but his honor would please to consider that they had not the least tincture of reason any more than the Yahoos in this country.

It put me to the pains of many circumlocutions to give my master a right idea of what I spoke; for their language doth not abound in variety of words, because their wants and passions are fewer than among us. But it is impossible to express his noble resentment at our savage treatment of the Houyhnhnm race; particularly after I had explained the manner and use of castrating horses among us, to hinder them from propagating their kind, and to render them more servile. He said, if it were possible there could be any country where Yahoos alone were endued with reason, they certainly must be the governing animal, because reason will in time always prevail against brutal strength. But, considering the frame of our bodies, and especially of mine, he thought no

---

1. Noble.

creature of equal bulk was so ill-contrived for employing that reason in the
common offices of life; whereupon he desired to know whether those among
whom I lived resembled me or the Yahoos of his country. I assured him that I
was as well shaped as most of my age; but the younger and the females were
much more soft and tender, and the skins of the latter generally as white as
milk. He said I differed indeed from other Yahoos, being much more cleanly,
and not altogether so deformed; but in point of real advantage, he thought I
differed for the worse. That my nails were of no use either to my fore or hinder
feet; as to my forefeet, he could not properly call them by that name, for he
never observed me to walk upon them; that they were too soft to bear the
ground; that I generally went with them uncovered, neither was the covering
I sometimes wore on them of the same shape, or so strong as that on my feet
behind. That I could not walk with any security; for if either of my hinder feet
slipped, I must inevitably fall. He then began to find fault with other parts of
my body; the flatness of my face, the prominence of my nose, my eyes placed
directly in front, so that I could not look on either side without turning my
head; that I was not able to feed myself without lifting one of my forefeet to
my mouth; and therefore nature had placed those joints to answer that necessity. He knew not what could be the use of those several clefts and divisions
in my feet behind; that these were too soft to bear the hardness and sharpness
of stones without a covering made from the skin of some other brute; that my
whole body wanted a fence against heat and cold, which I was forced to put
on and off every day with tediousness and trouble. And lastly, that he observed
every animal in his country naturally to abhor the Yahoos, whom the weaker
avoided, and the stronger drove from them. So that supposing us to have the
gift of reason, he could not see how it were possible to cure that natural antipathy which every creature discovered against us; nor consequently, how we
could tame and render them serviceable. However, he would (as he said)
debate the matter no farther, because he was more desirous to know my own
story, the country where I was born, and the several actions and events of my
life before I came hither.

I assured him how extremely desirous I was that he should be satisfied in
every point; but I doubted much whether it would be possible for me to
explain myself on several subjects whereof his honor could have no conception, because I saw nothing in his country to which I could resemble them.
That however, I would do my best, and strive to express myself by similitudes,
humbly desiring his assistance when I wanted proper words; which he was
pleased to promise me.

I said, my birth was of honest parents, in an island called England, which
was remote from this country, as many days journey as the strongest of his
honor's servants could travel in the annual course of the sun. That I was bred
a surgeon, whose trade it is to cure wounds and hurts in the body, got by
accident or violence. That my country was governed by a female man, whom
we called a queen. That I left it to get riches, whereby I might maintain myself
and family when I should return. That in my last voyage, I was Commander
of the ship and had about fifty Yahoos under me, many of which died at sea,
and I was forced to supply them by others picked out from several nations.
That our ship was twice in danger of being sunk; the first time by a great
storm, and the second, by striking against a rock. Here my master interposed,
by asking me, how I could persuade strangers out of different countries to

venture with me, after the losses I had sustained, and the hazards I had run. I said, they were fellows of desperate fortunes, forced to fly from the places of their birth, on account of their poverty or their crimes. Some were undone by lawsuits; others spent all they had in drinking, whoring, and gaming; others fled for treason; many for murder, theft, poisoning, robbery, perjury, forgery, coining false money; for committing rapes or sodomy; for flying from their colors, or deserting to the enemy; and most of them had broken prison. None of these durst return to their native countries for fear of being hanged, or of starving in a jail; and therefore were under a necessity of seeking a livelihood in other places.

During this discourse, my master was pleased often to interrupt me. I had made use of many circumlocutions in describing to him the nature of the several crimes, for which most of our crew had been forced to fly their country. This labor took up several days conversation before he was able to comprehend me. He was wholly at a loss to know what could be the use or necessity of practicing those vices. To clear up which I endeavored to give him some ideas of the desire of power and riches; of the terrible effects of lust, intemperance, malice, and envy. All this I was forced to define and describe by putting of cases, and making suppositions. After which, like one whose imagination was struck with something never seen or heard of before, he would lift up his eyes with amazement and indignation. Power, government, war, law, punishment, and a thousand other things had no terms, wherein that language could express them; which made the difficulty almost insuperable to give my master any conception of what I meant; but being of an excellent understanding, much improved by contemplation and converse, he at last arrived at a competent knowledge of what human nature in our parts of the world is capable to perform; and desired I would give him some particular account of that land, which we call Europe, especially, of my own country.

CHAPTER 5. *The Author, at his master's commands, informs him of the state of England. The causes of war among the princes of Europe. The Author begins to explain the English Constitution.*

The reader may please to observe that the following extract of many conversations I had with my master contains a summary of the most material points, which were discoursed at several times for above two years; his honor often desiring fuller satisfaction as I farther improved in the Houyhnhnm tongue. I laid before him, as well as I could, the whole state of Europe; I discoursed of trade and manufactures, of arts and sciences; and the answers I gave to all the questions he made, as they arose upon several subjects, were a fund of conversation not to be exhausted. But I shall here only set down the substance of what passed between us concerning my own country, reducing it into order as well as I can, without any regard to time or other circumstances, while I strictly adhere to truth. My only concern is that I shall hardly be able to do justice to my master's arguments and expressions; which must needs suffer by my want of capacity, as well as by a translation into our barbarous English.

In obedience therefore to his honor's commands, I related to him the Revolution under the Prince of Orange; the long war with France entered into by the said Prince, and renewed by his successor the present queen; wherein the greatest powers of Christendom were engaged, and which still continued. I computed at his request, that about a million of Yahoos might have been killed in the whole progress of it; and perhaps a hundred or more cities taken, and five times as many ships burned or sunk.[2]

He asked me what were the usual causes or motives that made one country to go to war with another. I answered, they were innumerable; but I should only mention a few of the chief. Sometimes the ambition of princes, who never think they have land or people enough to govern; sometimes the corruption of ministers, who engage their master in a war in order to stifle or divert the clamor of the subjects against their evil administration. Difference in opinions hath cost many millions of lives; for instance, whether flesh be bread, or bread be flesh; whether the juice of a certain berry be blood or wine; whether whistling be a vice or a virtue; whether it be better to kiss a post, or throw it into the fire; what is the best color for a coat, whether black, white, red, or grey; and whether it should be long or short, narrow or wide, dirty or clean;[3] with many more. Neither are any wars so furious and bloody, or of so long continuance, as those occasioned by difference in opinion, especially if it be in things indifferent.[4]

Sometimes the quarrel between two princes is to decide which of them shall dispossess a third of his dominions, where neither of them pretend to any right. Sometimes one prince quarreleth with another, for fear the other should quarrel with him. Sometimes a war is entered upon, because the enemy is too strong, and sometimes because he is too weak. Sometimes our neighbors want the things which we have, or have the things which we want; and we both fight, till they take ours or give us theirs. It is a very justifiable cause of war to invade a country after the people have been wasted by famine, destroyed by pestilence, or embroiled by factions amongst themselves. It is justifiable to enter into a war against our nearest ally, when one of his towns lies convenient for us, or a territory of land, that would render our dominions round and compact. If a prince send forces into a nation, where the people are poor and ignorant, he may lawfully put half of them to death, and make slaves of the rest, in order to civilize and reduce them from their barbarous way of living. It is a very kingly, honorable, and frequent practice, when one prince desires the assistance of another to secure him against an invasion, that the assistant, when he hath driven out the invader, should seize on the dominions himself, and kill, imprison, or banish the prince he came to relieve. Alliance by blood or marriage is a sufficient cause of war between princes; and the nearer the kindred is, the greater is their disposition to quarrel. Poor nations are hungry, and rich nations are proud; and pride and hunger will ever be at variance. For these reasons, the trade of a soldier is held the most honorable of all others: because a soldier is a Yahoo hired to kill in cold blood as many of his own species, who have never offended him, as possibly he can.

There is likewise a kind of beggarly princes in Europe, not able to make war by themselves, who hire out their troops to richer nations for so much a

---

2. Gulliver relates recent English history: the Glorious Revolution (1688–89) and the War of Spanish Succession (1703–13). He greatly exaggerates the casualties in the war.
3. Gulliver refers to the religious controversies of the Reformation and Counter-Reformation: the doctrine of transubstantiation, the use of music in church services, the veneration of the crucifix, and the wearing of priestly vestments.
4. Of little consequence.

day to each man; of which they keep three fourths to themselves, and it is the best part of their maintenance; such are those in many northern parts of Europe.[5]

"What you have told me," said my master, "upon the subject of war, doth indeed discover most admirably the effects of that reason you pretend to. However, it is happy that the shame is greater than the danger; and that Nature hath left you utterly uncapable of doing much mischief; for your mouths lying flat with your faces, you can hardly bite each other to any purpose, unless by consent. Then, as to the claws upon your feet before and behind, they are so short and tender, that one of our Yahoos would drive a dozen of yours before him. And therefore in recounting the numbers of those who have been killed in battle, I cannot but think that you have *said the thing which is not*."

I could not forbear shaking my head and smiling a little at his ignorance. And, being no stranger to the art of war, I gave him a description of cannons, culverins, muskets, carabines, pistols, bullets, powder, swords, bayonets, battles, sieges, retreats, attacks, undermines, countermines, bombardments, sea fights; ships sunk with a thousand men; twenty thousand killed on each side; dying groans, limbs flying in the air; smoke, noise, confusion, trampling to death under horses' feet; flight, pursuit, victory; fields strewed with carcasses left for food to dogs, and wolves, and birds of prey; plundering, stripping, ravishing, burning, and destroying. And, to set forth the valor of my own dear countrymen, I assured him that I had seen them blow up a hundred enemies at once in a siege, and as many in a ship; and beheld the dead bodies drop down in pieces from the clouds, to the great diversion of all the spectators.

I was going on to more particulars, when my master commanded me silence. He said, whoever understood the nature of Yahoos might easily believe it possible for so vile an animal, to be capable of every action I had named, if their strength and cunning equaled their malice. But, as my discourse had increased his abhorrence of the whole species, so he found it gave him a disturbance in his mind, to which he was wholly a stranger before. He thought his ears being used to such abominable words, might by degrees admit them with less detestation. That, although he hated the Yahoos of this country, yet he no more blamed them for their odious qualities, than he did a *gnnayh* (a bird of prey) for its cruelty, or a sharp stone for cutting his hoof. But, when a creature pretending to reason could be capable of such enormities, he dreaded lest the corruption of that faculty might be worse than brutality itself. He seemed therefore confident, that instead of reason, we were only possessed of some quality fitted to increase our natural vices; as the reflection from a troubled stream returns the image of an ill-shapen body, not only larger, but more distorted.

He added that he had heard too much upon the subject of war, both in this and some former discourses. There was another point which a little perplexed him at present. I had said that some of our crew left their country on account of being ruined by law: that I had already explained the meaning of the word; but he was at a loss how it should come to pass, that the law which was intended for every man's preservation, should be any man's ruin. Therefore he desired to be farther satisfied what I meant by law, and the dispensers

5. A satiric glance at George I, who, as elector of Hanover, had dealt in this trade.

thereof, according to the present practice in my own country; because he thought Nature and Reason were sufficient guides for a reasonable animal, as we pretended to be, in showing us what we ought to do, and what to avoid.

I assured his honor that law was a science wherein I had not much conversed, further than by employing advocates, in vain, upon some injustices that had been done me. However, I would give him all the satisfaction I was able.

I said there was a society of men among us, bred up from their youth in the art of proving by words multiplied for the purpose, that white is black, and black is white, according as they are paid. To this society all the rest of the people are slaves.

"For example. If my neighbor hath a mind to my cow, he hires a lawyer to prove that he ought to have my cow from me. I must then hire another to defend my right; it being against all rules of law that any man should be allowed to speak for himself. Now in this case, I who am the true owner lie under two great disadvantages. First, my lawyer being practiced almost from his cradle in defending falsehood is quite out of his element when he would be an advocate for justice, which as an office unnatural, he always attempts with great awkwardness, if not with ill-will. The second disadvantage is that my lawyer must proceed with great caution, or else he will be reprimanded by the judges, and abhorred by his brethren, as one who would lessen the practice of the law. And therefore I have but two methods to preserve my cow. The first is to gain over my adversary's lawyer with a double fee; who will then betray his client, by insinuating that he hath justice on his side. The second way is for my lawyer to make my cause appear as unjust as he can; by allowing the cow to belong to my adversary; and this if it be skillfully done, will certainly bespeak the favor of the bench.

"Now, your honor is to know that these judges are persons appointed to decide all controversies of property, as well as for the trial of criminals; and picked out from the most dextrous lawyers who are grown old or lazy; and having been biased all their lives against truth and equity, lie under such a fatal necessity of favoring fraud, perjury, and oppression, that I have known some of them to have refused a large bribe from the side where justice lay, rather than injure the faculty,[6] by doing anything unbecoming their nature or their office.

"It is a maxim among these lawyers, that whatever hath been done before may legally be done again; and therefore they take special care to record all the decisions formerly made against common justice and the general reason of mankind. These, under the name of *precedents*, they produce as authorities to justify the most iniquitous opinions; and the judges never fail of directing accordingly.

"In pleading, they studiously avoid entering into the merits of the cause; but are loud, violent, and tedious in dwelling upon all circumstances which are not to the purpose. For instance, in the case already mentioned, they never desire to know what claim or title my adversary hath to my cow; but whether the said cow were red or black; her horns long or short; whether the field I graze her in be round or square; whether she were milked at home or abroad;

6. Profession.

what diseases she is subject to, and the like. After which they consult precedents, adjourn the cause, from time to time, and in ten, twenty, or thirty years come to an issue.

"It is likewise to be observed, that this society hath a peculiar cant and jargon of their own, that no other mortal can understand, and wherein all their laws are written, which they take special care to multiply; whereby they have wholly confounded the very essence of truth and falsehood, of right and wrong; so that it will take thirty years to decide whether the field, left me by my ancestors for six generations, belong to me, or to a stranger three hundred miles off.

"In the trial of persons accused for crimes against the state, the method is much more short and commendable: the judge first sends to sound the disposition of those in power; after which he can easily hang or save the criminal, strictly preserving all the forms of law."

Here my master interposing said it was a pity that creatures endowed with such prodigious abilities of mind as these lawyers, by the description I gave of them, must certainly be, were not rather encouraged to be instructors of others in wisdom and knowledge. In answer to which, I assured his honor that in all points out of their own trade, they were usually the most ignorant and stupid generation among us, the most despicable in common conversation, avowed enemies to all knowledge and learning; and equally disposed to pervert the general reason of mankind, in every other subject of discourse as in that of their own profession.

CHAPTER 6. *A continuation of the state of England, under Queen Anne. The character of a first minister in the courts of Europe.*

My master was yet wholly at a loss to understand what motives could incite this race of lawyers to perplex, disquiet, and weary themselves by engaging in a confederacy of injustice, merely for the sake of injuring their fellow animals; neither could he comprehend what I meant in saying they did it for hire. Whereupon I was at much pains to describe to him the use of money, the materials it was made of, and the value of the metals; that when a Yahoo had got a great store of his precious substance, he was able to purchase whatever he had a mind to; the finest clothing, the noblest houses, great tracts of land, the most costly meats and drinks; and have his choice of the most beautiful females. Therefore since money alone was able to perform all these feats, our Yahoos thought they could never have enough of it to spend or to save, as they found themselves inclined from their natural bent either to profusion or avarice. That the rich man enjoyed the fruit of the poor man's labor, and the latter were a thousand to one in proportion to the former. That the bulk of our people was forced to live miserably, by laboring every day for small wages to make a few live plentifully. I enlarged myself much on these and many other particulars to the same purpose, but his honor was still to seek,[7] for he went upon a supposition that all animals had a title to their share in the productions of the earth; and especially those who presided over the rest. Therefore he desired I would let him know what these costly meats were, and how any of us happened to want[8] them. Whereupon I enumerated as many

7. Still did not understand.   8. Lack.

sorts as came into my head, with the various methods of dressing them, which could not be done without sending vessels by sea to every part of the world, as well for liquors to drink, as for sauces, and innumerable other conveniencies. I assured him, that this whole globe of earth must be at least three times gone round, before one of our better female Yahoos could get her breakfast, or a cup to put it in. He said, "That must needs be a miserable country which cannot furnish food for its own inhabitants." But what he chiefly wondered at, was how such vast tracts of ground as I described, should be wholly without fresh water, and the people put to the necessity of sending over the sea for drink. I replied that England (the dear place of my nativity) was computed to produce three times the quantity of food, more than its inhabitants are able to consume, as well as liquors extracted from grain, or pressed out of the fruit of certain trees, which made excellent drink; and the same proportion in every other convenience of life. But, in order to feed the luxury and intemperance of the males, and the vanity of the females, we sent away the greatest part of our necessary things to other countries, from whence in return we brought the materials of diseases, folly, and vice, to spend among ourselves. Hence it follows of necessity, that vast numbers of our people are compelled to seek their livelihood by begging, robbing, stealing, cheating, pimping, forswearing, flattering, suborning, forging, gaming, lying, fawning, hectoring, voting, scribbling, star gazing, poisoning, whoring, canting, libeling, freethinking, and the like occupations; every one of which terms, I was at much pains to make him understand.

That, wine was not imported among us from foreign countries, to supply the want of water or other drinks, but because it was a sort of liquid which made us merry, by putting us out of our senses; diverted all melancholy thoughts, begat wild extravagant imaginations in the brain, raised our hopes, and banished our fears; suspended every office of reason for a time, and deprived us of the use of our limbs, until we fell into a profound sleep; although it must be confessed, that we always awaked sick and dispirited; and that the use of this liquor filled us with diseases, which made our lives uncomfortable and short.

But beside all this, the bulk of our people supported themselves by furnishing the necessities or conveniencies of life to the rich, and to each other. For instance, when I am at home and dressed as I ought to be, I carry on my body the workmanship of an hundred tradesmen; the building and furniture of my house employ as many more; and five times the number to adorn my wife.

I was going on to tell him of another sort of people, who get their livelihood by attending the sick; having upon some occasions informed his honor that many of my crew had died of diseases. But here it was with the utmost difficulty that I brought him to apprehend what I meant. He could easily conceive that a Houyhnhnm grew weak and heavy a few days before his death; or by some accident might hurt a limb. But that nature, who worketh all things to perfection, should suffer any pains to breed in our bodies, he thought impossible; and desired to know the reason of so unaccountable an evil. I told him, we fed on a thousand things which operated contrary to each other; that we eat when we were not hungry, and drank without the provocation of thirst; that we sat whole nights drinking strong liquors without eating a bit, which disposed us to sloth, inflamed our bodies, and precipitated or prevented digestion. That, prostitute female Yahoos acquired a certain malady, which bred rottenness in the bones of those who fell into their embraces; that this and many other diseases were propagated from father to son; so that great numbers come into the world with complicated maladies upon them; that it would be endless to give him a catalogue of all diseases incident to human bodies; for they could not be fewer than five or six hundred, spread over every limb, and joint; in short, every part, external and intestine, having diseases appropriated to each. To remedy which, there was a sort of people bred up among us, in the profession or pretense of curing the sick. And because I had some skill in the faculty, I would in gratitude to his honor let him know the whole mystery and method by which they proceed.

Their fundamental is that all diseases arise from repletion; from whence they conclude, that a great evacuation of the body is necessary, either through the natural passage, or upwards at the mouth. Their next business is, from herbs, minerals, gums, oils, shells, salts, juices, seaweed, excrements, barks of trees, serpents, toads, frogs, spiders, dead men's flesh and bones, birds, beasts and fishes, to form a composition for smell and taste the most abominable, nauseous, and detestable, that they can possibly contrive, which the stomach immediately rejects with loathing, and this they call a vomit. Or else from the same storehouse, with some other poisonous additions, they command us to take in at the orifice above or below (just as the physician then happens to be disposed) a medicine equally annoying and disgustful to the bowels; which relaxing the belly, drives down all before it; and this they call a purge, or a clyster. For nature (as the physicians allege) having intended the superior anterior orifice only for the intromission of solids and liquids, and the inferior posterior for ejection, these artists ingeniously considering that in all diseases nature is forced out of her seat; therefore to replace her in it, the body must be treated in a manner directly contrary, by interchanging the use of each orifice; forcing solids and liquids in at the anus, and making evacuations at the mouth.

But, besides real diseases, we are subject to many that are only imaginary, for which the physicians have invented imaginary cures; these have their several names, and so have the drugs that are proper for them; and with these our female Yahoos are always infested.

One great excellency in this tribe is their skill at prognostics, wherein they seldom fail; their predictions in real diseases, when they rise to any degree of malignity, generally portending death, which is always in their power, when recovery is not, and therefore, upon any unexpected signs of amendment, after they have pronounced their sentence, rather than be accused as false prophets, they know how to approve[9] their sagacity to the world by a seasonable dose.

They are likewise of special use to husbands and wives, who are grown weary of their mates; to eldest sons, to great ministers of state, and often to princes.

I had formerly upon occasion discoursed with my master upon the nature of government in general, and particularly of our own excellent constitution, deservedly the wonder and envy of the whole world. But having here accidently mentioned a minister of state, he commanded me some time after to inform him what species of Yahoo I particularly meant by that appellation.

I told him that a first or chief minister of state, whom I intended to describe,

9. Prove.

was a creature wholly exempt from joy and grief, love and hatred, pity and anger; at least makes use of no other passions but a violent desire of wealth, power, and titles; that he applies his words to all uses, except to the indication of his mind; that he never tells a truth, but with an intent that you should take it for a lie; nor a lie, but with a design that you should take it for a truth; that those he speaks worst of behind their backs are in the surest way to preferment; and whenever he begins to praise you to others or to yourself, you are from that day forlorn. The worst mark you can receive is a promise, especially when it is confirmed with an oath; after which every wise man retires, and gives over all hopes.

There are three methods by which a man may rise to be chief minister: the first is by knowing how with prudence to dispose of a wife, a daughter, or a sister; the second, by betraying or undermining his predecessor; and the third is by a furious zeal in public assemblies against the corruptions of the court. But a wise prince would rather choose to employ those who practice the last of these methods; because such zealots prove always the most obsequious and subservient to the will and passions of their master. That, these ministers having all employments at their disposal, preserve themselves in power by bribing the majority of a senate or great council; and at last by an expedient called an Act of Indemnity[1] (whereof I described the nature to him) they secure themselves from after reckonings, and retire from the public, laden with the spoils of the nation.

The palace of a chief minister is a seminary to breed up others in his own trade; the pages, lackies, and porter, by imitating their master, become ministers of state in their several districts, and learn to excel in the three principal ingredients, of insolence, lying, and bribery. Accordingly, they have a subaltern court paid to them by persons of the best rank; and sometimes by the force of dexterity and impudence, arrive through several gradations to be successors to their lord.

He is usually governed by a decayed wench, or favorite footman, who are the tunnels through which all graces are conveyed, and may properly be called, in the last resort, the governors of the kingdom.

One day, my master, having heard me mention the nobility of my country, was pleased to make me a compliment which I could not pretend to deserve: that, he was sure, I must have been born of some noble family, because I far exceeded in shape, color, and cleanliness, all the Yahoos of his nation, although I seemed to fail in strength, and agility, which must be imputed to my different way of living from those other brutes; and besides, I was not only endowed with the faculty of speech, but likewise with some rudiments of reason, to a degree, that with all his acquaintance I passed for a prodigy.

He made me observe, that among the Houyhnhnms, the white, the sorrel, and the iron grey were not so exactly shaped as the bay, the dapple grey, and the black; nor born with equal talents of mind, or a capacity to improve them; and therefore continued always in the condition of servants, without ever aspiring to match out of their own race, which in that country would be reckoned monstrous and unnatural.

I made his honor my most humble acknowledgments for the good opinion

---

1. An act passed at each session of Parliament to protect ministers of state who in good faith might have acted illegally.

he was pleased to conceive of me; but assured him at the same time, that my birth was of the lower sort, having been born of plain, honest parents, who were just able to give me a tolerable education; that, nobility among us was altogether a different thing from the idea he had of it; that, our young noblemen are bred from their childhood in idleness and luxury; that, as soon as years will permit, they consume their vigor, and contract odious diseases among lewd females; and when their fortunes are almost ruined, they marry some woman of mean birth, disagreeable person, and unsound constitution, merely for the sake of money, whom they hate and despise. That, the productions of such marriages are generally scrofulous, rickety or deformed children; by which means the family seldom continues above three generations, unless the wife take care to provide a healthy father among her neighbors, or domestics, in order to improve and continue the breed. That a weak diseased body, a meager countenance, and sallow complexion are the true marks of noble blood; and a healthy robust appearance is so disgraceful in a man of quality, that the world concludes his real father to have been a groom or a coachman. The imperfections of his mind run parallel with those of his body; being a composition of spleen, dullness, ignorance, caprice, sensuality, and pride.

Without the consent of this illustrious body, no law can be enacted, repealed, or altered, and these nobles have likewise the decision of all our possessions without appeal.

CHAPTER 7. *The Author's great love of his native country. His master's observations upon the constitution and administration of England, as described by the Author, with parallel cases and comparisons. His master's observations upon human nature.*

The reader may be disposed to wonder how I could prevail on myself to give so free a representation of my own species, among a race of mortals who were already too apt to conceive the vilest opinion of humankind, from that entire congruity betwixt me and their Yahoos. But I must freely confess that the many virtues of those excellent quadrupeds placed in opposite view to human corruptions had so far opened my eyes, and enlarged my understanding, that I began to view the actions and passions of man in a very different light; and to think the honor of my own kind not worth managing;[2] which, besides, it was impossible for me to do before a person of so acute a judgment as my master, who daily convinced me of a thousand faults in myself, whereof I had not the least perception before, and which with us would never be numbered even among human infirmities. I had likewise learned from his example an utter detestation of all falsehood or disguise; and truth appeared so amiable to me, that I determined upon sacrificing everything to it.

Let me deal so candidly with the reader as to confess that there was yet a much stronger motive for the freedom I took in my representation of things. I had not been a year in this country, before I contracted such a love and veneration for the inhabitants, that I entered on a firm resolution never to return to humankind, but to pass the rest of my life among these admirable Houyhnhnms in the contemplation and practice of every virtue; where I could have no example or incitement to vice. But it was decreed by fortune, my

2. Taking care of.

perpetual enemy, that so great a felicity should not fall to my share. However, it is now some comfort to reflect that in what I said of my countrymen, I extenuated their faults as much as I durst before so strict an examiner; and upon every article, gave as favorable a turn as the matter would bear. For, indeed, who is there alive that will not be swayed by his bias and partiality to the place of his birth?

I have related the substance of several conversations I had with my master, during the greatest part of the time I had the honor to be in his service; but have indeed for brevity sake omitted much more than is here set down.

When I had answered all his questions, and his curiosity seemed to be fully satisfied; he sent for me one morning early, and commanding me to sit down at some distance (an honor which he had never before conferred upon me), he said he had been very seriously considering my whole story, as far as it related both to myself and my country; that, he looked upon us as a sort of animals to whose share, by what accident he could not conjecture, some small pittance of reason had fallen, whereof we made no other use than by its assistance to aggravate our natural corruptions, and to acquire new ones which nature had not given us. That we disarmed ourselves of the few abilities she had bestowed; had been very successful in multiplying our original wants, and seemed to spend our whole lives in vain endeavors to supply them by our own inventions. That, as to myself, it was manifest I had neither the strength or agility of a common Yahoo; that I walked infirmly on my hinder feet; had found out a contrivance to make my claws of no use or defense, and to remove the hair from my chin, which was intended as a shelter from the sun and the weather. Lastly, that I could neither run with speed, nor climb trees like my brethren (as he called them) the Yahoos in this country.

That our institutions of government and law were plainly owing to our gross defects in reason, and by consequence, in virtue; because reason alone is sufficient to govern a rational creature; which was therefore a character we had no pretense to challenge, even from the account I had given of my own people; although he manifestly perceived, that in order to favor them, I had concealed many particulars, and often *said the thing which was not*.

He was the more confirmed in this opinion, because he observed that I agreed in every feature of my body with other Yahoos, except where it was to my real disadvantage in point of strength, speed, and activity, the shortness of my claws, and some other particulars where Nature had no part; so, from the representation I had given him of our lives, our manners, and our actions, he found as near a resemblance in the disposition of our minds. He said the Yahoos were known to hate one another more than they did any different species of animals; and the reason usually assigned was the odiousness of their own shapes, which all could see in the rest, but not in themselves. He had therefore begun to think it not unwise in us to cover our bodies, and by that invention, conceal many of our deformities from each other, which would else be hardly supportable. But he now found he had been mistaken; and that the dissensions of those brutes in his country were owing to the same cause with ours, as I had described them. For, if (said he) you throw among five Yahoos as much food as would be sufficient for fifty, they will instead of eating peaceably, fall together by the ears, each single one impatient to have all to itself; and therefore a servant was usually employed to stand by while they were feeding abroad, and those kept at home were tied at a distance from each other. That, if a cow died of age or accident, before a Houyhnhnm could secure it for his own Yahoos, those in the neighborhood would come in herds to seize it, and then would ensue such a battle as I had described, with terrible wounds made by their claws on both sides, although they seldom were able to kill one another, for want of such convenient instruments of death as we had invented. At other times the like battles have been fought between the Yahoos of several neighborhoods without any visible cause; those of one district watching all opportunities to surprise the next before they are prepared. But if they find their project hath miscarried, they return home, and for want of enemies, engage in what I call a civil war among themselves.

That, in some fields of his country, there are certain shining stones of several colors, whereof the Yahoos are violently fond; and when part of these stones are fixed in the earth, as it sometimes happeneth, they will dig with their claws for whole days to get them out, and carry them away, and hide them by heaps in their kennels; but still looking round with great caution, for fear their comrades should find out their treasure. My master said he could never discover the reason of this unnatural appetite, or how these stones could be of any use to a Yahoo; but now he believed it might proceed from the same principle of avarice, which I had ascribed to mankind. That he had once, by way of experiment, privately removed a heap of these stones from the place where one of his Yahoos had buried it, whereupon, the sordid animal missing his treasure, by his loud lamenting brought the whole herd to the place, there miserably howled, then fell to biting and tearing the rest; began to pine away, would neither eat nor sleep, nor work, till he ordered a servant privately to convey the stones into the same hole, and hide them as before; which when his Yahoo had found, he presently recovered his spirits and good humor; but took care to remove them to a better hiding place; and hath ever since been a very serviceable brute.

My master farther assured me, which I also observed myself, that in the fields where these shining stones abound, the fiercest and most frequent battles are fought, occasioned by perpetual inroads of the neighboring Yahoos.

He said it was common when two Yahoos discovered such a stone in a field, and were contending which of them should be the proprietor, a third would take the advantage, and carry it away from them both; which my master would needs contend to have some resemblance with our suits at law; wherein I thought it for our credit not to undeceive him; since the decision he mentioned was much more equitable than many decrees among us; because the plaintiff and defendant there lost nothing beside the stone they contended for; whereas our courts of equity would never have dismissed the cause while either of them had anything left.

My master continuing his discourse said there was nothing that rendered the Yahoos more odious, than their undistinguished appetite to devour everything that came in their way, whether herbs, roots, berries, corrupted flesh of animals, or all mingled together; and it was peculiar in their temper, that they were fonder of what they could get by rapine or stealth at a greater distance, than much better food provided for them at home. If their prey held out, they would eat till they were ready to burst, after which nature had pointed out to them a certain root that gave them a general evacuation.

There was also another kind of root very juicy, but something rare and difficult to be found, which the Yahoos sought for with much eagerness, and would suck it with great delight; it produced the same effects that wine hath upon us. It would make them sometimes hug, and sometimes tear one another; they would howl and grin, and chatter, and reel, and tumble, and then fall asleep in the mud.

I did indeed observe that the Yahoos were the only animals in this country subject to any diseases; which however, were much fewer than horses have among us, and contracted not by any ill treatment they meet with, but by the nastiness and greediness of that sordid brute. Neither has their language any more than a general appellation for those maladies; which is borrowed from the name of the beast, and called *Hnea Yahoo,* or the Yahoo's Evil; and the cure prescribed is a mixture of their own dung and urine, forcibly put down the Yahoo's throat. This I have since often known to have been taken with success, and do here freely recommend it to my countrymen, for the public good, as an admirable specific against all diseases produced by repletion.

As to learning, government, arts, manufactures, and the like, my master confessed he could find little or no resemblance between the Yahoos of that country and those in ours. For he only meant to observe what parity there was in our natures. He had heard indeed some curious Houyhnhnms observe that in most herds there was a sort of ruling Yahoo (as among us there is generally some leading or principal stag in a park) who was always more deformed in body, and mischievous in disposition, than any of the rest. That this leader had usually a favorite as like himself as he could get, whose employment was to lick his master's feet and posteriors, and drive the female Yahoos to his kennel; for which he was now and then rewarded with a piece of ass's flesh. This favorite is hated by the whole herd; and therefore to protect himself, keeps always near the person of his leader. He usually continues in office till a worse can be found; but the very moment he is discarded, his successor, at the head of all the Yahoos in that district, young and old, male and female, come in a body, and discharge their excrements upon him from head to foot. But how far this might be applicable to our courts and favorites, and ministers of state, my master said I could best determine.

I durst make no return to this malicious insinuation, which debased human understanding below the sagacity of a common hound, who hath judgment enough to distinguish and follow the cry of the ablest dog in the pack, without being ever mistaken.

My master told me there were some qualities remarkable in the Yahoos, which he had not observed me to mention, or at least very slightly, in the accounts I had given him of humankind. He said, those animals, like other brutes, had their females in common; but in this they differed, that the she-Yahoo would admit the male while she was pregnant; and that the hes would quarrel and fight with the females as fiercely as with each other. Both which practices were such degrees of infamous brutality, that no other sensitive crea-ture ever arrived at.

Another thing he wondered at in the Yahoos was their strange disposition to nastiness and dirt; whereas there appears to be a natural love of cleanliness in all other animals. As to the two former accusations, I was glad to let them pass without any reply, because I had not a word to offer upon them in defense of my species, which otherwise I certainly had done from my own inclinations. But I could have easily vindicated humankind from the imputation of singu-larity upon the last article, if there had been any swine in that country (as unluckily for me there were not) which although it may be a sweeter quadruped than a Yahoo, cannot I humbly conceive in justice pretend to more cleanliness; and so his honor himself must have owned, if he had seen their filthy way of feeding, and their custom of wallowing and sleeping in the mud.

My master likewise mentioned another quality, which his servants had discovered in several Yahoos, and to him was wholly unaccountable. He said, a fancy would sometimes take a Yahoo, to retire into a corner, to lie down and howl, and groan, and spurn away all that came near him, although he were young and fat, and wanted neither food nor water; nor did the servants imagine what could possibly ail him. And the only remedy they found was to set him to hard work, after which he would infallibly come to himself. To this I was silent out of partiality to my own kind; yet here I could plainly discover the true seeds of spleen,[3] which only seizeth on the lazy, the luxurious, and the rich; who, if they were forced to undergo the same regimen, I would undertake for the cure.

His Honor had farther observed, that a female Yahoo would often stand behind a bank or a bush, to gaze on the young males passing by, and then appear, and hide, using many antic gestures and grimaces; at which time it was observed, that she had a most offensive smell; and when any of the males advanced, would slowly retire, looking back, and with a counterfeit show of fear, run off into some convenient place where she knew the male would follow her.

At other times, if a female stranger came among them, three or four of her own sex would get about her, and stare and chatter, and grin, and smell her all over; and then turn off with gestures that seemed to express contempt and disdain.

Perhaps my master might refine a little in these speculations, which he had drawn from what he observed himself, or had been told by others; however, I could not reflect without some amazement, and much sorrow, that the rudiments of lewdness, coquetry, censure, and scandal, should have place by instinct in womankind.

I expected every moment that my master would accuse the Yahoos of those unnatural appetites in both sexes, so common among us. But Nature it seems hath not been so expert a schoolmistress; and these politer pleasures are entirely the productions of art and reason, on our side of the globe.

CHAPTER 8. *The Author relateth several particulars of the Yahoos. The great virtues of the Houyhnhnms. The education and exercises of their youth. Their general assembly.*

As I ought to have understood human nature much better than I supposed it possible for my master to do, so it was easy to apply the character he gave of the Yahoos to myself and my countrymen; and I believed I could yet make farther discoveries from my own observation. I therefore often begged his honor to let me go among the herds of Yahoos in the neighborhood; to which he always very graciously consented, being perfectly convinced that the hatred I bore those brutes would never suffer me to be corrupted by them; and his honor ordered one of his servants, a strong sorrel nag, very honest and good-

3. Hypochondria.

natured, to be my guard; without whose protection I durst not undertake such adventures. For I have already told the reader how much I was pestered by those odious animals upon my first arrival. I afterwards failed very narrowly three or four times of falling into their clutches, when I happened to stray at any distance without my hanger. And I have reason to believe, they had some imagination that I was of their own species, which I often assisted myself, by stripping up my sleeves, and shewing my naked arms and breast in their sight, when my protector was with me; at which times they would approach as near as they durst, and imitate my actions after the manner of monkeys, but ever with great signs of hatred; as a tame jackdaw with cap and stockings is always persecuted by the wild ones, when he happens to be got among them.

They are prodigiously nimble from their infancy; however, I once caught a young male of three years old, and endeavored by all marks of tenderness to make it quiet; but the little imp fell a squalling, scratching, and biting with such violence, that I was forced to let it go; and it was high time, for a whole troop of old ones came about us at the noise; but finding the cub was safe (for away it ran) and my sorrel nag being by, they durst not venture near us. I observed the young animal's flesh to smell very rank, and the stink was some- what between a weasel and a fox, but much more disagreeable. I forgot another circumstance (and perhaps I might have the reader's pardon, if it were wholly omitted) that while I held the odious vermin in my hands, it voided its filthy excrements of a yellow liquid substance, all over my clothes; but by good fortune there was a small brook hard by, where I washed myself as clean as I could; although I durst not come into my master's presence until I were suffi- ciently aired.

By what I could discover, the Yahoos appear to be the most unteachable of all animals, their capacities never reaching higher than to draw or carry bur- dens. Yet I am of opinion, this defect ariseth chiefly from a perverse, restive disposition. For they are cunning, malicious, treacherous and revengeful. They are strong and hardy, but of a cowardly spirit, and by consequence inso- lent, abject, and cruel. It is observed that the red-haired of both sexes are more libidinous and mischievous than the rest, whom yet they much exceed in strength and activity.

The Houyhnhnms keep the Yahoos for present use in huts not far from the house; but the rest are sent abroad to certain fields, where they dig up roots, eat several kinds of herbs, and search about for carrion, or sometimes catch weasels and *luhimuhs* (a sort of wild rat) which they greedily devour. Nature hath taught them to dig deep holes with their nails on the side of a rising ground, wherein they lie by themselves; only the kennels of the females are larger, sufficient to hold two or three cubs.

They swim from their infancy like frogs, and are able to continue long under water, where they often take fish, which the females carry home to their young. And upon this occasion, I hope the reader will pardon my relating an odd adventure.

Being one day abroad with my protector the sorrel nag, and the weather exceeding hot, I entreated him to let me bathe in a river that was near. He consented, and I immediately stripped myself stark naked, and went down softly into the stream. It happened that a young female Yahoo standing behind a bank, saw the whole proceeding; and inflamed by desire, as the nag and I conjectured, came running with all speed, and leaped into the water within five yards of the place where I bathed. I was never in my life so terribly frighted; the nag was grazing at some distance, not suspecting any harm. She embraced me after a most fulsome manner; I roared as loud as I could, and the nag came galloping towards me, whereupon she quitted her grasp, with the utmost reluctancy, and leaped upon the opposite bank, where she stood gazing and howling all the time I was putting on my clothes.

This was matter of diversion to my master and his family, as well as of mortification to myself. For now I could no longer deny that I was a real Yahoo, in every limb and feature, since the females had a natural propensity to me as one of their own species; neither was the hair of this brute of a red color (which might have been some excuse for an appetite a little irregular) but black as a sloe, and her countenance did not make an appearance altogether so hideous as the rest of the kind; for I think, she could not be above eleven years old.

Having already lived three years in this country, the reader I suppose will expect that I should, like other travelers, give him some account of the manners and customs of its inhabitants, which it was indeed my principal study to learn.

As these noble Houyhnhnms are endowed by Nature with a general disposition to all virtues, and have no conceptions or ideas of what is evil in a rational creature; so their grand maxim is to cultivate reason, and to be wholly governed by it. Neither is reason among them a point problematical as with us, where men can argue with plausibility on both sides of a question; but strikes you with immediate conviction; as it must needs do where it is not mingled, obscured, or discolored by passion and interest. I remember it was with extreme difficulty that I could bring my master to understand the meaning of the word "opinion," or how a point could be disputable; because reason taught us to affirm or deny only where we are certain; and beyond our knowledge we cannot do either. So that controversies, wranglings, disputes, and positiveness in false or dubious propositions are evils unknown among the Houyhnhnms. In the like manner when I used to explain to him our several systems of natural philosophy,[4] he would laugh that a creature pretending to reason should value itself upon the knowledge of other people's conjectures, and in things, where that knowledge, if it were certain, could be of no use. Wherein he agreed entirely with the sentiments of Socrates, as Plato delivers them, which I mention as the highest honor I can do that prince of philosophers. I have often since reflected what destruction such a doctrine would make in the libraries of Europe; and how many paths to fame would be then shut up in the learned world.

Friendship and benevolence are the two principal virtues among the Houyhnhnms; and these not confined to particular objects, but universal to the whole race. For a stranger from the remotest part is equally treated with the nearest neighbor, and wherever he goes, looks upon himself as at home. They preserve decency and civility in the highest degrees, but are altogether ignorant of ceremony. They have no fondness for their colts or foals; but the care they take in educating them proceedeth entirely from the dictates of reason. And I observed my master to show the same affection to his neighbor's issue that he had for his own. They will have it that Nature teaches them to love

4. Science.

the whole species, and it is reason only that maketh a distinction of persons, where there is a superior degree of virtue.

When the matron Houyhnhnms have produced one of each sex, they no longer accompany with their consorts, except they lose one of their issue by some casualty, which very seldom happens; but in such a case they meet again; or when the like accident befalls a person whose wife is past bearing, some other couple bestows on him one of their own colts, and then go together a second time, until the mother be pregnant. This caution is necessary to prevent the country from being overburdened with numbers. But the race of inferior Houyhnhnms bred up to be servants is not so strictly limited upon this article; these are allowed to produce three of each sex, to be domestics in the noble families.

In their marriages they are exactly careful to choose such colors as will not make any disagreeable mixture in the breed. Strength is chiefly valued in the male, and comeliness in the female; not upon the account of love, but to preserve the race from degenerating; for, where a female happens to excel in strength, a consort is chosen with regard to comeliness. Courtship, love, presents, jointures, settlements, have no place in their thoughts, or terms whereby to express them in their language. The young couple meet and are joined, merely because it is the determination of their parents and friends; it is what they see done every day; and they look upon it as one of the necessary actions in a reasonable being. But the violation of marriage, or any other unchastity, was never heard of; and the married pair pass their lives with the same friendship and mutual benevolence that they bear to all others of the same species who come in their way, without jealousy, fondness, quarreling, or discontent.

In educating the youth of both sexes, their method is admirable, and highly deserveth our imitation. These are not suffered to taste a grain of oats, except upon certain days, till eighteen years old; nor milk, but very rarely; and in summer they graze two hours in the morning, and as many in the evening, which their parents likewise observe; but the servants are not allowed above half that time; and a great part of the grass is brought home, which they eat at the most convenient hours when they can be best spared from work.

Temperance, industry, exercise, and cleanliness are the lessons equally enjoined to the young ones of both sexes; and my master thought it monstrous in us to give the females a different kind of education from the males, except in some articles of domestic management; whereby, as he truly observed, one half of our natives were good for nothing but bringing children into the world; and to trust the care of their children to such useless animals, he said was yet a greater instance of brutality.

But the Houyhnhnms train up their youth to strength, speed, and hardiness, by exercising them in running races up and down steep hills, or over hard stony grounds; and when they are all in a sweat, they are ordered to leap over head and ears into a pond or a river. Four times a year the youth of certain districts meet to show their proficiency in running, and leaping, and other feats of strength or agility; where the victor is rewarded with a song made in his or her praise. On this festival the servants drive a herd of Yahoos into the field, laden with hay, and oats, and milk for a repast to the Houyhnhnms; after which these brutes are immediately driven back again, for fear of being noisome to the assembly.

Every fourth year, at the vernal equinox, there is a representative council of the whole nation, which meets in a plain about twenty miles from our house, and continueth about five or six days. Here they inquire into the state and condition of the several districts; whether they abound or be deficient in hay or oats, or cows or Yahoos? And wherever there is any want (which is but seldom) it is immediately supplied by unanimous consent and contribution. Here likewise the regulation of children is settled: as for instance, if a Houyhnhnm hath two males, he changeth one of them with another who hath two females, and when a child hath been lost by any casualty, where the mother is past breeding, it is determined what family in the district shall breed another to supply the loss.

CHAPTER 9. *A grand debate at the general assembly of the Houyhnhnms, and how it was determined. The learning of the Houyhnhnms. Their buildings. Their manner of burials. The defectiveness of their language.*

One of these grand assemblies was held in my time, about three months before my departure, whither my master went as the representative of our district. In this council was resumed their old debate, and indeed, the only debate that ever happened in their country; whereof my master after his return gave me a very particular account.

The question to be debated was whether the Yahoos should be exterminated from the face of the earth. One of the members for the affirmative offered several arguments of great strength and weight, alleging that, as the Yahoos were the most filthy, noisome, and deformed animal which nature ever produced, so they were the most restive and indocible,[5] mischievous, and malicious; they would privately suck the teats of the Houyhnhnms' cows; kill and devour their cats, trample down their oats and grass, if they were not continually watched; and commit a thousand other extravagancies. He took notice of a general tradition, that Yahoos had not been always in their country, but that many ages ago, two of these brutes appeared together upon a mountain; whether produced by the heat of the sun upon corrupted mud and slime, or from the ooze and froth of the sea, was never known. That these Yahoos engendered, and their brood in a short time grew so numerous as to overrun and infest the whole nation. That the Houyhnhnms to get rid of this evil, made a general hunting, and at last enclosed the whole herd; and destroying the older, every Houyhnhnm kept two young ones in a kennel, and brought them to such a degree of tameness as an animal so savage by nature can be capable of acquiring, using them for draught and carriage. That there seemed to be much truth in this tradition, and that those creatures could not be *ylnh-niamshy* (or aborigines of the land) because of the violent hatred the Houyhnhnms as well as all other animals bore them; which although their evil disposition sufficiently deserved, could never have arrived at so high a degree, if they had been aborigines, or else they would have long since been rooted out. That the inhabitants taking a fancy to use the service of the Yahoos, had very imprudently neglected to cultivate the breed of asses, which were a comely animal, easily kept, more tame and orderly, without any offensive smell, strong enough for labor, although they yield to the other in agility of

5. Unteachable.

body; and if their braying be no agreeable sound, it is far preferable to the horrible howlings of the Yahoos.

Several others declared their sentiments to the same purpose, when my master proposed an expedient to the assembly, whereof he had indeed borrowed the hint from me. He approved of the tradition, mentioned by the honorable member, who spoke before; and affirmed, that the two Yahoos said to be first seen among them, had been driven thither over the sea; that coming to land, and being forsaken by their companions, they retired to the mountains, and degenerating by degrees, became in process of time much more savage than those of their own species in the country from whence these two originals came. The reason of his assertion was that he had now in his possession a certain wonderful Yahoo (meaning myself) which most of them had heard of, and many of them had seen. He then related to them how he first found me; that my body was all covered with an artificial composure of the skins and hairs of other animals; that I spoke in a language of my own, and had thoroughly learned theirs; that I had related to him the accidents which brought me thither; that when he saw me without my covering, I was an exact Yahoo in every part, only of a whiter color, less hairy and with shorter claws. He added how I had endeavored to persuade him that in my own and other countries the Yahoos acted as the governing, rational animal, and held the Houyhnhnms in servitude; that he observed in me all the qualities of a Yahoo, only a little more civilized by some tincture of reason, which however was in a degree as far inferior to the Houyhnhnm race as the Yahoos of their country were to me; that among other things, I mentioned a custom we had of castrating Houyhnhnms when they were young, in order to render them tame; that the operation was easy and safe; that it was no shame to learn wisdom from brutes, as industry is taught by the ant, and building by the swallow (for so I translate the world *lyhannh*, although it be a much larger fowl). That this invention might be practiced upon the younger Yahoos here, which, besides rendering them tractable and fitter for use, would in an age put an end to the whole species without destroying life. That in the meantime the Houyhnhnms should be exhorted to cultivate the breed of asses, which, as they are in all respects more valuable brutes, so they have this advantage, to be fit for service at five years old, which the other are not till twelve.

This was all my master thought fit to tell me at that time, of what passed in the grand council. But he was pleased to conceal one particular, which related personally to myself, whereof I soon felt the unhappy effect, as the reader will know in its proper place, and from whence I date all the succeeding misfortunes of my life.

The Houyhnhnms have no letters, and consequently, their knowledge is all traditional. But there happening few events of any moment among a people so well united, naturally disposed to every virtue, wholly governed by reason, and cut off from all commerce with other nations, the historical part is easily preserved without burdening their memories. I have already observed that they are subject to no diseases, and therefore can have no need of physicians. However, they have excellent medicines composed of herbs, to cure accidental bruises and cuts in the pastern or frog of the foot by sharp stones, as well as other maims and hurts in the several parts of the body.

They calculate the year by the revolution of the sun and the moon, but use no subdivisions into weeks. They are well enough acquainted with the motions of those two luminaries, and understand the nature of eclipses; and this is the utmost progress of their astronomy.

In poetry they must be allowed to excel all other mortals; wherein the justness of their similes, and the minuteness, as well as exactness of their descriptions, are indeed inimitable. Their verses abound very much in both of these, and usually contain either some exalted notions of friendship and benevolence, or the praises of those who were victors in races and other bodily exercises. Their buildings, although very rude and simple, are not inconvenient, but well contrived to defend them from all injuries of cold and heat. They have a kind of tree, which at forty years old loosens in the root, and falls with the first storm; it grows very straight, and being pointed like stakes with a sharp stone (for the Houyhnhnms know not the use of iron), they stick them erect in the ground about ten inches asunder, and then weave in oat straw, or sometimes wattles, betwixt them. The roof is made after the same manner, and so are the doors.

The Houyhnhnms use the hollow part between the pastern and the hoof of their forefeet as we do our hands, and this with greater dexterity than I could at first imagine. I have seen a white mare of our family thread a needle (which I lent her on purpose) with that joint. They milk their cows, reap their oats, and do all the work which requires hands in the same manner. They have a kind of hard flints, which by grinding against other stones they form into instruments that serve instead of wedges, axes, and hammers. With tools made of these flints, they likewise cut their hay, and reap their oats, which there groweth naturally in several fields. The Yahoos draw home the sheaves in carriages, and the servants tread them in certain covered huts, to get out the grain, which is kept in stores. They make a rude kind of earthen and wooden vessels, and bake the former in the sun.

If they can avoid casualties, they die only of old age, and are buried in the obscurest places that can be found, their friends and relations expressing neither joy nor grief at their departure; nor does the dying person discover the least regret that he is leaving the world, any more than if he were upon returning home from a visit to one of his neighbors; I remember my master having once made an appointment with a friend and his family to come to his house upon some affair of importance; on the day fixed, the mistress and her two children came very late; she made two excuses, first for her husband, who, as she said, happened that very morning to *lhnuwnh*. The word is strongly expressive in their language, but not easily rendered into English; it signifies, *to retire to his first Mother*. Her excuse for not coming sooner was that her husband dying late in the morning, she was a good while consulting her servants about a convenient place where his body should be laid; and I observed she behaved herself at our house, as cheerfully as the rest. She died about three months after.

They live generally to seventy or seventy-five years, very seldom to fourscore; some weeks before their death they feel a gradual decay, but without pain. During this time they are much visited by their friends, because they cannot go abroad with their usual ease and satisfaction. However, about ten days before their death, which they seldom fail in computing, they return the visits that have been made by those who are nearest in the neighborhood, being carried in a convenient sledge drawn by Yahoos; which vehicle they use, not only upon this occasion, but when they grow old, upon long journeys, or when they are lamed by any accident. And therefore when the dying Houyhnhnms return those visits, they take a solemn leave of their friends, as if they were going to some remote part of the country, where they designed to pass the rest of their lives.

I know not whether it may be worth observing, that the Houyhnhnms have no word in their language to express anything that is evil, except what they borrow from the deformities or ill qualities of the Yahoos. Thus they denote the folly of a servant, an omission of a child, a stone that cuts their feet, a continuance of foul or unseasonable weather, and the like, by adding to each the epithet of Yahoo. For instance, *hhnm Yahoo, whnaholm Yahoo, ynlhmnd-wihlma Yahoo,* and an ill-contrived house, *ynholmhnmrohlnw Yahoo.*

I could with great pleasure enlarge farther upon the manners and virtues of this excellent people; but intending in a short time to publish a volume by itself expressly upon that subject, I refer the reader thither. And in the meantime, proceed to relate my own sad catastrophe.

CHAPTER 10. *The Author's economy, and happy life among the Houyhnhnms. His great improvement in virtue, by conversing with them. Their conversations. The Author hath notice given him by his master that he must depart from the country. He falls into a swoon for grief, but submits. He contrives and finishes a canoe, by the help of a fellow servant, and puts to sea at a venture.*

I had settled my little economy to my own heart's content. My master had ordered a room to be made for me after their manner, about six yards from the house; the sides and floors of which I plastered with clay, and covered with rush mats of my own contriving; I had beaten hemp, which there grows wild, and made of it a sort of ticking; this I filled with the feathers of several birds I had taken with springes made of Yahoos' hairs, and were excellent food. I had worked two chairs with my knife, the sorrel nag helping me in the grosser and more laborious part. When my clothes were worn to rags, I made myself others with the skins of rabbits, and of a certain beautiful animal about the same size, called *nnuhnoh,* the skin of which is covered with a fine down. Of these I likewise made very tolerable stockings. I soled my shoes with wood which I cut from a tree, and fitted to the upper leather, and when this was worn out, I supplied it with the skins of Yahoos, dried in the sun. I often got honey out of hollow trees, which I mingled with water, or eat it with my bread. No man could more verify the truth of these two maxims, that *Nature is very easily satisfied;* and, that *Necessity is the mother of invention.* I enjoyed perfect health of body, and tranquility of mind; I did not feel the treachery or inconstancy of a friend, nor the inquiries of a secret or open enemy. I had no occasion of bribing, flattering, or pimping to procure the favor of any great man, or of his minion. I wanted no fence against fraud or oppression; here was neither physician to destroy my body, nor lawyer to ruin my fortune; no informer to watch my words and actions, or forge accusations against me for hire; here were no gibers, censurers, backbiters, pickpockets, highwaymen, housebreakers, attorneys, bawds, buffoons, gamesters, politicians, wits, splenetics, tedious talkers, controvertists, ravishers, murderers, robbers, virtuosos;[6] no

6. Savants; those who pursue special interests in the arts or sciences.

leaders or followers of party and faction; no encouragers to vice, by seducement or examples; no dungeons, axes, gibbets, whipping posts, or pillories; no cheating shopkeepers or mechanics; no pride, vanity or affectation; no fops, bullies, drunkards, strolling whores, or poxes; no ranting, lewd, expensive wives; no stupid, proud pedants; no importunate, overbearing, quarrelsome, noisy, roaring, empty, conceited, swearing companions; no scoundrels raised from the dust upon the merit of their vices; or nobility thrown into it on account of their virtues; no lords, fiddlers, judges, or dancing masters.

I had the favor of being admitted to several Houyhnhnms, who came to visit or dine with my master; where his honor graciously suffered me to wait in the room, and listen to their discourse. Both he and his company would often descend to ask me questions, and receive my answers. I had also sometimes the honor of attending my master in his visits to others. I never presumed to speak, except in answer to a question; and then I did it with inward regret, because it was a loss of so much time for improving myself; but I was infinitely delighted with the station of an humble auditor in such conversations, where nothing passed but what was useful, expressed in the fewest and most significant words; where (as I have already said) the greatest decency was observed, without the least degree of ceremony; where no person spoke without being pleased himself, and pleasing his companions; where there was no interruption, tediousness, heat, or difference of sentiments. They have a notion, that when people are met together, a short silence doth much improve conversation; this I found to be true; for during those little intermissions of talk, new ideas would arise in their minds, which very much enlivened the discourse. Their subjects are generally on friendship and benevolence, on order and economy; sometimes upon the visible operations of nature, or ancient traditions; upon the bounds and limits of virtue; upon the unerring rules of reason; or upon some determinations, to be taken at the next great assembly; and often upon the various excellencies of poetry. I may add, without vanity, that my presence often gave them sufficient matter for discourse, because it afforded my master an occasion of letting his friends into the history of me and my country, upon which they were all pleased to descant in a manner not very advantageous to human kind; and for that reason I shall not repeat what they said; only I may be allowed to observe that his honor, to my great admiration, appeared to understand the nature of Yahoos much better than myself. He went through all our vices and follies, and discovered many which I had never mentioned to him; by only supposing what qualities a Yahoo of their country, with a small proportion of reason, might be capable of exerting; and concluded, with too much probability, how vile as well as miserable such a creature must be.

I freely confess, that all the little knowledge I have of any value was acquired by the lectures I received from my master, and from hearing the discourses of him and his friends; to which I should be prouder to listen, than to dictate to the greatest and wisest assembly in Europe. I admired the strength, comeliness, and speed of the inhabitants; and such a constellation of virtues in such amiable persons produced in me the highest veneration. At first, indeed, I did not feel that natural awe which the Yahoos and all other animals bear towards them; but it grew upon me by degrees, much sooner than I imagined, and was mingled with a respectful love and gratitude, that they would condescend to distinguish me from the rest of my species.

When I thought of my family, my friends, my countrymen, or human race in general, I considered them as they really were, Yahoos in shape and disposition, perhaps a little more civilized, and qualified with the gift of speech; but making no other use of reason than to improve and multiply those vices, whereof their brethren in this country had only the share that nature allotted them. When I happened to behold the reflection of my own form in a lake or fountain, I turned away my face in horror and detestation of myself, and could better endure the sight of a common Yahoo than of my own person. By conversing with the Houyhnhnms, and looking upon them with delight, I fell to imitate their gait and gesture, which is now grown into a habit; and my friends often tell me in a blunt way, that I trot like a horse; which, however, I take for a great compliment. Neither shall I disown, that in speaking I am apt to fall into the voice and manner of the Houyhnhnms, and hear myself ridiculed on that account without the least mortification.

In the midst of this happiness, when I looked upon myself to be fully settled for life, my master sent for me one morning a little earlier than his usual hour. I observed by his countenance that he was in some perplexity, and at a loss how to begin what he had to speak. After a short silence, he told me, he did not know how I would take what he was going to say; that, in the last general assembly, when the affair of the Yahoos was entered upon, the representatives had taken offense at his keeping a Yahoo (meaning myself) in his family more like a Houyhnhnm than a brute animal. That he was known frequently to converse with me, as if he could receive some advantage of pleasure in my company; that such a practice was not agreeable to reason or nature, or a thing ever heard of before among them. The assembly did therefore exhort him, either to employ me like the rest of my species, or command me to swim back to the place from whence I came. That the first of these expedients was utterly rejected by all the Houyhnhnms who had ever seen me at his house or their own; for, they alleged, that because I had some rudiments of reason, added to the natural pravity[7] of those animals, it was to be feared, I might be able to seduce them into the woody and mountainous parts of the country, and bring them in troops by night to destroy the Houyhnhnms' cattle, as being naturally of the ravenous kind, and averse from labor.

My master added that he was daily pressed by the Houyhnhnms of the neighborhood to have the assembly's exhortation executed, which he could not put off much longer. He doubted[8] it would be impossible for me to swim to another country; and therefore wished I would contrive some sort of vehicle resembling those I had described to him, that might carry me on the sea; in which work I should have the assistance of his own servants, as well as those of his neighbors. He concluded that for his own part he could have been content to keep me in his service as long as I lived; because he found I had cured myself of some bad habits and dispositions, by endeavoring, as far as my inferior nature was capable, to imitate the Houyhnhnms.

I should here observe to the reader, that a decree of the general assembly in this country is expressed by the word *hnhloayn*, which signifies an exhortation, as near as I can render it; for they have no conception how a rational creature can be compelled, but only advised, or exhorted; because no person can disobey reason without giving up his claim to be a rational creature.

7. Corruption.   8. Feared.

I was struck with the utmost grief and despair at my master's discourse; and being unable to support the agonies I was under, I fell into a swoon at his feet; when I came to myself, he told me that he concluded I had been dead (for these people are subject to no such imbecilities of nature). I answered, in a faint voice, that death would have been too great an happiness; that although I could not blame the assembly's exhortation, or the urgency of his friends; yet in my weak and corrupt judgment, I thought it might consist with reason to have been less rigorous. That I could not swim a league, and probably the nearest land to theirs might be distant above an hundred; that many materials, necessary for making a small vessel to carry me off, were wholly wanting in this country, which, however, I would attempt in obedience and gratitude to his honor, although I concluded the thing to be impossible, and therefore looked on myself as already devoted[9] to destruction. That the certain prospect of an unnatural death was the least of my evils; for, supposing I should escape with life by some strange adventure, how could I think with temper[1] of passing my days among Yahoos, and relapsing into my old corruptions, for want of examples to lead and keep me within the paths of virtue. That I knew too well upon what solid reasons all the determinations of the wise Houyhnhnms were founded, not to be shaken by arguments of mine, a miserable Yahoo; and therefore after presenting him with my humble thanks for the offer of his servants' assistance in making a vessel, and desiring a reasonable time for so difficult a work, I told him I would endeavor to preserve a wretched being; and, if ever I returned to England, was not without hopes of being useful to my own species by celebrating the praises of the renowned Houyhnhnms, and proposing their virtues to the imitation of mankind.

My master in a few words made me a very gracious reply, allowed me the space of two months to finish my boat, and ordered the sorrel nag, my fellow servant (for so at this distance I may presume to call him), to follow my instructions, because I told my master that his help would be sufficient, and I knew he had a tenderness for me.

In his company my first business was to go to that part of the coast where my rebellious crew had ordered me to be set on shore. I got upon a height, and looking on every side into the sea, fancied I saw a small island towards the northeast; I took out my pocket glass, and could then clearly distinguish it about five leagues off, as I computed; but it appeared to the sorrel nag to be only a blue cloud; for, as he had no conception of any country besides his own, so he could not be as expert in distinguishing remote objects at sea, as we who so much converse in that element.

After I had discovered this island, I considered no farther; but resolved, it should, if possible, be the first place of my banishment, leaving the consequence to fortune.

I returned home, and consulting with the sorrel nag, we went into a copse at some distance, where I with my knive, and he with a sharp flint fastened very artificially,[2] after their manner, to a wooden handle, cut down several oak wattles about the thickness of a walking staff, and some larger pieces. But I shall not trouble the reader with a particular description of my own mechanics; let it suffice to say, that in six weeks time, with the help of the sorrel nag,

9. Doomed.
1. Equanimity.
2. Artfully.

who performed the parts that required most labor, I finished a sort of Indian canoe; but much larger, covering it with the skins of Yahoos, well stitched together, with hempen threads of my own making. My sail was likewise composed of the skins of the same animal; but I made use of the youngest I could get, the older being too tough and thick; and I likewise provided myself with four paddles. I laid in a stock of boiled flesh, of rabbits and fowls; and took with me two vessels, one filled with milk, and the other with water.

I tried my canoe in a large pond near my master's house, and then corrected in it what was amiss, stopping all the chinks with Yahoo's tallow, till I found it staunch, and able to bear me and my freight. And when it was as complete as I could possibly make it, I had it drawn on a carriage very gently by Yahoos, to the seaside, under the conduct of the sorrel nag and another servant.

When all was ready, and the day came for my departure, I took leave of my master and lady, and the whole family, my eyes flowing with tears and my heart quite sunk with grief. But his honor, out of curiosity, and perhaps (if I may speak it without vanity) partly out of kindness, was determined to see me in my canoe; and got several of his neighboring friends to accompany him. I was forced to wait above an hour for the tide, and then observing the wind very fortunately bearing towards the island to which I intended to steer my course, I took a second leave of my master; but as I was going to prostrate myself to kiss his hoof, he did me the honor to raise it gently to my mouth. I am not ignorant how much I have been censured for mentioning this last particular. Detractors are pleased to think it improbable that so illustrious a person should descend to give so great a mark of distinction to a creature so inferior as I. Neither have I forgot how apt some travelers are to boast of extraordinary favors they have received. But, if these censurers were better acquainted with the noble and courteous disposition of the Houyhnhnms, they would soon change their opinion. I paid my respects to the rest of the Houyhnhnms in his honor's company; then getting into my canoe, I pushed off from shore.

CHAPTER 11. *The Author's dangerous voyage. He arrives at New Holland, hoping to settle there. Is wounded with an arrow by one of the natives. Is seized and carried by force into a Portuguese ship. The great civilities of the Captain. The Author arrives at England.*

I began this desperate voyage on February 15, 1714 / 5,[3] at 9 o'clock in the morning. The wind was very favorable; however, I made use at first only of my paddles; but considering I should soon be weary, and that the wind might probably chop about, I ventured to set up my little sail, and thus, with the help of the tide, I went at the rate of a league and a half an hour, as near as I could guess. My master and his friends continued on the shore, till I was almost out of sight; and I often heard the sorrel nag (who always loved me) crying out, "*Hnuy illa nyha maiah Yahoo*" ("Take care of thyself, gentle Yahoo").

My design was, if possible, to discover some small island uninhabited, yet sufficient by my labor to furnish me with necessaries of life, which I would have thought a greater happiness than to be first minister in the politest court

3. I.e., 1715, by modern dating. The year began on March 25.

of Europe, so horrible was the idea I conceived of returning to live in the society and under the government of Yahoos. For in such a solitude as I desired, I could at least enjoy my own thoughts, and reflect with delight on the virtues of those inimitable Houyhnhnms, without any opportunity of degenerating into the vices and corruptions of my own species.

The reader may remember what I related when my crew conspired against me, and confined me to my cabin, how I continued there several weeks, without knowing what course we took; and when I was put ashore in the longboat, how the sailors told me with oaths, whether true or false, that they knew not in what part of the world we were. However, I did then believe us to be about 10 degrees southward of the Cape of Good Hope, or about 45 degrees southern latitude, as I gathered from some general words I overheard among them, being I supposed to the southeast in their intended voyage to Madagascar. And although this were but little better than conjecture, yet I resolved to steer my course eastward, hoping to reach the southwest coast of New Holland, and perhaps some such island as I desired, lying westward of it. The wind was full west, and by six in the evening I computed I had gone eastward at least eighteen leagues; when I spied a very small island about half a league off, which I soon reached. It was nothing but a rock with one creek, naturally arched by the force of tempests. Here I put in my canoe, and climbing a part of the rock, I could plainly discover land to the east, extending from south to north. I lay all night in my canoe; and repeating my voyage early in the morning, I arrived in seven hours to the southeast point of New Holland. This confirmed me in the opinion I have long entertained, that the maps and charts place this country at least three degrees more to the east than it really is; which thought I communicated many years ago to my worthy friend Mr. Herman Moll,[4] and gave him my reasons for it, although he hath rather chosen to follow other authors.

I saw no inhabitants in the place where I landed; and being unarmed, I was afraid of venturing far into the country. I found some shellfish on the shore, and eat them raw, not daring to kindle a fire, for fear of being discovered by the natives. I continued three days feeding on oysters and limpets, to save my own provisions; and I fortunately found a brook of excellent water, which gave me great relief.

On the fourth day, venturing out early a little too far, I saw twenty or thirty natives upon a height, not above five hundred yards from me. They were stark naked, men, women, and children round a fire, as I could discover by the smoke. One of them spied me, and gave notice to the rest; five of them advanced towards me, leaving the women and children at the fire. I made what haste I could to the shore, and getting into my canoe, shoved off; the savages observing me retreat, ran after me; and before I could get far enough into the sea, discharged an arrow, which wounded me deeply on the inside of my left knee. (I shall carry the mark to my grave.) I apprehended the arrow might be poisoned; and paddling out of the reach of their darts (being a calm day) I made a shift to suck the wound, and dress it as well as I could.

I was at a loss what to do, for I durst not return to the same landing place, but stood to the north, and was forced to paddle; for the wind, although very gentle, was against me, blowing northwest. As I was looking about for a secure

4. A famous contemporary map maker.

landing place, I saw a sail to the north northeast, which appearing every minute more visible, I was in some doubt whether I should wait for them or no; but at last my detestation of the Yahoo race prevailed; and turning my canoe, I sailed and paddled together to the south, and got into the same creek from whence I set out in the morning, choosing rather to trust myself among these barbarians than live with European Yahoos. I drew up my canoe as close as I could to the shore, and hid myself behind a stone by the little brook, which, as I have already said, was excellent water.

The ship came within half a league of this creek, and sent out her longboat with vessels to take in fresh water (for the place it seems was very well known), but I did not observe it until the boat was almost on shore; and it was too late to seek another hiding place. The seamen at their landing observed my canoe, and rummaging it all over, easily conjectured that the owner could not be far off. Four of them well armed searched every cranny and lurking hole, till at last they found me flat on my face behind the stone. They gazed a while in admiration at my strange uncouth dress; my coat made of skins, my wooden-soled shoes, and my furred stockings; from whence, however, they concluded I was not a native of the place, who all go naked. One of the seamen in Portuguese bid me rise, and asked who I was. I understood that language very well, and getting upon my feet, said I was a poor Yahoo, banished from the Houyhnhnms, and desired they would please to let me depart. They admired to hear me answer them in their own tongue, and saw by my complexion I must be an European; but were at a loss to know what I meant by Yahoos and Houyhnhnms, and at the same time fell a laughing at my strange tone in speaking, which resembled the neighing of a horse. I trembled all the while betwixt fear and hatred; I again desired leave to depart, and was gently moving to my canoe; but they laid hold on me, desiring to know what country I was of? whence I came? with many other questions. I told them I was born in England, from whence I came about five years ago, and then their country and ours was at peace. I therefore hoped they would not treat me as an enemy, since I meant them no harm, but was a poor Yahoo, seeking some desolate place where to pass the remainder of his unfortunate life.

When they began to talk, I thought I never heard or saw any thing so unnatural; for it appeared to me as monstrous as if a dog or a cow should speak in England, or a Yahoo in Houyhnhnmland. The honest Portuguese were equally amazed at my strange dress, and the odd manner of delivering my words, which however they understood very well. They spoke to me with great humanity, and said they were sure their Captain would carry me *gratis* to Lisbon, from whence I might return to my own country; that two of the seamen would go back to the ship, to inform the Captain of what they had seen, and receive his orders; in the meantime, unless I would give my solemn oath not to fly, they would secure me by force. I thought it best to comply with their proposal. They were very curious to know my story, but I gave them very little satisfaction; and they all conjectured, that my misfortunes had impaired my reason. In two hours the boat, which went laden with vessels of water, returned with the Captain's commands to fetch me on board. I fell on my knees to preserve my liberty; but all was in vain, and the men having tied me with cords, heaved me into the boat, from whence I was taken into the ship, and from thence into the Captain's cabin.

His name was Pedro de Mendez; he was a very courteous and generous person; he entreated me to give some account of myself, and desired to know what I would eat or drink; said I should be used as well as himself, and spoke so many obliging things, that I wondered to find such civilities from a Yahoo. However, I remained silent and sullen; I was ready to faint at the very smell of him and his men. At last I desired something to eat out of my own canoe; but he ordered me a chicken and some excellent wine, and then directed that I should be put to bed in a very clean cabin. I would not undress myself, but lay on the bedclothes; and in half an hour stole out, when I thought the crew was at dinner; and getting to the side of the ship, was going to leap into the sea, and swim for my life, rather than continue among Yahoos. But one of the seamen prevented me, and having informed the Captain, I was chained to my cabin.

After dinner Don Pedro came to me, and desired to know my reason for so desperate an attempt; assured me he only meant to do me all the service he was able; and spoke so very movingly, that at last I descended to treat him like an animal which had some little portion of reason. I gave him a very short relation of my voyage; of the conspiracy against me by my own men; of the country where they set me on shore, and of my five years residence there. All which he looked upon as if it were a dream or a vision; whereat I took great offense; for I had quite forgot the faculty of lying, so peculiar to Yahoos in all countries where they preside, and consequently the disposition of suspecting truth in others of their own species. I asked him whether it were the custom of his country to *say the thing that was not?* I assured him I had almost forgot what he meant by falsehood; and if I had lived a thousand years in Houylnhnhnmland, I should never have heard a lie from the meanest servant. That I was altogether indifferent whether he believed me or no; but however, in return for his favors, I would give so much allowance to the corruption of his nature, as to answer any objection he would please to make; and he might easily discover the truth.

The Captain, a wise man, after many endeavors to catch me tripping in some part of my story, at last began to have a better opinion of my veracity. But he added that since I professed so inviolable an attachment to truth, I must give him my word of honor to bear him company in this voyage without attempting anything against my life; or else he would continue me a prisoner till we arrived at Lisbon. I gave him the promise he required; but at the same time protested that I would suffer the greatest hardships rather than return to live among Yahoos.

Our voyage passed without any considerable accident. In gratitude to the Captain I sometimes sat with him at his earnest request, and strove to conceal my antipathy against humankind, although it often broke out; which he suffered to pass without observation. But the greatest part of the day, I confined myself to my cabin, to avoid seeing any of the crew. The Captain had often entreated me to strip myself of my savage dress, and offered to lend me the best suit of clothes he had. This I would not be prevailed on to accept, abhorring to cover myself with anything that had been on the back of a Yahoo. I only desired he would lend me two clean shirts, which having been washed since he wore them, I believed would not so much defile me. These I changed every second day, and washed them myself.

We arrived at Lisbon, Nov. 5, 1715. At our landing, the Captain forced me to cover myself with his cloak, to prevent the rabble from crowding about me.

I was conveyed to his own house; and at my earnest request, he led me up to the highest room backwards.[5] I conjured him to conceal from all persons what I had told him of the Houyhnhnms; because the least hint of such a story would not only draw numbers of people to see me, but probably put me in danger of being imprisoned, or burned by the Inquisition. The Captain persuaded me to accept a suit of clothes newly made; but I would not suffer the tailor to take my measure; however, Don Pedro being almost of my size, they fitted me well enough. He accoutered me with other necessaries, all new, which I aired for twenty-four hours before I would use them.

The Captain had no wife, nor above three servants, none of which were suffered to attend at meals; and his whole deportment was so obliging, added to very good human understanding, that I really began to tolerate his company. He gained so far upon me, that I ventured to look out of the back window. By degrees I was brought into another room, from whence I peeped into the street, but drew my head back in a fright. In a week's time he seduced me down to the door. I found my terror gradually lessened, but my hatred and contempt seemed to increase. I was at last bold enough to walk the street in his company, but kept my nose well stopped with rue, or sometimes with tobacco.

In ten days, Don Pedro, to whom I had given some account of my domestic affairs, put it upon me as a point of honor and conscience that I ought to return to my native country, and live at home with my wife and children. He told me there was an English ship in the port just ready to sail, and he would furnish me with all things necessary. It would be tedious to repeat his arguments, and my contradictions. He said it was altogether impossible to find such a solitary island as I had desired to live in; but I might command in my own house, and pass my time in a manner as recluse as I pleased.

I complied at last, finding I could not do better. I left Lisbon the 24th day of November, in an English merchantman, but who was the Master I never inquired. Don Pedro accompanied me to the ship, and lent me twenty pounds. He took kind leave of me, and embraced me at parting; which I bore as well as I could. During this last voyage I had no commerce with the Master, or any of his men; but pretending I was sick kept close in my cabin. On the fifth of December, 1715, we cast anchor in the Downs about nine in the morning, and at three in the afternoon I got safe to my house at Redriff.

My wife and family received me with great surprise and joy, because they concluded me certainly dead; but I must freely confess, the sight of them filled me only with hatred, disgust, and contempt; and the more, by reflecting on the near alliance I had to them. For although since my unfortunate exile from the Houyhnhnm country, I had compelled myself to tolerate the sight of Yahoos, and to converse with Don Pedro de Mendez; yet my memory and imaginations were perpetually filled with the virtues and ideas of those exalted Houyhnhnms. And when I began to consider that by copulating with one of the Yahoo species, I had become a parent of more, it struck me with the utmost shame, confusion, and horror.

As soon as I entered the house, my wife took me in her arms, and kissed me; at which, having not been used to the touch of that odious animal for so many years, I fell in a swoon for almost an hour. At the time I am writing, it is

5. At the rear.

five years since my last return to England. During the first year I could not
endure my wife or children in my presence, the very smell of them was intolerable; much less could I suffer them to eat in the same room. To this hour they
dare not presume to touch my bread, or drink out of the same cup; neither
was I ever able to let one of them take me by the hand. The first money I laid
out was to buy two young stone-horses,[6] which I keep in a good stable, and
next to them the groom is my greatest favorite; for I feel my spirits revived by
the smell he contracts in the stable. My horses understand me tolerably well;
I converse with them at least four hours every day. They are strangers to bridle
or saddle; they live in great amity with me, and friendship to each other.

CHAPTER 12. *The Author's veracity. His design in publishing this work. His
censure of those travelers who swerve from the truth. The Author clears himself
from any sinister ends in writing. His native country commended. The right of
the crown to those countries described by the Author is justified. The difficulty
of conquering them. The Author takes his last leave of the reader; proposeth his
manner of living for the future; gives good advice, and concludeth.*

Thus gentle reader, I have given thee a faithful history of my travels for
sixteen years, and above seven months; wherein I have not been so studious
of ornament as of truth. I could perhaps like others have astonished thee with
strange improbable tales; but I rather chose to relate plain matter of fact in the
simplest manner and style; because my principal design was to inform, and
not to amuse thee.

It is easy for us who travel into remote countries, which are seldom visited
by Englishmen or other Europeans, to form descriptions of wonderful animals
both at sea and land. Whereas a traveler's chief aim should be to make men
wiser and better, and to improve their minds by the bad as well as good example of what they deliver concerning foreign places.

I could heartily wish a law were enacted, that every traveler, before he were
permitted to publish his voyages, should be obliged to make oath before the
Lord High Chancellor that all he intended to print was absolutely true to the
best of his knowledge; for then the world would no longer be deceived as it
usually is, while some writers, to make their works pass the better upon the
public, impose the grossest falsities on the unwary reader. I have perused several books of travels with great delight in my younger days; but, having since
gone over most parts of the globe, and been able to contradict many fabulous
accounts from my own observation, it hath given me a great disgust against
this part of reading, and some indignation to see the credulity of mankind so
impudently abused. Therefore, since my acquaintance were pleased to think
my poor endeavors might not be unacceptable to my country, I imposed on
myself as a maxim, never to be swerved from, that I would *strictly adhere to
truth*; neither indeed can I be ever under the least temptation to vary from it,
while I retain in my mind the lectures and example of my noble master, and
the other illustrious Houyhnhnms, of whom I had so long the honor to be an
humble hearer.

6. Stallions.

——Nec si miserum Fortuna Sinonem
Finxit, vanum etiam, mendacemque improba finget.[7]

I know very well how little reputation is to be got by writings which require neither genius nor learning, nor indeed any other talent, except a good memory, or an exact *Journal*. I know likewise, that writers of travels, like dictionary-makers, are sunk into oblivion by the weight and bulk of those who come last, and therefore lie uppermost. And it is highly probable that such travelers who shall hereafter visit the countries described in this work of mine, may be detecting my errors (if there be any) and adding many new discoveries of their own, jostle me out of vogue, and stand in my place, making the world forget that ever I was an author. This indeed would be too great a mortification if I wrote for fame; but, as my sole intention was the PUBLIC GOOD, I cannot be altogether disappointed. For, who can read the virtues I have mentioned in the glorious Houyhnhnms, without being ashamed of his own vices, when he considers himself as the reasoning, governing animal of his country? I shall say nothing of those remote nations where Yahoos preside; amongst which the least corrupted are the Brobdingnagians, whose wise maxims in morality and government it would be our happiness to observe. But I forbear descanting further, and rather leave the judicious reader to his own remarks and applications.

I am not a little pleased that this work of mine can possibly meet with no censurers; for what objections can be made against a writer who relates only plain facts that happened in such distant countries, where we have not the least interest with respect either to trade or negotiations? I have carefully avoided every fault with which common writers of travels are often too justly charged. Besides, I meddle not the least with any party, but write without passion, prejudice, or ill-will against any man or number of men whatsoever. I write for the noblest end, to inform and instruct mankind, over whom I may, without breach of modesty, pretend to some superiority, from the advantages I received by conversing so long among the most accomplished Houyhnhnms. I write without any view towards profit or praise. I never suffer a word to pass that may look like a reflection, or possibly give the least offense even to those who are most ready to take it. So that, I hope, I may with justice pronounce myself an Author perfectly blameless; against whom the tribes of answerers, considerers, observers, reflectors, detecters, remarkers will never be able to find matter for exercising their talents.

I confess it was whispered to me that I was bound in duty as a subject of England, to have given in a memorial[8] to a secretary of state, at my first coming over; because, whatever lands are discovered by a subject, belong to the Crown. But I doubt whether our conquests in the countries I treat of would be as easy as those of Ferdinando Cortez over the naked Americans. The Lilliputians, I think, are hardly worth the charge of a fleet and army to reduce them; and I question whether it might be prudent or safe to attempt the Brobdingnagians; or, whether an English army would be much at their ease with the Flying Island over their heads. The Houyhnhnms, indeed, appear not to be so well prepared for war, a science to which they are perfect strangers, and

---

7. Virgil, "nor if Fortune had moulded Sinon for misery, will she also in spite mould him as false and lying" (*Aeneid* 2.79–80).

8. Statement of facts for government use.

especially against missive weapons. However, supposing myself to be a minister of state, I could never give my advice for invading them. Their prudence, unanimity, unacquaintedness with fear, and their love of their country would amply supply all defects in the military art. Imagine twenty thousand of them breaking into the midst of an European army, confounding the ranks, overturning the carriages, battering the warriors' faces into mummy, by terrible yerks[9] from their hinder hoofs: for they would well deserve the character given to Augustus, *Recalcitrat undique tutus*.[1] But instead of proposals for conquering that magnanimous nation, I rather wish they were in a capacity or disposition to send a sufficient number of their inhabitants for civilizing Europe; by teaching us the first principles of Honor, Justice, Truth, Temperance, public Spirit, Fortitude, Chastity, Friendship, Benevolence, and Fidelity. The names of all which virtues are still retained among us in most languages, and are to be met with in modern as well as ancient authors, which I am able to assert from my own small reading.

But I had another reason which made me less forward to enlarge his majesty's dominions by my discoveries: to say the truth, I had conceived a few scruples with relation to the distributive justice of princes upon those occasions. For instance, a crew of pirates are driven by a storm they know not whither; at length a boy discovers land from the topmast; they go on shore to rob and plunder; they see an harmless people, are entertained with kindness, they give the country a new name, they take formal possession of it for the king, they set up a rotten plank or a stone for a memorial, they murder two or three dozen of the natives, bring away a couple more by force for a sample, return home, and get their pardon. Here commences a new dominion acquired with a title by Divine Right. Ships are sent with the first opportunity; the natives driven out or destroyed, their princes tortured to discover their gold; a free license given to all acts of inhumanity and lust; the earth reeking with the blood of its inhabitants: and this execrable crew of butchers employed in so pious an expedition is a *modern colony* sent to convert and civilize an idolatrous and barbarous people.

But this description, I confess, doth by no means affect the British nation, who may be an example to the whole world for their wisdom, care, and justice in planting colonies; their liberal endowments for the advancement of religion and learning; their choice of devout and able pastors to propagate Christianity; their caution in stocking their provinces with people of sober lives and conversations from this the Mother Kingdom; their strict regard to the distribution of justice, in supplying the civil administration through all their colonies with officers of the greatest abilities, utter strangers to corruption: and to crown all, by sending the most vigilant and virtuous governors, who have no other views than the happiness of the people over whom they preside, and the honor of the king their master.

But, as those countries which I have described do not appear to have any desire of being conquered, and enslaved, murdered, or driven out by colonies, nor abound either in gold, silver, sugar, or tobacco, I did humbly conceive they were by no means proper objects of our zeal, our valor, or our interest.

---

9. Kicks. "Mummy": pulp.
1. Horace, "he kicks backward, at every point on his

guard" (*Satires* 2.1.20).

However, if those whom it may concern, think fit to be of another opinion, I am ready to depose, when I shall be lawfully called, that no European did ever visit these countries before me. I mean, if the inhabitants ought to be believed.

But, as to the formality of taking possession in my sovereign's name, it never came once into my thoughts; and if it had, yet as my affairs then stood, I should perhaps in point of prudence and self-preservation have put it off to a better opportunity.

Having thus answered the only objection that can be raised against me as a traveler, I here take a final leave of my courteous readers, and return to enjoy my own speculations in my little garden at Redriff; to apply those excellent lessons of virtue which I learned among the Houyhnhnms; to instruct the Yahoos of my own family as far as I shall find them docible animals; to behold my figure often in a glass, and thus if possible habituate myself by time to tolerate the sight of a human creature; to lament the brutality of Houyhnhnms in my own country, but always treat their persons with respect, for the sake of my noble master, his family, his friends, and the whole Houyhnhnm race, whom these of ours have the honor to resemble in all their lineaments, however their intellectuals came to degenerate.

I began last week to permit my wife to sit at dinner with me, at the farthest end of a long table; and to answer (but with the utmost brevity) the few questions I ask her. Yet the smell of a Yahoo continuing very offensive, I always keep my nose well stopped with rue, lavender, or tobacco leaves. And although it be hard for a man late in life to remove old habits, I am not altogether out of hopes in some time to suffer a neighbor Yahoo in my company, without the apprehensions I am yet under of his teeth or his claws.

My reconcilement to the Yahoo kind in general might not be so difficult, if they would be content with those vices and follies only which nature hath entitled them to. I am not in the least provoked at the sight of a lawyer, a pickpocket, a colonel, a fool, a lord, a gamester, a politician, a whoremonger, a physician, an evidence,[2] a suborner, an attorney, a traitor, or the like: this is all according to the due course of things. But when I behold a lump of deformity, and diseases both in body and mind, smitten with *pride*, it immediately breaks all the measures of my patience; neither shall I be ever able to comprehend how such an animal and such a vice could tally together. The wise and virtuous Houyhnhnms, who abound in all excellencies that can adorn a rational creature, have no name for this vice in their language, which hath no terms to express anything that is evil, except those whereby they describe the detestable qualities of their Yahoos, among which they were not able to distinguish this of pride, for want of thoroughly understanding human nature, as it showeth itself in other countries, where that animal presides. But I, who had more experience, could plainly observe some rudiments of it among the wild Yahoos.

But the Houyhnhnms, who live under the government of reason, are no more proud of the good qualities they possess, than I should be for not wanting a leg or an arm, which no man in his wits would boast of, although he must be miserable without them. I dwell the longer upon this subject from the

---

2. Witness.

desire I have to make the society of an English Yahoo by any means not insupportable; and therefore I here entreat those who have any tincture of this absurd vice, that they will not presume to appear in my sight.

1726, 1735

A Modest Proposal[1]

FOR PREVENTING THE CHILDREN OF POOR PEOPLE IN IRELAND FROM BEING A BURDEN TO THEIR PARENTS OR COUNTRY, AND FOR MAKING THEM BENEFICIAL TO THE PUBLIC

It is a melancholy object to those who walk through this great town[2] or travel in the country, when they see the streets, the roads, and cabin doors, crowded with beggars of the female sex, followed by three, four, or six children, all in rags and importuning every passenger for an alms. These mothers, instead of being able to work for their honest livelihood, are forced to employ all their time in strolling to beg sustenance for their helpless infants, who, as they grow up, either turn thieves for want of work, or leave their dear native country to fight for the Pretender in Spain, or sell themselves to the Barbadoes.[3]

I think it is agreed by all parties that this prodigious number of children in the arms, or on the backs, or at the heels of their mothers, and frequently of their fathers, is in the present deplorable state of the kingdom a very great additional grievance; and therefore whoever could find out a fair, cheap, and easy method of making these children sound, useful members of the commonwealth would deserve so well of the public as to have his statue set up for a preserver of the nation.

But my intention is very far from being confined to provide only for the children of professed beggars; it is of a much greater extent, and shall take in the whole number of infants at a certain age who are born of parents in effect as little able to support them as those who demand our charity in the streets.

As to my own part, having turned my thoughts for many years upon this important subject, and maturely weighed the several schemes of other projectors,[4] I have always found them grossly mistaken in their computation. It is true, a child just dropped from its dam may be supported by her milk for a solar year, with little other nourishment; at most not above the value of two

---

1. *A Modest Proposal* is an example of Swift's favorite satiric devices used with superb effect. Irony (from the deceptive adjective *modest* in the title to the very last sentence) pervades the piece. A rigorous logic deduces ghastly arguments from a shocking premise so quietly assumed that readers assent before they are aware of what that assent implies. Parody, at which Swift is adept, allows him to glance sardonically at the by then familiar figure of the benevolent humanitarian (forerunner of the modern sociologist, social worker, and economic planner) concerned to correct a social evil by means of a theoretically conceived plan. The proposer, as naive as he is apparently logical and kindly, ignores and therefore emphasizes for the reader the enormity of his plan. The whole is an elaboration of a rather trite metaphor: "The English are devouring the Irish." But there is nothing trite about the pamphlet, which expresses in Swift's most controlled style his pity for the oppressed, ignorant, populous, and hungry Catholic peasants of Ireland and his anger at the rapacious English absentee landlords, who were bleeding the country white with the silent approbation of Parliament, ministers, and the crown.
2. Dublin.
3. James Francis Edward Stuart (1688–1766), the son of James II, was claimant ("Pretender") to the throne of England from which the Glorious Revolution had barred his succession. Catholic Ireland was loyal to him, and Irishmen joined him in his exile on the Continent. Because of the poverty in Ireland, many Irishmen emigrated to the West Indies and other British colonies in America; they paid their passage by binding themselves to work for a stated period for one of the planters.
4. Devisers of schemes.

shillings, which the mother may certainly get, or the value in scraps, by her lawful occupation of begging; and it is exactly at one year old that I propose to provide for them in such a manner as instead of being a charge upon their parents or the parish, or wanting food and raiment for the rest of their lives, they shall on the contrary contribute to the feeding, and partly to the clothing, of many thousands.

There is likewise another great advantage in my scheme, that it will prevent those voluntary abortions, and that horrid practice of women murdering their bastard children, alas, too frequent among us, sacrificing the poor innocent babes, I doubt, more to avoid the expense than the shame, which would move tears and pity in the most savage and inhuman breast.

The number of souls in this kingdom[5] being usually reckoned one million and a half, of these I calculate there may be about two hundred thousand couple whose wives are breeders; from which number I subtract thirty thousand couples who are able to maintain their own children, although I apprehend there cannot be so many under the present distresses of the kingdom; but this being granted, there will remain an hundred and seventy thousand breeders. I again subtract fifty thousand for those women who miscarry, or whose children die by accident or disease within the year. There only remain an hundred and twenty thousand children of poor parents annually born. The question therefore is, how this number shall be reared and provided for, which, as I have already said, under the present situation of affairs, is utterly impossible by all the methods hitherto proposed. For we can neither employ them in handicraft or agriculture; we neither build houses (I mean in the country) nor cultivate land. They can very seldom pick up a livelihood by stealing till they arrive at six years old, except where they are of towardly parts;[6] although I confess they learn the rudiments much earlier, during which time they can however be looked upon only as probationers, as I have been informed by a principal gentleman in the county of Cavan, who protested to me that he never knew above one or two instances under the ages of six, even in a part of the kingdom so renowned for the quickest proficiency in that art.

I am assured by our merchants that a boy or a girl before twelve years old is no salable commodity; and even when they come to this age they will not yield above three pounds, or three pounds and half a crown at most on the Exchange; which cannot turn to account either to the parents or the kingdom, the charge of nutriment and rags having been at least four times that value.

I shall now therefore humbly propose my own thoughts, which I hope will not be liable to the least objection.

I have been assured by a very knowing American of my acquaintance in London, that a young healthy child well nursed is at a year old a most delicious, nourishing, and wholesome food, whether stewed, roasted, baked, or boiled; and I make no doubt that it will equally serve in a fricassee or a ragout.[7]

I do therefore humbly offer it to public consideration that of the hundred and twenty thousand children, already computed, twenty thousand may be reserved for breed, whereof only one fourth part to be males, which is more than we allow to sheep, black cattle, or swine; and my reason is that these children are seldom the fruits of marriage, a circumstance not much regarded

5. Ireland.
6. Promising abilities.

7. A highly seasoned meat stew.

by our savages, therefore one male will be sufficient to serve four females. That the remaining hundred thousand may at a year old be offered in sale to the persons of quality and fortune through the kingdom, always advising the mother to let them suck plentifully in the last month, so as to render them plump and fat for a good table. A child will make two dishes at an entertainment for friends; and when the family dines alone, the fore or hind quarter will make a reasonable dish, and seasoned with a little pepper or salt will be very good boiled on the fourth day, especially in winter.

I have reckoned upon a medium that a child just born will weigh twelve pounds, and in a solar year if tolerably nursed increaseth to twenty-eight pounds.

I grant this food will be somewhat dear, and therefore very proper for landlords, who, as they have already devoured most of the parents, seem to have the best title to the children.

Infant's flesh will be in season throughout the year, but more plentiful in March, and a little before and after. For we are told by a grave author, an eminent French physician,[8] that fish being a prolific diet, there are more children born in Roman Catholic countries about nine months after Lent than at any other season; therefore, reckoning a year after Lent, the markets will be more glutted than usual, because the number of popish infants is at least three to one in this kingdom; and therefore it will have one other collateral advantage, by lessening the number of Papists among us.

I have already computed the charge of nursing a beggar's child (in which list I reckon all cottagers, laborers, and four fifths of the farmers) to be about two shillings per annum, rags included; and I believe no gentleman would repine to give ten shillings for the carcass of a good fat child, which, as I have said, will make four dishes of excellent nutritive meat, when he hath only some particular friend or his own family to dine with him. Thus the squire will learn to be a good landlord, and grow popular among the tenants; the mother will have eight shillings net profit, and be fit for the work till she produces another child.

Those who are more thrifty (as I must confess the times require) may flay the carcass; the skin of which artificially[9] dressed will make admirable gloves for ladies, and summer boots for fine gentlemen.

As to our city of Dublin, shambles[1] may be appointed for this purpose in the most convenient parts of it, and butchers we may be assured will not be wanting; although I rather recommend buying the children alive, and dressing them hot from the knife as we do roasting pigs.

A very worthy person, a true lover of his country, and whose virtues I highly esteem, was lately pleased in discoursing on this matter to offer a refinement upon my scheme. He said that many gentlemen of this kingdom, having of late destroyed their deer, he conceived that the want of venison might be well supplied by the bodies of young lads and maidens, not exceeding fourteen years of age nor under twelve, so great a number of both sexes in every county being now ready to starve for want of work and service; and these to be disposed of by their parents, if alive, or otherwise by their nearest relations. But with due deference to so excellent a friend and so deserving a patriot, I cannot

8. François Rabelais (ca. 1494–1553), a humorist and   9. Skillfully.
a satirist, by no means grave.   1. Slaughterhouses.

be altogether in his sentiments; for as to the males, my American acquaintance assured me from frequent experience that their flesh was generally tough and lean, like that of our schoolboys, by continual exercise, and their taste disagreeable; and to fatten them would not answer the charge. Then as to the females, it would, I think with humble submission, be a loss to the public, because they soon would become breeders themselves; and besides, it is not improbable that some scrupulous people might be apt to censure such a practice (although indeed very unjustly) as a little bordering upon cruelty; which I confess, hath always been with me the strongest objection against any project, how well soever intended.

But in order to justify my friend, he confessed that this expedient was put into his head by the famous Psalmanazar,[2] a native of the island Formosa, who came from thence to London above twenty years ago, and in conversation told my friend that in his country when any young person happened to be put to death, the executioner sold the carcass to persons of quality as a prime dainty; and that in his time the body of a plump girl of fifteen, who was crucified for an attempt to poison the emperor, was sold to his Imperial Majesty's prime minister of state, and other great mandarins of the court, in joints from the gibbet, at four hundred crowns. Neither indeed can I deny that if the same use were made of several plump young girls in this town, who without one single groat to their fortunes cannot stir abroad without a chair, and appear at the playhouse and assemblies in foreign fineries which they never will pay for, the kingdom would not be the worse.

Some persons of a desponding spirit are in great concern about that vast number of poor people who are aged, diseased, or maimed, and I have been desired to employ my thoughts what course may be taken to ease the nation of so grievous an encumbrance. But I am not in the least pain upon that matter, because it is very well known that they are every day dying and rotting by cold and famine, and filth and vermin, as fast as can be reasonably expected. And as to the younger laborers, they are now in almost as hopeful a condition. They cannot get work, and consequently pine away for want of nourishment to a degree that if at any time they are accidentally hired to common labor, they have not strength to perform it; and thus the country and themselves are happily delivered from the evils to come.

I have too long digressed, and therefore shall return to my subject. I think the advantages by the proposal which I have made are obvious and many, as well as of the highest importance.

For first, as I have already observed, it would greatly lessen the number of Papists, with whom we are yearly overrun, being the principal breeders of the nation as well as our most dangerous enemies; and who stay at home on purpose to deliver the kingdom to the Pretender, hoping to take their advantage by the absence of so many good Protestants, who have chosen rather to leave their country than stay at home and pay tithes against their conscience to an Episcopal curate.

Secondly, the poorer tenants will have something valuable of their own, which by law may be made liable to distress,[3] and help to pay their landlord's

2. George Psalmanazar (ca. 1679–1763), a famous impostor. A Frenchman, he imposed himself on English bishops, noblemen, and scientists as a Formosan. He wrote an entirely fictitious account of Formosa, in which he described human sacrifices and cannibalism.
3. Distraint, i.e., the seizing, through legal action, of property for the payment of debts and other obligations.

rent, their corn and cattle being already seized and money a thing unknown.

Thirdly, whereas the maintenance of an hundred thousand children, from two years old and upwards, cannot be computed at less than ten shillings a piece per annum, the nation's stock will be thereby increased fifty thousand pounds per annum, besides the profit of a new dish introduced to the tables of all gentlemen of fortune in the kingdom who have any refinement in taste. And the money will circulate among ourselves, the goods being entirely of our own growth and manufacture.

Fourthly, the constant breeders, besides the gain of eight shillings sterling per annum by the sale of their children, will be rid of the charge of maintaining them after the first year.

Fifthly, this food would likewise bring great custom to taverns, where the vintners will certainly be so prudent as to procure the best receipts for dressing it to perfection, and consequently have their houses frequented by all the fine gentlemen, who justly value themselves upon their knowledge in good eating; and a skillful cook, who understands how to oblige his guests, will contrive to make it as expensive as they please.

Sixthly, this would be a great inducement to marriage, which all wise nations have either encouraged by rewards or enforced by laws and penalties. It would increase the care and tenderness of mothers toward their children, when they were sure of a settlement for life to the poor babes, provided in some sort by the public, to their annual profit instead of expense. We should see an honest emulation among the married women, which of them could bring the fattest child to the market. Men would become as fond of their wives during the time of their pregnancy as they are now of their mares in foal, their cows in calf, or sows when they are ready to farrow; nor offer to beat or kick them (as is too frequent a practice) for fear of a miscarriage.

Many other advantages might be enumerated. For instance, the addition of some thousand carcasses in our exportation of barreled beef, the propagation of swine's flesh, and improvement in the art of making good bacon, so much wanted among us by the great destruction of pigs, too frequent at our tables, which are no way comparable in taste or magnificence to a well-grown, fat, yearling child, which roasted whole will make a considerable figure at a lord mayor's feast or any other public entertainment. But this and many others I omit, being studious of brevity.

Supposing that one thousand families in this city would be constant customers for infants' flesh, besides others who might have it at merry meetings, particularly weddings and christenings, I compute that Dublin would take off annually about twenty thousand carcasses, and the rest of the kingdom (where probably they will be sold somewhat cheaper) the remaining eighty thousand.

I can think of no one objection that will probably be raised against this proposal, unless it should be urged that the number of people will be thereby much lessened in the kingdom. This I freely own, and it was indeed one principal design in offering it to the world. I desire the reader will observe, that I calculate my remedy for this one individual kingdom of Ireland and for no other that ever was, is, or I think ever can be upon earth. Therefore let no man talk to me of other expedients: of taxing our absentees at five shillings a pound: of using neither clothes nor household furniture except what is of our own growth and manufacture: of utterly rejecting the materials and instruments that promote foreign luxury: of curing the expensiveness of pride, vanity, idleness, and gaming in our women: of introducing a vein of parsimony, prudence, and temperance: of learning to love our country, in the want of which we differ even from Laplanders and the inhabitants of Topinamboo:[4] of quitting our animosities and factions, nor acting any longer like the Jews, who were murdering one another at the very moment their city was taken:[5] of being a little cautious not to sell our country and conscience for nothing: of teaching landlords to have at least one degree of mercy toward their tenants: lastly, of putting a spirit of honesty, industry, and skill into our shopkeepers; who, if a resolution could now be taken to buy only our native goods, would immediately unite to cheat and exact upon us in the price, the measure, and the goodness, nor could ever yet be brought to make one fair proposal of just dealing, though often and earnestly invited to it.[6]

Therefore I repeat, let no man talk to me of these and the like expedients, till he hath at least some glimpse of hope that there will ever be some hearty and sincere attempt to put them in practice.

But as to myself, having been wearied out for many years with offering vain, idle, visionary thoughts, and at length utterly despairing of success, I fortunately fell upon this proposal, which, as it is wholly new, so it hath something solid and real, of no expense and little trouble, full in our own power, and whereby we can incur no danger in disobliging England. For this kind of commodity will not bear exportation, the flesh being of too tender a consistence to admit a long continuance in salt, although perhaps I could name a country which would be glad to eat up our whole nation without it.[7]

After all, I am not so violently bent upon my own opinion as to reject any offer proposed by wise men, which shall be found equally innocent, cheap, easy, and effectual. But before something of that kind shall be advanced in contradiction to my scheme, and offering a better, I desire the author or authors will be pleased maturely to consider two points. First, as things now stand, how they will be able to find food and raiment for an hundred thousand useless mouths and backs. And secondly, there being a round million of creatures in human figure throughout this kingdom, whose sole subsistence put into a common stock would leave them in debt two millions of pounds sterling, adding those who are beggars by profession to the bulk of farmers, cottagers, and laborers, with their wives and children who are beggars in effect; I desire those politicians who dislike my overture, and may perhaps be so bold to attempt an answer, that they will first ask the parents of these mortals whether they would not at this day think it a great happiness to have been sold for food at a year old in the manner I prescribe, and thereby have avoided such a perpetual sense of misfortunes as they have since gone through by the oppression of landlords, the impossibility of paying rent without money or trade, the want of common sustenance, with neither house nor clothes to cover them from the inclemencies of the weather, and the most inevitable prospect of entailing the like or greater miseries upon their breed forever.

I profess, in the sincerity of my heart, that I have not the least personal

---

4. I.e., even Laplanders love their frozen, infertile country and the savage tribes of Brazil love their jungle more than the Anglo-Irish love Ireland.
5. During the siege of Jerusalem by Roman Emperor Titus, who captured and destroyed the city in A.D. 70, the city was torn by bloody fights between factions of

fanatics.
6. Swift himself had made all these proposals in various pamphlets. In editions printed during his lifetime the various proposals were italicized to indicate that Swift is no longer being ironic.
7. I.e., England.

interest in endeavoring to promote this necessary work, having no other motive than the public good of my country, by advancing our trade, providing for infants, relieving the poor, and giving some pleasure to the rich. I have no children by which I can propose to get a single penny; the youngest being nine years old, and my wife past childbearing.

1729

ALEXANDER POPE
1688–1744

1711:   *An Essay on Criticism.*
1712:   First version of *The Rape of the Lock.*
1713–26:   Translating Homer, editing Shakespeare.
1728:   *The Dunciad* begins Pope's career as major verse satirist.
1733–34:   *An Essay on Man* begins his career as ethical and philosophical poet.

Alexander Pope is the only important writer of his generation who was solely a man of letters. Because he could not, as a Roman Catholic, attend a university, vote, or hold public office, he was excluded from the sort of patronage that was freely bestowed by statesmen on most writers during the reign of Anne. This disadvantage he turned into a positive good, for the translation of Homer's *Iliad* and *Odyssey*, which he undertook for profit as well as for fame, gave him ample means to live the life of an independent suburban gentleman. After 1718 he lived hospitably in his villa by the Thames at Twickenham (then pronounced *Twit'nam*), entertaining his friends and converting his five acres of land into a diminutive landscape garden. Almost exactly a century earlier, William Shakespeare had earned enough to retire to a country estate at Stratford—but he had been an actor-manager as well as a playwright; Pope was the first English writer to demonstrate that literature alone could be a gainful profession.

Ill health plagued Pope almost from birth. Delicate as a child, he was early stunted and deformed by tuberculosis of the spine. His father, a well-to-do London merchant, retired from business in the year of the poet's birth, and about 1700 acquired a small property at Binfield in Windsor Forest. In rural surroundings, as the boy's health improved, he early acquired his lifelong taste for natural beauty and for gardening. There he completed by wide reading the desultory schooling that both his ill health and his religion had made inevitable, and encouraged by his father, he began also to develop his precocious talent for poetry. But Pope was never to enjoy good health; in later life he was troubled by violent headaches, and he suffered from easily exacerbated nerves, perhaps a price he had to pay for the sensitive and ardent temperament that helped make him one of our greatest poets.

Pope's first striking success as a poet was *An Essay on Criticism* (1711), which earned him the fame of Joseph Addison's approval and the notoriety of an intemperate personal attack from the critic John Dennis, who was angered by a casual reference to himself in the poem. *The Rape of the Lock*, both in its original shorter version of 1712 and in its more elaborate version of 1714, established the author as a master not only of metrics and of language but also of witty, urbane satire. In

An Essay on Criticism, Pope had excelled all his predecessors in writing a didactic poem after the example of Horace; in the *Rape*, he had written the most brilliant mock epic in the language. But there was another vein in Pope's youthful poetry, much of which, concerned as it is with natural beauty and love, reveals a temperament that in a later poet might have been called "Romantic." The *Pastorals* (1709), Pope's first publication, and *Windsor Forest* (1713; much of it was written earlier) abound in visual imagery and descriptive passages of ideally ordered nature; they remind us that Pope was an amateur painter. The *Elegy to the Memory of an Unfortunate Lady*, published in the collected poems of 1717, presents the high heroics of romantic love. And even the long task of translating Homer, the "dull duty" of editing Shakespeare, and in middle age, his preoccupation with ethical and satirical poetry did not extinguish this side of Pope's nature and art. He learned to subordinate, but he did not cease to use, this sensitive awareness of visual beauty in his later poetry.

Pope's early poetry brought him to the attention of literary men, with whom he began to associate in the masculine world of coffeehouse and tavern. His fragile health never permitted him to live the rakish life that he would have liked, but it did not prevent his enjoying the company of some of the most distinguished authors of the time. Between 1706 and 1711 he came to know, among many others, William Congreve; William Walsh, the critic and poet; and Richard Steele and Joseph Addison. As it happened, all were Whigs. Pope could readily ignore politics in the excitement of taking his place among the leading wits of the town. But after the fall of the Whigs in 1710 and the formation of the Tory government under Robert Harley (later earl of Oxford) and Henry St. John (later Viscount Bolingbroke) party loyalties bred bitterness among the wits as among the politicians.

By 1712, Pope had made the acquaintance of another group of writers, all Tories, who soon became his intimate friends: Jonathan Swift, by then the close associate of Harley and St. John and the principal propagandist for their policies; Dr. John Arbuthnot, physician to the queen, a learned scientist, a wit, and a man of humanity and integrity; John Gay, the poet, who in 1728 was to produce *The Beggar's Opera*, the greatest theatrical success of the century; and the poet Thomas Parnell. It was among these men that Pope was to find his lifelong friends, and it was through them that he became the friend and admirer of Oxford and later the intimate of Bolingbroke. In 1714 this group, at the instigation of Pope, formed a club that was to cooperate in a scheme for satirizing all sorts of false learning and pedantry. The friends proposed to write jointly the biography of a learned fool whom they named Martinus Scriblerus (Martin the Scribbler), whose life and opinions would be a running commentary on whatever they considered the abuses of learning and the follies of the learned. Some amusing episodes were later rewritten and published as the *Memoirs of Martinus Scriblerus* (1741). The real importance of the club, however, is that it fostered a satiric temper that was to find unexpected expression in such mature works of the friends as *Gulliver's Travels*, *The Dunciad*, and even, perhaps, *The Beggar's Opera*.

"The life of a wit is a warfare on earth," said Pope, generalizing from his own experience. His very success as a poet (and his astonishing precocity brought him success very early) made enemies among less-talented writers, who were to plague him in pamphlets, verse satires, and squibs in the journals throughout his entire literary career. He was attacked for his writings, his religion, and his physical deformity. Though he smarted under the jibes of his detractors, he was a fighter who struck back, always giving better than he got. Pope's literary warfare began in 1713, when he announced his intention of translating the *Iliad* and sought subscribers to a deluxe edition of the work. Subscribers came in droves, but the Whig writers who surrounded Addison at Button's Coffee House did all they could through anonymous attacks to hinder the success of the venture. The eventual success of the first published installment of his *Iliad* in 1715 did not obliterate Pope's just resentment against Addison and his "little senate," and this resentment found expression in the damaging portrait of Addison (under the name of Atticus), which, years after it was written, was included in Pope's *Epistle to Dr. Arbuthnot* (1735), lines 193–214. The not unjustified attacks on Pope's edition of Shakespeare (1725), especially those by the learned Shakespeare scholar Lewis Theobald (Pope always spelled and pronounced the name "Tibbald" in his satires), led to Theobald's appearance as king of the dunces in *The Dunciad* (1728). In this impressive poem Pope stigmatized his literary enemies as agents of all that he disliked and feared in the literary tendencies of his time—the vulgarization of taste and the arts consequent on the rapid growth of the reading public and the development of journalism, magazines, and other popular and cheap publications, which spread scandal, sensationalism, and political partisanship—in short the new commercial spirit of the nation that was corrupting not only the arts but, as Pope saw it, the national life itself.

In the 1730s Pope moved on to philosophical, ethical, and political subjects in *An Essay on Man*, the *Epistles to Several Persons*, and the *Imitations of Horace*. The reigns of George I and George II appeared to him, as to Swift and other Tories, a period of rapid moral, political, and cultural deterioration. The agents of decay seemed in one way or another related to the spread of moneyed (as opposed to landed) wealth, which accounted for the political corruption encouraged by Sir Robert Walpole and the court party, and the increasing influence in all aspects of the national life of a vulgar class of *nouveaux riches*. Pope assumed the role of the champion of traditional civilization: of right reason, humanistic learning, sound art, good taste, and public virtue. It was fortunate that most of his enemies happened to illustrate various degrees of unreason, pedantry, bad art, vulgar taste, and at best, indifferent morals.

The satirist traditionally deals in generally prevalent evils and generally observable human types, not with particular individuals. So too with Pope; the bulk of his satire can be read and enjoyed without much biographical information. Usually in the later satires, as in the earlier *Rape*, he used fictional or type names, although he most often had an individual in mind—Sappho, Atossa, Atticus, Sporus—and when he named individuals (as he consistently did in *The Dunciad* and occasionally elsewhere), his purpose was to raise his victims to the bad eminence of typifying some sort of obliquity. To judge and censure the age, Pope also created the *I* of the satires (not identical with Alexander Pope of Twickenham). This fictional or semifictional figure is the detached observer, somewhat removed from the City, town, and court, the centers of corruption; he is the friend of the virtuous, whose friendship for him testifies to his integrity; he is fond of peace, country life, the arts, morality, and truth; and he detests their opposites that flourish in the great world. In such an age, Pope implies, it is impossible for such a man—honest, truthful, blunt—not to write satire.

Pope was a master of style. From first to last, his verse is notable for its rhythmic variety, despite the apparently rigid metrical unit—the heroic couplet—in which he wrote; for the precision of meaning and the harmony (or the expressive disharmony, when necessary) of his language; and for the union of maximum conciseness with maximum complexity. Something of Pope's metrical variety and verbal harmony can be observed in even so short a passage as lines 71–76 of the pastoral *Summer* (1709), lines so lyrical that, in *Semele*, Handel set them to music. In the passage quoted below (as also in the following quotation), only those rhetorical stresses that distort the normal iambic flow of the verse have been marked; internal pauses within the line are indicated by single and double bars, alliteration and assonance by italics.

> Óh déign to visit our *forsaken seats*,
>
> The mossy *fountains* ‖ and the green *retreats!*
>
> Where'er yóu wálk ‖ cóol gáles shall *fan* the *glade*,
>
> Trées whére yóu sít ‖ shall crowd into a shade:
>
> Where'er yóu tŕead ‖ the blushing *flowers* shall rise,
>
> And all thíngs *flóurish* where yóu túrn your eyes.

Pope has attained metrical variety by the free substitution of trochees and spondees for the normal iambs; he has achieved rhythmic variety by arranging phrases and clauses (units of syntax and logic) of different lengths within single lines and couplets, so that the passage moves with the sinuous fluency of thought and feeling; and he not only has chosen musical combinations of words but has also subtly modulated the harmony of the passage by unobtrusive patterns of alliteration and assonance.

Contrast with this pastoral passage lines 16–25 of the *Epilogue to the Satires, Dialogue* 2 (1738), in which Pope is not making music, but is imitating actual conversation so realistically that the metrical pattern and the integrity of the couplet and individual line seem to be destroyed (though in fact they are very much present). In a dialogue with a friend who warns him that his satire is too personal, indeed mere libel, the poet-satirist replies:

> Yé státesmen, | priests of one religion all!
>
> Yé trádesmen vile ‖ in army, court, or hall!
>
> Yé réverend atheists. ‖ F. Scandal! | name them, | Who?
>
>   P. Why that's the thing you bid me not to do.
>
> Whó stárved a sister, ‖ who foreswore a debt,
>
> Í néver named; ‖ the town's inquiring yet.
>
> The poisoning dame— | F. Yóu méan— | P. I don't— | F. Yóu dó.
>
>   P. Sée, nów Í kéep the secret, ‖ and nót yóu!
>
> The bribing statesman— | F. Hóld, ‖ tóo hígh you go.
>
>   P. The bribed elector— ‖ F. There you stoop tóo lów.

In such a passage the language and rhythms of poetry merge with the language and rhythms of impassioned living speech.

A fine example of Pope's ability to derive the maximum of meaning from the most economic use of language and image is the description of the manor house in which lives old Cotta, the miser (*Epistle to Lord Bathurst*, lines 187–196):

> Like some lone Chartreuse stands the good old Hall,
> Silence without, and fasts within the wall;
> No raftered roofs with dance and tabor sound,
> No noontide bell invites the country round;
> Tenants with sighs the smokeless towers survey,
> And turn the unwilling steeds another way;
> Benighted wanderers, the forest o'er,
> Curse the saved candle and unopening door;
> While the gaunt mastiff growling at the gate,
> Affrights the beggar whom he longs to eat.

The first couplet of this passage, which associates the "Hall," symbol of English rural hospitality, with the Grande Chartreuse, the monastery in the French Alps, which, though a place of "silence" and "fasts" for the monks, afforded food and shelter to all travelers, clashes forcefully with the dismal details of Cotta's miserly dwelling, and the meaning of the scene is concentrated in the grotesque image of the last couplet: the half-starved watchdog and the frightened beggar confronting each other in mutual hunger.

But there is another sort of variety within Pope's work as a whole that derives from the poet's respect for the idea that the different kinds of literature have their different and appropriate styles. Thus *An Essay on Criticism*, an informal discussion of literary theory, is written, like Horace's *Art of Poetry* (a similarly didactic poem), in a plain style, the easy language of well-bred talk. *The Rape of the Lock*, being "a heroi-comical poem" (that is, a comic poem that treats trivial material in an epic style), employs the lofty heroic language that John Dryden had perfected in his translation of Virgil and introduces amusing parodies of passages in *Paradise Lost*; parodies later raised to truly Miltonic sublimity and complexity by the conclusion of *The Dunciad. Eloisa to Abelard* renders the brooding, passionate voice of its heroine in a declamatory language, given to sudden outbursts and shifts of tone, that recalls the stage. The grave epistles that make up *An Essay on Man*, a philosophical discussion of such majestic themes as the Creator and His creation, the universe, human nature, society, and happiness, are written in a stately forensic language and tone and constantly employ the traditional rhetorical figures. The *Imitations of Horace*, and above all, the *Epistle to Dr. Arbuthnot*, his finest poem "in the Horatian way," reveal Pope's final mastery of the plain style of Horace's epistles and satires and justify his image of himself as the heir of the Roman poet. In short, no other poet of the century can equal Pope in the range of his materials, the diversity of his poetic styles, and his mastery of the poet's craft.

An Essay on Criticism   There is no pleasanter introduction to the canons of taste in the English Augustan age than Pope's *An Essay on Criticism*. As Addison said in his review in *Spectator* 253, it assembles the "most known and most received observations on the subject of literature and criticism." Pope was attempting to do for his time what Horace, in his *Art of Poetry*, and what Nicolas Boileau (French poet of the age of Louis XIV), in his *L'Art Poétique*, had done for theirs. Horace is not only one of Pope's instructors in the principles of criticism but he is also Pope's model in this poem, especially in the simple, conversational language, the tone of well-bred ease, and the deliberately plain style.

In framing his critical creed, Pope did not try for novelty: he wished merely to give to generally accepted doctrines pleasing and memorable expression and make them useful to modern poets. Here one meets the key words of neoclassical criticism: *wit, Nature, ancients, rules,* and *genius. Wit* in the poem is a word of many meanings—a clever remark or the man who makes it, a conceit, liveliness of mind, inventiveness, fancy, genius, a genius, and poetry itself, among others. *Nature* is an equally ambiguous word, meaning not "things out there," or "the outdoors," but most important that which is representative, universal, permanent in human experience as opposed to the idiosyncratic, the individual, the temporary. In line 21, *Nature* comes close to meaning "intuitive knowledge." In line 52, it means that half-personified power manifested in the cosmic order, which in its modes of working is a model for art. The reverence felt by most Augustans for the works of the great writers of ancient Greece and Rome raised the question how far the authority of these *ancients* extended. Were their works to be received as models to be conscientiously imitated? Were the *rules* received from them or deducible from their works to be accepted as prescriptive laws or merely convenient guides? Was individual *genius* to be bound by what has been conventionally held to be *Nature*, by the authority of the *ancients*, and by the legalistic pedantry of *rules*? Or could it go its own way?

In part 1 of the *Essay*, Pope constructs a harmonious system in which he effects a compromise among all these conflicting forces—a compromise that is typically eighteenth century in spirit. Part 2 analyzes the causes of faulty criticism. Part 3 characterizes the good critic and praises the great critics of the past.

An Essay on Criticism

Part 1

'Tis hard to say, if greater want of skill
Appear in writing or in judging ill;
But of the two less dangerous is the offense
To tire our patience than mislead our sense.
Some few in that, but numbers err in this,   5
Ten censure[1] wrong for one who writes amiss;
A fool might once himself alone expose,
Now one in verse makes many more in prose.
  'Tis with our judgments as our watches, none
Go just alike, yet each believes his own.   10
In poets as true genius is but rare,
True taste as seldom is the critic's share;
Both must alike from Heaven derive their light,
These born to judge, as well as those to write.
Let such teach others who themselves excel,   15
And censure freely who have written well.
Authors are partial to their wit, 'tis true,
But are not critics to their judgment too?
  Yet if we look more closely, we shall find
Most have the seeds of judgment in their mind: 20
Nature affords at least a glimmering light;
The lines, though touched but faintly, are drawn right.
But as the slightest sketch, if justly traced, ⎫
Is by ill coloring but the more disgraced, ⎬
So by false learning is good sense defaced: ⎭   25
Some are bewildered in the maze of schools,
And some made coxcombs[2] Nature meant but fools.
In search of wit these lose their common sense,
And then turn critics in their own defense:
Each burns alike, who can, or cannot write,   30
Or with a rival's or an eunuch's spite.
All fools have still an itching to deride,
And fain would be upon the laughing side.
If Maevius[3] scribble in Apollo's spite,
There are who judge still worse than he can write.   35
  Some have at first for wits, then poets passed,
Turned critics next, and proved plain fools at last.

---

1. Judge.
2. Superficial pretenders to learning.

3. A silly poet alluded to contemptuously by Virgil in *Eclogue* 3 and by Horace in *Epode* 10.

Some neither can for wits nor critics pass,
As heavy mules are neither horse nor ass.
Those half-learn'd witlings, numerous in our isle,   40
As half-formed insects on the banks of Nile;[4]
Unfinished things, one knows not what to call,
Their generation's so equivocal:
To tell[5] them would a hundred tongues require,
Or one vain wit's, that might a hundred tire.   45
    But you who seek to give and merit fame,
And justly bear a critic's noble name,
Be sure yourself and your own reach to know,
How far your genius, taste, and learning go;
Launch not beyond your depth, but be discreet,   50
And mark that point where sense and dullness meet.
    Nature to all things fixed the limits fit,
And wisely curbed proud man's pretending wit.
As on the land while here the ocean gains,
In other parts it leaves wide sandy plains;   55
Thus in the soul while memory prevails,
The solid power of understanding fails;
Where beams of warm imagination play,
The memory's soft figures melt away.
One science[6] only will one genius fit,   60
So vast is art, so narrow human wit.
Not only bounded to peculiar arts,
But oft in those confined to single parts,
Like kings we lose the conquests gained before,
By vain ambition still to make them more;   65
Each might his several province well command,
Would all but stoop to what they understand.
    First follow Nature, and your judgment frame
By her just standard, which is still the same;
Unerring Nature, still divinely bright,   70
One clear, unchanged, and universal light,
Life, force, and beauty must to all impart,
At once the source, and end, and test of art.
Art from that fund each just supply provides,
Works without show, and without pomp presides.   75
In some fair body thus the informing soul
With spirits feeds, with vigor fills the whole,
Each motion guides, and every nerve sustains;
Itself unseen, but in the effects remains.
Some, to whom Heaven in wit has been profuse,   80
Want as much more to turn it to its use;
For wit and judgment often are at strife,
Though meant each other's aid, like man and wife.
'Tis more to guide than spur the Muse's steed,
Restrain his fury than provoke his speed;   85
The wingèd courser, like a generous[7] horse,

4. The ancients believed that many forms of life were spontaneously generated in the fertile mud of the Nile.
5. Reckon, count.
6. Branch of learning.
7. Spirited, highly bred. "Wingèd courser": Pegasus, associated with the Muses and poetic inspiration.

Shows most true mettle when you check his course.
      Those rules of old discovered, not devised,
Are Nature still, but Nature methodized;
Nature, like liberty, is but restrained   90
By the same laws which first herself ordained.
      Hear how learn'd Greece her useful rules indites,
When to repress and when indulge our flights:
High on Parnassus' top her sons she showed,
And pointed out those arduous paths they trod;   95
Held from afar, aloft, the immortal prize,
And urged the rest by equal steps to rise.
Just precepts thus from great examples given,
She drew from them what they derived from Heaven.
The generous critic fanned the poet's fire,   100
And taught the world with reason to admire.
Then criticism the Muse's handmaid proved,
To dress her charms, and make her more beloved:
But following wits from that intention strayed,
Who could not win the mistress, wooed the maid;   105
Against the poets their own arms they turned,
Sure to hate most the men from whom they learned.
So modern 'pothecaries, taught the art
By doctors's bills[8] to play the doctor's part,
Bold in the practice of mistaken rules,   110
Prescribe, apply, and call their masters fools.
Some on the leaves of ancient authors prey,
Nor time nor moths e'er spoiled so much as they.
Some dryly plain, without invention's aid,
Write dull receipts[9] how poems may be made.   115
These leave the sense their learning to display,
And those explain the meaning quite away.
      You then whose judgment the right course would steer,
Know well each ancient's proper character;
His fable, subject, scope[1] in every page;   120
Religion, country, genius of his age:
Without all these at once before your eyes,
Cavil you may, but never criticize.
Be Homer's works your study and delight,
Read them by day, and meditate by night;   125
Thence form your judgment, thence your maxims bring,
And trace the Muses upward to their spring.
Still with itself compared, his text peruse;
And let your comment be the Mantuan Muse.
      When first young Maro[2] in his boundless mind   130
A work to outlast immortal Rome designed,
Perhaps he seemed above the critic's law,
And but from Nature's fountains scorned to draw;

8. Prescriptions.
9. Formulas for preparing a dish; recipes. Pope himself wrote an amusing burlesque, *Receipt to Make an
Epic Poem*, first published in the *Guardian* 78 (1713).
1. Aim or purpose. "Fable": plot or story of a play or
poem.

2. Virgil. He was born in a village adjacent to Mantua
in Italy, hence "Mantuan Muse." His epic, the *Aeneid*,
was modeled on Homer's *Iliad* and *Odyssey* and was
considered to be a refinement on the Greek poems.
Thus it could be thought of as a commentary ("comment") on Homer's poems.

But when to examine every part he came,
Nature and Homer were, he found, the same. 135
Convinced, amazed, he checks the bold design, ⎤
And rules as strict his labored work confine }
As if the Stagirite[3] o'erlooked each line. ⎦
Learn hence for ancient rules a just esteem;
To copy Nature is to copy them. 140
 Some beauties yet no precepts can declare,
For there's a happiness as well as care.[4]
Music resembles poetry, in each ⎤
Are nameless graces which no methods teach, }
And which a master hand alone can reach. ⎦ 145
If, where the rules not far enough extend
(Since rules were made but to promote their end)
Some lucky license answers to the full
The intent proposed, that license is a rule.
Thus Pegasus, a nearer way to take, 150
May boldly deviate from the common track.
Great wits sometimes may gloriously offend,
And rise to faults true critics dare not mend;
From vulgar bounds with brave disorder part,
And snatch a grace beyond the reach of art, 155
Which, without passing through the judgment, gains
The heart, and all its end at once attains.
In prospects thus, some objects please our eyes, ⎤
Which out of Nature's common order rise, }
The shapeless rock, or hanging precipice. ⎦ 160
But though the ancients thus their rules invade
(As kings dispense with laws themselves have made)
Moderns, beware! or if you must offend
Against the precept, ne'er transgress its end;
Let it be seldom, and compelled by need; 165
And have at least their precedent to plead.
The critic else proceeds without remorse,
Seizes your fame, and puts his laws in force.
 I know there are, to whose presumptuous thoughts
Those freer beauties, even in them, seem faults.[5] 170
Some figures monstrous and misshaped appear,
Considered singly, or beheld too near,
Which, but proportioned to their light or place,
Due distance reconciles to form and grace.
A prudent chief not always must display 175
His powers in equal ranks and fair array,
But with the occasion and the place comply,
Conceal his force, nay seem sometimes to fly.
Those oft are stratagems which errors seem,
Nor is it Homer nods, but we that dream. 180
 Still green with bays each ancient altar stands

---

3. Aristotle, native of Stagira, from whose *Poetics* later critics formulated strict rules for writing tragedy and the epic.
4. I.e., no rules ("precepts") can explain ("declare") some beautiful effects in a work of art that can be the result only of inspiration or good luck ("happiness"), not of painstaking labor ("care").
5. Pronounced *fawts*.

Above the reach of sacrilegious hands,
Secure from flames, from envy's fiercer rage,
Destructive war, and all-involving age.
See, from each clime the learn'd their incense bring!   185
Here in all tongues consenting[6] paeans ring!
In praise so just let every voice be joined,[7]
And fill the general chorus of mankind.
Hail, bards triumphant! born in happier days,
Immortal heirs of universal praise!   190
Whose honors with increase of ages grow,
As streams roll down, enlarging as they flow;
Nations unborn your mighty names shall sound,
And worlds applaud that must not yet be found!
Oh, may some spark of your celestial fire,   195
The last, the meanest of your sons inspire
(That on weak wings, from far, pursues your flights,
Glows while he reads, but trembles as he writes)
To teach vain wits a science little known,
To admire superior sense, and doubt their own!   200

Part 2

Of all the causes which conspire to blind
Man's erring judgment, and misguide the mind,
What the weak head with strongest bias rules,
Is pride, the never-failing vice of fools.
Whatever Nature has in worth denied,   205
She gives in large recruits[8] of needful pride;
For as in bodies, thus in souls, we find
What wants in blood and spirits, swelled with wind:
Pride, where wit fails, steps in to our defense,
And fills up all the mighty void of sense.   210
If once right reason drives that cloud away,
Truth breaks upon us with resistless day.
Trust not yourself: but your defects to know,
Make use of every friend—and every foe.
A little learning is a dangerous thing;   215
Drink deep, or taste not the Pierian spring.[9]
There shallow draughts intoxicate the brain,
And drinking largely sobers us again.
Fired at first sight with what the Muse imparts,
In fearless youth we tempt[1] the heights of arts,   220
While from the bounded level of our mind
Short views we take, nor see the lengths behind;
But more advanced, behold with strange surprise
New distant scenes of endless science rise!
So pleased at first the towering Alps we try,   225
Mount o'er the vales, and seem to tread the sky,
The eternal snows appear already past,

6. Agreeing, concurring.
7. Pronounced *jined*.
8. Supplies.

9. The spring in Pieria on Mt. Olympus, sacred to
the Muses.
1. Attempt.

And the first clouds and mountains seem the last;
But, those attained, we tremble to survey
The growing labors of the lengthened way,   230
The increasing prospect tires our wandering eyes,
Hills peep o'er hills, and Alps on Alps arise!
   A perfect judge will read each work of wit
With the same spirit that its author writ:
Survey the whole, nor seek slight faults to find   235
Where Nature moves, and rapture warms the mind;
Nor lose, for that malignant dull delight,
The generous pleasure to be charmed with wit.
But in such lays as neither ebb nor flow,
Correctly cold, and regularly low,   240
That, shunning faults, one quiet tenor keep,
We cannot blame indeed—but we may sleep.
In wit, as nature, what affects our hearts
Is not the exactness of peculiar parts;
'Tis not a lip, or eye, we beauty call,   245
But the joint force and full result of all.
Thus when we view some well-proportioned dome[2]
(The world's just wonder, and even thine, O Rome!),
No single parts unequally surprise,
All comes united to the admiring eyes: 250
No monstrous height, or breadth, or length appear;
The whole at once is bold and regular.
   Whoever thinks a faultless piece to see,
Thinks what ne'er was, nor is, nor e'er shall be.
In every work regard the writer's end,   255
Since none can compass more than they intend;
And if the means be just, the conduct true,
Applause, in spite of trivial faults, is due.
As men of breeding, sometimes men of wit,
To avoid great errors must the less commit,   260
Neglect the rules each verbal critic lays,
For not to know some trifles is a praise.
Most critics, fond of some subservient art,
Still make the whole depend upon a part:
They talk of principles, but notions prize,   265
And all to one loved folly sacrifice.
   Once on a time La Mancha's knight,[3] they say,
A certain bard encountering on the way,
Discoursed in terms as just, with looks as sage,
As e'er could Dennis,[4] of the Grecian stage;   270
Concluding all were desperate sots and fools
Who durst depart from Aristotle's rules.
Our author, happy in a judge so nice,
Produced his play, and begged the knight's advice;

---

2. The dome of St. Peter's, designed by Michelangelo.
3. Don Quixote. The story comes not from Cervantes'
novel, but from a spurious sequel to it by Don Alonzo
Fernandez de Avellaneda.
4. John Dennis (1657–1734), though one of the lead-

ing critics of the time, was frequently ridiculed by the
wits for his irascibility and his rather solemn pomposity. Pope apparently did not know Dennis personally,
but his jibe at him in part 3 of this poem incurred the
critic's lasting animosity.

Made him observe the subject and the plot, 275
The manners, passions, unities; what not?
All which exact to rule were brought about,
Were but a combat in the lists left out.
"What! leave the combat out?" exclaims the knight.
"Yes, or we must renounce the Stagirite." 280
"Not so, by Heaven!" he answers in a rage,
"Knights, squires, and steeds must enter on the stage."
"So vast a throng the stage can ne'er contain."
"Then build a new, or act it in a plain."
    Thus critics of less judgment than caprice, 285
Curious, not knowing, not exact, but nice,[5]
Form short ideas, and offend in arts
(As most in manners), by a love to parts.
    Some to conceit[6] alone their taste confine,
And glittering thoughts struck out at every line; 290
Pleased with a work where nothing's just or fit,
One glaring chaos and wild heap of wit.
Poets, like painters, thus unskilled to trace
The naked nature and the living grace,
With gold and jewels cover every part, 295
And hide with ornaments their want of art.
True wit is Nature to advantage dressed,
What oft was thought, but ne'er so well expressed;
Something whose truth convinced at sight we find,
That gives us back the image of our mind. 300
As shades more sweetly recommend the light,
So modest plainness sets off sprightly wit;
For works may have more wit than does them good,
As bodies perish through excess of blood.
    Others for language all their care express, 305
And value books, as women men, for dress.
Their praise is still—the style is excellent;
The sense they humbly take upon content.[7]
Words are like leaves; and where they most abound,
Much fruit of sense beneath is rarely found. 310
False eloquence, like the prismatic glass,
Its gaudy colors spreads on every place;[8]
The face of Nature we no more survey,
All glares alike, without distinction gay.
But true expression, like the unchanging sun, 315
Clears and improves whate'er it shines upon;
It gilds all objects, but it alters none.
Expression is the dress of thought, and still
Appears more decent as more suitable.
A vile conceit in pompous words expressed 320
Is like a clown[9] in regal purple dressed:

5. Minutely accurate, overrefined. "Curious": laboriously carefully.
6. Pointed wit, ingenuity and extravagance, or affectation in the use of figures, especially similes and metaphors.
7. Mere acquiescence.

8. A very up-to-date scientific reference. Newton's *Optics*, which dealt with the prism and the spectrum, had been published in 1704, though his theories had been known earlier.
9. Rustic, boor.

For different styles with different subjects sort,
As several garbs with country, town, and court.
Some by old words to fame have made pretense,
Ancients in phrase, mere moderns in their sense.   325
Such labored nothings, in so strange a style,
Amaze the unlearn'd, and make the learned smile;
Unlucky as Fungoso[1] in the play,
These sparks with awkward vanity display
What the fine gentleman wore yesterday;   330
And but so mimic ancient wits at best,
As apes our grandsires in their doublets dressed.
In words as fashions the same rule will hold,
Alike fantastic if too new or old:
Be not the first by whom the new are tried,   335
Nor yet the last to lay the old aside.
   But most by numbers[2] judge a poet's song,
And smooth or rough with them is right or wrong.
In the bright Muse though thousand charms conspire,
Her voice is all these tuneful fools admire,   340
Who haunt Parnassus but to please their ear,
Not mend their minds; as some to church repair,
Not for the doctrine, but the music there.
These equal syllables alone require,
Though oft the ear the open vowels tire,[3]   345
While expletives[4] their feeble aid do join,
And ten low words oft creep in one dull line:
While they ring round the same unvaried chimes,
With sure returns of still expected rhymes;
Where'er you find "the cooling western breeze,"   350
In the next line, it "whispers through the trees";
If crystal streams "with pleasing murmurs creep,"
The reader's threatened (not in vain) with "sleep";
Then, at the last and only couplet fraught
With some unmeaning thing they call a thought,   355
A needless Alexandrine[5] ends the song
That, like a wounded snake, drags its slow length along.
Leave such to tune their own dull rhymes, and know
What's roundly smooth or languishingly slow;
And praise the easy vigor of a line   360
Where Denham's strength and Waller's sweetness join.[6]
True ease in writing comes from art, not chance,
As those move easiest who have learned to dance.
'Tis not enough no harshness gives offense,
The sound must seem an echo to the sense.   365
Soft is the strain when Zephyr gently blows,

---

1. A character in Ben Jonson's comedy *Every Man out of His Humor* (1599).
2. Versification.
3. In lines 345–357 Pope cleverly contrives to make his own metrics or diction illustrate the faults that he is exposing.
4. Words used merely to achieve the necessary number of feet in a line of verse.

5. A line of verse containing six iambic feet; it is illustrated in the next line.
6. Dryden, whom Pope echoes here, considered Sir John Denham (1615–1669) and Edmund Waller (1606–1687) to have been the principal shapers of the closed pentameter couplet. He had distinguished the "strength" of the one and the "sweetness" of the other.

And the smooth stream in smoother numbers flows;
But when loud surges lash the sounding shore,
The hoarse, rough verse should like the torrent roar.
When Ajax strives some rock's vast weight to throw, 370
The line too labors, and the words move slow;
Not so when swift Camilla scours the plain,
Flies o'er the unbending corn, and skims along the main.
Hear how Timotheus'[7] varied lays surprise,
And bid alternate passions fall and rise! 375
While at each change the son of Libyan Jove[8]
Now burns with glory, and then melts with love;
Now his fierce eyes with sparkling fury glow,
Now sighs steal out, and tears begin to flow:
Persians and Greeks like turns of nature[9] found 380
And the world's victor stood subdued by sound!
The power of music all our hearts allow,
And what Timotheus was, is Dryden now.
    Avoid extremes; and shun the fault of such
Who still are pleased too little or too much. 385
At every trifle scorn to take offense:
That always shows great pride, or little sense.
Those heads, as stomachs, are not sure the best,
Which nauseate all, and nothing can digest.
Yet let not each gay turn thy rapture move; 390
For fools admire, but men of sense approve:[1]
As things seem large which we through mists descry,
Dullness is ever apt to magnify.
    Some foreign writers, some our own despise;
The ancients only, or the moderns prize. 395
Thus wit, like faith, by each man is applied
To one small sect, and all are damned beside.
Meanly they seek the blessing to confine,
And force that sun but on a part to shine,
Which not alone the southern wit sublimes,[2] 400
But ripens spirits in cold northern climes;
Which from the first has shone on ages past,
Enlights the present, and shall warm the last;
Though each may feel increases and decays,
And see now clearer and now darker days. 405
Regard not then if wit be old or new,
But blame the false and value still the true.
    Some ne'er advance a judgment of their own,
But catch the spreading notion of the town;
They reason and conclude by precedent, 410
And own stale nonsense which they ne'er invent.
Some judge of authors' names, not works, and then
Nor praise nor blame the writings, but the men.
Of all this servile herd the worst is he

7. The musician in Dryden's *Alexander's Feast*. Pope retells the story of that poem in the following lines.
8. Alexander the Great.
9. Alternations of feelings.

1. Judge favorably only after due deliberation. "Admire": wonder.
2. Raises up, purifies.

That in proud dullness joins with quality,[3]   415
A constant critic at the great man's board,
To fetch and carry nonsense for my lord.
What woeful stuff this madrigal would be
In some starved hackney sonneteer[4] or me!
But let a lord once own the happy lines,   420
How the wit brightens! how the style refines!
Before his sacred name flies every fault,
And each exalted stanza teems with thought!
    The vulgar thus through imitation err;
As oft the learn'd by being singular;   425
So much they scorn the crowd, that if the throng
By chance go right, they purposely go wrong.
So schismatics[5] the plain believers quit,
And are but damned for having too much wit.
Some praise at morning what they blame at night,   430
But always think the last opinion right.
A Muse by these is like a mistress used,
This hour she's idolized, the next abused;
While their weak heads like towns unfortified,
'Twixt sense and nonsense daily change their side.   435
Ask them the cause; they're wiser still, they say;
And still tomorrow's wiser than today.
We think our fathers fools, so wise we grow;
Our wiser sons, no doubt, will think us so.
Once school divines[6] this zealous isle o'erspread;   440
Who knew most sentences was deepest read.
Faith, Gospel, all seemed made to be disputed,
And none had sense enough to be confuted.
Scotists and Thomists now in peace remain
Amidst their kindred cobwebs in Duck Lane.[7]   445
If faith itself has different dresses worn,
What wonder modes in wit should take their turn?
Oft, leaving what is natural and fit,
The current folly proves the ready wit;
And authors think their reputation safe,   450
Which lives as long as fools are pleased to laugh.
    Some valuing those of their own side or mind,
Still make themselves the measure of mankind:
Fondly[8] we think we honor merit then,
When we but praise ourselves in other men.   455
Parties in wit attend on those of state,
And public faction doubles private hate.
Pride, Malice, Folly against Dryden rose,
In various shapes of parsons, critics, beaux;
But sense survived, when merry jests were past;   460

3. People of high rank.
4. Hireling poet.
5. Those who have divided the church on points of
theology. Pope stressed the first syllable, the pronunciation approved by Johnson in his *Dictionary*.
6. The medieval theologians, such as the followers of
Duns Scotus and St. Thomas Aquinas mentioned below. "Sentences" alludes to Peter Lombard's *Book of
Sentences*, a book esteemed by Scholastic philosophers.
7. Street where publishers' remainders and second-
hand books were sold.
8. Foolishly.

For rising merit will buoy up at last.
Might he return and bless once more our eyes,
New Blackmores and new Milbourns must arise.[9]
Nay, should great Homer lift his awful head,
Zoilus[1] again would start up from the dead.   465
Envy will merit, as its shade, pursue,
But like a shadow, proves the substance true;
For envied wit, like Sol eclipsed, makes known
The opposing body's grossness, not its own.
When first that sun too powerful beams displays,   470
It draws up vapors which obscure its rays;
But even those clouds at last adorn its way,
Reflect new glories, and augment the day.
     Be thou the first true merit to befriend;
His praise is lost who stays till all commend.   475
Short is the date, alas! of modern rhymes,
And 'tis but just to let them live betimes.
No longer now that golden age appears,
When patriarch wits survived a thousand years:
Now length of fame (our second life) is lost,   480
And bare threescore is all even that can boast;
Our sons their fathers' failing language see,
And such as Chaucer is, shall Dryden be.[2]
So when the faithful pencil has designed
Some bright idea of the master's mind,   485
Where a new world leaps out at his command,
And ready Nature waits upon his hand;
When the ripe colors soften and unite,
And sweetly melt into just shade and light;
When mellowing years their full perfection give,   490
And each bold figure just begins to live,
The treacherous colors the fair art betray,
And all the bright creation fades away!
     Unhappy wit, like most mistaken things,
Atones not for that envy which it brings.   495
In youth alone its empty praise we boast,
But soon the short-lived vanity is lost;
Like some fair flower the early spring supplies,
That gaily blooms, but even in blooming dies.
What is this wit, which must our cares employ?   500
The owner's wife, that other men enjoy;
Then most our trouble still when most admired,
And still the more we give, the more required;
Whose fame with pains we guard, but lose with ease,
Sure some to vex, but never all to please;   505
'Tis what the vicious fear, the virtuous shun,
By fools 'tis hated, and by knaves undone!

9. Sir Richard Blackmore, physician and poet, had attacked Dryden for the immorality of his plays; the Rev. Luke Milbourn had attacked his translation of Virgil.
1. A Greek critic of the 4th century B.C., who wrote a book of carping criticism of Homer.
2. The radical changes that took place in the English language between the death of Chaucer in 1400 and the death of Dryden in 1700 suggested that in another three hundred years Dryden would be unintelligible. Latin seemed the only means of attaining enduring fame.

If wit so much from ignorance undergo,
Ah, let not learning too commence its foe!
Of old those met rewards who could excel,   510
And such were praised who but endeavored well;
Though triumphs were to generals only due,
Crowns were reserved to grace the soldiers too.[3]
Now they who reach Parnassus' lofty crown
Employ their pains to spurn some others down;   515
And while self-love each jealous writer rules,
Contending wits become the sport of fools;
But still the worst with most regret commend,
For each ill author is as bad a friend.
To what base ends, and by what abject ways,   520
Are mortals urged through sacred[4] lust of praise!
Ah, ne'er so dire a thirst of glory boast,
Nor in the critic let the man be lost!
Good nature and good sense must ever join;
To err is human, to forgive divine.   525
    But if in noble minds some dregs remain
Not yet purged off, of spleen and sour disdain,
Discharge that rage on more provoking crimes,
Nor fear a dearth in these flagitious[5] times.
No pardon vile obscenity should find,   530
Though wit and art conspire to move your mind;
But dullness with obscenity must prove
As shameful sure as impotence in love.
In the fat age of pleasure, wealth, and ease
Sprung the rank weed, and thrived with large increase: 535
When love was all an easy monarch's[6] care,
Seldom at council, never in a war;
Jilts[7] ruled the state, and statesmen farces writ;
Nay, wits had pensions, and young lords had wit;
The fair sat panting at a courtier's play,   540
And not a mask[8] went unimproved away;
The modest fan was lifted up no more,
And virgins smiled at what they blushed before.
The following license of a foreign reign
Did all the dregs of bold Socinus drain;[9]   545
Then unbelieving priests reformed the nation,
And taught more pleasant methods of salvation;
Where Heaven's free subjects might their rights dispute,
Lest God himself should seem too absolute;
Pulpits their sacred satire learned to spare,   550
And Vice admired to find a flatterer there!
Encouraged thus, wit's Titans braved the skies,
And the press groaned with licensed blasphemies.
These monsters, critics! with your darts engage,

3. To celebrate Roman victories, valiant soldiers were decorated with a variety of crowns.
4. Accursed. The phrase imitates Virgil's *auri sacra fames,* "accursed hunger for gold" (*Aeneid* 3.57).
5. Scandalously wicked.
6. Charles II. The concluding lines of part 2 discuss the corruption of wit and poetry under this monarch.
7. Mistresses of the king.
8. A woman wearing a mask.
9. Socinus was the name of two Italian theologians of the 16th century who denied the divinity of Jesus. The "foreign reign" refers to William III, a Dutchman.

Here point your thunder, and exhaust your rage!   555
Yet shun their fault, who, scandalously nice,
Will needs mistake an author into vice;
All seems infected that the infected spy,
As all looks yellow to the jaundiced eye.

Part 3

Learn then what morals critics ought to show,   560
For 'tis but half a judge's task, to know.
'Tis not enough, taste, judgment, learning, join;
In all you speak, let truth and candor[1] shine:
That not alone what to your sense is due
All may allow; but seek your friendship too.   565
Be silent always when you doubt your sense;
And speak, though sure, with seeming diffidence:
Some positive, persisting fops we know,
Who, if once wrong, will needs be always so;
But you, with pleasure own your errors past,   570
And make each day a critic[2] on the last.
'Tis not enough, your counsel still be true;
Blunt truths more mischief than nice falsehoods do;
Men must be taught as if you taught them not,
And things unknown proposed as things forgot.   575
Without good breeding, truth is disapproved;
That only makes superior sense beloved.
Be niggards of advice on no pretense;
For the worst avarice is that of sense.
With mean complacence[3] ne'er betray your trust,   580
Nor be so civil as to prove unjust.
Fear not the anger of the wise to raise;
Those best can bear reproof, who merit praise.
'Twere well might critics still this freedom take;
But Appius reddens at each word you speak,   585
And stares, tremendous! with a threatening eye,
Like some fierce tyrant in old tapestry.[4]
Fear most to tax an honorable fool,
Whose right it is, uncensured to be dull;
Such, without wit, are poets when they please,   590
As without learning they can take degrees.[5]
Leave dangerous truths to unsuccessful satyrs,
And flattery to fulsome dedicators,
Whom, when they praise, the world believes no more,
Than when they promise to give scribbling o'er.   595
'Tis best sometimes your censure to restrain,
And charitably let the dull be vain:

1. Kindness, impartiality.
2. Critique.
3. Softness of manners; desire of pleasing.
4. This picture was taken to himself by John Dennis, a furious old critic by profession, who, upon no other provocation, wrote against this Essay and its author, in a manner perfectly lunatic ... [Pope's note, 1744].

Pope *did* intend to ridicule Dennis, whose *Appius and Virginia* had failed on the stage in 1709 and who was known for his stare and his use of the word *tremendous* (see line 270 above).
5. Satires. "Degrees": honorary degrees were granted to unqualified men of rank.

Your silence there is better than your spite,
For who can rail so long as they can write?
Still humming on, their drowsy course they keep,   600
And lashed so long, like tops, are lashed asleep.[6]
False steps but help them to renew the race,
As, after stumbling, jades[7] will mend their pace.
What crowds of these, impenitently bold,
In sounds and jingling syllables grown old,   605
Still run on poets, in a raging vein,
Even to the dregs and squeezings of the brain,
Strain out the last dull droppings of their sense,
And rhyme with all the rage of impotence.
      Such shameless bards we have, and yet 'tis true,   610
There are as mad, abandoned critics too.
The bookful blockhead, ignorantly read,
With loads of learned lumber[8] in his head,
With his own tongue still edifies his ears,
And always listening to himself appears.   615
All books he reads, and all he reads assails,
From Dryden's *Fables* down to Durfey's *Tales*.[9]
With him, most authors steal their works, or buy;
Garth did not write his own *Dispensary*.[1]
Name a new play, and he's the poet's friend,   620
Nay showed his faults—but when would poets mend?
No place so sacred from such fops is barred,
Nor is Paul's church more safe than Paul's churchyard:[2]
Nay, fly to altars; *there* they'll talk you dead:
For fools rush in where angels fear to tread.   625
Distrustful sense with modest caution speaks, ⎤
It still looks home, and short excursions makes; ⎬
But rattling nonsense in full volleys breaks, ⎦
And never shocked, and never turned aside,
Bursts out, resistless, with a thundering tide.   630
      But where's the man, who counsel can bestow,
Still pleased to teach, and yet not proud to know?
Unbiased, or[3] by favor, or by spite:
Not dully prepossessed, nor blindly right;
Though learned, well-bred; and though well-bred, sincere;   635
Modestly bold, and humanly severe:
Who to a friend his faults can freely show,
And gladly praise the merit of a foe?
Blessed with a taste exact, yet unconfined;
A knowledge both of books and humankind;   640
Gen'rous converse;[4] a soul exempt from pride;
And love to praise, with reason on his side?

---

6. Tops "sleep" when they spin so rapidly that they seem not to move.
7. Worthless, worn-out horses.
8. Rubbish.
9. Dryden's *Fables* (1700), a set of translations, were among his most admired works; Thomas D'Urfey's *Tales* (1704) were notorious potboilers.
1. Samuel Garth (1661–1719), who had been accused of plagiarizing his mock-epic poem *The Dispensary* (1699) was admired and defended by Pope.
2. Booksellers' district near St. Paul's Cathedral, whose aisles were used as a place to meet and do business.
3. Either.
4. Well-bred conversation.

Such once were critics; such the happy few,
Athens and Rome in better ages knew.
The mighty Stagirite[5] first left the shore,   645
Spread all his sails, and durst the deeps explore;
He steered securely, and discovered far,
Led by the light of the Maeonian star.[6]
Poets, a race long unconfined, and free,
Still fond and proud of savage liberty,   650
Received his laws; and stood convinced 'twas fit,
Who conquered nature, should preside o'er wit.
   Horace still charms with graceful negligence,
And without method talks us into sense;
Will, like a friend, familiarly convey   655
The truest notions in the easiest[7] way.
He, who supreme in judgment, as in wit,
Might boldly censure, as he boldly writ,
Yet judged with coolness, though he sung with fire;
His precepts teach but what his works inspire.   660
Our critics take a contrary extreme,
They judge with fury, but they write with fle'me.[8]
Nor suffers Horace more in wrong translations
By wits, than critics[9] in as wrong quotations.
   See Dionysius[1] Homer's thoughts refine,   665
And call new beauties forth from every line!
   Fancy and art in gay Petronius[2] please,
The scholar's learning, with the courtier's ease.
   In grave Quintilian's[3] copious work, we find
The justest rules, and clearest method joined: 670
Thus useful arms in magazines[4] we place,
All ranged in order, and disposed with grace,
But less to please the eye, than arm the hand,
Still fit for use, and ready at command.
   Thee, bold Longinus! all the nine[5] inspire,   675
And bless their critic with a poet's fire.
An ardent judge, who, zealous in his trust,
With warmth gives sentence, yet is always just;
Whose own example strengthens all his laws,
And is himself that great sublime he draws.   680
   Thus long succeeding critics justly reigned,
License repressed, and useful laws ordained.
Learning and Rome alike in empire grew;
And arts still followed where her eagles[6] flew;
From the same foes, at last, both felt their doom,   685

---

5. Aristotle, whose *Poetics* founded the art of literary criticism, was born at Stagira.
6. Homer, who was supposed to have been born in Maeonia.
7. Least formal.
8. Phlegmatically.
9. I.e., than by critics. Phrases from Horace's *Art of Poetry* were quoted incessantly by critics.
1. Dionysius of Halicarnassus (1st century B.C.) wrote an important treatise on the artistic arrangement of words.

2. Author of the *Satyricon* (1st century A.D.).
3. Author of the *Institutio Oratoria* (ca. 95 A.D.), a famous treatise on rhetoric. Here as elsewhere, Pope's terms of praise are drawn from the author he is praising.
4. Storehouses or arsenals.
5. The Muses. "Longinus": supposed author of the influential treatise *On the Sublime* (1st century A.D.), greatly in vogue at the time of Pope.
6. Emblems on the standards of the Roman army.

And the same age saw learning fall, and Rome.
With tyranny, then superstition joined,
As that the body, this enslaved the mind;
Much was believed, but little understood,
And to be dull was construed to be good;   690
A second deluge learning thus o'errun,
And the monks finished what the Goths begun.[7]
    At length Erasmus, that great, injured name
(The glory of the priesthood, and the shame!),[8]
Stemmed the wild torrent of a barb'rous age,   695
And drove those holy Vandals off the stage.
    But see! each Muse, in Leo's golden days,
Starts from her trance, and trims her withered bays![9]
Rome's ancient Genius, o'er its ruins spread,
Shakes off the dust, and rears his reverend head.   700
Then sculpture and her sister-arts revive;
Stones leaped to form, and rocks began to live;
With sweeter notes each rising temple rung;
A Raphael painted, and a Vida[1] sung.
Immortal Vida: on whose honored brow   705
The poet's bays and critic's ivy grow:
Cremona now shall ever boast thy name,
As next in place to Mantua, next in fame![2]
    But soon by impious arms from Latium[3] chased,
Their ancient bounds the banished Muses passed;   710
Thence arts o'er all the northern world advance,
But critic-learning flourished most in France:
The rules a nation, born to serve, obeys;
And Boileau still in right of Horace sways.[4]
But we, brave Britons, foreign laws despised,   715
And kept unconquered—and uncivilized;
Fierce for the liberties of wit, and bold,
We still defied the Romans, as of old.
Yet some there were, among the sounder few
Of those who less presumed, and better knew,   720
Who durst assert the juster ancient cause,
And here restored wit's fundamental laws.
Such was the Muse, whose rules and practice tell,
"Nature's chief masterpiece is writing well."[5]
Such was Roscommon,[6] not more learned than good,   725
With manners gen'rous as his noble blood;
To him the wit of Greece and Rome was known,

---

7. Pope thought that the Scholastic theologians of the Middle Ages were "holy Vandals" who had "sacked" learning as the Goths and Vandals had sacked Rome.
8. Erasmus (1466–1536), the great humanist scholar, was the "glory of the priesthood" because of his goodness and learning, and its "shame" because he was persecuted.
9. The wreath of poetry. Leo X, pope from 1513 to 1521, was notable for his encouragement of artists.
1. M. Hieronymus Vida, an excellent Latin poet, who writ an Art of Poetry in verse. He flourished in the time of Leo the Tenth [Pope's note]. Raphael (1483–1520) painted many of his greatest works under the patronage of Leo X.
2. Vida came from Cremona, near Mantua, the birthplace of Virgil, his favorite poet.
3. Italy. German and Spanish troops sacked Rome in 1527.
4. Boileau's L'Art Poétique (1674) regularized and modernized the lessons of Horace's Art of Poetry.
5. Quoted from an Essay on Poetry by John Sheffield, duke of Buckingham (1648–1721), who had befriended the young Pope.
6. Wentworth Dillon, earl of Roscommon, wrote the important Essay on Translated Verse (1684).

And every author's merit, but his own.
Such late was Walsh—the Muse's[7] judge and friend,
Who justly knew to blame or to commend; 730
To failings mild, but zealous for desert;
The clearest head, and the sincerest heart.
This humble praise, lamented shade! receive,
This praise at least a grateful Muse may give:
The Muse, whose early voice you taught to sing, 735
Prescribed her heights, and pruned her tender wing,
(Her guide now lost) no more attempts to rise,
But in low numbers[8] short excursions tries:
Content, if hence the unlearned their wants may view,
The learned reflect on what before they knew: 740
Careless of censure, nor too fond of fame;
Still pleased to praise, yet not afraid to blame;
Averse alike to flatter, or offend;
Not free from faults, nor yet too vain to mend.

1709   1711

The Rape of the Lock

The Rape of the Lock is based on an actual episode that provoked a quarrel between two prominent Catholic families. Pope's friend John Caryll, to whom the poem is addressed (line 3), suggested that Pope write it, in the hope that a little laughter might serve to soothe ruffled tempers. Lord Petre had cut off a lock of hair from the head of the lovely Arabella Fermor (often spelled "Farmer" and doubtless so pronounced), much to the indignation of the lady and her relatives. In its original version of two cantos and 334 lines, published in 1712, The Rape of the Lock was a great success. In 1713 a new version was undertaken against the advice of Addison, who considered the poem perfect as it was first written. Pope greatly expanded the earlier version, adding the delightful "machinery" (i.e., the supernatural agents in epic action) of the Sylphs, Belinda's toilet, the card game, and the visit to the Cave of Spleen in canto 4. In 1717, with the addition of Clarissa's speech on good humor, the poem assumed its final form.

With delicate fancy and playful wit, Pope elaborated the trivial episode that occasioned the poem into the semblance of an epic in miniature, the most nearly perfect heroicomical poem in English. The poem abounds in parodies and echoes of the Iliad, the Aeneid, and Paradise Lost, thus constantly forcing the reader to compare small things with great. The familiar devices of epic are observed, but the incidents or characters are beautifully proportioned to the scale of mock epic. The Rape tells of war, but it is the drawing-room war between the sexes; it has its heroes and heroines, but they are beaux and belles; it has its supernatural characters ("machinery"), but they are Sylphs (borrowed, as Pope tells us in his engaging dedicatory letter, from Rosicrucian lore)—creatures of the air, the souls of dead coquettes, with tasks appropriate to their nature—or the Gnome Umbriel, once a prude on earth; it has its epic game, played on the "velvet plain" of the card table, its feasting heroes, who sip coffee and gossip, and its battle, fought with the clichés of compliment and conceits, with frowns and angry glances, with snuff and bodkin; it has the traditional epic journey to the underworld—here the Cave of Spleen, emblematic of the ill nature of female hypochondriacs. And Pope creates

7. The "Muse" here is Pope himself. William Walsh (1663–1708), whom Dryden once called "the best critic of our nation," had advised Pope to work at be- coming the first great "correct" poet in English.
8. Humble verses.

a world in which these actions take place, a world that is dense with beautiful objects: brocades, ivory and tortoise shell, cosmetics and diamonds, lacquered furniture, silver teapot, delicate chinaware. It is a world that is constantly in motion and that sparkles and glitters with light, whether the light of the sun or of Belinda's eyes or that light into which the "fluid" bodies of the Sylphs seem to dissolve as they flutter in shrouds and around the mast of Belinda's ship. Though Pope laughs at this world and its creatures—and remembers that a grimmer, darker world surrounds it (3.19–24 and 5.145–48)—he makes us very much aware of its beauty and charm.

The epigraph may be translated, "I was unwilling, Belinda, to ravish your locks; but I rejoice to have conceded this to your prayers" (Martial, *Epigrams* 12.84.1–2). Pope substituted his heroine for Martial's Polytimus. The epigraph is intended to suggest that the poem was published at Miss Fermor's request.

The Rape of the Lock

An Heroi-Comical Poem

Nolueram, Belinda, tuos violare capillos;
sed juvat hoc precibus me tribuisse tuis.
— MARTIAL

TO MRS. ARABELLA FERMOR

MADAM,

It will be in vain to deny that I have some regard for this piece, since I dedicate it to you. Yet you may bear me witness, it was intended only to divert a few young ladies, who have good sense and good humor enough to laugh not only at their sex's little unguarded follies, but at their own. But as it was communicated with the air of a secret, it soon found its way into the world. An imperfect copy having been offered to a bookseller, you had the good nature for my sake to consent to the publication of one more correct; this I was forced to, before I had executed half my design, for the machinery was entirely wanting to complete it.

The machinery, Madam, is a term invented by the critics, to signify that part which the deities, angels, or demons are made to act in a poem; for the ancient poets are in one respect like many modern ladies: let an action be never so trivial in itself, they always make it appear of the utmost importance. These machines I determined to raise on a very new and odd foundation, the Rosicrucian[1] doctrine of spirits.

I know how disagreeable it is to make use of hard words before a lady; but 'tis so much the concern of a poet to have his works understood, and particularly by your sex, that you must give me leave to explain two or three difficult terms.

The Rosicrucians are a people I must bring you acquainted with. The best account I know of them is in a French book called *Le Comte de Gabalis*,[2] which both in its title and size is so like a novel, that many of the fair sex have read it for one by mistake. According to these gentlemen, the four elements are inhabited by spirits, which they call Sylphs, Gnomes, Nymphs, and Salamanders. The Gnomes or Demons of earth delight in mischief; but the

---

1. A system of arcane philosophy introduced into England from Germany in the 17th century.

2. By the Abbé de Montfaucon de Villars, published in 1670.

Sylphs, whose habitation is in the air, are the best-conditioned creatures imaginable. For they say, any mortals may enjoy the most intimate familiarities with these gentle spirits, upon a condition very easy to all true adepts, an inviolate preservation of chastity.

As to the following cantos, all the passages of them are as fabulous as the vision at the beginning, or the transformation at the end (except the loss of your hair, which I always mention with reverence). The human persons are as fictitious as the airy ones; and the character of Belinda, as it is now managed, resembles you in nothing but in beauty.

If this poem had as many graces as there are in your person, or in your mind, yet I could never hope it should pass through the world half so uncensured as you have done. But let its fortune be what it will, mine is happy enough, to have given me this occasion of assuring you that I am, with the truest esteem,

MADAM,
Your most obedient, humble servant,
A. POPE

Canto 1

What dire offense from amorous causes springs,
What mighty contests rise from trivial things,
I sing—This verse to Caryll, Muse! is due:
This, even Belinda may vouchsafe to view:
Slight is the subject, but not so the praise,   5
If she inspire, and he approve my lays.
    Say what strange motive, Goddess! could compel
A well-bred lord to assault a gentle belle?
Oh, say what stranger cause, yet unexplored,
Could make a gentle belle reject a lord?   10
In tasks so bold can little men engage,
And in soft bosoms dwells such mighty rage?
    Sol through white curtains shot a timorous ray,
And oped those eyes that must eclipse the day.
Now lapdogs give themselves the rousing shake,   15
And sleepless lovers, just at twelve, awake:
Thrice rung the bell, the slipper knocked the ground,
And the pressed watch[3] returned a silver sound.
Belinda still her downy pillow pressed,
Her guardian Sylph prolonged the balmy rest.   20
'Twas he had summoned to her silent bed
The morning dream that hovered o'er her head.
A youth more glittering than a birthnight beau[4]
(That even in slumber caused her cheek to glow)
Seemed to her ear his winning lips to lay,   25
And thus in whispers said, or seemed to say:
    "Fairest of mortals, thou distinguished care
Of thousand bright inhabitants of air!

---

3. A watch that chimes the hour and the quarter hour when the stem is pressed down. "Knocked the ground": summons to a maid.

4. Courtiers wore especially fine clothes on the sovereign's birthday.

If e'er one vision touched thy infant thought,
Of all the nurse and all the priest have taught,   30
Of airy elves by moonlight shadows seen,
The silver token, and the circled green,[5]
Or virgins visited by angel powers,
With golden crowns and wreaths of heavenly flowers,
Hear and believe! thy own importance know,   35
Nor bound thy narrow views to things below.
Some secret truths, from learned pride concealed,
To maids alone and children are revealed:
What though no credit doubting wits may give?
The fair and innocent shall still believe.   40
Know, then, unnumbered spirits round thee fly,
The light militia of the lower sky:
These, though unseen, are ever on the wing,
Hang o'er the box, and hover round the Ring.[6]
Think what an equipage thou hast in air,   45
And view with scorn two pages and a chair.[7]
As now your own, our beings were of old,
And once enclosed in woman's beauteous mold;
Thence, by a soft transition, we repair
From earthly vehicles to these of air.   50
Think not, when woman's transient breath is fled,
That all her vanities at once are dead:
Succeeding vanities she still regards,
And though she plays no more, o'erlooks the cards.
Her joy in gilded chariots, when alive,   55
And love of ombre,[8] after death survive.
For when the Fair in all their pride expire,
To their first elements[9] their souls retire:
The sprites of fiery termagants in flame
Mount up, and take a Salamander's name.[1]   60
Soft yielding minds to water glide away,
And sip, with Nymphs, their elemental tea.[2]
The graver prude sinks downward to a Gnome,
In search of mischief still on earth to roam.
The light coquettes in Sylphs aloft repair,   65
And sport and flutter in the fields of air.
    "Know further yet; whoever fair and chaste
Rejects mankind, is by some Sylph embraced:
For spirits, freed from mortal laws, with ease
Assume what sexes and what shapes they please.[3]   70
What guards the purity of melting maids,

5. According to popular belief fairies skim off the cream from jugs of milk left standing overnight and leave a coin ("silver token") in payment. Rings of bright green grass, which are common in England even in winter, were held to be due to the round dances of fairies.
6. The "box" in the theater and the fashionable circular drive ("Ring") in Hyde Park.
7. Sedan chair.
8. The popular card game (see n. 4, p. 1084).
9. The four elements out of which all things were be-

lieved to have been made were fire, water, earth, and air. One or another of these elements was supposed to be predominant in both the physical and psychological makeup of each human being. In this context they are spoken of as "humors."
1. Each element was inhabited by a spirit, as the following lines explain. The salamander is a lizardlike animal, in antiquity believed to live in fire.
2. Pronounce *tay*.
3. Cf. *Paradise Lost* 1.427–431 (p. 675); this is one of many allusions to that poem in the *Rape*.

In courtly balls, and midnight masquerades,
Safe from the treacherous friend, the daring spark,
The glance by day, the whisper in the dark,
When kind occasion prompts their warm desires,   75
When music softens, and when dancing fires?
'Tis but their Sylph, the wise Celestials know,
Though Honor is the word with men below.
    "Some nymphs there are, too conscious of their face,
For life predestined to the Gnomes' embrace.   80
These swell their prospects and exalt their pride,
When offers are disdained, and love denied:
Then gay ideas⁴ crowd the vacant brain,
While peers, and dukes, and all their sweeping train,
And garters, stars, and coronets appear,   85
And in soft sounds, 'your Grace'⁵ salutes their ear.
'Tis these that early taint the female soul,
Instruct the eyes of young coquettes to roll,
Teach infant cheeks a bidden blush to know,
And little hearts to flutter at a beau.   90
    "Oft, when the world imagine women stray,
The Sylphs through mystic mazes guide their way,
Through all the giddy circle they pursue,
And old impertinence⁶ expel by new.
What tender maid but must a victim fall   95
To one man's treat, but for another's ball?
When Florio speaks, what virgin could withstand,
If gentle Damon did not squeeze her hand?
With varying vanities, from every part,
They shift the moving toyshop⁷ of their heart;   100
Where wigs with wigs, with sword-knots sword-knots strive,
Beaux banish beaux, and coaches coaches drive.
This erring mortals levity may call;
Oh, blind to truth! the Sylphs contrive it all.
    "Of these am I, who thy protection claim,   105
A watchful sprite, and Ariel is my name.
Late, as I ranged the crystal wilds of air,
In the clear mirror of thy ruling star
I saw, alas! some dread event impend,
Ere to the main this morning sun descend,   110
But Heaven reveals not what, or how, or where:
Warned by the Sylph, O pious maid, beware!
This to disclose is all thy guardian can:
Beware of all, but most beware of Man!"
    He said; when Shock,⁸ who thought she slept too long,   115
Leaped up, and waked his mistress with his tongue.
'Twas then, Belinda, if report say true,
Thy eyes first opened on a billet-doux;
Wounds, charms, and ardors were no sooner read,
But all the vision vanished from thy head.   120

4. Showy images.
5. A duchess. "Garters, stars, and coronets": emblems
of nobility.
6. Trifle.
7. A shop stocked with baubles and trifles.
8. A long-haired poodle, Belinda's lapdog.

And now, unveiled, the toilet stands displayed,
Each silver vase in mystic order laid.
First, robed in white, the nymph intent adores,
With head uncovered, the cosmetic powers.
A heavenly image in the glass appears;   125
To that she bends, to that her eyes she rears.
The inferior priestess, at her altar's side,
Trembling begins the sacred rites of Pride.
Unnumbered treasures ope at once, and here
The various offerings of the world appear;   130
From each she nicely culls with curious toil,
And decks the goddess with the glittering spoil.
This casket India's glowing gems unlocks,
And all Arabia breathes from yonder box.
The tortoise here and elephant unite,   135
Transformed to combs, the speckled and the white.
Here files of pins extend their shining rows,
Puffs, powders, patches, Bibles,[9] billet-doux.
Now awful Beauty puts on all its arms;
The fair each moment rises in her charms,   140
Repairs her smiles, awakens every grace,
And calls forth all the wonders of her face;
Sees by degrees a purer blush arise,
And keener lightnings quicken in her eyes.
The busy Sylphs surround their darling care,   145
These set the head, and those divide the hair,
Some fold the sleeve, whilst others plait the gown;
And Betty's[1] praised for labors not her own.

Canto 2

Not with more glories, in the ethereal plain,
The sun first rises o'er the purpled main,
Than, issuing forth, the rival of his beams
Launched on the bosom of the silver Thames.
Fair nymphs and well-dressed youths around her shone,   5
But every eye was fixed on her alone.
On her white breast a sparkling cross she wore,
Which Jews might kiss, and infidels adore.
Her lively looks a sprightly mind disclose,
Quick as her eyes, and as unfixed as those: 10
Favors to none, to all she smiles extends;
Oft she rejects, but never once offends.
Bright as the sun, her eyes the gazers strike,
And, like the sun, they shine on all alike.
Yet graceful ease, and sweetness void of pride,   15
Might hide her faults, if belles had faults to hide:
If to her share some female errors fall,
Look on her face, and you'll forget 'em all.

---

9. It has been suggested that Pope intended here not   1. Belinda's maid, the "inferior priestess" mentioned
"Bibles," but "bibelots" (trinkets), but this interpreta-   in line 127.
tion has not gained wide acceptance.

This nymph, to the destruction of mankind,
Nourished two locks which graceful hung behind   20
In equal curls, and well conspired to deck
With shining ringlets her smooth ivory neck.
Love in these labyrinths his slaves detains,
And mighty hearts are held in slender chains.
With hairy springes[2] we the birds betray,   25
Slight lines of hair surprise the finny prey,
Fair tresses man's imperial race ensnare,
And beauty draws us with a single hair.
     The adventurous Baron the bright locks admired,
He saw, he wished, and to the prize aspired.   30
Resolved to win, he meditates the way,
By force to ravish, or by fraud betray;
For when success a lover's toil attends,
Few ask if fraud or force attained his ends.
     For this, ere Phoebus rose, he had implored   35
Propitious Heaven, and every power adored,
But chiefly Love—to Love an altar built,
Of twelve vast French romances, neatly gilt.
There lay three garters, half a pair of gloves,
And all the trophies of his former loves.   40
With tender billet-doux he lights the pyre,
And breathes three amorous sighs to raise the fire.
Then prostrate falls, and begs with ardent eyes
Soon to obtain, and long possess the prize:
The powers gave ear, and granted half his prayer,   45
The rest the winds dispersed in empty air.
     But now secure the painted vessel glides,
The sunbeams trembling on the floating tides,
While melting music steals upon the sky,
And softened sounds along the waters die.   50
Smooth flow the waves, the zephyrs gently play,
Belinda smiled, and all the world was gay.
All but the Sylph—with careful thoughts oppressed,
The impending woe sat heavy on his breast.
He summons straight his denizens of air;   55
The lucid squadrons round the sails repair:
Soft o'er the shrouds aërial whispers breathe
That seemed but zephyrs to the train beneath.
Some to the sun their insect-wings unfold,
Waft on the breeze, or sink in clouds of gold.   60
Transparent forms too fine for mortal sight,
Their fluid bodies half dissolved in light,
Loose to the wind their airy garments flew,
Thin glittering textures of the filmy dew,
Dipped in the richest tincture of the skies,   65
Where light disports in ever-mingling dyes,
While every beam new transient colors flings,
Colors that change whene'er they wave their wings.

---

2. Snares; pronounced *sprin-jez*.

Amid the circle, on the gilded mast,
Superior by the head was Ariel placed;   70
His purple[3] pinions opening to the sun,
He raised his azure wand, and thus begun:
   "Ye Sylphs and Sylphids, to your chief give ear!
Fays, Fairies, Genïi, Elves, and Daemons, hear!
Ye know the spheres and various tasks assigned   75
By laws eternal to the aërial kind.
Some in the fields of purest ether play,
And bask and whiten in the blaze of day.
Some guide the course of wandering orbs on high,
Or roll the planets through the boundless sky.   80
Some less refined, beneath the moon's pale light
Pursue the stars that shoot athwart the night,
Or suck the mists in grosser air below,
Or dip their pinions in the painted bow,
Or brew fierce tempests on the wintry main,   85
Or o'er the glebe[4] distill the kindly rain.
Others on earth o'er human race preside,
Watch all their ways, and all their actions guide:
Of these the chief the care of nations own,
And guard with arms divine the British Throne.   90
   "Our humbler province is to tend the Fair,
Not a less pleasing, though less glorious care:
To save the powder from too rude a gale,
Nor let the imprisoned essences exhale;
To draw fresh colors from the vernal flowers;   95
To steal from rainbows e'er they drop in showers
A brighter wash;[5] to curl their waving hairs,
Assist their blushes, and inspire their airs,
Nay oft, in dreams invention we bestow,
To change a flounce, or add a furbelow.   100
   "This day black omens threat the brightest fair,
That e'er deserved a watchful spirit's care;
Some dire disaster, or by force or slight,
But what, or where, the Fates have wrapped in night:
Whether the nymph shall break Diana's law,[6]   105
Or some frail china jar receive a flaw,
Or stain her honor, or her new brocade,
Forget her prayers, or miss a masquerade,
Or lose her heart, or necklace, at a ball;
Or whether Heaven has doomed that Shock must fall.   110
Haste, then, ye spirits! to your charge repair:
The fluttering fan be Zephyretta's care;
The drops[7] to thee, Brillante, we consign;
And, Momentilla, let the watch be thine;

---

3. In 18th-century poetic diction the word might
mean bloodred, purple, or simply (as is likely here)
brightly colored. The word derives from Virgil, *Eclogue* 9, 40, *purpureum.* An example of the Latinate
nature of some poetic diction of the period.

4. Cultivated field.
5. Cosmetic lotion.
6. Diana was the goddess of chastity.
7. Diamond earrings. Observe the appropriateness of
the names of the Sylphs to their assigned functions.

Do thou, Crispissa,[8] tend her favorite Lock;   115
Ariel himself shall be the guard of Shock.
    "To fifty chosen Sylphs, of special note,
We trust the important charge, the petticoat;
Oft have we known that sevenfold fence to fail,
Though stiff with hoops, and armed with ribs of whale.   120
Form a strong line about the silver bound,
And guard the wide circumference around.
    "Whatever spirit, careless of his charge,
His post neglects, or leaves the fair at large,
Shall feel sharp vengeance soon o'ertake his sins,   125
Be stopped in vials, or transfixed with pins,
Or plunged in lakes of bitter washes lie,
Or wedged whole ages in a bodkin's[9] eye;
Gums and pomatums shall his flight restrain,
While clogged he beats his silken wings in vain,   130
Or alum styptics with contracting power
Shrink his thin essence like a riveled[1] flower:
Or, as Ixion[2] fixed, the wretch shall feel
The giddy motion of the whirling mill,
In fumes of burning chocolate shall glow,   135
And tremble at the sea that froths below!"
    He spoke; the spirits from the sails descend;
Some, orb in orb, around the nymph extend;
Some thread the mazy ringlets of her hair;
Some hang upon the pendants of her ear: 140
With beating hearts the dire event they wait,
Anxious, and trembling for the birth of Fate.

Canto 3

    Close by those meads, forever crowned with flowers,
Where Thames with pride surveys his rising towers,
There stands a structure of majestic frame,
Which from the neighboring Hampton takes its name.[3]
Here Britain's statesmen oft the fall foredoom   5
Of foreign tyrants and of nymphs at home;
Here thou, great Anna! whom three realms obey,
Dost sometimes counsel take—and sometimes tea.
    Hither the heroes and the nymphs resort,
To taste awhile the pleasures of a court;   10
In various talk the instructive hours they passed,
Who gave the ball, or paid the visit last;
One speaks the glory of the British Queen,
And one describes a charming Indian screen;
A third interprets motions, looks, and eyes;   15
At every word a reputation dies.

8. From Latin *crispere*, "to curl."
9. A blunt needle with a large eye, used for drawing ribbon through eyelets in the edging of women's garments.
1. To "rivel" is to "contract into wrinkles and corruga-

tions" (Johnson's *Dictionary*).
2. In the Greek myth Ixion was punished in the underworld by being bound on an everturning wheel.
3. Hampton Court, the royal palace, about fifteen miles up the Thames from London.

Snuff, or the fan, supply each pause of chat,
With singing, laughing, ogling, and all that.
    Meanwhile, declining from the noon of day,
The sun obliquely shoots his burning ray;   20
The hungry judges soon the sentence sign,
And wretches hang that jurymen may dine;
The merchant from the Exchange returns in peace,
And the long labors of the toilet cease.
Belinda now, whom thirst of fame invites,   25
Burns to encounter two adventurous knights,
At ombre[4] singly to decide their doom,
And swells her breast with conquests yet to come.
Straight the three bands prepare in arms to join,
Each band the number of the sacred nine.   30
Soon as she spreads her hand, the aërial guard
Descend, and sit on each important card:
First Ariel perched upon a Matadore,
Then each according to the rank they bore;
For Sylphs, yet mindful of their ancient race,   35
Are, as when women, wondrous fond of place.
    Behold, four Kings in majesty revered,
With hoary whiskers and a forky beard;
And four fair Queens whose hands sustain a flower,
The expressive emblem of their softer power;   40
Four Knaves in garbs succinct,[5] a trusty band,
Caps on their heads, and halberts in their hand,
And parti-colored troops, a shining train,
Draw forth to combat on the velvet plain.
    The skillful nymph reviews her force with care;   45
"Let Spades be trumps!" she said, and trumps they were.
    Now move to war her sable Matadores,
In show like leaders of the swarthy Moors.
Spadillio first, unconquerable lord!
Led off two captive trumps, and swept the board.   50
As many more Manillio forced to yield,
And marched a victor from the verdant field.
Him Basto followed, but his fate more hard
Gained but one trump and one plebeian card.
With his broad saber next, a chief in years,   55
The hoary Majesty of Spades appears,
Puts forth one manly leg, to sight revealed,
The rest his many-colored robe concealed.
The rebel Knave, who dares his prince engage,
Proves the just victim of his royal rage.   60

4. The game of ombre that Belinda plays against the baron and another young man is too complicated for complete explication here. Pope has carefully arranged the cards so that Belinda wins. The baron's hand is strong enough to be a threat, but the third player's is of little account. The hand is played exactly according to the rules of ombre, and Pope's description of the cards is equally accurate. Each player holds nine cards (line 30). The "Matadores" (line 33), when spades are trumps, are "Spadillio" (line 49), the ace of spades; "Manillio" (line 51), the two of spades; "Basto" (line 53), the ace of clubs; Belinda holds all three of these. (For a more complete description of ombre, see *The Rape of the Lock and Other Poems*, ed. Geoffrey Tillotson, in the Twickenham Edition of Pope's poems, vol. 2, Appendix C.)
5. Girded up.

Even mighty Pam,[6] that kings and queens o'erthrew
And mowed down armies in the fights of loo,
Sad chance of war! now destitute of aid,
Falls undistinguished by the victor Spade.
    Thus far both armies to Belinda yield;   65
Now to the Baron fate inclines the field.
His warlike amazon her host invades,
The imperial consort of the crown of Spades.
The Club's black tyrant first her victim died,
Spite of his haughty mien and barbarous pride.   70
What boots the regal circle on his head,
His giant limbs, in state unwieldy spread?
That long behind he trails his pompous robe,
And of all monarchs only grasps the globe?
    The Baron now his Diamonds pours apace;   75
The embroidered King who shows but half his face,
And his refulgent Queen, with powers combined,
Of broken troops an easy conquest find.
Clubs, Diamonds, Hearts, in wild disorder seen,
With throngs promiscuous strew the level green.   80
Thus when dispersed a routed army runs,
Of Asia's troops, and Afric's sable sons,
With like confusion different nations fly,
Of various habit, and of various dye,
The pierced battalions disunited fall   85
In heaps on heaps; one fate o'erwhelms them all.
    The Knave of Diamonds tries his wily arts,
And wins (oh, shameful chance!) the Queen of Hearts.
At this, the blood the virgin's cheek forsook,
A livid paleness spreads o'er all her look;   90
She sees, and trembles at the approaching ill,
Just in the jaws of ruin, and Codille.[7]
And now (as oft in some distempered state)
On one nice trick depends the general fate.
An Ace of Hearts steps forth: the King unseen   95
Lurked in her hand, and mourned his captive Queen.
He springs to vengeance with an eager pace,
And falls like thunder on the prostrate Ace.
The nymph exulting fills with shouts the sky,
The walls, the woods, and long canals reply.   100
    O thoughtless mortals! ever blind to fate,
Too soon dejected, and too soon elate:
Sudden these honors shall be snatched away,
And cursed forever this victorious day.
    For lo! the board with cups and spoons is crowned,   105
The berries crackle, and the mill turns round;[8]
On shining altars of Japan[9] they raise

6. The knave of clubs, the highest trump in the game
of loo.
7. The term applied to losing a hand at cards.
8. I.e., coffee is roasted and ground.

9. I.e., small, lacquered tables. The word *altars* suggests the ritualistic character of coffee drinking in Belinda's world.

The silver lamp; the fiery spirits blaze:
From silver spouts the grateful liquors glide,
While China's earth receives the smoking tide.   110
At once they gratify their scent and taste,
And frequent cups prolong the rich repast.
Straight hover round the fair her airy band;
Some, as she sipped, the fuming liquor fanned,
Some o'er her lap their careful plumes displayed,   115
Trembling, and conscious of the rich brocade.
Coffee (which makes the politician wise,
And see through all things with his half-shut eyes)
Sent up in vapors to the Baron's brain
New stratagems, the radiant Lock to gain.   120
Ah, cease, rash youth! desist ere 'tis too late,
Fear the just Gods, and think of Scylla's fate![1]
Changed to a bird, and sent to flit in air,
She dearly pays for Nisus' injured hair!
    But when to mischief mortals bend their will,   125
How soon they find fit instruments of ill!
Just then, Clarissa drew with tempting grace
A two-edged weapon from her shining case:
So ladies in romance assist their knight,
Present the spear, and arm him for the fight.   130
He takes the gift with reverence, and extends
The little engine on his fingers' ends;
This just behind Belinda's neck he spread,
As o'er the fragrant steams she bends her head.
Swift to the Lock a thousand sprites repair,   135
A thousand wings, by turns, blow back the hair,
And thrice they twitched the diamond in her ear,
Thrice she looked back, and thrice the foe drew near.
Just in that instant, anxious Ariel sought
The close recesses of the virgin's thought;   140
As on the nosegay in her breast reclined,
He watched the ideas rising in her mind,
Sudden he viewed, in spite of all her art,
An earthly lover lurking at her heart.
Amazed, confused, he found his power expired,   145
Resigned to fate, and with a sigh retired.
    The Peer now spreads the glittering forfex[2] wide,
To enclose the Lock; now joins it, to divide.
Even then, before the fatal engine closed,
A wretched Sylph too fondly interposed;   150
Fate urged the shears, and cut the Sylph in twain
(But airy substance soon unites again):
The meeting points the sacred hair dissever
From the fair head, forever and forever!
    Then flashed the living lightning from her eyes,   155

1. Scylla, daughter of Nisus, was turned into a sea bird because, for the sake of her love for Minos of Crete, who was besieging her father's city of Megara, she cut from her father's head the purple lock on which his safety depended. She is not the Scylla of "Scylla and Charybdis."
2. Scissors.

And screams of horror rend the affrighted skies.
Not louder shrieks to pitying heaven are cast,
When husbands, or when lapdogs breathe their last;
Or when rich china vessels fallen from high,
In glittering dust and painted fragments lie!   160
"Let wreaths of triumph now my temples twine,"
The victor cried, "the glorious prize is mine!
While fish in streams, or birds delight in air,
Or in a coach and six the British fair,
As long as *Atalantis*[3] shall be read,   165
Or the small pillow grace a lady's bed,
While visits shall be paid on solemn days,
When numerous wax-lights in bright order blaze,
While nymphs take treats, or assignations give,
So long my honor, name, and praise shall live!   170
     "What time would spare, from steel receives its date,
And monuments, like men, submit to fate!
Steel could the labor of the Gods destroy,
And strike to dust the imperial towers of Troy;
Steel could the works of mortal pride confound,   175
And hew triumphal arches to the ground.
What wonder then, fair nymph! thy hairs should feel,
The conquering force of unresisted steel?"

Canto 4

     But anxious cares the pensive nymph oppressed,
And secret passions labored in her breast.
Not youthful kings in battle seized alive,
Not scornful virgins who their charms survive,
Not ardent lovers robbed of all their bliss,   5
Not ancient ladies when refused a kiss,
Not tyrants fierce that unrepenting die,
Not Cynthia when her manteau's[4] pinned awry,
E'er felt such rage, resentment, and despair,
As thou, sad virgin! for thy ravished hair.   10
     For, that sad moment, when the Sylphs withdrew
And Ariel weeping from Belinda flew,
Umbriel,[5] a dusky, melancholy sprite
As ever sullied the fair face of light,
Down to the central earth, his proper scene,   15
Repaired to search the gloomy Cave of Spleen.[6]
     Swift on his sooty pinions flits the Gnome,
And in a vapor reached the dismal dome.
No cheerful breeze this sullen region knows,
The dreaded east is all the wind that blows.   20
Here in a grotto, sheltered close from air,
And screened in shades from day's detested glare,
She sighs forever on her pensive bed,

3. Delariviere Manley's *New Atalantis* (1709) was notorious for its thinly concealed allusions to contemporary scandals.

4. Negligee or loose robe.
5. The name suggests shade and darkness.
6. Ill humor.

Pain at her side, and Megrim[7] at her head.
   Two handmaids wait the throne: alike in place			25
But differing far in figure and in face.
Here stood Ill-Nature like an ancient maid,
Her wrinkled form in black and white arrayed;
With store of prayers for mornings, nights, and noons,
Her hand is filled; her bosom with lampoons.			30
   There Affectation, with a sickly mien,
Shows in her cheek the roses of eighteen,
Practiced to lisp, and hang the head aside,
Faints into airs, and languishes with pride,
On the rich quilt sinks with becoming woe,			35
Wrapped in a gown, for sickness and for show.
The fair ones feel such maladies as these,
When each new nightdress gives a new disease.
   A constant vapor[8] o'er the palace flies,
Strange phantoms rising as the mists arise;			40
Dreadful as hermit's dreams in haunted shades,
Or bright as visions of expiring maids.
Now glaring fiends, and snakes on rolling spires,[9]
Pale specters, gaping tombs, and purple fires;
Now lakes of liquid gold, Elysian scenes,			45
And crystal domes, and angels in machines.[1]
   Unnumbered throngs on every side are seen
Of bodies changed to various forms by Spleen.
Here living teapots stand, one arm held out,
One bent; the handle this, and that the spout:			50
A pipkin[2] there, like Homer's tripod, walks;
Here sighs a jar, and there a goose pie talks;
Men prove with child, as powerful fancy works,
And maids, turned bottles, call aloud for corks.
   Safe passed the Gnome through this fantastic band,			55
A branch of healing spleenwort[3] in his hand.
Then thus addressed the Power: "Hail, wayward Queen!
Who rule the sex to fifty from fifteen:
Parent of vapors and of female wit,
Who give the hysteric or poetic fit,			60
On various tempers act by various ways,
Make some take physic, others scribble plays;
Who cause the proud their visits to delay,
And send the godly in a pet to pray.
A nymph there is that all your power disdains,			65
And thousands more in equal mirth maintains.
But oh! if e'er thy Gnome could spoil a grace,
Or raise a pimple on a beauteous face,

7. Headache.
8. Emblematic of "the vapors," a fashionable hypochondria, melancholy, or peevishness.
9. Coils.
1. Mechanical devices used in the theaters for spectacular effects. The catalog of hallucinations draws on the sensational stage effects popular with contemporary audiences.

2. An earthen pot. In *Iliad* 18.373–377, Vulcan furnishes the gods with self-propelling "tripods" (three-legged stools).
3. An herb, efficacious against the spleen. Pope alludes to the golden bough that Aeneas and the Cumaean sybil carry with them for protection into the underworld in *Aeneid* 6.

Like citron-waters[4] matrons' cheeks inflame,
Or change complexions at a losing game;   70
If e'er with airy horns[5] I planted heads,
Or rumpled petticoats, or tumbled beds,
Or caused suspicion when no soul was rude,
Or discomposed the headdress of a prude,
Or e'er to costive lapdog gave disease,   75
Which not the tears of brightest eyes could ease,
Hear me, and touch Belinda with chagrin:[6]
That single act gives half the world the spleen."
        The Goddess with a discontented air
Seems to reject him though she grants his prayer.   80
A wondrous bag with both her hands she binds,
Like that where once Ulysses held the winds;[7]
There she collects the force of female lungs,
Sighs, sobs, and passions, and the war of tongues.
A vial next she fills with fainting fears,   85
Soft sorrows, melting griefs, and flowing tears.
The Gnome rejoicing bears her gifts away,
Spreads his black wings, and slowly mounts to day.
        Sunk in Thalestris'[8] arms the nymph he found,
Her eyes dejected and her hair unbound.   90
Full o'er their heads the swelling bag he rent,
And all the Furies issued at the vent.
Belinda burns with more than mortal ire,
And fierce Thalestris fans the rising fire.
"O wretched maid!" she spread her hands, and cried   95
(While Hampton's echoes, "Wretched maid!" replied),
"Was it for this you took such constant care
The bodkin, comb, and essence to prepare?
For this your locks in paper durance bound,
For this with torturing irons wreathed around?   100
For this with fillets strained your tender head,
And bravely bore the double loads of lead?[9]
Gods! shall the ravisher display your hair,
While the fops envy, and the ladies stare!
Honor forbid! at whose unrivaled shrine   105
Ease, pleasure, virtue, all, our sex resign.
Methinks already I your tears survey,
Already hear the horrid things they say,
Already see you a degraded toast,
And all your honor in a whisper lost!   110
How shall I, then, your helpless fame defend?
'Twill then be infamy to seem your friend!
And shall this prize, the inestimable prize,

4. Brandy flavored with orange or lemon peel.
5. The symbol of the cuckold, the man whose wife has been unfaithful to him; here "airy," because they exist only in the jealous suspicions of the husband, the victim of the mischievous Umbriel.
6. Ill humor.
7. Aeolus (later conceived of as god of the winds) gave Ulysses a bag containing all the winds adverse to his voyage home. When his ship was in sight of Ithaca, his companions opened the bag and the storms that ensued drove Ulysses far away (*Odyssey* 10.19ff.).
8. The name is borrowed from a queen of the Amazons, hence a fierce and warlike woman.
9. The frame on which the elaborate coiffures of the day were arranged.

Exposed through crystal to the gazing eyes,
And heightened by the diamond's circling rays,   115
On that rapacious hand forever blaze?
Sooner shall grass in Hyde Park Circus grow,
And wits take lodgings in the sound of Bow;[1]
Sooner let earth, air, sea, to chaos fall,
Men, monkeys, lapdogs, parrots, perish all!"   120
    She said; then raging to Sir Plume repairs,
And bids her beau demand the precious hairs
(Sir Plume of amber snuffbox justly vain,
And the nice conduct of a clouded cane).
With earnest eyes, and round unthinking face,   125
He first the snuffbox opened, then the case,
And thus broke out—"My Lord, why, what the devil!
Z——ds! damn the lock! 'fore Gad, you must be civil!
Plague on 't! 'tis past a jest—nay prithee, pox!
Give her the hair"—he spoke, and rapped his box.   130
    "It grieves me much," replied the Peer again,
"Who speaks so well should ever speak in vain.
But by this Lock, this sacred Lock I swear
(Which never more shall join its parted hair;
Which never more its honors shall renew,   135
Clipped from the lovely head where late it grew),
That while my nostrils draw the vital air,
This hand, which won it, shall forever wear."
He spoke, and speaking, in proud triumph spread
The long-contended honors[2] of her head.   140
    But Umbriel, hateful Gnome, forbears not so;
He breaks the vial whence the sorrows flow.
Then see! the nymph in beauteous grief appears,
Her eyes half languishing, half drowned in tears;
On her heaved bosom hung her drooping head,   145
Which with a sigh she raised, and thus she said:
    "Forever cursed be this detested day,
Which snatched my best, my favorite curl away!
Happy! ah, ten times happy had I been,
If Hampton Court these eyes had never seen!   150
Yet am not I the first mistaken maid,
By love of courts to numerous ills betrayed.
Oh, had I rather unadmired remained
In some lone isle, or distant northern land;
Where the gilt chariot never marks the way,   155
Where none learn ombre, none e'er taste bohea![3]
There kept my charms concealed from mortal eye,
Like roses that in deserts bloom and die.
What moved my mind with youthful lords to roam?
Oh, had I stayed, and said my prayers at home!   160
'Twas this the morning omens seemed to tell;

1. A person born within sound of the bells of St. Mary-   2. Ornaments, hence locks; a Latinism.
le-Bow in Cheapside is said to be a cockney. No fash-   3. A costly sort of tea.
ionable wit would have so vulgar an address.

Thrice from my trembling hand the patch box[4] fell;
The tottering china shook without a wind,
Nay, Poll sat mute, and Shock was most unkind!
A Sylph too warned me of the threats of fate,   165
In mystic visions, now believed too late!
See the poor remnants of these slighted hairs!
My hands shall rend what e'en thy rapine spares.
These in two sable ringlets taught to break,
Once gave new beauties to the snowy neck.   170
The sister lock now sits uncouth, alone,
And in its fellow's fate foresees its own;
Uncurled it hangs, the fatal shears demands,
And tempts once more thy sacrilegious hands.
Oh, hadst thou, cruel! been content to seize   175
Hairs less in sight, or any hairs but these!"

Canto 5

She said: the pitying audience melt in tears.
But Fate and Jove had stopped the Baron's ears.
In vain Thalestris with reproach assails,
For who can move when fair Belinda fails?
Not half so fixed the Trojan[5] could remain,   5
While Anna begged and Dido raged in vain.
Then grave Clarissa graceful waved her fan;
Silence ensued, and thus the nymph began:
  "Say, why are beauties praised and honored most,
The wise man's passion, and the vain man's toast?   10
Why decked with all that land and sea afford,
Why angels called, and angel-like adored?
Why round our coaches crowd the white-gloved beaux,
Why bows the side box from its inmost rows?
How vain are all these glories, all our pains,   15
Unless good sense preserve what beauty gains;
That men may say when we the front box grace,
'Behold the first in virtue as in face!'
Oh! if to dance all night, and dress all day,
Charmed the smallpox, or chased old age away,   20
Who would not scorn what housewife's cares produce,
Or who would learn one earthly thing of use?
To patch, nay ogle, might become a saint,
Nor could it sure be such a sin to paint.
But since, alas! frail beauty must decay,   25
Curled or uncurled, since locks will turn to gray;
Since painted, or not painted, all shall fade,
And she who scorns a man must die a maid;
What then remains but well our power to use,
And keep good humor still whate'er we lose?   30

4. A box to hold the ornamental patches of court plaster worn on the face by both sexes.
5. Aeneas, who forsook Dido at the bidding of the
gods, despite her reproaches and the supplications of
her sister Anna. Virgil compares him to a steadfast oak
that withstands a storm (*Aeneid* 4.437–443).

And trust me, dear, good humor can prevail
When airs, and flights, and screams, and scolding fail.
Beauties in vain their pretty eyes may roll;
Charms strike the sight, but merit wins the soul."[6]
    So spoke the dame, but no applause ensued;   35
Belinda frowned, Thalestris called her prude.
"To arms, to arms!" the fierce virago cries,
And swift as lightning to the combat flies.
All side in parties, and begin the attack;
Fans clap, silks rustle, and tough whalebones crack;   40
Heroes' and heroines' shouts confusedly rise,
And bass and treble voices strike the skies.
No common weapons in their hands are found,
Like Gods they fight, nor dread a mortal wound.
    So when bold Homer makes the Gods engage,   45
And heavenly breasts with human passions rage;
'Gainst Pallas, Mars; Latona, Hermes arms;
And all Olympus rings with loud alarms:
Jove's thunder roars, heaven trembles all around,
Blue Neptune storms, the bellowing deeps resound: 50
Earth shakes her nodding towers, the ground gives way,
And the pale ghosts start at the flash of day!
    Triumphant Umbriel on a sconce's[7] height
Clapped his glad wings, and sat to view the fight:
Propped on the bodkin spears, the sprites survey   55
The growing combat, or assist the fray.
    While through the press enraged Thalestris flies,
And scatters death around from both her eyes,
A beau and witling perished in the throng,
One died in metaphor, and one in song.   60
"O cruel nymph! a living death I bear,"
Cried Dapperwit, and sunk beside his chair.
A mournful glance Sir Fopling upwards cast,
"Those eyes are made so killing"—was his last.
Thus on Maeander's flowery margin lies   65
The expiring swan, and as he sings he dies.
    When bold Sir Plume had drawn Clarissa down,
Chloe stepped in, and killed him with a frown;
She smiled to see the doughty hero slain,
But, at her smile, the beau revived again.   70
    Now Jove suspends his golden scales in air,
Weighs the men's wits against the lady's hair;
The doubtful beam long nods from side to side;
At length the wits mount up, the hairs subside.
    See, fierce Belinda on the Baron flies,   75
With more than usual lightning in her eyes;
Nor feared the chief the unequal fight to try,
Who sought no more than on his foe to die.
    But this bold lord with manly strength endued,

6. The speech is a close parody of Pope's own transla-   *Iliad* (12.371–396).
tion of the speech of Sarpedon to Glaucus, first pub-   7. Candlestick fastened on the wall.
lished in 1709 and slightly revised in his version of the

She with one finger and a thumb subdued:　　　　　　　　　80
Just where the breath of life his nostrils drew,
A charge of snuff the wily virgin threw;
The Gnomes direct, to every atom just,
The pungent grains of titillating dust.
Sudden, with starting tears each eye o'erflows,　　　　　85
And the high dome re-echoes to his nose.
　"Now meet thy fate," incensed Belinda cried,
And drew a deadly bodkin[8] from her side.
(The same, his ancient personage to deck,
Her great-great-grandsire wore about his neck,　　　　90
In three seal rings; which after, melted down,
Formed a vast buckle for his widow's gown:
Her infant grandame's whistle next it grew,
The bells she jingled, and the whistle blew;
Then in a bodkin graced her mother's hairs,　　　　　95
Which long she wore, and now Belinda wears.)
　"Boast not my fall," he cried, "insulting foe!
Thou by some other shalt be laid as low.
Nor think to die dejects my lofty mind:
All that I dread is leaving you behind!　　　　　　　100
Rather than so, ah, let me still survive,
And burn in Cupid's flames—but burn alive."
　"Restore the Lock!" she cries; and all around
"Restore the Lock!" the vaulted roofs rebound.
Not fierce Othello in so loud a strain　　　　　　　105
Roared for the handkerchief that caused his pain.[9]
But see how oft ambitious aims are crossed,
And chiefs contend till all the prize is lost!
The lock, obtained with guilt, and kept with pain,
In every place is sought, but sought in vain:　　　　110
With such a prize no mortal must be blessed,
So Heaven decrees! with Heaven who can contest?
　Some thought it mounted to the lunar sphere,
Since all things lost on earth are treasured there.
There heroes' wits are kept in ponderous vases,　　　115
And beaux' in snuffboxes and tweezer cases.
There broken vows and deathbed alms are found,
And lovers' hearts with ends of riband bound,
The courtier's promises, and sick man's prayers,
The smiles of harlots, and the tears of heirs,　　　　120
Cages for gnats, and chains to yoke a flea,
Dried butterflies, and tomes of casuistry.
　But trust the Muse—she saw it upward rise,
Though marked by none but quick, poetic eyes
(So Rome's great founder to the heavens withdrew,[1]　125
To Proculus alone confessed in view);
A sudden star, it shot through liquid air,
And drew behind a radiant trail of hair.

8. Here, an ornamental hairpin shaped like a dagger.　snatched to heaven in a storm cloud while reviewing
9. *Othello* 3.4.　　　　　　　　　　　　　　　　his army in the Campus Martius (Livy 1.16).
1. Romulus, the "founder" and first king of Rome, was

Not Berenice's locks first rose so bright,[2]
The heavens bespangling with disheveled light.   130
The Sylphs behold it kindling as it flies,
And pleased pursue its progress through the skies.
    This the beau monde shall from the Mall[3] survey,
And hail with music its propitious ray.
This the blest lover shall for Venus take,   135
And send up vows from Rosamonda's Lake.[4]
This Partridge soon shall view in cloudless skies,
When next he looks through Galileo's eyes;[5]
And hence the egregious wizard shall foredoom
The fate of Louis, and the fall of Rome.   140
    Then cease, bright nymph! to mourn thy ravished hair,
Which adds new glory to the shining sphere!
Not all the tresses that fair head can boast
Shall draw such envy as the Lock you lost.
For, after all the murders of your eye,   145
When, after millions slain, yourself shall die:
When those fair suns shall set, as set they must,
And all those tresses shall be laid in dust,
This Lock the Muse shall consecrate to fame,
And 'midst the stars inscribe Belinda's name.   150
1712   1714

Ode on Solitude[1]

Happy the man whose wish and care
    A few paternal acres bound,
Content to breathe his native air,
            In his own ground.

Whose herds with milk, whose fields with bread,   5
    Whose flocks supply him with attire,
Whose trees in summer yield him shade,
            In winter fire.

Blest, who can unconcernedly find
    Hours, days, and years slide soft away,   10
In health of body, peace of mind,
            Quiet by day,

Sound sleep by night; study and ease,
    Together mixed; sweet recreation;
And innocence, which most does please   15
            With meditation.

2. Berenice, the wife of Ptolemy III, dedicated a lock
of her hair to the gods to ensure her husband's safe
return from war. It was turned into a constellation.
3. A walk laid out by Charles II in St. James's Park
(London), a resort for strollers of all sorts.
4. In St. James's Park; associated with unhappy lovers.
5. I.e., a telescope. "Partridge": John Partridge, an as-

trologer whose annually published predictions had
been amusingly satirized by Swift and other wits in
1708.
1. The hint for this poem was taken from Horace's
well-known *Epode* 2, which praises the simplicity and
innocence of country life, a favorite literary theme in
Pope's time.

Thus let me live, unseen, unknown;
　　Thus unlamented let me die;
Steal from the world, and not a stone
　　　　　　Tell where I lie.   20

ca. 1700–09   1717, 1736

Epistle to Miss Blount[1]

On Her Leaving the Town, After the Coronation

As some fond virgin, whom her mother's care
Drags from the town to wholesome country air,
Just when she learns to roll a melting eye,
And hear a spark,[2] yet think no danger nigh;
From the dear man unwilling she must sever,   5
Yet takes one kiss before she parts forever:
Thus from the world fair Zephalinda[3] flew,
Saw others happy, and with sighs withdrew;
Not that their pleasures caused her discontent;
She sighed not that they stayed, but that she went.   10
　　She went, to plain-work,[4] and to purling brooks,
Old-fashioned halls, dull aunts, and croaking rooks:
She went from opera, park, assembly, play,
To morning walks, and prayers three hours a day;
To part her time 'twixt reading and bohea,[5]   15
To muse, and spill her solitary tea,
Or o'er cold coffee trifle with the spoon,
Count the slow clock, and dine exact at noon;[6]
Divert her eyes with pictures in the fire,
Hum half a tune, tell stories to the squire;   20
Up to her godly garret after seven,
There starve and pray, for that's the way to heaven.
　　Some squire, perhaps, you take delight to rack,
Whose game is whist, whose treat a toast in sack;
Who visits with a gun, presents you birds,   25
Then gives a smacking buss, and cries—"No words!"
Or with his hounds comes hollowing from the stable,
Makes love with nods and knees beneath a table;
Whose laughs are hearty, though his jests are coarse,
And loves you best of all things—but his horse.   30
　　In some fair evening, on your elbow laid,
You dream of triumphs in the rural shade;
In pensive thought recall the fancied scene,
See coronations rise on every green:
Before you pass the imaginary sights   35
Of lords and earls and dukes and gartered knights,

1. Teresa Blount, sister of Pope's lifelong friend Martha Blount. The "coronation" was that of George I (1714).
2. A fop, a beau.
3. A fanciful name adopted by Miss Blount.
4. "Needlework, as distinguished from embroidery"
(Johnson's *Dictionary*).
5. A costly sort of tea.
6. The fashionable hour for dining in London was three or four o'clock. A noon dinner is a sign of old-fashioned rusticity.

While the spread fan o'ershades your closing eyes;
Then give one flirt,[7] and all the vision flies.
Thus vanish scepters, coronets, and balls,
And leave you in lone woods, or empty walls.   40
    So when your slave,[8] at some dear idle time
(Not plagued with headaches or the want of rhyme)
Stands in the streets, abstracted from the crew,
And while he seems to study, thinks of you;
Just when his fancy points[9] your sprightly eyes,   45
Or sees the blush of soft Parthenia[1] rise,
Gay[2] pats my shoulder, and you vanish quite;
Streets, chairs, and coxcombs rush upon my sight;
Vexed to be still in town, I knit my brow,
Look sour, and hum a tune—as you may now.   50

                                                                1717

An Essay on Man   Pope's philosophical poem, *An Essay on Man*, is a fragment of an ambitious but never completed scheme for what the poet referred to
as his "ethic work," which was to have been a large survey of human nature,
society, and morals. The work is dedicated to Henry St. John (pronounced *Sín-
jun*), Viscount Bolingbroke (1678–1751), the brilliant, though erratic, secretary of
state in the Tory ministry of 1710–14, whom Pope had come to know through
Jonathan Swift. After the accession of George I he fled to France, attainted of
treason, but was pardoned and allowed to return in 1723. He settled near Pope at
Dawley farm and a close friendship developed between the two men. In their
conversations Bolingbroke, who fancied himself a philosopher, helped Pope to
formulate the optimistic system that is expounded in this poem. Yet it is clear that
the poem would have been pretty much what it is had the two men never met,
for it expresses doctrines widely circulated and generally accepted at the time by
enlightened minds throughout Europe. The *Essay* gives memorable expression
to ideas about the nature of the universe and our place in it, ideas on which
eighteenth-century optimism rested.
    Pope's purpose is to "vindicate the ways of God to man," a phrase that con-
sciously echoes *Paradise Lost* 1.26. Like John Milton, Pope faces the problem of
the existence of evil in a world presumed to be the creation of a good God. *Paradise Lost* is biblical in content, Christian in doctrine; *An Essay on Man* avoids all
specifically Christian doctrines, not because Pope disbelieved them, but because
"man," the subject of the poem, includes millions who never heard of Christianity,
and Pope is concerned with the universal. Milton tells a mythological story. Pope
writes in abstract terms.
    The *Essay* is divided into four epistles. In the first Pope asserts the essential
order and goodness of the universe and the rightness of our place in it. The other
epistles deal with how we may emulate in our nature and in society the cosmic
harmony revealed in the first epistle. The second seeks to show how we may attain
a psychological harmony that can become the basis of a virtuous life through the
cooperation of self-love and the passions (both necessary to our complete humanity) with reason, the controller and director. The third is concerned with the
individual in society, which, it teaches, was created through the cooperation of
self-love (the egoistic drives that motivate us) and social love (our dependence on

7. I.e., opens and closes her fan with a jerk.   1. Martha Blount.
8. I.e., Pope.   2. John Gay, the poet.
9. Notices.

others, our inborn benevolence). The fourth is concerned with happiness, which lies within the reach of all, for it is dependent on virtue, which becomes possible when—though only when—self-love is transmuted into love of others and love of God. Such, in brief summary, are Pope's main ideas, expressed in many phrases so memorable that they have detached themselves from the poem and become part of daily speech.

From An Essay on Man

TO HENRY ST. JOHN, LORD BOLINGBROKE

Epistle 1. Of the Nature and State of Man,
With Respect to the Universe

> Awake, my St. John! leave all meaner things
> To low ambition, and the pride of kings.
> Let us (since life can little more supply
> Than just to look about us and to die)
> Expatiate free[1] o'er all this scene of man;   5
> A mighty maze! but not without a plan;
> A wild, where weeds and flowers promiscuous shoot,
> Or garden, tempting with forbidden fruit.
> Together let us beat this ample field,
> Try what the open, what the covert yield;   10
> The latent tracts, the giddy heights, explore
> Of all who blindly creep, or sightless soar;
> Eye Nature's walks, shoot folly as it flies,
> And catch the manners living as they rise;
> Laugh where we must, be candid[2] where we can;   15
> But vindicate the ways of God to man.
>
>   1. Say first, of God above, or man below,
> What can we reason, but from what we know?
> Of man, what see we but his station here,
> From which to reason, or to which refer?   20
> Through worlds unnumbered though the God be known,
> 'Tis ours to trace him only in our own.
> He, who through vast immensity can pierce,
> See worlds on worlds compose one universe,
> Observe how system into system runs,   25
> What other planets circle other suns,
> What varied being peoples every star,
> May tell why Heaven has made us as we are.
> But of this frame the bearings, and the ties,
> The strong connections, nice dependencies,   30
> Gradations just, has thy pervading soul
> Looked through? or can a part contain the whole?
>   Is the great chain, that draws all to agree,
> And drawn supports, upheld by God, or thee?[3]

1. Range freely.
2. Kindly.

3. For the chain of being, see lines 207–258 below.

2. Presumptuous man! the reason wouldst thou find,   35
Why formed so weak, so little, and so blind?
First, if thou canst, the harder reason guess,
Why formed no weaker, blinder, and no less!
Ask of thy mother earth, why oaks are made
Taller or stronger than the weeds they shade?   40
Or ask of yonder argent fields above,
Why Jove's satellites[4] are less than Jove?
      Of systems possible, if 'tis confessed
That Wisdom Infinite must form the best,
Where all must full or not coherent be,   45
And all that rises, rise in due degree;
Then, in the scale of reasoning life, 'tis plain,
There must be, somewhere, such a rank as man:
And all the question (wrangle e'er so long)
Is only this, if God has placed him wrong?   50
      Respecting man, whatever wrong we call,
May, must be right, as relative to all.
In human works, though labored on with pain,
A thousand movements scarce one purpose gain;
In God's, one single can its end produce;   55
Yet serves to second too some other use.
So man, who here seems principal alone,
Perhaps acts second to some sphere unknown,
Touches some wheel, or verges to some goal;
'Tis but a part we see, and not a whole.   60
      When the proud steed shall know why man restrains
His fiery course, or drives him o'er the plains;
When the dull ox, why now he breaks the clod,
Is now a victim, and now Egypt's god:
Then shall man's pride and dullness comprehend   65
His actions', passions', being's use and end;
Why doing, suffering, checked, impelled; and why
This hour a slave, the next a deity.
      Then say not man's imperfect, Heaven in fault;
Say rather, man's as perfect as he ought;   70
His knowledge measured to his state and place,
His time a moment, and a point his space.
If to be perfect in a certain sphere,[5]
What matter, soon or late, or here or there?
The blest today is as completely so,   75
As who began a thousand years ago.

      3. Heaven from all creatures hides the book of Fate,
All but the page prescribed, their present state:
From brutes what men, from men what spirits know:
Or who could suffer being here below?   80
The lamb thy riot dooms to bleed today,
Had he thy reason, would he skip and play?
Pleased to the last, he crops the flowery food,

4. In his *Dictionary*, Johnson notes and condemns   5. I.e., in one's "state and place."
Pope's giving this word four syllables, as in Latin.

And licks the hand just raised to shed his blood.
O blindness to the future! kindly given,   85
That each may fill the circle marked by Heaven:
Who sees with equal eye, as God of all,
A hero perish, or a sparrow fall,
Atoms or systems[6] into ruin hurled,
And now a bubble burst, and now a world.   90
   Hope humbly then; with trembling pinions soar;
Wait the great teacher Death, and God adore!
What future bliss, he gives not thee to know,
But gives that hope to be thy blessing now.
Hope springs eternal in the human breast: 95
Man never is, but always to be blest:
The soul, uneasy and confined from home,
Rests and expatiates in a life to come.
   Lo! the poor Indian, whose untutored mind
Sees God in clouds, or hears him in the wind;   100
His soul proud Science never taught to stray
Far as the solar walk, or milky way;
Yet simple Nature to his hope has given,
Behind the cloud-topped hill, an humbler heaven;
Some safer world in depth of woods embraced,   105
Some happier island in the watery waste,
Where slaves once more their native land behold,
No fiends torment, no Christians thirst for gold!
To be, contents his natural desire,
He asks no angel's wing, no seraph's fire;   110
But thinks, admitted to that equal sky,
His faithful dog shall bear him company.

   4. Go, wiser thou! and, in thy scale of sense,
Weigh thy opinion against Providence;
Call imperfection what thou fancy'st such,   115
Say, here he gives too little, there too much;
Destroy all creatures for thy sport or gust,[7]
Yet cry, if man's unhappy, God's unjust;
If man alone engross not Heaven's high care,
Alone made perfect here, immortal there: 120
Snatch from his hand the balance and the rod,
Rejudge his justice, be the God of God!
   In pride, in reasoning pride, our error lies;
All quit their sphere, and rush into the skies.
Pride still is aiming at the blest abodes,   125
Men would be angels, angels would be gods.
Aspiring to be gods, if angels fell,
Aspiring to be angels, men rebel:
And who but wishes to invert the laws
Of order, sins against the Eternal Cause.   130

   5. Ask for what end the heavenly bodies shine,
Earth for whose use? Pride answers, " 'Tis for mine:

---

6. Solar systems.   7. "Sense of tasting" (Johnson's *Dictionary*).

For me kind Nature wakes her genial power,
Suckles each herb, and spreads out every flower;
Annual for me, the grape, the rose renew   135
The juice nectareous, and the balmy dew;
For me, the mine a thousand treasures brings;
For me, health gushes from a thousand springs;
Seas roll to waft me, suns to light me rise;
My footstool earth, my canopy the skies."   140
      But errs not Nature from this gracious end,
From burning suns when livid deaths descend,
When earthquakes swallow, or when tempests sweep
Towns to one grave, whole nations to the deep?
"No," 'tis replied, "the first Almighty Cause   145
Acts not by partial, but by general laws;
The exceptions few; some change since all began,
And what created perfect?"—Why then man?
If the great end be human happiness,
Then Nature deviates; and can man do less?   150
As much that end a constant course requires
Of showers and sunshine, as of man's desires;
As much eternal springs and cloudless skies,
As men forever temperate, calm, and wise.
If plagues or earthquakes break not Heaven's design,   155
Why then a Borgia, or a Catiline?[8]
Who knows but he whose hand the lightning forms,
Who heaves old ocean, and who wings the storms,
Pours fierce ambition in a Caesar's mind,
Or turns young Ammon[9] loose to scourge mankind?   160
From pride, from pride, our very reasoning springs;
Account for moral, as for natural things:
Why charge we Heaven in those, in these acquit?
In both, to reason right is to submit.
      Better for us, perhaps, it might appear,   165
Were there all harmony, all virtue here;
That never air or ocean felt the wind;
That never passion discomposed the mind:
But ALL subsists by elemental strife;
And passions are the elements of life.   170
The general ORDER, since the whole began,
Is kept in Nature, and is kept in man.

      6. What would this man? Now upward will he soar,
And little less than angel, would be more;
Now looking downwards, just as grieved appears   175
To want the strength of bulls, the fur of bears.
Made for his use all creatures if he call,
Say what their use, had he the powers of all?
Nature to these, without profusion, kind,

8. The Renaissance Italian family of the Borgias was notorious for its crimes: ruthless lust for power, cruelty, rapaciousness, treachery, and murder (especially by poisoning); Cesare Borgia (1476–1507), son of Pope Alexander VI, is here referred to. Lucius Sergius Cati- line (ca. 108–62 B.C.), an ambitious, greedy, and cruel conspirator against the Roman state, was denounced in Cicero's famous orations before the senate and in the Forum.
9. Alexander the Great.

The proper organs, proper powers assigned;   180
Each seeming want compènsated of course,
Here with degrees of swiftness, there of force;
All in exact proportion to the state;
Nothing to add, and nothing to abate.
Each beast, each insect, happy in its own;   185
Is Heaven unkind to man, and man alone?
Shall he alone, whom rational we call,
Be pleased with nothing, if not blessed with all?
    The bliss of man (could pride that blessing find)
Is not to act or think beyond mankind;   190
No powers of body or of soul to share,
But what his nature and his state can bear.
Why has not man a microscopic eye?
For this plain reason, man is not a fly.
Say what the use, were finer optics given,   195
To inspect a mite, not comprehend the heaven?
Or touch, if tremblingly alive all o'er,
To smart and agonize at every pore?
Or quick effluvia[1] darting through the brain,
Die of a rose in aromatic pain?   200
If nature thundered in his opening ears,
And stunned him with the music of the spheres,
How would he wish that Heaven had left him still
The whispering zephyr, and the purling rill?
Who finds not Providence all good and wise,   205
Alike in what it gives, and what denies?

    7. Far as creation's ample range extends,
The scale of sensual,[2] mental powers ascends:
Mark how it mounts, to man's imperial race,
From the green myriads in the peopled grass: 210
What modes of sight betwixt each wide extreme,
The mole's dim curtain, and the lynx's beam:[3]
Of smell, the headlong lioness between,
And hound sagacious[4] on the tainted green:
Of hearing, from the life that fills the flood,   215
To that which warbles through the vernal wood:
The spider's touch, how exquisitely fine!
Feels at each thread, and lives along the line:
In the nice[5] bee, what sense so subtly true
From poisonous herbs extracts the healing dew: 220
How instinct varies in the groveling swine,
Compared, half-reasoning elephant, with thine!
'Twixt that, and reason, what a nice barrier,[6]
Forever separate, yet forever near!
Remembrance and reflection how allied;   225

1. According to the philosophy of Epicurus (adopted
by Robert Boyle, the chemist, and other 17th-century
scientists), the senses are stirred to perception by being
bombarded through the pores by steady streams of "effluvia," incredibly thin and tiny—but material—images of the objects that surround us.

2. Sensory.
3. One of several early theories of vision held that the
eye casts a beam of light that makes objects visible.
4. Quick of scent.
5. Exact, accurate.
6. Pronounced ba-réer.

What thin partitions sense from thought divide:
And middle natures, how they long to join,
Yet never pass the insuperable line!
Without this just gradation, could they be
Subjected, these to those, or all to thee?   230
The powers of all subdued by thee alone,
Is not thy reason all these powers in one?

    8. See, through this air, this ocean, and this earth,
All matter quick, and bursting into birth.
Above, how high progressive life may go!   235
Around, how wide! how deep extend below!
Vast Chain of Being! which from God began,
Natures ethereal, human, angel, man,
Beast, bird, fish, insect, what no eye can see,
No glass can reach! from Infinite to thee,   240
From thee to nothing. — On superior powers
Were we to press, inferior might on ours:
Or in the full creation leave a void,
Where, one step broken, the great scale's destroyed:
From Nature's chain whatever link you strike,   245
Tenth or ten thousandth, breaks the chain alike.
    And, if each system in gradation roll
Alike essential to the amazing whole,
The least confusion but in one, not all
That system only, but the whole must fall.   250
Let earth unbalanced from her orbit fly,
Planets and suns run lawless through the sky,
Let ruling angels from their spheres be hurled,
Being on being wrecked, and world on world,
Heaven's whole foundations to their center nod,   255
And Nature tremble to the throne of God:
All this dread ORDER break — for whom? for thee?
Vile worm! — oh, madness, pride, impiety!

    9. What if the foot, ordained the dust to tread,
Or hand, to toil, aspired to be the head?   260
What if the head, the eye, or ear repined
To serve mere engines to the ruling Mind?[7]
Just as absurd, to mourn the tasks or pains,
The great directing MIND of ALL ordains.
    All are but parts of one stupendous whole,   265
Whose body Nature is, and God the soul;
That, changed through all, and yet in all the same,
Great in the earth, as in the ethereal frame,
Warms in the sun, refreshes in the breeze,
Glows in the stars, and blossoms in the trees,   270
Lives through all life, extends through all extent,
Spreads undivided, operates unspent,
Breathes in our soul, informs our mortal part,

---

7. Cf. 1 Corinthians 12.14–26.

As full, as perfect, in a hair as heart;
As full, as perfect, in vile man that mourns,   275
As the rapt seraph that adores and burns;
To him no high, no low, no great, no small;
He fills, he bounds, connects, and equals all.

10. Cease then, nor ORDER imperfection name:
Our proper bliss depends on what we blame.   280
Know thy own point: this kind, this due degree
Of blindness, weakness, Heaven bestows on thee.
Submit—In this, or any other sphere,
Secure to be as blest as thou canst bear:
Safe in the hand of one disposing Power,   285
Or in the natal, or the mortal hour.
All Nature is but art, unknown to thee;
All chance, direction, which thou canst not see;
All discord, harmony not understood;
All partial evil, universal good: 290
And, spite of pride, in erring reason's spite,
One truth is clear: Whatever IS, is RIGHT.

From *Epistle 2. Of the Nature and State of Man With
Respect to Himself, as an Individual*

1. Know then thyself, presume not God to scan;
The proper study of mankind is Man.
Placed on this isthmus of a middle state,
A being darkly wise, and rudely great:
With too much knowledge for the skeptic side,   5
With too much weakness for the Stoic's pride,
He hangs between; in doubt to act, or rest,
In doubt to deem himself a god, or beast;
In doubt his mind or body to prefer,
Born but to die, and reasoning but to err;   10
Alike in ignorance, his reason such,
Whether he thinks too little, or too much:
Chaos of thought and passion, all confused;
Still by himself abused, or disabused;
Created half to rise, and half to fall;   15
Great lord of all things, yet a prey to all;
Sole judge of truth, in endless error hurled:
The glory, jest, and riddle of the world!

*   *   *   1733

Epistle 2. To a Lady   This is one of four poems that Pope grouped together
under the title *Epistles to Several Persons* but that have usually been known by the
less appropriate title *Moral Essays*. They were conceived as parts of Pope's ambitious "ethic work," of which only the first part, *An Essay on Man*, was completed.
Epistle 1 treats the characters of men and *Epistle* 2, the characters of women. The
other two epistles are concerned with the use of riches, a subject that engaged

Pope's attention during the 1730s, because he distrusted the influence on private morals and public life of the rapidly growing wealth of England under the first Hanoverians.

Epistle 2 combines two literary forms: the satire on women, and the verse letter to a particular person—here Martha Blount (1690–1763), Pope's closest female friend, whose remark in line 2 sets the theme of the poem. The first section (to line 198) sketches a portrait gallery of ladies that illustrates their inconsistency and volatility. As an amateur painter, Pope is fascinated by the problem of catching such contrary types: the affected, the soft-natured, the cunning, the whimsical, the witty, and the silly. The next part of the poem (lines 199–248) develops Pope's favorite theory of the ruling passion—the idea that each person is driven by a single irresistible desire—and argues that women are limited to two passions: love of pleasure and love of power. The final part (line 249 to the end) describes an ideal woman, good-natured, sensible, and well balanced, who is identified with Martha Blount herself.

Like every satire on women, *Epistle* 2 is shaped by antifeminist stereotypes: women are fickle, frail, and subordinate to men. Yet much of the poem undermines those prejudices by showing the real difficulties of women's lives. "By man's oppression cursed," they waste their talents on trivial pursuits and "die of nothing but a rage to live." The poem shares that restlessness. If women are full of contradictions, so are Pope's couplets, torn between sympathy and satiric bite. The poet finds himself strangely attracted to what he disapproves, and many female readers, then and now, have felt the same way about the poem.

Epistle 2. To a Lady

OF THE CHARACTERS OF WOMEN

Nothing so true as what you once let fall,
"Most women have no characters at all."
Matter too soft a lasting mark to bear,
And best distinguished by black, brown, or fair.
    How many pictures[1] of one nymph we view,   5
All how unlike each other, all how true!
Arcadia's countess, here, in ermined pride,
Is, there, Pastora by a fountain side.
Here Fannia, leering on her own good man,
And there, a naked Leda with a swan.[2]   10
Let then the fair one beautifully cry,
In Magdalen's loose hair and lifted eye,
Or dressed in smiles of sweet Cecilia shine,[3]
With simpering angels, palms, and harps divine;
Whether the charmer sinner it, or saint it,   15
If folly grow romantic,[4] I must paint it.
    Come then, the colors and the ground prepare!
Dip in the rainbow, trick[5] her off in air;

1. Ladies of the 17th and 18th centuries were often painted in the costumes and attitudes of fanciful, mythological, or historical characters.
2. Leda was seduced by Zeus, who approached her in the form of a swan.
3. St. Mary Magdalen and St. Cecilia were often painted in the manner described.
4. Extravagant.
5. Sketch. "The ground": the first coatings of paint on the canvas before the figures in the picture are sketched in.

Choose a firm cloud, before it fall, and in it
Catch, ere she change, the Cynthia[6] of this minute.   20
    Rufa, whose eye quick-glancing o'er the park,
Attracts each light gay meteor of a spark,
Agrees as ill with Rufa studying Locke,[7]
As Sappho's diamonds with her dirty smock,
Or Sappho at her toilet's greasy task,[8]   25
With Sappho fragrant at an evening masque:
So morning insects that in muck begun,
Shine, buzz, and flyblow[9] in the setting sun.
    How soft is Silia! fearful to offend,
The frail one's advocate, the weak one's friend: 30
To her, Calista proved her conduct nice,
And good Simplicius asks of her advice.
Sudden, she storms! she raves! You tip the wink,
But spare your censure; Silia does not drink.
All eyes may see from what the change arose,   35
All eyes may see—a pimple on her nose.
    Papillia,[1] wedded to her amorous spark,
Sighs for the shades—"How charming is a park!"
A park is purchased, but the fair he sees
All bathed in tears—"Oh, odious, odious trees!"   40
    Ladies, like variegated tulips, show;
'Tis to their changes half their charms we owe;
Their happy spots the nice admirer take,
Fine by defect, and delicately weak.
'Twas thus Calypso[2] once each heart alarmed,   45
Awed without virtue, without beauty charmed;
Her tongue bewitched as oddly as her eyes,
Less wit than mimic, more a wit than wise;
Strange graces still, and stranger flights she had,
Was just not ugly, and was just not mad;   50
Yet ne'er so sure your passion to create,
As when she touched the brink of all we hate.
    Narcissa's[3] nature, tolerably mild,
To make a wash,[4] would hardly stew a child;
Has even been proved to grant a lover's prayer,   55
And paid a tradesman once to make him stare,
Gave alms at Easter, in a Christian trim,
And made a widow happy, for a whim.
Why then declare good nature is her scorn,
When 'tis by that alone she can be borne?   60
Why pique all mortals, yet affect a name?
A fool to pleasure, yet a slave to fame:

6. One of the names of Diana, goddess of the moon, a notoriously changeable heavenly body.
7. John Locke, author of *An Essay Concerning Human Understanding*.
8. Lady Mary Wortley Montagu, though beautiful as a young woman, became notorious for her slatternly appearance and personal uncleanliness. Both Sappho and Montagu were poets.
9. Deposit their eggs.

1. The name comes from Latin for "butterfly."
2. The name is borrowed from the fascinating goddess who detained Odysseus on her island for seven years after the fall of Troy, thus preventing his return to his kingdom, Ithaca.
3. Type of extreme self-love. Narcissus, a beautiful youth, fell in love with his own image when he saw it reflected in a fountain.
4. Cosmetic lotion.

Now deep in Taylor and the *Book of Martyrs*,[5]
Now drinking citron with his Grace and Chartres.[6]
Now conscience chills her, and now passion burns;   65
And atheism and religion take their turns;
A very heathen in the carnal part,
Yet still a sad, good Christian at her heart.
    See Sin in state, majestically drunk;
Proud as a peeress, prouder as a punk;   70
Chaste to her husband, frank[7] to all beside,
A teeming mistress, but a barren bride.
What then? let blood and body bear the fault,
Her head's untouched, that noble seat of thought:
Such this day's doctrine—in another fit   75
She sins with poets through pure love of wit.
What has not fired her bosom or her brain?
Caesar and Tallboy, Charles[8] and Charlemagne.
As Helluo,[9] late dictator of the feast,
The nose of hautgout,[1] and the tip of taste,   80
Criticked your wine, and analyzed your meat,
Yet on plain pudding deigned at home to eat;
So Philomedé,[2] lecturing all mankind
On the soft passion, and the taste refined,
The address, the delicacy—stoops at once,   85
And makes her hearty meal upon a dunce.
    Flavia's a wit, has too much sense to pray;
To toast our wants and wishes, is her way;
Nor asks of God, but of her stars, to give
The mighty blessing, "while we live, to live."   90
Then all for death, that opiate of the soul!
Lucretia's dagger, Rosamonda's bowl.[3]
Say, what can cause such impotence of mind?
A spark too fickle, or a spouse too kind.
Wise wretch! with pleasures too refined to please,   95
With too much spirit to be e'er at ease,
With too much quickness ever to be taught,
With too much thinking to have common thought:
You purchase pain with all that joy can give,
And die of nothing but a rage to live.   100
    Turn then from wits; and look on Simo's mate,
No ass so meek, no ass so obstinate:

---

5. Jeremy Taylor, 17th-century Anglican divine, whose *Holy Living and Holy Dying* was often reprinted in the 18th century. John Foxe's *Acts and Monuments*, usually referred to as Foxe's *Book of Martyrs*, was a household book in most Protestant families in the 17th and 18th centuries. A record of the Protestants who perished for their faith under the persecution of Mary Tudor (1553–58), it was instrumental in keeping anti-Catholic sentiments alive.
6. Francis Chartres was a debauchee often mentioned by Pope. "His Grace" is usually said to be the duke of Wharton, an old enemy of Swift's and a notorious libertine. "Citron": citron water, brandy flavored with lemon or orange peels.
7. Licentious. "Punk": harlot.

8. "Charles," as F. W. Bateson points out, was a generic name for a footman in the period. "Tallboy": a crude young man in Richard Brome's comedy *The Jovial Crew* (1641) or the opera adapted from the play (1731).
9. Latin for "glutton."
1. "Anything with a strong relish or strong scent, as overkept venison" (Johnson's *Dictionary*).
2. The name is Pope's adaptation of a Greek epithet meaning "laughter-loving," frequently applied to Aphrodite, the goddess of love.
3. Lucretia, violated by Tarquin, committed suicide; according to tradition, the "fair Rosamonda," mistress of Henry II, was forced by Queen Eleanor to drink poison.

Or her, that owns her faults, but never mends,
Because she's honest, and the best of friends:
Or her, whose life the Church and scandal share,   105
Forever in a passion, or a prayer:
Or her, who laughs at hell, but (like her Grace)
Cries, "Ah! how charming, if there's no such place!"
Or who in sweet vicissitude appears
Of mirth and opium, ratafie[4] and tears,   110
The daily anodyne, and nightly draught,
To kill those foes to fair ones, time and thought.
Woman and fool are two hard things to hit,
For true no-meaning puzzles more than wit.
    But what are these to great Atossa's mind?[5]   115
Scarce once herself, by turns all womankind!
Who, with herself, or others, from her birth
Finds all her life one warfare upon earth:
Shines in exposing knaves, and painting fools,
Yet is whate'er she hates and ridicules.   120
No thought advances, but her eddy brain
Whisks it about, and down it goes again.
Full sixty years the world has been her trade,
The wisest fool much time has ever made.
From loveless youth to unrespected age,   125
No passion gratified except her rage.
So much the fury still outran the wit,
The pleasure missed her, and the scandal hit.
Who breaks with her, provokes revenge from hell,
But he's a bolder man who dares be well:[6]   130
Her every turn with violence pursued,
Nor more a storm her hate than gratitude:
To that each passion turns, or soon or late;
Love, if it makes her yield, must make her hate:
Superiors? death! and equals? what a curse!   135
But an inferior not dependent? worse.
Offend her, and she knows not to forgive;
Oblige her, and she'll hate you while you live:
But die, and she'll adore you—Then the bust
And temple rise—then fall again to dust.   140
Last night, her lord was all that's good and great;
A knave this morning, and his will a cheat.
Strange! by the means defeated of the ends,
By spirit robbed of power, by warmth of friends,
By wealth of followers! without one distress   145
Sick of herself through very selfishness!
Atossa, cursed with every granted prayer,
Childless with all her children, wants an heir.
To heirs unknown descends the unguarded store,
Or wanders, Heaven-directed, to the poor.   150

4. "A fine liquor, prepared from the kernels of apricots and spirits" (Johnson's *Dictionary*).
5. Atossa, daughter of Cyrus, emperor of Persia (d. 529 B.C.). If the duchess of Buckinghamshire is alluded to, the name is appropriate, for she was the natural daughter of James II.
6. Be in her favor.

Pictures like these, dear Madam, to design,
Asks no firm hand, and no unerring line;
Some wandering touches, some reflected light,
Some flying stroke alone can hit 'em right:
For how should equal colors do the knack?[7]   155
Chameleons who can paint in white and black?
    "Yet Chloe sure was formed without a spot—"
Nature in her then erred not, but forgot.
"With every pleasing, every prudent part,
Say, what can Chloe want?"—She wants a heart.   160
She speaks, behaves, and acts just as she ought;
But never, never, reached one generous thought.
Virtue she finds too painful an endeavor,
Content to dwell in decencies forever.
So very reasonable, so unmoved,   165
As never yet to love, or to be loved.
She, while her lover pants upon her breast,
Can mark[8] the figures on an Indian chest;
And when she sees her friend in deep despair,
Observes how much a chintz exceeds mohair.   170
Forbid it Heaven, a favor or a debt
She e'er should cancel—but she may forget.
Safe is your secret still in Chloe's ear;
But none of Chloe's shall you ever hear.
Of all her dears she never slandered one,   175
But cares not if a thousand are undone.
Would Chloe know if you're alive or dead?
She bids her footman put it in her head.
Chloe is prudent—Would you too be wise?
Then never break your heart when Chloe dies.   180
    One certain portrait may (I grant) be seen,
Which Heaven has varnished out, and made a *Queen:*[9]
The same forever! and described by all
With truth and goodness, as with crown and ball.
Poets heap virtues, painters gems at will,   185
And show their zeal, and hide their want of skill.
'Tis well—but, artists! who can paint or write,
To draw the naked is your true delight.
That robe of quality so struts and swells,
None see what parts of Nature it conceals: 190
The exactest traits of body or of mind,
We owe to models of an humble kind.
If Queensberry[1] to strip there's no compelling,
'Tis from a handmaid we must take a Helen.
From peer or bishop 'tis no easy thing   195
To draw the man who loves his God, or king:
Alas! I copy (or my draft would fail)
From honest Mah'met or plain Parson Hale.[2]

7. Do the trick.
8. Pay attention to.
9. Pope refers as usual to Queen Caroline with disapprobation.
1. The duchess of Queensberry, whom Pope valued

because of her kindness to his friend John Gay, had
been a famous beauty.
2. Mahomet, a Turkish servant of George I. Dr. Stephen Hales, an Anglican clergyman and friend of
Pope.

But grant, in public men sometimes are shown,
A woman's seen in private life alone: 200
Our bolder talents in full light displayed;
Your virtues open fairest in the shade.
Bred to disguise, in public 'tis you hide;
There, none distinguish 'twixt your shame or pride,
Weakness or delicacy; all so nice,   205
That each may seem a virtue, or a vice.
      In men, we various ruling passions find;
In women, two almost divide the kind;
Those, only fixed, they first or last obey,
The love of pleasure, and the love of sway.   210
      That, Nature gives; and where the lesson taught
Is but to please, can pleasure seem a fault?
Experience, this; by man's oppression cursed,
They seek the second not to lose the first.
      Men, some to business, some to pleasure take;   215
But every woman is at heart a rake;
Men, some to quiet, some to public strife;
But every lady would be queen for life.
      Yet mark the fate of a whole sex of queens!
Power all their end, but beauty all the means: 220
In youth they conquer, with so wild a rage,
As leaves them scarce a subject in their age:
For foreign glory, foreign joy, they roam;
No thought of peace or happiness at home.
But wisdom's triumph is well-timed retreat,   225
As hard a science to the fair as great!
Beauties, like tyrants, old and friendless grown,
Yet hate repose, and dread to be alone,
Worn out in public, weary every eye,
Nor leave one sigh behind them when they die.   230
      Pleasures the sex, as children birds, pursue,
Still out of reach, yet never out of view,
Sure, if they catch, to spoil the toy at most,
To covet flying, and regret when lost:
At last, to follies youth could scarce defend,   235
It grows their age's prudence to pretend;
Ashamed to own they gave delight before,
Reduced to feign it, when they give no more:
As hags hold sabbaths, less for joy than spite,
So these their merry, miserable night;[3]   240
Still round and round the ghosts of beauty glide,
And haunt the places where their honor died.
      See how the world its veterans rewards!
A youth of frolics, an old age of cards;
Fair to no purpose, artful to no end,   245
Young without lovers, old without a friend;
A fop their passion, but their prize a sot;
Alive, ridiculous, and dead, forgot!

3. I.e., evenings on which ladies entertained guests. "Sabbaths": obscene rites popularly supposed to be held by witches ("hags").

Ah friend! to dazzle let the vain design;
To raise the thought, and touch the heart be thine!   250
That charm shall grow, while what fatigues the Ring[4]
Flaunts and goes down, an unregarded thing:
So when the sun's broad beam has tired the sight,
All mild ascends the moon's more sober light,
Serene in virgin modesty she shines,   255
And unobserved the glaring orb declines.
    Oh! blest with temper, whose unclouded ray
Can make tomorrow cheerful as today;
She, who can love a sister's charms, or hear
Sighs for a daughter with unwounded ear;   260
She, who ne'er answers till a husband cools,
Or, if she rules him, never shows she rules;
Charms by accepting, by submitting sways,
Yet has her humor most, when she obeys;
Lets fops or fortune fly which way they will;   265
Disdains all loss of tickets or Codille;[5]
Spleen, vapors, or smallpox, above them all,
And mistress of herself, though China[6] fall.
    And yet, believe me, good as well as ill,
Woman's at best a contradiction still.   270
Heaven, when it strives to polish all it can
Its last best work, but forms a softer man;
Picks from each sex, to make the favorite blest,
Your love of pleasure, our desire of rest:
Blends, in exception to all general rules,   275
Your taste of follies, with our scorn of fools:
Reserve with frankness, art with truth allied,
Courage with softness, modesty with pride;
Fixed principles, with fancy ever new;
Shakes all together, and produces—you.   280
    Be this a woman's fame: with this unblest,
Toasts live a scorn, and queens may die a jest.
This Phoebus promised (I forget the year)
When those blue eyes first opened on the sphere;
Ascendant Phoebus watched that hour with care,   285
Averted half your parents' simple prayer;
And gave you beauty, but denied the pelf
That buys your sex a tyrant o'er itself.
The generous god, who wit and gold refines,
And ripens spirits as he ripens mines,[7]   290
Kept dross for duchesses, the world shall know it,
To you gave sense, good humor, and a poet.

                                                              1735, 1744

4. The fashionable drive in Hyde Park.
5. The loss of a hand at the card games of ombre or
quadrille. "Tickets": i.e., lottery tickets.
6. Pope refers punningly to the chinaware that fashionable women collected enthusiastically.

7. Phoebus Apollo, as god of poetry, "ripens wit"; as
god of the sun, he "ripens mines," for respectable scientific theory held that the sun's rays mature precious
metals in the earth.

Epistle to Dr. Arbuthnot   Dr. John Arbuthnot (1667–1735), to whom Pope addressed his best-known verse epistle, was distinguished both as a physician and as a man of wit. He had been one of the liveliest members of the Martinus Scriblerus Club, helping his friends to create the character and shape the career of the learned pedant whose memoirs the club had undertaken to write.

Pope had long been meditating such a poem, which was to be both an attack on his detractors and a defense of his own character and career. In his usual way, he had jotted down hints, lines, couplets, and fragments over a period of two decades, but the poem might never have been completed had it not been for two events: Arbuthnot, from his deathbed, wrote to urge Pope to continue his abhorrence of vice and to express it in his writings and, during 1733, Pope was the victim of two bitter attacks by "persons of rank and fortune," as the "Advertisement" has it. The *Verses Addressed to the Imitator of Horace* was the work of Lady Mary Wortley Montagu, helped by her friend Lord Hervey (pronounced *Harvey*), a close friend and confidant of Queen Caroline. *An Epistle to a Doctor of Divinity from a Nobleman at Hampton Court* was the work of Lord Hervey alone. Montagu, it must be admitted, had provocation enough, especially in Pope's recent reference to her in *The First Satire of the Second Book of Horace*, lines 83–84, but Hervey had little to complain of beyond occasional covert references to him as "Lord Fanny." At any rate, the two scurrilous attacks goaded Pope into action, and the poem was completed by the end of the summer of 1734.

The epistle is a masterpiece of poetic rhetoric. The very fact that it is addressed to Arbuthnot, a man who had the general approbation of the world because of his kindliness and probity, in some degree seems to guarantee the integrity of the *I* of the poem and to diminish the moral stature of his enemies. This acquisition of virtue through association, an effective stroke, is supported by every device of persuasive rhetoric—reasonable argument and emotional appeals, subtly suggestive imagery, and superbly controlled shifts in tone and style—which help to sway the reader's judgment to the side of the speaker. The poem opens in the flat language of commonplace prose discourse, tinged with a wry humor and a tone of exasperation: "Shut, shut the door, good John! (fatigued, I said)" and as it progresses it rises or falls in language and style according to the emotions that the speaker expresses—anger, contempt, amusement, sarcasm, mock self-pity, indignation, hatred, affection, gratitude, and tenderness—to return at the end to the homely tone of the opening.

It is not clear that Pope intended the poem to be thought of as a dialogue, as it has usually been printed since Warburton's edition of 1751. The original edition, while suggesting interruptions in the flow of the monologue, kept entirely to the form of a letter. The introduction of the friend, who speaks from time to time, of course converts the original letter into a dramatic dialogue.

Epistle to Dr. Arbuthnot

Advertisement
TO THE FIRST PUBLICATION OF THIS *Epistle*

This paper is a sort of bill of complaint, begun many years since, and drawn up by snatches, as the several occasions offered. I had no thoughts of publishing it, till it pleased some persons of rank and fortune (the authors of *Verses to the Imitator of Horace*, and of an *Epistle to a Doctor of Divinity from a Nobleman at Hampton Court*) to attack, in a very extraordinary manner, not only my writings (of which, being public, the public is judge) but my person, morals, and family, whereof, to those who know me not, a truer information may be requisite. Being divided between the necessity to say something of myself, and my own laziness to undertake so awkward a task, I thought it the shortest way to put the last hand to this epistle. If it have anything pleasing, it will be that by which I am most desirous to please, the truth and the sentiment; and if anything offensive, it will be only to those I am least sorry to offend, the vicious or the ungenerous.

Many will know their own pictures in it, there being not a circumstance but what is true; but I have, for the most part, spared their names, and they may escape being laughed at, if they please.

I would have some of them know, it was owing to the request of the learned and candid friend to whom it is inscribed, that I make not as free use of theirs as they have done of mine. However, I shall have this advantage, and honor, on my side, that whereas, by their proceeding, any abuse may be directed at any man, no injury can possibly be done by mine, since a nameless character can never be found out, but by its truth and likeness. P.

P. Shut, shut the door, good John![1] (fatigued, I said),
Tie up the knocker, say I'm sick, I'm dead.
The Dog Star[2] rages! nay 'tis past a doubt
All Bedlam,[3] or Parnassus, is let out:
Fire in each eye, and papers in each hand,   5
They rave, recite, and madden round the land.
    What walls can guard me, or what shades can hide?
They pierce my thickets, through my grot[4] they glide,
By land, by water, they renew the charge,
They stop the chariot, and they board the barge.   10
No place is sacred, not the church is free;
Even Sunday shines no Sabbath day to me:
Then from the Mint[5] walks forth the man of rhyme,
Happy! to catch me just at dinner time.
    Is there a parson, much bemused in beer,   15
A maudlin poetess, a rhyming peer,
A clerk foredoomed his father's soul to cross,
Who pens a stanza when he should engross?[6]
Is there who, locked from ink and paper,[7] scrawls
With desperate charcoal round his darkened walls?   20
All fly to Twit'nam,[8] and in humble strain
Apply to me to keep them mad or vain.
Arthur,[9] whose giddy son neglects the laws,
Imputes to me and my damned works the cause:
Poor Cornus[1] sees his frantic wife elope,   25
And curses wit, and poetry, and Pope.

1. John Serle, Pope's gardener.
2. Sirius, associated with the period of greatest heat (and hence of madness) because it sets with the sun in late summer. August, in ancient Rome, was the season for reciting poetry.
3. Bethlehem Hospital for the insane, in London.
4. The subterranean passage under the road that separated his house at Twickenham from his garden became, in Pope's hands, a romantic grotto ornamented with shells and mirrors.
5. A place in Southwark where debtors were free from arrest (they could not be arrested anywhere on Sundays).

6. Write out legal documents.
7. Is there some madman who, locked up without ink or paper. . . ?
8. I.e., Twickenham, Pope's villa on the bank of the Thames, a few miles above Hampton Court.
9. Arthur Moore, whose son, James Moore Smythe, dabbled in literature. Moore Smythe had earned Pope's enmity by using in one of his plays some unpublished lines from Pope's Epistle 2. To a Lady in spite of Pope's objections.
1. Latin for "horn," the traditional emblem of the cuckold.

Friend to my life (which did not you prolong,
The world had wanted many an idle song)
What drop or nostrum[2] can this plague remove?
Or which must end me, a fool's wrath or love?   30
A dire dilemma! either way I'm sped,[3]
If foes, they write, if friends, they read me dead.
Seized and tied down to judge, how wretched I!
Who can't be silent, and who will not lie.
To laugh were want of goodness and of grace,   35
And to be grave exceeds all power of face.
I sit with sad civility, I read
With honest anguish and an aching head,
And drop at last, but in unwilling ears,
This saving counsel, "Keep your piece nine years."[4]   40
    "Nine years!" cries he, who high in Drury Lane,[5]
Lulled by soft zephyrs through the broken pane,
Rhymes ere he wakes, and prints before term[6] ends,
Obliged by hunger and request of friends:
"The piece, you think, is incorrect? why, take it,   45
I'm all submission, what you'd have it, make it."
    Three things another's modest wishes bound,
My friendship, and a prologue, and ten pound.
    Pitholeon[7] sends to me: "You know his Grace,
I want a patron; ask him for a place."   50
Pitholeon libeled me—"but here's a letter
Informs you, sir, 'twas when he knew no better.
Dare you refuse him? Curll[8] invites to dine,
He'll write a *Journal*, or he'll turn divine."[9]
Bless me! a packet.—" 'Tis a stranger sues,   55
A virgin tragedy, an orphan Muse."
If I dislike it, "Furies, death, and rage!"
If I approve, "Commend it to the stage."
There (thank my stars) my whole commission ends,
The players and I are, luckily, no friends.   60
Fired that the house reject him, " 'Sdeath, I'll print it,
And shame the fools—Your interest, sir, with Lintot!"[1]
Lintot, dull rogue, will think your price too much.
"Not, sir, if you revise it, and retouch."
All my demurs but double his attacks;   65
At last he whispers, "Do; and we go snacks."[2]
Glad of a quarrel, straight I clap the door,
"Sir, let me see your works and you no more."
    'Tis sung, when Midas' ears began to spring

2. Medicine.
3. "Destroyed; killed" (Johnson's *Dictionary*).
4. The advice of Horace in *Art of Poetry* (line 388).
5. I.e., living in a garret in Drury Lane, site of one of the theaters and the haunt of the profligate.
6. One of the four annual periods in which the law courts are in session and with which the publishing season coincided.
7. A foolish poet of Rhodes, who pretended much to Greek [Pope's note]. He is Leonard Welsted, who translated Longinus and had attacked and slandered

Pope (see line 375).
8. Edmund Curll, shrewd and disreputable bookseller, published pirated works, works falsely ascribed to reputable writers, scandalous biographies, and other ephemera. Pope had often attacked him and had assigned to him a low role in *The Dunciad*.
9. I.e., he will attack Pope in the *London Journal* or write a treatise on theology, as Welsted in fact did.
1. Bernard Lintot, publisher of Pope's Homer and other early works.
2. Go shares.

(Midas, a sacred person and a king),   70
His very minister who spied them first,
(Some say his queen) was forced to speak, or burst.[3]
And is not mine, my friend, a sorer case,
When every coxcomb perks them in my face?
        A. Good friend, forbear! you deal in dangerous things.   75
I'd never name queens, ministers, or kings;
Keep close to ears, and those let asses prick;
'Tis nothing——P. Nothing? if they bite and kick?
Out with it, *Dunciad!* let the secret pass,
That secret to each fool, that he's an ass: 80
The truth once told (and wherefore should we lie?)
The queen of Midas slept, and so may I.
        You think this cruel? take it for a rule,
No creature smarts so little as a fool.
Let peals of laughter, Codrus! round thee break,   85
Thou unconcerned canst hear the mighty crack.
Pit, box, and gallery in convulsions hurled,
Thou stand'st unshook amidst a bursting world.
Who shames a scribbler? break one cobweb through,
He spins the slight, self-pleasing thread anew: 90
Destroy his fib or sophistry, in vain;
The creature's at his dirty work again,
Throned in the center of his thin designs,
Proud of a vast extent of flimsy lines.
Whom have I hurt? has poet yet or peer   95
Lost the arched eyebrow or Parnassian sneer?
And has not Colley still his lord and whore?
His butchers Henley?[4] his freemasons Moore?
Does not one table Bavius still admit?
Still to one bishop Philips[5] seem a wit?   100
Still Sappho[6]——A. Hold! for god's sake—you'll offend.
No names—be calm—learn prudence of a friend.
I too could write, and I am twice as tall;
But foes like these!——P. One flatterer's worse than all.
Of all mad creatures, if the learn'd are right,   105
It is the slaver kills, and not the bite.
A fool quite angry is quite innocent:
Alas! 'tis ten times worse when they repent.

        One dedicates in high heroic prose,
And ridicules beyond a hundred foes;   110
One from all Grub Street[7] will my fame defend,

And, more abusive, calls himself my friend.
This prints my letters,[8] that expects a bribe,
And others roar aloud, "Subscribe, subscribe!"[9]
    There are, who to my person pay their court: 115
I cough like Horace, and, though lean, am short;
Ammon's great son one shoulder had too high,
Such Ovid's nose,[1] and "Sir! you have an eye—"
Go on, obliging creatures, make me see
All that disgraced my betters met in me.   120
Say for my comfort, languishing in bed,
"Just so immortal Maro[2] held his head":
And when I die, be sure you let me know
Great Homer died three thousand years ago.

    Why did I write? what sin to me unknown   125
Dipped me in ink, my parents', or my own?
As yet a child, nor yet a fool to fame,
I lisped in numbers, for the numbers came.
I left no calling for this idle trade,
No duty broke, no father disobeyed.   130
The Muse but served to ease some friend, not wife,
To help me through this long disease, my life,
To second, Arbuthnot! thy art and care,
And teach the being you preserved, to bear.[3]

    A. But why then publish? P. Granville the polite,   135
And knowing Walsh, would tell me I could write;
Well-natured Garth inflamed with early praise,
And Congreve loved, and Swift endured my lays;
The courtly Talbot, Somers, Sheffield, read;
Even mitered Rochester would nod the head,   140
And St. John's self (great Dryden's friends before)
With open arms received one poet more.[4]
Happy my studies, when by these approved!
Happier their author, when by these beloved!
From these the world will judge of men and books,   145
Not from the Burnets, Oldmixons, and Cookes.[5]
    Soft were my numbers; who could take offense
While pure description held the place of sense?
Like gentle Fanny's[6] was my flowery theme,
A painted mistress, or a purling stream.   150

---

8. In 1726 Curll had surreptitiously acquired and published without permission some of Pope's letters to Henry Cromwell.
9. To ensure the financial success of a work, the public was often asked to "subscribe" to it by taking a certain number of copies before printing was undertaken. Pope's Homer was published in this manner.
1. Ovid's family name, Naso, suggests the Latin word *nasus* ("nose"), hence the pun. "Great son": Alexander the Great.
2. Virgil.
3. Endure.
4. The purpose of this list is to establish Pope as the successor of Dryden and thus to place him far above

his Grub Street persecutors. George Granville, Lord Lansdowne, poet and statesman; William Walsh, poet and critic; Sir Samuel Garth, physician and mock epic poet; William Congreve, the playwright; the statesmen Charles Talbot, duke of Shrewsbury; Lord Sommers; John Sheffield, duke of Buckinghamshire; and Francis Atterbury, bishop of Rochester, had all been associated with Dryden in his later years and had all encouraged the young Pope.
5. Thomas Burnet, John Oldmixon, and Thomas Cooke: Pope identifies them in a note as "authors of secret and scandalous history."
6. John, Lord Hervey, whom Pope satirizes in the character of Sporus (lines 305–333).

Yet then did Gildon draw his venal quill;[7]
I wished the man a dinner, and sat still.
Yet then did Dennis[8] rave in furious fret;
I never answered, I was not in debt.
If want provoked, or madness made them print,   155
I waged no war with Bedlam or the Mint.
    Did some more sober critic come abroad?
If wrong, I smiled; if right, I kissed the rod.
Pains, reading, study are their just pretense,
And all they want is spirit, taste, and sense.   160
Commas and points they set exactly right,
And 'twere a sin to rob them of their mite.
Yet ne'er one sprig of laurel graced these ribalds,
From slashing Bentley down to piddling Tibbalds.[9]
Each wight who reads not, and but scans and spells,   165
Each word-catcher that lives on syllables,
Even such small critics some regard may claim,
Preserved in Milton's or in Shakespeare's name.
Pretty! in amber to observe the forms
Of hairs, or straws, or dirt, or grubs, or worms!   170
The things, we know, are neither rich nor rare,
But wonder how the devil they got there.
    Were others angry? I excused them too;
Well might they rage; I gave them but their due.
A man's true merit 'tis not hard to find;   175
But each man's secret standard in his mind,
That casting weight[1] pride adds to emptiness,
This, who can gratify? for who can guess?
The bard[2] whom pilfered pastorals renown,
Who turns a Persian tale for half a crown,   180
Just writes to make his barrenness appear,
And strains from hard-bound brains eight lines a year:
He, who still wanting, though he lives on theft,
Steals much, spends little, yet has nothing left;
And he who now to sense, now nonsense leaning,   185
Means not, but blunders round about a meaning:
And he whose fustian's so sublimely bad,
It is not poetry, but prose run mad:
All these, my modest satire bade translate,
And owned that nine such poets made a Tate.[3]   190

7. Charles Gildon, minor critic and scribbler, who, Pope believed, early attacked him at the instigation of Addison; hence "venal quill."
8. John Dennis (see *An Essay on Criticism*, n. 4, p. 1071).
9. Richard Bentley (1662–1742), the eminent classical scholar, seemed to both Pope and Swift the perfect type of the pedant: he is called "slashing" because, in his edition of *Paradise Lost* (1732), he had set in square brackets all passages that he disliked on the grounds they had been slipped into the poem without the blind poet's knowledge. Lewis Theobald (1688–1744), whose minute learning in Elizabethan literature had enabled him to expose Pope's defects as an editor of Shakespeare in 1726. Pope made him king of the Dunces in *The Dunciad* of 1728.
1. The weight that turns the scale; here, the "deciding factor."
2. Ambrose Philips, Pope's rival in pastoral poetry in 1709, when their pastorals were published in Tonson's 6th *Miscellany*. Philips had also translated some Persian tales (cf. line 100).
3. Nahum Tate (1652–1715), poet laureate (1692–1715). His popular rewriting of Shakespeare's *King Lear* provided a happy ending; he wrote most of part 2 of *Absalom and Achitophel*. The line refers to the old adage that it takes nine tailors to make one man.

How did they fume, and stamp, and roar, and chafe!
And swear, not Addison himself was safe.
   Peace to all such! but were there one whose fires
True Genius kindles, and fair Fame inspires;
Blessed with each talent and each art to please,   195
And born to write, converse, and live with ease:
Should such a man, too fond to rule alone,
Bear, like the Turk, no brother near the throne;
View him with scornful, yet with jealous eyes,
And hate for arts that caused himself to rise;   200
Damn with faint praise, assent with civil leer,
And without sneering, teach the rest to sneer;
Willing to wound, and yet afraid to strike,
Just hint a fault, and hesitate dislike;
Alike reserved to blame or to commend,   205
A timorous foe, and a suspicious friend;
Dreading even fools; by flatterers besieged,
And so obliging that he ne'er obliged;
Like Cato, give his little senate[4] laws,
And sit attentive to his own applause;   210
While wits and Templars[5] every sentence raise,
And wonder with a foolish face of praise—
Who but must laugh, if such a man there be?
Who would not weep, if Atticus[6] were he?
   What though my name stood rubric on the walls   215
Or plastered posts, with claps,[7] in capitals?
Or smoking forth, a hundred hawkers' load,
On wings of winds came flying all abroad?
I sought no homage from the race that write;
I kept, like Asian monarchs, from their sight: 220
Poems I heeded (now berhymed so long)
No more than thou, great George! a birthday song.
I ne'er with wits or witlings passed my days
To spread about the itch of verse and praise;
Nor like a puppy daggled through the town   225
To fetch and carry sing-song up and down;
Nor at rehearsals sweat, and mouthed, and cried,
With handkerchief and orange at my side;
But sick of fops, and poetry, and prate,
To Bufo left the whole Castalian[8] state.   230
   Proud as Apollo on his forkèd hill,[9]
Sat full-blown Bufo, puffed by every quill;
Fed with soft dedication all day long,
Horace and he went hand in hand in song.

---

4. Addison's tragedy *Cato* had been a sensational success in 1713. Pope had written the prologue, in which
occurs the line, "While Cato gives his little senate
laws." The satirical reference here is to Addison in the
role of arbiter of taste among his friends and admirers,
mostly Whigs, at Button's Coffee House. It was these
people who had worked against the success of Pope's
Homer.
5. Law students.

6. Pope's satiric pseudonym for Addison; Atticus (109–
32 B.C.) was a wealthy man of letters and a friend of
Cicero, known as a wise and disinterested man.
7. Posters. "Rubric": in red letters.
8. The Castalian spring on Mt. Parnassus was sacred
to Apollo and the Muses. "Bufo": a type of tasteless
patron of the arts. (*Bufo* means "toad" in Latin.)
9. Mt. Parnassus had two peaks, one sacred to Apollo,
one to Bacchus.

His library (where busts of poets dead   235
And a true Pindar stood without a head)
Received of wits an undistinguished race,
Who first his judgment asked, and then a place:
Much they extolled his pictures, much his seat,[1]
And flattered every day, and some days eat: 240
Till grown more frugal in his riper days,
He paid some bards with port, and some with praise;
To some a dry rehearsal was assigned,
And others (harder still) he paid in kind.
Dryden alone (what wonder?) came not nigh;   245
Dryden alone escaped this judging eye:
But still the great have kindness in reserve;
He helped to bury whom he helped to starve.
    May some choice patron bless each gray goose quill!
May every Bavius have his Bufo still!   250
So when a statesman wants a day's defense,
Or envy holds a whole week's war with sense,
Or simple pride for flattery makes demands,
May dunce by dunce be whistled off my hands!
Blessed be the great! for those they take away,   255
And those they left me—for they left me Gay;[2]
Left me to see neglected genius bloom,
Neglected die, and tell it on his tomb;
Of all thy blameless life the sole return
My verse, and Queensberry weeping o'er thy urn!   260
Oh, let me live my own, and die so too!
("To live and die is all I have to do")[3]
Maintain a poet's dignity and ease,
And see what friends, and read what books I please;
Above a patron, though I condescend   265
Sometimes to call a minister my friend.
I was not born for courts or great affairs;
I pay my debts, believe, and say my prayers,
Can sleep without a poem in my head,
Nor know if Dennis be alive or dead.   270
    Why am I asked what next shall see the light?
Heavens! was I born for nothing but to write?
Has life no joys for me? or (to be grave)
Have I no friend to serve, no soul to save?
"I found him close with Swift"—"Indeed? no doubt"   275
Cries prating Balbus, "something will come out."
'Tis all in vain, deny it as I will.
"No, such a genius never can lie still,"
And then for mine obligingly mistakes
The first lampoon Sir Will or Bubo[4] makes.   280

1. Estate. Pronounced *sate* and rhymed in next line with "eat" *(ate)*.
2. John Gay (1685–1732), author of *The Beggar's Opera* and other delightful works, dear friend of Swift and Pope. His failure to obtain patronage from the court intensified Pope's hostility to the Whig administration and the queen. Gay spent the last years of his life under the protection of the duke and duchess of Queensberry.
3. A quotation from John Denham's poem *Of Prudence*.
4. *Sir William Yonge, Whig politician and poetaster. George Bubb ("Bubo") Dodington, a Whig patron of letters.*

Poor guiltless I! and can I choose but smile,
When every coxcomb knows me by my style?
   Cursed be the verse, how well soe'er it flow,
That tends to make one worthy man my foe,
Give virtue scandal, innocence a fear,   285
Or from the soft-eyed virgin steal a tear!
But he who hurts a harmless neighbor's peace,
Insults fallen worth, or beauty in distress,
Who loves a lie, lame slander helps about,
Who writes a libel, or who copies out: 290
That fop whose pride affects a patron's name,
Yet absent, wounds an author's honest fame;
Who can your merit selfishly approve,
And show the sense of it without the love;
Who has the vanity to call you friend,   295
Yet wants the honor, injured, to defend;
Who tells whate'er you think, whate'er you say,
And, if he lie not, must at least betray:
Who to the dean and silver bell can swear,
And sees at Cannons what was never there:[5]   300
Who reads but with a lust to misapply,
Make satire a lampoon, and fiction, lie:
A lash like mine no honest man shall dread,
But all such babbling blockheads in his stead.
   Let Sporus[6] tremble—— A. What? that thing of silk,   305
Sporus, that mere white curd of ass's milk?[7]
Satire or sense, alas! can Sporus feel?
Who breaks a butterfly upon a wheel?
   P. Yet let me flap this bug with gilded wings,
This painted child of dirt, that stinks and stings;   310
Whose buzz the witty and the fair annoys,
Yet wit ne'er tastes, and beauty ne'er enjoys;
So well-bred spaniels civilly delight
In mumbling of the game they dare not bite.
Eternal smiles his emptiness betray,   315
As shallow streams run dimpling all the way.
Whether in florid impotence he speaks,
And, as the prompter breathes, the puppet squeaks;
Or at the ear of Eve,[8] familiar toad,
Half froth, half venom, spits himself abroad,   320
In puns, or politics, or tales, or lies,
Or spite, or smut, or rhymes, or blasphemies.
His wit all seesaw between *that* and *this*,
Now high, now low, now master up, now miss,
And he himself one vile antithesis.   325
Amphibious thing! that acting either part,

---

5. *Pope's enemies had accused him of satirizing Cannons, the ostentatious estate of the duke of Chandos, in his description of Timon's villa in the Epistle to Burlington. This Pope quite justly denied. The bell of Timon's chapel was of silver, and there preached a dean who "never mentions Hell to ears polite."*
6. John, Lord Hervey, effeminate courtier and confidant of Queen Caroline (see headnote "Epistle to Dr. Arbuthnot," p. 1111). The original Sporus was a boy, whom the Emperor Nero publicly married (see Suetonius's life of Nero in *The Twelve Caesars*).
7. "Ass's milk" was drunk by invalids.
8. The queen; the allusion is to *Paradise Lost* (4.799–809).

The trifling head or the corrupted heart,
Fop at the toilet, flatterer at the board,
Now trips a lady, and now struts a lord.
Eve's tempter thus the rabbins[9] have expressed,   330
A cherub's face, a reptile all the rest;
Beauty that shocks you, parts that none will trust,
Wit that can creep, and pride that licks the dust.
　　Not fortune's worshiper, nor fashion's fool,
Not lucre's madman, nor ambition's tool,   335
Not proud, nor servile, be one poet's praise,
That if he pleased, he pleased by manly ways:
That flattery, even to kings, he held a shame,
And thought a lie in verse or prose the same:
That not in fancy's maze he wandered long,   340
But stooped[1] to truth, and moralized his song:
That not for fame, but virtue's better end,
He stood the furious foe, the timid friend,
The damning critic, half approving wit,
The coxcomb hit, or fearing to be hit;   345
Laughed at the loss of friends he never had,
The dull, the proud, the wicked, and the mad;
The distant threats of vengeance on his head,
The blow unfelt, the tear he never shed;
The tale revived, the lie so oft o'erthrown,   350
The imputed trash, and dullness not his own;
The morals blackened when the writings 'scape,
The libeled person, and the pictured shape;[2]
Abuse on all he loved, or loved him, spread,
A friend in exile, or a father dead;   355
The whisper, that to greatness still too near,
Perhaps yet vibrates on his Sovereign's ear—
Welcome for thee, fair virtue! all the past:
For thee, fair virtue! welcome even the last!
　　A. But why insult the poor, affront the great?   360
P. A knave's a knave to me in every state:
Alike my scorn, if he succeed or fail,
Sporus at court, or Japhet[3] in a jail,
A hireling scribbler, or a hireling peer,
Knight of the post[4] corrupt, or of the shire,   365
If on a pillory, or near a throne,
He gain his prince's ear, or lose his own.
　　Yet soft by nature, more a dupe than wit,
Sappho can tell you how this man was bit:[5]
This dreaded satirist Dennis will confess   370
Foe to his pride, but friend to his distress:[6]

---

9. Scholars of and authorities on Jewish law and doctrine.
1. The falcon is said to "stoop" to its prey when it swoops down and seizes it in flight.
2. Pope's deformity was frequently ridiculed and occasionally caricatured.
3. Japhet Crook, a notorious forger.

4. One who lives by selling false evidence.
5. Taken in; deceived. "Sappho": Lady Mary Wortley Montagu.
6. Pope wrote the prologue to Cibber's *Provoked Husband* (1728) when that play was performed for Dennis's benefit, shortly before the old critic died.

So humble, he has knocked at Tibbald's door,
Has drunk with Cibber, nay, has rhymed for Moore.
Full ten years slandered, did he once reply?
Three thousand suns went down on Welsted's lie.   375
To please a mistress one aspersed his life;
He lashed him not, but let her be his wife.
Let Budgell charge low Grub Street on his quill,
And write whate'er he pleased, except his will;[7]
Let the two Curlls of town and court,[8] abuse   380
His father, mother, body, soul, and muse.
Yet why? that father held it for a rule,
It was a sin to call our neighbor fool;
That harmless mother thought no wife a whore:
Hear this, and spare his family, James Moore!   385
Unspotted names, and memorable long,
If there be force in virtue, or in song.
    Of gentle blood (part shed in honor's cause,
While yet in Britain honor had applause)
Each parent sprung—— A. What fortune, pray?—— P. Their own,   390
And better got than Bestia's[9] from the throne.
Born to no pride, inheriting no strife,
Nor marrying discord in a noble wife,
Stranger to civil and religious rage,
The good man walked innoxious through his age.   395
No courts he saw, no suits would ever try,
Nor dared an oath,[1] nor hazarded a lie.
Unlearn'd, he knew no schoolman's subtle art,
No language but the language of the heart.
By nature honest, by experience wise,   400
Healthy by temperance, and by exercise;
His life, though long, to sickness passed unknown,
His death was instant, and without a groan.
Oh, grant me thus to live, and thus to die!
Who sprung from kings shall know less joy than I.   405
    O friend! may each domestic bliss be thine!
Be no unpleasing melancholy mine:
Me, let the tender office long engage,
To rock the cradle of reposing age,
With lenient arts extend a mother's breath,   410
Make languor smile, and smooth the bed of death,
Explore the thought, explain the asking eye,
And keep a while one parent from the sky![2]
On cares like these if length of days attend,
May Heaven, to bless those days, preserve my friend,   415

7. Eustace Budgell attacked the *Grub Street Journal* for publishing what he took to be a squib by Pope charging him with having forged the will of Dr. Matthew Tindal.
8. I.e., the publisher and Lord Hervey.
9. Probably the duke of Marlborough, whose vast fortune was made through the favor of Queen Anne. The actual Bestia was a corrupt Roman consul.

1. As a Catholic, Pope's father refused to take the Oaths of Allegiance and Supremacy and the oath against the Pope. He thus rendered himself vulnerable to the many repressive anti-Catholic laws then in force.
2. Pope was a tender and devoted son. His mother had died in 1733, and the earliest version of these lines dates from 1731, when the poet was nursing her through a serious illness.

Preserve him social, cheerful, and serene,
And just as rich as when he served a Queen![3]
A. Whether that blessing be denied or given,
Thus far was right—the rest belongs to Heaven.

                                                                    1735

The Dunciad: Book the Fourth

The fourth book of *The Dunciad*, Pope's last major work, was originally intended as a continuation of *An Essay on Man*. To Jonathan Swift, the spiritual ancestor of the poem, Pope confided in 1736 that he was at work on a series of epistles on the uses of human reason and learning, to conclude with "a satire against the misapplication of all these, exemplified by pictures, characters, and examples." But the epistles never appeared; instead, the satire grew until it took their place. As Pope surveyed England in his last years, the complex literary and social order that had sustained him seemed to be crumbling. It was a time for desperate measures, for satire. And the means of retribution was at hand, in the structure of Pope's own *Dunciad*, the long work that had already impaled so many enemies.

The first *Dunciad*, published in three books in 1728, is a mock-epic reply to Pope's critics and other petty authors. Its hero and victim, Lewis Theobald, had attacked Pope's edition of Shakespeare (1725); other victims had offended Pope either by personal abuse or simply by ineptitude. Inspired by Dryden's *Mac Flecknoe*, *The Dunciad* celebrates the triumph of the hordes of Grub Street. Indeed, so many obscure hacks were mentioned that a *Dunciad Variorum* (1729) was soon required, in which mock-scholarly notes identify the victims, "since it is only in this monument that they must expect to survive." But a modern reader need not catch every reference to enjoy the dazzling wit of the poem, or the sheer sense of fun with which Pope remakes the London literary world into a tiny insane fairground of his own.

The New Dunciad (1742), however, plays a far more serious game: here Pope takes aim at the rot of the whole social fabric. The satire goes deep, and works at many levels, which for convenience, may be divided into four. (1) Politics: From 1721 to 1742 England had been ruled by the Whig supremacy of Robert Walpole, first minister. To Pope and his circle, the immensely powerful Walpole (no friend of poets) seemed a crass and greedy vulgarian, like his monarch George II. It is no accident, in the kingdom of *The Dunciad*, that Dulness personified sits on a throne. (2) Society: Just as the action of the *Aeneid* had been the removal of the empire of Troy to Latium, the action of *The Dunciad*, according to Pope, is "the removal of the empire of Dulness from the City of London to the polite world, Westminster"; that is, the abdication of civility in favor of commerce and financial interests. In modern England, authors write for money, and ministers govern for profit; conspicuous consumption (especially the consumption of paper by scribblers) has replaced the old values of the yeoman and the aristocrat. In 1743, Pope revised the original *Dunciad*, substituting the actor and poet laureate Colley Cibber for Theobald as the hero and incorporating *The New Dunciad* as the fourth book (the version printed here). Dulness, he implies, has achieved her final triumph; Cibber is laureate in England. (3) Education: The word *dunce* is derived from the Scholastic philosopher John Duns Scotus (ca. 1265–1308), whose name had come to stand for silly and useless subtlety, logical hair splitting. Pope, as an heir of the Renaissance, believes that the central subject of education must always be its relevance for human behavior: "The proper study of mankind is Man," and

---

3. Pope alludes to the fact that Arbuthnot, a man of strict probity, left the queen's service no wealthier than when he entered it.

moral philosophy, the relation of individuals to each other and to the world, should be the teacher's first and last concern. By contrast, Dunces waste their time on grammar (words alone) or the "science" of the collector (things alone); they never comprehend that word and thing, like spirit and matter, are essentially dead unless they join. (4) Religion: At its deepest level, the subject of *The Dunciad* is the undoing of God's creation. Many passages from the fourth book echo *Paradise Lost*, and one of Pope's starting places seems to be Satan's threat to return the world to its original darkness, chaos, and ancient night (*Paradise Lost* 2.968–987). *The Dunciad* ends in a great apocalypse, with a yawn that signals the death of *Logos*; as words have become meaningless, so has the whole creation, which the Lord called forth with words. Here Pope invokes, with terrifying intensity, the old idea that God was the first poet, whose poem was the world, and suggests that the sickness of the word has infected all nature. But there is one consolation: out of non-art itself, out of matter without spirit and substance without essence, the poet creates his own final artistic triumph, and makes a poem.

From The Dunciad

From *Book the Fourth*

Yet, yet a moment, one dim ray of light
Indulge, dread Chaos, and eternal Night!
Of darkness visible[1] so much be lent,
As half to show, half veil the deep intent.
Ye Powers![2] whose mysteries restored I sing, 5
To whom Time bears me on his rapid wing,
Suspend a while your force inertly strong,
Then take at once the poet and the song.
   Now flamed the Dog-star's[3] unpropitious ray,
Smote every brain, and withered every bay,[4] 10
Sick was the sun, the owl forsook his bower,
The moon-struck prophet felt the madding hour:
Then rose the seed[5] of Chaos, and of Night,
To blot out Order, and extinguish Light,
Of dull and venal a new world to mold, 15
And bring Saturnian days of lead and gold.[6]
   She mounts the throne: her head a cloud concealed,
In broad effulgence all below revealed,
('Tis thus aspiring Dulness ever shines)
Soft on her lap her Laureate son[7] reclines. 20
   Beneath her foot-stool, Science groans in chains,
And Wit dreads exile, penalties and pains.
There foamed rebellious Logic, gagged and bound,
There, stripped, fair Rhetoric languished on the ground;
His blunted arms by Sophistry are born, 25
And shameless Billingsgate[8] her robes adorn.

1. Cf. *Paradise Lost* 1.63 (p. 666).
2. Chaos and Night, invoked in place of the Muse, because "the restoration of their empire is the action of the poem" [Pope's note].
3. Sirius, associated with the heat of summer and the madness of poets (see *Epistle to Dr. Arbuthnot*, line 3, p. 1112).
4. The laurel, whose garlands are bestowed on poets.
5. The Goddess Dulness.
6. Saturn ruled during the golden age; the new age of "gold" will be reestablished by the dull and venal.
7. Colley Cibber, the poet laureate.
8. Fishmarket slang, which now covers the noble science of rhetoric.

Morality, by her false guardians drawn,
Chicane in furs, and Casuistry in lawn,[9]
Gasps, as they straighten at each end the cord,
And dies, when Dulness gives her Page[1] the word.   30

*   *   *

[THE EDUCATOR]

Now crowds on crowds around the Goddess press,   135
Each eager to present the first address.[2]
Dunce scorning dunce beholds the next advance,
But fop shows fop superior complaisance.
When lo! a specter[3] rose, whose index-hand
Held forth the virtue of the dreadful wand;   140
His beavered brow a birchen garland wears,[4]
Dropping with infant's blood, and mother's tears.
O'er every vein a shuddering horror runs;
Eton and Winton shake through all their sons.
All flesh is humbled, Westminster's bold race[5]   145
Shrink, and confess the Genius[6] of the place:
The pale boy-Senator yet tingling stands,
And holds his breeches close with both his hands.
    Then thus. "Since Man from beast by words is known,
Words are Man's province, words we teach alone.   150
When reason doubtful, like the Samian letter,[7]
Points him two ways, the narrower is the better.
Placed at the door of learning, youth to guide,
We never suffer it to stand too wide.
To ask, to guess, to know, as they commence,   155
As fancy opens the quick springs of sense,
We ply the memory, we load the brain,
Bind rebel wit, and double chain on chain,
Confine the thought, to exercise the breath;[8]
And keep them in the pale of words till death.   160
Whate'er the talents, or howe'er designed,
We hang one jingling padlock on the mind:
A poet the first day, he dips his quill;
And what the last? a very poet still.
Pity! the charm works only in our wall,   165
Lost, lost too soon in yonder House or Hall."[9]

*   *   *

9. Chicanery (legal trickery) wears the ermine robe of a judge; casuistry wears the linen sleeves of a bishop.
1. Sir Francis Page, a notorious hanging judge; or court page, used to strangle criminals in Turkey; or page of writing on which a dull author "kills" moral sentiments.
2. The goddess, newly enthroned, is receiving petitions and congratulations.
3. The ghost of Dr. Busby, stern headmaster of Westminster School.
4. He wears a hat (beaver) and a garland of birch twigs, used for flogging. "Wand": cane used for beating.
5. Alumni of Westminster School, with a play on the justices and members of Parliament who meet at Westminster Hall.
6. I.e., admit that Dr. Busby is the presiding deity (Genius).
7. The letter Y, which Pythagoras (a native of Samos) used as an emblem of the different roads of virtue and vice.
8. Students are taught only to recite the classic poets by heart.
9. The House of Commons and Westminster Hall, where law cases were heard. The eloquence learned by rote disappears on occasions for public speaking.

[THE CARNATION AND THE BUTTERFLY]

Then thick as locusts blackening all the ground,
A tribe,[1] with weeds and shells fantastic crowned,
Each with some wondrous gift approached the Power,
A nest, a toad, a fungus, or a flower.   400
But far the foremost, two, with earnest zeal,
And aspect ardent to the throne appeal.
    The first thus opened: "Hear thy suppliant's call,
Great Queen, and common mother of us all!
Fair from its humble bed I reared this flower,   405
Suckled, and cheer'd, with air, and sun, and shower,
Soft on the paper ruff its leaves I spread,
Bright with the gilded button tipped its head,
Then throned in glass, and named it CAROLINE:[2]
Each maid cried, charming! and each youth, divine!   410
Did Nature's pencil ever blend such rays,
Such varied light in one promiscuous blaze?
Now prostrate! dead! behold that Caroline:
No maid cries, charming! and no youth, divine!
And lo the wretch! whose vile, whose insect lust   415
Laid this gay daughter of the Spring in dust.
Oh punish him, or to th' Elysian shades
Dismiss my soul, where no carnation fades."
    He ceased, and wept. With innocence of mien,
The accused stood forth, and thus addressed the Queen.   420
    "Of all th' enameled race,[3] whose silvery wing
Waves to the tepid zephyrs of the spring,
Or swims along the fluid atmosphere,
Once brightest shined this child of heat and air.
I saw, and started from its vernal bower   425
The rising game, and chased from flower to flower.
It fled, I followed; now in hope, now pain;
It stopped, I stopped; it moved, I moved again.
At last it fixed, 'twas on what plant it pleased,
And where it fixed, the beauteous bird[4] I seized: 430
Rose or carnation was below my care;
I meddle, Goddess! only in my sphere.
I tell the naked fact without disguise,
And, to excuse it, need but show the prize;
Whose spoils this paper offers to your eye,   435
Fair even in death! this peerless Butterfly."
    "My sons!" she answered, "both have done your parts;
Live happy both, and long promote our arts.
But hear a mother, when she recommends
To your fraternal care, our sleeping friends.   440
The common soul, of heaven's more frugal make,
Serves but to keep fools pert, and knaves awake:
A drowsy watchman, that just gives a knock,

1. The Virtuosi, or amateur scientists and collectors.   tion.
2. Queen Caroline, an enthusiastic gardener, is an ap-   3. Colored insects.
propriate choice to lend her name to the perfect carna-   4. Insect.

And breaks our rest, to tell us what's a clock.[5]
Yet by some object every brain is stirred;   445
The dull may waken to a hummingbird;
The most recluse, discreetly opened, find
Congenial matter in the cockle-kind;[6]
The mind, in metaphysics at a loss,
May wander in a wilderness of moss;   450
The head that turns at super-lunar things,
Poised with a tail, may steer on Wilkins' wings.[7]
    "O! would the Sons of Men once think their eyes
And reason given them but to study *flies!*[8]
See Nature in some partial narrow shape,   455
And let the Author of the whole escape:
Learn but to trifle; or, who most observe,
To wonder at their Maker, not to serve."

                              *   *   *

[THE TRIUMPH OF DULNESS]

    Then blessing all,[9] "Go children of my care!
To practice now from theory repair.   580
All my commands are easy, short, and full:
My sons! be proud, be selfish, and be dull.
Guard my prerogative, assert my throne:
This nod confirms each privilege your own.
The cap and switch be sacred to his Grace;[1]   585
With staff and pumps[2] the Marquis lead the race;
From stage to stage the licensed[3] Earl may run,
Paired with his fellow-charioteer the sun;
The learned baron butterflies design,
Or draw to silk Arachne's subtle line;[4]   590
The Judge to dance his brother Sergeant[5] call;
The Senator at cricket urge the ball;
The Bishop stow (pontific luxury!)
An hundred souls of turkeys in a pie;[6]
The sturdy squire to Gallic masters[7] stoop,   595
And drown his lands and manors in a soup.
Others import yet nobler arts from France,
Teach kings to fiddle, and make senates dance.
Perhaps more high some daring son may soar,[8]
Proud to my list to add one monarch more;   600

5. In the 18th-century, watchmen kept guard in the
streets and announced the hours.
6. Cockleshells, popular with collectors, as were hum-
mingbirds and varieties of moss.
7. John Wilkins (1614–1672), one of the founders of
the Royal Society, had speculated "that a man may be
able to fly, by the application of wings to his own
body."
8. Cf. *An Essay on Man* (p. 1101): 1.189–196: "Say
what the use, were finer optics given, / To inspect a
mite, not comprehend the heaven?"
9. Having conferred her titles, Dulness bids each of
the rulers of England to indulge in the triviality closest
to his heart.
1. His Grace, a duke who loves horse racing, is to use

the cap and switch of a jockey.
2. Footmen, who wore pumps (low-cut shoes for running), were matched in races.
3. The license required by the owner of a stagecoach;
also privileged or licentious.
4. A spiderweb.
5. A lawyer or legislative officer. Formal ceremonies at
the Inns of Court are said to have resembled a country
dance, "a call of sergeants."
6. According to Pope, a hundred turkeys had been
"not unfrequently deposited in one Pye in the Bishopric of Durham."
7. French chefs.
8. A bold, direct attack on Walpole.

And nobly conscious, Princes are but things
Born for First Ministers, as slaves for kings,
Tyrant supreme! shall three estates command,
And MAKE ONE MIGHTY DUNCIAD OF THE LAND!"
    More she had spoke, but yawned—All Nature nods: 605
What mortal can resist the yawn of Gods?
Churches and chapels instantly it reached;
(St. James's first, for leaden Gilbert[9] preached)
Then catched the schools; the Hall scarce kept awake;
The Convocation gaped,[1] but could not speak: 610
Lost was the Nation's Sense,[2] nor could be found,
While the long solemn unison went round:
Wide, and more wide, it spread o'er all the realm;
Even Palinurus[3] nodded at the helm:
The vapor mild o'er each committee crept;   615
Unfinished treaties in each office slept;
And chiefless armies dozed out the campaign;
And navies yawned for orders on the main.
    O Muse! relate (for you can tell alone,
Wits have short memories, and dunces none)   620
Relate, who first, who last resigned to rest;
Whose heads she partly, whose completely blessed;
What charms could faction, what ambition lull,
The venal quiet, and entrance the dull;
'Till drowned was sense, and shame, and right, and wrong—   625
O sing, and hush the nations with thy song!

. . . .

    In vain, in vain,—the all-composing Hour
Resistless falls: The Muse obeys the Power.
She comes! she comes![4] the sable throne behold
Of Night primeval, and of Chaos old!   630
Before her, Fancy's gilded clouds decay,
And all its varying rainbows die away.
Wit shoots in vain its momentary fires,
The meteor drops, and in a flash expires.
As one by one, at dread Medea's strain,   635
The sickening stars fade off the ethereal plain;[5]
As Argus' eyes by Hermes' wand oppressed,
Closed one by one to everlasting rest;[6]
Thus at her felt approach, and secret might,
Art after Art goes out, and all is Night.   640
See skulking Truth to her old cavern fled,[7]
Mountains of casuistry heaped o'er her head!
Philosophy, that leaned on Heaven before,

---

9. Dr. John Gilbert, dean of Exeter.
1. The Convocation, an assembly of clergy consulting on ecclesiastical affairs, had been adjourned since 1717.
2. A term for Parliament.
3. The pilot of Aeneas's ship; here Walpole.
4. Having triumphed in the contemporary world of affairs, Dulness (like her antitype Christ) has a Second

Coming, a prophetic vision in which she extinguishes the light of the arts and sciences.
5. In Seneca's *Medea*, the stars obey the curse of Medea, a magician and avenger.
6. Argus, Hera's hundred-eyed watchman, was charmed to sleep and slain by Hermes.
7. Alluding to the saying of Democritus, that Truth lay at the bottom of a deep well [Pope's note].

Shrinks to her second cause,[8] and is no more.
Physic[9] of Metaphysic begs defense,   645
And Metaphysic calls for aid on Sense!
See Mystery[1] to Mathematics fly!
In vain! they gaze, turn giddy, rave, and die.
Religion blushing veils her sacred fires,
And unawares Morality expires.   650
Nor public flame, nor private, dares to shine;
Nor human spark is left, nor glimpse divine!
Lo! thy dread Empire, CHAOS! is restored;
Light dies before thy uncreating word:[2]
Thy hand, great Anarch! lets the curtain fall;   655
And Universal Darkness buries All.

                                                                      1743

8. Science (philosophy) no longer accepts God as the
first cause or final explanation of how all things came
to be; instead, it accepts only the second or material
cause and tries to account for all things by physical
principles alone.

9. Natural science in general.
1. A religious truth known only through divine revelation.
2. Cf. God's first creating words in Genesis, "Let there
be light."

SAMUEL JOHNSON
1709–1784

1737:   Settles in London.
1747–55:   At work on the *Dictionary*.
1762:   Pensioned by the Crown.
1765:   Edition of Shakespeare.
1779, 1781:   *Lives of the Poets*.

Samuel Johnson was famous as a talker in his own time, and his conversation (preserved by James Boswell and others) has been famous ever since. But his wisdom survives above all in his writings: a few superb poems; the grave *Rambler* essays, which established his reputation as a stylist and a moralist; the lessons about life in *Rasselas* and the *Lives of the Poets*; and literary criticism that ranks among the best in English. The virtues of the talk and the writings are the same. They come hot from a mind well stored with knowledge, searingly honest, humane, and quick to seize the unexpected but appropriate image of truth. Johnson's wit is timeless, for it deals with the great facts of human experience, with hope and happiness and loss and duty and the fear of death. Whatever topic he addresses, whatever the form in which he writes, he holds to one commanding purpose: to see life as it is.

Two examples must suffice here. When Anna Williams wondered why a man should make a beast of himself through drunkenness, Johnson answered that "he who makes a beast of himself gets rid of the pain of being a man." In this reply Williams's tired metaphor is so charged with an awareness of the dark aspects of human life that it comes almost unbearably alive. Such moments characterize Johnson's writings as well. For instance, in reviewing the book of a fatuous would-be philosopher who blandly explained away the pains of poverty by declaring that a kindly providence compensates the poor by making them more hopeful, more healthy, more capable of relishing small pleasures, and less sensitive to small annoyances than the rich, Johnson retorted: "The poor indeed are insensible of many little vexations which sometimes embitter the possessions and pollute the enjoyments of the rich. They are not pained by casual incivility, or mortified by the mutilation of a compliment; but this happiness is like that of a malefactor who ceases to feel the cords that bind him when the pincers are tearing his flesh."

Johnson had himself known the pains of poverty. During his boyhood and youth, his father's financial circumstances steadily worsened, so that he was forced to leave Oxford before he had taken a degree. An early marriage to a well-to-do widow, Elizabeth ("Tetty") Porter, more than twenty years older than he, enabled him to open a school. But the school failed, and he moved to London to make his way as a writer. The years between 1737, when he first arrived there with his pupil David Garrick (later to become the leading actor of his generation), and 1755, when the publication of the *Dictionary* established his reputation, were often difficult. He supported himself at first as best he could by doing hack work for the *Gentleman's Magazine*, but gradually his own original writings began to attract attention.

In 1747 Johnson published the *Plan* of his *Dictionary*, and the next seven years were occupied in compiling it—although he had been sanguine enough to count on finishing it in three years. When in 1748 Dr. Adams, a friend from Oxford days, questioned his ability to carry out such a work alone in so short a time, and reminded him that the *Dictionary* of the French Academy had been compiled by forty academicians working for forty years, Johnson replied with humorous jingoism: "Sir, thus it is. This is the proportion. Let me see; forty times forty is sixteen hundred. As three to sixteen hundred, so is the proportion of an Englishman to a Frenchman."

Johnson's achievement in compiling the *Dictionary* becomes even greater when it is realized that he was writing some of his best essays and poems during the same period, for although the booksellers who published the *Dictionary* paid him what was then the large sum of £1,575, it was not enough to enable him to support his household, buy materials, and pay the wages of the six assistants whom he employed year by year until the task was accomplished. He therefore had to exert himself to earn more money by writing. Thus, in 1749, his early tragedy *Irene* (pronounced I-re-nĕ) was produced at long last by his old friend Garrick, by then the manager of Drury Lane. The play was not a success, though Johnson made some profit from it. In the same year appeared his finest poem, *The Vanity of Human Wishes*. With the *Rambler* (1750–52) and the *Idler* (1758–60), two series of periodical essays, Johnson found a devoted audience, but his pleasure in success was tempered by the death of his wife in 1752. He never remarried.

Boswell said of the *Rambler* essays that "in no writings whatever can be found more bark and steel [i.e., quinine and iron] for the mind." Moral strength and health; the importance of applying reason to experience; the test of virtue by what we do, not what we say or "feel"; faith in God: these are the centers to which Johnson's moral writings always return. What Johnson uniquely offers us is the quality of his understanding of the human condition, based on wide reading but always ultimately referred to his own passionate and often anguished experience. Such understanding had to be fought for again and again.

Johnson is thought of as the great generalizer, but what gives his generalizations strength is that they are rooted in the particulars of his self-knowledge. He had constantly to fight against what he called "filling the mind" with illusions, in order to avoid the call of duty, his own black melancholy, and the realities of life. The portrait (largely a self-portrait) of Sober in *Idler* 31 is revealing: he occupies his idle hours with crafts and hobbies and has now taken up chemistry—he "sits and counts the drops as they come from his retort, and forgets that, whilst a drop is falling, a moment flies away." So clear a vision is some distance away from the secure ease of the Addisonian essay.

His theme of themes is expressed in the title of his poem *The Vanity of Human Wishes,* by which Johnson means the dangerous but all-pervasive illusion of what we now call wishful thinking, the feverish intrusion of desires and hopes that distort reality and lead to false expectations. Almost all of Johnson's major writings — verse satire, moral essay, or the prose fable *Rasselas* (1759) — express this theme. In *Rasselas* it is called "the hunger of imagination, which preys upon life," the seeing of things as one would like them to be, rather than as they are. The travelers who are the fable's protagonists pursue supposed guarantees of happiness; they reflect our naive hopefulness, against the accumulation of contrary experience, that one choice of life will make us happy forever.

During this time of great activity, Johnson developed his characteristic style: the rotund periods, proceeding through balanced or parallel words; phrases or clauses moving to carefully controlled rhythms, in language that is characteristically general, often Latinate, and frequently polysyllabic. It is a style at the opposite extreme from Jonathan Swift's simplicity or Joseph Addison's neatness. In Johnson's writings this style never becomes obscure or turgid, for even a very complex sentence reveals — as it should — the structure of the thought, and the learned words are always precisely used. While reading early scientists to collect words for the *Dictionary,* he developed a new vocabulary: for example, *obtund, exuberate, fugacity,* and *frigorific.* But he used many of these strange words in conversation as well as in his writings, often with a peculiarly Johnsonian felicity, describing the operations of the mind with a scientific precision.

After Johnson received his pension in 1762, he no longer had to write for a living, and because he held that "no man but a blockhead" ever wrote for any other reason, he produced as little as he decently could during the last twenty years of his life. His edition of Shakespeare, long delayed, was published in 1765, with its fine preface and its fascinating notes. His last important work is the *Lives of the Poets,* which came out in two parts in 1779 and 1781. These biographical and critical prefaces were commissioned by a group of booksellers who had joined together to publish a large collection of the English poets and who wished to give their venture the prestige that it would acquire if Johnson took part in it. The poets to be included (except for four insisted on by Johnson) were selected by the booksellers according to current fashions. We have, therefore, a collection that begins with Abraham Cowley and John Milton and ends with Thomas Gray and that omits poets whom we regard as "standard," such as Geoffrey Chaucer, Edmund Spenser, Sir Philip Sidney, John Donne, and Andrew Marvell.

In the *Lives of the Poets* and in the earlier *Life of Richard Savage* (1744), Johnson did much to advance the art of biography in England. The public had long been familiar with biography as panegyric or as scandalous memoir, and therefore Johnson's insistence on truth, even about the subject's defects, and on concrete, often minute, details was a new departure, disliked by many readers. "The biographical part of literature is what I love most," Johnson said, for he found every biography useful in revealing human nature and the way we all live. His insistence on truth in biography (and knowing that Boswell intended to write his life, he insisted that he should write it truthfully) was due to his conviction that the more truthful such a work is the more useful it will be to all of us who are concerned with the business of living.

The ideal poet, according to Johnson, has a genius for making the familiar things we see every day seem new. The same might be said of Johnson himself as a critic. He is our great champion, in criticism, of common sense and the common reader. Without denying the right of the poet to flights of imagination, he also insists that poems must make sense, please readers, and help us not only to understand the world but to cope with it. Johnson holds poems to the truth, as he sees it: the principles of nature, logic, religion, and morality. Not even Shakespeare can be excused when "he sacrifices virtue to convenience" and "seems to write without any moral purpose." Yet Johnson is no worshiper of authority or mere "correctness." As a critic he is always the empiricist, testing theory, as he tested all notions, by experience. His determination to judge literature by its truth to life, not by abstract rules, is perfectly illustrated by his treatment of the doctrine of the three unities in the Preface to Shakespeare. Johnson is never afraid to state the obvious, whether the lack of human interest in *Paradise Lost* or Shakespeare's temptation by puns. But at its best, as in the praise of Milton or Shakespeare, his criticism engages some of the deepest questions about literature: why it endures, and how it helps us to endure.

The Vanity of Human Wishes   This poem is an imitation of Juvenal's *Satire 10*. Although it closely follows the order and the ideas of the Latin poem, it remains a very personal work, for Johnson has used the Roman Stoic's satire as a means of expressing his own sense of the tragic and comic in human life. He has tried to reproduce in English verse the qualities he thought especially Juvenalian: stateliness, pointed sentences, and declamatory grandeur. The poem is difficult because of the extreme compactness of the style: every line is forced to convey the greatest possible amount of meaning. Johnson's poetic theory demanded that the poet should deal in the general rather than the particular (cf. his phrase "the grandeur of generality"), but he certainly did not intend that the general should become the merely abstract: observe, for example, how he makes abstract nouns concrete, active, and dramatic by using them as subjects of active and dramatic verbs: "Hate *dogs* their flight, and Insult *mocks* their end" (line 78). But the difficulty of the poem is also related to its theme, the difficulty of seeing anything clearly on this earth. In a world of blindness and illusion, human beings must struggle to find a point of view that will not deceive them, and a happiness that can last.

The Vanity of Human Wishes

In Imitation of the Tenth Satire of Juvenal

Let Observation, with extensive view,
Survey mankind, from China to Peru;
Remark each anxious toil, each eager strife,
And watch the busy scenes of crowded life;
Then say how hope and fear, desire and hate   5
O'erspread with snares the clouded maze of fate,
Where wavering man, betrayed by venturous pride
To tread the dreary paths without a guide,
As treacherous phantoms in the mist delude,
Shuns fancied ills, or chases airy good;   10
How rarely Reason guides the stubborn choice,
Rules the bold hand, or prompts the suppliant voice;
How nations sink, by darling schemes oppressed,
When Vengeance listens to the fool's request.
Fate wings with every wish the afflictive dart,   15
Each gift of nature, and each grace of art;
With fatal heat impetuous courage glows,

With fatal sweetness elocution flows,
Impeachment stops the speaker's powerful breath,
And restless fire precipitates on death.   20
    But scarce observed, the knowing and the bold
Fall in the general massacre of gold;
Wide-wasting pest! that rages unconfined,
And crowds with crimes the records of mankind;
For gold his sword the hireling ruffian draws,   25
For gold the hireling judge distorts the laws;
Wealth heaped on wealth, nor truth nor safety buys,
The dangers gather as the treasures rise.
    Let History tell where rival kings command,
And dubious title shakes the madded land,   30
When statutes glean the refuse of the sword,
How much more safe the vassal than the lord;
Low skulks the hind beneath the rage of power,
And leaves the wealthy traitor[1] in the Tower,
Untouched his cottage, and his slumbers sound,   35
Though Confiscation's vultures hover round.
    The needy traveler, serene and gay,
Walks the wild heath, and sings his toil away.
Does envy seize thee? crush the upbraiding joy,
Increase his riches and his peace destroy;   40
New fears in dire vicissitude invade,
The rustling brake[2] alarms, and quivering shade,
Nor light nor darkness bring his pain relief,
One shows the plunder, and one hides the thief.
    Yet still one general cry the skies assails,   45
And gain and grandeur load the tainted gales;
Few know the toiling statesman's fear or care,
The insidious rival and the gaping heir.
    Once more, Democritus,[3] arise on earth,
With cheerful wisdom and instructive mirth,   50
See motley life in modern trappings dressed,
And feed with varied fools the eternal jest:
Thou who couldst laugh where Want enchained Caprice,
Toil crushed Conceit, and man was of a piece;
Where Wealth unloved without a mourner died;   55
And scarce a sycophant was fed by Pride;
Where ne'er was known the form of mock debate,
Or seen a new-made mayor's unwieldy state;
Where change of favorites made no change of laws,
And senates heard before they judged a cause;   60
How wouldst thou shake at Britain's modish tribe,
Dart the quick taunt, and edge the piercing gibe?
Attentive truth and nature to descry,
And pierce each scene with philosophic eye.
To thee were solemn toys or empty show   65

---

1. Johnson first wrote "bonny traitor," recalling the Jacobite uprising of 1745 and the execution of four of its Scot leaders. "Hind": peasant.
2. Thicket.

3. A Greek philosopher of the late 5th century B.C., remembered as the "laughing philosopher" because men's follies only moved him to mirth.

The robes of pleasure and the veils of woe:
All aid the farce, and all thy mirth maintain,
Whose joys are causeless, or whose griefs are vain.
　　Such was the scorn that filled the sage's mind,
Renewed at every glance on human kind;   70
How just that scorn ere yet thy voice declare,
Search every state, and canvass every prayer.
　　Unnumbered suppliants crowd Preferment's gate,
Athirst for wealth, and burning to be great;
Delusive Fortune hears the incessant call,   75
They mount, they shine, evaporate, and fall.
On every stage the foes of peace attend,
Hate dogs their flight, and Insult mocks their end.
Love ends with hope, the sinking statesman's door
Pours in the morning worshiper no more;[4]   80
For growing names the weekly scribbler lies,
To growing wealth the dedicator flies;
From every room descends the painted face,
That hung the bright palladium[5] of the place;
And smoked in kitchens, or in auctions sold,   85
To better features yields the frame of gold;
For now no more we trace in every line
Heroic worth, benevolence divine:
The form distorted justifies the fall,
And Detestation rids the indignant wall.   90
　　But will not Britain hear the last appeal,
Sign her foes' doom, or guard her favorites' zeal?
Through Freedom's sons no more remonstrance rings,
Degrading nobles and controlling kings;
Our supple tribes repress their patriot throats,   95
And ask no questions but the price of votes;
With weekly libels and septennial ale,[6]
Their wish is full to riot and to rail.
　　In full-blown dignity, see Wolsey[7] stand,
Law in his voice, and fortune in his hand: 100
To him the church, the realm, their powers consign,
Through him the rays of regal bounty shine;
Turned by his nod the stream of honor flows,
His smile alone security bestows:
Still to new heights his restless wishes tower,   105
Claim leads to claim, and power advances power;
Till conquest unresisted ceased to please,
And rights submitted, left him none to seize.
At length his sovereign frowns—the train of state
Mark the keen glance, and watch the sign to hate.   110

---

4. Statesmen gave interviews and received friends and petitioners at levees, or morning receptions.
5. An image of Pallas Athena, which fell from heaven and was preserved at Troy. Not until it was stolen by Diomedes could the city fall to the Greeks.
6. Ministers and even the king freely bought support by bribing Members of Parliament, who in turn won elections by buying votes. "Weekly libels": politically motivated lampoons published in the weekly newspapers. "Septennial ale": the ale given away by candidates at parliamentary elections, held at least every seven years.
7. Thomas Cardinal Wolsey (ca. 1475–1530), lord chancellor and favorite of Henry VIII. Shakespeare dramatized his fall in *Henry VIII.*

Where'er he turns, he meets a stranger's eye,
His suppliants scorn him, and his followers fly;
At once is lost the pride of awful state,
The golden canopy, the glittering plate,
The regal palace, the luxurious board,   115
The liveried army, and the menial lord.
With age, with cares, with maladies oppressed,
He seeks the refuge of monastic rest.
Grief aids disease, remembered folly stings,
And his last sighs reproach the faith of kings.   120
　　Speak thou, whose thoughts at humble peace repine,
Shall Wolsey's wealth, with Wolsey's end be thine?
Or liv'st thou now, with safer pride content,
The wisest justice on the banks of Trent?
For why did Wolsey, near the steeps of fate,   125
On weak foundations raise the enormous weight?
Why but to sink beneath misfortune's blow,
With louder ruin to the gulfs below?
　　What gave great Villiers[8] to the assassin's knife,
And fixed disease on Harley's closing life?   130
What murdered Wentworth, and what exiled Hyde,
By kings protected and to kings allied?
What but their wish indulged in courts to shine,
And power too great to keep or to resign?
　　When first the college rolls receive his name,   135
The young enthusiast quits his ease for fame;
Through all his veins the fever of renown
Burns from the strong contagion of the gown:
O'er Bodley's dome his future labors spread,
And Bacon's[9] mansion trembles o'er his head.   140
Are these thy views? proceed, illustrious youth,
And Virtue guard thee to the throne of Truth!
Yet should thy soul indulge the generous heat,
Till captive Science yields her last retreat;
Should Reason guide thee with her brightest ray,   145
And pour on misty Doubt resistless day;
Should no false kindness lure to loose delight,
Nor praise relax, nor difficulty fright;
Should tempting Novelty thy cell refrain,
And Sloth effuse her opiate fumes in vain;   150
Should Beauty blunt on fops her fatal dart,
Nor claim the triumph of a lettered heart;
Should no disease thy torpid veins invade,
Nor Melancholy's phantoms haunt thy shade;
Yet hope not life from grief or danger free,   155

8. George Villiers, first duke of Buckingham, favorite of James I and Charles I, was assassinated in 1628. Mentioned in the following lines are Robert Harley, earl of Oxford, chancellor of the exchequer and later lord treasurer under Queen Anne (1710–14), impeached and imprisoned by the Whigs in 1715; Thomas Wentworth, earl of Strafford, intimate and adviser of Charles I, impeached by the Long Parliament and executed 1641; and Edward Hyde, earl of Clarendon ("to kings allied" because his daughter married James, duke of York), lord chancellor under Charles II (impeached in 1667, he fled to the Continent).
9. Roger Bacon (ca. 1214–1294), scientist and philosopher, taught at Oxford, where his study, according to tradition, would collapse when a man greater than he should appear at Oxford. "Bodley's dome": the Bodleian Library, Oxford.

Nor think the doom of man reversed for thee:
Deign on the passing world to turn thine eyes,
And pause a while from letters, to be wise;
There mark what ills the scholar's life assail,
Toil, envy, want, the patron,[1] and the jail.   160
See nations slowly wise, and meanly just,
To buried merit raise the tardy bust.
If dreams yet flatter, once again attend,
Hear Lydiat's life, and Galileo's[2] end.
    Nor deem, when Learning her last prize bestows,   165
The glittering eminence exempt from foes;
See when the vulgar 'scapes, despised or awed,
Rebellion's vengeful talons seize on Laud.[3]
From meaner minds though smaller fines content,
The plundered palace, or sequestered rent;[4]   170
Marked out by dangerous parts he meets the shock,
And fatal Learning leads him to the block:
Around his tomb let Art and Genius weep,
But hear his death, ye blockheads, hear and sleep.
    The festal blazes, the triumphal show,   175
The ravished standard, and the captive foe,
The senate's thanks, the gazette's pompous tale,
With force resistless o'er the brave prevail.
Such bribes the rapid Greek[5] o'er Asia whirled,
For such the steady Romans shook the world;   180
For such in distant lands the Britons shine,
And stain with blood the Danube or the Rhine;
This power has praise that virtue scarce can warm,
Till fame supplies the universal charm.
Yet Reason frowns on War's unequal game,   185
Where wasted nations raise a single name,
And mortgaged states their grandsires' wreaths regret
From age to age in everlasting debt;
Wreaths which at last the dear-bought right convey
To rust on medals, or on stones decay.   190
    On what foundation stands the warrior's pride?
How just his hopes, let Swedish Charles[6] decide;
A frame of adamant, a soul of fire,
No dangers fright him, and no labors tire;
O'er love, o'er fear, extends his wide domain,   195
Unconquered lord of pleasure and of pain;
No joys to him pacific scepters yield,
War sounds the trump, he rushes to the field;
Behold surrounding kings their powers combine,

1. In the 1st edition, "garret." For the reason of the change see Boswell's *Life of Johnson*.
2. Galileo (1564–1642), the famous astronomer, was imprisoned as a heretic by the Inquisition in 1633; he died blind. Thomas Lydiat (1572–1646), Oxford scholar, died impoverished because of his Royalist sympathies.
3. Appointed archbishop of Canterbury by Charles I, William Laud followed rigorously High Church policies and was executed by order of the Long Parliament in 1645.
4. During the Commonwealth, the estates of many Royalists were pillaged and their incomes confiscated ("sequestered") by the state.
5. Alexander the Great.
6. Charles XII of Sweden (1682–1718). Defeated by the Russians at Pultowa (1709), he escaped to Turkey and tried to form an alliance against Russia with the sultan. Returning to Sweden, he attacked Norway and was killed in the attack on Fredrikshald.

And one capitulate, and one resign;[7]   200
Peace courts his hand, but spreads her charms in vain;
"Think nothing gained," he cries, "till naught remain,
On Moscow's walls till Gothic standards fly,
And all be mine beneath the polar sky."
The march begins in military state,   205
And nations on his eye suspended wait;
Stern Famine guards the solitary coast,
And Winter barricades the realms of Frost;
He comes, nor want nor cold his course delay—
Hide, blushing Glory, hide Pultowa's day: 210
The vanquished hero leaves his broken bands,
And shows his miseries in distant lands;
Condemned a needy supplicant to wait,
While ladies interpose, and slaves debate.
But did not Chance at length her error mend?   215
Did no subverted empire mark his end?
Did rival monarchs give the fatal wound?
Or hostile millions press him to the ground?
His fall was destined to a barren strand,
A petty fortress, and a dubious hand;   220
He left the name at which the world grew pale,
To point a moral, or adorn a tale.
      All times their scenes of pompous woes afford,
From Persia's tyrant to Bavaria's lord.[8]
In gay hostility, and barbarous pride,   225
With half mankind embattled at his side,
Great Xerxes comes to seize the certain prey,
And starves exhausted regions in his way;
Attendant Flattery counts his myriads o'er,
Till counted myriads soothe his pride no more;   230
Fresh praise is tried till madness fires his mind,
The waves he lashes, and enchains the wind;
New powers are claimed, new powers are still bestowed,
Till rude resistance lops the spreading god;
The daring Greeks deride the martial show,   235
And heap their valleys with the gaudy foe;
The insulted sea with humbler thought he gains,
A single skiff to speed his flight remains;
The encumbered oar scarce leaves the dreaded coast
Through purple billows and a floating host.   240
      The bold Bavarian, in a luckless hour,
Tries the dread summits of Caesarean power,
With unexpected legions bursts away,
And sees defenseless realms receive his sway;
Short sway! fair Austria spreads her mournful charms,   245
The queen, the beauty, sets the world in arms;
From hill to hill the beacon's rousing blaze

---

7. Frederick IV of Denmark capitulated to Charles in 1700; Augustus II of Poland resigned his throne to Charles in 1704.
8. The Elector Charles Albert caused the War of the Austrian Succession (1740–48) when he contested the crown of the empire with Maria Theresa ("Fair Austria" in line 245). "Persia's tyrant": Xerxes invaded Greece and was totally defeated in the sea battle off Salamis, 480 B.C.

Spreads wide the hope of plunder and of praise;
The fierce Croatian, and the wild Hussar,[9]
With all the sons of ravage crowd the war;   250
The baffled prince in honor's flattering bloom
Of hasty greatness finds the fatal doom;
His foes' derision, and his subjects' blame,
And steals to death from anguish and from shame.
    Enlarge my life with multitude of days!   255
In health, in sickness, thus the suppliant prays;
Hides from himself his state, and shuns to know,
That life protracted is protracted woe.
Time hovers o'er, impatient to destroy,
And shuts up all the passages of joy;   260
In vain their gifts the bounteous seasons pour,
The fruit autumnal, and the vernal flower;
With listless eyes the dotard views the store,
He views, and wonders that they please no more;
Now pall the tasteless meats, and joyless wines,   265
And Luxury with sighs her slave resigns.
Approach, ye minstrels, try the soothing strain,
Diffuse the tuneful lenitives[1] of pain:
No sounds, alas! would touch the impervious ear,
Though dancing mountains witnessed Orpheus[2] near;   270
Nor lute nor lyre his feeble powers attend,
Nor sweeter music of a virtuous friend,
But everlasting dictates crowd his tongue,
Perversely grave, or positively wrong.
The still returning tale, and lingering jest,   275
Perplex the fawning niece and pampered guest,
While growing hopes scarce awe the gathering sneer,
And scarce a legacy can bribe to hear;
The watchful guests still hint the last offense,
The daughter's petulance, the son's expense,   280
Improve his heady rage with treacherous skill,
And mold his passions till they make his will.
    Unnumbered maladies his joints invade,
Lay siege to life and press the dire blockade;
But unextinguished avarice still remains,   285
And dreaded losses aggravate his pains;
He turns, with anxious heart and crippled hands,
His bonds of debt, and mortgages of lands;
Or views his coffers with suspicious eyes,
Unlocks his gold, and counts it till he dies.   290
    But grant, the virtues of a temperate prime
Bless with an age exempt from scorn or crime;
An age that melts with unperceived decay,
And glides in modest innocence away;
Whose peaceful day Benevolence endears,   295
Whose night congratulating Conscience cheers;

9. Hungarian light cavalry.
1. Medicines that relieve pain.

2. A legendary poet who played on the lyre so beautifully that wild beasts were spellbound.

The general favorite as the general friend:
Such age there is, and who shall wish its end?
   Yet even on this her load Misfortune flings,
To press the weary minutes' flagging wings;   300
New sorrow rises as the day returns,
A sister sickens, or a daughter mourns.
Now kindred Merit fills the sable bier,
Now lacerated Friendship claims a tear;
Year chases year, decay pursues decay,   305
Still drops some joy from withering life away;
New forms arise, and different views engage,
Superfluous lags the veteran[3] on the stage,
Till pitying Nature signs the last release,
And bids afflicted Worth retire to peace.   310
   But few there are whom hours like these await,
Who set unclouded in the gulfs of Fate.
From Lydia's monarch[4] should the search descend,
By Solon cautioned to regard his end,
In life's last scene what prodigies surprise,   315
Fears of the brave, and follies of the wise!
From Marlborough's eyes the streams of dotage flow,
And Swift[5] expires a driveler and a show.
   The teeming mother, anxious for her race,
Begs for each birth the fortune of a face: 320
Yet Vane could tell what ills from beauty spring;
And Sedley[6] cursed the form that pleased a king.
Ye nymphs of rosy lips and radiant eyes,
Whom Pleasure keeps too busy to be wise,
Whom Joys with soft varieties invite,   325
By day the frolic, and the dance by night;
Who frown with vanity, who smile with art,
And ask the latest fashion of the heart;
What care, what rules your heedless charms shall save,
Each nymph your rival, and each youth your slave?   330
Against your fame with Fondness Hate combines,
The rival batters, and the lover mines.
With distant voice neglected Virtue calls,
Less heard and less, the faint remonstrance falls;
Tired with contempt, she quits the slippery reign,   335
And Pride and Prudence take her seat in vain.
In crowd at once, where none the pass defend,
The harmless freedom, and the private friend.
The guardians yield, by force superior plied:
To Interest, Prudence; and to Flattery, Pride.   340
Now Beauty falls betrayed, despised, distressed,
And hissing Infamy proclaims the rest.

---

3. A veteran of life, not of war.
4. Croesus, the wealthy and fortunate king, was warned by Solon not to count himself happy until he ceased to live. He lost his crown to Cyrus the Great of Persia.
5. Jonathan Swift, who passed the last four years of his life in utter senility. John Churchill, duke of Marlborough, England's brilliant general during most of the War of the Spanish Succession (1702–13).
6. Catherine Sedley, mistress of James II. Anne Vane, mistress of Frederick, prince of Wales (son of George II).

Where then shall Hope and Fear their objects find?
Must dull Suspense corrupt the stagnant mind?
Must helpless man, in ignorance sedate,   345
Roll darkling down the torrent of his fate?
Must no dislike alarm, no wishes rise,
No cries invoke the mercies of the skies?
Inquirer, cease; petitions yet remain,
Which Heaven may hear, nor deem religion vain.   350
Still raise for good the supplicating voice,
But leave to Heaven the measure and the choice.
Safe in his power, whose eyes discern afar
The secret ambush of a specious prayer.
Implore his aid, in his decisions rest,   355
Secure, whate'er he gives, he gives the best.
Yet when the sense of sacred presence fires,
And strong devotion to the skies aspires,
Pour forth thy fervors for a healthful mind,
Obedient passions, and a will resigned;   360
For love, which scarce collective man can fill;[7]
For patience sovereign o'er transmuted ill;
For faith, that panting for a happier seat,
Counts death kind Nature's signal of retreat:
These goods for man the laws of Heaven ordain,   365
These goods he grants, who grants the power to gain;
With these celestial Wisdom calms the mind,
And makes the happiness she does not find.

                                                                    1749

On the Death of Dr. Robert Levet[1]

Condemned to Hope's delusive mine,
    As on we toil from day to day,
By sudden blasts, or slow decline,
    Our social comforts drop away.

Well tried through many a varying year,   5
    See Levet to the grave descend;
Officious,[2] innocent, sincere,
    Of every friendless name the friend.

Yet still he fills Affection's eye,
    Obscurely wise, and coarsely kind;   10
Nor, lettered Arrogance, deny
    Thy praise to merit unrefined.

When fainting Nature called for aid,
    And hovering Death prepared the blow,

---

7. Which humankind as a whole can hardly overtask.
1. An unlicensed physician, who lived in Johnson's house for many years and who died in 1782. His practice was among the very poor. Boswell wrote: "He was of a strange grotesque appearance, stiff and formal in his manner, and seldom said a word while any company was present."
2. "Kind, doing good offices" (Johnson's *Dictionary*).

    His vigorous remedy displayed   15
        The power of art without the show.

    In Misery's darkest caverns known,
        His useful care was ever nigh,
    Where hopeless Anguish poured his groan,
        And lonely Want retired to die.   20

    No summons mocked by chill delay,
        No petty gain disdained by pride,
    The modest wants of every day
        The toil of every day supplied.

    His virtues walked their narrow round,   25
        Nor made a pause, nor left a void;
    And sure the Eternal Master found
        The single talent well employed.[3]

    The busy day, the peaceful night,
        Unfelt, uncounted, glided by;   30
    His frame was firm, his powers were bright,
        Though now his eightieth year was nigh.

    Then with no throbbing fiery pain,
        No cold gradations of decay,
    Death broke at once the vital chain,   35
        And freed his soul the nearest way.

                                      1783

Translation of Horace, *Odes*, Book 4.7[1]

    The snow dissolved no more is seen,
    The fields, and woods, behold, are green,
    The changing year renews the plain,
    The rivers know their banks again,
    The spritely nymph and naked grace[2]   5
    The mazy dance together trace.
    The changing year's successive plan
    Proclaims mortality to man.
    Rough winter's blasts to spring give way,
    Spring yields to summer's sovereign ray,   10
    Then summer sinks in autumn's reign,
    And winter chills the world again.
    Her losses soon the moon supplies,
    But wretched man, when once he lies
    Where Priam[3] and his sons are laid,   15

3. In the parable of the talents (Matthew 25.14–30), Jesus suggests that salvation will be granted to those who make good use of their abilities, however small.
1. Johnson composed this translation the month be-fore his death.
2. One of the Three Graces, emblematic of beauty.
3. Last king of Troy, slain with his sons at the end of the Trojan War.

Is naught but ashes and a shade.
Who knows if Jove who counts our score
Will toss us in a morning more?
What with your friend you nobly share
At least you rescue from your heir.   20
Not you, Torquatus, boast of Rome,
When Minos once has fixed your doom,[4]
Or eloquence, or splendid birth,
Or virtue shall replace on earth.
Hippolytus[5] unjustly slain   25
Diana calls to life in vain,
Nor can the might of Theseus rend
The chains of hell that hold his friend.[6]

1784

Rasselas   Johnson wrote *Rasselas* in January 1759, during the evenings of one week, a remarkable instance of his ability to write rapidly and brilliantly under the pressure of necessity. His mother lay dying in Lichfield. Her son, famous for his *Dictionary*, was nonetheless oppressed by poverty and in great need of ready money with which to make her last days comfortable, pay her funeral expenses, and settle her small debts. He was paid £100 for the first edition of *Rasselas*, but not in time to attend her deathbed or her funeral.

Rasselas is a philosophical fable cast in the popular form of an Oriental tale, a type of fiction that owed its popularity to the vogue of the *Arabian Nights*, first translated into English in the early eighteenth century. Because the work is a fable, we should not approach it as a novel: psychologically credible characters and a series of intricately involved actions that lead to a necessary resolution and conclusion are not to be found in *Rasselas*. Instead we are meant to reflect on the ideas and to savor the melancholy resonance and intelligence of the stately prose that expresses them. Johnson arranges the incidents of the fable to test a variety of possible solutions to a problem: What choice of life will bring us happiness? (*The Choice of Life* was his working title for the book.) Many ways of life are examined in turn, and each is found wanting. Johnson does not pretend to have solved the problem. Rather, he locates the sources of discontent in a basic principle of human nature: the "hunger of imagination which preys incessantly upon life" (chapter 32) and which lures us to "listen with credulity to the whispers of fancy and pursue with eagerness the phantoms of hope" (chapter 1). The tale is a gentle satire on one of the perennial topics of satirists: the folly of all of us who stubbornly cling to our illusions despite the evidence of experience. *Rasselas* is not all darkness and gloom, for Johnson's theme invites comic as well as tragic treatment, and some of the episodes evoke that laughter of the mind that is the effect of high comedy. In its main theme, however—the folly of cherishing the dream of ever attaining unalloyed happiness in a world that can never wholly satisfy our desires—and in many of the sayings of its characters, especially of the sage Imlac, *Rasselas* expresses some of Johnson's own deepest convictions.

4. Sentence. L. Manlius Torquatus, a friend of Horace and an advocate, is represented as pleading his case before Minos, judge of the dead.
5. Phaedra, wife of Theseus, falsely accused his chaste son Hippolytus of rape. Theseus brought about the death of his son, and even Diana, goddess of chastity, could not restore him.
6. Pirithous, held prisoner with Theseus in hell.

The History of Rasselas, Prince of Abyssinia

Chapter 1. Description of a Palace in a Valley

Ye who listen with credulity to the whispers of fancy, and pursue with eagerness the phantoms of hope; who expect that age will perform the promises of youth, and that the deficiencies of the present day will be supplied by the morrow—attend to the history of Rasselas, prince of Abyssinia.

Rasselas was the fourth son of the mighty emperor in whose dominions the Father of Waters[1] begins his course; whose bounty pours down the streams of plenty, and scatters over half the world the harvests of Egypt.

According to the custom which has descended from age to age among the monarchs of the torrid zone, Rasselas was confined in a private palace, with the other sons and daughters of Abyssinian royalty, till the order of succession should call him to the throne.

The place which the wisdom or policy of antiquity had destined for the residence of the Abyssinian princes was a spacious valley[2] in the kingdom of Amhara, surrounded on every side by mountains, of which the summits overhang the middle part. The only passage by which it could be entered was a cavern that passed under a rock, of which it has long been disputed whether it was the work of nature or of human industry. The outlet of the cavern was concealed by a thick wood, and the mouth which opened into the valley was closed with gates of iron, forged by the artificers of ancient days, so massy that no man could, without the help of engines, open or shut them.

From the mountains on every side rivulets descended that filled all the valley with verdure and fertility, and formed a lake in the middle, inhabited by fish of every species, and frequented by every fowl whom nature has taught to dip the wing in water. This lake discharged its superfluities by a stream, which entered a dark cleft of the mountain on the northern side, and fell with dreadful noise from precipice to precipice till it was heard no more.

The sides of the mountains were covered with trees, the banks of the brooks were diversified with flowers; every blast shook spices from the rocks, and every month dropped fruits upon the ground. All animals that bite the grass, or browse the shrub, whether wild or tame, wandered in this extensive circuit, secured from beasts of prey by the mountains which confined them. On one part were flocks and herds feeding in the pastures, on another all the beasts of chase frisking in the lawns; the sprightly kid was bounding on the rocks, the subtle monkey frolicking in the trees, and the solemn elephant reposing in the shade. All the diversities of the world were brought together, the blessings of nature were collected, and its evils extracted and excluded.

The valley, wide and fruitful, supplied its inhabitants with the necessaries of life, and all delights and superfluities were added at the annual visit which the emperor paid his children, when the iron gate was opened to the sound of music, and during eight days everyone that resided in the valley was required to propose whatever might contribute to make seclusion pleasant, to fill up the vacancies of attention, and lessen the tediousness of time. Every desire was

---

1. The Nile.
2. Johnson had read of the Happy Valley in the Portuguese Jesuit Father Lobo's book on Abyssinia, which he translated in 1735. The description in this and the immediately following paragraphs illustrates well enough Johnson's preference for the "general" over the "particular" (see chap. 10). It owes something to the description of the Garden in *Paradise Lost* 4, and Coleridge's *Kubla Khan* owes something to it.

immediately granted. All the artificers of pleasure were called to gladden the festivity; the musicians exerted the power of harmony, and the dancers showed their activity before the princes, in hope that they should pass their lives in this blissful captivity, to which those only were admitted whose performance was thought able to add novelty to luxury. Such was the appearance of security and delight which this retirement afforded, that they to whom it was new always desired that it might be perpetual; and as those on whom the iron gate had once closed were never suffered to return, the effect of longer experience could not be known. Thus every year produced new schemes of delight and new competitors for imprisonment.

The palace stood on an eminence, raised about thirty paces above the surface of the lake. It was divided into many squares or courts, built with greater or less magnificence according to the rank of those for whom they were designed. The roofs were turned into arches of massy stone, joined with a cement that grew harder by time, and the building stood from century to century, deriding the solstitial rains and equinoctial hurricanes, without need of reparation.

This house, which was so large as to be fully known to none but some ancient officers, who successively inherited the secrets of the place, was built as if suspicion herself had dictated the plan. To every room there was an open and secret passage; every square had a communication with the rest, either from the upper stories by private galleries, or by subterranean passages from the lower apartments. Many of the columns had unsuspected cavities, in which a long race of monarchs had reposited their treasures. They then closed up the opening with marble, which was never to be removed but in the utmost exigencies of the kingdom, and recorded their accumulations in a book, which was itself concealed in a tower, not entered but by the emperor, attended by the prince who stood next in succession.

Chapter 2. The Discontent of Rasselas in the Happy Valley

Here the sons and daughters of Abyssinia lived only to know the soft vicissitudes of pleasure and repose, attended by all that were skillful to delight, and gratified with whatever the senses can enjoy. They wandered in gardens of fragrance, and slept in the fortresses of security. Every art was practiced to make them pleased with their own condition. The sages who instructed them told them of nothing but the miseries of public life, and described all beyond the mountains as regions of calamity, where discord was always raging, and where man preyed upon man.

To heighten their opinion of their own felicity, they were daily entertained with songs, the subject of which was the *happy valley*. Their appetites were excited by frequent enumerations of different enjoyments, and revelry and merriment was the business of every hour, from the dawn of morning to the close of even.

These methods were generally successful; few of the princes had ever wished to enlarge their bounds, but passed their lives in full conviction that they had all within their reach that art or nature could bestow, and pitied those whom fate had excluded from this seat of tranquility, as the sport of chance and the slaves of misery.

Thus they rose in the morning and lay down at night, pleased with each other and with themselves; all but Rasselas, who, in the twenty-sixth year of his age, began to withdraw himself from their pastimes and assemblies, and to delight in solitary walks and silent meditation. He often sat before tables covered with luxury, and forgot to taste the dainties that were placed before him; he rose abruptly in the midst of the song, and hastily retired beyond the sound of music. His attendants observed the change, and endeavored to renew his love of pleasure. He neglected their officiousness, repulsed their invitations, and spent day after day on the banks of rivulets sheltered with trees, where he sometimes listened to the birds in the branches, sometimes observed the fish playing in the stream, and anon cast his eyes upon the pastures and mountains filled with animals, of which some were biting the herbage, and some sleeping among the bushes.

This singularity of his humor made him much observed. One of the sages, in whose conversation he had formerly delighted, followed him secretly, in hope of discovering the cause of his disquiet. Rasselas, who knew not that anyone was near him, having for some time fixed his eyes upon the goats that were browsing among the rocks, began to compare their condition with his own.

"What," said he, "makes the difference between man and all the rest of the animal creation? Every beast that strays beside me has the same corporal necessities with myself; he is hungry, and crops the grass, he is thirsty, and drinks the stream, his thirst and hunger are appeased, he is satisfied, and sleeps; he rises again, and he is hungry, he is again fed, and is at rest. I am hungry and thirsty like him, but when thirst and hunger cease, I am not at rest; I am, like him, pained with want, but am not, like him, satisfied with fullness. The intermediate hours are tedious and gloomy; I long again to be hungry that I may again quicken my attention. The birds peck the berries or the corn, and fly away to the groves, where they sit in seeming happiness on the branches, and waste their lives in tuning one unvaried series of sounds. I likewise can call the lutanist and the singer, but the sounds that pleased me yesterday weary me today, and will grow yet more wearisome tomorrow. I can discover within me no power of perception which is not glutted with its proper pleasure, yet I do not feel myself delighted. Man has surely some latent sense for which this place affords no gratification, or he has some desires distinct from sense, which must be satisfied before he can be happy."

After this he lifted up his head, and seeing the moon rising, walked towards the palace. As he passed through the fields, and saw the animals around him, "Ye," said he, "are happy, and need not envy me that walk thus among you, burthened with myself; nor do I, ye gentle beings, envy your felicity, for it is not the felicity of man. I have many distresses from which ye are free; I fear pain when I do not feel it; I sometimes shrink at evils recollected, and sometimes start at evils anticipated. Surely the equity of Providence has balanced peculiar sufferings with peculiar enjoyments."

With observations like these the prince amused himself as he returned, uttering them with a plaintive voice, yet with a look that discovered him to feel some complacence in his own perspicacity, and to receive some solace of the miseries of life from consciousness of the delicacy with which he felt, and the eloquence with which he bewailed them. He mingled cheerfully in the diversions of the evening, and all rejoiced to find that his heart was lightened.

Chapter 3. The Wants of Him That Wants Nothing

On the next day his old instructor, imagining that he had now made himself acquainted with his disease of mind, was in the hope of curing it by counsel, and officiously sought an opportunity of conference, which the prince, having long considered him as one whose intellects were exhausted, was not very willing to afford. "Why," said he, "does this man thus intrude upon me; shall I be never suffered to forget those lectures which pleased only while they were new, and to become new again must be forgotten?" He then walked into the wood, and composed himself to his usual meditations; when, before his thoughts had taken any settled form, he perceived his pursuer at his side, and was at first prompted by his impatience to go hastily away; but, being unwilling to offend a man whom he had once reverenced and still loved, he invited him to sit down with him on the bank.

The old man, thus encouraged, began to lament the change which had been lately observed in the prince, and to inquire why he so often retired from the pleasures of the palace, to loneliness and silence. "I fly from pleasure," said the prince, "because pleasure has ceased to please; I am lonely because I am miserable, and am unwilling to cloud with my presence the happiness of others." "You, sir," said the sage, "are the first who has complained of misery in the *happy valley*. I hope to convince you that your complaints have no real cause. You are here in full possession of all that the emperor of Abyssinia can bestow; here is neither labor to be endured nor danger to be dreaded, yet here is all that labor or danger can procure or purchase. Look round and tell me which of your wants is without supply; if you want nothing, how are you unhappy?"

"That I want nothing," said the prince, "or that I know not what I want, is the cause of my complaint; if I had any known want, I should have a certain wish; that wish would excite endeavor, and I should not then repine to see the sun move so slowly towards the western mountain, or lament when the day breaks, and sleep will no longer hide me from myself. When I see the kids and the lambs chasing one another, I fancy that I should be happy if I had something to pursue. But, possessing all that I can want, I find one day and one hour exactly like another, except that the latter is still more tedious than the former. Let your experience inform me how the day may now seem as short as in my childhood, while nature was yet fresh and every moment showed me what I never had observed before. I have already enjoyed too much; give me something to desire."

The old man was surprised at this new species of affliction and knew not what to reply, yet was unwilling to be silent. "Sir," said he, "if you had seen the miseries of the world you would know how to value your present state." "Now," said the prince, "you have given me something to desire. I shall long to see the miseries of the world, since the sight of them is necessary to happiness."

Chapter 4. The Prince Continues to Grieve and Muse

At this time the sound of music proclaimed the hour of repast, and the conversation was concluded. The old man went away sufficiently discontented to find that his reasonings had produced the only conclusion which they were intended to prevent. But in the decline of life shame and grief are of short duration; whether it be that we bear easily what we have born long, or that, finding ourselves in age less regarded, we less regard others; or, that we look with slight regard upon afflictions, to which we know that the hand of death is about to put an end.

The prince, whose views were extended to a wider space, could not speedily quiet his emotions. He had been before terrified at the length of life which nature promised him, because he considered that in a long time much must be endured; he now rejoiced in his youth, because in many years much might be done.

This first beam of hope, that had been ever darted into his mind, rekindled youth in his cheeks, and doubled the luster of his eyes. He was fired with the desire of doing something, though he knew not yet with distinctness, either end or means.

He was now no longer gloomy and unsocial; but, considering himself as master of a secret stock of happiness, which he could enjoy only by concealing it, he affected to be busy in all schemes of diversion, and endeavored to make others pleased with the state of which he himself was weary. But pleasures never can be so multiplied or continued, as not to leave much of life unemployed; there were many hours, both of the night and day, which he could spend without suspicion in solitary thought. The load of life was much lightened: he went eagerly into the assemblies, because he supposed the frequency of his presence necessary to the success of his purposes; he retired gladly to privacy, because he had now a subject of thought.

His chief amusement was to picture to himself that world which he had never seen; to place himself in various conditions; to be entangled in imaginary difficulties, and to be engaged in wild adventures: but his benevolence always terminated his projects in the relief of distress, the detection of fraud, the defeat of oppression, and the diffusion of happiness.

Thus passed twenty months of the life of Rasselas. He busied himself so intensely in visionary bustle, that he forgot his real solitude; and, amidst hourly preparations for the various incidents of human affairs, neglected to consider by what means he should mingle with mankind.

One day, as he was sitting on a bank, he feigned to himself an orphan virgin robbed of her little portion[3] by a treacherous lover, and crying after him for restitution and redress. So strongly was the image impressed upon his mind, that he started up in the maid's defense, and ran forward to seize the plunderer with all the eagerness of real pursuit. Fear naturally quickens the flight of guilt. Rasselas could not catch the fugitive with his utmost efforts; but, resolving to weary, by perseverance, him whom he could not surpass in speed, he pressed on till the foot of the mountain stopped his course.

Here he recollected himself, and smiled at his own useless impetuosity. Then raising his eyes to the mountain, "This," said he, "is the fatal obstacle that hinders at once the enjoyment of pleasure, and the exercise of virtue. How long is it that my hopes and wishes have flown beyond this boundary of my life, which yet I never have attempted to surmount!"

Struck with this reflection, he sat down to muse, and remembered, that

3. Money or goods.

since he first resolved to escape from his confinement, the sun had passed twice over him in his annual course. He now felt a degree of regret with which he had never been before acquainted. He considered how much might have been done in the time which had passed, and left nothing real behind it. He compared twenty months with the life of man. "In life," said he, "is not to be counted the ignorance of infancy, or imbecility of age. We are long before we are able to think, and we soon cease from the power of acting. The true period of human existence may be reasonably estimated as forty years, of which I have mused away the four and twentieth part. What I have lost was certain, for I have certainly possessed it; but of twenty months to come who can assure me?"

The consciousness of his own folly pierced him deeply, and he was long before he could be reconciled to himself. "The rest of my time," said he, "has been lost by the crime or folly of my ancestors, and the absurd institutions of my country; I remember it with disgust, yet without remorse: but the months that have passed since new light darted into my soul, since I formed a scheme of reasonable felicity, have been squandered by my own fault. I have lost that which can never be restored: I have seen the sun rise and set for twenty months, an idle gazer on the light of heaven. In this time the birds have left the nest of their mother, and committed themselves to the woods and to the skies: the kid has forsaken the teat, and learned by degrees to climb the rocks in quest of independent sustenance. I only have made no advances, but am still helpless and ignorant. The moon, by more than twenty changes, admonished me of the flux of life; the stream that rolled before my feet upbraided my inactivity. I sat feasting on intellectual luxury, regardless alike of the examples of the earth, and the instructions of the planets. Twenty months are past, who shall restore them!"

These sorrowful meditations fastened upon his mind; he passed four months in resolving to lose no more time in idle resolves, and was awakened to more vigorous exertion by hearing a maid, who had broken a porcelain cup, remark that what cannot be repaired is not to be regretted.

This was obvious; and Rasselas reproached himself that he had not discovered it, having not known, or not considered, how many useful hints are obtained by chance, and how often the mind, hurried by her own ardor to distant views, neglects the truths that lie open before her. He, for a few hours, regretted his regret, and from that time bent his whole mind upon the means of escaping from the valley of happiness.

Chapter 5. The Prince Meditates His Escape

He now found that it would be very difficult to effect that which it was very easy to suppose effected. When he looked round about him, he saw himself confined by the bars of nature which had never yet been broken, and by the gate, through which none that once had passed it were ever able to return. He was now impatient as an eagle in a grate.[4] He passed week after week in clambering the mountains, to see if there was any aperture which the bushes might conceal, but found all the summits inaccessible by their prominence.

4. Barred cage.

The iron gate he despaired to open; for it was not only secured with all the power of art, but was always watched by successive sentinels, and was by its position exposed to the perpetual observation of all the inhabitants.

He then examined the cavern through which the waters of the lake were discharged; and, looking down at a time when the sun shone strongly upon its mouth, he discovered it to be full of broken rocks, which, though they permitted the stream to flow through many narrow passages, would stop any body of solid bulk. He returned discouraged and dejected; but, having now known the blessing of hope, resolved never to despair.

In these fruitless searches he spent ten months. The time, however, passed cheerfully away: in the morning he rose with new hope, in the evening applauded his own diligence, and in the night slept sound after his fatigue. He met a thousand amusements which beguiled his labor, and diversified his thoughts. He discerned the various instincts of animals, and properties of plants, and found the place replete with wonders, of which he purposed to solace himself with the contemplation, if he should never be able to accomplish his flight; rejoicing that his endeavors, though yet unsuccessful, had supplied him with a source of inexhaustible enquiry.

But his original curiosity was not yet abated; he resolved to obtain some knowledge of the ways of men. His wish still continued, but his hope grew less. He ceased to survey any longer the walls of his prison, and spared to search by new toils for interstices which he knew could not be found, yet determined to keep his design always in view, and lay hold on any expedient that time should offer.

Chapter 6. A Dissertation on the Art of Flying

Among the artists that had been allured into the happy valley, to labor for the accommodation and pleasure of its inhabitants, was a man eminent for his knowledge of the mechanic powers, who had contrived many engines[5] both of use and recreation. By a wheel, which the stream turned, he forced the water into a tower, whence it was distributed to all the apartments of the palace. He erected a pavillion in the garden, around which he kept the air always cool by artificial showers. One of the groves, appropriated to the ladies, was ventilated by fans, to which the rivulet that run through it gave a constant motion; and instruments of soft music were placed at proper distances, of which some played by the impulse of the wind, and some by the power of the stream.

This artist was sometimes visited by Rasselas, who was pleased with every kind of knowledge, imagining that the time would come when all his acquisitions should be of use to him in the open world. He came one day to amuse himself in his usual manner, and found the master busy in building a sailing chariot: he saw that the design was practicable upon a level surface, and with expressions of great esteem solicited its completion. The workman was pleased to find himself so much regarded by the prince, and resolved to gain yet higher honors. "Sir," said he, "you have seen but a small part of what the mechanic sciences can perform. I have been long of opinion, that, instead of the tardy

---

5. Machines. "Mechanic powers": the forces that cause things to move.

conveyance of ships and chariots, man might use the swifter migration of wings; that the fields of air are open to knowledge, and that only ignorance and idleness need crawl upon the ground."

This hint rekindled the prince's desire of passing the mountains; having seen what the mechanist had already performed, he was willing to fancy that he could do more; yet resolved to inquire further before he suffered hope to afflict him by disappointment. "I am afraid," said he to the artist, "that your imagination prevails over your skill, and that you now tell me rather what you wish than what you know. Every animal has his element assigned him; the birds have the air, and man and beasts the earth." "So," replied the mechanist, "fishes have the water, in which yet beasts can swim by nature, and men by art. He that can swim needs not despair to fly: to swim is to fly in a grosser fluid, and to fly is to swim in a subtler. We are only to proportion our power of resistance to the different density of the matter through which we are to pass. You will be necessarily upborn by the air, if you can renew any impulse upon it, faster than the air can recede from the pressure."

"But the exercise of swimming," said the prince, "is very laborious; the strongest limbs are soon wearied; I am afraid the act of flying will be yet more violent, and wings will be of no great use, unless we can fly further than we can swim."

"The labor of rising from the ground," said the artist "will be great, as we see it in the heavier domestic fowls; but, as we mount higher, the earth's attraction, and the body's gravity, will be gradually diminished, till we shall arrive at a region where the man will float in the air without any tendency to fall: no care will then be necessary, but to move forwards, which the gentlest impulse will effect. You, Sir, whose curiosity is so extensive, will easily conceive with what pleasure a philosopher, furnished with wings, and hovering in the sky, would see the earth, and all its inhabitants, rolling beneath him, and presenting to him successively, by its diurnal motion, all the countries within the same parallel. How must it amuse the pendent spectator to see the moving scene of land and ocean, cities and deserts! To survey with equal security the marts of trade, and the fields of battle; mountains infested by barbarians, and fruitful regions gladdened by plenty, and lulled by peace! How easily shall we then trace the Nile through all his passage; pass over to distant regions, and examine the face of nature from one extremity of the earth to the other!"

"All this," said the prince, "is much to be desired, but I am afraid that no man will be able to breathe in these regions of speculation and tranquility. I have been told, that respiration is difficult upon lofty mountains, yet from these precipices, though so high as to produce great tenuity of the air, it is very easy to fall: therefore I suspect, that from any height, where life can be supported, there may be danger of too quick descent."

"Nothing," replied the artist, "will ever be attempted, if all possible objections must be first overcome. If you will favor my project I will try the first flight at my own hazard. I have considered the structure of all volant[6] animals, and find the folding continuity of the bat's wings most easily accommodated to the human form. Upon this model I shall begin my task tomorrow, and in

6. Able to fly.

a year expect to tower into the air beyond the malice or pursuit of man. But I will work only on this condition, that the art shall not be divulged, and that you shall not require me to make wings for any but ourselves."

"Why," said Rasselas, "should you envy others so great an advantage? All skill ought to be exerted for universal good; every man has owed much to others, and ought to repay the kindness that he has received."

"If men were all virtuous," returned the artist, "I should with great alacrity teach them all to fly. But what would be the security of the good, if the bad could at pleasure invade them from the sky? Against an army sailing through the clouds neither walls, nor mountains, nor seas, could afford any security. A flight of northern savages might hover in the wind, and light at once with irresistible violence upon the capital of a fruitful region that was rolling under them. Even this valley, the retreat of princes, the abode of happiness, might be violated by the sudden descent of some of the naked nations that swarm on the coast of the southern sea."

The prince promised secrecy, and waited for the performance, not wholly hopeless of success. He visited the work from time to time, observed its progress, and remarked many ingenious contrivances to facilitate motion, and unite levity with strength. The artist was every day more certain that he should leave vultures and eagles behind him, and the contagion of his confidence seized upon the prince.

In a year the wings were finished, and, on a morning appointed, the maker appeared furnished for flight on a little promontory: he waved his pinions a while to gather air, then leaped from his stand, and in an instant dropped into the lake. His wings, which were of no use in the air, sustained him in the water, and the prince drew him to land, half dead with terror and vexation.

Chapter 7. The Prince Finds a Man of Learning

The prince was not much afflicted by this disaster, having suffered himself to hope for a happier event, only because he had no other means of escape in view. He still persisted in his design to leave the happy valley by the first opportunity.

His imagination was now at a stand; he had no prospect of entering into the world; and, notwithstanding all his endeavors to support himself, discontent by degrees preyed upon him, and he began again to lose his thoughts in sadness, when the rainy season, which in these countries is periodical, made it inconvenient to wander in the woods.

The rain continued longer and with more violence than had been ever known; the clouds broke on the surrounding mountains, and the torrents streamed into the plain on every side, till the cavern was too narrow to discharge the water. The lake overflowed its banks, and all the level of the valley was covered with the inundation. The eminence, on which the palace was built, and some other spots of rising ground, were all that the eye could now discover. The herds and flocks left the pastures, and both the wild beasts and the tame retreated to the mountains.

This inundation confined all the princes to domestic amusements, and the attention of Rasselas was particularly seized by a poem, which Imlac rehearsed,[7] upon the various conditions of humanity. He commanded the

7. Recited.

poet to attend him in his apartment, and recite his verses a second time; then entering into familiar talk, he thought himself happy in having found a man who knew the world so well, and could so skillfully paint the scenes of life. He asked a thousand questions about things, to which, though common to all other mortals, his confinement from childhood had kept him a stranger. The poet pitied his ignorance, and loved his curiosity, and entertained him from day to day with novelty and instruction, so that the prince regretted the necessity of sleep, and longed till the morning should renew his pleasure.

As they were sitting together, the prince commanded Imlac to relate his history, and to tell by what accident he was forced, or by what motive induced, to close his life in the happy valley. As he was going to begin his narrative, Rasselas was called to a concert, and obliged to restrain his curiosity till the evening.

Chapter 8. The History of Imlac

The close of the day is, in the regions of the torrid zone, the only season of diversion and entertainment, and it was therefore midnight before the music ceased, and the princesses retired. Rasselas then called for his companion and required him to begin the story of his life.

"Sir," said Imlac, "my history will not be long: the life that is devoted to knowledge passes silently away, and is very little diversified by events. To talk in public, to think in solitude, to read and to hear, to inquire, and answer inquiries, is the business of a scholar. He wanders about the world without pomp or terror, and is neither known nor valued but by men like himself.

"I was born in the kingdom of Goiama, at no great distance from the fountain of the Nile. My father was a wealthy merchant, who traded between the inland countries of Africk and the ports of the red sea. He was honest, frugal and diligent, but of mean sentiments, and narrow comprehension: he desired only to be rich, and to conceal his riches, lest he should be spoiled[8] by the governors of the province."

"Surely," said the prince, "my father must be negligent of his charge, if any man in his dominions dares take that which belongs to another. Does he not know that kings are accountable for injustice permitted as well as done? If I were emperor, not the meanest of my subjects should be oppressed with impunity. My blood boils when I am told that a merchant durst not enjoy his honest gains for fear of losing them by the rapacity of power. Name the governor who robbed the people, that I may declare his crimes to the emperor."

"Sir," said Imlac, "your ardor is the natural effect of virtue animated by youth: the time will come when you will acquit your father, and perhaps hear with less impatience of the governor. Oppression is, in the Abyssinian dominions, neither frequent nor tolerated; but no form of government has been yet discovered, by which cruelty can be wholly prevented. Subordination supposes power on one part and subjection on the other; and if power be in the hands of men, it will sometimes be abused. The vigilance of the supreme magistrate may do much, but much will still remain undone. He can never know all the crimes that are committed, and can seldom punish all that he knows."

---

8. Robbed.

"This," said the prince, "I do not understand, but I had rather hear thee than dispute. Continue thy narration."

"My father," proceeded Imlac "originally intended that I should have no other education, than such as might qualify me for commerce; and discovering in me great strength of memory, and quickness of apprehension, often declared his hope that I should be some time the richest man in Abyssinia."

"Why," said the prince, "did thy father desire the increase of his wealth, when it was already greater than he durst discover or enjoy? I am unwilling to doubt thy veracity, yet inconsistencies cannot both be true."

"Inconsistencies," answered Imlac, "cannot both be right, but, imputed to man, they may both be true. Yet diversity is not inconsistency. My father might expect a time of greater security. However, some desire is necessary to keep life in motion, and he, whose real wants are supplied, must admit those of fancy."

"This," said the prince, "I can in some measure conceive. I repent that I interrupted thee."

"With this hope," proceeded Imlac, "he sent me to school; but when I had once found the delight of knowledge, and felt the pleasure of intelligence[9] and the pride of invention, I began silently to despise riches, and determined to disappoint the purpose of my father, whose grossness of conception raised my pity. I was twenty years old before his tenderness would expose me to the fatigue of travel, in which time I had been instructed, by successive masters, in all the literature of my native country. As every hour taught me something new, I lived in a continual course of gratifications; but, as I advanced towards manhood, I lost much of the reverence with which I had been used to look on my instructors; because, when the lesson was ended, I did not find them wiser or better than common men.

"At length my father resolved to initiate me in commerce, and, opening one of his subterranean treasuries, counted out ten thousand pieces of gold. 'This, young man,' said he, 'is the stock with which you must negotiate. I began with less than the fifth part, and you see how diligence and parsimony have increased it. This is your own to waste or to improve. If you squander it by negligence or caprice, you must wait for my death before you will be rich: if, in four years, you double your stock, we will thenceforward let subordination cease, and live together as friends and partners; for he shall always be equal with me, who is equally skilled in the art of growing rich.'

"We laid our money upon camels, concealed in bales of cheap goods, and travelled to the shore of the red sea. When I cast my eye on the expanse of waters my heart bounded like that of a prisoner escaped. I felt an unextinguishable curiosity kindle in my mind, and resolved to snatch this opportunity of seeing the manners of other nations, and of learning sciences unknown in Abyssinia.

"I remembered that my father had obliged me to the improvement of my stock, not by a promise which I ought not to violate, but by a penalty which I was at liberty to incur; and therefore determined to gratify my predominant desire, and by drinking at the fountains of knowledge, to quench the thirst of curiosity.

9. Information or knowledge.

"As I was supposed to trade without connection with my father, it was easy for me to become acquainted with the master of a ship, and procure a passage to some other country. I had no motives of choice to regulate my voyage; it was sufficient for me that, wherever I wandered, I should see a country which I had not seen before. I therefore entered a ship bound for Surat,[1] having left a letter for my father declaring my intention.

Chapter 9. The History of Imlac Continued

"When I first entered upon the world of waters, and lost sight of land, I looked round about me with pleasing terror, and thinking my soul enlarged by the boundless prospect, imagined that I could gaze round for ever without satiety; but, in a short time, I grew weary of looking on barren uniformity, where I could only see again what I had already seen. I then descended into the ship, and doubted for a while whether all my future pleasures would not end like this in disgust and disappointment. Yet, surely, said I, the ocean and the land are very different; the only variety of water is rest and motion, but the earth has mountains and valleys, deserts and cities: it is inhabited by men of different customs and contrary opinions; and I may hope to find variety in life, though I should miss it in nature.

"With this thought I quieted my mind; and amused myself during the voyage, sometimes by learning from the sailors the art of navigation, which I have never practiced, and sometimes by forming schemes for my conduct in different situations, in not one of which I have been ever placed.

"I was almost weary of my naval amusements when we landed safely at Surat. I secured my money, and purchasing some commodities for show, joined myself to a caravan that was passing into the inland country. My companions, for some reason or other, conjecturing that I was rich, and, by my inquiries and admiration, finding that I was ignorant, considered me as a novice whom they had a right to cheat, and who was to learn at the usual expense the art of fraud. They exposed me to the theft of servants, and the exaction of officers,[2] and saw me plundered upon false pretences, without any advantage to themselves, but that of rejoicing in the superiority of their own knowledge."

"Stop a moment," said the prince. "Is there such depravity in man, as that he should injure another without benefit to himself? I can easily conceive that all are pleased with superiority; but your ignorance was merely accidental, which, being neither your crime nor your folly, could afford them no reason to applaud themselves; and the knowledge which they had, and which you wanted, they might as effectually have shown by warning, as betraying you."

"Pride," said Imlac, "is seldom delicate, it will please itself with very mean advantages; and envy feels not its own happiness, but when it may be compared with the misery of others. They were my enemies because they grieved to think me rich, and my oppressors because they delighted to find me weak."

"Proceed," said the prince: "I doubt not of the facts which you relate, but imagine that you impute them to mistaken motives."

"In this company," said Imlac, "I arrived at Agra, the capital of Indostan, the city in which the great Mogul commonly resides. I applied myself to the language of the country, and in a few months was able to converse with the

---

1. A port in India.   2. Officials or agents.

learned men; some of whom I found morose and reserved, and others easy and communicative; some were unwilling to teach another what they had with difficulty learned themselves; and some showed that the end of their studies was to gain the dignity of instructing.

"To the tutor of the young princes I recommended myself so much, that I was presented to the emperor as a man of uncommon knowledge. The emperor asked me many questions concerning my country and my travels; and though I cannot now recollect any thing that he uttered above the power of a common man, he dismissed me astonished at his wisdom, and enamored of his goodness.

"My credit was now so high, that the merchants, with whom I had traveled, applied to me for recommendations to the ladies of the court. I was surprised at their confidence of solicitation, and gently reproached them with their practices on the road. They heard me with cold indifference, and showed no tokens of shame or sorrow.

"They then urged their request with the offer of a bribe; but what I would not do for kindness I would not do for money; and refused them, not because they had injured me, but because I would not enable them to injure others; for I knew they would have made use of my credit to cheat those who should buy their wares.

"Having resided at Agra till there was no more to be learned, I traveled into Persia, where I saw many remains of ancient magnificence, and observed many new accommodations[3] of life. The Persians are a nation eminently social, and their assemblies afforded me daily opportunities of remarking characters and manners, and of tracing human nature through all its variations.

"From Persia I passed into Arabia, where I saw a nation at once pastoral and warlike; who live without any settled habitation; whose only wealth is their flocks and herds; and who have yet carried on, through all ages, an hereditary war with all mankind, though they neither covet nor envy their possessions.

Chapter 10. Imlac's History Continued.
A Dissertation upon Poetry

"Wherever I went, I found that poetry was considered as the highest learning, and regarded with a veneration somewhat approaching to that which man would pay to the angelic nature. And yet it fills me with wonder that, in almost all countries, the most ancient poets are considered as the best: whether it be that every other kind of knowledge is an acquisition gradually attained, and poetry is a gift conferred at once; or that the first poetry of every nation surprised them as a novelty, and retained the credit by consent which it received by accident at first; or whether, as the province of poetry is to describe nature and passion, which are always the same, the first writers took possession of the most striking objects for description and the most probable occurrences for fiction, and left nothing to those that followed them, but transcription of the same events, and new combinations of the same images—whatever be the reason, it is commonly observed that the early writers are in possession of

3. "Conveniences, things requisite to ease or refreshment" (Johnson's *Dictionary*).

nature, and their followers of art; that the first excel in strength and invention, and the latter in elegance and refinement.

"I was desirous to add my name to this illustrious fraternity. I read all the poets of Persia and Arabia, and was able to repeat by memory the volumes that are suspended in the mosque of Mecca. But I soon found that no man was ever great by imitation. My desire of excellence impelled me to transfer my attention to nature and to life. Nature was to be my subject, and men to be my auditors: I could never describe what I had not seen; I could not hope to move those with delight or terror, whose interests and opinions I did not understand.

"Being now resolved to be a poet, I saw everything with a new purpose; my sphere of attention was suddenly magnified; no kind of knowledge was to be overlooked. I ranged mountains and deserts for images and resemblances, and pictured upon my mind every tree of the forest and flower of the valley. I observed with equal care the crags of the rock and the pinnacles of the palace. Sometimes I wandered along the mazes of the rivulet, and sometimes watched the changes of the summer clouds. To a poet nothing can be useless. Whatever is beautiful, and whatever is dreadful, must be familiar to his imagination; he must be conversant with all that is awfully vast or elegantly little. The plants of the garden, the animals of the wood, the minerals of the earth, and meteors of the sky, must all concur to store his mind with inexhaustible variety: for every idea[4] is useful for the enforcement or decoration of moral or religious truth; and he who knows most will have most power of diversifying his scenes, and of gratifying his reader with remote allusions and unexpected instruction.

"All the appearances of nature I was therefore careful to study, and every country which I have surveyed has contributed something to my poetical powers."

"In so wide a survey," said the prince, "you must surely have left much unobserved. I have lived till now within the circuit of these mountains, and yet cannot walk abroad without the sight of something which I have never beheld before, or never heeded."

"The business of a poet," said Imlac, "is to examine, not the individual, but the species; to remark general properties and large appearances; he does not number the streaks of the tulip, or describe the different shades in the verdure of the forest. He is to exhibit in his portraits of nature such prominent and striking features as recall the original to every mind, and must neglect the minuter discriminations, which one may have remarked and another have neglected, for those characteristics which are alike obvious to vigilance and carelessness.

"But the knowledge of nature is only half the task of a poet; he must be acquainted likewise with all the modes of life. His character requires that he estimate the happiness and misery of every condition; observe the power of all the passions in all their combinations, and trace the changes of the human mind, as they are modified by various institutions and accidental influences of climate or custom, from the sprightliness of infancy to the despondence of decrepitude. He must divest himself of the prejudices of his age or country; he must consider right and wrong in their abstracted and invariable state; he

---

4. Mental image.

must disregard present laws and opinions, and rise to general and transcendental[5] truths, which will always be the same. He must, therefore, content himself
with the slow progress of his name, contemn the applause of his own time,
and commit his claims to the justice of posterity. He must write as the interpreter of nature and the legislator of mankind, and consider himself as presiding over the thoughts and manners of future generations, as a being superior
to time and place.

"His labor is not yet at an end; he must know many languages and many
sciences; and, that his style may be worthy of his thoughts, must by incessant
practice familiarize to himself every delicacy of speech and grace of harmony."

Chapter 11. Imlac's Narrative Continued. A Hint on Pilgrimage

Imlac now felt the enthusiastic fit, and was proceeding to aggrandize his
own profession, when the prince cried out: "Enough! thou hast convinced me
that no human being can ever be a poet. Proceed with thy narration."

"To be a poet," said Imlac, "is indeed very difficult." "So difficult," returned
the prince, "that I will at present hear no more of his labors. Tell me whither
you went when you had seen Persia."

"From Persia," said the poet, "I traveled through Syria, and for three years
resided in Palestine, where I conversed with great numbers of the northern
and western nations of Europe, the nations which are now in possession of
all power and all knowledge, whose armies are irresistible, and whose fleets
command the remotest parts of the globe. When I compared these men with
the natives of our own kingdom, and those that surround us, they appeared
almost another order of beings. In their countries it is difficult to wish for
anything that may not be obtained; a thousand arts, of which we never heard,
are continually laboring for their convenience and pleasure; and whatever
their own climate has denied them is supplied by their commerce."

"By what means," said the prince, "are the Europeans thus powerful, or
why, since they can so easily visit Asia and Africa for trade or conquest, cannot
the Asiatics and Africans invade their coasts, plant colonies in their ports, and
give laws to their natural princes? The same wind that carries them back
would bring us thither."

"They are more powerful, sir, than we," answered Imlac, "because they are
wiser; knowledge will always predominate over ignorance, as man governs the
other animals. But why their knowledge is more than ours, I know not what
reason can be given, but the unsearchable will of the Supreme Being."

"When," said the prince with a sigh, "shall I be able to visit Palestine, and
mingle with this mighty confluence of nations? Till that happy moment shall
arrive, let me fill up the time with such representations as thou canst give me.
I am not ignorant of the motive that assembles such numbers in that place,
and cannot but consider it as the center of wisdom and piety, to which the
best and wisest men of every land must be continually resorting."

"There are some nations," said Imlac, "that send few visitants to Palestine;
for many numerous and learned sects in Europe concur to censure pilgrimage
as superstitious, or deride it as ridiculous."

---

5. "General; pervading many particulars" (Johnson's *Dictionary*).

"You know," said the prince, "how little my life has made me acquainted with diversity of opinions. It will be too long to hear the arguments on both sides; you, that have considered them, tell me the result."

"Pilgrimage," said Imlac, "like many other acts of piety, may be reasonable or superstitious, according to the principles upon which it is performed. Long journeys in search of truth are not commanded. Truth, such as is necessary to the regulation of life, is always found where it is honestly sought. Change of place is no natural cause of the increase of piety, for it inevitably produces dissipation of mind. Yet, since men go every day to view the fields where great actions have been performed, and return with stronger impressions of the event, curiosity of the same kind may naturally dispose us to view that country whence our religion had its beginning; and I believe no man surveys those awful scenes without some confirmation of holy resolutions. That the Supreme Being may be more easily propitiated in one place than in another is the dream of idle superstition, but that some places may operate upon our own minds in an uncommon manner is an opinion which hourly experience will justify. He who supposes that his vices may be more successfully combated in Palestine, will, perhaps, find himself mistaken, yet he may go thither without folly; he who thinks they will be more freely pardoned, dishonors at once his reason and religion."

"These," said the prince, "are European distinctions. I will consider them another time. What have you found to be the effect of knowledge? Are those nations happier than we?"

"There is so much infelicity," said the poet, "in the world that scarce any man has leisure from his own distresses to estimate the comparative happiness of others. Knowledge is certainly one of the means of pleasure, as is confessed by the natural desire which every mind feels of increasing its ideas. Ignorance is mere privation, by which nothing can be produced; it is a vacuity in which the soul sits motionless and torpid for want of attraction; and, without knowing why, we always rejoice when we learn, and grieve when we forget. I am therefore inclined to conclude that if nothing counteracts the natural consequence of learning, we grow more happy as our minds take a wider range.

"In enumerating the particular comforts of life, we shall find many advantages on the side of the Europeans. They cure wounds and diseases with which we languish and perish. We suffer inclemencies of weather which they can obviate. They have engines for the despatch of many laborious works, which we must perform by manual industry. There is such communication between distant places that one friend can hardly be said to be absent from another. Their policy removes all public inconveniences; they have roads cut through their mountains, and bridges laid upon their rivers. And, if we descend to the privacies of life, their habitations are more commodious, and their possessions are more secure."

"They are surely happy," said the prince, "who have all these conveniencies, of which I envy none so much as the facility with which separated friends interchange their thoughts."

"The Europeans," answered Imlac, "are less unhappy than we, but they are not happy. Human life is everywhere a state in which much is to be endured, and little to be enjoyed."

Chapter 12. The Story of Imlac Continued

"I am not yet willing," said the prince, "to suppose that happiness is so parsimoniously distributed to mortals; nor can believe but that, if I had the choice of life, I should be able to fill every day with pleasure. I would injure no man, and should provoke no resentment: I would relieve every distress, and should enjoy the benedictions of gratitude. I would choose my friends among the wise, and my wife among the virtuous; and therefore should be in no danger from treachery, or unkindness. My children should, by my care, be learned and pious, and would repay to my age what their childhood had received. What would dare to molest him who might call on every side to thousands enriched by his bounty, or assisted by his power? And why should not life glide quietly away in the soft reciprocation of protection and reverence? All this may be done without the help of European refinements, which appear by their effects to be rather specious than useful. Let us leave them and pursue our journey."

"From Palestine," said Imlac, "I passed through many regions of Asia; in the more civilized kingdoms as a trader, and among the barbarians of the mountains as a pilgrim. At last I began to long for my native country, that I might repose after my travels, and fatigues, in the places where I had spent my earliest years, and gladden my old companions with the recital of my adventures. Often did I figure to myself those, with whom I had sported away the gay hours of dawning life, sitting round me in its evening, wondering at my tales, and listening to my counsels.

"When this thought had taken possession of my mind, I considered every moment as wasted which did not bring me nearer to Abyssinia. I hastened into Egypt, and, notwithstanding my impatience, was detained ten months in the contemplation of its ancient magnificence, and in enquiries after the remains of its ancient learning. I found in Cairo a mixture of all nations; some brought thither by the love of knowledge, some by the hope of gain, and many by the desire of living after their own manner without observation, and of lying hid in the obscurity of multitudes: for, in a city, populous as Cairo, it is possible to obtain at the same time the gratifications of society, and the secrecy of solitude.

"From Cairo I traveled to Suez, and embarked on the red sea, passing along the coast till I arrived at the port from which I had departed twenty years before. Here I joined myself to a caravan and re-entered my native country.

"I now expected the caresses of my kinsmen, and the congratulations of my friends, and was not without hope that my father, whatever value he had set upon riches, would own with gladness and pride a son who was able to add to the felicity and honor of the nation. But I was soon convinced that my thoughts were vain. My father had been dead fourteen years, having divided his wealth among my brothers, who were removed to some other provinces. Of my companions the greater part was in the grave, of the rest some could with difficulty remember me, and some considered me as one corrupted by foreign manners.

"A man used to vicissitudes is not easily dejected. I forgot, after a time, my disappointment, and endeavored to recommend myself to the nobles of the kingdom: they admitted me to their tables, heard my story, and dismissed me. I opened a school, and was prohibited to teach. I then resolved to sit down in the quiet of domestic life, and addressed a lady that was fond of my conversation, but rejected my suit, because my father was a merchant.

"Wearied at last with solicitation and repulses, I resolved to hide myself for ever from the world, and depend no longer on the opinion or caprice of others. I waited for the time when the gate of the *happy valley* should open, that I might bid farewell to hope and fear: the day came; my performance was distinguished with favor, and I resigned myself with joy to perpetual confinement."

"Hast thou here found happiness at last?" said Rasselas. "Tell me without reserve; art thou content with thy condition? or, dost thou wish to be again wandering and inquiring? All the inhabitants of this valley celebrate their lot, and, at the annual visit of the emperor, invite others to partake of their felicity."

"Great prince," said Imlac, "I shall speak the truth: I know not one of all your attendants who does not lament the hour when he entered this retreat. I am less unhappy than the rest, because I have a mind replete with images, which I can vary and combine at pleasure. I can amuse my solitude by the renovation of the knowledge which begins to fade from my memory, and by recollection of the accidents of my past life. Yet all this ends in the sorrowful consideration, that my acquirements are now useless, and that none of my pleasures can be again enjoyed. The rest, whose minds have no impression but of the present moment, are either corroded by malignant passions, or sit stupid in the gloom of perpetual vacancy."

"What passions can infest those," said the prince, "who have no trials? We are in a place where impotence precludes malice, and where all envy is repressed by community[6] of enjoyments."

"There may be community," said Imlac, "of material possessions, but there can never be community of love or of esteem. It must happen that one will please more than another; he that knows himself despised will always be envious; and still more envious and malevolent, if he is condemned to live in the presence of those who despise him. The invitations, by which they allure others to a state which they feel to be wretched, proceed from the natural malignity of hopeless misery. They are weary of themselves, and of each other, and expect to find relief in new companions. They envy the liberty which their folly has forfeited, and would gladly see all mankind imprisoned like themselves.

"From this crime, however, I am wholly free. No man can say that he is wretched by my persuasion. I look with pity on the crowds who are annually soliciting admission to captivity, and wish that it were lawful for me to warn them of their danger."

"My dear Imlac," said the prince, "I will open to thee my whole heart. I have long meditated an escape from the happy valley. I have examined the mountains on every side, but find myself insuperably barred: teach me the way to break my prison; thou shalt be the companion of my flight, the guide of my rambles, the partner of my fortune, and my sole director in the *choice of life.*"

"Sir," answered the poet, "your escape will be difficult, and, perhaps, you may soon repent your curiosity. The world, which you figure to yourself

6. Joint possession.

smooth and quiet as the lake in the valley, you will find a sea foaming with tempests, and boiling with whirlpools: you will be sometimes overwhelmed by the waves of violence, and sometimes dashed against the rocks of treachery. Amidst wrongs and frauds, competitions and anxieties, you will wish a thousand times for these seats of quiet, and willingly quit hope to be free from fear."

"Do not seek to deter me from my purpose," said the prince: "I am impatient to see what thou hast seen; and, since thou art thyself weary of the valley, it is evident, that thy former state was better than this. Whatever be the consequence of my experiment, I am resolved to judge with my own eyes of the various conditions of men, and then to make deliberately my *choice of life.*"

"I am afraid," said Imlac, "you are hindered by stronger restraints than my persuasions; yet, if your determination is fixed, I do not counsel you to despair. Few things are impossible to diligence and skill."

Chapter 13. Rasselas Discovers the Means of Escape

The prince now dismissed his favorite to rest, but the narrative of wonders and novelties filled his mind with perturbation. He revolved all that he had heard, and prepared innumerable questions for the morning.

Much of his uneasiness was now removed. He had a friend to whom he could impart his thoughts, and whose experience could assist him in his designs. His heart was no longer condemned to swell with silent vexation. He thought that even the *happy valley* might be endured with such a companion, and that, if they could range the world together, he should have nothing further to desire.

In a few days the water was discharged, and the ground dried. The prince and Imlac then walked out together to converse without the notice of the rest. The prince, whose thoughts were always on the wing, as he passed by the gate, said, with a countenance of sorrow, "Why art thou so strong, and why is man so weak?"

"Man is not weak," answered his companion; "knowledge is more than equivalent to force. The master of mechanics laughs at strength. I can burst the gate, but cannot do it secretly. Some other expedient must be tried."

As they were walking on the side of the mountain, they observed that the conies,[7] which the rain had driven from their burrows, had taken shelter among the bushes, and formed holes behind them, tending upwards in an oblique line. "It has been the opinion of antiquity," said Imlac, "that human reason borrowed many arts from the instinct of animals; let us, therefore, not think ourselves degraded by learning from the coney. We may escape by piercing the mountain in the same direction. We will begin where the summit hangs over the middle part, and labor upward till we shall issue out beyond the prominence."

The eyes of the prince, when he heard this proposal, sparkled with joy. The execution was easy, and the success certain.

No time was now lost. They hastened early in the morning to choose a place proper for their mine. They clambered with great fatigue among crags

7. Rabbits.

and brambles, and returned without having discovered any part that favored their design. The second and the third day were spent in the same manner, and with the same frustration. But, on the fourth, they found a small cavern, concealed by a thicket, where they resolved to make their experiment.

Imlac procured instruments proper to hew stone and remove earth, and they fell to their work on the next day with more eagerness than vigor. They were presently exhausted by their efforts, and sat down to pant upon the grass. The prince, for a moment, appeared to be discouraged. "Sir," said his companion, "practice will enable us to continue our labor for a longer time; mark, however, how far we have advanced, and you will find that our toil will some time have an end. Great works are performed, not by strength, but perseverance: yonder palace was raised by single stones, yet you see its height and spaciousness. He that shall walk with vigor three hours a day will pass in seven years a space equal to the circumference of the globe."

They returned to their work day after day, and, in a short time, found a fissure in the rock, which enabled them to pass far with very little obstruction. This Rasselas considered as a good omen. "Do not disturb your mind," said Imlac, "with other hopes or fears than reason may suggest: if you are pleased with prognostics of good, you will be terrified likewise with tokens of evil, and your whole life will be a prey to superstition. Whatever facilitates our work is more than an omen, it is a cause of success. This is one of those pleasing surprises which often happen to active resolution. Many things difficult to design prove easy to performance."

Chapter 14. Rasselas and Imlac Receive an Unexpected Visit

They had now wrought their way to the middle, and solaced their toil with the approach of liberty, when the prince, coming down to refresh himself with air, found his sister Nekayah standing before the mouth of the cavity. He started and stood confused, afraid to tell his design, and yet hopeless to conceal it. A few moments determined him to repose on her fidelity, and secure her secrecy by a declaration without reserve.

"Do not imagine," said the princess, "that I came hither as a spy: I had long observed from my window, that you and Imlac directed your walk every day towards the same point, but I did not suppose you had any better reason for the preference than a cooler shade, or more fragrant bank; nor followed you with any other design than to partake of your conversation. Since then not suspicion but fondness has detected you, let me not lose the advantage of my discovery. I am equally weary of confinement with yourself, and not less desirous of knowing what is done or suffered in the world. Permit me to fly with you from this tasteless tranquility, which will yet grow more loathsome when you have left me. You may deny me to accompany you, but cannot hinder me from following."

The prince, who loved Nekayah above his other sisters, had no inclination to refuse her request, and grieved that he had lost an opportunity of showing his confidence by a voluntary communication. It was therefore agreed that she should leave the valley with them; and that, in the mean time, she should watch, lest any other straggler should, by chance or curiosity, follow them to the mountain.

At length their labor was at an end; they saw light beyond the prominence, and, issuing to the top of the mountain, beheld the Nile, yet a narrow current, wandering beneath them.

The prince looked round with rapture, anticipated all the pleasures of travel, and in thought was already transported beyond his father's dominions. Imlac, though very joyful at his escape, had less expectation of pleasure in the world, which he had before tried, and of which he had been weary.

Rasselas was so much delighted with a wider horizon, that he could not soon be persuaded to return into the valley. He informed his sister that the way was open, and that nothing now remained but to prepare for their departure.

Chapter 15. The Prince and Princess Leave the Valley, and See Many Wonders

The prince and princess had jewels sufficient to make them rich whenever they came into a place of commerce, which, by Imlac's direction, they hid in their clothes, and, on the night of the next full moon, all left the valley. The princess was followed only by a single favorite, who did not know whither she was going.

They clambered through the cavity, and began to go down on the other side. The princess and her maid turned their eyes towards every part, and, seeing nothing to bound their prospect, considered themselves as in danger of being lost in a dreary vacuity. They stopped and trembled. "I am almost afraid," said the princess, "to begin a journey of which I cannot perceive an end, and to venture into this immense plain where I may be approached on every side by men whom I never saw." The prince felt nearly the same emotions, though he thought it more manly to conceal them.

Imlac smiled at their terrors, and encouraged them to proceed; but the princess continued irresolute till she had been imperceptibly drawn forward too far to return.

In the morning they found some shepherds in the field, who set milk and fruits before them. The princess wondered that she did not see a palace ready for her reception, and a table spread with delicacies; but, being faint and hungry, she drank the milk and ate the fruits, and thought them of a higher flavor than the products of the valley.

They traveled forward by easy journeys, being all unaccustomed to toil or difficulty, and knowing, that though they might be missed, they could not be pursued. In a few days they came into a more populous region, where Imlac was diverted with the admiration which his companions expressed at the diversity of manners, stations and employments.

Their dress was such as might not bring upon them the suspicion of having any thing to conceal, yet the prince, wherever he came, expected to be obeyed, and the princess was frighted, because those that came into her presence did not prostrate themselves before her. Imlac was forced to observe them with great vigilance, lest they should betray their rank by their unusual behavior, and detained them several weeks in the first village to accustom them to the sight of common mortals.

By degrees the royal wanderers were taught to understand that they had for a time laid aside their dignity, and were to expect only such regard as liberality and courtesy could procure. And Imlac, having, by many admonitions, prepared them to endure the tumults of a port, and the ruggedness of the commercial race, brought them down to the seacoast.

The prince and his sister, to whom every thing was new, were gratified equally at all places, and therefore remained for some months at the port without any inclination to pass further. Imlac was content with their stay, because he did not think it safe to expose them, unpracticed in the world, to the hazards of a foreign country.

At last he began to fear lest they should be discovered, and proposed to fix a day for their departure. They had no pretensions to judge for themselves, and referred the whole scheme to his direction. He therefore took passage in a ship to Suez; and, when the time came, with great difficulty prevailed on the princess to enter the vessel. They had a quick and prosperous voyage, and from Suez traveled by land to Cairo.

Chapter 16. *They Enter Cairo, and Find Every Man Happy*

As they approached the city, which filled the strangers with astonishment, "This," said Imlac to the prince, "is the place where travelers and merchants assemble from all the corners of the earth. You will here find men of every character and every occupation. Commerce is here honorable. I will act as a merchant, and you shall live as strangers, who have no other end of travel than curiosity. It will soon be observed that we are rich; our reputation will procure us access to all whom we shall desire to know; you will see all the conditions of humanity, and enable yourself at leisure to make your *choice of life.*"

They now entered the town, stunned by the noise, and offended by the crowds. Instruction had not yet so prevailed over habit, but that they wondered to see themselves pass undistinguished along the street, and met by the lowest of the people without reverence or notice. The princess could not at first bear the thought of being leveled with the vulgar,[8] and for some days continued in her chamber, where she was served by her favorite, Pekuah, as in the palace of the valley.

Imlac, who understood traffic,[9] sold part of the jewels the next day, and hired a house, which he adorned with such magnificence that he was immediately considered as a merchant of great wealth. His politeness attracted many acquaintance, and his generosity made him courted by many dependents. His table was crowded by men of every nation, who all admired his knowledge, and solicited his favor. His companions, not being able to mix in the conversation, could make no discovery of their ignorance or surprise, and were gradually initiated in the world as they gained knowledge of the language.

The prince had, by frequent lectures, been taught the use and nature of money; but the ladies could not for a long time comprehend what the merchants did with small pieces of gold and silver, or why things of so little use should be received as equivalent to the necessaries of life.

They studied the language two years, while Imlac was preparing to set before them the various ranks and conditions of mankind. He grew acquainted with all who had anything uncommon in their fortune or conduct. He frequented the voluptuous and the frugal, the idle and the busy, the merchants and the men of learning.

---

8. Ordinary people.   9. Commerce.

The prince being now able to converse with fluency, and having learned the caution necessary to be observed in his intercourse with strangers, began to accompany Imlac to places of resort, and to enter into all assemblies, that he might make his *choice of life*.

For some time he thought choice needless, because all appeared to him equally happy. Wherever he went he met gaiety and kindness, and heard the song of joy or the laugh of carelessness. He began to believe that the world overflowed with universal plenty, and that nothing was withheld either from want or merit; that every hand showered liberality, and every heart melted with benevolence: "And who then," says he, "will be suffered to be wretched?"

Imlac permitted the pleasing delusion, and was unwilling to crush the hope of inexperience, till one day, having sat awhile silent, "I know not," said the prince, "what can be the reason that I am more unhappy than any of our friends. I see them perpetually and unalterably cheerful, but feel my own mind restless and uneasy. I am unsatisfied with those pleasures which I seem most to court; I live in the crowds of jollity, not so much to enjoy company as to shun myself, and am only loud and merry to conceal my sadness."

"Every man," said Imlac, "may, by examining his own mind, guess what passes in the minds of others; when you feel that your own gaiety is counterfeit, it may justly lead you to suspect that of your companions not to be sincere. Envy is commonly reciprocal. We are long before we are convinced that happiness is never to be found, and each believes it possessed by others, to keep alive the hope of obtaining it for himself. In the assembly where you passed the last night, there appeared such sprightliness of air, and volatility of fancy, as might have suited beings of an higher order, formed to inhabit serener regions, inaccessible to care or sorrow; yet, believe me, prince, there was not one who did not dread the moment when solitude should deliver him to the tyranny of reflection."

"This," said the prince, "may be true of others, since it is true of me; yet, whatever be the general infelicity of man, one condition is more happy than another, and wisdom surely directs us to take the least evil in the *choice of life*."

"The causes of good and evil," answered Imlac, "are so various and uncertain, so often entangled with each other, so diversified by various relations, and so much subject to accidents which cannot be foreseen, that he who would fix his condition upon incontestable reasons of preference must live and die inquiring and deliberating."

"But, surely," said Rasselas, "the wise men, to whom we listen with reverence and wonder, chose that mode of life for themselves which they thought most likely to make them happy."

"Very few," said the poet, "live by choice. Every man is placed in his present condition by causes which acted without his foresight, and with which he did not always willingly cooperate; and therefore you will rarely meet one who does not think the lot of his neighbor better than his own."

"I am pleased to think," said the prince, "that my birth has given me at least one advantage over others, by enabling me to determine for myself. I have here the world before me. I will review it at leisure; surely happiness is somewhere to be found."

Chapter 17. The Prince Associates with Young Men
of Spirit and Gaiety

Rasselas rose next day, and resolved to begin his experiments upon life. "Youth," cried he, "is the time of gladness: I will join myself to the young men, whose only business is to gratify their desires, and whose time is all spent in a succession of enjoyments."

To such societies he was readily admitted, but a few days brought him back weary and disgusted. Their mirth was without images,[1] their laughter without motive; their pleasures were gross and sensual, in which the mind had no part; their conduct was at once wild and mean; they laughed at order and at law, but the frown of power dejected, and the eye of wisdom abashed them.

The prince soon concluded, that he should never be happy in a course of life of which he was ashamed. He thought it unsuitable to a reasonable being to act without a plan, and to be sad or cheerful only by chance. "Happiness," said he, "must be something solid and permanent, without fear and without uncertainty."

But his young companions had gained so much of his regard by their frankness and courtesy, that he could not leave them without warning and remonstrance. "My friends," said he, "I have seriously considered our manners and our prospects, and find that we have mistaken our own interest. The first years of man must make provision for the last. He that never thinks never can be wise. Perpetual levity must end in ignorance; and intemperance, though it may fire the spirits for an hour, will make life short or miserable. Let us consider that youth is of no long duration, and that in maturer age, when the enchantments of fancy shall cease, and phantoms of delight dance no more about us, we shall have no comforts but the esteem of wise men, and the means of doing good. Let us, therefore, stop, while to stop is in our power: let us live as men who are sometime to grow old, and to whom it will be the most dreadful of all evils not to count their past years but by follies, and to be reminded of their former luxuriance of health only by the maladies which riot has produced."

They stared a while in silence one upon another, and, at last, drove him away by a general chorus of continued laughter.

The consciousness that his sentiments were just, and his intentions kind, was scarcely sufficient to support him against the horror of derision. But he recovered his tranquillity, and pursued his search.

Chapter 18. The Prince Finds a Wise and Happy Man

As he was one day walking in the street, he saw a spacious building which all were, by the open doors, invited to enter: he followed the stream of people, and found it a hall or school of declamation, in which professors read lectures to their auditory. He fixed his eye upon a sage raised above the rest, who discoursed with great energy on the government of the passions. His look was venerable, his action graceful, his pronunciation clear, and his diction elegant. He showed with great strength of sentiment and variety of illustration that human nature is degraded and debased, when the lower faculties predom-

---

1. Ideas.

inate over the higher; that when fancy, the parent of passion, usurps the dominion of the mind, nothing ensues but the natural effect of unlawful government, perturbation, and confusion; that she betrays the fortresses of the intellect to rebels, and excites her children to sedition against reason, their lawful sovereign. He compared reason to the sun, of which the light is constant, uniform and lasting; and fancy to a meteor, of bright but transitory luster, irregular in its motion, and delusive in its direction.

He then communicated the various precepts given from time to time for the conquest of passion, and displayed the happiness of those who had obtained the important victory, after which man is no longer the slave of fear, nor the fool of hope; is no more emaciated by envy, inflamed by anger, emasculated by tenderness, or depressed by grief; but walks on calmly through the tumults or the privacies of life, as the sun pursues alike his course through the calm or the stormy sky.

He enumerated many examples of heroes immovable by pain or pleasure, who looked with indifference on those modes or accidents to which the vulgar give the names of good and evil. He exhorted his hearers to lay aside their prejudices, and arm themselves against the shafts of malice or misfortune, by invulnerable patience; concluding that this state only was happiness, and that this happiness was in everyone's power.

Rasselas listened to him with the veneration due to the instructions of a superior being, and, waiting for him at the door, humbly implored the liberty of visiting so great a master of true wisdom. The lecturer hesitated a moment, when Rasselas put a purse of gold into his hand, which he received with a mixture of joy and wonder.

"I have found," said the prince at his return to Imlac, "a man who can teach all that is necessary to be known; who, from the unshaken throne of rational fortitude, looks down on the scenes of life changing beneath him. He speaks, and attention watches his lips. He reasons, and conviction closes his periods. This man shall be my future guide; I will learn his doctrines, and imitate his life."

"Be not too hasty," said Imlac, "to trust or to admire the teachers of morality: they discourse like angels, but they live like men."

Rasselas, who could not conceive how any man could reason so forcibly without feeling the cogency of his own arguments, paid his visit in a few days, and was denied admission. He had now learned the power of money, and made his way by a piece of gold to the inner apartment, where he found the philosopher in a room half darkened, with his eyes misty and his face pale. "Sir," said he, "you are come at a time when all human friendship is useless; what I suffer cannot be remedied, what I have lost cannot be supplied. My daughter, my only daughter, from whose tenderness I expected all the comforts of my age, died last night of a fever. My views, my purposes, my hopes are at an end; I am now a lonely being, disunited from society."

"Sir," said the prince, "mortality is an event by which a wise man can never be surprised; we know that death is always near, and it should therefore always be expected." "Young man," answered the philosopher, "you speak like one that has never felt the pangs of separation." "Have you then forgot the precepts," said Rasselas, "which you so powerfully enforced? Has wisdom no strength to arm the heart against calamity? Consider that external things are naturally variable, but truth and reason are always the same." "What comfort," said the mourner, "can truth and reason afford me? Of what effect are they now, but to tell me that my daughter will not be restored?"

The prince, whose humanity would not suffer him to insult misery with reproof, went away, convinced of the emptiness of rhetorical sound, and the inefficacy of polished periods and studied sentences.[2]

Chapter 19. A Glimpse of Pastoral Life

He was still eager upon the same inquiry; and having heard of a hermit that lived near the lowest cataract of the Nile, and filled the whole country with the fame of his sanctity, resolved to visit his retreat, and inquire whether that felicity which public life could not afford was to be found in solitude; and whether a man whose age and virtue made him venerable could teach any peculiar art of shunning evils, or enduring them.

Imlac and the princess agreed to accompany him, and, after the necessary preparations, they began their journey. Their way lay through fields, where shepherds tended their flocks and the lambs were playing upon the pasture. "This," said the poet, "is the life which has been often celebrated for its innocence and quiet; let us pass the heat of the day among the shepherds' tents, and know whether all our searches are not to terminate in pastoral simplicity."

The proposal pleased them, and they induced the shepherds, by small presents and familiar questions, to tell their opinion of their own state. They were so rude and ignorant, so little able to compare the good with the evil of the occupation, and so indistinct in their narratives and descriptions, that very little could be learned from them. But it was evident that their hearts were cankered with discontent; that they considered themselves as condemned to labor for the luxury of the rich, and looked up with stupid malevolence toward those that were placed above them.

The princess pronounced with vehemence that she would never suffer these envious savages to be her companions, and that she should not soon be desirous of seeing any more specimens of rustic happiness; but could not believe that all the accounts of primeval pleasures were fabulous, and was yet in doubt whether life had anything that could be justly preferred to the placid gratifications of fields and woods. She hoped that the time would come, when, with a few virtuous and elegant companions, she could gather flowers planted by her own hand, fondle the lambs of her own ewe, and listen, without care, among brooks and breezes, to one of her maidens reading in the shade.

Chapter 20. The Danger of Prosperity

On the next day they continued their journey, till the heat compelled them to look round for shelter. At a small distance they saw a thick wood, which they no sooner entered than they perceived that they were approaching the habitations of men. The shrubs were diligently cut away to open walks where the shades were darkest; the boughs of opposite trees were artificially interwoven; seats of flowery turf were raised in vacant spaces, and a rivulet, that wantoned along the side of a winding path, had its banks sometimes opened

---

2. Maxims or moral axioms. "Periods": complete sentences.

into small basins, and its stream sometimes obstructed by little mounds of stone heaped together to increase its murmurs.

They passed slowly through the wood, delighted with such unexpected accommodations, and entertained each other with conjecturing what, or who, he could be, that, in those rude and unfrequented regions, had leisure and art for such harmless luxury.

As they advanced, they heard the sound of music, and saw youths and virgins dancing in the grove; and, going still further, beheld a stately palace built upon a hill surrounded with woods. The laws of eastern hospitality allowed them to enter, and the master welcomed them like a man liberal and wealthy.

He was skilful enough in appearances soon to discern that they were no common guests, and spread his table with magnificence. The eloquence of Imlac caught his attention, and the lofty courtesy of the princess excited his respect. When they offered to depart he entreated their stay, and was the next day still more unwilling to dismiss them than before. They were easily persuaded to stop, and civility grew up in time to freedom and confidence.

The prince now saw all the domestics cheerful, and all the face of nature smiling round the place, and could not forbear to hope that he should find here what he was seeking; but when he was congratulating the master upon his possessions, he answered with a sigh, "My condition has indeed the appearance of happiness, but appearances are delusive. My prosperity puts my life in danger; the Bassa of Egypt is my enemy, incensed only by my wealth and popularity. I have been hitherto protected against him by the princes of the country; but, as the favor of the great is uncertain, I know not how soon my defenders may be persuaded to share the plunder with the Bassa. I have sent my treasures into a distant country, and, upon the first alarm, am prepared to follow them. Then will my enemies riot in my mansion, and enjoy the gardens which I have planted."

They all joined in lamenting his danger, and deprecating his exile; and the princess was so much disturbed with the tumult of grief and indignation, that she retired to her apartment. They continued with their kind inviter a few days longer, and then went forward to find the hermit.

Chapter 21. The Happiness of Solitude. The Hermit's History

They came on the third day, by the direction of the peasants, to the hermit's cell: it was a cavern in the side of a mountain, over-shadowed with palm-trees; at such a distance from the cataract, that nothing more was heard than a gentle uniform murmur, such as composed the mind to pensive meditation, especially when it was assisted by the wind whistling among the branches. The first rude essay of nature had been so much improved by human labor, that the cave contained several apartments, appropriated to different uses, and often afforded lodging to travelers, whom darkness or tempests happened to overtake.

The hermit sat on a bench at the door, to enjoy the coolness of the evening. On one side lay a book with pens and papers, on the other mechanical instruments of various kinds. As they approached him unregarded, the princess observed that he had not the countenance of a man that had found, or could teach, the way to happiness.

They saluted him with great respect, which he repaid like a man not unaccustomed to the forms of courts. "My children," said he, "if you have lost your way, you shall be willingly supplied with such conveniencies for the night as this cavern will afford. I have all that nature requires, and you will not expect delicacies in a hermit's cell."

They thanked him, and, entering, were pleased with the neatness and regularity of the place. The hermit set flesh and wine before them, though he fed only upon fruits and water. His discourse was cheerful without levity, and pious without enthusiasm.[3] He soon gained the esteem of his guests, and the princess repented of her hasty censure.

At last Imlac began thus: "I do not now wonder that your reputation is so far extended; we have heard at Cairo of your wisdom, and came hither to implore your direction for this young man and maiden in the *choice of life*."

"To him that lives well," answered the hermit, "every form of life is good; nor can I give any other rule for choice, than to remove from all apparent evil."

"He will remove most certainly from evil," said the prince, "who shall devote himself to that solitude which you have recommended by your example."

"I have indeed lived fifteen years in solitude," said the hermit, "but have no desire that my example should gain any imitators. In my youth I professed arms, and was raised by degrees to the highest military rank. I have traversed wide countries at the head of my troops, and seen many battles and sieges. At last, being disgusted by the preferment of a younger officer, and feeling that my vigor was beginning to decay, I resolved to close my life in peace, having found the world full of snares, discord, and misery. I had once escaped from the pursuit of the enemy by the shelter of this cavern, and therefore chose it for my final residence. I employed artificers to form it into chambers, and stored it with all that I was likely to want.

"For some time after my retreat, I rejoiced like a tempest-beaten sailor at his entrance into the harbor, being delighted with the sudden change of the noise and hurry of war, to stillness and repose. When the pleasure of novelty went away, I employed my hours in examining the plants which grow in the valley, and the minerals which I collected from the rocks. But that inquiry is now grown tasteless and irksome. I have been for some time unsettled and distracted: my mind is disturbed with a thousand perplexities of doubt, and vanities of imagination, which hourly prevail upon me, because I have no opportunities of relaxation or diversion. I am sometimes ashamed to think that I could not secure myself from vice, but by retiring from the exercise of virtue, and begin to suspect that I was rather impelled by resentment, than led by devotion, into solitude. My fancy riots in scenes of folly, and I lament that I have lost so much, and have gained so little. In solitude, if I escape the example of bad men, I want likewise the counsel and conversation of the good. I have been long comparing the evils with the advantages of society, and resolve to return into the world tomorrow. The life of a solitary man will be certainly miserable, but not certainly devout."

They heard his resolution with surprise, but, after a short pause, offered to conduct him to Cairo. He dug up a considerable treasure which he had hid

---

3. "A vain belief of private revelation; a vain confidence of divine favor or communication" (Johnson's *Dictionary*).

among the rocks, and accompanied them to the city, on which, as he approached it, he gazed with rapture.

Chapter 22. The Happiness of a Life Led According to Nature

Rasselas went often to an assembly of learned men, who met at stated times to unbend their minds and compare their opinions. Their manners were somewhat coarse, but their conversation was instructive, and their disputations acute, though sometimes too violent, and often continued till neither controvertist remembered upon what question they began. Some faults were almost general among them; everyone was desirous to dictate to the rest, and everyone was pleased to hear the genius or knowledge of another depreciated.

In this assembly Rasselas was relating his interview with the hermit, and the wonder with which he heard him censure a course of life which he had so deliberately chosen, and so laudably followed. The sentiments of the hearers were various. Some were of opinion that the folly of his choice had been justly punished by condemnation to perpetual perserverance. One of the youngest among them, with great vehemence, pronounced him an hypocrite. Some talked of the right of society to the labor of individuals, and considered retirement as a desertion of duty. Others readily allowed that there was a time when the claims of the public were satisfied, and when a man might properly sequester himself, to review his life and purify his heart.

One, who appeared more affected with the narrative than the rest, thought it likely that the hermit would in a few years go back to his retreat, and perhaps, if shame did not restrain, or death intercept him, return once more from his retreat into the world. "For the hope of happiness," said he, "is so strongly impressed that the longest experience is not able to efface it. Of the present state, whatever it be, we feel and are forced to confess the misery; yet when the same state is again at a distance, imagination paints it as desirable. But the time will surely come when desire will be no longer our torment, and no man shall be wretched but by his own fault."

"This," said a philosopher who had heard him with tokens of great impatience, "is the present condition of a wise man. The time is already come when none are wretched but by their own fault. Nothing is more idle than to inquire after happiness, which nature has kindly placed within our reach. The way to be happy is to live according to nature, in obedience to that universal and unalterable law with which every heart is originally impressed; which is not written on it by precept, but engraven by destiny, not instilled by education, but infused at our nativity. He that lives according to nature will suffer nothing from the delusions of hope, or importunities of desire; he will receive and reject with equability of temper, and act or suffer as the reason of things shall alternately prescribe. Other men may amuse themselves with subtle definitions, or intricate ratiocination. Let them learn to be wise by easier means; let them observe the hind of the forest, and the linnet of the grove; let them consider the life of animals, whose motions are regulated by instinct; they obey their guide, and are happy. Let us therefore, at length, cease to dispute, and learn to live; throw away the encumbrance of precepts, which they who utter them with so much pride and pomp do not understand, and carry with us this simple and intelligible maxim, that deviation from nature is deviation from happiness."

When he had spoken, he looked round him with a placid air, and enjoyed the consciousness of his own beneficence. "Sir," said the prince with great modesty, "as I, like all the rest of mankind, am desirous of felicity, my closest attention has been fixed upon your discourse. I doubt not the truth of a position which a man so learned has so confidently advanced. Let me only know what it is to live according to nature."

"When I find young men so humble and so docile," said the philosopher, "I can deny them no information which my studies have enabled me to afford. To live according to nature, is to act always with due regard to the fitness arising from the relations and qualities of causes and effects; to concur with the great and unchangeable scheme of universal felicity; to co-operate with the general disposition and tendency of the present system of things."

The prince soon found that this was one of the sages whom he should understand less as he heard him longer. He therefore bowed and was silent; and the philosopher, supposing him satisfied, and the rest vanquished, rose up and departed with the air of a man that had co-operated with the present system.

Chapter 23. The Prince and his Sister Divide between Them the Work of Observation

Rasselas returned home full of reflections, doubtful how to direct his future steps. Of the way to happiness he found the learned and simple equally ignorant; but, as he was yet young, he flattered himself that he had time remaining for more experiments, and further inquiries. He communicated to Imlac his observations and his doubts, but was answered by him with new doubts, and remarks that gave him no comfort. He therefore discoursed more frequently and freely with his sister, who had yet the same hope with himself, and always assisted him to give some reason why, though he had been hitherto frustrated, he might succeed at last.

"We have hitherto," said she, "known but little of the world: we have never yet been either great or mean. In our own country, though we had royalty, we had no power, and in this we have not yet seen the private recesses of domestic peace. Imlac favors not our search, lest we should in time find him mistaken. We will divide the task between us: you shall try what is to be found in the splendor of courts, and I will range the shades of humbler life. Perhaps command and authority may be the supreme blessings, as they afford most opportunities of doing good: or, perhaps, what this world can give may be found in the modest habitations of middle fortune; too low for great designs, and too high for penury and distress."

Chapter 24. The Prince Examines the Happiness of High Stations

Rasselas applauded the design, and appeared next day with a splendid retinue at the court of the Bassa. He was soon distinguished for his magnificence, and admitted, as a prince whose curiosity had brought him from distant countries, to an intimacy with the great officers, and frequent conversation with the Bassa himself.

He was at first inclined to believe, that the man must be pleased with his own condition, whom all approached with reverence, and heard with obedience, and who had the power to extend his edicts to a whole kingdom. "There can be no pleasure," said he, "equal to that of feeling at once the joy of thousands all made happy by wise administration. Yet, since, by the law of subordination, this sublime delight can be in one nation but the lot of one, it is surely reasonable to think that there is some satisfaction more popular[4] and accessible, and that millions can hardly be subjected to the will of a single man, only to fill his particular breast with incommunicable content."

These thoughts were often in his mind, and he found no solution of the difficulty. But as presents and civilities gained him more familiarity, he found that almost every man who stood high in employment hated all the rest, and was hated by them, and that their lives were a continual succession of plots and detections, stratagems and escapes, faction and treachery. Many of those, who surrounded the Bassa, were sent only to watch and report his conduct; every tongue was muttering censure and every eye was searching for a fault.

At last the letters of revocation arrived, the Bassa was carried in chains to Constantinople, and his name was mentioned no more.

"What are we now to think of the prerogatives of power," said Rasselas to his sister; "is it without any efficacy to good? or, is the subordinate degree only dangerous, and the supreme safe and glorious? Is the Sultan the only happy man in his dominions? or, is the Sultan himself subject to the torments of suspicion, and the dread of enemies?"

In a short time the second Bassa was deposed. The Sultan, that had advanced him, was murdered by the Janisaries,[5] and his successor had other views and different favorites.

Chapter 25. The Princess Pursues Her Inquiry with More Diligence than Success

The princess, in the mean time, insinuated herself into many families; for there are few doors, through which liberality, joined with good humor, cannot find its way. The daughters of many houses were airy[6] and cheerful, but Nekayah had been too long accustomed to the conversation of Imlac and her brother to be much pleased with childish levity and prattle which had no meaning. She found their thoughts narrow, their wishes low, and their merriment often artificial. Their pleasures, poor as they were, could not be preserved pure, but were embittered by petty competitions and worthless emulation. They were always jealous of the beauty of each other; of a quality to which solicitude can add nothing, and from which detraction can take nothing away. Many were in love with triflers like themselves, and many fancied that they were in love when in truth they were only idle. Their affection was seldom fixed on sense or virtue, and therefore seldom ended but in vexation. Their grief, however, like their joy, was transient; everything floated in their mind unconnected with the past or future, so that one desire easily gave way to another, as a second stone cast into the water effaces and confounds the circles of the first.

With these girls she played as with inoffensive animals, and found them proud of her countenance,[7] and weary of her company.

---

4. Common.
5. Guards of the Turkish ruler.
6. "Gay; sprightly; full of mirth" (Johnson's Dic-

tionary).
7. Patronage, favor.

But her purpose was to examine more deeply, and her affability easily persuaded the hearts that were swelling with sorrow to discharge their secrets in her ear: and those whom hope flattered, or prosperity delighted, often courted her to partake their pleasures.

The princess and her brother commonly met in the evening in a private summer-house on the bank of the Nile, and related to each other the occurrences of the day. As they were sitting together, the princess cast her eyes upon the river that flowed before her. "Answer," said she, "great father of waters, thou that rollest thy floods through eighty nations, to the invocations of the daughter of thy native king. Tell me if thou waterest, through all thy course, a single habitation from which thou dost not hear the murmurs of complaint?"

"You are then," said Rasselas, "not more successful in private houses than I have been in courts." "I have, since the last partition of our provinces,"[8] said the princess, "enabled myself to enter familiarly into many families, where there was the fairest show of prosperity and peace, and know not one house that is not haunted by some fury that destroys its quiet.

"I did not seek ease among the poor, because I concluded that there it could not be found. But I saw many poor whom I had supposed to live in affluence. Poverty has, in large cities, very different appearances: it is often concealed in splendor, and often in extravagance. It is the care of a very great part of mankind to conceal their indigence from the rest: they support themselves by temporary expedients, and every day is lost in contriving for the morrow.

"This, however, was an evil, which, though frequent, I saw with less pain, because I could relieve it. Yet some have refused my bounties; more offended with my quickness to detect their wants, than pleased with my readiness to succor them: and others, whose exigencies compelled them to admit my kindness, have never been able to forgive their benefactress. Many, however, have been sincerely grateful without the ostentation of gratitude, or the hope of other favors."

Chapter 26. The Princess Continues Her Remarks upon Private Life

Nekayah, perceiving her brother's attention fixed, proceeded in her narrative.

"In families where there is or is not poverty, there is commonly discord. If a kingdom be, as Imlac tells us, a great family, a family likewise is a little kingdom, torn with factions and exposed to revolutions. An unpracticed observer expects the love of parents and children to be constant and equal; but this kindness seldom continues beyond the years of infancy: in a short time the children become rivals to their parents. Benefits are allayed[9] by reproaches, and gratitude debased by envy.

"Parents and children seldom act in concert; each child endeavors to appropriate the esteem or fondness of the parents, and the parents, with yet less temptation, betray each other to their children. Thus, some place their confidence in the father, and some in the mother, and by degrees the house is filled with artifices and feuds.

8. Division of our responsibilities.
9. To allay is "to joint anything to another, so as to abate its predominant qualities" (Johnson's *Dictionary*).

"The opinions of children and parents, of the young and the old, are naturally opposite, by the contrary effects of hope and despondence, of expectation and experience, without crime or folly on either side. The colors of life in youth and age appear different, as the face of nature in spring and winter. And how can children credit the assertions of parents, which their own eyes show them to be false?

"Few parents act in such a manner as much to enforce their maxims by the credit of their lives. The old man trusts wholly to slow contrivance and gradual progression; the youth expects to force his way by genius, vigor, and precipitance. The old man pays regard to riches, and the youth reverences virtue. The old man deifies prudence; the youth commits himself to magnanimity and chance. The young man, who intends no ill, believes that none is intended, and therefore acts with openness and candor; but his father, having suffered the injuries of fraud, is impelled to suspect, and too often allured to practice it. Age looks with anger on the temerity of youth, and youth with contempt on the scrupulosity[1] of age. Thus parents and children, for the greatest part, live on to love less and less; and, if those whom nature has thus closely united are the torments of each other, where shall we look for tenderness and consolation?"

"Surely," said the prince, "you must have been unfortunate in your choice of acquaintance: I am unwilling to believe that the most tender of all relations is thus impeded in its effects by natural necessity."

"Domestic discord," answered she, "is not inevitably and fatally necessary, but yet is not easily avoided. We seldom see that a whole family is virtuous; the good and evil cannot well agree, and the evil can yet less agree with one another. Even the virtuous fall sometimes to variance, when their virtues are of different kinds, and tending to extremes. In general, those parents have most reverence who most deserve it; for he that lives well cannot be despised.

"Many other evils infest private life. Some are the slaves of servants whom they have trusted with their affairs. Some are kept in continual anxiety to the caprice of rich relations, whom they cannot please, and dare not offend. Some husbands are imperious, and some wives perverse; and, as it is always more easy to do evil than good, though the wisdom or virtue of one can very rarely make many happy, the folly or vice of one may often make many miserable."

"If such be the general effect of marriage," said the prince, "I shall for the future think it dangerous to connect my interest with that of another, lest I should be unhappy by my partner's fault."

"I have met," said the princess, "with many who live single for that reason; but I never found that their prudence ought to raise envy. They dream away their time without friendship, without fondness, and are driven to rid themselves of the day, for which they have no use, by childish amusements, or vicious delights. They act as beings under the constant sense of some known inferiority that fills their minds with rancor, and their tongues with censure. They are peevish at home, and malevolent abroad; and, as the outlaws of human nature, make it their business and their pleasure to disturb that society which debars them from its privileges. To live without feeling or exciting sympathy, to be fortunate without adding to the felicity of others, or afflicted without tasting the balm of pity, is a state more gloomy than solitude; it is not

1. "Fear of acting in any manner" (Johnson's *Dictionary*).

retreat but exclusion from mankind. Marriage has many pains, but celibacy has no pleasures."

"What then is to be done?" said Rasselas; "the more we inquire, the less we can resolve. Surely he is most likely to please himself that has no other inclination to regard."

Chapter 27. Disquisition upon Greatness

The conversation had a short pause. The prince, having considered his sister's observations, told her, that she had surveyed life with prejudice, and supposed misery where she did not find it. "Your narrative," says he, "throws yet a darker gloom upon the prospects of futurity: the predictions of Imlac were but faint sketches of the evils painted by Nekayah. I have been lately convinced that quiet is not the daughter of grandeur, or of power: that her presence is not to be bought by wealth, nor enforced by conquest. It is evident, that as any man acts in a wider compass, he must be more exposed to opposition from enmity or miscarriage from chance; whoever has many to please or to govern, must use the ministry of many agents, some of whom will be wicked, and some ignorant; by some he will be misled, and by others betrayed. If he gratifies one he will offend another: those that are not favored will think themselves injured; and, since favors can be conferred but upon few, the greater number will be always discontented."

"The discontent," said the princess, "which is thus unreasonable, I hope that I shall always have spirit to despise, and you, power to repress."

"Discontent," answered Rasselas, "will not always be without reason under the most just or vigilant administration of public affairs. None, however attentive, can always discover that merit which indigence or faction may happen to obscure; and none, however powerful, can always reward it. Yet, he that sees inferior desert[2] advanced above him, will naturally impute that preference to partiality or caprice; and, indeed, it can scarcely be hoped that any man, however magnanimous by nature, or exalted by condition, will be able to persist for ever in fixed and inexorable justice of distribution: he will sometimes indulge his own affections, and sometimes those of his favorites; he will permit some to please him who can never serve him; he will discover in those whom he loves qualities which in reality they do not possess; and to those, from whom he receives pleasure, he will in his turn endeavor to give it. Thus will recommendations sometimes prevail which were purchased by money, or by the more destructive bribery of flattery and servility.

"He that has much to do will do something wrong, and of that wrong must suffer the consequences; and, if it were possible that he should always act rightly, yet when such numbers are to judge of his conduct, the bad will censure and obstruct him by malevolence, and the good sometimes by mistake.

"The highest stations cannot therefore hope to be the abodes of happiness, which I would willingly believe to have fled from thrones and palaces to seats of humble privacy and placid obscurity. For what can hinder the satisfaction, or intercept the expectations, of him whose abilities are adequate to his employments, who sees with his own eyes the whole circuit of his influence,

---

2. Merit; one deserving reward.

who chooses by his own knowledge all whom he trusts, and whom none are tempted to deceive by hope or fear? Surely he has nothing to do but to love and to be loved, to be virtuous and to be happy."

"Whether perfect happiness would be procured by perfect goodness," said Nekayah, "this world will never afford an opportunity of deciding. But this, at least, may be maintained, that we do not always find visible happiness in proportion to visible virtue. All natural and almost all political evils, are incident alike to the bad and good: they are confounded in the misery of a famine, and not much distinguished in the fury of a faction; they sink together in a tempest, and are driven together from their country by invaders. All that virtue can afford is quietness of conscience, a steady prospect of a happier state; this may enable us to endure calamity with patience; but remember that patience must suppose pain."

Chapter 28. Rasselas and Nekayah Continue Their Conversation

"Dear princess," said Rasselas, "you fall into the common errors of exaggeratory declamation, by producing, in a familiar disquisition,[3] examples of national calamities, and scenes of extensive misery, which are found in books rather than in the world, and which, as they are horrid, are ordained to be rare. Let us not imagine evils which we do not feel, nor injure life by misrepresentations. I cannot bear that querulous eloquence which threatens every city with a siege like that of Jerusalem,[4] that makes famine attend on every flight of locusts, and suspends pestilence on the wing of every blast that issues from the south.

"On necessary and inevitable evils, which overwhelm kingdoms at once, all disputation is vain: when they happen they must be endured. But it is evident, that these bursts of universal distress are more dreaded than felt: thousands and ten thousands flourish in youth, and wither in age, without the knowledge of any other than domestic evils, and share the same pleasures and vexations whether their kings are mild or cruel, whether the armies of their country pursue their enemies, or retreat before them. While courts are disturbed with intestine[5] competitions, and ambassadors are negotiating in foreign countries, the smith still plies his anvil, and the husbandman drives his plow forward; the necessaries of life are required and obtained, and the successive business of the seasons continues to make its wonted revolutions.

"Let us cease to consider what, perhaps, may never happen, and what, when it shall happen, will laugh at human speculation. We will not endeavor to modify the motions of the elements, or to fix the destiny of kingdoms. It is our business to consider what beings like us may perform; each laboring for his own happiness, by promoting within his circle, however narrow, the happiness of others.

"Marriage is evidently the dictate of nature; men and women were made to be companions of each other, and therefore I cannot be persuaded but that marriage is one of the means of happiness."

"I know not," said the princess, "whether marriage be more than one of the innumerable modes of human misery. When I see and reckon the various

3. Family discussion of a question.
4. In 70 A.D. the Romans, under Titus, besieged and

destroyed Jerusalem.
5. Internal, domestic.

forms of connubial infelicity, the unexpected causes of lasting discord, the diversities of temper, the oppositions of opinion, the rude collisons of contrary desire where both are urged by violent impulses, the obstinate contests of disagreeing virtues, where both are supported by consciousness of good intention, I am sometimes disposed to think with the severer casuists of most nations, that marriage is rather permitted than approved, and that none, but by the instigation of a passion too much indulged, entangle themselves with indissoluble compacts."

"You seem to forget," replied Rasselas, "that you have, even now, represented celibacy as less happy than marriage. Both conditions may be bad, but they cannot both be worst. Thus it happens when wrong opinions are entertained, that they mutually destroy each other, and leave the mind open to truth."

"I did not expect," answered the princess, "to hear that imputed to falsehood which is the consequence only of frailty. To the mind, as to the eye, it is difficult to compare with exactness objects vast in their extent, and various in their parts. Where we see or conceive the whole at once we readily note the discriminations and decide the preference: but of two systems, of which neither can be surveyed by any human being in its full compass of magnitude and multiplicity of complication, where is the wonder, that judging of the whole by parts, I am alternately affected by one and the other as either presses on my memory or fancy? We differ from ourselves just as we differ from each other, when we see only part of the question, as in the multifarious relations of politics and morality: but when we perceive the whole at once, as in numerical computations, all agree in one judgment, and none ever varies his opinion."

"Let us not add," said the prince, "to the other evils of life, the bitterness of controversy, nor endeavor to vie with each other in subtleties of argument. We are employed in a search, of which both are equally to enjoy the success, or suffer by the miscarriage. It is therefore fit that we assist each other. You surely conclude too hastily from the infelicity of marriage against its institution; will not the misery of life prove equally that life cannot be the gift of heaven? The world must be peopled by marriage, or peopled without it."

"How the world is to be peopled," returned Nekayah, "is not my care, and needs not be yours. I see no danger that the present generation should omit to leave successors behind them: we are not now inquiring for the world, but for ourselves."

Chapter 29. The Debate on Marriage Continued

"The good of the whole," says Rasselas, "is the same with the good of all its parts. If marriage be best for mankind it must be evidently best for individuals, or a permanent and necessary duty must be the cause of evil, and some must be inevitably sacrificed to the convenience of others. In the estimate which you have made of the two states, it appears that the incommodities of a single life are, in a great measure, necessary and certain, but those of the conjugal state accidental and avoidable.

"I cannot forbear to flatter myself that prudence and benevolence will make marriage happy. The general folly of mankind is the cause of general complaint. What can be expected but disappointment and repentance from a

choice made in the immaturity of youth, in the ardor of desire, without judgment, without foresight, without inquiry after conformity of opinions, similarity of manners, rectitude of judgment, or purity of sentiment.

"Such is the common process of marriage. A youth and maiden meeting by
chance, or brought together by artifice, exchange glances, reciprocate civilities, go home, and dream of one another. Having little to divert attention, or
diversify thought, they find themselves uneasy when they are apart, and therefore conclude that they shall be happy together. They marry, and discover
what nothing but voluntary blindness had before concealed; they wear out life
in altercations, and charge nature with cruelty.

"From those early marriages proceeds likewise the rivalry of parents and
children: the son is eager to enjoy the world before the father is willing to
forsake it, and there is hardly room at once for two generations. The daughter
begins to bloom before the mother can be content to fade, and neither can
forbear to wish for the absence of the other.

"Surely all these evils may be avoided by that deliberation and delay which
prudence prescribes to irrevocable choice. In the variety and jollity of youthful
pleasures life may be well enough supported without the help of a partner.
Longer time will increase experience, and wider views will allow better opportunities of inquiry and selection: one advantage, at least, will be certain; the
parents will be visibly older than their children."

"What reason cannot collect," said Nekayah, "and what experiment has not
yet taught, can be known only from the report of others. I have been told that
late marriages are not eminently happy. This is a question too important to be
neglected, and I have often proposed it to those, whose accuracy of remark,
and comprehensiveness of knowledge, made their suffrages[6] worthy of regard.
They have generally determined that it is dangerous for a man and woman to
suspend their fate upon each other, at a time when opinions are fixed, and
habits are established; when friendships have been contracted on both sides,
when life has been planned into method, and the mind has long enjoyed the
contemplation of its own prospects.

"It is scarcely possible that two traveling through the world under the conduct of chance should have been both directed to the same path, and it will
not often happen that either will quit the track which custom has made pleasing. When the desultory levity of youth has settled into regularity, it is soon
succeeded by pride ashamed to yield, or obstinacy delighting to contend. And
even though mutual esteem produces mutual desire to please, time itself, as it
modifies unchangeably the external mien, determines likewise the direction
of the passions, and gives an inflexible rigidity to the manners. Long customs
are not easily broken: he that attempts to change the course of his own life
very often labors in vain; and how shall we do that for others which we are
seldom able to do for ourselves?"

"But surely," interposed the prince, "you suppose the chief motive of choice
forgotten or neglected. Whenever I shall seek a wife, it shall be my first question, whether she be willing to be led by reason?"

"Thus it is," said Nekayah, "that philosophers are deceived. There are a
thousand familiar[7] disputes which reason never can decide; questions that
elude investigation, and make logic ridiculous; cases where something must

6. Opinions.   7. Domestic.

be done, and where little can be said. Consider the state of mankind, and inquire how few can be supposed to act upon any occasions, whether small or great, with all the reasons of action present to their minds. Wretched would be the pair above all names of wretchedness, who should be doomed to adjust by reason every morning all the minute detail of a domestic day.

"Those who marry at an advanced age will probably escape the encroach-ments of their children; but, in diminution of this advantage, they will be likely to leave them, ignorant and helpless, to a guardian's mercy: or, if that should not happen, they must at least go out of the world before they see those whom they love best either wise or great.

"From their children, if they have less to fear, they have less also to hope, and they lose, without equivalent, the joys of early love, and the convenience of uniting with manners pliant and minds susceptible of new impressions, which might wear away their dissimilitudes by long cohabitation, as soft bod-ies, by continual attrition, conform their surfaces to each other.

"I believe it will be found that those who marry late are best pleased with their children, and those who marry early with their partners."

"The union of these two affections," said Rasselas, "would produce all that could be wished. Perhaps there is a time when marriage might unite them, a time neither too early for the father, nor too late for the husband."

"Every hour," answered the princess, "confirms my prejudice in favor of the position so often uttered by the mouth of Imlac, 'That nature sets her gifts on the right hand and on the left.' Those conditions, which flatter hope and attract desire, are so constituted that, as we approach one, we recede from another. There are goods so opposed that we cannot seize both, but, by too much prudence, may pass between them at too great a distance to reach either. This is often the fate of long consideration; he does nothing who endeavors to do more than is allowed to humanity. Flatter not yourself with contrarieties of pleasure. Of the blessings set before you make your choice, and be content. No man can taste the fruits of autumn, while he is delighting his scent with the flowers of the spring: no man can, at the same time, fill his cup from the source and from the mouth of the Nile."

Chapter 30. Imlac Enters, and Changes the Conversation

Here Imlac entered, and interrupted them. "Imlac," said Rasselas, "I have been taking from the princess the dismal history of private life, and am almost discouraged from further search."

"It seems to me," said Imlac, "that while you are making the choice of life, you neglect to live. You wander about a single city, which, however large and diversified, can now afford few novelties, and forget that you are in a country, famous among the earliest monarchies for the power and wisdom of its inhab-itants; a country where the sciences first dawned that illuminate the world, and beyond which the arts cannot be traced of civil society or domestic life.

"The old Egyptians have left behind them monuments of industry and power before which all European magnificence is confessed to fade away. The ruins of their architecture are the schools of modern builders, and from the wonders which time has spared we may conjecture, though uncertainly, what it has destroyed."

"My curiosity," said Rasselas, "does not very strongly lead me to survey piles of stone, or mounds of earth; my business is with man. I came hither not to measure fragments of temples, or trace choked aqueducts, but to look upon the various scenes of the present world."

"The things that are now before us," said the princess, "require attention, and deserve it. What have I to do with the heroes or the monuments of ancient times? with times which never can return, and heroes, whose form of life was different from all that the present condition of mankind requires or allows."

"To know anything," returned the poet, "we must know its effects; to see men we must see their works, that we may learn what reason has dictated, or passion has incited, and find what are the most powerful motives of action. To judge rightly of the present we must oppose it to the past; for all judgment is comparative, and of the future nothing can be known. The truth is, that no mind is much employed upon the present: recollection and anticipation fill up almost all our moments. Our passions are joy and grief, love and hatred, hope and fear. Of joy and grief the past is the object, and the future of hope and fear; even love and hatred respect the past, for the cause must have been before the effect.

"The present state of things is the consequence of the former, and it is natural to inquire what were the sources of the good that we enjoy, or of the evil that we suffer. If we act only for ourselves, to neglect the study of history is not prudent: if we are entrusted with the care of others, it is not just. Ignorance, when it is voluntary, is criminal; and he may properly be charged with evil who refused to learn how he might prevent it.

"There is no part of history so generally useful as that which relates the progress of the human mind, the gradual improvement of reason, the successive advances of science, the vicissitudes of learning and ignorance, which are the light and darkness of thinking beings, the extinction and resuscitation of arts, and all the revolutions of the intellectual world. If accounts of battles and invasions are peculiarly the business of princes, the useful or elegant arts are not to be neglected; those who have kingdoms to govern, have understandings to cultivate.

"Example is always more efficacious than precept. A soldier is formed in war, and a painter must copy pictures. In this, contemplative life has the advantage: great actions are seldom seen, but the labors of art are always at hand for those who desire to know what art has been able to perform.

"When the eye or the imagination is struck with any uncommon work the next transition of an active mind is to the means by which it was performed. Here begins the true use of such contemplation; we enlarge our comprehension by new ideas, and perhaps recover some art lost to mankind, or learn what is less perfectly known in our own country. At least we compare our own with former times, and either rejoice at our improvements, or, what is the first motion towards good, discover our defects."

"I am willing," said the prince, "to see all that can deserve my search."

"And I," said the princess, "shall rejoice to learn something of the manners of antiquity."

"The most pompous monument of Egyptian greatness, and one of the most bulky works of manual industry," said Imlac, "are the pyramids; fabrics[8] raised

8. Buildings.

before the time of history, and of which the earliest narratives afford us only uncertain traditions. Of these the greatest is still standing, very little injured by time."

"Let us visit them tomorrow," said Nekayah. "I have often heard of the Pyramids, and shall not rest, till I have seen them within and without with my own eyes."

Chapter 31. *They Visit the Pyramids*

The resolution being thus taken, they set out the next day. They laid tents upon their camels, being resolved to stay among the pyramids till their curiosity was fully satisfied. They traveled gently, turned aside to everything remarkable, stopped from time to time and conversed with the inhabitants, and observed the various appearances of towns ruined and inhabited, of wild and cultivated nature.

When they came to the great pyramid, they were astonished at the extent of the base, and the height of the top. Imlac explained to them the principles upon which the pyramidal form was chosen for a fabric intended to coextend its duration with that of the world; he showed that its gradual diminution gave it such stability as defeated all the common attacks of the elements, and could scarcely be overthrown by earthquakes themselves, the least resistible of natural violence. A concussion that should shatter the pyramid would threaten the dissolution of the continent.

They measured all its dimensions, and pitched their tents at its foot. Next day they prepared to enter its interior apartments, and having hired the common guides, climbed up to the first passage, when the favorite of the princess, looking into the cavity, stepped back and trembled. "Pekuah," said the princess, "of what art thou afraid?" "Of the narrow entrance," answered the lady, "and of the dreadful gloom. I dare not enter a place which must surely be inhabited by unquiet souls. The original possessors of these dreadful vaults will start up before us, and perhaps shut us in forever." She spoke, and threw her arms round the neck of her mistress.

"If all your fear be of apparitions," said the prince, "I will promise you safety. There is no danger from the dead; he that is once buried will be seen no more."

"That the dead are seen no more," said Imlac, "I will not undertake to maintain, against the concurrent and unvaried testimony of all ages, and of all nations. There is no people, rude or learned, among whom apparitions of the dead are not related and believed. This opinion, which perhaps prevails as far as human nature is diffused, could become universal only by its truth; those that never heard of one another would not have agreed in a tale which nothing but experience can make credible. That it is doubted by single cavilers can very little weaken the general evidence; and some who deny it with their tongues confess it by their fears.

"Yet I do not mean to add new terrors to those which have already seized upon Pekuah. There can be no reason why specters should haunt the pyramid more than other places, or why they should have power or will to hurt innocence and purity. Our entrance is no violation of their privileges; we can take nothing from them, how then can we offend them?"

"My dear Pekuah," said the princess, "I will always go before you, and Imlac shall follow you. Remember that you are the companion of the princess of Abyssinia."

"If the princess is pleased that her servant should die," returned the lady, "let her command some death less dreadful than enclosure in this horrid cavern. You know I dare not disobey you; I must go if you command me, but if I once enter, I never shall come back."

The princess saw that her fear was too strong for expostulation or reproof, and, embracing her, told her that she should stay in the tent till their return. Pekuah was yet not satisfied, but entreated the princess not to pursue so dreadful a purpose as that of entering the recesses of the pyramid. "Though I cannot teach courage," said Nekayah, "I must not learn cowardice, nor leave at last undone what I came hither only to do."

Chapter 32. They Enter the Pyramid

Pekuah descended to the tents, and the rest entered the pyramid. They passed through the galleries, surveyed the vaults of marble, and examined the chest in which the body of the founder is supposed to have been reposited. They then sat down in one of the most spacious chambers to rest a while before they attempted to return.

"We have now," said Imlac, "gratified our minds with an exact view of the greatest work of man, except the wall of China.

"Of the wall it is very easy to assign the motive. It secured a wealthy and timorous nation from the incursions of barbarians, whose unskillfulness in arts made it easier for them to supply their wants by rapine than by industry, and who from time to time poured in upon the habitations of peaceful commerce, as vultures descend upon domestic fowl. Their celerity and fierceness made the wall necessary, and their ignorance made it efficacious.

"But for the pyramids, no reason has ever been given adequate to the cost and labor of the work. The narrowness of the chambers proves that it could afford no retreat from enemies, and treasures might have been reposited at far less expense with equal security. It seems to have been erected only in compliance with that hunger of imagination which preys incessantly upon life, and must be always appeased by some employment. Those who have already all that they can enjoy must enlarge their desires. He that has built for use till use is supplied, must begin to build for vanity, and extend his plan to the utmost power of human performance, that he may not be soon reduced to form another wish.

"I consider this mighty structure as a monument of the insufficiency of human enjoyments. A king, whose power is unlimited, and whose treasures surmount all real and imaginary wants, is compelled to solace, by the erection of a pyramid, the satiety of dominion and tastelessness of pleasures, and to amuse the tediousness of declining life by seeing thousands laboring without end, and one stone, for no purpose, laid upon another. Whoever thou art, that, not content with a moderate condition, imaginest happiness in royal magnificence, and dreamest that command or riches can feed the appetite of novelty with perpetual gratifications, survey the pyramids, and confess thy folly!"

Chapter 33. *The Princess Meets with an Unexpected Misfortune*

They rose up, and returned through the cavity at which they had entered, and the princess prepared for her favorite a long narrative of dark labyrinths, and costly rooms, and of the different impressions which the varieties of the way had made upon her. But when they came to their train, they found every one silent and dejected: the men discovered[9] shame and fear in their countenances, and the women were weeping in the tents.

What had happened they did not try to conjecture, but immediately inquired. "You had scarcely entered into the pyramid," said one of the attendants, "when a troop of Arabs rushed upon us: we were too few to resist them, and too slow to escape. They were about to search the tents, set us on our camels, and drive us along before them, when the approach of some Turkish horsemen put them to flight; but they seized the lady Pekuah with her two maids, and carried them away: the Turks are now pursuing them by our instigation, but I fear they will not be able to overtake them."

The princess was overpowered with surprise and grief. Rasselas, in the first heat of his resentment, ordered his servants to follow him, and prepared to pursue the robbers with his saber in his hand. "Sir," said Imlac, "what can you hope from violence or valor? the Arabs are mounted on horses trained to battle and retreat; we have only beasts of burden. By leaving our present station we may lose the princess, but cannot hope to regain Pekuah."

In a short time the Turks returned, having not been able to reach the enemy. The princess burst out into new lamentations, and Rasselas could scarcely forbear to reproach them with cowardice; but Imlac was of opinion, that the escape of the Arabs was no addition to their misfortune, for, perhaps, they would have killed their captives rather than have resigned them.

Chapter 34. *They Return to Cairo without Pekuah*

There was nothing to be hoped from longer stay. They returned to Cairo repenting of their curiosity, censuring the negligence of the government, lamenting their own rashness which had neglected to procure a guard, imagining many expedients by which the loss of Pekuah might have been prevented, and resolving to do something for her recovery, though none could find any thing proper to be done.

Nekayah retired to her chamber, where her women attempted to comfort her, by telling her that all had their troubles, and that lady Pekuah had enjoyed much happiness in the world for a long time, and might reasonably expect a change of fortune. They hoped that some good would befall her wheresoever she was, and that their mistress would find another friend who might supply her place.

The princess made them no answer, and they continued the form of condolence, not much grieved in their hearts that the favorite was lost.

Next day the prince presented to the Bassa a memorial[1] of the wrong which he had suffered, and a petition for redress. The Bassa threatened to punish the robbers, but did not attempt to catch them, nor, indeed, could any account or description be given by which he might direct the pursuit.

---

9. Revealed, betrayed. "Train": retinue.   1. Statement of facts.

It soon appeared that nothing would be done by authority. Governors, being accustomed to hear of more crimes than they can punish, and more wrongs than they can redress, set themselves at ease by indiscriminate negligence, and presently[2] forget the request when they lose sight of the petitioner.

Imlac then endeavored to gain some intelligence by private agents. He found many who pretended to an exact knowledge of all the haunts of the Arabs, and to regular correspondence with their chiefs, and who readily undertook the recovery of Pekuah. Of these, some were furnished with money for their journey, and came back no more; some were liberally paid for accounts which a few days discovered to be false. But the princess would not suffer any means, however improbable, to be left untried. While she was doing something she kept her hope alive. As one expedient failed, another was suggested; when one messenger returned unsuccessful, another was dispatched to a different quarter.

Two months had now passed, and of Pekuah nothing had been heard; the hopes which they had endeavored to raise in each other grew more languid, and the princess, when she saw nothing more to be tried, sunk down inconsolable in hopeless dejection. A thousand times she reproached herself with the easy compliance by which she permitted her favorite to stay behind her. "Had not my fondness," said she, "lessened my authority, Pekuah had not dared to talk of her terrors. She ought to have feared me more than specters. A severe look would have overpowered her; a peremptory command would have compelled obedience. Why did foolish indulgence prevail upon me? Why did I not speak and refuse to hear?"

"Great princess," said Imlac, "do not reproach yourself for your virtue, or consider that as blameable by which evil has accidentally been caused. Your tenderness for the timidity of Pekuah was generous and kind. When we act according to our duty, we commit the event to him by whose laws our actions are governed, and who will suffer none to be finally punished for obedience. When, in prospect of some good, whether natural or moral, we break the rules prescribed us, we withdraw from the direction of superior wisdom, and take all consequences upon ourselves. Man cannot so far know the connection of causes and events, as that he may venture to do wrong in order to do right. When we pursue our end by lawful means, we may always console our miscarriage by the hope of future recompense. When we consult only our own policy, and attempt to find a nearer way to good, by overleaping the settled boundaries of right and wrong, we cannot be happy even by success, because we cannot escape the consciousness of our fault; but, if we miscarry, the disappointment is irremediably embittered. How comfortless is the sorrow of him, who feels at once the pangs of guilt, and the vexation of calamity which guilt has brought upon him?

"Consider, princess, what would have been your condition, if the lady Pekuah had entreated to accompany you, and, being compelled to stay in the tents, had been carried away; or how would you have borne the thought, if you had forced her into the pyramid, and she had died before you in agonies of terror."

"Had either happened," said Nekayah, "I could not have endured life till

2. Immediately.

now: I should have been tortured to madness by the remembrance of such cruelty, or must have pined away in abhorrence of myself."

"This at least," said Imlac, "is the present reward of virtuous conduct, that no unlucky consequence can oblige us to repent it."

Chapter 35. The Princess Languishes for Want of Pekuah

Nekayah, being thus reconciled to herself, found that no evil is insupportable but that which is accompanied with consciousness of wrong. She was, from that time, delivered from the violence of tempestuous sorrow, and sunk into silent pensiveness and gloomy tranquillity. She sat from morning to evening recollecting all that had been done or said by her Pekuah, treasured up with care every trifle on which Pekuah had set an accidental value, and which might recall to mind any little incident or careless conversation. The sentiments of her, whom she now expected to see no more, were treasured in her memory as rules of life, and she deliberated to no other end than to conjecture on any occasion what would have been the opinion and counsel of Pekuah.

The women, by whom she was attended, knew nothing of her real condition, and therefore she could not talk to them but with caution and reserve. She began to remit[3] her curiosity, having no great care to collect notions which she had no convenience of uttering. Rasselas endeavored first to comfort and afterwards to divert her; he hired musicians, to whom she seemed to listen, but did not hear them, and procured masters to instruct her in various arts, whose lectures, when they visited her again, were again to be repeated. She had lost her taste of pleasure and her ambition of excellence. And her mind, though forced into short excursions, always recurred to the image of her friend.

Imlac was every morning earnestly enjoined to renew his inquiries, and was asked every night whether he had yet heard of Pekuah, till not being able to return the princess the answer that she desired, he was less and less willing to come into her presence. She observed his backwardness, and commanded him to attend her. "You are not," said she, "to confound impatience with resentment, or to suppose that I charge you with negligence, because I repine at your unsuccessfulness. I do not much wonder at your absence; I know that the unhappy are never pleasing, and that all naturally avoid the contagion of misery. To hear complaints is wearisome alike to the wretched and the happy; for who would cloud by adventitious grief the short gleams of gaiety which life allows us? or who, that is struggling under his own evils, will add to them the miseries of another?

"The time is at hand, when none shall be disturbed any longer by the sighs of Nekayah: my search after happiness is now at an end. I am resolved to retire from the world with all its flatteries and deceits, and will hide myself in solitude, without any other care than to compose my thoughts, and regulate my hours by a constant succession of innocent occupations, till, with a mind purified from all earthly desires, I shall enter into that state, to which all are hastening, and in which I hope again to enjoy the friendship of Pekuah."

"Do not entangle your mind," said Imlac, "by irrevocable determinations,

3. Slacken.

nor increase the burden of life by a voluntary accumulation of misery: the weariness of retirement will continue or increase when the loss of Pekuah is forgotten. That you have been deprived of one pleasure is no very good reason for rejection of the rest."

"Since Pekuah was taken from me," said the princess, "I have no pleasure to reject or to retain. She that has no one to love or trust has little to hope. She wants the radical principle of happiness. We may, perhaps, allow that what satisfaction this world can afford, must arise from the conjunction of wealth, knowledge and goodness: wealth is nothing but as it is bestowed, and knowledge nothing but as it is communicated: they must therefore be imparted to others, and to whom could I now delight to impart them? Goodness affords the only comfort which can be enjoyed without a partner, and goodness may be practised in retirement."

"How far solitude may admit goodness, or advance it, I shall not," replied Imlac, "dispute at present. Remember the confession of the pious hermit. You will wish to return into the world, when the image of your companion has left your thoughts." "That time," said Nekayah, "will never come. The generous frankness, the modest obsequiousness,[4] and the faithful secrecy of my dear Pekuah, will always be more missed, as I shall live longer to see vice and folly."

"The state of a mind oppressed with a sudden calamity," said Imlac, "is like that of the fabulous inhabitants of the new created earth, who, when the first night came upon them, supposed that day never would return. When the clouds of sorrow gather over us, we see nothing beyond them, nor can imagine how they will be dispelled: yet a new day succeeded to the night, and sorrow is never long without a dawn of ease. But they who restrain themselves from receiving comfort, do as the savages would have done, had they put out their eyes when it was dark. Our minds, like our bodies, are in continual flux; something is hourly lost, and something acquired. To lose much at once is inconvenient to either, but while the vital powers remain uninjured, nature will find the means of reparation. Distance has the same effect on the mind as on the eye, and while we glide along the stream of time, whatever we leave behind us is always lessening, and that which we approach increasing in magnitude. Do not suffer life to stagnate; it will grow muddy for want of motion: commit yourself again to the current of the world; Pekuah will vanish by degrees; you will meet in your way some other favorite, or learn to diffuse yourself in general conversation."

"At least," said the prince, "do not despair before all remedies have been tried: the inquiry after the unfortunate lady is still continued, and shall be carried on with yet greater diligence, on condition that you will promise to wait a year for the event, without any unalterable resolution."

Nekayah thought this a reasonable demand, and made the promise to her brother, who had been advised by Imlac to require it. Imlac had, indeed, no great hope of regaining Pekuah, but he supposed, that if he could secure the interval of a year, the princess would be then in no danger of a cloister.

4. Obedience.

Chapter 36. Pekuah Is Still Remembered. The Progress of Sorrow

Nekayah, seeing that nothing was omitted for the recovery of her favorite, and having, by her promise, set her intention of retirement at a distance, began imperceptibly to return to common cares and common pleasures. She rejoiced without her own consent at the suspension of her sorrows, and sometimes caught herself with indignation in the act of turning away her mind from the remembrance of her, whom yet she resolved never to forget.

She then appointed a certain hour of the day for meditation on the merits and fondness of Pekuah, and for some weeks retired constantly at the time fixed, and returned with her eyes swollen and her countenance clouded. By degrees she grew less scrupulous, and suffered any important and pressing avocation to delay the tribute of daily tears. She then yielded to less occasions; sometimes forgot what she was indeed afraid to remember, and, at last, wholly released herself from the duty of periodical affliction.

Her real love of Pekuah was yet not diminished. A thousand occurrences brought her back to memory, and a thousand wants, which nothing but the confidence of friendship can supply, made her frequently regretted. She, therefore, solicited Imlac never to desist from inquiry, and to leave no art of intelligence untried, that, at least, she might have the comfort of knowing that she did not suffer by negligence or sluggishness. "Yet what," said she, "is to be expected from our pursuit of happiness, when we find the state of life to be such, that happiness itself is the cause of misery? Why should we endeavor to attain that, of which the possession cannot be secured? I shall henceforward fear to yield my heart to excellence, however bright, or to fondness, however tender, lest I should lose again what I have lost in Pekuah."

Chapter 37. The Princess Hears News of Pekuah

In seven months, one of the messengers, who had been sent away upon the day when the promise was drawn from the princess, returned, after many unsuccessful rambles, from the borders of Nubia, with an account that Pekuah was in the hands of an Arab chief, who possessed a castle or fortress on the extremity of Egypt. The Arab, whose revenue was plunder, was willing to restore her, with her two attendants, for two hundred ounces of gold.

The price was no subject of debate. The princess was in ecstasies when she heard that her favorite was alive, and might so cheaply be ransomed. She could not think of delaying for a moment Pekuah's happiness or her own, but entreated her brother to send back the messenger with the sum required. Imlac, being consulted, was not very confident of the veracity of the relator, and was still more doubtful of the Arab's faith, who might, if he were too liberally trusted, detain at once the money and the captives. He thought it dangerous to put themselves in the power of the Arab, by going into his district, and could not expect that the rover[5] would so much expose himself as to come into the lower country, where he might be seized by the forces of the Bassa.

It is difficult to negotiate where neither will trust. But Imlac, after some

5. Robber.

deliberation, directed the messenger to propose that Pekuah should be conducted by ten horsemen to the monastery of St. Anthony, which is situated in the deserts of Upper Egypt, where she should be met by the same number, and her ransom should be paid.

That no time might be lost, as they expected that the proposal would not be refused, they immediately began their journey to the monastery; and, when they arrived, Imlac went forward with the former messenger to the Arab's fortress. Rasselas was desirous to go with them, but neither his sister nor Imlac would consent. The Arab, according to the custom of his nation, observed the laws of hospitality with great exactness to those who put themselves into his power, and, in a few days, brought Pekuah with her maids, by easy journeys, to their place appointed, where receiving the stipulated price, he restored her with great respect to liberty and her friends, and undertook to conduct them back toward Cairo beyond all danger of robbery or violence.

The princess and her favorite embraced each other with transport too violent to be expressed, and went out together to pour the tears of tenderness in secret, and exchange professions of kindness and gratitude. After a few hours they returned into the refectory of the convent, where, in the presence of the prior and his brethren, the prince required of Pekuah the history of her adventures.

Chapter 38. *The Adventures of the Lady Pekuah*

"At what time, and in what manner, I was forced away," said Pekuah, "your servants have told you. The suddenness of the event struck me with surprise, and I was at first rather stupified than agitated with any passion of either fear or sorrow. My confusion was increased by the speed and tumult of our flight while we were followed by the Turks, who, as it seemed, soon despaired to overtake us, or were afraid of those whom they made a show of menacing.

"When the Arabs saw themselves out of danger they slackened their course, and, as I was less harassed by external violence, I began to feel more uneasiness in my mind. After some time we stopped near a spring shaded with trees in a pleasant meadow, where we were set upon the ground, and offered such refreshments as our masters were partaking. I was suffered to sit with my maids apart from the rest, and none attempted to comfort or insult us. Here I first began to feel the full weight of my misery. The girls sat weeping in silence, and from time to time looked on me for succor. I knew not to what condition we were doomed, nor could conjecture where would be the place of our captivity, or whence to draw any hope of deliverance. I was in the hands of robbers and savages, and had no reason to suppose that their pity was more than their justice, or that they would forbear the gratification of any ardor of desire, or caprice of cruelty. I, however, kissed my maids, and endeavored to pacify them by remarking, that we were yet treated with decency, and that, since we were now carried beyond pursuit, there was no danger of violence to our lives.

"When we were to be set again on horseback, my maids clung round me, and refused to be parted, but I commanded them not to irritate those who had us in their power. We traveled the remaining part of the day through an unfrequented and pathless country, and came by moonlight to the side of a hill, where the rest of the troop was stationed. Their tents were pitched, and their fires kindled, and our chief was welcomed as a man much beloved by his dependents.

"We were received into a large tent, where we found women who had attended their husbands in the expedition. They set before us the supper which they had provided, and I eat it rather to encourage my maids than to comply with any appetite of my own. When the meat was taken away they spread the carpets for repose. I was weary, and hoped to find in sleep that remission of distress which nature seldom denies. Ordering myself therefore to be undressed, I observed that the women looked very earnestly upon me, not expecting, I suppose, to see me so submissively attended. When my upper vest was taken off, they were apparently struck with the splendor of my clothes, and one of them timorously laid her hand upon the embroidery. She then went out, and, in a short time, came back with another woman, who seemed to be of higher rank, and greater authority. She did, at her entrance, the usual act of reverence, and, taking me by the hand, placed me in a smaller tent, spread with finer carpets, where I spent the night quietly with my maids.

"In the morning, as I was sitting on the grass, the chief of the troop came towards me: I rose up to receive him, and he bowed with great respect. 'Illustrious lady,' said he, 'my fortune is better than I had presumed to hope; I am told by my women that I have a princess in my camp.' 'Sir,' answered I, 'your women have deceived themselves and you; I am not a princess, but an unhappy stranger who intended soon to have left this country, in which I am now to be imprisoned for ever.' 'Whoever, or whencesoever, you are,' returned the Arab, 'your dress, and that of your servants, show your rank to be high, and your wealth to be great. Why should you, who can so easily procure your ransom, think yourself in danger of perpetual captivity? The purpose of my incursions is to increase my riches, or more properly to gather tribute. The sons of Ishmael[6] are the natural and hereditary lords of this part of the continent, which is usurped by late invaders, and low-born tyrants, from whom we are compelled to take by the sword what is denied to justice. The violence of war admits no distinction; the lance that is lifted at guilt and power will sometimes fall on innocence and gentleness.'

" 'How little,' said I, 'did I expect that yesterday it should have fallen upon me.'

" 'Misfortunes,' answered the Arab, 'should always be expected. If the eye of hostility could learn reverence or pity, excellence like yours had been exempt from injury. But the angels of affliction spread their toils alike for the virtuous and the wicked, for the mighty and the mean. Do not be disconsolate; I am not one of the lawless and cruel rovers of the desert; I know the rules of civil life: I will fix your ransom, give a passport to your messenger, and perform my stipulation with nice punctuality.'[7]

"You will easily believe that I was pleased with his courtesy; and finding that his predominant passion was desire of money, I began now to think my danger less, for I knew that no sum would be thought too great for the release of Pekuah. I told him that he should have no reason to charge me with ingratitude, if I was used with kindness, and that any ransom, which could be expected for a maid of common rank, would be paid, but that he must not

6. Arabs, who claim descent from Ishmael, a son of Abraham.   7. Scrupulous exactness. "Civil": civilized.

persist to rate me as a princess. He said, he would consider what he should demand, and then, smiling, bowed and retired.

"Soon after the women came about me, each contending to be more officious[8] than the other, and my maids themselves were served with reverence. We traveled onward by short journeys. On the fourth day the chief told me, that my ransom must be two hundred ounces of gold, which I not only promised him, but told him, that I would add fifty more, if I and my maids were honorably treated.

"I never knew the power of gold before. From that time I was the leader of the troop. The march of every day was longer or shorter as I commanded, and the tents were pitched where I chose to rest. We now had camels and other conveniencies for travel, my own women were always at my side, and I amused myself with observing the manners of the vagrant nations,[9] and with viewing remains of ancient edifices with which these deserted countries appear to have been, in some distant age, lavishly embellished.

"The chief of the band was a man far from illiterate: he was able to travel by the stars or the compass, and had marked in his erratic expeditions such places as are most worthy the notice of a passenger.[1] He observed to me, that buildings are always best preserved in places little frequented, and difficult of access: for, when once a country declines from its primitive splendor, the more inhabitants are left, the quicker ruin will be made. Walls supply stones more easily than quarries, and palaces and temples will be demolished to make stables of granite, and cottages of porphyry.

Chapter 39. The Adventures of Pekuah Continued

"We wandered about in this manner for some weeks, whether, as our chief pretended, for my gratification, or, as I rather suspected, for some convenience of his own. I endeavored to appear contented where sullenness and resentment would have been of no use, and that endeavor conduced much to the calmness of my mind; but my heart was always with Nekayah, and the troubles of the night much overbalanced the amusements of the day. My women, who threw all their cares upon their mistress, set their minds at ease from the time when they saw me treated with respect, and gave themselves up to the incidental alleviations of our fatigue without solicitude or sorrow. I was pleased with their pleasure, and animated with their confidence. My condition had lost much of its terror, since I found that the Arab ranged the country merely to get riches. Avarice is an uniform and tractable vice: other intellectual distempers are different in different constitutions of mind; that which sooths the pride of one will offend the pride of another; but to the favor of the covetous there is a ready way, bring money and nothing is denied.

"At last we came to the dwelling of our chief, a strong and spacious house built with stone in an island of the Nile, which lies, as I was told, under the tropic. 'Lady,' said the Arab, 'you shall rest after your journey a few weeks in this place, where you are to consider yourself as sovereign. My occupation is war: I have therefore chosen this obscure residence, from which I can issue unexpected, and to which I can retire unpursued. You may now repose in

8. Ready to serve.   1. Traveler.
9. Nomads.

security: here are few pleasures, but here is no danger.' He then led me into the inner apartments, and seating me on the richest couch, bowed to the ground. His women, who considered me as a rival, looked on me with malignity; but being soon informed that I was a great lady detained only for my ransom, they began to vie with each other in obsequiousness and reverence.

"Being again comforted with new assurances of speedy liberty, I was for some days diverted from impatience by the novelty of the place. The turrets overlooked the country to a great distance, and afforded a view of many windings of the stream. In the day I wandered from one place to another as the course of the sun varied the splendor of the prospect, and saw many things which I had never seen before. The crocodiles and river-horses[2] are common in this unpeopled region, and I often looked upon them with terror, though I knew that they could not hurt me. For some time I expected to see mermaids and tritons, which, as Imlac has told me, the European travelers have stationed in the Nile, but no such beings ever appeared, and the Arab, when I inquired after them, laughed at my credulity.

"At night the Arab always attended me to a tower set apart for celestial observations, where he endeavored to teach me the names and courses of the stars. I had no great inclination to this study, but an appearance of attention was necessary to please my instructor, who valued himself for his skill, and, in a little while, I found some employment requisite to beguile the tediousness of time, which was to be passed always amidst the same objects. I was weary of looking in the morning on things from which I had turned away weary in the evening: I therefore was at last willing to observe the stars rather than do nothing, but could not always compose my thoughts, and was very often thinking on Nekayah when others imagined me contemplating the sky. Soon after the Arab went upon another expedition, and then my only pleasure was to talk with my maids about the accident by which we were carried away, and the happiness that we should all enjoy at the end of our captivity."

"There were women in your Arab's fortress," said the princess, "why did you not make them your companions, enjoy their conversation, and partake their diversions? In a place where they found business or amusement, why should you alone sit corroded with idle melancholy? or why could not you bear for a few months that condition to which they were condemned for life?"

"The diversions of the women," answered Pekuah, "were only childish play, by which the mind accustomed to stronger operations could not be kept busy. I could do all which they delighted in doing by powers merely sensitive,[3] while my intellectual faculties were flown to Cairo. They ran from room to room as a bird hops from wire to wire in his cage. They danced for the sake of motion, as lambs frisk in a meadow. One sometimes pretended to be hurt that the rest might be alarmed, or hid herself that another might seek her. Part of their time passed in watching the progress of light bodies that floated on the river, and part in marking the various forms into which clouds broke in the sky.

"Their business was only needlework, in which I and my maids sometimes helped them; but you know that the mind will easily straggle from the fingers, nor will you suspect that captivity and absence from Nekayah could receive solace from silken flowers.

2. Hippopotamuses.   son's *Dictionary*).
3. "Having sense or perception, but not reason" (John-

"Nor was much satisfaction to be hoped from their conversation: for of what could they be expected to talk? They had seen nothing; for they had lived from early youth in that narrow spot: of what they had not seen they could have no knowledge, for they could not read. They had no ideas but of the few things that were within their view, and had hardly names for anything but their clothes and their food. As I bore a superior character, I was often called to terminate their quarrels, which I decided as equitably as I could. If it could have amused me to hear the complaints of each against the rest, I might have been often detained by long stories, but the motives of their animosity were so small that I could not listen without intercepting the tale."

"How," said Rasselas, "can the Arab, whom you represented as a man of more than common accomplishments, take any pleasure in his seraglio, when it is filled only with women like these. Are they exquisitely beautiful?"

"They do not," said Pekuah, "want that unaffecting and ignoble beauty which may subsist without spriteliness or sublimity, without energy of thought or dignity of virtue. But to a man like the Arab such beauty was only a flower casually plucked and carelessly thrown away. Whatever pleasures he might find among them, they were not those of friendship or society. When they were playing about him he looked on them with inattentive superiority: when they vied for his regard he sometimes turned away disgusted. As they had no knowledge, their talk could take nothing from the tediousness of life: as they had no choice, their fondness, or appearance of fondness, excited in him neither pride nor gratitude; he was not exalted in his own esteem by the smiles of a woman who saw no other man, nor was much obliged by that regard, of which he could never know the sincerity, and which he might often perceive to be exerted not so much to delight him as to pain a rival. That which he gave, and they received, as love, was only a careless distribution of superfluous time, such love as man can bestow upon that which he despises, such as has neither hope nor fear, neither joy nor sorrow."

"You have reason, lady, to think yourself happy," said Imlac, "that you have been thus easily dismissed. How could a mind, hungry for knowledge, be willing, in an intellectual famine, to lose such a banquet as Pekuah's conversation?"

"I am inclined to believe," answered Pekuah, "that he was for some time in suspense; for, notwithstanding his promise, whenever I proposed to dispatch a messenger to Cairo, he found some excuse for delay. While I was detained in his house he made many incursions into the neighboring countries, and, perhaps, he would have refused to discharge me, had his plunder been equal to his wishes. He returned always courteous, related his adventures, delighted to hear my observations, and endeavored to advance my acquaintance with the stars. When I importuned him to send away my letters, he soothed me with professions of honor and sincerity; and, when I could be no longer decently denied, put his troop again in motion, and left me to govern in his absence. I was much afflicted by this studied procrastination, and was sometimes afraid that I should be forgotten; that you would leave Cairo, and I must end my days in an island of the Nile.

"I grew at last hopeless and dejected, and cared so little to entertain him, that he for a while more frequently talked with my maids. That he should fall in love with them, or with me, might have been equally fatal, and I was not much pleased with the growing friendship. My anxiety was not long; for, as I recovered some degree of cheerfulness, he returned to me, and I could not forbear to despise my former uneasiness.

"He still delayed to send for my ransom, and would, perhaps, never have determined, had not your agent found his way to him. The gold, which he would not fetch, he could not reject when it was offered. He hastened to prepare for our journey hither, like a man delivered from the pain of an intestine conflict. I took leave of my companions in the house, who dismissed me with cold indifference."

Nekayah, having heard her favorite's relation, rose and embraced her, and Rasselas gave her an hundred ounces of gold, which she presented to the Arab for the fifty that were promised.

Chapter 40. The History of a Man of Learning

They returned to Cairo, and were so well pleased at finding themselves together, that none of them went much abroad. The prince began to love learning, and one day declared to Imlac, that he intended to devote himself to science,[4] and pass the rest of his days in literary solitude.

"Before you make your final choice," answered Imlac, "you ought to examine its hazards, and converse with some of those who are grown old in the company of themselves. I have just left the observatory of one of the most learned astronomers in the world, who has spent forty years in unwearied attention to the motions and appearances of the celestial bodies, and has drawn out his soul in endless calculations. He admits a few friends once a month to hear his deductions and enjoy his discoveries. I was introduced as a man of knowledge worthy of his notice. Men of various ideas and fluent conversation are commonly welcome to those whose thoughts have been long fixed upon a single point, and who find the images of other things stealing away. I delighted him with my remarks, he smiled at the narrative of my travels, and was glad to forget the constellations, and descend for a moment into the lower world.

"On the next day of vacation I renewed my visit, and was so fortunate as to please him again. He relaxed from that time the severity of his rule, and permitted me to enter at my own choice. I found him always busy, and always glad to be relieved. As each knew much which the other was desirous of learning, we exchanged our notions with great delight. I perceived that I had every day more of his confidence, and always found new cause of admiration in the profundity of his mind. His comprehension is vast, his memory capacious and retentive, his discourse is methodical, and his expression clear.

"His integrity and benevolence are equal to his learning. His deepest researches and most favorite studies are willingly interrupted for any opportunity of doing good by his counsel or his riches. To his closest retreat, at his most busy moments, all are admitted that want his assistance: 'For though I exclude idleness and pleasure, I will never,' says he, 'bar my doors against charity. To man is permitted the contemplation of the skies, but the practice of virtue is commanded.'"

"Surely," said the princess, "this man is happy."

"I visited him," said Imlac, "with more and more frequency, and was every

4. Knowledge.

time more enamored of his conversation: he was sublime without haughtiness, courteous without formality, and communicative without ostentation. I was at first, great princess, of your opinion, thought him the happiest of mankind, and often congratulated him on the blessing that he enjoyed. He seemed to hear nothing with indifference but the praises of his condition, to which he always returned a general answer, and diverted the conversation to some other topic.

"Amidst this willingness to be pleased, and labor to please, I had quickly reason to imagine that some painful sentiment pressed upon his mind. He often looked up earnestly towards the sun, and let his voice fall in the midst of his discourse. He would sometimes, when we were alone, gaze upon me in silence with the air of a man who longed to speak what he was yet resolved to suppress. He would often send for me with vehement injunctions of haste, though, when I came to him, he had nothing extraordinary to say. And sometimes, when I was leaving him, he would call me back, pause a few moments and then dismiss me.

Chapter 41. The Astronomer Discovers the Cause of his Uneasiness

"At last the time came when the secret burst his reserve. We were sitting together last night in the turret of his house, watching the emersion of a satellite of Jupiter. A sudden tempest clouded the sky, and disappointed our observation. We sat a while silent in the dark, and then he addressed himself to me in these words: 'Imlac, I have long considered thy friendship as the greatest blessing of my life. Integrity without knowledge is weak and useless, and knowledge without integrity is dangerous and dreadful. I have found in thee all the qualities requisite for trust, benevolence, experience, and fortitude. I have long discharged an office which I must soon quit at the call of nature, and shall rejoice in the hour of imbecility[5] and pain to devolve it upon thee.'

"I thought myself honored by this testimony, and protested that whatever could conduce to his happiness would add likewise to mine.

" 'Hear, Imlac, what thou wilt not without difficulty credit. I have possessed for five years the regulation of weather, and the distribution of the seasons: the sun has listened to my dictates, and passed from tropic to tropic by my direction; the clouds, at my call, have poured their waters, and the Nile has overflowed at my command; I have restrained the rage of the dog-star, and mitigated the fervors of the crab.[6] The winds alone, of all the elemental powers, have hitherto refused my authority, and multitudes have perished by equinoctial tempests which I found myself unable to prohibit or restrain. I have administered this great office with exact justice, and made to the different nations of the earth an impartial dividend of rain and sunshine. What must have been the misery of half the globe, if I had limited the clouds to particular regions, or confined the sun to either side of the equator?'

---

5. Feebleness.
6. The fourth sign of the zodiac (Cancer). "The dog-   star": Sirius was supposed to cause the heat ("dog days") of summer.

Chapter 42. The Opinion of the Astronomer Is Explained and Justified

"I suppose he discovered in me, through the obscurity of the room, some tokens of amazement and doubt, for, after a short pause, he proceeded thus:

" 'Not to be easily credited will neither surprise nor offend me; for I am, probably, the first of human beings to whom this trust has been imparted. Nor do I know whether to deem this distinction a reward or punishment; since I have possessed it I have been far less happy than before, and nothing but the consciousness of good intention could have enabled me to support the weariness of unremitted vigilance.'

" 'How long, Sir, said I, has this great office been in your hands?'

" 'About ten years ago,' said he, 'my daily observations of the changes of the sky led me to consider, whether, if I had the power of the seasons, I could confer greater plenty upon the inhabitants of the earth. This contemplation fastened on my mind, and I sat days and nights in imaginary dominion, pouring upon this country and that the showers of fertility, and seconding every fall of rain with a due proportion of sunshine. I had yet only the will to do good, and did not imagine that I should ever have the power.

" 'One day as I was looking on the fields withering with heat, I felt in my mind a sudden wish that I could send rain on the southern mountains, and raise the Nile to an inundation. In the hurry of my imagination I commanded rain to fall, and, by comparing the time of my command, with that of the inundation, I found that the clouds had listened to my lips.'

" 'Might not some other cause,' said I, 'produce this concurrence? the Nile does not always rise on the same day.'

" 'Do not believe,' said he with impatience, 'that such objections could escape me: I reasoned long against my own conviction, and labored against truth with the utmost obstinacy. I sometimes suspected myself of madness, and should not have dared to impart this secret but to a man like you, capable of distinguishing the wonderful from the impossible, and the incredible from the false.'

" 'Why, Sir,' said I, 'do you call that incredible, which you know, or think you know, to be true?'

" 'Because,' said he, 'I cannot prove it by any external evidence; and I know too well the laws of demonstration to think that my conviction ought to influence another, who cannot, like me, be conscious of its force. I therefore shall not attempt to gain credit by disputation. It is sufficient that I feel this power, that I have long possessed, and every day exerted it. But the life of man is short, the infirmities of age increase upon me, and the time will soon come when the regulator of the year must mingle with the dust. The care of appointing a successor has long disturbed me; the night and the day have been spent in comparisons of all the characters which have come to my knowledge, and I have yet found none so worthy as thyself.

Chapter 43. The Astronomer Leaves Imlac His Directions

" 'Hear therefore, what I shall impart, with attention, such as the welfare of a world requires. If the task of a king be considered as difficult, who has the care only of a few millions, to whom he cannot do much good or harm, what

must be the anxiety of him, on whom depends the action of the elements, and
the great gifts of light and heat!—Hear me therefore with attention.

"'I have diligently considered the position of the earth and sun, and formed
innumerable schemes in which I changed their situation. I have sometimes
turned aside the axis of the earth, and sometimes varied the ecliptic of the
sun: but I have found it impossible to make a disposition by which the world
may be advantaged; what one region gains, another loses by any imaginable
alteration, even without considering the distant parts of the solar system with
which we are unacquainted. Do not, therefore, in thy administration of the
year, indulge thy pride by innovation; do not please thyself with thinking that
thou canst make thyself renowned to all future ages, by disordering the seasons. The memory of mischief is no desirable fame. Much less will it become
thee to let kindness or interest prevail. Never rob other countries of rain to
pour it on thine own. For us the Nile is sufficient.'

"I promised that when I possessed the power, I would use it with inflexible
integrity, and he dismissed me, pressing my hand. 'My heart,' said he, 'will be
now at rest, and my benevolence will no more destroy my quiet: I have found
a man of wisdom and virtue, to whom I can cheerfully bequeath the inheritance of the sun.'"

The prince heard this narration with very serious regard, but the princess
smiled, and Pekuah convulsed herself with laughter. "Ladies," said Imlac, "to
mock the heaviest of human afflictions is neither charitable nor wise. Few can
attain this man's knowledge, and few practice his virtues; but all may suffer
his calamity. Of the uncertainties of our present state, the most dreadful and
alarming is the uncertain continuance of reason."

The princess was recollected, and the favorite was abashed. Rasselas, more
deeply affected, inquired of Imlac, whether he thought such maladies of the
mind frequent, and how they were contracted.

Chapter 44. The Dangerous Prevalence[7] of Imagination

"Disorders of intellect," answered Imlac, "happen much more often than
superficial observers will easily believe. Perhaps, if we speak with rigorous
exactness, no human mind is in its right state. There is no man whose imagination does not sometimes predominate over his reason, who can regulate his
attention wholly by his will, and whose ideas will come and go at his command. No man will be found in whose mind airy notions do not sometimes
tyrannize, and force him to hope or fear beyond the limits of sober probability.
All power of fancy over reason is a degree of insanity; but while this power is
such as we can control and repress, it is not visible to others, nor considered
as any depravation of the mental faculties; it is not pronounced madness but
when it comes ungovernable, and apparently influences speech or action.

"To indulge the power of fiction, and send imagination out upon the wing,
is often the sport of those who delight too much in silent speculation. When
we are alone we are not always busy; the labor of excogitation is too violent to
last long; the ardor of inquiry will sometimes give way to idleness or satiety.
He who has nothing external that can divert him must find pleasure in his
own thoughts, and must conceive himself what he is not; for who is pleased

7. Predominance.

with what he is? He then expatiates in boundless futurity, and culls from all imaginable conditions that which for the present moment he should most desire, amuses his desires with impossible enjoyments, and confers upon his pride unattainable dominion. The mind dances from scene to scene, unites all pleasures in all combinations, and riots in delights which nature and fortune, with all their bounty, cannot bestow.

"In time, some particular train of ideas fixes the attention; all other intellectual gratifications are rejected; the mind, in weariness or leisure, recurs constantly to the favorite conception, and feasts on the luscious falsehood, whenever she is offended with the bitterness of truth. By degrees the reign of fancy is confirmed; she grows first imperious, and in time despotic. Then fictions begin to operate as realities, false opinions fasten upon the mind, and life passes in dreams of rapture or of anguish.

"This, sir, is one of the dangers of solitude, which the hermit has confessed not always to promote goodness, and the astronomer's misery has proved to be not always propitious to wisdom."

"I will no more," said the favorite, "imagine myself the queen of Abyssinia. I have often spent the hours which the princess gave to my own disposal, in adjusting ceremonies and regulating the court; I have repressed the pride of the powerful, and granted the petitions of the poor; I have built new palaces in more happy situations, planted groves upon the tops of mountains, and have exulted in the beneficence of royalty, till, when the princess entered, I had almost forgotten to bow down before her."

"And I," said the princess, "will not allow myself any more to play the shepherdess in my waking dreams. I have often soothed my thoughts with the quiet and innocence of pastoral employments, till I have in my chamber heard the winds whistle, and the sheep bleat; sometimes freed the lamb entangled in the thicket, and sometimes with my crook encountered the wolf. I have a dress like that of the village maids, which I put on to help my imagination, and a pipe on which I play softly, and suppose myself followed by my flocks."

"I will confess," said the prince, "an indulgence of fantastic delight more dangerous than yours. I have frequently endeavored to image the possibility of a perfect government, by which all wrong should be restrained, all vice reformed, and all the subjects preserved in tranquility and innocence. This thought produced innumerable schemes of reformation, and dictated many useful regulations and salutary edicts. This has been the sport, and sometimes the labor, of my solitude; and I start, when I think with how little anguish I once supposed the death of my father and my brothers."

"Such," says Imlac, "are the effects of visionary schemes; when we first form them, we know them to be absurd, but familiarize them by degrees, and in time lose sight of their folly."

Chapter 45. They Discourse with an Old Man

The evening was now far past, and they rose to return home. As they walked along the bank of the Nile, delighted with the beams of the moon quivering on the water, they saw at a small distance an old man, whom the prince had often heard in the assembly of the sages. "Yonder," said he, "is one whose years have calmed his passions, but not clouded his reason. Let us close the disquisitions of the night by inquiring what are his sentiments of his own state, that we may know whether youth alone is to struggle with vexation, and whether any better hope remains for the latter part of life."

Here the sage approached and saluted them. They invited him to join their walk, and prattled a while, as acquaintance that had unexpectedly met one another. The old man was cheerful and talkative, and the way seemed short in his company. He was pleased to find himself not disregarded, accompanied them to their house, and, at the prince's request, entered with them. They placed him in the seat of honor, and set wine and conserves before him.

"Sir," said the princess, "an evening walk must give to a man of learning like you pleasures which ignorance and youth can hardly conceive. You know the qualities and the causes of all that you behold, the laws by which the river flows, the periods in which the planets perform their revolutions. Everything must supply you with contemplation, and renew the consciousness of your own dignity."

"Lady," answered he, "let the gay and the vigorous expect pleasure in their excursions; it is enough that age can obtain ease. To me the world has lost its novelty; I look round, and see what I remember to have seen in happier days. I rest against a tree, and consider that in the same shade I once disputed upon the annual overflow of the Nile with a friend who is now silent in the grave. I cast my eyes upward, fix them on the changing moon, and think with pain on the vicissitudes of life. I have ceased to take much delight in physical truth; for what have I to do with those things which I am soon to leave?"

"You may at least recreate[8] yourself," said Imlac, "with the recollection of an honorable and useful life, and enjoy the praise which all agree to give you."

"Praise," said the sage with a sigh, "is to an old man an empty sound. I have neither mother to be delighted with the reputation of her son, nor wife to partake the honors of her husband. I have outlived my friends and my rivals. Nothing is now of much importance; for I cannot extend my interest beyond myself. Youth is delighted with applause, because it is considered as the earnest of some future good, and because the prospect of life is far extended; but to me, who am now declining to decrepitude, there is little to be feared from the malevolence of men, and yet less to be hoped from their affection or esteem. Something they may yet take away, but they can give me nothing. Riches would now be useless, and high employment would be pain. My retrospect of life recalls to my view many opportunities of good neglected, much time squandered upon trifles, and more lost in idleness and vacancy. I leave many great designs unattempted, and many great attempts unfinished. My mind is burthened with no heavy crime, and therefore I compose myself to tranquility; endeavor to abstract my thoughts from hopes and cares which, though reason knows them to be vain, still try to keep their old possession of the heart; expect,[9] with serene humility, that hour which nature cannot long delay; and hope to possess, in a better state, that happiness which here I could not find, and that virtue which here I have not attained."

He arose and went away, leaving his audience not much elated with the hope of long life. The prince consoled himself with remarking that it was not reasonable to be disappointed by this account; for age had never been considered as the season of felicity, and if it was possible to be easy in decline and

8. Refresh.   9. Await.

weakness, it was likely that the days of vigor and alacrity might be happy; that the noon of life might be bright, if the evening could be calm.

The princess suspected that age was querulous and malignant, and delighted to repress the expectations of those who had newly entered the world. She had seen the possessors of estates look with envy on their heirs, and known many who enjoy pleasure no longer than they can confine it to themselves.

Pekuah conjectured that the man was older than he appeared, and was willing to impute his complaints to delirious dejection; or else supposed that he had been unfortunate, and was therefore discontented. "For nothing," said she, "is more common than to call our own condition the condition of life."

Imlac, who had no desire to see them depressed, smiled at the comforts which they could so readily procure to themselves, and remembered that, at the same age, he was equally confident of unmingled prosperity, and equally fertile of consolatory expedients. He forbore to force upon them unwelcome knowledge, which time itself would too soon impress. The princess and her lady retired; the madness of the astronomer hung upon their minds, and they desired Imlac to enter upon his office, and delay next morning the rising of the sun.

Chapter 46. The Princess and Pekuah Visit the Astronomer

The princess and Pekuah, having talked in private of Imlac's astronomer, thought his character at once so amiable and so strange, that they could not be satisfied without a nearer knowledge, and Imlac was requested to find the means of bringing them together.

This was somewhat difficult; the philosopher had never received any visits from women, though he lived in a city that had in it many Europeans who followed the manners of their own countries, and many from other parts of the world that lived there with European liberty. The ladies would not be refused, and several schemes were proposed for the accomplishment of their design. It was proposed to introduce them as strangers in distress, to whom the sage was always accessible; but, after some deliberation, it appeared, that by this artifice, no acquaintance could be formed, for their conversation would be short, and they could not decently importune him often. "This," said Rasselas, "is true; but I have yet a stronger objection against the misrepresentation of your state. I have always considered it as treason against the great republic of human nature, to make any man's virtues the means of deceiving him, whether on great or little occasions. All imposture weakens confidence and chills benevolence. When the sage finds that you are not what you seemed, he will feel the resentment natural to a man who, conscious of great abilities, discovers that he has been tricked by understandings meaner than his own, and, perhaps, the distrust, which he can never afterwards wholly lay aside, may stop the voice of counsel, and close the hand of charity; and where will you find the power of restoring his benefactions to mankind, or his peace to himself?"

To this no reply was attempted, and Imlac began to hope that their curiosity would subside; but next day Pekuah told him, she had now found an honest pretense for a visit to the astronomer, for she would solicit permission to continue under him the studies in which she had been initiated by the Arab, and the princess might go with her either as a fellow-student, or because a woman could not decently come alone. "I am afraid," said Imlac, "that he will be soon weary of your company: men advanced far in knowledge do not love to repeat the elements of their art, and I am not certain, that even of the elements, as he will deliver them connected with inferences, and mingled with reflections, you are a very capable auditress." "That," said Pekuah, "must be my care: I ask of you only to take me thither. My knowledge is, perhaps, more than you imagine it, and by concurring always with his opinions I shall make him think it greater than it is."

The astronomer, in pursuance of this resolution, was told, that a foreign lady, traveling in search of knowledge, had heard of his reputation, and was desirous to become his scholar. The uncommonness of the proposal raised at once his surprise and curiosity, and when, after a short deliberation, he consented to admit her, he could not stay without impatience till the next day.

The ladies dressed themselves magnificently, and were attended by Imlac to the astronomer, who was pleased to see himself approached with respect by persons of so splendid an appearance. In the exchange of the first civilities he was timorous and bashful; but when the talk became regular, he recollected his powers, and justified the character which Imlac had given. Inquiring of Pekuah what could have turned her inclination towards astronomy, he received from her a history of her adventure at the pyramid, and of the time passed in the Arab's island. She told her tale with ease and elegance, and her conversation took possession of his heart. The discourse was then turned to astronomy: Pekuah displayed what she knew: he looked upon her as a prodigy of genius, and entreated her not to desist from a study which she had so happily begun.

They came again and again, and were every time more welcome than before. The sage endeavored to amuse them, that they might prolong their visits, for he found his thoughts grow brighter in their company; the clouds of solicitude vanished by degrees, as he forced himself to entertain them, and he grieved when he was left at their departure to his old employment of regulating the seasons.

The princess and her favorite had now watched his lips for several months, and could not catch a single word from which they could judge whether he continued, or not, in the opinion of his preternatural commission. They often contrived to bring him to an open declaration, but he easily eluded all their attacks, and on which side soever they pressed him escaped from them to some other topic.

As their familiarity increased they invited him often to the house of Imlac, where they distinguished him by extraordinary respect. He began gradually to delight in sublunary pleasures. He came early and departed late; labored to recommend himself by assiduity and compliance; excited their curiosity after new arts, that they might still want his assistance; and when they made any excursion of pleasure or inquiry, entreated to attend them.

By long experience of his integrity and wisdom, the prince and his sister were convinced that he might be trusted without danger; and lest he should draw any false hopes from the civilities which he received, discovered to him their condition, with the motives of their journey, and required his opinion on the choice of life.

"Of the various conditions which the world spreads before you, which you shall prefer," said the sage, "I am not able to instruct you. I can only tell that I have chosen wrong. I have passed my time in study without experience; in the attainment of sciences which can, for the most part, be but remotely useful to mankind. I have purchased knowledge at the expense of all the common comforts of life: I have missed the endearing elegance of female friendship, and the happy commerce of domestic tenderness. If I have obtained any pre-rogatives above other students, they have been accompanied with fear, dis-quiet, and scrupulosity; but even of these prerogatives, whatever they were, I have, since my thoughts have been diversified by more intercourse with the world, begun to question the reality. When I have been for a few days lost in pleasing dissipation, I am always tempted to think that my inquiries have ended in error, and that I have suffered much, and suffered it in vain."

Imlac was delighted to find that the sage's understanding was breaking through its mists, and resolved to detain him from the planets till he should forget his task of ruling them, and reason should recover its original influence.

From this time the astronomer was received into familiar friendship, and partook of all their projects and pleasures: his respect kept him attentive, and the activity of Rasselas did not leave much time unengaged. Something was always to be done; the day was spent in making observations which furnished talk for the evening, and the evening was closed with a scheme for the morrow.

The sage confessed to Imlac, that since he had mingled in the gay tumults of life, and divided his hours by a succession of amusements, he found the conviction of his authority over the skies fade gradually from his mind, and began to trust less to an opinion which he never could prove to others, and which he now found subject to variation from causes in which reason had no part. "If I am accidentally left alone for a few hours," said he, "my inveterate persuasion rushes upon my soul, and my thoughts are chained down by some irresistible violence, but they are soon disentangled by the prince's conversa-tion, and instantaneously released at the entrance of Pekuah. I am like a man habitually afraid of specters, who is set at ease by a lamp, and wonders at the dread which harassed him in the dark, yet, if his lamp be extinguished, feels again the terrors which he knows that when it is light he shall feel no more. But I am sometimes afraid lest I indulge my quiet by criminal negligence, and voluntarily forget the great charge with which I am intrusted. If I favor myself in a known error, or am determined by my own ease in a doubtful question of this importance, how dreadful is my crime!"

"No disease of the imagination," answered Imlac, "is so difficult of cure, as that which is complicated with the dread of guilt: fancy and conscience then act interchangeably upon us, and so often shift their places, that the illusions of one are not distinguished from the dictates of the other. If fancy presents images not moral or religious, the mind drives them away when they give it pain, but when melancholic notions take the form of duty, they lay hold on the faculties without opposition, because we are afraid to exclude or banish them. For this reason the superstitious are often melancholy, and the melan-choly almost always superstitious.

"But do not let the suggestions of timidity overpower your better reason: the danger of neglect can be but as the probability of the obligation, which, when you consider it with freedom, you find very little, and that little growing every day less. Open your heart to the influence of the light, which, from time to time, breaks in upon you: when scruples importune you, which you in your lucid moments know to be vain, do not stand to parley, but fly to business or to Pekuah, and keep this thought always prevalent, that you are only one atom of the mass of humanity, and have neither such virtue nor vice, as that you should be singled out for supernatural favors or afflictions."

Chapter 47. The Prince Enters, and Brings a New Topic

"All this," said the astronomer, "I have often thought, but my reason has been so long subjugated by an uncontrollable and overwhelming idea, that it durst not confide in its own decisions. I now see how fatally I betrayed my quiet, by suffering chimeras to prey upon me in secret; but melancholy shrinks from communication, and I never found a man before, to whom I could impart my troubles, though I had been certain of relief. I rejoice to find my own sentiments confirmed by yours, who are not easily deceived, and can have no motive or purpose to deceive. I hope that time and variety will dissipate the gloom that has so long surrounded me, and the latter part of my days will be spent in peace."

"Your learning and virtue," said Imlac, "may justly give you hopes."

Rasselas then entered with the princess and Pekuah, and inquired whether they had contrived any new diversion for the next day. "Such," said Nekayah, "is the state of life, that none are happy but by the anticipation of change: the change itself is nothing; when we have made it, the next wish is to change again. The world is not yet exhausted; let me see something tomorrow which I never saw before."

"Variety," said Rasselas, "is so necessary to content, that even the happy valley disgusted me by the recurrence of its luxuries; yet I could not forbear to reproach myself with impatience, when I saw the monks of St. Anthony support without complaint, a life, not of uniform delight, but uniform hardship."

"Those men," answered Imlac, "are less wretched in their silent convent than the Abyssinian princes in their prison of pleasure. Whatever is done by the monks is incited by an adequate and reasonable motive. Their labor supplies them with necessaries; it therefore cannot be omitted, and is certainly rewarded. Their devotion prepares them for another state, and reminds them of its approach, while it fits them for it. Their time is regularly distributed; one duty succeeds another, so that they are not left open to the distraction of unguided choice, nor lost in the shades of listless inactivity. There is a certain task to be performed at an appropriated hour; and their toils are cheerful, because they consider them as acts of piety, by which they are always advancing towards endless felicity."

"Do you think," said Nekayah, "that the monastic rule is a more holy and less imperfect state than any other? May not he equally hope for future happiness who converses openly with mankind, who succors the distressed by his charity, instructs the ignorant by his learning, and contributes by his industry to the general system of life; even though he should omit some of the mortifications which are practiced in the cloister, and allow himself such harmless delights as his condition may place within his reach?"

"This," said Imlac, "is a question which has long divided the wise, and perplexed the good. I am afraid to decide on either part. He that lives well in the world is better than he that lives well in a monastery. But perhaps everyone is not able to stem the temptations of public life; and if he cannot conquer, he may properly retreat. Some have little power to do good, and have likewise little strength to resist evil. Many are weary of their conflicts with adversity, and are willing to eject those passions which have long busied them in vain. And many are dismissed by age and diseases from the more laborious duties of society. In monasteries the weak and timorous may be happily sheltered, the weary may repose, and the penitent may meditate. Those retreats of prayer and contemplation have something so congenial to the mind of man, that, perhaps, there is scarcely one that does not purpose to close his life in pious abstraction with a few associates serious as himself."

"Such," said Pekuah, "has often been my wish, and I have heard the princess declare, that she should not willingly die in a crowd."

"The liberty of using harmless pleasures," proceeded Imlac, "will not be disputed; but it is still to be examined what pleasures are harmless. The evil of any pleasure that Nekayah can image is not in the act itself, but in its consequences. Pleasure, in itself harmless, may become mischievous, by endearing to us a state which we know to be transient and probatory,[1] and withdrawing our thoughts from that, of which every hour brings us nearer to the beginning, and of which no length of time will bring us to the end. Mortification is not virtuous in itself, nor has any other use, but that it disengages us from the allurements of sense. In the state of future perfection, to which we all aspire, there will be pleasure without danger, and security without restraint."

The princess was silent, and Rasselas, turning to the astronomer, asked him, whether he could not delay her retreat, by showing her something which she had not seen before.

"Your curiosity," said the sage, "has been so general, and your pursuit of knowledge so vigorous, that novelties are not now very easily to be found: but what you can no longer procure from the living may be given by the dead. Among the wonders of this country are the catacombs, or the ancient repositories, in which the bodies of the earliest generations were lodged, and where, by the virtue of the gums which embalmed them, they yet remain without corruption."

"I know not," said Rasselas, "what pleasure the sight of the catacombs can afford; but, since nothing else is offered, I am resolved to view them, and shall place this with many other things which I have done, because I would do something."

They hired a guard of horsemen, and the next day visited the catacombs. When they were about to descend into the sepulchral caves, "Pekuah," said the princess, "we are now again invading the habitations of the dead; I know that you will stay behind; let me find you safe when I return." "No, I will not be left," answered Pekuah; "I will go down between you and the prince."

They then all descended, and roved with wonder through the labyrinth of subterraneous passages, where the bodies were laid in rows on either side.

1. Serving as a trial or test.

Chapter 48. Imlac Discourses on the Nature of the Soul

"What reason," said the prince, "can be given, why the Egyptians should thus expensively preserve those carcasses which some nations consume with fire, others lay to mingle with the earth, and all agree to remove from their sight, as soon as decent rites can be performed?"

"The original of ancient customs," said Imlac, "is commonly unknown; for the practice often continues when the cause has ceased; and concerning superstitious ceremonies it is vain to conjecture; for what reason did not dictate reason cannot explain. I have long believed that the practice of embalming arose only from tenderness to the remains of relations or friends, and to this opinion I am more inclined, because it seems impossible that this care should have been general: had all the dead been embalmed, their repositories must in time have been more spacious than the dwellings of the living. I suppose only the rich or honorable were secured from corruption, and the rest left to the course of nature.

"But it is commonly supposed that the Egyptians believed the soul to live as long as the body continued undissolved, and therefore tried this method of eluding death."

"Could the wise Egyptians," said Nekayah, "think so grossly of the soul? If the soul could once survive its separation, what could it afterwards receive or suffer from the body?"

"The Egyptians would doubtless think erroneously," said the astronomer, "in the darkness of heathenism, and the first dawn of philosophy. The nature of the soul is still disputed amidst all our opportunities of clearer knowledge: some yet say, that it may be material, who, nevertheless, believe it to be immortal."

"Some," answered Imlac, "have indeed said that the soul is material, but I can scarcely believe that any man has thought it, who knew how to think; for all the conclusions of reason enforce the immateriality of mind, and all the notices of sense and investigations of science concur to prove the unconsciousness of matter.

"It was never supposed that cogitation is inherent in matter, or that every particle is a thinking being. Yet if any part of matter be devoid of thought, what part can we suppose to think? Matter can differ from matter only in form, density, bulk, motion, and direction of motion: to which of these, however varied or combined, can consciousness be annexed? To be round or square, to be solid or fluid, to be great or little, to be moved slowly or swiftly one way or another, are modes of material existence, all equally alien from the nature of cogitation. If matter be once without thought, it can only be made to think by some new modification, but all the modifications which it can admit are equally unconnected with cogitative powers."

"But the materialists," said the astronomer, "urge that matter may have qualities with which we are unacquainted."

"He who will determine," returned Imlac, "against that which he knows, because there may be something which he knows not; he that can set hypothetical possibility against acknowledged certainty, is not to be admitted among reasonable beings. All that we know of matter is, that matter is inert, senseless and lifeless; and if this conviction cannot be opposed but by referring us to something that we know not, we have all the evidence that human intellect can admit. If that which is known may be overruled by that which is unknown, no being, not omniscient, can arrive at certainty."

"Yet let us not," said the astronomer, "too arrogantly limit the Creator's power."

"It is no limitation of omnipotence," replied the poet, "to suppose that one thing is not consistent with another, that the same proposition cannot be at once true and false, that the same number cannot be even and odd, that cogitation cannot be conferred on that which is created incapable of cogitation."

"I know not," said Nekayah, "any great use of this question. Does that immateriality, which, in my opinion, you have sufficiently proved, necessarily include eternal duration?"

"Of immateriality," said Imlac, "our ideas are negative, and therefore obscure. Immateriality seems to imply a natural power of perpetual duration as a consequence of exemption from all causes of decay: whatever perishes, is destroyed by the solution of its contexture,[2] and separation of its parts; nor can we conceive how that which has no parts, and therefore admits no solution, can be naturally corrupted or impaired."

"I know not," said Rasselas, "how to conceive anything without extension: what is extended must have parts, and you allow, that whatever has parts may be destroyed."

"Consider your own conceptions," replied Imlac, "and the difficulty will be less. You will find substance without extension. An ideal form is no less real than material bulk: yet an ideal form has no extension. It is no less certain, when you think on a pyramid, that your mind possesses the idea of a pyramid, than that the pyramid itself is standing. What space does the idea of a pyramid occupy more than the idea of a grain of corn? or how can either idea suffer laceration? As is the effect such is the cause; as thought is, such is the power that thinks; a power impassive and indiscerptible."[3]

"But the Being," said Nekayah, "whom I fear to name, the Being which made the soul, can destroy it."

"He, surely, can destroy it," answered Imlac, "since, however unperishable, it receives from a superior nature its power of duration. That it will not perish by any inherent cause of decay, or principle of corruption, may be shown by philosophy; but philosophy can tell no more. That it will not be annihilated by him that made it, we must humbly learn from higher authority."

The whole assembly stood a while silent and collected. "Let us return," said Rasselas, "from this scene of mortality. How gloomy would be these mansions of the dead to him who did not know that he shall never die; that what now acts shall continue its agency, and what now thinks shall think on for ever. Those that lie here stretched before us, the wise and the powerful of ancient times, warn us to remember the shortness of our present state: they were, perhaps, snatched away while they were busy, like us, in the choice of life."

"To me," said the princess, "the choice of life is become less important; I hope hereafter to think only on the choice of eternity."

They then hastened out of the caverns, and, under the protection of their guard, returned to Cairo.

---

2. Dissolution of its structure.   3. Not to be separated.

Chapter 49. The Conclusion, in Which Nothing Is Concluded

It was now the time of the inundation of the Nile: a few days after their visit to the catacombs, the river began to rise.

They were confined to their house. The whole region being under water gave them no invitation to any excursions, and being well supplied with materials for talk, they diverted themselves with comparisons of the different forms of life which they had observed, and with various schemes of happiness which each of them had formed.

Pekuah was never so much charmed with any place as the convent of St. Anthony, where the Arab restored her to the princess, and wished only to fill it with pious maidens, and to be made prioress of the order; she was weary of expectation and disgust,[4] and would gladly be fixed in some unvariable state.

The princess thought that, of all sublunary things, knowledge was the best: she desired first to learn all sciences, and then purposed to found a college of learned women, in which she would preside, that, by conversing with the old and educating the young, she might divide her time between the acquisition and communication of wisdom, and raise up for the next age models of prudence, and patterns of piety.

The prince desired a little kingdom, in which he might administer justice in his own person, and see all the parts of government with his own eyes; but he could never fix the limits of his dominion, and was always adding to the number of his subjects.

Imlac and the astronomer were contented to be driven along the stream of life, without directing their course to any particular port.

Of these wishes that they had formed, they well knew that none could be obtained. They deliberated a while what was to be done, and resolved, when the inundation should cease, to return to Abyssinia.[5]

1759

Rambler No. 4

[On Fiction]

Saturday, *March* 31, 1750

Simul et jucunda et idonea dicere vitae.
—HORACE, *Art of Poetry*, 334
And join both profit and delight in one.
—CREECH

The works of fiction with which the present generation seems more particularly delighted are such as exhibit life in its true state, diversified only by accidents that daily happen in the world, and influenced by passions and qualities which are really to be found in conversing with mankind.

This kind of writing may be termed, not improperly, the comedy of romance, and is to be conducted nearly by the rules of comic poetry. Its prov-

4. Aversion.
5. Probably not, as is often suggested, to the Happy Valley, which the travelers earlier fled as a prison. Presumably the travelers return, with whatever wisdom they have gained but also with their cherished illusions, to share the common destiny of humankind.

ince is to bring about natural events by easy means, and to keep up curiosity without the help of wonder: it is therefore precluded from the machines[1] and expedients of the heroic romance, and can neither employ giants to snatch away a lady from the nuptial rites, nor knights to bring her back from captivity; it can neither bewilder its personages in deserts, nor lodge them in imaginary castles.

I remember a remark made by Scaliger upon Pontanus,[2] that all his writings are filled with the same images; and that if you take from him his lilies and his roses, his satyrs and his dryads, he will have nothing left that can be called poetry. In like manner, almost all the fictions of the last age will vanish if you deprive them of a hermit and a wood, a battle and a shipwreck.

Why this wild strain of imagination found reception so long in polite and learned ages, it is not easy to conceive; but we cannot wonder that while readers could be procured, the authors were willing to continue it; for when a man had by practice gained some fluency of language, he had no further care than to retire to his closet, let loose his invention, and heat his mind with incredibilities; a book was thus produced without fear of criticism, without the toil of study, without knowledge of nature, or acquaintance with life.

The task of our present writers is very different; it requires, together with that learning which is to be gained from books, that experience which can never be attained by solitary diligence, but must arise from general converse and accurate observation of the living world. Their performances have, as Horace expresses it, *plus oneris quanto veniae minus,*[3] little indulgence, and therefore more difficulty. They are engaged in portraits of which everyone knows the original, and can detect any deviation from exactness of resemblance. Other writings are safe, except from the malice of learning, but these are in danger from every common reader; as the slipper ill executed was censured by a shoemaker who happened to stop in his way at the Venus of Apelles.[4]

But the fear of not being approved as just copiers of human manners is not the most important concern that an author of this sort ought to have before him. These books are written chiefly to the young, the ignorant, and the idle, to whom they serve as lectures of conduct, and introductions into life. They are the entertainment of minds unfurnished with ideas, and therefore easily susceptible of impressions; not fixed by principles, and therefore easily following the current of fancy; not informed by experience, and consequently open to every false suggestion and partial account.

That the highest degree of reverence should be paid to youth, and that nothing indecent should be suffered to approach their eyes or ears, are precepts extorted by sense and virtue from an ancient writer by no means eminent for chastity of thought.[5] The same kind, though not the same degree, of caution, is required in everything which is laid before them, to secure them from unjust prejudices, perverse opinions, and incongruous combinations of images.

1. The technical term in neoclassical critical theory for the supernatural agents who intervene in human affairs in epic and tragedy.
2. Julius Caesar Scaliger (1484–1558) criticized the Latin poems of the Italian poet Jovianus Pontanus (1426–1503).
3. *Epistles* 2.1.170.

4. According to Pliny the Younger (*Naturalis Historia* 35.85), the Greek painter Apelles of Kos (4th century B.C.) corrected the drawing of a sandal after hearing a shoemaker criticize it as faulty, but when the flattered artisan dared to find fault with the drawing of a leg, the artist bade him "stick to his last."
5. Juvenal, *Satires* 14.1–58.

In the romances formerly written, every transaction and sentiment was so remote from all that passes among men that the reader was in very little danger of making any applications to himself; the virtues and crimes were equally beyond his sphere of activity; and he amused himself with heroes and with traitors, deliverers and persecutors, as with beings of another species, whose actions were regulated upon motives of their own, and who had neither faults nor excellencies in common with himself.

But when an adventurer is leveled with the rest of the world, and acts in such scenes of the universal drama as may be the lot of any other man, young spectators fix their eyes upon him with closer attention, and hope, by observing his behavior and success, to regulate their own practices when they shall be engaged in the like part.

For this reason these familiar histories may perhaps be made of greater use than the solemnities of professed morality, and convey the knowledge of vice and virtue with more efficacy than axioms and definitions. But if the power of example is so great as to take possession of the memory by a kind of violence, and produce effects almost without the intervention of the will, care ought to be taken that when the choice is unrestrained, the best examples only should be exhibited; and that which is likely to operate so strongly should not be mischievous or uncertain in its effects.

The chief advantage which these fictions have over real life is that their authors are at liberty, though not to invent, yet to select objects, and to cull from the mass of mankind those individuals upon which the attention ought most to be employed; as a diamond, though it cannot be made, may be polished by art, and placed in such situation as to display that luster which before was buried among common stones.

It is justly considered as the greatest excellency of art to imitate nature; but it is necessary to distinguish those parts of nature which are most proper for imitation: greater care is still required in representing life, which is so often discolored by passion or deformed by wickedness. If the world be promiscuously[6] described, I cannot see of what use it can be to read the account; or why it may not be as safe to turn the eye immediately upon mankind as upon a mirror which shows all that presents itself without discrimination.

It is therefore not a sufficient vindication of a character that it is drawn as it appears; for many characters ought never to be drawn: nor of a narrative that the train of events is agreeable to observation and experience; for that observation which is called knowledge of the world will be found much more frequently to make men cunning than good. The purpose of these writings is surely not only to show mankind, but to provide that they may be seen hereafter with less hazard; to teach the means of avoiding the snares which are laid by Treachery for Innocence, without infusing any wish for that superiority with which the betrayer flatters his vanity; to give the power of counteracting fraud without the temptation to practice it; to initiate youth by mock encounters in the art of necessary defense, and to increase prudence without impairing virtue.

Many writers, for the sake of following nature, so mingle good and bad qualities in their principal personages that they are both equally conspicuous; and as we accompany them through their adventures with delight, and are led

6. Indiscriminately.

by degrees to interest ourselves in their favor, we lose the abhorrence of their faults because they do not hinder our pleasure, or perhaps regard them with some kindness for being united with so much merit.

There have been men indeed splendidly wicked, whose endowments threw a brightness on their crimes, and whom scarce any villainy made perfectly detestable because they never could be wholly divested of their excellencies; but such have been in all ages the great corrupters of the world, and their resemblance ought no more to be preserved than the art of murdering without pain.

Some have advanced, without due attention to the consequences of this notion, that certain virtues have their correspondent faults, and therefore that to exhibit either apart is to deviate from probability. Thus men are observed by Swift to be "grateful in the same degree as they are resentful." This principle, with others of the same kind, supposes man to act from a brute impulse, and pursue a certain degree of inclination without any choice of the object; for, otherwise, though it should be allowed that gratitude and resentment arise from the same constitution of the passions, it follows not that they will be equally indulged when reason is consulted; yet, unless that consequence be admitted, this sagacious maxim becomes an empty sound, without any relation to practice or to life.

Nor is it evident that even the first motions to these effects are always in the same proportion. For pride, which produces quickness of resentment, will obstruct gratitude by unwillingness to admit that inferiority which obligation implies; and it is very unlikely that he who cannot think he receives a favor will acknowledge or repay it.

It is of the utmost importance to mankind that positions of this tendency should be laid open and confuted; for while men consider good and evil as springing from the same root, they will spare the one for the sake of the other, and in judging, if not of others at least of themselves, will be apt to estimate their virtues by their vices. To this fatal error all those will contribute who confound the colors of right and wrong, and, instead of helping to settle their boundaries, mix them with so much art that no common mind is able to disunite them.

In narratives where historical veracity has no place, I cannot discover why there should not be exhibited the most perfect idea of virtue; of virtue not angelical, nor above probability (for what we cannot credit, we shall never imitate), but the highest and purest that humanity can reach, which, exercised in such trials as the various revolutions of things shall bring upon it, may, by conquering some calamities and enduring others, teach us what we may hope, and what we can perform. Vice (for vice is necessary to be shown) should always disgust; nor should the graces of gaiety, nor the dignity of courage, be so united with it as to reconcile it to the mind. Wherever it appears, it should raise hatred by the malignity of its practices, and contempt by the meanness of its stratagems: for while it is supported by either parts or spirit, it will be seldom heartily abhorred. The Roman tyrant was content to be hated if he was but feared;[7] and there are thousands of the readers of romances willing to be thought wicked if they may be allowed to be wits. It is therefore to be steadily inculcated that virtue is the highest proof of understanding, and the

---

7. The Emperor Tiberius (see Suetonius's *Lives of the Caesars*).

only solid basis of greatness; and that vice is the natural consequence of narrow thoughts; that it begins in mistake, and ends in ignominy.

Rambler No. 60

[Biography]

Saturday, *October* 13, 1750

—*Quid sit pulchrum, quid turpe, quid utile, quid non,*
Plenius ac melius Chrysippo et Crantore dicit.
—HORACE, *Epistles*, 1.2. 3–4

Whose works the beautiful and base contain,
Of vice and virtue more instructive rules,
Than all the sober sages of the schools.
—FRANCIS

All joy or sorrow for the happiness or calamities of others is produced by an
act of the imagination, that realizes the event, however fictitious, or approximates it, however remote, by placing us, for a time, in the condition of
him whose fortune we contemplate; so that we feel, while the deception lasts,
whatever motions would be excited by the same good or evil happening to
ourselves.

Our passions are therefore more strongly moved, in proportion as we can
more readily adopt the pains or pleasure proposed to our minds, by recognizing them as once our own, or considering them as naturally incident to our
state of life. It is not easy for the most artful writer to give us an interest in
happiness or misery, which we think ourselves never likely to feel, and with
which we have never yet been made acquainted. Histories of the downfall of
kingdoms, and revolutions of empires, are read with great tranquility; the
imperial tragedy pleases common auditors only by its pomp of ornament, and
grandeur of ideas; and the man whose faculties have been engrossed by business, and whose heart never fluttered but at the rise or fall of stocks, wonders
how the attention can be seized, or the affections agitated, by a tale of love.

Those parallel circumstances, and kindred images to which we readily conform our minds, are, above all other writings, to be found in narratives of the
lives of particular persons; and therefore no species of writing seems more
worthy of cultivation than biography, since none can be more delightful or
more useful, none can more certainly enchain the heart by irresistible interest,
or more widely diffuse instruction to every diversity of condition.

The general and rapid narratives of history, which involve a thousand fortunes in the business of a day, and complicate innumerable incidents in one
great transaction, afford few lessons applicable to private life, which derives its
comforts and its wretchedness from the right or wrong management of things,
which nothing but their frequency makes considerable, *Parva si non fiunt*
quotidie, says Pliny,[1] and which can have no place in those relations which
never descend below the consultation of senates, the motions of armies, and
the schemes of conspirators.

---

1. Pliny the Younger, *Epistles* 3.1. Johnson translates the phrase in the preceding clause.

I have often thought that there has rarely passed a life of which a judicious and faithful narrative would not be useful. For, not only every man has in the mighty mass of the world great numbers in the same condition with himself, to whom his mistakes and miscarriages, escapes and expedients, would be of immediate and apparent use; but there is such an uniformity in the state of man, considered apart from adventitious and separable decorations and disguises, that there is scarce any possibility of good or ill, but is common to humankind. A great part of the time of those who are placed at the greatest distance by fortune, or by temper, must unavoidably pass in the same manner; and though, when the claims of nature are satisfied, caprice, and vanity, and accident, begin to produce discriminations and peculiarities, yet the eye is not very heedful or quick, which cannot discover the same causes still[2] terminating their influence in the same effects, though sometimes accelerated, sometimes retarded, or perplexed by multiplied combinations. We are all prompted by the same motives, all deceived by the same fallacies, all animated by hope, obstructed by danger, entangled by desire, and seduced by pleasure.

It is frequently objected to relations of particular lives, that they are not distinguished by any striking or wonderful vicissitudes. The scholar who passed his life among his books, the merchant who conducted only his own affairs, the priest whose sphere of action was not extended beyond that of his duty, are considered as no proper objects of public regard, however they might have excelled in their several stations, whatever might have been their learning, integrity, and piety. But this notion arises from false measures of excellence and dignity, and must be eradicated by considering, that in the esteem of uncorrupted reason, what is of most use is of most value.

It is, indeed, not improper to take honest advantages of prejudice, and to gain attention by a celebrated name; but the business of the biographer is often to pass slightly over those performances and incidents, which produce vulgar greatness, to lead the thoughts into domestic privacies, and display the minute details of daily life, where exterior appendages are cast aside, and men excel each other only by prudence and by virtue. The account of Thuanus[3] is, with great propriety, said by its author to have been written, that it might lay open to posterity the private and familiar character of that man, *cujus ingenium et candorem ex ipsius scriptis sunt olim semper miraturi*, whose candor and genius will to the end of time be by his writings preserved in admiration.

There are many invisible circumstances which, whether we read as inquirers after natural or moral knowledge, whether we intend to enlarge our science, or increase our virtue, are more important than public occurrences. Thus Sallust, the great master of nature, has not forgot, in his account of Catiline,[4] to remark that *his walk was now quick, and again slow,* as an indication of a mind revolving something with violent commotion. Thus the story of Melancthon[5] affords a striking lecture on the value of time, by informing us that when he made an appointment, he expected not only the hour, but the minute to be fixed, that the day might not run out in the idleness of suspense; and all the plans and enterprises of De Witt are now of less impor-

---

2. Always
3. Jacques-Auguste de Thou (1553–1617), an important French historian, of whom Nicholas Rigault wrote a brief biography, a sentence of which Johnson quotes and translates below.

4. Sallust, a Roman historian of the 1st century B.C., wrote an account of Catiline's conspiracy against the Roman state.
5. Camerarius wrote a life of Melancthon, a German theologian of the 16th century.

tance to the world, than that part of his personal character, which represents him as careful of his health, and negligent of his life.[6]

But biography has often been allotted to writers who seem very little acquainted with the nature of their task, or very negligent about the performance. They rarely afford any other account than might be collected from public papers, but imagine themselves writing a life when they exhibit a chronological series of actions or preferments; and so little regard the manners or behavior of their heroes, that more knowledge may be gained of a man's real character, by a short conversation with one of his servants, than from a formal and studied narrative, begun with his pedigree, and ended with his funeral.

If now and then they condescend to inform the world of particular facts, they are not always so happy as to select the most important. I know not well what advantage posterity can receive from the only circumstance by which Tickell has distinguished Addison from the rest of mankind, the irregularity of his pulse:[7] nor can I think myself overpaid for the time spent in reading the life of Malherbe, by being enabled to relate, after the learned biographer,[8] that Malherbe had two predominant opinions; one, that the looseness of a single woman might destroy all her boast of ancient descent; the other, that the French beggars made use very improperly and barbarously of the phrase *noble gentleman*, because either word included the sense of both.

There are, indeed, some natural reasons why these narratives are often written by such as were not likely to give much instruction or delight, and why most accounts of particular persons are barren and useless. If a life be delayed till interest and envy are at an end, we may hope for impartiality, but must expect little intelligence;[9] for the incidents which give excellence to biography are of a volatile and evanescent kind, such as soon escape the memory, and are rarely transmitted by tradition. We know how few can portray a living acquaintance, except by his most prominent and observable particularities, and the grosser features of his mind; and it may be easily imagined how much of this little knowledge may be lost in imparting it, and how soon a succession of copies will lose all resemblance of the original.

If the biographer writes from personal knowledge, and makes haste to gratify the public curiosity, there is danger lest his interest, his fear, his gratitude, or his tenderness, overpower his fidelity, and tempt him to conceal, if not to invent. There are many who think it an act of piety to hide the faults or failings of their friends, even when they can no longer suffer by their detection; we therefore see whole ranks of characters adorned with uniform panegyric, and not to be known from one another, but by extrinsic and casual circumstances. "Let me remember," says Hale, "when I find myself inclined to pity a criminal, that there is likewise a pity due to the country."[1] If we owe regard to the memory of the dead, there is yet more respect to be paid to knowledge, to virtue, and to truth.

6. Sir William Temple, characterizing the Dutch statesman John De Witt.
7. From Thomas Tickell's preface to Addision's *Works* (1721).
8. The life of the French poet François de Malherbe

(1555–1628) was written by Honorat de Racan.
9. Information.
1. From Gilbert Burnet's *Life and Death of Sir Matthew Hale* (1682).

A Dictionary of the English Language   Before Johnson, no standard dictionary of the English language existed. The want had troubled speakers of English for some time, both because Italian and French academies had produced major dictionaries of their own tongues and because, in the absence of any authority, English seemed likely to change utterly from one generation to another. Many eighteenth-century authors feared that their own language would soon become obsolete: as Alexander Pope wrote in *An Essay on Criticism*,

> Our sons their fathers' failing language see,
> And such as Chaucer is, shall Dryden be.

A dictionary could help retard such change, and commercially it would be a book that everyone would need to buy. In 1746 a group of London publishers commissioned Johnson, still an unknown author, to undertake the project. He hoped to finish it in three years; it took him nine. But the quantity and quality of work he accomplished, aided only by six part-time assistants, made him famous as "Dictionary Johnson." The *Dictionary* remained a standard reference book for one hundred years.

Johnson's achievement is notable in three respects: its size (forty thousand words), the wealth of illustrative quotations, and the excellence of the definitions. No earlier English dictionary rivaled the scope of Johnson's two large folio volumes. About 114,000 quotations, gathered from the best English writers from Sidney to the eighteenth century, exemplify the usage of words as well as their meanings. Above all, it was the definitions, however, that established the authority of Johnson's *Dictionary*. A small selection is only too likely to concentrate on a few amusing or notorious definitions, but the great majority are full, clear, and totally free from eccentricity. Indeed, many of them are still repeated in modern dictionaries. Language, Johnson knew, cannot be fixed once and for all; many of the words he defines have radically changed meaning since the eighteenth century. Yet Johnson did more than any person of his time to preserve the ideal of a standard English.

From A Dictionary of the English Language

From *Preface*

✳   ✳   ✳

A large work is difficult because it is large, even though all its parts might singly be performed with facility; where there are many things to be done, each must be allowed its share of time and labor, in the proportion only which it bears to the whole; nor can it be expected that the stones which form the dome of a temple should be squared and polished like the diamond of a ring.

Of the event of this work, for which, having labored it with so much application, I cannot but have some degree of parental fondness, it is natural to form conjectures. Those who have been persuaded to think well of my design will require that it should fix our language, and put a stop to those alterations which time and chance have hitherto been suffered to make in it without opposition. With this consequence I will confess that I flattered myself for a while;[1] but now begin to fear that I have indulged expectation which neither

---

1. Johnson's *Plan* (1747) had called for "a dictionary by which the pronunciation of our language may be fixed, and its attainment facilitated; by which its purity may be preserved, its use ascertained, and its duration lengthened."

reason nor experience can justify. When we see men grow old and die at a certain time one after another, from century to century, we laugh at the elixir that promises to prolong life to a thousand years; and with equal justice may the lexicographer be derided, who being able to produce no example of a nation that has preserved their words and phrases from mutability, shall imagine that his dictionary can embalm his language and secure it from corruption and decay, that it is in his power to change sublunary nature, or clear the world at once from folly, vanity, and affectation.

With this hope, however, academies have been instituted, to guard the avenues of their languages, to retain fugitives, and repulse intruders; but their vigilance and activity have hitherto been vain; sounds are too volatile and subtle for legal restraints; to enchain syllables, and to lash the wind, are equally the undertakings of pride, unwilling to measure its desires by its strength. The French language has visibly changed under the inspection of the academy;[2] the style of Amelot's translation of father Paul is observed by Le Courayer to be *un peu passé*;[3] and no Italian will maintain that the diction of any modern writer is not perceptibly different from that of Boccace, Machiavel, or Caro.[4]

Total and sudden transformations of a language seldom happen; conquests and migrations are now very rare: but there are other causes of change, which, though slow in their operation, and invisible in their progress, are perhaps as much superior to human resistance as the revolutions of the sky, or intumescence[5] of the tide. Commerce, however necessary, however lucrative, as it depraves the manners, corrupts the language; they that have frequent intercourse with strangers, to whom they endeavour to accommodate themselves, must in time learn a mingled dialect, like the jargon which serves the traffickers[6] on the Mediterranean and Indian coasts. This will not always be confined to the exchange, the warehouse, or the port, but will be communicated by degrees to other ranks of the people, and be at last incorporated with the current speech.

There are likewise internal causes equally forcible. The language most likely to continue long without alteration would be that of a nation raised a little, and but a little, above barbarity, secluded from strangers, and totally employed in procuring the conveniencies of life; either without books, or, like some of the Mahometan countries, with very few: men thus busied and unlearned, having only such words as common use requires, would perhaps long continue to express the same notions by the same signs. But no such constancy can be expected in a people polished by arts, and classed by subordination, where one part of the community is sustained and accommodated by the labor of the other. Those who have much leisure to think, will always be enlarging the stock of ideas, and every increase of knowledge, whether real or fancied, will produce new words, or combinations of words. When the mind is unchained from necessity, it will range after convenience; when it is left at large in the fields of speculation, it will shift opinions; as any custom is

---

2. The French academy, founded to purify the French language, had produced a dictionary in 1694; but revisions were necessary within a few years.
3. "A bit old-fashioned." Le Courayer's translation (1736) of Father Paolo Sarpi's *History of the Council of Trent* superseded Amelot's (1683).

4. Like Boccaccio (1313–1375) and Machiavelli (1469–1527), Annibale Caro (1507–1566) was a classic Italian stylist whose work had preceded the dictionary published in 1612 by the Italian academy.
5. Swelling.
6. Traders.

disused, the words that expressed it must perish with it; as any opinion grows popular, it will innovate speech in the same proportion as it alters practice.

As by the cultivation of various sciences, a language is amplified, it will be more furnished with words deflected from their original sense; the geometrician will talk of a courtier's zenith, or the eccentric virtue of a wild hero, and the physician of sanguine expectations and phlegmatic delays.[7] Copiousness of speech will give opportunities to capricious choice, by which some words will be preferred, and others degraded; vicissitudes of fashion will enforce the use of new, or extend the signification of known terms. The tropes[8] of poetry will make hourly encroachments, and the metaphorical will become the current sense: pronunciation will be varied by levity or ignorance, and the pen must at length comply with the tongue; illiterate writers will at one time or other, by public infatuation, rise into renown, who, not knowing the original import of words, will use them with colloquial licentiousness, confound distinction, and forget propriety. As politeness increases, some expressions will be considered as too gross and vulgar for the delicate, others as too formal and ceremonious for the gay and airy; new phrases are therefore adopted, which must, for the same reasons, be in time dismissed. Swift, in his petty treatise on the English language,[9] allows that new words must sometimes be introduced, but proposes that none should be suffered to become obsolete. But what makes a word obsolete, more than general agreement to forbear it? and how shall it be continued, when it conveys an offensive idea, or recalled again into the mouths of mankind, when it has once by disuse become unfamiliar, and by unfamiliarity unpleasing.

There is another cause of alteration more prevalent than any other, which yet in the present state of the world cannot be obviated. A mixture of two languages will produce a third distinct from both, and they will always be mixed, where the chief part of education, and the most conspicuous accomplishment, is skill in ancient or in foreign tongues. He that has long cultivated another language, will find its words and combinations crowd upon his memory; and haste or negligence, refinement or affectation, will obtrude borrowed terms and exotic expressions.

The great pest of speech is frequency of translation. No book was ever turned from one language into another, without imparting something of its native idiom; this is the most mischievous and comprehensive innovation; single words may enter by thousands, and the fabric of the tongue continue the same, but new phraseology changes much at once; it alters not the single stones of the building, but the order[1] of the columns. If an academy should be established for the cultivation of our style, which I, who can never wish to see dependence multiplied, hope the spirit of English liberty will hinder or destroy, let them, instead of compiling grammars and dictionaries, endeavor with all their influence to stop the license of translators, whose idleness and ignorance, if it be suffered to proceed, will reduce us to babble a dialect of France.

If the changes that we fear be thus irresistible, what remains but to acqui-

7. "Zenith" (the point of the sky directly overhead) and "eccentric" (deviating from the center) were originally astronomical and geometrical terms. "Sanguine" and "phlegmatic" once referred only to the physiological predominance of blood or phlegm.
8. "A change of a word from its original signification" (Johnson's Dictionary).
9. A Proposal for Correcting, Improving, and Ascertaining the English Tongue (1712). "Petty": little.
1. Architectural mode (Doric, etc.), which determines the style and proportions of columns.

esce with silence, as in the other insurmountable distresses of humanity? It remains that we retard what we cannot repel, that we palliate what we cannot cure. Life may be lengthened by care, though death cannot be ultimately defeated: tongues, like governments, have a natural tendency to degeneration; we have long preserved our constitution, let us make some struggles for our language.

In hope of giving longevity to that which its own nature forbids to be immortal, I have devoted this book, the labor of years, to the honor of my country, that we may no longer yield the palm of philology without a contest to the nations of the continent. The chief glory of every people arises from its authors: whether I shall add anything by my own writings to the reputation of English literature, must be left to time. Much of my life has been lost under the pressures of disease; much has been trifled away; and much has always been spent in provision for the day that was passing over me; but I shall not think my employment useless or ignoble, if by my assistance foreign nations, and distant ages, gain access to the propagators of knowledge, and understand the teachers of truth; if my labors afford light to the repositories of science, and add celebrity to Bacon, to Hooker, to Milton, and to Boyle.[2]

When I am animated by this wish, I look with pleasure on my book, however defective; and deliver it to the world with the spirit of a man that has endeavored well. That it will immediately become popular I have not promised to myself: a few wild blunders and risible absurdities, from which no work of such multiplicity was ever free, may for a time furnish folly with laughter, and harden ignorance in contempt; but useful diligence will at last prevail, and there never can be wanting some who distinguish desert;[3] who will consider that no dictionary of a living tongue ever can be perfect, since while it is hastening to publication, some words are budding, and some falling away; that a whole life cannot be spent upon syntax and etymology, and that even a whole life would not be sufficient; that he, whose design includes whatever language can express, must often speak of what he does not understand; that a writer will sometimes be hurried by eagerness to the end, and sometimes faint with weariness under a task, which Scaliger compares to the labors of the anvil and the mine;[4] that what is obvious is not always known, and what is known is not always present; that sudden fits of inadvertency will surprise vigilance, slight avocations[5] will reduce attention, and casual eclipses of the mind will darken learning; and that the writer shall often in vain trace his memory at the moment of need, for that which yesterday he knew with intuitive readiness, and which will come uncalled into his thoughts tomorrow.

In this work, when it shall be found that much is omitted, let it not be forgotten that much likewise is performed; and though no book was ever spared out of tenderness to the author, and the world is little solicitous to know whence proceeded the faults of that which it condemns; yet it may gratify curiosity to inform it, that the *English Dictionary* was written with little assistance of the learned, and without any patronage of the great; not in the soft obscurities of retirement, or under the shelter of academic bowers, but amidst

2. Richard Hooker wrote *The Laws of Ecclesiastical Polity* (1594–97), a famous defense of the Church of England. Robert Boyle (1627–1691) was a leading physicist and chemist. "Science": knowledge.
3. Merit.

4. Joseph Justus Scaliger (1540–1609), a great scholar and lexicographer, wrote Latin verses suggesting that criminals should be condemned to lexicography.
5. Whatever calls one aside.

inconvenience and distraction, in sickness and in sorrow: and it may repress the triumph of malignant criticism to observe, that if our language is not here fully displayed, I have only failed in an attempt which no human powers have hitherto completed. If the lexicons of ancient tongues, now immutably fixed, and comprised in a few volumes, be yet, after the toil of successive ages, inadequate and delusive; if the aggregated knowledge and cooperating diligence of the Italian academicians did not secure them from the censure of Beni;[6] if the embodied critics of France, when fifty years had been spent upon their work, were obliged to change its economy,[7] and give their second edition another form, I may surely be contented without the praise of perfection, which, if I could obtain, in this gloom of solitude, what would it avail me? I have protracted my work till most of those whom I wished to please have sunk into the grave,[8] and success and miscarriage are empty sounds: I therefore dismiss it with frigid tranquility, having little to fear or hope from censure or from praise.

[Some Definitions: A Small Anthology][9]

ANTHO'LOGY. *n.*
1. A collection of flowers.

To CANT. *v.*
   To talk in the jargon of particular professions, or in any kind of formal affected language, or with a peculiar and studied tone of voice.
> Men *cant* endlessly about *materia forma;* and hunt chimeras by rules of art, or dress up ignorance in words of bulk or sound, which may stop up the mouth of inquiry.—*Glanville's Scepsis Scientifica.*

ENTHU'SIASM. *n.*
1. A vain belief of private revelation; a vain confidence of divine favor or communication.
> *Enthusiasm* is founded neither on reason nor divine revelation, but rises from the conceits of a warmed or overweening brain.—*Locke.*

GE'NIUS. *n.*
1. The protecting or ruling power of men, places, or things.
> And as I awake, sweet music breathe,
> Sent by some spirit to mortals good,
> Or th' unseen *genius* of the wood.—*Milton.*

2. A man endowed with superior faculties.
3. Mental power or faculties.
4. Disposition of nature by which anyone is qualified for some peculiar employment.
5. Nature; disposition.

IMA'GINATION. *n.*
1. Fancy; the power of forming ideal pictures; the power of representing things absent to one's self or others.
2. Conception; image in the mind; idea.
3. Contrivance; scheme.

LEXICO'GRAPHER. *n.*
   A writer of dictionaries; a harmless drudge, that busies himself in tracing the original, and detailing the signification of words.

---

6. Paolo Beni's *L'Anticrusca* (1612) violently attacked the first edition of the *Vocabolario* (the Italian dictionary).
7. Organization.
8. Johnson's wife had died three years earlier.
9. Johnson's definitions include etymologies and illustrative quotations, some of which are omitted in this selection.

MELANCHO'LY. *n.*

1. A disease, supposed to proceed from a redundance of black bile.
2. A kind of madness, in which the mind is always fixed on one object.
3. A gloomy, pensive, discontented temper.

NA'TURE. *n.*

1. An imaginary being supposed to preside over the material and animal world.

> Thou, *nature*, art my goddess; to thy law
> My services are bound. —*Shakespeare.*

2. The native state or properties of anything, by which it is discriminated from others.
3. The constitution of an animated body.
4. Disposition of mind; temper.
5. The regular course of things.
6. The compass of natural existence.
7. Natural affection, or reverence; native sensations.
8. The state or operation of the material world.
9. Sort; species.
10. Sentiments or images adapted to nature, or comfortable to truth and reality.
11. Physics; the science which teaches the qualities of things.

> *Nature* and *nature's* laws lay hid in night,
> God said, Let Newton be, and all was light. —*Pope.*

NE'TWORK. *n.*

Anything reticulated or decussated, at equal distances, with interstices between the intersections.

OATS. *n.*

A grain, which in England is generally given to horses, but in Scotland supports the people.

PA'STERN. *n.*

1. The knee of an horse.[1]

PA'TRON. *n.*

1. One who countenances, supports, or protects. Commonly a wretch who supports with insolence, and is paid with flattery.

PE'NSION. *n.*

An allowance made to anyone without an equivalent. In England it is generally understood to mean pay given to a state hireling for treason to his country.[2]

SA'TIRE. *n.*

A poem in which wickedness or folly is censured. Proper *satire* is distinguished, by the generality of the reflections, from a *lampoon*, which is aimed against a particular person; but they are too frequently confounded.

TO'RY. *n.*

One who adheres to the ancient constitution of the state, and the apostolical hierarchy of the church of England, opposed to a whig.

> The knight is more a *tory* in the country than the town, because it more advances his interest. —*Addison.*

---

1. "A lady once asked him how he came to define *Pastern* the *knee* of a horse: instead of making an elaborate defense, as she expected, he at once answered, 'Ignorance, Madam, pure ignorance' " (Boswell).
2. In 1762 Johnson was awarded a pension, but he did not revise the definition in later editions.

WHIG. *n.*

2. The name of a faction.

> Whoever has a true value for church and state, should avoid the extremes of *whig* for the sake of the former, and the extremes of tory on the account of the latter. — *Swift.*

WIT. *n.*

1. The powers of the mind; the mental faculties; the intellects. This is the original signification.

2. Imagination; quickness of fancy.

3. Sentiments produced by quickness of fancy.

4. A man of fancy.

5. A man of genius.

6. Sense; judgment.

7. In the plural. Sound mind; intellect not crazed.

8. Contrivance; stratagem; power of expedients.

1755

The Preface to Shakespeare   This, the finest piece of Shakespeare criticism in the eighteenth century, is the culmination of a critical tradition that began with Nicholas Rowe's edition of the plays in 1709 (indeed with John Dryden's critical remarks on Shakespeare) and that was continued by subsequent editors, notably Alexander Pope, Lewis Theobald, and William Warburton. Johnson's topics are in the main the conventional ones of eighteenth-century Shakespeare criticism: Shakespeare as the poet of nature, not of learning; as the creator of memorable characters; and as a poet who supremely expresses and evokes the passions. Johnson follows this tradition in weighing Shakespeare's poetic virtues against his faults and finding that the virtues outweigh the faults. The *Preface* takes a fresh look not only at the plays but at the first principles of criticism. It is most original when Johnson attacks and dismisses the long-standing reverence in critical theory for the unities of time and place. By appealing to the experience of the playgoer, he demonstrates that, thanks to the imagination of the spectator, the playwright need not contain the action within a period of twenty-four hours or restrict it to one place throughout the drama.

Johnson's edition of Shakespeare also contained footnotes and brief introductions to each of the plays. We reprint here his afterwords on the two *Henry IV* plays.

From The Preface to Shakespeare

[*Shakespeare's Excellence. General Nature*]

That praises are without reason lavished on the dead, and that the honors due only to excellence are paid to antiquity, is a complaint likely to be always continued by those who, being able to add nothing to truth, hope for eminence from the heresies of paradox; or those who, being forced by disappointment upon consolatory expedients, are willing to hope from posterity what the present age refuses, and flatter themselves that the regard which is yet denied by envy will be at last bestowed by time.

Antiquity, like every other quality that attracts the notice of mankind, has undoubtedly votaries that reverence it not from reason but from prejudice.

Some seem to admire indiscriminately whatever has been long preserved, without considering that time has sometimes cooperated with chance; all perhaps are more willing to honor past than present excellence; and the mind contemplates genius through the shades of age, as the eye surveys the sun through artificial opacity. The great contention of criticism is to find the faults of the moderns and the beauties of the ancients. While an author is yet living we estimate his powers by his worst performance; and when he is dead we rate them by his best.

To works, however, of which the excellence is not absolute and definite, but gradual and comparative; to works not raised upon principles demonstrative and scientific, but appealing wholly to observation and experience, no other test can be applied than length of duration and continuance of esteem. What mankind have long possessed they have often examined and compared; and if they persist to value the possession, it is because frequent comparisons have confirmed opinion in its favor. As among the works of nature no man can properly call a river deep or a mountain high, without the knowledge of many mountains and many rivers; so in the productions of genius, nothing can be styled excellent till it has been compared with other works of the same kind. Demonstration[1] immediately displays its power and has nothing to hope or fear from the flux of years; but works tentative and experimental must be estimated by their proportion to the general and collective ability of man, as it is discovered in a long succession of endeavors. Of the first building that was raised, it might be with certainty determined that it was round or square, but whether it was spacious or lofty must have been referred to time. The Pythagorean scale of numbers[2] was at once discovered to be perfect; but the poems of Homer we yet know not to transcend the common limits of human intelligence, but by remarking that nation after nation, and century after century, has been able to do little more than transpose his incidents, new name his characters, and paraphrase his sentiments.

The reverence due to writings that have long subsisted arises, therefore, not from any credulous confidence in the superior wisdom of past ages, or gloomy persuasion of the degeneracy of mankind, but is the consequence of acknowledged and indubitable positions, that what has been longest known has been most considered, and what is most considered is best understood.

The poet of whose works I have undertaken the revision may now begin to assume the dignity of an ancient and claim the privilege of established fame and prescriptive veneration. He has long outlived his century, the term commonly fixed as the test of literary merit.[3] Whatever advantages he might once derive from personal allusions, local customs, or temporary opinions, have for many years been lost; and every topic of merriment or motive of sorrow which the modes of artificial life afforded him now only obscure the scenes which they once illuminated. The effects of favor and competition are at an end; the tradition of his friendships and his enmities has perished; his works support no opinion with arguments nor supply any faction with invectives; they can neither indulge vanity nor gratify malignity; but are read without any other reason than the desire of pleasure, and are therefore praised only as pleasure is obtained; yet, thus unassisted by interest or passion, they have passed through

---

1. "The highest degree of deducible or argumental evidence" (Johnson's *Dictionary*).
2. Pythagoras discovered the ratios that determine the
principal intervals of the musical scale.
3. Horace, *Epistles* 2.1.39.

variations of taste and changes of manners, and, as they devolved from one generation to another, have received new honors at every transmission.

But because human judgment, though it be gradually gaining upon certainty, never becomes infallible, and approbation, though long continued, may yet be only the approbation of prejudice or fashion, it is proper to inquire by what peculiarities of excellence Shakespeare has gained and kept the favor of his countrymen.

Nothing can please many, and please long, but just representations of general nature. Particular manners can be known to few, and therefore few only can judge how nearly they are copied. The irregular combinations of fanciful invention may delight awhile by that novelty of which the common satiety of life sends us all in quest; but the pleasures of sudden wonder are soon exhausted, and the mind can only repose on the stability of truth.

Shakespeare is, above all writers, at least above all modern writers, the poet of nature, the poet that holds up to his readers a faithful mirror of manners and of life. His characters are not modified by the customs of particular places, unpracticed by the rest of the world; by the peculiarities of studies or professions, which can operate but upon small numbers; or by the accidents of transient fashions or temporary opinions: they are the genuine progeny of common humanity, such as the world will always supply and observation will always find. His persons act and speak by the influence of those general passions and principles by which all minds are agitated and the whole system of life is continued in motion. In the writings of other poets a character is too often an individual: in those of Shakespeare it is commonly a species.

It is from this wide extension of design that so much instruction is derived. It is this which fills the plays of Shakespeare with practical axioms and domestic wisdom. It was said of Euripides[4] that every verse was a precept; and it may be said of Shakespeare that from his works may be collected a system of civil and economical prudence. Yet his real power is not shown in the splendor of particular passages, but by the progress of his fable[5] and the tenor of his dialogue; and he that tries to recommend him by select quotations will succeed like the pedant in Hierocles[6] who, when he offered his house to sale, carried a brick in his pocket as a specimen.

It will not easily be imagined how much Shakespeare excels in accommodating his sentiments to real life but by comparing him with other authors. It was observed of the ancient schools of declamation that the more diligently they were frequented, the more was the student disqualified for the world, because he found nothing there which he should ever meet in any other place. The same remark may be applied to every stage but that of Shakespeare. The theater, when it is under any other direction, is peopled by such characters as were never seen, conversing in a language which was never heard, upon topics which will never arise in the commerce of mankind. But the dialogue of this author is often so evidently determined by the incident which produces it, and is pursued with so much ease and simplicity, that it seems scarcely to claim the merit of fiction, but to have been gleaned by diligent selection out of common conversation and common occurrences.

4. The Greek tragic poet (ca. 480–406 B.C.). The observation is Cicero's.
5. Plot. "The series or contexture of events which constitute a poem epic or dramatic" (Johnson's *Diction-*

ary).
6. Hierocles of Alexandria, a Greek philosopher of the 5th century A.D.

Upon every other stage the universal agent is love, by whose power all good and evil is distributed and every action quickened or retarded. To bring a lover, a lady, and a rival into the fable; to entangle them in contradictory obligations, perplex them with oppositions of interest, and harass them with violence of desires inconsistent with each other; to make them meet in rapture, and part in agony; to fill their mouths with hyperbolical joy and outrageous sorrow; to distress them as nothing human ever was distressed; to deliver them as nothing human ever was delivered, is the business of a modern dramatist. For this, probability is violated, life is misrepresented, and language is depraved. But love is only one of many passions; and as it has no great influence upon the sum of life, it has little operation in the dramas of a poet who caught his ideas from the living world and exhibited only what he saw before him. He knew that any other passion, as it was regular or exorbitant, was a cause of happiness or calamity.

Characters thus ample and general were not easily discriminated and preserved; yet perhaps no poet ever kept his personages more distinct from each other. I will not say with Pope that every speech may be assigned to the proper speaker,[7] because many speeches there are which have nothing characteristical; but perhaps though some may be equally adapted to every person, it will be difficult to find that any can be properly transferred from the present possessor to another claimant. The choice is right when there is reason for choice.

Other dramatists can only gain attention by hyperbolical or aggravated characters, by fabulous and unexampled excellence or depravity, as the writers of barbarous romances invigorated the reader by a giant and a dwarf: and he that should form his expectations of human affairs from the play or from the tale would be equally deceived. Shakespeare has no heroes; his scenes are occupied only by men, who act and speak as the reader thinks that he should himself have spoken or acted on the same occasion; even where the agency is supernatural, the dialogue is level with life. Other writers disguise the most natural passions and most frequent incidents so that he who contemplates them in the book will not know them in the world: Shakespeare approximates[8] the remote, and familiarizes the wonderful; the event which he represents will not happen, but, if it were possible, its effects would probably be such as he has assigned; and it may be said that he has not only shown human nature as it acts in real exigencies, but as it would be found in trials to which it cannot be exposed.

This therefore is the praise of Shakespeare, that his drama is the mirror of life; that he who has mazed his imagination in following the phantoms which other writers raise up before him, may here be cured of his delirious ecstasies by reading human sentiments in human language, by scenes from which a hermit may estimate the transactions of the world, and a confessor predict the progress of the passions.

[Shakespeare's Faults. The Three Dramatic Unities]

Shakespeare with his excellencies has likewise faults, and faults sufficient to obscure and overwhelm any other merit. I shall show them in the propor-

7. In the preface to his edition of Shakespeare's plays (1725).   8. Brings near.

tion in which they appear to me, without envious malignity or superstitious veneration. No question can be more innocently discussed than a dead poet's pretensions to renown; and little regard is due to that bigotry which sets candor[9] higher than truth.

His first defect is that to which may be imputed most of the evil in books or in men. He sacrifices virtue to convenience, and is so much more careful to please than to instruct that he seems to write without any moral purpose. From his writings indeed a system of social duty may be selected, for he that thinks reasonably must think morally, but his precepts and axioms drop casually from him; he makes no just distribution of good or evil, nor is always careful to show in the virtuous a disapprobation of the wicked; he carries his persons indifferently through right and wrong, and at the close dismisses them without further care, and leaves their examples to operate by chance. This fault the barbarity of his age cannot extenuate; for it is always a writer's duty to make the world better, and justice is a virtue independent on time or place.

The plots are often so loosely formed that a very slight consideration may improve them, and so carelessly pursued that he seems not always fully to comprehend his own design. He omits opportunities of instructing or delighting which the train of his story seems to force upon him, and apparently rejects those exhibitions which would be more affecting for the sake of those which are more easy.

It may be observed that in many of his plays the latter part is evidently neglected. When he found himself near the end of his work, and in view of his reward, he shortened the labor to snatch the profit. He therefore remits his efforts where he should most vigorously exert them, and his catastrophe is improbably produced or imperfectly represented.

He had no regard to distinction of time or place, but gives to one age or nation, without scruple, the customs, institutions, and opinions of another, at the expense not only of likelihood but of possibility. These faults Pope has endeavored, with more zeal than judgment, to transfer to his imagined interpolators. We need not wonder to find Hector quoting Aristotle, when we see the loves of Theseus and Hippolyta combined with the Gothic mythology of fairies.[1] Shakespeare, indeed, was not the only violator of chronology, for in the same age Sidney, who wanted not the advantages of learning, has, in his *Arcadia*, confounded the pastoral with the feudal times, the days of innocence, quiet, and security with those of turbulence, violence, and adventure.

In his comic scenes he is seldom very successful when he engages his characters in reciprocations of smartness and contests of sarcasm; their jests are commonly gross, and their pleasantry licentious; neither his gentlemen nor his ladies have much delicacy, nor are sufficiently distinguished from his clowns by any appearance of refined manners. Whether he represented the real conversation of his time is not easy to determine: the reign of Elizabeth is commonly supposed to have been a time of stateliness, formality, and reserve; yet perhaps the relaxations of that severity were not very elegant. There must, however, have been always some modes of gaiety preferable to others, and a writer ought to choose the best.

In tragedy his performance seems constantly to be worse as his labor is

9. Kindness.   *Night's Dream*, respectively.
1. In *Troilus and Cressida* 2.2.166 and in *Midsummer*

more. The effusions of passion, which exigence forces out, are for the most part striking and energetic; but whenever he solicits his invention, or strains his faculties, the offspring of his throes is tumor,[2] meanness, tediousness, and obscurity.

In narration he affects a disproportionate pomp of diction and a wearisome train of circumlocution, and tells the incident imperfectly in many words which might have been more plainly delivered in few. Narration in dramatic poetry is naturally tedious, as it is unanimated and inactive, and obstructs the progress of the action; it should therefore always be rapid and enlivened by frequent interruption. Shakespeare found it an encumbrance, and instead of lightening it by brevity, endeavored to recommend it by dignity and splendor.

His declamations or set speeches are commonly cold and weak, for his power was the power of nature; when he endeavored, like other tragic writers, to catch opportunities of amplification and, instead of inquiring what the occasion demanded, to show how much his stores of knowledge could supply, he seldom escapes without the pity or resentment of his reader.

It is incident to him to be now and then entangled with an unwieldy sentiment which he cannot well express, and will not reject; he struggles with it awhile, and, if it continues stubborn, comprises it in words such as occur, and leaves it to be disentangled and evolved[3] by those who have more leisure to bestow upon it.

Not that always where the language is intricate the thought is subtle, or the image always great where the line is bulky; the equality of words to things is very often neglected, and trivial sentiments and vulgar[4] ideas disappoint the attention, to which they are recommended by sonorous epithets and swelling figures.

But the admirers of this great poet have most reason to complain when he approaches nearest to his highest excellence, and seems fully resolved to sink them in dejection and mollify them with tender emotions by the fall of greatness, the danger of innocence, or the crosses of love. What he does best, he soon ceases to do. He is not long soft and pathetic without some idle conceit or contemptible equivocation. He no sooner begins to move than he counteracts himself; and terror and pity, as they are rising in the mind, are checked and blasted by sudden frigidity.

A quibble[5] is to Shakespeare what luminous vapors are to the traveler: he follows it at all adventures; it is sure to lead him out of his way, and sure to engulf him in the mire. It has some malignant power over his mind, and its fascinations are irresistible. Whatever be the dignity or profundity of his disquisitions, whether he be enlarging knowledge or exalting affection, whether he be amusing[6] attention with incidents, or enchaining it in suspense, let but a quibble spring up before him, and he leaves his work unfinished. A quibble is the golden apple for which he will always turn aside from his career[7] or stoop from his elevation. A quibble, poor and barren as it is, gave him such delight that he was content to purchase it by the sacrifice of

2. Inflated grandeur, false magnificence.
3. Unfolded.
4. "Mean; low; being of the common rate" (Johnson's Dictionary).
5. Pun.
6. "To entertain with tranquility; to fill with thoughts that engage the mind, without distracting it" (John-

son's Dictionary).
7. Course of action; the ground on which a race is run. In Greek legend Atalanta refused to marry any man who could not defeat her in a foot race. Hippomenes won her by dropping, as he ran, three of the golden apples of the Hesperides, which she paused to pick up.

reason, propriety, and truth. A quibble was to him the fatal Cleopatra for which he lost the world, and was content to lose it.

It will be thought strange that in enumerating the defects of this writer, I have not yet mentioned his neglect of the unities; his violation of those laws which have been instituted and established by the joint authority of poets and critics.

For his other deviations from the art of writing, I resign him to critical justice without making any other demand in his favor than that which must be indulged to all human excellence: that his virtues be rated with his failings. But from the censure which this irregularity may bring upon him I shall, with due reverence to that learning which I must oppose, adventure to try how I can defend him.

His histories, being neither tragedies nor comedies, are not subject to any of their laws; nothing more is necessary to all the praise which they expect than that the changes of action be so prepared as to be understood; that the incidents be various and affecting, and the characters consistent, natural, and distinct. No other unity is intended, and therefore none is to be sought.

In his other works he has well enough preserved the unity of action. He has not, indeed, an intrigue regularly perplexed and regularly unraveled: he does not endeavor to hide his design only to discover it, for this is seldom the order of real events, and Shakespeare is the poet of nature: but his plan has commonly what Aristotle requires,[8] a beginning, a middle, and an end; one event is concatenated with another, and the conclusion follows by easy consequence. There are, perhaps, some incidents that might be spared, as in other poets there is much talk that only fills up time upon the stage; but the general system makes gradual advances, and the end of the play is the end of expectation.

To the unities of time and place he has shown no regard; and perhaps a nearer view of the principles on which they stand will diminish their value and withdraw from them the veneration which, from the time of Corneille,[9] they have very generally received, by discovering that they have given more trouble to the poet than pleasure to the auditor.

The necessity of observing the unities of time and place arises from the supposed necessity of making the drama credible. The critics hold it impossible that an action of months or years can be possibly believed to pass in three hours; or that the spectator can suppose himself to sit in the theater while ambassadors go and return between distant kings, while armies are levied and towns besieged, while an exile wanders and returns, or till he whom they saw courting his mistress shall lament the untimely fall of his son. The mind revolts from evident falsehood, and fiction loses its force when it departs from the resemblance of reality.

From the narrow limitation of time necessarily arises the contraction of place. The spectator who knows that he saw the first act at Alexandria cannot suppose that he sees the next at Rome, at a distance to which not the dragons of Medea[1] could, in so short a time, have transported him; he knows with certainty that he has not changed his place; and he knows that place cannot change itself, that what was a house cannot become a plain, that what was Thebes can never be Persepolis.

8. Poetics 7.
9. Pierre Corneille (1606–1684), the French play-wright, discussed the unities in his Discours des trois

unités (1660).
1. According to legend, Medea fled the scene of her crimes in a chariot drawn by dragons.

Such is the triumphant language with which a critic exults over the misery
of an irregular poet, and exults commonly without resistance or reply. It is
time, therefore, to tell him by the authority of Shakespeare that he assumes,
as an unquestionable principle, a position which, while his breath is forming
it into words, his understanding pronounces to be false. It is false that any
representation is mistaken for reality; that any dramatic fable in its materiality
was ever credible or, for a single moment, was ever credited.

The objection arising from the impossibility of passing the first hour at
Alexandria and the next at Rome supposes that when the play opens the spectator really imagines himself at Alexandria, and believes that his walk to the
theater has been a voyage to Egypt, and that he lives in the days of Antony and
Cleopatra. Surely he that imagines this may imagine more. He that can take
the stage at one time for the palace of the Ptolemies may take it in half an
hour for the promontory of Actium. Delusion, if delusion be admitted, has no
certain limitation; if the spectator can be once persuaded that his old acquaintances are Alexander and Caesar, that a room illuminated with candles is the
plain of Pharsalia or the bank of Granicus, he is in a state of elevation above
the reach of reason or of truth, and from the heights of empyrean poetry may
despise the circumscriptions of terrestrial nature. There is no reason why a
mind thus wandering in ecstasy should count the clock, or why an hour
should not be a century in that calenture[2] of the brain that can make the stage
a field.

The truth is that the spectators are always in their senses, and know, from
the first act to the last, that the stage is only a stage, and that the players are
only players. They came to hear a certain number of lines recited with just
gesture and elegant modulation. The lines relate to some action, and an action
must be in some place; but the different actions that complete a story may be
in places very remote from each other; and where is the absurdity of allowing
that space to represent first Athens, and then Sicily, which was always known
to be neither Sicily nor Athens but a modern theater?

By supposition, as place is introduced, time may be extended; the time
required by the fable elapses, for the most part, between the acts; for, of so
much of the action as is represented, the real and poetical duration is the
same. If, in the first act, preparations for war against Mithridates are represented to be made in Rome, the event of the war may, without absurdity, be
represented, in the catastrophe, as happening in Pontus; we know that there
is neither war nor preparation for war; we know that we are neither in Rome
nor Pontus, that neither Mithridates nor Lucullus are before us. The drama
exhibits successive imitations of successive actions; and why may not the second imitation represent an action that happened years after the first, if it be so
connected with it that nothing but time can be supposed to intervene? Time
is, of all modes of existence, most obsequious[3] to the imagination; a lapse of
years is as easily conceived as a passage of hours. In contemplation we easily
contract the time of real actions, and therefore willingly permit it to be contracted when we only see their imitation.

It will be asked how the drama moves if it is not credited. It is credited with
all the credit due to a drama. It is credited, whenever it moves, as a just picture
of a real original; as representing to the auditor what he would himself feel if

2. A delirium produced by tropical heat, which causes   a green field.
sailors to leap into the sea under the delusion that it is   3. "Obedient; compliant" (Johnson's *Dictionary*).

he were to do or suffer what is there feigned to be suffered or to be done. The reflection that strikes the heart is not that the evils before us are real evils, but that they are evils to which we ourselves may be exposed. If there be any fallacy, it is not that we fancy the players, but that we fancy ourselves, unhappy for a moment; but we rather lament the possibility than suppose the presence of misery, as a mother weeps over her babe when she remembers that death may take it from her. The delight of tragedy proceeds from our consciousness of fiction; if we thought murders and treasons real, they would please no more.

Imitations produce pain or pleasure, not because they are mistaken for realities, but because they bring realities to mind. When the imagination is recreated[4] by a painted landscape, the trees are not supposed capable to give us shade or the fountains coolness; but we consider how we should be pleased with such fountains playing beside us and such woods waving over us. We are agitated in reading the history of *Henry the Fifth*; yet no man takes his book for the field of Agincourt. A dramatic exhibition is a book recited with concomitants that increase or diminish its effect. Familiar comedy is often more powerful on the theater than in the page; imperial tragedy is always less. The humor of Petruchio may be heightened by grimace; but what voice or what gesture can hope to add dignity or force to the soliloquy of Cato?[5]

A play read affects the mind like a play acted. It is therefore evident that the action is not supposed to be real; and it follows that between the acts a longer or shorter time may be allowed to pass, and that no more account of space or duration is to be taken by the auditor of a drama than by the reader of a narrative, before whom may pass in an hour the life of a hero or the revolutions of an empire.

Whether Shakespeare knew the unities and rejected them by design or deviated from them by happy ignorance, it is, I think, impossible to decide and useless to inquire. We may reasonably suppose that, when he rose to notice, he did not want[6] the counsels and admonitions of scholars and critics, and that he at last deliberately persisted in a practice which he might have begun by chance. As nothing is essential to the fable but unity of action, and as the unities of time and place arise evidently from false assumptions, and, by circumscribing the extent of the drama, lessen its variety, I cannot think it much to be lamented that they were not known by him, or not observed: nor, if such another poet could arise, should I very vehemently reproach him that his first act passed at Venice and his next in Cyprus.[7] Such violations of rules merely positive[8] become the comprehensive genius of Shakespeare, and such censures are suitable to the minute and slender criticism of Voltaire.

> Non usque adeo permiscuit imis
> Longus summa dies, ut non, si voce Metelli
> Serventur leges, malint a Caesare tolli.[9]

Yet when I speak thus slightly of dramatic rules, I cannot but recollect how much wit and learning may be produced against me; before such authorities I am afraid to stand: not that I think the present question one of those that are

---

4. Delighted.
5. Petruchio is the hero of Shakespeare's comedy *The Taming of the Shrew*. In Addison's tragedy *Cato* (5.1), the hero soliloquizes on immortality shortly before committing suicide.
6. Lack.

7. As is the case in *Othello*.
8. Arbitrary; not natural.
9. Lucan, *Pharsalia* 3.138–140: "The course of time has not wrought such confusion that the laws would not rather be trampled on by Caesar than saved by Metellus."

to be decided by mere authority, but because it is to be suspected that these precepts have not been so easily received but for better reasons than I have yet been able to find. The result of my inquiries, in which it would be ludicrous to boast of impartiality, is that the unities of time and place are not essential to a just drama, that though they may sometimes conduce to pleasure, they are always to be sacrificed to the nobler beauties of variety and instruction; and that a play written with nice observation of critical rules is to be contemplated as an elaborate curiosity, as the product of superfluous and ostentatious art, by which is shown rather what is possible than what is necessary.

He that without diminution of any other excellence shall preserve all the unities unbroken deserves the like applause with the architect who shall display all the orders of architecture in a citadel without any deduction for its strength; but the principal beauty of a citadel is to exclude the enemy, and the greatest graces of a play are to copy nature and instruct life.* * *

[Henry IV]

None of Shakespeare's plays are more read than the first and second parts of *Henry the Fourth*. Perhaps no author has ever in two plays afforded so much delight. The great events are interesting, for the fate of kingdoms depends upon them; the slighter occurrences are diverting, and, except one or two, sufficiently probable; the incidents are multiplied with wonderful fertility of invention, and the characters diversified with the utmost nicety of discernment, and the profoundest skill in the nature of man.

The prince, who is the hero both of the comic and tragic part, is a young man of great abilities and violent passions, whose sentiments are right, though his actions are wrong; whose virtues are obscured by negligence, and whose understanding is dissipated by levity. In his idle hours he is rather loose than wicked, and when the occasion forces out his latent qualities, he is great without effort, and brave without tumult. The trifler is roused into a hero, and the hero again reposes in the trifler. This character is great, original, and just.[1]

Percy is a rugged soldier, choleric, and quarrelsome, and has only the soldier's virtues, generosity and courage.

But Falstaff, unimitated, unimitable Falstaff, how shall I describe thee? Thou compound of sense and vice; of sense which may be admired but not esteemed, of vice which may be despised, but hardly detested. Falstaff is a character loaded with faults, and with those faults which naturally produce contempt. He is a thief, and a glutton, a coward, and a boaster, always ready to cheat the weak, and prey upon the poor; to terrify the timorous and insult the defenseless. At once obsequious and malignant, he satirizes in their absence those whom he lives by flattering. He is familiar with the prince only as an agent of vice, but of this familiarity he is so proud as not only to be supercilious and haughty with common men, but to think his interest of importance to the duke of Lancaster. Yet the man thus corrupt, thus despicable, makes himself necessary to the prince that despises him, by the most pleasing of all qualities, perpetual gaiety, by an unfailing power of exciting laughter, which is the more freely indulged, as his wit is not of the splendid or ambitious kind, but consists in easy escapes and sallies of levity, which

1. Accurate, well grounded.

make sport but raise no envy. It must be observed that he is stained with no enormous or sanguinary crimes, so that his licentiousness is not so offensive but that it may be borne for his mirth.

The moral to be drawn from this representation is that no man is more dangerous than he that with a will to corrupt, hath the power to please; and that neither wit nor honesty ought to think themselves safe with such a companion when they see Henry seduced by Falstaff.

From LIVES OF THE POETS

From Cowley[1]

[Metaphysical Wit]

Wit, like all other things subject by their nature to the choice of man, has its changes and fashions, and at different times takes different forms. About the beginning of the seventeenth century appeared a race of writers that may be termed the metaphysical poets,[2] of whom in a criticism on the works of Cowley it is not improper to give some account.

The metaphysical poets were men of learning, and to show their learning was their whole endeavor; but, unluckily resolving to show it in rhyme, instead of writing poetry they only wrote verses, and very often such verses as stood the trial of the finger better than of the ear; for the modulation was so imperfect that they were only found to be verses by counting the syllables.

If the father of criticism[3] has rightly denominated poetry *tekhnē mimētikè, an imitative art*, these writers will without great wrong lose their right to the name of poets, for they cannot be said to have imitated anything: they neither copied nature nor life; neither painted the forms of matter nor represented the operations of intellect.

Those however who deny them to be poets allow them to be wits. Dryden confesses of himself and his contemporaries that they fall below Donne in wit, but maintains that they surpass him in poetry.[4]

If wit be well described by Pope as being "that which has been often thought, but was never before so well expressed,"[5] they certainly never attained nor ever sought it, for they endeavored to be singular in their thoughts, and were careless of their diction. But Pope's account of wit is undoubtedly erroneous; he depresses it below its natural dignity, and reduces it from strength of thought to happiness of language.

If by a more noble and more adequate conception that be considered as wit which is at once natural and new, that which though not obvious is, upon its

---

1. Abraham Cowley (1618–1667) was much admired during the middle of the 17th century. His reputation began to decline before 1700, but he was remembered as a writer of false wit, especially in his love poems *The Mistress*.
2. Presumably Johnson took this now common designation from a hint in Dryden's *A Discourse Concerning the Original and Progress of Satire*. Dryden con-

demned Donne because "he affects the metaphysics . . . and perplexes the minds of the fair sex with nice speculations of philosophy, when he should engage their hearts, and entertain them with the softnesses of love" (*Essays*, ed. W. P. Ker, 2.19).
3. Aristotle in his *Poetics*.
4. *A Discourse . . . of Satire* (Ker 2.102).
5. *An Essay on Criticism*, lines 297–298.

first production, acknowledged to be just; if it be that which he that never found it, wonders how he missed; to wit of this kind the metaphysical poets have seldom risen. Their thoughts are often new, but seldom natural; they are not obvious, but neither are they just;[6] and the reader, far from wondering that he missed them, wonders more frequently by what perverseness of industry they were ever found.

But wit, abstracted from its effects upon the hearer, may be more rigorously and philosophically considered as a kind of *discordia concors*;[7] a combination of dissimilar images, or discovery of occult resemblances in things apparently unlike. Of wit, thus defined, they have more than enough. The most heterogeneous ideas are yoked by violence together; nature and art are ransacked for illustrations, comparisons, and allusions; their learning instructs, and their subtlety surprises; but the reader commonly thinks his improvement dearly bought, and, though he sometimes admires, is seldom pleased.

From this account of their compositions it will be readily inferred that they were not successful in representing or moving the affections. As they were wholly employed on something unexpected and surprising, they had no regard to that uniformity of sentiment which enables us to conceive and to excite the pains and the pleasure of other minds: they never inquired what on any occasion they should have said or done, but wrote rather as beholders than partakers of human nature; as beings looking upon good and evil, impassive and at leisure; as Epicurean deities making remarks on the actions of men and the vicissitudes of life, without interest and without emotion. Their courtship was void of fondness and their lamentation of sorrow. Their wish was only to say what they hoped had been never said before.

Nor was the sublime more within their reach than the pathetic; for they never attempted that comprehension and expanse of thought which at once fills the whole mind, and of which the first effect is sudden astonishment, and the second rational admiration. Sublimity is produced by aggregation, and littleness by dispersion. Great thoughts are always general, and consist in positions not limited by exceptions, and in descriptions not descending to minuteness. It is with great propriety that subtlety, which in its original import means exility[8] of particles, is taken in its metaphorical meaning for nicety of distinction. Those writers who lay on the watch for novelty could have little hope of greatness; for great things cannot have escaped former observation. Their attempts were always analytic: they broke every image into fragments, and could no more represent by their slender conceits and labored particularities the prospects of nature or the scenes of life, than he who dissects a sunbeam with a prism can exhibit the wide effulgence of a summer noon.

What they wanted however of the sublime they endeavored to supply by hyperbole;[9] their amplification had no limits: they left not only reason but fancy behind them, and produced combinations of confused magnificence that not only could not be credited, but could not be imagined.

Yet great labor directed by great abilities is never wholly lost: if they frequently threw away their wit upon false conceits, they likewise sometimes struck out unexpected truth: if their conceits were farfetched, they were often

6. Exact, proper.
7. Literally, "a harmonious discord." Johnson is himself being witty in using this phrase, a familiar philosophical concept denoting the general harmony of God's creation despite its manifold and often contra-

dictory particulars.
8. Thinness, smallness.
9. An image heightened beyond reality (see Johnson's *Dictionary*).

worth the carriage.[1] To write on their plan it was at least necessary to read and think. No man could be born a metaphysical poet, nor assume the dignity of a writer by descriptions copied from descriptions, by imitations borrowed from imitations, by traditional imagery and hereditary similes, by readiness of rhyme and volubility of syllables.

1779

From Milton[1]

[Lycidas]

One of the poems on which much praise has been bestowed is Lycidas; of which the diction is harsh,[2] the rhymes uncertain, and the numbers unpleasing. What beauty there is, we must therefore seek in the sentiments and images. It is not to be considered as the effusion of real passion; for passion runs not after remote allusions and obscure opinions. Passion plucks no berries from the myrtle and ivy, nor calls upon Arethuse and Mincius, nor tells of "rough satyrs and fauns with cloven heel." Where there is leisure for fiction there is little grief.

In this poem there is no nature, for there is no truth; there is no art, for there is nothing new. Its form is that of a pastoral, easy, vulgar, and therefore disgusting:[3] whatever images it can supply are long ago exhausted; and its inherent improbability always forces dissatisfaction on the mind. When Cowley tells of Hervey that they studied together, it is easy to suppose how much he must miss the companion of his labors and the partner of his discoveries;[4] but what image of tenderness can be excited by these lines!

> We drove afield, and both together heard
> What time the grayfly winds her sultry horn,
> Battening our flocks with the fresh dews of night.

We know that they never drove afield, and that they had no flocks to batten; and though it be allowed that the representation may be allegorical, the true meaning is so uncertain and remote that it is never sought because it cannot be known when it is found.

Among the flocks and copses and flowers appear the heathen deities, Jove and Phoebus, Neptune and Aeolus, with a long train of mythological imagery, such as a college easily supplies. Nothing can less display knowledge or less exercise invention than to tell how a shepherd has lost his companion and must now feed his flocks alone, without any judge of his skill in piping; and how one god asks another god what is become of Lycidas, and how neither

---

1. In the *Life of Addison,* Johnson wrote: "A simile may be compared to lines converging at a point, and is more excellent as the lines approach from greater distance."

1. Johnson's treatment of Milton as man and poet gave great offense to many ardent Miltonians in his own day and damaged his reputation as a critic in the following century. He did not admire Milton's character, and he detested his politics and religion. But no one has praised *Paradise Lost* more handsomely. Especially offensive in the 19th century was his attack on *Lycidas.*

Johnson disliked modern pastorals, recognizing that the tradition had been worn threadbare. His views on the genre may be read in *Rambler* no. 36 and no. 37.
2. This notorious word does not mean "unmelodious," but "strained, forced, affected, or labored."
3. I.e., displeasing, because its stale conventionality made it "vulgar" by putting it within the reach of the many.
4. Cowley's *On the Death of Mr. William Hervey* (1656).

god can tell. He who thus grieves will excite no sympathy; he who thus praises will confer no honor.

This poem has yet a grosser fault. With these trifling fictions are mingled the most awful and sacred truths, such as ought never to be polluted with such irreverent combinations. The shepherd likewise is now a feeder of sheep, and afterwards an ecclesiastical pastor, a superintendent of a Christian flock. Such equivocations are always unskillful; but here they are indecent,[5] and at least approach to impiety, of which, however, I believe the writer not to have been conscious.

Such is the power of reputation justly acquired that its blaze drives away the eye from nice examination. Surely no man could have fancied that he read *Lycidas* with pleasure had he not known its author.

[*L'Allegro, Il Penseroso*]

Of the two pieces, *L'Allegro* and *Il Penseroso*, I believe opinion is uniform; every man that reads them, reads them with pleasure. The author's design is not, what Theobald[6] has remarked, merely to show how objects derived their colors from the mind, by representing the operation of the same things upon the gay and the melancholy temper, or upon the same man as he is differently disposed; but rather how, among the successive variety of appearances, every disposition of mind takes hold on those by which it may be gratified.

The *cheerful* man hears the lark in the morning; the *pensive* man hears the nightingale in the evening. The *cheerful* man sees the cock strut, and hears the horn and hounds echo in the wood; then walks "not unseen" to observe the glory of the rising sun or listen to the singing milkmaid, and view the labors of the plowman and the mower; then casts his eyes about him over scenes of smiling plenty, and looks up to the distant tower, the residence of some fair inhabitant: thus he pursues rural gaiety through a day of labor or of play, and delights himself at night with the fanciful narratives of superstitious ignorance.

The *pensive* man at one time walks "unseen" to muse at midnight, and at another hears the sullen curfew. If the weather drives him home he sits in a room lighted only by "glowing embers"; or by a lonely lamp outwatches the North Star to discover the habitation of separate souls, and varies the shades of meditation by contemplating the magnificent or pathetic scenes of tragic and epic poetry. When the morning comes, a morning gloomy with rain and wind, he walks into the dark trackless woods, falls asleep by some murmuring water, and with melancholy enthusiasm expects some dream of prognostication or some music played by aerial performers.

Both Mirth and Melancholy are solitary, silent inhabitants of the breast that neither receive nor transmit communication: no mention is therefore made of a philosophical friend or a pleasant companion. The seriousness does not arise from any participation of calamity, nor the gaiety from the pleasures of the bottle.

The man of *cheerfulness* having exhausted the country tries what "towered cities" will afford, and mingles with scenes of splendor, gay assemblies, and

5. Unbecoming, lacking in decorum.
6. Lewis Theobald (1688–1744), the editor of Shake- speare and the enemy of Pope.

nuptial festivities; but he mingles a mere spectator as, when the learned comedies of Jonson or the wild dramas of Shakespeare are exhibited, he attends the
theater.

The *pensive* man never loses himself in crowds, but walks the cloister or
frequents the cathedral. Milton probably had not yet forsaken the Church.

Both his characters delight in music; but he seems to think that cheerful
notes would have obtained from Pluto a complete dismission of Eurydice, of
whom solemn sounds only procured a conditional release.

For the old age of Cheerfulness he makes no provision; but Melancholy he
conducts with great dignity to the close of life. His Cheerfulness is without
levity, and his Pensiveness without asperity.

Through these two poems the images are properly selected and nicely distinguished, but the colors of the diction seem not sufficiently discriminated. I
know not whether the characters are kept sufficiently apart. No mirth can,
indeed, be found in his melancholy; but I am afraid that I always meet some
melancholy in his mirth. They are two noble efforts of imagination.

[*Paradise Lost*]

Those little pieces may be dispatched without much anxiety; a greater work
calls for greater care. I am now to examine *Paradise Lost,* a poem which,
considered with respect to design, may claim the first place, and with respect
to performance the second, among the productions of the human mind.

By the general consent of critics the first praise of genius is due to the writer
of an epic poem, as it requires an assemblage of all the powers which are
singly sufficient for other compositions. Poetry is the art of uniting pleasure
with truth, by calling imagination to the help of reason. Epic poetry undertakes to teach the most important truths by the most pleasing precepts, and
therefore relates some great event in the most affecting manner. History must
supply the writer with the rudiments of narration, which he must improve
and exalt by a nobler art, must animate by dramatic energy, and diversify by
retrospection and anticipation; morality must teach him the exact bounds and
different shades of vice and virtue; from policy and the practice of life he has
to learn the discriminations of character and the tendency of the passions,
either single or combined; and physiology must supply him with illustrations
and images. To put these materials to poetical use is required an imagination
capable of painting nature and realizing fiction. Nor is he yet a poet till he
has attained the whole extension of his language, distinguished all the delicacies of phrase, and all the colors of words, and learned to adjust their different
sounds to all the varieties of metrical modulation.

Bossu is of opinion that the poet's first work is to find a *moral,* which his
fable is afterwards to illustrate and establish.[7] This seems to have been the
process only of Milton: the moral of other poems is incidental and consequent; in Milton's only it is essential and intrinsic. His purpose was the most
useful and the most arduous: "to vindicate the ways of God to man"; to show
the reasonableness of religion, and the necessity of obedience to the Divine
Law.

---

7. Père le Bossu wrote a treatise on the epic poem, *Traité du Poëme Épique,* 1675, much admired during the late
17th and early 18th centuries.

To convey this moral there must be a *fable*, a narration artfully constructed, so as to excite curiosity and surprise expectation. In this part of his work Milton must be confessed to have equaled every other poet. He has involved in his account of the Fall of Man the events which preceded, and those that were to follow it: he has interwoven the whole system of theology with such propriety that every part appears to be necessary, and scarcely any recital is wished shorter for the sake of quickening the progress of the main action.

The subject of an epic poem is naturally an event of great importance. That of Milton is not the destruction of a city, the conduct of a colony, or the foundation of an empire. His subject is the fate of worlds, the revolutions of heaven and of earth; rebellion against the Supreme King raised by the highest order of created beings; the overthrow of their host and the punishment of their crime; the creation of a new race of reasonable creatures; their original happiness and innocence, their forfeiture of immortality, and their restoration to hope and peace.

Great events can be hastened or retarded only by persons of elevated dignity. Before the greatness displayed in Milton's poem all other greatness shrinks away. The weakest of his agents are the highest and noblest of human beings, the original parents of mankind; with whose actions the elements consented; on whose rectitude or deviation of will depended the state of terrestrial nature and the condition of all the future inhabitants of the globe.

Of the other agents in the poem, the chief are such as it is irreverence to name on slight occasions. The rest were lower powers;

> of which the least could wield
> Those elements, and arm him with the force
> Of all their regions;[8]

powers which only the control of Omnipotence restrains from laying creation waste, and filling the vast expanse of space with ruin and confusion. To display the motives and actions of beings thus superior, so far as human reason can examine them or human imagination represent them, is the task which this mighty poet has undertaken and performed.

In the examination of epic poems much speculation is commonly employed upon the *characters*. The characters in the *Paradise Lost* which admit of examination are those of angels and of man; of angels good and evil, of man in his innocent and sinful state.

Among the angels the virtue of Raphael is mild and placid, of easy condescension and free communication; that of Michael is regal and lofty, and, as may seem, attentive to the dignity of his own nature. Abdiel and Gabriel appear occasionally, and act as every incident requires; the solitary fidelity of Abdiel is very amiably painted.[9]

Of the evil angels the characters are more diversified. To Satan, as Addison observes, such sentiments are given as suit "the most exalted and most depraved being."[1] Milton has been censured by Clarke for the impiety which sometimes breaks from Satan's mouth. For there are thoughts, as he justly remarks, which no observation of character can justify, because no good man would willingly permit them to pass, however transiently, through his own

---

8. *Paradise Lost* 6.221. 1. *Spectator* 303.
9. *Paradise Lost* 5.803ff.

mind.[2] To make Satan speak as a rebel, without any such expressions as might taint the reader's imagination, was indeed one of the great difficulties in Milton's undertaking, and I cannot but think that he has extricated himself with great happiness. There is in Satan's speeches little that can give pain to a pious ear. The language of rebellion cannot be the same with that of obedience. The malignity of Satan foams in haughtiness and obstinacy; but his expressions are commonly general, and no otherwise offensive than as they are wicked.

The other chiefs of the celestial rebellion are very judiciously discriminated in the first and second books; and the ferocious character of Moloch appears, both in the battle and the council, with exact consistency.

To Adam and Eve are given during their innocence such sentiments as innocence can generate and utter. Their love is pure benevolence and mutual veneration; their repasts are without luxury and their diligence without toil. Their addresses to their Maker have little more than the voice of admiration and gratitude. Fruition left them nothing to ask, and Innocence left them nothing to fear.

But with guilt enter distrust and discord, mutual accusation, and stubborn self-defense; they regard each other with alienated minds, and dread their Creator as the avenger of their transgression. At last they seek shelter in his mercy, soften to repentance, and melt in supplication. Both before and after the Fall the superiority of Adam is diligently sustained.

Of the *probable* and the *marvelous*,[3] two parts of a vulgar epic poem which immerge the critic in deep consideration, the *Paradise Lost* requires little to be said. It contains the history of a miracle, of Creation and Redemption; it displays the power and the mercy of the Supreme Being: the probable therefore is marvelous, and the marvelous is probable. The substance of the narrative is truth; and as truth allows no choice, it is, like necessity, superior to rule. To the accidental or adventitious parts, as to every thing human, some slight exceptions may be made. But the main fabric is immovably supported.

It is justly remarked by Addison[4] that this poem has, by the nature of its subject, the advantage above all others, that it is universally and perpetually interesting. All mankind will, through all ages, bear the same relation to Adam and to Eve, and must partake of that good and evil which extend to themselves.

Of the *machinery*, so called from *theòs apò mēkhanēs*[5] by which is meant the occasional interposition of supernatural power, another fertile topic of critical remarks, here is no room to speak, because every thing is done under the immediate and visible direction of Heaven; but the rule is so far observed that no part of the action could have been accomplished by any other means.

Of *episodes*[6] I think there are only two, contained in Raphael's relation of the war in heaven and Michael's prophetic account of the changes to happen in this world. Both are closely connected with the great action; one was necessary to Adam as a warning, the other as a consolation.

To the completeness or *integrity* of the design nothing can be objected; it has distinctly and clearly what Aristotle requires, a beginning, a middle, and

2. John Clarke, *Essay upon Study* (1731).
3. Actions in an epic poem that are wonderful because they exceed the probable.
4. *Spectator* 273.
5. Aristotle, *Poetics* 15.10. *Deus ex machina*, the intervention of supernatural powers into the affairs of humans.
6. Incidental but related narratives within an epic poem. Johnson is citing *Paradise Lost* 5.577ff. and 11.334ff.

an end. There is perhaps no poem of the same length from which so little can be taken without apparent mutilation. Here are no funeral games, nor is there any long description of a shield. The short digressions at the beginning of the third, seventh, and ninth books might doubtless be spared; but superfluities so beautiful who would take away? or who does not wish that the author of the *Iliad* had gratified succeeding ages with a little knowledge of himself? Perhaps no passages are more frequently or more attentively read than those extrinsic paragraphs; and since the end of poetry is pleasure, that cannot be unpoetical with which all are pleased.

The questions, whether the action of the poem be strictly *one*,[7] whether the poem can be properly termed *heroic*, and who is the hero, are raised by such readers as draw their principles of judgment rather from books than from reason. Milton, though he entitled *Paradise Lost* only a "poem," yet calls it himself "heroic song."[8] Dryden, petulantly and indecently, denies the heroism of Adam because he was overcome; but there is no reason why the hero should not be unfortunate except established practice, since success and virtue do not go necessarily together. Cato is the hero of Lucan, but Lucan's authority will not be suffered by Quintilian to decide. However, if success be necessary, Adam's deceiver was at last crushed; Adam was restored to his Maker's favor, and therefore may securely resume his human rank.

After the scheme and fabric of the poem must be considered its component parts, the sentiments, and the diction.

The *sentiments*, as expressive of manners or appropriated to characters, are for the greater part unexceptionably just. Splendid passages containing lessons of morality or precepts of prudence occur seldom. Such is the original formation of this poem that as it admits no human manners till the Fall, it can give little assistance to human conduct. Its end is to raise the thoughts above sublunary cares or pleasures. Yet the praise of that fortitude, with which Abdiel maintained his singularity of virtue against the scorn of multitudes, may be accommodated to all times; and Raphael's reproof of Adam's curiosity after the planetary motions, with the answer returned by Adam, may be confidently opposed to any rule of life which any poet has delivered.[9]

The thoughts which are occasionally called forth in the progress are such as could only be produced by an imagination in the highest degree fervid and active, to which materials were supplied by incessant study and unlimited curiosity. The heat of Milton's mind might be said to sublimate his learning, to throw off into his work the spirit of science,[1] unmingled with its grosser parts.

He had considered creation in its whole extent, and his descriptions are therefore learned. He had accustomed his imagination to unrestrained indulgence, and his conceptions therefore were extensive. The characteristic quality of his poem is sublimity. He sometimes descends to the elegant, but his element is the great. He can occasionally invest himself with grace; but his natural port is gigantic loftiness. He can please when pleasure is required; but it is his peculiar power to astonish.

He seems to have been well acquainted with his own genius, and to know what it was that Nature had bestowed upon him more bountifully than upon

7. I.e., a single action dealing with a single character.
8. *Paradise Lost* 9.25.
9. *Paradise Lost* 8.65ff.
1. Knowledge.

others; the power of displaying the vast, illuminating the splendid, enforcing the awful, darkening the gloomy, and aggravating the dreadful: he therefore chose a subject on which too much could not be said, on which he might tire his fancy without the censure of extravagance.

*   *   *

The defects and faults of *Paradise Lost*, for faults and defects every work of man must have, it is the business of impartial criticism to discover. As in displaying the excellence of Milton I have not made long quotations, because of selecting beauties there had been no end, I shall in the same general manner mention that which seems to deserve censure; for what Englishman can take delight in transcribing passages, which, if they lessen the reputation of Milton, diminish in some degree the honor of our country?

*   *   *

The plan of *Paradise Lost* has this inconvenience, that it comprises neither human actions nor human manners. The man and woman who act and suffer are in a state which no other man or woman can ever know. The reader finds no transaction in which he can be engaged, beholds no condition in which he can by any effort of imagination place himself; he has, therefore, little natural curiosity or sympathy.

We all, indeed, feel the effects of Adam's disobedience; we all sin like Adam, and like him must all bewail our offenses; we have restless and insidious enemies in the fallen angels, and in the blessed spirits we have guardians and friends; in the Redemption of mankind we hope to be included: in the description of heaven and hell we are surely interested, as we are all to reside hereafter either in the regions of horror or of bliss.

But these truths are too important to be new: they have been taught to our infancy; they have mingled with our solitary thoughts and familiar conversation, and are habitually interwoven with the whole texture of life. Being therefore not new they raise no unaccustomed emotion in the mind: what we knew before, we cannot learn; what is not unexpected, cannot surprise.

Of the ideas suggested by these awful scenes, from some we recede with reverence, except when stated hours require their association; and from others we shrink with horror, or admit them only as salutary inflictions, as counterpoises to our interests and passions. Such images rather obstruct the career of fancy than incite it.

Pleasure and terror are indeed the genuine sources of poetry; but poetical pleasure must be such as human imagination can at least conceive, and poetical terror such as human strength and fortitude may combat. The good and evil of Eternity are too ponderous for the wings of wit; the mind sinks under them in passive helplessness, content with calm belief and humble adoration.

Known truths however may take a different appearance, and be conveyed to the mind by a new train of intermediate images. This Milton has undertaken, and performed with pregnancy and vigor of mind peculiar to himself. Whoever considers the few radical positions which the Scriptures afforded him will wonder by what energetic operation he expanded them to such extent and ramified them to so much variety, restrained as he was by religious reverence from licentiousness of fiction.

Here is a full display of the united force of study and genius; of a great accumulation of materials, with judgment to digest and fancy to combine them: Milton was able to select from nature or from story, from ancient fable or from modern science, whatever could illustrate or adorn his thoughts. An accumulation of knowledge impregnated his mind, fermented by study and exalted by imagination.

*   *   *

But original deficience cannot be supplied. The want of human interest is always felt. *Paradise Lost* is one of the books which the reader admires and lays down, and forgets to take up again. None ever wished it longer than it is. Its perusal is a duty rather than a pleasure. We read Milton for instruction, retire harassed and overburdened, and look elsewhere for recreation; we desert our master, and seek for companions.

*   *   *

Dryden remarks that Milton has some flats among his elevations.[2] This is only to say that all the parts are not equal. In every work one part must be for the sake of others; a palace must have passages, a poem must have transitions. It is no more to be required that wit should always be blazing than that the sun should always stand at noon. In a great work there is a vicissitude[3] of luminous and opaque parts, as there is in the world a succession of day and night. Milton, when he has expatiated in the sky, may be allowed sometimes to revisit earth; for what other author ever soared so high or sustained his flight so long?

*   *   *

The highest praise of genius is original invention. Milton cannot be said to have contrived the structure of an epic poem, and therefore owes reverence to that vigor and amplitude of mind to which all generations must be indebted for the art of poetical narration, for the texture of the fable, the variation of incidents, the interposition of dialogue, and all the stratagems that surprise and enchain attention. But of all the borrowers from Homer Milton is perhaps the least indebted. He was naturally a thinker for himself, confident of his own abilities and disdainful of help or hindrance; he did not refuse admission to the thoughts or images of his predecessors, but he did not seek them. From his contemporaries he neither courted nor received support; there is in his writings nothing by which the pride of other authors might be gratified or favor gained, no exchange of praise or solicitation of support. His great works were performed under discountenance and in blindness, but difficulties vanished at his touch; he was born for whatever is arduous; and his work is not the greatest of heroic poems, only because it is not the first.

1779

From *Pope*

[*Pope's Intellectual Character. Pope and Dryden Compared*]

Of his intellectual character, the constituent and fundamental principle was good sense, a prompt and intuitive perception of consonance and propri-

---

2. Preface to *Sylvae*; see W. P. Ker (ed.), *Essays*, 1.268.   3. Change.

ety. He saw immediately, of his own conceptions, what was to be chosen, and what to be rejected; and, in the works of others, what was to be shunned, and what was to be copied.

But good sense alone is a sedate and quiescent quality, which manages its possessions well, but does not increase them; it collects few materials for its own operations, and preserves safety, but never gains supremacy. Pope had likewise genius; a mind active, ambitious, and adventurous, always investigating, always aspiring; in its widest searches still longing to go forward, in its highest flights still wishing to be higher; always imagining something greater than it knows, always endeavoring more than it can do.

To assist these powers, he is said to have had great strength and exactness of memory. That which he had heard or read was not easily lost; and he had before him not only what his own meditation suggested, but what he had found in other writers that might be accommodated to his present purpose.

These benefits of nature he improved by incessant and unwearied diligence; he had recourse to every source of intelligence, and lost no opportunity of information; he consulted the living as well as the dead; he read his compositions to his friends, and was never content with mediocrity when excellence could be attained. He considered poetry as the business of his life, and however he might seem to lament his occupation, he followed it with constancy: to make verses was his first labor, and to mend them was his last.

From his attention to poetry he was never diverted. If conversation offered anything that could be improved, he committed it to paper; if a thought, or perhaps an expression more happy than was common, rose to his mind, he was careful to write it; an independent distich was preserved for an opportunity of insertion, and some little fragments have been found containing lines, or parts of lines, to be wrought upon at some other time.

He was one of those few whose labor is their pleasure; he was never elevated to negligence, nor wearied to impatience; he never passed a fault unamended by indifference, nor quitted it by despair. He labored his works first to gain reputation, and afterwards to keep it.

Of composition there are different methods. Some employ at once memory and invention, and, with little intermediate use of the pen, form and polish large masses by continued meditation, and write their productions only when, in their own opinion, they have completed them. It is related of Virgil[1] that his custom was to pour out a great number of verses in the morning, and pass the day in retrenching exuberances and correcting inaccuracies. The method of Pope, as may be collected from his translation, was to write his first thoughts in his first words, and gradually to amplify, decorate, rectify, and refine them.

With such faculties and such dispositions, he excelled every other writer in *poetical prudence*; he wrote in such a manner as might expose him to few hazards. He used almost always the same fabric of verse; and, indeed, by those few essays which he made of any other, he did not enlarge his reputation. Of this uniformity the certain consequence was readiness and dexterity. By perpetual practice, language had in his mind a systematical arrangement; having always the same use for words, he had words so selected and combined as to be ready at his call. This increase of facility he confessed himself to have perceived in the progress of his translation.

1. By Suetonius in his brief life of the poet.

But what was yet of more importance, his effusions were always voluntary, and his subjects chosen by himself. His independence secured him from drudging at a task, and laboring upon a barren topic: he never exchanged praise for money, nor opened a shop of condolence or congratulation. His poems, therefore, were scarce ever temporary. He suffered coronations and royal marriages to pass without a song, and derived no opportunities from recent events, nor any popularity from the accidental disposition of his readers. He was never reduced to the necessity of soliciting the sun to shine upon a birthday, of calling the Graces and Virtues to a wedding, or of saying what multitudes have said before him. When he could produce nothing new, he was at liberty to be silent.

His publications were for the same reason never hasty. He is said to have sent nothing to the press till it had lain two years under his inspection: it is at least certain that he ventured nothing without nice examination. He suffered the tumult of imagination to subside, and the novelties of invention to grow familiar. He knew that the mind is always enamored of its own productions, and did not trust his first fondness. He consulted his friends, and listened with great willingness to criticism; and, what was of more importance, he consulted himself, and let nothing pass against his own judgment.

He professed to have learned his poetry from Dryden, whom, whenever an opportunity was presented, he praised through his whole life with unvaried liberality; and perhaps his character may receive some illustration, if he be compared with his master.

Integrity of understanding and nicety of discernment were not allotted in a less proportion to Dryden than to Pope. The rectitude of Dryden's mind was sufficiently shown by the dismission of his poetical prejudices, and the rejection of unnatural thoughts and rugged numbers. But Dryden never desired to apply all the judgment that he had. He wrote, and professed to write, merely for the people; and when he pleased others, he contented himself. He spent no time in struggles to rouse latent powers; he never attempted to make that better which was already good, nor often to mend what he must have known to be faulty. He wrote, as he tells us, with very little consideration; when occasion or necessity called upon him, he poured out what the present moment happened to supply, and, when once it had passed the press, ejected it from his mind; for when he had no pecuniary interest, he had no further solicitude.

Pope was not content to satisfy; he desired to excel, and therefore always endeavored to do his best: he did not court the candor,[2] but dared the judgment of his reader, and, expecting no indulgence from others, he showed none to himself. He examined lines and words with minute and punctilious observation, and retouched every part with indefatigable diligence, till he had left nothing to be forgiven.

For this reason he kept his pieces very long in his hands, while he considered and reconsidered them. The only poems which can be supposed to have been written with such regard to the times as might hasten their publication were the two satires of *Thirty-Eight*; of which Dodsley[3] told me that they were brought to him by the author, that they might be fairly copied. "Almost every line," he said, "was then written twice over; I gave him a clean transcript,

---

2. Kindness, sweetness of temper.   3. Robert Dodsley, the publisher.

which he sent some time afterwards to me for the press, with almost every line written twice over a second time."

His declaration, that his care for his works ceased at their publication, was not strictly true. His parental attention never abandoned them; what he found amiss in the first edition, he silently corrected in those that followed. He appears to have revised the *Iliad*, and freed it from some of its imperfections; and the *Essay on Criticism* received many improvements after its first appearance. It will seldom be found that he altered without adding clearness, elegance, or vigor. Pope had perhaps the judgment of Dryden; but Dryden certainly wanted the diligence of Pope.

In acquired knowledge, the superiority must be allowed to Dryden, whose education was more scholastic, and who before he became an author had been allowed more time for study, with better means of information. His mind has a larger range, and he collects his images and illustrations from a more extensive circumference of science. Dryden knew more of man in his general nature, and Pope in his local manners. The notions of Dryden were formed by comprehensive speculation, and those of Pope by minute attention. There is more dignity in the knowledge of Dryden, and more certainty in that of Pope.

Poetry was not the sole praise of either; for both excelled likewise in prose; but Pope did not borrow his prose from his predecessor. The style of Dryden is capricious and varied, that of Pope is cautious and uniform; Dryden obeys the motions of his own mind, Pope constrains his mind to his own rules of composition; Dryden is sometimes vehement and rapid; Pope is always smooth, uniform, and gentle. Dryden's page is a natural field, rising into inequalities, and diversified by the varied exuberance of abundant vegetation; Pope's is a velvet lawn, shaven by the scythe, and leveled by the roller.

Of genius, that power which constitutes a poet; that quality without which judgment is cold and knowledge is inert; that energy which collects, combines, amplifies, and animates; the superiority must, with some hesitation, be allowed to Dryden. It is not to be inferred that of this poetical vigor Pope had only a little, because Dryden had more; for every other writer since Milton must give place to Pope; and even of Dryden it must be said that if he has brighter paragraphs, he has not better poems. Dryden's performances were always hasty, either excited by some external occasion, or extorted by domestic necessity; he composed without consideration, and published without correction. What his mind could supply at call, or gather in one excursion, was all that he sought, and all that he gave. The dilatory caution of Pope enabled him to condense his sentiments, to multiply his images, and to accumulate all that study might produce, or chance might supply. If the flights of Dryden therefore are higher, Pope continues longer on the wing. If of Dryden's fire the blaze is brighter, of Pope's the heat is more regular and constant. Dryden often surpasses expectation, and Pope never falls below it. Dryden is read with frequent astonishment, and Pope with perpetual delight.

This parallel will, I hope, when it is well considered, be found just; and if the reader should suspect me, as I suspect myself, of some partial fondness for the memory of Dryden, let him not too hastily condemn me; for meditation and inquiry may, perhaps, show him the reasonableness of my determination.

1781

Lyric Poets of the Eighteenth Century

The eighteenth century is usually considered an age in which lyric poetry wasted away; and that may be true if we think of lyrics as songs, or as brief expressions of feelings, made for music. Most eighteenth-century poets aimed at a different sort of verse—more flexible, less formulaic. Traditional forms like the sonnet, closely tied to courtly conventions and the influence of Italy and France, seemed artificial to modern English readers. Not everyone knew how to sing a madrigal, but hymns were set to music in which a whole congregation could join. For the first time in history, moreover, most ordinary people could read and write. Hence the market for poetry changed; Prior and Pope were the first English poets to make a living exclusively by selling their poems, not by pleasing a king or a patron. Eighteenth-century poets reached out to a larger public with experimental, open forms, and wrote new kinds of lyrics.

Variety was especially prized. If university poets tended to imitate the classics, less privileged men and women dealt with the problems of daily life in occasional, often humorous verse. There was even a fad for "natural" poets: a thresher, a shoemaker, a milkmaid, and eventually a plowman, Robert Burns. Poets looked at the world around them for inspiration. One popular form, represented by Finch's "Nocturnal Reverie," Gray's "Elegy," and Collins's "Ode to Evening," explores the "pensive pleasures" of the mind by brooding on the English landscape. Despite their lack of personal display, such poems foreshadow the absorption with nature and the self on which the Romantics would build—a poetry of "sensibility." But no one mode can circumscribe the eighteenth-century lyric. Many experiments that started then live on in modern verse.

ANNE FINCH,
COUNTESS OF WINCHILSEA
1661–1720

Born into an ancient country family, Anne Kingsmill became a maid of honor at the court of Charles II. There she met Colonel Heneage Finch; in 1684 they married. During the short reign of James II they prospered at court, but at the king's fall in 1688 they were forced to retire, eventually settling on a beautiful family estate at Eastwell, in Kent, near the south coast of England. Here Colonel Finch became, in 1712, earl of Winchilsea, and here Lady Winchilsea wrote most of her poems, influenced, she said, by "the solitude and security of the country," and by "objects naturally inspiring soft and poetical imaginations." Her *Miscellany Poems on Several Occasions, Written by a Lady* were published in 1713; one poem, *The Spleen,* a description of the mysterious melancholic illness from which she and many other fashionable people suffered, achieved some fame. But her larger

reputation only began a century later, when Wordsworth praised her for keeping
her eye on external nature and for a style "often admirable, chaste, tender, and
vigorous."

The Introduction[1]

Did I my lines intend for public view,
How many censures would their faults pursue!
Some would, because such words they do affect,
Cry they're insipid, empty, uncorrect.
And many have attained, dull and untaught,   5
The name of wit, only by finding fault.[2]
True judges might condemn their want of wit;
And all might say, they're by a woman writ.
Alas! a woman that attempts the pen,
Such an intruder on the rights of men,   10
Such a presumptuous creature is esteemed,
The fault can by no virtue be redeemed.
They tell us we mistake our sex and way;
Good breeding, fashion, dancing, dressing, play
Are the accomplishments we should desire;   15
To write, or read, or think, or to enquire,
Would cloud our beauty, and exhaust our time,
And interrupt the conquests of our prime;
Whilst the dull manage of a servile house
Is held by some our utmost art and use.   20
       Sure 'twas not ever thus, nor are we told
Fables,[3] of women that excelled of old;
To whom, by the diffusive hand of heaven,
Some share of wit and poetry was given.
On that glad day on which the Ark[4] returned,   25
The holy pledge for which the land had mourned,
The joyful tribes attend it on the way,
The Levites do the sacred charge convey,
Whilst various instruments before it play;
Here holy virgins in the concert join,[5]   30
The louder notes to soften and refine,
And with alternate verse[6] complete the hymn divine.
       Lo! the young poet,[7] after God's own heart,
By Him inspired and taught the Muses' art,
Returned from conquest a bright chorus meets.   35
That sing his slain ten thousand in the streets.[8]
In such loud numbers[9] they his acts declare,
Proclaim the wonders of his early war,

1. This preface to Winchilsea's work was never published during her lifetime, for reasons explained in the
poem itself.
2. Pronounced *fawt*.
3. Idle stories or lies.
4. The Ark of the Covenant, restored to Jerusalem by
David (1 Chronicles 15).
5. Pronounced *jine*.

6. A series of couplets. The choir of virgins, not mentioned in Chronicles, is imagined by Winchilsea as
chanting every other line, responsively, as in some of
the Psalms.
7. David.
8. 1 Samuel 18.6–7.
9. Measures of music and verse.

That Saul upon the vast applause does frown,
And feels its mighty thunder shake the crown.   40
What can the threatened judgment now prolong?[1]
Half of the kingdom is already gone;
The fairest half, whose influence guides the rest,
Have David's empire o'er their hearts confessed.
    A woman here leads fainting Israel on,   45
She fights, she wins, she triumphs with a song,[2]
Devout, majestic, for the subject fit,
And far above her arms, exalts her wit,
Then to the peaceful, shady palm withdraws,
And rules the rescued nation with her laws.   50
    How are we fallen! fallen by mistaken rules,
And education's, more than nature's fools;
Debarred from all improvements of the mind,
And to be dull, expected and designed;[3]
And if some one would soar above the rest,   55
With warmer fancy and ambition pressed,
So strong the opposing faction still appears,
The hopes to thrive can ne'er outweigh the fears.
Be cautioned, then, my Muse, and still retired;
Nor be despised, aiming to be admired;   60
Conscious of wants, still with contracted wing,
To some few friends and to thy sorrows sing.
For groves of laurel thou wert never meant;
Be dark enough thy shades, and be thou there content.

1689?   1903

A Nocturnal Reverie

In such a night,[1] when every louder wind
Is to its distant cavern safe confined;
And only gentle Zephyr fans his wings,
And lonely Philomel,[2] still waking, sings;
Or from some tree, famed for the owl's delight,   5
She, hollowing clear, directs the wanderer right:
In such a night, when passing clouds give place,
Or thinly veil the heavens' mysterious face;
When in some river, overhung with green,
The waving moon and trembling leaves are seen;   10
When freshened grass now bears itself upright,
And makes cool banks to pleasing rest invite,
Whence springs the woodbind, and the bramble-rose,
And where the sleepy cowslip sheltered grows;
Whilst now a paler hue the foxglove takes,   15
Yet checkers still with red the dusky brakes:

1. What can now stave off the threatened judgment? Saul's doom ("judgment") had been prophesied: God would replace him with a better king.
2. The prophet and judge Deborah sang to praise the Lord for the victory she herself had brought about (Judges 4–5).

3. Marked out, intended.
1. This phrase, repeated twice below, echoes the same repeated phrase in the night piece that opens act 5 of *The Merchant of Venice*.
2. The nightingale.

When scattered glow-worms, but in twilight fine,
Show trivial beauties watch their hour to shine;
Whilst Salisbury[3] stands the test of every light,
In perfect charms, and perfect virtue bright: 20
When odors, which declined repelling day,
Through temperate air uninterrupted stray;
When darkened groves their softest shadows wear,
And falling waters we distinctly hear;
When through the gloom more venerable shows   25
Some ancient fabric,[4] awful in repose,
While sunburnt hills their swarthy looks conceal,
And swelling haycocks thicken up the vale:
When the loosed horse now, as his pasture leads,
Comes slowly grazing through the adjoining meads,   30
Whose stealing pace, and lengthened shade we fear,
Till torn-up forage in his teeth we hear:
When nibbling sheep at large pursue their food,
And unmolested kine rechew the cud;
When curlews cry beneath the village walls,   35
And to her straggling brood the partridge calls;
Their shortlived jubilee the creatures keep,
Which but endures, whilst tyrant man does sleep;
When a sedate content the spirit feels,
And no fierce light disturbs, whilst it reveals;   40
But silent musings urge the mind to seek
Something, too high for syllables to speak;
Till the free soul to a composedness charmed,
Finding the elements of rage disarmed,
O'er all below a solemn quiet grown,   45
Joys in the inferior world,[5] and thinks it like her own:
In such a night let me abroad remain,
Till morning breaks, and all's confused again;
Our cares, our toils, our clamors are renewed,
Or pleasures, seldom reached, again pursued.   50

                                                                    1713

MATTHEW PRIOR
1664–1721

Matthew Prior was a public man. His career as a diplomat culminated in his
negotiating for Oxford's Tory ministry the Treaty of Utrecht (1713), which ended
the War of the Spanish Succession. But after the fall of the Tories in 1714, he was
recalled from Paris and placed under house arrest for over a year, in the futile
hope that he would trump up evidence that Oxford was a traitor. Upon his release
Prior found himself out of place and broken in fortune. But the extraordinary
success of such friends as Swift and Pope in collecting subscriptions for his *Poems*

3. Probably Lady Salisbury, the daughter of a friend.
The sense is that this lady differs from others more trivial, who like glowworms look fine only one hour a day.

4. Edifice.
5. The world of nature (compared to the world of the
soul).

on *Several Occasions* (1718) secured him a profit of four thousand guineas, a very large sum at that time, which enabled him to end his life in comfort. Prior's poetry was the by-product of a busy life—"the fruits of [his] vacant hours," as he once wrote. As a lyric poet he stands at the end of the long tradition of *vers de société*, such as was written by what Alexander Pope called the "mob of gentlemen who wrote with ease" at the courts of Charles and James. But his grace and simplicity are the effects of studied art. William Cowper admired Prior's ability to "make verse speak the language of prose, without being prosaic—to marshal the words of it in such an order as they might naturally take in falling from the lips of an extemporary speaker, yet without meanness, harmoniously, elegantly, and without seeming to displace a syllable for the sake of the rhyme."

A True Maid

> "No, no; for my virginity,
>   When I lose that," says Rose, "I'll die."
> "Behind the elms, last night," cried Dick,
>   "Rose, were you not extremely sick?"

                                                                          1718

A Better Answer

To Cloe Jealous

Dear Cloe, how blubbered is that pretty face!
  Thy cheek all on fire, and thy hair all uncurled!
Prithee quit this caprice; and (as old Falstaff says)
  Let us e'en talk a little like folks of this world.[1]

How canst thou presume thou hast leave to destroy   5
  The beauties which Venus but lent to thy keeping?
Those looks were designed to inspire love and joy;
  More ord'nary eyes may serve people for weeping.

To be vexed at a trifle or two that I writ,
  Your judgment at once and my passion you wrong: 10
You take that for fact which will scarce be found wit:
  Od's life! must one swear to the truth of a song?

What I speak, my fair Cloe, and what I write, shows
  The difference there is betwixt nature and art;
I court others in verse, but I love thee in prose;   15
  And they have my whimsies, but thou hast my heart.

The god of us verse-men (you know, child) the Sun,
  How after his journeys he sets up his rest;
If at morning o'er earth 'tis his fancy to run,
  At night he reclines on his Thetis's breast.[2]   20

1. Cf. 2 *Henry IV* 5.3.101–102.
2. Apollo, god of poetry and of the sun, is said to recline at night on the breast of Thetis, one of the Nereids or sea spirits, because the sun seems to sink into the western ocean.

So when I am wearied with wandering all day,
    To thee, my delight, in the evening I come;
No matter what beauties I saw in my way—
    They were but my visits, but thou art my home.

Then finish, dear Cloe, this pastoral war;   25
    And let us like Horace and Lydia agree:[3]
For thou art a girl as much brighter than her,
    As he was a poet sublimer than me.

                                                                    1718

3. In Horace, *Odes* 3.9, the poet, who has been dallying with a girl named Cloe, makes up with Lydia, his former love.

LADY MARY WORTLEY MONTAGU
1689–1762

In her early teens Lady Mary Pierrepont did something that well-bred young women were not supposed to do: she secretly taught herself Latin. The act reveals many traits that would characterize her as a mature woman: curiosity, love of learning, intelligence, ambition, and independence of mind. The eldest daughter of a wealthy Whig peer, she grew up amid a glittering London circle that included Addison, Steele, Congreve, and later Pope and Gay. But she was not content to live the life of a dutiful aristocratic daughter. Unlike most women in her time, she married for love, and when her husband, Edward Wortley Montagu, was appointed ambassador to Constantinople in 1716, she took the opportunity of traveling through Europe, studying the language and customs of Turkey, and even visiting harems; her "Turkish Letters," published in 1763, would establish her as one of the great letter writers in English. She also pioneered in introducing smallpox inoculation to England. Returning home in 1718, she spent unhappy years that included bitter political quarrels with Pope (who satirized her as "Sappho" in *Epistle 2. To a Lady*) and the gradual failure of her marriage. Then she fell in love with a young Italian author, Francesco Algarotti. In 1739 she traveled to Italy hoping to see him; but the passion that had kindled in their letters was quenched when he failed to join her. She spent the rest of her life abroad, and died soon after returning to London in 1762. Montagu is remembered chiefly for her letters, but was also admired in her own time as a poet. Her verse, though often casual, reveals the strong mind of a woman who is not willing to accept the stereotypes imposed on her by men and who insists on preserving her freedom of choice. Her sexual candor and punishing wit demand respect; and the poems, like Montagu herself, are never dull.

The Lover: A Ballad

At length, by so much importunity pressed,
Take, (Molly),[1] at once, the inside of my breast;

1. Molly Skerrett, a friend of Lady Mary, was the mistress of Sir Robert Walpole. The ideal "lover" of the title, however, is not to be identified with any particular person.

This stupid indifference so often you blame
Is not owing to nature, to fear, or to shame;
I am not as cold as a Virgin in lead,[2]   5
Nor is Sunday's sermon so strong in my head;
I know but too well how time flies along,
That we live but few years and yet fewer are young.

But I hate to be cheated, and never will buy
Long years of repentance for moments of joy.   10
Oh was there a man (but where shall I find
Good sense and good nature so equally joined?)
Would value his pleasure, contribute to mine,
Not meanly would boast, nor lewdly design,[3]
Not over severe, yet not stupidly vain,   15
For I would have the power though not give the pain;

No pedant yet learnèd, not rakehelly gay
Or laughing because he has nothing to say,
To all my whole sex obliging and free,
Yet never be fond of any but me;   20
In public preserve the decorums are just,
And show in his eyes he is true to his trust,
Then rarely approach, and respectfully bow,
Yet not fulsomely pert, nor yet foppishly low.

But when the long hours of public are past   25
And we meet with champagne and a chicken at last,
May every fond pleasure that hour endear,
Be banished afar both discretion and fear,
Forgetting or scorning the airs of the crowd
He may cease to be formal, and I to be proud,   30
Till lost in the joy we confess that we live,
And he may be rude, and yet I may forgive.

And that my delight may be solidly fixed,
Let the friend and the lover be handsomely mixed,
In whose tender bosom my soul might confide,   35
Whose kindness can sooth me, whose counsel could guide.
From such a dear lover as here I describe
No danger should fright me, no millions should bribe;
But till this astonishing creature I know,
As I long have lived chaste, I will keep myself so.   40

I never will share with the wanton coquette,
Or be caught by a vain affectation of wit.
The toasters and songsters may try all their art
But never shall enter the pass of my heart.
I loathe the lewd rake, the dressed fopling despise;   45
Before such pursuers the nice[4] virgin flies;

---

2. I.e., an image of the Virgin Mary, either as a leaden   3. Plot.
statue or as a stained-glass window framed in lead.   4. Fastidious.

And as Ovid has sweetly in parables told
We harden like trees, and like rivers are cold.[5]

                                                                                    1747

Epistle from Mrs. Yonge to Her Husband[1]

Think not this paper comes with vain pretense
To move your pity, or to mourn th' offense.
Too well I know that hard obdurate heart;
No softening mercy there will take my part,
Nor can a woman's arguments prevail,   5
When even your patron's wise example fails.[2]
But this last privilege I still retain;
Th' oppressed and injured always may complain.
    Too, too severely laws of honor bind
The weak submissive sex of womankind.   10
If sighs have gained or force compelled our hand,
Deceived by art, or urged by stern command,
Whatever motive binds the fatal tie,
The judging world expects our constancy.
    Just heaven! (for sure in heaven does justice reign,   15
Though tricks below that sacred name profane)
To you appealing I submit my cause,
Nor fear a judgment from impartial laws.
All bargains but conditional[3] are made;
The purchase void, the creditor unpaid;   20
Defrauded servants are from service free;
A wounded slave regains his liberty.
For wives ill used no remedy remains,
To daily racks condemned, and to eternal chains.
    From whence is this unjust distinction grown?   25
Are we not formed with passions like your own?
Nature with equal fire our souls endued,
Our minds as haughty, and as warm our blood;
O'er the wide world your pleasures you pursue, ⎫
The change is justified by something new;   ⎬   30
But we must sigh in silence—and be true.   ⎭

5. In Ovid's *Metamorphoses*, Daphne, to escape Apollo, was turned into a laurel, and Arethusa, escaping Alpheus, became a fountain.

1. In 1724 the notorious libertine William Yonge, separated from his wife, Mary, discovered that she (like him) had committed adultery. He sued her lover, Colonel Norton, for damages and collected £1,500. Later that year, according to the law of the time, he petitioned the Houses of Parliament for a divorce. The case was tried in public, Mrs. Yonge's love letters were read aloud, and two men testified that they had found her and Norton "together in naked bed." Yonge was granted the divorce, his wife's dowry, and the greater part of her fortune.

    Though the *Epistle* is obviously based on this sensational affair, it is also a work of imagination. Like Pope's *Eloisa to Abelard*—to which the author himself

called Montagu's attention—it takes the form of a heroic epistle, the passionate outcry of an abandoned woman. The poet, entering into the feelings of Mary Yonge, justifies her conduct with reasons both of the heart and head. The objects of her attack include the institution of marriage, which binds wives in "eternal chains"; the double standard of morality, which requires chastity from women but not men; the hypocrisy of society, which condemns the very behavior it secretly lusts after; and the craven greed and cruelty of the husband himself. But 18th-century women seldom dared to speak like this in public, and the *Epistle* was not published until the 1970s.

2. Sir Robert Walpole, William Yonge's friend at court, was rumored to tolerate his own wife's infidelities.

3. Only conditionally.

Our sex's weakness you expose and blame
(Of every prattling fop the common theme),
Yet from this weakness you suppose is due
Sublimer virtue than your Cato[4] knew.   35
Had heaven designed us trials so severe,
It would have formed our tempers then to bear.
   And I have borne (oh what have I not borne!)
The pang of jealousy, the insults of scorn.
Wearied at length, I from your sight remove,   40
And place my future hopes in secret love.
In the gay bloom of glowing youth retired,
I quit the woman's joy to be admired,
With that small pension your hard heart allows,
Renounce your fortune, and release your vows.   45
To custom (though unjust) so much is due;
I hide my frailty from the public view.
My conscience clear, yet sensible of shame,
My life I hazard, to preserve my fame.
And I prefer this low inglorious state   ⎫   50
To vile dependence on the thing I hate — ⎬
But you pursue me to this last retreat.   ⎭
Dragged into light, my tender crime is shown
And every circumstance of fondness known.
Beneath the shelter of the law you stand,   55
And urge my ruin with a cruel hand,
While to my fault thus rigidly severe,
Tamely submissive to the man you fear.[5]
   This wretched outcast, this abandoned wife,
Has yet this joy to sweeten shameful life: 60
By your mean conduct, infamously loose,
You are at once my accuser and excuse.
Let me be damned by the censorious prude
(Stupidly dull, or spiritually lewd),
My hapless case will surely pity find   65
From every just and reasonable mind.
When to the final sentence I submit,
The lips condemn me, but their souls acquit.
   No more my husband, to your pleasures go,
The sweets of your recovered freedom know.   70
Go: court the brittle friendship of the great,
Smile at his board, or at his levee[6] wait;
And when dismissed, to madam's toilet fly,
More than her chambermaids, or glasses,[7] lie,
Tell her how young she looks, how heavenly fair, 75
Admire the lilies and the roses there.
Your high ambition may be gratified,
Some cousin of her own be made your bride,

4. The asceticism and self-discipline of the Roman statesman Cato had been emphasized in Addison's famous tragedy *Cato* (1713).
5. I.e., Walpole. Montagu suggests that the whole political establishment of England takes sides against Mary Yonge.
6. Morning reception of visitors. "Board": dining table.
7. Mirrors. It was fashionable for women like Lady Walpole to receive visitors during the last stages of dressing (their "toilet").

And you the father of a glorious race
Endowed with Ch——l's strength and Low——r's face.[8]   80

1724   1972

8. General Churchill was rumored to have had an affair with Lady Walpole; Antony Lowther was a notorious gallant. The author implies that William Yonge's
next wife may be as untrue as his first. Mary Yonge
remarried immediately after her divorce; five years
later Yonge himself (whose divorce had made him
rich) married the daughter of a baron.

THOMAS GRAY
1716–1771

The man who wrote the English poem most loved by what Samuel Johnson called
"the common reader" was oddly enough a scholarly recluse who lived the quiet
life of a university professor in the stagnant atmosphere of mid-eighteenth-century
Cambridge, where toward the end of his life he held the professorship of modern
history without feeling called on to give a single lecture. He was educated at Eton,
where he made intimate friends—Richard West; Thomas Ashton; and Horace
Walpole, the son of the prime minister. After four years at Cambridge he left
without a degree to make the grand tour of France and Italy as Walpole's guest.
The death of West in 1742 desolated Gray, and memories of West haunt much of
his verse. He spent the rest of his life in Cambridge, pursuing his studies and
writing delightful letters as well as a handful of poems—including two high-flown
Pindaric odes, *The Progress of Poesy* (1754) and *The Bard* (1757).

Most of Gray's poems take part in a contemporary reaction against the finish of
Pope's couplets; poets sought a new style, at once intimate and prophetic. Gray
held that "the language of the age is never the language of poetry," and often uses
archaic diction and distorted syntax. But the *Elegy Written in a Country Church-
yard* stands alone in his work. It balances Latinate phrases with living English
speech, and the learning of a scholar with a common humanity that everyone can
share. Johnson, who did not usually like Gray's poetry, acknowledged that the
Elegy would live forever:

> The Churchyard abounds with images which find a mirror in every mind,
> and with sentiments to which every bosom returns an echo. The four stanzas
> beginning "Yet even these bones" are to me original: I have never seen the
> notions in any other place; yet he that reads them here, persuades himself
> that he has always felt them. Had Gray written often thus, it had been vain to
> blame, and useless to praise him.

Ode on the Death of a Favorite Cat[1]

Drowned in a Tub of Goldfishes

'Twas on a lofty vase's side,
Where China's gayest art had dyed
The azure flowers that blow;[2]

1. Selima, one of Horace Walpole's cats, had recently
drowned in a china cistern. Gray wrote this memorial
at Walpole's request.
2. Bloom.

Demurest of the tabby kind,
The pensive Selima reclined,   5
    Gazed on the lake below.

Her conscious tail her joy declared;
The fair round face, the snowy beard,
    The velvet of her paws,
Her coat, that with the tortoise vies,   10
Her ears of jet, and emerald eyes,
    She saw; and purred applause.

Still had she gazed; but 'midst the tide
Two angel forms were seen to glide,
    The genii of the stream: 15
Their scaly armor's Tyrian[3] hue
Through richest purple to the view
    Betrayed a golden gleam.

The hapless nymph with wonder saw:
A whisker first and then a claw,   20
    With many an ardent wish,
She stretched in vain to reach the prize.
What female heart can gold despise?
    What cat's averse to fish?

Presumptuous maid! with looks intent   25
Again she stretched, again she bent,
    Nor knew the gulf between.
(Malignant Fate sat by and smiled)
The slippery verge her feet beguiled,
    She tumbled headlong in.   30

Eight times emerging from the flood
She mewed to every watery god,
    Some speedy aid to send.
No dolphin came, no nereid stirred:
Nor cruel Tom, nor Susan[4] heard.   35
    A favorite has no friend!

From hence, ye beauties, undeceived,
Know, one false step is ne'er retrieved,
    And be with caution bold.
Not all that tempts your wandering eyes   40
And heedless hearts is lawful prize;
    Nor all that glisters gold.

1747   1748

---

3. Purple.   sea nymph.
4. "Tom" and "Susan" are servants' names. "Nereid":

Elegy Written in a Country Churchyard

The curfew tolls the knell of parting day,
  The lowing herd wind slowly o'er the lea,
The plowman homeward plods his weary way,
  And leaves the world to darkness and to me.

Now fades the glimmering landscape on the sight,   5
  And all the air a solemn stillness holds,
Save where the beetle wheels his droning flight,
  And drowsy tinklings lull the distant folds;

Save that from yonder ivy-mantled tower
  The moping owl does to the moon complain   10
Of such, as wandering near her secret bower,
  Molest her ancient solitary reign.

Beneath those rugged elms, that yew tree's shade,
  Where heaves the turf in many a moldering heap,
Each in his narrow cell forever laid,   15
  The rude[1] forefathers of the hamlet sleep.

The breezy call of incense-breathing Morn,
  The swallow twittering from the straw-built shed,
The cock's shrill clarion, or the echoing horn,[2]
  No more shall rouse them from their lowly bed.   20

For them no more the blazing hearth shall burn,
  Or busy housewife ply her evening care;
No children run to lisp their sire's return,
  Or climb his knees the envied kiss to share.

Oft did the harvest to their sickle yield,   25
  Their furrow oft the stubborn glebe[3] has broke;
How jocund did they drive their team afield!
  How bowed the woods beneath their sturdy stroke!

Let not Ambition mock their useful toil,
  Their homely joys, and destiny obscure;   30
Nor Grandeur hear with a disdainful smile
  The short and simple annals of the poor.

The boast of heraldry,[4] the pomp of power,
  And all that beauty, all that wealth e'er gave,
Awaits alike the inevitable hour.   35
  The paths of glory lead but to the grave.

Nor you, ye proud, impute to these the fault,
  If Memory o'er their tomb no trophies[5] raise,

1. Untaught.
2. The hunter's horn.
3. Soil, turf.

4. Noble birth.
5. An ornamental or symbolic group of figures depicting the achievements of the deceased.

Where through the long-drawn aisle and fretted[6] vault
   The pealing anthem swells the note of praise.   40

Can storied urn or animated[7] bust
   Back to its mansion call the fleeting breath?
Can Honor's voice provoke[8] the silent dust,
   Or Flattery soothe the dull cold ear of Death?

Perhaps in this neglected spot is laid   45
   Some heart once pregnant with celestial fire;
Hands that the rod of empire might have swayed,
   Or waked to ecstasy the living lyre.

But Knowledge to their eyes her ample page
   Rich with the spoils of time did ne'er unroll;   50
Chill Penury repressed their noble rage,
   And froze the genial current of the soul.

Full many a gem of purest ray serene,
   The dark unfathomed caves of ocean bear:
Full many a flower is born to blush unseen,   55
   And waste its sweetness on the desert air.

Some village Hampden,[9] that with dauntless breast
   The little tyrant of his fields withstood;
Some mute inglorious Milton here may rest,
   Some Cromwell guiltless of his country's blood.   60

The applause of listening senates to command,
   The threats of pain and ruin to despise,
To scatter plenty o'er a smiling land,
   And read their history in a nation's eyes,

Their lot forbade: nor circumscribed alone   65
   Their growing virtues, but their crimes confined;
Forbade to wade through slaughter to a throne,
   And shut the gates of mercy on mankind,

The struggling pangs of conscious truth to hide,
   To quench the blushes of ingenuous shame,   70
Or heap the shrine of Luxury and Pride
   With incense kindled at the Muse's flame.

Far from the madding crowd's ignoble strife,
   Their sober wishes never learned to stray;
Along the cool sequestered vale of life   75
   They kept the noiseless tenor of their way.

---

6. Decorated with intersecting lines in relief.
7. Lifelike. "Storied urn": a funeral urn with an epitaph or pictured story inscribed on it.
8. Call forth.
9. John Hampden (1594–1643), who, both as a private
citizen and as a Member of Parliament, zealously defended the rights of the people against the autocratic
policies of Charles I. A gallant soldier, he was mortally
wounded in a skirmish near Oxford.

Yet even these bones from insult to protect
    Some frail memorial still erected nigh,
With uncouth rhymes and shapeless sculpture decked,[1]
    Implores the passing tribute of a sigh.   80

Their name, their years, spelt by the unlettered Muse,
    The place of fame and elegy supply:
And many a holy text around she strews,
    That teach the rustic moralist to die.

For who to dumb Forgetfulness a prey,   85
    This pleasing anxious being e'er resigned,
Left the warm precincts of the cheerful day,
    Nor cast one longing lingering look behind?

On some fond breast the parting soul relies,
    Some pious drops the closing eye requires;   90
Even from the tomb the voice of Nature cries,
    Even in our ashes live their wonted fires.

For thee, who mindful of the unhonored dead
    Dost in these lines their artless tale relate;
If chance, by lonely contemplation led,   95
    Some kindred spirit shall inquire thy fate,

Haply some hoary-headed swain may say,
    "Oft have we seen him at the peep of dawn
Brushing with hasty steps the dews away
    To meet the sun upon the upland lawn.   100

"There at the foot of yonder nodding beech
    That wreathes its old fantastic roots so high,
His listless length at noontide would he stretch,
    And pore upon the brook that babbles by.

"Hard by yon wood, now smiling as in scorn,   105
    Muttering his wayward fancies he would rove,
Now drooping, woeful wan, like one forlorn,
    Or crazed with care, or crossed in hopeless love.

"One morn I missed him on the customed hill,
    Along the heath and near his favorite tree;   110
Another came; nor yet beside the rill,
    Nor up the lawn, nor at the wood was he;

"The next with dirges due in sad array
    Slow through the churchway path we saw him borne.
Approach and read (for thou canst read) the lay,   115
    Graved on the stone beneath yon aged thorn."

---

1. Cf. "the storied urn or animated bust" dedicated inside the church to "the proud" (line 41).

The Epitaph

Here rests his head upon the lap of Earth
    A youth to Fortune and to Fame unknown.
Fair Science[2] frowned not on his humble birth,
    And Melancholy marked him for her own.   120

Large was his bounty, and his soul sincere,
    Heaven did a recompense as largely send:
He gave to Misery all he had, a tear,
    He gained from Heaven ('twas all he wished) a friend.

No farther seek his merits to disclose,   125
    Or draw his frailties from their dread abode
(There they alike in trembling hope repose),
    The bosom of his Father and his God.

ca. 1742–50   1751

2. Learning.

WILLIAM COLLINS
1721–1759

William Collins was born in Chichester and educated at Winchester and Oxford. Coming up to London from the university, he tried to establish himself as an author, but he was given rather to planning than to writing books. Samuel Johnson later remembered him affectionately as a man of learning who "loved fairies, genii, giants, and monsters" and who "delighted to rove through the meanders of enchantment." In 1746 Collins published *Odes on Several Descriptive and Allegorical Subjects*, his part in an undertaking, with his friend Joseph Warton, to create a new poetry, more lyrical and fanciful than that of Alexander Pope's generation. Collins's *Odes* address personified abstractions (Fear, Pity, the Passions), which are imagined as vivid presences that overwhelm the poet as he calls them to life. This quest for the sublime has impressed many later readers of Collins, though contemporaries often found his poems obscure. Inheriting some money, the poet traveled for a while, but fits of depression gradually deepened into total debility. He spent his last years in Chichester, forgotten by all but a small circle of loyal friends. By the end of the century, however, his reputation had grown; the Romantics admired his poems and felt akin to him. The *Ode to Evening*, which combines a chaste and cool classicism with a delicate feeling for landscape and mood, is one of the delightful poems of the century.

Ode Written in the Beginning of the Year 1746

How sleep the brave[1] who sink to rest
    By all their country's wishes blest!

1. Collins is presumably thinking of those who lost their lives defending England in 1745, when the Scotch Jacobites, led by Bonnie Prince Charlie, penetrated to within 127 miles of London.

When Spring, with dewy fingers cold,
Returns to deck their hallowed mold,
  She there shall dress a sweeter sod   5
  Than Fancy's feet have ever trod.

By fairy hands their knell is rung,
By forms unseen their dirge is sung;
There Honor comes, a pilgrim gray,
To bless the turf that wraps their clay,   10
And Freedom shall awhile repair,
To dwell a weeping hermit there!

                                                    1746

Ode to Evening[1]

If aught of oaten stop, or pastoral song,
May hope, chaste Eve, to soothe thy modest ear,
  Like thy own solemn springs,
  Thy springs and dying gales,
O nymph reserved, while now the bright-haired sun   5
Sits in yon western tent, whose cloudy skirts,
  With brede[2] ethereal wove,
  O'erhang his wavy bed:
Now air is hushed, save where the weak-eyed bat,
With short shrill shriek flits by on leathern wing,   10
  Or where the beetle winds
  His small but sullen horn,
As oft he rises 'midst the twilight path,
Against the pilgrim borne in heedless hum:
  Now teach me, maid composed,   15
  To breathe some softened strain,
Whose numbers, stealing through thy darkening vale,
May not unseemly with its stillness suit,
  As, musing slow, I hail
  Thy genial loved return!   20
For when thy folding-star[3] arising shows
His paly circlet, at his warning lamp
  The fragrant Hours, and elves
  Who slept in flowers the day,
And many a nymph who wreaths her brows with sedge,   25
And sheds the freshening dew, and, lovelier still,
  The pensive Pleasures sweet,
  Prepare thy shadowy car.
Then lead, calm vot'ress, where some sheety lake
Cheers the lone heath, or some time-hallowed pile   30
  Or upland fallows gray

---

1. Collins borrowed the metrical structure and the rhymeless lines of this ode from Milton's translation of Horace, *Odes* 1.5 (1673). The text printed here is based on the revised version, published in Dodsley's *Miscel-* *lany* (1748).
2. Embroidery.
3. The evening star, which signals the hour for herding the sheep into the sheepfold.

Reflect its last cool gleam.
But when chill blustering winds, or driving rain,
Forbid my willing feet, be mine the hut
   That from the mountain's side   35
   Views wilds, and swelling floods,
And hamlets brown, and dim-discovered spires,
And hears their simple bell, and marks o'er all
   Thy dewy fingers draw
   The gradual dusky veil.   40
While Spring shall pour his showers, as oft he wont,
And bathe thy breathing tresses, meekest Eve;
   While Summer loves to sport
   Beneath thy lingering light;
While sallow Autumn fills thy lap with leaves;   45
Or Winter, yelling through the troublous air,
   Affrights thy shrinking train,
   And rudely rends thy robes;
So long, sure-found beneath the sylvan shed,
Shall Fancy, Friendship, Science, rose-lipped Health,   50
   Thy gentlest influence own,
   And hymn thy favorite name!

                                             1746, 1748

WILLIAM COWPER
1731–1800

There are no saner poems in the language than William Cowper's, yet they were
written by a man who was periodically insane and who, for forty years, lived day to
day with the possibility of madness. After attempting suicide in 1763, he believed
that he was damned for having committed the unforgivable sin, the "sin against
the Holy Ghost." From then on, a refugee from life, he looked for hope in Evangelicalism; and found shelter, first in the pious family of the clergyman, Morley
Unwin, and after Unwin's death, with his widow, Mary Unwin, who cared for
Cowper until her death in 1796. Their move to rural Olney (pronounced Own-y)
in 1768 brought them under the influence of the Evangelical minister John Newton; with him Cowper wrote the famous Olney Hymns. But another attack of
madness, in 1773, not only frustrated his planned marriage to Mary Unwin but
left him convinced for the rest of his life that he had been cast out by God. He
never again attended services, and the main purpose of his life thereafter was to
divert his mind from numb despair by every possible innocent device. He gar-
dened, he kept pets, he walked, he wrote letters (some of the best of the century),
he conversed, he read—and he wrote poetry. When his work was published, it
brought him a measure of fame that his modest nature could never have hoped
for. In the small world and gentle musings of Cowper's major work, The Task
(1785), contemporaries recognized their own heartfelt concerns. No poet of the
century was more beloved.

The Castaway

Obscurest night involved the sky,
    The Atlantic billows roared,
When such a destined wretch as I,
    Washed headlong from on board,
Of friends, of hope, of all bereft,   5
His floating home forever left.

No braver chief[1] could Albion boast
    Than he with whom he went,
Nor ever ship left Albion's coast,
    With warmer wishes sent.   10
He loved them both, but both in vain,
Nor him beheld, nor her again.

Not long beneath the whelming brine,
    Expert to swim, he lay;
Nor soon he felt his strength decline,   15
    Or courage die away;
But waged with death a lasting strife,
Supported by despair of life.

He shouted; nor his friends had failed
    To check the vessel's course,   20
But so the furious blast prevailed,
    That, pitiless perforce,
They left their outcast mate behind,
And scudded still before the wind.

Some succor yet they could afford;   25
    And, such as storms allow,
The cask, the coop, the floated cord,
    Delayed not to bestow.
But he (they knew) nor ship, nor shore,
Whate'er they gave, should visit more.   30

Nor, cruel as it seemed, could he
    Their haste himself condemn,
Aware that flight, in such a sea,
    Alone could rescue them;
Yet bitter felt it still to die   35
Deserted, and his friends so nigh.

He long survives, who lives an hour
    In ocean, self-upheld;
And so long he, with unspent power,
    His destiny repelled;   40
And ever, as the minutes flew,
Entreated help, or cried, "Adieu!"

1. George, Lord Anson (1697–1762), in whose *Voyage* (1748), Cowper, years before writing this poem, had read the story of the sailor washed overboard in a storm.

At length, his transient respite past,
  His comrades, who before
Had heard his voice in every blast,   45
  Could catch the sound no more.
For then, by toil subdued, he drank
The stifling wave, and then he sank.

No poet wept him; but the page
  Of narrative sincere,   50
That tells his name, his worth, his age,
  Is wet with Anson's tear.
And tears by bards or heroes shed
Alike immortalize the dead.

I therefore purpose not, or dream,   55
  Descanting on his fate,
To give the melancholy theme
  A more enduring date:
But misery still delights to trace
Its semblance in another's case.   60

No voice divine the storm allayed,
  No light propitious shone,
When, snatched from all effectual aid,
  We perished, each alone;
But I beneath a rougher sea,   65
And whelmed in deeper gulfs than he.

1799   1803

The Romantic Period
1785-1830

THE POLITICAL BACKGROUND: REVOLUTION AND REACTION

Following a widespread practice of historians of English literature, we shall denote by the "Romantic period" the span between the year 1785, the midpoint of the decade in which Samuel Johnson died and Blake and Burns published their first poems, and 1830, by which time the major writers of the earlier century were either dead or no longer productive. This was a turbulent period, during which England experienced the ordeal of change from a primarily agricultural society, where wealth and power had been concentrated in the landholding aristocracy, to a modern industrial nation, in which the balance of economic power shifted to large-scale employers, who found themselves ranged against an immensely enlarging and increasingly restive working class. And this change occurred in a context of the American Revolution and then of the much more radical French Revolution, of wars, of economic cycles of inflation and depression, and of the constant threat to the social structure from imported revolutionary ideologies to which the ruling classes responded by heresy hunts and the repression of traditional liberties.

The early period of the French Revolution, marked by the Declaration of the Rights of Man and the storming of the Bastille to release imprisoned political offenders, evoked enthusiastic support from English liberals and radicals alike. Two influential books indicate the radical social thinking stimulated by the Revolution. Tom Paine's *Rights of Man* (1791–92) justified the French Revolution against Edmund Burke's attack in his *Reflections on the Revolution in France* (1790), and advocated for England a democratic republic which was to be achieved, if lesser pressures failed, by popular revolution. More important as an influence on Wordsworth, Shelley, and other poets was William Godwin's *Inquiry Concerning Political Justice* (1793), which foretold an inevitable but peaceful evolution of society to a final stage in which all property would be equally distributed and all government would wither away. Later, however, English sympathizers dropped off as the Revolution followed its increasingly grim and violent course: the accession to power by Jacobin extremists; the "September Massacres" of the imprisoned and helpless nobility in 1792, followed by the execution of the royal family; the invasion by the French Republic of the Rhineland and Netherlands, and its offer of armed assistance to all countries desiring to overthrow their governments, which brought England into the war against France; the guillotining of thousands in the Reign of Terror under Robespierre; and, after the execution in their turn of the men who had directed the Terror, the emergence of Napoleon first as dictator and then as emperor of France. As Wordsworth wrote in *The Prelude* (11.206–9),

> become Oppressors in their turn,
> Frenchmen had changed a war of self-defence
> For one of Conquest, losing sight of all
> Which they had struggled for. . . .

For Wordsworth and other English observers of liberal inclinations, these events posed a dilemma that became familiar again after the 1920s, in our parallel era of wars, revolutions, and the struggle by competing social ideologies—liberals had no side they could wholeheartedly espouse. Napoleon, the child and champion of the French Revolution, had become an archaggressor, a despot, and the founder of a new dynasty; yet almost all those who opposed him did so for the wrong reasons, with the result that his final defeat at Waterloo in 1815 proved to be the triumph, not of progress and reform, but of reactionary despotisms throughout continental Europe.

In England this period was one of harsh repressive measures. Public meetings were prohibited, habeas corpus was suspended for the first time in over a hundred years, and advocates of even moderate political change were charged with high treason in time of war. The outlook of the Napoleonic wars put an end to reform, and to almost all genuine political life in England, for nearly three decades.

Yet this was the very time when profound economic and social changes were creating a desperate need for corresponding changes in political arrangements, and new classes—manufacturing, rather than agricultural—were beginning to demand a power in government proportionate to their wealth. The "Industrial Revolution"—the shift in manufacturing that resulted from the invention of power-driven machinery to replace hand labor—had begun in the mid-eighteenth century with improvements in machines for processing textiles, and was given immense impetus when James Watt perfected the steam engine in 1765. In the succeeding decades steam replaced wind and water as the primary source of power in one after another type of manufacturing; and at once, after centuries of almost imperceptibly slow change, there began that ever-accelerating alteration in economic and social conditions which shows no signs of slowing down in the foreseeable future. A new laboring population massed in the sprawling mill towns that burgeoned in central and northern England. In rural communities the destruction of home industry was accompanied by a rapid growth of the process—lamented by Oliver Goldsmith in *The Deserted Village* as early as 1770—of enclosing the old open-field and communally worked farms into privately owned agricultural holdings. This process was by and large necessary for the more efficient methods of agriculture and animal breeding required to supply a growing population (although some of the land thus acquired was turned into vast private parks); in any case, it created a new landless class that either migrated to the industrial towns or remained as farm laborers, subsisting on starvation wages eked out by an inadequate dole. The landscape of England began to take on its modern appearance—the hitherto open rural areas subdivided into a checkerboard of fields enclosed by hedges and stone walls, with the factories of the industrial and trading cities casting a pall of smoke over vast areas of jerry-built houses and slum tenements. Meanwhile, the population was becoming increasingly polarized into what Disraeli later called the "Two Nations"—the two classes of capital and labor, the large owner or trader and the possessionless wageworker, the rich and the poor.

No attempt was made to regulate this shift from the old economic world to the new, not only because of inertia and the power of vested interests, but because even liberal reformers were dominated by the social philosophy of laissez-faire. This theory of "let alone" holds that the general welfare can be ensured only by the free operation of economic laws; the government must maintain a policy of strict noninterference and leave people to pursue their private interests. For the great majority of the laboring class the results of this policy were inadequate wages, long hours of work under harsh discipline in sordid conditions, and the large-scale employment of women and children for tasks that destroyed both the body and the spirit. Reports by investigating committees on the coal mines, where male and female children of ten or even five years of age were harnessed to heavy coal-sledges which they dragged by crawling on their hands and knees, read like scenes from Dante's *Inferno*. In 1815 the conclusion of the French war, when the enlargement of the working force by demobilized troops coincided with the fall in the wartime demand for goods, brought on the first modern industrial depression. Since the workers had no vote and were prevented by law from unionizing, their sole recourse was to petitions, protest meetings, agitation, and hunger riots, which only frightened the ruling class into more repressive measures. In addition the introduction of new machines resulted in technological unemployment, and this provoked sporadic attempts by dispossessed workers to destroy the machines. After one such outbreak the House of Lords—despite Lord Byron's eloquent protest—passed a bill (1812) making death the penalty for destroying the frames used for weaving in the stocking industry. In 1819 meetings of workers were organized to demand parliamentary reform. In August of that year, a huge but orderly assembly at St. Peter's Fields, Manchester, was wantonly charged by troops, who killed nine and severely injured hundreds more; this was the notorious "Peterloo Massacre," so named with ironic reference to the Battle of Waterloo. The event incited Shelley to write his great poems for the working class, *England in 1819, Song: "Men of England,"* and *To Sidmouth and Castlereagh*.

Suffering was largely confined to the poor, however, for all this while the landed classes, the industrialists, and many of the merchants prospered. In London the Regency period (1811–20) was for the leisure class a time of lavish display and moral laxity. In the provinces the gentry in their country houses carried on their familial and social concerns—reflected in the novels of Jane Austen—almost untouched by great national and international events.

As in earlier English history, women constituted a deprived class which cut across social classes, for they were widely regarded as inferior to men in intellect and in all but domestic talents. They were therefore provided limited schooling and no facilities for higher education, had only lowly vocations open to them, were subjected to a rigid code of sexual behavior, and possessed (especially after marriage) almost no legal rights. In the revolutionary period, women finally acquired a strong and eloquent champion. Mary Wollstonecraft wrote an early defense of the French Revolution, *A Vindication of the Rights of Men* (1790), and followed this two years later with *A Vindication of the Rights of Woman*, a founding classic of the women's movement. Wollstonecraft asserted that women possess equal intellectual capacity and talents with men, and demanded for them a greater share of social, educational, and vocational privileges. The cause of women's rights, however, was not taken up by effective proponents until the Victorian era, and even partial achievement of its aims was delayed until well along in the twentieth century.

But the pressures for reform in the privileges of men, as distinct from women, could not be eliminated in the early nineteenth century, especially since political disabilities were not limited to laborers. Gradually the working-class reformers acquired the support of the middle classes and the liberal Whigs. Finally, at a time of acute economic distress, and after unprecedented agitation and disorders that threatened to break out into revolution, the first Reform Bill was carried in 1832, amid widespread rejoicing. It eliminated the rotten boroughs (depopulated areas whose seats in Commons were at the disposal of a nobleman), redistributed parliamentary representation to include the new industrial cities, and extended the vote. Although about half the middle class, almost all the working class, and all women remained still without a franchise, the principle of the peaceful adjustment of conflicting interests by parliamentary majority had been firmly established, and reform was to go on until, by stages, England acquired universal adult suffrage.

"THE SPIRIT OF THE AGE"

Attempts at a single definition of Romanticism fall far short of matching the facts of a time that exceeds almost all other ages of English literature in the range and diversity of its achievements. Writers in Wordsworth's lifetime did not think of themselves as "Romantic"; the word was not applied until half a century later, by English historians. Contemporary critics and reviewers treated them as independent individuals, or else grouped them (often invidiously, but with some basis in fact) into a number of separate schools: "the Lake School" of Wordsworth, Coleridge, and Robert Southey; "the Cockney School," a derogatory term for the Londoners Leigh Hunt, Hazlitt, and associated writers, including John Keats; and "the Satanic School" of Byron, Shelley, and their followers.

Many of the major writers, however, did feel that there was something distinctive about their time—not a shared doctrine or literary quality, but a pervasive intellectual and imaginative climate, which some of them called "the spirit of the age." They had the sense that (as Keats said in one of his sonnets) "Great spirits now on earth are sojourning," and that there was evidence of that release of energy, experimental boldness, and creative power that marks a literary renaissance. In his *Defence of Poetry* Shelley claimed that the literature of the age "has arisen as it were from a new birth," and that "an electric life burns" within the words of its best writers which is "less their spirit than the spirit of the age." Shelley explained this literary spirit as an accompaniment of political and social revolution, and other writers agreed. Francis Jeffrey, the foremost conservative reviewer of the day, connected "the revolution in our literature" with "the agitations of the French Revolution, and the discussions as well as the hopes and terrors to which it gave occasion." William Hazlitt, who published a book of essays called *The Spirit of the Age*, described how in his early youth the French Revolution had seemed "the dawn of a new era, a new impulse had been given to men's minds." The new poetry of the school of Wordsworth, he maintained, "had its origin in the French Revolution. . . . It was a time of promise, a renewal of the world—and of letters."

The imagination of many Romantic writers was, indeed, preoccupied with the fact and idea of revolution. In the early period of the French Revolution all the leading English writers except Edmund Burke were in sympathy with it, and Robert Burns, William Blake, Wordsworth, Coleridge, Southey, and Mary Wollstonecraft were among its fervent adherents. Later, even after the first boundless expectations had been disappointed by the events in France, the younger writers, including Hazlitt, Hunt, Shelley, and Byron, felt that its example, when purged of its errors, still constituted humanity's best hope. The Revolution generated a pervasive feeling that this was an age of new beginnings when, by discarding inherited procedures and outworn customs, everything was possible, and not only in the political and social realm but in intellectual and literary enterprises as well. In his *Prelude* Wordsworth wrote the classic description of the spirit of the early 1790s, with "France standing on the top of golden hours, / And human nature seeming born again," so that "the whole Earth, / The beauty wore of promise." Something of this sense of limitless possibilities survived the shock of first disappointment at events in France and carried over to the year 1797, when Wordsworth and Coleridge, in excited daily communion, revolutionized, on grounds analogous to the politics of democracy, the theory and practice of poetry. The product of these discussions was the *Lyrical Ballads* of 1798.

POETIC THEORY AND POETIC PRACTICE

Wordsworth undertook to justify the new poetry by a critical manifesto, or statement of poetic principles, in the form of an extended Preface to the second edition of *Lyrical Ballads* in 1800, which he enlarged still further in the third edition of 1802. In it he set himself in opposition to the literary *ancien régime*, those writers of the preceding century who, in his view, had imposed on poetry artificial conventions that distorted its free and natural expression. Many of Wordsworth's later critical writings were attempts to clarify, buttress, or qualify points made in his first declaration. Coleridge declared that the Preface was "half a child of my own brain"; and although he soon developed doubts about some of Wordsworth's unguarded statements, and undertook to correct them in *Biographia Literaria* (1817), he did not question the rightness of Wordsworth's attempt to overturn the reigning tradition. In the course of the eighteenth century there had been increasing opposition to the tradition of Dryden, Pope, and Johnson, and especially in the 1740s and later, there had emerged many of the critical concepts, as well as a number of the poetic subjects and forms, that were later exploited by Wordsworth and his contemporaries. Wordsworth's Preface nevertheless deserves its reputation as a turning point in English literature, for Wordsworth gathered up isolated ideas, organized them into a coherent theory based on explicit critical principles, and made them the rationale for his own massive achievements as a poet. We can conveniently use the concepts in this influential essay as points of departure for a survey of distinctive elements in the theory and poetry of the Romantic period.

1. The Concept of Poetry and the Poet

Representative eighteenth-century theorists had regarded poetry as primarily an imitation of human life—in a frequent figure, "a mirror held up to nature"—that the poet artfully renders and puts into an order designed to instruct and give artistic pleasure to the reader. Wordsworth, on the other hand, repeatedly described all good poetry as, at the moment of composition, "the spontaneous overflow of powerful feelings." Reversing earlier theory, he thus located the source of a poem not in the outer world, but in the individual poet, and specified that the essential materials of a poem were not external people and events, but the inner feelings of the author, or external objects only after these have been transformed or irradiated by the author's feelings. Other Romantic theories, however diverse in other aspects, concurred on this crucial point by referring primarily to the mind, emotions, and imagination of the poet, instead of to the outer world as perceived by the senses, for the origin, content, and defining attributes of a poem. Many writers identified poetry (in metaphors parallel to Wordsworth's "overflow") as the "expression" or "utterance" or "exhibition" of emotion. Blake and Shelley described a poem as an embodiment of the poet's imaginative vision, which they opposed to the ordinary world of common experience. Coleridge, following German precedents, introduced into English criticism an organic theory of the imaginative process and the poetic product based on the model of the growth of a plant. That is, he conceived a great work of literature to be a self-originating and self-organizing process that begins with a seedlike idea in the poet's imagination, grows by assimilating both the poet's feelings and the diverse materials of sense-experience, and evolves into an organic whole in which the parts are integrally related to each other and to the whole.

In accord with the view that poetry expresses the poet's own feelings and temperament, the lyric poem written in the first person, earlier regarded as a minor kind, became a major Romantic form, and was often described as the most essentially poetic of all the genres. And in the Romantic lyric the "I" often is not a conventionally typical lyric speaker, such as the Petrarchan lover or Cavalier gallant of Elizabethan and seventeenth-century love poems, but has recognizable traits of the poet in his own person and circumstances. In the poems of Wordsworth, Coleridge, Shelley, and Keats the experiences and states of mind expressed by the lyric speaker often accord closely with the known facts of the poet's life and with the personal confessions in his letters and journals. Even in his ostensibly fictional writings (narrative and dramatic), Byron usually invites his readers to identify the hero with the author, whether the hero is presented romantically (as in *Childe Harold*, *Manfred*, and the Oriental tales) or in an ironic perspective (as in *Don Juan*). An extreme instance of this tendency to self-reference is Wordsworth's *Prelude*, which is a poem of epic length and epic seriousness about the growth of the poet's own mind.

The Prelude exemplifies two other important tendencies in the period. Like Blake, Coleridge in his early poems, and later on Shelley, Wordsworth presents himself as what he calls "a chosen son," or "Bard." That is, he assumes the persona and voice of a poet-prophet, modeled on Milton and the prophets in the Bible, and puts himself forward as a spokesman for traditional Western civilization at a time of profound crisis—a time, as Wordsworth said in book 2 of *The Prelude*, "of dereliction and dismay" and the "melancholy waste of hopes o'erthrown." As bards, Wordsworth and the other visionary poets set out to revise the Biblical promise of divine redemption by reconstituting the grounds of hope and pronouncing the coming of a time in which a renewed humanity will inhabit a renovated earth on which men and women will feel thoroughly at home. *The Prelude* also is an instance of a central literary form of English, as of European, Romanticism—a long work about the formation of the self, often centering on a crisis, and presented in the radical metaphor of an interior journey in quest of one's true identity and destined spiritual home. Other English examples of this form are Blake's *Milton*, the crucial episode of Asia's underground journey in Shelley's *Prometheus Unbound*, and Keats's *Endymion* and *The Fall of Hyperion*. There are equivalent developments in contemporary prose: the self-revelation in the personal essays of Lamb, Hazlitt, and Leigh Hunt, and the currency of spiritual autobiography, whether fictionalized (Thomas Carlyle's *Sartor Resartus*) or presented as fact (Coleridge's *Biographia Literaria*, Thomas De Quincey's *Confessions of an English Opium Eater* and *Autobiographic Sketches*).

2. Poetic Spontaneity and Freedom

Wordsworth defined good poetry not merely as the overflow but as "the *spontaneous* overflow" of feelings. In traditional aesthetic theory, poetry had been regarded as supremely an art—an art that in modern times is practiced by poets who have assimilated classical precedents, are aware of the "rules" governing the kind of poem they are writing, and (except for the felicities that, as Pope said, are "beyond the reach of art") deliberately employ tested means to achieve foreknown effects upon an audience. But to Wordsworth, although the composition of a poem originates from "emotion recollected in tranquillity" and may be preceded and followed by reflection, the immediate act of composition must be spontaneous—that is, arising from impulse, and free from all rules and the artful manipulation of means to foreseen ends—if the product is to be a genuine poem. Other important Romantic critics also voiced declarations of artistic independence from inherited precepts. Keats listed as an "axiom" that "if poetry comes not as naturally as the leaves to a tree it had better not come at all." Blake insisted that he wrote from "Inspiration and Vision" and that his long "prophetic" poem *Milton* was given to him by an agency not himself and "produced without Labor or Study." Shelley also maintained that it is "an error to assert that the finest passages of poetry are produced by labor and study," and suggested instead that they are the products of an unconscious creativity: "A great statue or picture grows under the power of the artist as a child in the mother's womb." "The definition of genius," Hazlitt remarked, "is that it acts unconsciously." The surviving manuscripts of the Romantic poets, however, as well as the testimony of observers, show that they worked and reworked their texts no less arduously—if perhaps more immediately under the impetus of first conception—than the poets of earlier ages. Coleridge, who believed that truth lies in a union of opposites, came closer to the facts of Romantic practice when he claimed that the act of composing poetry involves the psychological contraries "of passion and of will, of *spontaneous* impulse and of *voluntary* purpose."

The emphasis in this period on the free activity of the imagination is related to an insistence on the essential role of instinct, intuition, and the feelings of "the heart" to supplement the judgments of the purely logical faculty, "the head," whether in the province of artistic beauty, philosophical and religious truth, or moral goodness. "Deep thinking," Coleridge wrote, "is attainable only by a man of deep feeling, and all truth is a species of revelation"; hence, "a metaphysical solution that does not tell you something in the heart is grievously to be suspected as apocryphal."

3. Romantic "Nature Poetry"

In his Preface, Wordsworth wrote that "I have at all times endeavored to look steadily at my subject," and in a supplementary Essay he complained that from Dryden through Pope there is scarcely an image from external nature "from which it can be inferred that the eye of the poet had been steadily fixed on his object." A glance at the table of contents of any collection of Romantic poems will show the degree to which the natural scene has become a primary poetic subject, while Wordsworth, Shelley, and even more Coleridge and Keats, described natural phenomena with an accuracy of observation that had no earlier match in its ability to capture the sensuous nuance.

Because of the prominence of landscape in this period, "Romantic poetry" has to the popular mind become almost synonymous with "nature poetry." Neither Romantic theory nor practice, however, justifies the opinion that the aim of this poetry was description for its own sake. Wordsworth in fact insisted that the ability to observe and describe objects accurately, although a necessary, is not at all a sufficient condition for poetry, "as its exercise supposes all the higher qualities of the mind to be passive, and in a state of subjection to external objects." And while many of the great Romantic lyrics—Wordsworth's *Tintern Abbey* and *Ode: Intimations of Immortality*, Coleridge's *Frost at Midnight* and *Dejection*, Shelley's *Ode to the West Wind*, Keats's *Nightingale*—begin with an aspect or change of aspect in the natural scene, this serves only as stimulus to the most characteristic human activity, that of thinking. The longer Romantic "nature poems" are in fact usually meditative poems, in which the presented scene serves to raise an emotional problem or personal crisis whose development and resolution constitute the organizing principle of the poem. As Wordsworth said in his Prospectus to *The Recluse*, not nature but "the Mind of Man" is "my haunt, and the main region of my song."

In addition, Romantic poems habitually endow the landscape with human life, passion, and expressiveness. In part such descriptions represent the poetic equivalent of the metaphysical concept of nature, which had developed in deliberate revolt against the world views of the scientific philosophers of the seventeenth and eighteenth centuries, who represented the ultimate reality as a mechanical world consisting of physical particles in motion. What is needed in philosophy, Coleridge wrote, is "the substitution of life and intelligence . . . for the philosophy of mechanism, which, in everything that is most worthy of the human intellect, strikes *Death*." But for many Romantic poets it was a matter of immediate experience to respond to the outer universe as a living entity that participates in the feelings of the observer. James Thomson and other descriptive poets of the preceding century had depicted the created universe as giving direct access to God, and even as itself possessing the attributes of divinity. In *Tintern Abbey* and other poems Wordsworth exhibits toward the landscape attitudes and sentiments that human beings had earlier felt not only for God, but also for a father, a mother, or a beloved. Elsewhere, as in the great passage on crossing Simplon Pass (*The Prelude* 6.625ff.), Wordsworth also revives the ancient theological concept that God's creation constitutes a symbol system, a physical revelation parallel to the written Apocalypse, the Book of Revelation in the Bible—

> Characters of the great Apocalypse,
> The types and symbols of Eternity,
> Of first, and last, and midst, and without end.

This view that natural objects correspond to an inner or a spiritual world underlay a tendency, especially in Blake and Shelley, to write a symbolist poetry in which a rose, a sunflower, a mountain, a cave, or a cloud is presented as an object imbued with a significance beyond itself. "I always seek in what I see," Shelley said, "the likeness of something beyond the present and tangible object." And by Blake mere nature, as perceived by the physical eye and unhumanized by the imagination, was spurned "as the dirt upon my feet, no part of me."

4. The Glorification of the Commonplace

In two lectures on Wordsworth, Hazlitt declared that the school of poetry founded by Wordsworth was the literary equivalent of the French Revolution, translating political changes into poetical experiments. "Kings and queens were dethroned from their rank and station in legitimate tragedy or epic poetry, as they were decapitated elsewhere. . . . The paradox [these poets] set out with was that all things are by nature equally fit subjects for poetry; or that if there is any preference to be given, those that are the meanest and most unpromising are the best."

Hazlitt had in mind Wordsworth's statement that the aim of *Lyrical Ballads* was "to choose incidents and situations from common life" and to use a "selection of language really spoken by men," for which the source and model is "humble and rustic life." As Hazlitt shrewdly saw, this was more a social than a distinctively literary definition of the proper materials and language for poetry. Versifiers of the later decades of the eighteenth century had experimented with the simple treatment of simple subjects, and Robert Burns—like Wordsworth, a sympathizer with the French Revolution—had achieved great poetic success in the serious representation of humble life in a language really spoken by rustics. But Wordsworth underwrote his poetic practice by a theory that inverted the traditional hierarchy of poetic genres, subjects, and style by elevating humble and rustic life and the plain style, which in earlier theory were appropriate only to the lowly pastoral, into the principal subject and medium for poetry in general. And in his own practice, as Hazlitt also noted, Wordsworth went even further and turned for the subjects of his serious poems not only to humble people but to the ignominious, the outcast, the delinquent—to "convicts, female vagrants, gypsies . . . idiot boys and mad mothers," as well as to "peasants, peddlers, and village barbers." Hence the outrage of Lord Byron, who alone among his great contemporaries insisted that Dryden and Pope had laid out the proper road for poetry, and who—in spite of his liberalism in politics—maintained his literary allegiance both to aristocratic proprieties and to traditional poetic decorum:

> "Peddlers," and "Boats," and "Wagons"! Oh! ye shades
> Of Pope and Dryden, are we come to this?

But Hazlitt insisted that, in his democratization of poetry, Wordsworth was "the most original poet now living." And certainly Wordsworth in *Lyrical Ballads* was, in this respect, more radical than any of his contemporaries. He effected an immense enlargement of his readers' imaginative sympathies and brought into the province of serious literature a range of materials and interests which are still being explored by writers of the present day.

It should be noted, however, that Wordsworth's aim in *Lyrical Ballads* was not simply to represent the world as it is but, as he announced in his Preface, to throw over "situations from common life . . . a certain coloring of imagination, whereby ordinary things should be presented to the mind in an unusual aspect." As this passage indicates, Wordsworth's concern in his poetry was not only with "common life" but with "ordinary *things*"; no one can read his poems without noticing the extraordinary reverence with which he invests words that in earlier writers had been derogatory—words like "common," "ordinary," "everyday," "humble," whether applied to people or to objects in the visible scene. His aim throughout is to shatter the lethargy of custom so as to refresh our sense of wonder—indeed, of divinity—in the everyday, the commonplace, the trivial, and the lowly.

Samuel Johnson had said that "wonder is a pause of reason" and that "all wonder is the effect of novelty upon ignorance." But for many Romantic critics, to arouse in the sophisticated mind that sense of wonder presumed to be felt by the ignorant and the innocent was a primary power of imagination and a major function of poetry. Commenting on the special imaginative quality of Wordsworth's early poetry (*Biographia Literaria*, chapter 6), Coleridge remarked: "To combine the child's sense of wonder and novelty with the appearances, which every day for perhaps forty years had rendered familiar . . . this is the character and privilege of genius," and its prime service is to awaken in the reader "freshness of sensation" in the representation of "familiar objects." Poetry, said Shelley in his *Defence of Poetry*, "reproduces the common universe" but "purges from our inward sight the film of familiarity which obscures from us the wonder of our being," and "creates anew the universe, after it has been blunted by reiteration." And in Carlyle's *Sartor Resartus* (1833–34), the chief—indeed the only—effect of the conversion of the protagonist from despairing unbelief is that he is able to sustain a sense of the "Natural Supernaturalism" in ordinary experience and so overcome the "custom" which "blinds us to the miraculousness of daily-recurring miracles." The great power of the imagination, according to these Romantic writers, is that it makes the old world new again.

5. The Supernatural and "Strangeness in Beauty"

In most of his poems Coleridge, like Wordsworth, dealt with the everyday things of this world, and in *Frost at Midnight* he showed how well he too could achieve the effect of wonder in the familiar. But Coleridge tells us (*Biographia Literaria*, chapter 14) that according to the division of labor in *Lyrical Ballads*, his special function was to achieve wonder by a frank violation of natural laws and the ordinary course of events in poems of which "the incidents and agents were to be, in part at least, supernatural." And in *The Rime of the Ancient Mariner, Christabel*, and *Kubla Khan*, Coleridge opened up to poetry the realm of mystery and magic, in which materials from ancient folklore, superstition, and demonology are used to impress upon the reader the sense of occult powers and unknown modes of being. Such poems are usually set in the distant past or in faraway places, or both; the milieu of *Kubla Khan*, for example, exploits the exoticism both of the Middle Ages and of the Orient. Next to Coleridge, the greatest master of this Romantic mode—in which supernatural events have a deep psychological import—was John Keats. In *La Belle Dame sans Merci* and *The Eve of St. Agnes* he adapted the old forms of ballad and romance to modern sophisticated use and, like Coleridge, established a medieval setting for events that violate our sense of realism and the natural order. Hence the term *medieval revival*, frequently attached to the Romantic period, which comprehends also the ballad imitations and some of the verse tales and historical novels of Sir Walter Scott.

Another side of the tendency that Walter Pater later called "the addition of strangeness to beauty" was the Romantic interest in unusual modes of experience, of a kind that earlier writers had largely ignored as either too trivial or too aberrant for serious literary concern. Blake, Wordsworth, and Coleridge in their poetry explored visionary states of consciousness that are common among children but violate the standard categories of adult judgment. Coleridge was interested in mesmerism (what we now call hypnotism) and, like Blake and Shelley, studied the literature of the occult and the esoteric. Coleridge also shared with De Quincey a concern with dreams and nightmares; both authors exploited in their writings the altered consciousness and distorted perceptions they experienced under their addiction to opium. Byron made repeated use of the fascination with the forbidden and the appeal of the terrifying Satanic hero. And Keats was extraordinarily sensitive to the ambivalences of human experience—to the mingling, at their highest intensity, of pleasure and pain, to the destructive aspect of sexuality, and to the erotic quality of the longing for death. These phenomena had already been explored by eighteenth-century writers of terror tales and Gothic fiction, and later in the nineteenth century all of them, sometimes exaggerated to perversity, became the special literary province of Charles Baudelaire, Algernon Charles Swinburne, and writers of the European "Decadence."

INDIVIDUALISM, INFINITE STRIVING, AND NONCONFORMITY

Through the greater part of the eighteenth century, humans had for the most part been viewed as limited beings in a strictly ordered and essentially unchanging world. A variety of philosophical and religious systems in this century coincided in a distrust of radical innovation, a respect for the precedents established through the ages by the common sense of humanity, and the recommendation to set accessible goals and avoid extremes, whether in politics, intellect, morality, or art. Many of the great literary works of the period joined in attacking "pride," or aspirations beyond the limits natural to our species. "The bliss of man," Pope wrote in *An Essay on Man*, "(could pride that blessing find) / Is not to act or think beyond mankind."

> This kind, this due degree
> Of blindness, weakness, Heaven bestows on thee.
> Submit.

The Romantic period, the age of burgeoning free enterprise and revolutionary hope, was also an age of radical individualism in which both the philosophers and poets put an immensely higher estimate on human potentialities and powers. In German post-Kantian philosophy, which generated many of the characteristic ideas of European Romanticism, the human mind—what was called the "Subject" or "Ego"—took over various functions that had hitherto been the sole prerogative of Divinity. Most prominent was the rejection by philosophers of a central eighteenth-century concept of the mind as a mirrorlike recipient of a universe already created, and its replacement by the new concept of the mind as itself the creator of the universe it perceives. In a parallel fashion, the English founders of the new poetry also described the mind as creating its own experience. According to Blake, the mind creates its proper milieu only if it totally rejects the material world; in Coleridge and Wordsworth, however, the mind creates in collaboration with something given to it from without. Mind, wrote Coleridge in 1801, is "not passive" but "made in God's Image, and that too in the sublimest sense—the Image of the *Creator*." And Wordsworth declared in *The Prelude* (2.258–61) that the individual mind

> Doth, like an Agent of the one great Mind,
> Create, creator and receiver both,
> Working but in alliance with the works
> Which it beholds.

Many Romantic writers also agreed that the mind has access beyond sense to the transcendant and the infinite, through a special faculty they called either Reason or Imagination. In *The Prelude* (6.600ff.) Wordsworth describes a flash of imagination "that has revealed / The invisible world," and affirms:

> Our destiny, our being's heart and home,
> Is with infinitude, and only there;
> With hope it is, hope that can never die,
> Effort, and expectation, and desire,
> And something evermore about to be.

The desire beyond human limits that, to the moralists of the preceding age, had been an essential sin, or tragic error, now becomes a glory and a triumph: the human being refuses to submit to limitations and, though finite, persists in setting infinite, hence inaccessible, goals. Wordsworth characteristically goes on to declare that "under such banners militant, the soul / Seeks for no trophies, struggles for no spoils"; for him, the infinite striving ends in physical quietism and moral fortitude. But for other writers, especially in Germany, the proper human aim is ceaseless activity—a "*Streben nach dem Unendlichen*," a striving for the infinite. This view is epitomized by Goethe's Faust, who in his quest for the unattainable violates ordinary moral limits, yet wins salvation by his very insatiability, which never stoops to contentment with the possibilities offered by this finite world. Infinite longing—in Shelley's phrase, "the desire of the moth for a star"—was a recurrent theme also in the English literature of the day. "Less than everything," Blake announced, "cannot satisfy man." Shelley's *Alastor* and Keats's *Endymion* both represent the quest for an indefinable and inaccessible goal, and Byron's *Manfred* has for its hero a man whose "powers and will" reach beyond the limits of that human clay "which clogs the ethereal essence," so that "his aspirations / Have been beyond the dwellers of the earth."

In a parallel fashion, Romantic theorists of art rejected the neoclassic ideal of a limited intention, perfectly accomplished, in favor of "the glory of the imperfect," in which the very failures of artists attest the unlimited reach of their aims. And in their own work, Romantic writers deliberately put themselves in competition with the greatest of their predecessors and experimented boldly in poetic language, versification, and design. Especially in their longer poems they struck out in new directions, and in the space of a few decades produced an astonishing variety of forms constructed on novel principles of organization and style. Blake's symbolic lyrics and visionary "prophetic" poems; Coleridge's haunting ballad-narrative of sin and retribution, *The Rime of the Ancient Mariner*; Wordsworth's epiclike spiritual autobiography, *The Prelude*; Shelley's cosmic symbolic drama, *Prometheus Unbound*; Keats's great sequence of Odes on the irreconcilable conflict in basic human desires; Byron's ironic survey of all European civilization, *Don Juan*—one can say of each of them, as Shelley said of Byron's poem, that it was "something wholly new and relative to the age."

The great eighteenth-century writers had typically dealt with men and women as members of an organized, and usually an urban, society; of this society authors regarded themselves to be integral parts, its highest standards were those that they spoke for, and to it as their audience they addressed themselves. Some Romantic writers, on the other hand, deliberately isolated themselves from society in order to give scope to their individual vision. Wordsworth's projected masterwork he entitled *The Recluse*, and he described himself as "musing in solitude" on its subject, "the individual Mind that keeps her own / Inviolate retirement." And in almost all Wordsworth's poems, long or short, the words "single," "solitary," "by oneself," "alone" constitute a leitmotif; his imagination is released by the sudden apparition of a single figure or object, stark against a natural background. Coleridge also, and still more strikingly Byron and Shelley, represented a solitary protagonist who is separated from society because he has rejected it, or because it has rejected him. These last three poets introduced what became a persistent theme in many Victorian and modern writers—the theme of exile, of the disinherited mind that cannot find a spiritual home in its native land and society or anywhere in the modern world. The solitary Romantic nonconformist was sometimes represented as also a great sinner. Writers of that time were fascinated by the outlaws of myth, legend, or history—Cain, Satan, Faust, the Wandering Jew, or the great, flawed figure of Napoleon—about whom they wrote and on whom they modeled a number of their villains or their heroes. In Coleridge's *Ancient Mariner* (as in Wordsworth's *Guilt and Sorrow* and *Peter Bell*) the guilty outcast—"alone, alone, all, all alone"—is made to realize and expiate his sin against the community of living things so that he may reassume his place in the social order. But in Byron the violator of conventional laws and limits remains proudly unrepentant. His hero Manfred, a compound of guilt and superhuman greatness, cannot be defeated by death, successfully defying the demons who, in the tradition of Marlowe's *Dr. Faustus*, have come to drag his soul to hell: I "was my own destroyer, and will be / My own hereafter . . . / Back, ye baffled fiends!" A more reputable Romantic hero, who turns up frequently in Byron and other writers and is made the protagonist of Shelley's great lyrical drama, is the Prometheus of Greek mythology. He shares with Satan the status of superlative nonconformity, since he sets himself in opposition to deity itself; unlike Satan, however, he is the champion rather than the enemy of the human race.

APOCALYPTIC EXPECTATIONS

Nowhere is the Romantic combination of boundless aspiration and the reliance on the power of the individual mind and imagination more evident than in the literary treatment of the ultimate hope of humanity. The French Revolution had aroused in many sympathizers the millennial expectations that are profoundly rooted in Hebrew and Christian tradition. "Few persons but those who have lived in it," Robert Southey reminisced in 1824, "can conceive or comprehend what the memory of the French Revolution was, nor what a visionary world seemed to open upon those who were just entering it. Old things seemed passing away, and nothing was dreamt of but the regeneration of the human race." Southey's language—like that of Wordsworth, Coleridge, Hazlitt, and other writers when they described their early Revolutionary fervor—is biblical; and it reflects the extent to which, in England, the Revolution was championed by members of radical Protestant sects, who envisioned it on the model of biblical prophecy.

The Bible ends with the book of Apocalypse (literally, "Revelation"), prophesying a return of human beings to their lost Edenic felicity, first in the millennium ("a thousand years") of an earthly kingdom, then in the eternity of "a new heaven and a new earth"; this consummation of history is symbolized by a marriage between the New Jerusalem and Christ the Lamb. At the outbreak of the French Revolution, Joseph Priestley and other Unitarian leaders hailed that event as the stage preceding the millennium prophesied in Revelation. Coleridge and Wordsworth, in their early poems, also interpreted the Revolution as the violent preliminary to the new earth and heaven of apocalyptic prophecy. And Blake's *The French Revolution* (1791) and *America, a Prophecy* (1793) represented both these revolutions as apocalyptic portents of the last days of the fallen world.

When the later events in France dashed their faith in political revolution as a means to the millennium, a number of Romantic writers salvaged their apocalyptic hope by giving it a new interpretation. They transferred the agency of apocalypse from mass action to the individual mind—from a political to a spiritual revolution—and proposed that "the new earth and new heaven" of Revelation is available here, now, to all of us, if only we can make our visionary imagination triumph over our senses and sensebound understanding. Hence the extraordinary Romantic emphasis on a new way of *seeing* (which is regarded as the restoration of a lost earlier way of seeing) as the chief aim in life. Blake's "Prophetic Books," for example, all deal with some aspects of the Fall and Redemption, and represent apocalypse as the recovery of the imaginative vision of things as they really are, seen "through and not with the eye." "The Nature of my Work," Blake wrote, "is Visionary or Imaginative; it is an Endeavor to Restore what the Ancients called the Golden Age." This concept of the imaginative re-creation of the old earth continues to be expressed by Romantic poets in the original biblical metaphor of a marriage—although now it is not a marriage of the New Jerusalem with the Lamb, but a conjunction of the inner faculties into spiritual unity, or else a marriage between the mind and the external world. Coleridge put this latter version succinctly in *Dejection: An Ode*; it is the inner condition of "Joy," at life's highest moments, "Which, wedding nature to us, gives in dower / A new earth and new heaven." Wordsworth announced as his "high argument" in the Prospectus to *The Recluse* (the same theme serves as underpattern for *The Prelude*) that "Paradise, and groves Elysian" are not "a history only of departed things"—

> For the discerning intellect of Man
> When wedded to this goodly universe
> In love and holy passion, shall find these
> A simple produce of the common day.

In Shelley's *Prometheus Unbound*, Prometheus represents an archetypal humanity whose total change in moral being frees the imaginative capacity to envision, and to achieve, a regenerate world; the fourth act symbolizes this event in the mode of a marriage festival in which the whole cosmos participates.

Carlyle's *Sartor Resartus*, to mention one other example, is the history of an individual's savage spiritual crisis and conversion, which turns out to be the achievement of an individual apocalypse: "And I awoke to a new Heaven and a new Earth." But, as Carlyle goes on to indicate, this new earth is the old earth, seen by his protagonist as though miraculously re-created, because he has learned to substitute the "Imaginative" faculty for what Carlyle represents as the chief faculty of the eighteenth-century Enlightenment, the "Logical, Mensurative faculty," or "Understanding." Writing in 1830–31, at the close of the period historians have labeled "Romantic," Carlyle thus summed up the tendency of a generation of writers to retain the ancient faith in apocalypse, but to interpret it not as a change of the world, but as a change in our worldview.

THE FAMILIAR ESSAY

At the close of the eighteenth century, reviews and magazines were written largely by hacks who acceded to the political bias and financial interests of the publisher and advertisers. The essays they included were weak imitations of the type established nearly a century earlier by single-essay periodicals such as the *Tatler* and the *Spectator*. In 1802, however, the *Edinburgh Review* inaugurated the modern type of periodical publication. It allowed considerable latitude to its writers, set its literary standards high, and was able to meet these standards by paying its contributors rates good enough to command the best talents of the day.

The immediate success of this new enterprise stimulated the founding of rival reviews and magazines. (A "review," usually issued four times yearly, consisted primarily of essays on important books and discussions of contemporary issues; a "magazine" was a monthly publication that printed more miscellaneous materials, including a high proportion of original essays, poems, and stories.) In 1820 appeared the *London Magazine,* liberal in politics and contemporary in literary interests; in its short but notable career until 1829 it printed the work of a group of brilliant writers, including the three men who soon established themselves as the greatest essayists of the age—Lamb, Hazlitt, and De Quincey. These new periodicals not only elevated the essay in literary dignity and quality but revolutionized its form and substance. They competed strenuously for talent, paying well enough so that an author (at least one as prolific as Hazlitt) could earn a living as a freelance essayist. Since allotment of space was flexible, each topic could find its appropriate length, instead of being held to the Procrustean brevity of the earlier essays modeled on Addison and Steele; in consequence, the new essays tended to be from two to four times as long as the eighteenth-century form. And writers were treated as serious practitioners who were competent, within broad limits, to write as they pleased.

Under these new conditions the "familiar essay"—a commentary on a non-technical subject written in a relaxed and intimate manner—flourished, and in a fashion that to some degree paralleled the course of Romantic poetry. Each of the three major essayists was in fact closely associated with important poets and supported at least some of the new poetic developments in critical commentaries whose perceptiveness and discrimination render them durably valuable. Like the poets, these essayists were personal and subjective; their essays are often candidly autobiographical, reminiscent, self-analytic; and when the writers treated other matters than themselves, they tended to do so impressionistically, so that the material is seen reflected in the temperament of the essayist. The subject matter of the essays, like that of the poetry, exhibits an extension of range and sympathy far beyond the earlier limits of the leisure class and its fashionable concerns; the essays now dealt with clerks, chimney sweeps, poor relations, handball players, prizefighters, and murderers. Most strikingly, the essayists resemble the poets in rebelling against eighteenth-century conventions to revive prose forms long disused and to develop new prose styles and structural principles. The result was a notable variety of achievements, ranging from Hazlitt's hard-hitting plain style and seemingly casual order of topics, through Lamb's delicately contrived rhetoric and meticulously controlled organization, to De Quincey's elaborate experiments in applying to prose the rhythms, harmonies, and thematic structure of musical compositions.

THE DRAMA

Although favorable to the essay, literary conditions in the early nineteenth century were unfavorable in the extreme to writing for the stage. By a licensing act that was not repealed until 1843, only the Drury Lane and Covent Garden theaters had the right to produce "legitimate"—that is to say, spoken—drama; the other theaters were restricted by law to entertainments in which there could be no dialogue except to music, and so put on mainly dancing, pantomime, and various types of musical plays. The two monopoly theaters were vast and ill-lighted, and their audiences were noisy and unruly; as a result, actors played in a grandiose and orotund style. To succeed under such conditions, plays had also to be blatant and magniloquent, so that the drama of that period (fettered also by rigid moral and political censorship) tended to the extremes of either farce or melodrama. None of the plays written by the professional playwrights of the time is read nowadays; they survive mainly in the limbo of scholarly monographs on the history of the theater.

Nonetheless, attracted irresistibly by the example of their idolized Shakespeare, all the greatest Romantic poets, and many minor ones, tried their hand at poetic plays. Some of these were written as closet drama—Byron's *Manfred* and Shelley's *Prometheus Unbound*, for example—but others were expressly written for the stage. The poets, however, lacked experience with the hard necessities of the practical theater, and they were for the most part unable to throw off the artifice of an archaic style dominated by Elizabethan and Jacobean models.

Above all, the genius of an age which excelled in subjective or visionary literary forms was ill adapted to the theater, which is a peculiarly social genre that represents a variety of credible characters. Even Byron, the only important poet of his generation to produce major work in a literary kind that requires a highly developed social sensibility—satire—did not succeed as a practical dramatist. His stage plays, while readable, mainly exhibit various aspects of the Byronic hero; they lack theatrical vigor and variety, and their thin-skinned author wisely refused to let them be put on before the merciless and demonstrative audiences of his day. Coleridge achieved a minor hit with his tragedy *Remorse*, which ran for twenty nights at the Drury Lane in 1813. The most capable Romantic dramatist was, surprisingly, Shelley. In *The Cenci* (1820) Shelley, with great tact and genuine theatrical acumen, converts a true story of the Italian Renaissance—of a monstrous father who violates his daughter and is in turn murdered by her—into a powerful version of his own central fable of the instinctive desire of evil to destroy, by degrading, the defiant individual, and of the moral triumph of the unconquerable single spirit, even in death. The play was not staged, however, until long after Shelley's death.

THE NOVEL

Two new types of fiction were prominent in the late eighteenth century. One was the "Gothic novel," which had been inaugurated in 1764 by Horace Walpole's *Castle of Otranto: A Gothic Story*, and continued by Clara Reeve in *The Champion of Virtue: A Gothic Story* (1777). The term derives from the frequent setting of these tales in a gloomy castle of the Middle Ages, but it has been extended to a larger group of novels, set somewhere in the past, which exploit the possibilities of mystery and terror in sullen, craggy landscapes; decaying mansions with dank dungeons, secret passages, and stealthy ghosts; chilling supernatural phenomena; and, often, sexual persecution of a beautiful maiden by an obsessed and haggard villain. These novels opened up to later fiction the dark, irrational side of human nature—the savage egoism, the perverse impulses, and the nightmarish terrors that lie beneath the controlled and ordered surface of the conscious mind. Some of the most powerful and influential writings in the mode were by women—they doubtless afforded a fictional release for the submerged desires and compensatory fantasies of that rigidly restricted and disadvantaged class. In *The Mysteries of Udolpho* (1794), and better still in *The Italian* (1797), Ann Radcliffe developed the figure of the mysterious and solitary *homme fatal*, torturing others because he is himself tortured by unspeakable guilt, who, though a villain, usurps the place of the hero in the reader's interest. Matthew Gregory Lewis in *The Monk* (1797), which he wrote at the age of twenty, has a similar protagonist, and brings to the fore the elements of diabolism, sensuality, and sadistic perversion which were pungent but submerged components in Radcliffe's Gothic formula. Gothicism is apparent also in Romantic poetry: in Coleridge's medieval terror poem *Christabel*, in Byron's recurrent hero-villain, in the setting and descriptive passages of Keats's *Eve of St. Agnes*, and in Shelley's inclinations (fostered by his early love for Gothic tales and his own youthful trials in that form) toward the fantastic, the macabre, and the exploration of the unconscious mind and of such aberrations as incest.

The second fictional mode popular at the turn of the century was the novel of purpose, often written to propagate the new social and political theories current in the period of the French Revolution. The best examples combine didactic intention with elements of Gothic terror. William Godwin, the political philosopher, wrote *Caleb Williams* (1794) to illustrate the thesis that the lower classes are helplessly subject to the power and privilege of the ruling class, but he did so in the form of a chilling story about the relentless pursuit and persecution by a wealthy squire of his young secretary, who has come upon evidence that the squire has committed murder. Mary Shelley—Percy Shelley's wife and the daughter of Mary Wollstonecraft, author of *A Vindication of the Rights of Woman*—wrote a thematic novel of terror which not only is a literary classic but has become a popular myth. Her *Frankenstein* (1817) transforms a story about a fabricated monster into a powerful representation of the moral distortion imposed on an individual who, because he diverges from the norm, is rejected by society.

The Romantic period produced two major novelists, Jane Austen and Sir Walter Scott. Jane Austen (1775–1817) is one of the greatest of English novelists, yet she is the only important author who seems to be untouched by the political, intellectual, and artistic revolutions of her age. Charlotte Brontë, speaking for the Romantic sensibility, complained that Jane Austen's novels lack warmth, enthusiasm, energy; "she ruffles her reader by nothing vehement, disturbs him by nothing profound. The passions are perfectly unknown to her." But Austen deliberately elected to work within the circumference of her own experience—the life of provincial English gentlefolk—and to maintain the decorum of the novel of manners, based on such literary antecedents as the comedy of manners of William Congreve and Richard Brinsley Sheridan and the novels of the earlier women authors Fanny Burney and Maria Edgeworth. Within these elected limits both of subject and form, Austen achieved a fully particularized setting within which to examine and criticize the values men and women live by in their everyday social lives.

Sense and Sensibility and *Northanger Abbey* gently ridicule two later eighteenth-century deviations from the humanistic norm, the cult of sensibility and the taste for Gothic terrors. Austen's other novels, published between 1813 and 1818—*Mansfield Park, Persuasion,* and best of all, *Pride and Prejudice* and *Emma*—all deal with the subject of getting married. This was in fact a central preoccupation and problem for the young leisure-class lady of that age, who had no career open to her outside of domesticity; Austen, however, chose the subject because it provided her with the best realistic opportunities for testing her heroines' practical sense and moral integrity, their degree of knowledge of the world and of themselves, and their capacity to demonstrate grace under social and financial pressure.

Sir Walter Scott (1771–1832) was contemporary with Jane Austen, and admired her greatly, but his work in fiction was at an extreme from hers. In 1814, with the anonymous *Waverley,* he turned from narrative verse (in which Byron had displaced him in popularity) to narrative prose and managed to write almost thirty long works of fiction in the eighteen years before he died. They are in the mode that he himself defined as romance, "the interest of which turns upon marvelous and uncommon incidents," in contrast to the novel such as Jane Austen wrote, in which "the events are accommodated to the ordinary train of human events, and the modern state of society." Scott's originality lay in opening up to fiction the rich and lively realm of history; he sometimes alters the order of events for novelistic purposes, yet he maintains fidelity to the spirit of the past and a meticulous accuracy in antiquarian detail. His great series of Scottish novels, including *Guy Mannering, The Antiquary, Old Mortality, Rob Roy,* and (most enduringly) *The Heart of Midlothian,* are rooted in historical events from the seventeenth century up to his own time; *Ivanhoe* is set in thirteenth-century England and *Kenilworth* in the age of Elizabeth; and *Quentin Durward*, the best of his Continental romances, has for background the French Court of the fifteenth century.

Like Byron, Scott wrote with dash and grandiosity in a kind of sustained improvisation; his plotting is often loose, his romantic lovers pallid, and his kings and chieftains large-scale puppets. But in his great scenes of action there are a scope and sweep not to be exceeded in fiction until the appearance of Leo Tolstoy's *War and Peace* in the 1860s. And although, unlike his liberal Romantic contemporaries, Scott's political sympathies were aristocratic and feudal, his most vivid and convincing characters are members of the middle and lower classes. His tradesmen, servants, peasantry, social outcasts, and demented old women, speaking a rich Scottish vernacular (Scott's language, like Robert Burns's in verse, tended to become stilted and conventional when he wrote in standard English), make up a populous world in which each person is an individual, rooted in the circumstances of time and place and class and occupation.

Scott had an immense international vogue, equaling that of Byron and Goethe, and became the acknowledged master of some of the greatest nineteenth-century novelists, including Balzac and Tolstoy. Jane Austen, on the other hand, during her lifetime was admired only by a limited group of English readers. Her novels have, however, demonstrated greater staying power. Scott's combination of casualness in design and prodigality in detail puts off many readers who have formed their sensibilities on the well-made novel of the present century. But even after the achievements of such masters in the form as Henry James, Jane Austen remains the sovereign of the intricate, spare, and ironic art of the novel of manners.

TEXTS	CONTEXTS
1789 William Blake, *Songs of Innocence*	1789 Fall of the Bastille begins French Revolution
1790 Blake, *The Marriage of Heaven and Hell*	
1791 Thomas Paine, *The Rights of Man*	1791–92 William Wordsworth in France inspired by revolutionary ideals
1792 Mary Wollstonecraft, *A Vindication of the Rights of Woman*	
	1793 Execution of Louis XVI; Reign of Terror; war breaks out between England and France
1794 Blake, *Songs of Experience*	
	1795 Wordsworth and Samuel Taylor Coleridge meet
1798 Wordsworth and Coleridge publish *Lyrical Ballads* anonymously	
1800 Second edition of *Lyrical Ballads* with Wordsworth's *Preface* (revised for 1802 edition)	
	1804 Napoleon crowned emperor
	1805 Horatio Nelson defeats French fleet at Trafalgar
1807 Wordsworth, *Poems in Two Volumes*	1807 Britain abolishes slave trade
1808 Johann Wolfgang von Goethe, *Faust*, Part 1	
	1811–20 Regency: Prince of Wales rules as regent for George III
1812 George Gordon, Lord Byron, *Childe Harold's Pilgrimage*, Cantos 1 and 2	
1813 Jane Austen, *Pride and Prejudice*	
1814 Sir Walter Scott, *Waverley*	

Boldface titles indicate works in the anthology.

TEXTS	CONTEXTS
	1815 Battle of Waterloo
1816 Coleridge, *Christabel, Kubla Khan* • Byron, *Childe Harold*, Cantos 3 and 4	1816 Byron separates from his wife; leaves England, never to return
1818 John Keats, *Endymion* • Mary Shelley, *Frankenstein*	1818 Percy Bysshe Shelley marries Mary, daughter of the radical William Godwin and Mary Wollstonecraft; leaves England for Italy, never to return
1819 Byron, *Don Juan*, Cantos 1 and 2 • Shelley, *Prometheus Unbound, Ode to the West Wind*, and other major lyrics; *A Defence of Poetry* (published 1840) • Keats writes most of his major poems	1819 "Peterloo Massacre," in which troops fire on workers at a peaceful rally, inspires Shelley's *England in 1819* and *"Men of England"*
1820 Keats publishes the volume *Lamia, Isabella, The Eve of St. Agnes, and Other Poems*	1820–30 Reign of George IV
1821 Shelley, *Adonais*	1821 Keats dies in Rome
	1822 Shelley drowns sailing off the Italian coast
	1823–24 Byron joins the Greek war for liberation from the Turks; dies of fever in Greece
	1825 Opening of the first passenger railroad in Britain
	1827 Death of Blake
	1830–37 Reign of William IV
	1832 First Reform Bill redistributes parliamentary representation; extends franchise • Death of Scott
	1834 Death of Coleridge
1850 Wordsworth, *The Prelude*, published posthumously	1850 Death of Wordsworth

WILLIAM BLAKE
1757–1827

1783:   *Poetical Sketches*, his first book of poems.
1794:   *Songs of Innocence and of Experience.*
1804–20:   The two last and greatest "prophetic" poems, *Milton* and *Jerusalem.*

What William Blake called his "Spiritual Life" was as varied, free, and dramatic as his "Corporeal Life" was simple, limited, and unadventurous. His father was a London haberdasher. His only formal education was in art: at the age of ten he entered a drawing school and later studied for a time at the school of the Royal Academy of Arts. At fourteen he served as apprentice for seven years to a well-known engraver, James Basire, read widely in his free time, and began to try his hand at poetry. At twenty-four he married Catherine Boucher, daughter of a market gardener. She was then illiterate, but Blake taught her to read and to help him in his engraving and printing. In the early and somewhat sentimentalized biographies, Catherine is represented as an ideal wife for an unorthodox and impecunious genius. Blake, however, must have been a trying domestic partner, and his vehement attacks on the torment caused by a possessive, jealous female will, which reached their height in 1793 and remained prominent in his writings for another decade, probably reflect a troubled period at home. The couple was childless.

The Blakes for a time enjoyed a moderate prosperity while Blake gave drawing lessons, illustrated books, and engraved designs made by other artists. When the demand for his work slackened, Blake in 1800 moved to a cottage at Felpham, on the Sussex seacoast, under the patronage of the wealthy poetaster, biographer, and amateur of the arts, William Hayley, who with the best of narrow intentions tried to transform Blake into a conventional artist and breadwinner. But the caged eagle soon rebelled. Hayley, Blake wrote, "is the Enemy of my Spiritual Life while he pretends to be the Friend of my Corporeal."

At Felpham in 1803 occurred an event that left a permanent mark on Blake's mind and art. He had an altercation with one John Schofield, a private in the Royal Dragoons. Blake ordered the soldier out of his garden and, when the soldier replied with threats and curses against Blake and his wife, pushed him the fifty yards to the inn where he was quartered. Schofield brought charges that Blake had uttered seditious statements about King and country. Since England was at war with France, sedition was a hanging offense. Blake was acquitted—an event, according to a newspaper account, "which so gratified the auditory that the court was . . . thrown into an uproar by their noisy exultations." Nevertheless Schofield, his fellow soldier Cock, and other participants in the trial haunted Blake's imagination and were enlarged to demonic characters who play a sinister role in *Jerusalem*. The event exacerbated Blake's sense that ominous forces were at work in the contemporary world and led him to complicate the symbolic obliquities by which he veiled the unorthodoxy of his religious and moral opinions, as well as the radicalism of the many allusions to contemporary affairs that he worked into his poems.

After three years at Felpham, Blake moved back to London, determined to follow his "Divine Vision" though it meant a life of isolation, misunderstanding, and poverty. When his single great bid for public recognition, a one-man show put on in 1809, proved a total failure, Blake passed into almost complete obscurity. Only when he was in his sixties did he finally attract a small but devoted group of young painters who served as an audience for his work and his talk. Blake's old age was serene and self-confident, largely free from the bursts of irascibility with which he had earlier responded to the shallowness and blindness of the English public. He died in his seventieth year.

Blake's first book of poems, *Poetical Sketches*, which he had printed when he was twenty-six years old, showed his dissatisfaction with the reigning poetic tradition and his restless quest for new forms and techniques. For lyric models he turned back to the Elizabethan and early seventeenth-century poets, to the Ossianic poems, and to Collins, Thomas Chatterton, and other eighteenth-century writers outside the tradition of Pope; he also experimented with partial rhymes and novel rhythms and employed bold figures of speech that at times approximate symbols. In 1788 he began to experiment with relief etching, a method that he called "illuminated printing" and used to produce most of his books of poems. Working directly on a copper plate with pens, brushes, and an acid-resistant medium, he wrote the text in reverse (so that it would print in the normal order) and also drew the illustration; he then etched the plate in acid to eat away the untreated copper and leave the design standing in relief. The pages printed from such plates were colored by hand ("illuminated") in water colors and stitched together to make up a volume. This process was laborious and time-consuming, and Blake printed very few copies of his books; for example, of *Songs of Innocence and of Experience* twenty-eight copies (some of them incomplete) are known to exist; of *The Book of Thel*, sixteen; of *The Marriage of Heaven and Hell*, nine; and of *Jerusalem*, five.

It must be remembered that to read Blake's poem in a printed text is to see only an abstraction from an integral and mutually enlightening combination of words and design. In this mode of relief etching, he published *Songs of Innocence* (1789), then added supplementary poems and printed *Songs of Innocence and of Experience* in 1794. The two groups of poems represent the world as it is envisioned by what he calls "two contrary states of the human soul." In the best of the songs of experience, such as *The Tyger* and *London*, Blake achieved his mature lyric technique of compressed metaphor and symbol which explode into a multiplicity of references.

Gradually Blake's thinking about human history and his experience of life and suffering articulated themselves in the "Giant Forms" and their actions, which constitute a complete mythology. As Los said, speaking for all imaginative artists, "I must Create a System or be enslaved by another Man's." This coherent but constantly altering and enlarging system composed the subject matter, first of Blake's "minor prophecies," completed by 1795, and then of the major prophetic books on which he continued working until about 1820: *The Four Zoas, Milton*, and *Jerusalem*.

In his sixties Blake gave up poetry to devote himself to pictorial art. In the course of his life he produced hundreds of paintings and engravings, many of them illustrations for the work of other poets, including a representation of Chaucer's Canterbury pilgrims, a superb set of designs for the Book of Job, and a series of illustrations of Dante, on which he was still hard at work when he died. At the time of his death Blake was little known as an artist and almost entirely unknown as a poet. In the mid-nineteenth century he acquired a group of admirers among the Pre-Raphaelites, who regarded him as a precursor. Since the mid-1920s, Blake has finally come into his own, both in poetry and painting, as one of the most dedicated, intellectually challenging, and astonishingly original of artists.

The explication of Blake's cryptic prophetic books has been the preoccupation of many scholars. Blake wrote them in the persona, or "voice," of "the Bard! / Who Present, Past, & Future sees"—that is, as a British poet who follows Spenser, and especially Milton, in a lineage going back to the prophets of the Bible. "The Nature of my Work," he said, "is Visionary or Imaginative." What Blake meant by the key terms *vision* and *imagination*, however, is often misinterpreted by taking literally what he, speaking the traditional language of his great predecessors, intended in a figurative sense. "That which can be made Explicit to the Idiot," Blake declared, "is not worth my care." Blake was a born ironist who enjoyed mystifying his well-meaning but literal-minded friends and who took a defiant pleasure in shocking the dull and complacent "angels" of his day by being deliberately outrageous in representing his work and opinions.

Blake declared that "all he knew was in the Bible" and that "The Old & New Testaments are the Great Code of Art." This is an exaggeration of the truth that all his prophetic writings deal, in various formulations, with some aspects of the overall biblical plot of the creation and the Fall, the history of the generations of humanity in the fallen world, redemption, and the promise of a recovery of Eden and of a New Jerusalem. These events, however, Blake interprets in what he calls "the spiritual sense." For such a procedure he had considerable precedent, not in the neoplatonic and occult thinkers with whom some modern commentators align him, but in the "spiritual" interpreters of the Bible among the radical Protestant sects in seventeenth- and eighteenth-century England. In *The French Revolution, America: A Prophecy, Europe: A Prophecy,* and the trenchant prophetic satire *The Marriage of Heaven and Hell*—all of which Blake wrote in the early 1790s while he was an ardent supporter of the French Revolution—he, like Wordsworth, Coleridge, Southey, and a number of radical English theologians, represented the contemporary Revolution as the purifying violence that, according to biblical prophecy, was the portent of the imminent redemption of humanity and the world. In Blake's later poems, Orc, the fiery spirit of revolution, gives way as a central personage to Los, the type of the visionary imagination in the fallen world. Even in his early writings, however, Blake had represented historical revolution as correlative with a radical change effected within the mind and imagination of the individual, so that the replacement of Orc by Los does not indicate Blake's recantation of former beliefs, but a shift of emphasis from an apocalypse by revolution to an apocalypse by imagination.

BLAKE'S MATURE MYTH

Blake's first attempt to articulate his full myth of humanity's present, past, and future was *The Four Zoas,* begun in 1796 or 1797. A passage from the opening statement of its theme exemplifies the long verse line (what Blake called "the march of long resounding strong heroic verse") in which he wrote his Prophetic Books and will serve also to outline the myth, or visualizable imaginative form, in which Blake's thought embodied itself:

> Four Mighty Ones are in every Man; a Perfect Unity
> Cannot Exist, but from the Universal Brotherhood of Eden,
> The Universal Man. To Whom be Glory Evermore, Amen. . . .
> Los was the fourth immortal starry one, & in the Earth
> Of a bright Universe Empery attended day & night
> Days & nights of revolving joy, Urthona was his name
> In Eden; in the Auricular Nerves of Human life
> Which is the Earth of Eden, he his Emanations propagated. . . .
>   Daughter of Beulah, Sing
> His fall into Division & his Resurrection to Unity.

Blake's mythical premise, or starting point, is not a transcendent God but the "Universal Man" who is himself God and who incorporates the cosmos as well. (Blake elsewhere describes this founding image as "the Human Form Divine" and names him "Albion.") The fall, in this myth, is not the fall of humanity away from God but a falling apart of primal people, a "fall into Division." In this event the original sin is what Blake calls "Selfhood," the attempt of an isolated part to be self-sufficient. The breakup of the all-inclusive Universal Man in Eden into exiled parts, it is evident, identifies the Fall with the creation—the creation not only of man and of nature as we ordinarily know them but also of a sky god who is alien from humanity. Universal Man divides first into the "Four Mighty Ones" who are the Zoas, or chief powers and component aspects of humanity, and these in turn divide sexually into male Spectres and female Emanations. (Thus in the quoted passage the Zoa known in the unfallen state of Eden as Urthona, the imaginative power, separates into the form of Los in the fallen world.) In addition to Eden there are three successively lower "states" of being in the fallen world, which Blake calls Beulah (a pastoral condition of easy and relaxed innocence, without clash of "contraries"), Generation (the realm of common human experience, suffering, and conflicting contraries), and Ulro (Blake's hell, the lowest state, or limit, of bleak rationality, tyranny, static negation, and isolated Selfhood). The fallen world moves through the cycles of its history, successively approaching and falling away from redemption, until, by the agency of the Redeemer (who is equated with the human imagination and is most potently operative in the prophetic poet), it will culminate in an apocalypse. In terms of his controlling image of the Universal Man, Blake describes this apocalypse as a return to the original, undivided condition, "his Resurrection to Unity."

Although Blake did not know it, he shared with a number of contemporary German philosophers the point of view—it has in our own time become the prevailing point of view—that our fall (or the malaise of modern culture) is essentially a mode of psychic disintegration and of resultant alienation from oneself, one's world, and one's fellow human beings, and that our hope of recovery lies in a process of reintegration. As an imaginative poet, however, Blake does not present this view in abstract conceptual terms, but embodies it in picturable agents acting out an epic plot. What is confusing to many readers is that Blake uses different ways of representing the same vision of men and women in the world. For example, Blake alternates the representation of the Fall as the division of Primal Man with its representation as a catastrophic alteration, in individual human beings, from imaginative vision to physical eyesight. The result of this alteration was that the cosmos, which in the original mode of unified imaginative perception had been beheld as human and one, came to be seen as a multitude of isolated individuals in a dehumanized and alien nature. Conversely, the apocalypse toward which Blake—the imaginative artist who as an individual represents the mythical type-figure Los—is always working, is to enable all men and women to break through to a restored unity of vision. By such a vision all beings, together with the world they inhabit, will again be perceived as sharing the one life and the one humanity of that "Universal Brotherhood," the Human Form Divine, who is imaged as creating such a universe by the very act of so envisioning it.

Blake decries, in the form of the mythical being "Vala," what we ordinarily mean by "nature," the material universe perceived by the senses. It would, however, be a mistake to equate his views with ascetic otherworldliness. Blake does not look forward to a consummation that will wipe out the natural world and replace it by a transcendental substitute. He maintained, on the contrary, that we achieve redemption by liberating and intensifying the bodily senses—as he said, by "an improvement of sensual enjoyment"—and by attaining and sustaining that mode of vision that does not cancel the fallen world, but transfigures it, by revealing the lineaments of its eternal imaginative form. That is what Blake means when, in *A Vision of the Last Judgment*, he says that "The Nature of my Work is Visionary or Imaginative," and that in the moment of apocalyptic redemption "Error or Creation will be Burned Up & then & not till then Truth or Eternity will appear. It is Burnt up the Moment Men cease to behold it." Accordingly, in the apocalypse that concludes *Jerusalem*, the reunion of Albion the Universal Man with Jerusalem, his emanation, is accompanied by a freeing of man's senses and results in the recovery of a lost mode of vision that sees a nature which, because it is humanized, is a place where all individuals, united as One Man, can feel at home.

   Our text for all of Blake's writings is that of *The Complete Poetry and Prose of William Blake*, edited by David V. Erdman and Harold Bloom (revised edition, Berkeley, 1982). Blake's erratic spelling and punctuation have been altered when the original form might mislead the reader. The editors are grateful for the expert advice of Joseph Viscomi and Robert Essick in editing the selections from Blake.

From POETICAL SKETCHES[1]

To Spring[2]

O thou, with dewy locks, who lookest down
Thro' the clear windows of the morning; turn
Thine angel eyes upon our western isle,
Which in full choir hails thy approach, O Spring!

The hills tell each other, and the list'ning   5
Vallies hear; all our longing eyes are turned
Up to thy bright pavillions: issue forth,
And let thy holy feet visit our clime.

Come o'er the eastern hills, and let our winds
Kiss thy perfumed garments; let us taste   10
Thy morn and evening breath; scatter thy pearls
Upon our love-sick land that mourns for thee.

O deck her forth with thy fair fingers; pour
Thy soft kisses on her bosom; and put
Thy golden crown upon her languish'd head,   15
Whose modest tresses were bound up for thee!

                                                          1783

To the Evening Star

Thou fair-hair'd angel of the evening,
Now, while the sun rests on the mountains, light
Thy bright torch of love;[1] thy radiant crown
Put on, and smile upon our evening bed!
Smile on our loves; and, while thou drawest the   5
Blue curtains of the sky, scatter thy silver dew

---

1. *Poetical Sketches*, Blake's only volume of poems to be set in type, went to press in 1783, but was never put on sale. A preface written by an anonymous friend apologized for the poems on the grounds that they had been composed between the ages of twelve and twenty. Although, like the work of other youthful poets, they echo earlier writers (including Spenser, Shakespeare,

and Milton), many of them are radical experiments in metaphor, meter, and rhyme.
2. *Poetical Sketches* includes four poems, each in the form of an invocation to one of the four seasons. *To Spring* is thronged with echoes from the poetry of the Old Testament, as well as from Milton.
1. The evening star is Venus, goddess of love.

On every flower that shuts its sweet eyes
In timely sleep. Let thy west wind sleep on
The lake; speak silence with thy glimmering eyes,
And wash the dusk with silver. Soon, full soon,   10
Dost thou withdraw; then the wolf rages wide,
And the lion glares thro' the dun forest:
The fleeces of our flocks are cover'd with
Thy sacred dew: protect them with thine influence.[2]

                                                                    1783

Song

How sweet I roam'd from field to field,
    And tasted all the summer's pride,
'Till I the prince of love[1] beheld,
    Who in the sunny beams did glide!

He shew'd me lilies for my hair,   5
    And blushing roses for my brow;
He led me through his gardens fair,
    Where all his golden pleasures grow.

With sweet May dews my wings were wet,
    And Phoebus fir'd my vocal rage;[2]   10
He caught me in his silken net,
    And shut me in his golden cage.

He loves to sit and hear me sing,
    Then, laughing, sports and plays with me;
Then stretches out my golden wing,   15
    And mocks my loss of liberty.

                                                                    1783

To the Muses

Whether on Ida's[1] shady brow,
    Or in the chambers of the East,
The chambers of the sun, that now
    From antient melody have ceas'd;

Whether in Heav'n ye wander fair,   5
    Or the green corners of the earth,
Or the blue regions of the air,
    Where the melodious winds have birth;

Whether on chrystal rocks ye rove,
    Beneath the bosom of the sea   10

2. In astrology, the technical term for the occult power   2. Fervor, i.e., my strong desire to sing.
of stars over humans.   1. Mountain in southern Phrygia, celebrated in classi-
1. In Greek myth, Eros or Cupid.   cal mythology.

Wand'ring in many a coral grove,
Fair Nine,[2] forsaking Poetry!

How have you left the antient love
That bards of old enjoy'd in you![3]
The languid strings do scarcely move!   15
The sound is forc'd, the notes are few!

• • •   1783

All Religions Are One[1]

The Voice of one crying in the Wilderness[2]

The Argument. As the true method of knowledge is experiment the true faculty of knowing must be the faculty which experiences. This faculty I treat of.

PRINCIPLE 1st. That the Poetic Genius is the true Man, and that the body or outward form of Man is derived from the Poetic Genius. Likewise that the forms of all things are derived from their Genius, which by the Ancients was call'd an Angel & Spirit & Demon.

PRINCIPLE 2d. As all men are alike in outward form, So (and with the same infinite variety) all are alike in the Poetic Genius.

PRINCIPLE 3d. No man can think write or speak from his heart, but he must intend truth. Thus all sects of Philosophy are from the Poetic Genius, adapted to the weaknesses of every individual.

PRINCIPLE 4. As none by travelling over known lands can find out the unknown, So from already acquired knowledge Man could not acquire more. Therefore an universal Poetic Genius exists.

PRINCIPLE 5. The Religions of all Nations are derived from each Nation's different reception of the Poetic Genius, which is every where call'd the Spirit of Prophecy.

PRINCIPLE 6. The Jewish & Christian Testaments are An original derivation from the Poetic Genius. This is necessary from the confined nature of bodily sensation.

Principle 7th. As all men are alike (tho' infinitely various), So all Religions & as all similars have one source.

The true Man is the source, he being the Poetic Genius.

---

2. The Nine Muses.
3. The poem is Blake's lament, in the diction of later 18-century poetry, over the failure of the inspiration that had been manifested by the "bards," the older British poet-prophets.
1. This and the following two selections are early illuminated works, probably etched in 1788. They are directed both against 18th-century Deism or "natural religion" (which bases its religious tenets not on scriptural revelation, but on evidences of God in the natural or "organic" world) and against Christian orthodoxy, whose creed is based on a particular Scrip-

ture. In this selection Blake ironically accepts the Deistic view that all particular religions are variants of the one true religion, but rejects the Deists' "Argument" that this religion is grounded on reasoning from sense-experience. He attributes the one religion instead to the innate possession by all men of "Poetic Genius"—that is, of a capacity for imaginative vision.
2. Applied in the Gospels (e.g., Matthew 3.3) to John the Baptist, regarded as fulfilling the prophecy in Isaiah 39.3. Blake applies the phrase to himself, as a later prophetic voice in an alien time.

There Is No Natural Religion[1]

[a]

The Argument. Man has no notion of moral fitness but from Education. Naturally he is only a natural organ subject to Sense.

I. Man cannot naturally Percieve but through his natural or bodily organs.

II. Man by his reasoning power can only compare & judge of what he has already perciev'd.

III. From a perception of only 3 senses or 3 elements none could deduce a fourth or fifth.

IV. None could have other than natural or organic thoughts if he had none but organic perceptions.

V. Man's desires are limited by his perceptions; none can desire what he has not perciev'd.

VI. The desires & perceptions of man, untaught by any thing but organs of sense, must be limited to objects of sense.

There Is No Natural Religion[1]

[b]

I. Man's perceptions are not bounded by organs of perception; he percieves more than sense (tho' ever so acute) can discover.

II. Reason, or the ratio[2] of all we have already known, is not the same that it shall be when we know more.

[III lacking]

IV. The bounded is loathed by its possessor. The same dull round even of a universe would soon become a mill with complicated wheels.

V. If the many become the same as the few when possess'd, More! More! is the cry of a mistaken soul. Less than All cannot satisfy Man.

VI. If any could desire what he is incapable of possessing, despair must be his eternal lot.

VII. The desire of Man being Infinite, the possession is Infinite & himself Infinite.

Application. He who sees the Infinite in all things sees God. He who sees the Ratio only sees himself only.

Conclusion. If it were not for the Poetic or Prophetic character the Philosophic & Experimental would soon be at the ratio of all things, & stand still unable to do other than repeat the same dull round over again.

Therefore God becomes as we are, that we may be as he is.

1788

---

1. In this selection Blake presents his version of English empiricism, which derives all mental content (including the evidences from which, in "natural religion," reason is held to prove the existence of God) from perceptions by the physical senses.

1. In this third document Blake presents his assertions (in opposition to those in the preceding tract) that knowledge is not limited to the physical senses, but is as unbounded as the infinite desires of humankind and its godlike capacity for infinite vision.

2. In Latin *ratio* signifies both "reason" and "calculation." Blake applies the term derogatorily to the 18th-century concept of reason as a calculating faculty whose operations are limited to sense-perceptions.

From SONGS OF INNOCENCE AND OF EXPERIENCE[1]

SHEWING THE TWO CONTRARY STATES OF THE HUMAN SOUL

From *Songs of Innocence*

Introduction

Piping down the valleys wild
Piping songs of pleasant glee
On a cloud I saw a child,
And he laughing said to me,

"Pipe a song about a Lamb";   5
So I piped with merry chear;
"Piper pipe that song again" —
So I piped, he wept to hear.

"Drop thy pipe thy happy pipe
Sing thy songs of happy chear";   10
So I sung the same again
While he wept with joy to hear.

"Piper sit thee down and write
In a book that all may read" —
So he vanish'd from my sight.   15
And I pluck'd a hollow reed,

And I made a rural pen,
And I stain'd the water clear,
And I wrote my happy songs
Every child may joy to hear.   20

1789

The Ecchoing Green

The Sun does arise,
And make happy the skies.
The merry bells ring
To welcome the Spring.
The sky-lark and thrush,   5

---

1. *Songs of Innocence* was etched in 1789, and in 1794 was combined with additional poems under the title *Songs of Innocence and of Experience*; this collection was reprinted at various later times with varying arrangements of the poems. In his songs of innocence Blake assumes the stance that he is writing "happy songs / Every child may joy to hear," but they do not all depict an innocent and happy world; many of them incorporate injustice, evil, and suffering. These aspects of the fallen world, however, are represented as they appear to a "state" of the human soul that Blake calls "innocence," and which he expresses in a simple pastoral language, in the tradition of Isaac Watts's widely read *Divine Songs for Children* (1715). The vision of the same world, as it appears to the "contrary" state of the soul that Blake calls "experience," is an ugly and terrifying one of poverty, disease, prostitution, war, and social, institutional, and sexual repression, epitomized in the ghastly representation of modern London. Though each stands as an independent poem, a number of the songs of innocence have a matched counterpart, or "contrary," in the songs of experience. Thus *Infant Joy* is paired with *Infant Sorrow,* and the meek *Lamb* reveals its other aspect of divinity in the flaming, wrathful *Tyger.*

The birds of the bush,
Sing louder around,
To the bells' chearful sound.
While our sports shall be seen
On the Ecchoing Green.   10

Old John with white hair
Does laugh away care,
Sitting under the oak,
Among the old folk.
They laugh at our play,   15
And soon they all say:
"Such, such were the joys.
When we all, girls & boys,
In our youth-time were seen,
On the Ecchoing Green."   20

Till the little ones weary
No more can be merry
The sun does descend,
And our sports have an end:
Round the laps of their mothers,   25
Many sisters and brothers,
Like birds in their nest,
Are ready for rest;
And sport no more seen,
On the darkening Green.   30

1789

The Lamb

Little Lamb, who made thee?
  Dost thou know who made thee?
Gave thee life & bid thee feed,
By the stream & o'er the mead;
Gave thee clothing of delight,   5
Softest clothing wooly bright;
Gave thee such a tender voice,
Making all the vales rejoice!
  Little Lamb who made thee?
  Dost thou know who made thee?   10

  Little Lamb I'll tell thee,
  Little Lamb I'll tell thee!
He is callèd by thy name,
For he calls himself a Lamb;
He is meek & he is mild,   15
He became a little child;
I a child & thou a lamb,
We are callèd by his name.
  Little Lamb God bless thee.
  Little Lamb God bless thee.   20

1789

The Little Black Boy

My mother bore me in the southern wild,
And I am black, but O! my soul is white;
White as an angel is the English child,
But I am black as if bereav'd of light.

My mother taught me underneath a tree, 5
And sitting down before the heat of day,
She took me on her lap and kissèd me,
And pointing to the east, began to say:

"Look on the rising sun: there God does live
And gives his light, and gives his heat away; 10
And flowers and trees and beasts and men receive
Comfort in morning, joy in the noon day.

"And we are put on earth a little space,
That we may learn to bear the beams of love,
And these black bodies and this sun-burnt face 15
Is but a cloud, and like a shady grove.

"For when our souls have learn'd the heat to bear,
The cloud will vanish; we shall hear his voice,
Saying: 'Come out from the grove, my love & care,
And round my golden tent like lambs rejoice.' " 20

Thus did my mother say, and kissèd me;
And thus I say to little English boy:
When I from black and he from white cloud free,
And round the tent of God like lambs we joy,

I'll shade him from the heat till he can bear 25
To lean in joy upon our father's knee.
And then I'll stand and stroke his silver hair,
And be like him, and he will then love me.

1789

The Chimney Sweeper

When my mother died I was very young,
And my father sold me while yet my tongue
Could scarcely cry " 'weep! 'weep! 'weep! 'weep!"[1]
So your chimneys I sweep & in soot I sleep.

There's little Tom Dacre, who cried when his head 5
That curl'd like a lamb's back, was shav'd, so I said,
"Hush, Tom! never mind it, for when your head's bare,
You know that the soot cannot spoil your white hair."

1. The child's lisping attempt at the chimney sweeper's street cry, "Sweep! Sweep!"

And so he was quiet, & that very night,
As Tom was a-sleeping he had such a sight!   10
That thousands of sweepers, Dick, Joe, Ned, & Jack,
Were all of them lock'd up in coffins of black;

And by came an Angel who had a bright key,
And he open'd the coffins & set them all free;
Then down a green plain, leaping, laughing they run,   15
And wash in a river and shine in the Sun.

Then naked & white, all their bags left behind,
They rise upon clouds, and sport in the wind.
And the Angel told Tom, if he'd be a good boy,
He'd have God for his father & never want joy.   20

And so Tom awoke; and we rose in the dark
And got with our bags & our brushes to work.
Tho' the morning was cold, Tom was happy & warm;
So if all do their duty, they need not fear harm.

                                                    1789

The Divine Image

To Mercy, Pity, Peace, and Love,
All pray in their distress,
And to these virtues of delight
Return their thankfulness.

For Mercy, Pity, Peace, and Love,   5
Is God, our father dear:
And Mercy, Pity, Peace, and Love,
Is Man, his child and care.

For Mercy has a human heart,
Pity, a human face,
And Love, the human form divine,   10
And Peace, the human dress.

Then every man of every clime,
That prays in his distress,
Prays to the human form divine,
Love, Mercy, Pity, Peace.   15

And all must love the human form,
In heathen, Turk, or Jew.
Where Mercy, Love, & Pity dwell,
There God is dwelling too.   20

                                                    1789

Holy Thursday[1]

'Twas on a Holy Thursday, their innocent faces clean,
The children walking two & two, in red & blue & green;
Grey headed beadles[2] walkd before with wands as white as snow,
Till into the high dome of Paul's they like Thames' waters flow.

O what a multitude they seemd, these flowers of London town!　　　5
Seated in companies they sit with radiance all their own.
The hum of multitudes was there, but multitudes of lambs,
Thousands of little boys & girls raising their innocent hands.

Now like a mighty wind they raise to heaven the voice of song,
Or like harmonious thunderings the seats of heaven among.　　　10
Beneath them sit the agèd men, wise guardians of the poor;
Then cherish pity, lest you drive an angel from your door.[3]

ca. 1784　　　　　　　　　　　　　　　　　　　　　　　　1789

Nurse's Song

When the voices of children are heard on the green
And laughing is heard on the hill,
My heart is at rest within my breast
And everything else is still.

"Then come home my children, the sun is gone down　　　5
And the dews of night arise;
Come, come, leave off play, and let us away
Till the morning appears in the skies."

"No, no, let us play, for it is yet day
And we cannot go to sleep;　　　10
Besides, in the sky, the little birds fly
And the hills are all coverd with sheep."

"Well, well, go & play till the light fades away
And then go home to bed."
The little ones leaped & shouted & laugh'd　　　15
And all the hills ecchoèd.

ca. 1784　　　　　　　　　　　　　　　　　　　　　　　　1789

Infant Joy

"I have no name,
I am but two days old."

1. In the English church, the Thursday celebrating the ascension of Jesus (thirty-nine days after Easter). It was the custom on this day to march the poor (frequently orphaned) children from the charity schools of London to a service at St. Paul's Cathedral.

2. Lower church officers, one of whose duties is to keep order.

3. Cf. Hebrews 13.2: "Be not forgetful to entertain strangers: for thereby some have entertained angels unawares."

What shall I call thee?
"I happy am,
Joy is my name."   5
Sweet joy befall thee!

Pretty joy!
Sweet joy but two days old,
Sweet joy I call thee;
Thou dost smile,   10
I sing the while —
Sweet joy befall thee.

1789

From *Songs of Experience*

Introduction

Hear the voice of the Bard!
Who Present, Past, & Future sees;
Whose ears have heard
The Holy Word
That walk'd among the ancient trees;[1]   5

Calling the lapsèd Soul[2]
And weeping in the evening dew,
That might controll
The starry pole,
And fallen, fallen light renew![3]   10

"O Earth, O Earth, return!
Arise from out the dewy grass;
Night is worn,
And the morn
Rises from the slumberous mass.   15

"Turn away no more;
Why wilt thou turn away?
The starry floor
The watry shore[4]
Is giv'n thee till the break of day."   20

1794

---

1. Genesis 3.8: "And [Adam and Eve] heard the voice of the Lord God walking in the garden in the cool of the day." The Bard, or poet-prophet, whose imagination is not bound by time, has heard the voice of the Lord in Eden.
2. The syntax leaves it ambiguous whether it is "the Bard" or "the Holy Word" who calls to the fallen

("lapsèd") soul and to the fallen earth to stop the natural cycle of light and darkness.
3. The likely syntax is that "Soul" is the subject of "might controll."
4. In Blake's recurrent symbolism the starry sky ("floor") signifies rigid rational order, and the sea signifies chaos.

Earth's Answer[1]

Earth rais'd up her head,
From the darkness dread & drear.
Her light fled:
Stony dread!
And her locks cover'd with grey despair.   5

"Prison'd on watry shore
Starry Jealousy does keep my den,
Cold and hoar
Weeping o'er
I hear the Father of the ancient men.[2]   10

"Selfish father of men,
Cruel, jealous, selfish fear!
Can delight
Chain'd in night
The virgins of youth and morning bear?   15

"Does spring hide its joy
When buds and blossoms grow?
Does the sower
Sow by night,
Or the plowman in darkness plow?   20

"Break this heavy chain
That does freeze my bones around;
Selfish! vain!
Eternal bane!
That free Love with bondage bound."   25

                                                                            1794

The Clod & the Pebble

"Love seeketh not Itself to please,
Nor for itself hath any care;
But for another gives its ease,
And builds a Heaven in Hell's despair."

    So sang a little Clod of Clay,   5
    Trodden with the cattle's feet;
    But a Pebble of the brook,
    Warbled out these metres meet:

"Love seeketh only Self to please,
To bind another to its delight;   10

---

1. The Earth's answer explains why she, the natural world, cannot by her unaided endeavors renew the fallen light.
2. This is the character that Blake later named "Ur-izen" in his prophetic works. He is the tyrant who binds the mind to the natural world and also imposes a moral bondage on sexual desire and other modes of human energy.

Joys in another's loss of ease,
And builds a Hell in Heaven's despite."

1794

Holy Thursday

Is this a holy thing to see,
In a rich and fruitful land,
Babes reduced to misery,
Fed with cold and usurous hand?

Is that trembling cry a song?   5
Can it be a song of joy?
And so many children poor?
It is a land of poverty!

And their sun does never shine,
And their fields are bleak & bare,   10
And their ways are fill'd with thorns;
It is eternal winter there.

For where-e'er the sun does shine,
And where-e'er the rain does fall,
Babe can never hunger there,   15
Nor poverty the mind appall.

1794

The Chimney Sweeper

A little black thing among the snow
Crying " 'weep, 'weep," in notes of woe!
"Where are thy father & mother? say?"
"They are both gone up to the church to pray.

"Because I was happy upon the heath,   5
And smil'd among the winter's snow;
They clothed me in the clothes of death,
And taught me to sing the notes of woe.

"And because I am happy, & dance & sing,
They think they have done me no injury,   10
And are gone to praise God & his Priest & King,
Who make up a heaven of our misery."

1790–92   1794

Nurse's Song

When the voices of children are heard on the green
And whisperings are in the dale,

The days of my youth rise fresh in my mind,
My face turns green and pale.

Then come home my children, the sun is gone down   5
And the dews of night arise;
Your spring & your day are wasted in play,
And your winter and night in disguise.

1794

The Sick Rose

O Rose, thou art sick.
The invisible worm
That flies in the night
In the howling storm

Has found out thy bed   5
Of crimson joy,
And his dark secret love
Does thy life destroy.

1794

The Tyger[1]

Tyger! Tyger! burning bright
In the forests of the night,
What immortal hand or eye
Could frame thy fearful symmetry?

In what distant deeps or skies   5
Burnt the fire of thine eyes?
On what wings dare he aspire?
What the hand dare seize the fire?

And what shoulder, & what art,
Could twist the sinews of thy heart?   10
And when thy heart began to beat,
What dread hand? & what dread feet?

What the hammer? what the chain?
In what furnace was thy brain?
What the anvil? what dread grasp   15
Dare its deadly terrors clasp?

When the stars threw down their spears[2]
And water'd heaven with their tears,

1. For the author's revisions while composing *The Tyger*, see "Poems in Process" (pp. 2579–81).
2. "Threw down" is ambiguous and may signify that the stars either "surrendered" or "hurled down" their spears.

Did he smile his work to see?
Did he who made the Lamb make thee?   20

Tyger! Tyger! burning bright
In the forests of the night,
What immortal hand or eye
Dare frame thy fearful symmetry?

1790–92   1794

My Pretty Rose Tree

A flower was offerd to me;
Such a flower as May never bore,
But I said, "I've a Pretty Rose-tree,"
And I passed the sweet flower o'er.

Then I went to my Pretty Rose-tree,   5
To tend her by day and by night.
But my Rose turnd away with jealousy,
And her thorns were my only delight.

1794

Ah Sun-flower

Ah Sun-flower! weary of time,
Who countest the steps of the Sun,
Seeking after that sweet golden clime
Where the traveller's journey is done;

Where the Youth pined away with desire,   5
And the pale Virgin shrouded in snow,
Arise from their graves and aspire,
Where my Sun-flower wishes to go.

1794

The Garden of Love

I went to the Garden of Love,
And saw what I never had seen:
A Chapel was built in the midst,
Where I used to play on the green.

And the gates of this Chapel were shut,   5
And "Thou shalt not" writ over the door;
So I turn'd to the Garden of Love,
That so many sweet flowers bore,

And I saw it was filled with graves,
And tomb-stones where flowers should be;

And Priests in black gowns were walking their rounds,
And binding with briars my joys & desires.

1794

London

I wander thro' each charter'd[1] street,
Near where the charter'd Thames does flow,
And mark in every face I meet
Marks of weakness, marks of woe.

In every cry of every Man,   5
In every Infant's cry of fear,
In every voice, in every ban,[2]
The mind-forg'd manacles I hear:

How the Chimney-sweeper's cry
Every blackning Church appalls,   10
And the hapless Soldier's sigh
Runs in blood down Palace walls.

But most thro' midnight streets I hear
How the youthful Harlot's curse
Blasts the new-born Infant's tear,[3]   15
And blights with plagues the Marriage hearse.[4]

1794

The Human Abstract[1]

Pity would be no more,
If we did not make somebody Poor;
And Mercy no more could be,
If all were as happy as we;

And mutual fear brings peace,   normally positive[5]
Till the selfish loves increase;   = loving one'self
Then Cruelty knits a snare,   cruelty
And spreads his baits with care.

He sits down with holy fears,
And waters the ground with tears;
Then Humility takes its root   Humility = free   10
Underneath his foot.   not real H. just

[handwritten, mirror-written annotations in left margin:] If there were no poor it would become no need with Mercy / Humility from Cruelty and fear not result when

1. "Given liberty," but also, ironically, "preempted as private property, and rented out."
2. The various meanings of "ban" are relevant (political and legal prohibition, curse, public condemnation) as well as "banns" (marriage proclamation).
3. Most critics read this line as implying prenatal blindness, resulting from a parent's venereal disease (the "plagues" of line 16) by earlier infection from the harlot.

4. In the older sense of "hearse": converts the marriage bed into a bier. Or possibly, since the current sense of the word had also come into use in Blake's day, "converts the marriage coach into a funeral hearse."
1. The matched contrary to *The Divine Image* in *Songs of Innocence*. The virtues of the earlier poem, "Mercy, Pity, Peace, and Love," are now represented as possible marks for exploitation, cruelty, conflict, and hypocritical humility.

Soon spreads the dismal shade
Of Mystery over his head;
And the Catterpiller and Fly
Feed on the Mystery.

And it bears the fruit of Deceit,
Ruddy and sweet to eat;
And the Raven his nest has made
In its thickest shade.   20

The Gods of the earth and sea,
Sought thro' Nature to find this Tree,
But their search was all in vain:
There grows one in the Human Brain.

1790–92   1794

Handwritten marginalia:
= Mystery / religion / Organised religion
Implies that humility is really a front
this false H. leads to even greater deciet
Things breeding in the "ugly secrets"
God / Creator / sun & moon
Human brain = breeding ground of cruelty and other bad stuff

Infant Sorrow

My mother groand! my father wept.
Into the dangerous world I leapt,
Helpless, naked, piping loud;
Like a fiend hid in a cloud.

Struggling in my father's hands,   5
Striving against my swadling bands;
Bound and weary I thought best
To sulk upon my mother's breast.

1794

A Poison Tree

I was angry with my friend:
I told my wrath, my wrath did end.
I was angry with my foe:
I told it not, my wrath did grow.

And I waterd it in fears,   5
Night & morning with my tears;
And I sunnèd it with smiles,
And with soft deceitful wiles.

And it grew both day and night,
Till it bore an apple bright.   10
And my foe beheld it shine,
And he knew that it was mine,

And into my garden stole,
When the night had veild the pole;
In the morning glad I see   15
My foe outstretchd beneath the tree.

1794

To Tirzah[1]

Whate'er is Born of Mortal Birth
Must be consumèd with the Earth
To rise from Generation free;
Then what have I to do with thee?[2]

The Sexes sprung from Shame & Pride,   5
Blow'd[3] in the morn, in evening died;
But Mercy changd Death into Sleep;
The Sexes rose to work & weep.

Thou, Mother of my Mortal part,
With cruelty didst mould my Heart,   10
And with false self-deceiving tears
Didst bind my Nostrils, Eyes, & Ears.

Didst close my Tongue in senseless clay
And me to Mortal Life betray.
The Death of Jesus set me free;   15
Then what have I to do with thee?

                                      ca. 1805

A Divine Image[1]

Cruelty has a Human Heart
And Jealousy a Human Face,
Terror, the Human Form Divine,
And Secrecy, the Human Dress.

The Human Dress is forgèd Iron,   5
The Human Form, a fiery Forge,
The Human Face, a Furnace seal'd,
The Human Heart, its hungry Gorge.[2]

1790–91

• • •

The Book of Thel   Although Blake dated the etched poem 1789, its composition probably extended to 1791, so that he was working on it at the time he was writing the *Songs of Innocence* and some of the *Songs of Experience*. *The Book of*

---

1. Tirzah was the capital of the northern kingdom of Israel and is conceived by Blake in opposition to Jerusalem, capital of the southern kingdom of Judah, whose tribes had been redeemed from captivity. In this poem, which was added to late versions of *Songs of Experience*, Tirzah is represented as the mother—in the realm of material nature and "Generation"—of the mortal body, with its restrictive senses.
2. Echoing the words of Christ to his mother at the marriage in Cana, John 2.4: "Woman, what have I to do with thee? mine hour is not yet come."
3. Blossomed.
1. Blake omitted this poem from all but one copy of *Songs of Experience*, probably because *The Human Abstract* served as a more comprehensive and subtle contrary to *The Divine Image* in *Songs of Innocence*.
2. Maw, stomach.

Thel treats the same two "states"; now, however, Blake employs the narrative instead of the lyrical mode and embodies aspects of the developing myth which was fully enacted in his later prophetic books. And like the major prophecies, this poem is written in the fourteener, a long line of seven stresses.

Thel—her name probably derives from a Greek word for "wish" or "will" and suggests the timid failure of a desire to fulfill itself—is a virgin dwelling in the Vales of Har, which is equivalent to the sheltered condition of pastoral peace and innocence in Blake's *Songs of Innocence* and will develop into the "Beulah" of his prophetic books. In the fragile beauty of this realm of unrealized potentiality, Thel lives a two-dimensional mirror image of existence (plate 1, line 9). The Lily of the Valley and the Cloud try to comfort her by describing their content with their roles in the cycle of innocent existence. Thel, however, since she is a human potentiality, finds such comfort inapplicable to her condition of unfulfillment and uselessness, as a virgin without a male contrary and as a shepherdess whose sheep run no risks and need no care. The Clod of Clay then speaks for her child, the voiceless Worm, an emblem of phallic generation and a devourer of the mortal body in the fallen world; but the maternal Clay sees the role of the Worm, as well as her own, only from the perspective of essential ignorance: "But how this is, sweet maid, I know not, and I cannot know." In her capacity, however, as the substance from which is formed the mortal body of man, the Clay invites Thel to try the experiment of dying into embodied life. With an abrupt and brutal shift in language and tone, part 4 expresses the shock of the revelation to Thel of the world of Generation and Experience—a revelation from which she flees in terror back to her sheltered, if unfulfilling, paradise.

Some commentators propose that Thel is an unborn soul that shrinks from the ordeal of an embodied life in the material world. Others propose that Thel is a human virgin who shrinks from experiencing a life of adult sexuality. It is readily possible, however, to read Blake's little myth as comprehending both these areas of significance. The reader does not need to be an adept in Blakean mythology to recognize the broad symbolic reach of this poem in ordinary human experience— the elemental failure of nerve to meet the challenge of life as it is, the timid incapacity to risk the conflict, physicality, pain, and loss without which there is no possibility either of growth or of creativity.

The Book of Thel

PLATE 1[1]

THEL'S MOTTO

Does the Eagle know what is in the pit?
Or wilt thou go ask the Mole?
Can Wisdom be put in a silver rod?
Or Love in a golden bowl?[2]

1

The daughters of Mne[3] Seraphim led round their sunny flocks,
All but the youngest; she in paleness sought the secret air,

---

1. The plate numbers identify the page, each with its own pictorial design, as originally printed by Blake. These numbers are reproduced here because they are frequently used in references to Blake's writings.
2. Ecclesiastes 12.5–6 describes a time when "fears shall be in the way . . . and desire shall fail: because man goeth to his long home, and the mourners go about the streets: Or ever the silver cord be loosed, or

the golden bowl be broken." Blake presumably changed the silver cord to a rod in order to make it, with the golden bowl, a sexual symbol.
3. There has been much speculation about this curious term. It may be an abbreviation for the name "Mnetha," the goddess of the vales of Har in Blake's earlier poem *Tiriel*.

To fade away like morning beauty from her mortal day;
Down by the river of Adona[4] her soft voice is heard,
And thus her gentle lamentation falls like morning dew: 5

"O life of this our spring! why fades the lotus of the water?
Why fade these children of the spring? born but to smile & fall.
Ah! Thel is like a watry bow, and like a parting cloud,
Like a reflection in a glass, like shadows in the water,
Like dreams of infants, like a smile upon an infant's face,   10
Like the dove's voice, like transient day, like music in the air.
Ah! gentle may I lay me down, and gentle rest my head,
And gentle sleep the sleep of death, and gentle hear the voice
Of him that walketh in the garden in the evening time."[5]

The Lilly of the valley breathing in the humble grass   15
Answer'd the lovely maid and said: "I am a watry weed,
And I am very small, and love to dwell in lowly vales;
So weak, the gilded butterfly scarce perches on my head;
Yet I am visited from heaven, and he that smiles on all
Walks in the valley and each morn over me spreads his hand,   20
Saying: 'Rejoice, thou humble grass, thou new-born lilly flower,
Thou gentle maid of silent valleys and of modest brooks;
For thou shalt be clothed in light, and fed with morning manna,
Till summer's heat melts thee beside the fountains and the springs
To flourish in eternal vales.' Then why should Thel complain?   25

PLATE 2

Why should the mistress of the vales of Har utter a sigh?"

She ceasd & smild in tears, then sat down in her silver shrine.

Thel answerd: "O thou little virgin of the peaceful valley,
Giving to those that cannot crave, the voiceless, the o'ertired;
Thy breath doth nourish the innocent lamb, he smells thy milky
        garments,
He crops thy flowers, while thou sittest smiling in his face,   5
Wiping his mild and meekin[6] mouth from all contagious taints.
Thy wine doth purify the golden honey; thy perfume,
Which thou dost scatter on every little blade of grass that springs,
Revives the milkèd cow, & tames the fire-breathing steed.   10
But Thel is like a faint cloud kindled at the rising sun:
I vanish from my pearly throne, and who shall find my place?"

"Queen of the vales," the Lilly answered, "ask the tender cloud,
And it shall tell thee why it glitters in the morning sky,
And why it scatters its bright beauty thro' the humid air.   15
Descend, O little cloud, & hover before the eyes of Thel."

4. Possibly suggesting an equation of the Vales of Har   5. Genesis 3.8: "And they heard the voice of the Lord
to Spenser's Garden of Adonis in *The Faerie Queene*   God walking in the garden in the cool of the day."
3.6, as well as to the paradisal garden in Genesis (in   6. Humble.
line 14).

The Cloud descended, and the Lilly bowd her modest head,
And went to mind her numerous charge among the verdant grass.

PLATE 3

2

"O little Cloud," the virgin said, "I charge thee tell to me,
Why thou complainest not when in one hour thou fade away:
Then we shall seek thee but not find; ah, Thel is like to Thee.
I pass away, yet I complain, and no one hears my voice."

The Cloud then shew'd his golden head & his bright form emerg'd,   5
Hovering and glittering on the air before the face of Thel.

"O virgin, know'st thou not our steeds drink of the golden springs
Where Luvah[7] doth renew his horses? Look'st thou on my youth,
And fearest thou because I vanish and am seen no more,
Nothing remains? O maid, I tell thee, when I pass away,   10
It is to tenfold life, to love, to peace, and raptures holy:
Unseen descending, weigh my light wings upon balmy flowers,
And court the fair eyed dew, to take me to her shining tent;
The weeping virgin trembling kneels before the risen sun,
Till we arise link'd in a golden band, and never part,   15
But walk united, bearing food to all our tender flowers."

"Dost thou O little Cloud? I fear that I am not like thee;
For I walk through the vales of Har and smell the sweetest flowers,
But I feed not the little flowers; I hear the warbling birds,
But I feed not the warbling birds; they fly and seek their food;   20
But Thel delights in these no more, because I fade away,
And all shall say, 'Without a use this shining woman liv'd,
Or did she only live to be at death the food of worms?' "

The Cloud reclind upon his airy throne and answer'd thus:

"Then if thou art the food of worms, O virgin of the skies,   25
How great thy use, how great thy blessing! Every thing that lives
Lives not alone, nor for itself; fear not, and I will call
The weak worm from its lowly bed, and thou shalt hear its voice.
Come forth, worm of the silent valley, to thy pensive queen."

The helpless worm arose, and sat upon the Lilly's leaf,   30
And the bright Cloud saild on, to find his partner in the vale.

PLATE 4

3

Then Thel astonish'd view'd the Worm upon its dewy bed.

"Art thou a Worm? Image of weakness, art thou but a Worm?
I see thee like an infant wrapped in the Lilly's leaf;

7. The earliest mention in Blake's work of one of his "Giant Forms," the Zoas. Luvah is the mythical embodiment of the passional and sexual aspect of humankind. He is represented here, like the Greek Phoebus Apollo, as the driver of the chariot of the sun; he repairs to the Vales of Har simply in order to rest and water his horses. The cloud in this passage describes the cycle of water, from cloud to rain and (by the vaporizing action of the sun on water) back to the cloud.

Ah, weep not, little voice, thou can'st not speak, but thou can'st weep.
Is this a Worm? I see thee lay helpless & naked, weeping,   5
And none to answer, none to cherish thee with mother's smiles."

The Clod of Clay heard the Worm's voice, & raisd her pitying head;
She bow'd over the weeping infant, and her life exhal'd
In milky fondness; then on Thel she fix'd her humble eyes.

"O beauty of the vales of Har! we live not for ourselves;   10
Thou seest me the meanest thing, and so I am indeed;
My bosom of itself is cold, and of itself is dark,

PLATE 5

But he that loves the lowly, pours his oil upon my head,
And kisses me, and binds his nuptial bands around my breast,
And says: 'Thou mother of my children, I have lovèd thee,
And I have given thee a crown that none can take away.'
But how this is, sweet maid, I know not, and I cannot know;   5
I ponder, and I cannot ponder; yet I live and love."

The daughter of beauty wip'd her pitying tears with her white veil,
And said: "Alas! I knew not this, and therefore did I weep.
That God would love a Worm, I knew, and punish the evil foot
That, wilful, bruis'd its helpless form; but that he cherish'd it   10
With milk and oil I never knew; and therefore did I weep,
And I complaind in the mild air, because I fade away,
And lay me down in thy cold bed, and leave my shining lot."

"Queen of the vales," the matron Clay answered, "I heard thy sighs,
And all thy moans flew o'er my roof, but I have call'd them down.   15
Wilt thou, O Queen, enter my house? 'tis given thee to enter
And to return; fear nothing, enter with thy virgin feet."

PLATE 6
                                4
The eternal gates' terrific porter lifted the northern bar:[8]
Thel enter'd in & saw the secrets of the land unknown.
She saw the couches of the dead, & where the fibrous roots
Of every heart on earth infixes deep its restless twists:
A land of sorrows & of tears where never smile was seen.   5

She wanderd in the land of clouds thro' valleys dark, listning
Dolours & lamentations; waiting oft beside a dewy grave,
She stood in silence, listning to the voices of the ground,
Till to her own grave plot she came, & there she sat down,
And heard this voice of sorrow breathed from the hollow pit: 10

"Why cannot the Ear be closed to its own destruction?
Or the glistning Eye to the poison of a smile?

8. Homer, in *Odyssey* 13, described the Cave of the
Naiades, of which the northern gate is for mortals and
the southern gate for gods. The neoplatonist Porphyro
had allegorized it as an account of the descent of the
soul into matter and then its return.

Why are Eyelids stord with arrows ready drawn,
Where a thousand fighting men in ambush lie?
Or an Eye of gifts & graces, show'ring fruits & coinèd gold?   15
Why a Tongue impress'd with honey from every wind?
Why an Ear, a whirlpool fierce to draw creations in?
Why a Nostril wide inhaling terror, trembling, & affright?
Why a tender curb upon the youthful burning boy?
Why a little curtain of flesh on the bed of our desire?"[9]   20

The Virgin started from her seat, & with a shriek
Fled back unhinderd till she came into the vales of Har.

1789–91

Visions of the Daughters of Albion   This work, dated 1793 on the title page, is one of Blake's early illuminated books, and like his later and longer works is written in what Blake called "the long resounding strong heroic verse" of seven-foot lines. Unlike the timid heroine of _The Book of Thel_, the virgin Oothoon (probably pronounced as two syllables, "Oo-thoon") dares to break through into adult sexuality (symbolized by her plucking a marigold and placing it between her breasts) and sets out joyously to join her lover Theotormon, whose realm is the Atlantic Ocean. In her flight overseas she is waylaid and raped by Bromion in the figurative mode of a thunderstorm (1.16–17). The jealous Theotormon, condemning the victim as well as the rapist, binds the two "back to back" in a cave and sits weeping on the threshold. The rest of the work consists of monologues by the three characters, who remain fixed in these postures. Throughout this stage tableau the Daughters of Albion serve as the chorus who, in a recurrent refrain, echo the "woes" and "sighs" of Oothoon, but not her call to rebellion.

This simple drama is densely significant, for as Blake's compressed allusions indicate, the characters, events, and monologues have multiple meanings with diverse areas of application. Blake's abrupt opening word, which he etched in very large letters, is "Enslav'd," and the work as a whole embodies his view that contemporary men, and even more women, in a spiritual parallel to shackled black slaves, are in bondage to oppressive concepts and codes in all aspects of perception, thought, social institutions, and actions. As indicated by the refrain of the Daughters of Albion (that is, contemporary Englishwomen), Oothoon in one aspect represents the sexual disabilities and slavelike status of all women in a male-dominated society. But as "the soft soul of America" (1.3) she is also the revolutionary nation which had recently won political emancipation, yet tolerated an agricultural system that involved black slavery and acquiesced in the crass economic exploitation of her "soft American plains"; at the same time, Oothoon is herself represented in the situation of a black female slave who has been branded, whipped, raped, and impregnated by her master.

Correlatively, the speeches of the boastful Bromion show him to be not only a sexual exploiter of women and a cruel and acquisitive slave owner but also a general proponent of gaining mastery by the use of force in wars, in an oppressive legal system, and in a religious morality based on the fear of hell (4.19–24). Theotormon is represented as even more contemptible. Broken and paralyzed by the prohibitions of a puritanical religion, he denies any possibility of achieving "joys" in this life, despairs of the power of human intellection and imagination to

9. This catalog of the life of Generation and Experience runs through the various senses to end with touch, the primary sexual sense.

improve the human condition and, rationalizing his own incapacity, bewails Oothoon's daring to think and act other than he does.

Prominent in Oothoon's long and passionate oration that concludes the poem (plates 5–8) is her celebration of a free sexual life for both women and men. Blake, however, uses an open and generous sexuality not only to typify the realization of human potentialities in general but also to represent an outgoing altruism, in opposition to an enclosed self-centeredness, "the self-love that envies all." To such a suspicious egotism, Oothoon attributes the tyranny of uniform moral laws imposed on the variousness of human individuals, as well as selfish acquisitiveness that is at the root of the contemporary commercial system, institutional religion, a possessive love, and the insistence on property rights in another person that are established by the legal contract of a loveless marriage.

Blake's poem reflects some prominent circumstances of the years of its composition, 1791–93. This was not only the time when the revolutionary spirit had moved from America to France and effected reverberations in England, but also the time of sporadic rebellions by black slaves in the Western Hemisphere and of widespread debate in England about attempts in Parliament to abolish the slave trade. Blake himself, while composing the *Visions*, had illustrated the sadistic punishments inflicted on rebellious slaves in his engravings for J. G. Stedman's *A Narrative, of a Five Years' Expedition, against the Revolted Negroes of Surinam* (see David Erdman, *Blake: Prophet against Empire*, chapter 10). Blake's championing of women's liberation parallels some of the views expressed in the *Vindication of the Rights of Woman* published in 1792 by Mary Wollstonecraft, whom Blake knew and for whom he had illustrated a book the year before.

Visions of the Daughters of Albion

The Eye sees more than the Heart knows.

PLATE iii

The Argument

I loved Theotormon
And I was not ashamed
I trembled in my virgin fears
And I hid in Leutha's[1] vale!

I plucked Leutha's flower,   5
And I rose up from the vale;
But the terrible thunders tore
My virgin mantle in twain.

PLATE 1

Visions

ENSLAV'D, the Daughters of Albion weep: a trembling lamentation
Upon their mountains; in their valleys, sighs toward America.

---

1. In some poems by Blake, Leutha is represented as a female figure who is beautiful and seductive, but treacherous.

For the soft soul of America, Oothoon[2] wandered in woe,
Along the vales of Leutha seeking flowers to comfort her;
And thus she spoke to the bright Marygold of Leutha's vale: 5

"Art thou a flower! art thou a nymph! I see thee now a flower,
Now a nymph! I dare not pluck thee from thy dewy bed!"

The Golden nymph replied: "Pluck thou my flower Oothoon the mild.
Another flower shall spring, because the soul of sweet delight
Can never pass away." She ceas'd & closd her golden shrine.   10

Then Oothoon pluck'd the flower saying, "I pluck thee from thy bed,
Sweet flower, and put thee here to glow between my breasts,
And thus I turn my face to where my whole soul seeks."

Over the waves she went in wing'd exulting swift delight;
And over Theotormon's reign took her impetuous course.   15

Bromion rent her with his thunders. On his stormy bed
Lay the faint maid, and soon her woes appalld his thunders hoarse.

Bromion spoke: "Behold this harlot here on Bromion's bed,
And let the jealous dolphins sport around the lovely maid;
Thy soft American plains are mine, and mine thy north & south: 20
Stampt with my signet[3] are the swarthy children of the sun:
They are obedient, they resist not, they obey the scourge:
Their daughters worship terrors and obey the violent.

PLATE 2
Now thou maist marry Bromion's harlot, and protect the child
Of Bromion's rage, that Oothoon shall put forth in nine moons' time."[4]

Then storms rent Theotormon's limbs; he rolld his waves around,
And folded his black jealous waters round the adulterate pair;
Bound back to back in Bromion's caves terror & meekness dwell.   5

At entrance Theotormon sits wearing the threshold hard
With secret tears; beneath him sound like waves on a desart shore
The voice of slaves beneath the sun, and children bought with money,
That shiver in religious caves beneath the burning fires
Of lust, that belch incessant from the summits of the earth.   10

Oothoon weeps not: she cannot weep! her tears are locked up;
But she can howl incessant, writhing her soft snowy limbs,
And calling Theotormon's Eagles to prey upon her flesh.[5]

"I call with holy voice! kings of the sounding air,
Rend away this defiled bosom that I may reflect   15
The image of Theotormon on my pure transparent breast."

---

2. The name is adapted by Blake from a character in James Macpherson's pretended translations, in the 1760s, from the ancient British bard Ossian.
3. A small seal or stamp. The allusion is to the branding of black slaves by their owners.

4. Pregnancy enhanced the market value of a female slave in America.
5. The implied parallel is to Zeus's punishment of Prometheus for befriending the human race, by setting an eagle to devour his liver.

The Eagles at her call descend & rend their bleeding prey;
Theotormon severely smiles; her soul reflects the smile,
As the clear spring mudded with feet of beasts grows pure & smiles.

The Daughters of Albion hear her woes, & eccho back her sighs.   20

"Why does my Theotormon sit weeping upon the threshold,
And Oothoon hovers by his side, perswading him in vain?
I cry, 'Arise O Theotormon, for the village dog
Barks at the breaking day, the nightingale has done lamenting,
The lark does rustle in the ripe corn, and the Eagle returns   25
From nightly prey, and lifts his golden beak to the pure east,
Shaking the dust from his immortal pinions to awake
The sun that sleeps too long. Arise my Theotormon, I am pure;
Because the night is gone that clos'd me in its deadly black.'
They told me that the night & day were all that I could see;   30
They told me that I had five senses to inclose me up,
And they inclos'd my infinite brain into a narrow circle,
And sunk my heart into the Abyss, a red round globe hot burning,
Till all from life I was obliterated and erased.
Instead of morn arises a bright shadow, like an eye   35
In the eastern cloud,[6] instead of night a sickly charnel house,
That Theotormon hears me not! to him the night and morn
Are both alike: a night of sighs, a morning of fresh tears;

PLATE 3
And none but Bromion can hear my lamentations.

"With what sense is it that the chicken shuns the ravenous hawk?
With what sense does the tame pigeon measure out the expanse?
With what sense does the bee form cells? have not the mouse & frog
Eyes and ears and sense of touch? yet are their habitations   5
And their pursuits as different as their forms and as their joys.
Ask the wild ass why he refuses burdens, and the meek camel
Why he loves man; is it because of eye, ear, mouth, or skin,
Or breathing nostrils? No, for these the wolf and tyger have.
Ask the blind worm the secrets of the grave, and why her spires   10
Love to curl round the bones of death; and ask the rav'nous snake
Where she gets poison, & the wing'd eagle why he loves the sun,
And then tell me the thoughts of man, that have been hid of old.[7]

"Silent I hover all the night, and all day could be silent,
If Theotormon once would turn his loved eyes upon me.   15
How can I be defild when I reflect thy image pure?
Sweetest the fruit that the worm feeds on, & the soul prey'd on by woe,
The new wash'd lamb ting'd with the village smoke, & the bright swan

---

6. The contrast is between the physical sun perceived by the constricted ("inclos'd," line 32) sensible eye and "the breaking day" (line 24) of a new era perceived by Oothoon's liberated vision.

7. Oothoon implies that "thoughts" (powers of conceiving a liberated life in a better world) are as innate to human beings as instinctual patterns of behavior are to other species of living things.

By the red earth[8] of our immortal river: I bathe my wings,
And I am white and pure to hover round Theotormon's breast."   20

Then Theotormon broke his silence, and he answered:

"Tell me what is the night or day to one o'erflowd with woe?
Tell me what is a thought? & of what substance is it made?
Tell me what is a joy? & in what gardens do joys grow?
And in what rivers swim the sorrows? and upon what mountains   25

PLATE 4
Wave shadows of discontent? and in what houses dwell the wretched
Drunken with woe, forgotten, and shut up from cold despair?

"Tell me where dwell the thoughts, forgotten till thou call them forth?
Tell me where dwell the joys of old! & where the ancient loves?
And when will they renew again & the night of oblivion past?   5
That I might traverse times & spaces far remote and bring
Comforts into a present sorrow and a night of pain.
Where goest thou, O thought? to what remote land is thy flight?
If thou returnest to the present moment of affliction
Wilt thou bring comforts on thy wings and dews and honey and balm,   10
Or poison from the desart wilds, from the eyes of the envier?"

Then Bromion said, and shook the cavern with his lamentation:

"Thou knowest that the ancient trees seen by thine eyes have fruit;
But knowest thou that trees and fruits flourish upon the earth
To gratify senses unknown? trees beasts and birds unknown: 15
Unknown, not unpercievd, spread in the infinite microscope,
In places yet unvisited by the voyager, and in worlds
Over another kind of seas, and in atmospheres unknown?
Ah! are there other wars, beside the wars of sword and fire?
And are there other sorrows, beside the sorrows of poverty?   20
And are there other joys, beside the joys of riches and ease?
And is there not one law for both the lion and the ox?[9]
And is there not eternal fire, and eternal chains?
To bind the phantoms of existence from eternal life?"

Then Oothoon waited silent all the day and all the night,   25

PLATE 5
But when the morn arose, her lamentation renewd.
The Daughters of Albion hear her woes, & eccho back her sighs.

"O Urizen![1] Creator of men! mistaken Demon of heaven:
Thy joys are tears! thy labour vain, to form men to thine image.

---

8. "Red earth" is the etymological meaning of the Hebrew name "Adam" (cf. *The Marriage of Heaven and
Hell* 2.13, p. 1313). The "immortal river," accordingly,
may refer to the "river" that "went out of Eden" (Genesis 2.10).
9. The last line of *The Marriage of Heaven and Hell*

proclaims: "One Law for the Lion & Ox is Oppression."
1. This is the first occurrence of the name "Urizen" in
Blake. Oothoon's liberated vision recognizes the error
in the way God is conceived in conventional religion.

How can one joy absorb another? are not different joys   5
Holy, eternal, infinite! and each joy is a Love.

"Does not the great mouth laugh at a gift? & the narrow eyelids mock
At the labour that is above payment? and wilt thou take the ape
For thy councellor? or the dog for a schoolmaster to thy children?
Does he who contemns poverty, and he who turns with
    abhorrence   10
From usury, feel the same passion, or are they moved alike?
How can the giver of gifts experience the delights of the merchant?
How the industrious citizen the pains of the husbandman?
How different far the fat fed hireling with hollow drum,
Who buys whole corn fields into wastes,[2] and sings upon the
    heath: 15
How different their eye and ear! how different the world to them!
With what sense does the parson claim the labour of the farmer?
What are his nets & gins[3] & traps? & how does he surround him
With cold floods of abstraction, and with forests of solitude,
To build him castles and high spires, where kings & priests may dwell?   20
Till she who burns with youth, and knows no fixed lot, is bound
In spells of law to one she loaths; and must she drag the chain
Of life, in weary lust? must chilling murderous thoughts obscure
The clear heaven of her eternal spring? to bear the wintry rage
Of a harsh terror, driv'n to madness, bound to hold a rod   25
Over her shrinking shoulders all the day, & all the night
To turn the wheel of false desire, and longings that wake her womb
To the abhorred birth of cherubs in the human form
That live a pestilence & die a meteor & are no more;
Till the child dwell with one he hates, and do the deed he loaths,   30
And the impure scourge force his seed into its unripe birth
E'er yet his eyelids can behold the arrows of the day?[4]

"Does the whale worship at thy footsteps as the hungry dog?
Or does he scent the mountain prey, because his nostrils wide
Draw in the ocean? does his eye discern the flying cloud   35
As the raven's eye? or does he measure the expanse like the vulture?
Does the still spider view the cliffs where eagles hide their young?
Or does the fly rejoice because the harvest is brought in?
Does not the eagle scorn the earth & despise the treasures beneath?
But the mole knoweth what is there, & the worm shall tell it thee.   40
Does not the worm erect a pillar in the mouldering church yard,

PLATE 6
And a palace of eternity in the jaws of the hungry grave?
Over his porch these words are written: 'Take thy bliss O Man!
And sweet shall be thy taste & sweet thy infant joys renew!'

"Infancy, fearless, lustful, happy! nestling for delight
In laps of pleasure; Innocence! honest, open, seeking   5

---

2. Probably a compressed allusion both to the wealthy
landowner who converts fertile fields into a game preserve, and to the recruiting officer ("with hollow
drum") who strips the land of its agricultural laborers.

3. Snares.
4. The reference is to the begetting of children, both
in actual slavery and in the metaphoric slavery of a
loveless marriage, from generation to generation.

The vigorous joys of morning light, open to virgin bliss,
Who taught thee modesty, subtil modesty? Child of night & sleep,
When thou awakest wilt thou dissemble all thy secret joys,
Or wert thou not awake when all this mystery was disclos'd?
Then com'st thou forth a modest virgin, knowing to dissemble,   10
With nets found under thy night pillow to catch virgin joy,
And brand it with the name of whore, & sell it in the night,
In silence, ev'n without a whisper, and in seeming sleep.[5]
Religious dreams and holy vespers light thy smoky fires;
Once were thy fires lighted by the eyes of honest morn.   15
And does my Theotormon seek this hypocrite modesty,
This knowing, artful, secret, fearful, cautious, trembling hypocrite?
Then is Oothoon a whore indeed! and all the virgin joys
Of life are harlots, and Theotormon is a sick man's dream,
And Oothoon is the crafty slave of selfish holiness.   20

"But Oothoon is not so; a virgin fill'd with virgin fancies
Open to joy and to delight where ever beauty appears.
If in the morning sun I find it, there my eyes are fix'd

PLATE 7
In happy copulation; if in evening mild, wearied with work,
Sit on a bank and draw the pleasures of this free born joy.

"The moment of desire! the moment of desire! The virgin
That pines for man shall awaken her womb to enormous joys
In the secret shadows of her chamber; the youth shut up from   5
The lustful joy shall forget to generate & create an amorous image
In the shadows of his curtains and in the folds of his silent pillow.
Are not these the places of religion? the rewards of continence?
The self enjoyings of self denial? Why dost seek religion?
Is it because acts are not lovely, that thou seekest solitude,   10
Where the horrible darkness is impressed with reflections of desire?

"Father of Jealousy,[6] be thou accursed from the earth!
Why hast thou taught my Theotormon this accursed thing?
Till beauty fades from off my shoulders, darken'd and cast out,
A solitary shadow wailing on the margin of non-entity.   15

"I cry, Love! Love! Love! happy happy Love! free as the mountain wind!
Can that be Love, that drinks another as a sponge drinks water?
That clouds with jealousy his nights, with weepings all the day,
To spin a web of age around him, grey and hoary! dark!
Till his eyes sicken at the fruit that hangs before his sight.   20
Such is self-love that envies all! a creeping skeleton
With lamplike eyes watching around the frozen marriage bed.

"But silken nets and traps of adamant[7] will Oothoon spread,
And catch for thee girls of mild silver, or of furious gold;

5. Oothoon contrasts the natural, innocent sensuality
of an infant to the socially acquired, hypocritical modesty of the adult virgin; the latter is Theotormon's concept of female virtue.

6. I.e., Urizen (5.3), the false conceived God who pro-
hibits the satisfaction of human desires.
7. A legendary stone believed to be unbreakable. (The
name is derived from the Greek word for diamond.)

I'll lie beside thee on a bank & view their wanton play   25
In lovely copulation bliss on bliss with Theotormon:
Red as the rosy morning, lustful as the first born beam,
Oothoon shall view his dear delight, nor e'er with jealous cloud
Come in the heaven of generous love; nor selfish blightings bring.

"Does the sun walk in glorious raiment on the secret floor   30

PLATE 8
Where the cold miser spreads his gold? or does the bright cloud drop
On his stone threshold? does his eye behold the beam that brings
Expansion to the eye of pity? or will he bind himself
Beside the ox to thy hard furrow? does not that mild beam blot
The bat, the owl, the glowing tyger, and the king of night?   5
The sea fowl takes the wintry blast for a cov'ring to her limbs,
And the wild snake the pestilence to adorn him with gems & gold.
And trees & birds & beasts & men behold their eternal joy.
Arise you little glancing wings, and sing your infant joy!
Arise and drink your bliss, for every thing that lives is holy!"[8]   10

Thus every morning wails Oothoon, but Theotormon sits
Upon the margind ocean conversing with shadows dire.

The Daughters of Albion hear her woes, & eccho back her sighs.

1791–93   1793

The Marriage of Heaven and Hell

This, the most immediately accessible of Blake's longer works, is a vigorous, deliberately outrageous, and at times, comic onslaught against the timidly conventional and self-righteous members of society as well as against many of the stock opinions of orthodox Christian piety and morality. The seeming simplicity of Blake's satiric attitude, however, is deceptive.

Initially, Blake accepts the terminology of standard Christian morality ("what the religious call Good & Evil") but reverses its values. In this conventional use Evil, which is manifested by the class of beings called Devils and which consigns wrongdoers to the orthodox Hell, is everything associated with the body and its desires and consists essentially of energy, abundance, act, freedom. And conventional Good, which is manifested by Angels and guarantees its adherents a place in the orthodox Heaven, is associated with the Soul (regarded as entirely separate from the body) and consists of the contrary qualities of reason, restraint, passivity, and prohibition. Blandly adopting this current nomenclature, Blake elects to assume the diabolic persona—what he calls "the voice of the Devil"—and to utter "Proverbs of Hell." This ironic stance produces a vein of satire which is in the great eighteenth-century tradition of sustained ironic reversal, represented by works such as Jonathan Swift's *Modest Proposal*.

But the transvaluation of standard criteria is only a first stage in Blake's complex irony, designed to startle the reader into recognizing the inadequacy of conventional moral categories and stock responses. As he also says in the opening summary, "Without Contraries is no progression," and "Reason and Energy" are both

---

8. This last phrase is also the concluding line of "A Song of Liberty," appended to *The Marriage of Heaven and Hell*.

"necessary to Human existence." It turns out that Blake subordinates his satiric reversal of conventional values under a more inclusive point of view, according to which the real Good, as distinguished from the merely ironic Good, is not instinctual abandon but a "marriage," or union of the contraries, of desire and restraint, energy and reason, the promptings of Hell and the denials of Heaven—or as Blake calls these contraries, in the comprehensive terms he introduces in plate 16, "the Prolific" and "the Devouring." These two classes, he adds, "should be enemies," and "whoever tries to reconcile them seeks to destroy existence." When Blake speaks not as moral satirist but as serious moralist, the good life is that abundant and strenuous life he describes as the sustained tension, without victory or suppression, of co-present oppositions.

Blake was stimulated to write this unique work in response to the books of the visionary Swedish theologian Emanuel Swedenborg, whom he had at first admired but then had come to recognize as a conventional Angel in the disguise of a radical Devil. In plate 3 the writings of Swedenborg are described as the winding clothes Blake discards as he is resurrected from the tomb of his past self, as a poet-prophet who heralds the apocalyptic promise of his age. Blake wrote *The Marriage of Heaven and Hell* in the early 1790s, during the bright early years of the French Revolution, when he shared the expectations of a number of radical English writers, including the young poets Wordsworth, Coleridge, and Southey, that the revolution was the universal violence that had been predicted by the biblical prophets as a stage immediately preceding the millennium. The double role of *The Marriage* as both satire and revolutionary prophecy is made explicit in *A Song of Liberty*, which Blake etched in 1792 and added as a coda.

The Marriage of Heaven and Hell

PLATE 2

The Argument

Rintrah[1] roars & shakes his fires in the burdend air;
Hungry clouds swag[2] on the deep.

Once meek, and in a perilous path,
The just man kept his course along
The vale of death.   5
Roses are planted where thorns grow,
And on the barren heath
Sing the honey bees.

Then the perilous path was planted,
And a river, and a spring,   10
On every cliff and tomb;
And on the bleached bones
Red clay[3] brought forth;

1. Rintrah plays the role of the angry Old Testament prophet Elijah as well as of John the Baptist, the voice "crying in the wilderness" (Matthew 3), preparing the way for Christ the Messiah. It has been plausibly suggested that stanzas 2–5 summarize the course of biblical history to the present time. "Once" (line 3) refers to Old Testament history after the fall of man; "Then" (line 9) is the time of the birth of Christ. "Till" (line 14) identifies the era when Christianity was perverted into an institutional religion. "Now" (line 17) is the time of the wrathful portent of the French Revolution. In this final era, the hypocritical serpent represents the priest of the "angels" in the poem, while "the just man" is embodied in Blake himself, a raging poet and prophet in the guise of a devil.
2. Sag, hang down.
3. In Hebrew, the literal meaning of "Adam," or created man. The probable reference is to the birth of the Redeemer, the new Adam.

Till the villain left the paths of ease,
To walk in perilous paths, and drive   15
The just man into barren climes.

Now the sneaking serpent walks
In mild humility,
And the just man rages in the wilds
Where lions roam.   20

Rintrah roars & shakes his fires in the burdend air;
Hungry clouds swag on the deep.

PLATE 3

As a new heaven is begun, and it is now thirty-three years since its advent, the Eternal Hell revives.[4] And lo! Swedenborg is the Angel sitting at the tomb; his writings are the linen clothes folded up. Now is the dominion of Edom, & the return of Adam into Paradise; see Isaiah xxxiv & XXXV Chap.[5]

Without Contraries is no progression. Attraction and Repulsion, Reason and Energy, Love and Hate, are necessary to Human existence.

From these contraries spring what the religious call Good & Evil. Good is the passive that obeys Reason. Evil is the active springing from Energy.

Good is Heaven. Evil is Hell.

PLATE 4

The Voice of the Devil

All Bibles or sacred codes have been the causes of the following Errors:

1. That Man has two real existing principles; Viz: a Body & a Soul.

2. That Energy, calld Evil, is alone from the Body, & that Reason, calld Good, is alone from the Soul.

3. That God will torment Man in Eternity for following his Energies.

But the following Contraries to these are True:

1. Man has no Body distinct from his Soul; for that calld Body is a portion of Soul discernd by the five Senses, the chief inlets of Soul in this age.

2. Energy is the only life, and is from the Body; and Reason is the bound or outward circumference of Energy.

3. Energy is Eternal Delight.

4. The Swedish scientist and religious philosopher Emanuel Swedenborg (1688–1772) had predicted, on the basis of his visions, that the Last Judgment and the coming of the Kingdom of Heaven would occur in 1757. This was precisely the year of Blake's birth. Now, in 1790, Blake is thirty-three, the age at which Christ had been resurrected from the tomb; correspondingly, Blake rises from the tomb of his past life in his new role as imaginative artist who will redeem his age. But, Blake ironically comments, the works he will engrave in his resurrection will constitute the Eternal Hell, the contrary brought into simultaneous being by Swedenborg's limited New Heaven.

5. Isaiah 34 prophesies "the day of the Lord's vengeance," a time of violent destruction and bloodshed; Isaiah 35 prophesies the redemption to follow, in which "the desert shall . . . blossom as the rose," "in the wilderness shall waters break out, and streams in the desert," and "no lion shall be there," but "an highway shall be there . . . and it shall be called the way of holiness" (cf. "The Argument," lines 3–11, 20). Blake combines with these chapters Isaiah 63, in which "Edom" is the place from which comes the man whose garments are red with the blood he has spilled; for as he says, "the day of vengeance is in mine heart, and the year of my redeemed is come." Blake interprets this last phrase as predicting the time when Adam would regain his lost Paradise.

With reference to affairs in 1790, Edom can be taken to represent France, and the red man coming from Edom (to England) to be the spirit of the French Revolution, which Blake interprets as a portent of apocalyptic redemption and the recovery of Paradise.

PLATE 5

Those who restrain desire, do so because theirs is weak enough to be restrained; and the restrainer or reason usurps its place & governs the unwilling.

And being restraind, it by degrees becomes passive, till it is only the shadow of desire.

The history of this is written in *Paradise Lost*,[6] & the Governor or Reason is call'd Messiah.

And the original Archangel, or possessor of the command of the heavenly host, is calld the Devil or Satan, and his children are call'd Sin & Death.[7]

But in the Book of Job, Milton's Messiah is call'd Satan.[8]

For this history has been adopted by both parties.

It indeed appear'd to Reason as if Desire was cast out; but the Devil's account is, that the Messi[PL 6]ah fell, & formed a heaven of what he stole from the Abyss.

This is shewn in the Gospel, where he prays to the Father to send the comforter or Desire that Reason may have Ideas to build on;[9] the Jehovah of the Bible being no other than he who dwells in flaming fire. Know that after Christ's death, he became Jehovah.

But in Milton, the Father is Destiny, the Son, a Ratio of the five senses,[1] & the Holy-ghost, Vacuum!

Note. The reason Milton wrote in fetters when he wrote of Angels & God, and at liberty when of Devils & Hell, is because he was a true Poet and of the Devil's party without knowing it.

A Memorable Fancy[2]

As I was walking among the fires of hell, delighted with the enjoyments of Genius, which to Angels look like torment and insanity, I collected some of their Proverbs; thinking that as the sayings used in a nation mark its character, so the Proverbs of Hell shew the nature of Infernal wisdom better than any description of buildings or garments.

When I came home, on the abyss of the five senses, where a flat sided steep frowns over the present world, I saw a mighty Devil folded in black clouds, hovering on the sides of the rock; with cor[PL 7]roding fires he wrote the following sentence[3] now perceived by the minds of men, & read by them on earth:

> How do you know but ev'ry Bird that cuts the airy way,
> Is an immense world of delight, clos'd by your senses five?

6. What follows, to the end of this section, is Blake's "diabolical" reading of *Paradise Lost*.
7. Satan's giving birth to Sin and then incestuously begetting Death upon her is described in *Paradise Lost* 2.745ff.; the war in heaven, referred to three lines below, in which the Messiah defeated Satan and drove him out of heaven, is described in 6.824ff.
8. In the Book of Job, Satan plays the role of Job's moral accuser and physical tormentor.
9. Possibly John 14.16–17, where Christ says he "will pray the Father, and he shall give you another Comforter . . . even the Spirit of truth."
1. The Latin *ratio* means both "reason" and "sum."

Blake applies the term to the 18th-century view, following the empirical philosophy of John Locke, that the content of the mind, on which the faculty of reason operates, is limited to the sum of the experience acquired by the five senses.
2. A parody of what Swedenborg called "memorable relations" of his literal-minded visions of the eternal world.
3. The "mighty Devil" is Blake, as he sees himself reflected in the shiny plate on which he is etching this very passage with "corroding fires"—i.e., acid. See also the third from last sentence in plate 14.

Proverbs of Hell[4]

In seed time learn, in harvest teach, in winter enjoy.
Drive your cart and your plow over the bones of the dead.
The road of excess leads to the palace of wisdom.
Prudence is a rich ugly old maid courted by Incapacity.
He who desires but acts not, breeds pestilence.   5
The cut worm forgives the plow.
Dip him in the river who loves water.
A fool sees not the same tree that a wise man sees.
He whose face gives no light, shall never become a star.
Eternity is in love with the productions of time.   10
The busy bee has no time for sorrow.
The hours of folly are measur'd by the clock; but of wisdom, no clock can
     measure.
All wholsom food is caught without a net or a trap.
Bring out number, weight, & measure in a year of dearth.
No bird soars too high, if he soars with his own wings.   15
A dead body revenges not injuries.
The most sublime act is to set another before you.
If the fool would persist in his folly he would become wise.
Folly is the cloke of knavery.
Shame is Pride's cloke.   20

PLATE 8
Prisons are built with stones of Law, Brothels with bricks of Religion.
The pride of the peacock is the glory of God.
The lust of the goat is the bounty of God.
The wrath of the lion is the wisdom of God.
The nakedness of woman is the work of God.   25
Excess of sorrow laughs. Excess of joy weeps.
The roaring of lions, the howling of wolves, the raging of the stormy sea, and
     the destructive sword, are portions of eternity too great for the eye of man.
The fox condemns the trap, not himself.
Joys impregnate. Sorrows bring forth.
Let man wear the fell of the lion, woman the fleece of the sheep.   30
The bird a nest, the spider a web, man friendship.
The selfish smiling fool & the sullen frowning fool shall be both thought wise,
     that they may be a rod.
What is now proved was once only imagin'd.
The rat, the mouse, the fox, the rabbit watch the roots; the lion, the tyger, the
     horse, the elephant, watch the fruits.
The cistern contains; the fountain overflows.   35
One thought fills immensity.
Always be ready to speak your mind, and a base man will avoid you.
Every thing possible to be believ'd is an image of truth.
The eagle never lost so much time as when he submitted to learn of the crow.

4. A "diabolic" version of the Book of Proverbs in the Old Testament.

PLATE 9

The fox provides for himself, but God provides for the lion.   40
Think in the morning, Act in the noon, Eat in the evening, Sleep in the night.
He who has sufferd you to impose on him knows you.
As the plow follows words, so God rewards prayers.
The tygers of wrath are wiser than the horses of instruction.
Expect poison from the standing water.   45
You never know what is enough unless you know what is more than enough.
Listen to the fool's reproach! it is a kingly title!
The eyes of fire, the nostrils of air, the mouth of water, the beard of earth.
The weak in courage is strong in cunning.
The apple tree never asks the beech how he shall grow, nor the lion the horse,
     how he shall take his prey.   50
The thankful reciever bears a plentiful harvest.
If others had not been foolish, we should be so.
The soul of sweet delight can never be defil'd.
When thou seest an Eagle, thou seest a portion of Genius; lift up thy head!
As the catterpiller chooses the fairest leaves to lay her eggs on, so the priest
     lays his curse on the fairest joys.   55
To create a little flower is the labour of ages.
Damn braces; Bless relaxes.
The best wine is the oldest, the best water the newest.
Prayers plow not! Praises reap not!
Joys laugh not! Sorrows weep not!   60

PLATE 10

The head Sublime, the heart Pathos, the genitals Beauty, the hands & feet
     Proportion.
As the air to a bird or the sea to a fish, so is contempt to the contemptible.
The crow wish'd every thing was black, the owl that every thing was white.
Exuberance is Beauty.
If the lion was advised by the fox, he would be cunning.   65
Improvement makes strait roads, but the crooked roads without
     Improvement are roads of Genius.
Sooner murder an infant in its cradle than nurse unacted desires.
Where man is not, nature is barren.
Truth can never be told so as to be understood, and not be believ'd.
                    Enough! or Too much.   70

PLATE 11

     The ancient Poets animated all sensible objects with Gods or Geniuses,
calling them by the names and adorning them with the properties of woods,
rivers, mountains, lakes, cities, nations, and whatever their enlarged & numerous senses could perceive.
     And particularly they studied the genius of each city & country, placing it
under its mental deity.
     Till a system was formed, which some took advantage of & enslav'd the
vulgar by attempting to realize or abstract the mental deities from their
objects; thus began Priesthood,
     Choosing forms of worship from poetic tales.

And at length they pronounced that the Gods had ordered such things.
Thus men forgot that All deities reside in the human breast.

PLATE 12

A Memorable Fancy[5]

The Prophets Isaiah and Ezekiel dined with me, and I asked them how they
dared so roundly to assert that God spake to them; and whether they did not
think at the time that they would be misunderstood, & so be the cause of
imposition.

Isaiah answer'd: "I saw no God, nor heard any, in a finite organical perception; but my senses discover'd the infinite in every thing, and as I was then
perswaded, & remain confirm'd, that the voice of honest indignation is the
voice of God, I cared not for consequences, but wrote."

Then I asked: "Does a firm perswasion that a thing is so, make it so?"

He replied: "All poets believe that it does, & in ages of imagination this
firm perswasion removed mountains; but many are not capable of a firm perswasion of any thing."

Then Ezekiel said: "The philosophy of the East taught the first principles
of human perception. Some nations held one principle for the origin & some
another; we of Israel taught that the Poetic Genius (as you now call it) was the
first principle and all the others merely derivative, which was the cause of our
despising the Priests & Philosophers of other countries, and prophecying that
all Gods [PL 13] would at last be proved to originate in ours & to be the
tributaries of the Poetic Genius; it was this that our great poet, King David,
desired so fervently & invokes so pathetically, saying by this he conquers enemies & governs kingdoms; and we so loved our God, that we cursed in his
name all the deities of surrounding nations, and asserted that they had
rebelled; from these opinions the vulgar came to think that all nations would
at last be subject to the Jews."

"This," said he, "like all firm perswasions, is come to pass, for all nations
believe the Jews' code and worship the Jews' god, and what greater subjection
can be?"

I heard this with some wonder, & must confess my own conviction. After
dinner I ask'd Isaiah to favour the world with his lost works; he said none of
equal value was lost. Ezekiel said the same of his.

I also asked Isaiah what made him go naked and barefoot three years? He
answered, "the same that made our friend Diogenes, the Grecian."[6]

I then asked Ezekiel why he eat dung, & lay so long on his right & left
side?[7] He answered, "the desire of raising other men into a perception of the
infinite; this the North American tribes practise, & is he honest who resists his
genius or conscience only for the sake of present ease or gratification?"

PLATE 14

The ancient tradition that the world will be consumed in fire at the end of
six thousand years is true, as I have heard from Hell.

---

5. Blake parodies Swedenborg's accounts, in his *Mem-*
orable Relations, of his conversations with the inhabitants during his spiritual trips to heaven.
6. In Isaiah 20.2–3, the prophet, at the command of
the Lord, walked "naked and bare-foot" for three years.

Diogenes was the 4th-century Greek Cynic whose extreme repudiation of civilized customs gave rise to anecdotes that he had renounced clothing.
7. The Lord gave these instructions to the prophet
Ezekiel, 4.4–6.

For the cherub with his flaming sword is hereby commanded to leave his guard at the tree of life;[8] and when he does, the whole creation will be consumed, and appear infinite and holy, whereas it now appears finite & corrupt.

This will come to pass by an improvement of sensual enjoyment.

But first the notion that man has a body distinct from his soul is to be expunged; this I shall do, by printing in the infernal method, by corrosives, which in Hell are salutary and medicinal, melting apparent surfaces away, and displaying the infinite which was hid.[9]

If the doors of perception were cleansed every thing would appear to man as it is, infinite.

For man has closed himself up, till he sees all things thro' narrow chinks of his cavern.

PLATE 15

A Memorable Fancy

I was in a Printing house in Hell & saw the method in which knowledge is transmitted from generation to generation.

In the first chamber was a Dragon-Man, clearing away the rubbish from a cave's mouth; within, a number of Dragons were hollowing the cave.

In the second chamber was a Viper folding round the rock & the cave, and others adorning it with gold, silver, and precious stones.

In the third chamber was an Eagle with wings and feathers of air; he caused the inside of the cave to be infinite; around were numbers of Eagle-like men, who built palaces in the immense cliffs.

In the fourth chamber were Lions of flaming fire, raging around & melting the metals into living fluids.

In the fifth chamber were Unnam'd forms, which cast the metals into the expanse.

There they were receiv'd by Men who occupied the sixth chamber, and took the forms of books & were arranged in libraries.[1]

PLATE 16

The Giants who formed this world into its sensual existence, and now seem to live in it in chains, are in truth the causes of its life & the sources of all activity; but the chains are the cunning of weak and tame minds which have power to resist energy; according to the proverb, the weak in courage is strong in cunning.

Thus one portion of being is the Prolific, the other, the Devouring; to the Devourer it seems as if the producer was in his chains, but it is not so; he only takes portions of existence and fancies that the whole.

But the Prolific would cease to be Prolific unless the Devourer as a sea received the excess of his delights.[2]

Some will say, "Is not God alone the Prolific?" I answer, "God only Acts & Is, in existing beings or Men."

---

8. In Genesis 3.24, when the Lord drove Adam and Eve from the Garden of Eden, he had placed Cherubim and a flaming sword at the eastern end "to keep the way of the tree of life."
9. See p. 1315, n. 3.
1. In this "Memorable Fancy," Blake allegorizes his procedure in designing, etching, printing, and binding his works of imaginative genius.
2. The "Giants" in this section are human creative energies, called "the Prolific," in their relation to their indispensable contrary, "the Devourer."

These two classes of men are always upon earth, & they should be enemies; whoever tries [PL 17] to reconcile them seeks to destroy existence.

Religion is an endeavour to reconcile the two.

Note. Jesus Christ did not wish to unite but to separate them, as in the Parable of sheep and goats! & he says, "I came not to send Peace but a Sword."[3]

Messiah or Satan or Tempter was formerly thought to be one of the Antediluvians[4] who are our Energies.

A Memorable Fancy

An Angel came to me and said: "O pitiable foolish young man! O horrible! O dreadful state! consider the hot burning dungeon thou art preparing for thyself to all eternity, to which thou art going in such career."

I said: "Perhaps you will be willing to shew me my eternal lot, & we will contemplate together upon it and see whether your lot or mine is most desirable."

So he took me thro' a stable & thro' a church & down into the church vault at the end of which was a mill; thro' the mill we went, and came to a cave; down the winding cavern we groped our tedious way till a void boundless as a nether sky appeared beneath us, & we held by the roots of trees and hung over this immensity, but I said: "If you please, we will commit ourselves to this void, and see whether Providence is here also, if you will not I will." But he answered: "Do not presume, O young man, but as we here remain, behold thy lot which will soon appear when the darkness passes away."[5]

So I remaind with him sitting in the twisted [PL 18] root of an oak; he was suspended in a fungus which hung with the head downward into the deep.

By degrees we beheld the infinite Abyss, fiery as the smoke of a burning city; beneath us at an immense distance was the sun, black but shining; round it were fiery tracks on which revolv'd vast spiders, crawling after their prey, which flew, or rather swum in the infinite deep, in the most terrific shapes of animals sprung from corruption; & the air was full of them, & seemed composed of them; these are Devils, and are called Powers of the air. I now asked my companion which was my eternal lot? He said, "Between the black & white spiders."

But now, from between the black & white spiders a cloud and fire burst and rolled thro the deep, blackning all beneath, so that the nether deep grew black as a sea & rolled with a terrible noise. Beneath us was nothing now to be seen but a black tempest, till looking east between the clouds & the waves, we saw a cataract of blood mixed with fire, and not many stones' throw from us appeared and sunk again the scaly fold of a monstrous serpent. At last to the east, distant about three degrees, appeared a fiery crest above the waves. Slowly it reared like a ridge of golden rocks till we discovered two globes of

3. Matthew 10.34. The parable of the sheep and the goats is in Matthew 25.32–33.
4. Those who lived before Noah's Flood.
5. The "stable" is that where Jesus was born, which, allegorically, leads to the "church" founded in his name and to the "vault" where this institution effectually buried him. The "mill" in Blake is a symbol of mechanical and analytic philosophy; through this the pilgrims pass into the twisting cave of rationalistic the-

ology and descend to an underworld that is an empty abyss. The point of this Blakean equivalent of a carnival fun house is that only after you have thoroughly confused yourself by this tortuous approach, and only if you then (as in the next two paragraphs) stare at this topsy-turvy emptiness long enough, will the void gradually assume the semblance of the comic horrors of the fantasied hell of angelic orthodoxy.

crimson fire, from which the sea fled away in clouds of smoke. And now we saw it was the head of Leviathan; his forehead was divided into streaks of green & purple like those on a tyger's forehead; soon we saw his mouth & red gills hang just above the raging foam, tinging the black deep with beams of blood, advancing toward [PL 19] us with all the fury of a spiritual existence.

My friend the Angel climb'd up from his station into the mill. I remain'd alone, & then this appearance was no more, but I found myself sitting on a pleasant bank beside a river by moon light, hearing a harper who sung to the harp, & his theme was: "The man who never alters his opinion is like standing water, & breeds reptiles of the mind."

But I arose, and sought for the mill, & there I found my Angel, who surprised asked me how I escaped?

I answered: "All that we saw was owing to your metaphysics: for when you ran away, I found myself on a bank by moonlight hearing a harper. But now we have seen my eternal lot, shall I shew you yours? He laughd at my proposal; but I by force suddenly caught him in my arms, & flew westerly thro' the night, til we were elevated above the earth's shadow; then I flung myself with him directly into the body of the sun. Here I clothed myself in white, & taking in my hand Swedenborg's volumes, sunk from the glorious clime, and passed all the planets till we came to Saturn. Here I staid to rest & then leap'd into the void between Saturn & the fixed stars.[6]

"Here," said I, "is your lot, in this space, if space it may be calld." Soon we saw the stable and the church, & I took him to the altar and open'd the Bible, and lo! it was a deep pit, into which I descended, driving the Angel before me. Soon we saw seven houses of brick;[7] one we enterd; in it were a [PL 20] number of monkeys, baboons, & all of that species, chaind by the middle, grinning and snatching at one another, but withheld by the shortness of their chains. However, I saw that they sometimes grew numerous, and then the weak were caught by the strong, and with a grinning aspect, first coupled with & then devourd, by plucking off first one limb and then another till the body was left a helpless trunk. This, after grinning & kissing it with seeming fondness, they devour'd too; and here & there I saw one savourily picking the flesh off of his own tail. As the stench terribly annoyd us both, we went into the mill, & I in my hand brought the skeleton of a body, which in the mill was Aristotle's Analytics.[8]

So the Angel said: "Thy phantasy has imposed upon me, & thou oughtest to be ashamed."

I answered: "We impose on one another, & it is but lost time to converse with you whose works are only Analytics."

Opposition is true Friendship.

PLATE 21

I have always found that Angels have the vanity to speak of themselves as the only wise; this they do with a confident insolence sprouting from systematic reasoning.

6. In the Ptolemaic world picture Saturn was in the outermost planetary sphere; beyond it was the sphere of the fixed stars.
7. The "seven churches which are in Asia," to which John addresses the Book of Revelation 1.4. Blake now forces on the angel his own diabolic view of angelic biblical exegesis, theological speculation and disputation, and Hell.
8. Aristotle's treatises on logic.

Thus Swedenborg boasts that what he writes is new; tho' it is only the Contents or Index of already publish'd books.

A man carried a monkey about for a shew, & because he was a little wiser than the monkey, grew vain, and conceiv'd himself as much wiser than seven men. It is so with Swedenborg; he shews the folly of churches & exposes hypocrites, till he imagines that all are religious, & himself the single [PL 22] one on earth that ever broke a net.

Now hear a plain fact: Swedenborg has not written one new truth. Now hear another: he has written all the old falshoods.

And now hear the reason: He conversed with Angels who are all religious, & conversed not with Devils, who all hate religion, for he was incapable thro' his conceited notions.

Thus Swedenborg's writings are a recapitulation of all superficial opinions, and an analysis of the more sublime, but no further.

Have now another plain fact: Any man of mechanical talents may from the writings of Paracelsus or Jacob Behmen[9] produce ten thousand volumes of equal value with Swedenborg's, and from those of Dante or Shakespear, an infinite number.

But when he has done this, let him not say that he knows better than his master, for he only holds a candle in sunshine.

A Memorable Fancy

Once I saw a Devil in a flame of fire, who arose before an Angel that sat on a cloud, and the Devil utterd these words:

"The worship of God is, Honouring his gifts in other men, each according to his genius, and loving the [PL 23] greatest men best. Those who envy or calumniate great men hate God, for there is no other God."

The Angel hearing this became almost blue; but mastering himself, he grew yellow, & at last white, pink, & smiling, and then replied:

"Thou Idolater, is not God One? & is not he visible in Jesus Christ? and has not Jesus Christ given his sanction to the law of ten commandments, and are not all other men fools, sinners, & nothings?"

The Devil answer'd; "Bray a fool in a mortar with wheat, yet shall not his folly be beaten out of him.[1] If Jesus Christ is the greatest man, you ought to love him in the greatest degree. Now hear how he has given his sanction to the law of ten commandments: did he not mock at the sabbath, and so mock the sabbath's God?[2] murder those who were murderd because of him? turn away the law from the woman taken in adultery?[3] steal the labor of others to support him? bear false witness when he omitted making a defence before Pilate?[4] covet when he pray'd for his disciples, and when he bid them shake off the dust of their feet against such as refused to lodge them?[5] I tell you, no virtue can exist without breaking these ten commandments. Jesus was all virtue, and acted from im[PL 24]pulse, not from rules."

9. Jakob Boehme (1575–1624), a German shoemaker who developed a theosophical system that has had persisting influence both on theological and metaphysical speculation. Paracelsus (1493–1541), a Swiss physician and a pioneer in empirical medicine, was also a prominent theorist of the occult.
1. Proverbs 27.22: "Though thou shouldst bray a fool in a mortar among wheat with a pestle, yet will not his foolishness depart from him." "Bray": pound into small pieces.
2. Mark 2.27: "The sabbath was made for man."
3. Cf. John 7.2ff.
4. Cf. Matthew 35.13–14.
5. Matthew 10.4: "Whosoever shall not receive you . . . when ye depart . . . shake off the dust of your feet."

When he had so spoken, I beheld the Angel, who stretched out his arms embracing the flame of fire, & he was consumed and arose as Elijah.[6]

Note. This Angel, who is now become a Devil, is my particular friend; we often read the Bible together in its infernal or diabolical sense, which the world shall have if they behave well.

I have also The Bible of Hell,[7] which the world shall have whether they will or no.

One Law for the Lion & Ox is Oppression.

1790–93   1790–93

PLATE 25

A Song of Liberty[1]

1. The Eternal Female groand! it was heard over all the Earth.

2. Albion's[2] coast is sick, silent; the American meadows faint!

3. Shadows of Prophecy shiver along by the lakes and the rivers and mutter across the ocean. France, rend down thy dungeon![3]

4. Golden Spain, burst the barriers of old Rome!

5. Cast thy keys, O Rome,[4] into the deep down falling, even to eternity down falling,

6. And weep.[5]

7. In her trembling hands she took the new born terror, howling.

8. On those infinite mountains of light now barr'd out by the Atlantic sea,[6] the new born fire stood before the starry king![7]

9. Flag'd with grey brow'd snows and thunderous visages, the jealous wings wav'd over the deep.

10. The speary hand burned aloft, unbuckled was the shield, forth went the hand of jealousy among the flaming hair, and [PL 26] hurl'd the new born wonder thro' the starry night.

11. The fire, the fire, is falling!

12. Look up! look up! O citizen of London, enlarge thy countenance! O Jew, leave counting gold! return to thy oil and wine. O African! black African! (Go, wingèd thought, widen his forehead.)

13. The fiery limbs, the flaming hair, shot like the sinking sun into the western sea.

14. Wak'd from his eternal sleep, the hoary element[8] roaring fled away:

15. Down rushd, beating his wings in vain, the jealous king; his grey brow'd councellors, thunderous warriors, curl'd veterans, among helms, and shields, and chariots, horses, elephants; banners, castles, slings and rocks,

---

6. In II Kings 2.11 the prophet Elijah "went up by a whirlwind into heaven," borne by "a chariot of fire."

7. I.e., the poems and designs that Blake is working on.

1. Blake etched this poem in 1792 and sometimes bound it as an appendix to *The Marriage of Heaven and Hell*. It recounts the birth, manifested in the contemporary events in France, of the flaming Spirit of Revolution (whom Blake later called Orc), and describes his conflict with the tyrannical sky god (whom Blake later called Urizen). The poem ends with the portent of the Spirit of Revolution shattering the ten commandments, or prohibitions against political, religious, and moral liberty, and bringing in a free and

joyous new world.

2. England's.

3. The political prison, the Bastille, was destroyed by the French revolutionaries in 1789.

4. The keys of Rome, a symbol of Papal power.

5. John 11.35: "Jesus wept."

6. The legendary continent of Atlantis, sunk beneath the sea; Blake uses it to represent the condition before the fall.

7. Blake often uses the stars, in their fixed courses, as a symbol of the law-governed Newtonian universe.

8. The sea, which to Blake represents a devouring chaos, such as had swallowed Atlantis.

16. Falling, rushing, ruining! buried in the ruins, on Urthona's[9] dens;

17. All night beneath the ruins; then, their sullen flames faded, emerge round the gloomy king,

18. With thunder and fire, leading his starry hosts thro' the waste wilderness [PL 27] he promulgates his ten commands, glancing his beamy eyelids over the deep in dark dismay,

19. Where the son of fire in his eastern cloud, while the morning plumes her golden breast,

20. Spurning the clouds written with curses, stamps the stony law[1] to dust, loosing the eternal horses from the dens of night, crying:

"Empire is no more! and now the lion & wolf shall cease."[2]

Chorus

Let the Priests of the Raven of dawn, no longer in deadly black, with hoarse note curse the sons of joy. Nor his accepted brethren, whom, tyrant, he calls free, lay the bound or build the roof. Nor pale religious letchery call that virginity, that wishes but acts not!

For every thing that lives is Holy.

1792   1792

From BLAKE'S NOTEBOOK[1]

Mock on, Mock on, Voltaire, Rousseau

Mock on, Mock on, Voltaire, Rousseau;[2]
Mock on, Mock on, 'tis all in vain.
You throw the sand against the wind,
And the wind blows it back again;

And every sand becomes a Gem   5
Reflected in the beams divine;
Blown back, they blind the mocking Eye,
But still in Israel's paths they shine.

The Atoms of Democritus
And Newton's Particles of light[3]   10

9. In the later Prophetic Books, Urthona is the unfallen form of Los, who in the fallen world represents the poetic imagination, the agent working for the regeneration of humanity.
1. I.e., the Ten Commandments (verse 18), which the "finger of God" had written on "tables [tablets] of stone" (Exodus 31.18).
2. Cf. Isaiah's prophecy, 65.17–25, of "new heavens and a new earth," when "the wolf and the lamb shall feed together, and the lion shall eat straw like the bullock."
1. A commonplace book in which Blake drew sketches and jotted down verses and memoranda be-

tween the late 1780s and 1810. It is known as the Rossetti manuscript because it later came into the possession of the poet and painter Dante Gabriel Rossetti. These poems were first published in imperfect form in 1863, then transcribed from the manuscript by Geoffrey Keynes in 1935.
2. Blake regards both Voltaire and Rousseau as representing rationalism and Deism.
3. Newton in his Opticks hypothesized that light consisted of minute material particles. Democritus (460–362 B.C.) proposed that atoms were the ultimate components of the universe.

Are sands upon the Red sea shore,
Where Israel's tents do shine so bright.

Never pain to tell thy love

Never pain to tell thy love
Love that never told can be,
For the gentle wind does move
Silently, invisibly.

I told my love, I told my love,   5
I told her all my heart,
Trembling, cold, in ghastly fears—
Ah, she doth depart.

Soon as she was gone from me
A traveller came by   10
Silently, invisibly—
O, was no deny.

I askèd a thief

I askèd a thief to steal me a peach,
He turned up his eyes;
I ask'd a lithe lady to lie her down,
Holy & meek she cries.

As soon as I went   5
An angel came.
He wink'd at the thief
And smild at the dame—

And without one word said
Had a peach from the tree   10
And still as a maid
Enjoy'd the lady.

1796   . . .

And did those feet[1]

And did those feet in ancient time
Walk upon England's mountains green?
And was the holy Lamb of God
On England's pleasant pastures seen?

1. These quatrains occur in the preface to Blake's prophetic poem *Milton*. There is an ancient belief, still current in parts of England, that Jesus came to England with Joseph of Arimathea. Blake adapts the legend to his own conception of a spiritual Israel, in which the significance of biblical events is as relevant to England as to Palestine. By a particularly Blakean irony, this poem of mental war in the service of apocalyptic desire is widely used as a hymn by those of us whom Blake called "angels."

And did the Countenance Divine 5
Shine forth upon our clouded hills?
And was Jerusalem builded here,
Among those dark Satanic Mills?²

Bring me my Bow of burning gold,
Bring me my Arrows of desire, 10
Bring me my Spear; O clouds unfold!
Bring me my Chariot of fire!

I will not cease from Mental Fight,
Nor shall my Sword sleep in my hand,
Till we have built Jerusalem 15
In England's green & pleasant Land.

ca. 1804–10   ca. 1804–10

From A Vision of The Last Judgment¹

For the Year 1810
Additions to Blake's Catalogue of Pictures &ᶜ

The Last Judgment [will be] when all those are Cast away who trouble
Religion with Questions concerning Good & Evil or Eating of the Tree of
those Knowledges or Reasonings which hinder the Vision of God turning all
into a Consuming fire. When Imaginative Art & Science & all Intellectual
Gifts, all the Gifts of the Holy Ghost, are lookd upon as of no use & only
Contention remains to Man, then the Last Judgment begins, & its Vision is
seen by the Imaginative Eye of Every one according to the situation he holds.
    [PAGE 68] The Last Judgment is not Fable or Allegory but Vision. Fable or
Allegory are a totally distinct & inferior kind of Poetry. Vision, or Imagination,
is a Representation of what Eternally Exists, Really & Unchangeably. Fable or
Allegory is Formd by the daughters of Memory. Imagination is Surrounded
by the daughters of Inspiration, who in the aggregate are calld Jerusalem. [P
69] Fable is Allegory, but what Critics call The Fable is Vision itself. [P 68]
The Hebrew Bible & the Gospel of Jesus are not Allegory, but Eternal Vision,
or Imagination of All that Exists. Note here that Fable or Allegory is Seldom
without some Vision. *Pilgrim's Progress* is full of it, the Greek Poets the same;
but Allegory & Vision ought to be known as Two Distinct Things, & so calld
for the Sake of Eternal Life. Plato has made Socrates say that Poets & Prophets
do not know or Understand what they write or Utter; this is a most Pernicious

2. There may be an allusion here to industrial England, but the mill is primarily Blake's symbol for a
mechanistic and utilitarian world view, according to
which, as he said elsewhere, "the same dull round,
even of a universe" becomes "a mill with complicated
wheels."
1. In this essay Blake describes and comments on his
painting of the Last Judgment, now lost, which is said
to have measured seven by five feet and to have included a thousand figures. The text has been transcribed and rearranged, as the sequence of the pages
indicates, from the scattered fragments in Blake's Notebook. The opening and closing parts are reprinted here
as Blake's fullest, although cryptic, statements of what
he means by "vision." These sections deal with the relations of imaginative vision to allegory, Greek fable,
and the biblical story; to uncurbed human passion and
intellectual power; to conventional and coercive virtue; to what is seen by the "corporeal" eye; to the arts;
and to the Last Judgment and the apocalyptic redemption of humanity and of the created world—an apocalypse that is to be achieved through the triumph over
the bodily eye by human imagination, as manifested in
the creative artist.

Falshood. If they do not, pray is an inferior Kind to be calld Knowing? Plato confutes himself.[2]

The Last Judgment is one of these Stupendous Visions. I have represented it as I saw it. To different People it appears differently, as [P 69] every thing else does; for tho on Earth things seem Permanent, they are less permanent than a Shadow, as we all know too well.

The Nature of Visionary Fancy, or Imagination, is very little Known, & the Eternal nature & permanence of its ever Existent Images is considered as less permanent than the things of Vegetative & Generative Nature; yet the Oak dies as well as the Lettuce, but Its Eternal Image & Individuality never dies, but renews by its seed. Just so the Imaginative Image returns by the seed of Contemplative Thought. The Writings of the Prophets illustrate these conceptions of the Visionary Fancy by their various sublime & Divine Images as seen in the Worlds of Vision. * * *

Let it here be Noted that the Greek Fables originated in Spiritual Mystery [P 72] & Real Visions, Which are lost & clouded in Fable & Allegory, while the Hebrew Bible & the Greek Gospel are Genuine, Preservd by the Saviour's Mercy. The Nature of my Work is Visionary or Imaginative; it is an Endeavour to Restore what the Ancients calld the Golden Age.

[PAGE 69] This world of Imagination is the World of Eternity; it is the Divine bosom into which we shall all go after the death of the Vegetated body. This World of Imagination is Infinite & Eternal, whereas the world of Generation, or Vegetation, is Finite & Temporal. There Exist in that Eternal World the Permanent Realities of Every Thing which we see reflected in this Vegetable Glass of Nature.

All Things are comprehended in their Eternal Forms in the Divine [P 70] body of the Saviour, the True Vine of Eternity, The Human Imagination, who appeard to Me as Coming to Judgment among his Saints & throwing off the Temporal that the Eternal might be Establishd. Around him were seen the Images of Existences according to a certain order suited to my Imaginative Eye. * * *

[PAGE 87] Men are admitted into Heaven not because they have curbed & governd their Passions, or have No Passions, but because they have Cultivated their Understandings. The Treasures of Heaven are not Negations of Passion, but Realities of Intellect from which All the Passions Emanate Uncurbed in their Eternal Glory. The Fool shall not enter into Heaven, let him be ever so Holy. Holiness is not The price of Enterance into Heaven. Those who are cast out Are All Those who, having no Passions of their own because No Intellect, Have spent their lives in Curbing & Governing other People's by the Various arts of Poverty & Cruelty of all kinds. Wo Wo Wo to you Hypocrites! Even Murder the Courts of Justice, more merciful than the Church, are compelld to allow, is not done in Passion but in Cool Blooded Design & Intention.

The Modern Church Crucifies Christ with the Head Downwards.

[PAGE 92] Many persons such as Paine & Voltaire, with some of the Ancient Greeks, say: "We will not converse concerning Good & Evil; we will live in Paradise & Liberty."[3] You may do so in Spirit, but not in the Mortal Body as

---

2. In Plato's dialogue *Ion*, in which Socrates traps Ion into admitting that, since poets compose by inspiration, they do so without knowing what they are doing.
3. Blake represents Thomas Paine, author of *The Rights of Man* (1791), and Voltaire, the great author of

the French Enlightenment, as proponents of the possibility of restoring an earthly paradise by political revolution. Such had been Blake's own view in the early 1790s (see, e.g., *The Marriage of Heaven and Hell*, pp. 1312–24).

you pretend, till after the last Judgment; for in Paradise they have no Corporeal & Mortal Body—that originated with the Fall & was calld Death & cannot be removed but by a Last Judgment; while we are in the world of Mortality we Must Suffer. The Whole Creation Groans to be deliverd; there will always be as many Hypocrites born as Honest Men & they will always have superior Power in Mortal Things. You cannot have Liberty in this World without what you call Moral Virtue, & you cannot have Moral Virtue without the Slavery of that half of the Human Race who hate what you call Moral Virtue.

* * *

Thinking as I do that the Creator of this World is a very Cruel Being, & being a Worshipper of Christ, I cannot help saying: "The Son, O how unlike the Father!" First God Almighty comes with a Thump on the Head. Then Jesus Christ comes with a balm to heal it.

The Last Judgment is an Overwhelming of Bad Art & Science. Mental Things are alone Real; what is Calld Corporeal Nobody Knows of its dwelling Place; it is in Fallacy & its Existence an Imposture. Where is the Existence Out of Mind or Thought? Where is it but in the Mind of a Fool? Some People flatter themselves that there will be No Last Judgment, & [P 95] that Bad Art will be adopted & mixed with Good Art, That Error or Experiment will make a Part of Truth, & they Boast that it is its Foundation. These People flatter themselves; I will not Flatter them. Error is Created; Truth is Eternal. Error or Creation will be Burned Up, & then & not till then Truth or Eternity will appear. It is Burnt up the Moment Men cease to behold it. I assert for My self that I do not behold the Outward Creation & that to me it is hindrance & not Action; it is as the Dirt upon my feet, No part of Me. "What," it will be Questioned, "When the Sun rises, do you not see a round Disk of fire somewhat like a Guinea?" O no no, I see an Innumerable company of the Heavenly host crying "Holy Holy Holy is the Lord God Almighty." I question not my Corporeal or Vegetative Eye any more than I would Question a Window concerning a Sight: I look thro it & not with it.

1810   1810

WILLIAM WORDSWORTH
1770–1850

1791–92:	In France during the early period of the Revolution.
1797:	With his sister, Dorothy, at Alfoxden House, Somersetshire, near Coleridge at Nether Stowey.
1798:	First edition of *Lyrical Ballads*.
1799:	William and Dorothy settle at Grasmere, in the Lake District.
1800:	Second edition of *Lyrical Ballads* in two volumes, with the famous Preface.
1807:	*Poems in Two Volumes*; end of the great decade.

William Wordsworth was born in Cockermouth in West Cumberland, just on the northern fringe of the English Lake District. When his mother died, the eight-year-old boy was sent to school at Hawkshead, near Esthwaite Lake, in the heart of that thinly settled region which he and Coleridge were to transform into the poetic center of England. William and his three brothers boarded in the cottage of Ann Tyson, who gave the boys simple comfort, ample affection, and freedom to roam the countryside at will. A vigorous, unruly, and sometimes moody boy, William spent his free days and occasionally "half the night" in the sports and rambles described in the first two books of *The Prelude*, "drinking in" (to use one of his favorite metaphors) the natural sights and sounds, and getting to know the cottagers, shepherds, and solitary wanderers who moved through his imagination into his later poetry. He also found time to read voraciously in the books owned by his young headmaster, William Taylor, who encouraged him in his inclination to poetry.

John Wordsworth, the poet's father, died suddenly when William was thirteen, leaving to his five children mainly the substantial sum owed him by Lord Lonsdale, whom he had served as attorney and as steward of the huge Lonsdale estate. That harsh and litigious nobleman managed to keep from paying the debt until he died in 1802. Wordsworth was nevertheless able to go up to St. John's College, Cambridge, in 1787, where he found very little in the limited curriculum of that time to appeal to him. He took his degree in 1791 without distinction.

During the summer vacation of his third year at Cambridge (1790), Wordsworth and his closest college friend, the Welshman Robert Jones, journeyed on foot through France and the Alps (described in *The Prelude* 6) at the time when the French were joyously celebrating the first anniversary of the fall of the Bastille. Upon completing his course at Cambridge, Wordsworth spent four months in London, set off on another walking tour with Robert Jones through Wales (the time of the memorable ascent of Mount Snowdon in *The Prelude* 14), and then went back alone to France in order to master the language and qualify as a traveling tutor.

During his year in France (between November 1791 and December 1792) Wordsworth became a fervent "democrat" and proselyte of the French Revolution—which seemed to him, as to many other generous spirits, to promise a "glorious renovation"—and he had a love affair with Annette Vallon, the impetuous and warm-hearted daughter of a French surgeon at Blois. It seems clear that Wordsworth and Annette planned to marry, despite their difference in religion and political inclinations (Annette belonged to an old Catholic family whose sympathies were Royalist). But almost immediately after a daughter, Caroline, was born, lack of funds forced Wordsworth back to England. The outbreak of war between England and France made it impossible for him to rejoin Annette until they had drifted so far apart in sympathies that a permanent union no longer seemed desirable. Wordsworth's agonies of guilt, his divided loyalties between England and France, his gradual disillusion with the course of the Revolution in France—according to his account in *The Prelude* 10 and 11—brought him to the verge of an emotional breakdown, when "sick, wearied out with contrarieties," he "yielded up moral questions in despair." His suffering, his near-collapse, and the successful effort, after his sharp break with his past, to reestablish "a saving intercourse with my true self," are the experiences that underlie many of his greatest poems.

At this critical point a young friend, Raisley Calvert, died and left Wordsworth a sum of money just sufficient to enable him to live by his poetry. He settled in a rent-free cottage at Racedown, Dorsetshire, with his beloved sister, Dorothy, who now began her long career as confidante, inspirer, and secretary. At that same time Wordsworth met Samuel Taylor Coleridge; two years later he moved to Alfoxden House, Somersetshire, to be near Coleridge, who lived four miles away at Nether Stowey. Here, his recovery complete, he entered at the age of twenty-seven on the delayed springtime of his poetic career.

Even while he had been an undergraduate at Cambridge, Coleridge claimed that he had detected signs of genius in Wordsworth's rather conventional poem about his tour in the Alps, *Descriptive Sketches*, published in 1793. Now he hailed Wordsworth unreservedly as "the best poet of the age." The two men met almost daily, talked for hours about poetry, and composed prolifically. So close was their association that we find the same phrases occurring in poems by Wordsworth and Coleridge, as well as in the remarkable journals that Dorothy kept at the time; the two poets collaborated in some writings and freely traded thoughts and passages for others; and Coleridge even undertook to complete a few poems that Wordsworth had left unfinished.

The result of their joint efforts was a small volume, published anonymously in 1798, *Lyrical Ballads, with a Few Other Poems*. It opened with Coleridge's *Ancient Mariner*; included three other poems by Coleridge, a number of Wordsworth's verse anecdotes and psychological studies of humble people, and some lyrics in which Wordsworth celebrated impulses from a vernal wood; and closed with Wordsworth's great descriptive and meditative poem in blank verse (not a "lyrical ballad," but one of the "other poems" of the title), *Tintern Abbey*. No other book of poems in English more plainly announces a new literary departure. William Hazlitt said that when he heard Coleridge read some of these newly written poems aloud, "the sense of a new style and a new spirit in poetry came over me," with something of the effect "that arises from the turning up of the fresh soil, or of the first welcome breath of spring." The professional reviewers were less enthusiastic. Nevertheless *Lyrical Ballads* sold out in two years, and Wordsworth published under his own name a new edition, dated 1800, to which he added a second volume of poems, many of them written in homesickness during a long, cold, and friendless winter that he and Dorothy had spent in Goslar, Germany, 1798–99. In his famous Preface to this edition, planned, like so many of the poems, in close consultation with Coleridge, Wordsworth enunciated the principles of the new criticism that served as rationale for the new poetry. Notable among the other works written in this prolific period is his austere and powerful tragic poem *The Ruined Cottage*.

Late in 1799 Wordsworth and Dorothy moved back permanently to their native lakes, settling at Grasmere in the little house later named Dove Cottage. Coleridge, following them, rented Greta Hall at Keswick, thirteen miles away. In 1802 Wordsworth finally came into his father's inheritance and, after an amicable settlement with Annette Vallon, married Mary Hutchinson, a Lake Country woman whom he had known since childhood. The course of his existence after that time was broken by various disasters: the drowning in 1805 of his favorite brother, John, a sea captain whose ship was wrecked in a storm; the death of two of his five children in 1812; a growing estrangement from Coleridge, culminating in a bitter quarrel (1810) from which they were not completely reconciled for almost two decades; and from the 1830s on, the physical and mental decline of his sister, Dorothy. The life of his middle age, however, was one of steadily increasing prosperity and reputation, as well as of political and religious conservatism. In 1813 an appointment as Stamp Distributor (that is, revenue collector) for Westmorland was concrete evidence of his recognition as a national poet. Gradually his residences, as he moved into more and more commodious quarters, became standard stops for tourists; he was awarded honorary degrees and, in 1843, was appointed poet laureate. He died in 1850 at the age of eighty; only then did his executors publish his masterpiece, *The Prelude*, the autobiographical poem that he had written in two parts in 1799, expanded to its full length in 1805, and then continued to revise almost to the last decade of his long life.

Most of Wordsworth's greatest poetry had been written by 1807, when he published *Poems in Two Volumes*; and after *The Excursion* (1814) and the first collected edition of his poems (1815), although he continued to write voluminously, there is an overall decline in his powers as a poet. The causes of the decline have been much debated; an important one seems to be inherent in the very nature of his most characteristic writing. Wordsworth is above all the poet of the remembrance of things past, or as he himself put it, of "emotion recollected in tranquillity." Some object or event in the present triggers a sudden renewal of feelings he had experienced in youth; the result is a poem exhibiting the sharp discrepancy between what Wordsworth called "two consciousnesses": himself as he is now and himself as he once was. But the memory of one's early emotional experience is not an inexhaustible resource for poetry. As Basil Willey has remarked, Wordsworth as a poet "was living upon capital"; and he knew it. As he says in *The Prelude* 12, while describing the recurrence of "spots of time" from his memories of childhood:

> The days gone by
> Return upon me almost from the dawn
> Of life: the hiding places of Man's power
> Open; I would approach them, but they close.
> I see by glimpses now; when age comes on,
> May scarcely see at all.

The past that Wordsworth recollected was one of moments of intense experience, and of emotional turmoil which is ordered, in the calmer present, into a hard-won equilibrium. The result was a poetry of excitation in calm; genius, as Wordsworth said, is "born to thrive by interchange / Of peace and excitation" (*Prelude* 13.1–10). As time went on, however, the precarious equilibrium of his great creative period became a habit, and Wordsworth finally gained what, in the *Ode to Duty* (composed in 1804), he longed for, "a repose which ever is the same"—but at the expense of the agony and excitation which, under the calm surface, empowers his best and most characteristic poems.

Occasionally, in his middle and later life a jolting experience would revive the intensity of Wordsworth's remembered emotion, and also his earlier poetic strength. The moving sonnet *Surprised by Joy*, for example, was written in his forties at the abrupt realization that time was beginning to diminish his grief at the death some years earlier of his little daughter Catherine. And when Wordsworth was sixty-five years old, the sudden report of the death of James Hogg called up the memory of other and greater poets whom Wordsworth had loved and outlived; the result was his *Extempore Effusion*, written in a return to the simple quatrains of the early *Lyrical Ballads* and with a recovery of the great elegiac voice that had uttered the dirges to Lucy, thirty-five years before.

From LYRICAL BALLADS

We Are Seven[1]

————A simple Child,
That lightly draws its breath,
And feels its life in every limb,
What should it know of death?

---

1. "Written at Alfoxden in the spring of 1798. . . . The little girl who is the heroine I met within the area of Goodrich Castle [in the Wye Valley north of Tintern Abbey] in the year 1793" [Wordsworth's note]. Words- worth also tells us that he composed the last line of the last stanza first, and that Coleridge contributed the initial stanza.

I met a little cottage Girl: 5
She was eight years old, she said;
Her hair was thick with many a curl
That clustered round her head.

She had a rustic, woodland air,
And she was wildly clad: 10
Her eyes were fair, and very fair;
—Her beauty made me glad.

"Sisters and brothers, little Maid,
How many may you be?"
"How many? Seven in all," she said,   15
And wondering looked at me.

"And where are they? I pray you tell."
She answered, "Seven are we;
And two of us at Conway² dwell,
And two are gone to sea.   20

"Two of us in the church-yard lie,
My sister and my brother;
And, in the church-yard cottage, I
Dwell near them with my mother."

"You say that two at Conway dwell,   25
And two are gone to sea,
Yet ye are seven! I pray you tell,
Sweet Maid, how this may be."

Then did the little Maid reply,
"Seven boys and girls are we;   30
Two of us in the church-yard lie,
Beneath the church-yard tree."

"You run about, my little Maid,
Your limbs they are alive;
If two are in the church-yard laid,   35
Then ye are only five."

"Their graves are green, they may be seen,"
The little Maid replied,
"Twelve steps or more from my mother's door,
And they are side by side.   40

"My stockings there I often knit,
My kerchief there I hem;
And there upon the ground I sit,
And sing a song to them.

2. A seaport town in north Wales.

"And often after sun-set, Sir,   45
When it is light and fair,
I take my little porringer,[3]
And eat my supper there.

"The first that died was sister Jane;
In bed she moaning lay,   50
Till God released her of her pain;
And then she went away.

"So in the church-yard she was laid;
And, when the grass was dry,
Together round her grave we played,   55
My brother John and I.

"And when the ground was white with snow,
And I could run and slide,
My brother John was forced to go,
And he lies by her side."   60

"How many are you, then," said I,
"If they two are in heaven?"
Quick was the little Maid's reply,
"O Master! we are seven."

"But they are dead; those two are dead!   65
Their spirits are in heaven!"
'Twas throwing words away; for still
The little Maid would have her will,
And said, "Nay, we are seven!"

1798   1798

Lines Written in Early Spring

I heard a thousand blended notes,
While in a grove I sate reclined,
In that sweet mood when pleasant thoughts
Bring sad thoughts to the mind.

To her fair works did Nature link   5
The human soul that through me ran;
And much it grieved my heart to think
What man has made of man.

Through primrose tufts, in that green bower,
The periwinkle[1] trailed its wreaths,   10
And 'tis my faith that every flower
Enjoys the air it breathes.

3. Bowl for porridge.   (U.S. myrtle).
1. A trailing evergreen plant with small blue flowers

The birds around me hopped and played,
Their thoughts I cannot measure:—
But the least motion which they made,   15
It seemed a thrill of pleasure.

The budding twigs spread out their fan,
To catch the breezy air;
And I must think, do all I can,
That there was pleasure there.   20

If this belief from heaven be sent,
If such be Nature's holy plan,[2]
Have I not reason to lament
What man has made of man?

1798   1798

Expostulation and Reply[1]

"Why, William, on that old grey stone,
Thus for the length of half a day,
Why, William, sit you thus alone,
And dream your time away?

"Where are your books? that light bequeathed   5
To Beings else forlorn and blind!
Up! up! and drink the spirit breathed
From dead men to their kind.

"You look round on your Mother Earth,
As if she for no purpose bore you;   10
As if you were her first-born birth,
And none had lived before you!"

One morning thus, by Esthwaite lake,
When life was sweet, I knew not why,
To me my good friend Matthew spake,   15
And thus I made reply.

"The eye—it cannot choose but see;
We cannot bid the ear be still;
Our bodies feel, where'er they be,
Against or with our will.   20

2. The version of these two lines in the *Lyrical Ballads* of 1798 reads: "If I these thoughts may not prevent, / If such be of my creed the plan."
1. This and the following companion poem have often been attacked—and defended—as Wordsworth's solemn deliverance on the comparative merits of nature and of books. But they are a dialogue between two friends who rally one another by the usual device of overstating parts of a whole truth. Wordsworth said that the pieces originated in a conversation "with a friend who was somewhat unreasonably attached to modern books of moral philosophy," and also that the lore of "a wise passiveness" made the poem a favorite among Quakers.

"Nor less I deem that there are Powers
Which of themselves our minds impress;
That we can feed this mind of ours
In a wise passiveness.

"Think you, 'mid all this mighty sum   25
Of things for ever speaking,
That nothing of itself will come,
But we must still be seeking?

"—Then ask not wherefore, here, alone,
Conversing² as I may,   30
I sit upon this old grey stone,
And dream my time away."

Spring 1798   1798

The Tables Turned

An Evening Scene on the Same Subject

Up! up! my Friend, and quit your books;
Or surely you'll grow double:
Up! up! my Friend, and clear your looks;
Why all this toil and trouble?

The sun, above the mountain's head,   5
A freshening lustre mellow
Through all the long green fields has spread,
His first sweet evening yellow.

Books! 'tis a dull and endless strife:
Come, hear the woodland linnet,¹   10
How sweet his music! on my life,
There's more of wisdom in it.

And hark! how blithe the throstle² sings!
He, too, is no mean preacher:
Come forth into the light of things,   15
Let Nature be your Teacher.

She has a world of ready wealth,
Our minds and hearts to bless—
Spontaneous wisdom breathed by health,
Truth breathed by cheerfulness.   20

One impulse from a vernal wood
May teach you more of man,

2. In the old sense of "communing" (with the "things   1. A small finch, common in Europe.
for ever speaking").   2. The song thrush.

Of moral evil and of good,
Than all the sages can.

Sweet is the lore which Nature brings;   25
Our meddling intellect
Mis-shapes the beauteous forms of things:—
We murder to dissect.

Enough of Science and of Art;
Close up those barren leaves;   30
Come forth, and bring with you a heart
That watches and receives.

1798   1798

Lines[1]

Composed a Few Miles above Tintern Abbey, on Revisiting the Banks of the Wye during a Tour, July 13, 1798

Five years have past; five summers, with the length
Of five long winters! and again I hear
These waters, rolling from their mountain-springs
With a soft inland murmur.—Once again
Do I behold these steep and lofty cliffs,   5
That on a wild secluded scene impress
Thoughts of more deep seclusion; and connect
The landscape with the quiet of the sky.
The day is come when I again repose
Here, under this dark sycamore, and view   10
These plots of cottage-ground, these orchard-tufts,
Which at this season, with their unripe fruits,
Are clad in one green hue, and lose themselves
'Mid groves and copses. Once again I see
These hedge-rows, hardly hedge-rows, little lines   15
Of sportive wood run wild: these pastoral farms,
Green to the very door; and wreaths of smoke
Sent up, in silence, from among the trees!
With some uncertain notice, as might seem
Of vagrant dwellers in the houseless woods,   20
Or of some Hermit's cave, where by his fire
The Hermit sits alone.

1. "No poem of mine was composed under circumstances more pleasant for me to remember than this. I
began it upon leaving Tintern, after crossing the Wye,
and concluded it just as I was entering Bristol in the
evening, after a ramble of 4 or 5 days, with my sister.
Not a line of it was altered, and not any part of it written down till I reached Bristol" [Wordsworth's note].
The poem was printed as the last item in *Lyrical Ballads*.
  Wordsworth had first visited the Wye valley and the
ruins of Tintern Abbey, in Monmouthshire, while on
a solitary walking tour in Aug. 1793, when he was
twenty-three years old. The puzzling difference between the present landscape and the remembered "picture of the mind" (line 61) gives rise to an intricately
organized meditation, in which the poet reviews his
past, evaluates the present, and (through his sister as
intermediary) anticipates the future; he ends by
rounding back quietly on the scene that had been his
point of departure.

                    These beauteous forms,
Through a long absence, have not been to me
As is a landscape to a blind man's eye:
But oft, in lonely rooms, and 'mid the din   25
Of towns and cities, I have owed to them
In hours of weariness, sensations sweet,
Felt in the blood, and felt along the heart;
And passing even into my purer mind,
With tranquil restoration:—feelings too   30
Of unremembered pleasure: such, perhaps,
As have no slight or trivial influence
On that best portion of a good man's life,
His little, nameless, unremembered, acts
Of kindness and of love. Nor less, I trust,   35
To them I may have owed another gift,
Of aspect more sublime; that blessed mood,
In which the burthen of the mystery,
In which the heavy and the weary weight
Of all this unintelligible world,   40
Is lightened:—that serene and blessed mood,
In which the affections gently lead us on,—
Until, the breath of this corporeal frame
And even the motion of our human blood
Almost suspended, we are laid asleep   45
In body, and become a living soul:
While with an eye made quiet by the power
Of harmony, and the deep power of joy,
We see into the life of things.

                    If this
Be but a vain belief, yet, oh! how oft—   50
In darkness and amid the many shapes
Of joyless daylight; when the fretful stir
Unprofitable, and the fever of the world,
Have hung upon the beatings of my heart—
How oft, in spirit, have I turned to thee,   55
O sylvan Wye! thou wanderer thro' the woods,
How often has my spirit turned to thee!

    And now, with gleams of half-extinguished thought,
With many recognitions dim and faint,
And somewhat of a sad perplexity,   60
The picture of the mind revives again:
While here I stand, not only with the sense
Of present pleasure, but with pleasing thoughts
That in this moment there is life and food
For future years. And so I dare to hope,   65
Though changed, no doubt, from what I was when first
I came among these hills; when like a roe
I bounded o'er the mountains, by the sides
Of the deep rivers, and the lonely streams,

Wherever nature led: more like a man   70
Flying from something that he dreads, than one
Who sought the thing he loved. For nature then
(The coarser pleasures of my boyish days,
And their glad animal movements all gone by)
To me was all in all.—I cannot paint   75
What then I was. The sounding cataract
Haunted me like a passion: the tall rock,
The mountain, and the deep and gloomy wood,
Their colours and their forms, were then to me
An appetite; a feeling and a love,   80
That had no need of a remoter charm,
By thought supplied, nor any interest
Unborrowed from the eye.—That time is past,
And all its aching joys are now no more,
And all its dizzy raptures.[2] Not for this   85
Faint[3] I, nor mourn nor murmur; other gifts
Have followed; for such loss, I would believe,
Abundant recompense. For I have learned
To look on nature, not as in the hour
Of thoughtless youth; but hearing oftentimes   90
The still, sad music of humanity,
Nor harsh nor grating, though of ample power
To chasten and subdue. And I have felt
A presence that disturbs me with the joy
Of elevated thoughts; a sense sublime   95
Of something far more deeply interfused,
Whose dwelling is the light of setting suns,
And the round ocean and the living air,
And the blue sky, and in the mind of man:
A motion and a spirit, that impels   100
All thinking things, all objects of all thought,
And rolls through all things. Therefore am I still
A lover of the meadows and the woods,
And mountains; and of all that we behold
From this green earth; of all the mighty world   105
Of eye, and ear,—both what they half create,[4]
And what perceive; well pleased to recognise
In nature and the language of the sense,
The anchor of my purest thoughts, the nurse,
The guide, the guardian of my heart, and soul   110
Of all my moral being.

            Nor perchance,
If I were not thus taught, should I the more
Suffer my genial spirits[5] to decay:

2. Lines 66ff. contain Wordsworth's famed description of the three stages of his growing up, defined in terms of his evolving relations to the natural scene: the young boy's purely physical responsiveness (lines 73–74); the postadolescent's aching, dizzy, and equivocal passions—a love that is more like dread (lines 67–72, 75–85: this was his state of mind on the occasion of his first visit); his present state (lines 85ff.), in which for the first time he adds thought to sense.
3. Lose heart.
4. This view that the "creative sensibility" contributes to its own perceptions is often reiterated in *The Prelude*.
5. Creative powers. ("Genial" is here the adjectival form of the noun "genius.")

For thou art with me here upon the banks
Of this fair river; thou my dearest Friend,[6]   115
My dear, dear Friend; and in thy voice I catch
The language of my former heart, and read
My former pleasures in the shooting lights
Of thy wild eyes. Oh! yet a little while
May I behold in thee what I was once,   120
My dear, dear Sister! and this prayer I make,
Knowing that Nature never did betray
The heart that loved her; 'tis her privilege,
Through all the years of this our life, to lead
From joy to joy: for she can so inform   125
The mind that is within us, so impress
With quietness and beauty, and so feed
With lofty thoughts, that neither evil tongues,
Rash judgments, nor the sneers of selfish men,
Nor greetings where no kindness is, nor all   130
The dreary intercourse of daily life,
Shall e'er prevail against us, or disturb
Our cheerful faith, that all which we behold
Is full of blessings. Therefore let the moon
Shine on thee in thy solitary walk;   135
And let the misty mountain-winds be free
To blow against thee: and, in after years,
When these wild ecstasies shall be matured
Into a sober pleasure; when thy mind
Shall be a mansion for all lovely forms,   140
Thy memory be as a dwelling-place
For all sweet sounds and harmonies; oh! then,
If solitude, or fear, or pain, or grief,
Should be thy portion, with what healing thoughts
Of tender joy wilt thou remember me,   145
And these my exhortations! Nor, perchance—
If I should be where I no more can hear
Thy voice, nor catch from thy wild eyes these gleams
Of past existence[7]—wilt thou then forget
That on the banks of this delightful stream   150
We stood together; and that I, so long
A worshipper of Nature, hither came
Unwearied in that service; rather say
With warmer love—oh! with far deeper zeal
Of holier love. Nor wilt thou then forget,   155
That after many wanderings, many years
Of absence, these steep woods and lofty cliffs,
And this green pastoral landscape, were to me
More dear, both for themselves and for thy sake!

July 1798   1798

6. His sister, Dorothy.   earlier (see lines 116–19).
7. I.e., reminders of his own "past existence" five years

Preface to *Lyrical Ballads* (1802)   To the first edition of *Lyrical Ballads*, published jointly with Coleridge in 1798, Wordsworth prefixed an "Advertisement" which asserted that the major number of the poems were "to be considered as experiments" to determine "how far the language of conversation in the middle and lower classes of society is adapted to the purposes of poetic pleasure." In the second, two-volume edition of 1800 Wordsworth, relying in part on frequent conversations with Coleridge, expanded the Advertisement into a Preface that justified the new poetry not as experiments, but as exemplifying the principles of all good poetry. The Preface was enlarged for the third edition of *Lyrical Ballads*, published two years later; this last version of 1802 is the one that is reprinted here.

Although some of its individual ideas had antecedents in the later eighteenth century, the Preface as a whole deserves its reputation as a revolutionary manifesto about the nature of poetry. Like many radical statements, however, it claims to go back to the implicit principles that governed the great poetry of the past but have been perverted in recent practice. Most discussions of the Preface, following the lead of Coleridge in his *Biographia Literaria*, have focused on Wordsworth's assertions about the valid language of poetry, on which he bases his attack on the "poetic diction" of eighteenth-century poets. As Coleridge pointed out, Wordsworth's argument about this issue is far from clear. It is apparent, however, that Wordsworth undertook to overthrow the basic theory, as well as the reigning practice, of neoclassic poetry. That is, his Preface implicitly denies the traditional assumption that the poetic genres constitute a hierarchy, from epic and tragedy at the top down through comedy, satire, pastoral, to the short lyric at the lower reaches of the poetic scale; he also rejects the traditional principle of "decorum," according to which the subject matter (especially the social class of the protagonists) and the level of diction of a poem must conform to the status of the literary kind on the poetic scale.

When Wordsworth asserted in the Preface that he deliberately chose to represent "incidents and situations from common life," he translated his democratic sympathies into critical terms, justifying his use of peasants, children, outcasts, criminals, and idiot boys as serious subjects of poetic and even tragic concern. He also undertook to write in "a selection of language really used by men," on the grounds that there can be no "essential difference between the language of prose and metrical composition." In making this claim, Wordsworth subverted the neoclassic principle that, in many kinds of poem, the language must be elevated over standard speech by a special diction and by artful figures of speech, in order to match the language to the height and dignity of a particular genre. Wordsworth's own views about the valid language of poetry are based on the new premise that "all good poetry is the spontaneous overflow of powerful feelings" — spontaneous, that is, at the moment of composition, even though the process is influenced by prior thought and acquired poetic skill. The equivalence that Wordsworth claims, therefore, between the valid language of poems and the prose language "really spoken by men" is not one of vocabulary or of syntax, but an equivalence in emotional genesis — instead of consisting in contrived and artful constructions, both forms of language originate spontaneously, as the words and figures that, as Keats later put it, are "the true voice of feeling."

Wordsworth's assertions about the materials and diction of poetry have been greatly influential in expanding the range of serious literature to include the common people and ordinary things and events, as well as in justifying a poetry of sincerity rather than of artifice, expressed in the ordinary language of its time. But in the long view, other aspects of his Preface have been no less significant in establishing its importance, not only as a turning point in English criticism but also as a central document in modern culture. Wordsworth attributed to imaginative literature the primary role in keeping human beings emotionally alive and morally sensitive — that is, keeping them essentially human — in the modern era of

a technological and increasingly urban society, with its mass media and mass culture that threaten, as he foresaw, to blunt the mind's "discriminatory powers" and
to "reduce it to a state of almost savage torpor." However radical their particular
application by Wordsworth, the values that permeate his Preface are the central
humanistic values of the eighteenth-century Enlightenment—that is, the use, as a
standard, of elements that he represents as essential, simple, universal, and permanent in human nature.

From Preface to *Lyrical Ballads, with Pastoral and Other Poems* (1802)

[*The Subject and Language of Poetry*]

The first volume of these poems has already been submitted to general
perusal. It was published, as an experiment, which, I hoped, might be of some
use to ascertain, how far, by fitting to metrical arrangement a selection of the
real language of men in a state of vivid sensation, that sort of pleasure and that
quantity of pleasure may be imparted, which a poet may rationally endeavour
to impart.

I had formed no very inaccurate estimate of the probable effect of those
poems: I flattered myself that they who should be pleased with them would
read them with more than common pleasure: and, on the other hand, I was
well aware, that by those who should dislike them they would be read with
more than common dislike. The result has differed from my expectation in
this only, that I have pleased a greater number than I ventured to hope I
should please.

For the sake of variety, and from a consciousness of my own weakness, I
was induced to request the assistance of a friend, who furnished me with the
poems of the *Ancient Mariner*, the *Foster-Mother's Tale*, the *Nightingale*, and
the poem entitled *Love*. I should not, however, have requested this assistance,
had I not believed that the poems of my friend would in a great measure
have the same tendency as my own, and that, though there would be found a
difference, there would be found no discordance in the colours of our style;
as our opinions on the subject of poetry do almost entirely coincide.[1]

Several of my friends are anxious for the success of these poems from a
belief, that, if the views with which they were composed were indeed realized,
a class of poetry would be produced, well adapted to interest mankind permanently, and not unimportant in the multiplicity, and in the quality of its moral
relations: and on this account they have advised me to prefix a systematic
defence of the theory upon which the poems were written. But I was unwilling
to undertake the task, because I knew that on this occasion the reader would
look coldly upon my arguments, since I might be suspected of having been
principally influenced by the selfish and foolish hope of *reasoning* him into
an approbation of these particular poems: and I was still more unwilling to
undertake the task, because, adequately to display my opinions, and fully to

---

1. The "friend" of course is Coleridge. When he read
this Preface and the new poems included in the 1802
edition of *Lyrical Ballads*, Coleridge wrote to Robert
Southey that although Wordsworth's Preface of 1800
had been "half a child of my own brain," he now suspects that "there is a radical difference in our theoretical opinions respecting poetry—this I shall endeavour
to go to the bottom of." The results of this endeavor
are Coleridge's discussions, fifteen years later, of
Wordsworth's Preface in *Biographia Literaria*, chaps.
14 and 17.

enforce my arguments, would require a space wholly disproportionate to the nature of a preface. For to treat the subject with the clearness and coherence of which I believe it susceptible, it would be necessary to give a full account of the present state of the public taste in this country, and to determine how far this taste is healthy or depraved; which, again, could not be determined, without pointing out, in what manner language and the human mind act and re-act on each other, and without retracing the revolutions, not of literature alone, but likewise of society itself. I have therefore altogether declined to enter regularly upon this defence; yet I am sensible, that there would be some impropriety in abruptly obtruding upon the public, without a few words of introduction, poems so materially different from those upon which general approbation is at present bestowed.

It is supposed, that by the act of writing in verse an author makes a formal engagement that he will gratify certain known habits of association; that he not only thus apprizes the reader that certain classes of ideas and expressions will be found in his book, but that others will be carefully excluded. This exponent or symbol held forth by metrical language must in different eras of literature have excited very different expectations: for example, in the age of Catullus, Terence, and Lucretius and that of Statius or Claudian,[2] and in our own country, in the age of Shakespeare and Beaumont and Fletcher, and that of Donne and Cowley, or Dryden, or Pope. I will not take upon me to determine the exact import of the promise which by the act of writing in verse an author, in the present day, makes to his reader; but I am certain, it will appear to many persons that I have not fulfilled the terms of an engagement thus voluntarily contracted. They who have been accustomed to the gaudiness and inane phraseology of many modern writers, if they persist in reading this book to its conclusion, will, no doubt, frequently have to struggle with feelings of strangeness and awkwardness: they will look round for poetry, and will be induced to inquire by what species of courtesy these attempts can be permitted to assume that title. I hope therefore the reader will not censure me, if I attempt to state what I have proposed to myself to perform; and also (as far as the limits of a preface will permit) to explain some of the chief reasons which have determined me in the choice of my purpose: that at least he may be spared any unpleasant feeling of disappointment, and that I myself may be protected from the most dishonorable accusation which can be brought against an author, namely, that of an indolence which prevents him from endeavouring to ascertain what is his duty, or, when this duty is ascertained, prevents him from performing it.

The principal object, then, which I proposed to myself in these poems was to choose incidents and situations from common life, and to relate or describe them, throughout, as far as was possible, in a selection of language really used by men; and, at the same time, to throw over them a certain colouring of imagination, whereby ordinary things should be presented to the mind in an unusual way; and, further, and above all, to make these incidents and situations interesting by tracing in them, truly though not ostentatiously, the primary laws of our nature: chiefly, as far as regards the manner in which we

2. Wordsworth's implied contrast is between the naturalness and simplicity of the first three Roman poets (who wrote in the last two centuries B.C.) and the elaborate artifice of the last two Roman poets (Statius wrote in the 1st and Claudian in the 4th century A.D.).

associate ideas in a state of excitement.[3] Low and rustic life was generally chosen, because in that condition, the essential passions of the heart find a better soil in which they can attain their maturity, are less under restraint, and speak a plainer and more emphatic language; because in that condition of life our elementary feelings co-exist in a state of greater simplicity, and, consequently, may be more accurately contemplated, and more forcibly communicated; because the manners of rural life germinate from those elementary feelings; and, from the necessary character of rural occupations, are more easily comprehended; and are more durable; and lastly, because in that condition the passions of men are incorporated with the beautiful and permanent forms of nature. The language, too, of these men is adopted (purified indeed from what appear to be its real defects, from all lasting and rational causes of dislike or disgust) because such men hourly communicate with the best objects from which the best part of language is originally derived; and because, from their rank in society and the sameness and narrow circle of their intercourse, being less under the influence of social vanity they convey their feelings and notions in simple and unelaborated expressions. Accordingly, such a language, arising out of repeated experience and regular feelings, is a more permanent, and a far more philosophical language, than that which is frequently substituted for it by poets, who think that they are conferring honour upon themselves and their art, in proportion as they separate themselves from the sympathies of men, and indulge in arbitrary and capricious habits of expression, in order to furnish food for fickle tastes, and fickle appetites, of their own creation.[4]

I cannot, however, be insensible of the present outcry against the triviality and meanness both of thought and language, which some of my contemporaries have occasionally introduced into their metrical compositions; and I acknowledge, that this defect, where it exists, is more dishonorable to the writer's own character than false refinement or arbitrary innovation, though I should contend at the same time that it is far less pernicious in the sum of its consequences. From such verses the poems in these volumes will be found distinguished at least by one mark of difference, that each of them has a worthy *purpose*. Not that I mean to say, that I always began to write with a distinct purpose formally conceived; but I believe that my habits of meditation have so formed my feelings, as that my descriptions of such objects as strongly excite those feelings, will be found to carry along with them a *purpose*. If in this opinion I am mistaken, I can have little right to the name of a poet. For all good poetry is the spontaneous overflow of powerful feelings: but though this be true, poems to which any value can be attached, were never produced on any variety of subjects but by a man who, being possessed of more than usual organic sensibility, had also thought long and deeply. For our continued influxes of feeling are modified and directed by our thoughts, which are indeed the representatives of all our past feelings; and, as by contemplating the relation of these general representatives to each other we discover what is really important to men, so, by the repetition and continuance of this act, our feelings will be connected with important subjects, till at length, if we be

3. Cf. Coleridge's account of their plan in *Biographia Literaria*, the beginning of chap. 14.
4. It is worth while here to observe that the affecting

parts of Chaucer are almost always expressed in language pure and universally intelligible even to this day [Wordsworth's note].

originally possessed of much sensibility, such habits of mind will be produced, that, by obeying blindly and mechanically the impulses of those habits, we shall describe objects, and utter sentiments, of such a nature and in such connection with each other, that the understanding of the being to whom we address ourselves, if he be in a healthful state of association, must necessarily be in some degree enlightened, and his affections ameliorated.

I have said that each of these poems has a purpose. I have also informed my reader what this purpose will be found principally to be: namely, to illustrate the manner in which our feelings and ideas are associated in a state of excitement. But, speaking in language somewhat more appropriate, it is to follow the fluxes and refluxes of the mind when agitated by the great and simple affections of our nature. This object I have endeavored in these short essays to attain by various means; by tracing the maternal passion through many of its more subtile windings, as in the poems of the *Idiot Boy* and the *Mad Mother*; by accompanying the last struggles of a human being, at the approach of death, cleaving in solitude to life and society, as in the poem of the *Forsaken Indian*; by shewing, as in the stanzas entitled *We Are Seven*, the perplexity and obscurity which in childhood attend our notion of death, or rather our utter inability to admit that notion; or by displaying the strength of fraternal, or to speak more philosophically, of moral attachment when early associated with the great and beautiful objects of nature, as in *The Brothers*; or, as in the Incident of *Simon Lee*, by placing my reader in the way of receiving from ordinary moral sensations another and more salutary impression than we are accustomed to receive from them. It has also been part of my general purpose to attempt to sketch characters under the influence of less impassioned feelings, as in the *Two April Mornings*, *The Fountain*, *The Old Man Travelling*, *The Two Thieves*, &c., characters of which the elements are simple, belonging rather to nature than to manners, such as exist now, and will probably always exist, and which from their constitution may be distinctly and profitably contemplated. I will not abuse the indulgence of my reader by dwelling longer upon this subject; but it is proper that I should mention one other circumstance which distinguishes these poems from the popular poetry of the day; it is this, that the feeling therein developed gives importance to the action and situation, and not the action and situation to the feeling. My meaning will be rendered perfectly intelligible by referring my reader to the poems entitled *Poor Susan* and the *Childless Father*, particularly to the last stanza of the latter poem.

I will not suffer a sense of false modesty to prevent me from asserting, that I point my reader's attention to this mark of distinction, far less for the sake of these particular poems than from the general importance of the subject. The subject is indeed important! For the human mind is capable of being excited without the application of gross and violent stimulants; and he must have a very faint perception of its beauty and dignity who does not know this, and who does not further know, that one being is elevated above another, in proportion as he possesses this capability. It has therefore appeared to me, that to endeavour to produce or enlarge this capability is one of the best services in which, at any period, a writer can be engaged; but this service, excellent at all times, is especially so at the present day. For a multitude of causes, unknown to former times, are now acting with a combined force to blunt the discriminating powers of the mind, and, unfitting it for all voluntary exertion, to reduce it to a state of almost savage torpor. The most effective of these causes are the great national events which are daily taking place, and the increasing accumulation of men in cities, where the uniformity of their occupations produces a craving for extraordinary incident, which the rapid communication of intelligence hourly gratifies.[5] To this tendency of life and manners the literature and theatrical exhibitions of the country have conformed themselves. The invaluable works of our elder writers, I had almost said the works of Shakespeare and Milton, are driven into neglect by frantic novels, sickly and stupid German tragedies,[6] and deluges of idle and extravagant stories in verse. — When I think upon this degrading thirst after outrageous stimulation, I am almost ashamed to have spoken of the feeble effort with which I have endeavoured to counteract it; and, reflecting upon the magnitude of the general evil, I should be oppressed with no dishonorable melancholy, had I not a deep impression of certain inherent and indestructible qualities of the human mind, and likewise of certain powers in the great and permanent objects that act upon it which are equally inherent and indestructible; and did I not further add to this impression a belief, that the time is approaching when the evil will be systematically opposed, by men of greater powers, and with far more distinguished success.

Having dwelt thus long on the subjects and aim of these poems, I shall request the reader's permission to apprize him of a few circumstances relating to their *style*, in order, among other reasons, that I may not be censured for not having performed what I never attempted. The reader will find that personifications of abstract ideas rarely occur in these volumes; and, I hope, are utterly rejected as an ordinary device to elevate the style, and raise it above prose. I have proposed to myself to imitate, and, as far as is possible, to adopt the very language of men; and assuredly such personifications do not make any natural or regular part of that language. They are, indeed, a figure of speech occasionally prompted by passion, and I have made use of them as such; but I have endeavoured utterly to reject them as a mechanical device of style, or as a family language which writers in metre seem to lay claim to by prescription. I have wished to keep my reader in the company of flesh and blood, persuaded that by so doing I shall interest him. I am, however, well aware that others who pursue a different track may interest him likewise; I do not interfere with their claim, I only wish to prefer a different claim of my own. There will also be found in these volumes little of what is usually called poetic diction;[7] I have taken as much pains to avoid it as others ordinarily take to produce it; this I have done for the reason already alleged, to bring my language near to the language of men, and further, because the pleasure which I have proposed to myself to impart is of a kind very different from that which is supposed by many persons to be the proper object of poetry. I do not know how, without being culpably particular, I can give my reader a more exact notion of the style in which I wished these poems to be written than by informing him that I have at all times endeavoured to look steadily at my subject, consequently, I hope that there is in these poems little falsehood of

5. This was the period of the wars against France, of industrial urbanization, and of the rapid proliferation in England of daily newspapers.
6. Wordsworth had in mind the "Gothic" terror novels by writers such as Ann Radcliffe and Matthew Gregory Lewis, and the sentimental melodrama, then im-

mensely popular in England, of August von Kotzebue and his German contemporaries.
7. In the sense of words, phrases, and figures of speech not commonly used in conversation or prose that are regarded as especially appropriate to poetry.

description, and that my ideas are expressed in language fitted to their respective importance. Something I must have gained by this practice, as it is friendly to one property of all good poetry, namely, good sense; but it has necessarily cut me off from a large portion of phrases and figures of speech which from father to son have long been regarded as the common inheritance of poets. I have also thought it expedient to restrict myself still further, having abstained from the use of many expressions, in themselves proper and beautiful, but which have been foolishly repeated by bad poets, till such feelings of disgust are connected with them as it is scarcely possible by any art of association to overpower.

If in a poem there should be found a series of lines, or even a single line, in which the language, though naturally arranged and according to the strict laws of metre, does not differ from that of prose, there is a numerous class of critics, who, when they stumble upon these prosaisms as they call them, imagine that they have made a notable discovery, and exult over the poet as over a man ignorant of his own profession. Now these men would establish a canon of criticism which the reader will conclude he must utterly reject, if he wishes to be pleased with these volumes. And it would be a most easy task to prove to him, that not only the language of a large portion of every good poem, even of the most elevated character, must necessarily, except with reference to the metre, in no respect differ from that of good prose, but likewise that some of the most interesting parts of the best poems will be found to be strictly the language of prose, when prose is well written. The truth of this assertion might be demonstrated by innumerable passages from almost all the poetical writings, even of Milton himself. I have not space for much quotation; but, to illustrate the subject in a general manner, I will here adduce a short composition of Gray, who was at the head of those who by their reasonings have attempted to widen the space of separation betwixt prose and metrical composition, and was more than any other man curiously elaborate in the structure of his own poetic diction.[8]

> In vain to me the smiling mornings shine,
> And reddening Phoebus lifts his golden fire:
> The birds in vain their amorous descant join,
> Or cheerful fields resume their green attire:
> These ears, alas! for other notes repine;
> *A different object do these eyes require;*
> *My lonely anguish melts no heart but mine;*
> *And in my breast the imperfect joys expire;*
> Yet Morning smiles the busy race to cheer,
> And new-born pleasure brings to happier men;
> The fields to all their wonted tribute bear;
> To warm their little loves the birds complain.
> *I fruitless mourn to him that cannot hear*
> *And weep the more because I weep in vain.*

It will easily be perceived that the only part of this sonnet which is of any value is the lines printed in italics: it is equally obvious, that, except in the rhyme, and in the use of the single word "fruitless" for fruitlessly, which is so

---

8. Thomas Gray had written, in a letter to Richard West, that "the language of the age is never the language of poetry." The poem that follows is Gray's *Sonnet on the Death of Richard West*.

far a defect, the language of these lines does in no respect differ from that of prose.

By the foregoing quotation I have shewn that the language of prose may yet be well adapted to poetry; and I have previously asserted that a large portion of the language of every good poem can in no respect differ from that of good prose. I will go further. I do not doubt that it may be safely affirmed, that there neither is, nor can be, any essential difference between the language of prose and metrical composition. We are fond of tracing the resemblance between poetry and painting, and, accordingly, we call them sisters: but where shall we find bonds of connection sufficiently strict to typify the affinity betwixt metrical and prose composition? They both speak by and to the same organs; the bodies in which both of them are clothed may be said to be of the same substance, their affections are kindred and almost identical, not necessarily differing even in degree; poetry[9] sheds no tears "such as Angels weep,"[1] but natural and human tears; she can boast of no celestial ichor[2] that distinguishes her vital juices from those of prose; the same human blood circulates through the veins of them both.

* * *

["What Is a Poet?"]

Taking up the subject, then, upon general grounds, I ask what is meant by the word "poet"? What is a poet? To whom does he address himself? And what language is to be expected from him? He is a man speaking to men: a man, it is true, endued with more lively sensibility, more enthusiasm and tenderness, who has a greater knowledge of human nature, and a more comprehensive soul, than are supposed to be common among mankind; a man pleased with his own passions and volitions, and who rejoices more than other men in the spirit of life that is in him; delighting to contemplate similar volitions and passions as manifested in the goings-on of the universe, and habitually impelled to create them where he does not find them. To these qualities he has added a disposition to be affected more than other men by absent things as if they were present; an ability of conjuring up in himself passions, which are indeed far from being the same as those produced by real events, yet (especially in those parts of the general sympathy which are pleasing and delightful) do more nearly resemble the passions produced by real events, than any thing which, from the motions of their own minds merely, other men are accustomed to feel in themselves; whence, and from practice, he has acquired a greater readiness and power in expressing what he thinks and feels, and especially those thoughts and feelings which, by his own choice, or from the structure of his own mind, arise in him without immediate external excitement.

But, whatever portion of this faculty we may suppose even the greatest poet to possess, there cannot be a doubt but that the language which it will suggest

9. I here use the word "poetry" (though against my own judgment) as opposed to the word prose, and synonymous with metrical composition. But much confusion has been introduced into criticism by this contradistinction of poetry and prose, instead of the more philosophical one of poetry and matter of fact, or science. The only strict antithesis to prose is metre; nor is this, in truth, a *strict* antithesis; because lines and passages of metre so naturally occur in writing prose, that it would be scarcely possible to avoid them, even were it desirable [Wordsworth's note].
1. *Paradise Lost* 1.620.
2. In Greek mythology, the fluid in the veins of the gods.

to him, must, in liveliness and truth, fall far short of that which is uttered by men in real life, under the actual pressure of those passions, certain shadows of which the poet thus produces, or feels to be produced, in himself. However exalted a notion we would wish to cherish of the character of a poet, it is obvious, that, while he describes and imitates passions, his situation is altogether slavish and mechanical, compared with the freedom and power of real and substantial action and suffering. So that it will be the wish of the poet to bring his feelings near to those of the persons whose feelings he describes, nay, for short spaces of time perhaps, to let himself slip into an entire delusion, and even confound and identify his own feelings with theirs; modifying only the language which is thus suggested to him, by a consideration that he describes for a particular purpose, that of giving pleasure. Here, then, he will apply the principle on which I have so much insisted, namely, that of selection; on this he will depend for removing what would otherwise be painful or disgusting in the passion; he will feel that there is no necessity to trick out or to elevate nature: and, the more industriously he applies this principle, the deeper will be his faith that no words, which his fancy or imagination can suggest, will be to be compared with those which are the emanations of reality and truth.

But it may be said by those who do not object to the general spirit of these remarks, that, as it is impossible for the poet to produce upon all occasions language as exquisitely fitted for the passion as that which the real passion itself suggests, it is proper that he should consider himself as in the situation of a translator, who deems himself justified when he substitutes excellences of another kind for those which are unattainable by him, and endeavours occasionally to surpass his original, in order to make some amends for the general inferiority to which he feels that he must submit. But this would be to encourage idleness and unmanly despair. Further, it is the language of men who speak of what they do not understand; who talk of poetry as a matter of amusement and idle pleasure; who will converse with us as gravely about a *taste* for poetry, as they express it, as if it were a thing as indifferent as a taste for rope-dancing, or Frontiniac[3] or sherry. Aristotle, I have been told, hath said, that poetry is the most philosophic of all writing;[4] it is so: its object is truth, not individual and local, but general, and operative; not standing upon external testimony, but carried alive into the heart by passion; truth which is its own testimony, which gives strength and divinity to the tribunal to which it appeals, and receives them from the same tribunal. Poetry is the image of man and nature. The obstacles which stand in the way of the fidelity of the biographer and historian, and of their consequent utility, are incalculably greater than those which are to be encountered by the poet who has an adequate notion of the dignity of his art. The poet writes under one restriction only, namely, that of the necessity of giving immediate pleasure to a human being possessed of that information which may be expected from him, not as a lawyer, a physician, a mariner, an astronomer or a natural philosopher, but as a man. Except this one restriction, there is no object standing between the poet and the image of things; between this, and the biographer and historian there are a thousand.

3. A sweet wine made from muscat grapes.
4. Aristotle in fact said that "poetry is more philosophic than history, since its statements are of the na- ture of universals, whereas those of history are singulars" (*Poetics* 1451b).

Nor let this necessity of producing immediate pleasure be considered as a degradation of the poet's art. It is far otherwise. It is an acknowledgment of the beauty of the universe, an acknowledgment the more sincere because it is not formal, but indirect; it is a task light and easy to him who looks at the world in the spirit of love: further, it is a homage paid to the native and naked dignity of man, to the grand elementary principle of pleasure, by which he knows, and feels, and lives, and moves.[5] We have no sympathy but what is propagated by pleasure: I would not be misunderstood; but wherever we sympathize with pain it will be found that the sympathy is produced and carried on by subtle combinations with pleasure. We have no knowledge, that is, no general principles drawn from the contemplation of particular facts, but what has been built up by pleasure, and exists in us by pleasure alone. The man of science, the chemist and mathematician, whatever difficulties and disgusts they may have had to struggle with, know and feel this. However painful may be the objects with which the anatomist's knowledge is connected, he feels that his knowledge is pleasure; and where he has no pleasure he has no knowledge. What then does the poet? He considers man and the objects that surround him as acting and re-acting upon each other, so as to produce an infinite complexity of pain and pleasure; he considers man in his own nature and in his ordinary life as contemplating this with a certain quantity of immediate knowledge, with certain convictions, intuitions, and deductions which by habit become of the nature of intuitions; he considers him as looking upon this complex scene of ideas and sensations, and finding every where objects that immediately excite in him sympathies which, from the necessities of his nature, are accompanied by an overbalance of enjoyment.

To this knowledge which all men carry about with them, and to these sympathies in which without any other discipline than that of our daily life we are fitted to take delight, the poet principally directs his attention. He considers man and nature as essentially adapted to each other,[6] and the mind of man as naturally the mirror of the fairest and most interesting qualities of nature. And thus the poet, prompted by this feeling of pleasure which accompanies him through the whole course of his studies, converses with general nature with affections akin to those, which, through labour and length of time, the man of science has raised up in himself, by conversing with those particular parts of nature which are the objects of his studies. The knowledge both of the poet and the man of science is pleasure; but the knowledge of the one cleaves to us as a necessary part of our existence, our natural and unalienable inheritance; the other is a personal and individual acquisition, slow to come to us, and by no habitual and direct sympathy connecting us with our fellow-beings. The man of science seeks truth as a remote and unknown benefactor; he cherishes and loves it in his solitude: the poet, singing a song in which all human beings join with him, rejoices in the presence of truth as our visible friend and hourly companion. Poetry is the breath and finer spirit of all knowledge; it is the impassioned expression which is in the countenance of all science. Emphatically may it be said of the poet, as Shakespeare hath said of man, "that he looks before and after."[7] He is the rock of defence of human nature; an upholder and preserver, carrying everywhere with him relationship

---

5. A bold echo of the words of St. Paul, that in God "we live, and move, and have our being" (Acts 17.28).
6. On the mutual adaptation of man's mind and nature, see Wordsworth's Prospectus to *The Recluse*, p. 1399, lines 63–71.
7. *Hamlet* 4.4.37.

and love. In spite of difference of soil and climate, of language and manners, of laws and customs, in spite of things silently gone out of mind and things violently destroyed, the poet binds together by passion and knowledge the vast empire of human society, as it is spread over the whole earth, and over all time. The objects of the poet's thoughts are every where; though the eyes and senses of man are, it is true, his favorite guides, yet he will follow wheresoever he can find an atmosphere of sensation in which to move his wings. Poetry is the first and last of all knowledge—it is as immortal as the heart of man. If the labours of men of science should ever create any material revolution, direct or indirect, in our condition, and in the impressions which we habitually receive, the poet will sleep then no more than at present, but he will be ready to follow the steps of the man of science, not only in those general indirect effects, but he will be at his side, carrying sensation into the midst of the objects of the science itself. The remotest discoveries of the chemist, the botanist, or mineralogist, will be as proper objects of the poet's art as any upon which it can be employed, if the time should ever come when these things shall be familiar to us, and the relations under which they are contemplated by the followers of these respective sciences shall be manifestly and palpably material to us as enjoying and suffering beings.[8] If the time should ever come when what is now called science, thus familiarized to men, shall be ready to put on, as it were, a form of flesh and blood, the poet will lend his divine spirit to aid the transfiguration, and will welcome the being thus produced, as a dear and genuine inmate of the household of man.—It is not, then, to be supposed that any one, who holds that sublime notion of poetry which I have attempted to convey, will break in upon the sanctity and truth of his pictures by transitory and accidental ornaments, and endeavour to excite admiration of himself by arts, the necessity of which must manifestly depend upon the assumed meanness of his subject.

What I have thus far said applies to poetry in general; but especially to those parts of composition where the poet speaks through the mouth of his characters; and upon this point it appears to have such weight that I will conclude, there are few persons, of good sense, who would not allow that the dramatic parts of composition are defective, in proportion as they deviate from the real language of nature, and are coloured by a diction of the poet's own, either peculiar to him as an individual poet, or belonging simply to poets in general, to a body of men who, from the circumstance of their compositions being in metre, it is expected will employ a particular language.

It is not, then, in the dramatic parts of composition that we look for this distinction of language; but still it may be proper and necessary where the poet speaks to us in his own person and character. To this I answer by referring my reader to the description which I have before given of a poet. Among the qualities which I have enumerated as principally conducing to form a poet, is implied nothing differing in kind from other men, but only in degree. The sum of what I have there said is, that the poet is chiefly distinguished from other men by a greater promptness to think and feel without immediate external excitement, and a greater power in expressing such thoughts and feelings as are produced in him in that manner. But these passions and thoughts and

---

8. Wordsworth is at least right in anticipating the poetry of the machine; he himself wrote an early instance, the sonnet *Steamboats, Viaducts, and Railways*.

feelings are the general passions and thoughts and feelings of men. And with what are they connected? Undoubtedly with our moral sentiments and animal sensations, and with the causes which excite these; with the operations of the elements and the appearances of the visible universe; with storm and sunshine, with the revolutions of the seasons, with cold and heat, with loss of friends and kindred, with injuries and resentments, gratitude and hope, with fear and sorrow. These, and the like, are the sensations and objects which the poet describes, as they are the sensations of other men, and the objects which interest them. The poet thinks and feels in the spirit of the passions of men. How, then, can his language differ in any material degree from that of all other men who feel vividly and see clearly? It might be *proved* that it is impossible. But supposing that this were not the case, the poet might then be allowed to use a peculiar language, when expressing his feelings for his own gratification, or that of men like himself. But poets do not write for poets alone, but for men. Unless therefore we are advocates for that admiration which depends upon ignorance, and that pleasure which arises from hearing what we do not understand, the poet must descend from this supposed height, and, in order to excite rational sympathy, he must express himself as other men express themselves. * * *

["*Emotion Recollected in Tranquillity*"]

I have said that poetry is the spontaneous overflow of powerful feelings: it takes its origin from emotion recollected in tranquillity: the emotion is contemplated till by a species of reaction the tranquillity gradually disappears, and an emotion, kindred to that which was before the subject of contemplation, is gradually produced, and does itself actually exist in the mind. In this mood successful composition generally begins, and in a mood similar to this it is carried on; but the emotion, of whatever kind and in whatever degree, from various causes is qualified by various pleasures, so that in describing any passions whatsoever, which are voluntarily described, the mind will upon the whole be in a state of enjoyment. Now, if nature be thus cautious in preserving in a state of enjoyment a being thus employed, the poet ought to profit by the lesson thus held forth to him, and ought especially to take care, that whatever passions he communicates to his reader, those passions, if his reader's mind be sound and vigorous, should always be accompanied with an overbalance of pleasure. Now the music of harmonious metrical language, the sense of difficulty overcome, and the blind association of pleasure which has been previously received from works of rhyme or metre of the same or similar construction, an indistinct perception perpetually renewed of language closely resembling that of real life, and yet, in the circumstance of metre, differing from it so widely, all these imperceptibly make up a complex feeling of delight, which is of the most important use in tempering the painful feeling which will always be found intermingled with powerful descriptions of the deeper passions. This effect is always produced in pathetic and impassioned poetry; while, in lighter compositions, the ease and gracefulness with which the poet manages his numbers are themselves confessedly a principal source of the gratification of the reader. I might perhaps include all which it is *necessary* to say upon this subject by affirming, what few persons will deny, that, of two descriptions, either of passions, manners, or characters, each of them

1352 WILLIAM WORDSWORTH

equally well executed, the one in prose and the other in verse, the verse will be read a hundred times where the prose is read once. * * *

I know that nothing would have so effectually contributed to further the end which I have in view, as to have shewn of what kind the pleasure is, and how the pleasure is produced, which is confessedly produced by metrical composition essentially different from that which I have here endeavoured to recommend: for the reader will say that he has been pleased by such composition; and what can I do more for him? The power of any art is limited; and he will suspect, that, if I propose to furnish him with new friends, it is only upon condition of his abandoning his old friends. Besides, as I have said, the reader is himself conscious of the pleasure which he has received from such composition, composition to which he has peculiarly attached the endearing name of poetry; and all men feel an habitual gratitude, and something of an honorable bigotry for the objects which have long continued to please them: we not only wish to be pleased, but to be pleased in that particular way in which we have been accustomed to be pleased. There is a host of arguments in these feelings; and I should be the less able to combat them successfully, as I am willing to allow, that, in order entirely to enjoy the poetry which I am recommending, it would be necessary to give up much of what is ordinarily enjoyed. But, would my limits have permitted me to point out how this pleasure is produced, I might have removed many obstacles, and assisted my reader in perceiving that the powers of language are not so limited as he may suppose; and that it is possible that poetry may give other enjoyments, of a purer, more lasting, and more exquisite nature. This part of my subject I have not altogether neglected; but it has been less my present aim to prove, that the interest excited by some other kinds of poetry is less vivid, and less worthy of the nobler powers of the mind, than to offer reasons for presuming, that, if the object which I have proposed to myself were adequately attained, a species of poetry would be produced, which is genuine poetry; in its nature well adapted to interest mankind permanently, and likewise important in the multiplicity and quality of its moral relations.

From what has been said, and from a perusal of the poems, the reader will be able clearly to perceive the object which I have proposed to myself: he will determine how far I have attained this object; and, what is a much more important question, whether it be worth attaining; and upon the decision of these two questions will rest my claim to the approbation of the public.

1800, 1802

Strange fits of passion have I known[1]

Strange fits of passion have I known:
And I will dare to tell,
But in the Lover's ear alone,
What once to me befel.

1. This and the four following pieces are often grouped by editors as the "Lucy poems," even though *A slumber did my spirit seal* does not identify the "she" who is the subject of that poem. All but the last were written in 1799, while Wordsworth and his sister were in Germany, and homesick. There has been diligent speculation about the identity of Lucy, but it remains speculation; the one certainty is that she is not the girl of Wordsworth's *Lucy Gray*.

When she I loved looked every day   5
Fresh as a rose in June,
I to her cottage bent my way,
Beneath an evening moon.

Upon the moon I fixed my eye,
All over the wide lea;   10
With quickening pace my horse drew nigh
Those paths so dear to me.

And now we reached the orchard-plot;
And, as we climbed the hill,
The sinking moon to Lucy's cot   15
Came near, and nearer still.

In one of those sweet dreams I slept,
Kind Nature's gentlest boon!
And all the while my eyes I kept
On the descending moon.   20

My horse moved on; hoof after hoof
He raised, and never stopped:
When down behind the cottage roof,
At once, the bright moon dropped.

What fond and wayward thoughts will slide   25
Into a Lover's head!
"O mercy!" to myself I cried,
"If Lucy should be dead!"[2]

1799   1800

She dwelt among the untrodden ways[1]

She dwelt among the untrodden ways
    Beside the springs of Dove,[2]
A Maid whom there were none to praise
    And very few to love:

A violet by a mossy stone   5
    Half hidden from the eye!
—Fair as a star, when only one
    Is shining in the sky.

She lived unknown, and few could know
    When Lucy ceased to be;   10
But she is in her grave, and, oh,
    The difference to me!

1799   1800

2. An additional stanza in an earlier manuscript version demonstrates how a poem can be improved by omission of a passage that is, in itself, excellent poetry: "I told her this: her laughter light / Is ringing in my ears; / And when I think upon that night / My eyes are dim with tears."

1. For the author's revisions while composing this poem, see "Poems in Process" (pp. 2581–82).
2. There are several rivers by this name in England, including one in the Lake District.

Three years she grew

Three years she grew in sun and shower,
Then Nature said, "A lovelier flower
On earth was never sown;
This Child I to myself will take;
She shall be mine, and I will make   5
A Lady of my own.[1]

"Myself will to my darling be
Both law and impulse: and with me
The Girl, in rock and plain,
In earth and heaven, in glade and bower,   10
Shall feel an overseeing power
To kindle or restrain.

"She shall be sportive as the fawn
That wild with glee across the lawn
Or up the mountain springs;   15
And hers shall be the breathing balm,
And hers the silence and the calm
Of mute insensate things.

"The floating clouds their state shall lend
To her; for her the willow bend;   20
Nor shall she fail to see
Even in the motions of the Storm
Grace that shall mould the Maiden's form
By silent sympathy.

"The stars of midnight shall be dear   25
To her; and she shall lean her ear
In many a secret place
Where rivulets dance their wayward round,
And beauty born of murmuring sound
Shall pass into her face.   30

"And vital feelings of delight
Shall rear her form to stately height,
Her virgin bosom swell;
Such thoughts to Lucy I will give
While she and I together live   35
Here in this happy dell."

Thus Nature spake—the work was done—
How soon my Lucy's race was run!
She died, and left to me
This heath, this calm, and quiet scene;   40
The memory of what has been,
And never more will be.

1799   1800

1. I.e., Lucy was three years old at the time when Nature made this promise; line 37 makes clear that Lucy had reached the maturity foretold in the sixth stanza when she died.

A slumber did my spirit seal

A slumber did my spirit seal;
  I had no human fears:
She seemed a thing that could not feel
  The touch of earthly years.

No motion has she now, no force;   5
  She neither hears nor sees;
Rolled round in earth's diurnal[1] course,
  With rocks, and stones, and trees.

1799   1800

I travelled among unknown men

I travelled among unknown men,
  In lands beyond the sea;
Nor, England! did I know till then
  What love I bore to thee.

'Tis past, that melancholy dream!   5
  Nor will I quit thy shore
A second time; for still I seem
  To love thee more and more.

Among thy mountains did I feel
  The joy of my desire;   10
And she I cherished turned her wheel
  Beside an English fire.

Thy mornings showed, thy nights concealed
  The bowers where Lucy played;
And thine too is the last green field   15
  That Lucy's eyes surveyed.

ca. 1801   1807

Nutting[1]

——————It seems a day
(I speak of one from many singled out)
One of those heavenly days that cannot die;
When, in the eagerness of boyish hope,
I left our cottage-threshold, sallying forth   5
With a huge wallet o'er my shoulder slung,
A nutting-crook in hand; and turned my steps
Tow'rd some far-distant wood, a Figure quaint,
Tricked out in proud disguise of cast-off weeds[2]

1. Daily.
1. Wordsworth said that these lines, written in Germany in 1798, were "intended as part of a poem on my own mind [*The Prelude*], but struck out as not being wanted there." He published them in the second edition of *Lyrical Ballads*, 1800.
2. Clothes.

Which for that service had been husbanded,   10
By exhortation of my frugal Dame[3] —
Motley accoutrement, of power to smile
At thorns, and brakes, and brambles, —and, in truth,
More ragged than need was! O'er pathless rocks,
Through beds of matted fern, and tangled thickets,   15
Forcing my way, I came to one dear nook
Unvisited, where not a broken bough
Drooped with its withered leaves, ungracious sign
Of devastation; but the hazels rose
Tall and erect, with tempting clusters hung,   20
A virgin scene! —A little while I stood,
Breathing with such suppression of the heart
As joy delights in; and, with wise restraint
Voluptuous, fearless of a rival, eyed
The banquet; —or beneath the trees I sate   25
Among the flowers, and with the flowers I played;
A temper known to those, who, after long
And weary expectation, have been blest
With sudden happiness beyond all hope.
Perhaps it was a bower beneath whose leaves   30
The violets of five seasons re-appear
And fade, unseen by any human eye;
Where fairy water-breaks[4] do murmur on
For ever; and I saw the sparkling foam,
And—with my cheek on one of those green stones   35
That, fleeced with moss, under the shady trees,
Lay round me, scattered like a flock of sheep—
I heard the murmur and the murmuring sound,
In that sweet mood when pleasure loves to pay
Tribute to ease; and, of its joy secure,   40
The heart luxuriates with indifferent things,
Wasting its kindliness on stocks[5] and stones,
And on the vacant air. Then up I rose,
And dragged to earth both branch and bough, with crash
And merciless ravage: and the shady nook   45
Of hazels, and the green and mossy bower,
Deformed and sullied, patiently gave up
Their quiet being: and, unless I now
Confound my present feelings with the past,
Ere from the mutilated bower I turned   50
Exulting, rich beyond the wealth of kings,
I felt a sense of pain when I beheld
The silent trees, and saw the intruding sky. —
Then, dearest Maiden,[6] move along these shades
In gentleness of heart; with gentle hand   55
Touch—for there is a spirit in the woods.

1798   1800

---

3. Ann Tyson, with whom Wordsworth lodged while
at Hawkshead grammar school.
4. Places where the flow of a stream is broken by rocks.
5. Tree stumps. ("Stocks and stones" is a conventional

expression for "inanimate things.")
6. In a manuscript passage, originally intended to lead
up to *Nutting*, the maiden is called Lucy.

The Ruined Cottage   Wordsworth wrote *The Ruined Cottage* in 1797–98, but revised it several times before he finally published an expanded rendering of the story as book 1 of *The Excursion*, in 1814. Not until 1949 was *The Ruined Cottage*, as an independent poem, made available in the fifth volume of *The Poetical Works of William Wordsworth*, edited by Ernest de Selincourt and Helen Darbishire, who printed a version known as "MS. B." The version reprinted here is from "MS. D," dating 1799, as transcribed by James Butler in the Cornell Wordsworth volume, *"The Ruined Cottage" and "The Pedlar"* (1979).

This version is presented as one of Wordsworth's earliest and most impressive successes in verse narrative. In the story we confront the bleak facts of "a tale of silent suffering"—suffering that is undeserved, unrationalized, and irremissive. The event is "a common tale," and it poses the implicit question, What are we to make of human life, in which such things happen? By his verbal power and his narrative artistry, Wordsworth carries us along in imagination so that we, whatever our own beliefs, feel what it might be to master the fact of human suffering, unsupported by the creed of a beneficent power, whether in or out of nature.

The Ruined Cottage

First Part

'Twas summer and the sun was mounted high.
Along the south the uplands feebly glared
Through a pale steam, and all the northern downs
In clearer air ascending shewed far off
Their surfaces with shadows dappled o'er   5
Of deep embattled clouds: far as the sight
Could reach those many shadows lay in spots
Determined and unmoved, with steady beams
Of clear and pleasant sunshine interposed;
Pleasant to him who on the soft cool moss   10
Extends his careless limbs beside the root
Of some huge oak whose aged branches make
A twilight of their own, a dewy shade
Where the wren warbles while the dreaming man,
Half-conscious of that soothing melody,   15
With side-long eye looks out upon the scene,
By those impending branches made more soft,
More soft and distant. Other lot was mine.
Across a bare wide Common I had toiled
With languid feet which by the slipp'ry ground   20
Were baffled still, and when I stretched myself
On the brown earth my limbs from very heat
Could find no rest nor my weak arm disperse
The insect host which gathered round my face
And joined their murmurs to the tedious noise   25
Of seeds of bursting gorse that crackled round.
I rose and turned towards a group of trees
Which midway in that level stood alone,
And thither come at length, beneath a shade
Of clustering elms that sprang from the same root   30
I found a ruined house, four naked walls

That stared upon each other. I looked round
And near the door I saw an aged Man,
Alone, and stretched upon the cottage bench;
An iron-pointed staff lay at his side.   35
With instantaneous joy I recognized
That pride of nature and of lowly life,
The venerable Armytage, a friend
As dear to me as is the setting sun.
                            Two days before   40
We had been fellow-travellers. I knew
That he was in this neighbourhood and now
Delighted found him here in the cool shade.
He lay, his pack of rustic merchandize
Pillowing his head—I guess he had no thought   45
Of his way-wandering life. His eyes were shut;
The shadows of the breezy elms above
Dappled his face. With thirsty heat oppress'd
At length I hailed him, glad to see his hat
Bedewed with water-drops, as if the brim   50
Had newly scoop'd a running stream. He rose
And pointing to a sun-flower bade me climb
The [   ]¹ wall where that same gaudy flower
Looked out upon the road. It was a plot
Of garden-ground, now wild, its matted weeds   55
Marked with the steps of those whom as they pass'd,
The goose berry trees that shot in long lank slips,
Or currants hanging from their leafless stems
In scanty strings, had tempted to o'erleap
The broken wall. Within that cheerless spot,   60
Where two tall hedgerows of thick willow boughs
Joined in a damp cold nook, I found a well
Half-choked [with willow flowers and weeds.]²
I slaked my thirst and to the shady bench
Returned, and while I stood unbonneted   65
To catch the motion of the cooler air
The old Man said, "I see around me here
Things which you cannot see: we die, my Friend,
Nor we alone, but that which each man loved
And prized in his peculiar nook of earth   70
Dies with him or is changed, and very soon
Even of the good is no memorial left.
The Poets in their elegies and songs
Lamenting the departed call the groves,
They call upon the hills and streams to mourn,   75
And senseless rocks, nor idly; for they speak
In these their invocations with a voice
Obedient to the strong creative power
Of human passion. Sympathies there are
More tranquil, yet perhaps of kindred birth,   80
That steal upon the meditative mind

---

1. The brackets here and in later lines mark blank   2. Wordsworth penciled the bracketed phrase into a
spaces left unfilled in the manuscript.   gap left in the maniscript.

And grow with thought. Beside yon spring I stood
And eyed its waters till we seemed to feel
One sadness, they and I. For them a bond
Of brotherhood is broken: time has been   85
When every day the touch of human hand
Disturbed their stillness, and they ministered
To human comfort. When I stooped to drink,
A spider's web hung to the water's edge,
And on the wet and slimy foot-stone lay   90
The useless fragment of a wooden bowl;
It moved my very heart. The day has been
When I could never pass this road but she
Who lived within these walls, when I appeared,
A daughter's welcome gave me, and I loved her   95
As my own child. O Sir! the good die first,
And they whose hearts are dry as summer dust
Burn to the socket. Many a passenger
Has blessed poor Margaret for her gentle looks
When she upheld the cool refreshment drawn   100
From that forsaken spring, and no one came
But he was welcome, no one went away
But that it seemed she loved him. She is dead,
The worm is on her cheek, and this poor hut,
Stripp'd of its outward garb of household flowers,   105
Of rose and sweet-briar, offers to the wind
A cold bare wall whose earthy top is tricked
With weeds and the rank spear-grass. She is dead,
And nettles rot and adders sun themselves
Where we have sate together while she nurs'd   110
Her infant at her breast. The unshod Colt,
The wandring heifer and the Potter's ass,
Find shelter now within the chimney-wall
Where I have seen her evening hearth-stone blaze
And through the window spread upon the road   115
Its chearful light.—You will forgive me, Sir,
But often on this cottage do I muse
As on a picture, till my wiser mind
Sinks, yielding to the foolishness of grief.
    She had a husband, an industrious man,   120
Sober and steady; I have heard her say
That he was up and busy at his loom
In summer ere the mower's scythe had swept
The dewy grass, and in the early spring
Ere the last star had vanished. They who pass'd   125
At evening, from behind the garden-fence
Might hear his busy spade, which he would ply
After his daily work till the day-light
Was gone and every leaf and flower were lost
In the dark hedges. So they pass'd their days   130
In peace and comfort, and two pretty babes
Were their best hope next to the God in Heaven.
    —You may remember, now some ten years gone,

Two blighting seasons when the fields were left
With half a harvest.[3] It pleased heaven to add   135
A worse affliction in the plague of war:
A happy land was stricken to the heart;
'Twas a sad time of sorrow and distress:
A wanderer among the cottages,
I with my pack of winter raiment saw   140
The hardships of that season: many rich
Sunk down as in a dream among the poor,
And of the poor did many cease to be,
And their place knew them not. Meanwhile, abridg'd
Of daily comforts, gladly reconciled   145
To numerous self-denials, Margaret
Went struggling on through those calamitous years
With chearful hope: but ere the second autumn
A fever seized her husband. In disease
He lingered long, and when his strength returned   150
He found the little he had stored to meet
The hour of accident or crippling age
Was all consumed. As I have said, 'twas now
A time of trouble; shoals of artisans
Were from their daily labour turned away   155
To hang for bread on parish charity,
They and their wives and children—happier far
Could they have lived as do the little birds
That peck along the hedges or the kite
That makes her dwelling in the mountain rocks.   160
Ill fared it now with Robert, he who dwelt
In this poor cottage; at his door he stood
And whistled many a snatch of merry tunes
That had no mirth in them, or with his knife
Carved uncouth figures on the heads of sticks,   165
Then idly sought about through every nook
Of house or garden any casual task
Of use or ornament, and with a strange,
Amusing but uneasy novelty
He blended where he might the various tasks   170
Of summer, autumn, winter, and of spring.
But this endured not; his good-humour soon
Became a weight in which no pleasure was,
And poverty brought on a petted[4] mood
And a sore temper: day by day he drooped,   175
And he would leave his home, and to the town
Without an errand would he turn his steps
Or wander here and there among the fields.
One while he would speak lightly of his babes
And with a cruel tongue: at other times   180
He played with them wild freaks of merriment:

3. As James Butler points out in his introduction, Wordsworth is purposely distancing his story in time. The "two blighting seasons" in fact occurred in 1794–95, only a few years before Wordsworth wrote *The Ruined Cottage*, when a bad harvest was followed by one of the worst winters on record; much of the seed grain was destroyed in the ground, and the price of wheat nearly doubled.
4. Ill-tempered.

And 'twas a piteous thing to see the looks
Of the poor innocent children. 'Every smile,'
Said Margaret to me here beneath these trees,
'Made my heart bleed.' " At this the old Man paus'd   185
And looking up to those enormous elms
He said, " 'Tis now the hour of deepest noon,
At this still season of repose and peace,
This hour when all things which are not at rest
Are chearful, while this multitude of flies   190
Fills all the air with happy melody,
Why should a tear be in an old man's eye?
Why should we thus with an untoward mind
And in the weakness of humanity
From natural wisdom turn our hearts away,   195
To natural comfort shut our eyes and ears,
And feeding on disquiet thus disturb
The calm of Nature with our restless thoughts?"

END OF THE FIRST PART

Second Part

He spake with somewhat of a solemn tone:
But when he ended there was in his face   200
Such easy chearfulness, a look so mild
That for a little time it stole away
All recollection, and that simple tale
Passed from my mind like a forgotten sound.
A while on trivial things we held discourse,   205
To me soon tasteless. In my own despite
I thought of that poor woman as of one
Whom I had known and loved. He had rehearsed
Her homely tale with such familiar power,
With such a[n active]⁵ countenance, an eye   210
So busy, that the things of which he spake
Seemed present, and, attention now relaxed,
There was a heartfelt chillness in my veins.
I rose, and turning from that breezy shade
Went out into the open air and stood   215
To drink the comfort of the warmer sun.
Long time I had not stayed ere, looking round
Upon that tranquil ruin, I returned
And begged of the old man that for my sake
He would resume his story. He replied,   220
"It were a wantonness and would demand
Severe reproof, if we were men whose hearts
Could hold vain dalliance with the misery
Even of the dead, contented thence to draw
A momentary pleasure never marked   225
By reason, barren of all future good.
But we have known that there is often found

5. Wordsworth penciled the bracketed phrase into a gap left in the manuscript.

In mournful thoughts, and always might be found,
A power to virtue friendly; were't not so,
I am a dreamer among men, indeed   230
An idle dreamer. 'Tis a common tale,
By moving accidents[6] uncharactered,
A tale of silent suffering, hardly clothed
In bodily form, and to the grosser sense
But ill adapted, scarcely palpable   235
To him who does not think. But at your bidding
I will proceed.
           While thus it fared with them
To whom this cottage till that hapless year
Had been a blessed home, it was my chance
To travel in a country far remote,   240
And glad I was when, halting by yon gate
That leads from the green lane, again I saw
These lofty elm-trees. Long I did not rest:
With many pleasant thoughts I cheer'd my way
O'er the flat common. At the door arrived,   245
I knocked, and when I entered with the hope
Of usual greeting, Margaret looked at me
A little while, then turned her head away
Speechless, and sitting down upon a chair
Wept bitterly. I wist not what to do   250
Or how to speak to her. Poor wretch! at last
She rose from off her seat—and then, oh Sir!
I cannot tell how she pronounced my name:
With fervent love, and with a face of grief
Unutterably helpless, and a look   255
That seem'd to cling upon me, she enquir'd
If I had seen her husband. As she spake
A strange surprize and fear came to my heart,
Nor had I power to answer ere she told
That he had disappeared—just two months gone.   260
He left his house; two wretched days had passed,
And on the third by the first break of light,
Within her casement full in view she saw
A purse of gold.[7] 'I trembled at the sight,'
Said Margaret, 'for I knew it was his hand   265
That placed it there, and on that very day
By one, a stranger, from my husband sent,
The tidings came that he had joined a troop
Of soldiers going to a distant land.
He left me thus—Poor Man! he had not heart   270
To take a farewell of me, and he feared
That I should follow with my babes, and sink
Beneath the misery of a soldier's life.'
This tale did Margaret tell with many tears:

6. Othello speaks "of most disastrous chances: / Of moving accidents by flood and field, / Of hair-breadth 'scapes" (Othello 1.3.135).
7. The "bounty" that her husband had been paid for enlisting in the militia. The shortage of volunteers and England's sharply rising military needs had in some counties forced the bounty up from about £1 in 1757 to more than £16 in 1796 (J. R. Western, English Militia in the Eighteenth Century, 1965, p. 276).

And when she ended I had little power   275
To give her comfort, and was glad to take
Such words of hope from her own mouth as serv'd
To cheer us both: but long we had not talked
Ere we built up a pile of better thoughts,
And with a brighter eye she looked around   280
As if she had been shedding tears of joy.
We parted. It was then the early spring;
I left her busy with her garden tools;
And well remember, o'er that fence she looked,
And while I paced along the foot-way path   285
Called out, and sent a blessing after me
With tender chearfulness and with a voice
That seemed the very sound of happy thoughts.
    I roved o'er many a hill and many a dale
With this my weary load, in heat and cold,   290
Through many a wood, and many an open ground,
In sunshine or in shade, in wet or fair,
Now blithe, now drooping, as it might befal,
My best companions now the driving winds
And now the 'trotting brooks'[8] and whispering trees   295
And now the music of my own sad steps,
With many a short-lived thought that pass'd between
And disappeared. I came this way again
Towards the wane of summer, when the wheat
Was yellow, and the soft and bladed grass   300
Sprang up afresh and o'er the hay-field spread
Its tender green. When I had reached the door
I found that she was absent. In the shade
Where now we sit I waited her return.
Her cottage in its outward look appeared   305
As chearful as before; in any shew
Of neatness little changed, but that I thought
The honeysuckle crowded round the door
And from the wall hung down in heavier wreathes,
And knots of worthless stone-crop[9] started out   310
Along the window's edge, and grew like weeds
Against the lower panes. I turned aside
And stroll'd into her garden.—It was chang'd:
The unprofitable bindweed spread his bells
From side to side and with unwieldy wreaths   315
Had dragg'd the rose from its sustaining wall
And bent it down to earth; the border-tufts—
Daisy and thrift and lowly camomile
And thyme—had straggled out into the paths
Which they were used to deck. Ere this an hour   320
Was wasted. Back I turned my restless steps,
And as I walked before the door it chanced
A stranger passed, and guessing whom I sought
He said that she was used to ramble far.

8. The quotation is from Robert Burns (*To William*   9. A plant with yellow flowers that grows on walls and
Simpson, line 87).   rocks.

The sun was sinking in the west, and now   325
I sate with sad impatience. From within
Her solitary infant cried aloud.
The spot though fair seemed very desolate,
The longer I remained more desolate.
And, looking round, I saw the corner-stones,   330
Till then unmark'd, on either side the door
With dull red stains discoloured and stuck o'er
With tufts and hairs of wool, as if the sheep
That feed upon the commons thither came
Familiarly and found a couching-place   335
Even at her threshold. —The house-clock struck eight;
I turned and saw her distant a few steps.
Her face was pale and thin, her figure too
Was chang'd. As she unlocked the door she said,
'It grieves me you have waited here so long,   340
But in good truth I've wandered much of late
And sometimes, to my shame I speak, have need
Of my best prayers to bring me back again.'
While on the board she spread our evening meal
She told me she had lost her elder child,   345
That he for months had been a serving-boy
Apprenticed by the parish. 'I perceive
You look at me, and you have cause. Today
I have been travelling far, and many days
About the fields I wander, knowing this   350
Only, that what I seek I cannot find.
And so I waste my time: for I am changed;
And to myself,' said she, 'have done much wrong,
And to this helpless infant. I have slept
Weeping, and weeping I have waked; my tears   355
Have flow'd as if my body were not such
As others are, and I could never die.
But I am now in mind and in my heart
More easy, and I hope,' said she, 'that heaven
Will give me patience to endure the things   360
Which I behold at home.' It would have grieved
Your very heart to see her. Sir, I feel
The story linger in my heart. I fear
'Tis long and tedious, but my spirit clings
To that poor woman: so familiarly   365
Do I perceive her manner, and her look
And presence, and so deeply do I feel
Her goodness, that not seldom in my walks
A momentary trance comes over me;
And to myself I seem to muse on one   370
By sorrow laid asleep or borne away,
A human being destined to awake
To human life, or something very near
To human life, when he shall come again
For whom she suffered. Sir, it would have griev'd   375
Your very soul to see her: evermore

Her eye-lids droop'd, her eyes were downward cast;
And when she at her table gave me food
She did not look at me. Her voice was low,
Her body was subdued. In every act   380
Pertaining to her house-affairs appeared
The careless stillness which a thinking mind
Gives to an idle matter—still she sighed,
But yet no motion of the breast was seen,
No heaving of the heart. While by the fire   385
We sate together, sighs came on my ear;
I knew not how, and hardly whence they came.
I took my staff, and when I kissed her babe
The tears stood in her eyes. I left her then
With the best hope and comfort I could give;   390
She thanked me for my will, but for my hope
It seemed she did not thank me.
                                    I returned
And took my rounds along this road again
Ere on its sunny bank the primrose flower
Had chronicled the earliest day of spring.   395
I found her sad and drooping; she had learn'd
No tidings of her husband: if he lived
She knew not that he lived; if he were dead
She knew not he was dead. She seemed the same
In person [or]¹ appearance, but her house   400
Bespoke a sleepy hand of negligence;
The floor was neither dry nor neat, the hearth
Was comfortless [   ],
The windows too were dim, and her few books,
Which, one upon the other, heretofore   405
Had been piled up against the corner-panes
In seemly order, now with straggling leaves
Lay scattered here and there, open or shut
As they had chanced to fall. Her infant babe
Had from its mother caught the trick of grief   410
And sighed among its playthings. Once again
I turned towards the garden-gate and saw
More plainly still that poverty and grief
Were now come nearer to her: the earth was hard,
With weeds defaced and knots of withered grass;   415
No ridges there appeared of clear black mould,
No winter greenness; of her herbs and flowers
It seemed the better part were gnawed away
Or trampled on the earth; a chain of straw
Which had been twisted round the tender stem   420
Of a young apple-tree lay at its root;
The bark was nibbled round by truant sheep.
Margaret stood near, her infant in her arms,
And seeing that my eye was on the tree
She said, 'I fear it will be dead and gone   425
Ere Robert come again.' Towards the house

1. The word "or" here was erased; later manuscripts read "and."

Together we returned, and she inquired
If I had any hope. But for her Babe
And for her little friendless Boy, she said,
She had no wish to live, that she must die   430
Of sorrow. Yet I saw the idle loom
Still in its place. His Sunday garments hung
Upon the self-same nail, his very staff
Stood undisturbed behind the door. And when
I passed this way beaten by Autumn winds   435
She told me that her little babe was dead
And she was left alone. That very time,
I yet remember, through the miry lane
She walked with me a mile, when the bare trees
Trickled with foggy damps, and in such sort   440
That any heart had ached to hear her begg'd
That wheresoe'er I went I still would ask
For him whom she had lost. We parted then,
Our final parting, for from that time forth
Did many seasons pass ere I returned   445
Into this tract again.
                              Five tedious years
She lingered in unquiet widowhood,
A wife and widow. Needs must it have been
A sore heart-wasting. I have heard, my friend,
That in that broken arbour she would sit   450
The idle length of half a sabbath day —
There, where you see the toadstool's lazy head —
And when a dog passed by she still would quit
The shade and look abroad. On this old Bench
For hours she sate, and evermore her eye   455
Was busy in the distance, shaping things
Which made her heart beat quick. Seest thou that path?
(The green-sward now has broken its grey line)
There to and fro she paced through many a day
Of the warm summer, from a belt of flax   460
That girt her waist spinning the long-drawn thread
With backward steps. —Yet ever as there passed
A man whose garments shewed the Soldier's red,
Or crippled Mendicant in Sailor's garb,
The little child who sate to turn the wheel   465
Ceased from his toil, and she with faltering voice,
Expecting still to learn her husband's fate,
Made many a fond inquiry; and when they
Whose presence gave no comfort were gone by,
Her heart was still more sad. And by yon gate   470
Which bars the traveller's road she often stood
And when a stranger horseman came, the latch
Would lift, and in his face look wistfully,
Most happy if from aught discovered there
Of tender feeling she might dare repeat   475
The same sad question. Meanwhile her poor hut
Sunk to decay, for he was gone whose hand

At the first nippings of October frost
Closed up each chink and with fresh bands of straw
Chequered the green-grown thatch. And so she lived   480
Through the long winter, reckless and alone,
Till this reft house by frost, and thaw, and rain
Was sapped; and when she slept the nightly damps
Did chill her breast, and in the stormy day
Her tattered clothes were ruffled by the wind   485
Even at the side of her own fire. Yet still
She loved this wretched spot, nor would for worlds
Have parted hence; and still that length of road
And this rude bench one torturing hope endeared,
Fast rooted at her heart, and here, my friend,   490
In sickness she remained, and here she died,
Last human tenant of these ruined walls."
     The old Man ceased: he saw that I was mov'd;
From that low Bench, rising instinctively,
I turned aside in weakness, nor had power   495
To thank him for the tale which he had told.
I stood, and leaning o'er the garden-gate
Reviewed that Woman's suff'rings, and it seemed
To comfort me while with a brother's love
I blessed her in the impotence of grief.   500
At length [towards] the [Cottage I returned]²
Fondly, and traced with milder interest
That secret spirit of humanity
Which, 'mid the calm oblivious tendencies
Of nature, 'mid her plants, her weeds, and flowers,   505
And silent overgrowings, still survived.
The old man, seeing this, resumed and said,
"My Friend, enough to sorrow have you given,
The purposes of wisdom ask no more;
Be wise and chearful, and no longer read   510
The forms of things with an unworthy eye.
She sleeps in the calm earth, and peace is here.
I well remember that those very plumes,
Those weeds, and the high spear-grass on that wall,
By mist and silent rain-drops silver'd o'er,   515
As once I passed did to my heart convey
So still an image of tranquillity,
So calm and still, and looked so beautiful
Amid the uneasy thoughts which filled my mind,
That what we feel of sorrow and despair   520
From ruin and from change, and all the grief
The passing shews of being leave behind,
Appeared an idle dream that could not live
Where meditation was. I turned away
And walked along my road in happiness."   525
     He ceased. By this the sun declining shot
A slant and mellow radiance which began
To fall upon us where beneath the trees

2. The words inside the brackets were added in MS. E.

We sate on that low bench, and now we felt,
Admonished thus, the sweet hour coming on.   530
A linnet warbled from those lofty elms,
A thrush sang loud, and other melodies,
At distance heard, peopled the milder air.
The old man rose and hoisted up his load.
Together casting then a farewell look   535
Upon those silent walls, we left the shade
And ere the stars were visible attained
A rustic inn, our evening resting-place.

THE END

1797–ca.1799   1949

Michael[1]

A Pastoral Poem

If from the public way you turn your steps
Up the tumultuous brook of Green-head Ghyll,[2]
You will suppose that with an upright path
Your feet must struggle; in such bold ascent
The pastoral mountains front you, face to face.   5
But, courage! for around that boisterous brook
The mountains have all opened out themselves,
And made a hidden valley of their own.
No habitation can be seen; but they
Who journey thither find themselves alone   10
With a few sheep, with rocks and stones, and kites[3]
That overhead are sailing in the sky.
It is in truth an utter solitude;
Nor should I have made mention of this Dell
But for one object which you might pass by,   15
Might see and notice not. Beside the brook
Appears a straggling heap of unhewn stones!
And to that simple object appertains
A story—unenriched with strange events,
Yet not unfit, I deem, for the fireside,   20
Or for the summer shade. It was the first
Of those domestic tales that spake to me
Of Shepherds, dwellers in the valleys, men
Whom I already loved;—not verily
For their own sakes, but for the fields and hills   25
Where was their occupation and abode.

1. This poem is founded on the actual misfortunes of a family at Grasmere. Wordsworth wrote to Thomas Poole, on Apr. 9, 1801, that he had attempted to picture a man "agitated by two of the most powerful affections of the human heart; the parental affection, and the love of property, *landed* property, including the feelings of inheritance, home, and personal and family independence." The subtitle shows Wordsworth's shift of the term "pastoral" from aristocratic make-believe to the tragic suffering of people in what he called "humble and rustic life."
2. Greenhead Ghyll (a ghyll is a ravine forming the bed of a stream) is not far from Wordsworth's cottage at Grasmere. The other places named in the poem are also in that vicinity.
3. Hawks.

And hence this Tale, while I was yet a Boy
Careless of books, yet having felt the power
Of Nature, by the gentle agency
Of natural objects, led me on to feel   30
For passions that were not my own, and think
(At random and imperfectly indeed)
On man, the heart of man, and human life.
Therefore, although it be a history
Homely and rude, I will relate the same   35
For the delight of a few natural hearts;
And, with yet fonder feeling, for the sake
Of youthful Poets, who among these hills
Will be my second self when I am gone.

     Upon the forest-side in Grasmere Vale   40
There dwelt a Shepherd, Michael was his name;
An old man, stout of heart, and strong of limb.
His bodily frame had been from youth to age
Of an unusual strength: his mind was keen,
Intense, and frugal, apt for all affairs,   45
And in his shepherd's calling he was prompt
And watchful more than ordinary men.
Hence had he learned the meaning of all winds,
Of blasts of every tone; and, oftentimes,
When others heeded not, he heard the South   50
Make subterraneous music, like the noise
Of bagpipers on distant Highland hills.
The Shepherd, at such warning, of his flock
Bethought him, and he to himself would say,
"The winds are now devising work for me!"   55
And, truly, at all times, the storm, that drives
The traveller to a shelter, summoned him
Up to the mountains: he had been alone
Amid the heart of many thousand mists,
That came to him, and left him, on the heights.   60
So lived he till his eightieth year was past.
And grossly that man errs, who should suppose
That the green valleys, and the streams and rocks,
Were things indifferent to the Shepherd's thoughts.
Fields, where with cheerful spirits he had breathed   65
The common air; hills, which with vigorous step
He had so often climbed; which had impressed
So many incidents upon his mind
Of hardship, skill or courage, joy or fear;
Which, like a book, preserved the memory   70
Of the dumb animals, whom he had saved,
Had fed or sheltered, linking to such acts
The certainty of honourable gain;
Those fields, those hills—what could they less? had laid
Strong hold on his affections, were to him   75
A pleasurable feeling of blind love,
The pleasure which there is in life itself.

His days had not been passed in singleness.
His Helpmate was a comely matron, old—
Though younger than himself full twenty years.   80
She was a woman of a stirring life,
Whose heart was in her house: two wheels she had
Of antique form; this large, for spinning wool;
That small, for flax; and if one wheel had rest,
It was because the other was at work.   85
The Pair had but one inmate in their house,
An only Child, who had been born to them
When Michael, telling o'er his years, began
To deem that he was old,—in shepherd's phrase,
With one foot in the grave. This only Son,   90
With two brave sheep-dogs tried in many a storm,
The one of an inestimable worth,
Made all their household. I may truly say,
That they were as a proverb in the vale
For endless industry. When day was gone,   95
And from their occupations out of doors
The Son and Father were come home, even then,
Their labour did not cease; unless when all
Turned to the cleanly supper-board, and there,
Each with a mess of pottage and skimmed milk,   100
Sat round the basket piled with oaten cakes,
And their plain home-made cheese. Yet when the meal
Was ended, Luke (for so the Son was named)
And his old Father both betook themselves
To such convenient work as might employ   105
Their hands by the fire-side; perhaps to card
Wool for the Housewife's spindle, or repair
Some injury done to sickle, flail, or scythe,
Or other implement of house or field.

Down from the ceiling, by the chimney's edge,   110
That in our ancient uncouth country style
With huge and black projection overbrowed
Large space beneath, as duly as the light
Of day grew dim the Housewife hung a lamp;
An aged utensil, which had performed   115
Service beyond all others of its kind.
Early at evening did it burn—and late,
Surviving comrade of uncounted hours,
Which, going by from year to year, had found,
And left the couple neither gay perhaps   120
Nor cheerful, yet with objects and with hopes,
Living a life of eager industry.
And now, when Luke had reached his eighteenth year,
There by the light of his old lamp they sate,
Father and Son, while far into the night   125
The Housewife plied her own peculiar work,
Making the cottage through the silent hours

Murmur as with the sound of summer flies.
This light was famous in its neighbourhood,
And was a public symbol of the life   130
That thrifty Pair had lived. For, as it chanced,
Their cottage on a plot of rising ground
Stood single, with large prospect, north and south,
High into Easedale, up to Dunmail-Raise,
And westward to the village near the lake;   135
And from this constant light, so regular
And so far seen, the House itself, by all
Who dwelt within the limits of the vale,
Both old and young, was named THE EVENING STAR.

    Thus living on through such a length of years,   140
The Shepherd, if he loved himself, must needs
Have loved his Helpmate; but to Michael's heart
This son of his old age was yet more dear—
Less from instinctive tenderness, the same
Fond spirit that blindly works in the blood of all—   145
Than that a child, more than all other gifts
That earth can offer to declining man,
Brings hope with it, and forward-looking thoughts,
And stirrings of inquietude, when they
By tendency of nature needs must fail.   150
Exceeding was the love he bare to him,
His heart and his heart's joy! For oftentimes
Old Michael, while he was a babe in arms,
Had done him female service, not alone
For pastime and delight, as is the use   155
Of fathers, but with patient mind enforced
To acts of tenderness; and he had rocked
His cradle, as with a woman's gentle hand.

    And, in a later time, ere yet the Boy
Had put on boy's attire, did Michael love,   160
Albeit of a stern unbending mind,
To have the Young-one in his sight, when he
Wrought in the field, or on his shepherd's stool
Sate with a fettered sheep before him stretched
Under the large old oak, that near his door   165
Stood single, and, from matchless depth of shade,
Chosen for the Shearer's covert from the sun,
Thence in our rustic dialect was called
The CLIPPING TREE, a name which yet it bears.
There, while they two were sitting in the shade,   170
With others round them, earnest all and blithe,
Would Michael exercise his heart with looks
Of fond correction and reproof bestowed
Upon the Child, if he disturbed the sheep
By catching at their legs, or with his shouts   175
Scared them, while they lay still beneath the shears.

And when by Heaven's good grace the boy grew up
A healthy Lad, and carried in his cheek
Two steady roses that were five years old;
Then Michael from a winter coppice[4] cut   180
With his own hand a sapling, which he hooped
With iron, making it throughout in all
Due requisites a perfect shepherd's staff,
And gave it to the Boy; wherewith equipt
He as a watchman oftentimes was placed   185
At gate or gap, to stem or turn the flock;
And, to his office prematurely called,
There stood the urchin, as you will divine,
Something between a hindrance and a help;
And for this cause not always, I believe,   190
Receiving from his Father hire of praise;
Though nought was left undone which staff, or voice,
Or looks, or threatening gestures, could perform.

But soon as Luke, full ten years old, could stand
Against the mountain blasts; and to the heights,   195
Not fearing toil, nor length of weary ways,
He with his Father daily went, and they
Were as companions, why should I relate
That objects which the Shepherd loved before
Were dearer now? that from the Boy there came   200
Feelings and emanations—things which were
Light to the sun and music to the wind;
And that the old Man's heart seemed born again?

Thus in his Father's sight the Boy grew up:
And now, when he had reached his eighteenth year,   205
He was his comfort and his daily hope.

While in this sort the simple household lived
From day to day, to Michael's ear there came
Distressful tidings. Long before the time
Of which I speak, the Shepherd had been bound   210
In surety for his brother's son, a man
Of an industrious life, and ample means;
But unforeseen misfortunes suddenly
Had prest upon him; and old Michael now
Was summoned to discharge the forfeiture,   215
A grievous penalty, but little less
Than half his substance. This unlooked-for claim,
At the first hearing, for a moment took
More hope out of his life than he supposed
That any old man ever could have lost.   220
As soon as he had armed himself with strength
To look his trouble in the face, it seemed
The Shepherd's sole resource to sell at once
A portion of his patrimonial fields.

4. Grove of small trees.

Such was his first resolve; he thought again,   225
And his heart failed him. "Isabel," said he,
Two evenings after he had heard the news,
"I have been toiling more than seventy years,
And in the open sunshine of God's love
Have we all lived; yet if these fields of ours   230
Should pass into a stranger's hand, I think
That I could not lie quiet in my grave.
Our lot is a hard lot; the sun himself
Has scarcely been more diligent than I;
And I have lived to be a fool at last   235
To my own family. An evil man
That was, and made an evil choice, if he
Were false to us; and if he were not false,
There are ten thousand to whom loss like this
Had been no sorrow. I forgive him;—but   240
'Twere better to be dumb than to talk thus.

     "When I began, my purpose was to speak
Of remedies and of a cheerful hope.
Our Luke shall leave us, Isabel; the land
Shall not go from us, and it shall be free;   245
He shall possess it, free as is the wind
That passes over it. We have, thou know'st,
Another kinsman—he will be our friend
In this distress. He is a prosperous man,
Thriving in trade—and Luke to him shall go,   250
And with his kinsman's help and his own thrift
He quickly will repair this loss, and then
He may return to us. If here he stay,
What can be done? Where every one is poor,
What can be gained?"
                              At this the old Man paused,   255
And Isabel sat silent, for her mind
Was busy, looking back into past times.
There's Richard Bateman,[5] thought she to herself,
He was a parish-boy—at the church-door
They made a gathering for him, shillings, pence   260
And halfpennies, wherewith the neighbours bought
A basket, which they filled with pedlar's wares;
And, with this basket on his arm, the lad
Went up to London, found a master there,
Who, out of many, chose the trusty boy   265
To go and overlook his merchandise
Beyond the seas; where he grew wondrous rich,
And left estates and monies to the poor,
And, at his birth-place, built a chapel floored
With marble, which he sent from foreign lands.   270
These thoughts, and many others of like sort,
Passed quickly through the mind of Isabel,

5. The story alluded to here is well known in the country. The chapel is called Ings Chapel and is on the road
leading from Kendal to Ambleside [Wordsworth's note].

And her face brightened. The old Man was glad,
And thus resumed:—"Well, Isabel! this scheme
These two days, has been meat and drink to me.   275
Far more than we have lost is left us yet.
—We have enough—I wish indeed that I
Were younger;—but this hope is a good hope.
Make ready Luke's best garments, of the best
Buy for him more, and let us send him forth   280
To-morrow, or the next day, or to-night:
—If he *could* go, the Boy should go to-night."

Here Michael ceased, and to the fields went forth
With a light heart. The Housewife for five days
Was restless morn and night, and all day long   285
Wrought on with her best fingers to prepare
Things needful for the journey of her son.
But Isabel was glad when Sunday came
To stop her in her work: for, when she lay
By Michael's side, she through the last two nights   290
Heard him, how he was troubled in his sleep:
And when they rose at morning she could see
That all his hopes were gone. That day at noon
She said to Luke, while they two by themselves
Were sitting at the door, "Thou must not go: 295
We have no other Child but thee to lose,
None to remember—do not go away,
For if thou leave thy Father he will die."
The Youth made answer with a jocund voice;
And Isabel, when she had told her fears,   300
Recovered heart. That evening her best fare
Did she bring forth, and all together sat
Like happy people round a Christmas fire.

With daylight Isabel resumed her work;
And all the ensuing week the house appeared   305
As cheerful as a grove in Spring: at length
The expected letter from their kinsman came,
With kind assurances that he would do
His utmost for the welfare of the Boy;
To which, requests were added, that forthwith   310
He might be sent to him. Ten times or more
The letter was read over; Isabel
Went forth to show it to the neighbours round;
Nor was there at that time on English land
A prouder heart than Luke's. When Isabel   315
Had to her house returned, the old Man said,
"He shall depart to-morrow." To this word
The Housewife answered, talking much of things
Which, if at such short notice he should go,
Would surely be forgotten. But at length   320
She gave consent, and Michael was at ease.

Near the tumultuous brook of Green-head Ghyll,
In that deep valley, Michael had designed
To build a Sheep-fold;[6] and, before he heard
The tidings of his melancholy loss,   325
For this same purpose he had gathered up
A heap of stones, which by the streamlet's edge
Lay thrown together, ready for the work.
With Luke that evening thitherward he walked:
And soon as they had reached the place he stopped,   330
And thus the old Man spake to him: — "My Son,
To-morrow thou wilt leave me: with full heart
I look upon thee, for thou art the same
That wert a promise to me ere thy birth,
And all thy life hast been my daily joy.   335
I will relate to thee some little part
Of our two histories; 'twill do thee good
When thou art from me, even if I should touch
On things thou canst not know of. — After thou
First cam'st into the world — as oft befals   340
To new-born infants — thou didst sleep away
Two days, and blessings from thy Father's tongue
Then fell upon thee. Day by day passed on,
And still I loved thee with increasing love.
Never to living ear came sweeter sounds   345
Than when I heard thee by our own fire-side
First uttering, without words, a natural tune;
While thou, a feeding babe, didst in thy joy
Sing at thy Mother's breast. Month followed month,
And in the open fields my life was passed   350
And on the mountains; else I think that thou
Hadst been brought up upon thy Father's knees.
But we were playmates, Luke: among these hills,
As well thou knowest, in us the old and young
Have played together, nor with me didst thou   355
Lack any pleasure which a boy can know."
Luke had a manly heart; but at these words
He sobbed aloud. The old Man grasped his hand,
And said, "Nay, do not take it so — I see
That these are things of which I need not speak.   360
— Even to the utmost I have been to thee
A kind and a good Father: and herein
I but repay a gift which I myself
Received at others' hands; for, though now old
Beyond the common life of man, I still   365
Remember them who loved me in my youth.
Both of them sleep together: here they lived,
As all their Forefathers had done; and when
At length their time was come, they were not loth
To give their bodies to the family mould.   370

6. Pen for sheep. "A sheepfold in these mountains is an unroofed building of stone walls, with different divisions" [Wordsworth's note].

I wished that thou should'st live the life they lived:
But, 'tis a long time to look back, my Son,
And see so little gain from threescore years.
These fields were burthened[7] when they came to me;
Till I was forty years of age, not more   375
Than half of my inheritance was mine.
I toiled and toiled; God blessed me in my work,
And till these three weeks past the land was free.
—It looks as if it never could endure
Another Master. Heaven forgive me, Luke,   380
If I judge ill for thee, but it seems good
That thou should'st go."
                            At this the old Man paused;
Then, pointing to the stones near which they stood,
Thus, after a short silence, he resumed:
"This was a work for us; and now, my Son,   385
It is a work for me. But, lay one stone—
Here, lay it for me, Luke, with thine own hands.
Nay, Boy, be of good hope;—we both may live
To see a better day. At eighty-four
I still am strong and hale;—do thou thy part;   390
I will do mine.—I will begin again
With many tasks that were resigned to thee:
Up to the heights, and in among the storms,
Will I without thee go again, and do
All works which I was wont to do alone,   395
Before I knew thy face.—Heaven bless thee, Boy!
Thy heart these two weeks has been beating fast
With many hopes; it should be so—yes—yes—
I knew that thou could'st never have a wish
To leave me, Luke: thou hast been bound to me   400
Only by links of love: when thou art gone,
What will be left to us!—But, I forget
My purposes. Lay now the corner-stone,
As I requested; and hereafter, Luke,
When thou art gone away, should evil men   405
Be thy companions, think of me, my Son,
And of this moment; hither turn thy thoughts,
And God will strengthen thee: amid all fear
And all temptation, Luke, I pray that thou
May'st bear in mind the life thy Fathers lived,   410
Who, being innocent, did for that cause
Bestir them in good deeds. Now, fare thee well—
When thou return'st, thou in this place wilt see
A work which is not here: a covenant
'Twill be between us; but, whatever fate   415
Befal thee, I shall love thee to the last,
And bear thy memory with me to the grave."

    The Shepherd ended here; and Luke stooped down,
And, as his Father had requested, laid

7. Mortgaged.

The first stone of the Sheep-fold. At the sight 420
The old Man's grief broke from him; to his heart
He pressed his Son, he kissèd him and wept;
And to the house together they returned.
—Hushed was that House in peace, or seeming peace,
Ere the night fell:—with morrow's dawn the Boy 425
Began his journey, and when he had reached
The public way, he put on a bold face;
And all the neighbours, as he passed their doors,
Came forth with wishes and with farewell prayers,
That followed him till he was out of sight. 430

    A good report did from their Kinsman come,
Of Luke and his well-doing: and the Boy
Wrote loving letters, full of wondrous news,
Which, as the Housewife phrased it, were throughout
"The prettiest letters that were ever seen." 435
Both parents read them with rejoicing hearts.
So, many months passed on: and once again
The Shepherd went about his daily work
With confident and cheerful thoughts; and now
Sometimes when he could find a leisure hour 440
He to that valley took his way, and there
Wrought at the Sheep-fold. Meantime Luke began
To slacken in his duty; and, at length,
He in the dissolute city gave himself
To evil courses: ignominy and shame 445
Fell on him, so that he was driven at last
To seek a hiding-place beyond the seas.

    There is a comfort in the strength of love;
'Twill make a thing endurable, which else
Would overset the brain, or break the heart: 450
I have conversed with more than one who well
Remember the old Man, and what he was
Years after he had heard this heavy news.
His bodily frame had been from youth to age
Of an unusual strength. Among the rocks 455
He went, and still looked up to sun and cloud,
And listened to the wind; and, as before
Performed all kinds of labour for his sheep,
And for the land, his small inheritance.
And to that hollow dell from time to time 460
Did he repair, to build the Fold of which
His flock had need. 'Tis not forgotten yet
The pity which was then in every heart
For the old Man—and 'tis believed by all
That many and many a day he thither went, 465
And never lifted up a single stone.

    There, by the Sheep-fold, sometimes was he seen
Sitting alone, or with his faithful Dog,

Then old, beside him, lying at his feet.
The length of full seven years, from time to time,   470
He at the building of this Sheep-fold wrought,
And left the work unfinished when he died.
Three years, or little more, did Isabel
Survive her Husband: at her death the estate
Was sold, and went into a stranger's hand.   475
The Cottage which was named the EVENING STAR
Is gone—the ploughshare has been through the ground
On which it stood; great changes have been wrought
In all the neighbourhood:—yet the oak is left
That grew beside their door; and the remains   480
Of the unfinished Sheep-fold may be seen
Beside the boisterous brook of Green-head Ghyll.

Oct. 11–Dec. 9, 1800   1800

Resolution and Independence[1]

1

There was a roaring in the wind all night;
The rain came heavily and fell in floods;
But now the sun is rising calm and bright;
The birds are singing in the distant woods;
Over his own sweet voice the Stock-dove broods;   5
The Jay makes answer as the Magpie chatters;
And all the air is filled with pleasant noise of waters.

2

All things that love the sun are out of doors;
The sky rejoices in the morning's birth;
The grass is bright with rain-drops;—on the moors   10
The hare is running races in her mirth;
And with her feet she from the plashy earth
Raises a mist; that, glittering in the sun,
Runs with her all the way, wherever she doth run.

3

I was a Traveller then upon the moor;   15
I saw the hare that raced about with joy;
I heard the woods and distant waters roar;
Or heard them not, as happy as a boy:
The pleasant season did my heart employ:
My old remembrances went from me wholly;   20
And all the ways of men, so vain and melancholy.

4

But, as it sometimes chanceth, from the might
Of joy in minds that can no further go,
As high as we have mounted in delight
In our dejection do we sink as low;   25
To me that morning did it happen so;

1. Wordsworth himself tells us that "I was in the state of feeling described in the beginning of the poem, while crossing over Barton Fell from Mr. Clarkson's, at the foot of Ullswater, towards Askam. The image of the hare I then observed on the ridge of the Fell." He wrote the poem eighteen months after this event.

And fears and fancies thick upon me came;
Dim sadness—and blind thoughts, I knew not, nor could name.
5
I heard the sky-lark warbling in the sky;
And I bethought me of the playful hare: 30
Even such a happy Child of earth am I;
Even as these blissful creatures do I fare;
Far from the world I walk, and from all care;
But there may come another day to me—
Solitude, pain of heart, distress, and poverty.   35
6
My whole life I have lived in pleasant thought,
As if life's business were a summer mood;
As if all needful things would come unsought
To genial faith, still rich in genial good;
But how can He expect that others should   40
Build for him, sow for him, and at his call
Love him, who for himself will take no heed at all?
7
I thought of Chatterton,[2] the marvellous Boy,
The sleepless Soul that perished in his pride;
Of Him who walked in glory and in joy   45
Following his plough, along the mountain-side:[3]
By our own spirits are we deified:
We Poets in our youth begin in gladness;
But thereof come in the end despondency and madness.
8
Now, whether it were by peculiar grace,   50
A leading from above, a something given,
Yet it befel, that, in this lonely place,
When I with these untoward thoughts had striven,
Beside a pool bare to the eye of heaven
I saw a Man before me unawares: 55
The oldest man he seemed that ever wore grey hairs.
9
As a huge stone is sometimes seen to lie
Couched on the bald top of an eminence;
Wonder to all who do the same espy,
By what means it could thither come, and whence;   60
So that it seems a thing endued with sense:
Like a sea-beast crawled forth, that on a shelf
Of rock or sand reposeth, there to sun itself;
10
Such seemed this Man,[4] not all alive nor dead,
Nor all asleep—in his extreme old age: 65

2. Thomas Chatterton (1752–1770), a poet of great talent who, in his loneliness and dire poverty, poisoned himself at the age of seventeen and so became the prime Romantic symbol of neglected young genius.
3. Robert Burns, also considered at that time as a natural poet who died young and poor, without adequate recognition.
4. In Wordsworth's own analysis of this passage he says that the stone is endowed with something of life, the sea beast is stripped of some of its life to assimilate it to the stone, and the old man divested of enough life and motion to make "the two objects unite and coalesce in just comparison." He used the passage to demonstrate his theory of how the "conferring, the abstracting, and the modifying powers of the Imagination . . . are all brought into conjunction" (Preface to the *Poems* of 1815). Cf. Coleridge's brief definitions of the imagination in *Biographia Literaria*, chap. 13 (p. 1542).

His body was bent double, feet and head
Coming together in life's pilgrimage;
As if some dire constraint of pain, or rage
Of sickness felt by him in times long past,
A more than human weight upon his frame had cast.   70

11

Himself he propped, limbs, body, and pale face,
Upon a long grey staff of shaven wood:
And, still as I drew near with gentle pace,
Upon the margin of that moorish flood
Motionless as a cloud the old Man stood,   75
That heareth not the loud winds when they call;
And moveth all together, if it move at all.

12

At length, himself unsettling, he the pond
Stirred with his staff, and fixedly did look
Upon the muddy water, which he conned,   80
As if he had been reading in a book:
And now a stranger's privilege I took;
And, drawing to his side, to him did say,
"This morning gives us promise of a glorious day."

13

A gentle answer did the old Man make,   85
In courteous speech which forth he slowly drew:
And him with further words I thus bespake,
"What occupation do you there pursue?
This is a lonesome place for one like you."
Ere he replied, a flash of mild surprise   90
Broke from the sable orbs of his yet-vivid eyes.

14

His words came feebly, from a feeble chest,
But each in solemn order followed each,
With something of a lofty utterance drest—
Choice word and measured phrase, above the reach   95
Of ordinary men; a stately speech;
Such as grave Livers[5] do in Scotland use,
Religious men, who give to God and man their dues.

15

He told, that to these waters he had come
To gather leeches,[6] being old and poor: 100
Employment hazardous and wearisome!
And he had many hardships to endure:
From pond to pond he roamed, from moor to moor;
Housing, with God's good help, by choice or chance;
And in this way he gained an honest maintenance.   105

16

The old Man still stood talking by my side;
But now his voice to me was like a stream
Scarce heard; nor word from word could I divide;

---

5. Those who live gravely.
6. Leeches were used to draw blood for curative purposes. A leech gatherer, bare legged in shallow water,
stirred the water to attract them and, when they fastened themselves to his legs, picked them off.

And the whole body of the Man did seem
Like one whom I had met with in a dream;   110
Or like a man from some far region sent,
To give me human strength, by apt admonishment.
                    17
My former thoughts returned: the fear that kills;
And hope that is unwilling to be fed;
Cold, pain, and labour, and all fleshly ills;   115
And mighty Poets in their misery dead.
—Perplexed, and longing to be comforted,
My question eagerly did I renew,
"How is it that you live, and what is it you do?"
                    18
He with a smile did then his words repeat;   120
And said, that, gathering leeches, far and wide
He travelled; stirring thus about his feet
The waters of the pools where they abide.
"Once I could meet with them on every side;
But they have dwindled long by slow decay;   125
Yet still I persevere, and find them where I may."
                    19
While he was talking thus, the lonely place,
The old Man's shape, and speech—all troubled me:
In my mind's eye I seemed to see him pace
About the weary moors continually,   130
Wandering about alone and silently.
While I these thoughts within myself pursued,
He, having made a pause, the same discourse renewed.
                    20
And soon with this he other matter blended,
Cheerfully uttered, with demeanour kind,   135
But stately in the main; and when he ended,
I could have laughed myself to scorn to find
In that decrepit Man so firm a mind.
"God," said I, "be my help and stay[7] secure;
I'll think of the Leech-gatherer on the lonely moor!"   140
May 3–July 4, 1802   1807

I wandered lonely as a cloud

I wandered lonely as a cloud
That floats on high o'er vales and hills,
When all at once I saw a crowd,
A host, of golden daffodils;
Beside the lake, beneath the trees,   5
Fluttering and dancing in the breeze.

Continuous as the stars that shine
And twinkle on the milky way,

---

7. Support (a noun).

They stretched in never-ending line
Along the margin of a bay: 10
Ten thousand saw I at a glance,
Tossing their heads in sprightly dance.

The waves beside them danced; but they
Out-did the sparkling waves in glee:
A poet could not but be gay,   15
In such a jocund company:
I gazed—and gazed—but little thought
What wealth the show to me had brought:

For oft, when on my couch I lie
In vacant or in pensive mood,   20
They flash upon that inward eye
Which is the bliss of solitude;
And then my heart with pleasure fills,
And dances with the daffodils.

1804   1807

My heart leaps up

My heart leaps up when I behold
    A rainbow in the sky:
So was it when my life began;
So is it now I am a man;
So be it when I shall grow old,   5
    Or let me die!
The Child is father of the Man;
And I could wish my days to be
Bound each to each by natural piety.[1]

Mar. 26, 1802   1807

Ode: Intimations of Immortality   Wordsworth said about this *Ode* to Isabella Fenwick:

This was composed during my residence at Town End, Grasmere; two years
at least passed between the writing of the four first stanzas and the remaining
part. To the attentive and competent reader the whole sufficiently explains
itself; but there may be no harm in adverting here to particular feelings or
experiences of my own mind on which the structure of the poem partly rests.
Nothing was more difficult for me in childhood than to admit the notion of
death as a state applicable to my own being. I have said elsewhere [in the
opening stanza of *We Are Seven*]:

    —A simple child,
    That lightly draws its breath,

1. As distinguished from piety based on the Scriptures,
in which God makes the rainbow the token of his covenant with Noah and all his descendants (Genesis 9.12–

17). The religious sentiment that binds Wordsworth's
mature self to that of his childhood is a continuing
responsiveness to the miracle of ordinary things.

> And feels its life in every limb,
> What should it know of death! —

But it was not so much from [feelings] of animal vivacity that *my* difficulty came as from a sense of the indomitableness of the spirit within me. I used to brood over the stories of Enoch and Elijah, and almost to persuade myself that, whatever might become of others, I should be translated, in something of the same way, to heaven. With a feeling congenial to this, I was often unable to think of external things as having external existence, and I communed with all that I saw as something not apart from, but inherent in, my own immaterial nature. Many times while going to school have I grasped at a wall or tree to recall myself from this abyss of idealism to the reality. At that time I was afraid of such processes. In later periods of life I have deplored, as we have all reason to do, a subjugation of an opposite character, and have rejoiced over the remembrances, as is expressed in the lines —

> Obstinate questionings
> Of sense and outward things,
> Fallings from us, vanishings; etc.

To that dreamlike vividness and splendor which invest objects of sight in childhood, everyone, I believe, if he would look back, could bear testimony, and I need not dwell upon it here: but having in the Poem regarded it as presumptive evidence of a prior state of existence, I think it right to protest against a conclusion, which has given pain to some good and pious persons, that I meant to inculcate such a belief. It is far too shadowy a notion to be recommended to faith, as more than an element in our instincts of immortality. But let us bear in mind that, though the idea is not advanced in revelation, there is nothing there to contradict it, and the fall of Man presents an analogy in its favor. Accordingly, a pre-existent state has entered into the popular creeds of many nations; and, among all persons acquainted with classic literature, is known as an ingredient in Platonic philosophy. Archimedes said that he could move the world if he had a point whereon to rest his machine. Who has not felt the same aspirations as regards the world of his own mind? Having to wield some of its elements when I was impelled to write this Poem on the 'Immortality of the Soul,' I took hold of the notion of pre-existence as having sufficient foundation in humanity for authorizing me to make for my purpose the best use of it I could as a Poet. (Wordsworth)

As Wordsworth says, Plato held the doctrine that the soul is immortal and exists separately from the body both before birth and after death. But while the *Ode* proposes that the soul only gradually loses "the vision splendid" after birth, Plato maintained the contrary: that the knowledge of the eternal Ideas, which the soul had acquired by direct acquaintance, is totally lost at the instant of birth, and must be gradually "recollected" by philosophical discipline in the course of this life (*Phaedo* 73–77). Wordsworth's metaphorical use of the concept of preexistence in his poem resembles more closely the view of some neoplatonists that the glory of the unborn soul is gradually quenched by its descent into the darkness of matter.

Wordsworth was troubled by objections to the Christian heterodoxy of this apparent claim for the preexistence, as against the orthodox belief only in the survival, of the soul. He insisted that he did not intend to assert this as doctrine but only to use it as a poetic postulate, enabling him to deal "as a poet" with an experience to which everyone, as he says, "if he would look back, could bear testimony." This experience is the general human one: that the loss of youth involves the loss of a freshness and radiance investing all experience. Coleridge's *Dejection: An Ode*, which he wrote after he had heard the first four stanzas of

Wordsworth's poem, employs a similar figurative technique for a comparable, though more devastating, experience of loss. As with all poems so large and rich as this one of Wordsworth's, there are divergent interpretations of its purport, emphases, and organization. But most commentators agree that the poem offers two different perspectives on the fact that growing up is also a stage on the way to death, and almost all agree that it is one of the greatest instances of the very difficult form of the irregular English ode.

The original published version of this poem had as its title only "Ode," and then as epigraph *"Paulo maiora canamus"* ("Let us sing of somewhat higher things") from Virgil's *Eclogue 4.*

Ode

Intimations of Immortality from Recollections of Early Childhood

> The Child is Father of the Man;
> And I could wish my days to be
> Bound each to each by natural piety.[1]

1

There was a time when meadow, grove, and stream,
The earth, and every common sight,
　　To me did seem
　　Apparelled in celestial light,
The glory and the freshness of a dream.　　　　　　5
It is not now as it hath been of yore;—
　　Turn wheresoe'er I may,
　　　　By night or day,
The things which I have seen I now can see no more.

2

　　The Rainbow comes and goes,　　　　　　10
　　And lovely is the Rose,
　　The Moon doth with delight
Look round her when the heavens are bare,
　　Waters on a starry night
　　Are beautiful and fair;　　　　　　15
　　The sunshine is a glorious birth;
　　But yet I know, where'er I go,
That there hath past away a glory from the earth.

3

Now, while the birds thus sing a joyous song,
　　And while the young lambs bound　　　　　　20
　　　　As to the tabor's[2] sound,
To me alone there came a thought of grief:
A timely utterance[3] gave that thought relief,
　　　　And I again am strong:
The cataracts blow their trumpets from the steep;　　25

1. The concluding lines of Wordsworth's *My heart leaps up.*
2. A small drum often used to beat time for dancing.
3. Perhaps *My heart leaps up,* perhaps *Resolution and Independence,* perhaps not a poem at all.

No more shall grief of mine the season wrong;
I hear the Echoes through the mountains throng,
The Winds come to me from the fields of sleep,[4]
    And all the earth is gay;
        Land and sea   30
      Give themselves up to jollity,
        And with the heart of May
    Doth every Beast keep holiday;—
        Thou Child of Joy,
Shout round me, let me hear thy shouts, thou happy
    Shepherd-boy!   35

[handwritten margin note: nature having lost adornment of thought]

4

Ye blessed Creatures, I have heard the call
    Ye to each other make; I see
The heavens laugh with you in your jubilee;
    My heart is at your festival,
      My head hath its coronal,[5]   40
The fulness of your bliss, I feel—I feel it all.
      Oh evil day! if I were sullen
      While Earth herself is adorning,
        This sweet May-morning,
      And the Children are culling   45
        On every side,
    In a thousand valleys far and wide,
    Fresh flowers; while the sun shines warm,
And the Babe leaps up on his Mother's arm:—
      I hear, I hear, with joy I hear!   50
      —But there's a Tree, of many, one,
A single Field which I have looked upon,
Both of them speak of something that is gone:
        The Pansy at my feet
        Doth the same tale repeat: 55
Whither is fled the visionary gleam?
Where is it now, the glory and the dream?

5

Our birth is but a sleep and a forgetting:
The Soul that rises with us, our life's Star,[6]
      Hath had elsewhere its setting,   60
      And cometh from afar:
      Not in entire forgetfulness,
      And not in utter nakedness,
But trailing clouds of glory do we come
      From God, who is our home: 65
Heaven lies about us in our infancy!
Shades of the prison-house begin to close
    Upon the growing Boy,
But He beholds the light, and whence it flows,

---

4. Of the many suggested interpretations, the simplest is "from the fields where they were sleeping." Wordsworth often associated a rising wind with the revival of spirit and of poetic inspiration (see, e.g., the opening passage of *The Prelude*, pp. 1402–03).
5. Circlet of wildflowers, with which the shepherd boys trimmed their hats in May.
6. The sun, as metaphor for the soul.

He sees it in his joy;   70
The Youth, who daily farther from the east
    Must travel, still is Nature's Priest,
    And by the vision splendid
    Is on his way attended;
At length the Man perceives it die away,   75
And fade into the light of common day.

6

Earth fills her lap with pleasures of her own;
Yearnings she hath in her own natural kind,
And, even with something of a Mother's mind,
    And no unworthy aim,   80
    The homely[7] Nurse doth all she can
To make her Foster-child, her Inmate Man,
    Forget the glories he hath known,
And that imperial palace whence he came.

7

Behold the Child among his new-born blisses,   85
A six years' Darling of a pigmy size!
See, where 'mid work of his own hand he lies,
Fretted[8] by sallies of his mother's kisses,
With light upon him from his father's eyes!
See, at his feet, some little plan or chart,   90
Some fragment from his dream of human life,
Shaped by himself with newly-learnèd art;
    A wedding or a festival,
    A mourning or a funeral;
      And this hath now his heart,   95
    And unto this he frames his song:
      Then will he fit his tongue
To dialogues of business, love, or strife;
    But it will not be long
    Ere this be thrown aside,   100
    And with new joy and pride
The little Actor cons another part;
Filling from time to time his "humorous stage"[9]
With all the Persons, down to palsied Age,
That Life brings with her in her equipage;   105
    As if his whole vocation
    Were endless imitation.

8

Thou, whose exterior semblance doth belie
    Thy Soul's immensity;
Thou best Philosopher, who yet dost keep   110
Thy heritage, thou Eye among the blind,
That, deaf and silent, read'st the eternal deep,
Haunted for ever by the eternal mind,—

7. In the old sense, "simple and friendly."
8. "Irritated," or possibly in the old sense, "checkered over."
9. From a sonnet by the Elizabethan poet Samuel Daniel. In Daniel's age "humorous" meant "capricious," and also referred to the various characters and temperaments ("humors") represented in drama.

Mighty Prophet! Seer blest!
On whom those truths do rest,   115
Which we are toiling all our lives to find,
In darkness lost, the darkness of the grave;
Thou, over whom thy Immortality
Broods like the Day, a Master o'er a Slave,
A Presence which is not to be put by;   120
Thou little Child, yet glorious in the might
Of heaven-born freedom on thy being's height,
Why with such earnest pains dost thou provoke
The years to bring the inevitable yoke,
Thus blindly with thy blessedness at strife?   125
Full soon thy Soul shall have her earthly freight,
And custom lie upon thee with a weight,
Heavy as frost, and deep almost as life!
                            9
O joy! that in our embers
Is something that doth live,   130
That nature yet remembers
What was so fugitive!
The thought of our past years in me doth breed
Perpetual benediction: not indeed
For that which is most worthy to be blest;   135
Delight and liberty, the simple creed
Of Childhood, whether busy or at rest,
With new-fledged hope still fluttering in his breast: —
Not for these I raise
The song of thanks and praise;   140
But for those obstinate questionings
Of sense and outward things,
Fallings from us, vanishings;
Blank misgivings of a Creature
Moving about in worlds not realised,[1]   145
High instincts before which our mortal Nature
Did tremble like a guilty Thing surprised:
But for those first affections,
Those shadowy recollections,
Which, be they what they may,   150
Are yet the fountain light of all our day,
Are yet a master light of all our seeing;
Uphold us, cherish, and have power to make
Our noisy years seem moments in the being
Of the eternal Silence: truths that wake,   155
To perish never;
Which neither listlessness, nor mad endeavour,
Nor Man nor Boy,
Nor all that is at enmity with joy,
Can utterly abolish or destroy!   160
Hence in a season of calm weather

---

1. Not seeming real (see Wordsworth's comment in headnote "Ode: Intimations of Immortality").

Though inland far we be,
Our Souls have sight of that immortal sea
    Which brought us hither,
        Can in a moment travel thither,   165
And see the Children sport upon the shore,
And hear the mighty waters rolling evermore.

10

Then sing, ye Birds, sing, sing a joyous song!
        And let the young Lambs bound
        As to the tabor's sound!   170
We in thought will join your throng,
        Ye that pipe and ye that play,
        Ye that through your hearts to-day
        Feel the gladness of the May!
What though the radiance which was once so bright   175
Be now for ever taken from my sight,
    Though nothing can bring back the hour
Of splendour in the grass, of glory in the flower;
        We will grieve not, rather find
        Strength in what remains behind;   180
        In the primal sympathy
        Which having been must ever be;
        In the soothing thoughts that spring
        Out of human suffering;
        In the faith that looks through death,   185
In years that bring the philosophic mind.

11

And O, ye Fountains, Meadows, Hills, and Groves,
Forebode not any severing of our loves!
Yet in my heart of hearts I feel your might;
I only have relinquished one delight   190
To live beneath your more habitual sway.
I love the Brooks which down their channels fret,
Even more than when I tripped lightly as they;
The innocent brightness of a new-born Day
            Is lovely yet;   195
The Clouds that gather round the setting sun
Do take a sober colouring from an eye
That hath kept watch o'er man's mortality;
Another race hath been, and other palms are won.[2]
Thanks to the human heart by which we live,   200
Thanks to its tenderness, its joys, and fears,
To me the meanest flower that blows can give
Thoughts that do often lie too deep for tears.

1802–04   1807

---

2. In Greece foot races were often run for the prize of a branch or wreath of palm. Wordsworth's line echoes Paul, 1 Corinthians 9.24, who uses such races as a metaphor for life: "Know ye not that they which run in a race run all, but one receiveth the prize?"

Ode to Duty[1]

Jam non consilio bonus, sed more eò perductus, ut non tantum rectè facere possim, sed nisi rectè facere non possim.[2]

Stern Daughter of the Voice of God![3]
O Duty! if that name thou love
Who art a light to guide, a rod
To check the erring, and reprove;
Thou, who art victory and law   5
When empty terrors overawe;
From vain temptations dost set free;
And calm'st the weary strife of frail humanity!

There are who ask not if thine eye
Be on them; who, in love and truth,   10
Where no misgiving is, rely
Upon the genial sense[4] of youth:
Glad Hearts! without reproach or blot;
Who do thy work, and know it not:
Oh! if through confidence misplaced   15
They fail, thy saving arms, dread Power! around them cast.

Serene will be our days and bright,
And happy will our nature be,
When love is an unerring light,
And joy its own security.   20
And they a blissful course may hold
Even now, who, not unwisely bold,
Live in the spirit of this creed;
Yet seek thy firm support, according to their need.

I, loving freedom, and untried;   25
No sport of every random gust,
Yet being to myself a guide,
Too blindly have reposed my trust:
And oft, when in my heart was heard
Thy timely mandate, I deferred   30
The task, in smoother walks to stray;
But thee I now would serve more strictly, if I may.

1. "This Ode . . . is on the model of Gray's *Ode to Adversity* which is copied from Horace's *Ode to Fortune*. Many and many a time have I been twitted by my wife and sister for having forgotten this dedication of myself to the stern lawgiver" [Wordsworth's note].

In this poem, a striking departure from his earlier forms and ideas, Wordsworth abandons the descriptive-meditative pattern of his *Tintern Abbey* and *Ode: Intimations of Immortality* and reverts to the standard 18th-century form of an ode addressed to a personified abstraction. The poem also represents Wordsworth's reversion from his youthful reliance on natural impulse to a more orthodox ethical and religious tradition. It makes no reference to that "Nature" which earlier had constituted for Wordsworth "both law and impulse" and, in *Tintern Abbey*, had been called "The guide, the guardian of my heart, and soul / Of all my moral being" (lines 110–11).

2. "Now I am not good by conscious intent, but have been so trained by habit that I not only can act rightly but am unable to act other than rightly." Added in 1837, this epigraph is an adaptation from *Moral Epistles* 120.10 by Seneca (4 B.C.–A.D. 65), Stoic philosopher and writer of tragedies.

3. Cf. *Paradise Lost* 9.652–54: "God so commanded, and left that Command / Sole Daughter of his voice; the rest, we live / Law to ourselves, our Reason is our Law."

4. Innate vitality.

Through no disturbance of my soul,
Or strong compunction[5] in me wrought,
I supplicate for thy control;   35
But in the quietness of thought:
Me this unchartered freedom tires;
I feel the weight of chance-desires:
My hopes no more must change their name,
I long for a repose that ever is the same.   40

Stern Lawgiver! yet thou dost wear
The Godhead's most benignant grace;
Nor know we any thing so fair
As is the smile upon thy face:
Flowers laugh before thee on their beds   45
And fragrance in thy footing treads;
Thou dost preserve the stars from wrong;
And the most ancient heavens, through Thee, are fresh and strong.

To humbler functions, awful Power!
I call thee: I myself commend   50
Unto thy guidance from this hour;
Oh, let my weakness have an end!
Give unto me, made lowly wise,[6]
The spirit of self-sacrifice;
The confidence of reason give;   55
And in the light of truth thy Bondman let me live!
1804   1807

The Solitary Reaper[1]

Behold her, single in the field,
Yon solitary Highland Lass!
Reaping and singing by herself;
Stop here, or gently pass!
Alone she cuts and binds the grain,   5
And sings a melancholy strain;
O listen! for the Vale profound
Is overflowing with the sound.

No Nightingale did ever chaunt
More welcome notes to weary bands   10
Of travellers in some shady haunt,
Among Arabian sands:
A voice so thrilling ne'er was heard

5. In the older sense, "sting of conscience, or remorse."
6. Another echo from Milton, whose Christian-
humanist ethic pervades this ode. The angel Raphael
had advised Adam (*Paradise Lost* 8.173–74), "Be lowly
wise: / Think only what concerns thee and thy being."
1. One of the rare poems not based on Wordsworth's
own experience. The poet tells us that it was suggested

by a passage in Thomas Wilkinson's *Tours to the British
Mountains* (1824), which he had seen in manuscript:
"Passed a female who was reaping alone: she sung in
Erse [the Gaelic language of Scotland] as she bended
over her sickle; the sweetest human voice I ever heard:
her strains were tenderly melancholy, and felt delicious, long after they were heard no more."

In spring-time from the Cuckoo-bird,
Breaking the silence of the seas
Among the farthest Hebrides.   15

Will no one tell me what she sings?[2]—
Perhaps the plaintive numbers flow
For old, unhappy, far-off things,
And battles long ago: 20
Or is it some more humble lay,
Familiar matter of to-day?
Some natural sorrow, loss, or pain,
That has been, and may be again?

Whate'er the theme, the Maiden sang   25
As if her song could have no ending;
I saw her singing at her work,
And o'er the sickle bending;—
I listened, motionless and still;
And, as I mounted up the hill,   30
The music in my heart I bore,
Long after it was heard no more.

Nov. 5, 1805   1807

Elegiac Stanzas

*Suggested by a Picture of Peele Castle, in a Storm, Painted by Sir
George Beaumont*[1]

I was thy neighbour once, thou rugged Pile!
Four summer weeks I dwelt in sight of thee:
I saw thee every day; and all the while
Thy Form was sleeping on a glassy sea.

So pure the sky, so quiet was the air!   5
So like, so very like, was day to day!
Whene'er I looked, thy Image still was there;
It trembled, but it never passed away.

How perfect was the calm! it seemed no sleep;
No mood, which season takes away, or brings: 10
I could have fancied that the mighty Deep
Was even the gentlest of all gentle Things.

Ah! THEN, if mine had been the Painter's hand,
To express what then I saw; and add the gleam,

2. The poet does not understand Erse, the language in which she sings.
1. Sir George Beaumont, a wealthy landscape painter, was Wordsworth's patron and close friend. Peele Castle is on an island opposite Rampside, Lancashire, where Wordsworth had spent a month in 1794, twelve years before he saw Beaumont's painting. A current tendency is to interpret this poem as an expression of Wordsworth's loss of faith in nature. It should be noted, however, that the focus of the poem is not on an altered view of nature but on an altered knowledge of human life and on the moral values necessary to manage the inevitability of loss and suffering.

The light that never was, on sea or land,   15
The consecration, and the Poet's dream;

I would have planted thee, thou hoary Pile
Amid a world how different from this!
Beside a sea that could not cease to smile;
On tranquil land, beneath a sky of bliss.   20

Thou shouldst have seemed a treasure-house divine
Of peaceful years; a chronicle of heaven;—
Of all the sunbeams that did ever shine
The very sweetest had to thee been given.

A Picture had it been of lasting ease,   25
Elysian[2] quiet, without toil or strife;
No motion but the moving tide, a breeze,
Or merely silent Nature's breathing life.

Such, in the fond illusion of my heart,
Such Picture would I at that time have made: 30
And seen the soul of truth in every part,
A stedfast peace that might not be betrayed.

So once it would have been,—'tis so no more;
I have submitted to a new control:
A power is gone, which nothing can restore;   35
A deep distress hath humanised my Soul.[3]

Not for a moment could I now behold
A smiling sea, and be what I have been:
The feeling of my loss will ne'er be old;
This, which I know, I speak with mind serene.   40

Then, Beaumont, Friend! who would have been the Friend,
If he had lived, of Him whom I deplore,[4]
This work of thine I blame not, but commend;
This sea in anger, and that dismal shore.

O 'tis a passionate Work!—yet wise and well,   45
Well chosen is the spirit that is here;
That Hulk which labours in the deadly swell,
This rueful sky, this pageantry of fear!

And this huge Castle, standing here sublime,
I love to see the look with which it braves,   50
Cased in the unfeeling armour of old time,
The lightning, the fierce wind, and trampling waves.

2. Referring to Elysium, in classical mythology the
peaceful place where those favored by the gods dwelled
after death.
3. Captain John Wordsworth, William's brother, had
been drowned in a shipwreck on Feb. 5, 1805. He is
referred to in lines 41–42.
4. Mourn.

Farewell, farewell the heart that lives alone,
Housed in a dream, at distance from the Kind![5]
Such happiness, wherever it be known,   55
Is to be pitied; for 'tis surely blind.

But welcome fortitude, and patient cheer,
And frequent sights of what is to be borne!
Such sights, or worse, as are before me here.—
Not without hope we suffer and we mourn.   60
Summer 1806   1807

SONNETS

Composed upon Westminster Bridge, September 3, 1802[1]

Earth has not any thing to show more fair:
Dull would he be of soul who could pass by
A sight so touching in its majesty:
This City now doth, like a garment, wear
The beauty of the morning; silent, bare,   5
Ships, towers, domes, theatres, and temples lie
Open unto the fields, and to the sky;
All bright and glittering in the smokeless air.
Never did sun more beautifully steep
In his first splendour, valley, rock, or hill;   10
Ne'er saw I, never felt, a calm so deep!
The river glideth at his own sweet will:
Dear God! the very houses seem asleep;
And all that mighty heart is lying still!

1802   1807

It is a beauteous evening

It is a beauteous evening, calm and free,
The holy time is quiet as a Nun
Breathless with adoration; the broad sun
Is sinking down in its tranquillity;
The gentleness of heaven broods o'er the Sea: 5
Listen! the mighty Being is awake,
And doth with his eternal motion make
A sound like thunder—everlastingly.
Dear Child! dear Girl! that walkest with me here,[2]

---

5. Humankind.
1. The date of this experience was not Sept. 3, but July 31, 1802; its occasion was a trip to France. The conflict of feelings attending Wordsworth's brief return to France, where he had once been a revolutionist and

the lover of Annette Vallon, evoked a number of personal and political sonnets, among them the two that follow.
2. The girl walking with Wordsworth is Caroline, his natural daughter by Annette Vallon.

If thou appear untouched by solemn thought,   10
Thy nature is not therefore less divine:
Thou liest in Abraham's bosom[3] all the year;
And worshipp'st at the Temple's inner shrine,
God being with thee when we know it not.

Aug. 1802   1807

London, 1802[4]

Milton! thou should'st be living at this hour:
England hath need of thee: she is a fen
Of stagnant waters: altar, sword, and pen,
Fireside, the heroic wealth of hall and bower,
Have forfeited their ancient English dower   5
Of inward happiness. We are selfish men;
Oh! raise us up, return to us again;
And give us manners, virtue, freedom, power.
Thy soul was like a Star, and dwelt apart:
Thou hadst a voice whose sound was like the sea: 10
Pure as the naked heavens, majestic, free,
So didst thou travel on life's common way,
In cheerful godliness; and yet thy heart
The lowliest duties on herself did lay.

Sept. 1802   1807

The world is too much with us

The world is too much with us; late and soon,
Getting and spending, we lay waste our powers:
Little we see in Nature that is ours;
We have given our hearts away, a sordid boon![5]
This Sea that bares her bosom to the moon;   5
The winds that will be howling at all hours,
And are up-gathered now like sleeping flowers;
For this, for every thing, we are out of tune;
It moves us not.—Great God! I'd rather be
A Pagan suckled in a creed outworn;   10
So might I, standing on this pleasant lea,
Have glimpses that would make me less forlorn;
Have sight of Proteus rising from the sea;
Or hear old Triton[6] blow his wreathèd horn.

1802–04   1807

3. Where the souls destined for heaven rest after death.
Luke 16.22: "And it came to pass, that the beggar died,
and was carried by the angels into Abraham's bosom."
4. One of a series "written immediately after my return from France to London, when I could not but
be struck, as here described, with the vanity and parade of our own country . . . as contrasted with the
quiet, and I may say the desolation, that the revolution had produced in France" [Wordsworth's note].
5. Gift; it is the act of giving the heart away that is

sordid.
6. A sea deity, usually represented as blowing on a
conch shell. Proteus: an old man of the sea who (in
the *Odyssey*) could assume a variety of shapes. The
description of Proteus echoes *Paradise Lost* 3.603–04,
and that of Triton echoes Spenser's *Colin Clouts
Come Home Againe*, lines 244–45. Milton and
Spenser are the two English poets with whom Wordsworth most closely allied himself.

Surprised by joy[7]

Surprised by joy—impatient as the Wind
I turned to share the transport—Oh! with whom
But Thee, deep buried in the silent tomb,
That spot which no vicissitude can find?
Love, faithful love, recalled thee to my mind— 5
But how could I forget thee? Through what power,
Even for the least division of an hour,
Have I been so beguiled as to be blind
To my most grievous loss!—That thought's return
Was the worst pang that sorrow ever bore, 10
Save one, one only, when I stood forlorn,
Knowing my heart's best treasure was no more;
That neither present time, nor years unborn
Could to my sight that heavenly face restore.

1813–14   1815

Mutability[8]

From low to high doth dissolution climb,
And sink from high to low, along a scale
Of awful notes, whose concord shall not fail;
A musical but melancholy chime,
Which they can hear who meddle not with crime, 5
Nor avarice, nor over-anxious care.
Truth fails not; but her outward forms that bear
The longest date do melt like frosty rime,
That in the morning whitened hill and plain
And is no more; drop like the tower sublime 10
Of yesterday, which royally did wear
His crown of weeds, but could not even sustain
Some casual shout that broke the silent air,
Or the unimaginable touch of Time.

1821   1822

Steamboats, Viaducts, and Railways[9]

Motions and Means, on land and sea at war
With old poetic feeling, not for this,
Shall ye, by Poets even, be judged amiss!
Nor shall your presence, howsoe'er it mar
The loveliness of Nature, prove a bar 5

7. "This was in fact suggested by my daughter Catherine, long after her death" [Wordsworth's note]. Catherine Wordsworth died June 4, 1812, at the age of four.
8. This great sonnet was included in an otherwise rather pedestrian sequence, *Ecclesiastical Sonnets*, dealing with the history and ceremonies of the Church of England.

9. In late middle age Wordsworth demonstrates, as he had predicted in the Preface to *Lyrical Ballads*, that the poet will assimilate to his subject matter the "material revolution" produced by science. Unlike most poets, furthermore, he boldly accepts as evidences of human progress even the unlovely encroachments of technology on his beloved natural scene.

To the Mind's gaining that prophetic sense
Of future change, that point of vision, whence
May be discovered what in soul ye are.
In spite of all that beauty may disown
In your harsh features, Nature doth embrace　　　　　　10
Her lawful offspring in Man's art; and Time,
Pleased with your triumphs o'er his brother Space,
Accepts from your bold hands the proffered crown
Of hope, and smiles on you with cheer sublime.

1833　　　　　　　　　　　　　　　　　　　　　　　　　　1835

·　·　·

Extempore Effusion upon the Death of James Hogg[1]

When first, descending from the moorlands,
I saw the Stream of Yarrow[2] glide
Along a bare and open valley,
The Ettrick Shepherd[3] was my guide.

When last along its banks I wandered,　　　　　　　　5
Through groves that had begun to shed
Their golden leaves upon the pathways,
My steps the Border-minstrel[4] led.

The mighty Minstrel breathes no longer,
'Mid mouldering ruins low he lies;　　　　　　　　　10
And death upon the braes[5] of Yarrow,
Has closed the Shepherd-poet's eyes:

Nor has the rolling year twice measured,
From sign to sign, its stedfast course,
Since every mortal power of Coleridge　　　　　　　15
Was frozen at its marvellous source;

The rapt One, of the godlike forehead,
The heaven-eyed creature sleeps in earth:
And Lamb, the frolic and the gentle,
Has vanished from his lonely hearth.　　　　　　　　20

Like clouds that rake the mountain-summits,
Or waves that own no curbing hand,

1. Wordsworth's niece relates how he was deeply moved by finding unexpectedly in a newspaper an account of the death of the poet James Hogg. "Half an hour afterwards he came into the room where the ladies were sitting and asked Miss Hutchinson [his sister-in-law] to write down some lines which he had just composed." All the poets named here, several of Wordsworth's closest friends among them, had died between 1832 and 1835.
2. A river in the southeast of Scotland.
3. Hogg was known as the "Ettrick Shepherd" (he was born in Ettrick Forest and worked as a shepherd). He was discovered as a writer by Sir Walter Scott, and became well known as a poet, essayist, and editor.
4. Sir Walter Scott.
5. The sloping banks of a stream.

How fast has brother followed brother,
From sunshine to the sunless land!

Yet I, whose lids from infant slumber   25
Were earlier raised, remain to hear
A timid voice, that asks in whispers,
"Who next will drop and disappear?"

Our haughty life is crowned with darkness,
Like London with its own black wreath,   30
On which with thee, O Crabbe![6] forth-looking,
I gazed from Hampstead's breezy heath.

As if but yesterday departed,
Thou too art gone before; but why,
O'er ripe fruit, seasonably gathered,   35
Should frail survivors heave a sigh?

Mourn rather for that holy Spirit,
Sweet as the spring, as ocean deep;
For Her[7] who, ere her summer faded,
Has sunk into a breathless sleep.   40

No more of old romantic sorrows,
For slaughtered Youth or love-lorn Maid!
With sharper grief is Yarrow smitten,
And Ettrick mourns with her their Poet dead.

Nov. 21, 1835   1835

Prospectus
to *The Recluse*[1]

On Man, on Nature, and on Human Life,
Musing in solitude, I oft perceive
Fair trains of imagery before me rise,
Accompanied by feelings of delight

6. George Crabbe, the poet of rural and village life.
7. The poet Felicia Hemans, who died when only forty-two.
1. Through most of his poetic life Wordsworth labored intermittently at a long philosophic poem called *The Recluse*, which he intended to be his masterwork. As Wordsworth described this project in the Preface to *The Excursion* (1814), it was to consist of an autobiographical introduction (the poem now called *The Prelude*) and three long parts; of these three he completed only book 1 of part 1 ("Home at Grasmere") and part 2, called *The Excursion*. In the Preface to *The Excursion*, Wordsworth printed this long extract (the concluding section of "Home at Grasmere") to serve "as a kind of *Prospectus* of the design and scope of the whole Poem"—i.e., of the entire *Recluse*.
   The first version of this "Prospectus" may have been drafted as early as 1798 or 1800. In language resonant with echoes from *Paradise Lost*, Wordsworth an-

nounces an undertaking which he conceives to be no less inspired and sublime than Milton's. In it he will move higher than Milton's heaven and deeper than Milton's hell, past scenes evoking greater fear than hell and greater awe than Jehovah; but without ever leaving "the Mind of Man— / My haunt, and the main region of my song" (lines 40–41). And his "high argument" is that Paradise can be regained; not, however, as in Revelation 21 and in Milton, by the marriage between the New Jerusalem and Christ the Lamb but by a marriage between the "intellect of Man" and "this goodly universe," and the resulting new "creation . . . which they with blended might / Accomplish" (lines 52–71). In no other passage does Wordsworth reveal so clearly the extent to which he assimilates in his poetry the biblical scheme of Milton's epic—assigning, however, the active role, from creation to redemption, to the human faculties, in their interaction with the external universe.

Pure, or with no unpleasing sadness mixed;   5
And I am conscious of affecting thoughts
And dear remembrances, whose presence soothes
Or elevates the Mind, intent to weigh
The good and evil of our mortal state.
—To these emotions, whencesoe'er they come,   10
Whether from breath of outward circumstance,
Or from the Soul—an impulse to herself—
I would give utterance in numerous verse.[2]
Of Truth, of Grandeur, Beauty, Love, and Hope,
And melancholy Fear subdued by Faith;   15
Of blessed consolations in distress;
Of moral strength, and intellectual Power;
Of joy in widest commonalty spread;
Of the individual Mind that keeps her own
Inviolate retirement, subject there   20
To Conscience only, and the law supreme
Of that Intelligence which governs all—
I sing:—"fit audience let me find though few!"[3]

     So prayed, more gaining than he asked, the Bard—
In holiest mood. Urania,[4] I shall need   25
Thy guidance, or a greater Muse, if such
Descend to earth or dwell in highest heaven!
For I must tread on shadowy ground, must sink
Deep—and, aloft ascending, breathe in worlds
To which the heaven of heavens[5] is but a veil.   30
All strength—all terror, single or in bands,
That ever was put forth in personal form—
Jehovah—with his thunder, and the choir
Of shouting Angels, and the empyreal thrones[6]—
I pass them unalarmed. Not Chaos, not   35
The darkest pit of lowest Erebus,[7]
Nor aught of blinder vacancy, scooped out
By help of dreams—can breed such fear and awe
As fall upon us often when we look
Into our Minds, into the Mind of Man—   40
My haunt, and the main region of my song.
—Beauty—a living Presence of the earth,
Surpassing the most fair ideal Forms
Which craft of delicate Spirits hath composed
From earth's materials—waits upon my steps;   45
Pitches her tents before me as I move,
An hourly neighbour. Paradise, and groves

---

2. Harmonious verse; an echo of *Paradise Lost* 5.150.
The inspiring "breath of outward circumstance" (line
11) parallels the "correspondent breeze" in the opening passage of *The Prelude*.
3. *Paradise Lost* 7.31.
4. The Muse whom Milton had invoked in *Paradise
Lost* 7.1–39.

5. In *Paradise Lost* the dwelling place, beyond the visible heaven, of God and his angels.
6. Cf. *Paradise Lost* 2.430: "O progeny of Heaven, empyreal thrones!"
7. In classical myth, a dark region of the underworld;
often used as a name for hell by Christian writers.

Elysian,[8] Fortunate Fields—like those of old
Sought in the Atlantic Main—why should they be
A history only of departed things,   50
Or a mere fiction of what never was?
For the discerning intellect of Man,
When wedded to this goodly universe
In love and holy passion, shall find these
A simple produce of the common day.   55
—I, long before the blissful hour arrives,
Would chant, in lonely peace, the spousal[9] verse
Of this great consummation:—and, by words
Which speak of nothing more than what we are,
Would I arouse the sensual from their sleep   60
Of Death, and win the vacant and the vain
To noble raptures; while my voice proclaims
How exquisitely the individual Mind
(And the progressive powers perhaps no less
Of the whole species) to the external World   65
Is fitted:—and how exquisitely, too—
Theme this but little heard of among men—
The external World is fitted to the Mind;
And the creation (by no lower name
Can it be called) which they with blended might   70
Accomplish:—this is our high argument.[1]
—Such grateful haunts foregoing, if I oft
Must turn elsewhere—to travel near the tribes
And fellowships of men, and see ill sights
Of madding passions mutually inflamed;   75
Must hear Humanity in fields and groves
Pipe solitary anguish; or must hang
Brooding above the fierce confederate storm
Of sorrow, barricadoed[2] evermore
Within the walls of cities—may these sounds   80
Have their authentic comment; that even these
Hearing, I be not downcast or forlorn!—
Descend, prophetic Spirit! that inspir'st
The human Soul of universal earth,
Dreaming on things to come;[3] and dost possess   85
A metropolitan temple[4] in the hearts
Of mighty Poets; upon me bestow
A gift of genuine insight; that my Song
With star-like virtue in its place may shine,
Shedding benignant influence, and secure,   90
Itself, from all malevolent effect

---

8. Elysium, in Greek myth, was the place where mortals favored by the gods live a happy life after death.
It was sometimes identified with the "Islands of the
Blessed," reputed to be located far out in the western
sea—hence "sought in the Atlantic Main" (line 49).
See Horace, *Epodes* 16.
9. Marital; hence a "spousal verse" is an epithalamion —a poem written to celebrate a marriage.

1. Theme, as in *Paradise Lost* 1.24: "the height of this
great argument."
2. Barricaded, as in *Paradise Lost* 8.241: "Fast we
found, fast shut / The dismal gates, and barricadoed
strong."
3. Cf. Shakespeare, Sonnet 107: "the prophetic soul /
Of the wide world dreaming on things to come."
4. The primary church of a religion.

Of those mutations that extend their sway
Throughout the nether sphere![5]—And if with this
I mix more lowly matter; with the thing
Contemplated, describe the Mind and Man   95
Contemplating; and who, and what he was—
The transitory Being that beheld
This Vision; when and where, and how he lived;[6]—
Be not this labour useless. If such theme
May sort with highest objects, then—dread Power!   100
Whose gracious favour is the primal source
Of all illumination—may my Life
Express the image of a better time,
More wise desires, and simpler manners;—nurse
My Heart in genuine freedom:—all pure thoughts   105
Be with me;—so shall thy unfailing love
Guide, and support, and cheer me to the end!

ca. 1798–1814   1814

The Prelude

The Prelude is Wordsworth's crowning achievement, the greatest and most original long poem since Milton's *Paradise Lost*. Its existence, however, was unknown to the public until after Wordsworth's death in 1850. When, three months later, *The Prelude* was published from manuscript by Wordsworth's literary executors, its title was given to it by the poet's wife; Wordsworth himself had referred to it variously as "the poem to Coleridge," "the poem on the growth of my own mind," and "the poem on my own poetical education."

For some seventy-five years this posthumous publication of 1850 was the only known text of *The Prelude*. Then in 1926 Ernest de Selincourt, working from manuscripts, printed an earlier version of the poem that Wordsworth had completed in 1805. Since that time other scholars have established the existence of a still earlier and much shorter version of *The Prelude*, in two parts, which Wordsworth had composed in 1798–99. The following seems to have been the process of composition that produced the three principal versions of the poem:

1. The *Two-Part Prelude* of 1799. Wordsworth originally planned, early in 1798, to include an account of his development as a poet in his projected but never-completed philosophical poem *The Recluse* (see the Prospectus to *The Recluse*, p. 1397, n. 1). While living in Germany during the autumn and winter of 1798–99, he composed a number of passages about his early experiences with nature. What had been intended to be part of *The Recluse*, however, quickly evolved into an independent autobiographical poem, and by late 1799, when Wordsworth settled with his sister, Dorothy, at Grasmere, he had written a poem in two parts, 978 lines in length, which takes his life from infancy, through his years at Hawkshead School, to the age of seventeen. This poem corresponds, by and large, to the contents of books 1 and 2 of the later versions of *The Prelude*.

2. The 1805 *Prelude*. Late in 1801 Wordsworth began to expand the poem on his poetic life, and in 1804 he set to work intensively on the project. His initial plan was to write it in five books. Before he completed the five-book poem, however, he

---

5. In the Ptolemaic world picture, the spheres of the heavenly bodies were immutable, and only the earth (the "nether sphere," or region below the sphere of the moon) was subject to change. Cf. *Paradise Lost* 7.375

and 10.656–64.
6. Wordsworth thus justifies *The Prelude* and the autobiographical sections of *The Recluse*.

decided to enlarge it still further, to incorporate an account of his experiences in France and of his mental crisis after the failure of his hopes in the French Revolution, and to end the poem with his settlement at Grasmere and his taking up the great task of *The Recluse*. He completed this poem, in thirteen books, in May 1805. This is the version that Wordsworth read to Coleridge after the latter's return from Malta (see Coleridge's *To William Wordsworth*, pp. 1527–30).

3. The 1850 *Prelude*. For the next thirty-five years Wordsworth tinkered with the text, polishing the style and qualifying some of its radical statements about the divine sufficiency of the human mind in its communion with nature; he did not, however, in any essential way alter its subject matter or overall design. *The Prelude* that was published in July 1850 is in fourteen books and was printed from a fair copy; it incorporated Wordsworth's latest revisions, which had been made in 1839, as well as some alterations introduced by his literary executors. The selections printed here are from the manuscript of this final version. Our reasons for choosing this version are set forth in Jack Stillinger's "Textual Primitivism and the Editing of Wordsworth," *Studies in Romanticism* 28 (1989): 3–28.

When Wordsworth enlarged the two-part *Prelude* of 1799, he not only made it a poem of epic length but also heightened the style and introduced various thematic parallels with earlier epics, especially *Paradise Lost*. (For a central example, see Wordsworth's version of Milton's enterprise to "justify the ways of God to men," in 14.162–70, p. 1478, and 14.384–89, p. 1480.) The expanded poem, however, is a personal history that turns on a mental crisis and recovery, and for such a narrative design the chief prototype is not the classical or Christian epic, but the spiritual autobiography of crisis. St. Augustine's *Confessions* established this great Christian form late in the fourth century, and it has had an uninterrupted history in European literature ever since. Among the scores of prose versions of the spiritual autobiography are the Catholic Dante's *Vita Nuova (The New Life)* and the Puritan Bunyan's *Grace Abounding to the Chief of Sinners*. Its greatest poetic instance is Dante's *Divine Comedy*, an allegorical account of the narrator's spiritual journey from earth through hell, purgatory, and paradise, back to earth.

As in *The Divine Comedy*, and in Augustine's *Confessions* itself, Wordsworth's recurrent metaphor is that of a journey, whose end—as T. S. Eliot put it in *Four Quartets*, his adaptation of the same form—is in its beginning, and in which it turns out that the end of the journey is "to arrive where we started / And know the place for the first time" (see the Quartet *Little Gidding*, lines 241–42, p. 2488). Wordsworth's *Prelude* opens with a literal journey whose chosen goal (1.72, 106–07) is "a known Vale whither my feet should turn"—that is, the Vale of Grasmere. There are a number of later journeys, of which the most important are the crossing of the Alps in book 6 and, at the beginning of the final book, the ascent of Mount Snowdon, which culminates in a definitive vision. In the course of the poem, however, such literal journeys become the metaphoric vehicle for an interior journey in a quest, both within the poet's memory and in his poetic enterprise itself, for his lost early self and his proper spiritual home. The poem ends by adverting to its own beginning, and leaves the poet at home in the Vale of Grasmere, ready finally to begin his great enterprise, *The Recluse* (14.302–11, 374–85).

In reading *The Prelude* as autobiography, we too easily overlook its traditional aspects in both voice and form; and in our understandable preoccupation with its great poetic moments we are apt to neglect the artistry of its overall structure. Although the narrator is the actual Wordsworth, addressing himself both to his friend Coleridge and to the English people of his own troubled age, he adopts a personal and a prophetic stance that goes back through Milton and Spenser to the poets and prophets of the Bible. And although the separate episodes are events from Wordsworth's own life, he does not describe these events as they had seemed to him at the time, but as they are interpreted in distant retrospect, reordered in sequence, and shaped into the inherited design of crisis and recovery, from which the author emerges as a different self in a transformed world.

Wordsworth, however, changes the Christian spiritual history in a radical way: he converts what had earlier been the supernatural agencies of its providential plot into secular and humanistic terms. The true protagonist in Wordsworth's poem turns out, in fact, to be a power of his own mind, which is capable of transforming the natural world with which it interacts; he calls this power "Imagination." "This faculty," he reveals in the last book (14.193ff.), "hath been the feeding source / Of our long labor," and he goes on to say that the account of its appearance, development, loss, and restoration has constituted the submerged plot of the poem in its entirety. *The Prelude* has justly been called the greatest religious poem of the nineteenth century. Its religion, however, despite some pious phrases and passages that Wordsworth cautiously inserted into the 1850 text, is not an inherited creed, nor even a religion of Nature, but rather a faith in the redeeming power of "the mind of man" which, the closing lines declare, compared with the unchanging earth, is "In beauty exalted, as it is itself / Of quality and fabric more divine."

The text reprinted here is that established from the surviving printer's copy by W. J. B. Owen in the Cornell Wordsworth volume, *The Fourteen-Book Prelude* (1985).

From THE PRELUDE
or
GROWTH OF A POET'S MIND

AN AUTOBIOGRAPHICAL POEM

Book First
Introduction, Childhood, and School-time

O there is blessing in this gentle breeze,
A visitant that, while he fans my cheek,
Doth seem half-conscious of the joy he brings
From the green fields, and from yon azure sky.
Whate'er his mission, the soft breeze can come   5
To none more grateful than to me; escaped
From the vast City,[1] where I long have pined
A discontented Sojourner—Now free,
Free as a bird to settle where I will.
What dwelling shall receive me? in what vale   10
Shall be my harbour? underneath what grove
Shall I take up my home? and what clear stream
Shall with its murmur lull me into rest?
The earth is all before me:[2] with a heart
Joyous, nor scared at its own liberty,   15
I look about; and should the chosen guide

1. London. Wordsworth uses this city as a type representing a place of spiritual bondage from which he has finally escaped.
2. One of many echoes from *Paradise Lost*, where the line is applied to Adam and Eve as, at the conclusion of the poem, they begin their new life after being expelled from Eden: "The world was all before them" (12.646).

Be nothing better than a wandering cloud,
I cannot miss my way. I breathe again;
Trances of thought and mountings of the heart
Come fast upon me: it is shaken off,   20
That burthen of my own unnatural self,
The heavy weight of many a weary day
Not mine, and such as were not made for me.
Long months of peace (if such bold word accord
With any promises of human life),   25
Long months of ease and undisturbed delight
Are mine in prospect; whither shall I turn,
By road or pathway, or through trackless field,
Up hill or down, or shall some floating thing
Upon the River point me out my course?   30
Dear Liberty! Yet what would it avail,
But for a gift that consecrates the joy?
For I, methought, while the sweet breath of heaven
Was blowing on my body, felt, within,
A correspondent breeze, that gently moved   35
With quickening virtue,[3] but is now become
A tempest, a redundant[4] energy,
Vexing its own creation. Thanks to both,
And their congenial[5] powers that, while they join
In breaking up a long continued frost,   40
Bring with them vernal promises, the hope
Of active days urged on by flying hours;
Days of sweet leisure taxed with patient thought
Abstruse, nor wanting punctual service high,
Matins and vespers, of harmonious verse![6]   45
    Thus far, O Friend![7] did I, not used to make
A present joy the matter of a Song,[8]
Pour forth, that day, my soul in measured strains,
That would not be forgotten, and are here
Recorded:—to the open fields I told   50
A prophecy:—poetic numbers came
Spontaneously, to clothe in priestly robe
A renovated Spirit singled out,

3. Revivifying power. ("To quicken" is to give or
restore life.)
4. Abundant, exuberant.
5. Kindred.
6. I.e., verses equivalent to morning prayers (matins)
and evening prayers (vespers). The opening passage
(lines 1–45), which Wordsworth calls in book 7, line 4,
a "glad preamble," replaces the traditional epic device,
such as Milton had adopted in Paradise Lost, of an
opening prayer to the Muse for inspiration. To be
"inspired," in the literal sense, is to be breathed or
blown into by a divinity (in Latin spirare means both
"to breathe" and "to blow"). Wordsworth begins his
poem with a "blessing" from an outer "breeze," which
(lines 34–45) is called the "breath of heaven" and
evokes in him a correspondent inner breeze that sig-
nalizes a springlike revival of his spirit after a wintry

season, and also a burst of poetic power that he goes on
to equate (lines 50–54) with the utterances of biblical
prophets when inspired by the Holy Spirit. The revivifying breeze and breath, at once material and spiritual,
recurs later in The Prelude as a kind of leitmotif. It
also serves as the radical metaphor of other Romantic
poems such as Coleridge's Eolian Harp and Dejection:
An Ode, and Shelley's Ode to the West Wind.
7. Samuel Taylor Coleridge, to whom Wordsworth
addresses the whole of the Prelude. For Coleridge's
response, after the poem was read to him, see To William Wordsworth (pp. 1527–30).
8. In the Preface to Lyrical Ballads Wordsworth says
that his poetry usually originates in "emotion recollected in tranquillity"; hence not, as in the preceding
preamble, during the experience that it records.

Such hope was mine, for holy services:
My own voice cheered me, and, far more, the mind's   55
Internal echo of the imperfect sound;
To both I listened, drawing from them both
A chearful confidence in things to come.
   Content, and not unwilling now to give
A respite to this passion, I paced on   60
With brisk and eager steps; and came at length
To a green shady place where down I sate
Beneath a tree, slackening my thoughts by choice,
And settling into gentler happiness.
'Twas Autumn, and a clear and placid day,   65
With warmth, as much as needed, from a sun
Two hours declined towards the west, a day
With silver clouds, and sunshine on the grass,
And, in the sheltered and the sheltering grove,
A perfect stillness. Many were the thoughts   70
Encouraged and dismissed, till choice was made
Of a known Vale whither my feet should turn,[9]
Nor rest till they had reached the very door
Of the one Cottage which methought I saw.
No picture of mere memory ever looked   75
So fair; and while upon the fancied scene
I gazed with growing love, a higher power
Than Fancy gave assurance of some work
Of glory, there forthwith to be begun,
Perhaps too there performed.[1] Thus long I mused,   80
Nor e'er lost sight of what I mused upon,
Save where, amid the stately grove of Oaks,
Now here—now there—an acorn, from its cup
Dislodged, through sere leaves rustled, or at once
To the bare earth dropped with a startling sound.   85
   From that soft couch I rose not, till the sun
Had almost touched the horizon; casting then
A backward glance upon the curling cloud
Of city smoke, by distance ruralized,
Keen as a Truant or a Fugitive,   90
But as a Pilgrim resolute, I took,
Even with the chance equipment of that hour,
The road that pointed tow'rd the chosen Vale.
   It was a splendid evening: and my Soul
Once more made trial of her strength, nor lacked   95
Eolian visitations;[2] but the harp
Was soon defrauded, and the banded host
Of harmony dispersed in straggling sounds;
And lastly utter silence! "Be it so;

---

9. Grasmere, where Wordsworth settled with his sister, Dorothy, in December 1799. Wordsworth uses his walk to that "Vale" to symbolize a new stage in the journey of his life—a stage in which he returns to what he calls (in the title of the opening book of *The Recluse*, designed to follow *The Prelude*) "Home at Grasmere."

1. I.e., *The Recluse*, which Wordsworth planned to be his major poetic work.
2. Influences to which his soul responded as an Eolian harp responds to gusts of a breeze. For a description of this instrument, see Coleridge's *The Eolian Harp*, pp. 1484–85, n. 1.

Why think of any thing but present good?"   100
So, like a Home-bound Labourer, I pursued
My way, beneath the mellowing sun, that shed
Mild influence;[3] nor left in me one wish
Again to bend the sabbath of that time[4]
To a servile yoke. What need of many words?   105
A pleasant loitering journey, through three days
Continued, brought me to my hermitage.
I spare to tell of what ensued, the life
In common things,—the endless store of things
Rare, or at least so seeming, every day   110
Found all about me in one neighbourhood;
The self-congratulation,[5] and from morn
To night unbroken cheerfulness serene.
But speedily an earnest longing rose
To brace myself to some determined aim,   115
Reading or thinking; either to lay up
New stores, or rescue from decay the old
By timely interference: and therewith
Came hopes still higher, that with outward life
I might endue some airy phantasies   120
That had been floating loose about for years;
And to such Beings temperately deal forth
The many feelings that oppressed my heart.
That hope hath been discouraged; welcome light
Dawns from the East, but dawns—to disappear   125
And mock me with a sky that ripens not
Into a steady morning: if my mind,
Remembering the bold promise of the past,
Would gladly grapple with some noble theme,
Vain is her wish: where'er she turns, she finds   130
Impediments from day to day renewed.
      And now it would content me to yield up
Those lofty hopes awhile for present gifts
Of humbler industry. But, O dear Friend!
The Poet, gentle Creature as he is,   135
Hath, like the Lover, his unruly times,
His fits when he is neither sick nor well,
Though no distress be near him but his own
Unmanageable thoughts: his mind, best pleas'd
While she, as duteous as the Mother Dove,   140
Sits brooding,[6] lives not always to that end,
But, like the innocent Bird, hath goadings on
That drive her, as in trouble, through the groves:
With me is now such passion, to be blamed
No otherwise than as it lasts too long.   145

---

3. *Paradise Lost* 7.374–75: "The Pleiades [a cluster of
stars] before him danced / Shedding sweet influence."
"Influence" is an astrological term for the effect of stars
on human life.
4. That time of rest.

5. Self-rejoicing.
6. An echo of Milton's reference in *Paradise Lost* to
the original act of creation in his invocation to the
Holy Spirit: Thou "Dovelike satst brooding on the vast
Abyss / And mad'st it pregnant" (1.21–22).

When as becomes a Man who would prepare
For such an arduous Work, I through myself
Make rigorous inquisition, the report
Is often chearing; for I neither seem
To lack that first great gift, the vital Soul,   150
Nor general Truths, which are themselves a sort
Of Elements and Agents, Under-powers,
Subordinate helpers of the living Mind:
Nor am I naked of external things,
Forms, images, nor numerous other aids   155
Of less regard, though won perhaps with toil,
And needful to build up a Poet's praise.
Time, place, and manners do I seek, and these
Are found in plenteous store, but no where such
As may be singled out with steady choice: 160
No little band of yet remembered names
Whom I in perfect confidence might hope
To summon back from lonesome banishment,
And make them dwellers in the hearts of men
Now living, or to live in future years.   165
Sometimes the ambitious Power of choice, mistaking
Proud spring-tide swellings for a regular sea,
Will settle on some British theme, some old
Romantic Tale by Milton left unsung:[7]
More often turning to some gentle place   170
Within the groves of Chivalry, I pipe
To Shepherd Swains, or seated, harp in hand,
Amid reposing knights by a River side
Or fountain, listen to the grave reports
Of dire enchantments faced, and overcome   175
By the strong mind, and Tales of warlike feats
Where spear encountered spear, and sword with sword
Fought, as if conscious of the blazonry
That the shield bore, so glorious was the strife;
Whence inspiration for a song that winds   180
Through ever changing scenes of votive quest,[8]
Wrongs to redress, harmonious tribute paid
To patient courage and unblemished truth,
To firm devotion, zeal unquenchable,
And Christian meekness hallowing faithful loves.[9]   185
Sometimes, more sternly moved, I would relate
How vanquished Mithridates northward passed,
And, hidden in the cloud of years, became
Odin, the Father of a Race by whom
Perished the Roman Empire;[1] how the friends   190

---

7. In *Paradise Lost* 9.24–41 Milton relates that, in
seeking a subject for his epic poem, he rejected "fabled
Knights" and medieval romance.
8. A quest undertaken to fulfill a vow.
9. An echo of the prefatory statement to Spenser's
Faerie Queene, line 9: "Fierce warres and faithfull
loves shall moralize my song."
1. Mithridates VI, king of Pontus, was defeated by the
Roman Pompey in 66 B.C. In chap. 10 of his *Decline
and Fall of the Roman Empire*, Edward Gibbon associates him with Odin, a chieftain of the Goths, who
hoped to produce descendants who would wreak
revenge upon the conquering Romans. All the protagonists that Wordsworth considered for his poem were
heroes in fights against tyranny.

And followers of Sertorius, out of Spain
Flying, found shelter in the Fortunate Isles;
And left their usages, their arts, and laws
To disappear by a slow gradual death;
To dwindle and to perish, one by one,   195
Starved in those narrow bounds: but not the soul
Of Liberty, which fifteen hundred years
Survived, and, when the European came
With skill and power that might not be withstood,
Did, like a pestilence, maintain its hold,   200
And wasted down by glorious death that Race
Of natural Heroes;[2]—or I would record
How, in tyrannic times, some high-souled Man,
Unnamed among the chronicles of Kings,
Suffered in silence for truth's sake: or tell   205
How that one Frenchman, through continued force
Of meditation on the inhuman deeds
Of those who conquered first the Indian isles,
Went, single in his ministry, across
The Ocean;—not to comfort the Oppressed,   210
But, like a thirsty wind, to roam about,
Withering the Oppressor:[3]—how Gustavus sought
Help at his need in Dalecarlia's mines:[4]
How Wallace fought for Scotland,[5] left the name
Of Wallace to be found, like a wild flower,   215
All over his dear Country, left the deeds
Of Wallace, like a family of Ghosts,
To people the steep rocks and river banks,
Her natural sanctuaries, with a local soul
Of independence and stern liberty.   220
Sometimes it suits me better to invent
A Tale from my own heart, more near akin
To my own passions, and habitual thoughts,
Some variegated Story, in the main
Lofty, but the unsubstantial Structure melts   225
Before the very sun that brightens it,
Mist into air dissolving! Then, a wish,
My last and favourite aspiration, mounts,
With yearning, tow'rds some philosophic Song
Of Truth[6] that cherishes our daily life;   230
With meditations passionate, from deep
Recesses in man's heart, immortal verse
Thoughtfully fitted to the Orphean lyre;[7]

2. Sertorius, a Roman general allied with Mithridates, fought off the armies of Pompey and others until he was assassinated in 72 B.C. There is a legend that after his death his followers, to escape Roman tyranny, fled from Spain to the Canary Islands (known in ancient times as "the Fortunate Isles," line 192), where their descendants flourished until subjugated and decimated by invading Spaniards late in the 15th century.
3. "Dominique de Gourges, a French gentleman who went in 1568 to Florida to avenge the massacre of the French by the Spaniards there" [footnote in The Pre-

lude of 1850].
4. Gustavus I of Sweden; in the 16th century he mustered supporters in Dalecarlia, a mining district, to help free Sweden from the tyranny of Denmark.
5. William Wallace, the Scottish national hero, fought against the English until captured and executed in 1305.
6. I.e., The Recluse.
7. The lyre of Orpheus. In Greek myth Orpheus was able to enchant not only human listeners but the natural world by his singing and playing.

But from this awful burthen I full soon
Take refuge, and beguile myself with trust   235
That mellower years will bring a riper mind
And clearer insight. Thus my days are passed
In contradiction; with no skill to part
Vague longing, haply bred by want of power,
From paramount impulse—not to be withstood;   240
A timorous capacity from prudence;
From circumspection, infinite delay.[8]
Humility and modest awe themselves
Betray me, serving often for a cloke
To a more subtile selfishness; that now   245
Locks every function up in blank reserve,[9]
Now dupes me, trusting to an anxious eye
That with intrusive restlessness beats off
Simplicity, and self-presented truth.
    Ah! better far than this, to stray about   250
Voluptuously,[1] through fields and rural walks,
And ask no record of the hours, resigned
To vacant musing, unreproved neglect
Of all things, and deliberate holiday:
Far better never to have heard the name   255
Of zeal and just ambition, than to live
Baffled and plagued by a mind that every hour
Turns recreant to her task, takes heart again,
Then feels immediately some hollow thought
Hang like an interdict[2] upon her hopes.   260
This is my lot; for either still I find
Some imperfection in the chosen theme;
Or see of absolute accomplishment
Much wanting, so much wanting, in myself
That I recoil and droop, and seek repose   265
In listlessness from vain perplexity;
Unprofitably travelling toward the grave,
Like a false Steward who hath much received,
And renders nothing back.[3]
                                Was it for this[4]
That one, the fairest of all rivers, loved   270
To blend his murmurs with my Nurse's song;
And, from his alder shades and rocky falls,
And from his fords and shallows, sent a voice
That flowed along my dreams? For this didst Thou,
O Derwent! winding among grassy holms[5]   275
Where I was looking on, a Babe in arms,

---

8. The syntax is complex and inverted; in outline, the sense of lines 238–42 seems to be, to put it shortly: "With no ability ('skill') to distinguish between vague desire (perhaps resulting from lack of power) and ruling impulse; between timidity and prudence; between endless delay and carefulness ('circumspection')."
9. Absolute inaction.

1. Luxuriously, sensuously.
2. Prohibition (pronounced "interdite").
3. The reference is to the parable of the false steward in Matthew 25.14–30.
4. The *Two-Part Prelude* that Wordsworth wrote in 1798–99 begins at this point.
5. Flat ground next to a river.

Make ceaseless music, that composed my thoughts
To more than infant softness, giving me,
Amid the fretful dwellings of mankind,
A foretaste, a dim earnest, of the calm   280
That Nature breathes among the hills and groves?
    When he had left the mountains, and received
On his smooth breast the shadow of those Towers
That yet survive, a shattered Monument
Of feudal sway, the bright blue River passed   285
Along the margin of our Terrace Walk;[6]
A tempting Playmate whom we dearly loved.
O many a time have I, a five years' Child,
In a small mill-race severed from his stream,
Made one long bathing of a summer's day;   290
Basked in the sun, and plunged, and basked again,
Alternate all a summer's day, or scoured[7]
The sandy fields, leaping through flow'ry groves
Of yellow ragwort; or when rock and hill,
The woods and distant Skiddaw's[8] lofty height,   295
Were bronzed with deepest radiance, stood alone
Beneath the sky, as if I had been born
On Indian plains, and from my Mother's hut
Had run abroad in wantonness, to sport,
A naked Savage, in the thunder shower.   300
    Fair seed-time had my soul, and I grew up
Fostered alike by beauty and by fear;[9]
Much favoured in my birth-place, and no less
In that beloved Vale[1] to which erelong
We were transplanted—there were we let loose   305
For sports of wider range. Ere I had told
Ten birth-days, when among the mountain slopes
Frost, and the breath of frosty wind, had snapped
The last autumnal Crocus, 'twas my joy,
With store of Springes[2] o'er my Shoulder slung,   310
To range the open heights where woodcocks ran
Along the smooth green turf. Through half the night,
Scudding away from snare to snare, I plied
That anxious visitation;—moon and stars
Were shining o'er my head; I was alone,   315
And seemed to be a trouble to the peace
That dwelt among them. Sometimes it befel,
In these night-wanderings, that a strong desire
O'erpowered my better reason, and the Bird

6. The Derwent River flows by Cockermouth Castle and then past the garden terrace behind Wordsworth's father's house in Cockermouth, Cumberland.
7. Run swiftly over.
8. A mountain nine miles east of Cockermouth.
9. Wordsworth introduces here a dialectic that plays a central role in the evolution of *The Prelude*. He represents his mind, confronting nature, as fostered in its growth by two antithetic principles, one associated with love and the other with fear. These principles cor-respond to the two main categories, "the beautiful" and "the sublime," into which theorists of the landscape during the preceding century had classified the anti-thetic aspects of the natural scene (see, e.g., 1.351–56, 466–75, 546). In the concluding book (in 14.162–70), this antithesis is finally resolved (see p. 1478, n. 4).
1. The valley of Esthwaite, the location of Hawkshead, where Wordsworth attended school.
2. Bird snares.

Which was the Captive of another's toil[3]   320
Became my prey; and when the deed was done
I heard, among the solitary hills,
Low breathings coming after me, and sounds
Of undistinguishable motion, steps
Almost as silent as the turf they trod.   325
     Nor less, when Spring had warmed the cultured[4] Vale,
Roved we as plunderers where the Mother-bird
Had in high places built her lodge; though mean
Our object, and inglorious, yet the end[5]
Was not ignoble. Oh! when I have hung   330
Above the Raven's nest, by knots of grass
And half-inch fissures in the slippery rock
But ill-sustained; and almost (so it seemed)
Suspended by the blast that blew amain,
Shouldering the naked crag; Oh, at that time,   335
While on the perilous ridge I hung alone,
With what strange utterance did the loud dry wind
Blow through my ears! the sky seemed not a sky
Of earth, and with what motion moved the clouds!
     Dust as we are, the immortal Spirit grows   340
Like harmony in music; there is a dark
Inscrutable workmanship that reconciles
Discordant elements, makes them cling together
In one society. How strange that all
The terrors, pains, and early miseries,   345
Regrets, vexations, lassitudes, interfused
Within my mind, should e'er have borne a part,
And that a needful part, in making up
The calm existence that is mine when I
Am worthy of myself! Praise to the end!   350
Thanks to the means which Nature deigned to employ!
Whether her fearless visitings or those
That came with soft alarm like hurtless lightning
Opening the peaceful clouds, or she would use
Severer interventions, ministry   355
More palpable, as best might suit her aim.[6]
     One summer evening (led by her) I found
A little Boat tied to a Willow-tree
Within a rocky cave, its usual home.
Straight I unloosed her chain, and, stepping in,   360
Pushed from the shore. It was an act of stealth
And troubled pleasure, nor without the voice
Of mountain-echoes did my Boat move on,
Leaving behind her still, on either side,
Small circles glittering idly in the moon,   365
Until they melted all into one track
Of sparkling light. But now, like one who rows
(Proud of his skill) to reach a chosen point

3. "Snare," or "labor."
4. Cultivated.
5. Outcome.

6. A restatement of the double ministry of nature described in line 302; what follows is a second example of discipline by fear.

With an unswerving line, I fixed my view
Upon the summit of a craggy ridge, 370
The horizon's utmost boundary; for above
Was nothing but the stars and the grey sky.
She was an elfin Pinnace;[7] lustily
I dipped my oars into the silent lake;
And, as I rose upon the stroke, my boat 375
Went heaving through the Water like a swan:
When, from behind that craggy Steep, till then
The horizon's bound, a huge peak, black and huge,
As if with voluntary power instinct,[8]
Upreared its head.[9]—I struck, and struck again, 380
And, growing still in stature, the grim Shape
Towered up between me and the stars, and still,
For so it seemed, with purpose of its own
And measured motion, like a living Thing
Strode after me. With trembling oars I turned, 385
And through the silent water stole my way
Back to the Covert of the Willow-tree;
There, in her mooring-place, I left my Bark,—
And through the meadows homeward went, in grave
And serious mood; but after I had seen 390
That spectacle, for many days, my brain
Worked with a dim and undetermined sense
Of unknown modes of being; o'er my thoughts
There hung a darkness, call it solitude
Or blank desertion. No familiar Shapes 395
Remained, no pleasant images of trees,
Of sea or Sky, no colours of green fields,
But huge and mighty Forms, that do not live
Like living men, moved slowly through the mind
By day, and were a trouble to my dreams. 400
    Wisdom and Spirit of the Universe!
Thou Soul that art the eternity of thought,
That giv'st to forms and images a breath
And everlasting Motion! not in vain,
By day or star-light, thus from my first dawn 405
Of Childhood didst thou intertwine for me
The passions that build up our human Soul,
Not with the mean and vulgar[1] works of man,
But with high objects, with enduring things,
With life and nature, purifying thus 410
The elements of feeling and of thought,
And sanctifying, by such discipline,
Both pain and fear; until we recognize
A grandeur in the beatings of the heart.
    Nor was this fellowship vouchsafed to me 415

7. Small boat.
8. Endowed.
9. In order to direct his boat in a straight line, the rower (sitting facing the stern of the boat) has fixed his eye on a point on the ridge above the nearby shore, which blocks out the landscape behind. As he moves farther out, the black peak rises into his altering angle of vision and seems to stride closer with each stroke of the oars.
1. Commonplace.

With stinted kindness. In November days
When vapours, rolling down the valley, made
A lonely scene more lonesome; among woods
At noon, and 'mid the calm of summer nights,
When, by the margin of the trembling Lake,   420
Beneath the gloomy hills homeward I went
In solitude, such intercourse was mine:
Mine was it, in the fields both day and night,
And by the waters, all the summer long.
    —And in the frosty season, when the sun   425
Was set, and visible for many a mile,
The cottage windows blazed through twilight gloom,
I heeded not their summons;—happy time
It was indeed for all of us; for me
It was a time of rapture!—Clear and loud   430
The village Clock toll'd six—I wheeled about,
Proud and exulting like an untired horse
That cares not for his home.—All shod with steel,
We hissed along the polished ice, in games
Confederate, imitative of the chase   435
And woodland pleasures,—the resounding horn,
The Pack loud-chiming and the hunted hare.
So through the darkness and the cold we flew,
And not a voice was idle: with the din
Smitten, the precipices rang aloud;   440
The leafless trees and every icy crag
Tinkled like iron; while far distant hills
Into the tumult sent an alien sound
Of melancholy, not unnoticed while the stars,
Eastward, were sparkling clear, and in the west   445
The orange sky of evening died away.
Not seldom from the uproar I retired
Into a silent bay,—or sportively
Glanced sideway,[2] leaving the tumultous throng
To cut across the reflex[3] of a star   450
That fled, and, flying still before me, gleamed
Upon the glassy plain: and oftentimes,
When we had given our bodies to the wind,
And all the shadowy banks on either side
Came sweeping through the darkness, spinning still   455
The rapid line of motion, then at once
Have I, reclining back upon my heels,
Stopped short; yet still the solitary cliffs
Wheeled by me—even as if the earth had rolled
With visible motion her diurnal[4] round!   460
Behind me did they stretch in solemn train,[5]
Feebler and feebler, and I stood and watched
Till all was tranquil as a dreamless sleep.
    Ye presences of Nature, in the sky,

2. Moved off obliquely.   4. Daily.
3. Reflection.   5. Succession.

And on the earth! Ye visions of the hills!   465
And Souls of lonely places![6] can I think
A vulgar hope was yours when ye employed
Such ministry, when ye, through many a year,
Haunting me thus among my boyish sports,
On caves and trees, upon the woods and hills,   470
Impressed upon all forms the characters[7]
Of danger or desire; and thus did make
The surface of the universal earth
With triumph and delight, with hope and fear,
Work[8] like a sea?
                Not uselessly employed,   475
Might I pursue this theme through every change
Of exercise and play, to which the year
Did summon us in his delightful round.
   —We were a noisy crew; the sun in heaven
Beheld not vales more beautiful than ours,   480
Nor saw a Band in happiness and joy
Richer, or worthier of the ground they trod.
I could record with no reluctant voice
The woods of Autumn, and their hazel bowers
With milk-white clusters hung; the rod and line,   485
True symbol of hope's foolishness, whose strong
And unreproved enchantment led us on,
By rocks and pools shut out from every star
All the green summer, to forlorn cascades
Among the windings hid of mountain brooks.   490
  —Unfading recollections! at this hour
The heart is almost mine with which I felt,
From some hill-top on sunny afternoons,
The paper-Kite, high among fleecy clouds,
Pull at her rein, like an impatient Courser;   495
Or, from the meadows sent on gusty days,
Beheld her breast the wind, then suddenly
Dashed headlong, and rejected by the storm.
   Ye lowly Cottages in which we dwelt,
A ministration of your own was yours!   500
Can I forget you, being as ye were
So beautiful among the pleasant fields
In which ye stood? or can I here forget
The plain and seemly countenance with which
Ye dealt out your plain Comforts? Yet had ye   505
Delights and exultations of your own.
Eager and never weary, we pursued
Our home-amusements by the warm peat-fire
At evening, when with pencil, and smooth slate
In square divisions parcelled out, and all   510
With crosses and with cyphers scribbled o'er,

6. Wordsworth refers both to a single "Spirit" or   various parts of the universe.
"Soul" of the universe as a whole (e.g., lines 401–02)   7. Signs.
and to plural "Presences" and "Souls" inanimating the   8. Seethe.

We schemed and puzzled, head opposed to head,
In strife too humble to be named in verse;[9]
Or round the naked table, snow-white deal,[1]
Cherry, or maple, sate in close array,   515
And to the Combat, Lu or Whist, led on
A thick-ribbed Army, not as in the world
Neglected and ungratefully thrown by
Even for the very service they had wrought,
But husbanded through many a long campaign.   520
Uncouth assemblage was it, where no few
Had changed their functions; some, plebeian cards
Which Fate, beyond the promise of their birth,
Had dignified, and called to represent
The Persons of departed Potentates.   525
Oh, with what echoes on the board they fell!
Ironic diamonds; Clubs, Hearts, Diamonds, Spades,
A congregation piteously akin!
Cheap matter offered they to boyish wit,
Those sooty Knaves, precipitated down   530
With scoffs and taunts like Vulcan out of heaven;[2]
The paramount Ace, a moon in her eclipse,
Queens gleaming through their Splendor's last decay,
And Monarchs surly at the wrongs sustained
By royal visages.[3] Meanwhile abroad   535
Incessant rain was falling, or the frost
Raged bitterly, with keen and silent tooth;
And, interrupting oft that eager game,
From under Esthwaite's splitting fields of ice
The pent-up air, struggling to free itself,   540
Gave out to meadow-grounds and hills, a loud
Protracted yelling, like the noise of wolves
Howling in Troops along the Bothnic Main.[4]
        Nor, sedulous[5] as I have been to trace
How Nature by extrinsic passion first   545
Peopled the mind with forms sublime or fair[6]
And made me love them, may I here omit
How other pleasures have been mine, and joys
Of subtler origin; how I have felt,
Not seldom even in that tempestuous time,   550
Those hallowed and pure motions of the sense
Which seem, in their simplicity, to own
An intellectual[7] charm;—that calm delight
Which, if I err not, surely must belong

9. I.e., ticktacktoe. By his phrasing in this passage, Wordsworth pokes fun at 18th-century poetic diction, which avoided homely terms by using circumlocutions.
1. Pine, or fir.
2. Vulcan was the Roman god of fire and forge. His mother, Hera, when he was born lame, threw him down from Olympus, the abode of the gods.
3. Wordsworth implicitly parallels the boys' card games to the mock-epic description of the aristocratic game of ombre in Pope's The Rape of the Lock 3.37–98.
4. A northern gulf of the Baltic Sea.
5. Diligent.
6. The passion at first was "extrinsic" because it was felt not for nature itself but for nature as associated with the outdoor activities he loved. Wordsworth now goes on to distinguish other "subtler" pleasures, felt in the very process of sensing the natural objects.
7. Spiritual, as opposed to sense perceptions.

To those first-born[8] affinities that fit   555
Our new existence to existing things,
And, in our dawn of being, constitute
The bond of union between life and joy.
　　Yes, I remember when the changeful earth
And twice five summers on my mind had stamped   560
The faces of the moving year, even then
I held unconscious intercourse with beauty
Old as creation, drinking in a pure
Organic pleasure from the silver wreaths
Of curling mist, or from the level plain   565
Of waters, colored by impending[9] clouds.
　　The sands of Westmorland, the creeks and bays
Of Cumbria's[1] rocky limits, they can tell
How, when the Sea threw off his evening shade,
And to the Shepherd's hut on distant hills   570
Sent welcome notice of the rising moon,
How I have stood, to fancies such as these
A Stranger, linking with the Spectacle
No conscious memory of a kindred sight,
And bringing with me no peculiar sense   575
Of quietness or peace, yet have I stood,
Even while mine eye hath moved o'er many a league[2]
Of shining water, gathering, as it seemed,
Through every hair-breadth in that field of light,
New pleasure, like a bee among the flowers.   580
　　Thus oft amid those fits of vulgar[3] joy
Which, through all seasons, on a Child's pursuits
Are prompt Attendants; 'mid that giddy bliss
Which like a tempest works along the blood
And is forgotten: even then I felt   585
Gleams like the flashing of a shield,—the earth
And common face of Nature spake to me
Rememberable things; sometimes, 'tis true,
By chance collisions and quaint accidents
(Like those ill-sorted unions, work supposed   590
Of evil-minded fairies), yet not vain
Nor profitless, if haply they impressed
Collateral[4] objects and appearances,
Albeit lifeless then, and doomed to sleep
Until maturer seasons called them forth   595
To impregnate and to elevate the mind.
—And, if the vulgar joy by its own weight
Wearied itself out of the memory,
The scenes which were a witness of that joy
Remained, in their substantial lineaments   600
Depicted on the brain, and to the eye
Were visible, a daily sight: and thus

---

8. Innate.
9. Overhanging.
1. Cumberland's.

2. A league is approximately three miles.
3. Ordinary, commonplace.
4. Accompanying but subordinate.

By the impressive discipline of fear,
By pleasure and repeated happiness,
So frequently repeated, and by force   605
Of obscure feelings representative
Of things forgotten; these same scenes so bright,
So beautiful, so majestic in themselves,
Though yet the day was distant, did become
Habitually dear; and all their forms   610
And changeful colours by invisible links
Were fastened to the affections.[5]
                                    I began
My Story early, not misled, I trust,
By an infirmity of love for days
Disowned by memory,[6] fancying flowers where none,   615
Not even the sweetest, do or can survive
For him at least whose dawning day they cheered;
Nor will it seem to Thee, O Friend! so prompt
In sympathy, that I have lengthened out,
With fond and feeble tongue, a tedious tale.   620
Meanwhile, my hope has been, that I might fetch
Invigorating thoughts from former years;
Might fix the wavering balance of my mind,
And haply meet reproaches too, whose power
May spur me on, in manhood now mature,   625
To honorable toil. Yet should these hopes
Prove vain, and thus should neither I be taught
To understand myself, nor thou to know
With better knowledge how the heart was framed
Of him thou lovest, need I dread from thee   630
Harsh judgments, if the Song be loth to quit
Those recollected hours that have the charm
Of visionary things, those lovely forms
And sweet sensations that throw back our life,
And almost make remotest infancy   635
A visible scene, on which the sun is shining?
      One end at least hath been attained—my mind
Hath been revived; and, if this genial[7] mood
Desert me not, forthwith shall be brought down
Through later years the story of my life: 640
The road lies plain before me,—'tis a theme
Single, and of determined bounds; and hence
I chuse it rather, at this time, than work
Of ampler or more varied argument,
Where I might be discomfited and lost;   645
And certain hopes are with me that to thee
This labour will be welcome, honoured Friend!

5. Feelings.   no longer remember.
6. I.e., he hopes that he has not mistakenly attributed   7. Productive, creative.
his later thoughts and feelings to a time of life he can

Book Second
School-time continued

Thus far, O Friend! have we, though leaving much
Unvisited, endeavoured to retrace
The simple ways in which my childhood walked,
Those chiefly, that first led me to the love
Of rivers, woods, and fields. The passion yet   5
Was in its birth, sustained, as might befal,
By nourishment that came unsought; for still,
From week to week, from month to month, we lived
A round of tumult. Duly[1] were our games
Prolonged in summer till the day-light failed;   10
No chair remained before the doors, the bench
And threshold steps were empty; fast asleep
The Labourer, and the old Man who had sate,
A later Lingerer, yet the revelry
Continued, and the loud uproar; at last,   15
When all the ground was dark, and twinkling stars
Edged the black clouds, home and to bed we went,
Feverish, with weary joints and beating minds.
Ah! is there One who ever has been young
Nor needs a warning voice to tame the pride   20
Of intellect, and virtue's self-esteem?
One is there,[2] though the wisest and the best
Of all mankind, who covets not at times
Union that cannot be; who would not give,
If so he might, to duty and to truth   25
The eagerness of infantine desire?
A tranquillizing spirit presses now
On my corporeal frame, so wide appears
The vacancy between me and those days,
Which yet have such self-presence[3] in my mind,   30
That, musing on them, often do I seem
Two consciousnesses, conscious of myself
And of some other Being. A rude mass
Of native rock, left midway in the Square
Of our small market Village, was the goal   35
Or centre of these sports; and, when, returned
After long absence, thither I repaired,
Gone was the old grey stone, and in its place
A smart Assembly-room usurped the ground
That had been ours.[4] There let the fiddle scream,   40
And be ye happy! Yet, my Friends,[5] I know
That more than one of you will think with me
Of those soft starry nights, and that old Dame
From whom the Stone was named, who there had sate

1. Appropriately.
2. I.e., "Is there anyone . . . ?"
3. Actuality, existence.
4. The Hawkshead Town Hall, built in 1790.

5. Coleridge and John Wordsworth (William's brother), who had visited Hawkshead together with William in Nov. 1799.

And watched her table with its huckster's wares   45
Assiduous, through the length of sixty years.
—We ran a boisterous course, the year span round
With giddy motion. But the time approached
That brought with it a regular desire
For calmer pleasures, when the winning forms   50
Of Nature were collaterally attached[6]
To every scheme of holiday delight,
And every boyish sport, less grateful[7] else
And languidly pursued.
                     When summer came,
Our pastime was, on bright half-holidays,   55
To sweep along the plain of Windermere
With rival oars; and the selected bourne[8]
Was now an Island musical with birds
That sang and ceased not; now a sister isle,
Beneath the oaks' umbrageous[9] covert, sown   60
With lilies of the valley like a field;
And now a third small island, where survived,
In solitude, the ruins of a shrine
Once to our Lady dedicate, and served
Daily with chaunted rites.[1] In such a race,   65
So ended, disappointment could be none,
Uneasiness, or pain, or jealousy;
We rested in the Shade, all pleased alike,
Conquered and Conqueror. Thus the pride of strength,
And the vain-glory of superior skill,   70
Were tempered, thus was gradually produced
A quiet independence of the heart:
And, to my Friend who knows me, I may add,
Fearless of blame, that hence, for future days,
Ensued a diffidence and modesty;   75
And I was taught to feel, perhaps too much,
The self-sufficing power of solitude.
     Our daily meals were frugal, Sabine fare![2]
More than we wished we knew the blessing then
Of vigorous hunger—hence corporeal strength   80
Unsapped by delicate viands; for, exclude
A little weekly stipend,[3] and we lived
Through three divisions of the quartered year
In pennyless poverty. But now, to school
From the half-yearly holidays returned,   85
We came with weightier purses, that sufficed
To furnish treats more costly than the Dame
Of the old grey stone, from her scanty board, supplied.
Hence rustic dinners on the cool green ground,

---

6. Associated as an accompaniment.
7. Pleasing.
8. Destination.
9. Shaded.
1. The island of Lady Holm, former site of a chapel dedicated to the Virgin Mary.
2. Like the meals of the Roman poet Horace on his Sabine farm.

3. In his last year at school Wordsworth had an allowance of sixpence a week, and his younger brother Christopher, threepence. After the Midsummer and Christmas holidays (line 85), the boys received a larger sum, ranging up to a guinea.

Or in the woods, or by a river side,   90
Or shady fountains,[4] while among the leaves
Soft airs were stirring, and the mid-day sun
Unfelt shone brightly round us in our joy.
    Nor is my aim neglected if I tell
How sometimes, in the length of those half years,   95
We from our funds drew largely—proud to curb,
And eager to spur on, the gallopping Steed:
And with the cautious Inn-keeper, whose Stud
Supplied our want, we haply might employ
Sly subterfuges, if the Adventure's bound   100
Were distant, some famed Temple where of yore
The Druids worshipped,[5] or the antique Walls
Of that large Abbey which within the Vale
Of Nightshade, to St Mary's honour built,
Stands yet, a mouldering Pile, with fractured arch,   105
Belfry, and Images, and living Trees;
A holy Scene![6]—Along the smooth green Turf
Our Horses grazed:—to more than inland peace
Left by the west wind sweeping overhead
From a tumultuous ocean, trees and towers   110
In that sequestered Valley may be seen
Both silent and both motionless alike;
Such the deep shelter that is there, and such
The safeguard for repose and quietness.
    Our Steeds remounted, and the summons given,   115
With whip and spur we through the Chauntry[7] flew
In uncouth race, and left the cross-legged Knight
And the Stone-abbot, and that single Wren
Which one day sang so sweetly in the Nave
Of the old Church, that, though from recent Showers   120
The earth was comfortless, and, touched by faint
Internal breezes, sobbings of the place
And respirations, from the roofless walls
The shuddering ivy dripped large drops, yet still
So sweetly 'mid the gloom the invisible Bird   125
Sang to herself, that there I could have made
My dwelling-place, and lived for ever there
To hear such music. Through the Walls we flew,
And down the Valley, and, a circuit made
In wantonness of heart, through rough and smooth   130
We scampered homewards. Oh, ye rocks and streams,
And that still Spirit shed from evening air!
Even in this joyous time I sometimes felt
Your presence, when with slackened step we breathed[8]
Along the sides of the steep hills, or when,   135
Lighted by gleams of moonlight from the sea,
We beat with thundering hoofs the level sand.

4. Springs, streams.
5. The stone circle at Swinside, on the lower Duddon River, mistakenly believed at the time to have been a Druid temple.
6. Furness Abbey, some twenty miles south of Hawks-
head.
7. A chapel endowed for masses to be sung to the donor.
8. Stopped to let the horses catch their breath.

Midway on long Winander's Eastern shore,
Within the crescent of a pleasant Bay,
A Tavern[9] stood, no homely-featured House,   140
Primeval like its neighbouring Cottages;
But 'twas a splendid place, the door beset
With   Chaises,   Grooms,   and   Liveries,—and   within
Decanters, Glasses, and the blood-red Wine.
In ancient times, or ere the Hall was built   145
On the large Island,[1] had this Dwelling been
More worthy of a Poet's love, a Hut
Proud of its one bright fire and sycamore shade.
But, though the rhymes were gone that once inscribed
The threshold, and large golden characters   150
Spread o'er the spangled sign-board had dislodged
The old Lion, and usurped his place in slight
And mockery of the rustic Painter's hand,
Yet to this hour the spot to me is dear
With all its foolish pomp. The garden lay   155
Upon a slope surmounted by the plain
Of a small Bowling-green: beneath us stood
A grove, with gleams of water through the trees
And over the tree-tops; nor did we want
Refreshment, strawberries, and mellow cream.   160
There, while through half an afternoon we played
On the smooth platform, whether skill prevailed
Or happy blunder triumphed, bursts of glee
Made all the mountains ring. But ere night-fall,
When in our pinnace we returned, at leisure   165
Over the shadowy Lake, and to the beach
Of some small Island steered our course with one,
The Minstrel of our Troop,[2] and left him there,
And rowed off gently, while he blew his flute
Alone upon the rock,—Oh then the calm   170
And dead still water lay upon my mind
Even with a weight of pleasure, and the sky,
Never before so beautiful, sank down
Into my heart, and held me like a dream!
    Thus were my sympathies enlarged, and thus   175
Daily the common range of visible things
Grew dear to me: already I began
To love the sun; a boy I loved the sun,
Not as I since have loved him, as a pledge
And surety of our earthly life, a light   180
Which we behold, and feel we are alive;
Nor for his bounty to so many worlds,
But for this cause, that I had seen him lay
His beauty on the morning hills, had seen
The western mountain touch his setting orb,   185
In many a thoughtless hour, when, from excess

9. The tavern was the White Lion at Bowness.   2. Identified by Christopher Wordsworth, *Memoirs*
1. The Hall on Belle Isle in Lake Windermere had   (1857), as Robert Greenwood, who became Senior
been built in the early 1780s.   Fellow of Trinity College, Cambridge.

Of happiness, my blood appear'd to flow
For its own pleasure, and I breathed with joy;
And from like feelings, humble though intense,
To patriotic and domestic love   190
Analogous, the moon to me was dear;
For I would dream away my purposes,
Standing to gaze upon her while she hung
Midway between the hills, as if she knew
No other region; but belonged to thee,   195
Yea, appertained by a peculiar right
To thee, and thy grey huts,[3] thou one dear Vale!
   Those incidental charms which first attached
My heart to rural objects, day by day
Grew weaker, and I hasten on to tell   200
How Nature, intervenient[4] till this time
And secondary, now at length was sought
For her own sake. But who shall[5] parcel out
His intellect, by geometric rules,
Split like a province into round and square?   205
Who knows the individual hour in which
His habits were first sown, even as a seed?
Who that shall point, as with a wand, and say,
"This portion of the river of my mind
Came from yon fountain"? Thou, my friend! art one   210
More deeply read in thy own thoughts; to thee
Science[6] appears but what in truth she is,
Not as our glory and our absolute boast,
But as a succedaneum,[7] and a prop
To our infirmity. No officious slave   215
Art thou of that false secondary power[8]
By which we multiply distinctions, then
Deem that our puny boundaries are things
That we perceive, and not that we have made.
To thee, unblinded by these formal arts,   220
The unity of all hath been revealed;
And thou wilt doubt with me, less aptly skilled
Than many are to range the faculties
In scale and order, class the cabinet[9]
Of their sensations, and in voluble phrase[1]   225
Run through the history and birth of each
As of a single independent thing.
Hard task, vain hope, to analyse the mind,
If each most obvious and particular thought,
Not in a mystical and idle sense,   230
But in the words of reason deeply weighed,
Hath no beginning.
           Blest the infant Babe,

---

3. Cottages built of gray stones.
4. I.e., entering incidentally into his other concerns.
5. Is able to.
6. In the old sense of "learning."
7. In medicine, a drug substituted for a different drug.
Wordsworth, however, uses the term to signify a remedy, or palliative.
8. The analytic faculty, as opposed to the power to
apprehend "the unity of all" (line 221).
9. To classify, as if arranged in a display case.
1. In fluent phraseology.

(For with my best conjecture I would trace
Our Being's earthly progress) blest the Babe,
Nursed in his Mother's arms, who sinks to sleep   235
Rocked on his Mother's breast; who, when his soul
Claims manifest kindred with a human soul,
Drinks in the feelings of his Mother's eye![2]
For him, in one dear Presence, there exists
A virtue which irradiates and exalts   240
Objects through widest intercourse of sense.
No outcast he, bewildered and depressed;
Along his infant veins are interfused
The gravitation and the filial bond
Of nature that connect him with the world.   245
Is there a flower to which he points with hand
Too weak to gather it, already love
Drawn from love's purest earthly fount for him
Hath beautified that flower; already shades
Of pity cast from inward tenderness   250
Do fall around him upon aught that bears
Unsightly marks of violence or harm.
Emphatically such a Being lives,
Frail Creature as he is, helpless as frail,
An inmate of this active universe.   255
For feeling has to him imparted power
That through the growing faculties of sense
Doth, like an Agent of the one great Mind,
Create, creator and receiver both,
Working but in alliance with the works   260
Which it beholds.[3]—Such, verily, is the first
Poetic spirit of our human life,
By uniform control of after years
In most abated or suppressed, in some,
Through every change of growth and of decay,   265
Preeminent till death.
                    From early days,
Beginning not long after that first time
In which, a Babe, by intercourse of touch,
I held mute dialogues with my Mother's heart,[4]
I have endeavoured to display the means   270
Whereby this infant sensibility,
Great birth-right of our being, was in me
Augmented and sustained. Yet is a path
More difficult before me, and I fear
That, in its broken windings, we shall need   275
The chamois'[5] sinews, and the eagle's wing:
For now a trouble came into my mind

2. Like the modern psychologist, Wordsworth recognized the importance of earliest infancy in the development of the individual mind, although he had then to invent the terms with which to analyze the process.
3. The infant, in the sense of security and love shed by his mother's presence, perceives on outer things, what would otherwise be an alien world as a place to which he has a relationship like that of a son to a mother (lines 239–45). On such grounds Wordsworth asserts that the mind partially creates, by altering, the world it seems simply to perceive.
4. I.e., both infant and mother feel the pulse of the other's heart.
5. An agile species of antelope inhabiting mountainous regions of Europe.

From unknown causes. I was left alone,
Seeking the visible world, nor knowing why.
The props of my affections were removed,[6]   280
And yet the building stood, as if sustained
By its own spirit! All that I beheld
Was dear, and hence to finer influxes[7]
The mind lay open, to a more exact
And close communion. Many are our joys   285
In youth, but Oh! what happiness to live
When every hour brings palpable access
Of knowledge, when all knowledge is delight,
And sorrow is not there! The seasons came,
And every season, wheresoe'er I moved,   290
Unfolded transitory qualities
Which, but for this most watchful power of love,
Had been neglected, left a register
Of permanent relations, else unknown.[8]
Hence life, and change, and beauty; solitude   295
More active even than "best society,"[9]
Society made sweet as solitude
By inward concords, silent, inobtrusive;
And gentle agitations of the mind
From manifold distinctions, difference   300
Perceived in things where, to the unwatchful eye,
No difference is, and hence, from the same source,
Sublimer joy: for I would walk alone
Under the quiet stars, and at that time
Have felt whate'er there is of power in sound   305
To breathe an elevated mood, by form
Or Image unprofaned: and I would stand,
If the night blackened with a coming storm,
Beneath some rock, listening to notes that are
The ghostly[1] language of the ancient earth,   310
Or make their dim abode in distant winds.
Thence did I drink the visionary power;
And deem not profitless those fleeting moods
Of shadowy exultation: not for this,
That they are kindred to our purer mind   315
And intellectual life;[2] but that the soul,
Remembering how she felt, but what she felt
Remembering not, retains an obscure sense[3]
Of possible sublimity, whereto
With growing faculties she doth aspire,   320
With faculties still growing, feeling still

6. Wordsworth's mother had died the month before his eighth birthday. It is unclear from the context whether the "trouble" that came into his mind (line 277) refers to the loss of his mother, in whose arms he had established his initial relationship to the natural world, or to the mysterious processes of the continued development and diversification of this relationship.
7. Influences.
8. I.e., had it not been for the watchful power of love (line 292), the "transitory qualities" (291) would have been neglected, and the "permanent relations" now recorded in his memory would have been unknown.
9. A partial quotation of a line spoken by Adam to Eve in *Paradise Lost* 9.249: "For solitude sometimes is best society."
1. Disembodied.
2. I.e., not because they are related to the nonsensuous ("intellectual") aspect of our life.
3. Pronounced "ăn óbscūre sénse."

That, whatsoever point they gain, they yet
Have something to pursue.[4]
          And not alone
'Mid gloom and tumult, but no less 'mid fair
And tranquil scenes, that universal power   325
And fitness in the latent qualities
And essences of things, by which the mind
Is moved with feelings of delight, to me
Came strengthened with a superadded soul,
A virtue not its own.—My morning walks   330
Were early;—oft before the hours of School
I travelled round our little Lake, five miles
Of pleasant wandering; happy time! more dear
For this, that One was by my side, a Friend
Then passionately loved;[5] with heart how full   335
Would he peruse these lines! for many years
Have since flowed in between us, and, our minds
Both silent to each other, at this time
We live as if those hours had never been.
Nor seldom did I lift our Cottage latch   340
Far earlier, and ere one smoke-wreath had risen
From human dwelling, or the thrush, high perched,
Piped to the woods his shrill *reveillé*,[6] sate
Alone upon some jutting eminence
At the first gleam of dawn-light, when the Vale,   345
Yet slumbering, lay in utter solitude.
How shall I seek the origin, where find
Faith in the marvellous things which then I felt?
Oft in those moments such a holy calm
Would overspread my soul, that bodily eyes   350
Were utterly forgotten, and what I saw
Appeared like something in myself, a dream,
A prospect[7] in the mind.
          'Twere long to tell
What spring and autumn, what the winter snows,
And what the summer shade, what day and night,   355
Evening and morning, sleep and waking thought,
From sources inexhaustible, poured forth
To feed the spirit of religious love,
In which I walked with Nature. But let this
Be not forgotten, that I still retained   360
My first creative sensibility,[8]
That by the regular action of the world
My soul was unsubdued. A plastic[9] power
Abode with me, a forming hand, at times
Rebellious, acting in a devious mood,   365
A local Spirit of his own, at war
With general tendency, but, for the most,

4. Cf. the revelation, while crossing Simplon Pass, that
our destiny is with "something evermore about to be"
(6.604–08, p. 1445).
5. Identified as John Fleming in a note to the edition
of 1850.

6. Military parlance for a signal call.
7. Scene.
8. I.e., the creative perception manifested by the babe
in his mother's arms (lines 235ff.).
9. Shaping, formative.

Subservient strictly to external things
With which it communed. An auxiliar light
Came from my mind which on the setting sun   370
Bestowed new splendor; the melodious birds,
The fluttering breezes, fountains that ran on
Murmuring so sweetly in themselves, obeyed
A like dominion; and the midnight storm
Grew darker in the presence of my eye;   375
Hence my obeisance, my devotion hence,
And hence my transport.[1]
                          Nor should this, perchance,
Pass unrecorded, that I still[2] had loved
The exercise and produce of a toil
Than analytic industry to me   380
More pleasing, and whose character I deem
Is more poetic, as resembling more
Creative agency. The Song would speak
Of that interminable building reared
By observation of affinities   385
In objects where no brotherhood exists
To passive minds. My seventeenth year was come;
And, whether from this habit rooted now
So deeply in my mind, or from excess
Of the great social principle of life   390
Coercing all things into sympathy,
To unorganic Natures were transferred
My own enjoyments; or the Power of truth,
Coming in revelation, did converse
With things that really are;[3] I, at this time,   395
Saw blessings spread around me like a sea.
Thus while the days flew by and years passed on,
From Nature overflowing on my soul
I had received so much, that every thought
Was steeped in feeling; I was only then   400
Contented when with bliss ineffable
I felt the sentiment of Being spread
O'er all that moves, and all that seemeth still;
O'er all that, lost beyond the reach of thought
And human knowledge, to the human eye   405
Invisible, yet liveth to the heart;
O'er all that leaps, and runs, and shouts, and sings,
Or beats the gladsome air; o'er all that glides
Beneath the wave, yea, in the wave itself,
And mighty depth of waters. Wonder not   410
If high the transport, great the joy I felt,
Communing in this sort through earth and Heaven
With every form of Creature, as it looked
Towards the Uncreated with a countenance

1. Exaltation.
2. Always.
3. Wordsworth is careful to indicate that there are
alternative explanations for his sense that life pervades

the inorganic as well as the organic world: it may be
the result either of a way of perceiving habitual since
infancy or of a projection of his own inner life, or else
it may be the perception of an objective truth.

Of adoration, with an eye of love.[4]   415
One song they sang, and it was audible,
Most audible, then, when the fleshly ear,
O'ercome by humblest prelude of that strain,
Forgot her functions and slept undisturbed.
        If this be error, and another faith   420
Find easier access to the pious mind,[5]
Yet were I grossly destitute of all
Those human sentiments that make this earth
So dear, if I should fail with grateful voice
To speak of you, Ye Mountains, and Ye Lakes,   425
And sounding Cataracts, Ye Mists and Winds
That dwell among the Hills where I was born.
If in my Youth I have been pure in heart,
If, mingling with the world, I am content
With my own modest pleasures, and have lived,   430
With God and Nature communing, removed
From little enmities and low desires,
The gift is yours: if in these times of fear,
This melancholy waste[6] of hopes o'erthrown,
If, 'mid indifference and apathy   435
And wicked exultation, when good men,
On every side, fall off, we know not how,
To selfishness, disguised in gentle names
Of peace and quiet and domestic love,
Yet mingled, not unwillingly, with sneers   440
On visionary minds; if, in this time
Of dereliction and dismay,[7] I yet
Despair not of our Nature, but retain
A more than Roman confidence, a faith
That fails not, in all sorrow my support,   445
The blessing of my life, the gift is yours,
Ye Winds and sounding Cataracts, 'tis yours,
Ye Mountains! thine, O Nature! Thou hast fed
My lofty speculations; and in thee,
For this uneasy heart of ours, I find   450
A never-failing principle of joy
And purest passion.
                        Thou, my Friend! wert reared
In the great City, 'mid far other scenes;[8]
But we, by different roads, at length have gained
The self-same bourne. And for this cause to Thee   455
I speak, unapprehensive of contempt,
The insinuated scoff of coward tongues,
And all that silent language which so oft,
In conversation between Man and Man,

---

4. Wordsworth did not add lines 412–14, giving a
Christian frame to his experience of the "one life,"
until the last revision of *The Prelude*, 1839.
5. With lines 416–21 cf. *Tintern Abbey*, lines 43–50
(p. 1337).
6. Wasteland.
7. The era, some ten years after the outbreak of the

French Revolution, was one of violent reaction, in
which many earlier sympathizers were recanting their
radical beliefs.
8. A reminiscence of Coleridge's *Frost at Midnight*,
lines 51–52: "For I was reared / In the great city, pent
'mid cloisters dim."

Blots from the human countenance all trace   460
Of beauty and of love. For Thou hast sought
The truth in solitude, and, since the days
That gave thee liberty, full long desired,
To serve in Nature's Temple, thou hast been
The most assiduous of her Ministers,[9]   465
In many things my Brother, chiefly here
In this our deep devotion.
                                    Fare Thee well!
Health, and the quiet of a healthful mind,
Attend Thee! seeking oft the haunts of Men,
And yet more often living with thyself   470
And for thyself, so haply shall thy days
Be many, and a blessing to mankind.

From Book Third
Residence at Cambridge

[Experiences at St. John's College. The "Heroic Argument"]

It was a dreary Morning when the Wheels
Rolled over a wide plain o'erhung with clouds,
And nothing cheered our way till first we saw
The long-roof'd Chapel of King's College lift
Turrets, and pinnacles in answering files   5
Extended high above a dusky grove.
    Advancing, we espied upon the road
A Student, clothed in Gown and tasselled Cap,
Striding along, as if o'ertasked by Time
Or covetous of exercise and air.   10
He passed—nor was I Master of my eyes
Till he was left an arrow's flight behind.
As near and nearer to the Spot we drew,
It seemed to suck us in with an eddy's force;
Onward we drove beneath the Castle, caught,   15
While crossing Magdalene Bridge, a glimpse of Cam,[1]
And at the *Hoop* alighted, famous Inn![2]
    My Spirit was up, my thoughts were full of hope;
Some friends I had, acquaintances who there
Seemed friends, poor simple School-boys! now hung round   20
With honor and importance: in a world
Of welcome faces up and down I roved;
Questions, directions, warnings, and advice
Flowed in upon me, from all sides; fresh day
Of pride and pleasure! to myself I seemed   25
A man of business and expence, and went

9. Wordsworth may be recalling the conclusion of
Coleridge's *France: An Ode* (1798) where, disillusioned about the promise of liberty by the French Revolution, he writes that, while standing on a "sea-cliff's
verge," "O Liberty! my spirit felt thee there." Wordsworth added lines 461–64 some years after Coleridge's

death in 1834.
1. The river that flows through Cambridge.
2. Wordsworth renders some of his early college experiences, when he was a callow country boy (lines 34–
35), in a deliberately inflated, or mock-epic, manner.

From shop to shop, about my own affairs,
To Tutor or to Tailor, as befel,
From street to street, with loose and careless mind.
    I was the Dreamer, they the dream: I roamed   30
Delighted through the motley spectacle;
Gowns grave or gaudy, Doctors, Students, Streets,
Courts, Cloisters, flocks of Churches, gateways, towers.
Migration strange for a Stripling of the Hills,
A Northern Villager! As if the change   35
Had waited on some Fairy's wand, at once
Behold me rich in monies; and attired
In splendid garb, with hose of silk, and hair
Powdered like rimy[3] trees, when frost is keen.
My lordly dressing-gown, I pass it by,   40
With other signs of manhood that supplied
The lack of beard.—The weeks went roundly on
With invitations, suppers, wine and fruit,
Smooth housekeeping within, and all without
Liberal, and suiting Gentleman's array!   45
    The Evangelist St. John my Patron was;[4]
Three gothic Courts are his, and in the first
Was my abiding-place, a nook obscure!
Right underneath, the College Kitchens made
A humming sound, less tuneable than bees,   50
But hardly less industrious; with shrill notes
Of sharp command and scolding intermixed.
Near me hung Trinity's loquacious Clock,
Who never let the quarters, night or day,
Slip by him unproclaimed, and told the hours   55
Twice over, with a male and female voice.
Her pealing Organ was my neighbour too;
And from my pillow, looking forth by light
Of moon or favoring stars, I could behold
The Antechapel, where the Statue stood   60
Of Newton, with his prism,[5] and silent face:
The marble index of a Mind for ever
Voyaging through strange seas of Thought, alone.
    Of College labors, of the Lecturer's room
All studded round, as thick as chairs could stand,   65
With loyal Students faithful to their books,
Half-and-half Idlers, hardy Recusants,[6]
And honest Dunces—of important days,
Examinations when the man was weighed
As in a balance! of excessive hopes,   70
Tremblings withal, and commendable fears;
Small jealousies, and triumphs good or bad,
Let others, that know more, speak as they know.
Such glory was but little sought by me

3. Covered with rime, frosted over.
4. Wordsworth was a student at St. John's College, Cambridge University, 1787–91. Book 3 deals with his first year there.
5. In the west end of Trinity Chapel, adjoining St. John's College, stands Roubiliac's statue of Newton holding the prism with which he had conducted the experiments described in his *Optics*.
6. Those who refused to work at their studies.

And little won. Yet, from the first crude days   75
Of settling time in this untried abode,
I was disturbed at times by prudent thoughts,
Wishing to hope, without a hope; some fears
About my future worldly maintenance;[7]
And, more than all, a strangeness in the mind,   80
A feeling that I was not for that hour,
Nor for that place. But wherefore be cast down?
For (not to speak of Reason and her pure
Reflective acts to fix the moral law
Deep in the conscience; nor of Christian Hope   85
Bowing her head before her Sister Faith
As one far mightier),[8] hither I had come,
Bear witness, Truth, endowed with holy powers
And faculties, whether to work or feel.
Oft when the dazzling shew no longer new   90
Had ceased to dazzle, ofttimes did I quit
My Comrades, leave the Crowd, buildings and groves,
And as I paced alone the level fields
Far from those lovely sights and sounds sublime
With which I had been conversant, the mind   95
Drooped not, but there into herself returning
With prompt rebound, seemed fresh as heretofore.
At least I more distinctly recognized
Her native instincts; let me dare to speak
A higher language, say that now I felt   100
What independent solaces were mine
To mitigate the injurious sway of place
Or circumstance, how far soever changed
In youth, or *to* be changed in manhood's prime;
Or, for the few who shall be called to look   105
On the long shadows, in our evening years,
Ordained Precursors to the night of death.
As if awakened, summoned, roused, constrained,
I looked for universal things, perused
The common countenance of earth and sky;   110
Earth no where unembellished by some trace
Of that first paradise whence man was driven;
And sky whose beauty and bounty are expressed
By the proud name she bears, the name of heaven.
I called on both to teach me what they might;   115
Or, turning the mind in upon herself,
Pored, watched, expected, listened, spread my thoughts
And spread them with a wider creeping; felt
Incumbencies more awful,[9] visitings
Of the Upholder, of the tranquil Soul   120
That tolerates the indignities of Time;
And, from his centre of eternity

7. Wordsworth was troubled by the expectation of his family that he would be appointed a Fellow of St. John's College.
8. This pious qualification, lines 83–87, was added by Wordsworth in late revisions of *The Prelude*. In the version of 1805, he wrote: "I was a chosen son. / For hither I had come with holy powers / And faculties, whether to work or feel."
9. I.e., the weight of more awe-inspiring moods.

All finite motions overruling, lives
In glory immutable. But peace!—enough
Here to record I had ascended now   125
To such community with highest truth.
—A track pursuing, not untrod before,
From strict analogies by thought supplied,
Or consciousnesses not to be subdued,
To every natural form, rock, fruit or flower,   130
Even the loose stones that cover the high-way,
I gave a moral life; I saw them feel,
Or linked them to some feeling: the great mass
Lay bedded in a quickening¹ soul, and all
That I beheld respired with inward meaning.   135
Add, that whate'er of Terror or of Love
Or Beauty, Nature's daily face put on
From transitory passion, unto this
I was as sensitive as waters are
To the sky's influence: in a kindred mood   140
Of passion, was obedient as a lute
That waits upon the touches of the wind.²
Unknown, unthought of, yet I was most rich;
I had a world about me; 'twas my own,
I made it; for it only lived to me,   145
And to the God who sees into the heart.
Such sympathies, though rarely, were betrayed
By outward gestures and by visible looks:
Some called it madness—so, indeed, it was,
If child-like fruitfulness in passing joy,   150
If steady moods of thoughtfulness, matured
To inspiration, sort with such a name;
If prophecy be madness; if things viewed
By Poets in old time, and higher up
By the first men, earth's first inhabitants,   155
May in these tutored days no more be seen
With undisordered sight. But, leaving this,
It was no madness: for the bodily eye
Amid my strongest workings evermore
Was searching out the lines of difference   160
As they lie hid in all external forms,
Near or remote, minute or vast, an eye
Which from a tree, a stone, a withered leaf,
To the broad ocean, and the azure heavens
Spangled with kindred multitudes of Stars,   165
Could find no surface where its power might sleep;
Which spake perpetual logic to my Soul,
And by an unrelenting agency
Did bind my feelings, even as in a chain.
    And here, O friend! have I retraced my life   170
Up to an eminence, and told a tale
Of matters which not falsely may be called

---

1. Life-giving.   2. I.e., as a wind harp.

The glory of my Youth. Of genius, power,
Creation, and Divinity itself,
I have been speaking, for my theme has been   175
What passed within me. Not of outward things
Done visibly for other minds; words, signs,
Symbols, or actions, but of my own heart
Have I been speaking, and my youthful mind.
O Heavens! how awful is the might of Souls   180
And what they do within themselves, while yet
The yoke of earth is new to them, the world
Nothing but a wild field where they were sown.
This is, in truth, heroic argument,
This genuine prowess, which I wished to touch   185
With hand however weak,[3] but in the main
It lies far hidden from the reach of words.
Points have we, all of us, within our Souls,
Where all stand single: this I feel, and make
Breathings for incommunicable powers.[4]   190
But is not each a memory to himself?
And, therefore, now that we must quit this theme,
I am not heartless;[5] for there's not a man
That lives who hath not known his god-like hours,
And feels not what an empire we inherit,   195
As natural Beings, in the strength of Nature.
    No more:—for now into a populous plain
We must descend.—A Traveller I am
Whose tale is only of himself; even so,
So be it, if the pure of heart be prompt   200
To follow, and if Thou, O honored Friend!
Who in these thoughts art ever at my side,
Support, as heretofore, my fainting steps.[6]

                    *   *   *

    Thus in submissive idleness, my Friend,
The laboring time of Autumn, Winter, Spring,
Eight months! rolled pleasingly away—the ninth
Came and returned me to my native hills.   635

From Book Fourth
Summer Vacation[1]

[*The Walks with His Terrier. The Circuit of the Lake*]

    Among the favorites whom it pleased me well
To see again, was one, by ancient right

---

3. Wordsworth describes the innovative epic theme ("heroic argument") for his projected long poem. Cf. his Prospectus to *The Recluse*, lines 25–41 (p. 1398).
4. This obscure assertion may mean that he tries, inadequately, to express the inexpressible.
5. Disheartened.
6. The terms of this behest to Coleridge suggest the relation to Dante of Virgil, his guide in the *Inferno*.
1. Wordsworth returned to Hawkshead for his first summer vacation in 1788.

Our Inmate, a rough terrier of the hills,   95
By birth and call of nature pre-ordained
To hunt the badger, and unearth the fox,
Among the impervious crags; but having been
From youth our own adopted, he had passed
Into a gentler service. And when first   100
The boyish spirit flagged, and day by day
Along my veins I kindled with the stir,
The fermentation and the vernal heat
Of poesy, affecting private shades
Like a sick lover, then this Dog was used   105
To watch me, an attendant and a friend
Obsequious to my steps, early and late,
Though often of such dilatory walk
Tired, and uneasy at the halts I made.
A hundred times when, roving high and low,   110
I have been harrassed with the toil of verse,
Much pains and little progress, and at once
Some lovely Image in the Song rose up
Full-formed, like Venus rising from the Sea;[2]
Then have I darted forwards and let loose   115
My hand upon his back, with stormy joy;
Caressing him again, and yet again.
And when at evening on the public Way
I sauntered, like a river murmuring
And talking to itself, when all things else   120
Are still, the Creature trotted on before—
Such was his custom; but whene'er he met
A passenger[3] approaching, he would turn
To give me timely notice; and, straitway,
Grateful for that admonishment, I hushed   125
My voice, composed my gait, and with the air
And mien of one whose thoughts are free, advanced
To give and take a greeting, that might save
My name from piteous rumours, such as wait
On men suspected to be crazed in brain.   130
    Those walks, well worthy to be prized and loved,
Regretted! that word too was on my tongue,
But they were richly laden with all good,
And cannot be remembered but with thanks
And gratitude, and perfect joy of heart;   135
Those walks, in all their freshness, now came back,
Like a returning Spring. When first I made
Once more the circuit of our little Lake,
If ever happiness hath lodged with man,
That day consummate[4] happiness was mine,   140
Wide-spreading, steady, calm, contemplative.
The sun was set, or setting, when I left
Our cottage door, and evening soon brought on
A sober hour,—not winning or serene,

2. Aphrodite (the Roman Venus), goddess of love, was   3. A foot traveler.
born from the foam of the sea.   4. Perfect (pronounced "consúmmate").

For cold and raw the air was, and untuned: 145
But as a face we love is sweetest then
When sorrow damps it; or, whatever look
It chance to wear, is sweetest if the heart
Have fulness in herself, even so with me
It fared that evening. Gently did my Soul   150
Put off her veil, and, self-transmuted, stood
Naked, as in the presence of her God.[5]
While on I walked, a comfort seemed to touch
A heart that had not been disconsolate;
Strength came where weakness was not known to be,   155
At least not felt; and restoration came,
Like an intruder, knocking at the door
Of unacknowledged weariness. I took
The balance, and with firm hand weighed myself.
—Of that external scene which round me lay   160
Little, in this abstraction, did I see,
Remembered less; but I had inward hopes
And swellings of the Spirit: was rapt and soothed,
Conversed with promises; had glimmering views
How life pervades the undecaying mind,   165
How the immortal Soul with God-like power
Informs, creates, and thaws the deepest sleep[6]
That time can lay upon her; how on earth,
Man, if he do but live within the light
Of high endeavours, daily spreads abroad   170
His being armed with strength that cannot fail.
Nor was there want of milder thoughts, of love,
Of innocence, and holiday repose;
And more than pastoral quiet 'mid the stir
Of boldest projects; and a peaceful end   175
At last, or glorious, by endurance won.
Thus musing, in a wood I sate me down,
Alone, continuing there to muse; the slopes
And heights, meanwhile, were slowly overspread
With darkness; and before a rippling breeze   180
The long lake lengthened out its hoary line:
And in the sheltered coppice[7] where I sate,
Around me from among the hazel leaves,
Now here, now there, moved by the straggling wind,
Came ever and anon a breath-like sound,   185
Quick as the pantings of the faithful Dog,
The off and on Companion of my walk;
And such, at times, believing them to be,
I turned my head, to look if he were there;
Then into solemn thought I passed once more.   190

---

5. In Exodus 34.30–34, when Moses descended from Mt. Sinai, he wore a veil to hide from the Israelites the shining of his face, but removed the veil when, in privacy, he talked to God.
6. "Informs" and "creates" are probably to be read as intransitive verbs, while "thaws" has "sleep" for its direct object. "Sleep" Wordsworth uses, here and elsewhere in *The Prelude*, for the deadening effect of routine experience.
7. A clump of small trees and underbrush.

["The Surface of Past Time." The Walk Home from the Dance. The
Discharged Soldier]

As one who hangs down-bending from the side
Of a slow-moving boat, upon the breast
Of a still water, solacing himself
With such discoveries as his eye can make,
Beneath him, in the bottom of the deep,   260
Sees many beauteous sights, weeds, fishes, flowers,
Grots, pebbles, roots of trees, and fancies more;
Yet often is perplexed, and cannot part
The shadow from the substance, rocks and sky,
Mountains and clouds reflected in the depth   265
Of the clear flood, from things which there abide
In their true Dwelling: now is crossed by gleam
Of his own image, by a sun-beam now,
And wavering motions, sent he knows not whence,
Impediments that make his task more sweet—   270
Such pleasant office have we long pursued,
Incumbent o'er the surface of past time,
With like success, nor often have appeared
Shapes fairer, or less doubtfully discerned
Than these to which the Tale, indulgent Friend!   275
Would now direct thy notice.[8] Yet in spite
Of pleasure won and knowledge not withheld,
There was an inner falling off. I loved,
Loved deeply, all that had been loved before,
More deeply even than ever: but a swarm   280
Of heady schemes, jostling each other, gawds,[9]
And feast, and dance, and public revelry;
And sports, and games (too grateful in themselves,
Yet in themselves less grateful, I believe,
Than as they were a badge, glossy and fresh,   285
Of manliness and freedom) all conspired
To lure my mind from firm habitual quest
Of feeding pleasures;[1] to depress the zeal
And damp those daily yearnings which had once been mine—
A wild unworldly-minded youth, given up   290
To his own eager thoughts. It would demand
Some skill, and longer time than may be spared,
To paint these vanities, and how they wrought
In haunts where they, till now, had been unknown.
It seemed the very garments that I wore   295
Preyed on my strength, and stopped the quiet stream
Of self-forgetfulness.
            Yes, that heartless[2] chase
Of trivial pleasures was a poor exchange
For books and nature at that early age.

---

8. In this sustained simile Wordsworth describes his
endeavors to distinguish facts from fancies, and his
present self from his former self, in his remembrance
of things past.

9. Amusements, pastimes.
1. Pleasures that would nourish the mind.
2. Dispirited, without deep feeling.

'Tis true some casual knowledge might be gained   300
Of character or life; but at that time,
Of manners put to School[3] I took small note;
And all my deeper passions lay elsewhere.
Far better had it been to exalt the mind
By solitary Study; to uphold   305
Intense desire through meditative peace.
And yet, for chastisement of these regrets,
The memory of one particular hour
Doth here rise up against me.—'Mid a throng
Of Maids and Youths, old Men and Matrons staid,   310
A medley of all tempers,[4] I had passed
The night in dancing, gaiety, and mirth;
With din of instruments, and shuffling feet,
And glancing forms, and tapers glittering,
And unaimed prattle flying up and down—   315
Spirits upon the stretch, and here and there
Slight shocks of young love-liking interspersed,
Whose transient pleasure mounted to the head,
And tingled through the veins. Ere we retired
The cock had crowed; and now the eastern sky   320
Was kindling, not unseen from humble copse
And open field through which the pathway wound
That homeward led my steps. Magnificent
The Morning rose, in memorable pomp,
Glorious as e'er I had beheld; in front   325
The Sea lay laughing at a distance;—near,
The solid mountains shone bright as the clouds,
Grain-tinctured, drenched in empyrean[5] light;
And, in the meadows and the lower grounds,
Was all the sweetness of a common dawn;   330
Dews, vapours, and the melody of birds;
And Labourers going forth to till the fields.
    Ah! need I say, dear Friend, that to the brim
My heart was full: I made no vows, but vows
Were then made for me; bond unknown to me   335
Was given, that I should be, else sinning greatly,
A dedicated Spirit.[6] On I walked
In thankful blessedness which yet survives.
    Strange rendezvous my mind was at that time,
A party-colored shew of grave and gay,   340
Solid and light, short-sighted and profound;
Of inconsiderate habits and sedate,
Consorting in one mansion, unreproved.
The worth I knew of powers that I possessed,
Though slighted and too oft misused. Besides,   345
That summer, swarming as it did with thoughts
Transient and idle, lacked not intervals

3. Made a subject of systematic study.
4. Temperaments, types of character.
5. In ancient belief, the outer sphere of the universe, composed of pure fire. "Grain-tinctured": crimson colored.

6. Wordsworth describes later in *The Prelude* his discovery that the specific vocation to which he felt dedicated was to be the agent of a new kind of poetry (13.232ff.).

When Folly from the frown of fleeting Time
Shrunk, and the Mind experienced in herself
Conformity as just as that of old[7]   350
To the end and written spirit of God's works,
Whether held forth in Nature or in Man,
Through pregnant vision, separate or conjoined.
    When from our better selves we have too long
Been parted by the hurrying world, and droop,   355
Sick of its business, of its pleasures tired,
How gracious, how benign is Solitude!
How potent a mere image of her sway!
Most potent when impressed upon the mind
With an appropriate human centre—Hermit   360
Deep in the bosom of the Wilderness;
Votary[8] (in vast Cathedral, where no foot
Is treading and no other face is seen)
Kneeling at prayer; or Watchman on the top
Of Lighthouse beaten by Atlantic Waves;   365
Or as the soul of that great Power is met
Sometimes embodied on a public road,
When, for the night deserted, it assumes
A character of quiet more profound
Than pathless Wastes.
                     Once, when those summer Months   370
Were flown, and Autumn brought its annual shew
Of oars with oars contending, sails with sails,
Upon Winander's[9] spacious breast, it chanced
That—after I had left a flower-decked room
(Whose in-door pastime, lighted-up, survived   375
To a late hour) and spirits overwrought[1]
Were making night do penance for a day
Spent in a round of strenuous idleness—
My homeward course led up a long ascent
Where the road's watery surface, to the top   380
Of that sharp rising, glittered to the moon
And bore the semblance of another stream
Stealing with silent lapse[2] to join the brook
That murmured in the Vale. All else was still;
No living thing appeared in earth or air,   385
And, save the flowing Water's peaceful voice,
Sound was there none: but lo! an uncouth shape
Shewn by a sudden turning of the road,
So near, that, slipping back into the shade
Of a thick hawthorn, I could mark him well,   390
Myself unseen. He was of stature tall,

---

7. I.e., an immediacy of response similar to his mental experience before he indulged in these present distractions.
8. A person devoted to God's service.
9. Lake Windermere's.
1. Worked up to a high pitch. Wordsworth is describing a party at which the "pastime" had been dancing. The description of the meeting with the discharged soldier that follows was written in 1798 as an independent poem, which Wordsworth later incorporated in *The Prelude*.
2. Flowing. Wordsworth is remembering a description that his sister, Dorothy, had entered into her journal in Jan. 1798, a few days before he composed this passage: "The road to the village of Holford glittered like another stream."

A span[3] above man's *common* measure tall.
Stiff, lank, and upright;—a more meagre[4] man
Was never seen before by night or day.
Long were his arms, pallid his hands;—his mouth   395
Looked ghastly[5] in the moonlight. From behind,
A mile-stone propped him; I could also ken
That he was clothed in military garb,
Though faded, yet entire. Companionless,
No dog attending, by no staff sustained   400
He stood; and in his very dress appeared
A desolation, a simplicity
To which the trappings of a gaudy world
Make a strange background. From his lips erelong
Issued low muttered sounds, as if of pain   405
Or some uneasy thought; yet still his form
Kept the same awful steadiness;—at his feet
His shadow lay and moved not. From self-blame
Not wholly free, I watched him thus; at length
Subduing my heart's specious cowardice,[6]   410
I left the shady nook where I had stood,
And hailed him. Slowly, from his resting-place
He rose; and, with a lean and wasted arm
In measured gesture lifted to his head,
Returned my salutation: then resumed   415
His station as before; and when I asked
His history, the Veteran, in reply,
Was neither slow nor eager; but, unmoved,
And with a quiet uncomplaining voice,
A stately air of mild indifference,   420
He told, in few plain words, a Soldier's tale—
That in the Tropic Islands he had served,
Whence he had landed, scarcely three weeks past,
That on his landing he had been dismissed,
And now was travelling towards his native home.[7]   425
This heard, I said in pity, "Come with me."
He stooped, and straightway from the ground took up
An oaken staff, by me yet unobserved—
A staff which must have dropped from his slack hand
And lay till now neglected in the grass.   430
    Though weak his step and cautious, he appeared
To travel without pain, and I beheld,
With an astonishment but ill suppressed,
His ghastly figure moving at my side;
Nor could I, while we journeyed thus, forbear   435
To turn from present hardships to the past,
And speak of war, battle, and pestilence,
Sprinkling this talk with questions, better spared,
On what he might himself have seen or felt.

3. About nine inches (the distance between extended thumb and little finger).
4. Lean, emaciated.
5. Ghostly.
6. I.e., he had been deceiving himself in thinking that the motive for his delay was not cowardice.
7. The Tropic Islands are the West Indies. Tens of thousands of British soldiers serving there contracted tropical fevers and died, or else were rendered unfit for further service and discharged.

He all the while was in demeanour calm,   440
Concise in answer; solemn and sublime
He might have seemed, but that in all he said
There was a strange half-absence, as of one
Knowing too well the importance of his theme,
But feeling it no longer. Our discourse   445
Soon ended, and together on we passed,
In silence, through a wood, gloomy and still.
Up-turning then along an open field,
We reached a Cottage. At the door I knocked,
And earnestly to charitable care   450
Commended him, as a poor friendless Man
Belated, and by sickness overcome.
Assured that now the Traveller would repose
In comfort, I entreated, that henceforth
He would not linger in the public ways,   455
But ask for timely furtherance and help,
Such as his state required.—At this reproof,
With the same ghastly mildness in his look,
He said, "My trust is in the God of Heaven,
And in the eye of him who passes me."   460
    The Cottage door was speedily unbarred,
And now the Soldier touched his hat once more
With his lean hand; and, in a faltering voice
Whose tone bespake reviving interests
Till then unfelt, he thanked me; I returned   465
The farewell blessing of the patient Man,
And so we parted. Back I cast a look,
And lingered near the door a little space;
Then sought with quiet heart my distant home.
    This passed, and He who deigns to mark with care   470
By what rules governed, with what end in view
This Work proceeds, *he* will not wish for more.

From Book Fifth
Books

[*The Dream of the Arab*]

    * * * Oh! why hath not the Mind   45
Some element to stamp her image on
In nature somewhat nearer to her own?
Why gifted with such powers to send abroad
Her spirit, must it lodge in shrines so frail?[1]
    One day, when from my lips a like complaint   50
Had fallen in presence of a studious friend,
He with a smile made answer that in truth
'Twas going far to seek disquietude,

---

1. Wordsworth is describing his recurrent fear that some holocaust might wipe out all books, the frail and perishable repositories of all man's wisdom and poetry.

But, on the front of his reproof, confessed
That he himself had oftentimes given way   55
To kindred hauntings. Whereupon I told
That once in the stillness of a summer's noon,
While I was seated in a rocky cave
By the sea-side, perusing, so it chanced,
The famous history of the errant Knight   60
Recovered by Cervantes,[2] these same thoughts
Beset me, and to height unusual rose,
While listlessly I sate, and, having closed
The Book, had turned my eyes tow'rd the wide Sea.
On Poetry, and geometric truth,   65
And their high privilege of lasting life,
From all internal injury exempt,
I mused; upon these chiefly: and, at length,
My senses yielding to the sultry air,
Sleep seized me, and I passed into a dream.   70
I saw before me stretched a boundless plain,
Of sandy wilderness, all blank and void;
And as I looked around, distress and fear
Came creeping over me, when at my side,
Close at my side, an uncouth Shape appeared   75
Upon a Dromedary, mounted high.
He seemed an Arab of the Bedouin Tribes:[3]
A Lance he bore, and underneath one arm
A Stone; and, in the opposite hand, a Shell
Of a surpassing brightness. At the sight   80
Much I rejoiced, not doubting but a Guide
Was present, one who with unerring skill
Would through the desert lead me; and while yet
I looked, and looked, self-questioned what this freight
Which the New-comer carried through the Waste   85
Could mean, the Arab told me that the Stone
(To give it in the language of the Dream)
Was Euclid's Elements;[4] "and this," said he,
"This other," pointing to the Shell, "this book
Is something of more worth": and, at the word,   90
Stretched forth the Shell, so beautiful in shape,
In color so resplendent, with command
That I should hold it to my ear. I did so,—
And heard, that instant, in an unknown tongue,
Which yet I understood, articulate sounds,   95
A loud prophetic blast of harmony—
An Ode, in passion uttered, which foretold
Destruction to the Children of the Earth,
By Deluge now at hand. No sooner ceased
The Song than the Arab with calm look declared   100
That all would come to pass, of which the voice

2. I.e., *Don Quixote*. Wordsworth's dream involves all
the elements of the poet's last waking experience.
3. Mathematics had flourished among the Arabs—
hence the Arabian rider.

4. Euclid was a Greek mathematician; his celebrated
book on plane geometry and the theory of numbers
continued to be used as a textbook into the 19th century.

1440

WILLIAM WORDSWORTH

Had given forewarning, and that he himself
Was going then to bury those two Books:
The One that held acquaintance with the stars,
And wedded Soul to Soul in purest bond   105
Of Reason, undisturbed by space or time:
Th'other, that was a God, yea many Gods,
Had voices more than all the winds, with power
To exhilarate the Spirit, and to soothe,
Through every clime, the heart of human kind.   110
While this was uttering, strange as it may seem,
I wondered not, although I plainly saw
The One to be a Stone, the Other a Shell,
Nor doubted once but that they both were Books;
Having a perfect faith in all that passed.   115
Far stronger now grew the desire I felt
To cleave unto this Man; but when I prayed
To share his enterprize, he hurried on,
Reckless⁵ of me: I followed, not unseen,
For oftentimes he cast a backward look,   120
Grasping his twofold treasure. Lance in rest,
He rode, I keeping pace with him; and now
He to my fancy had become the Knight
Whose tale Cervantes tells; yet not the Knight,
But was an Arab of the desert, too,   125
Of these was neither, and was both at once.
His countenance, meanwhile, grew more disturbed,
And looking backwards when he looked, mine eyes
Saw, over half the wilderness diffused,
A bed of glittering light: I asked the cause.   130
"It is," said he, "the waters of the Deep
Gathering upon us"; quickening then the pace
Of the unwieldy Creature he bestrode,
He left me; I called after him aloud,—
He heeded not; but with his twofold charge   135
Still in his grasp, before me, full in view,
Went hurrying o'er the illimitable Waste
With the fleet waters of a drowning World
In chase of him; whereat I waked in terror;
And saw the Sea before me, and the Book,   140
In which I had been reading, at my side.

[The Boy of Winander]

There was a Boy;⁶—ye knew him well, Ye Cliffs
And Islands of Winander!—many a time
At evening, when the earliest stars began
To move along the edges of the hills,
Rising or setting, would he stand alone,   370
Beneath the trees, or by the glimmering lake;
And there, with fingers interwoven, both hands

5. Heedless.
6. In an early manuscript version of this passage

Wordsworth uses the first-person pronoun; the experience he describes was thus apparently his own.

Pressed closely palm to palm and to his mouth
Uplifted, he, as through an instrument,
Blew mimic hootings to the silent owls   375
That they might answer him.—And they would shout
Across the watery Vale, and shout again,
Responsive to his call,—with quivering peals,
And long halloos, and screams, and echoes loud
Redoubled and redoubled; concourse wild   380
Of jocund din! and when a lengthened pause
Of silence came, and baffled his best skill,
Then, sometimes, in that silence, while he hung
Listening, a gentle shock of mild surprize
Has carried far into his heart the voice   385
Of mountain torrents; or the visible scene
Would enter unawares into his mind
With all its solemn imagery, its rocks,
Its woods, and that uncertain heaven, received
Into the bosom of the steady lake.[7]   390
    This Boy was taken from his Mates, and died
In childhood, ere he was full twelve years old.
Fair is the Spot, most beautiful the Vale
Where he was born: the grassy Church-yard hangs
Upon a slope above the Village School;   395
And through that Church-yard when my way has led
On summer evenings, I believe that there
A long half-hour together I have stood
Mute—looking at the grave in which he lies!
    Even now appears before the mind's clear eye   400
That self-same Village Church; I see her sit
(The thronèd Lady whom erewhile we hailed)
On her green hill, forgetful of this Boy
Who slumbers at her feet, forgetful, too,
Of all her silent neighbourhood of graves,   405
And listening only to the gladsome sounds
That, from the rural School ascending, play
Beneath her, and about her. May she long
Behold a race of Young Ones like to those
With whom I herded! (easily, indeed,   410
We might have fed upon a fatter soil
Of Arts and Letters, but be that forgiven)
A race of *real* children; not too wise,
Too learnèd, or too good: but wanton, fresh,
And bandied up and down by love and hate;   415
Not unresentful where self-justified;
Fierce, moody, patient, venturous, modest, shy;
Mad at their sports like withered leaves in winds:
Though doing wrong and suffering, and full oft
Bending beneath our life's mysterious weight   420
Of pain, and doubt, and fear; yet yielding not
In happiness to the happiest upon earth.

---

7. Coleridge wrote of the last line and a half ("that uncertain heaven . . . . lake"): "Had I met these lines running wild in the deserts of Arabia, I should instantly have screamed out, 'Wordsworth.'"

Simplicity in habit, truth in speech,
Be these the daily strengtheners of their minds!
May books and nature be their early joy!   425
And knowledge, rightly honored with that name,
Knowledge not purchased by the loss of power!

["The Mystery of Words"]

Here must we pause; this only let me add,
From heart-experience, and in humblest sense
Of modesty, that he, who, in his youth,
A daily Wanderer among woods and fields,
With living Nature hath been intimate,   590
Not only in that raw unpractised time
Is stirred to extasy, as others are,
By glittering verse; but, further, doth receive,
In measure only dealt out to himself,
Knowledge and increase of enduring joy   595
From the great Nature that exists in works
Of mighty Poets.[8] Visionary Power
Attends the motions of the viewless[9] winds
Embodied in the mystery of words:
There darkness makes abode, and all the host   600
Of shadowy things work endless changes there,
As in a mansion like their proper home.
Even forms and substances are circumfused
By that transparent veil with light divine;
And, through the turnings intricate of verse,   605
Present themselves as objects recognized,
In flashes, and with glory not their own.
    Thus far a scanty record is deduced
Of what I owed to Books in early life;
Their later influence yet remains untold;   610
But as this work was taking in my mind
Proportions that seemed larger than had first
Been meditated, I was indisposed
To any further progress, at a time
When these acknowledgments were left unpaid.   615

From Book Sixth
Cambridge, and the Alps

["Human Nature Seeming Born Again"]

When the third summer freed us from restraint,[1]
A youthful Friend, he too a Mountaineer,

8. Having found a set of symbols in nature, Wordsworth now finds nature in the symbol systems of "mighty poets."
9. Invisible.
1. After reviewing briefly his second and third years at Cambridge, Wordsworth here describes his trip through France and Switzerland with a college friend, Robert Jones, during the succeeding summer vacation, in 1790. France was then in the "golden hours" of the early period of the Revolution; the fall of the Bastille had occurred on July 14 of the preceding year.

Not slow to share my wishes, took his staff,   325
And, sallying forth, we journeyed, side by side,
Bound to the distant Alps. A hardy slight
Did this unprecedented course imply
Of College studies and their set rewards;[2]
Nor had, in truth, the scheme been formed by me   330
Without uneasy forethought of the pain,
The censures, and ill-omening of those
To whom my worldly interests were dear.
But Nature then was Sovereign in my mind,
And mighty Forms, seizing a youthful fancy,   335
Had given a charter[3] to irregular hopes.
In any age of uneventful calm
Among the Nations, surely would my heart
Have been possessed by similar desire;
But Europe at that time was thrilled with joy,   340
France standing on the top of golden hours,
And human nature seeming born again.

[Crossing Simplon Pass]

* * * That very day,
From a bare ridge we also first beheld   525
Unveiled the summit of Mont Blanc, and grieved
To have a soulless image on the eye
Which had usurped upon a living thought
That never more could be.[4] The wondrous Vale
Of Chamouny[5] stretched far below, and soon   530
With its dumb cataracts, and streams of ice,
A motionless array of mighty waves,
Five rivers broad and vast, made rich amends,
And reconciled us to realities.
There small birds warble from the leafy trees,   535
The eagle soars high in the element;
There doth the Reaper bind the yellow sheaf,
The Maiden spread the hay-cock in the sun,
While Winter like a well-tamed lion walks,
Descending from the Mountain to make sport   540
Among the Cottages by beds of flowers.
   Whate'er in this wide circuit we beheld,
Or heard, was fitted to our unripe state
Of intellect and heart. With such a book
Before our eyes we could not chuse but read   545
Lessons of genuine brotherhood, the plain
And universal reason of mankind,
The truths of Young and Old. Nor, side by side
Pacing, two social Pilgrims, or alone

2. English universities allow much longer vacations than those in the United States, on the optimistic assumption that they will be used primarily for intensive study. Wordsworth is facing his final examinations in the next college year.
3. Privileged freedom.
4. The "image" is the actual sight of Mont Blanc, as against what the poet has imagined the famous Swiss mountain to be.
5. Chamonix, a valley in eastern France, north of Mont Blanc.

Each with his humour,[6] could we fail to abound   550
In dreams and fictions pensively composed,
Dejection taken up for pleasure's sake,
And gilded sympathies; the willow wreath,[7]
And sober posies[8] of funereal flowers
Gathered, among those solitudes sublime,   555
From formal gardens of the Lady Sorrow,
Did sweeten many a meditative hour.
   Yet still in me with those soft luxuries
Mixed something of stern mood, an under thirst
Of vigor seldom utterly allayed.   560
And from that source how different a sadness
Would issue, let one incident make known.
When from the Vallais we had turned, and clomb[9]
Along the Simplon's steep and rugged road,[1]
Following a band of Muleteers, we reached   565
A halting-place where all together took
Their noon-tide meal. Hastily rose our Guide,
Leaving *us* at the Board; awhile we lingered,
Then paced the beaten downward way that led
Right to a rough stream's edge and there broke off.   570
The only track now visible was one
That from the torrent's further brink held forth
Conspicuous invitation to ascend
A lofty mountain. After brief delay
Crossing the unbridged stream, that road we took   575
And clomb with eagerness, till anxious fears
Intruded, for we failed to overtake
Our Comrades gone before. By fortunate chance,
While every moment added doubt to doubt,
A Peasant met us, from whose mouth we learned   580
That to the Spot which had perplexed us first
We must descend, and there should find the road,
Which in the stony channel of the Stream
Lay a few steps, and then along its banks,
And that our future course, all plain to sight,   585
Was downwards, with the current of that Stream.
Loth to believe what we so grieved to hear,
For still we had hopes that pointed to the clouds,
We questioned him again, and yet again;
But every word that from the Peasant's lips   590
Came in reply, translated by our feelings,
Ended in this, *that we had crossed the Alps.*[2]
   Imagination—here the Power so called
Through sad incompetence of human speech—

6. Temperament, or state of mind.
7. Symbolizing sorrow. "Gilded": laid on like gilt; i.e., superficial.
8. Small bunches of flowers.
9. Climbed.
1. The Simplon Pass through the Alps.
2. As Dorothy Wordsworth baldly put it later on, "The ambition of youth was disappointed at these tidings." The visionary experience that follows (lines 593–617) occurred not in the Alps but at the time of writing the passage, as the 1805 text explicitly says: "Imagination! lifting up itself / Before the eye and progress of my Song."

That awful Power rose from the Mind's abyss   595
Like an unfathered vapour[3] that enwraps
At once some lonely Traveller. I was lost,
Halted without an effort to break through;
But to my conscious soul I now can say,
"I recognize thy glory"; in such strength   600
Of usurpation, when the light of sense
Goes out, but with a flash that has revealed
The invisible world, doth Greatness make abode,
There harbours, whether we be young or old;
Our destiny, our being's heart and home,   605
Is with infinitude, and only there;
With hope it is, hope that can never die,
Effort, and expectation, and desire,
And something evermore about to be.[4]
Under such banners militant the Soul   610
Seeks for no trophies, struggles for no spoils,
That may attest her prowess, blest in thoughts
That are their own perfection and reward,
Strong in herself, and in beatitude[5]
That hides her like the mighty flood of Nile   615
Poured from his fount of Abyssinian clouds
To fertilize the whole Egyptian plain.
    The melancholy slackening that ensued
Upon those tidings by the Peasant given
Was soon dislodged; downwards we hurried fast   620
And, with the half-shaped road, which we had missed,
Entered a narrow chasm. The brook and road
Were fellow-Travellers in this gloomy Strait,
And with them did we journey several hours
At a slow pace. The immeasurable height   625
Of woods decaying, never to be decayed,
The stationary blasts of waterfalls,
And in the narrow rent at every turn
Winds thwarting winds, bewildered and forlorn,
The torrents shooting from the clear blue sky,   630
The rocks that muttered close upon our ears,
Black drizzling crags that spake by the way-side
As if a voice were in them, the sick sight
And giddy prospect of the raving stream,
The unfettered clouds, and region of the Heavens,   635
Tumult and peace, the darkness and the light—
Were all like workings of one mind, the features
Of the same face, blossoms upon one tree,
Characters of the great Apocalypse,[6]

3. Sudden vapor from no apparent source.
4. At the time, Wordsworth had not been able to understand why he had felt such grievous disappointment at finding that he had already crossed the Alps, while still expecting to climb upward (lines 587–92). Now, a flash of vision reveals the symbolic significance of that experience: that the glory of humankind is to aim infinitely high, even though our capabilities are finite.
5. The ultimate blessedness or happiness.
6. The objects in this natural scene, exhibiting a coincidence of all opposites, are like the written words of the Apocalypse—i.e., of the Book of Revelation, the last book of the New Testament.

The types and symbols of Eternity,   640
Of first and last, and midst, and without end.[7]

From Book Seventh
Residence in London[1]

[*The Blind Beggar. Bartholomew Fair*]

As the black storm upon the mountain top
Sets off the sunbeam in the Valley, so   620
That huge fermenting Mass of human-kind
Serves as a solemn background or relief
To single forms and objects, whence they draw,
For feeling and contemplative regard,
More than inherent liveliness and power.   625
How oft amid those overflowing streets
Have I gone forward with the Crowd, and said
Unto myself, "The face of every one
That passes by me is a mystery!"
Thus have I looked, nor ceased to look, oppressed   630
By thoughts of what and whither, when and how,
Until the Shapes before my eyes became
A second-sight procession, such as glides
Over still mountains, or appears in dreams.
And once, far-travelled in such mood, beyond   635
The reach of common indication, lost
Amid the moving pageant, I was smitten
Abruptly with the view (a sight not rare)
Of a blind Beggar who, with upright face,
Stood propped against a Wall; upon his chest   640
Wearing a written paper to explain
His Story, whence he came, and who he was.
Caught by the spectacle, my mind turned round
As with the might of waters; an apt type
This Label seemed, of the utmost we can know   645
Both of ourselves and of the universe;
And on the Shape of that unmoving Man,
His steadfast face, and sightless eyes, I gazed
As if admonished from another world.
Though reared upon the base of outward things,   650
Structures like these the excited Spirit mainly
Builds for herself. Scenes different there are,
Full-formed, that take, with small internal help,
Possession of the faculties—the peace
That comes with night; the deep solemnity   655
Of Nature's intermediate hours of rest,
When the great tide of human life stands still,

---

7. Cf. Revelation 1.8: "I am Alpha and Omega, the beginning and the ending, saith the Lord"; the phrase is repeated in 21.6, after the fulfillment of the last things. In *Paradise Lost* 5.153–65 Milton says that the things created declare their Creator, and calls on all to extol "him first, him last, him midst, and without end." 1. Wordsworth spent three and a half months in London in 1791.

The business of the day to come—unborn,
Of that gone by—locked up as in the grave;[2]
The blended calmness of the heavens and earth,   660
Moonlight, and stars, and empty streets, and sounds
Unfrequent as in deserts: at late hours
Of winter evenings when unwholesome rains
Are falling hard, with people yet astir,
The feeble salutation from the voice   665
Of some unhappy woman, now and then
Heard as we pass; when no one looks about,
Nothing is listened to. But these, I fear,
Are falsely catalogued;[3] things that are, are not,
As the mind answers to them, or the heart   670
Is prompt or slow to feel. What say you, then,
To times when half the City shall break out
Full of one passion, vengeance, rage, or fear?
To executions,[4] to a Street on fire,
Mobs, riots, or rejoicings? From these sights   675
Take one, that annual Festival, the Fair
Holden where Martyrs suffered in past time,
And named of St. Bartholomew;[5] there see
A work completed to our hands, that lays,
If any spectacle on earth can do,   680
The whole creative powers of Man asleep!
For once the Muse's help will we implore,
And she shall lodge us, wafted on her wings,
Above the press and danger of the Crowd,
Upon some Shewman's platform. What a shock   685
For eyes and ears! what anarchy and din
Barbarian and infernal—a phantasma[6]
Monstrous in color, motion, shape, sight, sound!
Below, the open space, through every nook
Of the wide area, twinkles, is alive   690
With heads; the midway region and above
Is thronged with staring pictures, and huge scrolls,
Dumb proclamations of the Prodigies!
With chattering monkeys dangling from their poles,
And children whirling in their roundabouts;[7]   695
With those that stretch the neck, and strain the eyes;
And crack the voice in rivalship, the crowd
Inviting; with buffoons against buffoons
Grimacing, writhing, screaming, him who grinds
The hurdy-gurdy,[8] at the fiddle weaves,   700
Rattles the salt-box,[9] thumps the Kettle-drum;

---

2. The sonnet *Composed upon Westminster Bridge*
describes a similar response to London when its
"mighty heart is lying still."
3. I.e., mistakenly classified as scenes (lines 652–54)
whose effects on the perceiver depend but little on
contributions by the perceiving mind.
4. Executions were public events in England until
1868.
5. This huge fair was long held in Smithfield, the

place where, on St. Bartholomew's Day, Aug. 24, Protestants had been executed in Queen Mary's reign
(1553–58).
6. Fantasy of a disordered mind.
7. Merry-go-rounds.
8. A stringed instrument, sounded by a turning wheel
covered by rosin.
9. A wooden box, rattled and beaten with a stick.

And him who at the trumpet puffs his cheeks;
The silver-collared Negro with his timbrel;[1]
Equestrians, tumblers, women, girls, and boys,
Blue-breeched, pink-vested, with high-towering plumes.   705
—All moveables of wonder from all parts
And here, Albinos, painted-Indians, Dwarfs,
The Horse of Knowledge,[2] and the learned Pig,
The Stone-eater, the Man that swallows fire—
Giants, Ventriloquists, the Invisible-girl,   710
The Bust that speaks, and moves its goggling eyes,
The Wax-work, Clock-work, all the marvellous craft
Of modern Merlins,[3] Wild-beasts, Puppet-shews,
All out-o'th'-way, far-fetched, perverted things,
All freaks of Nature, all Promethean[4] thoughts   715
Of man; his dullness, madness, and their feats,
All jumbled up together, to compose
A Parliament of Monsters. Tents and Booths,
Meanwhile, as if the whole were one vast mill,
Are vomiting, receiving, on all sides,   720
Men, Women, three-years' Children, Babes in arms.
     Oh blank confusion! true epitome
Of what the mighty City is herself
To thousands upon thousands of her Sons,
Living amid the same perpetual whirl   725
Of trivial objects, melted and reduced
To one identity, by differences
That have no law, no meaning, and no end;
Oppression under which even highest minds
Must labour, whence the strongest are not free!   730
But though the picture weary out the eye,
By nature an unmanageable sight,
It is not wholly so to him who looks
In steadiness, who hath among least things
An undersense of greatest; sees the parts   735
As parts, but with a feeling of the whole.

                    *   *   *

This did I feel in London's vast Domain;
The Spirit of Nature was upon me there;
The Soul of Beauty and enduring life
Vouchsafed her inspirations; and diffused,
Through meagre lines and colours, and the press   770
Of self-destroying transitory things,
Composure, and ennobling harmony.

---

1. Tambourine.   romance.
2. A horse trained to tap out answers to numerical 4. Creative, or highly inventive. In Greek mythology
questions, etc.   Prometheus made man out of clay and taught him the
3. Magicians. Merlin was the magician in Arthurian arts.

From Book Eighth
Retrospect, Love of Nature leading
to Love of Man[1]

[The Shepherd in the Mist. Man Still Subordinate to Nature]

* * * A rambling School-boy, thus
I felt his presence in his own domain
As of a Lord and Master; or a Power
Or Genius,[2] under Nature, under God
Presiding; and severest solitude   260
Had more commanding looks when he was there.
When up the lonely brooks on rainy days
Angling I went, or trod the trackless hills
By mists bewildered, suddenly mine eyes
Have glanced upon him distant a few steps,   265
In size a Giant, stalking through thick fog,
His sheep like Greenland bears;[3] or, as he stepped
Beyond the boundary line of some hill-shadow,
His form hath flashed upon me, glorified
By the deep radiance of the setting sun:[4]   270
Or him have I descried in distant sky,
A solitary object and sublime,
Above all height! like an aerial cross
Stationed alone upon a spiry rock
Of the Chartreuse, for worship.[5] Thus was Man   275
Ennobled outwardly before my sight,
And thus my heart was early introduced
To an unconscious love and reverence
Of human nature; hence the human Form
To me became an index of delight,   280
Of grace, and honor, power, and worthiness.
Meanwhile this Creature, spiritual almost
As those of Books, but more exalted far;
Far more of an imaginative Form
Than the gay Corin of the groves, who lives   285
For his own fancies, or to dance by the hour
In coronal, with Phillis in the midst[6] —
Was, for the purposes of Kind,[7] a Man
With the most common; husband, father; learned,
Could teach, admonish, suffered with the rest   290

1. In this book Wordsworth reviews the first twenty-one years of his life in order to trace the transfer of his earlier feelings for nature to shepherds and other humble people who carry on their lonely duties almost as though they were animate parts of the landscape (cf. *Michael*, lines 1–39, pp. 1368–69). Wordsworth's central concern is to describe the early development in his relatively inexperienced mind of an image, or conceptual model, of the largeness, worth, and almost sacred dignity of generic Man (lines 256–81), an image that proved invulnerable to the acid bath of his later experience of the vulgarity, meanness, and evil of which individuals are capable (lines 317–22).
2. Presiding spirit.

3. Polar bears.
4. A "glory" is a mountain phenomenon in which the enlarged figure of a person is seen projected by the sun on the mist, with a radiance about its head. Cf. Coleridge's *Dejection: An Ode*, line 54 (p. 1525).
5. In his tour of the Alps, Wordsworth had been deeply impressed by the Chartreuse, a Carthusian monastery in the French Alps, with its soaring cross visible against the sky. There is an overtone here of the Christlike divinity investing the "common" man (line 289).
6. Corin and Phillis, dancing in their coronals, or wreaths of flowers, were stock characters in earlier pastoral literature.
7. I.e., in carrying out the tasks of humankind.

From vice and folly, wretchedness and fear;
Of this I little saw, cared less for it;
But something must have felt.
                                    Call ye these appearances
Which I beheld of Shepherds in my youth,
This sanctity of Nature given to man—   295
A shadow, a delusion, ye who pore
On the dead letter, miss the spirit of things;
Whose truth is not a motion or a shape
Instinct with vital functions, but a Block
Or waxen image which yourselves have made,   300
And ye adore. But blessed be the God
Of Nature and of Man, that this was so,
That men before my inexperienced eyes
Did first present themselves thus purified,
Removed, and to a distance that was fit.   305
And so we all of us in some degree
Are led to knowledge, whencesoever led
And howsoever; were it otherwise,
And we found evil fast as we find good
In our first years, or think that it is found,   310
How could the innocent heart bear up and live?
But doubly fortunate my lot; not here
Alone, that something of a better life
Perhaps was round me than it is the privilege
Of most to move in, but that first I looked   315
At Man through objects that were great or fair,
First communed with him by their help. And thus
Was founded a sure safeguard and defence
Against the weight of meanness, selfish cares,
Coarse manners, vulgar passions, that beat in   320
On all sides from the ordinary world
In which we traffic. Starting from this point,
I had my face turned tow'rd the truth, began
With an advantage furnished by that kind
Of prepossession without which the soul   325
Receives no knowledge that can bring forth good,
No genuine insight ever comes to her.
From the restraint of over-watchful eyes
Preserved, I moved about, year after year
Happy, and now most thankful, that my walk   330
Was guarded from too early intercourse
With the deformities of crowded life,
And those ensuing laughters and contempts
Self-pleasing, which, if we would wish to think
With a due reverence on earth's rightful Lord,   335
Here placed to be the Inheritor of heaven,[8]
Will not permit us; but pursue the mind
That to devotion willingly would rise,
Into the Temple, and the Temple's heart.[9]

8. This pious line was a later addition to the version of   9. I.e., into the devotional recesses of the innermost
1805.   mind.

Yet deem not, Friend, that human-kind with me   340
Thus early took a place preeminent;
Nature herself was at this unripe time
But secondary to my own pursuits
And animal activities, and all
Their trivial pleasures:[1] and when these had drooped   345
And gradually expired, and Nature, prized
For her own sake, became my joy, even then—
And upwards through late youth, until not less
Than two and twenty summers had been told—
Was Man in my affections and regards   350
Subordinate to her; her visible Forms
And viewless agencies: a passion she,
A rapture often, and immediate love
Ever at hand; *he* only a delight
Occasional, an accidental grace,   355
His hour being not yet come. * * *

From Book Ninth
Residence in France[1]

[*Paris and Orléans. Becomes a "Patriot"*]

Even as a River—partly (it might seem)
Yielding to old remembrances, and swayed
In part by fear to shape a way direct
That would engulph him soon in the ravenous Sea—
Turns, and will measure back his course, far back,   5
Seeking the very regions which he crossed
In his first outset; so have we, my Friend!
Turned and returned with intricate delay.
Or as a Traveller, who has gained the brow
Of some aerial Down,[2] while there he halts   10
For breathing-time, is tempted to review
The region left behind him; and if aught
Deserving notice have escaped regard,
Or been regarded with too careless eye,
Strives, from that height, with one, and yet one more   15
Last look, to make the best amends he may,
So have we lingered. Now we start afresh
With courage, and new hope risen on our toil.
Fair greetings to this shapeless eagerness,
Whene'er it comes! needful in work so long,   20
Thrice needful to the argument which now
Awaits us! Oh, how much unlike the past![3]

1. Cf. his account of the stages of his development in
lines 65–92 of *Tintern Abbey* (p. 1338, n. 2).
1. Wordsworth's second visit to France, while he was
twenty-one and twenty-two years of age (1791–92),
came during a crucial period of the French Revolution. This book deals with his stay at Paris, Orléans,
and Blois, when he developed his passionate partisanship for the French people and the revolutionary

cause.
2. Treeless high land.
3. This preface parallels in function Milton's preface
to the equivalent ninth book of *Paradise Lost*, in which
he announces that, having narrated the blameless life
of Adam and Eve in Eden, he "now must change /
Those notes to tragic," and tell of their fall. "Argument": theme.

    Free as a Colt, at pasture on the hill,
I ranged at large through London's wide Domain
Month after Month. Obscurely did I live,   25
Not seeking frequent intercourse with men
By literature, or elegance, or rank
Distinguished. Scarcely was a year thus spent[4]
Ere I forsook the crowded Solitude;
With less regret for its luxurious pomp   30
And all the nicely-guarded shews of Art,
Than for the humble Bookstalls in the Streets,
Exposed to eye and hand where'er I turned.
    —France lured me forth, the realm that I had crossed
So lately, journeying toward the snow-clad Alps.   35
But now relinquishing the scrip and staff[5]
And all enjoyment which the summer sun
Sheds round the steps of those who meet the day
With motion constant as his own, I went
Prepared to sojourn in a pleasant Town   40
Washed by the current of the stately Loire.[6]
    Through Paris lay my readiest course, and there
Sojourning a few days, I visited
In haste each spot, of old or recent fame,
The latter chiefly; from the field of Mars   45
Down to the suburbs of St. Anthony;
And from Mont Martyr southward to the Dome
Of Genevieve.[7] In both her clamorous Halls,
The National Synod and the Jacobins,[8]
I saw the Revolutionary Power   50
Toss like a Ship at anchor, rocked by storms;
The Arcades I traversed, in the Palace huge
Of Orleans,[9] coasted round and round the line
Of Tavern, Brothel, Gaming-house, and Shop,
Great rendezvous of worst and best, the walk   55
Of all who had a purpose, or had not;
I stared, and listened with a Stranger's ears
To Hawkers and Haranguers, hubbub wild!
And hissing Factionists, with ardent eyes,
In knots, or pairs, or single. Not a look   60
Hope takes, or Doubt or Fear are forced to wear,
But seemed there present, and I scanned them all,
Watched every gesture uncontrollable
Of anger, and vexation, and despite,
All side by side, and struggling face to face   65

4. His stay in London in fact lasted only four or five months, Jan.–May 1791.
5. The "scrip" (the bag or knapsack) and the "staff" are the traditional emblems of the foot pilgrim.
6. Orléans, on the Loire River, where Wordsworth stayed from Dec. 1791 until he moved to Blois early the next year.
7. The "field of Mars" (the Champ de Mars), where Louis XVI swore fidelity to the new constitution. "The suburbs of St. Anthony": Faubourg St. Antoine, near the Bastille, a working-class quarter and center of revo-

lutionary violence. "Mont Martyr": Montmartre, a hill on which revolutionary meetings were held. The "Dome of Geneviève" became the Panthéon, a burial place for notable Frenchmen.
8. The club of radical democratic revolutionists, named for the ancient convent of St. Jacques, their meeting place. "National Synod": the newly formed National Assembly.
9. The arcades in the courtyard of the Palais d'Orléans, a fashionable shopping center and Parisian rendezvous.

With Gaiety and dissolute Idleness.
—Where silent zephyrs sported with the dust
Of the Bastille,[1] I sate in the open sun,
And from the rubbish gathered up a stone
And pocketed the Relic in the guise   70
Of an Enthusiast; yet, in honest truth,
I looked for Something that I could not find,
Affecting more emotion than I felt;
For 'tis most certain that these various sights,
However potent their first shock, with me   75
Appeared to recompence the Traveller's pains
Less than the painted Magdalene of Le Brun,[2]
A Beauty exquisitely wrought, with hair
Dishevelled, gleaming eyes, and rueful cheek
Pale, and bedropp'd with everflowing tears.   80
    But hence to my more permanent Abode[3]
I hasten; there by novelties in speech,
Domestic manners, customs, gestures, looks,
And all the attire of ordinary life,
Attention was engrossed; and, thus amused,   85
I stood 'mid those concussions unconcerned,
Tranquil almost, and careless as a flower
Glassed in a green-house, or a Parlour shrub
That spreads its leaves in unmolested peace
While every bush and tree, the country through,   90
Is shaking to the roots; indifference this
Which may seem strange; but I was unprepared
With needful knowledge, had abruptly passed
Into a theatre whose stage was filled,
And busy with an action far advanced.   95
Like Others I had skimmed, and sometimes read
With care, the master pamphlets of the day;[4]
Nor wanted such half-insight as grew wild
Upon that meagre soil, helped out by talk
And public news; but having never seen   100
A Chronicle that might suffice to shew
Whence the main Organs[5] of the public Power
Had sprung, their transmigrations when and how
Accomplished, giving thus unto events
A form and body; all things were to me   105
Loose and disjointed, and the affections left
Without a vital interest. At that time,
Moreover, the first storm was overblown,
And the strong hand of outward violence
Locked up in quiet.[6] For myself, I fear   110

1. The political prison of the Bastille had been demolished, after it had been stormed and sacked on July 14,
1789.
2. A painting of the weeping Mary Magdalene by
Charles Le Brun (1619–1690), then regarded as a religious masterpiece.
3. In Orléans.
4. Wordsworth probably refers to the numerous English pamphlets (including Paine's Rights of Man, part

1, and Wollstonecraft's A Vindication of the Rights of
Men) published in response to Edmund Burke's attack
on the revolution, Reflections on the Revolution in
France (1790).
5. Institutions, instruments.
6. After the storming of the Bastille in 1789 there was
a period of calm until the massacre of three thousand
Royalists in Sept. 1792, after the deposition and imprisonment of Louis XVI.

Now, in connection with so great a Theme,
To speak (as I must be compelled to do)
Of one so unimportant; night by night
Did I frequent the formal haunts of men
Whom, in the City, privilege of birth   115
Sequestered from the rest: societies
Polished in Arts, and in punctilio[7] versed;
Whence, and from deeper causes, all discourse
Of good and evil of the time was shunned
With scrupulous care: but these restrictions soon   120
Proved tedious, and I gradually withdrew
Into a noisier world, and thus erelong
Became a Patriot;[8] and my heart was all
Given to the People, and my love was theirs.

From Book Tenth
France continued[1]

[The Revolution: Paris and England]

Cheared with this hope,[2] to Paris I returned;
And ranged, with ardor heretofore unfelt,
The spacious City, and in progress passed   50
The Prison where the unhappy Monarch lay,[3]
Associate with his Children and his Wife,
In Bondage; and the Palace[4] lately stormed,
With roar of Cannon, by a furious Host.
I crossed the Square (an empty Area then!)   55
Of the Carousel, where so late had lain
The Dead, upon the Dying heaped; and gazed
On this and other Spots, as doth a Man
Upon a Volume whose contents he knows
Are memorable, but from him locked up,   60
Being written in a tongue he cannot read;
So that he questions the mute leaves with pain,
And half-upbraids their silence. But, that night,
I felt most deeply in what world I was,
What ground I trod on, and what air I breathed.   65
High was my Room and lonely, near the roof
Of a large Mansion or Hotel,[5] a Lodge
That would have pleased me in more quiet times,
Nor was it wholly without pleasure, then.
With unextinguished taper I kept watch,   70
Reading at intervals; the fear gone by
Pressed on me almost like a fear to come.

---

7. The niceties of social manners.
8. I.e., became committed to the people's side in the Revolution.
1. At this period, Oct. 1792–Aug. 1794, Wordsworth's revolutionary enthusiasm was at its height.
2. I.e., that the moderates were now taking over and would eliminate further violence.

3. I.e., the "Temple" (it had once housed the religious Order of Templars), where Louis XVI was held prisoner.
4. The Tuileries; in front of this is the great square of "the Carousel" (line 56), where a number of the mob storming the palace had been killed.
5. A town house.

I thought of those September massacres,
Divided from me by one little month,
Saw them and touched;[6] the rest was conjured up   75
From tragic fictions, or true history,
Remembrances and dim admonishments.
The Horse is taught his manage,[7] and no Star
Of wildest course but treads back his own steps;
For the spent hurricane the air provides   80
As fierce a Successor; the tide retreats
But to return out of its hiding place
In the great Deep; all things have second birth;
The earthquake is not satisfied at once;
And in this way I wrought upon myself   85
Until I seemed to hear a voice that cried
To the whole City, "Sleep no more."[8] The Trance
Fled with the Voice to which it had given birth,
But vainly comments of a calmer mind
Promised soft peace and sweet forgetfulness.   90
The place, all hushed and silent as it was,
Appeared unfit for the repose of Night,
Defenceless as a wood where Tygers roam.

          * * * In this frame of mind,
Dragged by a chain of harsh necessity,
So seemed it,—now I thankfully acknowledge,
Forced by the gracious providence of Heaven—
To England I returned,[9] else (though assured   225
That I both was, and must be, of small weight,
No better than a Landsman on the deck
Of a ship struggling with a hideous storm)
Doubtless I should have then made common cause
With some who perished, haply perished too,[1]   230
A poor mistaken and bewildered offering,
Should to the breast of Nature have gone back
With all my resolutions, all my hopes,
A Poet only to myself, to Men
Useless, and even, belovèd Friend, a Soul   235
To thee unknown![2]

                    *   *   *

What then were my emotions, when in Arms
Britain put forth her free-born strength in league,
O pity and shame! with those confederate Powers?[3]   265

6. I.e., his imagination of the September massacres
was so vivid as to be palpable.
7. The French *manège*, the prescribed action and
paces of a trained horse.
8. *Macbeth* 2.2.34–36: "Methought I heard a voice
cry, 'Sleep no more! / Macbeth does murder sleep.'"
9. Forced by the "harsh necessity" of a lack of money,
Wordsworth returned to England late in 1792.
1. Wordsworth had allied his sympathies with the
party of the Girondins, almost all of whom were guillotined or committed suicide.

2. Wordsworth did not meet Coleridge, the "beloved
Friend," until 1795.
3. England joined the war against France in Feb.
1793. The great moral crisis that almost wrecked
Wordsworth's life began with this sudden split between
his profound attachments to the English land (the
development of which he had described in the early
books of *The Prelude*) and his later but heartfelt identification with the cause of the French Revolution. What
had seemed a single and coherent development suddenly became split into conflicting parts.

Not in my single self alone I found,
But in the minds of all ingenuous Youth,
Change and subversion from that hour. No shock
Given to my moral nature had I known
Down to that very moment; neither lapse   270
Nor turn of sentiment that might be named
A revolution, save at this one time;
All else was progress on the self-same path
On which, with a diversity of pace,
I had been travelling: this a stride at once   275
Into another region.—As a light
And pliant hare-bell swinging in the breeze
On some gray rock, its birth-place, so had I
Wantoned, fast rooted on the ancient tower
Of my beloved Country, wishing not   280
A happier fortune than to wither there.
Now was I from that pleasant station torn
And tossed about in whirlwind. I rejoiced,
Yea, afterwards, truth most painful to record!
Exulted, in the triumph of my Soul,   285
When Englishmen by thousands were o'erthrown,
Left without glory on the field, or driven,
Brave hearts, to shameful flight.[4] It was a grief,—
Grief call it not, 'twas any thing but that,—
A conflict of sensations without name,   290
Of which *he* only who may love the sight
Of a Village Steeple as I do can judge,
When, in the Congregation bending all
To their great Father, prayers were offered up,
Or praises, for our Country's victories,   295
And, 'mid the simple Worshippers, perchance
I only, like an uninvited Guest,
Whom no one owned, sate silent, shall I add,
Fed on the day of vengeance yet to come?

[*The Reign of Terror. Nightmares*]

—Domestic carnage now filled the whole year
With Feast-days;[5] old Men from the Chimney-nook,
The Maiden from the bosom of her Love,
The Mother from the Cradle of her Babe,
The Warrior from the Field, all perished, all,   360
Friends, enemies, of all parties, ages, ranks,
Head after head, and never heads enough
For those that bade them fall. They found their joy,
They made it, proudly eager as a Child
(If like desires of innocent little ones   365
May with such heinous appetites be compared),
Pleased in some open field to exercise

---

4. The French defeated the English in the battle of Hondschoote, Sept. 6, 1793.
5. I.e., festivals celebrated by human slaughter ("carnage"). Lines 356–63 give a description of the height of the Reign of Terror under Robespierre; in 1794, 1,376 people were guillotined in Paris in forty-nine days.

A toy that mimics with revolving wings
The motion of a windmill, though the air
Do of itself blow fresh and make the Vanes 370
Spin in his eyesight, *that* contents him not,
But, with the play-thing at arm's length, he sets
His front against the blast, and runs amain
That it may whirl the faster.

* * *

Most melancholy at that time, O Friend!
Were my day-thoughts, my nights were miserable;
Through months, through years, long after the last beat
Of those atrocities, the hour of sleep 400
To me came rarely charged with natural gifts,
Such ghastly Visions had I of despair
And tyranny, and implements of death,
And innocent victims sinking under fear,
And momentary hope, and worn-out prayer, 405
Each in his separate cell, or penned in crowds
For sacrifice, and struggling with forced mirth
And levity in dungeons where the dust
Was laid with tears. Then suddenly the scene
Changed, and the unbroken dream entangled me 410
In long orations which I strove to plead
Before unjust tribunals—with a voice
Labouring, a brain confounded, and a sense
Death-like of treacherous desertion, felt
In the last place of refuge, my own soul. 415

From Book Eleventh
France, concluded[1]

[*Retrospect:* "*Bliss Was It in That Dawn.*" *Recourse to* "*Reason's Naked Self*"]

O pleasant exercise of hope and joy![2] 105
For mighty were the Auxiliars which then stood
Upon our side, we who were strong in Love!
Bliss was it in that dawn to be alive,
But to be young was very Heaven! O times,
In which the meagre, stale, forbidding ways 110
Of custom, law, and statute, took at once
The attraction of a Country in Romance!
When Reason seemed the most to assert her rights,
When most intent on making of herself

---

1. Book 11 deals with the year from Aug. 1794 through Sept. 1795: Wordsworth's growing disillusionment with the French Revolution, his recourse to abstract theories of man and politics, his despair and nervous breakdown, and the beginning of his recovery when he moved from London to Racedown.
2. Wordsworth in this passage turns back to the summer of 1792, when his enthusiasm for the revolution was at its height.

A prime Enchantress—to assist the work   115
Which then was going forward in her name!
Not favored spots alone, but the whole earth
The beauty wore of promise—that which sets
(As at some moments might not be unfelt
Among the bowers of Paradise itself)   120
The budding rose above the rose full blown.[3]
What Temper[4] at the prospect did not wake
To happiness unthought of? The inert
Were roused, and lively natures rapt away![5]
They who had fed their Childhood upon dreams,   125
The play-fellows of Fancy, who had made
All powers of swiftness, subtilty, and strength
Their ministers,—who in lordly wise had stirred
Among the grandest objects of the Sense,
And dealt with whatsoever they found there   130
As if they had within some lurking right
To wield it;—they, too, who of gentle mood
Had watched all gentle motions, and to these
Had fitted their own thoughts, schemers more mild,
And in the region of their peaceful selves;—   135
Now was it that *both* found, the Meek and Lofty
Did both find helpers to their hearts' desire,
And stuff at hand, plastic[6] as they could wish,—
Were called upon to exercise their skill,
Not in Utopia,—subterranean Fields,—   140
Or some secreted Island, Heaven knows where!
But in the very world, which is the world
Of all of us,—the place where in the end
We find our happiness, or not at all!
     Why should I not confess that Earth was then   145
To me what an Inheritance new-fallen
Seems, when the first time visited, to one
Who thither comes to find in it his home?
He walks about and looks upon the spot
With cordial transport, moulds it and remoulds,   150
And is half-pleased with things that are amiss,
'Twill be such joy to see them disappear.
     An active partisan, I thus convoked[7]
From every object pleasant circumstance
To suit my ends; I moved among mankind   155
With genial feelings still[8] predominant;
When erring, erring on the better part,
And in the kinder spirit; placable,
Indulgent, as not uninformed that men
See as they have been taught, and that Antiquity[9]   160
Gives rights to error; and aware no less
That throwing off oppression must be work

3. A statement of the Romantic theme of the glory of the imperfect, which sets a higher value on promise than on achievement.
4. Temperament.
5. Enraptured; carried away by enthusiasm.
6. Malleable.
7. Called up.
8. Always.
9. Classical antiquity.

As well of licence as of liberty;
And above all, for this was more than all,
Not caring if the wind did now and then   165
Blow keen upon an eminence that gave
Prospect so large into futurity;
In brief, a Child of Nature, as at first,
Diffusing only those affections wider
That from the cradle had grown up with me,   170
And losing, in no other way than light
Is lost in light, the weak in the more strong.
    In the main outline, such, it might be said,
Was my condition, till with open war
Britain opposed the Liberties of France;[1]   175
This threw me first out of the pale[2] of love,
Soured, and corrupted, upwards to the source,
My sentiments; was not,[3] as hitherto,
A swallowing up of lesser things in great;
But change of them into their contraries;   180
And thus a way was opened for mistakes
And false conclusions, in degree as gross,
In kind more dangerous. What had been a pride
Was now a shame; my likings and my loves
Ran in new channels, leaving old ones dry,   185
And hence a blow that in maturer age
Would but have touched the judgement, struck more deep
Into sensations near the heart; meantime,
As from the first, wild theories were afloat
To whose pretensions sedulously urged[4]   190
I had but lent a careless ear, assured
That time was ready to set all things right,
And that the multitude so long oppressed
Would be oppressed no more.
                  But when events
Brought less encouragement, and unto these   195
The immediate proof of principles no more
Could be entrusted, while the events themselves,
Worn out in greatness, stripped of novelty,
Less occupied the mind; and sentiments
Could through my understanding's natural growth   200
No longer keep their ground, by faith maintained
Of inward consciousness, and hope that laid
Her hand upon her object; evidence
Safer, of universal application, such
As could not be impeached, was sought elsewhere.   205
    But now, become Oppressors in their turn,
Frenchmen had changed a war of self-defence
For one of Conquest, losing sight of all
Which they had struggled for:[5] and mounted up,

---

1. On Feb. 11, 1793, England declared war against France.
2. Enclosure.
3. I.e., there was not (in my sentiments). . . .
4. Diligently argued for.

5. In late 1794 and early 1795 French troops had successes in Spain, Italy, Holland, and Germany—even though, in the constitution written in 1790, they had renounced all foreign conquest.

Openly in the eye of Earth and Heaven,   210
The scale of Liberty.[6] I read her doom
With anger vexed, with disappointment sore,
But not dismayed, nor taking to the shame
Of a false Prophet. While resentment rose,
Striving to hide, what nought could heal, the wounds   215
Of mortified presumption, I adhered
More firmly to old tenets, and, to prove[7]
Their temper, strained them more; and thus, in heat
Of contest, did opinions every day
Grow into consequence, till round my mind   220
They clung, as if they were its life, nay more,
The very being of the immortal Soul.
      This was the time when, all things tending fast
To depravation, speculative schemes
That promised to abstract the hopes of Man   225
Out of his feelings, to be fixed thenceforth
For ever in a purer element,
Found ready welcome.[8] Tempting region *that*
For Zeal to enter and refresh herself,
Where passions had the privilege to work,   230
And never hear the sound of their own names:
But, speaking more in charity, the dream
Flattered the young, pleased with extremes, nor least
With that which makes our Reason's naked self
The object of its fervour. * * *   235

[Crisis, Breakdown, and Recovery]

I summoned my best skill, and toiled, intent
To anatomize[9] the frame of social life,   280
Yea, the whole body of society
Searched to its heart. Share with me, Friend! the wish
That some dramatic tale indued with shapes
Livelier, and flinging out less guarded words
Than suit the Work we fashion, might set forth   285
What then I learned, or think I learned, of truth,
And the errors into which I fell, betrayed
By present objects, and by reasonings false
From their beginnings, inasmuch as drawn
Out of a heart that had been turned aside   290
From Nature's way by outward accidents,
And which was thus confounded more and more,
Misguided and misguiding. So I fared,
Dragging all precepts, judgments, maxims, creeds,
Like culprits to the bar; calling the mind,   295

6. I.e., the desire for power now outweighed the love of liberty.
7. Test; the figure is that of testing a tempered steel sword.
8. I.e., schemes that undertook to separate ("abstract") people's hopes for future happiness from reliance on the emotional part of human nature, and instead to ground those hopes on their rational natures ("a purer element"). The allusion is primarily to William Godwin's *Inquiry Concerning Political Justice* (1793), which attempted to ground ethical and political principles, and the expectation of human progress, exclusively on rational principles.
9. Analyze.

Suspiciously, to establish in plain day
Her titles[1] and her honors, now believing,
Now disbelieving, endlessly perplexed
With impulse, motive, right and wrong, the ground
Of obligation, what the rule and whence   300
The sanction, till, demanding formal *proof*
And seeking it in every thing, I lost
All feeling of conviction, and, in fine,[2]
Sick, wearied out with contrarieties,
Yielded up moral questions in despair.   305
    This was the crisis of that strong disease,
This the soul's last and lowest ebb; I drooped,
Deeming our blessed Reason of least use
Where wanted most. * * *

        * * * Then it was,
Thanks to the bounteous Giver of all good!
That the beloved Woman[3] in whose sight   335
Those days were passed, now speaking in a voice
Of sudden admonition—like a brook
That does but *cross* a lonely road, and now
Seen, heard, and felt, and caught at every turn,
Companion never lost through many a league—   340
Maintained for me a saving intercourse
With my true self:[4] for, though bedimmed and changed
Both as a clouded and a waning moon,
She whispered still that brightness would return,
She in the midst of all preserved me still   345
A Poet, made me seek beneath that name,
And that alone, my office upon earth.
And lastly, as hereafter will be shewn,
If willing audience fail not, Nature's self,
By all varieties of human love   350
Assisted, led me back through opening day
To those sweet counsels between head and heart
Whence grew that genuine knowledge fraught with peace
Which, through the later sinkings of this cause,
Hath still upheld me, and upholds me now   355
In the catastrophe (for so they dream,
And nothing less), when, finally to close
And rivet down the gains of France, a Pope
Is summoned in, to crown an Emperor:[5]
This last opprobrium, when we see a people   360
That once looked up in faith, as if to Heaven
For manna, take a lesson from the Dog
Returning to his vomit. * * *

1. Legal entitlements.
2. In the end.
3. After a long separation Dorothy Wordsworth came
to live with her brother at Racedown in 1795, and
remained a permanent member of his household.
4. Dorothy and the renewed influence of nature (line
349) healed the inner fracture between his earlier

and later self, which Wordsworth had described in
10.268ff.
5. The ultimate blow to liberal hopes for France
occurred when on Dec. 2, 1804, Napoleon summoned
Pope Pius VII to officiate at the ceremony elevating
him to emperor. At the last moment, Napoleon took
the crown and donned it himself.

Book Twelfth
Imagination and Taste, how impaired and restored[1]

Long time have human ignorance and guilt
Detained us, on what spectacles of woe
Compelled to look, and inwardly oppressed
With sorrow, disappointment, vexing thoughts,
Confusion of the judgment, zeal decayed,   5
And, lastly, utter loss of hope itself
And things to hope for! Not with these began
Our Song, and not with these our Song must end.[2]
Ye motions of delight, that haunt the sides
Of the green hills; ye breezes and soft airs,   10
Whose subtile intercourse with breathing flowers,
Feelingly watched, might teach Man's haughty race
How without injury to take, to give
Without offence; ye who, as if to shew
The wondrous influence of power gently used,   15
Bend the complying heads of lordly pines,
And with a touch shift the stupendous clouds
Through the whole compass of the sky; ye brooks
Muttering along the stones, a busy noise
By day, a quiet sound in silent night;   20
Ye waves that out of the great deep steal forth
In a calm hour to kiss the pebbly shore,
Not mute, and then retire, fearing no storm;
And you, ye Groves, whose ministry it is
To interpose the covert of your shades,   25
Even as a sleep, between the heart of man
And outward troubles, between man himself,
Not seldom, and his own uneasy heart!
Oh that I had a music and a voice
Harmonious as your own, that I might tell   30
What Ye have done for me! The morning shines,
Nor heedeth Man's perverseness; Spring returns,
I saw the Spring return and could rejoice,
In common with the Children of her love
Piping on boughs, or sporting on fresh fields,   35
Or boldly seeking pleasure nearer heaven
On wings that navigate cerulean skies.
So neither were complacency[3] nor peace
Nor tender yearnings wanting for my good
Through those distracted times;[4] in Nature still   40
Glorying, I found a counterpoise in her,
Which, when the Spirit of evil reached its height,
Maintained for me a secret happiness.
    This Narrative, my Friend, hath chiefly told

---

1. Book 12 reviews the "impairment" and gradual recovery of Wordsworth's creative sensibility in response to the natural world.
2. The reference is back to the joyous preamble with which *The Prelude* began. Wordsworth goes on (line 10) to invoke the breeze described in the opening line of the poem.
3. Satisfaction.
4. I.e., the period of spiritual crisis that he had described in 11.293–309.

Of intellectual power,[5] fostering love,   45
Dispensing truth, and over men and things,
Where reason yet might hesitate, diffusing
Prophetic sympathies of genial faith.
So was I favored, such my happy lot,
Until that natural graciousness of mind   50
Gave way to overpressure from the times
And their disastrous issues. What availed,
When spells forbade the Voyager to land,
That fragrant notice of a pleasant shore
Wafted at intervals from many a bower   55
Of blissful gratitude and fearless peace?
Dare I avow that wish was mine to see,
And hope that future times *would* surely see,
The man to come parted as by a gulph
From him who had been, that I could no more   60
Trust the elevation which had made me one
With the great Family that still survives
To illuminate the abyss of ages past,
Sage, Warrior, Patriot, Hero?—for it seemed
That their best virtues were not free from taint   65
Of something false and weak, that could not stand
The open eye of Reason.[6] Then I said,
"Go to the Poets; they will speak to thee
More perfectly of purer Creatures; yet
If Reason be nobility in Man,   70
Can aught be more ignoble than the Man
Whom they delight in, blinded as he is
By prejudice, the miserable slave
Of low ambition, or distempered love?"
    In such strange passion (if I may once more   75
Review the past) I warred against myself,
A Bigot to a New Idolatry;
Like a cowled Monk who hath forsworn the world,
Zealously labour'd to cut off my heart
From all the sources of her former strength;   80
And as by simple waving of a Wand
The wizard instantaneously dissolves
Palace or grove, even so could I unsoul
As readily by syllogistic words[7]

---

5. The power of the integral mind (as distinguished from the limited capacity of "reason" alone, line 47).
6. This passage is both elliptical and contorted in its syntax. The fragrance wafted to the sailor from the shore—i.e., his remembered experiences of human feelings of gratitude and love (lines 54–56)—serves also as evidence of the shared emotions that had earlier united him to the family of past humanity (lines 61–63). The "spells" that prevented the sailor from landing on that shore (line 53) consist of his fascination with a limited mode of analytic reasoning, which engendered the hope that in the future people would be purely rational beings, hence utterly different from the feelingful, passionate creatures of the past (lines 58–60). This mode of reasoning, in addition, not only made

Wordsworth distrust the earlier emotional evidences of his unity with humanity but also led him to believe that the actions of even the greatest men recorded in human history were tainted, because they were motivated by feelings rather than by reason alone (lines 64–67).
    In his allusions to the rational "spells" and his hope for a new type of humanity Wordsworth is describing the period in his life when he had succumbed to the views of William Godwin's *Inquiry Concerning Political Justice* (1793), which derogated the role of the feelings and passions as motives and confidently anticipated a future in which the actions of humanity will be determined solely by dispassionate reason.
7. Logical reasoning.

Those mysteries of being which have made,   85
And shall continue evermore to make,
Of the whole human race one brotherhood.
    What wonder, then, if to a mind so far
Perverted, even the visible Universe
Fell under the dominion of a taste   90
Less Spiritual, with microscopic view
Was scanned, as I had scanned the moral world?[8]
    Oh Soul of Nature, excellent and fair!
That didst rejoice with me, with whom I too
Rejoiced, through early Youth, before the winds   95
And roaring waters, and in lights and shades
That marched and countermarched about the hills
In glorious apparition, powers on whom
I daily waited, now all eye and now
All ear; but never long without the heart   100
Employed, and Man's unfolding intellect!
Oh Soul of Nature! that, by laws divine
Sustained and governed, still dost overflow
With an impassioned life, what feeble ones
Walk on this earth! how feeble have I been   105
When thou wert in thy strength! Nor this through stroke
Of human suffering, such as justifies
Remissness and inaptitude of mind,
But through presumption;[9] even in pleasure pleased
Unworthily, disliking here, and there   110
Liking; by rules of mimic Art transferred
To things above all Art; but more,—for this,
Although a strong infection of the age,
Was never much my habit—giving way
To a comparison of scene with scene,   115
Bent overmuch on superficial things,
Pampering myself with meagre novelties
Of colour and proportion, to the moods
Of time and season, to the moral power,
The affections and the spirit of the Place,   120
Insensible.[1] Nor only did the love
Of sitting thus in judgment interrupt
My deeper feelings, but another cause,
More subtile and less easily explained,
That almost seems inherent in the Creature,   125
A twofold frame of body and of mind.
I speak in recollection of a time
When the bodily eye, in every stage of life
The most despotic of our senses, gained
Such strength in *me* as often held my mind   130
In absolute dominion. Gladly here,
Entering upon abstruser Argument,

8. I.e., the habit of logical analysis perverted his way of perceiving the natural world.
9. Presumptuousness, arrogance.
1. Unresponsive. Wordsworth has described his temporary participation in the cult of the picturesque— i.e., judging a natural scene by criteria derived from the "Art" of landscape painting (lines 111–12)—and then his acquired tendency to judge the comparative value of natural scenes by superficial, purely aesthetic criteria (lines 115–18).

Could I endeavour to unfold the means
Which Nature studiously employs to thwart
This tyranny, summons all the senses each   135
To counteract the other, and themselves,
And makes them all, and the Objects with which all
Are conversant, subservient in their turn
To the great ends of Liberty and Power.[2]
But leave we this: enough that my delights   140
(Such as they were) were sought insatiably.
Vivid the transport, vivid, though not profound;
I roamed from hill to hill, from rock to rock,
Still craving combinations of new forms,
New pleasure, wider empire for the sight,   145
Proud of her own endowments, and rejoiced
To lay the inner faculties asleep.
Amid the turns and counterturns, the strife
And various trials of our complex being,
As we grow up, such thraldom of that sense[3]   150
Seems hard to shun. And yet I knew a Maid,
A young Enthusiast, who escaped these bonds;[4]
Her eye was not the Mistress of her heart;
Far less did rules prescribed by passive taste
Or barren intermeddling subtleties   155
Perplex her mind; but, wise as women are
When genial circumstance[5] hath favoured them,
She welcomed what was given and craved no more;
Whate'er the scene presented to her view,
That was the best, to that she was attuned   160
By her benign simplicity of life
And through a perfect happiness of Soul
Whose variegated feelings were in this
Sisters, that they were each some new delight.
Birds in the bower, and lambs in the green field,   165
Could they have known her, would have loved; methought
Her very presence such a sweetness breathed
That flowers, and trees, and even the silent hills,
And every thing she looked on should have had
An intimation how she bore herself   170
Towards them and to all creatures. God delights
In such a being; for her common thoughts
Are piety, her life is gratitude.
    Even like this Maid, before I was called forth
From the retirement of my native hills,   175
I loved whate'er I saw: nor lightly loved,
But most intensely; never dreamt of aught
More grand, more fair, more exquisitely framed
Than those few nooks to which my happy feet

2. I.e., the ways in which Nature uses an individual's
other senses to counteract the tyranny of the eye—as
well as the tyranny of any other single sense—so as to
make all the senses (and the external objects they
enable us to perceive) subordinate to the free, creative
power of the human mind. Later in this book Wordsworth attributes this power of free creativity to the
imagination.
3. I.e., subservience to the sense of sight.
4. Mary Hutchinson, whom Wordsworth had known
since childhood and whom he married in 1802.
5. Beneficent conditions (of a woman's life).

Were limited. I had not at that time   180
Lived long enough, nor in the least survived
The first diviner influence of this world
As it appears to unaccustomed eyes.
Worshipping then among the depth of things
As piety ordained,⁶ could I submit   185
To measured admiration, or to aught
That should preclude humility and love?
I felt, observed, and pondered; did not judge,
Yea, never thought of judging; with the gift
Of all this glory filled and satisfied.   190
And afterwards, when through the gorgeous Alps
Roaming, I carried with me the same heart:⁷
In truth, the degradation,⁸ howsoe'er
Induced, effect in whatsoe'er degree
Of custom that prepares a partial scale   195
In which the little oft outweighs the great,
Or any other cause that hath been named;
Or lastly, aggravated by the times,
And their empassioned sounds,⁹ which well might make
The milder minstrelsies of rural scenes   200
Inaudible, was transient; I had known
Too forcibly, too early in my life,
Visitings of imaginative power
For this to last: I shook the habit off
Entirely and for ever, and again   205
In Nature's presence stood, as now I stand,
A sensitive Being, a *creative* Soul.
    There are in our existence spots of time,¹
That with distinct pre-eminence retain
A renovating virtue, whence, depressed   210
By false opinion and contentious thought,
Or aught of heavier or more deadly weight,
In trivial occupations, and the round
Of ordinary intercourse, our minds
Are nourished and invisibly repaired;   215
A virtue by which pleasure is inhanced,
That penetrates, enables us to mount,
When high, more high, and lifts us up when fallen.
This efficacious Spirit chiefly lurks
Among those passages of life that give   220
Profoundest knowledge how and to what point
The mind is lord and master—outward sense
The obedient Servant of her will. Such moments
Are scattered every where, taking their date

6. In the 1805 text: "As my soul bade me."
7. In his walk across the Alps in 1790, described in book 6.
8. I.e., the deterioration (of a full, unreflective response to nature) that he has described in lines 109–51.
9. I.e., by the high passions aroused by the French Revolution. Wordsworth speculates that these may have been a contributing factor in diminishing his attention and responsiveness to the natural world.

1. Moments of experience in which something ordinary (line 254) suddenly becomes profoundly significant; since this significance is bestowed by the perceiver, it demonstrates the freedom and creative power of the imaginative mind (lines 220–23, 275–77). The remembrance of such moments nourishes and repairs the mind in periods of depression or distraction when the imagination flags (lines 210–15).

From our first Childhood. I remember well   225
That once, while yet my inexperienced hand
Could scarcely hold a bridle, with proud hopes
I mounted, and we journied towards the hills:
An ancient Servant of my Father's house
Was with me, my encourager and Guide.   230
We had not travelled long ere some mischance
Disjoined me from my Comrade, and, through fear
Dismounting, down the rough and stony Moor
I led my horse, and, stumbling on, at length
Came to a bottom,[2] where in former times   235
A Murderer had been hung in iron chains.
The Gibbet mast[3] had mouldered down, the bones
And iron case were gone, but on the turf
Hard by, soon after that fell deed was wrought,
Some unknown hand had carved the Murderer's name.   240
The monumental Letters were inscribed
In times long past, but still from year to year,
By superstition of the neighbourhood,
The grass is cleared away, and to that hour
The characters were fresh and visible.   245
A casual glance had shewn them, and I fled,
Faultering and faint and ignorant of the road:
Then, reascending the bare common, saw
A naked Pool that lay beneath the hills,
The Beacon on its summit, and, more near,   250
A Girl who bore a Pitcher on her head,
And seemed with difficult steps to force her way
Against the blowing wind. It was in truth
An ordinary sight; but I should need
Colors and words that are unknown to man   255
To paint the visionary dreariness
Which, while I looked all round for my lost Guide,
Invested Moorland waste and naked Pool,
The Beacon crowning the lone eminence,
The Female and her garments vexed and tossed   260
By the strong wind.—When, in the blessed hours
Of early love, the loved One[4] at my side,
I roamed, in daily presence of this scene,
Upon the naked Pool and dreary Crags,
And on the melancholy Beacon, fell   265
A spirit of pleasure, and Youth's golden gleam;
And think ye not with radiance more sublime
For these remembrances, and for the power
They had left behind? So feeling comes in aid
Of feeling, and diversity of strength   270
Attends us, if but once we have been strong.
Oh! mystery of Man, from what a depth
Proceed thy honors! I am lost, but see
In simple child-hood something of the base

2. Valley.   criminals.
3. The post with a projecting arm used for hanging   4. Mary Hutchinson.

On which thy greatness stands; but this I feel,   275
That from thyself it comes, that thou must give,
Else never canst receive. The days gone by
Return upon me almost from the dawn
Of life: the hiding-places of Man's power
Open; I would approach them, but they close.   280
I see by glimpses now; when age comes on
May scarcely see at all, and I would give,
While yet we may, as far as words can give,
Substance and life to what I feel, enshrining,
Such is my hope, the spirit of the past   285
For future restoration. —Yet another
Of these memorials.
                    One Christmas-time,[5]
On the glad Eve of its dear holidays,
Feverish, and tired, and restless, I went forth
Into the fields, impatient for the sight   290
Of those led Palfreys[6] that should bear us home,
My Brothers and myself. There rose a Crag
That, from the meeting point of two highways
Ascending, overlooked them both, far stretched;
Thither, uncertain on which road to fix   295
My expectation, thither I repaired,
Scout-like, and gained the summit; 'twas a day
Tempestuous, dark, and wild, and on the grass
I sate, half-sheltered by a naked wall;
Upon my right hand couched a single sheep,   300
Upon my left a blasted hawthorn stood:
With those Companions at my side, I sate,
Straining my eyes intensely, as the mist
Gave intermitting prospect of the copse
And plain beneath. Ere we to School returned   305
That dreary time, ere we had been ten days
Sojourners in my Father's House, he died,[7]
And I and my three Brothers, Orphans then,
Followed his Body to the Grave. The Event,
With all the sorrow that it brought, appeared   310
A chastisement; and when I called to mind
That day so lately passed, when from the Crag
I looked in such anxiety of hope,
With trite reflections of morality,
Yet in the deepest passion, I bowed low   315
To God, who thus corrected my desires;
And afterwards, the wind and sleety rain
And all the business[8] of the Elements,
The single Sheep, and the one blasted tree,
And the bleak music of that old stone wall,   320
The noise of wood and water, and the mist
That on the line of each of those two Roads

5. In 1783; Wordsworth, aged thirteen, was at Hawks   7. John Wordsworth died on Dec. 30, 1783; William's
head School with two of his brothers.   mother had died five years earlier.
6. Small saddle horses.   8. Busy-ness; motions.

Advanced in such indisputable shapes;[9]
All these were kindred spectacles and sounds
To which I oft repaired, and thence would drink   325
As at a fountain; and on winter nights,
Down to this *very* time, when storm and rain
Beat on my roof, or haply at noon-day,
While in a grove I walk whose lofty trees,
Laden with summer's thickest foliage, rock   330
In a strong wind, some working of the spirit,
Some inward agitations, thence are brought,[1]
Whate'er their office, whether to beguile
Thoughts over-busy in the course they took,
Or animate an hour of vacant ease.   335

From Book Thirteenth
Subject concluded

[*Return to "Life's Familiar Face"*]

From Nature doth emotion come, and moods
Of calmness equally are Nature's gift:
This is her glory; these two attributes
Are sister horns that constitute her strength.[1]
Hence Genius,[2] born to thrive by interchange   5
Of peace and excitation, finds in her
His best and purest friend, from her receives
That energy by which he seeks the truth,
From her that happy stillness of the mind
Which fits him to receive it, when unsought.   10
   Such benefit the humblest intellects
Partake of, each in their degree: 'tis mine
To speak of what myself have known and felt.
Smooth task! for words find easy way, inspired
By gratitude and confidence in truth.   15
Long time in search of knowledge did I range
The field of human life, in heart and mind
Benighted, but the dawn beginning now
To reappear,[3] 'twas proved that not in vain
I had been taught to reverence a Power   20
That is the visible quality and shape
And image of right reason,[4] that matures
Her processes by steadfast laws, gives birth
To no impatient or fallacious hopes,
No heat of passion or excessive zeal,   25
No vain conceits,—provokes to no quick turns
Of self-applauding intellect,—but trains

9. Pronounced "indísputáble shápes"; i.e., shapes one did not dare question.
1. Another instance of Wordsworth's inner response to an outer breeze (cf. 1.33–38, p. 1403).
1. In the Old Testament, the horn of an animal signifies power.

2. A person capable of creativity.
3. I.e., he is beginning to recover from the spiritual crisis recorded in 11.293–309.
4. Wordsworth follows Milton's use of the term "right reason" to denote a human faculty that is inherently attuned to truth.

To meekness, and exalts by humble faith;[5]
Holds up before the mind, intoxicate
With present objects, and the busy dance   30
Of things that pass away, a temperate shew
Of objects that endure; and by this course
Disposes her, when over-fondly set
On throwing off incumbrances, to seek
In Man, and in the frame of social life,   35
Whate'er there is desireable and good
Of kindred permanence, unchanged in form
And function, or through strict vicissitude
Of life and death revolving. Above all
Were re-established now those watchful thoughts   40
Which (seeing little worthy or sublime
In what the Historian's pen so much delights
To blazon, Power and Energy detached
From moral purpose) early tutored me
To look with feelings of fraternal love   45
Upon the unassuming things that hold
A silent station in this beauteous world.[6]
      Thus moderated, thus composed, I found
Once more in Man an object of delight,
Of pure imagination, and of love;   50
And, as the horizon of my mind enlarged,
Again I took the intellectual eye[7]
For my Instructor, studious more to see
Great Truths, than touch and handle little ones.
Knowledge was given accordingly; my trust   55
Became more firm in feelings that had stood
The test of such a trial; clearer far
My sense of excellence—of right and wrong:
The promise of the present time retired
Into its true proportions; sanguine[8] schemes,   60
Ambitious projects, pleased me less; I sought
For present good in life's familiar face,
And built thereon my hopes of good to come.

[*Discovery of His Poetic Subject. Salisbury Plain.*
Sight of "a New World"]

Here, calling up to mind what then I saw,[9]   220
A youthful Traveller, and see daily now

5. In the text of 1805: "but lifts / The being into magnanimity."
6. Here Wordsworth begins his account of how he
came to feel bonds to, and to love, the silent, lowly,
common things whose celebration he considers to be
his special vocation as an innovative poet-prophet (see
lines 301–08).
7. Perception by the integral mind.
8. Optimistic. Wordsworth apparently refers back to
his earlier "ambitious projects" for a long poem,
described in 1.166–220, as well as to the optimistic
schemes for mankind that had been engendered by his
commitment to the French Revolution.
9. Wordsworth has described, as part of his imagina-

tive recovery, his learning to look again with sympathy
upon "the unassuming things that hold / A silent station in this beauteous world" (lines 46–47) and his
finding again "in Man an object of delight" (line 49).
Now he shows how, in reaction against his concern
with great actions detached from moral purpose that
constituted the French Revolution, he came to embrace the poetic doctrines of the Preface to *Lyrical Ballads*. That is, he will write of simple, lowly people,
whose patient endurance of suffering redounds to the
glory of humankind and who speak a language that is
the spontaneous overflow of powerful feelings (lines
263–64).

In the familiar circuit of my home,
Here might I pause and bend in reverence
To Nature, and the power of human minds,
To Men as they are Men within themselves.   225
How oft high service is performed within,
When all the external Man is rude in shew!
Not like a Temple rich with pomp and gold,
But a mere mountain Chapel that protects
Its simple Worshippers from sun and shower.   230
Of these, said I, shall be my song, of these,
If future years mature me for the task,
Will I record the praises, making Verse
Deal boldly with substantial things; in truth
And sanctity of passion speak of these,   235
That justice may be done, obeisance paid
Where it is due: thus haply shall I teach,
Inspire, through unadulterated[1] ears
Pour rapture, tenderness, and hope, my theme
No other than the very heart of Man   240
As found among the best of those who live
Not unexalted by religious faith,
Nor uninformed by Books, good books, though few,
In Nature's presence: thence may I select
Sorrow, that is not sorrow, but delight,   245
And miserable love that is not pain
To hear of, for the glory that redounds
Therefrom to human kind and what we are.
Be mine to follow with no timid step
Where knowledge leads me; it shall be my pride   250
That I have dared to tread this holy ground,
Speaking no dream, but things oracular,
Matter not lightly to be heard by those
Who to the letter of the outward promise
Do read the invisible Soul,[2] by Men adroit   255
In speech, and for communion with the world
Accomplished, minds whose faculties are then
Most active when they are most eloquent,
And elevated most, when most admired.
Men may be found of other mold than these,   260
Who are their own Upholders, to themselves
Encouragement, and energy, and will,
Expressing liveliest thoughts in lively words
As native passion dictates.[3] Others, too,
There are, among the walks of homely life,   265
Still higher, men for contemplation framed,
Shy, and unpractised in the strife of phrase,[4]
Meek men, whose very souls perhaps would sink
Beneath them, summoned to such intercourse:

1. Uncorrupted.
2. I.e., this doctrine will not be lightly accepted by those who judge inner worth by exterior seeming.
3. In his Preface to *Lyrical Ballads* of 1800, Wordsworth said that he chose characters from low and rustic life because in them "the essential passions of the heart . . . are less under restraint, and speak a plainer and more emphatic language."
4. The rhetoric of controversy.

Theirs is the language of the heavens, the power,   270
The thought, the image, and the silent joy;
Words are but under-agents in their Souls;
When they are grasping with their greatest strength
They do not breathe among them;[5] this I speak
In gratitude to God, who feeds our hearts   275
For his own service; knoweth, loveth us
When we are unregarded by the world.
   Also, about this time did I receive
Convictions still more strong than heretofore
Not only that the inner frame is good,   280
And graciously composed, but that, no less,
Nature for all conditions wants not power
To consecrate, if we have eyes to see,
The outside of her Creatures, and to breathe
Grandeur upon the very humblest face   285
Of human life. I felt that the array
Of act and circumstance, and visible form,
Is mainly, to the pleasure of the mind,
What passion makes them, that meanwhile the forms
Of Nature have a passion in themselves   290
That intermingles with those works of man
To which she summons him; although the works
Be mean, have nothing lofty of their own;
And that the Genius of the Poet hence
May boldly take his way among mankind   295
Wherever Nature leads, that he hath stood
By Nature's side among the Men of old,
And so shall stand for ever. Dearest Friend,
If thou partake the animating faith
That Poets, even as Prophets, each with each   300
Connected in a mighty scheme of truth,
Have each his own peculiar faculty,
Heaven's gift, a sense that fits him to perceive
Objects unseen before, thou wilt not blame
The humblest of this band[6] who dares to hope   305
That unto him hath also been vouchsafed
An insight, that in some sort he possesses
A Privilege, whereby a Work of his,
Proceeding from a source of untaught things,
Creative and enduring, may become   310
A Power like one of Nature's. To a hope
Not less ambitious once among the Wilds
Of Sarum's Plain[7] my youthful Spirit was raised;
There, as I ranged at will the pastoral downs[8]
Trackless and smooth, or paced the bare white roads   315
Lengthening in solitude their dreary line,
Time with his retinue of ages fled

5. I.e., even in the greatest strength of their intuitive
grasp, they do not utter words, which (line 272) are for
them merely subsidiary to the fullness of their response
to an experience.

6. Wordsworth himself.
7. Salisbury Plain, which Wordsworth crossed alone
on foot in the summer of 1793.
8. Open hills used to pasture sheep.

Backwards, nor checked his flight until I saw
Our dim Ancestral Past in Vision clear;[9]
Saw multitudes of men, and here and there   320
A single Briton clothed in Wolf-skin vest,
With shield and stone-axe, stride across the wold;[1]
The voice of Spears was heard, the rattling spear
Shaken by arms of mighty bone, in strength,
Long mouldered, of barbaric majesty.   325
I called on Darkness—but before the word
Was uttered, midnight darkness seemed to take
All objects from my sight; and lo! again
The Desart visible by dismal flames;
It is the Sacrificial Altar, fed   330
With living Men—how deep the groans! the voice
Of those that crowd the giant wicker thrills
The monumental hillocks,[2] and the pomp
Is for both worlds, the living and the dead.
At other moments (for through that wide waste   335
Three summer days I roamed) where'er the Plain
Was figured o'er with circles, lines, or mounds,
That yet survive, a work, as some divine,[3]
Shaped by the Druids, so to represent
Their knowledge of the heavens, and image forth   340
The constellations; gently was I charmed
Into a waking dream, a reverie
That with believing eyes, where'er I turned,
Beheld long-bearded Teachers with white wands
Uplifted, pointing to the starry sky   345
Alternately, and Plain below, while breath
Of music swayed their motions, and the Waste
Rejoiced with them and me in those sweet Sounds.
        This for the past, and things that may be viewed
Or fancied, in the obscurity of years   350
From monumental hints:[4] and thou, O Friend!
Pleased with some unpremeditated strains
That served those wanderings to beguile, hast said
That then and there my mind had exercised
Upon the vulgar forms of present things,   355
The actual world of our familiar days,
Yet higher power, had caught from them a tone,
An image, and a character, by books
Not hitherto reflected.[5] Call we this

9. Wordsworth shared the common, but mistaken, belief of his time that Stonehenge, the giant megalithic structure on Salisbury Plain, had been a temple of the Celtic priests, the Druids, and that the Druids had there performed the rite of human sacrifice; hence the imaginings and vision that he goes on to relate.
1. High open country.
2. The many bronze age burial mounds on Salisbury Plain. "Giant wicker": Aylett Sammes, in *Britannia Antiqua Illustrata* (1676), had described, as a rite of the ancient Britons, that they wove a huge wicker structure in the shape of a man, filled it with living humans, and set it afire.

3. Conjecture (a verb).
4. I.e., from what the monumental remains on Salisbury Plain suggested to him.
5. Wordsworth refers to an event that Coleridge narrates in *Biographia Literaria*, chap. 4. In Nov. 1795 Wordsworth had read to Coleridge a manuscript version of his poem *Adventures on Salisbury Plain*. What impressed Coleridge, as he tells us, was Wordsworth's "fine balance of truth in observing with the imaginative faculty in modifying the objects observed, and above all, the original gift of spreading . . . the depth and height of the ideal world, around forms, incidents, and situations of which, for the common view, custom

A partial judgement—and yet why? for *then*   360
We were as Strangers;[6] and I may not speak
Thus wrongfully of verse, however rude,
Which on thy young imagination, trained
In the great City, broke like light from far.
Moreover, each man's mind is to herself   365
Witness and judge; and I remember well
That in Life's every-day appearances
I seemed about this time to gain clear sight
Of a new world, a world, too, that was fit
To be transmitted and to other eyes   370
Made visible, as ruled by those fixed laws
Whence spiritual dignity originates,
Which do both give it being and maintain
A balance, an ennobling interchange
Of action from without, and from within;   375
The excellence, pure function, and best power
Both of the object seen, and eye that sees.

From Book Fourteenth
Conclusion

[The Vision on Mount Snowdon. Fear vs. Love Resolved. Imagination]

In one of those Excursions (may they ne'er
Fade from remembrance!), through the Northern tracts
Of Cambria ranging with a youthful Friend,
I left Bethgellert's huts at couching-time,
And westward took my way, to see the sun   5
Rise from the top of Snowdon.[1] To the door
Of a rude Cottage at the Mountain's base
We came, and rouzed the Shepherd who attends
The adventurous Stranger's steps, a trusty Guide;
Then, cheered by short refreshment, sallied forth.   10
—It was a close, warm, breezeless summer night,
Wan, dull, and glaring,[2] with a dripping fog
Low-hung and thick, that covered all the sky.
But, undiscouraged, we began to climb
The mountain-side. The mist soon girt us round,   15
And, after ordinary Travellers' talk
With our Conductor, pensively we sank

had bedimmed all the luster." "This," Coleridge concludes, "is the character and privilege of genius."
6. Though Coleridge and Wordsworth had met in
Sept. 1795, they did not become close friends until
1797. "Partial": biased (in Wordsworth's favor).
1. Wordsworth climbed Mt. Snowdon—the highest
peak in Wales ("Cambria"), and some ten miles from
the sea—with Robert Jones, the friend with whom he
had also tramped through the Alps (book 6). The climb
started from the village of Bethgelert at "couching-

time" (line 4), the time of night when the sheep lie
down to sleep. This event had taken place in 1791 (or
possibly 1793); Wordsworth presents it out of its chronological order to introduce at this point a great natural "type" or "emblem" (lines 66, 70) for the mind, and
especially for the activity of the imagination, whose
"restoration" he has described in the two preceding
books.
2. In north of England dialect, "glairie," applied to the
weather, means dull, rainy.

Each into commerce with his private thoughts:
Thus did we breast the ascent, and by myself
Was nothing either seen or heard that checked   20
Those musings or diverted, save that once
The Shepherd's Lurcher,[3] who, among the crags,
Had to his joy unearthed a Hedgehog, teased
His coiled-up Prey with barkings turbulent.
This small adventure, for even such it seemed   25
In that wild place, and at the dead of night,
Being over and forgotten, on we wound
In silence as before. With forehead bent
Earthward, as if in opposition set
Against an enemy, I panted up   30
With eager pace, and no less eager thoughts.
Thus might we wear a midnight hour away,
Ascending at loose distance each from each,
And I, as chanced, the foremost of the Band:
When at my feet the ground appeared to brighten,   35
And with a step or two seemed brighter still;
Nor was time given to ask, or learn, the cause;
For instantly a light upon the turf
Fell like a flash; and lo! as I looked up,
The Moon hung naked in a firmament   40
Of azure without cloud, and at my feet
Rested a silent sea of hoary mist.
A hundred hills their dusky backs upheaved
All over this still Ocean;[4] and beyond,
Far, far beyond, the solid vapours stretched,   45
In Headlands, tongues, and promontory shapes,
Into the main Atlantic, that appeared
To dwindle, and give up his majesty,
Usurped upon far as the sight could reach.
Not so the ethereal Vault; encroachment none   50
Was there, nor loss;[5] only the inferior stars
Had disappeared, or shed a fainter light
In the clear presence of the full-orbed Moon;
Who, from her sovereign elevation, gazed
Upon the billowy ocean, as it lay   55
All meek and silent, save that through a rift
Not distant from the shore whereon we stood,
A fixed, abysmal, gloomy breathing-place,
Mounted the roar of waters—torrents—streams
Innumerable, roaring with one voice!   60
Heard over earth and sea, and in that hour,
For so it seemed, felt by the starry heavens.
      When into air had partially dissolved
That Vision, given to Spirits of the night,
And three chance human Wanderers, in calm thought   65

---

3. A crossbred dog used to hunt hares.
4. In Milton's description of the creation of the world, "the mountains huge appear / Emergent, and their broad bare backs upheave / Into the clouds" (*Paradise*

Lost, 7.285–87).
5. The mist projected in various shapes over the Atlantic Ocean, but did not "encroach" on the heavens overhead.

Reflected, it appeared to me the type
Of a majestic Intellect, its acts
And its possessions, what it has and craves,
What in itself it is, and would become.
There I beheld the emblem of a Mind   70
That feeds upon infinity, that broods
Over the dark abyss, intent to hear
Its voices issuing forth to silent light
In one continuous stream; a mind sustained
By recognitions of transcendent power   75
In sense, conducting to ideal form;
In soul, of more than mortal privilege.[6]
One function, above all, of such a mind
Had Nature shadowed there, by putting forth,
'Mid circumstances awful and sublime,   80
That mutual domination which she loves
To exert upon the face of outward things,
So moulded, joined, abstracted; so endowed
With interchangeable supremacy,
That Men least sensitive see, hear, perceive,   85
And cannot chuse but feel. The power which all
Acknowledge when thus moved, which Nature thus
To bodily sense exhibits, is the express
Resemblance of that glorious faculty
That higher minds bear with them as their own.[7]   90
This is the very spirit in which they deal
With the whole compass of the universe:
They, from their native selves, can send abroad
Kindred mutations; for themselves create
A like existence; and whene'er it dawns   95
Created for them, catch it;—or are caught
By its inevitable mastery,
Like angels stopped upon the wing by sound
Of harmony from heaven's remotest spheres.
Them the enduring and the transient both   100
Serve to exalt; they build up greatest things
From least suggestions; ever on the watch,
Willing to work and to be wrought upon,
They need not extraordinary calls
To rouse them, in a world of life they live;   105
By sensible impressions not enthralled,
But, by their quickening impulse, made more prompt
To hold fit converse with the spiritual world,
And with the generations of mankind
Spread over time, past, present, and to come,   110
Age after age, till Time shall be no more.

6. The sense of lines 74–77 seems to be that the mind
of someone who is gifted beyond the ordinary lot of
mortals recognizes its power to transcend the senses by
converting sensory objects into ideal forms.
7. The "glorious faculty" is the imagination, which in
its exhibition of mastery over sense—through its power
to alter and re-create what is given to it in perception
(lines 93–105)—is analogous to that aspect of the outer
scene in which the ordinary landscape is transfigured
by the moonlit mist. Cf. the mind as "lord and master"
of outward sense in 12.221–23 (p. 1466).

Such minds are truly from the Deity,
For they are powers; and hence the highest bliss
That flesh can know is theirs,—the consciousness
Of whom they are, habitually infused   115
Through every image, and through every thought,
And all affections[8] by communion raised
From earth to heaven, from human to divine.
Hence endless occupation for the Soul,
Whether discursive or intuitive;[9]   120
Hence chearfulness for acts of daily life,
Emotions which best foresight need not fear,
Most worthy then of trust when most intense:
Hence, amid ills that vex, and wrongs that crush
Our hearts, if here the words of holy Writ   125
May with fit reverence be applied, that peace
Which passeth understanding,[1]—that repose
In moral judgements which from this pure source
Must come, or will by Man be sought in vain.
    Oh! who is he that hath his whole life long   130
Preserved, enlarged, this freedom in himself?
For this alone is genuine Liberty.
Where is the favoured Being who hath held
That course, unchecked, unerring, and untired,
In one perpetual progress smooth and bright?   135
—A humbler destiny have we retraced,
And told of lapse and hesitating choice,
And backward wanderings along thorny ways:
Yet, compassed round by Mountain Solitudes
Within whose solemn temple I received   140
My earliest visitations, careless then
Of what was given me; and which now I range
A meditative, oft a suffering Man,
Do I declare, in accents which, from truth
Deriving chearful confidence, shall blend   145
Their modulation with these vocal streams,
That, whatsoever falls my better mind
Revolving[2] with the accidents of life
May have sustained, that, howsoe'er misled,
Never did I, in quest of right and wrong,   150
Tamper with conscience from a private aim;
Nor was in any public hope the dupe
Of selfish passions; nor did ever yield,
Wilfully, to mean cares or low pursuits;
But shrunk with apprehensive jealousy   155
From every combination which might aid
The tendency, too potent in itself,

---

8. Feelings, emotions.
9. An echo of *Paradise Lost* 5.488. The "discursive" reason undertakes to reach truths through a logical sequence of premises, observations, and conclusions; the "intuitive" reason comprehends truths immediately.

1. Philippians 4.7: "The peace of God, which passeth all understanding." This passage of Christian piety was added by Wordsworth in a late revision.
2. An allusion to the ancient concept of fortune's revolving wheel.

Of use and custom to bow down the Soul
Under a growing weight of vulgar sense,
And substitute a universe of death[3]   160
For that which moves with light and life informed,
Actual, divine, and true. To fear and love,
To love as prime and chief, for there fear ends,
Be this ascribed; to early intercourse
In presence of sublime or beautiful forms   165
With the adverse principles of pain and joy—
Evil, as one is rashly named by men
Who know not what they speak. By love subsists
All lasting grandeur, by pervading love;
That gone, we are as dust.[4]—Behold the fields   170
In balmy spring-time full of rising flowers
And joyous Creatures; see that Pair, the lamb
And the lamb's Mother, and their tender ways
Shall touch thee to the heart; thou callest this love,
And not inaptly so, for love it is,   175
Far as it carries thee. In some green Bower
Rest, and be not alone, but have thou there
The One who is thy choice of all the world:
There linger, listening, gazing with delight
Impassioned, but delight how pitiable!   180
Unless this love by a still higher love
Be hallowed, love that breathes not without awe;
Love that adores, but on the knees of prayer,
By heaven inspired; that frees from chains the soul,
Bearing in union with the purest, best   185
Of earth-born passions, on the wings of praise,
A mutual tribute to the Almighty's Throne.[5]
    This spiritual love acts not, nor can exist
Without Imagination, which in truth
Is but another name for absolute power   190
And clearest insight, amplitude of mind,
And reason, in her most exalted mood.
This faculty hath been the feeding source
Of our long labor: we have traced the stream
From the blind cavern whence is faintly heard   195
Its natal murmur; followed it to light
And open day; accompanied its course
Among the ways of Nature; for a time
Lost sight of it, bewildered and engulphed;

3. Milton's description of hell in *Paradise Lost* 2.622–23: "A universe of death, which God by curse / Created evil. . . ."
4. Wordsworth's mind, he had said early in *The Prelude*, had been "fostered alike by beauty and by fear" (1.302 and n. 9, p. 1409); that is, by the opposing but equally necessary principles of the beautiful and the terrifying, or "sublime," aspects of nature. Now, in his conclusion, the principles of fear and pain are said to be mistakenly equated with "evil," and to be ultimately transcended by their "adverse principles" of love and

joy. This passage is equivalent to the theodicy of *Paradise Lost*, in which Milton justifies evil and pain ("the ways of God to men," 1.26) by reference to the fall and redemption; Wordsworth, however, translates this into a natural theodicy of the interaction of man's mind with the external world (cf. the Prospectus to *The Recluse*, lines 8–9, p. 1398 and n. 1, p. 1397).
5. In place of lines 182–87, the text of 1805 has: ". . . a love that comes into the heart / With awe and a diffusive sentiment. / Thy love is human merely: this proceeds / More from the brooding soul, and is divine."

Then given it greeting as it rose once more   200
In strength, reflecting from its placid breast
The works of man, and face of human life;
And lastly, from its progress have we drawn
Faith in life endless, the sustaining thought
Of human being, Eternity, and God.[6]   205
—Imagination having been our theme,
So also hath that intellectual love,
For they are each in each, and cannot stand
Dividually.[7]—Here must thou be, O Man!
Power to thyself; no Helper hast thou here;   210
Here keepest thou in singleness thy state;
No other can divide with thee this work;
No secondary hand can intervene
To fashion this ability; 'tis thine,
The prime and vital principle is thine   215
In the recesses of thy nature, far
From any reach of outward fellowship,
Else is not thine at all. * * *

[Conclusion: "The Mind of Man"]

And now, O Friend![8] this History is brought
To its appointed close: the discipline
And consummation of a Poet's mind
In every thing that stood most prominent   305
Have faithfully been pictured; we have reached
The time (our guiding object from the first)
When we may, not presumptuously, I hope,
Suppose my powers so far confirmed, and such
My knowledge, as to make me capable   310
Of building up a Work that shall endure.

                       * * * Having now
Told what best merits mention, further pains
Our present purpose seems not to require,
And I have other tasks. Recall to mind
The mood in which this labour was begun.   375
O Friend! the termination of my course
Is nearer now, much nearer; yet even then,
In that distraction, and intense desire,
I said unto the life which I had lived,
Where art thou? Hear I not a voice from thee   380
Which 'tis reproach to hear?[9] Anon I rose

---

6. The 1805 version reads: "The feeling of life endless, the great thought / By which we live, Infinity and God."
7. Separately.
8. Coleridge.
9. As he approaches the end, Wordsworth recalls the beginning of *The Prelude*. The reproachful voice is that which asked the question, "Was it for this?" in 1.269ff.

This query called forth a vision of his remembered life, which he proceeded to explore in search of both the sources of his poetic powers and the impediments to their fulfillment. The "Song" (line 384) describing this quest, which he then began, is the poem he is now completing.

As if on wings, and saw beneath me stretched
Vast prospect of the world which I had been
And was; and hence this Song, which like a Lark
I have protracted, in the unwearied heavens   385
Singing, and often with more plaintive voice
To earth attempered and her deep-drawn sighs,
Yet centering all in love, and in the end
All gratulant, if rightly understood.[1]

                          *   *   *

Oh! yet a few short years of useful life,
And all will be complete, thy[2] race be run,
Thy monument of glory will be raised;
Then, though, too weak to tread the ways of truth,   435
This Age fall back to old idolatry,
Though Men return to servitude as fast
As the tide ebbs, to ignominy and shame
By Nations sink together,[3] we shall still
Find solace—knowing what we have learnt to know,   440
Rich in true happiness if allowed to be
Faithful alike in forwarding a day
Of firmer trust, joint laborers in the Work
(Should Providence such grace to us vouchsafe)
Of their deliverance,[4] surely yet to come.   445
Prophets of Nature, we to them will speak
A lasting inspiration, sanctified
By reason, blest by faith: what we have loved
Others will love, and we will teach them how,
Instruct them how the mind of Man becomes   450
A thousand times more beautiful than the earth
On which he dwells, above this Frame of things
(Which 'mid all revolutions in the hopes
And fears of Men doth still remain unchanged)
In beauty exalted, as it is itself   455
Of quality and fabric more divine.[5]

1798–1839   1850

---

1. The poet finds that suffering and frustration are justified, when seen as part of the overall design of the life
he has just reviewed. The passage echoes the conclusion of Pope's theodicy (the justification of evil) in *An
Essay on Man*, 1.291–92: "All discord, harmony not
understood; / All partial evil, universal good." "Gratulant": expressing joy.
2. Coleridge's.
3. I.e., though men—whole nations of them together—sink to ignominy and shame.
4. In the 1805 text: "redemption." Wordsworth reaf-
firms his belief in a millennial outcome of human history, though he now bases that belief not on political
"revolutions" (cf. line 453) but on a revolution in the
mind of man.
5. Cf. Wordsworth's assertion that "the Mind of Man"
is "My haunt, and the main region of my song" in the
Prospectus to *The Recluse*, lines 40–41 (p. 1398).

SAMUEL TAYLOR COLERIDGE
1772–1834

1797:   At Nether Stowey, Somersetshire; the Wordsworths settle nearby,
at Alfoxden.

1798:   *Lyrical Ballads*, which includes *The Rime of the Ancient Mariner*
and several other poems by Coleridge.

1800:   Moves to Greta Hall, Keswick, thirteen miles from the Wordsworths at Grasmere.

1816:   Final residence at Highgate, near London, under the care of Dr.
James Gillman.

1817:   *Biographia Literaria.*

In *The Prelude* Wordsworth, recording his gratitude to the mountains, lakes, and winds "that dwell among the hills where I was born," commiserates with Coleridge because "thou, my Friend! wert reared / In the great City, 'mid far other scenes." Samuel Taylor Coleridge had in fact been born in the small town of Ottery St. Mary, in rural Devonshire, but on the death of his father he had been sent to school at Christ's Hospital, in London. He was a dreamy, enthusiastic, and extraordinarily precocious schoolboy; Charles Lamb, his schoolmate and lifelong friend, in his essay on Christ's Hospital has given us a vivid sketch of Coleridge's loneliness, his learning, and his eloquence. When in 1791 Coleridge went up to Jesus College, Cambridge, he was an accomplished scholar; but he found little intellectual stimulation at the university, fell into idleness, dissoluteness, and debt, and in despair fled to London and enlisted in the Light Dragoons under the alias of Silas Tomkyn Comberbache—probably the most inept cavalryman in the long history of the British army. Although rescued by his brothers and sent back to Cambridge, he left in 1794 without a degree.

In June 1794 Coleridge met Robert Southey, then a student at Oxford who, like himself, had poetic aspirations, was a radical in religion and politics, and sympathized with the republican experiment in France. Together the two young men planned to establish an ideal democratic community in America for which Coleridge coined the name "Pantisocracy," signifying an equal rule by all. A plausible American real-estate agent persuaded them that the ideal location would be on the banks of the Susquehanna, in Pennsylvania. Twelve men undertook to go; and since perpetuation of the scheme required offspring, hence wives, Coleridge dutifully became engaged to Sara Fricker, conveniently at hand as the sister of Southey's fiancée. The Pantisocracy scheme collapsed, but at Southey's insistence Coleridge went through with the marriage, "resolved," as he said, "but wretched." Later Coleridge's radicalism waned, and he became a conservative—a highly philosophical one—in politics, and a staunch Anglican in religion.

Despite its inauspicious beginning, Coleridge was at first happy in his marriage. In 1795 he met Wordsworth and at once judged him to be "the best poet of the age." When in 1797 Wordsworth brought his sister, Dorothy, to settle at Alfoxden, only three miles from the Coleridges at Nether Stowey, the period of intimate communication and poetic collaboration began that was the golden time of Coleridge's life. An annuity of £150, granted to Coleridge by Thomas and Josiah Wedgwood, sons of the founder of the famous pottery firm, came just in time to deflect him from assuming a post as a Unitarian minister. After their momentous joint publication of *Lyrical Ballads* in 1798, Coleridge and the Wordsworths spent a winter in Germany, where Coleridge attended the University of Göttingen and began the lifelong study of Kant and the post-Kantian German philosophers and critics that helped to alter profoundly his thinking about philosophy, religion, and aesthetics.

Back in England, Coleridge in 1800 followed the Wordsworths to the Lake District, settling at Greta Hall, Keswick. He had become gradually disaffected from his wife, and in 1799 he fell helplessly and hopelessly in love with Sara Hutchinson, whose sister, Mary, Wordsworth married three years later. All his life Coleridge had suffered from painful physical ailments; Wordsworth has described how sometimes, in a sudden spasm of agony, Coleridge would "throw himself down and writhe like a worm upon the ground." According to the standard medical prescription of the time, Coleridge had long been taking laudanum (opium dissolved in alcohol). In 1800–01 heavy dosages taken for attacks of rheumatism made opium a necessity to him, and Coleridge soon recognized that the drug was a worse evil than the diseases it did not cure. *Dejection: An Ode*, published in 1802, was Coleridge's despairing farewell to health, happiness, and poetic creativity. A two-year sojourn on the Mediterranean island of Malta, intended to restore his health, instead completed his decline. When he returned to England in the late summer of 1806 he was a broken man, an inveterate drug addict, estranged from his wife, suffering from agonies of remorse, and subject to terrifying nightmares of guilt and despair from which his own shrieks awakened him. A bitter quarrel with Wordsworth in 1810 marked the nadir of his life and expectations.

Under these conditions Coleridge's literary efforts, however sporadic and fragmentary, were little short of heroic. In 1808 he gave his first course of public lectures in London and, in the next eleven years, followed these with other series on both literary and philosophical topics. He wrote for newspapers and single-handedly undertook to write, publish, and distribute a periodical, *The Friend*, which lasted for some fourteen months after January 1809. A tragedy, *Remorse*, had in 1813 a very successful run of twenty performances at the Drury Lane Theatre. In 1816 he took up residence at Highgate, a northern suburb of London, under the supervision of the excellent and endlessly forbearing physician James Gillman, who managed to control, although not to eliminate, Coleridge's consumption of opium. The next three years were Coleridge's most sustained period of literary activity: while continuing to lecture and to write for the newspapers on a variety of subjects, he published *Biographia Literaria*, *Zapolya* (a drama), a book consisting of the essays in *The Friend* (revised and greatly enlarged), two collections of poems, and several important treatises on philosohical and religious subjects. In these last he undertook to establish a philosophical basis for the Trinitarian theology to which he had turned after his youthful period of Unitarianism.

The remaining years of his life, which he spent with Dr. and Mrs. Gillman, were quieter and happier than any he had known since the turn of the century. He came to a peaceful understanding with his wife and was reconciled with Wordsworth, with whom he toured the Rhineland in 1828. His rooms at Highgate became a center for friends, for the London literati, and for a steady stream of pilgrims from England and America. They came to hear one of the wonders of the age, the Sage of Highgate's conversation — or monologue — for even in his decline, Coleridge's talk never lost the almost incantatory power that Hazlitt has immortalized in *My First Acquaintance with Poets*. When he died, Coleridge left his friends with the sense that an incomparable intellect had vanished from the world. "The most *wonderful* man that I have ever known," Wordsworth declared, his voice breaking; and Charles Lamb: "His great and dear spirit haunts me. . . . Never saw I his likeness, nor probably the world can see again."

Coleridge's friends, however, abetted by his own merciless self-judgments, set current the opinion, still common, that he was great in promise but not in performance. Even in his buoyant youth he described his own character as "indolence capable of energies"; and it is true that while his mind was incessantly active and fertile, he lacked application and staying power. He also manifested early in life a profound sense of guilt and a need for public expiation. After drug addiction sapped his strength and will, even while it reinforced his emotional problems, he often adapted (or simply adopted) passages from other writers, with little or no acknowledgment, and sometimes in a context that seems designed at once to obfuscate his literary obligations and to reveal the subterfuge. Whatever the tangled motives for his procedure, Coleridge has repeatedly been charged with gross plagiarism, from his day to our own. After *The Rime of the Ancient Mariner*, most of the poems he completed were written, like the first version of *Dejection: An Ode*, in a spasm of intense effort. Writings that required sustained planning and application were either left unfinished or, like *Biographia Literaria*, made up of brilliant sections eked out with filler, sometimes lifted from other writers, in a desperate effort to meet a deadline. Many of his best speculations Coleridge merely confided to his notebooks and the ears of his friends, incorporated in letters, and poured out in the margins of his own and other people's books.

Even so, it is only when measured against his own potentialities that Coleridge's achievements appear limited. In opposition to the prevailing British philosophy of empiricism and associationism, Coleridge for most of his mature life expounded his views of the mind as creative in perception, intuitive in its discovery of the first premises of metaphysics and religion, and capable of a poetic re-creation of the world of sense by the fusing and formative power of the "secondary imagination." Within the decade after Coleridge died, John Stuart Mill, an acute student of contemporary thought, announced that Coleridge was one of "the two great seminal minds of England," the most important instigator and representative of the conservative intellectual movement of the day. Time has proved Mill's estimate of Coleridge to be just, for his influence is strongly evident in nineteenth-century English and American traditions of philosophical idealism, enlightened political conservatism, and liberal interpretations of Trinitarian theology. By present consensus, Coleridge is also one of the greatest and most influential of literary theorists; his ideas became central points of reference even in many of the New Critics of the middle of the present century who depreciated the Romantic poetry for which Coleridge, in his criticism, attempted to provide a rationale. Above all, Coleridge's writings in verse, although small in bulk, are the work of a major and extraordinarily innovative poet.

In the course of a few years, he wrote his poems of mystery and demonism, *The Rime of the Ancient Mariner*, *Christabel*, and *Kubla Khan*. No less impressive in their own way are the blank-verse poems of the lonely and meditative mind that, by an extension of his term for one of them, are often called "Conversation Poems"; in the best of these, *Frost at Midnight*, Coleridge perfected the characteristic pattern of integrally related description and meditation, which Wordsworth immediately used in *Tintern Abbey*. Coleridge himself adapted this pattern to the larger requirements of *Dejection: An Ode*, a high achievement in a genre in which few poets have been successful, the irregular English ode. The verse epistle *To William Wordsworth* is at once a most insightful comment about *The Prelude*, a superb tribute to a friend whom Coleridge thought the greatest poet since Milton, and a moving elegy on the death of his own poetic power. But even when he had mainly given up poetry, after 1805, Coleridge continued to write occasional short lyrics (represented below) that are remarkable for their quality, their diversity, and the extent to which they have been neglected by anthologists.

The Eolian Harp[1]

Composed at Clevedon, Somersetshire

My pensive Sara! thy soft cheek reclined
Thus on mine arm, most soothing sweet it is
To sit beside our Cot, our Cot o'ergrown
With white-flowered Jasmin, and the broad-leaved Myrtle,
(Meet emblems they of Innocence and Love!)   5
And watch the clouds, that late were rich with light,
Slow saddening round, and mark the star of eve
Serenely brilliant (such should Wisdom be)
Shine opposite! How exquisite the scents
Snatched from yon bean-field! and the world so hushed!   10
The stilly murmur of the distant Sea
Tells us of silence.

           And that simplest Lute,
Placed length-ways in the clasping casement, hark!
How by the desultory breeze caressed,
Like some coy maid half yielding to her lover,   15
It pours such sweet upbraiding, as must needs
Tempt to repeat the wrong! And now, its strings
Boldlier swept, the long sequacious[2] notes
Over delicious surges sink and rise,
Such a soft floating witchery of sound   70
As twilight Elfins make, when they at eve
Voyage on gentle gales from Fairy-Land,
Where Melodies round honey-dropping flowers,
Footless and wild, like birds of Paradise,[3]
Nor pause, nor perch, hovering on untamed wing!   25
O! the one Life within us and abroad,
Which meets all motion and becomes its soul,
A light in sound, a sound-like power in light,
Rhythm in all thought, and joyance everywhere—
Methinks, it should have been impossible   30
Not to love all things in a world so filled;
Where the breeze warbles, and the mute still air
Is Music slumbering on her instrument.

1. Named for Aeolus, god of the winds, the harp has strings stretched over a rectangular sounding box. The strings are tuned in unison. When placed in an opened window, the harp (also called "Eolian lute," "Eolian lyre," "wind harp") responds to the altering wind by sequences of musical chords. This instrument, which seems to voice nature's own music, was a favorite household furnishing in the period and was repeatedly alluded to in Romantic poetry. It served also as one of the recurrent Romantic images for the mind—either the mind in poetic inspiration, as in the last stanza of Shelley's *Ode to the West Wind* (p. 1702), or else the mind in perception, responding to an intellectual breeze by trembling into consciousness, as in this poem, lines 44–48. Coleridge, however, no sooner puts forward this concept than he retracts it, for it comes too close to the heresy of pantheism, which identifies God with the nature that, in the orthodox view, is His creation.

Coleridge wrote this poem to Sara Fricker, whom he married on Oct. 4, 1795, and took to a cottage at Clevedon, overlooking the Bristol Channel. He later several times expanded and altered the original version; the famous lines 26–29, for example, were not added until 1817. The poem was Coleridge's first achievement in the important Romantic form of the sustained blank-verse lyric of description and meditation, in the mode of conversation addressed to a silent auditor—a form that he perfected in *Frost at Midnight*, and that Wordsworth made use of in *Tintern Abbey*.

2. Successive.

3. Brilliantly colored birds found in New Guinea and adjacent islands. The native practice of removing the legs when preparing the skin led Europeans to believe that the birds were footless and spent their lives hovering in the air and feeding on nectar.

And thus, my Love! as on the midway slope
Of yonder hill I stretch my limbs at noon,   35
Whilst through my half-closed eyelids I behold
The sunbeams dance, like diamonds, on the main,
And tranquil muse upon tranquillity:
Full many a thought uncalled and undetained,
And many idle flitting phantasies,   40
Traverse my indolent and passive brain,
As wild and various as the random gales
That swell and flutter on this subject Lute!

And what if all of animated nature
Be but organic Harps diversely framed,   45
That tremble into thought, as o'er them sweeps
Plastic and vast, one intellectual breeze,
At once the Soul of each, and God of all?

But thy more serious eye a mild reproof
Darts, O belovèd Woman! nor such thoughts   50
Dim and unhallowed dost thou not reject,
And biddest me walk humbly with my God.
Meek Daughter in the family of Christ!
Well hast thou said and holily dispraised
These shapings of the unregenerate mind;   55
Bubbles that glitter as they rise and break
On vain Philosophy's aye-babbling spring.
For never guiltless may I speak of him,
The Incomprehensible! save when with awe
I praise him, and with Faith that inly *feels*;   60
Who with his saving mercies healèd me,
A sinful and most miserable man,
Wildered and dark, and gave me to possess
Peace, and this Cot, and thee, heart-honored Maid!

1795   1796

This Lime-Tree Bower My Prison

Addressed to Charles Lamb, of the India House, London

In the June of 1797 some long-expected friends paid a visit to the author's cottage; and on the morning of their arrival, he met with an accident, which disabled him from walking during the whole time of their stay. One evening, when they had left him for a few hours, he composed the following lines in the garden-bower.[1]

Well, they are gone, and here must I remain,
This lime-tree bower my prison! I have lost

1. The time was in fact July 1797; the visiting friends were William and Dorothy Wordsworth and Charles Lamb; the accident was the fault of Mrs. Coleridge— "dear Sara," Coleridge wrote, "accidentally emptied a skillet of boiling milk on my foot"; and the bower consisted of lime (i.e., linden) trees in the garden of Thomas Poole, next door to Coleridge's cottage at Nether Stowey. Coleridge related these facts in a letter to Robert Southey, July 17, 1797, in which he transcribed the first version of this fine "conversation poem."

Beauties and feelings, such as would have been
Most sweet to my remembrance even when age
Had dimmed mine eyes to blindness! They, meanwhile,   5
Friends, whom I never more may meet again,
On springy² heath, along the hill-top edge,
Wander in gladness, and wind down, perchance,
To that still roaring dell, of which I told;
The roaring dell, o'erwooded, narrow, deep,   10
And only speckled by the mid-day sun;
Where its slim trunk the ash from rock to rock
Flings arching like a bridge;—that branchless ash,
Unsunned and damp, whose few poor yellow leaves
Ne'er tremble in the gale, yet tremble still,   15
Fanned by the waterfall! and there my friends
Behold the dark green file of long lank weeds,
That all at once (a most fantastic sight!)
Still nod and drip beneath the dripping edge
Of the blue clay-stone.

                              Now, my friends emerge   20
Beneath the wide wide Heaven—and view again
The many-steepled tract magnificent
Of hilly fields and meadows, and the sea,
With some fair bark, perhaps, whose sails light up
The slip of smooth clear blue betwixt two Isles   25
Of purple shadow! Yes! they wander on
In gladness all; but thou, methinks, most glad,
My gentle-hearted Charles! for thou hast pined
And hungered after Nature, many a year,
In the great City pent,³ winning thy way   30
With sad yet patient soul, through evil and pain
And strange calamity!⁴ Ah! slowly sink
Behind the western ridge, thou glorious Sun!
Shine in the slant beams of the sinking orb,
Ye purple heath-flowers! richlier burn, ye clouds!   35
Live in the yellow light, ye distant groves!
And kindle, thou blue Ocean! So my friend
Struck with deep joy may stand, as I have stood,
Silent with swimming sense; yea, gazing round
On the wide landscape, gaze till all doth seem   40
Less gross than bodily; and of such hues
As veil the Almighty Spirit, when yet he makes
Spirits perceive his presence.

                              A delight
Comes sudden on my heart, and I am glad
As I myself were there! Nor in this bower,   45
This little lime-tree bower, have I not marked

---

2. *Elastic*, I mean [Coleridge's note].
3. Despite Coleridge's claim, Charles Lamb eminently preferred London over what he called "dead
Nature."

4. Some ten months earlier Charles Lamb's sister,
Mary, had stabbed their mother to death in a fit of
insanity.

Much that has soothed me. Pale beneath the blaze
Hung the transparent foliage; and I watched
Some broad and sunny leaf, and loved to see
The shadow of the leaf and stem above   50
Dappling its sunshine! And that walnut-tree
Was richly tinged, and a deep radiance lay
Full on the ancient ivy, which usurps
Those fronting elms, and now, with blackest mass
Makes their dark branches gleam a lighter hue   55
Through the late twilight: and though now the bat
Wheels silent by, and not a swallow twitters,
Yet still the solitary humblebee
Sings in the bean-flower! Henceforth I shall know
That Nature ne'er deserts the wise and pure;   60
No plot so narrow, be but Nature there,
No waste so vacant, but may well employ
Each faculty of sense, and keep the heart
Awake to Love and Beauty! and sometimes
'Tis well to be bereft of promised good,   65
That we may lift the soul, and contemplate
With lively joy the joys we cannot share.
My gentle-hearted Charles! when the last rook
Beat its straight path along the dusky air
Homewards, I blessed it! deeming its black wing   70
(Now a dim speck, now vanishing in light)
Had crossed the mighty Orb's dilated glory,
While thou stood'st gazing; or, when all was still,
Flew creeking o'er thy head, and had a charm
For thee, my gentle-hearted Charles, to whom   75
No sound is dissonant which tells of Life.

1797   1800

The Rime of the Ancient Mariner[1]

IN SEVEN PARTS

*Facile credo, plures esse Naturas invisibiles quam visibiles in rerum universitate.
Sed horum [sic] omnium familiam quis nobis enarrabit? et gradus et cognati-
ones et discrimina et singulorum munera? Quid agunt? quae loca habitant?
Harum rerum notitiam semper ambivit ingenium humanum, nunquam attigit.
Juvat, interea, non diffiteor, quandoque in animo, tanquam in tabulâ, majoris
et melioris mundi imaginem contemplari: ne mens assuefacta hodiernae vitae
minutiis se contrahat nimis, et tota subsidat in pusillas cogitationes. Sed veritati*

1. Coleridge describes the origin of this poem in the opening section of chap. 14 of *Biographia Literaria*. In a comment made to the Rev. Alexander Dyce in 1835 and in a note on *We Are Seven* dictated in 1843, Wordsworth added some details. The poem, based on a dream of Coleridge's friend Cruikshank, was originally planned as a collaboration between the two friends, to pay the expense of a walking tour they took with Dorothy Wordsworth in Nov. 1797. Before he dropped out of the enterprise, Wordsworth suggested the shooting of the albatross and the navigation of the ship by the dead men; he also contributed lines 13–16 and 226–27.

The version of *The Rime of the Ancient Mariner* printed in *Lyrical Ballads* (1798) contained many archaic words and spellings. In later editions Coleridge greatly improved the poem by pruning the archaisms and by other revisions; he also added the Latin epigraph and the marginal glosses.

interea invigilandum est, modusque servandus, ut certa ab incertis, diem a
nocte, distinguamus.

T. BURNET, *Archaeol. Phil.* p. 68.[2]

Argument

How a Ship, having first sailed to the Equator, was driven by storms to the
cold Country towards the South Pole; how the Ancient Mariner cruelly and
in contempt of the laws of hospitality killed a Seabird and how he was followed by many and strange Judgments: and in what manner he came back to
his own Country.

Part 1

An ancient Mariner
meeteth three Gal-
lants bidden to a
wedding feast, and
detaineth one.

It is an ancient Mariner
And he stoppeth one of three.
—"By thy long gray beard and glittering eye,
Now wherefore stopp'st thou me?

The Bridegroom's doors are opened wide,   5
And I am next of kin;
The guests are met, the feast is set:
May'st hear the merry din."

He holds him with his skinny hand,
"There was a ship," quoth he.   10
"Hold off! unhand me, graybeard loon!"
Eftsoons[3] his hand dropped he.

The Wedding-Guest is
spellbound by the eye
of the old seafaring
man, and constrained
to hear his tale.

He holds him with his glittering eye—
The Wedding-Guest stood still,
And listens like a three years' child: 15
The Mariner hath his will.[4]

The Wedding-Guest sat on a stone;
He cannot choose but hear;
And thus spake on that ancient man,
The bright-eyed Mariner.   20

"The ship was cheered, the harbor cleared,
Merrily did we drop
Below the kirk,[5] below the hill,
Below the lighthouse top.

2. "I readily believe that there are more invisible than visible Natures in the universe. But who will explain for us the family of all these beings, and the ranks and relations and distinguishing features and functions of each? What do they do? What places do they inhabit? The human mind has always sought the knowledge of these things, but never attained it. Meanwhile I do not deny that it is helpful sometimes to contemplate in the mind, as on a tablet, the image of a greater and better world, lest the intellect, habituated to the petty things of daily life, narrow itself and sink wholly into trivial thoughts. But at the same time we must be watchful for the truth and keep a sense of proportion, so that we may distinguish the certain from the uncertain, day from night." Adapted by Coleridge from Thomas Burnet, *Archaeologiae Philosophicae* (1692).
3. At once.
4. I.e., the Mariner has gained control of the will of the Wedding-Guest by hypnosis—or, as it was called in Coleridge's time, by "mesmerism."
5. Church.

The Mariner tells how
the ship sailed south-
ward with a good
wind and fair
weather, till it
reached the Line.

The Sun came up upon the left,   25
Out of the sea came he!
And he shone bright, and on the right
Went down into the sea.

Higher and higher every day,
Till over the mast at noon[6]—"   30
The Wedding-Guest here beat his breast,
For he heard the loud bassoon.

The Wedding-Guest
heareth the bridal
music; but the Mari-
ner continueth his
tale.

The bride hath paced into the hall,
Red as a rose is she;
Nodding their heads before her goes   35
The merry minstrelsy.

The Wedding-Guest he beat his breast,
Yet he cannot choose but hear;
And thus spake on that ancient man,
The bright-eyed Mariner.   40

The ship driven by a
storm toward the
South Pole.

"And now the STORM-BLAST came, and he
Was tyrannous and strong;
He struck with his o'ertaking wings,
And chased us south along.

With sloping masts and dipping prow,   45
As who pursued with yell and blow
Still treads the shadow of his foe,
And forward bends his head,
The ship drove fast, loud roared the blast,
And southward aye we fled.   50

And now there came both mist and snow,
And it grew wondrous cold:
And ice, mast-high, came floating by,
As green as emerald.

The land of ice, and
of fearful sounds
where no living thing
was to be seen.

And through the drifts the snowy clifts   55
Did send a dismal sheen:
Nor shapes of men nor beasts we ken—
The ice was all between.

The ice was here, the ice was there,
The ice was all around: 60
It cracked and growled, and roared and howled,
Like noises in a swound![7]

Till a great sea bird,
called the Albatross,
came through the
snow-fog, and was
received with great joy
and hospitality.

At length did cross an Albatross,
Thorough the fog it came;
As if it had been a Christian soul,   65
We hailed it in God's name.

6. The ship had reached the equator.   7. Swoon.

It ate the food it ne'er had eat,
And round and round it flew.
The ice did split with a thunder-fit;
The helmsman steered us through! 70

And a good south wind sprung up behind;
The Albatross did follow,
And every day, for food or play,
Came to the mariners' hollo!

In mist or cloud, on mast or shroud,[8] 75
It perched for vespers nine;
Whiles all the night, through fog-smoke white,
Glimmered the white Moon-shine."

"God save thee, ancient Mariner!
From the fiends, that plague thee thus!— 80
Why look'st thou so?"—With my crossbow
I shot the ALBATROSS.

Part 2

The Sun now rose upon the right:[9]
Out of the sea came he,
Still hid in mist, and on the left 85
Went down into the sea.

And the good south wind still blew behind,
But no sweet bird did follow,
Nor any day for food or play
Came to the mariners' hollo! 90

And I had done a hellish thing,
And it would work 'em woe:
For all averred, I had killed the bird
That made the breeze to blow.
Ah wretch! said they, the bird to slay, 95
That made the breeze to blow!

Nor dim nor red, like God's own head,
The glorious Sun uprist:
Then all averred, I had killed the bird
That brought the fog and mist. 100
'Twas right, said they, such birds to slay,
That bring the fog and mist.

The fair breeze blew, the white foam flew,
The furrow followed free;
We were the first that ever burst 105
Into that silent sea.

Gloss (left margin):
And lo! the Albatross proveth a bird of good omen, and followeth the ship as it returned northward through fog and floating ice.

The ancient Mariner inhospitably killeth the pious bird of good omen.

His shipmates cry out against the ancient Mariner, for killing the bird of good luck.

But when the fog cleared off, they justify the same, and thus make themselves accomplices in the crime.

The fair breeze continues; the ship enters the Pacific Ocean, and sails northward, even till it reaches the Line.[1]

8. Rope supporting the mast.
9. Having rounded Cape Horn, the ship heads north into the Pacific.
1. I.e., the equator. Unless it is simply an error (Coleridge misreading his own poem), this gloss anticipates the ship's later arrival at the equator, on its trip north

The ship hath been suddenly becalmed.

Down dropped the breeze, the sails dropped down,
'Twas sad as sad could be;
And we did speak only to break
The silence of the sea!   110

All in a hot and copper sky,
The bloody Sun, at noon,
Right up above the mast did stand,
No bigger than the Moon.

Day after day, day after day,   115
We stuck, nor breath nor motion;
As idle as a painted ship
Upon a painted ocean.

And the Albatross begins to be avenged.

Water, water, everywhere,
And all the boards did shrink;   120
Water, water, everywhere,
Nor any drop to drink.

The very deep did rot: O Christ!
That ever this should be!
Yea, slimy things did crawl with legs   125
Upon the slimy sea.

About, about, in reel and rout
The death-fires[2] danced at night;
The water, like a witch's oils,
Burnt green, and blue and white.   130

A Spirit had followed them; one of the invisible inhabitants of this planet, neither departed souls nor angels; concerning whom the learned Jew, Josephus, and the Platonic Constantinopolitan, Michael Psellus, may be consulted. They are very numerous, and there is no climate or element without one or more.

And some in dreams assurèd were
Of the Spirit that plagued us so;
Nine fathom deep he had followed us
From the land of mist and snow.

And every tongue, through utter drought,   135
Was withered at the root;
We could not speak, no more than if
We had been choked with soot.

The shipmates, in their sore distress, would fain throw the whole guilt on the ancient Mariner: in sign whereof they hang the dead sea bird round his neck.

Ah! well-a-day! what evil looks
Had I from old and young!   140
Instead of the cross, the Albatross
About my neck was hung.

---

from the region of the South Pole, as described in lines 381–84.

2. Usually glossed as the corposant, or St. Elmo's fire—an atmospheric electricity on a ship's mast or rigging—believed by superstitious sailors to portend disaster. Possibly the image is instead a type of oceanic *ignis fatuus* ("foolish fire") resulting from the decomposition of putrescent matter in the sea (see line 123).

Part 3

There passed a weary time. Each throat
Was parched, and glazed each eye.
A weary time! a weary time!   145
How glazed each weary eye,

The ancient Mariner
beholdeth a sign in   When looking westward, I beheld
the element afar off.   A something in the sky.

At first it seemed a little speck,
And then it seemed a mist;   150
It moved and moved, and took at last
A certain shape, I wist.[3]

A speck, a mist, a shape, I wist!
And still it neared and neared:
As if it dodged a water-sprite,[4]   155
It plunged and tacked and veered.

At its nearer
approach, it seemeth   With throats unslaked, with black lips baked,
him to be a ship; and   We could nor laugh nor wail;
at a dear ransom he   Through utter drought all dumb we stood!
freeth his speech from   I bit my arm, I sucked the blood,   160
the bonds of thirst.   And cried, A sail! a sail!

With throats unslaked, with black lips baked,
Agape they heard me call:
A flash of joy;   Gramercy![5] they for joy did grin,
And all at once their breath drew in,   165
As they were drinking all.

And horror follows.
For can it be a ship   See! see! (I cried) she tacks no more!
that comes onward   Hither to work us weal;[6]
without wind or tide?   Without a breeze, without a tide,
She steadies with upright keel!   170

The western wave was all aflame.
The day was well nigh done!
Almost upon the western wave
Rested the broad bright Sun;
When that strange shape drove suddenly   175
Betwixt us and the Sun.

It seemeth him but
the skeleton of a ship. And straight the Sun was flecked with bars,
(Heaven's Mother send us grace!)
As if through a dungeon grate he peered
With broad and burning face.   180

---

3. Knew.
4. A supernatural being that supervises the natural elements (but Coleridge may in fact have been using the

term to mean water-*spout*).
5. From the French *grand-merci,* "great thanks."
6. Benefit.

Alas! (thought I, and my heart beat loud)
And its ribs are seen How fast she nears and nears!
as bars on the face of Are those *her* sails that glance in the Sun,
the setting Sun. Like restless gossameres?[7]

The Specter-Woman Are those *her* ribs through which the Sun   185
and her Deathmate, Did peer, as through a grate?
and no other on board And is that Woman all her crew?
the skeleton ship. Is that a DEATH? and are there two?
Is DEATH that woman's mate?

Like vessel, like crew! Her lips were red, *her* looks were free,   190
Her locks were yellow as gold:
Her skin was as white as leprosy,
The Night-mare LIFE-IN-DEATH was she,
Who thicks man's blood with cold.

Death and Life-in- The naked hulk alongside came,   195
Death have diced for And the twain were casting dice;
the ship's crew, and "The game is done! I've won! I've won!"
she (the latter) win- Quoth she, and whistles thrice.
neth the ancient Mar-
iner.

No twilight within the The Sun's rim dips; the stars rush out:
courts of the Sun. At one stride comes the dark;   200
With far-heard whisper, o'er the sea,
Off shot the spectre-bark.

At the rising of the We listened and looked sideways up!
Moon, Fear at my heart, as at a cup,
My lifeblood seemed to sip!   205
The stars were dim, and thick the night,
The steersman's face by his lamp gleamed white;
From the sails the dew did drip—
Till clomb above the eastern bar
The hornèd Moon, with one bright star   210
Within the nether tip.[8]

One after another, One after one, by the star-dogged Moon,
Too quick for groan or sigh,
Each turned his face with a ghastly pang,
And cursed me with his eye.   215

His shipmates drop Four times fifty living men,
down dead. (And I heard nor sigh nor groan)
With heavy thump, a lifeless lump,
They dropped down one by one.

But Life-in-Death The souls did from their bodies fly—   220
begins her work on the They fled to bliss or woe!
ancient Mariner. And every soul, it passed me by,
Like the whizz of my crossbow!

7. Filmy cobwebs floating in the air.   8. An omen of impending evil.

Part 4

"I fear thee, ancient Mariner!
I fear thy skinny hand!
And thou art long, and lank, and brown,   225
As is the ribbed sea-sand.

I fear thee and thy glittering eye,
And thy skinny hand, so brown."—

Fear not, fear not, thou Wedding-Guest!   230
This body dropped not down.

Alone, alone, all, all alone,
Alone on a wide wide sea!
And never a saint took pity on
My soul in agony.   235

The many men, so beautiful!
And they all dead did lie:
And a thousand thousand slimy things
Lived on; and so did I.

I looked upon the rotting sea,   240
And drew my eyes away;
I looked upon the rotting deck,
And there the dead men lay.

I looked to heaven, and tried to pray;
But or ever a prayer had gushed,   245
A wicked whisper came, and made
My heart as dry as dust.

I closed my lids, and kept them close,
And the balls like pulses beat;
For the sky and the sea, and the sea and the sky   250
Lay like a load on my weary eye,
And the dead were at my feet.

The cold sweat melted from their limbs,
Nor rot nor reek did they:
The look with which they looked on me   255
Had never passed away.

An orphan's curse would drag to hell
A spirit from on high;
But oh! more horrible than that
Is the curse in a dead man's eye!   260
Seven days, seven nights, I saw that curse,
And yet I could not die.

The moving Moon went up the sky,
And nowhere did abide:

neying Moon, and the
stars that still sojourn,
yet still move onward;
and everywhere the
blue sky belongs to
them, and is their
appointed rest, and
their native country
and their own natural
homes, which they
enter unannounced,
as lords that are cer-
tainly expected and yet there is a silent joy at their arrival.

Softly she was going up,   265
And a star or two beside—

Her beams bemocked the sultry main,
Like April hoar-frost spread;
But where the ship's huge shadow lay,
The charmèd water burnt alway   270
A still and awful red.

By the light of the
Moon he beholdeth
God's creatures of the
great calm.

Beyond the shadow of the ship,
I watched the water snakes:
They moved in tracks of shining white,
And when they reared, the elfish light   275
Fell off in hoary flakes.

Within the shadow of the ship
I watched their rich attire:
Blue, glossy green, and velvet black,
They coiled and swam; and every track   280
Was a flash of golden fire.

Their beauty and
their happiness.

O happy living things! no tongue
Their beauty might declare:

He blesseth them in
his heart.

A spring of love gushed from my heart,
And I blessed them unaware: 285
Sure my kind saint took pity on me,
And I blessed them unaware.

The spell begins to
break.

The self-same moment I could pray;
And from my neck so free
The Albatross fell off, and sank   290
Like lead into the sea.

Part 5

Oh sleep! it is a gentle thing,
Beloved from pole to pole!
To Mary Queen the praise be given!
She sent the gentle sleep from Heaven,   295
That slid into my soul.

By grace of the holy
Mother, the ancient
Mariner is refreshed
with rain.

The silly[9] buckets on the deck,
That had so long remained,
I dreamt that they were filled with dew;
And when I awoke, it rained.   300

My lips were wet, my throat was cold,
My garments all were dank;

9. Simple, homely.

Sure I had drunken in my dreams,
And still my body drank.

I moved, and could not feel my limbs: 305
I was so light—almost
I thought that I had died in sleep,
And was a blessed ghost.

He heareth sounds And soon I heard a roaring wind:
and seeth strange It did not come anear;   310
sights and commo- But with its sound it shook the sails,
tions in the sky and That were so thin and sere.
the element.

The upper air burst into life!
And a hundred fire-flags sheen,[1]
To and fro they were hurried about!   315
And to and fro, and in and out,
The wan stars danced between.

And the coming wind did roar more loud,
And the sails did sigh like sedge;[2]
And the rain poured down from one black cloud;   320
The Moon was at its edge.

The thick black cloud was cleft, and still
The Moon was at its side:
Like waters shot from some high crag,
The lightning fell with never a jag,   325
A river steep and wide.

The bodies of the The loud wind never reached the ship,
ship's crew are inspir- Yet now the ship moved on!
ited, and the ship Beneath the lightning and the Moon
moves on; The dead men gave a groan.   330

They groaned, they stirred, they all uprose,
Nor spake, nor moved their eyes;
It had been strange, even in a dream,
To have seen those dead men rise.

The helmsman steered, the ship moved on;   335
Yet never a breeze up-blew;
The mariners all 'gan work the ropes,
Where they were wont to do;
They raised their limbs like lifeless tools—
We were a ghastly crew.   340

The body of my brother's son
Stood by me, knee to knee:

1. Shone. These fire-flags are probably St. Elmo's fire   also lightning.
(see p. 1491, n. 2), but Coleridge may be describing   2. A rushlike plant growing in wet soil.
the Aurora Australis, or Southern Lights, and possibly

The body and I pulled at one rope,
But he said nought to me.

*But not by the souls
of the men, nor by
dæmons[3] of earth or
middle air, but by a
blessed troop of
angelic spirits, sent
down by the invoca-
tion of the guardian
saint.*

"I fear thee, ancient Mariner!"   345
Be calm, thou Wedding Guest!
'Twas not those souls that fled in pain,
Which to their corses[4] came again,
But a troop of spirits blest:

For when it dawned—they dropped their arms,   350
And clustered round the mast;
Sweet sounds rose slowly through their mouths,
And from their bodies passed.

Around, around, flew each sweet sound,
Then darted to the Sun;   355
Slowly the sounds came back again,
Now mixed, now one by one.

Sometimes a-dropping from the sky
I heard the sky-lark sing;
Sometimes all little birds that are,   360
How they seemed to fill the sea and air
With their sweet jargoning![5]

And now 'twas like all instruments,
Now like a lonely flute;
And now it is an angel's song,   365
That makes the heavens be mute.

It ceased; yet still the sails made on
A pleasant noise till noon,
A noise like of a hidden brook
In the leafy month of June,   370
That to the sleeping woods all night
Singeth a quiet tune.

Till noon we quietly sailed on,
Yet never a breeze did breathe:
Slowly and smoothly went the ship,   375
Moved onward from beneath.

*The lonesome Spirit
from the South Pole
carries on the ship as
far as the Line, in obe-
dience to the angelic
troop, but still
requireth vengeance.*

Under the keel nine fathom deep,
From the land of mist and snow,
The spirit slid: and it was he
That made the ship to go.   380
The sails at noon left off their tune,
And the ship stood still also.

---

3. Supernatural beings halfway between mortals and   4. Corpses.
gods (the type of spirit that Coleridge describes in the   5. Warbling (Middle English).
gloss beside lines 131–34).

The Sun, right up above the mast,
Had fixed her to the ocean:
But in a minute she 'gan stir,   385
With a short uneasy motion—
Backwards and forwards half her length
With a short uneasy motion.

Then like a pawing horse let go,
She made a sudden bound: 390
It flung the blood into my head,
And I fell down in a swound.

The Polar Spirit's fellow dæmons, the invisible inhabitants of the element, take part in his wrong; and two of them relate, one to the other, that penance long and heavy for the ancient Mariner hath been accorded to the Polar Spirit, who returneth southward.

How long in that same fit I lay,
I have not[6] to declare;
But ere my living life returned,   395
I heard and in my soul discerned
Two voices in the air.

"Is it he?" quoth one, "Is this the man?
By him who died on cross,
With his cruel bow he laid full low   400
The harmless Albatross.

The spirit who bideth by himself
In the land of mist and snow,
He loved the bird that loved the man
Who shot him with his bow."   405

The other was a softer voice,
As soft as honeydew:
Quoth he, "The man hath penance done,
And penance more will do."

Part 6

FIRST VOICE
"But tell me, tell me! speak again,   410
Thy soft response renewing—
What makes that ship drive on so fast?
What is the ocean doing?"

SECOND VOICE
"Still as a slave before his lord,
The ocean hath no blast;   415
His great bright eye most silently
Up to the Moon is cast—

If he may know which way to go;
For she guides him smooth or grim.

6. I.e., have not the knowledge.

See, brother, see! how graciously   420
She looketh down on him."

FIRST VOICE

The Mariner hath been cast into a trance; for the angelic power caus-eth the vessel to drive northward faster than human life could endure.
"But why drives on that ship so fast,
Without or wave or wind?"

SECOND VOICE

"The air is cut away before,
And closes from behind.   425

Fly, brother, fly! more high, more high!
Or we shall be belated:
For slow and slow that ship will go,
When the Mariner's trance is abated."

The supernatural motion is retarded; the Mariner awakes, and his penance begins anew.
I woke, and we were sailing on   430
As in a gentle weather:
'Twas night, calm night, the moon was high;
The dead men stood together.

All stood together on the deck,
For a charnel-dungeon fitter: 435
All fixed on me their stony eyes,
That in the Moon did glitter.

The pang, the curse, with which they died,
Had never passed away:
I could not draw my eyes from theirs,   440
Nor turn them up to pray.

The curse is finally expiated.
And now this spell was snapped: once more
I viewed the ocean green,
And looked far forth, yet little saw
Of what had else been seen—   445

Like one, that on a lonesome road
Doth walk in fear and dread,
And having once turned round walks on,
And turns no more his head;
Because he knows, a frightful fiend   450
Doth close behind him tread.

But soon there breathed a wind on me,
Nor sound nor motion made:
Its path was not upon the sea,
In ripple or in shade.   455

It raised my hair, it fanned my cheek
Like a meadow-gale of spring—
It mingled strangely with my fears,
Yet it felt like a welcoming.

Swiftly, swiftly flew the ship,   460
Yet she sailed softly too:
Sweetly, sweetly blew the breeze—
On me alone it blew.

And the ancient Mari-   Oh! dream of joy! is this indeed
ner beholdeth his   The lighthouse top I see?   465
native country.   Is this the hill? is this the kirk?
Is this mine own countree?

We drifted o'er the harbor bar,
And I with sobs did pray—
O let me be awake, my God!   470
Or let me sleep alway.

The harbor bay was clear as glass,
So smoothly it was strewn!
And on the bay the moonlight lay,
And the shadow of the Moon.   475

The rock shone bright, the kirk no less,
That stands above the rock:
The moonlight steeped in silentness
The steady weathercock.

And the bay was white with silent light,   480
Till rising from the same,
The angelic spirits   Full many shapes, that shadows were,
leave the dead bodies,   In crimson colors came.

And appear in their   A little distance from the prow
own forms of light.   Those crimson shadows were: 485
I turned my eyes upon the deck—
Oh, Christ! what saw I there!

Each corse lay flat, lifeless and flat,
And, by the holy rood!
A man all light, a seraph[7] man,   490
On every corse there stood.

This seraph band, each waved his hand:
It was a heavenly sight!
They stood as signals to the land,
Each one a lovely light;   495

This seraph band, each waved his hand,
No voice did they impart—
No voice; but oh! the silence sank
Like music on my heart.

7. A shining celestial being, highest in the ranks of the angels. "Rood": cross.

But soon I heard the dash of oars,   500
I heard the Pilot's cheer;
My head was turned perforce away
And I saw a boat appear.

The Pilot and the Pilot's boy,
I heard them coming fast: 505
Dear Lord in Heaven! it was a joy
The dead men could not blast.

I saw a third—I heard his voice:
It is the Hermit good!
He singeth loud his godly hymns   510
That he makes in the wood.
He'll shrieve my soul, he'll wash away
The Albatross's blood.

Part 7

The Hermit of the
Wood, This Hermit good lives in that wood
Which slopes down to the sea.   515
How loudly his sweet voice he rears!
He loves to talk with marineres
That come from a far countree.

He kneels at morn, and noon, and eve—
He hath a cushion plump: 520
It is the moss that wholly hides
The rotted old oak-stump.

The skiff-boat neared: I heard them talk,
"Why, this is strange, I trow!
Where are those lights so many and fair,   525
That signal made but now?"

Approacheth the ship
with wonder. "Strange, by my faith!" the Hermit said—
"And they answered not our cheer!
The planks looked warped! and see those sails,
How thin they are and sere!   530
I never saw aught like to them,
Unless perchance it were

Brown skeletons of leaves that lag
My forest-brook along;
When the ivy tod[8] is heavy with snow,   535

And the owlet whoops to the wolf below,
That eats the she-wolf's young."

---

8. Clump of ivy.

"Dear Lord! it hath a fiendish look,"
(The Pilot made reply)
"I am a-feared"—"Push on, push on!"   540
Said the Hermit cheerily.

The boat came closer to the ship,
But I nor spake nor stirred;
The boat came close beneath the ship,
And straight a sound was heard.   545

The ship suddenly sinketh.

Under the water it rumbled on,
Still louder and more dread:
It reached the ship, it split the bay;
The ship went down like lead.

The ancient Mariner is saved in the Pilot's boat.

Stunned by that loud and dreadful sound,   550
Which sky and ocean smote,
Like one that hath been seven days drowned
My body lay afloat;
But swift as dreams, myself I found
Within the Pilot's boat.   555

Upon the whirl, where sank the ship,
The boat spun round and round;
And all was still, save that the hill
Was telling of the sound.

I moved my lips—the Pilot shrieked   560
And fell down in a fit;
The holy Hermit raised his eyes,
And prayed where he did sit.

I took the oars: the Pilot's boy,
Who now doth crazy go,   565
Laughed loud and long, and all the while
His eyes went to and fro.
"Ha! ha!" quoth he, "full plain I see,
The Devil knows how to row."

And now, all in my own countree,   570
I stood on the firm land!
The Hermit stepped forth from the boat,
And scarcely he could stand.

The ancient Mariner earnestly entreateth the Hermit to shrieve him; and the penance of life falls on him.

"O shrieve me, shrieve me, holy man!"
The Hermit crossed his brow.[9]   575
"Say quick," quoth he, "I bid thee say—
What manner of man art thou?"

Forthwith this frame of mine was wrenched
With a woeful agony,

9. Made the sign of the cross on his forehead. "Shrieve me": hear my confession and grant me absolution.

Which forced me to begin my tale;   580
And then it left me free.

*And ever and
anon throughout
his future life an
agony constrain-
eth him to travel
from land to
land;*

Since then, at an uncertain hour,
That agony returns:
And till my ghastly tale is told,
This heart within me burns.   585

I pass, like night, from land to land;
I have strange power of speech;
That moment that his face I see,
I know the man that must hear me:
To him my tale I teach.   590

What loud uproar bursts from that door!
The wedding-guests are there:
But in the garden-bower the bride
And bride-maids singing are:
And hark the little vesper bell,   595
Which biddeth me to prayer!

O Wedding-Guest! this soul hath been
Alone on a wide wide sea:
So lonely 'twas, that God himself
Scarce seemèd there to be.   600

O sweeter than the marriage feast,
'Tis sweeter far to me,
To walk together to the kirk
With a goodly company!—

To walk together to the kirk,   605
And all together pray,
While each to his great Father bends,
Old men, and babes, and loving friends
And youths and maidens gay!

*And to teach, by
his own example,
love and reverence to
all things that God
made and loveth.*

Farewell, farewell! but this I tell   610
To thee, thou Wedding-Guest!
He prayeth well, who loveth well
Both man and bird and beast.

He prayeth best, who loveth best
All things both great and small;   615
For the dear God who loveth us,
He made and loveth all.[1]

1. Coleridge said in 1830, answering the objection of the poet Anna Barbauld that the poem "lacked a moral": "I told her that in my own judgment the poem had too much; and that the only, or chief fault, if I might say so, was the obtrusion of the moral sentiment so openly on the reader as a principle or cause of action in a work of pure imagination. It ought to have had no more moral than the *Arabian Nights'* tale of the merchant's sitting down to eat dates by the side of a well and throwing the shells aside, and lo! a genie starts up and says he *must* kill the aforesaid merchant *because* one of the date shells had, it seems, put out the eye of the genie's son."

The Mariner, whose eye is bright,
Whose beard with age is hoar,
Is gone: and now the Wedding-Guest   620
Turned from the bridegroom's door.

He went like one that hath been stunned,
And is of sense forlorn:[2]
A sadder and a wiser man,
He rose the morrow morn.   625

1797   1798

Kubla Khan

Or, A Vision in a Dream. A Fragment

The following fragment is here published at the request of a poet of great
and deserved celebrity,[1] and, as far as the author's own opinions are concerned, rather as a psychological curiosity, than on the ground of any supposed
poetic merits.

In the summer of the year 1797, the author, then in ill health, had retired
to a lonely farmhouse between Porlock and Linton, on the Exmoor confines
of Somerset and Devonshire. In consequence of a slight indisposition, an anodyne had been prescribed, from the effects of which he fell asleep in his chair
at the moment that he was reading the following sentence, or words of the
same substance, in *Purchas's Pilgrimage:* "Here the Khan Kubla commanded
a palace to be built, and a stately garden thereunto. And thus ten miles of
fertile ground were inclosed with a wall."[2] The author continued for about
three hours in a profound sleep, at least of the external senses,[3] during which
time he has the most vivid confidence that he could not have composed less
than from two to three hundred lines; if that indeed can be called composition
in which all the images rose up before him as *things*, with a parallel production of the correspondent expressions, without any sensation or consciousness
of effort. On awaking he appeared to himself to have a distinct recollection of
the whole, and taking his pen, ink, and paper, instantly and eagerly wrote
down the lines that are here preserved. At this moment he was unfortunately
called out by a person on business from Porlock, and detained by him above
an hour, and on his return to his room, found, to his no small surprise and
mortification, that though he still retained some vague and dim recollection
of the general purport of the vision, yet, with the exception of some eight or
ten scattered lines and images, all the rest had passed away like the images on
the surface of a stream into which a stone has been cast, but, alas! without the
after restoration of the latter!

2. Forsaken.
1. Lord Byron.
2. "In Xamdu did Cublai Can build a stately Palace,
encompassing sixteene miles of plaine ground with a
wall, wherein are fertile Meddowes, pleasant Springs,
delightfull Streames, and all sorts of beasts of chase
and game, and in the middest thereof a sumptuous
house of pleasure, which may be removed from place
to place." From Samuel Purchas, *Purchas his Pilgrimage* (1613). The historical Kublai Khan founded the

Mongol dynasty in China in the 13th century.
3. In a note on a manuscript copy of *Kubla Khan*,
Coleridge gave a more precise account of the nature
of this "sleep": "This fragment with a good deal more,
not recoverable, composed, in a sort of reverie brought
on by two grains of opium, taken to check a dysentery,
at a farmhouse between Porlock and Linton, a quarter
of a mile from Culbone Church, in the fall of the year,
1797."

Then all the charm
Is broken—all that phantom world so fair
Vanishes, and a thousand circlets spread,
And each misshape[s] the other. Stay awhile,
Poor youth! who scarcely dar'st lift up thine eyes—
The stream will soon renew its smoothness, soon
The visions will return! And lo, he stays,
And soon the fragments dim of lovely forms
Come trembling back, unite, and now once more
The pool becomes a mirror.
    [From Coleridge's *The Picture; or, the Lover's Resolution,*
lines 91–100]

Yet from the still surviving recollections in his mind, the author has frequently purposed to finish for himself what had been originally, as it were,
given to him. Σαμερον αδιον ασω: but the tomorrow is yet to come.[4]

As a contrast to this vision, I have annexed a fragment of a very different
character, describing with equal fidelity the dream of pain and disease.[5]

In Xanadu did Kubla Khan
A stately pleasure dome decree:
Where Alph,[6] the sacred river, ran
Through caverns measureless to man
    Down to a sunless sea.   5
So twice five miles of fertile ground
With walls and towers were girdled round:
And there were gardens bright with sinuous rills,
Where blossomed many an incense-bearing tree;
And here were forests ancient as the hills,   10
Enfolding sunny spots of greenery.

But oh! that deep romantic chasm which slanted
Down the green hill athwart a cedarn cover!
A savage place! as holy and enchanted
As e'er beneath a waning moon was haunted   15
By woman wailing for her demon lover!
And from this chasm, with ceaseless turmoil seething,
As if this earth in fast thick pants were breathing,
A mighty fountain momently was forced:
Amid whose swift half-intermitted burst   20
Huge fragments vaulted like rebounding hail,
Or chaffy grain beneath the thresher's flail:
And 'mid these dancing rocks at once and ever
It flung up momently the sacred river.
Five miles meandering with a mazy motion   25

4. The Greek may be translated, "I shall sing a sweeter song today." In the edition of 1834 Coleridge changed the Greek word for "today" to "tomorrow." He was re-calling Theocritus, *Idyls* 1.145: "I shall sing a sweeter song on a later day."

    A number of Coleridge's assertions in this preface have been debated by critics: whether the poem was written in 1797 or later, whether it was actually com-posed in a "dream" or opium reverie, even whether it is a fragment or in fact complete. All critics agree, how-ever, that this visionary poem of demonic inspiration is much more than a mere "psychological curiosity."

5. Coleridge refers to *The Pains of Sleep.*

6. Derived probably from the Greek river Alpheus, which flows into the Ionian Sea. Its waters were fabled to rise again in Sicily as the fountain of Arethusa (see Milton's *Lycidas,* lines 85 and 132; pp. 648 and 649).

Through wood and dale the sacred river ran,
Then reached the caverns measureless to man,
And sank in tumult to a lifeless ocean:
And 'mid this tumult Kubla heard from far
Ancestral voices prophesying war!   30
    The shadow of the dome of pleasure
    Floated midway on the waves;
    Where was heard the mingled measure
    From the fountain and the caves.
It was a miracle of rare device,   35
A sunny pleasure dome with caves of ice!

    A damsel with a dulcimer
    In a vision once I saw:
    It was an Abyssinian maid,
    And on her dulcimer she played,   40
    Singing of Mount Abora.[7]
    Could I revive within me
    Her symphony and song,
    To such a deep delight 'twould win me,
That with music loud and long,   45
I would build that dome in air,
That sunny dome! those caves of ice!
And all who heard should see them there,
And all should cry, Beware! Beware!
His flashing eyes, his floating hair!   50
Weave a circle round him thrice,[8]
And close your eyes with holy dread,
For he on honeydew hath fed,
And drunk the milk of Paradise.[9]

ca. 1797–98   1816

Christabel[1]

Preface

    The first part of the following poem was written in the year 1797, at Stowey, in the county of Somerset. The second part, after my return from Germany, in the year 1800, at Keswick, Cumberland. It is probable that if the poem had been finished at either of the former periods, or if even the first and second part had been published in the year 1800, the impression of its originality would have been much greater than I dare at present expect. But for this I

7. Apparently a reminiscence of *Paradise Lost* 4.280–82: "where Abassin Kings their issue guard / Mount Amara (though this by some supposed / True Paradise) under the Ethiop line."
8. A magic ritual, to protect the inspired poet from intrusion.
9. Lines 50ff. echo in part the description, in Plato's *Ion* 533–34, of inspired poets, who are "like Bacchic maidens who draw milk and honey from the rivers when they are under the influence of Dionysus but not when they are in their right mind."

1. Coleridge had planned to publish *Christabel* in the 2nd edition of *Lyrical Ballads* (1800), but had not been able to complete the poem. When *Christabel* was finally published in 1816 in its present fragmentary state, he still had hopes of finishing it, for the Preface contained this sentence (deleted in the edition of 1834): "But as, in my very first conception of the tale, I had the whole present to my mind, with the wholeness, no less than the liveliness of a vision, I trust that I shall be able to embody in verse the three parts yet to come, in the course of the present year."

have only my own indolence to blame. The dates are mentioned for the exclusive purpose of precluding charges of plagiarism or servile imitation from myself. For there is amongst us a set of critics, who seem to hold that every possible thought and image is traditional; who have no notion that there are such things as fountains in the world, small as well as great; and who would therefore charitably derive every rill they behold flowing, from a perforation made in some other man's tank. I am confident, however, that as far as the present poem is concerned, the celebrated poets[2] whose writings I might be suspected of having imitated, either in particular passages, or in the tone and the spirit of the whole, would be among the first to vindicate me from the charge, and who, on any striking coincidence, would permit me to address them in this doggerel version of two monkish Latin hexameters.

> 'Tis mine and it is likewise yours;
> But an if this will not do;
> Let it be mine, good friend! for I
> Am the poorer of the two.

   I have only to add that the meter of Christabel is not, properly speaking, irregular, though it may seem so from its being founded on a new principle: namely, that of counting in each line the accents, not the syllables.[3] Though the latter may vary from seven to twelve, yet in each line the accents will be found to be only four. Nevertheless, this occasional variation in number of syllables is not introduced wantonly, or for the mere ends of convenience, but in correspondence with some transition in the nature of the imagery or passion.

Part 1

'Tis the middle of night by the castle clock,
And the owls have awakened the crowing cock;
Tu—whit! ——Tu—whoo!
And hark, again! the crowing cock,
How drowsily it crew.   5

Sir Leoline, the Baron rich,
Hath a toothless mastiff bitch;
From her kennel beneath the rock
She maketh answer to the clock,
Four for the quarters, and twelve for the hour;   10
Ever and aye, by shine and shower,
Sixteen short howls, not over loud;
Some say she sees my lady's shroud.

Is the night chilly and dark?
The night is chilly, but not dark.   15

---

2. Sir Walter Scott and Lord Byron, who had read and admired *Christabel* while it circulated in manuscript. Coleridge has in mind Scott's *Lay of the Last Minstrel* (1805) and Byron's *Siege of Corinth* (1816), which showed the influence of *Christabel*, especially in their meter.
3. Much of the older English versification, following the example of Anglo-Saxon poetry, had been based on stress, or "accent," and some of it shows as much freedom in varying the number of syllables as does *Christabel*. The poem, however, is a radical departure from the theory and practice of versification in the 18th century, which had been based on a recurrent number of syllables in each line.

The thin gray cloud is spread on high,
It covers but not hides the sky.
The moon is behind, and at the full;
And yet she looks both small and dull.
The night is chill, the cloud is gray: 20
'Tis a month before the month of May,
And the spring comes slowly up this way.

The lovely lady, Christabel,
Whom her father loves so well,
What makes her in the wood so late,   25
A furlong from the castle gate?
She had dreams all yesternight
Of her own betrothèd knight;
And she in the midnight wood will pray
For the weal⁴ of her lover that's far away.   30

She stole along, she nothing spoke.
The sighs she heaved were soft and low,
And naught was green upon the oak
But moss and rarest mistletoe:⁵
She kneels beneath the huge oak tree,   35
And in silence prayeth she.

The lady sprang up suddenly,
The lovely lady, Christabel!
It moaned as near, as near can be,
But what it is she cannot tell.—   40
On the other side it seems to be,
Of the huge, broad-breasted, old oak tree.

The night is chill; the forest bare;
Is it the wind that moaneth bleak?
There is not wind enough in the air   45
To move away the ringlet curl
From the lovely lady's cheek—
There is not wind enough to twirl
The one red leaf, the last of its clan,
That dances as often as dance it can,   50
Hanging so light, and hanging so high,
On the topmost twig that looks up at the sky.

Hush, beating heart of Christabel!
Jesu, Maria, shield her well!
She folded her arms beneath her cloak,   55
And stole to the other side of the oak.
          What sees she there?

There she sees a damsel bright,
Dressed in a silken robe of white,

---

4. Well-being.
5. In Celtic Britain the mistletoe (a parasitic plant) had been held in veneration when it was found grow-ing—as it rarely does—on an oak tree. (Its usual host is the apple tree.)

That shadowy in the moonlight shone: 60
The neck that made that white robe wan,
Her stately neck, and arms were bare;
Her blue-veined feet unsandaled were,
And wildly glittered here and there
The gems entangled in her hair.   65
I guess, 'twas frightful there to see
A lady so richly clad as she—
Beautiful exceedingly!

"Mary mother, save me now!"
Said Christabel, "And who art thou?"   70

The lady strange made answer meet,
And her voice was faint and sweet—
"Have pity on my sore distress,
I scarce can speak for weariness:
Stretch forth thy hand, and have no fear!"   75
Said Christabel, "How camest thou here?"
And the lady, whose voice was faint and sweet,
Did thus pursue her answer meet:—

"My sire is of a noble line,
And my name is Geraldine: 80
Five warriors seized me yestermorn,
Me, even me, a maid forlorn:
They choked my cries with force and fright,
And tied me on a palfrey white.
The palfrey was as fleet as wind,   85
And they rode furiously behind.
They spurred amain,[6] their steeds were white:
And once we crossed the shade of night.
As sure as Heaven shall rescue me,
I have no thought what men they be;   90
Nor do I know how long it is
(For I have lain entranced, I wis[7])
Since one, the tallest of the five,
Took me from the palfrey's back,
A weary woman, scarce alive.   95
Some muttered words his comrades spoke:
He placed me underneath this oak;
He swore they would return with haste;
Whither they went I cannot tell—
I thought I heard, some minutes past,   100
Sounds as of a castle bell.
Stretch forth thy hand," thus ended she,
"And help a wretched maid to flee."

Then Christabel stretched forth her hand,
And comforted fair Geraldine: 105

6. At top speed.   dle English adverb *ywis*, meaning "certainly."
7. I believe; Coleridge's misinterpretation of the Mid-

"O well, bright dame! may you command
The service of Sir Leoline;
And gladly our stout chivalry
Will he send forth and friends withal
To guide and guard you safe and free   110
Home to your noble father's hall."

She rose: and forth with steps they passed
That strove to be, and were not, fast.
Her gracious stars the lady blessed,
And thus spake on sweet Christabel: 115
"All our household are at rest,
The hall as silent as the cell;
Sir Leoline is weak in health,
And may not well awakened be,
But we will move as if in stealth,   120
And I beseech your courtesy,
This night, to share your couch with me."

They crossed the moat, and Christabel
Took the key that fitted well;
A little door she opened straight,   125
All in the middle of the gate;
The gate that was ironed within and without,
Where an army in battle array had marched out.
The lady sank, belike through pain,
And Christabel with might and main   130
Lifted her up, a weary weight,
Over the threshold of the gate:[8]
Then the lady rose again,
And moved, as she were not in pain.

So free from danger, free from fear,   135
They crossed the court: right glad they were.
And Christabel devoutly cried
To the lady by her side,
"Praise we the Virgin all divine
Who hath rescued thee from thy distress!"   140
"Alas, alas!" said Geraldine,
"I cannot speak for weariness."
So free from danger, free from fear,
They crossed the court: right glad they were.

Outside her kennel, the mastiff old   145
Lay fast asleep, in moonshine cold.
The mastiff old did not awake,
Yet she an angry moan did make!
And what can ail the mastiff bitch?
Never till now she uttered yell   150
Beneath the eye of Christabel.

---

8. According to legend, a witch cannot cross the threshold by her own power because it has been blessed against evil spirits.

Perhaps it is the owlet's scritch:
For what can ail the mastiff bitch?

They passed the hall, that echoes still,
Pass as lightly as you will!   155
The brands were flat, the brands were dying,
Amid their own white ashes lying;
But when the lady passed, there came
A tongue of light, a fit of flame;
And Christabel saw the lady's eye,   160
And nothing else saw she thereby,
Save the boss of the shield of Sir Leoline tall,
Which hung in a murky old niche in the wall.
"O softly tread," said Christabel,
"My father seldom sleepeth well."   165

Sweet Christabel her feet doth bare,
And jealous of the listening air
They steal their way from stair to stair,
Now in glimmer, and now in gloom,
And now they pass the Baron's room,   170
As still as death, with stifled breath!
And now have reached her chamber door;
And now doth Geraldine press down
The rushes[9] of the chamber floor.

The moon shines dim in the open air,   175
And not a moonbeam enters here.
But they without its light can see
The chamber carved so curiously,
Carved with figures strange and sweet,
All made out of the carver's brain,   180
For a lady's chamber meet:
The lamp with twofold silver chain
Is fastened to an angel's feet.

The silver lamp burns dead and dim;
But Christabel the lamp will trim.   185
She trimmed the lamp, and made it bright,
And left it swinging to and fro,
While Geraldine, in wretched plight,
Sank down upon the floor below.

"O weary lady, Geraldine,   190
I pray you, drink this cordial wine!
It is a wine of virtuous powers;
My mother made it of wild flowers."

"And will your mother pity me,
Who am a maiden most forlorn?"   195

---

9. Often used as a floor covering in the Middle Ages.

Christabel answered—"Woe is me!
She died the hour that I was born.
I have heard the gray-haired friar tell
How on her deathbed she did say,
That she should hear the castle bell   200
Strike twelve upon my wedding day.
O mother dear! that thou wert here!"
"I would," said Geraldine, "she were!"

But soon with altered voice, said she—
"Off, wandering mother! Peak and pine!   205
I have power to bid thee flee."
Alas! what ails poor Geraldine?
Why stares she with unsettled eye?
Can she the bodiless dead espy?
And why with hollow voice cries she,   210
"Off, woman, off! this hour is mine—
Though thou her guardian spirit be,
Off, woman, off! 'tis given to me."

Then Christabel knelt by the lady's side,
And raised to heaven her eyes so blue—   215
"Alas!" said she, "this ghastly ride—
Dear lady! it hath 'wildered you!"
The lady wiped her moist cold brow,
And faintly said, " 'tis over now!"

Again the wild-flower wine she drank: 220
Her fair large eyes 'gan glitter bright,
And from the floor whereon she sank,
The lofty lady stood upright:
She was most beautiful to see,
Like a lady of a far countrée.   225

And thus the lofty lady spake—
"All they who live in the upper sky,
Do love you, holy Christabel!
And you love them, and for their sake
And for the good which me befell,   230
Even I in my degree will try,
Fair maiden, to requite you well.
But now unrobe yourself; for I
Must pray, ere yet in bed I lie."

Quoth Christabel, "So let it be!"   235
And as the lady bade, did she.
Her gentle limbs did she undress,
And lay down in her loveliness.

But through her brain of weal and woe
So many thoughts moved to and fro,   240
That vain it were her lids to close;

So halfway from the bed she rose,
And on her elbow did recline
To look at the lady Geraldine.

Beneath the lamp the lady bowed,   245
And slowly rolled her eyes around;
Then drawing in her breath aloud,
Like one that shuddered, she unbound
The cincture[1] from beneath her breast:
Her silken robe, and inner vest,   250
Dropped to her feet, and full in view,
Behold! her bosom and half her side——
A sight to dream of, not to tell!
O shield her! shield sweet Christabel!

Yet Geraldine nor speaks nor stirs;   255
Ah! what a stricken look was hers!
Deep from within she seems halfway
To lift some weight with sick assay,[2]
And eyes the maid and seeks delay;
Then suddenly, as one defied,   260
Collects herself in scorn and pride,
And lay down by the maiden's side!—
And in her arms the maid she took,
          Ah well-a-day!
And with low voice and doleful look   265
These words did say:
"In the touch of this bosom there worketh a spell,
Which is lord of thy utterance, Christabel!
Thou knowest tonight, and wilt know tomorrow,
This mark of my shame, this seal of my sorrow;   270
          But vainly thou warrest,
             For this is alone in
          Thy power to declare,
             That in the dim forest
          Thou heard'st a low moaning,   275
And found'st a bright lady, surpassingly fair;
And didst bring her home with thee in love and in charity,
To shield her and shelter her from the damp air."

The Conclusion to Part 1

It was a lovely sight to see
The lady Christabel, when she   280
Was praying at the old oak tree.
          Amid the jaggèd shadows
          Of mossy leafless boughs,
          Kneeling in the moonlight,
          To make her gentle vows: 285
Her slender palms together pressed,

---

1. Belt.   2. Attempt.

Heaving sometimes on her breast;
Her face resigned to bliss or bale[3]—
Her face, oh call it fair not pale,
And both blue eyes more bright than clear,   290
Each about to have a tear.

With open eyes (ah woe is me!)
Asleep, and dreaming fearfully,
Fearfully dreaming, yet, I wis,
Dreaming that alone, which is—   295
O sorrow and shame! Can this be she,

The lady, who knelt at the old oak tree?
And lo! the worker of these harms,
That holds the maiden in her arms,
Seems to slumber still and mild,   300
As a mother with her child.

A star hath set, a star hath risen,
O Geraldine! since arms of thine
Have been the lovely lady's prison.
O Geraldine! one hour was thine—   305
Thou'st had thy will! By tairn[4] and rill,
The night birds all that hour were still.
But now they are jubilant anew,
From cliff and tower, tu—whoo! tu—whoo!
Tu—whoo! tu—whoo! from wood and fell![5]   310

And see! the lady Christabel
Gathers herself from out her trance;
Her limbs relax, her countenance
Grows sad and soft; the smooth thin lids
Close o'er her eyes; and tears she sheds—   315
Large tears that leave the lashes bright!
And oft the while she seems to smile
As infants at a sudden light!

Yea, she doth smile, and she doth weep,
Like a youthful hermitess,   320
Beauteous in a wilderness,
Who, praying always, prays in sleep.
And, if she move unquietly,
Perchance, 'tis but the blood so free
Comes back and tingles in her feet.   325
No doubt, she hath a vision sweet.
What if her guardian spirit 'twere,
What if she knew her mother near?
But this she knows, in joys and woes,
That saints will aid if men will call: 330
For the blue sky bends over all!

3. Evil, sorrow.   5. Elevated moor, or hill.
4. Tarn, a mountain pool.

Part 2

"Each matin bell," the Baron saith,
"Knells us back to a world of death."
These words Sir Leoline first said,
When he rose and found his lady dead: 335
These words Sir Leoline will say
Many a morn to his dying day!

And hence the custom and law began
That still at dawn the sacristan,[6]
Who duly pulls the heavy bell,   340
Five and forty beads must tell[7]
Between each stroke—a warning knell,
Which not a soul can choose but hear
From Bratha Head to Wyndermere.[8]

Saith Bracy the bard, "So let it knell!   345
And let the drowsy sacristan
Still count as slowly as he can!
There is no lack of such, I ween,
As well fill up the space between.
In Langdale Pike[9] and Witch's Lair,   350
And Dungeon Ghyll[1] so foully rent,
With ropes of rock and bells of air
Three sinful sextons' ghosts are pent,
Who all give back, one after t'other,
The death note to their living brother;   355
And oft too, by the knell offended,
Just as their one! two! three! is ended,
The devil mocks the doleful tale
With a merry peal from Borodale."

The air is still! through mist and cloud   360
That merry peal comes ringing loud;
And Geraldine shakes off her dread,
And rises lightly from the bed;
Puts on her silken vestments white,
And tricks her hair in lovely plight,[2]   365
And nothing doubting of her spell
Awakens the lady Christabel.
"Sleep you, sweet lady Christabel?
I trust that you have rested well."

And Christabel awoke and spied   370
The same who lay down by her side—
O rather say, the same whom she
Raised up beneath the old oak tree!
Nay, fairer yet! and yet more fair!

6. Sexton.
7. Pray while "telling" (keeping count on) the beads
of a rosary.
8. These and the following names are of localities in
the English Lake District.
9. Peak
1. Ravine forming the bed of a stream.
2. Plait.

For she belike hath drunken deep   375
Of all the blessedness of sleep!
And while she spake, her looks, her air
Such gentle thankfulness declare,
That (so it seemed) her girded vests
Grew tight beneath her heaving breasts.   380
"Sure I have sinned!" said Christabel,
"Now heaven be praised if all be well!"
And in low faltering tones, yet sweet,
Did she the lofty lady greet
With such perplexity of mind   385
As dreams too lively leave behind.

So quickly she rose, and quickly arrayed
Her maiden limbs, and having prayed
That He, who on the cross did groan,
Might wash away her sins unknown,   390
She forthwith led fair Geraldine
To meet her sire, Sir Leoline.

The lovely maid and the lady tall
Are pacing both into the hall,
And pacing on through page and groom,   395
Enter the Baron's presence-room.

The Baron rose, and while he pressed
His gentle daughter to his breast,
With cheerful wonder in his eyes
The lady Geraldine espies,   400
And gave such welcome to the same,
As might beseem so bright a dame!

But when he heard the lady's tale,
And when she told her father's name,
Why waxed Sir Leoline so pale,   405
Murmuring o'er the name again,
Lord Roland de Vaux of Tryermaine?

Alas! they had been friends in youth;
But whispering tongues can poison truth;
And constancy lives in realms above;   410
And life is thorny; and youth is vain;
And to be wroth with one we love
Doth work like madness in the brain.
And thus it chanced, as I divine,
With Roland and Sir Leoline.   415
Each spake words of high disdain
And insult to his heart's best brother:
They parted—ne'er to meet again!
But never either found another
To free the hollow heart from paining—   420
They stood aloof, the scars remaining,

Like cliffs which had been rent asunder;
A dreary sea now flows between—
But neither heat, nor frost, nor thunder,
Shall wholly do away, I ween,   425
The marks of that which once hath been.

Sir Leoline, a moment's space,
Stood gazing on the damsel's face:
And the youthful Lord of Tryermaine
Came back upon his heart again.   430

O then the Baron forgot his age,
His noble heart swelled high with rage;
He swore by the wounds in Jesu's side
He would proclaim it far and wide,
With trump and solemn heraldry,   435
That they, who thus had wronged the dame,
Were base as spotted infamy!
"And if they dare deny the same,
My herald shall appoint a week,
And let the recreant traitors seek   440
My tourney court—that there and then
I may dislodge their reptile souls
From the bodies and forms of men!"
He spake: his eye in lightning rolls!
For the lady was ruthlessly seized; and he kenned   445
In the beautiful lady the child of his friend!

And now the tears were on his face,
And fondly in his arms he took
Fair Geraldine, who met the embrace,
Prolonging it with joyous look.   450
Which when she viewed, a vision fell
Upon the soul of Christabel,
The vision of fear, the touch and pain!
She shrunk and shuddered, and saw again—
(Ah, woe is me! Was it for thee,   455
Thou gentle maid! such sights to see?)

Again she saw that bosom old,
Again she felt that bosom cold,
And drew in her breath with a hissing sound:
Whereat the Knight turned wildly round,   460
And nothing saw, but his own sweet maid
With eyes upraised, as one that prayed.

The touch, the sight, had passed away,
And in its stead that vision blest,
Which comforted her after-rest   465
While in the lady's arms she lay,
Had put a rapture in her breast,
And on her lips and o'er her eyes

Spread smiles like light!
             With new surprise,
"What ails then my belovèd child?"   470
The Baron said—His daughter mild
Made answer, "All will yet be well!"
I ween, she had no power to tell
Aught else: so mighty was the spell.

Yet he, who saw this Geraldine,   475
Had deemed her sure a thing divine:
Such sorrow with such grace she blended,
As if she feared she had offended
Sweet Christabel, that gentle maid!
And with such lowly tones she prayed   480
She might be sent without delay
Home to her father's mansion.
                      "Nay!
Nay, by my soul!" said Leoline.
"Ho! Bracy the bard, the charge be thine!
Go thou, with music sweet and loud,   485
And take two steeds with trappings proud,
And take the youth whom thou lov'st best
To bear thy harp, and learn thy song,
And clothe you both in solemn vest,
And over the mountains haste along,   490
Lest wandering folk, that are abroad,
Detain you on the valley road.

"And when he has crossed the Irthing flood,
My merry bard! he hastes, he hastes
Up Knorren Moor, through Halegarth Wood,   495
And reaches soon that castle good
Which stands and threatens Scotland's wastes.

"Bard Bracy! bard Bracy! your horses are fleet,
Ye must ride up the hall, your music so sweet,
More loud than your horses' echoing feet!   500
And loud and loud to Lord Roland call,
Thy daughter is safe in Langdale hall!
Thy beautiful daughter is safe and free—
Sir Leoline greets thee thus through me!
He bids thee come without delay   505
With all thy numerous array
And take thy lovely daughter home:
And he will meet thee on the way
With all his numerous array
White with their panting palfreys' foam: 510
And, by mine honor! I will say,
That I repent me of the day
When I spake words of fierce disdain
To Roland de Vaux of Tryermaine!—

For since that evil hour hath flown,   515
Many a summer's sun hath shone;
Yet ne'er found I a friend again
Like Roland de Vaux of Tryermaine."

The lady fell, and clasped his knees,
Her face upraised, her eyes o'erflowing;   520
And Bracy replied, with faltering voice,
His gracious Hail on all bestowing! —
"Thy words, thou sire of Christabel,
Are sweeter than my harp can tell;
Yet might I gain a boon of thee,   525
This day my journey should not be,
So strange a dream hath come to me,
That I had vowed with music loud
To clear yon wood from thing unblest,
Warned by a vision in my rest!   530
For in my sleep I saw that dove,
That gentle bird, whom thou dost love,
And call'st by thy own daughter's name —
Sir Leoline! I saw the same
Fluttering, and uttering fearful moan,   535
Among the green herbs in the forest alone.
Which when I saw and when I heard,
I wondered what might ail the bird;
For nothing near it could I see,
Save the grass and green herbs underneath the old tree.   540

"And in my dream methought I went
To search out what might there be found;
And what the sweet bird's trouble meant,
That thus lay fluttering on the ground.
I went and peered, and could descry   545
No cause for her distressful cry;
But yet for her dear lady's sake
I stooped, methought, the dove to take,
When lo! I saw a bright green snake
Coiled around its wings and neck.   550
Green as the herbs on which it couched,
Close by the dove's its head it crouched;
And with the dove it heaves and stirs,
Swelling its neck as she swelled hers!
I woke; it was the midnight hour,   555
The clock was echoing in the tower;
But though my slumber was gone by,
This dream it would not pass away —
It seems to live upon my eye!
And thence I vowed this selfsame day   560
With music strong and saintly song
To wander through the forest bare,
Lest aught unholy loiter there."

Thus Bracy said: the Baron, the while,
Half-listening heard him with a smile;   565
Then turned to Lady Geraldine,
His eyes made up of wonder and love;
And said in courtly accents fine,
"Sweet maid, Lord Roland's beauteous dove,
With arms more strong than harp or song,   570
Thy sire and I will crush the snake!"
He kissed her forehead as he spake,
And Geraldine in maiden wise
Casting down her large bright eyes,
With blushing cheek and courtesy fine   575
She turned her from Sir Leoline;
Softly gathering up her train,
That o'er her right arm fell again;
And folded her arms across her chest,
And couched her head upon her breast,   580
And looked askance at Christabel—
Jesu, Maria, shield her well!

A snake's small eye blinks dull and shy;
And the lady's eyes they shrunk in her head,
Each shrunk up to a serpent's eye,   585
And with somewhat of malice, and more of dread,
At Christabel she looked askance!—
One moment—and the sight was fled!
But Christabel in dizzy trance
Stumbling on the unsteady ground   590
Shuddered aloud, with a hissing sound;
And Geraldine again turned round,
And like a thing, that sought relief,
Full of wonder and full of grief,
She rolled her large bright eyes divine   595
Wildly on Sir Leoline.

The maid, alas! her thoughts are gone,
She nothing sees—no sight but one!
The maid, devoid of guile and sin,
I know not how, in fearful wise,   600
So deeply had she drunken in
That look, those shrunken serpent eyes,
That all her features were resigned
To this sole image in her mind:
And passively did imitate   605
That look of dull and treacherous hate!
And thus she stood, in dizzy trance,
Still picturing that look askance
With forced unconscious sympathy
Full before her father's view—   610
As far as such a look could be
In eyes so innocent and blue!

And when the trance was o'er, the maid
Paused awhile, and inly prayed:
Then falling at the Baron's feet,   615
"By my mother's soul do I entreat
That thou this woman send away!"
She said: and more she could not say:
For what she knew she could not tell,
O'ermastered by the mighty spell.   620

Why is thy cheek so wan and wild,
Sir Leoline? Thy only child
Lies at thy feet, thy joy, thy pride,
So fair, so innocent, so mild;
The same, for whom thy lady died!   625
O by the pangs of her dear mother
Think thou no evil of thy child!
For her, and thee, and for no other,
She prayed the moment ere she died:
Prayed that the babe for whom she died,   630
Might prove her dear lord's joy and pride!
     That prayer her deadly pangs beguiled,
               Sir Leoline!
     And wouldst thou wrong thy only child,
               Her child and thine?   635

Within the Baron's heart and brain
If thoughts, like these, had any share,
They only swelled his rage and pain,
And did but work confusion there.
His heart was cleft with pain and rage,   640
His cheeks they quivered, his eyes were wild,
Dishonoured thus in his old age;
Dishonoured by his only child,
And all his hospitality
To the wronged daughter of his friend   645
By more than woman's jealousy
Brought thus to a disgraceful end—
He rolled his eye with stern regard
Upon the gentle minstrel bard,
And said in tones abrupt, austere—   650
"Why, Bracy! dost thou loiter here?
I bade thee hence!" The bard obeyed;
And turning from his own sweet maid,
The agèd knight, Sir Leoline,
Led forth the lady Geraldine!   655

The Conclusion to Part 2

A little child, a limber elf,
Singing, dancing to itself,

A fairy thing with red round cheeks,
That always finds, and never seeks,
Makes such a vision to the sight   660
As fills a father's eyes with light;
And pleasures flow in so thick and fast
Upon his heart, that he at last
Must needs express his love's excess
With words of unmeant bitterness.   665
Perhaps 'tis pretty to force together
Thoughts so all unlike each other;
To mutter and mock a broken charm,
To dally with wrong that does no harm.
Perhaps 'tis tender too and pretty   670
At each wild word to feel within
A sweet recoil of love and pity.
And what, if in a world of sin
(O sorrow and shame should this be true!)
Such giddiness of heart and brain   675
Comes seldom save from rage and pain,
So talks as it's most used to do.

1797–1801   1816

Frost at Midnight[1]

The Frost performs its secret ministry,
Unhelped by any wind. The owlet's cry
Came loud—and hark, again! loud as before.
The inmates of my cottage, all at rest,
Have left me to that solitude, which suits   5
Abstruser musings: save that at my side
My cradled infant slumbers peacefully.
'Tis calm indeed! so calm, that it disturbs
And vexes meditation with its strange
And extreme silentness. Sea, hill, and wood,   10
This populous village! Sea, and hill, and wood,
With all the numberless goings-on of life,
Inaudible as dreams! the thin blue flame
Lies on my low-burnt fire, and quivers not;
Only that film,[2] which fluttered on the grate,   15
Still flutters there, the sole unquiet thing.
Methinks its motion in this hush of nature
Gives it dim sympathies with me who live,
Making it a companionable form,
Whose puny flaps and freaks the idling Spirit   20
By its own moods interprets, everywhere
Echo or mirror seeking of itself,
And makes a toy of Thought.

1. The scene is Coleridge's cottage at Nether Stowey;
the infant in line 7 is his son Hartley, then aged seventeen months.
2. "In all parts of the kingdom these films are called
strangers and supposed to portend the arrival of some
absent friend" [Coleridge's note]. The "film" is a piece
of soot fluttering on the bar of the grate.

　　　　　　　　　　But O! how oft,
How oft, at school, with most believing mind,
Presageful, have I gazed upon the bars,　　　　　　　　25
To watch that fluttering *stranger!* and as oft
With unclosed lids, already had I dreamt
Of my sweet birthplace,[3] and the old church tower,
Whose bells, the poor man's only music, rang
From morn to evening, all the hot fair-day,　　　　　　30
So sweetly, that they stirred and haunted me
With a wild pleasure, falling on mine ear
Most like articulate sounds of things to come!
So gazed I, till the soothing things, I dreamt,
Lulled me to sleep, and sleep prolonged my dreams!　　35
And so I brooded all the following morn,
Awed by the stern preceptor's face,[4] mine eye
Fixed with mock study on my swimming book:
Save if the door half opened, and I snatched
A hasty glance, and still my heart leaped up,　　　　　40
For still I hoped to see the *stranger's* face,
Townsman, or aunt, or sister more beloved,
My playmate when we both were clothed alike![5]

　　Dear Babe, that sleepest cradled by my side,
Whose gentle breathings, heard in this deep calm,　　45
Fill up the interspersèd vacancies
And momentary pauses of the thought!
My babe so beautiful! it thrills my heart
With tender gladness, thus to look at thee,
And think that thou shalt learn far other lore,　　　　50
And in far other scenes! For I was reared
In the great city, pent 'mid cloisters dim,
And saw nought lovely but the sky and stars.
But *thou*, my babe! shalt wander like a breeze
By lakes and sandy shores, beneath the crags　　　　55
Of ancient mountain, and beneath the clouds,
Which image in their bulk both lakes and shores
And mountain crags: so shalt thou see and hear
The lovely shapes and sounds intelligible
Of that eternal language, which thy God　　　　　　60
Utters, who from eternity doth teach
Himself in all, and all things in himself.
Great universal Teacher! he shall mold
Thy spirit, and by giving make it ask.

　　Therefore all seasons shall be sweet to thee,　　　65
Whether the summer clothe the general earth
With greenness, or the redbreast sit and sing
Betwixt the tufts of snow on the bare branch

3. Coleridge was born at Ottery St. Mary, Devonshire, but went to school in London, beginning at the age of nine.
4. The "stern preceptor" at Coleridge's school, Christ's Hospital, was the Rev. James Boyer, whom Coleridge describes in *Biographia Literaria*, chap. 1.
5. I.e., when both Coleridge and his sister Ann still wore infant clothes.

Of mossy apple tree, while the nigh thatch
Smokes in the sun-thaw; whether the eave-drops fall   70
Heard only in the trances of the blast,
Or if the secret ministry of frost
Shall hang them up in silent icicles,
Quietly shining to the quiet Moon.

Feb. 1798   1798

Dejection: An Ode[1]

> Late, late yestreen I saw the new Moon,
> With the old Moon in her arms;
> And I fear, I fear, my master dear!
> We shall have a deadly storm.
> *Ballad of Sir Patrick Spence*

1

Well! If the bard was weather-wise, who made
    The grand old ballad of Sir Patrick Spence,
    This night, so tranquil now, will not go hence
Unroused by winds, that ply a busier trade
Than those which mold yon cloud in lazy flakes,   5
Or the dull sobbing draft, that moans and rakes
Upon the strings of this Aeolian lute,[2]
    Which better far were mute.
For lo! the New-moon winter-bright!
And overspread with phantom light,   10
    (With swimming phantom light o'erspread
    But rimmed and circled by a silver thread)
I see the old Moon in her lap, foretelling
    The coming-on of rain and squally blast.
And oh! that even now the gust were swelling,   15
    And the slant night shower driving loud and fast!
Those sounds which oft have raised me, whilst they awed,
    And sent my soul abroad,
Might now perhaps their wonted[3] impulse give,
Might startle this dull pain, and make it move and live!   20

2

A grief without a pang, void, dark, and drear,
    A stifled, drowsy, unimpassioned grief,
Which finds no natural outlet, no relief,
    In word, or sigh, or tear—

O Lady!,[4] in this wan and heartless mood,   25
To other thoughts by yonder throstle wooed,
   All this long eve, so balmy and serene,
Have I been gazing on the western sky,
   And its peculiar tint of yellow green:
And still I gaze—and with how blank an eye!   30
And those thin clouds above, in flakes and bars,
That give away their motion to the stars;
Those stars, that glide behind them or between,
Now sparkling, now bedimmed, but always seen:
Yon crescent Moon, as fixed as if it grew   35
In its own cloudless, starless lake of blue;
I see them all so excellently fair,
I see, not feel, how beautiful they are!

3

     My genial[5] spirits fail;
     And what can these avail   40
To lift the smothering weight from off my breast?
     It were a vain endeavour,
     Though I should gaze forever
On that green light that lingers in the west:
I may not hope from outward forms to win   45
The passion and the life, whose fountains are within.

4

O Lady! we receive but what we give,
And in our life alone does Nature live:
Ours is her wedding garment, ours her shroud![6]
   And would we aught behold, of higher worth,   50
Than that inanimate cold world allowed
To the poor loveless ever-anxious crowd,
   Ah! from the soul itself must issue forth
A light, a glory,[7] a fair luminous cloud
     Enveloping the Earth—   55
And from the soul itself must there be sent
   A sweet and potent voice, of its own birth,
Of all sweet sounds the life and element!

5

O pure of heart! thou need'st not ask of me
What this strong music in the soul may be!   60
What, and wherein it doth exist,
This light, this glory, this fair luminous mist,
This beautiful and beauty-making power.
   Joy,[8] virtuous Lady! Joy that ne'er was given,
Save to the pure, and in their purest hour,   65

---

4. In the original version "Sara"—i.e., Sara Hutchinson. After intervening versions, in which the poem was addressed first to "William" (Wordsworth) and then to "Edmund," Coleridge introduced the noncommittal "Lady" in 1817.
5. In its old use as the adjectival form of *genius*: "My innate powers fail."
6. I.e., whether nature is experienced as "inanimate" (line 51) or in living interchange with the observer depends on the apathy or joyous vitality of the observer's own spirit.
7. Coleridge commonly used "glory" not in the sense of a halo, merely, but as a term for a mountain phenomenon in which a walker sees his own figure projected by the sun in the mist, enlarged, and with a circle of light around its head.
8. Coleridge often uses "Joy" for a sense of abounding vitality and of harmony between one's inner life and the life of nature. He sometimes calls the contrary "exsiccation," or spiritual dryness.

Life, and Life's effluence, cloud at once and shower,
Joy, Lady! is the spirit and the power,
Which wedding Nature to us gives in dower
    A new Earth and new Heaven,[9]
Undreamt of by the sensual and the proud—   70
Joy is the sweet voice, Joy the luminous cloud—
        We in ourselves rejoice!
And thence flows all that charms or ear or sight,
    All melodies the echoes of that voice,
All colors a suffusion from that light.   75

                    6
There was a time when, though my path was rough,
    This joy within me dallied with distress,
And all misfortunes were but as the stuff
    Whence Fancy made me dreams of happiness:
For hope grew round me, like the twining vine,   80
And fruits, and foliage, not my own, seemed mine.
But now afflictions bow me down to earth:
Nor care I that they rob me of my mirth;
        But oh! each visitation
Suspends what nature gave me at my birth,   85
    My shaping spirit of Imagination.
For not to think of what I needs must feel,
    But to be still and patient, all I can;
And haply by abstruse research to steal
    From my own nature all the natural man—   90
    This was my sole resource, my only plan:
Till that which suits a part infects the whole,
And now is almost grown the habit of my soul.

                    7
Hence, viper thoughts, that coil around my mind,
        Reality's dark dream!   95
I turn from you, and listen to the wind,
    Which long has raved unnoticed. What a scream
Of agony by torture lengthened out
That lute sent forth! Thou Wind, that rav'st without,
    Bare crag, or mountain tairn,[1] or blasted tree,   100
Or pine grove whither woodman never clomb,
Or lonely house, long held the witches' home,
    Methinks were fitter instruments for thee,
Mad lutanist! who in this month of showers,
Of dark-brown gardens, and of peeping flowers,   105
Mak'st devils' yule,[2] with worse than wintry song,
The blossoms, buds, and timorous leaves among.
    Thou actor, perfect in all tragic sounds!
Thou mighty poet, e'en to frenzy bold!
    What tell'st thou now about?   110

9. The sense becomes clearer if line 68 is punctuated in the way that Coleridge himself punctuated it when quoting the passage in one of his essays: "Which, wedding Nature to us, gives in dower." The idea is that "Joy" is the condition which (overcoming the alienation between mind and its milieu) marries us to "Nature," and gives by way of wedding portion ("dower") the experience of a renovated world.
1. Tarn, or mountain pool.
2. Christmas as, in a perverted form, it is celebrated by devils.

'Tis of the rushing of an host in rout,
　With groans, of trampled men, with smarting wounds—
At once they groan with pain, and shudder with the cold!
But hush! there is a pause of deepest silence!
　And all that noise, as of a rushing crowd,   115
With groans, and tremulous shudderings—all is over—
　It tells another tale, with sounds less deep and loud!
　　A tale of less affright,
　　And tempered with delight,
As Otway's[3] self had framed the tender lay—   120
　　'Tis of a little child
　　Upon a lonesome wild,
Not far from home, but she hath lost her way:
And now moans low in bitter grief and fear,
And now screams loud, and hopes to make her mother hear.   125

8

'Tis midnight, but small thoughts have I of sleep:
Full seldom may my friend such vigils keep!
Visit her, gentle Sleep! with wings of healing,
　And may this storm be but a mountain birth,[4]
May all the stars hang bright above her dwelling,   130
　Silent as though they watched the sleeping Earth!
　　With light heart may she rise,
　　Gay fancy, cheerful eyes,
　Joy lift her spirit, joy attune her voice;
To her may all things live, from pole to pole,   135
Their life the eddying of her living soul!
　O simple spirit, guided from above,
Dear Lady! friend devoutest of my choice,
Thus mayest thou ever, evermore rejoice.

Apr. 4, 1802   1802

To William Wordsworth

Composed on the Night after His Recitation of a Poem on the Growth of an Individual Mind[1]

Friend of the wise! and teacher of the good!
Into my heart have I received that lay
More than historic, that prophetic lay
Wherein (high theme by thee first sung aright)
Of the foundations and the building up   5
Of a Human Spirit thou hast dared to tell
What may be told, to the understanding mind

---

3. Thomas Otway (1652–1685), a dramatist noted for the pathos of his tragic passages. The poet originally named was "William," and the allusion was probably to Wordsworth's *Lucy Gray*.
4. Probably, "May this be a typical mountain storm, short though violent," although it is possible that Coleridge intended an allusion to Horace's phrase, "the mountain labored and brought forth a mouse."

1. This was the poem (later called *The Prelude*), addressed to Coleridge, that Wordsworth had completed in 1805. After Coleridge returned from Malta, very low in health and spirits, Wordsworth read the poem aloud to him during the evenings of almost two weeks. Coleridge wrote most of the present response immediately after the reading was completed, on Jan. 7, 1807.

Revealable; and what within the mind
By vital breathings secret as the soul
Of vernal growth, oft quickens in the heart   10
Thoughts all too deep for words![2] —

                                    Theme hard as high!
Of smiles spontaneous, and mysterious fears
(The first-born they of Reason and twin birth),
Of tides obedient to external force,
And currents self-determined, as might seem,   15
Or by some inner Power; of moments awful,
Now in thy inner life, and now abroad,
When power streamed from thee, and thy soul received
The light reflected, as a light bestowed—
Of fancies fair, and milder hours of youth,   20
Hyblean[3] murmurs of poetic thought
Industrious in its joy, in vales and glens
Native or outland, lakes and famous hills!
Or on the lonely high-road, when the stars
Were rising; or by secret mountain streams,   25
The guides and the companions of thy way!

Of more than Fancy, of the Social Sense
Distending wide, and man beloved as man,
Where France in all her towns lay vibrating
Like some becalmèd bark beneath the burst   30
Of Heaven's immediate thunder, when no cloud
Is visible, or shadow on the main.
For thou wert there, thine own brows garlanded,
Amid the tremor of a realm aglow,
Amid a mighty nation jubilant,   35
When from the general heart of human kind
Hope sprang forth like a full-born deity!
——Of that dear Hope afflicted and struck down,
So summoned homeward, thenceforth calm and sure
From the dread watchtower of man's absolute self,   40
With light unwaning on her eyes, to look
Far on—herself a glory to behold,
The Angel of the vision! Then (last strain)
Of Duty, chosen Laws controlling choice,
Action and joy!—An Orphic song[4] indeed,   45
A song divine of high and passionate thoughts
To their own music chaunted!

                                    O great bard!
Ere yet that last strain dying awed the air,

2. Wordsworth had described the effect on his mind
of the animating breeze ("vital breathings") in *The Pre-*
lude 1.1–44. "Thoughts . . . words" echoes the last line
of Wordsworth's *Intimations* ode. Coleridge goes on to
summarize the major themes and events of *The Pre-*
lude.
3. Sweet. Hybla, in ancient Sicily, was famous for its

honey.
4. As enchanting and oracular as the song of the legendary Orpheus. There may also be an allusion to the
Orphic mysteries, involving spiritual death and rebirth
(see lines 61–66). "The Angel of the vision" (line 43)
probably alludes to "the great vision of the guarded
mount" in Milton's *Lycidas*, line 161.

With stedfast eye I viewed thee in the choir
Of ever-enduring men. The truly great   50
Have all one age, and from one visible space
Shed influence! They, both in power and act,
Are permanent, and Time is not with them,
Save as it worketh for them, they in it.
Nor less a sacred roll, than those of old,   55
And to be placed, as they, with gradual fame
Among the archives of mankind, thy work
Makes audible a linkèd lay of Truth,
Of Truth profound a sweet continuous lay,
Not learnt, but native, her own natural notes!   60
Ah! as I listened with a heart forlorn,
The pulses of my being beat anew:
And even as Life returns upon the drowned,[5]
Life's joy rekindling roused a throng of pains —
Keen pangs of Love, awakening as a babe   65
Turbulent, with an outcry in the heart;
And fears self-willed, that shunned the eye of Hope;
And Hope that scarce would know itself from Fear;
Sense of past Youth, and Manhood come in vain,
And Genius given, and Knowledge won in vain;   70
And all which I had culled in wood-walks wild,
And all which patient toil had reared, and all,
Commune with thee had opened out — but flowers
Strewed on my corse, and borne upon my bier,
In the same coffin, for the self-same grave!   75

That way no more! and ill beseems it me,
Who came a welcomer in herald's guise,
Singing of Glory, and Futurity,
To wander back on such unhealthful road,
Plucking the poisons of self-harm! And ill   80
Such intertwine beseems triumphal wreaths
Strewed before thy advancing!

                              Nor do thou,
Sage bard! impair the memory of that hour
Of thy communion with my nobler mind[6]
By pity or grief, already felt too long!   85
Nor let my words import more blame than needs.
The tumult rose and ceased: for Peace is nigh
Where Wisdom's voice has found a listening heart.
Amid the howl of more than wintry storms,
The Halcyon[7] hears the voice of vernal hours   90
Already on the wing.

                    Eve following eve,[8]
Dear tranquil time, when the sweet sense of Home

5. A death-in-life is also described in, e.g., *Dejection:*
An Ode and *Epitaph*.
6. I.e., during the early association between the two
poets (1797–98).

7. A fabled bird, able to calm the sea where it nested
in winter.
8. The evenings during which Wordsworth read his
poem aloud.

Is sweetest! moments for their own sake hailed
And more desired, more precious, for thy song,
In silence listening, like a devout child,   95
My soul lay passive, by thy various strain
Driven as in surges now beneath the stars,
With momentary stars of my own birth,
Fair constellated foam, still darting off
Into the darkness; now a tranquil sea,   100
Outspread and bright, yet swelling to the moon.

And when—O friend! my comforter and guide!
Strong in thyself, and powerful to give strength!—
Thy long sustainèd song finally closed,
And thy deep voice had ceased—yet thou thyself   105
Wert still before my eyes, and round us both
That happy vision of belovèd faces—
Scarce conscious, and yet conscious of its close
I sate, my being blended in one thought
(Thought was it? or aspiration? or resolve?)   110
Absorbed, yet hanging still upon the sound—
And when I rose, I found myself in prayer.
1807   1817

Recollections of Love

1
How warm this woodland wild recess!
    Love surely hath been breathing here;
    And this sweet bed of heath, my dear!
Swells up, then sinks with faint caress,
    As if to have you yet more near.   5
2
Eight springs have flown since last I lay
    On seaward Quantock's heathy hills,[1]
    Where quiet sounds from hidden rills
Float here and there, like things astray,
    And high o'erhead the sky-lark shrills.   10
3
No voice as yet had made the air
    Be music with your name; yet why
    That asking look? that yearning sigh?
That sense of promise every where?
    Belovèd! flew your spirit by?   15
4
As when a mother doth explore
    The rose mark on her long-lost child,
    I met, I loved you, maiden mild!
As whom I long had loved before—
    So deeply had I been beguiled.   20

---

1. Near Nether Stowey, Somerset, where Coleridge had lived from 1796 to 1798.

5
You stood before me like a thought,
    A dream remembered in a dream.
    But when those meek eyes first did seem
To tell me, Love within you wrought—
    O Greta,[2] dear domestic stream!   25
6
Has not, since then, Love's prompture deep,
    Has not Love's whisper evermore
    Been ceaseless, as thy gentle roar?
Sole voice, when other voices sleep,
    Dear under-song in clamor's hour.   30

ca. 1807   1817

On Donne's Poetry[1]

With Donne, whose muse on dromedary[2] trots,
Wreathe iron pokers into true-love knots;
Rhyme's sturdy cripple, fancy's maze and clue,
Wit's forge and fire-blast, meaning's press and screw.

ca. 1818   1836

Work without Hope

Lines Composed 21st February 1825

All Nature seems at work. Slugs leave their lair—
The bees are stirring—birds are on the wing—
And Winter slumbering in the open air,
Wears on his smiling face a dream of Spring!
And I the while, the sole unbusy thing,   5
Nor honey make, nor pair, nor build, nor sing.

Yet well I ken the banks where amaranths[1] blow,
Have traced the fount whence streams of nectar flow.
Bloom, O ye amaranths! bloom for whom ye may,
For me ye bloom not! Glide, rich streams, away!   10
With lips unbrightened, wreathless brow, I stroll:
And would you learn the spells that drowse my soul?
Work without Hope draws nectar in a sieve,
And Hope without an object cannot live.

1825   1828

2. The river Greta, which flowed past Coleridge's home in Keswick, in the Lake District.
1. John Donne as a poet had been in eclipse for most of the 18th century. This terse and penetrating comment shows the Romantic poet's great, though ironi-

cally qualified, respect for the master of the metaphysical style.
2. The one-humped Arabian camel, trained for riding.
1. Mythical flowers that bloom perpetually.

Epitaph[1]

Stop, Christian passer-by!—Stop, child of God,
And read with gentle breast. Beneath this sod
A poet lies, or that which once seemed he.
O, lift one thought in prayer for S. T. C.;
That he who many a year with toil of breath   5
Found death in life, may here find life in death!
Mercy for praise—to be forgiven for[2] fame
He asked, and hoped, through Christ. Do thou the same!

1833   1834

Biographia Literaria   In March 1815 Coleridge was preparing a collected edition of his poems and planned to include "a general preface . . . on the principles of philosophic and genial criticism." Characteristically, the materials developed as Coleridge worked on them until, on July 29, he declared that the preface had been extended into a complete work, "an Autobiographia Literaria"; it was to consist of two main parts, "my literary life and opinions, as far as poetry and *poetical* criticism [are] concerned" and a critique of Wordsworth's theory of poetic diction. This work was ready by September 17, 1815, but the *Biographia Literaria*, in two volumes, was not published until July 1817. The delay was caused by a series of miscalculations by his printer, which forced Coleridge to add miscellaneous materials needed to eke out the length of his original manuscript.

The critique of Wordsworth's theory of diction, which Coleridge had been planning ever since 1802, when he had detected "a radical difference in our theoretical opinions respecting poetry," is long, detailed, and subtly reasoned. In the selection from chapter 17 Coleridge agrees with Wordsworth's general aim of reforming the artifices of modern poetic diction, but he sharply denies Wordsworth's claim that there is no essential difference between the language of poetry and the language really spoken by people. The other selections printed here are devoted mainly to the central principle of Coleridge's own critical theory, the distinction between the mechanical "fancy" and the organic "imagination." Thus the biographical section of the *Biographia* (chapters 1 and 4), dealing with the development of his poetic taste and theory, describes his gradual realization, climaxed by his first exposure to Wordsworth's poetry, "that fancy and imagination were two distinct and widely different faculties." The conclusion to chapter 13 tersely summarizes this distinction, and the definition of poetry, at the end of chapter 14, develops at somewhat greater length the nature of the process and products of the "synthetic and magical power . . . of imagination." These cryptic paragraphs have proved to be the most widely discussed, disputed, and influential passages ever written by an English critic.

1. Written by Coleridge the year before he died. One version that he sent in a letter had as a title: "Epitaph on a Poet little known, yet better known by the Initials of his name than by the Name Itself."
2. "For" in the sense of "instead of" [Coleridge's note].

From Biographia Literaria

From *Chapter 1*

[THE DISCIPLINE OF HIS TASTE AT SCHOOL][1]

At school I enjoyed the inestimable advantage of a very sensible, though at the same time a very severe master. He[2] early molded my taste to the preference of Demosthenes to Cicero, of Homer and Theocritus to Virgil, and again of Virgil to Ovid. He habituated me to compare Lucretius (in such extracts as I then read), Terence, and, above all, the chaster poems of Catullus not only with the Roman poets of the so-called silver and brazen ages but with even those of the Augustan era; and, on grounds of plain sense and universal logic, to see and assert the superiority of the former in the truth and nativeness both of their thoughts and diction. At the same time that we were studying the Greek tragic poets, he made us read Shakespeare and Milton as lessons; and they were the lessons, too, which required most time and trouble to *bring up*, so as to escape his censure. I learnt from him that poetry, even that of the loftiest and, seemingly, that of the wildest odes, had a logic of its own as severe as that of science; and more difficult, because more subtle, more complex, and dependent on more, and more fugitive, causes. In the truly great poets, he would say, there is a reason assignable, not only for every word, but for the position of every word; and I well remember that, availing himself of the synonyms to the Homer of Didymus,[3] he made us attempt to show, with regard to each, *why* it would not have answered the same purpose, and *wherein* consisted the peculiar fitness of the word in the original text.

In our own English compositions (at least for the last three years of our school education) he showed no mercy to phrase, metaphor, or image unsupported by a sound sense, or where the same sense might have been conveyed with equal force and dignity in plainer words. Lute, harp, and lyre, muse, muses, and inspirations, Pegasus, Parnassus, and Hippocrene were all an abomination to him. In fancy I can almost hear him now, exclaiming, "Harp? Harp? Lyre? Pen and ink, boy, you mean! Muse, boy, muse? Your nurse's daughter, you mean! Pierian spring? Oh, aye! the cloister pump, I suppose!" Nay, certain introductions, similes, and examples were placed by name on a list of interdiction. Among the similes there was, I remember, that of the manchineel fruit,[4] as suiting equally well with too many subjects, in which, however, it yielded the palm at once to the example of Alexander and Clytus,[5] which was equally good and apt whatever might be the theme. Was it ambition? Alexander and Clytus! Flattery? Alexander and Clytus! Anger? Drunkenness? Pride? Friendship? Ingratitude? Late repentance? Still, still Alexander and Clytus! At length, the praises of agriculture having been exemplified in the sagacious observation that, had Alexander been holding the plow, he would not have run his friend Clytus through with a spear, this tried and

---

1. Coleridge heads each chapter with a list of topics. In instances where we excerpt from chapters, we introduce these headings in brackets before the relevant selection.
2. "The Rev. James Bowyer, many years Head Master of the Grammar School, Christ's Hospital" [Coleridge's note].
3. Didymus of Alexandria (ca. 65 B.C.–A.D. 10) was the author of a commentary on the text of Homer.
4. Poisonous, though attractive in appearance.
5. Plutarch's *Life* of Alexander the Great relates that the king killed his friend Clytus in a drunken quarrel.

serviceable old friend was banished by public edict in *secula seculorum*.[6] I have sometimes ventured to think that a list of this kind or an *index expurgatorius*[7] of certain well-known and ever returning phrases, both introductory and transitional, including the large assortment of modest egoisms and flattering illeisms,[8] etc., etc., might be hung up in our law courts and both Houses of Parliament with great advantage to the public as an important saving of national time, an incalculable relief to his Majesty's ministers; but, above all, as insuring the thanks of country attorneys and their clients, who have private bills to carry through the House.

Be this as it may, there was one custom of our master's which I cannot pass over in silence, because I think it imitable and worthy of imitation. He would often permit our theme exercises, under some pretext of want of time, to accumulate till each lad had four or five to be looked over. Then placing the whole number *abreast* on his desk, he would ask the writer why this or that sentence might not have found as appropriate a place under this or that other thesis; and if no satisfying answer could be returned and two faults of the same kind were found in one exercise, the irrevocable verdict followed, the exercise was torn up, and another on the same subject to be produced, in addition to the tasks of the day. The reader will, I trust, excuse this tribute of recollection to a man whose severities, even now, not seldom furnish the dreams by which the blind fancy would fain interpret to the mind the painful sensations of distempered sleep; but neither lessen nor dim the deep sense of my moral and intellectual obligations. He sent us to the university excellent Latin and Greek scholars and tolerable Hebraists. Yet our classical knowledge was the least of the good gifts which we derived from his zealous and conscientious tutorage. He is now gone to his final reward, full of years and full of honors, even of those honors which were dearest to his heart as gratefully bestowed by that school, and still binding him to the interests of that school, in which he had been himself educated and to which during his whole life he was a dedicated thing. * * *

[BOWLES'S SONNETS]

I had just entered on my seventeenth year, when the sonnets of Mr. Bowles,[9] twenty in number, and just then published in a quarto pamphlet, were first made known and presented to me by a schoolfellow who had quitted us for the university and who, during the whole time that he was in our first form (or in our school language, a Grecian),[1] had been my patron and protector. I refer to Dr. Middleton, the truly learned and every way excellent Bishop of Calcutta. * * *

It was a double pleasure to me, and still remains a tender recollection, that I should have received from a friend so revered the first knowledge of a poet by whose works, year after year, I was so enthusiastically delighted and inspired. My earliest acquaintances will not have forgotten the undisciplined eagerness and impetuous zeal with which I laboured to make proselytes, not

6. Forever ("for centuries of centuries").
7. Index of things to be deleted.
8. Excessive use of the pronoun *he* (in Latin, *ille*).
9. William Lisle Bowles (1762–1850) published in 1789 two editions of a collection of sonnets setting

forth the meditations evoked from a traveler by the changing scene.
1. Gifted students in the final class at Christ's Hospital who were being prepared for a university.

only of my companions, but of all with whom I conversed, of whatever rank and in whatever place. As my school finances did not permit me to purchase copies, I made, within less than a year and a half, more than forty transcriptions, as the best presents I could offer to those who had in any way won my regard. And with almost equal delight did I receive the three or four following publications of the same author.

Though I have seen and known enough of mankind to be well aware that I shall perhaps stand alone in my creed, and that it will be well if I subject myself to no worse charge than that of singularity, I am not therefore deterred from avowing that I regard and ever have regarded the obligations of intellect among the most sacred of the claims of gratitude. A valuable thought, or a particular train of thoughts, gives me additional pleasure when I can safely refer and attribute it to the conversation or correspondence of another. My obligations to Mr. Bowles were indeed important and for radical good. At a very premature age, even before my fifteenth year, I had bewildered myself in metaphysics and in theological controversy. Nothing else pleased me. History and particular facts lost all interest in my mind. Poetry (though for a schoolboy of that age I was above par in English versification and had already produced two or three compositions which, I may venture to say without reference to my age, were somewhat above mediocrity, and which had gained me more credit than the sound good sense of my old master was at all pleased with), poetry itself, yea novels and romances, became insipid to me. In my friendless wanderings on our leave-days (for I was an orphan, and had scarce any connections in London), highly was I delighted if any passenger, especially if he were dressed in black,[2] would enter into conversation with me. For I soon found the means of directing it to my favorite subjects

> Of providence, fore-knowledge, will, and fate,
> Fixed fate, free will, fore-knowledge absolute,
> And found no end, in wandering mazes lost.[3]

This preposterous pursuit was, beyond doubt, injurious both to my natural powers and to the progress of my education. It would perhaps have been destructive had it been continued; but from this I was auspiciously withdrawn, partly indeed by an accidental introduction to an amiable family,[4] chiefly however by the genial influence of a style of poetry so tender and yet so manly, so natural and real, and yet so dignified and harmonious, as the sonnets, etc., of Mr. Bowles! Well were it for me, perhaps, had I never relapsed into the same mental disease; if I had continued to pluck the flower and reap the harvest from the cultivated surface, instead of delving in the unwholesome quicksilver mines of metaphysic depths. But if in after time I have sought a refuge from bodily pain and mismanaged sensibility in abstruse researches, which exercised the strength and subtlety of the understanding without awakening the feelings of the heart; still there was a long and blessed interval, during which my natural faculties were allowed to expand and my original tendencies to develop themselves: my fancy, and the love of nature, and the sense of beauty in forms and sounds.

2. I.e., if he were a clergyman.
3. *Paradise Lost* 2.559–61.

4. The family of Mary Evans, with whom Coleridge fell in love in 1788.

[COMPARISON BETWEEN THE POETS BEFORE AND SINCE MR. POPE]

The second advantage which I owe to my early perusal and admiration of these poems (to which let me add, though known to me at a somewhat later period, the *Lewesdon Hill* of Mr. Crow)[5] bears more immediately on my present subject. Among those with whom I conversed there were, of course, very many who had formed their taste and their notions of poetry from the writings of Mr. Pope and his followers: or to speak more generally, in that school of French poetry condensed and invigorated by English understanding which had predominated from the last century. I was not blind to the merits of this school, yet from inexperience of the world and consequent want of sympathy with the general subjects of these poems they gave me little pleasure, I doubtless undervalued the *kind*, and with the presumption of youth withheld from its masters the legitimate name of poets. I saw that the excellence of this kind consisted in just and acute observations on men and manners in an artificial state of society as its matter and substance, and in the logic of wit conveyed in smooth and strong epigrammatic couplets as its *form*. Even when the subject was addressed to the fancy or the intellect, as in the *Rape of the Lock* or the *Essay on Man*; nay, when it was a consecutive narration, as in that astonishing product of matchless talent and ingenuity, Pope's translation of the *Iliad*; still a *point* was looked for at the end of each second line, and the whole was as it were a sorites or, if I may exchange a logical for a grammatical metaphor, a *conjunction disjunctive*,[6] of epigrams. Meantime the matter and diction seemed to me characterized not so much by poetic thoughts as by thoughts *translated* into the language of poetry. On this last point I had occasion to render my own thoughts gradually more and more plain to myself by frequent amicable disputes concerning Darwin's *Botanic Garden*,[7] which for some years was greatly extolled, not only by the *reading* public in general, but even by those whose genius and natural robustness of understanding enabled them afterwards to act foremost in dissipating these "painted mists" that occasionally rise from the marshes at the foot of Parnassus. During my first Cambridge vacation I assisted a friend in a contribution for a literary society in Devonshire, and in this I remember to have compared Darwin's work to the Russian palace of ice, glittering, cold, and transitory. In the same essay too I assigned sundry reasons, chiefly drawn from a comparison of passages in the Latin poets with the original Greek from which they were borrowed, for the preference of Collins's odes to those of Gray, and of the simile in Shakespeare:

> How like a younker or a prodigal
> The scarfed bark puts from her native bay,
> Hugged and embraced by the strumpet wind!
> How like the prodigal doth she return,
> With over-weathered ribs and ragged sails,
> Lean, rent and beggared by the strumpet wind![8]

5. William Crow(e) (1745–1829) published in 1788 *Lewesdon Hill*, a long poem in blank verse that, like Bowles's sonnets, combined descriptions of the natural scene with associated moral and personal reflections.
6. A word that connects the parts of a sentence but expresses an alternative or opposition: "or," "but," "lest," etc. "Sorites": a sequence of interconnected syllogisms.
7. Published in 1789–91 by Erasmus Darwin (1731–1802); a long poem in closed couplets, presenting the science of botany in elaborate allegories.
8. *Merchant of Venice* 2.6.14–19.

to the imitation in the *Bard:*

> Fair laughs the morn, and soft the zephyr blows
> While proudly riding o'er the azure realm
> In gallant trim the gilded vessel goes;
> YOUTH on the prow, and PLEASURE at the helm;
> Regardless of the sweeping whirlwind's sway,
> That, hushed in grim repose, expects its evening prey.[9]

(In which, by the bye, the words "realm" and "sway" are rhymes dearly purchased.) I preferred the original, on the ground that in the imitation it depended wholly in the compositor's putting, or not putting, a small capital both in this and in many other passages of the same poet whether the words should be personifications or mere abstracts. I mention this because, in referring various lines in Gray to their original in Shakespeare and Milton, and in the clear perception how completely all the propriety was lost in the transfer, I was at that early period led to a conjecture which, many years afterwards, was recalled to me from the same thought having been started in conversation, but far more ably, and developed more fully, by Mr. Wordsworth; namely, that this style of poetry which I have characterized above as translations of prose thoughts into poetic language had been kept up by, if it did not wholly arise from, the custom of writing Latin verses and the great importance attached to these exercises in our public schools. Whatever might have been the case in the fifteenth century, when the use of the Latin tongue was so general among learned men that Erasmus is said to have forgotten his native language; yet in the present day it is not to be supposed that a youth can think in Latin, or that he can have any other reliance on the force or fitness of his phrases but the authority of the author from whence he had adopted them. Consequently he must first prepare his thoughts and then pick out from Virgil, Horace, Ovid, or perhaps more compendiously, from his *Gradus,*[1] halves and quarters of lines in which to embody them.

I never object to a certain degree of disputatiousness in a young man from the age of seventeen to that of four or five and twenty, provided I find him always arguing on one side of the question. The controversies occasioned by my unfeigned zeal for the honor of a favorite contemporary, then known to me only by his works, were of great advantage in the formation and establishment of my taste and critical opinions. In my defense of the lines running into each other instead of closing at each couplet, and of natural language, neither bookish nor vulgar, neither redolent of the lamp nor of the kennel, such as *I will remember thee;* instead of the same thought tricked up in the rag-fair finery of

> ——Thy image on her wing
> Before my FANCY'S eye shall MEMORY bring,

I had continually to adduce the meter and diction of the Greek poets from Homer to Theocritus inclusive; and still more of our elder English poets from Chaucer to Milton. Nor was this all. But as it was my constant reply to authori-

---

9. Thomas Gray, *The Bard* (1757).
1. *Gradus ad Parnassum* ("Stairway to Parnassus"), a dictionary of Latin words, synonyms, and descriptive epithets, illustrated from the Latin poets. It was long used as a school text in Latin composition.

ties brought against me from later poets of great name that no authority could avail in opposition to Truth, Nature, Logic, and the Laws of Universal Grammar; actuated too by my former passion for metaphysical investigations, I labored at a solid foundation on which permanently to ground my opinions in the component faculties of the human mind itself and their comparative dignity and importance. According to the faculty or source from which the pleasure given by any poem or passage was derived I estimated the merit of such poem or passage. As the result of all my reading and meditation, I abstracted two critical aphorisms, deeming them to comprise the conditions and criteria of poetic style: first, that not the poem which we have *read*, but that to which we *return* with the greatest pleasure, possesses the genuine power and claims the name of *essential* poetry. Second, that whatever lines can be translated into other words of the same language without diminution of their significance, either in sense of association or in any worthy feeling, are so far vicious in their diction. Be it however observed that I excluded from the list of worthy feelings the pleasure derived from mere novelty in the reader, and the desire of exciting wonderment at his powers in the author. Oftentimes since then, in perusing French tragedies, I have fancied two marks of admiration at the end of each line, as hieroglyphics of the author's own admiration at his own cleverness. Our genuine admiration of a great poet is a continuous undercurrent of feeling; it is everywhere present, but seldom anywhere as a separate excitement. I was wont boldly to affirm that it would be scarcely more difficult to push a stone out from the pyramids with the bare hand than to alter a word, or the position of a word, in Milton or Shakespeare (in their most important works at least), without making the author say something else, or something worse, than he does say. One great distinction I appeared to myself to see plainly, between even the characteristic faults of our elder poets and the false beauties of the moderns. In the former, from Donne to Cowley, we find the most fantastic out-of-the-way thoughts, but in the most pure and genuine mother English; in the latter, the most obvious thoughts, in language the most fantastic and arbitrary. Our faulty elder poets sacrificed the passion and passionate flow of poetry to the subtleties of intellect and to the starts of wit; the moderns to the glare and glitter of a perpetual yet broken and heterogeneous imagery, or rather to an amphibious something, made up half of image and half of abstract[2] meaning. The one sacrificed the heart to the head, the other both heart and head to point and drapery. * * *

From *Chapter 4*

[MR. WORDSWORTH'S EARLIER POEMS]

* * * During the last year of my residence at Cambridge, I became acquainted with Mr. Wordsworth's first publication, entitled *Descriptive Sketches*;[3] and seldom, if ever, was the emergence of an original poetic genius

2. I remember a ludicrous instance in the poem of a young tradesman: "No more will I endure Love's pleasing pain, / Or round my *heart's leg* tie his galling chain" [Coleridge's note].
3. Published 1793, the year before Coleridge left Cambridge; a long descriptive-meditative poem in closed couplets, recounting Wordsworth's walking tour in the Alps in 1790. Wordsworth describes the same tour in *The Prelude*, book 6.

above the literary horizon more evidently announced. In the form, style, and manner of the whole poem, and in the structure of the particular lines and periods, there is a harshness and acerbity connected and combined with words and images all a-glow which might recall those products of the vegetable world, where gorgeous blossoms rise out of the hard and thorny rind and shell within which the rich fruit was elaborating. The language was not only peculiar and strong, but at times knotty and contorted, as by its own impatient strength; while the novelty and struggling crowd of images, acting in conjunction with the difficulties of the style, demanded always a greater closeness of attention than poetry (at all events than descriptive poetry) has a right to claim. It not seldom therefore justified the complaint of obscurity. In the following extract I have sometimes fancied that I saw an emblem of the poem itself and of the author's genius as it was then displayed:

> 'Tis storm; and hid in mist from hour to hour,
> All day the floods a deepening murmur pour;
> The sky is veiled, and every cheerful sight:
> Dark is the region as with coming night;
> And yet what frequent bursts of overpowering light!
> Triumphant on the bosom of the storm,
> Glances the fire-clad eagle's wheeling form;
> Eastward, in long perspective glittering, shine
> The wood-crowned cliffs that o'er the lake recline;
> Wide o'er the Alps a hundred streams unfold,
> At once to pillars turned that flame with gold;
> Behind his sail the peasant strives to shun
> The West, that burns like one dilated sun,
> Where in a mighty crucible expire
> The mountains, glowing hot, like coals of fire.[4]

The poetic Psyche, in its process to full development, undergoes as many changes as its Greek namesake, the butterfly.[5] And it is remarkable how soon genius clears and purifies itself from the faults and errors of its earliest products; faults which, in its earliest compositions, are the more obtrusive and confluent because, as heterogeneous elements which had only a temporary use, they constitute the very *ferment* by which themselves are carried off. Or we may compare them to some diseases, which must work on the humors and be thrown out on the surface in order to secure the patient from their future recurrence. I was in my twenty-fourth year when I had the happiness of knowing Mr. Wordsworth personally;[6] and, while memory lasts, I shall hardly forget the sudden effect produced on my mind by his recitation of a manuscript poem which still remains unpublished, but of which the stanza and tone of style were the same as those of *The Female Vagrant* as originally printed in the first volume of the *Lyrical Ballads*.[7] There was here no mark of strained thought or forced diction, no crowd or turbulence of imagery, and, as the poet hath himself well described in his lines on revisiting the Wye, manly reflection and human associations had given both variety and an additional interest to

4. *Descriptive Sketches* (1815 version), lines 332ff.
5. In Greek, Psyche is the common name for the soul and the butterfly [Coleridge's note].
6. The meeting occurred in Sept. 1795.
7. *Salisbury Plain* (1793–94), which was left in manu-

script until Wordsworth published a revised version in 1842 under the title *Guilt and Sorrow*. An excerpt from *Salisbury Plain* was printed as *The Female Vagrant*, in *Lyrical Ballads* (1798).

natural objects which in the passion and appetite of the first love they had seemed to him neither to need or permit.[8] The occasional obscurities, which had risen from an imperfect control over the resources of his native language, had almost wholly disappeared, together with that worse defect of arbitrary and illogical phrases, at once hackneyed and fantastic, which hold so distinguished a place in the *technique* of ordinary poetry and will, more or less, alloy the earlier poems of the truest genius, unless the attention has been specifically directed to their worthlessness and incongruity. I did not perceive anything particular in the mere style of the poem alluded to during its recitation, except indeed such difference as was not separable from the thought and manner; and the Spenserian stanza which always, more or less, recalls to the reader's mind Spenser's own style, would doubtless have authorized in my then opinion a more frequent descent to the phrases of ordinary life than could, without an ill effect, have been hazarded in the heroic couplet. It was not however the freedom from false taste, whether as to common defects or to those more properly his own, which made so unusual an impression on my feelings immediately, and subsequently on my judgment. It was the union of deep feeling with profound thought; the fine balance of truth in observing with the imaginative faculty in modifying the objects observed; and above all the original gift of spreading the tone, the *atmosphere*, and with it the depth and height of the ideal world, around forms, incidents, and situations of which, for the common view, custom had bedimmed all the luster, had dried up the sparkle and the dewdrops. "To find no contradiction in the union of old and new, to contemplate the Ancient of Days and all his works with feelings as fresh as if all had then sprang forth at the first creative fiat, characterizes the mind that feels the riddle of the world and may help to unravel it. To carry on the feelings of childhood into the powers of manhood; to combine the child's sense of wonder and novelty with the appearances which every day for perhaps forty years had rendered familiar;

> With sun and moon and stars throughout the year,
> And man and woman;[9]

this is the character and privilege of genius, and one of the marks which distinguish genius from talents. And therefore it is the prime merit of genius, and its most unequivocal mode of manifestation, so to represent familiar objects as to awaken in the minds of others a kindred feeling concerning them, and that freshness of sensation which is the constant accompaniment of mental no less than of bodily convalescence. Who has not a thousand times seen snow fall on water? Who has not watched it with a new feeling from the time that he has read Burns' comparison of sensual pleasure

> To snow that falls upon a river
> A moment white—then gone forever![1]

In poems, equally as in philosophic disquisitions, genius produces the strongest impressions of novelty while it rescues the most admitted truths from the impotence caused by the very circumstance of their universal admission. Truths of all others the most awful and mysterious, yet being at the same time

---

8. Wordsworth's *Tintern Abbey*, lines 76ff.
9. Altered from Milton's sonnet *To Mr. Cyriack Skin-*
ner upon His Blindness.
1. Altered from Burns's *Tam o' Shanter*, lines 61–62.

of universal interest, are too often considered as *so* true, that they lose all the life and efficiency of truth and lie bedridden in the dormitory of the soul side by side with the most despised and exploded errors." *The Friend*, p. 76, no. 5.[2]

[ON FANCY AND IMAGINATION—THE INVESTIGATION OF THE DISTINCTION IMPORTANT TO THE FINE ARTS]

This excellence, which in all Mr. Wordsworth's writings is more or less predominant and which constitutes the character of his mind, I no sooner felt than I sought to understand. Repeated meditations led me first to suspect (and a more intimate analysis of the human faculties, their appropriate marks, functions, and effects, matured my conjecture into full conviction) that fancy and imagination were two distinct and widely different faculties, instead of being, according to the general belief, either two names with one meaning, or at furthest the lower and higher degree of one and the same power. It is not, I own, easy to conceive a more apposite translation of the Greek *phantasia* than the Latin *imaginatio*; but it is equally true that in all societies there exists an instinct of growth, a certain collective unconscious good sense working progressively to desynonymize those words originally of the same meaning which the conflux of dialects had supplied to the more homogeneous languages, as the Greek and German: and which the same cause, joined with accidents of translation from original works of different countries, occasion in mixed languages like our own. The first and most important point to be proved is, that two conceptions perfectly distinct are confused under one and the same word, and (this done) to appropriate that word exclusively to one meaning, and the synonym (should there be one) to the other. But if (as will be often the case in the arts and sciences) no synonym exists, we must either invent or borrow a word. In the present instance the appropriation had already begun and been legitimated in the derivative adjective: Milton had a highly *imaginative*, Cowley a very *fanciful*, mind. If therefore I should succeed in establishing the actual existence of two faculties generally different, the nomenclature would be at once determined. To the faculty by which I had characterized Milton we should confine the term *imagination*; while the other would be contra-distinguished as *fancy*. Now were it once fully ascertained that this division is no less grounded in nature than that of delirium from mania, or Otway's

Lutes, lobsters, seas of milk, and ships of amber,[3]

from Shakespeare's

What! have his daughters brought him to this pass?[4]

or from the preceding apostrophe to the elements, the theory of the fine arts and of poetry in particular could not, I thought, but derive some additional and important light. It would in its immediate effects furnish a torch of guidance to the philosophical critic, and ultimately to the poet himself. In energetic minds truth soon changes by domestication into power; and from directing in the discrimination and appraisal of the product becomes influen-

2. A periodical published by Coleridge (1809–10).
3. Thomas Otway, in *Venice Preserved* (1682), wrote

"laurels" in place of "lobsters" (5.2.151).
4. *King Lear* 3.4.59.

cive in the production. To admire on principle is the only way to imitate without loss of originality. * * *

From *Chapter* 13

[ON THE IMAGINATION, OR ESEMPLASTIC[5] POWER]

* * * The IMAGINATION, then, I consider either as primary, or secondary. The primary IMAGINATION I hold to be the living power and prime agent of all human perception, and as a repetition in the finite mind of the eternal act of creation in the infinite I AM. The secondary I consider as an echo of the former, coexisting with the conscious will, yet still as identical with the primary in the *kind* of its agency, and differing only in *degree*, and in the *mode* of its operation. It dissolves, diffuses, dissipates, in order to recreate; or where this process is rendered impossible, yet still, at all events, it struggles to idealize and to unify. It is essentially *vital*, even as all objects (*as* objects) are essentially fixed and dead.

FANCY, on the contrary, has no other counters to play with but fixities and definites. The fancy is indeed no other than a mode of memory emancipated from the order of time and space; and blended with, and modified by that empirical phenomenon of the will which we express by the word CHOICE. But equally with the ordinary memory it must receive all its materials ready made from the law of association.[6] * * *

Chapter 14

OCCASION OF THE LYRICAL BALLADS, AND THE OBJECTS ORIGINALLY
PROPOSED — PREFACE TO THE SECOND EDITION — THE ENSUING
CONTROVERSY, ITS CAUSES AND ACRIMONY — PHILOSOPHIC DEFINITIONS OF
A POEM AND POETRY WITH SCHOLIA.[7]

During the first year that Mr. Wordsworth and I were neighbours,[8] our conversations turned frequently on the two cardinal points of poetry, the power of exciting the sympathy of the reader by a faithful adherence to the truth of nature, and the power of giving the interest of novelty by the modifying colors of imagination.[9] The sudden charm which accidents of light and shade, which moonlight or sunset diffused over a known and familiar landscape, appeared to represent the practicability of combining both. These are the poetry of nature. The thought suggested itself (to which of us I do not recollect) that a series of poems might be composed of two sorts. In the one, the incidents and agents were to be, in part at least, supernatural; and the excellence aimed at was to consist in the interesting of the affections by the dramatic truth of such emotions as would naturally accompany such situations, supposing them real. And real in *this* sense they have been to every

---

5. Coleridge coined this word and used it to mean "molding into unity."
6. Coleridge conceives God's creation to be a continuing process, which has an analogy in the creative perception ("primary imagination") of all human minds. The creative process is repeated, or "echoed," on still a third level, by the "secondary imagination" of the poet, which dissolves the products of primary perception in order to shape them into a new and unified creation—the imaginative passage or poem. The "fancy," on the other hand, can only manipulate "fix-

ities and definites" that, linked by association, come to it ready-made from perception. Its products, therefore, are not re-creations (echoes of God's original creative process) but mosaic-like reassemblies of existing bits and pieces.
7. Additional remarks, after a philosophic demonstration.
8. At Nether Stowey and Alfoxden, Somerset, in 1797.
9. Cf. Wordsworth's account in his Preface to *Lyrical Ballads* (p. 1341).

human being who, from whatever source of delusion, has at any time believed himself under supernatural agency. For the second class, subjects were to be chosen from ordinary life; the characters and incidents were to be such as will be found in every village and its vicinity where there is a meditative and feeling mind to seek after them, or to notice them when they present themselves.

In this idea originated the plan of the *Lyrical Ballads*; in which it was agreed that my endeavours should be directed to persons and characters supernatural, or at least romantic; yet so as to transfer from our inward nature a human interest and a semblance of truth sufficient to procure for these shadows of imagination that willing suspension of disbelief for the moment, which constitutes poetic faith. Mr. Wordsworth, on the other hand, was to propose to himself as his object to give the charm of novelty to things of every day, and to excite a feeling analogous to the supernatural, by awakening the mind's attention from the lethargy of custom and directing it to the loveliness and the wonders of the world before us; an inexhaustible treasure, but for which, in consequence of the film of familiarity and selfish solicitude, we have eyes yet see not, ears that hear not, and hearts that neither feel nor understand.[1]

With this view I wrote *The Ancient Mariner*, and was preparing, among other poems, *The Dark Ladie*, and the *Christabel*, in which I should have more nearly realized my ideal than I had done in my first attempt. But Mr. Wordsworth's industry had proved so much more successful and the number of his poems so much greater, that my compositions, instead of forming a balance, appeared rather an interpolation of heterogeneous matter.[2] Mr. Wordsworth added two or three poems written in his own character, in the impassioned, lofty, and sustained diction which is characteristic of his genius. In this form the *Lyrical Ballads* were published; and were presented by him, as an *experiment*,[3] whether subjects which from their nature rejected the usual ornaments and extra-colloquial style of poems in general might not be so managed in the language of ordinary life as to produce the pleasurable interest which it is the peculiar business of poetry to impart. To the second edition[4] he added a preface of considerable length; in which, notwithstanding some passages of apparently a contrary import, he was understood to contend for the extension of this style to poetry of all kinds, and to reject as vicious and indefensible all phrases and forms of style that were not included in what he (unfortunately, I think, adopting an equivocal expression) called the language of *real* life. From this preface, prefixed to poems in which it was impossible to deny the presence of original genius, however mistaken its direction might be deemed, arose the whole long-continued controversy.[5] For from the conjunction of perceived power with supposed heresy I explain the inveteracy and in some instances, I grieve to say, the acrimonious passions with which the controversy has been conducted by the assailants.

Had Mr. Wordsworth's poems been the silly, the childish things which they were for a long time described as being; had they been really distinguished from the compositions of other poets merely by meanness of language and inanity of thought; had they indeed contained nothing more than what is

---

1. Cf. Isaiah 6.9–10.
2. The first edition of *Lyrical Ballads*, published anonymously in 1798, contained nineteen poems by Wordsworth, four by Coleridge.
3. *Experiments* was the word used by Wordsworth in
his "Advertisement" to the first edition.
4. Of 1800.
5. The controversy over Wordsworth's theory and poetical practice in the literary journals of the day.

found in the parodies and pretended imitations of them; they must have sunk at once, a dead weight, into the slough of oblivion, and have dragged the preface along with them. But year after year increased the number of Mr. Wordsworth's admirers. They were found too not in the lower classes of the reading public, but chiefly among young men of strong sensibility and meditative minds; and their admiration (inflamed perhaps in some degree by opposition) was distinguished by its intensity, I might almost say, by its *religious* fervor. These facts, and the intellectual energy of the author, which was more or less consciously felt where it was outwardly and even boisterously denied, meeting with sentiments of aversion to his opinions and of alarm at their consequences, produced an eddy of criticism which would of itself have borne up the poems by the violence with which it whirled them round and round. With many parts of this preface, in the sense attributed to them and which the words undoubtedly seem to authorize, I never concurred; but, on the contrary objected to them as erroneous in principle, and as contradictory (in appearance at least) both to other parts of the same preface and to the author's own practice in the greater number of the poems themselves. Mr. Wordsworth in his recent collection[6] has, I find, degraded this prefatory disquisition to the end of his second volume, to be read or not at the reader's choice. But he has not, as far as I can discover, announced any change in his poetic creed. At all events, considering it as the source of a controversy in which I have been honored more than I deserve by the frequent conjunction of my name with his, I think it expedient to declare once for all in what points I coincide with his opinions, and in what points I altogether differ. But in order to render myself intelligible I must previously, in as few words as possible, explain my ideas, first, of a POEM;

The office of philosophical *disquisition* consists in just *distinction;* while it is the privilege of the philosopher to preserve himself constantly aware that distinction is not division. In order to obtain adequate notions of any truth, we must intellectually separate its distinguishable parts; and this is the technical *process* of philosophy. But having so done, we must then restore them in our conceptions to the unity in which they actually coexist; and this is the *result* of philosophy. A poem contains the same elements as a prose composition; the difference therefore must consist in a different combination of them, in consequence of a different object proposed. According to the difference of the object will be the difference of the combination. It is possible that the object may be merely to facilitate the recollection of any given facts or observations by artificial arrangement; and the composition will be a poem, merely because it is distinguished from prose by meter, or by rhyme, or by both conjointly. In this, the lowest sense, a man might attribute the name of a poem to the well-known enumeration of the days in the several months:

> Thirty days hath September,
> April, June, and November, etc.

and others of the same class and purpose. And as a particular pleasure is found in anticipating the recurrence of sounds and quantities, all compositions that have this charm superadded, whatever be their contents, *may* be entitled poems.

6. *Poems*, 2 vols., 1815.

So much for the superficial *form*. A difference of object and contents supplies an additional ground of distinction. The immediate purpose may be the communication of truths; either of truth absolute and demonstrable, as in works of science; or of facts experienced and recorded, as in history. Pleasure, and that of the highest and most permanent kind, may *result* from the *attainment* of the end; but it is not itself the immediate end. In other works the communication of pleasure may be the immediate purpose; and though truth, either moral or intellectual, ought to be the *ultimate* end, yet this will distinguish the character of the author, not the class to which the work belongs. Blessed indeed is that state of society in which the immediate purpose would be baffled by the perversion of the proper ultimate end; in which no charm of diction or imagery could exempt the Bathyllus even of an Anacreon, or the Alexis of Virgil,[7] from disgust and aversion!

But the communication of pleasure may be the immediate object of a work not metrically composed; and that object may have been in a high degree attained, as in novels and romances. Would then the mere superaddition of meter, with or without rhyme, entitle *these* to the name of poems? The answer is that nothing can permanently please which does not contain in itself the reason why it is so, and not otherwise. If meter be superadded, all other parts must be made consonant with it. They must be such as to justify the perpetual and distinct attention to each part which an exact correspondent recurrence of accent and sound are calculated to excite. The final definition then, so deduced, may be thus worded. A poem is that species of composition which is opposed to works of science by proposing for its *immediate* object pleasure, not truth; and from all other species (having *this* object in common with it) it is discriminated by proposing to itself such delight from the *whole* as is compatible with a distinct gratification from each component *part*.

Controversy is not seldom excited in consequence of the disputants attaching each a different meaning to the same word; and in few instances has this been more striking than in disputes concerning the present subject. If a man chooses to call every composition a poem which is rhyme, or measure, or both, I must leave his opinion uncontroverted. The distinction is at least competent to characterize the writer's intention. If it were subjoined that the whole is likewise entertaining or affecting as a tale or as a series of interesting reflections, I of course admit this as another fit ingredient of a poem and an additional merit. But if the definition sought for be that of a *legitimate* poem, I answer it must be one the parts of which mutually support and explain each other; all in their proportion harmonizing with, and supporting the purpose and known influences of metrical arrangement. The philosophic critics of all ages coincide with the ultimate judgment of all countries in equally denying the praises of a just poem on the one hand to a series of striking lines or distichs,[8] each of which absorbing the whole attention of the reader to itself disjoins it from its context and makes it a separate whole, instead of a harmonizing part; and on the other hand, to an unsustained composition, from which the reader collects rapidly the general result unattracted by the component parts. The reader should be carried forward, not merely or chiefly by the mechanical impulse of curiosity, or by a restless desire to arrive at the final

---

7. The reference is to poems of homosexual love. "Bathyllus" was a beautiful boy praised by Anacreon, a Greek lyric poet (ca. 560–475 B.C.); "Alexis" was a young man loved by the shepherd Corydon in Virgil's *Eclogues* 2.
8. Pairs of lines.

solution; but by the pleasurable activity of mind excited by the attractions of the journey itself. Like the motion of a serpent, which the Egyptians made the emblem of intellectual power; or like the path of sound through the air; at every step he pauses and half recedes, and from the retrogressive movement collects the force which again carries him onward. "*Praecipitandus est* liber *spiritus*," says Petronius Arbiter most happily.[9] The epithet *liber* here balances the preceding verb; and it is not easy to conceive more meaning condensed in fewer words.

But if this should be admitted as a satisfactory character of a poem, we have still to seek for a definition of poetry. The writings of Plato, and Bishop Taylor, and the *Theoria Sacra* of Burnet,[1] furnish undeniable proofs that poetry of the highest kind may exist without meter, and even without the contradistinguishing objects of a poem. The first chapter of Isaiah (indeed a very large proportion of the whole book) is poetry in the most emphatic sense; yet it would be not less irrational than strange to assert that pleasure, and not truth, was the immediate object of the prophet. In short, whatever *specific* import we attach to the word poetry, there will be found involved in it, as a necessary consequence, that a poem of any length neither can be, nor ought to be, all poetry.[2] Yet if a harmonious whole is to be produced, the remaining parts must be preserved in *keeping* with the poetry; and this can be no otherwise effected than by such a studied selection and artificial arrangement as will partake of *one*, though not a *peculiar*, property of poetry. And this again can be no other than the property of exciting a more continuous and equal attention than the language of prose aims at, whether colloquial or written.

My own conclusions on the nature of poetry, in the strictest use of the word, have been in part anticipated in the preceding disquisition on the fancy and imagination. What is poetry? is so nearly the same question with, what is a poet? that the answer to the one is involved in the solution of the other. For it is a distinction resulting from the poetic genius itself, which sustains and modifies the images, thoughts, and emotions of the poet's own mind.

The poet, described in *ideal* perfection, brings the whole soul of man into activity, with the subordination of its faculties to each other, according to their relative worth and dignity. He diffuses a tone and spirit of unity that blends and (as it were) *fuses*, each into each, by that synthetic and magical power to which we have exclusively appropriated the name of imagination. This power, first put in action by the will and understanding and retained under their irremissive, though gentle and unnoticed, control (*laxis effertur habenis*[3]) reveals itself in the balance or reconciliation of opposite or discordant qualities:[4] of sameness, with difference; of the general, with the concrete; the idea, with the image; the individual, with the representative; the sense of novelty and freshness, with old and familiar objects; a more than usual state of emotion, with more than usual order; judgment ever awake and steady self-posses-

---

9. "The *free* spirit [of the poet] must be hurled onward." From the *Satyricon*, by the lively Roman satirist Petronius Arbiter (1st century A.D.).
1. Bishop Jeremy Taylor (1613–1667), author of *Holy Living* and *Holy Dying*; Thomas Burnet (1635?–1715), author of *The Sacred Theory of the Earth*. Coleridge greatly admired the elaborate and sonorous prose of both these writers; he took from a work by Burnet the Latin motto for *The Rime of the Ancient Mariner*.
2. Coleridge does not use the word *poetry* in the usual

way, as a term for the class of all metrical compositions, or of all "poems," but to designate those passages, whether in verse or prose, produced by the mind of genius in its supreme moments of imaginative activity.
3. I.e., driven with loosened reins.
4. Here Coleridge introduces the concept that the highest poetry incorporates and reconciles opposite or discordant elements; under the names of "irony" and "paradox," this concept became a primary criterion of the American New Critics.

sion, with enthusiasm and feeling profound or vehement; and while it blends and harmonizes the natural and the artificial, still subordinates art to nature; the manner to the matter; and our admiration of the poet to our sympathy with the poetry. "Doubtless," as Sir John Davies observes of the soul (and his words may with slight alteration be applied, and even more appropriately, to the poetic IMAGINATION):

> Doubtless this could not be, but that she turns
>   Bodies to spirit by sublimation strange,
> As fire converts to fire the things it burns,
>   As we our food into our nature change.
>
> From their gross matter she abstracts their forms,
>   And draws a kind of quintessence from things;
> Which to her proper nature she transforms,
>   To bear them light on her celestial wings.
>
> Thus does she, when from individual states
>   She doth abstract the universal kinds;
> Which then reclothed in divers names and fates
>   Steal access through our senses to our minds.[5]

Finally, GOOD SENSE is the BODY of poetic genius, FANCY its DRAPERY, MOTION its LIFE, and IMAGINATION the SOUL that is everywhere, and in each; and forms all into one graceful and intelligent whole.

From *Chapter 17*

[EXAMINATION OF THE TENETS PECULIAR TO MR. WORDSWORTH]

As far then as Mr. Wordsworth in his preface contended, and most ably contended, for a reformation in our poetic diction, as far as he has evinced the truth of passion, and the *dramatic* propriety of those figures and metaphors in the original poets which, stripped of their justifying reasons and converted into mere artifices of connection or ornament, constitute the characteristic falsity in the poetic style of the moderns; and as far as he has, with equal acuteness and clearness, pointed out the process by which this change was effected and the resemblances between that state into which the reader's mind is thrown by the pleasurable confusion of thought from an unaccustomed train of words and images and that state which is induced by the natural language of impassioned feeling, he undertook a useful task and deserves all praise, both for the attempt and for the execution. The provocations to this remonstrance in behalf of truth and nature were still of perpetual recurrence before and after the publication of this preface. * * *

My own differences from certain supposed parts of Mr. Wordsworth's theory ground themselves on the assumption that his words had been rightly interpreted, as purporting that the proper diction for poetry in general consists altogether in a language taken, with due exceptions, from the mouths of men in real life, a language which actually constitutes the natural conversation of men under the influence of natural feelings.[6] My objection is, first, that in

5. Adapted from John Davies' *Nosce Teipsum* ("Know Thyself"), a philosophical poem (1599).
6. Wordsworth, Preface to *Lyrical Ballads* (1800): "A selection of the real language of men in a state of vivid sensation. . . . Low and rustic life was generally chosen. . . . The language, too, of these men is adopted."

any sense this rule is applicable only to *certain* classes of poetry; secondly, that even to these classes it is not applicable, except in such a sense as hath never by anyone (as far as I know or have read) been denied or doubted; and, lastly, that as far as, and in that degree in which it is *practicable*, yet as a *rule* it is useless, if not injurious, and therefore either need not or ought not to be practiced. * * *

[RUSTIC LIFE (ABOVE ALL, *LOW* AND RUSTIC LIFE) ESPECIALLY
UNFAVORABLE TO THE FORMATION OF A HUMAN DICTION—THE BEST
PARTS OF LANGUAGE THE PRODUCTS OF PHILOSOPHERS, NOT CLOWNS[7] OR
SHEPHERDS]

As little can I agree with the assertion that from the objects with which the rustic hourly communicates the best part of language is formed. For first, if to communicate with an object implies such an acquaintance with it, as renders it capable of being discriminately reflected on; the distinct knowledge of an uneducated rustic would furnish a very scanty vocabulary. The few things, and modes of action, requisite for his bodily conveniences, would alone be individualized; while all the rest of nature would be expressed by a small number of confused general terms. Secondly, I deny that the words and combinations of words derived from the objects, with which the rustic is familiar, whether with distinct or confused knowledge, can be justly said to form the *best* part of language. It is more than probable that many classes of the brute creation possess discriminating sounds, by which they can convey to each other notices of such objects as concern their food, shelter, or safety. Yet we hesitate to call the aggregate of such sounds a language, otherwise than metaphorically. The best part of human language, properly so called, is derived from reflection on the acts of the mind itself. It is formed by a voluntary appropriation of fixed symbols to internal acts, to processes and results of imagination, the greater part of which have no place in the consciousness of uneducated man; though in civilized society, by imitation and passive remembrance of what they hear from their religious instructors and other superiors, the most uneducated share in the harvest which they neither sowed or reaped. * * *

[THE LANGUAGE OF MILTON AS MUCH THE LANGUAGE OF *REAL* LIFE, YEA,
INCOMPARABLY MORE SO THAN THAT OF THE COTTAGER]

Here let me be permitted to remind the reader that the positions which I controvert are contained in the sentences—"a selection of the REAL language of men"; "the language of these men (i.e., men in low and rustic life) I propose to myself to imitate, and as far as possible to adopt the very language of men." "Between the language of prose and that of metrical composition there neither is, nor can be any essential difference." It is against these exclusively that my opposition is directed.

I object, in the very first instance, to an equivocation in the use of the word "real." Every man's language varies according to the extent of his knowledge, the activity of his faculties, and the depth or quickness of his feelings. Every man's language has, first, its *individualities*; secondly, the common properties

7. Rustic people.

of the *class* to which he belongs; and thirdly, words and phrases of *universal* use. The language of Hooker, Bacon, Bishop Taylor, and Burke differs from the common language of the learned class only by the superior number and novelty of the thoughts and relations which they had to convey. The language of Algernon Sidney[8] differs not at all from that which every well-educated gentleman would wish to write, and (with due allowances for the undeliberate-ness and less connected train of thinking natural and proper to conversation) such as he would wish to talk. Neither one nor the other differ half as much from the general language of cultivated society as the language of Mr. Words-worth's homeliest composition differs from that of a common peasant. For "real" therefore we must substitute *ordinary*, or *lingua communis*.[9] And this, we have proved, is no more to be found in the phraseology of low and rustic life than in that of any other class. Omit the peculiarities of each, and the result of course must be common to all. And assuredly the omissions and changes to be made in the language of rustics before it could be transferred to any species of poem, except the drama or other professed imitation, are at least as numerous and weighty as would be required in adapting to the same pur-pose the ordinary language of tradesmen and manufacturers. Not to mention that the language so highly extolled by Mr. Wordsworth varies in every county, nay, in every village, according to the accidental character of the clergyman, the existence or nonexistence of schools; or even, perhaps, as the exciseman, publican, or barber happen to be, or not to be, zealous politicians and readers of the weekly newspaper *pro bono publico*.[1] Anterior to cultivation the *lingua communis* of every country, as Dante has well observed, exists every where in parts and no where as a whole.[2]

Neither is the case rendered at all more tenable by the addition of the words "in a state of excitement."[3] For the nature of a man's words, when he is strongly affected by joy, grief, or anger, must necessarily depend on the num-ber and quality of the general truths, conceptions, and images, and of the words expressing them, with which his mind had been previously stored. For the property of passion is not to *create*, but to set in increased activity. At least, whatever new connections of thoughts or images, or (which is equally, if not more than equally, the appropriate effect of strong excitement) whatever gen-eralizations of truth or experience the heat of passion may produce, yet the terms of their conveyance must have pre-existed in his former conversations, and are only collected and crowded together by the unusual stimulation. It is indeed very possible to adopt in a poem the unmeaning repetitions, habitual phrases, and other blank counters which an unfurnished or confused under-standing interposes at short intervals in order to keep hold of his subject which is still slipping from him, and to give him time for recollection; or in mere aid of vacancy, as in the scanty companies of a country stage the same player pops backwards and forwards, in order to prevent the appearance of empty spaces, in the procession of *Macbeth* or *Henry VIIIth*. But what assistance to the poet or ornament to the poem these can supply, I am at a loss to conjecture. Noth-ing assuredly can differ either in origin or in mode more widely from the

---

8. Algernon Sidney (1622–1683), republican soldier and statesmen, author of *Discourses Concerning Gov-ernment.*
9. The common language (Latin).
1. For the public welfare (Latin).

2. In *De vulgari eloquentia* ("On the Speech of the People") Dante discusses—and affirms—the fitness for poetry of the unlocalized Italian vernacular.
3. Wordsworth: "the manner in which we associate ideas in a state of excitement."

apparent tautologies of intense and turbulent feeling in which the passion is greater and of longer endurance than to be exhausted or satisfied by a single representation of the image or incident exciting it. Such repetitions I admit to be a beauty of the highest kind; as illustrated by Mr. Wordsworth himself from the song of Deborah. "At her feet he bowed, he fell, he lay down; at her feet he bowed, he fell; where he bowed, there he fell down dead."[4]

1815   1817

4. Judges 5.27. Cited by Wordsworth in a note to *The Thorn* as an example of the natural tautology of "impassioned feelings."

GEORGE GORDON, LORD BYRON
1788–1824

1812:	*Childe Harold,* cantos 1 and 2.
1813–14:	The Oriental tales, including *The Giaour, The Corsair, Lara.*
1816:	Separation from Lady Byron; leaves England, never to return.
1818:	Begins *Don Juan.*
1823:	Joins the Greek war for liberation from the Turks.

In his *History of English Literature,* written in the late 1850s, the French critic Hippolyte Taine gave only a few condescending pages to Wordsworth, Coleridge, Shelley, and Keats and then devoted a long enthusiastic chapter to Lord Byron, "the greatest and most English of these artists; he is so great and so English that from him alone we shall learn more truths of his country and of his age than from all the rest together." This comment reflects the fact that Byron had achieved an immense European reputation during his own lifetime, while his English contemporaries were admired only by coteries in England and America; through much of the nineteenth century he continued to be rated as one of the greatest of English poets and the very prototype of literary Romanticism. His influence was felt everywhere, not only among minor writers—in the two or three decades after his death, most European poets struck Byronic attitudes—but among the major poets and novelists (including Goethe in Germany, Balzac and Stendhal in France, Pushkin and Dostoevsky in Russia, and Melville in America), painters (especially Delacroix), and composers (especially Beethoven and Berlioz).

These facts may surprise the student who is aware of the recent, and still fairly common, estimate of Byron as the least consequential of the great Romantic poets, whose achievements have little in common with the distinctive innovations of Wordsworth, Coleridge, Keats, or Shelley. Only Shelley, among these writers, thought highly of either Byron or his work; while Byron spoke slightingly of all of them except Shelley and, in fact, insisted that, measured against the poetic practice of Alexander Pope, he and his contemporaries were "all in the wrong, one as much as another . . . we are upon a wrong revolutionary poetical system, or systems, not worth a damn in itself." Byron's masterpiece, *Don Juan,* is an instance of that favorite neoclassic type, a satire against modern civilization, and shares many of the aims and methods of Pope, Swift, Voltaire, and Sterne. Even Byron's lyrics are old-fashioned: many are in the eighteenth-century gentlemanly mode of witty extemporization and epigram (*Written after Swimming from Sestos to Abydos*) or continue the Cavalier tradition of the elaborate development of a compliment to a lady (*She walks in beauty* and *Stanzas for Music*).

Byron's chief claim to be considered an arch-Romantic is that he provided his age with what Taine called its "ruling personage; that is, the model that contemporaries invest with their admiration and sympathy." This personage is the "Byronic hero." He occurs in various guises in Byron's writings, but from the first sketch in the opening canto of *Childe Harold,* and in the verse romances and dramas that follow, his persistent character is that of a moody, passionate, and remorse-torn but unrepentant wanderer. In his developed form, as we find it in *Manfred,* he is an alien, mysterious, and gloomy spirit, immensely superior in his passions and powers to the common run of humanity, whom he regards with disdain. He harbors the torturing memory of an enormous, nameless guilt that drives him toward an inevitable doom. He is in his isolation absolutely self-reliant, inflexibly pursuing his own ends according to his self-generated moral code against any opposition, human or supernatural. And he exerts an attraction on other characters that is the more compelling because it involves their terror at his obliviousness to ordinary human concerns and values. This figure, infusing the archrebel in a nonpolitical form with a strong erotic interest, embodied the implicit yearnings of Byron's time, was imitated in life as well as in art, and helped shape the intellectual as well as the cultural history of the later nineteenth century. The literary descendants of the Byronic hero include Heathcliff in *Wuthering Heights,* Captain Ahab in *Moby-Dick,* and the hero of Pushkin's great poem *Eugene Onegin.* Bertrand Russell, in his *History of Western Philosophy,* gives a chapter to Byron—not because he was a systematic thinker but because "Byronism," the attitude of "Titanic cosmic self-assertion," established an outlook and a stance toward humanity and the world that entered nineteenth-century philosophy and eventually helped to form Nietzsche's concept of the Superman, the hero who stands outside the jurisdiction of the ordinary criteria of good and evil.

Byron's contemporaries insisted on identifying the author with his fictional characters. But Byron's letters and the testimony of his friends show that, except for recurrent moods of black depression, his own temperament was in many respects antithetic to that of his heroes. He was passionate and willful, but when in good humor, he could be very much a man of the world in the eighteenth-century style—gregarious, lively, tolerant, and a witty conversationalist capable of taking an ironic attitude toward his own activities as well as those of others. The aloof hauteur he exhibited in public was largely a mask to hide his diffidence when in a strange company; he possessed devoted friends, both men and women, and among them he was usually unassuming, companionable, sometimes even exuberant, and tactful; to his household dependents he was unfailingly generous and tenaciously loyal. But although Byronism was largely a fiction, produced by a collaboration between Byron's imagination and that of his public, the fiction was historically more important than the poet in his actual person.

Byron was descended from two aristocratic families, both of them colorful, violent, and dissolute. His grandfather was an admiral nicknamed "Foulweather Jack"; his great-uncle was the fifth Baron Byron, known to his rural neighbors as the "Wicked Lord," who was tried by his peers for killing his kinsman William Chaworth in a drunken duel; his father, Captain John Byron, was a rake and fortune hunter who rapidly dissipated the patrimony of two wealthy wives. Byron's mother was a Scotswoman, Catherine Gordon of Gight, the last descendant of a line of lawless Scottish lairds. After her husband died (Byron was then three), she brought up her son in near poverty in Aberdeen, where he was indoctrinated with the Calvinistic morality of Scottish Presbyterianism. Catherine Byron was an ill-educated and almost pathologically irascible woman who nevertheless had an abiding love for her son; they fought violently when together, but corresponded affectionately enough when apart, until her death in 1811.

When Byron was ten, the death of his great-uncle, preceded by that of more immediate heirs to the title, made him the sixth Lord Byron. In a fashion suitable to his new eminence he was sent to Harrow School, then to Trinity College, Cambridge. He had been born with a clubfoot, which was made worse by inept medical treatment, and this defect all his life caused him physical suffering and agonized embarrassment. His lameness made him avid for athletic prowess; he played cricket and made himself an expert boxer, fencer, and horseman and a powerful swimmer. He was also sexually precocious; when only seven, he fell in love with a little cousin, Mary Duff, and so violently that ten years later news of her marriage threw him into convulsions. Both at Cambridge and at his ancestral estate of Newstead, he engaged with more than ordinary zeal in the expensive pursuits and fashionable dissipations of a young Regency lord. As a result, despite a sizable and increasing income, he got into financial difficulties from which he did not entirely extricate himself until late in his life. In the course of his schooling he formed many close friendships, the most important with John Cam Hobhouse, a sturdy political liberal and commonsense moralist who exerted a steadying influence throughout Byron's turbulent life.

Despite his distractions at the university, Byron found time to try his hand at lyric verse, some of which was published in 1807 in a slim and conventional volume titled *Hours of Idleness*. This was treated with unmerited harshness by the pontifical *Edinburgh Review*, and Byron was provoked to write in reply his first important poem, *English Bards and Scotch Reviewers*, a vigorous satire in the couplet style of the late-eighteenth-century followers of Pope, in which he incorporated brilliant but tactless ridicule of all his major poetic contemporaries, including Scott, Wordsworth, and Coleridge.

After attaining his M.A. degree and his majority, Byron set out with Hobhouse in 1809 on a tour through Portugal and Spain to Malta, and then to little-known Albania, Greece, and Asia Minor. In this adventurous two-year excursion, he accumulated materials that he wove into most of his important poems, including his last work, *Don Juan*. The first literary product was *Childe Harold*, he wrote the opening two cantos while on the tour that the poem describes, published them in 1812 soon after his return to England and, in his own oft-quoted phrase, "awoke one morning and found myself famous." He became the celebrity of fashionable London, enjoying an unprecedented literary success, which he soon increased by his series of highly readable Near Eastern verse tales; in these the Byronic hero, in various embodiments, flaunts his misanthropy and undergoes a variety of violent and romantic adventures that current gossip attributed to the author himself. In his chronic shortage of money, Byron could well have used the huge income from these publications, but instead maintained his status as an aristocratic amateur by giving the royalties away. Occupying his inherited seat in the House of Lords, he also became briefly active on the extreme liberal side of the Whig party and spoke courageously in defense of the Nottingham weavers who, made desperate by technological unemployment, had resorted to destroying the new textile machines; he also supported other liberal measures, including that of Catholic Emancipation.

In the meantime he found himself besieged by women. He was extraordinarily handsome—"so beautiful a countenance," Coleridge wrote, "I scarcely ever saw . . . his eyes the open portals of the sun—things of light, and for light." Because of a constitutional tendency to obesity, however, Byron was able to maintain his beauty only by recurring again and again to a starvation diet of biscuits, soda water, and strong cathartics. Often as a result of female initiative rather than his own, Byron entered into a sequence of liaisons with ladies of fashion. One of these, the flamboyant, eccentric, and hysterical young Lady Caroline Lamb, caused him so much distress by her frenzied pursuit and public tantrums that Byron turned for relief to marriage with Annabella Milbanke, who was in every way Lady Caroline's opposite, for she was naive, unworldly, intellectual (with a special passion for mathematics), and not a little priggish; she persuaded herself that she could make

Byron over in her own image. This ill-starred marriage produced a daughter (Augusta Ada) and many scenes in which Byron, goaded by financial difficulties, behaved so frantically that his wife suspected his sanity; after only one year, the union ended in a legal separation. The final blow came when Lady Byron discovered her husband's incestuous relations with his half-sister, Augusta Leigh. The two had been raised apart, so that they were almost strangers when they met as adults. Byron also seems to have had one attribute in common with the Byronic hero: a compulsion to try forbidden experience—including, as we now know, homosexual love affairs—joined with a tendency to court his own destruction. Byron's affection for his sister, however guilty, was genuine and endured all through his life. This affair proved a delicious morsel even to the jaded palate of the dissolute Regency society; Byron was ostracized by all but a few friends and was finally forced to leave England forever on April 25, 1816.

Byron now resumed the travels incorporated in the third and fourth cantos of *Childe Harold*. At Geneva he lived for several months in close and intellectually fruitful relation to Shelley, who was accompanied by his wife, Mary Wollstonecraft Shelley, and by his wife's stepsister, Claire Clairmont—a misguided girl of seventeen who had forced herself on Byron while he was still in England and who in January 1817 bore him a daughter, Allegra. In the fall of 1817 Byron established himself in Venice, where he inaugurated various affairs that culminated in a period of frenzied debauchery that, he estimated, involved more than two hundred women. This period was also one of great literary creativity: often working through the later hours of the night, he finished his tragedy *Manfred*, wrote the fourth canto of *Childe Harold*, and after turning out *Beppo*, a short preview of the narrative style and stanza of *Don Juan*, began the composition of *Don Juan* itself. In the colloquial ottava rima, he finally learned to write poetry as well as he had written the prose of his superbly vivid, informative, and witty letters.

Exhausted and bored by promiscuity, Byron in 1819 settled into a placid and relatively faithful relationship with Teresa Guiccioli, the young wife of the elderly Count Alessandro Guiccioli; according to the Italian upper-class mores of the times, having contracted a marriage of convenience, she could now with propriety attach Byron to herself as a *cavaliere servente*. Through the countess's nationalistic family, the Gambas, Byron became involved in the Carbonari plot against Austrian control over northern Italy. When the Gambas were forced by the authorities to move to Pisa, Byron followed them there and, for the second time, joined Shelley. There grew up about the two friends the "Pisan Circle," which in addition to the Gambas included Shelley's wife, Mary, and his friends Thomas Medwin and Edward and Jane Williams, as well as the Greek nationalist leader Prince Mavrocordatos, the picturesque Irish Count Taaffe, and the flamboyant and mendacious adventurer Edward Trelawny, who seems to have stepped out of one of Byron's romances. The circle was gradually broken up, first by Shelley's anger over Byron's treatment of his daughter Allegra (Byron had sent the child to be brought up as a Catholic in an Italian convent, where she died of a fever in 1822); then by the expulsion of the Gambas, whom Byron followed to Genoa; and finally by the drowning of Shelley and Williams in July 1822.

Byron meanwhile had been steadily at work on a series of closet tragedies (including *Cain*, *Sardanapalus*, and *Marino Faliero*) and on his superb satire *The Vision of Judgment*. But increasingly he devoted himself to the continuation of *Don Juan*. He had always been diffident in his self-judgments and easily swayed by literary advice. But now, confident that he had at last found his métier and was accomplishing a masterpiece, he kept on, in spite of persistent objections against the supposed immorality of the poem by the English public, by his publisher John Murray, by his friends and well-wishers, and by his extremely decorous mistress, the Countess Guiccioli—by almost everyone, in fact, except the idealist Shelley, who thought *Juan* incomparably better than anything he himself could write and insisted "that every word of it is pregnant with immortality."

Byron finally broke off literature for action when he organized an expedition to assist in the Greek war for independence from the Turks. He knew too well the conditions in Greece, and had too skeptical an estimate of human nature, to entertain hope of success; but he was bored with love, with the domesticity of his relations to Teresa, and in some moods, with life itself. Also, because his own writings had helped to kindle European enthusiasm for the Greek cause, he now felt honor-bound to try what could be done. In the dismal, marshy town of Missolonghi he lived a Spartan existence, training troops whom he had himself subsidized and exhibiting great practical grasp and power of leadership amid a chaos of factionalism, intrigue, and military ineptitude. Worn out, he succumbed to a series of feverish attacks and died just after he had reached his thirty-sixth birthday. To this day Byron is revered by the Greek people as a national hero.

Students of Byron still feel, as his friends had felt, the magnetism of his volatile temperament. As Mary Shelley wrote six years after his death, when she read Thomas Moore's edition of his *Letters and Journals:* "The Lord Byron I find there is our Lord Byron—the fascinating—faulty—childish—philosophical being—daring the world—docile to a private circle—impetuous and indolent—gloomy and yet more gay than any other. . . . [I become] reconciled (as I used to in his lifetime) to those waywardnesses which annoyed me when he was away, through the delightful and buoyant tone of his conversation and manners." Of his inner discordances, Byron himself was well aware; he told his friend Lady Blessington: "I am so changeable, being everything by turns and nothing long—I am such a strange *mélange* of good and evil, that it would be difficult to describe me." Yet he remained faithful to his code: a determination always to tell the truth as he saw it about the world and about himself (his refusal to suppress or conceal any of his moods is in part what made him seem so contradictory) and a dedication to the freedom of nations and individuals. As he went on to say to Lady Blessington: "There are but two sentiments to which I am constant—a strong love of liberty, and a detestation of cant."

Our texts are taken from Jerome J. McGann's edition, *Lord Byron: The Complete Poetical Works* (Oxford, 1980–86).

Written after Swimming from Sestos to Abydos[1]

May 9, 1810

1

If in the month of dark December
  Leander, who was nightly wont
(What maid will not the tale remember?)
  To cross thy stream, broad Hellespont!

---

1. The Hellespont (now called the Dardanelles) is the narrow strait between Europe and Asia. In the ancient story, retold in Christopher Marlowe's *Hero and Leander,* young Leander of Abydos, on the Asian side, swam nightly to visit Hero, a priestess of the goddess Venus at Sestos, until he was drowned when he made the attempt in a storm. Byron and a young Lt. Ekenhead swam the Hellespont in the reverse direction on May 3, 1810. Byron alternated between complacency and humor in his many references to the event. In a note to the poem, he mentions that the distance was "upwards of four English miles, though the actual breadth is barely one. The rapidity of the current is such that no boat can row directly across. . . . The water was extremely cold, from the melting of the mountain snows."

2

If when the wintry tempest roared   5
    He sped to Hero, nothing loth,
And thus of old thy current pour'd,
    Fair Venus! how I pity both!

3

For *me*, degenerate modern wretch,
    Though in the genial month of May,   10
My dripping limbs I faintly stretch,
    And think I've done a feat to-day.

4

But since he cross'd the rapid tide,
    According to the doubtful story,
To woo,—and—Lord knows what beside,   15
    And swam for Love, as I for Glory;

5

'Twere hard to say who fared the best:
    Sad mortals! thus the Gods still plague you!
He lost his labour, I my jest:
    For he was drown'd, and I've the ague.   20

1810   1812

She walks in beauty[1]

1

She walks in beauty, like the night
    Of cloudless climes and starry skies;
And all that's best of dark and bright
    Meet in her aspect and her eyes:
Thus mellow'd to that tender light   5
    Which heaven to gaudy day denies.

2

One shade the more, one ray the less,
    Had half impair'd the nameless grace
Which waves in every raven tress,
    Or softly lightens o'er her face;   10
Where thoughts serenely sweet express
    How pure, how dear their dwelling place.

3

And on that cheek, and o'er that brow,
    So soft, so calm, yet eloquent,
The smiles that win, the tints that glow,   15
    But tell of days in goodness spent,
A mind at peace with all below,
    A heart whose love is innocent!

June 1814   1815

---

1. One of the lyrics in *Hebrew Melodies* (1815), written to be set to adaptations of traditional Jewish tunes
by the young musician Isaac Nathan. Byron wrote the
lines the morning after he had met his beautiful young
cousin by marriage, Mrs. Robert John Wilmot, who
wore a black mourning gown brightened with spangles.

When we two parted

1

When we two parted
  In silence and tears,
Half broken-hearted
  To sever for years,
Pale grew thy cheek and cold,   5
  Colder thy kiss;
Truly that hour foretold
  Sorrow to this.

2

The dew of the morning
  Sunk chill on my brow—   10
It felt like the warning
  Of what I feel now.
Thy vows are all broken,
  And light is thy fame;
I hear thy name spoken,   15
  And share in its shame.

3

They name thee before me,
  A knell to mine ear;
A shudder comes o'er me—
  Why wert thou so dear?   20
They know not I knew thee,
  Who knew thee too well:—
Long, long shall I rue thee,
  Too deeply to tell.

4

In secret we met—   25
  In silence I grieve,
That thy heart could forget,
  Thy spirit deceive.
If I should meet thee
  After long years,   30
How should I greet thee!—
  With silence and tears.

1815   1815

Stanzas for Music

There be none of Beauty's daughters
  With a magic like thee;
And like music on the waters
  Is thy sweet voice to me:
When, as if its sound were causing   5
The charmed ocean's pausing,
The waves lie still and gleaming,
And the lulled winds seem dreaming.

And the midnight moon is weaving
    Her bright chain o'er the deep;   10
Whose breast is gently heaving,
    As an infant's asleep.
So the spirit bows before thee,
To listen and adore thee;
With a full but soft emotion,   15
Like the swell of Summer's ocean.

1816   1816

Darkness[1]

I had a dream, which was not all a dream.
The bright sun was extinguish'd, and the stars
Did wander darkling[2] in the eternal space,
Rayless, and pathless, and the icy earth
Swung blind and blackening in the moonless air;   5
Morn came, and went—and came, and brought no day,
And men forgot their passions in the dread
Of this their desolation; and all hearts
Were chill'd into a selfish prayer for light:
And they did live by watchfires—and the thrones,   10
The palaces of crowned kings—the huts,
The habitations of all things which dwell,
Were burnt for beacons; cities were consumed,
And men were gathered round their blazing homes
To look once more into each other's face;   15
Happy were those who dwelt within the eye
Of the volcanos, and their mountain-torch:
A fearful hope was all the world contain'd;
Forests were set on fire—but hour by hour
They fell and faded—and the crackling trunks   20
Extinguish'd with a crash—and all was black.
The brows of men by the despairing light
Wore an unearthly aspect, as by fits
The flashes fell upon them; some lay down
And hid their eyes and wept; and some did rest   25
Their chins upon their clenched hands, and smiled;
And others hurried to and fro, and fed
Their funeral piles with fuel, and looked up
With mad disquietude on the dull sky,
The pall of a past world; and then again   30
With curses cast them down upon the dust,
And gnash'd their teeth and howl'd: the wild birds shriek'd,
And, terrified, did flutter on the ground,
And flap their useless wings; the wildest brutes
Came tame and tremulous; and vipers crawl'd   35

1. A powerfully imagined blank-verse description of the end of life on earth—a speculation hardly less com- mon in Byron's time than in ours.
2. In the dark.

And twined themselves among the multitude,
Hissing, but stingless—they were slain for food:
And War, which for a moment was no more,
Did glut himself again;—a meal was bought
With blood, and each sate sullenly apart   40
Gorging himself in gloom: no love was left;
All earth was but one thought—and that was death,
Immediate and inglorious; and the pang
Of famine fed upon all entrails—men
Died, and their bones were tombless as their flesh;   45
The meagre by the meagre were devoured,
Even dogs assail'd their masters, all save one,
And he was faithful to a corse, and kept
The birds and beasts and famish'd men at bay,
Till hunger clung³ them, or the dropping dead   50
Lured their lank jaws; himself sought out no food,
But with a piteous and perpetual moan,
And a quick desolate cry, licking the hand
Which answered not with a caress—he died.
The crowd was famish'd by degrees; but two   55
Of an enormous city did survive,
And they were enemies; they met beside
The dying embers of an altar-place,
Where had been heap'd a mass of holy things
For an unholy usage; they raked up,   60
And shivering scraped with their cold skeleton hands
The feeble ashes, and their feeble breath
Blew for a little life, and made a flame
Which was a mockery; then they lifted up
Their eyes as it grew lighter, and beheld   65
Each other's aspects—saw, and shriek'd, and died—
Even of their mutual hideousness they died,
Unknowing who he was upon whose brow
Famine had written Fiend. The world was void,
The populous and the powerful—was a lump,   70
Seasonless, herbless, treeless, manless, lifeless—
A lump of death—a chaos of hard clay.
The rivers, lakes, and ocean all stood still,
And nothing stirred within their silent depths;
Ships sailorless lay rotting on the sea,   75
And their masts fell down piecemeal; as they dropp'd
They slept on the abyss without a surge—
The waves were dead; the tides were in their grave,
The moon their mistress had expired before;
The winds were withered in the stagnant air,   80
And the clouds perish'd; Darkness had no need
Of aid from them—She was the universe.

1816   1816

3. Withered.

So, we'll go no more a roving[1]

1

So, we'll go no more a roving
    So late into the night,
Though the heart be still as loving,
    And the moon be still as bright.

2

For the sword outwears its sheath,   5
    And the soul wears out the breast,
And the heart must pause to breathe,
    And love itself have rest.

3

Though the night was made for loving,
    And the day returns too soon,   10
Yet we'll go no more a roving
    By the light of the moon.

1817   1830

When a man hath no freedom to fight for at home[1]

When a man hath no freedom to fight for at home,
    Let him combat for that of his neighbors;
Let him think of the glories of Greece and of Rome,
    And get knock'd on the head for his labours.

To do good to mankind is the chivalrous plan,   5
    And is always as nobly requited;
Then battle for freedom wherever you can,
    And, if not shot or hang'd, you'll get knighted.

Nov. 5, 1820   1830

Childe Harold's Pilgrimage   *Childe Harold* is a travelogue, narrated by a melancholy, passionate, well-read, and very eloquent tourist. Byron wrote most of the first two cantos while on the tour through Spain, Portugal, Albania, and Greece that these cantos describe; when he published them, in 1812, they made him at one stroke the best known and most talked about English poet. Byron took up *Childe Harold* again in 1816, during the European tour he made after the breakup of his marriage. Canto 3, published in 1816, moves through Belgium, up the Rhine, then to Switzerland and the Alps. Canto 4, published in 1818, describes the great cities and monuments of Italy.

    Byron chose for his poem the Spenserian stanza, and like James Thomson (in the *Castle of Indolence*) and other eighteenth-century predecessors, he attempted in the first canto to imitate, in a seriocomic fashion, the archaic language of his

---

1. Composed in the Lenten aftermath of a spell of feverish dissipation in the Carnival season in Venice, and included in a letter to Thomas Moore, Feb. 28, 1817. Byron wrote, "I find 'the sword wearing out the scabbard,' though I have but just turned the corner of twenty-nine." The poem is based on the refrain of a Scottish song, *The Jolly Beggar:* "And we'll gang nae mair a roving / Sae late into the nicht."

1. The ironist's attitude toward gratuitous enlistment in a foreign war for national freedom—a cause to which Byron gave his own life less than four years later.

Elizabethan model. (The word *Childe* itself is the ancient term for a young noble awaiting knighthood.) But he soon dropped the archaisms, and in the last two cantos he adapts Spenser's mellifluous stanza to his own assured and brassy magniloquence.

In the preface to his first two cantos, Byron had insisted that the narrator, Childe Harold, was "a fictitious character," merely "the child of imagination." But in the manuscript version of these cantos, he had himself called his hero "Childe Burun," the early form of his own family name. The world insisted on identifying the character as well as the travels of the protagonist with those of the author, and in the fourth canto Byron, abandoning the third-person *dramatis persona*, spoke out frankly in the first person.

In its shock tactics of apostrophes, imperatives, exclamations, hyperbole, and abrupt changes in subject, pace, and mood, the style of *Childe Harold* is without close parallel in English; to it Goethe applied the terms *Keckheit, Kühnheit, und Grandiosität:* "daring, dash, and grandiosity." It is no small feat in the author to have converted a meticulously accurate tourist's record of scenes, memorials, and museums into a dramatic and passionate experience. The result is like seeing Europe by flashes of lightning, for everything is presented not as it is in itself but as it affects the violent sensibility of that new cultural phenomenon, the Romantic Man of Feeling.

From CHILDE HAROLD'S PILGRIMAGE

A ROMAUNT[1]

From Canto 1

["Sin's Long Labyrinth"]

1

Oh, thou! in Hellas deem'd of heav'nly birth,
Muse! form'd or fabled at the minstrel's will!
Since sham'd full oft by later lyres on earth,
Mine dares not call thee from thy sacred hill:
Yet there I've wander'd by thy vaunted rill;   5
Yes! sigh'd o'er Delphi's long-deserted shrine,
Where, save that feeble fountain, all is still;
Nor mote my shell awake the weary Nine[2]
To grace so plain a tale—this lowly lay of mine.

2

Whilome[3] in Albion's isle there dwelt a youth,   10
Who ne in virtue's ways did take delight;
But spent his days in riot most uncouth,
And vex'd with mirth the drowsy ear of Night.
Ah, me! in sooth he was a shameless wight,
Sore given to revel and ungodly glee;   15
Few earthly things found favour in his sight
Save concubines and carnal companie,
And flaunting wassailers[4] of high and low degree.

---

1. A romance, or narrative of adventure.
2. The Muses, whose "vaunted rill" (line 5) was the Castalian spring. "Mote": may. "Shell": lyre (Hermes is fabled to have invented the lyre by stretching strings over the hollow of a tortoise shell).
3. Once upon a time.
4. Noisy, insolent drinkers (Byron is thought to refer to his own youthful carousing with friends at Newstead Abbey).

3

Childe Harold was he hight:—but whence his name
And lineage long, it suits me not to say;   20
Suffice it, that perchance they were of fame,
And had been glorious in another day:
But one sad losel[5] soils a name for aye,
However mighty in the olden time;
Nor all that heralds rake from coffin'd clay,   25
Nor florid prose, nor honied lies of rhyme
Can blazon evil deeds, or consecrate a crime.

4

Childe Harold bask'd him in the noon-tide sun,
Disporting there like any other fly;
Nor deem'd before his little day was done   30
One blast might chill him into misery.
But long ere scarce a third of his pass'd by,
Worse than adversity the Childe befell;
He felt the fulness of satiety:
Then loath'd he in his native land to dwell,   35
Which seem'd to him more lone than Eremite's[6] sad cell.

5

For he through Sin's long labyrinth had run,
Nor made atonement when he did amiss,
Had sigh'd to many though he lov'd but one,
And that lov'd one, alas! could ne'er be his.   40
Ah, happy she! to 'scape from him whose kiss
Had been pollution unto aught so chaste;
Who soon had left her charms for vulgar bliss,
And spoil'd her goodly lands to gild his waste,
Nor calm domestic peace had ever deign'd to taste.   45

6

And now Childe Harold was sore sick at heart,
And from his fellow bacchanals would flee;
'Tis said, at times the sullen tear would start,
But Pride congeal'd the drop within his ee:[7]
Apart he stalk'd in joyless reverie,   50
And from his native land resolv'd to go,
And visit scorching climes beyond the sea;
With pleasure drugg'd he almost long'd for woe,
And e'en for change of scene would seek the shades below.

From Canto 3

["*Once More Upon the Waters*"]

1

Is thy face like thy mother's, my fair child!
Ada![1] sole daughter of my house and heart?

---

5. Rascal. Byron's great-uncle, the fifth Lord Byron,
had killed a kinsman in a drunken duel.
6. A religious hermit.
7. Eye.

1. Byron's daughter Augusta Ada, born in Dec. 1816,
a month before her parents separated. Byron's "hope"
(line 5) had been for a reconciliation, but he was never
to see Ada again.

When last I saw thy young blue eyes they smiled,
And then we parted,—not as now we part,
But with a hope.—
                Awaking with a start,   5
The waters heave around me; and on high
The winds lift up their voices: I depart,
Whither I know not; but the hour's gone by,
When Albion's[2] lessening shores could grieve or glad mine eye.

2

Once more upon the waters! yet once more!   10
And the waves bound beneath me as a steed
That knows his rider. Welcome, to their roar!
Swift be their guidance, wheresoe'er it lead!
Though the strain'd mast should quiver as a reed,
And the rent canvas fluttering strew the gale,   15
Still must I on; for I am as a weed,
Flung from the rock, on Ocean's foam, to sail
Where'er the surge may sweep, the tempest's breath prevail.

3

In my youth's summer[3] I did sing of One,
The wandering outlaw of his own dark mind;   20
Again I seize the theme then but begun,
And bear it with me, as the rushing wind
Bears the cloud onwards: in that Tale I find
The furrows of long thought, and dried-up tears,
Which, ebbing, leave a sterile track behind,   25
O'er which all heavily the journeying years
Plod the last sands of life,—where not a flower appears.

4

Since my young days of passion—joy, or pain,
Perchance my heart and harp have lost a string,
And both may jar:[4] it may be, that in vain   30
I would essay as I have sung to sing.
Yet, though a dreary strain, to this I cling;
So that it wean me from the weary dream
Of selfish grief or gladness—so it fling
Forgetfulness around me—it shall seem   35
To me, though to none else, a not ungrateful theme.

5

He, who grown aged in this world of woe,
In deeds, not years, piercing the depths of life,
So that no wonder waits him; nor below
Can love, or sorrow, fame, ambition, strife,   40
Cut to his heart again with the keen knife
Of silent, sharp endurance: he can tell
Why thought seeks refuge in lone caves, yet rife
With airy images, and shapes which dwell
Still unimpair'd, though old, in the soul's haunted cell.   45

2. England's.
3. Byron wrote canto 1 at age twenty-one; he is now   twenty-eight.
                                             4. Sound discordant.

6

'Tis to create, and in creating live
A being more intense, that we endow
With form our fancy, gaining as we give
The life we image, even as I do now.
What am I? Nothing; but not so art thou,   50
Soul of my thought![5] with whom I traverse earth,
Invisible but gazing, as I glow
Mix'd with thy spirit, blended with thy birth,
And feeling still with thee in my crush'd feelings' dearth.

7

Yet must I think less wildly:—I *have* thought   55
Too long and darkly, till my brain became,
In its own eddy boiling and o'erwrought,
A whirling gulf of phantasy and flame:
And thus, untaught in youth my heart to tame,
My springs of life were poison'd. 'Tis too late!   60
Yet am I chang'd; though still enough the same
In strength to bear what time can not abate,
And feed on bitter fruits without accusing Fate.

8

Something too much of this:—but now 'tis past,
And the spell closes with its silent seal.[6]   65
Long absent HAROLD re-appears at last;
He of the breast which fain no more would feel,
Wrung with the wounds which kill not, but ne'er heal;
Yet Time, who changes all, had alter'd him
In soul and aspect as in age: years steal   70
Fire from the mind as vigour from the limb;
And life's enchanted cup but sparkles near the brim.

9

His had been quaff'd too quickly, and he found
The dregs were wormwood; but he fill'd again,
And from a purer fount, on holier ground,   75
And deem'd its spring perpetual; but in vain!
Still round him clung invisibly a chain
Which gall'd for ever, fettering though unseen,
And heavy though it clank'd not; worn with pain,
Which pined although it spoke not, and grew keen,   80
Entering with every step, he took, through many a scene.

10

Secure in guarded coldness, he had mix'd
Again in fancied safety with his kind,
And deem'd his spirit now so firmly fix'd
And sheath'd with an invulnerable mind,   85
That, if no joy, no sorrow lurk'd behind;
And he, as one, might midst the many stand
Unheeded, searching through the crowd to find
Fit speculation! such as in strange land
He found in wonder-works of God and Nature's hand.   90

5. I.e., Childe Harold, his literary creation.   ("spell").
6. I.e., he sets the seal of silence on his personal tale

11

But who can view the ripened rose, nor seek
To wear it? who can curiously behold
The smoothness and the sheen of beauty's cheek,
Nor feel the heart can never all grow old?
Who can contemplate Fame through clouds unfold   95
The star which rises o'er her steep, nor climb?
Harold, once more within the vortex, roll'd
On with the giddy circle, chasing Time,
Yet with a nobler aim than in his youth's fond[7] prime.

12

But soon he knew himself the most unfit   100
Of men to herd with Man; with whom he held
Little in common; untaught to submit
His thoughts to others, though his soul was quell'd
In youth by his own thoughts; still uncompell'd,
He would not yield dominion of his mind   105
To spirits against whom his own rebell'd;
Proud though in desolation; which could find
A life within itself, to breathe without mankind.

13

Where rose the mountains, there to him were friends;
Where roll'd the ocean, thereon was his home;   110
Where a blue sky, and glowing clime, extends,
He had the passion and the power to roam;
The desert, forest, cavern, breaker's foam,
Were unto him companionship; they spake
A mutual language, clearer than the tome   115
Of his land's tongue, which he would oft forsake
For Nature's pages glass'd[8] by sunbeams on the lake.

14

Like the Chaldean,[9] he could watch the stars,
Till he had peopled them with beings bright
As their own beams; and earth, and earth-born jars,   120
And human frailties, were forgotten quite:
Could he have kept his spirit to that flight
He had been happy; but this clay will sink
Its spark immortal, envying it the light
To which it mounts, as if to break the link   125
That keeps us from yon heaven which woos us to its brink.

15

But in Man's dwellings he became a thing
Restless and worn, and stern and wearisome,
Droop'd as a wild-born falcon with clipt wing,
To whom the boundless air alone were home: 130
Then came his fit again, which to o'ercome,
As eagerly the barr'd-up bird will beat
His breast and beak against his wiry dome
Till the blood tinge his plumage, so the heat
Of his impeded soul would through his bosom eat.   135

7. Foolish.
8. Made glassy.

9. A people of ancient Babylonia, expert in astronomy.

16

Self-exiled Harold wanders forth again,
With nought of hope left, but with less of gloom;
The very knowledge that he lived in vain,
That all was over on this side the tomb,
Had made Despair a smilingness assume,   140
Which, though 'twere wild,—as on the plundered wreck
When mariners would madly meet their doom
With draughts intemperate on the sinking deck,—
Did yet inspire a cheer, which he forbore to check.

[Waterloo]

17

Stop!—for thy tread is on an Empire's dust!   145
An Earthquake's spoil is sepulchered below!
Is the spot mark'd with no colossal bust?
Nor column trophied for triumphal show?
None; but the moral's truth tells simpler so,
As the ground was before, thus let it be;—   150
How that red rain hath made the harvest grow!
And is this all the world has gained by thee,
Thou first and last of fields! king-making Victory?

18

And Harold stands upon this place of skulls,
The grave of France, the deadly Waterloo![1]   155
How in an hour the power which gave annuls
Its gifts, transferring fame as fleeting too!
In "pride of place" here last the eagle flew,[2]
Then tore with bloody talon the rent plain,
Pierced by the shaft of banded nations through;   160
Ambition's life and labours all were vain;
He wears the shattered links of the world's broken chain.[3]

19

Fit retribution! Gaul[4] may champ the bit
And foam in fetters;—but is Earth more free?
Did nations combat to make One submit;   165
Or league to teach all kings true sovereignty?
What! shall reviving Thraldom again be
The patched-up idol of enlightened days?
Shall we, who struck the Lion down, shall we
Pay the Wolf homage? proffering lowly gaze   170
And servile knees to thrones? No; prove[5] before ye praise!

20

If not, o'er one fallen despot boast no more!
In vain fair cheeks were furrowed with hot tears
For Europe's flowers long rooted up before

1. Napoleon's defeat at Waterloo, near Brussels, had occurred only the year before, on June 18, 1815.
2. The eagle was the standard of Napoleon. "Pride of place" is a term from falconry meaning the highest point of flight (cf. *Macbeth* 2.4.12).
3. Napoleon was then a prisoner at St. Helena.

4. France. Byron, like Shelley and other liberals, saw the defeat of the Napoleonic tyranny as also a victory for tyrannous kings and the forces of extreme reaction throughout Europe.
5. Await the test (proof) of experience.

The trampler of her vineyards; in vain years   175
Of death, depopulation, bondage, fears,
Have all been borne, and broken by the accord
Of roused-up millions: all that most endears
Glory, is when the myrtle wreathes a sword
Such as Harmodius drew on Athens' tyrant lord.[6]   180

                              21
There was a sound of revelry by night,
And Belgium's capital had gathered then
Her Beauty and her Chivalry, and bright
The lamps shone o'er fair women and brave men;[7]
A thousand hearts beat happily; and when   185
Music arose with its voluptuous swell,
Soft eyes look'd love to eyes which spake again,
And all went merry as a marriage-bell;
But hush! hark! a deep sound strikes like a rising knell!

                              22
Did ye not hear it?—No; 'twas but the wind,   190
Or the car rattling o'er the stony street;
On with the dance! let joy be unconfined;
No sleep till morn, when Youth and Pleasure meet
To chase the glowing Hours with flying feet—
But, hark!—that heavy sound breaks in once more,   195
As if the clouds its echo would repeat;
And nearer, clearer, deadlier than before!
Arm! Arm! and out—it is—the cannon's opening roar!

                              23
Within a windowed niche of that high hall
Sate Brunswick's fated chieftain;[8] he did hear   200
That sound the first amidst the festival,
And caught its tone with Death's prophetic ear;
And when they smiled because he deem'd it near,
His heart more truly knew that peal too well
Which stretch'd his father on a bloody bier,   205
And roused the vengeance blood alone could quell:
He rush'd into the field, and, foremost fighting, fell.

                              24
Ah! then and there was hurrying to and fro,
And gathering tears, and tremblings of distress,
And cheeks all pale, which but an hour ago   210
Blush'd at the praise of their own loveliness;
And there were sudden partings, such as press
The life from out young hearts, and choking sighs
Which ne'er might be repeated; who could guess
If ever more should meet those mutual eyes,   215
Since upon nights so sweet such awful morn could rise?

---

6. In 514 B.C. Harmodius and Aristogeiton, hiding
their daggers in myrtle (symbol of love), killed Hippar-
chus, tyrant of Athens.
7. A famous ball, given by the duchess of Richmond
on the eve of the battle of Quatre Bras, which opened
the conflict at Waterloo.

8. The duke of Brunswick, nephew of George III of
England, was killed in the battle of Quatre Bras, just
as his father, commanding the Prussian army against
Napoleon, had been killed at Auerstedt in 1806 (line
205).

25

And there was mounting in hot haste: the steed,
The mustering squadron, and the clattering car,
Went pouring forward in impetuous speed,
And swiftly forming in the ranks of war;   220
And the deep thunder peal on peal afar;
And near, the beat of the alarming drum
Roused up the soldier ere the morning star;
While throng'd the citizens with terror dumb,
Or whispering, with white lips—"The foe! They come! they come!"   225

26

And wild and high the "Cameron's gathering" rose!
The war-note of Lochiel, which Albyn's[9] hills
Have heard, and heard, too, have her Saxon foes:—
How in the noon of night that pibroch[1] thrills,
Savage and shrill! But with the breath which fills   230
Their mountain-pipe, so fill the mountaineers
With the fierce native daring which instils
The stirring memory of a thousand years,
And Evan's, Donald's fame[2] rings in each clansman's ears!

27

And Ardennes[3] waves above them her green leaves,   235
Dewy with nature's tear-drops, as they pass,
Grieving, if aught inanimate e'er grieves,
Over the unreturning brave,—alas!
Ere evening to be trodden like the grass
Which now beneath them, but above shall grow   240
In its next verdure, when this fiery mass
Of living valour, rolling on the foe
And burning with high hope, shall moulder cold and low.

28

Last noon beheld them full of lusty life,
Last eve in Beauty's circle proudly gay,   245
The midnight brought the signal-sound of strife,
The morn the marshalling in arms,—the day
Battle's magnificently-stern array!
The thunder-clouds close o'er it, which when rent
The earth is covered thick with other clay,   250
Which her own clay shall cover, heaped and pent,
Rider and horse,—friend, foe,—in one red burial blent!

*   *   *

[Napoleon]

36

There sunk the greatest, nor the worst of men,[4]
Whose spirit antithetically mixt
One moment of the mightiest, and again

---

9. Scotland's. "Cameron's gathering": the clan song of the Camerons, whose chief was called "Lochiel," after his estate.
1. Bagpipe music, usually warlike in character.
2. Sir Evan and Donald Cameron, famous warriors in the Stuart cause in the 17th and 18th centuries.
3. A forested region covering parts of Belgium, France, and Luxembourg.
4. Napoleon, here portrayed with many of the characteristics of the Byronic hero.

On little objects with like firmness fixt,
Extreme in all things! hadst thou been betwixt,   320
Thy throne had still been thine, or never been;
For daring made thy rise as fall: thou seek'st
Even now to re-assume the imperial mien,
And shake again the world, the Thunderer of the scene!
                              37
Conqueror and captive of the earth art thou!   325
She trembles at thee still, and thy wild name
Was ne'er more bruited in men's minds than now
That thou art nothing, save the jest of Fame,
Who wooed thee once, thy vassal, and became
The flatterer of thy fierceness, till thou wert   330
A god unto thyself; nor less the same
To the astounded kingdoms all inert,
Who deem'd thee for a time whate'er thou didst assert.
                              38
Oh, more or less than man—in high or low,
Battling with nations, flying from the field;   335
Now making monarchs' necks thy footstool, now
More than thy meanest soldier taught to yield;
An empire thou couldst crush, command, rebuild,
But govern not thy pettiest passion, nor,
However deeply in men's spirits skill'd,   340
Look through thine own, nor curb the lust of war,
Nor learn that tempted Fate will leave the loftiest star.
                              39
Yet well thy soul hath brook'd the turning tide
With that untaught innate philosophy,
Which, be it wisdom, coldness, or deep pride,   345
Is gall and wormwood to an enemy.
When the whole host of hatred stood hard by,
To watch and mock thee shrinking, thou hast smiled
With a sedate and all-enduring eye;—
When Fortune fled her spoil'd and favourite child,   350
He stood unbowed beneath the ills upon him piled.
                              40
Sager than in thy fortunes; for in them
Ambition steel'd thee on too far to show
That just habitual scorn which could contemn
Men and their thoughts; 'twas wise to feel, not so   355
To wear it ever on thy lip and brow,
And spurn the instruments thou wert to use
Till they were turn'd unto thine overthrow:
'Tis but a worthless world to win or lose;
So hath it proved to thee, and all such lot[5] who choose.   360
                              41
If, like a tower upon a headlong rock,
Thou hadst been made to stand or fall alone,
Such scorn of man had help'd to brave the shock;

---

5. An inversion: "all who choose such lot" (i.e., who choose to play such a game of chance).

But men's thoughts were the steps which paved thy throne,
  Their admiration thy best weapon shone; 365
The part of Philip's son[6] was thine, not then
(Unless aside thy purple had been thrown)
Like stern Diogenes[7] to mock at men;
For sceptred cynics earth were far too wide a den.

42

But quiet to quick bosoms is a hell,
And *there* hath been thy bane; there is a fire 370
And motion of the soul which will not dwell
In its own narrow being, but aspire
Beyond the fitting medium of desire;
And, but once kindled, quenchless evermore, 375
Preys upon high adventure, nor can tire
Of aught but rest; a fever at the core,
Fatal to him who bears, to all who ever bore.

43

This makes the madmen who have made men mad
By their contagion; Conquerors and Kings, 380
Founders of sects and systems, to whom add
Sophists, Bards, Statesmen, all unquiet things
Which stir too strongly the soul's secret springs,
And are themselves the fools to those they fool;
Envied, yet how unenviable! what stings 385
Are theirs! One breast laid open were a school
Which would unteach mankind the lust to shine or rule:

44

Their breath is agitation, and their life
A storm whereon they ride, to sink at last,
And yet so nurs'd and bigotted to strife, 390
That should their days, surviving perils past,
Melt to calm twilight, they feel overcast
With sorrow and supineness, and so die;
Even as a flame unfed, which runs to waste
With its own flickering, or a sword laid by 395
Which eats into itself, and rusts ingloriously.

45

He who ascends to mountain-tops, shall find
The loftiest peaks most wrapt in clouds and snow;
He who surpasses or subdues mankind,
Must look down on the hate of those below. 400
Though high *above* the sun of glory glow,
And far *beneath* the earth and ocean spread,
Round him are icy rocks, and loudly blow
Contending tempests on his naked head,
And thus reward the toils which to those summits led.[8] 405

*   *   *

6. Alexander the Great, son of Philip of Macedon.
7. The Greek philosopher of Cynicism, contemporary
of Alexander. It is related that Alexander was so struck
by his independence of mind that he said, "If I were
not Alexander, I should wish to be Diogenes," hence
the allusion in lines 367 and 369.
8. In the stanzas here omitted, Harold is abruptly sent
sailing up the Rhine, meditating on the "thousand battles" that "have assailed thy banks."

52

Thus Harold inly said, and pass'd along,　　　　　　　　　460
Yet not insensibly to all which here
Awoke the jocund birds to early song
In glens which might have made even exile dear:
Though on his brow were graven lines austere,
And tranquil sternness which had ta'en the place　　　465
Of feelings fierier far but less severe,
Joy was not always absent from his face,
But o'er it in such scenes would steal with transient trace.

53

Nor was all love shut from him, though his days
Of passion had consumed themselves to dust.　　　　470
It is in vain that we would coldly gaze
On such as smile upon us; the heart must
Leap kindly back to kindness, though disgust
Hath wean'd it from all worldlings: thus he felt,
For there was soft remembrance, and sweet trust　　475
In one fond breast,[9] to which his own would melt,
And in its tenderer hour on that his bosom dwelt.

54

And he had learn'd to love,—I know not why,
For this in such as him seems strange of mood,—
The helpless looks of blooming infancy,　　　　　　480
Even in its earliest nurture; what subdued,
To change like this, a mind so far imbued
With scorn of man, it little boots to know;
But thus it was; and though in solitude
Small power the nipp'd affections have to grow,　　485
In him this glowed when all beside had ceased to glow.

55

And there was one soft breast, as hath been said,
Which unto his was bound by stronger ties
Than the church links withal; and, though unwed,
That love was pure, and, far above disguise,　　　490
Had stood the test of mortal enmities
Still undivided, and cemented more
By peril, dreaded most in female eyes;
But this was firm, and from a foreign shore
Well to that heart might his these absent greetings pour!　　495

*　*　*

[Switzerland]

68

Lake Leman[1] woos me with its crystal face,
The mirror where the stars and mountains view　　　645
The stillness of their aspect in each trace
Its clear depth yields of their far height and hue:
There is too much of man here, to look through

---

9. Commentators agree that the reference is to Byron's　　1. Lake Geneva, in Switzerland.
half-sister, Augusta Leigh.

With a fit mind the might which I behold;
But soon in me shall Loneliness renew   650
Thoughts hid, but not less cherish'd than of old,
Ere mingling with the herd had penn'd me in their fold.

69

To fly from, need not be to hate, mankind;
All are not fit with them to stir and toil,
Nor is it discontent to keep the mind   655
Deep in its fountain, lest it overboil
In the hot throng, where we become the spoil
Of our infection, till too late and long
We may deplore and struggle with the coil,[2]
In wretched interchange of wrong for wrong   660
'Midst a contentious world, striving where none are strong.

70

There, in a moment, we may plunge our years
In fatal penitence, and in the blight
Of our own soul, turn all our blood to tears,
And colour things to come with hues of Night;   665
The race of life becomes a hopeless flight
To those that walk in darkness: on the sea,
The boldest steer but where their ports invite,
But there are wanderers o'er Eternity
Whose bark drives on and on, and anchored ne'er shall be.   670

71

Is it not better, then, to be alone,
And love Earth only for its earthly sake?
By the blue rushing of the arrowy Rhone,
Or the pure bosom of its nursing lake,
Which feeds it as a mother who doth make   675
A fair but froward infant her own care,
Kissing its cries away as these awake;—
Is it not better thus our lives to wear,
Than join the crushing crowd, doom'd to inflict or bear?

72

I live not in myself, but I become   680
Portion of that around me; and to me,
High mountains are a feeling, but the hum
Of human cities torture: I can see
Nothing to loathe in nature, save to be
A link reluctant in a fleshly chain,   685
Class'd among creatures, when the soul can flee,
And with the sky, the peak, the heaving plain
Of ocean, or the stars, mingle, and not in vain.[3]

73

And thus I am absorb'd, and this is life:
I look upon the peopled desart past,   690
As on a place of agony and strife,

2. Tumult.
3. Byron had lived in close contact with Shelley at Geneva and had toured the lake with him. At that time,
he was introduced to concepts of nature in the poetry
of Wordsworth, whom Shelley had pressed on Byron's
attention; these ideas are reflected in canto 3, but the
voice is Byron's own. For his comment on being "half
mad" while writing canto 3, see his letter to Thomas
Moore, Jan. 28, 1817 (pp. 1659–62).

Where, for some sin, to Sorrow I was cast,
To act and suffer, but remount at last
With a fresh pinion; which I feel to spring,
Though young, yet waxing vigorous, as the blast   695
Which it would cope with, on delighted wing,
Spurning the clay-cold bonds which round our being cling.

                              74
And when, at length, the mind shall be all free
From what it hates in this degraded form,
Reft of its carnal life, save what shall be   700
Existent happier in the fly and worm,—
When elements to elements conform,
And dust is as it should be, shall I not
Feel all I see, less dazzling, but more warm?
The bodiless thought? the Spirit of each spot?   705
Of which, even now, I share at times the immortal lot?

                              75
Are not the mountains, waves, and skies, a part
Of me and of my soul, as I of them?
Is not the love of these deep in my heart
With a pure passion? should I not contemn   710
All objects, if compared with these? and stem
A tide of suffering, rather than forego
Such feelings for the hard and worldly phlegm
Of those whose eyes are only turn'd below,
Gazing upon the ground, with thoughts which dare not glow?   715

                              76
But this is not my theme; and I return
To that which is immediate, and require
Those who find contemplation in the urn,[4]
To look on One, whose dust was once all fire,
A native of the land where I respire   720
The clear air for a while—a passing guest,
Where he became a being,—whose desire
Was to be glorious; 'twas a foolish quest,
The which to gain and keep, he sacrificed all rest.[5]

                              77
Here the self-torturing sophist, wild Rousseau,   725
The apostle of affliction, he who threw
Enchantment over passion, and from woe
Wrung overwhelming eloquence, first drew
The breath which made him wretched; yet he knew
How to make madness beautiful, and cast   730
O'er erring deeds and thoughts, a heavenly hue
Of words, like sunbeams, dazzling as they past
The eyes, which o'er them shed tears feelingly and fast.

                              78
His love was passion's essence—as a tree
On fire by lightning; with ethereal flame   735

4. I.e., those who find matter for meditation in an urn
containing the ashes of the dead.
5. Jean-Jacques Rousseau, who had been born in Geneva in 1712. Byron's characterization is based on
Rousseau's novel *La Nouvelle Héloise*, as well as on his
Confessions.

Kindled he was, and blasted; for to be
Thus, and enamoured, were in him the same.
But his was not the love of living dame,
Nor of the dead who rise upon our dreams,
But of ideal beauty, which became   740
In him existence, and o'erflowing teems
Along his burning page, distempered though it seems.

                              *   *   *

                              85
Clear, placid Leman! thy contrasted lake,
With the wild world I dwelt in, is a thing
Which warns me, with its stillness, to forsake
Earth's troubled waters for a purer spring.   800
This quiet sail is as a noiseless wing
To waft me from distraction; once I loved
Torn ocean's roar, but thy soft murmuring
Sounds sweet as if a sister's voice reproved,
That I with stern delights should e'er have been so moved.   805
                              86
It is the hush of night, and all between
Thy margin and the mountains, dusk, yet clear,
Mellowed and mingling, yet distinctly seen,
Save darken'd Jura,⁶ whose capt heights appear
Precipitously steep; and drawing near,   810
There breathes a living fragrance from the shore,
Of flowers yet fresh with childhood; on the ear
Drops the light drip of the suspended oar,
Or chirps the grasshopper one good-night carol more;
                              87
He is an evening reveller, who makes   815
His life an infancy, and sings his fill;
At intervals, some bird from out the brakes,⁷
Starts into voice a moment, then is still.
There seems a floating whisper on the hill,
But that is fancy, for the starlight dews   820
All silently their tears of love instil,
Weeping themselves away, till they infuse
Deep into Nature's breast the spirit of her hues.
                              88
Ye stars! which are the poetry of heaven!
If in your bright leaves we would read the fate   825
Of men and empires, — 'tis to be forgiven,
That in our aspirations to be great,
Our destinies o'erleap their mortal state,
And claim a kindred with you; for ye are
A beauty and a mystery, and create   830
In us such love and reverence from afar,
That fortune, fame, power, life, have named themselves a star.

6. The mountain range between Switzerland and   7. Thickets.
France, visible from Lake Geneva.

89

All heaven and earth are still—though not in sleep,
But breathless, as we grow when feeling most;
And silent, as we stand in thoughts too deep:—   835
All heaven and earth are still: From the high host
Of stars, to the lull'd lake and mountain-coast,
All is concentered in a life intense,
Where not a beam, nor air, nor leaf is lost,
But hath a part of being, and a sense   840
Of that which is of all Creator and defence.

90

Then stirs the feeling infinite, so felt
In solitude, where we are *least* alone;
A truth, which through our being then doth melt
And purifies from self: it is a tone,   845
The soul and source of music, which makes known
Eternal harmony, and sheds a charm,
Like to the fabled Cytherea's zone,[8]
Binding all things with beauty;—'twould disarm
The spectre Death, had he substantial power to harm.   850

91

Not vainly did the early Persian make
His altar the high places and the peak
Of earth-o'ergazing mountains, and thus take
A fit and unwall'd temple, there to seek
The Spirit, in whose honour shrines are weak,   855
Uprear'd of human hands. Come, and compare
Columns and idol-dwellings, Goth or Greek,
With Nature's realms of worship, earth and air,
Nor fix on fond abodes to circumscribe thy prayer!

92

The sky is changed!—and such a change! Oh night,   860
And storm, and darkness, ye are wondrous strong,
Yet lovely in your strength, as is the light
Of a dark eye in woman! Far along,
From peak to peak, the rattling crags among
Leaps the live thunder! Not from one lone cloud,   865
But every mountain now hath found a tongue,
And Jura answers, through her misty shroud,
Back to the joyous Alps, who call to her aloud!

93

And this is in the night:—Most glorious night!
Thou wert not sent for slumber! let me be   870
A sharer in thy fierce and far delight,—
A portion of the tempest and of thee!
How the lit lake shines, a phosphoric sea,
And the big rain comes dancing to the earth!
And now again 'tis black,—and now, the glee   875
Of the loud hills shakes with its mountain-mirth,
As if they did rejoice o'er a young earthquake's birth.

---

8. The sash of Venus, which conferred the power to attract love.

94

Now, where the swift Rhone cleaves his way between
Heights which appear as lovers who have parted
In hate, whose mining depths so intervene,   880
That they can meet no more, though broken-hearted;
Though in their souls, which thus each other thwarted,
Love was the very root of the fond rage
Which blighted their life's bloom, and then departed:—
Itself expired, but leaving them an age   885
Of years all winters,—war within themselves to wage.

95

Now, where the quick Rhone thus hath cleft his way,
The mightiest of the storms hath ta'en his stand:
For here, not one, but many, make their play,
And fling their thunder-bolts from hand to hand,   890
Flashing and cast around: of all the band,
The brightest through these parted hills hath fork'd
His lightnings,—as if he did understand,
That in such gaps as desolation work'd,
There the hot shaft should blast whatever therein lurk'd.   895

96

Sky, mountains, river, winds, lake, lightnings! ye!
With night, and clouds, and thunder, and a soul
To make these felt and feeling, well may be
Things that have made me watchful; the far roll
Of your departing voices, is the knoll[9]   900
Of what in me is sleepless,—if I rest.
But where of ye, oh tempests! is the goal?
Are ye like those within the human breast?
Or do ye find, at length, like eagles, some high nest?

97

Could I embody and unbosom now   905
That which is most within me,—could I wreak
My thoughts upon expression, and thus throw
Soul, heart, mind, passions, feelings, strong or weak,
All that I would have sought, and all I seek,
Bear, know, feel, and yet breathe—into *one* word,   910
And that one word were Lightning, I would speak;
But as it is, I live and die unheard,
With a most voiceless thought, sheathing it as a sword.

98

The morn is up again, the dewy morn,
With breath all incense, and with cheek all bloom,   915
Laughing the clouds away with playful scorn,
And living as if earth contain'd no tomb,—
And glowing into day: we may resume
The march of our existence: and thus I,
Still on thy shores, fair Leman! may find room   920
And food for meditation, nor pass by
Much, that may give us pause, if pondered fittingly.

9. Knell (old form).

*   *   *

113

I have not loved the world, nor the world me;[1]
I have not flattered its rank breath, nor bow'd   1050
To its idolatries a patient knee,—
Nor coin'd my cheek to smiles,—nor cried aloud
In worship of an echo; in the crowd
They could not deem me one of such; I stood
Among them, but not of them; in a shroud   1055
Of thoughts which were not their thoughts, and still could,
Had I not filed[2] my mind, which thus itself subdued.

114

I have not loved the world, nor the world me,—
But let us part fair foes; I do believe,
Though I have found them not, that there may be   1060
Words which are things,—hopes which will not deceive,
And virtues which are merciful, nor weave
Snares for the failing: I would also deem
O'er others' griefs that some sincerely grieve;
That two, or one, are almost what they seem,—   1065
That goodness is no name, and happiness no dream.

115

My daughter! with thy name this song begun—
My daughter! with thy name thus much shall end—
I see thee not,—I hear thee not,—but none
Can be so wrapt in thee; thou art the friend   1070
To whom the shadows of far years extend:
Albeit my brow thou never should'st behold,
My voice shall with thy future visions blend,
And reach into thy heart,—when mine is cold,—
A token and a tone, even from thy father's mould.   1075

116

To aid thy mind's development,—to watch
Thy dawn of little joys,—to sit and see
Almost thy very growth,—to view thee catch
Knowledge of objects,—wonders yet to thee!
To hold thee lightly on a gentle knee,   1080
And print on thy soft cheek a parent's kiss,—
This, it should seem, was not reserv'd for me;
Yet this was in my nature:—as it is,
I know not what is there, yet something like to this.

117

Yet, though dull Hate as duty should be taught,   1085
I know that thou wilt love me; though my name
Should be shut from thee, as a spell still fraught
With desolation,—and a broken claim:
Though the grave closed between us,—'twere the same,
I know that thou wilt love me; though to drain   1090
My blood from out thy being, were an aim,

---

1. Harold utters this soliloquy as he stands at the summit of an Alpine pass, looking southward on Italy.

2. Defiled. In a note Byron refers to *Macbeth* 3.1.64 ("For Banquo's issue have I filed my mind").

And an attainment,—all would be in vain,—
Still thou would'st love me, still that more than life retain.
118
The child of love,—though born in bitterness,
And nurtured in convulsion,—of thy sire 1095
These were the elements,—and thine no less.
As yet such are around thee,—but thy fire
Shall be more tempered, and thy hope far higher.
Sweet be thy cradled slumbers! O'er the sea,
And from the mountains where I now respire, 1100
Fain would I waft such blessing upon thee,
As, with a sigh, I deem thou might'st have been to me!

The Vision of Judgment[1]

By Quevedo Redivivus[2]

SUGGESTED BY THE COMPOSITION SO ENTITLED BY THE AUTHOR OF
Wat Tyler

"A Daniel come to judgment! yea, a Daniel!
I thank thee, Jew, for teaching me that word."[3]

1
Saint Peter sat by the celestial gate,
    His keys were rusty, and the lock was dull,
So little trouble had been given of late;
    Not that the place by any means was full,
But since the Gallic era "eighty-eight,"[4] 5
    The devils had ta'en a longer, stronger pull,
And "a pull altogether," as they say
At sea—which drew most souls another way.

2
The angels all were singing out of tune,
    And hoarse with having little else to do, 10

1. Although originally an ardent supporter of the French Revolution, Robert Southey early became a Tory and in 1813 was appointed poet laureate. Four years after the appointment he was dismayed by the unauthorized publication of his radical poetical drama Wat Tyler, which he had written in 1794 but had prudently left in manuscript. Byron reminds him of it in the subtitle. When King George III died in 1820—Shelley in his sonnet England in 1819 had called him, accurately enough, "an old, mad, blind, despised, and dying king"—Southey did his official duty by writing A Vision of Judgment (1821). In this fulsome eulogy George III goes to heaven, confounds such detractors as John Wilkes and Junius, and obtains a testimonial of noble character from his old enemy George Washington. The vision ends with the king, beatified, ceremoniously admitted to heaven.

Byron, responding to reports that Southey was vilifying him, had ridiculed the poet in his "Dedication" to canto 1 of Don Juan. In the Preface to his Vision of Judgment, Southey then exhibited his bad judgment by denouncing Byron as head of the "Satanic School"

of poetry, combining "lascivious" passages with "a satanic spirit of pride and audacious impiety." Byron immediately responded with The Vision of Judgment, in which he purports to tell the true story of how, with the unwitting help of Southey, King George had really managed to get into heaven. The poem is in the genre of the satiric attack on literary "dunces" by Dryden and Pope but is written in the ottava rima stanza and the easy colloquial manner of Don Juan. In its quick, sure characterization, the pace and economy of its narrative, its inventiveness in detail, and above all the high spirits and unfailing good humor with which the author demolishes his opponent, this poem represents Byron the satirist at his masterful best.
2. "Quevedo Revived." Quevedo was a 17th-century Spanish author of Sueños, "Visions," written in prose and predominantly satirical in tone.
3. Quoted, not quite accurately, from The Merchant of Venice, 4.1.340–41.
4. The last year of the old regime in France, before the outbreak of the revolution in 1789.

Excepting to wind up the sun and moon,
   Or curb a runaway young star or two,
Or wild colt of a comet, which too soon
   Broke out of bounds o'er the ethereal blue,
Splitting some planet with its playful tail,   15
As boats are sometimes by a wanton whale.

3

The guardian seraphs had retired on high,
   Finding their charges past all care below;
Terrestrial business fill'd nought in the sky
   Save the recording angel's black bureau;   20
Who found, indeed, the facts to multiply
   With such rapidity of vice and woe,
That he had stripp'd off both his wings in quills,
And yet was in arrear of human ills.

4

His business so augmented of late years,   25
   That he was forced, against his will no doubt,
(Just like those cherubs, earthly ministers)
   For some resource to turn himself about,
And claim the help of his celestial peers,
   To aid him ere he should be quite worn out   30
By the increased demand for his remarks;
Six angels and twelve saints were named his clerks.

5

This was a handsome board—at least for heaven;
   And yet they had even then enough to do,
So many conquerors' cars were daily driven,   35
   So many kingdoms fitted up anew;
Each day too slew its thousands six or seven,
   Till at the crowning carnage, Waterloo,
They threw their pens down in divine disgust—
The page was so besmear'd with blood and dust.   40

6

This by the way; 'tis not mine to record
   What angels shrink from: even the very devil
On this occasion his own work abhorr'd,
   So surfeited with the infernal revel;
Though he himself had sharpen'd every sword,   45
   It almost quench'd his innate thirst of evil.
(Here Satan's sole good work deserves insertion—
'Tis, that he has both generals in reversion.)[5]

7

Let's skip a few short years of hollow peace,
   Which peopled earth no better, hell as wont,   50
And heaven none—they form the tyrant's lease
   With nothing but new names subscribed upon 't;
'Twill one day finish: meantime they increase,
   "With seven heads and ten horns," and all in front,

5. I.e., Satan has the legal right to the possession, after their deaths, of both Napoleon and Wellington, the commanding officers at the Battle of Waterloo.

Like Saint John's foretold beast;[6] but ours are born   55
Less formidable in the head than horn.
                              8
In the first year of freedom's second dawn[7]
    Died George the Third; although no tyrant, one
Who shielded tyrants, till each sense withdrawn
    Left him nor mental nor external sun: 60
A better farmer ne'er brush'd dew from lawn,
    A worse king never left a realm undone!
He died—but left his subjects still behind,
One half as mad—and t'other no less blind.
                              9
He died!—his death made no great stir on earth;   65
    His burial made some pomp; there was profusion
Of velvet, gilding, brass, and no great dearth
    Of aught but tears—save those shed by collusion;
For these things may be bought at their true worth:
    Of elegy there was the due infusion—   70
Bought also; and the torches, cloaks, and banners,
Heralds, and relics of old Gothic manners,
                              10
Form'd a sepulchral melo-drame. Of all
    The fools who flock'd to swell or see the show,
Who cared about the corpse? The funeral   75
    Made the attraction, and the black the woe.
There throbb'd not there a thought which pierced the pall;
    And when the gorgeous coffin was laid low,
It seem'd the mockery of hell to fold
The rottenness of eighty years in gold.   80
                              11
So mix his body with the dust! It might
    Return to what it *must* far sooner, were
The natural compound left alone to fight
    Its way back into earth, and fire, and air;
But the unnatural balsams[8] merely blight   85
    What nature made him at his birth, as bare
As the mere million's base unmummied clay—
Yet all his spices but prolong decay.
                              12
He's dead—and upper earth with him has done:
    He's buried; save the undertaker's bill,   90
Or lapidary scrawl,[9] the world is gone
    For him, unless he left a German will;
But where's the proctor who will ask his son?[1]
    In whom his qualities are reigning still,
Except that household virtue, most uncommon,   95
Of constancy to an unhandsome woman.

---

6. The Book of Revelation, purported to be by St.
John, describes such a beast (13.1).
7. The year 1820 was one of new revolutionary movements in Italy and other countries of Southern Europe.
8. Embalming fluids.
9. Inscription cut into a stone monument.

1. A King's Proctor is an official who intervenes in the
probate of a will when chicanery is suspected. Byron
alludes to the scandal that the will of George I, of the
German House of Hanover, had been hidden by his
son, George II, who was the grandfather of the late
George III.

13

"God save the king!" It is a large economy
   In God to save the like; but if he will
Be saving, all the better; for not one am I
   Of those who think damnation better still: 100
I hardly know too if not quite alone am I
   In this small hope of bettering future ill
By circumscribing, with some slight restriction,
The eternity of hell's hot jurisdiction.

14

I know this is unpopular; I know   105
   'Tis blasphemous; I know one may be damn'd
For hoping no one else may e'er be so;
   I know my catechism; I know we're cramm'd
With the best doctrines till we quite o'erflow;
   I know that all save England's church have shamm'd,   110
And that the other twice two hundred churches
And synagogues have made a *damn'd* bad purchase.

15

God help us all! God help me too! I am,
   God knows, as helpless as the devil can wish,
And not a whit more difficult to damn   115
   Than is to bring to land a late-hook'd fish,
Or to the butcher to purvey the lamb;
   Not that I'm fit for such a noble dish
As one day will be that immortal fry
Of almost every body born to die.   120

16

Saint Peter sat by the celestial gate,
   And nodded o'er his keys; when lo! there came
A wond'rous noise he had not heard of late—
   A rushing sound of wind, and stream, and flame;
In short, a roar of things extremely great,   125
   Which would have made aught save a saint exclaim;
But he, with first a start and then a wink,
Said, "There's another star gone out, I think!"

17

But ere he could return to his repose,
   A cherub flapp'd his right wing o'er his eyes—   130
At which Saint Peter yawn'd, and rubb'd his nose:
   "Saint porter," said the Angel, "prithee rise!"
Waving a goodly wing, which glow'd, as glows
   An earthly peacock's tail, with heavenly dyes;
To which the Saint replied, "Well, what's the matter?   135
Is Lucifer come back with all this clatter?"

18

"No," quoth the Cherub; "George the Third is dead."
   "And who *is* George the Third?" replied the Apostle;
"*What George? what Third?*" "The King of England," said
   The Angel. "Well! he won't find kings to jostle   140
Him on his way; but does he wear his head?
   Because the last we saw here had a tussle,

And ne'er would have got into heaven's good graces,
Had he not flung his head in all our faces.[2]

19

"He was, if I remember, king of France;   145
   That head of his, which could not keep a crown
On earth, yet ventured in my face to advance
   A claim to those of martyrs—like my own:
If I had had my sword, as I had once
   When I cut ears off, I had cut him down;[3]   150
But having but my *keys*, and not my brand,
I only knock'd his head from out his hand.

20

"And then he set up such a headless howl,
   That all the saints came out, and took him in;
And there he sits by Saint Paul, cheek by jowl;   155
   That fellow Paul—the parvenu! The skin
Of Saint Bartholomew,[4] which makes his cowl
   In heaven, and upon earth redeem'd his sin
So as to make a martyr, never sped
Better than did this weak and wooden head.   160

21

"But had it come up here upon its shoulders,
   There would have been a different tale to tell:
The fellow feeling in the saint's beholders
   Seems to have acted on them like a spell,
And so this very foolish head heaven solders   165
   Back on its trunk: it may be very well,
And seems the custom here to overthrow
Whatever has been wisely done below."

22

The Angel answer'd, "Peter! do not pout;
   The king who comes has head and all entire,   170
And never knew much what it was about—
   He did as doth the puppet—by its wire,
And will be judged like all the rest, no doubt:
   My business and your own is not to inquire
Into such matters, but to mind our cue—   175
Which is to act as we are bid to do."

23

While thus they spake, the angelic caravan,
   Arriving like a rush of mighty wind,
Cleaving the fields of space, as doth the swan
   Some silver stream (say Ganges, Nile, or Inde,   180
Or Thames, or Tweed) and midst them an old man
   With an old soul, and both extremely blind,
Halted before the gate, and in his shroud
Seated their fellow-traveller on a cloud.

---

2. Louis XVI, who had been guillotined in Jan. 1793.
3. When the officers came to take Jesus, "Simon Peter having a sword drew it, and smote the high priest's servant, and cut off his right ear" (John 18.10). "Brand"
(line 151): archaic for sword.
4. According to tradition, the martyred St. Bartholomew was flayed alive.

GEORGE GORDON, LORD BYRON

24

But bringing up the rear of this bright host   185
   A Spirit of a different aspect waved
His wings, like thunder-clouds above some coast
   Whose barren beach with frequent wrecks is paved;
His brow was like the deep when tempest-tost;
   Fierce and unfathomable thoughts engraved   190
Eternal wrath on his immortal face,
And *where* he gazed a gloom pervaded space.

25

As he drew near, he gazed upon the gate
   Ne'er to be entered more by him or sin,
With such a glance of supernatural hate,   195
   As made Saint Peter wish himself within;
He potter'd with his keys at a great rate,
   And sweated through his apostolic skin:
Of course his perspiration was but ichor,[5]
Or some such other spiritual liquor.   200

26

The very cherubs huddled altogether,
   Like birds when soars the falcon; and they felt
A tingling to the tip of every feather,
   And form'd a circle like Orion's belt
Around their poor old charge; who scarce knew whither   205
   His guards had led him, though they gently dealt
With royal manes[6] (for by many stories,
And true, we learn the angels all are Tories).

27

As things were in this posture, the gate flew
   Asunder, and the flashing of its hinges   210
Flung over space an universal hue
   Of many-coloured flame, until its tinges
Reach'd even our speck of earth, and made a new
   Aurora borealis spread its fringes
O'er the North Pole; the same seen, when ice-bound,   215
By Captain Parry's[7] crews, in "Melville's Sound."

28

And from the gate thrown open issued beaming
   A beautiful and mighty Thing of Light,
Radiant with glory, like a banner streaming
   Victorious from some world-o'erthrowing fight: 220
My poor comparisons must needs be teeming
   With earthly likenesses, for here the night
Of clay obscures our best conceptions, saving
Johanna Southcote,[8] or Bob Southey raving.

---

5. The fluid in the veins of the classical gods.
6. In Roman religion, spirits of the dead (pronounced *mä'nēz*).
7. Capt. William Edward Parry, in his account of his *Voyage in 1819–20*, in search of a northwest passage.
8. Joanna Southcott (1750–1814) was a servant girl who, claiming direct communications from the Almighty, became head of a religious sect. In 1813 she proclaimed that she was about to give birth to a son, Shiloh, who would redeem the world. The pregnancy turned out to be a tumor, of which she died the following year.

29

'Twas the archangel Michael: all men know   225
  The make of angels and archangels, since
There's scarce a scribbler has not one to show,
  From the fiends' leader to the angels' prince.
There also are some altar-pieces, though
  I really can't say that they much evince   230
One's inner notions of immortal spirits;
But let the connoisseurs explain *their* merits.

30

Michael flew forth in glory and in good;
  A goodly work of him from whom all glory
And good arise; the portal past—he stood;   235
  Before him the young cherubs and saint hoary,
(I say *young*, begging to be understood
  By looks, not years; and should be very sorry
To state, they were not older than Saint Peter,
But merely that they seem'd a little sweeter).   240

31

The cherubs and the saints bow'd down before
  That arch-angelic Hierarch, the first
Of Essences angelical, who wore
  The aspect of a god; but this ne'er nurst
Pride in his heavenly bosom, in whose core   245
  No thought, save for his Maker's service, durst
Intrude, however glorified and high;
He knew him but the viceroy of the sky.

32

He and the sombre silent Spirit met—
  They knew each other both for good and ill;   250
Such was their power, that neither could forget
  His former friend and future foe; but still
There was a high, immortal, proud regret
  In either's eye, as if 'twere less their will
Than destiny to make the eternal years   255
Their date of war, and their "Champ Clos"[9] the spheres.

33

But here they were in neutral space: we know
  From Job, that Satan hath the power to pay
A heavenly visit thrice a year or so;
  And that the "Sons of God," like those of clay,   260
Must keep him company;[1] and we might show,
  From the same book, in how polite a way
The dialogue is held between the Powers
Of Good and Evil—but 'twould take up hours.

34

And this is not a theologic tract,   265
  To prove with Hebrew and with Arabic
If Job be allegory or a fact,

---

9. "Enclosed field," the arena for knightly tournaments.
1. Job 1.6: "There was a day when the sons of God

came to present themselves before the Lord, and Satan
came also among them."

But a true narrative; and thus I pick
From out the whole but such and such an act
    As sets aside the slightest thought of trick.   270
'Tis every tittle true, beyond suspicion,
And accurate as any other vision.

35

The spirits were in neutral space, before
    The gate of heaven; like eastern thresholds is
The place where Death's grand cause is argued o'er,[2]   275
    And souls dispatched to that world or to this;
And therefore Michael and the other wore
    A civil aspect: though they did not kiss,
Yet still between his Darkness and his Brightness
There passed a mutual glance of great politeness.   280

36

The Archangel bowed, not like a modern beau,
    But with a graceful Oriental bend,
Pressing one radiant arm just where below
    The heart in good men is supposed to tend.
He turned as to an equal, not too low,   285
    But kindly; Satan met his ancient friend
With more hauteur, as might an old Castilian
Poor noble meet a mushroom rich civilian.[3]

37

He merely bent his diabolic brow
    An instant; and then raising it, he stood   290
In act to assert his right or wrong, and show
    Cause why King George by no means could or should
Make out a case to be exempt from woe
    Eternal, more than other kings, endued
With better sense and hearts, whom history mentions,   295
Who long have "paved hell with their good intentions."[4]

38

Michael began: "What wouldst thou with this man,
    Now dead, and brought before the Lord? What ill
Hath he wrought since his mortal race began,
    That thou can'st claim him: Speak! and do thy will,   300
If it be just: if in this earthly span
    He hath been greatly failing to fulfil
His duties as a king and mortal, say,
And he is thine; if not, let him have way."

39

"Michael!" replied the Prince of Air, "even here,   305
    Before the gate of him thou servest, must
I claim my subject; and will make appear
    That as he was my worshipper in dust,
So shall he be in spirit, although dear
    To thee and thine, because nor wine nor lust   310

---

2. The gateways of walled cities in the Middle East were sometimes used for public debates and to administer justice.
3. Byron contrasts ancient Spanish noblemen with nouveaux riches who spring up as rapidly as mushrooms.
4. An old English proverb.

Were of his weaknesses; yet on the throne
He reign'd o'er millions to serve me alone.
40
"Look to *our* earth, or rather *mine*; it was,
   Once, more thy master's: but I triumph not
In this poor planet's conquest, nor, alas!   315
   Need he thou servest envy me my lot:
With all the myriads of bright worlds which pass
   In worship round him, he may have forgot
Yon weak creation of such paltry things;
I think few worth damnation save their kings,   320
41
"And these but as a kind of quit-rent,[5] to
   Assert my right as lord; and even had
I such an inclination, 'twere (as you
   Well know) superfluous; they are grown so bad,
That hell has nothing better left to do   325
   Than leave them to themselves: so much more mad
And evil by their now internal curse,
Heaven cannot make them better, nor I worse.
42
"Look to the earth, I said, and say again:
   When this old, blind, mad, helpless, weak, poor worm,   330
Began in youth's first bloom and flush to reign,
   The world and he both wore a different form,
And much of earth and all the watery plain
   Of ocean called him king: through many a storm
His isles had floated on the abyss of Time;   335
For the rough virtues chose them for their clime.
43
"He came to his sceptre young; he leaves it old:
   Look to the state in which he found his realm,
And left it; and his annals too behold,
   How to a minion first he gave the helm;[6]   340
How grew upon his heart a thirst for gold,
   The beggar's vice, which can but overwhelm
The meanest hearts; and for the rest, but glance
Thine eye along America and France!
44
" 'Tis true, he was a tool from first to last   345
   (I have the workmen safe); but as a tool
So let him be consumed! From out the past
   Of ages, since mankind have known the rule
Of monarchs—from the bloody rolls amass'd
   Of sin and slaughter—from the Caesar's school,   350
Take the worst pupil; and produce a reign
More drench'd with gore, more cumber'd with the slain!
45
"He ever warr'd with freedom and the free:
   Nations as men, home subjects, foreign foes,

---

5. A fixed rent, paid in place of services to a feudal lord.

6. The unpopular earl of Bute, whom George III made prime minister in 1802.

So that[7] they utter'd the word 'Liberty!'   355
   Found George the Third their first opponent. Whose
History was ever stain'd as his will be
   With national and individual woes?
I grant his household abstinence; I grant
His neutral virtues, which most monarchs want;   360

46

"I know he was a constant consort; own
   He was a decent sire, and middling lord.
All this is much, and most upon a throne;
   As temperance, if at Apicius' board,[8]
Is more than at an anchorite's[9] supper shown.   365
   I grant him all the kindest can accord;
And this was well for him, but not for those
Millions who found him what oppression chose.

47

"The new world shook him off; the old yet groans
   Beneath what he and his prepared, if not   370
Completed: he leaves heirs on many thrones
   To all his vices, without what begot
Compassion for him—his tame virtues; drones
   Who sleep, or despots who have now forgot
A lesson which shall be re-taught them, wake   375
Upon the throne of Earth; but let them quake!

48

"Five millions of the primitive,[1] who hold
   The faith which makes ye great on earth, implored
A *part* of that vast *all* they held of old,—
   Freedom to worship—not alone your Lord,   380
Michael, but you, and you, Saint Peter! Cold
   Must be your souls, if you have not abhorr'd
The foe to Catholic participation
In all the licence of a Christian nation.

49

"True! he allow'd them to pray God; but as   385
   A consequence of prayer, refused the law
Which would have placed them upon the same base
   With those who did not hold the saints in awe."
But here Saint Peter started from his place,
   And cried, "You may the prisoner withdraw: 390
Ere Heaven shall ope her portals to this Guelf,[2]
While I am guard, may I be damn'd myself!

50

"Sooner will I with Cerberus[3] exchange
   My office (and *his* is no sinecure)
Than see this royal Bedlam bigot range   395

---

7. Provided that.
8. I.e., at the table of Apicius (a famed Roman gour-
met in the time of Augustus).
9. A religious hermit's.
1. The Irish Catholics. In 1795 George had opposed
the Catholic Emancipation Bill, which would have

given Roman Catholics the right to hold public offices
(line 383).
2. The House of Hanover was descended from the
German Guelphs.
3. The three-headed dog guarding the entrance to
Hades.

The azure fields of heaven, of that be sure!"
"Saint!" replied Satan, "you do well to avenge
    The wrongs he made your satellites endure;
And if to this exchange you should be given,
I'll try to coax *our* Cerberus up to heaven."   400

                        51
Here Michael interposed: "Good saint! and devil!
    Pray not so fast; you both out-run discretion.
Saint Peter! you were wont to be more civil:
    Satan! excuse this warmth of his expression,
And condescension to the vulgar's level: 405
    Even saints sometimes forget themselves in session.
Have you got more to say?"—"No!"—"If you please,
I'll trouble you to call your witnesses."

                        52
Then Satan turn'd and wav'd his swarthy hand,
    Which stirr'd with its electric qualities   410
Clouds farther off than we can understand,
    Although we find him sometimes in our skies;
Infernal thunder shook both sea and land
    In all the planets, and hell's batteries
Let off the artillery, which Milton mentions   415
As one of Satan's most sublime inventions.[4]

                        53
This was a signal unto such damn'd souls
    As have the privilege of their damnation
Extended far beyond the mere controls
    Of worlds past, present, or to come; no station   420
Is theirs particularly in the rolls
    Of hell assigned; but where their inclination
Or business carries them in search of game,
They may range freely—being damn'd the same.

                        54
They are proud of this—as very well they may,   425
    It being a sort of knighthood, or gilt key
Stuck in their loins;[5] or like to an "entré"
    Up the back stairs, or such free-masonry:
I borrow my comparisons from clay,
    Being clay myself. Let not those spirits be   430
Offended with such base low likenesses;
We know their posts are nobler far than these.

                        55
When the great signal ran from heaven to hell,—
    About ten million times the distance reckon'd
From our sun to its earth, as we can tell   435
    How much time it takes up, even to a second,
For every ray that travels to dispel
    The fogs of London; through which, dimly beacon'd,

---

4. In *Paradise Lost* 6.469ff. Satan announces his invention of the cannon for use in the war in heaven.

5. A gold key hung from the belt betokens certain official positions at the English court.

The weathercocks are gilt, some thrice a year,
If that the *summer* is not too severe:—

56

I say that I can tell——'twas half a minute;
    I know the solar beams take up more time
Ere, pack'd up for their journey, they begin it;
    But then their telegraph[6] is less sublime,
And if they ran a race, they would not win it
    'Gainst Satan's couriers bound for their own clime.
The sun takes up some years for every ray
To reach its goal—the devil not half a day.

57

Upon the verge of space, about the size
    Of half-a-crown, a little speck appear'd,
(I've seen a something like it in the skies
    In the Aegean, ere a squall); it near'd,
And, growing bigger, took another guise;
    Like an aërial ship it tack'd, and steer'd
Or *was* steer'd (I am doubtful of the grammar
Of the last phrase, which makes the stanza stammer;—

58

But take your choice); and then it grew a cloud,
    And so it was—a cloud of witnesses.
But such a cloud! No land ere saw a crowd
    Of locusts numerous as the heavens saw these;
They shadow'd with their myriads space; their loud
    And varied cries were like those of wild-geese,
(If nations may be liken'd to a goose)
And realized the phrase of "hell broke loose."[7]

59

Here crash'd a sturdy oath of stout John Bull,
    Who damn'd away his eyes as heretofore:
There Paddy brogued "by Jasus!"—"What's your wull?"
    The temperate Scot exclaim'd: the French ghost swore
In certain terms I shan't translate in full,
    As the first coachman will; and midst the roar
The voice of Jonathan was heard to express,
"*Our* President is going to war, I guess."[8]

60

Besides there were the Spaniard, Dutch, and Dane;
    In short, an universal shoal of shades
From Otaheite's Isle[9] to Salisbury Plain,
    Of all climes and professions, years and trades,
Ready to swear against the good king's reign,
    Bitter as clubs in cards are against spades;
All summon'd by this grand "subpoena," to
Try if kings mayn't be damn'd, like me or you.

440
445
450
455
460
465
470
475
480

6. In its original sense, any apparatus for transmitting signals at a distance.
7. *Paradise Lost* 4.918.
8. "Brother Jonathan" was the name applied to the United States and its citizens, now replaced by "Uncle Sam." The "I guess" was intended by Byron as an obvious Americanism. This was written during the troubled Anglo-American relations after the War of 1812.
9. The old name for Tahiti.

61

When Michael saw this host, he first grew pale,
   As angels can; next, like Italian twilight,
He turned all colours—as a peacock's tail,
   Or sunset streaming through a Gothic skylight
In some old abbey, or a trout not stale,   485
   Or distant lightning on the horizon *by* night,
Or a fresh rainbow, or a grand review
Of thirty regiments in red, green, and blue.

62

Then he address'd himself to Satan: "Why—
   My good old friend, for such I deem you, though   490
Our different parties make us fight so shy,
   I ne'er mistake you for a *personal* foe;
Our difference is *political*, and I
   Trust that, whatever may occur below,
You know my great respect for you; and this   495
Makes me regret whate'er you do amiss—

63

"Why, my dear Lucifer, would you abuse
   My call for witnesses? I did not mean
That you should half of earth and hell produce;
   'Tis even superfluous, since two honest, clean,   500
True testimonies are enough: we lose
   Our time, nay, our eternity, between
The accusation and defence: if we
Hear both, 'twill stretch our immortality."

64

Satan replied, "To me the matter is   505
   Indifferent, in a personal point of view:
I can have fifty better souls than this
   With far less trouble than we have gone through
Already; and I merely argued his
   Late Majesty of Britain's case with you   510
Upon a point of form: you may dispose
Of him; I've kings enough below, God knows!"

65

Thus spoke the Demon (late call'd "multifaced"
   By multo-scribbling Southey).[1] "Then we'll call
One or two persons of the myriads placed   515
   Around our congress, and dispense with all
The rest," quoth Michael: "Who may be so graced
   As to speak first? there's choice enough—who shall
It be?" Then Satan answered, "There are many;
But you may choose Jack Wilkes[2] as well as any." 520

66

A merry, cock-eyed, curious looking Sprite,
   Upon the instant started from the throng,

---

1. In *A Vision of Judgment* 5.70.
2. John Wilkes (1727–1797), noted libertine, wit, and courageous political radical who in 1764 was expelled from the House of Commons and driven into exile for his libelous attack on George III in his weekly periodical, *The North Briton*. He later came back to England, became lord mayor of London, and was triumphantly returned to Parliament.

Drest in a fashion now forgotten quite;
   For all the fashions of the flesh stick long
By people in the next world; where unite   525
   All the costumes since Adam's, right or wrong,
From Eve's fig-leaf down to the petticoat,
Almost as scanty, of days less remote.
67
The Spirit look'd around upon the crowds
   Assembled, and exclaim'd, "My friends of all   530
The spheres, we shall catch cold amongst these clouds;
   So let's to business: why this general call?
If those are freeholders I see in shrouds,
   And 'tis for an election that they bawl,
Behold a candidate with unturn'd-coat!   535
Saint Peter, may I count upon your vote?"
68
"Sir," replied Michael, "you mistake: these things
   Are of a former life, and what we do
Above is more august; to judge of kings
   Is the tribunal met; so now you know."   540
"Then I presume those gentlemen with wings,"
   Said Wilkes, "are cherubs; and that soul below
Looks much like George the Third; but to my mind
A good deal older—Bless me! is he blind?"
69
"He is what you behold him, and his doom   545
   Depends upon his deeds," the Angel said.
"If you have ought to arraign in him, the tomb
   Gives licence to the humblest beggar's head
To lift itself against the loftiest."—"Some,"
   Said Wilkes, "don't wait to see them laid in lead,   550
For such a liberty—and I, for one,
Have told them what I thought beneath the sun."
70
"*Above* the sun repeat, then, what thou hast
   To urge against him," said the Archangel. "Why,"
Replied the Spirit, "since old scores are past,   555
   Must I turn evidence? In faith, not I.
Besides, I beat him hollow at the last,
   With all his Lords and Commons:[3] in the sky
I don't like ripping up old stories, since
His conduct was but natural in a prince.   560
71
"Foolish, no doubt, and wicked, to oppress
   A poor unlucky devil without a shilling;
But then I blame the man himself much less
   Than Bute and Grafton,[4] and shall be unwilling
To see him punish'd here for their excess,   565
   Since they were both damn'd long ago, and still in

---

3. In 1782 Wilkes succeeded in getting the House of
Commons to erase the record of his expulsion.

4. The duke of Grafton, like the earl of Bute, was a
minister subservient to George III.

Their place below; for me, I have forgiven,
And vote his 'habeas corpus' into heaven."

72

"Wilkes," said the Devil, "I understand all this;
   You turn'd to half a courtier ere you died,[5]   570
And seem to think it would not be amiss
   To grow a whole one on the other side
Of Charon's ferry;[6] you forget that *his*
   Reign is concluded; whatsoe'er betide,
He won't be sovereign more: you've lost your labour   575
For at the best he will but be your neighbour.

73

"However, I knew what to think of it,
   When I beheld you in your jesting way
Flitting and whispering round about the spit
   Where Belial, upon duty for the day,   580
With Fox's lard was basting William Pitt,[7]
   His pupil; I knew what to think, I say:
That fellow even in hell breeds farther ills;
I'll have him *gagg'd*—'twas one of his own bills.[8]

74

"Call Junius!"[9] From the crowd a Shadow stalk'd,   585
   And at the name there was a general squeeze,
So that the very ghosts no longer walk'd
   In comfort, at their own aërial ease,
But were all ramm'd, and jamm'd (but to be balk'd,
   As we shall see) and jostled hands and knees,   590
Like wind compress'd and pent within a bladder,
Or like a human cholic, which is sadder.

75

The Shadow came! a tall, thin, gray-hair'd figure,
   That look'd as it had been a shade on earth;
Quick in its motions, with an air of vigour,   595
   But nought to mark its breeding or its birth:
Now it wax'd little, then again grew bigger,
   With now an air of gloom, or savage mirth;
But as you gazed upon its features, they
Changed every instant—to *what*, none could say.   600

76

The more intently the ghosts gazed, the less
   Could they distinguish whose the features were;
The Devil himself seem'd puzzled even to guess;
   They varied like a dream—now here, now there;

---

5. Wilkes in his latter years softened his opposition and moved in higher social circles.
6. In Greek mythology, Charon ferried the dead to the underworld across the river Styx.
7. Charles James Fox, statesman and political opponent of William Pitt, prime minister under George III, was notably corpulent.
8. The Alien and Sedition Bills of 1795 severely restricted freedom of speech and of the press.
9. Pseudonym of the writer of a brilliant series of let-

ters (1769–71) attacking supporters of George III and the king himself. His identity is an unsolved political mystery; among more than fifty possibilities proposed are Edmund Burke, John Horne Tooke, and Sir Philip Francis, mentioned in lines 631–32. When the letters were published as a book the title page read: *Letters of Junius, Stat Nominis Umbra* ("he stands, the shadow of a name"), hence the allusions (lines 593ff., 667). The Latin phrase is from Lucan's *Pharsalia* 1.135.

And several people swore from out the press,   605
    They knew him perfectly; and one could swear
He was his father; upon which another
Was sure he was his mother's cousin's brother:

77

Another, that he was a duke, or knight,
    An orator, a lawyer, or a priest,   610
A nabob,[1] a man-midwife; but the wight
    Mysterious changed his countenance at least
As oft as they their minds: though in full sight
    He stood, the puzzle only was increased;
The man was a phantasmagoria in   615
Himself—he was so volatile and thin!

78

The moment that you had pronounced him *one*,
    Presto! his face changed, and he was another;
And when that change was hardly well put on,
    It varied, till I don't think his own mother   620
(If that he had a mother) would her son
    Have known, he shifted so from one to t'other,
Till guessing from a pleasure grew a task,
At this epistolary "iron mask."[2]

79

For sometimes he like Cerberus would seem—   625
    "Three gentlemen at once," (as sagely says
Good Mrs. Malaprop);[3] then you might deem
    That he was not even *one*; now many rays
Were flashing round him; and now a thick steam
    Hid him from sight—like fogs on London days: 630
Now Burke, now Tooke, he grew to people's fancies,
And certes often like Sir Philip Francis

80

I've an hypothesis—'tis quite my own;
    I never let it out till now, for fear
Of doing people harm about the throne,   635
    And injuring some minister or peer
On whom the stigma might perhaps be blown;
    It is—my gentle public, lend thine ear!
'Tis, that what Junius we are wont to call,
Was *really, truly*, nobody at all.   640

81

I don't see wherefore letters should not be
    Written without hands, since we daily view
Them written without heads; and books we see
    Are fill'd as well without the latter too:
And really till we fix on somebody   645
    For certain sure to claim them as his due,

1. A man of great wealth, especially one who has returned to England with a fortune acquired in India.
2. "The Man in the Iron Mask" was a state prisoner in the reign of Louis XIV whose identity was thus concealed.
3. A character in R. B. Sheridan's *The Rivals* who comically misused words; the term *malapropism* derives from her name.

Their author, like the Niger's mouth,[4] will bother
The world to say if *there* be mouth or author.
82
"And who and what art thou?" the Archangel said.
   "For *that* you may consult my title-page,"   650
Replied this mighty Shadow of a Shade:
   "If I have kept my secret half an age,
I scarce shall tell it now."—"Canst thou upbraid,"
   Continued Michael, "George Rex, or allege
Aught further?" Junius answer'd, "You had better   655
First ask him for *his* answer to my letter:
83
"My charges upon record will outlast
   The brass of both his epitaph and tomb."
"Repent'st thou not," said Michael, "of some past
   Exaggeration? something which may doom   660
Thyself, if false, as him if true? Thou wast
   Too bitter—is it not so? in thy gloom
Of passion?" "Passion!" cried the Phantom dim,
"I loved my country, and I hated him.
84
"What I have written, I have written:[5] let   665
   The rest be on his head or mine!" So spoke
Old "Nominis Umbra"; and while speaking yet,
   Away he melted in celestial smoke.
Then Satan said to Michael, "Don't forget
   To call George Washington, and John Horne Tooke,[6]   670
And Franklin":—but at this time there was heard
A cry for room, though not a phantom stirr'd.
85
At length with jostling, elbowing, and the aid
   Of cherubim appointed to that post,
The devil Asmodeus[7] to the circle made   675
   His way, and look'd as if his journey cost
Some trouble. When his burden down he laid,
   "What's this?" cried Michael; "why, 'tis not a ghost?"
"I know it," quoth the incubus; "but he
Shall be one, if you leave the affair to me.   680
86
"Confound the Renegado! I have sprain'd
   My left wing, he's so heavy; one would think
Some of his works about his neck were chain'd.
   But to the point: while hovering o'er the brink
Of Skiddaw (where as usual it still rain'd),[8]   685
   I saw a taper, far below me, wink,

---

4. Several recent British expeditions to explore the course of the river Niger, in western Africa, had ended in failure.
5. Said by Pilate, John 19.22.
6. A prominent English opponent of the war against the American colonies (see p. 1591, n. 9).

7. The devil in Le Sage's *Le Diable Boiteux* ("The Lame Devil"), published in 1707, who carries Don Cleofas to the summit of San Salvador.
8. Mount Skiddaw, near Southey's home in the Lake District.

And stooping, caught this fellow at a libel—
No less on History than the Holy Bible.

87

"The former is the devil's scripture, and
   The latter yours, good Michael; so the affair   690
Belongs to all of us, you understand.
   I snatch'd him up just as you see him there,
And brought him off for sentence out of hand:
   I've scarcely been ten minutes in the air—
At least a quarter it can hardly be: 695
I dare say that his wife is still at tea."

88

Here Satan said, "I know this man of old,
   And have expected him for some time here;
A sillier fellow you will scarce behold,
   Or more conceited in his petty sphere: 700
But surely it was not worth while to fold
   Such trash below your wing, Asmodeus dear!
We had the poor wretch safe (without being bored
With carriage) coming of his own accord.

89

"But since he's here, let's see what he has done."   705
   "Done!" cried Asmodeus, "he anticipates
The very business you are now upon,
   And scribbles as if head clerk to the Fates.
Who knows to what his ribaldry may run,
   When such an ass as this, like Balaam's,[9] prates?"   710
"Let's hear," quoth Michael, "what he has to say;
You know we're bound to that in every way."

90

Now the Bard, glad to get an audience, which
   By no means often was his case below,
Began to cough, and hawk, and hem, and pitch   715
   His voice into that awful note of woe
To all unhappy hearers within reach
   Of poets when the tide of rhyme's in flow;
But stuck fast with his first hexameter,
Not one of all whose gouty feet would stir.   720

91

But ere the spavin'd dactyls[1] could be spurr'd
   Into recitative, in great dismay
Both cherubim and seraphim were heard
   To murmur loudly through their long array;
And Michael rose ere he could get a word   725
   Of all his founder'd verses under way,
And cried, "For God's sake stop, my friend! 'twere best—
'Non Di, non homines'[2]—you know the rest."

9. Balaam's ass was granted speech in Numbers
22.28ff.
1. Southey's A Vision of Judgment was written in dactylic hexameters, a very awkward measure in English.
A "spavined" horse is a lame one.

2. Horace, Art of Poetry lines 372–73: "mediocribus
esse poetis / Non homines, non di, non concessere col-
umnae" ("mediocrity in poets has never been tolerated
by either men, or gods, or booksellers").

92

A general bustle spread throughout the throng,
  Which seem'd to hold all verse in detestation;   730
The angels had of course enough of song
  When upon service; and the generation
Of ghosts had heard too much in life, not long
  Before, to profit by a new occasion;
The Monarch, mute till then, exclaim'd, "What! what!   735
Pye³ come again? No more—no more of that!"

93

The tumult grew, an universal cough
  Convulsed the skies, as during a debate,
When Castlereagh⁴ has been up long enough,
  (Before he was first minister of state,   740
I mean—the *slaves hear now*);⁵ some cried "off, off,"
  As at a farce; till grown quite desperate,
The Bard Saint Peter pray'd to interpose
(Himself an author)⁶ only for his prose.

94

The varlet was not an ill-favour'd knave;   745
  A good deal like a vulture in the face,
With a hook nose and a hawk's eye, which gave
  A smart and sharper looking sort of grace
To his whole aspect, which, though rather grave,
  Was by no means so ugly as his case;   750
But that indeed was hopeless as can be,
Quite a poetic felony "*de se.*"⁷

95

Then Michael blew his trump, and still'd the noise
  With one still greater, as is yet the mode
On earth besides; except some grumbling voice,   755
  Which now and then will make a slight inroad
Upon decorous silence, few will twice
  Lift up their lungs when fairly overcrow'd;
And now the Bard could plead his own bad cause,
With all the attitudes of self-applause.   760

96

He said—(I only give the heads)—he said,
  He meant no harm in scribbling; 'twas his way
Upon all topics; 'twas, besides, his bread,
  Of which he butter'd both sides; 'twould delay
Too long the assembly (he was pleased to dread)   765
  And take up rather more time than a day,
To name his works—he would but cite a few—
"Wat Tyler"—"Rhymes on Blenheim"—"Waterloo."

---

3. Henry James Pye, an inept and much ridiculed poet and Southey's predecessor as poet laureate.
4. Viscount Castlereagh was foreign secretary when Byron wrote his poem.
5. I.e., now that Castlereagh is prime minister, members of the House of Commons listen obsequiously.
6. The reference is to the first and second epistles of Peter, very short books in the New Testament.
7. "Upon himself": i.e., suicide.

97

He had written praises of a regicide;[8]
   He had written praises of all kings whatever;   770
He had written for republics far and wide,
   And then against them bitterer than ever;
For pantisocracy[9] he once had cried
   Aloud, a scheme less moral than 'twas clever;
Then grew a hearty antijacobin—   775
Had turn'd his coat—and would have turn'd his skin.

98

He had sung against all battles, and again
   In their high praise and glory: he had call'd
Reviewing "the ungentle craft,"[1] and then
   Become as base a critic as ere crawl'd—   780
Fed, paid, and pamper'd by the very men
   By whom his muse and morals had been maul'd:
He had written much blank verse, and blanker prose,
And more of both than any body knows.

99

He had written Wesley's life:—here, turning round   785
   To Satan, "Sir, I'm ready to write yours,
In two octavo volumes, nicely bound,
   With notes and preface, all that most allures
The pious purchaser; and there's no ground
   For fear, for I can choose my own reviewers: 790
So let me have the proper documents,
That I may add you to my other saints."

100

Satan bow'd, and was silent. "Well, if you,
   With amiable modesty, decline
My offer, what says Michael? There are few   795
   Whose memoirs could be render'd more divine.
Mine is a pen of all work; not so new
   As it was once, but I would make you shine
Like your own trumpet; by the way, my own
Has more of brass in it, and is as well blown.   800

101

"But talking about trumpets, here's my Vision!
   Now you shall judge, all people; yes, you shall
Judge with my judgment! and by my decision
   Be guided who shall enter heaven or fall!
I settle all these things by intuition,   805
   Times present, past, to come, heaven, hell, and all,
Like King Alfonso![2] When I thus see double,
I save the Deity some worlds of trouble."

---

8. In Southey's early poem on Henry Martin, one of the judges who had condemned Charles I to be beheaded.
9. An ideal community that Southey and Coleridge, in 1794–95, had planned to set up in the United States on the banks of the Susquehanna. The scheme was utopian but in no way immoral.

1. In Southey's *The Remains of Henry Kirke White*, vol. 1 (1808).
2. King Alphonso [of Castile, in the 13th century], speaking of the Ptolemean system, said that had he been consulted at the creation of the world, he would have spared the Maker some absurdities [Byron's note].

102

He ceased; and drew forth an MS; and no
   Persuasion on the part of devils, or saints,   810
Or angels, now could stop the torrent; so
   He read the first three lines of the contents;
But at the fourth, the whole spiritual show
   Had vanish'd, with variety of scents,
Ambrosial and sulphureous, as they sprang,   815
Like lightning, off from his "melodious twang."[3]

103

Those grand heroics acted as a spell:
   The angels stopp'd their ears and plied their pinions;
The devils ran howling, deafen'd, down to hell;
   The ghosts fled, gibbering, for their own dominions—   820
(For 'tis not yet decided where they dwell,
   And I leave every man to his opinions);
Michael took refuge in his trump—but, lo!
His teeth were set on edge, he could not blow!

104

Saint Peter, who has hitherto been known   825
   For an impetuous saint, upraised his keys,
And at the fifth line knock'd the Poet down;
   Who fell like Phaeton,[4] but more at ease,
Into his lake, for there he did not drown,
   A different web being by the Destinies   830
Woven for the Laureate's final wreath, whene'er
Reform shall happen either here or there.

105

He first sunk to the bottom—like his works,
   But soon rose to the surface—like himself;
For all corrupted things are buoy'd, like corks,
   By their own rottenness, light as an elf,   835
Or wisp that flits o'er a morass: he lurks,
   It may be, still, like dull books on a shelf,
In his own den, to scrawl some "Life" or "Vision,"
As Wellborn says—"the devil turn'd precisian."[5]   840

106

As for the rest, to come to the conclusion
   Of this true dream, the telescope is gone
Which kept my optics free from all delusion,
   And show'd me what I in my turn have shown:
All I saw farther in the last confusion,   845
   Was, that King George slipp'd into heaven for one;
And when the tumult dwindled to a calm,
I left him practising the hundredth psalm.[6]

1821   1822

---

3. John Aubrey in his *Miscellanies upon Various Subjects* (1696) had described a ghost that vanished "with a curious perfume, and most melodious twang."
4. Phaethon, son of Apollo, tried to drive his father's chariot, the sun. He could not control the horses and was struck down into the sea by a thunderbolt of Zeus. The satiric point is that Apollo is the god of poetry as well as of the sun.
5. A "precisian" is a Puritan. Spoken by Wellborn in Philip Massinger's play *A New Way to Pay Old Debts* (1626) 1.1.6.
6. Psalm 100 contains the relevant line "Enter into his gates with thanksgiving."

Don Juan   Byron began his masterpiece (pronounced in the English fashion, *Don Joó-un*) in July of 1818, published it in installments beginning with cantos 1 and 2 in 1819, and continued working on it almost until his death. He extemporized the poem from episode to episode; "I *have* no plan," he said, "I *had* no plan; but I had or have materials." The work was composed with remarkable speed (the 888 lines of canto 13, for example, were accomplished within a week), and it aims at the effect of improvisation and scope rather than of compression; it asks to be read rapidly, at a conversational pace.

The poem breaks off with the sixteenth canto, but even in its unfinished state *Don Juan* is the longest satirical poem, and indeed one of the longest poems of any kind, in English. Its hero, the Spanish libertine, had in the original legend been superhuman in his sexual energy and wickedness. Throughout Byron's version the unspoken but persistent joke is that this violent and archetypal *homme fatal* of European legend is in fact more acted on than active. Unfailingly amiable and well intentioned, he is guilty largely of youth, charm, and a courteous and compliant spirit. The women do all the rest.

The chief models for the poem were the Italian seriocomic versions of medieval chivalric romances; the genre had been introduced by Pulci in the fifteenth century and achieved its greatest success in Ariosto's *Orlando Furioso* (1532). From these writers Byron caught the mixed moods and violent oscillations between the sublime and the ridiculous as well as the easy, colloquial management of the complex ottava rima—an eight-line stanza in which the initial interlaced rhymes (*ababab*) build up to the comic turn in the pat couplet (*cc*). Byron was influenced in the English use of this Italian form by a mildly amusing poem published in 1817, under the pseudonym of "Whistlecraft," by his friend John Hookham Frere. Other recognizable antecedents of *Don Juan* are Jonathan Swift's *Gulliver's Travels* and Samuel Johnson's *Rasselas*, which had employed the naive traveler as a satiric device, and Laurence Sterne's novel *Tristram Shandy* with its comic exploitation of a narrative medium blatantly subject to the whimsy of the author. But even the most original literary works play variations on inherited conventions. Shelley at once recognized his friend's poem for what it was, "something wholly new and relative to the age."

Byron's most trusted literary advisers thought the poem unacceptably immoral, and John Murray took the precaution of printing the first two installments without identifying either Byron as the author or himself as the publisher. More recently, however, a common complaint has been not that *Don Juan* is immoral but that it is morally nihilistic—that the poem is destructive without limit, because it proposes no positive values as a base for the satire, but sees life, in the words of one critic, as "a strange meaningless pageant." Yet Byron himself insisted that *Don Juan* is "a *satire* on *abuses* of the present state of society" and "the most moral of poems." Although the final phrase exaggerates, it has a foundation of truth. What the poem most frequently attacks, in love, religion, and social relations, are very considerable vices—sham, hypocrisy, complacency, oppression, greed, and lust. Furthermore the satire constantly, though silently, assumes as moral positives the qualities of courage, loyalty, generosity, and, above all, candor; it merely implies that these virtues are excessively rare and that the modern world is not constituted to reward, to encourage, or even to recognize them when they make their appearance. And the poem is zestfully on the side of life, in its abundant variety. "As to 'Don Juan,'" Byron wrote elatedly to a friend, "confess—confess, you dog—and be candid. . . . it may be profligate—but is it not *life*, is it not *the thing*?" (see his letter to Douglas Kinnaird, Oct. 26, 1819).

It is a mistake to look to *Don Juan* primarily for the story. The controlling element is not the narrative but the narrator, and his temperament gives the work its unity. The poem is really an incessant monologue, in the course of which a story manages to be told. It opens with the first-person pronoun and immediately lets us into the storyteller's predicament: "I want a hero. . . ." The voice then goes on, for almost two thousand stanzas, with effortless volubility and bewildering shifts of mood and perspective, using the occasion of Juan's misadventures to confide to us the speaker's thoughts and devastating judgments upon the major institutions, activities, and values of Western society.

What Byron discovered in *Don Juan* was how to give literary expression to those aspects of his temperament that, in real life, his self-consciousness and reserve permitted him to display only in the security of a circle of intimate friends or in his wonderfully vivacious letters to people he trusted. The poet who in his brilliantly successful youth created the gloomy and misanthropic Byronic hero, in his later and sadder life created a character (not the hero, but the narrator of *Don Juan*) who is one of the great, and one of the most complex, comic inventions in literature.

From Don Juan

Fragment[1]

> I would to Heaven that I were so much Clay—
>   As I am blood—bone—marrow, passion—feeling—
> Because at least the past were past away—
>   And for the future—(but I write this reeling
> Having got drunk exceedingly to day   5
>   So that I seem to stand upon the ceiling)
> I say—the future is a serious matter—
> And so—for Godsake—Hock[2] and Soda water.

From Canto 1

[*Juan and Donna Julia*]

1

> I want a hero: an uncommon want,
>   When every year and month sends forth a new one,
> Till, after cloying the gazettes with cant,
>   The age discovers he is not the true one;
> Of such as these I should not care to vaunt,   5
>   I'll therefore take our ancient friend Don Juan,
> We all have seen him in the pantomime[1]
> Sent to the devil, somewhat ere his time.

*   *   *

5

> Brave men were living before Agamemnon[2]
>   And since, exceeding valorous and sage,

---

1. This stanza was written on the back of a page of the manuscript of canto 1. For the author's revisions while composing two stanzas of *Don Juan*, see "Poems in Process" (pp. 2582–83).
2. A white Rhine wine, from the German *Hochheimer*.

1. The Juan legend was a popular subject in English pantomime.
2. In Homer's *Iliad*, the king commanding the Greeks in the siege of Troy. This line is translated from a Latin ode by Horace.

A good deal like him too, though quite the same none;   35
    But then they shone not on the poet's page,
And so have been forgotten—I condemn none,
    But can't find any in the present age
Fit for my poem (that is, for my new one);
So, as I said, I'll take my friend Don Juan.   40

6

Most epic poets plunge in *"medias res,"*[3]
    (Horace makes this the heroic turnpike road)
And then your hero tells, whene'er you please,
    What went before—by way of episode,
While seated after dinner at his ease,   45
    Beside his mistress in some soft abode,
Palace, or garden, paradise, or cavern,
Which serves the happy couple for a tavern.

7

That is the usual method, but not mine—
    My way is to begin with the beginning;   50
The regularity of my design
    Forbids all wandering as the worst of sinning,
And therefore I shall open with a line
    (Although it cost me half an hour in spinning)
Narrating somewhat of Don Juan's father,   55
And also of his mother, if you'd rather.

8

In Seville was he born, a pleasant city,
    Famous for oranges and women—he
Who has not seen it will be much to pity,
    So says the proverb—and I quite agree;   60
Of all the Spanish towns is none more pretty,
    Cadiz perhaps—but that you soon may see:—
Don Juan's parents lived beside the river,
A noble stream, and call'd the Guadalquivir.

9

His father's name was Jóse[4]—*Don*, of course,   65
    A true Hidalgo, free from every stain
Of Moor or Hebrew blood, he traced his source
    Through the most Gothic gentlemen of Spain;
A better cavalier ne'er mounted horse,
    Or, being mounted, e'er got down again,   70
Than Jóse, who begot our hero, who
Begot—but that's to come——Well, to renew:

10

His mother was a learned lady, famed
    For every branch of every science known—
In every christian language ever named,   75
    With virtues equall'd by her wit alone,
She made the cleverest people quite ashamed,
    And even the good with inward envy groan,

---

3. Into the middle of things (Horace, *Art of Poetry* 148).   4. Normally "José"; Byron transferred the accent to keep his meter.

Finding themselves so very much exceeded
In their own way by all the things that she did.   80

11

Her memory was a mine: she knew by heart
    All Calderon and greater part of Lopé,[5]
So that if any actor miss'd his part
    She could have served him for the prompter's copy;
For her Feinagle's[6] were an useless art,   85
    And he himself obliged to shut up shop—he
Could never make a memory so fine as
That which adorn'd the brain of Donna Inez.

12

Her favourite science was the mathematical,
    Her noblest virtue was her magnanimity,   90
Her wit (she sometimes tried at wit) was Attic[7] all,
    Her serious sayings darken'd to sublimity;
In short, in all things she was fairly what I call
    A prodigy—her morning dress was dimity,
Her evening silk, or, in the summer, muslin,   95
And other stuffs, with which I won't stay puzzling.

13

She knew the Latin—that is, "the Lord's prayer,"
    And Greek—the alphabet—I'm nearly sure;
She read some French romances here and there,
    Although her mode of speaking was not pure;   100
For native Spanish she had no great care,
    At least her conversation was obscure;
Her thoughts were theorems, her words a problem,
As if she deem'd that mystery would ennoble 'em.

*   *   *

22

'Tis pity learned virgins ever wed
    With persons of no sort of education,   170
Or gentlemen, who, though well-born and bred,
    Grow tired of scientific conversation:
I don't choose to say much upon this head,
    I'm a plain man, and in a single station,
But—Oh! ye lords of ladies intellectual,   175
Inform us truly, have they not hen-peck'd you all?

23

Don Jóse and his lady quarrell'd—why,
    Not any of the many could divine,
Though several thousand people chose to try,
    'Twas surely no concern of theirs nor mine;   180
I loathe that low vice curiosity,
    But if there's any thing in which I shine

---

5. Lope de Vega and Calderón de la Barca, the great Spanish dramatists of the early 17th century.
6. Gregor von Feinagle, a German expert on the art of memory, who had lectured in England in 1811.
7. Athenian. The common phrase "Attic salt" signifies the famed wit of the Athenians.

'Tis in arranging all my friends' affairs.
Not having, of my own, domestic cares.

24

And so I interfered, and with the best   185
    Intentions, but their treatment was not kind;
I think the foolish people were possess'd,
    For neither of them could I ever find,
Although their porter afterwards confess'd—
    But that's no matter, and the worst's behind,   190
For little Juan o'er me threw, down stairs,
A pail of housemaid's water unawares.

25

A little curly-headed, good-for-nothing,
    And mischief-making monkey from his birth;
His parents ne'er agreed except in doting   195
    Upon the most unquiet imp on earth;
Instead of quarrelling, had they been but both in
    Their senses, they'd have sent young master forth
To school, or had him soundly whipp'd at home,
To teach him manners for the time to come.   200

26

Don Jóse and the Donna Inez led
    For some time an unhappy sort of life,
Wishing each other, not divorced, but dead;
    They lived respectably as man and wife,
Their conduct was exceedingly well-bred,   205
    And gave no outward signs of inward strife,
Until at length the smother'd fire broke out,
And put the business past all kind of doubt.

27

For Inez call'd some druggists and physicians,
    And tried to prove her loving lord was *mad*,[8]   210
But as he had some lucid intermissions,
    She next decided he was only *bad*;
Yet when they ask'd her for her depositions,
    No sort of explanation could be had,
Save that her duty both to man and God   215
Required this conduct—which seem'd very odd.

28

She kept a journal, where his faults were noted,
    And open'd certain trunks of books and letters,
All which might, if occasion served, be quoted;
    And then she had all Seville for abettors,   220
Besides her good old grandmother (who doted);
    The hearers of her case became repeaters,
Then advocates, inquisitors, and judges,
Some for amusement, others for old grudges.

---

8. Lady Byron had thought her husband might be insane and sought medical advice on the matter. This and other passages obviously allude to his wife, although Byron insisted that Donna Inez was not intended to be a caricature of Lady Byron.

29

And then this best and meekest woman bore   225
   With such serenity her husband's woes,
Just as the Spartan ladies did of yore,
   Who saw their spouses kill'd, and nobly chose
Never to say a word about them more —
   Calmly she heard each calumny that rose,   230
And saw *his* agonies with such sublimity,
That all the world exclaim'd "What magnanimity!"

        *   *   *

32

Their friends had tried at reconciliation,
   Then their relations, who made matters worse;   250
('Twere hard to say upon a like occasion
   To whom it may be best to have recourse —
I can't say much for friend or yet relation):
   The lawyers did their utmost for divorce,
But scarce a fee was paid on either side   255
Before, unluckily, Don Jóse died.

33

He died: and most unluckily, because,
   According to all hints I could collect
From counsel learned in those kinds of laws,
   (Although their talk's obscure and circumspect)   260
His death contrived to spoil a charming cause;
   A thousand pities also with respect
To public feeling, which on this occasion
Was manifested in a great sensation.

        *   *   *

37

Dying intestate, Juan was sole heir
   To a chancery suit, and messuages,[9] and lands,   290
Which, with a long minority and care,
   Promised to turn out well in proper hands:
Inez became sole guardian, which was fair,
   And answer'd but to nature's just demands;
An only son left with an only mother   295
Is brought up much more wisely than another.

38

Sagest of women, even of widows, she
   Resolved that Juan should be quite a paragon,
And worthy of the noblest pedigree:
   (His sire was of Castile, his dam from Arragon).   300
Then for accomplishments of chivalry,
   In case our lord the king should go to war again,
He learn'd the arts of riding, fencing, gunnery,
And how to scale a fortress — or a nunnery.

9. Houses and the adjoining lands. "Chancery suit": a suit in what was then the highest English court, notorious for its delays.

39

But that which Donna Inez most desired,   305
    And saw into herself each day before all
The learned tutors whom for him she hired,
    Was, that his breeding should be strictly moral;
Much into all his studies she inquired,
    And so they were submitted first to her, all,   310
Arts, sciences, no branch was made a mystery
To Juan's eyes, excepting natural history.[1]

40

The languages, especially the dead,
    The sciences, and most of all the abstruse,
The arts, at least all such as could be said   315
    To be the most remote from common use,
In all these he was much and deeply read;
    But not a page of anything that's loose,
Or hints continuation of the species,
Was ever suffer'd, lest he should grow vicious.   320

41

His classic studies made a little puzzle,
    Because of filthy loves of gods and goddesses,
Who in the earlier ages made a bustle,
    But never put on pantaloons or boddices;
His reverend tutors had at times a tussle,   325
    And for their Aeneids, Iliads, and Odysseys,
Were forced to make an odd sort of apology,
For Donna Inez dreaded the mythology.

42

Ovid's a rake, as half his verses show him,
    Anacreon's morals are a still worse sample,   330
Catullus scarcely has a decent poem,
    I don't think Sappho's Ode a good example,
Although Longinus tells us there is no hymn
    Where the sublime soars forth on wings more ample;[2]
But Virgil's songs are pure, except that horrid one   335
Beginning with *"Formosum Pastor Corydon."*[3]

43

Lucretius' irreligion[4] is too strong
    For early stomachs, to prove wholesome food;
I can't help thinking Juvenal[5] was wrong,
    Although no doubt his real intent was good,   340
For speaking out so plainly in his song,
    So much indeed as to be downright rude;
And then what proper person can be partial
To all those nauseous epigrams of Martial?

44

Juan was taught from out the best edition,   345
    Expurgated by learned men, who place,

---

1. Includes biology and physiology.
2. The Greek rhetorician Longinus praises a passage from Sappho in *On the Sublime* 10.
3. Virgil's *Eclogue* 2 begins: "The shepherd, Corydon, burned with love for the handsome Alexis."

4. In *De rerum natura* ("On the Nature of Things") Lucretius sets out to show that the universe can be explained without reference to any god.
5. The Latin satires of Juvenal attacked the corruption of Roman society in the 1st century A.D.

Judiciously, from out the schoolboy's vision,
   The grosser parts; but fearful to deface
Too much their modest bard by this omission,
   And pitying sore his mutilated case,   350
They only add them all in an appendix,[6]
Which saves, in fact, the trouble of an index.

            *   *   *

52
For my part I say nothing—nothing—but
   This I will say—my reasons are my own—   410
That if I had an only son to put
   To school (as God be praised that I have none)
'Tis not with Donna Inez I would shut
   Him up to learn his catechism alone,
No—No—I'd send him out betimes to college,   415
For there it was I pick'd up my own knowledge.

53
For there one learns—'tis not for me to boast,
   Though I acquired—but I pass over *that,*
As well as all the Greek I since have lost:
   I say that there's the place—but *"Verbum sat,"*[7]   420
I think I pick'd up too, as well as most,
   Knowledge of matters—but no matter *what*—
I never married—but, I think, I know
That sons should not be educated so.

54
Young Juan now was sixteen years of age,   425
   Tall, handsome, slender, but well knit; he seem'd
Active, though not so sprightly, as a page;
   And every body but his mother deem'd
Him almost man; but she flew in a rage,
   And bit her lips (for else she might have scream'd),   430
If any said so, for to be precocious
Was in her eyes a thing the most atrocious.

55
Amongst her numerous acquaintance, all
   Selected for discretion and devotion,
There was the Donna Julia, whom to call   435
   Pretty were but to give a feeble notion
Of many charms in her as natural
   As sweetness to the flower, or salt to ocean,
Her zone[8] to Venus, or his bow to Cupid,
(But this last simile is trite and stupid).   440

56
The darkness of her Oriental eye
   Accorded with her Moorish origin;
(Her blood was not all Spanish, by the by;
   In Spain, you know, this is a sort of sin).

---

6. Fact! There is, or was, such an edition, with all the
obnoxious epigrams of Martial placed by themselves at
the end [Byron's note].

7. A word [to the wise] is sufficient (Latin).
8. Belt or sash.

When proud Grenada fell, and, forced to fly,   445
　　Boabdil wept,[9] of Donna Julia's kin
Some went to Africa, some staid in Spain,
Her great great grandmamma chose to remain.
57
She married (I forget the pedigree)
　　With an Hidalgo,[1] who transmitted down   450
His blood less noble than such blood should be;
　　At such alliances his sires would frown,
In that point so precise in each degree
　　That they bred *in and in*, as might be shown,
Marrying their cousins—nay, their aunts and nieces,   455
Which always spoils the breed, if it increases.
58
This heathenish cross restored the breed again,
　　Ruin'd its blood, but much improved its flesh;
For, from a root the ugliest in Old Spain
　　Sprung up a branch as beautiful as fresh;   460
The sons no more were short, the daughters plain:
　　But there's a rumour which I fain would hush,
'Tis said that Donna Julia's grandmamma
Produced her Don more heirs at love than law.
59
However this might be, the race went on   465
　　Improving still through every generation,
Until it center'd in an only son,
　　Who left an only daughter; my narration
May have suggested that this single one
　　Could be but Julia (whom on this occasion   470
I shall have much to speak about), and she
Was married, charming, chaste,[2] and twenty-three.
60
Her eye (I'm very fond of handsome eyes)
　　Was large and dark, suppressing half its fire
Until she spoke, then through its soft disguise   475
　　Flash'd an expression more of pride than ire,
And love than either; and there would arise
　　A something in them which was not desire,
But would have been, perhaps, but for the soul
Which struggled through and chasten'd down the whole.   480
61
Her glossy hair was cluster'd o'er a brow
　　Bright with intelligence, and fair and smooth;
Her eyebrow's shape was like the aerial bow,
　　Her cheek all purple with the beam of youth,
Mounting, at times, to a transparent glow,   485
　　As if her veins ran lightning; she, in sooth,
Possess'd an air and grace by no means common:
Her stature tall—I hate a dumpy woman.

---

9. The last Moorish king of Granada (then a province   1. A Spanish nobleman of the lower class.
in Spain) wept when his capital fell to the Spaniards   2. I.e., faithful to her husband.
(1492).

62

Wedded she was some years, and to a man
　　Of fifty, and such husbands are in plenty;   490
And yet, I think, instead of such a ONE
　　'Twere better to have TWO of five and twenty,
Especially in countries near the sun:
　　And now I think on't, "mi vien in mente,"[3]
Ladies even of the most uneasy virtue   495
Prefer a spouse whose age is short of thirty.

63

'Tis a sad thing, I cannot choose but say,
　　And all the fault of that indecent sun,
Who cannot leave alone our helpless clay,
　　But will keep baking, broiling, burning on,   500
That howsoever people fast and pray
　　The flesh is frail, and so the soul undone:
What men call gallantry, and gods adultery,
Is much more common where the climate's sultry.

64

Happy the nations of the moral north!   505
　　Where all is virtue, and the winter season
Sends sin, without a rag on, shivering forth;
　　('Twas snow that brought St. Francis back to reason);
Where juries cast up what a wife is worth
　　By laying whate'er sum, in mulct,[4] they please on   510
The lover, who must pay a handsome price,
Because it is a marketable vice.

65

Alfonso was the name of Julia's lord,
　　A man well looking for his years, and who
Was neither much beloved, nor yet abhorr'd;   515
　　They lived together as most people do,
Suffering each other's foibles by accord,
　　And not exactly either one or two;
Yet he was jealous, though he did not show it,
For jealousy dislikes the world to know it.   520

*　*　*

69

Juan she saw, and, as a pretty child,   545
　　Caress'd him often, such a thing might be
Quite innocently done, and harmless styled,
　　When she had twenty years, and thirteen he;
But I am not so sure I should have smiled
　　When he was sixteen, Julia twenty-three,   550
These few short years make wondrous alterations,
Particularly amongst sun-burnt nations.

70

Whate'er the cause might be, they had become
　　Changed; for the dame grew distant, the youth shy,

---

3. It comes to my mind (Italian).　　　　　4. By way of a fine or legal penalty.

Their looks cast down, their greetings almost dumb,   555
    And much embarrassment in either eye;
There surely will be little doubt with some
    That Donna Julia knew the reason why,
But as for Juan, he had no more notion
Than he who never saw the sea of ocean.   560

                                71
Yet Julia's very coldness still was kind,
    And tremulously gentle her small hand
Withdrew itself from his, but left behind
    A little pressure, thrilling, and so bland
And slight, so very slight, that to the mind   565
    'Twas but a doubt; but ne'er magician's wand
Wrought change with all Armida's[5] fairy art
Like what this light touch left on Juan's heart.

                                72
And if she met him, though she smiled no more,
    She look'd a sadness sweeter than her smile,   570
As if her heart had deeper thoughts in store
    She must not own, but cherish'd more the while,
For that compression in its burning core;
    Even innocence itself has many a wile,
And will not dare to trust itself with truth,   575
And love is taught hypocrisy from youth.

                              *   *   *

                                75
Poor Julia's heart was in an awkward state;
    She felt it going, and resolved to make
The noblest efforts for herself and mate,   595
    For honour's, pride's, religion's, virtue's sake;
Her resolutions were most truly great,
    And almost might have made a Tarquin[6] quake;
She pray'd the Virgin Mary for her grace,
As being the best judge of a lady's case.   600

                                76
She vow'd she never would see Juan more,
    And next day paid a visit to his mother,
And look'd extremely at the opening door,
    Which, by the Virgin's grace, let in another;
Grateful she was, and yet a little sore—   605
    Again it opens, it can be no other,
'Tis surely Juan now—No! I'm afraid
That night the Virgin was no further pray'd.

                                77
She now determined that a virtuous woman
    Should rather face and overcome temptation,   610
That flight was base and dastardly, and no man
    Should ever give her heart the least sensation;

5. The sorceress who seduces Rinaldo in Torquato
Tasso's *Jerusalem Delivered*.
6. A member of a legendary family of Roman kings

noted for tyranny and cruelty; perhaps a reference specifically to Lucius Tarquinus, the villain of Shakespeare's *The Rape of Lucrece*.

That is to say, a thought beyond the common
  Preference, that we must feel upon occasion,
For people who are pleasanter than others,
But then they only seem so many brothers.   615

78

And even if by chance—and who can tell?
  The devil's so very sly—she should discover
That all within was not so very well,
  And, if still free, that such or such a lover   620
Might please perhaps, a virtuous wife can quell
  Such thoughts, and be the better when they're over;
And if the man should ask, 'tis but denial:
I recommend young ladies to make trial.

79

And then there are such things as love divine,   625
  Bright and immaculate, unmix'd and pure,
Such as the angels think so very fine,
  And matrons, who would be no less secure,
Platonic, perfect, "just such love as mine":
  Thus Julia said—and thought so, to be sure,   630
And so I'd have her think, were I the man
On whom her reveries celestial ran.

*   *   *

86

So much for Julia. Now we'll turn to Juan,
  Poor little fellow! he had no idea
Of his own case, and never hit the true one;
  In feelings quick as Ovid's Miss Medea,[7]
He puzzled over what he found a new one,   685
  But not as yet imagined it could be a
Thing quite in course, and not at all alarming,
Which, with a little patience, might grow charming.

*   *   *

90

Young Juan wander'd by the glassy brooks
  Thinking unutterable things; he threw
Himself at length within the leafy nooks   715
  Where the wild branch of the cork forest grew;
There poets find materials for their books,
  And every now and then we read them through,
So that their plan and prosody are eligible,
Unless, like Wordsworth, they prove unintelligible.   720

91

He, Juan (and not Wordsworth), so pursued
  His self-communion with his own high soul,
Until his mighty heart, in its great mood,
  Had mitigated part, though not the whole
Of its disease; he did the best he could   725

---

7. In *Metamorphoses* 7 Ovid tells the story of Medea's mad infatuation for Jason.

With things not very subject to control,
And turn'd, without perceiving his condition,
Like Coleridge, into a metaphysician.

92

He thought about himself, and the whole earth,
   Of man the wonderful, and of the stars,   730
And how the deuce they ever could have birth;
   And then he thought of earthquakes, and of wars,
How many miles the moon might have in girth,
   Of air-balloons, and of the many bars
To perfect knowledge of the boundless skies;   735
And then he thought of Donna Julia's eyes.

93

In thoughts like these true wisdom may discern
   Longings sublime, and aspirations high,
Which some are born with, but the most part learn
   To plague themselves withal, they know not why: 740
'Twas strange that one so young should thus concern
   His brain about the action of the sky;
If *you* think 'twas philosophy that this did,
I can't help thinking puberty assisted.

94

He pored upon the leaves, and on the flowers,   745
   And heard a voice in all the winds; and then
He thought of wood nymphs and immortal bowers,
   And how the goddesses came down to men:
He miss'd the pathway, he forgot the hours,
   And when he look'd upon his watch again,   750
He found how much old Time had been a winner—
He also found that he had lost his dinner.

*   *   *

103

'Twas on a summer's day—the sixth of June:—
   I like to be particular in dates,
Not only of the age, and year, but moon;
   They are a sort of post-house, where the Fates   820
Change horses, making history change its tune,
   Then spur away o'er empires and o'er states,
Leaving at last not much besides chronology,
Excepting the post-obits[8] of theology.

104

'Twas on the sixth of June, about the hour   825
   Of half-past six—perhaps still nearer seven,
When Julia sate within as pretty a bower
   As e'er held houri in that heathenish heaven
Described by Mahomet, and Anacreon Moore,[9]

---

8. I.e., postobit bonds (*post obitum*, "after death"
[Latin]): loans to an heir that fall due after the death of
the person whose estate he or she is to inherit. Byron's
meaning is probably that only theology purports to tell
us what rewards are due in heaven.

9. Byron's friend the poet Thomas Moore, who had
translated the *Odes* of Anacreon; Byron is alluding to
the tale of *Paradise and the Peri* in Moore's Oriental
poem *Lalla Rookh*.

To whom the lyre and laurels have been given,   830
With all the trophies of triumphant song—
He won them well, and may he wear them long!
                        105
She sate, but not alone; I know not well
    How this same interview had taken place,
And even if I knew, I should not tell—   835
    People should hold their tongues in any case;
No matter how or why the thing befell,
    But there were she and Juan, face to face—
When two such faces are so, 'twould be wise,
But very difficult, to shut their eyes.   840
                        106
How beautiful she look'd! her conscious[1] heart
    Glow'd in her cheek, and yet she felt no wrong.
Oh Love! how perfect is thy mystic art,
    Strengthening the weak, and trampling on the strong,
How self-deceitful is the sagest part   845
    Of mortals whom thy lure hath led along—
The precipice she stood on was immense,
So was her creed[2] in her own innocence.
                        107
She thought of her own strength, and Juan's youth,
    And of the folly of all prudish fears,   850
Victorious virtue, and domestic truth,
    And then of Don Alfonso's fifty years:
I wish these last had not occurr'd, in sooth,
    Because that number rarely much endears,
And through all climes, the snowy and the sunny,   855
Sounds ill in love, whate'er it may in money.

                    *   *   *

                        113
The sun set, and up rose the yellow moon:
    The devil's in the moon for mischief; they
Who call'd her CHASTE, methinks, began too soon
    Their nomenclature; there is not a day,   900
The longest, not the twenty-first of June,
    Sees half the business in a wicked way
On which three single hours of moonshine smile—
And then she looks so modest all the while.
                        114
There is a dangerous silence in that hour,   905
    A stillness, which leaves room for the full soul
To open all itself, without the power
    Of calling wholly back its self-control;
The silver light which, hallowing tree and tower,
    Sheds beauty and deep softness o'er the whole,   910
Breathes also to the heart, and o'er it throws
A loving languor, which is not repose.

---

1. Inwardly aware (of her feelings).   2. Belief.

115

And Julia sate with Juan, half embraced
    And half retiring from the glowing arm,
Which trembled like the bosom where 'twas placed;   915
    Yet still she must have thought there was no harm,
Or else 'twere easy to withdraw her waist;
    But then the situation had its charm,
And then—God knows what next—I can't go on;
I'm almost sorry that I e'er begun.   920

116

Oh Plato! Plato! you have paved the way,
    With your confounded fantasies, to more
Immoral conduct by the fancied sway
    Your system feigns o'er the controlless core
Of human hearts, than all the long array   925
    Of poets and romancers:—You're a bore,
A charlatan, a coxcomb—and have been,
At best, no better than a go-between.

117

And Julia's voice was lost, except in sighs,
    Until too late for useful conversation;   930
The tears were gushing from her gentle eyes,
    I wish, indeed, they had not had occasion,
But who, alas! can love, and then be wise?
    Not that remorse did not oppose temptation,
A little still she strove, and much repented,   935
And whispering "I will ne'er consent"—consented.

*   *   *

126

'Tis sweet to win, no matter how, one's laurels
    By blood or ink; 'tis sweet to put an end
To strife; 'tis sometimes sweet to have our quarrels,
    Particularly with a tiresome friend;
Sweet is old wine in bottles, ale in barrels;   1005
    Dear is the helpless creature we defend
Against the world; and dear the schoolboy spot
We ne'er forget, though there we are forgot.

127

But sweeter still than this, than these, than all,
    Is first and passionate love—it stands alone,   1010
Like Adam's recollection of his fall;
    The tree of knowledge has been pluck'd—all's known—
And life yields nothing further to recall
    Worthy of this ambrosial sin, so shown,
No doubt in fable, as the unforgiven   1015
Fire which Prometheus[3] filch'd for us from heaven.

*   *   *

---

3. The Titan Prometheus incurred the wrath of Zeus by stealing fire from heaven for humans.

133

Man's a phenomenon, one knows not what,
  And wonderful beyond all wondrous measure;
'Tis pity though, in this sublime world, that
  Pleasure's a sin, and sometimes sin's a pleasure;   1060
Few mortals know what end they would be at,
  But whether glory, power, or love, or treasure,
The path is through perplexing ways, and when
The goal is gain'd, we die, you know—and then—

134

What then?—I do not know, no more do you—   1065
  And so good night.—Return we to our story:
'Twas in November, when fine days are few,
  And the far mountains wax a little hoary,
And clap a white cape on their mantles blue;
  And the sea dashes round the promontory,   1070
And the loud breaker boils against the rock,
And sober suns must set at five o'clock.

135

'Twas, as the watchmen say, a cloudy night;
  No moon, no stars, the wind was low or loud
By gusts, and many a sparkling hearth was bright   1075
  With the piled wood, round which the family crowd;
There's something cheerful in that sort of light,
  Even as a summer sky's without a cloud:
I'm fond of fire, and crickets, and all that,
A lobster-salad, and champagne, and chat.   1080

136

'Twas midnight—Donna Julia was in bed,
  Sleeping, most probably—when at her door
Arose a clatter might awake the dead,
  If they had never been awoke before,
And that they have been so we all have read,   1085
  And are to be so, at the least, once more—
The door was fasten'd, but with voice and fist
First knocks were heard, then "Madam—Madam—hist!

137

"For God's sake, Madam—Madam—here's my master,
  With more than half the city at his back—   1090
Was ever heard of such a curst disaster!
  'Tis not my fault—I kept good watch—Alack!
Do, pray undo the bolt a little faster—
  They're on the stair just now, and in a crack
Will all be here; perhaps he yet may fly—   1095
Surely the window's not so *very* high!"

138

By this time Don Alfonso was arrived,
  With torches, friends, and servants in great number;
The major part of them had long been wived,
  And therefore paused not to disturb the slumber   1100
Of any wicked woman, who contrived

By stealth her husband's temples to encumber:[4]
Examples of this kind are so contagious,
Were one not punish'd, all would be outrageous.

139

I can't tell how, or why, or what suspicion   1105
  Could enter into Don Alfonso's head;
But for a cavalier of his condition[5]
  It surely was exceedingly ill-bred
Without a word of previous admonition,
  To hold a levee[6] round his lady's bed,   1110
And summon lackeys, arm'd with fire and sword,
To prove himself the thing he most abhorr'd.

140

Poor Donna Julia! starting as from sleep,
  (Mind—that I do not say—she had not slept)
Began at once to scream, and yawn, and weep;   1115
  Her maid Antonia, who was an adept,
Contrived to fling the bed-clothes in a heap,
  As if she had just now from out them crept:
I can't tell why she should take all this trouble
To prove her mistress had been sleeping double.   1120

141

But Julia mistress, and Antonia maid,
  Appear'd like two poor harmless women, who
Of goblins, but still more of men afraid,
  Had thought one man might be deterr'd by two,
And therefore side by side were gently laid,   1125
  Until the hours of absence should run through,
And truant husband should return, and say,
"My dear, I was the first who came away."

142

Now Julia found at length a voice, and cried,
  "In heaven's name, Don Alfonso, what d'ye mean?   1130
Has madness seized you? would that I had died
  Ere such a monster's victim I had been!
What may this midnight violence betide,
  A sudden fit of drunkenness or spleen?
Dare you suspect me, whom the thought would kill?   1135
Search, then, the room!"—Alfonso said, "I will."

143

He search'd, *they* search'd, and rummaged every where,
  Closet and clothes'-press, chest and window-seat,
And found much linen, lace, and seven pair
  Of stockings, slippers, brushes, combs, complete,   1140
With other articles of ladies fair,
  To keep them beautiful, or leave them neat:
Arras[7] they prick'd and curtains with their swords,
And wounded several shutters, and some boards.

---

4. Horns growing on the forehead was the traditional emblem of the cuckolded husband.
5. Rank.
6. Morning reception.
7. A tapestry hanging on a wall.

144

Under the bed they search'd, and there they found— 1145
    No matter what—it was not that they sought;
They open'd windows, gazing if the ground
    Had signs or footmarks, but the earth said nought;
And then they stared each others' faces round:
    'Tis odd, not one of all these seekers thought, 1150
And seems to me almost a sort of blunder,
Of looking *in* the bed as well as under.

145

During this inquisition Julia's tongue
    Was not asleep—"Yes, search and search," she cried,
"Insult on insult heap, and wrong on wrong! 1155
    It was for this that I became a bride!
For this in silence I have suffer'd long
    A husband like Alfonso at my side;
But now I'll bear no more, nor here remain,
If there be law, or lawyers, in all Spain. 1160

146

"Yes, Don Alfonso! husband now no more,
    If ever you indeed deserved the name,
Is't worthy of your years?—you have threescore,
    Fifty, or sixty—it is all the same—
Is't wise or fitting causeless to explore 1165
    For facts against a virtuous woman's fame?
Ungrateful, perjured, barbarous Don Alfonso,
How dare you think your lady would go on so?"

*   *   *

159

The Senhor Don Alfonso stood confused; 1265
    Antonia bustled round the ransack'd room,
And, turning up her nose, with looks abused
    Her master, and his myrmidons, of whom
Not one, except the attorney, was amused;
    He, like Achates,[8] faithful to the tomb, 1270
So there were quarrels, cared not for the cause,
Knowing they must be settled by the laws.

160

With prying snub-nose, and small eyes, he stood,
    Following Antonia's motions here and there,
With much suspicion in his attitude; 1275
    For reputations he had little care;
So that a suit or action were made good,
    Small pity had he for the young and fair,
And ne'er believed in negatives, till these
Were proved by competent false witnesses. 1280

161

But Don Alfonso stood with downcast looks,
    And, truth to say, he made a foolish figure;

8. The *fidus Achates* ("faithful Achates") of Virgil's *Aeneid*, whose loyalty to Aeneas has become proverbial.

When, after searching in five hundred nooks,
   And treating a young wife with so much rigour,
He gain'd no point, except some self-rebukes,   1285
   Added to those his lady with such vigour
Had pour'd upon him for the last half-hour,
Quick, thick, and heavy—as a thunder-shower.

162

At first he tried to hammer an excuse,
   To which the sole reply was tears, and sobs,   1290
And indications of hysterics, whose
   Prologue is always certain throes, and throbs,
Gasps, and whatever else the owners choose:—
   Alfonso saw his wife, and thought of Job's;[9]
He saw too, in perspective, her relations,   1295
And then he tried to muster all his patience.

163

He stood in act to speak, or rather stammer,
   But sage Antonia cut him short before
The anvil of his speech received the hammer,
   With "Pray sir, leave the room, and say no more,   1300
Or madam dies."—Alfonso mutter'd "D—n her,"
   But nothing else, the time of words was o'er;
He cast a rueful look or two, and did,
He knew not wherefore, that which he was bid.

164

With him retired his *"posse comitatus,"*[1]   1305
   The attorney last, who linger'd near the door,
Reluctantly, still tarrying there as late as
   Antonia let him—not a little sore
At this most strange and unexplain'd *"hiatus"*
   In Don Alfonso's facts, which just now wore   1310
An awkward look; as he resolved the case
The door was fasten'd in his legal face.

165

No sooner was it bolted, than—Oh shame!
   Oh sin! Oh sorrow! and Oh womankind!
How can you do such things and keep your fame,   1315
   Unless this world, and t'other too, be blind?
Nothing so dear as an unfilch'd good name!
   But to proceed—for there is more behind:
With much heart-felt reluctance be it said,
Young Juan slipp'd, half-smother'd, from the bed.   1320

166

He had been hid—I don't pretend to say
   How, nor can I indeed describe the where—
Young, slender, and pack'd easily, he lay,
   No doubt, in little compass, round or square;
But pity him I neither must nor may   1325
   His suffocation by that pretty pair;

---

9. Job's wife had advised her afflicted husband to "curse God, and die" (Job 2.9).
1. The complete form of the modern word *posse* (*posse* *comitatus* means literally "power of the county" [Latin], i.e., the body of citizens summoned by a sheriff to preserve order in the county).

'Twere better, sure, to die so, than be shut
With maudlin Clarence in his Malmsey butt.[2]

*   *   *

169
What's to be done? Alfonso will be back   1345
    The moment he has sent his fools away.
Antonia's skill was put upon the rack,
    But no device could be brought into play—
And how to parry the renew'd attack?
    Besides, it wanted but few hours of day: 1350
Antonia puzzled; Julia did not speak,
But press'd her bloodless lip to Juan's cheek.

170
He turn'd his lip to hers, and with his hand
    Call'd back the tangles of her wandering hair;
Even then their love they could not all command,   1355
    And half forgot their danger and despair:
Antonia's patience now was at a stand—
    "Come, come, 'tis no time now for fooling there,"
She whisper'd, in great wrath—"I must deposit
This pretty gentleman within the closet."   1360

*   *   *

173
Now, Don Alfonso entering, but alone,
    Closed the oration of the trusty maid:
She loiter'd, and he told her to be gone,
    An order somewhat sullenly obey'd;   1380
However, present remedy was none,
    And no great good seem'd answer'd if she staid:
Regarding both with slow and sidelong view,
She snuff'd the candle, curtsied, and withdrew.

174
Alfonso paused a minute—then begun   1385
    Some strange excuses for his late proceeding;
He would not justify what he had done,
    To say the best, it was extreme ill-breeding;
But there were ample reasons for it, none
    Of which he specified in this his pleading: 1390
His speech was a fine sample, on the whole,
Of rhetoric, which the learn'd call "*rigmarole.*"[3]

*   *   *

180
Alfonso closed his speech, and begg'd her pardon,
    Which Julia half withheld, and then half granted,
And laid conditions, he thought, very hard on,   1435
    Denying several little things he wanted:
He stood like Adam lingering near his garden,

2. The duke of Clarence, brother of Richard III, was   a cask ("butt") of malmsey, a sweet and aromatic wine.
reputed to have been assassinated by being drowned in   3. Illogical sequence of vague statements.

With useless penitence perplex'd and haunted,
Beseeching she no further would refuse,
When lo! he stumbled o'er a pair of shoes.   1440

181

A pair of shoes!—what then? not much, if they
    Are such as fit with lady's feet, but these
(No one can tell how much I grieve to say)
    Were masculine; to see them, and to seize,
Was but a moment's act.—Ah! Well-a-day!   1445
    My teeth begin to chatter, my veins freeze—
Alfonso first examined well their fashion,
And then flew out into another passion.

182

He left the room for his relinquish'd sword,
    And Julia instant to the closet flew,   1450
"Fly, Juan, fly! for heaven's sake—not a word—
    The door is open—you may yet slip through
The passage you so often have explored—
    Here is the garden-key—Fly—fly—Adieu!
Haste—haste!—I hear Alfonso's hurrying feet—   1455
Day has not broke—there's no one in the street."

183

None can say that this was not good advice,
    The only mischief was, it came too late;
Of all experience 'tis the usual price,
    A sort of income-tax laid on by fate: 1460
Juan had reach'd the room-door in a trice,
    And might have done so by the garden-gate,
But met Alfonso in his dressing-gown,
Who threaten'd death—so Juan knock'd him down.

184

Dire was the scuffle, and out went the light,   1465
    Antonia cried out "Rape!" and Julia "Fire!"
But not a servant stirr'd to aid the fight.
    Alfonso, pommell'd to his heart's desire,
Swore lustily he'd be revenged this night;
    And Juan, too, blasphemed an octave higher,   1470
His blood was up; though young, he was a Tartar,[4]
And not at all disposed to prove a martyr.

185

Alfonso's sword had dropp'd ere he could draw it,
    And they continued battling hand to hand,
For Juan very luckily ne'er saw it;   1475
    His temper not being under great command,
If at that moment he had chanced to claw it,
    Alfonso's days had not been in the land
Much longer.—Think of husbands', lovers' lives!
And how ye may be doubly widows—wives!   1480

186

Alfonso grappled to detain the foe,
    And Juan throttled him to get away,

---

4. A formidable opponent.

And blood ('twas from the nose) began to flow;
  At last, as they more faintly wrestling lay,
Juan contrived to give an awkward blow,   1485
  And then his only garment quite gave way;
He fled, like Joseph,[5] leaving it; but there,
I doubt, all likeness ends between the pair.

                    187

Lights came at length, and men, and maids, who found
  An awkward spectacle their eyes before;   1490
Antonia in hysterics, Julia swoon'd,
  Alfonso leaning, breathless, by the door;
Some half-torn drapery scatter'd on the ground,
  Some blood, and several footsteps, but no more:
Juan the gate gain'd, turn'd the key about,   1495
And liking not the inside, lock'd the out.

                    188

Here ends this canto.—Need I sing, or say,
  How Juan, naked, favour'd by the night,
Who favours what she should not, found his way,
  And reach'd his home in an unseemly plight?   1500
The pleasant scandal which arose next day,
  The nine days' wonder which was brought to light,
And how Alfonso sued for a divorce,
Were in the English newspapers, of course.

                    189

If you would like to see the whole proceedings,   1505
  The depositions, and the cause at full,
The names of all the witnesses, the pleadings
  Of counsel to nonsuit,[6] or to annul,
There's more than one edition, and the readings
  Are various, but they none of them are dull,   1510
The best is that in shorthand ta'en by Gurney,[7]
Who to Madrid on purpose made a journey.

                    190

But Donna Inez, to divert the train
  Of one of the most circulating scandals
That had for centuries been known in Spain,   1515
  Since Roderic's Goths, or older Genseric's Vandals,[8]
First vow'd (and never had she vow'd in vain)
  To Virgin Mary several pounds of candles;
And then, by the advice of some old ladies,
She sent her son to be embark'd at Cadiz.   1520

                    191

She had resolved that he should travel through
  All European climes, by land or sea,
To mend his former morals, or get new,
  Especially in France and Italy,

---

5. In Genesis 39.7ff. the chaste Joseph flees from the advances of Potiphar's wife, leaving "his garment in her hand."
6. Judgment against the plaintiff for failure to establish his case.
7. William B. Gurney (1777–1855), official shorthand writer for the houses of Parliament and a famous court reporter.
8. The Germanic tribes that overran Spain and other parts of Southern Europe in the 5th through 8th centuries, notorious for rape and violence.

(At least this is the thing most people do).   1525
   Julia was sent into a nunnery,
And there, perhaps, her feelings may be better
Shown in the following copy of her letter:

192

"They tell me 'tis decided; you depart:
   'Tis wise—'tis well, but not the less a pain;   1530
I have no further claim on your young heart,
   Mine was the victim, and would be again;
To love too much has been the only art
   I used;—I write in haste, and if a stain
Be on this sheet, 'tis not what it appears,   1535
My eyeballs burn and throb, but have no tears.

193

"I loved, I love you, for that love have lost
   State, station, heaven, mankind's, my own esteem,
And yet can not regret what it hath cost,
   So dear is still the memory of that dream;   1540
Yet, if I name my guilt, 'tis not to boast,
   None can deem harshlier of me than I deem:
I trace this scrawl because I cannot rest—
I've nothing to reproach, nor to request.

194

"Man's love is of his life a thing apart,
   'Tis woman's whole existence; man may range   1545
The court, camp, church, the vessel, and the mart,
   Sword, gown, gain, glory, offer in exchange
Pride, fame, ambition, to fill up his heart,
   And few there are whom these can not estrange; 1550
Man has all these resources, we but one,
To love again, and be again undone.

195

"My breast has been all weakness, is so yet;
   I struggle, but cannot collect my mind;
My blood still rushes where my spirit's set,   1555
   As roll the waves before the settled wind;
My brain is feminine, nor can forget—
   To all, except your image, madly blind;
As turns the needle[9] trembling to the pole
It ne'er can reach, so turns to you, my soul.   1560

196

"You will proceed in beauty, and in pride,
   Beloved and loving many; all is o'er
For me on earth, except some years to hide
   My shame and sorrow deep in my heart's core;
These I could bear, but cannot cast aside   1565
   The passion which still rends it as before,
And so farewell—forgive me, love me—No,
That word is idle now—but let it go.

---

9. Of a compass.

197

"I have no more to say, but linger still,
    And dare not set my seal upon this sheet,   1570
And yet I may as well the task fulfil,
    My misery can scarce be more complete:
I had not lived till now, could sorrow kill;
    Death flies the wretch who fain the blow would meet,
And I must even survive this last adieu,   1575
And bear with life, to love and pray for you!"

198

This note was written upon gilt-edged paper
    With a neat crow-quill, rather hard, but new;
Her small white fingers scarce could reach the taper,[1]
    But trembled as magnetic needles do,   1580
And yet she did not let one tear escape her;
    The seal a sunflower; *"Elle vous suit partout,"*[2]
The motto, cut upon a white cornelian;
The wax was superfine, its hue vermilion.

199

This was Don Juan's earliest scrape; but whether   1585
    I shall proceed with his adventures is
Dependent on the public altogether;
    We'll see, however, what they say to this,
Their favour in an author's cap's a feather,
    And no great mischief's done by their caprice;   1590
And if their approbation we experience,
Perhaps they'll have some more about a year hence.

200

My poem's epic, and is meant to be
    Divided in twelve books; each book containing,
With love, and war, a heavy gale at sea,   1595
    A list of ships, and captains, and kings reigning,
New characters; the episodes are three:
    A panorama view of hell's in training,
After the style of Virgil and of Homer,
So that my name of Epic's no misnomer.   1600

201

All these things will be specified in time,
    With strict regard to Aristotle's rules,
The *vade mecum*[3] of the true sublime,
    Which makes so many poets, and some fools;
Prose poets like blank-verse, I'm fond of rhyme,   1605
    Good workmen never quarrel with their tools;
I've got new mythological machinery,
And very handsome supernatural scenery.

202

There's only one slight difference between
    Me and my epic brethren gone before,   1610

---

1. The candle (in order to melt wax to seal the letter).
2. She follows you everywhere (French).
3. Handbook; literally "go with me" (Latin). Byron is deriding the neoclassic view that Aristotle's *Poetics* proposes "rules" for writing epic and tragedy.

And here the advantage is my own, I ween;
   (Not that I have not several merits more,
But this will more peculiarly be seen)
   They so embellish, that 'tis quite a bore
Their labyrinth of fables to thread through,   1615
Whereas this story's actually true.

203

If any person doubt it, I appeal
   To history, tradition, and to facts,
To newspapers, whose truth all know and feel,
   To plays in five, and operas in three acts;   1620
All these confirm my statement a good deal,
   But that which more completely faith exacts
Is, that myself, and several now in Seville,
Saw Juan's last elopement with the devil.[4]

204

If ever I should condescend to prose,   1625
   I'll write poetical commandments, which
Shall supersede beyond all doubt all those
   That went before; in these I shall enrich
My text with many things that no one knows,
   And carry precept to the highest pitch: 1630
I'll call the work "Longinus o'er a Bottle,
Or, Every Poet his *own* Aristotle."

205

Thou shalt believe in Milton, Dryden, Pope;[5]
   Thou shalt not set up Wordsworth, Coleridge, Southey;
Because the first is crazed beyond all hope,
   The second drunk, the third so quaint and mouthey: 1635
With Crabbe it may be difficult to cope,
   And Campbell's Hippocrene[6] is somewhat drouthy:
Thou shalt not steal from Samuel Rogers, nor—
Commit—flirtation with the muse of Moore.[7]   1640

206

Thou shalt not covet Mr. Sotheby's Muse,
   His Pegasus,[8] nor any thing that's his;
Thou shalt not bear false witness like "the Blues,"[9]
   (There's one, at least, is very fond of this);
Thou shalt not write, in short, but what I choose: 1645
   This is true criticism, and you may kiss—
Exactly as you please, or not, the rod,
But if you don't, I'll lay it on, by G—d!

207

If any person should presume to assert
   This story is not moral, first I pray   1650

---

4. The usual plays on the Juan legend ended with Juan in hell; an early 20th-century version is George Bernard Shaw's *Man and Superman.*
5. This is one of many passages, in prose and verse, in which Byron vigorously defended Dryden and Pope against his Romantic contemporaries.
6. Fountain on Mt. Helicon whose waters supposedly gave inspiration.
7. George Crabbe, whom Byron admired, was the author of *The Village* and other realistic poems of rural

life. Thomas Campbell, Samuel Rogers, and Thomas Moore were lesser poets of the Romantic period; the last two were close friends of Byron's.
8. The winged horse symbolizing poetic inspiration. William Sotheby, contemporary poet and translator, was a wealthy man (see line 1642).
9. I.e., bluestockings, a contemporary term for pedantic female intellectuals, among whom Byron numbered his wife (line 1644).

That they will not cry out before they're hurt,
    Then that they'll read it o'er again, and say,
(But, doubtless, nobody will be so pert)
    That this is not a moral tale, though gay;
Besides, in canto twelfth, I mean to show   1655
The very place where wicked people go.

                            *   *   *

                            213
But now at thirty years my hair is gray—
    (I wonder what it will be like at forty?
I thought of a peruke[1] the other day)
    My heart is not much greener; and, in short, I   1700
Have squander'd my whole summer while 'twas May,
    And feel no more the spirit to retort; I
Have spent my life, both interest and principal,
And deem not, what I deem'd, my soul invincible.
                            214
No more—no more—Oh! never more on me   1705
    The freshness of the heart can fall like dew,
Which out of all the lovely things we see
    Extracts emotions beautiful and new,
Hived in our bosoms like the bag o' the bee:
    Think'st thou the honey with those objects grew?   1710
Alas! 'twas not in them, but in thy power
To double even the sweetness of a flower.
                            215
No more—no more—Oh! never more, my heart,
    Canst thou be my sole world, my universe!
Once all in all, but now a thing apart,   1715
    Thou canst not be my blessing or my curse:
The illusion's gone for ever, and thou art
    Insensible, I trust, but none the worse,
And in thy stead I've got a deal of judgment,
Though heaven knows how it ever found a lodgement.   1720
                            216
My days of love are over, me no more
    The charms of maid, wife, and still less of widow,
Can make the fool of which they made before,
    In short, I must not lead the life I did do;
The credulous hope of mutual minds is o'er,   1725
    The copious use of claret is forbid too,
So for a good old gentlemanly vice,
I think I must take up with avarice.
                            217
Ambition was my idol, which was broken
    Before the shrines of Sorrow and of Pleasure;   1730
And the two last have left me many a token
    O'er which reflection may be made at leisure:
Now, like Friar Bacon's brazen head, I've spoken,

---

1. Wig.

"Time is, Time was, Time's past,"[2] a chymic treasure
Is glittering youth, which I have spent betimes—   1735
My heart in passion, and my head on rhymes.

218

What is the end of fame? 'tis but to fill
    A certain portion of uncertain paper:
Some liken it to climbing up a hill,
    Whose summit, like all hills', is lost in vapour;   1740
For this men write, speak, preach, and heroes kill,
    And bards burn what they call their "midnight taper,"
To have, when the original is dust,
A name, a wretched picture, and worse bust.[3]

219

What are the hopes of man? old Egypt's King   1745
    Cheops erected the first pyramid
And largest, thinking it was just the thing
    To keep his memory whole, and mummy hid;
But somebody or other rummaging,
    Burglariously broke his coffin's lid: 1750
Let not a monument give you or me hopes,
Since not a pinch of dust remains of Cheops.

220

But I, being fond of true philosophy,
    Say very often to myself, "Alas!
All things that have been born were born to die,   1755
    And flesh (which Death mows down to hay) is grass;
You've pass'd your youth not so unpleasantly,
    And if you had it o'er again—'twould pass—
So thank your stars that matters are no worse,
And read your Bible, sir, and mind your purse."   1760

221

But for the present, gentle reader! and
    Still gentler purchaser! the bard—that's I—
Must, with permission, shake you by the hand,
    And so your humble servant, and good bye!
We meet again, if we should understand   1765
    Each other; and if not, I shall not try
Your patience further than by this short sample—
'Twere well if others follow'd my example.

222

"Go, little book, from this my solitude!
    I cast thee on the waters, go thy ways!
And if, as I believe, thy vein be good,   1770
    The world will find thee after many days."
When Southey's read, and Wordsworth understood,
    I can't help putting in my claim to praise—
The four first rhymes are Southey's every line:[4]   1775
For God's sake, reader! take them not for mine.

2. Spoken by a bronze bust in Robert Greene's comedy *Friar Bacon and Friar Bungay* (1594). "Chymic":
alchemic, i.e., the "treasure" is counterfeit gold.
3. Byron was unhappy with the portrait bust of him
recently made by the Danish sculptor Thorwaldsen.
4. The lines occur in the last stanza of Southey's *Epilogue to the Lay of the Laureate.*

From Canto 2

[*The Shipwreck*]

8

But to our tale: the Donna Inez sent
  Her son to Cadiz only to embark;
To stay there had not answer'd her intent,
  But why?—we leave the reader in the dark—   60
'Twas for a voyage that the young man was meant,
  As if a Spanish ship were Noah's ark,
To wean him from the wickedness of earth,
And send him like a dove of promise forth.

9

Don Juan bade his valet pack his things   65
  According to direction, then received
A lecture and some money: for four springs
  He was to travel; and though Inez grieved,
(As every kind of parting has its stings)
  She hoped he would improve—perhaps believed: 70
A letter, too, she gave (he never read it)
Of good advice—and two or three of credit.

10

In the mean time, to pass her hours away,
  Brave Inez now set up a Sunday school
For naughty children, who would rather play   75
  (Like truant rogues) the devil, or the fool;
Infants of three years old were taught that day,
  Dunces were whipt, or set upon a stool:
The great success of Juan's education,
Spurr'd her to teach another generation.   80

11

Juan embark'd—the ship got under way,
  The wind was fair, the water passing rough;
A devil of a sea rolls in that bay,
  As I, who've cross'd it oft, know well enough;
And, standing upon deck, the dashing spray   85
  Flies in one's face, and makes it weather-tough:
And there he stood to take, and take again,
His first—perhaps his last—farewell of Spain.

12

I can't but say it is an awkward sight
  To see one's native land receding through   90
The growing waters; it unmans one quite,
  Especially when life is rather new:
I recollect Great Britain's coast looks white,
  But almost every other country's blue,
When gazing on them, mystified by distance,   95
We enter on our nautical existence.

*   *   *

17

And Juan wept, and much he sigh'd and thought,
　　While his salt tears dropp'd into the salt sea,　　　　　　　　　130
"Sweets to the sweet"; (I like so much to quote;
　　You must excuse this extract, 'tis where she,
The Queen of Denmark, for Ophelia brought
　　Flowers to the grave);[1] and sobbing often, he
Reflected on his present situation,　　　　　　　　　　　　　　135
And seriously resolved on reformation.

18

"Farewell, my Spain! a long farewell!" he cried,
　　"Perhaps I may revisit thee no more,
But die, as many an exiled heart hath died,
　　Of its own thirst to see again thy shore:　　　　　　　　　　140
Farewell, where Guadalquivir's waters glide!
　　Farewell, my mother! and, since all is o'er,
Farewell, too dearest Julia!,"—(here he drew
Her letter out again, and read it through).

19

"And oh! if e'er I should forget, I swear—　　　　　　　　　　145
　　But that's impossible, and cannot be—
Sooner shall this blue ocean melt to air,
　　Sooner shall earth resolve itself to sea,
Than I resign thine image, Oh! my fair!
　　Or think of any thing excepting thee;　　　　　　　　　　　150

A mind diseased no remedy can physic—"
(Here the ship gave a lurch, and he grew sea-sick.)

20

"Sooner shall heaven kiss earth"—(here he fell sicker)
　　"Oh, Julia! what is every other woe?—
(For God's sake let me have a glass of liquor,　　　　　　　　155
　　Pedro, Battista, help me down below.)
Julia, my love!—(you rascal, Pedro, quicker)—
　　Oh Julia!—(this curst vessel pitches so)—
Beloved Julia, hear me still beseeching!"
(Here he grew inarticulate with retching.)　　　　　　　　　　160

21

He felt that chilling heaviness of heart,
　　Or rather stomach, which, alas! attends,
Beyond the best apothecary's art,
　　The loss of love, the treachery of friends,
Or death of those we doat on, when a part　　　　　　　　　165
　　Of us dies with them as each fond hope ends:
No doubt he would have been much more pathetic,
But the sea acted as a strong emetic.[2]

*　　*　　*

1. *Hamlet* 5.1.243.
2. In stanzas 22–48 (here omitted) the ship, bound for　　　Leghorn, runs into a violent storm and is battered into a helpless, sinking wreck.

49

'Twas twilight, and the sunless day went down   385
    Over the waste of waters; like a veil,
Which, if withdrawn, would but disclose the frown
    Of one whose hate is masked but to assail;
Thus to their hopeless eyes the night was shown
    And grimly darkled o'er their faces pale,   390
And the dim desolate deep; twelve days had Fear
Been their familiar, and now Death was here.

50

Some trial had been making at a raft,
    With little hope in such a rolling sea,
A sort of thing at which one would have laugh'd,   395
    If any laughter at such times could be,
Unless with people who too much have quaff'd,
    And have a kind of wild and horrid glee,
Half epileptical, and half hysterical: —
Their preservation would have been a miracle.   400

51

At half-past eight o'clock, booms, hencoops, spars,
    And all things, for a chance, had been cast loose,
That still could keep afloat the struggling tars,
    For yet they strove, although of no great use:
There was no light in heaven but a few stars,   405
    The boats put off o'ercrowded with their crews;
She gave a heel, and then a lurch to port,
And, going down head foremost—sunk, in short.

52

Then rose from sea to sky the wild farewell,
    Then shriek'd the timid, and stood still the brave,   410
Then some leap'd overboard with dreadful yell,
    As eager to anticipate their grave;
And the sea yawn'd around her like a hell,
    And down she suck'd with her the whirling wave,
Like one who grapples with his enemy,   415
And strives to strangle him before he die.

53

And first one universal shriek there rush'd,
    Louder than the loud ocean, like a crash
Of echoing thunder; and then all was hush'd,
    Save the wild wind and the remorseless dash   420
Of billows; but at intervals there gush'd,
    Accompanied with a convulsive splash,
A solitary shriek, the bubbling cry
Of some strong swimmer in his agony.

⁂ ⁂ ⁂

56

Juan got into the long-boat, and there
    Contrived to help Pedrillo[3] to a place;
It seem'd as if they had exchanged their care,

3. Juan's tutor.

For Juan wore the magisterial face
Which courage gives, while poor Pedrillo's pair   445
   Of eyes were crying for their owner's case:
Battista, though (a name call'd shortly Tita),
Was lost by getting at some aqua-vita.[4]

57

Pedro, his valet, too, he tried to save,
   But the same cause, conducive to his loss,   450
Left him so drunk, he jump'd into the wave
   As o'er the cutter's edge he tried to cross,
And so he found a wine-and-watery grave;
   They could not rescue him although so close,
Because the sea ran higher every minute,   455
And for the boat—the crew kept crowding in it.

        *   *   *

66

'Tis thus with people in an open boat,
   They live upon the love of life, and bear
More than can be believed, or even thought,
   And stand like rocks the tempest's wear and tear;
And hardship still has been the sailor's lot,   525
   Since Noah's ark went cruising here and there;
She had a curious crew as well as cargo,
Like the first old Greek privateer, the Argo.[5]

67

But man is a carnivorous production,
   And must have meals, at least one meal a day;   530
He cannot live, like woodcocks, upon suction,[6]
   But, like the shark and tiger, must have prey:
Although his anatomical construction
   Bears vegetables in a grumbling way,
Your labouring people think beyond all question,   535
Beef, veal, and mutton, better for digestion.

68

And thus it was with this our hapless crew,
   For on the third day there came on a calm,
And though at first their strength it might renew,
   And lying on their weariness like balm,   540
Lull'd them like turtles sleeping on the blue
   Of ocean, when they woke they felt a qualm,
And fell all ravenously on their provision,
Instead of hoarding it with due precision.

        *   *   *

72

The seventh day,[7] and no wind—the burning sun
   Blister'd and scorch'd, and, stagnant on the sea,   570

---

4. Brandy.
5. In the Greek myth the *Argo* is the ship on which
Jason set out in quest of the Golden Fleece. Byron
ironically calls it a "privateer" (a private ship licensed
by a government in wartime to attack and pillage enemy vessels).

6. Woodcocks probe the turf with long flexible bills,
seeming to suck air as they feed.
7. On the fourth day the crew had killed and eaten
Juan's pet spaniel. Byron based the episode of cannibalism that follows on various historical accounts of
disasters at sea.

They lay like carcases; and hope was none,
    Save in the breeze that came not; savagely
They glared upon each other—all was done,
    Water, and wine, and food,—and you might see
The longings of the cannibal arise   575
(Although they spoke not) in their wolfish eyes.

                  73
At length one whisper'd his companion, who
    Whisper'd another, and thus it went round,
And then into a hoarser murmur grew,
    An ominous, and wild, and desperate sound,   580
And when his comrade's thought each sufferer knew,
    'Twas but his own, suppress'd till now, he found:
And out they spoke of lots for flesh and blood,
And who should die to be his fellow's food.

                  74
But ere they came to this, they that day shared   585
    Some leathern caps, and what remain'd of shoes;
And then they look'd around them, and despair'd,
    And none to be the sacrifice would choose;
At length the lots were torn up, and prepared,
    But of materials that must shock the Muse—   590
Having no paper, for the want of better,
They took by force from Juan Julia's letter.

                  75
The lots were made, and mark'd, and mix'd, and handed,
    In silent horror, and their distribution
Lull'd even the savage hunger which demanded,   595
    Like the Promethean vulture,[8] this pollution;
None in particular had sought or plann'd it,
    'Twas nature gnaw'd them to this resolution,
By which none were permitted to be neuter—
And the lot fell on Juan's luckless tutor.   600

                  76
He but requested to be bled to death:
    The surgeon had his instruments, and bled
Pedrillo, and so gently ebb'd his breath,
    You hardly could perceive when he was dead.
He died as born, a Catholic in faith,   605
    Like most in the belief in which they're bred,
And first a little crucifix he kiss'd,
And then held out his jugular and wrist.

                  77
The surgeon, as there was no other fee,
    Had his first choice of morsels for his pains;   610
But being thirstiest at the moment, he
    Preferr'd a draught from the fast-flowing veins:
Part was divided, part thrown in the sea,
    And such things as the entrails and the brains

---

8. Because Prometheus had stolen fire from heaven to give to humans, Zeus punished him by chaining him to a
mountain peak, where an eagle fed on his ever-renewing liver.

Regaled two sharks, who follow'd o'er the billow—   615
The sailors ate the rest of poor Pedrillo.
                              78
The sailors ate him, all save three or four,
    Who were not quite so fond of animal food;
To these was added Juan, who, before
    Refusing his own spaniel, hardly could   620
Feel now his appetite increased much more;
    'Twas not to be expected that he should,
Even in extremity of their disaster,
Dine with them on his pastor and his master.
                              79
'Twas better that he did not; for, in fact,   625
    The consequence was awful in the extreme;
For they, who were most ravenous in the act,
    Went raging mad—Lord! how they did blaspheme!
And foam and roll, with strange convulsions rack'd,
    Drinking salt-water like a mountain-stream,   630
Tearing, and grinning, howling, screeching, swearing,
And, with hyaena laughter, died despairing.

                          *   *   *

                             103
As they drew nigh the land, which now was seen
    Unequal in its aspect here and there,
They felt the freshness of its growing green,
    That waved in forest-tops, and smooth'd the air,   820
And fell upon their glazed eyes like a screen
    From glistening waves, and skies so hot and bare—
Lovely seem'd any object that should sweep
Away the vast, salt, dread, eternal deep.
                             104
The shore look'd wild, without a trace of man,   825
    And girt by formidable waves; but they
Were mad for land, and thus their course they ran,
    Though right ahead the roaring breakers lay:
A reef between them also now began
    To show its boiling surf and bounding spray,   830
But finding no place for their landing better,
They ran the boat for shore, and overset her.
                             105
But in his native stream, the Guadalquivir,
    Juan to lave his youthful limbs was wont;
And having learnt to swim in that sweet river,   835
    Had often turn'd the art to some account:
A better swimmer you could scarce see ever,
    He could, perhaps, have pass'd the Hellespont,
As once (a feat on which ourselves we prided)
Leander, Mr. Ekenhead, and I did.[9]   840

9. Like Leander in the myth, Byron and Lt. Ekenhead had swum the Hellespont on May 3, 1810. See *Written after Swimming from Sestos to Abydos* (p. 1554).

106

So here, though faint, emaciated, and stark,
    He buoy'd his boyish limbs, and strove to ply
With the quick wave, and gain, ere it was dark,
    The beach which lay before him, high and dry:
The greatest danger here was from a shark,   845
    That carried off his neighbour by the thigh;
As for the other two, they could not swim,
So nobody arrived on shore but him.

107

Nor yet had he arrived but for the oar,
    Which, providentially for him, was wash'd   850
Just as his feeble arms could strike no more,
    And the hard wave o'erwhelm'd him as 'twas dash'd
Within his grasp; he clung to it, and sore
    The waters beat while he thereto was lash'd;
At last, with swimming, wading, scrambling, he   855
Roll'd on the beach, half senseless, from the sea:

108

There, breathless, with his digging nails he clung
    Fast to the sand, lest the returning wave,
From whose reluctant roar his life he wrung,
    Should suck him back to her insatiate grave: 860
And there he lay, full length, where he was flung,
    Before the entrance of a cliff-worn cave,
With just enough of life to feel its pain,
And deem that it was saved, perhaps, in vain.

109

With slow and staggering effort he arose,   865
    But sunk again upon his bleeding knee
And quivering hand; and then he look'd for those
    Who long had been his mates upon the sea,
But none of them appear'd to share his woes,
    Save one, a corpse from out the famish'd three,   870
Who died two days before, and now had found
An unknown barren beach for burial ground.

110

And as he gazed, his dizzy brain spun fast,
    And down he sunk; and as he sunk, the sand
Swam round and round, and all his senses pass'd: 875
    He fell upon his side, and his stretch'd hand
Droop'd dripping on the oar, (their jury-mast)
    And, like a wither'd lily, on the land
His slender frame and pallid aspect lay,
As fair a thing as e'er was form'd of clay.   880

[Juan and Haidee]

111

How long in his damp trance young Juan lay
    He knew not, for the earth was gone for him,
And Time had nothing more of night nor day
    For his congealing blood, and senses dim;

And how this heavy faintness pass'd away   885
   He knew not, till each painful pulse and limb,
And tingling vein seem'd throbbing back to life,
For Death, though vanquish'd, still retired with strife.

112
His eyes he open'd, shut, again unclosed,
   For all was doubt and dizziness; methought   890
He still was in the boat, and had but dozed,
   And felt again with his despair o'erwrought,
And wish'd it death in which he had reposed,
   And then once more his feelings back were brought,
And slowly by his swimming eyes was seen   895
A lovely female face of seventeen.

113
'Twas bending close o'er his, and the small mouth
   Seem'd almost prying into his for breath;
And chafing him, the soft warm hand of youth
   Recall'd his answering spirits back from death;   900
And, bathing his chill temples, tried to soothe
   Each pulse to animation, till beneath
Its gentle touch and trembling care, a sigh
To these kind efforts made a low reply.

114
Then was the cordial pour'd, and mantle flung   905
   Around his scarce-clad limbs; and the fair arm
Raised higher the faint head which o'er it hung;
   And her transparent cheek, all pure and warm,
Pillow'd his death-like forehead; then she wrung
   His dewy curls, long drench'd by every storm;   910
And watch'd with eagerness each throb that drew
A sigh from his heaved bosom—and hers, too.

115
And lifting him with care into the cave,
   The gentle girl, and her attendant,—one
Young, yet her elder, and of brow less grave,   915
   And more robust of figure,—then begun
To kindle fire, and as the new flames gave
   Light to the rocks that roof'd them, which the sun
Had never seen, the maid, or whatsoe'er
She was, appear'd distinct, and tall, and fair.   920

116
Her brow was overhung with coins of gold,
   That sparkled o'er the auburn of her hair,
Her clustering hair, whose longer locks were roll'd
   In braids behind, and though her stature were
Even of the highest for a female mould,   925
   They nearly reach'd her heel; and in her air
There was a something which bespoke command,
As one who was a lady in the land.

117
Her hair, I said, was auburn; but her eyes
   Were black as death, their lashes the same hue,   930

Of downcast length, in whose silk shadow lies
    Deepest attraction, for when to the view
Forth from its raven fringe the full glance flies,
    Ne'er with such force the swiftest arrow flew;
'Tis as the snake late coil'd, who pours his length,   935
And hurls at once his venom and his strength.

*   *   *

123

And these two tended him, and cheer'd him both
    With food and raiment, and those soft attentions,
Which are (as I must own) of female growth,
    And have ten thousand delicate inventions: 980
They made a most superior mess of broth,
    A thing which poesy but seldom mentions,
But the best dish that e'er was cook'd since Homer's
Achilles order'd dinner for new comers.[1]

124

I'll tell you who they were, this female pair,   985
    Lest they should seem princesses in disguise;
Besides, I hate all mystery, and that air
    Of clap-trap, which your recent poets prize;
And so, in short, the girls they really were
    They shall appear before your curious eyes,   990
Mistress and maid; the first was only daughter
Of an old man, who lived upon the water.

125

A fisherman he had been in his youth,
    And still a sort of fisherman was he;
But other speculations were, in sooth,   995
    Added to his connection with the sea,
Perhaps not so respectable, in truth:
    A little smuggling, and some piracy,
Left him, at last, the sole of many masters
Of an ill-gotten million of piastres.[2]   1000

126

A fisher, therefore, was he—though of men,
    Like Peter the Apostle,[3]—and he fish'd
For wandering merchant vessels, now and then,
    And sometimes caught as many as he wish'd;
The cargoes he confiscated, and gain   1005
    He sought in the slave-market too, and dish'd
Full many a morsel for that Turkish trade,
By which, no doubt, a good deal may be made.

127

He was a Greek, and on his isle had built
    (One of the wild and smaller Cyclades)[4]   1010
A very handsome house from out his guilt,

1. A reference to the lavish feast with which Achilles entertained Ajax, Phoenix, and Ulysses (*Iliad* 9.193ff.).
2. Near Eastern coins.
3. Christ's words to Peter and Andrew, both fishermen: "Follow me, and I will make you fishers of men" (Matthew 4.19).
4. A group of islands in the Aegean Sea.

And there he lived exceedingly at ease;
Heaven knows what cash he got, or blood he spilt,
   A sad[5] old fellow was he, if you please,
But this I know, it was a spacious building,   1015
Full of barbaric carving, paint, and gilding.

128

He had an only daughter, call'd Haidee,
   The greatest heiress of the Eastern Isles;
Besides, so very beautiful was she,
   Her dowry was as nothing to her smiles: 1020
Still in her teens, and like a lovely tree
   She grew to womanhood, and between whiles
Rejected several suitors, just to learn
How to accept a better in his turn.

129

And walking out upon the beach, below   1025
   The cliff, towards sunset, on that day she found,
Insensible,—not dead, but nearly so,—
   Don Juan, almost famish'd, and half drown'd;
But being naked, she was shock'd, you know,
   Yet deem'd herself in common pity bound,   1030
As far as in her lay, "to take him in,
A stranger"[6] dying, with so white a skin.

130

But taking him into her father's house
   Was not exactly the best way to save,
But like conveying to the cat the mouse,   1035
   Or people in a trance into their grave;
Because the good old man had so much "νοῦς,"[7]
   Unlike the honest Arab thieves so brave,
He would have hospitably cured the stranger,
And sold him instantly when out of danger.   1040

131

And therefore, with her maid, she thought it best
   (A virgin always on her maid relies)
To place him in the cave for present rest:
   And when, at last, he open'd his black eyes,
Their charity increased about their guest;   1045
   And their compassion grew to such a size,
It open'd half the turnpike-gates to heaven—
(St. Paul says 'tis the toll which must be given).[8]

* * *

141

And Haidee met the morning face to face;
   Her own was freshest, though a feverish flush
Had dyed it with the headlong blood, whose race
   From heart to cheek is curb'd into a blush,
Like to a torrent which a mountain's base,   1125

---

5. In the playful sense: "wicked."
6. Cf. Matthew 25.35: "I was a stranger, and ye took me in."

7. Nous, "intelligence" (Greek); in England, pronounced so as to rhyme with *mouse*.
8. 1 Corinthians 13.13.

That overpowers some Alpine river's rush,
Checks to a lake, whose waves in circles spread;
Or the Red Sea—but the sea is not red.

142

And down the cliff the island virgin came,
   And near the cave her quick light footsteps drew,   1130
While the sun smiled on her with his first flame,
   And young Aurora[9] kiss'd her lips with dew,
Taking her for a sister; just the same
   Mistake you would have made on seeing the two,
Although the mortal, quite as fresh and fair,   1135
Had all the advantage too of not being air.

143

And when into the cavern Haidee stepp'd
   All timidly, yet rapidly, she saw
That like an infant Juan sweetly slept;
   And then she stopp'd, and stood as if in awe,   1140
(For sleep is awful) and on tiptoe crept
   And wrapt him closer, lest the air, too raw,
Should reach his blood, then o'er him still as death
Bent, with hush'd lips, that drank his scarce-drawn breath.

*   *   *

148

And she bent o'er him, and he lay beneath,
   Hush'd as the babe upon its mother's breast,
Droop'd as the willow when no winds can breathe,
   Lull'd like the depth of ocean when at rest,   1180
Fair as the crowning rose of the whole wreath,
   Soft as the callow cygnet[1] in its nest;
In short, he was a very pretty fellow,
Although his woes had turn'd him rather yellow.

149

He woke and gazed, and would have slept again,   1185
   But the fair face which met his eyes forbade
Those eyes to close, though weariness and pain
   Had further sleep a further pleasure made;
For woman's face was never form'd in vain
   For Juan, so that even when he pray'd   1190
He turn'd from grisly saints, and martyrs hairy,
To the sweet portraits of the Virgin Mary.

150

And thus upon his elbow he arose,
   And look'd upon the lady, in whose cheek
The pale contended with the purple rose,   1195
   As with an effort she began to speak;
Her eyes were eloquent, her words would pose,
   Although she told him, in good modern Greek,
With an Ionian accent, low and sweet,
That he was faint, and must not talk, but eat.   1200

*   *   *

9. The dawn.   1. Young swan.

168

And every day by day-break—rather early
　For Juan, who was somewhat fond of rest—
She came into the cave, but it was merely
　To see her bird reposing in his nest;　　　　　　　　　　1340
And she would softly stir his locks so curly,
　Without disturbing her yet slumbering guest,
Breathing all gently o'er his cheek and mouth,
As o'er a bed of roses the sweet south.[2]

169

And every morn his colour freshlier came,　　　　　　　　1345
　And every day help'd on his convalescence;
'Twas well, because health in the human frame
　Is pleasant, besides being true love's essence,
For health and idleness to passion's flame
　Are oil and gunpowder; and some good lessons　　　　　1350
Are also learnt from Ceres[3] and from Bacchus,
Without whom Venus will not long attack us.

170

While Venus fills the heart (without heart really
　Love, though good always, is not quite so good)
Ceres presents a plate of vermicelli,—　　　　　　　　　　1355
　For love must be sustain'd like flesh and blood,—
While Bacchus pours out wine, or hands a jelly:
　Eggs, oysters too, are amatory food;
But who is their purveyor from above
Heaven knows,—it may be Neptune, Pan, or Jove.　　　　1360

171

When Juan woke he found some good things ready,
　A bath, a breakfast, and the finest eyes
That ever made a youthful heart less steady,
　Besides her maid's, as pretty for their size;
But I have spoken of all this already—　　　　　　　　　　1365
　And repetition's tiresome and unwise,—
Well—Juan, after bathing in the sea,
Came always back to coffee and Haidee.

172

Both were so young, and one so innocent,
　That bathing pass'd for nothing; Juan seem'd　　　　　　1370
To her, as 'twere, the kind of being sent,
　Of whom these two years she had nightly dream'd,
A something to be loved, a creature meant
　To be her happiness, and whom she deem'd
To render happy; all who joy would win　　　　　　　　　　1375
Must share it,—Happiness was born a twin.

173

It was such pleasure to behold him, such
　Enlargement of existence to partake
Nature with him, to thrill beneath his touch,
　To watch him slumbering, and to see him wake:　　　　　1380

---

2. The south wind.　　　　　　　　　3. Goddess of the grain.

To live with him for ever were too much;
    But then the thought of parting made her quake:
He was her own, her ocean-treasure, cast
Like a rich wreck—her first love, and her last.

174

And thus a moon roll'd on, and fair Haidee   1385
    Paid daily visits to her boy, and took
Such plentiful precautions, that still he
    Remain'd unknown within his craggy nook;
At last her father's prows put out to sea,
    For certain merchantmen upon the look,   1390
Not as of yore to carry off an Io,[4]
But three Ragusan vessels, bound for Scio.[5]

175

Then came her freedom, for she had no mother,
    So that, her father being at sea, she was
Free as a married woman, or such other   1395
    Female, as where she likes may freely pass,
Without even the encumbrance of a brother,
    The freest she that ever gazed on glass:
I speak of christian lands in this comparison,
Where wives, at least, are seldom kept in garrison.   1400

176

Now she prolong'd her visits and her talk
    (For they must talk), and he had learnt to say
So much as to propose to take a walk,—
    For little had he wander'd since the day
On which, like a young flower snapp'd from the stalk,   1405
    Drooping and dewy on the beach he lay,—
And thus they walk'd out in the afternoon,
And saw the sun set opposite the moon.

177

It was a wild and breaker-beaten coast,
    With cliffs above, and a broad sandy shore,   1410
Guarded by shoals and rocks as by an host,
    With here and there a creek, whose aspect wore
A better welcome to the tempest-tost;
    And rarely ceas'd the haughty billow's roar,
Save on the dead long summer days, which make   1415
The outstretch'd ocean glitter like a lake.

178

And the small ripple spilt upon the beach
    Scarcely o'erpass'd the cream of your champagne,
When o'er the brim the sparkling bumpers reach,
    That spring-dew of the spirit! the heart's rain!   1420
Few things surpass old wine; and they may preach
    Who please,—the more because they preach in vain,—
Let us have wine and woman, mirth and laughter,
Sermons and soda water the day after.

---

4. Io, a mistress of Zeus persecuted by his jealous wife, Hera, was kidnapped by Phoenician merchants.   5. The Italian name for Chios, an island near Turkey. "Ragusan": Ragusa (or Dubrovnik) is an Adriatic port.

179

Man, being reasonable, must get drunk;   1425
   The best of life is but intoxication:
Glory, the grape, love, gold, in these are sunk
   The hopes of all men, and of every nation;
Without their sap, how branchless were the trunk
   Of life's strange tree, so fruitful on occasion: 1430
But to return,—Get very drunk; and when
You wake with head-ache, you shall see what then.

180

Ring for your valet—bid him quickly bring
   Some hock and soda-water, then you'll know
A pleasure worthy Xerxes the great king;[6]   1435
   For not the blest sherbet, sublimed with snow,
Nor the first sparkle of the desert-spring,
   Nor Burgundy in all its sunset glow,
After long travel, ennui, love, or slaughter,
Vie with that draught of hock and soda-water.   1440

181

The coast—I think it was the coast that I
   Was just describing—Yes, it *was* the coast—
Lay at this period quiet as the sky,
   The sands untumbled, the blue waves untost,
And all was stillness, save the sea-bird's cry,   1445
   And dolphin's leap, and little billow crost
By some low rock or shelve, that made it fret
Against the boundary it scarcely wet.

182

And forth they wandered, her sire being gone,
   As I have said, upon an expedition;   1450
And mother, brother, guardian, she had none,
   Save Zoe, who, although with due precision
She waited on her lady with the sun,
   Thought daily service was her only mission,
Bringing warm water, wreathing her long tresses,   1455
And asking now and then for cast-off dresses.

183

It was the cooling hour, just when the rounded
   Red sun sinks down behind the azure hill,
Which then seems as if the whole earth it bounded,
   Circling all nature, hush'd, and dim, and still,   1460
With the far mountain-crescent half surrounded
   On one side, and the deep sea calm and chill
Upon the other, and the rosy sky,
With one star sparkling through it like an eye.

184

And thus they wander'd forth, and hand in hand,   1465
   Over the shining pebbles and the shells,
Glided along the smooth and harden'd sand,
   And in the worn and wild receptacles

---

6. The 5th-century Persian king was said to have offered a reward to anyone who could discover a new kind of pleasure.

Work'd by the storms, yet work'd as it were plann'd,
   In hollow halls, with sparry roofs and cells, 1470
They turn'd to rest; and, each clasp'd by an arm,
   Yielded to the deep twilight's purple charm.
             185

They look'd up to the sky, whose floating glow
   Spread like a rosy ocean, vast and bright;
They gazed upon the glittering sea below, 1475
   Whence the broad moon rose circling into sight;
They heard the wave's splash, and the wind so low,
   And saw each other's dark eyes darting light
Into each other—and, beholding this,
Their lips drew near, and clung into a kiss; 1480
             186

A long, long kiss, a kiss of youth and love,
   And beauty, all concentrating like rays
Into one focus, kindled from above;
   Such kisses as belong to early days,
Where heart, and soul, and sense, in concert move, 1485
   And the blood's lava, and the pulse a blaze,
Each kiss a heart-quake,—for a kiss's strength,
I think, it must be reckon'd by its length.
             187

By length I mean duration; theirs endured
   Heaven knows how long—no doubt they never reckon'd; 1490
And if they had, they could not have secured
   The sum of their sensations to a second:
They had not spoken; but they felt allured,
   As if their souls and lips each other beckon'd,
Which, being join'd, like swarming bees they clung— 1495
Their hearts the flowers from whence the honey sprung.
             188

They were alone, but not alone as they
   Who shut in chambers think it loneliness;
The silent ocean, and the starlight bay,
   The twilight glow, which momently grew less, 1500
The voiceless sands, and dropping caves, that lay
   Around them, made them to each other press,
As if there were no life beneath the sky
Save theirs, and that their life could never die.
             189

They fear'd no eyes nor ears on that lone beach, 1505
   They felt no terrors from the night, they were
All in all to each other: though their speech
   Was broken words, they *thought* a language there,—
And all the burning tongues the passions teach
   Found in one sigh the best interpreter 1510
Of nature's oracle—first love,—that all
Which Eve has left her daughters since her fall.
            190

Haidee spoke not of scruples, ask'd no vows,
   Nor offer'd any; she had never heard

Of plight and promises to be a spouse,   1515
    Or perils by a loving maid incurr'd;
She was all which pure ignorance allows,
    And flew to her young mate like a young bird;
And, never having dreamt of falsehood, she
Had not one word to say of constancy.[7]   1520

191

She loved, and was beloved—she adored,
    And she was worshipp'd; after nature's fashion,
Their intense souls, into each other pour'd,
    If souls could die, had perish'd in that passion,—
But by degrees their senses were restored,   1525
    Again to be o'ercome, again to dash on;
And, beating 'gainst *his* bosom, Haidee's heart
Felt as if never more to beat apart.

192

Alas! they were so young, so beautiful,
    So lonely, loving, helpless, and the hour   1530
Was that in which the heart is always full,
    And, having o'er itself no further power,
Prompts deeds eternity can not annul,
    But pays off moments in an endless shower
Of hell-fire—all prepared for people giving   1535
Pleasure or pain to one another living.

193

Alas! for Juan and Haidee! they were
    So loving and so lovely—till then never,
Excepting our first parents, such a pair
    Had run the risk of being damn'd for ever;   1540
And Haidee, being devout as well as fair,
    Had, doubtless, heard about the Stygian river,[8]
And hell and purgatory—but forgot
Just in the very crisis she should not.

194

They look upon each other, and their eyes   1545
    Gleam in the moonlight; and her white arm clasps
Round Juan's head, and his around hers lies
    Half buried in the tresses which it grasps;
She sits upon his knee, and drinks his sighs,
    He hers, until they end in broken gasps;   1550
And thus they form a group that's quite antique,
Half naked, loving, natural, and Greek.

195

And when those deep and burning moments pass'd,
    And Juan sunk to sleep within her arms,
She slept not, but all tenderly, though fast,   1555
    Sustain'd his head upon her bosom's charms;
And now and then her eye to heaven is cast,
    And then on the pale cheek her breast now warms,

---

7. Byron said, with reference to Haidee: "I was, and am, penetrated with the conviction that women only know evil from men, whereas men have no criterion to judge of purity or goodness but woman."
8. The Styx, which flows through Hades.

Pillow'd on her o'erflowing heart, which pants
With all it granted, and with all it grants.   1560
196
An infant when it gazes on a light,
   A child the moment when it drains the breast,
A devotee when soars the Host[9] in sight,
   An Arab with a stranger for a guest,
A sailor when the prize has struck[1] in fight,   1565
   A miser filling his most hoarded chest,
Feel rapture; but not such true joy are reaping
As they who watch o'er what they love while sleeping.
197
For there it lies so tranquil, so beloved,
   All that it hath of life with us is living;   1570
So gentle, stirless, helpless, and unmoved,
   And all unconscious of the joy 'tis giving;
All it hath felt, inflicted, pass'd, and proved,
   Hush'd into depths beyond the watcher's diving;
There lies the thing we love with all its errors   1575
And all its charms, like death without its terrors.
198
The lady watch'd her lover—and that hour
   Of Love's, and Night's, and Ocean's solitude,
O'erflow'd her soul with their united power;
   Amidst the barren sand and rocks so rude   1580
She and her wave-worn love had made their bower,
   Where nought upon their passion could intrude,
And all the stars that crowded the blue space
Saw nothing happier than her glowing face.
199
Alas! the love of women! it is known   1585
   To be a lovely and a fearful thing;
For all of theirs upon that die is thrown,
   And if 'tis lost, life hath no more to bring
To them but mockeries of the past alone,
   And their revenge is as the tiger's spring,   1590
Deadly, and quick, and crushing; yet, as real
Torture is theirs, what they inflict they feel.
200
They are right; for man, to man so oft unjust,
   Is always so to women; one sole bond
Awaits them, treachery is all their trust;   1595
   Taught to conceal, their bursting hearts despond
Over their idol, till some wealthier lust
   Buys them in marriage—and what rests beyond?
A thankless husband, next a faithless lover,
Then dressing, nursing, praying, and all's over.   1600
201
Some take a lover, some take drams or prayers,
   Some mind their household, others dissipation,

---

9. The Eucharistic wafer.   1. Has lowered its flag in token of surrender.

Some run away, and but exchange their cares,
　Losing the advantage of a virtuous station;
Few changes e'er can better their affairs,　　　　　　　　　　　　　1605
　Theirs being an unnatural situation,
From the dull palace to the dirty hovel:
Some play the devil, and then write a novel.[2]

                    202
Haidee was Nature's bride, and knew not this;
　Haidee was Passion's child, born where the sun　　　　　　　　1610
Showers triple light, and scorches even the kiss
　Of his gazelle-eyed daughters; she was one
Made but to love, to feel that she was his
　Who was her chosen: what was said or done
Elsewhere was nothing—She had nought to fear,　　　　　　　　1615
Hope, care, nor love beyond, her heart beat *here*.

                    203
And oh! that quickening of the heart, that beat!
　How much it costs us! yet each rising throb
Is in its cause as its effect so sweet,
　That Wisdom, ever on the watch to rob　　　　　　　　　　　　1620
Joy of its alchymy, and to repeat
　Fine truths, even Conscience, too, has a tough job
To make us understand each good old maxim,
So good—I wonder Castlereagh[3] don't tax 'em.

                    204
And now 'twas done—on the lone shore were plighted　　　　　　1625
　Their hearts; the stars, their nuptial torches, shed
Beauty upon the beautiful they lighted:
　Ocean their witness, and the cave their bed,
By their own feelings hallow'd and united,
　Their priest was Solitude, and they were wed:　　　　　　　　1630
And they were happy, for to their young eyes
Each was an angel, and earth paradise.

                    * * *

                    208
But Juan! had he quite forgotten Julia?
　And should he have forgotten her so soon?
I can't but say it seems to me most truly a
　Perplexing question; but, no doubt, the moon　　　　　　　　　1660
Does these things for us, and whenever newly a
　Strong palpitation rises, 'tis her boon,
Else how the devil is it that fresh features
Have such a charm for us poor human creatures?

                    209
I hate inconstancy—I loathe, detest,　　　　　　　　　　　　　1665
　Abhor, condemn, abjure the mortal made
Of such quicksilver clay that in his breast
　No permanent foundation can be laid;

---

2. The impetuous and hysterical Lady Caroline
Lamb, having thrown herself at Byron and been after
a time rejected, incorporated incidents from the affair
in her novel *Glenarvon* (1816).
3. Robert Stewart, Viscount Castlereagh, British foreign secretary (1812–22).

Love, constant love, has been my constant guest,
    And yet last night, being at a masquerade,   1670
I saw the prettiest creature, fresh from Milan,
Which gave me some sensations like a villain.

210

But soon Philosophy came to my aid,
    And whisper'd "think of every sacred tie!"
"I will, my dear Philosophy!" I said,   1675
    "But then her teeth, and then, Oh heaven! her eye!
I'll just inquire if she be wife or maid,
    Or neither—out of curiosity."
"Stop!" cried Philosophy, with air so Grecian,
(Though she was masqued then as a fair Venetian).   1680

211

"Stop!" so I stopp'd.—But to return: that which
    Men call inconstancy is nothing more
Than admiration due where nature's rich
    Profusion with young beauty covers o'er
Some favour'd object; and as in the niche   1685
    A lovely statue we almost adore,
This sort of adoration of the real
Is but a heightening of the "beau ideal."[4]

212

'Tis the perception of the beautiful,
    A fine extension of the faculties,   1690
Platonic, universal, wonderful,
    Drawn from the stars, and filter'd through the skies,
Without which life would be extremely dull;
    In short, it is the use of our own eyes,
With one or two small senses added, just   1695
To hint that flesh is form'd of fiery dust.

213

Yet 'tis a painful feeling, and unwilling,
    For surely if we always could perceive
In the same object graces quite as killing
    As when she rose upon us like an Eve,   1700
'Twould save us many a heart-ache, many a shilling,
    (For we must get them anyhow, or grieve),
Whereas, if one sole lady pleased for ever,
How pleasant for the heart, as well as liver!

*   *   *

216

In the mean time, without proceeding more
    In this anatomy, I've finish'd now
Two hundred and odd stanzas as before,
    That being about the number I'll allow
Each canto of the twelve, or twenty-four;   1725
    And, laying down my pen, I make my bow,
Leaving Don Juan and Haidee to plead
For them and theirs with all who deign to read.

4. Ideal beauty.

From Canto 3

[Juan and Haidee]

1

Hail, Muse! *et cetera.*—We left Juan sleeping,
   Pillow'd upon a fair and happy breast,
And watch'd by eyes that never yet knew weeping,
   And loved by a young heart, too deeply blest
To feel the poison through her spirit creeping,   5
   Or know who rested there, a foe to rest
Had soil'd the current of her sinless years,
And turn'd her pure heart's purest blood to tears.

2

Oh, Love! what is it in this world of ours
   Which makes it fatal to be loved? Ah why   10
With cypress branches[1] hast thou wreathed thy bowers,
   And made thy best interpreter a sigh?
As those who dote on odours pluck the flowers,
   And place them on their breast—but place to die!
Thus the frail beings we would fondly cherish   15
Are laid within our bosoms but to perish.

3

In her first passion woman loves her lover,
   In all the others all she loves is love,
Which grows a habit she can ne'er get over,
   And fits her loosely—like an easy glove,   20
As you may find, whene'er you like to prove her:
   One man alone at first her heart can move;
She then prefers him in the plural number,
Not finding that the additions much encumber.

4

I know not if the fault be men's or theirs;   25
   But one thing's pretty sure; a woman planted[2]—
(Unless at once she plunge for life in prayers)—
   After a decent time must be gallanted;
Although, no doubt, her first of love affairs
   Is that to which her heart is wholly granted;   30
Yet there are some, they say, who have had *none*,
But those who have ne'er end with only *one*.

5

'Tis melancholy, and a fearful sign
   Of human frailty, folly, also crime,
That love and marriage rarely can combine,   35
   Although they both are born in the same clime;
Marriage from love, like vinegar from wine—
   A sad, sour, sober beverage—by time
Is sharpen'd from its high celestial flavour
Down to a very homely household savour.   40

1. Signifying sorrow.
2. Abandoned (from the French *planter là*, to leave in the lurch).

6

There's something of antipathy, as 'twere,
    Between their present and their future state;
A kind of flattery that's hardly fair
    Is used until the truth arrives too late—
Yet what can people do, except despair?   45
    The same things change their names at such a rate;
For instance—passion in a lover's glorious,
But in a husband is pronounced uxorious.

7

Men grow ashamed of being so very fond;
    They sometimes also get a little tired   50
(But that, of course, is rare), and then despond:
    The same things cannot always be admired,
Yet 'tis "so nominated in the bond,"[3]
    That both are tied till one shall have expired.
Sad thought! to lose the spouse that was adorning   55
Our days, and put one's servants into mourning.

8

There's doubtless something in domestic doings,
    Which forms, in fact, true love's antithesis;
Romances paint at full length people's wooings,
    But only give a bust of marriages;   60
For no one cares for matrimonial cooings,
    There's nothing wrong in a connubial kiss:
Think you, if Laura had been Petrarch's wife,
He would have written sonnets all his life?

9

All tragedies are finish'd by a death,   65
    All comedies are ended by a marriage;
The future states of both are left to faith,
    For authors fear description might disparage
The worlds to come of both, or fall beneath,
    And then both worlds would punish their miscarriage; 70
So leaving each their priest and prayer-book ready,
They say no more of Death or of the Lady.[4]

10

The only two that in my recollection
    Have sung of heaven and hell, or marriage, are
Dante and Milton, and of both the affection   75
    Was hapless in their nuptials, for some bar
Of fault or temper ruin'd the connexion
    (Such things, in fact, it don't ask much to mar);
But Dante's Beatrice and Milton's Eve
Were not drawn from their spouses, you conceive.   80

11

Some persons say that Dante meant theology
    By Beatrice, and not a mistress—I,
Although my opinion may require apology,

3. Spoken by Shylock in *The Merchant of Venice*   4. Alluding to a popular ballad, *Death and the Lady*.
4.1.259: "Is it so nominated in the bond?"

Deem this a commentator's phantasy,
Unless indeed it was from his own knowledge he	85
    Decided thus, and show'd good reason why;
I think that Dante's more abstruse ecstatics
Meant to personify the mathematics.

12

Haidee and Juan were not married, but
    The fault was theirs, not mine: it is not fair,	90
Chaste reader, then, in any way to put
    The blame on me, unless you wish they were;
Then if you'd have them wedded, please to shut
    The book which treats of this erroneous pair,
Before the consequences grow too awful;	95
'Tis angerous to read of loves unlawful.

13

Yet they were happy,—happy in the illicit
    Indulgence of their innocent desires;
But more imprudent grown with every visit,
    Haidee forgot the island was her sire's;	100
When we have what we like, 'tis hard to miss it,
    At least in the beginning, ere one tires;
Thus she came often, not a moment losing,
Whilst her piratical papa was cruising.

14

Let not his mode of raising cash seem strange,	105
    Although he fleeced the flags of every nation,
For into a prime minister but change
    His title, and 'tis nothing but taxation;
But he, more modest, took an humbler range
    Of life, and in an honester vocation	110
Pursued o'er the high seas his watery journey,
And merely practised as a sea-attorney.

15

The good old gentleman had been detain'd
    By winds and waves, and some important captures;
And, in the hope of more, at sea remain'd,	115
    Although a squall or two had damp'd his raptures,
By swamping one of the prizes; he had chain'd
    His prisoners, dividing them like chapters
In number'd lots; they all had cuffs and collars,
And averaged each from ten to a hundred dollars.	120

*   *   *

19

Then having settled his marine affairs,	145
    Despatching single cruisers here and there,
His vessel having need of some repairs,
    He shaped his course to where his daughter fair
Continued still her hospitable cares;
    But that part of the coast being shoal and bare,	150
And rough with reefs which ran out many a mile,
His port lay on the other side o' the isle.

20

And there he went ashore without delay,
   Having no custom-house nor quarantine
To ask him awkward questions on the way   155
   About the time and place where he had been:
He left his ship to be hove down next day,
   With orders to the people to careen;[5]
So that all hands were busy beyond measure,
In getting out goods, ballast, guns, and treasure.   160

*   *   *

27

He saw his white walls shining in the sun,
   His garden trees all shadowy and green;   210
He heard his rivulet's light bubbling run,
   The distant dog-bark; and perceived between
The umbrage of the wood so cool and dun
   The moving figures, and the sparkling sheen
Of arms (in the East all arm)—and various dyes   215
Of colour'd garbs, as bright as butterflies.

28

And as the spot where they appear he nears,
   Surprised at these unwonted signs of idling,
He hears—alas! no music of the spheres,
   But an unhallow'd, earthly sound of fiddling!   220
A melody which made him doubt his ears,
   The cause being past his guessing or unriddling;
A pipe, too, and a drum, and shortly after,
A most unoriental roar of laughter.

*   *   *

38

He did not know (Alas! how men will lie)
   That a report (especially the Greeks)
Avouch'd his death (such people never die),
   And put his house in mourning several weeks,   300
But now their eyes and also lips were dry;
   The bloom too had return'd to Haidee's cheeks.
Her tears too being return'd into their fount,
She now kept house upon her own account.

39

Hence all this rice, meat, dancing, wine, and fiddling,   305
   Which turn'd the isle into a place of pleasure;
The servants all were getting drunk or idling,
   A life which made them happy beyond measure.
Her father's hospitality seem'd middling,
   Compared with what Haidee did with his treasure;   310
'Twas wonderful how things went on improving,
While she had not one hour to spare from loving.

---

5. To tip a vessel on its side to clean and repair its hull.

40

Perhaps you think in stumbling on this feast
   He flew into a passion, and in fact
There was no mighty reason to be pleased;   315
   Perhaps you prophesy some sudden act,
The whip, the rack, or dungeon at the least,
   To teach his people to be more exact,
And that, proceeding at a very high rate,
He showed the royal *penchants* of a pirate.   320

41

You're wrong.—He was the mildest manner'd man
   That ever scuttled ship or cut a throat;
With such true breeding of a gentleman,
   You never could divine his real thought;
No courtier could, and scarcely woman can   325
   Gird more deceit within a petticoat;
Pity he loved adventurous life's variety,
He was so great a loss to good society.

              *   *   *

48

Not that he was not sometimes rash or so,
   But never in his real and serious mood;
Then calm, concentrated, and still, and slow,
   He lay coil'd like the boa in the wood;   380
With him it never was a word and blow,
   His angry word once o'er, he shed no blood,
But in his silence there was much to rue,
And his *one* blow left little work for *two*.

49

He ask'd no further questions, and proceeded   385
   On to the house, but by a private way,
So that the few who met him hardly heeded,
   So little they expected him that day;
If love paternal in his bosom pleaded
   For Haidee's sake, is more than I can say,   390
But certainly to one deem'd dead returning,
This revel seem'd a curious mode of mourning.

50

If all the dead could now return to life,
   (Which God forbid!) or some, or a great many,
For instance, if a husband or his wife   395
   (Nuptial examples are as good as any),
No doubt whate'er might be their former strife,
   The present weather would be much more rainy—
Tears shed into the grave of the connexion
Would share most probably its resurrection.   400

51

He enter'd in the house no more his home,
   A thing to human feelings the most trying,
And harder for the heart to overcome,
   Perhaps, than even the mental pangs of dying;

To find our hearthstone turn'd into a tomb,   405
   And round its once warm precincts palely lying
The ashes of our hopes, is a deep grief,
Beyond a single gentleman's belief.

52

He enter'd in the house—his home no more,
   For without hearts there is no home;—and felt   410
The solitude of passing his own door
   Without a welcome; *there* he long had dwelt,
There his few peaceful days Time had swept o'er,
   There his worn bosom and keen eye would melt
Over the innocence of that sweet child,   415
His only shrine of feelings undefiled.

53

He was a man of a strange temperament,
   Of mild demeanour though of savage mood,
Moderate in all his habits, and content
   With temperance in pleasure, as in food,   420
Quick to perceive, and strong to bear, and meant
   For something better, if not wholly good;
His country's wrongs and his despair to save her
Had stung him from a slave to an enslaver.

*   *   *

96

But let me to my story: I must own,
   If I have any fault, it is digression;
Leaving my people to proceed alone,
   While I soliloquize beyond expression;   860
But these are my addresses from the throne,
   Which put off business to the ensuing session:
Forgetting each omission is a loss to
The world, not quite so great as Ariosto.[6]

97

I know that what our neighbours call "*longueurs*,"[7]   865
   (We've not so good a *word*, but have the *thing*

In that complete perfection which ensures
   An epic from Bob Southey[8] every spring—)
Form not the true temptation which allures
   The reader; but 'twould not be hard to bring   870
Some fine examples of the *épopée*,[9]
To prove its grand ingredient is *ennui*.

98

We learn from Horace, Homer sometimes sleeps;[1]
   We feel without him: Wordsworth sometimes wakes,
To show with what complacency he creeps,   875

---

6. Byron warmly admired this poet, author of *Orlando Furioso* (1532), the greatest of the Italian chivalric romances.
7. Boringly wordy passages of verse or prose (French).
8. Robert Southey (1774–1843), poet laureate and au-thor of a number of epic-length narrative poems (see *The Vision of Judgment*, p. 1577).
9. Epic poem (French).
1. Horace, *Art of Poetry* 359: "Sometimes great Homer nods."

With his dear *"Waggoners,"*[2] around his lakes;
He wishes for "a boat" to sail the deeps—
    Of ocean?—No, of air; and then he makes
Another outcry for "a little boat,"
And drivels seas to set it well afloat.[3]   880

99

If he must fain sweep o'er the etherial plain,
    And Pegasus[4] runs restive in his "waggon,"
Could he not beg the loan of Charles's Wain?[5]
    Or pray Medea for a single dragon?[6]
Or if too classic for his vulgar brain,   885
    He fear'd his neck to venture such a nag on,
And he must needs mount nearer to the moon,
Could not the blockhead ask for a balloon?

100

"Pedlars,"[7] and "boats," and "waggons!" Oh! Ye shades
    Of Pope and Dryden, are we come to this?   890
That trash of such sort not alone evades
    Contempt, but from the bathos' vast abyss
Floats scumlike uppermost, and these Jack Cades[8]
    Of sense and song above your graves may hiss—
The "little boatman" and his "Peter Bell"   895
Can sneer at him who drew "Achitophel!"[9]

101

T' our tale.—The feast was over, the slaves gone,
    The dwarfs and dancing girls had all retired;
The Arab lore and poet's song were done,
    And every sound of revelry expired;   900
The lady and her lover, left alone,
    The rosy flood of twilight's sky admired;—
Ave Maria![1] o'er the earth and sea,
That heavenliest hour of Heaven is worthiest thee!

102

Ave Maria! blessed be the hour!   905
    The time, the clime, the spot, where I so oft
Have felt that moment in its fullest power
    Sink o'er the earth so beautiful and soft,
While swung the deep bell in the distant tower,
    Or the faint dying day-hymn stole aloft,   910
And not a breath crept through the rosy air,
And yet the forest leaves seem'd stirr'd with prayer.

2. A reference to Wordsworth's long narrative poem *The Waggoner* (1819).

3. In the prologue to his poem *Peter Bell* (1819), Wordsworth wishes for "a little boat, / In shape a very crescent-moon: / Fast through the clouds my boat can sail. . . ."

4. In Greek myth, the winged horse; he was said to have produced the fountain Hippocrene, sacred to the Muses, by stamping his hoof.

5. The constellation known in the United States as the Big Dipper.

6. When the Argonaut Jason abandoned Medea to take a new wife, she murdered their sons to punish her husband, then escaped in a chariot drawn by winged dragons.

7. Wordsworth's Peddler narrates the story of Margaret, from the early manuscript *The Ruined Cottage* (pp. 1357–68). Byron knew this story in the later form that Wordsworth incorporated into book 1 of *The Excursion* (1814).

8. Jack Cade was an adventurer who led an uprising against Henry VI in 1450.

9. I.e., John Dryden, author of *Absalom and Achitophel* (1681), whom Byron greatly admired. Wordsworth had derogated Dryden's poetry in the *Essay, Supplementary to the Preface* to his *Poems* (1815).

1. "Hail, Mary," the opening words of a Roman Catholic prayer. *Ave Maria* is sometimes used to refer to evening (or morning), because the prayer is part of the service at these times.

103

Ave Maria! 'tis the hour of prayer!
  Ave Maria! 'tis the hour of love!
Ave Maria! may our spirits dare   915
  Look up to thine and to thy Son's above!
Ave Maria! oh that face so fair!
  Those downcast eyes beneath the Almighty dove—
What though 'tis but a pictured image strike—
That painting is no idol, 'tis too like.   920

104

Some kinder casuists are pleased to say,
  In nameless print—that I have no devotion;
But set those persons down with me to pray,
  And you shall see who has the properest notion
Of getting into Heaven the shortest way;   925
  My altars are the mountains and the ocean,
Earth, air, stars,—all that springs from the great Whole,
Who hath produced, and will receive the soul.

* * *

From Canto 4

[*Juan and Haidee*]

3

As boy, I thought myself a clever fellow,
  And wish'd that others held the same opinion;
They took it up when my days grew more mellow,
  And other minds acknowledged my dominion: 20
Now my sere fancy "falls into the yellow
  Leaf,"[1] and imagination droops her pinion,
And the sad truth which hovers o'er my desk
Turns what was once romantic to burlesque.

4

And if I laugh at any mortal thing,   25
  'Tis that I may not weep; and if I weep,
'Tis that our nature cannot always bring
  Itself to apathy, for we must steep
Our hearts first in the depths of Lethe's spring[2]
  Ere what we least wish to behold will sleep: 30
Thetis baptized her mortal son in Styx;[3]
A mortal mother would on Lethe fix.

5

Some have accused me of a strange design
  Against the creed and morals of the land,
And trace it in this poem every line: 35
  I don't pretend that I quite understand

---

1. Cf. *Macbeth* 5.3.22–23: "My way of life / Is fall'n
into the sear, the yellow leaf."
2. Lethe, a river in Hades, brings oblivion of life.

3. The river in Hades into which the nymph Thetis
dipped Achilles, to make him invulnerable.

My own meaning when I would be *very* fine,
    But the fact is that I have nothing plann'd,
Unless it were to be a moment merry,
A novel word in my vocabulary.   40

6

To the kind reader of our sober clime
    This way of writing will appear exotic;
Pulci[4] was sire of the half-serious rhyme,
    Who sang when chivalry was more Quixotic,
And revell'd in the fancies of the time,   45
    True knights, chaste dames, huge giants, kings despotic;
But all these, save the last, being obsolete,
I chose a modern subject as more meet.

7

How I have treated it, I do not know;
    Perhaps no better than they have treated me   50
Who have imputed such designs as show
    Not what they saw, but what they wish'd to see;
But if it gives them pleasure, be it so,
    This is a liberal age, and thoughts are free:
Meantime Apollo plucks me by the ear,   55
And tells me to resume my story here.

*   *   *

26

Juan and Haidee gazed upon each other
    With swimming looks of speechless tenderness,
Which mix'd all feelings, friend, child, lover, brother,
    All that the best can mingle and express
When two pure hearts are pour'd in one another,   205
    And love too much, and yet can not love less;
But almost sanctify the sweet excess
By the immortal wish and power to bless.

27

Mix'd in each other's arms, and heart in heart,
    Why did they not then die?—they had lived too long   210
Should an hour come to bid them breathe apart;
    Years could but bring them cruel things or wrong,
The world was not for them, nor the world's art
    For beings passionate as Sappho's song;
Love was born *with* them, *in* them, so intense,   215
It was their very spirit—not a sense.

28

They should have lived together deep in woods,
    Unseen as sings the nightingale; they were
Unfit to mix in these thick solitudes
    Call'd social, haunts of Hate, and Vice, and Care: 220
How lonely every freeborn creature broods!
    The sweetest song-birds nestle in a pair;

---

4. Author of the *Morgante Maggiore*, prototype of the Italian seriocomic romance from which Byron derived the stanza and manner of *Don Juan* (see headnote "Don Juan," pp. 1598–99).

The eagle soars alone; the gull and crow
Flock o'er their carrion, just like men below.

29

Now pillow'd cheek to cheek, in loving sleep,   225
    Haidee and Juan their siesta took,
A gentle slumber, but it was not deep,
    For ever and anon a something shook
Juan, and shuddering o'er his frame would creep;
    And Haidee's sweet lips murmur'd like a brook   230
A wordless music, and her face so fair
Stirr'd with her dream as rose-leaves with the air;

30

Or as the stirring of a deep clear stream
    Within an Alpine hollow, when the wind
Walks o'er it, was she shaken by the dream,   235
    The mystical usurper of the mind—
O'erpowering us to be whate'er may seem
    Good to the soul which we no more can bind;
Strange state of being! (for 'tis still to be)
Senseless to feel, and with seal'd eyes to see.   240

31

She dream'd of being alone on the sea-shore,
    Chain'd to a rock; she knew not how, but stir
She could not from the spot, and the loud roar
    Grew, and each wave rose roughly, threatening her;
And o'er her upper lip they seem'd to pour,   245
    Until she sobb'd for breath, and soon they were
Foaming o'er her lone head, so fierce and high—
Each broke to drown her, yet she could not die.

32

Anon—she was released, and then she stray'd
    O'er the sharp shingles[5] with her bleeding feet,   250
And stumbled almost every step she made;
    And something roll'd before her in a sheet,
Which she must still pursue howe'er afraid;
    'Twas white and indistinct, nor stopp'd to meet
Her glance nor grasp, for still she gazed and grasp'd,   255
And ran, but it escaped her as she clasp'd.

33

The dream changed; in a cave she stood, its walls
    Were hung with marble icicles; the work
Of ages on its water-fretted halls,
    Where waves might wash, and seals might breed and lurk;   260
Her hair was dripping, and the very balls
    Of her black eyes seemed turn'd to tears, and murk
The sharp rocks look'd below each drop they caught,
Which froze to marble as it fell, she thought.

34

And wet, and cold, and lifeless at her feet,   265
    Pale as the foam that froth'd on his dead brow,

---

5. Loose pebbles.

Which she essay'd in vain to clear, (how sweet
   Were once her cares, how idle seem'd they now!)
Lay Juan, nor could aught renew the beat
   Of his quench'd heart; and the sea dirges low   270
Rang in her sad ears like a mermaid's song,
And that brief dream appear'd a life too long.

35

And gazing on the dead, she thought his face
   Faded, or alter'd into something new—
Like to her father's features, till each trace   275
   More like and like to Lambro's aspect grew—
With all his keen worn look and Grecian grace;
   And starting, she awoke, and what to view?
Oh! Powers of Heaven! what dark eye meets she there?
'Tis—'tis her father's—fix'd upon the pair!   280

36

Then shrieking, she arose, and shrieking fell,
   With joy and sorrow, hope and fear, to see
Him whom she deem'd a habitant where dwell
   The ocean-buried, risen from death, to be
Perchance the death of one she loved too well: 285
   Dear as her father had been to Haidee,
It was a moment of that awful kind—
I have seen such—but must not call to mind.

37

Up Juan sprung to Haidee's bitter shriek,
   And caught her falling, and from off the wall   290
Snatch'd down his sabre, in hot haste to wreak
   Vengeance on him who was the cause of all:
Then Lambro, who till now forbore to speak,
   Smiled scornfully, and said, "Within my call,
A thousand scimitars await the word;   295
Put up, young man, put up your silly sword."

38

And Haidee clung around him; "Juan, 'tis—
   'Tis Lambro—'tis my father! Kneel with me—
He will forgive us—yes—it must be—yes.
   Oh! dearest father, in this agony   300
Of pleasure and of pain—even while I kiss
   Thy garment's hem with transport, can it be
That doubt should mingle with my filial joy?
Deal with me as thou wilt, but spare this boy."

39

High and inscrutable the old man stood,   305
   Calm in his voice, and calm within his eye—
Not always signs with him of calmest mood:
   He look'd upon her, but gave no reply;
Then turn'd to Juan, in whose cheek the blood
   Oft came and went, as there resolved to die;   310
In arms, at least, he stood, in act to spring
On the first foe whom Lambro's call might bring.

40

"Young man, your sword"; so Lambro once more said:
    Juan replied, "Not while this arm is free."
The old man's cheek grew pale, but not with dread,   315
    And drawing from his belt a pistol, he
Replied, "Your blood be then on your own head."
    Then look'd close at the flint, as if to see
'Twas fresh—for he had lately used the lock[6]—
And next proceeded quietly to cock.   320

41

It has a strange quick jar upon the ear,
    That cocking of a pistol, when you know
A moment more will bring the sight to bear
    Upon your person, twelve yards off, or so;
A gentlemanly distance,[7] not too near,   325
    If you have got a former friend for foe;
But after being fired at once or twice,
The ear becomes more Irish, and less nice.[8]

42

Lambro presented, and one instant more
    Had stopp'd this Canto, and Don Juan's breath,   330
When Haidee threw herself her boy before;
    Stern as her sire: "On me," she cried, "let death
Descend—the fault is mine; this fatal shore
    He found—but sought not. I have pledged my faith;
I love him—I will die with him: I knew   335
Your nature's firmness—know your daughter's too."

43

A minute past, and she had been all tears,
    And tenderness, and infancy: but now
She stood as one who champion'd human fears—
    Pale, statue-like, and stern, she woo'd the blow;   340
And tall beyond her sex, and their compeers,[9]
    She drew up to her height, as if to show
A fairer mark; and with a fix'd eye scann'd
Her father's face—but never stopp'd his hand.

44

He gazed on her, and she on him; 'twas strange   345
    How like they look'd! the expression was the same;
Serenely savage, with a little change
    In the large dark eye's mutual-darted flame;
For she too was as one who could avenge,
    If cause should be—a lioness, though tame: 350
Her father's blood before her father's face
Boil'd up, and prov'd her truly of his race.

45

I said they were alike, their features and
    Their stature differing but in sex and years;

---

6. The part of the gun that explodes the charge.
7. I.e., dueling distance.
8. Finicky. Byron alludes to the propensity of hot-headed young Irishmen to fight duels.
9. I.e., she was the match in height of Lambro and Juan.

Even to the delicacy of their hand   355
    There was resemblance, such as true blood wears;
And now to see them, thus divided, stand
    In fix'd ferocity, when joyous tears,
And sweet sensations, should have welcomed both,
Show what the passions are in their full growth.   360

                              46
The father paused a moment, then withdrew
    His weapon, and replaced it; but stood still,
And looking on her, as to look her through,
    "Not I," he said, "have sought this stranger's ill;
Not I have made this desolation: few   365
    Would bear such outrage, and forbear to kill;
But I must do my duty—how thou hast
Done thine, the present vouches for the past.

                              47
"Let him disarm; or, by my father's head,
    His own shall roll before you like a ball!"   370
He raised his whistle, as the word he said,
    And blew; another answer'd to the call,
And rushing in disorderly, though led,
    And arm'd from boot to turban, one and all,
Some twenty of his train came, rank on rank;   375
He gave the word, "Arrest or slay the Frank."[1]

                              48
Then, with a sudden movement, he withdrew
    His daughter; while compress'd within his clasp,
'Twixt her and Juan interposed the crew;
    In vain she struggled in her father's grasp—   380
His arms were like a serpent's coil: then flew
    Upon their prey, as darts an angry asp,
The file of pirates; save the foremost, who
Had fallen, with his right shoulder half cut through.

                              49
The second had his cheek laid open; but   385
    The third, a wary, cool old sworder, took
The blows upon his cutlass, and then put
    His own well in; so well, ere you could look,
His man was floor'd, and helpless at his foot,
    With the blood running like a little brook   390
From two smart sabre gashes, deep and red—
One on the arm, the other on the head.

                              50
And then they bound him where he fell, and bore
    Juan from the apartment: with a sign
Old Lambro bade them take him to the shore,   395
    Where lay some ships which were to sail at nine.
They laid him in a boat, and plied the oar
    Until they reach'd some galliots,[2] placed in line;

1. Term used in the Near East to designate a Western   2. A small, fast galley, propelled by both oars and sails.
European.

On board of one of these, and under hatches,
They stow'd him, with strict orders to the watches.   400

51

The world is full of strange vicissitudes,
    And here was one exceedingly unpleasant:
A gentleman so rich in the world's goods,
    Handsome and young, enjoying all the present,
Just at the very time when he least broods   405
    On such a thing is suddenly to sea sent,
Wounded and chain'd, so that he cannot move,
And all because a lady fell in love.

                              *   *   *

56

Afric is all the sun's, and as her earth
    Her human clay is kindled; full of power
For good or evil, burning from its birth,
    The Moorish blood partakes the planet's hour,
And like the soil beneath it will bring forth: 445
    Beauty and love were Haidee's mother's dower;
But her large dark eye show'd deep Passion's force,
Though sleeping like a lion near a source.

57

Her daughter, temper'd with a milder ray,
    Like summer clouds all silvery, smooth, and fair,   450
Till slowly charged with thunder they display
    Terror to earth, and tempest to the air,
Had held till now her soft and milky way;
    But overwrought with passion and despair,
The fire burst forth from her Numidian³ veins,   455
Even as the Simoom⁴ sweeps the blasted plains.

58

The last sight which she saw was Juan's gore,
    And he himself o'ermaster'd and cut down;
His blood was running on the very floor
    Where late he trod, her beautiful, her own;   460
Thus much she view'd an instant and no more,—
    Her struggles ceased with one convulsive groan;
On her sire's arm, which until now scarce held
Her writhing, fell she like a cedar fell'd.

59

A vein had burst, and her sweet lips' pure dyes   465
    Were dabbled with the deep blood which ran o'er;
And her head droop'd as when the lily lies
    O'ercharged with rain: her summon'd handmaids bore
Their lady to her couch with gushing eyes;
    Of herbs and cordials they produced their store,   470
But she defied all means they could employ,
Like one life could not hold, nor death destroy.

3. North African.   4. A violent, hot, dust-laden desert wind.

60

Days lay she in that state unchanged, though chill
　With nothing livid,[5] still her lips were red;
She had no pulse, but death seem'd absent still;　　　　　　475
　No hideous sign proclaim'd her surely dead;
Corruption came not in each mind to kill
　All hope; to look upon her sweet face bred
New thoughts of life, for it seem'd full of soul,
She had so much, earth could not claim the whole.　　　　480

*　　*　　*

69

Twelve days and nights she wither'd thus; at last,　　　　545
　Without a groan, or sigh, or glance, to show
A parting pang, the spirit from her past:
　And they who watch'd her nearest could not know
The very instant, till the change that cast
　Her sweet face into shadow, dull and slow,　　　　　　550
Glazed o'er her eyes—the beautiful, the black—
Oh! to possess such lustre—and then lack!

70

She died, but not alone; she held within
　A second principle of life, which might
Have dawn'd a fair and sinless child of sin;　　　　　　555
　But closed its little being without light,
And went down to the grave unborn, wherein
　Blossom and bough lie wither'd with one blight;
In vain the dews of Heaven descend above
The bleeding flower and blasted fruit of love.　　　　　　560

71

Thus lived—thus died she; never more on her
　Shall sorrow light, or shame. She was not made
Through years or moons the inner weight to bear,
　Which colder hearts endure till they are laid
By age in earth; her days and pleasures were　　　　　　565
　Brief, but delightful—such as had not staid
Long with her destiny; but she sleeps well
By the sea shore, whereon she loved to dwell.

72

That isle is now all desolate and bare,
　Its dwellings down, its tenants past away;　　　　　　570
None but her own and father's grave is there,
　And nothing outward tells of human clay;
Ye could not know where lies a thing so fair,
　No stone is there to show, no tongue to say
What was; no dirge, except the hollow sea's,　　　　　　575
Mourns o'er the beauty of the Cyclades.

73

But many a Greek maid in a loving song
　Sighs o'er her name; and many an islander

---

5. I.e., though she was ashen pale.

With her sire's story makes the night less long;
   Valour was his, and beauty dwelt with her;   580
If she loved rashly, her life paid for wrong—
   A heavy price must all pay who thus err,
In some shape; let none think to fly the danger,
For soon or late Love is his own avenger.
              74

But let me change this theme, which grows too sad,   585
   And lay this sheet of sorrows on the shelf;
I don't much like describing people mad,
   For fear of seeming rather touch'd myself—
Besides I've no more on this head to add;
   And as my Muse is a capricious elf,   590
We'll put about, and try another tack
With Juan, left half-kill'd some stanzas back.[6]
1818–23   1819–24

Letters   Three thousand of Byron's letters have survived—a remarkable number for so short a life—and they include some of the freshest and liveliest in all of English literature. In general, they are our best single biographical source for the poet, providing running commentary on his day-to-day concerns and activities and giving us the clearest possible picture of his complex personality, a picture relatively (but not entirely) free of the posturings that pervade both the romantic poems and the satires. In addition, they are independently valuable for their charm, energy, and sheer brilliance. The selections below focus primarily on Byron's own poetry and his ideas about writers and literature, but they also represent his wide-ranging interests, as well as his powers of amusing anecdote and vivid description of the society of his time.

    Our texts are from Leslie A. Marchand's twelve-volume edition, *Byron's Letters and Journals* (1973–82).

LETTERS

To Thomas Moore[1]

[Childe Harold. A *Venetian Adventure*]

Venice, January 28th, 1817

    Your letter of the 8th is before me. The remedy for your plethora is simple—abstinence. I was obliged to have recourse to the like some years ago, I mean in point of *diet*, and, with the exception of some convivial weeks and

---

6. Juan's adventures continue. He is sold as a slave in Constantinople to an enamored Sultana; she disguises him as a girl and adds him to her husband's harem for convenience of access. Juan escapes, joins the Russian army that is besieging Ismail, and so distinguishes himself in the capture of the town that he is sent with despatches to St. Petersburg. There he becomes "manmistress" to the insatiable Catherine the Great; as the result of her assiduous attentions, he falls into a physi-

cal decline and, for a salutary change of scene and climate, is sent on a diplomatic mission to England. In canto 16, the last that Byron finished, he is in the middle of an amorous adventure while a guest at the medieval country mansion of an English nobleman, Lord Henry Amundeville, and his very beautiful wife.

1. Irish poet and a good friend of Byron since they met in 1811. Moore's *Life* of Byron in 1830 is the sole source for many of Byron's letters, including this one.

days, (it might be months, now and then), have kept to Pythagoras[2] ever since. For all this, let me hear that you are better. You must not *indulge* in "filthy beer," nor in porter, nor eat *suppers*—the last are the devil to those who swallow dinner. * [3]

I am truly sorry to hear of your father's misfortune[4]—cruel at any time, but doubly cruel in advanced life. However, you will, at least, have the satisfaction of doing your part by him, and, depend upon it, it will not be in vain. Fortune, to be sure, is a female, but not such a b * * as the rest (always excepting your wife and my sister from such sweeping terms); for she generally has some justice in the long run. I have no spite against her, though between her and Nemesis I have had some sore gauntlets to run—but then I have done my best to deserve no better. But to *you*, she is a good deal in arrear, and she will come round—mind if she don't: you have the vigour of life, of independence, of talent, spirit, and character all with you. What you can do for yourself, you have done and will do; and surely there are some others in the world who would not be sorry to be of use, if you would allow them to be useful, or at least attempt it.

I think of being in England in the spring. If there is a row, by the sceptre of King Ludd,[5] but I'll be one; and if there is none, and only a continuance of "this meek, piping time of peace,"[6] I will take a cottage a hundred yards to the south of your abode, and become your neighbour; and we will compose such canticles, and hold such dialogues, as shall be the terror of the *Times* (including the newspaper of that name), and the wonder, and honour, and praise, of the Morning Chronicle and posterity.

I rejoice to hear of your forthcoming in February[7]—though I tremble for the "magnificence," which you attribute to the new Childe Harold.[8] I am glad you like it; it is a fine indistinct piece of poetical desolation, and my favourite. I was half mad during the time of its composition, between metaphysics, mountains, lakes, love unextinguishable, thoughts unutterable, and the nightmare of my own delinquencies. I should, many a good day, have blown my brains out, but for the recollection that it would have given pleasure to my mother-in-law; and, even *then*, if I could have been certain to haunt her—but I won't dwell upon these trifling family matters.

Venice is in the *estro* of her carnival, and I have been up these last two nights at the ridotto[9] and the opera, and all that kind of thing. Now for an adventure. A few days ago a gondolier brought me a billet without a subscription, intimating a wish on the part of the writer to meet me either in gondola or at the island of San Lazaro, or at a third rendezvous, indicated in the note. "I know the country's disposition well"—in Venice "they do let Heaven see those tricks they dare not show," &c. &c.;[1] so, for all response, I said that neither of the three places suited me; but that I would either be at home at ten at night *alone*, or at the ridotto at midnight, where the writer might meet me

2. I.e., have eaten no flesh (the disciples of the Greek philosopher-mathematician Pythagoras were strict vegetarians).
3. These asterisks (as well as those in the next paragraph and near the end of the letter) are Moore's, representing omissions in his printed text.
4. Moore's father had been dismissed from his post as barrack-master at Dublin.
5. A mythical king of Britain.
6. *Richard III* 1.1.24.
7. Moore's Oriental romance *Lalla Rookh*.
8. Canto 3 of *Childe Harold's Pilgrimage* (1816).
9. An Italian social gathering. "Estro": fire, fervor.
1. *Othello* 3.3.201–203. The passage continues: "dare not show their husbands."

masked. At ten o'clock I was at home and alone (Marianna was gone with her husband to a conversazione),[2] when the door of my apartment opened, and in walked a well-looking and (for an Italian) *bionda*[3] girl of about nineteen, who informed me that she was married to the brother of my *amorosa*, and wished to have some conversation with me. I made a decent reply, and we had some talk in Italian and Romaic (her mother being a Greek of Corfu), when lo! in a very few minutes, in marches, to my very great astonishment, Marianna S[egati], *in propria persona*, and after making polite courtesy to her sister-in-law and to me, without a single word seizes her said sister-in-law by the hair, and bestows upon her some sixteen slaps, which would have made your ear ache only to hear their echo. I need not describe the screaming which ensued. The luckless visitor took flight. I seized Marianna, who, after several vain efforts to get away in pursuit of the enemy, fairly went into fits in my arms; and, in spite of reasoning, eau de Cologne, vinegar, half a pint of water, and God knows what other waters beside, continued so till past midnight.

After damning my servants for letting people in without apprizing me, I found that Marianna in the morning had seen her sister-in-law's gondolier on the stairs, and, suspecting that his apparition boded her no good, had either returned of her own accord, or been followed by her maids or some other spy of her people to the conversazione, from whence she returned to perpetrate this piece of pugilism. I had seen fits before, and also some small scenery of the same genus in and out of our island: but this was not all. After about an hour, in comes—who? why, Signor S[egati], her lord and husband, and finds me with his wife fainting upon the sofa, and all the apparatus of confusion, dishevelled hair, hats, handkerchiefs, salts, smelling-bottles—and the lady as pale as ashes without sense or motion. His first question was, "What is all this?" The lady could not reply—so I did. I told him the explanation was the easiest thing in the world; but in the mean time it would be as well to recover his wife—at least, her senses. This came about in due time of suspiration and respiration.

You need not be alarmed—jealousy is not the order of the day in Venice, and daggers are out of fashion; while duels, on love matters, are unknown— at least, with the husbands. But, for all this, it was an awkward affair; and though he must have known that I made love to Marianna, yet I believe he was not, till that evening, aware of the extent to which it had gone. It is very well known that almost all the married women have a lover; but it is usual to keep up the forms, as in other nations. I did not, therefore, know what the devil to say. I could not out with the truth, out of regard to her, and I did not choose to lie for my sake;—besides, the thing told itself. I thought the best way would be to let her explain it as she chose (a woman being never at a loss—the devil always sticks by them)—only determining to protect and carry her off, in case of any ferocity on the part of the Signor. I saw that he was quite calm. She went to bed, and next day—how they settled it, I know not, but settle it they did. Well—then I had to explain to Marianna about this never to be sufficiently confounded sister-in-law; which I did by swearing innocence, eternal constancy, &c. &c. * * * But the sister-in-law, very much discomposed with being treated in such wise, has (not having her own shame

2. An evening party. Marianna Segati, wife of a Vene-   3. Blonde (Italian).
tian draper, was Byron's current *amorosa*.

before her eyes) told the affair to half Venice, and the servants (who were summoned by the fight and the fainting) to the other half. But, here, nobody minds such trifles, except to be amused by them. I don't know whether you will be so, but I have scrawled a long letter out of these follies.

Believe me ever. &c.

To John Murray[1]

[Byron's Poems and the Poetry of the Day]

Sept 15th. 1817

Dear Sir—I enclose a sheet for correction if ever you get to another edition—you will observe that the blunder in printing makes it appear as if the Chateau was over St. Gingo—instead of being on the opposite shore of the lake over Clarens—so—separate the paragraphs otherwise my topography will seems as inaccurate as your typography on this occasion.[2]——The other day I wrote to convey my proposition with regard to the 4th & concluding Canto—I have gone over—& extended it to one hundred and fifty stanzas which is almost as long as the two first were originally—& longer by itself—than any of the smaller poems except the "Corsair"[3]—Mr. Hobhouse has made some very valuable & accurate notes of considerable length[4]—& you may be sure I will do for the text all that I can to finish with decency.—I look upon C[hild]e Harold as my best—and as I begun—I think of concluding with it—but I make no resolutions on that head—as I broke my former intention with regard to "the Corsair"—however—I fear that I shall never do better—& yet—not being thirty years of age for some moons to come—one ought to be progressive as far as Intellect goes for many a good year—but I have had a devilish deal of wear & tear of mind and body—in my time—besides having published too often & much already. God grant me some judgement! to do what may be most fitting in that & every thing else—for I doubt my own exceedingly.——I have read "Lallah Rookh"—but not with sufficient attention yet—for I ride about—& lounge—& ponder &—two or three other things—so that my reading is very desultory & not so attentive as it used to be.—I am very glad to hear of its popularity—for Moore is a very noble fellow in all respects—& will enjoy it without any of the bad feelings which Success—good or evil—sometimes engenders in the men of rhyme.—Of the poem itself I will tell you my opinion when I have mastered it—I say of the poem—for I don't like the prose at all—at all—and in the mean time the "Fire-worshippers" is the best and the "Veiled Prophet" the worst, of the volume.[5]——With regard to poetry in general I am convinced the more I think of it—that he and all of us—Scott—Southey—Wordsworth—Moore—Campbell—I—are all in the wrong—one as much as another—that we are upon a wrong revolutionary poetical system—or systems—not worth a damn in itself—& from which none but Rogers and

---

1. Byron's London publisher.
2. These changes, in Byron's prose note to *Childe Harold's Pilgrimage* (3.927), were made in the next edition.
3. *The Corsair* (1814) ran to 1,860 lines.
4. Hobhouse (see the next letter) wrote most of the notes that were printed with canto 4. Subsequently, he

expanded them into a separate book, *Historical Illustrations to the Fourth Canto of Childe Harold* (1818).
5. Two of the tales in Moore's *Lalla Rookh*. The work is mostly in verse, with some introductory and framing passages in prose.

Crabbe[6] are free—and that the present & next generations will finally be of this opinion.—I am the more confirmed in this—by having lately gone over some of our Classics—particularly *Pope*—whom I tried in this way—I took Moore's poems & my own & some others—& went over them side by side with Pope's—and I was really astonished (I ought not to have been so) and mortified—at the ineffable distance in point of sense—harmony—effect—and even *Imagination* Passion—& *Invention*—between the little Queen Anne's Man—& us of the lower Empire—depend upon it [it] is all Horace then, and Claudian[7] now among us—and if I had to begin again—I woulld model myself accordingly—Crabbe's the man—but he has got a coarse and impracticable subject—& Rogers the Grandfather of living Poetry—is retired upon half-pay, (I don't mean as a Banker)—

> Since pretty Miss Jaqueline[8]
> With her nose aquiline

and has done enough—unless he were to do as he did formerly.—

To John Cam Hobhouse and Douglas Kinnaird[1]

[Don Juan *and Indecency*]

Venice January 19th. 1819

Dear H. and dear K.—I approve and sanction all your legal proceedings with regard to my affairs, and can only repeat my thanks & approbation—if you put off the payments of debts "till *after* Lady Noel's[2] death"—it is well—if till *after* her damnation—better—for that will last forever—yet I hope not:—for her sake as well as the Creditors'—I am willing to believe in Purgatory.——With regard to the Poeshie—I will have no "cutting & slashing" as Perry[3] calls it—you may omit the stanzas on Castlereagh—indeed it is better—& the two "Bobs" at the end of the 3d. stanza of the dedication—which will leave "high" & "adry" good rhymes without any "*double* (or Single) Entendre"[4]—but no more—I appeal—not "to Philip fasting" but to Alexander drunk[5]—I appeal to Murray at his ledger—to the people—in short, Don Juan shall be an entire horse or none.—If the objection be to the indecency, the Age which applauds the "Bath Guide" & Little's poems[6]—& reads Fielding & Smollett still—may bear with that;—if to the poetry—I will take my chance.—I will not give way to all the Cant of Christendom—I have been cloyed with applause &

6. Samuel Rogers, the "banker poet," and George Crabbe, author of *The Village*. Cf. *Don Juan* 1.1633–40 (p. 1622).
7. Claudian Claudianus (370–410), the last poet of classical Rome, representing a marked decline from the poetry of Horace (65–8 B.C.).
8. A reference to Rogers's *Jacqueline*, a sentimental tale in tetrameters that was published with Byron's *Lara* in 1814.
1. Hobhouse was a close friend of Byron from Cambridge days and had accompanied the poet on the first year of his grand tour to the East in 1809. Kinnaird, who also had been at Cambridge, was Byron's banker and literary agent in London.
2. Byron's mother-in-law.
3. James Perry, editor of the *Morning Chronicle*.

4. The 136-line dedication to Southey was omitted entirely when the first two cantos of *Don Juan* were published anonymously in 1819. Stanza 3 ends in an outrageous sexual pun on Southey's first name ("dry bob" was slang for intercourse without emission), and several later stanzas attack Viscount Castlereagh, the British foreign secretary, as an "intellectual eunuch," a "cold-blooded, smooth-faced, placid miscreant."
5. A play on a phrase in Valerius Maximus, *Facta et dicta* 7.2: "appeal from Philip drunk to Philip sober." Philip of Macedon was the father of Alexander the Great.
6. "Thomas Little" was a pseudonym of Thomas Moore. Christopher Anstey's *New Bath Guide* (1766) was a humorous work in anapests describing the Blunderhead family at Bath.

sickened with abuse;—at present—I care for little but the Copyright,—I have imbibed a great love for money—let me have it—if Murray loses this time—he won't the next—he will be cautious—and I shall learn the decline of his customers by his epistolary indications. —— But in no case will I submit to have the poem mutilated.—There is another Canto written—but not copied—in two hundred & odd Stanzas,—if this succeeds—as to the prudery of the present day—what is it? are we more moral than when Prior[7] wrote—is there anything in Don Juan so strong as in Ariosto—or Voltaire—or Chaucer?— Tell Hobhouse—his letter to De Breme has made a great Sensation—and is to be published in the Tuscan & other Gazettes—Count R[izzo] came to consult with me about it last Sunday—we think of Tuscany—for Florence and Milan are in literary war—but the Lombard league is headed by Monti[8]—& would make a difficulty of insertion in the Lombard Gazettes— once published in the Pisan—it will find its way through Italy—by translation or reply. —— So Lauderdale has been telling a story![9]—I suppose this is my reward for presenting him at Countess Benzone's—& shewing him—what attention I could. —— Which "piece" does he mean?—since last year I have run the Gauntlet;—is it the Tarruscelli—the Da Mosti—the Spineda—the Lotti—the Rizzato—the Eleanora—the Carlotta—the Giulietta—the Alvisi— the Zambieri—The Eleanora da Bezzi—(who was the King of Naples' Gioaschino's mistress—at least one of them) the Theresina of Mazzurati—the Glettenheimer—& her Sister—the Luigia & her mother—the Fornaretta— the Santa—the Caligari—the Portiera [Vedova?]—the Bolognese figurante— the Tentora and her sister—cum multis aliis?[1]—some of them are Countesses—& some of them Cobblers wives—some noble—some middling—some low—& all whores—which does the damned old "Ladro—& porco fottuto"[2] mean?—I have had them all & thrice as many to boot since 1817—Since *he* tells a story about me—I will tell one about him;—when he landed at the *Custom house* from *Corfu*—he called for *"Post horses—directly"*—he was told that there were no horses except mine nearer than the Lido—unless he wished for the four bronze Coursers of St. Mark[3]—which were at his Service.—

I am yrs. ever—

Let me have H's Election[4] immediately—I mention it *last* as being what I was least likely to forget. ——

P.S.—Whatever Brain-money—you get on my account from Murray—pray remit me—I will never consent to pay away what I *earn*—that is *mine*—& what I get by my brains—I will spend on my b——ks—as long as I have a tester or a testicle remaining.—I shall not live long—& for that Reason—I must live while I can—so—let him disburse—& me receive—"for the Night cometh."[5]—— If I had but had twenty thousand a year I should not have been

---

7. Matthew Prior, a contemporary of Pope.
8. Ludovico di Breme wrote a defense of Italian writers against the criticism that had appeared in Hobhouse's *Historical Illustrations* (see the preceding letter); Hobhouse in turn sent Byron an answer to di Breme. Count Francesco Rizzo-Patarol was an acquaintance in Venice. Vincenzo Monti was a poet whom Byron and Hobhouse had met in Milan.
9. James Maitland, eighth earl of Lauderdale, who along with his "story" about Byron's love affairs had carried back to England the manuscripts of *Don Juan* (canto 1) and some other poems.

1. With many others (Latin).
2. Thief—and filthy pig (Italian).
3. The four gilded bronze statues above the portal of St. Mark's Basilica in Venice.
4. Hobhouse had begun campaigning for the Westminster seat in Parliament in November 1818 but was defeated the following March. He succeeded in a subsequent election in 1820.
5. John 9.4: "I must work the works of him that sent me, while it is day: the night cometh, when no man can work."

living now—but all men are not born with a silver or Gold Spoon in their mouths. —— My balance—also—my balance—& a Copyright—I have another Canto—too—ready—& then there will be my half year in June—recollect— I care for nothing but "monies".—January 20th. 1819.—You say nothing of Mazeppa[6]—did it arrive—with one other—besides that you mention?——

To Douglas Kinnaird
[Don Juan: *"Is It Not* Life?"]

Venice. Octr. 26th. [1819]

My dear Douglas—My late expenditure has arisen from living at a distance from Venice and being obliged to keep up two establishments, from frequent journeys—and buying some furniture and books as well as a horse or two— and not from any renewal of the EPICUREAN system[1] as you suspect. I have been faithful to my honest liaison with Countess Guiccioli[2]—and I can assure you that *She* has never cost me directly or indirectly a sixpence—indeed the circumstances of herself and family render this no merit.—I never offered her but one present—a broach of brilliants—and she sent it back to me with her *own hair* in it (I shall *not* say of *what part* but *that* is an Italian custom) and a note to say that she was not in the habit of receiving presents of that value— but hoped that I would not consider her sending it back as an affront—nor the value diminished by the enclosure.—I have not had a whore this half-year—confining myself to the strictest adultery. —— Why should you prevent Hanson from making a *peer*[3] if he likes it—I think the *"Garretting"* would be by far the best parliamentary privilege—I know of. —— Damn your delicacy.— It is a low commercial quality—and very unworthy a man who prefixes "hon-ourable" to his nomenclature. If you say that I must sign the bonds—I suppose that I must—but it is very iniquitous to make me pay my debts—you have no idea of the pain it gives one.—Pray do three things—get my property out of the *funds*—get Rochdale[4] sold—get me some information from Perry about *South America*[5]—and 4thly. ask Lady Noel not to live so very long.——As to Subscribing to Manchester—if I do that—I will write a letter to Burdett[6]—for publication—to accompany the Subscription—which shall be more radical than anything yet rooted—but I feel lazy.—I have thought of this for some time—but alas! the air of this cursed Italy enervates—and disfranchises the thoughts of a man after nearly four years of respiration—to say nothing of emission.—As to "Don Juan"—confess—confess—you dog—and be candid— that it is the sublime of *that there* sort of writing—it may be bawdy—but is it not good English?—it may be profligate—but is it not *life*, is it not *the thing?*—Could any man have written it—who has not lived in the world?— and tooled in a post-chaise? in a hackney coach? in a Gondola? against a wall?

6. Murray published *Mazeppa* in June 1819.
1. I.e., money spent on pleasures of the senses.
2. Byron mentions having fallen in love with Teresa Guiccioli ("a Romagnuola Countess from Ravenna— who is nineteen years old & has a Count of fifty") in a letter of Apr. 6, 1819. Their relationship lasted until Byron set sail for Greece in the summer of 1823.
3. I.e., being made a peer (of the realm). John Hanson, Byron's solicitor and agent before Kinnaird took

over his principal business affairs, never realized this ambition.
4. An estate that Byron had inherited in Lancashire.
5. Byron was considering the possibility of emigrating to South America, specifically to Venezuela.
6. Sir Francis Burdett, Member of Parliament for Westminster, a reformer and leader of opposition to the Tories.

in a court carriage? in a vis a vis?[7]—on a table?—and under it?—I have written about a hundred stanzas of a third Canto—but it is damned modest—the outcry has frightened me.—I had such projects for the Don—but the *Cant* is so much stronger than *Cunt*—now a days,—that the benefit of experience in a man who had well weighed the worth of both monosyllables—must be lost to despairing posterity.—After all what stuff this outcry is—Lalla Rookh and Little—are more dangerous than my burlesque poem can be—Moore has been here—we got tipsy together—and were very amicable—he is gone on to Rome—I put my life (in M.S.) into his hands[8]—(*not* for publication) you— or any body else may see it—at his return.—It only comes up to 1816.——He is a noble fellow—and looks quite fresh and poetical—nine years (the age of a poem's education) my Senior—he looks younger—this comes of marriage and being settled in the Country. I want to go to South America—I have written to Hobhouse all about it.—I wrote to my wife—three months ago— under care to Murray—has she got the letter—or is the letter got into Black-wood's magazine?——You ask after my Christmas pye—Remit it any how— *Circulars*[9] is the best—you are right about *income*—I must have it all—how the devil do I know that I may live a year or a month?—I wish I knew that I might regulate my spending in more ways than one.—As it is one always thinks that there is but a span.—A man may as well break or be damned for a large sum as a small one—I should be loth to pay the devil or any other creditor more than sixpence in the pound.—

[scrawl for signature]

P.S.—I recollect nothing of "Davies's landlord"—but what ever Davies *says*—I will *swear* to—and *that's* more than *he* would.—So pray pay—has he a landlady too?—perhaps I may owe her something.——With regard to the bonds I will sign them but—it goes against the grain.——As to the rest—you *can't* err—so long as you *don't* pay.——Paying is executor's or executioner's work.——You may write somewhat oftener—Mr. Galignani's messenger[1] gives the outline of your public affairs—but I see no results—you have no man yet—(always excepting Burdett—& you & H[obhouse] and the Gentlemanly leaven of your two-penny loaf of rebellion) don't forget however my charge of horse—and commission for the Midland Counties and by the holies!—You shall have your account in decimals.—Love to Hobby—but why leave the Whigs?——

To Percy Bysshe Shelley

[*Keats and Shelley*]

Ravenna, April 26th, 1821

The child continues doing well, and the accounts are regular and favour-able. It is gratifying to me that you and Mrs. Shelley do not disapprove of the step which I have taken, which is merely temporary.[1]

---

7. A light carriage for two persons sitting face to face.
8. Byron's famous memoirs, which were later sold to John Murray and burned in the publisher's office.
9. Letters of credit.
1. *Galignani's Messenger*, an English newspaper pub-

lished in Paris.
1. Byron had recently placed his four-year-old daugh-ter Allegra in a convent school near Ravenna, against the wishes of her mother, Mary Shelley's stepsister Claire Clairmont.

I am very sorry to hear what you say of Keats[2]—is it *actually* true? I did not think criticism had been so killing. Though I differ from you essentially in your estimate of his performances, I so much abhor all unnecessary pain, that I would rather he had been seated on the highest peak of Parnassus than have perished in such a manner. Poor fellow! though with such inordinate self-love he would probably have not been very happy. I read the review of "Endymion" in the Quarterly. It was severe,—but surely not so severe as many reviews in that and other journals upon others.

I recollect the effect on me of the Edinburgh on my first poem;[3] it was rage, and resistance, and redress—but not despondency nor despair. I grant that those are not amiable feelings; but, in this world of bustle and broil, and especially in the career of writing, a man should calculate upon his powers of *resistance* before he goes into the arena.

"Expect not life from pain nor danger free,
Nor deem the doom of man reversed for thee."[4]

You know my opinion of *that second-hand* school of poetry. You also know my high opinion of your own poetry,—because it is of *no* school. I read Cenci—but, besides that I think the *subject* essentially *un*dramatic, I am not an admirer of our old dramatists *as models.* I deny that the English have hitherto had a drama at all. Your Cenci, however, was a work of power, and poetry. As to *my* drama,[5] pray revenge yourself upon it, by being as free as I have been with yours.

I have not yet got your Prometheus, which I long to see. I have heard nothing of mine, and do not know that it is yet published. I have published a pamphlet on the Pope controversy, which you will not like. Had I known that Keats was dead—or that he was alive and so sensitive—I should have omitted some remarks upon his poetry, to which I was provoked by his *attack* upon *Pope,*[6] and my disapprobation of *his own* style of writing.

You want me to undertake a great Poem—I have not the inclination nor the power. As I grow older, the indifference—*not* to life, for we love it by instinct—but to the stimuli of life, increases. Besides, this late failure of the Italians[7] has latterly disappointed me for many reasons,—some public, some personal. My respects to Mrs. S.

Yours ever,

B

P.S.—Could not you and I contrive to meet this summer? Could not you take a run *alone*?

2. In a letter to Byron, Apr. 17, 1821: "Young Keats, whose 'Hyperion' showed so great a promise, died lately at Rome from the consequences of breaking a blood-vessel, in paroxysms of despair at the contemptuous attack on his book in the *Quarterly Review*" (see Shelley's *Adonais*, p. 1738).
3. The review of Byron's *Hours of Idleness* in the *Edinburgh Review* prompted him to write his first major satire, *English Bards and Scotch Reviewers* (1809).
4. Johnson, *The Vanity of Human Wishes*, lines 155–56 (Byron is quoting from memory).
5. *Marino Faliero*, published in London on Apr. 21, 1821. Shelley's *The Cenci* and *Prometheus Unbound* (next paragraph) were written in 1819 and published in 1820.

6. Keats attacked Augustan poetry (but not necessarily Pope) in *Sleep and Poetry*, lines 181–206. Byron's pamphlet, *Letter to ⁎⁎⁎⁎⁎⁎⁎⁎⁎ [John Murray], on the Rev. W. L. Bowles' Strictures on the Life and Writings of Pope,* had just appeared in London. His best-known comment on Keats, written a year and a half later, is canto 11, stanza 60 in *Don Juan,* beginning "John Keats, who was killed off by one critique" and ending "'Tis strange the mind, that very fiery particle, / Should let itself be snuffed out by an Article."
7. A planned uprising by the Carbonari, a secret revolutionary society into which Byron had been initiated by the father and brother of his mistress Teresa Guiccioli, failed in Feb. 1821.

PERCY BYSSHE SHELLEY
1792–1822

1811:   Is expelled from Oxford and elopes with Harriet Westbrook.
1818:   Leaves England for Italy, never to return.
1819:   The great year: *Prometheus Unbound, The Cenci,* and some of
         his best lyrics, including *Ode to the West Wind.*
1820:   Settles in Pisa and its vicinity; the "Pisan Circle."

Percy Bysshe Shelley, although a radical nonconformist in every aspect of his life and thought, emerged from a solidly conservative background. His ancestors had been Sussex aristocrats since early in the seventeenth century; his grandfather, Sir Bysshe Shelley, made himself the richest man in Horsham, Sussex; his father, Timothy Shelley, was a hardheaded and conventional Member of Parliament. Percy Shelley himself was in line for a baronetcy and, as befitted his station, was sent to be educated at Eton and Oxford. He was slight of build, eccentric in manner, and unskilled in sports or fighting and, as a consequence, was mercilessly baited by older and stronger boys. Even then he saw the petty tyranny of schoolmasters and schoolmates as representative of man's general inhumanity to man, and dedicated his life to a war against injustice and oppression. He describes the experience in the Dedication to *Laon and Cythna* (later called *The Revolt of Islam*):

> So without shame, I spake:—"I will be wise,
> And just, and free, and mild, if in me lies
> Such power, for I grow weary to behold
> The selfish and the strong still tyrannise
> Without reproach or check." I then controuled
> My tears, my heart grew calm, and I was meek and bold.

At Oxford in the autumn of 1810 Shelley's closest friend was Thomas Jefferson Hogg, a self-centered and self-confident young man who shared Shelley's love of philosophy and scorn of orthodoxy. The two collaborated on a pamphlet, *The Necessity of Atheism,* which claimed that God's existence cannot be proved on empirical grounds. Shelley refused to repudiate the document, as demanded by the authorities; to his great shock and grief, he was peremptorily expelled, terminating a university career that had lasted only six months. This event opened a breach between Shelley and his father that widened over the years.

Shelley went to London, where, eager for a test of his zeal for social justice, he took up the cause of Harriet Westbrook, the pretty and warmhearted daughter of a well-to-do tavern keeper, whose father, Shelley wrote to Hogg, "has persecuted her in a most horrible way by endeavoring to compel her to go to school." Harriet threw herself on Shelley's protection, and "gratitude and admiration," he wrote, "all demand that I shall love her *forever.*" He eloped with Harriet to Edinburgh and married her, against his conviction that marriage was a tyrannical and degrading social institution. He was then eighteen years of age, and his bride, sixteen. The young couple moved restlessly from place to place, living on a small allowance granted reluctantly by their families. In February 1812, accompanied by Harriet's sister Eliza, they traveled to Dublin to distribute Shelley's *Address to the Irish People* and otherwise take part in the movement for Catholic emancipation and for the amelioration of the oppressed and poverty-stricken people.

Back in London, Shelley became a disciple of the radical social philosopher William Godwin, author of the *Inquiry Concerning Political Justice*. In 1813 he printed privately his first important work, *Queen Mab*, a long prophetic poem set in the fantastic frame of the journey of a disembodied soul through space, to whom the fairy Mab reveals in visions the woeful past, the dreadful present, and the utopian future. Announcing that "there is no God!" Mab decries institutional religion and codified morality as the roots of social evil. She prophesies that, under the rule of the goddess Necessity, all institutions will wither away, and humanity will return to its natural condition of goodness and felicity.

In the following spring Shelley, who had drifted apart from Harriet, fell in love with the beautiful Mary Wollstonecraft Godwin, daughter of Mary Wollstonecraft and William Godwin. Acting according to his conviction that cohabitation without love is immoral, he abandoned Harriet, fled to France with Mary (taking along her stepsister, Claire Clairmont), and—still acting in accordance with his belief in nonexclusive love—invited Harriet to come live with them in the relationship of a sister. Shelley's elopement with Mary outraged her father, despite the facts that his theoretical views of marriage had been no less radical than Shelley's and that Shelley, himself in financial difficulties, had earlier taken over Godwin's very substantial debts. When he returned to London, Shelley found that the general public, his family, and most of his friends regarded him not only as an atheist and revolutionary but also as a gross immoralist. When two years later Harriet, pregnant by an unknown lover, drowned herself in a fit of despair, the courts denied Shelley the custody of their two children. Shelley married Mary Godwin and in 1818 moved to Italy; thereafter he saw himself in the role of an alien and outcast, scorned and rejected by the human race to whose welfare he had dedicated his powers and his life.

In Italy he resumed his restless existence, moving from town to town and house to house. His health was usually bad. Although the death of his grandfather in 1815 had provided a substantial income, he dissipated so much of it by his warmhearted but improvident support of William Godwin, Leigh Hunt, and other indigent pensioners that he was constantly short of money and harried by creditors. Within nine months, in 1818–19, Clara and William, the beloved children of Percy and Mary Shelley, both died. This tragedy threw Mary into a state of apathy and self-absorption that destroyed the earlier harmony of her relationship with her husband and from which even the birth of another son, Percy Florence, could not entirely rescue her.

In these desperate circumstances, in a state sometimes verging on despair, and knowing that he almost entirely lacked an audience, Shelley wrote his greatest works. In 1819 he completed his masterpiece, *Prometheus Unbound*, and a fine tragedy, *The Cenci*. He wrote also numerous lyric poems; a visionary call for a proletarian revolution, *The Mask of Anarchy*; a discerning and witty satire on Wordsworth, *Peter Bell the Third*; and a penetrating political essay, *A Philosophical View of Reform*. His works of the next two years include *A Defence of Poetry*; *Epipsychidion*, a rhapsodic vision of love as a union, beyond earthly limits, with what the title identifies as "the soul out of my soul"; *Adonais*, his noble elegy on the death of Keats; and *Hellas*, a lyrical drama evoked by the Greek war for liberation from the Turks, in which he again projected his vision of a coming golden age. These writings, unlike the early *Queen Mab*, are the products of a mind enlarged and chastened by tragic experience, deepened by incessant philosophical speculation, and richly stored with the harvest of his reading—which Shelley carried on, as his friend Hogg said, "in season and out of season, at table, in bed, and especially during a walk," until he became one of the most erudite of poets. His delight in scientific discoveries and speculations continued, but his earlier zest for Gothic terrors and the social theories of the radical eighteenth-century optimists gave way to an absorption in Greek tragedy, Milton's *Paradise Lost*, and the Bible.

Although he did not give up his hopes for a millennial future (he wore a ring with the motto *Il buon tempo verrà*—"the good time will come"), he now attributed the evils of present society to humanity's own moral failures and grounded the possibility of radical social reform on a prior reform of the moral and imaginative faculties through the redeeming power of love. Though often represented as a simpleminded doctrinaire, Shelley in fact possessed a complex and energetically inquisitive intelligence that never halted at a fixed mental position; his writings reflect stages in a ceaseless exploration.

The poems of Shelley's maturity also show the influence of his study of Plato and the Neoplatonists. Shelley found congenial the Platonic division of the cosmos into two worlds—the ordinary world of change, mortality, evil, and suffering and the criterion world of perfect and eternal Forms, of which the world of sense-experience is only a distant and illusory reflection. The earlier interpretations of Shelley as a downright Platonic idealist, however, have been drastically modified by modern investigations of his reading and writings. He was a close student of English empirical philosophy, which limits knowledge to valid reasoning on what is given in sense-experience, and within this tradition he felt a special affinity to the radical skepticism of David Hume. Shelley was indeed an idealist, but as C. E. Pulos has shown in *The Deep Truth: A Study of Shelley's Scepticism*, his was "a qualified idealism," holding provisionally to the ideas envisioned by an imagination that transcends experience, but refusing to assert that these ideas are anything more than high possibilities. As Shelley wrote, we quickly reach "the verge where words abandon us, and what wonder if we grow dizzy to look down the dark abyss of how little we know." Many of his major poems express his sense of the limits of certain knowledge and his refusal to let his intuitions and hopes harden into a philosophical or religious creed. To the skeptical idealism of the mature Shelley (see, for example, the notes to his great lyrics from *Hellas*), the hope in the ultimate redemption of life by love and imagination is not a certainty but a moral obligation. We must, he asserts, cling to hope because its contrary, despair about human possibility, is self-fulfilling, by ensuring the permanence of the conditions before which the mind has surrendered its aspirations. Hope does not guarantee achievement, but it keeps open the possibility of achievement and so releases the imaginative and creative powers that are its only available means.

When in 1820 the Shelleys settled finally at Pisa, he came closer to finding contentment than at any other time in his adult life. A group of friends, Shelley's "Pisan Circle," gathered around them, including for a while Lord Byron and the swashbuckling young Cornishman Edward Trelawny. Chief in Shelley's affections, however, were Edward Williams, a retired lieutenant of a cavalry regiment serving in India, and his charming common-law wife, Jane, with whom Shelley carried on a flirtation and to whom he addressed some of his best lyrics and verse letters. The end came suddenly, and in a way previsioned in the ecstatic last stanza of *Adonais*, in which he had described his spirit as a ship driven by a violent storm out into the dark unknown. On July 8, 1822, Shelley and Edward Williams were sailing their open boat, the *Don Juan*, from Leghorn to their summer house near Lerici, on the Gulf of Spezia. A violent squall blew up and swamped the boat. When several days later the bodies were washed ashore they were cremated, and Shelley's ashes were buried in the Protestant Cemetery at Rome, near the graves of John Keats and William Shelley, the poet's young son. He left unfinished *The Triumph of Life*, which was a new departure that, in the estimation of many readers, promised to be his greatest poem. Byron, who did not pay moral compliments lightly, wrote to John Murray at the time of Shelley's death: "You were all brutally mistaken about Shelley, who was, without exception, the *best* and least selfish man I ever knew. I never knew one who was not a beast in comparison."

To many critics of the mid-twentieth century (and despite the reverence toward him of W. B. Yeats, an admitted master of the poetry these critics most admired), Shelley was a favorite resort for supposed examples of intellectual and emotional immaturity, shoddy workmanship, and incoherent imagery. In recent years, however, he has been the subject of many sympathetic critics, whose studies have clarified the complex and coherent structure of his symbolism and have increasingly confirmed Wordsworth's recognition that "Shelley is one of the best *artists* of us all: I mean in workmanship of style." Shelley's expansion of the metrical and stanzaic resources of verse is without recent parallel in the history of English literature. Furthermore, his successful poems show an astonishing range of voice, from the controlled passion of *Ode to the West Wind*, through the calm and heroic dignity of the utterances of Prometheus, to the approximation to what is inexpressible in the description of Asia's transfiguration and in the visionary conclusion of *Adonais*. Most surprising, for a poet who almost entirely lacked an audience, is the assured urbanity, the effortless command of the tone and language of a cultivated man of the world, exemplified in passages that Shelley wrote all through his mature career and especially in the lyrics and verse letters that he composed during the last year of his life.

TEXTUAL NOTE

The publication of Shelley's writings has had a tangled history. Shelley had no chance to correct proofs for many of the poems published during his lifetime, especially those that appeared in periodicals, while a number of his poems were not printed until after his death. As a result, standard editions of Shelley's collected poems—and the selections and anthologies that have been based on these editions—have included numerous errors and deviations from the poet's probable intentions.

The texts below are those prepared by Donald H. Reiman and Sharon B. Powers for *Shelley's Poetry and Prose*, a Norton Critical Edition (1977); Reiman has also edited for this anthology a few poems not included in that edition. The texts are based on Shelley's extant holograph manuscripts and transcripts, on first editions of the various works, and on any later editions that may have incorporated the author's own changes; they also take advantage of specialized editions and textual studies by various Shelley scholars.

The detailed rationale is provided in Reiman and Powers's Textual Introduction to the Norton Critical Edition. Shelley's spellings have been kept (though in part regularized according to the poet's own preferred forms), as well as Shelley's punctuation of those texts that he himself prepared for printing. The modern reader should remember that Shelley's punctuation, in the common fashion of his time, was primarily rhetorical rather than syntactical. That is, a punctuation mark indicates a phrasal pause in the reading; there is an increasingly longer pause in the sequence: comma, semicolon, colon, period, and dash. Also, Shelley often relied on the natural pause at the end of a line of verse, where modern usage would call for a comma or other mark of punctuation.

Mutability

We are as clouds that veil the midnight moon;
    How restlessly they speed, and gleam, and quiver,
Streaking the darkness radiantly!—yet soon
    Night closes round, and they are lost for ever:

Or like forgotten lyres,[1] whose dissonant strings   5
　　Give various response to each varying blast,
To whose frail frame no second motion brings
　　One mood or modulation like the last.

We rest.—A dream has power to poison sleep;
　　We rise.—One wandering thought pollutes the day;   10
We feel, conceive or reason, laugh or weep;
　　Embrace fond woe, or cast our cares away:

It is the same!—For, be it joy or sorrow,
　　The path of its departure still is free:
Man's yesterday may ne'er be like his morrow;   15
　　Nought may endure but Mutability.

ca. 1814–15   1816

To Wordsworth[2]

Poet of Nature, thou hast wept to know
That things depart which never may return:
Childhood and youth, friendship and love's first glow,
Have fled like sweet dreams, leaving thee to mourn.
These common woes I feel. One loss is mine   5
Which thou too feel'st, yet I alone deplore.
Thou wert as a lone star, whose light did shine
On some frail bark in winter's midnight roar:
Thou hast like to a rock-built refuge stood
Above the blind and battling multitude: 10
In honoured poverty thy voice did weave
Songs consecrate to truth and liberty,—
Deserting these, thou leavest me to grieve,
Thus having been, that thou shouldst cease to be.

ca. 1814–15   1816

Alastor; or, The Spirit of Solitude   According to Shelley's friend Thomas
Love Peacock, the poet was "at a loss for a title, and I proposed that which he
adopted: Alastor, or the Spirit of Solitude. The Greek word *Alastor* is an evil
genius. . . . I mention the true meaning of the word because many have supposed
Alastor to be the name of the hero" (*Memoirs of Shelley*). Peacock's definition of
an *alastor* as "an *evil* genius" has compounded the problems that many readers
have found in interpreting this work: the term *evil* does not seem to fit the attitude
expressed within the poem toward the protagonist's solitary quest, the poem seems
to clash with some statements in Shelley's preface, and the first and second paragraphs within the preface seem inconsistent with each other. These problems,
however, are largely resolved if we recognize that, in this early achievement (he
was only twenty-three when he wrote *Alastor*), Shelley established his characteristic procedure of working with multiple perspectives. Both preface and poem

---

1. Wind harps.
2. Shelley's grieved comment on the poet of nature

and of social radicalism after his views had become
conservative.

explore alternative and conflicting possibilities in what Shelley calls "doubtful knowledge"—matters that are humanly essential but in which no certainty is humanly possible.

The first paragraph of the preface explains the "allegorical" plot. By "allegorical" Shelley means that the poem, like medieval and Renaissance allegories such as Dante's *Divine Comedy* and Spenser's *Faerie Queene*, represents a spiritual need and aspiration in the vehicle of a journey and quest in the physical world. Shelley's protagonist reaches a stage at which the natural objects within the world "cease to suffice," for he envisions a "Being," a female Other who will answer to all that is best in his own self and will fulfill the diverse requirements of his "intellectual faculties," "imagination," and "the functions of sense." He commits himself to the search for "a prototype" of this vision in the real world, but because his desires are infinite and the world's possibilities are limited, his quest is doomed to end in his early death.

The second paragraph proceeds to pass judgment on such a Poet in terms of the values of "actual men"—the requirements of human and social life in this world. Because the visionary Poet turned away from both human and natural community in search of the projected demands of his own psyche, his lot can be said to have been "avenged" by the *alastor*, the spirit of solitude, in the sense of "solitude" as alienation from both nature and humanity. The preface goes on, however, passionately to elevate the moral status of such a visionary over the status of a second class of "meaner spirits" who also "keep aloof from sympathies with their kind," but only because they ignobly lack any capacity to project their imagination beyond their own narrow selves, and so are "morally dead." The preface leaves open a possibility that Shelley proceeded to explore in *Prometheus Unbound* and other poems—the possibility that there exists a third class of persons who sustain an imaginative vision but undertake to realize it, not in self-centered solitude but by effecting a transformation in human nature, society, and milieu.

The diverse attitudes expressed within the poem itself are clarified, once we realize that the story is narrated—as the many echoes from Wordsworth in the opening invocation suggest—in the persona of a Wordsworthian poet for whom nature suffices both to the demands of his imagination and to his need for community. This narrator-poet proceeds to tell, with insight and compassion, but from his own perspective, the history of a nameless visionary Poet who, having himself passed through a Wordsworthian phase, then gives up everything in the quest for a goal beyond possibility.

In this early poem Shelley established a form, conceptual frame, and imagery for the Romantic quest that not only shaped his own later poems but also served as a paradigm for the writings of many other poets, from Byron's *Manfred* and Keats's *Endymion* and invocation to *The Fall of Hyperion* to the quest-poems of Shelley's later admirer William Butler Yeats.

Alastor; or, The Spirit of Solitude

Preface

The poem entitled "ALASTOR," may be considered as allegorical of one of the most interesting situations of the human mind. It represents a youth of uncorrupted feelings and adventurous genius led forth by an imagination inflamed and purified through familiarity with all that is excellent and majestic, to the contemplation of the universe. He drinks deep of the fountains of knowledge, and is still insatiate. The magnificence and beauty of the external world sinks profoundly into the frame of his conceptions, and affords to their modifications a variety not to be exhausted. So long as it is possible for his desires to point towards objects thus infinite and unmeasured, he is joyous, and tranquil, and self-possessed. But the period arrives when these objects cease to suffice. His mind is at length suddenly awakened and thirsts for intercourse with an intelligence similar to itself. He images to himself the Being whom he loves. Conversant with speculations of the sublimest and most perfect natures, the vision in which he embodies his own imaginations unites all of wonderful, or wise, or beautiful, which the poet, the philosopher, or the lover could depicture. The intellectual faculties, the imagination, the functions of sense, have their respective requisitions on the sympathy of corresponding powers in other human beings. The Poet is represented as uniting these requisitions, and attaching them to a single image.[1] He seeks in vain for a prototype of his conception. Blasted by his disappointment, he descends to an untimely grave.

The picture is not barren of instruction to actual men. The Poet's self-centred seclusion was avenged by the furies of an irresistible passion pursuing him to speedy ruin. But that Power which strikes the luminaries of the world with sudden darkness and extinction, by awakening them to too exquisite a perception of its influences, dooms to a slow and poisonous decay those meaner spirits that dare to abjure its dominion. Their destiny is more abject and inglorious as their delinquency is more contemptible and pernicious. They who, deluded by no generous error, instigated by no sacred thirst of doubtful knowledge, duped by no illustrious superstition, loving nothing on this earth, and cherishing no hopes beyond, yet keep aloof from sympathies with their kind, rejoicing neither in human joy nor mourning with human grief; these, and such as they, have their apportioned curse. They languish, because none feel with them their common nature. They are morally dead. They are neither friends, nor lovers, nor fathers, nor citizens of the world, nor benefactors of their country. Among those who attempt to exist without human sympathy, the pure and tender-hearted perish through the intensity and passion of their search after its communities, when the vacancy of their spirit suddenly makes itself felt. All else, selfish, blind, and torpid, are those unforeseeing multitudes who constitute, together with their own, the lasting misery and loneliness of the world. Those who love not their fellow-beings live unfruitful lives, and prepare for their old age a miserable grave.

> "The good die first,
> And those whose hearts are dry as summer dust,
> Burn to the socket!"[2]

December 14, 1815

---

1. Shelley's view that the object of love is an idealized antitype to all that is best within the self is clarified by a passage in his *Essay on Love*, which may have been written at about the time of *Alastor*: "We dimly see within our intellectual nature . . . the ideal prototype of every thing excellent or lovely that we are capable of conceiving as belonging to the nature of men. . . . [This is] a soul within our soul. . . . The discovery of its anti-type . . . in such proportion as the type within

demands; this is the invisible and unattainable point to which Love tends; and . . . without the possession of which there is no rest nor respite to the heart over which it rules."
2. Wordsworth, *The Excursion* 1.519–21; the passage occurs also in *The Ruined Cottage* 96–98, which Wordsworth reworked into the first book of *The Excursion* (1814).

Alastor; or, The Spirit of Solitude

Nondum amabam, et amare amabam, quærebam quid amarem, amans amare.—Confess. St. August.[3]

Earth, ocean, air, beloved brotherhood!
If our great Mother[4] has imbued my soul
With aught of natural piety[5] to feel
Your love, and recompense the boon with mine;[6]
If dewy morn, and odorous noon, and even,   5
With sunset and its gorgeous ministers,[7]
And solemn midnight's tingling silentness;
If autumn's hollow sighs in the sere wood,
And winter robing with pure snow and crowns
Of starry ice the grey grass and bare boughs;   10
If spring's voluptuous pantings when she breathes
Her first sweet kisses, have been dear to me;
If no bright bird, insect, or gentle beast
I consciously have injured, but still loved
And cherished these my kindred; then forgive   15
This boast, beloved brethren, and withdraw
No portion of your wonted favour now!

　 Mother of this unfathomable world!
Favour my solemn song, for I have loved
Thee ever, and thee only; I have watched   20
Thy shadow, and the darkness of thy steps,
And my heart ever gazes on the depth
Of thy deep mysteries. I have made my bed
In charnels and on coffins, where black death
Keeps record of the trophies won from thee,   25
Hoping to still these obstinate questionings[8]
Of thee and thine, by forcing some lone ghost,
Thy messenger, to render up the tale
Of what we are. In lone and silent hours,
When night makes a weird sound of its own stillness,   30
Like an inspired and desperate alchymist
Staking his very life on some dark hope,
Have I mixed awful talk and asking looks
With my most innocent love, until strange tears
Uniting with those breathless kisses, made   35
Such magic as compels the charmed night
To render up thy charge: . . . and, though ne'er yet
Thou hast unveil'd thy inmost sanctuary,
Enough from incommunicable dream,

3. St. Augustine, *Confessions* 3.1: "Not yet did I love, though I loved to love, seeking what I might love, loving to love." Augustine thus describes his state of mind when he was addicted to illicit sexual love; the true object of his desire, which compels the tortuous spiritual journey of his life, he later discovered to be the infinite and transcendent God.
4. Nature, invoked as the common mother of the elements and of the poet.

5. Wordsworth, *My heart leaps up*, lines 8–9: "And I could wish my days to be / Bound each to each by natural piety." Wordsworth also used these lines as the epigraph to his *Ode: Intimations of Immortality.*
6. I.e., with my love.
7. The sunset colors.
8. Wordsworth, *Ode: Intimations of Immortality,* lines 141–42: "those obstinate questionings / Of sense and outward things."

And twilight phantasms, and deep noonday thought,   40
Has shone within me, that serenely now
And moveless, as a long-forgotten lyre
Suspended in the solitary dome
Of some mysterious and deserted fane,[9]
I wait thy breath, Great Parent, that my strain   45
May modulate with murmurs of the air,
And motions of the forests and the sea,
And voice of living beings, and woven hymns
Of night and day, and the deep heart of man.[1]

    There was a Poet whose untimely tomb   50
No human hands with pious reverence reared,
But the charmed eddies of autumnal winds
Built o'er his mouldering bones a pyramid
Of mouldering leaves in the waste wilderness:—
A lovely youth,—no mourning maiden decked   55
With weeping flowers, or votive cypress wreath,[2]
The lone couch of his everlasting sleep:—
Gentle, and brave, and generous,—no lorn[3] bard
Breathed o'er his dark fate one melodious sigh:
He lived, he died, he sung, in solitude.   60
Strangers have wept to hear his passionate notes,
And virgins, as unknown he past, have pined
And wasted for fond love of his wild eyes.
The fire of those soft orbs has ceased to burn,
And Silence, too enamoured of that voice,   65
Locks its mute music in her rugged cell.

    By solemn vision, and bright silver dream,
His infancy was nurtured. Every sight
And sound from the vast earth and ambient air,
Sent to his heart its choicest impulses.   70
The fountains of divine philosophy
Fled not his thirsting lips, and all of great
Or good, or lovely, which the sacred past
In truth or fable consecrates, he felt
And knew. When early youth had past, he left   75
His cold fireside and alienated home
To seek strange truths in undiscovered lands.
Many a wide waste and tangled wilderness
Has lured his fearless steps; and he has bought
With his sweet voice and eyes, from savage men,   80
His rest and food. Nature's most secret steps
He like her shadow has pursued, where'er
The red volcano overcanopies

---

9. Temple. The narrator calls on the Mother, his natural muse, to make him her wind harp. Cf. the opening passage of Wordsworth's *Prelude* (pp. 1402–03), Coleridge's *Dejection: An Ode* (pp. 1524–27), and the conclusions of Shelley's *Ode to the West Wind* (p. 1700) and of *Adonais* (p. 1739).
1. Cf. Wordsworth, *Tintern Abbey* 94ff.: "A presence ... / Whose dwelling is ... the round ocean and the living air, / And the blue sky, and in the mind of man: / A motion and a spirit."
2. The cypress represented mourning. "Votive": offered to fulfill a vow to the gods.
3. Abandoned.

Its fields of snow and pinnacles of ice
With burning smoke, or where bitumen lakes[4]   85
On black bare pointed islets ever beat
With sluggish surge, or where the secret caves
Rugged and dark, winding among the springs
Of fire and poison, inaccessible
To avarice or pride, their starry domes   90
Of diamond and of gold expand above
Numberless and immeasurable halls,
Frequent[5] with crystal column, and clear shrines
Of pearl, and thrones radiant with chrysolite.[6]
Nor had that scene of ampler majesty   95
Than gems or gold, the varying roof of heaven
And the green earth lost in his heart its claims
To love and wonder; he would linger long
In lonesome vales, making the wild his home,
Until the doves and squirrels would partake   100
From his innocuous hand his bloodless food,[7]
Lured by the gentle meaning of his looks,
And the wild antelope, that starts whene'er
The dry leaf rustles in the brake,[8] suspend
Her timid steps to gaze upon a form   105
More graceful than her own.

                    His wandering step
Obedient to high thoughts, has visited
The awful ruins of the days of old:
Athens, and Tyre, and Balbec,[9] and the waste
Where stood Jerusalem, the fallen towers   110
Of Babylon, the eternal pyramids,
Memphis and Thebes,[1] and whatsoe'er of strange
Sculptured on alabaster obelisk,
Or jasper tomb, or mutilated sphinx,
Dark Æthiopia in her desert hills   115
Conceals. Among the ruined temples there,
Stupendous columns, and wild images
Of more than man, where marble dæmons watch
The Zodiac's brazen mystery,[2] and dead men
Hang their mute thoughts on the mute walls around,[3]   120
He lingered, poring on memorials
Of the world's youth, through the long burning day
Gazed on those speechless shapes, nor, when the moon
Filled the mysterious halls with floating shades
Suspended he that task, but ever gazed   125
And gazed, till meaning on his vacant mind

---

4. Lakes of pitch, flowing from a volcano.
5. Crowded.
6. An olive green stone.
7. Shelley was himself a vegetarian.
8. Thicket.
9. An ancient city in modern-day Lebanon. Tyre was once an important commercial city on the Phoenician coast.

1. The ancient capital of Upper Egypt. Memphis is the ruined capital of Lower Egypt.
2. In the temple of Isis at Denderah, Egypt, the Zodiac is represented on the ceiling. "Daemons": in Greek mythology demons were not evil spirits but minor deities, or attendant spirits.
3. I.e., by quotations inscribed in the stone.

Flashed like strong inspiration, and he saw
The thrilling secrets of the birth of time.

Meanwhile an Arab maiden brought his food,
Her daily portion, from her father's tent,   130
And spread her matting for his couch, and stole
From duties and repose to tend his steps:—
Enamoured, yet not daring for deep awe
To speak her love:—and watched his nightly sleep,
Sleepless herself, to gaze upon his lips   135
Parted in slumber, whence the regular breath
Of innocent dreams arose: then, when red morn
Made paler the pale moon, to her cold home
Wildered,[4] and wan, and panting, she returned.

The Poet wandering on, through Arabie   140
And Persia, and the wild Carmanian waste,[5]
And o'er the aërial mountains which pour down
Indus and Oxus[6] from their icy caves,
In joy and exultation held his way;
Till in the vale of Cashmire, far within   145
Its loneliest dell, where odorous plants entwine
Beneath the hollow rocks a natural bower,
Beside a sparkling rivulet he stretched
His languid limbs. A vision on his sleep
There came, a dream of hopes that never yet   150
Had flushed his cheek. He dreamed a veiled maid
Sate near him, talking in low solemn tones.
Her voice was like the voice of his own soul
Heard in the calm of thought; its music long,
Like woven sounds of streams and breezes, held   155
His inmost sense suspended in its web
Of many-coloured woof and shifting hues.
Knowledge and truth and virtue were her theme,
And lofty hopes of divine liberty,
Thoughts the most dear to him, and poesy,   160

Herself a poet.[7] Soon the solemn mood
Of her pure mind kindled through all her frame
A permeating fire: wild numbers then
She raised, with voice stifled in tremulous sobs
Subdued by its own pathos: her fair hands   165
Were bare alone, sweeping from some strange harp
Strange symphony, and in their branching veins
The eloquent blood told an ineffable tale.
The beating of her heart was heard to fill
The pauses of her music, and her breath   170
Tumultuously accorded with those fits

---

4. Astray, bewildered.
5. A desert in southern Persia.
6. Rivers in Asia.
7. The envisioned maiden embodies all three qualities

specified in the preface: intellect (line 158), imagination (lines 160–61), and the sexual and other "functions of sense" (lines 176ff.).

Of intermitted song. Sudden she rose,
As if her heart impatiently endured
Its bursting burthen: at the sound he turned,
And saw by the warm light of their own life   175
Her glowing limbs beneath the sinuous veil
Of woven wind, her outspread arms now bare,
Her dark locks floating in the breath of night,
Her beamy bending eyes, her parted lips
Outstretched, and pale, and quivering eagerly.   180
His strong heart sunk and sickened with excess
Of love. He reared his shuddering limbs and quelled
His gasping breath, and spread his arms to meet
Her panting bosom: . . . she drew back a while,
Then, yielding to the irresistible joy,   185
With frantic gesture and short breathless cry
Folded his frame in her dissolving arms.
Now blackness veiled his dizzy eyes, and night
Involved and swallowed up the vision; sleep,
Like a dark flood suspended in its course,   190
Rolled back its impulse on his vacant brain.

    Roused by the shock he started from his trance—
The cold white light of morning, the blue moon
Low in the west, the clear and garish hills,
The distinct valley and the vacant woods,   195
Spread round him where he stood. Whither have fled
The hues of heaven that canopied his bower
Of yesternight? The sounds that soothed his sleep,
The mystery and the majesty of Earth,
The joy, the exultation? His wan eyes   200
Gaze on the empty scene as vacantly
As ocean's moon looks on the moon in heaven.
The spirit of sweet human love has sent
A vision to the sleep of him who spurned
Her choicest gifts. He eagerly pursues   205
Beyond the realms of dream that fleeting shade;
He overleaps the bounds. Alas! alas!
Were limbs, and breath, and being intertwined
Thus treacherously? Lost, lost, for ever lost,
In the wide pathless desart of dim sleep,   210
That beautiful shape! Does the dark gate of death
Conduct to thy mysterious paradise,
O Sleep?[8] Does the bright arch of rainbow clouds,
And pendent mountains seen in the calm lake,
Lead only to a black and watery depth,   215
While death's blue vault, with loathliest vapours hung,
Where every shade which the foul grave exhales
Hides its dead eye from the detested day,
Conduct,[9] O Sleep, to thy delightful realms?
This doubt with sudden tide flowed on his heart,   220

8. I.e., is death the only access to this maiden of his
dream?

9. "Conduct" is a singular subjunctive verb; its subject
is "vault" (line 216).

The insatiate hope which it awakened, stung
His brain even like despair.
                    While day-light held
The sky, the Poet kept mute conference
With his still soul. At night the passion came,
Like the fierce fiend of a distempered dream,   225
And shook him from his rest, and led him forth
Into the darkness.—As an eagle grasped
In folds of the green serpent, feels her breast
Burn with the poison, and precipitates[1]
Through night and day, tempest, and calm, and cloud,   230
Frantic with dizzying anguish, her blind flight
O'er the wide aëry wilderness:[2] thus driven
By the bright shadow of that lovely dream,
Beneath the cold glare of the desolate night,
Through tangled swamps and deep precipitous dells,   235
Startling with careless step the moon-light snake,
He fled. Red morning dawned upon his flight,
Shedding the mockery of its vital hues
Upon his cheek of death. He wandered on
Till vast Aornos seen from Petra's steep[3]   240
Hung o'er the low horizon like a cloud;
Through Balk,[4] and where the desolated tombs
Of Parthian kings scatter to every wind
Their wasting dust, wildly he wandered on,
Day after day, a weary waste of hours,   245
Bearing within his life the brooding care
That ever fed on its decaying flame.
And now his limbs were lean; his scattered hair
Sered by the autumn of strange suffering
Sung dirges in the wind; his listless hand   250
Hung like dead bone within its withered skin;
Life, and the lustre that consumed it, shone
As in a furnace burning secretly
From his dark eyes alone. The cottagers,
Who ministered with human charity   255
His human wants, beheld with wondering awe
Their fleeting visitant. The mountaineer,
Encountering on some dizzy precipice
That spectral form, deemed that the Spirit of wind
With lightning eyes, and eager breath, and feet   260
Disturbing not the drifted snow, had paused
In its career: the infant would conceal
His troubled visage in his mother's robe
In terror at the glare of those wild eyes,
To remember their strange light in many a dream   265
Of after-times; but youthful maidens, taught
By nature, would interpret half the woe

1. Hastens.
2. The eagle and serpent locked in mortal combat is a
recurrent image in Shelley's poems (see *Prometheus
Unbound* 3.1.72–73, p. 1719).
3. Aornos is a high mountain and Petra ("the rock") a
mountain stronghold in the northern part of ancient
Arabia.
4. Bactria, in ancient Persia, is now part of Afghanistan. The Parthians (line 243) inhabited northern
Persia.

That wasted him, would call him with false names
Brother, and friend,[5] would press his pallid hand
At parting, and watch, dim through tears, the path   270
Of his departure from their father's door.

    At length upon the lone Chorasmian shore[6]
He paused, a wide and melancholy waste
Of putrid marshes. A strong impulse urged
His steps to the sea-shore. A swan was there,   275
Beside a sluggish stream among the reeds.
It rose as he approached, and with strong wings
Scaling the upward sky, bent its bright course
High over the immeasurable main.
His eyes pursued its flight.—"Thou hast a home,   280
Beautiful bird; thou voyagest to thine home,
Where thy sweet mate will twine her downy neck
With thine, and welcome thy return with eyes
Bright in the lustre of their own fond joy.
And what am I that I should linger here,   285
With voice far sweeter than thy dying notes,
Spirit more vast than thine, frame more attuned
To beauty, wasting these surpassing powers
In the deaf air, to the blind earth, and heaven
That echoes not my thoughts?" A gloomy smile   290
Of desperate hope wrinkled his quivering lips.
For sleep, he knew, kept most relentlessly
Its precious charge,[7] and silent death exposed,
Faithless perhaps as sleep, a shadowy lure,
With doubtful smile mocking its own strange charms.   295

    Startled by his own thoughts he looked around.
There was no fair fiend[8] near him, not a sight
Or sound of awe but in his own deep mind.
A little shallop[9] floating near the shore
Caught the impatient wandering of his gaze.   300
It had been long abandoned, for its sides
Gaped wide with many a rift, and its frail joints
Swayed with the undulations of the tide.
A restless impulse urged him to embark
And meet lone Death on the drear ocean's waste;   305
For well he knew that mighty Shadow loves
The slimy caverns of the populous deep.

    The day was fair and sunny; sea and sky
Drank its inspiring radiance, and the wind
Swept strongly from the shore, blackening the waves.   310
Following his eager soul, the wanderer

---

5. The maidens call him "false" (i.e., mistaken) names
signifying an affectionate earthly relationship instead
of his unearthly love.
6. The shore of Lake Aral, about 175 miles east of the
Caspian Sea.
7. I.e., the maiden in the sleeper's dream. The passage
goes on to express the skeptical fear that neither sleep
nor death may yield the Poet his desire.
8. Apparently he suspects there may have been an external agent luring him to the death described in the
preceding lines.
9. A small open boat.

Leaped in the boat, he spread his cloak aloft
On the bare mast, and took his lonely seat,
And felt the boat speed o'er the tranquil sea
Like a torn cloud before the hurricane.   315

    As one that in a silver vision floats
Obedient to the sweep of odorous winds
Upon resplendent clouds, so rapidly
Along the dark and ruffled waters fled
The straining boat.—A whirlwind swept it on,   320
With fierce gusts and precipitating force,
Through the white ridges of the chafed sea.
The waves arose. Higher and higher still
Their fierce necks writhed beneath the tempest's scourge
Like serpents struggling in a vulture's grasp.   325
Calm and rejoicing in the fearful war
Of wave running on wave, and blast on blast
Descending, and black flood on whirlpool driven
With dark obliterating course, he sate:
As if their genii were the ministers   330
Appointed to conduct him to the light
Of those beloved eyes, the Poet sate
Holding the steady helm. Evening came on,
The beams of sunset hung their rainbow hues
High 'mid the shifting domes of sheeted spray   335
That canopied his path o'er the waste deep;
Twilight, ascending slowly from the east,
Entwin'd in duskier wreaths her braided locks
O'er the fair front and radiant eyes of day;
Night followed, clad with stars. On every side   340
More horribly the multitudinous streams
Of ocean's mountainous waste to mutual war
Rushed in dark tumult thundering, as to mock
The calm and spangled sky. The little boat
Still fled before the storm; still fled, like foam   345
Down the steep cataract of a wintry river;
Now pausing on the edge of the riven wave;
Now leaving far behind the bursting mass
That fell, convulsing ocean. Safely fled—
As if that frail and wasted human form,   350
Had been an elemental god.[1]
                        At midnight
The moon arose: and lo! the etherial cliffs[2]
Of Caucasus, whose icy summits shone
Among the stars like sunlight, and around
Whose cavern'd base the whirlpools and the waves   355
Bursting and eddying irresistibly
Rage and resound for ever.—Who shall save?—
The boat fled on,—the boiling torrent drove,—
The crags closed round with black and jagged arms,

1. A god of one of the natural elements (see line 1).   2. I.e., cliffs high in the air.

The shattered mountain overhung the sea,   360
And faster still, beyond all human speed,
Suspended on the sweep of the smooth wave,
The little boat was driven. A cavern there
Yawned, and amid its slant and winding depths
Ingulphed the rushing sea. The boat fled on   365
With unrelaxing speed.—"Vision and Love!"
The Poet cried aloud, "I have beheld
The path of thy departure. Sleep and death
Shall not divide us long!"

                    The boat pursued
The winding of the cavern.[3] Day-light shone   370
At length upon that gloomy river's flow;
Now, where the fiercest war among the waves
Is calm, on the unfathomable stream
The boat moved slowly. Where the mountain, riven,
Exposed those black depths to the azure sky,   375
Ere yet the flood's enormous volume fell
Even to the base of Caucasus, with sound
That shook the everlasting rocks, the mass
Filled with one whirlpool all that ample chasm;
Stair above stair the eddying waters rose,   380
Circling immeasurably fast, and laved
With alternating dash the knarled roots
Of mighty trees, that stretched their giant arms
In darkness over it. I' the midst was left,
Reflecting, yet distorting every cloud,   385
A pool of treacherous and tremendous calm.
Seized by the sway of the ascending stream,
With dizzy swiftness, round, and round, and round,
Ridge after ridge the straining boat arose,
Till on the verge of the extremest curve,   390
Where, through an opening of the rocky bank,
The waters overflow, and a smooth spot
Of glassy quiet mid those battling tides
Is left, the boat paused shuddering.—Shall it sink
Down the abyss? Shall the reverting stress   395
Of that resistless gulph embosom it?
Now shall it fall?—A wandering stream of wind,
Breathed from the west, has caught the expanded sail,
And, lo! with gentle motion, between banks
Of mossy slope, and on a placid stream,   400
Beneath a woven grove it sails, and, hark!
The ghastly torrent mingles its far roar,
With the breeze murmuring in the musical woods.
Where the embowering trees recede, and leave
A little space of green expanse, the cove   405
Is closed by meeting banks, whose yellow flowers
For ever gaze on their own drooping eyes,

---

3. A boat beating upstream within a cave, like the eagle and serpent, is a recurrent Shelleyan image (see, e.g., *Prometheus Unbound* 2.98–110, p. 1717).

Reflected in the crystal calm. The wave
Of the boat's motion marred their pensive task,
Which nought but vagrant bird, or wanton wind,   410
Or falling spear-grass, or their own decay
Had e'er disturbed before. The Poet longed
To deck with their bright hues his withered hair,
But on his heart its solitude returned,
And he forbore.[4] Not the strong impulse hid   415
In those flushed cheeks, bent eyes, and shadowy frame,
Had yet performed its ministry: it hung
Upon his life, as lightning in a cloud
Gleams, hovering ere it vanish, ere the floods
Of night close over it.
                    The noonday sun   420
Now shone upon the forest, one vast mass
Of mingling shade, whose brown magnificence
A narrow vale embosoms. There, huge caves,
Scooped in the dark base of their aëry rocks
Mocking[5] its moans, respond and roar for ever.   425
The meeting boughs and implicated[6] leaves
Wove twilight o'er the Poet's path, as led
By love, or dream, or god, or mightier Death,
He sought in Nature's dearest haunt, some bank,
Her cradle, and his sepulchre. More dark   430
And dark the shades accumulate. The oak,
Expanding its immense and knotty arms,
Embraces the light beech. The pyramids
Of the tall cedar overarching, frame
Most solemn domes within, and far below.   435
Like clouds suspended in an emerald sky,
The ash and the acacia floating hang
Tremulous and pale. Like restless serpents, clothed
In rainbow and in fire, the parasites,
Starred with ten thousand blossoms, flow around   440
The grey trunks, and, as gamesome infants' eyes,
With gentle meanings, and most innocent wiles,
Fold their beams round the hearts of those that love,
These twine their tendrils with the wedded boughs
Uniting their close union; the woven leaves   445
Make net-work of the dark blue light of day,
And the night's noontide clearness, mutable
As shapes in the weird clouds. Soft mossy lawns
Beneath these canopies extend their swells,
Fragrant with perfumed herbs, and eyed with blooms   450
Minute yet beautiful. One darkest glen
Sends from its woods of musk-rose, twined with jasmine,
A soul-dissolving odour, to invite

4. Another recurrent image: flowers overhanging their own reflection. The "yellow flowers" (line 406), probably narcisssus, may signify, in this passage, the temptation of the Poet to be satisfied with the projection of his own earthly nature. But his need for a supermundane Other revives, and "the strong impulse" (line

415), his *alastor*, drives him on.
5. As often in Shelley, "mocking" has a double sense: mimicking, as well as ridiculing, the sounds of the forest (line 421).
6. Intertwined.

To some more lovely mystery. Through the dell,
Silence and Twilight here, twin-sisters, keep　　　　　　　455
Their noonday watch, and sail among the shades,
Like vaporous shapes half seen; beyond, a well,
Dark, gleaming, and of most translucent wave,
Images all the woven boughs above,
And each depending leaf, and every speck　　　　　　　460
Of azure sky, darting between their chasms;
Nor aught else in the liquid mirror laves
Its portraiture, but some inconstant star
Between one foliaged lattice twinkling fair,
Or, painted bird, sleeping beneath the moon,　　　　　　465
Or gorgeous insect floating motionless,
Unconscious of the day, ere yet his wings
Have spread their glories to the gaze of noon.

　　Hither the Poet came. His eyes beheld
Their own wan light through the reflected lines　　　　　470
Of his thin hair, distinct in the dark depth
Of that still fountain; as the human heart,
Gazing in dreams over the gloomy grave,
Sees its own treacherous likeness there. He heard
The motion of the leaves, the grass that sprung　　　　475
Startled and glanced and trembled even to feel
An unaccustomed presence, and the sound
Of the sweet brook that from the secret springs
Of that dark fountain rose. A Spirit seemed
To stand beside him—clothed in no bright robes　　　480
Of shadowy silver or enshrining light,
Borrowed from aught the visible world affords
Of grace, or majesty, or mystery;—
But, undulating woods, and silent well,
And leaping rivulet, and evening gloom　　　　　　　485
Now deepening the dark shades, for speech assuming
Held commune with him, as if he and it
Were all that was,—only . . . when his regard
Was raised by intense pensiveness, . . . two eyes,
Two starry eyes, hung in the gloom of thought,　　　490
And seemed with their serene and azure smiles
To beckon him.[7]

　　　　　　Obedient to the light
That shone within his soul, he went, pursuing
The windings of the dell.—The rivulet
Wanton and wild, through many a green ravine　　　495
Beneath the forest flowed. Sometimes it fell
Among the moss with hollow harmony
Dark and profound. Now on the polished stones
It danced; like childhood laughing as it went:
Then, through the plain in tranquil wanderings crept,　　500

---

7. The Poet sees the eyes of the maiden of his vision and, obedient to his inner light, resumes his quest (lines 491–93).

Reflecting every herb and drooping bud
That overhung its quietness.—"O stream!
Whose source is inaccessibly profound,
Whither do thy mysterious waters tend?
Thou imagest my life. Thy darksome stillness,   505
Thy dazzling waves, thy loud and hollow gulphs,
Thy searchless[8] fountain, and invisible course
Have each their type in me: and the wide sky,
And measureless ocean may declare as soon
What oozy cavern or what wandering cloud   510
Contains thy waters, as the universe
Tell where these living thoughts reside, when stretched
Upon thy flowers my bloodless limbs shall waste
I' the passing wind!"

         Beside the grassy shore
Of the small stream he went; he did impress   515
On the green moss his tremulous step, that caught
Strong shuddering from his burning limbs. As one
Roused by some joyous madness from the couch
Of fever, he did move; yet, not like him,
Forgetful of the grave, where, when the flame   520
Of his frail exultation shall be spent,
He must descend. With rapid steps he went
Beneath the shade of trees, beside the flow
Of the wild babbling rivulet; and now
The forest's solemn canopies were changed   525
For the uniform and lightsome[9] evening sky.
Grey rocks did peep from the spare moss, and stemmed
The struggling brook: tall spires of windlestrae[1]
Threw their thin shadows down the rugged slope,
And nought but knarled roots[2] of antient pines   530
Branchless and blasted, clenched with grasping roots
The unwilling soil. A gradual change was here,
Yet ghastly. For, as fast years flow away,
The smooth brow gathers, and the hair grows thin
And white, and where irradiate[3] dewy eyes   535
Had shone, gleam stony orbs:—so from his steps
Bright flowers departed, and the beautiful shade
Of the green groves, with all their odorous winds
And musical motions. Calm, he still pursued
The stream, that with a larger volume now   540
Rolled through the labyrinthine dell; and there
Fretted a path through its descending curves
With its wintry speed. On every side now rose
Rocks, which, in unimaginable forms,
Lifted their black and barren pinnacles   545
In the light of evening, and its precipice[4]

8. Undiscoverable.
9. Illuminated.
1. Scottish dialect for "windlestraw"—tall, dried stalks of grass.
2. Apparently an error for "trunks."
3. Used adjectivally: illumined, brilliant.
4. Headlong fall (of the stream, line 540).

Obscuring the ravine, disclosed above,
Mid toppling stones, black gulphs and yawning caves,
Whose windings gave ten thousand various tongues
To the loud stream. Lo! where the pass expands   550
Its stony jaws, the abrupt mountain breaks,
And seems, with its accumulated crags,
To overhang the world: for wide expand
Beneath the wan stars and descending moon
Islanded seas, blue mountains, mighty streams,   555
Dim tracts and vast, robed in the lustrous gloom
Of leaden-coloured even, and fiery hills
Mingling their flames with twilight, on the verge
Of the remote horizon. The near scene,
In naked and severe simplicity,   560
Made contrast with the universe. A pine,[5]
Rock-rooted, stretched athwart the vacancy
Its swinging boughs, to each inconstant blast
Yielding one only response, at each pause
In most familiar cadence, with the howl   565
The thunder and the hiss of homeless streams
Mingling its solemn song, whilst the broad river,
Foaming and hurrying o'er its rugged path,
Fell into that immeasurable void
Scattering its waters to the passing winds.   570

    Yet the grey precipice and solemn pine
And torrent, were not all;—one silent nook
Was there. Even on the edge of that vast mountain,
Upheld by knotty roots and fallen rocks,
It overlooked in its serenity   575
The dark earth, and the bending vault of stars.
It was a tranquil spot, that seemed to smile
Even in the lap of horror. Ivy clasped
The fissured stones with its entwining arms,
And did embower with leaves for ever green,   580
And berries dark, the smooth and even space
Of its inviolated floor, and here
The children of the autumnal whirlwind bore,
In wanton sport, those bright leaves, whose decay,
Red, yellow, or etherially pale,   585
Rivals the pride of summer. 'Tis the haunt
Of every gentle wind, whose breath can teach
The wilds to love tranquillity. One step,
One human step alone, has ever broken
The stillness of its solitude:—one voice   590
Alone inspired its echoes,—even that voice
Which hither came, floating among the winds,
And led the loveliest among human forms
To make their wild haunts the depository
Of all the grace and beauty that endued   595

5. Pine trees in Shelley often signify persistence and steadfastness amid change and vicissitudes.

Its motions, render up its majesty,
Scatter its music on the unfeeling storm,
And to the damp leaves and blue cavern mould,
Nurses of rainbow flowers and branching moss,
Commit the colours of that varying cheek,   600
That snowy breast, those dark and drooping eyes.

    The dim and horned moon[6] hung low, and poured
A sea of lustre on the horizon's verge
That overflowed its mountains. Yellow mist
Filled the unbounded atmosphere, and drank   605
Wan moonlight even to fulness: not a star
Shone, not a sound was heard; the very winds,
Danger's grim playmates, on that precipice
Slept, clasped in his embrace.—O, storm of death!
Whose sightless[7] speed divides this sullen night: 610
And thou, colossal Skeleton, that, still
Guiding its irresistible career
In thy devastating omnipotence,
Art king of this frail world, from the red field
Of slaughter, from the reeking hospital,   615
The patriot's sacred couch, the snowy bed
Of innocence, the scaffold and the throne,
A mighty voice invokes thee. Ruin calls
His brother Death. A rare and regal prey
He hath prepared, prowling around the world;   620
Glutted with which thou mayst repose, and men
Go to their graves like flowers or creeping worms,
Nor ever more offer at thy dark shrine
The unheeded tribute of a broken heart.

    When on the threshold of the green recess   625
The wanderer's footsteps fell, he knew that death
Was on him. Yet a little, ere it fled,
Did he resign his high and holy soul
To images of the majestic past,
That paused within his passive being now,   630
Like winds that bear sweet music, when they breathe
Through some dim latticed chamber. He did place
His pale lean hand upon the rugged trunk
Of the old pine. Upon an ivied stone
Reclined his languid head, his limbs did rest,   635
Diffused and motionless, on the smooth brink
Of that obscurest chasm;—and thus he lay,
Surrendering to their final impulses
The hovering powers of life. Hope and despair,
The torturers, slept; no mortal pain or fear   640
Marred his repose, the influxes of sense,
And his own being unalloyed by pain,
Yet feebler and more feeble, calmly fed

---

6. Crescent-shaped, with the points curved in.   7. Invisible, or perhaps "unseeing."

The stream of thought, till he lay breathing there
At peace, and faintly smiling:—his last sight   645
Was the great moon, which o'er the western line
Of the wide world her mighty horn suspended,
With whose dun[8] beams inwoven darkness seemed
To mingle. Now upon the jagged hills
It rests, and still as the divided frame   650
Of the vast meteor[9] sunk, the Poet's blood,
That ever beat in mystic sympathy
With nature's ebb and flow, grew feebler still:
And when two lessening points of light alone
Gleamed through the darkness, the alternate gasp   655
Of his faint respiration scarce did stir
The stagnate night:[1]—till the minutest ray
Was quenched, the pulse yet lingered in his heart.
It paused—it fluttered. But when heaven remained
Utterly black, the murky shades involved   660
An image, silent, cold, and motionless,
As their own voiceless earth and vacant air.
Even as a vapour fed with golden beams
That ministered on[2] sunlight, ere the west
Eclipses it, was now that wonderous frame—   665
No sense, no motion, no divinity—
A fragile lute, on whose harmonious strings
The breath of heaven did wander—a bright stream
Once fed with many-voiced waves—a dream
Of youth, which night and time have quenched for ever,   670
Still, dark, and dry, and unremembered now.

    O, for Medea's wondrous alchemy,
Which wheresoe'er it fell made the earth gleam
With bright flowers, and the wintry boughs exhale
From vernal blooms fresh fragrance![3] O, that God,   675
Profuse of poisons, would concede the chalice
Which but one living man has drained,[4] who now,
Vessel of deathless wrath, a slave that feels
No proud exemption in the blighting curse
He bears, over the world wanders for ever,   680
Lone as incarnate death! O, that the dream
Of dark magician in his visioned cave,[5]
Raking the cinders of a crucible
For life and power, even when his feeble hand
Shakes in its last decay, were the true law   685
Of this so lovely world! But thou art fled
Like some frail exhalation; which the dawn

8. Darkened, dimmed.
9. I.e., the moon; "meteor" was once used for any phenomenon within the earth's atmosphere.
1. The Poet's life ebbs in consonance with the descent
of the "horned moon," to the moment when only the
two "points of light"—its horns—show above the hills.
2. Attended, acted as a servant to. "Vapour": cloud.
3. Medea brewed a magic potion to rejuvenate the dying Aeson; where some of the potion spilled on the

ground, flowers sprang up (Ovid, *Metamorphoses*
7.275ff.).
4. The Wandering Jew; according to a medieval legend, he had taunted Christ on the way to His crucifixion and was condemned to wander the world, deathless,
until Christ's second coming.
5. Cave in which he has visions. The "dark magician"
is an alchemist attempting to produce the elixir of enduring life.

Robes in its golden beams,—ah! thou hast fled!
The brave, the gentle, and the beautiful,
The child of grace and genius. Heartless things   690
Are done and said i' the world, and many worms
And beasts and men live on, and mighty Earth
From sea and mountain, city and wilderness,
In vesper low or joyous orison,[6]
Lifts still its solemn voice:—but thou art fled—   695
Thou canst no longer know or love the shapes
Of this phantasmal scene, who have to thee
Been purest ministers, who are, alas!
Now thou art not. Upon those pallid lips
So sweet even in their silence, on those eyes   700
That image sleep in death, upon that form
Yet safe from the worm's outrage, let no tear
Be shed—not even in thought. Nor, when those hues
Are gone, and those divinest lineaments,
Worn by the senseless[7] wind, shall live alone   705
In the frail pauses of this simple strain,
Let not high verse, mourning the memory
Of that which is no more, or painting's woe
Or sculpture, speak in feeble imagery
Their own cold powers. Art and eloquence,   710
And all the shews o' the world are frail and vain
To weep a loss that turns their lights to shade.
It is a woe too "deep for tears,"[8] when all
Is reft at once, when some surpassing Spirit,
Whose light adorned the world around it, leaves   715
Those who remain behind, not sobs or groans,
The passionate tumult of a clinging hope;
But pale despair and cold tranquillity,
Nature's vast frame, the web of human things,
Birth and the grave, that are not as they were.   720
1815   1816

Mont Blanc[1]

Lines Written in the Vale of Chamouni

1

The everlasting universe of things
Flows through the mind, and rolls its rapid waves,
Now dark—now glittering—now reflecting gloom—

6. Prayer. "Vesper": evening prayer.
7. Unfeeling.
8. From the last line of Wordsworth's Ode: Intimations of Immortality: "Thoughts that do often lie too deep for tears."
1. Mont Blanc, near the French border with Italy, is the highest mountain in the Alps. When he conceived the poem, Shelley was standing on a bridge over the Arve River in the valley of Chamonix, in what is now southeastern France.
   Shelley wrote of this poem: "It was composed under

the immediate impression of the deep and powerful feelings excited by the objects which it attempts to describe; and, as an indisciplined overflowing of the soul, rests its claim to approbation on an attempt to imitate the untamable wildness and inaccessible solemnity from which those feelings sprang."
   Shelley's comment points to two important attributes of Mont Blanc. First, he attempts, as in other poems (supremely in Ode to the West Wind), to make the poem iconic or directly imitative of the alternating "wildness" and "solemnity" of the scene and the conso-

Now lending splendour, where from secret springs
The source of human thought its tribute brings   5
Of waters,—with a sound but half its own.
Such as a feeble brook will oft assume
In the wild woods, among the mountains lone,
Where waterfalls around it leap forever,
Where woods and winds contend, and a vast river   10
Over its rocks ceaselessly bursts and raves.

2

Thus thou, Ravine of Arve—dark, deep Ravine—
Thou many-coloured, many-voiced vale,
Over whose pines, and crags, and caverns sail
Fast cloud shadows and sunbeams: awful[2] scene,   15
Where Power in likeness of the Arve comes down
From the ice gulphs that gird his secret throne,
Bursting through these dark mountains like the flame
Of lightning through the tempest;—thou dost lie,
Thy giant brood of pines around thee clinging,   20
Children of elder time, in whose devotion
The chainless winds still come and ever came
To drink their odours, and their mighty swinging
To hear—an old and solemn harmony;
Thine earthly rainbows stretched across the sweep   25
Of the etherial waterfall, whose veil
Robes some unsculptured[3] image; the strange sleep
Which when the voices of the desart fail
Wraps all in its own deep eternity;—
Thy caverns echoing to the Arve's commotion,   30
A loud, lone sound no other sound can tame;
Thou art pervaded with that ceaseless motion,
Thou art the path of that unresting sound—
Dizzy Ravine! and when I gaze on thee
I seem as in a trance sublime and strange   35

To muse on my own separate phantasy,
My own, my human mind, which passively
Now renders and receives fast influencings,
Holding an unremitting interchange
With the clear universe of things around;[4]   40
One legion of wild thoughts, whose wandering wings
Now float above thy darkness, and now rest
Where that or thou art no unbidden guest,
In the still cave of the witch Poesy,[5]
Seeking among the shadows that pass by   45

---

nant thought and feelings it evokes. Second, this work belongs to the genre of the "local" poem, a descriptive-meditative presentation of a precisely identified landscape. In this respect it resembles Wordsworth's *Tintern Abbey*, the major influence on *Mont Blanc*. Shelley's poem, like Wordsworth's, poses the question of the significance of the interchange between nature and the human mind; he proposes, however, a very different answer to that question.

2. Awe-inspiring.
3. I.e., not formed by humans.
4. This passage is remarkably parallel to a passage Shelley could not have read in *The Prelude*, published in 1850, in which Wordsworth discovers, in the landscape viewed from Mount Snowdon, the "type" or "emblem" of the human mind in its interchange with nature (see *The Prelude* 14.63ff, p. 1475).
5. I.e., in the part of the mind that creates poetry.

Ghosts of all things that are, some shade of thee,
Some phantom, some faint image; till the breast
From which they fled recalls them, thou art there!⁶

3

Some say that gleams of a remoter world
Visit the soul in sleep,—that death is slumber,   50
And that its shapes the busy thoughts outnumber
Of those who wake and live.—I look on high;
Has some unknown omnipotence unfurled
The veil of life and death? or do I lie
In dream, and does the mightier world of sleep   55
Spread far around and inaccessibly
Its circles? For the very spirit fails,
Driven like a homeless cloud from steep to steep
That vanishes among the viewless⁷ gales!
Far, far above, piercing the infinite sky,   60
Mont Blanc appears,—still, snowy, and serene—
Its subject mountains their unearthly forms
Pile around it, ice and rock; broad vales between
Of frozen floods, unfathomable deeps,
Blue as the overhanging heaven, that spread   65
And wind among the accumulated steeps;
A desart peopled by the storms alone,
Save when the eagle brings some hunter's bone,
And the wolf tracts⁸ her there—how hideously
Its shapes are heaped around! rude, bare, and high,   70
Ghastly, and scarred, and riven.—Is this the scene
Where the old Earthquake-dæmon⁹ taught her young
Ruin? Were these their toys? or did a sea
Of fire, envelope once this silent snow?
None can reply—all seems eternal now.   75
The wilderness has a mysterious tongue
Which teaches awful doubt, or faith so mild,
So solemn, so serene, that man may be
But for such faith¹ with nature reconciled;
Thou hast a voice, great Mountain, to repeal   80
Large codes of fraud and woe; not understood
By all, but which² the wise, and great, and good
Interpret, or make felt, or deeply feel.

4

The fields, the lakes, the forests, and the streams,
Ocean, and all the living things that dwell   85
Within the dædal³ earth; lightning, and rain,
Earthquake, and fiery flood, and hurricane,

---

6. I.e., the thoughts (line 41) seek, in the poet's creative faculty, some shade, phantom, or image of the Arve; and when the breast, which has forgotten these images, recalls them again—there, suddenly, does the Arve exist.
7. Invisible.
8. Tracks, traces.
9. A "daemon" is a supernatural being, halfway between mortals and the gods. Here it represents the force that makes earthquakes.

1. I.e., "simply by holding such faith." In Shelley's balance of possibilities the landscape is equally capable of instilling such a Wordsworthian faith (in the possibility of reconciling humans and nature, lines 78–79) or the "awful" (i.e., "awesome") doubt (that nature is totally alien to human ends and values).
2. The reference is to "voice," line 80.
3. Intricately formed; derived from Daedalus, builder of the labyrinth in Crete.

The torpor of the year when feeble dreams
Visit the hidden buds, or dreamless sleep
Holds every future leaf and flower;—the bound   90
With which from that detested trance they leap;
The works and ways of man, their death and birth,
And that of him and all that his may be;
All things that move and breathe with toil and sound
Are born and die; revolve, subside and swell.   95
Power dwells apart in its tranquillity
Remote, serene, and inaccessible:
And *this*, the naked countenance of earth,
On which I gaze, even these primæval mountains
Teach the adverting mind. The glaciers creep   100
Like snakes that watch their prey, from their far fountains,
Slow rolling on; there, many a precipice,
Frost and the Sun in scorn of mortal power
Have piled: dome, pyramid, and pinnacle,
A city of death, distinct with many a tower   105
And wall impregnable of beaming ice.
Yet not a city, but a flood of ruin
Is there, that from the boundaries of the sky
Rolls its perpetual stream; vast pines are strewing
Its destined path, or in the mangled soil   110
Branchless and shattered stand: the rocks, drawn down
From yon remotest waste, have overthrown
The limits of the dead and living world,
Never to be reclaimed. The dwelling-place
Of insects, beasts, and birds, becomes its spoil;   115
Their food and their retreat for ever gone,
So much of life and joy is lost. The race
Of man, flies far in dread; his work and dwelling
Vanish, like smoke before the tempest's stream,
And their place is not known. Below, vast caves   120
Shine in the rushing torrents' restless gleam,
Which from those secret chasms in tumult welling[4]
Meet in the vale, and one majestic River,[5]
The breath and blood of distant lands, for ever
Rolls its loud waters to the ocean waves,   125
Breathes its swift vapours to the circling air.
                              5
Mont Blanc yet gleams on high:—the power is there,
The still and solemn power of many sights,
And many sounds, and much of life and death.
In the calm darkness of the moonless nights,   130
In the lone glare of day, the snows descend
Upon that Mountain; none beholds them there,
Nor when the flakes burn in the sinking sun,
Or the star-beams dart through them:—Winds contend
Silently there, and heap the snow with breath   135

4. This description (as well as that in lines 9–11)   *Khan*, lines 12–24.
seems to be an echo of Coleridge's description of the   5. The Arve, which flows into Lake Geneva.
chasm and sacred river in the recently published *Kubla*

Rapid and strong, but silently! Its home
The voiceless lightning in these solitudes
Keeps innocently, and like vapour broods
Over the snow. The secret strength of things
Which governs thought, and to the infinite dome   140
Of heaven is as a law, inhabits thee!
And what were thou,[6] and earth, and stars, and sea,
If to the human mind's imaginings
Silence and solitude were vacancy?

1816   1817

Hymn to Intellectual Beauty[1]

1

The awful shadow of some unseen Power
  Floats though unseen amongst us,—visiting
  This various world with as inconstant wing
As summer winds that creep from flower to flower.—
Like moonbeams that behind some piny mountain shower,[2]   5
  It visits with inconstant glance
  Each human heart and countenance;
Like hues and harmonies of evening,—
  Like clouds in starlight widely spread,—
  Like memory of music fled,—   10
  Like aught that for its grace may be
Dear, and yet dearer for its mystery.

2

Spirit of BEAUTY, that dost consecrate
  With thine own hues all thou dost shine upon
  Of human thought or form,—where art thou gone?   15
Why dost thou pass away and leave our state,
This dim vast vale of tears, vacant and desolate?
  Ask why the sunlight not forever
  Weaves rainbows o'er yon mountain river,
Why aught should fail and fade that once is shewn,   20
  Why fear and dream and death and birth
  Cast on the daylight of this earth
  Such gloom,—why man has such a scope
For love and hate, despondency and hope?

3

No voice from some sublimer world hath ever   25
  To sage or poet these responses given—
  Therefore the name of God and ghosts and Heaven,
Remain the records of their vain endeavour,[3]

---

6. Mont Blanc.
1. "Intellectual" means "nonsensible." "Intellectual
Beauty" is thus beyond access by sense experience; it
is simply postulated to account for occasional states of
awareness that lend splendor, grace, and truth both to
experience of the natural world and to people's moral
consciousness. To this mystery (stanzas 5–7) Shelley
had, at its early visitation, dedicated his powers, and to
it he now prays as he passes the noon of life (stanza 7).
2. "Shower" is a verb.
3. The names (line 27) are nothing better than guesses
at identifying the mystery by religious philosophers and
poets (line 26).

Frail spells—whose uttered charm might not avail to sever,
   From all we hear and all we see,   30
   Doubt, chance, and mutability.
Thy light alone—like mist o'er mountains driven,
   Or music by the night wind sent
   Through strings of some still instrument,[4]
   Or moonlight on a midnight stream,   35
Gives grace and truth to life's unquiet dream.

4

Love, Hope, and Self-esteem, like clouds depart
  And come, for some uncertain moments lent.
  Man were immortal, and omnipotent,
Didst thou, unknown and awful as thou art,   40
Keep with thy glorious train firm state within his heart.[5]
   Thou messenger of sympathies,
   That wax and wane in lovers' eyes—
Thou—that to human thought art nourishment,
   Like darkness to a dying flame!   45
   Depart not as thy shadow came,
   Depart not—lest the grave should be,
Like life and fear, a dark reality.

5

While yet a boy I sought for ghosts, and sped
  Through many a listening chamber, cave and ruin,   50
  And starlight wood, with fearful steps pursuing
Hopes of high talk with the departed dead.
I called on poisonous names with which our youth is fed;[6]
   I was not heard—I saw them not—
   When musing deeply on the lot   55
Of life, at that sweet time when winds are wooing
   All vital things that wake to bring
   News of buds and blossoming,—
   Sudden, thy shadow fell on me;
I shrieked, and clasped my hands in extacy!   60

6

I vowed that I would dedicate my powers
  To thee and thine—have I not kept the vow?
  With beating heart and streaming eyes, even now
I call the phantoms of a thousand hours
Each from his voiceless grave: they have in visioned bowers 65
   Of studious zeal or love's delight
   Outwatched with me the envious night[7]—
They know that never joy illumed my brow
   Unlinked with hope that thou wouldst free
   This world from its dark slavery,   70
   That thou—O awful LOVELINESS,
Wouldst give whate'er these words cannot express.

---

4. A wind harp.
5. I.e., "man would be immortal . . . if thou didst keep."
6. Lines 49–52 refer to Shelley's youthful experiments with magic. The "poisonous names" (line 53) are probably those in the prayers he had been taught as a child.
7. I.e., stayed up until the night, envious of their delight, had reluctantly departed.

7

The day becomes more solemn and serene
   When noon is past—there is a harmony
   In autumn, and a lustre in its sky,   75
Which through the summer is not heard or seen,
As if it could not be, as if it had not been!
     Thus let thy power, which like the truth
     Of nature on my passive youth
Descended, to my onward life supply   80
     Its calm—to one who worships thee,
     And every form containing thee,
     Whom, SPIRIT fair, thy spells did bind
To fear[8] himself, and love all human kind.

1816   1817

Ozymandias[1]

I met a traveller from an antique land,
Who said—"Two vast and trunkless legs of stone
Stand in the desert. . . . Near them, on the sand,
Half sunk a shattered visage lies, whose frown,
And wrinkled lip, and sneer of cold command,   5
Tell that its sculptor well those passions read
Which yet survive, stamped on these lifeless things,
The hand that mocked them, and the heart that fed;[2]
And on the pedestal, these words appear:
My name is Ozymandias, King of Kings,   10
Look on my Works, ye Mighty, and despair!
Nothing beside remains. Round the decay
Of that colossal Wreck, boundless and bare
The lone and level sands stretch far away."

1817   1818

Stanzas Written in Dejection—
December 1818, near Naples[1]

The Sun is warm, the sky is clear,
The waves are dancing fast and bright,
Blue isles and snowy mountains wear
The purple noon's transparent might,
The breath of the moist earth is light   5

8. Probably in the old sense: "to stand in awe of."
1. According to Diodorus Siculus, Greek historian of
the 1st century B.C., the largest statue in Egypt had the
inscription: "I am Ozymandias, king of kings; if anyone
wishes to know what I am and where I lie, let him
surpass me in some of my exploits." Ozymandias was
the Greek name for Ramses II of Egypt, 13th century
B.C.

2. "The hand" is the sculptor's, who had "mocked"
(both imitated and derided) the sculptured passions;
"the heart" is the king's, which has "fed" his passions.
1. Shelley's first wife, Harriet, had drowned herself;
Clara, his baby daughter with Mary Shelley, had just
died; and Shelley himself was plagued by ill health,
pain, financial worries, and the sense that he had failed
as a poet.

Around its unexpanded buds;
Like many a voice of one delight
The winds, the birds, the Ocean-floods;
The City's voice itself is soft, like Solitude's.

I see the Deep's untrampled floor   10
With green and purple seaweeds strown;
I see the waves upon the shore
Like light dissolved in star-showers, thrown;
I sit upon the sands alone;
The lightning of the noontide Ocean   15
Is flashing round me, and a tone
Arises from its measured motion,
How sweet! did any heart now share in my emotion.

Alas, I have nor hope nor health
Nor peace within nor calm around,   20
Nor that content surpassing wealth
The sage² in meditation found,
And walked with inward glory crowned;
Nor fame nor power nor love nor leisure—
Others I see whom these surround,   25
Smiling they live and call life pleasure:
To me that cup has been dealt in another measure.

Yet now despair itself is mild,
Even as the winds and waters are;
I could lie down like a tired child   30
And weep away the life of care
Which I have borne and yet must bear
Till Death like Sleep might steal on me,
And I might feel in the warm air
My cheek grow cold, and hear the Sea   35
Breathe o'er my dying brain its last monotony.

Some might lament that I were cold,
As I, when this sweet day is gone,³
Which my lost heart, too soon grown old,
Insults with this untimely moan—   40
They might lament,—for I am one
Whom men love not, and yet regret;
Unlike this day, which, when the Sun
Shall on its stainless glory set,
Will linger though enjoyed, like joy in Memory yet.   45

1818   1824

---

2. Probably the Roman emperor Marcus Aurelius
(2nd century A.D.), Stoic philosopher who wrote twelve
books of *Meditations*.
3. I.e., as I will lament this sweet day when it has gone.

A Song: "Men of England"[1]

Men of England, wherefore plough
For the lords who lay ye low?
Wherefore weave with toil and care
The rich robes your tyrants wear?

Wherefore feed and clothe and save   5
From the cradle to the grave
Those ungrateful drones who would
Drain your sweat—nay, drink your blood?

Wherefore, Bees of England, forge
Many a weapon, chain, and scourge,   10
That these stingless drones may spoil
The forced produce of your toil?

Have ye leisure, comfort, calm,
Shelter, food, love's gentle balm?
Or what is it ye buy so dear   15
With your pain and with your fear?

The seed ye sow, another reaps;
The wealth ye find, another keeps;
The robes ye weave, another wears;
The arms ye forge, another bears.   20

Sow seed—but let no tyrant reap:
Find wealth—let no impostor heap:
Weave robes—let not the idle wear:
Forge arms—in your defence to bear.

Shrink to your cellars, holes, and cells—   25
In halls ye deck another dwells.
Why shake the chains ye wrought? Ye see
The steel ye tempered glance on ye.

With plough and spade and hoe and loom
Trace your grave and build your tomb   30
And weave your winding-sheet—till fair
England be your Sepulchre.

1819   1839

England in 1819

An old, mad, blind, despised, and dying King;[1]
Princes, the dregs of their dull race, who flow

---

1. This and the two following poems were written at a time of turbulent unrest, after the return of troops from the Napoleonic Wars had precipitated a great economic depression. The *Song*, expressing Shelley's hope for a proletarian revolution, was originally planned as one of a series for workers; it has become, as the poet wished, a hymn of the British labor movement.

1. George III, who had been declared insane in 1811; he died in 1820.

Through public scorn,—mud from a muddy spring;
Rulers who neither see nor feel nor know,
But leechlike to their fainting country cling   5
Till they drop, blind in blood, without a blow.
A people starved and stabbed in th' untilled field;[2]
An army, whom liberticide and prey
Makes as a two-edged sword to all who wield;
Golden and sanguine laws[3] which tempt and slay;   10
Religion Christless, Godless—a book sealed;
A senate, Time's worst statute, unrepealed[4]—
Are graves from which a glorious Phantom[5] may
Burst, to illumine our tempestuous day.

1819   1839

The Indian Girl's Song[1] [The Indian Serenade]

I arise from dreams of thee
In the first sleep of night—
The winds are breathing low
And the stars are burning bright.
I arise from dreams of thee—   5
And a spirit in my feet
Has borne me—Who knows how?
To thy chamber window, sweet!—

The wandering airs they faint
On the dark silent stream—   10
The champak[2] odours fail
Like sweet thoughts in a dream;
The nightingale's complaint—
It dies upon her heart—
As I must die on thine   15
O beloved as thou art!

O lift me from the grass!
I die, I faint, I fail!
Let thy love in kisses rain
On my lips and eyelids pale.   20
My cheek is cold and white, alas!
My heart beats loud and fast.
Oh press it close to thine again
Where it will break at last.

1819   1822

2. Alluding to the "Peterloo Massacre" on Aug. 16, 1819; in St. Peter's field, near Manchester, a troop of cavalry had charged into a crowd attending a peaceful rally in support of parliamentary reform. "Peterloo" is an ironic combination of "St. Peter's" and "Waterloo."
3. Laws bought with gold, and leading to bloodshed.
4. The law imposing disabilities on Dissenters and Roman Catholics.

5. I.e., a revolution.
1. Usually titled *The Indian Serenade*. Shelley's title makes it clear that the poem is not a personal utterance but a dramatic lyric, sung by an imagined East Indian girl. It manifests the conventional extravagance of an Oriental love poem.
2. An Indian species of magnolia, bearing fragrant orange flowers.

Ode to the West Wind[1]

1

O wild West Wind, thou breath of Autumn's being,
Thou, from whose unseen presence the leaves dead
Are driven, like ghosts from an enchanter fleeing,

Yellow, and black, and pale, and hectic[2] red,
Pestilence-stricken multitudes: O Thou,   5
Who chariotest to their dark wintry bed

The winged seeds, where they lie cold and low,
Each like a corpse within its grave, until
Thine azure sister of the Spring[3] shall blow

Her clarion[4] o'er the dreaming earth, and fill   10
(Driving sweet buds like flocks to feed in air)
With living hues and odours plain and hill:

Wild Spirit, which art moving everywhere;
Destroyer and Preserver; hear, O hear!

2

Thou on whose stream, 'mid the steep sky's commotion,   15
Loose clouds like Earth's decaying leaves are shed,
Shook from the tangled boughs of Heaven and Ocean,[5]

Angels of rain and lightning: there are spread
On the blue surface of thine aery surge,
Like the bright hair uplifted from the head   20

Of some fierce Mænad,[6] even from the dim verge
Of the horizon to the zenith's height,
The locks of the approaching storm. Thou Dirge

Of the dying year, to which this closing night
Will be the dome of a vast sepulchre,   25
Vaulted with all thy congregated might

---

1. "This poem was conceived and chiefly written in a
wood that skirts the Arno, near Florence, and on a day
when that tempestuous wind, whose temperature is at
once mild and animating, was collecting the vapours
which pour down the autumnal rains" [Shelley's note].
As in other major Romantic poems—for example, the
opening of Wordsworth's *Prelude*, Coleridge's *Dejection: An Ode*, and the conclusion to Shelley's *Adonais*—the rising wind, linked with the cycle of the
seasons, is presented as the outer correspondent to an
inner change from apathy to spiritual vitality, and from
imaginative sterility to a burst of creative power that is
paralleled to the inspiration of the biblical prophets. In
Hebrew, Latin, Greek, and many other languages, the
words for *wind, breath, soul,* and *inspiration* are all
identical or related. Thus Shelley's west wind is a
"spirit" (the Latin *spiritus*: wind, breath, soul, and the
root word in "inspiration"), the "breath of Autumn's
being," which on earth, sky, and sea destroys in the
autumn to revivify in the spring. Around this central

image the poem weaves various cycles of death and
regeneration—vegetational, human, and divine.
    Shelley's fourteen-line stanza, developed from the
interlaced three-line units of the Italian *terza rima* (*aba
bcb cdc*, etc.), consists of a set of four such tercets,
closed by a couplet rhyming with the middle line of
the preceding tercet: *aba bcb cdc ded ee*.
2. Referring to the kind of fever that occurs in tuberculosis.
3. The west wind that will blow in the spring.
4. A high, shrill trumpet.
5. The fragmentary clouds ("leaves") are torn by the
wind from the larger and higher clouds ("boughs"),
which are formed by a union of air with vapor drawn
up by the sun from the ocean. "Angels" (line 18) suggests the old sense: "messengers," "harbingers."
6. A female votary who danced frenziedly in the worship of Dionysus (Bacchus), the Greek god of wine and
vegetation. As vegetation god, he was fabled to die in
the fall and to be resurrected in the spring.

Of vapours,[7] from whose solid atmosphere
Black rain and fire and hail will burst: O hear!

3

Thou who didst waken from his summer dreams
The blue Mediterranean, where he lay,   30
Lulled by the coil of his chrystalline streams,[8]

Beside a pumice isle in Baiæ's bay,[9]
And saw in sleep old palaces and towers
Quivering within the wave's intenser day,[1]

All overgrown with azure moss and flowers   35
So sweet, the sense faints picturing them! Thou
For whose path the Atlantic's level powers

Cleave themselves into chasms, while far below
The sea-blooms and the oozy woods which wear
The sapless foliage of the ocean, know   40

Thy voice, and suddenly grow grey with fear,
And tremble and despoil themselves:[2] O hear!

4

If I were a dead leaf thou mightest bear;
If I were a swift cloud to fly with thee;
A wave to pant beneath thy power, and share   45

The impulse of thy strength, only less free
Than thou, O Uncontrollable! If even
I were as in my boyhood, and could be

The comrade of thy wanderings over Heaven,
As then, when to outstrip thy skiey speed   50
Scarce seemed a vision; I would ne'er have striven

As thus with thee in prayer in my sore need.
Oh! lift me as a wave, a leaf, a cloud!
I fall upon the thorns of life! I bleed!

A heavy weight of hours has chained and bowed   55
One too like thee: tameless, and swift, and proud.

5

Make me thy lyre,[3] even as the forest is:
What if my leaves are falling like its own!
The tumult of thy mighty harmonies

Will take from both a deep, autumnal tone,   60
Sweet though in sadness. Be thou, Spirit fierce,
My spirit! Be thou me, impetuous one!

---

7. Clouds.
8. The currents that flow in the Mediterranean Sea,
sometimes with a visible difference in color.
9. West of Naples, the locale of imposing villas erected
by Roman emperors. "Pumice": a porous volcanic
stone.
1. Shelley once observed that, when reflected in wa-

ter, colors are "more vivid yet blended with more harmony."
2. The vegetation at the bottom of the sea . . . sympa-
thizes with that of the land in the change of seasons
[Shelley's note].
3. The Eolian lyre, which responds to the wind with
rising and falling musical chords.

Drive my dead thoughts over the universe
Like withered leaves to quicken a new birth!
And, by the incantation of this verse,   65

Scatter, as from an unextinguished hearth
Ashes and sparks, my words among mankind!
Be through my lips to unawakened Earth

The trumpet of a prophecy![4] O Wind,
If Winter comes, can Spring be far behind?   70

1819   1820

Prometheus Unbound   Shelley composed this work in Italy between the autumn of 1818 and the close of 1819 and published it the following summer. Upon its completion he wrote in a letter, "It is a drama, with characters and mechanism of a kind yet unattempted; and I think the execution is better than any of my former attempts." It is based on the *Prometheus Bound* of Aeschylus, which dramatizes the sufferings of Prometheus, unrepentant champion of humanity, who, because he had stolen fire from heaven, was condemned by Zeus to be chained to Mount Caucasus and to be tortured by a vulture feeding on his liver; in a lost sequel, Aeschylus reconciled Prometheus with his oppressor. Shelley continued Aeschylus' story but transformed it into a symbolic drama about the origin of evil and the possibility of overcoming it. In such earlier writings as *Queen Mab* Shelley had expressed his belief that injustice and suffering can be eliminated by an external revolution that will wipe out or radically reform the causes of evil, which are existing social, political, and religious institutions. Implicit in *Prometheus Unbound*, on the other hand, is the view that both the origin of evil and the possibility of reform are the moral responsibility of men and women themselves. Social chaos and wars are a gigantic projection of human moral disorder and inner division and conflict; tyrants are the outer representatives of the tyranny of our baser over our better elements; hatred for others is a product of self-contempt; and successful political reform is impossible unless we have first reformed our own nature at its roots, by substituting selfless love for divisive hate. Shelley thus incorporates into his secular myth (of universal regeneration by an apocalypse of the moral imagination of the human race) the ethical teaching of Christ on the Mount, as well as the highest classical morality represented in the *Prometheus* of Aeschylus. And Shelley warns (4.562ff.) that even should such a victory take place—the reintegration of splintered humanity, with a consequent restoration of moral and political order and a release of all our creative powers in art and science—the price of its continuation is an unremitting vigilance lest the serpent deep in human nature should break loose and start the cycle all over again.

Shelley writes in his preface that Prometheus is, "as it were, the type of the highest perfection of moral and intellectual nature." But he also warns that it is a mistake to suppose that the poem contains "a reasoned system on the theory of human life. Didactic poetry is my abhorrence." *Prometheus Unbound* is not a dramatized philosophical essay or a moral allegory but a large and intricate imaginative construction that involves premises about human nature and the springs of morality and creativity. The non-Christian poet Yeats called it one of "the sacred books of the world," and the Christian critic C. S. Lewis found in it poetic powers matched only by Dante.

4. A reference to the "clarion" of line 10, as well as an allusion to the last trumpet of the apocalypse in Revelation 11.15.

From PROMETHEUS UNBOUND

A *Lyrical Drama in Four Acts*

Audisne hæc Amphiarae, sub terram abdite?[1]

Preface

The Greek tragic writers, in selecting as their subject any portion of their national history or mythology, employed in their treatment of it a certain arbitrary discretion. They by no means conceived themselves bound to adhere to the common interpretation or to imitate in story as in title their rivals and predecessors. Such a system would have amounted to a resignation of those claims to preference over their competitors which incited the composition. The Agamemnonian story was exhibited on the Athenian theatre with as many variations as dramas.

I have presumed to employ a similar licence.—The *Prometheus Unbound* of Æschylus, supposed the reconciliation of Jupiter with his victim as the price of the disclosure of the danger threatened to his empire by the consummation of his marriage with Thetis. Thetis, according to this view of the subject, was given in marriage to Peleus, and Prometheus by the permission of Jupiter delivered from his captivity by Hercules.[2]—Had I framed my story on this model I should have done no more than have attempted to restore the lost drama of Æschylus; an ambition, which, if my preference to this mode of treating the subject had incited me to cherish, the recollection of the high comparison such an attempt would challenge, might well abate. But in truth I was averse from a catastrophe so feeble as that of reconciling the Champion with the Oppressor of mankind. The moral interest of the fable which is so powerfully sustained by the sufferings and endurance of Prometheus, would be annihilated if we could conceive of him as unsaying his high language, and quailing before his successful and perfidious adversary. The only imaginary being resembling in any degree Prometheus, is Satan; and Prometheus is, in my judgement, a more poetical character than Satan because, in addition to courage and majesty and firm and patient opposition to omnipotent force, he is susceptible of being described as exempt from the taints of ambition, envy, revenge, and a desire for personal aggrandisement, which in the Hero of *Paradise Lost*, interfere with the interest. The character of Satan engenders in the mind a pernicious casuistry which leads us to weigh his faults with his wrongs and to excuse the former because the latter exceed all measure. In the minds of those who consider that magnificent fiction with a religious feeling, it engenders something worse. But Prometheus is, as it were, the type of the highest perfection of moral and intellectual nature, impelled by the purest and the truest motives to the best and noblest ends.

1. Cicero, *Tusculan Disputations* 2.60: "Do you hear this, O Amphiaraus, concealed under the earth?" In Greek myth Amphiaraus was a seer; fleeing from an unsuccessful assault on Thebes, he was saved from his pursuers by Zeus, who by a thunderbolt opened a cleft in the earth that swallowed him up.

In his *Disputations* Cicero is arguing for the Stoic doctrine of the need to master pain and suffering. He quotes this line (a Latin translation from Aeschylus' lost drama *Epigoni*) in the course of an anecdote about

Dionysius of Heraclea, who, tormented by kidney stones, abjures the doctrine of his Stoic teacher Zeno that pain is not an evil. By way of reproof his fellow-Stoic Cleanthes strikes his foot on the ground and utters this line; Cicero interprets it as an appeal to Zeno the Stoic master (under the name of Amphiaraus).

2. Shelley's description of the subject of Aeschylus' lost drama, *Prometheus Unbound*, is a speculation based on surviving fragments.

This Poem was chiefly written upon the mountainous ruins of the Baths of Caracalla, among the flowery glades, and thickets of odoriferous blossoming trees which are extended in ever winding labyrinths upon its immense platforms and dizzy arches suspended in the air. The bright blue sky of Rome, and the effect of the vigorous awakening of spring in that divinest climate, and the new life with which it drenches the spirits even to intoxication, were the inspiration of this drama.

The imagery which I have employed will be found in many instances to have been drawn from the operations of the human mind, or from those external actions by which they are expressed. This is unusual in modern Poetry; although Dante and Shakespeare are full of instances of the same kind: Dante indeed more than any other poet and with greater success. But the Greek poets, as writers to whom no resource of awakening the sympathy of their contemporaries was unknown, were in the habitual use of this power, and it is the study of their works (since a higher merit would probably be denied me) to which I am willing that my readers should impute this singularity.

One word is due in candour to the degree in which the study of contemporary writings may have tinged my composition, for such has been a topic of censure with regard to poems far more popular, and indeed more deservedly popular than mine. It is impossible that any one who inhabits the same age with such writers as those who stand in the foremost ranks of our own, can conscientiously assure himself, that his language and tone of thought may not have been modified by the study of the productions of those extraordinary intellects. It is true, that, not the spirit of their genius, but the forms in which it has manifested itself, are due, less to the peculiarities of their own minds, than to the peculiarity of the moral and intellectual condition of the minds among which they have been produced. Thus a number of writers possess the form, whilst they want the spirit of those whom, it is alleged, they imitate; because the former is the endowment of the age in which they live, and the latter must be the uncommunicated lightning of their own mind.

The peculiar style of intense and comprehensive imagery which distinguishes the modern literature of England, has not been, as a general power, the product of the imitation of any particular writer. The mass of capabilities remains at every period materially the same; the circumstances which awaken it to action perpetually change. If England were divided into forty republics, each equal in population and extent to Athens, there is no reason to suppose but that, under institutions not more perfect than those of Athens, each would produce philosophers and poets equal to those who (if we except Shakespeare) have never been surpassed. We owe the great writers of the golden age of our literature to that fervid awakening of the public mind which shook to dust the oldest and most oppressive form of the Christian Religion. We owe Milton to the progress and developement of the same spirit; the sacred Milton was, let it ever be remembered, a Republican, and a bold enquirer into morals and religion. The great writers of our own age are, we have reason to suppose, the companions and forerunners of some unimagined change in our social condition or the opinions which cement it. The cloud of mind is discharging its collected lightning, and the equilibrium between institutions and opinions is now restoring, or is about to be restored.[3]

3. See Shelley's similar tribute to his great contemporaries in the concluding paragraph of his *Defence of Poetry* (pp. 1767–68).

As to imitation; Poetry is a mimetic art. It creates, but it creates by combination and representation. Poetical abstractions are beautiful and new, not because the portions of which they are composed had no previous existence in the mind of man or in nature, but because the whole produced by their combination has some intelligible and beautiful analogy with those sources of emotion and thought, and with the contemporary condition of them: one great poet is a masterpiece of nature, which another not only ought to study but must study. He might as wisely and as easily determine that his mind should no longer be the mirror of all that is lovely in the visible universe, as exclude from his contemplation the beautiful which exists in the writings of a great contemporary. The pretence of doing it would be a presumption in any but the greatest; the effect, even in him, would be strained, unnatural and ineffectual. A Poet, is the combined product of such internal powers as modify the nature of others, and of such external influences as excite and sustain these powers; he is not one, but both. Every man's mind is in this respect modified by all the objects of nature and art, by every word and every suggestion which he ever admitted to act upon his consciousness; it is the mirror upon which all forms are reflected, and in which they compose one form. Poets, not otherwise than philosophers, painters, sculptors and musicians, are in one sense the creators and in another the creations of their age. From this subjection the loftiest do not escape. There is a similarity between Homer and Hesiod, between Æschylus and Euripides, between Virgil and Horace, between Dante and Petrarch, between Shakespeare and Fletcher, between Dryden and Pope; each has a generic resemblance under which their specific distinctions are arranged. If this similarity be the result of imitation, I am willing to confess that I have imitated.

Let this opportunity be conceded to me of acknowledging that I have, what a Scotch philosopher characteristically terms, "a passion for reforming the world:"[4] what passion incited him to write and publish his book, he omits to explain. For my part I had rather be damned with Plato and Lord Bacon, than go to Heaven with Paley and Malthus.[5] But it is a mistake to suppose that I dedicate my poetical compositions solely to the direct enforcement of reform, or that I consider them in any degree as containing a reasoned system on the theory of human life. Didactic poetry is my abhorrence; nothing can be equally well expressed in prose that is not tedious and supererogatory in verse. My purpose has hitherto been simply to familiarise the highly refined imagination of the more select classes of poetical readers with beautiful idealisms of moral excellence; aware that until the mind can love, and admire, and trust, and hope, and endure, reasoned principles of moral conduct are seeds cast upon the highway of life which the unconscious passenger tramples into dust, although they would bear the harvest of his happiness. Should I live to accomplish what I purpose, that is, produce a systematical history of what appear to me to be the genuine elements of human society,[6] let not the advocates of

4. This phrase has been identified as the title of chap. 16 in *The Principles of Moral Science* (1805) by the Scottish writer Robert Forsyth.
5. Thomas Malthus's *An Essay on the Principle of Population* (1798) argued that the rate of increase in population will soon exceed the rate of increase in the food supply necessary to sustain it. William Paley wrote *Evidences of Christianity* (1794), which undertakes to prove that the design apparent in natural phenomena, and especially in the human body, entails the existence of God as the great Designer. Shelley ironically expresses his contempt for the doctrines of both these thinkers, which he conceives as arguments for accepting uncomplainingly the present state of the world.
6. Shelley did not live to write this history.

injustice and superstition flatter themselves that I should take Æschylus rather than Plato as my model.

The having spoken of myself with unaffected freedom will need little apology with the candid; and let the uncandid consider that they injure me less than their own hearts and minds by misrepresentation. Whatever talents a person may possess to amuse and instruct others, be they ever so inconsiderable, he is yet bound to exert them: if his attempt be ineffectual, let the punishment of an unaccomplished purpose have been sufficient; let none trouble themselves to heap the dust of oblivion upon his efforts; the pile they raise will betray his grave which might otherwise have been unknown.

Prometheus Unbound

From *Act* 1

SCENE: A *Ravine of Icy Rocks in the Indian Caucasus.* PROMETHEUS *is discovered bound to the Precipice.* PANTHEA *and* IONE *are seated at his feet. Time, Night. During the Scene, Morning slowly breaks.*

PROMETHEUS. Monarch of Gods and Dæmons,[1] and all Spirits
But One, who throng those bright and rolling Worlds
Which Thou and I alone of living things
Behold with sleepless eyes! regard this Earth
Made multitudinous with thy slaves, whom thou   5
Requitest for knee-worship, prayer and praise,
And toil, and hecatombs[2] of broken hearts,
With fear and self contempt and barren hope;
Whilst me, who am thy foe, eyeless in hate,[3]
Hast thou made reign and triumph, to thy scorn,   10
O'er mine own misery and thy vain revenge.—
Three thousand years of sleep-unsheltered hours
And moments—aye[4] divided by keen pangs
Till they seemed years, torture and solitude,
Scorn and despair,—these are mine empire:—   15
More glorious far than that which thou surveyest
From thine unenvied throne, O Mighty God!
Almighty, had I deigned[5] to share the shame
Of thine ill tyranny, and hung not here
Nailed to this wall of eagle-baffling mountain,   20
Black, wintry, dead, unmeasured; without herb,
Insect, or beast, or shape or sound of life.
Ah me, alas, pain, pain ever, forever!

No change, no pause, no hope!—Yet I endure.
I ask the Earth, have not the mountains felt?   25
I ask yon Heaven—the all-beholding Sun,
Has it not seen? The Sea, in storm or calm,

1. Prometheus is addressing Jupiter. "Daemons" are supernatural beings, intermediary between gods and mortals. The "One" in the next line is Demogorgon (see 2.4).
2. Large sacrificial offerings.
3. Blinded by hate.
4. Always.
5. I.e., you would have been all-powerful, if I had deigned.

Heaven's ever-changing Shadow, spread below—
Have its deaf waves not heard my agony?
Ah me, alas, pain, pain ever, forever!   30

The crawling glaciers pierce me with the spears
Of their moon-freezing chrystals; the bright chains
Eat with their burning cold into my bones.
Heaven's winged hound, polluting from thy lips
His beak in poison not his own, tears up   35
My heart;[6] and shapeless sights come wandering by,
The ghastly people of the realm of dream,
Mocking me: and the Earthquake-fiends are charged
To wrench the rivets from my quivering wounds
When the rocks split and close again behind;   40
While from their loud abysses howling throng
The genii of the storm, urging the rage
Of whirlwind, and afflict me with keen hail.
And yet to me welcome is Day and Night,
Whether one breaks the hoar frost of the morn,   45
Or starry, dim, and slow, the other climbs
The leaden-coloured East; for then they lead
Their wingless, crawling Hours, one among whom
—As some dark Priest hales[7] the reluctant victim—
Shall drag thee, cruel King, to kiss the blood   50
From these pale feet,[8] which then might trample thee
If they disdained not such a prostrate slave.
Disdain? Ah no! I pity thee.[9]—What Ruin
Will hunt thee undefended through wide Heaven!
How will thy soul, cloven to its depth with terror,   55
Gape like a Hell within! I speak in grief,
Not exultation, for I hate no more,
As then, ere misery made me wise.—The Curse
Once breathed on thee I would recall. Ye Mountains,
Whose many-voiced Echoes, through the mist   60
Of cataracts, flung the thunder of that spell!
Ye icy Springs, stagnant with wrinkling frost,
Which vibrated to hear me, and then crept
Shuddering through India! Thou serenest Air,
Through which the Sun walks burning without beams!   65
And ye swift Whirlwinds, who on poised wings
Hung mute and moveless o'er yon hushed abyss,
As thunder louder than your own made rock
The orbed world! If then my words had power
—Though I am changed so that aught evil wish   70
Is dead within, although no memory be
Of what is hate—let them not lose it now![1]
What was that curse? for ye all heard me speak.[2]

              *   *   *

6. The vulture, tearing daily at Prometheus' heart, was kissed by Jupiter by way of reward.
7. Drags. The Hours were represented in Greek myth and art by human figures with wings.
8. One of a number of implied parallels between the agony of Prometheus and the passion of Christ.
9. At this early point occurs the crisis of the action: the beginning of Prometheus' change of heart from hate to compassion, consummated in lines 303–05. The rest of the symbolic drama gradually unfolds the consequences of this moral triumph—of which Prometheus himself is unaware.
1. Let my words not lose their power now.
2. In the passage here omitted, none dares, for fear of the god's vengeance, to repeat the curse Prometheus had proclaimed against Jupiter. Prometheus is finally

PHANTASM

Fiend, I defy thee! with a calm, fixed mind,
 All that thou canst inflict I bid thee do;
Foul Tyrant both of Gods and Humankind,
 One only being shalt thou not subdue.   265
  Rain then thy plagues upon me here,
  Ghastly disease and frenzying fear;
  And let alternate frost and fire
  Eat into me, and be thine ire
Lightning and cutting hail and legioned forms   270
Of furies, driving by upon the wounding storms.

Aye, do thy worst. Thou art Omnipotent.
 O'er all things but thyself I gave thee power,
And my own will. Be thy swift mischiefs sent
 To blast mankind, from yon etherial tower.   275
  Let thy malignant spirit move
  Its darkness over those I love:
  On me and mine I imprecate[3]
  The utmost torture of thy hate
And thus devote to sleepless agony   280
This undeclining head while thou must reign on high.

But thou who art the God and Lord—O thou
 Who fillest with thy soul this world of woe,
To whom all things of Earth and Heaven do bow
 In fear and worship—all-prevailing foe!   285
  I curse thee! let a sufferer's curse
  Clasp thee, his torturer, like remorse,
  Till thine Infinity shall be
  A robe of envenomed agony;[4]
And thine Omnipotence a crown of pain   290
To cling like burning gold round thy dissolving brain.

Heap on thy soul by virtue of this Curse
 Ill deeds, then be thou damned, beholding good,
Both infinite as is the Universe,
 And thou, and thy self-torturing solitude.   295
  An awful Image of calm power
  Though now thou sittest, let the hour
  Come, when thou must appear to be
  That which thou art internally.
And after many a false and fruitless crime   300
Scorn track thy lagging fall through boundless space and time.
                              [*The Phantasm vanishes.*]
PROMETHEUS. Were these my words, O Parent?
THE EARTH.   They were thine.
PROMETHEUS. It doth repent me: words are quick and vain;

---

forced to call up the Phantasm of Jupiter himself, who, in the next excerpt, repeats the words of Prometheus' curse.
3. Invoke, pray for.

4. Like the poisoned shirt of the centaur Nessus, which consumed Hercules' flesh when he put it on. The next two lines allude to the mock crowning of Christ with a crown of thorns.

Grief for awhile is blind, and so was mine.
I wish no living thing to suffer pain.   305

THE EARTH

Misery, O misery to me,
That Jove at length should vanquish thee.[5]
Wail, howl aloud, Land and Sea,
The Earth's rent heart shall answer ye.
Howl, Spirits of the living and the dead,   310
Your refuge, your defence lies fallen and vanquished.

FIRST ECHO

Lies fallen and vanquished?

SECOND ECHO

Fallen and vanquished!

IONE[6]

Fear not—'tis but some passing spasm,
The Titan is unvanquished still.[7]   315

* * *

FURY. Behold, an emblem—those who do endure
Deep wrongs for man, and scorn and chains, but heap   595
Thousand-fold torment on themselves and him.
PROMETHEUS. Remit the anguish of that lighted stare—
Close those wan lips—let that thorn-wounded brow
Stream not with blood—it mingles with thy tears
Fix, fix those tortured orbs in peace and death   600
So thy sick throes shake not that crucifix,
So those pale fingers play not with thy gore.—
O horrible! Thy name I will not speak,
It hath become a curse.[8] I see, I see
The wise, the mild, the lofty and the just,   605
Whom thy slaves hate for being like to thee,
Some hunted by foul lies from their heart's home,
An early-chosen, late-lamented home,
As hooded ounces cling to the driven hind,[9]
Some linked to corpses in unwholesome cells: 610
Some—hear I not the multitude laugh loud?—
Impaled in lingering fire: and mighty realms
Float by my feet like sea-uprooted isles
Whose sons are kneaded down in common blood
By the red light of their own burning homes.   615
FURY. Blood thou canst see, and fire; and canst hear groans;

5. Earth mistakes mercy for submission and therefore
interprets Prometheus' moral victory as his defeat.
6. Ione, Panthea, and Asia (in the following scene) are
sisters and Oceanids—i.e., daughters of Oceanus.
7. In the omitted passage the herald Mercury, at Jupiter's command, brings a group of Furies (in Greek
myth, avengers of crimes against the gods) who tempt
Prometheus to despair by revealing the loathsome potentialities for evil in humankind's conscious and unconscious mind. In the climactic temptation a Fury

tears aside a veil to reveal a representation ("emblem,"
line 594) of the suffering Christ on the cross.
8. I.e., the name "Christ" has become, literally, a curse
word, and metaphorically, a curse to humankind, in
that His religion of love is used to justify religious wars
and bloody oppression.
9. Female deer. "Ounces": cheetahs, or leopards, used
in hunting (hoods were sometimes placed over their
eyes to make them easier to control).

Worse things, unheard, unseen, remain behind.
PROMETHEUS. Worse?
FURY.   In each human heart terror survives
The ravin it has gorged:[1] he loftiest fear
All that they would disdain to think were true: 620
Hypocrisy and custom make their minds
The fanes[2] of many a worship, now outworn.
They dare not devise good for man's estate
And yet they know not that they do not dare.
The good want power, but to weep barren tears.   625
The powerful goodness want: worse need for them.
The wise want love, and those who love want wisdom;
And all best things are thus confused to ill.
Many are strong and rich,—and would be just,—
But live among their suffering fellow men   630
As if none felt: they know not what they do.[3]
PROMETHEUS. Thy words are like a cloud of winged snakes
And yet, I pity those they torture not.
FURY. Thou pitiest them? I speak no more!   [Vanishes.]
PROMETHEUS.   Ah woe!
Ah woe! Alas! pain, pain ever, forever!   635
I close my tearless eyes, but see more clear
Thy works within my woe-illumed mind,
Thou subtle Tyrant![4] . . . Peace is in the grave—
The grave hides all things beautiful and good—
I am a God and cannot find it there,   640
Nor would I seek it: for, though dread revenge,
This is defeat, fierce King, not victory.
The sights with which thou torturest gird my soul
With new endurance, till the hour arrives
When they shall be no types of things which are.   645
PANTHEA. Alas! what sawest thou?
PROMETHEUS.   There are two woes:
To speak and to behold; thou spare me one.[5]
Names are there, Nature's sacred watchwords—they
Were borne aloft in bright emblazonry.[6]
The nations thronged around, and cried aloud   650
As with one voice, "Truth, liberty and love!"
Suddenly fierce confusion fell from Heaven
Among them—there was strife, deceit and fear;
Tyrants rushed in, and did divide the spoil.
This was the shadow of the truth I saw.   655
THE EARTH. I felt thy torture, Son, with such mixed joy
As pain and Virtue give.—To cheer thy state
I bid ascend those subtle and fair spirits
Whose homes are the dim caves of human thought
And who inhabit, as birds wing the wind,   660
Its world-surrounding ether;[7] they behold

---

1. The prey that it has greedily devoured.
2. Temples.
3. The Fury ironically echoes Christ's plea for forgiveness of his crucifiers: "Father, forgive them: for they
know not what they do" (Luke 23.24). Lines 625–28
are Shelley's comment on his own age of political reaction and oppression. This passage underlies Yeats's description of the troubled era after World War I in *The*

Second Coming, lines 3–8.
4. Jupiter (also addressed as "fierce King," line 642).
5. I.e., spare me the woe of speaking (about what I
have beheld).
6. As in a brilliant display of banners.
7. A medium, weightless and infinitely elastic, once
supposed to permeate the universe.

Beyond that twilight realm, as in a glass,
The future—may they speak comfort to thee!⁸

* * *

From *Act 2*

SCENE 4—*The Cave of* DEMOGORGON. ASIA *and* PANTHEA.⁹

PANTHEA. What veiled form sits on that ebon throne?
ASIA. The veil has fallen! . . .
PANTHEA.   I see a mighty Darkness
  Filling the seat of power; and rays of gloom
  Dart round, as light from the meridian Sun,
  Ungazed upon and shapeless—neither limb   5
  Nor form—nor outline;¹ yet we feel it is
  A living Spirit.
DEMOGORGON.   Ask what thou wouldst know.
ASIA. What canst thou tell?
DEMOGORGON.   All things thou dar'st demand.
ASIA. Who made the living world?
DEMOGORGON.   God.
ASIA.   Who made all
  That it contains—thought, passion, reason, will,   10
  Imagination?
DEMOGORGON. God, Almighty God.
ASIA. Who made that sense² which, when the winds of Spring
  In rarest visitation, or the voice
  Of one beloved heard in youth alone,
  Fills the faint eyes with falling tears, which dim   15
  The radiant looks of unbewailing flowers,
  And leaves this peopled earth a solitude
  When it returns no more?
DEMOGORGON.   Merciful God.
ASIA. And who made terror, madness, crime, remorse,
  Which from the links of the great chain of things   20
  To every thought within the mind of man
  Sway and drag heavily—and each one reels
  Under the load towards the pit of death;
  Abandoned hope, and love that turns to hate;
  And self-contempt, bitterer to drink than blood;   25
  Pain whose unheeded and familiar speech
  Is howling and keen shrieks, day after day;

8. The speech of the Earth ushers in a troop of spirits representing the noble and virtuous potentialities of the mind, on which rests the hope of a future felicity for humanity. "Glass": mirror.
9. Act 2 has opened with Asia—the feminine principle and embodiment of love, who was separated from Prometheus at the moment of his fall into divisive hate—in a lovely Indian valley at the first hour of the dawn of the spring season of redemption. Asia and her sister Panthea have been led, by a sweet and irresistible compulsion, first to the portal and then down into the depths of the cave of Demogorgon—the central enigma of Shelley's poem.
   Commentators have usually equated Demogorgon with necessity, but the interpretation is too confining.

More flexibly, he can be thought of as process, the inexorable way in which things evolve. But the ultimate mover of that process—the ultimate reason for the way things are—must remain, Shelley skeptically insists, a mystery beyond the limits of accessible knowledge. Demogorgon is ignorant of the principle that controls him and can give merely riddling answers to Asia's questions about the "why" of creation, good, and evil.
1. Echoing Milton's description of Death, *Paradise Lost* 2.666–73.
2. Presumably the sense by which one is aware of the "unseen Power" that Shelley calls "Intellectual Beauty" (see *Hymn to Intellectual Beauty*, stanza 2, p. 1694).

And Hell, or the sharp fear of Hell?[3]
DEMOGORGON.   He reigns.
ASIA. Utter his name—a world pining in pain
    Asks but his name; curses shall drag him down.   30
DEMOGORGON. He reigns.
ASIA.   I feel, I know it—who?
DEMOGORGON.   He reigns.
ASIA. Who reigns? There was the Heaven and Earth at first
    And Light and Love;—then Saturn,[4] from whose throne
    Time fell, an envious shadow; such the state
    Of the earth's primal spirits beneath his sway   35
    As the calm joy of flowers and living leaves
    Before the wind or sun has withered them
    And semivital worms; but he refused
    The birthright of their being, knowledge, power,
    The skill which wields the elements, the thought   40
    Which pierces this dim Universe like light,
    Self-empire and the majesty of love,
    For thirst of which they fainted. Then Prometheus
    Gave wisdom, which is strength, to Jupiter
    And with this law alone: "Let man be free,"   45
    Clothed him with the dominion of wide Heaven.
    To know nor faith nor love nor law, to be
    Omnipotent but friendless, is to reign;
    And Jove now reigned; for on the race of man
    First famine, and then toil, and then disease,   50
    Strife, wounds, and ghastly death unseen before,
    Fell; and the unseasonable seasons drove,
    With alternating shafts of frost and fire,
    Their shelterless, pale tribes to mountain caves;
    And in their desart[5] hearts fierce wants he sent   55
    And mad disquietudes, and shadows idle
    Of unreal good, which levied mutual war,
    So ruining the lair wherein they raged.
    Prometheus saw, and waked the legioned hopes
    Which sleep within folded Elysian flowers,   60
    Nepenthe, Moly, Amaranth,[6] fadeless blooms;
    That they might hide with thin and rainbow wings
    The shape of Death; and Love he sent to bind
    The disunited tendrils of that vine
    Which bears the wine of life, the human heart;   65
    And he tamed fire which, like some beast of prey,
    Most terrible, but lovely, played beneath
    The frown of man, and tortured to his will
    Iron and gold, the slaves and signs of power,
    And gems and poisons, and all subtlest forms,   70
    Hidden beneath the mountains and the waves.
    He gave man speech, and speech created thought,
    Which is the measure of the Universe;

---

3. The nouns "hope," "love," etc. (lines 24–28), are all objects of the verb "made" (line 19).
4. In Greek myth Saturn's reign was the golden age. In Shelley's version Saturn refused to grant mortals knowledge and science, so that it was an age of ignorant innocence in which the deepest human needs remained unfulfilled.
5. Empty, forsaken.
6. These are medicinal drugs and flowers in Greek myth. Asia is describing (lines 59–97) the various sciences and arts given to humans by Prometheus, the culture bringer.

And Science struck the thrones of Earth and Heaven
Which shook, but fell not; and the harmonious mind   75
Poured itself forth in all-prophetic song,
And music lifted up the listening spirit
Until it walked, exempt from mortal care,
Godlike, o'er the clear billows of sweet sound;
And human hands first mimicked and then mocked[7]   80
With moulded limbs more lovely than its own
The human form, till marble grew divine,
And mothers, gazing, drank the love men see
Reflected in their race, behold, and perish.[8]—
He told the hidden power of herbs and springs,   85
And Disease drank and slept—Death grew like sleep.—
He taught the implicated[9] orbits woven
Of the wide-wandering stars, and how the Sun
Changes his lair, and by what secret spell
The pale moon is transformed, when her broad eye   90
Gazes not on the interlunar[1] sea;
He taught to rule, as life directs the limbs,
The tempest-winged chariots of the Ocean,
And the Celt knew the Indian.[2] Cities then
Were built, and through their snow-like columns flowed   95
The warm winds, and the azure æther shone,
And the blue sea and shadowy hills were seen . . .
Such the alleviations of his state
Prometheus gave to man—for which he hangs
Withering in destined pain—but who rains down   100
Evil, the immedicable plague, which while
Man looks on his creation like a God
And sees that it is glorious, drives him on,
The wreck of his own will, the scorn of Earth,
The outcast, the abandoned, the alone?—   105
Not Jove: while yet his frown shook Heaven, aye when
His adversary from adamantine chains
Cursed him, he trembled like a slave. Declare
Who is his master? Is he too a slave?
DEMOGORGON. All spirits are enslaved which serve things evil: 110
Thou knowest if Jupiter be such or no.
ASIA. Whom calledst thou God?
DEMOGORGON.   I spoke but as ye speak—
For Jove is the supreme of living things.
ASIA. Who is the master of the slave?
DEMOGORGON.   —If the Abysm
Could vomit forth its secrets:—but a voice   115
Is wanting, the deep truth is imageless;[3]
For what would it avail to bid thee gaze
On the revolving world? what to bid speak
Fate, Time, Occasion, Chance and Change? To these
All things are subject but eternal Love.   120

7. I.e., sculptors first merely reproduced but later improved on ("mocked" in the sense of "heightened") the
beauty of the human form.
8. Expectant mothers looked at the beautiful statues
so that their children might, by prenatal influence, be
born with the beauty that makes beholders die of love.
9. Intertwined.

1. The phase between old and new moons, when the
moon is invisible.
2. The reference is to the ships in which the Celtic
(here, non–Greco-Roman) races of Europe were able
to sail to India.
3. I.e., ultimate truths can be neither known nor expressed.

ASIA. So much I asked before, and my heart gave
    The response thou hast given; and of such truths
    Each to itself must be the oracle.—
    One more demand . . . and do thou answer me
    As my own soul would answer, did it know   125
    That which I ask.—Prometheus shall arise
    Henceforth the Sun of this rejoicing world:
    When shall the destined hour arrive?
DEMOGORGON.   Behold![4]
ASIA. The rocks are cloven, and through the purple night
    I see Cars drawn by rainbow-winged steeds   130
    Which trample the dim winds—in each there stands
    A wild-eyed charioteer, urging their flight.
    Some look behind, as fiends pursued them there
    And yet I see no shapes but the keen stars:
    Others with burning eyes lean forth, and drink   135
    With eager lips the wind of their own speed,
    As if the thing they loved fled on before,
    And now—even now they clasped it; their bright locks
    Stream like a comet's flashing hair: they all
    Sweep onward.—
DEMOGORGON.   These are the immortal Hours   140
    Of whom thou didst demand.—One waits for thee.
ASIA. A Spirit with a dreadful countenance
    Checks its dark chariot by the craggy gulph.
    Unlike thy brethren, ghastly charioteer,
    What art thou? whither wouldst thou bear me? Speak!   145
SPIRIT. I am the shadow of a destiny
    More dread than is my aspect—ere yon planet
    Has set, the Darkness[5] which ascends with me
    Shall wrap in lasting night Heaven's kingless throne.
ASIA. What meanest thou?
PANTHEA.   That terrible shadow floats   150
    Up from its throne, as may the lurid[6] smoke
    Of earthquake-ruined cities o'er the sea.—
    Lo! it ascends the Car . . . the coursers fly
    Terrified; watch its path among the stars
    Blackening the night!
ASIA.   Thus I am answered—strange!   155
PANTHEA. See, near the verge[7] another chariot stays;
    An ivory shell inlaid with crimson fire
    Which comes and goes within its sculptured rim
    Of delicate strange tracery—the young Spirit
    That guides it, has the dovelike eyes of hope.   160
    How its soft smiles attract the soul!—as light
    Lures winged insects[8] through the lampless air.

SPIRIT
My coursers are fed with the lightning,
    They drink of the whirlwind's stream

4. Demogorgon's answer is a gesture: he points to the
approaching chariots ("Cars").
5. Demogorgon, who is ascending (lines 150–55) to
effect the dethronement of Jupiter.
6. Red-glaring.
7. Horizon.
8. The ancient image of the soul, or *psyche*, was a
moth. The chariot described here will carry Asia to a
reunion with Prometheus.

And when the red morning is brightning   165
   They bathe in the fresh sunbeam;
They have strength for their swiftness, I deem:
   Then ascend with me, daughter of Ocean.

I desire—and their speed makes night kindle;
   I fear—they outstrip the Typhoon;   170
Ere the cloud piled on Atlas[9] can dwindle
   We encircle the earth and the moon:
   We shall rest from long labours at noon:
   Then ascend with me, daughter of Ocean.

SCENE 5—*The Car pauses within a Cloud on the Top of a snowy Mountain.* ASIA, PANTHEA, *and the* SPIRIT OF THE HOUR.

SPIRIT

On the brink of the night and the morning
   My coursers are wont to respire,[1]
But the Earth has just whispered a warning
   That their flight must be swifter than fire:
   They shall drink the hot speed of desire!   5

ASIA. Thou breathest on their nostrils—but my breath
   Would give them swifter speed.
SPIRIT.   Alas, it could not.
PANTHEA. O Spirit! pause and tell whence is the light
   Which fills the cloud? the sun is yet unrisen.
SPIRIT. The sun will rise not until noon.[2]—Apollo   10
   Is held in Heaven by wonder—and the light
   Which fills this vapour, as the aerial hue
   Of fountain-gazing roses fills the water,
   Flows from thy mighty sister.
PANTHEA.   Yes, I feel . . .
ASIA. What is it with thee, sister? Thou art pale.   15
PANTHEA. How thou art changed! I dare not look on thee;
   I feel, but see thee not. I scarce endure
   The radiance of thy beauty.[3] Some good change
   Is working in the elements which suffer
   Thy presence thus unveiled.—The Nereids tell   20
   That on the day when the clear hyaline[4]
   Was cloven at thy uprise, and thou didst stand
   Within a veined shell,[5] which floated on
   Over the calm floor of the chrystal sea,
   Among the Ægean isles, and by the shores   25
   Which bear thy name, love, like the atmosphere
   Of the sun's fire filling the living world,
   Burst from thee, and illumined Earth and Heaven
   And the deep ocean and the sunless caves,

9. A mountain in North Africa that the Greeks regarded as so high that it supported the heavens.
1. Catch their breath.
2. Noon will be the time of the reunion of Prometheus and Asia.
3. In an earlier scene Panthea had envisioned in a dream the radiant and eternal inner form of Prometheus emerging through his "wound-worn limbs." The corresponding transfiguration of Asia, prepared for by her descent to the underworld, now takes place.
4. The glassy sea.
5. The story told by the Nereids (sea nymphs) serves to associate Asia with Aphrodite, goddess of love, emerging (as in Botticelli's painting) from the Mediterranean on a seashell.

And all that dwells within them; till grief cast   30
Eclipse upon the soul from which it came:
Such art thou now, nor is it I alone,
Thy sister, thy companion, thine own chosen one,
But the whole world which seeks thy sympathy.
Hearest thou not sounds i' the air which speak the love   35
Of all articulate beings? Feelest thou not
The inanimate winds enamoured of thee?—List!   [*Music.*]
ASIA. Thy words are sweeter than aught else but his
    Whose echoes they are—yet all love is sweet,
    Given or returned; common as light is love   40
    And its familiar voice wearies not ever.
    Like the wide Heaven, the all-sustaining air,
    It makes the reptile equal to the God . . .
    They who inspire it most are fortunate
    As I am now; but those who feel it most   45
    Are happier still, after long sufferings
    As I shall soon become.
PANTHEA.   List! Spirits speak.

                    VOICE (*in the air, singing*)[6]
    Life of Life! thy lips enkindle
        With their love the breath between them
    And thy smiles before they dwindle   50
        Make the cold air fire; then screen them
    In those looks where whoso gazes
    Faints, entangled in their mazes.

    Child of Light! thy limbs are burning
        Through the vest which seems to hide them   55
    As the radiant lines of morning
        Through the clouds ere they divide them,
    And this atmosphere divinest
    Shrouds thee wheresoe'er thou shinest.

    Fair are others;—none beholds thee   60
        But thy voice sounds low and tender
    Like the fairest, for it folds thee
        From the sight, that liquid splendour,
    And all feel, yet see thee never
    As I feel now, lost forever!   65

    Lamp of Earth! where'er thou movest
        Its dim shapes are clad with brightness
    And the souls of whom thou lovest
        Walk upon the winds with lightness
    Till they fail, as I am failing,   70
    Dizzy, lost . . . yet unbewailing!

                            ASIA
    My soul is an enchanted Boat
    Which, like a sleeping swan, doth float

6. The voice attempts to describe, in a dizzying whirl of optical paradoxes, what it feels like to look on the naked essence of love and beauty.

Upon the silver waves of thy sweet singing,
  And thine doth like an Angel sit   75
  Beside the helm conducting it
Whilst all the winds with melody are ringing.
  It seems to float ever—forever—
  Upon that many winding River
  Between mountains, woods, abysses,   80
  A Paradise of wildernesses,
Till like one in slumber bound
Borne to the Ocean, I float down, around,
Into a Sea profound, of ever-spreading sound.

  Meanwhile thy spirit lifts its pinions[7]   85
  In Music's most serene dominions,
Catching the winds that fan that happy Heaven.
  And we sail on, away, afar,
  Without a course—without a star—
But by the instinct of sweet Music driven   90
  Till, through Elysian garden islets
  By thee, most beautiful of pilots,
  Where never mortal pinnace[8] glided,
  The boat of my desire is guided—
Realms where the air we breathe is Love   95
Which in the winds and on the waves doth move,
Harmonizing this Earth with what we feel above.

  We have past Age's icy caves,
  And Manhood's dark and tossing waves
And Youth's smooth ocean, smiling to betray;   100
  Beyond the glassy gulphs we flee
  Of shadow-peopled Infancy,
Through Death and Birth to a diviner day,[9]
  A Paradise of vaulted bowers
  Lit by downward-gazing flowers   105
  And watery paths that wind between
  Wildernesses calm and green,
Peopled by shapes too bright to see,
And rest, having beheld—somewhat like thee,
Which walk upon the sea, and chaunt melodiously!   110

From *Act 3*

SCENE 1—*Heaven.* JUPITER *on his Throne;* THETIS *and the other Deities assembled.*

JUPITER. Ye congregated Powers of Heaven who share
  The glory and the strength of him ye serve,
  Rejoice! henceforth I am omnipotent.
  All else had been subdued to me—alone
  The soul of man, like unextinguished fire,   5
  Yet burns towards Heaven with fierce reproach and doubt

---

7. Wings.
8. Small boat.
9. Asia is describing what it feels like to be transfigured—in the image of moving backward in the stream of time, through youth and infancy and birth itself, in order to die to this life and be born again to a "diviner" existence.

And lamentation and reluctant prayer,
Hurling up insurrection, which might make
Our antique empire insecure, though built
On eldest faith, and Hell's coeval,[1] fear.   10
And though my curses through the pendulous[2] air
Like snow on herbless peaks, fall flake by flake
And cling to it[3]—though under my wrath's night
It climb the crags of life, step after step,
Which wound it, as ice wounds unsandalled feet,   15
It yet remains supreme o'er misery,
Aspiring . . . unrepressed; yet soon to fall:
Even now have I begotten a strange wonder,
That fatal Child,[4] the terror of the Earth,
Who waits but till the destined Hour arrive,   20
Bearing from Demogorgon's vacant throne
The dreadful might of ever living limbs
Which clothed that awful spirit unbeheld—
To redescend, and trample out the spark . . .[5]

Pour forth Heaven's wine, Idæan Ganymede,   25
And let it fill the dædal[6] cups like fire
And from the flower-inwoven soil divine
Ye all triumphant harmonies arise
As dew from Earth under the twilight stars;
Drink! be the nectar circling through your veins   30
The soul of joy, ye everliving Gods,
Till exultation burst in one wide voice
Like music from Elysian winds.—
                              And thou
Ascend beside me, veiled in the light
Of the desire which makes thee one with me,   35
Thetis, bright Image of Eternity!—
When thou didst cry, "Insufferable might![7]
God! spare me! I sustain not the quick flames,
The penetrating presence; all my being,
Like him whom the Numidian seps[8] did thaw   40
Into a dew with poison, is dissolved,
Sinking through its foundations"—even then
Two mighty spirits, mingling, made a third
Mightier than either—which unbodied now
Between us, floats, felt although unbeheld,   45
Waiting the incarnation, which ascends—
Hear ye the thunder of the fiery wheels
Griding[9] the winds?—from Demogorgon's throne.—
Victory! victory! Feel'st thou not, O World,

1. Of the same age.
2. Suspending.
3. "It" (as also in lines 14 and 16) is "the soul of man" (line 5).
4. The son of Jupiter and Thetis; Jupiter believes that he has begotten a child who will assume the bodily form of the conquered Demogorgon and then return to announce his victory and the defeat of the resistance of Prometheus.
5. The "spark" of Prometheus' defiance.
6. Skillfully wrought (from the name of the Greek craftsman Daedalus). Ganymede (line 25) had been seized on Mt. Ida by an eagle and carried to heaven to be Jupiter's cupbearer.
7. This description of the sexual union of Jupiter and Thetis is a grotesque parody of the reunion of Prometheus and Asia.
8. A serpent of Numidia (North Africa) whose bite was thought to cause putrefaction.
9. Cutting with a rasping sound.

The Earthquake of his chariot thundering up   50
Olympus?
    [*The Car of the* HOUR *arrives.* DEMOGORGON *descends and moves to-*
wards the Throne of JUPITER.]
        Awful Shape, what art thou? Speak!
DEMOGORGON. Eternity—demand no direr name.
  Descend, and follow me down the abyss;
  I am thy child,[1] as thou wert Saturn's child,
  Mightier than thee; and we must dwell together   55
  Henceforth in darkness.—Lift thy lightnings not.
  The tyranny of Heaven none may retain,
  Or reassume, or hold succeeding thee . . .
  Yet if thou wilt—as 'tis the destiny
  Of trodden worms to writhe till they are dead—   60
  Put forth thy might.
JUPITER.   Detested prodigy!
  Even thus beneath the deep Titanian prisons[2]
  I trample thee! . . . thou lingerest?
                  Mercy! mercy!
  No pity—no release, no respite! . . . Oh,
  That thou wouldst make mine enemy my judge.   65
  Even where he hangs, seared by my long revenge
  On Caucasus—he would not doom me thus.—
  Gentle and just and dreadless, is he not
  The monarch of the world?[3] what then art thou? . . .
  No refuge! no appeal—. . .
           Sink with me then—   70
  We two will sink in the wide waves of ruin
  Even as a vulture and a snake outspent
  Drop, twisted in inextricable fight,[4]
  Into a shoreless sea.—Let Hell unlock
  Its mounded Oceans of tempestuous fire,   75
  And whelm on them into the bottomless void
  The desolated world and thee and me,
  The conqueror and the conquered, and the wreck
  Of that for which they combated.
              Ai! Ai!
  The elements obey me not . . . I sink . . .   80
  Dizzily down—ever, forever, down—
  And, like a cloud, mine enemy above
  Darkens my fall with victory!—Ai! Ai!

From SCENE 4—*A Forest. In the Background a Cave.* PROME-
THEUS, ASIA, PANTHEA, IONE, *and the* SPIRIT OF THE EARTH.[5]

                  *   *   *

1. Ironically, and in a figurative sense: Demogorgon's function follows from Jupiter's actions.
2. After they overthrew the Titans, Jupiter and the Olympian gods imprisoned them in Tartarus, deep beneath the earth.
3. The ultimate irony: Jupiter appeals to those very qualities of Prometheus for which he has hitherto persecuted him, begging for a mercy that Prometheus has already granted him, but Prometheus' change from vengefulness to mercy is in fact the cause of Jupiter's present downfall.

4. The eagle (or vulture) and the snake locked in equal combat—a favorite Shelleyan image (cf. *Alastor*, lines 227–32, p. 1680).
5. After Jupiter's annihilation (described in scene 2), Hercules unbinds Prometheus, who is reunited with Asia and retires to a cave "where we will sit and talk of time and change / . . . ourselves unchanged." In the speech that concludes the act (reprinted here) the Spirit of the Hour describes what happened in the human world when he sounded the apocalyptic trumpet.

[*The* SPIRIT OF THE HOUR *enters.*]

PROMETHEUS. We feel what thou hast heard and seen—yet speak.
SPIRIT OF THE HOUR. Soon as the sound had ceased whose thunder filled
    The abysses of the sky, and the wide earth,
    There was a change . . . the impalpable thin air   100
    And the all-circling sunlight were transformed
    As if the sense of love dissolved in them
    Had folded itself round the sphered world.
    My vision then grew clear and I could see
    Into the mysteries of the Universe.[6]   105
    Dizzy as with delight I floated down,
    Winnowing the lightsome air with languid plumes,
    My coursers sought their birthplace in the sun
    Where they henceforth will live exempt from toil,
    Pasturing flowers of vegetable fire—   110
    And where my moonlike car will stand within
    A temple, gazed upon by Phidian forms,[7]
    Of thee, and Asia and the Earth, and me
    And you fair nymphs, looking the love we feel,
    In memory of the tidings it has borne,   115
    Beneath a dome fretted with graven flowers,
    Poised on twelve columns of resplendent stone
    And open to the bright and liquid sky.
    Yoked to it by an amphisbænic snake[8]
    The likeness of those winged steeds will mock[9]   120
    The flight from which they find repose.—Alas,
    Whither has wandered now my partial[1] tongue
    When all remains untold which ye would hear!—
    As I have said, I floated to the Earth:
    It was, as it is still, the pain of bliss   125
    To move, to breathe, to be; I wandering went
    Among the haunts and dwellings of mankind
    And first was disappointed not to see
    Such mighty change as I had felt within
    Expressed in outward things; but soon I looked,   130
    And behold! thrones were kingless, and men walked
    One with the other even as spirits do,
    None fawned, none trampled; hate, disdain or fear,
    Self-love or self-contempt on human brows
    No more inscribed, as o'er the gate of hell,   135
    "All hope abandon, ye who enter here";[2]
    None frowned, none trembled, none with eager fear
    Gazed on another's eye of cold command
    Until the subject of a tyrant's will
    Became, worse fate, the abject of his own[3]   140
    Which spurred him, like an outspent horse, to death.

6. I.e., the earth's atmosphere clarifies, no longer refracting the sunlight, and so allows the Spirit of the Hour to see what is happening on earth.
7. The crescent-shaped ("moonlike") chariot, its apocalyptic mission accomplished, will be frozen to stone, and will be surrounded by the sculptured forms of other agents in the drama. Phidias (5th century B.C.) was the noblest of Greek sculptors.
8. A mythical snake with a head at either end; it serves here as a symbolic warning that a reversal of the process is always possible.
9. "Imitate" and also, in their immobility, "mock at" the flight they represent.
1. "Biased," or possibly, "telling only part of the story."
2. The inscription over the gate of hell in Dante's *Inferno* 3.9.
3. I.e., he was so abjectly enslaved that his own will accorded with the tyrant's will.

None wrought his lips in truth-entangling lines
Which smiled the lie his tongue disdained to speak;
None with firm sneer trod out in his own heart
The sparks of love and hope, till there remained   145
Those bitter ashes, a soul self-consumed,
And the wretch crept, a vampire among men,
Infecting all with his own hideous ill.
None talked that common, false, cold, hollow talk
Which makes the heart deny the *yes* it breathes   150
Yet question that unmeant hypocrisy
With such a self-mistrust as has no name.
And women too, frank, beautiful and kind
As the free Heaven which rains fresh light and dew
On the wide earth, past: gentle, radiant forms,   155
From custom's evil taint exempt and pure;
Speaking the wisdom once they could not think,
Looking emotions once they feared to feel
And changed to all which once they dared not be,
Yet being now, made Earth like Heaven—nor pride   160
Nor jealousy nor envy nor ill shame,
The bitterest of those drops of treasured gall,
Spoilt the sweet taste of the nepenthe,[4] love.

Thrones, altars, judgement-seats and prisons; wherein
And beside which, by wretched men were borne   165
Sceptres, tiaras, swords and chains, and tomes
Of reasoned wrong glozed on[5] by ignorance,
Were like those monstrous and barbaric shapes,
The ghosts of a no more remembered fame,
Which from their unworn obelisks[6] look forth   170
In triumph o'er the palaces and tombs
Of those who were their conquerors, mouldering round.
Those imaged to the pride of Kings and Priests
A dark yet mighty faith, a power as wide
As is the world it wasted, and are now   175
But an astonishment; even so the tools
And emblems of its last captivity
Amid the dwellings of the peopled Earth,
Stand, not o'erthrown, but unregarded now.
And those foul shapes, abhorred by God and man—   180
Which under many a name and many a form
Strange, savage, ghastly, dark and execrable
Were Jupiter,[7] the tyrant of the world;
And which the nations panic-stricken served
With blood, and hearts broken by long hope, and love   185
Dragged to his altars soiled and garlandless
And slain amid men's unreclaiming tears,
Flattering the thing they feared, which fear was hate—
Frown, mouldering fast, o'er their abandoned shrines.

4. A drug (probably opium) that brings forgetfulness of pain and sorrow.
5. Annotated, explained.
6. The Egyptian obelisks (tapering shafts of stone), brought to Rome by its conquering armies, included hieroglyphs that—because they were still undeciph-
ered in Shelley's time—seemed "monstrous and barbaric shapes" (line 168).
7. The "foul shapes" (line 180) were statues of the gods who, whatever their names, were all really manifestations of Jupiter.

The painted veil, by those who were, called life,[8]   190
Which mimicked, as with colours idly spread,
All men believed and hoped, is torn aside—
The loathsome mask has fallen, the man remains
Sceptreless, free, uncircumscribed—but man:
Equal, unclassed, tribeless, and nationless,   195
Exempt from awe, worship, degree,—the King
Over himself; just, gentle, wise—but man:
Passionless? no—yet free from guilt or pain
Which were, for his will made, or suffered them,
Nor yet exempt, though ruling them like slaves,   200
From chance and death and mutability,
The clogs of that which else might oversoar
The loftiest star of unascended Heaven
Pinnacled dim in the intense inane.[9]

From *Act 4*[1]

SCENE—A *Part of the Forest near the Cave of* PROMETHEUS.

                              *   *   *

IONE.   Even whilst we speak
New notes arise . . . What is that awful sound?   185
PANTHEA. 'Tis the deep music of the rolling world,
Kindling within the strings of the waved air
Æolian modulations.[2]
IONE.   Listen too,
How every pause is filled with under-notes,
Clear, silver, icy, keen, awakening tones   190
Which pierce the sense and live within the soul
As the sharp stars pierce Winter's chrystal air
And gaze upon themselves within the sea.
PANTHEA. But see, where through two openings in the forest
Which hanging branches overcanopy,   195
And where two runnels of a rivulet
Between the close moss violet-inwoven
Have made their path of melody, like sisters
Who part with sighs that they may meet in smiles,
Turning their dear disunion to an isle   200
Of lovely grief, a wood of sweet sad thoughts;

8. I.e., which was thought to be life by men as they were before their regeneration.
9. I.e., a dim point in the extreme of empty space. The sense of lines 198–204 is if regenerate man were to be released from all earthly and biological impediments ("clogs"), he would become what even the stars are not—a pure ideal.
1. The original drama, completed in the spring of 1819, consisted of three acts. Later that year Shelley added a jubilant fourth act. In Revelation 21, the apocalyptic replacement of the old world by "a new heaven and new earth" had been symbolized by the marriage of the Lamb with the New Jerusalem. Shelley's fourth act, somewhat like the conclusion of Blake's *Jerusalem*, expands this figure into a cosmic epithalamion, representing a union of divided elements that enacts everywhere the reunion of Prometheus and Asia taking place offstage.
   Shelley's model is the Renaissance masque, which combines song and dance with spectacular displays. Panthea and Ione serve as commentators on the action, which is divided into three episodes. In the first episode, omitted here, the purified "Spirits of the human mind" unite in a ritual dance with the Hours of the glad new day. In the second episode (lines 194–318), there appear emblematic representations of the moon and the earth, each bearing an infant whose hour has come round at last; Shelley based this description in part on Ezekiel 1, the vision of the chariot of divine glory, which had traditionally been interpreted as a portent of apocalypse. The third episode (lines 319–502) is the bacchanalian dance of the love-intoxicated Moon around her brother and paramour, the rejuvenescent Earth. By way of coda (line 549 to the end), Demogorgon calls on all beings to hear his proclamation of the moral significance of this great drama of humanity's self-betrayal and self-redemption.
2. Evoking music like that of the Eolian harp.

Two visions of strange radiance float upon
The Ocean-like inchantment of strong sound
Which flows intenser, keener, deeper yet
Under the ground and through the windless air.   205
IONE. I see a chariot like that thinnest boat
In which the Mother of the Months is borne
By ebbing light into her western cave
When she upsprings from interlunar dreams,[3]
O'er which is curved an orblike canopy   210
Of gentle darkness, and the hills and woods
Distinctly seen through that dusk aery veil
Regard[4] like shapes in an enchanter's glass;
Its wheels are solid clouds, azure and gold,
Such as the genii of the thunderstorm   215
Pile on the floor of the illumined sea
When the Sun rushes under it; they roll
And move and grow as with an inward wind.
Within it sits a winged Infant, white
Its countenance, like the whiteness of bright snow,   220
Its plumes are as feathers of sunny frost,
Its limbs gleam white, through the wind-flowing folds
Of its white robe, woof of ætherial pearl.
Its hair is white,—the brightness of white light
Scattered in strings,[5] yet its two eyes are Heavens   225
Of liquid darkness, which the Deity
Within, seems pouring, as a storm is poured
From jagged clouds, out of their arrowy lashes,
Tempering the cold and radiant air around
With fire that is not brightness;[6] in its hand   230
It sways a quivering moonbeam, from whose point
A guiding power directs the chariot's prow
Over its wheeled clouds, which as they roll
Over the grass and flowers and waves, wake sounds
Sweet as a singing rain of silver dew.   235
PANTHEA. And from the other opening in the wood
Rushes with loud and whirlwind harmony
A sphere, which is as many thousand spheres,
Solid as chrystal, yet through all its mass
Flow, as through empty space, music and light: 240
Ten thousand orbs involving and involved,[7]
Purple and azure, white and green and golden,
Sphere within sphere, and every space between
Peopled with unimaginable shapes

3. I.e., the chariot is a thin crescent shape, like the new Moon, when it carries within it the outline of the old Moon ("Mother of the Months") to the cave where she is reborn during the "interlunar" period—i.e., when the Moon is entirely invisible.
4. Look, appear.
5. The infant resembles "one like unto the Son of man" in Revelation 1.13–14: "His head and his hairs were white like wool, as white as snow." The description that follows, of the light radiated from the infant's eyes, echoes the description in Ezekiel's vision, 1.27–28, of the "brightness round about" that "was the appearance of the likeness of the glory of the Lord."
6. Shelley knew, from the account by Sir Humphry

Davy, Herschel's discovery (1800) that there are what Herschel called "dark rays"—i.e., infrared radiation; Davy suggested that the moon gave off such rays.
7. The transparent sphere is an emblem of earth. The description of its spinning and that of its interior orbs echoes both Ezekiel 1.15–17—"the appearance of the wheels and their work . . . was as it were a wheel in the middle of a wheel"—and *Paradise Lost* 5.620–24, which describes the "mystical dance" of the angels in heaven, whose movements resemble the revolving spheres of the planets: "mazes intricate, / Eccentric, intervolved, yet regular / Then most, when most irregular they seem."

Such as ghosts dream dwell in the lampless deep   245
Yet each intertranspicuous,[8] and they whirl
Over each other with a thousand motions
Upon a thousand sightless[9] axles spinning
And with the force of self-destroying swiftness,
Intensely, slowly, solemnly roll on—   250
Kindling with mingled sounds, and many tones,
Intelligible words and music wild.—
With mighty whirl the multitudinous Orb
Grinds the bright brook into an azure mist
Of elemental subtlety, like light,   255
And the wild odour of the forest flowers,
The music of the living grass and air,
The emerald light of leaf-entangled beams
Round its intense, yet self-conflicting[1] speed,
Seem kneaded into one aerial mass   260
Which drowns the sense. Within the Orb itself,
Pillowed upon its alabaster arms
Like to a child o'erwearied with sweet toil,
On its own folded wings and wavy hair
The Spirit of the Earth is laid asleep,   265
And you can see its little lips are moving
Amid the changing light of their own smiles
Like one who talks of what he loves in dream—
IONE.   'Tis only mocking[2] the Orb's harmony . . . .
PANTHEA. And from a star upon its forehead, shoot,   270
    Like swords of azure fire, or golden spears
    With tyrant-quelling myrtle[3] overtwined,
    Embleming Heaven and Earth united now,
    Vast beams like spokes of some invisible wheel
    Which whirl as the Orb whirls, swifter than thought,   275
    Filling the abyss with sunlike lightenings,
    And perpendicular now, and now transverse,
    Pierce the dark soil, and as they pierce and pass
    Make bare the secrets of the Earth's deep heart,[4]
    Infinite mine of adamant[5] and gold,   280
    Valueless[6] stones and unimagined gems,
    And caverns on chrystalline columns poised
    With vegetable silver overspread,
    Wells of unfathomed fire, and watersprings
    Whence the great Sea, even as a child, is fed   285
    Whose vapours clothe Earth's monarch mountain-tops
    With kingly, ermine snow; the beams flash on
    And make appear the melancholy ruins
    Of cancelled cycles;[7] anchors, beaks of ships,
    Planks turned to marble, quivers, helms and spears   290
    And gorgon-headed targes,[8] and the wheels

---

8. Transparent, so that each can be seen through the others.
9. Invisible.
1. Because its component spheres are spinning in opposed directions.
2. Imitating.
3. The myrtle, sacred to Venus, symbolizes love.
4. I.e., the star on the infant's forehead radiates pene-

trating beams that (like modern X rays) reveal what lies beneath the surface of the earth.
5. Very hard rock.
6. Priceless.
7. I.e., of civilizations that flourished, then disappeared.
8. Shields embossed with a gorgon's head. "Helms": helmets.

Of scythed chariots,[9] and the emblazonry
Of trophies, standards and armorial beasts[1]
Round which Death laughed, sepulchred emblems
Of dead Destruction, ruin within ruin!   295
The wrecks beside of many a city vast,
Whose population which the Earth grew over
Was mortal but not human;[2] see, they lie,
Their monstrous works and uncouth skeletons,
Their statues, homes, and fanes;[3] prodigious shapes   300
Huddled in grey annihilation, split,
Jammed in the hard black deep; and over these
The anatomies[4] of unknown winged things,
And fishes which were isles of living scale,
And serpents, bony chains, twisted around   305
The iron crags, or within heaps of dust
To which the tortuous strength of their last pangs
Had crushed the iron crags;—and over these
The jagged alligator and the might
Of earth-convulsing behemoth,[5] which once   310
Were monarch beasts, and on the slimy shores
And weed-overgrown continents of Earth
Increased and multiplied like summer worms
On an abandoned corpse, till the blue globe
Wrapt Deluge round it like a cloak, and they   315
Yelled, gaspt and were abolished; or some God
Whose throne was in a Comet, past, and cried—
"Be not!"—and like my words they were no more.[6]

THE EARTH

The joy, the triumph, the delight, the madness,
The boundless, overflowing, bursting gladness,   320
The vaporous exultation, not to be confined![7]
     Ha! ha! the animation of delight
     Which wraps me, like an atmosphere of light,
And bears me as a cloud is borne by its own wind!

THE MOON

     Brother mine, calm wanderer,   325
     Happy globe of land and air,
Some Spirit[8] is darted like a beam from thee,
     Which penetrates my frozen frame
     And passes with the warmth of flame—
With love and odour and deep melody   330
     Through me, through me!—

9. Ancient war chariots sometimes had steel blades fastened to the wheels.
1. Animals in heraldic insignia.
2. That is, a prehuman race of beings that once overspread the earth.
3. Temples.
4. Skeletons.
5. The huge land animal described in Job 40.15–24.
6. According to the theory of "Catastrophism" proposed by G. F. Cuvier, *Researches on Fossil Bones* (1812), successive geologic layers of fossils are evidence of a sequence of catastrophes—volcanic upheavals and gigantic floods—each of which wiped out the

forms of life that then existed. Shelley proposes two hypotheses (lines 314–18): either such floods originated from some cataclysm on earth or else they were prodigious tides caused by the gravitational pull of a passing comet.
     In writing this passage, Shelley recalled Keats's *Endymion* 3.123–36, which described the remains on the ocean floor of extinct cultures and animal species.
7. Literally, the earth's gases are bursting out through its volcanoes.
8. Physically, the gravitational force exerted by the earth on the satellite moon.

THE EARTH

Ha! ha! the caverns of my hollow mountains,
My cloven fire-crags, sound-exulting fountains
Laugh with a vast and inextinguishable laughter.
    The Oceans and the Desarts and the Abysses   335
    And the deep air's unmeasured wildernesses
Answer from all their clouds and billows, echoing after.

    They cry aloud as I do—"Sceptred Curse,[9]
    Who all our green and azure Universe
Threatenedst to muffle round with black destruction, sending   340
    A solid cloud to rain hot thunderstones,
    And splinter and knead down my children's bones,
All I bring forth, to one void mass battering and blending,

    "Until each craglike tower and storied column,
    Palace and Obelisk and Temple solemn,   345
My imperial mountains crowned with cloud and snow and fire,
    My sea-like forests, every blade and blossom
    Which finds a grave or cradle in my bosom,
Were stamped by thy strong hate into a lifeless mire,

    "How art thou sunk, withdrawn, cover'd—drunk up   350
    By thirsty nothing, as the brackish[1] cup
Drained by a Desart-troop—a little drop for all;
    And from beneath, around, within, above,
    Filling thy void annihilation, Love
Bursts in like light on caves cloven by the thunderball."   355

THE MOON

    The snow upon my lifeless mountains
    Is loosened into living fountains,
    My solid Oceans flow and sing and shine
      A spirit from my heart bursts forth,
      It clothes with unexpected birth   360
    My cold bare bosom: Oh! it must be thine
        On mine, on mine!

    Gazing on thee I feel, I know,
    Green stalks burst forth, and bright flowers grow
And living shapes upon my bosom move: 365
      Music is in the sea and air,
      Winged clouds soar here and there,
    Dark with the rain new buds are dreaming of:
      'Tis Love, all Love!

THE EARTH

It interpenetrates my granite mass,   370
    Through tangled roots and trodden clay doth pass
Into the utmost leaves and delicatest flowers;

---

9. Jupiter.   1. Slightly salty.

Upon the winds, among the clouds 'tis spread,
  It wakes a life in the forgotten dead,
They breathe a spirit up from their obscurest bowers   375

And like a storm, bursting its cloudy prison
  With thunder and with whirlwind, has arisen
Out of the lampless caves of unimagined being,
  With earthquake shock and swiftness making shiver
  Thought's stagnant chaos, unremoved forever,   380
Till Hate and Fear and Pain, light-vanquished shadows, fleeing,

  Leave Man, who was a many-sided mirror
  Which could distort to many a shape of error
This true fair world of things—a Sea reflecting Love;
  Which over all his kind, as the Sun's Heaven   385
  Gliding o'er Ocean, smooth, serene and even,
Darting from starry depths radiance and light, doth move,

  Leave Man, even as a leprous child is left
  Who follows a sick beast to some warm cleft
Of rocks, through which the might of healing springs is poured: 390
  Then when it wanders home with rosy smile
  Unconscious, and its mother fears awhile
It is a Spirit—then weeps on her child restored.[2]

  Man, oh, not men![3] a chain of linked thought,
  Of love and might to be divided not,   395
Compelling the elements with adamantine stress—
  As the Sun rules,[4] even with a tyrant's gaze,
  The unquiet Republic of the maze
Of Planets, struggling fierce towards Heaven's free wilderness.

  Man, one harmonious Soul of many a soul   400
  Whose nature is its own divine controul
Where all things flow to all, as rivers to the sea;
  Familiar acts are beautiful through love;
  Labour and Pain and Grief in life's green grove
Sport like tame beasts—none knew how gentle they could be!   405

  His Will, with all mean passions, bad delights,
  And selfish cares, its trembling satellites,
A spirit ill to guide, but mighty to obey,
  Is as a tempest-winged ship, whose helm
  Love rules, through waves which dare not overwhelm,   410
Forcing Life's wildest shores to own its sovereign sway.

  All things confess his strength.—Through the cold mass
  Of marble and of colour his dreams pass;

---

2. A reminiscence of the legend of King Bladud of
Britain, who, a banished leper, was following a lost
swine and stumbled on a hot spring (now in the town
of Bath), which cured him.

3. Human society, once splintered by hate, is now
united by love into a single macrocosmic "Man."
4. By gravitational force.

Bright threads, whence mothers weave the robes their children wear;
   Language is a perpetual Orphic song,[5]   415
   Which rules with Dædal harmony a throng
Of thoughts and forms, which else senseless and shapeless were.

   The Lightning is his slave;[6] Heaven's utmost deep
   Gives up her stars, and like a flock of sheep
They pass before his eye, are numbered, and roll on!   420
   The Tempest is his steed,—he strides the air;
   And the abyss shouts from her depth laid bare,
"Heaven, hast thou secrets? Man unveils me; I have none."

THE MOON
   The shadow of white Death has past
   From my path in Heaven at last,   425
   A clinging shroud of solid frost and sleep—
     And through my newly-woven bowers
     Wander happy paramours
   Less mighty, but as mild as those who keep
     Thy vales more deep.   430

THE EARTH
   As the dissolving warmth of Dawn may fold
   A half-unfrozen dewglobe, green and gold
And chrystalline, till it becomes a winged mist
   And wanders up the vault of the blue Day,
   Outlives the noon, and on the Sun's last ray   435
Hangs o'er the Sea—a fleece of fire and amethyst—

THE MOON
   Thou art folded, thou art lying
   In the light which is undying
Of thine own joy and Heaven's smile divine;
   All suns and constellations shower   440
   On thee a light, a life, a power
Which doth array thy sphere—thou pourest thine
   On mine, on mine!

THE EARTH
   I spin beneath my pyramid of night[7]
   Which points into the Heavens, dreaming delight,   445
Murmuring victorious joy in my enchanted sleep;
   As a youth lulled in love-dreams, faintly sighing,
   Under the shadow of his beauty lying
Which round his rest a watch of light and warmth doth keep.

THE MOON
   As in the soft and sweet eclipse   450
   When soul meets soul on lovers' lips,

5. Like the music of Orpheus, which attracted and controlled beasts, rocks, and trees.
6. The Earth describes regenerate man's scientific and technological triumphs.
7. The conical shadow cast by the earth as it intercepts the sun's light.

High hearts are calm and brightest eyes are dull;
  So when thy shadow falls on me[8]
  Then am I mute and still,—by thee
Covered; of thy love, Orb most beautiful,   455
    Full, oh, too full!—

  Thou art speeding round the Sun,
  Brightest World of many a one,
  Green and azure sphere, which shinest
  With a light which is divinest   460
  Among all the lamps of Heaven
  To whom life and light is given;
  I, thy chrystal paramour,
    Borne beside thee by a power
  Like the polar Paradise,   465
  Magnet-like, of lovers' eyes;[9]
  I, a most enamoured maiden
  Whose weak brain is overladen
  With the pleasure of her love—
  Maniac-like around thee move,   470
  Gazing, an insatiate bride,
  On thy form from every side
  Like a Mænad round the cup
  Which Agave lifted up
  In the weird Cadmæan forest.[1]—   475
  Brother, wheresoe'er thou soarest
  I must hurry, whirl and follow
  Through the Heavens wide and hollow,
  Sheltered by the warm embrace
  Of thy soul, from hungry space,   480
  Drinking, from thy sense and sight
  Beauty, majesty, and might,
  As a lover or chameleon
  Grows like what it looks upon,
  As a violet's gentle eye   485
  Gazes on the azure sky
Until its hue grows like what it beholds,
  As a grey and watery mist
  Glows like solid amethyst
Athwart the western mountains it enfolds,   490
  When the sunset sleeps
    Upon its snow—

       THE EARTH
And the weak day weeps[2]
  That it should be so.
O gentle Moon, the voice of thy delight   495

---

8. In the eclipse of the moon, when it enters the earth's shadow.
9. As it circles the earth, the moon spins at a rate that keeps the same side constantly toward it.
1. The Maenads were female participants in the ec-static worship of Dionysus (Bacchus). Agave, daughter of King Cadmus, in a blind frenzy tore her own son Pentheus to bits when he was caught spying on the Dionysiac rites.
2. I.e., with the dew at nightfall.

Falls on me like thy clear and tender light
Soothing the seaman, borne the summer night
    Through isles forever calm;
O gentle Moon, thy chrystal accents pierce
The caverns of my Pride's deep Universe,   500
Charming the tyger Joy, whose tramplings fierce
    Made wounds, which need thy balm.

                        *   *   *

                        DEMOGORGON
Man, who wert once a despot and a slave,—
    A dupe and a deceiver,—a Decay,   550
A Traveller from the cradle to the grave
    Through the dim night of this immortal Day:

                        ALL
Speak—thy strong words may never pass away.

                        DEMOGORGON
This is the Day which down the void Abysm
At the Earth-born's spell[3] yawns for Heaven's Despotism,   555
    And Conquest is dragged Captive through the Deep;[4]
Love from its awful throne of patient power
In the wise heart, from the last giddy hour
    Of dread endurance, from the slippery, steep,
And narrow verge of crag-like Agony, springs   560
And folds over the world its healing wings.

Gentleness, Virtue, Wisdom and Endurance,—
These are the seals of that most firm assurance
    Which bars the pit over Destruction's strength;
And if, with infirm hand, Eternity,   565
Mother of many acts and hours, should free
    The serpent that would clasp her with his length[5]—
These are the spells by which to reassume
An empire o'er the disentangled Doom.[6]

To suffer woes which Hope thinks infinite;   570
To forgive wrongs darker than Death or Night;
    To defy Power which seems Omnipotent;
To love, and bear; to hope, till Hope creates
From its own wreck the thing it contemplates;
    Neither to change nor falter nor repent: 575
This, like thy glory, Titan! is to be
Good, great and joyous, beautiful and free;
This is alone Life, Joy, Empire and Victory.

1818–19   1820

---

3. Prometheus' spell—i.e., his magically effective
words of pity, in place of vengefulness.
4. Ephesians 4.8: "When [Christ] ascended up on
high, he led captivity captive."
5. A final reminder that the serpent incessantly struggles to break loose and start the cycle of humanity's fall
all over again. Felicity must continue to be earned.
6. Shelley's four cardinal virtues (line 562), which seal
the serpent in the pit, also constitute the magic formulas ("spells") by which to remaster him, should he
again break loose. These virtues are expanded on in
the concluding lines (570–75).

The Cloud

I bring fresh showers for the thirsting flowers,
    From the seas and streams;
I bear light shade for the leaves when laid
    In their noon-day dreams.
From my wings are shaken the dews that waken   5
    The sweet buds every one,
When rocked to rest on their mother's[1] breast,
    As she dances about the Sun.
I wield the flail of the lashing hail,
    And whiten the green plains under,   10
And then again I dissolve it in rain,
    And laugh as I pass in thunder.

I sift the snow on the mountains below,
    And their great pines groan aghast;
And all the night 'tis my pillow white,   15
    While I sleep in the arms of the blast.
Sublime on the towers of my skiey bowers,
    Lightning my pilot sits;
In a cavern under is fettered the thunder,
    It struggles and howls at fits;[2]   20
Over Earth and Ocean, with gentle motion,
    This pilot is guiding me,
Lured by the love of the genii that move
    In the depths of the purple sea;[3]
Over the rills, and the crags, and the hills,   25
    Over the lakes and the plains,
Wherever he dream, under mountain or stream,
    The Spirit he loves remains;
And I all the while bask in Heaven's blue smile,[4]
    Whilst he is dissolving in rains.   30

The sanguine Sunrise, with his meteor eyes,[5]
    And his burning plumes outspread,
Leaps on the back of my sailing rack,[6]
    When the morning star shines dead;
As on the jag of a mountain crag,   35
    Which an earthquake rocks and swings,
An eagle alit one moment may sit
    In the light of its golden wings.
And when Sunset may breathe, from the lit Sea beneath,
    Its ardours of rest and of love,   40
And the crimson pall[7] of eve may fall
    From the depth of Heaven above,

1. The earth's.
2. Fitfully.
3. I.e., atmospheric electricity, guiding the cloud (line 18), discharges as lightning when "lured" by the attraction of an opposite charge.
4. The upper part of the cloud remains exposed to the sun.
5. Bright as a burning meteor. The following line refers to the sun's corona.
6. High, broken clouds, driven by the wind.
7. Coverlet of rich material.

With wings folded I rest, on mine aëry nest,
   As still as a brooding dove.

That orbed maiden with white fire laden   45
   Whom mortals call the Moon,
Glides glimmering o'er my fleece-like floor,
   By the midnight breezes strewn;
And wherever the beat of her unseen feet,
   Which only the angels hear,   50
May have broken the woof,[8] of my tent's thin roof,
   The stars peep behind her, and peer;
And I laugh to see them whirl and flee,
   Like a swarm of golden bees,
When I widen the rent in my wind-built tent,   55
   Till the calm rivers, lakes, and seas,
Like strips of the sky fallen through me on high,
   Are each paved with the moon and these.[9]

I bind the Sun's throne with a burning zone[1]
   And the Moon's with a girdle of pearl;   60
The volcanos are dim and the stars reel and swim
   When the whirlwinds my banner unfurl.
From cape to cape, with a bridge-like shape,
   Over a torrent sea,
Sunbeam-proof, I hang like a roof—   65
   The mountains its columns be!
The triumphal arch, through which I march
   With hurricane, fire, and snow,
When the Powers of the Air, are chained to my chair,
   Is the million-coloured Bow;   70
The sphere-fire[2] above its soft colours wove
   While the moist Earth was laughing below.

I am the daughter of Earth and Water,
   And the nursling of the Sky;
I pass through the pores, of the ocean and shores;   75
   I change, but I cannot die—
For after the rain, when with never a stain
   The pavilion of Heaven is bare,
And the winds and sunbeams, with their convex gleams,
   Build up the blue dome of Air[3]—   80
I silently laugh at my own cenotaph,[4]
   And out of the caverns of rain,
Like a child from the womb, like a ghost from the tomb,
   I arise, and unbuild it again.—

1820   1820

---

8. Texture.
9. The stars reflected in the water.
1. Belt or sash.
2. The sunlight.
3. The blue color of the sky; the phenomenon, as
Shelley indicates, results from the way "sunbeams" are

filtered by the earth's atmosphere.
4. The memorial monument of the dead cloud is the
cloudless blue dome of the sky. (The point is that a
cenotaph is a monument that does not contain a
corpse.)

To a Sky-Lark[1]

Hail to thee, blithe Spirit!
  Bird thou never wert—
That from Heaven, or near it,
  Pourest thy full heart
In profuse strains of unpremeditated art.   5

Higher still and higher
  From the earth thou springest
Like a cloud of fire;
  The blue deep thou wingest,
And singing still dost soar, and soaring ever singest.   10

In the golden lightning
  Of the sunken Sun—
O'er which clouds are brightning,
  Thou dost float and run;
Like an unbodied joy whose race is just begun.   15

The pale purple even
  Melts around thy flight,
Like a star of Heaven
  In the broad day-light
Thou art unseen,—but yet I hear thy shrill delight,   20

Keen as are the arrows
  Of that silver sphere,[2]
Whose intense lamp narrows
  In the white dawn clear
Until we hardly see—we feel that it is there.   25

All the earth and air
  With thy voice is loud,
As when Night is bare
  From one lonely cloud
The moon rains out her beams—and Heaven is overflowed.   30

What thou art we know not;
  What is most like thee?
From rainbow clouds there flow not
  Drops so bright to see
As from thy presence showers a rain of melody.   35

Like a Poet hidden
  In the light of thought,
Singing hymns unbidden,
  Till the world is wrought
To sympathy with hopes and fears it heeded not: 40

1. The European skylark is a small bird that sings only in flight, often when it is too high to be visible. This bird, freed from the bonds of earth and soaring beyond the reach of all the physical senses except hearing, is made the emblem of a nonmaterial spirit of pure joy, beyond the possibility of human experience (see lines 15, 31).
2. The morning star.

Like a high-born maiden
  In a palace-tower,
Soothing her love-laden
  Soul in secret hour,
With music sweet as love—which overflows her bower: 45

Like a glow-worm golden
  In a dell of dew,
Scattering unbeholden
  Its aerial hue
Among the flowers and grass which screen it from the view: 50

Like a rose embowered
  In its own green leaves—
By warm winds deflowered—
  Till the scent it gives
Makes faint with too much sweet those heavy-winged thieves:[3]   55

Sound of vernal showers
  On the twinkling grass,
Rain-awakened flowers,
  All that ever was
Joyous, and clear and fresh, thy music doth surpass.   60

Teach us, Sprite[4] or Bird,
  What sweet thoughts are thine;
I have never heard
  Praise of love or wine
That panted forth a flood of rapture so divine: 65

Chorus Hymeneal[5]
  Or triumphal chaunt
Matched with thine would be all
  But an empty vaunt,
A thing wherein we feel there is some hidden want.   70

What objects are the fountains
  Of thy happy strain?
What fields or waves or mountains?
  What shapes of sky or plain?
What love of thine own kind? what ignorance of pain?   75

With thy clear keen joyance
  Languor cannot be—
Shadow of annoyance
  Never came near thee;
Thou lovest—but ne'er knew love's sad satiety.   80

Waking or asleep,
  Thou of death must deem

3. The "warm winds," line 53.   5. Marital (from Hymen, Greek god of marriage).
4. Spirit.

Things more true and deep
   Than we mortals dream,
Or how could thy notes flow in such a chrystal stream?   85

We look before and after,
   And pine for what is not—
Our sincerest laughter
   With some pain is fraught—
Our sweetest songs are those that tell of saddest thought.   90

Yet if we could scorn
   Hate and pride and fear;
If we were things born
   Not to shed a tear,
I know not how thy joy we ever should come near.   95

Better than all measures
   Of delightful sound—
Better than all treasures
   That in books are found—
Thy skill to poet were, thou Scorner of the ground!   100

Teach me half the gladness
   That thy brain must know,
Such harmonious madness
   From my lips would flow
The world should listen then—as I am listening now.   105

1820   1820

To —— [Music, when soft voices die]

Music, when soft voices die,
Vibrates in the memory.—
Odours, when sweet violets sicken,
Live within the sense they quicken.—

Rose leaves, when the rose is dead,   5
Are heaped for the beloved's bed[1]—
And so thy thoughts,[2] when thou art gone,
Love itself shall slumber on.

1821   1824

O World, O Life, O Time[1]

O World, O Life, O Time,
   On whose last steps I climb,
Trembling at that where I had stood before,

---

1. The bed of the dead rose.
2. I.e., my thoughts of thee.

1. For the author's revisions while composing this
poem, see "Poems in Process" (pp. 2583–85).

When will return the glory of your prime?
No more, O never more!   5

Out of the day and night
A joy has taken flight—
Fresh spring and summer [   ] and winter hoar
Move my faint heart with grief, but with delight
No more, O never more!   10

1824

Choruses from *Hellas*[1]

Worlds on worlds[2]

Worlds on worlds are rolling ever
    From creation to decay,
Like the bubbles on a river
    Sparkling, bursting, borne away.
    But *they*[3] are still immortal   5
    Who through Birth's orient[4] portal
And Death's dark chasm hurrying to and fro,
    Clothe their unceasing flight
    In the brief dust and light
Gathered around their chariots as they go;   10
    New shapes they still may weave,
    New Gods, new Laws receive,
Bright or dim are they as the robes they last
    On Death's bare ribs had cast.

    A Power from the unknown God,   15
    A Promethean Conqueror,[5] came;
Like a triumphal path he trod
    The thorns of death and shame.
    A mortal shape to him
    Was like the vapour dim   20
Which the orient planet animates with light;
    Hell, Sin, and Slavery came
    Like bloodhounds mild and tame,
Nor preyed, until their Lord had taken flight;

1. *Hellas,* a closet drama written in the autumn of 1821, was inspired by the Greek war for independence against the Turks. In his preface, Shelley declared that he viewed this revolution as auguring the final overthrow of all tyranny. The choruses below are sung by Greek captive women. The first chorus describes the entrance of Christ into the revolving cycle of history; the second chorus concludes the drama.
2. "The popular notions of Christianity are represented in this chorus as true in their relation to the worship they superseded . . . without considering their merits in a relation more universal. . . . The concluding verses indicate a progressive state of more or less exalted existence. . . . Let it not be supposed that I mean to dogmatise upon a subject [i.e., the problem of evil, and the possibility of its future elimination] upon which all men are equally ignorant. . . . That there is a true solution to the riddle, and that in our present state that solution is unattainable by us, are propositions that may be regarded as equally certain: meanwhile, as it is the province of the poet to attach himself to those ideas which exalt and ennoble humanity, let him be permitted to have conjectured the condition of that futurity towards which we are all impelled by an inextinguishable thirst for immortality" [Shelley's note].
3. The immortal "beings which inhabit the planets and . . . clothe themselves in matter" [Shelley's note].
4. Eastern.
5. Christ, whom Shelley compares with Prometheus, who brought fire and the arts of civilization to humankind.

The moon of Mahomet[6]   25
  Arose, and it shall set,
While blazoned as on Heaven's immortal noon
  The cross leads generations on.[7]

  Swift as the radiant shapes of sleep
    From one whose dreams are Paradise   30
  Fly, when the fond wretch wakes to weep,
    And Day peers forth with her blank eyes;
    So fleet, so faint, so fair,
    The Powers of earth and air
Fled from the folding star[8] of Bethlehem: 35
    Apollo, Pan, and Love,
    And even Olympian Jove
Grew weak, for killing Truth had glared on them;
    Our hills and seas and streams,
    Dispeopled of their dreams,   40
Their waters turned to blood, their dew to tears,
    Wailed for the golden years.

The world's great age[9]

  The world's great age begins anew,
    The golden years return,[1]
  The earth doth like a snake renew
    Her winter weeds[2] outworn;
Heaven smiles, and faiths and empires gleam   5
Like wrecks of a dissolving dream.

  A brighter Hellas rears its mountains
    From waves serener far,
  A new Peneus[3] rolls his fountains
    Against the morning-star,   10
Where fairer Tempe bloom, there sleep
Young Cyclads[4] on a sunnier deep.

  A loftier Argo[5] cleaves the main,
    Fraught with a later prize;
  Another Orpheus[6] sings again,   15

6. The crescent, emblem of Islam, which was founded six centuries after the birth of Christ.
7. The Roman emperor Constantine was converted to Christianity when he saw a bright cross imposed on the sun at noon.
8. The star of evening, the time when sheep are driven into the sheepfold. Shelley goes on to describe the pagan gods of earth and Olympus fleeing before the star of Bethlehem.
9. "Prophecies of wars, and rumours of wars, etc., may safely be made by poet or prophet in any age, but to anticipate however darkly a period of regeneration and happiness is a more hazardous exercise of the faculty which bards possess or fain. It will remind the reader ... of Isaiah and Virgil, whose ardent spirits ... saw the possible and perhaps approaching state of society in which the 'lion shall lie down with the lamb,' and 'omnis feret omnia tellus.' Let these great names be my authority and excuse" [Shelley's note]. The quotations are from Isaiah's millennial prophecy (e.g., chaps. 25, 45), and Virgil's prediction, in Eclogue 4, of a return of the golden age, when "all the earth will produce all things."
1. In Greek myth, the first period of history, when Saturn reigned, was the golden age.
2. Clothes (especially mourning garments) as well as dead vegetation.
3. The river that flows through the beautiful vale of Tempe (line 11).
4. The Cyclades, islands in the Aegean Sea.
5. On which Jason sailed in his quest for the Golden Fleece.
6. The legendary player on the lyre who was torn to pieces by the frenzied Thracian women while he was mourning the death of his wife, Eurydice.

And loves, and weeps, and dies;
A new Ulysses leaves once more
Calypso[7] for his native shore.

O, write no more the tale of Troy,
    If earth Death's scroll must be!   20
Nor mix with Laian[8] rage the joy
    Which dawns upon the free;
Although a subtler Sphinx renew
Riddles of death Thebes never knew.

Another Athens shall arise,   25
    And to remoter time
Bequeath, like sunset to the skies,
    The splendour of its prime,
And leave, if nought so bright may live,
All earth can take or Heaven can give.   30

Saturn and Love their long repose
    Shall burst, more bright and good
Than all who fell, than One who rose,
    Than many unsubdued;[9]
Not gold, not blood their altar dowers   35
But votive tears and symbol flowers.

O cease! must hate and death return?
    Cease! must men kill and die?
Cease! drain not to its dregs the urn
    Of bitter prophecy.   40
The world is weary of the past,
O might it die or rest at last!

1821   1822

Adonais   John Keats died in Rome on February 23, 1821, and was buried there
in the Protestant Cemetery. Shelley had met Keats, had invited him to be his guest
at Pisa, and had gradually come to recognize him as "among the writers of the
highest genius who have adorned our age" (Preface to *Adonais*). The name "Adonais" is derived from Adonis, the handsome youth who had been loved by the
goddess Venus and slain by a wild boar; the function of the beast in this poem is
attributed to the anonymous author of a vituperative review of Keats's *Endymion*
in the *Quarterly Review*, April 1818 (now known to be John Wilson Croker), whom
Shelley mistakenly believed to be responsible for Keats's illness and death.
    Shelley described *Adonais* in a letter as a "highly wrought piece of art." Its
artistry consists in part in the care with which it follows the conventions of the

7. The nymph deserted by Ulysses on his voyage back
from the Trojan War to his native Ithaca.
8. King Laius of Thebes was killed in a quarrel by his
son Oedipus, who did not recognize his father. Shortly
thereafter, Oedipus delivered Thebes from the ravages
of the Sphinx by answering its riddle (lines 23–24).
9. "Saturn and Love were among the deities of a real

or imaginary state of innocence and happiness. 'All'
those 'who fell' [are] the Gods of Greece, Asia, and
Egypt; the 'One who rose' [is] Jesus Christ . . . and the
'many unsubdued' [are] the monstrous objects of the
idolatry of China, India, the Antarctic islands, and the
native tribes of America" [Shelley's note].

pastoral elegy, established more than two thousand years earlier by the Greek Sicilian poets Theocritus, Bion, and Moschus—Shelley had himself translated into English Bion's *Lament for Adonis* and Moschus' *Lament for Bion*. We recognize the centuries-old poetic ritual in many verbal echoes and in such devices as the mournful and accusing invocation to a muse (stanzas 2–4), the sympathetic participation of nature in the grieving (stanzas 14–17), the procession of appropriate mourners (stanzas 30–35), the denunciation of unworthy practitioners of the pastoral or literary art (stanzas 17, 27–29, 36–37), and above all, in the turn from despair at the finality of human death (lines 1, 64, 190: "*He* will awake no more, oh, never more!") to consolation in the sudden and contradictory discovery that the grave is a gate to a higher existence (line 343: "Peace, peace! he is not dead, he doth not sleep").

Adonais

An Elegy on the Death of John Keats, Author of Endymion, Hyperion, etc.

[Thou wert the morning star among the living,
  Ere thy fair light had fled—
Now, having died, thou art as Hesperus, giving
  New splendour to the dead.][1]

1

I weep for Adonais—he is dead!
O, weep for Adonais! though our tears
Thaw not the frost which binds so dear a head!
And thou, sad Hour,[2] selected from all years
To mourn our loss, rouse thy obscure compeers,   5
And teach them thine own sorrow, say: with me
Died Adonais; till the Future dares
Forget the Past, his fate and fame shall be
An echo and a light unto eternity!

2

Where wert thou mighty Mother,[3] when he lay,   10
When thy Son lay, pierced by the shaft which flies
In darkness? where was lorn[4] Urania
When Adonais died? With veiled eyes,
'Mid listening Echoes, in her Paradise
She sate, while one,[5] with soft enamoured breath,   15
Rekindled all the fading melodies,
With which, like flowers that mock the corse[6] beneath,
He had adorned and hid the coming bulk of death.

1. Shelley prefixed to *Adonais* a Greek epigram, attributed to Plato; this is Shelley's own translation of the Greek. The planet Venus appears both as the morning star, Lucifer, and the evening star, Hesperus or Vesper. Shelley makes of this phenomenon a key symbol for Adonais' triumph over death, in stanzas 44–46.
2. Shelley follows the classical mode of personifying the hours, which mark the passage of time and turn of the seasons.
3. Urania. She had originally been the Muse of astronomy, but the name was also an epithet for Venus. Shelley converts Venus Urania, who in Greek myth had been the lover of Adonis, into the mother of Adonais.
4. Abandoned. "In darkness" alludes to the anonymity of the review of *Endymion*.
5. I.e., the echo of Keats's voice in his poems.
6. Corpse.

3

O, weep for Adonais—he is dead!
Wake, melancholy Mother, wake and weep!   20
Yet wherefore? Quench within their burning bed
Thy fiery tears, and let thy loud heart keep
Like his, a mute and uncomplaining sleep;
For he is gone, where all things wise and fair
Descend;—oh, dream not that the amorous Deep[7]   25
Will yet restore him to the vital air;
Death feeds on his mute voice, and laughs at our despair.

4

Most musical of mourners, weep again!
Lament anew, Urania!—He[8] died,
Who was the Sire of an immortal strain,   30
Blind, old, and lonely, when his country's pride,
The priest, the slave, and the liberticide,
Trampled and mocked with many a loathed rite
Of lust and blood; he went, unterrified,
Into the gulph of death; but his clear Sprite[9]   35
Yet reigns o'er earth; the third among the sons of light.[1]

5

Most musical of mourners, weep anew!
Not all to that bright station dared to climb;
And happier they their happiness who knew,
Whose tapers yet burn through that night of time   40
In which suns perished; others more sublime,
Struck by the envious wrath of man or God,
Have sunk, extinct in their refulgent prime;
And some yet live, treading the thorny road,
Which leads, through toil and hate, to Fame's serene abode.   45

6

But now, thy youngest, dearest one, has perished—
The nursling of thy widowhood, who grew,
Like a pale flower by some sad maiden cherished,
And fed with true love tears, instead of dew;[2]
Most musical of mourners, weep anew!   50
Thy extreme[3] hope, the loveliest and the last,
The bloom, whose petals nipt before they blew[4]
Died on the promise of the fruit, is waste;
The broken lily lies—the storm is overpast.

7

To that high Capital,[5] where kingly Death   55
Keeps his pale court in beauty and decay,
He came; and bought, with price of purest breath,
A grave among the eternal.—Come away!

---

7. Abyss.
8. Milton, regarded as precursor of the great poetic tradition in which Keats wrote. He had adopted Urania as the muse of *Paradise Lost*. Lines 31–35 describe Milton's life during the restoration of the Stuart monarchy.
9. Spirit.
1. The three are Milton and his great predecessors in epic poetry, Homer and Dante. The stanza following describes the lot of other poets, up to Shelley's own time.
2. An allusion to an incident in Keats's *Isabella*.
3. Last, as well as highest.
4. Bloomed.
5. Rome.

Haste, while the vault of blue Italian day
Is yet his fitting charnel-roof! while still   60
He lies, as if in dewy sleep he lay;
Awake him not! surely he takes his fill
Of deep and liquid rest, forgetful of all ill.

                            8
He will awake no more, oh, never more!—
Within the twilight chamber spreads apace,   65
The shadow of white Death, and at the door
Invisible Corruption waits to trace
His extreme way to her dim dwelling-place;
The eternal Hunger sits, but pity and awe
Soothe her pale rage, nor dares she to deface   70
So fair a prey, till darkness, and the law
Of change, shall 'oer his sleep the mortal curtain draw.

                            9
O, weep for Adonais!—The quick[6] Dreams,
The passion-winged Ministers of thought,
Who were his flocks,[7] whom near the living streams   75
Of his young spirit he fed, and whom he taught
The love which was its music, wander not,—
Wander no more, from kindling brain to brain,
But droop there, whence they sprung; and mourn their lot
Round the cold heart, where, after their sweet pain,   80
They ne'er will gather strength, or find a home again.

                            10
And one[8] with trembling hands clasps his cold head,
And fans him with her moonlight wings, and cries;
"Our love, our hope, our sorrow, is not dead;
See, on the silken fringe of his faint eyes,   85
Like dew upon a sleeping flower, there lies
A tear some Dream has loosened from his brain."
Lost Angel of a ruined Paradise!
She knew not 'twas her own; as with no stain
She faded, like a cloud which had outwept its rain.   90

                            11
One from a lucid[9] urn of starry dew
Washed his light limbs as if embalming them;
Another clipt her profuse locks, and threw
The wreath upon him, like an anadem,[1]
Which frozen tears instead of pearls begem;   95
Another in her wilful grief would break
Her bow and winged reeds, as if to stem
A greater loss with one which was more weak;
And dull the barbed fire against his frozen cheek.

                            12
Another Splendour on his mouth alit,   100
That mouth, whence it was wont to draw the breath

---

6. Living.
7. The products of Keats's imagination, figuratively
represented (according to pastoral convention) as his
sheep.

8. One of the Dreams (line 73).
9. Luminous.
1. A rich garland.

Which gave it strength to pierce the guarded wit,[2]
And pass into the panting heart beneath
With lightning and with music: the damp death
Quenched its caress upon his icy lips;   105
And, as a dying meteor stains a wreath
Of moonlight vapour, which the cold night clips,[3]
It flushed through his pale limbs, and past to its eclipse.

13

And others came . . . Desires and Adorations,
Winged Persuasions and veiled Destinies,   110
Splendours, and Glooms, and glimmering Incarnations
Of hopes and fears, and twilight Phantasies;
And Sorrow, with her family of Sighs,
And Pleasure, blind with tears, led by the gleam
Of her own dying smile instead of eyes,   115
Came in slow pomp;—the moving pomp might seem
Like pageantry of mist on an autumnal stream.

14

All he had loved, and moulded into thought,
From shape, and hue, and odour, and sweet sound,
Lamented Adonais. Morning sought   120
Her eastern watchtower, and her hair unbound,
Wet with the tears which should adorn the ground,
Dimmed the aerial eyes that kindle day;
Afar the melancholy thunder moaned,
Pale Ocean in unquiet slumber lay,   125
And the wild winds flew round, sobbing in their dismay.

15

Lost Echo sits amid the voiceless mountains,
And feeds her grief with his remembered lay,
And will no more reply to winds or fountains,
Or amorous birds perched on the young green spray,   130
Or herdsman's horn, or bell at closing day;
Since she can mimic not his lips, more dear
Than those for whose disdain she pined away
Into a shadow of all sounds:[4]—a drear
Murmur, between their songs, is all the woodmen hear.   135

16

Grief made the young Spring wild, and she threw down
Her kindling buds, as if she Autumn were,
Or they dead leaves; since her delight is flown
For whom should she have waked the sullen year?
To Phoebus was not Hyacinth so dear[5]   140
Nor to himself Narcissus, as to both
Thou Adonais: wan they stand and sere[6]
Amid the faint companions of their youth,
With dew all turned to tears; odour, to sighing ruth.[7]

2. The cautious intellect (of the listener).
3. Embraces.
4. Because of her unrequited love for Narcissus, who was enamored of his own reflection (line 141), the nymph Echo pined away until she was only a reflected sound.

5. Young Hyacinthus was loved by Phoebus Apollo, who accidentally killed him in a game of quoits. Apollo made the hyacinth flower spring from his blood.
6. Dried, withered.
7. Pity.

17

Thy spirit's sister, the lorn nightingale[8]   145
Mourns not her mate with such melodious pain;
Not so the eagle, who like thee could scale
Heaven, and could nourish in the sun's domain
Her mighty youth with morning,[9] doth complain,
Soaring and screaming round her empty nest,   150
As Albion[1] wails for thee: the curse of Cain
Light on his[2] head who pierced thy innocent breast,
And scared the angel soul that was its earthly guest!

18

Ah woe is me! Winter is come and gone,
But grief returns with the revolving year;   155
The airs and streams renew their joyous tone;
The ants, the bees, the swallows reappear;
Fresh leaves and flowers deck the dead Seasons' bier;
The amorous birds now pair in every brake,[3]
And build their mossy homes in field and brere;[4]   160
And the green lizard, and the golden snake,
Like unimprisoned flames, out of their trance awake.

19

Through wood and stream and field and hill and Ocean
A quickening life from the Earth's heart has burst
As it has ever done, with change and motion,   165
From the great morning of the world when first
God dawned on Chaos; in its stream immersed
The lamps of Heaven flash with a softer light;
All baser things pant with life's sacred thirst;
Diffuse themselves; and spend in love's delight,   170
The beauty and the joy of their renewed might.

20

The leprous corpse touched by this spirit tender
Exhales itself in flowers of gentle breath;
Like incarnations of the stars, when splendour
Is changed to fragrance, they illumine death   175
And mock the merry worm that wakes beneath;
Nought we know, dies. Shall that alone which knows
Be as a sword consumed before the sheath
By sightless[5] lightning?—th' intense atom glows
A moment, then is quenched in a most cold repose.   180

21

Alas! that all we loved of him should be,
But for our grief, as if it had not been,
And grief itself be mortal! Woe is me!
Whence are we, and why are we? of what scene
The actors or spectators? Great and mean   185
Meet massed in death, who lends what life must borrow.
As long as skies are blue, and fields are green,

8. To whom Keats had written *Ode to a Nightingale*.
9. In the legend, the aged eagle, to renew his youth, flies toward the sun until his old plumage is burned off and the film cleared from his eyes.
1. England.
2. The reviewer of *Endymion*.
3. Thicket.
4. Briar.
5. Invisible. The "sword" is the mind that knows; the "sheath" is its vehicle, the material body.

Evening must usher night, night urge the morrow,
Month follow month with woe, and year wake year to sorrow.

22

He will awake no more, oh, never more!   190
"Wake thou," cried Misery, "childless Mother, rise
Out of thy sleep, and slake,[6] in thy heart's core,
A wound more fierce than his with tears and sighs."
And all the Dreams that watched Urania's eyes,
And all the Echoes whom their sister's song[7]   195
Had held in holy silence, cried: "Arise!"
Swift as a Thought by the snake Memory stung,
From her ambrosial rest the fading Splendour[8] sprung.

23

She rose like an autumnal Night, that springs
Out of the East, and follows wild and drear   200
The golden Day, which, on eternal wings,
Even as a ghost abandoning a bier,
Had left the Earth a corpse. Sorrow and fear
So struck, so roused, so rapt Urania;
So saddened round her like an atmosphere   205
Of stormy mist; so swept her on her way
Even to the mournful place where Adonais lay.

24

Out of her secret Paradise she sped,
Through camps and cities rough with stone, and steel,
And human hearts, which to her aery tread   210
Yielding not, wounded the invisible
Palms of her tender feet where'er they fell:
And barbed tongues, and thoughts more sharp than they
Rent the soft Form they never could repel,
Whose sacred blood, like the young tears of May,   215
Paved with eternal flowers that undeserving way.

25

In the death chamber for a moment Death
Shamed by the presence of that living Might
Blushed to annihilation, and the breath
Revisited those lips, and life's pale light   220
Flashed through those limbs, so late her dear delight.
"Leave me not wild and drear and comfortless,
As silent lightning leaves the starless night!
Leave me not!" cried Urania: her distress
Roused Death: Death rose and smiled, and met her vain caress.   225

26

"Stay yet awhile! speak to me once again;
Kiss me, so long but as a kiss may live;
And in my heartless[9] breast and burning brain
That word, that kiss shall all thoughts else survive
With food of saddest memory kept alive,   230
Now thou art dead, as if it were a part

---

6. Assuage.   8. Urania.
7. I.e., the Echo in line 127.   9. Because her heart had been given to Adonais.

Of thee, my Adonais! I would give
  All that I am to be as thou now art!
But I am chained to Time, and cannot thence depart!

27

  "Oh gentle child, beautiful as thou wert,   235
  Why didst thou leave the trodden paths of men
Too soon, and with weak hands though mighty heart
  Dare the unpastured dragon in his den?[1]
  Defenceless as thou wert, oh where was then
Wisdom the mirrored shield, or scorn the spear?[2]   240
  Or hadst thou waited the full cycle, when
  Thy spirit should have filled its crescent sphere,[3]
The monsters of life's waste had fled from thee like deer.

28

  "The herded wolves, bold only to pursue;
  The obscene ravens, clamorous o'er the dead;   245
The vultures to the conqueror's banner true
  Who feed where Desolation first has fed,
  And whose wings rain contagion;—how they fled,
When like Apollo, from his golden bow,
  The Pythian of the age[4] one arrow sped   250
  And smiled!—The spoilers tempt no second blow,
They fawn on the proud feet that spurn them lying low.

29

  "The sun comes forth, and many reptiles spawn;
  He sets, and each ephemeral insect then
Is gathered into death without a dawn,   255
  And the immortal stars awake again;
  So is it in the world of living men:
A godlike mind soars forth, in its delight
  Making earth bare and veiling heaven,[5] and when
  It sinks, the swarms that dimmed or shared its light   260
Leave to its kindred lamps[6] the spirit's awful night."

30

  Thus ceased she: and the mountain shepherds came,
  Their garlands sere, their magic mantles rent;
The Pilgrim of Eternity,[7] whose fame
  Over his living head like Heaven is bent,   265
  An early but enduring monument,
Came, veiling all the lightnings of his song
  In sorrow; from her wilds Ierne sent
  The sweetest lyrist of her saddest wrong,[8]
And love taught grief to fall like music from his tongue.   270

1. I.e., the hostile reviewers.
2. The allusion is to Perseus, who had cut off Medusa's head while avoiding the direct sight of her (which would have turned him to stone) by looking only at her reflection in his shield.
3. I.e., when thy spirit, like the full moon, should have reached its maturity.
4. Byron, who had directed against critics of the age his satiric poem English Bards and Scotch Reviewers (1809). The allusion is to Apollo, called "the Pythian"
because he had slain the dragon Python.
5. As the sun reveals the earth but veils the other stars.
6. The other stars (i.e., creative minds), of lesser brilliance than the sun.
7. Byron, who had referred to his Childe Harold as one of the "wanderers o'er eternity" (3.669).
8. Thomas Moore (1779–1852), from Ireland ("Ierne"), who had written poems about the oppression of his native land.

31

Midst others of less note, came one frail Form,[9]
A phantom among men; companionless
As the last cloud of an expiring storm
Whose thunder is its knell; he, as I guess,
Had gazed on Nature's naked loveliness,   275
Actæon-like, and now he fled astray
With feeble steps o'er the world's wilderness,
And his own thoughts, along that rugged way,
Pursued, like raging hounds, their father and their prey.[1]

32

A pardlike[2] Spirit beautiful and swift—
A Love in desolation masked;—a Power   280
Girt round with weakness;—it can scarce uplift
The weight of the superincumbent hour;[3]
It is a dying lamp, a falling shower,
A breaking billow;—even whilst we speak   285
Is it not broken? On the withering flower
The killing sun smiles brightly: on a cheek
The life can burn in blood, even while the heart may break.

33

His head was bound with pansies overblown,
And faded violets, white, and pied, and blue;   290
And a light spear topped with a cypress cone,
Round whose rude shaft dark ivy tresses grew[4]
Yet dripping with the forest's noonday dew,
Vibrated, as the ever-beating heart
Shook the weak hand that grasped it; of that crew   295
He came the last, neglected and apart;
A herd-abandoned deer struck by the hunter's dart.

34

All stood aloof, and at his partial[5] moan
Smiled through their tears; well knew that gentle band
Who in another's fate now wept his own;   300
As in the accents of an unknown land,
He sung new sorrow; sad Urania scanned
The Stranger's mien, and murmured: "who art thou?"
He answered not, but with a sudden hand
Made bare his branded and ensanguined brow,   305
Which was like Cain's or Christ's[6]—Oh! that it should be so!

35

What softer voice is hushed over the dead?
Athwart what brow is that dark mantle thrown?
What form leans sadly o'er the white death-bed,

---

9. Shelley himself, represented in one of his aspects—like the Poet in *Alastor*, rather than the author of *Prometheus Unbound*.
1. Actaeon, while hunting, came upon the naked Diana bathing and, as a punishment, was turned into a stag and torn to pieces by his own hounds.
2. Leopardlike.
3. The heavy, overhanging hour of Keats's death.

4. Like the thyrsus, the leaf-entwined and cone-topped staff carried by Dionysus. The pansies are emblems of sorrowful thought. The cypress is an emblem of mourning.
5. Sympathetic.
6. His bloody ("ensanguined") brow bore a mark like that with which God had branded Cain for murdering Abel—or like that left by Christ's crown of thorns.

In mockery of monumental stone,[7]   310
The heavy heart heaving without a moan?
If it be He,[8] who, gentlest of the wise,
Taught, soothed, loved, honoured the departed one;
Let me not vex, with inharmonious sighs
The silence of that heart's accepted sacrifice.   315

36

Our Adonais has drunk poison—oh!
What deaf and viperous murderer could crown
Life's early cup with such a draught of woe?
The nameless worm[9] would now itself disown:
It felt, yet could escape the magic tone   320
Whose prelude held all envy, hate, and wrong,
But what was howling in one breast alone,
Silent with expectation of the song,[1]
Whose master's hand is cold, whose silver lyre unstrung.

37

Live thou, whose infamy is not thy fame!   325
Live! fear no heavier chastisement from me,
Thou noteless blot on a remembered name!
But be thyself, and know thyself to be!
And ever at thy season be thou free
To spill the venom when thy fangs o'erflow: 330
Remorse and Self-contempt shall cling to thee;
Hot Shame shall burn upon thy secret brow,
And like a beaten hound tremble thou shalt—as now.

38

Nor let us weep that our delight is fled
Far from these carrion kites[2] that scream below;   335
He wakes or sleeps with the enduring dead;
Thou canst not soar where he is sitting now.—
Dust to the dust! but the pure spirit shall flow
Back to the burning fountain whence it came,
A portion of the Eternal,[3] which must glow   340
Through time and change, unquenchably the same,
Whilst thy cold embers choke the sordid hearth of shame.

39

Peace, peace! he is not dead, he doth not sleep—
He hath awakened from the dream of life—
'Tis we, who lost in stormy visions, keep   345
With phantoms an unprofitable strife,
And in mad trance, strike with our spirit's knife
Invulnerable nothings.—We decay
Like corpses in a charnel; fear and grief
Convulse us and consume us day by day,   350
And cold hopes swarm like worms within our living clay.

---

7. In imitation of a memorial statue.
8. Leigh Hunt, close friend of both Keats and Shelley.
9. Snake; the anonymous reviewer.
1. The promise of later greatness in Keats's early poems "held . . . silent" the expression of all malignant feelings except the reviewer's.
2. Large birds of prey; a species of hawk.

3. Shelley adopts for this poem the neoplatonic view that all life and all forms emanate from the Absolute, the eternal One. The Absolute is imaged as both a radiant light source and an overflowing fountain, which circulates continuously through the dross of matter (stanza 43) and back to its source.

40

He has outsoared the shadow of our night;[4]
Envy and calumny and hate and pain,
And that unrest which men miscall delight,
Can touch him not and torture not again;   355
From the contagion of the world's slow stain
He is secure, and now can never mourn
A heart grown cold, a head grown grey in vain;
Nor, when the spirit's self has ceased to burn,
With sparkless ashes load an unlamented urn.   360

41

He lives, he wakes—'tis Death is dead, not he;
Mourn not for Adonais.—Thou young Dawn
Turn all thy dew to splendour, for from thee
The spirit thou lamentest is not gone;
Ye caverns and ye forests, cease to moan!   365
Cease ye faint flowers and fountains, and thou Air
Which like a mourning veil thy scarf hadst thrown
O'er the abandoned Earth, now leave it bare
Even to the joyous stars which smile on its despair![5]

42

He is made one with Nature: there is heard   370
His voice in all her music, from the moan
Of thunder, to the song of night's sweet bird;[6]
He is a presence to be felt and known
In darkness and in light, from herb and stone,
Spreading itself where'er that Power may move   375
Which has withdrawn his being to its own;
Which wields the world with never wearied love,
Sustains it from beneath, and kindles it above.

43

He is a portion of the loveliness
Which once he made more lovely: he doth bear   380
His part, while the one Spirit's plastic[7] stress
Sweeps through the dull dense world, compelling there,
All new successions to the forms they wear;
Torturing th' unwilling dross that checks its flight
To its own likeness, as each mass may bear;[8]   385
And bursting in its beauty and its might
From trees and beasts and men into the Heaven's light.

44

The splendours of the firmament of time
May be eclipsed, but are extinguished not;
Like stars to their appointed height they climb   390
And death is a low mist which cannot blot
The brightness it may veil.[9] When lofty thought

4. He has soared beyond the shadow cast by the earth as it intercepts the sun's light.
5. Shelley's science is, as usual, accurate: it is the envelope of air around the earth that, by diffusing and reflecting sunlight, veils the stars.
6. The nightingale, in allusion to Keats's *Ode to a Nightingale*.
7. Formative, shaping.
8. I.e., to the degree that a particular substance will permit.
9. The radiance of stars (i.e., of poets) persists, even when they are temporarily "eclipsed" by another heavenly body, or obscured by the veil of the earth's atmosphere.

Lifts a young heart above its mortal lair,
And love and life contend in it, for what
Shall be its earthly doom, the dead live there[1]   395
And move like winds of light on dark and stormy air.

45

The inheritors of unfulfilled renown[2]
Rose from their thrones, built beyond mortal thought,
Far in the Unapparent. Chatterton
Rose pale, his solemn agony had not   400
Yet faded from him; Sidney, as he fought
And as he fell and as he lived and loved
Sublimely mild, a Spirit without spot,
Arose; and Lucan, by his death approved:[3]
Oblivion as they rose shrank like a thing reproved.   405

46

And many more, whose names on Earth are dark
But whose transmitted effluence cannot die
So long as fire outlives the parent spark,
Rose, robed in dazzling immortality.
"Thou art become as one of us," they cry,   410
"It was for thee yon kingless sphere has long
Swung blind in unascended majesty,
Silent alone amid an Heaven of song.
Assume thy winged throne, thou Vesper of our throng!"[4]

47

Who mourns for Adonais? oh come forth   415
Fond wretch! and know thyself and him aright.
Clasp with thy panting soul the pendulous[5] Earth;
As from a centre, dart thy spirit's light
Beyond all worlds, until its spacious might
Satiate the void circumference: then shrink   420
Even to a point within our day and night;[6]
And keep thy heart light lest it make thee sink
When hope has kindled hope, and lured thee to the brink.

48

Or go to Rome, which is the sepulchre
O, not of him, but of our joy: 'tis nought   425
That ages, empires, and religions there
Lie buried in the ravage they have wrought;
For such as he can lend,—they[7] borrow not
Glory from those who made the world their prey;
And he is gathered to the kings of thought   430

1. I.e., in the thought of the "young heart." "Doom": destiny.
2. Poets who (like Keats) died young, before achieving their full measure of fame: Thomas Chatterton (1752–1770) committed suicide at seventeen, Sir Philip Sidney (1554–1586) died in battle at thirty-two, and the Roman poet Lucan (A.D. 39–65) killed himself at twenty-six to escape a sentence of death for having plotted against the tyrant Nero.
3. Justified, proved worthy.
4. Adonais assumes his place in the sphere of Vesper, the evening star, hitherto unoccupied ("kingless"), hence also "silent" amid the music of the other spheres.
5. Suspended, floating in space.
6. The poet bids the wretch who is foolish ("fond") enough to mourn Adonais to stretch his imagination so as to reach the poet's own cosmic viewpoint, and then allow it to contract ("shrink") back to its ordinary vantage point on earth—where, unlike Adonais in his heavenly place, we have an alternation of day and night.
7. Poets like Keats, who can bestow ("lend") glory, as opposed to the Roman conquerors, who borrowed glory from those they conquered.

Who waged contention with their time's decay,
And of the past are all that cannot pass away.

                    49

Go thou to Rome,—at once the Paradise,
The grave, the city, and the wilderness;
And where its wrecks like shattered mountains rise,   435
And flowering weeds, and fragrant copses[8] dress
The bones of Desolation's nakedness
Pass, till the Spirit of the spot shall lead
Thy footsteps to a slope of green access[9]
Where, like an infant's smile, over the dead,   440
A light of laughing flowers along the grass is spread.

                    50

And grey walls moulder round,[1] on which dull Time
Feeds, like slow fire upon a hoary brand;[2]
And one keen pyramid with wedge sublime,[3]

Pavilioning the dust of him who planned   445
This refuge for his memory, doth stand
Like flame transformed to marble; and beneath,
A field is spread, on which a newer band
Have pitched in Heaven's smile their camp of death
Welcoming him we lose with scarce extinguished breath.   450

                    51

Here pause: these graves are all too young as yet
To have outgrown the sorrow which consigned
Its charge to each; and if the seal is set,
Here, on one fountain of a mourning mind,[4]
Break it not thou! too surely shalt thou find   455
Thine own well full, if thou returnest home,
Of tears and gall. From the world's bitter wind
Seek shelter in the shadow of the tomb.
What Adonais is, why fear we to become?

                    52

The One remains, the many change and pass;   460
Heaven's light forever shines, Earth's shadows fly;
Life, like a dome of many-coloured glass,
Stains the white radiance of Eternity,
Until Death tramples it to fragments.[5]—Die,
If thou wouldst be with that which thou dost seek!   465
Follow where all is fled!—Rome's azure sky,
Flowers, ruins, statues, music, words, are weak
The glory they transfuse with fitting truth to speak.

---

8. Undergrowth. In Shelley's time the ruins of ancient Rome were overgrown with weeds and shrubbery.
9. The Protestant Cemetery, Keats's burial place. The next line is a glancing allusion to Shelley's three-year-old son, William, also buried there.
1. The wall of ancient Rome formed one boundary of the cemetery.
2. A burning log.
3. The tomb of Caius Cestius, a Roman tribune, just outside the cemetery.
4. Shelley's mourning for his son.
5. Earthly life colors ("stains") the pure white light of the One, which is the source of all light (see lines 339–40, n. 3). The azure sky, flowers, etc., of lines 466–68 exemplify earthly colors that, however beautiful, fall far short of the "glory" of the pure Light that they transmit but also refract ("transfuse").

53

Why linger, why turn back, why shrink, my Heart?
Thy hopes are gone before; from all things here   470
They have departed; thou shouldst now depart!
A light is past from the revolving year,
And man, and woman; and what still is dear
Attracts to crush, repels to make thee wither.
The soft sky smiles,—the low wind whispers near: 475
'Tis Adonais calls! oh, hasten thither,
No more let Life divide what Death can join together.

54

That Light whose smile kindles the Universe,
That Beauty in which all things work and move,
That Benediction which the eclipsing Curse   480
Of birth can quench not, that sustaining Love
Which through the web of being blindly wove
By man and beast and earth and air and sea,
Burns bright or dim, as each are mirrors of[6]
The fire for which all thirst;[7] now beams on me,   485
Consuming the last clouds of cold mortality.

55

The breath whose might I have invoked in song[8]
Descends on me; my spirit's bark is driven,
Far from the shore, far from the trembling throng
Whose sails were never to the tempest given;   490
The massy earth and sphered skies are riven!
I am borne darkly, fearfully, afar;
Whilst burning through the inmost veil of Heaven,
The soul of Adonais, like a star,
Beacons from the abode where the Eternal are.   495
1821   1821

A Dirge

Rough wind, that moanest loud
    Grief too sad for song;
Wild wind, when sullen cloud
    Knells all the night long;
Sad storm, whose tears are vain,   5
Bare woods, whose branches strain,
Deep caves and dreary main,—
    Wail, for the world's wrong!

1821   1824

---

6. I.e., according to the degree that each reflects.
7. The "thirst" of the human spirit is to return to the fountain and fire (the "burning fountain," line 339) which is its source.

8. Two years earlier Shelley had "invoked" (prayed to, and also asked for) "the breath of Autumn's being" in his *Ode to the West Wind*.

When the lamp is shattered

When the lamp is shattered
The light in the dust lies dead—
    When the cloud is scattered
The rainbow's glory is shed—
    When the lute is broken   5
Sweet tones are remembered not—
    When the lips have spoken
Loved accents are soon forgot.

    As music and splendour
Survive not the lamp and the lute,   10
    The heart's echoes render
No song when the spirit is mute—
    No song—but sad dirges
Like the wind through a ruined cell
    Or the mournful surges   15
That ring the dead seaman's knell.

    When hearts have once mingled
Love first leaves the well-built nest[1]—
    The weak one is singled
To endure what it once possest.   20
    O Love! who bewailest
The frailty of all things here,
    Why choose you the frailest[2]
For your cradle, your home and your bier?

    Its passions will rock thee   25
As the storms rock the ravens on high—
    Bright Reason will mock thee
Like the Sun from a wintry sky—
    From thy nest every rafter
Will rot, and thine eagle home[3]   30
    Leave thee naked to laughter
When leaves fall and cold winds come.

1822   1824

To Jane. The Invitation[1]

Best and brightest, come away—
Fairer far than this fair day
Which like thee to those in sorrow
Comes to bid a sweet good-morrow
To the rough year just awake   5

---

1. Love abandons first the sturdier heart.
2. I.e., the human heart.
3. Like the lofty, and therefore exposed, nest of the
eagle.
1. This invitation to an outdoor excursion exemplifies

Shelley's grace and urbanity, writing in the ancient tradition of the verse letter. "Jane" is Jane Williams, the
common-law wife of Edward Williams, Shelley's close
friend.

In its cradle on the brake.[2] —
The brightest hour of unborn spring
Through the winter wandering
Found, it seems, this halcyon[3] morn
To hoar February born;   10
Bending from Heaven in azure mirth
It kissed the forehead of the earth
And smiled upon the silent sea,
And bade the frozen streams be free
And waked to music all their fountains,   15
And breathed upon the frozen mountains,
And like a prophetess of May
Strewed flowers upon the barren way,
Making the wintry world appear
Like one on whom thou smilest, dear.   20

Away, away from men and towns
To the wild wood and the downs,
To the silent wilderness
Where the soul need not repress
Its music lest it should not find   25
An echo in another's mind,
While the touch of Nature's art
Harmonizes heart to heart. —
I leave this notice on my door
For each accustomed visitor —   30
"I am gone into the fields
To take what this sweet hour yields.
Reflexion, you may come tomorrow,
Sit by the fireside with Sorrow —
You, with the unpaid bill, Despair,   35
You, tiresome verse-reciter Care,
I will pay you in the grave,
Death will listen to your stave[4] —
Expectation too, be off!
To-day is for itself enough —   40
Hope, in pity mock not woe
With smiles, nor follow where I go;
Long having lived on thy sweet food,
At length I find one moment's good
After long pain — with all your love   45
This you never told me of."

Radiant Sister of the day,
Awake, arise and come away
To the wild woods and the plains
And the pools where winter-rains   50
Image all their roof of leaves,
Where the pine its garland weaves
Of sapless green and ivy dun

2. Thicket.   4. Stanza, set of verses.
3. Calm and peaceful.

Round stems that never kiss the Sun—
Where the lawns and pastures be 55
And the sandhills of the sea—
Where the melting hoar-frost wets
The daisy-star that never sets,
And wind-flowers, and violets
Which yet join not scent to hue 60
Crown the pale year weak and new,
When the night is left behind
In the deep east dun and blind
And the blue noon is over us,
And the multitudinous 65
Billows murmur at our feet
Where the earth and ocean meet,
And all things seem only one
In the universal Sun.—

1822   1824

A Defence of Poetry

In 1820 Shelley's good friend Thomas Love Peacock published an ironic essay, *The Four Ages of Poetry*, implicitly directed against the towering claims for poetry and the poetic imagination by his Romantic contemporaries. Peacock adopted the premise of Wordsworth and some other Romantic critics—that poetry in its origin was a primitive use of language and mind—but from this premise he proceeded to draw the conclusion that poetry has become a useless anachronism in this age of science and technology. Peacock was himself a poet as well as the best contemporary prose satirist, and Shelley saw the joke; but he also recognized that the view that Peacock, as a satirist, had only half-humorously assumed was very close to that actually held in his day by Utilitarian philosophers and material-minded laypersons who either attacked or contemptuously ignored the imaginative faculty and its achievements. He therefore undertook, as he good-humoredly wrote to Peacock, "to break a lance with you . . . in honor of my mistress Urania," even though he was only "the knight of the shield of shadow and the lance of gossamere." The result was A *Defence of Poetry*, planned to consist of three parts. The last two parts were never written, and even the existing section, written in 1821, remained unpublished until 1840, eighteen years after Shelley's death.

For many decades Shelley's *Defence* was regarded as one of the classic essays in literary criticism. Its reputation, however, diminished in the era of the New Criticism, during the middle decades of the twentieth century, when the chief interest was in applied commentary and the kind of critical theory that provides useful distinctions for the close analysis of particular literary texts. But Shelley's main enterprise, although different, is no less valid and a rarer achievement in the history of critical writings. His emphasis is on the universal and permanent forms, qualities, and values that all great poems, as products of imagination, possess in common—on those aspects, as he puts it, in which time, person, and place "are convertible with respect to the highest poetry without injuring it as poetry." Shelley's position thus parallels that of William Blake, and has analogues to that of archetypal criticism in our own time. More than this, Shelley extends the term *poet* to comprehend all the creative minds that break out of the limitations of their age and place to approximate what he regards as enduring and general forms of value—including not only writers in verse and prose but artists, legislators, and prophets as well as the founders of a new organization of society, morality, or religion.

The range of the *Defence* gives it importance as a ringing claim for the validity and indispensability of the visionary and creative imagination in all the great human concerns. No later writer has exceeded the cogency of Shelley's attack on our acquisitive society and its narrowly material concept of utility and progress. This bias has permitted the human race to make enormous progress in science and in material well-being without a proportionate development of our "poetical faculty," the moral imagination—with the result, as Shelley says, that "man, having enslaved the elements, remains himself a slave."

From A Defence of Poetry

or Remarks Suggested by an Essay Entitled "The Four Ages of Poetry"

According to one mode of regarding those two classes of mental action, which are called reason and imagination, the former may be considered as mind contemplating the relations borne by one thought to another, however produced; and the latter, as mind acting upon those thoughts so as to colour them with its own light, and composing from them, as from elements, other thoughts, each containing within itself the principle of its own integrity. The one[1] is the *to poiein*,[2] or the principle of synthesis, and has for its objects those forms which are common to universal nature and existence itself; the other is the *to logizein*,[3] or principle of analysis, and its action regards the relations of things, simply as relations; considering thoughts, not in their integral unity, but as the algebraical representations which conduct to certain general results. Reason is the enumeration of quantities already known; imagination is the perception of the value of those quantities, both separately and as a whole. Reason respects the differences, and imagination the similitudes of things. Reason is to Imagination as the instrument to the agent, as the body to the spirit, as the shadow to the substance.

Poetry, in a general sense, may be defined to be "the expression of the Imagination": and poetry is connate with the origin of man. Man is an instrument over which a series of external and internal impressions are driven, like the alternations of an ever-changing wind over an Æolian lyre,[4] which move it by their motion to ever-changing melody. But there is a principle within the human being, and perhaps within all sentient beings, which acts otherwise than in the lyre, and produces not melody, alone, but harmony, by an internal adjustment of the sounds or motions thus excited to the impressions which excite them. It is as if the lyre could accommodate its chords to the motions of that which strikes them, in a determined proportion of sound; even as the musician can accommodate his voice to the sound of the lyre. A child at play by itself will express its delight by its voice and motions; and every inflexion of tone and every gesture will bear exact relation to a corresponding antitype in

1. The imagination; "the other" (later in the sentence) is the reason.
2. Making. The Greek word from which the English term *poet* derives means "maker," and "maker" was often used as equivalent to "poet" by Renaissance critics

such as Sir Philip Sidney in his *Defence of Poesy*, which Shelley had carefully studied.
3. Calculating, reasoning.
4. A wind harp (see Coleridge, *The Eolian Harp*, pp. 1484–85).

the pleasurable impressions which awakened it; it will be the reflected image of that impression; and as the lyre trembles and sounds after the wind has died away, so the child seeks, by prolonging in its voice and motions the duration of the effect, to prolong also a consciousness of the cause. In relation to the objects which delight a child, these expressions are, what poetry is to higher objects. The savage (for the savage is to ages what the child is to years) expresses the emotions produced in him by surrounding objects in a similar manner; and language and gesture, together with plastic or pictorial imitation, become the image of the combined effect of those objects, and of his apprehension of them. Man in society, with all his passions and his pleasures, next becomes the object of the passions and pleasures of man; an additional class of emotions produces an augmented treasure of expressions; and language, gesture, and the imitative arts, become at once the representation and the medium, the pencil and the picture, the chisel and the statue, the chord and the harmony. The social sympathies, or those laws from which as from its elements society results, begin to develope themselves from the moment that two human beings coexist; the future is contained within the present as the plant within the seed; and equality, diversity, unity, contrast, mutual dependence, become the principles alone capable of affording the motives according to which the will of a social being is determined to action, inasmuch as he is social; and constitute pleasure in sensation, virtue in sentiment, beauty in art, truth in reasoning, and love in the intercourse of kind. Hence men, even in the infancy of society, observe a certain order in their words and actions, distinct from that of the objects and the impressions represented by them, all expression being subject to the laws of that from which it proceeds. But let us dismiss those more general considerations which might involve an enquiry into the principles of society itself, and restrict our view to the manner in which the imagination is expressed upon its forms.

In the youth of the world, men dance and sing and imitate natural objects, observing[5] in these actions, as in all others, a certain rhythm or order. And, although all men observe a similar, they observe not the same order, in the motions of the dance, in the melody of the song, in the combinations of language, in the series of their imitations of natural objects. For there is a certain order or rhythm belonging to each of these classes of mimetic representation, from which the hearer and the spectator receive an intenser and purer pleasure than from any other: the sense of an approximation to this order has been called taste, by modern writers. Every man in the infancy of art, observes an order which approximates more or less closely to that from which this highest delight results: but the diversity is not sufficiently marked, as that its gradations should be sensible, except in those instances where the predominance of this faculty of approximation to the beautiful (for so we may be permitted to name the relation between this highest pleasure and its cause) is very great. Those in whom it exists in excess are poets, in the most universal sense of the word; and the pleasure resulting from the manner in which they express the influence of society or nature upon their own minds, communicates itself to others, and gathers a sort of reduplication from that community. Their language is vitally metaphorical; that is, it marks the before unapprehended relations of

5. Following, obeying.

things, and perpetuates their apprehension, until the words which represent them, become through time signs for portions or classes of thoughts[6] instead of pictures of integral thoughts; and then if no new poets should arise to create afresh the associations which have been thus disorganized, language will be dead to all the nobler purposes of human intercourse. These similitudes or relations are finely said by Lord Bacon to be "the same footsteps of nature impressed upon the various subjects of the world"[7]—and he considers the faculty which perceives them as the storehouse of axioms common to all knowledge. In the infancy of society every author is necessarily a poet, because language itself is poetry; and to be a poet is to apprehend the true and the beautiful, in a word the good which exists in the relation, subsisting, first between existence and perception, and secondly between perception and expression. Every original language near to its source is in itself the chaos of a cyclic poem:[8] the copiousness of lexicography and the distinctions of grammar are the works of a later age, and are merely the catalogue and the form of the creations of Poetry.

But Poets, or those who imagine and express this indestructible order, are not only the authors of language and of music, of the dance and architecture and statuary and painting: they are the institutors of laws, and the founders of civil society and the inventors of the arts of life and the teachers, who draw into a certain propinquity with the beautiful and the true that partial apprehension of the agencies of the invisible world which is called religion.[9] Hence all original religions are allegorical, or susceptible of allegory, and like Janus[1] have a double face of false and true. Poets, according to the circumstances of the age and nation in which they appeared, were called in the earlier epochs of the world legislators or prophets:[2] a poet essentially comprises and unites both these characters. For he not only beholds intensely the present as it is, and discovers those laws according to which present things ought to be ordered, but he beholds the future in the present, and his thoughts are the germs' of the flower and the fruit of latest time. Not that I assert poets to be prophets in the gross sense of the word, or that they can foretell the form as surely as they foreknow the spirit of events: such is the pretence of superstition which would make poetry an attribute of prophecy, rather than prophecy an attribute of poetry. A Poet participates in the eternal, the infinite, and the one; as far as relates to his conceptions, time and place and number are not. The grammatical forms which express the moods of time, and the difference of persons and the distinction of place are convertible with respect to the highest poetry without injuring it as poetry, and the choruses of Æschylus, and the book of Job, and Dante's Paradise would afford, more than any other writings, examples of this fact, if the limits of this essay did not forbid citation. The creations of sculpture, painting, and music, are illustrations still more decisive.

Language, colour, form, and religious and civil habits of action are all the instruments and materials of poetry; they may be called poetry by that figure

6. I.e., abstract concepts.
7. Francis Bacon, De Augmentis Scientiarum ("On the Enlargement of the Sciences") 1.3.
8. A group of poems (e.g., "the Arthurian cycle") that deal with the same subject.
9. Here Shelley enlarges the scope of the term poetry to denote all the creative achievements, or imaginative

breakthroughs, of humankind, including noninstitutional religious insights.
1. Roman god of beginnings and endings, often represented by two heads facing opposite directions.
2. Sir Philip Sidney had pointed out, in his Defence of Poesy, that vates, the Roman term for "poet," signifies "a diviner, fore-seer, or Prophet."

of speech which considers the effect as a synonime of the cause. But poetry in a more restricted sense[3] expresses those arrangements of language, and especially metrical language, which are created by that imperial faculty, whose throne is curtained within the invisible nature of man. And this springs from the nature itself of language, which is a more direct representation of the actions and passions of our internal being, and is susceptible of more various and delicate combinations, than colour, form, or motion, and is more plastic and obedient to the controul of that faculty of which it is the creation. For language is arbitrarily produced by the Imagination and has relation to thoughts alone; but all other materials, instruments and conditions of art, have relations among each other, which limit and interpose between conception and expression. The former[4] is as a mirror which reflects, the latter as a cloud which enfeebles, the light of which both are mediums of communication. Hence the fame of sculptors, painters and musicians, although the intrinsic powers of the great masters of these arts, may yield in no degree to that of those who have employed language as the hieroglyphic of their thoughts, has never equalled that of poets in the restricted sense of the term; as two performers of equal skill will produce unequal effects from a guitar and a harp. The fame of legislators and founders of religions, so long as their institutions last, alone seems to exceed that of poets in the restricted sense; but it can scarcely be a question whether, if we deduct the celebrity which their flattery of the gross opinions of the vulgar usually conciliates, together with that which belonged to them in their higher character of poets, any excess will remain.

We have thus circumscribed the meaning of the word Poetry within the limits of that art which is the most familiar and the most perfect expression of the faculty itself. It is necessary however to make the circle still narrower, and to determine the distinction between measured and unmeasured language; for the popular division into prose and verse is inadmissible in accurate philosophy.

Sounds as well as thoughts have relation both between each other and towards that which they represent, and a perception of the order of those relations has always been found connected with a perception of the order of the relations of thoughts. Hence the language of poets has ever affected a certain uniform and harmonious recurrence of sound, without which it were not poetry, and which is scarcely less indispensable to the communication of its influence, than the words themselves, without reference to that peculiar order. Hence the vanity of translation; it were as wise to cast a violet into a crucible that you might discover the formal principle of its colour and odour, as seek to transfuse from one language into another the creations of a poet. The plant must spring again from its seed or it will bear no flower—and this is the burthen of the curse of Babel.[5]

An observation of the regular mode of the recurrence of this harmony in the language of poetical minds, together with its relation to music, produced metre, or a certain system of traditional forms of harmony of language. Yet it is by no means essential that a poet should accommodate his language to this traditional form, so that the harmony which is its spirit, be observed. The

3. I.e., restricted to specifically verbal poetry, as against the inclusive sense in which Shelley has been applying the term.
4. I.e., language, as opposed to the media of sculpture, painting, and music.

5. When the descendants of Noah, who spoke a single language, undertook to build the Tower of Babel that would reach heaven, God cut short the attempt by multiplying languages so that the builders could no longer communicate (see Genesis 11.1–9).

practise is indeed convenient and popular, and to be preferred, especially in such composition as includes much form and action: but every great poet must inevitably innovate upon the example of his predecessors in the exact structure of his peculiar versification. The distinction between poets and prose writers is a vulgar error. The distinction between philosophers and poets has been anticipated.[6] Plato was essentially a poet—the truth and splendour of his imagery and the melody of his language is the most intense that it is possible to conceive. He rejected the measure of the epic, dramatic, and lyrical forms, because he sought to kindle a harmony in thoughts divested of shape and action, and he forbore to invent any regular plan of rhythm which would include, under determinate forms, the varied pauses of his style. Cicero[7] sought to imitate the cadence of his periods but with little success. Lord Bacon was a poet.[8] His language has a sweet and majestic rhythm, which satisfies the sense, no less than the almost superhuman wisdom of his philosophy satisfies the intellect; it is a strain which distends, and then bursts the circumference of the hearer's mind, and pours itself forth together with it into the universal element with which it has perpetual sympathy. All the authors of revolutions in opinion are not only necessarily poets as they are inventors, nor even as their words unveil the permanent analogy of things by images which partici- pate in the life of truth; but as their periods are harmonious and rhythmical and contain in themselves the elements of verse; being the echo of the eternal music. Nor are those supreme poets, who have employed traditional forms of rhythm on account of the form and action of their subjects, less capable of perceiving and teaching the truth of things, than those who have omitted that form. Shakespeare, Dante and Milton (to confine ourselves to modern writers) are philosophers of the very loftiest power.

A poem is the very image of life expressed in its eternal truth. There is this difference between a story and a poem, that a story is a catalogue of detached facts, which have no other bond of connexion than time, place, circumstance, cause and effect; the other is the creation of actions according to the unchangeable forms of human nature, as existing in the mind of the creator, which is itself the image of all other minds. The one is partial, and applies only to a definite period of time, and a certain combination of events which can never again recur; the other is universal, and contains within itself the germ of a relation to whatever motives or actions have place in the possible varieties of human nature. Time, which destroys the beauty and the use of the story of particular facts, stript of the poetry which should invest them, aug- ments that of Poetry, and for ever develops new and wonderful applications of the eternal truth which it contains. Hence epitomes[9] have been called the moths of just history;[1] they eat out the poetry of it. The story of particular facts is as a mirror which obscures and distorts that which should be beautiful: Poetry is a mirror which makes beautiful that which is distorted.

The parts of a composition may be poetical, without the composition as a whole being a poem. A single sentence may be considered as a whole though it be found in a series of unassimilated portions; a single word even may be a spark of inextinguishable thought. And thus all the great historians, Herodotus,

6. I.e., in what Shelley has already said.
7. Marcus Tullius Cicero, the great Roman orator of the 1st century B.C.
8. See the *Filium Labyrinthi* and the *Essay on Death*

particularly [Shelley's note].
9. Abstracts, summaries.
1. By Bacon in *The Advancement of Learning* 2.2.4.

Plutarch, Livy,[2] were poets; and although the plan of these writers, especially that of Livy, restrained them from developing this faculty in its highest degree, they make copious and ample amends for their subjection, by filling all the interstices of their subjects with living images.

Having determined what is poetry, and who are poets, let us proceed to estimate its effects upon society.

Poetry is ever accompanied with pleasure: all spirits on which it falls, open themselves to receive the wisdom which is mingled with its delight. In the infancy of the world, neither poets themselves nor their auditors are fully aware of the excellence of poetry: for it acts in a divine and unapprehended manner, beyond and above consciousness; and it is reserved for future generations to contemplate and measure the mighty cause and effect in all the strength and splendour of their union. Even in modern times, no living poet ever arrived at the fulness of his fame; the jury which sits in judgement upon a poet, belonging as he does to all time, must be composed of his peers: it must be impanelled by Time from the selectest of the wise of many generations. A Poet is a nightingale, who sits in darkness and sings to cheer its own solitude with sweet sounds; his auditors are as men entranced by the melody of an unseen musician, who feel that they are moved and softened, yet know not whence or why. The poems of Homer and his contemporaries were the delight of infant Greece; they were the elements of that social system which is the column upon which all succeeding civilization has reposed. Homer embodied the ideal perfection of his age in human character; nor can we doubt that those who read his verses were awakened to an ambition of becoming like to Achilles, Hector and Ulysses: the truth and beauty of friendship, patriotism and persevering devotion to an object, were unveiled to the depths in these immortal creations: the sentiments of the auditors must have been refined and enlarged by a sympathy with such great and lovely impersonations, until from admiring they imitated, and from imitation they identified themselves with the objects of their admiration. Nor let it be objected, that these characters are remote from moral perfection, and that they can by no means be considered as edifying patterns for general imitation. Every epoch under names more or less specious has deified its peculiar errors; Revenge is the naked Idol of the worship of a semi-barbarous age; and Self-deceit is the veiled Image of unknown evil before which luxury and satiety lie prostrate. But a poet considers the vices of his contemporaries as the temporary dress in which his creations must be arrayed, and which cover without concealing the eternal proportions of their beauty. An epic or dramatic personage is understood to wear them around his soul, as he may the antient armour or the modern uniform around his body; whilst it is easy to conceive a dress more graceful than either. The beauty of the internal nature cannot be so far concealed by its accidental vesture, but that the spirit of its form shall communicate itself to the very disguise, and indicate the shape it hides from the manner in which it is worn. A majestic form and graceful motions will express themselves through the most barbarous and tasteless costume. Few poets of the highest class have chosen to exhibit the beauty of their conceptions in its naked truth and splen-

---

2. Herodotus (ca. 480–ca. 425 B.C.) wrote the first systematic history of Greece. Plutarch (ca. A.D. 46–ca. 120) wrote *Parallel Lives* (of eminent Greeks and Romans). Titus Livius (59 B.C.–A.D. 17) wrote an immense history of Rome.

dour; and it is doubtful whether the alloy of costume, habit, etc., be not necessary to temper this planetary music[3] for mortal ears.

The whole objection, however, of the immorality of poetry[4] rests upon a misconception of the manner in which poetry acts to produce the moral improvement of man. Ethical science[5] arranges the elements which poetry has created, and propounds schemes and proposes examples of civil and domestic life: nor is it for want of admirable doctrines that men hate, and despise, and censure, and deceive, and subjugate one another. But Poetry acts in another and diviner manner. It awakens and enlarges the mind itself by rendering it the receptacle of a thousand unapprehended combinations of thought. Poetry lifts the veil from the hidden beauty of the world, and makes familiar objects be as if they were not familiar; it reproduces[6] all that it represents, and the impersonations clothed in its Elysian light stand thenceforward in the minds of those who have once contemplated them, as memorials of that gentle and exalted content[7] which extends itself over all thoughts and actions with which it coexists. The great secret of morals is Love; or a going out of our own nature, and an identification of ourselves with the beautiful which exists in thought, action, or person, not our own. A man, to be greatly good, must imagine intensely and comprehensively; he must put himself in the place of another and of many others; the pains and pleasures of his species must become his own. The great instrument of moral good is the imagination;[8] and poetry administers to the effect by acting upon the cause. Poetry enlarges the circumference of the imagination by replenishing it with thoughts of ever new delight, which have the power of attracting and assimilating to their own nature all other thoughts, and which form new intervals and interstices whose void for ever craves fresh food. Poetry strengthens that faculty which is the organ of the moral nature of man, in the same manner as exercise strengthens a limb. A Poet therefore would do ill to embody his own conceptions of right and wrong, which are usually those of his place and time, in his poetical creations, which participate in neither. By this assumption of the inferior office of interpreting the effect, in which perhaps after all he might acquit himself but imperfectly, he would resign the glory in a participation in the cause.[9] There was little danger that Homer, or any of the eternal Poets, should have so far misunderstood themselves as to have abdicated this throne of their widest dominion. Those in whom the poetical faculty, though great, is less intense, as Euripides, Lucan, Tasso,[1] Spenser, have frequently affected[2] a moral aim, and the effect of their poetry is diminished in exact proportion to the degree in which they compel us to advert to this purpose.[3]

3. The music made by the revolving crystalline spheres of the planets, inaudible to human ears.
4. In the preceding paragraph Shelley has been implicitly dealing with the charge, voiced by Plato in his *Republic*, that poetry is immoral because it represents evil characters acting evilly.
5. Moral philosophy.
6. Produces anew, re-creates.
7. Contentment (pronounced *con-tént*).
8. Central to Shelley's theory is the concept (developed by 18th-century philosophers) of the sympathetic imagination—the faculty by which an individual is enabled to identify with the thoughts and feelings of others. Shelley claims that the faculty in poetry that enables us to share the joys and sufferings of invented characters is also the basis of all morality, for it compels us to feel for others as we feel for ourselves.
9. The "effect," or the explicit moral standards into which imaginative insights are translated at a particular time or place, is contrasted to the "cause" of all morality, the imagination itself.
1. Euripides (ca. 484–406 B.C.), Greek writer of tragedies. Lucan (A.D. 39–65), Roman poet, author of the *Pharsalia*. Tasso Torquato (1544–1595), Italian poet, author of *Jerusalem Delivered*, an epic poem about a crusade.
2. Assumed, adopted.
3. In the following omitted passage Shelley reviews the history of drama and poetry in relation to civilization and morality and proceeds to refute the charge that poets are less useful than "reasoners and merchants." He begins by defining *utility* in terms of pleasure, and then

* * *

It is difficult to define pleasure in its highest sense; the definition involving a number of apparent paradoxes. For, from an inexplicable defect of harmony in the constitution of human nature, the pain of the inferior is frequently connected with the pleasures of the superior portions of our being. Sorrow, terror, anguish, despair itself are often the chosen expressions of an approximation to the highest good. Our sympathy in tragic fiction depends on this principle; tragedy delights by affording a shadow of the pleasure which exists in pain. This is the source also of the melancholy which is inseparable from the sweetest melody. The pleasure that is in sorrow is sweeter than the pleasure of pleasure itself. And hence the saying, "It is better to go to the house of mourning, than to the house of mirth."[4] Not that this highest species of pleasure is necessarily linked with pain. The delight of love and friendship, the ecstasy of the admiration of nature, the joy of the perception and still more of the creation of poetry is often wholly unalloyed.

The production and assurance of pleasure in this highest sense is true utility. Those who produce and preserve this pleasure are Poets or poetical philosophers.

The exertions of Locke, Hume, Gibbon, Voltaire, Rousseau,[5] and their disciples, in favour of oppressed and deluded humanity, are entitled to the gratitude of mankind. Yet it is easy to calculate the degree of moral and intellectual improvement which the world would have exhibited, had they never lived. A little more nonsense would have been talked for a century or two; and perhaps a few more men, women, and children, burnt as heretics. We might not at this moment have been congratulating each other on the abolition of the Inquisition in Spain.[6] But it exceeds all imagination to conceive what would have been the moral condition of the world if neither Dante, Petrarch, Boccaccio, Chaucer, Shakespeare, Calderon, Lord Bacon, nor Milton, had ever existed; if Raphael and Michael Angelo had never been born; if the Hebrew poetry had never been translated; if a revival of the study of Greek literature had never taken place; if no monuments of antient sculpture had been handed down to us; and if the poetry of the religion of the antient world had been extinguished together with its belief. The human mind could never, except by the intervention of these excitements, have been awakened to the invention of the grosser sciences, and that application of analytical reasoning to the aberrations of society, which it is now attempted to exalt over the direct expression of the inventive and creative faculty itself.

We have more moral, political and historical wisdom, than we know how to reduce into practice; we have more scientific and economical knowledge than can be accommodated to the just distribution of the produce which it multiplies. The poetry in these systems of thought, is concealed by the accumulation of facts and calculating processes. There is no want of knowledge respecting what is wisest and best in morals, government, and political economy, or at least, what is wiser and better than what men now practise and

---

distinguishes between the lower (physical and material) and the higher (imaginative) pleasures.
4. Ecclesiastes 7.2.
5. In a note Shelley says that, although Peacock had classified Rousseau with these other thinkers of the

17th and 18th centuries, "he was essentially a poet. The others, even Voltaire, were mere reasoners."
6. The Inquisition had been suspended in 1820, the year before Shelley wrote this essay; it was not abolished permanently until 1834.

endure. But we let "*I dare not* wait upon *I would,* like the poor cat i' the adage."[7] We want the creative faculty to imagine that which we know; we want the generous impulse to act that which we imagine; we want the poetry of life: our calculations have outrun conception; we have eaten more than we can digest. The cultivation of those sciences which have enlarged the limits of the empire of man over the external world, has, for want of the poetical faculty, proportionally circumscribed those of the internal world; and man, having enslaved the elements, remains himself a slave. To what but a cultivation of the mechanical arts in a degree disproportioned to the presence of the creative faculty, which is the basis of all knowledge, is to be attributed the abuse of all invention for abridging and combining labour, to the exasperation of the inequality of mankind? From what other cause has it arisen that these inventions which should have lightened, have added a weight to the curse imposed on Adam? Poetry, and the principle of Self, of which money is the visible incarnation, are the God and Mammon of the world.[8]

The functions of the poetical faculty are two-fold; by one it creates new materials of knowledge, and power and pleasure; by the other it engenders in the mind a desire to reproduce and arrange them according to a certain rhythm and order which may be called the beautiful and the good. The cultivation of poetry is never more to be desired than at periods when, from an excess of the selfish and calculating principle, the accumulation of the materials of external life exceed the quantity of the power of assimilating them to the internal laws of human nature. The body has then become too unwieldy for that which animates it.

Poetry is indeed something divine. It is at once the centre and circumference of knowledge; it is that which comprehends all science, and that to which all science must be referred. It is at the same time the root and blossom of all other systems of thought; it is that from which all spring, and that which adorns all; and that which, if blighted, denies the fruit and the seed, and withholds from the barren world the nourishment and the succession of the scions of the tree of life. It is the perfect and consummate surface and bloom of things; it is as the odour and the colour of the rose to the texture of the elements which compose it, as the form and the splendour of unfaded beauty to the secrets of anatomy and corruption. What were Virtue, Love, Patriotism, Friendship etc.—what were the scenery of this beautiful Universe which we inhabit—what were our consolations on this side of the grave—and what were our aspirations beyond it—if Poetry did not ascend to bring light and fire from those eternal regions where the owl-winged faculty of calculation dare not ever soar? Poetry is not like reasoning, a power to be exerted according to the determination of the will. A man cannot say, "I will compose poetry." The greatest poet even cannot say it: for the mind in creation is as a fading coal which some invisible influence, like an inconstant wind, awakens to transitory brightness: this power arises from within, like the colour of a flower which fades and changes as it is developed, and the conscious portions of our natures are unprophetic either of its approach or its departure.[9] Could this influence

---

7. *Macbeth* 1.7.44–45.
8. Matthew 6.24: "Ye cannot serve God and Mammon."
9. This passage reiterates the ancient belief that the highest poetry is "inspired" and, therefore, occurs independently of the intention, effort, or consciousness of the poet. Unlike earlier critics, however, Shelley attributes such poetry not to a god or muse but to the unconscious depths of the poet's own mind.

be durable in its original purity and force, it is impossible to predict the great-ness of the results; but when composition begins, inspiration is already on the decline, and the most glorious poetry that has ever been communicated to the world is probably a feeble shadow of the original conception of the poet. I appeal to the greatest Poets of the present day, whether it be not an error to assert that the finest passages of poetry are produced by labour and study. The toil and the delay recommended by critics can be justly interpreted to mean no more than a careful observation of the inspired moments, and an artificial connexion of the spaces between their suggestions by the intertexture of con-ventional expressions; a necessity only imposed by the limitedness of the poeti-cal faculty itself. For Milton conceived the Paradise Lost as a whole before he executed it in portions. We have his own authority also for the Muse having "dictated" to him the "unpremeditated song,"[1] and let this be an answer to those who would allege the fifty-six various readings of the first line of the Orlando Furioso.[2] Compositions so produced are to poetry what mosaic is to painting. This instinct and intuition of the poetical faculty is still more observ-able in the plastic and pictorial arts: a great statue or picture grows under the power of the artist as a child in the mother's womb; and the very mind which directs the hands in formation is incapable of accounting to itself for the ori-gin, the gradations, or the media of the process.

Poetry is the record of the best and happiest[3] moments of the happiest and best minds. We are aware of evanescent visitations of thought and feeling sometimes associated with place or person, sometimes regarding our own mind alone, and always arising unforeseen and departing unbidden, but ele-vating and delightful beyond all expression: so that even in the desire and the regret they leave, there cannot but be pleasure, participating as it does in the nature of its object. It is as it were the interpenetration of a diviner nature through our own; but its footsteps are like those of a wind over a sea, where the coming calm erases, and whose traces remain only as on the wrinkled sand which paves it. These and corresponding conditions of being are experienced principally by those of the most delicate sensibility and the most enlarged imagination; and the state of mind produced by them is at war with every base desire. The enthusiasm of virtue, love, patriotism, and friendship is essentially linked with these emotions; and whilst they last, self appears as what it is, an atom to a Universe. Poets are not only subject to these experiences as spirits of the most refined organization, but they can colour all that they combine with the evanescent hues of this etherial world; a word, or a trait in the repre-sentation of a scene or a passion, will touch the enchanted chord, and reani-mate, in those who have ever experienced these emotions, the sleeping, the cold, the buried image of the past. Poetry thus makes immortal all that is best and most beautiful in the world; it arrests the vanishing apparitions which haunt the interlunations[4] of life, and veiling them or in language or in form sends them forth among mankind, bearing sweet news of kindred joy to those with whom their sisters abide—abide, because there is no portal of expression from the caverns of the spirit which they inhabit into the universe of things. Poetry redeems from decay the visitations of the divinity in man.

Poetry turns all things to loveliness; it exalts the beauty of that which is

---

1. *Paradise Lost* 9.21–24.
2. The epic poem by the 16th-century Italian poet Ari-osto, noted for his care in composition.

3. In the double sense of "most joyous" and "most apt or felicitous in invention."
4. The dark intervals between the old and new moons.

most beautiful, and it adds beauty to that which is most deformed; it marries exultation and horror, grief and pleasure, eternity and change; it subdues to union under its light yoke all irreconcilable things. It transmutes all that it touches, and every form moving within the radiance of its presence is changed by wondrous sympathy to an incarnation of the spirit which it breathes; its secret alchemy turns to potable gold[5] the poisonous waters which flow from death through life; it strips the veil of familiarity from the world, and lays bare the naked and sleeping beauty which is the spirit of its forms.

All things exist as they are perceived: at least in relation to the percipient. "The mind is its own place, and of itself can make a heaven of hell, a hell of heaven."[6] But poetry defeats the curse which binds us to be subjected to the accident of surrounding impressions. And whether it spreads its own figured curtain or withdraws life's dark veil from before the scene of things, it equally creates for us a being within our being. It makes us the inhabitants of a world to which the familiar world is a chaos. It reproduces the common universe of which we are portions and percipients, and it purges from our inward sight the film of familiarity which obscures from us the wonder of our being. It compels us to feel that which we perceive, and to imagine that which we know. It creates anew the universe after it has been annihilated in our minds by the recurrence of impressions blunted by reiteration.[7] It justifies that bold and true word of Tasso: *Non merita nome di creatore, se non Iddio ed il Poeta.*[8]

A Poet, as he is the author to others of the highest wisdom, pleasure, virtue and glory, so he ought personally to be the happiest, the best, the wisest, and the most illustrious of men. As to his glory, let Time be challenged to declare whether the fame of any other institutor of human life be comparable to that of a poet. That he is the wisest, the happiest, and the best, inasmuch as he is a poet, is equally incontrovertible: the greatest poets have been men of the most spotless virtue, of the most consummate prudence, and, if we could look into the interior of their lives, the most fortunate of men: and the exceptions, as they regard those who possessed the poetic faculty in a high yet inferior degree, will be found on consideration to confirm rather than destroy the rule. Let us for a moment stoop to the arbitration of popular breath, and usurping and uniting in our own persons the incompatible characters of accuser, witness, judge and executioner, let us decide without trial, testimony, or form that certain motives of those who are "there sitting where we dare not soar"[9] are reprehensible. Let us assume that Homer was a drunkard, that Virgil was a flatterer, that Horace was a coward, that Tasso was a madman, that Lord Bacon was a peculator, that Raphael was a libertine, that Spenser was a poet laureate.[1] It is inconsistent with this division of our subject to cite living poets, but Posterity has done ample justice to the great names now referred to. Their errors have been weighed and found to have been dust in the balance; if their sins "were as scarlet, they are now white as snow";[2] they have been washed in

---

5. Alchemists aimed to produce a drinkable ("potable") form of gold that would be an elixir of life, curing all diseases.
6. Satan's speech, *Paradise Lost* 1.254–55.
7. Shelley's version of a widespread Romantic doctrine that the poetic imagination transforms the familiar into the miraculous and recreates the old world into a new world. See, e.g., Coleridge's *Biographia Literaria* on "freshness of sensation," chap. 4 (p. 1540).
8. "No one merits the name of Creator except God

and the Poet." Quoted by Pierantonio Serassi in his *Life of Torquato Tasso* (1785).
9. *Paradise Lost* 4.829.
1. Charges that had in fact been made against these men. The use of "poet laureate" as a derogatory term was a dig at Robert Southey, who held that honor at the time of Shelley's writing. "Peculator": a misappropriator of public money. Raphael is the 16th-century Italian painter.
2. Isaiah 1.18.

the blood of the mediator and the redeemer Time. Observe in what a ludicrous chaos the imputations of real or fictitious crime have been confused in the contemporary calumnies against poetry and poets;[3] consider how little is, as it appears—or appears, as it is; look to your own motives, and judge not, lest ye be judged.

Poetry, as has been said, in this respect differs from logic, that it is not subject to the controul of the active powers of the mind, and that its birth and recurrence has no necessary connexion with consciousness or will. It is presumptuous to determine that these[4] are the necessary conditions of all mental causation, when mental effects are experienced insusceptible of being referred to them. The frequent recurrence of the poetical power, it is obvious to suppose, may produce in the mind an habit of order and harmony correlative with its own nature and with its effects upon other minds. But in the intervals of inspiration, and they may be frequent without being durable, a poet becomes a man, and is abandoned to the sudden reflux of the influences under which others habitually live. But as he is more delicately organized than other men, and sensible to pain and pleasure, both his own and that of others, in a degree unknown to them, he will avoid the one and pursue the other with an ardour proportioned to this difference. And he renders himself obnoxious to calumny,[5] when he neglects to observe the circumstances under which these objects of universal pursuit and flight have disguised themselves in one another's garments.

But there is nothing necessarily evil in this error, and thus cruelty, envy, revenge, avarice, and the passions purely evil, have never formed any portion of the popular imputations on the lives of poets.

I have thought it most favourable to the cause of truth to set down these remarks according to the order in which they were suggested to my mind, by a consideration of the subject itself, instead of following that of the treatise that excited me to make them public.[6] Thus although devoid of the formality of a polemical reply; if the view they contain be just, they will be found to involve a refutation of the doctrines of the Four Ages of Poetry, so far at least as regards the first division of the subject. I can readily conjecture what should have moved the gall of the learned and intelligent author of that paper; I confess myself, like him, unwilling to be stunned by the Theseids of the hoarse Codri of the day. Bavius and Mævius[7] undoubtedly are, as they ever were, insufferable persons. But it belongs to a philosophical critic to distinguish rather than confound.

The first part of these remarks has related to Poetry in its elements and principles; and it has been shewn, as well as the narrow limits assigned them would permit, that what is called poetry, in a restricted sense, has a common source with all other forms of order and of beauty according to which the materials of human life are susceptible of being arranged, and which is poetry in an universal sense.

The second part[8] will have for its object an application of these principles

3. Shelley alludes especially to the charges of immorality by contemporary reviewers against Lord Byron and himself.
4. I.e., consciousness or will. Shelley again proposes that some mental processes are unconscious—outside our control or awareness.
5. Exposed to slander.

6. Peacock's Four Ages of Poetry.
7. Would-be poets satirized by Virgil and Horace. "Theseids": epic poems about Theseus. Codrus (plural "Codri") was the Roman author of a long, dull Theseid attacked by Juvenal and others.
8. Shelley, however, completed only the first part.

to the present state of the cultivation of Poetry, and a defence of the attempt to idealize the modern forms of manners and opinions, and compel them into a subordination to the imaginative and creative faculty. For the literature of England, an energetic developement of which has ever preceded or accompanied a great and free developement of the national will, has arisen as it were from a new birth. In spite of the low-thoughted envy which would undervalue contemporary merit, our own will be a memorable age in intellectual achievements, and we live among such philosophers and poets as surpass beyond comparison any who have appeared since the last national struggle for civil and religious liberty.[9] The most unfailing herald, companion, and follower of the awakening of a great people to work a beneficial change in opinion or institution, is Poetry. At such periods there is an accumulation of the power of communicating and receiving intense and impassioned conceptions respecting man and nature. The persons in whom this power resides, may often, as far as regards many portions of their nature, have little apparent correspondence with that spirit of good of which they are the ministers. But even whilst they deny and abjure, they are yet compelled to serve, the Power which is seated upon the throne of their own soul. It is impossible to read the compositions of the most celebrated writers of the present day without being startled with the electric life which burns within their words. They measure the circumference and sound the depths of human nature with a comprehensive and all-penetrating spirit, and they are themselves perhaps the most sincerely astonished at its manifestations, for it is less their spirit than the spirit of the age.[1] Poets are the hierophants[2] of an unapprehended inspiration, the mirrors of the gigantic shadows which futurity casts upon the present, the words which express what they understand not; the trumpets which sing to battle, and feel not what they inspire: the influence which is moved not, but moves.[3] Poets are the unacknowledged legislators of the World.

1821   1840

9. In the age of Milton and the English Civil Wars.
1. By attributing to the great poets and philosophers of his time a shared "spirit of the age," Shelley anticipates what later historians were to identify as "the Romantic movement."
2. Priests who are expositors of sacred mysteries.
3. Aristotle had said that God is the "Unmoved Mover" of the universe.

JOHN KEATS
1795–1821

1817:   *Poems*, Keats's first book.
1818:   *Endymion: A Poetic Romance.*
1819:   Keats's *annus mirabilis*, in which he writes almost all his greatest poems.
1820:   Publishes the volume *Lamia, Isabella, The Eve of St. Agnes, and Other Poems.*

No major poet has had a less propitious origin. John Keats's father was head stableman at a London livery stable; he married his employer's daughter and inherited the business. Mrs. Keats, by all reports, was a strongly sensual woman and a rather casual but affectionate mother to her five children—John (the first born), his three brothers (one of whom died in infancy), and a sister. Keats was sent to the Reverend John Clarke's private school at Enfield, where he was a noisy, high-spirited boy; despite his small stature (when full-grown, he was barely over five feet in height), he distinguished himself in skylarking and fistfights. Here he had the good fortune to have as a teacher Charles Cowden Clarke, son of the headmaster, who later became a writer and editor; he encouraged Keats's passion for reading and, both at school and in the course of their later friendship, introduced him to Spenser and other poets, to music, and to the theater.

When Keats was eight his father was killed by a fall from a horse, and when he was fourteen his mother died of tuberculosis. Although the livery stable had pros-pered, and £8,000 had been left in trust to the children by Keats's grandmother, the estate remained tied up in the law courts for all of Keats's lifetime. The chil-dren's guardian, Richard Abbey, was an unimaginative and practical-minded busi-nessman; he took Keats out of school at the age of fifteen and bound him apprentice to Thomas Hammond, a surgeon and apothecary at Edmonton. In 1815 Keats carried on his medical studies at Guy's Hospital, London, and the next year qualified to practice as an apothecary-surgeon—but almost immediately, over his guardian's protests, he abandoned medicine for poetry.

This decision was influenced by Keats's friendship with Leigh Hunt, then editor of the *Examiner* and a leading political radical, poet, and prolific writer of criticism and periodical essays. Hunt, the first successful author of Keats's acquaintance, added his enthusiastic encouragement of Keats's poetic efforts to that of Clarke. More important, he introduced him to writers greater than Hunt himself, William Hazlitt, Charles Lamb, and Shelley, as well as to Benjamin Robert Haydon, painter of grandiose historical and religious canvases. Through Hunt, Keats also met John Hamilton Reynolds and then Charles Wentworth Dilke and Charles Brown, men who became his intimate friends and provided him with an essential circumstance for a fledgling poet, a sympathetic and appreciative audience.

The rapidity and sureness of Keats's development has no match. He did not even undertake poetry until his eighteenth year and, for the following few years, produced album verse that was at best merely competent and at times manifested an arch sentimentality. Suddenly, in 1816, he spoke out loud and bold in the sonnet *On First Looking into Chapman's Homer*. Later that same year he wrote *Sleep and Poetry*, in which he laid out for himself a program deliberately modeled on the careers of the greatest poets, asking only

> for ten years, that I may overwhelm
> Myself in poesy; so I may do the deed
> That my own soul has to itself decreed.

For even while his health was good, Keats felt a foreboding of early death and applied himself to his art with a desperate urgency. In 1817 he went on to compose *Endymion*, an ambitious undertaking of more than four thousand lines. It is a profuse allegory of a mortal's quest for an ideal feminine counterpart and a flawless happiness beyond earthly possibility; in a number of passages, however, it already exhibits the sure movement and phrasing of his mature poetic style. But Keats's critical judgment and aspiration exceeded his achievement: long before he com-pleted it, he declared impatiently that he carried on with the "slipshod" *Endymion* only as a poetic exercise and "trial of invention" and began to block out the more ambitious *Hyperion*, conceived on the model of Milton's *Paradise Lost* in that most demanding of forms, the epic poem. The extent of his success in achieving the Miltonic manner is one of the reasons why Keats left off before *Hyperion* was finished, for he recognized that he was uncommonly susceptible to poetic influ-ences and regarded this as a threat to his individuality. "I will write independently," he insisted. "The Genius of Poetry must work out its own salvation in a man." He had refused the chance of intimacy with Shelley "that I might have my own unfettered scope"; he had broken away from Leigh Hunt's influence lest he get "the reputation of Hunt's *élève* [pupil]"; now he shied away from domination by Milton's powerfully infectious style.

With the year 1818 began a series of disappointments and disasters that culminated in Keats's mortal illness. Sentimental legend used to fix the blame on two anonymous articles: a scurrilous attack on Keats as a member of the "Cockney School" (that is, Hunt's radical literary circle in London), which appeared in the heavily Tory *Blackwood's Magazine*, and a savage mauling of *Endymion* in the *Quarterly Review*. Shelley gave impetus to this myth by his description of Keats in *Adonais* as "a pale flower," and Byron, who knew even less about him, asserted that he was "snuffed out by an article." But in fact, Keats had the good sense to recognize that the attacks were motivated by Tory bias and class snobbery, and he had already passed his own severe judgment on *Endymion*: "My own domestic criticism," he said, "has given me pain without comparison beyond what *Blackwood* or the *Quarterly* could possibly inflict." More important was the financial distress of his brother George and his young bride, who had just emigrated to Kentucky and lost their money in an ill-advised investment; Keats, himself always short of funds, had now to turn to literary journeywork to eke out the family income. His younger brother Tom contracted tuberculosis, and the poet, in devoted attendance on him through the later months of 1818, helplessly watched him waste away until his death that December. In the summer of that year Keats had taken a strenuous walking tour in the English Lake District, Scotland, and Ireland; it was a glorious adventure but a totally exhausting one in wet, cold weather, and he returned in August with a chronically ulcerated throat made increasingly ominous by the shadow of the tuberculosis that had killed his mother and brother. And in the late fall of 1818 Keats fell unwillingly, helplessly in love with Fanny Brawne. This pretty, vivacious, and mildly flirtatious girl of eighteen had little interest in poetry, but she possessed an alert and sensible mind and loved Keats sincerely. They became engaged, but Keats's dedication to poetry, his poverty, and his growing illness made marriage impossible and love a torment.

In this period of acute distress and emotional turmoil, within five years of his first trying his hand at poetry, Keats achieved the culmination of his brief poetic career. Between January and September of 1819, masterpiece followed masterpiece in astonishing succession: *The Eve of St. Agnes, La Belle Dame sans Merci,* all of the "great odes," *Lamia,* and a sufficient number of fine sonnets to make him, with Wordsworth, the major Romantic craftsman in that form. All of these poems possess the distinctive qualities of the work of his maturity: a slow-paced, gracious movement; a concreteness of description in which all the senses—tactile, gustatory, kinetic, visceral, as well as visual and auditory—combine to give the total apprehension of an experience; an intense delight at the sheer existence of things outside himself, the poet seeming to lose his own identity in the fullness of identification with the object he contemplates; and a concentrated felicity of phrasing that reminded his friends, as it has many critics since, of the language of Shakespeare. Under the richly sensuous surface, we find Keats's characteristic presentation of all experience as a tangle of inseparable but irreconcilable opposites. He finds melancholy in delight and pleasure in pain; he feels the highest intensity of love as an approximation to death; he inclines equally toward a life of indolence and "sensation" and toward a life of thought; he is aware both of the attraction of an imaginative dream world without "disagreeables" and the remorseless pressure of the actual; he aspires at the same time for aesthetic detachment and for social responsibility.

His letters, no less remarkable than his poetry, show that Keats felt on his pulses the conflicts he dramatized in his major poems. Above all, they reveal him wrestling with the problem of evil and suffering—what to make of our lives in the discovery that "the world is full of misery and heartbreak, pain, sickness and oppression." To the end of his life, with stubborn courage, he refused to seek solace for the complexity and contradictions of experience either in the abstractions of inherited philosophical doctrines or the absolutes of a religious creed. At the close of his poetic career, in the latter part of 1819, Keats began to rework the epic *Hyperion* into the form of a dream vision that he called *The Fall of Hyperion.* In the introductory section of this fragment the poet is told by the prophetess Moneta that he has hitherto been merely a dreamer; he must know that

> The poet and the dreamer are distinct,
> Diverse, sheer opposite, antipodes,

and that the height of poetry can be reached only by

> those to whom the miseries of the world
> Are misery, and will not let them rest.

He was seemingly planning to undertake a new direction and subject matter, when death intervened.

On the night of February 3, 1820, he coughed up blood. He refused to evade the truth: "I cannot be deceived in that colour; that drop of blood is my death warrant. I must die." That spring and summer a series of hemorrhages rapidly weakened him. In the autumn he allowed himself to be persuaded to seek the milder climate of Italy in the company of Joseph Severn, a young painter, but these last months were only what he called "a posthumous existence." He died in Rome on February 23, 1821, and was buried in the Protestant Cemetery. At times the agony of his disease, the apparent frustration of his hopes for great poetic achievement, and the despair of his passion for Fanny Brawne combined to compel even Keats's brave spirit to bitterness, resentment, and jealousy, but he always recovered his gallantry. His last letter, written to Charles Brown, concludes: "I can scarcely bid you good bye even in a letter. I always made an awkward bow. God bless you! John Keats."

No one can read Keats's poems and letters without an undersense of the tragic waste of so extraordinary an intellect and genius cut off so early. What he might have done is beyond conjecture; what we do know is that his achievement, when he stopped writing at the age of twenty-four, greatly exceeds the accomplishment at the same age of Chaucer, Shakespeare, or Milton.

The texts here are taken from Jack Stillinger's edition, *The Poems of John Keats* (Cambridge, Mass., 1978).

On First Looking into Chapman's Homer[1]

　Much have I travell'd in the realms of gold,
　　And many goodly states and kingdoms seen;
　　Round many western islands have I been
　Which bards in fealty to Apollo hold.

---

1. Keats's former schoolteacher Charles Cowden Clarke introduced him to Homer in the robust translation of the Elizabethan poet George Chapman. They read through the night, and Keats walked home at dawn; this sonnet reached Clarke by the ten o'clock mail that same morning. That it was Balboa, not Cortez, who caught his first sight of the Pacific from the heights of Darien, in Panama, matters to history but not to poetry.

grey eye'd

Flora

discovery

Oft of one wide expanse had I been told
  That deep-brow'd Homer ruled as his demesne;[2]
Yet did I never breathe its pure serene[3]   5
Till I heard Chapman speak out loud and bold:
Then felt I like some watcher of the skies   *verb*
  When a new planet swims into his ken; ~ *understanding*   10
Or like stout Cortez when with eagle eyes
  He star'd at the Pacific—and all his men
Look'd at each other with a wild surmise—
  Silent, upon a peak in Darien.

Oct. 1816   1816

From Sleep and Poetry[1]

["O for Ten Years"]

O for ten years, that I may overwhelm
Myself in poesy; so I may do the deed
That my own soul has to itself decreed.
Then will I pass the countries that I see
In long perspective, and continually   100
Taste their pure fountains. First the realm I'll pass
Of Flora, and old Pan:[2] sleep in the grass,
Feed upon apples red, and strawberries,
And choose each pleasure that my fancy sees;
Catch the white-handed nymphs in shady places,   105
To woo sweet kisses from averted faces,—
Play with their fingers, touch their shoulders white
Into a pretty shrinking with a bite
As hard as lips can make it: till agreed,
A lovely tale of human life we'll read.   110
And one will teach a tame dove how it best
May fan the cool air gently o'er my rest;
Another, bending o'er her nimble tread,
Will set a green robe floating round her head,
And still will dance with ever varied ease,   115
Smiling upon the flowers and the trees:
Another will entice me on, and on
Through almond blossoms and rich cinnamon;
Till in the bosom of a leafy world

2. Realm, feudal possession.
3. Clear expanse of air.
1. At the early age of twenty-one, Keats set himself a regimen of poetic training modeled on the course followed by the greatest poets. Virgil had established the pattern of beginning with pastoral writing and proceeding gradually to the point at which he was ready to undertake the epic, and this pattern had been deliberately followed by Spenser and Milton. Keats's version of this program, as he describes it here, is to begin with the realm "of Flora, and old Pan" (line 102) and, within ten years, to climb up to the level of poetry dealing with "the agonies, the strife / Of human hearts" (lines 124–25). The latter achievement Keats found best represented among his contemporaries by Wordsworth and, less successfully, by Shelley; Keats's vision of the chariot of poesy (lines 125–154) parallels Shelley's allegorical visions. The program Keats set himself is illuminated by his analysis of Wordsworth's progress in his letter to J. H. Reynolds of May 3, 1818 (pp. 1820–22).
2. I.e., the carefree pastoral world. Flora was the Roman goddess of flowers; Pan, the Greek god of pastures, woods, and animal life.

We rest in silence, like two gems upcurl'd   120
In the recesses of a pearly shell.

   And can I ever bid these joys farewell?
Yes, I must pass them for a nobler life,
Where I may find the agonies, the strife
Of human hearts: for lo! I see afar,   125
O'er sailing the blue cragginess, a car[3]
And steeds with streamy manes—the charioteer
Looks out upon the winds with glorious fear:
And now the numerous tramplings quiver lightly
Along a huge cloud's ridge; and now with sprightly   130
Wheel downward come they into fresher skies,
Tipt round with silver from the sun's bright eyes.
Still downward with capacious whirl they glide;
And now I see them on a green-hill's side
In breezy rest among the nodding stalks.   135
The charioteer with wond'rous gesture talks
To the trees and mountains; and there soon appear
Shapes of delight, of mystery, and fear,
Passing along before a dusky space
Made by some mighty oaks: as they would chase   140
Some ever-fleeting music on they sweep.
Lo! how they murmur, laugh, and smile, and weep:
Some with upholden hand and mouth severe;
Some with their faces muffled to the ear
Between their arms; some, clear in youthful bloom,   145
Go glad and smilingly athwart the gloom;
Some looking back, and some with upward gaze;
Yes, thousands in a thousand different ways
Flit onward—now a lovely wreath of girls
Dancing their sleek hair into tangled curls;   150
And now broad wings. Most awfully intent,
The driver of those steeds is forward bent,
And seems to listen: O that I might know
All that he writes with such a hurrying glow.

   The visions all are fled—the car is fled   155
Into the light of heaven, and in their stead
A sense of real things comes doubly strong,
And, like a muddy stream, would bear along
My soul to nothingness: but I will strive
Against all doubtings, and will keep alive   160
The thought of that same chariot, and the strange
Journey it went.

*   *   *

Oct.–Dec. 1816   1817

---

3. This chariot, with its "charioteer" (line 127), represents the higher poetic imagination, which bodies forth the
matters "of delight, of mystery, and fear" (line 138) that characterize the grander poetic genres.

On Seeing the Elgin Marbles[1]

My spirit is too weak—mortality
   Weighs heavily on me like unwilling sleep,
   And each imagined pinnacle and steep
Of godlike hardship tells me I must die
Like a sick eagle looking at the sky.   5
   Yet 'tis a gentle luxury to weep
   That I have not the cloudy winds to keep
Fresh for the opening of the morning's eye.
Such dim-conceived glories of the brain
   Bring round the heart an undescribable feud;   10
So do these wonders a most dizzy pain,
   That mingles Grecian grandeur with the rude
Wasting of old time—with a billowy main—
A sun—a shadow of a magnitude.

Mar. 1 or 2, 1817   1817

From Endymion: A Poetic Romance[1]

"The stretched metre of an antique song"

INSCRIBED TO THE MEMORY OF THOMAS CHATTERTON

Preface

Knowing within myself the manner in which this Poem has been produced, it is not without a feeling of regret that I make it public.

What manner I mean, will be quite clear to the reader, who must soon perceive great inexperience, immaturity, and every error denoting a feverish attempt, rather than a deed accomplished. The two first books, and indeed the two last, I feel sensible are not of such completion as to warrant their passing the press; nor should they if I thought a year's castigation would do them any good;—it will not: the foundations are too sandy. It is just that this youngster should die away: a sad thought for me, if I had not some hope that while it is dwindling I may be plotting, and fitting myself for verses fit to live.

This may be speaking too presumptuously, and may deserve a punishment: but no feeling man will be forward to inflict it: he will leave me alone, with the conviction that there is not a fiercer hell than the failure in a great object.

1. Lord Elgin had brought to England in 1806 the marble statues and friezes that adorned the Parthenon at Athens; in 1816 they were purchased by the government for the British Museum. Keats's response to his first sight of these timeworn memorials of Grecian artistry is characteristically intense, mixed, and subtly analyzed.

1. This poem of more than four thousand lines (based on the classical myth of a mortal beloved by the goddess of the moon) tells of Endymion's long and agonized search for an immortal goddess whom he had seen in several visions. In the course of his wanderings he comes upon an Indian maid who had been abandoned by the followers of Bacchus and, to his utter despair, succumbs to a sensual passion for her, in apparent betrayal of his love for his heavenly ideal. In the resolution the Indian maid reveals that she is herself Cynthia (Diana), goddess of the moon, the celestial subject of his earlier visions.

The verse epigraph is adapted from Shakespeare's Sonnet 17, line 12: "And stretchèd meter of an antique song." Thomas Chatterton (1752–1770), to whom *Endymion* is inscribed, wrote a number of brilliant pseudoarchaic poems that he attributed to an imaginary 15th-century poet, Thomas Rowley. Keats described him as "the most English of poets except Shakespeare."

This is not written with the least atom of purpose to forestall criticisms of course, but from the desire I have to conciliate men who are competent to look, and who do look with a zealous eye, to the honour of English literature.

The imagination of a boy is healthy, and the mature imagination of a man is healthy; but there is a space of life between, in which the soul is in a ferment, the character undecided, the way of life uncertain, the ambition thick-sighted: thence proceeds mawkishness, and all the thousand bitters which those men I speak of must necessarily taste in going over the following pages.

I hope I have not in too late a day touched the beautiful mythology of Greece, and dulled its brightness: for I wish to try once more,[2] before I bid it farewel.

Teignmouth, April 10, 1818

From *Book 1*

[A THING OF BEAUTY]

A thing of beauty is a joy for ever:
Its loveliness increases; it will never
Pass into nothingness; but still will keep
A bower quiet for us, and a sleep
Full of sweet dreams, and health, and quiet breathing.   5
Therefore, on every morrow, are we wreathing
A flowery band to bind us to the earth,
Spite of despondence, of the inhuman dearth
Of noble natures, of the gloomy days,
Of all the unhealthy and o'er-darkened ways   10
Made for our searching: yes, in spite of all,
Some shape of beauty moves away the pall
From our dark spirits. Such the sun, the moon,
Trees old, and young sprouting a shady boon
For simple sheep; and such are daffodils   15
With the green world they live in; and clear rills
That for themselves a cooling covert make
'Gainst the hot season; the mid forest brake,[3]
Rich with a sprinkling of fair musk-rose blooms:
And such too is the grandeur of the dooms[4]   20
We have imagined for the mighty dead;
All lovely tales that we have heard or read:
An endless fountain of immortal drink,
Pouring unto us from the heaven's brink.[5]

Nor do we merely feel these essences   25
For one short hour; no, even as the trees
That whisper round a temple become soon

2. In *Hyperion*, which Keats was already planning.
3. Thicket.
4. Judgments.
5. The poet sets up, and searches to resolve, the basic opposition between the inevitably "mortal" pleasures in this life and the conceived possibility of "immortal"

delight. Thus "essences" (line 25) seem to be the things of beauty in this world, purged of the mutability that is inescapable in ordinary experience. The central passage dealing with this theme is in book 1, lines 777ff.

Dear as the temple's self, so does the moon,
The passion poesy, glories infinite,
Haunt us till they become a cheering light   30
Unto our souls, and bound to us so fast,
That, whether there be shine, or gloom o'ercast,
They alway must be with us, or we die.

Therefore, 'tis with full happiness that I
Will trace the story of Endymion.   35
The very music of the name has gone
Into my being, and each pleasant scene
Is growing fresh before me as the green
Of our own vallies. * * *

[THE "PLEASURE THERMOMETER"]

"Peona![6] ever have I long'd to slake
My thirst for the world's praises: nothing base,   770
No merely slumberous phantasm, could unlace
The stubborn canvas for my voyage prepar'd—
Though now 'tis tatter'd; leaving my bark bar'd
And sullenly drifting: yet my higher hope
Is of too wide, too rainbow-large a scope,   775
To fret at myriads of earthly wrecks.
Wherein lies happiness? In that which becks
Our ready minds to fellowship divine,
A fellowship with essence; till we shine,
Full alchemiz'd,[7] and free of space. Behold   780
The clear religion of heaven! Fold
A rose leaf round thy finger's taperness,
And soothe thy lips: hist, when the airy stress
Of music's kiss impregnates the free winds,
And with a sympathetic touch unbinds   785
Eolian[8] magic from their lucid wombs:
Then old songs waken from enclouded tombs;
Old ditties sigh above their father's grave;
Ghosts of melodious prophecyings rave
Round every spot where trod Apollo's foot;   790
Bronze clarions awake, and faintly bruit,[9]
Where long ago a giant battle was;

6. The sister to whom Endymion confides his troubles. Of lines 769–857, Keats wrote to his publisher, John Taylor: "When I wrote it, it was the regular stepping of the Imagination towards a Truth. My having written that Argument will perhaps be of the greatest Service to me of anything I ever did—It set before me at once the gradations of Happiness even like a kind of Pleasure Thermometer, and is my first step towards the chief attempt in the Drama—the playing of different Natures with Joy and Sorrow." The gradations on this "Pleasure Thermometer" mark the stages on the way to what Keats calls "happiness" (line 777)—his secular version of the religious concept of "felicity" that, in the orthodox view, is to be achieved by a surrender of oneself to God. For Keats, the way to happiness lies through a fusion of ourselves, first sensuously, with the lovely objects of nature and art (lines 781–97), then on a higher level, with other human beings through "love and friendship" (line 801) and, ultimately, sexual love. By this "self-destroying," or loss of personal identity through our imaginative identification with a beloved person outside ourselves, we escape from the material limits and the self-centered condition of ordinary experience, to achieve a "fellowship with essence," which is a kind of immortality within our mortal existence (line 844).

7. Transformed by alchemy from a base to a precious metal.

8. From Aeolus, god of winds.

9. Make a sound.

And, from the turf, a lullaby doth pass
In every place where infant Orpheus slept.
Feel we these things?—that moment have we stept   795
Into a sort of oneness, and our state
Is like a floating spirit's. But there are
Richer entanglements, enthralments far
More self-destroying, leading, by degrees,
To the chief intensity: the crown of these   800
Is made of love and friendship, and sits high
Upon the forehead of humanity.
All its more ponderous and bulky worth
Is friendship, whence there ever issues forth
A steady splendour; but at the tip-top   805
There hangs by unseen film, an orbed drop
Of light, and that is love: its influence,
Thrown in our eyes, genders a novel sense,
At which we start and fret; till in the end,
Melting into its radiance, we blend,   810
Mingle, and so become a part of it,—
Nor with aught else can our souls interknit
So wingedly: when we combine therewith,
Life's self is nourish'd by its proper pith,[1]
And we are nurtured like a pelican brood.[2]   815
Aye, so delicious is the unsating food,
That men, who might have tower'd in the van
Of all the congregated world, to fan
And winnow from the coming step of time
All chaff of custom, wipe away all slime   820
Left by men-slugs and human serpentry,
Have been content to let occasion die,
Whilst they did sleep in love's elysium.
And, truly, I would rather be struck dumb,
Than speak against this ardent listlessness: 825
For I have ever thought that it might bless
The world with benefits unknowingly;
As does the nightingale, upperched high,
And cloister'd among cool and bunched leaves—
She sings but to her love, nor e'er conceives   830
How tiptoe Night holds back her dark-grey hood.[3]
Just so may love, although 'tis understood
The mere commingling of passionate breath,
Produce more than our searching witnesseth:
What I know not: but who, of men, can tell   835
That flowers would bloom, or that green fruit would swell
To melting pulp, that fish would have bright mail,
The earth its dower of river, wood, and vale,
The meadows runnels, runnels pebble-stones,
The seed its harvest, or the lute its tones,   840

---

1. Its own elemental substance.
2. Young pelicans were once thought to feed on their mother's flesh. In a parallel way, our life is nourished by another's life, with which it fuses in love.
3. I.e., in order better to hear.

Tones ravishment, or ravishment its sweet,
If human souls did never kiss and greet?

    "Now, if this earthly love has power to make
Men's being mortal, immortal; to shake
Ambition from their memories, and brim   845
Their measure of content; what merest whim,
Seems all this poor endeavour after fame,
To one, who keeps within his stedfast aim
A love immortal, an immortal too.
Look not so wilder'd; for these things are true,   850
And never can be born of atomies[4]
That buzz about our slumbers, like brain-flies,
Leaving us fancy-sick. No, no, I'm sure,
My restless spirit never could endure
To brood so long upon one luxury,   855
Unless it did, though fearfully, espy
A hope beyond the shadow of a dream."

Apr.–Nov. 1817   1818

On Sitting Down to Read *King Lear* Once Again[1]

O golden-tongued Romance, with serene lute!
    Fair plumed syren, queen of far-away!
    Leave melodizing on this wintry day,
Shut up thine olden pages, and be mute.
Adieu! for, once again, the fierce dispute   5
    Betwixt damnation and impassion'd clay
    Must I burn through; once more humbly assay
The bitter-sweet of this Shakespearean fruit.
Chief Poet! and ye clouds of Albion,[2]
    Begetters of our deep eternal theme!   10
When through the old oak forest[3] I am gone,
    Let me not wander in a barren dream:
But, when I am consumed in the fire,
Give me new phoenix[4] wings to fly at my desire.

Jan. 22, 1818   1838

When I have fears that I may cease to be[1]

When I have fears that I may cease to be
    Before my pen has glean'd my teeming brain,

---

4. Mites; tiny flying insects.
1. Keats pauses, while revising *Endymion: A Poetic Romance*, to read again Shakespeare's great tragedy. The word "syren" (line 2) indicates Keats's feeling that "Romance" was enticing him from the poet's prime duty, to deal with "the agonies, the strife / Of human hearts" (*Sleep and Poetry*, lines 124–25).
2. Albion is the old Celtic name for England; *King*

Lear is set in Celtic Britain.
3. A reference either to *King Lear* or to *Endymion*.
4. The fabulous bird that periodically burns itself to death to rise anew from the ashes.
1. The first, and one of the most successful, of Keats's attempts at the sonnet in the Shakespearean rhyme scheme.

Before high piled books, in charactry,[2]
　　Hold like rich garners the full ripen'd grain;
When I behold, upon the night's starr'd face,   5
　　Huge cloudy symbols of a high romance,
And think that I may never live to trace
　　Their shadows, with the magic hand of chance;
And when I feel, fair creature of an hour,
　　That I shall never look upon thee more,   10
Never have relish in the fairy power
　　Of unreflecting love;—then on the shore
Of the wide world I stand alone, and think
Till love and fame to nothingness do sink.

Jan. 1818   1848

To Homer

Standing aloof in giant ignorance,
　　Of thee I hear and of the Cyclades,[1]
As one who sits ashore and longs perchance
　　To visit dolphin-coral in deep seas.
So wast thou blind;—but then the veil was rent,   5
　　For Jove uncurtain'd heaven to let thee live,
And Neptune made for thee a spumy tent,
　　And Pan made sing for thee his forest-hive;
Aye on the shores of darkness there is light,
　　And precipices show untrodden green,   10
There is a budding morrow in midnight,
　　There is a triple sight in blindness keen;
Such seeing hadst thou, as it once befel
To Dian, Queen of Earth, and Heaven, and Hell.[2]

1818   1848

The Eve of St. Agnes[1]

1

St. Agnes' Eve—Ah, bitter chill it was!
The owl, for all his feathers, was a-cold;
The hare limp'd trembling through the frozen grass,
And silent was the flock in woolly fold:

---

2. Characters; printed letters of the alphabet.
1. A group of islands in the Aegean Sea, off Greece;
Keats's allusion is to his ignorance of the Greek language.
2. In late pagan cults Diana was worshiped as a three-figured goddess, the deity of nature and of the moon as well as the queen of hell. The "triple sight" that blind Homer paradoxically commands is of these three regions and also of heaven, sea, and earth (the realms of Jove, Neptune, and Pan, lines 6–8).
1. St. Agnes, martyred ca. 303 at the age of thirteen, is the patron saint of virgins. Legend has it that if a chaste young woman performs the proper ritual, she will dream of her future husband on the evening before St. Agnes's Day, Jan. 21. Keats combines this superstition with the Romeo and Juliet theme of young love

thwarted by feuding families and tells the story in a sequence of evolving Spenserian stanzas. The luxurious product has been called "a colored dream," but it is a complexly meaningful dream, in which the strong contrasts of heat and cold, crimson and silver, youth and age, revelry and austere penance, sensuality and chastity, life and death, hell and heaven, assume symbolic values. They figure forth the extremes of spirituality and physicality that are involved in sexuality, the difference between the dream and the reality of passion, and the ambivalences at the center of both human love and the imagination. The poem is Keats's first complete success in sustained narrative. For the author's revisions while composing stanzas 26 and 30 of The Eve of St. Agnes, see "Poems in Process" (pp. 2585–86).

Numb were the Beadsman's[2] fingers, while he told   5
  His rosary, and while his frosted breath,
  Like pious incense from a censer old,
  Seem'd taking flight for heaven, without a death,
Past the sweet Virgin's picture, while his prayer he saith.

                                2

His prayer he saith, this patient, holy man;   10
  Then takes his lamp, and riseth from his knees,
  And back returneth, meagre, barefoot, wan,
  Along the chapel aisle by slow degrees:
  The sculptur'd dead, on each side, seem to freeze,
  Emprison'd in black, purgatorial rails: 15
  Knights, ladies, praying in dumb orat'ries,[3]
  He passeth by; and his weak spirit fails
To think[4] how they may ache in icy hoods and mails.

                                3

Northward he turneth through a little door,
  And scarce three steps, ere Music's golden tongue   20
  Flatter'd[5] to tears this aged man and poor;
  But no—already had his deathbell rung;
  The joys of all his life were said and sung:
  His was harsh penance on St. Agnes' Eve:
  Another way he went, and soon among   25
  Rough ashes sat he for his soul's reprieve,
And all night kept awake, for sinners' sake to grieve.

                                4

That ancient Beadsman heard the prelude soft;
  And so it chanc'd, for many a door was wide,
  From hurry to and fro. Soon, up aloft,   30
  The silver, snarling trumpets 'gan to chide:
  The level chambers, ready with their pride,[6]
  Were glowing to receive a thousand guests:
  The carved angels, ever eager-eyed,
  Star'd, where upon their heads the cornice rests,   35
With hair blown back, and wings put cross-wise on their breasts.

                                5

At length burst in the argent revelry,[7]
  With plume, tiara, and all rich array,
  Numerous as shadows haunting fairily
  The brain, new stuff'd, in youth, with triumphs gay   40
  Of old romance. These let us wish away,
  And turn, sole-thoughted, to one Lady there,
  Whose heart had brooded, all that wintry day,
  On love, and wing'd St. Agnes' saintly care,
As she had heard old dames full many times declare.   45

                                6

They told her how, upon St. Agnes' Eve,
  Young virgins might have visions of delight,

---

2. A "beadsman" is paid to pray for his benefactor. He
"tells" (counts) the beads of his rosary, to keep track of
his prayers.
3. Silent chapels.

4. I.e., when he thinks.
5. Beguiled, charmed.
6. Ostentation.
7. Silver-adorned revelers.

And soft adorings from their loves receive
Upon the honey'd middle of the night,
If ceremonies due they did aright;   50
As, supperless to bed they must retire,
And couch supine their beauties, lily white;
Nor look behind, nor sideways, but require
Of heaven with upward eyes for all that they desire.

7

Full of this whim was thoughtful Madeline: 55
The music, yearning like a god in pain,
She scarcely heard: her maiden eyes divine,
Fix'd on the floor, saw many a sweeping train
Pass by—she heeded not at all: in vain
Came many a tiptoe, amorous cavalier,   60
And back retir'd, not cool'd by high disdain;
But she saw not: her heart was otherwhere:
She sigh'd for Agnes' dreams, the sweetest of the year.

8

She danc'd along with vague, regardless eyes,
Anxious her lips, her breathing quick and short: 65
The hallow'd hour was near at hand: she sighs
Amid the timbrels,[8] and the throng'd resort
Of whisperers in anger, or in sport;
'Mid looks of love, defiance, hate, and scorn,
Hoodwink'd with faery fancy; all amort,[9]   70
Save to St. Agnes and her lambs unshorn,[1]
And all the bliss to be before to-morrow morn.

9

So, purposing each moment to retire,
She linger'd still. Meantime, across the moors,
Had come young Porphyro, with heart on fire   75
For Madeline. Beside the portal doors,
Buttress'd from moonlight,[2] stands he, and implores
All saints to give him sight of Madeline,
But for one moment in the tedious hours,
That he might gaze and worship all unseen;   80
Perchance speak, kneel, touch, kiss—in sooth such things have been.

10

He ventures in: let no buzz'd whisper tell:
All eyes be muffled, or a hundred swords
Will storm his heart, Love's fev'rous citadel:
For him, those chambers held barbarian hordes,   85
Hyena foemen, and hot-blooded lords,
Whose very dogs would execrations howl
Against his lineage: not one breast affords
Him any mercy, in that mansion foul,
Save one old beldame,[3] weak in body and in soul.   90

---

8. Small drums.
9. As though dead. "Hoodwinked": covered by a hood
or blindfolded.
1. On St. Agnes's Day it was the custom to offer lambs'
wool at the altar, to be made into cloth by nuns.

2. Sheltered from the moonlight by the buttresses (the
supports projecting from the wall).
3. Old (and usually, homely) woman; an ironic development in English from the French meaning, "lovely
lady."

11

Ah, happy chance! the aged creature came,
Shuffling along with ivory-headed wand,[4]
To where he stood, hid from the torch's flame,
Behind a broad hall-pillar, far beyond
The sound of merriment and chorus bland:[5]   95
He startled her; but soon she knew his face,
And grasp'd his fingers in her palsied hand,
Saying, "Mercy, Porphyro! hie thee from this place;
They are all here to-night, the whole blood-thirsty race!

12

"Get hence! get hence! there's dwarfish Hildebrand;   100
He had a fever late, and in the fit
He cursed thee and thine, both house and land:
Then there's that old Lord Maurice, not a whit
More tame for his gray hairs—Alas me! flit!
Flit like a ghost away."—"Ah, Gossip[6] dear,   105
We're safe enough; here in this arm-chair sit,
And tell me how"—"Good Saints! not here, not here;
Follow me, child, or else these stones will be thy bier."

13

He follow'd through a lowly arched way,
Brushing the cobwebs with his lofty plume,   110
And as she mutter'd "Well-a—well-a-day!"
He found him in a little moonlight room,
Pale, lattic'd, chill, and silent as a tomb.
"Now tell me where is Madeline," said he,
"O tell me, Angela, by the holy loom   115
Which none but secret sisterhood may see,
When they St. Agnes' wool are weaving piously."

14

"St. Agnes! Ah! it is St. Agnes' Eve—
Yet men will murder upon holy days:
Thou must hold water in a witch's sieve,[7]   120
And be liege-lord of all the Elves and Fays,
To venture so: it fills me with amaze
To see thee, Porphyro!—St. Agnes' Eve!
God's help! my lady fair the conjuror plays[8]
This very night: good angels her deceive!   125
But let me laugh awhile, I've mickle[9] time to grieve."

15

Feebly she laugheth in the languid moon,
While Porphyro upon her face doth look,
Like puzzled urchin on an aged crone
Who keepeth clos'd a wond'rous riddle-book,   130
As spectacled she sits in chimney nook.
But soon his eyes grew brilliant, when she told
His lady's purpose; and he scarce could brook[1]

4. Staff.
5. Soft.
6. In the old sense: "godmother," or "old friend."
7. A sieve made to hold water by witchcraft.
8. I.e., in her attempt to evoke the vision of her lover.
9. Much.
1. Ordinarily, "endure"; here Keats apparently uses it to mean "restrain."

Tears, at the thought of those enchantments cold,
And Madeline asleep in lap of legends old.   135
                                  16
Sudden a thought came like a full-blown rose,
Flushing his brow, and in his pained heart
Made purple riot: then doth he propose
A stratagem, that makes the beldame start:
"A cruel man and impious thou art: 140
Sweet lady, let her pray, and sleep, and dream
Alone with her good angels, far apart
From wicked men like thee. Go, go!—I deem
Thou canst not surely be the same that thou didst seem."
                                  17
"I will not harm her, by all saints I swear,"   145
Quoth Porphyro: "O may I ne'er find grace
When my weak voice shall whisper its last prayer,
If one of her soft ringlets I displace,
Or look with ruffian passion in her face:
Good Angela, believe me by these tears;   150
Or I will, even in a moment's space,
Awake, with horrid shout, my foemen's ears,
And beard them, though they be more fang'd than wolves and bears."
                                  18
"Ah! why wilt thou affright a feeble soul?
A poor, weak, palsy-stricken, churchyard thing,   155
Whose passing-bell[2] may ere the midnight toll;
Whose prayers for thee, each morn and evening,
Were never miss'd."—Thus plaining,[3] doth she bring
A gentler speech from burning Porphyro;
So woful, and of such deep sorrowing,   160
That Angela gives promise she will do
Whatever he shall wish, betide her weal or woe.
                                  19
Which was, to lead him, in close secrecy,
Even to Madeline's chamber, and there hide
Him in a closet, of such privacy   165
That he might see her beauty unespied,
And win perhaps that night a peerless bride,
While legion'd fairies pac'd the coverlet,
And pale enchantment held her sleepy-eyed.
Never on such a night have lovers met,   170
Since Merlin paid his Demon all the monstrous debt.[4]
                                  20
"It shall be as thou wishest," said the Dame:
"All cates[5] and dainties shall be stored there
Quickly on this feast-night: by the tambour frame[6]
Her own lute thou wilt see: no time to spare,   175
For I am slow and feeble, and scarce dare

2. Death knell.
3. Complaining.
4. Probably the episode in the Arthurian legends in
which Merlin, the magician, lost his life when the wily

Vivien turned one of his own spells against him.
5. Delicacies.
6. A drum-shaped embroidery frame.

On such a catering trust my dizzy head.
  Wait here, my child, with patience; kneel in prayer
  The while: Ah! thou must needs the lady wed,
Or may I never leave my grave among the dead."   180

21
So saying, she hobbled off with busy fear.
  The lover's endless minutes slowly pass'd;
  The dame return'd, and whisper'd in his ear
  To follow her; with aged eyes aghast
  From fright of dim espial. Safe at last,   185
  Through many a dusky gallery, they gain
  The maiden's chamber, silken, hush'd, and chaste;
  Where Porphyro took covert, pleas'd amain.[7]
His poor guide hurried back with agues in her brain.

22
Her falt'ring hand upon the balustrade,   190
  Old Angela was feeling for the stair,
  When Madeline, St. Agnes' charmed maid,
  Rose, like a mission'd spirit,[8] unaware:
  With silver taper's light, and pious care,
  She turn'd, and down the aged gossip led   195
  To a safe level matting. Now prepare,
  Young Porphyro, for gazing on that bed;
She comes, she comes again, like ring-dove fray'd[9] and fled.

23
Out went the taper as she hurried in;
  Its little smoke, in pallid moonshine, died: 200
  She clos'd the door, she panted, all akin
  To spirits of the air, and visions wide:
  No uttered syllable, or, woe betide!
  But to her heart, her heart was voluble,
  Paining with eloquence her balmy side;   205
  As though a tongueless nightingale should swell
Her throat in vain, and die, heart-stifled, in her dell.

24
A casement high and triple-arch'd there was,
  All garlanded with carven imag'ries
  Of fruits, and flowers, and bunches of knot-grass,   210
  And diamonded with panes of quaint device,
  Innumerable of stains and splendid dyes,
  As are the tiger-moth's deep-damask'd wings;
  And in the midst, 'mong thousand heraldries,
  And twilight saints, and dim emblazonings,   215
A shielded scutcheon blush'd with blood of queens and kings.[1]

25
Full on this casement shone the wintry moon,
  And threw warm gules[2] on Madeline's fair breast,
  As down she knelt for heaven's grace and boon;[3]

7. Mightily.
8. I.e., like an angel sent on a mission.
9. Frightened.
1. I.e., among the genealogical emblems ("herald-ries") and other devices ("emblazonings"), a heraldic shield signified by its colors that the family was of royal blood.
2. In heraldry, the color red.
3. Gift, blessing.

Rose-bloom fell on her hands, together prest,   220
And on her silver cross soft amethyst,
And on her hair a glory, like a saint:
She seem'd a splendid angel, newly drest,
Save wings, for heaven:—Porphyro grew faint:
She knelt, so pure a thing, so free from mortal taint.   225

                         26
Anon his heart revives: her vespers done,
Of all its wreathed pearls her hair she frees;
Unclasps her warmed jewels one by one;
Loosens her fragrant boddice; by degrees
Her rich attire creeps rustling to her knees: 230
Half-hidden, like a mermaid in sea-weed,
Pensive awhile she dreams awake, and sees,
In fancy, fair St. Agnes in her bed,
But dares not look behind, or all the charm is fled.

                         27
Soon, trembling in her soft and chilly nest,   235
In sort of wakeful swoon, perplex'd[4] she lay,
Until the poppied warmth of sleep oppress'd
Her soothed limbs, and soul fatigued away;
Flown, like a thought, until the morrow-day;
Blissfully haven'd both from joy and pain;   240
Clasp'd like a missal where swart Paynims pray;[5]
Blinded alike from sunshine and from rain,
As though a rose should shut, and be a bud again.

                         28
Stol'n to this paradise, and so entranced,
Porphyro gazed upon her empty dress,   245
And listen'd to her breathing, if it chanced
To wake into a slumberous tenderness;
Which when he heard, that minute did he bless,
And breath'd himself: then from the closet crept,
Noiseless as fear in a wide wilderness,   250
And over the hush'd carpet, silent, stept,
And 'tween the curtains peep'd, where, lo!—how fast she slept.

                         29
Then by the bed-side, where the faded moon
Made a dim, silver twilight, soft he set
A table, and, half anguish'd, threw thereon   255
A cloth of woven crimson, gold, and jet:—
O for some drowsy Morphean amulet![6]
The boisterous, midnight, festive clarion,[7]
The kettle-drum, and far-heard clarionet,
Affray his ears, though but in dying tone:—   260
The hall door shuts again, and all the noise is gone.

4. In a confused state between waking and sleeping.
5. Variously interpreted; perhaps: held tightly, cherished (or else kept shut, fastened with a clasp), like a Christian prayer book ("missal") in a land where the religion is that of dark-skinned pagans ("swart Paynims").
6. Sleep-producing charm.
7. High-pitched trumpet.

30

And still she slept an azure-lidded sleep,
    In blanched linen, smooth, and lavender'd,
While he from forth the closet brought a heap
    Of candied apple, quince, and plum, and gourd;[8]   265
With jellies soother than the creamy curd,
    And lucent syrops, tinct with cinnamon;
Manna and dates, in argosy transferr'd
    From Fez,[9] and spiced dainties, every one,
From silken Samarcand to cedar'd Lebanon.   270

31

These delicates he heap'd with glowing hand
    On golden dishes and in baskets bright
Of wreathed silver: sumptuous they stand
    In the retired quiet of the night,
Filling the chilly room with perfume light.—   275
    "And now, my love, my seraph[1] fair, awake!
Thou art my heaven, and I thine eremite:[2]
    Open thine eyes, for meek St. Agnes' sake,
Or I shall drowse beside thee, so my soul doth ache."

32

Thus whispering, his warm, unnerved arm   280
    Sank in her pillow. Shaded was her dream
By the dusk curtains:—'twas a midnight charm
    Impossible to melt as iced stream:
The lustrous salvers in the moonlight gleam;
    Broad golden fringe upon the carpet lies: 285
It seem'd he never, never could redeem
    From such a stedfast spell his lady's eyes;
So mus'd awhile, entoil'd in woofed phantasies.[3]

33

Awakening up, he took her hollow lute,—
    Tumultuous,—and, in chords that tenderest be,   290
He play'd an ancient ditty, long since mute,
    In Provence call'd, "La belle dame sans mercy":[4]
Close to her ear touching the melody;—
    Wherewith disturb'd, she utter'd a soft moan:
He ceased—she panted quick—and suddenly   295
    Her blue affrayed eyes wide open shone:
Upon his knees he sank, pale as smooth-sculptured stone.

34

Her eyes were open, but she still beheld,
    Now wide awake, the vision of her sleep:
There was a painful change, that nigh expell'd   300
    The blisses of her dream so pure and deep:
At which fair Madeline began to weep,
    And moan forth witless words with many a sigh;

8. Melon. According to the legend, the dream lover would bring the virgin a feast of delicacies.
9. I.e., jellies softer ("soother") than the curds of cream, clear ("lucent") syrups tinged with cinnamon, and sweet gums ("manna") and dates transported in a great merchant ship ("argosy") from Fez.

1. One of the highest order of angels.
2. Hermit, religious solitary.
3. Entangled in a weave of fantasies.
4. "The Lovely Lady without Pity," title of a work by the medieval poet Alain Chartier. Keats later adopted the title for his own ballad.

While still her gaze on Porphyro would keep;
Who knelt, with joined hands and piteous eye,   305
Fearing to move or speak, she look'd so dreamingly.

35

"Ah, Porphyro!" said she, "but even now
Thy voice was at sweet tremble in mine ear,
Made tuneable with every sweetest vow;
And those sad eyes were spiritual and clear: 310
How chang'd thou art! how pallid, chill, and drear!
Give me that voice again, my Porphyro,
Those looks immortal, those complainings dear!
Oh leave me not in this eternal woe,
For if thou diest, my love, I know not where to go."   315

36

Beyond a mortal man impassion'd far
At these voluptuous accents, he arose,
Ethereal, flush'd, and like a throbbing star
Seen mid the sapphire heaven's deep repose;
Into her dream he melted, as the rose   320
Blendeth its odour with the violet,—
Solution sweet: meantime the frost-wind blows
Like Love's alarum pattering the sharp sleet
Against the window-panes; St. Agnes' moon hath set.

37

'Tis dark: quick pattereth the flaw-blown[5] sleet: 325
"This is no dream, my bride, my Madeline!"
'Tis dark: the iced gusts still rave and beat:
"No dream, alas! alas! and woe is mine!
Porphyro will leave me here to fade and pine.—
Cruel! what traitor could thee hither bring?   330
I curse not, for my heart is lost in thine,
Though thou forsakest a deceived thing;—
A dove forlorn and lost with sick unpruned wing."

38

"My Madeline! sweet dreamer! lovely bride!
Say, may I be for aye thy vassal blest?   335
Thy beauty's shield, heart-shap'd and vermeil[6] dyed?
Ah, silver shrine, here will I take my rest
After so many hours of toil and quest,
A famish'd pilgrim,—saved by miracle.
Though I have found, I will not rob thy nest   340
Saving of thy sweet self; if thou think'st well
To trust, fair Madeline, to no rude infidel.

39

"Hark! 'tis an elfin-storm from faery land,
Of haggard[7] seeming, but a boon indeed:
Arise—arise! the morning is at hand;—   345
The bloated wassaillers[8] will never heed:—
Let us away, my love, with happy speed;
There are no ears to hear, or eyes to see,—

---

5. Gust-blown.
6. Vermilion.

7. Wild, untamed (originally, a wild hawk).
8. Drunken carousers.

Drown'd all in Rhenish and the sleepy mead:[9]
Awake! arise! my love, and fearless be,   350
For o'er the southern moors I have a home for thee."

40

She hurried at his words, beset with fears,
For there were sleeping dragons all around,
At glaring watch, perhaps, with ready spears—
Down the wide stairs a darkling[1] way they found.—   355
In all the house was heard no human sound.
A chain-droop'd lamp was flickering by each door;
The arras, rich with horseman, hawk, and hound,
Flutter'd in the besieging wind's uproar;
And the long carpets rose along the gusty floor.   360

41

They glide, like phantoms, into the wide hall;
Like phantoms, to the iron porch, they glide;
Where lay the Porter, in uneasy sprawl,
With a huge empty flaggon by his side:
The wakeful bloodhound rose, and shook his hide,   365
But his sagacious eye an inmate owns:[2]
By one, and one, the bolts full easy slide:—
The chains lie silent on the footworn stones;—
The key turns, and the door upon its hinges groans.

42

And they are gone: ay, ages long ago   370
These lovers fled away into the storm.
That night the Baron dreamt of many a woe,
And all his warrior-guests, with shade and form
Of witch, and demon, and large coffin-worm,
Were long be-nightmar'd. Angela the old   375
Died palsy-twitch'd, with meagre face deform;
The Beadsman, after thousand aves[3] told,
For aye unsought for slept among his ashes cold.

Jan.–Feb. 1819   1820

Bright star, would I were stedfast as thou art[1]

Bright star, would I were stedfast as thou art—
    Not in lone splendor hung aloft the night,
And watching, with eternal lids apart,
    Like nature's patient, sleepless eremite,[2]
The moving waters at their priestlike task   5
    Of pure ablution[3] round earth's human shores,

9. Rhine wine and the sleep-producing mead (a heavy fermented drink made with honey).
1. In the dark.
2. Acknowledges a member of the household.
3. The prayers beginning *Ave Maria* ("Hail Mary").
1. While on a tour of the Lake District in 1818, Keats had said that the austere scenes "refine one's sensual vision into a sort of north star which can never cease to be open lidded and steadfast over the wonders of the

great Power"; the thought developed into this sonnet. Keats drafted this poem in 1819, then copied it into his volume of Shakespeare's poems, at the end of Sept. or the beginning of Oct. 1820, while on the way to Italy, where he died.
2. Hermit, religious solitary.
3. Washing, as part of a religious rite.

Or gazing on the new soft-fallen mask
    Of snow upon the mountains and the moors;
No—yet still stedfast, still unchangeable,
    Pillow'd upon my fair love's ripening breast,   10
To feel for ever its soft swell and fall,
    Awake for ever in a sweet unrest,
Still, still to hear her tender-taken breath,
And so live ever—or else swoon to death.[4]

1819   1838

La Belle Dame sans Merci: A Ballad[1]

1

O what can ail thee, knight at arms,
    Alone and palely loitering?
The sedge has wither'd from the lake,
    And no birds sing.

2

O what can ail thee, knight at arms,   5
    So haggard and so woe-begone?
The squirrel's granary is full,
    And the harvest's done.

3

I see a lily on thy brow
    With anguish moist and fever dew,   10
And on thy cheeks a fading rose
    Fast withereth too.

4

I met a lady in the meads,
    Full beautiful, a fairy's child;
Her hair was long, her foot was light,   15
    And her eyes were wild.

5

I made a garland for her head,
    And bracelets too, and fragrant zone;[2]
She look'd at me as she did love,
    And made sweet moan.   20

6

I set her on my pacing steed,
    And nothing else saw all day long,
For sidelong would she bend, and sing
    A fairy's song.

---

4. In the earlier version: "Half passionless, and so swoon on to death."
1. The title, though not the subject, was taken from a medieval poem by Alain Chartier and means "The Lovely Lady without Pity." The story of a mortal destroyed by his love for a supernatural femme fatale has been told repeatedly in myth, fairy tale, and ballad, but never so hauntingly. Conducive to this effect is the suspension achieved by shortening to two stresses the final line of each stanza. We print here Keats's earlier version of the poem, as transcribed by Charles Brown. The version published in 1820, "Ah, what can ail thee, wretched wight," is a rare instance in which Keats weakened a poem by revision.

Keats imitates a frequent procedure of folk ballads by casting the poem into the dialogue form. The first three stanzas are addressed to the knight, and the rest of the poem is his reply.
2. Belt (of flowers).

7
She found me roots of relish sweet,   25
    And honey wild, and manna dew,
And sure in language strange she said—
    I love thee true.
8
She took me to her elfin grot,
    And there she wept, and sigh'd full sore,   30
And there I shut her wild wild eyes
    With kisses four.
9
And there she lulled me asleep,
    And there I dream'd—Ah! woe betide!
The latest³ dream I ever dream'd   35
    On the cold hill's side.
10
I saw pale kings, and princes too,
    Pale warriors, death pale were they all;
They cried—"La belle dame sans merci
    Hath thee in thrall!"   40
11
I saw their starv'd lips in the gloam
    With horrid warning gaped wide,
And I awoke and found me here
    On the cold hill's side.
12
And this is why I sojourn here,   45
    Alone and palely loitering,
Though the sedge is wither'd from the lake,
    And no birds sing.

Apr. 1819   1820

Ode to Psyche¹

O Goddess! hear these tuneless numbers, wrung
    By sweet enforcement and remembrance dear,
And pardon that thy secrets should be sung

    Even into thine own soft-conched² ear:
    Surely I dreamt to-day, or did I see   5

3. Last.
1. This poem initiated the sequence of great odes that Keats wrote in the spring of 1819. It is copied into the same journal-letter that included the *Sonnet to Sleep* and several other sonnets as well as a comment about "endeavoring to discover a better sonnet stanza than we have." It is therefore likely that Keats's experiments with sonnet schemes led to the development of the intricate and varied stanzas of his odes and also that he abandoned the sonnet on discovering the richer possibilities of the more spacious form. In his journal-letter, on Apr. 30, he said that of all his recent poems, *Psyche* "is the first and the only one with which I have taken even moderate pains. I have for the most part dashed

off my lines in a hurry. This I have done leisurely—I think it reads the more richly for it and will I hope encourage me to write other things in even a more peaceable and healthy spirit."
    In the story told by the Roman author Apuleius in the 2nd century, Psyche was a lovely mortal beloved by Cupid, "the winged boy," son of Venus. After various tribulations, imposed by Venus because she was jealous of Psyche's beauty, Psyche was wedded to Cupid and translated to heaven as an immortal. To this latter-day goddess, Keats in the last two stanzas promises to establish a place of worship within his own mind, with himself as poet-priest and prophet.
2. Soft and shaped like a seashell.

The winged Psyche with awaken'd eyes?[3]
I wander'd in a forest thoughtlessly,
    And, on the sudden, fainting with surprise,
Saw two fair creatures, couched side by side
        In deepest grass, beneath the whisp'ring roof   10
        Of leaves and trembled blossoms, where there ran
            A brooklet, scarce espied:
'Mid hush'd, cool-rooted flowers, fragrant-eyed,
    Blue, silver-white, and budded Tyrian,[4]
They lay calm-breathing on the bedded grass;   15
    Their arms embraced, and their pinions[5] too;
    Their lips touch'd not, but had not bade adieu,
As if disjoined by soft-handed slumber,
And ready still past kisses to outnumber
      At tender eye-dawn of aurorean love:[6]   20
            The winged boy I knew;
    But who wast thou, O happy, happy dove?
            His Psyche true!

O latest born and loveliest vision far
    Of all Olympus' faded hierarchy![7]   25
Fairer than Phoebe's sapphire-region'd star,[8]
    Or Vesper,[9] amorous glow-worm of the sky;
Fairer than these, though temple thou hast none,
        Nor altar heap'd with flowers;
Nor virgin-choir to make delicious moan   30
        Upon the midnight hours;
No voice, no lute, no pipe, no incense sweet
        From chain-swung censer teeming;
No shrine, no grove, no oracle, no heat
        Of pale-mouth'd prophet dreaming.   35

O brightest! though too late for antique vows,
    Too, too late for the fond believing lyre,
When holy were the haunted forest boughs,
    Holy the air, the water, and the fire;
Yet even in these days so far retir'd   40
      From happy pieties, thy lucent fans,[1]
      Fluttering among the faint Olympians,
I see, and sing, by my own eyes inspired.
So let me be thy choir, and make a moan
        Upon the midnight hours;   45
Thy voice, thy lute, thy pipe, thy incense sweet
        From swinged censer teeming;

---

3. Another of Keats's inquiries into the relation of dreams to poetic vision; see, e.g., *Sleep and Poetry* (pp. 1771–72), and the concluding lines of *Ode to a Nightingale* (p. 1773).
4. The purple dye anciently made in Tyre.
5. Wings.
6. Aurora was the goddess of the dawn.
7. The ranks of the classic gods of Mt. Olympus. "You must recollect that Psyche was not embodied as a goddess before the time of Apuleius the Platonist who lived after the Augustan age, and consequently the goddess was never worshiped or sacrificed to with any of the ancient fervor—and perhaps never thought of in the old religion" (Keats, journal-letter, Apr. 30, 1819).
8. The moon, supervised by the goddess Phoebe (Diana).
9. The evening star.
1. Shining wings.

Thy shrine, thy grove, thy oracle, thy heat
    Of pale-mouth'd prophet dreaming.

Yes, I will be thy priest, and build a fane[2]   50
    In some untrodden region of my mind,
Where branched thoughts, new grown with pleasant pain,
    Instead of pines shall murmur in the wind:
Far, far around shall those dark-cluster'd trees
    Fledge[2] the wild-ridged mountains steep by steep;[3]   55
And there by zephyrs, streams, and birds, and bees,
    The moss-lain Dryads[4] shall be lull'd to sleep;
And in the midst of this wide quietness
A rosy sanctuary will I dress
With the wreath'd trellis of a working brain,   60
    With buds, and bells, and stars without a name,
With all the gardener Fancy e'er could feign,
    Who breeding flowers, will never breed the same:
And there shall be for thee all soft delight
    That shadowy thought can win,   65
A bright torch, and a casement ope at night,
    To let the warm Love[5] in!

Apr. 1819   1820

Ode to a Nightingale[1]

1

My heart aches, and a drowsy numbness pains
    My sense, as though of hemlock[2] I had drunk,
Or emptied some dull opiate to the drains
    One minute past, and Lethe-wards[3] had sunk:
'Tis not through envy of thy happy lot,   5
    But being too happy in thine happiness,—
        That thou, light-winged Dryad of the trees,
            In some melodious plot
Of beechen green, and shadows numberless,
    Singest of summer in full-throated ease.   10

2

O, for a draught of vintage! that hath been
    Cool'd a long age in the deep-delved earth,
Tasting of Flora[4] and the country green,
    Dance, and Provençal song,[5] and sunburnt mirth!

2. Temple.
3. I.e., the trees shall stand, rank against rank, like layers of feathers.
4. Wood nymphs.
5. I.e., Cupid, god of love.
1. Charles Brown, with whom Keats was then living in Hampstead, wrote: "In the spring of 1819 a nightingale had built her nest near my house. Keats felt a tranquil and continual joy in her song; and one morning he took his chair from the breakfast table to the grass plot under a plum tree, where he sat for two or three hours. When he came into the house, I perceived he had some scraps of paper in his hand, and these he was quietly thrusting behind the books. On inquiry, I found those scraps, four or five in number, contained his poetic feeling on the song of our nightingale."
2. A poisonous herb, not the North American evergreen tree.
3. Toward Lethe, the river in Hades whose waters cause forgetfulness.
4. Roman goddess of flowers, or the flowers themselves.
5. Provence, in southern France, was in the late Middle Ages renowned for its troubadours, the writers and singers of love songs.

O for a beaker full of the warm South,   15
   Full of the true, the blushful Hippocrene,[6]
     With beaded bubbles winking at the brim,
        And purple-stained mouth;
   That I might drink, and leave the world unseen,
     And with thee fade away into the forest dim: 20

3

Fade far away, dissolve, and quite forget
   What thou among the leaves hast never known,
The weariness, the fever, and the fret
   Here, where men sit and hear each other groan;
Where palsy shakes a few, sad, last gray hairs,   25
   Where youth grows pale, and spectre-thin, and dies;[7]
     Where but to think is to be full of sorrow
        And leaden-eyed despairs,
   Where Beauty cannot keep her lustrous eyes,
     Or new Love pine at them beyond to-morrow.   30

4

Away! away! for I will fly to thee,
   Not charioted by Bacchus and his pards,
But on the viewless wings of Poesy,[8]
   Though the dull brain perplexes and retards:
Already with thee! tender is the night,   35
   And haply the Queen-Moon is on her throne,
     Cluster'd around by all her starry Fays;[9]
        But here there is no light,
   Save what from heaven is with the breezes blown
     Through verdurous[1] glooms and winding mossy ways.   40

5

I cannot see what flowers are at my feet,
   Nor what soft incense hangs upon the boughs,
But, in embalmed[2] darkness, guess each sweet
   Wherewith the seasonable month endows
The grass, the thicket, and the fruit-tree wild;   45
   White hawthorn, and the pastoral eglantine;[3]
     Fast fading violets cover'd up in leaves;
        And mid-May's eldest child,
   The coming musk-rose, full of dewy wine,
     The murmurous haunt of flies on summer eves.   50

6

Darkling[4] I listen; and, for many a time
   I have been half in love with easeful Death,
Call'd him soft names in many a mused[5] rhyme,
   To take into the air my quiet breath;

bro died recently

6. Fountain of the Muses on Mt. Helicon, hence the
waters of inspiration, here applied metaphorically to a
beaker of wine.
7. Keats's brother Tom, wasted by tuberculosis, had
died the preceding winter.
8. I.e., not by getting drunk on wine (the "vintage" of
stanza 2), but on the invisible ("viewless") wings of the
poetic imagination. (Bacchus, god of wine, was sometimes represented in a chariot drawn by "pards"—leopards.)

9. Fairies.
1. Green-foliaged.
2. Perfumed.
3. Sweetbrier, or honeysuckle.
4. In darkness.
5. Meditated. Two earlier poems ("rhymes") by Keats
that called on "easeful Death" are the sonnets *Why did
I laugh tonight? No voice will tell* and *Bright star, would
I were stedfast as thou art.*

Now more than ever seems it rich to die,   55
  To cease upon the midnight with no pain,
    While thou art pouring forth thy soul abroad
      In such an ecstasy!
Still wouldst thou sing, and I have ears in vain—
  To thy high requiem become a sod.   60

7

Thou wast not born for death, immortal Bird!
  No hungry generations tread thee down;
The voice I hear this passing night was heard
  In ancient days by emperor and clown:
Perhaps the self-same song that found a path   65
  Through the sad heart of Ruth,[6] when, sick for home,
    She stood in tears amid the alien corn;[7]
      The same that oft-times hath
Charm'd magic casements, opening on the foam
  Of perilous seas, in faery lands forlorn.   70

8

Forlorn! the very word is like a bell
  To toll me back from thee to my sole self!
Adieu! the fancy[8] cannot cheat so well
  As she is fam'd to do, deceiving elf.
Adieu! adieu! thy plaintive anthem[9] fades   75
  Past the near meadows, over the still stream,
    Up the hill-side; and now 'tis buried deep
      In the next valley-glades:
Was it a vision, or a waking dream?
  Fled is that music:—Do I wake or sleep?[1]   80

May 1819   1819

Ode on a Grecian Urn[1]

1

Thou still unravish'd bride of quietness,
  Thou foster-child of silence and slow time,
Sylvan[2] historian, who canst thus express
  A flowery tale more sweetly than our rhyme:
What leaf-fring'd legend haunts about thy shape
  Of deities or mortals, or of both,

6. The young widow in the biblical Book of Ruth.
7. I.e., wheat.
8. I.e., imagination, "the viewless wings of Poesy" of line 33.
9. Hymn.
1. See *Ode to Psyche* (p. 1790, n. 3).
1. This urn, with its sculptured reliefs of Dionysian ecstasies, panting young lovers in flight and pursuit, a pastoral piper under spring foliage, and the quiet procession of priest and townspeople, resembles parts of various vases, sculptures, and paintings, but it existed in all its particulars only in Keats's imagination. In the urn—which captures moments of intense experience in attitudes of grace and immobilizes them in mar-

ble—Keats found the perfect correlative for his concern with the longing for permanence in a world of change. The interpretation of the details with which he develops this concept, however, is hotly disputed, all the way from the opening phrase—is "still" an adverb ("as yet") or an adjective ("motionless")?—to the two concluding lines, which have already accumulated as much critical discussion as the "two-handed engine" in Milton's *Lycidas* or the cruxes in Shakespeare's plays. These disputes testify to the enigmatic richness of meaning in the five stanzas, as well as to the fact that the ode has become a central point of reference in the criticism of the English lyric.
2. Rustic, representing a woodland scene.

In Tempe or the dales of Arcady?[3]
   What men or gods are these? What maidens loth?
What mad pursuit? What struggle to escape?
   What pipes and timbrels? What wild ecstasy?

2

Heard melodies are sweet, but those unheard
   Are sweeter; therefore, ye soft pipes, play on;
Not to the sensual ear,[4] but, more endear'd,
   Pipe to the spirit ditties of no tone:
Fair youth, beneath the trees, thou canst not leave
   Thy song, nor ever can those trees be bare;
     Bold lover, never, never canst thou kiss,
Though winning near the goal—yet, do not grieve;
     She cannot fade, though thou hast not thy bliss,
   For ever wilt thou love, and she be fair!

3

Ah, happy, happy boughs! that cannot shed
   Your leaves, nor ever bid the spring adieu;
And, happy melodist, unwearied,
   For ever piping songs for ever new;
More happy love! more happy, happy love!
   For ever warm and still to be enjoy'd,
     For ever panting, and for ever young;
All breathing human passion far above,
   That leaves a heart high-sorrowful and cloy'd,
     A burning forehead, and a parching tongue.

4

Who are these coming to the sacrifice?
   To what green altar, O mysterious priest,
Lead'st thou that heifer lowing at the skies,
   And all her silken flanks with garlands drest?
What little town by river or sea shore,
   Or mountain-built with peaceful citadel,
     Is emptied of this folk, this pious morn?
And, little town, thy streets for evermore
   Will silent be; and not a soul to tell
     Why thou art desolate, can e'er return.

5

O Attic[5] shape! Fair attitude! with brede
   Of marble men and maidens overwrought,[6]
With forest branches and the trodden weed;
   Thou, silent form, dost tease us out of thought
As doth eternity: Cold Pastoral!
   When old age shall this generation waste,
     Thou shalt remain, in midst of other woe
Than ours, a friend to man, to whom thou say'st,

10

15

20

25

30

35

40

45

---

3. The valleys of Arcadia, a state in ancient Greece often used as a symbol of the pastoral ideal. "Tempe": a beautiful valley in Greece that has come to represent supreme rural beauty.
4. The ear of sense (as opposed to that of the "spirit," or imagination).
5. Greek. Attica was the region of Greece in which Athens was located.
6. Ornamented all over ("overwrought") with an interwoven pattern ("brede").

"Beauty is truth, truth beauty,"[7]—that is all
        Ye know on earth, and all ye need to know.   50

1819   1820

Ode on Melancholy   This is Keats's best-known statement of his recurrent
theme of the mingled contrarieties of life. The remarkable last stanza, in which
Melancholy becomes a veiled goddess in a mystery religion, implies that it is the
tragic human destiny that beauty, joy, and life itself owe not only their quality but
their value to the fact that they are transitory and turn into their opposites.
    The poem once had the following initial stanza, which Keats canceled in manu-
script:

        Though you should build a bark of dead men's bones,
            And rear a phantom gibbet for a mast,
        Stitch creeds together for a sail, with groans
            To fill it out, bloodstained and aghast;
        Although your rudder be a Dragon's tail,
            Long sever'd, yet still hard with agony,
                Your cordage large uprootings from the skull
        Of bald Medusa: certes you would fail
            To find the Melancholy, whether she
            Dreameth in any isle of Lethe dull.

                    Ode on Melancholy

                                1
        No, no, go not to Lethe,[1] neither twist
            Wolf's-bane, tight-rooted, for its poisonous wine;
        Nor suffer thy pale forehead to be kiss'd
            By nightshade, ruby grape of Proserpine;[2]
        Make not your rosary of yew-berries,[3]   5
            Nor let the beetle, nor the death-moth be
                Your mournful Psyche,[4] nor the downy owl
        A partner in your sorrow's mysteries;[5]
            For shade to shade will come too drowsily,
            And drown the wakeful anguish of the soul.[6]   10

7. The quotation marks around this phrase are found
in the volume of poems Keats published in 1820, but
there are no quotation marks in the version printed in
Annals of the Fine Arts that same year or in the transcripts of the poem made by Keats's friends. This
discrepancy has multiplied the diversity of critical
interpretations of the last two lines. Critics disagree
whether the whole of these lines is said by the urn, or
"Beauty is truth, truth beauty" by the urn and the rest
by the lyric speaker; whether the "ye" in the last line is
addressed to the lyric speaker, to the readers, to the
urn, or to the figures on the urn; whether "all ye know"
is that beauty is truth, or this plus the statement in lines
46–48; and whether "beauty is truth" is a profound
metaphysical proposition, an overstatement representing the limited point of view of the urn, or simply nonsensical.
1. The waters of forgetfulness in Hades.
2. The wife of Pluto and queen of the infernal regions.
"Nightshade" and "wolf's-bane" (line 2) are poisonous
plants.
3. A symbol of death.
4. In ancient times, Psyche (the soul) was sometimes
represented as a butterfly or moth, fluttering out of the
mouth of a dying man. The allusion may also be to the
death's-head moth, which has skull-like markings on
its back. The "beetle" of line 6 refers to replicas of the
large black beetle, the scarab, which were often placed
by Egyptians in their tombs as a symbol of resurrection.
5. Secret religious rites.
6. I.e., sorrow needs contrast to sustain its intensity.

2

But when the melancholy fit shall fall
   Sudden from heaven like a weeping cloud,
That fosters the droop-headed flowers all,
   And hides the green hill in an April shroud;
Then glut thy sorrow on a morning rose,   15
   Or on the rainbow of the salt sand-wave,
      Or on the wealth of globed peonies;
Or if thy mistress some rich anger shows,
   Emprison her soft hand, and let her rave,
   And feed deep, deep upon her peerless eyes.   20

3

She[7] dwells with Beauty—Beauty that must die;
   And Joy, whose hand is ever at his lips
Bidding adieu; and aching Pleasure nigh,
   Turning to poison while the bee-mouth sips:
Ay, in the very temple of Delight   25
   Veil'd Melancholy has her sovran shrine,
      Though seen of none save him whose strenuous tongue
Can burst Joy's grape against his palate fine;[8]
His soul shall taste the sadness of her might,
   And be among her cloudy trophies hung.[9]   30

1819   1820

Ode on Indolence[1]

"They toil not, neither do they spin."[2]

1

One morn before me were three figures seen,
   With bowed necks, and joined hands, side-faced;
And one behind the other stepp'd serene,
   In placid sandals, and in white robes graced:
They pass'd, like figures on a marble urn,   5
   When shifted round to see the other side;
      They came again: as when the urn once more
Is shifted round, the first seen shades return;
   And they were strange to me, as may betide
   With vases, to one deep in Phidian[3] lore.   10

2

How is it, shadows, that I knew ye not?
How came ye muffled in so hush a masque?

7. Usually taken to refer to Melancholy rather than to "thy mistress" in line 18.
8. Sensitive, subtly discriminative.
9. A reference to the Greek and Roman practice of hanging trophies in the temples of the gods.
1. On Mar. 19, 1819, Keats wrote to George and Georgiana Keats: "This morning I am in a sort of temper indolent and supremely careless. . . . Neither Poetry, nor Ambition, nor Love have any alertness of countenance as they pass by me: they seem rather like three figures on a greek vase—a Man and two women— whom no one but myself could distinguish in their disguisement. This is the only happiness; and is a rare instance of advantage in the body overpowering the Mind." The ode was probably written soon after this time, but was not published until 1848, long after the poet's death.
2. Matthew 6.28.
3. Phidias was the great Athenian sculptor of the 5th century B.C. who designed the marble sculptures for the Parthenon.

Was it a silent deep-disguised plot
   To steal away, and leave without a task
My idle days? Ripe was the drowsy hour;   15
   The blissful cloud of summer-indolence
      Benumb'd my eyes; my pulse grew less and less;
Pain had no sting, and pleasure's wreath no flower.
   O, why did ye not melt, and leave my sense
      Unhaunted quite of all but—nothingness?   20

3

A third time pass'd they by, and, passing, turn'd
   Each one the face a moment whiles to me;
Then faded, and to follow them I burn'd
   And ached for wings, because I knew the three:
The first was a fair maid, and Love her name;   25
   The second was Ambition, pale of cheek,
      And ever watchful with fatigued eye;
The last, whom I love more, the more of blame
   Is heap'd upon her, maiden most unmeek,—
      I knew to be my demon Poesy.   30

4

They faded, and, forsooth! I wanted wings:
   O folly! What is Love? and where is it?
And for that poor Ambition—it springs
   From a man's little heart's short fever-fit;
For Poesy!—no,—she has not a joy,—   35
   At least for me,—so sweet as drowsy noons,
      And evenings steep'd in honied indolence;
O, for an age so shelter'd from annoy,
   That I may never know how change the moons,
      Or hear the voice of busy common-sense!   40

5

A third time came they by;—alas! wherefore?
   My sleep had been embroider'd with dim dreams;
My soul had been a lawn besprinkled o'er
   With flowers, and stirring shades, and baffled beams:
The morn was clouded, but no shower fell,   45
   Though in her lids hung the sweet tears of May;
      The open casement press'd a new-leaved vine,
Let in the budding warmth and throstle's lay;
O shadows! 'twas a time to bid farewell!
      Upon your skirts had fallen no tears of mine.   50

6

So, ye three ghosts, adieu! Ye cannot raise
   My head cool-bedded in the flowery grass;
For I would not be dieted with praise,
   A pet-lamb in a sentimental farce![4]
Fade softly from my eyes, and be once more   55
   In masque-like figures on the dreamy urn;

---

4. In a letter of June 9, 1819, Keats wrote: "I have been very idle lately, very averse to writing; both from the overpowering idea of our dead poets and from abatement of my love of fame. I hope I am a little more of a Philosopher than I was, consequently a little less of a versifying Pet-lamb.... You will judge of my 1819 temper when I tell you that the thing I have most enjoyed this year has been writing an ode to Indolence."

Farewell! I yet have visions for the night,
And for the day faint visions there is store;
Vanish, ye phantoms, from my idle spright,[5]
Into the clouds, and never more return!　　　　　　　60
Spring 1819　　　　　　　　　　　　　　　　　　　　　1848

Lamia　　Keats cited as his source the following story in Robert Burton's *Anatomy of Melancholy* (1621): "One Menippus Lycius, a young man twenty-five years of age, that going betwixt Cenchreas and Corinth, met such a phantasm in the habit of a fair gentlewoman, which, taking him by the hand, carried him home to her house, in the suburbs of Corinth. . . . The young man, a philosopher, otherwise staid and discreet, able to moderate his passions, though not this of love, tarried with her a while to his great content, and at last married her, to whose wedding, amongst other guests, came Apollonius; who, by some probable conjectures, found her out to be a serpent, a lamia; and that all her furniture was, like Tantalus' gold, described by Homer, no substance but mere illusions. When she saw herself descried, she wept, and desired Apollonius to be silent, but he would not be moved, and thereupon she, plate, house, and all that was in it, vanished in an instant: many thousands took notice of this fact, for it was done in the midst of Greece."

In ancient demonology, a "lamia"—pronounced *lā'·mĭ·a*—was a monster in woman's form who preyed on human beings. There are various clues that Keats invested the ancient legend with allegorical significance (see especially 2.229–38). Its interpretation, however, and even the inclination of Keats's own sympathies in the contest between Lamia and Apollonius, have been disputed. It is possible that Keats simply failed to make up his mind, or wavered in the course of composition. It seems more likely, however, that he intended to present an inevitably fatal situation, in which no one is entirely blameless or blameworthy and no character is meant to monopolize either our sympathy or antipathy. Lamia is an enchantress, a liar, and a calculating expert in *amour;* but she apparently intends no harm, is genuinely in love, and is very beautiful. And both male protagonists exhibit culpable extremes. Lycius, though an attractive young lover, is gullible, a slave to his passions, and capable of gratuitous cruelty; while Apollonius, though realistically clear-sighted, is rigid, puritanical, and inhumane.

The poem, written between late June and early September 1819, is a return, after the Spenserian stanzas of *The Eve of St. Agnes,* to the pentameter couplets Keats had used in *Endymion: A Poetic Romance* and other early narrative poems. But Keats had in the meantime been studying John Dryden's closed and strong-paced couplets. The initial lines of Dryden's version of Boccaccio's story *Cymon and Iphigenia* will show the kind of narrative model that helped Keats make the technical transition from the fluent but sprawling gracefulness of the opening of *Endymion* to the vigor and economy of the opening of *Lamia:*

In that sweet isle where Venus keeps her court,
And every grace, and all the loves, resort;
Where either sex is formed of softer earth,
And takes the bent of pleasure from their birth;
There lived a Cyprian lord, above the rest
Wise, wealthy, with a numerous issue blessed. . . .

5. Spirit.

Lamia

Part 1

Upon a time, before the faery broods
Drove Nymph and Satyr from the prosperous woods,[1]
Before King Oberon's bright diadem,
Sceptre, and mantle, clasp'd with dewy gem,
Frighted away the Dryads and the Fauns   5
From rushes green, and brakes,[2] and cowslip'd lawns,
The ever-smitten Hermes empty left
His golden throne, bent warm on amorous theft:[3]
From high Olympus had he stolen light,
On this side of Jove's clouds, to escape the sight   10
Of his great summoner, and made retreat
Into a forest on the shores of Crete.
For somewhere in that sacred island dwelt
A nymph, to whom all hoofed Satyrs knelt;
At whose white feet the languid Tritons[4] poured   15
Pearls, while on land they wither'd and adored.
Fast by the springs where she to bathe was wont,
And in those meads where sometime she might haunt,
Were strewn rich gifts, unknown to any Muse,
Though Fancy's casket were unlock'd to choose.   20
Ah, what a world of love was at her feet!
So Hermes thought, and a celestial heat
Burnt from his winged heels to either ear,
That from a whiteness, as the lily clear,
Blush'd into roses 'mid his golden hair,   25
Fallen in jealous curls about his shoulders bare.[5]

From vale to vale, from wood to wood, he flew,
Breathing upon the flowers his passion new,
And wound with many a river to its head,
To find where this sweet nymph prepar'd her secret bed: 30
In vain; the sweet nymph might nowhere be found,
And so he rested, on the lonely ground,
Pensive, and full of painful jealousies
Of the Wood-Gods, and even the very trees.
There as he stood, he heard a mournful voice,   35
Such as once heard, in gentle heart, destroys
All pain but pity: thus the lone voice spake:
"When from this wreathed tomb shall I awake!
When move in a sweet body fit for life,
And love, and pleasure, and the ruddy strife   40
Of hearts and lips! Ah, miserable me!"

1. Nymphs and satyrs—like the dryads and fauns in line 5—were all minor classical deities of the woods and fields, said here to have been driven off by Oberon, king of the fairies, who were supernatural beings of the postclassical era.
2. Thickets.
3. Hermes (or Mercury), wing-footed messenger at the summons of Jove (line 11), was notoriously amorous.
4. Minor sea gods.
5. I.e., the curls clung jealously to his bare shoulders. This line is the first of a number of Alexandrines, a six-foot line, used to vary the metrical movement—a device that Keats learned from Dryden. Another such device is the triplet, occurring first in lines 61–63.

The God, dove-footed,[6] glided silently
Round bush and tree, soft-brushing, in his speed,
The taller grasses and full-flowering weed,
Until he found a palpitating snake,   45
Bright, and cirque-couchant[7] in a dusky brake.

She was a gordian[8] shape of dazzling hue,
Vermilion-spotted, golden, green, and blue;
Striped like a zebra, freckled like a pard,
Eyed like a peacock,[9] and all crimson barr'd;   50
And full of silver moons, that, as she breathed,
Dissolv'd, or brighter shone, or interwreathed
Their lustres with the gloomier tapestries—
So rainbow-sided, touch'd with miseries,
She seem'd, at once, some penanced lady elf,   55
Some demon's mistress, or the demon's self.
Upon her crest she wore a wannish[1] fire
Sprinkled with stars, like Ariadne's tiar:[2]
Her head was serpent, but ah, bitter-sweet!
She had a woman's mouth with all its pearls[3] complete: 60
And for her eyes: what could such eyes do there
But weep, and weep, that they were born so fair?
As Proserpine still weeps for her Sicilian air.[4]
Her throat was serpent, but the words she spake
Came, as through bubbling honey, for Love's sake,   65
And thus; while Hermes on his pinions lay,
Like a stoop'd falcon[5] ere he takes his prey.

    "Fair Hermes, crown'd with feathers, fluttering light,
I had a splendid dream of thee last night:
I saw thee sitting, on a throne of gold,   70
Among the Gods, upon Olympus old,
The only sad one; for thou didst not hear
The soft, lute-finger'd Muses chaunting clear,
Nor even Apollo when he sang alone,
Deaf to his throbbing throat's long, long melodious moan.   75
I dreamt I saw thee, robed in purple flakes,
Break amorous through the clouds, as morning breaks,
And, swiftly as a bright Phœbean dart,[6]
Strike for the Cretan isle; and here thou art!
Too gentle Hermes, hast thou found the maid?"   80
Whereat the star of Lethe[7] not delay'd
His rosy eloquence, and thus inquired:

6. I.e., quietly as a dove.
7. Lying in a circular coil.
8. Intricately twisted, like the knot tied by King Gordius, which no one could undo.
9. Having multicolored spots, like the "eyes" in a peacock's tail. "Pard": leopard.
1. Rather dark.
2. Ariadne, who was transformed into a constellation, had been represented in a painting by Titian wearing a symbolic crown, or tiara ("tiar"), of stars.
3. "Pearls" had become almost a synonym for teeth in

Elizabethan love poems.
4. Proserpine had been carried off to Hades by Pluto from the field of Enna, in Sicily.
5. "Stoop" is the term for the plunge of a falcon upon his prey.
6. A ray of Phoebus Apollo, god of the sun.
7. Hermes, when he appeared like a star on the banks of Lethe, in the darkness of Hades. (One of Hermes' offices was to guide the souls of the dead to the lower regions.)

"Thou smooth-lipp'd serpent, surely high inspired!
Thou beauteous wreath, with melancholy eyes,
Possess whatever bliss thou canst devise,   85
Telling me only where my nymph is fled,—
Where she doth breathe!" "Bright planet, thou hast said,"
Return'd the snake, "but seal with oaths, fair God!"
"I swear," said Hermes, "by my serpent rod,
And by thine eyes, and by thy starry crown!"   90
Light flew his earnest words, among the blossoms blown.
Then thus again the brilliance feminine:
"Too frail of heart! for this lost nymph of thine,
Free as the air, invisibly, she strays
About these thornless wilds; her pleasant days   95
She tastes unseen; unseen her nimble feet
Leave traces in the grass and flowers sweet;
From weary tendrils, and bow'd branches green,
She plucks the fruit unseen, she bathes unseen:
And by my power is her beauty veil'd   100
To keep it unaffronted, unassail'd
By the love-glances of unlovely eyes,
Of Satyrs, Fauns, and blear'd Silenus'[8] sighs.
Pale grew her immortality, for woe
Of all these lovers, and she grieved so   105
I took compassion on her, bade her steep
Her hair in weïrd[9] syrops, that would keep
Her loveliness invisible, yet free
To wander as she loves, in liberty.
Thou shalt behold her, Hermes, thou alone,   110
If thou wilt, as thou swearest, grant my boon!"
Then, once again, the charmed God began
An oath, and through the serpent's ears it ran
Warm, tremulous, devout, psalterian.[1]
Ravish'd, she lifted her Circean head,   115
Blush'd a live damask,[2] and swift-lisping said,
"I was a woman, let me have once more
A woman's shape, and charming as before.
I love a youth of Corinth—O the bliss!
Give me my woman's form, and place me where he is.   120
Stoop, Hermes, let me breathe upon thy brow,
And thou shalt see thy sweet nymph even now."
The God on half-shut feathers sank serene,
She breath'd upon his eyes, and swift was seen
Of both the guarded nymph near-smiling on the green.   125
It was no dream; or say a dream it was,
Real are the dreams of Gods, and smoothly pass
Their pleasures in a long immortal dream.
One warm, flush'd moment, hovering, it might seem
Dash'd by the wood-nymph's beauty, so he burn'd;   130

8. Silenus was a satyr, tutor of Bacchus, usually represented as drunk.
9. Magical: Keats makes the word a dissyllable.
1. Either "like a psalm" or "like the sound of the psaltery" (an ancient stringed instrument).
2. The color of a damask rose (large and fragrant pink
rose). "Circean": like that of Circe, the enchantress in
the *Odyssey*.

Then, lighting on the printless verdure, turn'd
To the swoon'd serpent, and with languid arm,
Delicate, put to proof the lythe Caducean charm.[3]
So done, upon the nymph his eyes he bent
Full of adoring tears and blandishment,   135
And towards her stept: she, like a moon in wane,
Faded before him, cower'd, nor could restrain
Her fearful sobs, self-folding like a flower
That faints into itself at evening hour:
But the God fostering her chilled hand,   140
She felt the warmth, her eyelids open'd bland,[4]
And, like new flowers at morning song of bees,
Bloom'd, and gave up her honey to the lees.[5]
Into the green-recessed woods they flew;
Nor grew they pale, as mortal lovers do.   145

        Left to herself, the serpent now began
To change; her elfin blood in madness ran,
Her mouth foam'd, and the grass, therewith besprent,[6]
Wither'd at dew so sweet and virulent;
Her eyes in torture fix'd, and anguish drear,   150
Hot, glaz'd, and wide, with lid-lashes all sear,
Flash'd phosphor and sharp sparks, without one cooling tear.
The colours all inflam'd throughout her train,
She writh'd about, convuls'd with scarlet pain:
A deep volcanian yellow took the place   155
Of all her milder-mooned body's grace;[7]
And, as the lava ravishes the mead,
Spoilt all her silver mail, and golden brede;[8]
Made gloom of all her frecklings, streaks and bars,
Eclips'd her crescents, and lick'd up her stars: 160
So that, in moments few, she was undrest
Of all her sapphires, greens, and amethyst,
And rubious-argent:[9] of all these bereft,
Nothing but pain and ugliness were left.
Still shone her crown; that vanish'd, also she   165
Melted and disappear'd as suddenly;
And in the air, her new voice luting soft,
Cried, "Lycius! gentle Lycius!"—Borne aloft
With the bright mists about the mountains hoar
These words dissolv'd: Crete's forests heard no more.   170

        Whither fled Lamia, now a lady bright,
A full-born beauty new and exquisite?
She fled into that valley they pass o'er
Who go to Corinth from Cenchreas' shore;[1]
And rested at the foot of those wild hills,   175

3. I.e., put to the test the magic of the flexible Cadu-
ceus (Hermes' official staff).
4. Softly.
5. Dregs.
6. Sprinkled.
7. I.e., the yellow of sulfur (thrown up by a volcano)
replaced her former silvery moon color.
8. Embroidery, interwoven pattern. "Mail": inter-
linked rings, as in a coat of armor.
9. Silvery red.
1. Cenchrea (Keats's "Cenchreas") was a harbor of
Corinth, in southern Greece.

The rugged founts of the Peræan rills,
And of that other ridge whose barren back
Stretches, with all its mist and cloudy rack,
South-westward to Cleone. There she stood
About a young bird's flutter from a wood,   180
Fair, on a sloping green of mossy tread,
By a clear pool, wherein she passioned[2]
To see herself escap'd from so sore ills,
While her robes flaunted with the daffodils.

    Ah, happy Lycius!—for she was a maid   185
More beautiful than ever twisted braid,
Or sigh'd, or blush'd, or on spring-flowered lea
Spread a green kirtle[3] to the minstrelsy:
A virgin purest lipp'd, yet in the lore
Of love deep learned to the red heart's core: 190
Not one hour old, yet of sciential brain
To unperplex bliss from its neighbour pain;
Define their pettish limits, and estrange
Their points of contact, and swift counterchange;[4]
Intrigue with the specious chaos,[5] and dispart   195
Its most ambiguous atoms with sure art;
As though in Cupid's college she had spent
Sweet days a lovely graduate, still unshent,
And kept his rosy terms[6] in idle languishment.

    Why this fair creature chose so fairily   200
By the wayside to linger, we shall see;
But first 'tis fit to tell how she could muse
And dream, when in the serpent prison-house,
Of all she list,[7] strange or magnificent:
How, ever, where she will'd, her spirit went;   205
Whether to faint Elysium, or where
Down through tress-lifting waves the Nereids[8] fair
Wind into Thetis' bower by many a pearly stair;
Or where God Bacchus drains his cups divine,
Stretch'd out, at ease, beneath a glutinous pine;   210
Or where in Pluto's gardens palatine
Mulciber's columns gleam in far piazzian line.[9]
And sometimes into cities she would send
Her dream, with feast and rioting to blend;
And once, while among mortals dreaming thus,   215
She saw the young Corinthian Lycius
Charioting foremost in the envious race,
Like a young Jove with calm uneager face,

2. Felt intense excitement.
3. Gown. "Lea": meadow.
4. I.e., of knowledgeable ("sciential") brain to disentangle ("unperplex") bliss from its closely related pain, to define their quarreled-over ("pettish") limits, and to separate out ("estrange") their points of contact and the swift changes of each condition into its opposite. Cf. Keats's *Ode on Melancholy*, lines 21–26 (p. 1796).
5. I.e., turn to her own artful purpose the seeming ("specious") chaos.
6. The terms spent studying in "Cupid's college." "Unshent": unspoiled.
7. Wished.
8. Sea nymphs, of whom Thetis (line 208, the mother of Achilles) was one.
9. I.e., columns made by Mulciber (Vulcan, god of fire and metalworking) gleam in long lines around open courts (piazzas). "Palatine": palatial.

And fell into a swooning love of him.
Now on the moth-time of that evening dim   220
He would return that way, as well she knew,
To Corinth from the shore; for freshly blew
The eastern soft wind, and his galley now
Grated the quaystones with her brazen prow
In port Cenchreas, from Egina isle   225
Fresh anchor'd; whither he had been awhile
To sacrifice to Jove, whose temple there
Waits with high marble doors for blood and incense rare.
Jove heard his vows, and better'd his desire;
For by some freakful chance he made retire   230
From his companions, and set forth to walk,
Perhaps grown wearied of their Corinth talk:
Over the solitary hills he fared,
Thoughtless at first, but ere eve's star appeared
His phantasy was lost, where reason fades,   235
In the calm'd twilight of Platonic shades.[1]
Lamia beheld him coming, near, more near—
Close to her passing, in indifference drear,
His silent sandals swept the mossy green;
So neighbour'd to him, and yet so unseen   240
She stood: he pass'd, shut up in mysteries,
His mind wrapp'd like his mantle, while her eyes
Follow'd his steps, and her neck regal white
Turn'd—syllabling thus, "Ah, Lycius bright,
And will you leave me on the hills alone?   245
Lycius, look back! and be some pity shown."
He did; not with cold wonder fearingly,
But Orpheus-like at an Eurydice;[2]
For so delicious were the words she sung,
It seem'd he had lov'd them a whole summer long: 250
And soon his eyes had drunk her beauty up,
Leaving no drop in the bewildering cup,
And still the cup was full,—while he, afraid
Lest she should vanish ere his lip had paid
Due adoration, thus began to adore;   255
Her soft look growing coy, she saw his chain so sure:
"Leave thee alone! Look back! Ah, Goddess, see
Whether my eyes can ever turn from thee!
For pity do not this sad heart belie[3]—
Even as thou vanishest so I shall die.   260
Stay! though a Naiad of the rivers, stay!
To thy far wishes will thy streams obey:
Stay! though the greenest woods be thy domain,
Alone they can drink up the morning rain:
Though a descended Pleiad,[4] will not one   265

1. I.e., he was absorbed in musing about the obscurities of Plato's philosophy.
2. As Orpheus looked at Eurydice in Hades. Orpheus
was allowed by Pluto to lead Eurydice back to earth on
condition that he not look back at her, but he could
not resist doing so, hence lost her once more.
3. Be false to.
4. One of the seven sisters composing the constellation Pleiades.

Of thine harmonious sisters keep in tune
Thy spheres, and as thy silver proxy shine?
So sweetly to these ravish'd ears of mine
Came thy sweet greeting, that if thou shouldst fade
Thy memory will waste me to a shade:—   270
For pity do not melt!"—"If I should stay,"
Said Lamia, "here, upon this floor of clay,
And pain my steps upon these flowers too rough,
What canst thou say or do of charm enough
To dull the nice⁵ remembrance of my home?   275
Thou canst not ask me with thee here to roam
Over these hills and vales, where no joy is,—
Empty of immortality and bliss!
Thou art a scholar, Lycius, and must know
That finer spirits cannot breathe below   280
In human climes, and live: Alas! poor youth,
What taste of purer air hast thou to soothe
My essence? What serener palaces,
Where I may all my many senses please,
And by mysterious sleights a hundred thirsts appease?   285
It cannot be—Adieu!" So said, she rose
Tiptoe with white arms spread. He, sick to lose
The amorous promise of her lone complain,
Swoon'd, murmuring of love, and pale with pain.
The cruel lady, without any show   290
Of sorrow for her tender favourite's woe,
But rather, if her eyes could brighter be,
With brighter eyes and slow amenity,
Put her new lips to his, and gave afresh
The life she had so tangled in her mesh: 295
And as he from one trance was wakening
Into another, she began to sing,
Happy in beauty, life, and love, and every thing,
A song of love, too sweet for earthly lyres,
While, like held breath, the stars drew in their panting fires. 300
And then she whisper'd in such trembling tone,
As those who, safe together met alone
For the first time through many anguish'd days,
Use other speech than looks; bidding him raise
His drooping head, and clear his soul of doubt,   305
For that she was a woman, and without
Any more subtle fluid in her veins
Than throbbing blood, and that the self-same pains
Inhabited her frail-strung heart as his.
And next she wonder'd how his eyes could miss   310
Her face so long in Corinth, where, she said,
She dwelt but half retir'd, and there had led
Days happy as the gold coin could invent
Without the aid of love; yet in content
Till she saw him, as once she pass'd him by,   315

5. Detailed, minutely accurate.

Where 'gainst a column he leant thoughtfully
At Venus' temple porch, 'mid baskets heap'd
Of amorous herbs and flowers, newly reap'd
Late on that eve, as 'twas the night before
The Adonian feast;[6] whereof she saw no more,   320
But wept alone those days, for why should she adore?
Lycius from death awoke into amaze,
To see her still, and singing so sweet lays;
Then from amaze into delight he fell
To hear her whisper woman's lore so well;   325
And every word she spake entic'd him on
To unperplex'd delight[7] and pleasure known.
Let the mad poets say whate'er they please
Of the sweets of Fairies, Peris,[8] Goddesses,
There is not such a treat among them all,   330
Haunters of cavern, lake, and waterfall,
As a real woman, lineal indeed
From Pyrrha's pebbles[9] or old Adam's seed.
Thus gentle Lamia judg'd, and judg'd aright,
That Lycius could not love in half a fright,   335
So threw the goddess off, and won his heart
More pleasantly by playing woman's part,
With no more awe than what her beauty gave,
That, while it smote, still guaranteed to save.
Lycius to all made eloquent reply,   340
Marrying to every word a twinborn sigh;
And last, pointing to Corinth, ask'd her sweet,
If 'twas too far that night for her soft feet.
The way was short, for Lamia's eagerness
Made, by a spell, the triple league decrease   345
To a few paces; not at all surmised
By blinded Lycius, so in her comprized.[1]
They pass'd the city gates, he knew not how,
So noiseless, and he never thought to know.

        As men talk in a dream, so Corinth all,   350
Throughout her palaces imperial,
And all her populous streets and temples lewd,[2]
Mutter'd, like tempest in the distance brew'd,
To the wide-spreaded night above her towers.
Men, women, rich and poor, in the cool hours,   355
Shuffled their sandals o'er the pavement white,
Companion'd or alone; while many a light
Flared, here and there, from wealthy festivals,
And threw their moving shadows on the walls,
Or found them cluster'd in the corniced shade   360
Of some arch'd temple door, or dusky colonnade.

6. The feast of Adonis, beloved by Venus.
7. I.e., delight not mixed with its neighbor, pain (see line 192).
8. Fairylike creatures in Persian mythology.
9. Descended from the pebbles with which, in Greek myth, Pyrrha and Deucalion repeopled the earth after the flood.
1. Bound up, absorbed.
2. Temples of Venus, whose worship sometimes involved ritual prostitution.

Muffling his face, of greeting friends in fear,
Her fingers he press'd hard, as one came near
With curl'd gray beard, sharp eyes, and smooth bald crown,
Slow-stepp'd, and robed in philosophic gown: 365
Lycius shrank closer, as they met and past,
Into his mantle, adding wings to haste,
While hurried Lamia trembled: "Ah," said he,
"Why do you shudder, love, so ruefully?
Why does your tender palm dissolve in dew?"—   370
"I'm wearied," said fair Lamia: "tell me who
Is that old man? I cannot bring to mind
His features:—Lycius! wherefore did you blind
Yourself from his quick eyes?" Lycius replied,
" 'Tis Apollonius sage, my trusty guide   375
And good instructor; but to-night he seems
The ghost of folly haunting my sweet dreams."

    While yet he spake they had arrived before
A pillar'd porch, with lofty portal door,
Where hung a silver lamp, whose phosphor glow   380
Reflected in the slabbed steps below,
Mild as a star in water; for so new,
And so unsullied was the marble hue,
So through the crystal polish, liquid fine,
Ran the dark veins, that none but feet divine   385
Could e'er have touch'd there. Sounds Æolian[3]
Breath'd from the hinges, as the ample span
Of the wide doors disclos'd a place unknown
Some time to any, but those two alone,
And a few Persian mutes, who that same year   390
Were seen about the markets: none knew where
They could inhabit; the most curious
Were foil'd, who watch'd to trace them to their house:
And but the flitter-winged verse must tell,
For truth's sake, what woe afterwards befel,   395
'Twould humour many a heart to leave them thus,
Shut from the busy world of more incredulous.

Part 2

Love in a hut, with water and a crust,
Is—Love, forgive us!—cinders, ashes, dust;
Love in a palace is perhaps at last
More grievous torment than a hermit's fast:—
That is a doubtful tale from faery land,   5
Hard for the non-elect to understand.
Had Lycius liv'd to hand his story down,
He might have given the moral a fresh frown,
Or clench'd it quite: but too short was their bliss
To breed distrust and hate, that make the soft voice hiss.   10
Besides, there, nightly, with terrific glare,

3. Like sounds from the wind harp (Aeolus is god of winds), which responds musically to a current of air.

Love, jealous grown of so complete a pair,
Hover'd and buzz'd his wings, with fearful roar,
Above the lintel of their chamber door,
And down the passage cast a glow upon the floor.   15

     For all this came a ruin: side by side
They were enthroned, in the even tide,
Upon a couch, near to a curtaining
Whose airy texture, from a golden string,
Floated into the room, and let appear   20
Unveil'd the summer heaven, blue and clear,
Betwixt two marble shafts:—there they reposed,
Where use had made it sweet, with eyelids closed,
Saving a tythe which love still open kept,
That they might see each other while they almost slept;   25
When from the slope side of a suburb hill,
Deafening the swallow's twitter, came a thrill
Of trumpets—Lycius started—the sounds fled,
But left a thought, a buzzing in his head.
For the first time, since first he harbour'd in   30
That purple-lined palace of sweet sin,
His spirit pass'd beyond its golden bourn
Into the noisy world almost forsworn.
The lady, ever watchful, penetrant,
Saw this with pain, so arguing a want   35
Of something more, more than her empery[4]
Of joys; and she began to moan and sigh
Because he mused beyond her, knowing well
That but a moment's thought is passion's passing bell.[5]
"Why do you sigh, fair creature?" whisper'd he: 40
"Why do you think?" return'd she tenderly:
"You have deserted me;—where am I now?
Not in your heart while care weighs on your brow:
No, no, you have dismiss'd me; and I go
From your breast houseless: ay, it must be so."   45
He answer'd, bending to her open eyes,
Where he was mirror'd small in paradise,
"My silver planet, both of eve and morn![6]
Why will you plead yourself so sad forlorn,
While I am striving how to fill my heart   50
With deeper crimson, and a double smart?
How to entangle, trammel up and snare
Your soul in mine, and labyrinth you there
Like the hid scent in an unbudded rose?
Ay, a sweet kiss—you see your mighty woes.[7]   55
My thoughts! shall I unveil them? Listen then!
What mortal hath a prize, that other men
May be confounded and abash'd withal,
But lets it sometimes pace abroad majestical,

4. Empire.   the evening star.
5. Death knell.   7. Playfully: "You see how great your troubles were!"
6. The planet Venus, which is both the morning and

And triumph, as in thee I should rejoice   60
Amid the hoarse alarm of Corinth's voice.
Let my foes choke, and my friends shout afar,
While through the thronged streets your bridal car
Wheels round its dazzling spokes."—The lady's cheek
Trembled; she nothing said, but, pale and meek,   65
Arose and knelt before him, wept a rain
Of sorrows at his words; at last with pain
Beseeching him, the while his hand she wrung,
To change his purpose. He thereat was stung,
Perverse, with stronger fancy to reclaim   70
Her wild and timid nature to his aim:
Besides, for all his love, in self despite,
Against his better self, he took delight
Luxurious in her sorrows, soft and new.
His passion, cruel grown, took on a hue   75
Fierce and sanguineous as 'twas possible
In one whose brow had no dark veins to swell.
Fine was the mitigated fury, like
Apollo's presence when in act to strike
The serpent—Ha, the serpent! certes, she   80
Was none. She burnt, she lov'd the tyranny,
And, all subdued, consented to the hour
When to the bridal he should lead his paramour.
Whispering in midnight silence, said the youth,
"Sure some sweet name thou hast, though, by my truth,   85
I have not ask'd it, ever thinking thee
Not mortal, but of heavenly progeny,
As still I do. Hast any mortal name,
Fit appellation for this dazzling frame?
Or friends or kinsfolk on the citied earth,   90
To share our marriage feast and nuptial mirth?"
"I have no friends," said Lamia, "no, not one;
My presence in wide Corinth hardly known:
My parents' bones are in their dusty urns
Sepulchred, where no kindled incense burns,   95
Seeing all their luckless race are dead, save me,
And I neglect the holy rite for thee.
Even as you list invite your many guests;
But if, as now it seems, your vision rests
With any pleasure on me, do not bid   100
Old Apollonius—from him keep me hid."
Lycius, perplex'd at words so blind and blank,
Made close inquiry; from whose touch she shrank,
Feigning a sleep; and he to the dull shade
Of deep sleep in a moment was betray'd.   105

    It was the custom then to bring away,
The bride from home at blushing shut of day,
Veil'd, in a chariot, heralded along
By strewn flowers, torches, and a marriage song,
With other pageants: but this fair unknown   110

Had not a friend. So being left alone,
(Lycius was gone to summon all his kin)
And knowing surely she could never win
His foolish heart from its mad pompousness,
She set herself, high-thoughted, how to dress   115
The misery in fit magnificence.
She did so, but 'tis doubtful how and whence
Came, and who were her subtle servitors.
About the halls, and to and from the doors,
There was a noise of wings, till in short space   120
The glowing banquet-room shone with wide-arched grace.
A haunting music, sole perhaps and lone
Supportress of the faery-roof, made moan
Throughout, as fearful the whole charm might fade.
Fresh carved cedar, mimicking a glade   125
Of palm and plantain, met from either side,
High in the midst, in honour of the bride:
Two palms and then two plantains, and so on,
From either side their stems branch'd one to one
All down the aisled place; and beneath all   130
There ran a stream of lamps straight on from wall to wall.
So canopied, lay an untasted feast
Teeming with odours. Lamia, regal drest,
Silently paced about, and as she went,
In pale contented sort of discontent,   135
Mission'd her viewless servants to enrich
The fretted[8] splendour of each nook and niche.
Between the tree-stems, marbled plain at first,
Came jasper pannels; then, anon, there burst
Forth creeping imagery of slighter trees,   140
And with the larger wove in small intricacies.
Approving all, she faded at self-will,
And shut the chamber up, close, hush'd and still,
Complete and ready for the revels rude,
When dreadful[9] guests would come to spoil her solitude.   145

    The day appear'd, and all the gossip rout.
O senseless Lycius! Madman! wherefore flout
The silent-blessing fate, warm cloister'd hours,
And show to common eyes these secret bowers?
The herd approach'd; each guest, with busy brain,   150
Arriving at the portal, gaz'd amain,[1]
And enter'd marveling: for they knew the street,
Remember'd it from childhood all complete
Without a gap, yet ne'er before had seen
That royal porch, that high-built fair demesne;[2]   155
So in they hurried all, maz'd, curious and keen:
Save one, who look'd thereon with eye severe,
And with calm-planted steps walk'd in austere;
'Twas Apollonius: something too he laugh'd,

---

8. Adorned with fretwork (interlaced patterns).   1. Intently.
9. Terrifying.   2. Estate.

As though some knotty problem, that had daft[3]   160
His patient thought, had now begun to thaw,
And solve and melt:—'twas just as he foresaw.

He met within the murmurous vestibule
His young disciple. "'Tis no common rule,
Lycius," said he, "for uninvited guest   165
To force himself upon you, and infest
With an unbidden presence the bright throng
Of younger friends; yet must I do this wrong,
And you forgive me." Lycius blush'd, and led
The old man through the inner doors broad-spread;   170
With reconciling words and courteous mien
Turning into sweet milk the sophist's spleen.

Of wealthy lustre was the banquet-room,
Fill'd with pervading brilliance and perfume:
Before each lucid pannel fuming stood   175
A censer fed with myrrh and spiced wood,
Each by a sacred tripod held aloft,
Whose slender feet wide-swerv'd upon the soft
Wool-woofed[4] carpets: fifty wreaths of smoke
From fifty censers their light voyage took   180
To the high roof, still mimick'd as they rose
Along the mirror'd walls by twin-clouds odorous.
Twelve sphered tables, by silk seats insphered,
High as the level of a man's breast rear'd
On libbard's[5] paws, upheld the heavy gold   185
Of cups and goblets, and the store thrice told
Of Ceres' horn,[6] and, in huge vessels, wine
Come from the gloomy tun with merry shine.
Thus loaded with a feast the tables stood,
Each shrining in the midst the image of a God.   190

When in an antichamber every guest
Had felt the cold full sponge to pleasure press'd,
By minist'ring slaves, upon his hands and feet,
And fragrant oils with ceremony meet
Pour'd on his hair, they all mov'd to the feast   195
In white robes, and themselves in order placed
Around the silken couches, wondering
Whence all this mighty cost and blaze of wealth could spring.

Soft went the music the soft air along,
While fluent Greek a vowel'd undersong   200
Kept up among the guests, discoursing low
At first, for scarcely was the wine at flow;
But when the happy vintage touch'd their brains,
Louder they talk, and louder come the strains

3. Baffled, bewildered.   6. The horn of plenty, overflowing with the products
4. Woven.   of Ceres, goddess of grain.
5. Leopard's.

Of powerful instruments:—the gorgeous dyes,   205
The space, the splendour of the draperies,
The roof of awful richness, nectarous cheer,
Beautiful slaves, and Lamia's self, appear,
Now, when the wine has done its rosy deed,
And every soul from human trammels freed,   210
No more so strange; for merry wine, sweet wine,
Will make Elysian shades not too fair, too divine.

    Soon was God Bacchus at meridian height;
Flush'd were their cheeks, and bright eyes double bright:
Garlands of every green, and every scent   215
From vales deflower'd, or forest-trees branch-rent,
In baskets of bright osier'd[7] gold were brought
High as the handles heap'd, to suit the thought
Of every guest; that each, as he did please,
Might fancy-fit his brows, silk-pillow'd at his ease.   220

    What wreath for Lamia? What for Lycius?
What for the sage, old Apollonius?
Upon her aching forehead be there hung
The leaves of willow and of adder's tongue;[8]
And for the youth, quick, let us strip for him   225
The thyrsus,[9] that his watching eyes may swim
Into forgetfulness; and, for the sage,
Let spear-grass and the spiteful thistle wage
War on his temples. Do not all charms fly
At the mere touch of cold philosophy?[1]   230
There was an awful[2] rainbow once in heaven:
We know her woof, her texture; she is given
In the dull catalogue of common things.
Philosophy will clip an Angel's wings,
Conquer all mysteries by rule and line,   235
Empty the haunted air, and gnomed mine[3]—
Unweave a rainbow, as it erewhile made
The tender-person'd Lamia melt into a shade.

    By her glad Lycius sitting, in chief place,
Scarce saw in all the room another face,   240
Till, checking his love trance, a cup he took
Full brimm'd, and opposite sent forth a look
'Cross the broad table, to beseech a glance
From his old teacher's wrinkled countenance,
And pledge him.[4] The bald-head philosopher   245
Had fix'd his eye, without a twinkle or stir

7. Plaited. An "osier" is a strip of willow used in weaving baskets.
8. A fern whose spikes resemble a serpent's tongue.
9. The vine-covered staff of Bacchus, used to signify drunkenness.
1. In the sense of "natural philosophy," or science. Benjamin Haydon tells in his *Autobiography* how, at a hard-drinking and high-spirited dinner party, Keats had agreed with Charles Lamb (to what extent jokingly, is not clear) that Newton's *Optics* "had destroyed all the poetry of the rainbow by reducing it to the prismatic colors."
2. Awe-inspiring.
3. Gnomes were guardians of mines.
4. Drink a toast to him.

Full on the alarmed beauty of the bride,
Brow-beating her fair form, and troubling her sweet pride.
Lycius then press'd her hand, with devout touch,
As pale it lay upon the rosy couch: 250
'Twas icy, and the cold ran through his veins;
Then sudden it grew hot, and all the pains
Of an unnatural heat shot to his heart.
"Lamia, what means this? Wherefore dost thou start?
Know'st thou that man?" Poor Lamia answer'd not.   255
He gaz'd into her eyes, and not a jot
Own'd[5] they the lovelorn piteous appeal:
More, more he gaz'd: his human senses reel:
Some hungry spell that loveliness absorbs;
There was no recognition in those orbs.   260
"Lamia!" he cried—and no soft-toned reply.
The many heard, and the loud revelry
Grew hush; the stately music no more breathes;
The myrtle[6] sicken'd in a thousand wreaths.
By faint degrees, voice, lute, and pleasure ceased;   265
A deadly silence step by step increased,
Until it seem'd a horrid presence there,
And not a man but felt the terror in his hair.
"Lamia!" he shriek'd; and nothing but the shriek
With its sad echo did the silence break.   270
"Begone, foul dream!" he cried, gazing again
In the bride's face, where now no azure vein
Wander'd on fair-spaced temples; no soft bloom
Misted the cheek; no passion to illume
The deep-recessed vision:—all was blight;   275
Lamia, no longer fair, there sat a deadly white.
"Shut, shut those juggling[7] eyes, thou ruthless man!
Turn them aside, wretch! or the righteous ban
Of all the Gods, whose dreadful images
Here represent their shadowy presences,   280
May pierce them on the sudden with the thorn
Of painful blindness; leaving thee forlorn,
In trembling dotage to the feeblest fright
Of conscience, for their long offended might,
For all thine impious proud-heart sophistries,   285
Unlawful magic, and enticing lies.
Corinthians! look upon that gray-beard wretch!
Mark how, possess'd, his lashless eyelids stretch
Around his demon eyes! Corinthians, see!
My sweet bride withers at their potency."   290
"Fool!" said the sophist, in an under-tone
Gruff with contempt; which a death-nighing moan
From Lycius answer'd, as heart-struck and lost,
He sank supine beside the aching ghost.
"Fool! Fool!" repeated he, while his eyes still   295
Relented not, nor mov'd; "from every ill

5. Acknowledged.   7. Deceiving, full of trickery.
6. Sacred to Venus, hence an emblem of love.

Of life have I preserv'd thee to this day,
And shall I see thee made a serpent's prey?"
Then Lamia breath'd death breath; the sophist's eye,
Like a sharp spear, went through her utterly,   300
Keen, cruel, perceant,[8] stinging: she, as well
As her weak hand could any meaning tell,
Motion'd him to be silent; vainly so,
He look'd and look'd again a level—No!
"A Serpent!" echoed he; no sooner said,   305
Than with a frightful scream she vanished:
And Lycius' arms were empty of delight,
As were his limbs of life, from that same night.
On the high couch he lay!—his friends came round—
Supported him—no pulse, or breath they found,   310
And, in its marriage robe, the heavy body wound.
July–Aug. 1819   1820

To Autumn[1]

1

Season of mists and mellow fruitfulness,
    Close bosom-friend of the maturing sun;
Conspiring with him how to load and bless
    With fruit the vines that round the thatch-eves run;
To bend with apples the moss'd cottage-trees,   5
    And fill all fruit with ripeness to the core;
        To swell the gourd, and plump the hazel shells
    With a sweet kernel; to set budding more,
And still more, later flowers for the bees,
Until they think warm days will never cease,   10
        For summer has o'er-brimm'd their clammy cells.

2

Who hath not seen thee oft amid thy store?
    Sometimes whoever seeks abroad may find
Thee sitting careless on a granary floor,
    Thy hair soft-lifted by the winnowing[2] wind;   15
Or on a half-reap'd furrow sound asleep,
    Drows'd with the fume of poppies, while thy hook[3]
        Spares the next swath and all its twined flowers:
And sometimes like a gleaner thou dost keep
    Steady thy laden head across a brook;   20
Or by a cyder-press, with patient look,
    Thou watchest the last oozings hours by hours.

3

Where are the songs of spring? Ay, where are they?
    Think not of them, thou hast thy music too,—
While barred clouds bloom the soft-dying day,

8. Piercing.
1. Two days after this serene and gracious ode was composed, Keats wrote to J. H. Reynolds: "I never liked stubble fields so much as now—Aye, better than the chilly green of the spring. Somehow a stubble plain looks warm—in the same way that some pictures look warm—this struck me so much in my Sunday's walk that I composed upon it."
2. To "winnow" is to fan the chaff from the grain.
3. Scythe.

And touch the stubble-plains with rosy hue;
Then in a wailful choir the small gnats mourn
Among the river sallows,[4] borne aloft
Or sinking as the light wind lives or dies;
And full-grown lambs loud bleat from hilly bourn;[5]   30
Hedge-crickets sing; and now with treble soft
The red-breast whistles from a garden-croft;[6]
And gathering swallows twitter in the skies.

Sept. 19, 1819   1820

Letters   Keats's letters serve as a running commentary on his life, reading, thinking, and writing. They demonstrate a remarkable intelligence, whose very lack of academic or philosophical training gives its expression a freedom from jargon and standard categories that is equally challenging and rewarding to the reader. Keats's early reputation as a poet of pure luxury, sensation, and art for art's sake has undergone a radical change since, in the twentieth century, critics began to pay close attention to his letters. For Keats thought hard and persistently about life and art, and any seed of an ethical or critical idea that he picked up from his intellectual contemporaries (Hazlitt, Coleridge, Wordsworth) instantly germinated and flourished in the rich soil of his imagination. What T. S. Eliot said about the Metaphysical poets applies equally to Keats in his letters: his "mode of feeling was directly and freshly altered by [his] reading and thought." And like Donne, he looked not only into the heart but, literally, "into the cerebral cortex, the nervous system, and the digestive tract." A number of Keats's casual comments on the poet and on poetry included below—especially those dealing with what we now call empathy and with "negative capability"—have become standard points of reference in aesthetic theory. But Keats himself regarded nothing that he said as ultimate; each statement constituted only a stage in his continuing exploration into what he called "the mystery."

The text below is that of the edition of the *Letters* by Hyder E. Rollins (1958), which reproduces the original manuscripts precisely, so that the reader may follow Keats's pen as, throwing spelling and grammar to the winds, it strains to keep up with the rush of his thoughts.

LETTERS

To Benjamin Bailey[1]

[The Authenticity of the Imagination]

[November 22, 1817]

My dear Bailey,
* * * O I wish I was as certain of the end of all your troubles as that of your momentary start about the authenticity of the Imagination. I am certain of nothing but of the holiness of the Heart's affections and the truth of Imagi-

---

4. Willows.
5. Region.
6. A "croft" is an enclosed plot of farmland.

1. One of Keats's closest friends. Keats had stayed with him the month before at Oxford, where Bailey was an undergraduate.

nation—What the imagination seizes as Beauty must be truth[2]—whether it existed before or not—for I have the same Idea of all our Passions as of Love they are all in their sublime, creative of essential Beauty—In a Word, you may know my favorite Speculation by my first Book and the little song[3] I sent in my last—which is a representation from the fancy of the probable mode of operating in these Matters—The Imagination may be compared to Adam's dream[4]—he awoke and found it truth. I am the more zealous in this affair, because I have never yet been able to perceive how any thing can be known for truth by consequitive reasoning[5]—and yet it must be—Can it be that even the greatest Philosopher ever ~~when~~ arrived at his goal without putting aside numerous objections—However it may be, O for a Life of Sensations[6] rather than of Thoughts! It is "a Vision in the form of Youth" a Shadow of reality to come—and this consideration has further conv[i]nced me for it has come as auxiliary to another favorite Speculation of mine, that we shall enjoy ourselves here after by having what we called happiness on Earth repeated in a finer tone and so repeated[7]—And yet such a fate can only befall those who delight in sensation rather than hunger as you do after Truth—Adam's dream will do here and seems to be a conviction that Imagination and its empyreal reflection is the same as human Life and its spiritual repetition. But as I was saying—the simple imaginative Mind may have its rewards in the repeti[ti]on of its own silent Working coming continually on the spirit with a fine suddenness—to compare great things with small—have you never by being surprised with an old Melody—in a delicious place—by a delicious voice, fe[l]t over again your very speculations and surmises at the time it first operated on your soul—do you not remember forming to yourself the singer's face more beautiful that[8] it was possible and yet with the elevation of the Moment you did not think so— even then you were mounted on the Wings of Imagination so high—that the Prototype must be here after—that delicious face you will see—What a time! I am continually running away from the subject—sure this cannot be exactly the case with a complex Mind—one that is imaginative and at the same time careful of its fruits—who would exist partly on sensation partly on thought— to whom it is necessary that years should bring the philosophic Mind[9]—such an one I consider your's and therefore it is necessary to your eternal Happiness that you not only ~~have~~ drink this old Wine of Heaven which I shall call the redigestion of our most ethereal Musings on Earth; but also increase in knowl- edge and know all things. I am glad to hear you are in a fair Way for Easter— you will soon get through your unpleasant reading and then!—but the world is full of troubles and I have not much reason to think myself pesterd with many—I think Jane or Marianne has a better opinion of me than I deserve— for really and truly I do not think my Brothers illness connected with mine— you know more of the real Cause than they do—nor have I any chance of

2. The phrase occurs in a poetic context at the close of *Ode on a Grecian Urn*. Try substituting "real," or "reality," where Keats uses the word *truth*.
3. The song was "O Sorrow," from book 4 of *Endymion*.
4. In *Paradise Lost* 8.452–90, Adam dreams that Eve has been created, and awakes to find her real. Adam also describes an earlier prefigurative dream in the same work, 8.283–311.
5. Consecutive reasoning—reasoning that moves by logical steps.
6. Probably not only sense experiences but also the intuitive perceptions of truths, as opposed to truth achieved by consecutive reasoning.
7. Cf. the "Pleasure Thermometer" in *Endymion* 1.777ff. (p. 1775).
8. For "than."
9. An echo of Wordsworth, *Ode: Intimations of Immortality*, line 187.

being rack'd as you have been[1]—you perhaps at one time thought there was such a thing as Worldly Happiness to be arrived at, at certain periods of time marked out—you have of necessity from your disposition been thus led away—I scarcely remember counting upon any Happiness—I look not for it if it be not in the present hour—nothing startles me beyond the Moment. The setting sun will always set me to rights—or if a Sparrow come before my Window I take part in its existince and pick about the Gravel. The first thing that strikes me on hea[r]ing a Misfortune having befallen another is this. "Well it cannot be helped.—he will have the pleasure of trying the resourses of his spirit, and I beg now my dear Bailey that hereafter should you observe any thing cold in me not to but[2] it to the account of heartlessness but abstraction—for I assure you I sometimes feel not the influence of a Passion or Affection during a whole week—and so long this sometimes continues I begin to suspect myself and the genuiness of my feelings at other times—thinking them a few barren Tragedy-tears. * * *

Your affectionate friend
John Keats—

To George and Thomas Keats

[Negative Capability]

[December 21, 27 (?), 1817]

My dear Brothers

I must crave your pardon for not having written ere this. * * * I spent Friday evening with Wells[1] & went the next morning to see *Death on the Pale horse*. It is a wonderful picture, when West's[2] age is considered; But there is nothing to be intense upon; no women one feels mad to kiss; no face swelling into reality. the excellence of every Art is its intensity, capable of making all disagreeables evaporate, from their being in close relationship with Beauty & Truth[3]—Examine King Lear & you will find this examplified throughout; but in this picture we have unpleasantness without any momentous depth of speculation excited, in which to bury its repulsiveness—The picture is larger than Christ rejected—I dined with Haydon[4] the sunday after you left, & had a very pleasant day, I dined too (for I have been out too much lately) with Horace Smith & met his two Brothers with Hill & Kingston & one Du Bois,[5] they only served to convince me, how superior humour is to wit in respect to enjoyment—These men say things which make one start, without making one feel, they are all alike; their manners are alike; they all know fashionables; they have a mannerism in their very eating & drinking, in their mere handling a

1. Keats's friends Jane and Mariane Reynolds feared that his ill health at this time threatened tuberculosis, from which his brother Tom was suffering. Bailey had recently experienced pain (been "racked") because of an unsuccessful love affair.
2. For "put."
1. Charles Wells, a former schoolmate of Tom Keats.
2. Benjamin West (1738–1820), painter of historical pictures, was an American who moved to England and became president of the Royal Academy. The "Christ Rejected" mentioned a few sentences farther on is also by West.
3. Keats's solution to a problem at least as old as Aristotle's *Poetics*: why do we take pleasure in the aesthetic representation of a subject that in life would be ugly or painful?
4. Keats's close friend Benjamin Haydon, painter of large-scale historical and religious pictures.
5. Horace Smith was one of the best-known literary wits of the day; the others mentioned were men of letters or of literary interests.

Decanter—They talked of Kean[6] & his low company—Would I were with that company instead of yours said I to myself! I know such like acquaintance will never do for me & yet I am going to Reynolds, on wednesday—Brown & Dilke[7] walked with me & back from the Christmas pantomime.[8] I had not a dispute but a disquisition with Dilke, on various subjects; several things dovetailed in my mind, & at once it struck me, what quality went to form a Man of Achievement especially in Literature & which Shakespeare possessed so enormously—I mean *Negative Capability*,[9] that is when man is capable of being in uncertainties, Mysteries, doubts, without any irritable reaching after fact & reason—Coleridge, for instance, would let go by a fine isolated verisimilitude caught from the Penetralium[1] of mystery, from being incapable of remaining content with half knowledge. This pursued through Volumes would perhaps take us no further than this, that with a great poet the sense of Beauty overcomes every other consideration, or rather obliterates all consideration.

Shelley's poem[2] is out & there are words about its being objected too, as much as Queen Mab was. Poor Shelley I think he has his Quota of good qualities, in sooth la!! Write soon to your most sincere friend & affectionate Brother

John

To John Hamilton Reynolds[1]

[*Wordsworth's Poetry*]

[February 3, 1818]

My dear Reynolds,

* * * It may be said that we ought to read our Contemporaries. that Wordsworth &c should have their due from us. but for the sake of a few fine imaginative or domestic passages, are we to be bullied into a certain Philosophy engendered in the whims of an Egotist[2]—Every man has his speculations, but every man does not brood and peacock over them till he makes a false coinage and deceives himself—Many a man can travel to the very bourne[3] of Heaven,

6. Edmund Kean, noted Shakespearean actor of the early 19th century.
7. Charles Wentworth Dilke, John Hamilton Reynolds, and Charles Armitage Brown were all writers and friends of Keats. Keats interrupted the writing of this letter after the dash; beginning with "Brown & Dilke" he is writing several days after the preceding sentences.
8. Christmas pantomimes were performed each year at Drury Lane and Covent Garden theaters.
9. This famous and elusive phrase has accumulated a heavy body of commentary. Two points may be offered here: (1) Keats is concerned with a central aesthetic question of his day: to distinguish between what was called the "objective" poet, who simply and impersonally presents material, and the "subjective" or "sentimental" poet, who presents material as it appears when viewed through the writer's personal interests, beliefs, and feelings. The poet of "negative capability" is the objective poet (see the letter to Reynolds, Feb. 3, 1818, below). (2) Keats goes on to propose that, within a poem, the presentation of subject matter in an artistic form that appeals to our "sense of Beauty" is enough,

independently of its truth or falsity when considered outside the poem.
1. The Latin *penetralia* signified the innermost and most secret parts of a temple.
2. *Laon and Cythna* (1817), which dealt with incest and had to be recalled by the author; Shelley revised and republished it as *The Revolt of Islam* (1818). *Queen Mab* (1813) was a youthful poem in which Shelley presented his radical program for the achievement of a millennial earthly state by the elimination of "kings, priests, and statesmen," and the reform of human institutions.
1. A close friend who was at this time an insurance clerk and also an able poet and man of letters.
2. Keats immensely admired Wordsworth, as succeeding letters will show, and learned more from him than from any poetic contemporary. He had reservations, however, about the subjective and didactic qualities of Wordsworth's poetry (see the letter to George and Thomas Keats, p. 1817)—reservations that, in some moods, he stated in unflattering terms.
3. Boundary.

and yet want confidence to put down his halfseeing. Sancho[4] will invent a Journey heavenward as well as any body. We hate poetry that has a palpable design upon us—and if we do not agree, seems to put its hand in its breeches pocket. Poetry should be great & unobtrusive, a thing which enters into one's soul, and does not startle it or amaze it with itself but with its subject.—How beautiful are the retired flowers! how would they lose their beauty were they to throng into the highway crying out, "admire me I am a violet! dote upon me I am a primrose! Modern poets differ from the Elizabethans in this. Each of the moderns like an Elector of Hanover governs his petty state, & knows how many straws are swept daily from the Causeways in all his dominions & has a continual itching that all the Housewives should have their coppers well scoured: the antients were ~~Emperors of large~~ Emperors of vast Provinces, they had only heard of the remote ones and scarcely cared to visit them.—I will cut all this—I will have no more of Wordsworth or Hunt[5] in particular—Why should we be of the tribe of Manasseh, when we can wander with Esau?[6] why should we kick against the Pricks, when we can walk on Roses? Why should we be owls, when we can be Eagles? Why be teased with "nice Eyed wagtails," when we have in sight "the Cherub Contemplation"?[7]—Why with Wordsworths "Matthew with a bough of wilding in his hand" when we can have Jacques "under an oak &c"[8]—The secret of the Bough of Wilding will run through your head faster than I can write it—Old Matthew spoke to him some years ago on some nothing, & because he happens in an Evening Walk to imagine the figure of the old man—he must stamp it down in black & white, and it is henceforth sacred—I don't mean to deny Wordsworth's grandeur & Hunt's merit, but I mean to say we need not be teazed with grandeur & merit—when we can have them uncontaminated & unobtrusive. Let us have the old Poets, & robin Hood[9] Your letter and its sonnets gave me more pleasure than will the 4th Book of Childe Harold[1] & the whole of any body's life & opinions. * * *

Y*r* sincere friend and Coscribbler
John Keats.

To John Taylor[1]

[*Keats's Axioms in Poetry*]

[February 27, 1818]

My dear Taylor,
    Your alteration strikes me as being a great improvement—the page looks much better. * * * It is a sorry thing for me that any one should have to overcome Prejudices in reading my Verses—that affects me more than any

4. Sancho Panza, the earthy squire in Cervantes' *Don Quixote*.
5. Leigh Hunt, a poet who earlier had strongly influenced Keats's style.
6. I.e., why should we carry on a conventional way of life (as did the tribe of Manasseh in Old Testament history) when we can become adventurers (like Esau, who sold his birthright in Genesis 25.29–34 and became an outlaw).
7. Milton, *Il Penseroso*, line 54. "Nice Eyed wagtails": from Hunt's *Nymphs*.

8. *As You Like It* 2.1.31. The Wordsworth phrase is from his poem *The Two April Mornings*. A "wilding" is a wild apple tree.
9. A reference to two sonnets on Robin Hood, written by Reynolds, which he had sent to Keats.
1. Canto 4 of Byron's *Childe Harold's Pilgrimage* was being eagerly awaited by English readers.
1. Partner in the publishing firm of Taylor and Hessey, to whom Keats wrote this letter while *Endymion* was being put through the press.

hypercriticism on any particular Passage. In *Endymion* I have most likely but moved into the Go-cart from the leading strings. In Poetry I have a few Axioms, and you will see how far I am from their Centre. 1st I think Poetry should surprise by a fine excess and not by Singularity—it should strike the Reader as a wording of his own highest thoughts, and appear almost a Remembrance—2nd Its touches of Beauty should never be half way therby making the reader breathless instead of content: the rise, the progress, the setting of imagery should like the Sun come natural natural too him—shine over him and set soberly although in magnificence leaving him in the Luxury of twilight—but it is easier to think what Poetry should be than to write it—and this leads me on to another axiom. That if Poetry comes not as naturally as the Leaves to a tree it had better not come at all. However it may be with me I cannot help looking into new countries with "O for a Muse of fire to ascend!"[2]—If *Endymion* serves me as a Pioneer perhaps I ought to be content. I have great reason to be content, for thank God I can read and perhaps understand Shakspeare to his depths, and I have I am sure many friends, who, if I fail, will attribute any change in my Life and Temper to Humbleness rather than to Pride—to a cowering under the Wings of great Poets rather than to a Bitterness that I am not appreciated. I am anxious to get Endymion printed that I may forget it and proceed. * * *

Your sincere and oblig^d friend

John Keats—

P.S. You shall have a sho[r]t *Preface* in good time—

To John Hamilton Reynolds

[*Milton, Wordsworth, and the Chambers of Human Life*]

[May 3, 1818]

My dear Reynolds.

* * * Were I to study physic or rather Medicine again,—I feel it would not make the least difference in my Poetry; when the Mind is in its infancy a Bias ~~in~~ is in reality a Bias, but when we have acquired more strength, a Bias becomes no Bias. Every department of knowledge we see excellent and calculated towards a great whole. I am so convinced of this, that I am glad at not having given away my medical Books, which I shall again look over to keep alive the little I know thitherwards; and moreover intend through you and Rice to become a sort of Pip-civilian.[1] An extensive knowledge is needful to thinking people—it takes away the heat and fever; and helps, by widening speculation, to ease the Burden of the Mystery:[2] a thing I begin to understand a little, and which weighed upon you in the most gloomy and true sentence in your Letter. The difference of high Sensations with and without knowledge appears to me this—in the latter case we are falling continually ten thousand fathoms deep and being blown up again without wings and with all [the]

---

2. Altered from *Henry V*, Prologue, line 1.
1. Apparently "a small-scale layman." James Rice, a lawyer, was one of Keats's favorite friends.
2. Wordsworth, *Tintern Abbey*, line 38. Here begins

Keats's remarkably insightful expansion of the significance of this and other phrases and passages in Wordsworth.

horror of a ~~Case~~ bare shoulderd Creature—in the former case, our shoulders are fledged,[3] and we go thro' the same ~~Fir~~ air and space without fear. * * *

You say "I fear there is little chance of any thing else in this life." You seem by that to have been going through with a more painful and acute ~~test~~ zest the same labyrinth that I have—I have come to the same conclusion thus far. My Branchings out therefrom have been numerous: one of them is the consider-ation of Wordsworth's genius and as a help, in the manner of gold being the meridian Line of worldly wealth,—how he differs from Milton.[4]—And here I have nothing but surmises, from an uncertainty whether Miltons apparently less anxiety for Humanity proceeds from his seeing further or no than Words-worth: And whether Wordsworth has in truth epic passions~~,~~ and martyrs him-self to the human heart, the main region of his song[5]—In regard to his genius alone—we find what he says true as far as we have experienced and we can judge no further but by larger experience—for axioms in philosophy are not axioms until they are proved upon our pulses: We read fine——things but never feel them to thee[6] full until we have gone the same steps as the Author.—I know this is not plain; you will know exactly my meaning when I say, that now I shall relish Hamlet more than I ever have done—Or, better—You are sensible no man can set down Venery[7] as a bestial or joyless thing until he is sick of it and therefore all philosophizing on it would be mere wording. Until we are sick, we understand not;—in fine, as Byron says, "Knowledge is Sorrow";[8] and I go on to say that "Sorrow is Wisdom"—and further for aught we can know for certainty! "Wisdom is folly." * * *

I will return to Wordsworth—whether or no he has an extended vision or a circumscribed grandeur—whether he is an eagle in his nest, or on the wing—And to be more explicit and to show you how tall I stand by the giant, I will put down a simile of human life as far as I now perceive it; that is, to the point to which I say we both have arrived at—Well—I compare human life to a large Mansion of Many Apartments, two of which I can only describe, the doors of the rest being as yet shut upon me—The first we step into we call the infant or thoughtless Chamber, in which we remain as long as we do not think—We remain there a long while, and notwithstanding the doors of the second Chamber remain wide open, showing a bright appearance, we care not to hasten to it; but are at length imperceptibly impelled by the awakening of the thinking principle—within us—we no sooner get into the second Chamber, which I shall call the Chamber of Maiden-Thought,[9] than we become intoxicated with the light and the atmosphere, we see nothing but pleasant wonders, and think of delaying there for ever in delight: However among the effects this breathing is father of is that tremendous one of sharpen-ing one's vision into the ~~head~~ heart and nature of Man—of convincing ones nerves that the World is full of Misery and Heartbreak, Pain, Sickness and oppression—whereby This Chamber of Maiden Thought becomes gradually darken'd and at the same time on all sides of it many doors are set open—but all dark—all leading to dark passages—We see not the ballance of good and evil. We are in a Mist—We are now in that state—We feel the "burden of the

---

3. Grow wings.
4. I.e., as gold is the standard of material wealth (in the way that the meridian line of Greenwich Observa-tory, England, is the reference for measuring degrees of longitude), so Milton is the standard of poetic value, by which we may measure Wordsworth.

5. Cf. Prospectus to *The Recluse*, line 41 (p. 000).
6. For "the."
7. Sexual indulgence.
8. *Manfred* 1.1.10: "Sorrow is knowledge."
9. I.e., innocent thought, with the implication (as in "maiden voyage") of a first undertaking.

Mystery," To this point was Wordsworth come, as far as I can conceive when he wrote "Tintern Abbey" and it seems to me that his Genius is explorative of those dark Passages. Now if we live, and go on thinking, we too shall explore them. he is a Genius and superior [to] us, in so far as he can, more than we, make discoveries, and shed a light in them—Here I must think Wordsworth is deeper than Milton—though I think it has depended more upon the general and gregarious advance of intellect, than individual greatness of Mind—From the Paradise Lost and the other Works of Milton, I hope it is not too presuming, even between ourselves to say, his Philosophy, human and divine, may be tolerably understood by one not much advanced in years, In his time englishmen were just emancipated from a great superstition—and Men had got hold of certain points and resting places in reasoning which were too newly born to be doubted, and too much ~~oppressed~~ opposed by the Mass of Europe not to be thought etherial and authentically divine—who could gainsay his ideas on virtue, vice, and Chastity in Comus, just at the time of the dismissal of Cod-pieces[1] and a hundred other disgraces? who would not rest satisfied with his hintings at good and evil in the Paradise Lost, when just free from the inquisition and burrning in Smithfield?[2] The Reformation produced such immediate and ~~greats~~ benefits, that Protestantism was considered under the immediate eye of heaven, and its own remaining Dogmas and superstitions, then, as it were, regenerated, constituted those resting places and seeming sure points of Reasoning—from that I have mentioned, Milton, whatever he may have thought in the sequel,[3] appears to have been content with these by his writings—He did not think into the human heart, as Wordsworth has done—Yet Milton as a Philosop[h]er, had sure as great powers as Wordsworth—What is then to be inferr'd? O many things—It proves there is really a grand march of intellect—, It proves that a mighty providence subdues the mightiest Minds to the service of the time being, whether it be in human Knowledge or Religion— * * * Tom[4] has spit a leetle blood this afternoon, and that is rather a damper—but I know—the truth is there is something real in the World Your third Chamber of Life shall be a lucky and a gentle one—stored with the wine of love—and the Bread of Friendship— * * *

> Your affectionate friend
> John Keats.

To Richard Woodhouse[1]

[A Poet Has No Identity]

[October 27, 1818]

My dear Woodhouse,

   Your Letter gave me a great satisfaction; more on account of its friendliness, than any relish of that matter in it which is accounted so acceptable in the

---

1. In the 15th and 16th centuries, the codpiece was a flap, often ornamental, that covered an opening in the front of men's breeches.
2. An open place northwest of the walls of the City of London where, in the 16th century, heretics were burned.

3. Later on.
4. Keats's younger brother, then eighteen, who was dying of tuberculosis.
1. A young lawyer with literary interests who early recognized Keats's talents and prepared, or preserved, manuscript copies of many of his poems and letters.

"genus irritabile"[2] The best answer I can give you is in a clerklike manner to make some observations on two principle points, which seem to point like indices into the midst of the whole pro and con, about genius, and views and atchievements and ambition and cœtera. 1ˢᵗ As to the poetical Character itself, (I mean that sort of which, if I am any thing, I am a Member; that sort distinguished from the wordsworthian or egotistical sublime; which is a thing per se and stands alone) it is not itself—it has no self—it is every thing and nothing—It has no character—it enjoys light and shade; it lives in gusto, be it foul or fair, high or low, rich or poor, mean or elevated—It has as much delight in conceiving an Iago as an Imogen.[3] What shocks the virtuous philosop[h]er, delights the camelion[4] Poet. It does no harm from its relish of the dark side of things any more than from its taste for the bright one; because they both end in speculation.[5] A Poet is the most unpoetical of any thing in existence; because he has no Identity—he is continually in for[6]—and filling some other Body—The Sun, the Moon, the Sea and Men and Women who are creatures of impulse are poetical and have about them an unchangeable attribute—the poet has none; no identity—he is certainly the most unpoetical of all God's Creatures. If then he has no self, and if I am a Poet, where is the Wonder that I should say I would ~~right~~ write no more? Might I not at that very instant [have] been cogitating on the Characters of saturn and Ops?[7] It is a wretched thing to confess; but is a very fact that not one word I ever utter can be taken for granted as an opinion growing out of my identical nature—how can it, when I have no nature? When I am in a room with People if I ever am free from speculating on creations of my own brain, then not myself goes home to myself: but the identity of every one in the room begins to to press upon me[8] that, I am in a very little time an[ni]hilated—not only among Men; it would be the same in a Nursery of children: I know not whether I make myself wholly understood: I hope enough so to let you see that no dependence is to be placed on what I said that day.

In the second place I will speak of my views, and of the life I purpose to myself—I am ambitious of doing the world some good: if I should be spared that may be the work of maturer years—in the interval I will assay to reach to as high a summit in Poetry as the nerve[9] bestowed upon me will suffer. The faint conceptions I have of Poems to come brings the blood frequently into my forehead—All I hope is that I may not lose all interest in human affairs— that the solitary indifference I feel for applause even from the finest Spirits, will not blunt any acuteness of vision I may have. I do not think it will—I feel assured I should write from the mere yearning and fondness I have for the Beautiful even if my night's labours should be burnt every morning and no eye ever shine upon them. But even now I am perhaps not speaking from myself; but from some character in whose soul I now live. I am sure however

2. "The irritable race," a phrase Horace had applied to poets (*Epistles* 2.2.102).
3. Iago is the villain in Shakespeare's *Othello* and Imogen the virtuous heroine in his *Cymbeline*.
4. The chameleon is a lizard that camouflages itself by changing its color to match its surroundings.
5. Possibly "in contemplation"—i.e., without affecting our practical judgment or actions.
6. Instead of "in for," Keats may have intended to write "informing."
7. Characters in Keats's *Hyperion*. Woodhouse had recently written Keats to express concern at a remark by the poet that, because former writers had preempted the best poetic materials and styles, there was nothing new left for the modern poet.
8. Perhaps "so to press upon me."
9. Sinew.

that this next sentence is from myself. I feel your anxiety, good opinion and friendliness in the highest degree, and am

Your's most sincerely

John Keats

To George and Georgiana Keats[1]

["The Vale of Soul-Making"]

[February 14–May 3, 1819]

My dear Brother & Sister—

    * * * I have this moment received a note from Haslam[2] in which he expects the death of his Father who has been for some time in a state of insensibility—his mother bears up he says very well—I shall go to twon[3] tommorrow to see him. This is the world—thus we cannot expect to give way many hours to pleasure—Circumstances are like Clouds continually gathering and bursting—While we are laughing the seed of some trouble is put into he the wide arable land of events—while we are laughing it sprouts is[4] grows and suddenly bears a poison fruit which we must pluck—Even so we have leisure to reason on the misfortunes of our friends; our own touch us too nearly for words. Very few men have ever arrived at a complete disinterestedness of Mind: very few have been influenced by a pure desire of the benefit of others—in the greater part of the Benefactors of & to Humanity some meretricious motive has sullied their greatness—some melodramatic scenery has facinated them—From the manner in which I feel Haslam's misfortune I perceive how far I am from any humble standard of disinterestedness—Yet this feeling ought to be carried to its highest pitch, as there is no fear of its ever injuring society—which it would do I fear pushed to an extremity—For in wild nature the Hawk would loose his Breakfast of Robins and the Robin his of Worms The Lion must starve as well as the swallow—The greater part of Men make their way with the same instinctiveness, the same unwandering eye from their purposes, the same animal eagerness as the Hawk—The Hawk wants a Mate, so does the Man—look at them both they set about it and procure on[e] in the same manner—They want both a nest and they both set about one in the same manner—they get their food in the same manner—The noble animal Man for his amusement smokes his pipe—the Hawk balances about the Clouds—that is the only difference of their leisures. This it is that makes the Amusement of Life—to a speculative Mind. I go among the Feilds and catch a glimpse of a stoat[5] or a fieldmouse peeping out of the withered grass—the creature hath a purpose and its eyes are bright with it—I go amongst the buildings of a city and I see a Man hurrying along—to what? The Creature has a purpose and his eyes are bright with it. But then as Wordsworth says, "we have all one human heart"[6]—there is an ellectric fire in human nature tending to purify—so that among these human creature[s] there is continually

1. Keats's brother and his wife, who had emigrated to Louisville, Kentucky, in 1818. This is part of a long letter that Keats wrote over a period of several months. The date of this first extract is March 19.

2. William Haslam, a young businessman and close friend.

3. For "town."

4. For "it."

5. A weasel.

6. *The Old Cumberland Beggar*, line 153.

some birth of new heroism—The pity is that we must wonder at it: as we should at finding a pearl in rubbish—I have no doubt that thousands of people never heard of have had hearts comp[l]etely disinterested: I can remember but two—Socrates and Jesus—their Histories evince it—What I heard a little time ago, Taylor observe with respect to Socrates, may be said of Jesus—That he was so great as man that though he transmitted no writing of his own to posterity, we have his Mind and his sayings and his greatness handed to us by others. It is to be lamented that the history of the latter was written and revised by Men interested in the pious frauds of Religion. Yet through all this I see his splendour. Even here though I myself am pursueing the same instinctive course as the veriest human animal you can think of—I am however young writing at random—straining at particles of light in the midst of a great darkness—without knowing the bearing of any one assertion of any one opinion. Yet may I not in this be free from sin?[7] May there not be superior beings amused with any graceful, though instinctive attitude my mind my[8] fall into, as I am entertained with the alertness of a Stoat or the anxiety of a Deer? Though a quarrel in the streets is a thing to be hated, the energies displayed in it are fine; the commonest Man shows a grace in his quarrel—By a superior being our reasoning[s] may take the same tone—though erroneous they may be fine—This is the very thing in which consists poetry; and if so it is not so fine a thing as philosophy—For the same reason that an eagle is not so fine a thing as a truth—Give me this credit—Do you not think I strive—to know myself? Give me this credit—and you will not think that on my own accou[n]t I repeat Milton's lines

> "How charming is divine Philosophy
> Not harsh and crabbed as dull fools suppose
> But musical as is Apollo's lute"—[9]

No—no for myself—feeling grateful as I do to have got into a state of mind to relish them properly—Nothing ever becomes real till it is experienced—Even a Proverb is no proverb to you till your Life has illustrated it— * * *

* * * I have been reading lately two very different books Robertson's America and Voltaire's Siecle De Louis xiv[1] It is like walking arm and arm between Pizarro and the great-little Monarch.[2] In How lementabl[e] a case do we see the great body of the people in both instances: in the first, where Men might seem to inherit quiet of Mind from unsophisticated senses; from uncontamination of civilisation; and especially from their being as it were estranged from the mutual helps of Society and its mutual injuries—and thereby more immediately under the Protection of Providence—even there they had mortal pains to bear as bad; or even worse than Baliffs,[3] Debts and Poverties of civi-

---

7. Keats speculates that though his instinctive course is not, any more than an animal's, "disinterested" (free from selfish interests), it may still, like an animal's, be natural, hence innocent and possessed of an innate grace and beauty. He further supposes that this may be the nature of poetry, also, as distinguished from the deliberate and self-conscious process of philosophical reasoning (cf. the letter to George and Thomas Keats on "Negative Capability," begun on December 21, 1817, p. 1817).
8. For "may."

9. *Comus*, lines 475–77.
1. Voltaire, *Le Siècle de Louis XIV*, 5 vols. (1751); William Robertson, *The History of America* (1777—Keats was reading the 10th ed., 4 vols., 1803). In this second extract from the journal-letter Keats is writing toward the end of April (on the 21st or 28th).
2. Francisco Pizarro, the Spanish explorer whose exploits are described in Robertson's *America*. The "Monarch" is Louis XIV.
3. Bailiffs: officers of the law whose duties included making arrests for bad debts.

lised Life—The whole appears to resolve into this—that Man is originally "a poor forked creature"[4] subject to the same mischances as the beasts of the forest, destined to hardships and disquietude of some kind or other. If he improves by degrees his bodily accommodations and comforts—at each stage, at each accent there are waiting for him a fresh set of annoyances—he is mortal and there is still a heaven with its Stars abov[e] his head. The most interesting question that can come before us is, How far by the persevering endeavours of a seldom appearing Socrates Mankind may be made happy—I can imagine such happiness carried to an extreme—but what must it end in?—Death—and who could in such a case bear with death—the whole troubles of life which are now frittered away in a series of years, would the[n] be accumulated for the last days of a being who instead of hailing its approach, would leave this world as Eve left Paradise—But in truth I do not at all believe in this sort of perfectibility—the nature of the world will not admit of it—the inhabitants of the world will correspond to itself—Let the fish philosophise the ice away from the Rivers in winter time and they shall be at continual play in the tepid delight of summer. Look at the Poles and at the sands of Africa, Whirlpools and volcanoes—Let men exterminate them and I will say that they may arrive at earthly Happiness—The point at which Man may arrive is as far as the paralel state in inanimate nature and no further—For instance suppose a rose to have sensation, it blooms on a beautiful morning it enjoys itself—but there comes a cold wind, a hot sun—it can not escape it, it cannot destroy its annoyances—they are as native to the world as itself: no more can man be happy in spite, the world[l]y elements will prey upon his nature—The common cognomen of this world among the misguided and superstitious is "a vale of tears" from which we are to be redeemed by a certain arbitrary interposition of God and taken to Heaven—What a little circumscribe[d] straightened notion! Call the world if you Please "The vale of Soul-making" Then you will find out the use of the world (I am speaking now in the highest terms for human nature admitting it to be immortal which I will here take for granted for the purpose of showing a thought which has struck me concerning it) I say "Soul making" Soul as distinguished from an Intelligence—There may be intelligences or sparks of the divinity in millions—but they are not Souls ~~the~~ till they acquire identities, till each one is personally itself. I[n]telligences are atoms of perception—they know and they see and they are pure, in short they are God—how then are Souls to be made? How then are these sparks which are God to have identity given them—so as ever to possess a bliss peculiar to each ones individual existence? How, but by the medium of a world like this? This point I sincerely wish to consider because I think it a grander system of salvation than the chrysteain religion—or rather it is a system of Spirit-creation[5]—This is effected by three grand materials acting the one upon the

4. *King Lear* 3.4.94–95. Lear says: "Unaccommodated man is no more but such a poor, bare, forked animal as thou art."
5. Keats is struggling for an analogy that will embody his solution to the ancient riddle of evil, as an alternative to what he understands to be the Christian view: that evil exists as a test of the individual's merit of salvation in heaven and this world is only a proving ground for a later and better life. Keats proposes that the func-

tion of the human experience of sorrow and pain is to feed and discipline the formless and unstocked "intelligence" that we possess at birth and thus to shape it into a rich and coherent "identity," or "soul." This result provides a justification ("salvation") for our suffering in terms of our earthly life itself: that is, experience is its own reward. The passage is analogous to what Wordsworth says in the last two stanzas of his *Ode: Intimations of Immortality*.

other for a series of years—These three Materials are the *Intelligence*—the *human heart* (as distinguished from intelligence or Mind) and the *World* or *Elemental space* suited for the proper action of *Mind and Heart* on each other for the purpose of forming the *Soul* or *Intelligence destined to possess the sense of Identity*. I can scarcely express what I but dimly perceive—and yet I think I perceive it—that you may judge the more clearly I will put it in the most homely form possible—I will call the *world* a School instituted for the purpose of teaching little children to read—I will call the *human heart* the *horn Book*[6] used in that School—and I will call the *Child able to read, the Soul* made from that *school* and its *hornbook*. Do you not see how necessary a World of Pains and troubles is to school an Intelligence and make it a soul? A Place where the heart must feel and suffer in a thousand diverse ways! Not merely is the Heart a Hornbook, It is the Minds Bible, it is the Minds experience, it is the teat from which the Mind or intelligence sucks its identity—As various as the Lives of Men are—so various become their souls, and thus does God make individual beings, Souls, Identical Souls of the sparks of his own essence—This appears to me a faint sketch of a system of Salvation which does not affront our reason and humanity—I am convinced that many difficulties which christians labour under would vanish before it—There is one wh[i]ch even now Strikes me—the Salvation of Children—In them the Spark or intelligence returns to God without any identity—it having had no time to learn of, and be altered by, the heart—or seat of the human Passions—It is pretty generally suspected that the chr[i]stian scheme has been coppied from the ancient persian and greek Philosophers. Why may they not have made this simple thing even more simple for common apprehension by introducing Mediators and Personages in the same manner as in the hethen mythology abstractions are personified—Seriously I think it probable that this System of Soul-making—may have been the Parent of all the more palpable and personal Schemes of Redemption, among the Zoroastrians the Christians and the Hindoos. For as one part of the human species must have their carved Jupiter; so another part must have the palpable and named Mediatior and saviour, their Christ their Oromanes and their Vishnu[7]—If what I have said should not be plain enough, as I fear it may not be, I will but[8] you in the place where I began in this series of thoughts—I mean, I began by seeing how man was formed by circumstances—and what are circumstances?—but touchstones of his heart—? and what are touch stones?—but proovings of his hearrt?—and what are proovings of his heart but fortifiers or alterers of his nature? and what is his altered nature but his soul?—and what was his soul before it came into the world and had These provings and alterations and perfectionings?—An intelligences—without Identity—and how is this Identity to be made? Through the medium of the Heart? And how is the heart to become this Medium but in a world of Circumstances?—There now I think what with Poetry and Theology you may thank your Stars that my pen is not very long winded— * * *

This is the 3^d of May & every thing is in delightful forwardness; the violets

---

6. A child's primer, which used to consist of a sheet of paper mounted on thin wood, protected by a sheet of transparent horn.

7. The deity who creates and preserves the world, in Hindu belief. Oromanes (Ahriman) was the principle of evil, locked in a persisting struggle with Ormazd, the principle of good, in the Zoroastrian religion.

8. For "put."

are not withered, before the peeping of the first rose; You must let me know every thing, how parcels go & come, what papers you have, & what Newspapers you want, & other things—God bless you my dear Brother & Sister

Your ever Affectionate Brother

John Keats—

To Fanny Brawne

[*Fanny Brawne as Keats's "Fair Star"*]

[July 25, 1819]

My sweet Girl,

I hope you did not blame me much for not obeying your request of a Letter on Saturday: we have had four in our small room playing at cards night and morning leaving me no undisturb'd opportunity to write. Now Rice and Martin are gone I am at liberty. Brown to my sorrow confirms the account you give of your ill health. You cannot conceive how I ache to be with you: how I would die for one hour— —for what is in the world? I say you cannot conceive; it is impossible you should look with such eyes upon me as I have upon you: it cannot be. Forgive me if I wander a little this evening, for I have been all day employ'd in a very abstr[a]ct Poem[1] and I am in deep love with you— two things which must excuse me. I have, believe me, not been an age in letting you take possession of me; the very first week I knew you I wrote myself your vassal; but burnt the Letter as the very next time I saw you I thought you manifested some dislike to me. If you should ever feel for Man at the first sight what I did for you, I am lost. Yet I should not quarrel with you, but hate myself if such a thing were to happen—only I should burst if the thing were not as fine as a Man as you are as a Woman. Perhaps I am too vehement, then fancy me on my knees, especially when I mention a part of you Letter which hurt me; you say speaking of Mr. Severn[2] "but you must be satisfied in knowing that I admired you much more than your friend." My dear love, I cannot believe there ever was or ever could be any thing to admire in me especially as far as sight goes—I cannot be admired, I am not a thing to be admired. You are, I love you; all I can bring you is a swooning admiration of your Beauty. I hold that place among Men which snub-nos'd brunettes with meeting eyebrows do among women—they are trash to me—unless I should find one among them with a fire in her heart like the one that burns in mine. You absorb me in spite of myself—you alone: for I look not forward with any pleasure to what is call'd being settled in the world; I tremble at domestic cares— yet for you I would meet them, though if it would leave you the happier I would rather die than do so. I have two luxuries to brood over in my walks, your Loveliness and the hour of my death. O that I could have possession of them both in the same minute. I hate the world: it batters too much the wings of my self-will, and would I could take a sweet poison from your lips to send me out of it. From no others would I take it. I am indeed astonish'd to find myself so careless of all cha[r]ms but yours—remembring as I do the time when even a bit of ribband was a matter of interest with me. What softer words

1. Probably *Hyperion*.
2. Joseph Severn, who later looked after Keats during   his mortal illness in Rome.

can I find for you after this—what it is I will not read. Nor will I say more here, but in a Postscript answer any thing else you may have mentioned in your Letter in so many words—for I am distracted with a thousand thoughts. I will imagine you Venus tonight and pray, pray, pray to your star like a Hethen.[3]

Your's ever, fair Star,
John Keats.

To Percy Bysshe Shelley[1]

["Load Every Rift with Ore"]

[August 16, 1820]

My dear Shelley,

I am very much gratified that you, in a foreign country, and with a mind almost over occupied, should write to me in the strain of the Letter beside me. If I do not take advantage of your invitation it will be prevented by a circumstance I have very much at heart to prophesy[2]—There is no doubt that an english winter would put an end to me, and do so in a lingering hateful manner, therefore I must either voyage or journey to Italy as a soldier marches up to a battery. My nerves at present are the worst part of me, yet they feel soothed when I think that come what extreme may, I shall not be destined to remain in one spot long enough to take a hatred of any four particular bed-posts. I am glad you take any pleasure in my poor Poem;[3]—which I would willingly take the trouble to unwrite, if possible, did I care so much as I have done about Reputation. I received a copy of the Cenci,[4] as from yourself from Hunt. There is only one part of it I am judge of; the Poetry, and dramatic effect, which by many spirits now a days is considered the mammon. A modern work it is said must have a purpose,[5] which may be the God—an artist must serve Mammon—he must have "self concentration" selfishness perhaps. You I am sure will forgive me for sincerely remarking that you might curb your magnanimity and be more of an artist, and "load every rift"[6] of your subject with ore. The thought of such discipline must fall like cold chains upon you, who perhaps never sat with your wings furl'd for six Months together. And is not this extraordina[r]y talk for the writer of Endymion? whose mind was like a pack of scattered cards—I am pick'd up and sorted to a pip.[7] My Imagination is a Mon-astry and I am its Monk—you must explain my metap[cs8] to yourself. I am in expectation of Prometheus[9] every day. Could I have my own wish for its interest effected you would have it still in manuscript—or be but now putting an end to the second act. I remember you

---

3. See Keats's sonnet *Bright star* (p. 1787) for parallels to this and other remarks in the present letter.
1. Written in reply to a letter urging Keats (who was ill) to spend the winter with the Shelleys in Pisa.
2. His own death.
3. Keats's *Endymion*, Shelley had written, contains treasures, "though treasures poured forth with indistinct profusion." Keats here responds with advice in kind.
4. Shelley's blank-verse tragedy, *The Cenci*, had been published in the spring of 1820.

5. Wordsworth had said this in his Preface to *Lyrical Ballads*. For "Mammon" see Matthew 6.24 and Luke 16.13: "Ye cannot serve God and mammon."
6. Spenser, *The Faerie Queene* 2.7.28: "With rich metall loaded every rifte."
7. Perfectly ordered; all the suits in the deck matched up ("pips" are the conventional spots on playing cards).
8. Metaphysics.
9. *Prometheus Unbound*, of which Shelley had promised Keats a copy.

advising me not to publish my first-blights, on Hampstead heath—I am returning advice upon your hands. Most of the Poems in the volume I send you[1] have been written above two years, and would never have been publish'd but from a hope of gain; so you see I am inclined enough to take your advice now. I must exp[r]ess once more my deep sense of your kindness, adding my sincere thanks and respects for M[rs] Shelley. In the hope of soon seeing you I remain

> most sincerely yours,
> John Keats—

To Charles Brown[1]

[Keats's Last Letter]

> Rome. 30 November 1820.

My dear Brown,

'Tis the most difficult thing in the world to me to write a letter. My stomach continues so bad, that I feel it worse on opening any book,—yet I am much better than I was in Quarantine.[2] Then I am afraid to encounter the proing and conning of any thing interesting to me in England. I have an habitual feeling of my real life having past, and that I am leading a posthumous existence. God knows how it would have been—but it appears to me—however, I will not speak of that subject. I must have been at Bedhampton nearly at the time you were writing to me from Chichester—how unfortunate—and to pass on the river too! There was my star predominant![3] I cannot answer any thing in your letter, which followed me from Naples to Rome, because I am afraid to look it over again. I am so weak (in mind) that I cannot bear the sight of any hand writing of a friend I love so much as I do you. Yet I ride the little horse,—and, at my worst, even in Quarantine, summoned up more puns, in a sort of desperation, in one week than in any year of my life. There is one thought enough to kill me—I have been well, healthy, alert &c, walking with her[4]—and now—the knowledge of contrast, feeling for light and shade, all that information (primitive sense) necessary for a poem are great enemies to the recovery of the stomach. There, you rogue, I put you to the torture,—but you must bring your philosophy to bear—as I do mine, really—or how should I be able to live? D[r] Clarke is very attentive to me; he says, there is very little the matter with my lungs, but my stomach, he says, is very bad. I am well disappointed in hearing good news from George,—for it runs in my head we shall all die young. I have not written to x x x x x yet,[5] which he must think very neglectful; being anxious to send him a good account of my health, I have delayed it from week to week. If I recover, I will do all in my power to correct the mistakes made during sickness; and if I should not, all my faults will be forgiven. I shall write to x x x to-morrow, or next day. I will write to

---

1. Keats's volume of 1820, including *Lamia*, *The Eve of St. Agnes*, and the odes. When Shelley drowned, he had this small book open in his pocket.
1. Written to Keats's friend Charles Armitage Brown from the house on the Spanish Stairs, in the Piazza di Spagna, where Keats was being tended in his mortal illness by the devoted Joseph Severn.
2. When it landed at Naples, Keats's ship had been quarantined for ten miserably hot days.
3. *The Winter's Tale* 1.2.201–02: "It is a bawdy planet, that will strike / Where 'tis predominant."
4. Fanny Brawne.
5. Charles Brown, whose manuscript transcription is the only text for this letter, substituted crosses for the names of Keats's friends to conceal their identities.

x x x x x in the middle of next week. Severn is very well, though he leads so dull a life with me. Remember me to all friends, and tell x x x x I should not have left London without taking leave of him, but from being so low in body and mind. Write to George as soon as you receive this, and tell him how I am, as far as you can guess;—and also a note to my sister—who walks about my imagination like a ghost—she is so like Tom.[6] I can scarcely bid you good bye even in a letter. I always made an awkward bow.

God bless you!
John Keats.

---

6. Keats's youngest brother, whom Fanny, his only sister, closely resembled, had died of tuberculosis on Dec. 1, 1818. George was John Keats's younger brother.

The Victorian Age
1830-1901

1832:	The First Reform Bill.
1837:	Victoria becomes queen.
1846:	The Corn Laws repealed.
1850:	Tennyson succeeds Wordsworth as Poet Laureate.
1851:	The Great Exhibition in London.
1859:	Charles Darwin's *Origin of Species* published.
1870–71:	Franco-Prussian War.
1901:	Death of Victoria.

AN AGE OF EXPANSION

In 1897 Mark Twain was visiting London during the Diamond Jubilee celebrations honoring the sixtieth anniversary of Queen Victoria's coming to the throne. "British history is two thousand years old," Twain observed, "and yet in a good many ways the world has moved farther ahead since the Queen was born than it moved in all the rest of the two thousand put together." And if the whole world had "moved" during that long lifetime and reign of Victoria's, it was in her own country itself that the change was most marked and dramatic, a change that brought England to its highest point of development as a world power.

In the eighteenth century the pivotal city of Western civilization had been Paris; by the second half of the nineteenth century this center of influence had shifted to London, a city that expanded from about two million inhabitants when Victoria came to the throne to six and a half million at the time of her death. The rapid growth of London is one of the many indications of the most important development of the age: the shift from a way of life based on the ownership of land to a modern urban economy based on trade and manufacturing. "We have been living, as it were, the life of three hundred years in thirty" was the impression formed by Dr. Thomas Arnold during the early stages of England's industrialization. By the end of the century—after the resources of steam power had been more fully exploited for fast railways and iron ships, for looms, printing presses, and farmers' combines, and after the introduction of the telegraph, intercontinental cable, photography, anesthetics, and universal compulsory education—a late Victorian could look back with astonishment on these developments during his or her lifetime. Walter Besant, one of these late Victorians, observed that so completely transformed were "the mind and habits of the ordinary Englishman" by 1897, "that he would not, could he see him, recognize his own grandfather."

Because England was the first country to become industrialized, its transformation was an especially painful one: it experienced a host of social and economic problems consequent to rapid and unregulated industrialization. England also experienced an enormous increase in wealth. An early start enabled England to capture markets all over the globe. Cotton and other manufactured products were exported in English ships, a merchant fleet whose size was without parallel in other countries. The profits gained from trade led also to extensive capital investments in all continents. England gained particular profit from the development of its own colonies, which, by 1890, comprised more than a quarter of all the territory on the surface of the earth. After England had become the world's workshop, London became, from 1870 on, the world's banker. By the end of the century England was the world's foremost imperial power.

The effect of these developments on Victorian character has been described by the historian David Thomson. The period, he says in *England and the Nineteenth Century* (1950), "is one of strenuous activity and dynamic change, of ferment of ideas and recurrent social unrest, of great inventiveness and expansion."

The reactions of Victorian writers to the fast-paced expansion of England were various. Thomas Babington Macaulay (1800–1859) relished the spectacle as wholly delightful. During the prosperous 1850s Macaulay's essays and histories, with their recitations of the statistics of industrial growth, constituted a Hymn to Progress as well as a celebration of the superior qualities of the English people— "the greatest and most highly civilized people that ever the world saw." And later in the century there were lesser jingoists whose writings confidently pointed out the reasons for further national self-congratulation. More representative, perhaps, was Tennyson, whose capacity to relish industrial change was only sporadic. Much of the time he felt instead that leadership in commerce and industry was being paid for at a terrible price in human happiness. In his experience and that of others a so-called progress had been gained only by abandoning the traditional rhythms of life and traditional patterns of human relationships that had sustained us for centuries. In the melancholy poetry of Matthew Arnold this note is often struck:

> For what wears out the life of mortal men?
> 'Tis that from change to change their being rolls;
> 'Tis that repeated shocks, again, again,
> Exhaust the energy of strongest souls.

An occasional ride on a roller coaster may be exhilarating, but to be chained aboard for a lifetime is a nightmare.

Accounts of the Victorian state of mind can be wildly contradictory when interpretations focus on one side of this set of attitudes and exclude the other. To restore focus, it can be said that although most perceptive Victorians did share a sense of satisfaction in the industrial and political preeminence of England during the period, they also suffered from an anxious sense of something lost, a sense too of being displaced persons in a world made alien by technological changes that had been exploited too quickly for the adaptive powers of the human psyche. In this respect, as in many others, the Victorians may remind us of their English-speaking counterparts in America during the second half of the twentieth century who have taken over a leading position in the Western world with similar mixed feelings of satisfaction and anxiety.

DIFFERENT CRITICAL REACTIONS TO THE VICTORIAN AGE

To suggest a similarity between the Victorians and ourselves (a similarity, not an identity) hardly seems remarkable. In the earlier decades of the twentieth century, however, writers took pains to separate themselves from the Victorians. It was then the fashion for most literary critics to treat their Victorian predecessors as somewhat absurd creatures, stuffily complacent prigs with whose way of life they had little in common. Writers of the Georgian period (1911–36) took great delight in puncturing overinflated Victorian balloons, as Lytton Strachey, a member of Virginia Woolf's circle, did in *Eminent Victorians* (1918). A subtler example occurs in Woolf's *Orlando*, a delightful fictionalized survey of English literature from Elizabethan times to 1928, in which the Victorians are presented in terms of dampness, rain, and proliferating vegetation:

Ivy grew in unparalleled profusion. Houses that had been of bare stone were
smothered in greenery. . . . And just as the ivy and the evergreen rioted in the
damp earth outside, so did the same fertility show itself within. The life of the
average woman was a succession of childbirths. . . . Giant cauliflowers towered deck above deck till they rivaled . . . the elm trees themselves. Hens laid
incessantly eggs of no special tint. . . . The whole sky itself as it spread wide
above the British Isles was nothing but a vast feather bed.

  This witty description not only identifies a distinguishing quality of Victorian
life and literature—a superabundant energy—but reveals that the author of the
passage did not admire such energy. In fact, she felt terrified by it as if it might
smother her. Woolf was the daughter of Sir Leslie Stephen (1832–1904), himself
an eminent Victorian. In her later life, when assessing her father's powerful personality, Woolf recorded in her diary that she herself could never have become a
writer if he had not died when he did. Growing up under such towering shadows,
she and her generation felt an understandable need to mock their predecessors.
Also illustrative is the novelist Ford Madox Ford (1873–1939). In his reminiscences *Portraits from Life*, Ford recalled his feelings of terror when he confronted
the works of Carlyle and Ruskin, which he likened to an overpowering range of
high mountains. The mid-Victorians, he wrote, were "a childish nightmare to me."
  The Georgian reaction against the Victorians is now only a matter of the history
of taste, but its aftereffects still sometimes crop up when the term *Victorian* is
employed in an exclusively pejorative sense, as prudish or old-fashioned. Contemporary historians and critics now find the Victorian period a richly complex example of a society struggling with the issues and problems we identify with
modernism. But even to give the period the single designation *Victorian* suggests
a problem. The period takes its name, of course, from what was felt to be the
unifying presence of its monarch, who gave symbolic representation to the moral
virtue and national pride with which her subjects identified their epoch. For a
period almost seventy years in length, however, we can hardly expect generalizations to be uniformly applicable. It is therefore helpful to subdivide the age into
three phases: Early Victorian (1830–48), Mid-Victorian (1848–70), and Late Victorian (1870–1901). It may also be convenient to subdivide the Late phase by
considering the final decade, the nineties, as a bridge between two centuries.

THE EARLY PERIOD (1830–48): A TIME OF TROUBLES

  In his *Social History of Britain* (1988) F. M. R. Thompson notes that in
the autumn of 1830 the Liverpool and Manchester Railway opened, becoming
"the first locomotive-operated public line in the world." This decisive event in
England's technological development coincided with the opening of the Reform
Parliament, which two years later was to transform England's class structure. "The
two events," Thompson adds, "were not unconnected." That is, the Reform Bill of
1832 was passed in response to the demands of the middle classes, who were
gradually taking control of England's economy and who were also committed to
technological and industrial change.
  More precisely, the Reform Bill of 1832 extended the right to vote to all males
owning property worth £10 or more in annual rent. In effect the voting public
hereafter included the lower middle classes but not the working classes, who did
not obtain the vote until 1867 when a second Reform Bill was passed. Even more
important than the extension of the franchise was the virtual abolition in 1832
of an archaic electoral system whereby some of the new industrial cities were
unrepresented in Parliament while "rotten boroughs" (communities that had
become depopulated) elected the nominees of the local squire. Because it broke
up the monopoly of power that the conservative landowners had so long enjoyed
(the Tory party had been in office almost continuously from 1783 until 1830), the
Reform Bill represents the beginning of a new age. Yet this celebrated piece of

legislation could hardly be expected to solve all the economic, social, and political problems that had been building up while England was developing into a modern democratic and industrialized state. The changeover was in fact a painful one, attended with discord and conflict. This early period came to be called the Time of Troubles. In the early 1840s a severe depression, with widespread unemployment, led to rioting. Even without the provocation of unemployment, conditions in the new industrial and coal-mining areas were terrible enough to create fears of revolution. Workers and their families in the slums of such cities as Manchester lived in horribly crowded, unsanitary housing, and the conditions under which women and children toiled in mines and factories were unimaginably brutal. Elizabeth Barrett's poem *The Cry of the Children* (1843) may strike us as exaggerated, but it was based on reliable evidence concerning children of five years of age who dragged heavy tubs of coal through low-ceilinged mine passages for sixteen hours a day. Life in early Victorian mines and factories was much like Thomas Hobbes's "state of nature"—"poor, nasty, brutish, and short."

The owners of mines and factories regarded themselves as innocent of blame for such conditions, for they were wedded to an economic theory of laissez-faire, which assumed that unregulated working conditions would ultimately benefit everyone. A sense of the seemingly hopeless complexity of the situation during the Hungry 1840s is provided by an entry for 1842 in the diary of the statesman Charles Greville, an entry written at the same time that Carlyle was making his contribution to the "Condition of England Question," *Past and Present.* Conditions in the north of England, Greville reports, were "appalling."

> There is an immense and continually increasing population, no adequate demand for labor, . . . no confidence, but a universal alarm, disquietude, and discontent. Nobody can sell anything. . . . Certainly I have never seen . . . so serious a state of things as that which now stares us in the face; and this after thirty years of uninterrupted peace, and the most ample scope afforded for the development of all our resources. . . . One remarkable feature in the present condition of affairs is that nobody can account for it, and nobody pretends to be able to point out any remedy.

In reality many remedies were being pointed out. One of the most striking was put forward by the Chartists, a large organization of workingmen. In 1838 the organization drew up a "People's Charter" advocating the extension of the right to vote, the use of secret balloting, and other legislative reforms. For ten years the Chartist leaders engaged in agitation to have their program adopted by Parliament. Their fiery speeches, addressed to large mobs of discontented people, alarmed those who were not themselves suffering from hunger. In *Locksley Hall* Tennyson seems to have had the Chartist mobs in mind when he pictured the threat posed by this time of troubles: "Slowly comes a hungry people, as a lion, creeping nigher, / Glares at one that nods and winks behind a slowly-dying fire." Although in the eyes of posterity the Chartist program seems an eminently reasonable one, legislators in the 1840s were not ready to accept it. More immediately feasible was the agitation to abolish the high tariffs on imported grains, tariffs known as the Corn Laws (the word *corn* in England refers to wheat and other grains). These high tariffs had been established to protect English farm products from having to compete with low-priced products imported from abroad. Landowners and farmers fought to keep these tariffs in force so that high prices for their wheat would be ensured, but the rest of the population suffered severely from the exorbitant price of bread or, in years of bad crops, from scarcity of food. In 1845 serious crop failures in England and the outbreak of potato blight in Ireland convinced Sir Robert Peel, the Tory prime minister, that traditional protectionism must be abandoned. In 1846 the Corn Laws were repealed by Parliament, and the way was paved for the introduction of a system of Free Trade whereby goods could be imported with the payment of only minimal tariff duties. Although Free Trade did not eradicate the slums of Manchester, it worked well for many years and helped to relieve the major crisis of the Victorian economy. In 1848, when armed revolutions were exploding violently in every country in Europe, England was relatively unaffected. A large Chartist demonstration in London seemed to threaten revolution, but it came to nothing. The next two decades were relatively calm and prosperous.

This Time of Troubles left its mark on some early Victorian literature. "Insurrection is a most sad necessity," Carlyle writes in his *Past and Present*, "and governors who wait for that to instruct them are surely getting into the fatalest courses." A similar refrain runs through Carlyle's history *The French Revolution* (1837). Memories of the French Reign of Terror lasted longer than memories of Trafalgar and Waterloo, memories freshened by later outbreaks of civil strife, "the red fool-fury of the Seine" as Tennyson described one of the violent overturnings of government in France. It is the novelists of the 1840s and early 1850s, however, who show the most marked response to the industrial and political scene. Vivid records of these conditions are to be found in the fiction of Charles Kingsley (1819–1875), Elizabeth Gaskell (1810–1865), and Benjamin Disraeli (1804–1881), a novelist who became prime minister. For his novel *Sybil* (1845), Disraeli chose an appropriate subtitle, *The Two Nations*—a phrase that pointed out the line dividing the England of the rich from the other nation, the England of the poor.

THE MID-VICTORIAN PERIOD (1848–70): ECONOMIC PROSPERITY AND RELIGIOUS CONTROVERSY

In the decades following the Time of Troubles some Victorian writers, such as Dickens, continued to make critical attacks on the shortcomings of the Victorian social scene. Even more critical and indignant than Dickens was John Ruskin, who abandoned the criticism of art during this period to expose the faults of Victorian industry and commerce, as in his *The Stones of Venice* (1853), which combines a history of architecture with stern prophecies about the doom of technological culture, or in his attacks on laissez-faire economics in *Unto This Last* (1862). Generally speaking, however, the "solid substance" of the novels of Anthony Trollope (1815–1882)—as Robert Adams has described it—is a more characteristic reflection of the mid-Victorian attitude toward the social and political scene than are Ruskin's lamentations. As Adams said of Trollope in 1983: "His books are solidly put together, as befits the world of fixed values and stable institutions that he describes; aided, perhaps, by a bit of nostalgia, they have regained in our time some of the popularity they had in their own." Overall, this second phase of the Victorian period had many harassing problems, but it was a time of prosperity. On the whole its institutions worked well. Even the badly bungled war against Russia in the Crimea (1854–56) did not seriously affect the growing sense of satisfaction that the challenging difficulties of the 1840s had been solved or would be solved by English wisdom and energy. The monarchy was proving its worth in a modern setting. The queen and her husband, Prince Albert, were themselves models of middle-class domesticity and devotion to duty. The aristocracy was discovering that Free Trade was enriching rather than impoverishing their estates; agriculture flourished together with trade and industry. And through a succession of Factory Acts in Parliament, which restricted child labor and limited hours of employment, the condition of the working classes was also being gradually improved. When we speak of Victorian complacency or stability or optimism, we are usually referring to this mid-Victorian phase—"The Age of Improvement," as the historian Asa Briggs has called it. "Of all the decades in our history," writes G. M. Young, "a wise man would choose the eighteen-fifties to be young in."

In 1851 Prince Albert opened the Great Exhibition in Hyde Park, where a gigantic glass greenhouse, the Crystal Palace, had been erected to display the exhibits of modern industry and science. The Crystal Palace was one of the first buildings constructed according to modern architectural principles in which materials

such as glass and iron are employed for purely functional ends (much late Victorian furniture, on the other hand, with its fantastic and irrelevant ornamentation,
was constructed according to the opposite principle). The building itself, as well
as the exhibits, symbolized the triumphant feats of Victorian technology. As Benjamin Disraeli wrote to a friend in 1862: "It is a privilege to live in this age of
rapid and brilliant events. What an error to consider it a utilitarian age. It is one
of infinite romance."

Pride in technological progress, however, is only one element of the mid-
Victorian period. Equally significant is the conflict between religion and science.
This conflict was not, of course, altogether a new one. Tennyson's In Memoriam
(1850), like much mid-Victorian literature, carries on the religious debates of earlier decades. These debates, in their previous form, had been generally between
the Utilitarians, the followers of Jeremy Bentham (1772–1832), and the philosophical conservatives, the followers of Samuel Taylor Coleridge. As John Stuart Mill
demonstrates in his excellent essays on Bentham and Coleridge, these two writers
divided between them the allegiance of all thoughtful people in England. Bentham and his disciples were reformers of a distinctive cast of mind. Their aim was
to test all institutions in the light of human reason to determine whether such
institutions were useful—that is, whether they contributed to the greatest happiness of the greatest numbers. This "Utilitarian" test was an extremely effective
method of correcting inefficiencies in government administration: the drastic
remodeling of the Civil Service in Victorian England was a tribute to Benthamite
thinking. But such a test, if applied to a long-established institution like the
Church of England, or to religious belief in general, could have, and did have,
disruptive effects. Was religious belief useful for the needs of a reasonable person?
To the Benthamites the answer was evident: religious belief was merely an out-
moded superstition. This answer was emphatically stated in a letter by Harriet
Martineau (1802–1876), a Utilitarian writer and freethinker: "There is no theory
of a God, of an author of Nature, of an origin of the universe, which is not utterly
repugnant to my faculties; which is not (to my feelings) so irreverent as to make
me blush; so misleading as to make me mourn."

Opponents of Utilitarianism, including Coleridge, argued that Bentham's view
of human nature was unrealistically narrow, that people had always needed a faith
as profoundly as they had needed food, and that if reason seemed to demonstrate
the irrelevance of religion then reason must be an inadequate mode of arriving at
truth. These anti-Utilitarians were of two types. The first were those such as Carlyle, who abandoned institutional Christianity yet sought to retain some sort of
substitute religious belief—a quest that is vividly described in his spiritual autobiography Sartor Resartus. Others, led by John Henry Newman, argued that only a
powerful, dogmatic, and traditional religious institution could withstand the
attacks of irreverent thinkers of the Benthamite stamp. In the 1830s and 1840s
(before he was converted to Roman Catholicism), Newman became the leader of
an impressive crusade to strengthen the Church of England. The movement he
headed is known under various names including "The Oxford Movement,"
because it originated at Oxford University, and "Tractarianism," because Newman
and his conservative followers developed their arguments in defense of a High
Church in a series of pamphlets or tracts. Whatever name it went by, Newman's
campaign produced a lively controversy. When Arthur Hugh Clough and Matthew Arnold were at Oxford in the early 1840s, the university was seething with
religious debates, which were to have a marked effect on the poetry written by
both men in the 1850s.

In mid-Victorian England these controversies continued, but with an added
intensification. Leadership in the anticlerical position passed gradually from the
Utilitarians to some of the leaders of science, in particular to Thomas Henry Huxley, who popularized the theories of Charles Darwin. Although many English
scientists were themselves individuals of strong religious convictions, the impact

of their scientific discoveries seemed consistently damaging to established faiths. Complaining about the "flimsiness" of his own religious faith in 1851, Ruskin exclaimed: "If only the Geologists would let me alone, I could do very well, but those dreadful hammers! I hear the clink of them at the end of every cadence of the Bible verses."

The damage lamented by Ruskin was effected in two ways. First the scientific attitude of mind was applied toward a study of the Bible itself. This kind of investigation, developed especially in Germany, was known as the "Higher Criticism." Instead of treating the Bible as a sacredly infallible document, scientifically minded scholars examined it as a mere text of history and presented evidence about its composition that believers, especially in Protestant countries, found disconcerting, to say the least. A noteworthy example of such Higher Criticism studies was David Friedrich Strauss's *Das Leben Jesu*, which was translated by George Eliot in 1846 as *The Life of Jesus*. The second kind of damage was effected by the view of humanity implicit in the discoveries of geology and astronomy, the new and "Terrible Muses" of literature, as Tennyson called them in a late poem. Geology, by extending the history of the earth backward millions of years, reduced the stature of the human race in time. John Tyndall, an eminent physicist, said in an address at Belfast in 1874 that in the eighteenth century people had an "unwavering trust" in the "chronology of the Old Testament" but in Victorian times they had to become accustomed to

> the idea that not for six thousand, nor for sixty thousand, nor for six thousand thousand, but for aeons embracing untold millions of years, this earth has been the theater of life and death. The riddle of the rocks has been read by the geologist and paleontologist, from sub-Cambrian depths to the deposits thickening over the sea bottoms of today. And upon the leaves of that stone book are . . . stamped the characters, plainer and surer than those formed by the ink of history, which carry the mind back into abysses of past time.

The discoveries of astronomers, by extending a knowledge of stellar distances to dizzying expanses, were likewise disconcerting. Carlyle's friend John Sterling remarked in a letter of 1837 how geology "gives one the same sort of bewildering view of the abysmal extent of Time that Astronomy does of Space." To Tennyson's speaker in *Maud* (1855) the stars are "innumerable" tyrants of "iron skies." They are "Cold fires, yet with power to burn and brand / His nothingness into man."

In the mid-Victorian period, biology reduced humankind even further into "nothingness." Darwin's great treatise *The Origin of Species* (1859) was interpreted by the nonscientific public in a variety of ways. Some chose to assume that evolution was synonymous with progress, but most readers recognized that Darwin's theory of natural selection conflicted not only with the concept of creation derived from the Bible but also with long-established assumptions of the values attached to humanity's special role in the world. Darwin's later treatise *The Descent of Man* (1871) raised more explicitly the haunting question of our identification with the animal kingdom. If the principle of survival of the fittest was accepted as the key to conduct, there remained the inquiry: fittest for what? As John Fowles noted in 1968, Darwin's theories made the Victorians feel "infinitely isolated." "By the 1860s the great iron structures of their philosophies, religions, and social stratifications were already beginning to look dangerously corroded to the more perspicacious."

Disputes about evolutionary science, like the disputes about the Oxford Movement, are a reminder that beneath the placidly prosperous surface of the mid-Victorian age there were serious conflicts and anxieties. In the same year as the Great Exhibition, with its celebration of the triumphs of trade and industry, Charles Kingsley wrote, "The young men and women of our day are fast parting from their parents and each other; the more thoughtful are wandering either

towards Rome, towards sheer materialism, or towards an unchristian and unphilo-
sophic spiritualism."

The third phase of the Victorian age is more difficult to categorize. At first
glance its point of view seems merely an extension of mid-Victorianism, whose
golden glow lingered on through the Jubilee years of 1887 and 1897 (years celebrating the fiftieth and sixtieth anniversaries of the queen's accession) down to
1914. For many Victorians, this final phase of the century was a time of serenity
and security, the age of house parties and long weekends in the country. In the
amber of Henry James's prose is immortalized a sense of the comfortable pace of
these pleasant, well-fed gatherings. Life in London, too, was for many an exhilarating heyday. In *My Life and Loves* the Irish-American Frank Harris (1854–1931),
often a severe critic of the English scene, records his recollections of the gaiety of
London in the 1880s: "London: who would give even an idea of its varied delights:
London, the center of civilization, the queen city of the world without a peer in
the multitude of its attractions, as superior to Paris as Paris is to New York." Yet as
the leading social critic of the 1860s, Matthew Arnold, had tried to show, there
were anomalies in the seemingly smooth-working institutions of mid-Victorian
England, and after 1870 flaws became evident. Some of the flaws developed out
of issues of long standing such as relations with the Irish, and, a related issue, the
status of Roman Catholics in England. The "Irish Question," as it was called,
became especially divisive in the 1880s when Home Rule for Ireland became a
topic of heated debate—a proposed reform that was unsuccessfully advocated by
Prime Minister Gladstone and other leaders. And outside of England were other
developments that challenged Victorian stability and security. The sudden emergence of Bismarck's Germany after the defeat of France in 1871 was progressively
to confront England with powerful threats to its naval and military position and
also to its exclusive preeminence in trade and industry. The recovery of the United
States after the Civil War likewise provided new and serious competition not only
in industry but also in agriculture. As the westward expansion of railroads in the
United States and Canada opened up the vast, grain-rich prairies, the typical
English farmer had to confront lower grain prices and a dramatically different
scale of productivity that England could not match. In 1873 and 1874 such severe
economic depressions occurred that the rate of emigration rose to an alarming
degree. Another threat to the domestic balance of power was the growth of labor
as a political and economic force. In 1867, under Disraeli's guidance, a second
Reform Bill had been passed that extended the right to vote to sections of the
working classes, and this, together with the subsequent development of trade
unions, made labor a political force to be reckoned with. The Labor party represented a wide variety of shades of socialism. Some labor leaders were disciples of
the Tory-socialism of John Ruskin and shared his idealistic conviction that the
middle-class economic and political system, with its distrust of state interference,
was irresponsible and immoral. Other labor leaders had been influenced instead
by the revolutionary theories of Karl Marx and Friedrich Engels as expounded in
their *Communist Manifesto* of 1847 and in Marx's *Capital* (1867, 1885, 1895).
Perhaps the first English author of note to be connected with Marxism was the
poet and painter William Morris. Morris, himself a man of some independent
means, was too much of an individualist to follow Marx in every respect, but he
did share with Marx a conviction that utopia could be achieved only after the
working classes had, by revolution, taken control of government and industry.

In much of the literature of this final phase of Victorianism we can sense an
overall change of attitudes. Some of the late Victorian writers expressed the change
openly by simply attacking the major mid-Victorian idols. Samuel Butler (1835–
1902), for example, set about demolishing Darwin, Tennyson, and Prime Minister
Gladstone, figures whose aura of authority reminded him of his own father. For

the more worldly and casual-mannered Prime Minister Disraeli, on the other hand, Butler could express considerable admiration: "Earnestness was his greatest danger, but if he did not quite overcome it (as who indeed can? it is the last enemy that shall be subdued), he managed to veil it with a fair amount of success." In his novel *The Way of All Flesh*, much of which was written in the 1870s, Butler satirized family life, in particular the tyrannical self-righteousness of a Victorian father, his own father (a clergyman) serving as his model. Butler's open revolt was perhaps premature. More typical were Walter Pater and his followers, writers who concluded that the striving of their predecessors was ultimately pointless, that the answers to our problems are not to be found, and that our role is to enjoy the fleeting moments of beauty in "this short day of frost and sun." It is symptomatic of this shift in point of view that Edward FitzGerald's beautiful translation of the *Rubáiyát of Omar Khayyám* (1859), with its melancholy theme that life's problems are insoluble, went virtually unnoticed in the 1860s but became a popular favorite in subsequent decades.

THE NINETIES

The changes in attitude that had begun cropping up in the 1870s became much more conspicuous in the final decade of the century and give the nineties a special aura of notoriety. Of course the changes were not in evidence everywhere. Throughout the empire at its outposts in India and Africa, the English were building railways and administering governments with the same strenuous energy as in the mid-Victorian period. The stories of Kipling and Conrad variously record the struggles of such people. Also embodying the task of sustaining an empire were the soldiers and sailors who fought in various colonial wars, most notably in the war against the Boers in South Africa (1899–1902). But back in England, Victorian standards were breaking down on several fronts. One colorful embodiment of changing values was Victoria's son and heir, Edward, Prince of Wales, who was entering his fiftieth year as the nineties began. A pleasure-seeking, easygoing person, Edward was the antithesis of his father, Prince Albert, an earnest-minded intellectual who had devoted his life to hard work and to administrative responsibilities. Edward's carryings-on were a favorite topic for newspaper articles, one of which noted how this father of five children "openly maintained scandalous relations with ballet dancers and chorus singers." The familiar epithet "Gay Nineties," however inadequate to characterize the decade, evokes the rakish life-style of Victoria's son.

Much of the writing of the decade illustrates a breakdown of a different sort. Melancholy, not gaiety, is characteristic of its spirit. Artists of the nineties, representing the Aesthetic movement, were very much aware of living at the end of a great century and often cultivated a deliberately *fin-de-siècle* ("end-of-century") pose. A studied languor, a weary sophistication, a search for new ways of titillating jaded palates can be found in both the poetry and the prose of the period. *The Yellow Book*, a periodical that ran from 1894 to 1897, is generally taken to represent the aestheticism of the nineties. The startling black-and-white drawings and designs of its art editor, Aubrey Beardsley (1872–1898), the prose of George Moore and Max Beerbohm, and the poetry of Ernest Dowson illustrate different aspects of the movement. In 1893, an Austrian critic, Max Nordau, summed up what seemed to him to be happening, in a book that was as sensational as its title: *Degeneration.*

From the perspective of the twentieth century, however, it is easy to see in the nineties the beginning of the modernist movement in literature; a number of the great writers of the twentieth century—Yeats, Hardy, Conrad, Shaw—were already publishing. In his essay "The Nineties," Helmut Gerber offers a useful generalization (applicable to the 1790s as well as to the 1890s) on this point. According to Gerber it seems "that at the ends of centuries . . . human beings, but artists in particular, are infected by a sense of death, decay, agony, old gods falling, cultural decline, on the one hand, or by a sense of regeneration . . . on the other."

In Dickens's *David Copperfield* (1850) the hero affirms: "I have always been thoroughly in earnest." Forty-five years later Oscar Wilde's comedy *The Importance of Being Earnest* turns this typical mid-Victorian word *earnest* into a pun, a key joke in this comic spectacle of earlier Victorian values being turned upside down. As Richard Le Gallienne (a novelist of the nineties) remarked in *The Romantic Nineties* (1926): "Wilde made dying Victorianism laugh at itself, and it may be said to have died of the laughter."

EARNESTNESS, RESPECTABILITY, AND THE EVANGELICALS

Wilde's decades, the 1880s and 1890s, which took such delight in lampooning the quality of earnestness, show how important it was to the previous decades. Why has the term *earnest* been so often applied to the typical Victorian writers? It should be noted that the quality of earnestness (or as some historians call it, more appropriately, "eagerness") was not strained. It did not exclude high spirits and humor. An age that relished the comic genius of Dickens and Thackeray, the grotesque humor of Browning and Carlyle, the nonsensical whimsy of Edward Lear and Lewis Carroll, was not exclusively dedicated to mere solemnity. As Peter Ackroyd affirmed in his biography of Dickens, "There never was a period so capable of laughing at itself." Nevertheless, the general Victorian preference for earnestness of spirit was firmly rooted and can best be accounted for by distinguishing it not from what came after but from what went before it.

The connections between literature in the Romantic and Victorian ages are close. Victorian poets as different as Browning and Swinburne show the strong influence of Shelley. Tennyson frequently writes in the tradition of Keats; Arnold, in that of Wordsworth. Many other instances of such continuity and influence may be cited. Most Victorian writers, both in poems and in essays, grappled with the same religious issues that had been a central concern for Wordsworth, Blake, and Shelley. As M. H. Abrams demonstrates in *Natural Supernaturalism* (1971), the post-Romantics from Tennyson through Yeats continued the Romantic endeavor to salvage "the cardinal values of their religious heritage by reconstituting them in a way that would make them intellectually acceptable, as well as emotionally pertinent, for the time being."

A dividing point, however, may be observed in Carlyle's well-known advice to his contemporaries in 1834: "Close thy *Byron*; open thy *Goethe*." Carlyle's advice could be interpreted in two ways. The first is with reference to literary forms. A Victorian writer might avoid the wild excesses, the lack of controlled form of much Romantic writing; Byron himself foresaw that such a reformation was necessary. "We are all on a wrong tack ('Lakers' and all)," he wrote. "Our successors will have to go back to the riding school . . . and learn to ride the great horse." Some of Byron's Victorian successors ignored his prediction; they too rode Pegasus bareback as casually as he had done. Yet several Victorian poets, Tennyson in particular, do fulfill Byron's prediction. The energy of Romantic literature persists, but it is channeled into a stricter concern for disciplined forms. It is significant that the Romantic poet most influential in the Victorian age was Keats, the most form-conscious of the Romantics, rather than Byron.

Carlyle himself was not primarily concerned with a chastening of literary forms. He was saying, in effect: "Stop moping. There is work to be done, work that requires the earnest efforts of all of us." A similar message was made, also in 1834, by the popular novelist Edward Bulwer-Lytton (1803–1873) in his *England and the English*. "When Byron passed away," Lytton reported, ". . . we turned to the actual and practical career of life: we awoke from the morbid, the dreaming, 'the moonlight and dimness of the mind,' and by a natural reaction addressed ourselves to the active and daily objects which lay before us."

And to address themselves to the "actual and practical" meant for the Victorians that their "natural reaction" was directed not only against the excesses of Romanticism but also against the life-style of many of Byron's aristocratic contemporaries who had flourished in the previous decades and who had embodied the worldly code of the Regency, with its preference for a happy-go-lucky enjoyment of the physical pleasures of life, for fox hunting and hard drinking and lounging. Lord Melbourne, Victoria's first prime minister, embodied such a view of life and found himself out of place under the new dispensation—an "autumn rose" as Strachey called him. Carlyle's gospel, on the other hand, was soon to be extremely timely for the new generation. From 1830 on there developed what the historian Arnold Toynbee called a "challenge." The earnest strivings of the Victorians provided the needed "response." A speech made by the heroine of *Jane Eyre* sums up these developments. After she refuses to accept a proposal to become the mistress of the loose-living Mr. Rochester, and he is bewailing his lonely lot, Jane Eyre advises him sternly: "Mr. Rochester . . . we are born to strive and endure—you as well as I: do so."

A further indication of the timeliness of Carlyle's call to action in *Sartor Resartus* is its Evangelical tone. In its strictest sense *Evangelical* refers to part of a branch of the Church of England called the Low Church. Zealously dedicated to good causes (they were responsible for the emancipation of all the slaves in the British empire as early as 1833), advocates of a strict puritan code of morality, and righteously censorious of worldliness in others, the Evangelicals became a powerful and active minority in the early part of the nineteenth century. Much of their power depended on the fact that their view of life and religion was virtually identical with that of a much larger group, the Nonconformists—that is, the Baptists, Methodists, Congregationalists, and other Protestant sects that did not conform to the tenets of the Established Church (the Church of England has been, in effect, a state church). When united for action with this large group of sects—Dissenters as they were called, a group whose membership included a generous proportion of those successful in business—the Evangelicals were a formidable force.

Finally, the term *Evangelical* has been loosely applied to cover any kind of enthusiastic concern for reform. It is thus used to describe anyone infected with the *spirit* of the Evangelical movement even though he or she does not subscribe to its ethical code or its beliefs. Victorian earnestness may therefore be explained partly as responding to a challenging situation and partly as rooted in an active religious movement that left its stamp on agnostics as well as on believers. George Eliot is an example of this Evangelical legacy. After having abandoned Christianity and having flouted convention by living for years with a married man, she devoted her novels to painstaking analyses of problems of conscience and moral choice. It would be difficult to name a Victorian writer of any consequence who remained an Evangelical in the true sense of the term; it would be equally difficult to name one who was not affected by what Evangelicalism stood for.

The code of puritanism and respectability advocated by the Nonconformists and Evangelicals is symbolized by the joyless Victorian Sunday. In 1837, a new Sunday Observance Bill (strenuously opposed by Charles Dickens) was introduced into Parliament. Although the bill did not quite pass, the Sober Sunday ritual became established by custom if not by law. To later generations, even more repressive was the puritans' standard of sexual behavior, with its intense concern for female innocence—or, as its opponents contended, for female ignorance. Yet the puritanism of middle-class sexual morality was only one element of an elaborately codified sexual culture, with an extravagant pornography the underside of its prudishness. Victorians were as preoccupied with the fallen woman as they were with the innocent maiden and wife. There was in fact a significant growth in prostitution during the period; in 1850, eight thousand prostitutes were known by the police to be operating in London. Numerous reformers were involved in efforts to "rescue" prostitutes, among them figures as disparate as Charles Dickens, Prime Minister William Gladstone, and Christina Rossetti.

The middle-class puritan code was largely derived from the Old Testament, but it also reflected commercial experience in which sobriety, hard work, and a joyless abstention from worldly pleasures paid off, paradoxically enough, in worldly success. Intermixed with this ascetic code was an insistence on respectability—an insistence reflecting the insecurity of a newly powerful class in a fluid society, a class anxious to have a fixed set of manners by which to live and to measure themselves and the families of others. Hence developed the phenomenon of "Mrs. Grundyism": conformity in its worst sense—that is, external conformity.

It is against this background that John Stuart Mill's essay *On Liberty* (1859) should be read. The status of liberty in Victorian England was actually one of the most outstanding achievements of the age. For Continental agitators of the left, right, or center in politics, Victorian England was the land of freedom, an asylum where the police officer (who was unarmed) was a friendly protector instead of an instrument of tyranny. To this asylum flocked General Torrijos (whose plot against the Spanish monarchy involved Tennyson); Mazzini, the Italian nationalist; Louis Napoleon of France; Kossuth, the Hungarian patriot; Prince Metternich of Austria; and Karl Marx himself, whose major work, *Capital*, was conceived in the Reading Room of the British Museum. The Victorian achievement in religious as well as political freedom is also impressive. Atheist orators such as Charles Bradlaugh enjoyed the privilege of addressing large audiences. In 1844, Friedrich Engels (not usually friendly toward the English scene) observed: "England is unquestionably the freest—that is, the least unfree—country in the world, North America not excepted."

Under such circumstances, why did Mill consider liberty a problem? Mill was inspired by his experience that individuality is threatened not merely by political tyrannies or entrenched religions. It is threatened also by the less tangible pressures exerted by society itself, in particular by the middle-class conventions that weighed on the nonconformist in society rather than on the Nonconformist in religion. In Hardy's late-Victorian novel *Jude the Obscure*, which contributed to the breakdown of the puritan code in literature, it is revealing that when Sue Bridehead resolves to leave her husband she justifies her action by citing a passage from Mill's *On Liberty*.

THE ROLE OF WOMEN IN VICTORIAN LIFE AND LITERATURE

Hardy's heroine might also have cited a later treatise by Mill on a different aspect of liberty: *The Subjection of Women* (1869), in which he boldly challenged long-established assumptions about women's roles in society. Like Mary Wollstonecraft's *A Vindication of the Rights of Women* (1792), Mill's treatise brings libertarian arguments for reform in the privileges of men to apply to the status of women. It was not only the political revolutions of the times, however, that provided a basis for change in woman's position but the Industrial Revolution as well. The explosive growth of the textile industries brought hundreds of thousands of lower-class women into factory jobs with grueling working conditions. In its disruption of family life and in its similarity to male labor, women's factory work presented an increasing challenge to traditional ideas of woman's sphere. In quite a different way, however, the strains of modernization motivated a renewed emphasis on home and family that enforced the separation for the middle class between men's work and women's work. All of these changes brought to the fore what Victorians called the "Woman Question," which concerned issues of sexual inequality in politics, economic life, education, and social intercourse. In the political arena, it was abundantly evident that women continued to rank as second-class citizens. Like millions of working-class men, they could not vote or hold office except the highest office of queen (and Victoria was, in general, an antifeminist). Petitions to Parliament advocating women's suffrage were introduced as early as the 1840s, but women did not get the vote until 1918. Less prolonged was the agitation to allow married women to own and handle their own property, which culminated successfully in the passing of the Married Women's Property Acts

(1870–1908). The Factory Acts, which had been passed earlier, corrected some of the worst aspects of women's employment in the mines and factories, including the reduction of the sixteen-hour day; in this instance, however, the argument for reform was based not on women's equality but on the earlier chivalric view of their comparative frailty of physique.

In addition to pressuring Parliament for legal reform, feminists worked to enlarge educational opportunities for women. In 1837 none of England's three universities was open to women. Tennyson's long poem *The Princess* (1847), with its fantasy of a women's college from whose precincts all males are excluded, was inspired by contemporary discussions of the need for women to obtain an education more advanced than that provided by the popular finishing schools such as Miss Pinkerton's Academy in Thackeray's *Vanity Fair*. Although by the end of the poem, Princess Ida has repented of her Amazonian scheme, she and the prince look forward to a future in which man will be "more of woman, she of man." The poem reflects a climate of opinion that led in 1848 to the establishment of the first women's college in London, an example later recommended by Thomas Henry Huxley, a strong advocate of advanced education for women. By the end of Victoria's reign, women could take degrees at twelve universities or university colleges and could study, although not earn a degree, at Oxford and Cambridge.

There was also agitation for improved employment opportunities for women. Writers as diverse as Charlotte Brontë, Elizabeth Barrett Browning, and Florence Nightingale complained that middle-class women were taught trivial accomplishments in order to fill up days in which there was nothing important to do. The problem of nothing to do was acute in quite a different way for what contemporary journalists called "surplus" or "redundant" women, that is, the women in the population who remained unmarried because of the imbalance in numbers between the sexes. Such women (of whom there were approximately half a million in mid-Victorian England) had few employment opportunities, none of them attractive or profitable. Emigration was frequently proposed as a solution to the problem, but the number of single female emigrants was never high enough to affect significantly the population imbalance. Bad working conditions and underemployment drove thousands of women into prostitution, which became increasingly professionalized in the nineteenth century. The only occupation at which an unmarried middle-class woman could earn a living and maintain some claim to gentility was that of a governess, but a governess could expect no security of employment, minimal wages, and an ambiguous status, somewhere between servant and family member, that isolated her within the household. Perhaps because the governess so clearly indicated the precariousness of the unmarried middle-class woman's status in Victorian England, the governess novel, of which the most famous examples are *Jane Eyre* and *Vanity Fair*, became a popular genre through which to explore woman's role in society.

As such novels indicate, Victorian society was preoccupied not only with legal and economic limitations on women's lives but with the very nature of woman. In *The Subjection of Women* John Stuart Mill argues that "what is now called the nature of women is eminently an artificial thing—the result of forced repression in some directions, unnatural stimulation in others." In Tennyson's *The Princess* the king voices a more traditional view of woman's role:

> Man for the field and woman for the hearth:
> Man for the sword and for the needle she:
> Man with the head and woman with the heart:
> Man to command and woman to obey.

The king's relegation of women to the hearth and heart reflects an ideology that claimed that woman had a special nature peculiarly fit for her domestic role. Most aptly epitomized by the title of Coventry Patmore's immensely popular poem *The*

Angel in the House (1854–62), this concept of womanhood stressed woman's purity and selflessness. Protected and enshrined within the home, her role was to create a place of peace where man could take refuge from the difficulties of modern life. In *Of Queen's Gardens* John Ruskin writes:

> This is the true nature of home—it is the place of Peace; the shelter, not only from all injury, but from all terror, doubt, and division. In so far as it is not this, it is not home; so far as the anxieties of the outer life penetrate into it, and the inconsistently-minded, unknown, unloved, or hostile society of the outer world is allowed either by husband or wife to cross the threshold, it ceases to be home; it is then only a part of that outer world which you have roofed over, and lighted fire in. But so far as it is a sacred place, a vestal temple, a temple of the hearth watched over by Household Gods, . . . so far it vindicates the name, and fulfills the praise, of home.

Such an exalted conception of home placed great pressure on the woman who ran it to be, in Ruskin's words, "enduringly, incorruptibly good; instinctively, infallibly wise—wise, not for self-development, but for self-renunciation." It is easy to recognize the oppressive aspects of this ideology. Paradoxically, however, it was used not only by antifeminists, eager to keep woman in her place, but by some feminists as well, in justifying the special contribution that woman could make to public life.

In his preface to *The Portrait of a Lady* (1881) Henry James writes: "Millions of presumptuous girls, intelligent or not intelligent, daily affront their destiny, and what is it open to their destiny to *be*, at the most, that we should make an ado about it?" Every major Victorian novelist makes the "ado" that James describes in addressing the question of woman's vocation. Ultimately, as Victorian novels illustrate, the basic problem was not only political, economic, and educational. It was how women were regarded, and regarded themselves, as members of a society. In the final pages of our section "Victorian Issues," the vigorous debate about the problem is represented under the title "The Woman Question."

THE DIVERSITY OF VICTORIAN LITERATURE

The weight of the puritan code on the literature of early- and mid-Victorian England was, as we might expect, considerable. It was most evident in the novels, for novels were commonly read aloud in family gatherings, and the need to avoid topics that might cause embarrassment to young girls established taboos that novelists could not dare ignore, although they might sometimes skillfully circumvent them. Thackeray and others offered protests, but it was not until near the end of the century or later that the novelists broke clear of those restrictions. The poets and essayists fared better. When Browning was writing *The Ring and the Book* he was obviously unconcerned about whether his poem might raise blushes on prudish cheeks, and Swinburne's *Poems and Ballads* flouts the taboos in the manner of the French poets whom he admired (of his Victorian contemporaries Swinburne remarked that "their ears are the chastest part about them"). Both volumes appeared in the 1860s at the same time as Matthew Arnold's essays attacking the narrowness of the puritan middle-class mind.

Too much can be made of the importance of these taboos as literary conventions in the Victorian age. A much more significant kind of expectation of the Victorian audience from its writers, one that they were themselves inclined to comply with, was the desire on the part of readers to be guided and edified. The newly expanding reading public, despite its air of solid confidence, wanted help from its authors, and its authors were understandably flattered by the request. Only a few, such as Dante Gabriel Rossetti, ignored it; the others all exhibited, in varying degrees, an air of prophecy and mission. Carlyle in his lectures *On Heroes* identifies the writer or "Poet" such as Shakespeare with the great prophets such as Muhammad, and in his own writings it is evident that he sought to make his mark as a seer rather than as a mere man of letters. The very high status that even Matthew Arnold claimed for literature is evident in his statement that "most of what now passes with us for religion and philosophy will be replaced by poetry." Perhaps nonfiction prose writers like Carlyle or Ruskin provide the best examples of the Victorians' strong commitment to a didactic mission. Poets, however, were more ambivalent. Tennyson, here as in most instances, is more representative. To provide firm guidance in problems of science and religion and the destiny of nations and daily life was a task that sometimes appealed to Tennyson and sometimes appalled him. As we might expect, several of his poems are concerned with the dilemma of writers' divided duty toward their public and their art—a dilemma that has become even more acute in the twentieth century as the reading public has further expanded.

The existence of this dilemma may help to explain another characteristic of Victorian literature: its variety both in style and in subject matter. Variety is in part a symptom of the Victorian writers' bold independence and their zest for literary experiment for its own sake, but it is also a symptom of an absence of any final general agreement concerning the function of literature and art in a democratic society. Writers and their audiences might usually agree that instruction was a desirable attribute of a work of literature, but what was to constitute the instruction and what was the appropriate mode in which to convey it?

It is among the poets that the search for appropriate modes is most evident. All of them seem driven to experiment in a variety of ways. In versification, although making considerable use of traditional forms such as the sonnet, most of them preferred experimenting with new or unusual metrical patterns, as did Robert Browning, Swinburne, Gerard Manley Hopkins, and later, Thomas Hardy. In line with their metrical experiments are their experiments in the art of narrative poetry. The chief challenge facing the writer of a "modern poem," according to Dwight Culler, has been "not steam but the novel," and the development of poetic narrative in the Victorian age bears out his point. As the novel emerged as one of the dominant forms of literature, the poets sought new ways of telling stories in verse; examples of such attempts include Tennyson's *Maud*, Elizabeth Barrett Browning's *Aurora Leigh*, and Robert Browning's *The Ring and the Book*. George Meredith, William Morris, and Emily Brontë, novelists as well as poets, were especially aware that poetry can offer unusual resources for the writer of narratives, as demonstrated by the compression and intensification of Morris's early poems or Meredith's *Modern Love*. Others, in particular Arthur Hugh Clough, sought to write narrative poems as if they were novels, poems that are long, casual in tone, and usually prosaic in style.

To illustrate the diversity of styles in Victorian writing, two poems may be compared. Tennyson's *Tithonus* is in the grand manner of English poetry, the culmination of a poetic tradition, emphasizing beautiful cadences and vowel sounds:

> The woods decay, the woods decay and fall,
> The vapors weep their burthen to the ground,
> Man comes and tills the field and lies beneath,
> And after many a summer dies the swan.

In Browning's *The Bishop Orders His Tomb*, the colloquial tone of the speaker, as he hisses his hatred of a rival, seems to belong to a different century: "Shrewd was that snatch from out the corner south / He graced his carrion with, God curse the same!" And if we ignore the stylistic differences here and concentrate on a possible similarity—that both poems, like many Victorian writings, evoke the past of myth and history—what is to be done to align these works with other works of the same period? What resemblance is there to Dickens's *Oliver Twist* (1838), for example, with its realistic scenes of a sordid workhouse, or to Carlyle's *Past and Present* (1843) with its idiosyncratic manner of exposing the sufferings of the Victorian poor, or to John Ruskin's *Modern Painters* (1843) with its rhapsodic celebrations of alpine scenery and romantic sunsets? As a result, most candid literary historians admit that although we may confidently identify the distinguishing characteristics of individual Victorian writers, of a Browning, a Dickens, or a Newman, it is extremely difficult to devise satisfactory statements about Victorian literature that are generally applicable to most or all of these writers. This admission is distressing to tidy minds, but in itself it tells us something distinctive about Victorian literature as a whole.

What we can perhaps isolate is what Jerome Buckley calls the "temper" of Victorian literature, a state of mind and emotion already described in this introduction as an eager or earnest response to the expanding horizons of nineteenth-century life. We also encounter some frequently recurring subjects in Victorian literature, including a preoccupation with humanity's relationship to God and an acute awareness of time, past, present, and future. Among the poets (and the novelists as well) one topic that links their writings together is love—for love, given the concern with gender roles and with sexual morality, is as prominent in Victorian poetry as it had been in the time of John Donne and his followers. Although the Victorian poets, unlike their seventeenth-century predecessors, rarely made witty proposals for gathering rosebuds, they explored other aspects of love relationships, such as the timeless equilibrium of lovers pictured by D. G. Rossetti or the poignant experience of isolation by Arnold and Christina Rossetti or the hostility of partners of a shattered marriage in Meredith's *Modern Love*. All these aspects, and more, are present in the poetry of Robert Browning, and his comprehensive exploration of such relationships links him to his contemporaries. In reviewing Browning's volume *Men and Women*, William Morris (himself a fine love poet) praised some of the monologues dealing with religious issues, but added that these, "as it is in all art, in all life," however fine, were "but a supplement to the love-poems."

VICTORIAN PROSE

If Victorian poets and novelists write extensively of love and personal relationships, there is also a large body of writings in which these subjects are relatively subordinate, writings categorized as nonfictional prose. Although the term is clumsy and also not quite exact (the Victorians themselves did not use the term but instead referred to history, biography, theology, criticism), it has its uses not only to distinguish these prose writers from the novelists but also to indicate the centrality of argument and persuasion to Victorian intellectual life. Some of the major Victorian writers of nonfictional prose are Thomas Carlyle, John Henry Cardinal Newman, John Stewart Mill, John Ruskin, Matthew Arnold, and Thomas Henry Huxley.

On behalf of their kinds of writing, Pater argued, in his essay *Style* (1889), that prose was "the special and opportune art of the modern world." His contention was not that prose is superior to verse but that it more readily conveys the "chaotic variety and complexity" of modern life, the "incalculable" intellectual diversity of the "master currents of the present time." Whether prose is a more appropriate medium than verse to communicate the chaotic variety of an age remains a matter of dispute, but what Pater says of the age itself would be much more generally agreed on. Toward this condition of their age the Victorian writers of nonfictional prose responded in a variety of ways and in a variety of styles. All sought in their distinctive manners to create some sort of order out of the chaos. Pater himself, coming to maturity late in the century, differs from the others in his distaste for controversy. By writing critical essays celebrating a beautifully ordered world of art and literature, Pater sought to rise above the flux and chaos that he saw as characteristic of his century. His predecessors were more engaged in shaping and reconstructing the social order. All of them use prose primarily as an instrument of persuasion and argument. On a wide range of controversial topics—religious, political, and aesthetic—they seek to convince a reader to share their convictions and values. Their modes of persuasion differ. Mill and Huxley rely on clear reasoning, logical argument, and the kind of lucid style favored by essayists of the eighteenth century, uncolored by the emotional heightening of romanticism. Carlyle and Ruskin, in much of their writing, seem closer to the seventeenth century than to the eighteenth. Their "polyphonic" style, as it has been called, has affinities with the prose rhythms of Sir Thomas Browne and Robert Burton. It is a style that also appeals to the eye as well as the ear, and by a combination of vivid effects, plays on the feelings of the reader. Poetic passages in Newman and Arnold also play on our feelings, but much of their writing is less mannered and more in the relatively straightforward vein of Mill and Huxley.

However various their styles, all of these Victorian prose writers were linked by a common concern for the fate of humanity in an industrial, democratic, and increasingly secularized society. Of their interlocking debates on education, leadership, and the role of science and religion, C. F. Harrold aptly says: "What they wrote constitutes a fascinating chapter in the history of the English mind, and also provides a perspective for viewing much that continues to perplex the world. Above all, a survey of their beliefs and assumptions will illuminate the richness of their prose, a prose which is often highly allusive, sometimes deceptively simple, and always susceptible to fresh and profitable interpretation as the symbol of their thought and the eloquent expression of their convictions."

VICTORIAN DRAMA AND THEATER

If the Victorian age can lay claim to greatness for its poetry, its prose, and its novels, it would be difficult to make such a high claim for its plays, at least until the final decade of the century. Here we must distinguish between play writing on the one hand and theatrical activity on the other. For the theater itself, throughout the period, was a flourishing and popular institution, in which were performed not merely conventional dramas but a rich variety of theatrical entertainments, many with lavish spectacular effects—burlesques, extravaganzas, highly scenic and altered versions of Shakespeare's plays, melodramas, pantomimes, and musicals. Robert Corrigan gives figures that suggest the extent of the popularity of such entertainment: "In the decade between 1850 and 1860 the number of theaters built throughout the country was doubled, and in the middle of the sixties, in London alone, 150,000 would be attending the theater on any given day. Only when we realize that the theatre was to Victorian England what television is to us today will we be able to comprehend both its wide appeal and its limited artistic achievement." As might be expected, the soaring popularity of Victorian stage performances lured some of the major writers of the age, such as Tennyson and Browning and Henry James, to try their hands at writing plays, but the results were disappointing. Successful plays on stage were written by lesser lights of literature (except for the remarkable comic operas of W. S. Gilbert and Arthur Sullivan). New Victorian plays, as Robertson Davies comments, "are extremely numerous, and they are, in the main, undistinguished by literary merit, though many of them are not nearly so bad as people who have not studied them suppose." Davies's book *The Mirror of Nature* (1983) is an important corrective to the formerly established practice of dismissing all Victorian plays as deplorable melodramas. In any event, in the 1890s appeared the lively dramatic masterpieces of Oscar Wilde and George Bernard Shaw; no apologies are thereafter required.

THE VICTORIAN NOVEL

It will be obvious that any estimate of Victorian literature has to take into account the outstanding achievements of the Victorian novelists. From the time of Charles Dickens (1812–1870), early in the period (his first novel, *Pickwick Papers*, was published in the same year as Victoria became queen), to the final decade when the late novels of Thomas Hardy (1840–1928) such as *Tess of the D'Urbervilles* (1891) appeared, a long line of novelists continued to turn out monumental masterpieces that delighted their contemporaries and that continue to delight readers today.

After Dickens's epoch-making early novels had appeared on the scene in the 1830s, each subsequent decade featured the emergence of new novelists of stature such as Charlotte Brontë (1816–1855) and Emily Brontë (1818–1848) in the 1840s, and William Makepeace Thackeray (1811–1863), whose prominence in the 1850s was a challenge to Dickens's continued preeminence and popularity. In the 1860s, Anthony Trollope (1815–1882) established himself as a portraitist of mid-Victorian society, and in the 1870s, George Eliot (1819–1880) published what is generally regarded as her finest novel, *Middlemarch* (1872), although she had already established her reputation earlier with *Adam Bede* (1859) and *The Mill on the Floss* (1860). In the 1880s, George Meredith (1828–1909)—a less well known novelist today—finally began to receive adequate attention from the critics and public for novels he had published earlier such as *The Ordeal of Richard Feverel* (1859). In addition to these major novelists from Dickens to Hardy, several note-worthy names may be cited of writers who contributed to the rich variety of the Victorian novel, such as Elizabeth Gaskell (1810–1865), Wilkie Collins (1824–1889), and George Gissing (1857–1903).

Often these novelists confront the same issues and employ similar styles as their contemporaries among the poets and essayists (the stylistic affinities between Browning and Dickens, for example, are striking). One significant difference, however, is that the novelists for the most part do not share the preoccupation of the Victorian poets and essayists with humanity's relationship to God. Like their greatest predecessors—Fielding, Richardson, and Austen—most of the Victorian novelists were primarily concerned with people in society and with those aspects of experience categorized by the title of Lionel Trilling's essay "Manners, Morals and the Novel," to which we can add an additional topic—Money. Typically these stories center on the struggles of a protagonist, male or female, to find himself or herself in relation to other men and women, in love or marriage, with family or neighbors, or with associates in his or her working career. Occasionally such a search may take on quasi-religious dimensions, as in the later novels of Thomas Hardy or in Emily Brontë's *Wuthering Heights* (1847), and more indirectly, in George Eliot's novels, with their persistent concern with the role of free will and fate in the lives of their characters. On the whole, however, the major Victorian novelists were less occupied with people's relation to God than with their relation to other people.

And for the most part, the other people were the reader's contemporaries. The historical novel, as established by Sir Walter Scott, remained popular throughout the post-Romantic period, but it was a form especially congenial to the lesser novelists, such as Bulwer-Lytton (*The Last Days of Pompeii*, 1834) or Charles Reade (*The Cloister and the Hearth*, 1861). While the major novelists occasionally tried their hand at historical fiction, their preference was for the contemporary or the recent past. Whether the story was set in the rural landscapes of Eliot's Warwickshire and Hardy's Wessex, Trollope's cathedral towns, or Dickens's fogbound London, readers expected a representation of daily nineteenth-century life that would be recognizably familiar to them.

To satisfy such expectations they were provided with a rich fare. Dickens was praised by Walter Bagehot for having described London "like a special correspondent for posterity." His contemporaries and successors among the novelists were also skillful reporters, and most of them were more scrupulously concerned with detailed realism than he had been. Disputes about the degree of Dickens's realism have persisted among critical readers from his day to ours, but what is now generally recognized is that he was much more than a brilliant reporter, and that the heightening and stylization of his novels produce effects like poetic drama that are very different from straightforward realism. "Every writer of fiction," he said, "although he may not adopt the dramatic form, writes, in effect, for the stage."

The attitude to this aspect of his writing by other novelists is of crucial importance in understanding how the Victorian novel developed. Among Dickens's rivals and successors there was a common agreement that the stagey aspect of his novels was his most glaring fault, and each of the novelists in turn set out to correct that fault by an example of what he or she believed was a more realistic representation of life. Thackeray's masterpiece *Vanity Fair* (1848) has to a modern reader many mannerisms of its own but is much less blatantly mannered than a characteristic Dickens novel. "The Art of Novels," Thackeray affirmed in a letter, "*is* to represent nature: to convey as strongly as possible the sentiment of reality." In Thackeray's disciple, Anthony Trollope (and later in the naturalistic narratives of George Gissing, a lesser figure), there is a similar reduction of stagelike scenes and effects. In George Eliot this reaction against novelistic theatricalism took a more influential turn: she set out to explore what the theatrical writer rarely explores—the inner lives of her characters. Early in the twentieth century, the young D. H. Lawrence, beginning his career as a novelist, remarked to a friend: "You see, it was really George Eliot who started it all, and how wild they all were with her for doing it. It was she who started putting all the action inside. Before, you know, with Fielding and the others, it had been outside. Now I wonder which is right?" Lawrence himself decided, as a practicing novelist, that Fielding and his Victorian followers could be as right as George Eliot, but most early-twentieth-century novelists preferred to follow Eliot's example and concentrate on the inner lives of their characters, and critical readers, adapting their tastes to the new mode, were disposed at that time to undervalue Victorian novels that had portrayed people acting rather than people recollecting, or reflecting, or trying to come to a decision.

Contributing to this underevaluation of the Victorian achievement was the assumption that novels published in serial form (as Victorian novels had usually been published) must be slapdash productions altogether deficient in art, or as Henry James characterized them, "large loose baggy monsters." James's affectionate derogation is applicable to such a novel as Dickens's early *Pickwick Papers*, but it does not apply at all to some of Dickens's later novels such as *Bleak House* (a masterpiece of narrative construction), Eliot's *Middlemarch* (1872), Hardy's *Jude the Obscure* (1895), or the tight and intricate plotting of Wilkie Collins's detective novel *The Moonstone* (1868). Serial publication, as later critics have come to recognize, did not necessarily preclude artful storytelling, and it had advantages to offset the possible disadvantages of fragmentation. Publication by installments challenged the novelists to sustain the interest of their readers; in every single number they had to entertain them or, to use the traditional critical term, to provide delight. Like actors or public speakers, the Victorian novelists had a sense, during the very process of writing their books, of how their audience was responding to their performance. And it was an audience that offered a special challenge because of its exceptional diversity; Victorian readers ranged from the sophisticated and well-read lawyer to the semiliterate household servant. The present-day division of the novel-reading public into highbrow, middlebrow, and lowbrow existed only in embryonic form in the Victorian age and did not become a significant controlling influence on the novelist until late in the century.

This popular genre is thus especially representative of all but the religious attitudes that have been emphasized in this account of the Victorian period: the earnest sense of responsibility, the occasional lapses of taste, and the overflowing creative energy of its writers. Near the end of his life, Thackeray drew a comparison between himself and Dickens: "I am played out. All I can do now is to bring out my old puppets. . . . But, if he live to be ninety, Dickens will still be creating new characters. In his art that man is marvelous." Wrung from a novelist whose own writings occupy more than twenty thick volumes, this compliment is quintessentially Victorian.

TEXTS	CONTEXTS
1832 Alfred, Lord Tennyson, *The Lady of Shalott, The Lotos-Eaters*	1832 First Reform Bill redistributes parliamentary representation; extends franchise to some middle-class voters • Lyell's *Principles of Geology* challenges creationist belief about the age of the earth
	1837 Victoria becomes queen
	1838 "People's Charter," calling for further reforms favoring the working class, issued by "Chartist" movement
1842 Tennyson, *Poems (Ulysses)* • Robert Browning, *Dramatic Lyrics (My Last Duchess)*	
	1845–46 Potato famine in Ireland; mass emigration to North America
1846 George Eliot, translation of German *Das Leben Jesu (The Life of Jesus)*, a work applying historical criticism to Bible	1846 Repeal of "Corn Laws," high tariff on grain protecting landowners but causing hardship and civil disturbance among the poor • Browning marries Elizabeth Barrett; they move to Italy
1847 Charlotte Brontë, *Jane Eyre* • Emily Brontë, *Wuthering Heights*	
1848 William Makepeace Thackeray, *Vanity Fair*	1848 Karl Marx and Friedrich Engels, *The Communist Manifesto* • Revolutions on the Continent; Second Republic is established in France
1850 Tennyson, *In Memoriam*	1850 Tennyson succeeds Wordsworth as Poet Laureate
	1851 Great Exhibition of industry and science at Crystal Palace
1853 Matthew Arnold, *Poems*	
1854 Dickens, *Hard Times*	1854 Crimean War with Russia • Florence Nightingale organizes contingent of nurses to care for the sick and wounded

Boldface titles indicate works in the anthology.

TEXTS	CONTEXTS
1855 R. Browning, *Men and Women* (***Fra Lippo Lippi, Andrea del Sarto***)	
1857 E. B. Browning, ***Aurora Leigh***	1857 Indian Mutiny
1859 Charles Darwin, *Origin of Species* • Tennyson, *Idylls of the King* (Books 1–4)	
1860 Dickens, *Great Expectations*	
	1861–65 American Civil War
1862 Christina Rossetti, ***Goblin Market***	
1864 Browning, *Dramatis Personae* (***Abt Vogler, Rabbi Ben Ezra***)	
	1867 Second Reform Bill extends vote to working class males • Marx, *Capital*
	1868 Opening of Suez Canal
1869 Arnold, ***Culture and Anarchy***	
	1870–71 Victory in Franco-Prussian War makes Germany a world power
1872 Eliot, *Middlemarch*	
	1877 Victoria made Empress of India • Gerard Manley Hopkins joins Jesuit order
1891 Thomas Hardy, *Tess of the D'Urbervilles*	
	1895 Oscar Wilde arrested and imprisoned for homosexuality
	1899–1902 Boer War secures British control of South Africa
	1901 Death of Queen Victoria; succession of Edward VII
1918 Hopkins, *Poems*, published posthumously	

ELIZABETH BARRETT BROWNING
1806–1861

During her lifetime, Elizabeth Barrett Browning was England's most famous woman poet. Passionately admired by contemporaries as diverse as Ruskin, Swinburne, and Emily Dickinson for her moral and emotional ardor and her energetic engagement with the issues of her day, she was more famous than her husband, Robert Browning, at the time of her death. Her work fell into disrepute with the modernist reaction against what was seen as the inappropriate didacticism and rhetorical excess of Victorian poetry, but recently, scholars interested in her exploration of what it means to be a woman poet have initiated a revaluation of her work.

Barrett Browning received an unusual education for a woman of her time. Availing herself of her brother's tutor, she studied Latin and Greek. She read voraciously in history, philosophy, and literature and began to write poetry from an early age—her first volume of poetry was published when she was thirteen. But as her intellectual and literary powers matured, her personal life became increasingly circumscribed both by ill health and by a tyrannically protective father, who had forbidden any of his eleven children to marry. By the age of thirty-nine, Elizabeth Barrett was a prominent woman of letters who lived in semiseclusion as an invalid in her father's house, where she occasionally received visitors in her room. One of these visitors was Robert Browning, who, moved by his admiration of her poetry, wrote to tell her "I do as I say, love these books with all my heart—and I love you too." He thereby initiated a courtship that culminated in 1846 in their secret marriage and elopement to Italy, for which her father never forgave her. Once in Italy, she regained much health and strength, bearing and raising a son, Pen, to whom she was ardently devoted, and becoming deeply involved in Italian nationalist politics. She and her husband made their home in Florence, at the house called Casa Guidi, where she died in 1861.

Barrett Browning's poetry is characterized by a fervent moral sensibility. In her early work, she tended to use the visionary modes of Romantic narrative poetry, but she turned increasingly to contemporary topics, particularly liberal causes of her day. For example, in 1843, when government investigations had exposed the exploitation of children employed in coal mines and factories, she wrote *The Cry of the Children*, of which the following stanza is typical:

> "For oh," say the children, "we are weary,
>   And we cannot run or leap;
> If we cared for any meadows, it were merely
>   To drop down in them and sleep.
> Our knees tremble sorely in the stooping,
>   We fall upon our faces, trying to go;
> And, underneath our heavy eyelids drooping,
>   The reddest flower would look as pale as snow.
> For, all day, we drag our burden tiring
>   Through the coal dark, underground;
> Or, all day, we drive the wheels of iron
>   In the factories round and round."

In later poems she took up the cause of Italian nationalism, which, the critic Sandra M. Gilbert has recently argued, provided her a subject through which to enact her own struggle for poetic identity.

For many years Elizabeth Barrett Browning was best known for her *Sonnets from the Portuguese*, a sequence of forty-four sonnets in which she recorded the stages of her love for Robert Browning, a sequence she presented under the guise of a translation from the Portuguese language. But increasingly, her verse novel *Aurora Leigh* (1857) has attracted critical attention. The poem depicts the growth of a woman poet and is thus, as Cora Kaplan observes, the first work in English by a woman writer in which the heroine herself is an author. When Barrett Browning first envisioned the poem, she wrote, "My chief *intention* just now is the writing of a sort of novel-poem . . . running into the midst of our conventions, and rushing into drawing-rooms and the like 'where angels fear to tread'; and so, meeting face to face and without mask the Humanity of the age, and speaking the truth as I conceive of it out plainly." The poem is a female *Prelude* (cf. Wordsworth, *The Prelude*, p. 1400), a portrait of the artist as a young woman committed to a socially inclusive realist art. It is a daring work both in its presentation of social issues concerning women and in its claims for Aurora's poetic vocation; on her twentieth birthday, in order to pursue her career as a poet, Aurora refuses a proposal of marriage from her cousin Romney, who wants her to be his helpmate in the liberal causes he has embraced. Later in the poem, she rescues a fallen woman and takes her to Italy, where they settle together and confront a chastened Romney.

Immensely popular in its own day, *Aurora Leigh* had extravagant admirers (like Ruskin, who asserted that it was the greatest poem written in English) and critics who found fault with both its poetry and its morality. With its crowded canvas and melodramatic plot, it seems closer to the novel than to poetry, but it is important to view the poem in the context of the debate about appropriate poetic subjects that engaged other Victorian poets. Unlike Arnold, who believed that the present age had not produced actions heroic enough to be the subjects of a great poetry, and unlike Tennyson, who used Arthurian legend to represent contemporary concerns, Barrett Browning felt that the present age contained the materials for an epic poetry. Virginia Woolf writes that "Elizabeth Barrett was inspired by a flash of true genius when she rushed into the drawing-room and said that here, where we live and work, is the true place for the poet." And whatever its faults, *Aurora Leigh* succeeds in giving us what Woolf describes as "a sense of life in general, of people who are unmistakably Victorian, wrestling with the problems of their own time, all brightened, intensified, and compacted by the fire of poetry. . . . Aurora Leigh, with her passionate interest in social questions, her conflict as artist and woman, her longing for knowledge and freedom, is the true daughter of her age."

To George Sand[1]

A Desire

Thou large-brained woman and large-hearted man,
Self-called George Sand! whose soul, amid the lions
Of thy tumultuous senses, moans defiance
And answers roar for roar, as spirits can:
I would some mild miraculous thunder ran   5

1. French Romantic novelist (1804–1876), famous for her unconventional ideas and behavior. Elizabeth Barrett Browning discovered her writing when she was an invalid, "a prisoner," and asserts that George Sand, together with Balzac, "kept the color in my life." Barrett Browning defended Sand's genius to her less-sympathetic friends, who were critical of Sand's morality; she writes to her friend Mary Russell Mitford, a contemporary novelist and dramatist, "She is eloquent as a fallen angel. . . . A true woman of genius!—but of a womanhood tired of itself, and scorned by *her*, while she bears it burning above her head."

Above the applauded circus,[2] in appliance
Of thine own nobler nature's strength and science,
Drawing two pinions, white as wings of swan,
From thy strong shoulders, to amaze the place
With holier light! that thou to woman's claim   10
And man's, mightst join beside the angel's grace
Of a pure genius sanctified from blame,
Till child and maiden pressed to thine embrace
To kiss upon thy lips a stainless fame.

1844

To George Sand

A Recognition

True genius, but true woman! dost deny
The woman's nature with a manly scorn,
And break away the gauds[1] and armlets worn
By weaker women in captivity?
Ah, vain denial! that revolted cry   5
Is sobbed in by a woman's voice forlorn,—
Thy woman's hair, my sister, all unshorn
Floats back dishevelled strength in agony,
Disproving thy man's name: and while before
The world thou burnest in a poet-fire,   10
We see thy woman-heart beat evermore
Through the large flame. Beat purer, heart, and higher,
Till God unsex thee on the heavenly shore
Where unincarnate spirits purely aspire!

1844

From Sonnets from the Portuguese

21

Say over again, and yet once over again,
That thou dost love me. Though the word repeated
Should seem "a cuckoo song,"[1] as thou dost treat it,
Remember, never to the hill or plain,
Valley and wood, without her cuckoo strain   5
Comes the fresh Spring in all her green completed.
Belovèd, I, amid the darkness greeted
By a doubtful spirit voice, in that doubt's pain
Cry, "Speak once more—thou lovest!" Who can fear
Too many stars, though each in heaven shall roll,   10
Too many flowers, though each shall crown the year?
Say thou dost love me, love me, love me—toll

---

2. A Roman spectacle in which Christians were martyred by fighting lions.

1. Ornaments.

1. The cuckoo has a repeating call.

The silver iterance![2]—only minding, Dear,
To love me also in silence with thy soul.

22

When our two souls stand up erect and strong,
Face to face, silent, drawing nigh and nigher,
Until the lengthening wings break into fire
At either curvèd point—what bitter wrong
Can the earth do to us, that we should not long   5
Be here contented? Think. In mounting higher,
The angels would press on us and aspire
To drop some golden orb of perfect song
Into our deep, dear silence. Let us stay
Rather on earth, Belovèd,—where the unfit   10
Contrarious moods of men recoil away
And isolate pure spirits, and permit
A place to stand and love in for a day,
With darkness and the death-hour rounding it.

32

The first time that the sun rose on thine oath
To love me, I looked forward to the moon
To slacken all those bonds which seemed too soon
And quickly tied to make a lasting troth.
Quick-loving hearts, I thought, may quickly loathe;   5
And, looking on myself, I seemed not one
For such man's love!—more like an out-of-tune
Worn viol, a good singer would be wroth
To spoil his song with, and which, snatched in haste,
Is laid down at the first ill-sounding note.   10
I did not wrong myself so, but I placed
A wrong on *thee*. For perfect strains may float
'Neath master-hands, from instruments defaced—
And great souls, at one stroke, may do and dote.

43

How do I love thee? Let me count the ways.
I love thee to the depth and breadth and height
My soul can reach, when feeling out of sight
For the ends of Being and ideal Grace.
I love thee to the level of everyday's   5
Most quiet need, by sun and candlelight.
I love thee freely, as men strive for Right;
I love thee purely, as they turn from Praise.
I love thee with the passion put to use
In my old griefs, and with my childhood's faith.   10
I love thee with a love I seemed to lose

2. Repetition.

With my lost saints—I love thee with the breath,
Smiles, tears, of all my life!—and, if God choose,
I shall but love thee better after death.

1845–47   1850

A Year's Spinning

1

He listened at the porch that day,
    To hear the wheel go on, and on;
And then it stopped, ran back away,
    While through the door he brought the sun:
    But now my spinning is all done.   5

2

He sat beside me, with an oath
    That love ne'er ended, once begun;
I smiled—believing for us both,
    What was the truth for only one:
    And now my spinning is all done.   10

3

My mother cursed me that I heard
    A young man's wooing as I spun:
Thanks, cruel mother, for that word—
    For I have, since, a harder known!
    And now my spinning is all done.   15

4

I thought—O God!—my first-born's cry
    Both voices to mine ear would drown:
I listened in mine agony—
    It was the *silence* made me groan!
    And now my spinning is all done.   20

5

Bury me 'twixt my mother's grave,
    (Who cursed me on her death-bed lone)
And my dead baby's (God it save!)
    Who, not to bless me, would not moan.
    And now my spinning is all done.   25

6

A stone upon my heart and head,
    But no name written on the stone!
Sweet neighbours, whisper low instead,
    "This sinner was a loving one—
    And now her spinning is all done."   30

7

And let the door ajar remain,
    In case he should pass by anon;
And leave the wheel out very plain,—
    That HE, when passing in the sun,
    May see the spinning is all done.   35

1850

From Aurora Leigh

From *Book* 1

[THE FEMININE EDUCATION OF AURORA LEIGH][1]

Then, land!—then, England! oh, the frosty cliffs[2]
Looked cold upon me. Could I find a home
Among those mean red houses through the fog?
And when I heard my father's language first
From alien lips which had no kiss for mine   255
I wept aloud, then laughed, then wept, then wept,
And some one near me said the child was mad
Through much sea-sickness. The train swept us on:
Was this my father's England? the great isle?
The ground seemed cut up from the fellowship   260
Of verdure, field from field,[3] as man from man;
The skies themselves looked low and positive,
As almost you could touch them with a hand,
And dared to do it they were so far off
From God's celestial crystals;[4] all things blurred   265
And dull and vague. Did Shakespeare and his mates
Absorb the light here?—not a hill or stone
With heart to strike a radiant colour up
Or active outline on the indifferent air.

I think I see my father's sister stand   270
Upon the hall-step of her country-house
To give me welcome. She stood straight and calm,
Her somewhat narrow forehead braided tight
As if for taming accidental thoughts
From possible pulses;[5] brown hair pricked with gray   275
By frigid use of life (she was not old,
Although my father's elder by a year),
A nose drawn sharply, yet in delicate lines;
A close mild mouth, a little soured about
The ends, through speaking unrequited loves   280
Or peradventure niggardly half-truths;
Eyes of no colour,—once they might have smiled,
But never, never have forgot themselves
In smiling; cheeks, in which was yet a rose
Of perished summers, like a rose in a book,   285
Kept more for ruth[6] than pleasure,—if past bloom,
Past fading also.
                    She had lived, we'll say,
A harmless life, she called a virtuous life,

---

1. *Aurora Leigh*, the only child of an Italian mother and an English father, has been raised in Italy by her father since her mother's death when Aurora was four years old. When she was thirteen her father also died, and the orphaned girl has been sent to England to live with her father's maiden sister, who is to be responsible for the girl's education.
2. The white chalk cliffs at Dover.
3. English fields were separated from each other by hedgerows.
4. Perhaps a reference to the ancient notion that the sky was composed of several crystalline spheres orbiting around the earth.
5. I.e., pulsation in her temples from excitement.
6. Remorse.

A quiet life, which was not life at all
(But that, she had not lived enough to know),   290
Between the vicar and the county squires,
The lord-lieutenant[7] looking down sometimes
From the empyrean to assure their souls
Against chance vulgarisms, and, in the abyss,
The apothecary,[8] looked on once a year   295
To prove their soundness of humility.
The poor-club[9] exercised her Christian gifts
Of knitting stockings, stitching petticoats,
Because we are of one flesh, after all,
And need one flannel[1] (with a proper sense   300
Of difference in the quality)—and still
The book-club, guarded from your modern trick
Of shaking dangerous questions from the crease,[2]
Preserved her intellectual. She had lived
A sort of cage-bird life, born in a cage,   305
Accounting that to leap from perch to perch
Was act and joy enough for any bird.
Dear heaven, how silly are the things that live
In thickets, and eat berries!
                    I, alas,
A wild bird scarcely fledged, was brought to her cage,   310
And she was there to meet me. Very kind.
Bring the clean water, give out the fresh seed.

She stood upon the steps to welcome me,
Calm, in black garb. I clung about her neck,—
Young babes, who catch at every shred of wool   315
To draw the new light closer, catch and cling
Less blindly. In my ears my father's word
Hummed ignorantly, as the sea in shells,
"Love, love, my child." She, black there with my grief,
Might feel my love— she was his sister once—   320
I clung to her. A moment she seemed moved,
Kissed me with cold lips, suffered me to cling,
And drew me feebly through the hall into
The room she sat in.
                   There, with some strange spasm
Of pain and passion, she wrung loose my hands   325
Imperiously, and held me at arm's length,
And with two grey-steel naked-bladed eyes
Searched through my face,—ay, stabbed it through and through,
Through brows and cheeks and chin, as if to find
A wicked murderer in my innocent face,   330
If not here, there perhaps. Then, drawing breath,
She struggled for her ordinary calm—
And missed it rather,—told me not to shrink,

7. Governor of the county.
8. Pharmacist, who in England at the time could pre-
scribe as well as sell medicine.
9. Club devoted to making things for the poor.
1. Flannel petticoat.

2. The fold between two pages of a book, which had
to be cut to open the pages. Presumably more modern
books revealed more dangerous material when the
crease was cut.

As if she had told me not to lie or swear, —
"She loved my father and would love me too   335
As long as I deserved it." Very kind.

I understood her meaning afterward;
She thought to find my mother in my face,
And questioned it for that. For she, my aunt,
Had loved my father truly, as she could,   340
And hated, with the gall of gentle souls,
My Tuscan[3] mother who had fooled away
A wise man from wise courses, a good man
From obvious duties, and, depriving her,
His sister, of the household precedence,   345
Had wronged his tenants, robbed his native land,
And made him mad, alike by life and death,
In love and sorrow. She had pored[4] for years
What sort of woman could be suitable
To her sort of hate, to entertain it with,   350
And so, her very curiosity
Became hate too, and all the idealism
She ever used in life was used for hate,
Till hate, so nourished, did exceed at last
The love from which it grew, in strength and heat,   355
And wrinkled her smooth conscience with a sense
Of disputable virtue (say not, sin)
When Christian doctrine was enforced at church.

And thus my father's sister was to me
My mother's hater. From that day she did   360
Her duty to me (I appreciate it
In her own word as spoken to herself),
Her duty, in large measure, well pressed out
But measured always. She was generous, bland,
More courteous than was tender, gave me still   365
The first place, —as if fearful that God's saints
Would look down suddenly and say "Herein
You missed a point, I think, through lack of love."
Alas, a mother never is afraid
Of speaking angerly to any child,   370
Since love, she knows, is justified of love.

And I, I was a good child on the whole,
A meek and manageable child. Why not?
I did not live, to have the faults of life:
There seemed more true life in my father's grave   375
Than in all England. Since *that* threw me off
Who fain would cleave (his latest will, they say,
Consigned me to his land), I only thought
Of lying quiet there where I was thrown
Like sea-weed on the rocks, and suffering her   380

3. From Tuscany, a region in central Italy.   4. I.e., pored over.

To prick me to a pattern with her pin,[5]
Fibre from fibre, delicate leaf from leaf,
And dry out from my drowned anatomy
The last sea-salt left in me.
　　　　　　So it was.
I broke the copious curls upon my head　　　　　　　　385
In braids, because she liked smooth-ordered hair.
I left off saying my sweet Tuscan words
Which still at any stirring of the heart
Came up to float across the English phrase
As lilies (*Bene* or *Che che*[6]), because　　　　　　　390
She liked my father's child to speak his tongue.
I learnt the collects[7] and the catechism,
The creeds,[8] from Athanasius back to Nice,
The Articles, the Tracts *against* the times[9]
(By no means Buonaventure's "Prick of Love"[1]),　　　395
And various popular synopses of
Inhuman doctrines never taught by John,[2]
Because she liked instructed piety.
I learnt my complement of classic French
(Kept pure of Balzac and neologism[3])　　　　　　　400
And German also, since she liked a range
Of liberal education,—tongues,[4] not books.
I learnt a little algebra, a little
Of the mathematics,—brushed with extreme flounce
The circle of the sciences, because　　　　　　　　　405
She misliked women who are frivolous.
I learnt the royal genealogies
Of Oviedo,[5] the internal laws
Of the Burmese empire,—by how many feet
Mount Chimborazo outsoars Teneriffe,　　　　　　410
What navigable river joins itself
To Lara, and what census of the year five
Was taken at Klagenfurt,[6]—because she liked
A general insight into useful facts.
I learnt much music,—such as would have been　　　415
As quite impossible in Johnson's day[7]
As still it might be wished—fine sleights of hand
And unimagined fingering, shuffling off
The hearer's soul through hurricanes of notes

5. As in embroidery.
6. No, no, indeed; *Bene:* it is well.
7. Seasonal opening prayers in the Anglican church service.
8. Articles of Christian faith such as those proclaimed at the early church council held at Nicaea.
9. In the 1830s leaders of the conservative High Church party, such as John Henry Newman, had published *Tracts for the Times,* which expounded arguments against efforts by liberals to modernize the Anglican church. Aurora's version of the title is hence ironic. "Articles": the thirty-nine articles are the principles of faith of the Church of England.
1. St. Buonaventure's doctrine that the power of the heart to love leads to higher illumination than the power of the mind to reason.

2. I.e., the author of the gospel.
3. A new word or expression. Balzac (1799–1850), a French novelist whose realism made him improper reading for a young lady.
4. Languages.
5. A 16th-century Spanish historian who wrote a book on the genealogies of the grandees of Spain.
6. A town in Austria. "Lara": a town in Spain on the river Arlanza. "Mount Chimborazo": one of the highest peaks of the Andes. "Teneriffe": a mountain in the Canary Islands.
7. An allusion to the story about Samuel Johnson, who, when told how difficult a piece of music was that a young lady was playing, replied, "I would it had been impossible."

To a noisy Tophet;[8] and I drew . . . costumes   420
From French engravings, nereids[9] neatly draped
(With smirks of simmering godship): I washed in[1]
Landscapes from nature (rather say, washed out).
I danced the polka and Cellarius,[2]
Spun glass, stuffed birds, and modeled flowers in wax,   425
Because she liked accomplishments in girls.
I read a score of books on womanhood
To prove, if women do not think at all,
They may teach thinking (to a maiden aunt
Or else the author),—books that boldly assert   430
Their right of comprehending husband's talk
When not too deep, and even of answering
With pretty "may it please you," or "so it is,"—
Their rapid insight and fine aptitude,
Particular worth and general missionariness,   435
As long as they keep quiet by the fire
And never say "no" when the world says "ay,"
For that is fatal,—their angelic reach
Of virtue, chiefly used to sit and darn,
And fatten household sinners,—their, in brief,   440
Potential faculty in everything
Of abdicating power in it: she owned
She liked a woman to be womanly,
And English women, she thanked God and sighed
(Some people always sigh in thanking God),   445
Were models to the universe. And last
I learnt cross-stitch,[3] because she did not like
To see me wear the night with empty hands
A-doing nothing. So, my shepherdess
Was something after all (the pastoral saints   450
Be praised for't), leaning lovelorn with pink eyes
To match her shoes, when I mistook the silks;
Her head uncrushed by that round weight of hat
So strangely similar to the tortoise shell
Which slew the tragic poet.[4]
                        By the way,   455
The works of women are symbolical.
We sew, sew, prick our fingers, dull our sight,
Producing what? A pair of slippers, sir,
To put on when you're weary—or a stool
To stumble over and vex you . . . "curse that stool!"   460
Or else at best, a cushion, where you lean
And sleep, and dream of something we are not
But would be for your sake. Alas, alas!
This hurts most, this—that, after all, we are paid
The worth of our work, perhaps.
                         In looking down   465

8. Hell.
9. Sea nymphs.
1. As in painting with watercolors.
2. A kind of waltz.
3. As in needlepoint.

4. According to tradition, the Greek playwright Aeschylus was killed by an eagle, who, mistaking his bald head for a stone, dropped a tortoise on it to break the shell.

Those years of education (to return)
I wonder if Brinvilliers suffered more
In the water-torture[5] . . . flood succeeding flood
To drench the incapable throat and split the veins . . .
Than I did. Certain of your feebler souls   470
Go out in such a process; many pine
To a sick, inodorous light; my own endured:
I had relations in the Unseen, and drew
The elemental nutriment and heat
From nature, as earth feels the sun at nights,   475
Or as a babe sucks surely in the dark.
I kept the life thrust on me, on the outside
Of the inner life with all its ample room
For heart and lungs, for will and intellect,
Inviolable by conventions. God,   480
I thank thee for that grace of thine!
                        At first
I felt no life which was not patience,—did
The thing she bade me, without heed to a thing
Beyond it, sat in just the chair she placed,
With back against the window, to exclude   485
The sight of the great lime-tree on the lawn,[6]
Which seemed to have come on purpose from the woods
To bring the house a message,—ay, and walked
Demurely in her carpeted low rooms,
As if I should not, harkening my own steps,   490
Misdoubt I was alive. I read her books,
Was civil to her cousin, Romney Leigh,
Gave ear to her vicar, tea to her visitors,
And heard them whisper, when I changed a cup
(I blushed for joy at that),—"The Italian child,   495
For all her blue eyes and her quiet ways,
Thrives ill in England: she is paler yet
Than when we came the last time; she will die."

From *Book 2*

[AURORA'S ASPIRATIONS][7]

Times followed one another. Came a morn
I stood upon the brink of twenty years,
And looked before and after, as I stood
Woman and artist,—either incomplete,
Both credulous of completion. There I held   5
The whole creation in my little cup,
And smiled with thirsty lips before I drank

5. Marie Marguerite, marquise de Brinvilliers, a celebrated criminal who was beheaded in 1676, was tortured by having water forced down her throat.
6. Perhaps a reference to Coleridge's *This Lime-Tree
Bower My Prison*, in which the lime tree becomes the
vehicle of a realization that Nature never deserts the
wise and pure even when they seem to be cut off from
her most beautiful vistas.

7. Stifled by her aunt's oppressive conventionality,
Aurora has found three sources of comfort and inspiration: poetic aspirations, fostered by the discovery of her
father's library; the beauty of the natural world; and
the intellectual companionship of her cousin Romney
Leigh, an idealistic young man troubled by the misery
of the poor and inspired by contemporary notions of
social reform.

"Good health to you and me, sweet neighbour mine,
And all these peoples."
                    I was glad, that day;
The June was in me, with its multitudes   10
Of nightingales all singing in the dark,
And rosebuds reddening where the calyx⁸ split.
I felt so young, so strong, so sure of God!
So glad, I could not choose be very wise!
And, old at twenty, was inclined to pull   15
My childhood backward in a childish jest
To see the face of't once more, and farewell!
In which fantastic mood I bounded forth
At early morning,—would not wait so long
As even to snatch my bonnet by the strings,   20
But, brushing a green trail across the lawn
With my gown in the dew, took will and away
Among the acacias of the shrubberies,
To fly my fancies in the open air
And keep my birthday, till my aunt awoke   25
To stop good dreams. Meanwhile I murmured on
As honeyed bees keep humming to themselves,
"The worthiest poets have remained uncrowned
Till death has bleached their foreheads to the bone;
And so with me it must be unless I prove   30
Unworthy of the grand adversity,
And certainly I would not fail so much.
What, therefore, if I crown myself to-day
In sport, not pride, to learn the feel of it,
Before my brows be numbed as Dante's own   35
To all the tender pricking of such leaves?
Such leaves! what leaves?"
                    I pulled the branches down
To choose from.
          "Not the bay!⁹ I choose no bay
(The fates deny us if we are overbold),
Nor myrtle—which means chiefly love; and love   40
Is something awful which one dares not touch
So early o' mornings. This verbena strains
The point of passionate fragrance; and hard by,
This guelder-rose,¹ at far too slight a beck
Of the wind; will toss about her flower-apples.   45
Ah—there's my choice,—that ivy on the wall,
That headlong ivy! not a leaf will grow
But thinking of a wreath. Large leaves, smooth leaves,
Serrated like my vines, and half as green.
I like such ivy, bold to leap a height   50
'Twas strong to climb; as good to grow on graves
As twist about a thyrsus;² pretty too

---

8. The protective outer leaves covering a flower or
bud.
9. A type of laurel tree whose leaves the ancient Greeks
used to honor athletic champions; subsequently, a sym-

bol of poetic achievement.
1. Cranberry tree.
2. Staff twined with ivy, carried by Dionysus in Greek
myth.

(And that's not ill) when twisted round a comb."
Thus speaking to myself, half singing it,
Because some thoughts are fashioned like a bell   55
To ring with once being touched, I drew a wreath
Drenched, blinding me with dew, across my brow,
And fastening it behind so, turning faced
... My public!—cousin Romney—with a mouth
Twice graver than his eyes.
                I stood there fixed,—   60
My arms up, like the caryatid,[3] sole
Of some abolished temple, helplessly
Persistent in a gesture which derides
A former purpose. Yet my blush was flame,
As if from flax, not stone.
              "Aurora Leigh,   65
The earliest of Auroras!"[4]
             Hand stretched out
I clasped, as shipwrecked men will clasp a hand,
Indifferent to the sort of palm. The tide
Had caught me at my pastime, writing down
My foolish name too near upon the sea   70
Which drowned me with a blush as foolish. "You,
My cousin!"
         The smile died out in his eyes
And dropped upon his lips, a cold dead weight,
For just a moment, "Here's a book I found!
No name writ on it—poems, by the form;   75
Some Greek upon the margin,—lady's Greek
Without the accents. Read it? Not a word.
I saw at once the thing had witchcraft in't,
Whereof the reading calls up dangerous spirits:
I rather bring it to the witch."
              "My book.   80
You found it" ...
          "In the hollow by the stream
That beech leans down into—of which you said
The Oread in it has a Naiad's[5] heart
And pines for waters."
          "Thank you."
              "Thanks to *you*
My cousin! that I have seen you not too much   85
Witch, scholar, poet, dreamer, and the rest,
To be a woman also."
          With a glance
The smile rose in his eyes again and touched
The ivy on my forehead, light as air.
I answered gravely "Poets needs must be   90
Or men or women—more's the pity."
             "Ah,

---

3. Supporting architectural column in the shape of a woman.
4. Aurora, Roman goddess of the dawn; used poetically to signify dawn itself.
5. Water nymph. "Oread": tree nymph.

But men, and still less women, happily,
Scarce need be poets. Keep to the green wreath,
Since even dreaming of the stone and bronze
Brings headaches, pretty cousin, and defiles   95
The clean white morning dresses."
                              "So you judge!
Because I love the beautiful I must
Love pleasure chiefly, and be overcharged
For ease and whiteness! well, you know the world,
And only miss your cousin, 'tis not much.   100
But learn this; I would rather take my part
With God's Dead, who afford to walk in white
Yet spread His glory, than keep quiet here
And gather up my feet from even a step
For fear to soil my gown in so much dust.   105
I choose to walk at all risks. — Here, if heads
That hold a rhythmic thought, must ache perforce,
For my part I choose headaches, — and to-day's
My birthday,"
                  "Dear Aurora, choose instead
To cure them. You have balsams."[6]
                              "I perceive.   110
The headache is too noble for my sex.
You think the heartache would sound decenter,
Since that's the woman's special, proper ache,
And altogether tolerable, except
To a woman."   115

[AURORA'S REJECTION OF ROMNEY][7]

                              There he glowed on me
With all his face and eyes. "No other help?"
Said he — "no more than so?"
                              "What help?" I asked.   345
"You'd scorn my help, — as Nature's self, you say,
Has scorned to put her music in my mouth
Because a woman's. Do you now turn round
And ask for what a woman cannot give?"

"For what she only can, I turn and ask,"   350
He answered, catching up my hands in his,
And dropping on me from his high-eaved brow
The full weight of his soul, — "I ask for love,
And that, she can; for life in fellowship
Through bitter duties — that, I know she can;   355
For wifehood — will she?"

6. Balms.
7. Romney and Aurora have been arguing about whether art, particularly a young woman's poetry, is useful in a world that, according to Romney, is full of human suffering. Romney claims that women have no faculty of generalizing and are therefore doomed to be trivial poets and ineffectual social reformers. Aurora is quick to agree that to be merely a poetaster would be intolerable to her, but while she admires Romney's lofty concern for humanity, she remains untempted to join forces with him.

"Now," I said, "may God
Be witness 'twixt us two!" and with the word,
Meseemed[8] I floated into a sudden light
Above his stature,—"am I proved too weak
To stand alone, yet strong enough to bear   360
Such leaners on my shoulder? poor to think,
Yet rich enough to sympathise with thought?
Incompetent to sing, as blackbirds can,
Yet competent to love, like HIM?"

              I paused;
Perhaps I darkened, as the lighthouse will   365
That turns upon the sea. "It's always so.
Anything does for a wife."

            "Aurora, dear,
And dearly honoured,"—he pressed in at once
With eager utterance,—"you translate me ill.
I do not contradict my thought of you   370
Which is most reverent, with another thought
Found less so. If your sex is weak for art
(And I, who said so, did but honour you
By using truth in courtship), it is strong
For life and duty. Place your fecund heart   375
In mine, and let us blossom for the world
That wants love's colour in the grey of time.
My talk, meanwhile, is arid to you, ay,
Since all my talk can only set you where
You look down coldly on the arena-heaps   380
Of headless bodies, shapeless, indistinct!
The Judgment-Angel scarce would find his way
Through such a heap of generalised distress
To the individual man with lips and eyes,
Much less Aurora. Ah, my sweet, come down,   385
And hand in hand we'll go where yours shall touch
These victims, one by one! till, one by one,
The formless, nameless trunk of every man
Shall seem to wear a head with hair you know,
And every woman catch your mother's face   390
To melt you into passion."

            "I am a girl,"
I answered slowly; "you do well to name
My mother's face. Though far too early, alas,
God's hand did interpose 'twixt it and me,
I know so much of love as used to shine   395
In that face and another. Just so much;
No more indeed at all. I have not seen
So much love since, I pray you pardon me,
As answers even to make a marriage with
In this cold land of England. What you love   400
Is not a woman, Romney, but a cause:
You want a helpmate, not a mistress, sir,

---

8. I.e., it seemed to me (a deliberate archaism).

A wife to help your ends,—in her no end.
Your cause is noble, your ends excellent,
But I, being most unworthy of these and that,   405
Do otherwise conceive of love. Farewell."

"Farewell, Aurora? you reject me thus?"
He said.
        "Sir, you were married long ago.
You have a wife already whom you love,
Your social theory. Bless you both, I say.   410
For my part, I am scarcely meek enough
To be the handmaid of a lawful spouse.
Do I look a Hagar,[9] think you?"
           "So you jest."

"Nay, so, I speak in earnest," I replied.
"You treat of marriage too much like, at least,   415
A chief apostle: you would bear with you
A wife . . . a sister . . . shall we speak it out?
A sister of charity."
        "Then, must it be
Indeed farewell? And was I so far wrong
In hope and in illusion, when I took   420
The woman to be nobler than the man,
Yourself the noblest woman, in the use
And comprehension of what love is,—love,
That generates the likeness of itself
Through all heroic duties? so far wrong,   425
In saying bluntly, venturing truth on love,
'Come, human creature, love and work with me,'—
Instead of 'Lady, thou art wondrous fair,
'And, where the Graces walk before, the Muse
'Will follow at the lightning of their eyes,   430
'And where the Muse walks, lovers need to creep:
'Turn round and love me, or I die of love.' "

With quiet indignation I broke in.
"You misconceive the question like a man,
Who sees a woman as the complement   435
Of his sex merely. You forget too much
That every creature, female as the male,
Stands single in responsible act and thought
As also in birth and death. Whoever says
To a loyal woman, 'Love and work with me,'   440
Will get fair answers if the work and love,
Being good themselves, are good for her—the best
She was born for. Women of a softer mood,
Surprised by men when scarcely awake to life,
Will sometimes only hear the first word, love,   445
And catch up with it any kind of work,

9. In Genesis 16, Sarah's maidservant, who bore a child, Ishmael, by Sarah's husband, Abraham.

Indifferent, so that dear love go with it.
I do not blame such women, though, for love,
They pick much oakum;[1] earth's fanatics make
Too frequently heaven's saints. But *me* your work　　　　　450
Is not the best for,—nor your love the best,
Nor able to commend the kind of work
For love's sake merely. Ah, you force me, sir,
To be overbold in speaking of myself:
I too have my vocation,—work to do,　　　　　455
The heavens and earth have set me since I changed
My father's face for theirs, and, though your world
Were twice as wretched as you represent,
Most serious work, most necessary work
As any of the economists'. Reform,　　　　　460
Make trade a Christian possibility,
And individual right no general wrong;
Wipe out earth's furrows of the Thine and Mine,
And leave one green for men to play at bowls,[2]
With innings for them all! . . . What then, indeed,　　　　　465
If mortals are not greater by the head
Than any of their prosperities? what then,
Unless the artist keep up open roads
Betwixt the seen and unseen,—bursting through
The best of your conventions with his best,　　　　　470
The speakable, imaginable best
God bids him speak, to prove what lies beyond
Both speech and imagination? A starved man
Exceeds a fat beast: we'll not barter, sir,
The beautiful for barley.—And, even so,　　　　　475
I hold you will not compass your poor ends
Of barley-feeding and material ease,
Without a poet's individualism
To work your universal. It takes a soul,
To move a body: it takes a high-souled man,　　　　　480
To move the masses, even to a cleaner stye:
It takes the ideal, to blow a hair's-breadth off
The dust of the actual.—Ah, your Fouriers[3] failed,
Because not poets enough to understand
That life develops from within.——For me,　　　　　485
Perhaps I am not worthy, as you say,
Of work like this: perhaps a woman's soul
Aspires, and not creates: yet we aspire,
And yet I'll try out your perhapses, sir,
And if I fail . . . why, burn me up my straw[4]　　　　　490
Like other false works—I'll not ask for grace;
Your scorn is better, cousin Romney. I
Who love my art, would never wish it lower
To suit my stature. I may love my art.

---

1. Fiber derived by untwisting (picking) old rope, a task frequently assigned to workhouse inmates.
2. A game of skill played on a smooth lawn with weighted wooden balls.
3. François Marie Charles Fourier (1772–1837), a French political theorist who advocated communal property as a basis for social harmony.
4. I.e., destroy my poetry (a deliberate archaism).

You'll grant that even a woman may love art,   495
Seeing that to waste true love on anything
Is womanly, past question."

From *Book 5*

[POETS AND THE PRESENT AGE]

The critics say that epics have died out
With Agamemnon and the goat-nursed gods;[5]   140
I'll not believe it. I could never deem,
As Payne Knight[6] did (the mythic mountaineer
Who travelled higher than he was born to live,
And showed sometimes the goitre[7] in his throat
Discoursing of an image seen through fog),   145
That Homer's heroes measured twelve feet high.
They were but men:—his Helen's hair turned grey
Like any plain Miss Smith's who wears a front;[8]
And Hector's infant whimpered at a plume[9]
As yours last Friday at a turkey-cock.   150
All actual heroes are essential men,
And all men possible heroes: every age,
Heroic in proportions, double-faced,
Looks backward and before, expects a morn
And claims an epos.[1]
                    Ay, but every age   155
Appears to souls who live in 't (ask Carlyle)[2]
Most unheroic. Ours, for instance, ours:
The thinkers scout it, and the poets abound
Who scorn to touch it with a finger-tip:
A pewter age,[3]—mixed metal, silver-washed;   160
An age of scum, spooned off the richer past,
An age of patches for old gaberdines,[4]
An age of mere transition,[5] meaning nought
Except that what succeeds must shame it quite
If God please. That's wrong thinking, to my mind,   165
And wrong thoughts make poor poems.
                    Every age,
Through being beheld too close, is ill-discerned
By those who have not lived past it. We'll suppose
Mount Athos carved, as Alexander schemed,

5. Zeus was nursed by a goat.
6. Richard Payne Knight (1750–1824), a classical phi-
lologist, who, upon England's acquisition of the Parthenon marbles, claimed that Lord Elgin had wasted
his labor because they were not all Greek.
7. A disease often contracted in high mountain areas
because of the low iodine content of the water.
8. A piece of false hair worn by women over the forehead.
9. In an episode in the *Iliad*, Hector tries to take his
infant son in his arms, but the child clings to his nurse,
frightened of his father's helmet and crest.

1. An epic poem.
2. In *Heroes and Hero-Worship* (1841), Carlyle argues
that the present age needs a renewed perception of the
heroic.
3. An allusion to the convention, which originates in
Hesiod, of describing civilization's decline through a
succession of ages named for increasingly less precious
materials, i.e., the Golden Age, the Silver Age, the
Bronze Age.
4. Coats made of gabardine.
5. In *The Spirit of the Age* (1831) John Stuart Mill
calls the present age "an age of transition."

To some colossal statue of a man.[6]   170
The peasants, gathering brushwood in his ear,
Had guessed as little as the browsing goats
Of form or feature of humanity
Up there,—in fact, had travelled five miles off
Or ere the giant image broke on them,   175
Full human profile, nose and chin distinct,
Mouth, muttering rhythms of silence up the sky
And fed at evening with the blood of suns;
Grand torso,—hand, that flung perpetually
The largesse of a silver river down   180
To all the country pastures. 'Tis even thus
With times we live in,—evermore too great
To be apprehended near.
                          But poets should
Exert a double vision; should have eyes
To see near things as comprehensively   185
As if afar they took their point of sight,
And distant things as intimately deep
As if they touched them. Let us strive for this.
I do distrust the poet who discerns
No character or glory in his times,   190
And trundles back his soul five hundred years,
Past moat and drawbridge, into a castle-court,
To sing—oh, not of lizard or of toad
Alive i' the ditch there,—'twere excusable,
But of some black chief, half knight, half sheep-lifter,   195
Some beauteous dame, half chattel and half queen,
As dead as must be, for the greater part,
The poems made on their chivalric bones;
And that's no wonder: death inherits death.

Nay, if there's room for poets in this world   200
A little overgrown (I think there is),
Their sole work is to represent the age,
Their age, not Charlemagne's,[7]—this live, throbbing age,
That brawls, cheats, maddens, calculates, aspires,
And spends more passion, more heroic heat,   205
Betwixt the mirrors of its drawing-rooms,
Than Roland[8] with his knights at Roncesvalles.
To flinch from modern varnish, coat or flounce,
Cry out for togas and the picturesque,
Is fatal,—foolish too. King Arthur's self   210
Was commonplace to Lady Guenever;
And Camelot to minstrels seemed as flat
As Fleet Street[9] to our poets.
                          Never flinch,

---

6. Dionocrates, a sculptor, is said to have suggested to Alexander that Mt. Athos be carved into the statue of a conqueror with a city in his left hand and a basin in his right, where all the waters of the region could be collected and used to water the pasture lands below.
7. Frankish conqueror (768–814), who created a European empire.
8. Legendary medieval hero, whose adventures are told in the epic poem *Chanson de Roland.*
9. Street in London, a center for book shops and newspaper and publishing offices.

But still, unscrupulously epic, catch
Upon the burning lava of a song   215
The full-veined, heaving, double-breasted Age:
That, when the next shall come, the men of that
May touch the impress with reverent hand, and say
"Behold,—behold the paps[1] we all have sucked!
This bosom seems to beat still, or at least   220
It sets ours beating: this is living art,
Which thus presents and thus records true life."

1853–56   1857

A Musical Instrument

1

What was he doing, the great god Pan,[1]
   Down in the reeds by the river?
Spreading ruin and scattering ban,[2]
Splashing and paddling with hoofs of a goat,
And breaking the golden lilies afloat   5
   With the dragon-fly on the river.

2

He tore out a reed, the great god Pan,
   From the deep cool bed of the river:
The limpid water turbidly ran,
And the broken lilies a-dying lay,   10
And the dragon-fly had fled away,
   Ere he brought it out of the river.

3

High on the shore sat the great god Pan
   While turbidly flowed the river;
And hacked and hewed as a great god can,   15
With his hard bleak steel at the patient reed,
Till there was not a sign of the leaf indeed
   To prove it fresh from the river.

4

He cut it short, did the great god Pan,
   (How tall it stood in the river!)   20
Then drew the pith,[3] like the heart of a man,
Steadily from the outside ring,
And notched the poor dry empty thing
   In holes, as he sat by the river.

5

"This is the way," laughed the great god Pan   25
   (Laughed while he sat by the river),
"The only way, since gods began
To make sweet music, they could succeed."

1. Breasts.
1. God of woods, fields, and flocks, having a human body with goat's legs, horns, and ears. According to legend, a nymph, Syrinx, when escaping from Pan's pursuit of her, was metamorphosed into a reed in a stream. One version of the legend (the one used here) has Pan making this single reed into a shepherd's pipe, in shape like a flute. In another version, he makes a pipe out of seven reeds in a row, an invention named in honor of the nymph.
2. Curses, malediction.
3. Central tissue.

Then, dropping his mouth to a hole in the reed,
   He blew in power by the river.   30
6
Sweet, sweet, sweet, O Pan!
   Piercing sweet by the river!
Blinding sweet, O great god Pan!
The sun on the hill forgot to die,
And the lilies revived, and the dragon-fly   35
   Came back to dream on the river.
7
Yet half a beast is the great god Pan,
   To laugh as he sits by the river,
Making a poet out of a man:
The true gods sigh for the cost and pain,—   40
For the reed which grows nevermore again
   As a reed with the reeds in the river.

1860   1860

Mother and Poet[1]

(Turin, After News from Gaeta, 1861)

1

DEAD! One of them shot by the sea in the east,
   And one of them shot in the west by the sea.
Dead! both my boys! When you sit at the feast
   And are wanting a great song for Italy free,
     Let none look at *me*!   5
2
Yet I was a poetess only last year,
   And good at my art, for a woman, men said;
But *this* woman, *this*, who is agonised here,
   —The east sea and west sea rhyme on in her head
     For ever instead.   10
3
What art can a woman be good at? Oh, vain!
   What art *is* she good at, but hurting her breast
With the milk-teeth of babes, and a smile at the pain?
   Ah boys, how you hurt! you were strong as you pressed,
     And I proud, by that test.   15
4
What art's for a woman? To hold on her knees
   Both darlings! to feel all their arms round her throat,
Cling, strangle a little! to sew by degrees
   And 'broider the long-clothes and neat little coat;
     To dream and to doat.   20
5
To teach them . . . It stings there! *I* made them indeed
   Speak plain the word *country*. *I* taught them, no doubt,

---

1. The speaker is the Italian poet and patriot Laura Savio of Turin, both of whose sons were killed in the struggle for the unification of Italy, one in the attack on the fortress at Ancona, the other at the siege of Gaeta, the last stronghold of the Neapolitan government.

That a country's a thing men should die for at need.
   I prated of liberty, rights, and about
      The tyrant cast out.   25

6

And when their eyes flashed . . . O my beautiful eyes! . . .
   I exulted; nay, let them go forth at the wheels
Of the guns, and denied not. But then the surprise
   When one sits quite alone! Then one weeps, then one kneels!
      God, how the house feels!   30

7

At first, happy news came, in gay letters moiled[2]
   With my kisses,—of camp-life and glory, and how
They both loved me; and, soon coming home to be spoiled
   In return would fan off every fly from my brow
      With their green laurel-bough.[3]   35

8

Then was triumph at Turin: "Ancona was free!"
   And some one came out of the cheers in the street,
With a face pale as stone, to say something to me.
   My Guido was dead! I fell down at his feet,
      While they cheered in the street.   40

9

I bore it; friends soothed me; my grief looked sublime
   As the ransom of Italy. One boy remained
To be leant on and walked with, recalling the time
   When the first grew immortal, while both of us strained
      To the height he had gained.   45

10

And letters still came, shorter, sadder, more strong,
   Writ now but in one hand, "I was not to faint,—
One loved me for two—would be with me ere long:
   And *Viva l'Italia!*—*he* died for, our saint,
      Who forbids our complaint."   50

11

My Nanni would add, "he was safe, and aware
   Of a presence that turned off the balls,[4]—was imprest
It was Guido himself, who knew what I could bear,
   And how 'twas impossible, quite dispossessed
      To live on for the rest."   55

12

On which, without pause, up the telegraph line
   Swept smoothly the next news from Gaeta:—*Shot.*
Tell his mother. Ah, ah, "his," "their" mother,—not "mine,"
   No voice says "My mother" again to me. What!
      You think Guido forgot?   60

13

Are souls straight so happy that, dizzy with Heaven,
   They drop earth's affections, conceive not of woe?
I think not. Themselves were too lately forgiven

---

2. Moistened.
3. A laurel crown is the conventional mark of a poet's fame.
4. Cannon balls.

Through THAT Love and Sorrow which reconciled so
    The Above and Below.   65

14

O Christ of the five wounds, who look'dst through the dark
    To the face of thy mother! consider, I pray,
How we common mothers stand desolate, mark,
    Whose sons, not being Christs, die with eyes turned away
        And no last word to say!   70

15

Both boys dead? but that's out of nature. We all
    Have been patriots, yet each house must always keep one.
'Twere imbecile, hewing out roads to a wall;
    And, when Italy's made, for what end is it done
        If we have not a son?   75

16

Ah, ah, ah! when Gaeta's taken, what then?
    When the fair wicked queen sits no more at her sport
Of the fire-balls of death crashing souls out of men?
    When the guns of Cavalli with final retort
        Have cut the game short?[5]   80

17

When Venice and Rome keep their new jubilee,[6]
    When your flag takes all heaven for its white, green, and red,
When *you* have your country from mountain to sea,
    When King Victor has Italy's crown on his head,
        (And *I* have my Dead)—   85

18

What then? Do not mock me. Ah, ring your bells low,
    And burn your lights faintly! *My* country is *there*,
Above the star pricked by the last peak of snow:
    My Italy's THERE, with my brave civic Pair,
        To disfranchise despair!   90

19

Forgive me. Some women bear children in strength,
    And bite back the cry of their pain in self-scorn;
But the birth-pangs of nations will wring us at length
    Into wail such as this—and we sit on forlorn
        When the man-child is born.   95

20

Dead! One of them shot by the sea in the east,
    And one of them shot in the west by the sea.
Both! both my boys! If in keeping the feast
    You want a great song for your Italy free,
        Let none look at *me*!   100

1861   1862

---

5. Cavalli was the general commanding the siege of Gaeta. "The fair wicked queen" was Maria, wife of Francis II, the last ruler of the Neapolitan government, who retreated to Gaeta.
6. The celebration when they too will have been united with the rest of Italy under King Victor Emmanuel. In 1861, when the poem was written, they were the two cities that were still independent of the new state.

ALFRED, LORD TENNYSON
1809–1892

1830:   *Poems, Chiefly Lyrical.*
1833:   Death of Arthur Hallam.
1842:   *Poems.*
1850:   *In Memoriam.* Tennyson appointed poet laureate.
1859:   *Idylls of the King* (first four books).

Whether or not Alfred Tennyson was the greatest of the Victorian poets, as affirmed by many critics today, there is no doubt that in his own lifetime he was the most popular of poets. On the bookshelves of almost every family of readers in England and the United States, from 1850 onward, were the works of a man who had incontestably gained the title that Walt Whitman longed for: "The Poet of the People" (Whitman, in fact, called Tennyson, colorfully, "the Boss"). Popularity inevitably provided provocation for a reaction in the decades following his death. In the course of repudiating their Victorian predecessors, the Edwardians and Georgians established the fashion of making fun of Tennyson's great achievements. Samuel Butler (1835–1902), who anticipated early twentieth-century tastes, has a characteristic entry in his *Notebooks:* "Talking it over, we agreed that Blake was no good because he learnt Italian at sixty in order to study Dante, and we knew Dante was no good because he was so fond of Virgil, and Virgil was no good because Tennyson ran him, and as for Tennyson—well, Tennyson goes without saying." In the second half of the twentieth century, Butler's confident assumption that Tennyson's poetry was simply contemptible no longer "goes without saying." The delights to be found in this superb "lord of language"—as Tennyson himself addresses his favorite predecessor, Virgil—have been rediscovered, and Tennyson's stature as one of the major poets of any age has been reestablished. In 1892, the year of his death, he himself had made an accurate prophecy of his changing status in his lines on *Poets and Critics:*

> What is true at last will tell:
> Few at first will place thee well;
> Some too low would have thee shine,
> Some too high—no fault of thine—
> Hold thine own, and work thy will!

Like his poetry, Tennyson's life and character have been reassessed in the twentieth century. To many of his contemporaries he seemed a remote wizard, secure in his laureate's robes, a man whose life had been sheltered, marred only by the loss of his best friend in youth. During much of his career Tennyson may have been isolated, but his was not a sheltered life in the real sense of the word. Although he grew up in a parsonage, it was not the kind of parsonage one encounters in the novels of Jane Austen. It was a household dominated by frictions and loyalties and broodings over ancestral inheritances, in which the children showed marked strains of instability and eccentricity.

Alfred was the fourth son in a family of twelve children. One of his brothers had to be confined to an insane asylum for life; another was long a victim of the opium habit; another had violent quarrels with his father, the Reverend Dr. George Tennyson, who had become a drunkard. On one occasion Dr. Tennyson summoned a constable to have his son Frederick evicted from the household. On another, armed with knife and loaded gun, he threatened to kill the young man. This father, a man of considerable learning, had himself been born the eldest son of a wealthy landowner and had therefore expected to be heir to his family's estates. Instead he was disinherited in favor of his younger brother and had to make his own livelihood by joining the clergy, a profession that he disliked. After George Tennyson had settled in a small rectory in Somersby, his brooding sense of dissatisfaction led to increasingly violent bouts of drunkenness, despite which he was nevertheless still able to serve as tutor for his sons in classical and modern languages to prepare them for entering the university.

Before leaving this strange household for Cambridge, Alfred had already demonstrated a flair for writing verse — precocious exercises in the manner of Milton or Byron or the Elizabethan dramatists. He had even published a volume in 1827, in collaboration with his brother Charles, *Poems by Two Brothers*. This feat drew him to the attention of a group of gifted undergraduates at Cambridge, the "Apostles," who encouraged him to devote his life to poetry. Up until this time, the young man had known scarcely anyone outside the circle of his own family. Despite his massive frame and powerful physique, he was painfully shy, and the friendships he found at Cambridge as well as the intellectual and political discussions in which he participated served to give him confidence and to widen his horizons as a poet. The most important of these friendships was with Arthur Hallam, a leader of the Apostles, who later became engaged to Tennyson's sister. Hallam's sudden death, in 1833, seemed an overwhelming calamity to his friend. Not only the long elegy *In Memoriam* but many of Tennyson's other poems are tributes to this early friendship.

Alfred's career at Cambridge was interrupted and finally broken off in 1831 by family dissensions and financial need, and he returned home to study and practice the craft of poetry. His early volumes (1830 and 1832) were attacked as "obscure" or "affected" by some of the reviewers. Tennyson suffered acutely under hostile criticism, but he also profited from it. His volume of 1842 demonstrated a remarkable advance in taste and technical excellence, and in 1850 he at last attained fame and full critical recognition with *In Memoriam*. In the same year, he became poet laureate in succession to Wordsworth. The struggle during the previous twenty years had been made especially painful by the long postponement of his marriage to Emily Sellwood, with whom he had fallen in love in 1836 but could not marry, because of poverty, until 1850.

His life thereafter was a comfortable one. He was as popular as Byron had been, and his fame lasted for much longer. The earnings from his poetry (sometimes exceeding £10,000 a year) enabled him to purchase a house in the country and to enjoy the kind of seclusion he liked. His notoriety was enhanced, like that of George Bernard Shaw and Walt Whitman, by his colorful appearance. Huge and shaggy, in cloak and broad-brimmed hat, gruff in manner as a farmer, he impressed everyone as what is called a "character." The pioneering photographer Julia Cameron, who took magnificent portraits of him, called him "the most beautiful old man on earth." He also had a booming voice, when reading his poetry, that electrified listeners much as Dylan Thomas electrified audiences in the twentieth century: "mouthing out his hollow o's and a's, / Deep-chested music." Moreover, for many Victorian readers, he seemed not only a great poetical phrase maker and a striking individual but also a wise man whose occasional pronouncements on politics or world affairs represented the national voice itself. In 1884 he accepted a peerage. In 1892 he died and was buried in Westminster Abbey.

It is often said that success was bad for Tennyson, and that after *In Memoriam* his poetic power seriously declined. That in his last forty-two years certain of his mannerisms became accentuated is true. One of the difficulties of his dignified blank verse was, as he said himself, that it is hard to describe commonplace objects and "at the same time to retain poetical elevation." This difficulty is evident, for example, in *Enoch Arden* (1864), a long blank verse narrative of everyday life in a fishing village, in which a basketful of fish is ornately described as "Enoch's ocean spoil / In ocean-smelling osier." In others of his later poems, those dealing with national affairs, there is also an increased shrillness of tone—a mannerism accentuated by Tennyson's realizing that like Dickens he had a vast public behind him to back up his pronouncements.

It is foolish, however, to try to shelve all of Tennyson's later productions. In 1855 he published his experimental monologue *Maud*, perhaps his finest long poem. In its portrayal of the speaker's hope for a redeeming love and his despair and bitterness over the social ills surrounding him, *Maud* reflects Tennyson's preoccupation with the relationship of the role of women to modern civilization. In 1859 he published four books of his *Idylls of the King*, a large-scale epic that occupied most of his energies in the second half of his career. Concerned, as *Maud* is, with gender and society, the *Idylls* uses the body of Arthurian legend to construct a vision of the rise and fall of civilization. In this civilization, women at once inspire men's highest efforts and sow the seeds of their destruction. The *Idylls* provides Tennyson's most extensive social vision, one whose concern with medieval ideals of social community, heroism, and courtly love and whose despairing sense of the cycles of historical change typifies much social thought of the age. About the quality of this late poem, finally completed, in twelve books, in 1888, there is some disagreement. Some readers have criticized it for its prettiness and complacency—mere "lollipops," as Carlyle called it. In any event, even if this ambitious epic does not always show Tennyson in his best vein, there is no sign of decline in his late lyrics. The eighty-year-old poet who wrote *Crossing the Bar* had certainly not lost his touch.

The problem of Tennyson's development is really of more significance for the period before 1850 rather than afterward. W. H. Auden stated that Tennyson had "the finest ear, perhaps, of any English poet." The interesting point is that Tennyson did not "have" such an ear: he developed it. Studies of the original versions of his poems in the 1830 and 1832 volumes demonstrate not only that his taste was uncertain at the outset of his career but that his sense of meter was originally unreliable. The harmonics he was to achieve from 1842 onward had to be learned just as a pianist with a weak left hand has to overcome his or her weakness by constant exercise. Like Chaucer or Keats or Pope, Tennyson studied his predecessors assiduously to perfect his technique. Anyone wanting to learn the traditional craft of English verse can study with profit the various stages of revision that such poems as *The Lotos-Eaters* were subjected to by this painstaking and artful poet. Some lines of 1988 by the American poet Karl Shapiro effectively characterize Tennyson's accomplishments in these areas:

> Long-lived, the very image of English Poet,
> Whose songs still break out tears in the generations,
> Whose poetry for practitioners still astounds,
> Who crafted his life and letters like a watch.

If the early Tennyson was uncertain of meter, he had other skills that were immediately in evidence. One of these was a capacity for linking scenery to states of mind. As early as 1835, J. S. Mill identified the special kind of scene painting to be found in early poems such as *Mariana*: ". . . not the power of producing that rather vapid species of composition usually termed descriptive poetry . . . but the power of *creating* scenery, in keeping with some state of human feeling so fitted to it as to be the embodied symbol of it, and to summon up the state of feeling itself, with a force not to be surpassed by anything but reality."

The state of feeling to which Tennyson was most intensely drawn was a melancholy isolation, often portrayed through the consciousness of an abandoned woman, as in *Mariana*. Tennyson's absorption with such emotions in his early poetry evoked considerable criticism. His friend R. C. Trench warned him, "Tennyson, we cannot live in Art," and Mill urged him to "cultivate, and with no half devotion, philosophy as well as poetry." Advice of this kind Tennyson was already predisposed to heed. The death of Hallam, the religious uncertainties that he had himself experienced, together with his own extensive study of writings by geologists, astronomers, and biologists, led him to confront many of the religious issues that bewildered his and later generations. The result was *In Memoriam* (1850), a long elegy written over a period of seventeen years, embodying the poet's reflections on our relation to God and to nature.

Was Tennyson intellectually equipped to deal with the great questions raised in *In Memoriam*? The answer may depend on a reader's religious and philosophical presuppositions. Some, such as T. H. Huxley, considered Tennyson an intellectual giant, a thinker who had mastered the scientific thought of his century and fully confronted the issues it raised. Others dismissed Tennyson, in this phase, as a lightweight. Auden went so far as to call him the "stupidest" of English poets. He went on to say, "There was little about melancholia that he didn't know; there was little else that he did." Perhaps T. S. Eliot's evaluation of *In Memoriam* is the more accurate: the poem, he wrote, is remarkable not "because of the quality of its faith but because of the quality of its doubt." Tennyson's mind was slow, ponderous, brooding; for the composition of *In Memoriam* such qualities of mind were assets, not liabilities. In these terms we can understand when Tennyson's poetry really fails to measure up: it is when he writes of events of the moment over which his thoughts and feelings have had no time to brood. Several of his poems are what he himself called "newspaper verse." They are letters to the editor, in effect, with the ephemeral heat and simplicity we expect of such productions. *The Charge of the Light Brigade*, inspired by a report in the *Times* of a cavalry charge at Balaclava during the Crimean War, is one of the best of his productions in this category.

Tennyson's poems of contemporary events were inevitably popular in his own day. So too were those poems in which, as in *Locksley Hall*, he dipped into the future. The technological changes wrought by Victorian inventors and engineers fascinated him. Sometimes they gave him an assurance of human progress as swaggeringly exultant as that of Macaulay. At other times the horrors of industrialism's by-products in the slums, the bloodshed of war, the greed of the newly rich, destroyed his hopes that humanity was evolving upward. Such a late poem as *The Dawn* embodies an attitude that he found in Virgil: "Thou majestic in thy sadness at the doubtful doom of human kind."

For despite Tennyson's fascination with technological developments, he was essentially a poet of the countryside, a man whose whole being was conditioned by the recurring rhythms of rural rather than urban life. He had the country dweller's awareness of traditional roots and sense of the past. It is appropriate that most of his best poems are about the past, not about the present or future. Even in his childhood, Tennyson said that "the words 'far, far away' had always a strange charm for me"; he was haunted by what he called "the passion of the past." The past became his great theme, whether it be his own past (as in *In the Valley of Cauteretz*), his country's past (as in *The Idylls of the King*), the past of humankind, the past of the world itself:

> There rolls the deep where grew the tree.
> O earth, what changes hast thou seen!
> There where the long street roars hath been
> The stillness of the central sea.

Tennyson is the first major writer to express this awareness of the vast extent of geological time that has haunted human consciousness since Victorian scientists exposed the history of the earth's crust. In his more usual vein, however, it is the recorded past of humankind that inspires him, the classical past in particular. Classical themes, as Douglas Bush has noted, "generally banished from his mind what was timid, parochial, sentimental . . . and evoked his special gifts and most authentic emotions, his rich and wistful sense of the past, his love of nature, and his power of style."

One returns, finally then, to the question of language. At the time of his death, a critic complained that Tennyson was merely "a discoverer of words rather than of ideas." The same complaint has been made by George Bernard Shaw and others—not about Tennyson but about Shakespeare.

Mariana[1]

"Mariana in the moated grange."
Measure for Measure

With blackest moss the flower-plots
    Were thickly crusted, one and all;
The rusted nails fell from the knots
    That held the pear to the gable wall.
The broken sheds looked sad and strange: 5
    Unlifted was the clinking latch;
    Weeded and worn the ancient thatch
Upon the lonely moated grange.
        She only said, "My life is dreary,
            He cometh not," she said;   10
        She said, "I am aweary, aweary,
            I would that I were dead!"

Her tears fell with the dews at even;
    Her tears fell ere the dews were dried;
She could not look on the sweet heaven,[2]   15
    Either at morn or eventide.
After the flitting of the bats,
    When thickest dark did trance[3] the sky,
    She drew her casement curtain by,
And glanced athwart the glooming flats.   20
        She only said, "The night is dreary,
            He cometh not," she said;
        She said, "I am aweary, aweary,
            I would that I were dead!"

Upon the middle of the night,   25
    Waking she heard the nightfowl crow;
The cock sung out an hour ere light;
    From the dark fen the oxen's low
Came to her; without hope of change,

---

1. Mariana, in Shakespeare's *Measure for Measure* 3.1.277), waits in a grange (an outlying farmhouse) for her lover, who has deserted her.

2. Cf. Virgil, *Aeneid* 4.451, in which Dido "is weary of gazing on the arch of heaven."

3. Traverse [noted by R. W. Hill].

In sleep she seemed to walk forlorn,   30
　　Till cold winds woke the gray-eyed morn
About the lonely moated grange.
　　　She only said, "The day is dreary,
　　　　He cometh not," she said;
　　　She said, "I am aweary, aweary,   35
　　　　I would that I were dead!"

About a stonecast from the wall
　　A sluice with blackened waters slept,
And o'er it many, round and small,
　　The clustered marish-mosses[4] crept.   40
Hard by a poplar shook alway,
　　All silver-green with gnarlèd bark:
For leagues no other tree did mark
The level waste, the rounding gray.
　　　She only said, "My life is dreary,   45
　　　　He cometh not," she said;
　　　She said, "I am aweary, aweary,
　　　　I would that I were dead!"

And ever when the moon was low,
　　And the shrill winds were up and away,   50
In the white curtain, to and fro,
　　She saw the gusty shadow sway.
But when the moon was very low,
　　And wild winds bound within their cell,[5]
The shadow of the poplar fell   55
Upon her bed, across her brow.
　　　She only said, "The night is dreary,
　　　　He cometh not," she said;
　　　She said, "I am aweary, aweary,
　　　　I would that I were dead!"   60

All day within the dreamy house,
　　The doors upon their hinges creaked;
The blue fly sung in the pane; the mouse
　　Behind the moldering wainscot shrieked,[6]
Or from the crevice peered about.   65
　　Old faces glimmered through the doors,
　　Old footsteps trod the upper floors,
Old voices called her from without.
　　　She only said, "My life is dreary,
　　　　He cometh not," she said;   70
　　　She said, "I am aweary, aweary,
　　　　I would that I were dead!"

The sparrow's chirrup on the roof,
　　The slow clock ticking, and the sound

---

4. The little marsh-moss lumps that float on the surface of water [Tennyson's note].
5. According to Virgil, Aeolus, god of winds, kept the winds imprisoned in a cave (cf. *Aeneid* 1.50–59).
6. Cf. T. S. Eliot, *Four Quartets: East Coker* lines 11–13: "And a time for the wind . . . to shake the wainscot where the fieldmouse trots / And to shake the tattered arras."

Which to the wooing wind aloof   75
  The poplar made, did all confound
Her sense; but most she loathed the hour
  When the thick-moted sunbeam lay
  Athwart the chambers, and the day
Was sloping toward his western bower.   80
    Then, said she, "I am very dreary,
      He will not come," she said;
    She wept, "I am aweary, aweary,
      Oh God, that I were dead!"

                                        1830

The Lady of Shalott

Part 1

On either side the river lie
Long fields of barley and of rye,
That clothe the wold[1] and meet the sky;
And through the field the road runs by
    To many-towered Camelot;   5
And up and down the people go,
Gazing where the lilies blow[2]
Round an island there below,
    The island of Shalott.

Willows whiten, aspens quiver,   10
Little breezes dusk and shiver
Through the wave that runs forever
By the island in the river
    Flowing down to Camelot.
Four gray walls, and four gray towers,   15
Overlook a space of flowers,
And the silent isle imbowers
    The Lady of Shalott.

By the margin, willow-veiled,
Slide the heavy barges trailed   20
By slow horses; and unhailed
The shallop[3] flitteth silken-sailed
    Skimming down to Camelot:
But who hath seen her wave her hand?
Or at the casement seen her stand?   25
Or is she known in all the land,
    The Lady of Shalott?

Only reapers, reaping early
In among the bearded barley,

---

1. Rolling plain.   3. A light open boat.
2. Bloom.

Hear a song that echoes cheerly   30
From the river winding clearly,
        Down to towered Camelot;
And by the moon the reaper weary,
Piling sheaves in uplands airy,
Listening, whispers " 'Tis the fairy   35
        Lady of Shalott."

Part 2

There she weaves by night and day
A magic web with colors gay.
She has heard a whisper say,
A curse is on her if she stay   40
        To look down to Camelot.
She knows not what the curse may be,
And so she weaveth steadily,
And little other care hath she,
        The Lady of Shalott.   45

And moving through a mirror clear[4]
That hangs before her all the year,
Shadows of the world appear.
There she sees the highway near
        Winding down to Camelot;   50
There the river eddy whirls,
And there the surly village churls,
And the red cloaks of market girls,
        Pass onward from Shalott.

Sometimes a troop of damsels glad,   55
An abbot on an ambling pad,[5]
Sometimes a curly shepherd lad,
Or long-haired page in crimson clad,
        Goes by to towered Camelot;
And sometimes through the mirror blue   60
The knights come riding two and two:
She hath no loyal knight and true,
        The Lady of Shalott.

But in her web she still delights
To weave the mirror's magic sights,   65
For often through the silent nights
A funeral, with plumes and lights
        And music, went to Camelot;
Or when the moon was overhead,
Came two young lovers lately wed: 70
"I am half sick of shadows," said
        The Lady of Shalott.

---

4. Weavers used mirrors, placed facing their looms, to   5. Easy-paced horse.
see the progress of their work.

Part 3

A bowshot from her bower eaves,
He rode between the barley sheaves,
The sun came dazzling through the leaves,   75
And flamed upon the brazen greaves[6]
    Of bold Sir Lancelot.
A red-cross knight[7] forever kneeled
To a lady in his shield,
That sparkled on the yellow field,   80
    Beside remote Shalott.

The gemmy bridle glittered free,
Like to some branch of stars we see
Hung in the golden Galaxy.
The bridle bells rang merrily   85
    As he rode down to Camelot;
And from his blazoned baldric[8] slung
A mighty silver bugle hung,
And as he rode his armor rung,
    Beside remote Shalott.   90

All in the blue unclouded weather
Thick-jeweled shone the saddle leather,
The helmet and the helmet-feather
Burned like one burning flame together,
    As he rode down to Camelot;   95
As often through the purple night,
Below the starry clusters bright,
Some bearded meteor, trailing light,
    Moves over still Shalott.

His broad clear brow in sunlight glowed;   100
On burnished hooves his war horse trode;
From underneath his helmet flowed
His coal-black curls as on he rode,
    As he rode down to Camelot.
From the bank and from the river   105
He flashed into the crystal mirror,
"Tirra lirra," by the river
    Sang Sir Lancelot.

She left the web, she left the loom,
She made three paces through the room,   110
She saw the water lily bloom,
She saw the helmet and the plume,
    She looked down to Camelot.
Out flew the web and floated wide;
The mirror cracked from side to side;   115

6. Armor protecting the leg below the knee.   8. A richly decorated sash worn diagonally across the
7. Cf. *The Faerie Queene* 1 (p. 280) and 3.2.17–25.   breast.

"The curse is come upon me," cried
The Lady of Shalott.

Part 4

In the stormy east wind straining,
The pale yellow woods were waning,
The broad stream in his banks complaining,   120
Heavily the low sky raining
    Over towered Camelot;
Down she came and found a boat
Beneath a willow left afloat,
And round about the prow she wrote   125
The Lady of Shalott.

And down the river's dim expanse
Like some bold seër in a trance,
Seeing all his own mischance—
With a glassy countenance   130
    Did she look to Camelot.
And at the closing of the day
She loosed the chain, and down she lay;
The broad stream bore her far away,
    The Lady of Shalott.   135

Lying, robed in snowy white
That loosely flew to left and right—
The leaves upon her falling light—
Through the noises of the night
    She floated down to Camelot;   140
And as the boat-head wound along
The willowy hills and fields among,
They heard her singing her last song,
    The Lady of Shalott.

Heard a carol, mournful, holy,   145
Chanted loudly, chanted lowly,
Till her blood was frozen slowly,
And her eyes were darkened wholly,[9]
    Turned to towered Camelot.
For ere she reached upon the tide   150
The first house by the waterside,
Singing in her song she died,
    The Lady of Shalott.

Under tower and balcony,
By garden wall and gallery,   155
A gleaming shape she floated by,
Dead-pale between the houses high,
    Silent into Camelot.

9. In the 1832 version this line read: "And her smooth face sharpened slowly." George Eliot informed Tennyson that she preferred the earlier version.

Out upon the wharfs they came,
Knight and burgher, lord and dame,   160
And round the prow they read her name,
    The Lady of Shalott.

Who is this? and what is here?
And in the lighted palace near
Died the sound of royal cheer;   165
And they crossed themselves for fear,
    All the knights at Camelot:
But Lancelot mused a little space;
He said, "She has a lovely face;
God in his mercy lend her grace,   170
    The Lady of Shalott."

1831–32   1832, 1842

The Lotos-Eaters[1]

"Courage!" he[2] said, and pointed toward the land,
"This mounting wave will roll us shoreward soon."
In the afternoon they came unto a land[3]
In which it seemèd always afternoon.
All round the coast the languid air did swoon,   5
Breathing like one that hath a weary dream.
Full-faced above the valley stood the moon;
And, like a downward smoke, the slender stream
Along the cliff to fall and pause and fall did seem.

A land of streams! some, like a downward smoke,   10
Slow-dropping veils of thinnest lawn,[4] did go;
And some through wavering lights and shadows broke,
Rolling a slumbrous sheet of foam below.
They saw the gleaming river seaward flow
From the inner land; far off, three mountaintops,   15
Three silent pinnacles of aged snow,
Stood sunset-flushed; and, dewed with showery drops,
Up-clomb the shadowy pine above the woven copse.

The charmèd sunset lingered low adown
In the red West; through mountain clefts the dale   20

---

1. Based on a short episode from the *Odyssey* (9.82–97) in which the weary Greek veterans of the Trojan War are tempted by a desire to abandon their long voyage homeward. As Odysseus later reported: "On the tenth day we set foot on the land of the lotos-eaters who eat a flowering food. . . . I sent forth certain of my company [who] . . . mixed with the men of the lotos-eaters who gave . . . them of the lotos to taste. Now whosoever of them did eat the honey-sweet fruit of the lotos had no more wish to bring tidings nor to come back, but there he chose to abide . . . forgetful of his homeward way."

Tennyson expands Homer's brief account into an elaborate picture of weariness and the desire for rest and death. The descriptions in the first stanzas are similar to *Faerie Queene* 2.6, and employ the same stanza form. The final section derives, in part, from Lucretius' conception of the gods in *De rerum natura*.
2. Odysseus (or Ulysses).
3. The repetition of "land" from line 1 was deliberate; Tennyson said that this "no rhyme" was "lazier" in its effect. Cf. "afternoon" (lines 3–4) and the rhyming of "adown" and "down" (lines 19 and 21).
4. A fine, thin linen.

Was seen far inland, and the yellow down[5]
Bordered with palm, and many a winding vale
And meadow, set with slender galingale;[6]
A land where all things always seemed the same!
And round about the keel with faces pale,   25
Dark faces pale against that rosy flame,
The mild-eyed melancholy Lotos-eaters came.

Branches they bore of that enchanted stem,
Laden with flower and fruit, whereof they gave
To each, but whoso did receive of them   30
And taste, to him the gushing of the wave
Far far away did seem to mourn and rave
On alien shores; and if his fellow spake,
His voice was thin, as voices from the grave;
And deep-asleep he seemed, yet all awake,   35
And music in his ears his beating heart did make.

They sat them down upon the yellow sand,
Between the sun and moon upon the shore;
And sweet it was to dream of Fatherland,
Of child, and wife, and slave; but evermore   40
Most weary seemed the sea, weary the oar,
Weary the wandering fields of barren foam,
Then some one said, "We will return no more";
And all at once they sang, "Our island home[7]
Is far beyond the wave; we will no longer roam."   45

Choric Song[8]

1

There is sweet music here that softer falls
Than petals from blown roses on the grass,
Or night-dews on still waters between walls
Of shadowy granite, in a gleaming pass;
Music that gentlier on the spirit lies,   50
Than tired eyelids upon tired eyes;[9]
Music that brings sweet sleep down from the blissful skies.
Here are cool mosses deep,
And through the moss the ivies creep,
And in the stream the long-leaved flowers weep,   55
And from the craggy ledge the poppy hangs in sleep.

2

Why are we weighed upon with heaviness,
And utterly consumed with sharp distress,
While all things else have rest from weariness?
All things have rest: why should we toil alone,   60
We only toil, who are the first of things,

---

5. An open plain on high ground.
6. A plant resembling tall coarse grass.
7. Ithaca.
8. Sung by the mariners.

9. Tennyson wanted the word to be pronounced as *tie-yerd* rather than *tier'd* or *tire-èd*, thus "making the word neither monosyllable or disyllabic, but a dreamy child of the two."

And make perpetual moan,
Still from one sorrow to another thrown;
Nor ever fold our wings,
And cease from wanderings,   65
Nor steep our brows in slumber's holy balm;
Nor harken what the inner spirit sings,
"There is no joy but calm!" —
Why should we only toil, the roof and crown of things?[1]

                              3
Lo! in the middle of the wood,   70
The folded leaf is wooed from out the bud
With winds upon the branch, and there
Grows green and broad, and takes no care,
Sun-steeped at noon, and in the moon
Nightly dew-fed; and turning yellow   75
Falls, and floats adown the air.
Lo! sweetened with summer light,
The full-juiced apple, waxing over-mellow,
Drops in a silent autumn night.
All its allotted length of days   80
The flower ripens in its place,
Ripens and fades, and falls, and hath no toil,
Fast-rooted in the fruitful soil.

                              4
Hateful is the dark blue sky,
Vaulted o'er the dark blue sea.   85
Death is the end of life; ah, why
Should life all labor be?
Let us alone. Time driveth onward fast,
And in a little while our lips are dumb.
Let us alone. What is it that will last?   90
All things are taken from us, and become
Portions and parcels of the dreadful past.
Let us alone. What pleasure can we have
To war with evil? Is there any peace
In ever climbing up the climbing wave?   95
All things have rest, and ripen toward the grave
In silence — ripen, fall, and cease:
Give us long rest or death, dark death, or dreamful ease.[2]

                              5
How sweet it were, hearing the downward stream,
With half-shut eyes ever to seem   100
Falling asleep in a half-dream!
To dream and dream, like yonder amber light,
Which will not leave the myrrh-bush on the height;
To hear each other's whispered speech;
Eating the Lotos day by day,   105
To watch the crisping[3] ripples on the beach,

---

1. Cf. *Faerie Queene* 2.6.17: "Why then dost thou, O
man, that of them all / Art Lord, and eke of nature Sov-
ereaine, / Wilfully . . . wast thy joyous houres in needlesse paine?"

2. Cf. *Faerie Queen* 1.9.40: "Sleepe after toyle, port
after stormie seas, / Ease after warre, death after life
does greatly please."
3. Curling.

And tender curving lines of creamy spray;
To lend our hearts and spirits wholly
To the influence of mild-minded melancholy;
To muse and brood and live again in memory,   110
With those old faces of our infancy
Heaped over with a mound of grass,
Two handfuls of white dust, shut in an urn of brass!

6

Dear is the memory of our wedded lives,
And dear the last embraces of our wives   115
And their warm tears; but all hath suffered change;
For surely now our household hearths are cold,
Our sons inherit us, our looks are strange,
And we should come like ghosts to trouble joy.
Or else the island princes[4] overbold   120
Have eat our substance, and the minstrel sings
Before them of the ten years' war in Troy,
And our great deeds, as half-forgotten things.
Is there confusion in the little isle?
Let what is broken so remain.   125
The Gods are hard to reconcile;
'Tis hard to settle order once again.
There *is* confusion worse than death,
Trouble on trouble, pain on pain,
Long labor unto aged breath,   130
Sore tasks to hearts worn out by many wars
And eyes grown dim with gazing on the pilot-stars.

7

But, propped on beds of amaranth and moly,[5]
How sweet—while warm airs lull us, blowing lowly—
With half-dropped eyelid still,   135
Beneath a heaven dark and holy,
To watch the long bright river drawing slowly
His waters from the purple hill—
To hear the dewy echoes calling
From cave to cave through the thick-twined vine—   140
To watch the emerald-colored water falling
Through many a woven acanthus[6] wreath divine!
Only to hear and see the far-off sparkling brine,
Only to hear were sweet, stretched out beneath the pine.

8

The Lotos blooms below the barren peak,   145
The Lotos blows by every winding creek;
All day the wind breathes low with mellower tone;
Through every hollow cave and alley lone
Round and round the spicy downs the yellow Lotos dust is blown.
We have had enough of action, and of motion we,   150
Rolled to starboard, rolled to larboard, when the surge was seething free,
Where the wallowing monster spouted his foam-fountains in the sea.

---

4. Penelope's suitors.
5. A flower with magical properties mentioned by Homer. "Amaranth": a legendary unfading flower.

6. A plant resembling a thistle. Its leaves were the model for ornaments on Corinthian columns.

Let us swear an oath, and keep it with an equal mind,
In the hollow Lotos land to live and lie reclined
On the hills like Gods together, careless of mankind.   155
For they lie beside their nectar, and the bolts[7] are hurled
Far below them in the valleys, and the clouds are lightly curled
Round their golden houses, girdled with the gleaming world;
Where they smile in secret, looking over wasted lands,
Blight and famine, plague and earthquake, roaring deeps and fiery sands, 160
Clanging fights, and flaming towns, and sinking ships, and praying hands.
But they smile, they find a music centered in a doleful song
Steaming up, a lamentation and an ancient tale of wrong,
Like a tale of little meaning though the words are strong;
Chanted from an ill-used race of men that cleave the soil,   165
Sow the seed, and reap the harvest with enduring toil,
Storing yearly little dues of wheat, and wine and oil;
Till they perish and they suffer—some, 'tis whispered—down in hell
Suffer endless anguish, others in Elysian valleys dwell,
Resting weary limbs at last on beds of asphodel.[8]   170
Surely, surely, slumber is more sweet than toil, the shore
Than labor in the deep mid-ocean, wind and wave and oar;
O, rest ye, brother mariners, we will not wander more.

                                                          1832, 1842

Ulysses[1]

    It little profits that an idle king,
By this still hearth, among these barren crags,
Matched with an aged wife, I mete and dole
Unequal laws[2] unto a savage race,
That hoard, and sleep, and feed,[3] and know not me.   5

    I cannot rest from travel; I will drink
Life to the lees. All times I have enjoyed
Greatly, have suffered greatly, both with those
That loved me, and alone; on shore, and when
Through scudding drifts[4] the rainy Hyades   10
Vexed the dim sea. I am become a name;
For always roaming with a hungry heart
Much have I seen and known—cities of men
And manners, climates, councils, governments,

---

7. Thunderbolts.
8. A yellow lilylike flower supposed to grow in the Elysian valleys.
1. According to Dante, after the fall of Troy, Ulysses never returned to his island home of Ithaca. Instead he persuaded some of his followers to seek new experiences by a voyage of exploration westward out beyond the Strait of Gibraltar. In his inspiring speech to his aging crew he said: "Consider your origin: you were not made to live as brutes, but to pursue virtue and knowledge" (*Inferno* 26). Tennyson modified Dante's version by combining it with Homer's account (*Odyssey* 19–24). Thus Tennyson has Ulysses make his speech in Ithaca some time after his return home to

his reunion with his wife, Penelope, and his son, Telemachus, and, presumably, his resumption of administrative responsibilities involved in governing his kingdom.
    Tennyson himself stated that this poem expressed his own "need of going forward and braving the struggle of life" after the death of Hallam.
2. Measure out rewards and punishments.
3. Cf. *Hamlet* 4.4.33–35: "What is a man, / If his chief good . . . / Be but to sleep and feed? a beast, no more."
4. Driving showers of spray and rain; the "Hyades" are a group of stars whose rising was assumed to be followed by rain.

Myself not least, but honored of them all —   15
And drunk delight of battle with my peers,
Far on the ringing plains of windy Troy,
I am a part of all that I have met;
Yet all experience is an arch wherethrough
Gleams that untraveled world whose margin fades   20
Forever and forever when I move.
How dull it is to pause, to make an end,
To rust unburnished, not to shine in use![5]
As though to breathe were life! Life piled on life
Were all too little, and of one to me   25
Little remains; but every hour is saved
From that eternal silence, something more,
A bringer of new things; and vile it were
For some three suns to store and hoard myself,
And this gray spirit yearning in desire   30
To follow knowledge like a sinking star,
Beyond the utmost bound of human thought.

       This is my son, mine own Telemachus,
To whom I leave the scepter and the isle —
Well-loved of me, discerning to fulfill   35
This labor, by slow prudence to make mild
A rugged people, and through soft degrees
Subdue them to the useful and the good.
Most blameless is he, centered in the sphere
Of common duties, decent not to fail   40
In offices of tenderness, and pay
Meet adoration to my household gods,
When I am gone. He works his work, I mine.

       There lies the port; the vessel puffs her sail;
There gloom the dark, broad seas. My mariners,   45
Souls that have toiled, and wrought, and thought with me —
That ever with a frolic welcome took
The thunder and the sunshine, and opposed
Free hearts, free foreheads — you and I are old;
Old age hath yet his honor and his toil.   50
Death closes all; but something ere the end,
Some work of noble note, may yet be done,
Not unbecoming men that strove with Gods.
The lights begin to twinkle from the rocks;
The long day wanes; the slow moon climbs; the deep   55
Moans round with many voices. Come, my friends,
'Tis not too late to seek a newer world.
Push off, and sitting well in order smite
The sounding furrows; for my purpose holds
To sail beyond the sunset, and the baths   60
Of all the western stars,[6] until I die.

---

5. Cf. Ulysses' speech in *Troilus and Cressida* 3.3.
150–153: "Perseverance, dear my lord, / Keeps honour
bright; to have done, is to hang / Quite out of fashion,
like a rusty mail / in monumental mockery."

6. The outer ocean or river that, in Greek cosmology,
surrounded the flat circle of the earth and into which
the stars descended.

It may be that the gulfs will wash us down;
It may be we shall touch the Happy Isles,[7]
And see the great Achilles, whom we knew.
Though much is taken, much abides; and though   65
We are not now that strength which in old days
Moved earth and heaven, that which we are, we are—
One equal temper of heroic hearts,
Made weak by time and fate, but strong in will
To strive, to seek, to find, and not to yield.   70

1833   1842

Tithonus[1]

    The woods decay, the woods decay and fall,
The vapors weep their burthen to the ground,
Man comes and tills the field and lies beneath,
And after many a summer dies the swan.[2]
Me only cruel immortality   5
Consumes; I wither slowly in thine arms,[3]
Here at the quiet limit of the world,
A white-haired shadow roaming like a dream
The ever-silent spaces of the East,
Far-folded mists, and gleaming halls of morn.   10
    Alas! for this gray shadow, once a man—
So glorious in his beauty and thy choice,
Who madest him thy chosen, that he seemed
To his great heart none other than a God!
I asked thee, "Give me immortality."   15
Then didst thou grant mine asking with a smile,
Like wealthy men who care not how they give.
But thy strong Hours indignant worked their wills,
And beat me down and marred and wasted me,
And though they could not end me, left me maimed   20
To dwell in presence of immortal youth,
Immortal age beside immortal youth,
And all I was in ashes. Can thy love,
Thy beauty, make amends, though even now,
Close over us, the silver star,[4] thy guide,   25
Shines in those tremulous eyes that fill with tears
To hear me? Let me go; take back thy gift.
Why should a man desire in any way
To vary from the kindly race of men,
Or pass beyond the goal of ordinance[5]   30

---

7. In Greek myth the Islands of the Blessed, a paradise of perpetual summer, were thought to be located in the far-western ocean. They were peopled by great heroes who, without having died, had been translated there by the gods and made immortal. In later versions of the myth, the heroes became immortal after their deaths. Achilles, who had been killed at Troy, would have been one of these heroes.

1. Tithonus, a Trojan prince, was loved by the goddess of the dawn, Eos or Aurora, who obtained for him the gift of living forever but neglected to obtain for him the gift of everlasting youth.
2. Some species of swans live for at least fifty years.
3. I.e., the arms of Aurora.
4. The morning star that precedes the dawn.
5. What is decreed or ordained as human destiny.

Where all should pause, as is most meet for all?
    A soft air fans the cloud apart; there comes
A glimpse of that dark world where I was born.
Once more the old mysterious glimmer steals
From thy pure brows, and from thy shoulders pure,   35
And bosom beating with a heart renewed.
Thy cheek begins to redden through the gloom,
Thy sweet eyes brighten slowly close to mine,
Ere yet they blind the stars, and the wild team[6]
Which love thee, yearning for thy yoke, arise,   40
And shake the darkness from their loosened manes,
And beat the twilight into flakes of fire.
    Lo! ever thus thou growest beautiful
In silence, then before thine answer given
Departest, and thy tears are on my cheek.   45
    Why wilt thou ever scare me with thy tears,
And make me tremble lest a saying learnt,
In days far-off, on that dark earth, be true?
"The Gods themselves cannot recall their gifts."
    Ay me! ay me! with what another heart   50
In days far-off, and with what other eyes
I used to watch—if I be he that watched—
The lucid outline forming round thee; saw
The dim curls kindle into sunny rings;
Changed with thy mystic change, and felt my blood   55
Glow with the glow that slowly crimsoned all
Thy presence and thy portals, while I lay,
Mouth, forehead, eyelids, growing dewy-warm
With kisses balmier than half-opening buds
Of April, and could hear the lips that kissed   60
Whispering I knew not what of wild and sweet,
Like that strange song I heard Apollo sing,
While Ilion like a mist rose into towers.[7]
    Yet hold me not forever in thine East;
How can my nature longer mix with thine?   65
Coldly thy rosy shadows bathe me, cold
Are all thy lights, and cold my wrinkled feet
Upon thy glimmering thresholds, when the steam
Floats up from those dim fields about the homes
Of happy men that have the power to die,   70
And grassy barrows of the happier dead.
Release me, and restore me to the ground.
Thou seest all things, thou wilt see my grave;
Thou wilt renew thy beauty morn by morn,
I earth in earth forget these empty courts,   75
And thee returning on thy silver wheels.

1833, 1859   1860

6. The horses that draw Aurora's chariot into the sky   7. The walls of Troy (Ilion) were supposed to have
at daybreak.   been built to the strains of Apollo's music.

Break, Break, Break

Break, break, break,
   On thy cold gray stones, O Sea!
And I would that my tongue could utter
   The thoughts that arise in me.

O, well for the fisherman's boy,   5
   That he shouts with his sister at play!
O, well for the sailor lad,
   That he sings in his boat on the bay!

And the stately ships go on
   To their haven under the hill;   10
But O for the touch of a vanished hand,
   And the sound of a voice that is still!

Break, break, break,
   At the foot of thy crags, O Sea!
But the tender grace of a day that is dead   15
   Will never come back to me.

1834   1842

The Eagle: A Fragment

He clasps the crag with crooked hands;
Close to the sun in lonely lands,
Ringed with the azure world, he stands.

The wrinkled sea beneath him crawls:
He watches from his mountain walls,   5
And like a thunderbolt he falls.

1851

Locksley Hall[1]

Comrades, leave me here a little, while as yet 'tis early morn;
Leave me here, and when you want me, sound upon the bugle horn.

'Tis the place, and all around it, as of old, the curlews call,
Dreary gleams[2] about the moorland flying over Locksley Hall;

Locksley Hall, that in the distance overlooks the sandy tracts,   5
And the hollow ocean-ridges roaring into cataracts.

1. The situation in this poem—of a young man's being jilted by a woman who chose to marry a wealthy land-owner—may have been suggested to Tennyson by the experience of his brother Frederick, a hot-tempered man who had fallen in love with his cousin Julia Tennyson and who was similarly unsuccessful. It may also have been inspired by Tennyson's own frustrated courtship of Rosa Baring, who rejected the young poet in favor of a wealthy suitor. Concerning the ranting tone of the speaker (a tone accentuated by the heavily marked trochaic meter), Tennyson said: "The whole poem represents young life, its good side, its deficiencies, and its yearnings."
2. Tennyson stated that "gleams" does not refer to "curlews" flying but to streaks of light.

Many a night from yonder ivied casement, ere I went to rest,
Did I look on great Orion sloping slowly to the west.

Many a night I saw the Pleiads,[3] rising through the mellow shade,
Glitter like a swarm of fireflies tangled in a silver braid.   10

Here about the beach I wandered, nourishing a youth sublime
With the fairy tales of science, and the long result of time;

When the centuries behind me like a fruitful land reposed;
When I clung to all the present for the promise that it closed;[4]

When I dipped into the future far as human eye could see,   15
Saw the vision of the world and all the wonder that would be.—

In the spring a fuller crimson comes upon the robin's breast;
In the spring the wanton lapwing gets himself another crest;

In the spring a livelier iris changes on the burnished dove;[5]
In the spring a young man's fancy lightly turns to thoughts of love. 20

Then her cheek was pale and thinner than should be for one so young,
And her eyes on all my motions with a mute observance hung.

And I said, "My cousin Amy, speak, and speak the truth to me,
Trust me, cousin, all the current of my being sets to thee."

On her pallid cheek and forehead came a color and a light,   25
As I have seen the rosy red flushing in the northern night.

And she turned—her bosom shaken with a sudden storm of sighs—
All the spirit deeply dawning in the dark of hazel eyes—

Saying, "I have hid my feelings, fearing they should do me wrong";
Saying, "Dost thou love me, cousin?" weeping, "I have loved thee long." 30

Love took up the glass of Time, and turned it in his glowing hands;
Every moment, lightly shaken, ran itself in golden sands.

Love took up the harp of Life, and smote on all the chords with might;
Smote the chord of Self, that, trembling, passed in music out of sight.

Many a morning on the moorland did we hear the copses ring,   35
And her whisper thronged my pulses with the fullness of the spring.

Many an evening by the waters did we watch the stately ships,
And our spirits rushed together at the touching of the lips.

O my cousin, shallow-hearted! O my Amy, mine no more!
O the dreary, dreary moorland! O the barren, barren shore!   40

3. The Pleiades, a seven-starred constellation.   5. The rainbowlike colors of a dove's throat plumage
4. Enclosed.   are intensified in the mating season.

Falser than all fancy fathoms, falser than all songs have sung,
Puppet to a father's threat, and servile to a shrewish tongue!

Is it well to wish thee happy?—having known me—to decline
On a range of lower feelings and a narrower heart than mine!

Yet it shall be; thou shalt lower to his level day by day,   45
What is fine within thee growing coarse to sympathize with clay.

As the husband is, the wife is; thou art mated with a clown,[6]
And the grossness of his nature will have weight to drag thee down.

He will hold thee, when his passion shall have spent its novel force,
Something better than his dog, a little dearer than his horse.[7]   50

What is this? his eyes are heavy; think not they are glazed with wine.
Go to him, it is thy duty; kiss him, take his hand in thine.

It may be my lord is weary, that his brain is overwrought;
Soothe him with thy finer fancies, touch him with thy lighter thought.

He will answer to the purpose, easy things to understand—   55
Better thou wert dead before me, though I slew thee with my hand!

Better thou and I were lying, hidden from the heart's disgrace,
Rolled in one another's arms, and silent in a last embrace.

Cursed be the social wants that sin against the strength of youth!
Cursed be the social lies that warp us from the living truth!   60

Cursed be the sickly forms that err from honest Nature's rule!
Cursed be the gold that gilds the straitened[8] forehead of the fool!

Well—'tis well that I should bluster!—Hadst thou less unworthy proved—
Would to God—for I had loved thee more than ever wife was loved.

Am I mad, that I should cherish that which bears but bitter fruit?   65
I will pluck it from my bosom, though my heart be at the root.

Never, though my mortal summers to such length of years should come
As the many-wintered crow[9] that leads the clanging rookery home.

Where is comfort? in division of the records of the mind?
Can I part her from herself, and love her, as I knew her, kind?   70

I remember one that perished; sweetly did she speak and move;
Such a one do I remember, whom to look at was to love.

Can I think of her as dead, and love her for the love she bore?
No—she never loved me truly; love is love for evermore.

---

6. Boor.
7. Cf. Scott's *Ivanhoe*, chap. 29: "His war-horse—his
hunting hound are dearer to him than the despised
Jewess!"
8. Narrowed.
9. A rook, a long-lived bird.

Comfort? comfort scorned of devils! this is truth the poet[1] sings,   75
That a sorrow's crown of sorrow is remembering happier things.

Drug thy memories, lest thou learn it, lest thy heart be put to proof,
In the dead unhappy night, and when the rain is on the roof.

Like a dog, he hunts in dreams, and thou art staring at the wall,
Where the dying night-lamp flickers, and the shadows rise and fall.   80

Then a hand shall pass before thee, pointing to his drunken sleep,
To thy widowed[2] marriage-pillows, to the tears that thou wilt weep.

Thou shalt hear the "Never, never," whispered by the phantom years.
And a song from out the distance in the ringing of thine ears;

And an eye shall vex thee, looking ancient kindness on thy pain.   85
Turn thee, turn thee on thy pillow; get thee to thy rest again.

Nay, but Nature brings thee solace; for a tender voice will cry.
'Tis a purer life than thine, a lip to drain thy trouble dry.
Baby lips will laugh me down; my latest rival brings thee rest.
Baby fingers, waxen touches, press me from the mother's breast.   90

O, the child too clothes the father with a dearness not his due.
Half is thine and half is his; it will be worthy of the two.

O, I see thee old and formal, fitted to thy petty part,
With a little hoard of maxims preaching down a daughter's heart.

"They were dangerous guides the feelings—she herself was not exempt—   95
Truly, she herself had suffered"—Perish in thy self-contempt!

Overlive it—lower yet—be happy! wherefore should I care?
I myself must mix with action, lest I wither by despair.

What is that which I should turn to, lighting upon days like these?
Every door is barred with gold, and opens but to golden keys.   100

Every gate is thronged with suitors, all the markets overflow.
I have but an angry fancy; what is that which I should do?

I had been content to perish, falling on the foeman's ground,
When the ranks are rolled in vapor, and the winds are laid with sound.[3]

But the jingling of the guinea helps the hurt that Honor feels,   105
And the nations do but murmur, snarling at each other's heels.

Can I but relive in sadness? I will turn that earlier page.
Hide me from my deep emotion, O thou wondrous Mother-Age![4]

1. Dante's *Inferno* 5.121–123.
2. Presumably figurative. Her marriage having become a mockery, she is widowed.
3. It was once believed that the firing of artillery stilled the winds.
4. A happier past at life's beginning, which generated a more confident anticipation of the future (see also line 185).

Make me feel the wild pulsation that I felt before the strife,
When I heard my days before me, and the tumult of my life;   110

Yearning for the large excitement that the coming years would yield,
Eager-hearted as a boy when first he leaves his father's field,

And at night along the dusky highway near and nearer drawn,
Sees in heaven the light of London flaring like a dreary dawn;

And his spirit leaps within him to be gone before him then,   115
Underneath the light he looks at, in among the throngs of men;

Men, my brothers, men the workers, ever reaping something new;
That which they have done but earnest[5] of the things that they shall do.

For I dipped into the future, far as human eye could see,
Saw the Vision of the world, and all the wonder that would be;   120

Saw the heavens fill with commerce, argosies of magic sails,[6]
Pilots of the purple twilight, dropping down with costly bales;

Heard the heavens fill with shouting, and there rained a ghastly dew
From the nations' airy navies grappling in the central blue;

Far along the world-wide whisper of the south wind rushing warm,   125
With the standards of the peoples plunging through the thunderstorm;

Till the war drum throbbed no longer, and the battle flags were furled
In the Parliament of man, the Federation of the world.

There the common sense of most shall hold a fretful realm in awe,
And the kindly earth shall slumber, lapped in universal law.   130

So I triumphed ere my passion sweeping through me left me dry,
Left me with the palsied heart, and left me with the jaundiced eye;

Eye, to which all order festers, all things here are out of joint.
Science moves, but slowly, slowly, creeping on from point to point;

Slowly comes a hungry people, as a lion, creeping nigher,   135
Glares at one that nods and winks behind a slowly-dying fire.

Yet I doubt not through the ages one increasing purpose runs,
And the thoughts of men are widened with the process of the suns.

What is that to him that reaps not harvest of his youthful joys,
Though the deep heart of existence beat forever like a boy's?   140

Knowledge comes, but wisdom lingers, and I linger on the shore,
And the individual withers, and the world is more and more.

5. Pledge.   6. Probably airships, such as balloons.

Knowledge comes, but wisdom lingers, and he bears a laden breast,
Full of sad experience, moving toward the stillness of his rest.

Hark, my merry comrades call me, sounding on the bugle horn,   145
They to whom my foolish passion were a target for their scorn.

Shall it not be scorn to me to harp on such a moldered string?
I am shamed through all my nature to have loved so slight a thing.

Weakness to be wroth with weakness! woman's pleasure, woman's pain—
Nature made them blinder motions bounded in a shallower brain.   150

Woman is the lesser man, and all thy passions, matched with mine,
Are as moonlight unto sunlight, and as water unto wine—

Here at least, where nature sickens, nothing. Ah, for some retreat
Deep in yonder shining Orient, where my life began to beat.

Where in wild Mahratta-battle[7] fell my father evil-starred—   155
I was left a trampled orphan, and a selfish uncle's ward.

Or to burst all links of habit—there to wander far away,
On from island unto island at the gateways of the day.

Larger constellations burning, mellow moons and happy skies,
Breadths of tropic shade and palms in cluster, knots of Paradise.   160

Never comes the trader, never floats an European flag,
Slides the bird o'er lustrous woodland, swings the trailer[8] from the crag;

Droops the heavy-blossomed bower, hangs the heavy-fruited tree—
Summer isles of Eden lying in dark purple spheres of sea.

There methinks would be enjoyment more than in this march of mind,   165
In the steamship, in the railway, in the thoughts that shake mankind.

There the passions cramped no longer shall have scope and breathing space;
I will take some savage woman, she shall rear my dusky race.

Iron-jointed, supple-sinewed, they shall dive, and they shall run,
Catch the wild goat by the hair, and hurl their lances in the sun;   170

Whistle back the parrot's call, and leap the rainbows of the brooks,
Not with blinded eyesight poring over miserable books—

Fool, again the dream, the fancy! but I *know* my words are wild,
But I count the gray barbarian lower than the Christian child.

I, to herd with narrow foreheads, vacant of our glorious gains,   175
Like a beast with lower pleasures, like a beast with lower pains!

---

7. A reference to wars waged by a Hindu people   8. Vine.
against the British forces in India (1803 and 1817).

Mated with a squalid savage—what to me were sun or clime?
I the heir of all the ages, in the foremost files of time—

I that rather held it better men should perish one by one,
Than that earth should stand at gaze like Joshua's moon in Ajalon![9]   180

Not in vain the distance beacons. Forward, forward let us range,
Let the great world spin forever down the ringing grooves[1] of change.

Through the shadow of the globe we sweep into the younger day;
Better fifty years of Europe than a cycle of Cathay.[2]

Mother-Age—for mine I knew not—help me as when life begun;   185
Rift the hills, and roll the waters, flash the lightnings, weigh the sun.

O, I see the crescent promise of my spirit hath not set.
Ancient founts of inspiration well through all my fancy yet.

Howsoever these things be, a long farewell to Locksley Hall!
Now for me the woods may wither, now for me the roof-tree fall.   190

Comes a vapor from the margin, blackening over heath and holt,
Cramming all the blast before it, in its breast a thunderbolt.

Let it fall on Locksley Hall, with rain or hail, or fire or snow;
For the mighty wind arises, roaring seaward, and I go.
1837–38   1842

From THE PRINCESS[1]

Sweet and Low

Sweet and low, sweet and low,
   Wind of the western sea,
Low, low, breathe and blow,
   Wind of the western sea!
Over the rolling waters go,   5
Come from the dying moon, and blow,
   Blow him again to me;
While my little one, while my pretty one, sleeps.

Sleep and rest, sleep and rest,
   Father will come to thee soon;   10

9. At the command of Joshua, the sun and moon stood still while the Israelites completed the slaughter of their enemies in the valley of Ajalon (Joshua 10.12–13).
1. Railroad tracks. Tennyson at one time had the impression that train wheels ran in grooved rails.
2. China, regarded in the 19th century as a static, unprogressive country.

1. *The Princess* (1847), a long narrative poem, contains interludes in which occasional songs are sung. The six of these in our selection, some of which first appeared in later editions of the poem, rank among the finest of Tennyson's lyrics, and various 19th- and 20th-century composers have set them to music.

Rest, rest, on mother's breast,
  Father will come to thee soon;
Father will come to his babe in the nest,
  Silver sails all out of the west
    Under the silver moon;   15
  Sleep, my little one, sleep, my pretty one, sleep.

1849   1850

The Splendor Falls

The splendor falls on castle walls
  And snowy summits old in story;
The long light shakes across the lakes,
  And the wild cataract leaps in glory.
Blow, bugle, blow, set the wild echoes flying,   5
Blow, bugle; answer, echoes, dying, dying, dying.

O, hark, O, hear! how thin and clear,
  And thinner, clearer, farther going!
O, sweet and far from cliff and scar[2]
  The horns of Elfland faintly blowing!   10
Blow, let us hear the purple glens replying,
Blow, bugle; answer, echoes, dying, dying, dying.

O love, they die in yon rich sky,
  They faint on hill or field or river;
Our echoes roll from soul to soul,   15
  And grow forever and forever.
Blow, bugle, blow, set the wild echoes flying,
And answer, echoes, answer, dying, dying, dying.

                                                                 1850

Tears, Idle Tears[3]

  Tears, idle tears, I know not what they mean,
Tears from the depth of some divine despair
Rise in the heart, and gather to the eyes,
In looking on the happy autumn-fields,
And thinking of the days that are no more.   5

  Fresh as the first beam glittering on a sail,
That brings our friends up from the underworld,
Sad as the last which reddens over one
That sinks with all we love below the verge;
So sad, so fresh, the days that are no more.   10

2. Mountainside.
3. Tennyson commented: "This song came to me on the yellowing autumn-tide at Tintern Abbey, full for me of its bygone memories." This locale would be for him associated both with Wordsworth's *Tintern Abbey* and with memories of Hallam, who was buried across the Bristol Channel in this area. "It is what I have always felt even from a boy, and what as a boy I called the 'passion of the past.' And it is so always with me now; it is the distance that charms me in the landscape, the picture and the past, and not the immediate today in which I move."

Ah, sad and strange as in dark summer dawns
The earliest pipe of half-awakened birds
To dying ears, when unto dying eyes
The casement slowly grows a glimmering square;
So sad, so strange, the days that are no more.   15

Dear as remembered kisses after death,
And sweet as those by hopeless fancy feigned
On lips that are for others; deep as love,
Deep as first love, and wild with all regret;
O Death in Life, the days that are no more!   20

                                                                  1847

Ask Me No More

Ask me no more: the moon may draw the sea;
    The cloud may stoop from heaven and take the shape,
    With fold to fold, of mountain or of cape;
But O too fond, when have I answered thee?
                    Ask me no more.   5

Ask me no more: what answer should I give?
    I love not hollow cheek or faded eye:
    Yet, O my friend, I will not have thee die!
Ask me no more, lest I should bid thee live;
                    Ask me no more.   10

Ask me no more: thy fate and mine are sealed;
    I strove against the stream and all in vain;
    Let the great river take me to the main.
No more, dear love, for at a touch I yield;
                    Ask me no more.   15

1849   1850

Now Sleeps the Crimson Petal

Now sleeps the crimson petal, now the white;
Nor waves the cypress in the palace walk;
Nor winks the gold fin in the porphyry font.
The firefly wakens; waken thou with me.

Now droops the milk-white peacock like a ghost,   5
And like a ghost she glimmers on to me.

Now lies the Earth all Danaë[4] to the stars,
And all thy heart lies open unto me.

---

4. Danaë, a Greek princess, was confined in a metal tower by her father to prevent suitors from coming near her. Zeus, however, succeeded in visiting her in the form of a shower of gold. Their offspring was the hero Perseus.

Now slides the silent meteor on, and leaves
A shining furrow, as thy thoughts in me.   10

Now folds the lily all her sweetness up,
And slips into the bosom of the lake.
So fold thyself, my dearest, thou, and slip
Into my bosom and be lost in me.

1847

Come Down, O Maid[5]

Come down, O maid, from yonder mountain height.
What pleasure lives in height (the shepherd sang),
In height and cold, the splendor of the hills?
But cease to move so near the heavens, and cease
To glide a sunbeam by the blasted pine,   5
To sit a star upon the sparkling spire;
And come, for Love is of the valley, come,
For Love is of the valley, come thou down
And find him; by the happy threshold, he,
Or hand in hand with Plenty in the maize,   10
Or red with spirted purple of the vats,
Or foxlike in the vine;[6] nor cares to walk
With Death and Morning on the Silver Horns,[7]
Nor wilt thou snare him in the white ravine,
Nor find him dropped upon the firths of ice,[8]   15
That huddling slant in furrow-cloven falls
To roll the torrent out of dusky doors.[9]
But follow; let the torrent dance thee down
To find him in the valley; let the wild
Lean-headed eagles yelp alone, and leave   20
The monstrous ledges there to slope, and spill
Their thousand wreaths of dangling water-smoke,
That like a broken purpose waste in air.
So waste not thou, but come; for all the vales
Await thee; azure pillars of the hearth[1]   25
Arise to thee; the children call, and I
Thy shepherd pipe, and sweet is every sound,
Sweeter thy voice, but every sound is sweet;
Myriads of rivulets hurrying through the lawn,
The moan of doves in immemorial elms,   30
And murmuring of innumerable bees.

1847

---

5. Written during Tennyson's visit to the Swiss Alps in 1846, after he had seen Mt. Jungfrau ("The Maiden").
6. Cf. the Song of Solomon 2.15.
7. Mountain peaks.
8. Glaciers.

9. Heaps of rock and refuse at the base of a glacier through which the mountain torrent forces its way down to the valley below.
1. Columns of smoke from the houses in the valley.

["The Woman's Cause Is Man's"][2]

"Blame not thyself too much," I said, "nor blame
Too much the sons of men and barbarous laws;   240
These were the rough ways of the world till now.
Henceforth thou hast a helper, me, that know
The woman's cause is man's: they rise or sink
Together, dwarfed or godlike, bond or free:
For she that out of Lethe scales with man   245
The shining steps of Nature, shares with man
His nights, his days, moves with him to one goal,
Stays all the fair young planet in her hands—
If she be small, slight-natured, miserable,
How shall men grow? but work no more alone!   250
Our place is much: as far as in us lies
We two will serve them both in aiding her—
Will clear away the parasitic forms
That seem to keep her up but drag her down—
Will leave her space to burgeon out of all   255
Within her—let her make herself her own
To give or keep, to live and learn and be
All that not harms distinctive womanhood.
For woman is not undevelopt man,
But diverse: could we make her as the man,   260
Sweet Love were slain: his dearest bond is this,
Not like to like, but like in difference.
Yet in the long years liker must they grow;
The man be more of woman, she of man;
He gain in sweetness and in moral height,   265
Nor lose the wrestling thews that throw the world;
She mental breadth, nor fail in childward care,
Nor lose the childlike in the larger mind;
Till at the last she set herself to man,
Like perfect music unto noble words;   270
And so these twain, upon the skirts of Time,
Sit side by side, full-summed in all their powers,
Dispensing harvest, sowing the To-be,
Self-reverent each and reverencing each,
Distinct in individualities,   275
But like each other even as those who love.
Then comes the statelier Eden back to men:
Then reign the world's great bridals, chaste and calm:
Then springs the crowning race of humankind.
May these things be!"
                          Sighing she spoke "I fear   280
They will not."
                     Dear, but let us type them now

---

2. *The Princess* tells the story of a prince who courts the young and beautiful Princess Ida, who has established a university from which men are excluded; she has also vowed she will never marry. At the end she is persuaded that her feminist experiment was a failure, but the prince assures her that ideal relations between men and women may be achieved in the future. Our selection, covering the prince's key speech, is from book 7.

> In our own lives, and this proud watchword rest
> Of equal; seeing either sex alone
> Is half itself, and in true marriage lies
> Nor equal, nor unequal. each fulfils   285
> Defect in each, and always thought in thought,
> Purpose in purpose, will in will, they grow,
> The single pure and perfect animal,
> The two-celled heart beating, with one full stroke,
> Life."
>   And again sighing she spoke: "A dream   290
>   That once was mine! what woman taught you this?"

1839–47   1847

In Memoriam A. H. H. Like most of Tennyson's writings, *In Memoriam* shows his debt to earlier poetry. In its celebration of male friendship, as Christopher Ricks has shown, the poem has many affinities with Shakespeare's *Sonnets*, and as an elegy it is, of course, in the tradition of Milton's *Lycidas* and Shelley's *Adonais*. Its structure, however, is strikingly different. Resembling a song cycle more than a symphony, it is made up of individual lyric units, seemingly self-sustaining, that may be enjoyed by themselves even though the full pleasure to be derived from each component depends on its relationship to the poem as a whole. The circumstances of the poem's composition help to explain how this new kind of elegy was evolved. The sudden death of Arthur Hallam at the age of twenty-two had a profound effect on Tennyson. The young poet had cherished Hallam not only as his closest friend and the fiancé of his sister but as an all-wise counselor on whose judgment he depended for guidance. This fatherly prop having been pulled away, Tennyson was overwhelmed with doubts about the meaning of life and humanity's role in the universe, doubts reinforced by his own study of geology and other sciences. As a kind of poetic diary recording the variety of his feelings and reflections he began to compose a series of lyrics. These "short swallow-flights of song," as he calls them, written at intervals over a period of seventeen years, were later arranged into one long elegy in which a progressive development from despair to some sort of hope, as in section 95, is recorded.

Some of the early sections of the poem resemble traditional pastoral elegies, including those portraying the voyage during which Hallam's body was brought to England for burial (sections 9 to 15 and 19). Other early sections portraying the speaker's loneliness, in which even Christmas festivities seem joyless (sections 28 to 30), are more distinctive. With the passage of time, indicated by anniversaries and by recurring changes of the seasons, the speaker comes to accept the loss and to assert his belief in life and in an afterlife. In particular the recurring Christmases (sections 28, 78, 104) indicate the stages of his development, yet the pattern of progress in the poem is not a simple unimpeded movement upward. Dramatic conflicts recur throughout. Thus the most intense expression of doubt occurs not at the beginning of *In Memoriam* but as late as sections 54, 55, and 56.

The quatrain form in which the whole poem is written is usually called the "*In Memoriam* stanza," although it had been occasionally used by earlier poets. So rigid a form taxed Tennyson's ingenuity in achieving variety, but it is one of several means by which the diverse parts of the poem are knitted together.

The introductory section, consisting of eleven stanzas, is commonly referred to as the "Prologue," although Tennyson did not assign a title to it. It was written in 1849 after the rest of the poem was complete.

From In Memoriam A. H. H.

Strong Son of God, immortal Love,[2]
  Whom we, that have not seen thy face,
  By faith, and faith alone, embrace,
Believing where we cannot prove;[3]

Thine are these orbs[4] of light and shade;   5
  Thou madest Life in man and brute;
  Thou madest Death; and lo, thy foot
Is on the skull which thou hast made.

Thou wilt not leave us in the dust:
  Thou madest man, he knows not why,   10
  He thinks he was not made to die;
And thou hast made him: thou art just.

Thou seemest human and divine,
  The highest, holiest manhood, thou.
  Our wills are ours, we know not how;   15
Our wills are ours, to make them thine.

Our little systems[5] have their day;
  They have their day and cease to be;
  They are but broken lights of thee,
And thou, O Lord, art more than they.   20

We have but faith: we cannot know,
  For knowledge is of things we see;
  And yet we trust it comes from thee,
A beam in darkness: let it grow.

Let knowledge grow from more to more,   25
  But more of reverence in us dwell;
  That mind and soul, according well,
May make one music as before,[6]

But vaster. We are fools and slight;
  We mock thee when we do not fear: 30
  But help thy foolish ones to bear;
Help thy vain worlds to bear thy light.

Forgive what seemed my sin in me,
  What seemed my worth since I began;

1. Died 1833.
2. For the first line of the poem, cf. George Herbert, *Love:* "Immortal Love, Author of this great frame, / Sprung from that beauty which can never fade, / How hath Man parceled out Thy glorious name, / And thrown it on the dust which Thou hast made?" [R. W. Hill's note].
3. Cf. John 20.24–29, in which Jesus rebukes Thomas for his doubts concerning the Resurrection: "Blessed are they that have not seen, and yet have believed."
4. The sun and moon (according to Tennyson's note).
5. Systems of religion and philosophy.
6. As in the days of fixed religious faith.

For merit lives from man to man,   35
And not from man, O Lord, to thee.

Forgive my grief for one removed,
     Thy creature, whom I found so fair.
       I trust he lives in thee, and there
I find him worthier to be loved.   40

Forgive these wild and wandering cries,
     Confusions of a wasted[7] youth;
       Forgive them where they fail in truth,
And in thy wisdom make me wise.

1849

1

I held it truth, with him who sings
     To one clear harp in divers tones,[8]
       That men may rise on stepping stones
Of their dead selves to higher things.

But who shall so forecast the years   5
     And find in loss a gain to match?
       Or reach a hand through time to catch
The far-off interest of tears?

Let Love clasp Grief lest both be drowned,
     Let darkness keep her raven gloss.   10
       Ah, sweeter to be drunk with loss,
To dance with Death, to beat the ground,

Than that the victor Hours should scorn
     The long result of love, and boast,
       "Behold the man that loved and lost,   15
But all he was is overworn."

2

Old yew, which graspest at the stones
     That name the underlying dead,
       Thy fibers net the dreamless head,
Thy roots are wrapped about the bones.

The seasons bring the flower again,   5
     And bring the firstling to the flock;
       And in the dusk of thee the clock
Beats out the little lives of men.

O, not for thee the glow, the bloom,
     Who changest not in any gale,   10

---

7. Desolated.   8. Identified by Tennyson as Goethe.

Nor branding summer suns avail
To touch thy thousand years of gloom;[9]

And gazing on thee, sullen tree,
    Sick for[1] thy stubborn hardihood,
    I seem to fail from out my blood   15
And grow incorporate into thee.

3

O Sorrow, cruel fellowship,
    O Priestess in the vaults of Death,
    O sweet and bitter in a breath,
What whispers from thy lying lip?

"The stars," she whispers, "blindly run;   5
    A web is woven across the sky;
    From out waste places comes a cry,
And murmurs from the dying sun;

"And all the phantom, Nature, stands—
    With all the music in her tone,   10
    A hollow echo of my own—
A hollow form with empty hands."

And shall I take a thing so blind,
    Embrace her[2] as my natural good;
    Or crush her, like a vice of blood,   15
Upon the threshold of the mind?

4

To Sleep I give my powers away;
    My will is bondsman to the dark;
    I sit within a helmless bark,
And with my heart I muse and say:

O heart, how fares it with thee now,   5
    That thou should fail from thy desire,
    Who scarcely darest to inquire,
"What is it makes me beat so low?"

Something it is which thou hast lost,
    Some pleasure from thine early years.   10
    Break thou deep vase of chilling tears,
That grief hath shaken into frost![3]

9. The ancient yew tree, growing in the grounds near the clock tower and church where Hallam was to be buried, seems neither to blossom in spring nor to change from its dark mournful color in summer. "Thousand years": cf. Book of Common Prayer Psalm 90: "For a thousand years in Thy sight are but as yesterday when it is past, and as a watch in the night."

1. Envying or longing to share.
2. I.e., sorrow.
3. Water can be brought below freezing-point and not turn into ice—if it be kept still; but if it be moved suddenly it turns into ice and may break a vase [Tennyson's note].

Such clouds of nameless trouble cross
    All night below the darkened eyes;
    With morning wakes the will, and cries,   15
"Thou shalt not be the fool of loss."

5

I sometimes hold it half a sin
    To put in words the grief I feel;
    For words, like Nature, half reveal
And half conceal the Soul within.

But, for the unquiet heart and brain,   5
    A use in measured language lies;
    The sad mechanic exercise,
Like dull narcotics, numbing pain.[4]

In words, like weeds,[5] I'll wrap me o'er,
    Like coarsest clothes against the cold;
    But that large grief which these enfold   10
Is given in outline and no more.

6

One writes, that "Other friends remain,"
    That "Loss is common to the race"—
    And common is the commonplace,
And vacant chaff well meant for grain.

That loss is common would not make   5
    My own less bitter, rather more:
    Too common! Never morning wore
To evening, but some heart did break.

O father, wheresoe'er thou be,
    Who pledgest[6] now thy gallant son;   10
    A shot, ere half thy draft be done,
Hath stilled the life that beat from thee.

O mother, praying God will save
    Thy sailor—while thy head is bowed,
    His heavy-shotted hammock-shroud   15
Drops in his vast and wandering grave.

Ye know no more than I who wrought
    At that last hour to please him well;[7]
    Who mused on all I had to tell,
And something written, something thought;   20

---

4. Cf. Keats, *Ode to a Nightingale*, lines 1–3: "A
drowsy numbness pains / My sense, as though of hem-
lock I had drunk, / Or emptied some dull opiate to the
drains" [noted by Susan Shatto].
5. Garments.

6. Toasts.
7. According to Tennyson's son, his father had discovered that he had been writing a letter to Hallam during
the very hour when his friend died.

Expecting still his advent home;
  And ever met him on his way
    With wishes, thinking, "here today,"
Or "here tomorrow will he come."

O somewhere, meek, the unconscious dove,   25
  That sittest ranging[8] golden hair;
    And glad to find thyself so fair,
Poor child, that waitest for thy love!

For now her father's chimney glows
  In expectation of a guest;   30
    And thinking "this will please him best,"
She takes a riband or a rose;

For he will see them on tonight;
  And with the thought her color burns;
    And, having left the glass, she turns   35
Once more to set a ringlet right;

And, even when she turned, the curse
  Had fallen, and her future Lord
    Was drowned in passing through the ford,
Or killed in falling from his horse.   40

O what to her shall be the end?
  And what to me remains of good?
    To her, perpetual maidenhood,
And unto me no second friend.

7

Dark house,[9] by which once more I stand
  Here in the long unlovely street,
    Doors, where my heart was used to beat
So quickly, waiting for a hand,

A hand that can be clasped no more—   5
  Behold me, for I cannot sleep,
    And like a guilty thing I creep
At earliest morning to the door.

He is not here;[1] but far away
  The noise of life begins again,   10
    And ghastly through the drizzling rain
On the bald street breaks the blank day.

8

A happy lover who has come
  To look on her that loves him well,

---

8. Arranging.
9. The house on Wimpole Street, in London, where
Hallam had lived.

1. Perhaps evoking the words of the angel at Jesus'
empty tomb in Luke 24.6: "He is not here, but is risen."

Who 'lights and rings the gateway bell,
And learns her gone and far from home;

He saddens, all the magic light   5
  Dies off at once from bower and hall,
  And all the place is dark, and all
The chambers emptied of delight:

So find I every pleasant spot
  In which we two were wont to meet,   10
  The field, the chamber, and the street,
For all is dark where thou art not.

Yet as that other, wandering there
  In those deserted walks, may find
  A flower beat with rain and wind,   15
Which once she fostered up with care;

So seems it in my deep regret,
  O my forsaken heart, with thee
  And this poor flower of poesy
Which little cared for fades not yet.   20

But since it pleased a vanished eye,[2]
  I go to plant it on his tomb,
  That if it can it there may bloom,
Or dying, there at least may die.

                         9

Fair ship, that from the Italian shore
  Sailest the placid ocean-plains
  With my lost Arthur's loved remains,
Spread thy full wings, and waft him o'er.

So draw him home to those that mourn   5
  In vain; a favorable speed
  Ruffle thy mirrored mast, and lead
Through prosperous floods his holy urn.

All night no ruder air perplex
  Thy sliding keel, till Phosphor,[3] bright   10
  As our pure love, through early light
Shall glimmer on the dewey decks.

Sphere all your lights around, above;
  Sleep, gentle heavens, before the prow;
  Sleep, gentle winds, as he sleeps now,   15
My friend, the brother of my love;

2. Hallam expressed enthusiasm for Tennyson's early   3. The morning star.
poetry in a review written in 1831.

My Arthur, whom I shall not see
    Till all my widowed race be run;
    Dear as the mother to the son,
More than my brothers are to me.   20

10

I hear the noise about thy keel;
    I hear the bell struck in the night;
    I see the cabin window bright;
I see the sailor at the wheel.

Thou bring'st the sailor to his wife,   5
    And traveled men from foreign lands;
    And letters unto trembling hands;
And, thy dark freight, a vanished life.

So bring him; we have idle dreams;
    This look of quiet flatters thus   10
    Our home-bred fancies. O, to us,
The fools of habit, sweeter seems

To rest beneath the clover sod,
    That takes the sunshine and the rains,
    Or where the kneeling hamlet drains   15
The chalice of the grapes of God;[4]

Than if with thee the roaring wells
    Should gulf him fathom-deep in brine,
    And hands so often clasped in mine,
Should toss with tangle[5] and with shells.   20

11

Calm is the morn without a sound,
    Calm as to suit a calmer grief,
    And only through the faded leaf
The chestnut pattering to the ground;

Calm and deep peace on this high wold,[6]   5
    And on these dews that drench the furze,
    And all the silvery gossamers
That twinkle into green and gold;

Calm and still light on yon great plain
    That sweeps with all its autumn bowers,   10
    And crowded farms and lessening towers,
To mingle with the bounding main;

---

4. Referring to a burial inside a church building rather
than in the churchyard.

5. Seaweed.
6. Open countryside.

Calm and deep peace in this wide air,
  These leaves that redden to the fall,
  And in my heart, if calm at all,   15
If any calm, a calm despair;

Calm on the seas, and silver sleep,
  And waves that sway themselves in rest,
  And dead calm in that noble breast
Which heaves but with the heaving deep.[7]   20

12

Lo, as a dove when up she springs
  To bear through Heaven a tale of woe,
  Some dolorous message knit below
The wild pulsation of her wings;

Like her I go; I cannot stay;   5
  I leave this mortal ark behind,[8]
  A weight of nerves without a mind,
And leave the cliffs, and haste away

O'er ocean-mirrors rounded large,
  And reach the glow of southern skies,   10
  And see the sails at distance rise,
And linger weeping on the marge,

And saying; "Comes he thus, my friend?
  Is this the end of all my care?"
  And circle moaning in the air: 15
"Is this the end? Is this the end?"

And forward dart again, and play
  About the prow, and back return
  To where the body sits, and learn
That I have been an hour away.   20

13

Tears of the widower, when he sees
  A late-lost form that sleep reveals,
  And moves his doubtful arms, and feels
Her place is empty, fall like these;

Which weep a loss forever new,   5
  A void where heart on heart reposed;

---

7. It is now the autumn of 1833, and the poet imagines that Hallam's body was already being brought back by ship to England. The date of the actual voyage seems to have been later in the year.
8. According to Christopher Ricks, the account of the imagined flight of the soul refers to Genesis 8.8, when Noah first sends a dove from the ark to discover whether the flood has subsided, "but the dove found no rest for the sole of her foot, and she returned unto him into the ark, for the waters were on the face of the earth."

And, where warm hands have pressed and
   closed,
Silence, till I be silent too;

Which weep the comrade of my choice,
   An awful thought, a life removed,   10
   The human-hearted man I loved,
A Spirit, not a breathing voice.

Come, Time, and teach me, many years,
   I do not suffer in a dream;
   For now so strange do these things seem,   15
Mine eyes have leisure for their tears,

My fancies time to rise on wing,
   And glance about the approaching sails,
   As though they brought but merchants'
     bales,
And not the burthen that they bring.[9]   20

14

If one should bring me this report,
   That thou[1] hadst touched the land today,
   And I went down unto the quay;[2]
And found thee lying in the port;

And standing, muffled round with woe,   5
   Should see thy passengers in rank
   Come stepping lightly down the plank
And beckoning unto those they know;

And if along with these should come
   The man I held as half divine,   10
   Should strike a sudden hand in mine,
And ask a thousand things of home;

And I should tell him all my pain,
   And how my life had drooped of late,
   And he should sorrow o'er my state   15
And marvel what possessed my brain;

And I perceived no touch of change,
   No hint of death in all his frame,
   But found him all in all the same,
I should not feel it to be strange.   20

15

Tonight the winds begin to rise
   And roar from yonder dropping day;

9. The poet asks Time to teach him to confront the
"awful" fact of what has happened (line 10) so that he
will not delude himself by fancying the ship is bearing
only merchandise and not the body of his friend.

1. I.e., the ship.
2. By 1850 the accepted pronunciation of "quay"
would rhyme with *key*, but Tennyson reverts to an earlier pronunciation, *kay*.

The last red leaf is whirled away,
The rooks are blown about the skies;

The forest cracked, the waters curled,   5
    The cattle huddled on the lea;
    And wildly dashed on tower and tree
The sunbeam strikes along the world:

And but for fancies, which aver
    That all thy motions gently pass   10
    Athwart a plane of molten glass,
I scarce could brook the strain and stir

That makes the barren branches loud;
    And but for fear it is not so,
    The wild unrest that lives in woe   15
Would dote and pore on yonder cloud

That rises upward always higher,
    And onward drags a laboring breast,
    And topples round the dreary west,
A looming bastion fringed with fire.   20

                    *   *   *

19

The Danube to the Severn[3] gave
    The darkened heart that beat no more;
    They laid him by the pleasant shore,
And in the hearing of the wave.

There twice a day the Severn fills;   5
    The salt sea water passes by,
    And hushes half the babbling Wye,[4]
And makes a silence in the hills.

The Wye is hushed nor moved along,
    And hushed my deepest grief of all,   10
    When filled with tears that cannot fall,
I brim with sorrow drowning song.

The tide flows down, the wave again
    Is vocal in its wooded walls;
    My deeper anguish also falls,   15
And I can speak a little then.

                    *   *   *

3. Hallam died at Vienna on the Danube. His burial place is on the banks of the Severn, a tidal river in the southwest of England.
4. The water of the Wye River, a tributary of the Severn, is dammed up as the tide flows in, and its sound is silenced until, with the turn of the tide, its "wave" once more becomes "vocal" (lines 13–14); these stanzas were written at Tintern Abbey in the Wye River country.

21

I sing to him that rests below,
   And, since the grasses round me wave,
   I take the grasses of the grave,[5]
And make them pipes whereon to blow.

The traveler hears me now and then,   5
   And sometimes harshly will he speak:
   "This fellow would make weakness weak,
And melt the waxen hearts of men."

Another answers: "Let him be,
   He loves to make parade of pain,   10
   That with his piping he may gain
The praise that comes to constancy."

A third is wroth: "Is this an hour
   For private sorrow's barren song,
   When more and more the people throng   15
The chairs and thrones of civil power?

"A time to sicken and to swoon,
   When Science reaches forth her arms[6]
   To feel from world to world, and charms
Her secret from the latest moon?"[7]   20

Behold, ye speak an idle thing;
   Ye never knew the sacred dust.
   I do but sing because I must,
And pipe but as the linnets sing:

And one is glad; her note is gay,   25
   For now her little ones have ranged;
   And one is sad; her note is changed,
Because her brood is stolen away.

22

The path by which we twain did go,
   Which led by tracts that pleased us well,
   Through four sweet years arose and fell,
From flower to flower, from snow to snow;

And we with singing cheered the way,   5
   And, crowned with all the season lent,
   From April on to April went,
And glad at heart from May to May.

---

5. The poet assumes that the burial was in the church-
yard; in fact, Hallam's body was interred in a vault inside St. Andrews church at Clevedon, Somersetshire,
on January 3, 1834 (see section 10, lines 11–16).

6. Astronomical instruments such as telescopes.
7. Probably alluding to the discovery in 1846 of the
planet Neptune and its moon.

But where the path we walked began
  To slant the fifth autumnal slope,[8]   10
  As we descended following Hope,
There sat the Shadow feared of man;

Who broke our fair companionship,
  And spread his mantle dark and cold,
  And wrapped thee formless in the fold,   15
And dulled the murmur on thy lip,

And bore thee where I could not see
  Nor follow, though I walk in haste,
  And think that somewhere in the waste
The Shadow sits and waits for me.   20

23

Now, sometimes in my sorrow shut,
  Or breaking into song by fits,
  Alone, alone, to where he sits,
The Shadow cloaked from head to foot,

Who keeps the keys of all the creeds,   5
  I wander, often falling lame,
  And looking back to whence I came,
Or on to where the pathway leads;

And crying, How changed from where it ran
  Through lands where not a leaf was dumb,
  But all the lavish hills would hum   10
The murmur of a happy Pan;

When each by turns was guide to each,
  And Fancy light from Fancy caught,
  And Thought leapt out to wed with Thought   15
Ere Thought could wed itself with Speech;

And all we met was fair and good,
  And all was good that Time could bring,
  And all the secret of the Spring
Moved in the chambers of the blood;   20

And many an old philosophy
  On Argive heights[9] divinely sang,
  And round us all the thicket rang
To many a flute of Arcady.[1]

8. Hallam died in early autumn (September 15, 1833) in the fifth year of the friendship.
9. Argos, a Greek city renowned for its music.
1. A sheep-raising region in Greece associated with pastoral poetry.

24

And was the day of my delight
  As pure and perfect as I say?
  The very source and fount of day
Is dashed with wandering isles of night.[2]

If all was good and fair we met,   5
  This earth had been the Paradise
  It never looked to human eyes
Since our first sun arose and set.

And is it that the haze of grief
  Makes former gladness loom so great?   10
  The lowness of the present state,
That sets the past in this relief?

Or that the past will always win
  A glory from its being far,
  And orb into the perfect star   15
We saw not when we moved therein?[3]

25

I know that this was Life—the track
  Whereon with equal feet we fared;
  And then, as now, the day prepared
The daily burden for the back.

But this it was that made me move   5
  As light as carrier birds in air;
  I loved the weight I had to bear,
Because it needed help of Love;

Nor could I weary, heart or limb,
  When mighty Love would cleave in twain   10
  The lading[4] of a single pain,
And part it, giving half to him.

26

Still onward winds the dreary way;
  I with it, for I long to prove
  No lapse of moons can canker Love,
Whatever fickle tongues may say.

And if that eye which watches guilt   5
  And goodness, and hath power to see

2. Moving spots on the sun.
3. The poet speculates whether past experiences seem so much more "pure and perfect" (line 2) than present ones because they are far distant from us in time just as our planet earth would have the deceptive appearance of being a perfect orb if we viewed it from a great distance in space, as from another planet (cf. *Locksley Hall Sixty Years After*, lines 187–192).
4. Burden.

Within the green the mouldered tree,
And towers fallen as soon as built—

O, if indeed that eye foresee
   Or see—in Him is no before—   10
   In more of life true life no more
And Love the indifference to be,

Then might I find, ere yet the morn
   Breaks hither over Indian seas,
   That Shadow waiting with the keys,   15
To shroud me from my proper scorn.[5]

27

I envy not in any moods
   The captive void of noble rage,
   The linnet born within the cage,
That never knew the summer woods;

I envy not the beast that takes   5
   His license in the field of time,
   Unfettered by the sense of crime,
To whom a conscience never wakes;

Nor, what may count itself as blest,
   The heart that never plighted troth   10
   But stagnates in the weeds of sloth;
Nor any want-begotten rest.[6]

I hold it true, whate'er befall;
   I feel it, when I sorrow most;
   'Tis better to have loved and lost   15
Than never to have loved at all.

28

The time draws near the birth of Christ.[7]
   The moon is hid, the night is still;
   The Christmas bells from hill to hill
Answer each other in the mist.

Four voices of four hamlets round,   5
   From far and near, on mead and moor,
   Swell out and fail, as if a door
Were shut between me and the sound;

---

5. The Deity, being outside time, sees (rather than foresees) whether or not the rest of life ("more of life," line 11) will be pointless. If pointless then the way for the speaker to deal with his self-scorn ("proper scorn") might be to seek death.

6. Complacency resulting from some deficiency or "want."

7. The first Christmas after Hallam's death (1833); the setting is Tennyson's family home in Lincolnshire.

Each voice four changes[8] on the wind,
   That now dilate, and now decrease,   10
   Peace and goodwill, goodwill and peace,
Peace and goodwill, to all mankind.

This year I slept and woke with pain,
   I almost wished no more to wake,
   And that my hold on life would break   15
Before I heard those bells again;

But they my troubled spirit rule,
   For they controlled me when a boy;
   They bring me sorrow touched with joy,
The merry, merry bells of Yule.   20

29

With such compelling cause to grieve
   As daily vexes household peace,
   And chains regret to his decease,
How dare we keep our Christmas eve;

Which brings no more a welcome guest   5
   To enrich the threshold of the night
   With showered largess of delight
In dance and song and game and jest?

Yet go, and while the holly boughs
   Entwine the cold baptismal font,   10
   Make one wreath more for Use and Wont,[9]
That guard the portals of the house;

Old sisters of a day gone by,
   Gray nurses, loving nothing new;
   Why should they miss their yearly due   15
Before their time? They too will die.

30

With trembling fingers did we weave
   The holly round the Christmas hearth;
   A rainy cloud possessed the earth,
And sadly fell our Christmas eve.

At our old pastimes in the hall   5
   We gamboled, making vain pretense
   Of gladness, with an awful sense
Of one mute Shadow watching all.

We paused: the winds were in the beech;
   We heard them sweep the winter land;   10

---

8. Different sequences in which church bells are pealed.

9. Personifying the spirits who expect customary observances of the Christmas season to be followed.

And in a circle hand-in-hand
Sat silent, looking each at each.

Then echo-like our voices rang;
   We sung, though every eye was dim,
   A merry song we sang with him   15
Last year; impetuously we sang.

We ceased; a gentler feeling crept
   Upon us: surely rest is meet.[1]
   "They rest," we said, "their sleep is sweet,"[2]
And silence followed, and we wept.   20

Our voices took a higher range;
   Once more we sang: "They do not die
   Nor lose their mortal sympathy,
Nor change to us, although they change;

"Rapt[3] from the fickle and the frail   25
   With gathered power, yet the same,
   Pierces the keen seraphic flame
From orb to orb,[4] from veil to veil."

Rise, happy morn, rise, holy morn,
   Draw forth the cheerful day from night: 30
   O Father, touch the east, and light
The light that shone when Hope was born.

*   *   *

34

My own dim life should teach me this,
   That life shall live forevermore,
   Else earth is darkness at the core,
And dust and ashes all that is;

This round of green, this orb of flame,   5
   Fantastic beauty; such as lurks
   In some wild poet, when he works
Without a conscience or an aim.[5]

What then were God to such as I?
   'Twere hardly worth my while to choose   10
   Of things all mortal, or to use
A little patience ere I die;

'Twere best at once to sink to peace,
   Like birds the charming serpent draws,[6]

1. Proper or appropriate.
2. Cf. Proverbs 3.24: "Yea, thou shalt lie down, and thy sleep shall be sweet."
3. Carried away from.
4. The angelic spirit ("flame") of the dead moves from star to star.
5. Perhaps Thomas Lovell Beddoes, a brilliantly promising but erratic poet, admired by Tennyson. Beddoes committed suicide in 1849.
6. Some snakes are reputed to capture their prey by casting a charm.

To drop head-foremost in the jaws   15
Of vacant darkness and to cease.

35

Yet if some voice that man could trust
    Should murmur from the narrow house,
    "The cheeks drop in, the body bows;
Man dies, nor is there hope in dust";

Might I not say? "Yet even here,   5
    But for one hour, O Love, I strive
    To keep so sweet a thing alive."
But I should turn mine ears and hear

The moanings of the homeless sea,
    The sound of streams that swift or slow   10
    Draw down Aeonian hills,[7] and sow
The dust of continents to be;

And Love would answer with a sigh,
    "The sound of that forgetful shore
    Will change my sweetness more and more,   15
Half-dead to know that I shall die."

O me, what profits it to put
    An idle case? If Death were seen
    At first as Death, Love had not been,
Or been in narrowest working shut,   20

Mere fellowship of sluggish moods,
    Or in his coarsest Satyr-shape
    Had bruised the herb and crushed the grape,
And basked and battened in the woods.[8]

*   *   *

39

Old warder of these buried bones,
    And answering now my random stroke
    With fruitful cloud and living smoke,
Dark yew, that graspest at the stones

And dippest toward the dreamless head,   5
    To thee too comes the golden hour
    When flower is feeling after flower;[9]
But Sorrow—fixed upon the dead,

7. Hills that are eons old, seemingly everlasting.
8. Lines 18ff. may be paraphrased: if we knew death to be final and that no afterlife were possible, love could not exist except on a primitive or bestial level. Cf. Corinthians 15.32: "If the dead are not raised, let us eat and drink, for tomorrow we die."

9. The ancient yew tree in the graveyard was described in section 2 as never changing. Now the poet discovers that in the flowering season, if the tree is struck ("my random stroke," line 2), it gives off a cloud of golden pollen.

And darkening the dark graves of men —
   What whispered from her lying lips?   10
   Thy gloom is kindled at the tips,[1]
And passes into gloom again.

*   *   *

47

That each, who seems a separate whole,
   Should move his rounds,[2] and fusing all
   The skirts[3] of self again, should fall
Remerging in the general Soul,

Is faith as vague as all unsweet.   5
   Eternal form shall still divide
   The eternal soul from all beside;
And I shall know him when we meet;

And we shall sit at endless feast,
   Enjoying each the other's good.   10
   What vaster dream can hit the mood
Of Love on earth? He seeks at least

Upon the last and sharpest height,
   Before the spirits fade away,
   Some landing place, to clasp and say,   15
"Farewell! We lose ourselves in light."

48

If these brief lays, of Sorrow born,
   Were taken to be such as closed
   Grave doubts and answers here proposed,
Then these were such as men might scorn.

Her[4] care is not to part and prove;   5
   She takes, when harsher moods remit,
   What slender shade of doubt may flit,
And makes it vassal unto love;

And hence, indeed, she sports with words,
   But better serves a wholesome law,   10
   And holds it sin and shame to draw
The deepest measure from the chords;

Nor dare she trust a larger lay,
   But rather loosens from the lip
   Short swallow-flights of song, that dip   15
Their wings in tears, and skim away.

*   *   *

1. Only the tips of the yew branches are in flower.   3. Outer edges or fringes.
2. I.e., go through the customary circuit of life.   4. I.e., Sorrow's.

50

Be near me when my light is low,
    When the blood creeps, and the nerves prick
    And tingle; and the heart is sick,
And all the wheels of being slow.

Be near me when the sensuous frame   5
    Is racked with pangs that conquer trust;
    And Time, a maniac scattering dust,
And Life, a Fury slinging flame.

Be near me when my faith is dry,
    And men the flies of latter spring,   10
    That lay their eggs, and sting and sing
And weave their petty cells and die.

Be near me when I fade away,
    To point the term of human strife,
    And on the low dark verge of life   15
The twilight of eternal day.

                    *   *   *

54

O, yet we trust that somehow good
    Will be the final goal of ill,
    To pangs of nature, sins of will,
Defects of doubt, and taints of blood;

That nothing walks with aimless feet;   5
    That not one life shall be destroyed,
    Or cast as rubbish to the void,
When God hath made the pile complete;

That not a worm is cloven in vain;
    That not a moth with vain desire   10
    Is shriveled in a fruitless fire,
Or but subserves another's gain.

Behold, we know not anything;
    I can but trust that good shall fall
    At last—far off—at last, to all,   15
And every winter change to spring.

So runs my dream; but what am I?
    An infant crying in the night;
    An infant crying for the light,
And with no language but a cry.   20

55

The wish, that of the living whole
    No life may fail beyond the grave,

Derives it not from what we have
The likest God within the soul?

Are God and Nature then at strife,   5
    That Nature lends such evil dreams?
    So careful of the type[5] she seems,
So careless of the single life,

That I, considering everywhere
    Her secret meaning in her deeds,   10
    And finding that of fifty seeds
She often brings but one to bear,

I falter where I firmly trod,
    And falling with my weight of cares
    Upon the great world's altar-stairs   15
That slope through darkness up to God,

I stretch lame hands of faith, and grope,
    And gather dust and chaff, and call
    To what I feel is Lord of all,
And faintly trust the larger hope.[6]   20

56

"So careful of the type?" but no.
    From scarpèd[7] cliff and quarried stone
    She[8] cries, "A thousand types are gone;
I care for nothing, all shall go.

"Thou makest thine appeal to me: 5
    I bring to life, I bring to death;
    The spirit does but mean the breath:
I know no more." And he, shall he,

Man, her last work, who seemed so fair,
    Such splendid purpose in his eyes,   10
    Who rolled the psalm to wintry skies,
Who built him fanes[9] of fruitless prayer,

Who trusted God was love indeed
    And love Creation's final law—
    Though Nature, red in tooth and claw   15
With ravine, shrieked against his creed—

Who loved, who suffered countless ills,
    Who battled for the True, the Just,
    Be blown about the desert dust,
Or sealed within the iron hills?[1]   20

5. Species.
6. As expressed in lines 1–2 of this section.
7. Cut away so that the strata are exposed.

8. I.e., Nature.
9. Temples.
1. Preserved like fossils in rock.

No more? A monster then, a dream,
  A discord. Dragons of the prime,
  That tare[2] each other in their slime,
Were mellow music matched with[3] him.

O life as futile, then, as frail!   25
  O for thy voice to soothe and bless!
  What hope of answer, or redress?
Behind the veil, behind the veil.

57

Peace; come away:[4] the song of woe
  Is after all an earthly song.
  Peace; come away: we do him wrong
To sing so wildly: let us go.

Come; let us go: your cheeks are pale;   5
  But half my life I leave behind.
  Methinks my friend is richly shrined;
But I shall pass, my work will fail.

Yet in these ears, till hearing dies,
  One set slow bell will seem to toll   10
  The passing of the sweetest soul
That ever looked with human eyes.

I hear it now, and o'er and o'er,
  Eternal greetings to the dead;
  And "Ave,[5] Ave, Ave," said,   15
"Adieu, adieu," forevermore.

58

In those sad words I took farewell.
  Like echoes in sepulchral halls,
  As drop by drop the water falls
In vaults and catacombs, they fell;

And, falling, idly broke the peace   5
  Of hearts that beat from day to day,
  Half-conscious of their dying clay,
And those cold crypts where they shall cease.

The high Muse answered: "Wherefore grieve
  Thy brethren with a fruitless tear?   10
  Abide a little longer here,
And thou shalt take a nobler leave."

---

2. Tore (archaic).   sister and Hallam's fiancée.
3. In comparison with.   5. Hail.
4. Perhaps addressed to Emily Tennyson, the poet's

59

O Sorrow, wilt thou live with me
    No casual mistress, but a wife,
    My bosom friend and half of life;
As I confess it needs must be?

O Sorrow, wilt thou rule my blood,   5
    Be sometimes lovely like a bride,
    And put thy harsher moods aside,
If thou wilt have me wise and good?

My centered passion cannot move,
    Nor will it lessen from today;   10
    But I'll have leave at times to play
As with the creature of my love;

And set thee forth, for thou art mine,
    With so much hope for years to come,
    That, howsoe'er I know thee, some   15
Could hardly tell what name were thine.

*   *   *

64

Dost thou[6] look back on what hath been,
    As some divinely gifted man,
    Whose life in low estate began
And on a simple village green;

Who breaks his birth's invidious bar,   5
    And grasps the skirts of happy chance,
    And breasts the blows of circumstance,
And grapples with his evil star;

Who makes by force his merit known
    And lives to clutch the golden keys,[7]   10
    To mold a mighty state's decrees,
And shape the whisper of the throne;

And moving up from high to higher,
    Becomes on Fortune's crowning slope
    The pillar of a people's hope,   15
The center of a world's desire;

Yet feels, as in a pensive dream,
    When all his active powers are still,
    A distant dearness in the hill,
A secret sweetness in the stream,   20

6. I.e., Hallam.   7. Badges of high public office.

The limit of his narrower fate,
  While yet beside its vocal springs
  He played at counselors and kings,
With one that was his earliest mate;

Who plows with pain his native lea   25
  And reaps the labor of his hands,
  Or in the furrow musing stands:
"Does my old friend remember me?"

* * *

67

When on my bed the moonlight falls,
  I know that in thy place of rest
  By that broad water of the west[8]
There comes a glory on the walls:

Thy marble bright in dark appears,   5
  As slowly steals a silver flame
  Along the letters of thy name,
And o'er the number of thy years.

The mystic glory swims away,
  From off my bed the moonlight dies;   10
  And closing eaves of wearied eyes
I sleep till dusk is dipped in gray;

And then I know the mist is drawn
  A lucid veil from coast to coast,
  And in the dark church like a ghost   15
Thy tablet glimmers to the dawn.

* * *

70

I cannot see the features right,
  When on the gloom I strive to paint
  The face I know; the hues are faint
And mix with hollow masks of night;

Cloud-towers by ghostly masons wrought,   5
  A gulf that ever shuts and gapes,
  A hand that points, and pallèd shapes
In shadowy thoroughfares of thought;

And crowds that stream from yawning doors,
  And shoals of puckered faces drive;   10
  Dark bulks that tumble half alive,
And lazy lengths on boundless shores;

8. The Severn River.

Till all at once beyond the will
  I hear a wizard music roll,
  And through a lattice on the soul   15
Looks thy fair face and makes it still.

71

Sleep, kinsman thou to death and trance
  And madness, thou[9] has forged at last
  A night-long present of the past
In which we went through summer France.[1]

Hadst thou such credit with the soul?   5
  Then bring an opiate trebly strong,
  Drug down the blindfold sense of wrong,
That so my pleasure may be whole;

While now we talk as once we talked
  Of men and minds, the dust of change,   10
  The days that grow to something strange,
In walking as of old we walked

Beside the river's wooded reach,
  The fortress, and the mountain ridge,
  The cataract flashing from the bridge,   15
The breaker breaking on the beach.

72

Risest thou thus, dim dawn, again,[2]
  And howlest, issuing out of night,
  With blasts that blow the poplar white,
And lash with storm the streaming pane?

Day, when my crowned estate[3] begun   5
  To pine in that reverse of doom,[4]
  Which sickened every living bloom,
And blurred the splendor of the sun;

Who usherest in the dolorous hour
  With thy quick tears that make the rose   10
  Pull sideways, and the daisy close
Her crimson fringes to the shower;

Who mightst have heaved a windless flame
  Up the deep East, or, whispering, played
  A checker-work of beam and shade   15
Along the hills, yet looked the same,

---

9. I.e., sleep.
1. In the summer of 1830, Hallam and Tennyson went
through southern France en route to Spain.
2. September 15, 1834, the first anniversary of Hal-

lam's death.
3. State of happiness.
4. The reversal or disaster that doom brought upon
him when Hallam died.

As wan, as chill, as wild as now;
    Day, marked as with some hideous crime,
    When the dark hand struck down through time,
And canceled nature's best: but thou,   20

Lift as thou mayst thy burthened brows
    Through clouds that drench the morning star,
    And whirl the ungarnered sheaf afar,
And sow the sky with flying boughs,

And up thy vault with roaring sound   25
    Climb thy thick noon, disastrous day;
    Touch thy dull goal of joyless gray,
And hide thy shame beneath the ground.

                    *   *   *

                    75

I leave thy praises unexpressed
    In verse that brings myself relief,
    And by the measure of my grief
I leave thy greatness to be guessed.

What practice howsoe'er expert   5
    In fitting aptest words to things,
    Or voice the richest-toned that sings,
Hath power to give thee as thou wert?

I care not in these fading days
    To raise a cry that lasts not long,   10
    And round thee with the breeze of song
To stir a little dust of praise.

Thy leaf has perished in the green,
    And, while we breathe beneath the sun,
    The world which credits what is done   15
Is cold to all that might have been.

So here shall silence guard thy fame;
    But somewhere, out of human view,
    Whate'er thy hands are set to do
Is wrought with tumult of acclaim.   20

                    *   *   *

                    78

Again at Christmas[5] did we weave
    The holly round the Christmas hearth;
    The silent snow possessed the earth,
And calmly fell our Christmas eve.

---

5. The second Christmas (1834) after Hallam's death.

The yule clog[6] sparkled keen with frost,   5
    No wing of wind the region swept,
    But over all things brooding slept
The quiet sense of something lost.

As in the winters left behind,
    Again our ancient games had place,   10
    The mimic picture's[7] breathing grace,
And dance and song and hoodman-blind.[8]

Who showed a token of distress?
    No single tear, no mark of pain—
    O sorrow, then can sorrow wane?   15
O grief, can grief be changed to less?

O last regret, regret can die!
    No—mixed with all this mystic frame,
    Her[9] deep relations are the same,
But with long use her tears are dry.   20

*   *   *

82

I wage not any feud with Death
    For changes wrought on form and face;
    No lower life that earth's embrace
May breed with him can fright my faith.

Eternal process moving on,   5
    From state to state the spirit walks;
    And these are but the shattered stalks,
Or ruined chrysalis of one.

Nor blame I Death, because he bare
    The use of virtue out of earth;   10
    I know transplanted human worth
Will bloom to profit, otherwhere.

For this alone on Death I wreak
    The wrath that garners in my heart:[1]
    He put our lives so far apart   15
We cannot hear each other speak.

83

Dip down upon the northern shore,
    O sweet new-year[2] delaying long;
Thou doest expectant Nature wrong;
    Delaying long, delay no more.

---

6. Log.
7. A game in which the participants pose in the manner of some famous statue or painting and the spectators try to guess what work of art is being mimicked.
8. The player in the game of Blindman's Buff who wears a blindfold or hood.
9. I.e., Sorrow's.
1. Cf. *Othello* 4.2.57: "But there where I have garnered up my heart."
2. Spring of 1835.

What stays thee from the clouded noons,   5
   Thy sweetness from its proper place?
   Can trouble live with April days,
Or sadness in the summer moons?

Bring orchis, bring the foxglove spire,
   The little speedwell's[3] darling blue,   10
   Deep tulips dashed with fiery dew,
Laburnums, dropping-wells of fire.

O thou, new-year, delaying long,
   Delayest the sorrow in my blood,
   That longs to burst a frozen bud   15
And flood a fresher throat with song.

84

When I contemplate all alone
   The life that had been thine below,
   And fix my thoughts on all the glow
To which thy crescent would have grown,

I see thee sitting crowned with good,   5
   A central warmth diffusing bliss
   In glance and smile, and clasp and kiss,
On all the branches of thy blood;

Thy blood, my friend, and partly mine;
   For now the day was drawing on,   10
   When thou shouldst link thy life with one
Of mine own house, and boys of thine

Had babbled "Uncle" on my knee;
   But that remorseless iron hour
   Made cypress of her orange flower,[4]   15
Despair of hope, and earth of thee.

I seem to meet their least desire,
   To clap their cheeks, to call them mine.
   I see their unborn faces shine
Beside the never-lighted fire.   20

I see myself an honored guest,
   Thy partner in the flowery walk
   Of letters, genial table talk,
Or deep dispute, and graceful jest;

While now thy prosperous labor fills   25
   The lips of men with honest praise,

3. A blue spring flower.
4. Orange blossoms are associated with brides—here the poet's sister Emily Tennyson, to whom Hallam had been engaged.

And sun by sun the happy days
Descend below the golden hills

With promise of a morn as fair;
  And all the train of bounteous hours   30
  Conduct, by paths of growing powers,
To reverence and the silver hair;

Till slowly worn her earthly robe,
  Her lavish mission richly wrought,
  Leaving great legacies of thought,   35
Thy spirit should fail from off the globe;

What time mine own might also flee,
  As linked with thine in love and fate,
  And, hovering o'er the dolorous strait
To the other shore, involved in thee,   40

Arrive at last the blessed goal,
  And He that died in Holy Land
  Would reach us out the shining hand,
And take us as a single soul.

What reed was that on which I leant?   45
  Ah, backward fancy, wherefore wake
  The old bitterness again, and break
The low beginnings of content?

* * *

86

Sweet after showers, ambrosial air,
  That rollest from the gorgeous gloom
  Of evening over brake and bloom
And meadow, slowly breathing bare

The round of space,[5] and rapt below   5
  Through all the dewy-tasseled wood,
  And shadowing down the hornèd flood[6]
In ripples, fan my brows and blow

The fever from my cheek, and sigh
  The full new life that feeds thy breath   10
  Throughout my frame, till Doubt and Death,
Ill brethren, let the fancy fly

From belt to belt of crimson seas
  On leagues of odor streaming far,
  To where in yonder orient star   15
A hundred spirits whisper "Peace."

---

5. Air that is slowly clearing the clouds from the sky.   6. Between two promontories [Tennyson's note].

87

I passed beside the reverend walls[7]
   In which of old I wore the gown;
   I roved at random through the town,
And saw the tumult of the halls;

And heard once more in college fanes   5
   The storm their high-built organs make,
   And thunder-music, rolling, shake
The prophet blazoned on the panes;

And caught once more the distant shout,
   The measured pulse of racing oars   10
   Among the willows; paced the shores
And many a bridge, and all about

The same gray flats again, and felt
   The same, but not the same; and last
   Up that long walk of limes I passed   15
To see the rooms in which he dwelt.

Another name was on the door.
   I lingered; all within was noise
   Of songs, and clapping hands, and boys
That crashed the glass and beat the floor;   20

Where once we held debate, a band
   Of youthful friends,[8] on mind and art,
   And labor, and the changing mart,
And all the framework of the land;

When one would aim an arrow fair,   25
   But send it slackly from the string;
   And one would pierce an outer ring,
And one an inner, here and there;

And last the master bowman, he,
   Would cleave the mark. A willing ear   30
   We lent him. Who but hung to hear
The rapt oration flowing free

From point to point, with power and grace
   And music in the bounds of law,[9]
   To those conclusions when we saw   35
The God within him light his face,

And seem to lift the form, and glow
   In azure orbits heavenly-wise;

7. Of Trinity College, Cambridge University.
8. The "Apostles," an undergraduate club to which Tennyson and Hallam had belonged.
9. An essay presented by Arthur Hallam at Cambridge in 1831 provides an example of his skill in theological argument while still an undergraduate (cf. *The Writings of Arthur Hallam*, edited by T. H. V. Motter, 1943, pp. 198–213).

And over those ethereal eyes
The bar of Michael Angelo?[1]   40

88

Wild bird, whose warble, liquid sweet,
　　Rings Eden through the budded quicks,[2]
　　O tell me where the senses mix,
O tell me where the passions meet,

Whence radiate: fierce extremes employ   5
　　Thy spirits in the darkening leaf,[3]
　　And in the midmost heart of grief
Thy passion clasps a secret joy;

And I—my harp would prelude woe—
　　I cannot all command the strings;   10
　　The glory of the sum of things
Will flash along the chords and go.

89

Witch elms that counterchange the floor
　　Of this flat lawn with dusk and bright;[4]
　　And thou, with all thy breadth and height
Of foliage, towering sycamore;

How often, hither wandering down,   5
　　My Arthur found your shadows fair,
　　And shook to all the liberal air
The dust and din and steam of town!

He brought an eye for all he saw;
　　He mixed in all our simple sports;   10
　　They pleased him, fresh from brawling courts
And dusty purlieus of the law.[5]

O joy to him in this retreat,
　　Immantled in ambrosial dark,
　　To drink the cooler air, and mark   15
The landscape winking through the heat!

O sound to rout the brood of cares,
　　The sweep of scythe in morning dew,
　　The gust that round the garden flew,
And tumbled half the mellowing pears!   20

---

1. Hallam, like Michelangelo, had a prominent ridge of bone above his eyes.
2. Hawthorn hedges. The "wild bird" is presumably a nightingale.
3. Cf. Keats's *Ode to a Nightingale* (lines 10 and 60, pp. 1791 and 1793).
4. Shadows of the elm tree checker the lawn at Somersby, the Tennysons' country home.
5. Hallam became a law student in London after leaving Cambridge.

O bliss, when all in circle drawn
    About him, heart and ear were fed
    To hear him, as he lay and read
The Tuscan poets[6] on the lawn!

Or in the all-golden afternoon   25
    A guest, or happy sister, sung,
    Or here she brought the harp and flung
A ballad to the brightening moon.

Nor less it pleased in livelier moods,
    Beyond the bounding hill to stray,   30
    And break the livelong summer day
With banquet in the distant woods;

Whereat we glanced from theme to theme,
    Discussed the books to love or hate,
    Or touched the changes of the state,   35
Or threaded some Socratic dream;[7]

But if I praised the busy town,
    He loved to rail against it still,
    For "ground in yonder social mill
We rub each other's angles down,   40

"And merge," he said, "in form and gloss
    The picturesque of man and man."
    We talked: the stream beneath us ran,
The wine-flask lying couched in moss,

Or cooled within the glooming wave;   45
    And last, returning from afar,
    Before the crimson-circled star[8]
Had fallen into her father's grave,

And brushing ankle-deep in flowers,
    We heard behind the woodbine veil   50
    The milk that bubbled in[9] the pail,
And buzzings of the honeyed hours.

                    *   *   *

                    91

When rosy plumelets tuft the larch,
    And rarely[1] pipes the mounted thrush,
    Or underneath the barren bush
Flits by the sea-blue bird[2] of March;

6. I.e., Petrarch and Dante.
7. I.e., worked our way through some discourse of Socrates (as recorded by Plato).
8. Venus, which will sink into the west as the sun has done. According to the nebular hypothesis, planets condensed out of the sun's atmosphere; in this sense the sun is the "father" of planets.
9. Into.
1. Exquisitely.
2. The kingfisher.

Come, wear the form by which I know   5
  Thy spirit in time among thy peers;
  The hope of unaccomplished years
Be large and lucid round thy brow.

When summer's hourly-mellowing change
  May breathe, with many roses sweet,   10
  Upon the thousand waves of wheat
That ripple round the lowly grange,

Come; not in watches of the night,
  But where the sunbeam broodeth warm,
  Come, beauteous in thine after form,   15
And like a finer light in light.

* * *

93

I shall not see thee. Dare I say
  No spirit ever brake the band
  That stays him from the native land
Where first he walked when clasped in clay?[3]

No visual shade of someone lost,   5
  But he, the Spirit himself, may come
  Where all the nerve of sense is numb,
Spirit to Spirit, Ghost to Ghost.

Oh, therefore from thy sightless[4] range
  With gods in unconjectured bliss,   10
  Oh, from the distance of the abyss
Of tenfold-complicated change,

Descend, and touch, and enter; hear
  The wish too strong for words to name,
  That in this blindness of the frame[5]   15
My Ghost may feel that thine is near.

94

How pure at heart and sound in head,
  With what divine affections bold
  Should be the man whose thought would hold
An hour's communion with the dead.

In vain shalt thou, or any, call   5
  The spirits from their golden day,
  Except, like them, thou too canst say,
My spirit is at peace with all.

3. I.e., when he was alive and clothed in flesh.   5. The living body.
4. Invisible.

They haunt the silence of the breast,
    Imaginations calm and fair,   10
      The memory like a cloudless air,
The conscience as a sea at rest;

But when the heart is full of din,
    And doubt beside the portal waits,
      They can but listen at the gates,   15
And hear the household jar within.

95

By night we lingered on the lawn,
    For underfoot the herb was dry;
      And genial warmth; and o'er the sky
The silvery haze of summer drawn;

And calm that let the tapers burn   5
    Unwavering: not a cricket chirred;
      The brook alone far off was heard,
And on the board the fluttering urn.[6]

And bats went round in fragrant skies,
    And wheeled or lit the filmy shapes[7]   10
      That haunt the dusk, with ermine capes
And woolly breasts and beaded eyes;

While now we sang old songs that pealed
    From knoll to knoll, where, couched at ease,
      The white kine[8] glimmered, and the trees   15
Laid their dark arms[9] about the field.

But when those others, one by one,
    Withdrew themselves from me and night,
      And in the house light after light
Went out, and I was all alone,   20

A hunger seized my heart; I read
    Of that glad year which once had been,
      In those fallen leaves which kept their green,
The noble letters of the dead.

And strangely on the silence broke   25
    The silent-speaking words, and strange
      Was love's dumb cry defying change
To test his worth; and strangely spoke

The faith, the vigor, bold to dwell
    On doubts that drive the coward back,   30

6. Urn to boil water for tea or coffee, heated by a flut-   moths.
tering flame.   8. Cows.
7. The white-winged night moths called ermine   9. Cast the shadows of their branches.

And keen through wordy snares to track
Suggestion to her inmost cell.

So word by word, and line by line,
 The dead man touched me from the past,
 And all at once it seemed at last   35
The[1] living soul was flashed on mine.

And mine in this was wound, and whirled
 About empyreal heights of thought,
 And came on that which is, and caught
The deep pulsations of the world,   40

Aeonian music[2] measuring out
 The steps of Time—the shocks of Chance—
 The blows of Death. At length my trance
Was canceled, stricken through with doubt.[3]

Vague words! but ah, how hard to frame   45
 In matter-molded forms of speech,
 Or even for intellect to reach
Through memory that which I became.

Till now the doubtful dusk revealed
 The knolls once more where, couched at ease,   50
 The white kine glimmered, and the trees
Laid their dark arms about the field;

And sucked from out the distant gloom
 A breeze began to tremble o'er
 The large leaves of the sycamore,   55
And fluctuate all the still perfume,

And gathering freshlier overhead,
 Rocked the full-foliaged elms, and swung
 The heavy-folded rose, and flung
The lilies to and fro, and said,   60

"The dawn, the dawn," and died away;
 And East and West, without a breath,
 Mixed their dim lights, like life and death,
To broaden into boundless day.

1. It was "His" in the 1st edition, and also in the 1st edition, line 37 read, "And mine in his was wound."
2. The music of the universe that has pulsated for eons.
3. In a letter of 1874, replying to an inquiry about his experience of mystical trances, Tennyson wrote: "A kind of waking trance I have frequently had, quite up from boyhood, when I have been all alone. This has generally come upon me through repeating my own name two or three times to myself silently, till all at once, as it were out of the intensity of the conscious-ness of individuality, the individuality itself seemed to dissolve and fade away into boundless being, and this not a confused state, but the clearest of the clearest, the surest of the surest, the weirdest of the weirdest, utterly beyond words, where death was an almost laughable impossibility, the loss of personality (if so it were) seeming no extinction but the only true life. . . . This might . . . be the state which St. Paul describes, 'Whether in the body I cannot tell, or whether out of the body I cannot tell.' . . . I am ashamed of my feeble description. Have I not said the state is utterly beyond words? But in a moment, when I come back to my normal state of 'sanity,' I am ready to fight for *mein liebes Ich* [my dear self], and hold that it will last for aeons of aeons" (*Alfred Lord Tennyson, A Memoir*, 1897, 1, 320).

96

You say, but with no touch of scorn,
　　Sweet-hearted, you,[4] whose light blue eyes
　　Are tender over drowning flies,
You tell me, doubt is Devil-born.

I know not: one[5] indeed I knew   5
　　In many a subtle question versed,
　　Who touched a jarring lyre at first,
But ever strove to make it true;

Perplexed in faith, but pure in deeds,
　　At last he beat his music out.   10
　　There lives more faith in honest doubt,
Believe me, than in half the creeds.

He fought his doubts and gathered strength,
　　He would not make his judgment blind,
　　He faced the specters of the mind   15
And laid them; thus he came at length

To find a stronger faith his own,
　　And Power was with him in the night,
　　Which makes the darkness and the light,
And dwells not in the light alone,   20

But in the darkness and the cloud,[6]
　　As over Sinaï's peaks of old,
　　While Israel made their gods of gold,
Although the trumpet blew so loud.

＊　＊　＊

99

Risest thou thus, dim dawn, again,[7]
　　So loud with voices of the birds,
　　So thick with lowings of the herds,
Day, when I lost the flower of men;

Who tremblest through thy darkling red   5
　　On yon swollen brook that bubbles fast[8]
　　By meadows breathing of the past,
And woodlands holy to the dead;

Who murmurest in the foliage eaves
　　A song that slights the coming care,[9]   10

4. A woman of simple faith.
5. I.e., Hallam.
6. Cf. Exodus 19.16–25. After veiling Mt. Sinai in a "cloud" of smoke, God addressed Moses from the darkness.
7. September 15, 1835, the second anniversary of Hallam's death.
8. I.e., reflections of the clouded red light of dawn quiver on the surface of the fast-moving water.
9. I.e., disregards future events such as death or the coming of autumn (cf. Shelley, Ode to the West Wind, p. 1700).

And Autumn laying here and there
A fiery finger on the leaves;

Who wakenest with thy balmy breath
    To myriads on the genial earth,
    Memories of bridal, or of birth,[1]   15
And unto myriads more, of death.

Oh, wheresoever those[2] may be,
    Betwixt the slumber of the poles,
    Today they count as kindred souls;
They know me not, but mourn with me.   20

*   *   *

103

On that last night before we went
    From out the doors where I was bred,[3]
    I dreamed a vision of the dead,
Which left my after-morn content.

Methought I dwelt within a hall,   5
    And maidens with me; distant hills
    From hidden summits fed with rills
A river sliding by the wall.

The hall with harp and carol rang.
    They sang of what is wise and good   10
    And graceful. In the center stood
A statue veiled, to which they sang;

And which, though veiled, was known to me,
    The shape of him I loved, and love
    Forever. Then flew in a dove   15
And brought a summons from the sea;

And when they learnt that I must go,
    They wept and wailed, but led the way
    To where the little shallop[4] lay
At anchor in the flood below;   20

And on by many a level mead,
    And shadowing bluff that made the banks,
    We glided winding under ranks
Of iris and the golden reed;

And still as vaster grew the shore   25
    And rolled the floods in grander space,

---

1. Cf. *Epilogue*, lines 117–128 (p. 1953).
2. I.e., the "myriads" who remember death.
3. In 1837 Tennyson and his family moved away from their home in Lincolnshire, which had been closely associated with his friendship with Hallam. In section 104 the move seems to occur in 1835, the year of the third Christmas after Hallam's death.
4. A light open boat.

The maidens gathered strength and grace
And presence, lordlier than before;

And I myself, who sat apart
    And watched them, waxed in every limb;   30
I felt the thews of Anakim,[5]
The pulses of a Titan's[6] heart;

As one would sing the death of war,
    And one would chant the history
    Of that great race which is to be,[7]   35
And one the shaping of a star;

Until the forward-creeping tides
    Began to foam, and we to draw
    From deep to deep, to where we saw
A great ship lift her shining sides.[8]   40

The man we loved was there on deck,
    But thrice as large as man he bent
    To greet us. Up the side I went,
And fell in silence on his neck;

Whereat those maidens with one mind   45
    Bewailed their lot; I did them wrong:
    "We served thee here," they said, "so long,
And wilt thou leave us now behind?"

So rapt[9] I was, they could not win
    An answer from my lips, but he   50
    Replying, "Enter likewise ye
And go with us:" they entered in.

And while the wind began to sweep
    A music out of sheet and shroud,
    We steered her toward a crimson cloud   55
That landlike slept along the deep.

104

The time draws near the birth of Christ;[1]
    The moon is hid, the night is still;
    A single church below the hill
Is pealing, folded in the mist.

A single peal of bells below,   5
    That wakens at this hour of rest

5. Plural of *Anak*; a reference to the giant sons of Anak (cf. Numbers 13.33).
6. Giants of Greek mythology.
7. See the account of the "crowning race" in *Epilogue*, lines 128–144 (p. 1953–54).
8. Cf. *Morte d'Arthur*, lines 255–322, in which Bedivere is left behind as Arthur's barge, the ship of death, sails away. In the present dream vision not only is the speaker taken aboard but also his companions, who represent the creative arts of this world—"all the human powers and talents that do not pass with life but go along with it," as Tennyson said of this passage.
9. Entranced.
1. See p. 1942, n. 3.

A single murmur in the breast,
That these are not the bells I know.

Like strangers' voices here they sound,
    In lands where not a memory strays,   10
    Nor landmark breathes of other days,
But all is new unhallowed ground.

105

Tonight ungathered let us leave
    This laurel, let this holly stand:[2]
    We live within the stranger's land,
And strangely falls our Christmas eve.

Our father's dust is left alone   5
    And silent under other snows:
    There in due time the woodbine blows,
The violet comes, but we are gone.

No more shall wayward grief abuse
    The genial hour with mask and mime;   10
    For change of place, like growth of time,
Has broke the bond of dying use.

Let cares that petty shadows cast,
    By which our lives are chiefly proved,
    A little spare the night I loved,   15
And hold it solemn to the past.

But let no footstep beat the floor,
    Nor bowl of wassail mantle warm;[3]
    For who would keep an ancient form
Through which the spirit breathes no more?   20

Be neither song, nor game, nor feast;
    Nor harp be touched, nor flute be blown;
    No dance, no motion, save alone
What lightens in the lucid east

Of rising worlds[4] by yonder wood.   25
    Long sleeps the summer in the seed;
    Run out your measured arcs, and lead
The closing cycle rich in good.

106

Ring out, wild bells, to the wild sky,
    The flying cloud, the frosty light:

---

2. Cf. section 29, in which the family in their former
home still continued to gather holly. In the new home,
in "stranger's land," the customary observances lapse.

3. I.e., no bowl of hot punch warms the mantelpiece.
4. The scintillating motion of the stars that rise [Ten-
nyson's note].

The year is dying in the night;
Ring out, wild bells, and let him die.

Ring out the old, ring in the new,   5
  Ring, happy bells, across the snow:
  The year is going, let him go;
Ring out the false, ring in the true.

Ring out the grief that saps the mind,
  For those that here we see no more;   10
  Ring out the feud of rich and poor,
Ring in redress to all mankind.

Ring out a slowly dying cause,
  And ancient forms of party strife;
  Ring in the nobler modes of life,   15
With sweeter manners, purer laws.

Ring out the want, the care, the sin,
  The faithless coldness of the times:
  Ring out, ring out my mournful rhymes,
But ring the fuller minstrel in.   20

Ring out false pride in place and blood,
  The civic slander and the spite;
  Ring in the love of truth and right,
Ring in the common love of good.

Ring out old shapes of foul disease;   25
  Ring out the narrowing lust of gold;
  Ring out the thousand wars of old,
Ring in the thousand years of peace.

Ring in the valiant man and free,
  The larger heart, the kindlier hand;   30
  Ring out the darkness of the land,
Ring in the Christ that is to be.[5]

107

It is the day when he was born.[6]
  A bitter day that early sank
  Behind a purple-frosty bank
Of vapor, leaving night forlorn.

The time admits not flowers or leaves   5
  To deck the banquet. Fiercely flies

---

5. These allusions to the second coming of Christ and to the millennium are derived from Revelation 20, but Tennyson has interpreted the biblical account in his own way. He once told his son of his conviction that "the forms of Christian religion would alter; but that the spirit of Christ would still grow from more to more."
6. February 1.

The blast of North and East, and ice
Makes daggers at the sharpened eaves,

And bristles all the brakes and thorns
  To yon hard crescent, as she hangs   10
  Above the wood which grides[7] and clangs
Its leafless ribs and iron horns

Together, in the drifts[8] that pass
  To darken on the rolling brine
  That breaks the coast. But fetch the wine,   15
Arrange the board and brim the glass;

Bring in great logs and let them lie,
  To make a solid core of heat;
  Be cheerful-minded, talk and treat
Of all things even as he were by;   20

We keep the day. With festal cheer,
  With books and music, surely we
  Will drink to him, whate'er he be,
And sing the songs he loved to hear.

108

I will not shut me from my kind,
  And, lest I stiffen into stone,
  I will not eat my heart alone,
Nor feed with sighs a passing wind:

What profit lies in barren faith,   5
  And vacant yearning, though with might
  To scale the heaven's highest height,
Or dive below the wells of Death?

What find I in the highest place,
  But mine own phantom chanting hymns?   10
  And on the depths of death there swims
The reflex of a human face.[9]

I'll rather take what fruit may be
  Of sorrow under human skies:
  'Tis held that sorrow makes us wise,   15
Whatever wisdom sleep with thee.[1]

109

Heart-affluence in discursive talk
  From household fountains never dry;

---

7. Clashes with a strident noise.
8. Either cloud-drifts or clouds of snow.

9. I.e., his own face.
1. Hallam.

The critic clearness of an eye
That saw through all the Muses' walk;[2]

Seraphic intellect and force   5
    To seize and throw the doubts of man;
    Impassioned logic, which outran
The hearer in its fiery course;

High nature amorous of the good,
    But touched with no ascetic gloom;   10
    And passion pure in snowy bloom
Through all the years of April blood;

A love of freedom rarely felt,
    Of freedom in her regal seat
    Of England; not the schoolboy heat,   15
The blind hysterics of the Celt;[3]

And manhood fused with female grace
    In such a sort, the child would twine
    A trustful hand, unasked, in thine,
And find his comfort in thy face;   20

All these have been, and thee mine eyes
    Have looked on: if they looked in vain,
    My shame is greater who remain,
Nor let thy wisdom make me wise.

                        *   *   *

115

Now fades the last long streak of snow,
    Now burgeons every maze of quick
    About the flowering squares,[4] and thick
By ashen roots the violets blow.

Now rings the woodland loud and long,   5
    The distance takes a lovelier hue,
    And drowned in yonder living blue
The lark becomes a sightless song.

Now dance the lights on lawn and lea,
    The flocks are whiter down the vale,   10
    And milkier every milky sail
On winding stream or distant sea;

Where now the seamew pipes, or dives
    In yonder greening gleam, and fly
    The happy birds, that change their sky   15
To build and brood, that live their lives

---

2. The realm of art and literature.   tion of 1789 (see also section 127, lines 7–8).
3. In particular the French at the time of the revolu-   4. Fields. "Quick": hawthorn hedges.

From land to land; and in my breast
  Spring wakens too, and my regret
  Becomes an April violet,
And buds and blossoms like the rest.   20

*   *   *

118

Contèmplate all this work of Time,
  The giant laboring in his youth;
  Nor dream of human love and truth,
As dying Nature's earth and lime;[5]

But trust that those we call the dead   5
  Are breathers of an ampler day
  For ever nobler ends. They[6] say,
The solid earth whereon we tread

In tracts of fluent heat began,
  And grew to seeming-random forms,   10
  The seeming prey of cyclic storms,
Till at the last arose the man;

Who throve and branched from clime to clime,
  The herald of a higher race,
  And of himself in higher place   15
If so he type[7] this work of time

Within himself, from more to more;
  Or, crowned with attributes of woe
  Like glories, move his course, and show
That life is not as idle ore,   20

But iron dug from central gloom,
  And heated hot with burning fears,
  And dipped in baths of hissing tears,
And battered with the shocks of doom

To shape and use. Arise and fly   25
  The reeling Faun, the sensual feast;
  Move upward, working out the beast,
And let the ape and tiger die.

119

Doors, where my heart was used to beat
  So quickly, not as one that weeps
  I come once more; the city sleeps;
I smell the meadow in the street;

5. "Alluding to the materialistic analysis of living matter into chemicals and simpler compounds" [cited by
Susan Shatto].

6. Geologists and astronomers.
7. Emulate, prefigure as a type.

I hear a chirp of birds; I see   5
   Betwixt the black fronts long-withdrawn
   A light blue lane of early dawn,
And think of early days and thee,

And bless thee, for thy lips are bland,
   And bright the friendship of thine eye;   10
   And in my thoughts with scarce a sigh
I take the pressure of thine hand.

120

I trust I have not wasted breath:
   I think we are not wholly brain,
   Magnetic mockeries;[8] not in vain,
Like Paul[9] with beasts, I fought with Death;

Not only cunning casts in clay: 5
   Let Science prove we are, and then
   What matters Science unto men,
At least to me? I would not stay.

Let him, the wiser man who springs
   Hereafter, up from childhood shape   10
   His action like the greater ape,
But I was *born* to other things.

121

Sad Hesper[1] o'er the buried sun
   And ready, thou, to die with him,
   Thou watchest all things ever dim
And dimmer, and a glory done.

The team is loosened from the wain,[2]   5
   The boat is drawn upon the shore;
   Thou listenest to the closing door,
And life is darkened in the brain.

Bright Phosphor,[3] fresher for the night,
   By thee the world's great work is heard   10
   Beginning, and the wakeful bird;
Behind thee comes the greater light.[4]

The market boat is on the stream,
   And voices hail it from the brink;
   Thou hear'st the village hammer clink,   15
And see'st the moving of the team.

---

8. Mechanisms operated by responses to electrical forces.
9. 1 Corinthians 15.32.
1. Evening star.
2. Hay wagon.
3. Morning star.
4. Cf. Genesis 1.16: "The greater light to rule the day."

Sweet Hesper-Phosphor, double name[5]
  For what is one, the first, the last,
  Thou, like my present and my past,
Thy place is changed; thou art the same.   20

* * *

123

There rolls the deep where grew the tree.
  O earth, what changes hast thou seen!
  There where the long street roars hath been
The stillness of the central sea.[6]

The hills are shadows, and they flow   5
  From form to form, and nothing stands;
  They melt like mist, the solid lands,
Like clouds they shape themselves and go.

But in my spirit will I dwell,
  And dream my dream, and hold it true;   10
  For though my lips may breathe adieu,
I cannot think the thing farewell.

124

That which we dare invoke to bless;
  Our dearest faith; our ghastliest doubt;
  He, They, One, All; within, without;
The Power in darkness whom we guess—

I found Him not in world or sun,   5
  Or eagle's wing, or insect's eye,[7]
  Nor through the questions men may try,
The petty cobwebs we have spun.

If e'er when faith had fallen asleep,
  I heard a voice, "believe no more,"   10
  And heard an ever-breaking shore
That tumbled in the Godless deep,

A warmth within the breast would melt
  The freezing reason's colder part,
  And like a man in wrath the heart   15
Stood up and answered, "I have felt."

No, like a child in doubt and fear:
  But that blind clamor made me wise;

5. The planet Venus is both evening star and morning star.
6. Cf. a passage from Sir Charles Lyell's *The Principles of Geology* (1832), a book well known to Tennyson. In discussing the "interchange of sea and land" that has occurred "on the surface of our globe" Lyell remarks: "In the Mediterranean alone, many flourishing inland towns and a still greater number of ports now stand where the sea rolled its waves since the era when civilized nations first grew in Europe."
7. He does not discover satisfactory proof of God's existence in the 18th-century argument that because objects in nature are designed there must exist a designer.

Then was I as a child that cries,
But, crying, knows his father near;   20

And what I am beheld again
    What is, and no man understands;
    And out of darkness came the hands
That reach through nature, molding men.

*   *   *

126

Love is and was my lord and king,
    And in his presence I attend
    To hear the tidings of my friend,
Which every hour his couriers bring.

Love is and was my king and lord,   5
    And will be, though as yet I keep
    Within the court on earth, and sleep
Encompassed by his faithful guard,

And hear at times a sentinel
    Who moves about from place to place,   10
    And whispers to the worlds of space,
In the deep night, that all is well.

127

And all is well, though faith and form[8]
    Be sundered in the night of fear;
    Well roars the storm to those that hear
A deeper voice across the storm,

Proclaiming social truth shall spread,   5
    And justice, even though thrice again
    The red fool-fury of the Seine
Should pile her barricades with dead.[9]

But ill for him that wears a crown,[1]
    And him, the lazar,[2] in his rags!   10
    They tremble, the sustaining crags;
The spires of ice are toppled down,

And molten up, and roar in flood;
    The fortress crashes from on high,
    The brute earth lightens[3] to the sky,   15
And the great Aeon[4] sinks in blood,

8. Traditional institutions through which faith was formerly expressed, such as the church.
9. Revolutionary uprisings in France, in each of which a king lost his throne (line 9): in 1789 against Louis XVI, in 1830 against Charles X, and in 1848 against Louis Philippe. The third (line 6) would have been a prophecy if, as Tennyson recollected, section 126 was finished at a date earlier than 1848.
1. Cf. 2 Henry IV 3.1.31: "Uneasy lies the head that wears the crown."
2. Pauper suffering from disease.
3. Is lit up by fire.
4. A vast tract of time, here perhaps modern Western civilization.

And compassed by the fires of hell,
   While thou, dear spirit, happy star,
   O'erlook'st the tumult from afar,
And smilest, knowing all is well.   20

*   *   *

129

Dear friend, far off, my lost desire,
   So far, so near in woe and weal,
   O loved the most, when most I feel
There is a lower and a higher;

Known and unknown, human, divine;   5
   Sweet human hand and lips and eye;
   Dear heavenly friend that canst not die,
Mine, mine, forever, ever mine;

Strange friend, past, present, and to be;
   Loved deeplier, darklier understood;   10
   Behold, I dream a dream of good,
And mingle all the world with thee.

130

Thy voice is on the rolling air
   I hear thee where the waters run;
   Thou standest in the rising sun,
And in the setting thou art fair.

What art thou then? I cannot guess;   5
   But though I seem in star and flower
   To feel thee some diffusive power,
I do not therefore love thee less.

My love involves the love before;
   My love is vaster passion now;   10
   Tho' mix'd with God and Nature thou,
I seem to love thee more and more.

Far off thou art, but ever nigh;
   I have thee still, and I rejoice;
   I prosper, circled with thy voice;   15
I shall not lose thee tho' I die.

131

O living will[5] that shalt endure
   When all that seems shall suffer shock,
   Rise in the spiritual rock,[6]
Flow through our deeds and make them pure,

---

5. Tennyson later commented that he meant here the   6. Christ (cf. 1 Corinthians 10.4).
moral will of humankind.

That we may lift from out of dust   5
   A voice as unto him that hears,
   A cry above the conquered years
To one that with us works, and trust,

With faith that comes of self-control,
   The truths that never can be proved   10
   Until we close with all we loved,
And all we flow from, soul in soul.

From Epilogue[7]

*   *   *

And rise, O moon, from yonder down,
   Till over down and over dale   110
   All night the shining vapor sail
And pass the silent-lighted town,

The white-faced halls, the glancing rills,
   And catch at every mountain head,
   And o'er the friths[8] that branch and spread   115
Their sleeping silver through the hills;

And touch with shade the bridal doors,
   With tender gloom the roof, the wall;
   And breaking let the splendor fall
To spangle all the happy shores   120

By which they rest, and ocean sounds,
   And, star and system rolling past,
   A soul shall draw from out the vast
And strike his being into bounds,

And, moved through life of lower phase,   125
   Result in man,[9] be born and think,
   And act and love, a closer link
Betwixt us and the crowning race

Of those that, eye to eye, shall look
   On knowledge; under whose command   130
   Is Earth and Earth's, and in their hand
Is Nature like an open book;

No longer half-akin to brute,
   For all we thought and loved and did,
   And hoped, and suffered, is but seed   135
Of what in them is flower and fruit;

---

7. The *Epilogue* describes the wedding day of Tennyson's sister Cecilia to Edmund Lushington. At the conclusion (reprinted here) the speaker reflects on the moonlit wedding night and the kind of offspring that will result from their union.
8. Inlets of the sea.

9. A child will be conceived and will develop in embryo through various stages. This development is similar to human evolution from the animal to the human level and perhaps to a future higher stage of development.

Whereof the man that with me trod
  This planet was a noble type
  Appearing ere the times were ripe,
That friend of mine who lives in God,   140

That God, which ever lives and loves,
  One God, one law, one element,
  And one far-off divine event,
To which the whole creation moves.

1833–50   1850

The Charge of the Light Brigade[1]

1

Half a league, half a league,
Half a league onward,
All in the valley of Death
  Rode the six hundred.
"Forward the Light Brigade!   5
Charge for the guns!" he said.
Into the valley of Death
  Rode the six hundred.[2]

2

"Forward, the Light Brigade!"
Was there a man dismayed?   10
Not though the soldier knew
  Someone had blundered.
Theirs not to make reply,
Theirs not to reason why,
Theirs but to do and die.   15
Into the valley of Death
  Rode the six hundred.

3

Cannon to right of them,
Cannon to left of them,
Cannon in front of them   20
  Volleyed and thundered;
Stormed at with shot and shell,
Boldly they rode and well,
Into the jaws of Death,
Into the mouth of hell   25
  Rode the six hundred.

4

Flashed all their sabers bare,
Flashed as they turned in air
Sab'ring the gunners there,

1. During the Crimean War, owing to confusion of orders, a brigade of British cavalry charged some entrenched batteries of Russian artillery. This blunder cost the lives of three-quarters of the six hundred horsemen engaged (see Cecil Woodham-Smith, *The Reason Why*, 1954). Tennyson rapidly composed his "ballad" (as he called the poem) after reading an account of the battle in a newspaper.
2. In the recording Tennyson made of this poem, "hundred" sounds like "hunderd"—a Lincolnshire pronunciation that reinforces the rhyme with "thundered," etc.

Charging an army, while   30
    All the world wondered.
Plunged in the battery smoke
Right through the line they broke;
Cossack and Russian
Reeled from the saber stroke   35
    Shattered and sundered.
Then they rode back, but not,
    Not the six hundred.

5

Cannon to right of them,
Cannon to left of them,   40
Cannon behind them
    Volleyed and thundered;
Stormed at with shot and shell,
While horse and hero fell.
They that had fought so well   45
Came through the jaws of Death,
Back from the mouth of hell,
All that was left of them,
    Left of six hundred.

6

When can their glory fade?   50
O the wild charge they made!
    All the world wondered.
Honor the charge they made!
Honor the Light Brigade,
    Noble six hundred!   55

1854   1854

From Maud[1]

Part 1

6

*   *   *

5

Ah, what shall I be at fifty
Should Nature keep me alive,   220
If I find the world so bitter

---

1. Tennyson described this experimental long poem as a "monodrama," in which a speaker tells his story in a sequence of short lyrics, in varying meters—a method that requires the reader to fill in the events of the action on the evidence of the speaker's shifting emotional states. The speaker is a young man, living alone in the country, whose disillusionment after his father's suicide has left him full of a bitterness that borders on madness. He is restored to sanity and intense happiness when he discovers that Maud, the beautiful daughter of a local landowner, accepts his love for her. Our selections focus on the stages of this love affair. In the early sections he is fearful of love itself ("And most of all would I flee from the cruel madness of love"), and he is suspicious that Maud is stony hearted and will make a fool of him. When she accepts his proposal, he is, at first, deliriously exultant but, later, serene and secure. Subsequent sections of the poem (not printed here) show how the resolution of his problems is shattered when he loses Maud after killing her brother in a duel. Eventually he finds a fresh resolution by enlisting to fight against Russia in the Crimean War.

    Tennyson called the poem "a little *Hamlet*, the history of a morbid, poetic soul, under the blighting influence of a recklessly speculative age."

When I am but twenty-five?
Yet, if she were not a cheat,
If Maud were all that she seemed,
And her smile were all that I dreamed,[2]   225
Then the world were not so bitter
But a smile could make it sweet.

*   *   *

8

Perhaps the smile and tender tone
Came out of her pitying womanhood,
For am I not, am I not, here alone
So many a summer since she died,   255
My mother, who was so gentle and good?
Living alone in an empty house,
Here half-hid in the gleaming wood,
Where I hear the dead at midday moan,
And the shrieking rush of the wainscot mouse,   260
And my own sad name in corners cried,
When the shiver of dancing leaves is thrown
About its echoing chambers wide,
Till a morbid hate and horror have grown
Of a world in which I have hardly mixed,   265
And a morbid eating lichen fixed
On a heart half turned to stone.

*   *   *

10

I have played with her when a child;
She remembers it now we meet.
Ah, well, well, well, I *may* be beguiled
By some coquettish deceit.
Yet, if she were not a cheat,   280
And Maud were all that she seemed,
And her smile had all that I dreamed,
Then the world were not so bitter
But a smile could make it sweet.

8

She came to the village church,
And sat by a pillar alone;
An angel watching an urn
Wept over her, carved in stone;
And once, but once, she lifted her eyes,   305
And suddenly, sweetly, strangely blushed
To find they were met by my own;
And suddenly, sweetly, my heart beat stronger
And thicker, until I heard no longer
The snowy-banded, dilettante,   310

---

2. On a previous day he had encountered Maud and was surprised by her smiling at him.

Delicate-handed priest intone;
And thought, is it pride? and mused and sighed,
"No surely, now it cannot be pride."

11

1

O let the solid ground
  Not fail beneath my feet
Before my life has found   400
  What some have found so sweet;
Then let come what come may,
What matter if I go mad,
I shall have had my day.

2

Let the sweet heavens endure,   405
  Not close and darken above me
Before I am quite quite sure
  That there is one to love me;
Then let come what come may
To a life that has been so sad,   410
I shall have had my day.

12

1

Birds in the high Hall-garden
  When twilight was falling,
Maud, Maud, Maud, Maud,
  They were crying and calling.   415

2

Where was Maud? in our wood;
  And I, who else, was with her,
Gathering woodland lilies,
  Myriads blow together.

3

Birds in our wood[3] sang   420
  Ringing through the valleys,
Maud is here, here, here
  In among the lilies.

4

I kissed her slender hand,
  She took the kiss sedately;   425
Maud is not seventeen,
  But she is tall and stately.

5

I to cry out on pride
  Who have won her favor!
O Maud were sure of Heaven   430
  If lowliness[4] could save her.

3. The wood in the valley of the speaker's small country estate. Here the "little birds" (as Tennyson called
them in a note) are responding, in a sort of duet, to the
caws of the rooks in the garden of Maud's family estate.
4. Meekness.

6

I know the way she went
    Home with her maiden posy,
For her feet have touched the meadows
    And left the daisies rosy.[5]   435

7

Birds in the high Hall-garden
    Were crying and calling to her,
Where is Maud, Maud, Maud?
    One is come to woo her.

8

Look, a horse at the door,   440
    And little King Charley snarling,[6]
Go back, my lord, across the moor,
    You are not her darling.

16

*   *   *

3

Catch not my breath, O clamorous heart,
Let not my tongue be a thrall to my eye,
For I must tell her before we part,
I must tell her, or die.[7]   570

18

1

I have led her home, my love, my only friend.
There is none like her, none.   600
And never yet so warmly ran my blood
And sweetly, on and on
Calming itself to the long-wished-for end.
Full to the banks, close on the promised good.

2

None like her, none.   605
Just now the dry-tongued laurels' pattering talk
Seemed her light foot along the garden walk,
And shook my heart to think she comes once more.
But even then I heard her close the door;
The gates of heaven are closed, and she is gone.   610

3

There is none like her, none,
Nor will be when our summers have deceased.
O, art thou[8] sighing for Lebanon
In the long breeze that streams to thy delicious East,
Sighing for Lebanon,
Dark cedar, though thy limbs have here increased,   615
Upon a pastoral slope as fair,

5. As Tennyson explained: "If you tread on the daisy [English variety], it turns up a rosy underside."
6. Maud's dog snarls at the aristocratic visitor who is the speaker's rival for Maud's hand.
7. He is about to propose to Maud, who will accept him.

8. The vast old cedar tree in Maud's garden, addressed in a fourteen-line question about its ancestry on Mt. Lebanon in Syria and its ultimate ancestry in Eden (cf. Song of Solomon 5.15).

And looking to the South and fed
With honeyed rain and delicate air,
And haunted by the starry head   620
Of her whose gentle will has changed my fate,
And made my life a perfumed altar-flame;
And over whom thy darkness must have spread
With such delight as theirs of old, thy great
Forefathers of the thornless garden, there   625
Shadowing the snow-limbed Eve from whom she came?

4

Here will I lie, while these long branches sway,
And you fair stars that crown a happy day
Go in and out as if at merry play,
Who am no more so all forlorn   630
As when it seemed far better to be born
To labor and the mattock-hardened hand
Than nursed at ease and brought to understand
A sad astrology,⁹ the boundless plan
That makes you tyrants in your iron skies,   635
Innumerable, pitiless, passionless eyes,
Cold fires, yet with power to burn and brand
His nothingness into man.

5

But now shine on, and what care I,
Who in this stormy gulf have found a pearl   640
The countercharm of space and hollow sky,¹
And do accept my madness, and would die
To save from some slight shame one simple girl?—

6

Would die, for sullen-seeming Death may give
More life to Love than is or ever was   645
In our low world, where yet 'tis sweet to live.
Let no one ask me how it came to pass;
It seems that I am happy, that to me
A livelier emerald twinkles in the grass,
A purer sapphire melts into the sea.   650

7

Not die, but live a life of truest breath,
And teach true life to fight with mortal wrongs.
O, why should Love, like men in drinking songs,
Spice his fair banquet with the dust of death?²
Make answer, Maud my bliss,   655
Maud made my Maud by that long loving kiss,
Life of my life, wilt thou not answer this?
"The dusky strand of Death inwoven here
With dear Love's tie, makes Love himself more dear."

8

Is that enchanted moan only the swell   660
Of the long waves that roll in yonder bay?

---

9. Astronomy.
1. Something that calms his former fears of the vast-
ness of space revealed by modern astronomy.

2. I.e., why do we try to intensify the experience of
love by linking it with death?

And hark the clock within, the silver knell
Of twelve sweet hours that passed in bridal white,
And died to live, long as my pulses play;
But now by this my love has closed her sight   665
And given false death[3] her hand, and stolen away
To dreamful wastes where footless fancies dwell
Among the fragments of the golden day.
May nothing there her maiden grace affright!
Dear heart, I feel with thee the drowsy spell.   670
My bride to be, my evermore delight,
My own heart's heart, my ownest own, farewell;
It is but for a little space I go.
And ye[4] meanwhile far over moor and fell
Beat to the noiseless music of the night!   675
Has our whole earth gone nearer to the glow
Of your soft splendors that you look so bright?
I have climbed nearer out of lonely hell.
Beat, happy stars, timing with things below,
Beat with my heart more blest than heart can tell,   680
Blest, but for some dark undercurrent woe
That seems to draw—-but it shall not be so;
Let all be well, be well.

*   *   *

Part 2

4[5]

1
O that 'twere possible
After long grief and pain
To find the arms of my true love
Round me once again!
2
When I was wont to meet her   145
In the silent woody places
By the home that gave me birth,
We stood tranced in long embraces
Mixt with kisses sweeter sweeter
Than anything on earth.   150
3
A shadow flits before me,
Not thou, but like to thee:
Ah Christ, that it were possible
For one short hour to see
The souls we loved, that they might tell us   155
What and where they be.
4
It leads me forth at evening,
It lightly winds and steals

3. Sleep.
4. I.e., the stars.
5. This excerpt was originally a separate lyric, written in 1833–34 and published in 1837. Tennyson wrote that a friend "begged me to weave a story round this poem, and so *Maud* came into being." The lyric expresses the speaker's longing for reunion with Maud, who has died by this point in the poem.

In a cold white robe before me,
When all my spirit reels   160
At the shouts, the leagues of lights
And the roaring of the wheels.

                           *   *   *

                                                                 1855

In the Valley of Cauteretz[1]

All along the valley, stream that flashest white,
Deepening thy voice with the deepening of the night,[2]
All along the valley, where thy waters flow,
I walked with one I loved two and thirty years ago.
All along the valley, while I walked today,   5
The two and thirty years were a mist that rolls away;
For all along the valley, down thy rocky bed,
Thy living voice to me was as the voice of the dead,
And all along the valley, by rock and cave and tree,
The voice of the dead was a living voice to me.   10

1861   1864

Idylls of the King   When John Milton was considering subjects suitable for an epic poem, one of those he entertained was the story of the Christian British king Arthur, a semilegendary leader of about A.D. 500 who fought off the heathen Saxon invaders who had swarmed into Britain after the withdrawal of the Roman legions. Tennyson likewise saw that the Arthurian story had epic potential and selected it for his lifework as "the greatest of all poetical subjects." At intervals, during a period of fifty years, he labored over the twelve books that make up his *Idylls of the King,* completing the work in 1888.

The principal source of Tennyson's stories of Arthur and his knights was Sir Thomas Malory's *Morte Darthur,* a version that Malory translated into English prose from French sources in 1470. As Talbot Donaldson has suggested, one basis of the appeal of the Arthurian stories, like the legends of Robin Hood and stories of the American West, is that all three represent the struggle of individuals to restore order in situations of chaos and anarchy, a task performed in the face of seemingly overwhelming odds. The individual stories in Tennyson's *Idylls* have the same basic appeal, but the overall design of the whole poem is more ambitious and impressive. The *Idylls of the King* represent the rise and fall of a civilization. They imply that after two thousand years of Christianity, Western civilization may be going through a cycle in which it must confront the possibilities of a renewal in the future or an apocalyptic extinction. The first book, *The Coming of Arthur,* introduces the basic myth of a springtime hero transforming a wasteland and inspiring faith and hope in the highest values of civilized life among his devoted followers. Succeeding books move through summer and autumn and culminate

---

1. A valley in the French Pyrenees visited by Tennyson and Hallam in 1830 and revisited by Tennyson in 1861. Hallam himself had earlier described Cauteretz as a place of "waters in all shapes," including "the impetuous cataract, fraying its way" and the "little blue lake whose deep, cold waters are fed eternally from neighboring glaciers." Tennyson said of this poem: "I like the little piece as well as anything I have written."
2. Lady Tennyson's journal reports how the noisy mountain stream affected her husband: "We had noticed the deepening of the Voice in the night."

in the bleak wintry scene of Arthur's last battle in which his order perishes in a
civil war; the leader of the enemy forces is his own nephew, Sir Modred.

Throughout the later books of the *Idylls* the forces of opposition grow in
strength, and disaffections infect leading figures of the Round Table itself. The
most glaring example is the adulterous relationship between Guinevere, Arthur's
"sumptuous" queen (as Tennyson once described her), and the king's chief lieutenant and friend, Sir Lancelot. Many other fallings away subsequently come to
light, such as the perfidious betrayal by Sir Gawain in *Pelleas and Ettarre*, and the
cynical conduct of Sir Tristram, whose story is told in the bitter tenth book, *The
Last Tournament*. Even Merlin, Arthur's trusted magician and counselor, becomes
corrupted and can perform no further offices for the king (*Merlin and Vivien*).
These accumulating signs of decline and fall figure prominently in the following
late idyll.

From Idylls of the King

The Passing of Arthur[1]

That story which the bold Sir Bedivere,[2]
First made and latest left of all the knights,
Told, when the man was no more than a voice
In the white winter of his age, to those
With whom he dwelt, new faces, other minds.   5

    For on their march to westward, Bedivere,
Who slowly paced among the slumbering host,
Heard in his tent the moanings of the King:

    "I found Him in the shining of the stars,
I marked Him in the flowering of His fields,   10
But in His ways with men I find Him not.
I waged His wars, and now I pass and die.
O me! for why is all around us here
As if some lesser god had made the world,
But had not force to shape it as he would,   15
Till the High God behold it from beyond,
And enter it, and make it beautiful?
Or else as if the world were wholly fair,
But that these eyes of men are dense and dim,
And have not power to see it as it is: 20
Perchance, because we see not to the close;—
For I, being simple, thought to work His will,
And have but stricken with the sword in vain;
And all whereon I leaned in wife and friend
Is traitor to my peace, and all my realm   25
Reels back into the beast, and is no more.

1. The principal source of this final idyll was Malory's *Morte Darthur* 21.4–5. Preceding the action of
this idyll, Arthur had been in France with his nephew
Gawain fighting against the forces of Lancelot. Learning at that time of the gathering of an army against
him in England, under the leadership of his nephew

Modred, Arthur returned there to engage in his last
battle. Upon landing at Dover, Gawain was slain.
2. A knight who had long been close to the king,
described in *The Coming of Arthur*: "Bedivere, the
first of all his knights / knighted by Arthur at his
crowning."

My God, thou hast forgotten me in my death:[3]
Nay—God my Christ—I pass but shall not die."

Then, ere that last weird battle in the west,
There came on Arthur sleeping, Gawain killed   30
In Lancelot's war, the ghost of Gawain blown
Along a wandering wind, and past his ear
Went shrilling. "Hollow, hollow all delight!
Hail, King! tomorrow thou shalt pass away.
Farewell! there is an isle of rest for thee.   35
And I am blown along a wandering wind,
And hollow, hollow, hollow all delight."
And fainter onward, like wild birds that change
Their season in the night and wail their way
From cloud to cloud, down the long wind the dream   40
Shrilled; but in going mingled with dim cries
Far in the moonlit haze among the hills,
As of some lonely city sacked by night,
When all is lost, and wife and child with wail
Pass to new lords; and Arthur woke and called,   45
"Who spake? A dream. O light upon the wind,
Thine, Gawain, was the voice—are these dim cries
Thine? or doth all that haunts the waste and wild
Mourn, knowing it will go along with me?"

This heard the bold Sir Bedivere and spake: 50
"O me, my King, let pass whatever will,
Elves, and the harmless glamor of the field;[4]
But in their stead thy name and glory cling
To all high places like a golden cloud
Forever: but as yet thou shalt not pass.   55
Light was Gawain in life, and light in death
Is Gawain, for the ghost is as the man;
And care not thou for dreams from him, but rise—
I hear the steps of Modred in the west,
And with him many of thy people, and knights   60
Once thine, whom thou hast loved, but grosser grown
Than heathen, spitting at their vows and thee.
Right well in heart they know thee for the King.
Arise, go forth and conquer as of old."

Then spake King Arthur to Sir Bedivere: 65
"Far other is this battle in the west
Whereto we move, than when we strove in youth,
And brake the petty kings, and fought with Rome,
Or thrust the heathen from the Roman wall,
And shook him through the north. Ill doom is mine   70
To war against my people and my knights.
The king who fights his people fights himself.

3. Cf. Matthew 27.46: "My God, my God, why hast thou forsaken me?"
4. Tennyson said the reference is to "the legends which cluster round the King's name." One legend told of the elves' bestowing gifts on Arthur as a child.

And they thy knights, who loved me once, the stroke
That strikes them dead is as my death to me.
Yet let us hence, and find or feel a way   75
Through this blind haze, which ever since I saw
One lying in the dust at Almesbury,[5]
Hath folded in the passes of the world."

   Then rose the King and moved his host by night,
And ever pushed Sir Modred, league by league,   80
Back to the sunset bound of Lyonnesse[6]—
A land of old upheaven from the abyss
By fire, to sink into the abyss again;
Where fragments of forgotten peoples dwelled,
And the long mountains ended in a coast   85
Of ever-shifting sand, and far away
The phantom circle of a moaning sea.
There the pursuer could pursue no more,
And he that fled no further fly the King;
And there, that day when the great light of heaven   90
Burned at his lowest in the rolling year,
On the waste sand by the waste sea they closed.
Nor ever yet had Arthur fought a fight
Like this last, dim, weird battle of the west.
A deathwhite mist slept over sand and sea: 95
Whereof the chill, to him who breathed it, drew
Down with his blood, till all his heart was cold
With formless fear; and even on Arthur fell
Confusion, since he saw not whom he fought.
For friend and foe were shadows in the mist,   100
And friend slew friend not knowing whom he slew;
And some had visions out of golden youth,
And some beheld the faces of old ghosts
Look in upon the battle; and in the mist
Was many a noble deed, many a base,   105
And chance and craft and strength in single fights,
And ever and anon with host to host
Shocks, and the splintering spear, the hard mail hewn,
Shield-breakings, and the clash of brands, the crash
Of battleaxes on shattered helms, and shrieks   110
After the Christ, of those who falling down
Looked up for heaven, and only saw the mist;
And shouts of heathen and the traitor knights,
Oaths, insult, filth, and monstrous blasphemies,
Sweat, writhings, anguish, laboring of the lungs   115
In that close mist, and cryings for the light,
Moans of the dying, and voices of the dead.

   Last, as by some one deathbed after wail
Of suffering, silence follows, or through death

---

5. The convent to which Guinevere had withdrawn;   6. Legendary land extending west from Cornwall,
during the king's farewell visit to her there, she had   that sank into the sea.
lain in the dust at his feet.

Or deathlike swoon, thus over all that shore,   120
Save for some whisper of the seething seas,
A dead hush fell; but when the dolorous day
Grew drearier toward twilight falling, came
A bitter wind, clear from the North, and blew
The mist aside, and with that wind the tide   125
Rose, and the pale King glanced across the field
Of battle: but no man was moving there;
Nor any cry of Christian heard thereon,
Nor yet of heathen; only the wan wave
Brake in among dead faces, to and fro   130
Swaying the helpless hands, and up and down
Tumbling the hollow helmets of the fallen,
And shivered brands that once had fought with Rome,
And rolling far along the gloomy shores
The voice of days of old and days to be.   135

    Then spake King Arthur to Sir Bedivere,
And whiter than the mist that all day long
Had held the field of battle was the King:

    "Hearest thou this great voice that shakes the world,
And wastes the narrow realm whereon we move,   140
And beats upon the faces of the dead,
My dead, as though they had not died for me? —
O Bedivere, for on my heart hath fallen
Confusion, till I know not what I am,
Nor whence I am, nor whether I be King.   145
Behold, I seem but King among the dead."

    Then spake the bold Sir Bedivere: "My King,
King everywhere! and so the dead have kings,
There also will I worship thee as King.
Yet still thy life is whole, and still I live   150
Who love thee; but who hates thee, he that brought
The heathen back among us, yonder stands,
Modred, unharmed, the traitor of thine house."

    Then spake the King: "My house hath been my doom.
But call not thou this traitor of my house   155
Who hath but dwelled beneath one roof with me.
My house are rather they who sware my vows,
Yea, even while they brake them, owned me King.
And well for thee, saying in my dark hour,
When all the purport of my throne hath failed,   160
That quick or dead thou holdest me for King.
King am I, whatsoever be their cry;
And one last act of kinghood shalt thou see
Yet, ere I pass." And uttering this the King
Made at the man: then Modred smote his liege   165
Hard on that helm which many a heathen sword
Had beaten thin; while Arthur at one blow,

Striking the last stroke with Excalibur,
Slew him, and all but slain himself, he fell.

So all day long the noise of battle rolled   170
Among the mountains by the winter sea;
Until King Arthur's Table, man by man,
Had fallen in Lyonnesse about their lord,
King Arthur. Then, because his wound was deep,
The bold Sir Bedivere uplifted him,   175
And bore him to a chapel nigh the field,
A broken chancel with a broken cross,
That stood on a dark strait of barren land:
On one side lay the Ocean, and on one
Lay a great water, and the moon was full.   180

Then spake King Arthur to Sir Bedivere:
"The sequel of today unsolders all
The goodliest fellowship of famous knights
Whereof this world holds record. Such a sleep
They sleep—the men I loved. I think that we   185
Shall never more, at any future time,
Delight our souls with talk of knightly deeds,
Walking about the gardens and the halls
Of Camelot, as in the days that were.
I perish by this people which I made,—   190
Though Merlin sware that I should come again
To rule once more;[7] but, let what will be, be,
I am so deeply smitten through the helm
That without help I cannot last til morn.
Thou therefore take my brand[8] Excalibur,   195
Which was my pride: for thou rememberest how
In those old days, one summer noon, an arm
Rose up from out the bosom of the lake,
Clothed in white samite,[9] mystic, wonderful,
Holding the sword—and how I rowed across   200
And took it, and have worn it, like a king;
And, wheresoever I am sung or told
In aftertime, this also shall be known:
But now delay not: take Excalibur,
And fling him far into the middle mere:[1]   205
Watch what thou seëst, and lightly[2] bring me word."

To him replied the bold Sir Bedivere:
"It is not meet, Sir King, to leave thee thus,
Aidless, alone, and smitten through the helm—
A little thing may harm a wounded man;   210
Yet I thy hest[3] will all perform at full,
Watch what I see, and lightly bring thee word."

7. Cf. Malory, *Morte Darthur* 21.7: "Some men yet   9. A rich, heavy silk.
say in many parts of England that King Arthur is not   1. Middle of the lake.
dead, but by the will of our Lord in another place. And 2. Quickly.
men say that he will come again."   3. Command.
8. Sword.

So saying, from the ruined shrine he stepped,
And in the moon athwart the place of tombs,
Where lay the mighty bones of ancient men,   215
Old knights, and over them the sea-wind sang
Shrill, chill, with flakes of foam. He, stepping down
By zigzag paths, and juts of pointed rock,
Came on the shining levels of the lake.

There drew he forth the brand Excalibur,   220
And o'er him, drawing it, the winter moon,
Brightening the skirts of a long cloud, ran forth
And sparkled keen with frost against the hilt:
For all the haft twinkled with diamond sparks,
Myriads of topaz-lights, and jacinth-work[4]   225
Of subtlest jewelry. He gazed so long
That both his eyes were dazzled as he stood,
This way and that dividing the swift mind,
In act to throw: but at the last it seemed
Better to leave Excalibur concealed   230
There in the many-knotted waterflags,
That whistled stiff and dry about the marge.
So strode he back slow to the wounded King.

Then spake King Arthur to Sir Bedivere:
"Hast thou performed my mission which I gave?   235
What is it thou hast seen? or what hast heard?"

And answer made the bold Sir Bedivere:
"I heard the ripple washing in the reeds,
And the wild water lapping on the crag."

To whom replied King Arthur, faint and pale: 240
"Thou hast betrayed thy nature and thy name.
Not rendering true answer, as beseemed
Thy fëalty, nor like a noble knight:
For surer sign had followed, either hand,
Or voice, or else a motion of the mere.   245
This is a shameful thing for men to lie.
Yet now, I charge thee, quickly go again,
As thou art lief[5] and dear, and do the thing
I bade thee, watch, and lightly bring me word."

Then went Sir Bedivere the second time   250
Across the ridge, and paced beside the mere,
Counting the dewy pebbles, fixed in thought;
But when he saw the wonder of the hilt,
How curiously and strangely chased,[6] he smote
His palms together, and he cried aloud: 255

4. "Jacinth": a red gem.   6. Adorned. "Curiously": skillfully.
5. Beloved.

"And if indeed I cast the brand away,
Surely a precious thing, one worthy note,
Should thus be lost forever from the earth,
Which might have pleased the eyes of many men.
What good should follow this, if this were done?   260
What harm, undone? Deep harm to disobey,
Seeing obedience is the bond of rule.
Were it well to obey then, if a king demand
An act unprofitable, against himself?
The King is sick, and knows not what he does.   265
What record, or what relic of my lord
Should be to aftertime, but empty breath
And rumors of a doubt? But were this kept,
Stored in some treasure-house of mighty kings,
Some one might show it at a joust of arms,   270
Saying, 'King Arthur's sword, Excalibur,
Wrought by the lonely maiden of the Lake.
Nine years she wrought it, sitting in the deeps
Upon the hidden bases of the hills.'
So might some old man speak in the aftertime   275
To all the people, winning reverence.
But now much honor and much fame were lost."

    So spake he, clouded with his own conceit,[7]
And hid Excalibur the second time,
And so strode back slow to the wounded king.   280

    Then spoke King Arthur, breathing heavily:
"What is it thou hast seen? or what hast heard?"

    And answer made the bold Sir Bedivere:
"I heard the water lapping on the crag,
And the long ripple washing in the reeds."   285

    To whom replied King Arthur, much in wrath:
"Ah, miserable and unkind, untrue,
Unknightly, traitor-hearted! Woe is me!
Authority forgets a dying king,
Laid widowed of the power in his eye   290
That bowed the will. I see thee what thou art,
For thou, the latest-left of all my knights,
In whom should meet the offices of all,
Thou wouldst betray me for the precious hilt;
Either from lust of gold, or like a girl   295
Valuing the giddy pleasure of the eyes.
Yet, for a man may fail in duty twice,
And the third time may prosper, get thee hence:
But, if thou spare to fling Excalibur,
I will arise and slay thee with my hands."   300

7. Vain and foolish fancies.

Then quickly rose Sir Bedivere, and ran,
And, leaping down the ridges lightly, plunged
Among the bullrush beds, and clutched the sword,
And strongly wheeled and threw it. The great brand
Made lightnings in the splendor of the moon,   305
And flashing round and round and whirled in an arch,
Shot like a streamer of the northern morn,[8]
Seen where the moving isles of winter shock[9]
By night, with noises of the Northern Sea.
So flashed and fell the brand Excalibur: 310
But ere he dipped the surface, rose an arm
Clothed in white samite, mystic, wonderful,
And caught him by the hilt, and brandished him
Three times, and drew him under in the mere.
And lightly went the other to the King.   315

Then spoke King Arthur, drawing thicker breath:
"Now see I by thine eyes that this is done.
Speak out: what is it thou hast heard, or seen?"

And answer made the bold Sir Bedivere:
"Sir King, I closed mine eyelids, lest the gems   320
Should blind my purpose, for I never saw,
Nor shall see, here or elsewhere, till I die,
Not though I live three lives of mortal men,
So great a miracle as yonder hilt.
Then with both hands I flung him, wheeling him;   325
But when I looked again, behold an arm,
Clothed in white samite, mystic, wonderful,
That caught him by the hilt, and brandished him
Three times, and drew him under in the mere."

And answer made King Arthur, breathing hard: 330
"My end draws nigh; 'tis time that I were gone.
Make broad thy shoulders to receive my weight,
And bear me to the margin; yet I fear
My wound hath taken cold, and I shall die."

So saying, from the pavement he half rose,   335
Slowly, with pain, reclining on his arm,
And looking wistfully with wide blue eyes
As in a picture. Him Sir Bedivere
Remorsefully regarded through his tears,
And would have spoken, but he found not words;   340
Then took with care, and kneeling on one knee,
O'er both his shoulders drew the languid hands,
And rising bore him through the place of tombs.

But, as he walked, King Arthur panted hard,
Like one that feels a nightmare on his bed   345

8. The northern lights.   9. I.e., where the icebergs collide.

When all the house is mute. So sighed the King,
Muttering and murmuring at his ear, "Quick, quick!
I fear it is too late, and I shall die."
But the other swiftly strode from ridge to ridge,
Clothed with his breath, and looking, as he walked,   350
Larger than human on the frozen hills.
He heard the deep behind him, and a cry
Before. His own thought drove him like a goad.
Dry clashed his harness in the icy caves
And barren chasms, and all to left and right   355
The bare black cliff clanged round him, as he based
His feet on juts of slippery crag that rang
Sharp-smitten with the dint of armèd heels —
And on a sudden, lo! the level lake,
And the long glories of the winter moon.   360

      Then saw they how there hove a dusky barge,
Dark as a funeral scarf from stem to stern,
Beneath them; and descending they were ware
That all the decks were dense with stately forms,
Black-stoled, black-hooded, like a dream — by these   365
Three Queens with crowns of gold: and from them rose
A cry that shivered to the tingling stars,
And, as it were one voice, an agony
Of lamentation, like a wind that shrills
All night in a waste land, where no one comes,   370
Or hath come, since the making of the world.

      Then murmured Arthur, "Place me in the barge."
So to the barge they came. There those three Queens
Put forth their hands, and took the King, and wept.
But she, that rose the tallest of them all   375
And fairest, laid his head upon her lap,
And loosed the shattered casque,[1] and chafed his hands,
And called him by his name, complaining loud,
And dropping bitter tears against a brow
Striped with dark blood: for all his face was white   380
And colorless, and like the withered moon
Smote by the fresh beam of the springing east;
And all his greaves and cuisses[2] dashed with drops
Of onset;[3] and the light and lustrous curls —
That made his forehead like a rising sun   385
High from the daïs-throne — were parched with dust;
Or, clotted into points and hanging loose,
Mixed with the knightly growth that fringed his lips.
So like a shattered column lay the King;
Not like that Arthur who, with lance in rest,   390
From spur to plume a star of tournament,
Shot through the lists at Camelot, and charged
Before the eyes of ladies and of kings.

1. Helmet.   armor to protect the leg below the knee.
2. Armor to protect the front of the thighs. "Greaves":   3. Blood from battle.

Then loudly cried the bold Sir Bedivere:
"Ah! my Lord Arthur, whither shall I go?   395
Where shall I hide my forehead and my eyes?
For now I see the true old times are dead,
When every morning brought a noble chance,
And every chance brought out a noble knight.
Such times have been not since the light that led   400
The holy Elders[4] with the gift of myrrh.
But now the whole Round Table is dissolved
Which was an image of the mighty world,
And I, the last, go forth companionless,
And the days darken round me, and the years,   405
Among new men, strange faces, other minds."

And slowly answered Arthur from the barge:
"The old order changeth, yielding place to new,
And God fulfills himself in many ways,
Lest one good custom should corrupt the world.   410
Comfort thyself: what comfort is in me?
I have lived my life, and that which I have done
May He within himself make pure! but thou,
If thou shouldst never see my face again,
Pray for my soul. More things are wrought by prayer   415
Than this world dreams of. Wherefore, let thy voice
Rise like a fountain for me night and day.
For what are men better than sheep or goats
That nourish a blind life within the brain,
If, knowing God, they lift not hands of prayer   420
Both for themselves and those who call them friend?
For so the whole round earth is every way
Bound by gold chains about the feet of God.
But now farewell. I am going a long way
With these thou seëst—if indeed I go   425
(For all my mind is clouded with a doubt)—
To the island-valley of Avilion;[5]
Where falls not hail, or rain, or any snow,
Nor ever wind blows loudly: but it lies
Deep-meadowed, happy, fair with orchard lawns   430
And bowery hollows crowned with summer sea,
Where I will heal me of my grievous wound."

So said he, and the barge with oar and sail
Moved from the brink, like some full-breasted swan
That, fluting a wild carol ere her death,   435
Ruffles her pure cold plume, and takes the flood
With swarthy webs. Long stood Sir Bedivere
Revolving many memories, till the hull
Looked one black dot against the verge of dawn,
And on the mere the wailing died away.   440

4. I.e., the star that guided the three kings ("Elders") to the Christ child at Bethlehem.
5. Avalon, in Celtic mythology and medieval ro-mance, the Vale of the Blessed where heroes enjoyed life after death.

But when that moan had passed for evermore,
The stillness of the dead world's winter dawn
Amazed him, and he groaned, "The King is gone."
And therewithal came on him the weird rhyme,[6]
"From the great deep to the great deep he goes."   445

Whereat he slowly turned and slowly clomb
The last hard footstep of that iron crag;
Thence marked the black hull moving yet, and cried,
"He passes to be King among the dead,
And after healing of his grievous wound   450
He comes again; but—if he come no more—
O me, be yon dark Queens in yon black boat,
Who shrieked and wailed, the three whereat we gazed
On that high day, when, clothed with living light,
They stood before his throne in silence, friends   455
Of Arthur, who should help him at his need?"

Then from the dawn it seemed there came, but faint
As from beyond the limit of the world,
Like the last echo born of a great cry,
Sounds, as if some fair city were one voice   460
Around a king returning from his wars.

Thereat once more he moved about, and clomb
Even to the highest he could climb, and saw,
Straining his eyes beneath an arch of hand,
Or thought he saw, the speck that bare the King,   465
Down that long water opening on the deep
Somewhere far off, pass on and on, and go
From less to less and vanish into light.
And the new sun rose bringing the new year.

1833–69   1869

Northern Farmer[1]

New Style

1

Doss't thou 'ear my 'erse's[2] legs, as they canters awaäy?
Proputty,[3] proputty, proputty—that's what I 'ears 'em saäy.
Proputty, proputty, proputty—Sam, thou's an ass for thy paaïns:
Theer's moor sense i' one o' 'is legs, nor in all thy braaïns.

---

6. A mysterious prophecy in verse had been spoken by
Merlin concerning Arthur's birth: "Sun, rain, and sun!
and where is he who knows? From the great deep to
the great deep he goes" (*The Coming of Arthur*, lines
409–410).
1. This monologue exemplifies the diversity of Tennyson's talents. A passionate attachment to land and
property, which was portrayed sympathetically by
Wordsworth in *Michael*, is here represented humorously. The harsh common sense of the farmer's atti-

tude toward love and marriage is reinforced by his jaw-
breaking north English dialect.
    This is the second of a pair of monologues in dialect.
In the first, *Northern Farmer: Old Style*, the speaker is
a bailiff who has spent his life supervising the farm-
lands of a wealthy squire. In the second, the "new
style" farmer is himself an independent landowner.
2. Horse's.
3. Property.

2

Woä—theer's a craw[4] to pluck wi' tha, Sam: yon's parson's 'ouse—   5
Dosn't thou knaw that a man mun be eäther a man or a mouse?
Time to think on it then; for thou'll be twenty to weeäk.[5]
Proputty, proputty—woä then woä—let ma 'ear mysèn[6] speäk.

3

Me an' thy muther, Sammy, 'as beän a-talkin' o' thee;
Thou's beän talkin' to muther, an' she beän a tellin' it me.   10
Thou'll not marry for munny—thou's sweet upo' parson's lass—
Noä—thou'll marry for luvv—an' we boäth on us thinks tha an ass.

4

Seeäd her todaäy goä by—Saäint's-daäy—they was ringing the bells.
She's a beauty thou thinks—an' soä is scoors o' gells,[7]
Them as 'as munny an' all—wot's a beauty?—the flower as blaws.   15
But proputty, proputty sticks, an' proputty, proputty graws.

5

Do'ant be stunt:[8] taäke time; I knaws what maäkes tha sa mad.
Warn't I craäzed fur the lasses mysèn when I wur a lad?
But I knawed a Quaäker feller as often 'as towd[9] ma this:
"Doänt thou marry for munny, but goä wheer munny is!"   20

6

An' I went wheer munny war; an' thy muther coom to 'and,
Wi' lots o' munny laaïd by, an' a nicetish bit o' land.
Maäybe she warn't a beauty:—I niver giv it a thowt—
But warn't she as good to cuddle an' kiss as a lass as 'ant nowt?[1]

7

Parson's lass 'ant nowt, an' she weänt 'a nowt[2] when 'e's deäd,   25
Mun be a guvness,[3] lad, or summut, and addle[4] her breäd:
Why? fur 'e's nobbut[5] a curate, an' weänt niver get hissèn clear,
An' 'e maäde the bed as 'e ligs on afoor 'e coomed to the shere.[6]

8

An' thin 'e coomed to the parish wi' lots o' Varsity debt,
Stook to his taaïl they did, an' 'e 'ant got shut on 'em[7] yet.   30
An' 'e ligs on 'is back i' the grip,[8] wi' noan to lend 'im a shuvv,
Woorse nor a far-weltered yowe:[9] fur, Sammy, 'e married fur luvv.

9

Luvv? what's luvv? thou can luvv thy lass an' 'er munny too,
Maäkin' 'em goä togither, as they've good right to do.
Couldn' I luvv thy muther by cause o' 'er munny laaïd by?   35
Naäy—fur I luvved 'er a vast sight moor fur it: reäson why.

10

Ay an' thy muther says thou wants to marry the lass,
Cooms of a gentleman burn:[1] an' we boäth on us think tha an ass.
Woä then, proputty, wiltha?—an ass as near as mays nowt[2]—
Woä then, wiltha? dangtha!—the bees is as fell as owt.[3]   40

4. Crow.
5. This week.
6. Myself.
7. Scores of girls.
8. Stubborn.
9. Told.
1. Has nothing.
2. Won't have anything.
3. Must be a governess.

4. Earn.
5. Nothing but.
6. Shire. "Ligs": lies.
7. Rid of them.
8. Ditch.
9. Ewe lying on her back.
1. Born.
2. Makes nothing.
3. The flies are as mean as anything.

11

Breäk me a bit o' the esh[4] for his 'eäd, lad, out o' the fence!
Gentleman burn! what's gentleman burn? is it shillins an' pence?
Proputty, proputty's ivrything 'ere, an', Sammy, I'm blest
If it isn't the saäme oop yonder, fur them as 'as it's the best.

12

Tis'n them as 'as munny as breäks into 'ouses an' steäls,   45
Them as 'as coäts to their backs an' taäkes their regular meäls.
Noä, but it's them as niver knaws wheer a meäl's to be 'ad.
Taäke my word for it, Sammy, the poor in a loomp is bad.

13

Them or thir feythers, tha sees, mun 'a beän a laäzy lot,
Fur work mun 'a gone to the gittin' whiniver munny was got.   50
Feyther 'ad ammost nowt; leästways 'is munny was 'id.
But 'e tued an' moiled[5] 'issèn deäd, an' 'e died a good un, 'e did.

14

Loök thou theer wheer Wrigglesby beck[6] cooms out by the 'ill!
Feyther run oop[7] to the farm, an' I runs oop to the mill;
An' I'll run oop to the brig,[8] an' that thou'll live to see;   55
And if thou marries a good un I'll leäve the land to thee.

15

Thim's my noätions, Sammy, wheerby I meäns to stick;
But if thou marries a bad un, I'll leäve the land to Dick.—
Coom oop, propputty, proputty—that's what I 'ears 'im saäy—
Proputty, proputty, proputty—canter an' canter awaäy.   60
1865   1869

Flower in the Crannied Wall

Flower in the crannied wall,
I pluck you out of the crannies,
I hold you here, root and all, in my hand,
Little flower—but if I could understand
What you are, root and all, and all in all,   5
I should know what God and man is.

1869

"Frater Ave atque Vale"[1]

Row us out from Desenzano,[2] to your Sirmione row!
So they rowed, and there we landed—"O venusta Sirmio!"
There to me through all the groves of olive in the summer glow,
There beneath the Roman ruin where the purple flowers grow,

4. A branch of ash leaves (to keep the flies off the horse's head).
5. Toiled and drudged.
6. Brook.
7. I.e., father's property ran up.
8. Bridge.
1. "Brother, hail and farewell," a line from an elegy by the Roman poet Catullus on the death of his brother (101.10). Tennyson himself had recently lost his brother Charles.
2. A town on Lake Garda in Italy, which Tennyson visited in 1880. "Sirmione" is a beautiful peninsula jutting into the lake, on which Catullus had his summer home. Catullus' poem in honor of the locality includes the phrase "O venusta Sirmio!" ("O lovely Sirmio!").

Came that "Ave atque Vale" of the Poet's hopeless woe,   5
Tenderest of Roman poets nineteen hundred years ago,
"Frater Ave atque Vale"—as we wandered to and fro
Gazing at the Lydian[3] laughter of the Garda Lake below
Sweet Catullus's all-but-island olive-silvery Sirmio!

1880   1883

The Dawn

"You are but children."
—EGYPTIAN PRIEST TO SOLON

Red of the Dawn!
Screams of a babe in the red-hot palms of a Moloch[1] of Tyre,
    Man with his brotherless dinner on man in the tropical wood,
    Priests in the name of the Lord passing souls through fire to the fire,
Head-hunters and boats of Dahomey[2] that float upon human blood!   5

Red of the Dawn!
Godless fury of peoples, and Christless frolic of kings,
    And the bolt of war dashing down upon cities and blazing farms,
    For Babylon was a child newborn, and Rome was a babe in arms,
And London and Paris and all the rest are as yet but in leading strings.   10

Dawn not Day,
While scandal is mouthing a bloodless name at *her* cannibal feast,
    And rake-ruined bodies and souls go down in a common wreck,
    And the Press of a thousand cities is prized for it smells of the beast,
Or easily violates virgin Truth for a coin or a check.   15

Dawn not Day!
Is it Shame, so few should have climbed from the dens in the level below,
    Men, with a heart and a soul, no slaves of a four-footed will?
    But if twenty million of summers are stored in the sunlight still,
We are far from the noon of man, there is time for the race to grow.   20

Red of the Dawn!
Is it turning a fainter red? So be it, but when shall we lay
    The Ghost of the Brute that is walking and haunting us yet, and be free?
    In a hundred, a thousand winters? Ah, what will *our* children be?
The men of a hundred thousand, a million summers away?   25

1892

3. The Etruscans, who settled near Lake Garda, were thought to be descended from the Lydians of Asia Minor.
1. A god to whom children were sacrificed as burnt offerings.
2. West African country in which the custom of human sacrifice may have persisted in the 19th century. In 1870, Tennyson reported in a conversation: "On the accession of a king in Dahomey, enough women victims were killed to float a small canoe with their blood." In 1892, after a war, Dahomey became a French colony.

Crossing the Bar[1]

Sunset and evening star,
  And one clear call for me!
And may there be no moaning of the bar,[2]
  When I put out to sea,

But such a tide as moving seems asleep, 5
  Too full for sound and foam,
When that which drew from out the boundless deep
  Turns again home.

Twilight and evening bell,
  And after that the dark! 10
And may there be no sadness of farewell,
  When I embark;

For though from out our bourne[3] of Time and Place
  The flood may bear me far,
I hope to see my Pilot face to face[4] 15
  When I have crossed the bar.

1889   1889

1. Although not the last poem written by Tennyson, *Crossing the Bar* appears, at his request, as the final poem in all collections of his work.
2. Mournful sound of the ocean beating on a sand bar at the mouth of a harbor.
3. Boundary.
4. The expression "face to face" also occurs in two lines of section 131 of *In Memoriam* not used but left in manuscript: "And come to look on those we loved / And That which made us, face to face."

ROBERT BROWNING
1812–1889

1846:   Marriage to Elizabeth Barrett and residence in Italy.
1855:   *Men and Women* published.
1861:   Death of Elizabeth Barrett Browning.
1868–69: *The Ring and the Book* published.

During the years of his marriage Robert Browning was sometimes referred to as "Mrs. Browning's husband." Elizabeth Barrett, who has been regarded in the twentieth century as a lesser figure, was at that time a famous poet while her husband was a relatively unknown experimenter whose poems were greeted with misunderstanding or indifference. Not until the 1860s did he at last gain a public and become recognized as the rival or equal of Tennyson. In the twentieth century his reputation has persisted but in an unusual way: his poetry is admired by two groups of readers widely different in tastes. To one group, his work is a moral tonic. Such readers appreciate him as a man who lived bravely and as a writer who showed life to be a joyful battle, the imperfections of this world being remedied, under the dispensations of an all-loving God, by the perfections of the next. Typical of this group are the Browning societies that have flourished in England and

America. Members of these societies usually regard their poet as a wise philosopher and religious teacher who resolved the doubts that had troubled Arnold and
Tennyson and that have continued to trouble later generations of less confident
writers.

A second group of readers enjoy Browning less for his attempt to solve problems
of religious doubt than for his attempt to solve the problems of how poetry should
be written. Such poets as Ezra Pound and Robert Lowell have valued him as a
major artist; they have recognized that more than any other nineteenth-century
poet (even including Hopkins), it was Browning who energetically hacked through
a trail that has subsequently become the main road of twentieth-century poetry. In
Poetry and the Age (1953) Randall Jarrell remarked how "the dramatic monologue,
which once had depended for its effect upon being a departure from the norm of
poetry, now became in one form or another the norm." Later poets such as Richard Howard in the United States are especially close to Browning's mode. In 1969,
Howard dedicated a volume of monologues to Browning: "to the great poet of
otherness . . . who said, as I should like to say, 'I'll tell my state as though 'twere
none of mine.'" And George Macbeth, in 1987, ranked Browning as "the most
effective creator of character in English, after Dickens and Shakespeare."

The dramatic monologue, as Browning uses it, separates the speaker from the
poet in such a way that the reader must work through the words of the speaker to
discover the meaning of the poet. For example, in the well-known early monologue *My Last Duchess*, we listen to the duke as he speaks of his dead wife as if
we were overhearing a man talking into the telephone in a booth adjacent to ours.
From his one-sided conversation we piece together the situation, both past and
present, and we infer what sort of woman the duchess really was and what sort of
man the duke is. Ultimately, we may also infer what the poet himself thinks of the
speaker he has created. In this poem, it is fairly easy to reach such a judgment,
although the pleasure of the poem results from our reconstruction of a story quite
different from the one the duke thinks he is telling. Many of Browning's poems
are far less stable, and it is difficult to discern the relationship of the poet to his
speaker. In reading *A Grammarian's Funeral*, for example, can we be sure that the
central character is a hero? Or is he merely a fool? In *"Childe Roland to the Dark
Tower Came"* is the speaker describing a phantasmagoric landscape of his own
paranoid imagining or is the poem a fable of courage and defiance in a modern
wasteland? Browning has not made the answers easy for us.

In addition to his experiments with the dramatic monologue, Browning also
experimented with language and syntax. The grotesque rhymes and jaw-breaking
diction that he often employs have been repugnant to some critics; George Santayana, for instance, dismissed him as a clumsy barbarian. But to those who appreciate Browning, the incongruities of language are not literally incongruous but
functional, a humorous and appropriate counterpart to an imperfect world. Ezra
Pound's tribute to "Old Hippety-Hop o' the accents," as he addresses Browning, is
both affectionate and memorable:

> Heart that was big as the bowels of Vesuvius
> Words that were winged as her sparks in eruption,
> Eagled and thundered as Jupiter Pluvius
> Sound in your wind past all signs o' corruption.

This capacity to attract the admiration of such a diversity of readers, sophisticated
and unsophisticated, is one of several ways in which Browning's writings can be
likened to those of Dickens and Shakespeare.

The personal life of Robert Browning falls into three phases: his years as a child
and young bachelor, as a husband, and as a widower. Each of these phases is most
appropriately considered in relation to his development as a poet.

He was born in Camberwell, a London suburb, within a few months of the births of Dickens and Thackeray. His father, a bank clerk, was a learned man with an extensive library. His mother was a kindly, religious-minded woman, interested in music, whose love for her brilliant son was warmly reciprocated. Until the time of his marriage, at the age of thirty-four, Browning was rarely absent from his parents' home. He attended a boarding school near Camberwell, traveled a little (to Russia and Italy), and was a student at the University of London for a short period, but he preferred to pursue his education at home, where he was tutored in foreign languages, music, boxing, and horsemanship and where he read omnivorously. From this unusual education he acquired a store of knowledge on which to draw for the background of his poems.

The "obscurity" of which his contemporaries complained in his earlier poetry may be partly accounted for by the circumstances of Browning's education. He was inclined to assume that his out-of-the-ordinary learning was generally shared by educated readers. Often it was not. But the obscurity of such poems as *Sordello* (1840) is attributable not only to the nature of Browning's learning but to the poet's anxious desire to avoid exposing himself too explicitly before his readers. His first poem, *Pauline*, published when he was twenty-one, had been modeled on the example of Shelley, the most personal of poets. When a review by John Stuart Mill pointed out that the young author was parading a "morbid state" of self-worship, Browning was overwhelmed with embarrassment. He resolved to avoid confessional writings thereafter.

One way of reducing the personal element in his poetry was to write plays instead of soul-searching narratives or lyrics. In 1836, encouraged by the actor W. C. Macready, Browning began work on his first play, *Strafford*, a historical tragedy that lasted only four nights when it was produced in London in 1837. For ten years, the young writer struggled to produce other plays that would better hold the attention of an audience, but as stage productions they all remained failures. Browning nevertheless profited from this otherwise disheartening experience. Writing dialogue for actors led him to explore another form more congenial to his genius, the dramatic monologue, a form that enabled him through imaginary speakers to avoid explicit autobiography and yet did not demand that these speakers act out their story with the speed or the simplifications that stage production demands. As William Irvine notes: "In Browning's monologues, murderers recollect, but do not commit, their murders." His first collection of such monologues, *Dramatic Lyrics*, appeared in 1842. Unlike Tennyson's volume, appearing the same year, *Dramatic Lyrics* was as poorly received by reviewers and public as Browning's plays had been.

Browning's resolution to avoid the subjective manner of Shelley did not preclude his being influenced by the earlier poet in other ways. At fourteen, when he first discovered Shelley's works, he became an atheist and liberal. Although he grew away from the atheism, after a struggle, and also the extreme phases of his liberalism, he retained from Shelley's influence something permanent and more difficult to define: an ardent dedication to ideals (often undefined ideals) and an energetic striving toward goals (often undefined goals). This quality of aspiration is much more mixed with earthiness—even worldliness—in Browning's character than in Shelley's. To soar upward on a skylark's wing was not to Browning's taste. He is more like Robert Frost's swinger of birches who climbs a tree toward heaven but is anxious to swing down to earth again before getting too far away.

Yet the element of worldliness should not obscure from us Browning's ardent romanticism. His love affair with Elizabeth Barrett was romantic in several of the senses of that hard-worked adjective. It is easy to see why the well-known story of their courtship has been retold by novelists, dramatists, and movie producers, for the situation had the dramatic ingredients of Browning's own favorite story of St. George rescuing the maiden from the dragon. Almost everything seemed unpropitious when Browning met Elizabeth Barrett in 1845. She was six years older than he was, a semi-invalid, jealously guarded by her possessively tyrannical father. But love, as the poet was to say later, is best, and love swept aside all obstacles. After their elopement to Italy, the former semi-invalid was soon enjoying good health and a full life. The husband likewise seemed to thrive during the years of this remarkable marriage. Like many English poets, he was especially at ease in the warm lands of the Mediterranean. His most memorable volume of poems, *Men and Women* (1855), reflects his enjoyment of Italy: its picturesque landscapes and lively street scenes as well as its monuments from the past—its Renaissance past in particular, a period of expanding energies that was congenial to his own expansive temperament.

The happy fifteen-year sojourn in Italy ended in 1861 with Elizabeth's death. The widower returned to London with his son. During the twenty-eight years remaining to him, the quantity of verse he produced did not diminish. Nor, during the first decade, did it decrease in quality. *Dramatis Personae* (1864) is a volume containing some of his finest monologues, such as *Caliban upon Setebos*. And in 1868 he published his greatest single poem, *The Ring and the Book*, which was inspired by his discovery of an old book of legal records concerning a murder trial in seventeenth-century Rome. His poem tells the story of a brutally sadistic husband, Count Guido Francheschini (who has much in common with the duke in *My Last Duchess*). The middle-aged Guido grows dissatisfied with his young wife, Pompilia, and accuses her of having adulterous relations with a handsome priest who, like St. George, had tried to rescue her from the dragon's den in which her husband confined her. Eventually Guido stabs his wife to death and is himself executed. In a series of twelve books, Browning retells this tale of violence, presenting it from the contrasting points of view of participants and spectators. Because of its vast scale, *The Ring and the Book* is like a Victorian novel, but in its experiments with multiple points of view it anticipates later novels such as Conrad's *Lord Jim* (1900). (Unlike Tennyson's major long poem, *The Idylls of the King*, Browning's twelve monologues do not lend themselves to excerpting.)

After *The Ring and the Book* several more volumes appeared. In general, Browning's writings during the last two decades of his life suffer from a certain mechanical repetition of mannerism and an excess of argumentation—faults into which he may have been led by the unqualified enthusiasm of his admirers, for it was during this period that he gained his great following. When he died, in 1889, he was buried in Westminster Abbey.

During these London years, Browning became abundantly fond of social life. He dined at the homes of friends and at clubs, where he enjoyed port wine and conversation. He would talk loudly and emphatically about many topics—except his own poetry, about which he was usually reticent. His reticence bothered many of his admirers. American women visiting in London, after having looked forward to meeting the author whose poems had inspired them to higher things, were disappointed—almost appalled—when they met the man at a dinner party. He did not "look like a poet." His late poem *House* may show why he gave such an impression. Behind the facade of the hearty diner-out, Browning could live and think as he pleased, just as he had discovered in writing his monologues the advantage, for him, of indirect speaking. Each speaker of monologue provides a mask for the poet.

Despite his bursts of outspokenness, Browning's character is thus not so clearly known to us as that of Tennyson or Arnold or Carlyle. Hardy once said that Browning's character seemed to him "*the* literary puzzle of the nineteenth century." To solve the puzzle one biographer, Betty Miller, has tried to show that Browning was not such a happy and confident person as he is usually represented to have been, an impression that can be reinforced by the note of desperation in such poems as "*Childe Roland.*" And although later biographies correct the eccentricities of this interpretation, they also demonstrate that Browning was a complex figure. Like Yeats, he was a poet preoccupied with masks. On the occasion of his burial in Westminster Abbey, his friend Henry James reflected that many oddities and many great writers have been buried there, "but none of the odd ones have been so great and none of the great ones been so odd."

Just as Browning's character is harder to identify than that of Tennyson, so also are his poems more difficult to relate to the age in which they were written than are the sometimes topical poems of Tennyson. Our first impression may be that there is no connection whatever. Bishops and painters of the Renaissance, physicians of the Roman empire, musicians of eighteenth-century Germany—as we explore this gallery of talking portraits we seem to be in a world of time long past, remote from the world of steam engines and disputes about human beings' descent from the ape.

Yet our first impression is misleading. Many of these portraits explore problems that confronted Browning's contemporaries, especially problems of faith and doubt, good and evil, and problems of the function of the artist in modern life. *Caliban upon Setebos,* for example, is a highly topical critique of Darwinism and of natural (as opposed to supernatural) religions. Browning's own attitude toward these topics is partially concealed because of his use of speakers and of settings from earlier ages, yet we do encounter certain recurrent religious assumptions that we can safely assign to the poet himself. The most recurrent is that God has created an imperfect world as a kind of testing ground, a "vale of soul-making," as Keats had said. It followed, for Browning's purposes, that the human soul must be immortal and that heaven itself be perfect. As Abt Vogler affirms: "On the earth the broken arcs; in the heaven, a perfect round." Armed with such a faith, Browning sometimes gives the impression that he was himself untroubled by the doubts that gnawed at the hearts of Arnold and Clough and Tennyson. The "evidence" presented by historical criticism of the Bible he could dismiss because of its perspective being limited and partial. We therefore need to trust in the truth of feeling and aspiration.

This kind of religious conviction attracts many readers who expect poetry to provide uplift and reassurances. Other readers find it an insurmountable obstacle, as fatuous as Macaulay's faith in progress. To what extent our capacity to enjoy the writings of authors is hindered if their religious positions seem repellent to us is one of the most important problems in modern criticism. The problem is much too vast to explore here, but there is at least room to insert a qualifying clause to modify the indictment that Browning's critics too hastily draw up against his cheerful religious position. A blind optimist might be simply unreadable, but Browning's optimism was not blind. Few writers, in fact, seem to have been more aware of the existence of evil. His gallery of villains—murderers, sadistic husbands, mean and petty manipulators—is an extraordinary one. Nothing is more essential to a fair-minded study of his poetry than our recognition that his apparent optimism is consistently being tested by his bringing to light the evils of human nature. Readers who prefer to dispose of his writings by pinning them down in a formulated phrase, instead of reading them with attention, invariably cite the following lines as summing up all of Browning:

> God's in his heaven—
> All's right with the world!

But if we turn to the poem in which these lines appear, we have to modify our formulation. *Pippa Passes* is a collection of sordid tales such as one encounters on the front page of the most lurid style of newspaper. The heroine, who works in a sweatshop 364 days a year, is about to be sent to Rome as a prostitute; a man and woman living in adultery have just murdered the woman's husband; a waspish set of bohemians have tricked a youth into marriage. Because Pippa's innocence seems to counteract the sordidness of the other scenes, we may say afterward that God is in his heaven. But that all's right with the world is merely affirmed by the girl; the poem does not show it.

A second aspect of Browning's poetry that separates it from the Victorian age is its style. The most representative Victorian poets such as Tennyson or Dante Gabriel Rossetti write in the manner of Keats, Milton, Spenser, and of classical poets such as Virgil. Theirs is the central stylistic tradition in English poetry, one that favors smoothly polished texture, elevated diction and subjects, and pleasing liquidity of sound. Browning draws from a different tradition, more colloquial and discordant, a tradition that includes the poetry of John Donne, the soliloquies of Shakespeare, the comic verse of the early nineteenth-century poet Thomas Hood, and certain features of the narrative style of Chaucer. Of most significance are Browning's affinities with Donne. Both poets sacrifice, on occasion, the pleasures of harmony and of a consistent elevation of tone by using a harshly discordant style and unexpected juxtapositions that startle us into an awareness of a world of every-day realities and trivialities. Readers who dislike this kind of poetry in Browning or in Donne argue that it suffers from prosiness. Oscar Wilde once described the novelist George Meredith as "a prose Browning." And so, he added, was Browning. Wilde's joke may help us to relate Browning to his contemporaries. For if Browning seems out of step with other Victorian poets, he is by no means out of step with his contemporaries in prose. The grotesque, which plays such a prominent role in the style and subject matter of Carlyle and Dickens and in the aesthetic theories of John Ruskin, is equally prominent in Browning's verse:

> Fee, faw, fum! bubble and squeak!
> Blessedest Thursday's the fat of the week.
> Rumble and tumble, sleek and rough,
> Stinking and savory, smug and gruff.

These opening lines of *Holy-Cross Day* display a kind of noisy jocularity in pre-senting a situation of grave seriousness similar to that used by Carlyle in his *Sartor Resartus*. It was fitting that Browning and Carlyle remained good friends, even though the elder writer kept urging Browning to give up verse in favor of prose.

The link between Browning and the Victorian prose writers is not limited to style. With the later generation of Victorian novelists, George Eliot, George Mere-dith, and Henry James, Browning shares a central preoccupation. Like Eliot in particular, he was interested in exposing the devious ways in which our minds work and the complexity of our motives. "My stress lay on incidents in the develop-ment of a human soul," he wrote; "little else is worth study." His psychological insights can be illustrated in such poems as *The Bishop Orders His Tomb* or *Dîs Aliter Visum*. Although these are spoken monologues, not inner monologues in the manner of James Joyce, the insight into the workings of the mind is similarly acute. As in reading Joyce, we must be on our guard to follow the rapid shifts of the speakers' mental processes as jumps are made from one cluster of associations to another. A further challenge for the reader of Browning is to identify what has been left out. As was remarked in a letter by the 1890s poet Ernest Dowson, Brown-ing's "masterpieces in verse" demonstrate both "subtlety" and "the tact of omis-sion." *My Last Duchess*, he added, "is pure Henry James."

But Browning's role as a forerunner of twentieth-century literature should not blind us to his essential Victorianism. Energy is the most characteristic aspect of his writing and of the man (Turgenev compared Browning's handshake to an elec-tric shock). And energy is perhaps the most characteristic aspect of Victorian litera-ture in general. Often, of course, such energy was misdirected. Gerard Manley

Hopkins identified this failing precisely when he complained of Browning's "Broad Church" way of talking, like "a man bouncing up from table with his mouth full of bread and cheese and saying that he meant to stand no blasted nonsense." At its best, however, such buoyancy is a virtue imparting a creative vitality to all of Browning's writings.

Porphyria's Lover[1]

The rain set early in tonight,
    The sullen wind was soon awake,
It tore the elm-tops down for spite,
    And did its worst to vex the lake:
    I listened with heart fit to break.   5
When glided in Porphyria; straight
    She shut the cold out and the storm,
And kneeled and made the cheerless grate
    Blaze up, and all the cottage warm;
    Which done, she rose, and from her form   10
Withdrew the dripping cloak and shawl,
    And laid her soiled gloves by, untied
Her hat and let the damp hair fall,
    And, last, she sat down by my side
    And called me. When no voice replied,   15
She put my arm about her waist,
    And made her smooth white shoulder bare,
And all her yellow hair displaced,
    And, stooping, made my cheek lie there,
    And spread, o'er all, her yellow hair,   20
Murmuring how she loved me—she
    Too weak, for all her heart's endeavor,
To set its struggling passion free
    From pride, and vainer ties dissever,
    And give herself to me forever.   25
But passion sometimes would prevail,
    Nor could tonight's gay feast restrain
A sudden thought of one so pale
    For love of her, and all in vain:
    So, she was come through wind and rain.   30
Be sure I looked up at her eyes
    Happy and proud; at last I knew
Porphyria worshiped me: surprise
    Made my heart swell, and still it grew
    While I debated what to do.   35
That moment she was mine, mine, fair,
    Perfectly pure and good: I found
A thing to do, and all her hair
    In one long yellow string I wound
    Three times her little throat around,   40
And strangled her. No pain felt she;

1. One of a pair of monologues originally published under the title *Madhouse Cells*, a title that emphasized the abnormal state of mind of the speaker.

I am quite sure she felt no pain.
As a shut bud that holds a bee,
    I warily oped her lids: again
    Laughed the blue eyes without a stain.   45
And I untightened next the tress
    About her neck; her cheek once more
Blushed bright beneath my burning kiss:
    I propped her head up as before,
    Only, this time my shoulder bore   50
Her head, which droops upon it still:
    The smiling rosy little head,
So glad it has its utmost will,
    That all it scorned at once is fled,
    And I, its love, am gained instead!   55
Porphyria's love: she guessed not how
    Her darling one wish would be heard.
And thus we sit together now,
    And all night long we have not stirred,
    And yet God has not said a word!   60

1834   1836, 1842

Soliloquy of the Spanish Cloister[1]

1

Gr-r-r—there go, my heart's abhorrence!
    Water your damned flowerpots, do!
If hate killed men, Brother Lawrence,
    God's blood, would not mine kill you!
What? your myrtle bush wants trimming?   5
    Oh, that rose has prior claims—
Needs its leaden vase filled brimming?
    Hell dry you up with its flames!

2

At the meal we sit together:
    Salve tibi![2] I must hear   10
Wise talk of the kind of weather,
    Sort of season, time of year:
Not a plenteous cork crop: scarcely
    Dare we hope oak-galls,[3] *I doubt:*
What's the Latin name for "parsley"?   15
    What's the Greek name for Swine's Snout?[4]

3

Whew! We'll have our platter burnished,
    Laid with care on our own shelf!
With a fire-new spoon we're furnished,
    And a goblet for ourself,   20
Rinsed like something sacrificial

---

1. No period of history is specified in this poem.
2. "Hail to thee!" This and other speeches in italics in this stanza are the words of Brother Lawrence.
3. Abnormal outgrowths on oak trees, used for tan-
ning.
4. In the 19th century, "Swine's Snout" meant dandelion.

Ere 'tis fit to touch our chaps[5]—
Marked with L. for our initial!
    (He-he! There his lily snaps!)
4

Saint, forsooth! While brown Dolores   25
    Squats outside the Convent bank
With Sanchicha, telling stories,
    Steeping tresses in the tank,
Blue-black, lustrous, thick like horsehairs,
    —Can't I see his dead eye glow,   30
Bright as 'twere a Barbary corsair's?[6]
    (That is, if he'd let it show!)
5
When he finishes refection,[7]
    Knife and fork he never lays
Cross-wise, to my recollection,   35
    As do I, in Jesu's praise.
I the Trinity illustrate,
    Drinking watered orange pulp—
In three sips the Arian[8] frustrate;
    While he drains his at one gulp.   40
6
Oh, those melons? If he's able
    We're to have a feast! so nice!
One goes to the Abbot's table,
    All of us get each a slice.
How go on your flowers? None double?   45
    Not one fruit-sort can you spy?
Strange!—And I, too, at such trouble,
    Keep them close-nipped on the sly!
7
There's a great text in Galatians,[9]
    Once you trip on it, entails   50
Twenty-nine distinct damnations,
    One sure, if another fails:
If I trip him just a-dying,
    Sure of heaven as sure can be,
Spin him round and send him flying   55
    Off to hell, a Manichee?[1]
8
Or, my scrofulous French novel
    On gray paper with blunt type!
Simply glance at it, you grovel
    Hand and foot in Belial's gripe: 60
If I double down its pages
    At the woeful sixteenth print,

---

5. Jaws.
6. Pirate of the Barbary Coast of northern Africa, renowned for fierceness and lechery.
7. Dinner.
8. Heretical followers of Arius (256–336), who denied the doctrine of the Trinity.
9. The speaker hopes to obtain Lawrence's damnation by luring him into a heresy, this to be accomplished

by exposing him to the difficult task of interpreting "Galatians" in an unswervingly orthodox way. In Galatians 5.15–23, St. Paul specifies an assortment of "works of the flesh" that lead to damnation, which could make up a total of "twenty-nine" (line 51).
1. A heretic, a follower of the Persian prophet of the 3rd century, Mani.

When he gathers his greengages,
   Ope a sieve and slip it in't?
         9
Or, there's Satan!—one might venture   65
   Pledge one's soul to him,[2] yet leave
Such a flaw in the indenture
   As he'd miss till, past retrieve,
Blasted lay that rose-acacia
   We're so proud of! *Hy, Zy, Hine* . . .[3]   70
'St, there's Vespers! *Plena gratiâ*
   Ave, Virgo![4] Gr-r-r—you swine!

ca. 1839   1842

My Last Duchess[1]

FERRARA

That's my last Duchess painted on the wall,
Looking as if she were alive. I call
That piece a wonder, now: Frà Pandolf's[2] hands
Worked busily a day, and there she stands.
Will 't please you sit and look at her? I said   5
"Frà Pandolf" by design, for never read
Strangers like you that pictured countenance,
The depth and passion of its earnest glance,
But to myself they turned (since none puts by
The curtain I have drawn for you, but I)   10
And seemed as they would ask me, if they durst,
How such a glance came there; so, not the first
Are you to turn and ask thus. Sir, 'twas not
Her husband's presence only, called that spot
Of joy into the Duchess' cheek: perhaps   15
Frà Pandolf chanced to say "Her mantle laps
Over my lady's wrist too much," or "Paint
Must never hope to reproduce the faint
Half-flush that dies along her throat": such stuff
Was courtesy, she thought, and cause enough   20
For calling up that spot of joy. She had
A heart—how shall I say?—too soon made glad,
Too easily impressed; she liked whate'er
She looked on, and her looks went everywhere.
Sir, 'twas all one! My favor at her breast,   25
The dropping of the daylight in the West,

---

2. The speaker would pledge his own soul to Satan in return for blasting Lawrence and his "rose-acacia" (line 69), but the pledge would be so cleverly worded that the speaker himself would not have to pay his debt to Satan. There would be an escape clause, a "flaw in the indenture," for himself.
3. Perhaps the opening of a mysterious curse against Lawrence.
4. "Full of grace, Hail, Virgin!" The speaker's twisted state of mind may be reflected in his mixed-up version of the prayer to Mary: "Ave, Maria, gratia plena."
1. The poem is based on incidents in the life of Alfonso II, duke of Ferrara in Italy, whose first wife, Lucrezia, a young woman, died in 1561 after three years of marriage. Following her death, the duke negotiated through an agent to marry a niece of the count of Tyrol. Browning represents the duke as addressing this agent.
2. Brother Pandolf, an imaginary painter.

The bough of cherries some officious fool
Broke in the orchard for her, the white mule
She rode with round the terrace—all and each
Would draw from her alike the approving speech,   30
Or blush, at least. She thanked men—good! but thanked
Somehow—I know not how—as if she ranked
My gift of a nine-hundred-years-old name
With anybody's gift. Who'd stoop to blame
This sort of trifling? Even had you skill   35
In speech—(which I have not)—to make your will
Quite clear to such an one, and say, "Just this
Or that in you disgusts me; here you miss,
Or there exceed the mark"—and if she let
Herself be lessoned so, nor plainly set   40
Her wits to yours, forsooth, and made excuse
—E'en then would be some stooping; and I choose
Never to stoop. Oh sir, she smiled, no doubt,
Whene'er I passed her; but who passed without
Much the same smile? This grew; I gave commands;   45
Then all smiles stopped together. There she stands
As if alive. Will 't please you rise? We'll meet
The company below, then. I repeat,
The Count your master's known munificence
Is ample warrant that no just pretense   50
Of mine for dowry will be disallowed;
Though his fair daughter's self, as I avowed
At starting, is my object. Nay, we'll go
Together down, sir. Notice Neptune, though,
Taming a sea horse, thought a rarity,   55
Which Claus of Innsbruck[3] cast in bronze for me!

1842   1842

Home-Thoughts, from Abroad

1

Oh, to be in England
Now that April's there,
And whoever wakes in England
Sees, some morning, unaware,
That the lowest boughs and the brushwood sheaf   5
Round the elm-tree bole are in tiny leaf,
While the chaffinch sings on the orchard bough
In England—now!

2

And after April, when May follows,
And the whitethroat builds, and all the swallows!   10
Hark, where my blossomed peartree in the hedge
Leans to the field and scatters on the clover
Blossoms and dewdrops—at the bent spray's edge—

---

3. An unidentified or imaginary sculptor. The count of Tyrol had his capital at Innsbruck.

That's the wise thrush; he sings each song twice over,
Lest you should think he never could recapture   15
The first fine careless rapture!
And though the fields look rough with hoary dew,
All will be gay when noontide wakes anew
The buttercups, the little children's dower
—Far brighter than this gaudy melon-flower!   20

ca. 1845   1845

Home-Thoughts, from the Sea

Nobly, nobly Cape Saint Vincent[1] to the northwest died away;
Sunset ran, one glorious blood-red, reeking into Cadiz Bay;
Bluish 'mid the burning water, full in face Trafalgar[2] lay;
In the dimmest northeast distance dawned Gibraltar grand and gray;
"Here and here did England help me: how can I help England?" —say,   5
Whoso turns as I, this evening, turn to God to praise and pray,
While Jove's planet[3] rises yonder, silent over Africa.

1844   1845

The Bishop Orders His Tomb at Saint Praxed's Church[1]

Rome, 15—

Vanity, saith the preacher, vanity![2]
Draw round my bed: is Anselm keeping back?
Nephews—sons mine . . . ah God, I know not! Well—
She, men would have to be your mother once,
Old Gandolf envied me, so fair she was!   5
What's done is done, and she is dead beside,
Dead long ago, and I am Bishop since,
And as she died so must we die ourselves,
And thence ye may perceive the world's a dream.
Life, how and what is it? As here I lie   10
In this state chamber, dying by degrees,

1. Off the coast of Portugal, scene of British naval victory under Admiral Nelson (1797).
2. A cape in Spain, where Nelson won his great victory over Napoleon's fleets (1805).
3. Jupiter.
1. In *Fra Lippo Lippi*, Browning represents the dawn of the Renaissance in Italy, with its fresh zest for human experiences in this world. In the present monologue, he portrays a later stage of the Renaissance when such worldliness, full-blown, had infected even some of the leading clergy of Italy. Browning's portrait of the dying bishop is, however, not primarily a satire against corruption in the church. It is a brilliant exposition of the workings of a mind, a mind that has been conditioned by special historical circumstances. The Victo-

rian historian of art John Ruskin said of this poem: "I know of no other piece of modern English, prose or poetry, in which there is so much told, as in these lines, of the Renaissance spirit—its worldliness, inconsistency, pride, hypocrisy, ignorance of itself, love of art, of luxury, and of good Latin. It is nearly all that I have said of the central Renaissance in thirty pages of the *Stones of Venice*, put into as many lines, Browning's also being the antecedent work."
St. Praxed's Church was named in honor of St. Praxedes, a Roman virgin of the 2nd century who gave her riches to poor Christians. Both the bishop and his predecessor, Gandolf, are imaginary persons.
2. Cf. Ecclesiastes 1.2.

Hours and long hours in the dead night, I ask
"Do I live, am I dead?" Peace, peace seems all.
Saint Praxed's ever was the church for peace;
And so, about this tomb of mine. I fought   15
With tooth and nail to save my niche, ye know:
—Old Gandolf cozened[3] me, despite my care;
Shrewd was that snatch from out the corner south
He graced his carrion with, God curse the same!
Yet still my niche is not so cramped but thence   20
One sees the pulpit o' the epistle side,[4]
And somewhat of the choir, those silent seats,
And up into the aery dome where live
The angels, and a sunbeam's sure to lurk:
And I shall fill my slab of basalt[5] there,   25
And 'neath my tabernacle[6] take my rest,
With those nine columns round me, two and two,
The odd one at my feet where Anselm stands:
Peach-blossom marble all, the rare, the ripe
As fresh-poured red wine of a mighty pulse.[7]   30
—Old Gandolf with his paltry onion-stone,[8]
Put me where I may look at him! True peach,
Rosy and flawless: how I earned the prize!
Draw close: that conflagration of my church
—What then? So much was saved if aught were missed!   35
My sons, ye would not be my death? Go dig
The white-grape vineyard where the oil-press stood,
Drop water gently till the surface sink,
And if ye find . . . Ah God, I know not, I! . . .
Bedded in store of rotten fig leaves soft,   40
And corded up in a tight olive-frail,[9]
Some lump, ah God, of *lapis lazuli*,[1]
Big as a jew's head cut off at the nape,[2]
Blue as a vein o'er the Madonna's breast . . .
Sons, all have I bequeathed you, villas, all,   45
That brave Frascati[3] villa with its bath,
So, let the blue lump poise between my knees,
Like God the Father's globe on both his hands
Ye worship in the Jesu Church[4] so gay,
For Gandolf shall not choose but see and burst!   50
Swift as a weaver's shuttle fleet our years:[5]
Man goeth to the grave, and where is he?
Did I say basalt for my slab, sons? Black[6]—

3. Cheated.
4. The Epistles of the New Testament are read from the right-hand side of the altar (as one faces it).
5. Dark-colored igneous rock.
6. Stone canopy or tentlike roof, presumably supported by the "nine columns" under which the sculptured effigy of the bishop would lie on the "slab of basalt."
7. Browning uses "pulse" in the special sense of a pulpy mash of fermented grapes from which a strong wine might be poured off. In a later poem, the *Epilogue to Pacchiarotto*, he likens such wine to "viscous blood" that has been "squeezed gold" from the "pulp"
of the grapes.
8. An inferior marble that peels in layers.
9. Basket for holding olives.
1. Valuable bright blue stone.
2. Perhaps a reference to the head of John the Baptist, cut off at the request of Salomé.
3. Suburb of Rome, used as a resort by wealthy Italians.
4. Il Gesù, a Jesuit church in Rome. On the altar of this church the figure of an angel (rather than God) holds a huge lump of lapis lazuli in his hands.
5. Cf. Job 7.6.
6. Black marble.

'Twas ever antique-black I meant! How else
Shall ye contrast my frieze[7] to come beneath?   55
The bas-relief in bronze ye promised me,
Those Pans and Nymphs ye wot of, and perchance
Some tripod, thyrsus, with a vase or so,
The Saviour at his sermon on the mount,
Saint Praxed in a glory, and one Pan   60
Ready to twitch the Nymph's last garment off,
And Moses with the tables[8] . . . but I know
Ye mark me not! What do they whisper thee,
Child of my bowels, Anselm? Ah, ye hope
To revel down my villas while I gasp   65
Bricked o'er with beggar's moldy travertine[9]
Which Gandolf from his tomb-top chuckles at!
Nay, boys, ye love me—all of jasper, then!
'Tis jasper ye stand pledged to, lest I grieve
My bath must needs be left behind, alas!   70
One block, pure green as a pistachio nut,
There's plenty jasper somewhere in the world—
And have I not Saint Praxed's ear to pray
Horses for ye, and brown Greek manuscripts,
And mistresses with great smooth marbly limbs?   75
—That's if ye carve my epitaph aright,
Choice Latin, picked phrase, Tully's[1] every word,
No gaudy ware like Gandolf's second line—
Tully, my masters? Ulpian[2] serves his need!
And then how I shall lie through centuries,   80
And hear the blessed mutter of the mass,
And see God made and eaten all day long,[3]
And feel the steady candle flame, and taste
Good strong thick stupefying incense-smoke!
For as I lie here, hours of the dead night,   85
Dying in state and by such slow degrees,
I fold my arms as if they clasped a crook,[4]
And stretch my feet forth straight as stone can point,
And let the bedclothes, for a mortcloth,[5] drop
Into great laps and folds of sculptor's-work: 90
And as yon tapers dwindle, and strange thoughts
Grow, with a certain humming in my ears,
About the life before I lived this life,
And this life too, popes, cardinals, and priests,
Saint Praxed at his sermon on the mount,[6]   95

7. Continuous band of sculpture.
8. The "bas-relief" (or sculpture in which the figures do not project far from the background surface) would consist of a mixture of pagan and religious scenes (lines 57–62). Among the former would be a "tripod," on which priestesses at the Oracle of Delphi sat to make their prophecies, and a "thyrsus," a long staff carried in processions in honor of Bacchus, the god of wine. The religious scenes would include St. Praxedes with her halo ("a glory") and Moses with the stone tablets ("tables") on which the Ten Commandments were written. Such intermingling of pagan and Christian traditions, characteristic of the Renaissance, had been attacked in 1841 in *Contrasts*, a book on architecture by A. W. Pugin, a Roman Catholic.
9. Italian limestone.
1. A familiar name for Marcus Tullius Cicero, whose writing was the model, during the Renaissance, of classical Latin prose.
2. Late Latin prose writer, not considered a model of good style.
3. Reference to the doctrine of transubstantiation.
4. Bishop's staff or crozier.
5. Rich cloth spread over a dead body or coffin.
6. The bishop is confusing St. Praxed (a woman) with Christ—an indication that his mind is wandering.

Your tall pale mother with her talking eyes,
And new-found agate urns as fresh as day,
And marble's language, Latin pure, discreet
—Aha, ELUCESCEBAT[7] quoth our friend?
No Tully, said I, Ulpian at the best!   100
Evil and brief hath been my pilgrimage.[8]
All *lapis*, all, sons! Else I give the Pope
My villas! Will ye ever eat my heart?
Ever your eyes were as a lizard's quick,
They glitter like your mother's for my soul,   105
Or ye would heighten my impoverished frieze,
Pierce out its starved design, and fill my vase
With grapes, and add a vizor and a Term,[9]
And to the tripod ye would tie a lynx
That in his struggle throws the thyrsus down,   110
To comfort me on my entablature[1]
Whereon I am to lie till I must ask
"Do I live, am I dead?" There, leave me, there!
For ye have stabbed me with ingratitude
To death—ye wish it—God, ye wish it! Stone—   115
Gritstone,[2] a-crumble! Clammy squares which sweat
As if the corpse they keep were oozing through—
And no more *lapis* to delight the world!
Well go! I bless ye. Fewer tapers there,
But in a row: and, going, turn your backs   120
—Aye, like departing altar-ministrants,
And leave me in my church, the church for peace,
That I may watch at leisure if he leers—
Old Gandolf, at me, from his onion-stone,
As still he envied me, so fair she was!   125

1844   1845

Meeting at Night[1]

1

The gray sea and the long black land;
And the yellow half-moon large and low;
And the startled little waves that leap
In fiery ringlets from their sleep,
As I gain the cove with pushing prow,   5
And quench its speed i' the slushy sand.

2

Then a mile of warm sea-scented beach;
Three fields to cross till a farm appears;
A tap at the pane, the quick sharp scratch

---

7. Word from Gandolf's epitaph meaning "he was illustrious." The bishop considers the form of the verb
to be in "gaudy" bad taste. If the epitaph had been
copied from Cicero instead of from Ulpian, the word
would have been *elucebat*.
8. Cf. Genesis 47.9.
9. Statue of Terminus, the Roman god of boundaries,

usually represented without arms. "Vizor": part of a
helmet, often represented in sculpture.
1. Horizontal platform supporting a statue or effigy.
2. Coarse sandstone such as that used for grindstones.
1. This poem and the one that follows it appeared
originally under the single title *Night and Morning*.
The speaker in both is a man.

And blue spurt of a lighted match,   10
And a voice less loud, through its joys and fears,
Than the two hearts beating each to each!

                                                        1845

Parting at Morning

Round the cape of a sudden came the sea,
And the sun looked over the mountain's rim:
And straight was a path of gold for him,[1]
And the need of a world of men for me.

                                                        1845

A Toccata of Galuppi's[1]

1

Oh, Galuppi, Baldassaro, this is very sad to find!
I can hardly misconceive you; it would prove me deaf and blind;
But although I take your meaning, 'tis with such a heavy mind!

2

Here you come with your old music, and here's all the good it brings.
What, they lived once thus at Venice where the merchants were the kings,   5
Where Saint Mark's is, where the Doges used to wed the sea with rings?[2]

3

Aye, because the sea's the street there; and 'tis arched by . . . what you call
. . . Shylock's bridge[3] with houses on it, where they kept the carnival:
I was never out of England—it's as if I saw it all.

4

Did young people take their pleasure when the sea was warm in May?   10
Balls and masks[4] begun at midnight, burning ever to midday,
When they made up fresh adventures for the morrow, do you say?

5

Was a lady such a lady, cheeks so round and lips so red—
On her neck the small face buoyant, like a bellflower on its bed,
O'er the breast's superb abundance where a man might base his head?   15

6

Well, and it was graceful of them—they'd break talk off and afford
—She, to bite her mask's black velvet—he, to finger on his sword,
While you sat and played toccatas, stately at the clavichord?[5]

---

1. I.e., the sun.

1. There are three speakers in this short poem. The first is a 19th-century scientist in England who is listening to a musical composition by Baldassaro Galuppi (1706–1785), a Venetian. The music evokes for this scientist the voice of the dead composer (the third speaker) who comments on the pointless and butterfly-like frivolity of his 18th-century contemporaries. The second group of voices is made up of comments by members of Galuppi's audience as they respond to the different moods of his clavichord playing during a party that the scientist imagines to have taken place in Venice.

A "toccata" is defined in Grove's *Dictionary of Music* as a "touch-piece, or a composition intended to exhibit the touch and execution of the performer." The same authority states that "no particular composition was taken as the basis of the poem."

2. An annual ceremony in which the doge, the Venetian chief magistrate, threw a ring into the water to symbolize the bond between his city, with its maritime empire, and the sea.

3. The Rialto, a bridge over the Grand Canal.

4. Masquerades.

5. A keyboard instrument in which the strings are struck by metal hammers. As a mechanism, it resembles a piano, but the sound is more like that of a harpsichord.

7

What? Those lesser thirds so plaintive, sixths diminished, sigh on sigh,
Told them something? Those suspensions, those solutions—"Must we die?" 20
Those commiserating sevenths[6]—"Life might last! we can but try!"

8

"Were you happy?"—"Yes."—"And are you still as happy?"—"Yes. And you?"
—"Then, more kisses!"—"Did I stop them, when a million seemed so few?"
Hark, the dominant's persistence till it must be answered to!

9

So, an octave struck the answer. Oh, they praised you, I dare say!   25
"Brave Galuppi! that was music; good alike at grave and gay!
I can always leave off talking when I hear a master play!"

10

Then they left you for their pleasure: till in due time, one by one,
Some with lives that came to nothing, some with deeds as well undone,
Death stepped tacitly and took them where they never see the sun.   30

11

But when I sit down to reason, think to take my stand nor swerve,
While I triumph o'er a secret wrung from nature's close reserve,
In you come with your cold music till I creep through every nerve.

12

Yes, you, like a ghostly cricket, creaking where a house was burned:
"Dust and ashes, dead and done with, Venice spent what Venice earned.   35
The soul, doubtless, is immortal—where a soul can be discerned.

13

"Yours for instance: you know physics, something of geology,
Mathematics are your pastime; souls shall rise in their degree;
Butterflies may dread extinction—you'll not die, it cannot be!

14

"As for Venice and her people, merely born to bloom and drop,   40
Here on earth they bore their fruitage, mirth and folly were the crop:
What of soul was left, I wonder, when the kissing had to stop?

15

"Dust and ashes!" So you creak it, and I want[7] the heart to scold.
Dear dead women, with such hair, too—what's become of all the gold
Used to hang and brush their bosoms? I feel chilly and grown old.   45
ca. 1847   1855

Love Among the Ruins[1]

1

Where the quiet-colored end of evening smiles,
          Miles and miles
On the solitary pastures where our sheep
          Half-asleep

---

6. This term and others in these lines all refer to the technical devices used by Galuppi to produce alternating moods in his music, conflict in each instance being resolved into harmony. Thus the "dominant" (the fifth note of the scale), after being persistently sounded, is answered by a resolving chord (lines 24–25).
7. Lack.

1. The ruins may be those of such cities as Babylon or Nineveh or one of the Etruscan cities of Italy. The unusual stanza used in this poem was invented by Browning. The contrast between past and present, which is the core of the poem, is reinforced by devoting one half of each stanza to the past and the other half to the present.

Tinkle homeward through the twilight, stray or stop   5
    As they crop—
Was the site once of a city great and gay
    (So they say),
Of our country's very capital, its prince
    Ages since   10
Held his court in, gathered councils, wielding far
    Peace or war.

2

Now—the country does not even boast a tree,
    As you see,
To distinguish slopes of verdure, certain rills   15
    From the hills
Intersect and give a name to (else they run
    Into one),
Where the domed and daring palace shot its spires
    Up like fires   20
O'er the hundred-gated circuit of a wall
    Bounding all,
Made of marble, men might march on nor be pressed,
    Twelve abreast.

3

And such plenty and perfection, see, of grass   25
    Never was!
Such a carpet as, this summertime, o'erspreads
    And embeds
Every vestige of the city, guessed alone,
    Stock or stone—   30
Where a multitude of men breathed joy and woe
    Long ago;
Lust of glory pricked their hearts up, dread of shame
    Struck them tame;
And that glory and that shame alike, the gold   35
    Bought and sold.

4

Now—the single little turret that remains
    On the plains,
By the caper overrooted, by the gourd
    Overscored,   40
While the patching houseleek's[2] head of blossom winks
    Through the chinks—
Marks the basement whence a tower in ancient time
    Sprang sublime,
And a burning ring, all round, the chariots traced   45
    As they raced,
And the monarch and his minions and his dames
    Viewed the games.

5

And I know, while thus the quiet-colored eve
    Smiles to leave   50

---

2. Common European plant, with petals clustered in the shape of rosettes.

To their folding, all our many-tinkling fleece
    In such peace,
And the slopes and rills in undistinguished gray
    Melt away—
That a girl with eager eyes and yellow hair   55
    Waits me there
In the turret whence the charioteers caught soul
    For the goal,
When the king looked, where she looks now, breathless, dumb
    Till I come.   60

6

But he looked upon the city, every side,
    Far and wide,
All the mountains topped with temples, all the glades'
    Colonnades,
All the causeys,[3] bridges, aqueducts—and then,   65
    All the men!
When I do come, she will speak not, she will stand,
    Either hand
On my shoulder, give her eyes the first embrace
    Of my face,   70
Ere we rush, ere we extinguish sight and speech
    Each on each.

7

In one year they sent a million fighters forth
    South and north,
And they built their gods a brazen pillar high   75
    As the sky,
Yet reserved a thousand chariots in full force—
    Gold, of course.
Oh heart! oh blood that freezes, blood that burns!
    Earth's returns   80
For whole centuries of folly, noise, and sin!
    Shut them in,
With their triumphs and their glories and the rest!
    Love is best.

1853   1855

"Childe Roland to the Dark Tower Came"[1]

(See Edgar's Song in "Lear")

1

My first thought was, he lied in every word,
    That hoary cripple, with malicious eye

---

3. Causeways or roads raised above low ground.
1. Browning stated that this poem "came upon me as a kind of dream," and that it was written in one day. Although the poem was among those of his own writings that pleased him most, he was reluctant to explain what the dream (or nightmare) signified. He once agreed with a friend's suggestion that the meaning might be expressed in the statement: "He that endureth to the end shall be saved." Most readers have responded to the poem in this way, finding in the story of Roland's quest an inspiring expression of defiance and courage. Other readers find the poem to be more expressive of despair than of enduring hope, and it is at least true that the landscape is as grim and night-

Askance[2] to watch the working of his lie
On mine, and mouth scarce able to afford
Suppression of the glee, that pursed and scored   5
    Its edge, at one more victim gained thereby.

2

What else should he be set for, with his staff?
    What, save to waylay with his lies, ensnare
    All travelers who might find him posted there,
And ask the road? I guessed what skull-like laugh   10
Would break, what crutch 'gin write my epitaph
    For pastime in the dusty thoroughfare,

3

If at his counsel I should turn aside
    Into that ominous tract which, all agree,
    Hides the Dark Tower. Yet acquiescingly   15
I did turn as he pointed: neither pride
Nor hope rekindling at the end descried,
    So much as gladness that some end might be.

4

For, what with my whole world-wide wandering,
    What with my search drawn out through years, my hope   20
    Dwindled into a ghost not fit to cope
With that obstreperous joy success would bring,
I hardly tried now to rebuke the spring
    My heart made, finding failure in its scope.

5

As when a sick man very near to death   25
    Seems dead indeed, and feels begin and end
    The tears and takes the farewell of each friend,
And hears one bid the other go, draw breath
Freelier outside ("since all is o'er," he saith,
    "And the blow fallen no grieving can amend"),   30

6

While some discuss if near the other graves
    Be room enough for this, and when a day
    Suits best for carrying the corpse away,
With care about the banners, scarves and staves:
And still the man hears all, and only craves   35
    He may not shame such tender love and stay.

7

Thus, I had so long suffered in this quest,
    Heard failure prophesied so oft, been writ
    So many times among "The Band"—to wit,
The knights who to the Dark Tower's search addressed   40
Their steps—that just to fail as they, seemed best,
    And all the doubt was now—should I be fit?

---

marelike as in such 20th-century writings as T. S. Eliot's *Hollow Men* or Franz Kafka's *Penal Colony*. It has been said of *"Childe Roland"* that every reader can be his own allegorist.

The lines from Shakespeare's *King Lear* 3.4 (lines 163–65), from which the title is taken, are spoken when Lear is about to enter a hovel on the heath, and Edgar, feigning madness, chants the fragment of a song reminiscent of quests and challenges in fairy tales: "Child Rowland to the dark tower came, / His word was still,—Fie, foh, and fum, / I smell the blood of a British man." A "childe" is a youth of gentle birth, usually a candidate for knighthood.

2. Squinting sidewise.

8

So, quiet as despair, I turned from him,
   That hateful cripple, out of his highway
   Into the path he pointed. All the day   45
Had been a dreary one at best, and dim
Was settling to its close, yet shot one grim
   Red leer to see the plain catch its estray.[3]

9

For mark! no sooner was I fairly found
   Pledged to the plain, after a pace or two,   50
   Than, pausing to throw backward a last view
O'er the safe road, 'twas gone; gray plain all round:
Nothing but plain to the horizon's bound.
   I might go on; naught else remained to do.

10

So, on I went. I think I never saw   55
   Such starved ignoble nature; nothing throve:
   For flowers—as well expect a cedar grove!
But, cockle, spurge,[4] according to their law
Might propagate their kind, with none to awe,
   You'd think; a burr had been a treasure trove.   60

11

No! penury, inertness and grimace,
   In some strange sort, were the land's portion. "See
   Or shut your eyes," said Nature peevishly,
"It nothing skills: I cannot help my case;
'Tis the Last Judgment's fire must cure this place,   65
   Calcine[5] its clods and set my prisoners free."

12

If there pushed any ragged thistle stalk
   Above its mates, the head was chopped; the bents[6]
   Were jealous else. What made those holes and rents
In the dock's[7] harsh swarth leaves, bruised as to balk   70
All hope of greenness? 'tis a brute must walk
   Pashing their life out, with a brute's intents.

13

As for the grass, it grew as scant as hair
   In leprosy; thin dry blades pricked the mud
   Which underneath looked kneaded up with blood.   75
One stiff blind horse, his every bone a-stare,
Stood stupefied, however he came there:
   Thrust out past service from the devil's stud!

14

Alive? he might be dead for aught I know,
   With that red gaunt and colloped[8] neck a-strain,   80
   And shut eyes underneath the rusty mane;
Seldom went such grotesqueness with such woe;
I never saw a brute I hated so;
   He must be wicked to deserve such pain.

---

3. Literally, a domestic animal that has strayed away from its home.
4. A bitter-juiced weed. "Cockle": a weed that bears burrs.
5. Turn to powder by heat.
6. Coarse, stiff grasses.
7. Coarse plant.
8. Ridged.

15

I shut my eyes and turned them on my heart.   85
    As a man calls for wine before he fights,
    I asked one draught of earlier, happier sights,
Ere fitly I could hope to play my part.
Think first, fight afterwards—the soldier's art:
    One taste of the old time sets all to rights.   90

16

Not it! I fancied Cuthbert's reddening face
    Beneath its garniture of curly gold,
    Dear fellow, till I almost felt him fold
An arm in mine to fix me to the place,
That way he used. Alas, one night's disgrace!   95
    Out went my heart's new fire and left it cold.

17

Giles then, the soul of honor—there he stands
    Frank as ten years ago when knighted first.
    What honest man should dare (he said) he durst.
Good—but the scene shifts—faugh! what hangman hands   100
Pin to his breast a parchment? His own bands
    Read it. Poor traitor, spit upon and cursed!

18

Better this present than a past like that;
    Back therefore to my darkening path again!
    No sound, no sight as far as eye could strain.   105
Will the night send a howlet[9] or a bat?
I asked: when something on the dismal flat
    Came to arrest my thoughts and change their train.

19

A sudden little river crossed my path
    As unexpected as a serpent comes.   110
    No sluggish tide congenial to the glooms;
This, as it frothed by, might have been a bath
For the fiend's glowing hoof—to see the wrath
    Of its black eddy bespate[1] with flakes and spumes.

20

So petty yet so spiteful! All along,   115
    Low scrubby alders kneeled down over it;
    Drenched willows flung them headlong in a fit
Of mute despair, a suicidal throng:
The river which had done them all the wrong,
    Whate'er that was, rolled by, deterred no whit.   120

21

Which, while I forded—good saints, how I feared
    To set my foot upon a dead man's cheek,
    Each step, or feel the spear I thrust to seek
For hollows, tangled in his hair or beard!
—It may have been a water rat I speared,   125
    But, ugh! it sounded like a baby's shriek.

9. Owl.   1. Bespattered.

22

Glad was I when I reached the other bank.
    Now for a better country. Vain presage!
    Who were the strugglers, what war did they wage,
Whose savage trample thus could pad the dank   130
Soil to a plash? Toads in a poisoned tank,
    Or wild cats in a red-hot iron cage—

23

The fight must so have seemed in that fell cirque.[2]
    What penned them there, with all the plain to choose?
    No footprint leading to that horrid mews,[3]   135
None out of it. Mad brewage set to work
Their brains, no doubt, like galley slaves the Turk
    Pits for his pastime, Christians against Jews.

24

And more than that—a furlong on—why, there!
    What bad use was that engine for, that wheel,   140
    Or brake,[4] not wheel—that harrow fit to reel
Men's bodies out like silk? with all the air
Of Tophet's[5] tool, on earth left unaware,
    Or brought to sharpen its rusty teeth of steel.

25

Then came a bit of stubbed ground, once a wood,   145
    Next a marsh, it would seem, and now mere earth
    Desperate and done with; (so a fool finds mirth,
Makes a thing and then mars it, till his mood
Changes and off he goes!) within a rood[6]
    Bog, clay and rubble, sand and stark black dearth.   150

26

Now blotches rankling, colored gay and grim,
    Now patches where some leanness of the soil's
    Broke into moss or substances like boils;
Then came some palsied oak, a cleft in him
Like a distorted mouth that splits its rim   155
    Gaping at death, and dies while it recoils.

27

And just as far as ever from the end!
    Naught in the distance but the evening, naught
    To point my footstep further! At the thought,
A great black bird, Apollyon's[7] bosom friend,   160
Sailed past, nor beat his wide wing dragon-penned[8]
    That brushed my cap—perchance the guide I sought.

28

For, looking up, aware I somehow grew,
    'Spite of the dusk, the plain had given place
    All round to mountains—with such name to grace

---

2. Dreadful arena.
3. Enclosed stable yard.
4. A toothed machine used for separating the fibers of flax or hemp. Here an instrument of torture.
5. Hell's. Cf. Jeremiah 19.4–5.

6. Quarter acre of land.
7. In Revelation 9.11 Apollyon is "an angel of the bottomless pit." In Bunyan's *Pilgrim's Progress*, he is a hideous "monster"; "he had wings like a dragon."
8. With wings or pinions like those of a dragon.

Mere ugly heights and heaps now stolen in view.
How thus they had surprised me—solve it, you!
   How to get from them was no clearer case.
29
Yet half I seemed to recognize some trick
   Of mischief happened to me, God knows when—   170
   In a bad dream perhaps. Here ended, then,
Progress this way. When, in the very nick
Of giving up, one time more, came a click
   As when a trap shuts—you're inside the den!
30
Burningly it came on me all at once,   175
   This was the place! those two hills on the right,
   Crouched like two bulls locked horn in horn in fight;
While to the left, a tall scalped mountain . . . Dunce,
Dotard, a-dozing at the very nonce,[9]
   After a life spent training for the sight!   180
31
What in the midst lay but the Tower itself?
   The round squat turret, blind as the fool's heart,[1]
   Built of brown stone, without a counterpart
In the whole world. The tempest's mocking elf
Points to the shipman thus the unseen shelf   185
   He strikes on, only when the timbers start.
32
Not see? because of night perhaps?—why, day
   Came back again for that! before it left,
   The dying sunset kindled through a cleft:
The hills, like giants at a hunting, lay,   190
Chin upon hand, to see the game at bay—
   "Now stab and end the creature—to the heft!"[2]
33
Not hear? when noise was everywhere! it tolled
   Increasing like a bell. Names in my ears
   Of all the lost adventurers my peers—   195
How such a one was strong, and such was bold,
And such was fortunate, yet each of old
   Lost, lost! one moment knelled the woe of years.
34
There they stood, ranged along the hillsides, met
   To view the last of me, a living frame   200
   For one more picture! in a sheet of flame
I saw them and I knew them all. And yet
Dauntless the slug-horn[3] to my lips I set,
   And blew. *"Childe Roland to the Dark Tower came."*

1852   1855

9. Moment.
1. Cf. Psalms 14.1: "the fool hath said in his heart, There is no God."
2. Handle of dagger or sword.
3. This Scottish word meant the war cry or slogan (*slug-horn*) of a clan about to engage in battle, but in 1770, the poet Chatterton was misled into using it to mean a kind of trumpet or horn. Browning followed Chatterton's example, although the original meaning would also be relevant here.

Fra Lippo Lippi[1]

I am poor brother Lippo, by your leave!
You need not clap your torches to my face.
Zooks,[2] what's to blame? you think you see a monk!
What, 'tis past midnight, and you go the rounds,
And here you catch me at an alley's end   5
Where sportive ladies leave their doors ajar?
The Carmine's[3] my cloister: hunt it up,
Do—harry out, if you must show your zeal,
Whatever rat, there, haps on his wrong hole,
And nip each softling of a wee white mouse,   10
Weke, weke, that's crept to keep him company!
Aha, you know your betters! Then, you'll take
Your hand away that's fiddling on my throat,
And please to know me likewise. Who am I?
Why, one, sir, who is lodging with a friend   15
Three streets off—he's a certain . . . how d'ye call?
Master—a . . . Cosimo of the Medici,[4]
I' the house that caps the corner. Boh! you were best!
Remember and tell me, the day you're hanged,
How you affected such a gullet's gripe![5]   20
But you,[6] sir, it concerns you that your knaves
Pick up a manner nor discredit you:
Zooks, are we pilchards,[7] that they sweep the streets
And count fair prize what comes into this net?
He's Judas to a tittle, that man is![8]   25
Just such a face! Why, sir, you make amends.
Lord, I'm not angry! Bid your hangdogs go
Drink out this quarter-florin to the health
Of the munificent House that harbors me
(And many more beside, lads! more beside!)   30
And all's come square again. I'd like his face—
His, elbowing on his comrade in the door
With the pike and lantern—for the slave that holds
John Baptist's head a-dangle by the hair
With one hand ("Look you, now," as who should say)   35
And his weapon in the other, yet unwiped!
It's not your chance to have a bit of chalk,
A wood-coal or the like? or you should see!
Yes, I'm the painter, since you style me so.
What, brother Lippo's doings, up and down,   40
You know them and they take you? like enough!

1. This monologue portrays the dawn of the Renaissance in Italy at a point when the medieval attitude
toward life and art was about to be displaced by a fresh
appreciation of earthly pleasures. It was from Giorgio
Vasari's *Lives of the Painters* that Browning derived
most of his information about the life of the Florentine
painter and friar Lippo Lippi (1406–1469), but the theory of art propounded by Lippi in the poem was developed by the poet himself.
2. A shortened version of *Gadzooks,* a mild oath now
obscure in meaning but perhaps resembling a phrase
still in use: "God's truth."
3. Santa Maria del Carmine, a church and cloister of
the Carmelite order of friars to which Lippi belonged.
4. Lippi's patron, banker and virtual ruler of Florence.
5. I.e., how you had the arrogance to choke the gullet
of someone with my connections.
6. The officer in charge of the patrol of policemen or
watchmen.
7. Small fish.
8. I.e., one of the watchmen has a face that would
serve as a model for a painting of Judas.

I saw the proper twinkle in your eye—
'Tell you, I liked your looks at very first.
Let's sit and set things straight now, hip to haunch.
Here's spring come, and the nights one makes up bands   45
To roam the town and sing out carnival,[9]
And I've been three weeks shut within my mew,[1]
A-painting for the great man, saints and saints
And saints again. I could not paint all night—
Ouf! I leaned out of window for fresh air.   50
There came a hurry of feet and little feet,
A sweep of lute-strings, laughs, and whiffs of song—
Flower o' the broom,
Take away love, and our earth is a tomb!
Flower o' the quince,   55
I let Lisa go, and what good in life since?[2]
Flower o' the thyme—and so on. Round they went.
Scarce had they turned the corner when a titter
Like the skipping of rabbits by moonlight—three slim shapes,
And a face that looked up . . . zooks, sir, flesh and blood,   60
That's all I'm made of! Into shreds it went,
Curtain and counterpane and coverlet,
All the bed-furniture—a dozen knots,
There was a ladder! Down I let myself,
Hands and feet, scrambling somehow, and so dropped,   65
And after them. I came up with the fun
Hard by Saint Laurence,[3] hail fellow, well met—
Flower o' the rose,
If I've been merry, what matter who knows!
And so as I was stealing back again   70
To get to bed and have a bit of sleep
Ere I rise up tomorrow and go work
On Jerome knocking at his poor old breast
With his great round stone to subdue the flesh,[4]
You snap me of the sudden. Ah, I see!   75
Though your eye twinkles still, you shake your head—
Mine's shaved—a monk, you say—the sting's in that!
If Master Cosimo announced himself,
Mum's the word naturally; but a monk!
Come, what am I a beast for? tell us, now!   80
I was a baby when my mother died
And father died and left me in the street.
I starved there, God knows how, a year or two
On fig skins, melon parings, rinds and shucks,
Refuse and rubbish. One fine frosty day,   85
My stomach being empty as your hat,
The wind doubled me up and down I went.
Old Aunt Lapaccia trussed me with one hand

---

9. Season of revelry before the commencement of Lent.
1. Private den.
2. This and other interspersed flower songs are called *stornelli* in Italy.

3. San Lorenzo, a church in Florence.
4. A picture of St. Jerome (ca. 340–420), whose ascetic observances were hardly a congenial subject for such a painter as Lippi.

(Its fellow was a stinger as I knew),
And so along the wall, over the bridge,   90
By the straight cut to the convent. Six words there,
While I stood munching my first bread that month:
"So, boy, you're minded," quoth the good fat father
Wiping his own mouth, 'twas refection time⁵—
"To quit this very miserable world?   95
Will you renounce" . . . "the mouthful of bread?" thought I;
By no means! Brief, they made a monk of me;
I did renounce the world, its pride and greed,
Palace, farm, villa, shop, and banking house,
Trash, such as these poor devils of Medici   100
Have given their hearts to—all at eight years old.
Well, sir, I found in time, you may be sure,
'Twas not for nothing—the good bellyful,
The warm serge and the rope that goes all round,
And day-long blessed idleness beside!   105
"Let's see what the urchin's fit for"—that came next.
Not overmuch their way, I must confess.
Such a to-do! They tried me with their books:
Lord, they'd have taught me Latin in pure waste!
Flower o' the clove,   110
All the Latin I construe is "amo," I love!
But, mind you, when a boy starves in the streets
Eight years together, as my fortune was,
Watching folk's faces to know who will fling
The bit of half-stripped grape bunch he desires,   115
And who will curse or kick him for his pains—
Which gentleman processional and fine,
Holding a candle to the Sacrament,
Will wink and let him lift a plate and catch
The droppings of the wax to sell again,   120
Or holla for the Eight⁶ and have him whipped—
How say I?—nay, which dog bites, which lets drop
His bone from the heap of offal in the street—
Why, soul and sense of him grow sharp alike,
He learns the look of things, and none the less   125
For admonition from the hunger-pinch.
I had a store of such remarks, be sure,
Which, after I found leisure, turned to use.
I drew men's faces on my copybooks,
Scrawled them within the antiphonary's marge,⁷   130
Joined legs and arms to the long music-notes,
Found eyes and nose and chin for A's and B's,
And made a string of pictures of the world
Betwixt the ins and outs of verb and noun,
On the wall, the bench, the door. The monks looked black.   135
"Nay," quoth the Prior,⁸ "turn him out, d' ye say?
In no wise. Lose a crow and catch a lark.
What if at last we get our man of parts,

---

5. Mealtime.   7. Margin of music book used for choral singing.
6. Florentine magistrates.   8. Head of a Carmelite convent.

We Carmelites, like those Camaldolese
And Preaching Friars,[9] to do our church up fine   140
And put the front on it that ought to be!"
And hereupon he bade me daub away.
Thank you! my head being crammed, the walls a blank,
Never was such prompt disemburdening.
First, every sort of monk, the black and white,   145
I drew them, fat and lean: then, folk at church,
From good old gossips waiting to confess
Their cribs of barrel droppings, candle ends—
To the breathless fellow at the altar-foot,
Fresh from his murder, safe and sitting there   150
With the little children round him in a row
Of admiration, half for his beard and half
For that white anger of his victim's son
Shaking a fist at him with one fierce arm,
Signing himself with the other because of Christ   155
(Whose sad face on the cross sees only this
After the passion[1] of a thousand years)
Till some poor girl, her apron o'er her head
(Which the intense eyes looked through), came at eve
On tiptoe, said a word, dropped in a loaf,   160
Her pair of earrings and a bunch of flowers
(The brute took growling), prayed, and so was gone.
I painted all, then cried "'Tis ask and have;
Choose, for more's ready!"—laid the ladder flat,
And showed my covered bit of cloister wall.   165
The monks closed in a circle and praised loud
Till checked, taught what to see and not to see,
Being simple bodies—"That's the very man!
Look at the boy who stoops to pat the dog!
That woman's like the Prior's niece who comes   170
To care about his asthma: it's the life!"
But there my triumph's straw-fire flared and funked;[2]
Their betters took their turn to see and say:
The Prior and the learned pulled a face
And stopped all that in no time. "How? what's here?   175
Quite from the mark of painting, bless us all!
Faces, arms, legs and bodies like the true
As much as pea and pea! it's devil's game!
Your business is not to catch men with show,
With homage to the perishable clay,   180
But lift them over it, ignore it all,
Make them forget there's such a thing as flesh.
Your business is to paint the souls of men—
Man's soul, and it's a fire, smoke . . . no, it's not . . .
It's vapor done up like a newborn babe—   185
(In that shape when you die it leaves your mouth)
It's . . . well, what matters talking, it's the soul!
Give us no more of body than shows soul!

9. Benedictine and Dominican religious orders, re-   1. Sufferings.
spectively.   2. Went up in smoke.

Here's Giotto,[3] with his Saint a-praising God,
That sets us praising—why not stop with him?   190
Why put all thoughts of praise out of our head
With wonder at lines, colors, and what not?
Paint the soul, never mind the legs and arms!
Rub all out, try at it a second time.
Oh, that white smallish female with the breasts,   195
She's just my niece . . . Herodias,[4] I would say—
Who went and danced and got men's heads cut off!
Have it all out!" Now, is this sense, I ask?
A fine way to paint soul, by painting body
So ill, the eye can't stop there, must go further   200
And can't fare worse! Thus, yellow does for white
When what you put for yellow's simply black,
And any sort of meaning looks intense
When all beside itself means and looks naught.
Why can't a painter lift each foot in turn,   205
Left foot and right foot, go a double step,
Make his flesh liker and his soul more like,
Both in their order? Take the prettiest face,
The Prior's niece . . . patron-saint—is it so pretty
You can't discover if it means hope, fear,   210
Sorrow or joy? won't beauty go with these?
Suppose I've made her eyes all right and blue,
Can't I take breath and try to add life's flash,
And then add soul and heighten them threefold?
Or say there's beauty with no soul at all—   215
(I never saw it—put the case the same—)
If you get simple beauty and naught else,
You get about the best thing God invents:
That's somewhat: and you'll find the soul you have missed,
Within yourself, when you return him thanks.   220
"Rub all out!" Well, well, there's my life, in short,
And so the thing has gone on ever since.
I'm grown a man no doubt, I've broken bounds:
You should not take a fellow eight years old
And make him swear to never kiss the girls.   225
I'm my own master, paint now as I please—
Having a friend, you see, in the Corner-house![5]
Lord, it's fast holding by the rings in front—
Those great rings serve more purposes than just
To plant a flag in, or tie up a horse!   230
And yet the old schooling sticks, the old grave eyes
Are peeping o'er my shoulder as I work,
The heads shake still—"It's art's decline, my son!
You're not of the true painters, great and old;
Brother Angelico's the man, you'll find;   235

---

3. Great Florentine painter (1276–1337), whose stylized pictures of religious subjects were admired as
models of pre-Renaissance art.
4. Herodias, also called Salomé, had the same name
as her mother, Herodias, sister-in-law of King Herod.

The daughter's dance coincided with the beheading of
John the Baptist, who had aroused her mother's displeasure (cf. Matthew 14.1–2).
5. The Medici palace.

Brother Lorenzo stands his single peer:[6]
Fag on at flesh, you'll never make the third!"
Flower o' the pine,
You keep your mistr . . . manners, and I'll stick to mine!
I'm not the third, then: bless us, they must know!   240
Don't you think they're the likeliest to know,
They with their Latin? So, I swallow my rage,
Clench my teeth, suck my lips in tight, and paint
To please them—sometimes do and sometimes don't;
For, doing most, there's pretty sure to come   245
A turn, some warm eve finds me at my saints—
A laugh, a cry, the business of the world—
(Flower o' the peach,
Death for us all, and his own life for each!)
And my whole soul revolves, the cup runs over,   250
The world and life's too big to pass for a dream,
And I do these wild things in sheer despite,
And play the fooleries you catch me at,
In pure rage! The old mill-horse, out at grass
After hard years, throws up his stiff heels so,   255
Although the miller does not preach to him
The only good of grass is to make chaff.[7]
What would men have? Do they like grass or no—
May they or mayn't they? all I want's the thing
Settled forever one way. As it is,   260
You tell too many lies and hurt yourself:
You don't like what you only like too much,
You do like what, if given you at your word,
You find abundantly detestable.
For me, I think I speak as I was taught;   265
I always see the garden and God there
A-making man's wife: and, my lesson learned,
The value and significance of flesh,
I can't unlearn ten minutes afterwards.

You understand me: I'm a beast, I know.   270
But see, now—why, I see as certainly
As that the morning star's about to shine,
What will hap some day. We've a youngster here
Comes to our convent, studies what I do,
Slouches and stares and lets no atom drop: 275
His name is Guidi[8]—he'll not mind the monks—
They call him Hulking Tom, he lets them talk—
He picks my practice up—he'll paint apace,
I hope so—though I never live so long,
I know what's sure to follow. You be judge!   280
You speak no Latin more than I, belike;

6. Fra Angelico (1387–1455) and Lorenzo Monaco (1370–1425), whose paintings were in the approved traditional manner.
7. Straw.
8. Guidi or Masaccio (1401–1428), a painter who may have been Lippi's master rather than his pupil, al-though Browning, in a letter to the press in 1870, argued that Lippi had been born earlier. Like Lippi, Masaccio was in revolt against the medieval theory of art. His frescoes in the chapel of Santa Maria del Carmine are considered his masterpiece.

However, you're my man, you've seen the world
—The beauty and the wonder and the power,
The shapes of things, their colors, lights and shades,
Changes, surprises—and God made it all!   285
—For what? Do you feel thankful, aye or no,
For this fair town's face, yonder river's line,
The mountain round it and the sky above,
Much more the figures of man, woman, child,
These are the frame to? What's it all about?   290
To be passed over, despised? or dwelt upon,
Wondered at? oh, this last of course!—you say.
But why not do as well as say—paint these
Just as they are, careless what comes of it?
God's works—paint any one, and count it crime   295
To let a truth slip. Don't object, "His works
Are here already; nature is complete:
Suppose you reproduce her—(which you can't)
There's no advantage! You must beat her, then."
For, don't you mark? we're made so that we love   300
First when we see them painted, things we have passed
Perhaps a hundred times nor cared to see;
And so they are better, painted—better to us,
Which is the same thing. Art was given for that;
God uses us to help each other so,   305
Lending our minds out. Have you noticed, now,
Your cullion's⁹ hanging face? A bit of chalk,
And trust me but you should, though! How much more,
If I drew higher things with the same truth!
That were to take the Prior's pulpit-place,   310
Interpret God to all of you! Oh, oh,
It makes me mad to see what men shall do
And we in our graves! This world's no blot for us,
Nor blank; it means intensely, and means good:
To find its meaning is my meat and drink.   315
"Aye, but you don't so instigate to prayer!"
Strikes in the Prior: "when your meaning's plain
It does not say to folk—remember matins,
Or, mind you fast next Friday!" Why, for this
What need of art at all? A skull and bones,   320
Two bits of stick nailed crosswise, or, what's best,
A bell to chime the hour with, does as well.
I painted a Saint Laurence¹ six months since
At Prato, splashed the fresco² in fine style:
"How looks my painting, now the scaffold's down?"   325
I ask a brother: "Hugely," he returns—
"Already not one phiz of your three slaves
Who turn the Deacon off his toasted side,
But it's scratched and prodded to our heart's content,
The pious people have so eased their own   330

9. Rascal's.
1. A scene representing the fiery martyrdom of St.
Laurence.

2. A "fresco" is painted quickly on fresh plaster over a
surface of bricks. "Prato": a town near Florence.

With coming to say prayers there in a rage:
We get on fast to see the bricks beneath.
Expect another job this time next year,
For pity and religion grow i' the crowd—
Your painting serves its purpose!" Hang the fools!   335

    —That is—you'll not mistake an idle word
Spoke in a huff by a poor monk, God wot,
Tasting the air this spicy night which turns
The unaccustomed head like Chianti wine!
Oh, the church knows! don't misreport me, now!   340
It's natural a poor monk out of bounds
Should have his apt word to excuse himself:
And hearken how I plot to make amends.
I have bethought me: I shall paint a piece
. . . There's for you! Give me six months, then go, see   345
Something in Sant' Ambrogio's!³ Bless the nuns!
They want a cast o' my office.⁴ I shall paint
God in the midst, Madonna and her babe,
Ringed by a bowery flowery angel brood,
Lilies and vestments and white faces, sweet   350
As puff on puff of grated orris-root⁵
When ladies crowd to Church at midsummer.
And then i' the front, of course a saint or two—
Saint John, because he saves the Florentines,
Saint Ambrose, who puts down in black and white   355
The convent's friends and gives them a long day,
And Job, I must have him there past mistake,
The man of Uz (and Us without the z,
Painters who need his patience). Well, all these
Secured at their devotion, up shall come   360
Out of a corner when you least expect,
As one by a dark stair into a great light,
Music and talking, who but Lippo! I!—
Mazed, motionless and moonstruck—I'm the man!
Back I shrink—what is this I see and hear?   365
I, caught up with my monk's things by mistake,
My old serge gown and rope that goes all round,
I, in this presence, this pure company!
Where's a hole, where's a corner for escape?
Then steps a sweet angelic slip of a thing   370
Forward, puts out a soft palm—"Not so fast!"
—Addresses the celestial presence, "nay—
He made you and devised you, after all,
Though he's none of you! Could Saint John there draw—
His camel-hair⁶ make up a painting-brush?   375
We come to brother Lippo for all that,

---

3. A convent church in Florence.
4. Sample of my work. The completed painting, which Browning saw in Florence, is Lippi's *Coronation of the Virgin.*
5. Powder (like talcum) made from sweet-smelling roots of a flower.
6. Cf. Mark 1.6: "And John was clothed with camel's hair."

Iste perfecit opus!"[7] So, all smile—
I shuffle sideways with my blushing face
Under the cover of a hundred wings
Thrown like a spread of kirtles[8] when you're gay   380
And play hot cockles,[9] all the doors being shut,
Till, wholly unexpected, in there pops
The hothead husband! Thus I scuttle off
To some safe bench behind, not letting go
The palm of her, the little lily thing   385
That spoke the good word for me in the nick,
Like the Prior's niece . . . Saint Lucy, I would say.
And so all's saved for me, and for the church
A pretty picture gained. Go, six months hence!
Your hand, sir, and good-by: no lights, no lights!   390
The street's hushed, and I know my own way back,
Don't fear me! There's the gray beginning. Zooks!

ca. 1853   1855

The Last Ride Together

1

I said—Then, dearest, since 'tis so,
Since now at length my fate I know,
Since nothing all my love avails,
Since all, my life seemed meant for, fails,
    Since this was written and needs must be—   5
My whole heart rises up to bless
Your name in pride and thankfulness!
Take back the hope you gave—I claim
Only a memory of the same,
  —And this beside, if you will not blame,   10
    Your leave for one more last ride with me.

2

My mistress bent that brow of hers;
Those deep dark eyes where pride demurs
When pity would be softening through,
Fixed me a breathing-while or two   15
    With life or death in the balance: right!
The blood replenished me again;
My last thought was at least not vain:
I and my mistress, side by side
Shall be together, breathe and ride,   20
So, one day more am I deified.
    Who knows but the world may end tonight?

3

Hush! if you saw some western cloud
All billowy-bosomed, over-bowed

---

7. "This man made the work!" In this painting, as later completed, these words appear beside a figure that Browning took to be Lippi's self-portrait.
8. Skirts.
9. A game in which a player wears a blindfold.

By many benedictions—sun's   25
And moon's and evening star's at once—
    And so, you, looking and loving best,
Conscious grew, your passion drew
Cloud, sunset, moonrise, star-shine too,
Down on you, near and yet more near,   30
Till flesh must fade for heaven was here!—
Thus leant she and lingered[1]—joy and fear!
    Thus lay she a moment on my breast.
4

Then we began to ride. My soul
Smoothed itself out, a long-cramped scroll   35
Freshening and fluttering in the wind.
Past hopes already lay behind.
    What need to strive with a life awry?
Had I said that, had I done this,
So might I gain, so might I miss.   40
Might she have loved me? just as well
She might have hated, who can tell!
Where had I been now if the worst befell?
    And here we are riding, she and I.
5

Fail I alone, in words and deeds?   45
Why, all men strive and who succeeds?
We rode; it seemed my spirit flew,
Saw other regions, cities new,
    As the world rushed by on either side.
I thought—All labor, yet no less   50
Bear up beneath their unsuccess.
Look at the end of work, contrast
The petty done, the undone vast,
This present of theirs with the hopeful past!
    I hoped she would love me; here we ride.   55
6

What hand and brain went ever paired?
What heart alike conceived and dared?
What act proved all its thought had been?
What will but felt the fleshly screen?
    We ride and I see her bosom heave.   60
There's many a crown for who can reach.
Ten lines, a statesman's life in each![2]
The flag stuck on a heap of bones,
A soldier's doing! what atones?
They scratch his name on the Abbey stones.[3]   65
    My riding is better, by their leave.
7

What does it all mean, poet? Well,
Your brains beat into rhythm, you tell

---

1. Before she mounts her horse.
2. If a man tries hard enough, he may be crowned with what seems to be success. He might become, for example, an eminent "statesman." Yet his only me-morial would be a short sketch of his career ("ten lines") in some history or biographical dictionary.
3. I.e., he is honored by burial in Westminster Abbey.

What we felt only; you expressed
You hold things beautiful the best,   70
   And pace them in rhyme so, side by side.
'Tis something, nay 'tis much: but then,
Have you yourself what's best for men?
Are you—poor, sick, old ere your time—
Nearer one whit your own sublime   75
Than we who never have turned a rhyme?
   Sing, riding's a joy! For me, I ride.
8

And you, great sculptor—so, you gave
A score of years to Art, her slave,
And that's your Venus, whence we turn   80
To yonder girl that fords the burn!⁴
   You acquiesce, and shall I repine?
What, man of music, you grown gray
With notes and nothing else to say,
Is this your sole praise from a friend,   85
"Greatly his opera's strains intend,
But in music we know how fashions end!"
   I gave my youth; but we ride, in fine.⁵
9

Who knows what's fit for us? Had fate
Proposed bliss here should sublimate   90
My being—had I signed the bond—
Still one must lead some life beyond,
   Have a bliss to die with, dim-descried.
This foot once planted on the goal,
This glory-garland round my soul,   95
Could I descry such? Try and test!
I sink back shuddering from the quest.
Earth being so good, would Heaven seem best?⁶
   Now, Heaven and she are beyond this ride.
10

And yet—she has not spoke so long!   100
What if heaven be that, fair and strong
At life's best, with our eyes upturned
Whither life's flower is first discerned,
   We, fixed so, ever should so abide?
What if we still ride on, we two   105
With life forever old yet new,
Changed not in kind but in degree,
The instant made eternity—
And heaven just prove that I and she
   Ride, ride together, forever ride?   110

1855

---

4. Crosses the brook.
5. In short.
6. If fate had decreed that he could possess his mistress fully, life on earth would have been so blissful that heaven could offer nothing for him to look forward to after death. Hence (he argues) to preserve "a bliss to die with" (line 93), it is better that she never really became his on earth.

Andrea del Sarto[1]

(called "The Faultless Painter")

But do not let us quarrel any more,
No, my Lucrezia; bear with me for once:
Sit down and all shall happen as you wish.
You turn your face, but does it bring your heart?
I'll work then for your friend's friend, never fear,   5
Treat his own subject after his own way,
Fix his own time, accept too his own price,
And shut the money into this small hand
When next it takes mine. Will it? tenderly?
Oh, I'll content him—but tomorrow, Love!   10
I often am much wearier than you think,
This evening more than usual, and it seems
As if—forgive now—should you let me sit
Here by the window with your hand in mine
And look a half-hour forth on Fiesole,[2]   15
Both of one mind, as married people use,
Quietly, quietly the evening through,
I might get up tomorrow to my work
Cheerful and fresh as ever. Let us try.
Tomorrow, how you shall be glad for this!   20
Your soft hand is a woman of itself,
And mine the man's bared breast she curls inside.
Don't count the time lost, neither; you must serve
For each of the five pictures we require:
It saves a model. So! keep looking so—   25
My serpentining beauty, rounds on rounds![3]
—How could you ever prick those perfect ears,
Even to put the pearl there! oh, so sweet—
My face, my moon, my everybody's moon,
Which everybody looks on and calls his,   30
And, I suppose, is looked on by in turn,
While she looks—no one's: very dear, no less.[4]
You smile? why, there's my picture ready made,
There's what we painters call our harmony!

1. This portrait of Andrea del Sarto (1486–1531) was derived from a biography written by his pupil Giorgio Vasari, author of *The Lives of the Painters*. Vasari's account seeks to explain why his Florentine master, one of the most skillful painters of the Renaissance, never altogether fulfilled the promise he had shown early in his career and why he had never arrived (in Vasari's opinion) at the level of such artists as Raphael. Vasari noted that Andrea suffered from "a certain timidity of mind . . . which rendered it impossible that those evidences of ardor and animation, which are proper to the more exalted character, should ever appear in him."

Browning also follows Vasari's account of Andrea's marriage to a beautiful widow, Lucrezia, "an artful woman who made him do as she pleased in all things." Vasari reports that Andrea's "immoderate love for her soon caused him to neglect the studies de-manded by his art" and that this infatuation had "more influence over him than the glory and honor towards which he had begun to make such hopeful advances."

Browning's poem has often been praised for its exposition of a paradoxical theory of success and failure, but it has other qualities as well. Its slow-paced, enervated blank verse, its setting of a quiet evening in autumn, its comparative lack of the movement and noise that we expect in Browning's energetic verse create a unity of impression that is unobtrusive yet effective.
2. A suburb on the hills overlooking Florence.
3. Coils of hair like the coils of a serpent.
4. Her affections are centered on no one person, not even on her husband, yet she is nevertheless dear to him.

A common grayness silvers everything[5]—   35
All in a twilight, you and I alike
—You, at the point of your first pride in me
(That's gone you know)—but I, at every point;
My youth, my hope, my art, being all toned down
To yonder sober pleasant Fiesole.   40
There's the bell clinking from the chapel top;
That length of convent wall across the way
Holds the trees safer, huddled more inside;
The last monk leaves the garden; days decrease,
And autumn grows, autumn in everything.   45
Eh? the whole seems to fall into a shape
As if I saw alike my work and self
And all that I was born to be and do,
A twilight-piece. Love, we are in God's hand.
How strange now, looks the life he makes us lead;   50
So free we seem, so fettered fast we are!
I feel he laid the fetter: let it lie!
This chamber for example—turn your head—
All that's behind us! You don't understand
Nor care to understand about my art,   55
But you can hear at least when people speak:
And that cartoon,[6] the second from the door
—It is the thing, Love! so such things should be—
Behold Madonna!—I am bold to say.
I can do with my pencil what I know,   60
What I see, what at bottom of my heart
I wish for, if I ever wish so deep—
Do easily, too—when I say, perfectly,
I do not boast, perhaps: yourself are judge,
Who listened to the Legate's[7] talk last week,   65
And just as much they used to say in France.
At any rate 'tis easy, all of it!
No sketches first, no studies, that's long past:
I do what many dream of, all their lives,
—Dream? strive to do, and agonize to do,   70
And fail in doing. I could count twenty such
On twice your fingers, and not leave this town,
Who strive—you don't know how the others strive
To paint a little thing like that you smeared
Carelessly passing with your robes afloat—   75
Yet do much less, so much less, Someone[8] says
(I know his name, no matter)—so much less!
Well, less is more, Lucrezia: I am judged.
There burns a truer light of God in them,
In their vexed beating stuffed and stopped-up brain,   80
Heart, or whate'er else, than goes on to prompt
This low-pulsed forthright craftsman's hand of mine.
Their works drop groundward, but themselves, I know,

---

5. The predominant color in many of Andrea's paint-   7. A deputy of the pope.
ings is silver gray.   8. Probably Michelangelo (1475–1564).
6. Drawing.

Reach many a time a heaven that's shut to me,
Enter and take their place there sure enough,   85
Though they come back and cannot tell the world.
My works are nearer heaven, but I sit here.
The sudden blood of these men! at a word—
Praise them, it boils, or blame them, it boils too.
I, painting from myself and to myself,   90
Know what I do, am unmoved by men's blame
Or their praise either. Somebody remarks
Morello's[9] outline there is wrongly traced,
His hue mistaken; what of that? or else,
Rightly traced and well ordered; what of that?   95
Speak as they please, what does the mountain care?
Ah, but a man's reach should exceed his grasp,
Or what's a heaven for? All is silver-gray
Placid and perfect with my art: the worse!
I know both what I want and what might gain,   100
And yet how profitless to know, to sigh
"Had I been two, another and myself,
Our head would have o'erlooked the world!"[1] No doubt.
Yonder's a work now, of that famous youth
The Urbinate[2] who died five years ago.   105
('Tis copied, George Vasari sent it me.[3])
Well, I can fancy how he did it all,
Pouring his soul, with kings and popes to see,
Reaching, that heaven might so replenish him,
Above and through his art—for it gives way;   110
That arm is wrongly put—and there again—
A fault to pardon in the drawing's lines,
Its body, so to speak: its soul is right,
He means right—that, a child may understand.
Still, what an arm! and I could alter it: 115
But all the play, the insight and the stretch—
Out of me, out of me! And wherefore out?
Had you enjoined them on me, given me soul,
We might have risen to Rafael, I and you!
Nay, Love, you did give all I asked, I think—   120
More than I merit, yes, by many times.
But had you—oh, with the same perfect brow,
And perfect eyes, and more than perfect mouth,
And the low voice my soul hears, as a bird
The fowler's pipe,[4] and follows to the snare—   125
Had you, with these the same, but brought a mind!
Some women do so. Had the mouth there urged
"God and the glory! never care for gain.
The present by the future, what is that?
Live for fame, side by side with Agnolo!"[5]   130

9. A mountain peak outside Florence.
1. I.e., if I had been both an aspiring, dedicated, and
soul-conscious artist as well as a faultless craftsman, the
combination would have been unsurpassable! See also
line 140 ("we half-men").
2. Raphael (1483–1520), born at Urbino.

3. In saying that the painting is a copy, Andrea may
perhaps be concerned to prevent Lucrezia from selling
it.
4. Whistle or call used by hunters to lure wild fowl
into range.
5. Michelangelo.

Rafael is waiting: up to God, all three!"
I might have done it for you. So it seems:
Perhaps not. All is as God overrules.
Beside, incentives come from the soul's self;
The rest avail not. Why do I need you?   135
What wife had Rafael, or has Agnolo?
In this world, who can do a thing, will not;
And who would do it, cannot, I perceive:
Yet the will's somewhat—somewhat, too, the power—
And thus we half-men struggle. At the end,   140
God, I conclude, compensates, punishes.
'Tis safer for me, if the award be strict,
That I am something underrated here.
Poor this long while, despised, to speak the truth.
I dared not, do you know, leave home all day,   145
For fear of chancing on the Paris lords.
The best is when they pass and look aside;
But they speak sometimes; I must bear it all.
Well may they speak! That Francis,[6] that first time,
And that long festal year at Fontainebleau!   150
I surely then could sometimes leave the ground,
Put on the glory, Rafael's daily wear,
In that humane great monarch's golden look—
One finger in his beard or twisted curl
Over his mouth's good mark that made the smile,   155
One arm about my shoulder, round my neck,
The jingle of his gold chain in my ear,
I painting proudly with his breath on me,
All his court round him, seeing with his eyes,
Such frank French eyes, and such a fire of souls   160
Profuse, my hand kept plying by those hearts—
And, best of all, this, this, this face beyond,
This in the background, waiting on my work,
To crown the issue with a last reward!
A good time, was it not, my kingly days?   165
And had you not grown restless . . . but I know—
'Tis done and past; 'twas right, my instinct said;
Too live the life grew, golden and not gray,
And I'm the weak-eyed bat no sun should tempt
Out of the grange whose four walls make his world.[7]   170
How could it end in any other way?
You called me, and I came home to your heart.
The triumph was—to reach and stay there; since
I reached it ere the triumph, what is lost?
Let my hands frame your face in your hair's gold,   175
You beautiful Lucrezia that are mine!

6. King Francis I of France had invited Andrea to his
court at Fontainebleau and warmly encouraged him
in his painting. On returning to Florence, however,
Andrea is reputed to have stolen some funds entrusted
to him by Francis, and to please Lucrezia he built a
house with the money. Now he is afraid of being insulted by "Paris lords" on the streets.
7. The bat, a creature of evening, thrives best in the
confines of the "four walls" of a farm building
("grange"). See also line 261, in which Andrea thinks
of heaven as a place of four walls.

"Rafael did this, Andrea painted that;
The Roman's is the better when you pray,
But still the other's Virgin was his wife—"
Men will excuse me. I am glad to judge   180
Both pictures in your presence; clearer grows
My better fortune, I resolve to think.
For, do you know, Lucrezia, as God lives,
Said one day Agnolo, his very self,
To Rafael . . . I have known it all these years . . .   185
(When the young man was flaming out his thoughts
Upon a palace wall for Rome to see,
Too lifted up in heart because of it)
"Friend, there's a certain sorry little scrub
Goes up and down our Florence, none cares how,   190
Who, were he set to plan and execute
As you are, pricked on by your popes and kings,
Would bring the sweat into that brow of yours!"
To Rafael's—And indeed the arm is wrong.
I hardly dare . . . yet, only you to see,   195
Give the chalk here—quick, thus the line should go!
Aye, but the soul! he's Rafael! rub it out!
Still, all I care for, if he spoke the truth,
(What he? why, who but Michel Agnolo?
Do you forget already words like those?)   200
If really there was such a chance, so lost—
Is, whether you're—not grateful—but more pleased.
Well, let me think so. And you smile indeed!
This hour has been an hour! Another smile?
If you would sit thus by me every night   205
I should work better, do you comprehend?
I mean that I should earn more, give you more.
See, it is settled dusk now; there's a star;
Morello's gone, the watch-lights show the wall,
The cue-owls[8] speak the name we call them by.   210
Come from the window, love—come in, at last,
Inside the melancholy little house
We built to be so gay with. God is just.
King Francis may forgive me: oft at nights
When I look up from painting, eyes tired out,   215
The walls become illumined, brick from brick
Distinct, instead of mortar, fierce bright gold,
That gold of his I did cement them with!
Let us but love each other. Must you go?
That Cousin here again? he waits outside?   220
Must see you—you, and not with me? Those loans?
More gaming debts to pay?[9] you smiled for that?
Well, let smiles buy me! have you more to spend?
While hand and eye and something of a heart

---

8. An owl whose cry sounds like the Italian word *ciù*.
9. Lucrezia's "Cousin" (or lover or friend) owes gambling debts to a creditor. Andrea has already contracted

(lines 5–10) to pay off these debts by painting some
pictures according to the creditor's specifications. Now
he agrees to pay off further debts.

Are left me, work's my ware, and what's it worth?   225
I'll pay my fancy. Only let me sit
The gray remainder of the evening out,
Idle, you call it, and muse perfectly
How I could paint, were I but back in France,
One picture, just one more—the Virgin's face,   230
Not yours this time! I want you at my side
To hear them—that is, Michel Agnolo—
Judge all I do and tell you of its worth.
Will you? Tomorrow, satisfy your friend.
I take the subjects for his corridor,   235
Finish the portrait out of hand—there, there,
And throw him in another thing or two
If he demurs; the whole should prove enough
To pay for this same Cousin's freak. Beside,
What's better and what's all I care about,   240
Get you the thirteen scudi[1] for the ruff!
Love, does that please you? Ah, but what does he,
The Cousin! What does he to please you more?

    I am grown peaceful as old age tonight.
I regret little, I would change still less.   245
Since there my past life lies, why alter it?
The very wrong to Francis!—it is true
I took his coin, was tempted and complied,
And built this house and sinned, and all is said.
My father and my mother died of want.[2]   250
Well, had I riches of my own? you see
How one gets rich! Let each one bear his lot.
They were born poor, lived poor, and poor they died:
And I have labored somewhat in my time
And not been paid profusely. Some good son   255
Paint my two hundred pictures—let him try!
No doubt, there's something strikes a balance. Yes,
You loved me quite enough, it seems tonight.
This must suffice me here. What would one have?
In heaven, perhaps, new chances, one more chance—   260
Four great walls in the New Jerusalem,[3]
Meted on each side by the angel's reed,[4]
For Leonard,[5] Rafael, Agnolo and me
To cover—the three first without a wife,
While I have mine! So—still they overcome   265
Because there's still Lucrezia—as I choose.

    Again the Cousin's whistle! Go, my Love.

ca. 1853   1855

1. Italian coins.   3. Cf. Revelation 21.10–21.
2. According to Vasari, Andrea's infatuation for Lu-   4. Measuring rod.
crezia prompted him to stop supporting his poverty-   5. Leonardo da Vinci (1452–1519).
stricken parents.

Two in the Campagna[1]

1

I wonder do you feel today
    As I have felt since, hand in hand,
We sat down on the grass, to stray
    In spirit better through the land,
This morn of Rome and May?   5

2

For me, I touched a thought, I know,
    Has tantalized me many times,
(Like turns of thread the spiders throw
    Mocking across our path) for rhymes
To catch at and let go.   10

3

Help me to hold it! First it left
    The yellowing fennel,[2] run to seed
There, branching from the brickwork's cleft,
    Some old tomb's ruin: yonder weed
Took up the floating weft,[3]   15

4

Where one small orange cup amassed
    Five beetles—blind and green they grope
Among the honey-meal: and last,
    Everywhere on the grassy slope
I traced it. Hold it fast!   20

5

The champaign[4] with its endless fleece
    Of feathery grasses everywhere!
Silence and passion, joy and peace,
    An everlasting wash of air—
Rome's ghost since her decease.   25

6

Such life here, through such lengths of hours,
    Such miracles performed in play,
Such primal naked forms of flowers,
    Such letting nature have her way
While heaven looks from its towers!   30

7

How say you? Let us, O my dove,
    Let us be unashamed of soul,
As earth lies bare to heaven above!
    How is it under our control
To love or not to love?   35

8

I would that you were all to me,
    You that are just so much, no more.
Nor yours nor mine, nor slave nor free!

---

1. The Campagna is the name for the level plains and pasture lands near Rome where the ruins of ancient cities are overrun with wildflowers.
2. A yellow-flowered plant from which a pungent spice is derived.
3. Threads crossing from side to side of a web.
4. Here, the Campagna.

Where does the fault lie? What the core
O' the wound, since wound must be? 40

9

I would I could adopt your will,
    See with your eyes, and set my heart
Beating by yours, and drink my fill
    At your soul's springs—your part my part
In life, for good and ill. 45

10

No. I yearn upward, touch you close,
    Then stand away. I kiss your cheek,
Catch your soul's warmth—I pluck the rose
    And love it more than tongue can speak—
Then the good minute goes. 50

11

Already how am I so far
    Out of that minute? Must I go
Still like the thistle-ball, no bar,
    Onward, whenever light winds blow,
Fixed by no friendly star?[5] 55

12

Just when I seemed about to learn!
    Where is the thread now? Off again!
The old trick! Only I discern—
    Infinite passion, and the pain
Of finite hearts that yearn. 60

1854 1855

A Grammarian's Funeral[1]

Shortly After the Revival of Learning in Europe

Let us begin and carry up this corpse,
    Singing together.
Leave we the common crofts, the vulgar thorpes[2]
    Each in its tether[3]
Sleeping safe on the bosom of the plain, 5
    Cared for till cock-crow:
Look out if yonder be not day again
    Rimming the rock-row!
That's the appropriate country; there, man's thought,
    Rarer, intenser, 10

5. Cf. Shakespeare's Sonnet 116 (p. 477).
1. The speaker is one of the students who are bearing the body of their scholarly master to the mountaintop for burial. The student's defense of the dead grammarian's idealistic dedication to knowledge and faith in a future life is expressed in some of the harshest-sounding and most laborious verse ever written by Browning. It is this grotesque combination of opposites (soaring idealism in conjunction with harsh or petty realities) that gives A Grammarian's Funeral its distinctive tone.

No model for the grammarian has been specifically identified. Browning seems to have had in mind the kind of early Renaissance scholar whose devotion to the Greek language made it possible for others to enjoy the more recognizably significant aspects of the revival of learning.
2. Villages. "Crofts": small tracts of land farmed by peasants.
3. Restricted to a narrow sphere like an animal tied to a stake.

Self-gathered for an outbreak, as it ought,
  Chafes in the censer.
Leave we the unlettered plain its herd and crop;[4]
  Seek we sepulture[5]
On a tall mountain, cities to the top,   15
  Crowded with culture!
All the peaks soar, but one the rest excels;
  Clouds overcome it;
No! yonder sparkle is the citadel's
  Circling its summit.   20
Thither our path lies; wind we up the heights:
  Wait ye the warning?
Our low life was the level's and the night's;
  He's for the morning.
Step to a tune, square chests, erect each head,   25
  'Ware[6] the beholders!
This is our master, famous, calm, and dead,
  Borne on our shoulders.

Sleep, crop and herd! sleep, darkling thorpe and croft,
  Safe from the weather!   30
He, whom we convoy to his grave aloft,
  Singing together,
He was a man born with thy face and throat,
  Lyric Apollo![7]
Long he lived nameless: how should spring take note   35
  Winter would follow?
Till lo, the little touch, and youth was gone!
  Cramped and diminished,
Moaned he, "New measures, other feet anon!
  My dance is finished?"   40
No, that's the world's way: (keep the mountain-side,
  Make for the city!)
He knew the signal, and stepped on with pride
  Over men's pity;
Left play for work, and grappled with the world   45
  Bent on escaping:
"What's in the scroll," quoth he, "thou keepest furled?
  Show me their shaping,
Theirs who most studied man, the bard and sage —
  Give!" — So, he gowned him,[8]   50
Straight got by heart that book to its last page:
  Learned, we found him.
Yea, but we found him bald too, eyes like lead,
  Accents uncertain:
"Time to taste life," another would have said,   55
  "Up with the curtain!"
This man said rather, "Actual life comes next?"

---

4. Flatlands at the base of the mountain that are populated by illiterate shepherds and peasants.
5. Burial place.

6. I.e., beware, or look out for.
7. God of music and embodiment of male beauty.
8. Dressed in academic gown; became a scholar.

Patience a moment!
Grant I have mastered learning's crabbed text,
  Still there's the comment.[9]   60
Let me know all! Prate not of most or least,
  Painful or easy!
Even to the crumbs I'd fain eat up the feast,
  Aye, nor feel queasy."
Oh, such a life as he resolved to live,   65
  When he had learned it,
When he had gathered all books had to give!
  Sooner, he spurned it.
Image the whole, then execute the parts—
  Fancy the fabric   70
Quite, ere you build, ere steel strike fire from quartz,
  Ere mortar dab brick!

(Here's the town gate reached: there's the market place
  Gaping before us.)
Yea, this in him was the peculiar grace   75
  (Hearten our chorus!)
That before living he'd learn how to live—
  No end to learning:
Earn the means first—God surely will contrive
  Use for our earning.   80
Others mistrust and say, "But time escapes:
  Live now or never!"
He said, "What's time? Leave Now for dogs and apes!
  Man has Forever."
Back to his book then: deeper drooped his head: 85
  Calculus[1] racked him:
Leaden before, his eyes grew dross of lead:
  Tussis[2] attacked him.
"Now, master, take a little rest!"—not he!
  (Caution redoubled,   90
Step two abreast, the way winds narrowly!)
  Not a whit troubled
Back to his studies, fresher than at first,
  Fierce as a dragon
He (soul-hydroptic[3] with a sacred thirst)   95
  Sucked at the flagon.
Oh, if we draw a circle premature,
  Heedless of far gain,
Greedy for quick returns of profit, sure
  Bad is our bargain!   100
Was it not great? did not he throw on God
  (He loves the burthen)—
God's task to make the heavenly period
  Perfect the earthen?
Did not he magnify the mind, show clear   105

9. Commentaries or annotations on a text.   2. A cough.
1. A stone such as a gallstone.   3. Insatiably soul thirsty.

Just what it all meant?
He would not discount life, as fools do here,
    Paid by installment.
He ventured neck or nothing—heaven's success
    Found, or earth's failure: 110
"Wilt thou trust death or not?" He answered "Yes:
    Hence with life's pale lure!"
That low man seeks a little thing to do,
    Sees it and does it:
This high man, with a great thing to pursue,   115
    Dies ere he knows it.
That low man goes on adding one to one,
    His hundred's soon hit:
This high man, aiming at a million,
    Misses an unit.[4]   120
That, has the world here—should he need the next,
    Let the world mind him!
This, throws himself on God, and unperplexed
    Seeking shall find him.
So, with the throttling hands of death at strife,   125
    Ground he at grammar;
Still, through the rattle, parts of speech were rife:
    While he could stammer
He settled *Hoti's* business—let it be!—
    Properly based *Oun*—   130
Gave us the doctrine of the enclitic *De*,[5]
    Dead from the waist down.
Well, here's the platform, here's the proper place:
    Hail to your purlieus,
All ye highfliers of the feathered race,   135
    Swallows and curlews!
Here's the top peak; the multitude below
    Live, for they can, there:
This man decided not to Live but Know—
    Bury this man there?   140
Here—here's his place, where meteors shoot, clouds form,
    Lightnings are loosened,
Stars come and go! Let joy break with the storm,
    Peace let the dew send!
Lofty designs must close in like effects: 145
    Loftily lying,
Leave him—still loftier than the world suspects,
    Living and dying.

ca. 1854   1855

---

4. A small item such as some trifling worldly pleasure.

5. "*Hoti*," "*Oun*," and "*De*" are Greek particles meaning "that," "then," and "toward." An unaccented word such as *de* is "enclitic" when it affects the accentuation of a word adjacent to it. In a letter of 1863, Browning commented to Tennyson that he wanted his grammarian to have been working on "the biggest of the littlenesses."

A Woman's Last Word

1

Let's contend no more, Love,
　　Strive nor weep:
All be as before, Love,
　　—Only sleep!

2

What so wild as words are?   5
　　I and thou
In debate, as birds are,
　　Hawk on bough!

3

See the creature stalking
　　While we speak!   10
Hush and hide the talking,
　　Cheek on cheek!

4

What so false as truth is,
　　False to thee?
Where the serpent's tooth is   15
　　Shun the tree—

5

Where the apple reddens
　　Never pry—
Lest we lose our Edens,
　　Eve and I.   20

6

Be a god and hold me
　　With a charm!
Be a man and fold me
　　With thine arm!

7

Teach me, only teach, Love!   25
　　As I ought
I will speak thy speech, Love,
　　Think thy thought—

8

Meet, if thou require it,
　　Both demands,   30
Laying flesh and spirit
　　In thy hands.

9

That shall be tomorrow
　　Not tonight:
I must bury sorrow   35
　　Out of sight:

10

—Must a little weep, Love
　　(Foolish me!),
And so fall asleep, Love,
　　Loved by thee.   40

1855

Caliban upon Setebos   Two closely related controversies of the Victorian period led Browning to write this poem (the title of which means "Caliban's thoughts about Setebos"). The first, stimulated by Darwin, was concerned with humanity's origins and our relation to other animals (the poem teems with animal life; in 295 lines, as Park Honan has shown, there are sixty-three references to animals). Caliban, the half-man and half-monster of Shakespeare's *Tempest*, provided the poet with a model of how the mind of a primitive creature may operate. The second controversy concerned the nature of God and God's responsibility for the existence of suffering in the world. Like many humans, Caliban thinks of God's nature as similar to his own. His anthropomorphic conception of the deity, whom he calls Setebos, is confined to what he has observed of life on his island and to what he has observed of himself. From the former derives his "natural theology," that is, his identifying the character of God from evidences provided by nature rather than from the evidence of supernatural revelation. From the latter, his observation of his own character, derives Caliban's conception of God's willful power. Caliban himself admires power and thinks of God in Calvinistic terms as a being who selects at random some creatures who are to be saved and others who are to be condemned to suffer.

An obstacle for the reader is Caliban's use of the third-person pronoun. He says that he "never speaks his mind save housed as now"—that is, he thinks if he is adequately hidden under the slush in his cave, the deity will not catch him thinking; he may remind us of the hero of George Orwell's *Nineteen Eighty-Four* (1949) trying to evade the Thought Police. But to make especially sure of not being caught, Caliban refers to himself in the third person. Thus " 'Will sprawl" means "Caliban will sprawl" (an apostrophe before the verb usually indicates that Caliban himself is the implied subject). When he feels that Setebos will not hear him, he then slips into the first person (e.g., line 56 or 68). The deity is also referred to in the third person but with an initial capital letter ("He").

Caliban upon Setebos

Or Natural Theology in the Island

"Thou thoughtest that I was altogether such a one as thyself."[1]

['Will sprawl, now that the heat of day is best,
Flat on his belly in the pit's much mire,
With elbows wide, fists clenched to prop his chin.
And, while he kicks both feet in the cool slush,
And feels about his spine small eft-things[2] course,   5
Run in and out each arm, and make him laugh:
And while above his head a pompion plant,[3]
Coating the cave-top as a brow its eye,
Creeps down to touch and tickle hair and beard,
And now a flower drops with a bee inside,   10
And now a fruit to snap at, catch and crunch—
He looks out o'er yon sea which sunbeams cross
And recross till they weave a spider web
(Meshes of fire, some great fish breaks at times)
And talks to his own self, howe'er he please,   15

1. Psalms 50.21. The speaker is God.   3. Pumpkin plant.
2. Water lizards.

Touching that other, whom his dam[4] called God.
Because to talk about Him, vexes—ha,
Could He but know! and time to vex is now,
When talk is safer than in wintertime.
Moreover Prosper[5] and Miranda sleep   20
In confidence he drudges at their task,
And it is good to cheat the pair, and gibe,
Letting the rank tongue blossom into speech.]

Setebos, Setebos, and Setebos!
'Thinketh, He dwelleth i' the cold o' the moon.   25

'Thinketh He made it, with the sun to match,
But not the stars; the stars came otherwise;
Only made clouds, winds, meteors, such as that:
Also this isle, what lives and grows thereon,
And snaky sea which rounds and ends the same.   30

'Thinketh, it came of being ill at ease:
He hated that He cannot change His cold,
Nor cure its ache. 'Hath spied an icy fish
That longed to 'scape the rock-stream where she lived,
And thaw herself within the lukewarm brine   35
O' the lazy sea her stream thrusts far amid,
A crystal spike 'twixt two warm walls of wave;[6]
Only, she ever sickened, found repulse
At the other kind of water, not her life,
(Green-dense and dim-delicious, bred o' the sun)   40
Flounced back from bliss she was not born to breathe,
And in her old bounds buried her despair,
Hating and loving warmth alike: so He.

'Thinketh, He made thereat the sun, this isle,
Trees and the fowls here, beast and creeping thing.   45
Yon otter, sleek-wet, black, lithe as a leech;
Yon auk,[7] one fire-eye in a ball of foam,
That floats and feeds; a certain badger brown
He hath watched hunt with that slant white-wedge eye
By moonlight; and the pie[8] with the long tongue   50
That pricks deep into oakwarts for a worm,
And says a plain word when she finds her prize,
But will not eat the ants; the ants themselves
That build a wall of seeds and settled stalks
About their hole—He made all these and more,   55
Made all we see, and us, in spite: how else?
He could not, Himself, make a second self
To be His mate; as well have made Himself:
He would not make what he mislikes or slights,

---

4. Caliban's mother, Sycorax.
5. Prospero the magician, who is Caliban's master in
The Tempest. Miranda is Prospero's daughter.
6. I.e., the thin stream of cold water that is driven

into the warm ocean like a spike between walls.
7. Sea bird.
8. Magpie.

An eyesore to Him, or not worth His pains: 60
But did, in envy, listlessness, or sport,
Make what Himself would fain, in a manner, be—
Weaker in most points, stronger in a few,
Worthy, and yet mere playthings all the while,
Things He admires and mocks too—that is it.   65
Because, so brave, so better though they be,
It nothing skills if He begin to plague.⁹
Look now, I melt a gourd-fruit into mash,
Add honeycomb and pods, I have perceived,
Which bite like finches when they bill and kiss—   70
Then, when froth rises bladdery,¹ drink up all,
Quick, quick, till maggots scamper through my brain;
Last, throw me on my back i' the seeded thyme,
And wanton, wishing I were born a bird.
Put case, unable to be what I wish,   75
I yet could make a live bird out of clay:
Would not I take clay, pinch my Caliban
Able to fly?—for, there, see, he hath wings,
And great comb like the hoopoe's² to admire,
And there, a sting to do his foes offense,   80
There, and I will that he begin to live,
Fly to yon rock-top, nip me off the horns
Of griggs³ high up that make the merry din,
Saucy through their veined wings, and mind me not.
In which feat, if his leg snapped, brittle clay,   85
And he lay stupid-like—why, I should laugh;
And if he, spying me, should fall to weep,
Beseech me to be good, repair his wrong,
Bid his poor leg smart less or grow again—
Well, as the chance were, this might take or else   90
Not take my fancy: I might hear his cry,
And give the mankin three sound legs for one,
Or pluck the other off, leave him like an egg,
And lessoned he was mine and merely clay.
Were this no pleasure, lying in the thyme,   95
Drinking the mash, with brain become alive,
Making and marring clay at will? So He.

'Thinketh, such shows nor right nor wrong in Him,
Nor kind, nor cruel: He is strong and Lord.
'Am strong myself compared to yonder crabs   100
That march now from the mountain to the sea;
'Let twenty pass, and stone the twenty-first,
Loving not, hating not, just choosing so.
'Say, the first straggler that boasts purple spots
Shall join the file, one pincer twisted off;   105
'Say, this bruised fellow shall receive a worm,

---

9. I.e., our superior virtues are of no help to us if   2. Bird with bright plumage.
God elects to inflict plagues on us.   3. Grasshoppers.
1. Bubbly.

And two worms he whose nippers end in red;
As it likes me each time, I do: so He.

Well then, 'supposeth He is good i' the main,
Placable if His mind and ways were guessed,   110
But rougher than His handiwork, be sure!
Oh, He hath made things worthier than Himself,
And envieth that, so helped, such things do more
Than He who made them! What consoles but this?
That they, unless through Him, do naught at all,   115
And must submit: what other use in things?
'Hath cut a pipe of pithless elder-joint
That, blown through, gives exact the scream o' the jay
When from her wing you twitch the feathers blue:
Sound this, and little birds that hate the jay   120
Flock within stone's throw, glad their foe is hurt:
Put case such pipe could prattle and boast forsooth,
"I catch the birds, I am the crafty thing,
I make the cry my maker cannot make
With his great round mouth; he must blow through mine!"   125
Would not I smash it with my foot? So He.

But wherefore rough, why cold and ill at ease?
Aha, that is a question! Ask, for that,
What knows—the something over Setebos
That made Him, or He, may be, found and fought,   130
Worsted, drove off and did to nothing,[4] perchance.
There may be something quiet o'er His head,
Out of His reach, that feels nor joy nor grief,
Since both derive from weakness in some way.
I joy because the quails come; would not joy   135
Could I bring quails here when I have a mind:
This Quiet, all it hath a mind to, doth.
'Esteemeth stars the outposts of its couch,
But never spends much thought nor care that way.
It may look up, work up—the worse for those   140
It works on! 'Careth but for Setebos[5]
The many-handed as a cuttlefish,
Who, making Himself feared through what He does,
Looks up, first, and perceives he cannot soar
To what is quiet and hath happy life;   145
Next looks down here, and out of very spite
Makes this a bauble-world to ape yon real,
These good things to match those as hips[6] do grapes.
'Tis solace making baubles, aye, and sport.
Himself peeped late, eyed Prosper at his books   150
Careless and lofty, lord now of the isle:
Vexed, 'stitched a book of broad leaves, arrow-shaped,
Wrote thereon, he knows what, prodigious words;

4. Completely overcame.   the other deity—the Quiet.
5. Caliban's concern is to appease only Setebos, not   6. Hard fruits produced by wild roses.

Has peeled a wand and called it by a name;
Weareth at whiles for an enchanter's robe   155
The eyed skin of a supple oncelot;[7]

And hath an ounce[8] sleeker than youngling mole,
A four-legged serpent he makes cower and couch,
Now snarl, now hold its breath and mind his eye,
And saith she is Miranda and my wife: 160
'Keeps for his Ariel[9] a tall pouch-bill crane
He bids go wade for fish and straight disgorge;
Also a sea beast, lumpish, which he snared,
Blinded the eyes of, and brought somewhat tame,
And split its toe-webs, and now pens the drudge   165
In a hole o' the rock and calls him Caliban;
A bitter heart that bides its time and bites.
'Plays thus at being Prosper in a way,
Taketh his mirth with make-believes: so He.

His dam held that the Quiet made all things   170
Which Setebos vexed only: 'holds not so.
Who made them weak, meant weakness He might vex.
Had He meant other, while His hand was in,
Why not make horny eyes no thorn could prick,
Or plate my scalp with bone against the snow,   175
Or overscale my flesh 'neath joint and joint,
Like an orc's[1] armor? Aye—so spoil His sport!
He is the One now: only He doth all.

'Saith, He may like, perchance, what profits Him.
Aye, himself loves what does him good; but why?   180
'Gets good no otherwise. This blinded beast
Loves whoso places flesh-meat on his nose,
But, had he eyes, would want no help, but hate
Or love, just as it liked him: He hath eyes.
Also it pleaseth Setebos to work,   185
Use all His hands, and exercise much craft,
By no means for the love of what is worked.
'Tasteth, himself, no finer good i' the world
When all goes right, in this safe summertime,
And he wants little, hungers, aches not much,   190
Than trying what to do with wit and strength.
'Falls to make something: 'piled yon pile of turfs,
And squared and stuck there squares of soft white chalk,
And, with a fish-tooth, scratched a moon on each,
And set up endwise certain spikes of tree,   195
And crowned the whole with a sloth's skull a-top,
Found dead i' the woods, too hard for one to kill.

---

7. Browning may have invented this term from the
Spanish *oncela* or from the French *ocelot*. Both words
signify a leopard or spotted wildcat.
8. A large, ferocious leopard, six or seven feet in
length.
9. In *The Tempest*, a spirit who serves Prospero.
1. Killer whale.

No use at all i' the work, for work's sole sake;
'Shall some day knock it down again: so He.

'Saith He is terrible: watch His feats in proof!   200
One hurricane will spoil six good months' hope.
He hath a spite against me, that I know,
Just as He favors Prosper, who knows why?
So it is, all the same, as well I find.
'Wove wattles half the winter, fenced them firm   205
With stone and stake to stop she-tortoises
Crawling to lay their eggs here: well, one wave,
Feeling the foot of Him upon its neck,
Gaped as a snake does, lolled out its large tongue,
And licked the whole labor flat; so much for spite.   210
'Saw a ball[2] flame down late (yonder it lies)
Where, half an hour before, I slept i' the shade:
Often they scatter sparkles: there is force!
'Dug up a newt He may have envied once
And turned to stone, shut up inside a stone.   215
Please Him and hinder this?—What Prosper does?[3]
Aha, if He would tell me how! Not He!
There is the sport: discover how or die!
All need not die, for of the things o' the isle
Some flee afar, some dive, some run up trees;   220
Those at His mercy—why, they please Him most
When . . . when . . . well, never try the same way twice!
Repeat what act has pleased, He may grow wroth.
You must not know His ways, and play Him off,
Sure of the issue. 'Doth the like himself: 225
'Spareth a squirrel that it nothing fears
But steals the nut from underneath my thumb,
And when I threat, bites stoutly in defense:
'Spareth an urchin[4] that contrariwise
Curls up into a ball, pretending death   230
For fright at my approach: the two ways please.
But what would move my choler more than this,
That either creature counted on its life
Tomorrow and next day and all days to come,
Saying, forsooth, in the inmost of its heart,   235
"Because he did so yesterday with me,
And otherwise with such another brute,
So must he do henceforth and always."—Aye?
Would teach the reasoning couple what "must" means!
'Doth as he likes, or wherefore Lord? So He.   240

'Conceiveth all things will continue thus,
And we shall have to live in fear of Him
So long as He lives, keeps His strength: no change,
If He have done His best, make no new world

---

2. Meteorite.   thus prevent my being punished as the newt was?
3. I.e., shall I please Setebos, as Prospero does, and   4. Hedgehog.

To please Him more, so leave off watching this—   245
If He surprise not even the Quiet's self
Some strange day—or, suppose, grow into it
As grubs grow butterflies: else, here are we,
And there is He, and nowhere help at all.
'Believeth with the life, the pain shall stop.   250
His dam held different, that after death
He both plagued enemies and feasted friends:
Idly![5] He doth His worst in this our life,
Giving just respite lest we die through pain,
Saving last pain for worst—with which, an end.   255
Meanwhile, the best way to escape His ire
Is, not to seem too happy. 'Sees, himself,
Yonder two flies, with purple films and pink,
Bask on the pompion-bell above: kills both.
'Sees two black painful beetles roll their ball   260
On head and tail as if to save their lives:
Moves them the stick away they strive to clear.

Even so, 'would have Him misconceive, suppose
This Caliban strives hard and ails no less,
And always, above all else, envies Him;   265
Wherefore he mainly dances on dark nights,
Moans in the sun, gets under holes to laugh,
And never speaks his mind save housed as now:
Outside, 'groans, curses. If He caught me here,
O'erheard this speech, and asked "What chucklest at?"   270
'Would, to appease Him, cut a finger off,
Or of my three kid yearlings burn the best,
Or let the toothsome apples rot on tree,
Or push my tame beast for the orc to taste:
While myself lit a fire, and made a song   275
And sung it, *"What I hate, be consecrate*
To celebrate Thee and Thy state, no mate
For Thee; what see for envy in poor me?"
Hoping the while, since evils sometimes mend,
Warts rub away and sores are cured with slime,   280
That some strange day, will either the Quiet catch
And conquer Setebos, or likelier He
Decrepit may doze, doze, as good as die.

[What, what? A curtain o'er the world at once!
Crickets stop hissing; not a bird—or, yes,   285
There scuds His raven that has told Him all!
It was fool's play this prattling! Ha! The wind
Shoulders the pillared dust, death's house o' the move,[6]
And fast invading fires begin! White blaze—

5. I.e., Caliban thinks his mother's opinion was wrong   6. The whirlwind stirs up a column of dust that Cali-
or idle. God's sport with humankind is confined to this   ban associates with a house of death.
world: there is no afterlife.

A tree's head snaps—and there, there, there, there, there,   290
    His thunder follows! Fool to gibe at Him!
Lo! 'Lieth flat and loveth Setebos!
'Maketh his teeth meet through his upper lip,
Will let those quails fly, will not eat this month
One little mess of whelks,[7] so he may 'scape!]   295
ca. 1860   1864

Prospice[1]

Fear death?—to feel the fog in my throat,
    The mist in my face,
When the snows begin, and the blasts denote
    I am nearing the place,
The power of the night, the press of the storm,   5
    The post of the foe;
Where he stands, the Arch Fear in a visible form,
    Yet the strong man must go:
For the journey is done and the summit attained,
    And the barriers fall,   10
Though a battle's to fight ere the guerdon be gained,
    The reward of it all.
I was ever a fighter, so—one fight more,
    The best and the last!
I would hate that death bandaged my eyes, and forbore,   15
    And bade me creep past.
No! let me taste the whole of it, fare like my peers
    The heroes of old,
Bear the brunt, in a minute pay glad life's arrears
    Of pain, darkness, and cold.   20
For sudden the worst turns the best to the brave,
    The black minute's at end,
And the elements' rage, the fiend-voices that rave,
    Shall dwindle, shall blend,
Shall change, shall become first a peace out of pain,   25
    Then a light, then thy breast,
O thou soul of my soul![2] I shall clasp thee again,
    And with God be the rest!
ca. 1861   1864

Abt Vogler[1]

*(After he has Been Extemporizing Upon the Musical Instrument of His
Invention)*

1

Would that the structure brave, the manifold music I build,
    Bidding my organ obey, calling its keys to their work,

---

7. Shellfish.
1. The title means "Look forward."
2. Browning's wife.

1. Georg Joseph Vogler (1749–1814), a German priest
and musician, held the honorary title of *Abbé* or *Abt.*
As a composer, teacher, and designer of musical instru-

Claiming each slave of the sound, at a touch, as when Solomon willed
    Armies of angels that soar, legions of demons that lurk,
Man, brute, reptile, fly—alien of end and of aim,   5
    Adverse, each from the other heaven-high, hell-deep removed—
Should rush into sight at once as he named the ineffable Name,[2]
    And pile him a palace straight, to pleasure the princess[3] he loved!

2

Would it might tarry like his, the beautiful building of mine,
    This which my keys in a crowd pressed and importuned to raise!   10
Ah, one and all, how they helped, would dispart now and now combine,
    Zealous to hasten the work, heighten their master his praise!
And one would bury his brow with a blind plunge down to hell,
    Burrow awhile and build, broad on the roots of things,
Then up again swim into sight, having based me my palace well,   15
    Founded it, fearless of flame, flat on the nether springs.

3

And another would mount and march, like the excellent minion he was,
    Aye, another and yet another, one crowd but with many a crest,
Raising my rampired walls of gold as transparent as glass,
    Eager to do and die, yield each his place to the rest: 20
For higher still and higher (as a runner tips with fire,
    When a great illumination surprises a festal night—
Outlining round and round Rome's dome from space to spire)[4]
    Up, the pinnacled glory reached, and the pride of my soul was in sight.

4

In sight? Not half! for it seemed, it was certain, to match man's birth,   25
    Nature in turn conceived, obeying an impulse as I;
And the emulous heaven yearned down, made effort to reach the earth,
    As the earth had done her best, in my passion, to scale the sky:
Novel splendors burst forth, grew familiar and dwelt with mine,
    Not a point nor peak but found and fixed its wandering star;   30
Meteor-moons, balls of blaze: and they did not pale nor pine,
    For earth had attained to heaven, there was no more near nor far.

5

Nay more; for there wanted not who walked in the glare and glow,
    Presences plain in the place; or, fresh from the Protoplast,[5]
Furnished for ages to come, when a kindlier wind should blow,   35
    Lured now to begin and live, in a house to their liking at last;
Or else the wonderful Dead who have passed through the body and gone,
    But were back once more to breathe in an old world worth their new:

---

ments he was well known in his own day, but he was most famous as an extemporizer at the organ. Browning's soliloquy represents Vogler at the organ joyfully improvising a piece of music and then reflecting on the ephemeral existence of such a unique work of art and of its possible relation to God's purposes in heaven and on earth.

    A characteristic feature of *Abt Vogler* is the use of exceptionally long sentences, densely packed with details, which may evoke for us the effects of rolling organ music. The resulting movement is markedly different from the brisk staccato rhythms of *A Toccata of Galuppi's.*

    The "musical instrument of his invention" is a com-
pact organ called the Orchestrion.

2. According to Jewish legend King Solomon (because he possessed a seal inscribed with the "ineffable Name" of God) had the power of compelling the demons of earth and air to perform his bidding.

3. Pharaoh's daughter (1 Kings 7.8).

4. On festival nights the dome of St. Peter's in Rome is illuminated by a series of lights ignited by a torchbearer.

5. The original or archetypal form of a species. The "presences" from this source are beings of the future, not yet existing, who are "lured" into life by the music (line 36).

What never had been, was now; what was, as it shall be anon;
    And what is—shall I say, matched both? for I was made perfect too.   40

6

All through my keys that gave their sounds to a wish of my soul,
    All through my soul that praised as its wish flowed visibly forth,
All through music and me! For think, had I painted the whole,
    Why, there it had stood, to see, nor the process so wonderworth:
Had I written the same, made verse—still, effect proceeds from cause,   45
    Ye know why the forms are fair, ye hear how the tale is told;
It is all triumphant art, but art in obedience to laws,
    Painter and poet are proud in the artist-list enrolled—

7

But here is the finger of God, a flash of the will that can,
    Existent behind all laws, that made them and, lo, they are!   50
And I know not if, save in this, such gift be allowed to man,
    That out of three sounds he frame, not a fourth sound, but a star.[6]
Consider it well: each tone of our scale in itself is naught;
    It is everywhere in the world—loud, soft, and all is said:
Give it to me to use! I mix it with two in my thought: 55
    And, there! Ye have heard and seen: consider and bow the head!

8

Well, it is gone at last, the palace of music I reared;
    Gone! and the good tears start, the praises that come too slow;
For one is assured at first, one scarce can say that he feared,
    That he even gave it a thought, the gone thing was to go.   60
Never to be again! But many more of the kind
    As good, nay, better perchance: is this your comfort to me?
To me, who must be saved because I cling with my mind
    To the same, same self, same love, same God: aye, what was, shall be.

9

Therefore to whom turn I but to thee, the ineffable Name?   65
    Builder and maker, thou, of houses not made with hands![7]
What, have fear of change from thee who art ever the same?
    Doubt that thy power can fill the heart that thy power expands?
There shall never be one lost good! What was, shall live as before;
    The evil is null, is naught, is silence implying sound;   70
What was good shall be good, with, for evil, so much good more;
    On the earth the broken arcs; in the heaven, a perfect round.

10

All we have willed or hoped or dreamed of good shall exist;
    Not its semblance, but itself; no beauty, nor good, nor power
Whose voice has gone forth, but each survives for the melodist   75
    When eternity affirms the conception of an hour.
The high that proved too high, the heroic for earth too hard,
    The passion that left the ground to lose itself in the sky,
Are music sent up to God by the lover and the bard;
    Enough that he heard it once: we shall hear it by-and-by.   80

---

6. I.e., the musician's combining of three notes into a new harmonic unit is a creative act as miraculous as the creation of a star.

7. Cf. 2 Corinthians 5.1, in which St. Paul speaks of "a building of God, an house not made with hands, eternal in the heavens."

11

And what is our failure here but a triumph's evidence
    For the fullness of the days? Have we withered or agonized?
Why else was the pause prolonged but that singing might issue thence?
    Why rushed the discords in but that harmony should be prized?
Sorrow is hard to bear, and doubt is slow to clear,   85
    Each sufferer says his say, his scheme of the weal and woe:
But God has a few of us whom he whispers in the ear;
    The rest may reason and welcome: 'tis we musicians know.

12

Well, it is earth with me; silence resumes her reign:
    I will be patient and proud, and soberly acquiesce.   90
Give me the keys. I feel for the common chord again,
    Sliding by semitones, till I sink to the minor—yes,
And I blunt it into a ninth,[8] and I stand on alien ground,
    Surveying awhile the heights I rolled from into the deep;
Which, hark, I have dared and done, for my resting place is found,   95
    The C Major[9] of this life: so, now I will try to sleep.

                                                    1864

Rabbi Ben Ezra[1]

1

        Grow old along with me!
        The best is yet to be,
The last of life, for which the first was made:
        Our times are in His hand
        Who saith, "A whole I planned,
Youth shows but half; trust God: see all nor be afraid!"   5

2

        Not that, amassing flowers,
        Youth sighed, "Which rose make ours,
Which lily leave and then as best recall?"
        Not that, admiring stars,   10
        It yearned, "Nor Jove, nor Mars;
Mine be some figured flame which blends, transcends them all!"

3

        Not for such hopes and fears
        Annulling youth's brief years,
Do I remonstrate: folly wide the mark!   15
        Rather I prize the doubt
        Low kinds exist without,
Finished and finite clods, untroubled by a spark.

4

        Poor vaunt of life indeed,
        Were man but formed to feed   20
On joy, to solely seek and find and feast:
        Such feasting ended, then

8. A discord that requires resolution.
9. A key without sharps or flats, representing the plane
of ordinary life.
1. The speaker, Abraham Ibn Ezra (ca. 1092–1167),
was an eminent biblical scholar of Spain, but Browning makes little attempt to present him as a distinct
individual or to relate him to the age in which he lived.
Unlike the more characteristic monologues, *Rabbi Ben
Ezra* is not dramatic but declamatory.

As sure an end to men;
Irks care the crop-full bird? Frets doubt the maw-crammed beast?[2]

5

Rejoice we are allied   25
To That which doth provide
And not partake, effect and not receive!
A spark disturbs our clod;
Nearer we hold of God
Who gives, than of His tribes that take, I must believe.   30

6

Then, welcome each rebuff
That turns earth's smoothness rough,
Each sting that bids nor sit nor stand but go!
Be our joys three parts pain!
Strive, and hold cheap the strain;   35
Learn, nor account the pang; dare, never grudge the throe![3]

7

For thence—a paradox
Which comforts while it mocks—
Shall life succeed in that it seems to fail:
What I aspired to be,   40
And was not, comforts me:
A brute I might have been, but would not sink i' the scale.

8

What is he but a brute
Whose flesh has soul to suit,
Whose spirit works lest arms and legs want play?   45
To man, propose this test—
Thy body at its best,
How far can that project thy soul on its lone way?

9

Yet gifts should prove their use:
I own the Past profuse   50
Of power each side, perfection every turn:
Eyes, ears took in their dole,
Brain treasured up the whole;
Should not the heart beat once, "How good to live and learn"?

10

Not once beat, "Praise be Thine!   55
I see the whole design,
I, who saw power, see now love perfect too:
Perfect I call Thy plan:
Thanks that I was a man!
Maker, remake, complete—I trust what Thou shalt do!"   60

11

For pleasant is this flesh;
Our soul, in its rose-mesh[4]
Pulled ever to the earth, still yearns for rest;
Would we some prize might hold

---

2. I.e., does care disturb a bird whose gullet ("crop")   3. Anguish.
is full of food? Does doubt trouble an animal whose   4. The body, which holds the soul in its net.
stomach ("maw") is full?

To match those manifold   65
Possessions of the brute—gain most, as we did best!

                            12
        Let us not always say,
        "Spite of this flesh today
I strove, made head, gained ground upon the whole!"
        As the bird wings and sings,   70
        Let us cry, "All good things
Are ours, nor soul helps flesh more, now, than flesh helps soul!"

                            13
        Therefore I summon age
        To grant youth's heritage,
Life's struggle having so far reached its term: 75
        Thence shall I pass, approved
        A man, for aye removed
From the developed brute; a god though in the germ.

                            14
        And I shall thereupon
        Take rest, ere I be gone   80
Once more on my adventure brave and new;[5]
        Fearless and unperplexed,
        When I wage battle next,
What weapons to select, what armor to indue.[6]

                            15
        Youth ended, I shall try   85
        My gain or loss thereby;
Leave the fire ashes,[7] what survives is gold:
        And I shall weigh the same,
        Give life its praise or blame:
Young, all lay in dispute; I shall know, being old.   90

                            16
        For note, when evening shuts,
        A certain moment cuts
The deed off, calls the glory from the gray:
        A whisper from the west
        Shoots—"Add this to the rest,   95
Take it and try its worth: here dies another day."

                            17
        So, still within this life,
        Though lifted o'er its strife,
Let me discern, compare, pronounce at last,
        "This rage was right i' the main,   100
        That acquiescence vain:
The Future I may face now I have proved the Past."

                            18
        For more is not reserved
        To man, with soul just nerved
To act tomorrow what he learns today: 105
        Here, work enough to watch
        The Master work, and catch
Hints of the proper craft, tricks of the tool's true play.

5. In the next life.   7. If the fire leaves ashes.
6. Put on.

19

As it was better, youth
    Should strive, through acts uncouth,   110
Toward making, than repose on aught found made:
    So, better, age, exempt
    From strife, should know, than tempt[8]
Further. Thou waitedst age: wait death nor be afraid!

20

Enough now, if the Right   115
    And Good and Infinite
Be named here, as thou callest thy hand thine own,
    With knowledge absolute,
    Subject to no dispute
From fools that crowded youth, nor let thee feel alone.[9]   120

21

Be there, for once and all,
    Severed great minds from small,
Announced to each his station in the Past!
    Was I, the world arraigned,[1]
    Were they, my soul disdained,   125
Right? Let age speak the truth and give us peace at last!

22

Now, who shall arbitrate?
    Ten men love what I hate,
Shun what I follow, slight what I receive;
    Ten, who in ears and eyes   130
    Match me: we all surmise,
They this thing, and I that: whom shall my soul believe?

23

Not on the vulgar mass
    Called "work," must sentence pass,
Things done, that took the eye and had the price;   135
    O'er which, from level stand,
    The low world laid its hand,
Found straightway to its mind, could value in a trice:

24

But all, the world's coarse thumb
    And finger failed to plumb,   140
So passed in making up the main account;
    All instincts immature,
    All purposes unsure,
That weighed not as his work, yet swelled the man's amount:

25

Thoughts hardly to be packed   145
    Into a narrow act,
Fancies that broke through language and escaped;
    All I could never be,

---

8. Attempt.
9. Stanzas 20 and 21 affirm that in age we can more readily think independently than in youth. Maturity enables us to ignore the pressure of having to conform to the thinking of the crowd of small-minded people.
1. I.e., was I, whom the world arraigned.

All, men ignored in me,
This, I was worth to God, whose wheel[2] the pitcher shaped.   150
                                    26
          Aye, note that Potter's wheel,
          That metaphor! and feel
Why time spins fast, why passive lies our clay—
          Thou, to whom fools propound,[3]
          When the wine makes its round,   155
"Since life fleets, all is change; the Past gone, seize today!"
                                    27
          Fool! All that is, at all,
          Lasts ever, past recall;
Earth changes, but thy soul and God stand sure:
          What entered into thee,   160
          That was, is, and shall be:
Time's wheel runs back or stops: Potter and clay endure.
                                    28
          He fixed thee 'mid this dance
          Of plastic circumstance,
This Present, thou, forsooth, wouldst fain arrest:[4]   165
          Machinery just meant
          To give thy soul its bent,
Try thee and turn thee forth, sufficiently impressed.
                                    29
          What though the earlier grooves
          Which ran the laughing loves   170
Around thy base,[5] no longer pause and press?
          What though, about thy rim,
          Skull-things in order grim
Grow out, in graver mood, obey the sterner stress?
                                    30
          Look not thou down but up!   175
          To uses of a cup,
The festal board, lamp's flash, and trumpet's peal,
          The new wine's foaming flow,
          The Master's lips a-glow!
Thou, heaven's consummate cup, what need'st thou with earth's wheel?   180
                                    31
          But I need, now as then,
          Thee, God, who moldest men;
And since, not even while the whirl was worst,
          Did I—to the wheel of life
          With shapes and colors rife,   185
Bound dizzily—mistake my end, to slake Thy thirst:
                                    32
          So, take and use Thy work:
          Amend what flaws may lurk,
What strain o' the stuff, what warpings past the aim!

2. The potting-wheel on which the speaker's highest qualities of soul were shaped into an enduring "pitcher" by God. Cf. Isaiah 64.8.
3. Perhaps addressed to Omar Khayyám, whose poem, *The Rubáiyát,* urged men to eat, drink, and be merry.
Edward FitzGerald's translation of Omar's poem had appeared in 1859.
4. I.e., you would be glad to stop ("arrest") time at this present point of your life.
5. Base of the clay pitcher.

My times be in Thy hand!   190
    Perfect the cup as planned!
Let age approve of youth, and death complete the same!
ca. 1862   1864

Epilogue to *Asolando*[1]

At the midnight in the silence of the sleep-time,
    When you[2] set your fancies free,
Will they pass to where—by death, fools think, imprisoned—
Low he lies who once so loved you, whom you loved so,
        —Pity me?   5

Oh to love so, be so loved, yet so mistaken!
    What had I on earth to do
With the slothful, with the mawkish, the unmanly?
Like the aimless, helpless, hopeless, did I drivel
        —Being—who?   10

One who never turned his back but marched breast forward,
    Never doubted clouds would break,
Never dreamed, though right were worsted, wrong would triumph,
Held we fall to rise, are baffled to fight better,
        Sleep to wake.   15

No, at noonday in the bustle of man's work-time
    Greet the unseen[3] with a cheer!
Bid him forward, breast and back as either should be,
"Strive and thrive!" cry, "Speed—fight on, fare ever
        There as here!"   20
1889   1890

1. The final poem in *Asolando*, a volume published   it's the simple truth," he added, "and as it's true, it shall
on the day of Browning's death. Browning is said to   stand."
have recognized that because the third stanza sounded   2. Any loved person who survives the speaker.
"like bragging" he ought to consider canceling it. "But 3. The speaker, after he is dead.

MATTHEW ARNOLD
1822–1888

How is a full and enjoyable life to be lived in a modern industrial society? This was the recurrent topic in the poetry and prose of Matthew Arnold. In his poetry the question itself is raised; in his prose some answers are attempted. Arnold's mode of posing such questions may not always satisfy us, and his answers may sometimes be simply wrong. What is less excusable, as he himself said of Ruskin, is that he could be not only wrong but dogmatic when he was wrong. On the whole, however, his writings have fared well with posterity. "The misapprehensiveness of his age is exactly what a poet is sent to remedy," wrote Browning. Oddly enough it is to Arnold's work rather than to Browning's that the statement seems more appropriate. And its applicability to Arnold has persisted from Victorian times to ours, in part because the "misapprehensiveness" has also persisted.

Matthew Arnold was born in Laleham, a village in the valley of the Thames. That his childhood was spent in the vicinity of a river seems appropriate, for clear-flowing streams were later to appear in his poems as symbols of serenity. At six, Arnold was moved to Rugby School, where his father, Dr. Thomas Arnold, had become headmaster. As a clergyman Dr. Arnold was a leader of the liberal or Broad Church and hence one of the principal opponents of John Henry Newman. As a headmaster he became famous as an educational reformer, a teacher who instilled into his pupils an earnest preoccupation with moral and social issues and also an awareness of the connection between liberal studies and modern life. At Rugby his eldest son, Matthew, was directly exposed to the powerful force of the father's mind and character. The son's attitude toward this force was a mixture of attraction and repulsion. That he was permanently influenced by his father is evident in his poems and in his writings on religion and politics, but like many sons of clergymen, he made a determined effort in his youth to be different. At Oxford he behaved like a character from one of Evelyn Waugh's early novels. Elegantly and colorfully dressed, alternately languid or merry in manner, he attracted attention as a dandy whose irreverent jokes irritated his more solemn undergraduate friends and acquaintances. "His manner displeases, from its seeming foppery," wrote Charlotte Brontë after talking with the young man. "The shade of Dr. Arnold," she added, "seemed to me to frown on his young representative." With Rugby School's standards of earnestness, thus, the son of Dr. Arnold appeared to have no connection. Even his studies did not seem to occupy him seriously. By a session of cramming, he managed to earn second-class honors in his final examinations, a near disaster that was redeemed by his election to a fellowship at Oriel College.

Arnold's biographers usually dismiss his youthful frivolity of spirit as a temporary pose or mask, but it was more. It remained to color his prose style, brightening his most serious criticism with geniality and wit. For most readers the jauntiness of his prose is a virtue, although for others it is offensive. Anyone suspicious of urbanity and irony would applaud Whitman's sour comment that Arnold is "one of the dudes of literature." A more appropriate estimate of his manner is provided by Arnold's own description of Sainte-Beuve as a critic: "a critic of measure, not exuberant; of the center, not provincial . . . with gay and amiable temper, his manner as good as his matter—the *critique souriant* [smiling critic]."

Unlike Tennyson or Carlyle, Arnold had to confine his writing and reading to his spare time. In 1847 he took the post of private secretary to Lord Lansdowne, and in 1851, the year of his marriage, he became an inspector of schools, a position that he held for thirty-five years. Although his work as an inspector may have reduced his output as a writer, it had several advantages. His extensive traveling in England took him to the homes of the more ardently Protestant middle classes, and when he criticized the dullness of middle-class life (as he often did), Arnold knew his subject intimately. His position also led to travel on the Continent to study the schools of Europe. As a critic of English education, he was thus able to make helpful comparisons and to draw on a stock of fresh ideas in the same way as in his literary criticism he used his knowledge of French, German, Italian, and classical literatures to measure the achievements of English writers. Despite the monotony of much of his work as an inspector, Arnold became convinced of its importance. It was work that contributed to what he regarded as the most important need of his century: the development of a satisfactory system of education for the middle classes.

In 1849, Arnold published *The Strayed Reveler*, the first of his volumes of poetry. Eight years later, as a tribute to his poetic achievement, he was elected to the professorship of poetry at Oxford, a part-time position that he held for ten years. Later, like Dickens and Thackeray before him, Arnold toured America to make money by lecturing. The reception accorded his lectures was varied. Sometimes his audiences were indifferent, but it is of interest to learn from the *Washington Post* of his stunning success in that city, where, following a two-hour address, the great African-American leader Frederick Douglass "moved that a tremendous vote of thanks be tendered to the speaker." For his two visits (1883 and 1886), there was the further inducement of seeing his daughter Lucy, who had married an American. Two years after his second visit to the United States, Arnold died of a sudden heart attack.

Arnold's career as a writer can be divided roughly into four periods. In the 1850s most of his poems appeared; in the 1860s, his literary criticism and social criticism; in the 1870s, his religious and educational writings; and in the 1880s, his second set of essays in literary criticism.

About his career as a poet, two questions are repeatedly asked. The first is whether his poetry is as effective as or better than his prose; the second is why he virtually stopped writing poetry after 1860. The first has, of course, been variously answered. Many would endorse Tennyson's request in a letter: "Tell Mat not to write any more of those prose things like *Literature and Dogma*, but to give us something like his *Thyrsis, Scholar Gypsy*, or *Forsaken Merman*." At the opposite extreme is a recent critic, J. D. Jump, who has a high regard for Arnold's prose but considers only one of the poems (*Dover Beach*) to have merit. Such readers complain, and with good cause, of Arnold's bad habits as a poet: for example, his excessive reliance on italics instead of on meter as a method of emphasizing the meaning of a line. Or they cite the prosy flatness with which he opens his fine sonnet *To a Friend:* "Who prop, thou ask'st, in these bad days, my mind?" Contrariwise, when Arnold leaves the flat plane of versified reflections and attempts to scale the heights of what he called "the grand style," there is a different kind of uncertainty that becomes evident, as in *Sohrab and Rustum*, in the overelaborated similes. Yet the success of such lovely poems as *Thyrsis* is more than enough to overcome the indictments of the critics. Often, as in *Thyrsis*, he is at his best as a poet of nature. Settings of seashore or river or mountaintop provide something more than picturesque backdrops for these poems; they function to draw the meaning together. A concern for rendering outdoor nature may seem a curious accomplishment for so sophisticated a writer, but as his contemporaries noted, Arnold is in this respect, as in several others, similar to Thomas Gray.

Arnold's own verdict on the qualities of his poetry is a reasonable one. In a letter to his mother, in 1869, he writes: "My poems represent, on the whole, the main movement of mind of the last quarter of a century, and thus they will probably have their day as people become conscious to themselves of what that movement of mind is, and interested in the literary productions which reflect it. It might be fairly urged that I have less poetical sentiment than Tennyson, and less intellectual vigor and abundance than Browning; yet, because I have perhaps more of a fusion of the two than either of them, and have more regularly applied that fusion to the main line of modern development, I am likely enough to have my turn, as they have had theirs."

The emphasis in the letter on "movement of mind" suggests that Arnold's poetry and prose should be studied together. Such an approach can be fruitful provided that it does not obscure the important difference between Arnold the poet and

Arnold the critic. T. S. Eliot once said of his own writings that "in one's prose reflections one may be legitimately occupied with ideals, whereas in the writing of verse, one can deal only with actuality." Arnold's writings provide a nice verification of Eliot's seeming paradox. As a poet he usually records his own experiences, his own feelings of loneliness and isolation as a lover, his longing for a serenity that he cannot find, his melancholy sense of the passing of youth (more than for many men, Arnold's thirtieth birthday was an awesome landmark after which he felt, he said, "three parts iced over"). Above all he records his despair in a universe in which humanity's role seemed as incongruous as it was later to seem to Thomas Hardy. In a memorable passage of his *Stanzas from the Grande Chartreuse*, he describes himself as "wandering between two worlds, one dead, / The other powerless to be born." And addressing the representatives of a faith that seems to him dead, he cries: "Take me, cowled forms, and fence me round, / Till I possess my soul again."

As a poet, then, like T. S. Eliot and W. H. Auden, Arnold provides a record of a sick individual in a sick society. This was "actuality" as he experienced it—an actuality, like Eliot's and Auden's, representative of his era. As a prose writer, a formulator of "ideals," he seeks a different role. It is the role of what Auden calls the "healer" of a sick society, or as he himself called Goethe, the "Physician of the iron age." And in this difference we have a clue to the question previously raised: why did Arnold virtually abandon the writing of poetry and shift into criticism? Among other reasons, he abandoned it because he was dissatisfied with the kind of poetry he himself was writing.

In one of his excellent letters to his friend Arthur Hugh Clough in the 1850s (letters that provide the best insight we have into Arnold's mind and tastes) this note of dissatisfaction is struck: "I am glad you like the *Gypsy Scholar*—but what does it *do* for you? Homer *animates*—Shakespeare *animates*—in its poor way I think *Sohrab and Rustum animates*—the *Gypsy Scholar* at best awakens a pleasing melancholy. But this is not what we want." It is evident that early in his career Arnold had evolved a theory of what poetry should do for its readers, a theory based, in part, on his impression of what classical poetry had achieved. To help make life bearable, poetry, in Arnold's view, must bring joy. As he says in the preface to his *Poems* in 1853, it must "inspirit and rejoice the reader"; it must "convey a charm, and infuse delight." Such a demand does not exclude tragic poetry but does exclude works "in which suffering finds no vent in action; in which a continual state of mental distress is prolonged." Of Charlotte Brontë's novel *Villette* he says witheringly: "The writer's mind contains nothing but hunger, rebellion, and rage. . . . No fine writing can hide this thoroughly, and it will be fatal to her in the long run." Judged by such a standard, most nineteenth-century poems, including *Empedocles on Etna* and others by Arnold, were unsatisfactory. And when Arnold tried himself to write poems that would meet his own requirements—*Sohrab and Rustum* or *Balder Dead*—he was not at his best. By the late 1850s he thus found himself at a dead end. By turning aside to literary criticism he was able partially to escape the dilemma. In his prose his melancholy and "morbid" personality was subordinated to the resolutely cheerful and purposeful character he had created for himself by an effort of will.

Arnold's two volumes of *Essays in Criticism* (1865 and 1888) repeatedly show how authors as different as Marcus Aurelius, Tolstoy, Homer, and Wordsworth provide the virtues he sought in his reading. Among these virtues was plainness of style. Although he could on occasion recommend the richness of language of such poets as Keats or Tennyson—their "natural magic" as he himself called it—Arnold's usual preference was for literature that was unadorned. And beyond stylistic excellences the principal virtue he admired as a critic was what he called the quality of "high seriousness." Given a world in which formal religion appeared to be of subordinate importance, it became increasingly important to Arnold that the poet must be a serious thinker who could offer guidance for his readers. Arnold's attitude toward religion helps to account for his finally asking perhaps too much from literature. Excessive expectations underlie his most glaring blunder as a critic: his solemnly inadequate discussion of Chaucer's lack of high seriousness in *The Study of Poetry*.

In *The Function of Criticism*, it is apparent that Arnold regarded good literary criticism, as he regarded literature itself, as a potent force in producing what he conceived as a civilized society. From a close study of this basic essay one could forecast the third stage of his career: his excursion into the criticism of society that was to culminate in *Culture and Anarchy* (1869) and *Friendship's Garland* (1871).

Arnold's starting point as a critic of society is different from that of Carlyle and John Ruskin. The older prophets attacked the Victorian middle classes on the grounds of their materialism, their selfish indifference to the sufferings of the poor—their immorality, in effect. Arnold argued instead that the "Philistines," as he called them, were not so much wicked as ignorant, narrow-minded, and suffering from the dullness of their private lives. This novel analysis was reinforced by Arnold's conviction that the world of the future, both in England and America, would be a middle-class world, a world dominated therefore by a class inadequately equipped for leadership and inadequately equipped to enjoy civilized living.

To establish this point, Arnold employed cajolery, satire, and even quotations from the newspapers with considerable effect. He also employed memorable catchwords (such as "sweetness and light") that sometimes pose an obstacle to understanding the complexities of his position. His view of civilization, for example, was pared down to a four-point formula of the four "powers": conduct, intellect and knowledge, beauty, social life and manners. The formula was simple and workable. Applying it to French or American civilizations, he had a scale by which to show up the virtues of different countries as well as their inadequacies. Applying the formula to his own country, Arnold usually awarded the Victorian middle classes an "A" in the first category (of conduct) but a failing grade in the other three categories.

Arnold's relentless exposure of middle-class narrow-mindedness eventually led him into the arena of religious controversy. As a critic of religious institutions he was arguing, in effect, that just as the middle classes did not know how to lead full lives, so also did they not know how to read the Bible intelligently or attend church intelligently. Of the Christian religion, he remarked that there are two things "that surely must be clear to anybody with eyes in his head. One is, that men cannot do without it; the other that they cannot do with it as it is." His three full-length studies of the Bible, including *Literature and Dogma* (1873), are best considered in this way as a postscript to his social criticism. The Bible, to Arnold, was a great work of literature like the *Odyssey*, and the Church of England was a great national institution like Parliament. Both Bible and church must be preserved not because historical Christianity was credible but because both, when properly understood, were agents of what he called "culture"—they contributed to making humanity more civilized.

The term *culture* is perhaps Arnold's most familiar catchword, although what he meant by it has sometimes been misunderstood. For him the term connotes the qualities of an open-minded intelligence (as described in *The Function of Criticism*)—a refusal to take things on authority. In this respect, Arnold appears close to T. H. Huxley and J. S. Mill. But the word also connotes a full awareness of humanity's past and a capacity to enjoy the best works of art, literature, history, and philosophy that have come down to us from that past. As a way of viewing life in all its aspects, including the social, political, and religious, culture represents for Arnold the most effective way of curing the ills of a sick society. It is his principal prescription.

To attempt to define culture brings one to a final aspect of Arnold's career as a critic: his writings on education, in which he sought to make cultural values, as he said, "prevail." Most obviously these writings comprise his reply to Huxley in his admirably reasoned essay *Literature and Science*, as well as his volumes of official reports written as an inspector of schools. Less obviously, they comprise all his prose. At the core of these writings is his belief that good education is *the* crucial need. Arnold was essentially a great teacher. He has the faults of a teacher: a tendency to repeat himself, to lean too hard on formulated phrases, and he displays something of the lectern manner at times. He also has the great teacher's virtues, in particular the virtue of skillfully conveying to us the conviction on which all his arguments are based. This conviction is that the humanist tradition of which he is the expositor can enable the individual man or woman to live life more fully as well as to change the course of society. He believes that a democratic society can only thrive if its citizens become educated in what he saw as the great Western tradition, "the best that is known and thought." These values, which some readers find elitist, make Arnold both timely and controversial. It is for these values Arnold fought. He boxed with the gloves on—kid gloves, his opponents used to say—and he provided a lively exhibition of footwork that is a pleasure in itself for us to witness. Yet the gracefulness of the display should not obscure the fact that he is landing hard blows squarely on his opponents.

Although his lifelong attacks against the inadequacies of puritanism make Arnold one of the most anti-Victorian figures of the Victorian age, there is an assumption behind his attacks that is itself characteristically Victorian. This assumption is that the puritan middle classes *can* be changed, that they are, as we would more clumsily say, educable. In 1852, writing to Clough on the subject of equality (a political objective in which he believed by conviction if not by instinct), he observed: "I am more and more convinced that the world tends to become more comfortable for the mass, and more uncomfortable for those of any natural gift or distinction—and it is as well perhaps that it should be so—for hitherto the gifted have astonished and delighted the world, but not trained or inspired or in any real way changed it." Arnold's gifts as a poet and critic enabled him to do both: to delight the world and also to change it.

To a Friend

Who prop, thou ask'st in these bad days, my mind?—
He much, the old man,[1] who, clearest-souled of men,
Saw The Wide Prospect, and the Asian Fen,
And Tmolus hill, and Smyrna bay, though blind.

Much he, whose friendship I not long since won,   5
That halting slave, who in Nicopolis
Taught Arrian,[2] when Vespasian's brutal son[3]
Cleared Rome of what most shamed him. But be his

My special thanks, whose even-balanced soul,
From first youth tested up to extreme old age,   10
Business could not make dull, nor passion wild;

1. Homer, who was reputed to have been born in Smyrna, a seaport of what is now Turkey. From Smyrna he saw across the sea to Europe ("The Wide Prospect") as well as to the nearby marshes ("Fen") and mountain ranges ("Tmolus hill") of Asia Minor.
2. Epictetus, a lame philosopher who was exiled to Ni- copolis where he taught Stoicism to Arrian, a Greek historian.
3. I.e., Emperor Domitian (81–96). Because the philosophers had "shamed" him, he had ordered their expulsion from Rome.

Who saw life steadily, and saw it whole;
The mellow glory of the Attic stage,
Singer of sweet Colonus,[4] and its child.

1848   1849

The Forsaken Merman[1]

Come, dear children, let us away;
Down and away below!
Now my brothers call from the bay,
Now the great winds shoreward blow,
Now the salt tides seaward flow;   5
Now the wild white horses play,
Champ and chafe and toss in the spray.
Children dear, let us away!
This way, this way!

Call her once before you go—   10
Call once yet!
In a voice that she will know:
"Margaret! Margaret!"
Children's voices should be dear
(Call once more) to a mother's ear;   15
Children's voices, wild with pain—
Surely she will come again!
Call her once and come away;
This way, this way!
"Mother dear, we cannot stay!   20
The wild white horses foam and fret."
Margaret! Margaret!

Come, dear children, come away down;
Call no more!
One last look at the white-walled town,   25
And the little gray church on the windy shore,
Then come down!
She will not come though you call all day;
Come away, come away!

Children dear, was it yesterday   30
We heard the sweet bells over the bay?
In the caverns where we lay,
Through the surf and through the swell,
The far-off sound of a silver bell?
Sand-strewn caverns, cool and deep,   35
Where the winds are all asleep;
Where the spent lights quiver and gleam,
Where the salt weed sways in the stream,

---

4. Sophocles (496–406 B.C.), a native of Colonus, sang
of his town in his *Oedipus at Colonus.*
1. For a comparison of Arnold's skillful telling of this
story with the Danish version from which he derived
it, see C. B. Tinker and H. F. Lowry, *The Poetry of
Matthew Arnold: A Commentary* (1940) 129–132.

Where the sea beasts, ranged all round,
Feed in the ooze of their pasture ground;   40
Where the sea snakes coil and twine,
Dry their mail and bask in the brine;
Where great whales come sailing by,
Sail and sail, with unshut eye,
Round the world for ever and aye?   45
When did music come this way?
Children dear, was it yesterday?

Children dear, was it yesterday
(Call yet once) that she went away?
Once she sate with you and me,   50
On a red gold throne in the heart of the sea,
And the youngest sate on her knee.
She combed its bright hair, and she tended it well,
When down swung the sound of a far-off bell.
She sighed, she looked up through the clear green sea;   55
She said: "I must go, for my kinsfolk pray
In the little gray church on the shore today.
'Twill be Easter time in the world—ah me!
And I lose my poor soul, Merman! here with thee."
I said: "Go up, dear heart, through the waves;   60
Say thy prayer, and come back to the kind sea-caves!"
She smiled, she went up through the surf in the bay.
Children dear, was it yesterday?

    Children dear, were we long alone?
"The sea grows stormy, the little ones moan;   65
Long prayers," I said, "in the world they say;
Come!" I said; and we rose through the surf in the bay.
We went up the beach, by the sandy down
Where the sea-stocks bloom, to the white-walled town;
Through the narrow paved streets, where all was still,   70
To the little gray church on the windy hill.
From the church came a murmur of folk at their prayers,
But we stood without in the cold blowing airs.
We climbed on the graves, on the stones worn with rains,
And we gazed up the aisle through the small leaded panes.   75
She sate by the pillar; we saw her clear:
"Margaret, hist! come quick, we are here!
Dear heart," I said, "we are long alone;
The sea grows stormy, the little ones moan."
But, ah, she gave me never a look,   80
For her eyes were sealed to the holy book!
Loud prays the priest; shut stands the door.
Come away, children, call no more!
Come away, come down, call no more!

    Down, down, down!   85
Down to the depths of the sea!
She sits at her wheel in the humming town,

Singing most joyfully.
Hark what she sings: "O joy, O joy,
For the humming street, and the child with its toy!   90
For the priest, and the bell, and the holy well;
For the wheel where I spun,
And the blessed light of the sun!"
And so she sings her fill,
Singing most joyfully,   95
Till the spindle drops from her hand,
And the whizzing wheel stands still.
She steals to the window, and looks at the sand,
And over the sand at the sea;
And her eyes are set in a stare;   100
And anon there breaks a sigh,
And anon there drops a tear,
From a sorrow-clouded eye,
And a heart sorrow-laden,
A long, long sigh;   105
For the cold strange eyes of a little Mermaiden
And the gleam of her golden hair.

    Come away, away children;
Come children, come down!
The hoarse wind blows coldly;   110
Lights shine in the town.
She will start from her slumber
When gusts shake the door;
She will hear the winds howling,
Will hear the waves roar.   115
We shall see, while above us
The waves roar and whirl,
A ceiling of amber,
A pavement of pearl.
Singing: "Here came a mortal,   120
But faithless was she!
And alone dwell forever
The kings of the sea."

    But, children, at midnight,
When soft the winds blow,   125
When clear falls the moonlight,
When spring tides are low;
When sweet airs come seaward
From heaths starred with broom,
And high rocks throw mildly   130
On the blanched sands a gloom;
Up the still, glistening beaches,
Up the creek we will hie,
Over banks of bright seaweed
The ebb-tide leaves dry.   135
We will gaze, from the sand-hills,
At the white, sleeping town;

At the church on the hillside—
And then come back down.
Singing: "There dwells a loved one,   140
But cruel is she!
She left lonely forever
The kings of the sea."

                                                                        1849

Isolation. To Marguerite[1]

We were apart; yet, day by day,
I bade my heart more constant be.
I bade it keep the world away,
And grow a home for only thee;
Nor feared but thy love likewise grew,   5
Like mine, each day, more tried, more true.

The fault was grave! I might have known,
What far too soon, alas! I learned—
The heart can bind itself alone,
And faith may oft be unreturned.   10
Self-swayed our feelings ebb and swell—
Thou lov'st no more—Farewell! Farewell!

Farewell!—and thou, thou lonely heart,[2]
Which never yet without remorse
Even for a moment didst depart   15
From thy remote and spherèd course
To haunt the place where passions reign—
Back to thy solitude again!

Back with the conscious thrill of shame
Which Luna[3] felt, that summer night,   20
Flash through her pure immortal frame,
When she forsook the starry height
To hang over Endymion's sleep
Upon the pine-grown Latmian steep.
 Yet she, chaste queen, had never proved   25
How vain a thing is mortal love,
Wandering in Heaven, far removed.
But thou hast long had place to prove
This truth—to prove, and make thine own:
"Thou hast been, shalt be, art, alone."   30

Or, if not quite alone, yet they
Which touch thee are unmating things—

1. Addressed to a woman Arnold is reputed to have met in Switzerland in the 1840s. It has been commonly assumed that she was French or Swiss, but some recent biographies speculate she might have been Mary Claude, a woman Arnold knew in England at this same period, who, although English, had connections with Germany and had translated German prose and verse.
2. Presumably the speaker's heart, not Marguerite's.
3. Luna (or Diana), the goddess of chastity and of the moon, fell in love with Endymion, a handsome shepherd, whom she discovered asleep on Mt. Latmos.

Ocean and clouds and night and day;
Lorn autumns and triumphant springs;
And life, and others' joy and pain,   35
And love, if love, of happier men.

Of happier men—for they, at least,
Have *dreamed* two human hearts might blend
In one, and were through faith released
From isolation without end   40
Prolonged; nor knew, although not less
Alone than thou, their loneliness.

1849   1857

To Marguerite—Continued

Yes! in the sea of life enisled,
With echoing straits between us thrown,
Dotting the shoreless watery wild,
We mortal millions live *alone*.
The islands feel the enclasping flow,   5
And then their endless bounds they know.

But when the moon their hollows lights,
And they are swept by balms of spring,
And in their glens, on starry nights,
The nightingales divinely sing;   10
And lovely notes, from shore to shore,
Across the sounds and channels pour—

Oh! then a longing like despair
Is to their farthest caverns sent;
For surely once, they feel, we were   15
Parts of a single continent!
Now round us spreads the watery plain—
Oh might our marges meet again!

Who ordered that their longing's fire
Should be, as soon as kindled, cooled?   20
Who renders vain their deep desire?—
A God, a God their severance ruled!
And bade betwixt their shores to be
The unplumbed, salt, estranging sea.

1849   1852

The Buried Life

Light flows our war of mocking words, and yet,
Behold, with tears mine eyes are wet!
I feel a nameless sadness o'er me roll.
Yes, yes, we know that we can jest,

We know, we know that we can smile!   5
But there's a something in this breast,
To which thy light words bring no rest,
And thy gay smiles no anodyne.
Give me thy hand, and hush awhile,
And turn those limpid eyes on mine,   10 .
And let me read there, love! thy inmost soul.

Alas! is even love too weak
To unlock the heart, and let it speak?
Are even lovers powerless to reveal
To one another what indeed they feel?   15
I knew the mass of men concealed
Their thoughts, for fear that if revealed
They would by other men be met
With blank indifference, or with blame reproved;
I knew they lived and moved   20
Tricked in disguises, alien to the rest
Of men, and alien to themselves—and yet
The same heart beats in every human breast!

But we, my love!—doth a like spell benumb
Our hearts, our voices?—must we too be dumb?   25

Ah! well for us, if even we,
Even for a moment, can get free
Our heart, and have our lips unchained;
For that which seals them hath been deep-ordained!

Fate, which foresaw   30
How frivolous a baby man would be—
By what distractions he would be possessed,
How he would pour himself in every strife,
And well-nigh change his own identity—
That it might keep from his capricious play   35
His genuine self, and force him to obey
Even in his own despite his being's law,
Bade through the deep recesses of our breast
The unregarded river of our life
Pursue with indiscernible flow its way;   40
And that we should not see
The buried stream, and seem to be
Eddying at large in blind uncertainty,
Though driving on with it eternally.

But often, in the world's most crowded streets,[1]   45
But often, in the din of strife,
There rises an unspeakable desire
After the knowledge of our buried life;

1. This passage, like many others in Arnold's poetry,   "But oft, in lonely rooms, and 'mid the din / Of towns
illustrates the impact on his writings of Wordsworth. In   and cities, I have owed to them, / In hours of weariness,
this instance cf. Wordsworth's *Tintern Abbey* 25–27:   sensations sweet."

A thirst to spend our fire and restless force
In tracking out our true, original course;
A longing to inquire   50
Into the mystery of this heart which beats
So wild, so deep in us—to know
Whence our lives come and where they go.
And many a man in his own breast then delves,
But deep enough, alas! none ever mines.   55
And we have been on many thousand lines,
And we have shown, on each, spirit and power;
But hardly have we, for one little hour,
Been on our own line, have we been ourselves—   60
Hardly had skill to utter one of all
The nameless feelings that course through our breast,
But they course on forever unexpressed.
And long we try in vain to speak and act
Our hidden self, and what we say and do   65
Is eloquent, is well—but 'tis not true!
And then we will no more be racked
With inward striving, and demand
Of all the thousand nothings of the hour
Their stupefying power;   70
Ah yes, and they benumb us at our call!
Yet still, from time to time, vague and forlorn,
From the soul's subterranean depth upborne
As from an infinitely distant land,
Come airs, and floating echoes, and convey   75
A melancholy into all our day.[2]

Only—but this is rare—
When a beloved hand is laid in ours,
When, jaded with the rush and glare
Of the interminable hours,   80
Our eyes can in another's eyes read clear,
When our world-deafened ear
Is by the tones of a loved voice caressed—
A bolt is shot back somewhere in our breast,
And a lost pulse of feeling stirs again.   85
The eye sinks inward, and the heart lies plain,
And what we mean, we say, and what we would, we know.
A man becomes aware of his life's flow,
And hears its winding murmur; and he sees
The meadows where it glides, the sun, the breeze.   90

And there arrives a lull in the hot race
Wherein he doth forever chase
That flying and elusive shadow, rest.
An air of coolness plays upon his face,
And an unwonted calm pervades his breast.   95
And then he thinks he knows

2. Cf. Wordworth's *Ode: Intimations of Immortality*, lines 149–151: "Those shadowy recollections, / Which, be they what they may, / Are yet the fountain light of all our day."

The hills where his life rose,
And the sea where it goes.

1852

Memorial Verses[1]

April 1850

Goethe in Weimar sleeps, and Greece,
Long since, saw Byron's struggle cease.
But one such death remained to come;
The last poetic voice is dumb—
We stand today by Wordsworth's tomb.   5

When Byron's eyes were shut in death,
We bowed our head and held our breath.
He taught us little; but our soul
Had *felt* him like the thunder's roll.
With shivering heart the strife we saw   10
Of passion with eternal law;
And yet with reverential awe
We watched the fount of fiery life
Which served for that Titanic strife.
When Goethe's death was told, we said: 15
Sunk, then, is Europe's sagest head.
Physician of the iron age,
Goethe has done his pilgrimage.
He took the suffering human race,
He read each wound, each weakness clear;   20
And struck his finger on the place,
And said: *Thou ailest here, and here!*
He looked on Europe's dying hour
Of fitful dream and feverish power;
His eye plunged down the weltering strife,   25
The turmoil of expiring life—
He said: *The end is everywhere,*
Art still has truth, take refuge there!
And he was happy, if to know
Causes of things, and far below   30
His feet to see the lurid flow
Of terror, and insane distress,
And headlong fate, be happiness.

And Wordsworth!—Ah, pale ghosts, rejoice!
For never has such soothing voice   35

---

1. This elegy was written shortly after Wordsworth had died in April 1850, at the age of eighty. Arnold had known the poet as a man and deeply admired his writings—as is evident not only in this poem but in his late essay, *Wordsworth*. Byron, who died in Greece in 1824, had affected Arnold profoundly in his youth, but later that strenuous "Titanic" (line 14) poetry seemed to him less satisfactory, its value limited by its lack of serenity. His final verdict on Byron can be encountered in his essay in *Essays in Criticism: Second Series*. Goethe, who died in 1832, was regarded by Arnold as a great philosophical poet and the most significant man of letters of the early 19th century.

Been to your shadowy world conveyed,
Since erst, at morn, some wandering shade
Heard the clear song of Orpheus[2] come
Through Hades, and the mournful gloom.
Wordsworth has gone from us—and ye,   40
Ah, may ye feel his voice as we!
He too upon a wintry clime
Had fallen—on this iron time
Of doubts, disputes, distractions, fears.
He found us when the age had bound   45
Our souls in its benumbing round;
He spoke, and loosed our heart in tears.
He laid us as we lay at birth
On the cool flowery lap of earth,
Smiles broke from us and we had ease;   50
The hills were round us, and the breeze
Went o'er the sunlit fields again;
Our foreheads felt the wind and rain.
Our youth returned; for there was shed
On spirits that had long been dead,   55
Spirits dried up and closely furled,
The freshness of the early world.

Ah! since dark days still bring to light
Man's prudence and man's fiery might,
Time may restore us in his course   60
Goethe's sage mind and Byron's force;
But where will Europe's latter hour
Again find Wordsworth's healing power?
Others will teach us how to dare,
And against fear our breast to steel;   65
Others will strengthen us to bear—
But who, ah! who, will make us feel?
The cloud of mortal destiny,
Others will front it fearlessly—
But who, like him, will put it by?   70

Keep fresh the grass upon his grave
O Rotha,[3] with thy living wave!
Sing him thy best! for few or none
Hears thy voice right, now he is gone.

1850   1850

The Scholar Gypsy   The story of a seventeenth-century student who left
Oxford and joined a band of gypsies had made a strong impression on Arnold. In
the poem he wistfully imagines that the spirit of this scholar is still to be encountered in the Cumner countryside near Oxford, having achieved immortality by a

2. By means of his beautiful music, Orpheus won his
way through Hades in his search for the shade of his

dead wife, Eurydice.
3. A river near Wordsworth's burial place.

serene pursuit of the secret of human existence. Like Keats's nightingale, the scholar has escaped "the weariness, the fever, and the fret" of modern life.

At the outset, the poet addresses a shepherd who has been helping him in his search for traces of the scholar. The shepherd is addressed as *you*. After line 61, with the shift to *thou* and *thy*, the person addressed is the scholar himself, and the poet thereafter sometimes uses the pronoun *we* to indicate he is speaking for all humanity of later generations.

About the setting Arnold wrote to his brother Tom on May 15, 1857: "You alone of my brothers are associated with that life at Oxford, the *freest* and most delightful part, perhaps, of my life, when with you and Clough and Walrond I shook off all the bonds and formalities of the place, and enjoyed the spring of life and that unforgotten Oxfordshire and Berkshire country. Do you remember a poem of mine called 'The Scholar Gipsy'? It was meant to fix the remembrance of those delightful wanderings of ours in the Cumner Hills."

The passage from Joseph Glanvill's *Vanity of Dogmatizing* (1661) that inspired the poem was included by Arnold as a note:

> There was very lately a lad in the University of Oxford, who was by his poverty forced to leave his studies there; and at last to join himself to a company of vagabond gypsies. Among these extravagant people, by the insinuating subtilty of his carriage, he quickly got so much of their love and esteem as that they discovered to him their mystery. After he had been a pretty while exercised in the trade, there chanced to ride by a couple of scholars, who had formerly been of his acquaintance. They quickly spied out their old friend among the gypsies; and he gave them an account of the necessity which drove him to that kind of life, and told them that the people he went with were not such imposters as they were taken for, but that they had a traditional kind of learning among them, and could do wonders by the power of imagination, their fancy binding that of others: that himself had learned much of their art, and when he had compassed the whole secret, he intended, he said, to leave their company, and give the world an account of what he had learned.

The Scholar Gypsy

Go, for they call you, shepherd, from the hill;
  Go, shepherd, and untie the wattled cotes!¹
    No longer leave thy wistful flock unfed,
  Nor let thy bawling fellows rack their throats,
    Nor the cropped herbage shoot another head.   5
      But when the fields are still,
  And the tired men and dogs all gone to rest,
    And only the white sheep are sometimes seen
    Cross and recross the strips of moon-blanched green,
  Come, shepherd, and again begin the quest!   10

Here, where the reaper was at work of late—
  In this high field's dark corner, where he leaves
    His coat, his basket, and his earthen cruse,²
  And in the sun all morning binds the sheaves,
    Then here, at noon, comes back his stores to use—   15
      Here will I sit and wait,

---

1. Sheepfolds woven from sticks.   2. Pot or jug for carrying his drink.

While to my ear from uplands far away
  The bleating of the folded[3] flocks is borne,
    With distant cries of reapers in the corn[4]—
      All the live murmur of a summer's day.   20

Screened is this nook o'er the high, half-reaped field,
  And here till sundown, shepherd! will I be.
    Through the thick corn the scarlet poppies peep,
    And round green roots and yellowing stalks I see
      Pale pink convolvulus in tendrils creep;   25
        And air-swept lindens yield
Their scent, and rustle down their perfumed showers
  Of bloom on the bent grass[5] where I am laid,
    And bower me from the August sun with shade;
      And the eye travels down to Oxford's towers.   30

And near me on the grass lies Glanvill's book—
  Come, let me read the oft-read tale again!
    The story of the Oxford scholar poor,
    Of pregnant parts[6] and quick inventive brain,
      Who, tired of knocking at preferment's door,   35
        One summer morn forsook
His friends, and went to learn the gypsy lore,
  And roamed the world with that wild brotherhood,
    And came, as most men deemed, to little good,
      But came to Oxford and his friends no more.   40

But once, years after, in the country lanes,
  Two scholars, whom at college erst he knew,
    Met him, and of his way of life inquired;
    Whereat he answered, that the gypsy crew,
      His mates, had arts to rule as they desired   45
        The workings of men's brains,
And they can bind them to what thoughts they will.
  "And I," he said, "the secret of their art,
    When fully learned, will to the world impart;
      But it needs heaven-sent moments for this skill."   50

This said, he left them, and returned no more.—
  But rumors hung about the countryside,
    That the lost Scholar long was seen to stray,
    Seen by rare glimpses, pensive and tongue-tied,
      In hat of antique shape, and cloak of grey,   55
        The same the gypsies wore.
Shepherds had met him on the Hurst[7] in spring;
  At some lone alehouse in the Berkshire moors,
    On the warm ingle-bench, the smock-frocked boors[8]
      Had found him seated at their entering,   60

3. Penned up.
4. Grain or wheat.
5. A stiff kind of grass.
6. Teeming with ideas.

7. A hill near Oxford. All the place-names in the poem
(except those in the final two stanzas) refer to the countryside near Oxford.
8. Rustics. "Ingle-bench": fireside bench.

But, 'mid their drink and clatter, he would fly.
  And I myself seem half to know thy looks,
    And put the shepherds, wanderer! on thy trace;
  And boys who in lone wheatfields scare the rooks[9]
    I ask if thou hast passed their quiet place;   65
      Or in my boat I lie
  Moored to the cool bank in the summer heats,
    'Mid wide grass meadows which the sunshine fills,
    And watch the warm, green-muffled Cumner hills,
  And wonder if thou haunt'st their shy retreats.   70

For most, I know, thou lov'st retired ground!
  Thee at the ferry Oxford riders blithe,
    Returning home on summer nights, have met
  Crossing the stripling Thames[1] at Bab-lock-hithe,
    Trailing in the cool stream thy fingers wet,   75
      As the punt's rope chops round;[2]
  And leaning backward in a pensive dream,
    And fostering in thy lap a heap of flowers
    Plucked in shy fields and distant Wychwood bowers,
  And thine eyes resting on the moonlit stream.   80

And then they land, and thou art seen no more!—
  Maidens, who from the distant hamlets come
    To dance around the Fyfield elm in May,
  Oft through the darkening fields have seen thee roam,
    Or cross a stile into the public way.   85
      Oft thou hast given them store
  Of flowers—the frail-leafed, white anemone,
    Dark bluebells drenched with dews of summer eves,
    And purple orchises with spotted leaves—
  But none hath words she can report of thee.   90

And, above Godstow Bridge, when hay time's here
  In June, and many a scythe in sunshine flames,
    Men who through those wide fields of breezy grass
  Where black-winged swallows haunt the glittering Thames,
    To bathe in the abandoned lasher pass,[3]   95
      Have often passed thee near
  Sitting upon the river bank o'ergrown;
    Marked thine outlandish garb, thy figure spare,
    Thy dark vague eyes, and soft abstracted air—
  But, when they came from bathing, thou wast gone!   100

At some lone homestead in the Cumner hills,
  Where at her open door the housewife darns,

---

9. Boys hired to frighten crows away from eating wheat grains.
1. The narrow upper reaches of the river before it broadens out to its full width.
2. The scholar's flat-bottomed boat ("punt") is tied up by a rope at the riverbank near the ferry crossing like the speaker's boat (in the previous stanza), which was "moored to the cool bank." The motion of the boat as it is stirred by the current of the river causes the chopping sound of the rope in the water.
3. Water that spills over a dam or weir.

Thou hast been seen, or hanging on a gate
To watch the threshers in the mossy barns.
   Children, who early range these slopes and late   105
      For cresses from the rills,
Have known thee eying, all an April day,
   The springing pastures and the feeding kine;
   And marked thee, when the stars come out and shine,
Through the long dewy grass move slow away.   110

In autumn, on the skirts of Bagley Wood—
   Where most the gypsies by the turf-edged way
      Pitch their smoked tents, and every bush you see
   With scarlet patches tagged and shreds of grey,
      Above the forest ground called Thessaly—   115
         The blackbird, picking food,
   Sees thee, nor stops his meal, nor fears at all;
      So often has he known thee past him stray,
      Rapt, twirling in thy hand a withered spray,
   And waiting for the spark from heaven to fall.   120

And once, in winter, on the causeway chill
   Where home through flooded fields foot-travelers go,
      Have I not passed thee on the wooden bridge,
   Wrapped in thy cloak and battling with the snow,
      Thy face tow'rd Hinksey and its wintry ridge?   125
         And thou hast climbed the hill,
   And gained the white brow of the Cumner range;
      Turned once to watch, while thick the snowflakes fall,
      The line of festal light in Christ Church hall[4]—
   Then sought thy straw in some sequestered grange.   130

But what—I dream! Two hundred years are flown
   Since first thy story ran through Oxford halls,
      And the grave Glanvill did the tale inscribe
   That thou wert wandered from the studious walls
      To learn strange arts, and join a gypsy tribe;   135
         And thou from earth art gone
   Long since, and in some quiet churchyard laid—
      Some country nook, where o'er thy unknown grave
      Tall grasses and white flowering nettles wave,
   Under a dark, red-fruited yew tree's shade.   140

—No, no, thou hast not felt the lapse of hours!
   For what wears out the life of mortal men?
      'Tis that from change to change their being rolls;
   'Tis that repeated shocks, again, again,
      Exhaust the energy of strongest souls   145
         And numb the elastic powers.
   Till having used our nerves with bliss and teen,[5]

---

4. The dining hall of an Oxford college.   5. Vexation.

And tired upon a thousand schemes our wit,
    To the just-pausing Genius[6] we remit
        Our worn-out life, and are—what we have been.   150

Thou hast not lived, why should'st thou perish, so?
    Thou hadst *one* aim, *one* business, *one* desire;
        Else wert thou long since numbered with the dead!
Else hadst thou spent, like other men, thy fire!
    The generations of thy peers are fled,   155
        And we ourselves shall go;
But thou possessest an immortal lot,
    And we imagine thee exempt from age
    And living as thou liv'st on Glanvill's page,
Because thou hadst—what we, alas! have not.   160

For early didst thou leave the world, with powers
    Fresh, undiverted to the world without,
        Firm to their mark, not spent on other things;
Free from the sick fatigue, the languid doubt,
    Which much to have tried, in much been baffled, brings.   165
        O life unlike to ours!
Who fluctuate idly without term or scope,
    Of whom each strives, nor knows for what he strives,
        And each half[7] lives a hundred different lives;
Who wait like thee, but not, like thee, in hope.   170

Thou waitest for the spark from heaven! and we,
    Light half-believers of our casual creeds,
        Who never deeply felt, nor clearly willed,
Whose insight never has borne fruit in deeds,
    Whose vague resolves never have been fulfilled;   175
        For whom each year we see
Breeds new beginnings, disappointments new;
    Who hesitate and falter life away,
    And lose tomorrow the ground won today—
Ah! do not we, wanderer! await it too?   180

Yes, we await it!—but it still delays,
    And then we suffer! and amongst us one,[8]
        Who most has suffered, takes dejectedly
His seat upon the intellectual throne;
    And all his store of sad experience he   185
        Lays bare of wretched days;
Tells us his misery's birth and growth and signs,
    And how the dying spark of hope was fed,
    And how the breast was soothed, and how the head,
And all his hourly varied anodynes.   190

6. Perhaps the spirit of the universe, which pauses   8. Probably Goethe, although possibly referring to
briefly to receive back the life given to us.   Tennyson, whose *In Memoriam* had appeared in 1850.
7. An adverb modifying "lives."

This for our wisest! and we others pine,
　And wish the long unhappy dream would end,
　　And waive all claim to bliss, and try to bear;
　With close-lipped patience for our only friend,
　　Sad patience, too near neighbor to despair—　　　　195
　　　But none has hope like thine!
Thou through the fields and through the woods dost stray,
　Roaming the countryside, a truant boy,
　　Nursing thy project in unclouded joy,
And every doubt long blown by time away.　　　　　　200

O born in days when wits were fresh and clear,
　And life ran gaily as the sparkling Thames;
　　Before this strange disease of modern life,
　With its sick hurry, its divided aims,
　　Its heads o'ertaxed, its palsied hearts, was rife—　　205
　　　Fly hence, our contact fear!
Still fly, plunge deeper in the bowering wood!
　Averse, as Dido[9] did with gesture stern
　　From her false friend's approach in Hades turn,
Wave us away, and keep thy solitude!　　　　　　　　210

Still nursing the unconquerable hope,
　Still clutching the inviolable shade,
　　With a free, onward impulse brushing through,
　By night, the silvered branches of the glade—
　　Far on the forest skirts, where none pursue.　　　　215
　　　On some mild pastoral slope
Emerge, and resting on the moonlit pales
　Freshen thy flowers as in former years
　　With dew, or listen with enchanted ears,
From the dark dingles,[1] to the nightingales!　　　　　220

But fly our paths, our feverish contact fly!
　For strong the infection of our mental strife,
　　Which, though it gives no bliss, yet spoils for rest;
　And we should win thee from thy own fair life,
　　Like us distracted, and like us unblest.　　　　　　225
　　　Soon, soon thy cheer would die,
Thy hopes grow timorous, and unfixed thy powers,
　And thy clear aims be cross and shifting made;
　　And then thy glad perennial youth would fade,
Fade, and grow old at last, and die like ours.　　　　230

Then fly our greetings, fly our speech and smiles!
　—As some grave Tyrian trader, from the sea,
　　Descried at sunrise an emerging prow
　Lifting the cool-haired creepers stealthily,
　　The fringes of a southward-facing brow　　　　　　235

9. Dido committed suicide after her lover, Aeneas, deserted her. When he later encountered her in Hades, she turned sternly away from him.　1. Small deep valleys.

    Among the Aegean isles;
And saw the merry Grecian coaster come,
    Freighted with amber grapes, and Chian wine,
    Green, bursting figs, and tunnies[2] steeped in brine—
And knew the intruders on his ancient home,   240

The young lighthearted masters of the waves—
    And snatched his rudder, and shook out more sail;
    And day and night held on indignantly
O'er the blue Midland waters with the gale,
    Betwixt the Syrtes[3] and soft Sicily,   245
      To where the Atlantic raves
Outside the western straits; and unbent sails
    There, where down cloudy cliffs, through sheets of foam,
    Shy traffickers, the dark Iberians[4] come;
And on the beach undid his corded bales.[5]   250

                                            1853

Dover Beach

    The sea is calm tonight.
    The tide is full, the moon lies fair
    Upon the straits—on the French coast the light
    Gleams and is gone; the cliffs of England stand,
    Glimmering and vast, out in the tranquil bay.   5
    Come to the window, sweet is the night air!
    Only, from the long line of spray
    Where the sea meets the moon-blanched land,
    Listen! you hear the grating roar[1]
    Of pebbles which the waves draw back, and fling,   10
    At their return, up the high strand,
    Begin, and cease, and then again begin,
    With tremulous cadence slow, and bring
    The eternal note of sadness in.

    Sophocles long ago   15
    Heard it on the Aegean, and it brought

2. Tuna fish.
3. Shoals off the coast of North Africa.
4. Dark inhabitants of Spain and Portugal—perhaps associated with gypsies.
5. The elaborate simile of the final two stanzas has been variously interpreted. The trader from Tyre is disconcerted when, peering out through the foliage ("fringes," line 235) that screens his hiding place, he sees noisy intruders entering his harbor. Like the Scholar Gypsy, when similarly intruded on by hearty extroverts, he resolves to flee and seek a new home.
    The reference (line 249) to the Iberians as "shy traffickers" (traders) is explained by Kenneth Allott as having been derived from Herodotus' History (4.196). Herodotus describes a distinctive method of selling goods established by Carthaginian merchants who used to sail through the Strait of Gibraltar to trade with the inhabitants of the coast of West Africa. The Carthaginians would leave bales of their merchandise on display along the beaches and, without having seen their prospective customers, would return to their ships. The shy natives would then come down from their inland hiding places and set gold beside the bales they wished to buy. When the natives withdrew in their turn, the Carthaginians would return to the beach and decide whether payments were adequate, a process repeated until agreement was reached. On the Atlantic coasts this method of bargaining persisted into the 19th century. As William Beloe, a translator of Herodotus, noted in 1844: "In this manner they transact their exchange without seeing one another, or without the least instance of dishonesty . . . on either side." For the solitary Tyrian trader such a procedure, with its avoidance of "contact" (line 221), would have been especially appropriate.

1. Cf. Wordsworth, It Is a Beauteous Evening, lines 6–8: "Listen! the mighty Being is awake, / And doth with his eternal motion make / A sound like thunder—everlastingly."

Into his mind the turbid ebb and flow
Of human misery;[2] we
Find also in the sound a thought,
Hearing it by this distant northern sea.   20

The Sea of Faith
Was once, too, at the full, and round earth's shore
Lay like the folds of a bright girdle furled.[3]
But now I only hear
Its melancholy, long, withdrawing roar,   25
Retreating, to the breath
Of the night wind, down the vast edges drear
And naked shingles[4] of the world.

Ah, love, let us be true
To one another! for the world, which seems   30
To lie before us like a land of dreams,
So various, so beautiful, so new,
Hath really neither joy, nor love, nor light,
Nor certitude, nor peace, nor help for pain;
And we are here as on a darkling plain   35
Swept with confused alarms of struggle and flight,
Where ignorant armies[5] clash by night.

ca. 1851   1867

Stanzas from the Grande Chartreuse[1]

Through Alpine meadows soft-suffused
With rain, where thick the crocus blows,
Past the dark forges long disused,
The mule track from Saint Laurent goes.
The bridge is crossed, and slow we ride,   5
Through forest, up the mountainside.

The autumnal evening darkens round,
The wind is up, and drives the rain;
While, hark! far down, with strangled sound

2. Some of Sophocles' plays include episodes featuring "human misery" which may have influenced Arnold's lines. Editors cite as possible sources: *Antigone* (lines 583 ff.); *Oedipus at Colonus* (lines 120 ff.); and especially *The Women of Trachis* (lines 112 ff.).
3. This difficult line means, in general, that at high tide the sea envelops the land closely. Its forces are "gathered" up (to use Wordsworth's term for it) like the "folds" of bright clothing ("girdle") that have been compressed ("furled"). At ebb tide, as the sea retreats, it is unfurled and spread out. It still surrounds the shoreline but not as an "enclasping flow" (as in *To Marguerite—Continued*).
4. Beaches covered with pebbles.
5. Perhaps alluding to battles in Arnold's own time such as occurred during the revolutions of 1848 in Europe, or at the Siege of Rome by the French in 1849 (the date of composition of the poem is unknown, al-

though generally assumed to be 1851.) But the passage also refers back to another battle, one that occurred more than two thousand years earlier when an Athenian army was attempting an invasion of Sicily at nighttime. As this "night battle" was described by Thucydides in his *History of the Peloponnesian War* (vii, Ch.44), the invaders became confused by darkness and slaughtered many of their own men. Hence "ignorant armies."
1. A monastery situated high in the French Alps. It was established in 1084 by St. Bruno, founder of the Carthusians (line 30), whose austere regimen of solitary contemplation, fasting, and religious exercises (lines 37–44) had remained virtually unchanged for centuries. Arnold visited the site on September 7, 1851, accompanied by his bride. His account may be compared with that by Wordsworth (*Prelude* 6.416–488), who had made a similar visit in 1790.

Doth the Dead Guier's[2] stream complain,   10
Where that wet smoke, among the woods,
Over his boiling cauldron broods.

Swift rush the spectral vapors white
Past limestone scars[3] with ragged pines,
Showing—then blotting from our sight!—   15
Halt—through the cloud-drift something shines!
High in the valley, wet and drear,
The huts of Courrerie appear.

Strike leftward! cries our guide; and higher
Mounts up the stony forest way.   20
At last the encircling trees retire;
Look! through the showery twilight grey
What pointed roofs are these advance?—
A palace of the Kings of France?

Approach, for what we seek is here!   25
Alight, and sparely sup, and wait
For rest in this outbuilding near;
Then cross the sward and reach that gate.
Knock; pass the wicket! Thou art come
To the Carthusians' world-famed home.   30

The silent courts, where night and day
Into their stone-carved basins cold
The splashing icy fountains play—
The humid corridors behold!
Where, ghostlike in the deepening night,   35
Cowled forms brush by in gleaming white.

The chapel, where no organ's peal
Invests the stern and naked prayer—
With penitential cries they kneel
And wrestle; rising then, with bare   40
And white uplifted faces stand,
Passing the Host from hand to hand;[4]

Each takes, and then his visage wan
Is buried in his cowl once more.
The cells!—the suffering Son of Man   45
Upon the wall—the knee-worn floor—
And where they sleep, that wooden bed,
Which shall their coffin be, when dead![5]

2. The Guiers Mort River flows down from the monastery and joins the Guiers Vif in the valley below. Wordsworth speaks of the two rivers as "the sister streams of Life and Death."
3. Precipices.
4. Arnold, during his short visit, may not actually have witnessed the service of the Mass in the monastery. The consecrated wafer ("the Host") is not passed from the hand of the officiating priest to the hands of the communicant (as is the practice in Arnold's own Anglican church) but placed, instead, on the tongue of the communicant (who kneels rather than stands). See C. B. Tinker and H. F. Lowry, *The Poetry of Matthew Arnold: A Commentary* (1940) 249–251.
5. A Carthusian is buried on a wooden plank but does not sleep in a coffin.

The library, where tract and tome
Not to feed priestly pride are there,   50
To hymn the conquering march of Rome,
Nor yet to amuse, as ours are!
They paint of souls the inner strife,
Their drops of blood, their death in life.

The garden, overgrown—yet mild,   55
See, fragrant herbs[6] are flowering there!
Strong children of the Alpine wild
Whose culture is the brethren's care;
Of human tasks their only one,
And cheerful works beneath the sun.   60

Those halls, too, destined to contain
Each its own pilgrim-host of old,
From England, Germany, or Spain—
All are before me! I behold
The House, the Brotherhood austere!   65
—And what am I, that I am here?

For rigorous teachers seized my youth,
And purged its faith, and trimmed its fire,
Showed me the high, white star of Truth,
There bade me gaze, and there aspire.   70
Even now their whispers pierce the gloom:
What dost thou in this living tomb?

Forgive me, masters of the mind![7]
At whose behest I long ago
So much unlearnt, so much resigned—   75
I come not here to be your foe!
I seek these anchorites, not in ruth,[8]
To curse and to deny your truth;

Not as their friend, or child, I speak!
But as, on some far northern strand,   80
Thinking of his own Gods, a Greek
In pity and mournful awe might stand
Before some fallen Runic stone—[9]
For both were faiths, and both are gone.

Wandering between two worlds, one dead,   85
The other powerless to be born,
With nowhere yet to rest my head,
Like these, on earth I wait forlorn.

---

6. From which the liqueur Chartreuse is manufactured. Sales of this liqueur provide the principal revenues for upkeep of the monastery.
7. Writers whose insistence on testing religious beliefs
in the light of fact and reason persuaded Arnold that
faith in Christianity (especially in the Roman Catholic
or Anglo Catholic forms) was no longer tenable in the
modern world.
8. Remorse for having adopted the rationalist view of
Christianity.
9. A monument inscribed in Teutonic letters (runes),
emblematic of a Nordic religion that has become extinct. The relic reminds the Greek that his own religion
is likewise dying and will soon be extinct.

Their faith, my tears, the world deride—
I come to shed them at their side.   90

Oh, hide me in your gloom profound,
Ye solemn seats of holy pain!
Take me, cowled forms, and fence me round,
Till I possess my soul again;
Till free my thoughts before me roll,   95
Not chafed by hourly false control!

For the world cries your faith is now
But a dead time's exploded dream;
My melancholy, sciolists[1] say,
Is a passed mode, an outworn theme—   100
As if the world had ever had
A faith, or sciolists been sad!

Ah, if it *be* passed, take away,
At least, the restlessness, the pain;
Be man henceforth no more a prey   105
To these out-dated stings again!
The nobleness of grief is gone—
Ah, leave us not the fret alone!

But—if you[2] cannot give us ease—
Last of the race of them who grieve   110
Here leave us to die out with these
Last of the people who believe!
Silent, while years engrave the brow;
Silent—the best are silent now.

Achilles[3] ponders in his tent,   115
The kings of modern thought[4] are dumb;
Silent they are, though not content,
And wait to see the future come.
They have the grief men had of yore,
But they contend and cry no more.   120

Our fathers[5] watered with their tears
This sea of time whereon we sail,
Their voices were in all men's ears
Who passed within their puissant hail.
Still the same ocean round us raves,   125
But we stand mute, and watch the waves.

1. Superficial-minded persons who pretend to know the answers to all questions.
2. It is not clear whether the speaker has resumed addressing his "rigorous teachers" (line 67) or (as would seem more likely) a combination of the sciolists, who scorn the speaker's melancholy, and the worldly, who scorn the faith of the monks. See his address to the "sons of the world" (lines 161–168).
3. Achilles, until the death of Patroclus, refused to participate in the Trojan war, hence similar to modern intellectual leaders who refuse to speak out about their frustrated sense of alienation.
4. Variously but never satisfactorily identified as Newman or Carlyle (the latter was said to have preached the gospel of silence in forty volumes). Another advocate of stoical silence was the French poet Alfred de Vigny (1797–1863).
5. Predecessors among the Romantic writers such as Byron.

For what availed it, all the noise
And outcry of the former men?—
Say, have their sons achieved more joys,
Say, is life lighter now than then?   130
The sufferers died, they left their pain—
The pangs which tortured them remain.

What helps it now, that Byron bore,
With haughty scorn which mocked the smart,
Through Europe to the Aetolian shore[6]   135
The pageant of his bleeding heart?
That thousands counted every groan,
And Europe made his woe her own?

What boots it, Shelley! that the breeze
Carried thy lovely wail away,   140
Musical through Italian trees
Which fringe thy soft blue Spezzian bay?[7]
Inheritors of thy distress
Have restless hearts one throb the less?

Or are we easier, to have read,   145
O Obermann![8] the sad, stern page,
Which tells us how thou hidd'st thy head
From the fierce tempest of thine age
In the lone brakes of Fontainebleau,
Or chalets near the Alpine snow?   150

Ye slumber in your silent grave!
The world, which for an idle day
Grace to your mood of sadness gave,
Long since hath flung her weeds[9] away.
The eternal trifler[1] breaks your spell;   155
But we—we learnt your lore too well!

Years hence, perhaps, may dawn an age,
More fortunate, alas! than we,
Which without hardness will be sage,
And gay without frivolity.   160
Sons of the world, oh, speed those years;
But, while we wait, allow our tears!

Allow them! We admire with awe
The exulting thunder of your race;
You give the universe your law,   165
You triumph over time and space!
Your pride of life, your tireless powers,
We laud them, but they are not ours.

6. Region in Greece where Byron died.
7. The Gulf of Spezzia in Italy, where Shelley was
drowned.
8. Melancholy hero of *Obermann* (1804), a novel by
the French writer Senancour.
9. Mourning clothes.
1. The sciolist, as in line 99.

We are like children reared in shade
Beneath some old-world abbey wall,   170
Forgotten in a forest glade,
And secret from the eyes of all.
Deep, deep the greenwood round them waves,
Their abbey, and its close[2] of graves!

But, where the road runs near the stream,   175
Oft through the trees they catch a glance
Of passing troops in the sun's beam—
Pennon, and plume, and flashing lance!
Forth to the world those soldiers fare,
To life, to cities, and to war!   180

And through the wood, another way,
Faint bugle notes from far are borne,
Where hunters gather, staghounds bay,[3]
Round some fair forest-lodge at morn.
Gay dames are there, in sylvan green;   185
Laughter and cries—those notes between!

The banners flashing through the trees
Make their blood dance and chain their eyes;
That bugle music on the breeze
Arrests them with a charmed surprise.   190
Banner by turns and bugle woo:
Ye shy recluses, follow too!

O children, what do ye reply?—
"Action and pleasure, will ye roam
Through these secluded dells to cry   195
And call us?—but too late ye come!
Too late for us your call ye blow,
Whose bent was taken long ago.

"Long since we pace this shadowed nave;
We watch those yellow tapers shine,   200
Emblems of hope over the grave,
In the high altar's depth divine;
The organ carries to our ear
Its accents of another sphere.[4]

"Fenced early in this cloistral round   205
Of reverie, of shade, of prayer,
How should we grow in other ground?
How can we flower in foreign air?
—Pass, banners, pass, and bugles, cease;
And leave our desert to its peace!"   210

1852(?)   1855

---

2. Enclosure.
3. Cf. the contrast between recluses and hunters in
The Scholar Gypsy, lines 71–81 (p. 2055).

4. The organ music is from the abbey in the greenwood (line 174), as contrasted with the monastery on
the mountaintop in which there is no organ (line 37).

Thyrsis[1]

A Monody, to Commemorate the Author's Friend, Arthur Hugh Clough, Who Died at Florence, 1861

How changed is here each spot man makes or fills!
  In the two Hinkseys[2] nothing keeps the same;
    The village street its haunted mansion lacks,
    And from the sign is gone Sibylla's name,[3]
      And from the roofs the twisted chimney stacks—   5
      Are ye too changed, ye hills?
  See, 'tis no foot of unfamiliar men
    Tonight from Oxford up your pathway strays!
    Here came I often, often, in old days—
  Thyrsis and I; we still had Thyrsis then.   10

Runs it not here, the track by Childsworth Farm,
  Past the high wood, to where the elm tree crowns
    The hill behind whose ridge the sunset flames?
  The signal-elm, that looks on Ilsley Downs,
    The Vale, the three lone weirs, the youthful Thames?—   15
      This winter eve is warm,
  Humid the air! leafless, yet soft as spring,
    The tender purple spray on copse and briers!
    And that sweet city with her dreaming spires,
  She needs not June for beauty's heightening,   20

Lovely all times she lies, lovely tonight!—
  Only, methinks, some loss of habit's power
    Befalls me wandering through this upland dim.
  Once passed I blindfold here, at any hour;
    Now seldom come I, since I came with him.   25
      That single elm tree bright
  Against the west—I miss it! is it gone?
    We prized it dearly; while it stood, we said,
    Our friend, the Gypsy Scholar, was not dead;
  While the tree lived, he in these fields lived on.   30

Too rare, too rare, grow now my visits here,
  But once I knew each field, each flower, each stick;
    And with the countryfolk acquaintance made
  By barn in threshing time, by new-built rick.

1. In the 1840s, at Oxford, Clough had been one of Arnold's closest friends. After the death of this fellow poet twenty years later, Arnold revisited the Thames valley countryside that they had explored together. The familiar scenes prompted him to review the changes wrought by time on the ideals shared in his Oxford days with Clough, ideals symbolized, in part, by a distant elm and by the story of the Scholar Gypsy. The survival of these ideals in the face of the difficulties of modern life is the subject of this elegy. Unlike Tennyson in such elegies as In Memoriam, Arnold rarely touches here on other kinds of immortality.

As a framework for his elegy, Arnold draws on the same Greek and Latin pastoral tradition from which Milton's Lycidas and Shelley's Adonais were derived. Hence Clough is referred to by one of the traditional names for a shepherd poet, Thyrsis, and Arnold himself as Corydon. The sense of distancing that results from this traditional elegiac mode is reduced considerably by the realism of the setting with its bleak wintry landscape at twilight, a landscape that is brightened, in turn, by evocations of the return of hopeful springtime.

2. The villages of North Hinksey and South Hinksey.
3. Sibylla Kerr had been the proprietress of a tavern in South Hinksey.

Here, too, our shepherd pipes we first assayed.   35
    Ah me! this many a year
My pipe is lost, my shepherd's holiday!
    Needs must I lose them, needs with heavy heart
    Into the world and wave of men depart;
But Thyrsis of his own will went away.[4]   40

It irked him to be here, he could not rest.
    He loved each simple joy the country yields,
      He loved his mates; but yet he could not keep,[5]
    For that a shadow loured on the fields,
      Here with the shepherds and the silly[6] sheep.   45
        Some life of men unblest
    He knew, which made him droop, and filled his head.
      He went; his piping took a troubled sound
      Of storms[7] that rage outside our happy ground;
    He could not wait their passing, he is dead.   50

So, some tempestuous morn in early June,
    When the year's primal burst of bloom is o'er,
      Before the roses and the longest day—
    When garden walks and all the grassy floor
      With blossoms red and white of fallen May   55
        And chestnut flowers are strewn—
    So have I heard the cuckoo's parting cry,
      From the wet field, through the vexed garden trees,
      Come with the volleying rain and tossing breeze:
    The bloom is gone, and with the bloom go I!   60

Too quick despairer, wherefore wilt thou go?
    Soon will the high Midsummer pomps come on,
      Soon will the musk carnations break and swell,
    Soon shall we have gold-dusted snapdragon,
      Sweet-William with his homely cottage-smell,   65
        And stocks in fragrant blow;
    Roses that down the alleys shine afar,
      And open, jasmine-muffled lattices,
      And groups under the dreaming garden trees,
    And the full moon, and the white evening star.   70

He hearkens not! light comer, he is flown!
    What matters it? next year he will return,
      And we shall have him in the sweet spring days,
    With whitening hedges, and uncrumpling fern,
      And bluebells trembling by the forest ways,   75
        And scent of hay new-mown.
    But Thyrsis never more we swains shall see,
      See him come back, and cut a smoother reed,

---

4. Arnold left Oxford out of the necessity for earning a   5. Stay.
living; Clough left as a matter of principle when in   6. Innocent.
1848 he resigned a fellowship rather than subscribe to   7. Religious and political controversies.
the creed of the Anglican church.

And blow a strain the world at last shall heed—
For Time, not Corydon, hath conquered thee!   80

Alack, for Corydon no rival now!—
  But when Sicilian shepherds lost a mate,
    Some good survivor with his flute would go,
  Piping a ditty sad for Bion's fate;[8]
    And cross the unpermitted ferry's flow,[9]   85
      And relax Pluto's brow,
  And make leap up with joy the beauteous head
    Of Proserpine, among whose crownèd hair
    Are flowers first opened on Sicilian air,
  And flute his friend, like Orpheus, from the dead.[1]   90

O easy access to the hearer's grace
  When Dorian shepherds[2] sang to Proserpine!
    For she herself had trod Sicilian fields,
  She knew the Dorian water's gush divine,
    She knew each lily white which Enna yields,[3]   95
      Each rose with blushing face;
  She loved the Dorian pipe, the Dorian strain.
    But ah, of our poor Thames she never heard!
    Her foot the Cumner cowslips never stirred;
  And we should tease her with our plaint in vain!   100

Well! wind-dispersed and vain the words will be,
  Yet, Thyrsis, let me give my grief its hour
    In the old haunt, and find our tree-topped hill!
  Who, if not I, for questing here hath power?
    I know the wood which hides the daffodil,   105
      I know the Fyfield tree,
  I know what white, what purple fritillaries[4]
    The grassy harvest of the river fields,
    Above by Ensham, down by Sandford, yields,
  And what sedged brooks are Thames's tributaries;   110

I know these slopes; who knows them if not I?—
  But many a dingle[5] on the loved hillside,
    With thorns once studded, old, white-blossomed trees,
  Where thick the cowslips grew, and far descried
    High towered the spikes of purple orchises,   115
      Hath since our day put by
  The coronals of that forgotten time;
    Down each green bank hath gone the plowboy's team,
    And only in the hidden brookside gleam
  Primroses, orphans of the flowery prime.   120

8. Moschus, a Greek poet, composed a pastoral elegy upon the death of the poet Bion in Sicily.
9. The river Styx across which the dead were ferried to the underworld where Pluto ruled with his queen, Proserpine. In spring, Proserpine's returning above ground in Sicily would cause the flowers to blossom.
1. Orpheus' music enabled him to enter the "unpermitted" realms of the dead and to bring his wife, Eurydice, back with him to the land of the living.
2. The Dorian Greeks had colonized Sicily, the home of pastoral poetry.
3. From a meadow near Enna, a Sicilian town, Proserpine had been carried off to the underworld by Pluto (or Dis).
4. Flowers commonly found in moist meadows.
5. Small deep valley.

Where is the girl, who by the boatman's door,
   Above the locks, above the boating throng,
     Unmoored our skiff when through the Wytham flats,
   Red loosestrife[6] and blond meadowsweet among
     And darting swallows and light water-gnats,   125
      We tracked the shy Thames shore?
   Where are the mowers, who, as the tiny swell
     Of our boat passing heaved the river grass,
     Stood with suspended scythe to see us pass?—
   They all are gone, and thou art gone as well!   130

Yes, thou art gone! and round me too the night
   In ever-nearing circle weaves her shade.
     I see her veil draw soft across the day,
   I feel her slowly chilling breath invade
     The cheek grown thin, the brown hair sprent[7] with grey;   135
      I feel her finger light
   Laid pausefully upon life's headlong train;
     The foot less prompt to meet the morning dew,
     The heart less bounding at emotion new,
   And hope, once crushed, less quick to spring again.   140

And long the way appears, which seemed so short
   To the less practiced eye of sanguine youth;
     And high the mountaintops, in cloudy air,
   The mountaintops where is the throne of Truth,
     Tops in life's morning sun so bright and bare!   145
      Unbreachable the fort
   Of the long-battered world uplifts its wall;
     And strange and vain the earthly turmoil grows,
     And near and real the charm of thy repose,
   And night as welcome as a friend would fall.   150

But hush! the upland hath a sudden loss
   Of quiet!—Look, adown the dusk hillside,
     A troop of Oxford hunters going home,
   As in old days, jovial and talking, ride!
     From hunting with the Berkshire hounds they come.   155
      Quick! let me fly, and cross
   Into yon farther field!—'Tis done; and see,
     Backed by the sunset, which doth glorify
     The orange and pale violet evening sky,
   Bare on its lonely ridge, the Tree! the Tree!   160

I take the omen! Eve lets down her veil,
   The white fog creeps from bush to bush about,
     The west unflushes, the high stars grow bright,
   And in the scattered farms the lights come out.
     I cannot reach the signal-tree tonight,   165
      Yet, happy omen, hail!

6. Flowers that grow on banks of streams.   7. Sprinkled.

Hear it from thy broad lucent Arno vale[8]
(For there thine earth-forgetting eyelids keep
The morningless and unawakening sleep
Under the flowery oleanders pale),   170

Hear it, O Thyrsis, still our tree is there! —
Ah, vain! These English fields, this upland dim,
These brambles pale with mist engarlanded,
That lone, sky-pointing tree, are not for him;
To a boon southern country he is fled,   175
And now in happier air,
Wandering with the great Mother's[9] train divine
(And purer or more subtle soul than thee,
I trow, the mighty Mother doth not see)
Within a folding of the Apennine,[1]   180

Thou hearest the immortal chants of old! —
Putting his sickle to the perilous grain
In the hot cornfield of the Phrygian king,[2]
For thee the Lityerses song again
Young Daphnis with his silver voice doth sing;   185
Sings his Sicilian fold,
His sheep, his hapless love, his blinded eyes —
And how a call celestial round him rang,
And heavenward from the fountain brink he sprang,
And all the marvel of the golden skies.   190

There thou art gone, and me thou leavest here
Sole in these fields! yet will I not despair.
Despair I will not, while I yet descry
'Neath the mild canopy of English air
That lonely tree against the western sky.   195
Still, still these slopes, 'tis clear,
Our Gypsy Scholar haunts, outliving thee!
Fields where soft sheep from cages pull the hay,
Woods with anemones in flower till May,
Know him a wanderer still; then why not me?   200

A fugitive and gracious light he seeks,
Shy to illumine; and I seek it too.
This does not come with houses or with gold,

---

8. Clough was buried in Florence, which is situated in the valley of the Arno River.
9. Demeter (whose name may mean Earth Mother) was worshiped as the goddess of agriculture. The "immortal chants" (line 181) would be sung in her honor by her followers, members of the "train divine" (line 177).
1. Mountains near Florence.
2. Arnold includes a note from Servius's commentary on Virgil's *Eclogues*: "Daphnis, the ideal Sicilian shepherd of Greek pastoral poetry, was said to have followed into Phrygia his mistress Piplea, who had been carried off by robbers, and to have found her in the power of the king of Phrygia, Lityerses. Lityerses used to make strangers try a contest with him in reaping

corn, and to put them to death if he overcame them. Hercules arrived in time to save Daphnis, took upon himself the reaping contest with Lityerses, overcame him, and slew him. The Lityerses song connected with this tradition was, like the Linus song, one of the early plaintive strains of Greek popular poetry, and used to be sung by corn reapers. Other traditions represented Daphnis as beloved by a nymph who exacted from him an oath to love no one else. He fell in love with a princess, and was struck blind by the jealous nymph. Mercury, who was his father, raised him to heaven, and made a fountain spring up in the place from which he ascended. At this fountain the Sicilians offered yearly sacrifices."

With place, with honor, and a flattering crew;
  'Tis not in the world's market bought and sold—   205
    But the smooth-slipping weeks
Drop by, and leave its seeker still untired;
  Out of the heed of mortals he is gone,
  He wends unfollowed, he must house alone;
Yet on he fares, by his own heart inspired.   210

Thou too, O Thyrsis, on like quest wast bound;
  Thou wanderedst with me for a little hour!
    Men gave thee nothing; but this happy quest,
If men esteemed thee feeble, gave thee power,
    If men procured thee trouble, gave thee rest.   215
    And this rude Cumner ground,
Its fir-topped Hurst, its farms, its quiet fields,
  Here cam'st thou in thy jocund youthful time,
  Here was thine height of strength, thy golden prime!
And still the haunt beloved a virtue yields.   220

What though the music of thy rustic flute
  Kept not for long its happy, country tone;
    Lost it too soon, and learnt a stormy note[3]
Of men contention-tossed, of men who groan,
    Which tasked thy pipe too sore, and tired thy throat—   225
    It failed, and thou wast mute!
Yet hadst thou always visions of our light,
  And long with men of care thou couldst not stay,
  And soon thy foot resumed its wandering way,
Left human haunt, and on alone till night.   230

Too rare, too rare, grow now my visits here!
  'Mid city noise, not, as with thee of yore,
    Thyrsis! in reach of sheep-bells is my home.
—Then through the great town's harsh, heart-wearying roar,
    Let in thy voice a whisper often come,   235
      To chase fatigue and fear:
Why faintest thou? I wandered till I died.
  Roam on! The light we sought is shining still.
  Dost thou ask proof? Our tree yet crowns the hill,
Our Scholar travels yet the loved hillside.   240
                             1866

Growing Old[1]

  What is it to grow old?
  Is it to lose the glory of the form,
  The luster of the eye?

---

3. Clough's poetry often dealt with contemporary religious problems.
1. This poem may have been prompted as a rejoinder to Browning's enthusiastic picture of old age in *Rabbi Ben Ezra* (1864).

Is it for beauty to forego her wreath?
—Yes, but not this alone.   5

Is it to feel our strength—
Not our bloom only, but our strength—decay?
Is it to feel each limb
Grow stiffer, every function less exact,
Each nerve more loosely strung?   10

Yes, this, and more; but not
Ah, 'tis not what in youth we dreamed 'twould be!
'Tis not to have our life
Mellowed and softened as with sunset glow,
A golden day's decline.   15

'Tis not to see the world
As from a height, with rapt prophetic eyes,
And heart profoundly stirred;
And weep, and feel the fullness of the past,
The years that are no more.   20

It is to spend long days
And not once feel that we were ever young;
It is to add, immured
In the hot prison of the present, month
To month with weary pain.   25

It is to suffer this,
And feel but half, and feebly, what we feel.
Deep in our hidden heart
Festers the dull remembrance of a change,
But no emotion—none.   30

It is—last stage of all—
When we are frozen up within, and quite
The phantom of ourselves,
To hear the world applaud the hollow ghost
Which blamed the living man.   35

                                                                            1867

From The Function of Criticism at the Present Time[1]

Many objections have been made to a proposition which, in some remarks
of mine on translating Homer,[2] I ventured to put forth; a proposition about
criticism, and its importance at the present day. I said: "Of the literature of

---

1. This essay served as an introduction to *Essays in Criticism* (1865). As a declaration of intentions it can serve as a standard for measuring his total accomplishment in criticism. The essay makes us aware that criticism, for Arnold, meant a great deal more than casual book reviewing or mere censoriousness. He was not a Utilitarian, yet his object in this essay is to show that

good criticism is useful. Creative writers, he argues, can profit in a special way from good criticism, but all of us can also derive from it benefits of the greatest value. In particular, we may develop a civilized attitude of mind in which to examine the social, political, aesthetic, and religious problems that confront us.
2. *On Translating Homer* (1861).

France and Germany, as of the intellect of Europe in general, the main effort, for now many years, has been a critical effort; the endeavor, in all branches of knowledge, theology, philosophy, history, art, science, to see the object as in itself it really is." I added, that owing to the operation in English literature of certain causes, "almost the last thing for which one would come to English literature is just that very thing which now Europe most desires—criticism"; and that the power and value of English literature was thereby impaired. More than one rejoinder declared that the importance I here assigned to criticism was excessive, and asserted the inherent superiority of the creative effort of the human spirit over its critical effort. And the other day, having been led by a Mr. Shairp's excellent notice of Wordsworth[3] to turn again to his biography, I found, in the words of this great man, whom I, for one, must always listen to with the profoundest respect, a sentence passed on the critic's business, which seems to justify every possible disparagement of it. Wordsworth says in one of his letters:

> The writers in these publications (the Reviews), while they prosecute their inglorious employment, cannot be supposed to be in a state of mind very favorable for being affected by the finer influences of a thing so pure as genuine poetry.

And a trustworthy reporter of his conversation quotes a more elaborate judgment to the same effect:

> Wordsworth holds the critical power very low, infinitely lower than the inventive; and he said today that if the quantity of time consumed in writing critiques on the works of others were given to original composition, of whatever kind it might be, it would be much better employed; it would make a man find out sooner his own level, and it would do infinitely less mischief. A false or malicious criticism may do much injury to the minds of others; a stupid invention, either in prose or verse, is quite harmless.

It is almost too much to expect of poor human nature, that a man capable of producing some effect in one line of literature, should, for the greater good of society, voluntarily doom himself to impotence and obscurity in another. Still less is this to be expected from men addicted to the composition of the "false or malicious criticism" of which Wordsworth speaks. However, everybody would admit that a false or malicious criticism had better never have been written. Everybody, too, would be willing to admit, as a general proposition, that the critical faculty is lower than the inventive. But is it true that criticism is really, in itself, a baneful and injurious employment; is it true that all time given to writing critiques on the works of others would be much better employed if it were given to original composition, of whatever kind this may be? Is it true that Johnson had better have gone on producing more *Irenes*[4]

---

3. J. C. Shairp's essay *Wordsworth: The Man and the Poet* was published in 1864. Arnold comments in a footnote: "I cannot help thinking that a practice, common in England during the last century, and still followed in France, of printing a notice of this kind—a notice by a competent critic—to serve as an introduction to an eminent author's works, might be revived among us with advantage. To introduce all succeeding editions of Wordsworth, Mr. Shairp's notice might, it seems to me, excellently serve; it is written from the point of view of an admirer, nay, of a disciple, and that is right; but then the disciple must be also, as in this case he is, a critic, a man of letters, not, as too often happens, some relation or friend with no qualification for his task except affection for his author."

4. *Irene* is the name of a clumsy play by Samuel Johnson.

instead of writing his *Lives of the Poets*; nay, is it certain that Wordsworth himself was better employed in making his Ecclesiastical Sonnets than when he made his celebrated Preface[5] so full of criticism, and criticism of the works of others? Wordsworth was himself a great critic, and it is to be sincerely regretted that he has not left us more criticism; Goethe was one of the greatest of critics, and we may sincerely congratulate ourselves that he has left us so much criticism. Without wasting time over the exaggeration which Wordsworth's judgment on criticism clearly contains, or over an attempt to trace the causes—not difficult, I think, to be traced—which may have led Wordsworth to this exaggeration, a critic may with advantage seize an occasion for trying his own conscience, and for asking himself of what real service, at any given moment, the practice of criticism either is or may be made to his own mind and spirit, and to the minds and spirits of others.

The critical power is of lower rank than the creative. True; but in assenting to this proposition, one or two things are to be kept in mind. It is undeniable that the exercise of a creative power, that a free creative activity, is the highest function of man; it is proved to be so by man's finding in it his true happiness. But it is undeniable, also, that men may have the sense of exercising this free creative activity in other ways than in producing great works of literature or art; if it were not so, all but a very few men would be shut out from the true happiness of all men. They may have it in well-doing, they may have it in learning, they may have it even in criticizing. This is one thing to be kept in mind. Another is, that the exercise of the creative power in the production of great works of literature or art, however high this exercise of it may rank, is not at all epochs and under all conditions possible; and that therefore labor may be vainly spent in attempting it, which might with more fruit be used in preparing for it, in rendering it possible. This creative power works with elements, with materials; what if it has not those materials, those elements, ready for its use? In that case it must surely wait till they are ready. Now, in literature—I will limit myself to literature, for it is about literature that the question arises—the elements with which the creative power works are ideas; the best ideas on every matter which literature touches, current at the time. At any rate we may lay it down as certain that in modern literature no manifestation of the creative power not working with these can be very important or fruitful. And I say *current* at the time, not merely accessible at the time; for creative literary genius does not principally show itself in discovering new ideas, that is rather the business of the philosopher. The grand work of literary genius is a work of synthesis and exposition, not of analysis and discovery; its gift lies in the faculty of being happily inspired by a certain intellectual and spiritual atmosphere, by a certain order of ideas, when it finds itself in them; of dealing divinely with these ideas, presenting them in the most effective and attractive combinations—making beautiful works with them, in short. But it must have the atmosphere, it must find itself amidst the order of ideas, in order to work freely; and these it is not so easy to command. This is why great creative epochs in literature are so rare, this is why there is so much that is unsatisfactory in the productions of many men of real genius; because, for the creation of a masterwork of literature two powers must concur, the power of the man and the power of the moment, and the man is not enough without the moment; the

5. The preface to *Lyrical Ballads* (1800). "The Ecclesiastical Sonnets" are a sonnet sequence by Wordsworth, usually regarded as minor verse.

creative power has, for its happy exercise, appointed elements, and those elements are not in its own control.

Nay, they are more within the control of the critical power. It is the business of the critical power, as I said in the words already quoted, "in all branches of knowledge, theology, philosophy, history, art, science, to see the object as in itself it really is." Thus it tends, at last, to make an intellectual situation of which the creative power can profitably avail itself. It tends to establish an order of ideas, if not absolutely true, yet true by comparison with that which it displaces; to make the best ideas prevail. Presently these new ideas reach society, the touch of truth is the touch of life, and there is a stir and growth everywhere; out of this stir and growth come the creative epochs of literature.

Or, to narrow our range, and quit these considerations of the general march of genius and of society—considerations which are apt to become too abstract and impalpable—everyone can see that a poet, for instance, ought to know life and the world before dealing with them in poetry; and life and the world being in modern times very complex things, the creation of a modern poet, to be worth much, implies a great critical effort behind it; else it must be a comparatively poor, barren, and short-lived affair. This is why Byron's poetry had so little endurance in it, and Goethe's so much; both Byron and Goethe had a great productive power, but Goethe's was nourished by a great critical effort providing the true materials for it, and Byron's was not; Goethe knew life and the world, the poet's necessary subjects, much more comprehensively and thoroughly than Byron. He knew a great deal more of them, and he knew them much more as they really are.

It has long seemed to me that the burst of creative activity in our literature, through the first quarter of this century, had about it in fact something premature; and that from this cause its productions are doomed, most of them, in spite of the sanguine hopes which accompanied and do still accompany them, to prove hardly more lasting than the productions of far less splendid epochs. And this prematureness comes from its having proceeded without having its proper data, without sufficient materials to work with. In other words, the English poetry of the first quarter of this century, with plenty of energy, plenty of creative force, did not know enough. This makes Byron so empty of matter, Shelley so incoherent, Wordsworth even, profound as he is, yet so wanting in completeness and variety. Wordsworth cared little for books, and disparaged Goethe. I admire Wordsworth, as he is, so much that I cannot wish him different; and it is vain, no doubt, to imagine such a man different from what he is, to suppose that he *could* have been different. But surely the one thing wanting to make Wordsworth an even greater poet than he is—his thought richer, and his influence of wider application—was that he should have read more books, among them, no doubt, those of that Goethe whom he disparaged without reading him.

But to speak of books and reading may easily lead to a misunderstanding here. It was not really books and reading that lacked to our poetry at this epoch: Shelley had plenty of reading, Coleridge had immense reading. Pindar and Sophocles—as we all say so glibly, and often with so little discernment of the real import of what we are saying—had not many books; Shakespeare was no deep reader. True; but in the Greece of Pindar and Sophocles, in the England of Shakespeare, the poet lived in a current of ideas in the highest degree animating and nourishing to the creative power; society was, in the fullest measure, permeated by fresh thought, intelligent and alive. And this state of things is the true basis for the creative power's exercise, in this it finds its data, its materials, truly ready for its hand; all the books and reading in the world are only valuable as they are helps to this. Even when this does not actually exist, books and reading may enable a man to construct a kind of semblance of it in his own mind, a world of knowledge and intelligence in which he may live and work. This is by no means an equivalent to the artist for the nationally diffused life and thought of the epochs of Sophocles or Shakespeare; but, besides that it may be a means of preparation for such epochs, it does really constitute, if many share in it, a quickening and sustaining atmosphere of great value. Such an atmosphere the many-sided learning and the long and widely combined critical effort of Germany formed for Goethe, when he lived and worked. There was no national glow of life and thought there as in the Athens of Pericles[6] or the England of Elizabeth. That was the poet's weakness. But there was a sort of equivalent for it in the complete culture and unfettered thinking of a large body of Germans. That was his strength. In the England of the first quarter of this century there was neither a national glow of life and thought, such as we had in the age of Elizabeth, nor yet a culture and a force of learning and criticism such as were to be found in Germany. Therefore the creative power of poetry wanted, for success in the highest sense, materials and a basis; a thorough interpretation of the world was necessarily denied to it.

At first sight it seems strange that out of the immense stir of the French Revolution and its age should not have come a crop of works of genius equal to that which came out of the stir of the great productive time of Greece, or out of that of the Renascence, with its powerful episode the Reformation. But the truth is that the stir of the French Revolution took a character which essentially distinguished it from such movements as these. These were, in the main, disinterestedly intellectual and spiritual movements; movements in which the human spirit looked for its satisfaction in itself and in the increased play of its own activity. The French Revolution took a political, practical character. The movement, which went on in France under the old *régime*, from 1700 to 1789, was far more really akin than that of the Revolution itself to the movement of the Renascence; the France of Voltaire and Rousseau told far more powerfully upon the mind of Europe than the France of the Revolution. Goethe reproached this last expressly with having "thrown quiet culture back." Nay, and the true key to how much in our Byron, even in our Wordsworth, is this!—that they had their source in a great movement of feeling, not in a great movement of mind. The French Revolution, however—that object of so much blind love and so much blind hatred—found undoubtedly its motive power in the intelligence of men, and not in their practical sense; this is what distinguishes it from the English Revolution of Charles the First's time. This is what makes it a more spiritual event than our Revolution, an event of much more powerful and worldwide interest, though practically less successful; it appeals to an order of ideas which are universal, certain, permanent. 1789 asked of a thing, Is it rational? 1642 asked of a thing, Is it legal? or, when it went furthest, Is it according to conscience? This is the English fashion, a

---

6. Pericles (d. 429 B.C.), the leading statesman of Athens during a period of the city's most outstanding achievements in art, literature, and politics.

fashion to be treated, within its own sphere, with the highest respect; for its success, within its own sphere, has been prodigious. But what is law in one place is not law in another; what is law here today is not law even here tomorrow; and as for conscience, what is binding on one man's conscience is not binding on another's. The old woman who threw her stool at the head of the surpliced minister in St. Giles's Church at Edinburgh[7] obeyed an impulse to which millions of the human race may be permitted to remain strangers. But the prescriptions of reason are absolute, unchanging, of universal validity; *to count by tens is the easiest way of counting*—that is a proposition of which everyone, from here to the Antipodes, feels the force; at least I should say so if we did not live in a country where it is not impossible that any morning we may find a letter in the *Times* declaring that a decimal coinage is an absurdity.[8] That a whole nation should have been penetrated with an enthusiasm for pure reason, and with an ardent zeal for making its prescriptions triumph, is a very remarkable thing, when we consider how little of mind, or anything so worthy and quickening as mind, comes into the motives which alone, in general, impel great masses of men. In spite of the extravagant direction given to this enthusiasm, in spite of the crimes and follies in which it lost itself, the French Revolution derives from the force, truth, and universality of the ideas which it took for its law, and from the passion with which it could inspire a multitude for these ideas, a unique and still living power; it is—it will probably long remain—the greatest, the most animating event in history. And as no sincere passion for the things of the mind, even though it turn out in many respects an unfortunate passion, is ever quite thrown away and quite barren of good, France has reaped from hers one fruit—the natural and legitimate fruit though not precisely the grand fruit she expected: she is the country in Europe where *the people* is most alive.

But the mania for giving an immediate political and practical application to all these fine ideas of the reason was fatal. Here an Englishman is in his element: on this theme we can all go on for hours. And all we are in the habit of saying on it has undoubtedly a great deal of truth. Ideas cannot be too much prized in and for themselves, cannot be too much lived with; but to transport them abruptly into the world of politics and practice, violently to revolutionize this world to their bidding—that is quite another thing. There is the world of ideas and there is the world of practice; the French are often for suppressing the one and the English the other; but neither is to be suppressed. A member of the House of Commons said to me the other day: "That a thing is an anomaly, I consider to be no objection to it whatever." I venture to think he was wrong; that a thing is an anomaly *is* an objection to it, but absolutely and in the sphere of ideas: it is not necessarily, under such and such circumstances, or at such and such a moment, an objection to it in the sphere of politics and practice. Joubert[9] has said beautifully: "*C'est la force et le droit qui règlent toutes choses dans le monde; la force en attendant le droit.*"—"Force and right are the governors of this world; force till right is ready." *Force till*

7. In 1637 rioting broke out in Scotland against a new kind of church service prescribed by Charles I. The riot was started by an old woman hurling a stool at a clergyman.
8. In 1863 a proposal in Parliament to introduce the French decimal system for weights and measures had provoked articles in the *Times* defending the English system (of ounces and pounds or inches and feet) as more practical.
9. Joseph Joubert (1754–1824), French moralist about whom Arnold wrote one of his *Essays in Criticism*.

right is ready; and till right is ready, force, the existing order of things, is justified, is the legitimate ruler. But right is something moral, and implies inward recognition, free assent of the will; we are not ready for right—*right*, so far as we are concerned, is *not ready*—until we have attained this sense of seeing it and willing it. The way in which for us it may change and transform force, the existing order of things, and become, in its turn, the legitimate ruler of the world, should depend on the way in which, when our time comes, we see it and will it. Therefore for other people enamored of their own newly discerned right, to attempt to impose it upon us as ours, and violently to substitute their right for our force, is an act of tyranny, and to be resisted. It sets at nought the second great half of our maxim, *force till right is ready*. This was the grand error of the French Revolution; and its movement of ideas, by quitting the intellectual sphere and rushing furiously into the political sphere, ran, indeed a prodigious and memorable course, but produced no such intellectual fruit as the movement of ideas of the Renascence, and created, in opposition to itself, what I may call an *epoch of concentration*. The great force of that epoch of concentration was England; and the great voice of that epoch of concentration was Burke.[1] It is the fashion to treat Burke's writings on the French Revolution as superannuated and conquered by the event; as the eloquent but unphilosophical tirades of bigotry and prejudice. I will not deny that they are often disfigured by the violence and passion of the moment, and that in some directions Burke's view was bounded, and his observation therefore at fault. But on the whole, and for those who can make the needful corrections, what distinguishes these writings is their profound, permanent, fruitful, philosophical truth. They contain the true philosophy of an epoch of concentration, dissipate the heavy atmosphere which its own nature is apt to engender round it, and make its resistance rational instead of mechanical.

But Burke is so great because, almost alone in England, he brings thought to bear upon politics, he saturates politics with thought. It is his accident that his ideas were at the service of an epoch of concentration, not of an epoch of expansion; it is his characteristic that he so lived by ideas, and had such a source of them welling up within him, that he could float even an epoch of concentration and English Tory politics with them. It does not hurt him that Dr. Price[2] and the Liberals were enraged with him; it does not even hurt him that George the Third and the Tories were enchanted with him. His greatness is that he lived in a world which neither English Liberalism nor English Toryism is apt to enter—the world of ideas, not the world of catchwords and party habits. So far is it from being really true of him that he "to party gave up what was meant for mankind,"[3] that at the very end of his fierce struggle with the French Revolution, after all his invectives against its false pretensions, hollowness, and madness, with his sincere convictions of its mischievousness, he can close a memorandum on the best means of combating it, some of the last pages[4] he ever wrote—the *Thoughts on French Affairs*, in December 1791—with these striking words:

---

1. Edmund Burke (1729–1797), prominent statesman and author of *Reflections on the French Revolution* (1790), which expressed the conservative opposition to revolutionary theories.
2. Richard Price (1723–1791), a prorevolutionary clergyman who was an opponent of Burke's.

3. From Oliver Goldsmith's poem *Retaliation* (1774).
4. Arnold was mistaken; Burke continued to write for another six years after 1791. According to Arnold's editor, R. H. Super, the mistake was caused by misunderstanding a passage in one of Burke's letters.

The evil is stated, in my opinion, as it exists. The remedy must be where power, wisdom, and information, I hope, are more united with good intentions than they can be with me. I have done with this subject, I believe, forever. It has given me many anxious moments for the last two years. *If a great change is to be made in human affairs, the minds of men will be fitted to it; the general opinions and feelings will draw that way. Every fear, every hope will forward it; and then they who persist in opposing this mighty current in human affairs, will appear rather to resist the decrees of Providence itself, than the mere designs of men. They will not be resolute and firm, but perverse and obstinate.*

That return of Burke upon himself has always seemed to me one of the finest things in English literature, or indeed in any literature. That is what I call living by ideas: when one side of a question has long had your earnest support, when all your feelings are engaged, when you hear all round you no language but one, when your party talks this language like a steam engine and can imagine no other—still to be able to think, still to be irresistibly carried, if so it be, by the current of thought to the opposite side of the question, and, like Balaam,[5] to be unable to speak anything *but what the Lord has put in your mouth.* I know nothing more striking, and I must add that I know nothing more un-English.

For the Englishman in general is like my friend the Member of Parliament, and believes, point-blank, that for a thing to be an anomaly is absolutely no objection to it whatever. He is like the Lord Auckland of Burke's day, who, in a memorandum on the French Revolution, talks of certain "miscreants, assuming the name of philosophers, who have presumed themselves capable of establishing a new system of society." The Englishman has been called a political animal, and he values what is political and practical so much that ideas easily become objects of dislike in his eyes, and thinkers, "miscreants," because ideas and thinkers have rashly meddled with politics and practice. This would be all very well if the dislike and neglect confined themselves to ideas transported out of their own sphere, and meddling rashly with practice; but they are inevitably extended to ideas as such, and to the whole life of intelligence; practice is everything, a free play of the mind is nothing. The notion of the free play of the mind upon all subjects being a pleasure in itself, being an object of desire, being an essential provider of elements without which a nation's spirit, whatever compensations it may have for them, must, in the long run, die of inanition, hardly enters into an Englishman's thoughts. It is noticeable that the word *curiosity,* which in other languages is used in a good sense, to mean, as a high and fine quality of man's nature, just this disinterested love of a free play of the mind on all subjects, for its own sake— it is noticeable, I say, that this word has in our language no sense of the kind, no sense but a rather bad and disparaging one. But criticism, real criticism, is essentially the exercise of this very quality. It obeys an instinct prompting it to try to know the best that is known and thought in the world, irrespectively of practice, politics, and everything of the kind; and to value knowledge and thought as they approach this best, without the intrusion of any other considerations whatever. This is an instinct for which there is, I think, little original sympathy in the practical English nature, and what there was of it has under-

5. Cf. Numbers 22.38.

gone a long benumbing period of blight and suppression in the epoch of concentration which followed the French Revolution.

But epochs of concentration cannot well endure forever; epochs of expansion, in the due course of things, follow them. Such an epoch of expansion seems to be opening in this country. In the first place all danger of a hostile forcible pressure of foreign ideas upon our practice has long disappeared; like the traveler in the fable, therefore, we begin to wear our cloak a little more loosely.[6] Then, with a long peace, the ideas of Europe steal gradually and amicably in, and mingle, though in infinitesimally small quantities at a time, with our own notions. Then, too, in spite of all that is said about the absorbing and brutalizing influence of our passionate material progress, it seems to me indisputable that this progress is likely, though not certain, to lead in the end to an apparition of intellectual life; and that man, after he has made himself perfectly comfortable and has now to determine what to do with himself next, may begin to remember that he has a mind, and that the mind may be made the source of great pleasure. I grant it is mainly the privilege of faith, at present, to discern this end to our railways, our business, and our fortune-making; but we shall see if, here as elsewhere, faith is not in the end the true prophet. Our ease, our traveling, and our unbounded liberty to hold just as hard and securely as we please to the practice to which our notions have given birth, all tend to beget an inclination to deal a little more freely with these notions themselves, to canvass them a little, to penetrate a little into their real nature. Flutterings of curiosity, in the foreign sense of the word, appear amongst us, and it is in these that criticism must look to find its account. Criticism first; a time of true creative activity, perhaps—which, as I have said, must inevitably be preceded amongst us by a time of criticism—hereafter, when criticism has done its work.

It is of the last importance that English criticism should clearly discern what rule for its course, in order to avail itself of the field now opening to it, and to produce fruit for the future, it ought to take. The rule may be summed up in one word—*disinterestedness*.[7] And how is criticism to show disinterestedness? By keeping aloof from what is called "the practical view of things"; by resolutely following the law of its own nature, which is to be a free play of the mind on all subjects which it touches. By steadily refusing to lend itself to any of those ulterior, political, practical considerations about ideas, which plenty of people will be sure to attach to them, which perhaps ought often to be attached to them, which in this country at any rate are certain to be attached to them quite sufficiently, but which criticism has really nothing to do with. Its business is, as I have said, simply to know the best that is known and thought in the world, and by in its turn making this known, to create a current of true and fresh ideas. Its business is to do this with inflexible honesty, with due ability; but its business is to do no more, and to leave alone all questions of practical consequences and applications, questions which will never fail to have due prominence given to them. Else criticism, besides being really false to its own nature, merely continues in the old rut which it has hitherto followed in this country, and will certainly miss the chance now given to it. For what is at present the bane of criticism in this country? It is that practical

---

6. See Aesop's fable of the wind and the sun.
7. This key word in Arnold's argument connotes inde-
pendence and objectivity of mind. It should not be confused, as it often is, with mere lack of interest.

considerations cling to it and stifle it. It subserves interests not its own. Our organs of criticism are organs of men and parties having practical ends to serve, and with them those practical ends are the first thing and the play of mind the second; so much play of mind as is compatible with the prosecution of those practical ends is all that is wanted. An organ like the *Revue des Deux Mondes*,[8] having for its main function to understand and utter the best that is known and thought in the world, existing, it may be said, as just an organ for a free play of the mind, we have not. But we have the *Edinburgh Review*, existing as an organ of the old Whigs, and for as much play of mind as may suit its being that; we have the *Quarterly Review*, existing as an organ of the Tories, and for as much play of mind as may suit its being that; we have the *British Quarterly Review*, existing as an organ of the political Dissenters, and for as much play of mind as may suit its being that; we have the *Times*, existing as an organ of the common, satisfied, well-to-do Englishman, and for as much play of mind as may suit its being that. And so on through all the various fractions, political and religious, of our society; every fraction has, as such, its organ of criticism, but the notion of combining all fractions in the common pleasure of a free disinterested play of mind meets with no favor. Directly this play of mind wants to have more scope, and to forget the pressure of practical considerations a little, it is checked, it is made to feel the chain. We saw this the other day in the extinction, so much to be regretted, of the *Home and Foreign Review*.[9] Perhaps in no organ of criticism in this country was there so much knowledge, so much play of mind; but these could not save it. The *Dublin Review* subordinates play of mind to the practical business of English and Irish Catholicism, and lives. It must needs be that men should act in sects and parties, that each of these sects and parties should have its organ, and should make this organ subserve the interests of its action; but it would be well, too, that there should be a criticism, not the minister of these interests, not their enemy, but absolutely and entirely independent of them. No other criticism will ever attain any real authority or make any real way towards its end—the creating a current of true and fresh ideas.

It is because criticism has so little kept in the pure intellectual sphere, has so little detached itself from practice, has been so directly polemical and controversial, that it has so ill accomplished, in this country, its best spiritual work, which is to keep man from a self-satisfaction which is retarding and vulgarizing, to lead him towards perfection, by making his mind dwell upon what is excellent in itself, and the absolute beauty and fitness of things. A polemical practical criticism makes men blind even to the ideal imperfection of their practice, makes them willingly assert its ideal perfection, in order the better to secure it against attack; and clearly this is narrowing and baneful for them. If they were reassured on the practical side, speculative considerations of ideal perfection they might be brought to entertain, and their spiritual horizon would thus gradually widen. Sir Charles Adderley[1] says to the Warwickshire farmers:

> Talk of the improvement of breed! Why, the race we ourselves represent, the men and women, the old Anglo-Saxon race, are the best breed

8. An international magazine of exceptionally high quality, founded in Paris in 1829.
9. A liberal Catholic periodical, founded in 1862, which ceased publication in 1864.
1. Conservative politician and wealthy landowner (1814–1905).

in the whole world. . . . The absence of a too enervating climate, too unclouded skies, and a too luxurious nature, has produced so vigorous a race of people, and has rendered us so superior to all the world.

Mr. Roebuck[2] says to the Sheffield cutlers:

> I look around me and ask what is the state of England? Is not property safe? Is not every man able to say what he likes? Can you not walk from one end of England to the other in perfect security? I ask you whether, the world over or in past history, there is anything like it? Nothing. I pray that our unrivaled happiness may last.

Now obviously there is a peril for poor human nature in words and thoughts of such exuberant self-satisfaction, until we find ourselves safe in the streets of the Celestial City.

> Das wenige verschwindet leicht dem Blicke
> Der vorwärts sieht, wie viel noch übrig bleibt — [3]

says Goethe; "the little that is done seems nothing when we look forward and see how much we have yet to do." Clearly this is a better line of reflection for weak humanity, so long as it remains on this earthly field of labor and trial.

But neither Sir Charles Adderley nor Mr. Roebuck is by nature inaccessible to considerations of this sort. They only lose sight of them owing to the controversial life we all lead, and the practical form which all speculation takes with us. They have in view opponents whose aim is not ideal, but practical; and in their zeal to uphold their own practice against these innovators, they go so far as even to attribute to this practice an ideal perfection. Somebody has been wanting to introduce a six-pound franchise, or to abolish church-rates,[4] or to collect agricultural statistics by force, or to diminish local self-government. How natural, in reply to such proposals, very likely improper or ill-timed, to go a little beyond the mark and to say stoutly, "Such a race of people as we stand, so superior to all the world! The old Anglo-Saxon race, the best breed in the whole world! I pray that our unrivaled happiness may last! I ask you whether, the world over or in past history, there is anything like it?" And so long as criticism answers this dithyramb by insisting that the old Anglo-Saxon race would be still more superior to all others if it had no church-rates, or that our unrivaled happiness would last yet longer with a six-pound franchise, so long will the strain, "The best breed in the whole world!" swell louder and louder, everything ideal and refining will be lost out of sight, and both the assailed and their critics will remain in a sphere, to say the truth, perfectly unvital, a sphere in which spiritual progression is impossible. But let criticism leave church-rates and the franchise alone, and in the most candid spirit, without a single lurking thought of practical innovation, confront with our dithyramb this paragraph on which I stumbled in a newspaper immediately after reading Mr. Roebuck:

> A shocking child murder has just been committed at Nottingham. A girl named Wragg left the workhouse there on Saturday morning with

2. John Arthur Roebuck (1801–1879), radical politician and representative in Parliament for the industrial city of Sheffield.
3. Goethe, Iphigenie auf Tauris 1.2.91–92.

4. Taxes supporting the Church of England. "Six-pound franchise": a radical proposal to extend the right to vote to anyone owning land worth £6 annual rent.

her young illegitimate child. The child was soon afterwards found dead on Mapperly Hills, having been strangled. Wragg is in custody.

Nothing but that; but, in juxtaposition with the absolute eulogies of Sir Charles Adderley and Mr. Roebuck, how eloquent, how suggestive are those few lines! "Our old Anglo-Saxon breed, the best in the whole world!"—how much that is harsh and ill-favored there is in this best! *Wragg!* If we are to talk of ideal perfection, of "the best in the whole world," has anyone reflected what a touch of grossness in our race, what an original shortcoming in the more delicate spiritual perceptions, is shown by the natural growth amongst us of such hideous names—Higginbottom, Stiggins, Bugg! In Ionia and Attica they were luckier in this respect than "the best race in the world"; by the Ilissus[5] there was no Wragg, poor thing! And "our unrivaled happiness"—what an element of grimness, bareness, and hideousness mixes with it and blurs it; the workhouse, the dismal Mapperly Hills[6]—how dismal those who have seen them will remember—the gloom, the smoke, the cold, the strangled illegitimate child! "I ask you whether, the world over or in past history, there is anything like it?" Perhaps not, one is inclined to answer; but at any rate, in that case, the world is very much to be pitied. And the final touch—short, bleak and inhuman: *Wragg is in custody.* The sex lost in the confusion of our unrivaled happiness; or (shall I say?) the superfluous Christian name lopped off by the straightforward vigor of our old Anglo-Saxon breed! There is profit for the spirit in such contrasts as this; criticism serves the cause of perfection by establishing them. By eluding sterile conflict, by refusing to remain in the sphere where alone narrow and relative conceptions have any worth and validity, criticism may diminish its momentary importance, but only in this way has it a chance of gaining admittance for those wider and more perfect conceptions to which all its duty is really owed. Mr. Roebuck will have a poor opinion of an adversary who replies to his defiant songs of triumph only by murmuring under his breath, *Wragg is in custody;* but in no other way will these songs of triumph be induced gradually to moderate themselves, to get rid of what in them is excessive and offensive, and to fall into a softer and truer key.

It will be said that it is a very subtle and indirect action which I am thus prescribing for criticism, and that, by embracing in this manner the Indian virtue of detachment and abandoning the sphere of practical life, it condemns itself to a slow and obscure work. Slow and obscure it may be, but it is the only proper work of criticism. The mass of mankind will never have any ardent zeal for seeing things as they are; very inadequate ideas will always satisfy them. On these inadequate ideas reposes, and must repose, the general practice of the world. That is as much as saying that whoever sets himself to see things as they are will find himself one of a very small circle; but it is only by this small circle resolutely doing its own work that adequate ideas will ever get current at all. The rush and roar of practical life will always have a dizzying and attracting effect upon the most collected spectator, and tend to draw him into its vortex; most of all will this be the case where that life is so powerful as it is in England. But it is only by remaining collected, and refusing to lend himself to the point of view of the practical man, that the critic can do the

---

5. A stream in Attica, Greece.
6. Adjacent to the coal-mining and industrial area of Nottingham (later associated with the writings of D. H. Lawrence).

practical man any service, and it is only by the greatest sincerity in pursuing his own course, and by at last convincing even the practical man of his sincerity, that he can escape misunderstandings which perpetually threaten him.

For the practical man is not apt for fine distinctions, and yet in these distinctions truth and the highest culture greatly find their account. But it is not easy to lead a practical man—unless you reassure him as to your practical intentions, you have no chance of leading him—to see that a thing which he has always been used to look at from one side only, which he greatly values, and which, looked at from that side, quite deserves, perhaps, all the prizing and admiring which he bestows upon it—that this thing, looked at from another side, may appear much less beneficent and beautiful, and yet retain all its claims to our practical allegiance. Where shall we find language innocent enough, how shall we make the spotless purity of our intentions evident enough, to enable us to say to the political Englishman that the British Constitution itself, which, seen from the practical side, looks such a magnificent organ of progress and virtue, seen from the speculative side—with its compromises, its love of facts, its horror of theory, its studied avoidance of clear thoughts—that, seen from this side, our august Constitution sometimes looks—forgive me, shade of Lord Somers![7]—a colossal machine for the manufacture of Philistines?[8] How is Cobbett[9] to say this and not be misunderstood, blackened as he is with the smoke of a lifelong conflict in the field of political practice? how is Mr. Carlyle to say it and not be misunderstood, after his furious raid into this field with his *Latter-day Pamphlets?* how is Mr. Ruskin, after his pugnacious political economy?[1] I say, the critic must keep out of the region of immediate practice in the political, social, humanitarian sphere if he wants to make a beginning for that more free speculative treatment of things, which may perhaps one day make its benefits felt even in this sphere, but in a natural and thence irresistible manner.

* * *

If I have insisted so much on the course which criticism must take where politics and religion are concerned, it is because, where these burning matters are in question, it is most likely to go astray. I have wished, above all, to insist on the attitude which criticism should adopt towards things in general; on its right tone and temper of mind. But then comes another question as to the subject matter which literary criticism should most seek. Here, in general, its course is determined for it by the idea which is the law of its being; the idea of a disinterested endeavor to learn and propagate the best that is known and thought in the world, and thus to establish a current of fresh and true ideas. By the very nature of things, as England is not all the world, much of the best that is known and thought in the world cannot be of English growth, must be foreign; by the nature of things, again, it is just this that we are least likely to know, while English thought is streaming in upon us from all sides, and takes excellent care that we shall not be ignorant of its existence. The English critic of literature, therefore, must dwell much on foreign thought, and with particu-

---

7. John Somers (1651–1716), statesman responsible for formulating the Declaration of Rights.
8. The unenlightened middle classes, whose opposition to the defenders of culture is parallel to the biblical tribe that fought against the people of Israel, "the children of light." Arnold's repeated use of this parallel

has established the term in our language.
9. William Cobbett (1762–1835), vehement reformer whose political position anticipated that of Dickens.
1. Reference to *Unto this Last* (1862), in which Ruskin shifted from art criticism to an attack on traditional theories of economics.

lar heed on any part of it, which, while significant and fruitful in itself, is for any reason specially likely to escape him. Again, judging is often spoken of as the critic's one business, and so in some sense it is; but the judgment which almost insensibly forms itself in a fair and clear mind, along with fresh knowledge, is the valuable one; and thus knowledge, and ever fresh knowledge, must be the critic's great concern for himself. And it is by communicating fresh knowledge, and letting his own judgment pass along with it—but insensibly, and in the second place, not the first, as a sort of companion and clue, not as an abstract lawgiver—that the critic will generally do most good to his readers. Sometimes, no doubt, for the sake of establishing an author's place in literature, and his relation to a central standard (and if this is not done, how are we to get at our *best in the world?*) criticism may have to deal with a subject matter so familiar that fresh knowledge is out of the question, and then it must be all judgment; an enunciation and detailed application of principles. Here the great safeguard is never to let oneself become abstract, always to retain an intimate and lively consciousness of the truth of what one is saying, and, the moment this fails us, to be sure that something is wrong. Still under all circumstances, this mere judgment and application of principles is, in itself, not the most satisfactory work to the critic; like mathematics, it is tautological, and cannot well give us, like fresh learning, the sense of creative activity.

But stop, some one will say; all this talk is of no practical use to us whatever; this criticism of yours is not what we have in our minds when we speak of criticism; when we speak of critics and criticism, we mean critics and criticism of the current English literature of the day; when you offer to tell criticism its function, it is to this criticism that we expect you to address yourself. I am sorry for it, for I am afraid I must disappoint these expectations. I am bound by my own definition of criticism: *a disinterested endeavor to learn and propagate the best that is known and thought in the world.* How much of current English literature comes into this "best that is known and thought in the world"? Not very much I fear; certainly less, at this moment, than of the current literature of France or Germany. Well, then, am I to alter my definition of criticism, in order to meet the requirements of a number of practicing English critics, who, after all, are free in their choice of a business? That would be making criticism lend itself just to one of those alien practical considerations, which, I have said, are so fatal to it. One may say, indeed, to those who have to deal with the mass—so much better disregarded—of current English literature, that they may at all events endeavor, in dealing with this, to try it, so far as they can, by the standard of the best that is known and thought in the world; one may say, that to get anywhere near this standard, every critic should try and possess one great literature, at least, besides his own; and the more unlike his own, the better. But, after all, the criticism I am really concerned with—the criticism which alone can much help us for the future, the criticism which, throughout Europe, is at the present day meant, when so much stress is laid on the importance of criticism and the critical spirit—is a criticism which regards Europe as being, for intellectual and spiritual purposes, one great confederation, bound to a joint action and working to a common result, and whose members have, for their proper outfit, a knowledge of Greek, Roman, and Eastern antiquity, and of one another. Special, local, and temporary advantages being put out of account, that modern nation will in the intellectual and spiritual sphere make most progress, which most thoroughly carries out this program. And what is that but saying that we too, all of us, as individuals, the more thoroughly we carry it out, shall make the more progress?

There is so much inviting us!—what are we to take? what will nourish us in growth towards perfection? That is the question which, with the immense field of life and of literature lying before him, the critic has to answer; for himself first, and afterwards for others. In this idea of the critic's business the essays brought together in the following pages have had their origin; in this idea, widely different as are their subjects, they have, perhaps, their unity.

I conclude with what I said at the beginning: to have the sense of creative activity is the great happiness and the great proof of being alive, and it is not denied to criticism to have it; but then criticism must be sincere, simple, flexible, ardent, ever widening its knowledge. Then it may have, in no contemptible measure, a joyful sense of creative activity; a sense which a man of insight and conscience will prefer to what he might derive from a poor, starved, fragmentary, inadequate creation. And at some epochs no other creation is possible.

Still, in full measure, the sense of creative activity belongs only to genuine creation; in literature we must never forget that. But what true man of letters ever can forget it? It is no such common matter for a gifted nature to come into possession of a current of true and living ideas, and to produce amidst the inspiration of them, that we are likely to underrate it. The epochs of Aeschylus and Shakespeare make us feel their pre-eminence. In an epoch like those is, no doubt, the true life of literature; there is the promised land, towards which criticism can only beckon. That promised land it will not be ours to enter, and we shall die in the wilderness: but to have desired to enter it, to have saluted it from afar, is already, perhaps, the best distinction among contemporaries; it will certainly be the best title to esteem with posterity.

1864, 1865

From Culture and Anarchy[1]

From *Chapter 1. Sweetness and Light*

The impulse of the English race towards moral development and self-conquest has nowhere so powerfully manifested itself as in Puritanism. Nowhere has Puritanism found so adequate an expression as in the religious organiza-

---

1. As a critic of social life, Arnold sought to test Victorian institutions according to whether they seemed to him civilized. A characteristic quality of the civilized state of mind is summed up, for his purposes, in his formula "sweetness and light," a phrase suggesting reasonableness of temper and intellectual insight. Arnold derived the phrase from a fable contrasting the spider with the bee in Swift's *Battle of the Books*. The spider (representing a narrow, self-centered, and uncultured mind) spins out of itself "nothing at all but flybane and cobweb." The bee (representing a cultured mind that has drawn nourishment from the humanist tradition) ranges far and wide and brings to its hive honey and also wax out of which candles may be made. Therefore the bee, Swift says, furnishes humankind "with the two noblest of things, which are sweetness and light."

The following excerpts illustrate aspects of Arnold's indictment of the middle classes for their lack of sweetness and light. The first and third expose the narrowness and dullness of middle-class Puritan religious institutions in both the 17th and 19th centuries. The second, *Doing As One Likes*, shows the limitations of the middle-class political bias and the irresponsibility of laissez-faire. Here Arnold is most close to Carlyle and Ruskin. These three extracts indicate why it has been said that Matthew Arnold discovered the foibles of Main Street fifty years before Sinclair Lewis exposed them in his novels of American life.

tion of the Independents.[2] The modern Independents have a newspaper, the *Nonconformist*, written with great sincerity and ability. The motto, the standard, the profession of faith which this organ of theirs carries aloft, is: "The Dissidence of Dissent and the Protestantism of the Protestant religion." There is sweetness and light, and an ideal of complete harmonious human perfection! One need not go to culture and poetry to find language to judge it. Religion, with its instinct for perfection, supplies language to judge it, language, too, which is in our mouths every day. "Finally, be of one mind, united in feeling," says St. Peter.[3] There is an ideal which judges the Puritan ideal: "The Dissidence of Dissent and the Protestantism of the Protestant religion!" And religious organizations like this are what people believe in, rest in, would give their lives for! Such, I say, is the wonderful virtue of even the beginnings of perfection, of having conquered even the plain faults of our animality, that the religious organization which has helped us to do it can seem to us something precious, salutary, and to be propagated, even when it wears such a brand of imperfection on its forehead as this. And men have got such a habit of giving to the language of religion a special application, of making it a mere jargon, that for the condemnation which religion itself passes on the shortcomings of their religious organizations they have no ear; they are sure to cheat themselves and to explain this condemnation away. They can only be reached by the criticism which culture, like poetry, speaking of language not to be sophisticated, and resolutely testing these organizations by the ideal of a human perfection complete on all sides, applies to them.

But men of culture and poetry, it will be said, are again and again failing, and failing conspicuously, in the necessary first stage to a harmonious perfection, in the subduing of the great obvious faults of our animality, which it is the glory of these religious organizations to have helped us to subdue. True, they do often so fail. They have often been without the virtues as well as the faults of the Puritan; it has been one of their dangers that they so felt the Puritan's faults that they too much neglected the practice of his virtues. I will not, however, exculpate them at the Puritan's expense. They have often failed in morality, and morality is indispensable. And they have been punished for their failure, as the Puritan has been rewarded for his performance. They have been punished wherein they erred; but their ideal of beauty, of sweetness and light, and a human nature complete on all its sides, remains the true ideal of perfection still; just as the Puritan's ideal of perfection remains narrow and inadequate, although for what he did well he has been richly rewarded. Notwithstanding the mighty results of the Pilgrim Fathers' voyage, they and their standard of perfection are rightly judged when we figure to ourselves Shakespeare or Virgil—souls in whom sweetness and light, and all that in human nature is most humane, were eminent—accompanying them on their voyage, and think what intolerable company Shakespeare and Virgil would have found them! In the same way let us judge the religious organizations which we see all around us. Do not let us deny the good and the happiness which they have accomplished; but do not let us fail to see clearly that their idea of human perfection is narrow and inadequate, and that the Dissidence of Dissent and the Protestantism of the Protestant religion will never bring humanity

2. A 17th-century Puritan group (of which Cromwell was an adherent), allied with the Congregationalists.   3. 1 Peter 3.8.

to its true goal. As I said with regard to wealth: Let us look at the life of those who live in and for it—so I say with regard to the religious organizations. Look at the life imaged in such a newspaper as the *Nonconformist*—a life of jealousy of the Establishment,[4] disputes, tea-meetings, openings of chapels, sermons; and then think of it as an ideal of a human life completing itself on all sides, and aspiring with all its organs after sweetness, light, and perfection!

From *Chapter 2. Doing As One Likes*

*   *   *

When I began to speak of culture, I insisted on our bondage to machinery, on our proneness to value machinery as an end in itself, without looking beyond it to the end for which alone, in truth, it is valuable. Freedom, I said, was one of those things which we thus worshiped in itself, without enough regarding the ends for which freedom is to be desired. In our common notions and talk about freedom, we eminently show our idolatry of machinery. Our prevalent notion is—and I quoted a number of instances to prove it—that it is a most happy and important thing for a man merely to be able to do as he likes. On what he is to do when he is thus free to do as he likes, we do not lay so much stress. Our familiar praise of the British Constitution under which we live, is that it is a system of checks—a system which stops and paralyzes any power in interfering with the free action of individuals. To this effect Mr. Bright,[5] who loves to walk in the old ways of the Constitution, said forcibly in one of his great speeches, what many other people are every day saying less forcibly, that the central idea of English life and politics is *the assertion of personal liberty*. Evidently this is so; but evidently, also, as feudalism, which with its ideas, and habits of subordination was for many centuries silently behind the British Constitution, dies out, and we are left with nothing but our system of checks, and our notion of its being the great right and happiness of an Englishman to do as far as possible what he likes, we are in danger of drifting towards anarchy. We have not the notion, so familiar on the Continent and to antiquity, of *the State*—the nation in its collective and corporate character, entrusted with stringent powers for the general advantage, and controlling individual wills in the name of an interest wider than that of individuals. We say, what is very true, that this notion is often made instrumental to tyranny; we say that a State is in reality made up of the individuals who compose it, and that every individual is the best judge of his own interests. Our leading class is an aristocracy, and no aristocracy likes the notion of a State-authority greater than itself, with a stringent administrative machinery superseding the decorative inutilities of lord-lieutenancy, deputy-lieutenancy, and the *posse comitatus*,[6] which are all in its own hands. Our middle class, the great representative of trade and Dissent, with its maxims of every man for himself in business, every man for himself in religion, dreads a powerful administration which might somehow interfere with it; and besides, it has its own decorative inutilities of vestrymanship and guardianship, which are to this class what lord-lieutenancy and the county magistracy are to the aristo-

---

4. The Church of England or the Established Church.
5. John Bright, 19th-century orator and reformer.
6. "Power of the county": a feudal method of enforc-

ing law by local authorities instead of by agencies of the central government.

cratic class, and a stringent administration might either take these functions out of its hands, or prevent its exercising them in its own comfortable, independent manner, as at present.

Then as to our working class. This class, pressed constantly by the hard daily compulsion of material wants, is naturally the very center and stronghold of our national idea, that it is man's ideal right and felicity to do as he likes. I think I have somewhere related how M. Michelet[7] said to me of the people of France, that it was "a nation of barbarians civilized by the conscription." He meant that through their military service the idea of public duty and of discipline was brought to the mind of these masses, in other respects so raw and uncultivated. Our masses are quite as raw and uncultivated as the French; and so far from their having the idea of public duty and of discipline, superior to the individual's self-will, brought to their mind by a universal obligation of military service, such as that of the conscription—so far from their having this, the very idea of a conscription is so at variance with our English notion of the prime right and blessedness of doing as one likes, that I remember the manager of the Clay Cross works in Derbyshire told me during the Crimean war, when our want of soldiers was much felt and some people were talking of a conscription, that sooner than submit to a conscription the population of that district would flee to the mines, and lead a sort of Robin Hood life underground.

For a long time, as I have said, the strong feudal habits of subordination and deference continued to tell upon the working class. The modern spirit has now almost entirely dissolved those habits, and the anarchical tendency of our worship of freedom in and for itself, of our superstitious faith, as I say, in machinery, is becoming very manifest. More and more, because of this our blind faith in machinery, because of our want of light to enable us to look beyond machinery to the end for which machinery is valuable, this and that man, and this and that body of men, all over the country, are beginning to assert and put in practice an Englishman's right to do what he likes; his right to march where he likes, meet where he likes, enter where he likes, hoot as he likes, threaten as he likes, smash as he likes.[8] All this, I say, tends to anarchy; and though a number of excellent people, and particularly my friends of the Liberal or progressive party, as they call themselves, are kind enough to reassure us by saying that these are trifles, that a few transient outbreaks of rowdyism signify nothing, that our system of liberty is one which itself cures all the evils which it works, that the educated and intelligent classes stand in overwhelming strength and majestic repose, ready, like our military force in riots, to act at a moment's notice—yet one finds that one's Liberal friends generally say this because they have such faith in themselves and their nostrums, when they shall return, as the public welfare requires, to place and power. But this faith of theirs one cannot exactly share, when one has so long had them and their nostrums at work, and see that they have not prevented our coming to our present embarrassed condition. And one finds, also, that the outbreaks of rowdyism tend to become less and less of trifles, to become more frequent rather than less frequent; and that meanwhile our educated and intelligent classes remain in their majestic repose, and somehow or other,

7. Jules Michelet (1798–1874), French historian.
8. A reference to the riots of 1866 in which a London mob demolished the iron railings enclosing Hyde Park.

whatever happens, their overwhelming strength, like our military force in riots, never does act.

How indeed, *should* their overwhelming strength act, when the man who gives an inflammatory lecture, or breaks down the park railings, or invades a Secretary of State's office, is only following an Englishman's impulse to do as he likes; and our own conscience tells us that we ourselves have always regarded this impulse as something primary and sacred? Mr. Murphy[9] lectures at Birmingham, and showers on the Catholic population of that town "words," says the Home Secretary, "only fit to be addressed to thieves or murderers." What then? Mr. Murphy has his own reasons of several kinds. He suspects the Roman Catholic Church of designs upon Mrs. Murphy; and he says if mayors and magistrates do not care for their wives and daughters, he does. But, above all, he is doing as he likes; or, in worthier language, asserting his personal liberty. "I will carry out my lectures if they walk over my body as a dead corpse, and I say to the Mayor of Birmingham that he is my servant while I am in Birmingham, and as my servant he must do his duty and protect me." Touching and beautiful words, which find a sympathetic chord in every British bosom! The moment it is plainly put before us that a man is asserting his personal liberty, we are half disarmed; because we are believers in freedom, and not in some dream of a right reason to which the assertion of our freedom is to be subordinated. Accordingly, the Secretary of State had to say that although the lecturer's language was "only fit to be addressed to thieves or murderers," yet, "I do not think he is to be deprived, I do not think that anything I have said could justify the inference that he is to be deprived, of the right of protection in a place built by him for the purpose of these lectures; because the language was not language which afforded grounds for a criminal prosecution." No, nor to be silenced by Mayor, or Home Secretary, or any administrative authority on earth, simply on their notion of what is discreet and reasonable! This is in perfect consonance with our public opinion, and with our national love for the assertion of personal liberty.

* * *

From *Chapter 5. Porro Unum Est Necessarium*[1]

* * *

* * * Sweetness and light evidently have to do with the bent or side in humanity which we call Hellenic. Greek intelligence has obviously for its essence the instinct for what Plato calls the true, firm, intelligible law of things; the law of light, of seeing things as they are. Even in the natural sciences, where the Greeks had not time and means adequately to apply this instinct, and where we have gone a great deal further than they did, it is this instinct which is the root of the whole matter and the ground of all our success; and this instinct the world has mainly learnt of the Greeks, inasmuch as they are humanity's most signal manifestation of it. Greek art, again, Greek beauty, have their root in the same impulse to see things as they really are,

---

9. An orator whose inflammatory anti-Catholic public speech *The Errors of the Roman Church* led to rioting in Birmingham and other cities in 1867.
1. "But one thing is needful" (Luke 10.42). This chapter develops a contrast established in chap. 4 between

Hebraism (Puritan morality and energetic devotion to work) and *Hellenism* (cultivation of the aesthetic and intellectual understanding of life). The Puritan middle classes, according to Arnold, think that the "one thing needful" is the Hebraic form of virtue.

inasmuch as Greek art and beauty rest on fidelity to nature—the *best* nature—
and on a delicate discrimination of what this best nature is. To say we work
for sweetness and light, then, is only another way of saying that we work for
Hellenism. But, oh! cry many people, sweetness and light are not enough; you
must put strength or energy along with them, and make a kind of trinity of
strength, sweetness and light, and then, perhaps, you may do some good. That
is to say, we are to join Hebraism, strictness of the moral conscience, and
manful walking by the best light we have, together with Hellenism, inculcate
both, and rehearse the praises of both.

Or, rather, we may praise both in conjunction, but we must be careful to
praise Hebraism most. "Culture," says an acute, though somewhat rigid critic,
Mr. Sidgwick,[2] "diffuses sweetness and light. I do not undervalue these blessings, but religion gives fire and strength, and the world wants fire and strength
even more than sweetness and light." By religion, let me explain, Mr. Sidgwick here means particularly that Puritanism on the insufficiency of which I
have been commenting and to which he says I am unfair. Now, no doubt, it
is possible to be a fanatical partisan of light and the instincts which push us to
it, a fanatical enemy of strictness of moral conscience and the instincts which
push us to it. A fanaticism of this sort deforms and vulgarizes the well-known
work, in some respects so remarkable, of the late Mr. Buckle.[3] Such a fanaticism carries its own mark with it, in lacking sweetness; and its own penalty, in
that, lacking sweetness, it comes in the end to lack light too. And the Greeks—
the great exponents of humanity's bent for sweetness and light united, of its
perception that the truth of things must be at the same time beauty—singu-
larly escaped the fanaticism which we moderns, whether we Hellenize or
whether we Hebraize, are so apt to show. They arrived—though failing, as has
been said, to give adequate practical satisfaction to the claims of man's moral
side—at the idea of a comprehensive adjustment of the claims of both the
sides in man, the moral as well as the intellectual, of a full estimate of both,
and of a reconciliation of both; an idea which is philosophically of the greatest
value, and the best of lessons for us moderns. So we ought to have no difficulty
in conceding to Mr. Sidgwick that manful walking by the best light one has—
fire and strength as he calls it—has its high value as well as culture, the
endeavor to see things in their truth and beauty, the pursuit of sweetness and
light. But whether at this or that time, and to this or that set of persons, one
ought to insist most on the praises of fire and strength, or on the praises of
sweetness and light, must depend, one would think, on the circumstances and
needs of that particular time and those particular persons. And all that we
have been saying, and indeed any glance at the world around us, shows that
with us, with the most respectable and strongest part of us, the ruling force is
now, and long has been, a Puritan force—the care for fire and strength, strictness of conscience, Hebraism, rather than the care for sweetness and light,
spontaneity of consciousness, Hellenism.

Well, then, what is the good of our now rehearsing the praises of fire and
strength to ourselves, who dwell too exclusively on them already? When Mr.
Sidgwick says so broadly, that the world wants fire and strength even more

2. Henry Sidgwick (1838–1900), philosopher, whose   3. Henry Thomas Buckle (1821–1862), author of *A*
article on Arnold appeared in *Macmillan's Magazine*   *History of Civilization.*
(August 1867).

than sweetness and light, is he not carried away by a turn for broad generalization? does he not forget that the world is not all of one piece, and every piece with the same needs at the same time? It may be true that the Roman world at the beginning of our era, or Leo the Tenth's Court at the time of the Reformation, or French society in the eighteenth century,[4] needed fire and strength even more than sweetness and light. But can it be said that the Barbarians who overran the empire needed fire and strength even more than sweetness and light; or that the Puritans needed them more; or that Mr. Murphy, the Birmingham lecturer, and the Rev. W. Cattle[5] and his friends, need them more?

The Puritan's great danger is that he imagines himself in possession of a rule telling him the *unum necessarium*, or one thing needful, and that he then remains satisfied with a very crude conception of what this rule really is and what it tells him, thinks he has now knowledge and henceforth needs only to act, and, in this dangerous state of assurance and self-satisfaction, proceeds to give full swing to a number of the instincts of his ordinary self. Some of the instincts of his ordinary self he has, by the help of his rule of life, conquered; but others which he has not conquered by this help he is so far from perceiving to need subjugation, and to be instincts of an inferior self, that he even fancies it to be his right and duty, in virtue of having conquered a limited part of himself, to give unchecked swing to the remainder. He is, I say, a victim of Hebraism, of the tendency to cultivate strictness of conscience rather than spontaneity of consciousness. And what he wants is a larger conception of human nature, showing him the number of other points at which his nature must come to its best, besides the points which he himself knows and thinks of. There is no *unum necessarium*, or one thing needful, which can free human nature from the obligation of trying to come to its best at all these points. The real *unum necessarium* for us is to come to our best at all points. Instead of our "one thing needful," justifying in us vulgarity, hideousness, ignorance, violence—our vulgarity, hideousness, ignorance, violence, are really so many touchstones which try our one thing needful, and which prove that in the state, at any rate, in which we ourselves have it, it is not all we want. And as the force which encourages us to stand staunch and fast by the rule and ground we have is Hebraism, so the force which encourages us to go back upon this rule, and to try the very ground on which we appear to stand, is Hellenism—a turn for giving our consciousness free play and enlarging its range. And what I say is, not that Hellenism is always for everybody more wanted than Hebraism, but that for the Rev. W. Cattle at this particular moment, and for the great majority of us his fellow countrymen, it is more wanted.

*   *   *

1868, 1869

From The Study of Poetry[1]

"The future of poetry is immense, because in poetry, where it is worthy of its high destinies, our race, as time goes on, will find an ever surer and surer stay. There is not a creed which is not shaken, not an accredited dogma which is not shown to be questionable, not a received tradition which does not threaten to dissolve. Our religion has materialized itself in the fact, in the supposed fact; it has attached its emotion to the fact, and now the fact is failing it. But for poetry the idea is everything; the rest is a world of illusion, of divine illusion. Poetry attaches its emotion to the idea; the idea *is* the fact. The strongest part of our religion today is its unconscious poetry."

Let me be permitted to quote these words of my own, as uttering the thought which should, in my opinion, go with us and govern us in all our study of poetry. In the present work[2] it is the course of one great contributory stream to the world-river of poetry that we are invited to follow. We are here invited to trace the stream of English poetry. But whether we set ourselves, as here, to follow only one of the several streams that make the mighty river of poetry, or whether we seek to know them all, our governing thought should be the same. We should conceive of poetry worthily, and more highly than it has been the custom to conceive of it. We should conceive of it as capable of higher uses, and called to higher destinies, than those which in general men have assigned to it hitherto. More and more mankind will discover that we have to turn to poetry to interpret life for us, to console us, to sustain us. Without poetry, our science will appear incomplete; and most of what now passes with us for religion and philosophy will be replaced by poetry. Science, I say, will appear incomplete without it. For finely and truly does Wordsworth call poetry "the impassioned expression which is in the countenance of all science";[3] and what is a countenance without its expression? Again, Wordsworth finely and truly calls poetry "the breath and finer spirit of all knowledge": our religion, parading evidences such as those on which the popular mind relies now; our philosophy, pluming itself on its reasonings about causation and finite and infinite being; what are they but the shadows and dreams and false shows of knowledge? The day will come when we shall wonder at ourselves for having trusted to them, for having taken them seriously; and the more we perceive their hollowness, the more we shall prize "the breath and finer spirit of knowledge" offered to us by poetry.

But if we conceive thus highly of the destinies of poetry, we must also set our standard for poetry high, since poetry, to be capable of fulfilling such

---

1. Aside from its vindication of the importance of literature, this essay is an interesting example of the variety of Arnold's own reading. To know literature in only one language seemed to him not to know literature. His personal *Notebooks* show that throughout his active life he continued to read books in French, German, Italian, Latin, and Greek. His favorite authors in these languages are used by him as a means of testing English poetry. The testing is sometimes a severe one. Readers may also protest that despite Arnold's own wit, his essay is limited by an incomplete recognition of the values of comic literature, a shortcoming abundantly

evident in the discussion of Chaucer. Nevertheless, whether we agree or disagree with some of Arnold's verdicts, we can be attracted by the combination of traditionalism and impressionism on which these verdicts are based, and we can enjoy the memorable phrasemaking in which the verdicts are expressed. *The Study of Poetry* has been extraordinarily potent in shaping literary tastes in England and in America.
2. An anthology of English poetry for which this essay served as the introduction.
3. Preface to *Lyrical Ballads.*

high destinies, must be poetry of a high order of excellence. We must accustom ourselves to a high standard and to a strict judgment. * * *

The best poetry is what we want; the best poetry will be found to have a power of forming, sustaining, and delighting us, as nothing else can. A clearer, deeper sense of the best in poetry, and of the strength and joy to be drawn from it, is the most precious benefit which we can gather from a poetical collection such as the present. And yet in the very nature and conduct of such a collection there is inevitably something which tends to obscure in us the consciousness of what our benefit should be, and to distract us from the pursuit of it. We should therefore steadily set it before our minds at the outset, and should compel ourselves to revert constantly to the thought of it as we proceed.

Yes; constantly in reading poetry, a sense for the best, the really excellent, and of the strength and joy to be drawn from it, should be present in our minds and should govern our estimate of what we read. But this real estimate, the only true one, is liable to be superseded, if we are not watchful, by two other kinds of estimate, the historic estimate and the personal estimate, both of which are fallacious. A poet or a poem may count to us historically, they may count to us on grounds personal to ourselves, and they may count to us really. They may count to us historically. The course of development of a nation's language, thought, and poetry, is profoundly interesting; and by regarding a poet's work as a stage in this course of development we may easily bring ourselves to make it of more importance as poetry than in itself it really is, we may come to use a language of quite exaggerated praise in criticizing it; in short, to overrate it. So arises in our poetic judgments the fallacy caused by the estimate which we may call historic. Then, again, a poet or a poem may count to us on grounds personal to ourselves. Our personal affinities, likings, and circumstances, have great power to sway our estimate of this or that poet's work, and to make us attach more importance to it as poetry than in itself it really possesses, because to us it is, or has been, of high importance. Here also we overrate the object of our interest, and apply to it a language of praise which is quite exaggerated. And thus we get the source of a second fallacy in our poetic judgments—the fallacy caused by an estimate which we may call personal.

* * *

* * * The historic estimate is likely in especial to affect our judgment and our language when we are dealing with ancient poets; the personal estimate when we are dealing with poets our contemporaries, or at any rate modern. The exaggerations due to the historic estimate are not in themselves, perhaps, of very much gravity. Their report hardly enters the general ear; probably they do not always impose even on the literary men who adopt them. But they lead to a dangerous abuse of language. So we hear Caedmon,[4] amongst our own poets, compared to Milton. I have already noticed the enthusiasm of one accomplished French critic for "historic origins."[5] Another eminent French critic, M. Vitet, comments upon that famous document of the early poetry of

---

4. A 7th-century Old English poet.
5. Charles d'Héricault, a critic cited earlier, in a passage omitted here. Arnold had mildly reprimanded

him for his "historical" bias in praising a 15th-century poet, Clément Marot, at the expense of such classical 17th-century poets as Racine.

his nation, the *Chanson de Roland*.[6] It is indeed a most interesting document. The *joculator* or *jongleur*[7] Taillefer, who was with William the Conqueror's army at Hastings, marched before the Norman troops, so said the tradition, singing "of Charlemagne and of Roland and of Oliver, and of the vassals who died at Roncevaux"; and it is suggested that in the *Chanson de Roland* by one Turoldus or *Théroulde*, a poem preserved in a manuscript of the twelfth century in the Bodleian Library at Oxford, we have certainly the matter, perhaps even some of the words, of the chant which Taillefer sang. The poem has vigor and freshness; it is not without pathos. But M. Vitet is not satisfied with seeing in it a document of some poetic value, and of very high historic and linguistic value; he sees in it a grand and beautiful work, a monument of epic genius. In its general design he finds the grandiose conception, in its details he finds the constant union of simplicity with greatness, which are the marks, he truly says, of the genuine epic, and distinguish it from the artificial epic of literary ages. One thinks of Homer; this is the sort of praise which is given to Homer, and justly given. Higher praise there cannot well be, and it is the praise due to epic poetry of the highest order only, and to no other. Let us try, then, the *Chanson de Roland* at its best. Roland, mortally wounded, lays himself down under a pine tree, with his face turned towards Spain and the enemy—

> De plusurs choses à remembrer li prist,
> De tantes teres cume li bers cunquist,
> De dulce France, des humes de sun lign,
> De Carlemagne sun seignor ki l'nurrit.[8]

That is primitive work, I repeat, with an undeniable poetic quality of its own. It deserves such praise, and such praise is sufficient for it. But now turn to Homer—

> Hōs pháto toùs d'ēdē kátechen phusízoos aîa
> ēn Lakedaímoni aûthi phílē en patrídi gaíē.[9]

We are here in another world, another order of poetry altogether; here is rightly due such supreme praise as that which M. Vitet gives to the *Chanson de Roland*. If our words are to have any meaning, if our judgments are to have any solidity, we must not heap that supreme praise upon poetry of an order immeasurably inferior.

Indeed there can be no more useful help for discovering what poetry belongs to the class of the truly excellent, and can therefore do us most good, than to have always in one's mind lines and expressions of the great masters, and to apply them as a touchstone to other poetry. Of course we are not to require this other poetry to resemble them; it may be very dissimilar. But if we have any tact we shall find them, when we have lodged them well in our minds, an infallible touchstone for detecting the presence or absence of high poetic quality, and also the degree of this quality, in all other poetry which we

6. An 11th-century epic poem in Old French that tells of the wars of Charlemagne against the Moors in Spain and of the bravery of the French leaders Roland and Oliver.
7. Minstrel.
8. "Then began he to call many things to remembrance—all the lands which his valor conquered and pleasant France, and the men of his lineage, and Charlemagne his liege lord who nourished him." *Chanson de Roland* 3.939–42 [Arnold's note].
9. "So said she; they long since in Earth's soft arms were reposing, / There, in their own dear land, their fatherland, Lacedaemon." *Iliad* 3.243–44 (translated by Dr. Hawtrey) [Arnold's note].

may place beside them. Short passages, even single lines, will serve our turn quite sufficiently. Take the two lines which I have just quoted from Homer, the poet's comment on Helen's mention of her brothers—or take his

> A deilō, tí sphōi dómen Pēlēi ánakti
> thnētō? humeis d'estòn agērō t' athanátō te.
> ē hina dustēnoisi met' andrásin alge' echēton[1]

the address of Zeus to the horses of Peleus—or take finally his

> Kaì sé géron, tò prìn mèn akoúomen olbion eînai:[2]

the words of Achilles to Priam, a suppliant before him. Take that incomparable line and a half of Dante, Ugolino's tremendous words—

> Io no piangeva; sì dentro impietrai.
> Piangevan elli . . .[3]

take the lovely words of Beatrice to Virgil—

> Io son fatta da Dio, sua mercè, tale,
> Che la vostra miseria non mi tange,
> Nè fiamma d'esto incendio non m'assale . . .[4]

take the simple, but perfect, single line—

> In la sua volontade è nostra pace.[5]

Take of Shakespeare a line or two of Henry the Fourth's expostulation with sleep—

> Wilt thou upon the high and giddy mast
> Seal up the shipboy's eyes, and rock his brains
> In cradle of the rude imperious surge . . .[6]

and take, as well, Hamlet's dying request to Horatio—

> If thou didst ever hold me in thy heart,
> Absent thee from felicity awhile,
> And in this harsh world draw thy breath in pain,
> To tell my story . . .[7]

Take of Milton that Miltonic passage—

> Darkened so, yet shone
> Above them all the archangel; but his face
> Deep scars of thunder had intrenched, and care
> Sat on his faded cheek . . .[8]

add two such lines as—

> And courage never to submit or yield
> And what is else not to be overcome . . .[9]

---

1. "Ah, unhappy pair, why gave we you to King Peleus, to a mortal? but ye are without old age, and immortal. Was it that with men born to misery ye might have sorrow?" *Iliad* 17.443–45 [Arnold's note].
2. "Nay, and thou too, old man, in former days wast, as we hear, happy." *Iliad* 14.543 [Arnold's note].
3. "I wailed not, so of stone I grew within; they wailed." *Inferno* 33.49–50 [Arnold's note].
4. "Of such sort hath God, thanked be His mercy, made me, that your misery toucheth me not, neither doth the flame of this fire strike me." *Inferno* 2.91–93 [Arnold's note].
5. "In His will is our peace." *Paradiso* 3.85 [Arnold's note].
6. 2 *Henry IV* 3.1.18–20.
7. *Hamlet* 5.2.357–360.
8. *Paradise Lost* 1.599–602.
9. *Paradise Lost* 1.108–109.

and finish with the exquisite close to the loss of Proserpine, the loss

> . . . which cost Ceres all that pain
> To seek her through the world.[1]

These few lines, if we have tact and can use them, are enough even of themselves to keep clear and sound our judgments about poetry, to save us from fallacious estimates of it, to conduct us to a real estimate.

The specimens I have quoted differ widely from one another, but they have in common this: the possession of the very highest poetical quality. If we are thoroughly penetrated by their power, we shall find that we have acquired a sense enabling us, whatever poetry may be laid before us, to feel the degree in which a high poetical quality is present or wanting there. Critics give themselves great labor to draw out what in the abstract constitutes the characters of a high quality of poetry. It is much better simply to have recourse to concrete examples—to take specimens of poetry of the high, the very highest quality, and to say: The characters of a high quality of poetry are what is expressed *there.* They are far better recognized by being felt in the verse of the master, than by being perused in the prose of the critic. Nevertheless if we are urgently pressed to give some critical account of them, we may safely, perhaps, venture on laying down, not indeed how and why the characters arise, but where and in what they arise. They are in the matter and substance of the poetry, and they are in its manner and style. Both of these, the substance and matter on the one hand, the style and manner on the other, have a mark, an accent, of high beauty, worth, and power. But if we are asked to define this mark and accent in the abstract, our answer must be: No, for we should thereby be darkening the question, not clearing it. The mark and accent are as given by the substance and matter of that poetry, by the style and manner of that poetry, and of all other poetry which is akin to it in quality.

Only one thing we may add as to the substance and matter of poetry, guiding ourselves by Aristotle's profound observation that the superiority of poetry over history consists in its possessing a higher truth and a higher seriousness (philosophōteron kai spoudaióteron).[2] Let us add, therefore, to what we have said, this: that the substance and matter of the best poetry acquire their special character from possessing, in an eminent degree, truth and seriousness. We may add yet further, what is in itself evident, that to the style and manner of the best poetry their special character, their accent, is given by their diction, and, even yet more, by their movement. And though we distinguish between the two characters, the two accents, of superiority, yet they are nevertheless vitally connected one with the other. The superior character of truth and seriousness, in the matter and substance of the best poetry, is inseparable from the superiority of diction and movement marking its style and manner. The two superiorities are closely related, and are in steadfast proportion one to the other. So far as high poetic truth and seriousness are wanting to a poet's matter and substance, so far also, we may be sure, will a high poetic stamp of diction and movement be wanting to his style and manner. In proportion as this high stamp of diction and movement, again, is absent from a poet's style and manner, we shall find, also, that high poetic truth and seriousness are absent from his substance and matter.

---

1. *Paradise Lost* 4.271–272.   2. Aristotle, *Poetics* 9.

So stated, these are but dry generalities; their whole force lies in their application. And I could wish every student of poetry to make the application of them for himself. Made by himself, the application would impress itself upon his mind far more deeply than made by me. Neither will my limits allow me to make any full application of the generalities above propounded; but in the hope of bringing out, at any rate, some significance in them, and of establishing an important principle more firmly by their means, I will, in the space which remains to me, follow rapidly from the commencement the course of our English poetry with them in my view.

*   *   *

Chaucer's * * * poetical importance does not need the assistance of the historic estimate; it is real. He is a genuine source of joy and strength, which is flowing still for us and will flow always. He will be read, as time goes on, far more generally than he is read now. His language is a cause of difficulty for us; but so also, and I think in quite as great a degree, is the language of Burns. In Chaucer's case, as in that of Burns, it is a difficulty to be unhesitatingly accepted and overcome.

If we ask ourselves wherein consists the immense superiority of Chaucer's poetry over the romance poetry—why it is that in passing from this to Chaucer we suddenly feel ourselves to be in another world, we shall find that his superiority is both in the substance of his poetry and in the style of his poetry. His superiority in substance is given by his large, free, simple, clear yet kindly view of human life—so unlike the total want, in the romance poets, of all intelligent command of it. Chaucer has not their helplessness; he has gained the power to survey the world from a central, a truly human point of view. We have only to call to mind the Prologue to *The Canterbury Tales.* The right comment upon it is Dryden's: "It is sufficient to say, according to the proverb, that *here is God's plenty.*" And again: "He is a perpetual fountain of good sense."[3] It is by a large, free, sound representation of things, that poetry, this high criticism of life, has truth of substance; and Chaucer's poetry has truth of substance.

Of his style and manner, if we think first of the romance poetry and then of Chaucer's divine liquidness of diction, his divine fluidity of movement, it is difficult to speak temperately. They are irresistible, and justify all the rapture with which his successors speak of his "gold dewdrops of speech."[4] Johnson misses the point entirely when he finds fault with Dryden for ascribing to Chaucer the first refinement of our numbers, and says that Gower[5] also can show smooth numbers and easy rhymes. The refinement of our numbers means something far more than this. A nation may have versifiers with smooth numbers and easy rhymes, and yet may have no real poetry at all. Chaucer is the father of our splendid English poetry; he is our "well of English undefiled,"[6] because by the lovely charm of his diction, the lovely charm of his movement, he makes an epoch and founds a tradition. In Spenser, Shakespeare, Milton, Keats, we can follow the tradition of the liquid diction, the fluid movement, of Chaucer; at one time it is his liquid diction of which in

---

3. Both quotations are from Dryden's preface to his *Fables Ancient and Modern* (1700).
4. *The Life of Our Lady,* a poem by John Lydgate (ca. 1370–ca.1451).

5. John Gower (ca. 1325–1408), friend of Chaucer and author of the *Confessio Amantis,* a long poem in octosyllabic couplets.
6. Said of Chaucer by Spenser, *Faerie Queene* 4.2.32.

these poets we feel the virtue, and at another time it is his fluid movement.
And the virtue is irresistible.

Bounded as is my space, I must yet find room for an example of Chaucer's
virtue, as I have given examples to show the virtue of the great classics. I feel
disposed to say that a single line is enough to show the charm of Chaucer's
verse; that merely one line like this—

O martyr souded[7] in virginitee!

has a virtue of manner and movement such as we shall not find in all the verse
of romance poetry—but this is saying nothing. The virtue is such as we shall
not find, perhaps, in all English poetry, outside the poets whom I have named
as the special inheritors of Chaucer's tradition. A single line, however, is too
little if we have not the strain of Chaucer's verse well in our memory; let us
take a stanza. It is from *The Prioress's Tale*, the story of the Christian child
murdered in a Jewry—

> My throte is cut unto my nekke-bone
> Saidè this child, and as by way of kinde
> I should have deyd, yea, longè time agone;
> But Jesu Christ, as ye in bookès finde,
> Will that his glory last and be in minde,
> And for the worship of his mother dere
> Yet may I sing O *Alma* loud and clere.

Wordsworth has modernized this Tale, and to feel how delicate and evanescent is the charm of verse, we have only to read Wordsworth's first three lines
of this stanza after Chaucer's—

> My throat is cut unto the bone, I trow,
> Said this young child, and by the law of kind
> I should have died, yea, many hours ago.

The charm is departed. It is often said that the power of liquidness and fluidity
in Chaucer's verse was dependent upon a free, a licentious dealing with language, such as is now impossible; upon a liberty, such as Burns too enjoyed,
of making words like *neck, bird*, into a dissyllable by adding to them, and
words like *cause, rhyme*, into a dissyllable by sounding the *e* mute. It is true
that Chaucer's fluidity is conjoined with this liberty, and is admirably served
by it; but we ought not to say that it was dependent upon it. It was dependent
upon his talent. Other poets with a like liberty do not attain to the fluidity of
Chaucer; Burns himself does not attain to it. Poets, again, who have a talent
akin to Chaucer's, such as Shakespeare or Keats, have known how to attain to
his fluidity without the like liberty.

And yet Chaucer is not one of the great classics. His poetry transcends and
effaces, easily and without effort, all the romance poetry of Catholic Christendom; it transcends and effaces all the English poetry contemporary with it,
it transcends and effaces all the English poetry subsequent to it down to the
age of Elizabeth. Of such avail is poetic truth of substance, in its natural and
necessary union with poetic truth of style. And yet, I say, Chaucer is not one
of the great classics. He has not their accent. What is wanting to him is sug-

---

7. "The French *soudé*: soldered, fixed fast" [Arnold's note]. The line is from *The Canterbury Tales, The Prioress's
Tale* (line 127): Chaucer wrote "souded to" rather than "souded in."

gested by the mere mention of the name of the first great classic of Christendom, the immortal poet who died eighty years before Chaucer—Dante. The accent of such verse as

In la sua volontade è nostra pace . . .

is altogether beyond Chaucer's reach; we praise him, but we feel that this accent is out of the question for him. It may be said that it was necessarily out of the reach of any poet in the England of that stage of growth. Possibly; but we are to adopt a real, not a historic, estimate of poetry. However we may account for its absence, something is wanting, then, to the poetry of Chaucer, which poetry must have before it can be placed in the glorious class of the best. And there is no doubt what that something is. It is the spoudaiótes, the high and excellent seriousness, which Aristotle assigns as one of the grand virtues of poetry. The substance of Chaucer's poetry, his view of things and his criticism of life, has largeness, freedom, shrewdness, benignity; but it has not this high seriousness. Homer's criticism of life has it, Dante's has it, Shakespeare's has it. It is this chiefly which gives to our spirits what they can rest upon; and with the increasing demands of our modern ages upon poetry, this virtue of giving us what we can rest upon will be more and more highly esteemed. A voice from the slums of Paris, fifty or sixty years after Chaucer, the voice of poor Villon[8] out of his life of riot and crime, has at its happy moments (as, for instance, in the last stanza of *La Belle Heaulmière*)[9] more of this important poetic virtue of seriousness than all the productions of Chaucer. But its apparition in Villon, and in men like Villon, is fitful; the greatness of the great poets, the power of their criticism of life, is that their virtue is sustained.

To our praise, therefore, of Chaucer as a poet there must be this limitation: he lacks the high seriousness of the great classics, and therewith an important part of their virtue. Still, the main fact for us to bear in mind about Chaucer is his sterling value according to that real estimate which we firmly adopt for all poets. He has poetic truth of substance, though he has not high poetic seriousness, and corresponding to his truth of substance he has an exquisite virtue of style and manner. With him is born our real poetry.

For my present purpose I need not dwell on our Elizabethan poetry, or on the continuation and close of this poetry in Milton. We all of us profess to be agreed in the estimate of this poetry; we all of us recognize it as great poetry, our greatest, and Shakespeare and Milton as our poetical classics. The real estimate, here, has universal currency. With the next age of our poetry divergency and difficulty begin. An historic estimate of that poetry has established itself; and the question is, whether it will be found to coincide with the real estimate.

The age of Dryden, together with our whole eighteenth century which followed it, sincerely believed itself to have produced poetical classics of its own,

8. François Villon (1431–1484), French poet and vagabond.
9. The name *Heaulmière* is said to be derived from a headdress (helm) worn as a mask by courtesans. In Villon's ballad, a poor old creature of this class laments her days of youth and beauty. The last stanza of the ballad runs thus—"*Ainsi le bon temps regretons / Entre nous, pauvres vieilles sottes, / Assises bas, à croppetons, / Tout en ung tas comme pelottes; / A petit feu de* chenevottes / Tost allumées, tost estaincles, / Et jadis fusmes si mignottes! / Ainsi en prend à maintz et maintes.*" [It may be translated:] "Thus amongst ourselves we regret the good time, poor silly old things, low-seated on our heels, all in a heap like so many balls; by a little fire of hemp stalks, soon lighted, soon spent. And once we were such darlings! So fares it with many and many a one" [Arnold's note].

and even to have made advance, in poetry, beyond all its predecessors. Dryden regards as not seriously disputable the opinion "that the sweetness of English verse was never understood or practiced by our fathers."[1] Cowley could see nothing at all in Chaucer's poetry. Dryden heartily admired it, and, as we have seen, praised its matter admirably; but of its exquisite manner and movement all he can find to say is that "there is the rude sweetness of a Scotch tune in it, which is natural and pleasing, though not perfect."[2] Addison, wishing to praise Chaucer's numbers, compares them with Dryden's own. And all through the eighteenth century, and down even into our own times, the stereotyped phrase of approbation for good verse found in our early poetry has been, that it even approached the verse of Dryden, Addison, Pope, and Johnson.

Are Dryden and Pope poetical classics? Is the historic estimate, which represents them as such, and which has been so long established that it cannot easily give way, the real estimate? Wordsworth and Coleridge, as is well known, denied it; but the authority of Wordsworth and Coleridge does not weigh much with the young generation, and there are many signs to show that the eighteenth century and its judgments are coming into favor again. Are the favorite poets of the eighteenth century classics?

It is impossible within my present limits to discuss the question fully. And what man of letters would not shrink from seeming to dispose dictatorially of the claims of two men who are, at any rate, such masters in letters as Dryden and Pope; two men of such admirable talent, both of them, and one of them, Dryden, a man, on all sides, of such energetic and genial power? And yet, if we are to gain the full benefit from poetry, we must have the real estimate of it. I cast about for some mode of arriving, in the present case, at such an estimate without offense. And perhaps the best way is to begin, as it is easy to begin, with cordial praise.

When we find Chapman, the Elizabethan translator of Homer, expressing himself in his preface thus: "Though truth in her very nakedness sits in so deep a pit, that from Gades to Aurora and Ganges few eyes can sound her, I hope yet those few here will so discover and confirm that, the date being out of her darkness in this morning of our poet, he shall now gird his temples with the sun," we pronounce that such a prose is intolerable. When we find Milton writing: "And long it was not after, when I was confirmed in this opinion, that he, who would not be frustrate of his hope to write well hereafter in laudable things, ought himself to be a true poem"[3]—we pronounce that such a prose has its own grandeur, but that it is obsolete and inconvenient. But when we find Dryden telling us: "What Virgil wrote in the vigor of his age, in plenty and at ease, I have undertaken to translate in my declining years; struggling with wants, oppressed with sickness, curbed in my genius, liable to be misconstrued in all I write"[4]—then we exclaim that here at last we have the true English prose, a prose such as we would all gladly use if we only knew how. Yet Dryden was Milton's contemporary.

But after the Restoration the time had come when our nation felt the imperious need of a fit prose. So, too, the time had likewise come when our nation felt the imperious need of freeing itself from the absorbing preoccupation

---

1. *Essay on Dramatic Poesy.* Cowley (next sentence) is Abraham Cowley (1618–1667), the poet.
2. Preface to his *Fables.*

3. *Apology for Smectymnuus.*
4. *Postscript to the Reader* in his translation of Virgil.

which religion in the Puritan age had exercised. It was impossible that this freedom should be brought about without some negative excess, without some neglect and impairment of the religious life of the soul; and the spiritual history of the eighteenth century shows us that the freedom was not achieved without them. Still, the freedom was achieved; the preoccupation, an undoubtedly baneful and retarding one if it had continued, was got rid of. And as with religion amongst us at that period, so it was also with letters. A fit prose was a necessity; but it was impossible that a fit prose should establish itself amongst us without some touch of frost to the imaginative life of the soul. The needful qualities for a fit prose are regularity, uniformity, precision, balance. The men of letters, whose destiny it may be to bring their nation to the attainment of a fit prose, must of necessity, whether they work in prose or in verse, give a predominating, an almost exclusive attention to the qualities of regularity, uniformity, precision, balance. But an almost exclusive attention to these qualities involves some repression and silencing of poetry.

We are to regard Dryden as the puissant and glorious founder, Pope as the splendid high priest, of our age of prose and reason, of our excellent and indispensable eighteenth century. For the purposes of their mission and destiny their poetry, like their prose, is admirable. Do you ask me whether Dryden's verse, take it almost where you will, is not good?

> A milk-white Hind, immortal and unchanged,
> Fed on the lawns and in the forest ranged.[5]

I answer: Admirable for the purposes of the inaugurator of an age of prose and reason. Do you ask me whether Pope's verse, take it almost where you will, is not good?

> To Hounslow Heath I point, and Banstead Down;
> Thence comes your mutton, and these chicks my own.[6]

I answer: Admirable for the purposes of the high priest of an age of prose and reason. But do you ask me whether such verse proceeds from men with an adequate poetic criticism of life, from men whose criticism of life has a high seriousness, or even, without that high seriousness, has poetic largeness, freedom, insight, benignity? Do you ask me whether the application of ideas to life in the verse of these men, often a powerful application, no doubt, is a powerful *poetic* application? Do you ask me whether the poetry of these men has either the matter or the inseparable manner of such an adequate poetic criticism; whether it has the accent of

> Absent thee from felicity awhile . . .

or of

> And what is else not to be overcome . . .

or of

> O martyr souded in virginitee!

I answer: It has not and cannot have them; it is the poetry of the builders of an age of prose and reason. Though they may write in verse, though they may

---

5. *The Hind and the Panther* 1.1–2.   6. *Imitations of Horace*, Satire 2.2.143–144.

in a certain sense be masters of the art of versification, Dryden and Pope are not classics of our poetry, they are classics of our prose.

Gray is our poetical classic of that literature and age; the position of Gray is singular, and demands a word of notice here. He has not the volume or the power of poets who, coming in times more favorable, have attained to an independent criticism of life. But he lived with the great poets, he lived, above all, with the Greeks, through perpetually studying and enjoying them; and he caught their poetic point of view for regarding life, caught their poetic manner. The point of view and the manner are not self-sprung in him, he caught them of others; and he had not the free and abundant use of them. But whereas Addison and Pope never had the use of them, Gray had the use of them at times. He is the scantiest and frailest of classics in our poetry, but he is a classic.[7]

* * *

At any rate the end to which the method and the estimate are designed to lead, and from leading to which, if they do lead to it, they get their whole value—the benefit of being able clearly to feel and deeply to enjoy the best, the truly classic, in poetry—is an end, let me say it once more at parting, of supreme importance. We are often told that an era is opening in which we are to see multitudes of a common sort of readers, and masses of a common sort of literature; that such readers do not want and could not relish anything better than such literature, and that to provide it is becoming a vast and profitable industry. Even if good literature entirely lost currency with the world, it would still be abundantly worth while to continue to enjoy it by oneself. But it never will lose currency with the world, in spite of momentary appearances; it never will lose supremacy. Currency and supremacy are insured to it, not indeed by the world's deliberate and conscious choice, but by something far deeper—by the instinct of self-preservation in humanity.

1880

7. After Gray, the only other poet discussed by Arnold is Burns. We have omitted this evaluation. In it Arnold concludes that "Burns, like Chaucer, comes short of the high seriousness of the great classics."

CHRISTINA ROSSETTI
1830–1894

Referring to the title of George Gissing's novel about women who choose not to marry, the critic Jerome McGann calls Christina Rossetti "one of nineteenth-century England's greatest 'Odd Women.'" Her life had little apparent incident. She was the youngest child in the Rossetti family. Her father was an exiled Italian patriot who wrote poetry and commentaries on Dante that tried to show evidence in his poems of mysterious ancient conspiracies; her mother was an Anglo-Italian who had worked as a governess. Their household was a lively gathering place for Italian exiles, full of conversation of politics and culture, which encouraged Christina, like her brothers Dante Gabriel and William Michael, to develop an early love for art and literature and to draw and write poetry from a very early age. When she was an adolescent, her life changed dramatically: her father became a permanent invalid, the family's economic situation worsened, and her own health deterio-rated. At this point, she, her mother, and her sister became intensely involved with the Anglo-Catholic movement within the Church of England. For the rest of her life, Christina Rossetti governed herself by strict religious principles, giving up the-ater, opera, and chess; on two occasions, she canceled plans for marriage because of religious scruples, breaking her first engagement when her fiancé reverted to Roman Catholicism and ultimately refusing to marry a second suitor because he seemed insufficiently concerned with religion. She lived a quiet life, occupying herself with charitable work—including ten years of volunteer service at a peniten-tiary for fallen women—with caring for her family, and with writing poetry.

   Christina Rossetti's first volume of poetry, *Goblin Market and Other Poems* (1862), contains all the different poetic modes that mark her achievement—pure lyric, narrative fable, ballad, and the devotional verse to which she increasingly turned in her later years. The most remarkable poem in the book is the title piece, which early established its popularity as a seemingly simple moral fable for children. Later readers have likened it to Coleridge's *Rime of the Ancient Mariner* and have detected in it a complex representation of the religious themes of temptation and sin, and of redemption by vicarious suffering; the fruit that tempts Laura, however, is clearly not from the Tree of Knowledge but from an orchard of sensual delights. In its deceptively simple style, *Goblin Market*, like many of her poems, demonstrates her affinity with the early aims of the Pre-Raphaelite group, but her work as a whole resists this classification. A conscious-ness of gender often leads her to criticize the conventional representation of women in Pre-Raphaelite art, as in her sonnet *In An Artist's Studio*, and a stern religious vision controls the sensuous impulses typical of Pre-Raphaelite poetry and painting. Virginia Woolf has described the distinctive combination of sensu-ousness and religious severity in Rossetti's work.

> Your poems are full of gold dust and "sweet geraniums' varied brightness"; your eye noted incessantly how rushes are "velvet headed," and lizards have a "strange metallic mail"—your eye, indeed, observed with a sensual pre-Raphaelite intensity that must have surprised Christina the Anglo-Catholic. But to her you owed perhaps the fixity and sadness of your muse. . . . No sooner have you feasted on beauty with your eyes than your mind tells you that beauty is vain and beauty passes. Death, oblivion, and rest lap round your songs with their dark wave.

   William Michael Rossetti wrote of his sister, "She was replete with the spirit of self-postponement." Christina Rossetti was a poet who created, in Sandra M. Gil-bert and Susan Gubar's term, "an aesthetics of renunciation." She writes a poetry of deferral, of deflection, of negation, whose very denials and constraints give her a powerful way to articulate a poetic self in critical relationship to the little that the world offers. Like Emily Dickinson, she often, as in *Winter: My Secret*, uses a coy playfulness and sardonic wit to reduce the self but at the same time to preserve for it a secret inner space. And like Dickinson, she wrote many poems of an extraordinarily pure lyric beauty that made Virginia Woolf remark, "Your instinct was so sure, so direct, so intense that it produced poems that sing like music in one's ears—like a melody by Mozart or an air by Gluck."

Song

She sat and sang alway
   By the green margin of a stream,

Watching the fishes leap and play
   Beneath the glad sunbeam.

I sat and wept away   5
   Beneath the moon's most shadowy beam,
Watching the blossoms of the May
   Weep leaves into the stream.

I wept for memory;
   She sang for hope that is so fair: 10
My tears were swallowed by the sea;
   Her songs died on the air.

1848   1862

Song

When I am dead, my dearest,
   Sing no sad songs for me;
Plant thou no roses at my head,
   Nor shady cypress tree:
Be the green grass above me   5
   With showers and dewdrops wet;
And if thou wilt, remember,
   And if thou wilt, forget.

I shall not see the shadows,
   I shall not feel the rain;   10
I shall not hear the nightingale
   Sing on, as if in pain:
And dreaming through the twilight
   That doth not rise nor set,
Haply I may remember,   15
   And haply may forget.

1848   1862

After Death

The curtains were half drawn, the floor was swept
   And strewn with rushes, rosemary and may[1]
Lay thick upon the bed on which I lay,
Where thro' the lattice ivy-shadows crept.
He leaned above me, thinking that I slept   5
   And could not hear him; but I heard him say:
   "Poor child, poor child": and as he turned away
Came a deep silence, and I knew he wept.
He did not touch the shroud, or raise the fold
   That hid my face, or take my hand in his,   10
   Or ruffle the smooth pillows for my head:

---

1. Flowers associated with death.

He did not love me living; but once dead
He pitied me; and very sweet it is
To know he still is warm tho' I am cold.

1849   1862

Dead Before Death

Ah! changed and cold, how changed and very cold!
    With stiffened smiling lips and cold calm eyes:
    Changed, yet the same; much knowing, little wise;
This was the promise of the days of old!
Grown hard and stubborn in the ancient mould,   5
    Grown rigid in the sham of lifelong lies:
    We hoped for better things as years would rise,
But it is over as a tale once told.
All fallen the blossom that no fruitage bore,
    All lost the present and the future time,   10
All lost, all lost, the lapse that went before:
So lost till death shut-to the opened door,
    So lost from chime to everlasting chime,
So cold and lost for ever evermore.

1854   1862

Cobwebs

It is a land with neither night nor day,
    Nor heat nor cold, nor any wind, nor rain,
    Nor hills nor valleys; but one even plain
Stretches thro' long unbroken miles away:
While thro' the sluggish air a twilight grey   5
    Broodeth; no moons or seasons wax and wane,
    No ebb and flow are there along the main,
No bud-time no leaf-falling, there for aye:—
No ripple on the sea, no shifting sand,
    No beat of wings to stir the stagnant space,   10
No pulse of life thro' all the loveless land:
And loveless sea; no trace of days before,
    No guarded home, no toil-won resting place,
No future hope no fear for evermore.

1855   1896

A Triad

Three sang of love together: one with lips
    Crimson, with cheeks and bosom in a glow,
Flushed to the yellow hair and finger tips;
    And one there sang who soft and smooth as snow
Bloomed like a tinted hyacinth at a show;   5

And one was blue with famine after love,
   Who like a harpstring snapped rang harsh and low
The burden of what those were singing of.
One shamed herself in love; one temperately
   Grew gross in soulless love, a sluggish wife;   10
One famished died for love. Thus two of three
   Took death for love and won him after strife;
One droned in sweetness like a fattened bee:
   All on the threshold, yet all short of life.

1856   1862

In An Artist's Studio[1]

One face looks out from all his canvases,
   One selfsame figure sits or walks or leans;
   We found her hidden just behind those screens,
That mirror gave back all her loveliness.
A queen in opal or in ruby dress,   5
   A nameless girl in freshest summer-greens,
   A saint, an angel; — every canvass means
The same one meaning, neither more nor less.
He feeds upon her face by day and night,
   And she with true kind eyes looks back on him   10
Fair as the moon and joyful as the light:
   Not wan with waiting, not with sorrow dim;
Not as she is, but was when hope shone bright;
   Not as she is, but as she fills his dream.

1856   1896

A Birthday

My heart is like a singing bird
   Whose nest is in a watered shoot;
My heart is like an apple tree
   Whose boughs are bent with thickset fruit;
My heart is like a rainbow shell   5
   That paddles in a halcyon[1] sea;
My heart is gladder than all these
   Because my love is come to me.

Raise me a dais of silk and down;
   Hang it with vair[2] and purple dyes;   10
Carve it in doves and pomegranates,
   And peacocks with a hundred eyes;
Work it in gold and silver grapes,
   In leaves and silver fleurs-de-lys;

1. William Michael Rossetti, the younger of Christina's older brothers, noted, "The reference is apparently
to our brother's studio, and to his constantly repeated
heads of the lady whom he afterwards married, Miss
Siddal."
1. Tranquil.
2. Squirrel fur.

Because the birthday of my life   15
Is come, my love is come to me.

1857   1862

An Apple-Gathering

I plucked pink blossoms from mine apple tree
    And wore them all that evening in my hair:
Then in due season when I went to see
        I found no apples there.

With dangling basket all along the grass   5
    As I had come I went the selfsame track:
My neighbours mocked me while they saw me pass
        So empty-handed back.

Lilian and Lilias smiled in trudging by,
    Their heaped-up basket teazed me like a jeer;   10
Sweet-voiced they sang beneath the sunset sky,
        Their mother's home was near.

Plump Gertrude passed me with her basket full,
    A stronger hand than hers helped it along;
A voice talked with her thro' the shadows cool   15
        More sweet to me than song.

Ah Willie, Willie, was my love less worth
    Than apples with their green leaves piled above?
I counted rosiest apples on the earth
        Of far less worth than love.   20

So once it was with me you stooped to talk
    Laughing and listening in this very lane:
To think that by this way we used to walk
        We shall not walk again!

I let my neighbours pass me, ones and twos   25
    And groups; the latest said the night grew chill,
And hastened: but I loitered, while the dews
        Fell fast I loitered still.

1857   1862

Winter: My Secret

I tell my secret? No indeed, not I:
Perhaps some day, who knows?
But not today; it froze, and blows, and snows,
And you're too curious: fie!
You want to hear it? well: 5
Only, my secret's mine, and I won't tell.

Or, after all, perhaps there's none:
Suppose there is no secret after all,
But only just my fun.
Today's a nipping day, a biting day;   10
In which one wants a shawl,
A veil, a cloak, and other wraps:
I cannot ope to every one who taps,
And let the draughts come whistling thro' my hall;
Come bounding and surrounding me,   15
Come buffeting, astounding me,
Nipping and clipping thro' my wraps and all.
I wear my mask for warmth: who ever shows
His nose to Russian snows
To be pecked at by every wind that blows?   20
You would not peck? I thank you for good will,
Believe, but leave that truth untested still.

Spring's an expansive time: yet I don't trust
March with its peck of dust,
Nor April with its rainbow-crowned brief showers,   25
Nor even May, whose flowers
One frost may wither thro' the sunless hours.

Perhaps some languid summer day,
When drowsy birds sing less and less,
And golden fruit is ripening to excess,   30
If there's not too much sun nor too much cloud,
And the warm wind is neither still nor loud,
Perhaps my secret I may say,
Or you may guess.

1857   1862

Up-Hill

Does the road wind up-hill all the way?
  Yes, to the very end.
Will the day's journey take the whole long day?
  From morn to night, my friend.

But is there for the night a resting-place?   5
  A roof for when the slow dark hours begin.
May not the darkness hide it from my face?
  You cannot miss that inn.

Shall I meet other wayfarers at night?
  Those who have gone before.   10
Then must I knock, or call when just in sight?
  They will not keep you standing at that door.

Shall I find comfort, travel-sore and weak?
  Of labour you shall find the sum.

Will there be beds for me and all who seek?   15
Yea, beds for all who come.

1858   1862

Goblin Market

Morning and evening
Maids heard the goblins cry:
"Come buy our orchard fruits,
Come buy, come buy:
Apples and quinces,   5
Lemons and oranges,
Plump unpecked cherries,
Melons and raspberries,
Bloom-down-cheeked peaches,
Swart-headed mulberries,   10
Wild free-born cranberries,
Crab-apples, dewberries,
Pine-apples, blackberries,
Apricots, strawberries; —
All ripe together   15
In summer weather, —
Morns that pass by,
Fair eves that fly;
Come buy, come buy:
Our grapes fresh from the vine,   20
Pomegranates full and fine,
Dates and sharp bullaces,
Rare pears and greengages,
Damsons[1] and bilberries,
Taste them and try: 25
Currants and gooseberries,
Bright-fire-like barberries,
Figs to fill your mouth,
Citrons from the South,
Sweet to tongue and sound to eye;   30
Come buy, come buy."

Evening by evening
Among the brookside rushes,
Laura bowed her head to hear,
Lizzie veiled her blushes: 35
Crouching close together
In the cooling weather,
With clasping arms and cautioning lips,
With tingling cheeks and finger tips.
"Lie close," Laura said,   40
Pricking up her golden head:
"We must not look at goblin men,

---

1. "Bullaces," "greengages," and "damsons" are varieties of plums.

We must not buy their fruits:
Who knows upon what soil they fed
Their hungry thirsty roots?"   45
"Come buy," call the goblins
Hobbling down the glen.
"Oh," cried Lizzie, "Laura, Laura,
You should not peep at goblin men."
Lizzie covered up her eyes,   50
Covered close lest they should look;
Laura reared her glossy head,
And whispered like the restless brook:
"Look, Lizzie, look, Lizzie,
Down the glen tramp little men.   55
One hauls a basket,
One bears a plate,
One lugs a golden dish
Of many pounds weight.
How fair the vine must grow   60
Whose grapes are so luscious;
How warm the wind must blow
Thro' those fruit bushes."
"No," said Lizzie: "No, no, no;
Their offers should not charm us,   65
Their evil gifts would harm us."
She thrust a dimpled finger
In each ear, shut eyes and ran:
Curious Laura chose to linger
Wondering at each merchant man.   70
One had a cat's face,
One whisked a tail,
One tramped at a rat's pace,
One crawled like a snail,
One like a wombat prowled obtuse and furry,   75
One like a ratel[2] tumbled hurry skurry.
She heard a voice like voice of doves
Cooing all together:
They sounded kind and full of loves
In the pleasant weather.   80

Laura stretched her gleaming neck
Like a rush-imbedded swan,
Like a lily from the beck,[3]
Like a moonlit poplar branch,
Like a vessel at the launch   85
When its last restraint is gone.

Backwards up the mossy glen
Turned and trooped the goblin men,
With their shrill repeated cry,
"Come buy, come buy."   90

2. South African mammal resembling a badger (pro-   3. Small brook.
nounced "ray-tell").

When they reached where Laura was
They stood stock still upon the moss,
Leering at each other,
Brother with queer brother;
Signalling each other,   95
Brother with sly brother.
One set his basket down,
One reared his plate;
One began to weave a crown
Of tendrils, leaves and rough nuts brown   100
(Men sell not such in any town);
One heaved the golden weight
Of dish and fruit to offer her:
"Come buy, come buy," was still their cry.
Laura stared but did not stir,   105
Longed but had no money:
The whisk-tailed merchant bade her taste
In tones as smooth as honey,
The cat-faced purr'd,
The rat-paced spoke a word   110
Of welcome, and the snail-paced even was heard;
One parrot-voiced and jolly
Cried "Pretty Goblin" still for "Pretty Polly;"—
One whistled like a bird.

But sweet-tooth Laura spoke in haste: 115
"Good folk, I have no coin;
To take were to purloin:
I have no copper in my purse,
I have no silver either,
And all my gold is on the furze   120
That shakes in windy weather
Above the rusty heather."
"You have much gold upon your head,"
They answered all together:
"Buy from us with a golden curl."   125
She clipped a precious golden lock,
She dropped a tear more rare than pearl,
Then sucked their fruit globes fair or red:
Sweeter than honey from the rock.
Stronger than man-rejoicing wine,   130
Clearer than water flowed that juice;
She never tasted such before,
How should it cloy with length of use?
She sucked and sucked and sucked the more
Fruits which that unknown orchard bore;   135
She sucked until her lips were sore;
Then flung the emptied rinds away
But gathered up one kernel-stone,
And knew not was it night or day
As she turned home alone.   140

Lizzie met her at the gate
Full of wise upbraidings:
"Dear, you should not stay so late,
Twilight is not good for maidens;
Should not loiter in the glen   145
In the haunts of goblin men.
Do you not remember Jeanie,
How she met them in the moonlight,
Took their gifts both choice and many,
Ate their fruits and wore their flowers   150
Plucked from bowers
Where summer ripens at all hours?
But ever in the noonlight
She pined and pined away;
Sought them by night and day,   155
Found them no more but dwindled and grew grey;
Then fell with the first snow,
While to this day no grass will grow
Where she lies low:
I planted daisies there a year ago   160
That never blow.
You should not loiter so."
"Nay, hush," said Laura:
"Nay, hush, my sister:
I ate and ate my fill,   165
Yet my mouth waters still;
Tomorrow night I will
Buy more:" and kissed her:
"Have done with sorrow;
I'll bring you plums tomorrow   170
Fresh on their mother twigs,
Cherries worth getting;
You cannot think what figs
My teeth have met in,
What melons icy-cold   175
Piled on a dish of gold
Too huge for me to hold,
What peaches with a velvet nap,
Pellucid grapes without one seed:
Odorous indeed must be the mead   180
Whereon they grow, and pure the wave they drink
With lilies at the brink,
And sugar-sweet their sap."

Golden head by golden head,
Like two pigeons in one nest   185
Folded in each other's wings,
They lay down in their curtained bed:
Like two blossoms on one stem,
Like two flakes of new-fall'n snow,
Like two wands of ivory   190

Tipped with gold for awful[4] kings.
Moon and stars gazed in at them,
Wind sang to them lullaby,
Lumbering owls forbore to fly,
Not a bat flapped to and fro   195
Round their rest:
Cheek to cheek and breast to breast
Locked together in one nest.

Early in the morning
When the first cock crowed his warning,   200
Neat like bees, as sweet and busy,
Laura rose with Lizzie:
Fetched in honey, milked the cows,
Aired and set to rights the house,
Kneaded cakes of whitest wheat,   205
Cakes for dainty mouths to eat,
Next churned butter, whipped up cream,
Fed their poultry, sat and sewed;
Talked as modest maidens should:
Lizzie with an open heart,   210
Laura in an absent dream,
One content, one sick in part;
One warbling for the mere bright day's delight,
One longing for the night.

At length slow evening came: 215
They went with pitchers to the reedy brook;
Lizzie most placid in her look,
Laura most like a leaping flame.
They drew the gurgling water from its deep;
Lizzie plucked purple and rich golden flags,   220
Then turning homewards said: "The sunset flushes
Those furthest loftiest crags;
Come, Laura, not another maiden lags,
No wilful squirrel wags,
The beasts and birds are fast asleep."   225
But Laura loitered still among the rushes
And said the bank was steep.

And said the hour was early still,
The dew not fall'n, the wind not chill:
Listening ever, but not catching   230
The customary cry,
"Come buy, come buy,"
With its iterated jingle
Of sugar-baited words:
Not for all her watching   235
Once discerning even one goblin
Racing, whisking, tumbling, hobbling;
Let alone the herds

4. Awe-inspiring.

That used to tramp along the glen,
In groups or single,   240
Of brisk fruit-merchant men.
Till Lizzie urged, "O Laura, come;
I hear the fruit-call but I dare not look:
You should not loiter longer at this brook:
Come with me home.   245
The stars rise, the moon bends her arc,
Each glowworm winks her spark,
Let us get home before the night grows dark:
For clouds may gather
Tho' this is summer weather,   250
Put out the lights and drench us thro';
Then if we lost our way what should we do?"

Laura turned cold as stone
To find her sister heard that cry alone,
That goblin cry,   255
"Come buy our fruits, come buy."
Must she then buy no more such dainty fruit?
Must she no more such succous⁵ pasture find,
Gone deaf and blind?
Her tree of life drooped from the root: 260
She said not one word in her heart's sore ache;
But peering thro' the dimness, nought discerning,
Trudged home, her pitcher dripping all the way;
So crept to bed, and lay
Silent till Lizzie slept;   265
Then sat up in a passionate yearning,
And gnashed her teeth for baulked desire, and wept
As if her heart would break.

Day after day, night after night,
Laura kept watch in vain   270
In sullen silence of exceeding pain.
She never caught again the goblin cry:
"Come buy, come buy;"—
She never spied the goblin men
Hawking their fruits along the glen: 275
But when the noon waxed bright
Her hair grew thin and gray;
She dwindled, as the fair full moon doth turn
To swift decay and burn
Her fire away.   280

One day remembering her kernel-stone
She set it by a wall that faced the south;
Dewed it with tears, hoped for a root,
Watched for a waxing shoot,
But there came none;   285
It never saw the sun,

5. Juicy or succulent.

It never felt the trickling moisture run:
While with sunk eyes and faded mouth
She dreamed of melons, as a traveller sees
False waves in desert drouth   290
With shade of leaf-crowned trees,
And burns the thirstier in the sandful breeze.

She no more swept the house,
Tended the fowls or cows,
Fetched honey, kneaded cakes of wheat,   295
Brought water from the brook:
But sat down listless in the chimney-nook
And would not eat.

Tender Lizzie could not bear
To watch her sister's cankerous care   300
Yet not to share.
She night and morning
Caught the goblins' cry:
"Come buy our orchard fruits,
Come buy, come buy:" —   305
Beside the brook, along the glen,
She heard the tramp of goblin men,
The voice and stir
Poor Laura could not hear;
Longed to buy fruit to comfort her,   310
But feared to pay too dear.
She thought of Jeanie in her grave,
Who should have been a bride;
But who for joys brides hope to have
Fell sick and died   315
In her gay prime,
In earliest Winter time,
With the first glazing rime,
With the first snow-fall of crisp Winter time.

Till Laura dwindling   320
Seemed knocking at Death's door:
Then Lizzie weighed no more
Better and worse;
But put a silver penny in her purse,
Kissed Laura, crossed the heath with clumps of furze   325
At twilight, halted by the brook:
And for the first time in her life
Began to listen and look.

Laughed every goblin
When they spied her peeping: 330
Came towards her hobbling,
Flying, running, leaping,
Puffing and blowing,
Chuckling, clapping, crowing,

Clucking and gobbling,   335
Mopping and mowing,
Full of airs and graces,
Pulling wry faces,
Demure grimaces,
Cat-like and rat-like,   340
Ratel- and wombat-like,
Snail-paced in a hurry,
Parrot-voiced and whistler,
Helter skelter, hurry skurry,
Chattering like magpies,   345
Fluttering like pigeons,
Gliding like fishes,—
Hugged her and kissed her,
Squeezed and caressed her:
Stretched up their dishes,   350
Panniers, and plates:
"Look at our apples
Russet and dun,
Bob at our cherries,
Bite at our peaches,   355
Citrons and dates,
Grapes for the asking,
Pears red with basking
Out in the sun,
Plums on their twigs;   360
Pluck them and suck them,
Pomegranates, figs."—

"Good folk," said Lizzie,
Mindful of Jeanie:
"Give me much and many:"—   365
Held out her apron,
Tossed them her penny.
"Nay, take a seat with us,
Honour and eat with us,"
They answered grinning: 370
"Our feast is but beginning.
Night yet is early,
Warm and dew-pearly,
Wakeful and starry:
Such fruits as these   375
No man can carry;
Half their bloom would fly,
Half their dew would dry,
Half their flavour would pass by.
Sit down and feast with us,   380
Be welcome guest with us,
Cheer you and rest with us."—
"Thank you," said Lizzie: "But one waits
At home alone for me:
So without further parleying,   385

If you will not sell me any
Of your fruits tho' much and many,
Give me back my silver penny
I tossed you for a fee."—
They began to scratch their pates,   390
No longer wagging, purring,
But visibly demurring,
Grunting and snarling.
One called her proud,
Cross-grained, uncivil;   395
Their tones waxed loud,
Their looks were evil.
Lashing their tails
They trod and hustled her,
Elbowed and jostled her,   400
Clawed with their nails,
Barking, mewing, hissing, mocking,
Tore her gown and soiled her stocking,
Twitched her hair out by the roots,
Stamped upon her tender feet,   405
Held her hands and squeezed their fruits
Against her mouth to make her eat.

White and golden Lizzie stood,
Like a lily in a flood,—
Like a rock of blue-veined stone   410
Lashed by tides obstreperously,—
Like a beacon left alone
In a hoary roaring sea,
Sending up a golden fire,—
Like a fruit-crowned orange-tree   415
White with blossoms honey-sweet
Sore beset by wasp and bee,—
Like a royal virgin town
Topped with gilded dome and spire
Close beleaguerred by a fleet   420
Mad to tug her standard down.

One may lead a horse to water,
Twenty cannot make him drink.
Tho' the goblins cuffed and caught her,
Coaxed and fought her,   425
Bullied and besought her,
Scratched her, pinched her black as ink,
Kicked and knocked her,
Mauled and mocked her,
Lizzie uttered not a word;   430
Would not open lip from lip
Lest they should cram a mouthful in:
But laughed in heart to feel the drip
Of juice that syruped all her face,
And lodged in dimples of her chin,   435

And streaked her neck which quaked like curd.
At last the evil people
Worn out by her resistance
Flung back her penny, kicked their fruit
Along whichever road they took,   440
Not leaving root or stone or shoot;
Some writhed into the ground,
Some dived into the brook
With ring and ripple,
Some scudded on the gale without a sound,   445
Some vanished in the distance.
In a smart, ache, tingle,
Lizzie went her way;
Knew not was it night or day;
Sprang up the bank, tore thro' the furze,   450
Threaded copse and dingle,
And heard her penny jingle
Bouncing in her purse,
Its bounce was music to her ear.
She ran and ran   455
As if she feared some goblin man
Dogged her with gibe or curse
Or something worse:
But not one goblin skurried after,
Nor was she pricked by fear;   460
The kind heart made her windy-paced
That urged her home quite out of breath with haste
And inward laughter.

She cried "Laura," up the garden,
"Did you miss me?   465
Come and kiss me.
Never mind my bruises,
Hug me, kiss me, suck my juices
Squeezed from goblin fruits for you,
Goblin pulp and goblin dew.   470
Eat me, drink me, love me;
Laura, make much of me:
For your sake I have braved the glen
And had to do with goblin merchant men."

Laura started from her chair,   475
Flung her arms up in the air,
Clutched her hair:
"Lizzie, Lizzie, have you tasted
For my sake the fruit forbidden?
Must your light like mine be hidden,   480
Your young life like mine be wasted,
Undone in mine undoing
And ruined in my ruin,
Thirsty, cankered, goblin-ridden?"—
She clung about her sister,   485

Kissed and kissed and kissed her:
Tears once again
Refreshed her shrunken eyes,
Dropping like rain
After long sultry drouth;   490
Shaking with aguish fear, and pain,
She kissed and kissed her with a hungry mouth.

Her lips began to scorch,
That juice was wormwood to her tongue,
She loathed the feast: 495
Writhing as one possessed she leaped and sung,
Rent all her robe, and wrung
Her hands in lamentable haste,
And beat her breast.
Her locks streamed like the torch   500
Borne by a racer at full speed,
Or like the mane of horses in their flight,
Or like an eagle when she stems[6] the light
Straight toward the sun,
Or like a caged thing freed,   505
Or like a flying flag when armies run.

Swift fire spread thro' her veins, knocked at her heart,
Met the fire smouldering there
And overbore its lesser flame;
She gorged on bitterness without a name: 510
Ah! fool, to choose such part
Of soul-consuming care!
Sense failed in the mortal strife:
Like the watch-tower of a town
Which an earthquake shatters down,   515
Like a lightning-stricken mast,
Like a wind-uprooted tree
Spun about,
Like a foam-topped waterspout
Cast down headlong in the sea,   520
She fell at last;
Pleasure past and anguish past,
Is it death or is it life?

Life out of death.
That night long Lizzie watched by her,   525
Counted her pulse's flagging stir,
Felt for her breath,
Held water to her lips, and cooled her face
With tears and fanning leaves:
But when the first birds chirped about their eaves,   530
And early reapers plodded to the place
Of golden sheaves,
And dew-wet grass

6. Breasts or makes headway against.

Bowed in the morning winds so brisk to pass,
And new buds with new day   535
Opened of cup-like lilies on the stream,
Laura awoke as from a dream,
Laughed in the innocent old way,
Hugged Lizzie but not twice or thrice;
Her gleaming locks showed not one thread of grey,   540
Her breath was sweet as May
And light danced in her eyes.

Days, weeks, months, years
Afterwards, when both were wives
With children of their own;   545
Their mother-hearts beset with fears,
Their lives bound up in tender lives;
Laura would call the little ones
And tell them of her early prime,
Those pleasant days long gone   550
Of not-returning time:
Would talk about the haunted glen,
The wicked, quaint fruit-merchant men,
Their fruits like honey to the throat
But poison in the blood;   555
(Men sell not such in any town:)
Would tell them how her sister stood
In deadly peril to do her good,
And win the fiery antidote:
Then joining hands to little hands   560
Would bid them cling together,
"For there is no friend like a sister
In calm or stormy weather;
To cheer one on the tedious way,
To fetch one if one goes astray,   565
To lift one if one totters down,
To strengthen whilst one stands."

1859   1862

"No, Thank You, John"

I never said I loved you, John:
    Why will you teaze me day by day,
And wax a weariness to think upon
    With always "do" and "pray"?

You know I never loved you, John;   5
    No fault of mine made me your toast:
Why will you haunt me with a face as wan
    As shows an hour-old ghost?

I dare say Meg or Moll would take
    Pity upon you, if you'd ask: 10

And pray don't remain single for my sake
    Who can't perform that task.

I have no heart?—Perhaps I have not;
    But then you're mad to take offence
That I don't give you what I have not got: 15
    Use your own common sense.

Let bygones be bygones:
    Don't call me false, who owed not to be true:
I'd rather answer "No" to fifty Johns
    Than answer "Yes" to you.   20

Let's mar our pleasant days no more,
    Song-birds of passage, days of youth:
Catch at today, forget the days before:
    I'll wink at your untruth.

Let us strike hands as hearty friends;   25
    No more, no less; and friendship's good:
Only don't keep in view ulterior ends,
    And points not understood

In open treaty. Rise above
    Quibbles and shuffling off and on: 30
Here's friendship for you if you like; but love,—
    No, thank you, John.

1860   1862

Promises Like Pie-Crust

Promise me no promises,
    So will I not promise you:
Keep we both our liberties,
    Never false and never true:
Let us hold the die uncast,   5
    Free to come as free to go:
For I cannot know your past,
    And of mine what can you know?

You, so warm, may once have been
    Warmer towards another one: 10
I, so cold, may once have seen
    Sunlight, once have felt the sun:
Who shall show us if it was
    Thus indeed in time of old?
Fades the image from the glass,   15
    And the fortune is not told.

If you promised, you might grieve
    For lost liberty again:

If I promised, I believe
    I should fret to break the chain.   20
Let us be the friends we were,
    Nothing more but nothing less:
Many thrive on frugal fare
    Who would perish of excess.

1861   1896

In Progress

Ten years ago it seemed impossible
    That she should ever grow so calm as this,
    With self-remembrance in her warmest kiss
And dim dried eyes like an exhausted well.
Slow-speaking when she has some fact to tell,   5
    Silent with long-unbroken silences,
    Centred in self yet not unpleased to please,
Gravely monotonous like a passing bell.
Mindful of drudging daily common things,
    Patient at pastime, patient at her work,   10
        Wearied perhaps but strenuous certainly.
        Sometimes I fancy we may one day see
    Her head shoot forth seven stars from where they lurk
And her eyes lightnings and her shoulders wings.

1862   1896

A Life's Parallels

    Never on this side of the grave again,
        On this side of the river,
    On this side of the garner of the grain,
        Never,—

    Ever while time flows on and on and on,   5
        That narrow noiseless river,
    Ever while corn bows heavy-headed, wan,
        Ever,—

    Never despairing, often fainting, rueing,
        But looking back, ah never!   10
    Faint yet pursuing, faint yet still pursuing
        Ever.

1881

From Later Life

17

Something this foggy day, a something which
    Is neither of this fog nor of today,

Has set me dreaming of the winds that play
Past certain cliffs, along one certain beach,
    And turn the topmost edge of waves to spray: 5
    Ah pleasant pebbly strand so far away,
So out of reach while quite within my reach,
    As out of reach as India or Cathay!
I am sick of where I am and where I am not,
    I am sick of foresight and of memory,   10
    I am sick of all I have and all I see,
        I am sick of self, and there is nothing new;
Oh weary impatient patience of my lot!—
        Thus with myself: how fares it, Friends, with you?

1881

Cardinal Newman[1]

In the grave, whither thou goest

O weary Champion of the Cross, lie still:
    Sleep thou at length the all-embracing sleep:
    Long was thy sowing-day, rest now and reap:
Thy fast was long, feast now thy spirit's fill.
Yea, take thy fill of love, because thy will   5
    Chose love not in the shallows but the deep:
    Thy tides were springtides, set against the neap[2]
Of calmer souls: thy flood rebuked their rill.
Now night has come to thee—please God, of rest:
    So some time must it come to every man;   10
    To first and last, where many last are first.
Now fixed and finished thine eternal plan,
    Thy best has done its best, thy worst its worst:
Thy best its best, Please God, thy best its best.

1890

Sleeping at Last

Sleeping at last, the trouble & tumult over,
    Sleeping at last, the struggle & horror past,
Cold & white out of sight of friend & of lover
        Sleeping at last.

No more a tired heart downcast or overcast,   5
No more pangs that wring or shifting fears that hover,
    Sleeping at last in a dreamless sleep locked fast.

Fast asleep.   Singing birds in their leafy cover
    Cannot wake her, nor shake her the gusty blast.

---

1. Written on the occasion of the death of John Henry
Newman. The epigraph is from Ecclesiastes 9.10.
    2. Tides that do not rise to the high-water mark of the
spring tides.

Under the purple thyme and the purple clover   10
Sleeping at last.

1896

GERARD MANLEY HOPKINS
1844–1889

1866:   Converts to Roman Catholic church.
1877:   Ordained a Jesuit priest.
1918:   Posthumous publication of his poems.

It has been said that the most important date in Gerard Manley Hopkins's career was 1918, twenty-nine years after his death, for it was then that the first publication of his poems made them accessible to the world of readers. During his lifetime, these remarkable poems, most of them celebrating the wonders of God's creation, had been known only to a small circle of friends, including his literary executor, the poet Robert Bridges, who waited until 1918 before releasing them to a publisher. Partly because his work was first made public in a twentieth-century volume, but especially because of his striking experiments in meter and diction, Hopkins was widely hailed as a pioneering figure of "modern" literature, miraculously unconnected with his fellow Victorian poets (who during the 1920s and 1930s were largely out of fashion among critical readers). And this way of classifying and evaluating his writings has long persisted. In 1936 a substantial selection of his poems led off *The Faber Book of Modern Verse*, one of the most influential anthologies of the century, featuring poets such as W. H. Auden, Dylan Thomas, and T. S. Eliot (the only one whose selections occupy more pages than those allotted to Hopkins). And the first four editions of *The Norton Anthology of English Literature* (1962–1979) grouped Hopkins with these same twentieth-century poets. To reclassify him is not to repudiate his earlier reputation as a "modern" but rather to suggest that his work can be better understood and appreciated if it is restored to the Victorian world out of which it developed.

Hopkins was born near London into a large and cultivated family in comfortable circumstances. After a brilliant career at Highgate School, he entered Oxford in 1863, where he was exposed to a variety of Victorian ways of thinking, both secular and religious. Among influential leaders at Oxford was Matthew Arnold, professor of poetry, but more important for Hopkins was his tutor, Walter Pater, an aesthetician whose emphasis on the intense apprehension of sensuous beauty struck a responsive chord in Hopkins. At Oxford he was also exposed to the Broad Church theology of one of the tutors at his college (Balliol), Benjamin Jowett. But Hopkins became increasingly attracted first to the High Church movement represented at Oxford by Edward Pusey, and then to Roman Catholicism. Profoundly influenced by John Henry Newman's conversion to Rome and by subsequent conversations with Newman himself, Hopkins entered the Roman Catholic church in 1866. The estrangement from his family that resulted from his conversion was very painful for him; his parents' letters to him were so "terrible" (he reported to Newman) that he could not bear to "read them twice." And this alienation was heightened by his decision not only to become a Roman Catholic but to become a priest and, in particular, a Jesuit priest, for in the eyes of many Victorian Protestants, the Jesuit order was regarded with a special distrust. For the rest of his life, Hopkins served as a priest and teacher in various places, among them Oxford, Liverpool, and Lancashire. In 1884 he was appointed professor of classics at University College in Dublin, where Newman had served as rector in the 1850s and where James Joyce would be enrolled as a student at the turn of the century.

At school and at Oxford in the early 1860s, Hopkins had written poems in the vein of Keats. He burned most of these early writings after his conversion (although drafts survive), for he believed that his vocation must require renouncing such personal satisfactions as the writing of poems. Only after his superiors in the church encouraged him to do so did he resume writing poetry, but during the seven years of silence, as his letters show, he had been thinking about experimenting with what he called a "new rhythm." The result, in 1876, was his rhapsodic lyric-narrative, *The Wreck of the Deutschland*, a long ode about the wreck of a ship in which five Franciscan nuns were drowned. The style of the poem was so distinctive that the editor of the Jesuit magazine to which he had submitted it "dared not print it," as Hopkins himself reported. During the remaining fourteen years of his life, Hopkins continued to write poems but seldom submitted them for publication, partly because he was convinced that poetic fame was incompatible with his religious vocation but also because of a fear that readers would be discouraged by the eccentricity of his work.

Hopkins's sense of his own singularity gives us an indication of the organizing structure of his poetry. Drawing on the theology of Duns Scotus, a medieval philosopher, he felt that everything in the universe was characterized by what he called *inscape*, the distinctive design that constitutes individual identity. This identity is not static but dynamic. Each being in the universe "selves," that is, enacts its identity. And the human being, the most highly selved, the most individually distinctive being in the universe, recognizes the inscape of other beings in an act that Hopkins calls *instress*, the apprehension of an object in an intense thrust of energy toward it that enables one to realize its specific distinctiveness. Ultimately, the instress of inscape leads one to Christ, for the individual identity of any object is the stamp of divine creation on it. In the act of instress, therefore, the human being becomes a celebrant of the divine, at once recognizing God's creation and enacting his or her own God-given identity within it.

Poetry for Hopkins enacts this celebration. It is instress, and it realizes the inscape of its subject in its own distinctive design. Hopkins wrote, "But as air, melody, is what strikes me most of all in music and design in painting, so design, pattern or what I am in the habit of calling 'inscape' is what I above all aim at in poetry." To create inscape, Hopkins seeks to give each poem a unique design that captures the initial inspiration when he is "caught" by his subject. Many of the characteristics of Hopkins's style—his disruption of conventional syntax, his coining and compounding of words, his use of ellipsis and repetition—can be understood as ways of representing the stress and action of the brain in moments of inspiration. He creates compounds to represent the unique interlocking of the characteristics of an object—"piece-bright," "dapple-dawn-drawn," "blue-bleak." He omits syntactical connections to fuse qualities more intensely—"the dearest freshness deep down things." He creates puns to suggest how God's creation rhymes and chimes in a divine patterning. He violates conventional syntactic order to represent the shape of mental experience. In the act of imaginative apprehension, a language particular to the moment generates itself.

Hopkins also uses a new rhythm to give each poem its distinctive design. In the new metric system he created, which he called *sprung rhythm*, lines have a given number of stresses, but the number and placement of unstressed syllables is highly variable. Hopkins rarely marks all the intended stresses, only those that readers might not anticipate. To indicate stressed syllables, Hopkins often uses both the stress (´) and the "great stress" (″). A curved line marks an "outride"—one or more syllables added to a foot but not counted in the scansion of the line; they indicate a stronger stress on the preceding syllable and a short pause after the outride. Here, for example, is the scansion for the first three lines of *The Windhover*:

> I caúght this mórning mórning's mínion, kíng-
> dom of dáylight's daúphin, dapple-dawn-drawn Fálcon, in his ríding
> Of the rólling level underneáth him steady aír, and stríding

Hopkins argued that sprung rhythm was the natural rhythm of common speech and written prose, as well as of music. He found a model for it in Old English poetry and in nursery rhymes, but he claimed that it had not been used in English poetry since the Elizabethan Age.

The density and difficulty that result from Hopkins's unconventional rhythm and syntax make his poetry seem modern, but his concern with the imagination's shaping of the natural world puts him very much in the Romantic tradition, and his creation of a rough and difficult style, designed to capture the mind's own motion, resembles the style of Browning. "A horrible thing has happened to me," Hopkins wrote in 1864, "I have begun to *doubt* Tennyson." He goes on to criticize Tennyson for using the grand style as a smooth and habitual poetic speech. Like Swinburne, Pater, and Henry James as well as Browning, Hopkins displays a new mannerism, characteristic of the latter part of the nineteenth century, which paradoxically combines an elaborate aestheticism with a more complex representation of consciousness.

In Hopkins's early poetry, his singular apprehension of the beauty of individual objects always brings him to an ecstatic illumination of the presence of God. But in his late poems, the so-called terrible sonnets, his distinctive individuality comes to isolate him from the God who made him thus. Hopkins wrote, "To me there is no resemblance: searching nature, I taste *self* but at one tankard, that of my own being." In the terrible sonnets, Hopkins confronts the solipsism to which his own stress on individuality seems to lead him. Like the mad speakers of so many Victorian dramatic monologues, he cannot escape a world solely of his own imagining. Yet even these poems of despair, which seem so distinctively modern, reflect a traditional religious vision, the dark night of the soul as described by earlier religious writers such as St. Ignatius Loyola, the founder of the Jesuit order.

In his introduction to *The Oxford Book of Modern Verse*, Yeats calls Hopkins's poetry "a last development of poetical diction." Yeats's remark indicates the anomaly that Hopkins's work poses. Perhaps it is only appropriate for a writer who stressed the uniqueness of inscape to strike us with the individuality of his achievement.

God's Grandeur

> The world is charged with the grandeur of God.
> It will flame out, like shining from shook foil;[1]
> It gathers to a greatness, like the ooze of oil
> Crushed.[2] Why do men then now not reck his rod?
> Generations have trod, have trod, have trod;   5

---

1. Hopkins explained this image in a letter: "I mean foil in its sense of leaf or tinsel. . . . Shaken goldfoil gives off broad glares like sheet lightning and also, and this is true of nothing else, owing to its zigzag dints and creasings and network of small many cornered facets, a sort of fork lightning too."
2. I.e., from the crushing of olives.

And all is seared with trade; bleared, smeared with toil;
And wears man's smudge and shares man's smell: the soil
Is bare now, nor can foot feel, being shod.

And for[3] all this, nature is never spent;
There lives the dearest freshness deep down things;   10
And though the last lights off the black West went
Oh, morning, at the brown brink eastward, springs—
Because the Holy Ghost over the bent
World broods with warm breast and with ah! bright wings.

1877   1918

The Starlight Night

Look at the stars! look, look up at the skies!
O look at all the fire-folk sitting in the air!
The bright boroughs, the circle-citadels there!
Down in dim woods the diamond delves![1] the elves'-eyes!
The grey lawns cold where gold, where quickgold[2] lies!   5
Wind-beat whitebeam! airy abeles[3] set on a flare!
Flake-doves sent floating forth at a farmyard scare!—
Ah well! it is all a purchase, all is a prize.

Buy then! bid then!—What?—Prayer, patience, alms, vows.
Look, look: a May-mess,[4] like on orchard boughs!   10
Look! March-bloom, like on mealed-with-yellow sallows![5]
These are indeed the barn; withindoors house
The shocks. This piece-bright paling[6] shuts the spouse
Christ home, Christ and his mother and all his hallows.[7]

1877   1918

As Kingfishers Catch Fire

As kingfishers catch fire, dragonflies draw flame;
As tumbled over rim in roundy wells
Stones ring; like each tucked[1] string tells, each hung bell's
Bow swung finds tongue to fling out broad its name;
Each mortal thing does one thing and the same: 5
Deals out that being indoors[2] each one dwells;
Selves[3]—goes itself; *myself* it speaks and spells,
Crying *What I do is me: for that I came.*

3. Despite.
1. Quarries.
2. Coined by analogy with quicksilver. The starlight
night resembles the lawns below it where the dew, reflecting the starlight, looks like gold.
3. White poplars.
4. A profusion of growing things such as May blossoms.
5. Willows, here with yellow spots like meal.
6. Picket fence. "Shocks": sheaves of grain.
7. Saints.
1. Plucked.
2. Within.
3. Fulfills its individuality.

Í say more: the just man justices;[4]
    Kéeps gráce: thát keeps all his goings graces;   10
Acts in God's eye what in God's eye he is—
    Chríst. For Christ plays in ten thousand places,
Lovely in limbs, and lovely in eyes not his
    To the Father through the features of men's faces.

1877   1918

Spring

Nothing is so beautiful as Spring—
    When weeds, in wheels, shoot long and lovely and lush;
    Thrush's eggs look little low heavens, and thrush
Through the echoing timber does so rinse and wring
The ear, it strikes like lightnings to hear him sing;   5
    The glassy peartree leaves and blooms, they brush
    The descending blue; that blue is all in a rush
With richness; the racing lambs too have fair their fling.

What is all this juice and all this joy?
    A strain of the earth's sweet being in the beginning   10
In Eden garden.—Have, get, before it cloy,

    Before it cloud, Christ, lord, and sour with sinning,
Innocent mind and Mayday in girl and boy,
    Most, O maid's child,[1] thy choice and worthy the winning.

1877   1918

The Windhover:[1]

To Christ our Lord

I caught this morning morning's minion,[2] king-
    dom of daylight's dauphin,[3] dapple-dawn-drawn Falcon, in his riding
    Of the rolling level underneath him steady air, and striding
High there, how he rung upon the rein of a wimpling[4] wing
In his ecstasy! then off, off forth on swing,   5
    As a skate's heel sweeps smooth on a bow-bend: the hurl and gliding
Rebuffed the big wind. My heart in hiding
Stirred for a bird,—the achieve of, the mastery of the thing!

Brute beauty and valour and act, oh, air, pride, plume, here
    Buckle![5] AND the fire that breaks from thee then, a billion   10
Times told lovelier, more dangerous, O my chevalier![6]

4. Acts in a just manner.
1. Jesus, son of the Virgin Mary.
1. Kestrel, a small falcon noted for hovering in the air.
2. Darling.
3. A prince who is heir to the French throne.
4. Rippling. "Rung upon the rein": circled at the end of a rein.
5. The verb can be read as imperative or indicative. All three meanings are relevant: to prepare for action, to fasten together, to collapse.
6. Knight.

No wonder of it: shéer plód makes plough down sillion[7]
  Shine, and blue-bleak embers, ah my dear,
    Fall, gall[8] themselves, and gash gold-vermilion.
1877   1918

Pied[1] Beauty

Glory be to God for dappled things—
  For skies of couple-colour as a brinded[2] cow;
    For rose-moles all in stipple upon trout that swim;
Fresh-firecoal chestnut-falls,[3] finches' wings;
  Landscape plotted and pieced—fold, fallow, and plough;[4]   5
  And áll trádes, their gear and tackle and trim.[5]

All things counter, original, spare,[6] strange;
  Whatever is fickle, freckled (who knows how?)
    With swift, slow; sweet, sour; adazzle, dim;
He fathers-forth whose beauty is past change: 10
                              Praise him.
1877   1918

Hurrahing in Harvest

Summer ends now; now, barbarous in beauty, the stooks[1] rise
Around; up above, what wind-walks! what lovely behavior
Of silk-sack clouds! has wilder, wilful-wavier
Meal-drift moulded ever and melted across skies?

I walk, I lift up, I lift up heart, eyes,   5
Down all that glory in the heavens to glean our Saviour;
And, éyes, heárt, what looks, what lips yet gave you a
Rapturous love's greeting of realer, of rounder replies?

And the azurous hung hills are his world-wielding shoulder
Majestic—as a stallion stalwart, very-violet-sweet!—   10
These things, these things were here and but the beholder
Wanting; which two when they once meet,
The heart rears wings bold and bolder
And hurls for him, O half hurls earth for him off under his feet.
1877   1918

Binsey Poplars

felled 1879

My aspens dear, whose airy cages quelled,
  Quelled or quenched in leaves the leaping sun,

---

7. The ridge between two furrows of a plowed field.
8. Break the surface of.
1. Of two or more colors in blotches, variegated.
2. Brownish orange in color with streaks of gray.
3. I.e., freshly fallen chestnuts, bright as coals.
4. Divided into fields used as pastures ("fold"), lying

fallow, or plowed for cultivation. The landscape thus
appears like patches of different colors.
5. Equipment.
6. Rare. "Counter": contrary.
1. Sheaves of grain.

All felled, felled, are all felled;
Of a fresh and following folded rank
    Not spared, not one   5
    That dandled a sandalled
  Shadow that swam or sank
On meadow and river and wind-wandering
  weed-winding bank.

  O if we but knew what we do   10
    When we delve[1] or hew—
  Hack and rack[2] the growing green!
    Since country is so tender
  To touch, her being só slender,
  That, like this sleek and seeing ball[3]   15
  But a prick will make no eye at all,

  Where we, even where we mean
    To mend her we end her,
    When we hew or delve:
After-comers cannot guess the beauty been.   20
  Ten or twelve, only ten or twelve
    Strokes of havoc únselve[4]
    The sweet especial scene,
  Rural scene, a rural scene,
  Sweet especial rural scene.   25

1879   1918

Duns Scotus's Oxford[1]

Towery city and branchy between towers;
Cuckoo-echoing, bell-swarmèd, lark-charmèd, rook-racked, river-rounded;
The dapple-eared lily below thee; that country and town did
Once encounter in, here coped[2] and poisèd powers;

Thou hast a base and brickish skirt[3] there, sours   5
That neighbour-nature thy grey beauty is grounded
Best in; graceless growth, thou hast confounded
Rural rural keeping[4]—folk, flocks, and flowers.

Yet ah! this air I gather and I release
He lived on; these weeds and waters, these walls are what   10
He haunted who of all men most sways my spirits to peace;

1. Dig.
2. Torture.
3. The eye.
4. Rob it of self.
1. Duns Scotus, the 13th-century theologian, lectured at Oxford about 1301. His idea that individuality is the final perfection of any creature influenced Hopkins's conception of inscape. When Hopkins came on two of Scotus's commentaries in 1872, he wrote that he was immediately "flush with a new stroke of enthusiasm

. . . when I took in any inscape of the sky or sea I thought of Scotus."
2. Set off against one another.
3. Redbrick housing developments and industrial complexes, built in the 19th century on the north edge of Oxford, are in marked contrast with the "gray" stone buildings of the medieval city.
4. The "brickish skirt" has destroyed the way in which the rural landscape and the old city have tended and preserved each other.

Of realty[5] the rarest-veinèd unraveller; a not
Rivalled insight, be rival Italy or Greece;
Who fired France for Mary without spot.[6]

1879   1918

Felix Randal

Felix Randal the farrier,[1] O is he dead then? my duty all ended,
Who have watched his mould of man, big-boned and hardy-handsome
Pining, pining, till time when reason rambled in it and some
Fatal four disorders, fleshed there, all contended?

Sickness broke him. Impatient, he cursed at first, but mended   5
Being anointed[2] and all; though a heavenlier heart began some
Months earlier, since I had our sweet reprieve and ransom[3]
Tendered to him. Ah well, God rest him all road ever[4] he offended!

This seeing the sick endears them to us, us too it endears.
My tongue had taught thee comfort, touch had quenched thy tears,   10
Thy tears that touched my heart, child, Felix, poor Felix Randal;

How far from then forethought of, all thy more boisterous years,
When thou at the random[5] grim forge, powerful amidst peers,
Didst fettle[6] for the great grey drayhorse his bright and battering sandal!

1880   1918

Spring and Fall:

to a young child

Márgarét, áre you gríeving
Over Goldengrove unleaving?
Leáves, líke the things of man, you
With your fresh thoughts care for, can you?
Áh! ás the heart grows older   5
It will come to such sights colder
By and by, nor spare a sigh
Though worlds of wanwood leafmeal[1] lie;
And yet you *will* weep and know why.
Now no matter, child, the name: 10
Sórrow's spríngs áre the same.
Nor mouth had, no nor mind, expressed
What heart heard of, ghost[2] guessed:

5. Reality.
6. In Paris, Scotus was the first to defend the doctrine of the Immaculate Conception, that Mary was born without original sin.
1. Blacksmith.
2. In Extreme Unction, the sacrament for the dying.
3. Holy Communion preceded by confession and absolution.
4. In whatever way.
5. Built with stones of irregular size and shape.
6. Prepare.
1. Wan forest with scattered leaves. "Leafmeal" is coined by analogy with piecemeal.
2. Spirit.

It ís the blight man was born for,
It is Margaret you mourn for.   15
1880   1918

[Carrion Comfort]¹

Not, I'll not, carrion comfort, Despair, not feast on thee,²
Not untwist—slack they may be—these last strands of man
In me ór, most weary, cry *I can no more*. I can;
Can something, hope, wish day come, not choose not to be.

But ah, but O thou terrible, why wouldst thou rude on me   5
Thy wring-world right foot rock?³ lay a lionlimb against me? scan
With darksome devouring eyes my bruisèd bones? and fan,
O in turns of tempest, me heaped there; me frantic to avoid thee and flee?

Why? That my chaff might fly; my grain lie, sheer and clear.
Nay in all that toil, that coil,⁴ since (seems) I kissed the rod,   10
Hand rather,⁵ my heart lo! lapped strength, stole joy, would laugh, chéer.
Cheer whom though? The Hero whose heaven-handling flung me, fóot tród
Me? or me that fought him? O which one? is it each one? That night, that
    year
Of now done darkness I wretch lay wrestling with (my God!) my God.
1885   1918

No Worst, There Is None

No worst, there is none. Pitched past pitch of grief,
More pangs will, schooled at forepangs, wilder wring.
Comforter, where, where is your comforting?
Mary, mother of us, where is your relief?
My cries heave, herds-long;¹ huddle in a main, a chief-   5
woe, world-sorrow; on an age-old anvil wince and sing—
Then lull, then leave off. Fury had shrieked "No ling-
ering! Let me be fell: force² I must be brief."
O the mind, mind has mountains; cliffs of fall
Frightful, sheer, no-man-fathomed. Hold them cheap   10
May who ne'er hung there. Nor does long our small
Durance³ deal with that steep or deep. Here! creep,
Wretch, under a comfort serves in a whirlwind: all
Life death does end and each day dies with sleep.
1885   1918

---

1. The title of this poem was supplied by Bridges. It is one of the "terrible sonnets," as are the three following poems.
2. The satisfaction of giving in to despair as a kind of "comfort" is implicitly likened to a vulture's satisfaction in feasting on dead flesh.
3. I.e., why wouldst thou roughly against me rock thy right foot that wrings the world?
4. Tumult.
5. I.e., the hand that wields the rod.

1. Like the succession of cries made by cattle that have been following one another in a long line.
2. Perforce. "Fell": fierce.
3. Endurance.

GERARD MANLEY HOPKINS

I Wake and Feel the Fell of Dark, Not Day

I wake and feel the fell[1] of dark, not day.
What hours, O what black hoürs we have spent
This night! what sights you, heart, saw; ways you went!
And more must, in yet longer light's delay.

With witness I speak this. But where I say   5
Hours I mean years, mean life. And my lament
Is cries countless, cries like dead letters[2] sent
To dearest him that lives alas! away.

I am gall, I am heartburn. God's most deep decree
Bitter would have me taste: my taste was me;   10
Bones built in me, flesh filled, blood brimmed the curse.

Selfyeast of spirit a dull dough sours. I see
The lost are like this, and their scourge to be
As I am mine, their sweating selves; but worse.

1885   1918

Thou Art Indeed Just, Lord

*Justus quidem tu es, Domine, si disputem tecum; verumtamen
justa loquar ad te: Quare via impiorum prosperatur? &c.*[1]

Thou art indeed just, Lord, if I contend
With thee; but, sir, so what I plead is just.
Why do sinners' ways prosper? and why must
Disappointment all I endeavour end?

Wert thou my enemy, O thou my friend,   5
How wouldst thou worse, I wonder, than thou dost
Defeat, thwart me? Oh, the sots and thralls of lust
Do in spare hours more thrive than I that spend,

Sir, life upon thy cause. See, banks and brakes[2]
Now, leavèd how thick! lacèd they are again   10
With fretty chervil,[3] look, and fresh wind shakes

Them; birds build—but not I build; no, but strain,
Time's eunuch, and not breed one work that wakes.
Mine, O thou lord of life, send my roots rain.

1889   1918

---

1. Bitterness. Cf. *Faerie Queene* 3.11.2: "Untroubled
of vile feare, or bitter fell."
2. Letters undelivered or returned to the sender by the
post office.
1. "Righteous art thou, O Lord, when I plead with
thee: yet let me talk with thee of thy judgments:

Wherefore doth the way of the wicked prosper?" (Jeremiah 12.1). The Latin was Hopkins's title. For the author's revisions while composing this poem, see
"Poems in Process" (p. 2587).
2. Thickets.
3. A kind of herb, related to parsley.

The Twentieth Century

HISTORICAL BACKGROUND

The period, which for convenience we call "the twentieth century," begins really with the late nineteenth, when the sense of the passing of a major phase of English history was already in the air. Queen Victoria's Jubilee in 1887 and, even more, her Diamond Jubilee in 1897 were felt even by contemporaries to mark the end of an era. As the nineteenth century drew to a close, there were many manifestations of a weakening of traditional stabilities. The aesthetic movement, with its insistence on "art for art's sake," assaulted the assumptions about the nature and function of art held by ordinary middle-class readers, deliberately, provocatively. It helped to widen the breach between artists and writers on the one hand and the "Philistine" public on the other—a breach an earlier symptom of which was Matthew Arnold's war on the Philistines in *Culture and Anarchy* and that was later to result in the "alienation of the artist," which has since become a commonplace of criticism. This breach was more than a purely English matter. From France came the tradition of the bohemian life that scorned the limits imposed by conventional ideas of respectability, together with other notions of the artist as rejecting and rejected by ordinary society, which in different ways fostered the view of the alienated artist. The life and work of the French symbolist poets in France, the early novels of Thomas Mann in Germany (especially *Buddenbrooks*, 1901), and James Joyce's *Portrait of the Artist as a Young Man* (1916) show some of the very different ways in which this attitude revealed itself in literature all over Europe. In England, the growth of popular education as a result of the Education Act of 1870, which finally made elementary education compulsory and universal, led to the rapid emergence of a large, unsophisticated literary public at whom new kinds of journalism, in particular the cheap "yellow press," were directed. A public that was literate but not in any real sense educated increased steadily throughout the nineteenth century, and one result of this was the splitting up of the audience for literature into "highbrows," "lowbrows," and "middlebrows." Although in earlier periods there had been different kinds of audience for different kinds of writing, the split now developed with unprecedented speed and to an unprecedented degree because of the mass production of "popular" literature for the semiliterate. The fragmentation of the reading public now merged with the artist's war on the Philistine (and indeed was one of the causes of that war in the first place) to widen the gap between popular art and art esteemed only by the sophisticated and the expert.

Another manifestation—or at least accompaniment—of the end of the Victorian age was the rise of various kinds of pessimism and stoicism. The novels and poetry of Thomas Hardy show one kind of pessimism (and it *was* pessimism, even if

Hardy himself repudiated the term), and the poems of A. E. Housman show another variety, while a real or affected stoicism is to be found not only in these writers but also in many minor writers of the last decade of the nineteenth century and the first decade of the twentieth. Examples of this stoicism—the determination to stand for human dignity by enduring bravely, with a stiff upper lip, whatever fate may bring—range from Robert Louis Stevenson's essays and the rhetorically assertive poems of the editor and journalist W. E. Henley, to Rudyard Kipling's *Jungle Books* and many of his short stories, the last stanza of Housman's *The Chestnut Casts His Flambeaux* ("Bear them we can, and if we can we must") and W. B. Yeats's "They know that Hamlet and Lear are gay."

Although the high tide of anti-Victorianism was marked by the publication in 1918 of that classic of ironic debunking, *Eminent Victorians* by Lytton Strachey (1880–1932), the criticism of the normal attitudes and preconceptions of the Victorian middle classes first became really violent in the last two decades of the nineteenth century. No one could have been more savage in attacks on the Victorian conceptions of the family, education, and religion than Samuel Butler, whose novel *The Way of All Flesh* (completed in 1884, posthumously published in 1903) is still the bitterest indictment in English literature of the Victorian way of life. The chorus of questioning of Victorian assumptions grew ever louder as the century drew to an end; sounding prominently in it was the voice of the young Bernard Shaw, one of Butler's greatest admirers. The position of women, too, was rapidly changing during this period. The Married Woman's Property Act of 1882, which allowed married women to own property in their own right; the admission of women to the universities at different times during the latter part of the century; the fight for women's suffrage, which was not won until 1918 (and not fully won until 1928)—these events marked a change in the attitude toward women and in the part they played in the national life as well as in the relation between the sexes, which is reflected in a variety of ways in the literature of the period.

The Boer War (1899–1902), fought by the British to establish political and economic control over the Boer republics of South Africa, marked both the high point of and the reaction against British imperialism. It was a war against which many British intellectuals protested and one that the British in the end were slightly ashamed of having won. The development of the British Empire into the British Commonwealth (an association of self-governing countries) continued in fits and starts throughout the first half of the twentieth century, with imperialist and anti-imperialist sentiment often meeting head on; writers as far apart as Kipling and E. M. Forster occupied themselves with the problem. The Irish question also caused a great deal of excitement from the beginning of the period until well into the 1920s. A steadily rising Irish nationalism protested with increasing violence against the political subordination of Ireland to the British Crown and government. In World War I some Irish nationalists sought German help in rebelling against Britain, and this exacerbated feeling on both sides. No one can fully understand Yeats or Joyce without some awareness of the Irish struggle for independence, the feelings of Anglo-Irish literary people on this burning topic, and the way in which the Irish literary revival of the late nineteenth and early twentieth centuries (with which Yeats was much concerned) reflected a determination to achieve a vigorous national life culturally even if the road seemed blocked politically.

Edwardian England (1901–10) was very conscious of being no longer Victorian. Edward VII stamped his extrovert and self-indulgent character on the decade in which he reigned. It was a vulgar age of conspicuous enjoyment by those who could afford it, and writers and artists kept well away from implication in high society (although there were some conspicuous exceptions): in general, there was no equivalent in this period of Queen Victoria's interest in Tennyson. The alienation of artists and intellectuals was proceeding apace. From 1910 (when George

V came to the throne) until war broke out in August 1914, Britain achieved a temporary equilibrium between Victorian earnestness and Edwardian flashiness; in retrospect that Georgian period seems peculiarly golden, the last phase of assurance and stability before the old order throughout Europe broke up in violence with results that are still with us. Yet even then, under the surface, there was restlessness and experimentation. If this was the age of Rupert Brooke, it was also the age of T. S. Eliot's first experiments in a radically new kind of poetry.

Edwardian as a term applied to English cultural history suggests a period in which the social and economic stabilities of the Victorian age—country houses with numerous servants, a flourishing and confident middle class, a strict hierarchy of social classes—remained unimpaired, though on the level of ideas there was a sense of change and liberation. *Georgian* refers largely to the lull before the storm of World War I. That war, as our selection of the war poets makes clear, produced some major shifts in attitude.

The postwar disillusion of the 1920s was, it might be said, a spiritual matter, just as Eliot's Waste Land was a spiritual and not a literal wasteland. Depression and unemployment in the early 1930s, followed by the rise of Hitler and the cruel shadow of Fascism and Nazism over Europe, with its threat of another war, represented another sort of wasteland that produced another sort of effect on poets and novelists. The impotence of capitalist governments in the face of Hitlerism combined with economic dislocation to turn the majority of young intellectuals (and not only intellectuals) in the 1930s to the political Left. The 1930s were the red decade, because only the Left seemed to offer any solution. The early poetry of W. H. Auden and his contemporaries cried out for "the death of the old gang" (in Auden's phrase) and a clean sweep politically and economically, while the right-wing army's rebellion against the left-wing republican government in Spain, which started in the summer of 1936 and soon led to full-scale civil war, was regarded as a rehearsal for an inevitable second world war and thus further emphasized the inadequacy of politicians. Yet though all this is reflected passionately in the literature of the period, particularly in the poetry, it was not accompanied by any interesting developments in technique; many younger writers were more anxious to express their attitudes than to construct new kinds of works of art. The outbreak of World War II in September 1939, following very shortly on Hitler's pact with Russia, which shocked and disillusioned so many of the young left-wing writers, marked the sudden end of the red decade; the concern of writers in Britain now was to maintain their integrity and indeed their existence in what was from the beginning expected to be a long and destructive war. This they did surprisingly well, but nevertheless the struggle brought inevitable exhaustion, and winning a war, Great Britain lost an empire. India, long the jewel in the imperial Crown, came to independence in 1947 and, although India and the newly formed Muslim state of Pakistan elected to remain within the British Commonwealth, other former dominions did not. The Irish Republic withdrew from the Commonwealth in 1949, and the Republic of South Africa in 1961. While Britain was engaged in a painful reappraisal of its place in the world, countries that had lost the war—West Germany and Japan—were, in economic terms, winning the peace that followed.

Less obvious, but no less significant for English literature, were changes on the national scene. London, as the capital of the empire, had long dominated the culture as well as the politics and the economy of the British Isles. London spoke for Britain in the impeccable southern English intonations of the radio announcers of the state-owned British Broadcasting Corporation (known as the BBC), but from the 1960s this changed. Regional dialects were admitted to the air waves. Regional radio and television stations sprang up. The Arts Council, which had subsidized the nation's drama, literature, music, painting, and plastic arts from London, delegated much of its grant-giving responsibility to regional arts councils.

This gave a new confidence to writers and artists outside London and has since contributed to a notable renaissance of regional literature. At its best, this builds on the native tradition of Yeats and Hardy, transcending the narrowly provincial to achieve a true universality.

POETRY

The years leading up to World War I saw the start of a poetic revolution. The imagist movement, influenced by the philosopher-poet T. E. Hulme's insistence on hard, clear, precise images and encouraged by the modernist American poet Ezra Pound, who was then living in London, fought against romantic fuzziness and facile emotionalism in poetry. The movement developed simultaneously on both sides of the Atlantic, and its early members included Amy Lowell, Richard Aldington, H. D. (Hilda Doolittle), John Gould Fletcher, and F. S. Flint. As Flint explained in an article in March 1913, imagists insisted on "direct treatment of the 'thing,' whether subjective or objective," on the avoidance of all words "that did not contribute to the presentation," and on a freer metrical movement than a strict adherence to "the sequence of a metronome" could allow. All this encouraged precision in imagery and freedom of rhythmic movement, but more was required for the production of poetry of any real scope and interest. Imagism went in for the short, sharply etched, descriptive lyric, but it had no technique for the production of longer and more complex poems. Other new ideas about poetry helped to provide this technique. Sir Herbert Grierson's great edition of the poems of John Donne in 1912 both reflected and helped to encourage a new enthusiasm for seventeenth-century Metaphysical poetry. The revival of interest in Metaphysical wit brought with it a desire on the part of some pioneering poets to introduce into their poetry a much higher degree of intellectual complexity than had been found among the Victorians or the Georgians. The full subtlety of French symbolist poetry also now came to be appreciated; it had been admired in the 1890s, but for its dreamy suggestiveness rather than for its imagistic precision and complexity. At the same time a need was felt to bring poetic language and rhythms closer to those of conversation or at least to spice the formalities of poetic utterance with echoes of the colloquial and even the slangy. Irony, which made possible several levels of discourse simultaneously, and wit, with the use of puns (banished from serious poetry for more than two hundred years), helped to achieve that union of thought and passion that T. S. Eliot, in his review of Grierson's anthology of Metaphysical poetry (1921), saw as characteristic of the Metaphysicals and wished to bring back into modern poetry. A new critical and a new creative movement in poetry went hand in hand, with Eliot the high priest of both. It was Eliot who extended the scope of Imagism by bringing the English Metaphysicals and the French symbolists (as well as the English Jacobean dramatists) to the rescue, thus adding new criteria of complexity and allusiveness to the criteria of concreteness and precision stressed by the Imagists. It was Eliot, too, who introduced into modern English and American poetry the kind of irony achieved by shifting suddenly from the formal to the colloquial or by oblique allusions to objects or ideas that contrasted sharply with those carried by the surface meaning of the poem. Thus between, say, 1911 (the first year of the Georgian poets) and 1922 (the year of the publication of The Waste Land) a major revolution occurred in English — and for that matter American — poetic theory and practice — one that determined the way in which most serious poets and critics now think about their art. This revolution was by no means an isolated literary phenomenon. Writers on both sides of the English Channel were influenced by the French impressionist, post-impressionist, and cubist painters' radical reexamination of the nature of reality. Pound wrote books about the French sculptor Henri Gaudier-Brzeska and the American composer George Antheil. Wilfred Owen wrote in 1918: "I suppose I am doing in poetry what the advanced composers are doing in music"; and Eliot, while writing *The Waste Land* three years later, was so impressed by a performance of the composer Igor Stravinsky's *Le Sacre du Printemps (The Rite of Spring)* that he stood up at the end and cheered.

The posthumous publication by Robert Bridges in 1918 of the poetry of Gerard Manley Hopkins encouraged experimentation in language and rhythms. Hopkins combined absolute precision of the individual image with a complex ordering of images and a new kind of metrical patterning. The young poets of the early 1930s— Auden, Stephen Spender, C. Day Lewis—were much influenced by Hopkins as well as by Eliot (then the presiding genius of modern English and American poetry) and by a variety of other poets from the sixteenth-century John Skelton to Wilfred Owen.

Meanwhile the remarkable career of Yeats, stretching across the whole modern period, showed how a truly great poet can reflect the varying developments of his or her age yet maintain an unmistakably individual accent. Beginning among the aesthetes of the 1890s, turning later to a more tough and spare ironic language without losing his characteristic verbal magic, working out his own notions of symbolism and bringing them in different ways into his poetry, developing in his full maturity a rich symbolic and Metaphysical poetry with its own curiously haunting cadences and its imagery both shockingly realistic and movingly sugges-tive, Yeats's work is itself a history of English poetry between 1890 and 1939. Yet he is always Yeats, unique and inimitable—without doubt the greatest English-speaking poet of his age.

In his poem *Remembering the Thirties*, Donald Davie declared: "A neutral tone is nowadays preferred." That tone—the coolly clinical tone of Auden—dominated the poetry of the decade, but as it ended and World War II began, a neutral tone gave way to the vehemence of what came to be known as the New Apocalypse. The poets of this movement, the most notable of whom was Dylan Thomas, owed something of their audacity and violence to the example of the French surrealist poets and painters, who sought to express, often by free association, the operation of the subconscious mind. Many of these, such as Salvador Dali and Pablo Picasso, were both poets and painters, whose poetry was introduced to English readers in translations and in *A Short History of Surrealism* (1936) by David Gascoyne, one of the poets of the New Apocalypse. With the coming of the 1950s, however, the pendulum swung back again. A new generation of poets that included Donald Davie, Thom Gunn, and Philip Larkin reacted against what seemed to them the verbal excesses of Dylan Thomas, Edith Sitwell, and others. "The Movement," as this new group came to be called, aimed once again for a neutral tone, a purity of diction, in which to render an unpretentious fidelity to experience. Larkin, its most notable exponent, explicitly rejected the imported modernism of Pound and Eliot in favor of a native tradition represented in this century by Hardy. That tradition now flourishes in the work of Tony Harrison and Seamus Heaney. Other of the younger poets, following the example of Craig Raine and taking their name—the Martian School—from his poem *A Martian Sends a Postcard Home* once again look to the painters for their inspiration. *Look* is the operative word, for the eye is paramount in their poetry, an eye that sees the world with the freshness of a child or a painter or a visitor from Mars and records what it sees with an often exuberant wit.

In 1912, Edward Marsh introduced the first of his anthologies of *Georgian Poetry* with the claim that "English poetry is now once again putting on a new strength and beauty." That claim can be made with more justice today, and per-haps with more justice than it could have been made at any point in the years between.

FICTION

The years 1912 to 1930 were the Heroic Age of the modern novel, the age of Joseph Conrad, James Joyce, D. H. Lawrence, Virginia Woolf, and E. M. Forster. One can trace three major influences on the changes in attitude and technique in the fiction of this period. The first is the novelists' realization that the general background of belief that united them with their public in a common sense of what was significant in experience had disappeared. The public values of the Victorian novel, in which major crises of plot could be shown through changes in the social or financial or marital status of the chief characters, gave way to more personally conceived notions of value, dependent on the novelists' own intuitions and sensibilities rather than on public agreement. "To believe that your impressions hold good for others," Woolf once wrote (discussing Jane Austen), "is to be released from the cramp and confinement of personality." Modern novelists could no longer believe this: they had to fall back on personality, drawing their criteria of significance in human affairs (and thus their principles of selection) from their own intuitions, so that they needed to find ways of convincing readers that their own sense of what was significant in experience was truly valid. A new technical burden was thus imposed on the novelist's prose, for it had now to build up a world of values instead of drawing on an existing world of values. Woolf tried to solve the problem by using some of the devices of poetry to suggest the novelist's own sense of value and vision of the world. Joyce, on the other hand, made no attempt to convey a single personal attitude but reacted to the breakdown of public values by employing a kind of writing so multiple in its implications that it conveyed numerous points of view simultaneously, the author remaining totally objective and committed to none of them—a mode that required remarkable technical virtuosity.

The second influence on the changes in attitude and technique in the modern novel was a new view of time; time was not a series of chronological moments to be presented by the novelist in sequence with an occasional deliberate retrospect ("this reminded him of," "she recalled that") but a continuous flow in the consciousness of the individual, with the "already" continuously merging into the "not yet" and retrospect merging into anticipation. This influence is closely bound up with a third: the new notions of the nature of consciousness, which derived in a general way from the pioneer explorations of the subconscious by Sigmund Freud (1856–1939) and Carl Jung (1875–1961), but were also part of the spirit of the age and discernible even in those novelists who had not read either of these psychologists. Consciousness is multiple; the past is always present in it at some level and is continually coloring one's present reaction. Marcel Proust in France, in his great novel sequence *Remembrance of Things Past* (1913–28), had explored the ways in which the past impinges on the present and consciousness is determined by memory. The view that we *are* our memories, that our present is the sum of our past, that if we dig into the human consciousness we can tell the whole truth about people without waiting for a chronological sequence of time to take them through a series of testing circumstances, inevitably led to a technical revolution in the novel. For now, by exploring in depth into consciousness and memory rather than proceeding lengthwise along the dimension of time, a novelist could write a novel concerned ostensibly with only one day of the protagonist's life (Joyce's *Ulysses* and Woolf's *Mrs. Dalloway*). This view of multiple levels of consciousness existing simultaneously, coupled with the view of time as a constant flow rather than a series of separate moments, meant that novelists preferred to plunge into the consciousness of their characters in order to tell their stories rather than to provide external frameworks of chronological narrative. The "stream-of-consciousness" technique, in which the author tries to render directly the very fabric of a character's consciousness without reporting it in formal, quoted remarks, was developed in the 1920s as an important new technique of the English novel. It made for more difficult reading, at least for those accustomed only to the methods of the older English novel. No "porch" was constructed at the front of the novel to put the reader in possession of necessary preliminary information: such information emerged, as the novel progressed, from the consciousness of each character as it responded to the present with echoes of its past. No conventional signposts were put up to tell readers where they were, for that was believed to interfere with the immediacy of the impression. But once readers learn how to find their way in this unsignposted territory, they are rewarded by new delicacies of perception and new subtleties of presentation.

Concentration on the stream of consciousness and on the association of ideas within the individual consciousness led inevitably to stress on the essential loneliness of the individual. For all consciousnesses are unique and isolated, and if this unique, private world is the real world in which we live, if the public values to which we must pay lip service in the social world in which we move are not the real values that give meaning to our personalities, then we are all condemned to live in the prison of our own incommunicable consciousness. How is true communication possible in such a world? The public gestures imposed on us by society never correspond to our real inward needs. They are conventional in the bad sense, mechanical, imposing a crude standardization on the infinite subtlety of experience. If we do try to give out a sign from our real selves, that sign is bound to be misunderstood when read by some other self in the light of that self's quite other personality. The theme of such modern fiction is thus the possibility of love, the establishment of emotional communication, in a community of private consciousnesses. This is, in different ways, the theme of Joyce, of Lawrence, of Woolf, of Forster, and (on a rather different scale and not always so directly) of Conrad. The search for communion and the inescapable isolation of Leopold Bloom in *Ulysses* is symbolic of the human condition as seen by the modern novelist. Similar investigations of this basic condition are Forster's explorations of the conventions that seem to be helps to living but that in fact prevent true human contacts, and Woolf's projection of the relation between the self's need for privacy and the self's need for genuine communication. The theme of all Lawrence's novels is human relationships, the ideal of which he restlessly explored with shifting emphasis throughout his career; such relationships can be all too easily distorted by the mechanical conventions of society, by notions of respectability or propriety, by all the shams and frauds of middle-class life, by the demands of power or money or success. One might almost say that the greatest modern novels are about the difficulty, and at the same time the inevitability, of being human. The dilemma of the human condition is never really solved in these novels; but knowledge that the dilemma is shared—a knowledge so brilliantly conveyed in *Ulysses* and so wryly proffered by Forster—can both illuminate and comfort.

Not all the novelists of the period, of course, were concerned with these themes or employed the new techniques appropriate to them. The "documentary" novelists, such as Arnold Bennett and John Galsworthy (and, in at least some of his novels, H. G. Wells), presented, often with great skill, the changing social scene, showing considerable insight and sympathy in recording aspects of it through the behavior of their imagined characters. Woolf called these writers "materialists," maintaining that they were content to deal with externals and did not go on to explore those aspects of consciousness, of our true inward life, in which human reality resides. She was perhaps judging unfairly, by standards that were not applicable to their sort of fiction, but modern criticism has on the whole agreed with her.

The short story in this century has benefited from the new techniques of exploration in depth. A great consciousness of the symbolic uses to which objects and incidents can be put and a greater subtlety in the ways in which patterns of suggestiveness are built up below the quietly realistic surface can be found in the short stories of writers so different from each other as Joyce, Katherine Mansfield, Lawrence, Forster, Doris Lessing, Edna O'Brien, and Susan Hill. Mansfield learned from the Russian short-story writer Anton Chekhov (1860–1904) how to use the casual-seeming incidents of ordinary life in such a way as to set up haunting overtones of meaning. The apparently inconsequential surface masking the carefully organized substructure is found in much modern fiction (perhaps most of all in *Ulysses*): it is one of the results of the coming together, in the novel and the short story, of realism and symbolism, of contemporary probability and timeless significance. These things, of course, come together in great fiction of all ages, but modern writers contrive their coexistence with greater self-consciousness than their predecessors.

DRAMA

Modern drama begins in a sense with the witty drawing-room comedies of Oscar Wilde; yet Wilde founded no dramatic school. His wit was personal and generative of paradoxes for their own sake, unlike the wit of Restoration comedy, which reflected an attitude to the relation between the sexes that was part of a view of society held by a whole (if a small) social class. Bernard Shaw brought still another kind of wit into drama—not Wilde's light-hearted sparkle or yet the assured sophistication of the Restoration dramatists but the provocative paradox that was meant to tease and disturb, to challenge the complacency of the audience. Shaw's discussion plays were given dramatic life through the mastery of theatrical techniques, which he learned during his years as a dramatic critic. In his general attitudes he represents the anti-Victorianism of the late Victorians; his long life should not obscure the fact that his first—and some of his best—plays belong to the 1890s. Other attempts by twentieth-century dramatists to debate social questions on the stage—by John Galsworthy, for example—deserve respect for their humanity and intelligence and sometimes for their theatrical craftsmanship, but they lack Shaw's verbal and intellectual brilliance and his superb capacity to entertain.

We must turn to Ireland to find another really impressive variety of dramatic activity. The Irish Literary Theatre was founded in 1899, with Yeats's early play *The Countess Cathleen* as its first production. The founders—Yeats, Lady Gregory, George Moore, and Edward Martyn—wanted to make a contribution to an Irish literary revival, but they were influenced also by the Independent Theatre in London, founded in 1891 by J. T. Grein in order to encourage new developments in the drama. In 1902 the Irish Literary Theatre was able to maintain a permanent all-Irish company and changed its name to the Irish National Theatre, which moved in 1904 to the Abbey Theatre, by which name it has since been known. Many of the plays produced at the Abbey Theatre were only of local and ephemeral interest. But J. M. Synge's use of the speech and imagination of Irish country people, Yeats's powerful symbolic use of themes from old Irish legend, and Sean O'Casey's use of the Irish civil war as a background for plays combining tragic melodrama, humor of character, and irony of circumstance brought new kinds of vitality to the theater. T. S. Eliot attempted with considerable success to revive a ritual poetic drama in England with his *Murder in the Cathedral* (1935). His later attempts to combine religious symbolism with the box-office appeal of an entertaining society comedy (as in *The Cocktail Party*, 1950), although impressive technical achievements, were not wholly successful: the combination of contemporary social chatter with profound religious symbolism produces both an unevenness of tone and disturbing shifts in levels of realism. Elsewhere in modern drama the conflict between realism and symbolism (first clearly seen in works by the great Norwegian playwright Henrik Ibsen, 1828–1906) is acted out in a variety of ways.

In spite of the achievements of Shaw, Yeats, and Eliot, it cannot be said of the drama, as it can of poetry and fiction in the first half of the century, that a technical revolution occurred that changed the whole course of literary history with respect to that particular literary form. The reformers of the 1890s invoked the name of Ibsen: like Shaw they saw him as essentially a critic of middle-class society rather than (as critics tend to see him today) as an essentially poetic dramatist experimenting with symbolic modes of expression. This may be the reason why the influence of Ibsen soon petered out in run-of-the-mill plays of humanitarian social concern. The staple of the London West End theater remained social comedy stiffened by occasional irony and sweetened by sentimentality (Noel Coward, 1899–1973, was one of the best, as well as most successful, purveyors of this sort of fare). The cleverly contrived sentimentalities of J. M. Barrie (1860–1937) were highly popular in their day; Barrie's plays showed a great theatrical skill and a determined cunning in the exploitation of the audience's reaction. That audience consisted for the most part of tired Philistines, and it was they who determined what was to be a box-office success.

The course of British and Irish drama during the first half of the century may have been less revolutionary than developments in poetry and fiction over the same period, but its revolution was to come, and since the end of World War II it has been the major area of literary innovation. There is no accounting for the emergence of genius. In the history of cultural movements, it appears sporadically and less often singly than in constellations, as if it were the property of great "stars" to attract lesser. A factor in the emergence of such a constellation in twentieth-century British and Irish drama has been the role played by the BBC in commissioning and promoting new work. Wartime verse plays, written for radio by Louis MacNeice and other poets, helped prepare the audience that in the late 1940s and early 1950s rapturously received the verse plays of Christopher Fry (1907–). It seemed that these were about to bring a new kind of poetic life into English drama. But Fry's exuberantly witty use of metaphor soon lost its appeal, and by the late 1950s a very different kind of drama brought vitality to the British theater. John Osborne's *Look Back in Anger* was produced at the Royal Court Theatre in 1956. Angrily, violently, and in an unadorned and sometimes brutally colloquial dialogue, it thrust on the audience the revelation of psychological and social problems left unresolved, or even exacerbated, by the welfare state. *The Entertainer* (1957) was similar in its brash virtuosity; Osborne's third play, *Luther* (1960), shows him moving out of a preoccupation with a restricted part of the contemporary social scene to wider concerns and a freer use of imagination. Arnold Wesker was another Royal Court discovery and became the most prominent of the so-called kitchen sink playwrights. In a trilogy that began with *Chicken Soup with Barley* (1958), he explored, although less stridently than Osborne, related social and psychological problems. Joan Littlewood's Theatre Workshop introduced another kind of vigorous new theatricalism, with an impromptu-seeming kind of play made up of numerous small scenes: distinctive examples are Brendan Behan's *The Quare Fellow* (1956) and Shelagh Delaney's *A Taste of Honey* (1958). Another significant factor in the recent resurgence of British drama has been the interaction of such innovative directors as Peter Brook and Peter Hall with the outstanding playwrights of the period and with several generations of superlative actors.

It is clear, however, that the major star in the constellation of playwrights that has emerged in the last three decades is Samuel Beckett. Friend and amanuensis of the major star of an earlier literary constellation, James Joyce, Beckett changed the course of English drama with his first play, written in French in 1948 and translated by the author himself as *Waiting for Godot* (1953), which strongly influenced a younger group of playwrights that includes Harold Pinter, South African Athol Fugard, and Tom Stoppard. These, now at the height of their powers, have benefited from the variety of outlets for their work—large stage, small stage, film, radio, and television—and have helped to make London once again the capital city of the theater world.

TEXTS	CONTEXTS
1898 Hardy, *Wessex Poems* • Shaw, **Mrs. Warren's Profession**	
	1899 William Butler Yeats and others found the Irish National Theater
	1901–10 Reign of Edward VII: the "Edwardian" era
1902 Conrad, **Heart of Darkness**	
	1905 Albert Einstein publishes theory of special relativity
	1910–36 Reign of George V
1914 Joyce, *Dubliners* (**The Dead**) • Hardy, *Satires of Circumstances* (**Channel Firing, The Walk**, etc.)	1914–18 World War I
	1916 Easter Uprising in Dublin, commemorated by Yeats, **Easter 1916**
1917 Eliot, **The Love Song of J. Alfred Prufrock**	
	1918 Armistice • Franchise Act grants vote to women over thirty
1920 Lawrence, *Women in Love*	1920 Treaty of Versailles • League of Nations formed
1921 Yeats, *Michael Robartes and the Dancer* (**Easter 1916, The Second Coming, A Prayer for My Daughter**)	1921 Formation of Irish Free State with Northern Ireland (Ulster) remaining part of Great Britain
1922 Katherine Mansfield, *The Garden-Party and Other Stories* • Joyce, *Ulysses* (**Proteus, Lestrygonians**); Eliot, **The Waste Land**	
	1923 Yeats receives Nobel Prize
	1925 Shaw receives Nobel Prize
1927 Virginia Woolf, *To the Lighthouse*	1927 Eliot becomes British citizen; joins Anglican Church
1928 Yeats, *The Tower* (**Sailing to Byzantium, Among School Children**)	

Boldface titles indicate works in the anthology.

TEXTS	CONTEXTS
1929 Woolf, *A Room of One's Own*	1929 Stock market crash; the Great Depression begins
	1933 Adolf Hitler comes to power in Germany
1936–39 Yeats, *Last Poems (**The Circus Animals' Desertion, Under Ben Bulben**)*	1936–39 Spanish Civil War; George Orwell, W. H. Auden, and Louis MacNeice go to Spain to support the Republican side
	1936 Edward VIII succeeds George V but abdicates in favor of his brother, crowned as George VI
1939 Auden, *In Memory of W. B. Yeats*	1939–45 World War II
	1940 Fall of France • Battle of Britain
	1941–45 The Holocaust
1942 Eliot, *Four Quartets (**Little Gidding**)*	
1945 Auden, *Collected Poems*	
1946 Dylan Thomas, *Deaths and Entrances*, containing his major poems	
	1947 India and Pakistan become independent nations
	1948 Eliot receives Nobel Prize
	1950 Apartheid laws passed in South Africa
	1952 George VI dies; accession of Elizabeth II
1955 Samuel Beckett, *Waiting for Godot*	
1958 Beckett, ***Endgame***	
	1969 Apollo moon-landing • Beckett receives Nobel Prize

THOMAS HARDY
1840–1928

1872–96:   Career as novelist, ending with *Jude the Obscure*.
1898:   *Wessex Poems*, first collection of poetry.

Thomas Hardy was born near Dorchester, in that area of southwest England that he was to make the "Wessex" of his novels. He attended local schools until the age of fifteen, when he was apprenticed to a Dorchester architect with whom he worked for six years. In 1861 he went to London to continue his studies and to practice as an architect. Meanwhile he was completing his general education informally through his own erratic reading and was becoming more and more interested in both fiction and poetry. After some early attempts at writing both short stories and poems, he decided to concentrate on fiction. His first novel was rejected by the publishers in 1868 on the recommendation of George Meredith, who nevertheless advised Hardy to write another. The result was *Desperate Remedies*, published anonymously in 1871, followed the next year by his first real success (also published anonymously), *Under the Greenwood Tree*. Hardy's career as a novelist was now well launched; he gave up his architectural work and produced a series of novels that ended with *Jude the Obscure* in 1896. The hostile reception of this novel sent him back to poetry. His remarkable epic-drama of the Napoleonic Wars, *The Dynasts*, came out in three parts between 1903 and 1908; after this he wrote mostly lyric poetry.

Hardy's novels, set in a predominantly rural "Wessex," show the forces of nature outside and inside individuals combining to shape human destiny. Against a background of immemorial agricultural labor, with ancient monuments such as Stonehenge or an old Roman amphitheater reminding us of the human past, he presents characters at the mercy of their own passions or finding temporary salvation in the age-old rhythms of rural work or rural recreation. Men and women in Hardy's fiction are not masters of their fates; they are at the mercy of the indifferent forces that manipulate their behavior and their relations with others, but they can achieve dignity through endurance and heroism through simple strength of character. The characteristic Victorian novelist—e.g., Dickens and Thackeray—was concerned with the behavior and problems of people in a given social milieu, which were described in detail; Hardy preferred to go directly for the elemental in human behavior with a minimum of contemporary social detail. Most of Hardy's novels are tragic, although *Under the Greenwood Tree* has an idyllic character possessed by no other of his novels. But even here the happy ending is achieved only by ending the story with the marriage of the hero and heroine and refusing to go further; the texture of the narrative, for all its moments of gaiety and charm, has already suggested the bitter ironies of which life is capable. His later work explores those ironies with sometimes an almost malevolent staging of coincidence to emphasize the disparity between human desire and ambition on the one hand and what fate has in store for the characters on the other. But fate is not a wholly external force. Men and women are driven by the demands of their own nature as much as by anything from outside them. *Tess of the D'Urbervilles* (1891) is the story of an intelligent and sensitive girl, daughter of a poor family, driven to murder and so to death by hanging, by a concatenation of events and circumstances so bitterly ironic that many readers find it the darkest of Hardy's novels, while others would award that distinction to *Jude the Obscure*, the disturbingly powerful account of an ambitious rustic trapped between his intellect and his sensuality and as a result delivered to destruction.

Hardy himself denied that he was a pessimist, calling himself a "meliorist," i.e., one who believes that the world may be made better by human effort. But there is little sign of meliorism in either his most important novels or his lyric poetry. In his poems—which alone are represented here because no extract could do justice to Hardy's power as a novelist—many of his characteristic attitudes and ideas and many of his favorite situations can be found. A number of his poems are verse anecdotes illustrating the perversity of fate, the disastrous or ironic coincidence. But his best poems go beyond this mood to present with quiet gravity and a carefully controlled elegiac feeling some aspect of human sorrow or loss or frustration or regret, always projected through a particular, fully realized situation. *Hap* shows Hardy in the characteristic mood of complaining about the irony of human destiny in a universe ruled by chance, but a poem such as *The Walk* (one of a group of poems written after the death of his first wife in 1912) gives, with remarkable power, concrete embodiment to a sense of loss. That power—we see it also in *A Broken Appointment*—is achieved through a kind of verbal as well as an emotional integrity. Hardy's poetry, like his prose, often has a self-taught air about it; both can be odd or pretentious or awkward or clumsy. But at their best both his poetry and his prose have an air of persuasive authenticity. The association of a given emotion with particular visual memories in *Neutral Tones*, for example, is impressive because it carries such extraordinary conviction, and it carries that conviction because the rhythms and rhymes are handled so as to suggest the kind of utterance actually wrung from the poet (consider, e.g., the curious dead fall of "They had fallen from an ash, and were gray"). At the same time, Hardy will use an antique or a poetic word or phrase ("thereby," "a-wing") if it fits in with the movement of the poem and keeps him from having to stop and search for something more deft: the result is an effect not of artificiality but of spontaneity. Hardy's use of ballad rhythms often helps to give an elemental quality to his poetry, suggesting that this incident or situation, carefully particularized though it is, nevertheless stands for some profound and recurring themes in human experience.

The sadness in Hardy—his inability to believe in the government of the world by a benevolent God, his sense of the waste and frustration involved in human life, his insistent irony when faced with moral or metaphysical questions—is part of the late Victorian mood. We can see something like it in A. E. Housman, and there is an earlier version of Victorian pessimism in Edward FitzGerald's *Rubáiyát of Omar Khayyám*, published when Hardy was nineteen. What has been termed "the disappearance of God" affected him more deeply than many of his contemporaries, because until he was twenty-five he seriously considered entering the church. Yet his characteristic themes and attitudes cannot be related simply to the reaction to new scientific and philosophical ideas (Darwin's theory of evolution, for example) that we see in so many forms in late-nineteenth-century literature. The favorite poetic mood of both Tennyson and Arnold was also an elegiac one (e.g., in Tennyson's *Break, Break, Break* and Arnold's *Dover Beach*), but this is not Hardy's mood. The sad-sweet cadences of Victorian self-pity are not to be found in Hardy's poetry, which is sterner, as though braced by a long look at the worst. It is this sternness—sometimes amounting to ruggedness—together with his verbal and emotional integrity, his refusal ever to surrender to mere poetic fashion, his quietly searching individual accent, that has helped to bring about the steady rise in Hardy's poetic reputation, so that today he is regarded not only as a distinguished novelist but also as a great English poet.

Hap[1]

If but some vengeful god would call to me
From up the sky, and laugh: "Thou suffering thing,
Know that thy sorrow is my ecstasy,
That thy love's loss is my hate's profiting!"

Then would I bear it, clench myself, and die,   5
Steeled by the sense of ire unmerited;
Half-eased in that a Powerfuller than I
Had willed and meted[2] me the tears I shed.

But not so. How arrives it joy lies slain,
And why unblooms the best hope ever sown?   10
—Crass Casualty obstructs the sun and rain,
And dicing Time for gladness casts a moan. . . .
These purblind Doomsters[3] had as readily strown
Blisses about my pilgrimage as pain.

1866   1898

The Impercipient

(At a Cathedral Service)

That with this bright believing band
        I have no claim to be,
That faiths by which my comrades stand
        Seem fantasies to me,
And mirage-mists their Shining Land,   5
        Is a strange destiny.

Why thus my soul should be consigned
        To infelicity,
Why always I must feel as blind
        To sights my brethren see,   10
Why joys they have found I cannot find,
        Abides a mystery.

Since heart of mine knows not that ease
        Which they know; since it be
That He who breathes All's Well to these   15
        Breathes no All's-Well to me,
My lack might move their sympathies
        And Christian charity!

I am like a gazer who should mark
        An inland company   20
Standing upfingered, with, "Hark! hark!
        The glorious distant sea!"

1. I.e., chance (as also "Casualty," line 11).   3. Half-blind judges.
2. Allotted, given.

And feel, "Alas, 'tis but yon dark
    And wind-swept pine to me!"

Yet I would bear my shortcomings   25
    With meet tranquillity,
But for the charge that blessed things
    I'd liefer not have be.
O, doth a bird beshorn of wings
    Go earth-bound wilfully!   30

• • •

Enough. As yet disquiet clings
    About us. Rest shall we.

1898

Neutral Tones

We stood by a pond that winter day,
And the sun was white, as though chidden of God,
And a few leaves lay on the starving sod;
    —They had fallen from an ash, and were gray.

Your eyes on me were as eyes that rove   5
Over tedious riddles of years ago;
And some words played between us to and fro
    On which lost the more by our love.

The smile on your mouth was the deadest thing
Alive enough to have strength to die;   10
And a grin of bitterness swept thereby
    Like an ominous bird a-wing. . .

Since then, keen lessons that love deceives,
And wrings with wrong, have shaped to me
Your face, and the God-curst sun, and a tree,   15
    And a pond edged with grayish leaves.

1867   1898

I Look into My Glass[1]

I look into my glass,
And view my wasting skin,
And say, "Would God it came to pass
My heart had shrunk as thin!"

For then, I, undistrest   5
By hearts grown cold to me,

1. Mirror.

Could lonely wait my endless rest
With equanimity.

But Time, to make me grieve,
Part steals, lets part abide;   10
And shakes this fragile frame at eve
With throbbings of noontide.

1898

A Broken Appointment

You did not come,
And marching Time drew on, and wore me numb.—
Yet less for loss of your dear presence there
Than that I thus found lacking in your make
That high compassion which can overbear   5
Reluctance for pure lovingkindness' sake
Grieved I, when, as the hope-hour stroked its sum,
    You did not come.

You love not me,
And love alone can lend you loyalty;   10
—I know and knew it. But, unto the store
Of human deeds divine in all but name,
Was it not worth a little hour or more
To add yet this: Once you, a woman, came
To soothe a time-torn man; even though it be   15
    You love not me?

1902

Drummer Hodge

1

They throw in Drummer Hodge, to rest
    Uncoffined—just as found:
His landmark is a kopje-crest
    That breaks the veldt[1] around;
And foreign constellations west[2]   5
    Each night above his mound.

2

Young Hodge the Drummer never knew—
    Fresh from his Wessex home—
The meaning of the broad Karoo,[3]

---

1. South African Dutch (Afrikaans) word for a plain or prairie. "Kopje-crest": Afrikaans for a small hill. The poem is a lament for an English soldier killed in the Boer War (1899–1902).

2. Set. The "foreign constellations" are those visible only in the Southern Hemisphere.
3. A dry tableland region in South Africa (usually spelled "Karroo").

10

The Bush,[4] the dusty loam,
And why uprose to nightly view
    Strange stars amid the gloam.
3
Yet portion of that unknown plain
    Will Hodge for ever be;
His homely Northern breast and brain   15
    Grow to some Southern tree,
And strange-eyed constellations reign
    His stars eternally.

1899   1902

The Darkling[1] Thrush

I leant upon a coppice gate[2]
    When Frost was spectre-gray,
And Winter's dregs made desolate
    The weakening eye of day.
The tangled bine-stems[3] scored the sky   5
    Like strings of broken lyres,
And all mankind that haunted nigh
    Had sought their household fires.

The land's sharp features seemed to be
    The Century's corpse outleant,[4]   10
His crypt the cloudy canopy,
    The wind his death-lament.
The ancient pulse of germ and birth
    Was shrunken hard and dry,
And every spirit upon earth   15
    Seemed fervourless as I.

At once a voice arose among
    The bleak twigs overhead
In a full-hearted evensong
    Of joy illimited;   20
An aged thrush, frail, gaunt, and small,
    In blast-beruffled plume,
Had chosen thus to fling his soul
    Upon the growing gloom.

So little cause for carolings   25
    Of such ecstatic sound
Was written on terrestrial things
    Afar or nigh around,
That I could think there trembled through

---

4. British colonial word for an uncleared area of land.   3. Twining stems of shrubs.
1. In the dark.   4. Leaning out (of its coffin); i.e., the 19th century was
2. Gate leading to a small wood or thicket.   dead. This poem was written on December 31, 1900.

His happy good-night air   30
Some blessed Hope, whereof he knew
And I was unaware.

1900   1901

The Ruined Maid

"O 'Melia, my dear, this does everything crown!
Who could have supposed I should meet you in Town?
And whence such fair garments, such prosperi-ty?" —
"O didn't you know I'd been ruined?" said she.

— "You left us in tatters, without shoes or socks,   5
Tired of digging potatoes, and spudding up docks;[1]
And now you've gay bracelets and bright feathers three!" —
"Yes: that's how we dress when we're ruined," said she.

— "At home in the barton[2] you said 'thee' and 'thou,'
And 'thik oon,' and 'theäs oon,' and 't'other'; but now   10
Your talking quite fits 'ee for high compa-ny!" —
"Some polish is gained with one's ruin," said she.

— "Your hands were like paws then, your face blue and bleak
But now I'm bewitched by your delicate cheek,
And your little gloves fit as on any la-dy!" —   15
"We never do work when we're ruined," said she.

— "You used to call home-life a hag-ridden dream,
And you'd sigh, and you'd sock;[3] but at present you seem
To know not of megrims[4] or melancho-ly!" —
"True. One's pretty lively when ruined," said she.   20

— "I wish I had feathers, a fine sweeping gown,
And a delicate face, and could strut about Town!" —
"My dear—a raw country girl, such as you be,
Cannot quite expect that. You ain't ruined," said she.

1866   1901

Channel Firing[1]

That night your great guns, unawares,
Shook all our coffins as we lay,

---

1. Digging up a species of thick-rooted weed.
2. Farmyard.
3. Sigh.
4. Low spirits.

1. Written in April 1914, when Anglo-German naval rivalry was growing steadily more acute; the title refers to gunnery practice in the English Channel. Four months later (August 4), World War I broke out.

And broke the chancel[2] window-squares,
We thought it was the Judgment-day

And sat upright. While drearisome   5
Arose the howl of wakened hounds:
The mouse let fall the altar-crumb,
The worms drew back into the mounds,

The glebe cow[3] drooled. Till God called, "No;
It's gunnery practice out at sea   10
Just as before you went below;
The world is as it used to be:

"All nations striving strong to make
Red war yet redder. Mad as hatters
They do no more for Christès[4] sake   15
Than you who are helpless in such matters.

"That this is not the judgment-hour
For some of them's a blessed thing,
For if it were they'd have to scour
Hell's floor for so much threatening. . . .   20

"Ha, ha. It will be warmer when
I blow the trumpet (if indeed
I ever do; for you are men,
And rest eternal sorely need)."

So down we lay again. "I wonder,   25
Will the world ever saner be,"
Said one, "than when He sent us under
In our indifferent century!"

And many a skeleton shook his head.
"Instead of preaching forty year,"   30
My neighbour Parson Thirdly said,
"I wish I had stuck to pipes and beer."

Again the guns disturbed the hour,
Roaring their readiness to avenge,
As far inland as Stourton Tower,   35
And Camelot, and starlit Stonehenge.[5]

1914   1914

2. Part of church nearest to the altar.
3. I.e., cow on a small plot of land belonging to a church (a "glebe" is a small field).
4. The archaic spelling and pronunciation suggest a ballad note of doom.
5. The sound of guns preparing for war across the

Channel reaches Alfred's ("Stourten") Tower (near Stourton in Dorset), commemorating King Alfred's defeat of a Danish invasion in 879; also the site of his court at Camelot (supposedly near Glastonbury) and the famous prehistoric stone circle of Stonehenge on Salisbury Plain.

The Convergence of the Twain

(Lines on the Loss of the Titanic*)*[1]

1

In a solitude of the sea
Deep from human vanity,
And the Pride of Life that planned her, stilly couches she.

2

Steel chambers, late the pyres
Of her salamandrine fires,[2]   5
Cold currents thrid,[3] and turn to rhythmic tidal lyres.

3

Over the mirrors meant
To glass the opulent
The sea-worm crawls—grotesque, slimed, dumb, indifferent.

4

Jewels in joy designed   10
To ravish the sensuous mind
Lie lightless, all their sparkles bleared and black and blind.

5

Dim moon-eyed fishes near
Gaze at the gilded gear
And query: "What does this vaingloriousness down here?" . . .   15

6

Well: while was fashioning
This creature of cleaving wing,
The Immanent Will[4] that stirs and urges everything

7

Prepared a sinister mate
For her—so gaily great—   20
A Shape of Ice, for the time far and dissociate.

8

And as the smart ship grew
In stature, grace, and hue,
In shadowy silent distance grew the Iceberg too.

9

Alien they seemed to be: 25
No mortal eye could see
The intimate welding of their later history,

10

Or sign that they were bent
By paths coincident
On being anon twin halves of one august event,   30

1. The *Titanic* was the largest and most luxurious ocean liner of the day. Considered unsinkable, it sank with great loss of life on April 15, 1912, on the ship's maiden voyage, from Southampton to the United States, after colliding with an iceberg.
2. Probably "fires in which nothing could survive" (although, since the salamander is a lizardlike animal supposed to be able to live in fire, "salamandrine" usually means "able to resist or to live in fire").
3. A variant form of the verb "thread."
4. The force (blind, but slowly gaining consciousness throughout history) that drives the world, according to Hardy's philosophy.

11
Till the Spinner of the Years
Said "Now!" And each one hears,
And consummation comes, and jars two hemispheres.

1912   1912, 1914

Ah, Are You Digging on My Grave?

"Ah, are you digging on my grave
    My loved one?—planting rue?"[1]
— "No: yesterday he went to wed
One of the brightest wealth has bred.
'It cannot hurt her now,' he said,   5
    'That I should not be true.' "

"Then who is digging on my grave?
    My nearest dearest kin?"
— "Ah, no; they sit and think, 'What use!
What good will planting flowers produce?   10
No tendance of her mound can loose
    Her spirit from Death's gin.' "[2]

"But some one digs upon my grave?
    My enemy?—prodding sly?"
— "Nay: when she heard you had passed the Gate   15
That shuts on all flesh soon or late,
She thought you no more worth her hate,
    And cares not where you lie."

"Then, who is digging on my grave?
    Say—since I have not guessed!"   20
— "O it is I, my mistress dear,
Your little dog, who still lives near,
And much I hope my movements here
    Have not disturbed your rest?"

"Ah, yes! *You* dig upon my grave . . .   25
    Why flashed it not on me
That one true heart was left behind!
What feeling do we ever find
To equal among human kind
    A dog's fidelity!"   30

"Mistress, I dug upon your grave
    To bury a bone, in case
I should be hungry near this spot
When passing on my daily trot.

1. A yellow-flowered herb, traditionally an emblem of   2. Trap.
sorrow (*rue* is also an archaic word for "sorrow").

I am sorry, but I quite forgot   35
    It was your resting-place."

                                                                  1914

Under the Waterfall

"Whenever I plunge my arm, like this,
In a basin of water, I never miss
The sweet sharp sense of a fugitive day
Fetched back from its thickening shroud of gray.
            Hence the only prime   5
            And real love-rhyme
            That I know by heart,
            And that leaves no smart,
Is the purl of a little valley fall
About three spans wide and two spans tall   10
Over a table of solid rock,
And into a scoop of the self-same block;
The purl of a runlet that never ceases
In stir of kingdoms, in wars, in peaces;
With a hollow boiling voice it speaks   15
And has spoken since hills were turfless peaks."

"And why gives this the only prime
Idea to you of a real love-rhyme?
And why does plunging your arm in a bowl
Full of spring water, bring throbs to your soul?"   20

"Well, under the fall, in a crease of the stone,
Though where precisely none ever has known,
Jammed darkly, nothing to show how prized,
And by now with its smoothness opalized,
            Is a drinking-glass: 25
            For, down that pass
            My lover and I
            Walked under a sky
Of blue with a leaf-wove awning of green,
In the burn of August, to paint the scene,   30
And we placed our basket of fruit and wine
By the runlet's rim, where we sat to dine;
And when we had drunk from the glass together,
Arched by the oak-copse from the weather,
I held the vessel to rinse in the fall,   35
Where it slipped, and sank, and was past recall,
Though we stooped and plumbed the little abyss
With long bared arms. There the glass still is.
And, as said, if I thrust my arm below
Cold water in basin or bowl, a throe[1]   40
From the past awakens a sense of that time,

---

1. Violent pang.

And the glass we used, and the cascade's rhyme.
The basin seems the pool, and its edge
The hard smooth face of the brook-side ledge,
And the leafy pattern of china-ware   45
The hanging plants that were bathing there.

"By night, by day, when it shines or lours,
There lies intact that chalice of ours,
And its presence adds to the rhyme of love
Persistently sung by the fall above.   50
No lip has touched it since his and mine
In turns therefrom sipped lovers' wine."

        1914

The Walk

You did not walk with me
Of late to the hill-top tree
    By the gated ways,
    As in earlier days;
You were weak and lame,   5
    So you never came,
And I went alone, and I did not mind,
Not thinking of you as left behind.

I walked up there to-day
Just in the former way: 10
    Surveyed around
    The familiar ground
    By myself again:
    What difference, then?
Only that underlying sense   15
Of the look of a room on returning thence.

1912–13   1914

The Voice

Woman much missed, how you call to me, call to me,
Saying that now you are not as you were
When you had changed from the one who was all to me,
But as at first, when our day was fair.

Can it be you that I hear? Let me view you, then,   5
Standing as when I drew near to the town
Where you would wait for me: yes, as I knew you then,
Even to the original air-blue gown!

Or is it only the breeze, in its listlessness
Travelling across the wet mead to me here,   10

You being ever dissolved to wan wistlessness,[1]
Heard no more again far or near?

    Thus I; faltering forward,
    Leaves around me falling,
Wind oozing thin through the thorn from norward,[2]   15
    And the woman calling.

December 1912   1914

The Workbox

"See, here's the workbox, little wife,
    That I made of polished oak."
He was a joiner,[1] of village life;
    She came of borough folk.[2]

He holds the present up to her   5
    As with a smile she nears
And answers to the profferer,
    "'Twill last all my sewing years!"

"I warrant it will. And longer too.
    'Tis a scantling[3] that I got   10
Off poor John Wayward's coffin, who
    Died of they knew not what.

"The shingled pattern that seems to cease
    Against your box's rim
Continues right on in the piece   15
    That's underground with him.

"And while I worked it made me think
    Of timber's varied doom;
One inch where people eat and drink,
    The next inch in a tomb.   20

"But why do you look so white, my dear,
    And turn aside your face?
You knew not that good lad, I fear,
    Though he came from your native place?"

"How could I know that good young man,   25
    Though he came from my native town,
When he must have left far earlier than
    I was a woman grown?"

"Ah, no. I should have understood!
    It shocked you that I gave   30

1. Inattention.   2. Townspeople.
2. Northward.   3. Small piece of wood.
1. Carpenter.

To you one end of a piece of wood
  Whose other is in a grave?"

"Don't, dear, despise my intellect,
  Mere accidental things
Of that sort never have effect   35
  On my imaginings."

Yet still her lips were limp and wan,
  Her face still held aside,
As if she had known not only John,
  But known of what he died.   40

                                       1914

During Wind and Rain

They sing their dearest songs—
He, she, all of them—yea,
Treble and tenor and bass,
  And one to play;
With the candles mooning each face. . . .   5
  Ah, no; the years O!
How the sick leaves reel down in throngs!

They clear the creeping moss—
Elders and juniors—aye,
Making the pathways neat   10
  And the garden gay;
And they build a shady seat. . . .
  Ah, no; the years, the years;
See, the white storm-birds wing across.

They are blithely breakfasting all—   15
Men and maidens—yea,
Under the summer tree,
  With a glimpse of the bay,
While pet fowl come to the knee. . . .
  Ah, no; the years O!   20
And the rotten rose is ript from the wall.

They change to a high new house,
He, she, all of them—aye,
Clocks and carpets and chairs
  On the lawn all day,   25
And brightest things that are theirs. . . .
  Ah, no; the years, the years;
Down their carved names the rain-drop ploughs.

                                       1917

In Time of "The Breaking of Nations"[1]

1

Only a man harrowing clods
    In a slow silent walk
With an old horse that stumbles and nods
    Half asleep as they stalk.

2

Only thin smoke without flame   5
    From the heaps of couch-grass;
Yet this will go onward the same
    Though Dynasties pass.

3

Yonder a maid and her wight[2]
    Come whispering by: 10
War's annals will cloud into night
    Ere their story die.

1915   1916

He Never Expected Much

[or]
A Consideration
[*A reflection*] *on My Eighty-Sixth Birthday*

Well, World, you have kept faith with me,
    Kept faith with me;
Upon the whole you have proved to be
    Much as you said you were.
Since as a child I used to lie   5
Upon the leaze[1] and watch the sky,
Never, I own, expected I
    That life would all be fair.

'Twas then you said, and since have said,
    Times since have said,   10
In that mysterious voice you shed
    From clouds and hills around:
"Many have loved me desperately,
Many with smooth serenity,
While some have shown contempt of me   15
    Till they dropped underground.

"I do not promise overmuch,
    Child; overmuch;
Just neutral-tinted haps[2] and such,"
    You said to minds like mine.   20
Wise warning for your credit's sake!

---

1. Cf. "Thou art my battle axe and weapon of war: for   2. Man.
with thee will I break in pieces the nations" (Jeremiah   1. Pasture.
51.20). The poem was written during World War I.   2. Happenings.

Which I for one failed not to take,
And hence could stem such strain and ache
As each year might assign.

1926

1928

BERNARD SHAW
1856–1950

1876:   Settles in London.
1892:   *Widowers' Houses* produced.
1898:   Publication of *Plays Pleasant and Unpleasant.*
1923:   *Saint Joan.*

George Bernard Shaw was born in Dublin of English stock, one of the galaxy of the Anglo-Irish (they include Jonathan Swift, Richard Brinsley Sheridan, Edmund Burke, and W. B. Yeats) who have contributed so brilliantly to English literature. He settled in London in 1876 and began his literary career as a writer of unsuccessful novels. He soon became interested in social reform and added his original voice to that of other reformers of the time. His interest in music (his mother was a music teacher) led him into journalism as a music critic, and in 1895 he became drama critic for the *Saturday Review.*

Shaw's training in music and dramatic criticism, his interest in social reform, his admiration for Wagner and Isben (both looked at askance by the conservative), and the influence of Samuel Butler (author of *Erewhon* and *The Way of All Flesh* and the great satirist of Victorian life and thought) all helped to make him a playwright who on the one hand knew all the conventional tricks of the theater and on the other was determined to use the drama as a means of shaking theater audiences out of their complacencies, hypocrisies, and thoughtless acquiescence in all kinds of social evil.

Shaw's first play, *Widowers' Houses*, dealt in a characteristically provocative manner with the problem of slum landlordism: even here, with a subject easily compartmentalized into moral blacks and whites, Shaw's technique of reversal and inversion kept revealing new aspects of the problem, so that, instead of merely condemning the landlord, the audience is forced to comprehend the entire complex of social and economic conditions that produced the problem. *Mrs. Warren's Profession*, written in 1893, was for a long time banned from the public theater because of its concern with the taboo subject of prostitution; it is not, however, simply about prostitution, but about well-meaning brothel keepers and the laws of supply and demand, which it explores with boldness and wit, again substituting the revelation of causes and consequences for simple moral indignation. In 1898 Shaw published *Plays Pleasant and Unpleasant*, with long provocative prefaces attacking a great variety of things, including theatrical censorship; the plays included *arms and the Man, Candida, The Man of Destiny*, and (among the "unpleasant") *Widowers' Houses* and *Mrs. Warren's Profession*. Among his later plays, *John Bull's Other Island* (1904) is a characteristic contribution to the discussion of Ireland's grievances against the English; *Man and Superman* (1904) is an ambitious attempt to project through comedy his views of how the Life Force works in ordinary life and contains some brilliant scenes, although the play as a whole is rather too long and too talkative; *The Doctor's Dilemma* (1906) exposes both doctors and artists while exploring some of the moral problems in which they can become involved; *Major Barbara* (1907) shows Shaw's characteristic admiration of success and energy and his contempt for those evangelists who attempt to promote religion by giving soup to the poor instead of trying to convert the strong and successful. *Pygmalion* (1912) is a brilliant exploration of the relation between social class and accent in England, which was subsequently made into the popular musical *My Fair Lady*. *Heartbreak House* (1919) suggests the Russian dramatist Anton Chekhov (1860–1904) in its depiction of the imminent collapse of a civilization, but it is essentially Shavian, and the finest example of what Eric Bentley has called the "disquisitory" Shavian play, based on the interplay of ideas in dialogue. *Back to Methuselah* (1921) is an ambitious play about the working of the Life Force in human destiny that lacks the true Shavian sparkle, while *Saint Joan* (1923) interprets the life of the French saint in a mischievously Shavian manner.

Shaw's preface to *Mrs. Warren's Profession* attacks the confusions and contradictions involved in censorship of plays and contains an eloquent plea for the recognition of the seriousness and morality of his play. The play was written, he tells us, "to draw attention to the truth that prostitution is caused, not by female depravity and male licentiousness, but simply by underpaying, undervaluing, and overworking women so shamefully that the poorest of them are forced to resort to prostitution to keep body and soul together." He argues that Mrs. Warren's defense of herself in the play is

> valid and unanswerable. . . . But it is no defense at all of the vice which she organizes. It is no defense of an immoral life to say that the alternative offered by society collectively to women is a miserable life, starved, overworked, fetid, ailing, ugly. Though it is quite natural and *right* for Mrs. Warren to choose what is, according to her lights, the least immoral alternative, it is none the less infamous of society to offer such alternatives. For the alternatives offered are not morality and immorality, but two sorts of immorality. The man who cannot see that starvation, overwork, dirt, and disease are as anti-social as prostitution—that they are the vices and crimes of a nation, and not merely its misfortunes—is (to put it as politely as possible) a hopeless Private Person.

(This is Shaw's way of saying that such a man is a hopeless idiot: the word "idiot" comes from the Greek *idiotes*, "a private person," as distinct from one interested in public affairs.) Another theme of the play is the emergence of the "new woman," independent and sure of herself, represented by Vivie.

Shaw was an ardent believer in spelling reform and, while awaiting a reformed alphabet and phonetic spelling, introduced some minor simplifications in his own spelling that he insisted on his publishers' retaining. These simplifications (omission of the apostrophe in a number of contractions, and the use of widely spaced letters rather than italics to indicate emphasis, for example) are retained in the text here printed.

Mrs. Warren's Profession

Act 1

Summer afternoon in a cottage garden on the eastern slope of a hill a little south of Haslemere in Surrey. Looking up the hill, the cottage is seen in the left hand corner of the garden, with its thatched roof and porch, and a large latticed window to the left of the porch. A paling completely shuts in the garden, except for a gate on the right. The common rises uphill beyond the paling to the sky line. Some folded canvas garden chairs are leaning against the side bench in the porch. A lady's bicycle is propped against the wall, under the window. A little to the right of the porch a hammock is slung from two posts. A big canvas umbrella, stuck in the ground, keeps the sun off the hammock, in which a young lady lies reading and making notes, her head towards the cottage and her feet towards the gate. In front of the hammock, and within reach of her hand, is a common kitchen chair, with a pile of serious-looking books and a supply of writing paper on it.

A gentleman walking on the common comes into sight from behind the cottage. He is hardly past middle age, with something of the artist about him, unconventionally but carefully dressed, and clean-shaven except for a moustache, with an eager susceptible face and very amiable and considerate manners. He has silky black hair, with waves of grey and white in it. His eyebrows are white, his moustache black. He seems not certain of his way. He looks over the paling; takes stock of the place; and sees the young lady.

THE GENTLEMAN. [*taking off his hat*] I beg your pardon. Can you direct me to Hindhead View—Mrs Alison's?

THE YOUNG LADY. [*glancing up from her book*] This is Mrs Alison's. [*She resumes her work.*]

THE GENTLEMAN. Indeed! Perhaps—may I ask are you Miss Vivie Warren?

THE YOUNG LADY. [*sharply, as she turns on her elbow to get a good look at him*] Yes.

THE GENTLEMAN. [*daunted and conciliatory*] I'm afraid I appear intrusive. My name is Praed. [VIVIE *at once throws her books upon the chair, and gets out of the hammock.*] Oh, pray dont let me disturb you.

VIVIE. [*striding to the gate and opening it for him*] Come in, Mr Praed. [*He comes in.*] Glad to see you. [*She proffers her hand and takes his with a resolute and hearty grip. She is an attractive specimen of the sensible, able, highly-educated young middle-class Englishwoman. Age 22. Prompt, strong, confident, self-possessed. Plain business-like dress, but not dowdy. She wears a chatelaine[1] at her belt, with a fountain pen and a paper knife among its pendants.*]

PRAED. Very kind of you indeed, Miss Warren. [*She shuts the gate with a vigorous slam. He passes in to the middle of the garden, exercising his fingers, which are slightly numbed by her greeting.*] Has your mother arrived?

VIVIE. [*quickly, evidently scenting aggression*] Is she coming?

PRAED. [*surprised*] Didnt you expect us?

VIVIE. No.

PRAED. Now, goodness me, I hope Ive not mistaken the day. That would be just like me, you know. Your mother arranged that she was to come down from London and that I was to come over from Horsham to be introduced to you.

VIVIE. [*not at all pleased*] Did she? Hm! My mother has rather a trick of taking me by surprise—to see how I behave myself when she's away, I suppose. I fancy I shall take my mother very much by surprise one of these days, if she makes arrangements that concern me without consulting me beforehand. She hasnt come.

PRAED. [*embarrassed*] I'm really very sorry.

VIVIE. [*throwing off her displeasure*] It's not your fault, Mr Praed, is it? And I'm very glad youve come. You are the only one of my mother's friends I have ever asked her to bring to see me.

---

1. Clasp or hook.

PRAED. [*relieved and delighted*] Oh, now this is really very good of you, Miss Warren!

VIVIE. Will you come indoors; or would you rather sit out here and talk?

PRAED. It will be nicer out here, dont you think?

VIVIE. Then I'll go and get you a chair. [*She goes to the porch for a garden chair.*]

PRAED. [*following her*] Oh, pray, pray! Allow me. [*He lays hands on the chair.*]

VIVIE. [*letting him take it*] Take care of your fingers: theyre rather dodgy things, those chairs. [*She goes across to the chair with the books on it; pitches them into the hammock; and brings the chair forward with one swing.*]

PRAED. [*who has just unfolded his chair*] Oh, now d o let me take that hard chair. I like hard chairs.

VIVIE. So do I. Sit down, Mr Praed. [*This invitation she gives with genial peremptoriness, his anxiety to please her clearly striking her as a sign of weakness of character on his part. But he does not immediately obey.*]

PRAED. By the way, though, hadnt we better go to the station to meet your mother?

VIVIE. [*coolly*] Why? She knows the way.

PRAED. [*disconcerted*] Er—I suppose she does. [*He sits down.*]

VIVIE. Do you know, you are just like what I expected. I hope you are disposed to be friends with me.

PRAED. [*again beaming*] Thank you, my d e a r Miss Warren: thank you. Dear me! I'm glad your mother hasnt spoilt you!

VIVIE. How?

PRAED. Well, in making you too conventional. You know, my dear Miss Warren, I am a born anarchist. I hate authority. It spoils the relations between parent and child: even between mother and daughter. Now I was always afraid that your mother would strain her authority to make you very conventional. It's such a relief to find that she hasnt.

VIVIE. Oh! have I been behaving unconventionally?

PRAED. Oh no; oh dear no. At least not conventionally unconventionally, you understand. [*She nods and sits down. He goes on, with a cordial outburst.*] But it was so charming of you to say that you were disposed to be friends with me! You modern young ladies are splendid: perfectly splendid!

VIVIE. [*dubiously*] Eh? [*Watching him with dawning disappointment as to the quality of his brains and character.*]

PRAED. When I was your age, young men and women were afraid of each other: there was no good fellowship. Nothing real. Only gallantry copied out of novels, and as vulgar and affected as it could be. Maidenly reserve! gentlemanly chivalry! always saying no when you meant yes! simple purgatory for shy and sincere souls.

VIVIE. Yes, I imagine there must have been a frightful waste of time. Especially women's time.

PRAED. Oh, waste of life, waste of everything. But things are improving. Do you know, I have been in a positive state of excitement about meeting you ever since your magnificent achievements at Cambridge: a thing unheard of in my day. It was perfectly splendid, you tieing with the third wrangler.[2] Just the right place, you know. The first wrangler is always a dreamy, morbid fellow, in whom the thing is pushed to the length of a disease.

VIVIE. It doesnt pay. I wouldnt do it again for the same money.

PRAED. [*aghast*] The same money!

---

2. A unique Cambridge term denoting distinction in the final honors examination (known as the tripos) leading to an A.B. in mathematics. The person who achieved the top mark was the senior wrangler; then came the junior wrangler, and then the third wrangler.

VIVIE. I did it for £50.

PRAED. Fifty pounds!

VIVIE. Yes. Fifty pounds. Perhaps you dont know how it was. Mrs. Latham, my
tutor at Newnham,[3] told my mother that I could distinguish myself in the
mathematical tripos if I went in for it in earnest. The papers were full just
then of Phillipa Summers beating the senior wrangler. You remember
about it, of course.

PRAED. [shakes his head energetically]!!!

VIVIE. Well anyhow she did; and nothing would please my mother but that I
should do the same thing. I said flatly it was not worth my while to face the
grind since I was not going in for teaching; but I offered to try for fourth
wrangler, or thereabouts for £50. She closed with me at that, after a little
grumbling; and I was better than my bargain. But I wouldn't do it again for
that. £200 would have been nearer the mark.

PRAED. [much damped] Lord bless me! Thats a very practical way of looking at
it.

VIVIE. Did you expect to find me an unpractical person?

PRAED. But surely it's practical to consider not only the work these honors cost,
but also the culture they bring.

VIVIE. Culture! My dear Mr Praed: do you know what the mathematical tripos
means? It means grind, grind, grind for six to eight hours a day at mathematics, and nothing but mathematics. I'm supposed to know something about
science; but I know nothing except the mathematics it involves. I can make
calculations for engineers, electricians, insurance companies, and so on;
but I know next to nothing about engineering or electricity or insurance. I
dont even know arithmetic well. Outside mathematics, lawn-tennis, eating,
sleeping, cycling, and walking, I'm a more ignorant barbarian than any
woman could possibly be who hadnt gone in for the tripos.

PRAED. [revolted] What a monstrous, wicked, rascally system! I knew it! I felt
at once that it meant destroying all that makes womanhood beautiful.

VIVIE. I dont object to it on that score in the least. I shall turn it to very good
account, I assure you.

PRAED. Pooh! In what way?

VIVIE. I shall set up in chambers in the City, and work at actuarial calculations
and conveyancing. Under cover of that I shall do some law, with one eye
on the Stock Exchange all the time. Ive come down here by myself to read
law: not for a holiday, as my mother imagines. I hate holidays.

PRAED. You make my blood run cold. Are you to have no romance, no beauty
in your life?

VIVIE. I don't care for either, I assure you.

PRAED. You cant mean that.

VIVIE. Oh yes I do. I like working and getting paid for it. When I'm tired of
working, I like a comfortable chair, a cigar, a little whisky, and a novel with
a good detective story in it.

PRAED. [rising in a frenzy of repudiation] I dont believe it. I am an artist; and I
cant believe it: I refuse to believe it. It's only that you havnt discovered yet
what a wonderful world art can open up to you.

VIVIE. Yes I have. Last May I spent six weeks in London with Honoria Fraser.
Mamma thought we were doing a round of sightseeing together; but I was
really at Honoria's chambers in Chancery Lane[4] every day, working away at
actuarial calculations for her, and helping her as well as a greenhorn could.
In the evenings we smoked and talked, and never dreamt of going out
except for exercise. And I never enjoyed myself more in my life. I cleared

---

3. Women's college at Cambridge University.   4. I.e., office in the legal quarter of London.

all my expenses, and got initiated into the business without a fee into the bargain.

PRAED. But bless my heart and soul, Miss Warren, do you call that discovering art?

VIVIE. Wait a bit. That wasnt the beginning. I went up to town on an invitation from some artistic people in Fitzjohn's Avenue: one of the girls was a Newnham chum. They took me to the National Gallery—

PRAED. [approving] Ah!! [He sits down, much relieved.]

VIVIE. [continuing]—to the Opera—

PRAED. [still more pleased] Good!

VIVIE. —and to a concert where the band played all the evening: Beethoven and Wagner and so on. I wouldn't go through that experience again for anything you could offer me. I held out for civility's sake until the third day; and then I said, plump out, that I couldnt stand any more of it, and went off to Chancery Lane. N o w you know the sort of perfectly splendid modern young lady I am. How do you think I shall get on with my mother?

PRAED. [startled] Well, I hope—er—

VIVIE. It's not so much what you hope as what you believe, that I want to know.

PRAED. Well, frankly, I am afraid your mother will be a little disappointed. Not from any shortcoming on your part, you know: I dont mean that. But you are so different from her ideal.

VIVIE. Her what?!

PRAED. Her ideal.

VIVIE. Do you mean her ideal of ME?

PRAED. Yes.

VIVIE. What on earth is it like?

PRAED. Well, you must have observed, Miss Warren, that people who are dissatisfied with their own bringing-up generally think that the world would be all right if everybody were to be brought up quite differently. Now your mother's life has been—er—I suppose you know—

VIVIE. Dont suppose anything, Mr Praed. I hardly know my mother. Since I was a child I have lived in England, at school or college, or with people paid to take charge of me. I have been boarded out all my life. My mother has lived in Brussels or Vienna and never let me go to her. I only see her when she visits England for a few days. I dont complain: it's been very pleasant; for people have been very good to me; and there has always been plenty of money to make things smooth. But dont imagine I know anything about my mother. I know far less than you do.

PRAED. [very ill at ease] In that case—[He stops, quite at a loss. Then, with a forced attempt at gaiety] But what nonsense we are talking! Of course you and your mother will get on capitally. [He rises, and looks abroad at the view.] What a charming little place you have here!

VIVIE. [unmoved] Rather a violent change of subject, Mr Praed. Why wont my mother's life bear being talked about?

PRAED. Oh, you really mustnt say that. Isnt it natural that I should have a certain delicacy in talking to my old friend's daughter about her behind her back? You and she will have plenty of opportunity of talking about it when she comes.

VIVIE. No: s h e wont talk about it either. [rising] However, I daresay you have good reasons for telling me nothing. Only, mind this, Mr Praed. I expect there will be a battle royal when my mother hears of my Chancery Lane project.

PRAED. [ruefully] I'm afraid there will.

VIVIE. Well, I shall win, because I want nothing but my fare to London to start

there to-morrow earning my own living by devilling[5] for Honoria. Besides,
I have no mysteries to keep up; and it seems she has. I shall use that advantage over her if necessary.

PRAED. [*greatly shocked*] Oh no! No, pray. Youd not do such a thing.

VIVIE. Then tell me why not.

PRAED. I really cannot. I appeal to your good feeling. [*She smiles at his sentimentality.*] Besides you may be too bold. Your mother is not to be trifled
with when she's angry.

VIVIE. You cant frighten me, Mr Praed. In that month at Chancery Lane I had
opportunities of taking the measure of one or two women v e r y like my
mother. You may back me to win. But if I hit harder in my ignorance than
I need, remember that it is you who refuse to enlighten me. Now, let us
drop the subject. [*She takes her chair and replaces it near the hammock with
the same vigorous swing as before.*]

PRAED. [*taking a desperate resolution*] One word, Miss Warren. I had better
tell you. It's very difficult; but—

[MRS WARREN *and* SIR GEORGE CROFTS *arrive at the gate.* MRS WARREN *is between 40 and 50, formerly pretty, showily dressed in a brilliant hat and a gay
blouse fitting tightly over her bust and flanked by fashionable sleeves, Rather
spoilt and domineering, and decidedly vulgar, but, on the whole, a genial and
fairly presentable old blackguard of a woman.*

CROFTS *is a tall powerfully-built man of about 50, fashionably dressed in the
style of a young man. Nasal voice, reedier than might be expected from his
strong frame. Clean-shaven bulldog jaws, large flat ears, and thick neck: gentlemanly combination of the most brutal types of city man, sporting man, and man
about town.*]

VIVIE. Here they are. [*coming to them as they enter the garden*] How do, mater?
Mr Praed's been here this half hour waiting for you.

MRS WARREN. Well, if youve been waiting, Praddy, it's your own fault: I
thought youd have the gumption to know I was coming by the 3.10 train.
Vivie: put your hat on, dear: youll get sunburnt. Oh, I forgot to introduce
you. Sir George Crofts: my little Vivie.

[CROFTS *advances to* VIVIE *with his most courtly manner. She nods, but makes
no motion to shake hands.*]

CROFTS. May I shake hands with a young lady whom I have known by reputation very long as the daughter of one of my oldest friends?

VIVIE. [*who has been looking him up and down sharply*] If you like. [*She takes
his tenderly proffered hand and gives it a squeeze that makes him open his
eyes; then turns away, and says to her mother*] Will you come in, or shall I
get a couple more chairs? [*She goes into the porch for the chairs.*]

MRS WARREN. Well George, what do you think of her?

CROFTS. [*ruefully*] She has a powerful fist. Did you shake hands with her,
Praed?

PRAED. Yes: it will pass off presently.

CROFTS. I hope so. [VIVIE *reappears with two more chairs. He hurries to her
assistance.*] Allow me.

MRS WARREN. [*patronizingly*] Let Sir George help you with the chairs, dear.

VIVIE. [*pitching them into his arms*] Here you are. [*She dusts her hands and
turns to* MRS WARREN.] Youd like some tea, wouldnt you?

MRS WARREN. [*sitting in* PRAED'*s chair and fanning herself*] I'm dying for a
drop to drink.

VIVIE. I'll see about it. [*She goes into the cottage.*]

---

5. Acting as assistant to a barrister (trial lawyer) as a way of gaining legal experience.

[SIR GEORGE *has by this time managed to unfold a chair and plant it beside* MRS WARREN, *on her left. He throws the other on the grass and sits down, looking dejected and rather foolish, with the handle of his stick in his mouth.* PRAED, *still very uneasy, fidgets about the garden on their right.*]

MRS WARREN. [*to* PRAED, *looking at* CROFTS] Just look at him, Praddy: he looks cheerful, dont he? He's been worrying my life out these three years to have that little girl of mine shewn to him; and now that Ive done it, he's quite out of countenance. [*briskly*] Come! sit up, George; and take your stick out of your mouth. [CROFTS *sulkily obeys.*]

PRAED. I think, you know—if you dont mind my saying so—that we had better get out of the habit of thinking of her as a little girl. You see she has really distinguished herself; and I'm not sure, from what I have seen of her, that she is not older than any of us.

MRS WARREN. [*greatly amused*] Only listen to him, George! Older than any of us! Well, she has been stuffing you nicely with her importance.

PRAED. But young people are particularly sensitive about being treated in that way.

MRS WARREN. Yes; and young people have to get all that nonsense taken out of them, and a good deal more besides. Dont you interfere, Praddy: I know how to treat my own child as well as you do. [PRAED, *with a grave shake of his head, walks up the garden with his hands behind his back.* MRS WARREN *pretends to laugh, but looks after him with perceptible concern. Then she whispers to* CROFTS] Whats the matter with him? What does he take it like that for?

CROFTS. [*morosely*] Youre afraid of Praed.

MRS WARREN. What! Me! Afraid of dear old Praddy! Why, a fly wouldnt be afraid of him.

CROFTS. Y o u r e afraid of him.

MRS WARREN. [*angry*] I'll trouble you to mind your own business, and not try any of your sulks on me. I'm not afraid of y o u, anyhow. If you cant make yourself agreeable, youd better go home. [*She gets up, and turning her back on him, finds herself face to face with* PRAED.] Come, Praddy, I know it was only your tender-heartedness. Youre afraid I'll bully her.

PRAED. My dear Kitty: you think I'm offended. Dont imagine that: pray dont. But you know I often notice things that escape you; and though you never take my advice, you sometimes admit afterwards that you ought to have taken it.

MRS WARREN. Well, what do you notice now?

PRAED. Only that Vivie is a grown woman. Pray, Kitty, treat her with every respect.

MRS WARREN. [*with genuine amazement*] Respect! Treat my own daughter with respect! What next, pray!

VIVIE. [*appearing at the cottage door and calling to* MRS WARREN] Mother: will you come to my room before tea?

MRS WARREN. Yes, dearie. [*She laughs indulgently at* PRAED's *gravity, and pats him on the cheek as she passes him on her way to the porch.*] Dont be cross, Praddy. [*She follows* VIVIE *into the cottage.*]

CROFTS. [*furtively*] I say, Praed.

PRAED. Yes.

CROFTS. I want to ask you a rather particular question.

PRAED. Certainly. [*He takes* MRS WARREN's *chair and sits close to* CROFTS.]

CROFTS. Thats right: they might hear us from the window. Look here: did Kitty ever tell you who that girl's father is?

PRAED. Never.

CROFTS. Have you any suspicion of who it might be?

PRAED. None.

CROFTS. [*not believing him*] I know, of course, that you perhaps might feel bound not to tell if she had said anything to you. But it's very awkward to be uncertain about it now that we shall be meeting the girl every day. We dont exactly know how we ought to feel towards her.

PRAED. What difference can that make? We take her on her own merits. What does it matter who her father was?

CROFTS. [*suspiciously*] Then you know who he was?

PRAED. [*with a touch of temper*] I said no just now. Did you not hear me?

CROFTS. Look here, Praed. I ask you as a particular favor. If you do know [*Movement of protest from* PRAED.]—I only say, if you know you might at least set my mind at rest about her. The fact is, I feel attracted.

PRAED. [*sternly*] What do you mean?

CROFTS. Oh, dont be alarmed: it's quite an innocent feeling. Thats what puzzles me about it. Why, for all I know, *I* might be her father.

PRAED. You! Impossible!

CROFTS. [*catching him up cunningly*] You know for certain that I'm not?

PRAED. I know nothing about it, I tell you, any more than you. But really, Crofts—oh no, it's out of the question. Theres not the least resemblance.

CROFTS. As to that, theres no resemblance between her and her mother that I can see. I suppose she's not y o u r daughter, is she?

PRAED. [*rising indignantly*] Really, Crofts—!

CROFTS. No offence, Praed. Quite allowable as between two men of the world.

PRAED. [*recovering himself with an effort and speaking gently and gravely*] Now listen to me, my dear Crofts. [*He sits down again.*] I have nothing to do with that side of Mrs Warren's life, and never had. She has never spoken to me about it; and of course I have never spoken to her about it. Your delicacy will tell you that a handsome woman needs s o m e friends who are not— well, not on that footing with her. The effect of her own beauty would become a torment to her if she could not escape from it occasionally. You are probably on much more confidential terms with Kitty than I am. Surely you can ask her the question yourself.

CROFTS. I have asked her, often enough. But she's so determined to keep the child all to herself that she would deny that it ever had a father if she could. [*rising*] I'm thoroughly uncomfortable about it, Praed.

PRAED. [*rising also*] Well, as you are, at all events, old enough to be her father, I dont mind agreeing that we both regard Miss Vivie in a parental way, as a young girl whom we are bound to protect and help. What do you say?

CROFTS. [*aggressively*] I'm no older than you, if you come to that.

PRAED. Yes you are, my dear fellow: you were born old. I was born a boy: Ive never been able to feel the assurance of a grown-up man in my life. [*He folds his chair and carries it to the porch.*]

MRS WARREN. [*calling from within the cottage*] Prad-dee! George! Tea-ea-ea-ea!

CROFTS. [*hastily*] She's calling us. [*He hurries in.*]

[PRAED *shakes his head bodingly, and is following* CROFTS *when he is hailed by a young gentleman who has just appeared on the common, and is making for the gate. He is pleasant, pretty, smartly dressed, cleverly good-for-nothing, not long turned 20, with a charming voice and agreeably disrespectful manners. He carries a light sporting magazine rifle.*]

THE YOUNG GENTLEMAN. Hallo! Praed!

PRAED. Why, Frank Gardner! [FRANK *comes in and shakes hands cordially.*] What on earth are you doing here?

FRANK. Staying with my father.

PRAED. The Roman father?[6]

FRANK. He's rector here. I'm living with my people this autumn for the sake of economy. Things came to a crisis in July: the Roman father had to pay my debts. He's stony broke in consequence; and so am I. What are you up to in these parts? Do you know the people here?

PRAED. Yes: I'm spending the day with a Miss Warren.

FRANK. [enthusiastically] What! Do you know Vivie? Isnt she a jolly girl? I'm teaching her to shoot with this. [putting down the rifle] I'm so glad she knows you: youre just the sort of fellow she ought to know. [He smiles, and raises the charming voice almost to a singing tone as he exclaims] It's e v e r so jolly to find you here, Praed.

PRAED. I'm an old friend of her mother. Mrs Warren brought me over to make her daughter's acquaintance.

FRANK. The mother! Is s h e here?

PRAED. Yes: inside, at tea.

MRS WARREN. [calling from within] Prad-dee-ee-ee-eee! The tea-cake'll be cold.

PRAED. [calling] Yes, Mrs Warren. In a moment. Ive just met a friend here.

MRS WARREN. A what?

PRAED. [louder] A friend.

MRS WARREN. Bring him in.

PRAED. All right. [to FRANK] Will you accept the invitation?

FRANK. [incredulous, but immensely amused] Is that Vivie's mother?

PRAED. Yes.

FRANK. By jove! What a lark! Do you think she'll like me?

PRAED. Ive no doubt youll make yourself popular, as usual. Come in and try. [Moving towards the house.]

FRANK. Stop a bit. [seriously] I want to take you into my confidence.

PRAED. Pray dont. It's only some fresh folly, like the barmaid at Redhill.

FRANK. It's ever so much more serious than that. You say youve only just met Vivie for the first time?

PRAED. Yes.

FRANK. [rhapsodically] Then you can have no idea what a girl she is. Such character! Such sense! And her cleverness! Oh, my eye, Praed, but I can tell you she is clever! And—need I add?—she loves me.

CROFTS. [putting his head out of the window] I say, Praed: what are you about? D o come along. [He disappears.]

FRANK. Hallo! Sort of chap that would take a prize at a dog show, aint he? Who's he?

PRAED. Sir George Crofts, an old friend of Mrs Warren's. I think we had better come in.

[On their way to the porch they are interrupted by a call from the gate. Turning, they see an elderly clergyman looking over it.]

THE CLERGYMAN. [calling] Frank!

FRANK. Hallo! [to PRAED] The Roman father. [to the clergyman] Yes, gov'nor: all right: presently. [to PRAED] Look here, Praed: youd better go in to tea. I'll join you directly.

PRAED. Very good. [He goes into the cottage.]

[The clergyman remains outside the gate, with his hands on the top of it. The REV. SAMUEL GARDNER, a beneficed clergyman of the Established Church, is over 50. Externally he is pretentious, booming, noisy, important. Really he is that obsolescent social phenomenon the fool of the family dumped on the

---

6. Not "Roman Catholic" (he is a Church of England priest) but a father with a Roman sense of duty. The word is used ironically.

Church by his father, the patron, clamorously asserting himself as father and clergyman without being able to command respect in either capacity.]

REV. SAMUEL. Well, sir. Who are your friends here, if I may ask?

FRANK. Oh, it's all right, gov'nor! Come in.

REV. SAMUEL. No sir; not until I know whose garden I am entering.

FRANK. It's all right. It's Miss Warren's.

REV. SAMUEL. I have not seen her at church since she came.

FRANK. Of course not: she's a third wrangler. Ever so intellectual. Took a higher degree than you did; so why should she go to hear you preach?

REV. SAMUEL. Dont be disrespectful, sir.

FRANK. Oh, it dont matter: nobody hears us. Come in. [*He opens the gate, unceremoniously pulling his father with it into the garden.*] I want to introduce you to her. Do you remember the advice you gave me last July, gov'nor?

REV. SAMUEL. [*severely*] Yes, I advised you to conquer your idleness and flippancy, and to work your way into an honorable profession and live on it and not upon me.

FRANK. No; thats what you thought of afterwards. What you actually said was that since I had neither brains nor money, I'd better turn my good looks to account by marrying somebody with both. Well, look here. Miss Warren has brains: you cant deny that.

REV. SAMUEL. Brains are not everything.

FRANK. No, of course not: theres the money—

REV. SAMUEL. [*interrupting him austerely*] I was not thinking of money, sir. I was speaking of higher things. Social position, for instance.

FRANK. I dont care a rap about that.

REV. SAMUEL. But I do, sir.

FRANK. Well, nobody wants you to marry her. Anyhow, she has what amounts to a high Cambridge degree; and she seems to have as much money as she wants.

REV. SAMUEL. [*sinking into a feeble vein of humor*] I greatly doubt whether she has as much money as y o u will want.

FRANK. Oh, come; I havnt been so very extravagant. I live ever so quietly; I dont drink; I dont bet much; and I never go regularly on the razzle-dazzle as you did when you were my age.

REV. SAMUEL. [*booming hollowly*] Silence, sir.

FRANK. Well, you told me yourself, when I was making ever such an ass of myself about the barmaid at Redhill, that you once offered a woman £50 for the letters you wrote to her when—

REV. SAMUEL. [*terrified*] Sh-sh-sh, Frank, for heaven's sake! [*He looks round apprehensively. Seeing no one within earshot he plucks up courage to boom again, but more subduedly.*] You are taking an ungentlemanly advantage of what I confided to you for your own good, to save you from an error you would have repented all your life long. Take warning by your father's follies, sir; and dont make them an excuse for your own.

FRANK. Did you ever hear the story of the Duke of Wellington and his letters?

REV. SAMUEL. No, sir; and I dont want to hear it.

FRANK. The old Iron Duke didnt throw away £50: not he. He just wrote: "Dear Jenny: publish and be damned! Yours affectionately, Wellington." Thats what you should have done.

REV. SAMUEL. [*piteously*] Frank, my boy: when I wrote those letters I put myself into that woman's power. When I told you about them I put myself, to some extent, I am sorry to say, in your power. She refused my money with these words, which I shall never forget. "Knowledge is power" she said; "and I never sell power." Thats more than twenty years ago; and she has never made use of her power or caused me a moment's uneasiness. You are behaving worse to me than she did, Frank.

FRANK. Oh yes I dare say! Did you ever preach at her the way you preach at me every day?

REV. SAMUEL. [*wounded almost to tears*] I leave you sir. You are incorrigible. [*He turns towards the gate.*]

FRANK. [*utterly unmoved*] Tell them I shant be home to tea, will you, gov'nor, like a good fellow? [*He moves towards the cottage door and is met by* PRAED *and* VIVIE *coming out.*]

VIVIE. [*to* FRANK] Is that your father, Frank? I do so want to meet him.

FRANK. Certainly. [*calling after his father*] Gov'nor. Youre wanted. [*The parson turns at the gate, fumbling nervously at his hat.* PRAED *crosses the garden to the opposite side, beaming in anticipation of civilities.*] My father: Miss Warren.

VIVIE. [*going to the clergyman and shaking his hand*] Very glad to see you here, Mr Gardner. [*calling to the cottage*] Mother: come along: youre wanted.

[MRS WARREN *appears on the threshold, and is immediately transfixed recognizing the clergyman.*]

VIVIE. [*continuing*] Let me introduce—

MRS WARREN. [*swooping on the* REVEREND SAMUEL] Why, it's Sam Gardner, gone into the Church! Well, I never! Dont you know us, Sam? This is George Crofts, as large as life and twice as natural. Dont you remember me?

REV. SAMUEL. [*very red*] I really—er—

MRS WARREN. Of course you do. Why, I have a whole album of your letters still: I came across them only the other day.

REV. SAMUEL. [*miserably confused*] Miss Vavasour, I believe.

MRS WARREN. [*correcting him quickly in a loud whisper*] Tch! Nonsense! Mrs Warren: dont you see my daughter there?

Act 2

Inside the cottage after nightfall. Looking eastward from within instead of westward from without, the latticed window, with its curtains drawn, is now seen in the middle of the front wall of the cottage, with the porch door to the left of it. In the left-hand side wall is the door leading to the kitchen. Farther back against the same wall is a dresser with a candle and matches on it, and FRANK's *rifle standing beside them, with the barrel resting in the plate-rack. In the centre a table stands with a lighted lamp on it.* VIVIE's *books and writing materials are on a table to the right of the window, against the wall. The fireplace is on the right, with a settle: there is no fire. Two of the chairs are set right and left of the table.*

The cottage door opens, shewing a fine starlit night without; and MRS WARREN, *her shoulders wrapped in a shawl borrowed from* VIVIE, *enters, followed by* FRANK, *who throws his cap on the window seat. She has had enough of walking, and gives a gasp of relief as she unpins her hat; takes it off; sticks the pin through the crown; and puts it on the table.*

MRS WARREN. O Lord! I dont know which is the worst of the country, the walking or the sitting at home with nothing to do. I could do with a whisky and soda now very well, if only they had such a thing in this place.

FRANK. Perhaps Vivie's got some.

MRS WARREN. Nonsense! What would a young girl like her be doing with such things! Never mind: it dont matter. I wonder how she passes her time here! I'd a good deal rather be in Vienna.

FRANK. Let me take you there. [*He helps her to take off her shawl, gallantly giving her shoulders a very perceptible squeeze as he does so.*]

MRS WARREN. Ah! would you? I'm beginning to think youre a chip of the old block.

FRANK. Like the gov'nor, eh? [*He hangs the shawl on the nearest chair, and sits down.*]

MRS WARREN. Never you mind. What do you know about such things? Youre only a boy. [*She goes to the hearth, to be farther from temptation.*]

FRANK. Do come to Vienna with me? It'd be ever such larks.

MRS WARREN. No, thank you. Vienna is no place for you—at least not until youre a little older. [*She nods at him to emphasize this piece of advice. He makes a mock-piteous face, belied by his laughing eyes. She looks at him; then comes back to him.*] Now, look here, little boy [*taking his face in her hands and turning it up to her*]; I know you through and through by your likeness to your father, better than you know yourself. Dont you go taking any silly ideas into your head about me. Do you hear?

FRANK. [*gallantly wooing her with his voice*] Cant help it, my dear Mrs Warren: it runs in the family.

[*She pretends to box his ears; then looks at the pretty laughing upturned face for a moment, tempted. At last she kisses him, and immediately turns away, out of patience with herself.*]

MRS WARREN. There! I shouldnt have done that. I am wicked. Never you mind, my dear: it's only a motherly kiss. Go and make love to Vivie.

FRANK. So I have.

MRS WARREN. [*turning on him with a sharp note of alarm in her voice*] What!

FRANK. Vivie and I are ever such chums.

MRS WARREN. What do you mean? Now see here: I wont have any young scamp tampering with my little girl. Do you hear? I wont have it.

FRANK. [*quite unabashed*] My dear Mrs Warren: dont you be alarmed. My intentions are honorable: ever so honorable; and your little girl is jolly well able to take care of herself. She dont need looking after half so much as her mother. She aint so handsome, you know.

MRS WARREN. [*taken aback by his assurance*] Well, you have got a nice healthy two inches thick of cheek all over you. I dont know where you got it. Not from your father, anyhow.

CROFTS. [*in the garden*] The gipsies, I suppose?

REV. SAMUEL. [*replying*] The broomsquires[7] are far worse.

MRS WARREN. [*to* FRANK] S-sh! Remember! youve had your warning.

[CROFTS *and the* REVEREND SAMUEL *come in from the garden, the clergyman continuing his conversation as he enters.*]

REV. SAMUEL. The perjury at the Winchester assizes[8] is deplorable.

MRS WARREN. Well? What became of you two? And wheres Praddy and Vivie?

CROFTS. [*putting his hat on the settle and his stick in the chimney corner*] They went up the hill. We went to the village. I wanted a drink. [*He sits down on the settle, putting his legs up along the seat.*]

MRS WARREN. Well, she oughtnt to go off like that without telling me. [*to* FRANK] Get your father a chair, Frank: where are your manners? [*Frank springs up and gracefully offers his father his chair; and then takes another from the wall and sits down at the table, in the middle, with his father on his*

---

7. Small country landowners.   8. Law courts.

right and MRS WARREN *on his left.*] George: where are you going to stay to-night? You cant stay here. And whats Praddy going to do?

CROFTS. Gardner'll put me up.

MRS WARREN. Oh no doubt youve taken care of yourself! But what about Praddy?

CROFTS. Dont know. I suppose he can sleep at the inn.

MRS WARREN. Havnt you room for him, Sam?

REV. SAMUEL. Well—er—you see, as rector here, I am not free to do as I like. Er—what is Mr Praed's social position?

MRS. WARREN. Oh, he's all right: he's an architect. What an old stick-in-the-mud you are, Sam!

FRANK. Yes, it's all right, gov'nor. He built that place down in Wales for the Duke. Caernarvon Castle they call it. You must have heard of it. [*He winks with lightning smartness at* MRS WARREN, *and regards his father blandly.*]

REV. SAMUEL. Oh, in that case, of course we shall only be too happy. I suppose he knows the Duke personally.

FRANK. Oh, ever so intimately! We can stick him in Georgina's old room.

MRS WARREN. Well, thats settled. Now if those two would only come in and let us have supper. Theyve no right to stay out after dark like this.

CROFTS. [*aggressively*] What harm are they doing you?

MRS WARREN. Well, harm or not, I dont like it.

FRANK. Better not wait for them, Mrs Warren. Praed will stay out as long as possible. He has never known before what it is to stray over the heath on a summer night with my Vivie.

CROFTS. [*sitting up in some consternation*] I say, you know! Come!

REV. SAMUEL. [*rising, startled out of his professional manner into real force and sincerity*] Frank, once for all, it's out of the question. Mrs Warren will tell you that it's not to be thought of.

CROFTS. Of course not.

FRANK. [*with enchanting placidity*] Is that so, Mrs Warren?

MRS WARREN. [*reflectively*] Well, Sam, I dont know. If the girl wants to get married, no good can come of keeping her unmarried.

REV. SAMUEL. [*astounded*] But married to him!—your daughter to my son! Only think: it's impossible.

CROFTS. Of course it's impossible. Dont be a fool, Kitty.

MRS WARREN. [*nettled*] Why not? Isnt my daughter good enough for your son?

REV. SAMUEL. But surely, my dear Mrs Warren, you know the reasons—

MRS WARREN. [*defiantly*] I know no reasons. If you know any, you can tell them to the lad, or to the girl, or to your congregation, if you like.

REV. SAMUEL. [*collapsing helplessly into his chair*] You know very well that I couldnt tell anyone the reasons. But my boy will believe me when I tell him there a r e reasons.

FRANK. Quite right, Dad: he will. But has your boy's conduct ever been influenced by your reasons?

CROFTS. You cant marry her: and thats all about it. [*He gets up and stands on the hearth, with his back to the fireplace, frowning determinedly.*]

MRS WARREN. [*turning on him sharply*] What have you got to do with it, pray?

FRANK. [*with his prettiest lyrical cadence*] Precisely what I was going to ask, myself, in my own graceful fashion.

CROFTS. [*to* MRS WARREN] I suppose you dont want to marry the girl to a man younger than herself and without either a profession or twopence to keep her on. Ask Sam, if you dont believe me. [*to the parson*] How much more money are you going to give him?

REV. SAMUEL. Not another penny. He has had his patrimony; and he spent the last of it in July. [MRS WARREN'S *face falls.*]

CROFTS. [*watching her*] There! I told you. [*He resumes his place on the settle and puts up his legs on the seat again, as if the matter were finally disposed of.*]

FRANK. [*plaintively*] This is ever so mercenary. Do you suppose Miss Warren's going to marry for money? If we love one another—

MRS WARREN. Thank you. Your love's a pretty cheap commodity, my lad. If you have no means of keeping a wife, that settles it: you cant have Vivie.

FRANK. [*much amused*] What do y o u say, gov'nor, eh?

REV. SAMUEL. I agree with Mrs Warren.

FRANK. And good old Crofts has already expressed his opinion.

CROFTS. [*turning angrily on his elbow*] Look here: I want none of y o u r cheek.

FRANK. [*pointedly*] I'm ever so sorry to surprise you, Crofts, but you allowed yourself the liberty of speaking to me like a father a moment ago. One father is enough, thank you.

CROFTS. [*contemptuously*] Yah! [*He turns away again.*]

FRANK. [*rising*] Mrs Warren: I cannot give my Vivie up, even for your sake.

MRS WARREN. [*muttering*] Young scamp!

FRANK. [*continuing*] And as you no doubt intend to hold out other prospects to her, I shall lose no time in placing my case before her. [*They stare at him; and he begins to declaim gracefully*]

> He either fears his fate too much,
> Or his deserts are small,
> That dares not put it to the touch
> To gain or lose it all.[9]

[*The cottage door opens whilst he is reciting; and* VIVIE *and* PRAED *come in. He breaks off.* PRAED *puts his hat on the dresser. There is an immediate improvement in the company's behavior.* CROFTS *takes down his legs from the settle and pulls himself together as* PRAED *joins him at the fireplace.* MRS WARREN *loses her ease of manner and takes refuge in querulousness.*]

MRS WARREN. Wherever have you been, Vivie?

VIVIE. [*taking off her hat and throwing it carelessly on the table*] On the hill.

MRS WARREN. Well, you shouldnt go off like that without letting me know. How could I tell what had become of you? And night coming on too!

VIVIE. [*going to the door of the kitchen and opening it, ignoring her mother*] Now, about supper? [*All rise except* MRS WARREN.] We shall be rather crowded in here, I'm afraid.

MRS WARREN. Did you hear what I said, Vivie?

VIVIE. [*quietly*] Yes, mother. [*reverting to the supper difficulty*] How many are we? [*counting*] One, two, three, four, five, six. Well, two will have to wait until the rest are done: Mrs Alison has only plates and knives for four.

PRAED. Oh, it doesnt matter about me. I—

VIVIE. You have had a long walk and are hungry, Mr Praed: you shall have your supper at once. I can wait myself. I want one person to wait with me. Frank: are you hungry?

FRANK. Not the least in the world. Completely off my peck, in fact.

MRS WARREN. [*to* CROFTS] Neither are you, George. You can wait.

CROFTS. Oh, hang it. Ive eaten nothing since tea-time. Cant Sam do it?

FRANK. Would you starve my poor father?

REV. SAMUEL. [*testily*] Allow me to speak for myself, sir. I am perfectly willing to wait.

VIVIE. [*decisively*] Theres no need. Only two are wanted. [*she opens the door*

---

9. From the poem *My Dear and Only Love*, by the marquis of Montrose (1612–1650).

of the kitchen] Will you take my mother in, Mr Gardner. [*The parson takes*
MRS WARREN; *and they pass into the kitchen.* PRAED *and* CROFTS *follow. All
except* PRAED *clearly disapprove of the arrangement, but do not know how to
resist it.* VIVIE *stands at the door looking in at them.*] Can you squeeze past
to that corner, Mr Praed: it's rather a tight fit. Take care of your coat against
the white-wash: thats right. Now, are you all comfortable?

PRAED. [*within*] Quite, thank you.

MRS WARREN. [*within*] Leave the door open, dearie. [VIVIE *frowns; but* FRANK
*checks her with a gesture, and steals to the cottage door, which he softly sets
wide open.*] Oh Lor, what a draught! Youd better shut it, dear.

[VIVIE *shuts it with a slam, and then, noting with disgust that her mother's
hat and shawl are lying about, takes them tidily to the window seat, whilst*
FRANK *noiselessly shuts the cottage door.*]

FRANK. [*exulting*] Aha! Got rid of em. Well, Vivvums: what do you think of
my guvernor?

VIVIE. [*preoccupied and serious*] Ive hardly spoken to him. He doesnt strike me
as being a particularly able person.

FRANK. Well, you know, the old man is not altogether such a fool as he looks.
You see, he was shoved into the Church rather; and in trying to live up to
it he makes a much bigger ass of himself than he really is. I dont dislike
him as much as you might expect. He means well. How do you think youll
get on with him?

VIVIE. [*rather grimly*] I dont think my future life will be much concerned with
him, or with any of that old circle of my mother's, except perhaps Praed.
[*she sits down on the settle*] What do you think of my mother?

FRANK. Really and truly?

VIVIE. Yes, really and truly.

FRANK. Well, she's ever so jolly. But she's rather a caution, isn't she? And
Crofts! Oh my eye, Crofts! [*He sits beside her.*]

VIVIE. What a lot, Frank!

FRANK. What a crew!

VIVIE. [*with intense contempt for them*] If I thought that *I* was like that—that I
was going to be a waster, shifting along from one meal to another with no
purpose, and no character, and no grit in me, I'd open an artery and bleed
to death without one moment's hesitation.

FRANK. Oh no, you wouldnt. Why should they take any grind when they can
afford not to? I wish I had their luck. No: what I object to is their form. It
isnt the thing: it's slovenly, ever so slovenly.

VIVIE. Do you think your form will be any better when youre as old as Crofts,
if you dont work?

FRANK. Of course I do. Ever so much better. Vivvums mustnt lecture: her little
boy's incorrigible. [*He attempts to take her face caressingly in his hands.*]

VIVIE. [*striking his hands down sharply*] Off with you: Vivvums is not in a
humor for petting her little boy this evening. [*She rises and comes forward
to the other side of the room.*]

FRANK. [*following her*] How unkind!

VIVIE. [*stamping at him*] Be serious. I'm serious.

FRANK. Good. Let us talk learnedly. Miss Warren: do you know that all the
most advanced thinkers are agreed that half the diseases of modern civilization are due to starvation of the affections in the young. Now, I—

VIVIE. [*cutting him short*] You are very tiresome. [*she opens the inner door*]
Have you room for Frank there? He's complaining of starvation.

MRS. WARREN. [*within*] Of course there is. [*clatter of knives and glasses as she
moves the things on the table*] Here! theres room now beside me. Come
along, Mr Frank.

FRANK. Her little boy will be ever so even with his Vivvums for this. [*He passes into the kitchen.*]

MRS WARREN. [*within*] Here, Vivie: come on you too, child. You must be famished. [*She enters, followed by* CROFTS, *who holds the door open for* VIVIE *with marked deference. She goes out without looking at him; and he shuts the door after her.*] Why, George, you cant be done: youve eaten nothing. Is there anything wrong with you?

CROFTS. Oh, all I wanted was a drink. [*He thrusts his hands in his pockets, and begins prowling about the room, restless and sulky.*]

MRS WARREN. Well, I like enough to eat. But a little of that cold beef and cheese and lettuce goes a long way. [*With a sigh of only half repletion she sits down lazily on the settle.*]

CROFTS. What do you go encouraging that young pup for?

MRS WARREN. [*on the alert at once*] Now see here, George: what are you up to about that girl? Ive been watching your way of looking at her. Remember: I know you and what your looks mean.

CROFTS. Theres no harm in looking at her, is there?

MRS WARREN. I'd put you out and pack you back to London pretty soon if I saw any of your nonsense. My girl's little finger is more to me than your whole body and soul. [CROFTS *receives this with a sneering grin.* MRS WARREN, *flushing a little at her failure to impose on him in the character of a theatrically devoted mother, adds in a lower key*] Make your mind easy: the young pup has no more chance than you have.

CROFTS. Maynt a man take an interest in a girl?

MRS WARREN. Not a man like you.

CROFTS. How old is she?

MRS WARREN. Never you mind how old she is.

CROFTS. Why do you make such a secret of it?

MRS WARREN. Because I choose.

CROFTS. Well, I'm not fifty yet; and my property is as good as ever it was—

MRS WARREN. [*interrupting him*] Yes; because youre as stingy as youre vicious.

CROFTS. [*continuing*] And a baronet isnt to be picked up every day. No other man in my position would put up with you for a mother-in-law. Why shouldnt she marry me?

MRS WARREN. You!

CROFTS. We three could live together quite comfortably. I'd die before her and leave her a bouncing widow with plenty of money. Why not? It's been growing in my mind all the time Ive been walking with that fool inside there.

MRS WARREN. [*revolted*] Yes; it's the sort of thing that would grow in your mind. [*He halts in his prowling; and the two look at one another, she steadfastly, with a sort of awe behind her contemptuous disgust: he stealthily, with a carnal gleam in his eye and a loose grin.*]

CROFTS. [*suddenly becoming anxious and urgent as he sees no sign of sympathy in her*] Look here, Kitty: youre a sensible woman: you neednt put on any moral airs. I'll ask no more questions; and you need answer none. I'll settle the whole property on her; and if you want a cheque for yourself on the wedding day, you can name any figure you like—in reason.

MRS WARREN. So it's come to that with you, George, like all the other worn-out old creatures!

CROFTS. [*savagely*] Damn you!

[*Before she can retort the door of the kitchen is opened; and the voices of the others are heard returning.* CROFTS, *unable to recover his presence of mind, hurries out of the cottage. The clergyman appears at the kitchen door.*]

REV. SAMUEL. [*looking around*] Where is Sir George?

MRS WARREN. Gone out to have a pipe. [*The clergyman takes his hat from the table, and joins* MRS WARREN *at the fireside. Meanwhile* VIVIE *comes in, followed by* FRANK, *who collapses into the nearest chair with an air of extreme exhaustion.* MRS WARREN *looks round at* VIVIE *and says, with her affectation of maternal patronage even more forced than usual*] Well, dearie: have you had a good supper?

VIVIE. You know what Mrs Alison's suppers are. [*she turns to* FRANK *and pets him*] Poor Frank! was all the beef gone? did it get nothing but bread and cheese and ginger beer? [*seriously, as if she had done quite enough trifling for one evening*] Her butter is really awful. I must get some down from the stores.

FRANK. Do, in heaven's name!

[VIVIE *goes to the writing-table and makes a memorandum to order the butter.* PRAED *comes in from the kitchen, putting up his handkerchief, which he has been using as a napkin.*]

REV. SAMUEL. Frank, my boy: it is time for us to be thinking of home. Your mother does not know yet that we have visitors.

PRAED. I'm afraid we're giving trouble.

FRANK. [*rising*] Not the least in the world; my mother will be delighted to see you. She's a genuinely intellectual artistic woman; and she sees nobody here from one year's end to another except the gov'nor; so you can imagine how jolly dull it pans out for her. [*to his father*] Y o u r e not intellectual or artistic are you, pater? So take Praed home at once; and I'll stay here and entertain Mrs Warren. Youll pick up Crofts in the garden. He'll be excellent company for the bull-pup.

PRAED. [*taking his hat from the dresser, and coming close to* FRANK] Come with us, Frank. Mrs Warren has not seen Miss Vivie for a long time; and we have prevented them from having a moment together yet.

FRANK. [*quite softened, and looking at* PRAED *with romantic admiration*] Of course. I forgot. Ever so thanks for reminding me. Perfect gentleman, Praddy. Always were. My ideal through life. [*he rises to go, but pauses a moment between the two older men, and puts his hand on* PRAED's *shoulder*] Ah, if you had only been my father instead of this unworthy old man! [*He puts his other hand on his father's shoulder.*]

REV. SAMUEL. [*blustering*] Silence, sir, silence; you are profane.

MRS. WARREN. [*laughing heartily*] You should keep him in better order, Sam. Goodnight. Here: take George his hat and stick with my compliments.

REV. SAMUEL. [*taking them*] Goodnight. [*They shake hands. As he passes* VIVIE *he shakes hands with her also and bids her goodnight. Then, in booming command, to* FRANK] Come along, sir, at once. [*He goes out.*]

MRS WARREN. Byebye, Praddy.

PRAED. Byebye, Kitty.

[*They shake hands affectionately and go out together, she accompanying him to the garden gate.*]

FRANK. [*to* VIVIE] Kissums?

VIVIE. [*fiercely*] No. I hate you. [*She takes a couple of books and some paper from the writing-table, and sits down with them at the middle table, at the end next the fireplace.*]

FRANK. [*grimacing*] Sorry. [*He goes for his cap and rifle.* MRS WARREN *returns. He takes her hand*] Goodnight, d e a r Mrs Warren. [*He kisses her hand. She snatches it away, her lips tightening, and looks more than half disposed to box his ears. He laughs mischievously and runs off, clapping-to the door behind him.*]

MRS WARREN. [*resigning herself to an evening of boredom now that the men are gone*] Did you ever in your life hear anyone rattle on so? Isnt he a tease?

[*She sits at the table.*] Now that I think of it, dearie, dont you go on encouraging him. I'm sure he's a regular good-for-nothing.

VIVIE. [*rising to fetch more books*] I'm afraid so. Poor Frank! I shall have to get rid of him; but I shall feel sorry for him, though he's not worth it. That man Crofts does not seem to me to be good for much either: is he? [*She throws the books on the table rather roughly.*]

MRS WARREN. [*galled by* VIVIE's *indifference*] What do you know of men, child, to talk that way about them? Youll have to make up your mind to see a good deal of Sir George Crofts, as he's a friend of mine.

VIVIE. [*quite unmoved*] Why? [*She sits down and opens a book.*] Do you expect that we shall be much together? You and I, I mean?

MRS WARREN. [*staring at her*] Of course: until youre married. Youre not going back to college again.

VIVIE. Do you think my way of life would suit you? I doubt it.

MRS WARREN. Y o u r way of life! What do you mean?

VIVIE. [*cutting a page of her book with the paper knife on her chatelaine*] Has it really never occurred to you, mother, that I have a way of life like other people?

MRS WARREN. What nonsense is this youre trying to talk? Do you want to shew your independence, now that youre a great little person at school? Dont be a fool, child.

VIVIE. [*indulgently*] Thats all you have to say on the subject, is it, mother?

MRS WARREN. [*puzzled, then angry*] Dont you keep on asking me questions like that. [*violently*] Hold your tongue. [VIVIE *works on, losing no time, and saying nothing.*] You and your way of life, indeed! What next? [*She looks at* VIVIE *again. No reply.*] Your way of life will be what I please, so it will. [*another pause*] Ive been noticing these airs in you ever since you got that tripos or whatever you call it. If you think I'm going to put up with them youre mistaken; and the sooner you find it out, the better. [*muttering*] All I have to say on the subject, indeed! [*again raising her voice angrily*] Do you know who youre speaking to, Miss?

VIVIE. [*looking across at her without raising her head from her book*] No. Who are you? What are you?

MRS WARREN. [*rising breathless*] You young imp!

VIVIE. Everybody knows my reputation, my social standing, and the profession I intend to pursue. I know nothing about you. What is that way of life which you invite me to share with you and Sir George Crofts, pray?

MRS WARREN. Take care. I shall do something I'll be sorry for after, and you too.

VIVIE. [*putting aside her books with cool decision*] Well, let us drop the subject until you are better able to face it. [*looking critically at her mother*] You want some good walks and a little lawn tennis to set you up. You are shockingly out of condition: you were not able to manage twenty yards uphill today without stopping to pant; and your wrists are mere rolls of fat. Look at mine. [*She holds out her wrists.*]

MRS. WARREN. [*after looking at her helplessly, begins to whimper*] Vivie—

VIVIE. [*springing up sharply*] Now pray dont begin to cry. Anything but that. I really cannot stand whimpering. I will go out of the room if you do.

MRS WARREN. [*piteously*] Oh, my darling, how can you be so hard on me? Have I no rights over you as your mother?

VIVIE. Are you my mother?

MRS WARREN. [*appalled*] Am I your mother! Oh, Vivie!

VIVIE. Then where are our relatives? my father? our family friends? You claim the rights of a mother: the right to call me fool and child; to speak to me as no woman in authority over me at college dare speak to me; to dictate my way of life; and to force on me the acquaintance of a brute whom anyone can see to be the most vicious sort of London man about town. Before I give myself the trouble to resist such claims, I may as well find out whether they have any real existence.

MRS WARREN. [*distracted, throwing herself on her knees*] Oh no, no. Stop, stop. I am your mother: I swear it. Oh, you cant mean to turn on me—my own child! It's not natural. You believe me, dont you? Say you believe me.

VIVIE. Who was my father?

MRS WARREN. You dont know what youre asking. I cant tell you.

VIVIE. [*determinedly*] Oh yes you can, if you like. I have a right to know; and you know very well that I have that right. You can refuse to tell me, if you please; but if you do, you will see the last of me tomorrow morning.

MRS WARREN. Oh, it's too horrible to hear you talk like that. You wouldnt— you c o u l d n t leave me.

VIVIE. [*ruthlessly*] Yes, without a moment's hesitation, if you trifle with me about this. [*shivering with disgust*] How can I feel sure that I may not have the contaminated blood of that brutal waster in my veins?

MRS WARREN. No, no. On my oath it's not he, nor any of the rest that you have ever met. I'm certain of that, at least.

[VIVIE's *eyes fasten sternly on her mother as the significance of this flashes on her.*]

VIVIE. [*slowly*] You are certain of that, a t l e a s t. Ah! You mean that that is all you are certain of. [*thoughtfully*] I see. [MRS WARREN *buries her face in her hands.*] Dont do that, mother: you know you dont feel it a bit. [MRS WARREN *takes down her hands and looks up deplorably at* VIVIE, *who takes out her watch and says*] Well, that is enough for tonight. At what hour would you like breakfast? Is half-past eight too early for you?

MRS WARREN. [*wildly*] My God, what sort of woman are you?

VIVIE. [*coolly*] The sort the world is mostly made of, I should hope. Otherwise I dont understand how it gets its business done. Come [*taking her mother by the wrist, and pulling her up pretty resolutely*]: pull yourself together. Thats right.

MRS WARREN. [*querulously*] Youre very rough with me, Vivie.

VIVIE. Nonsense. What about bed? It's past ten.

MRS WARREN. [*passionately*] Whats the use of my going to bed? Do you think I could sleep?

VIVIE. Why not? I shall.

MRS WARREN. You! youve no heart. [*She suddenly breaks out vehemently in her natural tongue—the dialect of a woman of the people—with all her affectations of maternal authority and conventional manners gone, and an overwhelming inspiration of true conviction and scorn in her.*] Oh, I wont bear it: I wont put up with the injustice of it. What right have you to set yourself up above me like this? You boast of what you are to me—to m e, who gave you the chance of being what you are. What chance had I! Shame on you for a bad daughter and a stuck-up prude!

VIVIE. [*sitting down with a shrug, no longer confident; for her replies, which have sounded sensible and strong to her so far, now begin to ring rather woodenly and even priggishly against the new tone of her mother*] Dont think for a moment I set myself above you in any way. You attacked me with the conventional authority of a mother: I defended myself with the conventional superiority of a respectable woman. Frankly, I am not going to stand any of your nonsense; and when you drop it I shall not expect you to stand any of mine. I shall always respect your right to your own opinions and your own way of life.

MRS WARREN. My own opinions and my own way of life! Listen to her talking!

Do you think I was brought up like you? able to pick and choose my own way of life? Do you think I did what I did because I liked it, or thought it right, or wouldnt rather have gone to college and been a lady if I'd had the chance?

VIVIE. Everybody has some choice, mother. The poorest girl alive may not be able to choose between being Queen of England or Principal of Newnham; but she can choose between ragpicking and flower-selling, according to her taste. People are always blaming their circumstances for what they are. I dont believe in circumstances. The people who get on in this world are the people who get up and look for the circumstances they want, and, if they cant find them, make them.

MRS WARREN. Oh, it's easy to talk, very easy, isnt it? Here! would you like to know what my circumstances were?

VIVIE. Yes: you had better tell me. Wont you sit down?

MRS WARREN. Oh, I'll sit down: dont you be afraid. [*She plants her chair farther forward with brazen energy, and sits down.* VIVIE *is impressed in spite of herself.*] D'you know what your gran'mother was?

VIVIE. No.

MRS WARREN. No you dont. I do. She called herself a widow and had a fried-fish shop down by the Mint, and kept herself and four daughters out of it. Two of us were sisters: that was me and Liz; and we were both good-looking and well made. I suppose our father was a well-fed man: mother pretended he was a gentleman; but I dont know. The other two were only half sisters: undersized, ugly, starved looking, hard working, honest poor creatures: Liz and I would have half-murdered them if mother hadnt half-murdered us to keep our hands off them. They were the respectable ones. Well, what did they get by their respectability? I'll tell you. One of them worked in a whitelead factory twelve hours a day for nine shillings a week until she died of lead poisoning. She only expected to get her hands a little paralyzed; but she died. The other was always held up to us as a model because she married a Government laborer in the Deptford victualling yard, and kept his room and the three children neat and tidy on eighteen shillings a week—until he took to drink. That was worth being respectable for, wasnt it?

VIVIE. [*now thoughtfully attentive*] Did you and your sister think so?

MRS WARREN. Liz didnt, I can tell you: she had more spirit. We both went to a church school—that was part of the ladylike airs we gave ourselves to be superior to the children that knew nothing and went nowhere—and we stayed there until Liz went out one night and never came back. I know the school-mistress thought I'd soon follow her example; for the clergyman was always warning me that Lizzie'd end by jumping off Waterloo Bridge. Poor fool: that was all he knew about it! But I was more afraid of the whitelead factory than I was of the river; and so would you have been in my place. That clergyman got me a situation as a scullery maid in a temperance restaurant where they sent out for anything you liked. Then I was waitress; and then I went to the bar at Waterloo station: fourteen hours a day serving drinks and washing glasses for four shillings a week and my board. That was considered a great promotion for me. Well, one cold, wretched night, when I was so tired I could hardly keep myself awake, who should come up for a half of Scotch but Lizzie, in a long fur cloak, elegant and comfortable, with a lot of sovereigns in her purse.

VIVIE. [*grimly*] My aunt Lizzie!

MRS WARREN. Yes; and a very good aunt to have, too. She's living down at Winchester now, close to the cathedral, one of the most respectable ladies there. Chaperones girls at the county ball, if you please. No river for Liz, thank you! You remind me of Liz a little: she was a first-rate business woman—saved money from the beginning—never let herself look too like what she was—never lost her head or threw away a chance. When she saw I'd grown up good-looking she said to me across the bar "What are you doing there, you little fool? wearing out your health and your appearance for other people's profit!" Liz was saving money then to take a house for herself in Brussels; and she thought we two could save faster than one. So she lent me some money and gave me a start; and I saved steadily and first paid her back, and then went into business with her as her partner. Why shouldnt I have done it? The house in Brussels was real high class: a much better place for a woman to be in than the factory where Anne Jane got poisoned. None of our girls were ever treated as I was treated in the scullery of that temperance place, or at the Waterloo bar, or at home. Would you have had me stay in them and become a worn out old drudge before I was forty?

VIVIE. [*intensely interested by this time*] No; but why did you choose that business? Saving money and good management will succeed in any business.

MRS WARREN. Yes, saving money. But where can a woman get the money to save in any other business? Could you save out of four shillings a week and keep yourself dressed as well? Not you. Of course, if youre a plain woman and cant earn anything more; or if you have a turn for music, or the stage, or newspaper writing; thats different. But neither Liz nor I had any turn for such things: all we had was our appearance and our turn for pleasing men. Do you think we were such fools as to let other people trade in our good looks by employing us as shopgirls, or barmaids, or waitresses, when we could trade in them ourselves and get all the profits instead of starvation wages? Not likely.

VIVIE. You were certainly quite justified—from the business point of view.

MRS WARREN. Yes; or any other point of view. What is any respectable girl brought up to do but to catch some rich man's fancy and get the benefit of his money by marrying him?—as if a marriage ceremony could make any difference in the right or wrong of the thing! Oh! the hypocrisy of the world makes me sick! Liz and I had to work and save and calculate just like other people; elseways we should be as poor as any good-for-nothing drunken waster of a woman that thinks her luck will last for ever. [*with great energy*] I despise such people: theyve no character; and if theres a thing I hate in a woman, it's want of character.

VIVIE. Come now, mother: frankly! Isnt it part of what you call character in a woman that she should greatly dislike such a way of making money?

MRS WARREN. Why, of course. Everybody dislikes having to work and make money; but they have to do it all the same. I'm sure Ive often pitied a poor girl; tired out and in low spirits, having to try to please some man that she doesnt care two straws for—some half-drunken fool that thinks he's making himself agreeable when he's teasing and worrying and disgusting a woman so that hardly any money could pay her for putting up with it. But she has to bear with disagreeables and take the rough with the smooth, just like a nurse in a hospital or anyone else. It's not work that any woman would do for pleasure, goodness knows; though to hear the pious people talk you would suppose it was a bed of roses.

VIVIE. Still, you consider it worth while. It pays.

MRS WARREN. Of course it's worth while to a poor girl, if she can resist temptation and is good-looking and well conducted and sensible. It's far better than any other employment open to her. I always thought that oughtnt to be. It c a n t be right, Vivie, that there shouldnt be better opportunities for women. I stick to that: it's wrong. But it's so, right or wrong; and a girl must make the best of it. But of course it's not worth while for a lady. If you took to it youd be a fool; but I should have been a fool if I'd taken to anything else.

VIVIE. [*more and more deeply moved*] Mother; suppose we were both as poor as you were in those wretched old days, are you quite sure that you wouldnt advise me to try the Waterloo bar, or marry a laborer, or even go into the factory?

MRS WARREN. [*indignantly*] Of course not. What sort of mother do you take me for! How could you keep your self-respect in such starvation and slavery? And whats a woman worth? whats life worth? without self-respect! Why am I independent and able to give my daughter a first-rate education, when other women that had just as good opportunities are in the gutter? Because I always knew how to respect myself and control myself. Why is Liz looked up to in a cathedral town? The same reason. Where would we be now if we'd minded the clergyman's foolishness? Scrubbing floors for one and sixpence a day and nothing to look forward to but the workhouse infirmary. Dont you be led astray by people who dont know the world, my girl. The only way for a woman to provide for herself decently is for her to be good to some man that can afford to be good to her. If she's in his own station of life, let her make him marry her; but if she's far beneath him she cant expect it: why should she? it wouldn't be for her own happiness. Ask any lady in London society that has daughters; and she'll tell you the same, except that I tell you straight and she'll tell you crooked. Thats all the difference.

VIVIE. [*fascinated, gazing at her*] My dear mother; you are a wonderful woman: you are stronger than all England. And are you really and truly not one wee bit doubtful—or—or—ashamed?

MRS WARREN. Well, of course, dearie, it's only good manners to be ashamed of it; it's expected from a woman. Women have to pretend to feel a great deal that they dont feel. Liz used to be angry with me for plumping out the truth about it. She used to say that when every woman could learn enough from what was going on in the world before her eyes, there was no need to talk about it to her. But then Liz was such a perfect lady! She had the true instinct of it; while I was always a bit of a vulgarian. I used to be so pleased when you sent me your photos to see that you were growing up like Liz: youve just her ladylike, determined way. But I cant stand saying one thing when everyone knows I mean another. Whats the use in such hypocrisy? If people arrange the world that way for women, theres no good pretending it's arranged the other way. No: I never was a bit ashamed really. I consider I had a right to be proud of how we managed everything so respectably, and never had a word against us, and how the girls were so well taken care of. Some of them did very well: one of them married an ambassador. But of course now I darent talk about such things: whatever would they think of us! [*she yawns*] Oh dear! I do believe I'm getting sleepy after all. [*She stretches herself lazily, thoroughly relieved by her explosion, and placidly ready for her night's rest.*]

VIVIE. I believe it is I who will not be able to sleep now. [*She goes to the dresser and lights the candle. Then she extinguishes the lamp, darkening the room a good deal.*] Better let in some fresh air before locking up. [*She opens the cottage door, and finds that it is broad moonlight.*] What a beautiful night! Look! [*She draws aside the curtains of the window. The landscape is seen bathed in the radiance of the harvest moon rising over Blackdown.*]

MRS WARREN. [*with a perfunctory glance at the scene*] Yes, dear; but take care you dont catch your death of cold from the night air.

VIVIE. [*contemptuously*] Nonsense.

MRS WARREN. [*querulously*] Oh yes: everything I say is nonsense, according to you.

VIVIE. [*turning to her quickly*] No: really that is not so, mother. You have got completely the better of me tonight, though I intended it to be the other way. Let us be good friends now.

MRS WARREN. [*shaking her head a little ruefully*] So it has been the other way. But I suppose I must give in to it. I always got the worst of it from Liz; and now I suppose it'll be the same with you.

VIVIE. Well, never mind. Come: goodnight, dear old mother. [*She takes her mother in her arms.*]

MRS WARREN. [*fondly*] I brought you up well, didnt I, dearie?

VIVIE. You did.

MRS WARREN. And youll be good to your poor old mother for it, wont you?

VIVIE. I will, dear. [*kissing her*] Goodnight.

MRS WARREN. [*with unction*] Blessings on my own dearie darling! a mother's blessing!

[*She embraces her daughter protectingly, instinctively looking upward for divine sanction.*]

Act 3

In the Rectory garden next morning, with the sun shining from a cloudless sky. The garden wall has a five-barred wooden gate, wide enough to admit a carriage, in the middle. Beside the gate hangs a bell on a coiled spring, communicating with a pull outside. The carriage drive comes down the middle of the garden and then swerves to its left, where it ends in a little gravelled circus opposite the Rectory porch. Beyond the gate is seen the dusty high road, parallel with the wall, bounded on the farther side by a strip of turf and an unfenced pine wood. On the lawn, between the house and the drive, is a clipped yew tree, with a garden bench in its shade. On the opposite side the garden is shut in by a box hedge; and there is a sundial on the turf, with an iron chair near it. A little path leads off through the box hedge, behind the sundial.

FRANK, seated on the chair near the sundial, on which he has placed the morning papers, is reading The Standard. His father comes from the house, red-eyed and shivery, and meets FRANK's eye with misgiving.

FRANK. [*looking at his watch*] Half-past eleven. Nice hour for a rector to come down to breakfast!

REV. SAMUEL. Dont mock, Frank: dont mock. I am a little—er—[*shivering*]—

FRANK. Off color?

REV. SAMUEL. [*repudiating the expression*] No, sir: u n w e l l this morning. Wheres your mother?

FRANK. Dont be alarmed: she's not here. Gone to town by the 11.13 with Bessie. She left several messages for you. Do you feel equal to receiving them now, or shall I wait til youve breakfasted?

REV. SAMUEL. I h a v e breakfasted, sir. I am surprised at your mother going to town when we have people staying with us. Theyll think it very strange.

FRANK. Possibly she has considered that. At all events, if Crofts is going to stay here, and you are going to sit up every night with him until four, recalling the incidents of your fiery youth, it is clearly my mother's duty, as a prudent housekeeper, to go up to the stores and order a barrel of whisky and few hundred siphons.

REV. SAMUEL. I did not observe that Sir George drank excessively.

FRANK. You were not in a condition to, gov'nor.

REV. SAMUEL. Do you mean to say that *I*—?

FRANK. [*calmly*] I never saw a beneficed clergyman less sober. The anecdotes you told about your past career were so awful that I really dont think Praed would have passed the night under your roof if it hadnt been for the way my mother and he took to one another.

REV. SAMUEL. Nonsense, sir. I am Sir George Croft's host. I must talk to him about something; and he has only one subject. Where is Mr Praed now?

FRANK. He is driving my mother and Bessie to the station.

REV. SAMUEL. Is Crofts up yet?

FRANK. Oh, long ago. He hasnt turned a hair: he's in much better practice than you. Has kept it up ever since, probably. He's taken himself off somewhere to smoke.

[*FRANK resumes his paper. The parson turns disconsolately towards the gate; then comes back irresolutely.*]

REV. SAMUEL. Er—Frank.

FRANK. Yes.

REV. SAMUEL. Do you think the Warrens will expect to be asked here after yesterday afternoon?

FRANK. Theyve been asked already.

REV. SAMUEL. [*appalled*] What!!!

FRANK. Crofts informed us at breakfast that you told him to bring Mrs Warren and Vivie over here today, and to invite them to make this house their home. My mother then found she must go to town by the 11.13 train.

REV. SAMUEL. [*with despairing vehemence*] I never gave any such invitation. I never thought of such a thing.

FRANK. [*compassionately*] How do you know, gov'nor, what you said and thought last night?

PRAED. [*coming in through the hedge*] Good morning.

REV. SAMUEL. Good morning. I must apologize for not having met you at breakfast. I have a touch of—of—

FRANK. Clergyman's sore throat, Praed. Fortunately not chronic.

PRAED. [*changing the subject*] Well, I must say your house is in a charming spot here. Really most charming.

REV. SAMUEL. Yes: it is indeed. Frank will take you for a walk, Mr Praed, if you like. I'll ask you to excuse me: I must take the opportunity to write my sermon while Mrs Gardner is away and you are all amusing yourselves. You wont mind, will you?

PRAED. Certainly not. Dont stand on the slightest ceremony with me.

REV. SAMUEL. Thank you. I'll—er—er—[*He stammers his way to the porch and vanishes into the house.*]

PRAED. Curious thing it must be writing a sermon every week.

FRANK. Ever so curious, if he did it. He buys em. He's gone for some soda water.

PRAED. My dear boy: I wish you would be more respectful to your father. You know you can be so nice when you like.

FRANK. My dear Praddy: you forget that I have to live with the governor. When two people live together—it doesnt matter whether theyre father and son or husband and wife or brother and sister—they cant keep up the polite humbug thats so easy for ten minutes on an afternoon call. Now the governor, who unites to many admirable domestic qualities the irresoluteness of a sheep and the pompousness and aggressiveness of a jackass—

PRAED. No, pray, pray, my dear Frank, remember! He is your father.

FRANK. I give him due credit for that. [*rising and flinging down his paper*] But just imagine his telling Crofts to bring the Warrens over here! He must have been ever so drunk. You know, my dear Praddy, my mother wouldnt stand Mrs Warren for a moment. Vivie mustnt come here until she's gone back to town.

PRAED. But your mother doesnt know anything about Mrs Warren, does she? [*He picks up the paper and sits down to read it.*]

FRANK. I don't know. Her journey to town looks as if she did. Not that my mother would mind in the ordinary way: she has stuck like a brick to lots of women who had got into trouble. But they were all nice women. Thats what makes the real difference. Mrs Warren, no doubt, has her merits; but she's ever so rowdy; and my mother simply wouldnt put up with her. So— hallo! [*This exclamation is provoked by the reappearance of the clergyman, who comes out of the house in haste and dismay.*]

REV. SAMUEL. Frank: Mrs Warren and her daughter are coming across the heath with Crofts: I saw them from the study windows. What am I to say about your mother?

FRANK. Stick on your hat and go out and say how delighted you are to see them; and that Frank's in the garden; and that mother and Bessie have been called to the bedside of a sick relative, and were ever so sorry they couldnt stop; and that you hope Mrs Warren slept well; and—and—say any blessed thing except the truth, and leave the rest to Providence.

REV. SAMUEL. But how are we to get rid of them afterwards?

FRANK. Theres no time to think of that now. Here! [*He bounds into the house.*]

REV. SAMUEL. He's so impetuous. I dont know what to do with him, Mr Praed.

FRANK. [*returning with clerical felt hat, which he claps on his father's head*] Now: off with you. [*rushing him through the gate*] Praed and I'll wait here, to give the thing an unpremeditated air. [*The clergyman, dazed but obedient, hurries off.*]

FRANK. We must get the old girl back to town somehow, Praed. Come! Honestly, dear Praddy, do you like seeing them together?

PRAED. Oh, why not?

FRANK. [*his teeth on edge*] Dont it make your flesh creep ever so little? that wicked old devil, up to every villainy under the sun, I'll swear, and Vivie— ugh!

PRAED. Hush, pray. Theyre coming.

[*The clergyman and* CROFTS *are seen coming along the road, followed by* MRS WARREN *and* VIVIE *walking affectionately together.*]

FRANK. Look: she actually has her arm round the old woman's waist. It's her right arm: she began it. She's gone sentimental, by God! Ugh! ugh! Now do you feel the creeps? [*The clergyman opens the gate; and* MRS WARREN *and* VIVIE *pass him and stand in the middle of the garden looking at the house.* FRANK, *in an ecstasy of dissimulation, turns gaily to* MRS WARREN, *exclaiming*] Ever so delighted to see you, Mrs Warren. This quiet old rectory garden becomes you perfectly.

MRS WARREN. Well, I never! Did you hear that, George? He says I look well in a quiet old rectory garden.

REV. SAMUEL. [*still holding the gate for* CROFTS, *who loafs through it, heavily bored*] You look well everywhere, Mrs Warren.

FRANK. Bravo, gov'nor! Now look here: lets have a treat before lunch. First lets see the church. Everyone has to do that. It's a regular old thirteenth century church, you know: the gov'nor's ever so fond of it, because he got up a restoration fund and had it completely rebuilt six years ago. Praed will be able to shew its points.

PRAED. [*rising*] Certainly, if the restoration has left any to shew.

REV. SAMUEL. [*mooning hospitably at them*] I shall be pleased, I'm sure, if Sir George and Mrs Warren really care about it.

MRS WARREN. Oh, come along and get it over.

CROFTS. [*turning back towards the gate*] Ive no objection.

REV. SAMUEL. Not that way. We go through the fields, if you dont mind. Round here. [*He leads the way by the little path through the box hedge.*]

CROFTS. Oh, all right. [*He goes with the parson.*]

[PRAED *follows with* MRS WARREN. VIVIE *does not stir: she watches them until they have gone, with all the lines of purpose in her face marking it strongly.*]

FRANK. Aint you coming?

VIVIE. No. I want to give you a warning, Frank. You were making fun of my mother just now when you said that about the rectory garden. That is barred in future. Please treat my mother with as much respect as you treat your own.

FRANK. My dear Viv: she wouldnt appreciate it: the two cases require different treatment. But what on earth has happened to you? Last night we were perfectly agreed as to your mother and her set. This morning I find you attitudinizing sentimentally with your arm round your parent's waist.

VIVIE. [*flushing*] Attitudinizing!

FRANK. That was how it struck me. First time I ever saw you do a second-rate thing.

VIVIE. [*controlling herself*] Yes, Frank: there has been a change; but I dont think it a change for the worse. Yesterday I was a little prig.

FRANK. And today?

VIVIE. [*wincing; then looking at him steadily*] Today I know my mother better than you do.

FRANK. Heaven forbid!

VIVIE. What do you mean?

FRANK. Viv: theres a freemasonry among thoroughly immoral people that you know nothing of. Youve too much character. T h a t s the bond between your mother and me: thats why I know her better than youll ever know her.

VIVIE. You are wrong: you know nothing about her. If you knew the circumstances against which my mother had to struggle—

FRANK. [*adroitly finishing the sentence for her*] I should know why she is what she is, shouldnt I? What difference would that make? Circumstances or no circumstances, Viv, you wont be able to stand your mother.

VIVIE. [*very angrily*] Why not?

FRANK. Because she's an old wretch, Viv. If you ever put your arm round her waist in my presence again, I'll shoot myself there and then as a protest against an exhibition which revolts me.

VIVIE. Must I choose between dropping your acquaintance and dropping my mother's?

FRANK. [*gracefully*] That would put the old lady at ever such a disadvantage. No, Viv: your infatuated little boy will have to stick to you in any case. But he's all the more anxious that you shouldnt make mistakes. It's no use, Viv: your mother's impossible. She may be a good sort; but she's a bad lot, a very bad lot.

VIVIE. [*hotly*] Frank—! [*He stands his ground. She turns away and sits down on the bench under the yew tree, struggling to recover her self-command. Then she says*] Is she to be deserted by all the world because she's what you call a bad lot? Has she no right to live?

FRANK. No fear of that, Viv: s h e wont ever be deserted. [*He sits on the bench beside her.*]

VIVIE. But I am to desert her, I suppose.

FRANK. [*babyishly, lulling her and making love to her with his voice*] Mustnt go live with her. Little family group of mother and daughter wouldnt be a success. Spoil our little group.

VIVIE. [*falling under the spell*] What little group?

FRANK. The babes in the wood: Vivie and little Frank. [*He nestles against her like a weary child.*] Lets go and get covered up with leaves.

VIVIE. [*rhythmically, rocking him like a nurse*] Fast asleep, hand in hand, under the trees.

FRANK. The wise little girl with her silly little boy.

VIVIE. The dear little boy with his dowdy little girl.

FRANK. Ever so peaceful, and relieved from the imbecility of the little boy's father and the questionableness of the little girl's—

VIVIE. [*smothering the word against her breast*] Sh-sh-sh-sh! little girl wants to forget all about her mother. [*They are silent for some moments, rocking one another. Then* VIVIE *wakes up with a shock, exclaiming*] What a pair of fools we are! Come: sit up. Gracious! your hair. [*She smoothes it.*] I wonder do all grown up people play in that childish way when nobody is looking. I never did it when I was a child.

FRANK. Neither did I. You are my first playmate. [*He catches her hand to kiss it, but checks himself to look round first. Very unexpectedly, he sees* CROFTS *emerging from the box hedge.*] Oh damn!

VIVIE. Why damn, dear?

FRANK. [*whispering*] Sh! Here's this brute Crofts. [*He sits farther away from her with an unconcerned air.*]

CROFTS. Could I have a few words with you, Miss Vivie?

VIVIE. Certainly.

CROFTS. [*to* FRANK] Youll excuse me, Gardner. Theyre waiting for you in the church, if you don't mind.

FRANK. [*rising*] Anything to oblige you, Crofts—except church. If you should happen to want me, Vivvums, ring the gate bell. [*He goes into the house with unruffled suavity.*]

CROFTS. [*watching him with a crafty air as he disappears, and speaking to* VIVIE *with an assumption of being on privileged terms with her*] Pleasant young fellow that, Miss Vivie. Pity he has no money, isnt it?

VIVIE. Do you think so?

CROFTS. Well, whats he to do? No profession. No property. Whats he good for?

VIVIE. I realize his disadvantages, Sir George.

CROFTS. [*a little taken aback at being so precisely interpreted*] Oh, it's not that. But while we're in this world we're in it; and money's money. [*Vivie does not answer.*] Nice day, isnt it?

VIVIE. [*with scarcely veiled contempt for this effort at conversation*] Very.

CROFTS. [*with brutal good humor, as if he liked her pluck*] Well, thats not what I came to say. [*sitting down beside her*] Now listen, Miss Vivie. I'm quite aware that I'm not a young lady's man.

VIVIE. Indeed, Sir George?

CROFTS. No; and to tell you the honest truth I dont want to be either. But when I say a thing I mean it; when I feel a sentiment I feel it in earnest; and what I value I pay hard money for. Thats the sort of man I am.

VIVIE. It does you great credit, I'm sure.

CROFTS. Oh, I dont mean to praise myself. I have my faults, Heaven knows: no man is more sensible of that than I am. I know I'm not perfect: thats one of the disadvantages of being a middle-aged man; for I'm not a young man, and I know it. But my code is a simple one, and, I think, a good one. Honor between man and man; fidelity between man and woman; and no cant about this religion or that religion, but an honest belief that things are making for good on the whole.

VIVIE. [*with biting irony*] "A power, not ourselves, that makes for righteousness," eh?

CROFTS. [*taking her seriously*] Oh certainly. Not ourselves, of course. You understand what I mean. Well, now as to practical matters. You may have an idea that Ive flung my money about; but I havnt: I'm richer today than when I first came into the property. Ive used my knowledge of the world to invest my money in ways that other men have overlooked; and whatever else I may be, I'm a safe man from the money point of view.

VIVIE. It's very kind of you to tell me all this.

CROFTS. Oh well, come, Miss Vivie: you neednt pretend you dont see what I'm driving at. I want to settle down with a Lady Crofts. I suppose you think me very blunt, eh?

VIVIE. Not at all: I am much obliged to you for being so definite and businesslike. I quite appreciate the offer: the money, the position, L a d y C r o f t s, and so on. But I think I will say no, if you don't mind. I'd rather not. [*She rises, and strolls across to the sundial to get out of his immediate neighborhood.*]

CROFTS. [*not at all discouraged, and taking advantage of the additional room left him on the seat to spread himself comfortably, as if a few preliminary refusals were part of the inevitable routine of courtship*] I'm in no hurry. It was only just to let you know in case young Gardner should try to trap you. Leave the question open.

VIVIE. [*sharply*] My no is final. I wont go back from it.

[CROFTS *is not impressed. He grins; leans forward with his elbows on his knees to prod with his stick at some unfortunate insect in the grass; and looks cunningly at her. She turns away impatiently.*]

CROFTS. I'm a good deal older than you. Twenty-five years; quarter of a century. I shant live for ever; and I'll take care that you shall be well off when I'm gone.

VIVIE. I am proof against even that inducement, Sir George. Dont you think youd better take your answer? There is not the slightest chance of my altering it.

CROFTS. [*rising after a final slash at a daisy, and coming nearer to her*] Well, no matter. I could tell you some things that would change your mind fast enough; but I wont, because I'd rather win you by honest affection. I was a good friend to your mother: ask her whether I wasnt. She'd never have made the money that paid for your education if it hadnt been for my advice and help, not to mention the money I advanced her. There are not many men would have stood by her as I have. I put not less than £40,000 into it, from first to last.

VIVIE. [*staring at him*] Do you mean to say you were my mother's business partner?

CROFTS. Yes. Now just think of all the trouble and the explanations it would save if we were to keep the whole thing in the family, so to speak. Ask your mother whether she'd like to have to explain all her affairs to a perfect stranger.

VIVIE. I see no difficulty, since I understand that the business is wound up, and the money invested.

CROFTS. [*stopping short, amazed*] Wound up! Wind up a business thats paying 35 per cent in the worst years! Not likely. Who told you that?

VIVIE. [*her color quite gone*] Do you mean that it is still—? [*She stops abruptly, and puts her hand on the sundial to support herself. Then she gets quickly to the iron chair and sits down.*] What business are you talking about?

CROFTS. Well, the fact is it's not what would be considered exactly a high-class business in my set—the county set, you know—our set it will be if you think better of my offer. Not that theres any mystery about it: dont think that. Of course you know by your mother's being in it that it's perfectly straight and honest. Ive known her for many years; and I can say of her that she'd cut off her hands sooner than touch anything that was not what it ought to be. I'll tell you all about it if you like. I dont know whether youve found in travelling how hard it is to find a really comfortable private hotel.

VIVIE. [sickened, averting her face] Yes: go on.

CROFTS. Well, thats all it is. Your mother has a genius for managing such things. We've got two in Brussels, one in Ostend, one in Vienna, and two in Budapest. Of course there are others besides ourselves in it; but we hold most of the capital; and your mother's indispensable as managing director. Youve noticed, I daresay, that she travels a good deal. But you see you cant mention such things in society. Once let out the word hotel and everybody says you keep a public-house. You wouldnt like people to say that of your mother, would you? Thats why we're so reserved about it. By the way, youll keep it to yourself, wont you? Since it's been a secret so long, it had better remain so.

VIVIE. And this is the business you invite me to join you in?

CROFTS. Oh, no. My wife shant be troubled with business. Youll not be in it more than youve always been.

VIVIE. I always been! What do you mean?

CROFTS. Only that youve always lived on it. It paid for your education and the dress you have on your back. Dont turn up your nose at business, Miss Vivie: where would your Newnhams and Girtons[1] be without it?

VIVIE. [rising, almost beside herself] Take care. I know what this business is.

CROFTS. [staring, with a suppressed oath] Who told you?

VIVIE. Your partner. My mother.

CROFTS. [black with rage] The old—

VIVIE. Just so.

[He swallows the epithet and stands for a moment swearing and raging foully to himself. But he knows that his cue is to be sympathetic. He takes refuge in generous indignation.]

CROFTS. She ought to have had more consideration for you. I'd never have told you.

VIVIE. I think you would probably have told me when we were married; it would have been a convenient weapon to break me in with.

CROFTS. [quite sincerely] I never intended that. On my word as a gentleman I didnt.

[VIVIE wonders at him. Her sense of the irony of his protest cools and braces her. She replies with contemptuous self-possession.]

VIVIE. It does not matter. I suppose you understand that when we leave here today our acquaintance ceases.

CROFTS. Why? Is it for helping your mother?

VIVIE. My mother was a very poor woman who had no reasonable choice but to do as she did. You were a rich gentleman; and you did the same for the sake of 35 per cent. You are a pretty common sort of scoundrel, I think. That is my opinion of you.

CROFTS. [after a stare: not at all displeased, and much more at ease on these frank terms than on their former ceremonious ones] Ha! ha! ha! ha! Go it, little missie, go it: it doesnt hurt me and it amuses you. Why the devil shouldnt I invest my money that way? I take the interest on my capital like

_____

1. Girton, like Newnham, is a women's college at Cambridge University.

other people: I hope you dont think I dirty my own hands with the work. Come! you wouldnt refuse the acquaintance of my mother's cousin the Duke of Belgravia because some of the rents he gets are earned in queer ways. You wouldnt cut the Archbishop of Canterbury, I suppose, because the Ecclesiastical Commissioners have a few publicans and sinners among their tenants. Do you remember your Crofts scholarship at Newnham? Well, that was founded by my brother the M.P.[2] He gets his 22 per cent out of a factory with 600 girls in it, and not one of them getting wages enough to live on. How d'ye suppose they manage when they have no family to fall back on? Ask your mother. And do you expect me to turn my back on 35 per cent when all the rest are pocketing what they can, like sensible men? No such fool! If youre going to pick and choose your acquaintances on moral principles, youd better clear out of this country, unless you want to cut yourself out of all decent society.

VIVIE. [*conscience stricken*] You might go on to point out that I myself never asked where the money I spent came from. I believe I am just as bad as you.

CROFTS. [*greatly reassured*] Of course you are; and a very good thing too! What harm does it do after all? [*rallying her jocularly*] So you dont think me such a scoundrel now you come to think it over. Eh?

VIVIE. I have shared profits with you; and I admitted you just now to the familiarity of knowing what I think of you.

CROFTS. [*with serious friendliness*] To be sure you did. You wont find me a bad sort: I dont go in for being superfine intellectually; but Ive plenty of honest human feeling; and the old Crofts breed comes out in a sort of instinctive hatred of anything low, in which I'm sure youll sympathize with me. Believe me, Miss Vivie, the world isnt such a bad place as the croakers make out. As long as you dont fly openly in the face of society, society doesnt ask any inconvenient questions; and it makes precious short work of the cads who do. There are no secrets better kept than the secrets everybody guesses. In the class of people I can introduce you to, no lady or gentleman would so far forget themselves as to discuss my business affairs or your mother's. No man can offer you a safer position.

VIVIE. [*studying him curiously*] I suppose you really think youre getting on famously with me.

CROFTS. Well, I hope I may flatter myself that you think better of me than you did at first.

VIVIE. [*quietly*] I hardly find you worth thinking about at all now. When I think of the society that tolerates you, and the laws that protect you! when I think of how helpless nine out of ten young girls would be in the hands of you and my mother! the unmentionable woman and her capitalist bully —

CROFTS. [*livid*] Damn you!

VIVIE. You need not. I feel among the damned already.

[*She raises the latch of the gate to open it and go out. He follows her and puts his hand heavily on the top bar to prevent its opening.*]

CROFTS. [*panting with fury*] Do you think I'll put up with this from you, you young devil?

VIVIE. [*unmoved*] Be quiet. Some one will answer the bell. [*Without flinching a step she strikes the bell with the back of her hand. It clangs harshly; and he starts back involuntarily. Almost immediately* FRANK *appears at the porch with his rifle.*]

FRANK. [*with cheerful politeness*] Will you have the rifle, Viv; or shall I operate?

VIVIE. Frank: have you been listening?

FRANK. [*coming down into the garden*] Only for the bell, I assure you; so that

2. Member of Parliament.

you shouldn't have to wait. I think I shewed great insight into your character Crofts.

CROFTS. For two pins I'd take that gun from you and break it across your head.

FRANK. [*stalking him cautiously*] Pray dont. I'm ever so careless in handling firearms. Sure to be a fatal accident, with a reprimand from the coroner's jury for my negligence.

VIVIE.. Put the rifle away, Frank: it's quite unnecessary.

FRANK. Quite right, Viv. Much more sportsmanlike to catch him in a trap. [CROFTS, *understanding the insult, makes a threatening movement.*] Crofts: there are fifteen cartridges in the magazine here; and I am a dead shot at the present distance and at an object of your size.

CROFTS. Oh, you neednt be afraid. I'm not going to touch you.

FRANK. Ever so magnanimous of you under the circumstances! Thank you!

CROFTS. I'll tell you this before I go. It may interest you, since youre so fond of one another. Allow me, Mister Frank, to introduce you to your half-sister, the eldest daughter of the Reverend Samuel Gardner. Miss Vivie: your half-brother. Good morning. [*He goes out through the gate and along the road.*]

FRANK. [*after a pause of stupefaction, raising the rifle*] Youll testify before the coroner that it's an accident, Viv. [*He takes aim at the retreating figure of* CROFTS. VIVIE *seizes the muzzle and pulls it round against her breast.*]

VIVIE. Fire now. You may.

FRANK. [*dropping his end of the rifle hastily*] Stop! take care. [*She lets go. It falls on the turf.*] Oh, youve given your little boy such a turn. Suppose it had gone off! ugh! [*He sinks on the garden seat, overcome.*]

VIVIE. Suppose it had: do you think it would not have been a relief to have some sharp physical pain tearing through me?

FRANK. [*coaxingly*] Take it ever so easy, dear Viv. Remember; even if the rifle scared that fellow into telling the truth for the first time in his life, that only makes us the babes in the wood in earnest. [*He holds out his arms to her.*] Come and be covered up with leaves again.

VIVIE. [*with a cry of disgust*] Ah, not that, not that. You make all my flesh creep.

FRANK. Why, whats the matter?

VIVIE. Goodbye. [*She makes for the gate.*]

FRANK. [*jumping up*] Hallo! Stop! Viv! Viv! [*She turns in the gateway.*] Where are you going to? Where shall we find you?

VIVIE. At Honoria Fraser's chambers, 67 Chancery Lane, for the rest of my life. [*She goes off quickly in the opposite direction to that taken by* CROFTS.]

FRANK. But I say—wait—dash it! [*He runs after her.*]

Act 4

HONORIA FRASER's *chambers in Chancery Lane. An office at the top of New Stone Buildings, with a plate-glass window, distempered walls, electric light, and a patent stove. Saturday afternoon. The chimneys of Lincoln's Inn[3] and the western sky beyond are seen through the window. There is a double writing table in the middle of the room, with a cigar box, ash pans, and a portable electric reading lamp almost snowed up in heaps of papers and books. This table has knee holes and chairs right and left and is very untidy. The clerk's desk, closed and tidy, with its high stool, is against the wall, near a door communicating with the inner rooms. In the opposite wall is the door leading to the public corridor. Its upper panel is of opaque glass, lettered in black on the outside,*

---

3. One of the four legal societies in London collectively known as the Inns of Court.

FRASER AND WARREN. *A baize screen hides the corner between this door and the window.*

FRANK, *in a fashionable light-colored coaching suit, with his stick, gloves, and white hat in his hands, is pacing up and down the office. Somebody tries the door with a key.*

FRANK. [*calling*] Come in. It's not locked.

[VIVIE *comes in, in her hat and jacket. She stops and stares at him.*]

VIVIE. [*sternly*] What are you doing here?

FRANK. Waiting to see you. Ive been here for hours. Is this the way you attend to your business? [*He puts his hat and stick on the table, and perches himself with a vault on the clerk's stool, looking at her with every appearance of being in a specially restless, teasing flippant mood.*]

VIVIE. Ive been away exactly twenty minutes for a cup of tea. [*She takes off her hat and jacket and hangs them up behind the screen.*] How did you get in?

FRANK. The staff had not left when I arrived. He's gone to play cricket on Primrose Hill.[4] Why dont you employ a woman, and give your sex a chance?

VIVIE. What have you come for?

FRANK. [*springing off the stool and coming close to her*] Viv: lets go and enjoy the Saturday half-holiday somewhere, like the staff. What do you say to Richmond,[5] and then a music hall, and a jolly supper?

VIVIE. Cant afford it. I shall put in another six hours work before I go to bed.

FRANK. Cant afford it, cant we? Aha! Look here. [*He takes out a handful of sovereigns and makes them chink.*] Gold, Viv: gold!

VIVIE. Where did you get it?

FRANK. Gambling, Viv: gambling. Poker.

VIVIE. Pah! It's meaner than stealing it. No: I'm not coming. [*She sits down to work at the table, with her back to the glass door, and begins turning over the papers.*]

FRANK. [*remonstrating piteously*] But, my dear Viv, I want to talk to you ever so seriously.

VIVIE. Very well: sit down in Honoria's chair and talk here. I like ten minutes chat after tea. [*He murmurs.*] No use groaning: I'm inexorable. [*He takes the opposite seat disconsolately.*] Pass that cigar box, will you?

FRANK. [*pushing the cigar box across*] Nasty womanly habit. Nice men dont do it any longer.

VIVIE. Yes: they object to the smell in the office; and weve had to take to cigarets. See! [*She opens the box and takes out a cigaret, which she lights. She offers him one; but he shakes his head with a wry face. She settles herself comfortably in her chair, smoking.*] Go ahead.

FRANK. Well, I want to know what youve done—what arrangements youve made.

VIVIE. Everything was settled twenty minutes after I arrived here. Honoria has found the business too much for her this year; and she was on the point of sending for me and proposing a partnership when I walked in and told her I hadnt a farthing in the world. So I installed myself and packed her off for a fortnight's holiday. What happened at Haslemere when I left?

FRANK. Nothing at all. I said youd gone to town on particular business.

VIVIE. Well?

FRANK. Well, either they were too flabbergasted to say anything, or else Crofts had prepared your mother. Anyhow, she didnt say anything; and Crofts didnt say anything; and Praddy only stared. After tea they got up and went;

---

4. A park in northwest London.   5. A residential suburb in southwest London.

and Ive not seen them since.

VIVIE. [*nodding placidly with one eye on a wreath of smoke*] Thats all right.

FRANK. [*looking round disparagingly*] Do you intend to stick in this confounded place?

VIVIE. [*blowing the wreath decisively away, and sitting straight up*] Yes. These two days have given me back all my strength and self-possession. I will never take a holiday again as long as I live.

FRANK. [*with a very wry face*] Mps! You look quite happy. And as hard as nails.

VIVIE. [*grimly*] Well for me that I am!

FRANK. [*rising*] Look here, Viv: we must have an explanation. We parted the other day under a complete misunderstanding. [*He sits on the table, close to her.*]

VIVIE. [*putting away the cigaret*] Well: clear it up.

FRANK. You remember what Crofts said?

VIVIE. Yes.

FRANK. That revelation was supposed to bring about a complete change in the nature of our feeling for one another. It placed us on the footing of brother and sister.

VIVIE. Yes.

FRANK. Have you ever had a brother?

VIVIE. No.

FRANK. Then you dont know what being brother and sister feels like? Now I have lots of sisters; and the fraternal feeling is quite familiar to me. I assure you my feeling for you is not the least in the world like it. The girls will go their way; I will go mine; and we shant care if we never see one another again. Thats brother and sister. But as to you, I cant be easy if I have to pass a week without seeing you. Thats not brother and sister. It's exactly what I felt an hour before Crofts made his revelation. In short, dear Viv, it's love's young dream.

VIVIE. [*bitingly*] The same feeling, Frank, that brought your father to my mother's feet. Is that it?

FRANK. [*so revolted that he slips off the table for a moment*] I very strongly object, Viv, to have my feelings compared to any which the Reverend Samuel is capable of harboring; and I object still more to a comparison of you to your mother. [*resuming his perch*] Besides, I dont believe the story. I have taxed my father with it, and obtained from him what I consider tantamount to a denial.

VIVIE. What did he say?

FRANK. He said he was sure there must be some mistake.

VIVIE. Do you believe him?

FRANK. I am prepared to take his word as against Crofts'.

VIVIE. Does it make any difference? I mean in your imagination or conscience; for of course it makes no real difference.

FRANK. [*shaking his head*] None whatever to m e.

VIVIE. Nor to me.

FRANK. [*staring*] But this is ever so surprising! [*he goes back to his chair*] I thought our whole relations were altered in your imagination and conscience, as you put it, the moment those words were out of the brute's muzzle.

VIVIE. No: it was not that. I didnt believe him. I only wish I could.

FRANK. Eh?

VIVIE. I think brother and sister would be a very suitable relation for us.

FRANK. You really mean that?

VIVIE. Yes. It's the only relation I care for, even if we could afford any other. I mean that.

FRANK. [*raising his eyebrows like one on whom a new light has dawned, and rising with quite an effusion of chivalrous sentiment*] My dear Viv: why didnt you say so before? I am ever so sorry for persecuting you. I understand, of course.

VIVIE. [*puzzled*] Understand what?

FRANK. Oh, I'm not a fool in the ordinary sense: only in the Scriptural sense of doing all the things the wise man declared to be folly, after trying them himself on the most extensive scale. I see I am no longer Vivvum's little boy. Dont be alarmed: I shall never call you Vivvums again—at least unless you get tired of your new little boy, whoever he may be.

VIVIE. My new little boy!

FRANK. [*with conviction*] Must be a new little boy. Always happens that way. No other way, in fact.

VIVIE. None that you know of, fortunately for you.

[*Someone knocks at the door.*]

FRANK. My curse upon yon caller, whoe'er he be!

VIVIE. It's Praed. He's going to Italy and wants to say goodbye. I asked him to call this afternoon. Go and let him in.

FRANK. We can continue our conversation after his departure for Italy. I'll stay him out. [*He goes to the door and opens it.*] How are you, Praddy? Delighted to see you. Come in.

[PRAED, *dressed for travelling, comes in, in high spirits.*]

PRAED. How do you do, Miss Warren? [*She presses his hand cordially, though a certain sentimentality in his high spirits jars on her.*] I start in an hour from Holborn Viaduct.[6] I wish I could persuade you to try Italy.

VIVIE. What for?

PRAED. Why, to saturate yourself with beauty and romance, of course.

[VIVIE, *with a shudder, turns her chair to the table, as if the work waiting for her were a support to her.* PRAED *sits opposite to her.* FRANK *places a chair near* VIVIE, *and drops lazily and carelessly into it, talking at her over his shoulder.*]

FRANK. No use, Praddy. Viv is a little Philistine. She is indifferent to my romance, and insensible to my beauty.

VIVIE. Mr Praed: once for all, there is no beauty and no romance in life for me. Life is what it is; and I am prepared to take it as it is.

PRAED. [*enthusiastically*] You will not say that if you come with me to Verona and on to Venice. You will cry with delight at living in such a beautiful world.

FRANK. This is most eloquent, Praddy. Keep it up.

PRAED. Oh, I assure you I have cried—I shall cry again, I hope—at fifty! At your age, Miss Warren, you would not need to go so far as Verona. Your spirits would absolutely fly up at the mere sight of Ostend. You would be charmed with the gaiety, the vivacity, the happy air of Brussels.

VIVIE. [*springing up with an exclamation of loathing*] Agh!

PRAED. [*rising*] Whats the matter?

FRANK. [*rising*] Hallo, Viv!

VIVIE. [*to* PRAED, *with deep reproach*] Can you find no better example of your beauty and romance than Brussels to talk to me about?

PRAED. [*puzzled*] Of course it's very different from Verona. I dont suggest for a moment that—

VIVIE. [*bitterly*] Probably the beauty and romance come to much the same in both places.

PRAED. [*completely sobered and much concerned*] My dear Miss Warren: I— [*looking inquiringly at* FRANK] Is anything the matter?

---

6. A road bridge in the City of London.

FRANK. She thinks your enthusiasm frivolous, Praddy. She's had ever such a serious call.

VIVIE. [*sharply*] Hold your tongue, Frank. Dont be silly.

FRANK. [*sitting down*] Do you call this good manners, Praed?

PRAED. [*anxious and considerate*] Shall I take him away, Miss Warren? I feel sure we have disturbed you at your work.

VIVIE. Sit down: I'm not ready to go back to work yet. [PRAED *sits.*] You both think I have an attack of nerves. Not a bit of it. But there are two subjects I want dropped, if you dont mind. One of them [*to* FRANK] is love's young dream in any shape or form: the other [*to* PRAED] is the romance and beauty of life, especially Ostend and the gaiety of Brussels. You are welcome to any illusions you may have left on these subjects: I have none. If we three are to remain friends, I must be treated as a woman of business, permanently single [*to* FRANK] and permanently unromantic [*to* PRAED].

FRANK. I also shall remain permanently single until you change your mind. Praddy: change the subject. Be eloquent about something else.

PRAED. [*diffidently*] I'm afraid theres nothing else in the world that I c a n talk about. The Gospel of Art is the only one I can preach. I know Miss Warren is a great devotee of the Gospel of Getting On; but we cant discuss that without hurting your feelings, Frank, since you are determined not to get on.

FRANK. Oh, dont mind my feelings. Give me some improving advice by all means: it does me ever so much good. Have another try to make a successful man of me, Viv. Come; lets have it all: energy, thrift, foresight, self-respect, character. Dont you hate people who have no character, Viv?

VIVIE. [*wincing*] Oh, stop, stop: let us have no more of that horrible cant. Mr Praed: if there are really only those two gospels in the world, we had better all kill ourselves; for the same taint is in both, through and through.

FRANK. [*looking critically at her*] There is a touch of poetry about you today, Viv, which has hitherto been lacking.

PRAED. [*remonstrating*] My dear Frank: arnt you a little unsympathetic?

VIVIE. [*merciless to herself*] No: it's good for me. It keeps me from being sentimental.

FRANK. [*bantering her*] Checks your strong natural propensity that way, dont it?

VIVIE. [*almost hysterically*] Oh yes; go on: dont spare me. I was sentimental for one moment in my life—beautifully sentimental—by moonlight; and now—

FRANK. [*quickly*] I say, Viv: take care. Dont give yourself away.

VIVIE. Oh, do you think Mr Praed does not know all about my mother? [*turning on* PRAED] You had better have told me that morning, Mr Praed. You are very old fashioned in your delicacies, after all.

PRAED. Surely it is you who are a little old fashioned in your prejudices, Miss Warren, I feel bound to tell you, speaking as an artist, and believing that the most intimate human relationships are far beyond and above the scope of the law, that though I know that your mother is an unmarried woman, I do not respect her the less on that account. I respect her more.

FRANK. [*airily*] Hear! Hear!

VIVIE. [*staring at him*] Is that a l l you know?

PRAED. Certainly that is all.

VIVIE. Then you neither of you know anything. Your guesses are innocence itself compared to the truth.

PRAED. [*rising, startled and indignant, and preserving his politeness with an effort*] I hope not. [*more emphatically*] I hope not, Miss Warren.

FRANK. [*whistles*] Whew!

VIVIE. You are not making it easy for me to tell you, Mr Praed.

PRAED. [*his chivalry drooping before their conviction*] If there is anything worse—that is, anything else—are you sure you are right to tell us, Miss Warren?

VIVIE. I am sure that if I had the courage I should spend the rest of my life in telling everybody—stamping and branding it into them until they all felt their part in its abomination as I feel mine. There is nothing I despise more than the wicked convention that protects these things by forbidding a woman to mention them. And yet I cant tell you. The two infamous words that describe what my mother is are ringing in my ears and struggling on my tongue; but I cant utter them: the shame of them is too horrible for me. [*She buries her face in her hands. The two men, astonished, stare at one another and then at her. She raises her head again desperately and snatches a sheet of paper and a pen*] Here: let me draft you a prospectus.

FRANK. Oh, she's mad. Do you hear, Viv? mad. Come! pull yourself together.

VIVIE. You shall see. [*She writes*] "Paid up capital: not less than £40,000 standing in the name of Sir George Crofts, Baronet, the chief shareholder. Premises at Brussels, Ostend, Vienna and Budapest. Managing director: Mrs Warren"; and now dont let us forget her qualifications: the two words. [*She writes the words and pushes the paper to them.*] There! Oh no: dont read it: dont! [*She snatches it back and tears it to pieces; then seizes her head in her hands and hides her face on the table.*]

[FRANK, *who has watched the writing over his shoulder, and opened his eyes very widely at it, takes a card from his pocket; scribbles the two words on it; and silently hands it to* PRAED, *who reads it with amazement, and hides it hastily in his pocket.*]

FRANK. [*whispering tenderly*] Viv, dear: thats all right. I read what you wrote: so did Praddy. We understand. And we remain, as this leaves us at present, yours ever so devotedly.

PRAED. We do indeed, Miss Warren. I declare you are the most splendidly courageous woman I ever met.

[*This sentimental compliment braces* VIVIE. *She throws it away from her with an impatient shake, and forces herself to stand up, though not without some support from the table.*]

FRANK. Dont stir, Viv, if you dont want to. Take it easy.

VIVIE. Thank you. You can always depend on me for two things: not to cry and not to faint. [*She moves a few steps towards the door of the inner room, and stops close to* PRAED *to say*] I shall need much more courage than that when I tell my mother that we have come to the parting of the ways. Now I must go into the next room for a moment to make myself neat again, if you dont mind.

PRAED. Shall we go away?

VIVIE. No; I shall be back presently. Only for a moment. [*She goes into the other room,* PRAED *opening the door for her.*]

PRAED. What an amazing revelation! I'm extremely disappointed in Crofts: I am indeed.

FRANK. I'm not in the least. I feel he's perfectly accounted for at last. But what a facer for me, Praddy! I cant marry her now.

PRAED. [*sternly*] Frank! [*The two look at one another, Frank unruffled, Praed deeply indignant.*] Let me tell you, Gardner, that if you desert her now you will behave very despicably.

FRANK. Good old Praddy! Ever chivalrous! But you mistake: it's not the moral aspect of the case: it's the money aspect. I really cant bring myself to touch the old woman's money now.

PRAED. And was that what you were going to marry on?

FRANK. What else? I havnt any money, nor the smallest turn for making it. If I married Viv now she would have to support me; and I should cost her more than I am worth.

PRAED. But surely a clever bright fellow like you can make something by your own brains.

FRANK. Oh yes, a little. [He takes out his money again.] I made all that yesterday in an hour and a half. But I made it in a highly speculative business. No, dear Praddy: even if Bessie and Georgina marry millionaires and the governor dies after cutting them off with a shilling, I shall have only four hundred a year. And he wont die until he's three score and ten: he hasnt originality enough. I shall be on short allowance for the next twenty years. No short allowance for Viv, if I can help it. I withdraw gracefully and leave the field to the gilded youth of England. So thats settled. I shant worry her about it: I'll just send her a little note after we're gone. She'll understand.

PRAED. [grasping his hand] Good fellow, Frank! I heartily beg your pardon. But must you never see her again?

FRANK. Never see her again! Hang it all, be reasonable. I shall come along as often as possible, and be her brother. I can n o t understand the absurd consequences you romantic people expect from the most ordinary transactions. [A knock at the door.] I wonder who this is. Would you mind opening the door? If it's a client it will look more respectable than if I appeared.

PRAED. Certainly. [He goes to the door and opens it. FRANK sits down in VIVIE's chair to scribble a note.] My dear Kitty: come in: come in.

[MRS WARREN comes in, looking apprehensively round for VIVIE. She has done her best to make herself matronly and dignified. The brilliant hat is replaced by a sober bonnet, and the gay blouse covered by a costly black silk mantle. She is pitiably anxious and ill at ease: evidently panic-stricken.]

MRS. WARREN. [to FRANK] What! Y o u r e here, are you?

FRANK. [turning in his chair from his writing, but not rising] Here, and charmed to see you. You come like a breath of spring.

MRS WARREN. Oh, get out with your nonsense. [in a low voice] Wheres Vivie?

[FRANK points expressively to the door of the inner room, but says nothing.]

MRS WARREN. [sitting down suddenly and almost beginning to cry] Praddy: wont she see me, dont you think?

PRAED. My dear Kitty: dont distress yourself. Why should she not?

MRS WARREN. Oh, you never can see why not: youre too innocent. Mr Frank: did she say anything to you?

FRANK. [folding his note] She m u s t see you, if [very expressively] you wait til she comes in.

MRS WARREN. [frightened] Why shouldnt I wait?

[FRANK looks quizzically at her; puts his note carefully on the inkbottle, so that VIVIE cannot fail to find it when next she dips her pen; then rises and devotes his attention entirely to her.]

FRANK. My dear Mrs Warren: suppose you were a sparrow—ever so tiny and pretty a sparrow hopping in the roadway—and you saw a steam roller coming in your direction, would you wait for it?

MRS WARREN. Oh, dont bother me with your sparrows. What did she run away from Haslemere like that for?

FRANK. I'm afraid she'll tell you if you rashly await her return.

MRS WARREN. Do you want me to go away?

FRANK. No: I always want you to stay. But I a d v i s e you to go away.

MRS WARREN. What! and never see her again!

FRANK. Precisely.

MRS WARREN. [*crying again*] Praddy: dont let him be cruel to me. [*She hastily checks her tears and wipes her eyes.*] She'll be so angry if she sees Ive been crying.

FRANK. [*with a touch of real compassion in his airy tenderness*] You know that Praddy is the soul of kindness, Mrs Warren. Praddy: what do y o u say? Go or stay?

PRAED. [*to* MRS WARREN] I really should be very sorry to cause you unnecessary pain; but I think perhaps you had better not wait. The fact is—[VIVIE *is heard at the inner door.*]

FRANK. Sh! Too late. She's coming.

MRS WARREN. Dont tell her I was crying. [VIVIE *comes in. She stops gravely on seeing* MRS WARREN, *who greets her with hysterical cheerfulness.*] Well, dearie. So here you are at last.

VIVIE. I am glad you have come: I want to speak to you. You said you were going, Frank, I think.

FRANK. Yes. Will you come with me, Mrs Warren? What do you say to a trip to Richmond, and the theatre in the evening? There is safety in Richmond. No steam roller there.

VIVIE. Nonsense, Frank. My mother will stay here.

MRS WARREN. [*scared*] I dont know: perhaps I'd better go. We're disturbing you at your work.

VIVIE. [*with quiet decision*] Mr. Praed: please take Frank away. Sit down, mother. [MRS WARREN *obeys helplessly.*]

PRAED. Come, Frank. Goodbye, Miss Vivie.

VIVIE. [*shaking hands*] Goodbye. A pleasant trip.

PRAED. Thank you: thank you. I hope so.

FRANK. [*to* MRS WARREN] Goodbye: youd ever so much better have taken my advice. [*He shakes hands with her. Then airily to* VIVIE] Byebye, Viv.

VIVIE. Goodbye. [*He goes out gaily without shaking hands with her.*]

PRAED. [*sadly*] Goodbye, Kitty.

MRS WARREN. [*sniveling*]—oobye!

[PRAED *goes.* VIVIE, *composed and extremely grave, sits down in Honoria's chair, and waits for her mother to speak.* MRS WARREN, *dreading a pause, loses no time in beginning.*]

MRS. WARREN. Well, Vivie, what did you go away like that for without saying a word to me? How could you do such a thing! And what have you done to poor George? I wanted him to come with me; but he shuffled out of it. I could see that he was quite afraid of you. Only fancy: he wanted me not to come. As if [*trembling*] I should be afraid of you, dearie. [VIVIE's *gravity deepens.*] But of course I told him it was all settled and comfortable between us, and that we were on the best of terms. [*She breaks down.*] Vivie: whats the meaning of this? [*She produces a commercial envelope, and fumbles at the enclosure with trembling fingers.*] I got it from the bank this morning.

VIVIE. It is my month's allowance. They sent it to me as usual the other day. I simply sent it back to be placed to your credit, and asked them to send you the lodgment receipt. In future I shall support myself.

MRS WARREN. [*not daring to understand*] Wasnt it enough? Why didnt you tell me? [*with a cunning gleam in her eye*] I'll double it: I was intending to double it. Only let me know how much you want.

VIVIE. You know very well that that has nothing to do with it. From this time I go my own way in my own business and among my own friends. And you will go yours. [*She rises.*] Goodbye.

MRS WARREN. [*rising, appalled*] Goodbye?

VIVIE. Yes: Goodbye. Come: dont let us make a useless scene: you understand perfectly well. Sir George Crofts has told me the whole business.

MRS WARREN. [*angrily*] Silly old— [*She swallows an epithet, and turns white at the narrowness of her escape from uttering it.*]

VIVIE. Just so.

MRS WARREN. He ought to have his tongue cut out. But I thought it was ended: you said you didnt mind.

VIVIE. [*steadfastly*] Excuse me: I d o mind.

MRS WARREN. But I explained—

VIVIE. You explained how it came about. You did not tell me that it is still going on. [*She sits.*]

[MRS WARREN, *silenced for a moment, looks forlornly at* VIVIE, *who waits, secretly hoping that the combat is over. But the cunning expression comes back into* MRS WARREN's *face; and she bends across the table, sly and urgent, half whispering.*]

MRS WARREN. Vivie: do you know how rich I am?

VIVIE. I have no doubt you are very rich.

MRS WARREN. But you dont know all that that means: youre too young. It means a new dress every day; it means theatres and balls every night; it means having the pick of all the gentlemen in Europe at your feet; it means a lovely house and plenty of servants; it means the choicest of eating and drinking; it means everything you like, everything you want, everything you can think of. And what are you here? A mere drudge, toiling and moiling early and late for your bare living and two cheap dresses a year. Think over it. [*soothingly*] Youre shocked, I know. I can enter into your feelings; and I think they do you credit; but trust me, nobody will blame you: you may take my word for that. I know what young girls are; and I know youll think better of it when youve turned it over in your mind.

VIVIE. So thats how it's done, is it? You must have said all that to many a woman, mother, to have it so pat.

MRS WARREN. [*passionately*] What harm am I asking you to do? [VIVIE *turns away contemptuously.* MRS WARREN *continues desperately.*] Vivie: listen to me: you dont understand: youve been taught wrong on purpose: you dont know what the world is really like.

VIVIE. [*arrested*] Taught wrong on purpose! What do you mean?

MRS WARREN. I mean that youre throwing away all your chances for nothing. You think that people are what they pretend to be: that the way you were taught at school and college to think right and proper is the way things really are. But it's not: it's all only a pretence, to keep the cowardly slavish common run of people quiet. Do you want to find that out, like other women, at forty, when youve thrown yourself away and lost your chances; or wont you take it in good time now from your own mother, that loves you and swears to you that it's truth: gospel truth? [*urgently*] Vivie: the big people, the clever people, the managing people, all know it. They do as I do, and think what I think. I know plenty of them. I know them to speak to, to introduce you to, to make friends of for you. I dont mean anything wrong; thats what you dont understand: your head is full of ignorant ideas about me. What do the people that taught you know about life or about people like me? When did they ever meet me, or speak to me, or let anyone tell them about me? the fools! Would they ever have done anything for you if I hadnt paid them? Havnt I told you that I want you to be respectable? Havnt I brought you up to be respectable? And how can you keep it up without my money and my influence and Lizzie's friends? Cant you see that youre cutting your own throat as well as breaking my heart in turning your back on me?

VIVIE. I recognize the Crofts philosophy of life, mother. I heard it all from him that day at the Gardners'.

MRS WARREN. You think I want to force that played-out old sot on you! I dont, Vivie: on my oath I dont.

VIVIE. It would not matter if you did: you would not succeed. [MRS WARREN *winces, deeply hurt by the implied indifference towards her affectionate intention.* VIVIE, *neither understanding this nor concerning herself about it, goes on calmly.*] Mother: you dont at all know the sort of person I am. I dont object to Crofts more than to any other coarsely built man of his class. To tell you the truth, I rather admire him for being strong-minded enough to enjoy himself in his own way and make plenty of money instead of living the usual shooting, hunting, dining-out, tailoring, loafing life of his set merely because all the rest do it. And I'm perfectly aware that if I'd been in the same circumstances as my aunt Liz, I'd have done exactly what she did. I dont think I'm more prejudiced or straitlaced than you: I think I'm less. I'm certain I'm less sentimental. I know very well that fashionable morality is all a pretence, and that if I took your money and devoted the rest of my life to spending it fashionably, I might be as worthless and vicious as the silliest woman could possibly want to be without having a word said to me about it. But I dont want to be worthless. I shouldnt enjoy trotting about the park to advertize my dressmaker and carriage builder, or being bored at the opera to shew off a shopwindowful of diamonds.

MRS WARREN. [*bewildered*] But—

VIVIE. Wait a moment: Ive not done. Tell me why you continue your business now that you are independent of it. Your sister, you told me, has left all that behind her. Why dont you do the same?

MRS WARREN. Oh, it's all very easy for Liz: she likes good society, and has the air of being a lady. Imagine me in a cathedral town! Why, the very rooks in the trees would find me out even if I could stand the dulness of it. I must have work and excitement, or I should go melancholy mad. And what else is there for me to do? The life suits me: I'm fit for it and not for anything else. If I didnt do it somebody else would; so I dont do any real harm by it. And then it brings in money; and I like making money. No; it's no use: I cant give it up—not for anybody. But what need you know about it? I'll never mention it. I'll keep Crofts away. I'll not trouble you much: you see I have to be constantly running about from one place to another. Youll be quit of me altogether when I die.

VIVIE. No: I am my mother's daughter. I am like you: I must have work, and must make more money than I spend. But my work is not your work, and my way not your way. We must part. It will not make much difference to us: instead of meeting one another for perhaps a few months in twenty years we shall never meet: thats all.

MRS WARREN. [*her voice stifled in tears*] Vivie: I meant to have been more with you: I did indeed.

VIVIE. It's no use, mother: I am not to be changed by a few cheap tears and entreaties any more than you are, I daresay.

MRS WARREN. [*wildly*] Oh, you call a mother's tears cheap.

VIVIE. They cost you nothing; and you ask me to give you the peace and quietness of my whole life in exchange for them. What use would my company be to you if you could get it? What have we two in common that could make either of us happy together?

MRS WARREN. [*lapsing recklessly into her dialect*] We're mother and daughter. I want my daughter. Ive a right to you. Who is to care for me when I'm old? Plenty of girls have taken to me like daughters and cried at leaving me; but I let them all go because I had you to look forward to. I kept myself lonely for you. Youve no right to turn on me now and refuse to do your duty as a daughter.

VIVIE. [*jarred and antagonized by the echo of the slums in her mother's voice*] My duty as a daughter! I thought we should come to that presently. Now once for all, mother, you want a daughter and Frank wants a wife. I dont want a mother; and I dont want a husband. I have spared neither Frank nor myself in sending him about his business. Do you think I will spare y o u ?

MRS WARREN. [*violently*] Oh, I know the sort you are: no mercy for yourself or anyone else. *I* know. My experience has done that for me anyhow: I can tell the pious, canting, hard, selfish woman when I meet her. Well, keep yourself to yourself: *I* dont want you. But listen to this. Do you know what I would do with you if you were a baby again? aye, as sure as there's a Heaven above us.

VIVIE. Strangle me, perhaps.

MRS WARREN. No: I'd bring you up to be a real daughter to me, and not what you are now, with your pride and your prejudices and the college education you stole from me: yes, stole: deny it if you can: what was it but stealing? I'd bring you up in my own house, I would.

VIVIE. [*quietly*] In one of your own houses.

MRS WARREN. [*screaming*] Listen to her! listen to how she spits on her mother's grey hairs! Oh, may you live to have your own daughter tear and trample on you as you have trampled on me. And you will: you will. No woman ever had luck with a mother's curse on her.

VIVIE. I wish you wouldnt rant, mother. It only hardens me. Come: I suppose I am the only young woman you ever had in your power that you did good to. Dont spoil it all now.

MRS WARREN. Yes, Heaven forgive me, it's true; and you are the only one that ever turned on me. Oh, the injustice of it! the injustice! the injustice! I always wanted to be a good woman. I tried honest work; and I was slave-driven until I cursed the day I ever heard of honest work. I was a good mother; and because I made my daughter a good woman she turns me out as if I was a leper. Oh, if I only had my life to live over again! I'd talk to that lying clergyman in the school. From this time forth, so help me Heaven in my last hour, I'll do wrong and nothing but wrong. And I'll prosper on it.

VIVIE. Yes: it's better to choose your line and go through with it. If I had been you, mother, I might have done as you did; but I should not have lived one life and believed in another. You are a conventional woman at heart. That is why I am bidding you goodbye now. I am right, am I not?

MRS WARREN. [*taken aback*] Right to throw away all my money?

VIVIE. No: right to get rid of you? I should be a fool not to! Isnt that so?

MRS WARREN. [*sulkily*] Oh well, yes, if you come to that, I suppose you are. But Lord help the world if everybody took to doing the right thing! And now I'd better go than stay where I'm not wanted. [*She turns to the door.*]

VIVIE. [*kindly*] Wont you shake hands?

MRS WARREN. [*after looking at her fiercely for a moment with a savage impulse to strike her*] No, thank you. Goodbye.

VIVIE. [*matter-of-factly*] Goodbye. [MRS WARREN *goes out, slamming the door behind her. The strain on* VIVIE's *face relaxes; her grave expression breaks up into one of joyous content; her breath goes out in a half sob, half laugh of intense relief. She goes buoyantly to her place at the writing-table; pushes the electric lamp out of the way; pulls over a great sheaf of papers; and is in the act of dipping her pen in the ink when she finds* FRANK's *note. She opens it unconcernedly and reads it quickly, giving a little laugh at some quaint turn of expression in it*] And goodbye, Frank. [*She tears the note up and tosses the pieces into the wastepaper basket without a second thought. Then she goes at her work with a plunge, and soon becomes absorbed in its figures.*]

1893   1898

JOSEPH CONRAD
1857–1924

1875–94:	Career as a seaman.
1895:	*Almayer's Folly*.
1904:	*Nostromo*.

Joseph Conrad was born Jozef Teodor Konrad Nalecz Korzeniowski in Poland (then under Russian rule), son of a Polish patriot who suffered exile in Russia for his Polish nationalist activities and died in 1869, leaving Conrad to be brought up by a maternal uncle. At the age of fifteen he amazed his family and friends by announcing his passionate desire to go to sea; he was eventually allowed to go to Marseilles in 1874, and from there he made a number of voyages on French merchant ships to Martinique and the West Indies. In 1878 he signed on an English ship that brought him to the east coast English port of Lowestoft, where (still as an ordinary seaman) he joined the crew of a small coasting vessel plying between Lowestoft and Newcastle. In six voyages between these two ports he learned English. Thus launched on a career in the British merchant service, Conrad sailed on a variety of British ships to the Orient and elsewhere and eventually gained his master's certificate in 1886, the year when he became a naturalized British subject. He received his first command in 1888, and in 1890 took a steamboat up the Congo River in nightmarish circumstances (described in *Heart of Darkness*) that produced severe illness and permanently haunted his imagination. In the early 1890s he was already thinking of turning some of his Malayan experiences into English fiction, and in 1892–93, when serving as first mate on the *Torrens* sailing from London to Adelaide, he revealed to a sympathetic passenger that he had begun a novel (*Almayer's Folly*), while on the return journey he impressed the young John Galsworthy, who was on board, with his conversation. Although possessed of a master's certificate, Conrad found it difficult to get the kind of job as master that he wished, and occasionally he had to serve in lesser capacities. His difficulty in obtaining a command, together with the interest aroused by *Almayer's Folly* when it was published in 1895, helped to turn him away from the sea to a career as a writer. He settled in London and in 1896 married an English woman; this son of a Polish patriot turned merchant seaman turned writer was henceforth an English novelist.

Conrad was for a long time regarded as a sea writer whose exotic descriptions of eastern landscapes and exploitation of the romantic atmosphere of Malaya and other unfamiliar regions gave his work a special kind of richness and splendor. But this is only one, and not in the last analysis the most important, aspect of his work. More and more Conrad used the sea and the circumstances of life on shipboard or in remote eastern settlements as means of exploring certain profound moral ambiguities in human experience. In *The Nigger of the "Narcissus"* (1897) he shows how a dying black seaman corrupts the morale of a ship's crew by the very fact that his plight produces sympathy, thus symbolically presenting one of his commonest themes—the necessity and at the same time the dangers of human contact. In *Lord Jim* (1900), using the device of an intermediate narrator, he probes the meaning of a gross failure of duty on the part of a romantic and idealistic young sailor, and by presenting the hero's history from a series of different points of view keeps the moral questioning continuing to the end. The use of intermediate narrators and multiple points of view is common in Conrad; it is his favorite way of suggesting the complexity of experience and the difficulty of judging human actions.

This notion of the difficulty of true communion, coupled with the idea that communion can be unexpectedly forced on us—sometimes with someone who may be on the surface our moral opposite, so that we can at times be compelled into a mysterious recognition of our opposite as our true self—is found in many of Conrad's works; it provides one of the underlying themes of *The Secret Sharer* (1912). This story can be enjoyed for the clarity and power with which Conrad renders the atmosphere of the Gulf of Siam as felt by a young sea captain on taking on his first command, but it also uses situation and incident symbolically to suggest some of the paradoxes of identity and sympathy.

Other stories and novels explore the ways in which the codes we live by are tested in moments of crisis, revealing either their inadequacy or our own. Imagination can corrupt (as with Lord Jim) or save (as in *The Shadow-Line*, 1917), and there are times when total lack of it can see a man through (Captain MacWhirr in *Typhoon*, 1902), though a similar lack in other circumstances can render a man comically ridiculous (Captain Mitchell in *Nostromo*, 1904).

Nostromo, a profound and subtle study of the corrupting effects of politics and "material interests" on personal relationships (set in an imaginary South American republic), is often regarded as Conrad's greatest work. His two other political novels—*The Secret Agent* (1906) and *Under Western Eyes* (1911)—have also recently come into their own. The latter is the story of a Russian student who becomes involuntarily associated with antigovernment violence in czarist Russia and is irresistibly maneuvered by circumstances into a position where, although a government spy, he has to pretend to be a revolutionary among revolutionaries. This is the ultimate in human loneliness and incommunicability—when you must consistently pretend to be the opposite of what you are. It is a story of Dostoyevskian power, and shows a very different Conrad from the picturesque sea-dreamer portrayed by the earlier critics. Conrad was as much a pessimist as Hardy, but he projected his pessimism in subtler ways. He was also a great master of English prose, an astonishing fact when we realize that he was twenty-one before he learned any English, and that to the end of his life he spoke English with a thick foreign accent.

Heart of Darkness

Heart of Darkness   This story is derived from Conrad's personal experience in the Congo in 1890. Like Marlow, the narrator of the story, Conrad had as a child determined one day to visit the heart of Africa. "It was in 1868, when nine years old or thereabouts, that while looking at a map of Africa at the time and putting my finger on the blank space then representing the unsolved mystery of that continent, I said to myself with absolute assurance and an amazing audacity which are no longer in my character now: 'When I grow up I shall go *there*' " (*A Personal Record*, 1912).

Conrad was promised a job as a Congo River pilot through the influence of his distant cousin Marguerite Poradowska, who lived in Brussels and knew important officials of the Belgian company that exploited the Congo. At this time the Congo, although nominally an independent state, the Congo Free State (État Indépendent du Congo), was virtually the personal property of Leopold II, king of the Belgians, who made a fortune out of it. Later, the appalling abuses involved in the naked colonial exploitation that went on in the Congo were exposed to public view, and international criticism compelled the setting up of a committee of inquiry in 1904. What Conrad saw in 1890 shocked him profoundly and shook his view of the moral basis of all exploring and trading in newly discovered countries and indeed of civilization in general. "*Heart of Darkness* is experience, too," Conrad wrote in his 1917 "Author's Note," "but it is experience pushed a little (and only very little) beyond the actual facts of the case for the perfectly legitimate, I believe, purpose of bringing it home to the minds and bosoms of the readers." And later he told Edward Garnett: "Before the Congo I was just a mere animal."

Conrad arrived in Africa in May 1890 and made his way up the Congo River very much as described in *Heart of Darkness*. At Kinshasa (which Conrad spells Kinchassa) on Stanley Pool, which he reached after an exhausting two hundred-mile trek from Matadi, near the mouth of the river, Conrad was much taken aback to learn that the steamer of which he was to be captain had been damaged and was undergoing repairs. He was sent as supernumerary on another steamer to learn the river. This other steamer was sent to Stanley Falls to collect and bring back to Kinshasa one Georges Antoine Klein, an agent of the company who had fallen gravely ill and who in fact died on board. Klein was the original of Kurtz. Conrad himself then fell seriously ill and eventually returned to London in January 1891 without ever having actually served as a Congo River pilot, the job for which he went out to Africa. The Congo experience permanently impaired his health: it also permanently haunted his imagination. The nightmare atmosphere of *Heart of Darkness* is an accurate reflection of Conrad's own response to his traumatic experience.

The theme of the story is partly the "choice of nightmares" facing the white man in the Congo—either to become like the wholly commercially minded manager, who sees Africa, its people, and its resources solely as instruments of financial gain or to become like Kurtz, the self-tortured and corrupted idealist. The manager is a "hollow man" (T. S. Eliot quoted from this story in his poem of that title); his only objections to Kurtz are commercial, not moral; Kurtz's methods are "unsound" and would therefore lose the company money. Kurtz finally recognizes the moral horror of his having succumbed to the dark temptations that African life posed for the white man. "He had summed up—he had judged." But the story also has other levels of meaning, and the counterpointing of Western civilization in Europe with what that civilization has done in Africa (see the concluding interview between Marlow and Kurtz's "intended"—based on a real interview between Conrad and the dead Klein's fiancée) throws out several of these.

Heart of Darkness

1

The *Nellie*, a cruising yawl, swung to her anchor without a flutter of the sails, and was at rest. The flood had made, the wind was nearly calm, and being bound down the river, the only thing for it was to come to and wait for the turn of the tide.

The sea-reach of the Thames stretched before us like the beginning of an interminable waterway. In the offing the sea and the sky were welded together without a joint, and in the luminous space the tanned sails of the barges drifting up with the tide seemed to stand still in red clusters of canvas sharply peaked, with gleams of varnished sprits. A haze rested on the low shores that ran out to sea in vanishing flatness. The air was dark above Gravesend,[1] and farther back still seemed condensed into a mournful gloom, brooding motionless over the biggest, and the greatest, town on earth.

The Director of Companies was our captain and our host. We four affec-

---

1. River port on the south bank of the Thames twenty-four miles east (downriver) of London.

tionately watched his back as he stood in the bows looking to seaward. On the whole river there was nothing that looked half so nautical. He resembled a pilot, which to a seaman is trustworthiness personified. It was difficult to real- ise his work was not out there in the luminous estuary, but behind him, within the brooding gloom.

Between us there was, as I have already said somewhere, the bond of the sea. Besides holding our hearts together through long periods of separation, it had the effect of making us tolerant of each other's yarns—and even convic- tions. The Lawyer—the best of old fellows—had, because of his many years and many virtues, the only cushion on deck, and was lying on the only rug. The Accountant had brought out already a box of dominoes, and was toy- ing architecturally with the bones. Marlow sat cross-legged right aft, leaning against the mizzenmast. He had sunken cheeks, a yellow complexion, a straight back, an ascetic aspect, and, with his arms dropped, the palms of hands outwards, resembled an idol. The Director, satisfied the anchor had good hold, made his way aft and sat down amongst us. We exchanged a few words lazily. Afterwards there was silence on board the yacht. For some reason or other we did not begin that game of dominoes. We felt meditative, and fit for nothing but placid staring. The day was ending in a serenity of still and exquisite brilliance. The water shone pacifically; the sky, without a speck, was a benign immensity of unstained light; the very mist on the Essex marshes was like a gauzy and radiant fabric, hung from the wooded rises inland, and drap- ing the low shores in diaphanous folds. Only the gloom to the west, brooding over the upper reaches, became more sombre every minute, as if angered by the approach of the sun.

And at last, in its curved and imperceptible fall, the sun sank low, and from glowing white changed to a dull red without rays and without heat, as if about to go out suddenly, stricken to death by the touch of that gloom brooding over a crowd of men.

Forthwith a change came over the waters, and the serenity became less brilliant but more profound. The old river in its broad reach rested unruffled at the decline of day, after ages of good service done to the race that peopled its banks, spread out in the tranquil dignity of a waterway leading to the utter- most ends of the earth. We looked at the venerable stream not in the vivid flush of a short day that comes and departs for ever, but in the august light of abiding memories. And indeed nothing is easier for a man who has, as the phrase goes, "followed the sea" with reverence and affection, than to evoke the great spirit of the past upon the lower reaches of the Thames. The tidal current runs to and fro in its unceasing service, crowded with memories of men and ships it has borne to the rest of home or to the battles of the sea. It had known and served all the men of whom the nation is proud, from Sir Francis Drake to Sir John Franklin,[2] knights all, titled and untitled—the great knights-errant of the sea. It had borne all the ships whose names are like jewels flashing in the night of time, from the *Golden Hind* returning with her round flanks full of treasure, to be visited by the Queen's Highness and thus pass out of the gigantic tale, to the *Erebus* and *Terror*, bound on other conquests—and

2. Sir John Franklin (1786–1847), Arctic explorer who in 1845 commanded an expedition consisting of the ships *Erebus* and *Terror* in search of the Northwest pas- sage. The ships never returned. Sir Francis Drake (ca. 1540–1596), Elizabethan naval hero and explorer, sailed around the world on his ship *The Golden Hind.* Queen Elizabeth knighted Drake on board his ship, loaded with captured Spanish treasure, on his return.

that never returned. It had known the ships and the men. They had sailed from Deptford, from Greenwich, from Erith—the adventurers and the settlers; kings' ships and the ships of men on 'Change; captains, admirals, the dark "interlopers"[3] of the Eastern trade, and the commissioned "generals" of East India fleets. Hunters for gold or pursuers of fame, they all had gone out on that stream, bearing the sword, and often the torch, messengers of the might within the land, bearers of a spark from the sacred fire. What greatness had not floated on the ebb of that river into the mystery of an unknown earth! . . . The dreams of men, the seed of commonwealths, the germs of empires.

The sun set; the dusk fell on the stream, and lights began to appear along the shore. The Chapman lighthouse, a three-legged thing erect on a mud-flat, shone strongly. Lights of ships moved in the fairway[4]—a great stir of lights going up and going down. And farther west on the upper reaches the place of the monstrous town was still marked ominously on the sky, a brooding gloom in sunshine, a lurid glare under the stars.

"And this also," said Marlow suddenly, "has been one of the dark places of the earth."

He was the only man of us who still "followed the sea." The worst that could be said of him was that he did not represent his class. He was a seaman, but he was a wanderer too, while most seamen lead, if one may so express it, a sedentary life. Their minds are of the stay-at-home order, and their home is always with them—the ship; and so is their country—the sea. One ship is very much like another, and the sea is always the same. In the immutability of their surroundings the foreign shores, the foreign faces, the changing immensity of life, glide past, veiled not by a sense of mystery but by a slightly disdainful ignorance; for there is nothing mysterious to a seaman unless it be the sea itself, which is the mistress of his existence and as inscrutable as Destiny. For the rest, after his hours of work, a casual stroll or a casual spree on shore suffices to unfold for him the secret of a whole continent, and generally he finds the secret not worth knowing. The yarns of seamen have a direct simplicity, the whole meaning of which lies within the shell of a cracked nut. But Marlow was not typical (if his propensity to spin yarns be excepted), and to him the meaning of an episode was not inside like a kernel but outside, enveloping the tale which brought it out only as a glow brings out a haze, in the likeness of one of these misty halos that sometimes are made visible by the spectral illumination of moonshine.

His remark did not seem at all surprising. It was just like Marlow. It was accepted in silence. No one took the trouble to grunt even; and presently he said, very slow:

"I was thinking of very old times, when the Romans first came here, nineteen hundred years ago—the other day. . . . Light came out of this river since—you say Knights? Yes; but it is like a running blaze on a plain, like a flash of lightning in the clouds. We live in the flicker—may it last as long as the old earth keeps rolling! But darkness was here yesterday. Imagine the feel-

---

3. Private ships muscling in on the monopoly of the East India Company, which was founded in 1600, lost its trading monopoly in 1813, and transferred its governmental functions to the Crown in 1858. "Deptford," on the south bank of the Thames, on the eastern edge of London, was once an important dockyard.

"Greenwich" is on the south bank of the Thames immediately east of Deptford. "Erith" is eight miles farther east. " 'Change": the Stock Exchange.
4. Navigable part of a river, through which ships enter and depart.

ings of a commander of a fine—what d'ye call 'em?—trireme[5] in the Mediterranean, ordered suddenly to the north; run overland across the Gauls in a hurry; put in charge of one of these craft the legionaries—a wonderful lot of handy men they must have been too—used to build, apparently by the hundred, in a month or two, if we may believe what we read. Imagine him here— the very end of the world, a sea the colour of lead, a sky the colour of smoke, a kind of ship about as rigid as a concertina—and going up this river with stores, or orders, or what you like. Sandbanks, marshes, forests, savages—precious little to eat fit for a civilised man, nothing but Thames water to drink. No Falernian wine here, no going ashore. Here and there a military camp lost in a wilderness, like a needle in a bundle of hay—cold, fog, tempests, disease, exile, and death—death skulking in the air, in the water, in the bush. They must have been dying like flies here. Oh yes—he did it. Did it very well, too, no doubt, and without thinking much about it either, except afterwards to brag of what he had gone through in his time, perhaps. They were men enough to face the darkness. And perhaps he was cheered by keeping his eye on a chance of promotion to the fleet at Ravenna[6] by and by, if he had good friends in Rome and survived the awful climate. Or think of a decent young citizen in a toga—perhaps too much dice, you know—coming out here in the train of some prefect, or tax-gatherer, or trader, even, to mend his fortunes. Land in a swamp, march through the woods, and in some inland post feel the savagery, the utter savagery, had closed round him—all that mysterious life of the wilderness that stirs in the forest, in the jungles, in the hearts of wild men. There's no initiation either into such mysteries. He has to live in the midst of the incomprehensible, which is also detestable. And it has a fascination, too, that goes to work upon him. The fascination of the abomination—you know. Imagine the growing regrets, the longing to escape, the powerless disgust, the surrender, the hate."

He paused.

"Mind," he began again, lifting one arm from the elbow, the palm of the hand outwards, so that, with his legs folded before him, he had the pose of a Buddha preaching in European clothes and without a lotus-flower—"Mind, none of us would feel exactly like this. What saves us is efficiency—the devotion to efficiency. But these chaps were not much account, really. They were no colonists; their administration was merely a squeeze, and nothing more, I suspect. They were conquerors, and for that you want only brute force—nothing to boast of, when you have it, since your strength is just an accident arising from the weakness of others. They grabbed what they could get for the sake of what was to be got. It was just robbery with violence, aggravated murder on a great scale, and men going at it blind—as is very proper for those who tackle a darkness. The conquest of the earth, which mostly means the taking it away from those who have a different complexion or slightly flatter noses than ourselves, is not a pretty thing when you look into it too much. What redeems it is the idea only. An idea at the back of it; not a sentimental pretence but an idea; and an unselfish belief in the idea—something you can set up, and bow down before, and offer a sacrifice to. . . ."

---

5. Ancient Greek and Roman galley with three ranks of oars.
6. A city in northern Italy once directly on the Adriatic

Sea and an important naval station in Roman times. It is now about six miles from the sea, connected with it by a canal.

He broke off. Flames glided in the river, small green flames, red flames, white flames, pursuing, overtaking, joining, crossing each other—then separating slowly or hastily. The traffic of the great city went on in the deepening night upon the sleepless river. We looked on, waiting patiently—there was nothing else to do till the end of the flood; but it was only after a long silence, when he said, in a hesitating voice, "I suppose you fellows remember I did once turn fresh-water sailor for a bit," that we knew we were fated, before the ebb began to run, to hear about one of Marlow's inconclusive experiences.

"I don't want to bother you much with what happened to me personally," he began, showing in this remark the weakness of many tellers of tales who seem so often unaware of what their audience would best like to hear; "yet to understand the effect of it on me you ought to know how I got out there, what I saw, how I went up that river to the place where I first met the poor chap. It was the farthest point of navigation and the culminating point of my experience. It seemed somehow to throw a kind of light on everything about me— and into my thoughts. It was sombre enough too—and pitiful—not extraordinary in any way—not very clear either. No, not very clear. And yet it seemed to throw a kind of light.

"I had then, as you remember, just returned to London after a lot of Indian Ocean, Pacific, China Seas—a regular dose of the East—six years or so, and I was loafing about, hindering you fellows in your work and invading your homes, just as though I had got a heavenly mission to civilise you. It was very fine for a time, but after a bit I did get tired of resting. Then I began to look for a ship—I should think the hardest work on earth. But the ships wouldn't even look at me. And I got tired of that game too.

"Now when I was a little chap I had a passion for maps. I would look for hours at South America, or Africa, or Australia, and lose myself in all the glories of exploration. At that time there were many blank spaces on the earth, and when I saw one that looked particularly inviting on a map (but they all look that) I would put my finger on it and say, When I grow up I will go there. The North Pole was one of these places, I remember. Well, I haven't been there yet, and shall not try now. The glamour's off. Other places were scattered about the Equator, and in every sort of latitude all over the two hemispheres. I have been in some of them, and . . . well, we won't talk about that. But there was one yet—the biggest, the most blank, so to speak—that I had a hankering after.

"True, by this time it was not a blank space any more. It had got filled since my boyhood with rivers and lakes and names. It had ceased to be a blank space of delightful mystery—a white patch for a boy to dream gloriously over. It had become a place of darkness. But there was in it one river especially, a mighty big river, that you could see on the map, resembling an immense snake uncoiled, with its head in the sea, its body at rest curving afar over a vast country, and its tail lost in the depths of the land. And as I looked at the map of it in a shop-window, it fascinated me as a snake would a bird—a silly little bird. Then I remembered there was a big concern, a Company for trade on that river. Dash it all! I thought to myself, they can't trade without using some kind of craft on that lot of fresh water—steamboats! Why shouldn't I try to get charge of one? I went on along Fleet Street, but could not shake off the idea. The snake had charmed me.

"You understand it was a Continental concern, that Trading Society; but I have a lot of relations living on the Continent, because it's cheap and not so nasty as it looks, they say.

"I am sorry to own I began to worry them. This was already a fresh departure for me. I was not used to get things that way, you know. I always went my own road and on my own legs where I had a mind to go. I wouldn't have believed it of myself; but, then—you see—I felt somehow I must get there by hook or by crook. So I worried them. The men said, 'My dear fellow,' and did nothing. Then—would you believe it?—I tried the women. I, Charlie Marlow, set the women to work—to get a job. Heavens! Well, you see, the notion drove me. I had an aunt, a dear enthusiastic soul. She wrote: 'It will be delightful. I am ready to do anything, anything for you. It is a glorious idea. I know the wife of a very high personage in the Administration, and also a man who has lots of influence with,' etc. etc. She was determined to make no end of fuss to get me appointed skipper of a river steamboat, if such was my fancy.

"I got my appointment—of course; and I got it very quick. It appears the Company had received news that one of their captains had been killed in a scuffle with the natives. This was my chance, and it made me the more anxious to go. It was only months and months afterwards, when I made the attempt to recover what was left of the body, that I heard the original quarrel arose from a misunderstanding about some hens. Yes, two black hens. Fresleven—that was the fellow's name, a Dane—thought himself wronged somehow in the bargain, so he went ashore and started to hammer the chief of the village with a stick. Oh, it didn't surprise me in the least to hear this, and at the same time to be told that Fresleven was the gentlest, quietest creature that ever walked on two legs. No doubt he was; but he had been a couple of years already out there engaged in the noble cause, you know, and he probably felt the need at last of asserting his self-respect in some way. Therefore he whacked the old nigger mercilessly, while a big crowd of his people watched him, thunderstruck, till some man—I was told the chief's son—in desperation at hearing the old chap yell, made a tentative jab with a spear at the white man—and of course it went quite easy between the shoulder-blades. Then the whole population cleared into the forest, expecting all kinds of calamities to happen, while, on the other hand, the steamer Fresleven commanded left also in a bad panic, in charge of the engineer, I believe. Afterwards nobody seemed to trouble much about Fresleven's remains, till I got out and stepped into his shoes. I couldn't let it rest, though; but when an opportunity offered at last to meet my predecessor, the grass growing through his ribs was tall enough to hide his bones. They were all there. The supernatural being had not been touched after he fell. And the village was deserted, the huts gaped black, rotting, all askew within the fallen enclosures. A calamity had come to it, sure enough. The people had vanished. Mad terror had scattered them, men, women, and children, through the bush, and they had never returned. What became of the hens I don't know either. I should think the cause of progress got them, anyhow. However, through this glorious affair I got my appointment, before I had fairly begun to hope for it.

"I flew around like mad to get ready, and before forty-eight hours I was crossing the Channel to show myself to my employers, and sign the contract. In a very few hours I arrived in a city that always makes me think of a whited sepulchre. Prejudice no doubt. I had no difficulty in finding the Company's offices. It was the biggest thing in the town, and everybody I met was full of it. They were going to run an oversea empire, and make no end of coin by trade.

"A narrow and deserted street in deep shadow, high houses, innumerable windows with venetian blinds, a dead silence, grass sprouting between the stones, imposing carriage archways right and left, immense double doors standing ponderously ajar. I slipped through one of these cracks, went up a swept and ungarnished staircase, as arid as a desert, and opened the first door I came to. Two women, one fat and the other slim, sat on straw-bottomed chairs, knitting black wool. The slim one got up and walked straight at me — still knitting with downcast eyes — and only just as I began to think of getting out of her way, as you would for a somnambulist, stood still, and looked up. Her dress was as plain as an umbrella-cover, and she turned round without a word and preceded me into a waiting-room. I gave my name, and looked about. Deal table in the middle, plain chairs all round the walls, on one end a large shining map, marked with all the colours of a rainbow. There was a vast amount of red — good to see at any time, because one knows that some real work is done in there, a deuce of a lot of blue, a little green, smears of orange, and, on the East Coast, a purple patch, to show where the jolly pioneers of progress drink the jolly lager-beer. However, I wasn't going into any of these. I was going into the yellow. Dead in the centre. And the river was there — fascinating — deadly — like a snake. Ough! A door opened, a white-haired secretarial head, but wearing a compassionate expression, appeared, and a skinny forefinger beckoned me into the sanctuary. Its light was dim, and a heavy writing desk squatted in the middle. From behind that structure came out an impression of pale plumpness in a frockcoat. The great man himself. He was five feet six, I should judge, and had his grip on the handle-end of ever so many millions. He shook hands, I fancy, murmured vaguely, was satisfied with my French. *Bon voyage.*

"In about forty-five seconds I found myself again in the waiting-room with the compassionate secretary, who, full of desolation and sympathy, made me sign some document. I believe I undertook amongst other things not to disclose any trade secrets. Well, I am not going to.

"I began to feel slightly uneasy. You know I am not used to such ceremonies, and there was something ominous in the atmosphere. It was just as though I had been let into some conspiracy — I don't know — something not quite right; and I was glad to get out. In the outer room the two women knitted black wool feverishly. People were arriving, and the younger one was walking back and forth introducing them. The old one sat on her chair. Her flat cloth slippers were propped up on a foot-warmer, and a cat reposed on her lap. She wore a starched white affair on her head, had a wart on one cheek, and silver-rimmed spectacles hung on the tip of her nose. She glanced at me above the glasses. The swift and indifferent placidity of that look troubled me. Two youths with foolish and cheery countenances were being piloted over, and she threw at them the same quick glance of unconcerned wisdom. She seemed to know all about them and about me too. An eerie feeling came over me. She seemed uncanny and fateful. Often far away there I thought of these two, guarding the door of Darkness, knitting black wool as for a warm pall, one introducing, introducing continuously to the unknown, the other scrutinising the cheery and foolish faces with unconcerned old eyes. *Ave!* Old knitter of black wool. *Morituri te salutant.*[7] Not many of those she looked at ever saw her again—not half, by a long way.

"There was yet a visit to the doctor. 'A simple formality,' assured me the secretary, with an air of taking an immense part in all my sorrows. Accordingly a young chap wearing his hat over the left eyebrow, some clerk I suppose—there must have been clerks in the business, though the house was as still as a house in a city of the dead—came from somewhere upstairs, and led me forth. He was shabby and careless, with ink-stains on the sleeves of his jacket, and his cravat was large and billowy, under a chin shaped like the toe of an old boot. It was a little too early for the doctor, so I proposed a drink, and thereupon he developed a vein of joviality. As we sat over our vermuths he glorified the Company's business, and by and by I expressed casually my surprise at him not going out there. He became very cool and collected all at once. 'I am not such a fool as I look, quoth Plato to his disciples,' he said sententiously, emptied his glass with great resolution, and we rose.

"The old doctor felt my pulse, evidently thinking of something else the while. 'Good, good for there,' he mumbled, and then with a certain eagerness asked me whether I would let him measure my head. Rather surprised, I said Yes, when he produced a thing like callipers and got the dimensions back and front and every way, taking notes carefully. He was an unshaven little man in a threadbare coat like a gaberdine, with his feet in slippers, and I thought him a harmless fool. 'I always ask leave, in the interests of science, to measure the crania of those going out there,' he said. 'And when they come back too?' I asked. 'Oh, I never see them,' he remarked; 'and, moreover, the changes take place inside, you know.' He smiled, as if at some quiet joke. 'So you are going out there. Famous. Interesting too.' He gave me a searching glance, and made another note. 'Ever any madness in your family?' he asked, in a matter-of-fact tone. I felt very annoyed. 'Is that question in the interests of science too?' 'It would be,' he said, without taking notice of my irritation, 'interesting for science to watch the mental changes of individuals, on the spot, but . . .' 'Are you an alienist?'[8] I interrupted. 'Every doctor should be—a little,' answered that original imperturbably. 'I have a little theory which you Messieurs who go out there must help me to prove. This is my share in the advantages my country shall reap from the possession of such a magnificent dependency. The mere wealth I leave to others. Pardon my questions, but you are the first Englishman coming under my observation . . .' I hastened to assure him I was not in the least typical. 'If I were,' said I, 'I wouldn't be talking like this with you.' 'What you say is rather profound, and probably erroneous,' he said, with a laugh. 'Avoid irritation more than exposure to the sun. Adieu. How do you English say, eh? Good-bye. Ah! Good-bye. Adieu. In the tropics one must before everything keep calm.' . . . He lifted a warning forefinger. . . . '*Du calme, du calme. Adieu.*'

"One thing more remained to do—say good-bye to my excellent aunt. I found her triumphant. I had a cup of tea—the last decent cup of tea for many days—and in a room that most soothingly looked just as you would expect a lady's drawing-room to look, we had a long quiet chat by the fireside. In the course of these confidences it became quite plain to me I had been repre-

7. "Hail! . . . Those who are about to die salute you." The Roman gladiators' salute to the emperor on entering the arena.

8. Doctor who treats mental diseases. (The term has now been replaced by *psychiatrist*.)

sented to the wife of the high dignitary, and goodness knows to how many more people besides, as an exceptional and gifted creature—a piece of good fortune for the Company—a man you don't get hold of every day. Good heavens! and I was going to take charge of a two-penny-halfpenny river-steamboat with a penny whistle attached! It appeared, however, I was also one of the Workers, with a capital—you know. Something like an emissary of light, something like a lower sort of apostle. There had been a lot of such rot let loose in print and talk just about that time, and the excellent woman, living right in the rush of all that humbug, got carried off her feet. She talked about 'weaning those ignorant millions from their horrid ways,' till, upon my word, she made me quite uncomfortable. I ventured to hint that the Company was run for profit.

"'You forget, dear Charlie, that the labourer is worthy of his hire,' she said brightly. It's queer how out of touch with truth women are. They live in a world of their own, and there had never been anything like it, and never can be. It is too beautiful altogether, and if they were to set it up it would go to pieces before the first sunset. Some confounded fact we men have been living contentedly with ever since the day of creation would start up and knock the whole thing over.

"After this I got embraced, told to wear flannel, be sure to write often, and so on—and I left. In the street—I don't know why—a queer feeling came to me that I was an impostor. Odd thing that I, who used to clear out for any part of the world at twenty-four hours' notice, with less thought than most men give to the crossing of a street, had a moment—I won't say of hesitation, but of startled pause, before this commonplace affair. The best way I can explain it to you is by saying that, for a second or two, I felt as though, instead of going to the centre of a continent, I were about to set off for the centre of the earth.

"I left in a French steamer, and she called in every blamed port they have out there, for, as far as I could see, the sole purpose of landing soldiers and custom-house officers. I watched the coast. Watching a coast as it slips by the ship is like thinking about an enigma. There it is before you—smiling, frowning, inviting, grand, mean, insipid, or savage, and always mute with an air of whispering, Come and find out. This one was almost featureless, as if still in the making, with an aspect of monotonous grimness. The edge of a colossal jungle, so dark green as to be almost black, fringed with white surf, ran straight, like a ruled line, far, far away along a blue sea whose glitter was blurred by a creeping mist. The sun was fierce, the land seemed to glisten and drip with steam. Here and there greyish-whitish specks showed up clustered inside the white surf, with a flag flying above them perhaps—settlements some centuries old, and still no bigger than pin-heads on the untouched expanse of their background. We pounded along, stopped, landed soldiers; went on, landed custom-house clerks to levy toll in what looked like a God-forsaken wilderness, with a tin shed and a flag-pole lost in it; landed more soldiers—to take care of the custom-house clerks presumably. Some, I heard, got drowned in the surf; but whether they did or not, nobody seemed particularly to care. They were just flung out there, and on we went. Every day the coast looked the same, as though we had not moved; but we passed various places—trading places—with names like Gran' Bassam, Little Popo; names that seemed to belong to some sordid farce acted in front of a sinister back-cloth. The idleness of a passenger, my isolation amongst all these men with whom I had no point of contact, the oily and languid sea, the uniform sombreness of the coast, seemed to keep me away from the truth of things, within the toil of a mournful and senseless delusion. The voice of the surf heard now and then was a positive pleasure, like the speech of a brother. It was something natural, that had its reason, that had a meaning. Now and then a boat from the shore gave one a momentary contact with reality. It was paddled by black fellows. You could see from afar the white of their eyeballs glistening. They shouted, sang; their bodies streamed with perspiration; they had faces like grotesque masks—these chaps; but they had bone, muscle, a wild vitality, an intense energy of movement, that was as natural and true as the surf along their coast. They wanted no excuse for being there. They were a great comfort to look at. For a time I would feel I belonged still to a world of straightforward facts; but the feeling would not last long. Something would turn up to scare it away. Once, I remember, we came upon a man-of-war anchored off the coast. There wasn't even a shed there, and she was shelling the bush. It appears the French had one of their wars going on thereabouts. Her ensign dropped limp like a rag; the muzzles of the long six-inch guns stuck out all over the low hull; the greasy, slimy swell swung her up lazily and let her down, swaying her thin masts. In the empty immensity of earth, sky, and water, there she was, incomprehensible, firing into a continent. Pop, would go one of the six-inch guns; a small flame would dart and vanish, a little white smoke would disappear, a tiny projectile would give a feeble screech—and nothing happened. Nothing could happen. There was a touch of insanity in the proceeding, a sense of lugubrious drollery in the sight; and it was not dissipated by somebody on board assuring me earnestly there was a camp of natives—he called them enemies!—hidden out of sight somewhere.

"We gave her her letters (I heard the men in that lonely ship were dying of fever at the rate of three a day) and went on. We called at some more places with farcical names, where the merry dance of death and trade goes on in a still and earthy atmosphere as of an overheated catacomb; all along the formless coast bordered by dangerous surf, as if Nature herself had tried to ward off intruders; in and out of rivers, streams of death in life, whose banks were rotting into mud, whose waters, thickened into slime, invaded the contorted mangroves, that seemed to writhe at us in the extremity of an impotent despair. Nowhere did we stop long enough to get a particularised impression, but the general sense of vague and oppressive wonder grew upon me. It was like a weary pilgrimage amongst hints for nightmares.

"It was upward of thirty days before I saw the mouth of the big river. We anchored off the seat of the government. But my work would not begin till some two hundred miles farther on. So as soon as I could I made a start for a place thirty miles higher up.

"I had my passage on a little sea-going steamer. Her captain was a Swede, and knowing me for a seaman, invited me on the bridge. He was a young man, lean, fair, and morose, with lanky hair and a shuffling gait. As we left the miserable little wharf, he tossed his head contemptuously at the shore. 'Been living there?' he asked. I said, 'Yes.' 'Fine lot these government chaps—are they not?' he went on, speaking English with great precision and considerable bitterness. 'It is funny what some people will do for a few francs a month. I wonder what becomes of that kind when it goes up country?' I said to him I expected to see that soon. 'So-o-o!' he exclaimed. He shuffled athwart, keeping one eye ahead vigilantly. 'Don't be too sure,' he continued. 'The other day I took up a man who hanged himself on the road. He was a Swede, too.' 'Hanged himself! Why, in God's name?' I cried. He kept on looking out watchfully. 'Who knows? The sun too much for him, or the country perhaps.'

"At last we opened a reach. A rocky cliff appeared, mounds of turned-up earth by the shore, houses on a hill, others with iron roofs, amongst a waste of excavations, or hanging to the declivity. A continuous noise of the rapids above hovered over this scene of inhabited devastation. A lot of people, mostly black and naked, moved about like ants. A jetty projected into the river. A blinding sunlight drowned all this at times in a sudden recrudescence of glare. 'There's your Company's station,' said the Swede, pointing to three wooden barrack-like structures on the rocky slope. 'I will send your things up. Four boxes did you say? So. Farewell.'

"I came upon a boiler wallowing in the grass, then found a path leading up the hill. It turned aside for the boulders, and also for an undersized railway truck lying there on its back with its wheels in the air. One was off. The thing looked as dead as the carcass of some animal. I came upon more pieces of decaying machinery, a stack of rusty nails. To the left a clump of trees made a shady spot, where dark things seemed to stir feebly. I blinked, the path was steep. A horn tooted to the right, and I saw the black people run. A heavy and dull detonation shook the ground, a puff of smoke came out of the cliff, and that was all. No change appeared on the face of the rock. They were building a railway. The cliff was not in the way or anything; but this objectless blasting was all the work going on.

"A slight clinking behind me made me turn my head. Six black men advanced in a file, toiling up the path. They walked erect and slow, balancing small baskets full of earth on their heads, and the clink kept time with their footsteps. Black rags were wound round their loins, and the short ends behind waggled to and fro like tails. I could see every rib, the joints of their limbs like knots in a rope; each had an iron collar on his neck, and all were connected together with a chain whose bights swung between them, rhythmically clinking. Another report from the cliff made me think suddenly of that ship of war I had seen firing into a continent. It was the same kind of ominous voice; but these men could by no stretch of imagination be called enemies. They were called criminals, and the outraged law, like the bursting shells, had come to them, an insoluble mystery from the sea. All their meagre breasts panted together, the violently dilated nostrils quivered, the eyes stared stonily uphill. They passed me within six inches, without a glance, with that complete, deathlike indifference of unhappy savages. Behind this raw matter one of the reclaimed, the product of the new forces at work, strolled despondently, carrying a rifle by its middle. He had a uniform jacket with one button off, and seeing a white man on the path, hoisted his weapon to his shoulder with alacrity. This was simple prudence, white men being so much alike at a distance that he could not tell who I might be. He was speedily reassured, and with a large, white, rascally grin, and a glance at his charge, seemed to take me into partnership in his exalted trust. After all, I also was a part of the great cause of these high and just proceedings.

"Instead of going up, I turned and descended to the left. My idea was to let that chain-gang get out of sight before I climbed the hill. You know I am not particularly tender; I've had to strike and to fend off. I've had to resist and to attack sometimes—that's only one way of resisting—without counting the exact cost, according to the demands of such sort of life as I had blundered into. I've seen the devil of violence, and the devil of greed, and the devil of hot desire; but, by all the stars! these were strong, lusty, red-eyed devils, that swayed and drove men—men, I tell you. But as I stood on this hillside, I foresaw that in the blinding sunshine of that land I would become acquainted with a flabby, pretending, weak-eyed devil of a rapacious and pitiless folly. How insidious he could be, too, I was only to find out several months later and a thousand miles farther. For a moment I stood appalled, as though by a warning. Finally I descended the hill, obliquely, towards the trees I had seen.

"I avoided a vast artificial hole somebody had been digging on the slope, the purpose of which I found it impossible to divine. It wasn't a quarry or a sandpit, anyhow. It was just a hole. It might have been connected with the philanthropic desire of giving the criminals something to do. I don't know. Then I nearly fell into a very narrow ravine, almost no more than a scar in the hillside. I discovered that a lot of imported drainage-pipes for the settlement had been tumbled in there. There wasn't one that was not broken. It was a wanton smash-up. At last I got under the trees. My purpose was to stroll into the shade for a moment; but no sooner within than it seemed to me I had stepped into the gloomy circle of some Inferno. The rapids were near, and an uninterrupted, uniform, headlong, rushing noise filled the mournful stillness of the grove, where not a breath stirred, not a leaf moved, with a mysterious sound—as though the tearing pace of the launched earth had suddenly become audible.

"Black shapes crouched, lay, sat between the trees, leaning against the trunks, clinging to the earth, half coming out, half effaced within the dim light, in all the attitudes of pain, abandonment, and despair. Another mine on the cliff went off, followed by a slight shudder of the soil under my feet. The work was going on. The work! And this was the place where some of the helpers had withdrawn to die.

"They were dying slowly—it was very clear. They were not enemies, they were not criminals, they were nothing earthly now—nothing but black shadows of disease and starvation, lying confusedly in the greenish gloom. Brought from all the recesses of the coast in all the legality of time contracts, lost in uncongenial surroundings, fed on unfamiliar food, they sickened, became inefficient, and were then allowed to crawl away and rest. These moribund shapes were free as air—and nearly as thin. I began to distinguish the gleam of eyes under the trees. Then, glancing down, I saw a face near my hand. The black bones reclined at full length with one shoulder against the tree, and slowly the eyelids rose and the sunken eyes looked up at me, enormous and vacant, a kind of blind, white flicker in the depths of the orbs, which died out slowly. The man seemed young—almost a boy—but you know with them it's hard to tell. I found nothing else to do but to offer him one of my good Swede's ship's biscuits I had in my pocket. The fingers closed slowly on it and held—there was no other movement and no other glance. He had tied a bit of white worsted round his neck—Why? Where did he get it? Was it a badge— an ornament—a charm—a propitiatory act? Was there any idea at all connected with it? It looked startling round his black neck, this bit of white thread from beyond the seas.

"Near the same tree two more bundles of acute angles sat with their legs drawn up. One, with his chin propped on his knees, stared at nothing, in an intolerable and appalling manner: his brother phantom rested its forehead, as if overcome with a great weariness; and all about others were scattered in every pose of contorted collapse, as in some picture of a massacre or a pestilence. While I stood horror-struck, one of these creatures rose to his hands and knees, and went off on all-fours towards the river to drink. He lapped out of his hand, then sat up in the sunlight, crossing his shins in front of him, and after a time let his woolly head fall on his breastbone.

"I didn't want any more loitering in the shade, and I made haste towards the station. When near the buildings I met a white man, in such an unexpected elegance of get-up that in the first moment I took him for a sort of vision. I saw a high starched collar, white cuffs, a light alpaca jacket, snowy trousers, a clear necktie, and varnished boots. No hat. Hair parted, brushed, oiled, under a green-lined parasol held in a big white hand. He was amazing, and had a penholder behind his ear.

"I shook hands with this miracle, and I learned he was the Company's chief accountant, and that all the book-keeping was done at this station. He had come out for a moment, he said, 'to get a breath of fresh air.' The expression sounded wonderfully odd, with its suggestion of sedentary desk-life. I wouldn't have mentioned the fellow to you at all, only it was from his lips that I first heard the name of the man who is so indissolubly connected with the memories of that time. Moreover, I respected the fellow. Yes; I respected his collars, his vast cuffs, his brushed hair. His appearance was certainly that of a hairdresser's dummy; but in the great demoralisation of the land he kept up his appearance. That's backbone. His starched collars and got-up shirt-fronts were achievements of character. He had been out nearly three years; and, later, I could not help asking him how he managed to sport such linen. He had just the faintest blush, and said modestly, 'I've been teaching one of the native women about the station. It was difficult. She had a distaste for the work.' Thus this man had verily accomplished something. And he was devoted to his books, which were in apple-pie order.

"Everything else in the station was in a muddle,—heads, things, buildings. Strings of dusty niggers with splay feet arrived and departed; a stream of manufactured goods, rubbishy cottons, beads, and brass-wire set into the depths of darkness, and in return came a precious trickle of ivory.

"I had to wait in the station for ten days—an eternity. I lived in a hut in the yard, but to be out of the chaos I would sometimes get into the accountant's office. It was built of horizontal planks, and so badly put together that, as he bent over his high desk, he was barred from neck to heels with narrow strips of sunlight. There was no need to open the big shutter to see. It was hot there too; big flies buzzed fiendishly, and did not sting, but stabbed. I sat generally on the floor, while, of faultless appearance (and even slightly scented), perching on a high stool, he wrote, he wrote. Sometimes he stood up for exercise. When a truckle-bed with a sick man (some invalided agent from up country) was put in there, he exhibited a gentle annoyance. 'The groans of this sick person' he said, 'distract my attention. And without that it is extremely difficult to guard against clerical errors in this climate.'

"One day he remarked, without lifting his head, 'In the interior you will no doubt meet Mr. Kurtz.' On my asking who Mr. Kurtz was, he said he was a first-class agent; and seeing my disappointment at this information, he added slowly, laying down his pen, 'He is a very remarkable person.' Further questions elicited from him that Mr. Kurtz was at present in charge of a trading-post, a very important one, in the true ivory-country, at 'the very bottom of there. Sends in as much ivory as all the others put together . . .' He began to write again. The sick man was too ill to groan. The flies buzzed in a great peace.

"Suddenly there was a growing murmur of voices and a great tramping of feet. A caravan had come in. A violent babble of uncouth sounds burst out on the other side of the planks. All the carriers were speaking together, and in the midst of the uproar the lamentable voice of the chief agent was heard 'giving it up' tearfully for the twentieth time that day. . . . He rose slowly. 'What a frightful row,' he said. He crossed the room gently to look at the sick man, and returning, said to me, 'He does not hear.' 'What! Dead?' I asked, startled. 'No, not yet,' he answered, with great composure. Then, alluding with a toss of the head to the tumult in the station-yard, 'When one has got to make correct entries, one comes to hate those savages—hate them to the death.' He remained thoughtful for a moment. 'When you see Mr. Kurtz,' he went on, 'tell him from me that everything here'—he glanced at the desk—'is very satisfactory. I don't like to write to him—with those messengers of ours you never know who may get hold of your letter—at that Central Station.' He stared at me for a moment with his mild, bulging eyes. 'Oh, he will go far, very far,' he began again. 'He will be a somebody in the Administration before long. They, above—the Council in Europe, you know—mean him to be.'

"He turned to his work. The noise outside had ceased, and presently in going out I stopped at the door. In the steady buzz of flies the homeward-bound agent was lying flushed and insensible; the other, bent over his books, was making correct entries of perfectly correct transactions; and fifty feet below the doorstep I could see the still tree-tops of the grove of death.

"Next day I left that station at last, with a caravan of sixty men, for a two-hundred-mile tramp.

"No use telling you much about that. Paths, paths, everywhere; a stamped-in network of paths spreading over the empty land, through long grass, through burnt grass, through thickets, down and up chilly ravines, up and down stony hills ablaze with heat; and a solitude, a solitude, nobody, not a hut. The population had cleared out a long time ago. Well, if a lot of mysterious niggers armed with all kinds of fearful weapons suddenly took to travelling on the road between Deal and Gravesend, catching the yokels right and left to carry heavy loads for them, I fancy every farm and cottage thereabouts would get empty very soon. Only here the dwellings were gone too. Still, I passed through several abandoned villages. There's something pathetically childish in the ruins of grass walls. Day after day, with the stamp and shuffle of sixty pair of bare feet behind me, each pair under a 60-lb. load. Camp, cook, sleep, strike camp, march. Now and then a carrier dead in harness, at rest in the long grass near the path, with an empty water-gourd and his long staff lying by his side. A great silence around and above. Perhaps on some quiet night the tremor of far-off drums, sinking, swelling, a tremor vast, faint; a sound weird, appealing, suggestive, and wild—and perhaps with as profound a meaning as the sound of bells in a Christian country. Once a white man in an unbuttoned uniform, camping on the path with an armed escort of lank

Zanzibaris,[9] very hospitable and festive—not to say drunk. Was looking after the upkeep of the road, he declared. Can't say I saw any road or any upkeep, unless the body of a middle-aged negro, with a bullet-hole in the forehead, upon which I absolutely stumbled three miles farther on, may be considered as a permanent improvement. I had a white companion too, not a bad chap, but rather too fleshy and with the exasperating habit of fainting on the hot hillsides, miles away from the least bit of shade and water. Annoying, you know, to hold your own coat like a parasol over a man's head while he is coming-to. I couldn't help asking him once what he meant by coming there at all. 'To make money, of course. What do you think?' he said scornfully. Then he got fever, and had to be carried in a hammock slung under a pole. As he weighed sixteen stone[1] I had no end of rows with the carriers. They jibbed, ran away, sneaked off with their loads in the night—quite a mutiny. So, one evening, I made a speech in English with gestures, not one of which was lost to the sixty pairs of eyes before me, and the next morning I started the hammock off in front all right. An hour afterwards I came upon the whole concern wrecked in a bush—man, hammock, groans, blankets, horrors. The heavy pole had skinned his poor nose. He was very anxious for me to kill somebody, but there wasn't the shadow of a carrier near. I remembered the old doctor—'It would be interesting for science to watch the mental changes of individuals, on the spot.' I felt I was becoming scientifically interesting. However, all that is to no purpose. On the fifteenth day I came in sight of the big river again, and hobbled into the Central Station. It was on a back water surrounded by scrub and forest, with a pretty border of smelly mud on one side, and on the three others enclosed by a crazy fence of rushes. A neglected gap was all the gate it had, and the first glance at the place was enough to let you see the flabby devil was running that show. White men with long staves in their hands appeared languidly from amongst the buildings, strolling up to take a look at me, and then retired out of sight somewhere. One of them, a stout, excitable chap with black moustaches, informed me with great volubility and many digressions, as soon as I told him who I was, that my steamer was at the bottom of the river. I was thunderstruck. What, how, why? Oh, it was 'all right.' The 'manager himself' was there. All quite correct. 'Everybody had behaved splendidly! splendidly!'—'You must,' he said in agitation, 'go and see the general manager at once. He is waiting!'

"I did not see the real significance of that wreck at once. I fancy I see it now, but I am not sure—not at all. Certainly the affair was too stupid—when I think of it—to be altogether natural. Still . . . But at the moment it presented itself simply as a confounded nuisance. The steamer was sunk. They had started two days before in a sudden hurry up the river with the manager on board, in charge of some volunteer skipper, and before they had been out three hours they tore the bottom out of her on stones, and she sank near the south bank. I asked myself what I was to do there, now my boat was lost. As a matter of fact, I had plenty to do in fishing my command out of the river. I had to set about it the very next day. That, and the repairs when I brought the pieces to the station, took some months.

9. Natives of Zanzibar, an island off the east coast of Africa, once part of the sultanate of Zanzibar and a British protectorate, now part of the independent state of Tanzania. Zanzibaris were used as mercenaries throughout Africa.
1. One stone equals 14 pounds. The man weighed 224 pounds.

"My first interview with the manager was curious. He did not ask me to sit down after my twenty-mile walk that morning. He was commonplace in complexion, in feature, in manners, and in voice. He was of middle size and of ordinary build. His eyes, of the usual blue, were perhaps remarkably cold, and he certainly could make his glance fall on one as trenchant and heavy as an axe. But even at these times the rest of his person seemed to disclaim the intention. Otherwise there was only an indefinable, faint expression of his lips, something stealthy—a smile—not a smile—I remember it, but I can't explain. It was unconscious, this smile was, though just after he had said something it got intensified for an instant. It came at the end of his speeches like a seal applied on the words to make the meaning of the commonest phrase appear absolutely inscrutable. He was a common trader, from his youth up employed in these parts—nothing more. He was obeyed, yet he inspired neither love nor fear, nor even respect. He inspired uneasiness. That was it! Uneasiness. Not a definite mistrust—just uneasiness—nothing more. You have no idea how effective such a . . . a . . . faculty can be. He had no genius for organising, for initiative, or for order even. That was evident in such things as the deplorable state of the station. He had no learning, and no intelligence. His position had come to him—why? Perhaps because he was never ill. . . He had served three terms of three years out there . . . Because triumphant health in the general rout of constitutions is a kind of power in itself. When he went home on leave he rioted on a large scale—pompously. Jack ashore—with a difference—in externals only. This one could gather from his casual talk. He originated nothing, he could keep the routine going—that's all. But he was great. He was great by this little thing that it was impossible to tell what could control such a man. He never gave that secret away. Perhaps there was nothing within him. Such a suspicion made one pause—for out there there were no external checks. Once when various tropical diseases had laid low almost every 'agent' in the station, he was heard to say, 'Men who come out here should have no entrails.' He sealed the utterance with that smile of his, as though it had been a door opening into a darkness he had in his keeping. You fancied you had seen things—but the seal was on. When annoyed at meal-times by the constant quarrels of the white men about precedence, he ordered an immense round table to be made, for which a special house had to be built. This was the station's mess-room. Where he sat was the first place—the rest were nowhere. One felt this to be his unalterable conviction. He was neither civil nor uncivil. He was quiet. He allowed his 'boy'—an overfed young negro from the coast—to treat the white men, under his very eyes, with provoking insolence.

"He began to speak as soon as he saw me. I had been very long on the road. He could not wait. Had to start without me. The up-river stations had to be relieved. There had been so many delays already that he did not know who was dead and who was alive, and how they got on—and so on, and so on. He paid no attention to my explanations, and, playing with a stick of sealing-wax, repeated several times that the situation was 'very grave, very grave.' There were rumors that a very important station was in jeopardy, and its chief, Mr. Kurtz, was ill. Hoped it was not true. Mr. Kurtz was . . . I felt weary and irritable. Hang Kurtz, I thought. I interrupted him by saying I had heard of Mr. Kurtz on the coast. 'Ah! So they talk of him down there,' he murmured to himself. Then he began again, assuring me Mr. Kurtz was the best agent he had, an exceptional man, of the greatest importance to the Company; therefore I could understand his anxiety. He was, he said, 'very, very uneasy.' Certainly he fidgeted on his chair a good deal, exclaimed, 'Ah, Mr. Kurtz!' broke the stick of sealing-wax and seemed dumbfounded by the accident. Next thing he wanted to know 'how long it would take to' . . . I interrupted him again. Being hungry, you know, and kept on my feet too, I was getting savage. 'How can I tell?' I said, 'I haven't even seen the wreck yet—some months, no doubt.' All this talk seemed to me so futile. 'Some months,' he said. 'Well, let us say three months before we can make a start. Yes. That ought to do the affair.' I flung out of his hut (he lived all alone in a clay hut with a sort of verandah) muttering to myself my opinion of him. He was a chattering idiot. Afterwards I took it back when it was borne in upon me startlingly with what extreme nicety he had estimated the time requisite for the 'affair.'

"I went to work the next day, turning, so to speak, my back on that station. In that way only it seemed to me I could keep my hold on the redeeming facts of life. Still, one must look about sometimes; and then I saw this station, these men strolling aimlessly about in the sunshine of the yard. I asked myself sometimes what it all meant. They wandered here and there with their absurd long staves in their hands, like a lot of faithless pilgrims bewitched inside a rotten fence. The word 'ivory' rang in the air, was whispered, was sighed. You would think they were praying to it. A taint of imbecile rapacity blew through it all, like a whiff from some corpse. By Jove! I've never seen anything so unreal in my life. And outside, the silent wilderness surrounding this cleared speck on the earth struck me as something great and invincible, like evil or truth, waiting patiently for the passing away of this fantastic invasion.

"Oh, these months! Well, never mind. Various things happened. One evening a grass shed full of calico, cotton prints, beads, and I don't know what else, burst into a blaze so suddenly that you would have thought the earth had opened to let an avenging fire consume all that trash. I was smoking my pipe quietly by my dismantled steamer, and saw them all cutting capers in the light, with their arms lifted high, when the stout man with moustaches came tearing down to the river, a tin pail in his hand, assured me that everybody was 'behaving splendidly, splendidly,' dipped about a quart of water and tore back again. I noticed there was a hole in the bottom of his pail.

"I strolled up. There was no hurry. You see the thing had gone off like a box of matches. It had been hopeless from the very first. The flame had leaped high, driven everybody back, lighted up everything—and collapsed. The shed was already a heap of embers glowing fiercely. A nigger was being beaten near by. They said he had caused the fire in some way; be that as it may, he was screeching most horribly. I saw him, later, for several days, sitting in a bit of shade looking very sick and trying to recover himself: afterwards he arose and went out—and the wilderness without a sound took him into its bosom again. As I approached the glow from the dark I found myself at the back of two men, talking. I heard the name of Kurtz pronounced, then the words, 'take advantage of this unfortunate accident.' One of the men was the manager. I wished him a good evening. 'Did you ever see anything like it—eh? it is incredible,' he said, and walked off. The other man remained. He was a first-class agent, young, gentlemanly, a bit reserved, with a forked little beard and a hooked nose. He was standoffish with the other agents, and they on their side said he was the manager's spy upon them. As to me, I had hardly ever spoken to him before. We got into talk, and by and by we strolled away from the hissing ruins. Then he asked me to his room, which was in the main building of the station. He struck a match, and I perceived that this young aristocrat had not only a silver-mounted dressing-case but also a whole candle all to himself. Just at that time the manager was the only man supposed to have any right to candles. Native mats covered the clay walls; a collection of spears, assegais,[2] shields, knives, was hung up in trophies. The business entrusted to this fellow was the making of bricks—so I had been informed; but there wasn't a fragment of a brick anywhere in the station, and he had been there more than a year—waiting. It seems he could not make bricks without something, I don't know what—straw maybe. Anyway, it could not be found there, and as it was not likely to be sent from Europe, it did not appear clear to me what he was waiting for. An act of special creation perhaps. However, they were all waiting—all the sixteen or twenty pilgrims of them—for something; and upon my word it did not seem an uncongenial occupation, from the way they took it, though the only thing that ever came to them was disease—as far as I could see. They beguiled the time by backbiting and intriguing against each other in a foolish kind of way. There was an air of plotting about that station, but nothing came of it, of course. It was as unreal as everything else—as the philanthropic pretence of the whole concern, as their talk, as their government, as their show of work. The only real feeling was a desire to get appointed to a trading-post where ivory was to be had, so that they could earn percentages. They intrigued and slandered and hated each other only on that account—but as to effectually lifting a little finger— oh no. By heavens! there is something after all in the world allowing one man to steal a horse while another must not look at a halter. Steal a horse straight out. Very well. He has done it. Perhaps he can ride. But there is a way of looking at a halter that would provoke the most charitable of saints into a kick.

"I had no idea why he wanted to be sociable, but as we chatted in there it suddenly occurred to me the fellow was trying to get at something—in fact, pumping me. He alluded constantly to Europe, to the people I was supposed to know there—putting leading questions as to my acquaintances in the sepulchral city, and so on. His little eyes glittered like mica discs—with curiosity— though he tried to keep up a bit of superciliousness. At first I was astonished, but very soon I became awfully curious to see what he would find out from me. I couldn't possibly imagine what I had in me to make it worth his while. It was very pretty to see how he baffled himself, for in truth my body was full only of chills, and my head had nothing in it but that wretched steamboat business. It was evident he took me for a perfectly shameless prevaricator. At last he got angry, and, to conceal a movement of furious annoyance, he yawned. I rose. Then I noticed a small sketch in oils, on a panel, representing a woman, draped and blindfolded, carrying a lighted torch. The background was sombre—almost black. The movement of the woman was stately, and the effect of the torchlight on the face was sinister.

"It arrested me, and he stood by civilly, holding an empty half-pint champagne bottle (medical comforts) with the candle stuck in it. To my question he said Mr. Kurtz had painted this—in this very station more than a year

---

2. Slender iron-tipped spears.

ago—while waiting for means to go to his trading-post. 'Tell me, pray,' said I, 'who is this Mr. Kurtz?'

"'The chief of the Inner Station,' he answered in a short tone, looking away. 'Much obliged,' I said, laughing. 'And you are the brickmaker of the Central Station. Every one knows that.' He was silent for a while. 'He is a prodigy,' he said at last. 'He is an emissary of pity, and science, and progress, and devil knows what else. We want,' he began to declaim suddenly, 'for the guidance of the cause entrusted to us by Europe, so to speak, higher intelligence, wide sympathies, a singleness of purpose.' 'Who says that?' I asked. 'Lots of them,' he replied. 'Some even write that; and so *he* comes here, a special being, as you ought to know.' 'Why ought I to know?' I interrupted, really surprised. He paid no attention. 'Yes. To-day he is chief of the best station, next year he will be assistant-manager, two years more and . . . but I daresay you know what he will be in two years' time. You are of the new gang—the gang of virtue. The same people who sent him specially also recommended you. Oh, don't say no. I've my own eyes to trust.' Light dawned upon me. My dear aunt's influential acquaintances were producing an unexpected effect upon that young man. I nearly burst into a laugh. 'Do you read the Company's confidential correspondence?' I asked. He hadn't a word to say. It was great fun. 'When Mr. Kurtz,' I continued severely, 'is General Manager, you won't have the opportunity.'

"He blew the candle out suddenly, and we went outside. The moon had risen. Black figures strolled about listlessly, pouring water on the glow, whence proceeded a sound of hissing; steam ascended in the moonlight; the beaten nigger groaned somewhere. 'What a row the brute makes!' said the indefatigable man with the moustaches, appearing near us. 'Serve him right. Transgression—punishment—bang! Pitiless, pitiless. That's the only way. This will prevent all conflagrations for the future. I was just telling the manager . . .' He noticed my companion, and became crestfallen all at once. 'Not in bed yet,' he said, with a kind of servile heartiness; 'it's so natural. Ha! Danger—agitation.' He vanished. I went on to the river-side, and the other followed me. I heard a scathing murmur at my ear, 'Heap of muffs—go to.' The pilgrims could be seen in knots gesticulating, discussing. Several had still their staves in their hands. I verily believe they took these sticks to bed with them. Beyond the fence the forest stood up spectrally in the moonlight, and through the dim stir, through the faint sounds of that lamentable courtyard, the silence of the land went home to one's very heart—its mystery, its greatness, the amazing reality of its concealed life. The hurt nigger moaned feebly somewhere near by, and then fetched a deep sigh that made me mend my pace away from there. I felt a hand introducing itself under my arm. 'My dear sir,' said the fellow, 'I don't want to be misunderstood, and especially by you, who will see Mr. Kurtz long before I can have that pleasure. I wouldn't like him to get a false idea of my disposition. . . .'

"I let him run on, this papier-mâché Mephistopheles, and it seemed to me that if I tried I could poke my forefinger through him, and would find nothing inside but a little loose dirt, maybe. He, don't you see, had been planning to be assistant-manager by and by under the present man, and I could see that the coming of that Kurtz had upset them both not a little. He talked precipitately, and I did not try to stop him. I had my shoulders against the wreck of my steamer, hauled up on the slope like a carcass of some big river animal. The smell of mud, of primeval mud, by Jove! was in my nostrils, the high stillness of primeval forest was before my eyes; there were shiny patches on the black creek. The moon had spread over everything a thin layer of silver—over the rank grass, over the mud, upon the wall of matted vegetation standing higher than the wall of a temple, over the great river I could see through a sombre gap glittering, glittering, as it flowed broadly by without a murmur. All this was great, expectant, mute, while the man jabbered about himself. I wondered whether the stillness on the face of the immensity looking at us two were meant as an appeal or as a menace. What were we who had strayed in here? Could we handle that dumb thing, or would it handle us? I felt how big, how confoundedly big, was that thing that couldn't talk and perhaps was deaf as well. What was in there? I could see a little ivory coming out from there, and I had heard Mr. Kurtz was in there. I had heard enough about it too—God knows! Yet somehow it didn't bring any image with it—no more than if I had been told an angel or a fiend was in there. I believed it in the same way one of you might believe there are inhabitants in the planet Mars. I knew once a Scotch sailmaker who was certain, dead sure, there were people in Mars. If you asked him for some idea how they looked and behaved, he would get shy and mutter something about 'walking on all-fours.' If you as much as smiled, he would—though a man of sixty—offer to fight you. I would not have gone so far as to fight for Kurtz, but I went for him near enough to a lie. You know I hate, detest, and can't bear a lie, not because I am straighter than the rest of us, but simply because it appals me. There is a taint of death, a flavour of mortality in lies—which is exactly what I hate and detest in the world—what I want to forget. It makes me miserable and sick, like biting something rotten would do. Temperament, I suppose. Well, I went near enough to it by letting the young fool there believe anything he liked to imagine as to my influence in Europe. I became in an instant as much of a pretence as the rest of the bewitched pilgrims. This simply because I had a notion it somehow would be of help to that Kurtz whom at the time I did not see—you understand. He was just a word for me. I did not see the man in the name any more than you do. Do you see him? Do you see the story? Do you see anything? It seems to me I am trying to tell you a dream—making a vain attempt, because no relation of a dream can convey the dream-sensation, that commingling of absurdity, surprise, and bewilderment in a tremor of struggling revolt, that notion of being captured by the incredible which is of the very essence of dreams. . . ."

He was silent for a while.

". . . No, it is impossible; it is impossible to convey the life-sensation of any given epoch of one's existence—that which makes its truth, its meaning—its subtle and penetrating essence. It is impossible. We live, as we dream—alone. . . ."

He paused again as if reflecting, then added:

"Of course in this you fellows see more than I could then. You see me, whom you know. . . ."

It had become so pitch dark that we listeners could hardly see one another. For a long time already he, sitting apart, had been no more to us than a voice. There was not a word from anybody. The others might have been asleep, but I was awake. I listened, I listened on the watch for the sentence, for the word, that would give me the clue to the faint uneasiness inspired by this narrative that seemed to shape itself without human lips in the heavy night-air of the river.

"... Yes—I let him run on," Marlow began again, "and think what he pleased about the powers that were behind me. I did! And there was nothing behind me! There was nothing but that wretched, old, mangled steamboat I was leaning against, while he talked fluently about 'the necessity for every man to get on.' 'And when one comes out here, you conceive, it is not to gaze at the moon.' Mr. Kurtz was a 'universal genius,' but even a genius would find it easier to work with 'adequate tools—intelligent men.' He did not make bricks—why, there was a physical impossibility in the way—as I was well aware; and if he did secretarial work for the manager, it was because 'no sensible man rejects wantonly the confidence of his superiors.' Did I see it? I saw it. What more did I want? What I really wanted was rivets, by heaven! Rivets. To get on with the work—to stop the hole. Rivets I wanted. There were cases of them down at the coast—cases—piled up—burst—split! You kicked a loose rivet at every second step in that station yard on the hillside. Rivets had rolled into the grove of death. You could fill your pockets with rivets for the trouble of stooping down—and there wasn't one rivet to be found where it was wanted. We had plates that would do, but nothing to fasten them with. And every week the messenger, a lone negro, letter-bag on shoulder and staff in hand, left our station for the coast. And several times a week a coast caravan came in with trade goods—ghastly glazed calico that made you shudder only to look at it, glass beads value about a penny a quart, confounded spotted cotton handkerchiefs. And no rivets. Three carriers could have brought all that was wanted to set that steamboat afloat.

"He was becoming confidential now, but I fancy my unresponsive attitude must have exasperated him at last, for he judged it necessary to inform me he feared neither God nor devil, let alone any mere man. I said I could see that very well, but what I wanted was a certain quantity of rivets—and rivets were what really Mr. Kurtz wanted, if he had only known it. Now letters went to the coast every week.... 'My dear sir,' he cried, 'I write from dictation.' I demanded rivets. There was a way—for an intelligent man. He changed his manner; became very cold, and suddenly began to talk about a hippopotamus; wondered whether sleeping on board the steamer (I stuck to my salvage night and day) I wasn't disturbed. There was an old hippo that had the bad habit of getting out on the bank and roaming at night over the station grounds. The pilgrims used to turn out in a body and empty every rifle they could lay hands on at him. Some even had sat up o' nights for him. All his energy was wasted, though. 'That animal has a charmed life,' he said; 'but you can say this only of brutes in this country. No man—you apprehend me?—no man here bears a charmed life.' He stood there for a moment in the moonlight with his delicate hooked nose set a little askew, and his mica eyes glittering without a wink, then, with a curt Good-night, he strode off. I could see he was disturbed and considerably puzzled, which made me feel more hopeful than I had been for days. It was a great comfort to turn from that chap to my influential friend, the battered, twisted, ruined, tinpot steamboat. I clambered on board. She rang under my feet like an empty Huntley & Palmer biscuit-tin kicked along a gutter; she was nothing so solid in make, and rather less pretty in shape, but I had expended enough hard work on her to make me love her. No influential friend would have served me better. She had given me a chance to come out a bit—to find out what I could do. No, I don't like work. I had rather laze about and think of all the fine things that can be done. I don't like work—no man does—but I like what is in the work—the chance to find yourself. Your own reality—for yourself, not for others—what no other man can ever know. They can only see the mere show, and never can tell what it really means.

"I was not surprised to see somebody sitting aft, on the deck, with his legs dangling over the mud. You see I rather chummed with the few mechanics there were in that station, whom the other pilgrims naturally despised—on account of their imperfect manners, I suppose. This was the foreman—a boiler-maker by trade—a good worker. He was a lank, bony, yellow-faced man, with big intense eyes. His aspect was worried, and his head was as bald as the palm of my hand; but his hair in falling seemed to have stuck to his chin, and had prospered in the new locality, for his beard hung down to his waist. He was a widower with six young children (he had left them in charge of a sister of his to come out there), and the passion of his life was pigeon-flying. He was an enthusiast and a connoisseur. He would rave about pigeons. After work hours he used sometimes to come over from his hut for a talk about his children and his pigeons; at work, when he had to crawl in the mud under the bottom of the steamboat, he would tie up that beard of his in a kind of white serviette[3] he brought for the purpose. It had loops to go over his ears. In the evening he could be seen squatted on the bank rinsing that wrapper in the creek with great care, then spreading it solemnly on a bush to dry.

"I slapped him on the back and shouted 'We shall have rivets!' He scrambled to his feet exclaiming 'No! Rivets!' as though he couldn't believe his ears. Then in a low voice, 'You . . . eh?' I don't know why we behaved like lunatics. I put my finger to the side of my nose and nodded mysteriously. 'Good for you!' he cried, snapped his fingers above his head, lifting one foot. I tried a jig. We capered on the iron deck. A frightful clatter came out of that hulk, and the virgin forest on the other bank of the creek sent it back in a thundering roll upon the sleeping station. It must have made some of the pilgrims sit up in their hovels. A dark figure obscured the lighted doorway of the manager's hut, vanished, then, a second or so after, the doorway itself vanished too. We stopped, and the silence driven away by the stamping of our feet flowed back again from the recesses of the land. The great wall of vegetation, an exuberant and entangled mass of trunks, branches, leaves, boughs, festoons, motionless in the moonlight, was like a rioting invasion of soundless life, a rolling wave of plants, piled up, crested, ready to topple over the creek, to sweep every little man of us out of his little existence. And it moved not. A deadened burst of mighty splashes and snorts reached us from afar, as though an ichthyosaurus had been taking a bath of glitter in the great river. 'After all,' said the boiler-maker in a reasonable tone, 'why shouldn't we get the rivets?' Why not, indeed! I did not know of any reason why we shouldn't. 'They'll come in three weeks,' I said confidently.

"But they didn't. Instead of rivets there came an invasion, an infliction, a visitation. It came in sections during the next three weeks, each section headed by a donkey carrying a white man in new clothes and tan shoes, bowing from that elevation right and left to the impressed pilgrims. A quarrelsome

---

3. Table napkin.

band of footsore sulky niggers trod on the heels of the donkey; a lot of tents, camp-stools, tin boxes, white cases, brown bales would be shot down in the courtyard, and the air of mystery would deepen a little over the muddle of the station. Five such instalments came, with their absurd air of disorderly flight with the loot of innumerable outfit shops and provision stores, that, one would think, they were lugging, after a raid, into the wilderness for equitable division. It was an inextricable mess of things decent in themselves but that human folly made look like the spoils of thieving.

"This devoted band called itself the Eldorado Exploring Expedition, and I believe they were sworn to secrecy. Their talk, however, was the talk of sordid buccaneers: it was reckless without hardihood, greedy without audacity, and cruel without courage; there was not an atom of foresight or of serious intention in the whole batch of them, and they did not seem aware these things are wanted for the work of the world. To tear treasure out of the bowels of the land was their desire, with no more moral purpose at the back of it than there is in burglars breaking into a safe. Who paid the expenses of the noble enterprise I don't know; but the uncle of our manager was leader of that lot.

"In exterior he resembled a butcher in a poor neighbourhood, and his eyes had a look of sleepy cunning. He carried his fat paunch with ostentation on his short legs, and during the time his gang infested the station spoke to no one but his nephew. You could see these two roaming about all day long with their heads close together in an everlasting confab.

"I had given up worrying myself about the rivets. One's capacity for that kind of folly is more limited than you would suppose. I said Hang!—and let things slide. I had plenty of time for meditation, and now and then I would give some thought to Kurtz. I wasn't very interested in him. No. Still, I was curious to see whether this man, who had come out equipped with moral ideas of some sort, would climb to the top after all, and how he would set about his work when there."

2

"One evening as I was lying flat on the deck of my steamboat, I heard voices approaching—and there were the nephew and the uncle strolling along the bank. I laid my head on my arm again, and had nearly lost myself in a doze, when somebody said in my ear, as it were: 'I am as harmless as a little child, but I don't like to be dictated to. Am I the manager—or am I not? I was ordered to send him there. It's incredible.' . . . I became aware that the two were standing on the shore alongside the forepart of the steamboat, just below my head. I did not move; it did not occur to me to move: I was sleepy. 'It *is* unpleasant,' grunted the uncle. 'He has asked the Administration to be sent there,' said the other, 'with the idea of showing what he could do; and I was instructed accordingly. Look at the influence that man must have. Is it not frightful?' They both agreed it was frightful, then made several bizarre remarks: 'Make rain and fine weather—one man—the Council—by the nose'—bits of absurd sentences that got the better of my drowsiness, so that I had pretty near the whole of my wits about me when the uncle said, 'The climate may do away with this difficulty for you. Is he alone there?' 'Yes,' answered the manager; 'he sent his assistant down the river with a note to me in these terms: "Clear this poor devil out of the country, and don't bother sending more of that sort. I had rather be alone than have the kind of men you can dispose of with me." It was more than a year ago. Can you imagine such impudence?' 'Anything since then?' asked the other hoarsely. 'Ivory,' jerked the nephew; 'lots of it—prime sort—lots—most annoying, from him.' 'And with that?' questioned the heavy rumble. 'Invoice,' was the reply fired out, so to speak. Then silence. They had been talking about Kurtz.

"I was broad awake by this time, but, lying perfectly at ease, remained still, having no inducement to change my position. 'How did that ivory come all this way?' growled the elder man, who seemed very vexed. The other explained that it had come with a fleet of canoes in charge of an English half-caste clerk Kurtz had with him; that Kurtz had apparently intended to return himself, the station being by that time bare of goods and stores, but after coming three hundred miles, had suddenly decided to go back, which he started to do alone in a small dugout with four paddlers, leaving the half-caste to continue down the river with the ivory. The two fellows there seemed astounded at anybody attempting such a thing. They were at a loss for an adequate motive. As for me, I seemed to see Kurtz for the first time. It was a distinct glimpse: the dugout, four paddling savages, and the lone white man turning his back suddenly on the headquarters, on relief, on thoughts of home—perhaps; setting his face towards the depths of the wilderness, towards his empty and desolate station. I did not know the motive. Perhaps he was just simply a fine fellow who stuck to his work for its own sake. His name, you understand, had not been pronounced once. He was 'that man.' The half-caste, who, as far as I could see, had conducted a difficult trip with great prudence and pluck, was invariably alluded to as 'that scoundrel.' The 'scoundrel' had reported that the 'man' had been very ill—had recovered imperfectly. . . . The two below me moved away then a few paces, and strolled back and forth at some little distance. I heard: 'Military post—doctor—two hundred miles—quite alone now—unavoidable delays—nine months—no news—strange rumours.' They approached again, just as the manager was saying, 'No one, as far as I know, unless a species of wandering trader—a pestilential fellow, snapping ivory from the natives.' Who was it they were talking about now? I gathered in snatches that this was some man supposed to be in Kurtz's district, and of whom the manager did not approve. 'We will not be free from unfair competition till one of these fellows is hanged for an example,' he said. 'Certainly,' grunted the other; 'get him hanged! Why not? Anything—anything can be done in this country. That's what I say; nobody here, you understand, here, can endanger your position. And why? You stand the climate—you outlast them all. The danger is in Europe; but there before I left I took care to—' They moved off and whispered, then their voices rose again. 'The extraordinary series of delays is not my fault. I did my possible.'[4] The fat man sighed, 'Very sad.' 'And the pestiferous absurdity of his talk,' continued the other; 'he bothered me enough when he was here. "Each station should be like a beacon on the road towards better things, a centre for trade of course, but also for humanising, improving, instructing." Conceive you—that ass! And he wants to be manager! No, it's—' Here he got choked by excessive indignation, and I lifted my head the least bit. I was surprised to see how near they were—right under me. I could have spat upon their hats. They were

---

4. Conrad, who wrote and spoke French perfectly, sometimes slipped into a French usage when writing English. This is one of his Gallicisms, a literal rendering of *J'ai fait mon possible*.

looking on the ground, absorbed in thought. The manager was switching his leg with a slender twig: his sagacious relative lifted his head. 'You have been well since you came out this time?' he asked. The other gave a start. 'Who? I? Oh! Like a charm—like a charm. But the rest—oh, my goodness! All sick. They die so quick, too, that I haven't the time to send them out of the country—it's incredible!' 'H'm. Just so,' grunted the uncle. 'Ah! my boy, trust to this—I say, trust to this.' I saw him extend his short flipper of an arm for a gesture that took in the forest, the creek, the mud, the river—seemed to beckon with a dishonouring flourish before the sunlit face of the land a treacherous appeal to the lurking death, to the hidden evil, to the profound darkness of its heart. It was so startling that I leaped to my feet and looked back at the edge of the forest, as though I had expected an answer of some sort to that black display of confidence. You know the foolish notions that come to one sometimes. The high stillness confronted these two figures with its ominous patience, waiting for the passing away of a fantastic invasion.

"They swore aloud together—out of sheer fright, I believe—then, pretending not to know anything of my existence, turned back to the station. The sun was low; and leaning forward side by side, they seemed to be tugging painfully uphill their two ridiculous shadows of unequal length, that trailed behind them slowly over the tall grass without bending a single blade.

"In a few days the Eldorado Expedition went into the patient wilderness, that closed upon it as the sea closes over a diver. Long afterwards the news came that all the donkeys were dead. I know nothing as to the fate of the less valuable animals. They, no doubt, like the rest of us, found what they deserved. I did not inquire. I was then rather excited at the prospect of meeting Kurtz very soon. When I say very soon I mean it comparatively. It was just two months from the day we left the creek when we came to the bank below Kurtz's station.

"Going up that river was like travelling back to the earliest beginnings of the world, when vegetation rioted on the earth and the big trees were kings. An empty stream, a great silence, an impenetrable forest. The air was warm, thick, heavy, sluggish. There was no joy in the brilliance of sunshine. The long stretches of the waterway ran on, deserted, into the gloom of overshadowed distances. On silvery sandbanks hippos and alligators sunned themselves side by side. The broadening waters flowed through a mob of wooded islands; you lost your way on that river as you would in a desert, and butted all day long against shoals, trying to find the channel, till you thought yourself bewitched and cut off for ever from everything you had known once—somewhere—far away—in another existence perhaps. There were moments when one's past came back to one, as it will sometimes when you have not a moment to spare to yourself; but it came in the shape of an unrestful and noisy dream, remembered with wonder amongst the overwhelming realities of this strange world of plants, and water, and silence. And this stillness of life did not in the least resemble a peace. It was the stillness of an implacable force brooding over an inscrutable intention. It looked at you with a vengeful aspect. I got used to it afterwards; I did not see it any more; I had no time. I had to keep guessing at the channel; I had to discern, mostly by inspiration, the signs of hidden banks; I watched for sunken stones; I was learning to clap my teeth smartly before my heart flew out, when I shaved by a fluke some infernal sly old snag that would have ripped the life out of the tin-pot steamboat and drowned all the pilgrims; I had to keep a look-out for the signs of dead wood we could cut up in the night for next day's steaming. When you have to attend to things of that sort, to the mere incidents of the surface, the reality—the reality, I tell you—fades. The inner truth is hidden—luckily, luckily. But I felt it all the same; I felt often its mysterious stillness watching me at my monkey tricks, just as it watches you fellows performing on your respective tight-ropes for—what is it? half a crown a tumble—".

"Try to be civil, Marlow," growled a voice, and I knew there was at least one listener awake besides myself.

"I beg your pardon. I forgot the heartache which makes up the rest of the price. And indeed what does the price matter, if the trick be well done? You do your tricks very well. And I didn't do badly either, since I managed not to sink that steamboat on my first trip. It's a wonder to me yet. Imagine a blind-folded man set to drive a van over a bad road. I sweated and shivered over that business considerably, I can tell you. After all, for a seaman, to scrape the bottom of the thing that's supposed to float all the time under his care is the unpardonable sin. No one may know of it, but you never forget the thump—eh? A blow on the very heart. You remember it, you dream of it, you wake up at night and think of it—years after—and go hot and cold all over. I don't pretend to say that steamboat floated all the time. More than once she had to wade for a bit, with twenty cannibals splashing around and pushing. We had enlisted some of these chaps on the way for a crew. Fine fellows—cannibals—in their place. They were men one could work with, and I am grateful to them. And, after all, they did not eat each other before my face: they had brought along a provision of hippo-meat which went rotten, and made the mystery of the wilderness stink in my nostrils. Phoo! I can sniff it now. I had the manager on board and three or four pilgrims with their staves—all com-plete. Sometimes we came upon a station close by the bank, clinging to the skirts of the unknown, and the white men rushing out of a tumble-down hovel, with great gestures of joy and surprise and welcome, seemed very strange—had the appearance of being held there captive by a spell. The word 'ivory' would ring in the air for a while—and on we went again into the silence, along empty reaches, round the still bends, between the high walls of our winding way, reverberating in hollow claps the ponderous beat of the stern-wheel. Trees, trees, millions of trees, massive, immense, running up high; and at their foot, hugging the bank against the stream, crept the little begrimed steamboat, like a sluggish beetle crawling on the floor of a lofty portico. It made you feel very small, very lost, and yet it was not altogether depressing, that feeling. After all, if you were small, the grimy beetle crawled on—which was just what you wanted it to do. Where the pilgrims imagined it crawled to I don't know. To some place where they expected to get something, I bet! For me it crawled towards Kurtz—exclusively; but when the steam-pipes started leaking we crawled very slow. The reaches opened before us and closed behind, as if the forest had stepped leisurely across the water to bar the way for our return. We penetrated deeper and deeper into the heart of darkness. It was very quiet there. At night sometimes the roll of drums behind the curtain of trees would run up the river and remain sustained faintly, as if hovering in the air high over our heads, till the first break of day. Whether it meant war, peace, or prayer we could not tell. The dawns were heralded by the descent of a chill stillness; the woodcutters slept, their fires burned low; the snapping of a twig would make you start. We were wanderers on a prehistoric earth, on an earth that wore the aspect of an unknown planet. We could have fancied ourselves the first of men taking possession of an accursed inheritance, to be subdued at the cost of profound anguish and of excessive toil. But suddenly, as we struggled round a bend, there would be a glimpse of rush walls, of peaked grass-roofs, a burst of yells, a whirl of black limbs, a mass of hands clapping, of feet stamping, of bodies swaying, of eyes rolling, under the droop of heavy and motionless foliage. The steamer toiled along slowly on the edge of a black and incomprehensible frenzy. The prehistoric man was cursing us, praying to us, welcoming us—who could tell? We were cut off from the comprehension of our surroundings; we glided past like phantoms, wondering and secretly appalled, as sane men would be before an enthusiastic outbreak in a madhouse. We could not understand because we were too far and could not remember, because we were travelling in the night of first ages, of those ages that are gone, leaving hardly a sign—and no memories.

"The earth seemed unearthly. We are accustomed to look upon the shack-led form of a conquered monster, but there—there you could look at a thing monstrous and free. It was unearthly, and the men were— No, they were not inhuman. Well, you know, that was the worst of it—this suspicion of their not being inhuman. It would come slowly to one. They howled and leaped, and spun, and made horrid faces; but what thrilled you was just the thought of their humanity—like yours—the thought of your remote kinship with this wild and passionate uproar. Ugly. Yes, it was ugly enough; but if you were man enough you would admit to yourself that there was in you just the faintest trace of a response to the terrible frankness of that noise, a dim suspicion of there being a meaning in it which you—you so remote from the night of first ages—could comprehend. And why not? The mind of man is capable of anything—because everything is in it, all the past as well as all the future. What was there after all? Joy, fear, sorrow, devotion, valour, rage—who can tell?—but truth —truth stripped of its cloak of time. Let the fool gape and shudder—the man knows, and can look on without a wink. But he must at least be as much of a man as these on the shore. He must meet that truth with his own true stuff—with his own inborn strength. Principles? Principles won't do. Acquisitions, clothes, pretty rags—rags that would fly off at the first good shake. No; you want a deliberate belief. An appeal to me in this fiendish row— is there? Very well; I hear; I admit, but I have a voice too, and for good or evil mine is the speech that cannot be silenced. Of course, a fool, what with sheer fright and fine sentiments, is always safe. Who's that grunting? You wonder I didn't go ashore for a howl and a dance? Well, no—I didn't. Fine sentiments, you say? Fine sentiments be hanged! I had no time. I had to mess about with white-lead and strips of woollen blanket helping to put bandages on those leaky steam-pipes—I tell you. I had to watch the steering, and circumvent those snags, and get the tin-pot along by hook or by crook. There was surface-truth enough in these things to save a wiser man. And between whiles I had to look after the savage who was fireman. He was an improved specimen; he could fire up a vertical boiler. He was there below me, and, upon my word, to look at him was as edifying as seeing a dog in a parody of breeches and a feather hat, walking on his hind legs. A few months of training had done for that really fine chap. He squinted at the steam-gauge and at the water-gauge with an evident effort of intrepidity—and he had filed teeth too, the poor devil, and the wool of his pate shaved into queer patterns, and three ornamental scars on each of his cheeks. He ought to have been clapping his hands and stamping his feet on the bank, instead of which he was hard at work, a thrall to strange witchcraft, full of improving knowledge. He was useful because he had been instructed; and what he knew was this—that should the water in that transparent thing disappear, the evil spirit inside the boiler would get angry through the greatness of his thirst, and take a terrible vengeance. So he sweated and fired up and watched the glass fearfully (with an impromptu charm, made of rags, tied to his arm, and a piece of polished bone, as big as a watch, stuck flatways through his lower lip), while the wooded banks slipped past us slowly, the short noise was left behind, the interminable miles of silence—and we crept on, towards Kurtz. But the snags were thick, the water was treacherous and shallow, the boiler seemed indeed to have a sulky devil in it, and thus neither that fireman nor I had any time to peer into our creepy thoughts.

"Some fifty miles below the Inner Station we came upon a hut of reeds, an inclined and melancholy pole, with the unrecognisable tatters of what had been a flag of some sort flying from it, and a neatly stacked wood-pile. This was unexpected. We came to the bank, and on the stack of firewood found a flat piece of board with some faded pencil-writing on it. When deciphered it said: 'Wood for you. Hurry up. Approach cautiously.' There was a signature, but it was illegible—not Kurtz—a much longer word. Hurry up. Where? Up the river? 'Approach cautiously.' We had not done so. But the warning could not have been meant for the place where it could be only found after approach. Something was wrong above. But what—and how much? That was the question. We commented adversely upon the imbecility of that telegraphic style. The bush around said nothing, and would not let us look very far, either. A torn curtain of red twill hung in the doorway of the hut, and flapped sadly in our faces. The dwelling was dismantled; but we could see a white man had lived there not very long ago. There remained a rude table— a plank on two posts; a heap of rubbish reposed in a dark corner, and by the door I picked up a book. It had lost its covers, and the pages had been thumbed into a state of extremely dirty softness; but the back had been lovingly stitched afresh with white cotton thread, which looked clean yet. It was an extraordinary find. Its title was, An Inquiry into some Points of Seamanship, by a man Towser, Towson—some such name—Master in His Majesty's Navy. The matter looked dreary reading enough, with illustrative diagrams and repulsive tables of figures, and the copy was sixty years old. I handled this amazing antiquity with the greatest possible tenderness, lest it should dissolve in my hands. Within, Towson or Towser was inquiring earnestly into the breaking strain of ships' chains and tackle, and other such matters. Not a very enthralling book; but at the first glance you could see there a singleness of intention, an honest concern for the right way of going to work, which made these humble pages, thought out so many years ago, luminous with another than a professional light. The simple old sailor, with his talk of chains and purchases, made me forget the jungle and the pilgrims in a delicious sensation of having come upon something unmistakably real. Such a book being there was wonderful enough; but still more astounding were the notes pencilled in the margin, and plainly referring to the text. I couldn't believe my eyes! They were in cipher! Yes, it looked like cipher. Fancy a man lugging with him a book of that description into this nowhere and studying it—and making notes—in cipher at that! It was an extravagant mystery.

"I had been dimly aware for some time of a worrying noise, and when I lifted my eyes I saw the wood-pile was gone, and the manager, aided by all the pilgrims, was shouting at me from the river-side. I slipped the book into my pocket. I assure you to leave off reading was like tearing myself away from the shelter of an old and solid friendship.

"I started the lame engine ahead. 'It must be this miserable trader—this intruder,' exclaimed the manager, looking back malevolently at the place we had left. 'He must be English,' I said. 'It will not save him from getting into trouble if he is not careful,' muttered the manager darkly. I observed with assumed innocence that no man was safe from trouble in this world.

"The current was more rapid now, the steamer seemed at her last gasp, the stern-wheel flopped languidly, and I caught myself listening on tiptoe for the next beat of the float,[5] for in sober truth I expected the wretched thing to give up every moment. It was like watching the last flickers of a life. But still we crawled. Sometimes I would pick out a tree a little way ahead to measure our progress towards Kurtz by, but I lost it invariably before we got abreast. To keep the eyes so long on one thing was too much for human patience. The manager displayed a beautiful resignation. I fretted and fumed and took to arguing with myself whether or no I would talk openly with Kurtz; but before I could come to any conclusion it occurred to me that my speech or my silence, indeed any action of mine, would be a mere futility. What did it matter what any one knew or ignored? What did it matter who was manager? One gets sometimes such a flash of insight. The essentials of this affair lay deep under the surface, beyond my reach, and beyond my power of meddling.

"Towards the evening of the second day we judged ourselves about eight miles from Kurtz's station. I wanted to push on; but the manager looked grave, and told me the navigation up there was so dangerous that it would be advisable, the sun being very low already, to wait where we were till next morning. Moreover, he pointed out that if the warning to approach cautiously were to be followed, we must approach in daylight—not at dusk, or in the dark. This was sensible enough. Eight miles meant nearly three hours' steaming for us, and I could also see suspicious ripples at the upper end of the reach. Nevertheless, I was annoyed beyond expression at the delay, and most unreasonably too, since one night more could not matter much after so many months. As we had plenty of wood, and caution was the word, I brought up in the middle of the stream. The reach was narrow, straight, with high sides like a railway cutting. The dusk came gliding into it long before the sun had set. The current ran smooth and swift, but a dumb immobility sat on the banks. The living trees, lashed together by the creepers and every living bush of the undergrowth, might have been changed into stone, even to the slenderest twig, to the lightest leaf. It was not sleep—it seemed unnatural, like a state of trance. Not the faintest sound of any kind could be heard. You looked on amazed, and began to suspect yourself of being deaf—then the night came suddenly, and struck you blind as well. About three in the morning some large fish leaped, and the loud splash made me jump as though a gun had been fired. When the sun rose there was a white fog, very warm and clammy, and more

---

5. Automatic water-level regulator opening and closing a water-supply valve.

blinding than the night. It did not shift or drive; it was just there, standing all round you like something solid. At eight or nine, perhaps, it lifted as a shutter lifts. We had a glimpse of the towering multitude of trees, of the immense matted jungle, with the blazing little ball of the sun hanging over it—all perfectly still—and then the white shutter came down again, smoothly, as if sliding in greased grooves. I ordered the chain, which we had begun to heave in, to be paid out again. Before it stopped running with a muffled rattle, a cry, a very loud cry, as of infinite desolation, soared slowly in the opaque air. It ceased. A complaining clamour, modulated in savage discords, filled our ears. The sheer unexpectedness of it made my hair stir under my cap. I don't know how it struck the others: to me it seemed as though the mist itself had screamed, so suddenly, and apparently from all sides at once, did this tumultuous and mournful uproar arise. It culminated in a hurried outbreak of almost intolerably excessive shrieking, which stopped short, leaving us stiffened in a variety of silly attitudes, and obstinately listening to the nearly as appalling and excessive silence. 'Good God! What is the meaning—?' stammered at my elbow one of the pilgrims—a little fat man, with sandy hair and red whiskers, who wore side-spring boots, and pink pyjamas tucked into his socks. Two others remained open-mouthed a whole minute, then dashed into the little cabin, to rush out incontinently and stand darting scared glances, with Winchesters at 'ready' in their hands. What we could see was just the steamer we were on, her outlines blurred as though she had been on the point of dissolving, and a misty strip of water, perhaps two feet broad, around her—and that was all. The rest of the world was nowhere, as far as our eyes and ears were concerned. Just nowhere. Gone, disappeared; swept off without leaving a whisper or a shadow behind.

"I went forward, and ordered the chain to be hauled in short, so as to be ready to trip the anchor and move the steamboat at once if necessary. 'Will they attack?' whispered an awed voice. 'We will all be butchered in this fog,' murmured another. The faces twitched with the strain, the hands trembled slightly, the eyes forgot to wink. It was very curious to see the contrast of expressions of the white men and of the black fellows of our crew, who were as much strangers to that part of the river as we, though their homes were only eight hundred miles away. The whites, of course greatly discomposed, had besides a curious look of being painfully shocked by such an outrageous row. The others had an alert, naturally interested expression; but their faces were essentially quiet, even those of the one or two who grinned as they hauled at the chain. Several exchanged short, grunting phrases, which seemed to settle the matter to their satisfaction. Their headman, a young, broad-chested black, severely draped in dark-blue fringed cloths, with fierce nostrils and his hair all done up artfully in oily ringlets, stood near me. 'Aha!' I said, just for good fellowship's sake. 'Catch 'im,' he snapped, with a bloodshot widening of his eyes and a flash of sharp teeth—'catch 'im. Give 'im to us.' 'To you, eh?' I asked; 'what would you do with them?' 'Eat 'im!' he said curtly, and, leaning his elbow on the rail, looked out into the fog in a dignified and profoundly pensive attitude. I would no doubt have been properly horrified, had it not occurred to me that he and his chaps must be very hungry: that they must have been growing increasingly hungry for at least this month past. They had been engaged for six months (I don't think a single one of them had any clear idea of time, as we at the end of countless ages have. They still belonged to the beginnings of time—had no inherited experience to teach them, as it were), and of course, as long as there was a piece of paper written over in accordance with some farcical law or other made down the river, it didn't enter anybody's head to trouble how they would live. Certainly they had brought with them some rotten hippo-meat, which couldn't have lasted very long, anyway, even if the pilgrims hadn't, in the midst of a shocking hullaba-loo, thrown a considerable quantity of it overboard. It looked like a high-handed proceeding; but it was really a case of legitimate self-defence. You can't breathe dead hippo waking, sleeping, and eating, and at the same time keep your precarious grip on existence. Besides that, they had given them every week three pieces of brass wire, each about nine inches long; and the theory was they were to buy their provisions with that currency in river-side villages. You can see how *that* worked. There were either no villages, or the people were hostile, or the director, who like the rest of us fed out of tins, with an occasional old he-goat thrown in, didn't want to stop the steamer for some more or less recondite reasons. So, unless they swallowed the wire itself, or made loops of it to snare the fishes with, I don't see what good their extravagant salary could be to them. I must say it was paid with a regularity worthy of a large and honourable trading company. For the rest, the only thing to eat—though it didn't look eatable in the least—I saw in their possession was a few lumps of some stuff like half-cooked dough, of a dirty lavender colour, they kept wrapped in leaves, and now and then swallowed a piece of, but so small that it seemed done more for the look of the thing than for any serious purpose of sustenance. Why in the name of all the gnawing devils of hunger they didn't go for us—they were thirty to five—and have a good tuck-in for once, amazes me now when I think of it. They were big powerful men, with not much capacity to weigh the consequences, with courage, with strength, even yet, though their skins were no longer glossy and their muscles no longer hard. And I saw that something restraining, one of those human secrets that baffle probability, had come into play there. I looked at them with a swift quickening of interest—not because it occurred to me I might be eaten by them before very long, though I own to you that just then I perceived—in a new light, as it were—how unwholesome the pilgrims looked, and I hoped, yes, I positively hoped, that my aspect was not so—what shall I say?—so—unappetising: a touch of fantastic vanity which fitted well with the dream-sensation that per-vaded all my days at that time. Perhaps I had a little fever too. One can't live with one's finger everlastingly on one's pulse. I had often 'a little fever,' or a little touch of other things—the playful paw-strokes of the wilderness, the preliminary trifling before the more serious onslaught which came in due course. Yes; I looked at them as you would on any human being, with a curios-ity of their impulses, motives, capacities, weaknesses, when brought to the test of an inexorable physical necessity. Restraint! What possible restraint? Was it superstition, disgust, patience, fear—or some kind of primitive honour? No fear can stand up to hunger, no patient can wear it out, disgust simply does not exist where hunger is; and as to superstition, beliefs, and what you may call principles, they are less than chaff in a breeze. Don't you know the devilry of lingering starvation, its exasperating torment, its black thoughts, its sombre and brooding ferocity? Well, I do. It takes a man all his inborn strength to fight hunger properly. It's really easier to face bereavement, dishonour, and the perdition of one's soul—than this kind of prolonged hunger. Sad, but true.

And these chaps too had no earthly reason for any kind of scruple. Restraint! I would just as soon have expected restraint from a hyena prowling amongst the corpses of a battlefield. But there was the fact facing me—the fact dazzling, to be seen, like the foam on the depths of the sea, like a ripple on an unfathomable enigma, a mystery greater—when I thought of it—than the curious, inexplicable note of desperate grief in this savage clamour that had swept by us on the river-bank, behind the blind whiteness of the fog.

"Two pilgrims were quarrelling in hurried whispers as to which bank. 'Left.' 'No, no; how can you? Right, right, of course.' 'It is very serious,' said the manager's voice behind me; 'I would be desolated if anything should happen to Mr. Kurtz before we came up.' I looked at him, and had not the slightest doubt he was sincere. He was just the kind of man who would wish to preserve appearances. That was his restraint. But when he muttered something about going on at once, I did not even take the trouble to answer him. I knew, and he knew, that it was impossible. Were we to let go our hold of the bottom, we would be absolutely in the air—in space. We wouldn't be able to tell where we were going to—whether up or down stream, or across—till we fetched against one bank or the other—and then we wouldn't know at first which it was. Of course I made no move. I had no mind for a smash-up. You couldn't imagine a more deadly place for a shipwreck. Whether drowned at once or not, we were sure to perish speedily in one way or another. 'I authorise you to take all the risks,' he said, after a short silence. 'I refuse to take any,' I said shortly; which was just the answer he expected, though its tone might have surprised him. 'Well, I must defer to your judgment. You are captain,' he said, with marked civility. I turned my shoulder to him in sign of my appreciation, and looked into the fog. How long would it last? It was the most hopeless lookout. The approach to this Kurtz grubbing for ivory in the wretched bush was beset by as many dangers as though he had been an enchanted princess sleeping in a fabulous castle. 'Will they attack, do you think?' asked the manager, in a confidential tone.

"I did not think they would attack, for several obvious reasons. The thick fog was one. If they left the bank in their canoes they would get lost in it, as we would be if we attempted to move. Still, I had also judged the jungle of both banks quite impenetrable—and yet eyes were in it, eyes that had seen us. The river-side bushes were certainly very thick; but the undergrowth behind was evidently penetrable. However, during the short lift I had seen no canoes anywhere in the reach—certainly not abreast of the steamer. But what made the idea of attack inconceivable to me was the nature of the noise—of the cries we had heard. They had not the fierce character boding of immediate hostile intention. Unexpected, wild, and violent as they had been, they had given me an irresistible impression of sorrow. The glimpse of the steamboat had for some reason filled those savages with unrestrained grief. The danger, if any, I expounded, was from our proximity to a great human passion let loose. Even extreme grief may ultimately vent itself in violence—but more generally takes the form of apathy. . . .

"You should have seen the pilgrims stare! They had no heart to grin, or even to revile me; but I believe they thought me gone mad—with fright, maybe. I delivered a regular lecture. My dear boys, it was no good bothering. Keep a look-out? Well, you may guess I watched the fog for the signs of lifting as a cat watches a mouse; but for anything else our eyes were of no more use to us than if we had been buried miles deep in a heap of cotton-wool. It felt like it too—choking, warm, stifling. Besides, all I said, though it sounded extravagant, was absolutely true to fact. What we afterwards alluded to as an attack was really an attempt at repulse. The action was very far from being aggressive—it was not even defensive, in the usual sense: it was undertaken under the stress of desperation, and in its essence was purely protective.

"It developed itself, I should say, two hours after the fog lifted, and its commencement was at a spot, roughly speaking, about a mile and a half below Kurtz's station. We had just floundered and flopped round a bend, when I saw an islet, a mere grassy hummock of bright green, in the middle of the stream. It was the only thing of the kind; but as we opened the reach more, I perceived it was the head of a long sandbank, or rather of a chain of shallow patches stretching down the middle of the river. They were discoloured, just awash, and the whole lot was seen just under the water, exactly as a man's backbone is seen running down the middle of his back under the skin. Now, as far as I did see, I could go to the right or to the left of this. I didn't know either channel, of course. The banks looked pretty well alike, the depth appeared the same; but as I had been informed the station was on the west side, I naturally headed for the western passage.

"No sooner had we fairly entered it than I became aware it was much narrower than I had supposed. To the left of us there was the long uninterrupted shoal, and to the right a high steep bank heavily overgrown with bushes. Above the bush the trees stood in serried ranks. The twigs overhung the current thickly, and from distance to distance a large limb of some tree projected rigidly over the stream. It was then well on in the afternoon, the face of the forest was gloomy, and a broad strip of shadow had already fallen on the water. In this shadow we steamed up—very slowly, as you may imagine. I sheered her well inshore—the water being deepest near the bank, as the sounding-pole informed me.

"One of my hungry and forbearing friends was sounding in the bows just below me. This steamboat was exactly like a decked scow. On the deck there were two little teak-wood houses, with doors and windows. The boiler was in the fore-end, and the machinery right astern. Over the whole there was a light roof, supported on stanchions. The funnel projected through that roof, and in front of the funnel a small cabin built of light planks served for a pilot-house. It contained a couch, two camp-stools, a loaded Martini-Henry[6] leaning in one corner, a tiny table, and the steering-wheel. It had a wide door in front and a broad shutter at each side. All these were always thrown open, of course. I spent my days perched up there on the extreme fore-end of that roof, before the door. At night I slept, or tried to, on the couch. An athletic black belonging to some coast tribe, and educated by my poor predecessor, was the helmsman. He sported a pair of brass earrings, wore a blue cloth wrapper from the waist to the ankles, and thought all the world of himself. He was the most unstable kind of fool I had ever seen. He steered with no end of a swagger while you were by; but if he lost sight of you, he became instantly the prey of an abject funk, and would let that cripple of a steamboat get the upper hand of him in a minute.

"I was looking down at the sounding-pole, and feeling much annoyed to

6. Rifle combining the seven-grooved barrel of the Scottish gunmaker A. Henry with the block-action breech mechanism introduced by the Swiss inventor F. Martini.

see at each try a little more of it stick out of that river, when I saw my poleman give up the business suddenly, and stretch himself flat on the deck, without even taking the trouble to haul his pole in. He kept hold on it though, and it trailed in the water. At the same time the fireman, whom I could also see below me, sat down abruptly before his furnace and ducked his head. I was amazed. Then I had to look at the river mighty quick, because there was a snag in the fairway. Sticks, little sticks, were flying about—thick; they were whizzing before my nose, dropping below me, striking behind me against my pilot-house. All this time the river, the shore, the woods, were very quiet—perfectly quiet. I could only hear the heavy splashing thump of the stern-wheel and the patter of these things. We cleared the snag clumsily. Arrows, by Jove! We were being shot at! I stepped in quickly to close the shutter on the land-side. That fool-helmsman, his hands on the spokes, was lifting his knees high, stamping his feet, champing his mouth, like a reined-in horse. Confound him! And we were staggering within ten feet of the bank. I had to lean right out to swing the heavy shutter, and I saw a face amongst the leaves on the level with my own, looking at me very fierce and steady; and then suddenly, as though a veil had been removed from my eyes, I made out, deep in the tangled gloom, naked breasts, arms, legs, glaring eyes—the bush was swarming with human limbs in movement, glistening, of bronze colour. The twigs shook, swayed, and rustled, the arrows flew out of them, and then the shutter came to. 'Steer her straight,' I said to the helmsman. He held his head rigid, face forward; but his eyes rolled, he kept on lifting and setting down his feet gently, his mouth foamed a little. 'Keep quiet!' I said in a fury. I might just as well have ordered a tree not to sway in the wind. I darted out. Below me there was a great scuffle of feet on the iron deck; confused exclamations; a voice screamed, 'Can you turn back?' I caught sight of a V-shaped ripple on the water ahead. What? Another snag! A fusillade burst out under my feet. The pilgrims had opened with their Winchesters, and were simply squirting lead into that bush. A deuce of a lot of smoke came up and drove slowly forward. I swore at it. Now I couldn't see the ripple or the snag either. I stood in the doorway, peering, and the arrows came in swarms. They might have been poisoned, but they looked as though they wouldn't kill a cat. The bush began to howl. Our wood-cutters raised a warlike whoop; the report of a rifle just at my back deafened me. I glanced over my shoulder, and the pilot-house was yet full of noise and smoke when I made a dash at the wheel. The fool-nigger had dropped everything, to throw the shutter open and let off that Martini-Henry. He stood before the wide opening, glaring, and I yelled at him to come back, while I straightened the sudden twist out of that steamboat. There was no room to turn even if I had wanted to, the snag was somewhere very near ahead in that confounded smoke, there was no time to lose, so I just crowded her into the bank—right into the bank, where I knew the water was deep.

"We tore slowly along the overhanging bushes in a whirl of broken twigs and flying leaves. The fusillade below stopped short, as I had foreseen it would when the squirts got empty. I threw my head back to a glinting whizz that traversed the pilot-house, in at one shutter-hole and out at the other. Looking past that mad helmsman, who was shaking the empty rifle and yelling at the shore, I saw vague forms of men running bent double, leaping, gliding, distinct, incomplete, evanescent. Something big appeared in the air before the shutter, the rifle went overboard, and the man stepped back swiftly, looked at me over his shoulder in an extraordinary, profound, familiar manner, and fell upon my feet. The side of his head hit the wheel twice, and the end of what appeared a long cane clattered round and knocked over a little camp-stool. It looked as though after wrenching that thing from somebody ashore he had lost his balance in the effort. The thin smoke had blown away, we were clear of the snag, and looking ahead I could see that in another hundred yards or so I would be free to sheer off, away from the bank; but my feet felt so very warm and wet that I had to look down. The man had rolled on his back and stared straight up at me; both his hands clutched that cane. It was the shaft of a spear that, either thrown or lunged through the opening, had caught him in the side just below the ribs; the blade had gone in out of sight, after making a frightful gash; my shoes were full; a pool of blood lay very still, gleaming dark-red under the wheel; his eyes shone with an amazing lustre. The fusillade burst out again. He looked at me anxiously, gripping the spear like something precious, with an air of being afraid I would try to take it away from him. I had to make an effort to free my eyes from his gaze and attend to the steering. With one hand I felt above my head for the line of the steam whistle, and jerked out screech after screech hurriedly. The tumult of angry and warlike yells was checked instantly, and then from the depths of the woods went out such a tremulous and prolonged wail of mournful fear and utter despair as may be imagined to follow the flight of the last hope from the earth. There was a great commotion in the bush; the shower of arrows stopped, a few dropping shots rang out sharply—then silence, in which the languid beat of the stern-wheel came plainly to my ears. I put the helm hard a-starboard at the moment when the pilgrim in pink pyjamas, very hot and agitated, appeared in the doorway. 'The manager sends me—' he began in an official tone, and stopped short. 'Good God!' he said, glaring at the wounded man.

"We two whites stood over him, and his lustrous and inquiring glance enveloped us both. I declare it looked as though he would presently put to us some question in an understandable language; but he died without uttering a sound, without moving a limb, without twitching a muscle. Only in the very last moment, as though in response to some sign we could not see, to some whisper we could not hear, he frowned heavily, and that frown gave to his black death-mask an inconceivably sombre, brooding, and menacing expression. The lustre of inquiring glance faded swiftly into vacant glassiness. 'Can you steer?' I asked the agent eagerly. He looked very dubious; but I made a grab at his arm, and he understood at once I meant him to steer whether or no. To tell you the truth, I was morbidly anxious to change my shoes and socks. 'He is dead,' murmured the fellow, immensely impressed. 'No doubt about it,' said I, tugging like mad at the shoe-laces. 'And by the way, I suppose Mr. Kurtz is dead as well by this time.'

"For the moment that was the dominant thought. There was a sense of extreme disappointment, as though I had found out I had been striving after something altogether without a substance. I couldn't have been more disgusted if I had travelled all this way for the sole purpose of talking with Mr. Kurtz. Talking with . . . I flung one shoe overboard, and became aware that that was exactly what I had been looking forward to—a talk with Kurtz. I made the strange discovery that I had never imagined him as doing, you know, but as discoursing. I didn't say to myself, 'Now I will never see him,' or 'Now I will never shake him by the hand,' but, 'Now I will never hear him.' The man presented himself as a voice. Not of course that I did not connect him with some sort of action. Hadn't I been told in all the tones of jealousy and admiration that he had collected, bartered, swindled, or stolen more ivory than all the other agents together? That was not the point. The point was in his being a gifted creature, and that of all his gifts the one that stood out pre-eminently, that carried with it a sense of real presence, was his ability to talk, his words—the gift of expression, the bewildering, the illuminating, the most exalted and the most contemptible, the pulsating stream of light, or the deceitful flow from the heart of an impenetrable darkness.

"The other shoe went flying unto the devil-god of that river. I thought, By Jove! it's all over. We are too late; he has vanished—the gift has vanished, by means of some spear, arrow, or club. I will never hear that chap speak after all—and my sorrow had a startling extravagance of emotion, even such as I had noticed in the howling sorrow of these savages in the bush. I couldn't have felt more of lonely desolation somehow, had I been robbed of a belief or had missed my destiny in life. . . . Why do you sigh in this beastly way, somebody? Absurd? Well, absurd. Good Lord! mustn't a man ever—Here, give me some tobacco." . . .

There was a pause of profound stillness, then a match flared, and Marlow's lean face appeared, worn, hollow, with downward folds and dropped eyelids, with an aspect of concentrated attention; and as he took vigorous draws at his pipe, it seemed to retreat and advance out of the night in the regular flicker of the tiny flame. The match went out.

"Absurd!" he cried. "This is the worst of trying to tell . . . Here you all are, each moored with two good addresses, like a hulk with two anchors, a butcher round one corner, a policeman round another, excellent appetites, and temperature normal—you hear—normal from year's end to year's end. And you say, Absurd! Absurd be—exploded! Absurd! My dear boys, what can you expect from a man who out of sheer nervousness had just flung overboard a pair of new shoes? Now I think of it, it is amazing I did not shed tears. I am, upon the whole, proud of my fortitude. I was cut to the quick at the idea of having lost the inestimable privilege of listening to the gifted Kurtz. Of course I was wrong. The privilege was waiting for me. Oh yes, I heard more than enough. And I was right, too. A voice. He was very little more than a voice. And I heard—him—it—this voice—other voices—all of them were so little more than voices—and the memory of that time itself lingers around me, impalpable, like a dying vibration of one immense jabber, silly, atrocious, sordid, savage, or simply mean, without any kind of sense. Voices, voices—even the girl herself—now—"

He was silent for a long time.

"I laid the ghost of his gifts at last with a lie," he began suddenly. "Girl! What? Did I mention a girl? Oh, she is out of it—completely. They—the women I mean—are out of it—should be out of it. We must help them to stay in that beautiful world of their own, lest ours gets worse. Oh, she had to be out of it. You should have heard the disinterred body of Mr. Kurtz saying, 'My Intended.' You would have perceived directly then how completely she was out of it. And the lofty frontal bone of Mr. Kurtz! They say the hair goes on growing sometimes, but this—ah—specimen was impressively bald. The wilderness had patted him on the head, and, behold, it was like a ball—an ivory ball; it had caressed him, and—lo!—he had withered; it had taken him, loved him, embraced him, got into his veins, consumed his flesh, and sealed his soul to its own by the inconceivable ceremonies of some devilish initiation. He was its spoiled and pampered favourite. Ivory? I should think so. Heaps of it, stacks of it. The old mud shanty was bursting with it. You would think there was not a single tusk left either above or below the ground in the whole country. 'Mostly fossil,' the manager had remarked disparagingly. It was no more fossil than I am; but they call it fossil when it is dug up. It appears these niggers do bury the tusks sometimes—but evidently they couldn't bury this parcel deep enough to save the gifted Mr. Kurtz from his fate. We filled the steamboat with it, and had to pile a lot on the deck. Thus he could see and enjoy as long as he could see, because the appreciation of this favour had remained with him to the last. You should have heard him say, 'My ivory.' Oh yes, I heard him. 'My Intended, my ivory, my station, my river, my—' everything belonged to him. It made me hold my breath in expectation of hearing the wilderness burst into a prodigious peal of laughter that would shake the fixed stars in their places. Everything belonged to him—but that was a trifle. The thing was to know what he belonged to, how many powers of darkness claimed him for their own. That was the reflection that made you creepy all over. It was impossible—it was not good for one either—trying to imagine. He had taken a high seat amongst the devils of the land—I mean literally. You can't understand. How could you?—with solid pavement under your feet, surrounded by kind neighbours ready to cheer you or to fall on you, stepping delicately between the butcher and the policeman, in the holy terror of scandal and gallows and lunatic asylums—how can you imagine what particular region of the first ages a man's untrammelled feet may take him into by the way of solitude—utter solitude without a policeman—by the way of silence—utter silence, where no warning voice of a kind neighbour can be heard whispering of public opinion? These little things make all the great difference. When they are gone you must fall back upon your own innate strength, upon your own capacity for faithfulness. Of course you may be too much of a fool to go wrong—too dull even to know you are being assaulted by the powers of darkness. I take it, no fool ever made a bargain for his soul with the devil: the fool is too much of a fool, or the devil too much of a devil—I don't know which. Or you may be such a thunderingly exalted creature as to be altogether deaf and blind to anything but heavenly sights and sounds. Then the earth for you is only a standing place—and whether to be like this is your loss or your gain I won't pretend to say. But most of us are neither one nor the other. The earth for us is a place to live in, where we must put up with sights, with sounds, with smells, too, by Jove!—breathe dead hippo, so to speak, and not be contaminated. And there, don't you see? your strength comes in, the faith in your ability for the digging of unostentatious holes to bury the stuff in— your power of devotion, not to yourself, but to an obscure, back-breaking business. And that's difficult enough. Mind, I am not trying to excuse or even explain—I am trying to account to myself for—for—Mr. Kurtz—for the shade of Mr. Kurtz. This initiated wraith from the back of Nowhere honoured me with its amazing confidence before it vanished altogether. This was because it could speak English to me. The original Kurtz had been educated partly in England, and—as he was good enough to say himself—his sympathies were in the right place. His mother was half-English, his father was half-French. All Europe contributed to the making of Kurtz; and by and by I learned that, most appropriately, the International Society for the Suppression of Savage Customs had entrusted him with the making of a report, for its future guidance. And he had written it too. I've seen it. I've read it. It was eloquent, vibrating with eloquence, but too high-strung, I think. Seventeen pages of close writing he had found time for! But this must have been before his—let us say—nerves went wrong, and caused him to preside at certain midnight dances ending with unspeakable rites, which—as far as I reluctantly gathered from what I heard at various times—were offered up to him—do you understand?—to Mr. Kurtz himself. But it was a beautiful piece of writing. The opening paragraph, however, in the light of later information, strikes me now as ominous. He began with the argument that we whites, from the point of development we had arrived at, 'must necessarily appear to them [savages] in the nature of supernatural beings—we approach them with the might as of a deity,' and so on, and so on. 'By the simple exercise of our will we can exert a power for good practically unbounded,' etc. etc. From that point he soared and took me with him. The peroration was magnificent, though difficult to remember, you know. It gave me the notion of an exotic Immensity ruled by an august Benevolence. It made me tingle with enthusiasm. This was the unbounded power of eloquence—of words—of burning noble words. There were no practical hints to interrupt the magic current of phrases, unless a kind of note at the foot of the last page, scrawled evidently much later, in an unsteady hand, may be regarded as the exposition of a method. It was very simple, and at the end of that moving appeal to every altruistic sentiment it blazed at you, luminous and terrifying, like a flash of lightning in a serene sky: 'Exterminate all the brutes!' The curious part was that he had apparently forgotten all about that valuable postscriptum, because, later on, when he in a sense came to himself, he repeatedly entreated me to take good care of 'my pamphlet' (he called it), as it was sure to have in the future a good influence upon his career. I had full information about all these things, and, besides, as it turned out, I was to have the care of his memory. I've done enough for it to give me the indisputable right to lay it, if I choose, for an everlasting rest in the dust-bin of progress, amongst all the sweepings and, figuratively speaking, all the dead cats of civilisation. But then, you see, I can't choose. He won't be forgotten. Whatever he was, he was not common. He had the power to charm or frighten rudimentary souls into an aggravated witchdance in his honour; he could also fill the small souls of the pilgrims with bitter misgivings: he had one devoted friend at least, and he had conquered one soul in the world that was neither rudimentary nor tainted with self-seeking. No; I can't forget him, though I am not prepared to affirm the fellow was exactly worth the life we lost in getting to him. I missed my late helmsman awfully—I missed him even while his body was still lying in the pilot-house. Perhaps you will think it passing strange this regret for a savage who was no more account than a grain of sand in a black Sahara. Well, don't you see, he had done something, he had steered; for months I had him at my back—a help—an instrument. It was a kind of partnership. He steered for me—I had to look after him, I worried about his deficiencies, and thus a subtle bond had been created, of which I only became aware when it was suddenly broken. And the intimate profundity of that look he gave me when he received his hurt remains to this day in my memory—like a claim of distant kinship affirmed in a supreme moment.

"Poor fool! If he had only left that shutter alone. He had no restraint, no restraint—just like Kurtz—a tree swayed by the wind. As soon as I had put on a dry pair of slippers, I dragged him out, after first jerking the spear out of his side, which operation I confess I performed with my eyes shut tight. His heels leaped together over the little doorstep; his shoulders were pressed to my breast; I hugged him from behind desperately. Oh! he was heavy, heavy; heavier than any man on earth, I should imagine. Then without more ado I tipped him overboard. The current snatched him as though he had been a wisp of grass, and I saw the body roll over twice before I lost sight of it for ever. All the pilgrims and the manager were then congregated on the awning-deck about the pilot-house, chattering at each other like a flock of excited magpies, and there was a scandalised murmur at my heartless promptitude. What they wanted to keep that body hanging about for I can't guess. Embalm it, maybe. But I had also heard another, and a very ominous, murmur on the deck below. My friend the wood-cutters were likewise scandalised, and with a better show of reason—though I admit that the reason itself was quite inadmissible. Oh, quite! I had made up my mind that if my late helmsman was to be eaten, the fishes alone should have him. He had been a very second-rate helmsman while alive, but now he was dead he might have become a first-class temptation, and possibly cause some startling trouble. Besides, I was anxious to take the wheel, the man in pink pyjamas showing himself a hopeless duffer at the business.

"This I did directly the simple funeral was over. We were going half-speed, keeping right in the middle of the stream, and I listened to the talk about me. They had given up Kurtz, they had given up the station; Kurtz was dead, and the station had been burnt—and so on—and so on. The red-haired pilgrim was beside himself with the thought that at least this poor Kurtz had been properly revenged. 'Say! We must have made a glorious slaughter of them in the bush. Eh? What do you think? Say?' He positively danced, the bloodthirsty little gingery beggar.[7] And he had nearly fainted when he saw the wounded man! I could not help saying, 'You made a glorious lot of smoke, anyhow.' I had seen, from the way the tops of the bushes rustled and flew, that almost all the shots had gone too high. You can't hit anything unless you take aim and fire from the shoulder; but these chaps fired from the hip with their eyes shut. The retreat, I maintained—and I was right—was caused by the screeching of the steam-whistle. Upon this they forgot Kurtz, and began to howl at me with indignant protests.

"The manager stood by the wheel murmuring confidentially about the necessity of getting well away down the river before dark at all events, when I saw in the distance a clearing on the river-side and the outlines of some sort of building. 'What's this?' I asked. He clapped his hands in wonder. 'The station!' he cried. I edged in at once, still going half-speed.

"Through my glasses I saw the slope of a hill interspersed with rare trees and perfectly free from undergrowth. A long decaying building on the summit was half buried in the high grass; the large holes in the peaked roof gaped black from afar; the jungle and the woods made a background. There was no enclosure or fence of any kind; but there had been one apparently, for near the house half a dozen slim posts remained in a row, roughly trimmed, and with their upper ends ornamented with round carved balls. The rails, or what-

7. Redheaded rascal.

ever there had been between, had disappeared. Of course the forest surrounded all that. The river-bank was clear, and on the water side I saw a white man under a hat like a cart-wheel beckoning persistently with his whole arm. Examining the edge of the forest above and below, I was almost certain I could see movements—human forms gliding here and there. I steamed past prudently, then stopped the engines and let her drift down. The man on the shore began to shout, urging us to land. 'We have been attacked,' screamed the manager. 'I know—I know. It's all right,' yelled back the other, as cheerful as you please. 'Come along. It's all right. I am glad.'

"His aspect reminded me of something I had seen—something funny I had seen somewhere. As I manœuvred to get alongside, I was asking myself, 'What does this fellow look like?' Suddenly I got it. He looked like a harlequin. His clothes had been made of some stuff that was brown holland probably, but it was covered with patches all over, with bright patches, blue, red, and yellow—patches on the back, patches on the front, patches on elbows, on knees; coloured binding round his jacket, scarlet edging at the bottom of his trousers; and the sunshine made him look extremely gay and wonderfully neat withal, because you could see how beautifully all this patching had been done. A beardless, boyish face, very fair, no features to speak of, nose peeling, little blue eyes, smiles and frowns chasing each other over that open countenance like sunshine and shadow on a wind-swept plain. 'Look out, captain!' he cried; 'there's a snag lodged in here last night.' What! Another snag? I confess I swore shamefully. I had nearly holed my cripple, to finish off that charming trip. The harlequin on the bank turned his little pug nose up to me. 'You English?' he asked, all smiles. 'Are you?' I shouted from the wheel. The smiles vanished, and he shook his head as if sorry for my disappointment. Then he brightened up. 'Never mind!' he cried encouragingly. 'Are we in time?' I asked. 'He is up there,' he replied, with a toss of the head up the hill, and becoming gloomy all of a sudden. His face was like the autumn sky, overcast one moment and bright the next.

"When the manager, escorted by the pilgrims, all of them armed to the teeth, had gone to the house, this chap came on board. 'I say, I don't like this. These natives are in the bush,' I said. He assured me earnestly it was all right. 'They are simple people,' he added; 'well, I am glad you came. It took me all my time to keep them off.' 'But you said it was all right,' I cried. 'Oh, they meant no harm,' he said; and as I stared he corrected himself, 'Not exactly.' Then vivaciously, 'My faith, your pilot-house wants a clean up!' In the next breath he advised me to keep enough steam on the boiler to blow the whistle in case of any trouble. 'One good screech will do more for you than all your rifles. They are simple people,' he repeated. He rattled away at such a rate he quite overwhelmed me. He seemed to be trying to make up for lots of silence, and actually hinted, laughing, that such was the case. 'Don't you talk with Mr. Kurtz?' I said. 'You don't talk with that man—you listen to him,' he exclaimed with severe exaltation. 'But now—' He waved his arm, and in the twinkling of an eye was in the uttermost depths of despondency. In a moment he came up again with a jump, possessed himself of both my hands, shook them continuously, while he gabbled: 'Brother sailor . . . honour . . . pleasure . . . delight . . . introduce myself . . . Russian . . . son of an arch-priest . . . Government of Tambov . . . What? Tobacco! English tobacco; the excellent English tobacco! Now, that's brotherly. Smoke? Where's a sailor that does not smoke?'

"The pipe soothed him, and gradually I made out he had run away from school, had gone to sea in a Russian ship; ran away again; served some time in English ships; was now reconciled with the arch-priest. He made a point of that. 'But when one is young one must see things, gather experience, ideas; enlarge the mind.' 'Here!' I interrupted. 'You can never tell! Here I met Mr. Kurtz,' he said, youthfully solemn and reproachful. I held my tongue after that. It appears he had persuaded a Dutch trading-house on the coast to fit him out with stores and goods, and had started for the interior with a light heart, and no more idea of what would happen to him than a baby. He had been wandering about that river for nearly two years alone, cut off from everybody and everything. 'I am not so young as I look. I am twenty-five,' he said. 'At first old Van Shuyten would tell me to go to the devil,' he narrated with keen enjoyment; 'but I stuck to him, and talked and talked, till at last he got afraid I would talk the hind-leg off his favourite dog, so he gave me some cheap things and a few guns, and told me he hoped he would never see my face again. Good old Dutchman, Van Shuyten. I sent him one small lot of ivory a year ago, so that he can't call me a little thief when I get back. I hope he got it. And for the rest I don't care. I had some wood stacked for you. That was my old house. Did you see?'

"I gave him Towson's book. He made as though he would kiss me, but restrained himself. 'The only book I had left, and I thought I had lost it,' he said, looking at it ecstatically. 'So many accidents happen to a man going about alone, you know. Canoes get upset sometimes—and sometimes you've got to clear out so quick when the people get angry.' He thumbed the pages. 'You made notes in Russian?' I asked. He nodded. 'I thought they were written in cipher,' I said. He laughed, then became serious. 'I had lots of trouble to keep these people off,' he said. 'Did they want to kill you?' I asked. 'Oh no!' he cried, and checked himself. 'Why did they attack us?' I pursued. He hesitated, then said shamefacedly, 'They don't want him to go.' 'Don't they?' I said curiously. He nodded a nod full of mystery and wisdom. 'I tell you,' he cried, 'this man has enlarged my mind.' He opened his arms wide, staring at me with his little blue eyes that were perfectly round."

3

"I looked at him, lost in astonishment. There he was before me, in motley, as though he had absconded from a troupe of mimes, enthusiastic, fabulous. His very existence was improbable, inexplicable, and altogether bewildering. He was an insoluble problem. It was inconceivable how he had existed, how he had succeeded in getting so far, how he had managed to remain—why he did not instantly disappear. 'I went a little farther,' he said, 'then still a little farther—till I had gone so far that I don't know how I'll ever get back. Never mind. Plenty time. I can manage. You take Kurtz away quick—quick—I tell you.' The glamour of youth enveloped his particoloured rags, his destitution, his loneliness, the essential desolation of his futile wanderings. For months— for years—his life hadn't been worth a day's purchase; and there he was gallantly, thoughtlessly alive, to all appearance indestructible solely by the virtue of his few years and of his unreflecting audacity. I was seduced into something like admiration—like envy. Glamour urged him on, glamour kept him unscathed. He surely wanted nothing from the wilderness but space to breathe in and to push on through. His need was to exist, and to move onwards at the greatest possible risk, and with a maximum of privation. If the absolutely pure, uncalculating, unpractical spirit of adventure had ever ruled a human being, it ruled this be-patched youth. I almost envied him the possession of this modest and clear flame. It seemed to have consumed all thought of self so completely, that, even while he was talking to you, you forgot that it was he—the man before your eyes—who had gone through these things. I did not envy him his devotion to Kurtz, though. He had not meditated over it. It came to him, and he accepted it with a sort of eager fatalism. I must say that to me it appeared about the most dangerous thing in every way he had come upon so far.

"They had come together unavoidably, like two ships becalmed near each other, and lay rubbing sides at last. I suppose Kurtz wanted an audience, because on a certain occasion, when encamped in the forest, they had talked all night, or more probably Kurtz had talked. 'We talked of everything,' he said, quite transported at the recollection. 'I forgot there was such a thing as sleep. The night did not seem to last an hour. Everything! Everything! . . . Of love too.' 'Ah, he talked to you of love!' I said, much amused. 'It isn't what you think,' he cried, almost passionately. 'It was in general. He made me see things—things.'

"He threw his arms up. We were on deck at the time, and the head-man of my wood-cutters, lounging near by, turned upon him his heavy and glittering eyes. I looked around, and I don't know why, but I assure you that never, never before, did this land, this river, this jungle, the very arch of this blazing sky, appear to me so hopeless and so dark, so impenetrable to human thought, so pitiless to human weakness. 'And, ever since, you have been with him, of course?' I said.

"On the contrary. It appears their intercourse had been very much broken by various causes. He had, as he informed me proudly, managed to nurse Kurtz through two illnesses (he alluded to it as you would to some risky feat), but as a rule Kurtz wandered alone, far in the depths of the forest. 'Very often coming to this station, I had to wait days and days before he would turn up,' he said. 'Ah, it was worth waiting for!—sometimes.' 'What was he doing? exploring or what?' I asked. 'Oh yes, of course'; he had discovered lots of villages, a lake too—he did not know exactly in what direction; it was dangerous to inquire too much—but mostly his expeditions had been for ivory. 'But he had no goods to trade with by that time,' I objected. 'There's a good lot of cartridges left even yet,' he answered, looking away. 'To speak plainly, he raided the country,' I said. He nodded. 'Not alone, surely!' He muttered something about the villages round that lake. 'Kurtz got the tribe to follow him, did he?' I suggested. He fidgeted a little. 'They adored him,' he said. The tone of these words was so extraordinary that I looked at him searchingly. It was curious to see his mingled eagerness and reluctance to speak of Kurtz. The man filled his life, occupied his thoughts, swayed his emotions. 'What can you expect?' he burst out; 'he came to them with thunder and lightning, you know—and they had never seen anything like it—and very terrible. He could be very terrible. You can't judge Mr. Kurtz as you would an ordinary man. No, no, no! Now—just to give you an idea—I don't mind telling you, he wanted to shoot me too one day—but I don't judge him.' 'Shoot you!' I cried. 'What for?' 'Well, I had a small lot of ivory the chief of that village near my house gave me. You see I used to shoot game for them. Well, he wanted it, and wouldn't hear reason. He declared he would shoot me unless I gave him the ivory and then cleared out of the country, because he could do so, and had a fancy for it, and there was nothing on earth to prevent him killing whom he jolly well pleased. And it was true too. I gave him the ivory. What did I care! But I didn't clear out. No, no. I couldn't leave him. I had to be careful, of course, till we got friendly again for a time. He had his second illness then. Afterwards I had to keep out of the way; but I didn't mind. He was living for the most part in those villages on the lake. When he came down to the river, sometimes he would take to me, and sometimes it was better for me to be careful. This man suffered too much. He hated all this, and somehow he couldn't get away. When I had a chance I begged him to try and leave while there was time; I offered to go back with him. And he would say yes, and then he would remain; go off on another ivory hunt; disappear for weeks; forget himself amongst these people—forget himself—you know.' 'Why! he's mad,' I said. He protested indignantly. Mr. Kurtz couldn't be mad. If I had heard him talk, only two days ago, I wouldn't dare hint at such a thing. . . . I had taken up my binoculars while we talked, and was looking at the shore, sweeping the limit of the forest at each side and at the back of the house. The consciousness of there being people in that bush, so silent, so quiet—as silent and quiet as the ruined house on the hill—made me uneasy. There was no sign on the face of nature of this amazing tale that was not so much told as suggested to me in desolate exclamations, completed by shrugs, in interrupted phrases, in hints ending in deep sighs. The woods were unmoved, like a mask—heavy, like the closed door of a prison—they looked with their air of hidden knowledge, of patient expectation, of unapproachable silence. The Russian was explaining to me that it was only lately that Mr. Kurtz had come down to the river, bringing along with him all the fighting men of that lake tribe. He had been absent for several months—getting himself adored, I suppose—and had come down unexpectedly, with the intention to all appearance of making a raid either across the river or down stream. Evidently the appetite for more ivory had got the better of the—what shall I say?—less material aspirations. However, he had got much worse suddenly. 'I heard he was lying helpless, and so I came up—took my chance,' said the Russian. 'Oh, he is bad, very bad.' I directed my glass to the house. There were no signs of life, but there was the ruined roof, the long mud wall peeping above the grass, with three little square window-holes, no two of the same size; all this brought within reach of my hand, as it were. And then I made a brusque movement, and one of the remaining posts of that vanished fence leaped up in the field of my glass. You remember I told you I had been struck at the distance by certain attempts at ornamentation, rather remarkable in the ruinous aspect of the place. Now I had suddenly a nearer view, and its first result was to make me throw my head back as if before a blow. Then I went carefully from post to post with my glass, and I saw my mistake. These round knobs were not ornamental but symbolic; they were expressive and puzzling, striking and disturbing—food for thought and also for the vultures if there had been any looking down from the sky; but at all events for such ants as were industrious enough to ascend the pole. They would have been even more impressive, those heads on the stakes, if their faces had not been turned to the house. Only one, the first I had made out, was facing my way. I was not so shocked as you may think. The start back I had given was really nothing but a movement of surprise. I had expected to see a knob of wood there, you know. I returned deliberately to the first I had seen—and there it was, black, dried, sunken, with closed eyelids—a head that seemed to sleep at the top of that pole, and, with the shrunken dry lips showing a narrow white line of the teeth, was smiling too, smiling continuously at some endless and jocose dream of that eternal slumber.

"I am not disclosing any trade secrets. In fact the manager said afterwards that Mr. Kurtz's methods had ruined the district. I have no opinion on that point, but I want you clearly to understand that there was nothing exactly profitable in these heads being there. They only show that Mr. Kurtz lacked restraint in the gratification of his various lusts, that there was something wanting in him—some small matter which, when the pressing need arose, could not be found under his magnificent eloquence. Whether he knew of this deficiency himself I can't say. I think the knowledge came to him at last— only at the very last. But the wilderness had found him out early, and had taken on him a terrible vengeance for the fantastic invasion. I think it had whispered to him things about himself which he did not know, things of which he had no conception till he took counsel with this great solitude—and the whisper had proved irresistibly fascinating. It echoed loudly within him because he was hollow at the core. . . . I put down the glass, and the head that had appeared near enough to be spoken to seemed at once to have leaped away from me into inaccessible distance.

"The admirer of Mr. Kurtz was a bit crestfallen. In a hurried, indistinct voice he began to assure me he had not dared to take these—say, symbols— down. He was not afraid of the natives; they would not stir till Mr. Kurtz gave the word. His ascendancy was extraordinary. The camps of these people surrounded the place, and the chiefs came every day to see him. They would crawl . . . 'I don't want to know anything of the ceremonies used when approaching Mr. Kurtz,' I shouted. Curious, this feeling that came over me that such details would be more intolerable than those heads drying on the stakes under Mr. Kurtz's windows. After all, that was only a savage sight, while I seemed at one bound to have been transported into some lightless region of subtle horrors, where pure, uncomplicated savagery was a positive relief, being something that had a right to exist—obviously—in the sunshine. The young man looked at me with surprise. I suppose it did not occur to him that Mr. Kurtz was no idol of mine. He forgot I hadn't heard any of these splendid monologues on, what was it? on love, justice, conduct of life—or what not. If it had come to crawling before Mr. Kurtz, he crawled as much as the veriest savage of them all. I had no idea of the conditions, he said: these heads were the heads of rebels. I shocked him excessively by laughing. Rebels! What would be the next definition I was to hear? There had been enemies, criminals, workers—and these were rebels. Those rebellious heads looked very subdued to me on their sticks. 'You don't know how such a life tries a man like Kurtz,' cried Kurtz's last disciple. 'Well, and you?' I said. 'I! I! I am a simple man. I have no great thoughts. I want nothing from anybody. How can you compare me to . . . ?' His feelings were too much for speech, and suddenly he broke down. 'I don't understand,' he groaned. 'I've been doing my best to keep him alive, and that's enough. I had no hand in all this. I have no abilities. There hasn't been a drop of medicine or a mouthful of invalid food for months here. He was shamefully abandoned. A man like this, with such ideas. Shamefully! Shamefully! I—I—haven't slept for the last ten nights. . . .'

"His voice lost itself in the calm of the evening. The long shadows of the forest had slipped down hill while we talked, had gone far beyond the ruined hovel, beyond the symbolic row of stakes. All this was in the gloom, while we down there were yet in the sunshine, and the stretch of the river abreast of the clearing glittered in a still and dazzling splendour, with a murky and overshadowed bend above and below. Not a living soul was seen on the shore. The bushes did not rustle.

"Suddenly round the corner of the house a group of men appeared, as though they had come up from the ground. They waded waist-deep in the grass, in a compact body, bearing an improvised stretcher in their midst. Instantly, in the emptiness of the landscape, a cry arose whose shrillness pierced the still air like a sharp arrow flying straight to the very heart of the land; and, as if by enchantment, streams of human beings—of naked human beings—with spears in their hands, with bows, with shields, with wild glances and savage movements, were poured into the clearing by the dark-faced and pensive forest. The bushes shook, the grass swayed for a time, and then everything stood still in attentive immobility.

" 'Now, if he does not say the right thing to them we are all done for,' said the Russian at my elbow. The knot of men with the stretcher had stopped too, half-way to the steamer, as if petrified. I saw the man on the stretcher sit up, lank and with an uplifted arm, above the shoulders of the bearers. 'Let us hope that the man who can talk so well of love in general will find some particular reason to spare us this time,' I said. I resented bitterly the absurd danger of our situation, as if to be at the mercy of that atrocious phantom had been a dishonouring necessity. I could not hear a sound, but through my glasses I saw the thin arm extended commandingly, the lower jaw moving, the eyes of that apparition shining darkly far in its bony head that nodded with grotesque jerks. Kurtz—Kurtz—that means 'short' in German—don't it? Well, the name was as true as everything else in his life—and death. He looked at least seven feet long. His covering had fallen off, and his body emerged from it pitiful and appalling as from a winding-sheet. I could see the cage of his ribs all astir, the bones of his arm waving. It was as though an animated image of death carved out of old ivory had been shaking its hand with menaces at a motionless crowd of men made of dark and glittering bronze. I saw him open his mouth wide—it gave him a weirdly voracious aspect, as though he had wanted to swallow all the air, all the earth, all the men before him. A deep voice reached me faintly. He must have been shouting. He fell back suddenly. The stretcher shook as the bearers staggered forward again, and almost at the same time I noticed that the crowd of savages was vanishing without any perceptible movement of retreat, as if the forest that had ejected these beings so suddenly had drawn them in again as the breath is drawn in a long aspiration.

"Some of the pilgrims behind the stretcher carried his arms—two shot-guns, a heavy rifle, and a light revolver-carbine—the thunderbolts of that pitiful Jupiter. The manager bent over him murmuring as he walked beside his head. They laid him down in one of the little cabins—just a room for a bedplace and a camp-stool or two, you know. We had brought his belated correspondence, and a lot of torn envelopes and open letters littered his bed. His hand roamed feebly amongst these papers. I was struck by the fire of his eyes and the composed languor of his expression. It was not so much the exhaustion of disease. He did not seem in pain. This shadow looked satiated and calm, as though for the moment it had had its fill of all the emotions.

"He rustled one of the letters, and looking straight in my face said, 'I am glad.' Somebody had been writing to him about me. These special recommendations were turning up again. The volume of tone he emitted without effort, almost without the trouble of moving his lips, amazed me. A voice! a voice! It was grave, profound, vibrating, while the man did not seem capable of a whisper. However, he had enough strength in him—factitious no doubt—to very nearly make an end of us, as you shall hear directly.

"The manager appeared silently in the doorway; I stepped out at once and he drew the curtain after me. The Russian, eyed curiously by the pilgrims, was staring at the shore. I followed the direction of his glance.

"Dark human shapes could be made out in the distance, flitting indistinctly against the gloomy border of the forest, and near the river two bronze figures, leaning on tall spears, stood in the sunlight under fantastic head-dresses of spotted skins, warlike and still in statuesque repose. And from right to left along the lighted shore moved a wild and gorgeous apparition of a woman.

"She walked with measured steps, draped in striped and fringed cloths, treading the earth proudly, with a slight jingle and flash of barbarous ornaments. She carried her head high; her hair was done in the shape of a helmet; she had brass leggings to the knee, brass wire gauntlets to the elbow, a crimson spot on her tawny cheek, innumerable necklaces of glass beads on her neck; bizarre things, charms, gifts of witch-men, that hung about her, glittered and trembled at every step. She must have had the value of several elephant tusks upon her. She was savage and superb, wild-eyed and magnificent; there was something ominous and stately in her deliberate progress. And in the hush that had fallen suddenly upon the whole sorrowful land, the immense wilderness, the colossal body of the fecund and mysterious life seemed to look at her, pensive, as though it had been looking at the image of its own tenebrous and passionate soul.

"She came abreast of the steamer, stood still, and faced us. Her long shadow fell to the water's edge. Her face had a tragic and fierce aspect of wild sorrow and of dumb pain mingled with the fear of some struggling, half-shaped resolve. She stood looking at us without a stir, and like the wilderness itself, with an air of brooding over an inscrutable purpose. A whole minute passed, and then she made a step forward. There was a low jingle, a glint of yellow metal, a sway of fringed draperies, and she stopped as if her heart had failed her. The young fellow by my side growled. The pilgrims murmured at my back. She looked at us all as if her life had depended upon the unswerving steadiness of her glance. Suddenly she opened her bared arms and threw them up rigid above her head, as though in an uncontrollable desire to touch the sky, and at the same time the swift shadows darted out on the earth, swept around on the river, gathering the steamer into a shadowy embrace. A formidable silence hung over the scene.

"She turned away slowly, walked on, following the bank, and passed into the bushes to the left. Once only her eyes gleamed back at us in the dusk of the thickets before she disappeared.

" 'If she had offered to come aboard I really think I would have tried to shoot her,' said the man of patches nervously. 'I had been risking my life every day for the last fortnight to keep her out of the house. She got in one day and kicked up a row about those miserable rags I picked up in the storeroom to mend my clothes with. I wasn't decent. At least it must have been that, for she talked like a fury to Kurtz for an hour, pointing at me now and then. I don't understand the dialect of this tribe. Luckily for me, I fancy Kurtz felt too ill that day to care, or there would have been mischief. I don't understand. . . .No—it's too much for me. Ah, well, it's all over now.'

"At this moment I heard Kurtz's deep voice behind the curtain: 'Save me!—save the ivory, you mean. Don't tell me. Save *me*! Why, I've had to save you. You are interrupting my plans now. Sick! Sick! Not so sick as you would like to believe. Never mind. I'll carry my ideas out yet—I will return. I'll show you what can be done. You with your little peddling notions—you are interfering with me. I will return. I . . . '

"The manager came out. He did me the honour to take me under the arm and lead me aside. 'He is very low, very low,' he said. He considered it necessary to sigh, but neglected to be consistently sorrowful. 'We have done all we could for him—haven't we? But there is no disguising the fact, Mr. Kurtz has done more harm than good to the Company. He did not see the time was not ripe for vigorous action. Cautiously, cautiously—that's my principle. We must be cautious yet. The district is closed to us for a time. Deplorable! Upon the whole, the trade will suffer. I don't deny there is a remarkable quantity of ivory—mostly fossil. We must save it, at all events—but look how precarious the position is—and why? Because the method is unsound.' 'Do you,' said I, looking at the shore, 'call it "unsound method"?' 'Without doubt,' he exclaimed hotly, 'Don't you?' . . . 'No method at all,' I murmured after a while. 'Exactly,' he exulted. 'I anticipated this. Shows a complete want of judgment. It is my duty to point it out in the proper quarter.' 'Oh,' said I, 'that fellow—what's his name?—the brickmaker, will make a readable report for you.' He appeared confounded for a moment. It seemed to me I had never breathed an atmosphere so vile, and I turned mentally to Kurtz for relief—positively for relief. 'Nevertheless, I think Mr. Kurtz is a remarkable man,' I said with emphasis. He started, dropped on me a cold heavy glance, said very quietly, 'He *was*,' and turned his back on me. My hour of favour was over; I found myself lumped along with Kurtz as a partisan of methods for which the time was not ripe: I was unsound! Ah! but it was something to have at least a choice of nightmares.

"I had turned to the wilderness really, not to Mr. Kurtz, who, I was ready to admit, was as good as buried. And for a moment it seemed to me as if I also were buried in a vast grave full of unspeakable secrets. I felt an intolerable weight oppressing my breast, the smell of the damp earth, the unseen presence of victorious corruption, the darkness of an impenetrable night. . . . The Russian tapped me on the shoulder. I heard him mumbling and stammering something about 'brother seaman—couldn't conceal—knowledge of matters that would affect Mr. Kurtz's reputation.' I waited. For him evidently Mr. Kurtz was not in his grave; I suspect that for him Mr. Kurtz was one of the immortals. 'Well!' said I at last, 'speak out. As it happens, I am Mr. Kurtz's friend—in a way.'

"He stated with a good deal of formality that had we not been 'of the same profession,' he would have kept the matter to himself without regard to consequences. He suspected 'there was an active ill-will towards him on the part of these white men that—' 'You are right,' I said, remembering a certain conversation I had overheard. 'The manager thinks you ought to be hanged.' He showed a concern at this intelligence which amused me at first. 'I had better get out of the way quietly,' he said earnestly. 'I can do no more for Kurtz now, and they would soon find some excuse. What's to stop them? There's a military post three hundred miles from here.' 'Well, upon my word,' said I, 'perhaps you had better go if you have any friends amongst the savages near by.' 'Plenty,' he said. 'They are simple people—and I want nothing, you know.' He stood biting his lip, then: 'I don't want any harm to happen to these whites here, but of course I was thinking of Mr. Kurtz's reputation—but you are a brother seaman and—' 'All right,' said I, after a time. 'Mr. Kurtz's reputation is safe with me.' I did not know how truly I spoke.

"He informed me, lowering his voice, that it was Kurtz who had ordered the attack to be made on the steamer. 'He hated sometimes the idea of being taken away—and then again . . . But I don't understand these matters. I am a simple man. He thought it would scare you away—that you would give it up, thinking him dead. I could not stop him. Oh, I had an awful time of it this last month.' 'Very well,' I said. 'He is all right now.' 'Ye-e-es,' he muttered, not very convinced apparently. 'Thanks,' said I; 'I shall keep my eyes open.' 'But quiet—eh?' he urged anxiously. 'It would be awful for his reputation if anybody here—' I promised a complete discretion with great gravity. 'I have a canoe and three black fellows waiting not very far. I am off. Could you give me a few Martini-Henry cartridges?' I could, and did, with proper secrecy. He helped himself, with a wink at me, to a handful of my tobacco. 'Between sailors—you know—good English tobacco.' At the door of the pilot-house he turned round—'I say, haven't you a pair of shoes you could spare?' He raised one leg. 'Look.' The soles were tied with knotted strings sandal-wise under his bare feet. I rooted out an old pair, at which he looked with admiration before tucking it under his left arm. One of his pockets (bright red) was bulging with cartridges, from the other (dark blue) peeped 'Towson's Inquiry,' etc. etc. He seemed to think himself excellently well equipped for a renewed encounter with the wilderness. 'Ah! I'll never, never meet such a man again. You ought to have heard him recite poetry—his own too it was, he told me. Poetry!' He rolled his eyes at the recollection of these delights. 'Oh, he enlarged my mind!' 'Good-bye,' said I. He shook hands and vanished in the night. Sometimes I ask myself whether I had ever really seen him—whether it was possible to meet such a phenomenon! . . .

"When I woke up shortly after midnight his warning came to my mind with its hint of danger that seemed, in the starred darkness, real enough to make me get up for the purpose of having a look round. On the hill a big fire burned, illuminating fitfully a crooked corner of the station-house. One of the agents with a picket of a few of our blacks, armed for the purpose, was keeping guard over the ivory; but deep within the forest, red gleams that wavered, that seemed to sink and rise from the ground amongst confused columnar shapes of intense blackness, showed the exact position of the camp where Mr. Kurtz's adorers were keeping their uneasy vigil. The monotonous beating of a big drum filled the air with muffled shocks and a lingering vibration. A steady droning sound of many men chanting each to himself some weird incantation came out from the black, flat wall of the woods as the humming of bees comes out of a hive, and had a strange narcotic effect upon my half-awake senses. I believe I dozed off leaning over the rail, till an abrupt burst of yells, an overwhelming outbreak of a pent-up and mysterious frenzy, woke me up in a bewildered wonder. It was cut short all at once, and the low droning went on with an effect of audible and soothing silence. I glanced casually into the little cabin. A light was burning within, but Mr. Kurtz was not there.

"I think I would have raised an outcry if I had believed my eyes. But I didn't believe them at first—the thing seemed so impossible. The fact is I was completely unnerved by a sheer blank fright, pure abstract terror, unconnected with any distinct shape of physical danger. What made this emotion so overpowering was—how shall I define it?—the moral shock I received, as if something altogether monstrous, intolerable to thought and odious to the soul, had been thrust upon me unexpectedly. This lasted of course the merest fraction of a second, and then the usual sense of commonplace, deadly danger, the possibility of a sudden onslaught and massacre, or something of the kind, which I saw impending, was positively welcome and composing. It pacified me, in fact, so much, that I did not raise an alarm.

"There was an agent buttoned up inside an ulster and sleeping on a chair on deck within three feet of me. The yells had not awakened him; he snored very slightly; I left him to his slumbers and leaped ashore. I did not betray Mr. Kurtz—it was ordered I should never betray him—it was written I should be loyal to the nightmare of my choice. I was anxious to deal with this shadow by myself alone—and to this day I don't know why I was so jealous of sharing with any one the peculiar blackness of that experience.

"As soon as I got on the bank I saw a trail—a broad trail through the grass. I remember the exultation with which I said to myself, 'He can't walk—he is crawling on all-fours—I've got him.' The grass was wet with dew. I strode rapidly with clenched fists. I fancy I had some vague notion of falling upon him and giving him a drubbing. I don't know. I had some imbecile thoughts. The knitting old woman with the cat obtruded herself upon my memory as a most improper person to be sitting at the other end of such an affair. I saw a row of pilgrims squirting lead in the air out of Winchesters held to the hip. I thought I would never get back to the steamer, and imagined myself living alone and unarmed in the woods to an advanced age. Such silly things—you know. And I remember I confounded the beat of the drum with the beating of my heart, and was pleased at its calm regularity.

"I kept to the track though—then stopped to listen. The night was very clear; a dark blue space, sparkling with dew and starlight, in which black things stood very still. I thought I could see a kind of motion ahead of me. I was strangely cocksure of everything that night. I actually left the track and ran in a wide semicircle (I verily believe chuckling to myself) so as to get in front of that stir, of that motion I had seen—if indeed I had seen anything. I was circumventing Kurtz as though it had been a boyish game.

"I came upon him, and, if he had not heard me coming, I would have fallen over him too, but he got up in time. He rose, unsteady, long, pale, indistinct, like a vapour exhaled by the earth, and swayed slightly, misty and silent before me; while at my back the fires loomed between the trees, and the murmur of many voices issued from the forest. I had cut him off cleverly; but when actually confronting him I seemed to come to my senses, I saw the danger in its right proportion. It was by no means over yet. Suppose he began to shout? Though he could hardly stand, there was still plenty of vigour in his voice. 'Go away—hide yourself,' he said, in that profound tone. It was very awful. I glanced back. We were within thirty yards of the nearest fire. A black figure stood up, strode on long black legs, waving long black arms, across the glow. It had horns—antelope horns, I think—on its head. Some sorcerer, some witch-man no doubt: it looked fiend-like enough. 'Do you know what you are doing?' I whispered. 'Perfectly,' he answered, raising his voice for that single word: it sounded to me far off and yet loud, like a hail through a speaking-trumpet. If he makes a row we are lost, I thought to myself. This clearly was not a case for fisticuffs, even apart from the very natural aversion I had to beat that Shadow—this wandering and tormented thing. 'You will be lost,' I said—'utterly lost.' One gets sometimes such a flash of inspiration, you know. I did say the right thing, though indeed he could not have been more irretrievably lost than he was at this very moment, when the foundations of our intimacy were being laid—to endure—to endure—even to the end—even beyond.

" 'I had immense plans,' he muttered irresolutely. 'Yes,' said I; 'but if you try to shout I'll smash your head with—' There was not a stick or a stone near. 'I will throttle you for good,' I corrected myself. 'I was on the threshold of great things,' he pleaded, in a voice of longing, with a wistfulness of tone that made my blood run cold. 'And now for this stupid scoundrel—' 'Your success in Europe is assured in any case,' I affirmed steadily. I did not want to have the throttling of him, you understand—and indeed it would have been very little use for any practical purpose. I tried to break the spell—the heavy, mute spell of the wilderness—that seemed to draw him to its pitiless breast by the awakening of forgotten and brutal instincts, by the memory of gratified and monstrous passions. This alone, I was convinced, had driven him out to the edge of the forest, to the bush, towards the gleam of fires, the throb of drums, the drone of weird incantations; this alone had beguiled his unlawful soul beyond the bounds of permitted aspirations. And, don't you see, the terror of the position was not in being knocked on the head—though I had a very lively sense of that danger too—but in this, that I had to deal with a being to whom I could not appeal in the name of anything high or low. I had, even like the niggers, to invoke him—himself—his own exalted and incredible degradation. There was nothing either above or below him, and I knew it. He had kicked himself loose of the earth. Confound the man! he had kicked the very earth to pieces. He was alone, and I before him did not know whether I stood on the ground or floated in the air. I've been telling you what we said—repeating the phrases we pronounced—but what's the good? They were common everyday words—the familiar, vague sounds exchanged on every waking day of life. But what of that? They had behind them, to my mind, the terrific suggestiveness of words heard in dreams, of phrases spoken in nightmares. Soul! If anybody had ever struggled with a soul, I am the man. And I wasn't arguing with a lunatic either. Believe me or not, his intelligence was perfectly clear—concentrated, it is true, upon himself with horrible intensity, yet clear; and therein was my only chance—barring, of course, the killing him there and then, which wasn't so good, on account of unavoidable noise. But his soul was mad. Being alone in the wilderness, it had looked within itself, and, by heavens! I tell you, it had gone mad. I had—for my sins, I suppose, to go through the ordeal of looking into it myself. No eloquence could have been so withering to one's belief in mankind as his final burst of sincerity. He struggled with himself too. I saw it—I heard it. I saw the inconceivable mystery of a soul that knew no restraint, no faith, and no fear, yet struggling blindly with itself. I kept my head pretty well; but when I had him at last stretched on the couch, I wiped my forehead, while my legs shook under me as though I had carried half a ton on my back down that hill. And yet I had only supported him, his bony arm clasped round my neck—and he was not much heavier than a child.

"When next day we left at noon, the crowd, of whose presence behind the curtain of trees I had been acutely conscious all the time, flowed out of the woods again, filled the clearing, covered the slope with a mass of naked, breathing, quivering, bronze bodies. I steamed up a bit, then swung down-stream, and two thousand eyes followed the evolutions of the splashing, thumping, fierce river-demon beating the water with its terrible tail and breathing black smoke into the air. In front of the first rank, along the river, three men, plastered with bright red earth from head to foot, strutted to and fro restlessly. When we came abreast again, they faced the river, stamped their feet, nodded their horned heads, swayed their scarlet bodies; they shook towards the fierce river-demon a bunch of black feathers, a mangy skin with a pendent tail—something that looked like a dried gourd; they shouted periodi-cally together strings of amazing words that resembled no sounds of human language; and the deep murmurs of the crowd, interrupted suddenly, were like the responses of some satanic litany.

"We had carried Kurtz into the pilot-house: there was more air there. Lying on the couch, he stared through the open shutter. There was an eddy in the mass of human bodies, and the woman with helmeted head and tawny cheeks rushed out to the very brink of the stream. She put out her hands, shouted something, and all that wild mob took up the shout in a roaring chorus of articulated, rapid, breathless utterance.

" 'Do you understand this?' I asked.

"He kept on looking out past me with fiery, longing eyes, with a mingled expression of wistfulness and hate. He made no answer, but I saw a smile, a smile of indefinable meaning, appear on his colourless lips that a moment after twitched convulsively. 'Do I not?' he said slowly, gasping, as if the words had been torn out of him by a supernatural power.

"I pulled the string of the whistle, and I did this because I saw the pilgrims on deck getting out their rifles with an air of anticipating a jolly lark. At the sudden screech there was a movement of abject terror through that wedged mass of bodies. 'Don't! don't you frighten them away,' cried some one on deck disconsolately. I pulled the string time after time. They broke and ran, they leaped, they crouched, they swerved, they dodged the flying terror of the sound. The three red chaps had fallen flat, face down on the shore, as though they had been shot dead. Only the barbarous and superb woman did not so much as flinch, and stretched tragically her bare arms after us over the sombre and glittering river.

"And then that imbecile crowd down on the deck started their little fun, and I could see nothing more for smoke.

"The brown current ran swiftly out of the heart of darkness, bearing us down towards the sea with twice the speed of our upward progress; and Kurtz's life was running swiftly too, ebbing, ebbing out of his heart into the sea of inexorable time. The manager was very placid, he had no vital anxieties now, he took us both in with a comprehensive and satisfied glance: the 'affair' had come off as well as could be wished. I saw the time approaching when I would be left alone of the party of 'unsound method.' The pilgrims looked upon me with disfavour. I was, so to speak, numbered with the dead. It is strange how I accepted this unforeseen partnership, this choice of nightmares forced upon me in the tenebrous land invaded by these mean and greedy phantoms.

"Kurtz discoursed. A voice! a voice! It rang deep to the very last. It survived his strength to hide in the magnificent folds of eloquence the barren darkness of his heart. Oh, he struggled! he struggled! The wastes of his weary brain were haunted by shadowy images now—images of wealth and fame revolving obsequiously round his unextinguishable gift of noble and lofty expression. My Intended, my station, my career, my ideas—these were the subjects for the occasional utterances of elevated sentiments. The shade of the original Kurtz frequented the bedside of the hollow sham, whose fate it was to be buried presently in the mould of primeval earth. But both the diabolic love and the unearthly hate of the mysteries it had penetrated fought for the possession of that soul satiated with primitive emotions, avid of lying fame, of sham distinction, of all the appearances of success and power.

"Sometimes he was contemptibly childish. He desired to have kings meet him at railway stations on his return from some ghastly Nowhere, where he intended to accomplish great things. 'You show them you have in you something that is really profitable, and then there will be no limits to the recognition of your ability,' he would say. 'Of course you must take care of the motives—right motives—always.' The long reaches that were like one and the same reach, monotonous bends that were exactly alike, slipped past the steamer with their multitude of secular[8] trees looking patiently after this grimy fragment of another world, the forerunner of change, of conquest, of trade, of massacres, of blessings. I looked ahead—piloting. 'Close the shutter,' said Kurtz suddenly one day; 'I can't bear to look at this.' I did so. There was a silence. 'Oh, but I will wring your heart yet!' he cried at the invisible wilderness.

"We broke down—as I had expected—and had to lie up for repairs at the head of an island. This delay was the first thing that shook Kurtz's confidence. One morning he gave me a packet of papers and a photograph—the lot tied together with a shoe-string. 'Keep this for me,' he said. 'This noxious fool' (meaning the manager) 'is capable of prying into my boxes when I am not looking.' In the afternoon I saw him. He was lying on his back with closed eyes, and I withdrew quietly, but I heard him mutter, 'Live rightly, die, die . . .' I listened. There was nothing more. Was he rehearsing some speech in his sleep, or was it a fragment of a phrase from some newspaper article? He had been writing for the papers and meant to do so again, 'for the furthering of my ideas. It's a duty.'

"His was an impenetrable darkness. I looked at him as you peer down at a man who is lying at the bottom of a precipice where the sun never shines. But I had not much time to give him, because I was helping the engine-driver to take to pieces the leaky cylinders, to straighten a bent connecting-rod, and in other such matters. I lived in an infernal mess of rust, filings, nuts, bolts, spanners, hammers, ratchet-drills—things I abominate, because I don't get on

8. Centuries old.

with them. I tended the little forge we fortunately had aboard; I toiled wearily in a wretched scrap-heap—unless I had the shakes too bad to stand.

"One evening coming in with a candle I was startled to hear him say a little tremulously, 'I am lying here in the dark waiting for death.' The light was within a foot of his eyes. I forced myself to murmur, 'Oh, nonsense!' and stood over him as if transfixed.

"Anything approaching the change that came over his features I have never seen before, and hope never to see again. Oh, I wasn't touched. I was fascinated. It was as though a veil had been rent. I saw on that ivory face the expression of sombre pride, of ruthless power, of craven terror—of an intense and hopeless despair. Did he live his life again in every detail of desire, temptation, and surrender during that supreme moment of complete knowledge? He cried in a whisper at some image, at some vision—he cried out twice, a cry that was no more than a breath:

" 'The horror! The horror!'

"I blew the candle out and left the cabin. The pilgrims were dining in the mess-room, and I took my place opposite the manager, who lifted his eyes to give me a questioning glance, which I successfully ignored. He leaned back, serene, with that peculiar smile of his sealing the unexpressed depths of his meanness. A continuous shower of small flies streamed upon the lamp, upon the cloth, upon our hands and faces. Suddenly the manager's boy put his insolent black head in the doorway, and said in a tone of scathing contempt:

" 'Mistah Kurtz—he dead.'

"All the pilgrims rushed out to see. I remained, and went on with my dinner. I believe I was considered brutally callous. However, I did not eat much. There was a lamp in there—light, don't you know—and outside it was so beastly, beastly dark. I went no more near the remarkable man who had pronounced a judgment upon the adventures of his soul on this earth. The voice was gone. What else had been there? But I am of course aware that next day the pilgrims buried something in a muddy hole.

"And then they very nearly buried me.

"However, as you see, I did not go to join Kurtz there and then. I did not. I remained to dream the nightmare out to the end, and to show my loyalty to Kurtz once more. Destiny. My destiny! Droll thing life is—that mysterious arrangement of merciless logic for a futile purpose. The most you can hope from it is some knowledge of yourself—that comes too late—a crop of unextinguishable regrets. I have wrestled with death. It is the most unexciting contest you can imagine. It takes place in an impalpable greyness, with nothing underfoot, with nothing around, without spectators, without clamour, without glory, without the great desire of victory, without the great fear of defeat, in a sickly atmosphere of tepid scepticism, without much belief in your own right, and still less in that of your adversary. If such is the form of ultimate wisdom, then life is a greater riddle than some of us think it to be. I was within a hair's-breadth of the last opportunity for pronouncement, and I found with humiliation that probably I would have nothing to say. This is the reason why I affirm that Kurtz was a remarkable man. He had something to say. He said it. Since I had peeped over the edge myself, I understand better the meaning of his stare, that could not see the flame of the candle, but was wide enough to embrace the whole universe, piercing enough to penetrate all the hearts that beat in the darkness. He had summed up—he had judged. 'The horror!'

He was a remarkable man. After all, this was the expression of some sort of belief; it had candour, it had conviction, it had a vibrating note of revolt in its whisper, it had the appalling face of a glimpsed truth—the strange commingling of desire and hate. And it is not my own extremity I remember best—a vision of greyness without form filled with physical pain, and a careless contempt for the evanescence of all things—even of this pain itself. No! It is his extremity that I seem to have lived through. True, he had made that last stride, he had stepped over the edge, while I had been permitted to draw back my hesitating foot. And perhaps in this is the whole difference; perhaps all the wisdom, and all truth, and all sincerity, are just compressed into that inappreciable moment of time in which we step over the threshold of the invisible. Perhaps! I like to think my summing-up would not have been a word of careless contempt. Better his cry—much better. It was an affirmation, a moral victory paid for by innumerable defeats, by abominable terrors, by abominable satisfactions. But it was a victory! That is why I have remained loyal to Kurtz to the last, and even beyond, when a long time after I heard once more, not his own voice, but the echo of his magnificent eloquence thrown to me from a soul as translucently pure as a cliff of crystal.

"No, they did not bury me, though there is a period of time which I remember mistily, with a shuddering wonder, like a passage through some inconceivable world that had no hope in it and no desire. I found myself back in the sepulchral city resenting the sight of people hurrying through the streets to filch a little money from each other, to devour their infamous cookery, to gulp their unwholesome beer, to dream their insignificant and silly dreams. They trespassed upon my thoughts. They were intruders whose knowledge of life was to me an irritating pretence, because I felt so sure they could not possibly know the things I knew. Their bearing, which was simply the bearing of commonplace individuals going about their business in the assurance of perfect safety, was offensive to me like the outrageous flauntings of folly in the face of a danger it is unable to comprehend. I had no particular desire to enlighten them, but I had some difficulty in restraining myself from laughing in their faces, so full of stupid importance. I daresay I was not very well at that time. I tottered about the streets—there were various affairs to settle—grinning bitterly at perfectly respectable persons. I admit my behaviour was inexcusable, but then my temperature was seldom normal in these days. My dear aunt's endeavours to 'nurse up my strength' seemed altogether beside the mark. It was not my strength that wanted nursing, it was my imagination that wanted soothing. I kept the bundle of papers given me by Kurtz, not knowing exactly what to do with it. His mother had died lately, watched over, as I was told, by his Intended. A clean-shaven man, with an official manner and wearing gold-rimmed spectacles, called on me one day and made inquiries, at first circuitous, afterwards suavely pressing, about what he was pleased to denominate certain 'documents.' I was not surprised, because I had had two rows with the manager on the subject out there. I had refused to give up the smallest scrap out of that package, and I took the same attitude with the spectacled man. He became darkly menacing at last, and with much heat argued that the Company had the right to every bit of information about its 'territories.' And, said he, 'Mr. Kurtz's knowledge of unexplored regions must have been necessarily extensive and peculiar—owing to his great abilities and to the deplorable circumstances in which he had been placed: therefore—' I assured him Mr.

Kurtz's knowledge, however extensive, did not bear upon the problems of commerce or administration. He invoked then the name of science. 'It would be an incalculable loss if,' etc. etc. I offered him the report on the 'Suppression of Savage Customs,' with the postscriptum torn off. He took it up eagerly, but ended by sniffing at it with an air of contempt. 'This is not what we had a right to expect,' he remarked. 'Expect nothing else,' I said. 'There are only private letters.' He withdrew upon some threat of legal proceedings, and I saw him no more; but another fellow, calling himself Kurtz's cousin, appeared two days later, and was anxious to hear all the details about his dear relative's last moments. Incidentally he gave me to understand that Kurtz had been essentially a great musician. 'There was the making of an immense success,' said the man, who was an organist, I believe, with lank grey hair flowing over a greasy coat-collar. I had no reason to doubt his statement; and to this day I am unable to say what was Kurtz's profession, whether he ever had any—which was the greatest of his talents. I had taken him for a painter who wrote for the papers, or else for a journalist who could paint—but even the cousin (who took snuff during the interview) could not tell me what he had been—exactly. He was a universal genius—on that point I agreed with the old chap, who thereupon blew his nose noisily into a large cotton handkerchief and withdrew in senile agitation, bearing off some family letters and memoranda without importance. Ultimately a journalist anxious to know something of the fate of his 'dear colleague' turned up. This visitor informed me Kurtz's proper sphere ought to have been politics 'on the popular side.' He had furry straight eyebrows, bristly hair cropped short, an eyeglass on a broad ribbon, and, becoming expansive, confessed his opinion that Kurtz really couldn't write a bit— 'but heavens! how that man could talk! He electrified large meetings. He had faith—don't you see?—he had the faith. He could get himself to believe anything—anything. He would have been a splendid leader of an extreme party.' 'What party?' I asked. 'Any party,' answered the other. 'He was an— an—extremist.' Did I not think so? I assented. Did I know, he asked, with a sudden flash of curiosity, 'what it was that had induced him to go out there?' 'Yes,' said I, and forthwith handed him the famous Report for publication, if he thought fit. He glanced through it hurriedly, mumbling all the time, judged 'it would do,' and took himself off with this plunder.

"Thus I was left at last with a slim packet of letters and the girl's portrait. She struck me as beautiful—I mean she had a beautiful expression. I know that the sunlight can be made to lie too, yet one felt that no manipulation of light and pose could have conveyed the delicate shade of truthfulness upon those features. She seemed ready to listen without mental reservation, without suspicion, without a thought for herself. I concluded I would go and give her back her portrait and those letters myself. Curiosity? Yes; and also some other feeling perhaps. All that had been Kurtz's had passed out of my hands: his soul, his body, his station, his plans, his ivory, his career. There remained only his memory and his Intended—and I wanted to give that up too to the past, in a way—to surrender personally all that remained of him with me to that oblivion which is the last word of our common fate. I don't defend myself. I had no clear perception of what it was I really wanted. Perhaps it was an impulse of unconscious loyalty, or the fulfilment of one of those ironic necessities that lurk in the facts of human existence. I don't know. I can't tell. But I went.

"I thought his memory was like the other memories of the dead that accumulate in every man's life—a vague impress on the brain of shadows that had fallen on it in their swift and final passage; but before the high and ponderous door, between the tall houses of a street as still and decorous as a well-kept alley in a cemetery, I had a vision of him on the stretcher, opening his mouth voraciously, as if to devour all the earth with all its mankind. He lived then before me; he lived as much as he had ever lived—a shadow insatiable of splendid appearances, of frightful realities; a shadow darker than the shadow of the night, and draped nobly in the folds of a gorgeous eloquence. The vision seemed to enter the house with me—the stretcher, the phantom-bearers, the wild crowd of obedient worshippers, the gloom of the forests, the glitter of the reach between the murky bends, the beat of the drum, regular and muffled like the beating of a heart—the heart of a conquering darkness. It was a moment of triumph for the wilderness, an invading and vengeful rush which, it seemed to me, I would have to keep back alone for the salvation of another soul. And the memory of what I had heard him say afar there, with the horned shapes stirring at my back, in the glow of fires, within the patient woods, those broken phrases came back to me, were heard again in their ominous and terrifying simplicity. I remembered his abject pleading, his abject threats, the colossal scale of his vile desires, the meanness, the torment, the tempestuous anguish of his soul. And later on I seemed to see his collected languid manner, when he said one day, 'This lot of ivory now is really mine. The Company did not pay for it. I collected it myself at a very great personal risk. I am afraid they will try to claim it as theirs though. H'm. It is a difficult case. What do you think I ought to do—resist? Eh? I want no more than justice.' . . . He wanted no more than justice—no more than justice. I rang the bell before a mahogany door on the first floor, and while I waited he seemed to stare at me out of the glossy panel—stare with that wide and immense stare embracing, condemning, loathing all the universe. I seemed to hear the whispered cry, 'The horror! The horror!'

"The dusk was falling. I had to wait in a lofty drawing-room with three long windows from floor to ceiling that were like three luminous and bedraped columns. The bent gilt legs and backs of the furniture shone in indistinct curves. The tall marble fireplace had a cold and monumental whiteness. A grand piano stood massively in a corner; with dark gleams on the flat surfaces like a sombre and polished sarcophagus. A high door opened—closed. I rose.

"She came forward, all in black, with a pale head, floating towards me in the dusk. She was in mourning. It was more than a year since his death, more than a year since the news came; she seemed as though she would remember and mourn for ever. She took both my hands in hers and murmured, 'I had heard you were coming.' I noticed she was not very young—I mean not girlish. She had a mature capacity for fidelity, for belief, for suffering. The room seemed to have grown darker, as if all the sad light of the cloudy evening had taken refuge on her forehead. This fair hair, this pale visage, this pure brow, seemed surrounded by an ashy halo from which the dark eyes looked out at me. Their glance was guileless, profound, confident, and trustful. She carried her sorrowful head as though she were proud of that sorrow, as though she would say, I—I alone know how to mourn for him as he deserves. But while we were still shaking hands, such a look of awful desolation came upon her face that I perceived she was one of those creatures that are not the playthings of Time. For her he had died only yesterday. And, by Jove! the impression was so powerful that for me too he seemed to have died only yesterday—nay, this very minute. I saw her and him in the same instant of time—his death and her sorrow—I saw her sorrow in the very moment of his death. Do you understand? I saw them together—I heard them together. She had said, with a deep catch of the breath, 'I have survived'; while my strained ears seemed to hear distinctly, mingled with her tone of despairing regret, the summing-up whisper of his eternal condemnation. I asked myself what I was doing there, with a sensation of panic in my heart as though I had blundered into a place of cruel and absurd mysteries not fit for a human being to behold. She motioned me to a chair. We sat down. I laid the packet gently on the little table, and she put her hand over it. . . . 'You knew him well,' she murmured, after a moment of mourning silence.

" 'Intimacy grows quickly out there,' I said. 'I knew him as well as it is possible for one man to know another.'

" 'And you admired him,' she said. 'It was impossible to know him and not to admire him. Was it?'

" 'He was a remarkable man,' I said unsteadily. Then before the appealing fixity of her gaze, that seemed to watch for more words on my lips, I went on, 'It was impossible not to—'

" 'Love him,' she finished eagerly, silencing me into an appalled dumbness. 'How true! how true! But when you think that no one knew him so well as I! I had all his noble confidence. I knew him best.'

" 'You knew him best,' I repeated. And perhaps she did. But with every word spoken the room was growing darker, and only her forehead, smooth and white, remained illumined by the unextinguishable light of belief and love.

" 'You were his friend,' she went on. 'His friend,' she repeated, a little louder. 'You must have been, if he had given you this, and sent you to me. I feel I can speak to you—and oh! I must speak. I want you—you who have heard his last words—to know I have been worthy of him. . . . It is not pride. . . . Yes! I am proud to know I understood him better than any one on earth—he told me so himself. And since his mother died I have had no one—no one—to—to—'

"I listened. The darkness deepened. I was not even sure whether he had given me the right bundle. I rather suspect he wanted me to take care of another batch of his papers which, after his death, I saw the manager examining under the lamp. And the girl talked, easing her pain in the certitude of my sympathy; she talked as thirsty men drink. I had heard that her engagement with Kurtz had been disapproved by her people. He wasn't rich enough or something. And indeed I don't know whether he had not been a pauper all his life. He had given me some reason to infer that it was his impatience of comparative poverty that drove him out there.

" '. . . Who was not his friend who had heard him speak once?' she was saying. 'He drew men towards him by what was best in them.' She looked at me with intensity. 'It is the gift of the great,' she went on, and the sound of her low voice seemed to have the accompaniment of all the other sounds, full of mystery, desolation, and sorrow, I had ever heard—the ripple of the river, the soughing of the trees swayed by the wind, the murmurs of the crowds, the faint ring of incomprehensible words cried from afar, the whisper of a voice speaking from beyond the threshold of an eternal darkness. 'But you have heard him! You know!' she cried.

" 'Yes, I know,' I said with something like despair in my heart, but bowing my head before the faith that was in her, before that great and saving illusion that shone with an unearthly glow in the darkness, in the triumphant darkness from which I could not have defended her—from which I could not even defend myself.

" 'What a loss to me—to us!'—she corrected herself with beautiful generosity; then added in a murmur, 'To the world.' By the last gleams of twilight I could see the glitter of her eyes, full of tears—of tears that would not fall.

" 'I have been very happy—very fortunate—very proud,' she went on. 'Too fortunate. Too happy for a little while. And now I am unhappy for—for life.'

"She stood up; her fair hair seemed to catch all the remaining light in a glimmer of gold. I rose too.

" 'And of all this,' she went on mournfully, 'of all his promise, and of all his greatness, of his generous mind, of his noble heart, nothing remains—nothing but a memory. You and I—'

" 'We shall always remember him,' I said hastily.

" 'No!' she cried. 'It is impossible that all this should be lost—that such a life should be sacrificed to leave nothing—but sorrow. You know what vast plans he had. I knew of them too—I could not perhaps understand—but others knew of them. Something must remain. His words, at least, have not died.'

" 'His words will remain,' I said.

" 'And his example,' she whispered to herself. 'Men looked up to him—his goodness shone in every act. His example—'

" 'True,' I said; 'his example too. Yes, his example. I forgot that.'

" 'But I do not. I cannot—I cannot believe—not yet. I cannot believe that I shall never see him again, that nobody will see him again, never, never, never.'

"She put out her arms as if after a retreating figure, stretching them black and with clasped pale hands across the fading and narrow sheen of the window. Never see him! I saw him clearly enough then. I shall see this eloquent phantom as long as I live, and I shall see her too, a tragic and familiar Shade, resembling in this gesture another one, tragic also, and bedecked with powerless charms, stretching bare brown arms over the glitter of the infernal stream, the stream of darkness. She said suddenly very low, 'He died as he lived.'

" 'His end,' said I, with dull anger stirring in me, 'was in every way worthy of his life.'

" 'And I was not with him,' she murmured. My anger subsided before a feeling of infinite pity.

" 'Everything that could be done—' I mumbled.

" 'Ah, but I believed in him more than any one on earth—more than his own mother, more than—himself. He needed me! Me! I would have treasured every sigh, every word, every sign, every glance.'

"I felt like a chill grip on my chest. 'Don't,' I said, in a muffled voice.

" 'Forgive me. I—I—have mourned so long in silence—in silence. . . . You were with him—to the last? I think of his loneliness. Nobody near to understand him as I would have understood. Perhaps no one to hear. . . .'

" 'To the very end,' I said shakily. 'I heard his very last words. . . .' I stopped in a fright.

" 'Repeat them,' she murmured in a heart-broken tone. 'I want—I want—something—something—to—to live with.'

"I was on the point of crying at her, 'Don't you hear them?' The dusk was repeating them in a persistent whisper all around us, in a whisper that seemed to swell menacingly like the first whisper of a rising wind. 'The horror! The horror!'

" 'His last word—to live with,' she insisted. 'Don't you understand I loved him—I loved him—I loved him!'

"I pulled myself together and spoke slowly.

" 'The last word he pronounced was—your name.'

"I heard a light sigh and then my heart stood still, stopped dead short by an exulting and terrible cry, by the cry of inconceivable triumph and of unspeakable pain. 'I knew it—I was sure!' . . . She knew. She was sure. I heard her weeping; she had hidden her face in her hands. It seemed to me that the house would collapse before I could escape, that the heavens would fall upon my head. But nothing happened. The heavens do not fall for such a trifle. Would they have fallen, I wonder, if I had rendered Kurtz that justice which was his due? Hadn't he said he wanted only justice? But I couldn't. I could not tell her. It would have been too dark—too dark altogether. . . ."[9]

Marlow ceased, and sat apart, indistinct and silent, in the pose of a meditating Buddha. Nobody moved for a time. "We have lost the first of the ebb," said the Director suddenly. I raised my head. The offing was barred by a black bank of clouds, and the tranquil waterway leading to the uttermost ends of the earth flowed sombre under an overcast sky—seemed to lead into the heart of an immense darkness.

1899   1902

9. Writing to William Blackwood (editor of *Blackwood's Magazine*, where the story first appeared) in May 1902, Conrad referred to "the last pages of Heart of Darkness where the interview of the man and the girl locks in—as it were—the whole 30,000 words of narrative description into one suggestive view of a whole phase of life, and makes of that story something quite on another plane than an anecdote of a man who went mad in the Centre of Africa" (Joseph Conrad, *Letters to William Blackwood and David S. Meldrum*, ed. William Blackburn, 1958).

WILLIAM BUTLER YEATS
1865–1939

[margin notes:] Dublin = Nationalists / Revolutionary
Sligo = Gaelic / Mythology
London = Literary Btwt

1891:   Organization of the Rhymers' Club.
1899:   Launching of the Irish National Theatre.
1914:   *Responsibilities.*
1923:   Nobel Prize.
1928:   *The Tower.*

[margin note:] Maude Gonne

William Butler Yeats was born in Sandymount, Dublin. His father's family, of English stock, had been in Ireland for at least two hundred years; his mother's, the Pollexfens, hailing originally from Devon, had been for some generations in Sligo, in the west of Ireland. J. B. Yeats, his father, had abandoned law to take up painting, at which he made a somewhat precarious living. The Yeatses were in London from 1874 until 1883, when they returned to Ireland—to Howth, a few miles from

Dublin. On leaving high school in Dublin in 1883 Yeats decided to be an artist, with poetry as his avocation, and attended art school, but he soon left, to concentrate on poetry. His first published poems appeared in the *Dublin University Review* in 1885.

Yeats's father was a religious skeptic, but he believed in the "religion of art." Yeats himself, religious by temperament but unable to believe in Christian orthodoxy, sought all his life for traditions of esoteric thought that would compensate for a lost religion. This search led him to various kinds of mysticism, to folklore, theosophy, spiritualism, and neoplatonism—not in any strict chronological order, for he kept returning to and reworking earlier aspects of his thought. In middle life he elaborated a symbolic system of his own, based on a variety of sources, which enabled him to strengthen the pattern and coherence of his poetic imagery. The student of Yeats is constantly coming up against this willful and sometimes baffling esotericism that he cultivated sometimes playfully, sometimes earnestly, sometimes treating it as though it were a body of truths and sometimes as though it were a convenient language of symbols. Modern scholarship has traced most of Yeats's mystical and quasi-mystical ideas to sources that were common to William Blake and Percy Shelley and that sometimes go far back into pre-Platonic beliefs and traditions. But his greatness as a poet lies in his ability to communicate the power and significance of his symbols, by the way he expresses and organizes them, even to readers who know nothing of his system.

Yeats's childhood and young manhood were spent between Dublin, London, and Sligo, and each of these places contributed something to his poetic development. In London in the 1890s he met the important poets of the day, and in 1891 was one of the founders of the Rhymers' Club, whose members included Lionel Johnson, Ernest Dowson, and many other characteristic figures of the 1890s. Here he acquired ideas of poetry that were vaguely Pre-Raphaelite: he believed, in this early stage of his career, that a poet's language should be dreamy, evocative, and ethereal. From the countryside around Sligo he got something much more vigorous and earthy—a knowledge of the life of the peasantry and of their folklore. In Dublin he was influenced by the currents of Irish nationalism and, while often in disagreement with those who wished to use literature for crude political ends, he nevertheless learned to see his poetry as a contribution to a rejuvenated Irish culture. The three influences of Dublin, London, and Sligo did not develop in chronological order—he was going to and fro among these places throughout his early life—and we sometimes find a poem based on Sligo folklore in the midst of a group of dreamy poems written under the influence of the Rhymers' Club or an echo of Irish nationalist feeling in a lyric otherwise wholly Pre-Raphaelite in tone.

We can distinguish quite clearly, however, the main periods into which Yeats's poetic career falls. He began in the tradition of self-conscious Romanticism, which he learned from the London poets of the 1890s. Edmund Spenser and Shelley, and a little later Blake, were also important influences. One of his early verse plays ends with a song:

> The woods of Arcady are dead
> And over is their antique joy;
> Of old the world on dreaming fed;
> Grey Truth is now her painted toy.

About the same time he was writing poems (e.g., *The Stolen Child*) deriving from his Sligo experience, with a quiet precision of natural imagery, country place names, and themes from folklore. A little later—i.e., in the latter part of his first period—Dublin literary circles sent him to Standish O'Grady's *History of Ireland: Heroic Period*, where he found the great stories of the heroic age of Irish history, and to George Sigerson's and Douglas Hyde's translations of Gaelic poetry into "that dialect which gets from Gaelic its syntax and keeps its still partly Tudor vocabulary." Even when he plays with Neoplatonic ideas, as in *The Rose of the World* (also the product of the latter part of his early period), he can link them with Irish heroic themes and so give a dignity and a *style* to his imagery not normally associated with this sort of poetic dreaminess. Thus the heroic legends of old Ireland and the folk traditions of the modern Irish countryside provided Yeats with a stiffening for his early dreamlike imagery, which is why even his first, "nineties" phase is productive of interesting poems. *The Lake Isle of Innisfree*, spoiled for some by overanthologizing, is nevertheless a fine poem of its kind: it is the clarity and control shown in the handling of the imagery that keeps all romantic fuzziness out of it and gives it its haunting quality. In *The Man Who Dreamed of Faeryland* he makes something peculiarly effective out of the contrast between human activities and the strangeness of nature. In *The Madness of King Goll* the disturbing sense of the *otherness* of the natural world drives the king mad. (Such contrasts are common in the early Yeats; in his later poetry he tries to resolve what he called these "antinomies" in inclusive symbols; e.g., *Crazy Jane Talks with the Bishop*.)

It is important to realize that Yeats had a habit of revising his earlier poems in later printings, tightening up the language and getting rid of the more self-indulgent romantic imagery. The revised versions are found in his *Collected Poems*, which, therefore, present a somewhat muted picture of his poetic development. For the complete picture one should consult *The Variorum Edition* edited by Peter Allt and Russell K. Alspach (1957).

It was Irish nationalism that first sent Yeats in search of a consistently simpler and more popular style. He tells in one of his autobiographical essays how he sought for a style in which to express the elemental facts about Irish life and aspirations. This led him to the concrete image, as did Hyde's translations from Gaelic folk songs, in which "nothing . . . was abstract, nothing worn-out." But other forces were also working on him. In 1902 a friend gave him the works of the German philosopher Friedrich Nietzsche, to which he responded with great excitement, and it would seem that, in persuading Yeats, the passive love-poet, to get off his knees, Nietzsche's books prompted his search for a more active stance, a more masculine style. Looking back in 1906, he found that he had mistaken the poetic ideal. "Without knowing it, I had come to care for nothing but impersonal beauty. . . . We should ascend out of common interests, the thoughts of the newspapers, of the market place, but only so far as we can carry the normal, passionate, reasoning self, the personality as a whole." The result of the abandonment of "impersonal beauty," and of the desire to "carry the normal, passionate, reasoning self" into his poetry, is seen in the volumes of collected poems, *In the Seven Woods* (1903) and *The Green Helmet and Other Poems* (1910). *The Folly of Being Comforted* and *Adam's Curse* are from the former of these, and one can see immediately how Yeats here combines the colloquial with the formal. This is characteristic of his "second period."

By this time Yeats had met the beautiful actress and violent Irish nationalist Maud Gonne, with whom he was desperately in love for many years, but who persistently refused to marry him. The affair is reflected in many of the poems of his second period, notably *No Second Troy*, published in *The Green Helmet*. He had also met Lady Gregory, Irish writer and promoter of Irish literature, in 1896, and she invited him to spend the following summer at her country house, Coole Park, in Galway. Yeats spent many holidays with Lady Gregory and discovered the attractiveness of the "country house ideal," seeing in an aristocratic life of elegance and leisure in a great house a method of imposing order on chaos and a symbol of the Neoplatonic dance of life. He expresses this view many times in his poetry— e.g., at the end of *A Prayer for My Daughter*—and it became an important part of his complex of attitudes. The middle classes, with their Philistine money grubbing, he detested, and for his ideal characters he looked either below them, to peasants and beggars, or above them, to the aristocracy, for each of these had their own traditions and lived according to them.

It was under Lady Gregory's influence that Yeats became involved in the founding of the Irish National Theatre in 1899. This led to his active participation in problems of play production, which included political problems of censorship, economic problems of paying carpenters and actors, and other aspects of "theater business, management of men." All this had an effect on his style. The reactions of Dublin audiences did not encourage Yeats's trust in popular judgment, and his bitterness with the "Paudeens," middle-class shopkeepers—who seemed to him to be without any dignity, or understanding, or nobility of spirit—produced some of the most effective poems of his third or middle period. He was now becoming more and more of a national figure. Three public controversies had moved him to anger and to poetry; the first over the hounding of Parnell (*To a Shade*), the second over Synge's play *The Playboy of the Western World* in 1907, and the third over the Lane pictures (*September 1913*). In each, the cause for which he fought was defeated by representatives of the Roman Catholic middle class, and at last, bitterly turning his back on Ireland, Yeats moved to England. Then came the Easter Rising (*Easter 1916*), mounted by members of the class and religion that had so long opposed him. Persuaded by Gonne (whose estranged husband was one of the executed leaders of the rising) that "tragic dignity had returned to Ireland," Yeats himself returned. To mark his new commitment, he refurbished, occupied, and renamed "Thoor Ballylee" the Norman tower on Lady Gregory's land that was to become one of the central symbols of his later poetry. In 1922 he was appointed a senator of the recently established Irish Free State and served until 1928, playing an active part not only in promoting the arts but also in general political affairs, in which he supported the views of the Protestant landed class.

Meanwhile Yeats was responding in his own way to the change in poetic taste represented in the poetry and criticism of Ezra Pound and T. S. Eliot immediately before World War I. A gift for epigram had already begun to emerge in his poetry; in the volume titled *The Wild Swans at Coole* (1919) he has a poem citing Walter Savage Landor (the nineteenth-century poet who wrote some fine lapidary verse) and John Donne as masters. To the precision, and the combination of colloquial and formal, that he had achieved early in the century, he now added a "metaphysical" as well as an epigrammatic element, and this is seen in the later poems of his third period. He also continued his experiments with different kinds of rhythm. At the same time he was continuing his search for a language of symbols and pursuing his esoteric studies. Yeats married in 1917, and his wife proved so sympathetic to his imaginative needs that the automatic writing which for several years she produced (believed by Yeats to have been dictated by spirits) gave him the elements of a symbolic system that he later worked out in his book *A Vision* (1925, 1937) and that he used in all sorts of ways in much of his later poetry. The system was both a theory of the movements of history and a theory of the different types of personality, each movement and type being related in various complicated ways to a different phase of the moon. Some of Yeats's poetry is unintelligible without a knowledge of *A Vision*, but the better poems, such as the two on Byzantium, can be appreciated without such knowledge by the experienced reader who responds sensitively to the patterning of the imagery reinforced by the incantatory effect of the rhythms. Some criticism decries attempts by those who are not experts in the background of Yeats's esoteric thought to discuss his poetry and insists that only a detailed knowledge of Yeats's sources can yield his poetic meaning; but while it is true that some particular images do not yield all their significance to those who are ignorant of the background, it is also true that too literal a paraphrase of the symbolism in the light of the sources robs the poems of their power by reducing them to mere exercises in the use of a code.

The Tower (1928) and *The Winding Stair* (1933), from which the poems from *Sailing to Byzantium* through *After Long Silence* have been here selected, represent the mature Yeats at his very best—a realist-symbolist-Metaphysical poet with an uncanny power over words. These volumes represent his fourth and greatest period. Here, in his poems of the 1920s and 1930s, winding stairs, spinning tops, "gyres," spirals of all kinds, are important symbols; not only are they connected with Yeats's philosophy of history and of personality but they also serve as a means of resolving some of those contraries that had arrested him from the beginning. Life is a journey up a spiral staircase; as we grow older we cover the ground we have covered before, only higher up; as we look down the winding stair below us we measure our progress by the number of places where we were but no longer are. The journey is both repetitious and progressive; we go both round and upward. Through symbolic images of this kind Yeats explores the paradoxes of time and change, of growth and identity, of love and age, of life and art, of madness and wisdom.

The Byzantium poems show him trying to escape from the turbulence of life to the calm eternity of art. But in his fifth and final period he returned to the turbulence after (if only partly as a result of) undergoing the Steinach operation to increase his sexual potency in 1934, and his last poems have a controlled yet startling wildness. Yeats's return to life, to "the foul rag-and-bone shop of the heart," is one of the most impressive final phases of any poet's career. "I shall be a sinful man to the end, and think upon my deathbed of all the nights I wasted in my youth," he wrote in old age to a correspondent, and in one of his last letters he wrote: "When I try to put all into a phrase I say, 'Man can embody truth but he cannot know it.' . . . The abstract is not life and everywhere draws out its contradictions. You can refute Hegel but not the Saint or the Song of Sixpence." When he died in January 1939, he left a body of verse that, in variety and power, makes him beyond question the greatest twentieth-century poet of the English language.

The Stolen Child

Where dips the rocky highland
Of Sleuth Wood[1] in the lake,
There lies a leafy island
Where flapping herons wake
The drowsy water-rats;   5
There we've hid our faery vats,
Full of berries
And of reddest stolen cherries.
Come away, O human child!
To the waters and the wild   10
With a faery, hand in hand,
For the world's more full of weeping than you can understand.

Where the wave of moonlight glosses
The dim grey sands with light,
Far off by furthest Rosses   15
We foot it all the night,
Weaving olden dances,
Mingling hands and mingling glances

---

1. This and other places mentioned in the poem are in County Sligo, in northwestern Ireland, where Yeats spent much of his childhood.

Till the moon has taken flight;
To and fro we leap   20
And chase the frothy bubbles,
While the world is full of troubles
And is anxious in its sleep.
Come away, O human child!
To the waters and the wild   25
With a faery, hand in hand,
For the world's more full of weeping than you can understand.

Where the wandering water gushes
From the hills above Glen-Car,
In pools among the rushes   30
That scarce could bathe a star,
We seek for slumbering trout
And whispering in their ears
Give them unquiet dreams;
Leaning softly out   35
From ferns that drop their tears
Over the young streams.
Come away, O human child!
To the waters and the wild
With a faery, hand in hand,   40
For the world's more full of weeping than you can understand.

Away with us he's going,
The solemn-eyed:
He'll hear no more the lowing
Of the calves on the warm hillside   45
Or the kettle on the hob
Sing peace into his breast,
Or see the brown mice bob
Round and round the oatmeal-chest.
For he comes, the human child,   50
To the waters and the wild
With a faery, hand in hand,
From a world more full of weeping than he can understand.

                                                      1886, 1889

The Rose of the World[1]

Who dreamed that beauty passes like a dream?
For these red lips, with all their mournful pride,
Mournful that no new wonder may betide,
Troy passed away in one high funeral gleam,
And Usna's children died.[2]   5

1. The platonic idea of eternal beauty. "I notice upon reading these poems for the first time for several years that the quality symbolized as The Rose differs from the Intellectual Beauty of Shelley and of Spenser in that I have imagined it as suffering with man and not as something pursued and seen from afar" [Yeats, in 1925].

2. In Old Irish legend the Ulster warrior Naoise, son of Usna or Usnach (pronounced *Úskna,*) carried off the beautiful Deirdre, whom King Conchubar of Ulster had intended to marry, and with his two brothers took her to Scotland. Eventually Cochubar lured the four of them back to Ireland and killed the three brothers.

We and the labouring world are passing by:
Amid men's souls, that waver and give place
Like the pale waters in their wintry race,
Under the passing stars, foam of the sky,
Lives on this lonely face.   10

Bow down, archangels, in your dim abode:
Before you were, or any hearts to beat,
Weary and kind one lingered by His seat;
He made the world to be a grassy road
Before her wandering feet.   15

1892

The Lake Isle of Innisfree[1]

I will arise and go now, and go to Innisfree,
And a small cabin build there, of clay and wattles[2] made;
Nine bean-rows will I have there, a hive for the honey-bee,
And live alone in the bee-loud glade.

And I shall have some peace there, for peace comes dropping slow,   5
Dropping from the veils of the morning to where the cricket sings;
There midnight's all a glimmer, and noon a purple glow,
And evening full of the linnet's wings.

I will arise and go now, for always night and day
I hear lake water lapping with low sounds by the shore;   10
While I stand on the roadway, or on the pavements grey,
I hear it in the deep heart's core.

1890   1890, 1892

The Sorrow of Love

The brawling of a sparrow in the eaves,
The brilliant moon and all the milky sky,
And all that famous harmony of leaves,
Had blotted out man's image and his cry.

A girl arose that had red mournful lips   5
And seemed the greatness of the world in tears,
Doomed like Odysseus and the labouring ships
And proud as Priam murdered with his peers;[1]

1. Island in Lough Gill, County Sligo. "My father had read to me some passage out of [Thoreau's] *Walden*, and I planned to live some day in a cottage on a little island called Innisfree."
2. Stakes interwoven with twigs or branches.
1. Odysseus (whom the Romans called Ulysses), hero of Homer's *Odyssey*, which describes how, after having fought in the siege of Troy, he wandered for ten years before reaching his home, the Greek island of Ithaca. Priam was king of Troy at the time of the siege and was killed when the Greeks captured the city.

Arose, and on the instant clamorous eaves,
A climbing moon upon an empty sky,   10
And all that lamentation of the leaves,
Could but compose man's image and his cry.

1891   1892, 1925

When You Are Old[1]

When you are old and grey and full of sleep,
And nodding by the fire, take down this book,
And slowly read, and dream of the soft look
Your eyes had once, and of their shadows deep;

How many loved your moments of glad grace,   5
And loved your beauty with love false or true,
But one man loved the pilgrim soul in you,
And loved the sorrows of your changing face;

And bending down beside the glowing bars,[2]
Murmur, a little sadly, how Love fled   10
And paced upon the mountains overhead
And hid his face amid a crowd of stars.

October 1891   1892

Who Goes with Fergus?[1]

Who will go drive with Fergus now,
And pierce the deep wood's woven shade,
And dance upon the level shore?
Young man, lift up your russet brow,
And lift your tender eyelids, maid,   5
And brood on hopes and fear no more.

And no more turn aside and brood
Upon love's bitter mystery;
For Fergus rules the brazen cars,
And rules the shadows of the wood,   10
And the white breast of the dim sea
And all dishevelled wandering stars.

1893

---

1. A poem suggested by a sonnet of the 16th-century French poet Pierre de Ronsard; it begins "*Quand vous serez bien vieille, au soir, à la chandelle*" ("When you are old, sitting at evening by candle light") but ends very differently from Yeats's poem.
2. I.e., of the grate.

1. In a late version of this Irish heroic legend, Fergus, "king of the proud Red Branch Kings," gave up his throne voluntarily to Conchubar to learn by dreaming and meditating the bitter wisdom of the poet and philosopher.

The Man Who Dreamed of Faeryland

He stood among a crowd at Dromahair;[1]
His heart hung all upon a silken dress,
And he had known at last some tenderness,
Before earth took him to her stony care;
But when a man poured fish into a pile,   5
It seemed they raised their little silver heads,
And sang what gold morning or evening sheds
Upon a woven world-forgotten isle
Where people love beside the ravelled[2] seas;
That Time can never mar a lover's vows   10
Under that woven changeless roof of boughs:
The singing shook him out of his new ease.

He wandered by the sands of Lissadell;
His mind ran all on money cares and fears,
And he had known at last some prudent years   15
Before they heaped his grave under the hill;
But while he passed before a plashy place,
A lug-worm with its grey and muddy mouth
Sang that somewhere to north or west or south
There dwelt a gay, exulting, gentle race   20
Under the golden or the silver skies;
That if a dancer stayed his hungry foot
It seemed the sun and moon were in the fruit:
And at that singing he was no more wise.

He mused beside the well of Scanavin,   25
He mused upon his mockers: without fail
His sudden vengeance were a country tale,
When earthy night had drunk his body in;
But one small knot-grass growing by the pool
Sang where—unnecessary cruel voice—   30
Old silence bids its chosen race rejoice,
Whatever ravelled waters rise and fall
Or stormy silver fret the gold of day,
And midnight there enfold them like a fleece
And lover there by lover be at peace.   35
The tale drove his fine angry mood away.

He slept under the hill of Lugnagall;
And might have known at last unhaunted sleep
Under that cold and vapour-turbaned steep,
Now that the earth had taken man and all: 40
Did not the worms that spired about his bones
Proclaim with that unwearied, reedy cry
That God has laid His fingers on the sky,
That from those fingers glittering summer runs
Upon the dancer by the dreamless wave.   45

1. This and other place names in the poem refer to   2. Tangled, hence here "turbulent."
places in County Sligo.

Why should those lovers that no lovers miss
Dream, until God burn Nature with a kiss?
The man has found no comfort in the grave.

1891, 1892

The Secret Rose[1]

Far-off, most secret, and inviolate Rose,
Enfold me in my hour of hours; where those
Who sought thee in the Holy Sepulchre,
Or in the wine-vat, dwell beyond the stir
And tumult of defeated dreams; and deep   5
Among pale eyelids, heavy with the sleep
Men have named beauty. Thy great leaves enfold
The ancient beards, the helms of ruby and gold
Of the crowned Magi;[2] and the king whose eyes
Saw the Pierced Hands and Rood of elder rise   10
In Druid vapour and make the torches dim;
Till vain frenzy awoke and he died;[3] and him
Who met Fand walking among flaming dew
By a grey shore where the wind never blew,
And lost the world and Emer for a kiss;[4]   15
And him who drove the gods out of their liss,[5]
And till a hundred morns had flowered red
Feasted, and wept the barrows of his dead;
And the proud dreaming king[6] who flung the crown
And sorrow away, and calling bard and clown   20
Dwelt among wine-stained wanderers in deep woods;
And him who sold tillage, and house, and goods,
And sought through lands and islands numberless years,
Until he found, with laughter and with tears,
A woman of so shining loveliness   25

1. The Rose is a symbol of beauty (see *The Rose of the World*, p. 2268). Yeats reveals in an interesting note how he used his sources: "I find that I have unintentionally changed the old story of Conchubar's death. He did not see the Crucifixion in a vision but was told of it . . . I have imagined Cuchulain meeting Fand 'walking among the flaming dew,' because, I think, of something in Mr. Standish O'Grady's books. [See headnote "William Butler Yeats," p. 2263.] I have founded the man 'who drove the gods out of their liss,' or fort, upon something I have read about Caoilte after the battle of Gabhra, when almost all his companions were killed, driving the gods out of their liss, . . . I have founded 'the proud dreaming kind' upon Fergus, the son of Rogh, but when I wrote my poem here, and in the song in my early book, 'Who will drive with Fergus now?' I only knew him in Mr. Standish O'Grady, . . . I have founded 'him who sold tillage, and house, and goods,' upon something in 'The Red Pony,' a folktale in Mr. Larminie's *West Irish Folk Tales*. A young man 'saw a light before him on the high-road. When he came as far, there was an open box on the road, and a light coming up out of it. He took up the box. There was a lock of hair in it. Presently he had to go to become the servant of a king for his living. There were eleven boys. When they were going out into the stable at ten o'clock, each of them took a light but he. He took no candle at all with him. Each of them went into his own stable. When he went into his stable he opened the box. He left it in a hole in the wall. The light was great. It was twice as much as in the other stables.' The king hears of it, and makes him show him the box. The king says, 'You must go and bring me the woman to whom the hair belongs.' In the end the young man, and not the king, marries the woman."
2. The wise men from the east who came to do homage to the infant Jesus.
3. King Conchubar, in early Christian legend, is said to have died on the day of Christ's crucifixion in a fit of rage at hearing the news. Yeats (as his n. 1 explains) makes Conchubar see the crucifixion in a vision raised by the magic of the ancient Celtic priests, or Druids. The "Pierced Hands" are Christ's, and the "Rood" is the Cross.
4. The ancient Irish hero Cuchulain was seduced by Fand away from his wife, Emer.
5. Fort. This is Caoilte, legendary Irish hero and companion of Oisin, son of Finn, poet and warrior.
6. I.e., Fergus (see n. 1).

That men threshed corn at midnight by a tress,
A little stolen tress.[7] I, too, await
The hour of thy great wind of love and hate.
When shall the stars be blown about the sky,
Like the sparks blown out of a smithy, and die?   30
Surely thine hour has come, thy great wind blows,
Far-off, most secret, and inviolate Rose?

                                                      1896, 1897

The Folly of Being Comforted

One that is ever kind said yesterday:
"Your well-belovèd's hair has threads of grey,
And little shadows come about her eyes;
Time can but make it easier to be wise
Though now it seem impossible, and so   5
All that you need is patience."
                          Heart cries, "No,
I have not a crumb of comfort, not a grain.
Time can but make her beauty over again:
Because of that great nobleness of hers
The fire that stirs about her, when she stirs,   10
Burns but more clearly. O she had not these ways
When all the wild summer was in her gaze."

O heart! O heart! if she'd but turn her head,
You'd know the folly of being comforted.

                                                      1902, 1903

Adam's Curse[1]

We sat together at one summer's end,
That beautiful mild woman, your close friend,
And you and I, and talked of poetry.
I said: "A line will take us hours maybe;
Yet if it does not seem a moment's thought,   5
Our stitching and unstitching has been naught.
Better go down upon your marrow-bones
And scrub a kitchen pavement, or break stones
Like an old pauper, in all kinds of weather;
For to articulate sweet sounds together   10
Is to work harder than all these, and yet
Be thought an idler by the noisy set
Of bankers, schoolmasters, and clergymen
The martyrs call the world."

7. See n. 1.
1. To work for a living was the curse imposed by God
on Adam after the Fall (Genesis 3.17–19). The poem
reflects an incident in Yeats's passionate but hopeless
love for the beautiful revolutionary Maud Gonne (see
A. N. Jeffares, W. B. Yeats: Man and Poet, 1949, pp.
128–129).

                                    And thereupon
That beautiful mild woman for whose sake   15
There's many a one shall find out all heartache
On finding that her voice is sweet and low
Replied: "To be born woman is to know—
Although they do not talk of it at school—
That we must labour to be beautiful."   20

I said: "It's certain there is no fine thing
Since Adam's fall but needs much labouring.
There have been lovers who thought love should be
So much compounded of high courtesy
That they would sigh and quote with learned looks   25
Precedents out of beautiful old books;
Yet now it seems an idle trade enough."

We sat grown quiet at the name of love;
We saw the last embers of daylight die,
And in the trembling blue-green of the sky   30
A moon, worn as if it had been a shell
Washed by time's waters as they rose and fell
About the stars and broke in days and years.

I had a thought for no one's but your ears:
That you were beautiful, and that I strove   35
To love you in the old high way of love;
That it had all seemed happy, and yet we'd grown
As weary-hearted as that hollow moon.
November 1902   1902, 1903

No Second Troy

Why should I blame her[1] that she filled my days
With misery, or that she would of late
Have taught to ignorant men most violent ways,
Or hurled the little streets upon the great,
Had they but courage equal to desire?   5
What could have made her peaceful with a mind
That nobleness made simple as a fire,
With beauty like a tightened bow, a kind
That is not natural in an age like this,
Being high and solitary and most stern?   10
Why, what could she have done, being what she is?
Was there another Troy for her to burn?[2]
December 1908   1910

1. I.e., Gonne.   the first Troy.
2. Helen of Troy was the cause of the destruction of

The Fascination of What's Difficult[1]

The fascination of what's difficult
Has dried the sap out of my veins, and rent
Spontaneous joy and natural content
Out of my heart. There's something ails our colt
That must, as if it had not holy blood   5
Nor on Olympus leaped from cloud to cloud,
Shiver under the lash, strain, sweat and jolt
As though it dragged road-metal. My curse on plays
That have to be set up in fifty ways,
On the day's war with every knave and dolt,   10
Theatre business, management of men.
I swear before the dawn comes round again
I'll find the stable and pull out the bolt.

September 1909–March 1910   1910

September 1913[1]

What need you,[2] being come to sense,
But fumble in a greasy till
And add the halfpence to the pence
And prayer to shivering prayer, until
You have dried the marrow from the bone?   5
For men were born to pray and save:
Romantic Ireland's dead and gone,
It's with O'Leary[3] in the grave.

Yet they were of a different kind,
The names that stilled your childish play,   10
They have gone about the world like wind,
But little time had they to pray
For whom the hangman's rope was spun,
And what, God help us, could they save?
Romantic Ireland's dead and gone,   15
It's with O'Leary in the grave.

Was it for this the wild geese[4] spread
The grey wing upon every tide;

1. Written when Yeats was director-manager of the Abbey Theatre. "Subject. To complain of the fascination of what's difficult. It spoils spontaneity and pleasure, and wastes time. Repeat the line ending difficult three times and rhyme on bolt, exalt, colt, jolt" [Yeats's diary for September 1909].
1. Originally titled *Romance in Ireland (On Reading Much of the Correspondence against the Art Gallery)* and published in the *Irish Times* of September 8, 1913. Sir Hugh Lane, Lady Gregory's nephew, had offered his collection of French impressionist paintings to the city of Dublin, provided they were permanently housed in a suitable gallery. Fierce abuse of the paintings and of the proposed design of the gallery in the Dublin nationalist press caused Lane to send the pictures to the London National Gallery. (Lane was drowned in the *Lusitania* in 1915; after years of bitter court dispute over an unwitnessed codicil to his will bequeathing the paintings to Dublin, an arrangement was reached in 1959 for the pictures to hang first in Dublin and then in London, for five years at a time.)
2. I.e., members of the new and predominantly Roman Catholic middle class.
3. John O'Leary (1830–1907), Irish nationalist of great courage and integrity who, returning to Dublin in 1885 after five years' imprisonment and fifteen years' exile, drew Yeats and others to the nationalist cause.
4. Popular name for the Irishmen who, because of the penal laws against Catholics, were forced to flee to the Continent from 1691 until Catholic Emancipation in 1829. One hundred and twenty thousand fought in the armies of France, Spain, and Austria.

For this that all that blood was shed,
For this Edward Fitzgerald died,   20
And Robert Emmet and Wolfe Tone,[5]
All that delirium of the brave?
Romantic Ireland's dead and gone,
It's with O'Leary in the grave.

Yet could we turn the years again,   25
And call those exiles as they were
In all their loneliness and pain,
You'd cry, "Some woman's yellow hair
Has maddened every mother's son":
They weighed so lightly what they gave.   30
But let them be, they're dead and gone,
They're with O'Leary in the grave.

September 1913   1913

To a Shade[1]

If you have revisited the town, thin Shade,
Whether to look upon your monument
(I wonder if the builder has been paid)
Or happier-thoughted when the day is spent
To drink of that salt breath out of the sea   5
When grey gulls flit about instead of men,
And the gaunt houses put on majesty:
Let these content you and be gone again;
For they are at their old tricks yet.
                         A man[2]
Of your own passionate serving kind who had brought   10
In his full hands what, had they only known,
Had given their children's children loftier thought,
Sweeter emotion, working in their veins
Like gentle blood, has been driven from the place,
And insult heaped upon him for his pains,   15
And for his open-handedness, disgrace;
Your enemy, an old foul mouth, had set
The pack upon him.[3]
                    Go, unquiet wanderer,
And gather the Glasnevin[4] coverlet
About your head till the dust stops your ear,   20
The time for you to taste of that salt breath
And listen at the corners has not come;

5. Theobald Wolfe Tone (1763–1798), one of the chief founders of the United Irishmen (an Irish nationalist organization), committed suicide in prison in Dublin. Lord Edward Fitzgerald (1763–1798), British officer who, after being dismissed from the army for disloyal activities, joined the United Irishmen, was arrested, and died in prison. Robert Emmet (1778–1803) was also an Irish patriot, executed for treason after a heroic career.

1. The spirit of the great Irish nationalist leader Charles Stewart Parnell (1846–1891).
2. Sir Hugh Lane (see p. 2275, 2nd n. 1).
3. William Martin Murphy, proprietor of the *Irish Independent* and *Evening Herald*. He had opposed the Lane benefaction and had earlier supported those who led the attack on Parnell.
4. The cemetery where Parnell is buried.

You had enough of sorrow before death—
Away, away! You are safer in the tomb.
September 1913   1913

A Coat

I made my song a coat
Covered with embroideries
Out of old mythologies[1]
From heel to throat;
But the fools caught it,[2]   5
Wore it in the world's eyes
As though they'd wrought it.
Song, let them take it,
For there's more enterprise
In walking naked.   10

1912   1914

The Wild Swans at Coole[1]

The trees are in their autumn beauty,
The woodland paths are dry,
Under the October twilight the water
Mirrors a still sky;
Upon the brimming water among the stones   5
Are nine-and-fifty swans.

The nineteenth autumn has come upon me
Since I first made my count;[2]
I saw, before I had well finished,
All suddenly mount   10
And scatter wheeling in great broken rings
Upon their clamorous wings.

I have looked upon those brilliant creatures,
And now my heart is sore.
All's changed since I, hearing at twilight,   15
The first time on this shore,
The bell-beat of their wings above my head,
Trod with a lighter tread.

Unwearied still, lover by lover,[3]
They paddle in the cold   20

1. Gaelic legends, which Yeats had read in such translations as those of Standish O'Grady and James Clarence Mangan.
2. Probably a reference to the protégés of Æ [George
William Russell], among them Seamus O'Sullivan. Cf.
To a poet who would have me Praise certain Bad Poets,
Imitators of His and Mine.

1. Coole Park, Lady Gregory's country estate, where
Yeats was a frequent guest.
2. His first visit had been in 1897 (nineteen years earlier).
3. In Irish legend, the lovers Baile and Aillinn had
been changed into swans; also, the subject of Yeats's
poem Baile and Aillinn (1903).

Companionable streams or climb the air;
Their hearts have not grown old;
Passion or conquest, wander where they will,
Attend upon them still.

But now they drift on the still water,   25
Mysterious, beautiful;
Among what rushes will they build,
By what lake's edge or pool
Delight men's eyes when I awake some day
To find they have flown away?   30

October 1916   1917

Easter 1916[1]

I have met them at close of day
Coming with vivid faces
From counter or desk among grey
Eighteenth-century houses.
I have passed with a nod of the head   5
Or polite meaningless words,
Or have lingered awhile and said
Polite meaningless words,
And thought before I had done
Of a mocking tale or a gibe   10
To please a companion
Around the fire at the club,
Being certain that they and I
But lived where motley[2] is worn:
All changed, changed utterly: 15
A terrible beauty is born.

That woman's days were spent
In ignorant good-will,
Her nights in argument
Until her voice grew shrill.   20
What voice more sweet than hers
When, young and beautiful,
She rode to harriers?[3]
This man had kept a school
And rode our wingèd horse;[4]   25
This other his helper and friend

1. This title, with its resemblance to *September 1913*, suggests that the poem is a palinode (one in which the author retracts something said in a former poem). On Easter Monday of 1916, Irish nationalists launched a heroic but unsuccessful revolt against the British government; the week of street fighting that followed is known as the Easter Rebellion. As a result, a number of the nationalists were executed: Britain, at war with Germany, was in no mood to tolerate Irish agitation for independence—which was supported, for obvious reasons, by Germany. Yeats knew the chief rebels personally.
2. Jester's parti-colored costume.
3. Constance Gore-Booth (afterward Countess Markiewicz), a member of the Sligo county aristocracy. A gay and beautiful woman, she had annoyed Yeats by becoming an embittered nationalist.
4. Patrick Pearse, a schoolmaster, a leader in the movement to restore the Gaelic language in Ireland, and a poet (hence the reference to "our wingèd horse"—Pegasus, the horse of the Muses). "His helper and friend" was Thomas MacDonagh.

Was coming into his force;
He might have won fame in the end,
So sensitive his nature seemed,
So daring and sweet his thought.   30
This other man I had dreamed
A drunken, vainglorious lout.[5]
He had done most bitter wrong
To some who are near my heart,
Yet I number him in the song;   35
He, too, has resigned his part
In the casual comedy;
He, too, has been changed in his turn,
Transformed utterly:
A terrible beauty is born.   40

Hearts with one purpose alone
Through summer and winter seem
Enchanted to a stone
To trouble the living stream.
The horse that comes from the road,   45
The rider, the birds that range
From cloud to tumbling cloud,
Minute by minute they change;
A shadow of cloud on the stream
Changes minute by minute;   50
A horse-hoof slides on the brim,
And a horse plashes within it;
The long-legged moor-hens dive,
And hens to moor-cocks call;
Minute by minute they live: 55
The stone's in the midst of all.

Too long a sacrifice
Can make a stone of the heart.
O when may it suffice?
That is Heaven's part, our part   60
To murmur name upon name,
As a mother names her child
When sleep at last has come
On limbs that had run wild.
What is it but nightfall?   65
No, no, not night but death;
Was it needless death after all?
For England may keep faith
For all that is done and said.
We know their dream; enough   70
To know they dreamed and are dead;
And what if excess of love
Bewildered them till they died?
I write it out in a verse—

5. Major John MacBride. Gonne, to Yeats's great disgust, had married MacBride in 1903, only to be separated
from him after two years.

MacDonagh and MacBride   75
And Connolly[6] and Pearse
Now and in time to be,
Wherever green is worn,
Are changed, changed utterly:
A terrible beauty is born.   80

May–September 1916   1916, 1920

The Second Coming[1]

Turning and turning in the widening gyre
The falcon cannot hear the falconer;
Things fall apart; the center cannot hold;
Mere anarchy is loosed upon the world,
The blood-dimmed tide is loosed, and everywhere   5
The ceremony of innocence is drowned;
The best lack all conviction, while the worst
Are full of passionate intensity.[2]

Surely some revelation is at hand;
Surely the Second Coming is at hand.   10
The Second Coming! Hardly are those words out
When a vast image out of *Spiritus Mundi*[3]
Troubles my sight: somewhere in sands of the desert
A shape with lion body and the head of a man,
A gaze blank and pitiless as the sun,   15
Is moving its slow thighs, while all about it
Reel shadows of the indignant desert birds.
The darkness drops again; but now I know
That twenty centuries of stony sleep
Were vexed to nightmare by a rocking cradle,[4]   20
And what rough beast, its hour come round at last,
Slouches towards Bethlehem to be born?

January 1919   1920, 1921

A Prayer for My Daughter[1]

Once more the storm is howling, and half hid
Under this cradle-hood and coverlid

6. James Connolly, Pearse's partner in leading the insurrection. Like the other rebels named here, he was executed by firing squad.
1. This poem expresses Yeats's sense of the dissolution of the civilization of his time, the end of one cycle of history and the approach of another. He called each cycle of history a "gyre" (line 1)—literally a circular or spiral turn (Yeats pronounced it with a hard g). The birth of Christ brought to an end the cycle that had lasted from what Yeats called the "Babylonian mathematical starlight" (2000 B.C.) to the dissolution of Greco-Roman culture. "What if the irrational return?" Yeats asked in his prose work *A Vision*. "What if the circle begin again?" He speculates that "we may be about to accept the most implacable authority the world has known."

2. Lines 4–8 refer to the Russian Revolution of 1917. "The ceremony of innocence" suggests Yeats's view of ritual as the basis of civilized living. Cf. the last stanza of *A Prayer for My Daughter* (p. 2282).
3. The spirit or soul of the universe, with which all individual souls are connected through the "Great Memory," which Yeats held to be a universal subconscious in which the human race preserves its past memories. It is thus a source of symbolic images for the poet.
4. I.e., the cradle of the infant Christ.
1. Yeats's daughter, Anne Butler, was born on February 26, 1919, in Dublin and brought home to the refitted Norman tower of Thoor Ballylee (Ballylee Castle) in Galway, where Yeats lived; it is not far from Coole Park.

My child sleeps on. There is no obstacle
But Gregory's wood[2] and one bare hill
Whereby the haystack- and roof-levelling wind,   5
Bred on the Atlantic, can be stayed;
And for an hour I have walked and prayed
Because of the great gloom that is in my mind.

I have walked and prayed for this young child an hour
And heard the sea-wind scream upon the tower,   10
And under the arches of the bridge, and scream
In the elms above the flooded stream;
Imagining in excited reverie
That the future years had come,
Dancing to a frenzied drum,   15
Out of the murderous innocence of the sea.[3]

May she be granted beauty and yet not
Beauty to make a stranger's eye distraught,
Or hers before a looking-glass, for such,
Being made beautiful overmuch,   20
Consider beauty a sufficient end,
Lose natural kindness and maybe
The heart-revealing intimacy
That chooses right, and never find a friend.

Helen being chosen found life flat and dull   25
And later had much trouble from a fool,[4]
While that great Queen, that rose out of the spray,[5]
Being fatherless could have her way
Yet chose a bandy-leggèd smith for man.
It's certain that fine women eat   30
A crazy salad with their meat
Whereby the Horn of Plenty is undone.

In courtesy I'd have her chiefly learned;
Hearts are not had as a gift but hearts are earned
By those that are not entirely beautiful;   35
Yet many, that have played the fool
For beauty's very self, has charm made wise,
And many a poor man that has roved,
Loved and thought himself beloved,
From a glad kindness cannot take his eyes.   40

May she become a flourishing hidden tree
That all her thoughts may like the linnet[6] be,
And have no business but dispensing round
Their magnanimities of sound,
Not but in merriment begin a chase,   45

2. Originally part of the Gregory estate, which had once also included Thoor Ballylee.
3. A reference to Yeats's visions of the future (cf. *The Second Coming*, above).
4. Menelaus, the husband of Helen, whom she de-
serted in favor of Paris.
5. Venus, wife (in the *Odyssey* and later accounts) of Vulcan, "bandy-legged" god of fire and forge (line 29).
6. A small European songbird.

Nor but in merriment a quarrel.
O may she live like some green laurel
Rooted in one dear perpetual place.

My mind, because the minds that I have loved,
The sort of beauty that I have approved,   50
Prosper but little, has dried up of late,
Yet knows that to be choked with hate
May well be of all evil chances chief.
If there's no hatred in a mind
Assault and battery of the wind   55
Can never tear the linnet from the leaf.

An intellectual hatred is the worst,
So let her think opinions are accursed.
Have I not seen the loveliest woman born[7]
Out of the mouth of Plenty's horn,   60
Because of her opinionated mind
Barter that horn and every good
By quiet natures understood
For an old bellows full of angry wind?

Considering that, all hatred driven hence,   65
The soul recovers radical innocence
And learns at last that it is self-delighting,
Self-appeasing, self-affrighting,
And that its own sweet will is Heaven's will;
She can, though every face should scowl   70
And every windy quarter howl
Or every bellows burst, be happy still.

And may her bridegroom bring her to a house
Where all's accustomed, ceremonious;
For arrogance and hatred are the wares   75
Peddled in the thoroughfares.
How but in custom and in ceremony
Are innocence and beauty born?
Ceremony's a name for the rich horn,
And custom for the spreading laurel tree.   80

February–June 1919   1919, 1921

Sailing to Byzantium[1]

1

That is no country for old men. The young
In one another's arms, birds in the trees

---

7. Maud Gonne.
1. Yeats wrote in A Vision: "I think that if I could be given a month of antiquity and leave to spend it where I chose, I would spend it in Byzantium [modern Istanbul] a little before Justinian opened St. Sophia and closed the Academy of Plato [i.e., ca. A.D. 535]. . . . I think that in early Byzantium, maybe never before or since in recorded history, religious, aesthetic, and practical life were one, that architects and artificers . . . spoke to the multitude in gold and silver. The painter, the mosaic worker, the worker in gold and silver, the illuminator of sacred books were almost impersonal, almost perhaps without the consciousness of individual design, absorbed in their subject matter and that the vision of a whole people."

—Those dying generations—at their song,
The salmon-falls, the mackerel-crowded seas,
Fish, flesh, or fowl, commend all summer long   5
Whatever is begotten, born, and dies.
Caught in that sensual music all neglect
Monuments of unageing intellect.

2

An aged man is but a paltry thing,
A tattered coat upon a stick, unless   10
Soul clap its hands and sing, and louder sing
For every tatter in its mortal dress,
Nor is there singing school but studying
Monuments of its own magnificence;
And therefore I have sailed the seas and come   15
To the holy city of Byzantium.

3

O sages standing in God's holy fire
As in the gold mosaic of a wall,[2]
Come from the holy fire, perne in a gyre,[3]
And be the singing-masters of my soul.   20
Consume my heart away; sick with desire
And fastened to a dying animal
It knows not what it is; and gather me
Into the artifice of eternity.

4

Once out of nature I shall never take   25
My bodily form from any natural thing,
But such a form as Grecian goldsmiths make
Of hammered gold and gold enamelling
To keep a drowsy Emperor awake;[4]
Or set upon a golden bough to sing   30
To lords and ladies of Byzantium
Of what is past, or passing, or to come.

September 1926   1927

Leda and the Swan[1]

A sudden blow: the great wings beating still
Above the staggering girl, her thighs caressed

2. Yeats had in mind the mosaic frieze of the holy martyrs in the church of San Apollinare Nuovo at Ravenna, which he had visited in 1907.
3. I.e., whirl round in a spiral motion. "Perne" (or "pirn") is literally a bobbin, reel, or spool, on which something is wound. It became a favorite word of Yeats's, used as a verb meaning "to spin round"; he associated the spinning with the spinning of fate.
4. "I have read somewhere," Yeats wrote, "that in the Emperor's palace at Byzantium was a tree made of gold and silver, and artificial birds that sang." Cf. also Hans Christian Andersen's *Emperor's Nightingale*, which may have been in Yeats's mind at the time.
1. In Greek mythology Zeus visited Leda in the form of a swan. As a result of the union Leda gave birth to Helen and to Clytemnestra (wife of Agamemnon).

Yeats saw Zeus's visit to Leda as an "annunciation," marking the beginning of Greek civilization: "I imagine the annunciation that founded Greece as made to Leda, remembering that they showed in a Spartan temple, strung up to the roof as a holy relic, an unhatched egg of hers, and that from one of her eggs came love and from the other war" (*A Vision*). In the original Cuala Press edition Yeats noted: "I wrote *Leda and the Swan* because the editor of a political review asked me for a poem. I thought, 'After the individualist, demagogic movement, founded by Hobbes and popularized by the Encyclopedists and the French Revolution, we have a soil so exhausted that it cannot grow that crop again for centuries.' Then I thought, 'Nothing is now possible but some movement from above preceded by some violent annunciation.' My fancy began to play

By the dark webs, her nape caught in his bill,
He holds her helpless breast upon his breast.

How can those terrified vague fingers push   5
The feathered glory from her loosening thighs?
And how can body, laid in that white rush,
But feel the strange heart beating where it lies?

A shudder in the loins engenders there
The broken wall, the burning roof and tower[2]   10

And Agamemnon dead.Being so caught up,
So mastered by the brute blood of the air,
Did she put on his knowledge with his power
Before the indifferent beak could let her drop?

September 1923   1924, 1928

Among School Children

1

I walk through the long schoolroom questioning;
A kind old nun in a white hood replies;
The children learn to cipher and to sing,
To study reading-books and history,
To cut and sew, be neat in everything   5
In the best modern way—the children's eyes
In momentary wonder stare upon
A sixty-year-old smiling public man.

2

I dream of a Ledaean[1] body, bent
Above a sinking fire, a tale that she   10
Told of a harsh reproof, or trivial event
That changed some childish day to tragedy—
Told, and it seemed that our two natures blent
Into a sphere from youthful sympathy,
Or else, to alter Plato's parable,   15
Into the yolk and white of the one shell.[2]

3

And thinking of that fit of grief or rage
I look upon one child or t'other there
And wonder if she stood so at that age—

with Leda and the Swan for metaphor, and I began this poem; but as I wrote, bird and lady took such possession of the scene that all politics went out of it, and my friend tells me that his 'conservative readers would misunderstand the poem.'" For the author's revisions while composing this poem, see "Poems in Process" (p. 2588).

2. I.e., the destruction of Troy, caused by Helen's elopement with the Trojan Paris. Agamemnon was murdered by his wife, Clytemnestra, the other daughter of Leda and the Swan.

1. Adjective from "Leda," meaning "like Helen of

Troy" (Leda's daughter). The reference is to Maud Gonne (as also in lines 19–28).

2. In Plato's *Symposium* Aristophanes explains love by supposing that "the primeval man was round and had four hands and four feet, back and sides forming a circle, one head with two faces," and was subsequently divided into two. "After the division, the two parts of man, each desiring his other half, came together, and threw their arms about one another eager to grow into one." The fact that Helen was born from an egg (as the daughter of Leda and the Swan) suggests Yeats's image for such a union.

For even daughters of the swan can share   20
Something of every paddler's heritage—
And had that colour upon cheek or hair,
And thereupon my heart is driven wild:
She stands before me as a living child.

4

Her present image floats into the mind—   25
Did Quattrocento[3] finger fashion it
Hollow of cheek as though it drank the wind
And took a mess of shadows for its meat?
And I though never of Ledaean kind
Had pretty plumage once—enough of that,   30
Better to smile on all that smile, and show
There is a comfortable kind of old scarecrow.

5

What youthful mother, a shape upon her lap
Honey of generation had betrayed,
And that must sleep, shriek, struggle to escape   35
As recollection or the drug decide,[4]
Would think her son, did she but see that shape
With sixty or more winters on its head,
A compensation for the pang of his birth,
Or the uncertainty of his setting forth?   40

6

Plato thought nature but a spume that plays
Upon a ghostly paradigm of things;
Solider Aristotle played the taws
Upon the bottom of a king of kings;[5]
World-famous golden-thighed Pythagoras[6]   45
Fingered upon a fiddle-stick or strings
What a star sang and careless Muses heard:
Old clothes upon old sticks to scare a bird.[7]

7

Both nuns and mothers worship images,[8]
But those the candles light are not as those   50
That animate a mother's reveries,
But keep a marble or a bronze repose.
And yet they too break hearts—O Presences
That passion, piety or affection knows,

3. I.e., 15th century; a reference to Italian painters of the period.
4. "I have taken the 'honey of generation' from Porphyry's essay on 'The Cave of the Nymphs,' but find no warrant in Porphyry for considering it the 'drug' that destroys the 'recollection' of prenatal freedom" [Yeats's note]. Porphyry was a Neoplatonic philosopher of the 3rd century A.D. "Honey of generation," by blotting out the memory of prenatal happiness, "betrays" an infant to be born into this world. The infant will either "sleep" or "struggle to escape" (from this world) depending on whether the drug works or the recollection of blissful prenatal life overcomes the oblivion caused by the drug.
5. I.e., Plato thought nature was a mere appearance ("spume") veiling the ultimate spiritual and mathematical reality ("ghostly paradigm"). Aristotle was "sol-ider" in that he believed that form really inhered in the matter of nature and thus that nature itself had reality. Aristotle was tutor to Alexander the Great and disciplined him by applying the "taws" or strap.
6. Greek philosopher (early 6th century B.C.), interested in mathematics and the mathematical study of acoustics and music; his disciples, the Pythagoreans, developed a mystical philosophy of numerical relations and united the notions of astronomical and mathematical relations in the theory of the music of the spheres. Pythagoreans regarded their master with veneration as a god with a golden thigh.
7. A contemptuous description of the philosophies of Plato, Aristotle, and Pythagoras.
8. Nuns worship images of Christ or the Virgin; mothers worship their own inward images of their children.

And that all heavenly glory symbolise—   55
O self-born mockers of man's enterprise;
                              8
Labour is blossoming or dancing where
The body is not bruised to pleasure soul,
Nor beauty born out of its own despair,
Nor blear-eyed wisdom out of midnight oil.   60
O chestnut tree, great-rooted blossomer,
Are you the leaf, the blossom, or the bole?
O body swayed to music, O brightening glance,
How can we know the dancer from the dance?

June 1926   1927

A Dialogue of Self and Soul[1]

                              1

MY SOUL. I summon to the winding ancient stair;
     Set all your mind upon the steep ascent,
     Upon the broken, crumbling battlement,
     Upon the breathless starlit air,
     Upon the star that marks the hidden pole;   5
     Fix every wandering thought upon
     That quarter where all thought is done:
     Who can distinguish darkness from the soul?

MY SELF. The consecrated blade upon my knees
     Is Sato's ancient blade, still as it was,   10
     Still razor-keen, still like a looking-glass
     Unspotted by the centuries;
     That flowering, silken, old embroidery, torn
     From some court-lady's dress and round
     The wooden scabbard bound and wound,   15
     Can, tattered, still protect, faded adorn.

MY SOUL. Why should the imagination of a man
     Long past his prime remember things that are
     Emblematical of love and war?
     Think of ancestral night that can,   20
     If but imagination scorn the earth
     And intellect its wandering
     To this and that and t'other thing,
     Deliver from the crime of death and birth.

MY SELF. Montashigi, third of his family, fashioned it   25
     Five hundred years ago, about it lie
     Flowers from I know not what embroidery—
     Heart's purple—and all these I set

---

1. In a letter of October 2, 1923, Yeats wrote, "I am   make the Japanese sword and its silk covering my sym-
writing a new tower poem 'Sword and Tower,' which is   bol of life." The sword was a present from a friend,
a choice of rebirth rather than deliverance from birth. I   Junzo Sato.

For emblems of the day against the tower
Emblematical of the night,   30
And claim as by a soldier's right
A charter to commit the crime once more.

MY SOUL. Such fullness in that quarter overflows
    And falls into the basin of the mind
    That man is stricken deaf and dumb and blind,   35
    For intellect no longer knows
    Is from *Ought*, or *Knower* from the *Known* —
    That is to say, ascends to Heaven;
    Only the dead can be forgiven;
    But when I think of that my tongue's a stone.   40

2

MY SELF. A living man is blind and drinks his drop.
    What matter if the ditches are impure?
    What matter if I live it all once more?
    Endure that toil of growing up;
    The ignominy of boyhood; the distress   45
    Of boyhood changing into man;
    The unfinished man and his pain
    Brought face to face with his own clumsiness;

    The finished man among his enemies? —
    How in the name of Heaven can he escape   50
    That defiling and disfigured shape
    The mirror of malicious eyes
    Casts upon his eyes until at last
    He thinks that shape must be his shape?
    And what's the good of an escape   55
    If honour find him in the wintry blast?

    I am content to live it all again
    And yet again, if it be life to pitch
    Into the frog-spawn of a blind man's ditch,
    A blind man battering blind men;   60
    Or into that most fecund ditch of all,
    The folly that man does
    Or must suffer, if he woos
    A proud woman not kindred of his soul.

    I am content to follow to its source   65
    Every event in action or in thought;
    Measure the lot; forgive myself the lot!
    When such as I cast out remorse
    So great a sweetness flows into the breast
    We must laugh and we must sing,   70
    We are blest by everything,
    Everything we look upon is blest.

July–December 1927   1929

For Anne Gregory

"Never shall a young man,
Thrown into despair
By those great honey-coloured
Ramparts at your ear,
Love you for yourself alone   5
And not your yellow hair."

"But I can get a hair-dye
And set such colour there,
Brown, or black, or carrot,
That young men in despair   10
May love me for myself alone
And not my yellow hair."

"I heard an old religious man
But yesternight declare
That he had found a text to prove   15
That only God, my dear,
Could love you for yourself alone
And not your yellow hair."

September 1930   1931, 1932

Byzantium[1]

The unpurged images of day recede;
The Emperor's drunken soldiery are abed;
Night resonance recedes, night-walkers' song
After great cathedral gong;
A starlit or a moonlit dome[2] disdains   5
All that man is,
All mere complexities,
The fury and the mire of human veins.

Before me floats an image, man or shade,
Shade more than man, more image than a shade;   10
For Hades' bobbin bound in mummy-cloth
May unwind the winding path;[3]
A mouth that has no moisture and no breath
Breathless mouths may summon;
I hail the superhuman;   15
I call it death-in-life and life-in-death.

1. On October 4, 1930, Yeats sent his friend Sturge Moore a copy of *Byzantium*, saying, "The poem originates from a criticism of yours. You objected to the last verse of 'Sailing to Byzantium' because a bird made by a goldsmith was just as natural as anything else. That showed me that the idea needed exposition." The previous April, Yeats had noted in his diary: "Subject for a poem / Describe Byzantium as it is in the system towards the end of the first Christian millennium. A walking mummy; flames at the street corners where the soul is purified. Birds of hammered gold singing in the golden trees. In the harbour [dolphins] offering their backs to the wailing dead that they may carry them to paradise."
2. Of the great church of St. Sophia.
3. The spool of people's fate, which spins their destiny and which is symbolized by the wrappings around a mummy, may lead people, as it unwinds, to the realm of pure spirit.

Miracle, bird or golden handiwork,
More miracle than bird or handiwork,
Planted on the star-lit golden bough,[4]
Can like the cocks of Hades crow, 20
Or, by the moon embittered, scorn aloud
In glory of changeless metal
Common bird or petal
And all complexities of mire or blood.

At midnight on the Emperor's pavement flit 25
Flames that no faggot feeds, nor steel has lit,
Nor storm disturbs, flames begotten of flame,
Where blood-begotten spirits come
And all complexities of fury leave,
Dying into a dance, 30
An agony of trance,
An agony of flame[5] that cannot singe a sleeve.

Astraddle on the dolphin's mire and blood,[6]
Spirit after spirit! The smithies break the flood,
The golden smithies of the Emperor! 35
Marbles of the dancing floor
Break bitter furies of complexity,
Those images that yet
Fresh images beget,
That dolphin-torn, that gong-tormented sea. 40

September 1930   1932

Crazy Jane Talks with the Bishop[1]

I met the Bishop on the road
And much said he and I.
"Those breasts are flat and fallen now,
Those veins must soon be dry;
Live in a heavenly mansion, 5
Not in some foul sty."

"Fair and foul are near of kin,
And fair needs foul," I cried.
"My friends are gone, but that's a truth
Nor grave nor bed denied, 10

---

4. Part of the death-world of artifice and eternity; it is opposed to a real, living bough, which would be lighted by the sun or the moon. Reminiscent of the golden bough that guides Aeneas through the underworld in Virgil's *Aeneid*, it is also associated with the mystical tree of the esoteric Hebrew doctrine of the cabala, in whose branches "the birds lodge and build their nests; that is, the souls or angels have their place." The cock, that crows at dawn, appears on Roman tombstones as a herald of rebirth.
5. This phrase was suggested to Yeats by a Japanese Nō play, *Motomezuka*, wherein a young girl suffers from perpetual burning, which is a sense of her own guilt. A priest tells her that the flames will cease if she no longer believes in their reality; she finds herself incapable of disbelief, however, and the play ends in "the dance of her agony."
6. The dolphin, in ancient art, was a symbol of the soul in transit from one state to another.
1. One of a series of poems dealing with the paradox that wisdom may reside with fools and beggars (such as Jane) rather than with the respectable representatives of orthodoxy (such as the Bishop).

Learned in bodily lowliness
And in the heart's pride.

"A woman can be proud and stiff
When on love intent;
But Love has pitched his mansion in   15
The place of excrement;
For nothing can be sole or whole
That has not been rent."

November 1931   1932

After Long Silence[1]

Speech after long silence; it is right,
All other lovers being estranged or dead,
Unfriendly lamplight hid under its shade,
The curtains drawn upon unfriendly night,
That we descant and yet again descant   5
Upon the supreme theme of Art and Song:
Bodily decrepitude is wisdom; young
We loved each other and were ignorant.

November 1929   1932

Lapis Lazuli[1]

(For Harry Clifton)

I have heard that hysterical women say
They are sick of the palette and fiddle-bow,
Of poets that are always gay,
For everybody knows or else should know
That if nothing drastic is done   5
Aeroplane and Zeppelin will come out,
Pitch like King Billy[2] bomb-balls in
Until the town lie beaten flat.

All perform their tragic play,
There struts Hamlet, there is Lear,   10
That's Ophelia, that Cordelia;
Yet they, should the last scene be there,
The great stage curtain about to drop,
If worthy their prominent part in the play,
Do not break up their lines to weep.   15

1. For the author's revisions while composing this poem, see "Poems in Process" (p. 2590).
1. A deep blue stone. "I notice that you have much lapis lazuli; someone has sent me a present of a great piece carved by some Chinese sculptor into the semblance of a mountain with temple, trees, paths, and an ascetic and pupil about to climb the mountain. Ascetic, pupil, hard stone, eternal theme of the sensual east. The heroic cry in the midst of despair. But no, I am wrong, the east has its solutions always and therefore knows nothing of tragedy. It is we, not the east, that must raise the heroic cry" [Yeats to Dorothy Wellesley, July 6, 1935].
2. King William III (William of Orange), who defeated the army of King James II at the Battle of the Boyne in 1690.

They know that Hamlet and Lear are gay;
Gaiety transfiguring all that dread.
All men have aimed at, found and lost;
Black out; Heaven blazing into the head:
Tragedy wrought to its uttermost.   20
Though Hamlet rambles and Lear rages,
And all the drop-scenes drop at once
Upon a hundred thousand stages,
It cannot grow by an inch or an ounce.

On their own feet they came, or on shipboard,   25
Camel-back, horse-back, ass-back, mule-back,
Old civilisations put to the sword.
Then they and their wisdom went to rack:
No handiwork of Callimachus,[3]
Who handled marble as if it were bronze,   30
Made draperies that seemed to rise
When sea-wind swept the corner, stands;
His long lamp-chimney shaped like the stem
Of a slender palm, stood but a day;
All things fall and are built again,   35
And those that build them again are gay.

Two Chinamen, behind them a third,
Are carved in lapis lazuli,
Over them flies a long-legged bird,
A symbol of longevity;   40
The third, doubtless a serving-man,
Carries a musical instrument.

Every discolouration of the stone,
Every accidental crack or dent,
Seems a water-course or an avalanche,   45
Or lofty slope where it still snows
Though doubtless plum or cherry-branch
Sweetens the little half-way house
Those Chinamen climb towards, and I
Delight to imagine them seated there;   50
There, on the mountain and the sky,
On all the tragic scene they stare.
One asks for mournful melodies;
Accomplished fingers begin to play.
Their eyes mid many wrinkles, their eyes,   55
Their ancient, glittering eyes, are gay.

July 1936   1938

---

3. Greek sculptor (5th century B.C.), supposedly the originator of the Corinthian column and of the use of the running drill to imitate folds in drapery in statues. Yeats wrote of him: "With Callimachus pure Ionic revives again . . . and upon the only example of his work known to us, a marble chair, a Persian is represented, and may one not discover a Persian symbol in that bronze lamp, shaped like a palm . . . ? But he was an archaistic workman, and those who set him to work brought back public life to an older form" (A Vision).

Long-Legged Fly

That civilisation may not sink,
Its great battle lost,
Quiet the dog, tether the pony
To a distant post;
Our master Caesar[1] is in the tent   5
Where the maps are spread,
His eye fixed upon nothing,
A hand under his head.
Like a long-legged fly upon the stream
His mind moves upon silence.   10

That the topless towers be burnt
And men recall that face,
Move most gently if move you must
In this lonely place.
She[2] thinks, part woman, three parts a child,   15
That nobody looks; her feet
Practice a tinker shuffle
Picked up on a street.
Like a long-legged fly upon the stream
Her mind moves upon silence.   20

That girls at puberty may find
The first Adam in their thought,
Shut the door of the Pope's chapel,
Keep those children out.
There on that scaffolding reclines   25
Michael Angelo.[3]
With no more sound than the mice make
His hand moves to and fro.
Like a long-legged fly upon the stream
His mind moves upon silence.   30

November 1937   1939

The Circus Animals' Desertion

1

I sought a theme and sought for it in vain,
I sought it daily for six weeks or so.
Maybe at last, being but a broken man,
I must be satisfied with my heart, although
Winter and summer till old age began   5
My circus animals were all on show,

---

1. Emperor of Rome.
2. Helen of Troy, who precipitated the Trojan War. Cf. Marlowe, *Dr. Faustus:* "Was this the face that launched a thousand ships / And burnt the topless towers of Ilium?"
3. Michaelangelo (1475–1564) is painting *The Creation of Man* on the Sistine Chapel ceiling in the Vatican. Cf. *Under Ben Bulben* (p. 2294).

Those stilted boys, that burnished chariot,
Lion and woman and the Lord knows what.[1]

2

What can I but enumerate old themes?
First that sea-rider Oisin[2] led by the nose   10
Through three enchanted islands, allegorical dreams,
Vain gaiety, vain battle, vain repose,
Themes of the embittered heart, or so it seems,
That might adorn old songs or courtly shows;
But what cared I that set him on to ride,   15
I, starved for the bosom of his faery bride?

And then a counter-truth filled out its play,
The Countess Cathleen was the name I gave it;[3]
She, pity-crazed, had given her soul away,
But masterful Heaven had intervened to save it.   20
I thought my dear must her own soul destroy,
So did fanaticism and hate enslave it,
And this brought forth a dream and soon enough
This dream itself had all my thought and love.

And when the Fool and Blind Man stole the bread   25
Cuchulain fought the ungovernable sea;[4]
Heart-mysteries there, and yet when all is said
It was the dream itself enchanted me:
Character isolated by a deed
To engross the present and dominate memory.   30
Players and painted stage took all my love,
And not those things that they were emblems of.

3

Those masterful images because complete
Grew in pure mind, but out of what began?
A mound of refuse or the sweepings of a street,   35
Old kettles, old bottles, and a broken can,
Old iron, old bones, old rags, that raving slut
Who keeps the till. Now that my ladder's gone,
I must lie down where all the ladders start,
In the foul rag-and-bone shop of the heart.   40

1939

---

1. Yeats refers to the ancient Irish heroes of his early work ("those stilted boys"), the gilded carriage of his play The Unicorn from the Stars (1908), and "A Sphinx with woman breast and lion paw" in his poem The Double Vision of Michael Robartes.
2. In the long title-poem of Yeats's first book, The Wanderings of Oisin and Other Poems (1889), the legendary poet-warrior Oisin (pronounced Usheen) is bewitched by the beautiful fairy woman Niamh. He returns 150 years later to find his friends dead and Ireland Christian.
3. This play (1892), about an Irish countess who sells her soul to the devil to buy food for the starving peasantry but is taken up to heaven (for God "Looks always on the motive, not the deed"), was dedicated to Maud Gonne ("my dear," line 21) and inspired by her work on behalf of evicted peasants in the West of Ireland.
4. In Yeats's play On Baile's Strand (1904).

Under Ben Bulben[1]

1

Swear by what the sages spoke
Round the Mareotic Lake[2]
That the Witch of Atlas knew,
Spoke and set the cocks a-crow.

Swear by those horsemen, by those women   5
Complexion and form prove superhuman,[3]
That pale, long-visaged company
That air in immortality
Completeness of their passions won;
Now they ride the wintry dawn   10
Where Ben Bulben sets the scene.

Here's the gist of what they mean.

2

Many times man lives and dies
Between his two eternities,
That of race and that of soul,   15
And ancient Ireland knew it all.
Whether man die in his bed
Or the rifle knocks him dead,
A brief parting from those dear
Is the worst man has to fear.   20
Though grave-diggers' toil is long,
Sharp their spades, their muscles strong,
They but thrust their buried men
Back in the human mind again.

3

You that Mitchel's prayer have heard,   25
"Send war in our time, O Lord!"[4]
Know that when all words are said
And a man is fighting mad,
Something drops from eyes long blind,
He completes his partial mind,   30
For an instant stands at ease,

1. Mountain in Country Sligo, which Yeats had often
climbed as a boy. Nine years after he died in the south
of France, his body was brought home to Ireland and
buried in Drumcliff churchyard at the foot of Ben
Bulben.
2. Lake Mareotis, bordering the city of Alexandria
where a school of neo-Pythagorean philosophers flourished in the 1st century A.D. By Lake Mareotis also
flourished (3rd century A.D.) the Christian Neoplatonists, in whom Yeats was much interested. The lake is
mentioned in Shelley's poem *The Witch of Atlas*, a
poem that Yeats admired and interpreted in his own
way, seeing the witch as a symbol of timeless, absolute
beauty; hence what she "knew" and "spoke" and what
"set the cocks a-crow" can be related to the "miracle"
that "can like the cocks of Hades crow" in *Byzantium*
(lines 17–20, p. 2289).
3. The *sidhe*, or fairy folk, who were believed to ride
through the countryside near Ben Bulben.
4. John Mitchel (1815–1875), an Irish patriot imprisoned for his activities, wrote in his *Jail Journal*: "Give
us war in our time, O Lord!"

Laughs aloud, his heart at peace.
Even the wisest man grows tense
With some sort of violence
Before he can accomplish fate, 35
Know his work or choose his mate.

4

Poet and sculptor, do the work,
Nor let the modish painter shirk
What his great forefathers did,
Bring the soul of man to God. 40
Make him fill the cradles right.

Measurement began our might:
Forms a stark Egyptian thought,
Forms that gentler Phidias wrought[5]
Michael Angelo left a proof 45
On the Sistine Chapel roof,
Where but half-awakened Adam
Can disturb globe-trotting Madam
Till her bowels are in heat,[6]
Proof that there's a purpose set 50
Before the secret working mind:
Profane perfection of mankind.

Quattrocento[7] put in paint
On backgrounds for a God or Saint
Gardens where a soul's at ease; 55
Where everything that meets the eye,
Flowers and grass and cloudless sky,
Resemble forms that are or seem
When sleepers wake and yet still dream,
And when it's vanished still declare, 60
With only bed and bedstead there,

That heavens had opened.Gyres run on;
When that greater dream had gone
Calvert and Wilson, Blake and Claude,[8]
Prepared a rest for the people of God, 65
Palmer's phrase, but after that
Confusion fell upon our thought.

---

5. Greek sculptor (5th century B.C.), generally thought to have raised the classical ideal in art to its highest culmination. Yeats here itemizes steps in his history of knowledge and the arts, beginning with Babylonian mathematics ("measurement"), through "stark Egyptian thought," to the Renaissance of Michelangelo. Each of these steps is related to Yeats's cyclical theory of history.

6. Cf. Long-Legged Fly, p. 2292, stanza 3.

7. 15th-century Italian art.

8. Works by the five artists mentioned in lines 64–66 all provided images for Yeats's poetry: Edward Calvert, 19th-century wood engraver; Richard Wilson, 18th-century landscape painter; William Blake, "one of the great mythmakers and mask-makers"; Claude Lorrain, 17th-century landscape painter; and (in line 66) Samuel Palmer, 19th-century landscape painter and etcher, one of whose works was The Lonely Tower. Calvert, Blake, and Palmer knew one another and shared a view of the holiness of art.

5

Irish poets, learn your trade,
Sing whatever is well made,
Scorn the sort now growing up   70
All out of shape from toe to top,
Their unremembering hearts and heads
Base-born products of base beds.
Sing the peasantry, and then
Hard-riding country gentlemen,   75
The holiness of monks, and after
Porter-drinkers'[9] randy laughter;
Sing the lords and ladies gay
That were beaten into the clay
Through seven heroic centuries;   80
Cast your mind on other days
That we in coming days may be
Still the indomitable Irishry.

6

Under bare Ben Bulben's head
In Drumcliff churchyard Yeats is laid.   85
An ancestor was rector there[1]
Long years ago, a church stands near,
By the road an ancient cross.
No marble, no conventional phrase;
On limestone quarried near the spot   90
By his command these words are cut:
        Cast a cold eye
        On life, on death.
        Horseman, pass by!

September 1938   1939

From Reveries over Childhood and Youth[1]

[*The Yeats Family*]

Some six miles off towards Ben Bulben and beyond the Channel,[2] as we
call the tidal river between Sligo and the Rosses, and on top of a hill there was
a little square two-storied house covered with creepers and looking out upon
a garden where the box borders were larger than any I had ever seen, and
where I saw for the first time the crimson streak of the gladiolus and awaited
its blossom with excitement. Under one gable a dark thicket of small trees
made a shut-in mysterious place, where one played and believed that something was going to happen. My great-aunt Micky lived there. Micky was not

9. Drinkers of dark brown bitter beer.
1. The Rev. John Yeats (1774–1847) was rector of
Drumcliff from 1805.
1. Yeats wrote a variety of autobiographical essays between 1914 and 1928; these were originally published
separately and later collected as *The Autobiography of*

W. B. Yeats (1936, 1953). The selections given here
are from *Reveries over Childhood and Youth,* first
published in 1915, and *The Trembling of the Veil,* first
published in 1922.
2. Yeats's favorite County Sligo landscape. Cf. the
places named in *The Stolen Child* (p. 2267).

her right name for she was Mary Yeats and her father had been my great-grandfather, John Yeats, who had been Rector of Drumcliffe, a few miles further off, and died in 1847. She was a spare, high-coloured, elderly woman and had the oldest-looking cat I had ever seen, for its hair had grown into matted locks of yellowy white. She farmed and had one old man-servant, but could not have farmed at all, had not neighbouring farmers helped to gather in the crops, in return for the loan of her farm implements and "out of respect for the family," for as Johnny MacGurk, the Sligo barber said to me, "The Yeats's were always very respectable." She was full of family history; all her dinner-knives were pointed like daggers through much cleaning, and there was a little James the First cream-jug with the Yeats motto and crest, and on her dining-room mantel-piece a beautiful silver cup that had belonged to my great-great-grandfather, who had married a certain Mary Butler. It had upon it the Butler crest and had been already old at the date 1534, when the initials of some bride and bridegroom were engraved under the lip. All its history for generations was rolled up inside it upon a piece of paper yellow with age, until some caller took the paper to light his pipe.

Another family of Yeats, a widow and her two children on whom I called sometimes with my grandmother, lived near in a long low cottage, and owned a very fierce turkey-cock that did battle with their visitors; and some miles away lived the secretary to the Grand Jury and Land Agent, my great-uncle Mat Yeats and his big family of boys and girls; but I think it was only in later years that I came to know them well. I do not think any of these liked the Pollexfens, who were well off and seemed to them purse-proud, whereas they themselves had come down in the world. I remember them as very well-bred and very religious in the Evangelical way and thinking a good deal of Aunt Micky's old histories. There had been among our ancestors a King's County soldier, one of Marlborough's[3] generals, and when his nephew came to dine he gave him boiled pork, and when the nephew said he disliked boiled pork he had asked him to dine again and promised him something he would like better. However, he gave him boiled pork again and the nephew took the hint in silence. The other day as I was coming home from America, I met one of his descendants whose family has not another discoverable link with ours, and he too knew the boiled pork story and nothing else. We have the General's portrait, and he looks very fine in his armour and his long curly wig, and underneath it, after his name, are many honours that have left no tradition among us. Were we country people, we could have summarised his life in a legend. Other ancestors or great-uncles bore a part in Irish history; one saved the life of Sarsfield[4] at the battle of Sedgmoor; another, taken prisoner by King James's army, owed his to Sarsfield's gratitude; another, a century later, roused the gentlemen of Meath[5] against some local Jacquère,[6] and was shot dead upon a country road, and yet another "chased the United Irishmen[7] for a fortnight, fell into their hands and was hanged." The notorious Major Sirr,

3. John Churchill, duke of Marlborough (1650–1722), English general in the War of the Spanish Succession (1702–13).
4. Patrick Sarsfield (d. 1693), Irish Jacobite general who served in the battle of Sedgemoor (1685) when the duke of Monmouth, illegitimate son of Charles II who was claiming the throne from his uncle James II, was defeated and captured.
5. Maritime county in province of Leinster, in the east

of Ireland.
6. Peasant revolutionary. The "Jacquere" was a peasants' revolt (1358) against the nobles in northern France (the term derived from *Jacques Bonhomme*, the nobility's contemptuous name for a peasant).
7. The Irish society founded 1791 by Theobald Wolfe Tone that later was influential in causing the Irish rebellion of 1798.

who arrested Lord Edward Fitzgerald[8] and gave him the bullet wound he died of in the jail, was godfather to several of my great-great-grandfather's children; while to make a balance, my great-grandfather had been Robert Emmett's[9] friend and was suspected and imprisoned though but for a few hours. One great-uncle fell at New Orleans in 1813, while another, who became Governor of Penang,[1] led the forlorn hope at the taking of Rangoon, and even in the last generation of all there had been lives of some power and pleasure. An old man who had entertained many famous people, in his eighteenth-century house, where battlement and tower showed the influence of Horace Walpole,[2] had but lately, after losing all his money, drowned himself, first taking off his rings and chain and watch as became a collector of many beautiful things; and once to remind us of more passionate life, a gunboat put into Rosses, commanded by the illegitimate son of some great-uncle or other. Now that I can look at their miniatures, turning them over to find the name of soldier, or lawyer, or Castle official,[3] and wondering if they cared for good books or good music, I am delighted with all that joins my life to those who had power in Ireland or with those anywhere that were good servants and poor bargainers, but I cared nothing as a child for Micky's tales. I could see my grandfather's ships come up the bay or the river, and his sailors treated me with deference, and a ship's carpenter made and mended my toy boats and I thought that nobody could be so important as my grandfather. Perhaps, too, it is only now that I can value those more gentle natures so unlike his passion and violence. An old Sligo priest has told me how my great-grandfather John Yeats always went into his kitchen rattling the keys, so much did he fear finding some one doing wrong, and of a speech of his when the agent of the great landowner of his parish brought him from cottage to cottage to bid the women send their children to the Protestant school. All promised till they came to one who cried, "Child of mine will never darken your door." "Thank you, my woman," he said, "you are the first honest woman I have met to-day." My uncle, Mat Yeats, the Land Agent, had once waited up every night for a week to catch some boys who stole his apples and when he caught them had given them sixpence and told them not to do it again. Perhaps it is only fancy or the softening touch of the miniaturist that makes me discover in their faces some courtesy and much gentleness. Two eighteenth-century faces interest me the most, one that of a great-great-grandfather, for both have under their powdered curling wigs a half-feminine charm, and as I look at them I discover a something clumsy and heavy in myself. Yet it was a Yeats who spoke the only eulogy that turns my head: "We have ideas and no passions, but by marriage with a Pollexfen we have given a tongue to the sea cliffs."

Among the miniatures there is a larger picture, an admirable drawing by I know not what master, that is too harsh and merry for its company. He was a connection and close friend of my great-grandmother Corbet, and though we spoke of him as "Uncle Beattie" in our childhood, no blood relation. My

8. Fitzgerald (1763–1798) was a British officer who, after dismissal from the army for disloyal activities, joined the United Irishmen. Cf. *September 1913*, lines 19–22 (p. 2276).
9. Emmett (1778–1803) was an Irish patriot, hanged at Dublin for treason.
1. Island in Malaya. Rangoon, capital of Burma, was taken by the British in 1824.

2. The 18th-century English author whose pseudo-Gothic house, Strawberry Hill, much influenced subsequent Gothic architecture in England and elsewhere.
3. Official at Dublin Castle, where the viceroy (representing the British Crown) lived with his staff before Irish independence was achieved in 1922.

great-grandmother who died at ninety-three had many memories of him. He was the friend of Goldsmith and was accustomed to boast, clergyman though he was, that he belonged to a hunt-club of which every member but himself had been hanged or transported for treason, and that it was not possible to ask him a question he could not reply to with a perfectly appropriate blasphemy or indecency.

[An Irish Literature]

From these debates, from O'Leary's[4] conversation, and from the Irish books he lent or gave me has come all I have set my hand to since. I had begun to know a great deal about the Irish poets who had written in English. I read with excitement books I should find unreadable to-day, and found romance in lives that had neither wit nor adventure. I did not deceive myself, I knew how often they wrote a cold and abstract language, and yet I who had never wanted to see the houses where Keats and Shelley lived would ask everybody what sort of place Inchedony was, because Callanan[5] had named after it a bad poem in the manner of *Childe Harold*. Walking home from a debate, I remember saying to some college student, "Ireland cannot put from her the habits learned from her old military civilisation and from a church that prays in Latin. Those popular poets have not touched her heart, her poetry when it comes will be distinguished and lonely." O'Leary had once said to me, "Neither Ireland nor England knows the good from the bad in any art, but Ireland unlike England does not hate the good when it is pointed out to her." I began to plot and scheme how one might seal with the right image the soft wax before it began to harden. I had noticed that Irish Catholics among whom had been born so many political martyrs had not the good taste, the household courtesy and decency of the Protestant Ireland I had known, yet Protestant Ireland seemed to think of nothing but getting on in the world. I thought we might bring the halves together if we had a national literature that made Ireland beautiful in the memory, and yet had been freed from provincialism by an exacting criticism, an European pose.

1915

4. John O'Leary (d. 1907), an Irish nationalist, for whom Yeats had great respect. Cf. *September 1913*, lines 7–8: "Romantic Ireland's dead and gone, / It's with O'Leary in the grave."

5. Jeremiah John Callanan, Anglo-Irish poet, published *The Recluse of Inchedony and Other Poems* in 1830.

VIRGINIA WOOLF
1882–1941

1912: Marries Leonard Woolf.
1921: *Monday or Tuesday.*
1925: *Mrs. Dalloway.*

Virginia Woolf was born in London, daughter of Leslie (later Sir Leslie) Stephen, the Victorian critic, philosopher, biographer, and scholar. She grew up as a member of a large and talented family, educating herself in her father's magnificent library, meeting in childhood many eminent Victorians, learning Greek from Walter Pater's sister. After her father's death in 1904 she settled with her sister and two brothers in Bloomsbury, that district of London which later was to become associated with her and the group among whom she moved. The "Bloomsbury Group" included Lytton Strachey, the biographer; J. M. Keynes, the celebrated economist; Roger Fry, an art critic; and E. M. Forster. When her sister, Vanessa, a notable painter, married Clive Bell, an art critic, in 1907, she and her brother took together another house in Bloomsbury, and there they entertained their literary and artistic friends at evening gatherings where the conversation sparkled. Their intelligence was equaled by their frankness, notably on sexual topics, and the sexual life of Bloomsbury provided ample material for discussion. The painter Duncan Grant, for example, was at different times the lover of Maynard Keynes, Virginia Woolf's brother Adrian, and her sister, Vanessa, and he was the father of Vanessa's daughter, Angelica. Virginia was herself bisexual and, thirteen years after her marriage to the journalist and essayist Leonard Woolf, she fell passionately in love with the poet Vita [Victoria] Sackville-West, wife of the bisexual diplomat and author Harold Nicolson. Woolf's relationship with this aristocratic lesbian was to produce the most light-hearted and scintillating of her books, *Orlando* (1928). She was fortunate to have a husband as supportive emotionally as he was intellectually, and their marriage withstood this and other strains. Together they founded the Hogarth Press in 1917—a press that published some of the most interesting literature of our time, including Eliot's *Poems* (1919) and *Homage to John Dryden* (1924), the English translations of Freud, as well as her own novels. Her suicide in March 1941, resulting from her dread of World War II and her fear that she was about to lose her mind and become a burden on her husband, first revealed to the public that she had been subject to periods of nervous depression, particularly after finishing a book, and that underneath the liveliness and wit so well known among the Bloomsbury Group lay disturbing pyschological tensions.

Woolf came naturally into the profession of writing. She moved among writers and artists, and her world was from the beginning the cultured world of the middle-class and upper-middle-class London intelligentsia. She rebelled against what she called the "materialism" of such novelists as Arnold Bennett and John Galsworthy and sought a more delicate rendering of those aspects of consciousness in which she felt that the truth of human experience really lay. After two novels cast in traditional form, she developed her own style, which handled the "stream of consciousness" with a carefully modulated poetic flow and brought into prose fiction something of the rhythms and the imagery of lyric poetry. The sketches in which she explored the possibilities of moving between action and contemplation, between specific external events in time and delicate tracings of the flow of consciousness where the mind moves between retrospect and anticipation, were collected in *Monday or Tuesday* (1921). These were technical experiments, and they made possible those later novels in which her characteristic method is fully developed—*Jacob's Room* (1922); *Mrs. Dalloway* (1925), the first completely successful novel in her "new" style; *To the Lighthouse* (1927); *The Waves* (1931), the most stylized of her novels; and *Between the Acts* (1941), published after her death. She was a skilled exponent of the stream of consciousness technique in her novels, exploring with great subtlety problems of personal identity and personal relationships as well as the significance of time, change, and memory for human personality.

Woolf was increasingly concerned with the position of women, especially professional women, and the constrictions they suffered under. She wrote several cogent essays on the subject, notably in *A Room of One's Own* (1929) and *Three Guineas* (1938). Her novel *The Years* (1937) was originally to have included reflections on the position of women interspersed amid the action, but she later decided to publish them as a separate book, which became *Three Guineas.*

She also wrote a great many reviews and critical essays, collected in *The Common Reader* (1925) and *The Second Common Reader* (1932); informal and personal in tone, her criticism is suggestive rather than authoritative and has an engaging air of spontaneity. She is equally concerned with her own craft as a writer and with what it was like to be a quite different person living in a different age. At once more informal and more revealing are the six volumes of her *Letters* (1975–80) and five volumes of her *Diary* (1977–84). These, with their running commentary on her life and work, resemble the sketchbooks of a great painter and serve as a reminder that her writings, for all their variety, have the coherence found only in the work of the greatest writers.

The Mark on the Wall

Perhaps it was the middle of January in the present year that I first looked up and saw the mark on the wall. In order to fix a date it is necessary to remember what one saw. So now I think of the fire; the steady film of yellow light upon the page of my book; the three chrysanthemums in the round glass bowl on the mantelpiece. Yes, it must have been the winter time, and we had just finished our tea, for I remember that I was smoking a cigarette when I looked up and saw the mark on the wall for the first time. I looked up through the smoke of my cigarette and my eye lodged for a moment upon the burning coals, and that old fancy of the crimson flag flapping from the castle tower came into my mind, and I thought of the cavalcade of red knights riding up the side of the black rock. Rather to my relief the sight of the mark interrupted the fancy, for it is an old fancy, an automatic fancy, made as a child perhaps. The mark was a small round mark, black upon the white wall, about six or seven inches above the mantelpiece.

How readily our thoughts swarm upon a new object, lifting it a little way, as ants carry a blade of straw so feverishly, and then leave it. . . . If that mark was made by a nail, it can't have been for a picture, it must have been for a miniature—the miniature of a lady with white powdered curls, powder-dusted cheeks, and lips like red carnations. A fraud of course, for the people who had this house before us would have chosen pictures in that way—an old picture for an old room. That is the sort of people they were—very interesting people, and I think of them so often, in such queer places, because one will never see them again, never know what happened next. They wanted to leave this house because they wanted to change their style of furniture, so he said, and he was in process of saying that in his opinion art should have ideas behind it when we were torn asunder, as one is torn from the old lady about to pour out tea and the young man about to hit the tennis ball in the back garden of the suburban villa as one rushes past in the train.

But for that mark, I'm not sure about it; I don't believe it was made by a nail after all; it's too big, too round, for that. I might get up, but if I got up and looked at it, ten to one I shouldn't be able to say for certain; because once a thing's done, no one ever knows how it happened. Oh! dear me, the mystery of life; the inaccuracy of thought! The ignorance of humanity! To show how very little control of our possessions we have—what an accidental affair this living is after all our civilisation—let me just count over a few of the things lost in one lifetime, beginning, for that seems always the most mysterious of losses—what cat would gnaw, what rat would nibble—three pale blue canisters of book-binding tools? Then there were the bird cages, the iron hoops, the steel skates, the Queen Anne coal-scuttle, the bagatelle board, the hand organ—all gone, and jewels, too. Opals and emeralds, they lie about the roots of turnips. What a scraping paring affair it is to be sure! The wonder is that I've any clothes on my back, that I sit surrounded by solid furniture at this moment. Why, if one wants to compare life to anything, one must liken it to being blown through the Tube[1] at fifty miles an hour—landing at the other end without a single hairpin in one's hair! Shot out at the feet of God entirely naked! Tumbling head over heels in the asphodel meadows[2] like brown paper parcels pitched down a shoot in the post office! With one's hair flying back like the tail of a race-horse. Yes, that seems to express the rapidity of life, the perpetual waste and repair; all so casual, all so haphazard. . . .

But after life. The slow pulling down of thick green stalks so that the cup of the flower, as it turns over, deluges one with purple and red light. Why, after all, should one not be born there as one is born here, helpless, speechless, unable to focus one's eyesight, groping at the roots of the grass, at the toes of the Giants? As for saying which are trees, and which are men and women, or whether there are such things, that one won't be in a condition to do for fifty years or so. There will be nothing but spaces of light and dark, intersected by thick stalks, and rather higher up perhaps, rose-shaped blots of an indistinct colour—dim pinks and blues—which will, as time goes on, become more definite, become—I don't know what. . . .

And yet that mark on the wall is not a hole at all. It may even be caused by some round black substance, such as a small rose leaf, left over from the summer, and I, not being a very vigilant housekeeper—look at the dust on the mantelpiece, for example, the dust which, so they say, buried Troy three times over, only fragments of pots utterly refusing annihilation, as one can believe.

The tree outside the window taps very gently on the pane. . . . I want to think quietly, calmly, spaciously, never to be interrupted, never to have to rise from my chair, to slip easily from one thing to another, without any sense of hostility, or obstacle. I want to sink deeper and deeper, away from the surface, with its hard separate facts. To steady myself, let me catch hold of the first idea that passes . . . Shakespeare. . . . Well, he will do as well as another. A man who sat himself solidly in an arm-chair, and looked into the fire, so— A shower of ideas fell perpetually from some very high Heaven down through his mind. He leant his forehead on his hand, and people, looking in through the open door—for this scene is supposed to take place on a summer's evening—But how dull this is, this historical fiction! It doesn't interest me at all. I wish I could hit upon a pleasant track of thought, a track indirectly reflecting credit upon myself, for those are the pleasantest thoughts, and very frequent even in the minds of modest mouse-coloured people, who believe genuinely that they dislike to hear their own praises. They are not thoughts directly praising oneself; that is the beauty of them; they are thoughts like this:

"And then I came into the room. They were discussing botany. I said how I'd seen a flower growing on a dust heap on the site of an old house in

---

1. The London underground railway, or subway.   asphodel flowers grow in the Elysian fields).
2. I.e., heaven, the next world (in Greek mythology,

Kingsway.[3] The seed, I said, must have been sown in the reign of Charles the First. What flowers grew in the reign of Charles the First?" I asked— (But I don't remember the answer.) Tall flowers with purple tassels to them perhaps. And so it goes on. All the time I'm dressing up the figure of myself in my own mind, lovingly, stealthily, not openly adoring it, for if I did that, I should catch myself out, and stretch my hand at once for a book in self-protection. Indeed, it is curious how instinctively one protects the image of oneself from idolatry or any other handling that could make it ridiculous, or too unlike the original to be believed in any longer. Or is it not so very curious after all? It is a matter of great importance. Suppose the looking-glass smashes, the image disappears, and the romantic figure with the green of forest depths all about it is there no longer, but only that shell of a person which is seen by other people—what an airless, shallow, bald, prominent world it becomes! A world not to be lived in. As we face each other in omnibuses and underground railways we are looking into the mirror; that accounts for the vagueness, the gleam of glassiness, in our eyes. And the novelists in future will realize more and more the importance of these reflections, for of course there is not one reflection but an almost infinite number; those are the depths they will explore, those the phantoms they will pursue, leaving the description of reality more and more out of their stories, taking a knowledge of it for granted, as the Greeks did and Shakespeare perhaps—but these generalizations are very worthless. The military sound of the word is enough. It recalls leading articles, cabinet ministers—a whole class of things indeed which, as a child, one thought the thing itself, the standard thing, the real thing, from which one could not depart save at the risk of nameless damnation. Generalizations bring back somehow Sunday in London, Sunday afternoon walks, Sunday luncheons, and also ways of speaking of the dead, clothes, and habits—like the habit of sitting all together in one room until a certain hour, although nobody liked it. There was a rule for everything. The rule for tablecloths at that particular period was that they should be made of tapestry with little yellow compartments marked upon them, such as you may see in photographs of the carpets in the corridors of the royal palaces. Tablecloths of a different kind were not real tablecloths. How shocking, and yet how wonderful it was to discover that these real things, Sunday luncheons, Sunday walks, country houses, and tablecloths were not entirely real, were indeed half phantoms, and the damnation which visited the disbeliever in them was only a sense of illegitimate freedom. What now takes the place of those things I wonder, those real standard things? Men perhaps, should you be a woman; the masculine point of view which governs our lives, which sets the standard, which establishes Whitaker's Table of Precedency,[4] which has become, I suppose, since the war, half a phantom to many men and women, which soon, one may hope, will be laughed into the dustbin where the phantoms go, the mahogany sideboards and the Landseer[5] prints, Gods and Devils, Hell and so forth, leaving us all with an intoxicating sense of illegitimate freedom—if freedom exists. . . .

In certain lights that mark on the wall seems actually to project from the wall. Nor is it entirely circular. I cannot be sure, but it seems to cast a percepti-

---

3. Street in London.
4. *Whitaker's Almanack*, an annual compendium of information, prints a "Table of Precedency," which shows the order in which the various ranks in public life and society proceed on formal occasions.

5. Edwin Henry Landseer, 19th-century animal painter, reproductions of whose *Stag at Bay*, *Monarch of the Glen*, and similar paintings were often found in Victorian homes.

ble shadow, suggesting that if I ran my finger down that strip of the wall it would, at a certain point, mount and descend a small tumulus, a smooth tumulus like those barrows on the South Downs[6] which are, they say, either tombs or camps. Of the two I should prefer them to be tombs, desiring melancholy like most English people, and finding it natural at the end of a walk to think of the bones stretched beneath the turf. . . . There must be some book about it. Some antiquary must have dug up those bones and given them a name. . . . What sort of a man is an antiquary, I wonder? Retired Colonels for the most part, I daresay, leading parties of aged labourers to the top here, examining clods of earth and stone, and getting into correspondence with the neighbouring clergy, which, being opened at breakfast time, gives them a feeling of importance, and the comparison of arrow-heads necessitates cross-country journeys to the country towns, an agreeable necessity both to them and to their elderly wives, who wish to make plum jam or to clean out the study, and have every reason for keeping that great question of the camp or the tomb in perpetual suspension, while the Colonel himself feels agreeably philosophic in accumulating evidence on both sides of the question. It is true that he does finally incline to believe in the camp; and, being opposed, indites a pamphlet which he is about to read at the quarterly meeting of the local society when a stroke lays him low, and his last conscious thoughts are not of wife or child, but of the camp and that arrow-head there, which is now in the case at the local museum, together with the foot of a Chinese murderess, a handful of Elizabethan nails, a great many Tudor clay pipes, a piece of Roman pottery, and the wineglass that Nelson drank out of—proving I really don't know what.

No, no, nothing is proved, nothing is known. And if I were to get up at this very moment and ascertain that the mark on the wall is really—what shall we say?—the head of a gigantic old nail, driven in two hundred years ago, which has now, owing to the patient attrition of many generations of housemaids, revealed its head above the coat of paint, and is taking its first view of modern life in the sight of a white-walled fire-lit room, what should I gain?—Knowledge? Matter for further speculation? I can think sitting still as well as standing up. And what is knowledge? What are our learned men save the descendants of witches and hermits who crouched in caves and in woods brewing herbs, interrogating shrew-mice and writing down the language of the stars? And the less we honour them as our superstitions dwindle and our respect for beauty and health of mind increases. . . . Yes, one could imagine a very pleasant world. A quiet, spacious world, with the flowers so red and blue in the open fields. A world without professors or specialists or house-keepers with the profiles of policemen, a world which one could slice with one's thought as a fish slices the water with his fin, grazing the stems of the water-lilies, hanging suspended over nests of white sea eggs. . . . How peaceful it is down here, rooted in the centre of the world and gazing up through the grey waters, with their sudden gleams of light, and their reflections—if it were not for Whitaker's Almanack—if it were not for the Table of Precedency!

I must jump up and see for myself what that mark on the wall really is—a nail, a rose-leaf, a crack in the wood?

6. A range of low hills in southeastern England. "Barrows": mounds of earth or stones erected by prehistoric peoples, usually as burial places.

Here is nature once more at her old game of self-preservation. This train of thought, she perceives, is threatening mere waste of energy, even some collision with reality, for who will ever be able to lift a finger against Whitaker's Table of Precedency? The Archbishop of Canterbury is followed by the Lord High Chancellor; the Lord High Chancellor is followed by the Archbishop of York. Everybody follows somebody, such is the philosophy of Whitaker; and the great thing is to know who follows whom. Whitaker knows, and let that, so Nature counsels, comfort you, instead of enraging you; and if you can't be comforted, if you must shatter this hour of peace, think of the mark on the wall.

I understand Nature's game—her prompting to take action as a way of ending any thought that threatens to excite or to pain. Hence, I suppose, comes our slight contempt for men of action—men, we assume, who don't think. Still, there's no harm in putting a full stop to one's disagreeable thoughts by looking at a mark on the wall.

Indeed, now that I have fixed my eyes upon it, I feel that I have grasped a plank in the sea; I feel a satisfying sense of reality which at once turns the two Archbishops and the Lord High Chancellor to the shadows of shades. Here is something definite, something real. Thus, waking from a midnight dream of horror, one hastily turns on the light and lies quiescent, worshipping the chest of drawers, worshipping solidity, worshipping reality, worshipping the impersonal world which is a proof of some existence other than ours. That is what one wants to be sure of. . . . Wood is a pleasant thing to think about. It comes from a tree; and trees grow, and we don't know how they grow. For years and years they grow, without paying any attention to us, in meadows, in forests, and by the side of rivers—all things one likes to think about. The cows swish their tails beneath them on hot afternoons; they paint rivers so green that when a moorhen dives one expects to see its feathers all green when it comes up again. I like to think of the fish balanced against the stream like flags blown out; and of water-beetles slowly raising domes of mud upon the bed of the river. I like to think of the tree itself: first of the close dry sensation of being wood; then the grinding of the storm; then the slow, delicious ooze of sap; I like to think of it, too, on winter's nights standing in the empty field with all leaves close-furled, nothing tender exposed to the iron bullets of the moon, a naked mast upon an earth that goes tumbling, tumbling, all night long. The song of birds must sound very loud and strange in June; and how cold the feet of insects must feel upon it, as they make laborious progresses up the creases of the bark, or sun themselves upon the thin green awning of the leaves, and look straight in front of them with diamond-cut red eyes. . . . One by one the fibres snap beneath the immense cold pressure of the earth, then the last storm comes and, falling, the highest branches drive deep into the ground again. Even so, life isn't done with; there are a million patient, watchful lives still for a tree, all over the world, in bedrooms, in ships, on the pavement, living rooms, where men and women sit after tea, smoking cigarettes. It is full of peaceful thoughts, happy thoughts, this tree. I should like to take each one separately—but something is getting in the way. . . . Where was I? What has it all been about? A tree? A river? The Downs? Whitaker's Almanack? The fields of asphodel? I can't remember a thing. Everything's moving, falling, slipping, vanishing. . . . There is a vast upheaval of matter. Someone is standing over me and saying:

"I'm going out to buy a newspaper."

"Yes?"

"Though it's no good buying newspapers. . . . Nothing ever happens. Curse this war; God damn this war! . . . All the same, I don't see why we should have a snail on our wall."

Ah, the mark on the wall! It was a snail.

1921

Modern Fiction

In making any survey, even the freest and loosest, of modern fiction, it is difficult not to take it for granted that the modern practice of the art is somehow an improvement upon the old. With their simple tools and primitive materials, it might be said, Fielding[1] did well and Jane Austen even better, but compare their opportunities with ours! Their masterpieces certainly have a strange air of simplicity. And yet the analogy between literature and the process, to choose an example, of making motor cars scarcely holds good beyond the first glance. It is doubtful whether in the course of the centuries, though we have learnt much about making machines, we have learnt anything about making literature. We do not come to write better; all that we can be said to do is to keep moving, now a little in this direction, now in that, but with a circular tendency should the whole course of the track be viewed from a sufficiently lofty pinnacle. It need scarcely be said that we make no claim to stand, even momentarily, upon that vantage-ground. On the flat, in the crowd, half blind with dust, we look back with envy to those happier warriors, whose battle is won and whose achievements wear so serene an air of accomplishment that we can scarcely refrain from whispering that the fight was not so fierce for them as for us. It is for the historian of literature to decide; for him to say if we are now beginning or ending or standing in the middle of a great period of prose fiction, for down in the plain little is visible. We only know that certain gratitudes and hostilities inspire us; that certain paths seem to lead to fertile land, others to the dust and the desert; and of this perhaps it may be worth while to attempt some account.

Our quarrel, then, is not with the classics, and if we speak of quarrelling with Mr. Wells, Mr. Bennett, and Mr. Galsworthy;[2] it is partly that by the mere fact of their existence in the flesh their work has a living, breathing, everyday imperfection which bids us take what liberties with it we choose. But it is also true, that, while we thank them for a thousand gifts, we reserve our unconditional gratitude for Mr. Hardy, for Mr. Conrad, and in much lesser degree for the Mr. Hudson of *The Purple Land, Green Mansions*, and *Far Away and Long Ago*.[3] Mr. Wells, Mr. Bennett, and Mr. Galsworthy have excited so many hopes and disappointed them so persistently that our gratitude largely takes the form of thanking them for having shown us what they might have done but have not done; what we certainly could not do, but as certainly, perhaps, do not wish to do. No single phrase will sum up the charge or griev-

---

1. Henry Fielding (1707–1754), novelist.
2. John Galsworthy (1867–1933), H. G. Wells (1866–1946), Arnold Bennett (1867–1931), novelists.
3. W. H. Hudson (1841–1922), naturalist and writer,

was born in Argentina, though he later lived in London. *The Purple Land* (1885) is about South America; *Green Mansions* (1904), a novel set in South America, was his first real success.

ance which we have to bring against a mass of work so large in its volume and embodying so many qualities, both admirable and the reverse. If we tried to formulate our meaning in one word we should say that these three writers are materialists. It is because they are concerned not with the spirit but with the body that they have disappointed us, and left us with the feeling that the sooner English fiction turns its back upon them, as politely as may be, and marches, if only into the desert, the better for its soul. Naturally, no single word reaches the centre of three separate targets. In the case of Mr. Wells it falls notably wide of the mark. And yet even with him it indicates to our thinking the fatal alloy in his genius, the great clod of clay that has got itself mixed up with the purity of his inspiration. But Mr. Bennett is perhaps the worst culprit of the three, inasmuch as he is by far the best workman. He can make a book so well constructed and solid in its craftsmanship that it is diffi-cult for the most exacting of critics to see through what chink or crevice decay can creep in. There is not so much as a draught between the frames of the windows, or a crack in the boards. And yet—if life should refuse to live there? That is a risk which the creator of The Old Wives' Tale, George Cannon, Edwin Clayhanger,[4] and hosts of other figures, may well claim to have sur-mounted. His characters live abundantly, even unexpectedly, but it remains to ask how do they live, and what do they live for? More and more they seem to us, deserting even the well-built villa in the Five Towns,[5] to spend their time in some softly padded first-class railway carriage, pressing bells and but-tons innumerable; and the destiny to which they travel so luxuriously becomes more and more unquestionably an eternity of bliss spent in the very best hotel in Brighton.[6] It can scarcely be said of Mr. Wells that he is a materialist in the sense that he takes too much delight in the solidity of his fabric. His mind is too generous in its sympathies to allow him to spend much time in making things shipshape and substantial. He is a materialist from sheer goodness of heart, taking upon his shoulders the work that ought to have been discharged by Government officials, and in the plethora of his ideas and facts scarcely having leisure to realize, or forgetting to think important, the crudity and coarseness of his human beings. Yet what more damaging criticism can there be both of his earth and of his Heaven than that they are to be inhabited here and hereafter by his Joans and his Peters? Does not the inferiority of their natures tarnish whatever institutions and ideals may be provided for them by the generosity of their creator? Nor, profoundly though we respect the integrity and humanity of Mr. Galsworthy, shall we find what we seek in his pages.

If we fasten, then, one label on all these books, on which is one word, materialists, we mean by it that they write of unimportant things; that they spend immense skill and immense industry making the trivial and the transi-tory appear the true and the enduring.

We have to admit that we are exacting, and, further, that we find it difficult to justify our discontent by explaining what it is that we exact. We frame our question differently at different times. But it reappears most persistently as we drop the finished novel on the crest of a sigh—Is it worth while? What is the point of it all? Can it be that, owing to one of those little deviations which the human spirit seems to make from time to time, Mr. Bennett has come down

4. Characters in Arnold Bennett's novels; The Old Wives' Tale (1908) is his best-known novel.
5. The pottery towns of Staffordshire in which many of Bennett's novels and stories were set.
6. One-time fashionable seaside resort on the south-west coast of England.

with his magnificent apparatus for catching life just an inch or two on the wrong side? Life escapes; and perhaps without life nothing else is worth while. It is a confession of vagueness to have to make use of such a figure as this, but we scarcely better the matter by speaking, as critics are prone to do, of reality. Admitting the vagueness which afflicts all criticism of novels, let us hazard the opinion that for us at this moment the form of fiction most in vogue more often misses than secures the thing we seek. Whether we call it life or spirit, truth or reality, this, the essential thing, has moved off, or on, and refuses to be contained any longer in such ill-fitting vestments as we provide. Neverthe-less, we go on perseveringly, conscientiously, constructing our two and thirty chapters after a design which more and more ceases to resemble the vision in our minds. So much of the enormous labour of proving the solidity, the like-ness to life, of the story is not merely labour thrown away but labour misplaced to the extent of obscuring and blotting out the light of the conception. The writer seems constrained, not by his own free will but by some powerful and unscrupulous tyrant who has him in thrall, to provide a plot, to provide com-edy, tragedy, love interest, and an air of probability embalming the whole so impeccable that if all his figures were to come to life they would find them-selves dressed down to the last button of their coats in the fashion of the hour. The tyrant is obeyed; the novel is done to a turn. But sometimes, more and more often as time goes by, we suspect a momentary doubt, a spasm of rebel-lion, as the pages fill themselves in the customary way. Is life like this? Must novels be like this?

Look within and life, it seems, is very far from being "like this." Examine for a moment an ordinary mind on an ordinary day. The mind receives a myriad impressions—trivial, fantastic, evanescent, or engraved with the sharp-ness of steel. From all sides they come, an incessant shower of innumerable atoms; and as they fall, as they shape themselves into the life of Monday or Tuesday,[7] the accent falls differently from of old; the moment of importance came not here but there; so that, if a writer were a free man and not a slave, if he could write what he chose, not what he must, if he could base his work upon his own feeling and not upon convention, there would be no plot, no comedy, no tragedy, no love interest or catastrophe in the accepted style, and perhaps not a single button sewn on as the Bond Street[8] tailors would have it. Life is not a series of gig-lamps[9] symmetrically arranged; life is a luminous halo, a semi-transparent envelope surrounding us from the beginning of con-sciousness to the end. Is it not the task of the novelist to convey this varying, this unknown and uncircumscribed spirit, whatever aberration or complexity it may display, with as little mixture of the alien and external as possible? We are not pleading merely for courage and sincerity; we are suggesting that the proper stuff of fiction is a little other than custom would have us believe it.

It is, at any rate, in some such fashion as this that we seek to define the quality which distinguishes the work of several young writers, among whom Mr. James Joyce is the most notable, from that of their predecessors. They attempt to come closer to life, and to preserve more sincerely and exactly what interests and moves them, even if to do so they must discard most of the conventions which are commonly observed by the novelist. Let us record the

7. *Monday or Tuesday* was the title of the collection of experimental stories and sketches that Woolf brought out in 1921.
8. Fashionable shopping street in London.
9. Carriage lamps.

atoms as they fall upon the mind in the order in which they fall, let us trace the pattern, however disconnected and incoherent in appearance, which each sight or incident scores upon the consciousness. Let us not take it for granted that life exists more fully in what is commonly thought big than in what is commonly thought small. Anyone who has read *The Portrait of the Artist as a Young Man* or, what promises to be a far more interesting work, *Ulysses*,[1] now appearing in the *Little Review*, will have hazarded some theory of this nature as to Mr. Joyce's intention. On our part, with such a fragment before us, it is hazarded rather than affirmed; but whatever the intention of the whole, there can be no question but that it is of the utmost sincerity and that the result, difficult or unpleasant as we may judge it, is undeniably important. In contrast with those whom we have called materialists, Mr. Joyce is spiritual; he is concerned at all costs to reveal the flickerings of that innermost flame which flashes its messages through the brain, and in order to preserve it he disregards with complete courage whatever seems to him adventitious, whether it be probability, or coherence, or any other of these signposts which for generations have served to support the imagination of a reader when called upon to imagine what he can neither touch nor see. The scene in the cemetery,[2] for instance, with its brilliancy, its sordidity, its incoherence, its sudden lightning flashes of significance, does undoubtedly come so close to the quick of the mind that, on a first reading at any rate, it is difficult not to acclaim a masterpiece. If we want life itself, here surely we have it. Indeed, we find ourselves fumbling rather awkwardly if we try to say what else we wish, and for what reason a work of such originality yet fails to compare, for we must take high examples, with *Youth* or *The Mayor of Casterbridge*.[3] It fails because of the comparative poverty of the writer's mind, we might say simply and have done with it. But it is possible to press a little further and wonder whether we may not refer our sense of being in a bright yet narrow room, confined and shut in, rather than enlarged and set free, to some limitation imposed by the method as well as by the mind. Is it the method that inhibits the creative power? Is it due to the method that we feel neither jovial nor magnanimous, but centred in a self which, in spite of its tremor of susceptibility, never embraces or creates what is outside itself and beyond? Does the emphasis laid, perhaps didactically, upon indecency contribute to the effect of something angular and isolated? Or is it merely that in any effort of such originality it is much easier, for contemporaries especially, to feel what it lacks than to name what it gives? In any case it is a mistake to stand outside examining "methods". Any method is right, every method is right, that expresses what we wish to express, if we are writers; that brings us closer to the novelist's intention if we are readers. This method has the merit of bringing us closer to what we were prepared to call life itself; did not the reading of *Ulysses* suggest how much of life is excluded or ignored, and did it not come with a shock to open *Tristram Shandy* or even *Pendennis*[4] and be by them convinced that there are not only other aspects of life, but more important ones into the bargain.

However this may be, the problem before the novelist at present, as we suppose it to have been in the past, is to contrive means of being free to set

1. Written April, 1919 [Woolf's note].
2. The sixth episode ("Hades") of *Ulysses*, where Bloom goes to Paddy Dignam's funeral.
3. Stories by, respectively, Joseph Conrad and Thomas Hardy.
4. Novels by, respectively, Laurence Sterne (1713–1768) and William Makepeace Thackeray (1811–1863).

down what he chooses. He has to have the courage to say that what interests him is no longer "this" but "that": out of "that" alone must he construct his work. For the moderns "that", the point of interest, lies very likely in the dark places of psychology. At once, therefore, the accent falls a little differently; the emphasis is upon something hitherto ignored; at once a different outline of form becomes necessary, difficult for us to grasp, incomprehensible to our predecessors. No one but a modern, no one perhaps but a Russian, would have felt the interest of the situation which Tchekov[5] has made into the short story which he calls "Gusev." Some Russian soldiers lie ill on board a ship which is taking them back to Russia. We are given a few scraps of their talk and some of their thoughts; then one of them dies and is carried away; the talk goes on among the others for a time, until Gusev himself dies, and looking "like a carrot or a radish" is thrown overboard. The emphasis is laid upon such unexpected places that at first it seems as if there were no emphasis at all; and then, as the eyes accustom themselves to twilight and discern the shapes of things in a room we see how complete the story is, how profound, and how truly in obedience to his vision Tchekov has chosen this, that, and the other, and placed them together to compose something new. But it is impossible to say "this is comic," or "that is tragic," nor are we certain, since short stories, we have been taught, should be brief and conclusive, whether this, which is vague and inconclusive, should be called a short story at all.

The most elementary remarks upon modern English fiction can hardly avoid some mention of the Russian influence, and if the Russians are mentioned one runs the risk of feeling that to write of any fiction save theirs is waste of time. If we want understanding of the soul and heart where else shall we find it of comparable profundity? If we are sick of our own materialism the least considerable of their novelists has by right of birth a natural reverence for the human spirit. "Learn to make yourself akin to people. . . . But let this sympathy be not with the mind—for it is easy with the mind—but with the heart, with love towards them." In every great Russian writer we seem to discern the features of a saint, if sympathy for the sufferings of others, love towards them, endeavour to reach some goal worthy of the most exacting demands of the spirit constitute saintliness. It is the saint in them which confounds us with a feeling of our own irreligious triviality, and turns so many of our famous novels to tinsel and trickery. The conclusions of the Russian mind, thus comprehensive and compassionate, are inevitably, perhaps, of the utmost sadness. More accurately indeed we might speak of the inconclusiveness of the Russian mind. It is the sense that there is no answer, that if honestly examined life presents question after question which must be left to sound on and on after the story is over in hopeless interrogation that fills us with a deep, and finally it may be with a resentful, despair. They are right perhaps; unquestionably they see further than we do and without our gross impediments of vision. But perhaps we see something that escapes them, or why should this voice of protest mix itself with our gloom? The voice of protest is the voice of another and an ancient civilization which seems to have bred in us the instinct to enjoy and fight rather than to suffer and understand. English fiction from Sterne to Meredith[6] bears witness to our natural delight in humour and comedy, in the beauty of earth, in the activities of the intellect,

---

5. Anton Pavlovich Chekhov (1860–1904).   6. George Meredith (1828–1909), novelist.

and in the splendour of the body. But any deductions that we may draw from the comparison of two fictions so immeasurably far apart are futile save indeed as they flood us with a view of the infinite possibilities of the art and remind us that there is no limit to the horizon, and that nothing—no "method," no experiment, even of the wildest—is forbidden, but only falsity and pretence. "The proper stuff of fiction" does not exist; everything is the proper stuff of fiction, every feeling, every thought; every quality of brain and spirit is drawn upon; no perception comes amiss. And if we can imagine the art of fiction come alive and standing in our midst, she would undoubtedly bid us break her and bully her, as well as honour and love her, for so her youth is renewed and her sovereignty assured.

1925

From A Room of One's Own
[Shakespeare's Sister][1]

It was disappointing not to have brought back in the evening some important statement, some authentic fact. Women are poorer than men because—this or that. Perhaps now it would be better to give up seeking for the truth, and receiving on one's head an avalanche of opinion hot as lava, discoloured as dish-water. It would be better to draw the curtains; to shut out distractions; to light the lamp; to narrow the enquiry and to ask the historian, who records not opinions but facts, to describe under what conditions women lived, not throughout the ages, but in England, say in the time of Elizabeth.

For it is a perennial puzzle why no woman wrote a word of that extraordinary literature when every other man, it seemed, was capable of song or sonnet. What were the conditions in which women lived, I asked myself; for fiction, imaginative work that is, is not dropped like a pebble upon the ground, as science may be; fiction is like a spider's web, attached ever so lightly perhaps, but still attached to life at all four corners. Often the attachment is scarcely perceptible; Shakespeare's plays, for instance, seem to hang there complete by themselves. But when the web is pulled askew, hooked up at the edge, torn in the middle, one remembers that these webs are not spun in midair by incorporeal creatures, but are the work of suffering human beings, and are attached to grossly material things, like health and money and the houses we live in.

I went, therefore, to the shelf where the histories stand and took down one of the latest, Professor Trevelyan's *History of England*.[2] Once more I looked up Women, found "position of," and turned to the pages indicated. "Wife-beating," I read, "was a recognised right of man, and was practised without shame by high as well as low. . . . Similarly," the historian goes on, "the daughter who refused to marry the gentleman of her parents' choice was liable to be locked up, beaten and flung about the room, without any shock being inflicted

---

1. The selection is drawn from chapter 3 and from the conclusion to the final chapter. In chapter 2, the narrator has been to the library of the British Museum, trying in vain to find answers to questions about the different fates of men and women.

2. G. M. Trevelyan's *History of England* (1926) long held its place as the standard one-volume history of the country.

on public opinion. Marriage was not an affair of personal affection, but of family avarice, particularly in the 'chivalrous' upper classes. . . . Betrothal often took place while one or both of the parties was in the cradle, and marriage when they were scarcely out of the nurses' charge." That was about 1470, soon after Chaucer's time. The next reference to the position of women is some two hundred years later, in the time of the Stuarts. "It was still the exception for women of the upper and middle class to choose their own husbands, and when the husband had been assigned, he was lord and master, so far at least as law and custom could make him. Yet even so," Professor Trevelyan concludes, "neither Shakespeare's women nor those of authentic seventeenth-century memoirs, like the Verneys and the Hutchinsons,[3] seem wanting in personality and character." Certainly, if we consider it, Cleopatra must have had a way with her; Lady Macbeth, one would suppose, had a will of her own; Rosalind, one might conclude, was an attractive girl.[4] Professor Trevelyan is speaking no more than the truth when he remarks that Shakespeare's women do not seem wanting in personality and character. Not being a historian, one might go even further and say that women have burnt like beacons in all the works of all the poets from the beginning of time—Clytemnestra, Antigone, Cleopatra, Lady Macbeth, Phèdre, Cressida, Rosalind, Desdemona, the Duchess of Malfi, among the dramatists; then among the prose writers: Millamant, Clarissa, Becky Sharp, Anna Karenina, Emma Bovary, Madame de Guermantes[5]—the names flock to mind, nor do they recall women "lacking in personality and character." Indeed, if woman had no existence save in the fiction written by men, one would imagine her a person of the utmost importance, very various; heroic and mean; splendid and sordid; infinitely beautiful and hideous in the extreme; as great as a man, some think even greater.[6] But this is woman in fiction. In fact, as Professor Trevelyan points out, she was locked up, beaten and flung about the room.

A very queer, composite being thus emerges. Imaginatively she is of the highest importance; practically she is completely insignificant. She pervades poetry from cover to cover; she is all but absent from history. She dominates the lives of kings and conquerors in fiction; in fact she was the slave of any boy whose parents forced a ring upon her finger. Some of the most inspired words, some of the most profound thoughts in literature fall from her lips; in

---

3. "The ideal family life of the period [1640–50] that ended in such tragic political division has been recorded once for all in the *Memoirs of the Verney Family*" (Trevelyan, *History of England*). Lucy Hutchinson (b. 1628) wrote the biography of her husband, Col. John Hutchinson (1616–1684); it was first published in 1806.

4. These three Shakespearean heroines are, respectively, in *Antony and Cleopatra, Macbeth*, and *As You Like It*.

5. Characters in, respectively, Aeschylus' *Agamemnon*; Sophocles' *Antigone*; Shakespeare's *Antony and Cleopatra* and *Macbeth*; Racine's *Phèdre*; Shakespeare's *Troilus and Cressida, As You Like It*, and *Othello*; Webster's *The Duchess of Malfi*; Congreve's *Way of the World*; Richardson's *Clarissa*; Thackeray's *Vanity Fair*; Tolstoy's *Anna Karenina*; Flaubert's *Madame Bovary*; and Proust's *A la Récherche du Temps Perdu*.

6. "It remains a strange and almost inexplicable fact that in Athena's city, where women were kept in almost Oriental suppression as odalisques or drudges, the stage should yet have produced figures like Clytemnestra and Cassandra, Atossa and Antigone, Phèdre and Medea, and all the other heroines who dominate play after play of the 'misogynist' Euripides. But the paradox of this world where in real life a respectable woman could hardly show her face alone in the street, and yet on the stage woman equals or surpasses man, has never been satisfactorily explained. In modern tragedy the same predominance exists. At all events, a very cursory survey of Shakespeare's work (similarly with Webster, though not with Marlowe or Jonson) suffices to reveal how this dominance, this initiative of women, persists from Rosalind to Lady Macbeth. So too in Racine; six of his tragedies bear their heroines' names; and what male characters of his shall we set against Hermione and Andromaque, Bérénice and Roxane, Phèdre and Athalie? So again with Ibsen; what men shall we match with Solveig and Nora, Hedda and Hilda Wangel and Rebecca West?"—F. L. Lucas, *Tragedy*, pp. 114–15 [Woolf's note].

real life she could hardly read, could scarcely spell, and was the property of her husband.

It was certainly an odd monster that one made up by reading the historians first and the poets afterwards—a worm winged like an eagle; the spirit of life and beauty in a kitchen chopping up suet. But these monsters, however amusing to the imagination, have no existence in fact. What one must do to bring her to life was to think poetically and prosaically at one and the same moment, thus keeping in touch with fact—that she is Mrs. Martin, aged thirty-six, dressed in blue, wearing a black hat and brown shoes; but not losing sight of fiction either—that she is a vessel in which all sorts of spirits and forces are coursing and flashing perpetually. The moment, however, that one tries this method with the Elizabethan woman, one branch of illumination fails; one is held up by the scarcity of facts. One knows nothing detailed, nothing perfectly true and substantial about her. History scarcely mentions her. And I turned to Professor Trevelyan again to see what history meant to him. I found by looking at his chapter headings that it meant—

"The Manor Court and the Methods of Open-field Agriculture . . . The Cistercians and Sheep-farming . . . The Crusades . . . The University . . . The House of Commons . . . The Hundred Years' War . . . The Wars of the Roses . . . The Renaissance Scholars . . . The Dissolution of the Monasteries . . . Agrarian and Religious Strife . . . The Origin of English Sea-power . . . The Armada . . ." and so on. Occasionally an individual woman is mentioned, an Elizabeth, or a Mary; a queen or a great lady. But by no possible means could middle-class women with nothing but brains and character at their command have taken part in any one of the great movements which, brought together, constitute the historian's view of the past. Nor shall we find her in any collection of anecdotes. Aubrey[7] hardly mentions her. She never writes her own life and scarcely keeps a diary; there are only a handful of her letters in existence. She left no plays or poems by which we can judge her. What one wants, I thought—and why does not some brilliant student at Newnham or Girton supply it?—is a mass of information; at what age did she marry; how many children had she as a rule; what was her house like; had she a room to herself; did she do the cooking; would she be likely to have a servant? All these facts lie somewhere, presumably, in parish registers and account books; the life of the average Elizabethan woman must be scattered about somewhere, could one collect it and make a book of it. It would be ambitious beyond my daring, I thought, looking about the shelves for books that were not there, to suggest to the students of those famous colleges that they should re-write history, though I own that it often seems a little queer as it is, unreal, lop-sided; but why should they not add a supplement to history? calling it, of course, by some inconspicuous name so that women might figure there without impropriety? For one often catches a glimpse of them in the lives of the great, whisking away into the background, concealing, I sometimes think, a wink, a laugh, perhaps a tear. And, after all, we have lives enough of Jane Austen; it scarcely seems necessary to consider again the influence of the tragedies of Joanna Baillie[8] upon the poetry of Edgar Allan Poe; as for myself, I should not mind if the homes and haunts of Mary Russell Mitford[9] were closed to the

7. John Aubrey (1626–1697), diarist.
8. Baillie (1762–1851), poet and dramatist.

9. Mitford (1787–1855), poet and novelist, best known for her sketches of country life.

public for a century at least. But what I find deplorable, I continued, looking about the bookshelves again, is that nothing is known about women before the eighteenth century. I have no model in my mind to turn about this way and that. Here am I asking why women did not write poetry in the Elizabethan age, and I am not sure how they were educated; whether they were taught to write; whether they had sitting-rooms to themselves; how many women had children before they were twenty-one; what, in short, they did from eight in the morning till eight at night. They had no money evidently; according to Professor Trevelyan they were married whether they liked it or not before they were out of the nursery, at fifteen or sixteen very likely. It would have been extremely odd, even upon this showing, had one of them suddenly written the plays of Shakespeare, I concluded, and I thought of that old gentleman, who is dead now, but was a bishop, I think, who declared that it was impossible for any woman, past, present, or to come, to have the genius of Shakespeare. He wrote to the papers about it. He also told a lady who applied to him for information that cats do not as a matter of fact go to heaven, though they have, he added, souls of a sort. How much thinking those old gentlemen used to save one! How the borders of ignorance shrank back at their approach! Cats do not go to heaven. Women cannot write the plays of Shakespeare.

Be that as it may, I could not help thinking, as I looked at the works of Shakespeare on the shelf, that the bishop was right at least in this; it would have been impossible, completely and entirely, for any woman to have written the plays of Shakespeare in the age of Shakespeare. Let me imagine, since facts are so hard to come by, what would have happened had Shakespeare had a wonderfully gifted sister, called Judith, let us say. Shakespeare himself went, very probably—his mother was an heiress—to the grammar school, where he may have learnt Latin—Ovid, Virgil and Horace—and the elements of grammar and logic. He was, it is well known, a wild boy who poached rabbits, perhaps shot a deer, and had, rather sooner than he should have done, to marry a woman in the neighbourhood, who bore him a child rather quicker than was right. That escapade sent him to seek his fortune in London. He had, it seemed, a taste for the theatre; he began by holding horses at the stage door. Very soon he got work in the theatre, became a successful actor, and lived at the hub of the universe, meeting everybody, knowing everybody, practising his art on the boards, exercising his wits in the streets, and even getting access to the palace of the queen. Meanwhile his extraordinarily gifted sister, let us suppose, remained at home. She was as adventurous, as imaginative, as agog to see the world as he was. But she was not sent to school. She had no chance of learning grammar and logic, let alone of reading Horace and Virgil. She picked up a book now and then, one of her brother's perhaps, and read a few pages. But then her parents came in and told her to mend the stockings or mind the stew and not moon about with books and papers. They would have spoken sharply but kindly, for they were substantial people who knew the conditions of life for a woman and loved their daughter—indeed, more likely than not she was the apple of her father's eye. Perhaps she scribbled some pages up in an apple loft on the sly, but was careful to hide them or set fire to them. Soon, however, before she was out of her teens, she was to be betrothed to the son of a neighbouring wool-stapler.[1] She cried out that mar-

1. A stapler is a dealer in staple goods (i.e., established goods in trade and marketing); hence a wool-stapler is a dealer in wool (one of the "staple" products of 16th-century England).

riage was hateful to her, and for that she was severely beaten by her father. Then he ceased to scold her. He begged her instead not to hurt him, not to shame him in this matter of her marriage. He would give her a chain of beads or a fine petticoat, he said; and there were tears in his eyes. How could she disobey him? How could she break his heart? The force of her own gift alone drove her to it. She made up a small parcel of her belongings, let herself down by a rope one summer's night and took the road to London. She was not seventeen. The birds that sang in the hedge were not more musical than she was. She had the quickest fancy, a gift like her brother's, for the tune of words. Like him, she had a taste for the theatre. She stood at the stage door; she wanted to act, she said. Men laughed in her face. The manager—a fat, loose-lipped man—guffawed. He bellowed something about poodles dancing and women acting—no woman, he said, could possibly be an actress. He hinted—you can imagine what. She could get no training in her craft. Could she even seek her dinner in a tavern or roam the streets at midnight? Yet her genius was for fiction and lusted to feed abundantly upon the lives of men and women and the study of their ways. At last—for she was very young, oddly like Shakespeare the poet in her face, with the same grey eyes and rounded brows—at last Nick Greene the actor-manager took pity on her; she found herself with child by that gentleman and so—who shall measure the heat and violence of the poet's heart when caught and tangled in a woman's body?— killed herself one winter's night and lies buried at some cross-roads where the omnibuses now stop outside the Elephant and Castle.[2]

That, more or less, is how the story would run, I think, if a woman in Shakespeare's day had had Shakespeare's genius. But for my part, I agree with the deceased bishop, if such he was—it is unthinkable that any woman in Shakespeare's day should have had Shakespeare's genius. For genius like Shakespeare's is not born among labouring, uneducated, servile people. It was not born in England among the Saxons and the Britons. It is not born today among the working classes. How, then, could it have been born among women whose work began, according to Professor Trevelyan, almost before they were out of the nursery, who were forced to it by their parents and held to it by all the power of law and custom? Yet genius of a sort must have existed among women as it must have existed among the working classes. Now and again an Emily Brontë or a Robert Burns blazes out and proves its presence. But certainly it never got itself on to paper. When, however, one reads of a witch being ducked, of a woman possessed by devils, of a wise woman selling herbs, or even of a very remarkable man who had a mother, then I think we are on the track of a lost novelist, a suppressed poet, of some mute and inglori-ous[3] Jane Austen, some Emily Brontë who dashed her brains out on the moor or mopped and mowed about the highways crazed with the torture that her gift had put her to. Indeed, I would venture to guess that Anon, who wrote so many poems without signing them, was often a woman. It was a woman Edward Fitzgerald,[4] I think, suggested who made the ballads and the folk-songs, crooning them to her children, beguiling her spinning with them, or the length of the winter's night.

2. Suicides were buried at crossroads. The Elephant and Castle was a tavern south of the Thames where roads went off to different parts of southern England.
3. An echo of Thomas Gray's famous line about "some

mute inglorious Milton" in *Elegy Written in a Country Churchyard* (1751), line 59.
4. Fitzgerald (1809–1883), poet and translator.

This may be true or it may be false—who can say?—but what is true in it, so it seemed to me, reviewing the story of Shakespeare's sister as I had made it, is that any woman born with a great gift in the sixteenth century would certainly have gone crazed, shot herself, or ended her days in some lonely cottage outside the village, half witch, half wizard, feared and mocked at. For it needs little skill in psychology to be sure that a highly gifted girl who had tried to use her gift for poetry would have been so thwarted and hindered by other people, so tortured and pulled asunder by her own contrary instincts, that she must have lost her health and sanity to a certainty. No girl could have walked to London and stood at a stage door and forced her way into the presence of actor-managers without doing herself a violence and suffering an anguish which may have been irrational—for chastity may be a fetish invented by certain societies for unknown reasons—but were none the less inevitable. Chastity had then, it has even now, a religious importance in a woman's life, and has so wrapped itself round with nerves and instincts that to cut it free and bring it to the light of day demands courage of the rarest. To have lived a free life in London in the sixteenth century would have meant for a woman who was poet and playwright a nervous stress and dilemma which might well have killed her. Had she survived, whatever she had written would have been twisted and deformed, issuing from a strained and morbid imagination. And undoubtedly, I thought, looking at the shelf where there are no plays by women, her work would have gone unsigned. That refuge she would have sought certainly. It was the relic of the sense of chastity that dictated anonymity to women even so late as the nineteenth century. Currer Bell, George Eliot, George Sand,[5] all the victims of inner strife as their writings prove, sought ineffectively to veil themselves by using the name of a man. Thus they did homage to the convention, which if not implanted by the other sex was liberally encouraged by them (the chief glory of a woman is not to be talked of, said Pericles,[6] himself a much-talked-of man), that publicity in women is detestable. Anonymity runs in their blood. The desire to be veiled still possesses them.

*   *   *

I told you in the course of this paper that Shakespeare had a sister; but do not look for her in Sir Sidney Lee's[7] life of the poet. She died young— alas, she never wrote a word. She lies buried where the omnibuses now stop, opposite the Elephant and Castle. Now my belief is that this poet who never wrote a word and was buried at the crossroads still lives. She lives in you and in me, and in many other women who are not here tonight, for they are washing up the dishes and putting the children to bed. But she lives; for great poets do not die; they are continuing presences; they need only the opportunity to walk among us in the flesh. This opportunity, as I think, it is now coming within your power to give her. For my belief is that if we live another century or so—I am talking of the common life which is the real life and not of the little separate lives which we live as individuals—and have five hundred a year each of us and rooms of our own; if we have the habit of freedom and

5. Male pseudonyms, respectively, of Charlotte Brontë, Marian Evans, and Amandine-Aurore-Lucie Dupin.

6. Pericles (ca. 495–429 B.C.), Athenian statesman.
7. Lee (1859–1926), biographer and Shakespeare scholar, author of *Life of William Shakespeare* (1898).

the courage to write exactly what we think; if we escape a little from the common sitting-room and see human beings not always in their relation to each other but in relation to reality; and the sky, too, and the trees or whatever it may be in themselves; if we look past Milton's bogey,[8] for no human being should shut out the view; if we face the fact, for it is a fact, that there is no arm to cling to, but that we go alone and that our relation is to the world of reality and not only to the world of men and women, then the opportunity will come and the dead poet who was Shakespeare's sister will put on the body which she has so often laid down. Drawing her life from the lives of the unknown who were her forerunners, as her brother did before her, she will be born. As for her coming without that preparation, without that effort on our part, without that determination that when she is born again she shall find it possible to live and write her poetry, that we cannot expect, for that would be impossible. But I maintain that she would come if we worked for her, and that so to work, even in poverty and obscurity, is worth while.

1929

Professions for Women[1]

When your secretary invited me to come here, she told me that your Society is concerned with the employment of women and she suggested that I might tell you something about my own professional experiences. It is true I am a woman; it is true I am employed; but what professional experiences have I had? It is difficult to say. My profession is literature; and in that profession there are fewer experiences for women than in any other, with the exception of the stage—fewer, I mean, that are peculiar to women. For the road was cut many years ago—by Fanny Burney, by Aphra Behn, by Harriet Martineau,[2] by Jane Austen, by George Eliot—many famous women, and many more unknown and forgotten, have been before me, making the path smooth, and regulating my steps. Thus, when I came to write, there were very few material obstacles in my way. Writing was a reputable and harmless occupation. The family peace was not broken by the scratching of a pen. No demand was made upon the family purse. For ten and sixpence one can buy paper enough to write all the plays of Shakespeare—if one has a mind that way. Pianos and models, Paris, Vienna, and Berlin, masters and mistresses, are not needed by a writer. The cheapness of writing paper is, of course, the reason why women have succeeded as writers before they have succeeded in the other professions.

But to tell you my story—it is a simple one. You have only got to figure to yourselves a girl in a bedroom with a pen in her hand. She had only to move that pen from left to right—from ten o'clock to one. Then it occurred to her to do what is simple and cheap enough after all—to slip a few of those pages into an envelope, fix a penny stamp in the corner, and drop the envelope into the red box at the corner. It was thus that I became a journalist; and my effort was rewarded on the first day of the following month—a very glorious day it

---

8. Milton, with his unhappy first marriage, his campaign for freedom of divorce, and his deliberate subordination of Eve to Adam in *Paradise Lost*, was and often still is held to be (not altogether accurately) an example of what the present age calls a male chauvinist attitude to women.

1. A paper read to the Women's Service League [Woolf's note].
2. Martineau (1802–1876), economist, moralist, journalist, and novelist. Burney (1752–1840), author of *Evelina* and other novels. Behn (1640–1689), writer of romances and plays.

was for me—by a letter from an editor containing a cheque for one pound ten shillings and sixpence. But to show you how little I deserve to be called a professional woman, how little I know of the struggles and difficulties of such lives, I have to admit that instead of spending that sum upon bread and butter, rent, shoes and stockings, or butcher's bills, I went out and bought a cat—a beautiful cat, a Persian cat, which very soon involved me in bitter disputes with my neighbours.

What could be easier than to write articles and to buy Persian cats with the profits? But wait a moment. Articles have to be about something. Mine, I seem to remember, was about a novel by a famous man. And while I was writing this review, I discovered that if I were going to review books I should need to do battle with a certain phantom. And the phantom was a woman, and when I came to know her better I called her after the heroine of a famous poem, The Angel in the House.[3] It was she who used to come between me and my paper when I was writing reviews. It was she who bothered me and wasted my time and so tormented me that at last I killed her. You who come of a younger and happier generation may not have heard of her—you may not know what I mean by The Angel in the House. I will describe her as shortly as I can. She was intensely sympathetic. She was immensely charming. She was utterly unselfish. She excelled in the difficult arts of family life. She sacrificed herself daily. If there was chicken, she took the leg; if there was a draught she sat in it—in short she was so constituted that she never had a mind or a wish of her own, but preferred to sympathize always with the minds and wishes of others. Above all—I need not say it—she was pure. Her purity was supposed to be her chief beauty—her blushes, her great grace. In those days—the last of Queen Victoria—every house had its Angel. And when I came to write I encountered her with the very first words. The shadow of her wings fell on my page; I heard the rustling of her skirts in the room. Directly, that is to say, I took my pen in my hand to review that novel by a famous man, she slipped behind me and whispered: 'My dear, you are a young woman. You are writing about a book that has been written by a man. Be sympathetic; be tender; flatter; deceive; use all the arts and wiles of our sex. Never let anybody guess that you have a mind of your own. Above all, be pure.' And she made as if to guide my pen. I now record the one act for which I take some credit to myself, though the credit rightly belongs to some excellent ancestors of mine who left me a certain sum of money—shall we say five hundred pounds a year?—so that it was not necessary for me to depend solely on charm for my living. I turned upon her and caught her by the throat. I did my best to kill her. My excuse, if I were to be had up in a court of law, would be that I acted in self-defence. Had I not killed her she would have killed me. She would have plucked the heart out of my writing. For, as I found, directly I put pen to paper, you cannot review even a novel without having a mind of your own, without expressing what you think to be the truth about human relations, morality, sex. And all these questions, according to the Angel of the House, cannot be dealt with freely and openly by women; they must charm, they must conciliate, they must—to put it bluntly—tell lies if they are to succeed. Thus, whenever I felt the shadow of her wing or the radiance of her halo upon my page, I took up the inkpot and flung it at her. She died hard. Her fictitious nature was of great assistance to

3. By Coventry Patmore (1823–1896), published 1854–62.

her. It is far harder to kill a phantom than a reality. She was always creeping back when I thought I had despatched her. Though I flatter myself that I killed her in the end, the struggle was severe; it took much time that had better have been spent upon learning Greek grammar; or in roaming the world in search of adventures. But it was a real experience; it was an experience that was bound to befall all women writers at that time. Killing the Angel in the House was part of the occupation of a woman writer.

But to continue my story. The Angel was dead; what then remained? You may say that what remained was a simple and common object—a young woman in a bedroom with an inkpot. In other words, now that she had rid herself of falsehood, that young woman had only to be herself. Ah, but what is 'herself'? I mean, what is a woman? I assure you, I do not know. I do not believe that you know. I do not believe that anybody can know until she has expressed herself in all the arts and professions open to human skill. That indeed is one of the reasons why I have come here—out of respect for you, who are in process of showing us by your experiments what a woman is, who are in process of providing us, by your failures and successes, with that extremely important piece of information.

But to continue the story of my professional experiences. I made one pound ten and six by my first review; and I bought a Persian cat with the proceeds. Then I grew ambitious. A Persian cat is all very well, I said; but a Persian cat is not enough. I must have a motor-car. And it was thus that I became a novelist—for it is a very strange thing that people will give you a motor-car if you will tell them a story. It is a still stranger thing that there is nothing so delightful in the world as telling stories. It is far pleasanter than writing reviews of famous novels. And yet, if I am to obey your secretary and tell you my professional experiences as a novelist, I must tell you about a very strange experience that befell me as a novelist. And to understand it you must try first to imagine a novelist's state of mind. I hope I am not giving away professional secrets if I say that a novelist's chief desire is to be as unconscious as possible. He has to induce in himself a state of perpetual lethargy. He wants life to proceed with the utmost quiet and regularity. He wants to see the same faces, to read the same books, to do the same things day after day, month after month, while he is writing, so that nothing may break the illusion in which he is living—so that nothing may disturb or disquiet the mysterious nosings about, feelings round, darts, dashes, and sudden discoveries of that very shy and illusive spirit, the imagination. I suspect that this state is the same both for men and women. Be that as it may, I want you to imagine me writing a novel in a state of trance. I want you to figure to yourselves a girl sitting with a pen in her hand, which for minutes, and indeed for hours, she never dips into the inkpot. The image that comes to my mind when I think of this girl is the image of a fisherman lying sunk in dreams on the verge of a deep lake with a rod held out over the water. She was letting her imagination sweep unchecked round every rock and cranny of the world that lies submerged in the depths of our unconscious being. Now came the experience that I believe to be far commoner with women writers than with men. The line raced through the girl's fingers. Her imagination had rushed away. It had sought the pools, the depths, the dark places where the largest fish slumber. And then there was a smash. There was an explosion. There was foam and confusion. The imagination had dashed itself against something hard. The girl was roused from her dream. She was indeed in a state of the most acute and difficult distress. To speak without figure, she had thought of something, something about the body, about the passions which it was unfitting for her as a woman to say. Men, her reason told her, would be shocked. The consciousness of what men will say of a woman who speaks the truth about her passions had roused her from her artist's state of unconsciousness. She could write no more. The trance was over. Her imagination could work no longer. This I believe to be a very common experience with women writers—they are impeded by the extreme conventionality of the other sex. For though men sensibly allow themselves great freedom in these respects, I doubt that they realize or can control the extreme severity with which they condemn such freedom in women.

These then were two very genuine experiences of my own. These were two of the adventures of my professional life. The first—killing the Angel in the House—I think I solved. She died. But the second, telling the truth about my own experiences as a body, I do not think I solved. I doubt that any woman has solved it yet. The obstacles against her are still immensely powerful—and yet they are very difficult to define. Outwardly, what is simpler than to write books? Outwardly, what obstacles are there for a woman rather than for a man? Inwardly, I think, the case is very different; she has still many ghosts to fight, many prejudices to overcome. Indeed it will be a long time still, I think, before a woman can sit down to write a book without finding a phantom to be slain, a rock to be dashed against. And if this is so in literature, the freest of all professions for women, how is it in the new professions which you are now for the first time entering?

Those are the questions that I should like, had I time, to ask you. And indeed, if I have laid stress upon these professional experiences of mine, it is because I believe that they are, though in different forms, yours also. Even when the path is nominally open—when there is nothing to prevent a woman from being a doctor, a lawyer, a civil servant—there are many phantoms and obstacles, as I believe, looming in her way. To discuss and define them is I think of great value and importance; for thus only can the labour be shared, the difficulties be solved. But besides this, it is necessary also to discuss the ends and the aims for which we are fighting, for which we are doing battle with these formidable obstacles. Those aims cannot be taken for granted; they must be perpetually questioned and examined. The whole position, as I see it—here in this hall surrounded by women practising for the first time in history I know not how many different professions—is one of extraordinary interest and importance. You have won rooms of your own in the house hitherto exclusively owned by men. You are able, though not without great labour and effort, to pay the rent. You are earning your five hundred pounds a year. But this freedom is only a beginning; the room is your own, but it is still bare. It has to be furnished; it has to be decorated; it has to be shared. How are you going to furnish it, how are you going to decorate it? With whom are you going to share it, and upon what terms? These, I think are questions of the utmost importance and interest. For the first time in history you are able to ask them; for the first time you are able to decide for yourselves what the answers should be. Willingly would I stay and discuss those questions and answers—but not tonight. My time is up; and I must cease.

1942

Moments of Being: "Slater's Pins Have No Points"[1]

"Slater's pins have no points—don't you always find that?" said Miss Craye, turning round as the rose fell out of Fanny Wilmot's dress, and Fanny stooped with her ears full of the music, to look for the pin on the floor.

The words gave her an extraordinary shock, as Miss Craye struck the last chord of the Bach fugue. Did Miss Craye actually go to Slater's and buy pins then, Fanny Wilmot asked herself, transfixed for a moment? Did she stand at the counter waiting like anybody else, and was she given a bill with coppers wrapped in it, and did she slip them into her purse and then, an hour later, stand by her dressing table and take out the pins? What need had she of pins? For she was not so much dressed as cased, like a beetle compactly in its sheath, blue in winter, green in summer. What need had she of pins—Julia Craye—who lived, it seemed, in the cool, glassy world of Bach fugues, playing to herself what she liked and only consenting to take one or two pupils at the Archer Street College of Music (so the Principal, Miss Kingston, said) as a special favour to herself, who had "the greatest admiration for her in every way." Miss Craye was left badly off, Miss Kingston was afraid, at her brother's death. Oh, they used to have such lovely things, when they lived at Salisbury and her brother Julius was, of course, a very well-known man: a famous archaeologist. It was a great privilege to stay with them, Miss Kingston said ("My family had always known them—they were regular Salisbury[2] people," Miss Kingston said), but a little frightening for a child; one had to be careful not to slam the door or bounce into the room unexpectedly. Miss Kingston, who gave little character sketches like this on the first day of term while she received cheques and wrote out receipts for them, smiled here. Yes, she had been rather a tomboy; she had bounced in and set all those green Roman glasses and things jumping in their case. The Crayes were none of them married. The Crayes were not used to children. They kept cats. The cats, one used to feel, knew as much about the Roman urns and things as anybody.

"Far more than I did!" said Miss Kingston brightly, writing her name across the stamp, in her dashing, cheerful, full-bodied hand, for she had always been practical.

Perhaps then, Fanny Wilmot thought, looking for the pin, Miss Craye said that about "Slater's pins having no points," at a venture. None of the Crayes had ever married. She knew nothing about pins—nothing whatever. But she wanted to break the spell that had fallen on the house; to break the pane of glass which separated them from other people. When Polly Kingston, that merry little girl, had slammed the door and made the Roman vases jump, Julius, seeing that no harm was done (that would be his first instinct) looked, for the case was stood in the window, at Polly skipping home across the fields; looked with the look his sister often had, that lingering, desiring look.

"Stars, sun, moon," it seemed to say, "the daisy in the grass, fires, frost on the window pane, my heart goes out to you. But," it always seemed to add, "you break, you pass, you go." And simultaneously it covered the intensity of both these states of mind with "I can't reach you—I can't get at you," spoken wistfully, frustratedly. And the stars faded, and the child went.

That was the kind of spell, that was the glassy surface that Miss Craye

---

1. See Woolf's discussion of "moments of being and non-being" on pp. 2328–35. 2. Cathedral town in the south of England.

wanted to break by showing, when she had played Bach beautifully as a reward
to a favourite pupil (Fanny Wilmot knew that she was Miss Craye's favourite
pupil) that she too felt as other people felt about pins. Slater's pins had no
points.

Yes, the "famous archaeologist" had looked like that, too. "The famous archaeologist"—as she said that endorsing cheques, ascertaining the day of the
month, speaking so brightly and frankly, there was in Miss Kingston's voice an indescribable tone which hinted at something odd, something queer, in Julius Craye. It was the very same thing that was odd perhaps
in Julia too. One could have sworn, thought Fanny Wilmot, as she looked for
the pin, that at parties, meetings (Miss Kingston's father was a clergyman) she
had picked up some piece of gossip, or it might only have been a smile, or a
tone when his name was mentioned, which had given her "a feeling" about
Julius Craye. Needless to say, she had never spoken about it to anybody. Probably she scarcely knew what she meant by it. But whenever she spoke of Julius,
or heard him mentioned, that was the first thought that came to mind: there
was something odd about Julius Craye.

It was so that Julia looked too, as she sat half turned on the music stool,
smiling. It's on the field, it's on the pane, it's in the sky—beauty; and I can't
get at it; I can't have it—I, she seemed to add, with that little clutch of the
hand which was so characteristic, who adore it so passionately, would give the
whole world to possess it! And she picked up the carnation which had fallen
on the floor, while Fanny searched for the pin. She crushed it, Fanny felt,
voluptuously in her smooth, veined hands stuck about with water-coloured
rings set in pearls. The pressure of her fingers seemed to increase all that was
most brilliant in the flower; to set it off; to make it more frilled, fresh, immaculate. What was odd in her, and perhaps in her brother too, was that this crush
and grasp of the fingers was combined with a perpetual frustration. So it was
even now with the carnation. She had her hands on it; she pressed it; but she
did not possess it, enjoy it, not altogether.

None of the Crayes had married, Fanny Wilmot remembered. She had in
mind how one evening when the lesson had lasted longer than usual and it
was dark, Julia Craye had said, "It's the use of men, surely, to protect us,"
smiling at her that same odd smile, as she stood fastening her cloak, which
made her, like the flower, conscious to her finger tips of youth, and brilliance,
but, like the flower too, Fanny suspected, inhibited.

"Oh, but I don't want protection," Fanny had laughed, and when Julia
Craye, fixing on her that extraordinary look, had said she was not so sure of
that, Fanny positively blushed under the admiration in her eyes.

It was the only use of men, she had said. Was it for that reason then, Fanny
wondered, with her eyes on the floor, that she had never married? After all,
she had not lived all her life in Salisbury. "Much the nicest part of London,"
she had said once, "(but I'm speaking of fifteen or twenty years ago) is Kensington.[3] One was in the Gardens in ten minutes—it was like the heart of the
country. One could dine out in one's slippers without catching cold. Kensington—it was like a village then, you know," she had said.

Here she had broken off, to denounce acridly, the draughts in the Tubes.[4]

"It was the use of men," she had said, with a queer, wry acerbity. Did that

3. A fashionable London district with an elegant   4. London subway.
park—"the Gardens."

throw any light on the problem why she had not married? One could imagine every sort of scene in her youth, when with her good, blue eyes, her straight, firm nose, her piano playing, her rose flowering with chaste passion in the bosom of her muslin dress, she had attracted first the young men to whom such things, and the china tea-cups and the silver candlesticks, and the inlaid tables (for the Crayes had such nice things) were wonderful; young men not sufficiently distinguished; young men of the Cathedral town with ambitions. She had attracted them first, and then her brother's friends from Oxford or Cambridge. They would come down in the summer, row her up the river, continue the argument about Browning by letter, and arrange perhaps on the rare occasions when she stayed in London to show her—Kensington Gardens?

"Much the nicest part of London—Kensington. I'm speaking of fifteen or twenty years ago," she had said once. "One was in the Gardens in ten minutes—in the heart of the country." One could make that yield what one liked, Fanny Wilmot thought, single out for instance, Mr. Sherman, the painter, an old friend of hers; make him call for her by appointment one sunny day in June; take her to have tea under the trees. (They had met, too, at those parties to which one tripped in slippers without fear of catching a cold.) The aunt or other elderly relative was to wait there while they looked at the Serpentine. They looked at the Serpentine.[5] He may have rowed her across. They compared it with the Avon.[6] She would have considered the comparison very seriously, for views of rivers were important to her. She sat hunched a little, a little angular, though she was graceful then, steering. At the critical moment, for he had determined that she must speak now—it was his only chance of getting her alone—he was speaking with his head turned at an absurd angle, in his great nervousness, over his shoulder—at the very moment she interrupted fiercely. He would have them[7] into the Bridge, she cried. It was a moment of horror, of disillusionment, of revelation for both of them. I can't have it, I can't possess it, she thought. He could not see why she had come then. With a great splash of his oar he pulled the boat round. Merely to snub him? He rowed her back and said good-bye to her.

The setting of that scene could be varied as one chose, Fanny Wilmot reflected. (Where had that pin fallen?) It might be Ravenna—or Edinburgh, where she had kept house for her brother. The scene could be changed and the young man and the exact manner of it all; but one thing was constant— her refusal and her frown and her anger with herself afterwards and her argument, and her relief—yes, certainly her immense relief. The very next day perhaps she would get up at six, put on her cloak, and walk all the way from Kensington to the river. She was so thankful that she had not sacrificed her right to go and look at things when they are at their best—before people are up, that is to say. She could have her breakfast in bed if she liked. She had not sacrificed her independence.

Yes, Fanny Wilmot smiled, Julia had not endangered her habits. They remained safe, and her habits would have suffered if she had married. "They're ogres," she had said one evening, half laughing, when another pupil, a girl lately married, suddenly bethinking her that she would miss her husband, had rushed off in haste.

"They're ogres," she had said, laughing grimly. An ogre would have inter-

5. Artificial body of water in London's Hyde Park.   7. I.e., run them.
6. English river, near Shakespeare's birthplace.

fered perhaps with breakfast in bed; with walks at dawn down to the river. What would have happened (but one could hardly conceive this) had she had children? She took astonishing precautions against chills, fatigue, rich food, the wrong food, draughts, heated rooms, journeys in the Tube, for she could never determine which of these it was exactly that brought on those terrible headaches that gave her life the semblance of a battlefield. She was always engaged in outwitting the enemy, until it seemed as if the pursuit had its interest; could she have beaten the enemy finally she would have found life a little dull. As it was, the tug-of-war was perpetual—on one side the nightingale or the view which she loved with passion—yes, for views and birds she felt nothing less than passion; on the other, the damp path or the horrid long drag up a steep hill which would certainly make her good for nothing next day and bring on one of her headaches. When, therefore, from time to time, she managed her forces adroitly and brought off a visit to Hampton Court the week the crocuses (those glossy bright flowers were her favourites) were at their best, it was a victory. It was something that lasted; something that mattered for ever. She strung the afternoon on the necklace of memorable days, which was not too long for her to be able to recall this one or that one; this view, that city; to finger it, to feel it, to savour, sighing, the quality that made it unique.

"It was so beautiful last Friday," she said, "that I determined I must go there." So she had gone off to Waterloo on her great undertaking—to visit Hampton Court—alone. Naturally, but perhaps foolishly, one pitied her for the thing she never asked pity for (indeed she was reticent habitually, speaking of her health only as a warrior might speak of his foe)—one pitied her for always doing everything alone. Her brother was dead. Her sister was asthmatic. She found the climate of Edinburgh good for her. It was too bleak for Julia. Perhaps too she found the associations painful, for her brother, the famous archaeologist, had died there; and she had loved her brother. She lived in a little house off the Brompton Road entirely alone.

Fanny Wilmot saw the pin on the carpet; she picked it up. She looked at Miss Craye. Was Miss Craye so lonely? No, Miss Craye was steadily, blissfully, if only for a moment, a happy woman. Fanny had surprised her in a moment of ecstasy. She sat there, half turned away from the piano, with her hands clasped in her lap holding the carnation upright, while behind her was the sharp square of the window, uncurtained, purple in the evening, intensely purple after the brilliant electric lights which burnt unshaded in the bare music room. Julia Craye sitting hunched and compact holding her flower seemed to emerge out of the London night, seemed to fling it like a cloak behind her. It seemed in its bareness and intensity the effluence of her spirit, something she had made which surrounded her, which was her. Fanny stared.

All seemed transparent for a moment to the gaze of Fanny Wilmot, as if looking through Miss Craye, she saw the very fountain of her being spurt up in pure, silver drops. She saw back and back into the past behind her. She saw the green Roman vases stood in their case; heard the choristers playing cricket; saw Julia quietly descend the curving steps on to the lawn; saw her pour out tea beneath the cedar tree; softly enclose the old man's hand in hers; saw her going round and about the corridors of that ancient Cathedral dwelling place with towels in her hand to mark them;[8] lamenting as she went the pettiness of

---

8. I.e., mark them for the laundry.

daily life; and slowly ageing, and putting away clothes when summer came, because at her age they were too bright to wear; and tending her father's sickness; and cleaving her way ever more definitely as her will stiffened towards her solitary goal; travelling frugally; counting the cost and measuring out of her tight shut purse the sum needed for this journey, or for that old mirror; obstinately adhering whatever people might say in choosing her pleasures for herself. She saw Julia—

She saw Julia open her arms; saw her blaze; saw her kindle. Out of the night she burnt like a dead white star. Julia kissed her. Julia possessed her.

"Slater's pins have no points," Miss Craye said, laughing queerly and relaxing her arms, as Fanny Wilmot pinned the flower to her breast with trembling fingers.

1944

The Searchlight

The mansion of the eighteenth century Earl had been changed in the twentieth century into a Club. And it was pleasant, after dining in the great room with the pillars and the chandeliers under a glare of light to go out on to the balcony overlooking the Park. The trees were in full leaf, and had there been a moon, one could have seen the pink and cream coloured cockades on the chestnut trees. But it was a moonless night; very warm, after a fine summer's day.

Mr. and Mrs. Ivimey's party were drinking coffee and smoking on the balcony. As if to relieve them from the need of talking, to entertain them without any effort on their part, rods of light wheeled across the sky. It was peace then; the air force was practising; searching for enemy aircraft in the sky. After pausing to prod some suspected spot, the light wheeled, like the wings of a windmill, or again like the antennae of some prodigious insect and revealed here a cadaverous stone front; here a chestnut tree with all its blossoms riding; and then suddenly the light struck straight at the balcony, and for a second a bright disc shone—perhaps it was a mirror in a lady's hand-bag.

"Look!" Mrs Ivimey exclaimed.

The light passed. They were in darkness again.

"You'll never guess what *that* made me see!" she added. Naturally, they guessed.

"No, no, no," she protested. Nobody could guess; only she knew; only she could know, because she was the great-grand-daughter of the man himself. He had told her the story. What story? If they liked, she would try to tell it. There was still time before the play.

"But where do I begin?" she pondered. "In the year 1820? . . . It must have been about then that my great-grandfather was a boy. I'm not young myself"— no, but she was very well set up and handsome—"and he was a very old man when I was a child—when he told me the story. A very handsome old man," she explained, "with a shock of white hair, and blue eyes. He must have been a beautiful boy. But queer. . . . That was only natural—seeing how they lived. The name was Comber. They'd come down in the world. They'd been gentlefolk; they'd owned land up in Yorkshire. But when he was a boy only the tower was left. The house was nothing but a little farmhouse, standing in the middle of the fields. We saw it ten years ago and went over it. We had to leave the car and walk across the fields. There isn't any road to the house. It stands all alone, the grass grows right up to the gate . . . there were chickens pecking about, running in and out of the rooms. All gone to rack and ruin. I remember a stone fell from the tower suddenly." She paused. "There they lived," she went on, "the old man, the woman and the boy. She wasn't his wife, or the boy's mother. She was just a farm hand, a girl the old man had taken to live with him when his wife died. Another reason perhaps why nobody visited them— why the whole place was gone to rack and ruin. But I remember a coat of arms over the door; and books, old books, gone mouldy. He taught himself all he knew from books. He read and read, he told me, old books, books with maps hanging out from the pages. He dragged them up to the top of the tower—the rope's still there and the broken steps. There's a chair still in the window with the bottom fallen out; and the window swinging open, and the panes broken, and a view for miles and miles across the moors."

She paused as if she were up in the tower looking from the window that swung open.

"But we couldn't," she said, "find the telescope." In the dining-room behind them the clatter of plates grew louder. But Mrs Ivimey, on the balcony, seemed puzzled, because she could not find the telescope.

"Why a telescope?" someone asked her.

"Why? Because if there hadn't been a telescope," she laughed, "I shouldn't be sitting here now!"

And certainly she was sitting there now, a well set-up, middle-aged woman, with something blue over her shoulders.

"It must have been there," she resumed, "because, he told me, every night when the old people had gone to bed he sat at the window looking through the telescope at the stars. Jupiter, Aldebaran, Cassiopeia." She waved her hand at the stars that were beginning to show over the trees. It was growing darker. And the searchlight seemed brighter, sweeping across the sky, pausing here and there to stare at the stars.

"There they were," she went on, "the stars. And he asked himself, my grand-father—the boy, 'What are they? why are they? And who am I?' as one does, sitting alone, with no one to talk to, looking at the stars."

She was silent. They all looked at the stars that were coming out in the darkness over the trees. The stars seemed very permanent, very unchanging. The roar of London sank away. A hundred years seemed nothing. They felt that the boy was looking at the stars with them. They seemed to be with him, in the tower, looking out over the moors at the stars.

Then a voice behind them said:

"Right you are. Friday."

They all turned, shifted, felt dropped down on to the balcony again.

"Ah, but there was nobody to say that to him," she murmured. The couple rose and walked away.

"*He* was alone," she resumed. "It was a fine summer's day. A June day. One of those perfect summer days when everything seems to stand still in the heat. There were the chickens pecking in the farm-yard; the old horse stamping in the stable; the old man dozing over his glass. The woman scouring pails in the scullery. Perhaps a stone fell from the tower. It seemed as if the day would never end. And he had no one to talk to—nothing whatever to do. The whole world stretched before him. The moor rising and falling; the sky meeting the moor; green and blue, green and blue, for ever and ever."

In the half light, they could see that Mrs Ivimey was leaning over the balcony, with her chin propped on her hands, as if she were looking out over the moors from the top of a tower.

"Nothing but moor and sky, moor and sky, for ever and ever," she murmured.

Then she made a movement, as if she swung something into position.

"But what did the earth look like through the telescope?" she asked.

She made another quick little movement with her fingers as if she were twirling something.

"He focussed it," she said. "He focussed it upon the earth. He focussed it upon a dark mass of wood upon the horizon. He focussed it so that he could see . . . each tree . . . each tree separate . . . and the birds . . . rising and falling . . . and a stem of smoke . . . there . . . in the mist of the trees. . . . And then . . . lower . . . lower . . . (she lowered her eyes) . . . there was a house . . . a house among the trees . . . a farm house . . . every brick showed . . . and the tubs on either side of the door . . . with flowers in them blue, pink, hydrangeas perhaps . . ." She paused . . . "And then a girl came out of the house . . . wearing something blue upon her head . . . and stood there . . . feeding birds . . . pigeons . . . they came fluttering round her. . . . And then . . . look. . . . A man. . . . A man! He came round the corner. He seized her in his arms! They kissed . . . they kissed!"

Mrs. Ivimey opened her arms and closed them as if she were kissing someone.

"It was the first time he had seen a man kiss a woman—in his telescope—miles and miles away across the moors!"

She thrust something from her—the telescope presumably. She sat upright.

"So he ran down the stairs. He ran through the fields. He ran down lanes, out upon the high road, through woods. He ran for miles and miles, and just when the stars were showing above the trees he reached the house . . . covered with dust, streaming with sweat. . . ."

She stopped, as if she saw him.

"And then, and then . . . what did he do then? What did he say? And the girl . . ." they pressed her.

A shaft of light fell upon Mrs Ivimey as if someone had focussed the lens of a telescope upon her. (It was the air force, looking for enemy air craft.) She had risen. She had something blue on her head. She had raised her hand, as if she stood in a doorway, amazed.

"Oh the girl . . . She was my—" she hesitated, as if she were about to say "myself." But she remembered; and corrected herself. "She was my great-grandmother," she said.

She turned to look for her cloak. It was on a chair behind her.

"But tell us—what about the other man, the man who came round the corner?" they asked.

"That man? That man," Mrs. Ivimey murmured, stooping to fumble with her cloak, (the searchlight had left the balcony), "he, I suppose, vanished."

"The light," she added, gathering her things about her, "only falls here and there."

The searchlight had passed on. It was now focussed on the plain expanse of Buckingham Palace. And it was time they went on to the play.

1944

From A Sketch of the Past[1]
[Moments of Being and Non-Being]

—I begin: the first memory.

This was of red and purple flowers on a black ground—my mother's dress; and she was sitting either in a train or in an omnibus, and I was on her lap. I therefore saw the flowers she was wearing very close; and can still see purple and red and blue, I think, against the black; they must have been anemones, I suppose. Perhaps we were going to St Ives; more probably, for from the light it must have been evening, we were coming back to London. But it is more convenient artistically to suppose that we were going to St Ives, for that will lead to my other memory, which also seems to be my first memory, and in fact it is the most important of all my memories. If life has a base that it stands upon, if it is a bowl that one fills and fills and fills—then my bowl without a doubt stands upon this memory. It is of lying half asleep, half awake, in bed in the nursery at St Ives. It is of hearing the waves breaking, one, two, one, two, and sending a splash of water over the beach; and then breaking, one, two, one, two, behind a yellow blind. It is of hearing the blind draw its little acorn[2] across the floor as the wind blew the blind out. It is of lying and hearing this splash and seeing this light, and feeling, it is almost impossible that I should be here; of feeling the purest ecstasy I can conceive.

I could spend hours trying to write that as it should be written, in order to give the feeling which is even at this moment very strong in me. But I should fail (unless I had some wonderful luck); I dare say I should only succeed in having the luck if I had begun by describing Virginia herself.

Here I come to one of the memoir writer's difficulties—one of the reasons why, though I read so many, so many are failures. They leave out the person to whom things happened. The reason is that it is so difficult to describe any human being. So they say: "This is what happened"; but they do not say what the person was like to whom it happened. And the events mean very little unless we know first to whom they happened. Who was I then? Adeline Virginia Stephen, the second daughter of Leslie and Julia Prinsep Stephen, born on 25th January 1882, descended from a great many people, some famous, others obscure; born into a large connection, born not of rich parents, but of well-to-do parents, born into a very communicative, literate, letter writing, visiting, articulate, late nineteenth century world; so that I could if I liked to take the trouble, write a great deal here not only about my mother and father

1. The autobiographical essay from which this extract is taken was published in *Moments of Being*, ed. Jeanne Schulkind (1976). Woolf began it on April 18, 1939, as a relief from the labor of writing *Roger Fry: A Biography* (1940). The last date entered in the manuscript is November 17, 1940, some four months before her death. Under the shadow of approaching war, she gropes back for the bright memories of childhood, especially those associated with the Stephens' summer home, Talland House, at St. Ives in Cornwall, the setting for her novel *To the Lighthouse*.
2. I.e., the acorn-shaped button on the end of the blind cord.

but about uncles and aunts, cousins and friends. But I do not know how much of this, or what part of this, made me feel what I felt in the nursery at St Ives. I do not know how far I differ from other people. That is another memoir writer's difficulty. Yet to describe oneself truly one must have some standard of comparison; was I clever, stupid, good looking, ugly, passionate, cold—? Owing partly to the fact that I was never at school, never competed in any way with children of my own age, I have never been able to compare my gifts and defects with other people's. But of course there was one external reason for the intensity of this first impression: the impression of the waves and the acorn on the blind; the feeling, as I describe it sometimes to myself, of lying in a grape and seeing through a film of semi-transparent yellow—it was due partly to the many months we spent in London. The change of nursery was a great change. And there was the long train journey; and the excitement. I remember the dark; the lights; the stir of the going up to bed.

But to fix my mind upon the nursery—it had a balcony; there was a partition, but it joined the balcony of my father's and mother's bedroom. My mother would come out onto her balcony in a white dressing gown. There were passion flowers growing on the wall; they were great starry blossoms, with purple streaks, and large green buds, part empty, part full.

If I were a painter I should paint these first impressions in pale yellow, silver, and green. There was the pale yellow blind; the green sea; and the silver of the passion flowers. I should make a picture that was globular; semi-transparent. I should make a picture of curved petals; of shells; of things that were semi-transparent; I should make curved shapes, showing the light through, but not giving a clear outline. Everything would be large and dim; and what was seen would at the same time be heard; sounds would come through this petal or leaf—sounds indistinguishable from sights. Sound and sight seem to make equal parts of these first impressions. When I think of the early morning in bed I also hear the caw of rooks[3] falling from a great height. The sound seems to fall through an elastic, gummy air; which holds it up; which prevents it from being sharp and distinct. The quality of the air above Talland House seemed to suspend sound, to let it sink down slowly, as if it were caught in a blue gummy veil. The rooks cawing is part of the waves breaking—one, two, one, two—and the splash as the wave drew back and then it gathered again, and I lay there half awake, half asleep, drawing in such ecstasy as I cannot describe.

The next memory—all these colour-and-sound memories hang together at St Ives—was much more robust; it was highly sensual. It was later. It still makes me feel warm; as if everything were ripe; humming; sunny; smelling so many smells at once; and all making a whole that even now makes me stop— as I stopped then going down to the beach; I stopped at the top to look down at the gardens. They were sunk beneath the road. The apples were on a level with one's head. The gardens gave off a murmur of bees; the apples were red and gold; there were also pink flowers; and grey and silver leaves. The buzz, the croon, the smell, all seemed to press voluptuously against some membrane; not to burst it; but to hum round one such a complete rapture of pleasure that I stopped, smelt; looked. But again I cannot describe that rapture. It was rapture rather than ecstasy.

---

3. Black crows.

The strength of these pictures—but sight was always then so much mixed with sound that picture is not the right word—the strength anyhow of these impressions makes me again digress. Those moments—in the nursery, on the road to the beach—can still be more real than the present moment. This I have just tested. For I got up and crossed the garden. Percy was digging the asparagus bed; Louie was shaking a mat in front of the bedroom door.[4] But I was seeing them through the sight I saw here—the nursery and the road to the beach. At times I can go back to St Ives more completely than I can this morning. I can reach a state where I seem to be watching things happen as if I were there. That is, I suppose, that my memory supplies what I had forgotten, so that it seems as if it were happening independently, though I am really making it happen. In certain favourable moods, memories—what one has forgotten—come to the top. Now if this is so, is it not possible—I often wonder—that things we have felt with great intensity have an existence independent of our minds; are in fact still in existence? And if so, will it not be possible, in time, that some device will be invented by which we can tap them? I see it—the past—as an avenue lying behind; a long ribbon of scenes, emotions. There at the end of the avenue still, are the garden and the nursery. Instead of remembering here a scene and there a sound, I shall fit a plug into the wall;[5] and listen in to the past. I shall turn up August 1890. I feel that strong emotion must leave its trace; and it is only a question of discovering how we can get ourselves again attached to it, so that we shall be able to live our lives through from the start.

But the peculiarity of these two strong memories is that each was very simple. I am hardly aware of myself, but only of the sensation. I am only the container of the feeling of ecstasy, of the feeling of rapture. Perhaps this is characteristic of all childhood memories; perhaps it accounts for their strength. Later we add to feelings much that makes them more complex; and therefore less strong; or if not less strong, less isolated, less complete. But instead of analysing this, here is an instance of what I mean—my feeling about the looking-glass in the hall.

There was a small looking-glass in the hall at Talland House. It had, I remember, a ledge with a brush on it. By standing on tiptoe I could see my face in the glass. When I was six or seven perhaps, I got into the habit of looking at my face in the glass. But I only did this if I was sure that I was alone. I was ashamed of it. A strong feeling of guilt seemed naturally attached to it. But why was this so? One obvious reason occurs to me—Vanessa and I were both what was called tomboys; that is, we played cricket, scrambled over rocks, climbed trees, were said not to care for clothes and so on. Perhaps therefore to have been found looking in the glass would have been against our tomboy code. But I think that my feeling of shame went a great deal deeper. I am almost inclined to drag in my grandfather—Sir James, who once smoked a cigar, liked it, and so threw away his cigar and never smoked another. I am almost inclined to think that I inherited a streak of the puritan, of the Clapham Sect.[6] At any rate, the looking-glass shame has lasted all my life, long

4. The gardener and "daily help," respectively, at Monks House, the Woolfs' country home in Rodmell, Sussex.
5. I.e., as if plugging in a radio.
6. In marrying Jane Catherine Venn, Woolf's grandfather, James Stephen, had allied himself with the heart of the so-called Clapham sect. John and Henry Venn, respectively rector and curate of Clapham in South London, were prominent members of this evangelical society that, in the early 19th century, was instrumental in bringing about the abolition of the slave trade.

after the tomboy phase was over. I cannot now powder my nose in public. Everything to do with dress—to be fitted, to come into a room wearing a new dress—still frightens me; at least makes me shy, self-conscious, uncomfortable. "Oh to be able to run, like Julian Morrell,[7] all over the garden in a new dress", I thought not many years ago at Garsington; when Julian undid a parcel and put on a new dress and scampered round and round like a hare. Yet femininity was very strong in our family. We were famous for our beauty—my mother's beauty, Stella's beauty, gave me as early as I can remember, pride and plea-sure. What then gave me this feeling of shame, unless it were that I inherited some opposite instinct? My father was spartan, ascetic, puritanical. He had I think no feeling for pictures; no ear for music; no sense of the sound of words. This leads me to think that my—I would say 'our' if I knew enough about Vanessa, Thoby and Adrian[8]—but how little we know even about brothers and sisters—this leads me to think that my natural love for beauty was checked by some ancestral dread. Yet this did not prevent me from feeling ecstasies and raptures spontaneously and intensely and without any shame or the least sense of guilt, so long as they were disconnected with my own body. I thus detect another element in the shame which I had in being caught looking at myself in the glass in the hall. I must have been ashamed or afraid of my own body. Another memory, also of the hall, may help to explain this. There was a slab outside the dining room door for standing dishes upon. Once when I was very small Gerald Duckworth lifted me onto this, and as I sat there he began to explore my body.[9] I can remember the feel of his hand going under my clothes; going firmly and steadily lower and lower. I remember how I hoped that he would stop; how I stiffened and wriggled as his hand approached my private parts. But it did not stop. His hand explored my private parts too. I remember resenting, disliking it—what is the word for so dumb and mixed a feeling? It must have been strong, since I still recall it. This seems to show that a feeling about certain parts of the body; how they must not be touched; how it is wrong to allow them to be touched; must be instinctive. It proves that Virginia Stephen was not born on the 25th January 1882, but was born many thousands of years ago; and had from the very first to encounter instincts already acquired by thousands of ancestresses in the past.

And this throws light not merely on my own case, but upon the problem that I touched on the first page; why it is so difficult to give any account of the person to whom things happen. The person is evidently immensely compli-cated. Witness the incident of the looking-glass. Though I have done my best to explain why I was ashamed of looking at my own face I have only been able to discover some possible reasons; there may be others; I do not suppose that I have got at the truth; yet this is a simple incident; and it happened to me personally; and I have no motive for lying about it. In spite of all this, people write what they call "lives" of other people; that is, they collect a number of events, and leave the person to whom it happened unknown. Let me add a dream; for it may refer to the incident of the looking-glass. I dreamt that I was looking in a glass when a horrible face—the face of an animal—suddenly showed over my shoulder. I cannot be sure if this was a dream, or if it hap-

7. Daughter of Philip Morrell, Member of Parliament, and his wife, Ottoline, the celebrated literary hostess. Garsington Manor was their house in Oxfordshire.
8. Woolf's brothers and sister.

9. Woolf's half-brother and the subject of her autobio-graphical essay 22 *Hyde Park Gate*, written in 1920 and published in *Moments of Being* (1978).

pened. Was I looking in the glass one day when something in the background moved, and seemed to me alive? I cannot be sure. But I have always remembered the other face in the glass, whether it was a dream or a fact, and that it frightened me.

These then are some of my first memories. But of course as an account of my life they are misleading, because the things one does not remember are as important; perhaps they are more important. If I could remember one whole day I should be able to describe, superficially at least, what life was like as a child. Unfortunately, one only remembers what is exceptional. And there seems to be no reason why one thing is exceptional and another not. Why have I forgotten so many things that must have been, one would have thought, more memorable than what I do remember? Why remember the hum of bees in the garden going down to the beach, and forget completely being thrown naked by father into the sea? (Mrs Swanwick says she saw that happen.)[1]

This leads to a digression, which perhaps may explain a little of my own psychology; even of other people's. Often when I have been writing one of my so-called novels I have been baffled by this same problem; that is, how to describe what I call in my private shorthand—"non-being." Every day includes much more non-being than being. Yesterday for example, Tuesday the 18th of April, was [as] it happened a good day; above the average in "being." It was fine; I enjoyed writing these first pages; my head was relieved of the pressure of writing about Roger; I walked over Mount Misery[2] and along the river; and save that the tide was out, the country, which I notice very closely always, was coloured and shaded as I like—there were the willows, I remember, all plumy and soft green and purple against the blue. I also read Chaucer with pleasure; and began a book—the memoirs of Madame de la Fayette—which interested me. These separate moments of being were however embedded in many more moments of non-being. I have already forgotten what Leonard and I talked about at lunch; and at tea; although it was a good day the goodness was embedded in a kind of nondescript cotton wool. This is always so. A great part of every day is not lived consciously. One walks, eats, sees things, deals with what has to be done; the broken vacuum cleaner; ordering dinner; writing orders to Mabel;[3] washing; cooking dinner; bookbinding. When it is a bad day the proportion of non-being is much larger. I had a slight temperature last week; almost the whole day was non-being. The real novelist can somehow convey both sorts of being. I think Jane Austen can; and Trollope; perhaps Thackeray and Dickens and Tolstoy. I have never been able to do both. I tried—in *Night and Day*; and in *The Years*.[4] But I will leave the literary side alone for the moment.

As a child then, my days, just as they do now, contained a large proportion of this cotton wool, this non-being. Week after week passed at St Ives and nothing made any dint upon me. Then, for no reason that I know about, there was a sudden violent shock; something happened so violently that I have remembered it all my life. I will give a few instances. The first: I was fighting with Thoby on the lawn. We were pommelling each other with our fists. Just as I raised my fist to hit him, I felt: why hurt another person? I dropped my

---

1. In Mrs. Swanwick's autobiography, *I Have Been Young* (1935), she recalls having known Leslie Stephen at St. Ives: "We watched with delight his naked babies running about the beach or being towed into the sea between his legs, and their beautiful mother."

2. Two cottages on the hillside between Southease and Piddinghoe known locally as Mount Misery.
3. Instructions to the Woolfs' maid.
4. Novels published in 1919 and 1938, respectively.

hand instantly, and stood there, and let him beat me. I remember the feeling. It was a feeling of hopeless sadness. It was as if I became aware of something terrible; and of my own powerlessness. I slunk off alone, feeling horribly depressed. The second instance was also in the garden at St Ives. I was looking at the flower bed by the front door; "That is the whole," I said. I was looking at a plant with a spread of leaves; and it seemed suddenly plain that the flower itself was a part of the earth; that a ring enclosed what was the flower; and that was the real flower; part earth; part flower. It was a thought I put away as being likely to be very useful to me later. The third case was also at St Ives. Some people called Valpy had been staying at St Ives, and had left. We were waiting at dinner one night, when somehow I overheard my father or my mother say that Mr Valpy had killed himself. The next thing I remember is being in the garden at night and walking on the path by the apple tree. It seemed to me that the apple tree was connected with the horror of Mr Valpy's suicide. I could not pass it. I stood there looking at the grey-green creases of the bark— it was a moonlit night—in a trance of horror. I seemed to be dragged down, hopelessly, into some pit of absolute despair from which I could not escape. My body seemed paralysed.

These are three instances of exceptional moments. I often tell them over, or rather they come to the surface unexpectedly. But now that for the first time I have written them down, I realise something that I have never realised before. Two of these moments ended in a state of despair. The other ended, on the contrary, in a state of satisfaction. When I said about the flower "That is the whole," I felt that I had made a discovery. I felt that I had put away in my mind something that I should go back [to], to turn over and explore. It strikes me now that this was a profound difference. It was the difference in the first place between despair and satisfaction. This difference I think arose from the fact that I was quite unable to deal with the pain of discovering that people hurt each other; that a man I had seen had killed himself. The sense of horror held me powerless. But in the case of the flower I found a reason; and was thus able to deal with the sensation. I was not powerless. I was conscious—if only at a distance—that I should in time explain it. I do not know if I was older when I saw the flower than I was when I had the other two experiences. I only know that many of these exceptional moments brought with them a peculiar horror and a physical collapse; they seemed dominant; myself passive. This suggests that as one gets older one has a greater power through reason to provide an explanation; and that this explanation blunts the sledge-hammer force of the blow. I think this is true, because though I still have the peculiarity that I receive these sudden shocks, they are now always welcome; after the first surprise, I always feel instantly that they are particularly valuable. And so I go on to suppose that the shock-receiving capacity is what makes me a writer. I hazard the explanation that a shock is at once in my case followed by the desire to explain it. I feel that I have had a blow; but it is not, as I thought as a child, simply a blow from an enemy hidden behind the cotton wool of daily life; it is or will become a revelation of some order; it is a token of some real thing behind appearances; and I make it real by putting it into words. It is only by putting it into words that I make it whole; this wholeness means that it has lost its power to hurt me; it gives me, perhaps because by doing so I take away the pain, a great delight to put the severed parts together. Perhaps this is the strongest pleasure known to me. It is the rapture I get when in writing I seem to be discovering what belongs to what; making a scene come right; making a character come together. From this I reach what I might call a philosophy; at any rate it is a constant idea of mine; that behind the cotton wool is hidden a pattern; that we—I mean all human beings—are connected with this; that the whole world is a work of art; that we are parts of the work of art. *Hamlet* or a Beethoven quartet is the truth about this vast mass that we call the world. But there is no Shakespeare, there is no Beethoven; certainly and emphatically there is no God; we are the words; we are the music; we are the thing itself. And I see this when I have a shock.

This intuition of mine—it is so instinctive that it seems given to me, not made by me—has certainly given its scale to my life ever since I saw the flower in the bed by the front door at St Ives. If I were painting myself I should have to find some—rod, shall I say—something that would stand for the conception. It proves that one's life is not confined to one's body and what one says and does; one is living all the time in relation to certain background rods or conceptions. Mine is that there is a pattern hid behind the cotton wool. And this conception affects me every day. I prove this, now, by spending the morning writing, when I might be walking, running a shop, or learning to do something that will be useful if war comes. I feel that by writing I am doing what is far more necessary than anything else.

All artists I suppose feel something like this. It is one of the obscure elements in life that has never been much discussed. It is left out in almost all biographies and autobiographies, even of artists. Why did Dickens spend his entire life writing stories? What was his conception? I bring in Dickens partly because I am reading *Nicholas Nickleby* at the moment; also partly because it struck me, on my walk yesterday, that these moments of being of mine were scaffolding in the background; were the invisible and silent part of my life as a child. But in the foreground there were of course people; and these people were very like characters in Dickens. They were caricatures; they were very simple; they were immensely alive. They could be made with three strokes of the pen, if I could do it. Dickens owes his astonishing power to make characters alive to the fact that he saw them as a child sees them; as I saw Mr Wolstenholme; C. B. Clarke, and Mr Gibbs.

I name these three people because they all died when I was a child. Therefore they have never been altered. I see them exactly as I saw them then. Mr Wolstenholme was a very old gentleman who came every summer to stay with us. He was brown; he had a beard and very small eyes in fat cheeks; and he fitted into a brown wicker beehive chair as if it had been his nest. He used to sit in this beehive chair smoking and reading. He had only one characteristic—that when he ate plum tart he spurted the juice through his nose so that it made a purple stain on his grey moustache. This seemed enough to cause us perpetual delight. We called him "The Woolly One." By way of shading him a little I remember that we had to be kind to him because he was not happy at home; that he was very poor, yet once gave Thoby half a crown; that he had a son who was drowned in Australia; and I know too that he was a great mathematician. He never said a word all the time I knew him. But he still seems to me a complete character; and whenever I think of him I begin to laugh.

Mr Gibbs was perhaps less simple. He wore a tie ring; had a bald, benevolent head; was dry; neat; precise; and had folds of skin under his chin. He made father groan—"why can't you go—why can't you go?" And he gave Vanessa and myself two ermine skins, with slits down the middle out of which poured endless wealth—streams of silver. I also remember him lying in bed, dying; husky; in a night shirt; and showing us drawings by Retzsch.[5] The character of Mr Gibbs also seems to me complete and amuses me very much.

As for C. B. Clarke, he was an old botanist; and he said to my father "All you young botanists like Osmunda."[6] He had an aunt aged eighty who went for a walking tour in the New Forest. That is all—that is all I have to say about these three old gentlemen. But how real they were! How we laughed at them! What an immense part they played in our lives!

One more caricature comes into my mind; though pity entered into this one. I am thinking of Justine Nonon. She was immensely old. Little hairs sprouted on her long bony chin. She was a hunchback; and walked like a spider, feeling her way with her long dry fingers from one chair to another. Most of the time she sat in the arm-chair beside the fire. I used to sit on her knee; and her knee jogged up and down; and she sang in a hoarse cracked voice "Ron ron ron—et plon plon plon—" and then her knee gave and I was tumbled onto the floor. She was French; she had been with the Thackerays. She only came to us on visits. She lived by herself at Shepherd's Bush; and used to bring Adrian a glass jar of honey. I got the notion that she was extremely poor; and it made me uncomfortable that she brought this honey, because I felt she did it by way of making her visit acceptable. She said too: "I have come in my carriage and pair"—which meant the red omnibus. For this too I pitied her; also because she began to wheeze; and the nurses said she would not live much longer; and soon she died. That is all I know about her; but I remember her as if she were a completely real person, with nothing left out, like the three old men.

April 1939–November 1940   1976

The Legacy

"For Sissy Miller." Gilbert Clandon, taking up the pearl brooch that lay among a litter of rings and brooches on a little table in his wife's drawing-room, read the inscription: "For Sissy Miller, with my love."

It was like Angela to have remembered even Sissy Miller, her secretary. Yet how strange it was, Gilbert Clandon thought once more, that she had left everything in such order—a little gift of some sort for every one of her friends. It was as if she had foreseen her death. Yet she had been in perfect health when she left the house that morning, six weeks ago; when she stepped off the kerb in Piccadilly[1] and the car had killed her.

He was waiting for Sissy Miller. He had asked her to come; he owed her, he felt, after all the years she had been with them, this token of consideration. Yes, he went on, as he sat there waiting, it was strange that Angela had left everything in such order. Every friend had been left some little token of her affection. Every ring, every necklace, every little Chinese box—she had a pas-

5. Friedrich Retzsch (1779–1857), German engraver.   1. Street in the center of London.
6. Flowering ferns.

sion for little boxes—had a name on it. And each had some memory for him. This he had given her; this—the enamel dolphin with the ruby eyes—she had pounced upon one day in a back street in Venice. He could remember her little cry of delight. To him, of course, she had left nothing in particular, unless it were her diary. Fifteen little volumes, bound in green leather, stood behind him on her writing table. Ever since they were married, she had kept a diary. Some of their very few—he could not call them quarrels, say tiffs— had been about that diary. When he came in and found her writing, she always shut it or put her hand over it. "No, no, no," he could hear her say, "After I'm dead—perhaps." So she had left it him, as her legacy. It was the only thing they had not shared when she was alive. But he had always taken it for granted that she would outlive him. If only she had stopped one moment, and had thought what she was doing, she would be alive now. But she had stepped straight off the kerb, the driver of the car had said at the inquest. She had given him no chance to pull up. . . . Here the sound of voices in the hall interrupted him.

"Miss Miller, Sir," said the maid.

She came in. He had never seen her alone in his life, nor, of course, in tears. She was terribly distressed, and no wonder. Angela had been much more to her than an employer. She had been a friend. To himself, he thought, as he pushed a chair for her and asked her to sit down, she was scarcely distinguishable from any other woman of her kind. There were thousands of Sissy Millers—drab little women in black carrying attaché cases. But Angela, with her genius for sympathy, had discovered all sorts of qualities in Sissy Miller. She was the soul of discretion, so silent; so trustworthy, one could tell her anything, and so on.

Miss Miller could not speak at first. She sat there dabbing her eyes with her pocket handkerchief. Then she made an effort.

"Pardon me, Mr. Clandon," she said.

He murmured. Of course he understood. It was only natural. He could guess what his wife had meant to her.

"I've been so happy here," she said, looking round. Her eyes rested on the writing table behind him. It was here they had worked—she and Angela. For Angela had her share of the duties that fall to the lot of the wife of a prominent politician. She had been the greatest help to him in his career. He had often seen her and Sissy sitting at that table—Sissy at the typewriter, taking down letters from her dictation. No doubt Miss Miller was thinking of that, too. Now all he had to do was to give her the brooch his wife had left her. A rather incongruous gift it seemed. It might have been better to have left her a sum of money, or even the typewriter. But there it was—"For Sissy Miller, with my love." And, taking the brooch, he gave it her with the little speech that he had prepared. He knew, he said, that she would value it. His wife had often worn it. . . . And she replied, as she took it, almost as if she too had prepared a speech, that it would always be a treasured possession. . . . She had, he supposed, other clothes upon which a pearl brooch would not look quite so incongruous. She was wearing the little black coat and skirt that seemed the uniform of her profession. Then he remembered—she was in mourning, of course. She too had had her tragedy—a brother, to whom she was devoted, had died only a week or two before Angela. In some accident was it? He could remember only Angela telling him; Angela, with her genius for sympathy, had been terribly upset. Meanwhile Sissy Miller had risen. She was putting on her gloves. Evidently she felt that she ought not to intrude. But he could not let her go without saying something about her future. What were her plans? Was there any way in which he could help her?

She was gazing at the table, where she had sat at her typewriter, where the diary lay. And, lost in her memories of Angela, she did not at once answer his suggestion that he should help her. She seemed for a moment not to understand. So he repeated:

"What are your plans, Miss Miller?"

"My plans? Oh, that's all right, Mr. Clandon," she exclaimed. "Please don't bother yourself about me."

He took her to mean that she was in no need of financial assistance. It would be better, he realised, to make any suggestion of that kind in a letter. All he could do now was to say as he pressed her hand, "Remember, Miss Miller, if there's any way in which I can help you, it will be a pleasure. . . ." Then he opened the door. For a moment, on the threshold, as if a sudden thought had struck her, she stopped.

"Mr. Clandon," she said, looking straight at him for the first time, and for the first time he was struck by the expression, sympathetic yet searching, in her eyes. "If at any time," she was saying, "there's anything I can do to help you, remember, I shall feel it, for your wife's sake, a pleasure. . . ."

With that she was gone. Her words and the look that went with them were unexpected. It was almost as if she believed, or hoped, that he would have need of her. A curious, perhaps a fantastic idea occurred to him as he returned to his chair. Could it be, that during all those years when he had scarcely noticed her, she, as the novelists say, had entertained a passion for him? He caught his own reflection in the glass as he passed. He was over fifty; but he could not help admitting that he was still, as the looking-glass showed him, a very distinguished-looking man.

"Poor Sissy Miller!" he said, half laughing. How he would have liked to share that joke with his wife! He turned instinctively to her diary. "Gilbert," he read, opening it at random, "looked so wonderful. . . ." It was as if she had answered his question. Of course, she seemed to say, you're very attractive to women. Of course Sissy Miller felt that too. He read on. "How proud I am to be his wife!" And he had always been very proud to be her husband. How often when they dined out somewhere he had looked at her across the table and said to himself, She is the loveliest woman here! He read on. That first year he had been standing for Parliament. They had toured his constituency.[2] "When Gilbert sat down the applause was terrific. The whole audience rose and sang: 'For he's a jolly good fellow.' I was quite overcome." He remembered that, too. She had been sitting on the platform beside him. He could still see the glance she cast at him, and how she had tears in her eyes. And then? He turned the pages. They had gone to Venice. He recalled that happy holiday after the election. "We had ices at Florians."[3] He smiled—she was still such a child, she loved ices. "Gilbert gave me a most interesting account of the history of Venice. He told me that the Doges[4] . . ." she had written it all out in her schoolgirl hand. One of the delights of travelling with Angela had been that she was so eager to learn. She was so terribly ignorant, she used

2. Area represented by a Member of Parliament.   4. Chief magistrates in the Republic of Venice.
3. A café in the Piazza San Marco in Venice.

to say, as if that were not one of her charms. And then—he opened the next volume—they had come back to London. "I was so anxious to make a good impression. I wore my wedding dress." He could see her now sitting next old Sir Edward; and making a conquest of that formidable old man, his chief. He read on rapidly, filling in scene after scene from her scrappy fragments. "Dined at the House of Commons.[5] . . . To an evening party at the Love-groves. Did I realise my responsibility, Lady L. asked me, as Gilbert's wife?" Then as the years passed—he took another volume from the writing table—he had become more and more absorbed in his work. And she, of course, was more often alone. It had been a great grief to her, apparently, that they had had no children. "How I wish," one entry read, "that Gilbert had a son!" Oddly enough he had never much regretted that himself. Life had been so full, so rich as it was. That year he had been given a minor post in the govern-ment. A minor post only, but her comment was: "I am quite certain now that he will be Prime Minister!" Well, if things had gone differently, it might have been so. He paused here to speculate upon what might have been. Politics was a gamble, he reflected; but the game wasn't over yet. Not at fifty. He cast his eyes rapidly over more pages, full of the little trifles, the insignificant, happy, daily trifles that had made up her life.

He took up another volume and opened it at random. "What a coward I am! I let the chance slip again. But it seemed selfish to bother him about my own affairs, when he has so much to think about. And we so seldom have an evening alone." What was the meaning of that? Oh here was the explana-tion—it referred to her work in the East End. "I plucked up courage and talked to Gilbert at last. He was so kind, so good. He made no objection." He remembered that conversation. She had told him that she felt so idle, so use-less. She wished to have some work of her own. She wanted to do something—she had blushed so prettily, he remembered, as she said it sitting in that very chair—to help others. He had bantered her a little. Hadn't she enough to do looking after him, after her home? Still if it amused her of course he had no objection. What was it? Some district? Some committee? Only she must promise not to make herself ill. So it seemed that every Wednesday she went to Whitechapel. He remembered how he hated the clothes she wore on those occasions. But she had taken it very seriously it seemed. The diary was full of references like this: "Saw Mrs. Jones. . . . She has ten children. . . . Husband lost his arm in an accident. . . . Did my best to find a job for Lily." He skipped on. His own name occurred less frequently. His interest slackened. Some of the entries conveyed nothing to him. For example: "Had a heated argument about socialism with B. M." Who was B. M.? He could not fill in the initials; some woman, he supposed, that she had met on one of her committees. "B. M. made a violent attack upon the upper classes. . . . I walked back after the meeting with B. M. and tried to convince him. But he is so narrow-minded." So B. M. was a man—no doubt one of those "intellectuals" as they call themselves, who are so violent, as Angela said, and so narrow-minded. She had invited him to come and see her apparently. "B. M. came to dinner. He shook hands with Minnie!" That note of exclamation gave another twist to his mental picture. B. M. it seemed wasn't used to parlourmaids; he had shaken hands with Minnie. Presumably he was one of those tame working

5. Lower House of the British Parliament.

men who air their views in ladies' drawing-rooms. Gilbert knew the type, and had no liking for this particular specimen, whoever B. M. might be. Here he was again. "Went with B. M. to the Tower of London. . . . He said revolution is bound to come. . . . He said we live in a Fool's Paradise." That was just the kind of thing B. M. would say—Gilbert could hear him. He could also see him quite distinctly—a stubby little man, with a rough beard, red tie, dressed as they always did in tweeds, who had never done an honest day's work in his life. Surely Angela had the sense to see through him? He read on. "B. M. said some very disagreeable things about . . ." The name was carefully scratched out. "I told him I would not listen to any more abuse of . . ." Again the name was obliterated. Could it have been his own name? Was that why Angela covered the page so quickly when he came in? The thought added to his growing dislike of B. M. He had had the impertinence to discuss him in this very room. Why had Angela never told him? It was very unlike her to conceal anything; she had been the soul of candour. He turned the pages, picking out every reference to B. M. "B. M. told me the story of his childhood. His mother went out charring.[6] . . . When I think of it, I can hardly bear to go on living in such luxury. . . . Three guineas for one hat!" If only she had discussed the matter with him, instead of puzzling her poor little head about questions that were much too difficult for her to understand! He had lent her books. Karl Marx. "The Coming Revolution." The initials B. M., B. M., B. M., recurred repeatedly. But why never the full name? There was an informality, an intimacy in the use of initials that was very unlike Angela. Had she called him B. M. to his face? He read on. "B. M. came unexpectedly after dinner. Luckily, I was alone." That was only a year ago. "Luckily"—why luckily?—"I was alone." Where had he been that night? He checked the date in his engagement book. It had been the night of the Mansion House[7] dinner. And B. M. and Angela had spent the evening alone! He tried to recall that evening. Was she waiting up for him when he came back? Had the room looked just as usual? Were there glasses on the table? Were the chairs drawn close together? He could remember nothing—nothing whatever, nothing except his own speech at the Mansion House dinner. It became more and more inexplicable to him—the whole situation: his wife receiving an unknown man alone. Perhaps the next volume would explain. Hastily he reached for the last of the diaries—the one she had left unfinished when she died. There on the very first page was that cursed fellow again. "Dined alone with B. M. . . . He became very agitated. He said it was time we understood each other. . . . I tried to make him listen. But he would not. He threatened that if I did not . . ." the rest of the page was scored over. She had written "Egypt. Egypt. Egypt." over the whole page. He could not make out a single word; but there could be only one interpretation: the scoundrel had asked her to become his mistress. Alone in his room! The blood rushed to Gilbert Clandon's face. He turned the pages rapidly. What had been her answer? Initials had ceased. It was simply "he" now. "He came again. I told him I could not come to any decision. . . . I implored him to leave me." He had forced himself upon her in this very house? But why hadn't she told him? How could she have hesitated for an instant? Then: "I wrote him a letter." Then pages were left blank. Then there was this: "No answer to my letter." Then more blank pages; and

---

6. Working as a "charwoman" or house cleaner.   of London.
7. A banquet at the official residence of the lord mayor

then this. "He has done what he threatened." After that—what came after that? He turned page after page. All were blank. But there, on the very day before her death, was this entry: "Have I the courage to do it too?" That was the end.

Gilbert Clandon let the book slide to the floor. He could see her in front of him. She was standing on the kerb in Piccadilly. Her eyes stared; her fists were clenched. Here came the car. . . .

He could not bear it. He must know the truth. He strode to the telephone.

"Miss Miller!" There was silence. Then he heard someone moving in the room.

"Sissy Miller speaking"—her voice at last answered him.

"Who," he thundered, "is B. M.?"

He could hear the cheap clock ticking on her mantelpiece; then a long drawn sigh. Then at last she said:

"He was my brother."

He *was* her brother; her brother who had killed himself.

"Is there," he heard Sissy Miller asking, "anything that I can explain?"

"Nothing!" he cried. "Nothing!"

He had received his legacy. She had told him the truth. She had stepped off the kerb to rejoin her lover. She had stepped off the kerb to escape from him.

1940   1985

JAMES JOYCE
1882–1941

1914:   *Dubliners.*
1916:   *A Portrait of the Artist as a Young Man.*
1922:   *Ulysses.*
1939:   *Finnegans Wake.*

James Joyce was born in Dublin, son of a talented but feckless father who is accurately described by Stephen Dedalus in *A Portrait of the Artist as a Young Man* as a man who had in his time been "a medical student, an oarsman, a tenor, an amateur actor, a shouting politician, a small landlord, a small investor, a drinker, a good fellow, a storyteller, somebody's secretary, something in a distillery, a tax-gatherer, a bankrupt, and at present a praiser of his own past." The elder Joyce drifted steadily down the financial and social scale, his family moving from house to house, each one less genteel and more shabby than the previous. James Joyce's whole education was Catholic, from the age of six to the age of nine at Clongowes Wood College, and from eleven to sixteen at Belvedere College, Dublin. Both were Jesuit institutions, and were normal roads to the priesthood. He then studied modern languages at University College, Dublin.

From a comparatively early age Joyce regarded himself as a rebel against the shabbiness and Philistinism of Dublin. In his early youth he was very religious, but in his last year at Belvedere he began to reject his Catholic faith in favor of a literary mission that he saw as involving rebellion and exile. He refused to play any part in the nationalist or other popular activities of his fellow students, and he created some stir by his outspoken articles, one of which, on the Norwegian playwright Henrik Ibsen, appeared in the *Fortnightly Review* for April 1900. He taught himself Norwegian to be able to read Ibsen and to write to him. When an article by Joyce, significantly titled *The Day of the Rabblement,* was refused, on instructions of the faculty adviser, by the student magazine that had commissioned it, he had it printed privately. By 1902, when he received his A.B. degree, he was already committed to a career as exile and writer. For Joyce, as for his character Stephen Dedalus, the latter implied the former. To preserve his integrity, to avoid involvement in popular sentimentalities and dishonesties, and above all to be able to recreate with both total understanding and total objectivity the Dublin life he knew so well, he felt that he had to go abroad.

Joyce went to Paris after graduation, was recalled to Dublin by his mother's fatal illness, had a short spell there as a schoolteacher, then returned to the Continent in 1904 to teach English at Trieste and then at Zurich. He took with him Nora Barnacle, an uneducated Galway girl with no interest in literature; her native vivacity and peasant wit charmed Joyce, and the two lived in devoted companionship until Joyce's death, although they were not married until 1931. In 1920 Joyce settled in Paris, where he lived until December 1940, when the war forced him to take refuge in Switzerland; he died in Zurich a few weeks later.

Proud, obstinate, absolutely convinced of his genius, given to fits of sudden gaiety and of sudden silence, Joyce was not always an easy person to get along with, yet he never lacked friends, and throughout his thirty-six years on the Continent he was always the center of a literary circle. Life was hard at first. At Trieste he had very little money, and he did not improve matters by drinking heavily, a habit checked somewhat by his brother Stanislaus, who came out from Dublin to act (as Stanislaus put it much later) as his "brother's keeper." His financial position was much improved by the patronage of Mrs. Harold McCormick (Edith Rockefeller), who provided him with a monthly stipend from March 1917 until September 1919, when they quarreled, apparently because Joyce refused to submit to psychoanalysis by Carl Jung, who had been heavily endowed by Mrs. McCormick. The New York lawyer and art patron John Quinn, steered in Joyce's direction by Ezra Pound, also helped Joyce financially in 1917. A more permanent benefactor was the English feminist and editor Harriet Shaw Weaver, who not only subsidized Joyce generously from 1917 to the end of his life but occupied herself indefatigably with arrangements for publishing his work.

Joyce's almost lifelong exile from his native Ireland has something paradoxical about it. No writer has ever been more soaked in Dublin, its atmosphere, its history, its topography; in spite of doing most of his writing in Trieste, Zurich, and Paris, he wrote only and always about Dublin. He devised ways of expanding his accounts of Dublin, however, so that they became microcosms, small-scale models, of all human life, of all history, and of all geography. Indeed that was his life's work: to write about Dublin in such a way that he was writing about all of human experience.

Joyce began his career by writing a series of stories etching with extraordinary clarity aspects of Dublin life. But these stories—published as *Dubliners* in 1914— are more than sharp realistic sketches. In each, the detail is so chosen and organized that carefully interacting symbolic meanings are set up, and as a result, *Dubliners* is a book about human fate as well as a series of sketches of Dublin. Furthermore, the stories are presented in a particular order so that new meanings arise from the relation between them.

The last story in Dubliners, *The Dead,* was not part of the original draft of the book, but was added later, at a time when Joyce was preoccupied with the nature of artistic objectivity. A series of jolting events frees the protagonist, Gabriel, from his possessiveness and egotism; the view he attains at the end is the mood of supreme neutrality that Joyce saw as the beginning of artistic awareness. It is the view of art developed by Stephen Dedalus in A *Portrait of the Artist as a Young Man*. *Dubliners* represents Joyce's first phase: he had to come directly to terms with the life he had rejected, to see it for what it was and for what it meant. Next, he had to come to terms with the meaning of his own development as a man dedicated to writing. He did this by weaving his autobiography into a novel so finely chiseled and carefully organized, so stripped of everything superfluous, that each word contributes to the presentation of the theme: the parallel movement toward art and toward exile. A part of Joyce's first draft has been posthumously published under the original title of *Stephen Hero* (1944): a comparison between it and the final version that Joyce gave to the world, A *Portrait of the Artist as a Young Man* (1916), will show how carefully Joyce reworked and compressed his material for maximum effect. The *Portrait* is not literally true as autobiography, although it has many autobiographical elements, but it is representatively true not only of Joyce but of the relation between the artist and society in the modern world.

In the *Portrait* Stephen worked out a theory of art which considers that art moves from the lyrical form—which is the simplest, the personal expression of an instant of emotion—through the narrative form—no longer purely personal—to the dramatic—the highest and most perfect form, where "the artist, like the God of creation, remains within or behind or beyond or above his handiwork, invisible, refined out of existence, indifferent, paring his fingernails." This view of art, which involves the objectivity, even the exile, of the artist (even though the artist uses only the materials provided for him or her by his or her own life), is related to that held by the poets of the 1890s. More widely, it is related to the rejection by the artist of the ordinary world of middle-class values and activities that we see equally, though in different ways, in Matthew Arnold's war against the Philistines and in the concept (very un-Arnoldian) of the artist as bohemian. Joyce's career belongs to that long chapter in the history of the arts in Western civilization that begins with the artist's declaring independence and ends with his or her feeling inevitable "alienation." But if Joyce was alienated, as in certain ways he clearly was, he made his alienation serve his art: the kinds of writing represented by *Ulysses* and *Finnegans Wake* represent the most consummate craftsmanship put at the service of a humanely comic vision of all life. Some of Joyce's innovations in organization and style have been imitated by other writers, but these books are, and will probably remain, unique in our literature.

From the beginning, Joyce had trouble with the Philistines. Publication of *Dubliners* was held up for many years while he fought with both English and Irish publishers about certain words and phrases that they wished to eliminate. (It was the former who finally published the book.) His masterpiece *Ulysses* was banned in both Britain and America on its first appearance in 1922, its earlier serialization in the *Little Review* (March 1918–December 1920) having had to stop abruptly when the U.S. Post Office brought a charge of obscenity against it. Fortunately, Judge Woolsey's history-making decision in favor of *Ulysses* in a U.S. district court on December 6, 1933, resulted in the lifting of the ban and the free circulation of the work first in America and soon afterward in Britain.

ULYSSES

Ulysses is an account of one day in the lives of citizens of Dublin in the year 1904; it is thus the description of a limited number of events involving a limited number of people in a limited environment. Yet Joyce's ambition—which took him seven years to realize—is to make his action into a microcosm of all human experience. The events are not, therefore, told on a single level; the story is presented in such a manner that depth and implication are given to them and they become symbolic of the activity of the Individual in the World. The most obvious of the devices that Joyce employs to make clear the microcosmic aspect of his story is the parallel with Homer's *Odyssey*: every episode in *Ulysses* corresponds in some way to an episode in the *Odyssey*. Joyce regarded Homer's Ulysses as the most "complete" man in literature, a man who is shown in all his aspects—both coward and hero, cautious and reckless, weak and strong, husband and lover, father and son, sublime and ridiculous; so he makes his hero, Leopold Bloom, an Irish Jew, into a modern Ulysses, and by so doing helps to make him Everyman and to make Dublin the world.

The book opens at eight o'clock on the morning of June 16, 1904. Stephen Dedalus (the same character we saw in the *Portrait*, but this is two years after our last glimpse of him there) had been summoned back to Dublin by his mother's fatal illness and now lives in an old military tower on the shore with Buck Mulligan, a rollicking medical student, and an Englishman called Haines. In the first three episodes of *Ulysses*, which concentrate on Stephen, he is built up as an aloof, uncompromising artist, rejecting all advances by representatives of the normal world, the incomplete man, to be contrasted later with the complete Leopold Bloom, who is much more "normal" and conciliatory. After tracing Stephen through his early-morning activities and learning the main currents of his mind, we go, in the fourth episode, to the home of Bloom. We follow closely his every activity: attending a funeral, transacting his business, eating his lunch, walking through the Dublin streets, worrying about his wife's infidelity with Blazes Boylan—and at each point the contents of his mind, including retrospect and anticipation, are presented to the reader, until all his past history is revealed. Finally, Bloom and Stephen, who have just been missing each other all day, get together. By this time it is late, and Stephen, who has been drinking with some medical students, is the worse for liquor. Bloom, moved by a paternal feeling toward Stephen (his own son had died in infancy and in a symbolic way Stephen takes his place), follows him during subsequent adventures in the role of protector. The climax of the book comes when Stephen, far gone in drink, and Bloom, worn out with fatigue, succumb to a series of hallucinations where their subconscious and unconscious come to the surface in dramatic form and their whole personalities are revealed with a completeness and a frankness unique in literature. Then Bloom takes the unresponsive Stephen home and gives him a meal. After Stephen's departure Bloom retires to bed—it is now two in the morning on June 17—while his wife, Molly, representing the principles of sex and reproduction on which all human life is based, closes the book with a long monologue in which her experiences as woman are remembered.

On the level of realistic description, *Ulysses* pulses with life and can be enjoyed for its evocation of early twentieth-century Dublin. On the level of psychological exploration, it gives a profound and moving presentation of the personality and consciousness of Leopold Bloom and (to a lesser extent) Stephen Dedalus. On the level of style, it exhibits the most fascinating linguistic virtuosity. On a deeper symbolic level, the novel explores the paradoxes of human loneliness and sociability (for Bloom is both Jew and Dubliner, both exile and citizen, just as all of us are in a sense both exiles and citizens), and it explores the problems posed by the relations between parent and child, between the generations, and between the sexes. At the same time, through its use of themes from Homer, Dante, and Shakespeare and from literature, philosophy, and history, the book weaves a subtle pattern of allusion and suggestion that illuminates many aspects of human experience. The more one reads *Ulysses* the more one finds in it, but at the same time one does not need to probe into the symbolic meaning to relish both its literary artistry and its human feeling. At the forefront stands Leopold Bloom, from one point of view, a frustrated and confused outsider in the society in which he moves, from another, a champion of kindness and justice whose humane curiosity about his fellows redeems him from mere vulgarity and gives the book its positive human foundation.

Readers who come to *Ulysses* with expectations about the way the story is to be presented derived from their reading of Victorian novels or even of such twentieth-century novelists as Conrad and Lawrence will find much that is at first puzzling. Joyce presents the consciousness of his characters directly, without any explanatory comment that tells the reader whose consciousness is being rendered (this is the stream of consciousness method). He may move, in the same paragraph and without any sign that he is making such a transition, from a description of a character's action—e.g., Stephen walking along the shore or Bloom entering a restaurant—to an evocation of the character's mental response to this action. That response is always multiple: it derives partly from the character's immediate situation and partly from the whole complex of attitudes that his past history has created in him. To suggest this multiplicity, Joyce may vary his style, from the flippant to the serious or from a realistic description to a suggestive set of images that indicate what might be called the general tone of the character's consciousness. Past and present mingle in the texture of the prose because they mingle in the texture of consciousness, and this mingling can be indicated by puns, by sudden breaks into a new kind of style or a new kind of subject matter, or by some other device for keeping the reader constantly in sight of the shifting, kaleidoscopic nature of human awareness. With a little experience, the reader learns to follow the implications of Joyce's shifts in manner and content—even to follow that at first sight bewildering passage in the "Proteus" episode in which Stephen does not go to visit his uncle and aunt but, passing the road that leads to their house, imagines the kind of conversation that would take place in his home *if* he had gone to visit his uncle and had then returned home and reported that he had done so. *Ulysses* must not be approached as though it were a novel written in a traditional manner; all preconceptions must be set aside and we must follow wherever the author leads us and let the language tell us what it has to say without our troubling whether language is being used "properly" or not.

FINNEGANS WAKE

Joyce's last work, *Finnegans Wake*, was published in 1939; it took more than fourteen years to write, and Joyce considered it his masterpiece. In *Ulysses* he had made the symbolic aspect of the novel at least as important as the realistic aspect, but in *Finnegans Wake* he gave up realism altogether. This vast story of a symbolic Irishman's cosmic dream develops by enormous reverberating puns a continuous expansion of meaning, the elements in the puns deriving from every conceivable source in history, literature, mythology, and Joyce's personal experience. The whole book being (on one level at least) a dream, Joyce invents his own dream language in which words are combined, distorted, created by fitting together bits of other words, used with several different meanings at once, often drawn from several different languages at once, and fused in all sorts of ways to achieve whole clusters of meaning simultaneously. In fact, so many echoing suggestions can be found in every word or phrase that a full annotation of even a few pages would require a large book. It has taken the cooperative work of a number of devoted readers to make clear the complex interactions of the multiple puns and punclusters through which the ideas are projected, and every rereading reveals new meanings. It is true that many readers find the efforts of explication demanded by *Finegans Wake* too arduous; some, indeed, feel that the law of diminishing returns has now begun to operate, and that the effort of both author and reader is disproportionate. Nevertheless, the book has great beauty and fascination even for the casual reader. Students are advised to read aloud—or to listen to the record of Joyce reading aloud—the extract printed in this anthology, to appreciate the degree to which the rhythms of the prose assist in conveying the meaning.

To an even greater extent than *Ulysses, Finnegans Wake* aims at embracing all of human history. The title is from an Irish-American ballad about Tom Finnegan, a hod carrier who falls off a ladder when drunk and is apparently killed, but who revives when during the wake (the watch by the dead body) someone spills whiskey on him. The theme of death and resurrection, of cycles of change coming round in the course of history, is central to *Finnegans Wake*, which derives one of its main principles of organization from the cyclical theory of history put forward in 1725 by the Italian philosopher Giambattista Vico. Vico held that history passes through four phases: the divine or theocratic, when people are governed by their awe of the supernatural; the aristocratic (the "heroic age" reflected in Homer and in *Beowulf*); the democratic and individualistic; and the final stage of chaos, a fall into confusion startles humanity back into supernatural reverence and starts the process once again. Joyce, like Yeats, saw his own generation as in the final stage awaiting the shock that will bring humans back to the first.

A mere account of the narrative line of *Finnegans Wake* cannot, of course, give any idea of the content of the work. If one explains that it opens with Finnegan's fall, then introduces his successor Humphrey Chimpden Earwicker, who is Every-man, and whose dream constitutes the novel; that he is presented as having guilt feelings about an indecency he committed (or may have committed) in Phoenix Park, Dublin; that his wife, Anna Livia Plurabelle or ALP (who is also Eve, Iseult, Ireland, the river Liffey), changes her role just as he does; that he has two sons, Shem and Shaun (or Jerry and Kevin), who represent introvert and extrovert, artist and practical man, creator and popularizer, and symbolize this basic dichotomy in human nature by all kinds of metamorphoses; and if one adds that, in the four books into which *Finnegans Wake* is divided (after Vico's pattern), actions comic or grotesque or sad or tender or desperate or passionate or terribly ordinary (and very often several of these things at the same time) take place with all the shifting meanings of a dream, so that characters change into others or into inanimate objects and the setting keeps shifting—if we explain all this, we still have said very little about what makes *Finnegans Wake* what it is. The dreamer, whose initials HCE indicate his universality ("Here Comes Everybody"), is at the same time a particular person, who keeps a pub in Chapelizod, a Dublin suburb on the river Liffey near Phoenix Park. His mysterious misdemeanor in Phoenix Park is in a sense Original Sin: Earwicker is Adam as well as a primeval giant, the Hill of Howth, the Great Parent ("Haveth Childers Everywhere" is another expansion of HCE), and Man in History. Other characters who flit and change through the book, such as the Twelve Customers (who are also twelve jurymen and public opinion) and the Four Old Men (who are also judges, the authors of the four Gospels, and the four elements), help to weave the texture of multiple significance so characteristic of the work. But always it is the punning language, extending significance downward—rather than the plot, developing it lengthwise—that bears the main load of meaning.

The Dead

Lily, the caretaker's daughter, was literally run off her feet. Hardly had she brought one gentleman into the little pantry behind the office on the ground floor and helped him off with his overcoat than the wheezy hall-door bell clanged again and she had to scamper along the bare hallway to let in another guest. It was well for her she had not to attend to the ladies also. But Miss

Kate and Miss Julia had thought of that and had converted the bathroom upstairs into a ladies' dressing-room. Miss Kate and Miss Julia were there, gossiping and laughing and fussing, walking after each other to the head of the stairs, peering down over the banisters and calling down to Lily to ask her who had come.

It was always a great affair, the Misses Morkan's annual dance. Everybody who knew them came to it, members of the family, old friends of the family, the members of Julia's choir, any of Kate's pupils that were grown up enough and even some of Mary Jane's pupils too. Never once had it fallen flat. For years and years it had gone off in splendid style as long as anyone could remember; ever since Kate and Julia, after the death of their brother Pat, had left the house in Stoney Batter and taken Mary Jane, their only niece, to live with them in the dark gaunt house on Usher's Island, the upper part of which they had rented from Mr Fulham, the cornfactor[1] on the ground floor. That was a good thirty years ago if it was a day. Mary Jane, who was then a little girl in short clothes, was now the main prop of the household for she had the organ in Haddington Road. She had been through the Academy and gave a pupils' concert every year in the upper room of the Antient Concert Rooms.[2] Many of her pupils belonged to better-class families on the Kingstown and Dalkey line. Old as they were, her aunts also did their share. Julia, though she was quite grey, was still the leading soprano in Adam and Eve's, and Kate, being too feeble to go about much, gave music lessons to beginners on the old square piano in the back room. Lily, the caretaker's daughter, did house-maid's work for them. Though their life was modest they believed in eating well; the best of everything: diamond-bone sirloins, three-shilling tea and the best bottled stout.[3] But Lily seldom made a mistake in the orders so that she got on well with her three mistresses. They were fussy, that was all. But the only thing they would not stand was back answers.

Of course they had good reason to be fussy on such a night. And then it was long after ten o'clock and yet there was no sign of Gabriel and his wife. Besides they were dreadfully afraid that Freddy Malins might turn up screwed. They would not wish for worlds that any of Mary Jane's pupils should see him under the influence; and when he was like that it was sometimes very hard to man-age him. Freddy Malins always came late but they wondered what could be keeping Gabriel: and that was what brought them every two minutes to the banisters to ask Lily had Gabriel or Freddy come.

—O, Mr Conroy, said Lily to Gabriel when she opened the door for him, Miss Kate and Miss Julia thought you were never coming. Good-night, Mrs Conroy.

—I'll engage they did, said Gabriel, but they forget that my wife here takes three mortal hours to dress herself.

He stood on the mat, scraping the snow from his goloshes, while Lily led his wife to the foot of the stairs and called out:

—Miss Kate, here's Mrs Conroy.

Kate and Julia came toddling down the dark stairs at once. Both of them kissed Gabriel's wife, said she must be perished alive and asked was Gabriel with her.

---

1. Grain merchant.
2. Concert hall in Dublin; the academy was the Royal

Irish Academy of Music.
3. A dark brown malt liquor, akin to beer.

—Here I am as right as the mail, Aunt Kate! Go on up. I'll follow, called
out Gabriel from the dark.

He continued scraping his feet vigorously while the three women went
upstairs, laughing, to the ladies' dressing-room. A light fringe of snow lay like
a cape on the shoulders of his overcoat and like toecaps on the toes of his
goloshes; and, as the buttons of his overcoat slipped with a squeaking noise
through the snow-stiffened frieze, a cold fragrant air from out-of-doors escaped
from crevices and folds.

—Is it snowing again, Mr Conroy? asked Lily.

She had preceded him into the pantry to help him off with his overcoat.
Gabriel smiled at the three syllables she had given his surname and glanced
at her. She was a slim, growing girl, pale in complexion and with hay-coloured
hair. The gas in the pantry made her look still paler. Gabriel had known her
when she was a child and used to sit on the lowest step nursing a rag doll.

—Yes, Lily, he answered, and I think we're in for a night of it.

He looked up at the pantry ceiling, which was shaking with the stamping
and shuffling of feet on the floor above, listened for a moment to the piano
and then glanced at the girl, who was folding his overcoat carefully at the end
of a shelf.

—Tell me, Lily, he said in a friendly tone, do you still go to school?

—O no, sir, she answered. I'm done schooling this year and more.

—O, then, said Gabriel gaily, I suppose we'll be going to your wedding one
of these fine days with your young man, eh?

The girl glanced back at him over her shoulder and said with great bitterness:

—The men that is now is only all palaver and what they can get out of you.

Gabriel coloured as if he felt he had made a mistake and, without looking
at her, kicked off his goloshes and flicked actively with his muffler at his
patent-leather shoes.

He was a stout tallish young man. The high colour of his cheeks pushed
upwards even to his forehead where it scattered itself in a few formless patches
of pale red; and on his hairless face there scintillated restlessly the polished
lenses and the bright gilt rims of the glasses which screened his delicate and
restless eyes. His glossy black hair was parted in the middle and brushed in a
long curve behind his ears where it curled slightly beneath the groove left by
his hat.

When he had flicked lustre into his shoes he stood up and pulled his waistcoat down more tightly on his plump body. Then he took a coin rapidly from
his pocket.

—O Lily, he said, thrusting it into her hands, it's Christmas-time, isn't it?
Just . . . here's a little. . . .

He walked rapidly towards the door.

—O no, sir! cried the girl, following him. Really, sir, I wouldn't take it.

—Christmas-time! Christmas-time! said Gabriel, almost trotting to the stairs
and waving his hand to her in deprecation.

The girl, seeing that he had gained the stairs, called out after him:

—Well, thank you, sir.

He waited outside the drawing-room door until the waltz should finish,
listening to the skirts that swept against it and to the shuffling of feet. He was
still discomposed by the girl's bitter and sudden retort. It had cast a gloom

over him which he tried to dispel by arranging his cuffs and the bows of his tie. Then he took from his waistcoat pocket a little paper and glanced at the headings he had made for his speech. He was undecided about the lines from Robert Browning for he feared they would be above the heads of his hearers. Some quotation that they could recognise from Shakespeare or from the Melodies[4] would be better. The indelicate clacking of the men's heels and the shuffling of their soles reminded him that their grade of culture differed from his. He would only make himself ridiculous by quoting poetry to them which they could not understand. They would think that he was airing his superior education. He would fail with them just as he had failed with the girl in the pantry. He had taken up a wrong tone. His whole speech was a mistake from first to last, an utter failure.

Just then his aunts and his wife came out of the ladies' dressing-room. His aunts were two small plainly dressed old women. Aunt Julia was an inch or so taller. Her hair, drawn low over the tops of her ears, was grey; and grey also, with darker shadows, was her large flaccid face. Though she was stout in build and stood erect her slow eyes and parted lips gave her the appearance of a woman who did not know where she was or where she was going. Aunt Kate was more vivacious. Her face, healthier than her sister's, was all puckers and creases, like a shrivelled red apple, and her hair, braided in the same old-fashioned way, had not lost its ripe nut colour.

They both kissed Gabriel frankly. He was their favourite nephew, the son of their dead elder sister, Ellen, who had married T. J. Conroy of the Port and Docks.

—Gretta tells me you're not going to take a cab back to Monkstown to-night, Gabriel, said Aunt Kate.

—No, said Gabriel, turning to his wife, we had quite enough of that last year, hadn't we. Don't you remember, Aunt Kate, what a cold Gretta got out of it? Cab windows rattling all the way, and the east wind blowing in after we passed Merrion. Very jolly it was. Gretta caught a dreadful cold.

Aunt Kate frowned severely and nodded her head at every word.

—Quite right, Gabriel, quite right, she said. You can't be too careful.

—But as for Gretta there, said Gabriel, she'd walk home in the snow if she were let.

Mrs Conroy laughed.

—Don't mind him, Aunt Kate, she said. He's really an awful bother, what with green shades for Tom's eyes at night and making him do the dumb-bells, and forcing Eva to eat the stirabout.[5] The poor child! And she simply hates the sight of it! . . . O, but you'll never guess what he makes me wear now!

She broke out into a peal of laughter and glanced at her husband, whose admiring and happy eyes had been wandering from her dress to her face and hair. The two aunts laughed heartily too, for Gabriel's solicitude was a standing joke with them.

—Goloshes! said Mrs Conroy. That's the latest. Whenever it's wet underfoot I must put on my goloshes. To-night even he wanted me to put them on, but I wouldn't. The next thing he'll buy me will be a diving suit.

4. *Irish Melodies* by Dublin-born Thomas Moore (1779–1852), a collection of songs—words and music—that was extremely popular in late-19th- and early-   20th-century Ireland.
5. Porridge made by stirring oatmeal in boiling milk or water.

Gabriel laughed nervously and patted his tie reassuringly while Aunt Kate nearly doubled herself, so heartily did she enjoy the joke. The smile soon faded from Aunt Julia's face and her mirthless eyes were directed towards her nephew's face. After a pause she asked:

—And what are goloshes, Gabriel?

—Goloshes, Julia! exclaimed her sister. Goodness me, don't you know what goloshes are? You wear them over your . . . over your boots, Gretta, isn't it?

—Yes, said Mrs Conroy. Guttapercha things. We both have a pair now. Gabriel says everyone wears them on the continent.

—O, on the continent, murmured Aunt Julia, nodding her head slowly.

Gabriel knitted his brows and said, as if he were slightly angered:

—It's nothing very wonderful but Gretta thinks it very funny because she says the word reminds her of Christy Minstrels.[6]

—But tell me, Gabriel, said Aunt Kate, with brisk tact. Of course, you've seen about the room. Gretta was saying . . .

—O, the room is all right, replied Gabriel. I've taken one in the Gresham.[7]

—To be sure, said Aunt Kate, by far the best thing to do. And the children, Gretta, you're not anxious about them?

—O, for one night, said Mrs Conroy. Besides, Bessie will look after them.

—To be sure, said Aunt Kate again. What a comfort it is to have a girl like that, one you can depend on! There's that Lily, I'm sure I don't know what has come over her lately. She's not the girl she was at all.

Gabriel was about to ask his aunt some questions on this point but she broke off suddenly to gaze after her sister who had wandered down the stairs and was craning her neck over the banisters.

—Now, I ask you, she said, almost testily, where is Julia going? Julia! Julia! Where are you going?

Julia, who had gone halfway down one flight, came back and announced blandly:

—Here's Freddy.

At the same moment a clapping of hands and a final flourish of the pianist told that the waltz had ended. The drawing-room door was opened from within and some couples came out. Aunt Kate drew Gabriel aside hurriedly and whispered into his ear:

—Slip down, Gabriel, like a good fellow and see if he's all right, and don't let him up if he's screwed. I'm sure he's screwed. I'm sure he is.

Gabriel went to the stairs and listened over the banisters. He could hear two persons talking in the pantry. Then he recognised Freddy Malins' laugh. He went down the stairs noisily.

—It's such a relief, said Aunt Kate to Mrs Conroy, that Gabriel is here. I always feel easier in my mind when he's here. . . . Julia, there's Miss Daly and Miss Power will take some refreshment. Thanks for your beautiful waltz, Miss Daly. It made lovely time.

A tall wizen-faced man, with a stiff grizzled moustache and swarthy skin, who was passing out with his partner said:

6. Originally the name of a troupe of entertainers imitating Negroes, founded by George Christy of New York. By Joyce's time the meaning had become extended to any group with blackened faces who sang what were known as Negro melodies to banjo accompaniment, interspersed with jokes.
7. The Gresham Hotel, still one of the best hotels in Dublin.

—And may we have some refreshment, too, Miss Morkan?

—Julia, said Aunt Kate summarily, and here's Mr Browne and Miss Fur-long. Take them in, Julia, with Miss Daly and Miss Power.

—I'm the man for the ladies, said Mr Browne, pursing his lips until his moustache bristled and smiling in all his wrinkles. You know, Miss Morkan, the reason they are so fond of me is—

He did not finish his sentence, but, seeing that Aunt Kate was out of earshot, at once led the three young ladies into the back room. The middle of the room was occupied by two square tables placed end to end, and on these Aunt Julia and the caretaker were straightening and smoothing a large cloth. On the sideboard were arrayed dishes and plates, and glasses and bundles of knives and forks and spoons. The top of the closed square piano served also as a sideboard for viands and sweets. At a smaller sideboard in one corner two young men were standing, drinking hop-bitters.

Mr Browne led his charges thither and invited them all, in jest, to some ladies' punch, hot, strong and sweet. As they said they never took anything strong he opened three bottles of lemonade for them. Then he asked one of the young men to move aside, and, taking hold of the decanter, filled out for himself a goodly measure of whisky. The young men eyed him respectfully while he took a trial sip.

—God help me, he said, smiling, it's the doctor's orders.

His wizened face broke into a broader smile, and the three young ladies laughed in musical echo to his pleasantry, swaying their bodies to and fro, with nervous jerks of their shoulders. The boldest said:

—O, now, Mr Browne, I'm sure the doctor never ordered anything of the kind.

Mr Browne took another sip of his whisky and said, with sidling mimicry:

—Well, you see, I'm like the famous Mrs Cassidy, who is reported to have said: *Now, Mary Grimes, if I don't take it, make me take it, for I feel I want it.*

His hot face had leaned forward a little too confidentially and he had assumed a very low Dublin accent so that the young ladies, with one instinct, received his speech in silence. Miss Furlong, who was one of Mary Jane's pupils, asked Miss Daly what was the name of the pretty waltz she had played; and Mr Browne, seeing that he was ignored, turned promptly to the two young men who were more appreciative.

A red-faced young woman, dressed in pansy, came into the room, excitedly clapping her hands and crying:

—Quadrilles! Quadrilles![8]

Close on her heels came Aunt Kate, crying:

—Two gentlemen and three ladies, Mary Jane!

—O, here's Mr Bergin and Mr Kerrigan, said Mary Jane. Mr Kerrigan, will you take Miss Power? Miss Furlong, may I get you a partner, Mr Bergin. O, that'll just do now.

—Three ladies, Mary Jane, said Aunt Kate.

The two young gentlemen asked the ladies if they might have the pleasure, and Mary Jane turned to Miss Daly.

—O, Miss Daly, you're really awfully good, after playing for the last two dances, but really we're so short of ladies to-night.

---

8. A square dance usually performed by four couples.

—I don't mind in the least, Miss Morkan.

—But I've a nice partner for you, Mr Bartell D'Arcy, the tenor. I'll get him to sing later on. All Dublin is raving about him.

—Lovely voice, lovely voice! said Aunt Kate.

As the piano had twice begun the prelude to the first figure Mary Jane led her recruits quickly from the room. They had hardly gone when Aunt Julia wandered slowly into the room, looking behind her at something.

—What is the matter, Julia? asked Aunt Kate anxiously. Who is it?

Julia, who was carrying in a column of table-napkins, turned to her sister and said, simply, as if the question had surprised her:

—It's only Freddy, Kate, and Gabriel with him.

In fact right behind her Gabriel could be seen piloting Freddy Malins across the landing. The latter, a young man of about forty, was of Gabriel's size and build, with very round shoulders. His face was fleshy and pallid, touched with colour only at the thick hanging lobes of his ears and at the wide wings of his nose. He had coarse features, a blunt nose, a convex and receding brow, tumid and protruded lips. His heavy-lidded eyes and the disorder of his scanty hair made him look sleepy. He was laughing heartily in a high key at a story which he had been telling Gabriel on the stairs and at the same time rubbing the knuckles of his left fist backwards and forwards into his left eye.

—Good-evening, Freddy, said Aunt Julia.

Freddy Malins bade the Misses Morkan good-evening in what seemed an offhand fashion by reason of the habitual catch in his voice and then, seeing that Mr Browne was grinning at him from the sideboard, crossed the room on rather shaky legs and began to repeat in an undertone the story he had just told to Gabriel.

—He's not so bad, is he? said Aunt Kate to Gabriel.

Gabriel's brows were dark but he raised them quickly and answered:

—O no, hardly noticeable.

—Now, isn't he a terrible fellow! she said. And his poor mother made him take the pledge[9] on New Year's Eve. But come on, Gabriel, into the drawing-room.

Before leaving the room with Gabriel she signalled to Mr Browne by frowning and shaking her forefinger in warning to and fro. Mr Browne nodded in answer and, when she had gone, said to Freddy Malins:

—Now, then, Teddy, I'm going to fill you out a good glass of lemonade just to buck you up.

Freddy Malins, who was nearing the climax of his story, waved the offer aside impatiently but Mr Browne, having first called Freddy Malins' attention to a disarray in his dress, filled out and handed him a full glass of lemonade. Freddy Malins' left hand accepted the glass mechanically, his right hand being engaged in the mechanical readjustment of his dress. Mr Browne, whose face was once more wrinkling with mirth, poured out for himself a glass of whisky while Freddy Malins exploded, before he had well reached the climax of his story, in a kink of high-pitched bronchitic laughter and, setting down his untasted and overflowing glass, began to rub the knuckles of his left fist backwards and forwards into his left eye, repeating words of his last phrase as well as his fit of laughter would allow him.

9. Sign a solemn engagement not to drink alcohol.

Gabriel could not listen while Mary Jane was playing her Academy piece, full of runs and difficult passages, to the hushed drawing-room. He liked music but the piece she was playing had no melody for him and he doubted whether it had any melody for the other listeners, though they had begged Mary Jane to play something. Four young men, who had come from the refreshment-room to stand in the door-way at the sound of the piano, had gone away quietly in couples after a few minutes. The only persons who seemed to follow the music were Mary Jane herself, her hands racing along the key-board or lifted from it at the pauses like those of a priestess in momentary imprecation, and Aunt Kate standing at her elbow to turn the page.

Gabriel's eyes, irritated by the floor, which glittered with beeswax under the heavy chandelier, wandered to the wall above the piano. A picture of the balcony scene in *Romeo and Juliet* hung there and beside it was a picture of the two murdered princes in the Tower which Aunt Julia had worked in red, blue and brown wools when she was a girl. Probably in the school they had gone to as girls that kind of work had been taught, for one year his mother had worked for him as a birthday present a waistcoat of purple tabinet, with little foxes' heads upon it, lined with brown satin and having round mulberry buttons. It was strange that his mother had had no musical talent though Aunt Kate used to call her the brains carrier of the Morkan family. Both she and Julia had always seemed a little proud of their serious and matronly sister. Her photograph stood before the pierglass.[1] She held an open book on her knees and was pointing out something in it to Constantine who, dressed in a man-o'-war suit,[2] lay at her feet. It was she who had chosen the names for her sons for she was very sensible of the dignity of family life. Thanks to her, Constantine was now senior curate[3] in Balbriggan and, thanks to her, Gabriel himself had taken his degree in the Royal University. A shadow passed over his face as he remembered her sullen opposition to his marriage. Some slighting phrases she had used still rankled in his memory; she had once spoken of Gretta as being country cute and that was not true of Gretta at all. It was Gretta who had nursed her during all her last long illness in their house at Monkstown.

He knew that Mary Jane must be near the end of her piece for she was playing again the opening melody with runs of scales after every bar and while he waited for the end the resentment died down in his heart. The piece ended with a trill of octaves in the treble and a final deep octave in the bass. Great applause greeted Mary Jane as, blushing and rolling up her music nervously, she escaped from the room. The most vigorous clapping came from the four young men in the doorway who had gone away to the refreshment-room at the beginning of the piece but had come back when the piano had stopped.

Lancers[4] were arranged. Gabriel found himself partnered with Miss Ivors. She was a frank-mannered talkative young lady, with a freckled face and prominent brown eyes. She did not wear a low-cut bodice and the large brooch which was fixed in the front of her collar bore on it an Irish device.

When they had taken their places she said abruptly:

—I have a crow to pluck with you.

1. Large tall mirror.
2. Sailor suit, favorite wear for children of both sexes early in this century.
3. Clergyman appointed to assist a parish priest.
4. A square dance for four or more couples.

—With me? said Gabriel.

She nodded her head gravely.

—What is it? asked Gabriel, smiling at her solemn manner.

—Who is G. C.? answered Miss Ivors, turning her eyes upon him.

Gabriel coloured and was about to knit his brows, as if he did not understand, when she said bluntly:

—O, innocent Amy! I have found out that you write for *The Daily Express*. Now, aren't you ashamed of yourself?

—Why should I be ashamed of myself? asked Gabriel, blinking his eyes and trying to smile.

—Well, I'm ashamed of you, said Miss Ivors frankly. To say you'd write for a rag like that. I didn't think you were a West Briton.[5]

A look of perplexity appeared on Gabriel's face. It was true that he wrote a literary column every Wednesday in *The Daily Express*, for which he was paid fifteen shillings. But that did not make him a West Briton surely. The books he received for review were almost more welcome than the paltry cheque. He loved to feel the covers and turn over the pages of newly printed books. Nearly every day when his teaching in the college was ended he used to wander down the quays to the second-hand booksellers, to Hickey's on Bachelor's Walk, to Webb's, or Massey's on Aston's Quay, or to O'Clohissey's in the by-street. He did not know how to meet her charge. He wanted to say that literature was above politics. But they were friends of many years' standing and their careers had been parallel, first at the University and then as teachers: he could not risk a grandiose phrase with her. He continued blinking his eyes and trying to smile and murmured lamely that he saw nothing political in writing reviews of books.

When their turn to cross had come he was still perplexed and inattentive. Miss Ivors promptly took his hand in a warm grasp and said in a soft friendly tone:

—Of course, I was only joking. Come, we cross now.

When they were together again she spoke of the University question and Gabriel felt more at ease. A friend of hers had shown her his review of Browning's poems. That was how she had found out the secret: but she liked the review immensely. Then she said suddenly:

—O, Mr Conroy, will you come for an excursion to the Aran Isles[6] this summer? We're going to stay there a whole month. It will be splendid out in the Atlantic. You ought to come. Mr Clancy is coming, and Mr Kilkelly and Kathleen Kearney. It would be splendid for Gretta too if she'd come. She's from Connacht,[7] isn't she?

—Her people are, said Gabriel shortly.

—But you will come, won't you? said Miss Ivors, laying her warm hand eagerly on his arm.

—The fact is, said Gabriel, I have already arranged to go—

—Go where? asked Miss Ivors.

—Well, you know, every year I go for a cycling tour with some fellows and so—

---

5. One who denies a separate Irish nationality and sees Ireland as simply the western part of Great Britain.
6. Three small islands lying across the entrance to

Galway Bay, on the west coast of Ireland.
7. Connacht (or Connaught) is a region in the west of Ireland containing largely a poor peasant population.

—But where? asked Miss Ivors.

—Well, we usually go to France or Belgium or perhaps Germany, said Gabriel awkwardly.

—And why do you go to France and Belgium, said Miss Ivors, instead of visiting your own land?

—Well, said Gabriel, it's partly to keep in touch with the languages and partly for a change.

—And haven't you your own language to keep in touch with—Irish? asked Miss Ivors.

—Well, said Gabriel, if it comes to that, you know, Irish is not my language.

Their neighbours had turned to listen to the cross-examination. Gabriel glanced right and left nervously and tried to keep his good humour under the ordeal which was making a blush invade his forehead.

—And haven't you your own land to visit, continued Miss Ivors, that you know nothing of, your own people, and your own country?

—O, to tell you the truth, retorted Gabriel suddenly, I'm sick of my own country, sick of it!

—Why? asked Miss Ivors.

Gabriel did not answer for his retort had heated him.

—Why? repeated Miss Ivors.

They had to go visiting together and, as he had not answered her, Miss Ivors said warmly:

—Of course, you've no answer.

Gabriel tried to cover his agitation by taking part in the dance with great energy. He avoided her eyes for he had seen a sour expression on her face. But when they met in the long chain he was surprised to feel his hand firmly pressed. She looked at him from under her brows for a moment quizzically until he smiled. Then, just as the chain was about to start again, she stood on tiptoe and whispered into his ear:

—West Briton!

When the lancers were over Gabriel went away to a remote corner of the room where Freddy Malins' mother was sitting. She was a stout feeble old woman with white hair. Her voice had a catch in it like her son's and she stuttered slightly. She had been told that Freddy had come and that he was nearly all right. Gabriel asked her whether she had had a good crossing. She lived with her married daughter in Glasgow and came to Dublin on a visit once a year. She answered placidly that she had had a beautiful crossing and that the captain had been most attentive to her. She spoke also of the beautiful house her daughter kept in Glasgow, and of all the nice friends they had there. While her tongue rambled on Gabriel tried to banish from his mind all memory of the unpleasant incident with Miss Ivors. Of course the girl or woman, or whatever she was, was an enthusiast but there was a time for all things. Perhaps he ought not to have answered her like that. But she had no right to call him a West Briton before people, even in joke. She had tried to make him ridiculous before people, heckling him and staring at him with her rabbit's eyes.

He saw his wife making her way towards him through the waltzing couples. When she reached him she said into his ear:

—Gabriel, Aunt Kate wants to know won't you carve the goose as usual. Miss Daly will carve the ham and I'll do the pudding.

—All right, said Gabriel.

—She's sending in the younger ones first as soon as this waltz is over so that we'll have the table to ourselves.

—Were you dancing? asked Gabriel.

—Of course I was. Didn't you see me? What words had you with Molly Ivors?

—No words. Why? Did she say so?

—Something like that. I'm trying to get that Mr D'Arcy to sing. He's full of conceit, I think.

—There were no words, said Gabriel moodily, only she wanted me to go for a trip to the west of Ireland and I said I wouldn't.

His wife clasped her hands excitedly and gave a little jump.

—O, do go, Gabriel, she cried. I'd love to see Galway again.

—You can go if you like, said Gabriel coldly.

She looked at him for a moment, then turned to Mrs Malins and said:

—There's a nice husband for you, Mrs Malins.

While she was threading her way back across the room Mrs Malins, without adverting to the interruption, went on to tell Gabriel what beautiful places there were in Scotland and beautiful scenery. Her son-in-law brought them every year to the lakes and they used to go fishing. Her son-in-law was a splendid fisher. One day he caught a fish, a beautiful big big fish, and the man in the hotel boiled it for their dinner.

Gabriel hardly heard what she said. Now that supper was coming near he began to think again about his speech and about the quotation. When he saw Freddy Malins coming across the room to visit his mother Gabriel left the chair free for him and retired into the embrasure of the window. The room had already cleared and from the back room came the clatter of plates and knives. Those who still remained in the drawing-room seemed tired of dancing and were conversing quietly in little groups. Gabriel's warm trembling fingers tapped the cold pane of the window. How cool it must be outside! How pleasant it would be to walk out alone, first along by the river and then through the park! The snow would be lying on the branches of the trees and forming a bright cap on the top of the Wellington Monument. How much more pleasant it would be there than at the supper-table!

He ran over the headings of his speech: Irish hospitality, sad memories, the Three Graces,[8] Paris, the quotation from Browning. He repeated to himself a phrase he had written in his review: *One feels that one is listening to a thought-tormented music.* Miss Ivors had praised the review. Was she sincere? Had she really any life of her own behind all her propagandism? There had never been any ill-feeling between them until that night. It unnerved him to think that she would be at the supper-table, looking up at him while he spoke with her critical quizzing eyes. Perhaps she would not be sorry to see him fail in his speech. An idea came into his mind and gave him courage. He would say, alluding to Aunt Kate and Aunt Julia: *Ladies and Gentlemen, the generation which is now on the wane among us may have had its faults but for my part I think it had certain qualities of hospitality, of humour, of humanity, which the new and very serious and hypereducated generation that is growing up around*

8. In Greek mythology, three goddesses—Aglaia, splendor; Euphrosyne, festivity; and Thalia, rejoicing—who together represented loveliness and joy. Ga- briel is making a mental note to refer to his two aunts and Mary Jane in this complimentary way.

us seems to me to lack. Very good: that was one for Miss Ivors. What did he care that his aunts were only two ignorant old women?

A murmur in the room attracted his attention. Mr Browne was advancing from the door, gallantly escorting Aunt Julia, who leaned upon his arm, smiling and hanging her head. An irregular musketry of applause escorted her also as far as the piano and then, as Mary Jane seated herself on the stool, and Aunt Julia, no longer smiling, half turned so as to pitch her voice fairly into the room, gradually ceased. Gabriel recognised the prelude. It was that of an old song of Aunt Julia's—*Arrayed for the Bridal.*[9] Her voice, strong and clear in tone, attacked with great spirit the runs which embellish the air and though she sang very rapidly she did not miss even the smallest of the grace notes. To follow the voice, without looking at the singer's face, was to feel and share the excitement of swift and secure flight. Gabriel applauded loudly with all the others at the close of the song and loud applause was borne in from the invisible supper-table. It sounded so genuine that a little colour struggled into Aunt Julia's face as she bent to replace in the music-stand the old leather-bound songbook that had her initials on the cover. Freddy Malins, who had listened with his head perched sideways to hear her better, was still applauding when everyone else had ceased and talking animatedly to his mother who nodded her head gravely and slowly in acquiescence. At last, when he could clap no more, he stood up suddenly and hurried across the room to Aunt Julia whose hand he seized and held in both his hands, shaking it when words failed him or the catch in his voice proved too much for him.

—I was just telling my mother, he said, I never heard you sing so well, never. No, I never heard your voice so good as it is to-night. Now! Would you believe that now? That's the truth. Upon my word and honour that's the truth I never heard your voice sound so fresh and so . . . so clear and fresh, never.

Aunt Julia smiled broadly and murmured something about compliments as she released her hand from his grasp. Mr Browne extended his open hand towards her and said to those who were near him in the manner of a showman introducing a prodigy to an audience:

—Miss Julia Morkan, my latest discovery!

He was laughing very heartily at this himself when Freddy Malins turned to him and said:

—Well, Browne, if you're serious you might make a worse discovery. All I can say is I never heard her sing half so well as long as I am coming here. And that's the honest truth.

—Neither did I, said Mr Browne. I think her voice has greatly improved.

Aunt Julia shrugged her shoulders and said with meek pride:

—Thirty years ago I hadn't a bad voice as voices go.

—I often told Julia, said Aunt Kate emphatically, that she was simply thrown away in that choir. But she never would be said by me.

She turned as if to appeal to the good sense of the others against a refractory child while Aunt Julia gazed in front of her, a vague smile of reminiscence playing on her face.

—No, continued Aunt Kate, she wouldn't be said or led by anyone, slaving

---

9. This old song (beginning "Arrayed for the bridal, in beauty behold her") "is replete with long and complicated runs, requiring a sophisticated and gifted singer" (Bowen, *Musical Allusions in the Works of James Joyce,* 1974); the suggestion is that Aunt Julia was a really accomplished singer.

there in that choir night and day, night and day. Six o'clock on Christmas morning! And all for what?

—Well, isn't it for the honour of God, Aunt Kate? asked Mary Jane, twisting round on the piano-stool and smiling.

Aunt Kate turned fiercely on her niece and said:

—I know all about the honour of God, Mary Jane, but I think it's not at all honourable for the pope to turn out the women out of the choirs that have slaved there all their lives and put little whipper-snappers of boys over their heads. I suppose it is for the good of the Church if the pope does it. But it's not just, Mary Jane, and it's not right.

She had worked herself into a passion and would have continued in defence of her sister for it was a sore subject with her but Mary Jane, seeing that all the dancers had come back, intervened pacifically:

—Now, Aunt Kate, you're giving scandal to Mr Browne who is of the other persuasion.[1]

Aunt Kate turned to Mr Browne, who was grinning at this allusion to his religion, and said hastily:

—O, I don't question the pope's being right. I'm only a stupid old woman and I wouldn't presume to do such a thing. But there's such a thing as common everyday politeness and gratitude. And if I were in Julia's place I'd tell that Father Healy straight up to his face . . .

—And besides, Aunt Kate, said Mary Jane, we really are all hungry and when we are hungry we are all very quarrelsome.

—And when we are thirsty we are also quarrelsome, added Mr Browne.

—So that we had better go to supper, said Mary Jane, and finish the discussion afterwards.

On the landing outside the drawing-room Gabriel found his wife and Mary Jane trying to persuade Miss Ivors to stay for supper. But Miss Ivors, who had put on her hat and was buttoning her cloak, would not stay. She did not feel in the least hungry and she had already overstayed her time.

—But only for ten minutes, Molly, said Mrs Conroy. That won't delay you.

—To take a pick itself, said Mary Jane, after all your dancing.

—I really couldn't, said Miss Ivors.

—I am afraid you didn't enjoy yourself at all, said Mary Jane hopelessly.

—Ever so much, I assure you, said Miss Ivors, but you really must let me run off now.

—But how can you get home? asked Mrs Conroy.

—O, it's only two steps up the quay.

Gabriel hesitated a moment and said:

—If you will allow me, Miss Ivors, I'll see you home if you really are obliged to go.

But Miss Ivors broke away from them.

—I won't hear of it, she cried. For goodness sake go in to your suppers and don't mind me. I'm quite well able to take care of myself.

—Well, you're the comical girl, Molly, said Mrs Conroy frankly.

—*Beannacht libh*,[2] cried Miss Ivors, with a laugh, as she ran down the staircase.

1. I.e., Protestant.   2. Good-bye (Gaelic). Literally "blessing on you."

Mary Jane gazed after her, a moody puzzled expression on her face, while Mrs Conroy leaned over the banisters to listen for the hall-door. Gabriel asked himself was he the cause of her abrupt departure. But she did not seem to be in ill humour: she had gone away laughing. He stared blankly down the staircase.

At that moment Aunt Kate came toddling out of the supper-room, almost wringing her hands in despair.

—Where is Gabriel? she cried. Where on earth is Gabriel? There's everyone waiting in there, stage to let, and nobody to carve the goose!

—Here I am, Aunt Kate! cried Gabriel, with sudden animation, ready to carve a flock of geese, if necessary.

A fat brown goose lay at one end of the table and at the other end, on a bed of creased paper strewn with sprigs of parsley, lay a great ham, stripped of its outer skin and peppered over with crust crumbs, a neat paper frill round its shin and beside this was a round of spiced beef. Between these rival ends ran parallel lines of side-dishes: two little minsters of jelly, red and yellow; a shallow dish full of blocks of blancmange and red jam, a large green leaf-shaped dish with a stalk-shaped handle, on which lay bunches of purple raisins and peeled almonds, a companion dish on which lay a solid rectangle of Smyrna figs, a dish of custard topped with grated nutmeg, a small bowl full of chocolates and sweets wrapped in gold and silver papers and a glass vase in which stood some tall celery stalks. In the centre of the table there stood, as sentries to a fruit-stand which upheld a pyramid of oranges and American apples, two squat old-fashioned decanters of cut glass, one containing port and the other dark sherry. On the closed square piano a pudding in a huge yellow dish lay in waiting and behind it were three squads of bottles of stout and ale and minerals, drawn up according to the colours of their uniforms, the first two black, with brown and red labels, the third and smallest squad white, with transverse green sashes.

Gabriel took his seat boldly at the head of the table and, having looked to the edge of the carver, plunged his fork firmly into the goose. He felt quite at ease now for he was an expert carver and liked nothing better than to find himself at the head of a well-laden table.

—Miss Furlong, what shall I send you? he asked. A wing or a slice of the breast?

—Just a small slice of the breast.

—Miss Higgins, what for you?

—O, anything at all, Mr Conroy.

While Gabriel and Miss Daly exchanged plates of goose and plates of ham and spiced beef Lily went from guest to guest with a dish of hot floury potatoes wrapped in a white napkin. This was Mary Jane's idea and she had also suggested apple sauce for the goose but Aunt Kate had said that plain roast goose without apple sauce had always been good enough for her and she hoped she might never eat worse. Mary Jane waited on her pupils and saw that they got the best slices and Aunt Kate and Aunt Julia opened and carried across from the piano bottles of stout and ale for the gentlemen and bottles of minerals for the ladies. There was a great deal of confusion and laughter and noise, the noise of orders and counter-orders, of knives and forks, of corks and glass-stoppers. Gabriel began to carve second helpings as soon as he had finished the first round without serving himself. Everyone protested loudly so that he compromised by taking a long draught of stout for he had found the carving hot work. Mary Jane settled down quietly to her supper but Aunt Kate and Aunt Julia were still toddling round the table, walking on each other's heels, getting in each other's way and giving each other unheeded orders. Mr Browne begged of them to sit down and eat their suppers and so did Gabriel but they said there was time enough so that, at last, Freddy Malins stood up and, capturing Aunt Kate, plumped her down on her chair amid general laughter.

When everyone had been well served Gabriel said, smiling:

—Now, if anyone wants a little more of what vulgar people call stuffing let him or her speak.

A chorus of voices invited him to begin his own supper and Lily came forward with three potatoes which she had reserved for him.

—Very well, said Gabriel amiably, as he took another preparatory draught, kindly forget my existence, ladies and gentlemen, for a few minutes.

He set to his supper and took no part in the conversation with which the table covered Lily's removal of the plates. The subject of talk was the opera company which was then at the Theatre Royal. Mr Bartell D'Arcy, the tenor, a dark-complexioned young man with a smart moustache, praised very highly the leading contralto of the company but Miss Furlong thought she had a rather vulgar style of production. Freddy Malins said there was a negro chieftain singing in the second part of the Gaiety pantomime who had one of the finest tenor voices he had every heard.

—Have you heard him? he asked Mr Bartell D'Arcy across the table.

—No, answered Mr Bartell D'Arcy carelessly.

—Because, Freddy Malins explained, now I'd be curious to hear your opinion of him. I think he has a grand voice.

—It takes Teddy to find out the really good things, said Mr Browne familiarly to the table.

—And why couldn't he have a voice too? asked Freddy Malins sharply. Is it because he's only a black?

Nobody answered this question and Mary Jane led the table back to the legitimate opera. One of her pupils had given her a pass for *Mignon*.[3] Of course it was very fine, she said, but it made her think of poor Georgina Burns. Mr Browne could go back farther still, to the old Italian companies that used to come to Dublin—Tietjens, Ilma de Murzka, Campanini, the great Trebelli, Giuglini, Ravelli, Aramburo. Those were the days, he said, when there was something like singing to be heard in Dublin. He told too of how the top gallery of the old Royal used to be packed night after night, of how one night an Italian tenor had sung five encores to *Let Me Like a Soldier Fall*,[4] introducing a high C every time, and of how the gallery boys would sometimes in their enthusiasm unyoke the horses from the carriage of some great *prima donna* and pull her themselves through the streets to her hotel. Why did they never play the grand old operas now, he asked, *Dinorah, Lucrezia Borgia?*[5] Because they could not get the voices to sing them: that was why.

3. Opera by Ambroise Thomas first produced in Paris in 1866 and in London in 1870.
4. This song, from the opera *Maritana* by W. Wallace (it actually begins "Yes! let me like a soldier fall"), ends on middle C; it would be a piece of exhibitionism to end on a high C, as Joyce's father, who had a good voice, used to do. Joyce's brother Stanislaus remembered the song as insufferable rubbish. Mr. Browne is not to be taken seriously as a music critic.
5. *Lucrezia Borgia* is an opera by Donizetti, first produced at La Scala, Milan, in 1833. *Dinorah* is an opera by Meyerbeer, first produced in Paris in 1859.

—O, well, said Mr Bartell D'Arcy, I presume there are as good singers to-day as there were then.

—Where are they? asked Mr Browne defiantly.

—In London, Paris, Milan, said Mr Bartell d'Arcy warmly. I suppose Caruso,[6] for example, is quite as good, if not better than any of the men you have mentioned.

—Maybe so, said Mr Browne. But I may tell you I doubt it strongly.

—O, I'd give anything to hear Caruso sing, said Mary Jane.

—For me, said Aunt Kate, who had been picking a bone, there was only one tenor. To please me, I mean. But I suppose none of you ever heard of him.

—Who was he, Miss Morkan? asked Mr Bartell D'Arcy politely.

—His name, said Aunt Kate, was Parkinson. I heard him when he was in his prime and I think he had then the purest tenor voice that was ever put into a man's throat.

—Strange, said Mr Bartell d'Arcy. I never even heard of him.

—Yes, yes, Miss Morkan is right, said Mr Browne. I remember hearing of old Parkinson but he's too far back for me.

—A beautiful pure sweet mellow English tenor, said Aunt Kate with enthusiasm.

Gabriel having finished, the huge pudding was transferred to the table. The clatter of forks and spoons began again. Gabriel's wife served out spoonfuls of the pudding and passed the plates down the table. Midway down they were held up by Mary Jane, who replenished them with raspberry or orange jelly or with blancmange and jam. The pudding was of Aunt Julia's making and she received praises for it from all quarters. She herself said that it was not quite brown enough.

—Well, I hope, Miss Morkan, said Mr Browne, that I'm brown enough for you because, you know, I'm all brown.

All the gentlemen, except Gabriel, ate some of the pudding out of compliment to Aunt Julia. As Gabriel never ate sweets the celery had been left for him. Freddy Malins also took a stalk of celery and ate it with his pudding. He had been told that celery was a capital thing for the blood and he was just then under doctor's care. Mrs Malins, who had been silent all through the supper, said that her son was going down to Mount Melleray in a week or so. The table then spoke of Mount Melleray, how bracing the air was down there, how hospitable the monks were and how they never asked for a penny-piece from their guests.

—And do you mean to say, asked Mr Browne incredulously, that a chap can go down there and put up there as if it were a hotel and live on the fat of the land and then come away without paying a farthing?

—O, most people give some donation to the monastery when they leave, said Mary Jane.

—I wish we had an institution like that in our Church, said Mr Browne candidly.

He was astonished to hear that the monks never spoke, got up at two in the morning and slept in their coffins. He asked what they did it for.

—That's the rule of the order, said Aunt Kate firmly.

6. Enrico Caruso (1873–1921), the great Italian dramatic tenor.

—Yes, but why? asked Mr Browne.

Aunt Kate repeated that it was the rule, that was all. Mr Browne still seemed not to understand. Freddy Malins explained to him, as best he could, that the monks were trying to make up for the sins committed by all the sinners in the outside world. The explanation was not very clear for Mr Browne grinned and said:

—I like that idea very much but wouldn't a comfortable spring bed do them as well as a coffin?

—The coffin, said Mary Jane, is to remind them of their last end.

As the subject had grown lugubrious it was buried in a silence of the table during which Mrs Malins could be heard saying to her neighbour in an indistinct undertone:

—They are very good men, the monks, very pious men.

The raisins and almonds and figs and apples and oranges and chocolates and sweets were now passed about the table and Aunt Julia invited all the guests to have either port or sherry. At first Mr Bartell D'Arcy refused to take either but one of his neighbours nudged him and whispered something to him upon which he allowed his glass to be filled. Gradually as the last glasses were being filled the conversation ceased. A pause followed, broken only by the noise of the wine and by unsettlings of chairs. The Misses Morkan, all three, looked down at the tablecloth. Someone coughed once or twice and then a few gentlemen patted the table gently as a signal for silence. The silence came and Gabriel pushed back his chair and stood up.

The patting at once grew louder in encouragement and then ceased altogether. Gabriel leaned his ten trembling fingers on the tablecloth and smiled nervously at the company. Meeting a row of upturned faces he raised his eyes to the chandelier. The piano was playing a waltz tune and he could hear the skirts sweeping against the drawing-room door. People, perhaps, were standing in the snow on the quay outside, gazing up at the lighted windows and listening to the waltz music. The air was pure there. In the distance lay the park where the trees were weighted with snow. The Wellington Monument wore a gleaming cap of snow that flashed westward over the white field of Fifteen Acres.

He began:

—Ladies and Gentlemen.

—It has fallen to my lot this evening, as in years past, to perform a very pleasing task but a task for which I am afraid my poor powers as a speaker are all too inadequate.

—No, no! said Mr Browne.

—But, however that may be, I can only ask you to-night to take the will for the deed and to lend me your attention for a few moments while I endeavour to express to you in words what my feelings are on this occasion.

—Ladies and Gentlemen. It is not the first time that we have gathered together under this hospitable roof, around this hospitable board. It is not the first time that we have been the recipients—or perhaps, I had better say, the victims—of the hospitality of certain good ladies.

He made a circle in the air with his arm and paused. Everyone laughed or smiled at Aunt Kate and Aunt Julia and Mary Jane who all turned crimson with pleasure. Gabriel went on more boldly:

—I feel more strongly with every recurring year that our country has no tradition which does it so much honour and which it should guard so jealously as that of its hospitality. It is a tradition that is unique as far as my experience goes (and I have visited not a few places abroad) among the modern nations. Some would say, perhaps, that with us it is rather a failing than anything to be boasted of. But granted even that, it is, to my mind, a princely failing, and one that I trust will long be cultivated among us. Of one thing, at least, I am sure. As long as this one roof shelters the good ladies aforesaid—and I wish from my heart it may do so for many and many a long year to come—the tradition of genuine warm-hearted courteous Irish hospitality, which our forefathers have handed down to us and which we in turn must hand down to our descendants, is still alive among us.

A hearty murmur of assent ran round the table. It shot through Gabriel's mind that Miss Ivors was not there and that she had gone away discourteously: and he said with confidence in himself:

—Ladies and Gentlemen.

—A new generation is growing up in our midst, a generation actuated by new ideas and new principles. It is serious and enthusiastic for these new ideas and its enthusiasm, even when it is misdirected, is, I believe, in the main sincere. But we are living in a sceptical and, if I may use the phrase, a thought-tormented age: and sometimes I fear that this new generation, educated or hypereducated as it is, will lack those qualities of humanity, of hospitality, of kindly humour which belonged to an older day. Listening to-night to the names of all those great singers of the past it seemed to me, I must confess, that we were living in a less spacious age. Those days might, without exaggeration, be called spacious days: and if they are gone beyond recall let us hope, at least, that in gatherings such as this we shall still speak of them with pride and affection, still cherish in our hearts the memory of those dead and gone great ones whose fame the world will not willingly let die.

—Hear, hear! said Mr Browne loudly.

—But yet, continued Gabriel, his voice falling into a softer inflection, there are always in gatherings such as this sadder thoughts that will recur to our minds: thoughts of the past, of youth, of changes, of absent faces that we miss here to-night. Our path through life is strewn with many such sad memories: and were we to brood upon them always we could not find the heart to go on bravely with our work among the living. We have all of us living duties and living affections which claim, and rightly claim, our strenuous endeavours.

—Therefore, I will not linger on the past. I will not let any gloomy moralising intrude upon us here to-night. Here we are gathered together for a brief moment from the bustle and rush of our everyday routine. We are met here as friends, in the spirit of good-fellowship, as colleagues, also to a certain extent, in the true spirit of *camaraderie*, and as the guests of—what shall I call them?—the Three Graces of the Dublin musical world.

The table burst into applause and laughter at this sally. Aunt Julia vainly asked each of her neighbours in turn to tell her what Gabriel had said.

—He says we are the Three Graces, Aunt Julia, said Mary Jane.

Aunt Julia did not understand but she looked up, smiling, at Gabriel, who continued in the same vein:

—Ladies and Gentlemen.

—I will not attempt to play to-night the part that Paris played on another occasion. I will not attempt to choose between them. The task would be an invidious one and one beyond my poor powers. For when I view them in turn, whether it be our chief hostess herself, whose good heart, whose too good heart, has become a byword with all who know her, or her sister, who seems to be gifted with perennial youth and whose singing must have been a surprise and a revelation to us all to-night, or, last but not least, when I consider our youngest hostess, talented, cheerful, hard-working and the best of nieces, I confess, Ladies and Gentlemen, that I do not know to which of them I should award the prize.

Gabriel glanced down at his aunts and, seeing the large smile on Aunt Julia's face and the tears which had risen to Aunt Kate's eyes, hastened to his close. He raised his glass of port gallantly, while every member of the company fingered a glass expectantly, and said loudly:

—Let us toast them all three together. Let us drink to their health, wealth, long life, happiness and prosperity and may they long continue to hold the proud and self-won position which they hold in their profession and the position of honour and affection which they hold in our hearts.

All the guests stood up, glass in hand, and, turning towards the three seated ladies, sang in unison, with Mr Browne as leader:

> For they are jolly gay fellows,
> For they are jolly gay fellows,
> For they are jolly gay fellows,
> Which nobody can deny.

Aunt Kate was making frank use of her handkerchief and even Aunt Julia seemed moved. Freddy Malins beat time with his pudding-fork and the singers turned towards one another, as if in melodious conference, while they sang, with emphasis:

> Unless he tells a lie,
> Unless he tells a lie.

Then, turning once more towards their hostesses, they sang:

> For they are jolly gay fellows,
> For they are jolly gay fellows,
> For they are jolly gay fellows,
> Which nobody can deny.

The acclamation which followed was taken up beyond the door of the supper-room by many of the other guests and renewed time after time, Freddy Malins acting as officer with his fork on high.

The piercing morning air came into the hall where they were standing so that Aunt Kate said:

—Close the door, somebody. Mrs Malins will get her death of cold.

—Browne is out there, Aunt Kate, said Mary Jane.

—Browne is everywhere, said Aunt Kate, lowering her voice.

Mary Jane laughed at her tone.

—Really, she said archly, he is very attentive.

—He has been laid on here like the gas, said Aunt Kate in the same tone, all during the Christmas.

She laughed herself this time good-humouredly and then added quickly:

　—But tell him to come in, Mary Jane, and close the door. I hope to goodness he didn't hear me.

　At that moment the hall-door was opened and Mr Browne came in from
the doorstep, laughing as if his heart would break. He was dressed in a long
green overcoat with mock astrakhan cuffs and collar and wore on his head an
oval fur cap. He pointed down the snow-covered quay from where the sound
of shrill prolonged whistling was borne in.

　—Teddy will have all the cabs in Dublin out, he said.

　Gabriel advanced from the little pantry behind the office, struggling into
his overcoat and, looking round the hall, said:

　—Gretta not down yet?

　—She's getting on her things, Gabriel, said Aunt Kate.

　—Who's playing up there? asked Gabriel.

　—Nobody. They're all gone.

　—O no, Aunt Kate, said Mary Jane. Bartell D'Arcy and Miss O'Callaghan
aren't gone yet.

　—Someone is strumming at the piano, anyhow, said Gabriel.

　Mary Jane glanced at Gabriel and Mr Browne and said with a shiver:

　—It makes me feel cold to look at you two gentlemen muffled up like that.
I wouldn't like to face your journey home at this hour.

　—I'd like nothing better this minute, said Mr Browne stoutly, than a rattling
fine walk in the country or a fast drive with a good spanking goer between the
shafts.

　—We used to have a very good horse and trap[7] at home, said Aunt Julia
sadly.

　—The never-to-be-forgotten Johnny, said Mary Jane, laughing.

　Aunt Kate and Gabriel laughed too.

　—Why, what was wonderful about Johnny? asked Mr Browne.

　—The late lamented Patrick Morkan, our grandfather, that is, explained
Gabriel, commonly known in his later years as the old gentleman, was a glue-
boiler.

　—O, now, Gabriel, said Aunt Kate, laughing, he had a starch mill.

　—Well, glue or starch, said Gabriel, the old gentleman had a horse by the
name of Johnny. And Johnny used to work in the old gentleman's mill, walking round and round in order to drive the mill. That was all very well; but
now comes the tragic part about Johnny. One fine day the old gentleman
thought he'd like to drive out with the quality[8] to a military review in the park.

　—The Lord have mercy on his soul, said Aunt Kate compassionately.

　—Amen, said Gabriel. So the old gentleman, as I said, harnessed Johnny
and put on his very best tall hat and his very best stock collar and drive out in
grand style from his ancestral mansion somewhere near Back Lane, I think.

　Everyone laughed, even Mrs Malins, at Gabriel's manner and Aunt Kate
said:

　—O now, Gabriel, he didn't live in Back Lane, really. Only the mill was
there.

　—Out from the mansion of his forefathers, continued Gabriel, he drove
with Johnny. And everything went on beautifully until Johnny came in sight
of King Billy's statue: and whether he fell in love with the horse King Billy sits

---

7. A two-wheeled horse-drawn carriage on springs.　　　8. People of rank or high social position.

on or whether he thought he was back again in the mill, anyhow he began to walk round the statue.

Gabriel paced in a circle round the hall in his goloshes amid the laughter of the others.

—Round and round he went, said Gabriel, and the old gentleman, who was a very pompous old gentleman, was highly indignant. *Go on, sir! What do you mean, sir? Johnny! Johnny! Most extraordinary conduct! Can't understand the horse!*

The peals of laughter which followed Gabriel's imitation of the incident were interrupted by a resounding knock at the hall-door. Mary Jane ran to open it and let in Freddy Malins. Freddy Malins, with his hat well back on his head and his shoulders humped with cold, was puffing and steaming after his exertions.

—I could only get one cab, he said.

—O, we'll find another along the quay, said Gabriel.

—Yes, said Aunt Kate. Better not keep Mrs Malins standing in the draught.

Mrs Malins was helped down the front steps by her son and Mr Browne and, after many manœuvres, hoisted into the cab. Freddy Malins clambered in after her and spent a long time settling her on the seat, Mr Browne helping him with advice. At last she was settled comfortably and Freddy Malins invited Mr Browne into the cab. There was a good deal of confused talk, and then Mr Browne got into the cab. The cabman settled his rug over his knees, and bent down for the address. The confusion grew greater and the cabman was directed differently by Freddy Malins and Mr Browne, each of whom had his head out through a window of the cab. The difficulty was to know where to drop Mr Browne along the route and Aunt Kate, Aunt Julia and Mary Jane helped the discussion from the doorstep with cross-directions and contradictions and abundance of laughter. As for Freddy Malins he was speechless with laughter. He popped his head in and out of the window every moment, to the great danger of his hat, and told his mother how the discussion was progressing till at last Mr Browne shouted to the bewildered cabman above the din of everybody's laughter:

—Do you know Trinity College?

—Yes, sir, said the cabman.

—Well, drive bang up against Trinity College gates, said Mr Browne, and then we'll tell you where to go. You understand now?

—Yes, sir, said the cabman.

—Make like a bird for Trinity College.

—Right, sir, cried the cabman.

The horse was whipped up and the cab rattled off along the quay amid a chorus of laughter and adieus.

Gabriel had not gone to the door with the others. He was in a dark part of the hall gazing up the staircase. A woman was standing near the top of the first flight, in the shadow also. He could not see her face but he could see the terracotta and salmonpink panels of her skirt which the shadow made appear black and white. It was his wife. She was leaning on the banisters, listening to something. Gabriel was surprised at her stillness and strained his ear to listen also. But he could hear little save the noise of laughter and dispute on the front steps, a few chords struck on the piano and a few notes of a man's voice singing.

He stood still in the gloom of the hall, trying to catch the air that the voice was singing and gazing up at his wife. There was grace and mystery in her attitude as if she were a symbol of something. He asked himself what is a woman standing on the stairs in the shadow, listening to distant music, a symbol of. If he were a painter he would paint her in that attitude. Her blue felt hat would show off the bronze of her hair against the darkness and the dark panels of her skirt would show off the light ones. *Distant Music* he would call the picture if he were a painter.

The hall-door was closed; and Aunt Kate, Aunt Julia and Mary Jane came down the hall, still laughing.

—Well, isn't Freddy terrible? said Mary Jane. He's really terrible.

Gabriel said nothing but pointed up the stairs towards where his wife was standing. Now that the hall-door was closed the voice and the piano could be heard more clearly. Gabriel held up his hand for them to be silent. The song seemed to be in the old Irish tonality and the singer seemed uncertain both of his words and of his voice. The voice, made plaintive by distance and by the singer's hoarseness, faintly illuminated the cadence of the air with words expressing grief:

> O, the rain falls on my heavy locks
> And the dew wets my skin,
> My babe lies cold . . .

—O, exclaimed Mary Jane. It's Bartell D'Arcy singing and he wouldn't sing all the night. O, I'll get him to sing a song before he goes.

—O do, Mary Jane, said Aunt Kate.

Mary Jane brushed past the others and ran to the staircase but before she reached it the singing stopped and the piano was closed abruptly.

—O, what a pity! she cried. Is he coming down, Gretta?

Gabriel heard his wife answer yes and saw her come down towards them. A few steps behind her were Mr Bartell D'Arcy and Miss O'Callaghan.

—O, Mr D'Arcy, cried Mary Jane, it's downright mean of you to break off like that when we were all in raptures listening to you.

—I have been at him all the evening, said Miss O'Callaghan, and Mrs Conroy too and he told us he had a dreadful cold and couldn't sing.

—O, Mr D'Arcy, said Aunt Kate, now that was a great fib to tell.

—Can't you see that I'm as hoarse as a crow? said Mr D'Arcy roughly.

He went into the pantry hastily and put on his overcoat. The others, taken aback by his rude speech, could find nothing to say. Aunt Kate wrinkled her brows and made signs to the others to drop the subject. Mr D'Arcy stood swathing his neck carefully and frowning.

—It's the weather, said Aunt Julia, after a pause.

—Yes, everybody has colds, said Aunt Kate readily, everybody.

—They say, said Mary Jane, we haven't had snow like it for thirty years; and I read this morning in the newspapers that the snow is general all over Ireland.

—I love the look of snow, said Aunt Julia sadly.

—So do I, said Miss O'Callaghan. I think Christmas is never really Christmas unless we have the snow on the ground.

—But poor Mr D'Arcy doesn't like the snow, said Aunt Kate, smiling.

Mr D'Arcy came from the pantry, full swathed and buttoned, and in a repentant tone told them the history of his cold. Everyone gave him advice and said it was a great pity and urged him to be very careful of his throat in the night air. Gabriel watched his wife who did not join in the conversation. She was standing right under the dusty fanlight and the flame of the gas lit up the rich bronze of her hair which he had seen her drying at the fire a few days before. She was in the same attitude and seemed unaware of the talk about her. At last she turned towards them and Gabriel saw that there was colour on her cheeks and that her eyes were shining. A sudden tide of joy went leaping out of his heart.

—Mr D'Arcy, she said, what is the name of that song you were singing?

—It's called *The Lass of Aughrim*,[9] said Mr D'Arcy, but I couldn't remember it properly. Why? Do you know it?

—*The Lass of Aughrim*, she repeated. I couldn't think of the name.

—It's a very nice air, said Mary Jane. I'm sorry you were not in voice tonight.

—Now, Mary Jane, said Aunt Kate, don't annoy Mr D'Arcy. I won't have him annoyed.

Seeing that all were ready to start she shepherded them to the door where good-night was said:

—Well, good-night, Aunt Kate, and thanks for the pleasant evening.

—Good-night, Gabriel. Good-night, Gretta!

—Good-night, Aunt Kate, and thanks ever so much. Good-night, Aunt Julia.

—O, good-night, Gretta, I didn't see you.

—Good-night, Mr D'Arcy. Good-night, Miss O'Callaghan.

—Good-night, Miss Morkan.

—Good-night, again.

—Good-night, all. Safe home.

—Good-night. Good-night.

The morning was still dark. A dull yellow light brooded over the houses and the river; and the sky seemed to be descending. It was slushy underfoot; and only streaks and patches of snow lay on the roofs, on the parapets of the quay and on the area railings. The lamps were still burning redly in the murky air and, across the river, the palace of the Four Courts stood out menacingly against the heavy sky.

She was walking on before him with Mr Bartell D'Arcy, her shoes in a brown parcel tucked under one arm and her hands holding her skirt up from the slush. She had no longer any grace of attitude but Gabriel's eyes were still bright with happiness. The blood went bounding along his veins; and the thoughts went rioting through his brain, proud, joyful, tender, valorous.

She was walking on before him so lightly and so erect that he longed to run after her noiselessly, catch her by the shoulders and say something foolish and affectionate into her ear. She seemed to him so frail that he longed to defend her against something and then to be alone with her. Moments of their secret life together burst like stars upon his memory. A heliotrope envelope was lying beside his breakfast-cup and he was caressing it with his hand. Birds were twittering in the ivy and the sunny web of the curtain was shimmering along

9. An Irish version of a ballad about a girl deserted by her lover whom she later tries to find, bringing the baby she had by him. Other versions are called *Love Gregory* and *Lord Gregory* (the name of the deserting lover), *The Lass of Lochryan*, and *The Lass of Ocram*.

the floor: he could not eat for happiness. They were standing on the crowded platform and he was placing a ticket inside the warm palm of her glove. He was standing with her in the cold, looking in through a grated window at a man making bottles in a roaring furnace. It was very cold. Her face, fragrant in the cold air, was quite close to his; and suddenly she called out to the man at the furnace:

—Is the fire hot, sir?

But the man could not hear her with the noise of the furnace. It was just as well. He might have answered rudely.

A wave of yet more tender joy escaped from his heart and went coursing in warm flood along his arteries. Like the tender fires of stars moments of their life together, that no one knew of or would ever know of, broke upon and illumined his memory. He longed to recall to her those moments, to make her forget the years of their dull existence together and remember only their moments of ecstasy. For the years, he felt, had not quenched his soul or hers. Their children, his writing, her household cares had not quenched all their souls' tender fire. In one letter that he had written to her then he had said: *Why is it that words like these seem to me so dull and cold? Is it because there is no word tender enough to be your name?*

Like distant music these words that he had written years before were borne towards him from the past. He longed to be alone with her. When the others had gone away, when he and she were in their room in the hotel, then they would be alone together. He would call her softly:

—Gretta!

Perhaps she would not hear at once: she would be undressing. Then something in his voice would strike her. She would turn and look at him. . . .

At the corner of Winetavern Street they met a cab. He was glad of its rattling noise as it saved him from conversation. She was looking out of the window and seemed tired. The others spoke only a few words, pointing out some building or street. The horse galloped along wearily under the murky morning sky, dragging his old rattling box after his heels, and Gabriel was again in a cab with her, galloping to catch the boat, galloping to their honeymoon.

As the cab drove across O'Connell Bridge[1] Miss O'Callaghan said:

—They say you never cross O'Connell Bridge without seeing a white horse.

—I see a white man this time, said Gabriel.

—Where? asked Mr Bartell D'Arcy.

Gabriel pointed to the statue, on which lay patches of snow. Then he nodded familiarly to it and waved his hand.

—Good-night, Dan, he said gaily.

When the cab drew up before the hotel Gabriel jumped out and, in spite of Mr Bartell D'Arcy's protest, paid the driver. He gave the man a shilling over his fare. The man saluted and said:

—A prosperous New Year to you, sir.

—The same to you, said Gabriel cordially.

She leaned for a moment on his arm in getting out of the cab and while standing at the curbstone, bidding the others good-night. She leaned lightly on his arm, as lightly as when she had danced with him a few hours before.

---

1. Daniel O'Connell (1775–1847), Irish nationalist, statesman, and orator. His statue stands by O'Connell Bridge in Dublin.

He had felt proud and happy then, happy that she was his, proud of her grace and wifely carriage. But now, after the kindling again of so many memories, the first touch of her body, musical and strange and perfumed, sent through him a keen pang of lust. Under cover of her silence he pressed her arm closely to his side; and, as they stood at the hotel door, he felt that they had escaped from their lives and duties, escaped from home and friends and run away together with wild and radiant hearts to a new adventure.

An old man was dozing in a great hooded chair in the hall. He lit a candle in the office and went before them to the stairs. They followed him in silence, their feet falling in soft thuds on the thickly carpeted stairs. She mounted the stairs behind the porter, her head bowed in the ascent, her frail shoulders curved as with a burden, her skirt girt tightly about her. He could have flung his arms about her hips and held her still for his arms were trembling with desire to seize her and only the stress of his nails against the palms of his hands held the wild impulse of his body in check. The porter halted on the stairs to settle his guttering candle. They halted too on the steps below him. In the silence Gabriel could hear the falling of the molten wax into the tray and the thumping of his own heart against his ribs.

The porter led them along a corridor and opened a door. Then he set his unstable candle down on a toilet-table and asked at what hour they were to be called in the morning.

—Eight, said Gabriel.

The porter pointed to the tap of the electric-light and began a muttered apology but Gabriel cut him short.

—We don't want any light. We have light enough from the street. And I say, he added, pointing to the candle, you might remove that handsome article, like a good man.

The porter took up his candle again, but slowly for he was surprised by such a novel idea. Then he mumbled good-night and went out. Gabriel shot the lock to.

A ghostly light from the street lamp lay in a long shaft from one window to the door. Gabriel threw his overcoat and hat on a couch and crossed the room towards the window. He looked down into the street in order that his emotion might calm a little. Then he turned and leaned against a chest of drawers with his back to the light. She had taken off her hat and cloak and was standing before a large swinging mirror, unhooking her waist. Gabriel paused for a few moments, watching her, and then said:

—Gretta!

She turned away from the mirror slowly and walked along the shaft of light towards him. Her face looked so serious and weary that the words would not pass Gabriel's lips. No, it was not the moment yet.

—You looked tired, he said.

—I am a little, she answered.

—You don't feel ill or weak?

—No, tired: that's all.

She went on to the window and stood there, looking out. Gabriel waited again and then, fearing that diffidence was about to conquer him, he said abruptly:

—By the way, Gretta!

—What is it?

—You know that poor fellow Malins? he said quickly.

—Yes. What about him?

—Well, poor fellow, he's a decent sort of chap after all, continued Gabriel in a false voice. He gave me back that sovereign I lent him and I didn't expect it really. It's a pity he wouldn't keep away from that Browne, because he's not a bad fellow at heart.

He was trembling now with annoyance. Why did she seem so abstracted? He did not know how he could begin. Was she annoyed, too, about something? If she would only turn to him or come to him of her own accord! To take her as she was would be brutal. No, he must see some ardour in her eyes first. He longed to be master of her strange mood.

—When did you lend him the pound? she asked, after a pause.

Gabriel strove to restrain himself from breaking out into brutal language about the sottish Malins and his pound. He longed to cry to her from his soul, to crush her body against his, to overmaster her. But he said:

—O, at Christmas, when he opened that little Christmas-card shop in Henry Street.

He was in such a fever of rage and desire that he did not hear her come from the window. She stood before him for an instant, looking at him strangely. Then, suddenly raising herself on tiptoe and resting her hands lightly on his shoulders, she kissed him.

—You are a very generous person, Gabriel, she said.

Gabriel, trembling with delight at her sudden kiss and at the quaintness of her phrase, put his hands on her hair and began smoothing it back, scarcely touching it with his fingers. The washing had made it fine and brilliant. His heart was brimming over with happiness. Just when he was wishing for it she had come to him of her own accord. Perhaps her thoughts had been running with his. Perhaps she had felt the impetuous desire that was in him and then the yielding mood had come upon her. Now that she had fallen to him so easily he wondered why he had been so diffident.

He stood, holding her head between his hands. Then, slipping one arm swiftly about her body and drawing her towards him, he said softly:

—Gretta dear, what are you thinking about?

She did not answer nor yield wholly to his arm. He said again, softly:

—Tell me what it is, Gretta. I think I know what is the matter. Do I know?

She did not answer at once. Then she said in an outburst of tears:

—O, I am thinking about that song, The Lass of Aughrim.

She broke loose from him and ran to the bed and, throwing her arms across the bed-rail, hid her face. Gabriel stood stock-still for a moment in astonishment and then followed her. As he passed in the way of the cheval-glass he caught sight of himself in full length, his broad, well-filled shirt-front, the face whose expression always puzzled him when he saw it in a mirror and his glimmering gilt-rimmed eyeglasses. He halted a few paces from her and said:

—What about the song? Why does that make you cry?

She raised her head from her arms and dried her eyes with the back of her hand like a child. A kinder note than he had intended went into his voice.

—Why, Gretta? he asked.

—I am thinking about a person long ago who used to sing that song.

—And who was the person long ago? asked Gabriel, smiling.

—It was a person I used to know in Galway when I was living with my grandmother, she said.

The smile passed away from Gabriel's face. A dull anger began to gather again at the back of his mind and the dull fires of his lust began to glow angrily in his veins.

—Someone you were in love with? he asked ironically.

—It was a young boy I used to know, she answered, named Michael Furey. He used to sing that song, *The Lass of Aughrim*. He was very delicate.

Gabriel was silent. He did not wish her to think that he was interested in this delicate boy.

—I can see him so plainly, she said after a moment. Such eyes as he had: big dark eyes! And such an expression in them—an expression!

—O then, you were in love with him? said Gabriel.

—I used to go out walking with him, she said, when I was in Galway.

A thought flew across Gabriel's mind.

—Perhaps that was why you wanted to go to Galway with that Ivors girl? he said coldly.

She looked at him and asked in surprise:

—What for?

Her eyes made Gabriel feel awkward. He shrugged his shoulders and said:

—How do I know! To see him perhaps.

She looked away from him along the shaft of light towards the window in silence.

—He is dead, she said at length. He died when he was only seventeen. Isn't it a terrible thing to die so young as that?

—What was he? asked Gabriel, still ironically.

—He was in the gasworks, she said.

Gabriel felt humiliated by the failure of his irony and by the evocation of this figure from the dead, a boy in the gasworks. While he had been full of memories of their secret life together, full of tenderness and joy and desire, she had been comparing him in her mind with another. A shameful consciousness of his own person assailed him. He saw himself as a ludicrous figure, acting as a pennyboy for his aunts, a nervous well-meaning sentimentalist, orating to vulgarians and idealising his own clownish lusts, the pitiable fatuous fellow he had caught a glimpse of in the mirror. Instinctively he turned his back more to the light lest she might see the shame that burned upon his forehead.

He tried to keep up his tone of cold interrogation but his voice when he spoke was humble and indifferent.

—I suppose you were in love with this Michael Furey, Gretta, he said.

—I was great with him at that time, she said.

Her voice was veiled and sad. Gabriel, feeling now how vain it would be to try to lead her whither he had purposed, caressed one of her hands and said, also sadly:

—And what did he die of so young, Gretta? Consumption, was it?

—I think he died for me, she answered.

A vague terror seized Gabriel at this answer as if, at that hour when he had hoped to triumph, some impalpable and vindictive being was coming against him, gathering forces against him in its vague world. But he shook himself free of it with an effort of reason and continued to caress her hand. He did not question her again for he felt that she would tell him of herself. Her hand was warm and moist: it did not respond to his touch but he continued to caress it just as he had caressed her first letter to him that spring morning.

—It was in the winter, she said, about the beginning of the winter when I was going to leave my grandmother's and come up here to the convent. And he was ill at the time in his lodgings in Galway and wouldn't be let out and his people in Oughterard were written to. He was in decline, they said, or something like that. I never knew rightly.

She paused for a moment and sighed.

—Poor fellow, she said. He was very fond of me and he was such a gentle boy. We used to go out together, walking, you know, Gabriel, like the way they do in the country. He was going to study singing only for his health. He had a very good voice, poor Michael Furey.

—Well; and then? asked Gabriel.

—And then when it came to the time for me to leave Galway and come up to the convent he was much worse and I wouldn't be let see him so I wrote a letter saying I was going up to Dublin and would be back in the summer and hoping he would be better then.

She paused for a moment to get her voice under control and then went on:

—Then the night before I left I was in my grandmother's house in Nuns' Island, packing up, and I heard gravel thrown up against the window. The window was so wet I couldn't see so I ran downstairs as I was and slipped out the back into the garden and there was the poor fellow at the end of the garden, shivering.

—And did you not tell him to go back? asked Gabriel.

—I implored him to go home at once and told him he would get his death in the rain. But he said he did not want to live. I can see his eyes as well as well! He was standing at the end of the wall where there was a tree.

—And did he go home? asked Gabriel.

—Yes, he went home. And when I was only a week in the convent he died and he was buried in Oughterard where his people came from. O, the day I heard that, that he was dead!

She stopped, choking with sobs, and overcome by emotion, flung herself face downward on the bed, sobbing in the quilt. Gabriel held her hand for a moment longer, irresolutely, and then, shy of intruding on her grief, let it fall gently and walked quietly to the window.

She was fast asleep.

Gabriel, leaning on his elbow, looked for a few moments unresentfully on her tangled hair and half-open mouth, listening to her deep-drawn breath. So she had had that romance in her life: a man had died for her sake. It hardly pained him now to think how poor a part he, her husband, had played in her life. He watched her while she slept as though he and she had never lived together as man and wife. His curious eyes rested long upon her face and on her hair: and, as he thought of what she must have been then, in that time of her first girlish beauty, a strange friendly pity for her entered his soul. He did not like to say even to himself that her face was no longer beautiful but he knew that it was no longer the face for which Michael Furey had braved death.

Perhaps she had not told him all the story. His eyes moved to the chair over which she had thrown some of her clothes. A petticoat string dangled to the floor. One boot stood upright, its limp upper fallen down: the fellow of it lay upon its side. He wondered at his riot of emotions of an hour before. From what had it proceeded? From his aunt's supper, from his own foolish speech, from the wine and dancing, the merry-making when saying good-night in the hall, the pleasure of the walk along the river in the snow. Poor Aunt Julia! She, too, would soon be a shade with the shade of Patrick Morkan and his horse. He had caught that haggard look upon her face for a moment when she was singing *Arrayed for the Bridal*. Soon, perhaps, he would be sitting in that same drawing-room, dressed in black, his silk hat on his knees. The blinds would be drawn down and Aunt Kate would be sitting beside him, crying and blowing her nose and telling him how Julia had died. He would cast about in his mind for some words that might console her, and would find only lame and useless ones. Yes, yes: that would happen very soon.

The air of the room chilled his shoulders. He stretched himself cautiously along under the sheets and lay down beside his wife. One by one they were all becoming shades. Better pass boldly into that other world, in the full glory of some passion, than fade and wither dismally with age. He thought of how she who lay beside him had locked in her heart for so many years that image of her lover's eyes when he had told her that he did not wish to live.

Generous tears filled Gabriel's eyes. He had never felt like that himself towards any woman but he knew that such a feeling must be love. The tears gathered more thickly in his eyes and in the partial darkness he imagined he saw the form of a young man standing under a dripping tree. Other forms were near. His soul had approached that region where dwell the vast hosts of the dead. He was conscious of, but could not apprehend, their wayward and flickering existence. His own identity was fading out into a grey impalpable world: the solid world itself which these dead had one time reared and lived in was dissolving and dwindling.

A few light taps upon the pane made him turn to the window. It had begun to snow again. He watched sleepily the flakes, silver and dark, falling obliquely against the lamplight. The time had come for him to set out on his journey westward. Yes, the newspapers were right: snow was general all over Ireland. It was falling on every part of the dark central plain, on the treeless hills, falling softly upon the Bog of Allen[2] and, farther westward, softly falling into the dark mutinous Shannon waves. It was falling, too, upon every part of the lonely churchyard on the hill where Michael Furey lay buried. It lay thickly drifted on the crooked crosses and headstones, on the spears of the little gate, on the barren thorns. His soul swooned slowly as he heard the snow falling faintly through the universe and faintly falling, like the descent of their last end, upon all the living and the dead.

1914

---

2. The name given to many separate peat bogs between the rivers Liffey (which runs through Dublin) and Shannon (which runs through the central plain of Ireland.

From Ulysses[1]

[Proteus][2]

Ineluctable modality of the visible: at least that if no more, thought through my eyes.[3] Signatures of all things[4] I am here to read, seaspawn and seawrack, the nearing tide, that rusty boot. Snotgreen, bluesilver, rust: coloured signs. Limits of the diaphane.[5] But he adds: in bodies. Then he was aware of them bodies before of them coloured. How? By knocking his sconce against them, sure. Go easy. Bald he was and a millionaire, *maestro di color che sanno*.[6] Limit of the diaphane in. Why in? Diaphane, adiaphane.[7] If you can put your five fingers through it, it is a gate, if not a door. Shut your eyes and see.

Stephen closed his eyes to hear his boots crush crackling wrack and shells. You are walking through it howsomever. I am, a stride at a time. A very short space of time through very short times of space. Five, six: the *Nacheinander*.[8] Exactly: and that is the ineluctable modality of the audible. Open your eyes. No. Jesus! If I fell over a cliff that beetles o'er his base,[9] fell through the *Nebeneinander*[1] ineluctably. I am getting on nicely in the dark. My ash sword hangs at my side. Tap with it: they do.[2] My two feet in his boots[3] are at the ends of my legs, *nebeneinander*. Sounds solid: made by the mallet of *Los demiurgos*.[4] Am I walking into eternity along Sandymount strand? Crush, crack, crik, crick. Wild sea money. Dominie[5] Deasy kens them a'.

1. *Ulysses* was first published in book form on February 2, 1922, Joyce's fortieth birthday. The text given here has been collated with the 1932 Odyssey Press edition.
2. *Proteus* is so titled because of the deliberate analogies that exist between it and the description of Proteus in *Odyssey* 4. (Joyce did not title any of the episodes in *Ulysses*, but the names are his; he used them in correspondence and in talk with friends.)
   In Homer's *Odyssey*, Proteus is the changing sea god who continually alters his shape: when Telemachus, the son of Ulysses, asks Menelaus for help in finding his father, Menelaus tells him that he encountered Proteus by the seashore on the island of Pharos "in front of Egypt," and that, by holding on to him while he changed from one shape to another, he was able to force him to tell what had happened to Ulysses and the other Greek heroes of the Trojan war. In Joyce's narrative, Stephen Dedalus (who, like Homer's Telemachus, is looking for a father, but not in the literal "consubstantial" sense) is walking by the Dublin shore alone, "along Sandymount strand," speculating on the shifting shapes of things and the possibility of knowing truth by mere appearances.
   First Stephen meditates on the "modality of the visible" and on the mystical notion that God writes his signature on all His works; then on the "modality of the audible," closing his eyes and trying to know reality simply through the sense of hearing. As he continues his walk, the people and objects he sees mingle in his thoughts with memories of his past relations with his family, of his schooldays, his residence in Paris whence he was recalled by his mother's fatal illness, his feeling of guilt about his mother's death (he had refused to kneel down and pray at her bedside, because he considered it would be a betrayal of his integrity as an unbeliever), and a variety of speculations about life and reality often derived from mystical works he had read "in the stagnant bay of Marsh's library" (in Dublin). The highly theoretical, inquiring, musing, speculating mind of Stephen is in sharp contrast to the practical, humane, sensual, concrete imagination of the book's

real hero, Leopold Bloom, but there are also significant parallels between the streams of consciousness of the two. Some of the more important themes that emerge in Stephen's reverie are pointed out in the footnotes.
3. I.e., the sense of sight provides an unavoidable way ("ineluctable modality") of knowing reality, the knowledge thus provided being a kind of "thought through [the] eyes."
4. From Jackob Böhme (1575–1624), German mystic.
5. Transparency. Stephen is speculating on Aristotle's view of perception as developed in his *De Anima*.
6. There was a tradition that Aristotle was bald, with thin legs, small eyes, and a lisp. Aristotle is also traditionally supposed to have inherited considerable wealth and to have been presented with a fortune by his former pupil Alexander the Great. The Italian phrase is Dante's description of Aristotle in the *Inferno*, and means "the master of them that know."
7. What is not transparent (opposite of "diaphane").
8. "After one another." Stephen, with eyes shut, is now sensing reality through the sense of sound only: unlike sight, sound falls on the sense of hearing in chronological sequence, one sound after another.
9. "What if it tempt you toward the flood, my lord. / Or to the dreadful summit of the cliff / That beetles o'er his base into the sea" (*Hamlet* 1.4.69–71).
1. Beside one another.
2. I.e., Stephen is still walking with his eyes shut, tapping with his "ash sword" (the walking stick of ash wood he always carried), as "they" (i.e., blind people) do.
3. I.e., Buck Mulligan's. Stephen, lacking boots of his own, had borrowed a castoff pair of Mulligan's.
4. The Demiurge, supernatural being who made the world in subordination to God. The mystical notion of the Demiurge who created the world haunts Stephen's mind; it is the Demiurge who writes his signature on created objects and whose mallet fashioned them. The world, sensed by the ear only, "sounds solid," as though made by the Demiurge's hammer.
5. Schoolmaster; Mr. Deasy was the headmaster of the school where Stephen taught (the previous episode has

> *Won't you come to Sandymount,*
> *Madeline the mare?*

Rhythm begins, you see. I hear. A catalectic tetrameter[6] of iambs marching. No, agallop: *deline the mare.*

Open your eyes now. I will. One moment. Has all vanished since? If I open and am for ever in the black adiaphane. *Basta!*[7] I will see if I can see.

See now. There all the time without you: and ever shall be, world without end.

They came down the steps from Leahy's terrace prudently, *Frauenzimmer:*[8] and down the shelving shore flabbily, their splayed feet sinking in the silted sand. Like me, like Algy,[9] coming down to our mighty mother. Number one swung lourdily[1] her midwife's bag, the other's gamp[2] poked in the beach. From the liberties, out for the day. Mrs Florence MacCabe, relict of the late Patk MacCabe,[3] deeply lamented, of Bride Street. One of her sisterhood lugged me squealing into life. Creation from nothing. What has she in the bag? A misbirth with a trailing navelcord, hushed in ruddy wool. The cords of all link back, strandentwining cable of all flesh. That is why mystic monks. Will you be as gods? Gaze in your *omphalos.* Hello. Kinch here. Put me on to Edenville. Aleph, alpha: nought, nought, one.[4]

Spouse and helpmate of Adam Kadmon: Heva,[5] naked Eve. She had no navel. Gaze. Belly without blemish, bulging big, a buckler of taut vellum, no, whiteheaped corn, orient and immortal, standing from everlasting to everlasting. Womb of sin.[6]

Wombed in sin darkness I was too, made not begotten. By them, the man with my voice and my eyes and a ghostwoman with ashes on her breath.[7] They clasped and sundered, did the coupler's will. From before the ages He willed me and now may not will me away or ever. A *lex eterna*[8] stays about Him. Is that then the divine substance wherein Father and Son are consubstantial? Where is poor dear Arius[9] to try conclusions? Warring his life long on the

---

shown Stephen teaching). "Kens them a'": knows them all; Stephen is putting Deasy into a mock-Scottish folk song.

6. The first of the two lines of popular verse that have come into Stephen's head consists metrically of four iambic feet ("tetrameter") with the last foot unlike the first, not defective ("catalectic").

7. "Enough!" (Italian).

8. Here "midwives"; Stephen sees them coming from Leahy's Terrace, which runs by the beach.

9. Algernon Charles Swinburne, who wrote: "I will go back to the great sweet mother, / Mother and lover of men, the sea. / I will go down to her, I and none other" (*The Triumph of Time,* lines 1–3).

1. Heavily (coined by Stephen from the French *lourd*). Stephen, like Joyce, had studied modern languages at University College, Dublin, and his preoccupation with words and languages is part of his character as potential literary artist.

2. Umbrella; and perhaps reference to Mrs. Gamp, the nurse in Dickens's *Martin Chuzzlewit.*

3. Stephen imagines the first midwife is called Mrs. MacCabe. "Relict": widow.

4. Stephen is speculating on the mystical significance of the naval cord, seeing it as linking the generations, the combined navel cords stretching back to Adam and Eve. A mystic gazed in his *omphalos* (navel) to make contact with the first man. Stephen thinks of himself ("Kinch," his nickname) calling up Adam in "Eden-

ville" through his navel, using the line of linked navel cords as a telephone line. Adam's telephone number, "Aleph, alpha: nought, nought, one," begins with the first letters of the Hebrew and of the Greek alphabet to suggest the great primeval number.

5. Hebrew for Eve. Because she was not born in the regular way, but created from Adam's rib, she had no navel. "Adam Kadman": Adam the Beginner, so called in Hebrew cabalistic literature of the Middle Ages.

6. Stephen is led, through reflection on Eve's navelless "belly without blemish," to a recollection of the description of the original Eden (Paradise) by Thomas Traherne (ca. 1637–1674), from whose prose *Centuries of Meditation* he quotes: "The corn was orient and immortal wheat, which should never be reaped, nor was ever sown. I thought it had stood from everlasting to everlasting." But immediately afterward Stephen reflects that such language is inappropriate to Eve's body, as hers was the "womb of sin"—i.e., she first ate the fatal apple and brought forth sin.

7. Stephen is haunted by thoughts of his mother in this guise.

8. Eternal law. God's eternal law, Stephen reflects, willed his birth from the beginning. He then goes on to speculate on the nature of the divine substance and whether God the Father and God the Son are of the same substance ("consubstantial").

9. Third-century theologian who "tried conclusions" on this matter, maintaining that Christ was less divine

contransmagnificandjewbangtantiality.[1] Illstarred heresiarch.[2] In a Greek watercloset he breathed his last: *euthanasia*. With beaded mitre and with crozier, stalled upon his throne, widower of a widowed see, with upstiffed omophorion, with clotted hinderparts.

Airs romped round him, nipping and eager airs. They are coming, waves. The whitemaned seahorses, champing, brightwindbridled, the steeds of Mananaan.[3]

I mustn't forget his letter for the press. And after? The Ship, half twelve. By the way go easy with that money like a good young imbecile. Yes, I must.[4]

His pace slackened. Here. Am I going to aunt Sara's or not? My consubstantial father's voice. Did you see anything of your artist brother Stephen lately? No? Sure he's not down in Strasburg terrace with his aunt Sally? Couldn't he fly a bit higher than that, eh? And and and and tell us Stephen, how is uncle Si? O weeping God, the things I married into. De boys up in de hayloft. The drunken little costdrawer and his brother, the cornet player. Highly respectable gondoliers. And skeweyed Walter sirring his father, no less. Sir. Yes, sir. No, sir. Jesus wept: and no wonder, by Christ.[5]

I pull the wheezy bell of their shuttered cottage: and wait. They take me for a dun, peer out from a coign of vantage.[6]

—It's Stephen, sir.

—Let him in. Let Stephen in.

A bolt drawn back and Walter welcomes me.

—We thought you were someone else.

In his broad bed nuncle Richie, pillowed and blanketed, extends over the hillock of his knees a sturdy forearm. Cleanchested. He has washed the upper moiety.

—Morrow, nephew.

He lays aside the lapboard whereon he drafts his bills of costs for the eyes of master Goff and master Shapland Tandy, filing consents and common searches and a writ of *Duces Tecum*.[7] A bogoak frame over his bald head: Wilde's *Requiescat*.[8] The drone of his misleading whistle brings Walter back.

—Yes, sir?

—Malt[9] for Richie and Stephen, tell mother. Where is she?

—Bathing Crissie, sir.

than God (Arius' views were condemned as heretical by the Council of Nicaea in 325).

1. Ironic "portmanteau word" made up of terms connected with the Arian controversy—"consubstantial," "transubstantial" (of a substance that changes into another)—and with the facts of Christ's nature (e.g., "Jew"; Jesus was a Jew, as Leopold Bloom in a later episode reminds an anti-Semitic Irishman).

2. Arch-heretic. Arius died suddenly in Constantinople in 336. He was never a bishop, and Stephen's image of him at the moment of death in full episcopal attire seems to combine recollections of other early "heresiarchs." In an earlier reverie Stephen had conjured up in his mind "a horde of heresies fleeing with mitres awry." These heretics are connected in Stephen's mind with argument about the relation between God the Father and God the Son and so with the problem of the true nature of paternity, which haunts him constantly.

3. Mananaan MacLir, Celtic sea god; his steeds are the "whitemaned seahorses." ("White horses" is still the name in Britain for the white foam on top of waves.)

4. Mr. Deasy had given Stephen a letter to the press to be taken to the newspaper office. After that he has an appointment with Mulligan at The Ship, a tavern. "That money" is Mr. Deasy's last payment to him.

5. Stephen has been wondering whether to call on his uncle and aunt, Richie and Sara Goulding. He imagines his father interrogating him about the visit as if he had gone, and then pictures his cousins asking after his father, Simon Dedalus (his cousins' "uncle Si"). Simon is contemptuous of his wife's relations (Sara Goulding is his wife's sister). Stephen knows that any mention of them will bring on the familiar abuse of "the things I married into"—at best "highly respectable gondoliers" (from Gilbert and Sullivan's opera *The Gondoliers*). The scene that follows is also Stephen's purely imaginary picture of what the visit would be like.

6. Favorable corner.

7. "You shall take with you": opening words of a search warrant. Goulding was a law clerk with Messrs. Goff and Tandy.

8. Poem by Oscar Wilde.

9. Whisky.

Papa's little bedpal. Lump of love.

—No, uncle Richie. . .

—Call me Richie. Damn your lithia water. It lowers. Whusky!

—Uncle Richie, really. . . .

—Sit down or by the law Harry I'll knock you down.

Walter squints vainly for a chair.

—He has nothing to sit down on, sir.

—He has nowhere to put it, you mug. Bring in our chippendale chair. Would you like a bite of something? None of your damned lawdeedaw air here: the rich of a rasher fried with a herring? Sure? So much the better. We have nothing in the house but backache pills.

All'erta![1]

He drones bars of Ferrando's *aria di sortita*. The grandest number, Stephen, in the whole opera. Listen.

His tuneful whistle sounds again, finely shaded, with rushes of the air, his fists bigdrumming on his padded knees.

This wind is sweeter.

Houses of decay, mine, his and all. You told the Clongowes gentry you had an uncle a judge and an uncle a general in the army.[2] Come out of them, Stephen. Beauty is not there. Nor in the stagnant bay of Marsh's library where you read the fading prophecies of Joachim Abbas.[3] For whom? The hundredheaded rabble of the cathedral close.[4] A hater of his kind ran from them to the wood of madness, his mane foaming in the moon, his eyeballs stars. Houyhnhnm, horsenostrilled.[5] The oval equine faces, Temple, Buck Mulligan, Foxy Campbell. Lantern jaws. Abbas[6] father, furious dean, what offence laid fire to their brains? Paff! *Descende, calve, ut nimium decalveris.*[7] A garland of grey hair on his comminated head see him me clambering down to the footpace (*descende*), clutching a monstrance, basiliskeyed. Get down, bald poll! A choir gives back menace and echo, assisting about the altar's horns, the snorted Latin of jackpriests moving burly in their albs, tonsured and oiled and gelded, fat with the fat of kidneys of wheat.

And at the same instant perhaps a priest round the corner is elevating it. Dringdring! And two streets off another locking it into a pyx.[8] Dringadring! And in a ladychapel another taking housel all to his own cheek. Dringdring! Down, up, forward, back. Dan Occam[9] thought of that, invincible doctor. A

---

1. "Look out!" The first words of the *aria di sortita* (aria of a singer's entrance) sung by Ferrando, captain of the guard, in Verdi's opera *Il Trovatore*.
2. Stephen, reflecting on the steady social decline of his family, is remembering that, while at school at Clongowes Wood College, he had pretended to have important relations.
3. Abbot Joachim of Floris (the monastery of San Giovanni in Fiore, Italy), 12th-century mystic and theologian, whose prophetic work *Expositio in Apocalypsin* Stephen (i.e., Joyce) had read in Marsha's Library.
4. I.e., the precinct of a cathedral (Marsh's Library is in the close of St. Patrick's Cathedral).
5. St. Patrick's Close has recalled Jonathan Swift (who was dean of St. Patrick's). Stephen remembers Swift's misanthropy (he was "a hater of his kind") and his creation of the Houyhnhnms (noble horses) in book 4 of *Gulliver's Travels*. Then he thinks of people he knew who have horse faces.
6. Literally: "father."

7. "Go down, bald-head, lest you become even balder." This sentence, from Joachim's *Concordia* of the Old and New Testaments, is based on the mocking cry of the children to the prophet Elisha (2 Kings 2.23: "Go up, thou bald head"); Joachim saw Elisha as a forerunner of St. Benedict—both had shaven or baldish heads. Stephen goes on to imagine the "comminated" (threatened) head of Joachim descending, clutching a "monstrance" (receptacle in which the Host [consecrated bread or wafer] is exposed for adoration), in the midst of a nightmare church service.
8. Vessel in which the Host is kept. Stephen is imagining such a service, with himself officiating (he almost became a priest).
9. William of Occam or Ockham ("Dan" means "master"), 14th-century English theologian, who held that the individual thing is the reality and its name, the universal, an abstraction; he was concerned with hypostasis—the essential part of a thing as distinct from its attributes.

misty English morning the imp hypostasis tickled his brain. Bringing his host
down and kneeling he heard twine with his second bell the first bell in the
transept (he is lifting his) and, rising, heard (now I am lifting) their two bells
(he is kneeling) twang in diphthong.

Cousin Stephen, you will never be a saint.[1] Isle of saints.[2] You were awfully
holy, weren't you? You prayed to the Blessed Virgin that you might not have
a red nose. You prayed to the devil in Serpentine avenue that the fubsy widow
in front might lift her clothes still more from the wet street. O si, certo![3] Sell
your soul for that, do, dyed rags pinned round a squaw. More tell me, more
still! On the top of the Howth tram alone crying to the rain: Naked women!
What about that, eh?

What about what? What else were they invented for?

Reading two pages apiece of seven books every night, eh? I was young. You
bowed to yourself in the mirror, stepping forward to applause earnestly, striking
face. Hurray for the Goddamned idiot! Hray! No-one saw: tell no-one. Books
you were going to write with letters for titles. Have you read his F? O yes, but
I prefer Q. Yes, but W is wonderful. O yes, W. Remember your epiphanies[4]
on green oval leaves, deeply deep, copies to be sent if you died to all the great
libraries of the world, including Alexandria? Someone was to read them there
after a few thousand years, a mahamanvantara.[5] Pico della Mirandola[6] like.
Ay, very like a whale.[7] When one reads these strange pages of one long gone
one feels that one is at one with one who once. . .

The grainy sand had gone from under his feet. His boots trod again a damp
crackling mast, razorshells, squeaking pebbles, that on the unnumbered pebbles beats, wood sieved by the shipworm, lost Armada. Unwholesome sandflats
waited to suck his treading soles, breathing upward sewage breath. He coasted
them, walking warily. A porterbottle stood up, stogged to its waist, in the cakey
sand dough. A sentinel: isle of dreadful thirst.[8] Broken hoops on the shore; at
the land a maze of dark cunning nets; farther away chalkscrawled backdoors
and on the higher beach a dryingline with two crucified shirts. Ringsend:
wigwams of brown steersmen and master mariners. Human shells.

He halted. I have passed the way to aunt Sara's. Am I not going there?
Seems not. No-one about. He turned northeast and crossed the firmer sand
towards the Pigeonhouse.[9]

---

1. A parody of the words of Dryden to his distant relative Swift: "Cousin, you will never make a poet."
2. Ireland was called "insula sanctorum," ("isle of
saints") in the Middle Ages.
3. Oh yes, certainly!
4. Joyce's term for the prose poems he wrote as a
young man. An epiphany, he said, was the sudden "revelation of the whatness of a thing"—of a gesture, a
phrase, or a thought which he had experienced; he
attempted to express, in the writing, the moment at
which "the soul of the commonest object . . . seems to
us radiant." Stephen's recollection of early and exotic
literary ambitions is drawn directly from Joyce's own
ambitions at the same age.
5. Cycle of change and recurrence, in Indian mystical
thought. It is connected in Stephen's mind with the
constant ebb and flow of the sea by which he is
walking.
6. Fifteenth-century mystical philosopher; his Hep-
taplus is a mystical account of the creation, much
influenced by Jewish cabalistic thought.

7. Polonius to Hamlet (Hamlet 3.2.399) with reference to the changing shape of a cloud. The Protean
theme of constant change, of ebb and flow, and of
metempsychosis (i.e., transmigration of souls: a major
theme in Ulysses), is working in Stephen's mind. The
following sentence is a parody of an elegant, condescending modern essay on Pico or some other early
mystic.
8. The atmosphere of the sandflats reminds Stephen
of a desert island where people die of thirst. (The island
of Pharos, where Menelaus found Proteus, was an
"island of dreadful hunger.")
9. The Pigeon House in Ringsend, an old structure
built on a breakwater in Dublin Bay and which in the
course of time has served a great variety of purposes,
suggests to Stephen the Dove, which is the symbol of
the Holy Spirit, and this in turn suggests an irreverent
dialogue (supposedly between Joseph and Mary when
Mary is found to be pregnant: "Who has got you into
this wretched condition?" "It was the pigeon [i.e., the
Holy Dove], Joseph"). This he had picked up in Paris

—*Qui vous a mis dans cette fichue position?*
—*C'est le pigeon, Joseph.*

Patrice, home on furlough, lapped warm milk with me in the bar MacMahon. Son of the wild goose, Kevin Egan of Paris. My father's a bird, he lapped the sweet *lait chaud* with pink young tongue, plump bunny's face. Lap, *lapin.* He hopes to win in the *gros lots.* About the nature of women he read in Michelet. But he must send me *La Vie de Jésus* by M. Léo Taxil. Lent it to his friend.[1]

—*C'est tordant, vous savez. Moi, je suis socialiste. Je ne crois pas en l'existence de Dieu. Faut pas le dire à mon père.*

—*Il croit?*

—*Mon père, oui.*

Schluss.[2] He laps.

My Latin quarter hat. God, we simply must dress the character. I want puce gloves. You were a student, weren't you? Of what in the other devil's name? Paysayenn. P. C. N., you know: *physiques, chimiques et naturelles.*[3] Aha. Eating your groatsworth of *mou en civet,*[4] fleshpots of Egypt, elbowed by belching cabmen. Just say in the most natural tone: when I was in Paris, *boul'Mich',*[5] I used to. Yes, used to carry punched tickets to prove an alibi if they arrested you for murder somewhere. Justice. On the night of the seventeenth of February 1904 the prisoner was seen by two witnesses. Other fellow did it: other me. Hat, tie, overcoat, nose. *Lui, c'est moi.*[6] You seem to have enjoyed yourself.

Proudly walking. Whom were you trying to walk like? Forget: a dispossessed. With mother's money order, eight shillings, the banging door of the post office slammed in your face by the usher. Hunger toothache. *Encore deux minutes.* Look clock. Must get. *Fermé.* Hired dog! Shoot him to bloody bits with a bang shotgun, bits man spattered walls all brass buttons. Bits all khrrrrklak in place clack back. Not hurt? O, that's all right. Shake hands. See what I meant, see? O, that's all right. Shake a shake. O, that's all only all right.[7]

You were going to do wonders, what? Missionary to Europe after fiery Columbanus. Fiacre and Scotus on their creepystools[8] in heaven spilt from their

from the blasphemous M. Léo Taxil, whose book *La Vie de Jésus* ("The Life of Jesus") is mentioned in the next paragraph.

1. Stephen had first met Léo Taxil through Patrice, the son of "Kevin Egan of Paris," who in real life was the exiled nationalist Joseph Casey. The phrase "my father's a bird" comes from *The Song of the Cheerful Jesus,* a blasphemous poem by Buck Mulligan (actually Oliver Gogarty, who really wrote the poem); Stephen recalls Patrice reciting it as he drank warm milk (*"lait chaud"*), lapping it like a *"lapin"* (rabbit), and expressing the hope that he would win something substantial in the French national lottery (*gros lot:* "first prize"). Jules Michelet (1798–1874), French historian.

2. Conversation between Stephen and Patrice: "It's screamingly funny, you know. I'm a socialist myself. I don't believe in the existence of God. Mustn't tell my father." "He is a believer?" "My father, yes." "*Schluss*": end.

3. I.e., the faculty of physics, chemistry, and biology at the École de Médecine in Paris, where Stephen, like Joyce, took a premedical course for a short time. The

faculty was popularly known as "P. C. N." (pronounced "Paysayenn").

4. Stew.

5. Popular Parisian abbreviation for the Boulevard Saint Michel.

6. "He is me"—a parody of Louis XIV's remark "*L'état c'est moi*" (I am the state).

7. A recollection of the occasion when, desperate for money, Stephen had received a money order for eight shillings from his mother. Afflicted with both hunger and toothache, he had gone to cash it at the post office—which was closed, even though, as he expostulated with the man at the door, there were still two minutes (*"encore deux minutes"*) until the official closing time. In his retrospective rage he imagines himself shooting the "hired dog" to bits, and then in a revulsion of feeling has a mental reconciliation with him.

8. Low stools. "Columbanus": 6th-century Irish missionary on the Continent. "Fiacre": a 6th-century Irish saint. "Scotus": Duns Scotus (ca. 1265–1308), scholastic theologian and philosopher.

pintpots, loudlatinlaughing: *Euge! Euge!*[9] Pretending to speak broken English
as you dragged your valise, porter threepence, across the slimy pier at Newha-
ven. *Comment?* Rich booty you brought back; *Le Tutu*, five tattered numbers
of *Pantalon Blanc et Culotte Rouge*,[1] a blue French telegram, curiosity to
show:
    —Mother dying come home father.[2]
The aunt thinks you killed your mother. That's why she won't.[3]

> Then here's a health to Mulligan's aunt
> And I'll tell you the reason why.
> She always kept things decent in
> The Hannigan famileye.

His feet marched in sudden proud rhythm over the sand furrows, along by
the boulders of the south wall. He stared at them proudly, piled stone mam-
moth skulls. Gold light on sea, on sand, on boulders. The sun is there, the
slender trees, the lemon houses.

Paris rawly waking, crude sunlight on her lemon streets. Moist pith of farls[4]
of bread, the froggreen wormwood, her matin incense, court the air. Belluomo
rises from the bed of his wife's lover's wife, the kerchiefed housewife is astir, a
saucer of acetic acid in her hand. In Rodot's Yvonne and Madeleine newmake
their tumbled beauties, shattering with gold teeth *chaussons* of pastry, their
mouths yellowed with the *pus* of *flan breton*.[5] Faces of Paris men go by, their
wellpleased pleasers, curled *conquistadores*.[6]

Noon slumbers. Kevin Egan rolls gunpowder cigarettes through fingers
smeared with printer's ink,[7] sipping his green fairy as Patrice his white. About
us gobblers fork spiced beans down their gullets. *Un demi setier!*[8] A jet of
coffee steam from the burnished caldron. She serves me at his beck. *Il est
irlandais. Hollandais? Non fromage. Deux irlandais, nous, Irlande, vous savez?
Ah, oui!*[9] She thought you wanted a cheese *hollandais*. Your postprandial, do
you know that word? Postprandial. There was a fellow I knew once in Bar-
celona, queer fellow, used to call it his postprandial. Well: *slainte!*[1] Around
the slabbed tables the tangle of wined breaths and grumbling gorges. His
breath hangs over our saucestained plates, the green fairy's fang thrusting
between his lips. Of Ireland, the Dalcassians, of hopes, conspiracies, of Arthur
Griffith now.[2] To yoke me as his yokefellow, our crimes our common cause.
You're your father's son. I know the voice. His fustian shirt, sanguineflowered,
trembles its Spanish tassels at his secrets. M. Drumont,[3] famous journalist,
Drumont, know what he called queen Victoria? Old hag with the yellow

---

9. Well done!
1. Like the preceding name, name of French popular
periodical.
2. This telegram was actually received by Joyce in
Paris.
3. Stephen recalls Buck Mulligan's telling him that
his (Mulligan's) aunt disapproved of Stephen because,
by refusing to pray at his dying mother's bedside, he
had hastened her death. Stephen then tries to laugh
away his feeling of guilt by quoting mentally a (slightly
parodied) verse of a popular song.
4. Thin circular cakes.
5. Memories of a restaurant in Paris: "*chaussons*" are
pastry turnovers; "*flan breton*" is a pastry filled with custard.
6. Conquerors (Spanish).

7. Egan (i.e., Joseph Casey) became a typesetter for
the Parisian edition of the *New York Herald*.
8. Abusive Parisian slang for a liquid measure (about
one-fourth of a liter)—here, presumably, of wine or
beer.
9. He is Irish. Dutch? Not cheese. We are two
Irishmen, Ireland, you understand? Oh, yes!
1. Your health! (Gaelic).
2. Two extremes of Irish history. From the Dalcassian
line came the early kings of Munster (from A.D. 300
on). Arthur Griffith (1872–1922) was an Irish revolutionary leader, founder of the Sinn Fein ("We Ourselves") movement.
3. Edouard Drumont (1844–1917), French politician
and bitter anti-Semite.

teeth. *Vieille ogresse* with the *dents jaunes*. Maud Gonne, beautiful woman, *la Patrie*, M. Millevoye, Félix Faure,[4] know how he died? Licentious men. The *froeken, bonne à tout faire*,[5] who rubs male nakedness in the bath at Upsala. *Moi faire*, she said, *tous les messieurs*.[6] Not this *monsieur*, I said. Most licentious custom. Bath a most private thing. I wouldn't let my brother, not even my own brother, most lascivious thing. Green eyes, I see you. Fang, I feel. Lascivious people.

The blue fuse burns deadly between hands and burns clear. Loose tobacco shreds catch fire: a flame and acrid smoke light our corner. Raw facebones under his peep of day boy's hat. How the head centre got away, authentic version. Got up as a young bride, man, veil, orangeblossoms, drove out the road to Malahide. Did, faith. Of lost leaders, the betrayed, wild escapes. Disguises, clutched at, gone not here.[7]

Spurned lover. I was a strapping young gossoon[8] at that time, I tell you. I'll show you my likeness one day. I was, faith. Lover, for her love he prowled with colonel Richard Burke, tanist of his sept,[9] under the walls of Clerkenwell[1] and, crouching, saw a flame of vengeance hurl them upward in the fog. Shattered glass and toppling masonry. In gay Paree he hides, Egan of Paris, unsought by any save by me. Making his day's stations, the dingy printingcase, his three taverns, the Montmartre lair he sleeps short night in, *rue de la Goutte-d'Or*, damascened with flyblown faces of the gone. Loveless, landless, wifeless. She is quite nicey comfy without her outcast man,[2] madame in *rue Gît-le-Cœur*, canary and two buck lodgers. Peachy cheeks, a zebra skirt, frisky as a young thing's. Spurned and undespairing. Tell Pat[3] you saw me, won't you? I wanted to get poor Pat a job one time. *Mon fils*, soldier of France. I taught him to sing *The boys of Kilkenny are stout roaring blades*. Know that old lay? I taught Patrice that. Old Kilkenny: saint Canice, Strongbow's castle on the Nore.[4] Goes like this. O, O. He takes me, Napper Tandy,[5] by the hand.

> O, O the boys of
> Kilkenny. . .

Weak wasting hand on mine. They have forgotten Kevin Egan, not he them. Remembering thee, O Sion.[6]

He had come nearer the edge of the sea and wet sand slapped his boots. The new air greeted him, harping in wild nerves, wind of wild air of seeds of brightness. Here, I am not walking out to the Kish lightship, am I? He stood suddenly, his feet beginning to sink slowly in the quaking soil. Turn back.

Turning, he scanned the shore south, his feet sinking again slowly in new

---

4. Nineteenth-century French statesman. Maud Gonne, the beautiful actress and violent Irish nationalist whom Yeats loved. "La Patrie": journal edited by Lucien Millevoye, French nationalist deputy and Maud Gonne's lover.
5. Maid-of-all-work (French, translating the preceding Swedish word).
6. I do all the gentlemen (in broken French).
7. Another Protean theme of change. Egan had told Stephen of his cousin James Stephens's escape from prison disguised as a bride (Stephens was really the cousin of Casey, the original of Egan in this episode).
8. Boy.
9. Clan. "Tanist": successor-apparent to a Celtic chief.
1. District in east-central London. Stephen is recalling Egan's conversation about the Fenian violence in Lon-

don that necessitated his fleeing to France.
2. I.e., Egan's wife, who is "quite nicey comfy" in the metaphorical "rue Gît-le-Coeur" (i.e., the street where the heart lies dead) back home in Ireland.
3. Patrice, Egan's son.
4. Kilkenny is called after the Irish St. Canice (its Irish name is Cill Chainnigh), on the river Nore, where Strongbow (the second earl of Pembroke, who invaded Ireland in the 12th century), had his stronghold.
5. James Napper Tandy (1740–1803), Irish revolutionary hero of the song "The Wearing of the Green."
6. Cf. Psalm 137.1 (in the King James Bible): "we wept, when we remembered Zion." But "Zion" in the Douay (Roman Catholic) Bible, is spelled "Sion," and the Book of Common Prayer has "When we remembered thee, O Sion."

sockets. The cold domed room of the tower[7] waits. Through the barbicans[8] the shafts of light are moving ever, slowly ever as my feet are sinking, creeping duskward over the dial floor. Blue dusk, nightfall, deep blue night. In the darkness of the dome they wait, their pushedback chairs, my obelisk valise, around a board of abandoned platters. Who to clear it? He has the key.[9] I will not sleep there when this night comes. A shut door of a silent tower, entombing their blind bodies, the panthersahib and his pointer.[1] Call: no answer. He lifted his feet up from the suck and turned back by the mole of boulders. Take all, keep all. My soul walks with me, form of forms. So in the moon's midwatches I pace the path above the rocks, in sable silvered, hearing Elsinore's tempting flood.[2]

The flood is following me. I can watch it flow past from here. Get back then by the Poolbeg road to the strand there. He climbed over the sedge and eely oarweeds and sat on a stool of rock, resting his ashplant in a grike.

A bloated carcass of a dog lay lolled on bladderwrack. Before him the gunwale of a boat, sunk in sand. *Un coche ensablé*[3] Louis Veuillot called Gautier's[4] prose. These heavy sands are language tide and wind have silted here. And there, the stoneheaps of dead builders, a warren of weasel rats. Hide gold there. Try it. You have some. Sands and stones. Heavy of the past. Sir Lout's toys. Mind you don't get one bang on the ear. I'm the bloody well gigant rolls all them bloody well boulders, bones for my steppingstones. Feefawfum. I zmellz de bloodz oldz an Iridzman.[5]

A point, live dog, grew into sight running across the sweep of sand. Lord, is he going to attack me? Respect his liberty. You will not be master of others or their slave. I have my stick. Sit tight. From farther away, walking shoreward across from the crested tide, figures, two. The two maries. They have tucked it safe mong the bulrushes. Peekaboo. I see you. No, the dog. He is running back to them. Who?

Galleys of the Lochlanns[6] ran here to beach, in quest of prey, their blood-beaked prows riding low on a molten pewter surf. Dane vikings, torcs of tomahawks aglitter on their breasts when Malachi wore the collar of gold. A school of turlehide whales stranded in hot noon, spouting, hobbling in the shallows. Then from the starving cagework city a horde of jerkined dwarfs, my people, with flayers' knives, running, scaling, hacking in green blubbery whalemeat. Famine, plague and slaughters. Their blood is in me, their lusts my waves. I moved among them on the frozen Liffey, that I, a changeling, among the spluttering resin fires. I spoke to no-one: none to me.

The dog's bark ran towards him, stopped, ran back.[7] Dog of my enemy. I

7. Where Stephen lived with Buck Mulligan.
8. Outworks of a castle.
9. In the preceding episode, Mulligan asked for and got the key of the tower from Stephen.
1. I.e., Mulligan and the Englishman Haines, who lived with Stephen in the tower. Stephen thinks of them as calling for him in vain, because he has decided not to return.
2. Cf. *Hamlet* 1.2.242, where the ghost of Hamlet's murdered father is described as having a beard of "sable silver'd." Allusions to *Hamlet* occur often in *Ulysses*; in a later episode Stephen expounds the theory that Shakespeare is to be identified not with Hamlet himself but with his betrayed father.
3. A coach embedded in the sand.
4. Théophile Gautier, 19th-century French poet, nov-

elist, and critic. Veuillot, 19th-century French journalist.
5. Stephen is thinking of the boulders on the shore as the work of a large but clumsy giant ("Sir Lout"). "They [Sir Lout and his family] were giants right enough. . . . My Sir Lout has rocks in his mouth instead of teeth. He articulates badly" (Joyce to Frank Budgen, reported in Budgen's *James Joyce and the Making of Ulysses*, 1934).
6. Scandinavians (Gaelic). Stephen is meditating on the Vikings who settled Dublin; it was here that they came ashore, he thinks.
7. The dog in this and subsequent paragraphs keeps changing in appearance; he "is the mummer among beasts—the Protean animal" (Joyce to Budgen). Joyce himself was afraid of dogs.

just simply stood pale, silent, bayed about. *Terribilia meditans.*[8] A primrose doublet, fortune's knave, smiled on my fear. For that are you pining, the bark of their applause? Pretenders: live their lives. The Bruce's brother, Thomas Fitzgerald, silken knight, Perkin Warbeck, York's false scion, in breeches of silk of whiterose ivory, wonder of a day, and Lambert Simnel, with a tail of nans and sutlers, a scullion crowned.[9] All kings' sons. Paradise of pretenders then and now. He saved men from drowning[1] and you shake at a cur's yelping. But the courtiers who mocked Guido in Or san Michele were in their own house. House of . . . We don't want any of your medieval abstrusiosities. Would you do what he did? A boat would be near, a lifebuoy. *Natürlich,*[2] put there for you. Would you or would you not? The man that was drowned nine days ago off Maiden's rock. They are waiting for him now. The truth, spit it out. I would want to. I would try. I am not a strong swimmer. Water cold soft. When I put my face into it in the basin at Clongowes. Can't see! Who's behind me? Out quickly, quickly! Do you see the tide flowing quickly in on all sides, sheeting the lows of sands quickly, shellcocoacoloured? If I had land under my feet. I want his life still to be his, mine to be mine. A drowning man. His human eyes scream to me out of horror of his death. I . . . With him together down . . . I could not save her.[3] Waters: bitter death: lost.

A woman and a man. I see her skirties. Pinned up, I bet.

Their dog ambled about a bank of dwindling sand, trotting, sniffing on all sides. Looking for something lost in a past life. Suddenly he made off like a bounding hare, ears flung back, chasing the shadow of a lowskimming gull. The man's shrieked whistle struck his limp ears. He turned, bounded back, came nearer, trotted on twinkling shanks. On a field tenney a buck, trippant, proper, unattired.[4] At the lacefringe of the tide he halted with stiff forehoofs, seawardpointed ears. His snout lifted barked at the wavenoise, herds of seamorse. They serpented towards his feet, curling, unfurling many crests, every ninth, breaking, plashing, from far, from farther out, waves and waves.

Cocklepickers.[5] They waded a little way in the water and, stooping, soused their bags, and, lifting them again, waded out. The dog yelped running to them, reared up and pawed them, dropping on all fours, again reared up at them with mute bearish fawning. Unheeded he kept by them as they came towards the drier sand, a rag of wolf's tongue redpanting from his jaws. His speckled body ambled ahead of them and then loped off at a calf's gallop. The carcass lay on his path. He stopped, sniffed, stalked round it, brother, nosing closer, went round it, sniffing rapidly like a dog all over the dead dog's bedraggled fell. Dogskull, dogsniff, eyes on the ground, moves to one great goal. Ah, poor dogsbody. Here lies poor dogsbody's body.

—Tatters! Outofthat, you mongrel.

The cry brought him skulking back to his master and a blunt bootless kick sent him unscathed across a spit of sand, crouched in flight. He slunk back in

---

8. Meditating terrible things.
9. Stephen is meditating on pretenders (i.e., false claimants): the names here are those of pretenders who have figured in English history. This is the Proteus theme again—disguises and changes.
1. Mulligan had saved a man from drowning.
2. Of course.
3. A man had been drowned off the coast, and his body had not yet been recovered. As Stephen thinks of the horror of drowning he recalls once again his moth-

er's death.
4. At this point in its constantly changing appearance the dog looks like a heraldic animal and is described in the language of heraldry; this sentence means: "On an orange-brown (tawny) background, a buck, tripping, in natural colors, without horns."
5. Stephen recognizes the man and woman on the beach as gypsy cockle pickers (cockles are edible shellfish, like mussels).

a curve. Doesn't see me. Along by the edge of the mole he lolloped, dawdled, smelt a rock and from under a cocked hindleg pissed against it. He trotted forward and, lifting his hindleg, pissed quick short at an unsmelt rock. The simple pleasures of the poor. His hindpaws then scattered sand: then his fore-paws dabbled and delved. Something he buried there, his grandmother.[6] He rooted in the sand, dabbling, delving and stopped to listen to the air, scraped up the sand again with a fury of his claws, soon ceasing, a pard,[7] a panther, got in spousebreach,[8] vulturing the dead.

After he woke me last night same dream or was it? Wait. Open hallway. Street of harlots. Remember. Haroun al Raschid.[9] I am almosting it. That man led me, spoke. I was not afraid. The melon he had he held against my face. Smiled: creamfruit smell. That was the rule, said. In. Come. Red carpet spread. You will see who.

Shouldering their bags they trudged, the red Egyptians.[1] His blued feet out of turnedup trousers slapped the clammy sand, a dull brick muffler strangling his unshaven neck. With woman steps she followed: the ruffian and his stroll-ing mort.[2] Spoils slung at her back. Loose sand and shellgrit crusted her bare feet. About her windraw face her hair trailed. Behind her lord his helpmate, bing awast, to Romeville.[3] When night hides her body's flaws calling under her brown shawl from an archway where dogs have mired. Her fancyman is treating two Royal Dublins in O'Loughlin's of Blackpitts. Buss her, wap in rogues' rum lingo, for, O, my dimber wapping dell.[4] A shefiend's whiteness under her rancid rags. Fumbally's lane that night: the tanyard smells.

> White thy fambles, red thy gan
> And thy quarrons dainty is.
> Couch a hogshead with me then.
> In the darkmans clip and kiss.[5]

Morose delectation Aquinas tunbelly calls this, *frate porcospino*.[6] Unfallen Adam rode and not rutted. Call away let him:[7] *thy quarrons dainty is.* Lan-guage no whit worse than his. Monkwords, marybeads jabber on their girdles: roguewords, tough nuggets patter in their pockets.

Passing now.

A side-eye at my Hamlet hat. If I were suddenly naked here as I sit? I am not. Across the sands of all the world, followed by the sun's flaming sword, to

6. Reference to a joke Stephen had made to his pupils in school that morning about "the fox burying his grandmother under a hollybush." This has many sym-bolic reverberations throughout *Ulysses.* The buried grandmother suggests Stephen's mother, the church, and Ireland (the "Poor old Woman"), while the hol-lybush, evergreen tree of life, represents resurrection in which, in spite of his religious disbelief, Stephen is much interested and about which (as about metempsy-chosis) he is continually brooding.

7. Leopard or panther.

8. I.e., begotten in adultery.

9. Stephen's dream of the famous Caliph of Baghdad, of the "street of harlots" and of his meeting a man with a melon, foreshadows his meeting later in the day with Leopold Bloom and his visit to the brothel area of Dublin.

1. I.e., gypsies. As Stephen watches the gypsy cockle pickers with their dog he imagines their vagabond life and recalls fragments of gypsy speech and of thieves'

slang.

2. Gypsies' "freewoman" (i.e., a harlot). "Spoils": the association gypsy-Egyptian reminds Stephen of the Israelites "spoiling the Egyptians" (Exodus 12.36).

3. Go away to London.

4. Seventeenth-century thieves' slang. "Wapping dell": whore. "Buss": kiss. "Wap": copulate with. "Rum": good. "Dimber": pretty.

5. More thieves' slang. "Clip": kiss. "Fambles": hands. "Gan": mouth. "Quarrons": body. "Couch a hogs-head": come to bed. "Darkmans": night. These four lines and some of the phrases in the preceding para-graph are quoted from a song of the period, "The Rogue's Delight in Praise of His Strolling Mort" (cf. n. 1).

6. Brother porcupine (Italian), a reference to the fat ("tunbelly") but prickly philosopher, St. Thomas Aquinas.

7. The gypsy is calling his dog.

the west, trekking to evening lands. She trudges, schlepps, trains, drags, tras-
cines her load.[8] A tide westering, moondrawn, in her wake. Tides, myriadis-
landed, within her, blood not mine, *oinopa ponton*,[9] a winedark sea. Behold
the handmaid of the moon. In sleep the wet sign calls her hour, bids her rise.
Bridebed, childbed, bed of death, ghostcandled.[1] *Omnis caro ad te veniet.* He
comes, pale vampire, through storm his eyes, his bat sails bloodying the sea,
mouth to her mouth's kiss.[2]

Here. Put a pin in that chap, will you? My tablets.[3] Mouth to her kiss. No.
Must be two of em. Glue 'em well. Mouth to her mouth's kiss.

His lips lipped and mouthed fleshless lips of air: mouth to her womb.
Oomb, allwombing tomb.[4] His mouth moulded issuing breath, unspeeched:
ooeeehah: roar of cataractic planets, globed, blazing, roaring wayawayawaya-
wayawayaway. Paper. The banknotes, blast them. Old Deasy's letter. Here.
Thanking you for the hospitality tear the blank end off. Turning his back to
the sun he bent over far to a table of rock and scribbled words.[5] That's twice I
forgot to take slips from the library counter.

His shadow lay over the rocks as he bent, ending. Why not endless till the
farthest star? Darkly they are there behind this light, darkness shining in the
brightness, delta of Cassiopeia, worlds. Me sits there with his augur's rod of
ash, in borrowed sandals, by day beside a livid sea, unbeheld, in violet night
walking beneath a reign of uncouth stars.[6] I throw this ended shadow from
me, manshape ineluctable, call it back. Endless, would it be mine, form of
my form? Who watches me here? Who ever anywhere will read these written
words? Signs on a white field. Somewhere to someone in your flutiest voice.
The good bishop of Cloyne[7] took the veil of the temple out of his shovel hat:
veil of space with coloured emblems hatched on its field. Hold hard. Coloured on a flat: yes, that's right. Flat I see, then think distance, near, far, flat I
see, east, back. Ah, see now. Falls back suddenly, frozen in stereoscope. Click
does the trick. You find my words dark. Darkness is in our souls, do you not
think? Flutier. Our souls, shamewounded by our sins, cling to us yet more, a
woman to her lover clinging, the more the more.

She trusts me, her hand gentle, the longlashed eyes. Now where the blue
hell am I bringing her beyond the veil?[8] Into the ineluctable modality of the
ineluctable visuality. She, she, she. What she? The virgin at Hodges Figgis'
window on Monday looking in for one of the alphabet books you were going
to write. Keen glance you gave her. Wrist through the braided jess of her

8. All words suggesting moving or dragging. " 'I like
that crescendo of verbs,' he [Joyce] said. 'The irresistible tug of the tides' " (Budgen).
9. Winedark sea (Homer).
1. He is thinking of his mother again. The following
Latin (from the burial service) means: "All flesh will
come to thee."
2. Death comes like the Flying Dutchman in a phantom ship to give the fatal kiss.
3. Cf. *Hamlet* 1.5.107: "My tablets!"
4. Our understanding of Stephen's consciousness here
can be illuminated with reference to Blake's poem *The
Gates of Paradise*, which concludes: "The door of
death I open found / And the worm weaving in the
ground: / Thou'rt my mother from the womb, / Wife,
sister, daughter, to the tomb." Cf. also *Romeo and
Juliet* 2.3.9–10: "the earth that's nature's mother is her
tomb. / What is her burying ground that is her
womb."

5. Stephen tears off the blank end of Mr. Deasy's letter
to the press and writes a poem that will be quoted later
in the novel.
6. He imagines himself as the constellation Cassiopeia, supposed to represent the wife of Cepheus (an
Ethiopian king) seated in a chair and holding up her
arms. His ash walking stick he thinks of as an "augur's
[Roman soothsayer's] rod of ash."
7. George Berkeley (1685–1753), bishop of Cloyne (in
Ireland), who argued that the external world has no
objective reality but exists only in the mind of the perceiver. Stephen (as at the opening of this episode) is
experimenting again with ways of sensing reality.
8. "She" is Psyche, the soul, whom he is bringing from
"beyond the veil." But from metaphysical speculations
on reality and the soul Stephen is led (by the Psyche
association) to think of "the virgin at Hodges Figgis' [a
bookseller's] window."

sunshade. She lives in Leeson park with a grief and kickshaws, a lady of letters. Talk that to some else, Stevie: a pickmeup. Bet she wears those curse of God stays suspenders and yellow stockings, darned with lumpy wool. Talk about apple dumplings, *piuttosto*.[9] Where are your wits?

Touch me. Soft eyes. Soft soft soft hand. I am lonely here. O, touch me soon, now. What is that word known to all men? I am quiet here alone. Sad too. Touch, touch me.

He lay back at full stretch over the sharp rocks, cramming the scribbled note and pencil into a pocket, his hat tilted down on his eyes. That is Kevin Egan's movement I made, nodding for his nap, sabbath sleep. *Et vidit Deus. Et erant valde bona.*[1] Alo! Bonjour. Welcome as the flowers in May. Under its leaf he watched through peacocktwittering lashes the southing sun. I am caught in this burning scene. Pan's hour, the faunal noon. Among gumheavy serpentplants, milkoozing fruits, where on the tawny waters leaves lie wide. Pain is far.

And no more turn aside and brood.[2]

His gaze brooded on his broadtoed boots, a buck's castoffs, *nebeneinander.* He counted the creases of rucked leather wherein another's foot had nested warm. The foot that beat the ground in tripudium, foot I dislove. But you were delighted when Esther Osvalt's shoe went on you: girl I knew in Paris. *Tiens, quel petit pied!*[3] Staunch friend, a brother soul: Wilde's love that dare not speak its name. He now will leave me. And the blame? As I am. As I am. All or not at all.

In long lassoes from the Cock lake the water flowed full, covering green-goldenly lagoons of sand, rising, flowing. My ashplant will float away. I shall wait. No, they will pass on, passing chafing against the low rocks, swirling, passing. Better get this job over quick. Listen: a fourworded wavespeech: see-soo, hrss, rsseeiss ooos. Vehement breath of waters amid seasnakes, rearing horses, rocks. In cups of rocks it slops: flop, slop, slap: bounded in barrels. And, spent, its speech ceases. It flows purling, widely flowing, floating foam-pool, flower unfurling.

Under the upswelling tide he saw the writhing weeds lift languidly and sway reluctant arms, hising up their petticoats,[4] in whispering water swaying and upturning coy silver fronds. Day by day: night by night: lifted, flooded and let fall. Lord, they are weary: and, whispered to, they sigh. Saint Ambrose heard it, sigh of leaves and waves, waiting, awaiting the fullness of their times, *diebus ac noctibus iniurias patiens ingemiscit.*[5] To no end gathered; vainly then released, forthflowing, wending back: loom of the moon. Weary too in sight of lovers, lascivious men, a naked woman shining in her courts, she draws a toil of waters.

Five fathoms out there. Full fathom five thy father lies.[6] At one he said.

9. Rather, sooner.
1. Connecting two phrases from the Vulgate: "And God saw" (Genesis 1.4) and "And they were very good" (Genesis 1.31).
2. The first line of the second (and last) stanza of Yeats's poem *Who Goes with Fergus?* which is often in Stephen's mind. The line expresses for him the mood of noontide stillness and of lotos eating in a lush Oriental scene that overcomes him momentarily when he realizes that it is twelve o'clock, the hour of the Greek nature god Pan, "faunal noon." This Oriental lotos-

eating theme, which is associated also with Bloom, is important in the *Odyssey.*
3. Look, what a little foot!
4. A phrase from a vulgar song sung by Mulligan earlier that morning.
5. Night and day he patiently groaned forth his wrongs (St. Ambrose).
6. From Ariel's song (*The Tempest* 1.2.396). The theme of the drowned man is important in this episode (cf. the drowned sailor in Eliot's *Waste Land*).

Found drowned. High water at Dublin bar. Driving before it a loose drift of rubble, fanshoals of fishes, silly shells. A corpse rising salt-white from the undertow, bobbing landward a pace a pace a porpoise. There he is. Hook it quick. Sunk though he be beneath the watery floor. We have him. Easy now.

Bag of corpsegas sopping in foul brine. A quiver of minnows, fat of a spongy titbit, flash through the slits of his buttoned trouserfly. God becomes man becomes fish becomes barnacle goose becomes featherbed mountain. Dead breaths I living breathe, tread dead dust, devour a urinous offal from all dead. Hauled stark over the gunwhale he breathes upward the stench of his green grave, his leprous nosehole snoring to the sun.

A seachange[7] this, brown eyes saltblue. Seadeath, mildest of all deaths known to man. Old Father Ocean. *Prix de Paris:*[8] beware of imitations. Just you give it a fair trial. We enjoyed ourselves immensely.

Come. I thirst. Clouding over. No black clouds anywhere, are there?[9] Thunderstorm. Allbright he falls, proud lightning of the intellect, *Lucifer, dico, qui nescit occasum.*[1] No. My cockle hat and staff and hismy sandal shoon.[2] Where? To evening lands. Evening will find itself.

He took the hilt of his ashplant, lunging with it softly, dallying still. Yes, evening will find itself in me, without me. All days make their end. By the way next when is it? Tuesday will be the longest day. Of all the glad new year, mother,[3] the rum tum tiddledy tum. Lawn Tennyson,[4] gentleman poet. *Già.*[5] For the old hag with the yellow teeth. And Monsieur Drumont, gentleman journalist. *Già.* My teeth are very bad. Why, I wonder? Feel. That one is going too. Shells. Ought I go to a dentist, I wonder, with what money? That one. Toothless Kinch, the superman. Why is that, I wonder, or does it mean something perhaps?

My handkerchief. He threw it. I remember. Did I not take it up?

His hand groped vainly in his pockets. No, I didn't. Better buy one.

He laid the dry snot picked from his nostril on a ledge of rock, carefully. For the rest let look who will.

Behind. Perhaps there is someone.

He turned his face over a shoulder, rere regardant.[6] Moving through the air high spars of a threemaster, her sails brailed up on the crosstrees,[7] homing, upstream, silently moving, a silent ship.

7. Another quotation from Ariel's song (*The Tempest* 1.2.400).

8. Prize of Paris. The reference is probably to the Paris Exposition of 1889, where prizes were awarded in various categories of food, etc.; the prize-winning commodities bear the seal of the prize on the label (hence, "beware of imitations"). Stephen mentally awards the prize to death by drowning.

9. Stephen is looking up to make sure the sky does not threaten a thunderstorm; like Joyce, he hates thunder.

1. Lucifer, I say, who knows not his fall. Thunder and lightning recall the fall of Lucifer.

2. From Ophelia's mad song (*Hamlet* 4.5.23–26): "How should I your true-love know / From another one? / By his cockle hat and staff / And his sandal shoon." Ophelia, too, was drowned.

3. Cf. Tennyson, *The May Queen:* "You must wake and call me early, call me early, mother dear; /

Tomorrow 'ill be the happiest time of all the glad New Year."

4. Alfred, Lord Tennyson.

5. Of course!

6. Looking behind him (heraldic terminology). Stephen, as we leave him sitting by the shore, is described in a highly stylized, heraldic language.

7. When Budgen pointed out to Joyce that *crosstrees* was not the proper nautical term for the spars to which the sails are bent, Joyce thanked him but added: "But the word 'crosstrees' is essential. It comes in later on and I can't change it. After all, a yard is also a crosstree for the onlooking landlubber." Joyce later uses *crosstree* in a reference to the crucifixion of Christ, so that the suggestion here is of Stephen as both artist and martyr (as his name implies). But the ship is also a real ship, which arrived in Dublin on June 16, 1904.

[*Lestrygonians*][8]

Pineapple rock, lemon platt, butter scotch. A sugarsticky girl shovelling scoopfuls of creams for a christian brother. Some school treat. Bad for their tummies. Lozenge and comfit manufacturer to His Majesty the King. God. Save. Our. Sitting on his throne sucking red jujubes white.

A sombre Y. M. C. A. young man, watchful among the warm sweet fumes of Graham Lemon's, placed a throwaway in a hand of Mr Bloom.

Heart to heart talks.

Bloo . . . Me? No.

Blood of the Lamb.[9]

His slow feet walked him riverward, reading. Are you saved? All are washed in the blood of the lamb. God wants blood victim. Birth, hymen, martyr, war, foundation of a building, sacrifice, kidney burntoffering, druids' altars. Elijah is coming. Dr John Alexander Dowie,[1] restorer of the church in Zion, is coming.

Is coming! Is coming!! Is coming!!!
All heartily welcome.

Paying game. Torry and Alexander last year. Polygamy. His wife will put the stopper on that. Where was that ad some Birmingham firm the luminous crucifix. Our Saviour. Wake up in the dead of night and see him on the wall, hanging. Pepper's ghost idea.[2] Iron Nails Ran In.

Phosphorus it must be done with. If you leave a bit of codfish for instance. I could see the bluey silver over it. Night I went down to the pantry in the kitchen. Don't like all the smells in it waiting to rush out. What was it she[3] wanted? The Malaga raisins. Thinking of Spain. Before Rudy[4] was born. The phosphorescence, that bluey greeny. Very good for the brain.

From Butler's monument house corner he glanced along Bachelor's walk. Dedalus' daughter there still outside Dillon's auctionrooms. Must be selling off some old furniture. Knew her eyes at once from the father. Lobbing about

8. It is lunchtime in Dublin and Leopold Bloom, as he walks through the city in no great hurry (for he likes to linger and watch what goes on around him), thinks of food. The Lestrygonians in book 10 of the *Odyssey* are cannibals, and throughout this episode there are suggestions of the slaughter of living creatures for food or of food as something disgusting, which make somewhat tenuous contact with Homer's description of the cannibals spearing Ulysses' men for food; the parallel is not, however, profound or very important. What is most important about this episode is that it shows us Bloom's consciousness responding to the sights and sounds of Dublin. His humane curiosity, his desire to learn and to improve the human lot, his sympathetic concern for Mrs. Breen and Mrs. Purefoy, his feeding the gulls, his recollections of a happier time when his daughter was a baby and his relations with his wife, Molly, were thoroughly satisfactory, his interest in opera, his continuous shying away from thoughts of his wife's rendezvous with the dashing Blazes Boylan—all this helps to build up his character in depth and to differentiate him sharply from Stephen. Unlike Stephen, Bloom's consciousness is confined to simple puns and translations, his interest in poetry is obvious and sentimental; his interest in the nature of reality takes the form of half-forgotten fragments of science remaining in his mind from schooldays. Every-

thing about him is concrete, practical, sensual, and middlebrow or lowbrow, as distinct from the abstract, theoretical, esoteric speculations of Stephen in the *Proteus* episode. For example, when Stephen saw seagulls, he speculated on Daedalus and on flying as a symbol of the artist going into exile; when Bloom sees them, he thinks they must be hungry and buys a bun to feed them. There are parallels between their two streams of consciousness. Bloom's thoughts, in a sense, include Stephen's but in a popularized and even vulgarized form.
9. Bloom has been handed a religious leaflet ("throwaway") containing the phrase "Blood of the Lamb." He at first mistakes "Blood" for "Bloom."
1. Dowie (1847–1907), Scottish-American evangelist who established the "Christian Catholic Apostolic Church in Zion" (i.e., Zion City, IL) in 1901.
2. A dramatic troupe advertising themselves as "The original Pepper's Ghost! and Spectral Opera Company" was popular in the late 19th century; they seem to have specialized in ghostly special effects, possibly achieved through the use of phosphorescent material on their costumes.
3. I.e., Bloom's wife, Molly, born in Gibraltar.
4. Their son, who had died in infancy eleven years before.

waiting for him. Home always breaks up when the mother goes. Fifteen children he had. Birth every year almost. That's in their theology or the priest
won't give the poor woman the confession, the absolution. Increase and multiply. Did you ever hear such an idea? Eat you out of house and home. No
families themselves to feed. Living on the fat of the land. Their butteries and
larders. I'd like to see them do the black fast Yom Kippur.[5] Crossbuns. One
meal and a collation for fear he'd collapse on the altar. A housekeeper of one
of those fellows if you could pick it out of her. Never pick it out of her. Like
getting L s. d.[6] out of him. Does himself well. No guests. All for number one.
Watching his water. Bring your own bread and butter. His reverence. Mum's
the word.

Good Lord, that poor child's dress is in flitters. Underfed she looks too.
Potatoes and marge, marge and potatoes. It's after they feel it. Proof of the
pudding. Undermines the constitution.

As he set foot on O'Connell bridge a puffball of smoke plumed up from the
parapet. Brewery barge with export stout. England. Sea air sours it, I heard.
Be interesting some day get a pass through Hancock to see the brewery. Regular world in itself. Vats of porter, wonderful. Rats get in too. Drink themselves
bloated as big as a collie floating. Dead drunk on the porter. Drink till they
puke again like christians. Imagine drinking that! Rats: vats. Well of course if
we knew all the things.

Looking down he saw flapping strongly, wheeling between the gaunt quay-
walls, gulls. Rough weather outside. If I threw myself down? Reuben J's son
must have swallowed a good bellyful of that sewage.[7] One and eightpence too
much. Hhhhm. It's the droll way he comes out with the things. Knows how
to tell a story too.

They wheeled lower. Looking for grub. Wait.

He threw down among them a crumpled paper ball. Elijah thirtytwo feet
per sec is com.[8] Not a bit. The ball bobbed unheeded on the wake of swells,
floated under by the bridgepiers. Not such damn fools. Also the day I threw
that stale cake out of the Erin's King picked it up in the wake fifty yards astern.
Live by their wits. They wheeled, flapping.

> The hungry famished gull
> Flaps o'er the waters dull.

That is how poets write, the similar sounds. But then Shakespeare has no
rhymes: blank verse. The flow of the language it is. The thoughts. Solemn.

> Hamlet, I am thy father's spirit
> Doomed for a certain time to walk the earth.[9]

—Two apples a penny! Two for a penny!

His gaze passed over the glazed apples serried on her stand. Australians
they must be this time of year. Shiny peels: polishes them up with a rag or a
handkerchief.

5. Jewish Day of Atonement.
6. I.e., cash: L, s., d. are the abbreviations, respectively,
for pounds, shillings, and pence.
7. Reuben J. Dodd, Dublin solicitor (lawyer), whose
son had been rescued from the Liffey River by a man
to whom Reuben J. had given two shillings as a
reward—"one and eightpence too much," as Simon
Dedalus had remarked to Bloom earlier that morning

when they were discussing the incident. It is Dedalus's
comment that Bloom is thinking of in the following
sentences.
8. I.e., Elijah is coming, accelerating at the rate of
thirty-two feet per second per second, the acceleration
rate of falling bodies. ("Elijah is coming" is the legend
on the handbill Bloom is tossing away).
9. *Hamlet* 1.5.9–10 (slightly misquoted).

Wait. Those poor birds.

He halted again and bought from the old applewoman two Banbury cakes for a penny and broke the brittle paste and threw its fragments down into the Liffey. See that? The gulls swooped silently two, then all from their heights, pouncing on prey. Gone. Every morsel.

Aware of their greed and cunning he shook the powdery crumb from his hands. They never expected that. Manna.[1] Live on fishy flesh they have to, all seabirds, gulls, seagoose. Swans from Anna Liffey[2] swim down here sometimes to preen themselves. No accounting for tastes. Wonder what kind is swanmeat. Robinson Crusoe had to live on them.

They wheeled, flapping weakly. I'm not going to throw any more. Penny quite enough. Lot of thanks I get. Not even a caw. They spread foot and mouth disease too. If you cram a turkey, say, on chestnutmeal it tastes like that. Eat pig like pig. But then why is it that saltwater fish are not salty? How is that?

His eyes sought answer from the river and saw a rowboat rock at anchor on the treacly swells lazily its plastered board.

Kino's

11 / -

Trousers[3]

Good idea that. Wonder if he pays rent to the corporation. How can you own water really? It's always flowing in a stream, never the same, which in the stream of life we trace. Because life is a stream. All kinds of places are good for ads. That quack doctor for the clap used to be stuck up in all the greenhouses. Never see it now. Strictly confidential. Dr Hy Franks. Didn't cost him a red like Maginni the dancing master self advertisement. Got fellows to stick them up or stick them up himself for that matter on the q.t. running in to loosen a button. Flybynight. Just the place too. POST NO BILLS. POST NO PILLS.[4] Some chap with a dose burning him.

If he . . .

O!

Eh?

No. . . No.

No, no. I don't believe it. He wouldn't surely?

No, no.[5]

Mr Bloom moved forward, raising his troubled eyes. Think no more about that. After one. Timeball on the ballastoffice is down. Dunsink time. Fascinating little book that is of Sir Robert Ball's. Parallax. I never exactly under-

---

1. The divine food (small, round, and white) that the children of Israel ate in the wilderness (Exodus 16.14–15).

2. The Liffey flows from the Wicklow Mountains northeast and east to Dublin Bay.

3. I.e., eleven shillings ("11 /-") for Kino's Trousers. Bloom is a canvasser for advertisements: he receives commissions from newspapers for getting tradesmen to place advertisements with them.

4. The revised text edited by John Kidd (1993) reads, POST NO BILLS. POST 110 PILLS. "Post no bills" can mean either "do not affix any posters" or "mail no accounts." Bloom is punning to himself on the quack doctor's advertising (by posting bills), collecting his money (by mailing accounts), and sending pills to patients by mail.

5. Blazes Boylan, flashy philanderer, is due to call on Molly Bloom that afternoon, to discuss the program of a concert that he is managing for her (Molly is a singer). Bloom knows that Boylan and his wife will commit adultery together. Here it suddenly occurs to him that Boylan might give Molly a "dose" of venereal disease, but he puts the thought from him as incredible.

6. The "timeball on the ballastoffice" registers the official time of the observatory at Dunsink. Noticing that the timeball is down, which means that it is after one o'clock, Bloom is reminded of the observatory, then of the Irish astronomer Sir Robert Ball's popular book on astronomy, *The Story of the Heavens* (1886), and of the astronomical term "parallax" he found in the book but "never exactly understood."

stood.[6] There's a priest. Could ask him. Par it's Greek: parallel, parallax. Met him pike hoses[7] she called it till I told her about the transmigration. O rocks!

Mr Bloom smiled O rocks at two windows of the ballastoffice. She's right after all. Only big words for ordinary things on account of the sound. She's not exactly witty. Can be rude too. Blurt out what I was thinking. Still I don't know. She used to say Ben Dollard had a base barreltone voice. He has legs like barrels and you'd think he was singing into a barrel. Now isn't that wit? They used to call him big Ben. Not half as witty as calling him base barreltone. Appetite like an albatross. Get outside of a baron of beef. Powerful man he was at stowing away number one Bass.[8] Barrel of Bass. See? It all works out.

A procession of whitesmocked men marched slowly towards him along the gutter, scarlet sashes across their boards. Bargains. Like that priest they are this morning: we have sinned: we have suffered. He read the scarlet letters on their five tall white hats: H. E. L. Y. S. Wisdom Hely's. Y lagging behind drew a chunk of bread from under his foreboard, crammed it into his mouth and munched as he walked. Our staple food. Three bob a day, walking along the gutters, street after street. Just keep skin and bone together, bread and skilly. They are not Boyl: no: M'Glade's men. Doesn't bring in any business either. I suggested to him about a transparent showcart with two smart girls sitting inside writing letters, copybooks, envelopes, blottingpaper. I bet that would have caught on. Smart girls writing something catch the eye at once. Everyone dying to know what she's writing. Get twenty of them round you if you stare at nothing. Have a finger in the pie. Women too. Curiosity. Pillar of salt. Wouldn't have it of course because he didn't think of it himself first. Or the inkbottle I suggested with a false stain of black celluloid. His ideas for ads like Plumtree's potted under the obituaries, cold meat department. You can't lick 'em. What? Our envelopes. Hello! Jones, where are you going? Can't stop, Robinson, I am hastening to purchase the only reliable inkeraser *Kansell*, sold by Hely's Ltd, 85 Dame street. Well out of that ruck I am. Devil of a job it was collecting accounts of those convents. Tranquilla convent. That was a nice nun there, really sweet face. Wimple suited her small head. Sister? Sister? I am sure she was crossed in love by her eyes. Very hard to bargain with that sort of a woman. I disturbed her at her devotions that morning. But glad to communicate with the outside world. Our great day, she said. Feast of Our Lady of Mount Carmel. Sweet name too: caramel. She knew, I think she knew by the way she. If she had married she would have changed. I suppose they really were short of money. Fried everything in the best butter all the same. No lard for them. My heart's broke eating dripping. They like buttering themselves in and out. Molly tasting it, her veil up. Sister? Pat Claffey, the pawnbroker's daughter. It was a nun they say invented barbed wire.

He crossed Westmoreland street when apostrophe S had plodded by. Rover cycleshop. Those races are on today. How long ago is that? Year Phil Gilligan died. We were in Lombard street west. Wait, was in Thom's. Got the job in Wisdom Hely's year we married. Six years. Ten years ago: ninetyfour he died, yes that's right the big fire at Arnott's. Val Dillon was lord mayor. The Glencree dinner. Alderman Robert O'Reilly emptying the port into his soup before the flag fell, Bobbob lapping it for the inner alderman. Couldn't hear

7. Molly's way of pronouncing *metempsychosis*. When Bloom had explained metempsychosis to her that morning, she had exclaimed "O rocks" at the preten-tious term. He now mentally repeats "O rocks!" at the thought of the word *parallax*.
8. A popular British ale.

what the band played. For what we have already received may the Lord make us. Milly[9] was a kiddy then. Molly had that elephantgrey dress with the braided frogs. Mantailored with selfcovered buttons. She didn't like it because I sprained my ankle first day she wore choir picnic at the Sugarloaf. As if that. Old Goodwin's tall hat done up with some sticky stuff. Flies' picnic too. Never put a dress on her back like it. Fitted her like a glove, shoulder and hips. Just beginning to plump it out well. Rabbitpie we had that day. People looking after her.

Happy. Happier then. Snug little room that was with the red wallpaper, Dockrell's, one and ninepence a dozen. Milly's tubbing night. American soap I bought: elderflower. Cosy smell of her bathwater. Funny she looked soaped all over. Shapely too. Now photography.[1] Poor papa's daguerreotype atelier he told me of. Hereditary taste.

He walked along the curbstone.

Stream of life. What was the name of that priestlylooking chap was always squinting in when he passed? Weak eyes, woman. Stopped in Citron's saint Kevin's parade. Pen something. Pendennis? My memory is getting. Pen . . . ? Of course it's years ago. Noise of the trams probably. Well, if he couldn't remember the dayfather's name that he sees every day.

Bartell d'Arcy was the tenor, just coming out then. Seeing her home after practice. Conceited fellow with his waxedup moustache. Gave her that song *Winds that blow from the south.*

Windy night that was I went to fetch her there was that lodge meeting on about those lottery tickets after Goodwin's concert in the supperroom or oak-room of the Mansion house. He and I behind. Sheet of her music blew out of my hand against the High school railings. Lucky it didn't. Thing like that spoils the effect of a night for her. Professor Goodwin linking her in front. Shaky on his pins, poor old sot. His farewell concerts. Positively last appearance on any stage. May be for months and may be for never. Remember her laughing at the wind, her blizzard collar up. Corner of Harcourt road remember that gust. Brrfoo! Blew up all her skirts and her boa nearly smothered old Goodwin. She did get flushed in the wind. Remember when we got home raking up the fire and frying up those pieces of lap of mutton for her supper with the Chutney sauce she liked. And the mulled rum. Could see her in the bedroom from the hearth unclamping the busk of her stays: white.

Swish and soft flop her stays made on the bed. Always warm from her. Always liked to let her self out. Sitting there after till near two taking out her hairpins. Milly tucked up in beddyhouse. Happy. Happy. That was the night. . .

—O, Mr Bloom, how do you do?

—O, how do you do, Mrs Breen?[2]

—No use complaining. How is Molly those times? Haven't seen her for ages.

—In the pink, Mr Bloom said gaily, Milly has a position down in Mullingar, you know.

—Go away! Isn't that grand for her?

—Yes, in a photographer's there. Getting on like a house on fire. How are all your charges?

---

9. Bloom's fifteen-year-old daughter.   2. Mrs. Breen had been an old sweetheart of Bloom's.
1. Milly is working at a photographer's.

—All on the baker's list, Mrs Breen said.

How many has she? No other in sight.

—You're in black I see. You have no . . .

—No, Mr. Bloom said. I have just come from a funeral.

Going to crop up all day, I foresee. Who's dead, when and what did he die of? Turn up like a bad penny.

—O dear me, Mrs Breen said, I hope it wasn't any near relation.

May as well get her sympathy.

—Dignam, Mr Bloom said. An old friend of mine. He died quite suddenly, poor fellow. Heart trouble, I believe. Funeral was this morning.

> *Your funeral's tomorrow*
> *While you're coming through the rye.*
> *Diddlediddle dumdum*
> *Diddlediddle . . .*

—Sad to lose the old friends, Mrs Breen's womaneyes said melancholily.

Now that's quite enough about that. Just quietly: husband.

—And your lord and master?

Mrs Breen turned up her two large eyes. Hasn't lost them anyhow.

—O, don't be talking, she said. He's a caution to rattlesnakes. He's in there now with his lawbooks finding out the law of libel. He has me heartscalded. Wait till I show you.

Hot mockturtle vapour and steam of newbaked jampuffs rolypoly poured out from Harrison's. The heavy noonreek tickled the top of Mr Bloom's gullet. Want to make good pastry, butter, best flour, Demerara sugar, or they'd taste it with the hot tea. Or is it from her? A barefoot arab stood over the grating, breathing in the fumes. Deaden the gnaw of hunger that way. Pleasure or pain is it? Penny dinner. Knife and fork chained to the table.

Opening her handbag, chipped leather, hatpin: ought to have a guard on those things. Stick it in a chap's eye in the tram. Rummaging. Open. Money. Please take one. Devils if they lose sixpence. Raise Cain. Husband barging. Where's the ten shillings I gave you on Monday? Are you feeding your little brother's family? Soiled handkerchief: medicinebottle. Pastille that was fell. What is she? . . .

—There must be a new moon out, she said. He's always bad then.[3] Do you know what he did last night?

Her hand ceased to rummage. Her eyes fixed themselves on him, wide in alarm, yet smiling.

—What? Mr. Bloom asked.

Let her speak. Look straight in her eyes. I believe you. Trust me.

—Woke me up in the night, she said. Dream he had, a nightmare.

Indiges.

—Said the ace of spades[4] was walking up the stairs.

—The ace of spades! Mr Bloom said.

She took a folded postcard from her handbag.

—Read that, she said. He got it this morning.

—What is it? Mr Bloom asked, taking the card. U. P.?

---

3. Mr. Breen is mentally disturbed.   4. Symbol of death.

—U.p.: up, she said. Someone taking a rise out of him. It's a great shame for them whoever he is.

—Indeed it is, Mr Bloom said.

She took back the card, sighing.

—And now he's going round to Mr Menton's office. He's going to take an action for ten thousand pounds, he says.

She folded the card into her untidy bag and snapped the catch.

Same blue serge dress she had two years ago, the nap bleaching. Seen its best days. Wispish hair over her ears. And that dowdy toque: three old grapes to take the harm out of it. Shabby genteel. She used to be a tasty dresser. Lines round her mouth. Only a year or so older than Molly.

See the eye that woman gave her, passing. Cruel. The unfair sex.

He looked still at her, holding back behind his look his discontent. Pungent mockturtle oxtail mulligatawny. I'm hungry too. Flakes of pastry on the gusset of her dress: daub of sugary flour stuck to her cheek. Rhubarb tart with liberal fillings, rich fruit interior. Josie Powell that was. In Luke Doyle's long ago, Dolphin's Barn, the charades. U.p.: up.

Change the subject.

—Do you ever see anything of Mrs Beaufoy, Mr Bloom asked.

—Mina Purefoy? she said.

Philip Beaufoy I was thinking. Playgoers' Club[5] Matcham often thinks of the masterstroke. Did I pull the chain? Yes. The last act.

—Yes.

—I just called to ask on the way in is she over it. She's in the lying-in hospital in Holles street. Dr Horne got her in. She's three days bad now.

—O, Mr Bloom said. I'm sorry to hear that.

—Yes, Mrs Breen said. And a houseful of kids at home. It's a very stiff birth, the nurse told me.

—O, Mr Bloom said.

His heavy pitying gaze absorbed her news. His tongue clacked in compassion. Dth! Dth!

—I'm sorry to hear that, he said. Poor thing! Three days! That's terrible for her.

Mrs Breen nodded

—She was taken bad on the Tuesday . . .

Mr Bloom touched her funnybone gently, warning her.

—Mind! Let this man pass.

A bony form strode along the curbstone from the river, staring with a rapt gaze into the sunlight through a heavystringed glass. Tight as a skullpiece a tiny hat gripped his head. From his arm a folded dustcoat, a stick and an umbrella dangled to his stride.

—Watch him, Mr Bloom said. He always walks outside the lampposts. Watch!

—Who is he if it's a fair question? Mrs Breen asked. Is he dotty?

—His name is Cashel Boyle O'Connor Fitzmaurice Tisdall Farrell, Mr Bloom said smiling. Watch!

—He has enough of them, she said. Denis will be like that one of these days.

5. Bloom is thinking of the story *Matcham's Masterstroke*, by "Mr. Philip Beaufoy, Playgoers' Club, London," which he had read in the toilet that morning. He then mentally quotes the opening sentence.

She broke off suddenly.

—There he is, she said. I must go after him. Goodbye. Remember me to
Molly, won't you?

—I will, Mr Bloom said.

He watched her dodge through passers towards the shopfronts. Denis Breen
in skimpy frockcoat and blue canvas shoes shuffled out of Harrison's hugging
two heavy tomes to his ribs. Blown in from the bay. Like old times. He suffered
her to overtake him without surprise and thrust his dull grey beard towards
her, his loose jaw wagging as he spoke earnestly.

Meshuggah.[6] Off his chump.

Mr Bloom walked on again easily, seeing ahead of him in sunlight the tight
skullpiece, the dangling stick, umbrella, dustcoat. Going the two days. Watch
him! Out he goes again. One way of getting on in the world. And that other
old mosey lunatic in those duds. Hard time she must have with him.

U.p.: up. I'll take my oath that's Alf Bergan or Richie Goulding. Wrote it
for a lark in the Scotch house, I bet anything. Round to Menton's office. His
oyster eyes staring at the postcard. Be a feast for the gods.

He passed the *Irish Times*. There might be other answers lying there. Like
to answer them all. Good system for criminals. Code. At their lunch now.
Clerk with the glasses there doesn't know me. O, leave them there to simmer.
Enough bother wading through fortyfour of them. Wanted smart lady typist to
aid gentleman in literary work. I called you naughty darling because I do not
like that other world. Please tell me what is the meaning. Please tell me what
perfume does your wife. Tell me who made the world. The way they spring
those questions on you. And the other one Lizzie Twigg.[7] My literary efforts
have had the good fortune to meet with the approval of the eminent poet A.
E. (Mr Geo. Russell).[8] No time to do her hair drinking sloppy tea with a book
of poetry.

Best paper by long chalks for a small ad. Got the provinces now. Cook and
general, exc cuisine, housemaid kept. Wanted live man for spirit counter.
Resp. girl (R. C.) wishes to hear of post in fruit or pork shop. James Carlisle
made that. Six and a half per cent dividend. Made a big deal on Coates's
shares. Ca' canny. Cunning old Scotch hunks. All the toady news. Our gracious and popular vicereine.[9] Bought the *Irish Field* now. Lady Mountcashel
has quite recovered after her confinement and rode out with the Ward Union
staghounds at the enlargement yesterday at Rathoath. Uneatable fox. Pothunt-
ers too. Fear injects juices make it tender enough for them. Riding astride. Sit
her horse like a man. Weightcarrying huntress. No sidesaddle or pillion for
her, not for Joe. First to the meet and in at the death. Strong as a broodmare
some of those horsey women. Swagger around livery stables. Toss off a glass of
brandy neat while you'd say knife. That one at the Grosvenor this morning.
Up with her on the car: wishwish. Stonewall or fivebarred gate put her mount
to it. Think that pugnosed driver did it out of spite. Who is this she was like?

6. Mad (Yiddish).
7. Bloom is mentally quoting a letter written to him
by the typist Martha Clifford, with whom he is carrying
on a purely epistolary love affair (she had misspelled
word as *world*: "I do not like that other world"). Lizzie
Twigg was one of the other typists who had answered
his advertisement for a secretary "to aid gentleman in
literary work" (Bloom's pretext for beginning such an
affair).

8. A. E. (George Russell, 1867–1935), the Irish poet
mentioned as a reference by Lizzie Twigg when she
answered Bloom's advertisement, is later encountered
by Bloom with a woman who Bloom speculates might
be Lizzie.
9. Wife of the viceroy, who represented the British
Crown in Ireland; Bloom is thinking of the society column in the *Irish Times*.

O yes! Mrs Miriam Dandrade that sold me her old wraps and black under-clothes in the Shelbourne hotel. Divorced Spanish American. Didn't take a feather out of her my handling them. As if I was her clotheshorse. Saw her in the viceregal party when Stubbs the park ranger got me in with Whelan of the *Express*. Scavenging what the quality left. High tea. Mayonnaise I poured on the plums thinking it was custard. Her ears ought to have tingled for a few weeks after. Want to be a bull for her. Born courtesan. No nursery work for her, thanks.

Poor Mrs Purefoy! Methodist husband. Method in his madness. Saffron bun and milk and soda lunch in the educational dairy. Eating with a stop-watch, thirtytwo chews to the minute. Still his muttonchop whiskers grew. Supposed to be well connected. Theodore's cousin in Dublin Castle. One tony relative in every family. Hardy annuals he presents her with. Saw him out at the Three Jolly Topers marching along bareheaded and his eldest boy carrying one in a marketnet. The squallers. Poor thing! Then having to give the breast year after year all hours of the night. Selfish those t.t's[1] are. Dog in the manger. Only one lump of sugar in my tea, if you please.

He stood at Fleet street crossing. Luncheon interval a sixpenny at Rowe's? Must look up that ad in the national library.[2] An eightpenny in the Burton. Better. On my way.

He walked on past Bolton's Westmoreland house. Tea. Tea. Tea. I forgot to tap Tom Kernan.[3]

Sss. Dth, dth, dth! Three days imagine groaning on a bed with a vinegared handkerchief round her forehead, her belly swollen out. Phew! Dreadful sim-ply! Child's head too big: forceps. Doubled up inside her trying to butt its way out blindly, groping for the way out. Kill me that would. Lucky Molly got over hers lightly. They ought to invent something to stop that. Life with hard labour. Twilightsleep idea: queen Victoria was given that. Nine she had. A good layer. Old woman that lived in a shoe she had so many children. Sup-pose he was consumptive. Time someone thought about it instead of gassing about the what was it the pensive bosom of the silver effulgence. Flapdoodle to feed fools on. They could easily have big establishments. Whole thing quite painless out of all the taxes give every child born five quid at compound inter-est up to twentyone, five per cent is a hundred shillings and five tiresome pounds, multiply by twenty decimal system, encourage people to put by money save hundred and ten and a bit twentyone years want to work it out on paper come to a tidy sum, more than you think.

Not stillborn of course. They are not even registered. Trouble for nothing.

Funny sight two of them together, their bellies out. Molly and Mrs Moisel. Mothers' meeting. Phthisis retires for the time being, then returns. How flat they look after all of a sudden! Peaceful eyes. Weight off their mind. Old Mrs Thornton was a jolly old soul. All my babies, she said. The spoon of pap in her mouth before she fed them. O, that's nyumyum. Got her hand crushed by old Tom Wall's son. His first bow to the public. Head like a prize pumpkin. Snuffy Dr Murren. People knocking them up at all hours. For God's sake

1. Abbreviation of "Teetotallers," total abstainers from alcohol.
2. Bloom's goal, on his walk through Dublin, is the National Library, where he wants to look up an adver-tisement in a back number of the *Kilkenny People*.
3. A Dublin tea merchant and friend of Bloom's, whom Bloom had earlier intended to ask ("tap") for some tea.

doctor. Wife in her throes. Then keep them waiting months for their fee. To attendance on your wife. No gratitude in people. Humane doctors, most of them.

Before the huge high door of the Irish house of parliament a flock of pigeons flew. Their little frolic after meals. Who will we do it on? I pick the fellow in black. Here goes. Here's good luck. Must be thrilling from the air. Apjohn, myself and Owen Goldberg up in the trees near Goose green playing the monkeys. Mackerel they called me.

A squad of constables debouched from College street, marching in Indian file. Goosestep. Foodheated faces, sweating helmets, patting their truncheons. After their feed with a good load of fat soup under their belts. Policeman's lot is oft a happy one.[4] They split up into groups and scattered, saluting towards their beats. Let out to graze. Best moment to attack one in pudding time. A punch in his dinner. A squad of others, marching irregularly, rounded Trinity railings, making for the station. Bound for their troughs. Prepare to receive cavalry. Prepare to receive soup.

He crossed under Tommy Moore's roguish finger. They did right to put him up over a urinal: meeting of the waters.[5] Ought to be places for women. Running into cakeshops. Settle my hat straight. *There is not in this wide world a vallee.* Great song of Julia Morkan's. Kept her voice up to the very last. Pupil of Michael Balfe's wasn't she?

He gazed after the last broad tunic. Nasty customers to tackle. Jack Power could a tale unfold: father a G man. If a fellow gave them trouble being lagged they let him have it hot and heavy in the bridewell.[6] Can't blame them after all with the job they have especially the young hornies. That horsepoliceman the day Joe Chamberlain was given his degree in Trinity he got a run for his money.[7] My word he did! His horse's hoofs clattering after us down Abbey street. Luck I had the presence of mind to dive into Manning's or I was souped. He did come a wallop, by George. Must have cracked his skull on the cobblestones. I oughtn't to have got myself swept along with those medicals. And the Trinity jibs[8] in their mortarboards. Looking for trouble. Still I got to know that young Dixon who dressed that sting for me in the Mater and now he's in Holles street where Mrs Purefoy. Wheels within wheels. Police whistle in my ears still.All skedaddled. Why he fixed on me. Give me in charge. Right here it began.

—Up the Boers!

—Three cheers for De Wet![9]

—We'll hang Joe Chamberlain on a sourapple tree.

Silly billies: mob of young cubs yelling their guts out. Vinegar hill. The Butter exchange band. Few years' time half of them magistrates and civil servants. War comes on: into the army helterskelter: same fellows used to. Whether on the scaffold high.

Never know who you're talking to. Corny Kelleher he has Harvey Duff in his eye. Like that Peter or Denis or James Carey that blew the gaff on the

4. Cf. W. S. Gilbert, *Pirates of Penzance:* "The policeman's lot is not a happy one."
5. *The Meeting of the Waters* was a famous poem by the much-loved Irish poet Thomas Moore (1779–1852), whose statue Bloom now passes.
6. Prison.
7. When Joseph Chamberlain, the British colonial secretary, came to Dublin to receive an honorary degree from Trinity College, a group of medical students rioted against him and against the Boer War.
8. Trinity College students.
9. Boer general.

invincibles. Member of the corporation too. Egging raw youths on to get in the know. All the time drawing secret service pay from the castle.[1] Drop him like a hot potato. Why those plainclothes men are always courting slaveys. Easily twig a man used to uniform. Squarepushing up against a backdoor. Maul her a bit. Then the next thing on the menu. And who is the gentleman does be visiting there? Was the young master saying anything? Peeping Tom through the keyhole. Decoy duck. Hotblooded young student fooling round her fat arms ironing.

—Are those yours, Mary?

—I don't wear such things. . . Stop or I'll tell the missus on you. Out half the night.

—There are great times coming, Mary. Wait till you see.

—Ah, get along with your great times coming.

Barmaids too. Tobaccoshopgirls.

James Stephens'[2] idea was the best. He knew them. Circles of ten so that a fellow couldn't round on more than his own ring. Sinn Fein.[3] Back out you get the knife. Hidden hand. Stay in. The firing squad. Turnkey's daughter got him out of Richmond, off from Lusk. Putting up in the Buckingham Palace hotel under their very noses. Garibaldi.[4]

You must have a certain fascination: Parnell. Arthur Griffith[5] is a square-headed fellow but he has no go in him for the mob. Want to gas about our lovely land. Gammon and spinach. Dublin Bakery Company's tearoom. Debating societies. That republicanism is the best form of government. That the language question should take precedence of the economic question. Have your daughters inveigling them to your house. Stuff them up with meat and drink. Michaelmas goose. Here's a good lump of thyme seasoning under the apron for you. Have another quart of goosegrease before it gets too cold. Halffed enthusiasts. Penny roll and a walk with the band. No grace for the carver. The thought that the other chap pays best sauce in the world. Make themselves thoroughly at home. Show us over those apricots, meaning peaches. The not far distant day. Home Rule sun rising up in the northwest.[6]

His smile faded as he walked, a heavy cloud hiding the sun slowly, shadowing Trinity's surly front. Trams passed one another, ingoing, outgoing, clanging. Useless words. Things go on same; day after day: squads of police marching out, back: trams in, out. Those two loonies mooching about. Dignam carted off. Mina Purefoy swollen belly on a bed groaning to have a child tugged out of her. One born every second somewhere. Other dying every second. Since I fed the birds five minutes. Three hundred kicked the bucket. Other three hundred born, washing the blood off, all are washed in the blood of the lamb, bawling maaaaaa.

Cityful passing away, other cityful coming, passing away too: other coming on, passing on. Houses, lines of houses, streets, miles of pavements, piledup bricks, stones. Changing hands. This owner, that. Landlord never dies they

---

1. I.e., from the British government, whose representative lived at Dublin Castle.
2. Irish nationalist revolutionary.
3. Irish revolutionary movement; the Gaelic words mean "We Ourselves."
4. Bloom is thinking of a variety of nationalist conspirators who escaped from danger, among them the 19th-century Italian patriot and general Giuseppe Garibaldi.

5. Griffith (1872–1922), founder of the Sinn Fein. Charles Stewart Parnell (1846–1891), Irish nationalist political leader.
6. Reference to Griffith's comment on the *Freeman* masthead, which showed the sun rising in the northwest from behind the Bank of Ireland. Bloom has a *Freeman* in his pocket.

say. Other steps into his shoes when he gets his notice to quit. They buy the
place up with gold and still they have all the gold. Swindle in it somewhere.
Piled up in cities, worn away age after age. Pyramids in sand. Built on bread
and onions. Slaves Chinese wall. Babylon. Big stones left. Round towers. Rest
rubble, sprawling suburbs, jerrybuilt, Kerwan's mushroom houses built of
breeze. Shelter for the night.

No-one is anything.

This is the very worst hour of the day. Vitality. Dull, gloomy: hate this hour.
Feel as if I had been eaten and spewed.

Provost's house. The reverend Dr Salmon: tinned salmon. Well tinned in
there. Wouldn't live in it if they paid me. Hope they have liver and bacon
today. Nature abhors a vacuum.

The sun freed itself slowly and lit glints of light among the silverware in
Walter Sexton's window opposite by which John Howard Parnell[7] passed,
unseeing.

There he is: the brother. Image of him. Haunting face. Now that's a coincidence. Course hundreds of times you think of a person and don't meet him.
Like a man walking in his sleep. No-one knows him. Must be a corporation
meeting today. They say he never put on the city marshal's uniform since he
got the job. Charley Beulger used to come out on his high horse, cocked hat,
puffed, powdered and shaved. Look at the woebegone walk of him. Eaten a
bad egg. Poached eyes on ghost. I have a pain. Great man's brother: his brother's brother. He'd look nice on the city charger. Drop into the D. B. C. probably for his coffee, play chess there. His brother used men as pawns. Let them
all go to pot. Afraid to pass a remark on him. Freeze them up with that eye of
his. That's the fascination: the name. All a bit touched. Mad Fanny and his
other sister Mrs Dickinson driving about with scarlet harness. Bolt upright like
surgeon M'Ardle. Still David Sheehy beat him for south Meath. Apply for the
Chiltern Hundreds[8] and retire into public life. The patriot's banquet. Eating
orangepeels in the park. Simon Dedalus said when they put him in parliament
that Parnell would come back from the grave and lead him out of the House
of Commons by the arm.

—Of the twoheaded octopus, one of whose heads is the head upon which
the ends of the world have forgotten to come while the other speaks with a
Scotch accent. The tentacles . . .

They passed from behind Mr Bloom along the curbstone. Beard and bicycle. Young woman.

And there he is too. Now that's really a coincidence: second time. Coming
events cast their shadows before. With the approval of the eminent poet, Mr
Geo Russell. That might be Lizzie Twigg with him.[9] A. E.: what does that
mean? Initials perhaps. Albert Edward, Arthur Edmund, Alphonsus Eb Ed El
Esquire. What was he saying? The ends of the world with a Scotch accent.
Tentacles: octopus. Something occult: symbolism. Holding forth. She's taking
it all in. Not saying a word. To aid gentleman in literary work.

7. Parnell's brother.
8. The Stewardship of the Chiltern Hundreds (a tract
of land in central England owned by the British
Crown) is by a legal figment held to be an office of
profit under the Crown and is conferred on any Member of Parliament wishing to resign his seat, which by
law he cannot do, so long as he is duly qualified. A

Member of Parliament who accepts an office of profit
under the Crown must vacate his seat.
9. Bloom wonders whether the woman with A. E.
might be Lizzie Twigg and then goes on to speculate
on the meaning of "A. E." and on Russell's mystical
ideas.

His eyes followed the high figure in homespun, beard and bicycle, a listening woman at his side. Coming from the vegetarian. Only weggebobbles and fruit. Don't eat a beefsteak. If you do the eyes of that cow will pursue you through all eternity. They say it's healthier. Wind and watery though. Tried it. Keep you on the run all day. Bad as a bloater. Dreams all night. Why do they call that thing they gave me nutsteak? Nutarians. Fruitarians. To give you the idea you are eating rumpsteak. Absurd. Salty too. They cook in soda. Keep you sitting by the tap all night.

Her stockings are loose over her ankles. I detest that: so tasteless. Those literary etherial people they are all. Dreamy, cloudy, symbolistic. Esthetes they are. I wouldn't be surprised if it was that kind of food you see produces the like waves of the brain the poetical. For example one of those policemen sweating Irish stew into their shirts; you couldn't squeeze a line of poetry out of him. Don't know what poetry is even. Must be in a certain mood.

> The dreamy cloudy gull
> Waves o'er the waters dull.

He crossed at Nassau street corner and stood before the window of Yeates and Son, pricing the fieldglasses. Or will I drop into old Harris's and have a chat with young Sinclair? Wellmannered fellow. Probably at his lunch. Must get those old glasses of mine set right. Gœrz lenses six guineas. Germans making their way everywhere. Sell on easy terms to capture trade. Undercutting. Might chance on a pair in the railway lost property office. Astonishing the things people leave behind them in trains and cloakrooms. What do they be thinking about? Women too. Incredible. Last year travelling to Ennis had to pick up that farmer's daughter's bag and hand it to her at Limerick junction. Unclaimed money too. There's a little watch up there on the roof of the bank to test those glasses by.

His lids came down on the lower rims of his irides. Can't see it. If you imagine it's there you can almost see it. Can't see it.

He faced about and, standing between the awnings, held out his right hand at arm's length towards the sun. Wanted to try that often. Yes: completely. The tip of his little finger blotted out the sun's disk. Must be the focus where the rays cross. If I had black glasses. Interesting. There was a lot of talk about those sunspots when we were in Lombard street west. Terrific explosions they are. There will be a total eclipse this year: autumn some time.

Now that I come to think of it, that ball falls at Greenwich time. It's the clock is worked by an electric wire from Dunsink. Must go out there some first Saturday of the month. If I could get an introduction to professor Joly or learn up something about his family. That would do to: man always feels complimented. Flattery where least expected. Nobleman proud to be descended from some king's mistress. His foremother. Lay it on with a trowel. Cap in hand goes through the land. Not go in and blurt out what you know you're not to: what's parallax? Show this gentleman the door.

Ah.

His hand fell again to his side.

Never know anything about it. Waste of time. Gasballs spinning about, crossing each other, passing. Same old dingdong always. Gas, then solid, then world, then cold, then dead shell drifting around, frozen rock like that pineapple rock. The moon. Must be a new moon out, she said. I believe there is.

He went on by la maison Claire.

Wait. The full moon was the night we were Sunday fortnight exactly there is a new moon. Walking down by the Tolka. Not bad for a Fairview moon. She was humming. The young May moon she's beaming, love. He other side of her. Elbow, arm. He. Glowworm's la-amp is gleaming, love. Touch. Fingers. Asking. Answer. Yes.

Stop. Stop. If it was it was.[1] Must.

Mr Bloom, quickbreathing, slowlier walking passed Adam court.

With deep quiet relief, his eyes took note: this is street here middle of the day Bob Doran's bottle shoulders. On his annual bend, M'Coy said. They drink in order to say or do something or *cherchez la femme.*[2] Up in the Coombe with chummies and streetwalkers and then the rest of the year as sober as a judge.

Yes. Thought so. Sloping into the Empire. Gone. Plain soda would do him good. Where Pat Kinsella had his Harp theatre before Whitbread ran the Queen's.[3] Broth of a boy. Dion Boucicault[4] business with his harvestmoon face in a poky bonnet. Three Purty Maids from School. How time flies eh? Showing long red pantaloons under his skirts. Drinkers, drinking, laughed spluttering, their drink against their breath. More power, Pat. Coarse red: fun for drunkards: guffaw and smoke. Take off that white hat. His parboiled eyes. Where is he now? Beggar somewhere. The harp that once did starve us all.[5]

I was happier then. Or was that I? Or am I now I? Twentyeight I was. She twentythree when we left Lombard street west something changed. Could never like it again after Rudy. Can't bring back time. Like holding water in your hand. Would you go back to then? Just beginning then. Would you? Are you not happy in your home, you poor little naughty boy? Wants to sew on buttons for me. I must answer. Write it in the library.

Grafton street gay with housed awnings lured his senses. Muslin prints silk, dames and dowagers, jingle of harnesses, hoofthuds lowringing in the baking causeway. Thick feet that woman has in the white stockings. Hope the rain mucks them up on her. Countrybred chawbacon. All the beef to the heels were in. Always gives a woman clumsy feet. Molly looks out of plumb.

He passed, dallying, the windows of Brown Thomas, silk mercers. Cascades of ribbons. Flimsy China silks. A tilted urn poured from its mouth a flood of bloodhued poplin: lustrous blood. The huguenots brought that here. *La causa è santa!*[6] *Tara tara.* Great chorus that. *Tara.* Must be washed in rainwater. Meyerbeer. *Tara: bom bom bom.*

Pincushions. I'm a long time threatening to buy one. Stick them all over the place. Needles in window curtains.

He bared slightly his left forearm. Scrape: nearly gone. Not today anyhow. Must go back for that lotion. For her birthday perhaps. Junejuly augseptember eighth. Nearly three months off. Then she mightn't like it. Women won't pick up pins. Say it cuts lo.

Gleaming silks, petticoats on slim brass rails, rays of flat silk stockings.

1. Bloom is thinking again of his wife's infidelity.
2. Look for the woman (in the case).
3. The Queen's Theatre.
4. Irish-born American dramatist, manager, and actor.
5. A reference to the lack of financial success of the Harp Theatre through a punning reworking (almost worthy of Stephen Dedalus) of Moore's famous *Harp*

That Once Through Tara's Halls.
6. "The cause is sacred," chorus from Meyerbeer's opera *Les Huguenots,* which Bloom is recalling. The Huguenots were 16th- and 17th-century French Protestants, many of whom fled to Britain to escape persecution.

2402

Useless to go back. Had to be. Tell me all.

High voices. Sunwarm silk. Jingling harnesses. All for a woman, home and houses, silkwebs, silver, rich fruits, spicy from Jaffa. Agendath Netaim.[7] Wealth of the world.

A warm human plumpness settled down on his brain. His brain yielded. Perfume of embraces all him assailed. With hungered flesh obscurely, he mutely craved to adore.

Duke street. Here we are. Must eat. The Burton. Feel better then.

He turned Combridge's corner, still pursued. Jingling hoofthuds. Perfumed bodies, warm, full. All kissed, yielded: in deep summer fields, tangled pressed grass, in trickling hallways of tenements, along sofas, creaking beds.

—Jack, love!
—Darling!
—Kiss me, Reggy!
—My boy!
—Love![8]

His heart astir he pushed in the door of the Burton restaurant. Stink gripped his trembling breath: pungent meatjuice, slop of greens. See the animals feed.

Men, men, men.

Perched on high stools by the bar, hats shoved back, at the tables calling for more bread no charge, swilling, wolfing gobfuls of sloppy food, their eyes bulging, wiping wetted moustaches. A pallid suetfaced young man polished his tumbler knife fork and spoon with his napkin. New set of microbes. A man with an infant's saucestained napkin tucked round him shovelled gurgling soup down his gullet. A man spitting back on his plate: halfmasticated gristle: no teeth to chewchewchew it. Chump chop from the grill. Bolting to get it over. Sad booser's eyes. Bitten off more than he can chew. Am I like that? See ourselves as others see us. Hungry man is an angry man. Working tooth and jaw. Don't! O! A bone! That last pagan king of Ireland Cormac in the school-poem choked himself at Sletty southward of the Boyne.[9] Wonder what he was eating. Something galoptious. Saint Patrick converted him to Christianity. Couldn't swallow it all however.

—Roast beef and cabbage.
—One stew.

Smells of men. His gorge rose. Spaton sawdust, sweetish warmish ciga-rettesmoke, reek of plug, spilt beer, men's beery piss, the stale of ferment.

Couldn't eat a morsel here. Fellow sharpening knife and fork, to eat all before him, old chap picking his tootles. Slight spasm, full, chewing the cud. Before and after. Grace after meals. Look on this picture then on that. Scoffing up stewgravy with sopping sippets of bread. Lick it off the plate, man! Get out of this.

He gazed round the stooled and tabled eaters, tightening the wings of his nose.

—Two stouts here.

7. Planters' Company (Hebrew). Bloom recalls a leaflet, which he had seen that morning and is still carrying in his pocket, advertising an early Zionist settlement
8. Sensual images are leading Bloom to imagine love scenes from a sentimental novel. The Lestrygonians had used "the handsome daughter of Lestrygonian

Antiphates" as a decoy to lure Ulysses' men to her father, and Bloom is drawn by his sensual and sexual imagination to enter Burton's restaurant—only to be disgusted by the grossness of the atmosphere.
9. Bloom is recalling a "schoolpoem" about a legendary incident in Irish history.

—One corned and cabbage.

That fellow ramming a knifeful of cabbage down as if his life depended on it. Good stroke. Give me the fidgets to look. Safer to eat from his three hands. Tear it limb from limb. Second nature to him. Born with a silver knife in his mouth. That's witty, I think. Or no. Silver means born rich. Born with a knife. But then the allusion is lost.

An illgirt server gathered sticky clattering plates. Rock, the bailiff, standing at the bar blew the foamy crown from his tankard. Well up: it splashed yellow near his boot. A diner, knife and fork upright, elbows on table, ready for a second helping stared towards the food-lift across his stained square of newspaper. Other chap telling him something with his mouth full. Sympathetic listener. Table talk. I munched hum un thu Unchster Bunk un Munchday. Ha? Did you, faith?

Mr Bloom raised two fingers doubtfully to his lips. His eyes said:

—Not here. Don't see him.[1]

Out. I hate dirty eaters.

He backed towards the door. Get a light snack in Davy Byrne's. Stopgap. Keep me going. Had a good breakfast.

—Roast and mashed here.

—Pint of stout.

Every fellow for his own, tooth and nail. Gulp. Grub. Gulp. Gobstuff.

He came out into clearer air and turned back towards Grafton street. Eat or be eaten. Kill! Kill!

Suppose that communal kitchen years to come perhaps. All trotting down with porringers and tommycans to be filled. Devour contents in the street. John Howard Parnell example the provost of Trinity every mother's son don't talk of your provosts and provost of Trinity women and children, cabmen, priests, parsons, fieldmarshals, archbishops. From Ailesbury road, Clyde road, artisans' dwellings north Dublin union, lord mayor in his gingerbread coach, old queen in a bathchair. My plate's empty. After you with our incorporated drinking cup. Like sir Philip Crampton's fountain. Rub off the microbes with your handkerchief. Next chap rubs on a new batch with his. Father O'Flynn would make hares of them all. Have rows all the same. All for number one. Children fighting for the scrapings of the pot. Want a souppot as big as the Phoenix park. Harpooning flitches and hindquarters out of it. Hate people all round you. City Arms hotel *table d'hôte* she called it. Soup, joint and sweet. Never know whose thoughts you're chewing. Then who'd wash up all the plates and forks? Might be all feeding on tabloids that time. Teeth getting worse and worse.

After all there's a lot in that vegetarian fine flavour of things from the earth garlic, of course, it stinks Italian organgrinders crisp of onions mushrooms truffles. Pain to animal too. Pluck and draw fowl. Wretched brutes there at the cattlemarket waiting for the poleaxe to split their skulls open. Moo. Poor trembling calves. Meh. Staggering bob. Bubble and squeak. Butchers' buckets wobble lights. Give us that brisket off the hook. Plup. Rawhead and bloody bones. Flayed glasseyed sheep hung from their haunches, sheepsnouts bloodypapered snivelling nosejam on sawdust. Top and lashers going out. Don't maul them pieces, young one.

1. He pretends he is looking for someone he cannot see, so that he has an excuse to leave without eating.

Hot fresh blood they prescribe for decline. Blood always needed. Insidious. Lick it up smokinghot, thick sugary. Famished ghosts.

Ah, I'm hungry.

He entered Davy Byrne's. Moral pub. He doesn't chat. Stands a drink now and then. But in leapyear once in four. Cashed a cheque for me once.

What will I take now? He drew his watch. Let me see now. Shandygaff?

—Hello, Bloom, Nosey Flynn said from his nook.

—Hello, Flynn.

—How's things?

—Tiptop . . . Let me see. I'll take a glass of burgundy and . . . let me see.

Sardines on the shelves. Almost taste them by looking. Sandwich? Ham and his descendants mustered and bred there. Potted meats. What is home without Plumtree's potted meat? Incomplete. What a stupid ad! Under the obituary notices they stuck it. All up a plumtree. Dignam's potted mat. Cannibals would with lemon and rice. White missionary too salty. Like pickled pork. Expect the chief consumes the parts of honour. Ought to be tough from exercise. His wives in a row to watch the effect. *There was a right royal old nigger. Who ate or something the somethings of the reverend Mr MacTrigger.* With it an abode of bliss. Lord knows what concoction. Cauls mouldy tripes windpipes faked and minced up. Puzzle find the meat. Kosher. No meat and milk together. Hygiene that was what they call now, Yom Kippur fast spring cleaning of inside. Peace and war depend on some fellow's digestion. Religions. Christmas turkeys and geese. Slaughter of innocents. Eat, drink and be merry. Then casual wards full after. Heads bandaged. Cheese digests all but itself. Mighty cheese.

—Have you a cheese sandwich?

—Yes, sir.

Like a few olives too if they had them. Italian I prefer. Good glass of burgundy; take away that. Lubricate. A nice salad, cool as a cucumber. Tom Kernan can dress. Puts gusto into it. Pure olive oil. Milly served me that cutlet with a sprig of parsley. Take one Spanish onion. God made food, the devil the cooks. Devilled crab.

—Wife well?

—Quite well, thanks. . . A cheese sandwich, then. Gorgonzola, have you?

—Yes, sir.

Nosey Flynn sipped his grog.

—Doing any singing those times?

Look at his mouth. Could whistle in his own ear. Flap ears to match. Music. Knows as much about it as my coachman. Still better tell him. Does no harm. Free ad.

—She's engaged for a big tour end of this month. You may have heard perhaps.

—No. O, that's the style. Who's getting it up?

The curate[2] served.

—How much is that?

—Seven d., sir. . . Thank you, sir.

Mr Bloom cut his sandwich into slender strips. *Mr MacTrigger.* Easier than the dreamy creamy stuff. *His five hundred wives. Had the time of their lives.*

---

2. Bartender.

—Mustard, sir?

—Thank you.

He studded under each lifted strip yellow blobs. *Their lives.* I have it. *It grew bigger and bigger and bigger.*

—Getting it up? he said. Well, it's like a company idea, you see. Part shares and part profits.

—Ay, now I remember, Nosey Flynn said, putting his hand in his pocket to scratch his groin. Who is this was telling me? Isn't Blazes Boylan mixed up in it?

A warm shock of air heat of mustard hanched on Mr Bloom's heart. He raised his eyes and met the stare of a bilious clock. Two. Pub clock five minutes fast. Time going on. Hands moving. Two. Not yet.[3]

His midriff yearned then upward, sank within him, yearned more longly, longingly.

Wine.

He smellsipped the cordial juice and, bidding his throat strongly to speed it, set his wineglass delicately down.

—Yes, he said. He's the organiser in point of fact.

No fear: no brains.

Nosey Flynn snuffled and scratched. Flea having a good square meal.

—He had a good slice of luck, Jack Mooney was telling me, over that boxing match Myler Keogh won again that soldier in the Portobello barracks. By God, he had the little kipper down in the country Carlow he was telling me. . . .

Hope that dewdrop doesn't come down into his glass. No, snuffled it up.

—For near a month, man, before it came off. Sucking duck eggs by God till further orders. Keep him off the boose, see? O, by God, Blazes is a hairy chap.

Davy Byrne came forward from the hindbar in tuckstitched shirtsleeves, cleaning his lips with two wipes of his napkin. Herring's blush. Whose smile upon each feature plays with such and such replete. Too much fat on the parsnips.

—And here's himself and pepper on him, Nosey Flynn said. Can you give us a good one for the Gold cup?

—I'm off that, Mr Flynn, Davy Byrne answered. I never put anything on a horse.

—You're right there, Nosey Flynn said.

Mr Bloom ate his strips of sandwich, fresh clean bread, with relish of disgust, pungent mustard, the feety savour of green cheese. Sips of his wine soothed his palate. Not logwood that. Tastes fuller this weather with the chill off.

Nice quiet bar. Nice piece of wood in that counter. Nicely planed. Like the way it curves there.

—I wouldn't do anything at all in that line, Davy Byrne said. It ruined many a man, the same horses.

Vintners' sweepstake. Licensed for the sale of beer, wine and spirits for consumption on the premises. Heads I win tails you lose.

—True for you, Nosey Flynn said. Unless you're in the know. There's no

3. I.e., not yet time for Boylan to visit Molly.

straight sport going now. Lenehan gets some good ones. He's giving Sceptre today. Zinfandel's the favourite, lord Howard de Walden's, won at Epsom. Morny Cannon is riding him. I could have got seven to one against Saint Amant a fortnight before.

—That so? Davy Byrne said. . . .

He went towards the window and, taking up the petty cash book, scanned its pages.

—I could, faith, Nosey Flynn said, snuffling. That was a rare bit of horse-flesh. Saint Frusquin was her sire. She won in a thunderstorm, Rothschild's filly, with wadding in her ears. Blue jacket and yellow cap. Bad luck to big Ben Dollard and his John O'Gaunt. He put me off it. Ay.

He drank resignedly from his tumbler, running his fingers down the flutes.

—Ay, he said, sighing.

Mr Bloom, champing standing, looked upon his sigh. Nosey numbskull. Will I tell him that horse Lenehan?[4] He knows already. Better let him forget. Go and lose more. Fool and his money. Dewdrop coming down again. Cold nose he'd have kissing a woman. Still they might like. Prickly beards they like. Dogs' cold noses. Old Mrs Riordan with the rumbling stomach's Skye terrier in the City Arms hotel. Molly fondling him in her lap. O, the big doggybow-wowsywowsy!

Wine soaked and softened rolled pith of bread mustard a moment mawkish cheese. Nice wine it is. Taste it better because I'm not thirsty. Bath of course does that. Just a bite or two. Then about six o'clock I can. Six. Six. Time will be gone then. She. . .

Mild fire of wine kindled his veins. I wanted that badly. Felt so off colour. His eyes unhungrily saw shelves of tins, sardines, gaudy lobsters' claws. All the odd things people pick up for food. Out of shells, periwinkles with a pin, off trees, snails out of the ground the French eat, out of the sea with bait on a hook. Silly fish learn nothing in a thousand years. If you didn't know risky putting anything into your mouth. Poisonous berries. Johnny Magories. Roundness you think good. Gaudy colour warns you off. One fellow told another and so on. Try it on the dog first. Led on by the smell or the look. Tempting fruit. Ice cones. Cream. Instinct. Orangegroves for instance. Need artificial irrigation. Bleibtreustrasse.[5] Yes but what about oysters. Unsightly like a clot of phlegm. Filthy shells. Devil to open them too. Who found them out? Garbage, sewage they feed on. Fizz and Red bank oysters. Effect on the sexual. Aphrodis. He was in the Red bank this morning. Was he oyster old fish at table. Perhaps he young flesh in bed. No. June has no ar no oysters. But there are people like tainted game. Jugged hare. First catch your hare. Chinese eating eggs fifty years old, blue and green again. Dinner of thirty courses. Each dish harmless might mix inside. Idea for a poison mystery. That archduke Leopold was it. No. Yes, or was it Otto one of those Habsburgs? Or who was it used to eat the scruff off his own head? Cheapest lunch in town. Of course, aristocrats, then the others copy to be in the fashion. Milly too rock oil and flour. Raw pastry I like myself. Half the catch of oysters they throw back in the sea to keep up the price. Cheap. No-one would buy. Caviare. Do the grand. Hock in green glasses. Swell blowout. Lady this. Powdered bosom pearls. The

---

4. Bloom is wondering whether to pass on a tip from Lenehan, who wrote for the racing paper *Sport*.

5. The Berlin street that contained the offices of the "Planters' Company."

élite. Crème de la crème.[6] They want special dishes to pretend they're. Hermit with a platter of pulse keep down the stings of the flesh. Know me come eat with me. Royal sturgeon. High sheriff, Coffey, the butcher, right to venisons of the forest from his ex.[7] Send him back the half of a cow. Spread I saw down in the Master of the Rolls' kitchen area. Whitehatted *Chef* like a rabbi. Combustible duck. Curly cabbage *à la duchesse de Parme.* Just as well to write it on the bill of fare so you can know what you've eaten too many drugs spoil the broth. I know it myself. Dosing it with Edwards' desicated soup. Geese stuffed silly for them. Lobsters boiled alive. Do ptake some ptarmigan. Wouldn't mind being a waiter in a swell hotel. Tips, evening dress, halfnaked ladies. May I tempt you to a little more filleted lemon sole, miss Dubedat? Yes, do bedad. And she did bedad. Huguenot name I expect that. A miss Dubedat lived in Killiney, I remember. *Du, de la,* French. Still it's the same fish, perhaps old Micky Hanlon of Moore street ripped the guts out of making money, hand over fist, finger in fishes' gills, can't write his name on a cheque, think he was painting the landscape with his mouth twisted. Moooikill A Aitcha Ha. Ignorant as a kish of brogues,[8] worth fifty thousand pounds.

Stuck on the pane two flies buzzed, stuck.

Glowing wine on his palate lingered swallowed. Crushing in the winepress grapes of Burgundy. Sun's heat it is. Seems to a secret touch telling me memory. Touched his sense moistened remembered. Hidden under wild ferns on Howth. Below us bay sleeping sky. No sound. The sky. The bay purple by the Lion's head. Green by Drumleck. Yellowgreen towards Sutton. Fields of undersea, the lines faint brown in grass, buried cities. Pillowed on my coat she had her hair, earwigs in the heather scrub my hand under her nape, you'll toss me all. O wonder! Coolsoft with ointments her hand touched me, caressed: her eyes upon me did not turn away. Ravished over her I lay, full lips full open, kissed her mouth. Yum. Softly she gave me in my mouth the seedcake warm and chewed. Mawkish pulp her mouth had mumbled sweet and sour with spittle. Joy: I ate it: joy. Young life, her lips that gave me pouting. Soft, warm, sticky gumjelly lips. Flowers her eyes were, take me, willing eyes. Pebbles fell. She lay still. A goat. No-one. High on Ben Howth rhododendrons a nannygoat walking surefooted, dropping currants. Screened under ferns she laughed warmfolded. Wildly I lay on her, kissed her, eyes, her lips, her stretched neck, beating, woman's breasts full in her blouse of nun's veiling, fat nipples upright. Hot I tongued her. She kissed me. I was kissed. All yielding she tossed my hair. Kissed, she kissed me.[9]

Me. And me now.

Stuck, the flies buzzed.

His downcast eyes followed the silent veining of the oaken slab. Beauty: it curves: curves are beauty. Shapely goddesses, Venus, Juno: curves the world admires. Can see them library museum standing in the round hall, naked goddesses. Aids to digestion. They don't care what man looks. All to see. Never

---

6. Cream of the cream (i.e., the very best, socially).
7. All sturgeon caught in or off Britain were the property of the king, according to the ancient traditional rights to certain kinds of fish or game. Bloom goes on to imagine a Dublin butcher having a "right to venisons of the forest from his ex[cellency]"—i.e., the viceroy.
8. A basket of shoes.
9. Bloom is remembering when he first proposed to

Molly, on the Hill of Howth, near Dublin; Molly also recalls this in the final "Penelope" episode, which is her soliloquy: "we were lying among the rhododendrons on Howth head in the gray tweed suit and his straw hat the day I got him to propose to me yes . . . my God after that long kiss I near lost my breath . . . I saw he understood or felt what a woman is and I knew I could always get round him and I gave him all the pleasure I could leading him on."

speaking, I mean to say to fellows like Flynn. Suppose she did Pygmalion and Galatea[1] what would she say first? Mortal! Put you in your proper place. Quaffing nectar at mess with gods, golden dishes, all ambrosial. Not like a tanner lunch we have, boiled mutton, carrots and turnips, bottle of Allsop. Nectar, imagine it drinking electricity: god's food. Lovely forms of women sculped Junonian. Immortal lovely. And we stuffing food in one hole and out behind: food, chyle, blood, dung, earth, food: have to feed it like stoking an engine. They have no. Never looked. I'll look today. Keeper won't see. Bend down let something see if she.

Dribbling a quiet message from his bladder came to go to do not to do there to do. A man and ready he drained his glass to the lees and walked, to men too they gave themselves, manly conscious, lay with men lovers, a youth enjoyed her, to the yard.

When the sound of his boots had ceased Davy Byrne said from his book:

—What is this he is? Isn't he in the insurance line?

—He's out of that long ago, Nosey Flynn said. He does canvassing for the *Freeman.*

—I know him well to see, Davy Byrne said. Is he in trouble?

—Trouble? Nosey Flynn said. Not that I heard of. Why?

—I noticed he was in mourning.

—Was he? Nosey Flynn said. So he was, faith. I asked him how was all at home. You're right, by God. So he was.

—I never broach the subject, Davy Byrne said humanely, if I see a gentleman is in trouble that way. It only brings it up fresh in their minds.

—It's not the wife anyhow, Nosey Flynn said. I met him the day before yesterday and he coming out of that Irish farm dairy John Wyse Nolan's wife has in Henry street with a jar of cream in his hand taking it home to his better half. She's well nourished, I tell you. Plovers on toast.

—And is he doing for the *Freeman?* Davy Byrne said.

Nosey Flynn pursed his lips.

—He doesn't buy cream on the ads he picks up. You can make bacon of that.

—How so? Davy Byrne asked, coming from his book.

Nosey Flynn made swift passes in the air with juggling fingers. He winked.

—He's in the craft,[2] he said.

—Do you tell me so? Davy Byrne said.

—Very much so, Nosey Flynn said. Ancient free and accepted order. Light, life and love, by God. They give him a leg up. I was told that by a, well, I won't say who.

—Is that a fact?

—O, it's a fine order, Nosey Flynn said. They stick to you when you're down. I know a fellow was trying to get into it, but they're as close as damn it. By God they did right to keep the women out of it.

Davy Byrne smiledyawnednodded all in one:

—Iiiiiichaaaaaaach!

—There was one woman, Nosey Flynn said, hid herself in a clock to find out what they do be doing. But be damned but they smelt her out and swore

---

1. Pygmalion was the sculptor whose statue of Galatea came alive.
2. I.e., in the "free and accepted order" of Freema- sons, one of the oldest European secret societies; it was not in good repute in predominantly Roman Catholic countries like Ireland.

her in on the spot a master mason. That was one of the Saint Legers of Doner-
aile.

Davy Byrne, sated after his yawn, said with tearwashed eyes:

—And is that a fact? Decent quiet man he is. I often saw him in here and I
never once saw him, you know, over the line.

—God Almighty couldn't make him drunk, Nosey Flynn said firmly. Slips
off when the fun gets too hot. Didn't you see him look at his watch? Ah, you
weren't there. If you ask him to have a drink first thing he does he outs with
the watch to see what he ought to imbibe. Declare to God he does.

—There are some like that, Davy Byrne said. He's a safe man, I'd say.

—He's not too bad, Nosey Flynn said, snuffling it up. He has been known
to put his hand down too to help a fellow. Give the devil his due. O, Bloom
has his good points. But there's one thing he'll never do.

His hand scrawled a dry pen signature beside his grog.

—I know, Davy Byrne said.

—Nothing in black and white, Nosey Flynn said.

Paddy Leonard and Bantam Lyons came in. Tom Rochford followed frowning, a plaining hand on his claret waistcoat.

—Day, Mr Byrne.

—Day, gentlemen.

They paused at the counter.

—Who's standing? Paddy Leonard asked.

—I'm sitting anyhow, Nosey Flynn answered.

—Well, what'll it be? Paddy Leonard asked.

—I'll take a stone ginger, Bantam Lyons said.

—How much? Paddy Leonard cried. Since when, for God's sake? What's
yours, Tom?

—How is the main drainage? Nosey Flynn asked, sipping.

For answer Tom Rochford pressed his hand to his breastbone and hic-
cupped.

—Would I trouble you for a glass of fresh water, Mr Byrne? he said.

—Certainly, sir.

Paddy Leonard eyed his alemates.

—Lord love a duck, he said, look at what I'm standing drinks to! Cold water
and gingerpop! Two fellows that would suck whisky off a sore leg. He has
some bloody horse up his sleeve for the Gold cup. A dead snip.

—Zinfandel is it? Nosey Flynn asked.

Tom Rochford spilt powder from a twisted paper into the water set before
him.

—That cursed dyspepsia, he said before drinking.

—Breadsoda is very good, Davy Byrne said.

Tom Rochford nodded and drank.

—Is it Zinfandel?

—Say nothing, Bantam Lyons winked. I'm going to plunge five bob on my
own.

—Tell us if you're worth your salt and be damned to you, Paddy Leonard
said. Who gave it to you?

Mr Bloom on his way out raised three fingers in greeting.

—So long, Nosey Flynn said.

The others turned.

—That's the man now that gave it to me, Bantam Lyons whispered.

—Prrwht! Paddy Leonard said with scorn. Mr Byrne, sir, we'll take two of your small Jamesons[3] after that and a . . .

—Stone ginger, Davy Byrne added civilly.

—Ay, Paddy Leonard said. A suckingbottle for the baby.

Mr Bloom walked towards Dawson street, his tongue brushing his teeth smooth. Something green it would have to be: spinach say. Then with those Röntgen rays searchlight you could.

At Duke lane a ravenous terrier choked up a sick knuckly cud on the cobblestones and lapped it with new zest. Surfeit. Returned with thanks having fully digested the contents. First sweet then savoury. Mr Bloom coasted warily. Ruminants. His second course. Their upper jaw they move. Wonder if Tom Rochford will do anything with that invention of his. Wasting time explaining it to Flynn's mouth. Lean people long mouths. Ought to be a hall or a place where inventors could go in and invent free. Course then you'd have all the cranks pestering.

He hummed, prolonging in solemn echo, the closes of the bars:

> Don Giovanni, a cenar teco
> M'invitasti.[4]

Feel better. Burgundy. Good pick me up. Who distilled first? Some chap in the blues. Dutch courage. That *Kilkenny People* in the national library now I must.

Bare clean closestools, waiting, in the window of William Miller, plumber, turned back his thoughts. They could: and watch it all the way down, swallow a pin sometimes come out of the ribs years after, tour round the body, changing biliary duct, spleen squirting liver, gastric juice coils of intestines like pipes. But the poor buffer would have to stand all the time with his insides entrails on show. Science.

—*A cenar teco.*

What does that *teco* mean? Tonight perhaps.

> Don Giovanni, thou haste me invited
> To come to supper tonight,
> The rum the rumdum.

Doesn't go properly.

Keyes: two months if I get Nannetti[5] to. That'll be two pounds ten, about two pounds eight. Three Hynes owes me. Two eleven. Prescott's ad. Two fifteen. Five guineas about. On the pig's back.

Could buy one of those silk petticoats for Molly, colour of her new garters. Today. Today. Not think.[6]

Tour the south then. What about English wateringplaces? Brighton, Mar-

---

3. Brand of Irish whiskey.

4. Since Molly is a singer, Bloom is familiar with opera. Here he recalls the song sung by the Commendatore's statue in Mozart's *Don Giovanni* and translates accurately the Italian words he quotes, except for "*teco*" ("with you"). This opera supplies some of the key themes in *Ulysses*, and the famous duet between Don Giovanni and Zerlina. "*Là ci darèm la mano*" ("There we will join hands"), haunts Bloom's mind continually throughout the day. It is on the pro-

gram of Molly's concert that she is discussing with Boylan that afternoon, and Bloom associates it with her adultery with Boylan.

5. Proofreader and business manager of the *Freeman's Journal* and in charge of the advertising Bloom is trying to get for the paper. If he will add a complimentary reference to Keyes, a grocer, in a gossip column, Keyes promises to renew his advertisement, which means a commission for Bloom.

6. I.e., of Molly and Boylan.

gate. Piers by moonlight. Her voice floating out. Those lovely seaside girls. Against John Long's a drowsing loafer lounged in heavy thought, gnawing a crusted knuckle. Handy man wants job. Small wages. Will eat anything.

Mr Bloom turned at Gray's confectioner's window of unbought tarts and passed the reverend Thomas Connellan's bookstore. *Why I left the church of Rome?* Birds' Nest. Women run him. They say they used to give pauper children soup to change to protestants in the time of the potato blight. Society over the way papa went to for the conversion of poor jews. Same bait. *Why we left the church of Rome?*

A blind stripling stood tapping the curbstone with his slender cane. No tram in sight. Wants to cross.

—Do you want to cross? Mr Bloom asked.

The blind stripling did not answer. His wallface frowned weakly. He moved his head uncertainly.

—You're in Dawson street, Mr Bloom said. Molesworth street is opposite. Do you want to cross? There's nothing in the way.

The cane moved out trembling to the left. Mr Bloom's eye followed its line and saw again the dyeworks' van drawn up before Drago's. Where I saw his brillantined hair just when I was. Horse drooping. Driver in John Long's. Slaking his drouth.

—There's a van there, Mr Bloom said, but it's not moving. I'll see you across. Do you want to go to Molesworth street?

—Yes, the stripling answered. South Frederick street.

—Come, Mr Bloom said.

He touched the thin elbow gently: then took the limp seeing hand to guide it forward.

Say something to him. Better not do the condescending. They mistrust what you tell them. Pass a common remark.

—The rain kept off.

No answer.

Stains on his coat. Slobbers his food, I suppose. Tastes all different for him. Have to be spoonfed first. Like a child's hand, his hand. Like Milly's was. Sensitive. Sizing me up I daresay from my hand. Wonder if he has a name. Van. Keep his cane clear of the horse's legs tired drudge get his doze. That's right. Clear. Behind a bull: in front of a horse.

—Thanks, sir.

Knows I'm a man. Voice.

—Right now? First turn to the left.

The blind stripling tapped the curbstone and went on his way, drawing his cane back, feeling again.

Mr Bloom walked behind the eyeless feet, a flatcut suit of herringbone tweed. Poor young fellow! How on earth did he know that van was there? Must have felt it. See things in their foreheads perhaps. Kind of sense of volume. Weight would he feel it if something was removed. Feel a gap. Queer idea of Dublin he must have, tapping his way round by the stones. Could he walk in a beeline if he hadn't that cane? Bloodless pious face like a fellow going in to be a priest.

Penrose! That was that chap's name.

Look at all the things they can learn to do. Read with their fingers. Tune pianos. Or we are surprised they have any brains. Why we think a deformed

person or a hunchback clever if he says something we might say. Of course
the other senses are more. Embroider. Plait baskets. People ought to help.
Workbasket I could buy Molly's birthday. Hates sewing. Might take an objection. Dark men they call them.

Sense of smell must be stronger too. Smells on all sides bunched together.
Each person too. Then the spring, the summer: smells. Tastes. They say you
can't taste wines with your eyes shut or a cold in the head. Also smoke in the
dark they say get no pleasure.

And with a woman, for instance. More shameless not seeing. That girl passing the Stewart institution, head in the air. Look at me. I have them all on.
Must be strange not to see her. Kind of a form in his mind's eye. The voice
temperature when he touches her with fingers must almost see the lines, the
curves. His hands on her hair, for instance. Say it was black for instance.
Good. We call it black. Then passing over her white skin. Different feel perhaps. Feeling of white.

Postoffice. Must answer.[7] Fag[8] today. Send her a postal order two shillings
half a crown. Accept my little present. Stationer's just here too. Wait. Think
over it.

With a gentle finger he felt ever so slowly the hair combed back above his
ears. Again. Fibres of fine fine straw. Then gently his finger felt the skin of
his right cheek. Downy hair there too. Not smooth enough. The belly is the
smoothest. No-one about. There he goes into Frederick street. Perhaps to Lev-
enston's dancing academy piano. Might be settling my braces.

Walking by Doran's public house he slid his hand between waistcoat and
trousers and, pulling aside his shirt gently, felt a slack fold of his belly. But I
know it's whitey yellow. Want to try in the dark to see.

He withdrew his hand and pulled his dress to.

Poor fellow! Quite a boy. Terrible. Really terrible. What dreams would he
have, not seeing. Life a dream for him. Where is the justice being born that
way. All those women and children excursion beanfeast burned and drowned
in New York.[9] Holocaust. Karma they call that transmigration for sins you did
in a past life the reincarnation met him pike hoses.[1] Dear, dear, dear. Pity of
course: but somehow you can't cotton on to them someway.

Sir Frederick Falkiner going into the freemasons' hall. Solemn as Troy.
After his good lunch in Earlsfort terrace. Old legal cronies cracking a mag-
num. Tales of the bench and assizes and annals of the bluecoat school.[2] I
sentenced him to ten years. I suppose he'd turn up his nose at that stuff I
drank. Vintage wine for them, the year marked on a dusty bottle. Has his own
ideas of justice in the recorder's court. Wellmeaning old man. Police charge
sheets crammed with cases get their percentage manufacturing crime. Sends
them to the rightabout. The devil on moneylenders. Gave Reuben J. a great
strawcalling. Now he's really what they call a dirty jew. Power those judges
have. Crusty old topers in wigs. Bear with a sore paw. And may the Lord have
mercy on your soul.

Hello, placard. Mirus bazaar. His excellency the lord lieutenant. Sixteenth

---

7. Martha Clifford's letter.
8. Nuisance.
9. This terrible disaster on an excursion steamer on
the Hudson took place on June 15, 1904, and was
reported in the Dublin papers on June 16.
1. I.e., metempsychosis: Bloom is remembering again

their morning conversation on this subject, when
Molly exclaimed, "O rocks!"
2. Sir Frederick Falkiner wrote the history of the
"bluecoat school" in Oxmantown, Dublin. The Dublin bluecoat school was founded by Charles II for poor
children.

today it is. In aid of funds for Mercer's hospital. The *Messiah* was first given for that. Yes. Handel. What about going out there. Ballsbridge. Drop in on Keyes. No use sticking to him like a leech. Wear out my welcome. Sure to know someone on the gate.

Mr Bloom came to Kildare street. First I must. Library.

Straw hat in sunlight. Tan shoes. Turnedup trousers. It is. It is.[3]

His heart quopped softly. To the right. Museum. Goddesses. He swerved to the right.

Is it? Almost certain. Won't look. Wine in my face. Why did I? Too heady. Yes, it is. The walk. Not see. Not see. Get on.

Making for the museum gate with long windy strides he lifted his eyes. Handsome building. Sir Thomas Deane designed. Not following me?

Didn't see me perhaps. Light in his eyes.

The flutter of his breath came forth in short sighs. Quick. Cold statues: quiet there. Safe in a minute.

No, didn't see me. After two. Just at the gate.

My heart!

His eyes beating looked steadfastly at cream curves of stone. Sir Thomas Deane was the Greek architecture.

Look for something I.

His hasty hand went quick into a pocket, took out, read unfolded Agendath Netaim. Where did I?

Busy looking for.

He thrust back quickly Agendath.

Afternoon she said.

I am looking for that. Yes, that. Try all pockets. Handker. *Freeman.* Where did I? Ah, yes. Trousers. Purse. Potato. Where did I?

Hurry. Walk quietly. Moment more. My heart.

His hand looking for the where did I put found in his hip pocket soap lotion have to call tepid paper stuck. Ah, soap there! Yes. Gate.[4]

Safe!

1914–21   1922

Finnegans Wake   Because the meanings in *Finnegans Wake* are developed not by action but by language—a great network of multiple puns that echo themes back and forth throughout the book—the careful reading of a single passage, even out of context, will convey more than any summary of the "plot" (some discussion of the general plan of the work is given in the Joyce headnote). The particular passage selected here was one of Joyce's favorites, and there exists a phonograph recording of it made by himself. It consists of the closing pages of chapter 8 of book 1; the chapter was published separately as *Anna Livia Plurabelle* in 1928 and 1930, although the finished book omits this title.

The entire chapter is a dialogue, and the scene is the river Liffey: two washer-

---

3. Bloom catches a glimpse of Boylan and tries to avoid an encounter.

4. Anxious to avoid Boylan, Bloom pretends to admire the architecture of the Museum and National Library building, and then pretends to be looking for something in his pockets, where he finds the "Agendath Netaim" leaflet. He continues to search desperately in his pockets to avoid looking up and seeing Boylan, discovers the potato he carries as a remedy against rheumatism and a cake of soap he had bought that morning (the soap reminds him that he must call at the chemist's to collect a face lotion he had ordered for Molly). At last he goes through the National Library gate and feels safe.

women are washing in public the dirty linen of HCE and ALP (the "hero" and "heroine"; see headnote "James Joyce," p. 2340) and gossiping as they work. As this excerpt opens, it is growing dark; things become gradually less and less distinct, so that the washerwomen cannot be sure what the objects seen in the dusk really are. As it grows darker, the river becomes wider (we get nearer its mouth) and the wind rises, so that the women have more and more difficulty hearing each other. At last, as night falls, they become part of the landscape, an elm tree and a stone on the river bank. Toward the end of the dialogue they ask to hear a tale of Shem and Shaun (HCE's two sons), and this question points the way to book 2, which opens with the two boys (metamorphosed for the moment into Glugg and Chuff) playing in front of the tavern in the evening.

A complete annotation of even this brief passage is, of course, a physical impossibility in this anthology. The notes that are provided are intended to indicate the nature of what Joyce does with language and to enable the reader to see what is going on. But there are all sorts of suggestions built up in the language that are not referred to in the notes: all readers will find some for themselves.

From Finnegans Wake

From *Anna Livia Plurabelle*

* * * Well, you know or don't you kennet[1] or haven't I told you every telling has a taling and that's the he and the she of it. Look, look, the dusk is growing! My branches lofty are taking root. And my cold cher's[2] gone ashley. Fieluhr? Filou![3] What age is at? It saon[4] is late. 'Tis endless now senne[5] eye or erewone[6] last saw Waterhouse's clogh.[7] They took it asunder, I hurd thum sigh. When will they reassemble it? O, my back, my back, my bach![8] I'd want to go to Aches-les-Pains.[9] Pingpong! There's the Belle for Sexaloitez![10] And Concepta de Send-us-pray! Pang! Wring out the Clothes! Wring in the dew![11] Godavari,[12] vert the showers![13] And grant thaya grace! Aman. Will we spread them here now? Ay, we will. Flip! Spread on your bank and I'll spread mine on mine. Flep! It's what I'm doing. Spread! It's churning chill. Der went[14] is rising. I'll lay a few stones on the hostel sheets. A man and his bride embraced between them. Else I'd have sprinkled and folded them only. And I'll tie my butcher's apron here. It's suety yet. The strollers will pass it by. Six shifts, ten

1. Ken it ("know it") + Kennet (river in England). Rivers in *Finnegans Wake* symbolize the flow of life, and thousands of river names are suggested throughout the book in allusive pun combinations, as here.
2. Cold cheer (i.e., cold comfort) + cold chair + (perhaps) culture. "Gone ashley": gone to ashes. Going to ashes suggests the fiery death and rebirth of the mythical phoenix: from the ashes of the dead phoenix rises a new one. Modern culture, which can provide only cold cheer, is in the state of decay, the "going to ashes," which precedes the stage of rebirth into a new cultural cycle (according to Giambattista Vico's cyclical theory of history, which is important to *Finnegans Wake*). "Gone ashley" also means "turned into an ash tree" (i.e., it is so cold that the speaker feels herself turning into a tree).
3. "Pickpocket; thief" (French). "Fieluhr": *Viel Uhr?* ("What's the time?" German). From an old anecdote of a German soldier and a French soldier shouting at each other across the Rhine. They mishear each other

as the washerwomen will later.
4. Soon + Saône (river in France).
5. Since + Senne (river in Belgium).
6. E'er a one + *Erewhon* (novel by Samuel Butler—"Nowhere" spelled backward).
7. Waterhouse's clock, a well-known clock on Dame Street, Dublin.
8. "Brook" (German) + "dear" (Welsh).
9. Cf. Aix-les-Bains, France.
10. "Sachselüte," a Zurich fertility rite (literally, the ringing of six o'clock), which celebrates the burial of winter.
11. Tennyson, *In Memoriam:* "Ring out the old, ring in the new."
12. God of Eire + the name of a river in India.
13. "Vert": avert + *vert* ("green," French), for "the showers" make grass green.
14. *Der Wind* ("the wind," German) + Derwent (river in England).

kerchiefs, nine to hold to the fire and this for the code,[15] the convent napkins, twelve, one baby's shawl. Good mother Jossiph[16] knows, she said. Whose head? Mutter snores? Deataceas![17] Wharnow are alle her childer, say? In kingdome gone or power to come or gloria be to them farther? Allalivial, allalluvial![18] Some here, more no more, more again lost alla stranger.[19] I've heard tell that same brooch of the Shannons[20] was married into a family in Spain. And all the Dunders de Dunnes[21] in Markland's[22] Vineland beyond the Brendan's herring pool[23] takes number nine in yangsee's[24] hats. And one of Biddy's[25] beads went bobbing till she rounded up lost histereve[26] with a marigold and a cobbler's candle in a side strain of a main drain of a manzinahurries[27] off Bachelor's Walk. But all that's left to the last of the Meaghers[28] in the loup[29] of the years prefixed and between is one kneebuckle and two hooks in the front. Do you tell me that now? I do in troth. Orara por Orbe and poor Las Animals![30] Ussa, Ulla, we're umbas[31] all! Mezha, didn't you hear it a deluge of times, ufer[32] and ufer, respund to spond?[33] You deed, you deed! I need, I need! It's that irrawaddyng[34] I've stoke in my aars. It all but husheth the lethest zswound. Oronoko![35] What's your trouble? Is that the great Finn-leader[36] himself in his joakimono[37] on his statue riding the high horse there forehengist?[38] Father of Otters,[39] it is himself! Yonne there! Isset that? On Fallareen Common? You're thinking of Astley's Amphitheayter where the bobby restrained you making sugarstuck pouts to the ghostwhite horse of the

---

15. Cold + code (i.e., the code in which the book is written). The numbers in this sentence have special meanings indicated in other episodes.
16. Joseph + joss ("God," pidgin English) + gossip (which derives from "god-sib," Middle English, "god-parent").
17. A play on Deo gratias ("thanks be to God") and on Dea Tacita ("silent-goddess"), a name from Roman mythology.
18. Multiple punning—Anna Livia + all alive + la lluvia ("rain," Spanish) + alluvial—suggesting the mother-river-fertility associations of ALP. At least two other meanings are also present: All alive O! (street cry of shellfish vendors) + Alleluia (Vulgate Latin form of "Hallelujah").
19. Cf. à l'étranger ("abroad," French).
20. Ornament and branch of the Shannons (family and river).
21. The form of the name suggests an aristocratic Anglo-Norman family. "Dunder" suggests thunder; dun is an Irish word meaning "hill," "fort on a hill."
22. Borderland + land of the mark (i.e., land of money, or America; Markland's Vineland was one of Leif Ericson's names for America). Both King Mark of Cornwall (a character in the Tristan and Iseult story) and Mark of the Gospels are primary symbolic characters in Finnegans Wake.
23. The Atlantic Ocean; St. Brendan was an Irish monk who sailed out into the Atlantic to find the terrestrial paradise.
24. Yankees' + Yangtze (river in China). The de Dunnes have swollen heads now that they have emigrated to America.
25. Diminutive form of the name Bridget; St. Brigid (or Bridget) is a patron saint of Ireland. "Biddy" is also a term for an Irish maidservant.
26. Yester eve (last night) + eve of history. The sentence may be paraphrased: "Irish history got lost when she went off in a side branch of the main Roman Cath-

olic church, and Biddy (i.e., Ireland) landed herself in the dirt." There are also Freudian implications here.
27. A urinal + Manzanares (river in Spain).
28. Thomas Francis Meagher, Irish patriot and revolutionary, who was transported to Van Diemen's Land in 1849 and escaped to America in 1852.
29. Loop + loup ("wolf" and also "solitary man," French). Cf. Wolfe Tone, the ill-fated Irish revolutionist.
30. Ora pro nobis ("pray for us," Latin) + Orara (river in New South Wales) + pro orbe ("for the world," Latin) + Orbe (river in France). "Las Animas": "souls" (Spanish) + the name of a river in Colorado. The entire sentence may be read: "Pray for us and for all souls."
31. Umbra ("shade," Latin) + Umba (river in Africa). "Ussa," "Ulla," and "Mezha" are also river names; each contains a number of other meanings.
32. Bank (of river).
33. Spund ("bung," German).
34. A multiple pun: Irrawady (river in Burma) + irritating + wadding. This and the following sentence may be paraphrased: "It's that wadding I've stuck in my ears. It hushes the least sound."
35. Oroonoko (novel by Aphra Behn about a "noble savage," published ca. 1678) + Orinoco (river in Venezuela).
36. Fionn mac Cumhail (Finn MacCool), legendary hero of ancient Ireland.
37. Comic kimono. Joki is the Finnish word for river; the name Joachim is perhaps also implied.
38. Hengist was the Jute invader of England (with Horsa), ca. 449; he founded the kingdom of Kent.
39. Father of Waters (i.e., the Mississippi) + Father of Orders (i.e., Saint Patrick).
40. Philip Astley's Royal Amphitheatre was a famous late 18th-century English circus, specializing in trained horses. "Pepper's Ghost" was a popular circus act. One of the washerwomen has been reproving the

Peppers.[40] Throw the cobwebs from your eyes, woman, and spread your washing proper! It's well I know your sort of slop. Flap! Ireland sober is Ireland stiff.[41] Lord help you, Maria, full of grease, the load is with me! Your prayers. I sonht zo![42] Madammangut! Were you lifting your elbow, tell us, glazy cheeks, in Conway's Carrigacurra canteen? Was I what, hobbledyhips?[43] Flop! Your rere gait's creakorheuman bitts your butts disagrees.[44] Amn't I up since the damp dawn, marthared mary allacook, with Corrigan's pulse and varicoarse veins, my pramaxle smashed, Alice Jane in decline and my oneeyed mongrel twice run over, soaking and bleaching boiler rags, and sweating cold, a widow like me, for to deck my tennis champion son, the laundryman with the lavandier flannels? You won your limpopo[45] limp from the husky[46] hussars when Collars and Cuffs was heir to the town and your slur gave the stink to Carlow.[47] Holy Scamander,[48] I sar[49] it again! Near the golden falls. Icis on us! Seints of light! Zezere![50] Subdue your noise, you hamble creature! What is it but a blackburry growth or the dwyergray ass them four old codgers[51] owns. Are you meanam[52] Tarpey and Lyons and Gregory?[53] I meyne now, thank all, the four of them, and the roar of them, that draves[54] that stray in the mist and old Johnny MacDougal along with them. Is that the Poolbeg flasher beyant,[55] pharphar, or a fireboat coasting nyar[56] the Kishtna[57] or a glow I behold within a hedge or my Garry come back from the Indes? Wait till the honeying of the lune,[58] love! Die eve, little eve, die![59] We see that wonder in your eye. We'll meet again, we'll part once more. The spot I'll seek if the hour you'll find. My chart shines high where the blue milk's upset. Forgivemequick. I'm going! Bubye! And you, pluck your watch, forgetmenot. Your evenlode.[60] So save to jurna's[61] end! My sights are swimming thicker on me by the shadows to this place. I sow[62] home slowly now by own way, moyvalley way. Towy[63] I too, rathmine.

Ah, but she was the queer old skeowsha[64] anyhow, Anna Livia, trinkettoes! And sure he was the quare old buntz too, Dear Dirty Dumpling,[65] foosther-

---

other, who thought she saw the great Finn himself riding his high horse, by telling her that once before she had to be restrained by a policeman for making "sugarstuck pouts" at a circus horse.

41. The temperance reformer Father Matthew had as his slogan "Ireland sober is Ireland free."

42. I thought so + Izontzo (river in Italy).

43. Hobbledehoy + wobbly hips.

44. The sentence is a punning discussion of her hard work and ailments.

45. A river in south Africa.

46. Cf. *uisge* ("whisky," but literally "water [of life]," Gaelic).

47. I.e., "You got a slur on your reputation carrying on with soldiers in the Age of Elegance, and the scandal was all over Ireland" (ALP is being addressed and some of her many lovers are mentioned). "Carlow": a county in Ireland.

48. River near Troy, famous in classical legend.

49. I saw + Isar (river in Germany).

50. See there + Zezere (river in Portugal).

51. The Four Old Men, who represent, among other things, the authors of the Gospels, and the four elements.

52. Meaning + Menam (river in Thailand).

53. Tarpey, Lyons, Gregory, and MacDougal (next sentence) are the "four old codgers."

54. Drives + Drave (river in Hungary).

55. I.e., the Poolbeg Lighthouse beyond (this lighthouse is in Dublin Bay). "Pharphar": far far + Pharphar (river in Damascus) + *pharos* ("lighthouse," Greek).

56. Near + Nyar (river in India).

57. City in ancient Mesopotamia, traditionally the ruling city after the Flood + Krishna (Hindu god of joy) + Kistna (river in India) + the Kish lightship (in Dublin Bay).

58. Loon ("boy," Scottish) + *luna* ("moon," Latin). "Honeying of the lune": honeymoon, etc.

59. From a children's game in which a swing is allowed to slow down to the refrain "She's dead, little Eva, little Eva, she's dead."

60. Evening load + Evenlode (river in England).

61. Journey + Jurna (river in Brazil).

62. Sow (river in England).

63. Name of a river in Wales. Moy is the name of an Irish river, and Moyvalley and Rathmine are names of Dublin suburbs.

64. Old timer, in Dublin.

65. "Dumpling" suggests Humpty Dumpty, whose fall is one of the many involved in the vastly symbolic fall of Finnegan. The phrase "Dear Dirty Dublin" occurs in *Ulysses*.

66. Blond and dark Scandinavian invaders of Ireland.

father of fingalls[66] and dotthergills. Gammer and gaffer we're all their gang-sters. Hadn't he seven dams to wive him? And every dam had her seven crutches. And every crutch had its seven hues.[67] And each hue had a differing cry. Sudds[68] for me and supper for you and the doctor's bill for Joe John. Befor! Bifur![69] He married his markets, cheap by foul, I know, like any Etrur-ian Catholic Heathen, in their pinky limony creamy birnies[70] and their turkiss indienne mauves. But at milkidmass[71] who was the spouse? Then all that was was fair. Tys Elvenland![72] Teems of times and happy returns. The seim anew.[73] Ordovico or viricordo. Anna was, Livia is, Plurabelle's to be.[74] North-men's thing made southfolk's place but howmulty plurators made each one in person?[75] Latin me that, my trinity scholard, out of eure sanscreed into oure eryan![76] *Hircus Civis Eblanensis!*[77] He had buckgoat paps on him, soft ones for orphans. Ho,[78] Lord! Twins of his bosom. Lord save us! And ho! Hey? What all men. Hot? His tittering daughters of. Whawk?

Can't hear with the waters of. The chittering waters of. Flittering bats, fieldmice bawk talk. Ho! Are you not gone ahome? What Thom Malone? Can't hear with bawk of bats, all thim liffeying waters of. Ho, talk save us! My foos won't moos.[79] I feel as old as yonder elm. A tale told of Shaun or Shem? All Livia's daughter-sons. Dark hawks hear us. Night! Night! My ho head halls. I feel as heavy as yonder stone. Tell me of John or Shaun? Who were Shem and Shaun the living sons or daughters of? Night now! Tell, tell me, tell me, elm! Night night! Telmetale of stem or stone.[80] Beside the rivering waters of, hitherandthithering waters of. Night!

1923–38   1939

67. Colors of the rainbow (suggested a few lines later by "pinky limony creamy" and "turkiss indienne mauves"). In these sentences Joyce is parodying the nursery rhyme, "As I was going to St. Ives / I met a man with seven wives."
68. Suds (slang for beer) + soap suds + sudd (the floating vegetable matter that often obstructs naviga-tion on the White Nile).
69. Bifurcated creature! This image of man as a forked being suggests HCE (cf. "Etrurian Catholic Hea-then"). HCE's marital history, in his role as the Great Parent or generator, is one of the themes in this pas-sage.
70. Coats of mail.
71. Milking time + Michaelmas (September 29).
72. 'Tis the land of Elves + Tys Elv (Norway).
73. The same again + Seim (river in Ireland).
74. The Ordovices were an ancient British tribe in northern Wales, and Ordovician is a term for a geologi-cal period. "Ordovico" is also a pun on Vico and his order of historical phases. Joyce is suggesting the cycli-cal nature of things: the marital history of HCE is the history of ever-renewing life ("the seim anew"), and HCE's bride is Everywoman, past, present, and future ("Anna was, Livia is, Plurabelle's to be"). "Viricordo" is another verbal twist to Vico and his cycles, sug-gesting his *ricorso* ("recurrence," i.e., the fourth stage

of the cycle that brings back the first), as well as over-tones from the Latin *vir* (man) and *cor* (heart): the heart of the individual beats on, through all phases of civilization.
75. This sentence may be paraphrased: "The North-men's assembly (thing) is now in Suffolk Place, but how many ancestors went into the making of each one of us?"
76. I.e., out of your Sanskrit into your Aryan. "Sanscreed" has further punning meanings: *sans* screed (without script) + *sans* creed (without faith). Thus the phrase can read: "out of your illiteracy or faithlessness into Irish" (Eire-an). I.e., the greatest skep-tic must pause in reverence before the endless flow of life, represented by Irish history.
77. The Goat-Citizen of Dublin! (Latin). The goat is the symbol of lust and so of fecundity; "*Eblanensis*" is the adjective form of Eblana, the name given by the 3rd-century Alexandrian geographer Ptolemy to what may have been the site of the modern Dublin.
78. River (Chinese).
79. Move + *Moos* ("moss," German). Her foot ("foos") won't move; it is also turning to moss.
80. Stone and elm tree are important symbols in *Fin-negans Wake*. Signifying permanence and change, time and space, mercy and justice, they undergo many changes of symbolic meaning throughout the book.

D. H. LAWRENCE
1885–1930

1912:   Gives up school teaching for literature.
1915:   *The Rainbow,* first of the "new" novels.

David Herbert Lawrence was born in the Midland mining village of Eastwood, Nottinghamshire. His father was a miner; his mother, better educated than her husband and self-consciously genteel, fought all her married life to lift her children out of the working class. Lawrence was aware from an early age of the struggle between his parents; he was very much on his mother's side during his childhood, resenting his father's coarse and sometimes drunken behavior and allying himself with his mother's delicacy and refinement. After the death of an elder brother he became the center of his mother's emotional life and played in his own relation to her a loving and protective role. His mother's claims on him kept frustrating his relationships with women, and the personal problems and conflicts that resulted are presented in his first really distinguished novel, *Sons and Lovers* (1913), where, against a background of paternal coarseness and vitality conflicting with maternal refinement and gentility, he sets the theme of the demanding mother who has given up the prospect of achieving a true emotional life with her husband and turns to her sons with a stultifying and possessive love. Many years later Lawrence came to feel that he had misjudged his father, whose coarseness represented after all a genuine vitality and some wholeness of personality, even if these qualities were impoverished and distorted by the civilization in which he lived.

Spurred on by his mother, Lawrence escaped through education from the mining world of his father. He won a scholarship to Nottingham high school and later, after working first as a clerk and then as an elementary-school teacher (1902–6), studied for two years at Nottingham University College, where he obtained his teacher's certificate in 1908. Meanwhile he was reading on his own a great deal of literature and some philosophy and was working on his first novel, encouraged (as he was in all his early writing) by Jessie Chambers, the "Miriam" of *Sons and Lovers.* His first published work was a group of poems that appeared in the *English Review* for November 1909. The following February the same periodical published his first short story. He was now regarded in London literary circles as a promising young writer; his first novel, *The White Peacock* (1910), was received with respect. From 1908 to 1912 he taught school in Croydon, a southern suburb of London, but he gave this up after falling in love with Frieda von Richthofen, the German wife of a professor of French at Nottingham. They went to Germany together and married in 1914, after Frieda had been divorced by her first husband.

Abroad with Frieda, Lawrence finished *Sons and Lovers,* the autobiographical novel at which he had been working off and on for years. The war brought them back to England, where Frieda's German origins and Lawrence's fierce objection to the war gave him trouble with the authorities. More and more—especially after the banning of his next novel, *The Rainbow,* in 1915—Lawrence came to feel that the forces of modern civilization were arrayed against him. As soon as he could leave England after the war he sought refuge in Italy, Australia, Mexico, then again in Italy, and finally in the south of France, often desperately ill, restlessly searching for an ideal, or at least a tolerable, community in which to live. He died of tuberculosis in the south of France on March 2, 1930, at the age of forty-four.

Shortly before his death he had written:

> Give me the moon at my feet
> Put my feet upon the crescent, like a Lord!
> O let my ankles be bathed in moonlight, that I may go
> sure and moon-shod, cool and bright-footed
> towards my goal.
>
> For the sun is hostile, now
> his face is like the red lion . . .

In these elemental images he invoked his end, a gesture at once heroic and desperate. It was typical of him to symbolize his passing with reference to the sun and moon, for Lawrence was at home with such cosmic images as no other English writer except Blake has ever been; he was at home, one might say, with the universe, with all that is deep-rooted and elemental in the Individual and Nature, and at constant war with the mechanical and artificial, with the constraints and hypocrisies that civilization imposes on our fundamental selves. His most characteristic writings are essentially a record in symbolic terms of his explorations of human individuality and of all that hindered it and all that might fulfill it, whether in the natural world or in the world of other individuals.

This is not what the English novel is generally supposed to do, and Lawrence, with new things to say and a new way of using the novel form, was not easily or quickly appreciated. His early novels, *The White Peacock, The Trespasser,* and even the original and impressive *Sons and Lovers,* were more conventional in style and treatment; they aroused contemporary interest and even acclaim, and it appeared that he might be on his way to becoming one of the acknowledged and popular Georgian novelists. But with the publication of *The Rainbow* in 1915 the true, original Lawrence first emerged clearly, and the critics turned away in bewilderment and condemnation. *The Rainbow* was suppressed as indecent a month after its publication, and the war between Lawrence and the world of timid convention was on. The rest of his life, during which he produced about a dozen more novels and many poems, short stories, sketches, and miscellaneous articles, was, in his own words, "a savage enough pilgrimage," marked by incessant struggle and by moments of frustration and despair. Lawrence was one of those artists who had to create the taste by which they could be appreciated. He had no gift for explaining his attitude and literary technique in simple expository prose. He could explain himself only by performing, by operating in his own way as an artist, letting the work of art speak with its own voice and pulse with its own life. When he tried to talk *about* his ideas, instead of projecting them symbolically in art, he was often irritatingly and vaguely rhetorical. "Sense of truth," "supreme impulse" are phrases characteristic of Lawrence's belief in intuition, in the dark forces of the inner self, that must not be allowed to be swamped by the rational faculties but must be brought into a harmonious relation with them. It was a point of view—or rather, a perception, a passionate insight—that could not be convincingly expressed in argument but demanded direct projection in art.

The genteel culture of Lawrence's mother came more and more to represent death for Lawrence. In much of his later work, and especially in some of his short stories, he sets the deadening restrictiveness of middle-class conventional living against the forces of liberation that are often represented by an outsider—a peasant, a gypsy, a worker, a primitive of some kind, someone free by circumstance or personal effort. The recurring theme of his short stories—which contain some of his best work—is the distortion of love by possessiveness or gentility or a false romanticism or a false conception of the life of the artists, and the achievement of a living relation between a man and a woman against the pressure of class-feeling or tradition or habit or prejudice.

His two masterpieces, *The Rainbow* and *Women in Love* (both of which developed out of what was originally conceived as a single novel to be called *The Sisters*), are to be read as symbolic and dramatic poems in prose. In these novels Lawrence probes with both subtlety and power into various aspects of relationship—the relationship between humans and their environment, the relationship between the generations, the relationship between man and woman, the relationship between instinct and intellect, and above all the proper basis for the marriage relationship as he conceived it. Lawrence's view of marriage as a struggle derived from his own relationship with his strong-minded German-born wife, Frieda. There are more and bitterer lovers' quarrels in Lawrence's novels than anywhere else in English literature. Lawrence's "crockery-throwing" view of love could become tedious, except that, as he presents it, it is bound up with the deepest rhythms and most profound instincts of the man-woman relationship.

In *The Rainbow* and *Women in Love* Lawrence is developing a radically new kind of novel in which he explores kinds of human relationships with a combination of uncanny psychological precision and intense poetic feeling. They have an acute surface realism, a sharp sense of time and place, and brilliant topographical detail, and at the same time their high poetic symbolism, both of the total pattern of action and of incidents and objects within it, establishes a rhythm of meaning that is missed by those who read the novels with the conventional categories of "plot" and "characters" in mind. His next novel, *Aaron's Rod* (1922), is more uneven; in it Lawrence, employing many of his own experiences, explores problems of human relations under the question of moral and political leadership, which for a time obsessed him. He was concerned with the struggle for leadership in marriage as well as in politics. Two other novels on the theme of leadership, *Kangaroo* (1923), set in Australia, and *The Plumed Serpent* (1926), set in Mexico, similarly uneven, show him trying to give symbolic fictional form to his own problems and preoccupations. But *Kangaroo* in particular has its moments of uncanny perceptiveness, and it is extraordinary how Lawrence, drawing on his experiences during a short stay in Australia, was able to get beneath the skin of the country and evoke so much of the essential reality of both place and people.

It is hard to think of another English novelist whose best and most characteristic work makes such a disquieting assault on our normal patterns of thought and feeling. It is not simply that Lawrence is a rebel against convention—many writers have been that—or that his views are startling, though they sometimes are. It is rather that the whole response to life, and in particular to the problems posed by human relationships, that emerges from his novels and stories seems to come so profoundly from the deepest recesses of his being and, therefore, assault the deepest recesses of *our* being, that the challenge seems to go beyond that which is normally asserted by a work of art. It is difficult to escape the challenge; to make any attempt to respond fully to what he is saying is to be drawn into his world, forced to share his vision.

Although there are complex critical reasons for the posthumous triumph of this writer who was so much reviled in his lifetime, there is also a simple and striking reason that must not be forgotten. Lawrence had vision; he had a poetic sense of life; he had a keen ear and a piercing eye for every kind of vitality and color and sound in the world, for landscape—be it of England or Italy or New Mexico—for the individuality and concreteness of things in nature, and for the individuality and concreteness of people. His travel sketches are as impressive in their way as his novels; he seizes both on the symbolic incident and on the concrete reality, and each is interpreted in terms of the other. He looked at the world freshly, with his own eyes, avoiding formulas and clichés; and he forged for himself a kind of utterance that, at his best, was able to convey powerfully and vividly what his fresh, original vision showed him. This kind of originality has its drawbacks; he was sometimes shrill, sometimes repetitive, sometimes almost hysterical; some scenes in his novels are murky with unachieved symbolism or splutter with unresolved passion. But the great Lawrence remains.

This restless pilgrim with his uncanny perceptions into the depths of physical things, with his uncompromising honesty and originality in his view of human beings and the world, cannot be dismissed as merely a great eccentric. Nor is he a great prophet. He is essentially an artist; it is his *rendering* of life in his art, not his preaching about life's meaning, that matters.

Odor of Chrysanthemums

1

The small locomotive engine, Number 4, came clanking, stumbling down from Selston with seven full wagons. It appeared round the corner with loud threats of speed, but the colt that it startled from among the gorse,[1] which still flickered indistinctly in the raw afternoon, out-distanced it at a canter. A woman, walking up the railway line to Underwood, drew back into the hedge, held her basket aside, and watched the footplate of the engine advancing. The trucks[2] thumped heavily past, one by one, with slow inevitable movement, as she stood insignificantly trapped between the jolting black wagons and the hedge; then they curved away towards the coppice[3] where the withered oak leaves dropped noiselessly, while the birds, pulling at the scarlet hips beside the track, made off into the dusk that had already crept into the spinney.[4] In the open, the smoke from the engine sank and cleaved to the rough grass. The fields were dreary and forsaken, and in the marshy strip that led to the whim-sey,[5] a reedy pit pond, the fowls had already abandoned their run among the alders, to roost in the tarred fowl house. The pit bank loomed up beyond the pond, flames like red sores licking its ashy sides, in the afternoon's stagnant light. Just beyond rose the tapering chimneys and the clumsy black headstocks of Brinsley Colliery.[6] The two wheels were spinning fast up against the sky, and the winding engine rapped out its little spasms. The miners were being turned up.

The engine whistled as it came into the wide bay of railway lines beside the colliery, where rows of trucks stood in harbor.

Miners, single, trailing, and in groups, passed like shadows diverging home. At the edge of the ribbed level of sidings squat a low cottage, three steps down from the cinder track. A large bony vine clutched at the house, as if to claw down the tiled roof. Round the bricked yard grew a few wintry primroses. Beyond, the long garden sloped down to a bush-covered brook course. There were some twiggy apple trees, winter-crack trees, and ragged cabbages. Beside the path hung disheveled pink chrysanthemums, like pink cloths hung on bushes. A woman came stooping out of the felt-covered fowl house, halfway down the garden. She closed and padlocked the door, then drew herself erect, having brushed some bits from her white apron.

---

1. Also known as furze or whin, a prickly bush with yellow flowers common on heaths, moors, and hill-sides all over Britain.
2. Open freight cars.
3. A wood of small trees or shrubs.

4. Copse, thicket.
5. Machine for raising ore or water from a mine.
6. Coal mine. "Headstocks" support revolving parts of a machine.

She was a tall woman of imperious mien, handsome, with definite black eyebrows. Her smooth black hair was parted exactly. For a few moments she stood steadily watching the miners as they passed along the railway: then she turned towards the brook course. Her face was calm and set, her mouth was closed with disillusionment. After a moment she called:

"John!" There was no answer. She waited, and then said distinctly:

"Where are you?"

"Here!" replied a child's sulky voice from among the bushes. The woman looked piercingly through the dusk.

"Are you at that brook?" she asked sternly.

For answer the child showed himself before the raspberry canes that rose like whips. He was a small, sturdy boy of five. He stood quite still, defiantly.

"Oh!" said the mother, conciliated. "I thought you were down at that wet brook—and you remember what I told you——"

The boy did not move or answer.

"Come, come on in," she said more gently, "it's getting dark. There's your grandfather's engine coming down the line!"

The lad advanced slowly, with resentful, taciturn movement. He was dressed in trousers and waistcoat of cloth that was too thick and hard for the size of the garments. They were evidently cut down from a man's clothes.

As they went slowly towards the house he tore at the ragged wisps of chrysanthemums and dropped the petals in handfuls along the path.

"Don't do that—it does look nasty," said his mother. He refrained, and she, suddenly pitiful, broke off a twig with three or four wan flowers and held them against her face. When mother and son reached the yard her hand hesitated, and instead of laying the flower aside, she pushed it in her apron-band. The mother and son stood at the foot of the three steps looking across the bay of lines at the passing home of the miners. The trundle of the small train was imminent. Suddenly the engine loomed past the house and came to a stop opposite the gate.

The engine-driver, a short man with round gray beard, leaned out of the cab high above the woman.

"Have you got a cup of tea?" he said in a cheery, hearty fashion.

It was her father. She went in, saying she would mash.[7] Directly, she returned.

"I didn't come to see you on Sunday," began the little gray-bearded man.

"I didn't expect you," said his daughter.

The engine driver winced; then, reassuming his cheery, airy manner, he said:

"Oh, have you heard then? Well, and what do you think——?"

"I think it is soon enough," she replied.

At her brief censure the little man made an impatient gesture, and said coaxingly, yet with dangerous coldness:

"Well, what's a man to do? It's no sort of life for a man of my years, to sit at my own hearth like a stranger. And if I'm going to marry again it may as well be soon as late—what does it matter to anybody?"

The woman did not reply, but turned and went into the house. The man in the engine-cab stood assertive, till she returned with a cup of tea and a

---

7. Steep the tea.

piece of bread and butter on a plate. She went up the steps and stood near the footplate of the hissing engine.

"You needn't 'a' brought me bread an' butter," said her father. "But a cup of tea"—he sipped appreciatively—"it's very nice." He sipped for a moment or two, then: "I hear as Walter's got another bout on," he said.

"When hasn't he?" said the woman bitterly.

"I heerd tell of him in the Lord Nelson braggin' as he was going to spend that b—— afore he went: half a sovereign[8] that was."

"When?" asked the woman.

"A' Sat'day night—I know that's true."

"Very likely," she laughed bitterly. "He gives me twenty-three shillings."

"Aye, it's a nice thing, when a man can do nothing with his money but make a beast of himself!" said the gray-whiskered man. The woman turned her head away. Her father swallowed the last of his tea and handed her the cup.

"Aye, he sighed, wiping his mouth. "It's a settler,[9] it is——"

He put his hand on the lever. The little engine strained and groaned, and the train rumbled towards the crossing. The woman again looked across the metals. Darkness was settling over the spaces of the railway and trucks: the miners, in gray somber groups, were still passing home. The winding engine pulsed hurriedly, with brief pauses. Elizabeth Bates looked at the dreary flow of men, then she went indoors. Her husband did not come.

The kitchen was small and full of firelight; red coals piled glowing up the chimney mouth. All the life of the room seemed in the white, warm hearth and the steel fender reflecting the red fire. The cloth was laid for tea; cups glinted in the shadows. At the back, where the lowest stairs protruded into the room, the boy sat struggling with a knife and a piece of white wood. He was almost hidden in the shadow. It was half-past four. They had but to await the father's coming to begin tea. As the mother watched her son's sullen little struggle with the wood, she saw herself in his silence and pertinacity; she saw the father in her child's indifference to all but himself. She seemed to be occupied by her husband. He had probably gone past his home, slunk past his own door, to drink before he came in, while his dinner spoiled and wasted in waiting. She glanced at the clock, then took the potatoes to strain them in the yard. The garden and fields beyond the brook were closed in uncertain darkness. When she rose with the saucepan, leaving the drain streaming into the night behind her, she saw the yellow lamps were lit along the high road that went up the hill away beyond the space of the railway lines and the field.

Then again she watched the men trooping home, fewer now and fewer.

Indoors the fire was sinking and the room was dark red. The woman put her saucepan on the hob, and set a batter pudding near the mouth of the oven. Then she stood unmoving. Directly, gratefully, came quick young steps to the door. Someone hung on the latch a moment, then a little girl entered and began pulling off her outdoor things, dragging a mass of curls, just ripening from gold to brown, over her eyes with her hat.

Her mother chid her for coming late from school, and said she would have to keep her at home the dark winter days.

---

8. Gold coin worth twenty shillings. Half a sovereign is worth ten.   9. Crushing (or final) blow.

"Why, mother, it's hardly a bit dark yet. The lamp's not lighted, and my father's not home."

"No, he isn't. But it's a quarter to five! Did you see anything of him?"

The child became serious. She looked at her mother with large, wistful blue eyes.

"No, mother, I've never seen him. Why? Has he come up an' gone past, to Old Brinsley? He hasn't, mother, 'cos I never saw him."

"He'd watch that," said the mother bitterly, "he'd take care as you didn't see him. But you may depend upon it, he's seated in the Prince o' Wales. He wouldn't be this late."

The girl looked at her mother piteously.

"Let's have our teas, mother, should we?" said she.

The mother called John to table. She opened the door once more and looked out across the darkness of the lines. All was deserted: she could not hear the winding-engines.

"Perhaps," she said to herself, "he's stopped to get some ripping[1] done."

They sat down to tea. John, at the end of the table near the door, was almost lost in the darkness. Their faces were hidden from each other. The girl crouched against the fender slowly moving a thick piece of bread before the fire. The lad, his face a dusky mark on the shadow, sat watching her who was transfigured in the red glow.

"I do think it's beautiful to look in the fire," said the child.

"Do you?" said her mother. "Why?"

"It's so red, and full of little caves—and it feels so nice, and you can fair smell it."

"It'll want mending directly," replied her mother, "and then if your father comes he'll carry on and say there never is a fire when a man comes home sweating from the pit. A public house is always warm enough."

There was silence till the boy said complainingly: "Make haste, our Annie."

"Well, I am doing! I can't make the fire do it no faster, can I?"

"She keeps wafflin' it about so's to make 'er slow," grumbled the boy.

"Don't have such an evil imagination, child," replied the mother.

Soon the room was busy in the darkness with the crisp sound of crunching. The mother ate very little. She drank her tea determinedly, and sat thinking. When she rose her anger was evident in the stern unbending of her head. She looked at the pudding in the fender, and broke out:

"It *is* a scandalous thing as a man can't even come home to his dinner! If it's crozzled up to a cinder I don't see why I should care. Past his very door he goes to get to a public house, and here I sit with his dinner waiting for him——"

She went out. As she dropped piece after piece of coal on the red fire, the shadows fell on the walls, till the room was almost in total darkness.

"I canna see," grumbled the invisible John. In spite of herself, the mother laughed.

"You know the way to your mouth," she said. She set the dust pan outside the door. When she came again like a shadow on the hearth, the lad repeated, complaining sulkily:

---

1. Taking out or cutting away coal or stone (a mining and quarrying term).

"I canna see."

"Good gracious!" cried the mother irritably, "you're as bad as your father if it's a bit dusk!"

Nevertheless, she took a paper spill from a sheaf on the mantelpiece and proceeded to light the lamp that hung from the ceiling in the middle of the room. As she reached up, her figure displayed itself just rounding with maternity.

"Oh, mother——!" exclaimed the girl.

"What?" said the woman, suspended in the act of putting the lamp glass over the flame. The copper reflector shone handsomely on her, as she stood with uplifted arm, turning to face her daughter.

"You've got a flower in your apron!" said the child, in a little rapture at this unusual event.

"Goodness me!" exclaimed the woman, relieved. "One would think the house was afire." She replaced the glass and waited a moment before turning up the wick. A pale shadow was seen floating vaguely on the floor.

"Let me smell!" said the child, still rapturously, coming forward and putting her face to her mother's waist.

"Go along, silly!" said the mother, turning up the lamp. The light revealed their suspense so that the woman felt it almost unbearable. Annie was still bending at her waist. Irritably, the mother took the flowers out from her apron band.

"Oh, mother—don't take them out!" Annie cried, catching her hand and trying to replace the sprig.

"Such nonsense!" said the mother, turning away. The child put the pale chrysanthemums to her lips, murmuring:

"Don't they smell beautiful!"

Her mother gave a short laugh.

"No," she said, "not to me. It was chrysanthemums when I married him, and chrysanthemums when you were born, and the first time they ever brought him home drunk, he'd got brown chrysanthemums in his buttonhole."

She looked at the children. Their eyes and their parted lips were wondering. The mother sat rocking in silence for some time. Then she looked at the clock.

"Twenty minutes to six!" In a tone of fine bitter carelessness she continued: "Eh, he'll not come now till they bring him. There he'll stick! But he needn't come rolling in here in his pit dirt, for *I* won't wash him. He can lie on the floor——Eh, what a fool I've been, what a fool! And this is what I came here for, to this dirty hole, rats and all, for him to slink past his very door. Twice last week—he's begun now——"

She silenced herself and rose to clear the table.

While for an hour or more the children played, subduedly intent, fertile of imagination, united in fear of the mother's wrath, and in dread of their father's home-coming, Mrs. Bates sat in her rocking chair making a "singlet" of thick cream-colored flannel, which gave a dull wounded sound as she tore off the gray edge. She worked at her sewing with energy, listening to the children, and her anger wearied itself, lay down to rest, opening its eyes from time to time and steadily watching, its ears raised to listen. Sometimes even her anger quailed and shrank, and the mother suspended her sewing, tracing the foot-

steps that thudded along the sleepers outside; she would lift her head sharply
to bid the children "hush," but she recovered herself in time, and the footsteps
went past the gate, and the children were not flung out of their play-world.

But at last Annie sighed, and gave in. She glanced at her wagon of slippers,
and loathed the game. She turned plaintively to her mother.

"Mother!"—but she was inarticulate.

John crept out like a frog from under the sofa. His mother glanced up.

"Yes," she said, "just look at those shirt-sleeves!"

The boy held them out to survey them, saying nothing. Then somebody
called in a hoarse voice away down the line, and suspense bristled in the room,
till two people had gone by outside, talking.

"It is time for bed," said the mother.

"My father hasn't come," wailed Annie plaintively. But her mother was
primed with courage.

"Never mind. They'll bring him when he does come—like a log." She
meant there would be no scene. "And he may sleep on the floor till he wakes
himself. I know he'll not go to work tomorrow after this!"

The children had their hands and faces wiped with a flannel. They were
very quiet. When they had put on their nightdresses, they said their prayers,
the boy mumbling. The mother looked down at them, at the brown silken
bush of intertwining curls in the nape of the girl's neck, at the little black head
of the lad, and her heart burst with anger at their father, who caused all three
such distress. The children hid their faces in her skirts for comfort.

When Mrs. Bates came down, the room was strangely empty, with a tension
of expectancy. She took up her sewing and stitched for some time without
raising her head. Meantime her anger was tinged with fear.

2

The clock struck eight and she rose suddenly, dropping her sewing on her
chair. She went to the stair-foot door, opened it, listening. Then she went out,
locking the door behind her.

Something scuffled in the yard, and she started, though she knew it was
only the rats with which the place was over-run. The night was very dark. In
the great bay of railway lines, bulked with trucks, there was no trace of light,
only away back she could see a few yellow lamps at the pit top, and the red
smear of the burning pit bank on the night. She hurried along the edge of the
track, then, crossing the converging lines, came to the stile by the white gates,
whence she emerged on the road. Then the fear which had led her shrank.
People were walking up to New Brinsley; she saw the lights in the houses;
twenty yards farther on were the broad windows of the Prince of Wales, very
warm and bright, and the loud voices of men could be heard distinctly. What
a fool she had been to imagine that anything had happened to him! He was
merely drinking over there at the Prince of Wales. She faltered. She had never
yet been to fetch him, and she never would go. So she continued her walk
towards the long straggling line of houses, standing back on the highway. She
entered a passage between the dwellings.

"Mr. Rigley?—Yes! Did you want him? No, he's not in at this minute."

The raw-boned woman leaned forward from her dark scullery and peered at the other, upon whom fell a dim light through the blind of the kitchen window.

"Is it Mrs. Bates?" she asked in a tone tinged with respect.

"Yes. I wondered if your Master was at home. Mine hasn't come yet."

" 'Asn't 'e! Oh, Jack's been 'ome an' 'ad 'is dinner an' gone out. 'E's just gone for 'alf an hour afore bedtime. Did you call at the Prince of Wales?"

"No——"

"No, you didn't like——! It's not very nice." The other woman was indulgent. There was an awkward pause. "Jack never said nothink about—about your Master," she said.

"No!—I expect he's stuck in there!"

Elizabeth Bates said this bitterly, and with recklessness. She knew that the woman across the yard was standing at her door listening, but she did not care. As she turned:

"Stop a minute! I'll just go an' ask Jack if 'e knows anythink," said Mrs. Rigley.

"Oh no—I wouldn't like to put——!"

"Yes, I will, if you'll just step inside an' see as th' childer doesn't come downstairs and set theirselves afire."

Elizabeth Bates, murmuring a remonstrance, stepped inside. The other woman apologized for the state of the room.

The kitchen needed apology. There were little frocks and trousers and childish undergarments on the squab[2] and on the floor, and a litter of playthings everywhere. On the black American cloth[3] of the table were pieces of bread and cake, crusts, slops, and a teapot with cold tea.

"Eh, ours is just as bad," said Elizabeth Bates, looking at the woman, not at the house. Mrs. Rigley put a shawl over her head and hurried out, saying: "I shanna be a minute."

The other sat, noting with faint disapproval the general untidiness of the room. Then she fell to counting the shoes of various sizes scattered over the floor. There were twelve. She sighed and said to herself: "No wonder!"— glancing at the litter. There came the scratching of two pairs of feet on the yard, and the Rigleys entered. Elizabeth Bates rose. Rigley was a big man, with very large bones. His head looked particularly bony. Across his temple was a blue scar, caused by a wound got in the pit, a wound in which the coal dust remained blue like tattooing.

" 'Asna 'e come whoam yit?" asked the man, without any form of greeting, but with deference and sympathy. "I couldna say wheer he is—'e's non ower theer!"—he jerked his head to signify the Prince of Wales.

" 'E's 'appen gone up to th' Yew," said Mrs. Rigley.

There was another pause. Rigley had evidently something to get off his mind:

"Ah left 'im finishin' a stint," he began. "Loose-all[4] 'ad bin gone about ten minutes when we com'n away, an' I shouted: 'Are ter comin', Walt?' an' 'e said: 'Go on, Ah shanna be but a'ef a minnit,' so we com'n ter th' bottom, me an' Bowers, thinkin' as 'e wor just behint, an' 'ud come up i' th' next bantle[5]——"

2. Couch.
3. Oilcloth.
4. Signal for end of work.
5. Group.

He stood perplexed, as if answering a charge of deserting his mate. Elizabeth Bates, now again certain of disaster, hastened to reassure him:

"I expect 'e's gone up to th' Yew Tree, as you say. It's not the first time. I've fretted myself into a fever before now. He'll come home when they carry him."

"Ay, isn't it too bad!" deplored the other woman.

"I'll just step up to Dick's an' see if 'e *is* theer," offered the man, afraid of appearing alarmed, afraid of taking liberties.

"Oh, I wouldn't think of bothering you that far," said Elizabeth Bates, with emphasis, but he knew she was glad of his offer.

As they stumbled up the entry, Elizabeth Bates heard Rigley's wife run across the yard and open her neighbor's door. At this, suddenly all the blood in her body seemed to switch away from her heart.

"Mind!" warned Rigley. "Ah've said many a time as Ah'd fill up them ruts in this entry, sumb'dy 'll be breakin' their legs yit."

She recovered herself and walked quickly along with the miner.

"I don't like leaving the children in bed, and nobody in the house," she said.

"No, you dunna!" he replied courteously. They were soon at the gate of the cottage.

"Well, I shanna be many minnits. Dunna you be frettin' now, 'e'll be all right," said the butty.[6]

"Thank you very much, Mr. Rigley," she replied.

"You're welcome!" he stammered, moving away. "I shanna be many minnits."

The house was quiet. Elizabeth Bates took off her hat and shawl, and rolled back the rug. When she had finished, she sat down. It was a few minutes past nine. She was startled by the rapid chuff of the winding engine at the pit, and the sharp whirr of the brakes on the rope as it descended. Again she felt the painful sweep of her blood, and she put her hand to her side, saying aloud: "Good gracious! — it's only the nine o'clock deputy[7] going down," rebuking herself.

She sat still, listening. Half an hour of this, and she was wearied out.

"What am I working myself up like this for?" she said pitiably to herself, "I s'll only be doing myself some damage."

She took out her sewing again.

At a quarter to ten there were footsteps. One person! She watched for the door to open. It was an elderly woman, in a black bonnet and a black woolen shawl — his mother. She was about sixty years old, pale, with blue eyes, and her face all wrinkled and lamentable. She shut the door and turned to her daughter-in-law peevishly.

"Eh, Lizzie, whatever shall we do, whatever shall we do!" she cried.

Elizabeth drew back a little, sharply.

"What is it, mother?" she said.

The elder woman seated herself on the sofa.

"I don't know, child, I can't tell you!" — she shook her head slowly. Elizabeth sat watching her, anxious and vexed.

---

6. Workmate (cf. "buddy"). Among English coal miners it has the meaning of "a supervisor intermediary ers it has the meaning of "a supervisor intermediary between the employers and the men."
7. Minor coal-mine official.

"I don't know," replied the grandmother, sighing very deeply. "There's no end to my troubles, there isn't. The things I've gone through, I'm sure it's enough——!" She wept without wiping her eyes, the tears running.

"But, mother," interrupted Elizabeth, "what do you mean? What is it?"

The grandmother slowly wiped her eyes. The fountains of her tears were stopped by Elizabeth's directness. She wiped her eyes slowly.

"Poor child! Eh, you poor thing!" she moaned. "I don't know what we're going to do, I don't—and you as you are—it's a thing, it is indeed!"

Elizabeth waited.

"Is he dead?" she asked, and at the words her heart swung violently, though she felt a slight flush of shame at the ultimate extravagance of the question. Her words sufficiently frightened the old lady, almost brought her to herself.

"Don't say so, Elizabeth! We'll hope it's not as bad as that; no, may the Lord spare us that, Elizabeth. Jack Rigley came just as I was sittin' down to a glass afore going to bed, an' 'e said: ' 'Appen you'll go down th' line, Mrs. Bates. Walt's had an accident. 'Appen you'll go an' sit wi' 'er till we can get him home.' I hadn't time to ask him a word afore he was gone. An' I put my bonnet on an' come straight down, Lizzie. I thought to myself: 'Eh, that poor blessed child, if anybody should come an' tell her of a sudden, there's no knowin' what'll 'appen to 'er.' You mustn't let it upset you, Lizzie—or you know what to expect. How long is it, six months—or is it five, Lizzie? Ay!"— the old woman shook her head—"time slips on, it slips on! Ay!"

Elizabeth's thoughts were busy elsewhere. If he was killed—would she be able to manage on the little pension and what she could earn?—she counted up rapidly. If he was hurt—they wouldn't take him to the hospital—how tiresome he would be to nurse!—but perhaps she'd be able to get him away from the drink and his hateful ways. She would—while he was ill. The tears offered to come to her eyes at the picture. But what sentimental luxury was this she was beginning? She turned to consider the children. At any rate she was absolutely necessary for them. They were her business.

"Ay!" repeated the old woman, "it seems but a week or two since he brought me his first wages. Ay—he was a good lad, Elizabeth, he was, in his way. I don't know why he got to be such a trouble, I don't. He was a happy lad at home, only full of spirits. But there's no mistake he's been a handful of trouble, he has! I hope the Lord'll spare him to mend his ways. I hope so, I hope so. You've had a sight o' trouble with him, Elizabeth, you have indeed. But he was a jolly enough lad wi' me, he was, I can assure you. I don't know how it is. . . ."

The old woman continued to muse aloud, a monotonous irritating sound, while Elizabeth thought concentratedly, startled once, when she heard the winding engine chuff quickly, and the brakes skirr with a shriek. Then she heard the engine more slowly, and the brakes made no sound. The old woman did not notice. Elizabeth waited in suspense. The mother-in-law talked, with lapses into silence.

"But he wasn't your son, Lizzie, an' it makes a difference. Whatever he was, I remember him when he was little, an' I learned to understand him and to make allowances. You've got to make allowances for them——"

It was half-past ten, and the old woman was saying: "But it's trouble from beginning to end; you're never too old for trouble, never too old for that——" when the gate banged back, and there were heavy feet on the steps.

"I'll go, Lizzie, let me go," cried the old woman, rising. But Elizabeth was at the door. It was a man in pit clothes.

"They're bringin' 'im, Missis," he said. Elizabeth's heart halted a moment. Then it surged on again, almost suffocating her.

"Is he—is it bad?" she asked.

The man turned away, looking at the darkness:

"The doctor says 'e'd been dead hours. 'E saw 'im i' th' lamp-cabin."

The old woman, who stood just behind Elizabeth, dropped into a chair, and folded her hands, crying: "Oh, my boy, my boy!"

"Hush!" said Elizabeth, with a sharp twitch of a frown. "Be still, mother, don't waken th' children: I wouldn't have them down for anything!"

The old woman moaned softly, rocking herself. The man was drawing away. Elizabeth took a step forward.

"How was it?" she asked.

"Well, I couldn't say for sure," the man replied, very ill at ease. " 'E wor finishin' a stint an' th' butties 'ad gone, an' a lot o' stuff come down atop 'n 'im."

"And crushed him?" cried the widow, with a shudder.

"No," said the man, "it fell at th' back of 'im. 'E wor under th' face an' it niver touched 'im. It shut 'im in. It seems 'e wor smothered."

Elizabeth shrank back. She heard the old woman behind her cry:

"What?—what did 'e say it was?"

The man replied, more loudly: " 'E wor smothered!"

Then the old woman wailed aloud, and this relieved Elizabeth.

"Oh, mother," she said, putting her hand on the old woman, "don't waken th' children, don't waken th' children."

She wept a little, unknowing, while the old mother rocked herself and moaned. Elizabeth remembered that they were bringing him home, and she must be ready. "They'll lay him in the parlor," she said to herself, standing a moment pale and perplexed.

Then she lighted a candle and went into the tiny room. The air was cold and damp, but she could not make a fire, there was no fireplace. She set down the candle and looked round. The candlelight glittered on the luster-glasses, on the two vases that held some of the pink chrysanthemums, and on the dark mahogany. There was a cold, deathly smell of chrysanthemums in the room. Elizabeth stood looking at the flowers. She turned away, and calculated whether there would be room to lay him on the floor, between the couch and the chiffonier. She pushed the chairs aside. There would be room to lay him down and to step round him. Then she fetched the old red tablecloth, and another old cloth, spreading them down to save her bit of carpet. She shivered on leaving the parlor; so, from the dresser drawer she took a clean shirt and put it at the fire to air. All the time her mother-in-law was rocking herself in the chair and moaning.

"You'll have to move from there, mother," said Elizabeth. "They'll be bring-ing him in. Come in the rocker."

The old mother rose mechanically, and seated herself by the fire, continu-ing to lament. Elizabeth went into the pantry for another candle, and there, in the little penthouse under the naked tiles, she heard them coming. She stood still in the pantry doorway, listening. She heard them pass the end of the house, and come awkwardly down the three steps, a jumble of shuffling footsteps and muttering voices. The old woman was silent. The men were in the yard.

Then Elizabeth heard Matthews, the manager of the pit, say: "You go in first, Jim. Mind!"

The door came open, and the two women saw a collier backing into the room, holding one end of a stretcher, on which they could see the nailed pit boots of the dead man. The two carriers halted, the man at the head stooping to the lintel of the door.

"Wheer will you have him?" asked the manager, a short, white-bearded man.

Elizabeth roused herself and came from the pantry carrying the unlighted candle.

"In the parlor," she said.

"In there, Jim!" pointed the manager, and the carriers backed round into the tiny room. The coat with which they had covered the body fell off as they awkwardly turned through the two doorways, and the women saw their man, naked to the waist, lying stripped for work. The old woman began to moan in a low voice of horror.

"Lay th' stretcher at th' side," snapped the manager, "an' put 'im on th' cloths. Mind now, mind! Look you now——!"

One of the men had knocked off a vase of chrysanthemums. He stared awkwardly, then they set down the stretcher. Elizabeth did not look at her husband. As soon as she could get in the room, she went and picked up the broken vase and the flowers.

"Wait a minute!" she said.

The three men waited in silence while she mopped up the water with a duster.

"Eh, what a job, what a job, to be sure!" the manager was saying, rubbing his brow with trouble and perplexity. "Never knew such a thing in my life, never! He'd no business to ha' been left. I never knew such a thing in my life! Fell over him clean as a whistle, an' shut him in. Not four foot of space, there wasn't—yet it scarce bruised him."

He looked down at the dead man, lying prone, half naked, all grimed with coal dust.

"'Sphyxiated,' the doctor said. It is the most terrible job I've ever known Seems as if it was done o' purpose. Clean over him, an' shut 'im in, like a mouse-trap"—he made a sharp, descending gesture with his hand.

The colliers standing by jerked aside their heads in hopeless comment.

The horror of the thing bristled upon them all.

Then they heard the girl's voice upstairs calling shrilly: "Mother, mother—who is it? Mother, who is it?"

Elizabeth hurried to the foot of the stairs and opened the door:

"Go to sleep!" she commanded sharply. "What are you shouting about? Go to sleep at once—there's nothing——"

Then she began to mount the stairs. They could hear her on the boards, and on the plaster floor of the little bedroom. They could hear her distinctly:

"What's the matter now?—what's the matter with you, silly thing?"—her voice was much agitated, with an unreal gentleness.

"I thought it was some men come," said the plaintive voice of the child. "Has he come?"

"Yes, they've brought him. There's nothing to make a fuss about. Go to sleep now, like a good child."

They could hear her voice in the bedroom, they waited whilst she covered the children under the bedclothes.

"Is he drunk?" asked the girl, timidly, faintly.

"No! No—he's not! He—he's asleep."

"Is he asleep downstairs?"

"Yes—and don't make a noise."

There was silence for a moment, then the men heard the frightened child again:

"What's that noise?"

"It's nothing, I tell you, what are you bothering for?"

The noise was the grandmother moaning. She was oblivious of everything, sitting on her chair rocking and moaning. The manager put his hand on her arm and bade her "Sh—sh!!"

The old woman opened her eyes and looked at him. She was shocked by this interruption, and seemed to wonder.

"What time is it?" the plaintive thin voice of the child, sinking back unhappily into sleep, asked this last question.

"Ten o'clock," answered the mother more softly. Then she must have bent down and kissed the children.

Matthews beckoned to the men to come away. They put on their caps and took up the stretcher. Stepping over the body, they tiptoed out of the house. None of them spoke till they were far from the wakeful children.

When Elizabeth came down she found her mother alone on the parlor floor, leaning over the dead man, the tears dropping on him.

"We must lay him out," the wife said. She put on the kettle, then returning knelt at the feet, and began to unfasten the knotted leather laces. The room was clammy and dim with only one candle, so that she had to bend her face almost to the floor. At last she got off the heavy boots and put them away.

"You must help me now," she whispered to the old woman. Together they stripped the man.

When they arose, saw him lying in the naïve dignity of death, the women stood arrested in fear and respect. For a few moments they remained still, looking down, the old mother whimpering. Elizabeth felt countermanded. She saw him, how utterly inviolable he lay in himself. She had nothing to do with him. She could not accept it. Stooping, she laid her hand on him, in claim. He was still warm, for the mine was hot where he had died. His mother had his face between her hands, and was murmuring incoherently. The old tears fell in succession as drops from wet leaves; the mother was not weeping, merely her tears flowed. Elizabeth embraced the body of her husband, with cheek and lips. She seemed to be listening, inquiring, trying to get some connection. But she could not. She was driven away. He was impregnable.

She rose, went into the kitchen where she poured warm water into a bowl, brought soap and flannel and a soft towel. "I must wash him," she said.

Then the old mother rose stiffly, and watched Elizabeth as she carefully washed his face, carefully brushing his big blond moustache from his mouth with the flannel. She was afraid with a bottomless fear, so she ministered to him. The old woman, jealous, said:

"Let me wipe him!"—and she kneeled on the other side drying slowly as

Elizabeth washed, her big black bonnet sometimes brushing the dark head of her daughter-in-law. They worked thus in silence for a long time. They never forgot it was death, and the touch of the man's dead body gave them strange emotions, different in each of the women; a great dread possessed them both, the mother felt the lie was given to her womb, she was denied; the wife felt the utter isolation of the human soul, the child within her was a weight apart from her.

At last it was finished. He was a man of handsome body, and his face showed no traces of drink. He was blond, full fleshed, with fine limbs. But he was dead.

"Bless him," whispered his mother, looking always at his face, and speaking out of sheer terror. "Dear lad—bless him!" She spoke in a faint, sibilant ecstasy of fear and mother love.

Elizabeth sank down again to the floor, and put her face against his neck, and trembled and shuddered. But she had to draw away again. He was dead, and her living flesh had no place against his. A great dread and weariness held her: she was so unavailing. Her life was gone like this.

"White as milk he is, clear as a twelve-month baby, bless him, the darling!" the old mother murmured to herself. "Not a mark on him, clear and clean and white, beautiful as ever a child was made," she murmured with pride. Elizabeth kept her face hidden.

"He went peaceful, Lizzie—peaceful as sleep. Isn't he beautiful, the lamb? Ay—he must ha' made his peace, Lizzie. 'Appen he made it all right, Lizzie, shut in there. He'd have time. He wouldn't look like this if he hadn't made his peace. The lamb, the dear lamb. Eh, but he had a hearty laugh. I loved to hear it. He had the heartiest laugh, Lizzie, as a lad——"

Elizabeth looked up. The man's mouth was fallen back, slightly open under the cover of the moustache. The eyes, half shut, did not show glazed in the obscurity. Life with its smoky burning gone from him, had left him apart and utterly alien to her. And she knew what a stranger he was to her. In her womb was ice of fear, because of this separate stranger with whom she had been living as one flesh. Was this what it all meant—utter, intact separateness, obscured by heat of living? In dread she turned her face away. The fact was too deadly. There had been nothing between them, and yet they had come together, exchanging their nakedness repeatedly. Each time he had taken her, they had been two isolated beings, far apart as now. He was no more responsible than she. The child was like ice in her womb. For as she looked at the dead man, her mind, cold and detached, said clearly: "Who am I? What have I been doing? I have been fighting a husband who did not exist. He existed all the time. What wrong have I done? What was that I have been living with? There lies the reality, this man." And her soul died in her for fear: she knew she had never seen him, he had never seen her, they had met in the dark and had fought in the dark, not knowing whom they met or whom they fought. And now she saw, and turned silent in seeing. For she had been wrong. She had said he was something he was not; she had felt familiar with him. Whereas he was apart all the while, living as she never lived, feeling as she never felt.

In fear and shame she looked at his naked body, that she had known falsely. And he was the father of her children. Her soul was torn from her body and stood apart. She looked at his naked body and was ashamed, as if she had denied it. After all, it was itself. It seemed awful to her. She looked at his face, and she turned her own face to the wall. For his look was other than hers, his way was not her way. She had denied him what he was—she saw it now. She had refused him as himself. And this had been her life, and his life. She was grateful to death, which restored the truth. And she knew she was not dead.

And all the while her heart was bursting with grief and pity for him. What had he suffered? What stretch of horror for this helpless man! She was rigid with agony. She had not been able to help him. He had been cruelly injured, this naked man, this other being, and she could make no reparation. There were the children—but the children belonged to life. This dead man had nothing to do with them. He and she were only channels through which life had flowed to issue in the children. She was a mother—but how awful she knew it now to have been a wife. And he, dead now, how awful he must have felt it to be a husband. She felt that in the next world he would be a stranger to her. If they met there, in the beyond, they would only be ashamed of what had been before. The children had come, for some mysterious reason, out of both of them. But the children did not unite them. Now he was dead, she knew how eternally he was apart from her, how eternally he had nothing more to do with her. She saw this episode of her life closed. They had denied each other in life. Now he had withdrawn. An anguish came over her. It was finished then: it had become hopeless between them long before he died. Yet he had been her husband. But how little!

"Have you got his shirt, 'Lizabeth?"

Elizabeth turned without answering, though she strove to weep and behave as her mother-in-law expected. But she could not, she was silenced. She went into the kitchen and returned with the garment.

"It is aired," she said, grasping the cotton shirt here and there to try. She was almost ashamed to handle him; what right had she or anyone to lay hands on him; but her touch was humble on his body. It was hard work to clothe him. He was so heavy and inert. A terrible dread gripped her all the while: that he could be so heavy and utterly inert, unresponsive, apart. The horror of the distance between them was almost too much for her—it was so infinite a gap she must look across.

At last it was finished. They covered him with a sheet and left him lying, with his face bound. And she fastened the door of the little parlor, lest the children should see what was lying there. Then, with peace sunk heavy on her heart, she went about making tidy the kitchen. She knew she submitted to life, which was her immediate master. But from death, her ultimate master, she winced with fear and shame.

1911, 1914

The Horse-Dealer's Daughter

"Well, Mabel, and what are you going to do with yourself?" asked Joe, with foolish flippancy. He felt quite safe himself. Without listening for an answer, he turned aside, worked a grain of tobacco to the tip of his tongue, and spat it out. He did not care about anything, since he felt safe himself.

The three brothers and the sister sat round the desolate breakfast-table, attempting some sort of desultory consultation. The morning's post had given the final tap to the family fortunes, and all was over. The dreary dining-room itself, with its heavy mahogany furniture, looked as if it were waiting to be done away with.

But the consultation amounted to nothing. There was a strange air of ineffectuality about the three men, as they sprawled at table, smoking and reflecting vaguely on their own condition. The girl was alone, a rather short, sullen-looking young woman of twenty-seven. She did not share the same life as her brothers. She would have been good-looking, save for the impressive fixity of her face, "bull-dog," as her brothers called it.

There was a confused tramping of horses' feet outside. The three men all sprawled round in their chairs to watch. Beyond the dark holly bushes that separated the strip of lawn from the highroad, they could see a cavalcade of shire horses swinging out of their own yard, being taken for exercise. This was the last time. These were the last horses that would go through their hands. The young men watched with critical, callous look. They were all frightened at the collapse of their lives, and the sense of disaster in which they were involved left them no inner freedom.

Yet they were three fine, well-set fellows enough. Joe, the eldest, was a man of thirty-three, broad and handsome in a hot, flushed way. His face was red, he twisted his black moustache over a thick finger, his eyes were shallow and restless. He had a sensual way of uncovering his teeth when he laughed, and his bearing was stupid. Now he watched the horses with a glazed look of helplessness in his eyes, a certain stupor of downfall.

The great draught horses swung past. They were tied head to tail, four of them, and they heaved along to where a lane branched off from the highroad, planting their great hoofs floutingly in the fine black mud, swinging their great rounded haunches sumptuously, and trotting a few sudden steps as they were led into the lane, round the corner. Every movement showed a massive, slumbrous strength, and a stupidity which held them in subjection. The groom at the head looked back, jerking the leading rope. And the cavalcade moved out of sight up the lane, the tail of the last horse, bobbed up tight and stiff, held out taut from the swinging great haunches as they rocked behind the hedges in a motion-like sleep.

Joe watched with glazed hopeless eyes. The horses were almost like his own body to him. He felt he was done for now. Luckily he was engaged to a woman as old as himself, and therefore her father, who was steward of a neighboring estate, would provide him with a job. He would marry and go into harness. His life was over, he would be a subject animal now.

He turned uneasily aside, the retreating steps of the horses echoing in his ears. Then, with foolish restlessness, he reached for the scraps of bacon rind from the plates, and making a faint whistling sound, flung them to the terrier that lay against the fender. He watched the dog swallow them, and waited till the creature looked into his eyes. Then a faint grin came on his face, and in a high, foolish voice he said:

"You won't get much more bacon, shall you, you little b——?"

The dog faintly and dismally wagged its tail, then lowered its haunches, circled round, and lay down again.

There was another helpless silence at the table. Joe sprawled uneasily in his seat, not willing to go till the family conclave was dissolved. Fred Henry, the second brother, was erect, clean-limbed, alert. He had watched the passing of the horses with more *sang froid*. If he was an animal, like Joe, he was an animal which controls, not one which is controlled. He was master of any horse, and he carried himself with a well-tempered air of mastery. But he was not master of the situations of life. He pushed his coarse brown moustache upwards, off his lip, and glanced irritably at his sister, who sat impassive and inscrutable.

"You'll go and stop with Lucy for a bit, shan't you?" he asked. The girl did not answer.

"I don't see what else you can do," persisted Fred Henry.

"Go as a skivvy,"[1] Joe interpolated laconically.

The girl did not move a muscle.

"If I was her, I should go in for training for a nurse," said Malcolm, the youngest of them all. He was the baby of the family, a young man of twenty-two, with a fresh, jaunty *museau*.[2]

But Mabel did not take any notice of him. They had talked at her and round her for so many years, that she hardly heard them at all.

The marble clock on the mantelpiece softly chimed the half-hour, the dog rose uneasily from the hearth-rug and looked at the party at the breakfast-table. But still they sat in an ineffectual conclave.

"Oh, all right," said Joe suddenly, apropos of nothing. "I'll get a move on."

He pushed back his chair, straddled his knees with a downward jerk, to get them free, in horsey fashion, and went to the fire. Still he did not go out of the room; he was curious to know what the others would do or say. He began to charge his pipe, looking down at the dog and saying in a high, affected voice:

"Going wi' me? Going wi' me are ter? Tha'rt goin' further than tha counts on just now, dost hear?"

The dog faintly wagged his tail, the man stuck out his jaw and covered his pipe with his hands, and puffed intently, losing himself in the tobacco, looking down all the while at the dog with an absent brown eye. The dog looked up at him in mournful distrust. Joe stood with his knees stuck out, in real horsey fashion.

"Have you had a letter from Lucy?" Fred Henry asked of his sister.

"Last week," came the neutral reply.

"And what does she say?"

There was no answer.

"Does she *ask* you to go and stop there?" persisted Fred Henry.

"She says I can if I like."

"Well, then, you'd better. Tell her you'll come on Monday."

This was received in silence.

"That's what you'll do then, is it?" said Fred Henry, in some exasperation.

But she made no answer. There was a silence of futility and irritation in the room. Malcolm grinned fatuously.

"You'll have to make up your mind between now and next Wednesday," said Joe loudly, "or else find yourself lodgings on the curbstone."

The face of the young woman darkened, but she sat on immutable.

"Here's Jack Ferguson!" exclaimed Malcolm, who was looking aimlessly out of the window.

"Where?" exclaimed Joe loudly.

---

1. Servant girl. 2. Face (French slang).

"Just gone past."

"Coming in?"

Malcolm craned his neck to see the gate.

"Yes," he said.

There was a silence. Mabel sat on like one condemned, at the head of the table. Then a whistle was heard from the kitchen. The dog got up and barked sharply. Joe opened the door and shouted:

"Come on."

After a moment a young man entered. He was muffled up in overcoat and a purple woolen scarf, and his tweed cap, which he did not remove, was pulled down on his head. He was of medium height, his face was rather long and pale, his eyes looked tired.

"Hello, Jack! Well, Jack!" exclaimed Malcolm and Joe. Fred Henry merely said: "Jack."

"What's doing?" asked the newcomer, evidently addressing Fred Henry.

"Same. We've got to be out by Wednesday. Got a cold?"

"I have—got it bad, too."

"Why don't you stop in?"

"*Me* stop in? When I can't stand on my legs, perhaps I shall have a chance." The young man spoke huskily. He had a slight Scotch accent.

"It's a knockout, isn't it," said Joe, boisterously, "if a doctor goes round croaking with a cold. Looks bad for the patients, doesn't it?"

The young doctor looked at him slowly.

"Anything the matter with *you*, then?" he asked sarcastically.

"Not as I know of. Damn your eyes, I hope not. Why?"

"I thought you were very concerned about the patients, wondered if you might be one yourself."

"Damn it, no, I've never been patient to no flaming doctor, and hope I never shall be," returned Joe.

At this point Mabel rose from the table, and they all seemed to become aware of her existence. She began putting the dishes together. The young doctor looked at her, but did not address her. He had not greeted her. She went out of the room with the tray, her face impassive and unchanged.

"When are you off then, all of you?" asked the doctor.

"I'm catching the eleven-forty," replied Malcolm. "Are you goin' down wi' th' trap, Joe?"

"Yes, I've told you I'm going down wi' th' trap, haven't I?"

"We'd better be getting her in then. So long Jack, if I don't see you before I go," said Malcolm, shaking hands.

He went out, followed by Joe, who seemed to have his tail between his legs.

"Well, this is the devil's own," exclaimed the doctor, when he was left alone with Fred Henry. "Going before Wednesday, are you?"

"That's the orders," replied the other.

"Where, to Northampton?"

"That's it."

"The devil!" exclaimed Ferguson, with quiet chagrin.

And there was silence between the two.

"All settled up, are you?" asked Ferguson.

"About."

There was another pause.

"Well, I shall miss yer, Freddy, boy," said the young doctor.

"And I shall miss thee, Jack," returned the other.

"Miss you like hell," mused the doctor.

Fred Henry turned aside. There was nothing to say. Mabel came in again, to finish clearing the table.

"What are *you* going to do, then, Miss Pervin?" asked Ferguson. "Going to your sister's, are you?"

Mabel looked at him with her steady, dangerous eyes, that always made him uncomfortable, unsettling his superficial ease.

"No," she said.

"Well, what in the name of fortune *are* you going to do? Say what you mean to do," cried Fred Henry, with futile intensity.

But she only averted her head, and continued her work. She folded the white table cloth, and put on the chenille cloth.

"The sulkiest bitch that ever trod!" muttered her brother.

But she finished her task with perfectly impassive face, the young doctor watching her interestedly all the while. Then she went out.

Fred Henry stared after her, clenching his lips, his blue eyes fixing in sharp antagonism, as he made a grimace of sour exasperation.

"You could bray her into bits, and that's all you'd get out of her," he said, in a small, narrowed tone.

The doctor smiled faintly.

"What's she *going* to do, then?" he asked.

"Strike me if *I* know!" returned the other.

There was a pause. Then the doctor stirred.

"I'll be seeing you tonight, shall I?" he said to his friend.

"Ay—where's it to be? Are we going over to Jessdale?"

"I don't know. I've got such a cold on me. I'll come round to the Moon and Stars, anyway."

"Let Lizzie and May miss their night for once, eh?"

"That's it—if I feel as I do now."

"All's one——"

The two young men went through the passage and down to the back door together. The house was large, but it was servantless now, and desolate. At the back was a small bricked house yard and beyond that a big square, graveled fine and red, and having stables on two sides. Sloping, dank, winter-dark fields stretched away on the open sides.

But the stables were empty. Joseph Pervin, the father of the family, had been a man of no education, who had become a fairly large horse dealer. The stables had been full of horses, there was a great turmoil and come-and-go of horses and of dealers and grooms. Then the kitchen was full of servants. But of late things had declined. The old man had married a second time, to retrieve his fortunes. Now he was dead and everything was gone to the dogs, there was nothing but debt and threatening.

For months, Mabel had been servantless in the big house, keeping the home together in penury for her ineffectual brothers. She had kept house for ten years. But previously it was with unstinted means. Then, however brutal and coarse everything was, the sense of money had kept her proud, confident. The men might be foul-mouthed, the women in the kitchen might have had reputations, her brothers might have illegitimate children. But so long as there was money, the girl felt herself established, and brutally proud, reserved.

No company came to the house, save dealers and coarse men. Mabel had no associates of her own sex, after her sister went away. But she did not mind. She went regularly to church, she attended to her father. And she lived in the memory of her mother, who had died when she was fourteen, and whom she had loved. She had loved her father, too, in a different way, depending upon him, and feeling secure in him, until at the age of fifty-four, he married again. And then she had set hard against him. Now he had died and left them all hopelessly in debt.

She had suffered badly during the period of poverty. Nothing, however, could shake the curious, sullen, animal pride that dominated each member of the family. Now, for Mabel, the end had come. Still she would not cast about her. She would follow her own way just the same. She would always hold the keys of her own situation. Mindless and persistent, she endured from day to day. Why should she think? Why should she answer anybody? It was enough that this was the end, and there was no way out. She need not pass any more darkly along the main street of the small town, avoiding every eye. She need not demean herself any more, going into the shops and buying the cheapest food. This was at an end. She thought of nobody, not even of herself. Mindless and persistent, she seemed in a sort of ecstasy to be coming nearer to her fulfillment, her own glorification, approaching her dead mother, who was glorified.

In the afternoon, she took a little bag, with shears and sponge and a small scrubbing-brush, and went out. It was a gray, wintry day, with saddened, dark green fields and an atmosphere blackened by the smoke of foundries not far off. She went quickly, darkly along the causeway, heeding nobody, through the town to the churchyard.

There she always felt secure, as if no one could see her, although as a matter of fact she was exposed to the stare of everyone who passed along under the churchyard wall. Nevertheless, once under the shadow of the great looming church, among the graves, she felt immune from the world, reserved within the thick churchyard wall as in another country.

Carefully she clipped the grass from the grave, and arranged the pinky-white, small chrysanthemums in the tin cross. When this was done, she took an empty jar from a neighboring grave, brought water, and carefully, most scrupulously sponged the marble headstone and the coping-stone.

It gave her sincere satisfaction to do this. She felt in immediate contact with the world of her mother. She took minute pains, went through the park in a state bordering on pure happiness, as if in performing this task she came into a subtle, intimate connection with her mother. For the life she followed here in the world was far less real than the world of death she inherited from her mother.

The doctor's house was just by the church. Ferguson, being a mere hired assistant, was slave to the countryside. As he hurried now to attend to the out-patients in the surgery, glancing across the graveyard with his quick eye, he saw the girl at her task at the grave. She seemed so intent and remote, it was like looking into another world. Some mystical element was touched in him. He slowed down as he walked, watching her as if spellbound.

She lifted her eyes, feeling him looking. Their eyes met. And each looked away again at once, each feeling, in some way, found out by the other. He lifted his cap and passed on down the road. There remained distinct in his consciousness, like a vision, the memory of her face, lifted from the tombstone in the churchyard, and looking at him with slow, large, portentous eyes. It was portentous, her face. It seemed to mesmerize him. There was a heavy power in her eyes which laid hold of his whole being, as if he had drunk some powerful drug. He had been feeling weak and done before. Now the life came back into him, he felt delivered from his own fretted, daily self.

He finished his duties at the surgery as quickly as might be, hastily filling up the bottles of the waiting people with cheap drugs. Then, in perpetual haste, he set off again to visit several cases in another part of his round, before tea-time. At all times he preferred to walk if he could, but particularly when he was not well. He fancied the motion restored him.

The afternoon was falling. It was gray, deadened, and wintry, with a slow, moist, heavy coldness sinking in and deadening all the faculties. But why should he think or notice? He hastily climbed the hill and turned across the dark green fields, following the black cinder-track. In the distance, across a shallow dip in the country, the small town was clustered like smouldering ash, a tower, a spire, a heap of low, raw, extinct houses. And on the nearest fringe of the town, sloping into the dip, was Oldmeadow, the Pervins' house. He could see the stables and the outbuildings distinctly, as they lay towards him on the slope. Well, he would not go there many more times! Another resource would be lost to him, another place gone: the only company he cared for in the alien, ugly little town he was losing. Nothing but work, drudgery, constant hastening from dwelling to dwelling among the colliers and the iron-workers. It wore him out, but at the same time he had a craving for it. It was a stimulant to him to be in the homes of the working people, moving, as it were, through the innermost body of their life. His nerves were excited and gratified. He could come so near, into the very lives of the rough, inarticulate, powerfully emotional men and women. He grumbled, he said he hated the hellish hole. But as a matter of fact it excited him, the contact with the rough, strongly-feeling people was a stimulant applied direct to his nerves.

Below Oldmeadow, in the green, shallow, soddened hollow of fields, lay a square, deep pond. Roving across the landscape, the doctor's quick eye detected a figure in black passing through the gate of the field, down towards the pond. He looked again. It would be Mabel Pervin. His mind suddenly became alive and attentive.

Why was she going down there? He pulled up on the path on the slope above, and stood staring. He could just make sure of the small black figure moving in the hollow of the failing day. He seemed to see her in the midst of such obscurity, that he was like a clairvoyant, seeing rather with the mind's eye than with ordinary sight. Yet he could see her positively enough, whilst he kept his eye attentive. He felt, if he looked away from her, in the thick, ugly falling dusk, he would lose her altogether.

He followed her minutely as she moved, direct and intent, like something transmitted rather than stirring in voluntary activity, straight down the field towards the pond. There she stood on the bank for a moment. She never raised her head. Then she waded slowly into the water.

He stood motionless as the small black figure walked slowly and deliberately towards the center of the pond, very slowly, gradually moving deeper into the motionless water, and still moving forward as the water got up to her breast. Then he could see her no more in the dusk of the dead afternoon.

"There!" he exclaimed. "Would you believe it?"

And he hastened straight down, running over the wet, soddened fields, pushing through the hedges, down into the depression of callous wintry obscurity. It took him several minutes to come to the pond. He stood on the bank, breathing heavily. He could see nothing. His eyes seemed to penetrate the dead water. Yes, perhaps that was the dark shadow of her black clothing beneath the surface of the water.

He slowly ventured into the pond. The bottom was deep, soft clay, he sank in, and the water clasped dead cold round his legs. As he stirred he could smell the cold, rotten clay that fouled up into the water. It was objectionable in his lungs. Still, repelled and yet not heeding, he moved deeper into the pond. The cold water rose over his thighs, over his loins, upon his abdomen. The lower part of his body was all sunk in the hideous cold element. And the bottom was so deeply soft and uncertain, he was afraid of pitching with his mouth underneath. He could not swim, and was afraid.

He crouched a little, spreading his hands under the water and moving them round, trying to feel for her. The dead cold pond swayed upon his chest. He moved again, a little deeper, and again, with his hands underneath, he felt all around under the water. And he touched her clothing. But it evaded his fingers. He made a desperate effort to grasp it.

And so doing he lost his balance and went under, horribly, suffocating in the foul earthy water, struggling madly for a few moments. At last, after what seemed an eternity, he got his footing, rose again into the air and looked around. He gasped, and knew he was in the world. Then he looked at the water. She had risen near him. He grasped her clothing, and drawing her nearer, turned to take his way to land again.

He went very slowly, carefully, absorbed in the slow progress. He rose higher, climbing out of the pond. The water was now only about his legs; he was thankful, full of relief to be out of the clutches of the pond. He lifted her and staggered on to the bank, out of the horror of wet, gray clay.

He laid her down on the bank. She was quite unconscious and running with water. He made the water come from her mouth, he worked to restore her. He did not have to work very long before he could feel the breathing begin again in her; she was breathing naturally. He worked a little longer. He could feel her live beneath his hands; she was coming back. He wiped her face, wrapped her in his overcoat, looked round into the dim, dark gray world, then lifted her and staggered down the bank and across the fields.

It seemed an unthinkably long way, and his burden so heavy he felt he would never get to the house. But at last he was in the stable yard, and then in the house yard. He opened the door and went into the house. In the kitchen he laid her down on the hearth-rug and called. The house was empty. But the fire was burning in the grate.

Then again he kneeled to attend to her. She was breathing regularly, her eyes were wide open and as if conscious, but there seemed something missing in her look. She was conscious in herself, but unconscious of her surroundings.

He ran upstairs, took blankets from a bed, and put them before the fire to warm. Then he removed her saturated, earthy-smelling clothing, rubbed her dry with a towel, and wrapped her naked in the blankets. Then he went into the dining room, to look for spirits. There was a little whisky. He drank a gulp himself, and put some into her mouth.

The effect was instantaneous. She looked full into his face, as if she had been seeing him for some time, and yet had only just become conscious of him.

"Dr. Ferguson?" she said.

"What?" he answered.

He was divesting himself of his coat, intending to find some dry clothing upstairs. He could not bear the smell of the dead, clayey water, and he was mortally afraid for his own health.

"What did I do?" she asked.

"Walked into the pond," he replied. He had begun to shudder like one sick, and could hardly attend to her. Her eyes remained full on him, he seemed to be going dark in his mind, looking back at her helplessly. The shuddering became quieter in him, his life came back to him, dark and unknowing, but strong again.

"Was I out of my mind?" she asked, while her eyes were fixed on him all the time.

"Maybe, for the moment," he replied. He felt quiet, because his strength had come back. The strange fretful strain had left him.

"Am I out of my mind now?" she asked.

"Are you?" he reflected a moment. "No," he answered truthfully. "I don't see that you are." He turned his face aside. He was afraid now, because he felt dazed, and felt dimly that her power was stronger than his, in this issue. And she continued to look at him fixedly all the time. "Can you tell me where I shall find some dry things to put on?" he asked.

"Did you dive into the pond for me?" she asked.

"No," he answered. "I walked in. But I went in overhead as well."

There was silence for a moment. He hesitated. He very much wanted to go upstairs to get into dry clothing. But there was another desire in him. And she seemed to hold him. His will seemed to have gone to sleep, and left him, standing there slack before her. But he felt warm inside himself. He did not shudder at all, though his clothes were sodden on him.

"Why did you?" she asked.

"Because I didn't want you to do such a foolish thing," he said.

"It wasn't foolish," she said, still gazing at him as she lay on the floor, with a sofa cushion under her head. "It was the right thing to do. *I* knew best, then."

"I'll go and shift these wet things," he said. But still he had not the power to move out of her presence, until she sent him. It was as if she had the life of his body in her hands, and he could not extricate himself. Or perhaps he did not want to.

Suddenly she sat up. Then she became aware of her own immediate condition. She felt the blankets about her, she knew her own limbs. For a moment it seemed as if her reason were going. She looked round, with wild eye, as if seeking something. He stood still with fear. She saw her clothing lying scattered.

"Who undressed me?" she asked, her eyes resting full and inevitable on his face.

"I did," he replied, "to bring you round."

For some moments she sat and gazed at him awfully, her lips parted.

"Do you love me, then?" she asked.

He only stood and stared at her, fascinated. His soul seemed to melt.

She shuffled forward on her knees, and put her arms round him, round his legs, as he stood there, pressing her breasts against his knees and thighs, clutching him with strange, convulsive certainty, pressing his thighs against her, drawing him to her face, her throat, as she looked up at him with flaring, humble eyes of transfiguration, triumphant in first possession.

"You love me," she murmured, in strange transport, yearning and triumphant and confident. "You love me. I know you love me, I know."

And she was passionately kissing his knees, through the wet clothing, passionately and indiscriminately kissing his knees, his legs, as if unaware of everything.

He looked down at the tangled wet hair, the wild, bare, animal shoulders. He was amazed, bewildered, and afraid. He had never thought of loving her. He had never wanted to love her. When he rescued her and restored her, he was a doctor, and she was a patient. He had had no single personal thought of her. Nay, this introduction of the personal element was very distasteful to him, a violation of his professional honor. It was horrible to have her there embracing his knees. It was horrible. He revolted from it, violently. And yet—and yet—he had not the power to break away.

She looked at him again, with the same supplication of powerful love, and that same transcendent, frightening light of triumph. In view of the delicate flame which seemed to come from her face like a light, he was powerless. And yet he had never intended to love her. He had never intended. And something stubborn in him could not give way.

"You love me," she repeated, in a murmur of deep, rhapsodic assurance. "You love me."

Her hands were drawing him, drawing him down to her. He was afraid, even a little horrified. For he had, really, no intention of loving her. Yet her hands were drawing him towards her. He put out his hand quickly to steady himself, and grasped her bare shoulder. A flame seemed to burn the hand that grasped her soft shoulder. He had no intention of loving her: his whole will was against his yielding. It was horrible. And yet wonderful was the touch of her shoulders, beautiful the shining of her face. Was she perhaps mad? He had a horror of yielding to her. Yet something in him ached also.

He had been staring away at the door, away from her. But his hand remained on her shoulder. She had gone suddenly very still. He looked down at her. Her eyes were now wide with fear, with doubt, the light was dying from her face, a shadow of terrible grayness was returning. He could not bear the touch of her eyes' question upon him, and the look of death behind the question.

With an inward groan he gave way, and let his heart yield towards her. A sudden gentle smile came on his face. And her eyes, which never left his face, slowly, slowly filled with tears. He watched the strange water rise in her eyes, like some slow fountain coming up. And his heart seemed to burn and melt away in his breast.

He could not bear to look at her any more. He dropped on his knees and caught her head with his arms and pressed her face against his throat. She was very still. His heart, which seemed to have broken, was burning with a kind of agony in his breast. And he felt her slow, hot tears wetting his throat. But he could not move.

He felt the hot tears wet his neck and the hollows of his neck, and he remained motionless, suspended through one of man's eternities. Only now it had become indispensable to him to have her face pressed close to him; he could never let her go again. He could never let her head go away from the close clutch of his arm. He wanted to remain like that for ever, with his heart hurting him in a pain that was also life to him. Without knowing, he was looking down on her damp, soft brown hair.

Then, as it were suddenly, he smelt the horrid stagnant smell of that water. And at the same moment she drew away from him and looked at him. Her eyes were wistful and unfathomable. He was afraid of them, and he fell to kissing her, not knowing what he was doing. He wanted her eyes not to have that terrible, wistful, unfathomable look.

When she turned her face to him again, a faint delicate flush was glowing, and there was again dawning that terrible shining of joy in her eyes, which really terrified him, and yet which he now wanted to see, because he feared the look of doubt still more.

"You love me?" she said, rather faltering.

"Yes." The word cost him a painful effort. Not because it wasn't true. But because it was too newly true, the *saying* seemed to tear open again his newly torn heart. And he hardly wanted it to be true, even now.

She lifted her face to him, and he bent forward and kissed her on the mouth, gently, with the one kiss that is an eternal pledge. And as he kissed her his heart strained again in his breast. He never intended to love her. But now it was over. He had crossed over the gulf to her, and all that he had left behind had shriveled and become void.

After the kiss, her eyes again slowly filled with tears. She sat still, away from him, with her face drooped aside, and her hands folded in her lap. The tears fell very slowly. There was complete silence. He too sat there motionless and silent on the hearth rug. The strange pain of his heart that was broken seemed to consume him. That he should love her? That this was love! That he should be ripped open in this way! Him, a doctor! How they would all jeer if they knew! It was agony to him to think they might know.

In the curious naked pain of the thought he looked again to her. She was sitting there drooped into a muse. He saw a tear fall, and his heart flared hot. He saw for the first time that one of her shoulders was quite uncovered, one arm bare, he could see one of her small breasts; dimly, because it had become almost dark in the room.

"Why are you crying?" he asked, in an altered voice.

She looked up at him, and behind her tears the consciousness of her situation for the first time brought a dark look of shame to her eyes.

"I'm not crying, really," she said, watching him, half frightened.

He reached his hand, and softly closed it on her bare arm.

"I love you! I love you!" he said in a soft, low vibrating voice, unlike himself.

She shrank, and dropped her head. The soft, penetrating grip of his hand on her arm distressed her. She looked up at him.

"I want to go," she said. "I want to go and get you some dry things."

"Why?" he said. "I'm all right."

"But I want to go," she said. "And I want you to change your things."

He released her arm, and she wrapped herself in the blanket, looking at him, rather frightened. And still she did not rise.

"Kiss me," she said wistfully.

He kissed her, but briefly, half in anger.

Then, after a second, she rose nervously, all mixed up in the blanket. He watched her in her confusion as she tried to extricate herself and wrap herself up so that she could walk. He watched her relentlessly, as she knew. And as she went, the blanket trailing, and as he saw a glimpse of her feet and her white leg, he tried to remember her as she was when he had wrapped her in the blanket. But then he didn't want to remember, because she had been nothing to him then, and his nature revolted from remembering her as she was when she was nothing to him.

A tumbling muffled noise from within the dark house startled him. Then he heard her voice: "There are clothes." He rose and went to the foot of the stairs, and gathered up the garments she had thrown down. Then he came back to the fire, to rub himself down and dress. He grinned at his own appearance when he had finished.

The fire was sinking, so he put on coal. The house was now quite dark, save for the light of a street-lamp that shone in faintly from beyond the holly trees. He lit the gas with matches he found on the mantelpiece. Then he emptied the pockets of his own clothes, and threw all his wet things in a heap into the scullery. After which he gathered up her sodden clothes, gently, and put them in a separate heap on the copper-top in the scullery.

It was six o'clock on the clock. His own watch had stopped. He ought to go back to the surgery. He waited, and still she did not come down. So he went to the foot of the stairs and called:

"I shall have to go."

Almost immediately he heard her coming down. She had on her best dress of black voile, and her hair was tidy, but still damp. She looked at him—and in spite of herself, smiled.

"I don't like you in those clothes," she said.

"Do I look a sight?" he answered.

They were shy of one another.

"I'll make you some tea," she said.

"No, I must go."

"Must you?" And she looked at him again with the wide, strained, doubtful eyes. And again, from the pain of his breast, he knew how he loved her. He went and bent to kiss her, gently, passionately, with his heart's painful kiss.

"And my hair smells so horrible," she murmured in distraction. "And I'm so awful, I'm so awful! Oh no, I'm too awful." And she broke into bitter, heartbroken sobbing. "You can't want to love me, I'm horrible."

"Don't be silly, don't be silly," he said, trying to comfort her, kissing her, holding her in his arms. "I want you, I want to marry you, we're going to be married, quickly, quickly—tomorrow if I can."

But she only sobbed terribly, and cried:

"I feel awful. I feel awful. I feel I'm horrible to you."

"No, I want you, I want you," was all he answered, blindly, with that terrible intonation which frightened her almost more than her horror lest he should *not* want her.

1922

Why the Novel Matters

We have curious ideas of ourselves. We think of ourselves as a body with a spirit in it, or a body with a soul in it, or a body with a mind in it. *Mens sana in corpore sano.*[1] The years drink up the wine, and at last throw the bottle away, the body, of course, being the bottle.

It is a funny sort of superstition. Why should I look at my hand, as it so cleverly writes these words, and decide that it is a mere nothing compared to the mind that directs it? Is there really any huge difference between my hand and my brain? Or my mind? My hand is alive, it flickers with a life of its own. It meets all the strange universe in touch, and learns a vast number of things, and knows a vast number of things. My hand, as it writes these words, slips gaily along, jumps like a grasshopper to dot an *i*, feels the table rather cold, gets a little bored if I write too long, has its own rudiments of thought, and is just as much *me* as is my brain, my mind, or my soul. Why should I imagine that there is a *me* which is more *me* than my hand is? Since my hand is absolutely alive, me alive.

Whereas, of course, as far as I am concerned, my pen isn't alive at all. My pen *isn't me* alive. Me alive ends at my finger tips.

Whatever is me alive is me. Every tiny bit of my hands is alive, every little freckle and hair and fold of skin. And whatever is me alive is me. Only my fingernails, those ten little weapons between me and an inanimate universe, they cross the mysterious Rubicon[2] between me alive and things like my pen, which are not alive, in my own sense.

So, seeing my hand is all alive, and me alive, wherein is it just a bottle, or a jug, or a tin can, or a vessel of clay, or any of the rest of that nonsense? True, if I cut it it will bleed, like a can of cherries. But then the skin that is cut, and the veins that bleed, and the bones that should never be seen, they are all just as alive as the blood that flows. So the tin can business, or vessel of clay, is just bunk.

And that's what you learn, when you're a novelist. And that's what you are very liable *not* to know, if you're a parson, or a philosopher, or a scientist, or a stupid person. If you're a parson, you talk about souls in heaven. If you're a novelist, you know that paradise is in the palm of your hand, and on the end of your nose, because both are alive; and alive, and man alive, which is more than you can say, for certain, of paradise. Paradise is after life, and I for one am not keen on anything that is *after* life. If you are a philosopher, you talk about infinity, and the pure spirit which knows all things. But if you pick up a novel, you realize immediately that infinity is just a handle to this self-same jug of a body of mine; while as for knowing, if I find my finger in the fire, I know that fire burns, with a knowledge so emphatic and vital, it leaves Nir-

---

1. A healthy mind in a healthy body.
2. When Julius Caesar crossed the river Rubicon (near Rimini, Italy) in 49 B.C., in defiance of the Senate's orders, this indicated his intention of advancing against Pompey and thus involving the country in civil war. Hence to "cross the Rubicon" means to take an important and irrevocable decision.

vana[3] merely a conjecture. Oh, yes, my body, me alive, *knows,* and knows intensely. And as for the sum of all knowledge, it can't be anything more than an accumulation of all the things I know in the body, and you, dear reader, know in the body.

These damned philosophers, they talk as if they suddenly went off in steam, and were then much more important than they are when they're in their shirts. It is nonsense. Every man, philosopher included, ends in his own finger tips. That's the end of his man alive. As for the words and thoughts and sighs and aspirations that fly from him, they are so many tremulations in the ether, and not alive at all. But if the tremulations reach another man alive, he may receive them into his life, and his life may take on a new color, like a chameleon creeping from a brown rock on to a green leaf. All very well and good. It still doesn't alter the fact that the so-called spirit, the message or teaching of the philosopher or the saint, isn't alive at all, but just a tremulation upon the ether, like a radio message. All this spirit stuff is just tremulations upon the ether. If you, as man alive, quiver from the tremulation of the ether into new life, that is because you are man alive, and you take sustenance and stimulation into your alive man in a myriad ways. But to say that the message, or the spirit which is communicated to you, is more important than your living body, is nonsense. You might as well say that the potato at dinner was more important.

Nothing is important but life. And for myself, I can absolutely see life nowhere but in the living. Life with a capital L is only man alive. Even a cabbage in the rain is cabbage alive. All things that are alive are amazing. And all things that are dead are subsidiary to the living. Better a live dog than a dead lion. But better a live lion than a live dog. *C'est la vie!*

It seems impossible to get a saint, or a philosopher, or a scientist, to stick to this simple truth. They are all, in a sense, renegades. The saint wishes to offer himself up as spiritual food for the multitude. Even Francis of Assisi turns himself into a sort of angel-cake, of which anyone may take a slice. But an angel-cake is rather less than man alive. And poor St. Francis might well apologize to his body, when he is dying: "Oh, pardon me, my body, the wrong I did you through the years!" It was no wafer, for others to eat.

The philosopher, on the other hand, because he can think, decides that nothing but thoughts matter. It is as if a rabbit, because he can make little pills, should decide that nothing but little pills matter. As for the scientist, he has absolutely no use for me so long as I am man alive. To the scientist, I am dead. He puts under the microscope a bit of dead me, and calls it me. He takes me to pieces, and says first one piece, and then another piece, is me. My heart, my liver, my stomach have all been scientifically me, according to the scientist; and nowadays I am either a brain, or nerves, or glands, or something more up-to-date in the tissue line.

Now I absolutely flatly deny that I am a soul, or a body, or a mind, or an intelligence, or a brain, or a nervous system, or a bunch of glands, or any of the rest of these bits of me. The whole is greater than the part. And therefore, I, who am man alive, am greater than my soul, or spirit, or body, or mind, or consciousness, or anything else that is merely a part of me. I am a man, and alive. I am man alive, and as long as I can, I intend to go on being man alive.

3. In Buddhist theology, the extinction of the self and its desires and the attainment of perfect beatitude.

For this reason I am a novelist. And being a novelist, I consider myself superior to the saint, the scientist, the philosopher, and the poet, who are all great masters of different bits of man alive, but never get the whole hog.

The novel is the one bright book of life. Books are not life. They are only tremulations on the ether. But the novel as a tremulation can make the whole man alive tremble. Which is more than poetry, philosophy, science, or any other book-tremulation can do.

The novel is the book of life. In this sense, the Bible is a great confused novel. You may say, it is about God. But it is really about man alive. Adam, Eve, Sarai, Abraham, Isaac, Jacob, Samuel, David, Bath-Sheba, Ruth, Esther, Solomon, Job, Isaiah, Jesus, Mark, Judas, Paul, Peter: what is it but man alive, from start to finish? Man alive, not mere bits. Even the Lord is another man alive, in a burning bush, throwing the tablets of stone at Moses's head.

I do hope you begin to get my idea, why the novel is supremely important, as a tremulation on the ether. Plato makes the perfect ideal being tremble in me. But that's only a bit of me. Perfection is only a bit, in the strange make-up of man alive. The Sermon on the Mount makes the selfless spirit of me quiver. But that, too, is only a bit of me. The Ten Commandments set the old Adam shivering in me, warning me that I am a thief and a murderer, unless I watch it. But even the old Adam is only a bit of me.

I very much like all these bits of me to be set trembling with life and the wisdom of life. But I do ask that the whole of me shall tremble in its wholeness, some time or other.

And this, of course, must happen in me, living.

But as far as it can happen from a communication, it can only happen when a whole novel communicates itself to me. The Bible—but *all* the Bible—and Homer, and Shakespeare: these are the supreme old novels. These are all things to all men. Which means that in their wholeness they affect the whole man alive, which is the man himself, beyond any part of him. They set the whole tree trembling with a new access of life, they do not just stimulate growth in one direction.

I don't want to grow in any one direction any more. And, if I can help it, I don't want to stimulate anybody else into some particular direction. A particular direction ends in a *cul-de-sac*. We're in a *cul-de-sac* at present.

I don't believe in any dazzling revelation, or in any supreme Word. "The grass withereth, the flower fadeth, but the Word of the Lord shall stand for ever." That's the kind of stuff we've drugged ourselves with. As a matter of fact, the grass withereth, but comes up all the greener for that reason, after the rains. The flower fadeth, and therefore the bud opens. But the Word of the Lord, being man-uttered and a mere vibration on the ether, becomes staler and staler, more and more boring, till at last we turn a deaf ear and it ceases to exist, far more finally than any withered grass. It is grass that renews its youth like the eagle, not any Word.

We should ask for no absolutes, or absolute. Once and for all and for ever, let us have done with the ugly imperialism of any absolute. There is no absolute good, there is nothing absolutely right. All things flow and change, and even change is not absolute. The whole is a strange assembly of apparently incongruous parts, slipping past one another.

Me, man alive, I am a very curious assembly of incongruous parts. My yea! of today is oddly different from my yea! of yesterday. My tears of tomorrow will have nothing to do with my tears of a year ago. If the one I love remains unchanged and unchanging, I shall cease to love her. It is only because she changes and startles me into change and defies my inertia, and is herself staggered in her inertia by my changing, that I can continue to love her. If she stayed put, I might as well love the pepper pot.

In all this change, I maintain a certain integrity. But woe betide me if I try to put my finger on it. If I say of myself, I am this, I am that!—then, if I stick to it, I turn into a stupid fixed thing like a lamp-post. I shall never know wherein lies my integrity, my individuality, my me. I *can* never know it. It is useless to talk about my ego. That only means that I have made up an *idea* of myself, and that I am trying to cut myself out to pattern. Which is no good. You can cut your cloth to fit your coat, but you can't clip bits off your living body, to trim it down to your idea. True, you can put yourself into ideal corsets. But even in ideal corsets, fashions change.

Let us learn from the novel. In the novel, the characters can do nothing but *live*. If they keep on being good, according to pattern, or bad, according to pattern, or even volatile, according to pattern, they cease to live, and the novel falls dead. A character in a novel has got to live, or it is nothing.

We, likewise, in life have got to live, or we are nothing.

What we mean by living is, of course, just as indescribable as what we mean by *being*. Men get ideas into their heads, of what they mean by Life, and they proceed to cut life out to pattern. Sometimes they go into the desert to seek God, sometimes they go into the desert to seek cash, sometimes it is wine, woman, and song, and again it is water, political reform, and votes. You never know what it will be next: from killing your neighbor with hideous bombs and gas that tears the lungs, to supporting a Foundlings Home and preaching infinite Love, and being co-respondent in a divorce.

In all this wild welter, we need some sort of guide. It's no good inventing Thou Shalt Nots!

What then? Turn truly, honorably to the novel, and see wherein you are man alive, and wherein you are dead man in life. You may love a woman as man alive, and you may be making love to a woman as sheer dead man in life. You may eat your dinner as man alive, or as a mere masticating corpse. As man alive you may have shot at your enemy. But as a ghastly simulacrum of life you may be firing bombs into men who are neither your enemies nor your friends, but just things you are dead to. Which is criminal, when the things happen to be alive.

To be alive, to be man alive, to be whole man alive: that is the point. And at its best, the novel, and the novel supremely, can help you. It can help you not to be dead man in life. So much of a man walks about dead and a carcass in the street and house, today: so much of women is merely dead. Like a pianoforte with half the notes mute.

But the novel you can see, plainly, when the man goes dead, the woman goes inert. You can develop an instinct for life, if you will, instead of a theory of right and wrong, good and bad.

In life, there is right and wrong, good and bad, all the time. But what is right in one case is wrong in another. And in the novel you see one man becoming a corpse, because of his so-called goodness, another going dead because of his so-called wickedness. Right and wrong is an instinct: but an instinct of the whole consciousness in a man, bodily, mental, spiritual at once.

And only in the novel are *all* things given full play, or at least, they may be given full play, when we realize that life itself, and not inert safety, is the reason for living. For out of the full play of all things emerges the only thing that is anything, the wholeness of a man, the wholeness of a woman, man live, and live woman.

1936

Love on the Farm[1]

What large, dark hands are those at the window
Grasping in the golden light
Which weaves its way through the evening wind
 At my heart's delight?

Ah, only the leaves! But in the west   5
I see a redness suddenly come
Into the evening's anxious breast—
 'Tis the wound of love goes home!

The woodbine creeps abroad
Calling low to her lover: 10
 The sunlit flirt who all the day
 Has poised above her lips in play
 And stolen kisses, shallow and gay
 Of pollen, now has gone away—
 She woos the moth with her sweet, low word;   15
And when above her his moth-wings hover
Then her bright breast she will uncover
And yield her honey-drop to her lover.

Into the yellow, evening glow
Saunters a man from the farm below;   20
Leans, and looks in at the low-built shed
Where the swallow has hung her marriage bed.
 The bird lies warm against the wall.
 She glances quick her startled eyes
 Towards him, then she turns away   25
 Her small head, making warm display
 Of red upon the throat. Her terrors sway
 Her out of the nest's warm, busy ball,
 Whose plaintive cry is heard as she flies
 In one blue stoop from out the sties   30
 Into the twilight's empty hall.
Oh, water-hen, beside the rushes
Hide your quaintly scarlet blushes,
Still your quick tail, lie still as dead,
Till the distance folds over his ominous tread!   35

---

1. Called *Cruelty and Love* when first published in 1913 and *Love on the Farm* when it appeared in *Collected Poems* (1928).

The rabbit presses back her ears,
Turns back her liquid, anguished eyes
And crouches low; then with wild spring
Spurts from the terror of *his* oncoming;
To be choked back, the wire ring   40
Her frantic effort throttling:
     Piteous brown ball of quivering fears!
Ah, soon in his large, hard hands she dies,
And swings all loose from the swing of his walk!
Yet calm and kindly are his eyes   45
And ready to open in brown surprise
Should I not answer to his talk
Or should he my tears surmise.

I hear his hand on the latch, and rise from my chair
Watching the door open; he flashes bare   50
His strong teeth in a smile, and flashes his eyes
In a smile like triumph upon me; then careless-wise
He flings the rabbit soft on the table board
And comes towards me: ah! the uplifted sword
Of his hand against my bosom! and oh, the broad   55
Blade of his glance that asks me to applaud
His coming! With his hand he turns my face to him
And caresses me with his fingers that still smell grim
Of the rabbit's fur! God, I am caught in a snare!
I know not what fine wire is round my throat;   60
I only know I let him finger there
My pulse of life, and let him nose like a stoat
Who sniffs with joy before he drinks the blood.

And down his mouth comes to my mouth! and down
His bright dark eyes come over me, like a hood   65
Upon my mind! his lips meet mine, and a flood
Of sweet fire sweeps across me, so I drown
Against him, die, and find death good.

                                        1913, 1928

Piano[1]

Softly, in the dusk, a woman is singing to me;
Taking me back down the vista of years, till I see
A child sitting under the piano, in the boom of the tingling strings
And pressing the small, poised feet of a mother who smiles as she sings.

In spite of myself, the insidious mastery of song   5
Betrays me back, till the heart of me weeps to belong
To the old Sunday evenings at home, with winter outside
And hymns in the cozy parlor, the tinkling piano our guide.

1. For an earlier version of this poem, see "Poems in Process" (p. 2591).

So now it is vain for the singer to burst into clamor
With the great black piano appassionato. The glamor   10
Of childish days is upon me, my manhood is cast
Down in the flood of remembrance, I weep like a child for the past.

                                                                    1918

Bavarian Gentians[1]

Not every man has gentians in his house
in Soft September, at slow, Sad Michaelmas.

Bavarian gentians, big and dark, only dark
darkening the daytime torchlike with the smoking blueness of Pluto's[2] gloom,
ribbed and torchlike, with their blaze of darkness spread blue   5
down flattening into points, flattened under the sweep of white day
torch-flower of the blue-smoking darkness, Pluto's dark-blue daze,
black lamps from the halls of Dis, burning dark blue,
giving off darkness, blue darkness, as Demeter's pale lamps give off light,
lead me then, lead me the way.   10

Reach me a gentian, give me a torch
let me guide myself with the blue, forked torch of this flower
down the darker and darker stairs, where blue is darkened on blueness.
even where Persephone[3] goes, just now, from the frosted September
to the sightless realm where darkness was awake upon the dark   15
and Persephone herself is but a voice
or a darkness invisible enfolded in the deeper dark
of the arms Plutonic, and pierced with the passion of dense gloom,
among the splendor of torches of darkness, shedding darkness on the lost bride
    and her groom.

                                                                    1923

Snake

A snake came to my water trough
On a hot, hot day, and I in pajamas for the heat,
To drink there.

In the deep, strange-scented shade of the great dark carob tree
I came down the steps with my pitcher   5
And must wait, must stand and wait, for there he was at the trough before me.

1. Keith Sagar challenges the accepted view that this is the final version of the poem in "The Genesis of 'Bavarian Gentians,' " *The D. H. Lawrence Review* (Spring 1975): 47–53. He prefers the longer version printed in *The Collected Poems of D. H. Lawrence* (1964), ed. Vivian de Sola Pinto and Warren Roberts, 975.
2. Pluto was god of the underworld in classical mythology; he was also called "Dis" (line 8).

3. Bride of Pluto, who abducted her from the earth, and daughter of Demeter, goddess of the fruits of the earth (line 11). She was allowed to return to earth every spring but had to descend again to Hades in the autumn, "the frosted September." Demeter and Persephone were central figures in ancient fertility myths, where Persephone's annual descent and return were linked with the death and rebirth of vegetation.

He reached down from a fissure in the earth-wall in the gloom
And trailed his yellow-brown slackness soft-bellied down, over the edge of the
    stone trough
And rested his throat upon the stone bottom,
And where the water had dripped from the tap, in a small clearness,   10
He sipped with his straight mouth,
Softly drank through his straight gums, into his slack long body,
Silently.

Someone was before me at my water trough,
And I, like a second-comer, waiting.   15

He lifted his head from his drinking, as cattle do,
And looked at me vaguely, as drinking cattle do,
And flickered his two-forked tongue from his lips, and mused a moment,
And stooped and drank a little more,
Being earth-brown, earth-golden from the burning bowels of the earth   20
On the day of Sicilian July, with Etna smoking.

The voice of my education said to me
He must be killed,
For in Sicily the black black snakes are innocent, the gold are venomous.

And voices in me said, If you were a man   25
You would take a stick and break him now, and finish him off.

But must I confess how I liked him,
How glad I was he had come like a guest in quiet, to drink at my water trough
And depart peaceful, pacified, and thankless
Into the burning bowels of this earth?   30

Was it cowardice, that I dared not kill him?
Was it perversity, that I longed to talk to him?
Was it humility, to feel so honored?
I felt so honored.

And yet those voices: 35
If you were not afraid, you would kill him!

And truly I was afraid, I was most afraid,
But even so, honored still more
That he should seek my hospitality
From out the dark door of the secret earth.   40

He drank enough
And lifted his head, dreamily, as one who has drunken,
And flickered his tongue like a forked night on the air, so black,
Seeming to lick his lips,
And looked around like a god, unseeing, into the air,   45
And slowly turned his head,
And slowly, very slowly, as if thrice adream

Proceeded to draw his slow length curving round
And climb the broken bank of my wall-face.

And as he put his head into that dreadful hole,   50
And as he slowly drew up, snake-easing his shoulders, and entered further,
A sort of horror, a sort of protest against his withdrawing into that horrid black
     hole,
Deliberately going into the blackness, and slowly drawing himself after,
Overcame me now his back was turned.

I looked round, I put down my pitcher,   55
I picked up a clumsy log
And threw it at the water trough with a clatter.

I think it did not hit him;
But suddenly that part of him that was left behind convulsed in undignified
     haste,
Writhed like lightning, and was gone   60
Into the black hole, the earth-lipped fissure in the wall-front
At which, in the intense still noon, I stared with fascination.

And immediately I regretted it.
I thought how paltry, how vulgar, what a mean act!
I despised myself and the voices of my accursed human education.   65

And I thought of the albatross,[1]
And I wished he would come back, my snake.

For he seemed to me again like a king,
Like a king in exile, uncrowned in the underworld,
Now due to be crowned again.   70

And so, I missed my chance with one of the lords
Of life.
And I have something to expiate:
A pettiness.

                                                                            1923

How Beastly the Bourgeois Is

How beastly the bourgeois is
especially the male of the species—

Presentable, eminently presentable—
shall I make you a present of him?

Isn't he handsome? Isn't he healthy? Isn't he a fine specimen?   5
Doesn't he look the fresh clean Englishman, outside?
Isn't it God's own image? tramping his thirty miles a day

---

1. In Coleridge's *Ancient Mariner*.

after partridges, or a little rubber ball?
wouldn't you like to be like that, well off, and quite the thing?

Oh, but wait!   10
Let him meet a new emotion, let him be faced with another man's need,
let him come home to a bit of moral difficulty, let life face him with a new
     demand on his understanding
and then watch him go soggy, like a wet meringue.
Watch him turn into a mess, either a fool or a bully.
Just watch the display of him, confronted with a new demand on his
     intelligence,   15
a new life-demand.

How beastly the bourgeois is
especially the male of the species —

Nicely groomed, like a mushroom
standing there so sleek and erect and eyeable —   20
and like a fungus, living on the remains of bygone life
sucking his life out of the dead leaves of greater life than his own.

And even so, he's stale, he's been there too long.
Touch him, and you'll find he's all gone inside
just like an old mushroom, all wormy inside, and hollow   25
under a smooth skin and an upright appearance.

Full of seething, wormy, hollow feelings
rather nasty —
How beastly the bourgeois is!

Standing in their thousands, these appearances, in damp England   30
what a pity they can't all be kicked over
like sickening toadstools, and left to melt back, swiftly
into the soil of England.

                                              1929

T. S. ELIOT
1888–1965

<table>
<tr><td>1915:</td><td>Settles in London.</td></tr>
<tr><td>1917:</td><td>Prufrock and Other Observations.</td></tr>
<tr><td>1922:</td><td>The Waste Land.</td></tr>
<tr><td>1927:</td><td>Becomes British subject; confirmed in Anglican church.</td></tr>
<tr><td>1944:</td><td>Four Quartets.</td></tr>
</table>

Thomas Stearns Eliot was born in St. Louis, Missouri, of New England stock. He
entered Harvard in 1906, and was influenced there by the anti-Romanticism of
Irving Babbitt and the philosophical and critical interests of George Santayana, as

well as by the enthusiasm that prevailed in certain Harvard circles for Elizabethan and Jacobean literature, the Italian Renaissance, and Indian mystical philosophy. His philosophical studies included intensive work on the English idealist philosopher F. H. Bradley, on whom he eventually wrote his Harvard dissertation. (Bradley's emphasis on the private nature of individual experience, "a circle enclosed on the outside," had considerable influence on the private imagery of Eliot's poetry and on the view of the relation between the individual and other individuals reflected in much of his poetry.) Later, Eliot studied literature and philosophy in France and Germany, before going to England shortly after the outbreak of World War I in 1914. He studied Greek philosophy at Oxford, taught school in London, and then obtained a position with Lloyd's Bank. In 1915 he married an English writer, Vivienne Haigh-Wood, but the marriage was not a success. She was highly neurotic and in increasingly bad health. The strain told on Eliot, too. By November 1921 distress and worry had brought him to the verge of a nervous breakdown, and on medical advice, he went to recuperate in a Swiss sanitorium. Two months later he returned, pausing in Paris long enough to give Ezra Pound the manuscript of *The Waste Land*. Eliot left his wife in 1933, and she was eventually committed to a mental home where she died in 1947. Ten years later he married again and, for the eight years that remained to him, at last knew happiness.

Eliot started writing literary and philosophical reviews soon after settling in London. He wrote for the *Athenaeum* and the *Times Literary Supplement*, among other periodicals, and was assistant editor of the *Egoist* from 1917 to 1919. In 1922 he founded the influential quarterly *Criterion*, which he edited until it ceased publication in 1939. His poetry first appeared in 1915, when *The Love Song of J. Alfred Prufrock* was printed in *Poetry* magazine (Chicago) and a few other short poems were published in the short-lived periodical *Blast*. His first published collection of poems was *Prufrock and Other Observations*, 1917; two other small collections followed in 1919 and 1920; in 1922 *The Waste Land* appeared, first in the *Criterion* in October, then in the *Dial* (in America) in November, and finally in book form. *Poems 1909–25* (1925) collected these earlier poems. Meanwhile he was also publishing collections of his critical essays, notably *The Sacred Wood* in 1920 and *Homage to John Dryden* in 1924. *For Lancelot Andrewes* followed in 1928 and in 1932 he included most of these earlier essays with some new ones in *Selected Essays*. In 1925 he joined the London publishing firm of Faber and Gwyer, becoming a director when the firm became Faber and Faber. He became a British subject and joined the Church of England in 1927.

"Our civilization comprehends great variety and complexity, and this variety and complexity, playing upon a refined sensibility, must produce various and complex results. The poet must become more and more comprehensive, more allusive, more indirect, in order to force, to dislocate if necessary, language into his meaning." This remark, from Eliot's essay *The Metaphysical Poets* (1921), gives one clue to his poetic method from *Prufrock* through *The Waste Land*. In the tradition of the Georgian poets who were active when he settled in London, he saw an exhausted poetic mode being employed, with no verbal excitement or original craftsmanship. He sought to make poetry more subtle, more suggestive, and at the same time more precise. He had learned from the imagists the necessity of clear and precise images, and he learned, too, from the philosopher-poet T. E. Hulme and from his early supporter and adviser Ezra Pound to fear romantic softness and to regard the poetic medium rather than the poet's personality as the important factor. At the same time, the "hard, dry" images advocated by Hulme were not enough for him; he wanted wit, allusiveness, irony. He saw in the Metaphysical poets how wit and passion could be combined, and he saw in the French symbolists how an image could be both absolutely precise in what it referred to physically and at the same time endlessly suggestive in the meanings it set up because of its relationship to other images. The combination of precision, symbolic suggestion, and ironic mockery in the poetry of the late-nineteenth-century French poet Jules Laforgue attracted and influenced him, and he was influenced too by other nineteenth-century French poets: by Théophile Gautier's artful carving of impersonal shapes of meaning; by Charles Baudelaire's strangely evocative explorations of the symbolic suggestions of objects and images; by the symbolist poets Paul Verlaine, Arthur Rimbaud, and Stéphane Mallarmé. He also found in the Jacobean dramatists a flexible blank verse with overtones of colloquial movement: Middleton, Tourneur, Webster, and others, taught him as much—in the way of verse movement, imagery, the counterpointing of the accent of conversation and the note of terror—as either the Metaphysicals or the French symbolists.

Hulme's protests against the Romantic concept of poetry fitted in well enough with what Eliot had learned from Irving Babbitt at Harvard; yet for all his severity with such poets as Shelley, for all his conscious cultivation of a classical viewpoint and his insistence on order and discipline rather than on mere self-expression in art, one side of Eliot's poetic genius is, in one sense of the word, Romantic. The symbolist influence on his imagery, his interest in the evocative and the suggestive, such lines as "And fiddled whisper music on those strings / And bats with baby faces in the violet light / Whistled, and beat their wings," and such recurring images as the hyacinth girl and the rose garden, all show what could be called a Romantic element in his poetry. But it is combined with a dry ironic allusiveness, a play of wit, and a colloquial element, which are not normally found in poets of the Romantic tradition.

Eliot's real novelty—and the cause of much bewilderment when his poems first appeared—was his deliberate elimination of all merely connective and transitional passages, his building up of the total pattern of meaning through the immediate juxtaposition of images without overt explanation of what they are doing, together with his use of oblique references to other works of literature (some of them quite obscure to most readers of his time). *Prufrock* presents a symbolic landscape where the meaning emerges from the mutual interaction of the images, and that meaning is enlarged by echoes, often ironic, of Hesiod and Dante and Shakespeare. *The Waste Land* is a series of scenes and images with no author's voice intervening to tell us where we are, but with the implications developed through multiple contrasts and through analogies with older literary works often referred to in a distorted quotation or half-concealed allusion. Furthermore, the works referred to are not necessarily works that are central in the Western literary tradition: besides Dante and Shakespeare there are pre-Socratic philosophers; minor (as well as major) seventeenth-century poets and dramatists; works of anthropology, history, and philosophy; and other echoes of the poet's private reading. In a culture where there is no longer any assurance on the part of the poet that his or her public has a common cultural heritage, a common knowledge of works of the past, Eliot felt it necessary to build up his own body of references. It is this that marks the difference between Eliot's use of earlier literature and, say, Milton's. Both poets are difficult to the modern reader, who needs editorial assistance in recognizing and understanding many of the allusions—but Milton was drawing on a body of knowledge common to educated people in his day. Nevertheless, this aspect of Eliot can be exaggerated: the fact remains that the nature of his imagery together with the movement of his verse generally succeed in setting the tone he requires, in establishing the area of meaning to be developed, so that even a reader ignorant of most of the literary allusions can often get the feel of the poem and achieve some understanding of what it says.

Eliot's early poetry, until at least the middle 1920s, is mostly concerned in one way or another with the Waste Land, with aspects of the decay of culture in the modern Western world. After his formal acceptance of Anglican Christianity we find a penitential note in much of his verse, a note of quiet searching for spiritual peace, with considerable allusion to biblical, liturgical, and mystical religious literature and to Dante. *Ash Wednesday* (1930), a poem in six parts, much less fiercely concentrated in style than the earlier poetry, explores with gentle insistence a mood both penitential and questioning. The so-called Ariel poems (the title has nothing to do with their form or content) present or explore aspects of religious doubt or discovery or revelation, sometimes, as in *Marina*, using a purely secular imagery and sometimes, as in *Journey of the Magi*, drawing on biblical incident. In *Four Quartets* (of which the first, *Burnt Norton*, appeared in the *Collected Poems* of 1935, though all four were not completed until 1943, when they were published together) Eliot further explored essentially religious moods, dealing with the relation between time and eternity and the cultivation of that selfless passivity that can yield the moment of timeless revelation in the midst of time. The mocking irony, the savage humor, the deliberately startling juxtaposition of the sordid and the romantic give way in these later poems to a quieter poetic idiom, often still complexly allusive but never deliberately shocking.

Eliot's criticism was the criticism of a practicing poet who worked out in relation to his reading of older literature what he needed to hold and to admire. He lent the growing weight of his authority to that shift in literary taste that replaced Milton by Donne as the great seventeenth-century English poet and replaced Tennyson in the nineteenth century by Hopkins. His often-quoted description of the late seventeenth-century "dissociation of sensibility"—keeping wit and passion in separate compartments—which he saw as determining the course of English poetry throughout the eighteenth and nineteenth centuries, is both a contribution to the rewriting of English literary history and an explanation of what he was aiming at in his own poetry: the reestablishment of that *unified* sensibility he found in Donne and other early seventeenth-century poets and dramatists. His view of tradition, his dislike of the poetic exploitation of the author's own personality, his advocacy of what he called "orthodoxy," made him suspicious of what he considered eccentric geniuses such as Blake and D. H. Lawrence. On the other side, his dislike of the grandiloquent and his insistence on complexity and on the mingling of the formal with the conversational made him distrustful of the influence of Milton on English poetry. He considered himself "classicist in literature, royalist in politics, and Anglo-Catholic in religion" (*For Lancelot Andrewes*, 1928), in favor of order against chaos, tradition against eccentricity, authority against rampant individualism; yet his own poetry is in many respects untraditional and certainly highly individual in tone. His conservative and even authoritarian habit of mind alienated some who admire—and some whose own poetry has been much influenced by—his poetry.

Eliot's plays have all been, directly or indirectly, on religious themes. *Murder in the Cathedral* (1935) deals with the murder of Archbishop Thomas à Becket in an appropriately ritual manner, with much use of a chorus and with the central speech in the form of a sermon by the archbishop in his cathedral shortly before his murder. *The Family Reunion* (1939) deals with the problem of guilt and redemption in a modern upper-class English family; it makes a deliberate attempt to combine choric devices from Greek tragedy with a poetic idiom subdued to the accents of drawing-room conversation. In his three later plays, all written in the 1950s, *The Cocktail Party*, *The Confidential Clerk*, and *The Elder Statesman*, he achieved popular success by casting a serious religious theme in the form of a sophisticated modern social comedy, using a verse that is so conversational in movement that when spoken in the theater it does not sound like verse at all.

Critics differ on the degree to which Eliot succeeded in his last plays in combining box-office success with dramatic effectiveness. But there is no disagreement on his importance as one of the great renovators of the English poetic dialect, whose influence on a whole generation of poets, critics, and intellectuals generally was enormous. His range as a poet is limited, and his interest in the great middle ground of human experience (as distinct from the extremes of saint and sinner) deficient: but when in 1948 he was awarded the rare honor of the Order of Merit by King George VI and also gained the Nobel Prize in literature, his positive qualities were widely and fully recognized—his poetic cunning, his fine craftsmanship, his original accent, his historical and representative importance as *the* poet of the modern symbolist-Metaphysical tradition.

The Love Song of J. Alfred Prufrock[1]

> S'io credesse che mia risposta fosse
> A persona che mai tornasse al mondo,
> Questa fiamma staria senza piu scosse.
> Ma perciocche giammai di questo fondo
> Non torno vivo alcun, s'i'odo il vero,
> Senza tema d'infamia ti rispondo.[2]

Let us go then, you and I,
When the evening is spread out against the sky
Like a patient etherized upon a table;
Let us go, through certain half-deserted streets,
The muttering retreats   5
Of restless nights in one-night cheap hotels
And sawdust restaurants with oyster shells:
Streets that follow like a tedious argument
Of insidious intent
To lead you to an overwhelming question . . .   10

---

1. The title implies an ironic contrast between the romantic suggestions of "love song" and the dully prosaic name "J. Alfred Prufrock."
2. "If I thought that my reply would be to one who would ever return to the world, this flame would stay without further movement; but since none has ever returned alive from this depth, if what I hear is true, I answer you without fear of infamy" (Dante, *Inferno* 27.61–66). Guido da Montefeltro, shut up in his flame (the punishment given to false counselors), tells the shame of his evil life to Dante because he believes Dante will never return to earth to report it.

Oh, do not ask, "What is it?"
Let us go and make our visit.

    In the room the women come and go
Talking of Michelangelo.

    The yellow fog that rubs its back upon the windowpanes,   15
The yellow smoke that rubs its muzzle on the windowpanes
Licked its tongue into the corners of the evening,
Lingered upon the pools that stand in drains,
Let fall upon its back the soot that falls from chimneys,
Slipped by the terrace, made a sudden leap,   20
And seeing that it was a soft October night,
Curled once about the house, and fell asleep.

    And indeed there will be time[3]
For the yellow smoke that slides along the street,
Rubbing its back upon the windowpanes;   25
There will be time, there will be time
To prepare a face to meet the faces that you meet;
There will be time to murder and create,
And time for all the works and days of hands[4]
That lift and drop a question on your plate;   30
Time for you and time for me,
And time yet for a hundred indecisions,
And for a hundred visions and revisions,
Before the taking of a toast and tea.

    In the room the women come and go   35
Talking of Michelangelo.

    And indeed there will be time
To wonder, "Do I dare?" and, "Do I dare?"
Time to turn back and descend the stair,
With a bald spot in the middle of my hair—   40
(They will say: "How his hair is growing thin!")
My morning coat, my collar mounting firmly to the chin,
My necktie rich and modest, but asserted by a simple pin—
(They will say: "But how his arms and legs are thin!")
Do I dare   45
Disturb the universe?
In a minute there is time
For decisions and revisions which a minute will reverse.

    For I have known them all already, known them all—
Have known the evenings, mornings, afternoons,   50
I have measured out my life with coffee spoons;
I know the voices dying with a dying fall[5]

---

3. Cf. Andrew Marvell, *To His Coy Mistress*, line 1: "Had we but world enough, and time."
4. *Works and Days* is a poem about the farming year by Hesiod (8th century B.C.), Greek poet. Eliot's contrast is between useful agricultural labor and the futile

"works and days of hands" engaged in meaningless social gesturing.
5. Ironic recollection of Orsino's speech in *Twelfth Night* 1.1.4: "That strain again! It had a dying fall."

Beneath the music from a farther room.
    So how should I presume?

And I have known the eyes already, known them all—   55
The eyes that fix you in a formulated phrase,
And when I am formulated, sprawling on a pin,
When I am pinned and wriggling on the wall,
Then how should I begin
To spit out all the butt-ends of my days and ways?   60
    And how should I presume?

And I have known the arms already, known them all—
Arms that are braceleted and white and bare
(But in the lamplight, downed with light brown hair!)
Is it perfume from a dress   65
That makes me so digress?
Arms that lie along a table, or wrap about a shawl.
    And should I then presume?
    And how should I begin?

                    • • •

Shall I say, I have gone at dusk through narrow streets   70
And watched the smoke that rises from the pipes
Of lonely men in shirt-sleeves, leaning out of windows? . . .

I should have been a pair of ragged claws
Scuttling across the floors of silent seas.[6]

                    • • •

And the afternoon, the evening, sleeps so peacefully!   75
Smoothed by long fingers,
Asleep . . . tired . . . or it malingers,
Stretched on the floor, here beside you and me.
Should I, after tea and cakes and ices,
Have the strength to force the moment to its crisis?   80
But though I have wept and fasted, wept and prayed,
Though I have seen my head (grown slightly bald) brought in upon a platter,[7]
I am no prophet—and here's no great matter;
I have seen the moment of my greatness flicker,
And I have seen the eternal Footman hold my coat, and snicker,   85
And in short, I was afraid.

And would it have been worth it, after all,
After the cups, the marmalade, the tea,
Among the porcelain, among some talk of you and me,
Would it have been worth while,   90

6. I.e., he would have been better as a crab on the ocean bed. Perhaps, too, the motion of a crab suggests futility and growing old. Cf. *Hamlet* 2.2.205–206: "for you yourself, sir, should be old as I am, if, like a crab, you could go backward." 7. Like that of John the Baptist. See Mark 6.17–28 and Matthew 14.3–11.

To have bitten off the matter with a smile,
To have squeezed the universe into a ball[8]
To roll it toward some overwhelming question,
To say: "I am Lazarus,[9] come from the dead,
Come back to tell you all, I shall tell you all"—   95
If one, settling a pillow by her head,
    Should say: "That is not what I meant at all.
    That is not it, at all."

    And would it have been worth it, after all,
Would it have been worth while,   100
After the sunsets and the dooryards and the sprinkled streets,
After the novels, after the teacups, after the skirts that trail along the floor—
And this, and so much more?—
It is impossible to say just what I mean!
But as if a magic lantern threw the nerves in patterns on a screen: 105
Would it have been worth while
If one, settling a pillow or throwing off a shawl,
And turning toward the window, should say:
    "That is not it at all,
    That is not what I meant, at all."   110

                          .   .   .

    No! I am not Prince Hamlet, nor was meant to be;
Am an attendant lord, one that will do
To swell a progress,[1] start a scene or two,
Advise the prince; no doubt, an easy tool,
Deferential, glad to be of use,   115
Politic, cautious, and meticulous;
Full of high sentence,[2] but a bit obtuse;
At times, indeed, almost ridiculous—
Almost, at times, the Fool.

    I grow old . . . I grow old . . .   120
I shall wear the bottoms of my trousers rolled.

    Shall I part my hair behind? Do I dare to eat a peach?
I shall wear white flannel trousers, and walk upon the beach.
I have heard the mermaids singing, each to each.

I do not think that they will sing to me.   125

I have seen them riding seaward on the waves
Combing the white hair of the waves blown back
When the wind blows the water white and black.

8. Cf., Marvell, *To His Coy Mistress*, lines 41–44: "Let us roll all our strength and all / Our sweetness up into one ball, / And tear our pleasures with rough strife / Thorough the iron gates of life."
9. Cf. Luke 16.19–31 and John 11.1–44.

1. In the Elizabethan sense of a state journey made by a royal or noble person. Elizabethan plays sometimes showed such "progresses" crossing the stage.
2. In its older meanings: "opinions," "sententiousness."

We have lingered in the chambers of the sea
By sea-girls wreathed with seaweed red and brown　　　　130
Till human voices wake us, and we drown.
1910–11　　　　　　　　　　　　　　　　　　　1915, 1917

Sweeney Among the Nightingales

ómoi, péplegmai kairían plegén éso.[1]

Apeneck Sweeney spreads his knees
Letting his arms hang down to laugh,
The zebra stripes along his jaw
Swelling to maculate[2] giraffe.

The circles of the stormy moon　　　　　　　　　　　5
Slide westward toward the River Plate,[3]
Death and the Raven drift above
And Sweeney guards the hornèd gate.[4]

Gloomy Orion and the Dog
Are veiled;[5] and hushed the shrunken seas;　　　　　10
The person in the Spanish cape
Tries to sit on Sweeney's knees

Slips and pulls the tablecloth
Overturns a coffee cup,
Reorganized upon the floor　　　　　　　　　　　15
She yawns and draws a stocking up;

The silent man in mocha brown
Sprawls at the window sill and gapes;
The waiter brings in oranges
Bananas figs and hothouse grapes;　　　　　　　　20

The silent vertebrate in brown
Contracts and concentrates, withdraws;
Rachel *née* Rabinovitch
Tears at the grapes with murderous paws;

She and the lady in the cape　　　　　　　　　　　25
Are suspect, thought to be in league;
Therefore the man with heavy eyes
Declines the gambit, shows fatigue,

---

1. "Alas, I am struck with a mortal blow within" (Aeschylus, *Agamemnon*, line 1343). The voice of Agamemnon heard crying out from the palace as he is murdered by his wife, Clytemnestra.
2. Spotted, stained.
3. Estuary on the South American coast between Argentina and Uruguay, formed by the Uruguay and Paraná rivers.
4. The gates of horn, in Hades, through which true dreams come to the upper world.
5. "Orion" and "the Dog" are the constellations. For Sweeney and his lady friend, the gate of vision is blocked and the great myth-making constellations are "veiled."

Leaves the room and reappears
Outside the window, leaning in,   30
Branches of wistaria
Circumscribe a golden grin;

The host with someone indistinct
Converses at the door apart,
The nightingales are singing near   35
The Convent of the Sacred Heart,

And sang within the bloody wood
When Agamemnon cried aloud,[6]
And let their liquid siftings fall
To stain the stiff dishonored shroud.   40

1918, 1919

The Hippopotamus[1]

*And when this epistle is read among you, cause that
it be read also in the church of the Laodiceans.*[2]

The broad-backed hippopotamus
Rests on his belly in the mud;
Although he seems so firm to us
He is merely flesh and blood.

Flesh and blood is weak and frail,   5
Susceptible to nervous shock;
While the True Church can never fail
For it is based upon a rock.[3]

The hippo's feeble steps may err
In compassing material ends,   10
While the True Church need never stir
To gather in its dividends.

The 'potamus can never reach
The mango on the mango-tree;
But fruits of pomegranate and peach   15
Refresh the Church from over sea.

At mating time the hippo's voice
Betrays inflections hoarse and odd,

6. Agamemnon was not murdered in a "bloody wood,"
but in his bath. Eliot is here telescoping Agamemnon's
murder with the wood where Philomela, in Greek
myth, was ravished by her sister's husband, Terens (she
was subsequently turned into a nightingale), and also
with the "bloody wood" of Nemi, where in ancient
times the old priest was slain by his successor (as described in the first chapter of Sir James Frazer's *Golden
Bough*).
1. Cf. S. J. Stone's famous hymn "The Church's one

foundation" (*Hymns Ancient and Modern*, 2nd ed.,
1916, no. 215), with which this poem has a parodic
relation.
2. Colossians 4.16. The inhabitants of Laodicea, a city
in Asia Minor, were regarded by St. John as "lukewarm, and neither cold nor hot" (Revelation 3.16).
3. Jesus said to his disciple: "And I also say unto thee,
that thou art Peter [Greek, *Petros*], and upon this rock
[Greek, *petra*] I will build my church" (Matthew
16.18).

But every week we hear rejoice
The Church, at being one with God.[4]   20

The hippopotamus's day
Is passed in sleep; at night he hunts;
God works in a mysterious way—[5]
The Church can sleep and feed at once.

I saw the 'potamus take wing[6]   25
Ascending from the damp savannas,
And quiring angels round him sing
The praise of God, in loud hosannas.

Blood of the Lamb shall wash him clean
And him shall heavenly arms enfold,   30
Among the saints he shall be seen
Performing on a harp of gold.

He shall be washed as white as snow,
By all the martyr'd virgins kist,
While the True Church remains below   35
Wrapt in the old miasmal mist.

                                                        1920

The Waste Land   This is a poem about spiritual dryness, about the kind of
existence in which no regenerating belief gives significance and value to people's
daily activities, sex brings no fruitfulness, and death heralds no resurrection. Eliot
himself gives one of the main clues to the theme and structure of the poem in a
general note, in which he stated that "not only the title, but the plan and a good
deal of the symbolism of the poem were suggested by Miss Jessie L. Weston's book
on the Grail legend: *From Ritual to Romance*" (1920). He further acknowledged
a general indebtedness to Sir James Frazer's *Golden Bough* (13 volumes, 1890–
1915), "especially the . . . volumes *Adonis, Attis, Osiris*," in which Frazer deals
with ancient vegetation myths and fertility ceremonies. Weston's study, drawing
on material from Frazer and other anthropologists, traced the relationship of these
myths and rituals to Christianity and most especially to the legend of the Holy
Grail. She found an archetypal fertility myth in the story of the Fisher King whose
death, infirmity, or impotence (there are many forms of the myth) brought drought
and desolation to the land and failure of the power to reproduce themselves among
both humans and beasts. This symbolic Waste Land can be revived only if a
"questing knight" goes to the Chapel Perilous, situated in the heart of it, and there
asks certain ritual questions about the Grail (or Cup) and the Lance—originally
fertility symbols, female and male, respectively. The proper asking of these questions revives the king and restores fertility to the land. The relation of this original
Grail myth to fertility cults and rituals found in many different civilizations, and
represented by stories of a dying god who is later resurrected (e.g., Tammuz,
Adonis, Attis), shows their common origin in a response to the cyclical movement

---

4. The biblical Song of Solomon is traditionally interpreted as depicting Christ's marriage with His church.
5. Cf. William Cowper, *Olney Hymn* 35: "God moves
in a mysterious way / His wonders to perform; / He

plants his footsteps in the sea, / And rides upon the
storm."
6. Cf. Revelation 20.1: "And I saw an angel coming
down out of heaven."

of the seasons, with vegetation dying in winter to be resurrected again in the spring. Christianity, according to Weston, gave its own spiritual meaning to the myth; it "did not hesitate to utilize the already existing medium of instruction, but boldly identified the Deity of Vegetation, regarded as Life Principle, with the God of the Christian Faith." The Fisher King is related to the use of the fish symbol in early Christianity. Weston states "with certainty that the Fish is a Life symbol of immemorial antiquity, and that the title of Fisher has, from the earliest ages, been associated with the Deities who were held to be specially connected with the origin and preservation of Life." Eliot, following Weston, thus uses a great variety of mythological and religious material, both Occidental and Oriental, to paint a symbolic picture of the modern Waste Land and the need for regeneration. The terror of that life—its loneliness, emptiness, and irrational apprehensions—as well as its misuse of sexuality are vividly presented, but paradoxically, the poem ends with a benediction. Another significant general source for the poem is the composer Richard Wagner, some of whose operas (*Götterdämmerung* ["Twilight of the Gods"], *Parsifal*, *Rheingold*, and *Tristan and Isolde*) are drawn on.

The poem as published owed a great deal to the severe pruning of Ezra Pound; the original manuscript, with Pound's excisions and comments, provides fascinating information about the genesis and development of the poem. It was reproduced in facsimile in 1971, edited by Eliot's widow, Valerie Eliot, who also supplied notes supplementing those that Eliot himself added when the poem was first published in book form in 1925 and that are included with the present editors' footnotes to the poem.

The Waste Land

"Nam Sibyllam quidem Cumis ego ipse oculis meis vidi in ampulla pendere, et cum illi pueri dicerent: Σίβυλλα τί θέλεις; respondebat illa: ἀποθανεῖν θέλω."[1]

FOR EZRA POUND
il miglior fabbro[2]

1. The Burial of the Dead[3]

April is the cruelest month, breeding
Lilacs out of the dead land, mixing
Memory and desire, stirring
Dull roots with spring rain.
Winter kept us warm, covering   5
Earth in forgetful snow, feeding
A little life with dried tubers.
Summer surprised us, coming over the Starnbergersee[4]

1. From the *Satyricon* of Petronius (1st century A.D.): "For once I myself saw with my own eyes the Sibyl at Cumae hanging in a cage, and when the boys said to her 'Sibyl, what do you want?' she replied, 'I want to die.'" (The Greek may be transliterated, "Síbylla tí théleis?" and "apothanéin thélo.") The Cumaean Sibyl was the most famous of the Sibyls, the prophetic old women of Greek mythology; she guided Aeneas through Hades in the *Aeneid*. She had been granted immortality by Apollo, but because she forgot to ask for perpetual youth, she shrank into withered old age and her authority declined.
2. "The better craftsman," a tribute originally paid to the Provençal poet Arnaut Daniel in Dante's *Purgatorio* 26.117. Ezra Pound (1885–1972), American expatriate poet who was a key figure in the modern movement in poetry, helped Eliot with the final revisions.
3. The title comes from the Anglican burial service.
4. Lake a few miles south of Munich, where the "mad" King Ludwig II of Bavaria drowned in 1886 in mysterious circumstances. This romantic, melancholy king was a passionate admirer of Richard Wagner and

With a shower of rain; we stopped in the colonnade,
And went on in sunlight, into the Hofgarten,[5]   10
And drank coffee, and talked for an hour.
Bin gar keine Russin, stamm' aus Litauen, echt deutsch.[6]
And when we were children, staying at the archduke's,
My cousin's, he took me out on a sled,
And I was frightened. He said, Marie,   15
Marie, hold on tight. And down we went.
In the mountains, there you feel free.
I read, much of the night, and go south in the winter.

    What are the roots that clutch, what branches grow
Out of this stony rubbish? Son of man,[7]   20
You cannot say, or guess, for you know only
A heap of broken images, where the sun beats,
And the dead tree gives no shelter, the cricket no relief,[8]
And the dry stone no sound of water. Only
There is shadow under this red rock,[9]   25
(Come in under the shadow of this red rock),
And I will show you something different from either
Your shadow at morning striding behind you
Or your shadow at evening rising to meet you;
I will show you fear in a handful of dust.   30
        Frisch weht der Wind
        Der Heimat zu
        Mein Irisch Kind,
        Wo weilest du?[1]
"You gave me hyacinths first a year ago;   35
They called me the hyacinth girl."
—Yet when we came back, late, from the Hyacinth garden,
Yours arms full, and your hair wet, I could not
Speak, and my eyes failed, I was neither
Living nor dead, and I knew nothing,   40
Looking into the heart of light, the silence.
Oed' und leer das Meer.[2]

    Madame Sosostris,[3] famous clairvoyante,
Had a bad cold, nevertheless

---

especially of Wagner's opera *Tristan and Isolde*, which plays a significant part in *The Waste Land*. Ludwig's suffering of "death by water" in the Starnbergersee thus evokes a cluster of themes central to the poem. Eliot had met King Ludwig's second cousin Countess Marie Larisch and talked with her. Although he had probably not read the countess's book *My Past*, which discusses King Ludwig at length, he got information about her life and times from her in person, and the remarks made in lines 7–17 are hers. They distill a sense of romantic decadence that Eliot associates with this period of European history. Line 17 is a translation of the opening of a Bavarian folksong celebrating King Ludwig and lamenting his drowning.
5. A small public park in Munich.
6. I am not Russian at all; I come from Lithuania, a true German.
7. "Cf. Ezekiel 2.1" [Eliot's note]. Here God is addressing Ezekiel. God continues, "stand upon thy feet, and I will speak unto thee."

8. "Cf. Ecclesiastes 12.5" [Eliot's note]. The verse cited by Eliot is part of the preacher's picture of the desolation of old age, "when they shall be afraid of that which is high, and fears shall be in the way, and the almond tree shall flourish, and the grasshopper shall be a burden, and desire shall fail."
9. Cf. Isaiah 32.2: the "righteous king" "shall be . . . as rivers of water in a dry place, as the shadow of a great rock in a weary land."
1. "V. [see] *Tristan und Isolde*, 1, verses 5–8" [Eliot's note]. In Wagner's opera, a sailor recalls the girl he has left behind: "Fresh blows the wind to the homeland; my Irish child, where are you waiting?"
2. "Id. [Ibid] 3, verse 24" [Eliot's note]. In act 3 of *Tristan und Isolde*, Tristan lies dying. He is waiting for Isolde to come to him from Cornwall, but a shepherd, appointed to watch for her sail, can only report, "Waste and empty is the sea."
3. A mock Egyptian name (suggested to Eliot by "Sesostris, the Sorceress of Ecbatana," the name assumed

Is known to be the wisest woman in Europe,   45
With a wicked pack of cards.[4] Here, said she,
Is your card, the drowned Phoenician Sailor,[5]
(Those are pearls that were his eyes. Look!)
Here is Belladonna,[6] the Lady of the Rocks,
The lady of situations.   50
Here is the man with three staves,[7] and here the Wheel,[8]
And here is the one-eyed merchant,[9] and this card,
Which is blank, is something he carries on his back,
Which I am forbidden to see. I do not find
The Hanged Man.[1] Fear death by water.   55
I see crowds of people, walking round in a ring.
Thank you. If you see dear Mrs. Equitone,
Tell her I bring the horoscope myself:
One must be so careful these days.

    Unreal City,[2]   60
Under the brown fog of a winter dawn,
A crowd flowed over London Bridge, so many,[3]
I had not thought death had undone so many.
Sighs, short and infrequent, were exhaled,[4]
And each man fixed his eyes before his feet.   65

---

by a character in Aldous Huxley's novel *Crome Yellow* who dresses up as a gypsy to tell fortunes at a fair).

4. I.e., the deck of Tarot cards. The four suits of the Tarot pack, discussed by Jessie Weston in *From Ritual to Romance*, are the cup, lance, sword, and dish—the life symbols found in the Grail story. Weston noted that "today the Tarot has fallen somewhat into disrepute, being principally used for purposes of divination." Some of the cards mentioned in lines 46–56 are discussed by Eliot in his note to this passage: "I am not familiar with the exact constitution of the Tarot pack of cards, from which I have obviously departed to suit my own convenience. The Hanged Man, a member of the traditional pack, fits my purpose in two ways: because he is associated in my mind with the Hanged God of Frazer, and because I associate him with the hooded figure in the passage of the disciples to Emmaus in part 5. The Phoenician Sailor and the Merchant appear later; also the 'crowds of people,' and Death by Water is executed in part 4. The Man with Three Staves (an authentic member of the Tarot pack) I associate, quite arbitrarily, with the Fisher King himself."

5. See part 4. Phlebas the Phoenician and Mr. Eugenides, the Smyrna merchant—both of whom appear later in the poem—are different phases of the same symbolic character, here identified as the "Phoenician Sailor." Mr. Eugenides exports "currants" (line 210); the drowned Phlebas floats in the "current" (line 315). The line that follows is from Shakespeare's *Tempest* (1.2.398). Ariel's song to the shipwrecked Ferdinand, who was "sitting on a bank / Weeping again the King my father's wrack," when "this music crept by me on the waters." The song is about the supposed drowning of Ferdinand's father, Alonso. *The Waste Land* contains many references to *The Tempest*. Ferdinand is associated with Phlebas and Mr. Eugenides and, therefore, with the "drowned Phoenician Sailor."

6. Beautiful lady. The word also suggests Madonna (the Virgin Mary) and, therefore, the Madonna of the Rocks (as in Leonardo da Vinci's painting); the rocks

symbolize the church. Belladonna is also an eye cosmetic and a poison—the deadly nightshade. In the next line, the woman figure of the Virgin becomes "the lady of situations," foreshadowing the neurasthenic lady of intrigue in part 2.

7. Life-force symbol, associated by Eliot with the Fisher King.

8. I.e., the wheel of fortune, whose turning represents the reversals of human life.

9. I.e., Mr. Eugenides, "one-eyed" because the figure is in profile on the card and also as a suggestion of evil or crookedness.

1. On his card in the Tarot pack he is shown hanging from one foot from a T-shaped cross. He symbolizes the self-sacrifice of the fertility god who is killed in order that his resurrection may bring fertility once again to land and people.

2. "Cf. Baudelaire: '*Fourmillante cité, cité pleine de rêves, / Où le spectre en plein jour raccroche le passant*'" [Eliot's note]. The lines are quoted from *Les Sept Vieillards* ("The Seven Old Men") by Charles Baudelaire (1821–67); it is poem 93 of *Les Fleurs du Mal* ("The Flowers of Evil"). The lines may be translated: "Swarming city, city full of dreams, / Where the specter in broad daylight accosts the passerby."

3. "Cf. Inferno 3.55–57" [Eliot's note]. The note goes on to quote Dante's lines, which may be translated: "So long a train of people, / that I should never have believed / That death had undone so many." Dante, just outside the gate of hell, has seen "the wretched souls of those who lived without disgrace and without praise." In his essay on Baudelaire, Eliot argued that in a sense it was better to be positively evil than to be neither good nor evil.

4. "Cf. Inferno 4.25–27" [Eliot's note]. In Limbo, the first circle of hell, Dante has found the virtuous heathens, who lived before Christianity and are, therefore, eternally unable to achieve their desire of seeing God. Dante's lines, cited by Eliot, mean "Here, so far as I could tell by listening, / there was no lamentation except sighs, / which caused the eternal air to tremble."

Flowed up the hill and down King William Street,
To where Saint Mary Woolnoth kept the hours
With a dead sound on the final stroke of nine.[5]
There I saw one I knew, and stopped him, crying: "Stetson![6]
You who were with me in the ships at Mylae![7]   70
That corpse you planted last year in your garden,
Has it begun to sprout?[8] Will it bloom this year?
Or has the sudden frost disturbed its bed?
Oh keep the Dog far hence, that's friend to men,
Or with his nails he'll dig it up again![9]   75
You! hypocrite lecteur!—mon semblable—mon frère!"[1]

2. A Game of Chess[2]

The Chair she sat in, like a burnished throne,[3]
Glowed on the marble, where the glass
Held up by standards wrought with fruited vines
From which a golden Cupidon peeped out   80
(Another hid his eyes behind his wing)
Doubled the flames of sevenbranched candelabra
Reflecting light upon the table as
The glitter of her jewels rose to meet it,
From satin cases poured in rich profusion.   85
In vials of ivory and colored glass
Unstoppered, lurked her strange synthetic perfumes,
Unguent, powdered, or liquid—troubled, confused
And drowned the sense in odors; stirred by the air
That freshened from the window, these ascended   90
In fattening the prolonged candle flames,
Flung their smoke into the laquearia,[4]
Stirring the pattern on the coffered ceiling.
Huge sea-wood fed with copper
Burned green and orange, framed by the colored stone,   95
In which sad light a carvèd dolphin swam.

5. "A phenomenon which I have often noticed" [Eliot's note]. St. Mary Woolnoth is a church in the "Unreal City" of London (the financial district); the crowd is flowing across London Bridge to work in the City.
6. Presumably representing the "average businessman."
7. The battle of Mylae (260 B.C.) in the First Punic War, which, like World War I, was fought for economic reasons.
8. A distortion of the ritual death of the fertility god.
9. "Cf. the Dirge in Webster's White Devil" [Eliot's note]. In the play by John Webster (d. 1625), the dirge, sung by Cornelia, has the lines "But keep the wolf far thence, that's foe to men, / For with his nails he'll dig them up again." Eliot makes the "wolf" into a "dog," which is not a foe but a friend to humans. There may be a reference to Sirius, the Dog Star, which is important in Egyptian mythology as heralding the fertilizing floods of the Nile (this is discussed by Weston).
1. "V. Baudelaire, Preface to Fleurs du Mal" [Eliot's note]. The passage is the last line of the introductory poem Au Lecteur ("To the Reader") in Baudelaire's Fleurs du Mal; it may be translated: "Hypocrite reader!—my likeness—my brother!" Au Lecteur describes man as sunk in stupidity, sin, and evil, but the worst in "each man's foul menagerie of sin" is boredom, the "monstre délicat"—"You know him, reader."
2. The title suggests two plays by Thomas Middleton (1580–1627): A Game at Chess and, more significant, Women Beware Women, which has a scene in which a mother-in-law is distracted by a game of chess while her daughter-in-law is seduced: every move in the chess game represents a move in the seduction.
3. "Cf. Antony and Cleopatra, 2.2.190" [Eliot's note]. In Shakespeare's play, Enobarbus's famous description of the first meeting of Antony and Cleopatra begins, "The barge she sat in, like a burnish'd throne, / Burn'd on the water." Eliot's language in the opening lines of part 2 is full of ironic distortions of Enobarbus's speech.
4. "Laquearia. V. Aeneid, 1. 726" [Eliot's note]. Laquearia means "a paneled ceiling," and Eliot's note quotes the passage in the Aeneid that was his source for the word. The passage may be translated: "Blazing torches hang from the gold-paneled ceiling [laquearibus aureis], and torches conquer the night with flames." Virgil is describing the banquet given by Dido, queen of Carthage, for Aeneas, with whom she fell in love.

Above the antique mantel was displayed
As though a window gave upon the sylvan scene[5]
The change of Philomel,[6] by the barbarous king
So rudely forced; yet there the nightingale   100
Filled all the desert with inviolable voice
And still she cried, and still the world pursues,
"Jug Jug"[7] to dirty ears.
And other withered stumps of time
Were told upon the walls; staring forms   105
Leaned out, leaning, hushing the room enclosed.
Footsteps shuffled on the stair.
Under the firelight, under the brush, her hair
Spread out in fiery points
Glowed into words, then would be savagely still.   110

        "My nerves are bad tonight. Yes, bad. Stay with me.
Speak to me. Why do you never speak. Speak.
        What are you thinking of? What thinking? What?
I never know what you are thinking. Think."

        I think we are in rats' alley[8]   115
Where the dead men lost their bones.

        "What is that noise?"
                        The wind under the door.[9]
"What is that noise now? What is the wind doing?"
                        Nothing again nothing.   120
                                        "Do
You know nothing? Do you see nothing? Do you remember
Nothing?"

        I remember
Those are pearls that were his eyes.   125
"Are you alive, or not? Is there nothing in your head?"
                                        But
O O O O that Shakespeherian Rag—[1]
It's so elegant
So intelligent   130
"What shall I do now? What shall I do?"
"I shall rush out as I am, and walk the street
With my hair down, so. What shall we do tomorrow?
What shall we ever do?"
                        The hot water at ten.   135
And if it rains, a closed car at four.

---

5. "Sylvan scene. V. Milton, *Paradise Lost*, 4.140" [Eliot's note]. The phrase is part of the first description of Eden, which we see through Satan's eyes.
6. "V. Ovid, *Metamorphoses*, 6, Philomela" [Eliot's note]. The note is a reference to Ovid's version of the Greek myth of the rape of Philomela by "the barbarous king" Tereus, husband of her sister Procne. Philomela was transformed into a nightingale. Eliot's note for line 100 refers ahead to his elaboration of the nightingale's

song.
7. Conventional representation of nightingale's song in Elizabethan poetry.
8. "Cf. part 3, line 195" [Eliot's note].
9. "Cf. Webster: 'Is the wind in that door still?' " [Eliot's note]. The line cited in the note is from John Webster, *The Devil's Law Case* 3.2.162.
1. American ragtime song, which was a hit of Ziegfeld's Follies in 1912.

And we shall play a game of chess,[2]
Pressing lidless eyes and waiting for a knock upon the door.

When Lil's husband got demobbed,[3] I said—
I didn't mince my words, I said to her myself,   140
HURRY UP PLEASE ITS TIME[4]
Now Albert's coming back, make yourself a bit smart.
He'll want to know what you done with that money he gave you
To get yourself some teeth. He did, I was there.
You have them all out, Lil, and get a nice set,   145
He said, I swear, I can't bear to look at you.
And no more can't I, I said, and think of poor Albert,
He's been in the army four years, he wants a good time,
And if you don't give it him, there's others will, I said.
Oh is there, she said. Something o' that, I said.   150
Then I'll know who to thank, she said, and give me a straight look.
HURRY UP PLEASE ITS TIME
If you don't like it you can get on with it, I said.
Others can pick and choose if you can't.
But if Albert makes off, it won't be for lack of telling.   155
You ought to be ashamed, I said, to look so antique.
(And her only thirty-one.)
I can't help it, she said, pulling a long face,
It's them pills I took, to bring it off,[5] she said.
(She's had five already, and nearly died of young George.)   160
The chemist[6] said it would be all right, but I've never been the same.
You *are* a proper fool, I said.
Well, if Albert won't leave you alone, there it is, I said,
What you get married for if you don't want children?
HURRY UP PLEASE ITS TIME   165
Well, that Sunday Albert was home, they had a hot gammon,[7]
And they asked me in to dinner, to get the beauty of it hot—
HURRY UP PLEASE ITS TIME
HURRY UP PLEASE ITS TIME
Goonight Bill. Goonight Lou. Goonight May. Goonight.   170
Ta ta. Goonight. Goonight.
Good night, ladies, good night, sweet ladies, good night, good night.[8]

3. *The Fire Sermon*[9]

The river's tent is broken: the last fingers of leaf
Clutch and sink into the wet bank. The wind
Crosses the brown land, unheard. The nymphs are departed.   175

---

2. "Cf. the game of chess in Middleton's *Women Be-ware Women*" [Eliot's note]. The significance of this chess game is discussed in n. 2, p. 2469.
3. British slang for "demobilized" (discharged from the army).
4. The traditional call of the British bartender at closing time.
5. To have an abortion.

6. Druggist.
7. Ham or bacon.
8. Cf. the mad Ophelia's departing words (*Hamlet* 4.5.72). Ophelia, too, met "death by water."
9. The Fire Sermon was preached by the Buddha against the fires of lust and other passions that destroy people and prevent their regeneration (see also p. 2476, n. 2).

Sweet Thames, run softly, till I end my song.[1]
The river bears no empty bottles, sandwich papers,
Silk handkerchiefs, cardboard boxes, cigarette ends
Or other testimony of summer nights. The nymphs are departed.
And their friends, the loitering heirs of city directors;   180
Departed, have left no addresses.
By the waters of Leman I sat down and wept[2] . . .
Sweet Thames, run softly till I end my song,
Sweet Thames, run softly, for I speak not loud or long.
But at my back in a cold blast I hear[3]   185
The rattle of the bones, and chuckle spread from ear to ear.

A rat crept softly through the vegetation
Dragging its slimy belly on the bank
While I was fishing in the dull canal
On a winter evening round behind the gashouse   190
Musing upon the king my brother's wreck[4]
And on the king my father's death before him.
White bodies naked on the low damp ground
And bones cast in a little low dry garret,
Rattled by the rat's foot only, year to year.   195
But at my back from time to time I hear[5]
The sound of horns and motors, which shall bring
Sweeney to Mrs. Porter in the spring.[6]
O the moon shone bright on Mrs. Porter
And on her daughter   200
They wash their feet in soda water[7]
Et O ces voix d'enfants, chantant dans la coupole![8]

Twit twit twit
Jug jug jug jug jug jug
So rudely forc'd.   205
Tereu[9]

---

1. "V. Spenser, *Prothalamion*" [Eliot's note]. Eliot's line is the refrain from Spenser's marriage song, which is also set by the Thames in London—but a very different Thames from the modern littered river.
2. Cf. Psalms 137.1, in which the exiled Hebrews mourn for their homeland: "By the rivers of Babylon, there we sat down, yea, we wept, when we remembered Zion." Lake Leman is another name for Lake Geneva; Eliot wrote *The Waste Land* in Lausanne, by that lake. The common noun *leman* is an archaic word meaning, in the bad sense, an illicit sweetheart or mistress.
3. An ironic distortion of Andrew Marvell's *To His Coy Mistress*, lines 21–22: "But at my back I always hear / Time's wingèd chariot hurrying near." Cf. line 196.
4. "Cf. *The Tempest*, 1.2" [Eliot's note]. See line 48.
5. Cf. Marvell, *To His Coy Mistress* [Eliot's note].
6. "Cf. Day, *Parliament of Bees*: 'When of the sudden, listening, you shall hear, / A noise of horns and hunting, which shall bring / Actaeon to Diana in the spring, / Where all shall see her naked skin' " [Eliot's note]. Actaeon was changed to a stag and hunted to death after he saw Diana, the goddess of chastity, bath-

ing with her nymphs.
7. "I do not know the origin of the ballad from which these lines are taken: it was reported to me from Sydney, Australia" [Eliot's note]. One of the less bawdy versions of the song, which was popular among Australian troops in World War I, went as follows: "O the moon shines bright on Mrs. Porter / And on the daughter / Of Mrs. Porter. / They wash their feet in soda water / And so they oughter / To keep them clean."
8. "V. Verlaine, *Parsifal*" [Eliot's note]. The line is translated, "And O those children's voices singing in the dome!" Verlaine's sonnet describes Parsifal, the questing knight, resisting all sensual temptations to keep himself pure for the Grail; Wagner's Parsifal had his feet washed before entering the castle of the Grail.
9. "Tereu" is a reference to Tereus, who "rudely forc'd" Philomela; it was also one of the conventional words for a nightingale's song in Elizabethan poetry. Cf. the song from John Lyly's *Alexander and Campaspe* (1564): "Oh, 'tis the ravished nightingale. / Jug, jug, jug, jug, tereu! she cries," and lines 100ff.

Unreal City
Under the brown fog of a winter noon
Mr. Eugenides, the Smyrna[1] merchant
Unshaven, with a pocket full of currants   210
C.i.f.[2] London: documents at sight,
Asked me in demotic French[3]
To luncheon at the Cannon Street Hotel[4]
Followed by a weekend at the Metropole.

At the violet hour, when the eyes and back   215
Turn upward from the desk, when the human engine waits
Like a taxi throbbing waiting,
I Tiresias,[5] though blind, throbbing between two lives,
Old man with wrinkled female breasts, can see
At the violet hour, the evening hour that strives   220
Homeward, and brings the sailor home from sea,[6]
The typist home at teatime, clears her breakfast, lights
Her stove, and lays out food in tins.
Out of the window perilously spread
Her drying combinations touched by the sun's last rays,   225
On the divan are piled (at night her bed)
Stockings, slippers, camisoles, and stays.
I Tiresias, old man with wrinkled dugs
Perceived the scene, and foretold the rest—
I too awaited the expected guest.   230
He, the young man carbuncular,[7] arrives,
A small house agent's clerk, with one bold stare,
One of the low on whom assurance sits
As a silk hat on a Bradford[8] millionaire.

1. Seaport in western Turkey; here associated with Carthage and the ancient Phoenician and Syrian merchants (unlike those of modern Smyrna), who spread the old mystery cults. The sort of cult spread by Mr. Eugenides is indicated by his suggestion of "a weekend at the Metropole" (a luxury hotel at Brighton).
2. "The currants were quoted at a price 'carriage and insurance free to London'; and the Bill of Lading etc. were to be handed to the buyer upon payment of the sight draft" [Eliot's note].
3. Popular French.
4. Located near the station that was then chief terminus for travelers to the Continent, hence a favorite meeting place for businesspeople going or coming from abroad.
5. "Tiresias, although a mere spectator and not indeed a 'character,' is yet the most important personage in the poem, uniting all the rest. Just as the one-eyed merchant, seller of currants, melts into the Phoenician Sailor, and the latter is not wholly distinct from Ferdinand Prince of Naples, so all the women are one woman, and the two sexes meet in Tiresias. What Tiresias sees, in fact, is the substance of the poem. The whole passage from Ovid is of great anthropological interest" [Eliot's note]. The note then quotes the Latin text of Ovid's Metamorphoses that tells the story of Tiresias's change of sex. The Latin may be translated: "[The story goes that once Jove, having drunk a great deal,] jested with Juno. He said, 'Your pleasure in love is really greater than that enjoyed by men.' She denied

it; so they decided to seek the opinion of the wise Tiresias, for he knew both aspects of love. For once, with a blow of his staff, he had committed violence on two huge snakes as they copulated in the green forest; and—wonderful to tell—was turned from a man into a woman and thus spent seven years. In the eighth year he saw the same snakes again and said: 'If a blow struck at you is so powerful that it changes the sex of the giver, I will now strike at you again.' With these words he struck the snakes, and his former shape was restored to him and he became as he had been born. So he was appointed arbitrator in the playful quarrel, and supported Jove's statement. It is said that Saturnia [i.e., Juno] was quite disproportionately upset, and condemned the arbitrator to perpetual blindness. But the almighty father (for no god may undo what has been done by another god), in return for the sight that was taken away, gave him the power to know the future and so lightened the penalty paid by the honor."
6. "This may not appear as exact as Sappho's lines, but I had in mind the 'longshore' or 'dory' fisherman, who returns at nightfall" [Eliot's note]. Sappho's poem addressed Hesperus, the evening star, as the star that brings everyone home from work to evening rest; her poem is here distorted by Eliot. There is also an echo of Robert Louis Stevenson's Requiem, line 221: "Home is the sailor, home from sea."
7. Pimply.
8. Either the Yorkshire woolen manufacturing town, where many fortunes were made in World War I, or

The time is now propitious, as he guesses,   235
The meal is ended, she is bored and tired,
Endeavors to engage her in caresses
Which still are unreproved, if undesired.
Flushed and decided, he assaults at once;
Exploring hands encounter no defense;   240
His vanity requires no response,
And makes a welcome of indifference.
(And I Tiresias have foresuffered all
Enacted on this same divan or bed;
I who have sat by Thebes[9] below the wall   245
And walked among the lowest of the dead.)
Bestows one final patronizing kiss,
And gropes his way, finding the stairs unlit . . .

  She turns and looks a moment in the glass,
Hardly aware of her departed lover;   250
Her brain allows one half-formed thought to pass:
"Well now that's done: and I'm glad it's over."
When lovely woman stoops to folly and
Paces about her room again, alone,
She smoothes her hair with automatic hand,   255
And puts a record on the gramophone.[1]

  "This music crept by me upon the waters"[2]
And along the Strand, up Queen Victoria Street.
O City city, I can sometimes hear
Beside a public bar in Lower Thames Street,   260
The pleasant whining of a mandolin
And a clatter and a chatter from within
Where fishmen lounge at noon: where the walls
Of Magnus Martyr hold
Inexplicable splendor of Ionian white and gold.[3]   265

        The river sweats[4]
        Oil and tar
        The barges drift

---

the pioneer oil town of Bradford, Pennsylvania, the
home of one of Eliot's wealthy Harvard contemporaries, T. E. Hanley.
9. Tiresias lived in Thebes for many generations,
where he witnessed the tragic fates of Oedipus and
Creon; he prophesied in the market place by the wall
of Thebes.
1. "V. Goldsmith, the song in *The Vicar of Wakefield*"
[Eliot's note]. Olivia, a character in Oliver Goldsmith's
novel, sings the following song when she returns to the
place where she was seduced: "When lovely woman
stoops to folly / And finds too late that men betray /
What charm can soothe her melancholy, / What art
can wash her guilt away? / The only art her guilt to
cover, / To hide her shame from every eye, / To give
repentance to her lover / And wring his bosom—is to
die."
2. "V. *The Tempest*, as above" [Eliot's note]. Cf. line
48. The line is from Ferdinand's speech, continuing

after "weeping again the King my father's wrack."
3. "The interior of St. Magnus Martyr is to my mind
one of the finest among [Sir Christopher] Wren's inte-
riors" [Eliot's note]. In these lines, the "pleasant" music, the "fishmen" resting after labor, and the splendor
of the church interior all suggest a world of true values,
where work and relaxation are both real and take place
in a context of religious meaning. It is but a momentary glimpse of an almost lost world.
4. "The Song of the (three) Thames-daughters begins
here. From line 292 to 306 inclusive they speak in
turn. V. *Götterdämmerung*, 3.1: the Rhine-daughters"
[Eliot's note]. Eliot parallels the Thames-daughters
with the Rhine-maidens in Wagner's opera *Die Götterdämmerung* ("The Twilight of the Gods") who lament
that, with the gold of the Nibelungs stolen, the beauty
of the river is gone. The refrain in lines 277–278 is
borrowed from Wagner.

With the turning tide
Red sails   270
Wide
To leeward, swing on the heavy spar.
The barges wash
Drifting logs
Down Greenwich reach   275
Past the Isle of Dogs.[5]
      Weialala leia
      Wallala leialala

Elizabeth and Leicester[6]
Beating oars
The stern was formed   280
A gilded shell
Red and gold
The brisk swell
Rippled both shores   285
Southwest wind
Carried down stream
The peal of bells
White towers
      Weialala leia   290
      Wallala leialala

"Trams and dusty trees.
Highbury bore me. Richmond and Kew
Undid me.[7] By Richmond I raised my knees
Supine on the floor of a narrow canoe."   295

"My feet are at Moorgate,[8] and my heart
Under my feet. After the event
He wept. He promised 'a new start.'
I made no comment. What should I resent?"

"On Margate[9] Sands.   300
I can connect
Nothing with nothing.
The broken fingernails of dirty hands.
My people humble people who expect
Nothing."   305
      la la

5. Greenwich is a borough in London on the south side of the Thames; opposite is the Isle of Dogs (a peninsula): Eliot presumably intends a reference to the earlier theme of the Dog.
6. The fruitless love of Queen Elizabeth and the earl of Leicester (Sir Robert Dudley) is recalled in Eliot's note: "V. [J. A.] Froude, *Elizabeth*, Vol. 1, ch. 4, letter of De Quadra to Philip of Spain: 'In the afternoon we were in a barge, watching the games on the river. (The queen) was alone with Lord Robert and myself on the poop, when they began to talk nonsense, and went so far that Lord Robert at last said, as I was on the spot there was no reason why they should not be married if the queen pleased.'" Queen Elizabeth was born in the old Greenwich House, by the river, where Greenwich Hospital now stands.
7. "Cf. *Purgatorio*, 5.133" [Eliot's note]. The *Purgatorio* lines, which Eliot here parodies, may be translated: "Remember me, who am La Pia. / Siena made me, Maremma undid me." "Highbury": a residential London suburb. "Richmond": a pleasant part of London westward up the Thames, with boating and riverside hotels. "Kew": adjoining Richmond, has the famous Kew Gardens.
8. Slum area in east London.
9. Popular seaside resort on Thames estuary.

To Carthage then I came[1]

Burning burning burning burning[2]
O Lord Thou pluckest me out[3]
O Lord Thou pluckest   310

burning

4. Death by Water[4]

Phlebas the Phoenician, a fortnight dead,
Forgot the cry of gulls, and the deep sea swell
And the profit and loss.
                     A current under sea   315
Picked his bones in whispers. As he rose and fell
He passed the stages of his age and youth
Entering the whirlpool.
                     Gentile or Jew
O you who turn the wheel and look to windward,   320
consider Phlebas, who was once handsome and tall as you.

5. What the Thunder Said[5]

After the torchlight red on sweaty faces
After the frosty silence in the gardens
After the agony in stony places
The shouting and the crying   325
Prison and palace and reverberation
Of thunder of spring over distant mountains
He who was living is now dead[6]
We who were living are now dying
With a little patience   330

1. "V. St. Augustine's *Confessions*: 'to Carthage then I came, where a caldron of unholy loves sang all about mine ears'" [Eliot's note]. The passage from the *Confessions* quoted here occurs in St. Augustine's account of his youthful life of lust. Cf. line 92 and its note.
2. "The complete text of the Buddha's Fire Sermon (which corresponds in importance to the Sermon on the Mount) from which these words are taken, will be found translated in the late Henry Clarke Warren's *Buddhism in Translation* (Harvard Oriental Series)" [Eliot's note]. In the sermon, the Buddha instructs his priests that all things "are on fire. . . . The eye . . . is on fire; forms are on fire; eye-consciousness is on fire; impressions received by the eye are on fire; and whatever sensation, pleasant, unpleasant, or indifferent, originates in dependence on impressions received by the eye, that also is on fire. And with what are these on fire? With the fire of passion, say I, with the fire of hatred, with the fire of infatuation." For Christ's Sermon on the Mount see Matthew 5–7.
3. "From St. Augustine's *Confessions* again. The collocation of these two representatives of eastern and western asceticism, as the culmination of this part of the poem, is not an accident" [Eliot's note]. Cf. also Zechariah 3.2, where God, rebuking Satan, speaks of Joshua the high priest as "a brand plucked out of the fire."
4. This section has been interpreted in two ways: either it signifies death by water without resurrection (water *misused*) or it symbolizes the sacrificial death that precedes rebirth. It is true that Phlebas is purged of his commercial interests and vanities when he suffers a sea change, and Weston tells of the annual casting into the sea at Alexandria of an effigy of the head of Adonis—to be taken out after seven days by jubilant celebrators of the cult. The majority of interpreters, however, see Phlebas's drowning as a death by water that brings no resurrection, although there is a strange sense of peace in the death. Cf. line 47 and n. 5, p. 2468.
5. "In the first part of part 5 three themes are employed: the journey to Emmaus, the approach to the Chapel Perilous (see Miss Weston's book), and the present decay of eastern Europe" [Eliot's note]. The journey to Emmaus (see line 360 and n. 9, p. 2477) is a significant feature in the story of Christ, and in this section the Waste Land is more clearly related to that story. Christ is associated with the slain fertility god, but there is still no resurrection.
6. These lines, containing allusions to Christ's imprisonment and trial, and to Gethsemane and Golgotha, suggest the hopeless days between Good Friday and Easter, between the Crucifixion and the Resurrection—associated with the death of the Fisher King.

Here is no water but only rock
Rock and no water and the sandy road
The road winding above among the mountains
Which are mountains of rock without water
If there were water we should stop and drink   335
Amongst the rock one cannot stop or think
Sweat is dry and feet are in the sand
If there were only water amongst the rock
Dead mountain mouth of carious teeth that cannot spit
Here one can neither stand nor lie nor sit   340
There is not even silence in the mountains
But dry sterile thunder without rain
There is not even solitude in the mountains
But red sullen faces sneer and snarl
From doors of mudcracked houses   345
                         If there were water
   And no rock
   If there were rock
   And also water
   And water   350
   A spring
   A pool among the rock
   If there were the sound of water only
   Not the cicada[7]
   And dry grass singing   355
   But sound of water over a rock
   Where the hermit thrush[8] sings in the pine trees
   Drip drop drip drop drop drop drop
   But there is no water

Who is the third who walks always beside you?[9]   360
When I count, there are only you and I together
But when I look ahead up the white road
There is always another one walking beside you
Gliding wrapped in a brown mantle, hooded
I do not know whether a man or a woman   365
—But who is that on the other side of you?

   What is that sound high in the air[1]
Murmur of maternal lamentation

---

7. Grasshopper. Cf. the prophecy of Ecclesiastes, "the grasshopper shall be a burden, and desire shall fail." Cf. also line 23 and n. 8, p. 2467.

8. "This is . . . the hermit thrush which I have heard in Quebec County . . . Its 'water-dripping song' is justly celebrated" [Eliot's note].

9. "The following lines were stimulated by the account of one of the Antarctic expeditions (I forget which, but I think one of Shackleton's): it was related that the party of explorers, at the extremity of their strength, had the constant delusion that there was *one more member* than could actually be counted" [Eliot's note]. This reminiscence is associated with the journey of Christ's disciples to Emmaus given in Luke 24.13–

16: "And it came to pass, that, while they communed together and reasoned, Jesus himself drew near, and went with them. But their eyes were holden that they should not know him."

1. Eliot's note for lines 367–377 is: "Cf. Herman Hesse, *Blick ins Chaos* ["A Glimpse into Chaos"]." The note then quotes a passage from the German text, which is translated: "Already half of Europe, already at least half of Eastern Europe, on the way to Chaos, drives drunk in sacred infatuation along the edge of the precipice, sings drunkenly, as though hymn singing, as Dmitri Karamazov [in Dostoyevski's *Brothers Karamazov*] sang. The offended bourgeois laughs at the songs; the saint and the seer hear them with tears."

Who are those hooded hordes swarming
Over endless plains, stumbling in cracked earth 370
Ringed by the flat horizon only
What is the city over the mountains
Cracks and reforms and bursts in the violet air
Falling towers
Jerusalem Athens Alexandria 375
Vienna London
Unreal

    A woman drew her long black hair out tight
And fiddled whisper music on those strings
And bats with baby faces in the violet light 380
Whistled, and beat their wings
And crawled head downward down a blackened wall
And upside down in air were towers
Tolling reminiscent bells, that kept the hours
And voices singing out of empty cisterns and exhausted wells. 385

    In this decayed hole among the mountains
In the faint moonlight, the grass is singing
Over the tumbled graves, about the chapel
There is the empty chapel, only the wind's home.[2]
It has no windows, and the door swings, 390
Dry bones can harm no one.
Only a cock stood on the rooftree
Co co rico co co rico[3]
In a flash of lightning. Then a damp gust
Bringing rain 395

    Ganga[4] was sunken, and the limp leaves
Waited for rain, while the black clouds
Gathered far distant, over Himavant.[5]
The jungle crouched, humped in silence.
Then spoke the thunder 400
DA[6]
Datta: what have we given?
My friend, blood shaking my heart
The awful daring of a moment's surrender
Which an age of prudence can never retract 405
By this, and this only, we have existed
Which is not to be found in our obituaries

---

2. Suggesting the moment of near despair before the Chapel Perilous, when the questing knight sees nothing there but decay. This illusion of nothingness is the knight's final test.
3. The crowing of the cock signals the departure of ghosts and evil spirits. Cf. *Hamlet* 1.1.157ff.
4. The river Ganges.
5. I.e., snowy mountain; the name of a peak in the Himalayas.
6. " 'Datta, dayadhvam, damyata' (Give, sympathize, control). The fable of the meaning of the Thunder is found in the *Brihadaranyaka—Upanishad,* 5, 1" [El-

iot's note]. The Hindu fable referred to is that of gods, men, and demons each in turn asking of their father Prajapati, "Speak to us, O Lord." To each he replied with the one syllable "DA," and each group interpreted it in a different way: "*Datta,*" to give alms; "*Dayadhvam,*" to have compassion; "*Damyata,*" to practice self-control. The fable concludes, "This is what the divine voice, the Thunder, repeats when he says: DA, DA, DA: 'Control yourselves; give alms; be compassionate.' Therefore one should practice these three things: self-control, alms-giving, and compassion."

Or in memories draped by the beneficent spider[7]
Or under seals broken by the lean solicitor[8]
In our empty rooms   410
DA
Dayadhvam: I have heard the key[9]
Turn in the door once and turn once only
We think of the key, each in his prison
Thinking of the key, each confirms a prison   415
Only at nightfall, ethereal rumors
Revive for a moment a broken Coriolanus[1]
DA
Damyata: The boat responded
Gaily, to the hand expert with sail and oar   420
The sea was calm, your heart would have responded
Gaily, when invited, beating obedient
To controlling hands

                                I sat upon the shore
Fishing,[2] with the arid plain behind me   425
Shall I at least set my lands in order?[3]
London Bridge is falling down falling down falling down[4]
Poi s'ascose nel foco che gli affina[5]
Quando fiam uti chelidon[6] — O swallow swallow[7]
Le Prince d'Aquitaine à la tour abolie[8]   430

---

7. "Cf. Webster, *The White Devil*, 5.6: '. . . they'll re-marry / Ere the worm pierce your winding-sheet, ere the spider / Make a thin curtain for your epitaphs' " [Eliot's note].
8. Lawyer.
9. "Cf. *Inferno*, 33.46" [Eliot's note]. In this passage from the *Inferno* Ugolino recalls his imprisonment in the tower with his children, where they starved to death: "And I heard below the door of the horrible tower being locked up." Eliot implies that we cannot obey the command to sympathize because we are imprisoned within the circle of our own egotism. Eliot's note for this line goes on to quote F. H. Bradley, *Appearance and Reality*, p. 346, as follows: " 'My external sensations are no less private to myself than are my thoughts or my feelings. In either case my experience falls within my own circle, a circle closed on the outside; and, with all its elements alike, every sphere is opaque to the others which surround it. . . . In brief, regarded as an existence which appears in a soul, the whole world for each is peculiar and private to that soul.' "
1. Coriolanus, who acted out of pride rather than duty, is an obvious example of a man locked in the prison of his own self. He led the enemy against his native city out of injured pride (cf. Shakespeare, *Coriolanus*).
2. "V. Weston: *From Ritual to Romance*; chapter on the Fisher King" [Eliot's note].
3. Cf. Isaiah 38.1: "Thus saith the Lord, Set thine house in order; for thou shalt die, and not live." The inclusive "I," who sits in the symbolic act of fishing (seeking salvation, regeneration, eternity) with the Waste Land behind him, wonders how far he can order his affairs.
4. One of the later lines of this nursery rhyme is "Take the key and lock her up, my fair lady."
5. "V. *Purgatorio*, 26.148" [Eliot's note]. The note

goes on to quote lines 145–148 of the *Purgatorio*, in which Arnaut Daniel, the Provençal poet, addresses Dante: " 'Now I pray you, by that virtue which guides you to the summit of the stairway, be mindful in due time of my pain.' " Then (in the line Eliot quotes here) "he hid himself in the fire which refines them." The purgatorial vision of refining fire — as distinct from the fires of lust — represents one of the hopeful fragments shored up by the seeker for regeneration and order.
6. "V. *Pervigilium Veneris*. Cf. Philomela in parts 2 and 3" [Eliot's note]. The Latin phrase in the text means, "When shall I be as the swallow?" It comes from the *Pervigilium Veneris* ("Vigil of Venus"), an anonymous late Latin poem combining a hymn to Venus with a description of spring. In the last two stanzas of the *Pervigilium* occurs a recollection of the Tereus-Procne-Philomela myth (except that in this version the swallow is identified with Philomela); the anonymous poet's mood changes to one of sadness, combined with hope for renewal: "The maid of Tereus sings under the poplar shade, so that you would think musical trills of love came from her mouth and not a sister's complaint of a barbarous husband. . . . She sings, we are silent. When will my spring come? When shall I be as the swallow that I may cease to be silent? I have lost the Muse in silence, and Apollo regards me not."
7. Cf. Swinburne's *Itylus*, which begins, "Swallow, my sister, O sister swallow, / How can thine heart be full of spring?" and Tennyson's lyric in *The Princess*: "O Swallow, Swallow, flying, flying south."
8. "V. Gerard de Nerval, Sonnet *El Desdichado*" [Eliot's note]. The French line may be translated, "The Prince of Aquitaine in the ruined tower." One of the cards in the Tarot pack is "the tower struck by lightning."

T. S. ELIOT

These fragments I have shored against my ruins[9]
Why then Ile fit you. Hieronymo's mad againe.[1]
Datta. Dayadhvam. Damyata.
        Shantih   shantih   shantih[2]

1922

Journey of the Magi[1]

    "A cold coming we had of it,
Just the worst time of the year
For a journey, and such a long journey:
The ways deep and the weather sharp,
The very dead of winter."[2]   5
And the camels galled, sore-footed, refractory,
Lying down in the melting snow.
There were times we regretted
The summer palaces on slopes, the terraces,
And the silken girls bringing sherbet.   10
Then the camel men cursing and grumbling
And running away, and wanting their liquor and women,
And the night-fires going out, and the lack of shelters,
And the cities hostile and the towns unfriendly
And the villages dirty and charging high prices: 15
A hard time we had of it.
At the end we preferred to travel all night,
Sleeping in snatches,
With the voices singing in our ears, saying
That this was all folly.   20

    Then at dawn we came down to a temperate valley,
Wet, below the snow line, smelling of vegetation;
With a running stream and a water mill beating the darkness,
And three trees on the low sky,[3]
And an old white horse galloped away in the meadow.   25
Then we came to a tavern with vine-leaves over the lintel,

This may refer to the whole poem—fragments assembled by the speaker in the attempt to come to terms
with his situation.
1. "V. Kyd's *Spanish Tragedy*" [Eliot's note]. Subtitled
"Hieronymo's Mad Againe," Kyd's play (1594) is an
early example of the Elizabethan tragedy of revenge.
Hieronymo, driven mad by the murder of his son, has
his revenge when he is asked to write a court entertainment. He replies, "Why then Ile fit you!" (i.e., accommodate you), and assigns the parts in the entertainment so that, in the course of the action, his son's
murderers are killed.
2. "Shantih. Repeated as here, a formal ending to an
Upanishad. 'The Peace which passeth understanding'
is our equivalent to this word" [Eliot's note]. The
Upanishads are poetic dialogues on Hindu metaphysics, written after the Vedas, the ancient Hindu scriptures, and in part commenting on them. The fact that
the benediction is in a language so foreign to Western

tradition may indicate that the solution is willed, not
achieved.
1. One of the three wise men who came from the east
to Jerusalem to do homage to the infant Jesus (Matthew 2.1–12) is recalling in old age the meaning of the
experience.
2. Adapted from a passage in a Nativity sermon by the
17th-century divine Lancelot Andrewes: "A cold coming they had of it at this time of the year, just the worst
time of the year to take a journey, and specially a long
journey in. The ways deep, the weather sharp, the days
short, the sun farthest off, *in solstitio brumali*, 'the very
dead of winter.'"
3. The "three trees" suggest the three crosses, with
Christ crucified on the center one; the men "dicing for
pieces of silver" (line 27) suggest the soldiers dicing for
Christ's garments and Judas's betrayal of him for thirty
pieces of silver.

Six hands at an open door dicing for pieces of silver,[4]
And feet kicking the empty wineskins.
But there was no information, and so we continued
And arrived at evening, not a moment too soon   30
Finding the place; it was (you may say) satisfactory.

    All this was a long time ago, I remember,
And I would do it again, but set down
This set down
This: were we led all that way for   35
Birth or Death? There was a Birth, certainly,
We had evidence and no doubt. I had seen birth and death,
But had thought they were different; this Birth was
Hard and bitter agony for us, like Death, our death.
We returned to our places, these Kingdoms,   40
But no longer at ease here, in the old dispensation,
With an alien people clutching their gods.
I should be glad of another death.

                                                                    1927

Marina[1]

Quis hic locus, quae regio, quae mundi plaga?[2]

    What seas what shores what gray rocks and what islands
What water lapping the bow
And scent of pine and the woodthrush singing through the fog
What images return
O my daughter.   5

    Those who sharpen the tooth of the dog, meaning
Death
Those who glitter with the glory of the hummingbird, meaning
Death
Those who sit in the sty of contentment, meaning   10
Death
Those who suffer the ecstasy of the animals, meaning
Death

    Are become unsubstantial, reduced by a wind,
A breath of pine, and the woodsong fog   15
By this grace dissolved in place

---

4. "Why, for all of us, out of all that we have heard, seen, felt, in a lifetime, do certain images recur, charged with emotion, rather than others? . . . six ruffians seen through an open window playing cards at night at a small French railway junction where there was a water mill" (Eliot, *The Use of Poetry and the Use of Criticism*).
1. Pericles' daughter in Shakespeare's play *Pericles, Prince of Tyre*: she was born at sea, lost to her father, then as a young woman found by him again.
2. "What place is this, what country, what region of the world?" Spoken by Hercules on regaining sanity after having killed his children in his madness, in Seneca's play *Hercules Furens* ("The Mad Hercules"). This is a situation contrary to the one evoked in the poem. Eliot once wrote to a correspondent that he wished to achieve a "crisscross" between the scenes in the Senecan and the Shakespearean plays.

What is this face, less clear and clearer
The pulse in the arm, less strong and stronger—
Given or lent? more distant than stars and nearer than the eye

Whispers and small laughter between leaves and hurrying feet   20
Under sleep, where all the waters meet.

Bowsprit cracked with ice and paint cracked with heat.
I made this, I have forgotten
And remember.
The rigging weak and the canvas rotten   25
Between one June and another September.
Made this unknowing, half conscious, unknown, my own.
The garboard strake[3] leaks, the seams need calking.
This form, this face, this life
Living to live in a world of time beyond me; let me   30
Resign my life for this life, my speech for that unspoken,
The awakened, lips parted, the hope, the new ships.

What seas what shores what granite islands towards my timbers
And woodthrush calling through the fog
My daughter.   35
                                                                 1930

From FOUR QUARTETS

Little Gidding[1]

1

Midwinter spring is its own season
Sempiternal[2] though sodden towards sundown,
Suspended in time, between pole and tropic,
When the short day is brightest, with frost and fire,
The brief sun flames the ice, on pond and ditches,   5
In windless cold that is the heart's heat,
Reflecting in a watery mirror
A glare that is blindness in the early afternoon.
And glow more intense than blaze of branch, or brazier,

3. The planking nearest to the boat's keel—hence its most vital spot.
1. This is the fourth of Eliot's *Four Quartets*, four related poems each divided into five "movements" in a manner reminiscent of the structure of a quartet or a sonata and each dealing with some aspect of the relation of time and eternity, the meaning of history, the achievement of the moment of timeless insight. Although the *Four Quartets* constitute a unified sequence, they were each written separately and can be read as individual poems. "*Little Gidding* can be understood by itself, without reference to the preceding poems, which it yet so beautifully completes" (Helen Gardner). Each of the four is named after a place. Little Gidding is a village in Huntingdonshire where in 1625 Nicholas Ferrar established an Anglican religious community; it was broken up in 1647, toward the end of the civil war, by the victorious Puritans; the chapel, however, was rebuilt in the 19th century and still exists. Eliot wrote the poem in 1942, when he was taking his turn as a nighttime fire-watcher during the incendiary bombings of London in World War II, and he looks back at the history and meaning of Little Gidding from his own war experience in order to project its present significance.
2. Eternal, everlasting.

Stirs the dumb spirit: no wind, but pentecostal fire[3]   10
In the dark time of the year. Between melting and freezing
The soul's sap quivers. There is no earth smell
Or smell of living thing. This is the springtime
But not in time's covenant. Now the hedgerow
Is blanched for an hour with transitory blossom   15
Of snow, a bloom more sudden
Than that of summer, neither budding nor fading,
Not in the scheme of generation.
Where is the summer, the unimaginable
Zero summer?

       If you came this way,   20
Taking the route you would be likely to take
From the place you would be likely to come from,
If you came this way in may time, you would find the hedges
White again, in May, with voluptuary sweetness.
It would be the same at the end of the journey,   25
If you came at night like a broken king,[4]
If you came by day not knowing what you came for,
It would be the same, when you leave the rough road
And turn behind the pigsty to the dull façade
And the tombstone. And what you thought you came for   30
Is only a shell, a husk of meaning
From which the purpose breaks only when it is fulfilled
If at all. Either you had no purpose
Or the purpose is beyond the end you figured
And is altered in fulfillment. There are other places   35
Which also are the world's end, some at the sea jaws,
Or over a dark lake, in a desert or a city[5]—
But this is the nearest, in place and time,
Now and in England.

       If you came this way,
Taking any route, starting from anywhere,   40
At any time or at any season,
It would always be the same: you would have to put off
Sense and notion. You are not here to verify,
Instruct yourself, or inform curiosity
Or carry report. You are here to kneel   45
Where prayer has been valid. And prayer is more
Than an order of words, the conscious occupation
Of the praying mind, or the sound of the voice praying.
And what the dead had no speech for, when living,
They can tell you, being dead: the communication   50

3. On the Pentecost day after the death and resurrection of Christ, there appeared to His apostles "cloven tongues like as of fire . . . And they were all filled with the Holy Ghost" (Acts 2).
4. King Charles I visited Ferrar's community more than once and is said to have paid his last visit in secret after his final defeat at the battle of Naseby in the Civil War.

5. "The 'sea jaws' [Eliot] associated with Iona and St. Columba and with Lindisfarne and St. Cuthbert: the 'dark lake' with the lake of Glendalough and St. Kevin's hermitage in County Wicklow: the desert with the hermits of the Thebaid and St. Antony: the city with Padua and the other St. Antony" (Gardner, The Composition of Four Quartets, p. 163).

Of the dead is tongued with fire beyond the language of the living.
Here, the intersection of the timeless moment
Is England and nowhere. Never and always.

2

Ash on an old man's sleeve
Is all the ash the burnt roses leave.   55
Dust in the air suspended
Marks the place where a story ended.[6]
Dust inbreathed was a house—
The wall, the wainscot, and the mouse.
The death of hope and despair,   60
     This is the death of air.[7]

There are flood and drouth
Over the eyes and in the mouth,
Dead water and dead sand
Contending for the upper hand.   65
The parched eviscerate soil
Gapes at the vanity of toil,
Laughs without mirth.
     This is the death of earth.

Water and fire succeed   70
The town, the pasture, and the weed.
Water and fire deride
The sacrifice that we denied.
Water and fire shall rot
The marred foundations we forgot,   75
Of sanctuary and choir.
     This is the death of water and fire.

In the uncertain hour before the morning[8]
     Near the ending of interminable night
     At the recurrent end of the unending   80
After the dark dove with the flickering tongue[9]
     Had passed below the horizon of his homing
     While the dead leaves still rattled on like tin
Over the asphalt where no other sound was
     Between three districts whence the smoke arose   85
     I met one walking, loitering and hurried
As if blown towards me like the metal leaves
     Before the urban dawn wind unresisting.
     And as I fixed upon the down-turned face

6. Eliot wrote to a friend: "During the Blitz [bombing] the accumulated debris was suspended in the London air for hours after a bombing. Then it would slowly descend and cover one's sleeves and coat with a fine white ash."

7. "The death of air," like that of "earth" and of "water and fire" in the succeeding stanzas, recalls the theory of the creative strife of the four elements propounded by Heraclitus (Greek philosopher of 4th and 5th centuries B.C.): "Fire lives in the death of air; water lives in the death of earth; and earth lives in the death of water."

8. The pattern of indentation in the left margin of lines 78–149, their movement and elevated diction, are meant to suggest the *terza rima* or Dante's *Inferno*.

9. The German dive-bomber.

That pointed scrutiny with which we challenge   90
    The first-met stranger in the waning dusk
    I caught the sudden look of some dead master
Whom I had known, forgotten, half recalled
    Both one and many; in the brown baked features
    The eyes of a familiar compound ghost[1]   95
Both intimate and unidentifiable.
    So I assumed a double part, and cried
    And heard another's voice cry: "What! are *you* here?"
Although we were not. I was still the same,
    Knowing myself yet being someone other—   100
    And he a face still forming; yet the words sufficed
To compel the recognition they preceded.
    And so, compliant to the common wind,
    Too strange to each other for misunderstanding,
In concord at this intersection time   105
    Of meeting nowhere, no before and after,
    We trod the pavement in a dead patrol.
I said: "The wonder that I feel is easy,
    Yet ease is cause of wonder. Therefore speak:
    I may not comprehend, may not remember."   110
And he: "I am not eager to rehearse
    My thought and theory which you have forgotten.
    These things have served their purpose: let them be.
So with your own, and pray they be forgiven
    By others, as I pray you to forgive   115
    Both bad and good. Last season's fruit is eaten
And the fullfed beast shall kick the empty pail.
    For last year's words belong to last year's language
    And next year's words await another voice.
But, as the passage now presents no hindrance   120
    To the spirit unappeased and peregrine[2]
    Between two worlds become much like each other,
So I find words I never thought to speak
    In streets I never thought I should revisit
    When I left my body on a distant shore.[3]   125
Since our concern was speech, and speech impelled us
    To purify the dialect of the tribe[4]
    And urge the mind to aftersight and foresight,
Let me disclose the gifts reserved for age
    To set a crown upon your lifetime's effort.   130
    First, the cold friction of expiring sense
Without enchantment, offering no promise
    But bitter tastelessness of shadow fruit
    As body and soul begin to fall asunder.
Second, the conscious impotence of rage[5]   135

1. This encounter with a ghost "compounded" of W. B. Yeats and his fellow Irishman Jonathan Swift is modeled on Dante's meeting with Brunetto Latini (*Inferno* 15), closing with a direct translation of Dante's cry of horrified recognition: "*Siete voi qui, ser Brunetto?*" Cf. also Shakespeare's *Sonnet* 86, line 9: "that affable familiar ghost."
2. Foreign, wandering.

3. Yeats died on January 28, 1939, at Roquebrune in the south of France.
4. A rendering of the line "*Donner un sens plus pur aux mots de la tribu*" in Stéphane Mallarmé's sonnet *Le Tombeau d'Edgar Poe* ("The Tomb of Edgar Poe").
5. Cf. Yeats, *The Spur:* "You think it horrible that lust and rage / Should dance attention upon my old age."

At human folly, and the laceration
Of laughter at what ceases to amuse.[6]
And last, the rending pain of re-enactment
Of all that you have done, and been;[7] the shame
Of motives late revealed, and the awareness   140
Of things ill done and done to other's harm
    Which once you took for exercise of virtue.
    Then fools's approval stings, and honor stains.
From wrong to wrong the exasperated spirit
    Proceeds, unless restored by that refining fire[8]   145
    Where you must move in measure, like a dancer."[9]
The day was breaking. In the disfigured street
    He left me, with a kind of valediction,
    And faded on the blowing of the horn.[1]

                                        3

There are three conditions which often look alike   150
Yet differ completely, flourish in the same hedgerow:
Attachment to self and to things and to persons, detachment
From self and from things and from persons; and, growing between
    them, indifference
Which resembles the others as death resembles life,
Being between two lives—unflowering, between   155
The live and the dead nettle.[2] This is the use of memory:
For liberation—not less of love but expanding
Of love beyond desire, and so liberation
From the future as well as the past. Thus, love of a country
Begins as attachment to our own field of action   160
And comes to find that action of little importance
Though never indifferent. History may be servitude,
History may be freedom. See, now they vanish,
The faces and places, with the self which, as it could, loved them,
To become renewed, transfigured, in another pattern.   165

Sin is Behovely, but
All shall be well, and
All manner of thing shall be well.[3]
If I think, again, of this place,
And of people, not wholly commendable,   170

6. Cf. Yeats, *Swift's Epitaph* (translated from Swift's own Latin): "Savage indignation there / Cannot lacerate his breast."
7. Cf. Yeats, *The Man and the Echo:* "All that I have said and done, / Now that I am old and ill, / Turns into a question till / I lie awake night after night / And never get the answer right. / Did that play of mine send out / Certain men the English shot?"
8. Cf. *The Waste Land*, line 428 and n. 5, p. 2479; also the refining fire in Yeats's *Byzantium*, lines 25–32.
9. Cf. Yeats, *Among School Children*, line 64: "How can we know the dancer from the dance?"
1. Cf. *Hamlet* 1.2.157: "It faded on the crowing of the cock." The horn is the all-clear signal after an air raid (the dialogue has taken place between the dropping of the last bomb and the sounding of the all clear). Eliot called the section that ends with this line "the nearest equivalent to a canto of the *Inferno* or *Purgatorio*" that he could achieve and spoke of his intention to present "a parallel, by means of contrast, between the *Inferno* and the *Purgatorio* . . . and a hallucinated scene after an air raid."
2. Eliot wrote to a friend: "The dead nettle is the family of flowering plants of which the White Archangel is one of the commonest and closely resembles the stinging nettle and is found in its company."
3. A quotation from the 14th-century English mystic Dame Julian of Norwich: "Sin is behovabil [inevitable], but all shall be well and all shall be well and all manner of thing shall be well."

Of no immediate kin or kindness,
But some of peculiar genius,
All touched by a common genius,
United in the strife which divided them;
If I think of a king at nightfall,[4]   175
Of three men, and more, on the scaffold
And a few who died forgotten
In other places, here and abroad,
And of one who died blind and quiet[5]
Why should we celebrate   180
These dead men more than the dying?
It is not to ring the bell backward
Nor is it an incantation
To summon the specter of a Rose.
We cannot revive old factions   185
We cannot restore old policies
Or follow an antique drum.
These men, and those who opposed them
And those whom they opposed
Accept the constitution of silence   190
And are folded in a single party.
Whatever we inherit from the fortunate
We have taken from the defeated
What they had to leave us—a symbol:
A symbol perfected in death.   195
And all shall be well and
All manner of thing shall be well
By the purification of the motive
In the ground of our beseeching.[6]

4

The dove descending breaks the air   200
With flame of incandescent terror
Of which the tongues declare
The one discharge from sin and error.
The only hope, or else despair
    Lies in the choice of pyre or pyre—   205
    To be redeemed from fire by fire.

Who then devised the torment? Love.
Love is the unfamiliar Name
Behind the hands that wove
The intolerable shirt of flame[7]   210
Which human power cannot remove.
    We only live, only suspire
    Consumed by either fire or fire.

---

4. I.e., Charles I. He died "on the scaffold" in 1649, while his principal advisers, Archbishop Laud and Thomas Wentworth, earl of Strafford, were both executed earlier by the victorious parliamentary forces.
5. I.e., Milton.
6. Dame Julian of Norwich was instructed in a vision that "the ground of our beseeching" is love.
7. Out of love for her husband, Hercules, Deianira gave him the poisoned shirt of Nessus. She had been told that it would increase his love for her, but instead it so corroded his flesh that in his agony he mounted a funeral pyre and burned himself to death.

5

What we call the beginning is often the end
And to make an end is to make a beginning.   215
The end is where we start from. And every phrase
And sentence that is right (where every word is at home,
Taking its place to support the others,
The word neither diffident nor ostentatious,
And easy commerce of the old and the new,   220
The common word exact without vulgarity,
The formal word precise but not pedantic,
The complete consort[8] dancing together)
Every phrase and every sentence is an end and a beginning,
Every poem an epitaph. And any action   225
Is a step to the block, to the fire, down the sea's throat
Or to an illegible stone: and that is where we start.
We die with the dying:
See, they depart, and we go with them.
We are born with the dead: 230
See, they return, and bring us with them.
The moment of the rose and the moment of the yew tree
Are of equal duration. A people without history
Is not redeemed from time, for history is a pattern
Of timeless moments. So, while the light fails   235
On a winter's afternoon, in a secluded chapel
History is now and England.

With the drawing of this Love and the voice of this Calling[9]

We shall not cease from exploration
And the end of all our exploring   240
Will be to arrive where we started
And know the place for the first time.
Through the unknown, remembered gate
When the last of earth left to discover
Is that which was the beginning;   245
At the source of the longest river
The voice of the hidden waterfall
And the children in the apple tree
Not known, because not looked for
But heard, half-heard, in the stillness   250
Between two waves of the sea.[1]
Quick now, here, now, always—
A condition of complete simplicity
(Costing not less than everything)
And all shall be well and   255
All manner of thing shall be well

---

8. Company, also harmony of sounds.
9. This line is from the *Cloud of Unknowing*, an anonymous 14th-century mystical work.
1. The voices of the children in the apple tree symbolize the sudden moment of insight. Cf. the conclusion to *Burnt Norton* (the first of the *Four Quartets*), where the laughter of the children in the garden has a like meaning: "Sudden in a shaft of sunlight / Even while the dust moves / There rises the hidden laughter / Of children in the foliage / Quick now, here, now, always."

When the tongues of flame are in-folded
Into the crowned knot of fire
And the fire and the rose are one.
1942   1942, 1943

Tradition and the Individual Talent[1]

1

In English writing we seldom speak of tradition, though we occasionally
apply its name in deploring its absence. We cannot refer to "the tradition" or
to "a tradition"; at most, we employ the adjective in saying that the poetry of
So-and-so is "traditional" or even "too traditional." Seldom, perhaps, does the
word appear except in a phrase of censure. If otherwise, it is vaguely approba-
tive, with the implication, as to the work approved, of some pleasing archaeo-
logical reconstruction. You can hardly make the word agreeable to English
ears without this comfortable reference to the reassuring science of archaeol-
ogy.

Certainly the word is not likely to appear in our appreciations of living or
dead writers. Every nation, every race, has not only its own creative, but its
own critical turn of mind; and is even more oblivious of the shortcomings and
limitations of its critical habits than of those of its creative genius. We know,
or think we know, from the enormous mass of critical writing that has
appeared in the French language the critical method or habit of the French;
we only conclude (we are such unconscious people) that the French are
"more critical" than we, and sometimes even plume ourselves a little with the
fact, as if the French were the less spontaneous. Perhaps they are; but we
might remind ourselves that criticism is as inevitable as breathing, and that
we should be none the worse for articulating what passes in our minds when
we read a book and feel an emotion about it, for criticizing our own minds in
their work of criticism. One of the facts that might come to light in this process
is our tendency to insist, when we praise a poet, upon those aspects of his work
in which he least resembles anyone else. In these aspects or parts of his work
we pretend to find what is individual, what is the peculiar essence of the
man. We dwell with satisfaction upon the poet's difference from his predecessors, especially his immediate predecessors; we endeavor to find something
that can be isolated in order to be enjoyed. Whereas if we approach a poet
without this prejudice we shall often find that not only the best, but the most
individual parts of his work may be those in which the dead poets, his ancestors, assert their immortality most vigorously. And I do not mean the impres-
sionable period of adolescence, but the period of full maturity.

Yet if the only form of tradition, of handing down, consisted in following
the ways of the immediate generation before us in a blind or timid adherence
to its successes, "tradition" should positively be discouraged. We have seen
many such simple currents soon lost in the sand; and novelty is better than
repetition. Tradition is a matter of much wider significance. It cannot be
inherited, and if you want it you must obtain it by great labor. It involves, in

1. First published in the *Egoist* (1919) and later collected in *The Sacred Wood* (1920).

the first place, the historical sense, which we may call nearly indispensable to any one who would continue to be a poet beyond his twenty-fifth year; and the historical sense involves a perception, not only of the pastness of the past, but of its presence; the historical sense compels a man to write not merely with his own generation in his bones, but with a feeling that the whole of the literature of Europe from Homer and within it the whole of the literature of his own country has a simultaneous existence and composes a simultaneous order. This historical sense, which is a sense of the timeless as well as of the temporal and of the timeless and of the temporal together, is what makes a writer traditional. And it is at the same time what makes a writer most acutely conscious of his place in time, of his own contemporaneity.

No poet, no artist of any art, has his complete meaning alone. His significance, his appreciation is the appreciation of his relation to the dead poets and artists. You cannot value him alone; you must set him, for contrast and comparison, among the dead. I mean this as a principle of aesthetic, not merely historical, criticism. The necessity that he shall conform, that he shall cohere, is not one-sided; what happens when a new work of art is created is something that happens simultaneously to all the works of art which preceded it. The existing monuments form an ideal order among themselves, which is modified by the introduction of the new (the really new) work of art among them. The existing order is complete before the new work arrives; for order to persist after the supervention of novelty, the *whole* existing order must be, if ever so slightly, altered; and so the relations, proportions, values of each work of art toward the whole are readjusted; and this is conformity between the old and the new. Whoever has approved this idea of order, of the form of European, of English literature will not find it preposterous that the past should be altered by the present as much as the present is directed by the past. And the poet who is aware of this will be aware of great difficulties and responsibilities.

In a peculiar sense he will be aware also that he must inevitably be judged by the standards of the past. I say judged, not amputated, by them; not judged to be as good as, or worse or better than, the dead; and certainly not judged by the canons of dead critics. It is a judgment, a comparison, in which two things are measured by each other. To conform merely would be for the new work not really to conform at all; it would not be new, and would therefore not be a work of art. And we do not quite say that the new is more valuable because it fits in; but its fitting in is a test of its value—a test, it is true, which can only be slowly and cautiously applied, for we are none of us infallible judges of conformity. We say: it appears to conform, and is perhaps individual, or it appears individual, and may conform; but we are hardly likely to find that it is one and not the other.

To proceed to a more intelligible exposition of the relation of the poet to the past: he can neither take the past as a lump, an indiscriminate bolus,[2] nor can he form himself wholly on one or two private admirations, nor can he form himself wholly upon one preferred period. The first course is inadmissible, the second is an important experience of youth, and the third is a pleasant and highly desirable supplement. The poet must be very conscious of the main current, which does not at all flow invariably through the most distinguished reputations. He must be quite aware of the obvious fact that art never

---

2. A round mass of anything; a large pill.

improves, but that the material of art is never quite the same. He must be aware that the mind of Europe—the mind of his own country—a mind which he learns in time to be much more important than his own private mind—is a mind which changes, and that this change is a development which abandons nothing en route, which does not superannuate either Shakespeare, or Homer, or the rock drawing of the Magdalenian[3] draftsmen. That this development, refinement perhaps, complication certainly, is not, from the point of view of the artist, any improvement. Perhaps not even an improvement from the point of view of the psychologist or not to the extent which we imagine; perhaps only in the end based upon a complication in economics and machinery. But the difference between the present and the past is that the conscious present is an awareness of the past in a way and to an extent which the past's awareness of itself cannot show.

Someone said: "The dead writers are remote from us because we *know* so much more than they did." Precisely, and they are that which we know.

I am alive to a usual objection to what is clearly part of my program for the métier of poetry. The objection is that the doctrine requires a ridiculous amount of erudition (pedantry), a claim which can be rejected by appeal to the lives of poets in any pantheon. It will even be affirmed that much learning deadens or perverts poetic sensibility. While, however, we persist in believing that a poet ought to know as much as will not encroach upon his necessary receptivity and necessary laziness, it is not desirable to confine knowledge to whatever can be put into a useful shape for examinations, drawing rooms, or the still more pretentious modes of publicity. Some can absorb knowledge, the more tardy must sweat for it. Shakespeare acquired more essential history from Plutarch[4] than most men could from the whole British Museum. What is to be insisted upon is that the poet must develop or procure the consciousness of the past and that he should continue to develop this consciousness throughout his career.

What happens is a continual surrender of himself as he is at the moment to something which is more valuable. The progress of an artist is a continual self-sacrifice, a continual extinction of personality.

There remains to define this process of depersonalization and its relation to the sense of tradition. It is in this depersonalization that art may be said to approach the condition of science. I, therefore, invite you to consider, as a suggestive analogy, the action which takes place when a bit of finely filiated[5] platinum is introduced into a chamber containing oxygen and sulphur dioxide.

2

Honest criticism and sensitive appreciation are directed not upon the poet but upon the poetry. If we attend to the confused cries of the newspaper critics and the *susurrus*[6] of popular repetition that follows, we shall hear the names of poets in great numbers; if we seek not Blue-book[7] knowledge but the enjoy-

---

3. The most advanced culture of the European Paleolithic period (from discoveries at La Madeleine, France).
4. Plutarch (1st century A.D.), Greek biographer of Greek and Roman celebrities, from whose work Shake-

speare drew the plots of his Roman plays.
5. Drawn out like a thread.
6. Murmuring, buzzing.
7. British official government publication.

ment of poetry, and ask for a poem, we shall seldom find it. I have tried to
point out the importance of the relation of the poem to other poems by other
authors, and suggested the conception of poetry as a living whole of all the
poetry that has ever been written. The other aspect of this Impersonal theory
of poetry is the relation of the poem to its author. And I hinted, by an analogy,
that the mind of the mature poet differs from that of the immature one not
precisely in any valuation of "personality," not being necessarily more interesting, or having "more to say," but rather by being a more finely perfected
medium in which special, or very varied, feelings are at liberty to enter into
new combinations.

The analogy was that of the catalyst.[8] When the two gases previously mentioned are mixed in the presence of a filament of platinum, they form sulphurous acid. This combination takes place only if the platinum is present;
nevertheless the newly formed acid contains no trace of platinum, and the
platinum itself is apparently unaffected; has remained inert, neutral, and
unchanged. The mind of the poet is the shred of platinum. It may partly or
exclusively operate upon the experience of the man himself; but, the more
perfect the artist, the more completely separate in him will be the man who
suffers and the mind which creates; the more perfectly will the mind digest
and transmute the passions which are its material.

The experience, you will notice, the elements which enter the presence of
the transforming catalyst, are of two kinds: emotions and feelings. The effect
of a work of art upon the person who enjoys it is an experience different in
kind from any experience not of art. It may be formed out of one emotion, or
may be a combination of several; and various feelings, inhering for the writer
in particular words or phrases or images, may be added to compose the final
result. Or great poetry may be made without the direct use of any emotion
whatever: composed out of feelings solely. Canto XV of the *Inferno* (Brunetto
Latini)[9] is a working up of the emotion evident in the situation; but the effect,
though single as that of any work of art, is obtained by considerable complexity
of detail. The last quatrain gives an image, a feeling attaching to an image,
which "came," which did not develop simply out of what precedes, but which
was probably in suspension in the poet's mind until the proper combination
arrived for it to add itself to.[1] The poet's mind is in fact a receptacle for seizing
and storing up numberless feelings, phrases, images, which remain there until
all the particles which can unite to form a new compound are present
together.

If you compare several representative passages of the greatest poetry you see
how great is the variety of types of combination, and also how completely any
semi-ethical criterion of "sublimity" misses the mark. For it is not the "greatness," the intensity, of the emotions, the components, but the intensity of the
artistic process, the pressure, so to speak, under which the fusion takes place,
that counts. The episode of Paolo and Francesca[2] employs a definite emotion,

8. Substance that triggers a chemical change without itself being affected by the reaction.
9. Dante meets in Hell his old master Brunetto Latini, suffering eternal punishment for unnatural lust, yet still loved and admired by Dante, who addresses him with affectionate courtesy (see n. 1, below).
1. Dante's strange interview with Brunetto is over, and Brunetto moves off to continue his punishment: "Then

he turned round, and seemed like one of those / Who run for the green cloth [in the footrace] at Verona / In the field; and he seemed among them / Not the loser but the winner."
2. Illicit lovers whom Dante meets in the second circle of Hell (*Inferno* 5) and at whose punishment and sorrows he swoons with pity.

but the intensity of the poetry is something quite different from whatever intensity in the supposed experience it may give the impression of. It is no more intense, furthermore, than Canto XXVI,[3] the voyage of Ulysses, which has not the direct dependence upon an emotion. Great variety is possible in the process of transmutation of emotion: the murder of Agamemnon,[4] or the agony of Othello, gives an artistic effect apparently closer to a possible original than the scenes from Dante. In the *Agamemnon*, the artistic emotion approximates to the emotion of an actual spectator; in *Othello* to the emotion of the protagonist himself. But the difference between art and the event is always absolute; the combination which is the murder of Agamemnon is probably as complex as that which is the voyage of Ulysses. In either case there has been a fusion of elements. The ode of Keats contains a number of feelings which have nothing particular to do with the nightingale, but which the nightingale, partly, perhaps, because of its attractive name, and partly because of its reputation, served to bring together.

The point of view which I am struggling to attack is perhaps related to the metaphysical theory of the substantial unity of the soul: for my meaning is, that the poet has, not a "personality" to express, but a particular medium, which is only a medium and not a personality, in which impressions and experiences combine in peculiar and unexpected ways. Impressions and experiences which are important for the man may take no place in the poetry, and those which become important in the poetry may play quite a negligible part in the man, the personality.

I will quote a passage which is unfamiliar enough to be regarded with fresh attention in the light—or darkness—of these observations:

> And now methinks I could e'en chide myself
> For doting on her beauty, though her death
> Shall be revenged after no common action.
> Does the silkworm expend her yellow labors
> For thee? For thee does she undo herself?
> Are lordships sold to maintain ladyships
> For the poor benefit of a bewildering minute?
> Why does yon fellow falsify highways,
> And put his life between the judge's lips,
> To refine such a thing—keeps horse and men
> To beat their valors for her? . . .[5]

In this passage (as is evident if it is taken in its context) there is a combination of positive and negative emotions: an intensely strong attraction toward beauty and an equally intense fascination by the ugliness which is contrasted with it and which destroys it. This balance of contrasted emotion is in the dramatic situation to which the speech is pertinent, but that situation alone is inadequate to it. This is, so to speak, the structural emotion, provided by the drama. But the whole effect, the dominant tone, is due to the fact that a number of floating feelings, having an affinity to this emotion by no means superficially evident, have combined with it to give us a new art emotion.

It is not in his personal emotions, the emotions provoked by particular

---

3. Of the *Inferno*. Ulysses, suffering in Hell for "false counseling," tells Dante of his final voyage.
4. By his wife, Clytemnestra; the central action of Ae-
schylus' play *Agamemnon*.
5. From Cyril Tourneur, *The Revenger's Tragedy* 3.4 (1607).

events in his life, that the poet is in any way remarkable or interesting. His particular emotions may be simple, or crude, or flat. The emotion in his poetry will be a very complex thing, but not with the complexity of the emotions of people who have very complex or unusual emotions in life. One error, in fact, of eccentricity in poetry is to seek for new human emotions to express; and in this search for novelty in the wrong place it discovers the perverse. The business of the poet is not to find new emotions, but to use the ordinary ones and, in working them up into poetry, to express feelings which are not in actual emotions at all. And emotions which he has never experienced will serve his turn as well as those familiar to him. Consequently, we must believe that "emotion recollected in tranquility"[6] is an inexact formula. For it is neither emotion, nor recollection, nor, without distortion of meaning, tranquility. It is a concentration, and a new thing resulting from the concentration, of a very great number of experiences which to the practical and active person would not seem to be experiences at all; it is a concentration which does not happen consciously or of deliberation. These experiences are not "recollected," and they finally unite in an atmosphere which is "tranquil" only in that it is a passive attending upon the event. Of course this is not quite the whole story. There is a great deal, in the writing of poetry, which must be conscious and deliberate. In fact, the bad poet is usually unconscious where he ought to be conscious, and conscious where he ought to be unconscious. Both errors tend to make him "personal." Poetry is not a turning loose of emotion, but an escape from emotion; it is not the expression of personality, but an escape from personality. But, of course, only those who have personality and emotions know what it means to want to escape from these things.

3

o dé noús ísos Theióterón ti chaí apathés estin.[7]

   This essay proposes to halt at the frontier of metaphysics or mysticism, and confine itself to such practical conclusions as can be applied by the responsible person interested in poetry. To divert interest from the poet to the poetry is a laudable aim: for it would conduce to a juster estimation of actual poetry, good and bad. There are many people who appreciate the expression of sincere emotion in verse, and there is a smaller number of people who can appreciate technical excellence. But very few know when there is an expression of *significant* emotion, emotion which has its life in the poem and not in the history of the poet. The emotion of art is impersonal. And the poet cannot reach this impersonality without surrendering himself wholly to the work to be done. And he is not likely to know what is to be done unless he lives in what is not merely the present, but the present moment of the past, unless he is conscious, not of what is dead, but of what is already living.

1919, 1920

---

6. Wordsworth, "Preface," *Lyrical Ballads* (2nd ed., 1800). Wordsworth said that poetry "takes its origin from emotion recollected in tranquility."

7. Aristotle, *De Anima* ("On the Soul") 1.4: "The mind is doubtless something more divine and unimpressionable."

KATHERINE MANSFIELD
1888–1923

1918: *Prelude.*
1920: *Bliss and Other Stories.*
1922: *The Garden-Party and Other Stories.*

When she was thirty years old, Katherine Mansfield described the two motives of what she called her "writing game" with striking clarity and conviction: "One is joy," she explained in a letter to her husband, the critic J. Middleton Murry, adding that in this state of being "in some perfectly blissful way at peace," something like a flower "seems to open before my eyes." The other "kick off" consisted of "a cry against corruption" that she associated with the hopeless sense that "everything [is] doomed to disaster." Feeling divided about her identity as a London literary figure called Katherine Mansfield, she also lived a life of divided emotional loyalties and conflicting impulses. She came from a conventional Victorian family, but she lived the bohemian life of a New Woman. She repeatedly protested that she wanted nothing more than a home of her own, but she spent her life restlessly traveling from England to France and Italy, and back again. She said she adored her husband, but she never relinquished her close ties to her "wife," Ida Baker. Finally, and tragically, while she searched for spiritual health, she suffered from the debilitating consequences of the tuberculosis that killed her at the age of thirty-five.

Kathleen Mansfield Beauchamp was born in Wellington, New Zealand, to Harold Deauchamp, a respected businessman who became a prominent director of the Bank of New Zealand, and Annie (Dyer) Beauchamp. In 1903, the family traveled to London, where Kathleen and her sisters entered Queen's College, the first institution in England founded expressly for the higher education of women. At Queen's College, she met Ida Constance Baker, a motherless girl whose father was Mansfield's model for the tyrannical paterfamilias in *The Daughters of the Late Colonel*. In 1906, Kathleen unwillingly returned to New Zealand with her parents. By this time, she had written a number of poems, sketches, and stories and, after experimenting with different pen names, called herself Katherine Mansfield. She continued to read the fiction of Oscar Wilde, Elizabeth Robins, the Brontës, and Leo Tolstoy, and she was beginning to receive payment for vignettes appearing in *The Native Companion*, a New Zealand journal. In March 1907, her mother gave a garden party in their Wellington house; a fatal street accident involving a neighbor living in a poor quarter nearby almost spoiled the festive atmosphere of the day. (This incident was to form the basis of her story *The Garden-Party*, but Laura's sensibility as portrayed in that story is subtler and finer than anything the author appears to have felt at that time. The story, like so much of Mansfield's reworking of her New Zealand experiences in her last years, represents a kind of atonement for her younger self.)

While in New Zealand, she wrote love letters to the son of her Wellington music teacher, Tom Trowell, whose twin, Garnet, would become her fiancé on her return to England in July 1908. After Garnet's parents rejected the engagement, Katherine decided on the spur of the moment to marry a new acquaintance, George Bowden, but she left him the same evening. Shortly afterward she became pregnant by another man, and traveled with her mother to Germany, where she suffered a miscarriage. Her experiences in Germany are told in carefully observed sketches full of ironic detail in her first published book, *In a German Pension* (1911).

In 1910, she briefly resumed life with Bowden, who put her in touch with A. R. Orage, editor of the avant garde periodical *New Age*. There she published a number of her stories and sketches. After she sent one tale, *The Woman at the Store*, to a new review, *Rhythm*, she was visited by its literary editor, J. Middleton Murry, an Oxford undergarduate who became in 1912 first a lodger in her flat and then a lover. In 1918, after Mansfield and Bowden finally divorced, she and Murry married.

When she was not traveling of living on the Continent, Mansfield befriended a number of literary celebrities in London, including, most importantly, the novelists D. H. Lawrence and Virginia Woolf. The relationship with Lawrence was a strong but strange one that developed into a hatred by Lawrence of both Mansfield and Murray. Despite her sense that they were "unthinkably alike" not only in temperament but in their artistic efforts to capture the sensuous feeling of life, Mansfield later felt completely alienated by a shocking letter Lawrence wrote to her in 1920: "You revolt me, stewing in your consumption."

Equally significant to Mansfield was her relationship with Virginia Woolf. In 1917, the "Woolves" published *Prelude* at their Hogarth Press, and Mansfield and Woolf began visiting and writing to each other. Sometimes the older, wealthier Woolf criticized her bohemian promiscuity, but she nevertheless admitted that beyond Mansfield's "commonness" was an "inscrutable" intelligence. After Mansfield died, Woolf recorded in her diary that she had produced "the only writing I have ever been jealous of."

During all this time Mansfield was experimenting in technique and refining her art in an attempt to achieve a kind of short story that, by precision of style and imagery and a symbolic patterning of incident, would project insights into certain kinds of experience. The death in October 1915 of her much-loved brother, a soldier, sent her imagination back to their childhood days in New Zealand and in doing so gave a fresh charge and significance to her work. Writing with growing subtlety and sensitivity, she produced her best stories: *Prelude, Daughters of the Late Colonel, At the Bay*, and *The Garden-Party*. With the publication of *The Garden-Party and Other Stories* in February 1922, Mansfield's place as a master of the modern short story was assured. But she was by then gravely ill with tuberculosis and died suddenly in January 1923 at Fontainebleau, France, where she had sought a cure based on the methods of the controversial mystic George Ivanovich Gurdjieff.

Beginning in rebellion and ending in almost mystic acceptance, Mansfield proceeded through a variety of literary styles, but her best and most characteristic work was produced in the last years of her short life, when she was able to combine incident, image, symbol, and structure in a way comparable with, yet interestingly different from, Joyce's method in *Dubliners*. *Daughters of the Late Colonel* shows her working characteristically through suggestion rather than explicit development, with the subdued elegiac sense of wasted lives providing a note of potential tragedy, although the surface is restrained comedy. The meaning is achieved most of all through the atmosphere, built up through the accumulation of small strokes, none of which seems in itself more than a piece of shrewdly observed realistic detail. The ability to manipulate time is another quality Mansfield shows in some of her best work: she makes particular effective use of the unobtrusive flashback, where we find ourselves in an earlier phase of the action without quite knowing how we got there, although fully aware of its relevance to the total action and atmosphere.

The Daughters of the Late Colonel

1

The week after was one of the busiest weeks of their lives. Even when they went to bed it was only their bodies that lay down and rested; their minds went on, thinking things out, talking things over, wondering, deciding, trying to remember where . . .

Constantia lay like a statue, her hands by her sides, her feet just overlapping each other, the sheet up to her chin. She stared at the ceiling.

"Do you think father would mind if we gave his top hat to the porter?"

"The porter?" snapped Josephine. "Why ever the porter? What a very extraordinary idea!"

"Because," said Constantia slowly, "he must often have to go to funerals. And I noticed at—at the cemetery that he only had a bowler." She paused. "I thought then how very much he'd appreciate a top hat. We ought to give him a present, too. He was always very nice to father."

"But," cried Josephine, flouncing on her pillow and staring across the dark at Constantia, "father's head!" And suddenly, for one awful moment, she nearly giggled. Not, of course, that she felt in the least like giggling. It must have been habit. Years ago, when they had stayed awake at night talking, their beds had simply heaved. And now the porter's head, disappearing, popped out, like a candle, under father's hat. . . . The giggle mounted, mounted; she clenched her hands; she fought it down; she frowned fiercely at the dark and said "Remember" terribly sternly.

"We can decide tomorrow," she sighed.

Constantia had noticed nothing; she sighed.

"Do you think we ought to have our dressing gowns dyed as well?"

"Black?" almost shrieked Josephine.

"Well, what else?" said Constantia. "I was thinking—it doesn't seem quite sincere, in a way, to wear black out of doors and when we're fully dressed, and then when we're at home——"

"But nobody sees us," said Josephine. She gave the bedclothes such a twitch that both her feet became uncovered, and she had to creep up the pillows to get them well under again.

"Kate does," said Constantia. "And the postman very well might."

Josephine thought of her dark-red slippers, which matched her dressing gown, and of Constantia's favorite indefinite green ones which went with hers. Black! Two black dressing gowns and two pairs of black woolly slippers, creeping off to the bathroom like black cats.

"I don't think it's absolutely necessary," said she.

Silence. Then Constantia said, "We shall have to post the papers with the notice in them tomorrow to catch the Ceylon mail. . . . How many letters have we had up till now?"

"Twenty-three."

Josephine had replied to them all, and twenty-three times when she came to "We miss our dear father so much" she had broken down and had to use her handkerchief, and on some of them even to soak up a very light-blue tear with an edge of blotting paper. Strange! She couldn't have put it on—but twenty-three times. Even now, though, when she said over to herself sadly, "We miss our dear father so much" she could have cried if she'd wanted to.

"Have you got enough stamps?" came from Constantia.

"Oh, how can I tell?" said Josephine crossly. "What's the good of asking me that now?

"I was just wondering," said Constantia mildly.

Silence again. There came a little rustle, a scurry, a hop.

"A mouse," said Constantia.

"It can't be a mouse because there aren't any crumbs," said Josephine.

"But it doesn't know there aren't," said Constantia.

A spasm of pity squeezed her heart. Poor little thing! She wished she'd left a tiny piece of biscuit on the dressing table. It was awful to think of it not finding anything. What would it do?

"I can't think how they manage to live at all," she said slowly.

"Who?" demanded Josephine.

And Constantia said more loudly than she meant to, "Mice."

Josephine was furious. "Oh, what nonsense, Con!" she said. "What have mice got to do with it? You're asleep."

"I don't think I am," said Constantia. She shut her eyes to make sure. She was.

Josephine arched her spine, pulled up her knees, folded her arms so that her fists came under her ears, and pressed her cheek hard against the pillow.

2

Another thing which complicated matters was they had Nurse Andrews staying on with them that week. It was their own fault; they had asked her. It was Josephine's idea. On the morning—well, on the last morning, when the doctor had gone, Josephine had said to Constantia, "Don't you think it would be rather nice if we asked Nurse Andrews to stay on for a week as our guest?"

"Very nice," said Constantia.

"I thought," went on Josephine quickly, "I should just say this afternoon, after I've paid her, 'My sister and I would be very pleased, after all you've done for us, Nurse Andrews, if you would stay on for a week as our guest.' I'd have to put that in about being our guest in case——"

"Oh, but she could hardly expect to be paid!" cried Constantia.

"One never knows," said Josephine sagely.

Nurse Andrews had, of course, jumped at the idea. But it was a bother. It meant they had to have regular sit-down meals at the proper times, whereas if they'd been alone they could just have asked Kate if she wouldn't have minded bringing them a tray wherever they were. And meal times now that the strain was over were rather a trial.

Nurse Andrews was simply fearful about butter. Really they couldn't help feeling that about butter, at least, she took advantage of their kindness. And she had that maddening habit of asking for just an inch more bread to finish what she had on her plate, and then, at the last mouthful, absent-mindedly— of course it wasn't absent-mindedly—taking another helping. Josephine got very red when this happened, and she fastened her small, beadlike eyes on the tablecloth as if she saw a minute strange insect creeping through the web of it. But Constantia's long, pale face lengthened and set, and she gazed away—away—far over the desert, to where that line of camels unwound like a thread of wool. . . .

"When I was with Lady Tukes," said Nurse Andrews, "she had such a dainty little contrayvance for the buttah. It was a silvah Cupid balanced on the—on the bordah of a glass dish, holding a tayny fork. And when you wanted some buttah you simply pressed his foot and he bent down and speared you a piece. It was quite a gayme."

Josephine could hardly bear that. But "I think those things are very extravagant" was all she said.

"But whey?" asked Nurse Andrews, beaming through her eyeglasses. "No one, surely, would take more buttah than one wanted—would one?"

"Ring, Con," cried Josephine. She couldn't trust herself to reply.

And proud young Kate, the enchanted princess, came in to see what the old tabbies wanted now. She snatched away their plates of mock something or other and slapped down a white terrified blanc-mange.

"Jam, please, Kate," said Josephine kindly.

Kate knelt and burst open the sideboard, lifted the lid of the jam pot, saw it was empty, put it on the table, and stalked off.

"I'm afraid," said Nurse Andrews a moment later, "there isn't any."

"Oh, what a bother!" said Josephine. She bit her lip. "What had we better do?"

Constantia looked dubious. "We can't disturb Kate again," she said softly.

Nurse Andrews waited, smiling at them both. Her eyes wandered, spying at everything behind her eyeglasses. Constantia in despair went back to her camels. Josephine frowned heavily—concentrated. If it hadn't been for this idiotic woman she and Con would, of course, have eaten their blanc-mange without. Suddenly the idea came.

"I know," she said. "Marmalade. There's some marmalade in the sideboard. Get it, Con."

"I hope," laughed Nurse Andrews, and her laugh was like a spoon tinkling against a medicine glass—"I hope it's not very bittah marmalayde."

3

But, after all, it was not long now, and then she'd be gone for good. And there was no getting over the fact that she had been very kind to father. She had nursed him day and night at the end. Indeed, both Constantia and Josephine felt privately she had rather overdone the not leaving him at the very last. For when they had gone in to say good-bye Nurse Andrews had sat beside his bed the whole time, holding his wrist and pretending to look at her watch. It couldn't have been necessary. It was so tactless, too. Supposing father had wanted to say something—something private to them. Not that he had. Oh, far from it! He lay there, purple, a dark, angry purple in the face, and never even looked at them when they came in. Then, as they were standing there, wondering what to do, he had suddenly opened one eye. Oh, what a difference it would have made, what a difference to their memory of him, how much easier to tell people about it, if he had only opened both! But no—one eye only. It glared at them a moment and then . . . went out.

4

It had made it very awkward for them when Mr. Farolles, of St. John's, called the same afternoon.

"The end was quite peaceful, I trust?" were the first words he said as he glided towards them through the dark drawing room.

"Quite," said Josephine faintly. They both hung their heads. Both of them felt certain that eye wasn't at all a peaceful eye.

"Won't you sit down?" said Josephine.

"Thank you, Miss Pinner," said Mr. Farolles gratefully. He folded his coat-tails and began to lower himself into father's armchair, but just as he touched it he almost sprang up and slid into the next chair instead.

He coughed. Josephine clasped her hands; Constantia looked vague.

"I want you to feel, Miss Pinner," said Mr. Farolles, "and you, Miss Constantia, that I'm trying to be helpful. I want to be helpful to you both, if you will let me. These are the times," said Mr. Farolles, very simply and earnestly, "when God means us to be helpful to one another."

"Thank you very much, Mr. Farolles," said Josephine and Constantia.

"Not at all," said Mr. Farolles gently. He drew his kid gloves through his fingers and leaned forward. "And if either of you would like a little Communion, either or both of you, here *and* now, you have only to tell me. A little Communion is often very help—a great comfort," he added tenderly.

But the idea of a little Communion terrified them. What! In the drawing room by themselves—with no—no altar or anything! The piano would be much too high, thought Constantia, and Mr. Farolles could not possibly lean over it with the chalice. And Kate would be sure to come bursting in and interrupt them, thought Josephine. And supposing the bell rang in the middle? It might be somebody important—about their mourning. Would they get up reverently and go out, or would they have to wait . . . in torture?

"Perhaps you will send round a note by your good Kate if you would care for it later," said Mr. Farolles.

"Oh yes, thank you very much!" they both said.

Mr. Farolles got up and took his black straw hat from the round table.

"And about the funeral," he said softly. "I may arrange that—as your dear father's old friend and yours, Miss Pinner—and Miss Constantia?"

Josephine and Constantia got up too.

"I should like it to be quite simple," said Josephine firmly, "and not too expensive. At the same time, I should like——"

"A good one that will last," thought dreamy Constantia, as if Josephine were buying a nightgown. But of course Josephine didn't say that. "One suitable to our father's position." She was very nervous.

"I'll run round to our good friend Mr. Knight," said Mr. Farolles soothingly. "I will ask him to come and see you. I am sure you will find him very helpful indeed."

5

Well, at any rate, all that part of it was over, though neither of them could possibly believe that father was never coming back. Josephine had had a moment of absolute terror at the cemetery, while the coffin was lowered, to think that she and Constantia had done this thing without asking his permission. What would father say when he found out? For he was bound to find out sooner or later. He always did. "Buried. You two girls had me *buried*?" She heard his stick thumping. Oh, what would they say? What possible excuse could they make? It sounded such an appallingly heartless thing to do. Such a wicked advantage to take of a person because he happened to be helpless at the moment. The other people seemed to treat it all as a matter of course. They were strangers; they couldn't be expected to understand that father was the very last person for such a thing to happen to. No, the entire blame for it all would fall on her and Constantia. And the expense, she thought, stepping into the tight-buttoned cab. When she had to show him the bills. What would he say then?

She heard him absolutely roaring, "And do you expect me to pay for this gimcrack excursion of yours?"

"Oh," groaned poor Josephine aloud, "we shouldn't have done it, Con!"

And Constantia, pale as a lemon in all that blackness, said in a frightened whisper, "Done what, Jug?"

"Let them bu-bury father like that," said Josephine, breaking down and crying into her new, queer-smelling mourning handkerchief.

"But what else could we have done?" asked Constantia wonderingly. "We couldn't have kept him, Jug—we couldn't have kept him unburied. At any rate, not in a flat that size."

Josephine blew her nose; the cab was dreadfully stuffy.

"I don't know," she said forlornly. "It is all so dreadful. I feel we ought to have tried to, just for a time at least. To make perfectly sure. One thing's certain"—and her tears sprang out again—"father will never forgive us for this—never!"

6

Father would never forgive them. That was what they felt more than ever when, two mornings later, they went into his room to go through his things. They had discussed it quite calmly. It was even down on Josephine's list of things to be done. *Go through father's things and settle about them.* But that was a very different matter from saying after breakfast:

"Well, are you :eady, Con?"

"Yes, Jug—when you are."

"Then I think we'd better get it over."

It was dark in the hall. It had been a rule for years never to disturb father in the morning, whatever happened. And now they were going to open the door without knocking even. . . . Constantia's eyes were enormous at the idea; Josephine felt weak in the knees.

"You—you go first," she gasped, pushing Constantia.

But Constantia said, as she always had said on those occasions, "No, Jug, that's not fair. You're eldest."

Josephine was just going to say—what at other times she wouldn't have owned to for the world—what she kept for her very last weapon, "But you're tallest," when they noticed that the kitchen door was open, and there stood Kate. . . .

"Very stiff," said Josephine, grasping the door-handle and doing her best to turn it. As if anything ever deceived Kate!

It couldn't be helped. That girl was . . . Then the door was shut behind them, but—but they weren't in father's room at all. They might have suddenly walked through the wall by mistake into a different flat altogether. Was the door just behind them? They were too frightened to look. Josephine knew that if it was it was holding itself tight shut; Constantia felt that, like the doors in dreams, it hadn't any handle at all. It was the coldness which made it so awful. Or the whiteness—which? Everything was covered. The blinds were down, a cloth hung over the mirror, a sheet hid the bed, a huge fan of white paper filled the fireplace. Constantia timidly put out her hand; she almost expected a snowflake to fall. Josephine felt a queer tingling in her nose, as if her nose was freezing. Then a cab klop-klopped over the cobbles below, and the quiet seemed to shake into little pieces.

"I had better pull up a blind," said Josephine bravely.

"Yes, it might be a good idea," whispered Constantia.

They only gave the blind a touch, but it flew up and the cord flew after, rolling round the blind-stick, and the little tassel tapped as if trying to get free. That was too much for Constantia.

"Don't you think—don't you think we might put it off for another day?" she whispered.

"Why?" snapped Josephine, feeling, as usual, much better now that she knew for certain that Constantia was terrified. "It's got to be done. But I do wish you wouldn't whisper, Con."

"I didn't know I was whispering," whispered Constantia.

"And why do you keep on staring at the bed?" said Josephine, raising her voice almost defiantly. "There's nothing on the bed."

Oh, Jug, don't say so!" said poor Connie. "At any rate, not so loudly."

Josephine felt herself that she had gone too far. She took a wide swerve over to the chest of drawers, put out her hand, but quickly drew it back again.

"Connie!" she gasped, and she wheeled round and leaned with her back against the chest of drawers.

"Oh, Jug—what?"

Josephine could only glare. She had the most extraordinary feeling that she had just escaped something simply awful. But how could she explain to Constantia that father was in the chest of drawers? He was in the top drawer with his handkerchiefs and neckties, or in the next with his shirts and pajamas, or in the lowest of all with his suits. He was watching there, hidden away— just behind the door handle—ready to spring.

She pulled a funny old-fashioned face at Constantia, just as she used to in the old days when she was going to cry.

"I can't open," she nearly wailed.

"No, don't, Jug," whispered Constantia earnestly. "It's much better not to. Don't let's open anything. At any rate, not for a long time."

"But—but it seems so weak," said Josephine, breaking down.

"But why not be weak for once, Jug?" argued Constantia, whispering quite fiercely. "If it is weak." And her pale stare flew from the locked writing table— so safe—to the huge glittering wardrobe, and she began to breathe in a queer, panting way. "Why shouldn't we be weak for once in our lives, Jug? It's quite excusable. Let's be weak—be weak, Jug. It's much nicer to be weak than to be strong."

And then she did one of those amazingly bold things that she'd done about twice before in their lives; she marched over to the wardrobe, turned the key, and took it out of the lock. Took it out of the lock and held it up to Josephine, showing Josephine by her extraordinary smile that she knew what she'd done, she'd risked deliberately father being in there among his overcoats.

If the huge wardrobe had lurched forward, had crashed down on Constantia, Josephine wouldn't have been surprised. On the contrary, she would have thought it the only suitable thing to happen. But nothing happened. Only the room seemed quieter than ever, and bigger flakes of cold air fell on Josephine's shoulders and knees. She began to shiver.

"Come, Jug," said Constantia, still with that awful callous smile, and Josephine followed just as she had that last time, when Constantia had pushed Benny into the round pond.

7

But the strain told on them when they were back in the dining room. They sat down, very shaky, and looked at each other.

"I don't feel I can settle to anything," said Josephine, "until I've had something. Do you think we could ask Kate for two cups of hot water?"

"I really don't see why we shouldn't," said Constantia carefully. She was quite normal again. "I won't ring. I'll go to the kitchen door and ask her."

"Yes, do," said Josephine, sinking down into a chair. "Tell her, just two cups, Con, nothing else—on a tray."

"She needn't even put the jug on, need she?" said Constantia, as though Kate might very well complain if the jug had been there.

"Oh, no, certainly not! The jug's not at all necessary. She can pour it direct out of the kettle," cried Josephine, feeling that would be a labor-saving indeed.

Their cold lips quivered at the greenish brims. Josephine curved her small red hands round the cup; Constantia sat up and blew on the wavy stream, making it flutter from one side to the other.

"Speaking of Benny," said Josephine.

And though Benny hadn't been mentioned Constantia immediately looked as though he had.

"He'll expect us to send him something of father's, of course. But it's so difficult to know what to send to Ceylon."

"You mean things get unstuck so on the voyage," murmured Constantia.

"No, lost," said Josephine sharply. "You know there's no post. Only runners."

Both paused to watch a black man in white linen drawers running through the pale fields for dear life, with a large brown-paper parcel in his hands. Josephine's black man was tiny; he scurried along glistening like an ant. But there was something blind and tireless about Constantia's tall, thin fellow, which made him, she decided, a very unpleasant person indeed. . . . On the veranda, dressed all in white and wearing a cork helmet, stood Benny. His right hand shook up and down, as father's did when he was impatient. And behind him, not in the least interested, sat Hilda, the unknown sister-in-law. She swung in a cane rocker and flicked over the leaves of the *Tatler*.

"I think his watch would be the most suitable present," said Josephine.

Constantia looked up; she seemed surprised.

"Oh, would you trust a gold watch to a native?"

"But of course I'd disguise it," said Josephine. "No one would know it was a watch." She liked the idea of having to make a parcel such a curious shape that no one could possibly guess what it was. She even thought for a moment of hiding the watch in a narrow cardboard corset-box that she'd kept by her for a long time, waiting for it to come in for something. It was such beautiful firm cardboard. But, no, it wouldn't be appropriate for this occasion. It had lettering on it: *Medium Women's 28. Extra Firm Busks.* It would be almost too much of a surprise for Benny to open that and find father's watch inside.

"And of course it isn't as though it would be going—ticking, I mean," said Constantia, who was still thinking of the native love of jewelry. "At least," she added, "it would be very strange if after all that time it was."

<h1 style="text-align:center">8</h1>

Josephine made no reply. She had flown off on one of her tangents. She had suddenly thought of Cyril. Wasn't it more usual for the only grandson to have the watch? And then dear Cyril was so appreciative, and a gold watch meant so much to a young man. Benny, in all probability, had quite got out of the habit of watches; men so seldom wore waistcoats in those hot climates. Whereas Cyril in London wore them from year's end to year's end. And it would be so nice for her and Constantia, when he came to tea, to know it was there. "I see you've got on grandfather's watch, Cyril." It would be somehow so satisfactory.

Dear boy! What a blow his sweet, sympathetic little note had been! Of course they quite understood; but it was most unfortunate.

"It would have been such a point, having him," said Josephine.

"And he would have enjoyed it so," said Constantia, not thinking what she was saying.

However, as soon as he got back he was coming to tea with his aunties. Cyril to tea was one of their rare treats.

"Now, Cyril, you mustn't be frightened of our cakes. Your Auntie Con and I bought them at Buszard's this morning. We know what a man's appetite is. So don't be ashamed of making a good tea."

Josephine cut recklessly into the rich dark cake that stood for her winter gloves or the soling and heeling of Constantia's only respectable shoes. But Cyril was most unmanlike in appetite.

"I say, Aunt Josephine, I simply can't. I've only just had lunch, you know."

"Oh, Cyril, that can't be true! It's after four," cried Josephine. Constantia sat with her knife poised over the chocolate-roll.

"It is, all the same," said Cyril. "I had to meet a man at Victoria,[1] and he kept me hanging about till . . . there was only time to get lunch and to come on here. And he gave me—phew"—Cyril put his hand to his forehead—"a terrific blowout," he said.

It was disappointing—today of all days. But still he couldn't be expected to know.

"But you'll have a meringue, won't you, Cyril?" said Aunt Josephine. "These meringues were bought specially for you. Your dear father was so fond of them. We were sure you are, too."

---

1. London railroad station, connecting with the Channel ports.

"I *am*, Aunt Josephine," cried Cyril ardently. "Do you mind if I take half to begin with?"

"Not at all, dear boy; but we mustn't let you off with that."

"Is your dear father still so fond of meringues?" asked Auntie Con gently. She winced faintly as she broke through the shell of hers.

"Well, I don't quite know, Auntie Con," said Cyril breezily.

At that they both looked up.

"Don't know?" almost snapped Josephine. "Don't know a thing like that about your own father, Cyril?"

"Surely," said Auntie Con softly.

Cyril tried to laugh it off. "Oh, well," he said, "it's such a long time since — He faltered. He stopped. Their faces were too much for him.

"Even *so*," said Josephine.

And Auntie Con looked.

Cyril put down his teacup. "Wait a bit," he cried. "Wait a bit, Aunt Josephine. What am I thinking of?"

He looked up. They were beginning to brighten. Cyril slapped his knee.

"Of course," he said, "it was meringues. How could I have forgotten? Yes, Aunt Josephine, you're perfectly right. Father's most frightfully keen on meringues."

They didn't only beam. Aunt Josephine went scarlet with pleasure; Auntie Con gave a deep, deep sigh.

"And now, Cyril, you must come and see father," said Josephine. "He knows you were coming today."

"Right," said Cyril, very firmly and heartily. He got up from his chair; suddenly he glanced at the clock.

"I say, Auntie Con, isn't your clock a bit slow? I've got to meet a man at — at Paddington[2] just after five. I'm afraid I shan't be able to stay very long with grandfather."

"Oh, he won't expect you to stay *very* long!" said Aunt Josephine.

Constantia was still gazing at the clock. She couldn't make up her mind if it was fast or slow. It was one or the other, she felt almost certain of that. At any rate, it had been.

Cyril still lingered. "Aren't you coming along, Auntie Con?"

"Of course," said Josephine, "we shall all go. Come on, Con."

<h2 style="text-align:center">9</h2>

They knocked at the door, and Cyril followed his aunts into grandfather's hot, sweetish room.

"Come on," said Grandfather Pinner. "Don't hang about. What is it? What've you been up to?"

He was sitting in front of a roaring fire, clasping his stick. He had a thick rug over his knees. On his lap there lay a beautiful pale yellow silk handkerchief.

"It's Cyril, father," said Josephine shyly. And she took Cyril's hand and led him forward.

"Good afternoon, grandfather," said Cyril, trying to take his hand out of Aunt Josephine's. Grandfather Pinner shot his eyes at Cyril in the way he was

---

2. London railroad station, serving the west of England and Wales.

famous for. Where was Auntie Con? She stood on the other side of Aunt Josephine; her long arms hung down in front of her; her hands were clasped. She never took her eyes off grandfather.

"Well," said Grandfather Pinner, beginning to thump, "what have you got to tell me?"

What had he, what had he got to tell him? Cyril felt himself smiling like a perfect imbecile. The room was stifling, too.

But Aunt Josephine came to his rescue. She cried brightly, "Cyril says his father is still very fond of meringues, father dear."

"Eh?" said Grandfather Pinner, curving his hand like a purple meringue-shell over one ear.

Josephine repeated, "Cyril says his father is still very fond of meringues."

"Can't hear," said old Colonel Pinner. And he waved Josephine away with his stick, then pointed with his stick to Cyril. "Tell me what she's trying to say," he said.

(My God!) "Must I?" said Cyril, blushing and staring at Aunt Josephine.

"Do, dear," she smiled. "It will please him so much."

"Come on, out with it!" cried Colonel Pinner testily, beginning to thump again.

And Cyril leaned forward and yelled, "Father's still very fond of meringues."

At that Grandfather Pinner jumped as though he had been shot.

"Don't shout!" he cried. "What's the matter with the boy? *Meringues!* What about 'em?"

"Oh, Aunt Josephine, must we go on?" groaned Cyril desperately.

"It's quite all right, dear boy," said Aunt Josephine, as though he and she were at the dentist's together. "He'll understand in a minute." And she whispered to Cyril, "He's getting a bit deaf, you know." Then she leaned forward and really bawled at Grandfather Pinner, "Cyril only wanted to tell you, father dear, that *his* father is still very fond of meringues."

Colonel Pinner heard that time, heard and brooded, looking Cyril up and down.

"What an esstrordinary thing!" said old Grandfather Pinner. "What an esstrordinary thing to come all this way here to tell me!"

And Cyril felt it *was.*

"Yes, I shall send Cyril the watch," said Josephine.

"That would be very nice," said Constantia. "I seem to remember last time he came there was some little trouble about the time."

10

They were interrupted by Kate bursting through the door in her usual fashion, as though she had discovered some secret panel in the wall.

"Fried or boiled?" asked the bold voice.

Fried or boiled? Josephine and Constantia were quite bewildered for the moment. They could hardly take it in.

"Fried or boiled what, Kate?" asked Josephine, trying to begin to concentrate.

Kate gave a loud sniff. "Fish."

"Well, why didn't you say so immediately?" Josephine reproached her gently. "How could you expect us to understand, Kate? There are a great many things in this world, you know, which are fried or boiled." And after such a display of courage she said quite brightly to Constantia. "Which do you prefer, Con?"

"I think it might be nice to have it fried," said Constantia. "On the other hand, of course boiled fish is very nice. I think I prefer both equally well . . . Unless you . . . In that case——"

"I shall fry it," said Kate, and she bounced back, leaving their door open and slamming the door of her kitchen.

Josephine gazed at Constantia; she raised her pale eyebrows until they rippled away into her pale hair. She got up. She said in a very lofty, imposing way, "Do you mind following me me into the drawing room, Constantia? I've something of great importance to discuss with you."

For it was always to the drawing room they retired when they wanted to talk over Kate.

Josephine closed the door meaningly. "Sit down, Constantia," she said, still very grand. She might have been receiving Constantia for the first time. And Con looked round vaguely for a chair, as though she felt indeed quite a stranger.

"Now the question is," said Josephine, bending forward, "whether we shall keep her or not."

"That is the question," agreed Constantia.

"And this time," said Josephine firmly, "we must come to a definite decision."

Constantia looked for a moment as though she might begin going over all the other times, but she pulled herself together and said, "Yes, Jug."

"You see, Con," explained Josephine, "everything is so changed now." Constantia looked up quickly. "I mean," went on Josephine, "we're not dependent on Kate as we were." And she blushed faintly. "There's not father to cook for."

"That is perfectly true," agreed Constantia. "Father certainly doesn't want any cooking now, whatever else——"

Josephine broke in sharply. "You're not sleepy, are you, Con?"

"Sleepy, Jug?" Constantia was wide-eyed.

"Well, concentrate more," said Josephine sharply, and she returned to the subject. "What it comes to is, if we did"—and this she barely breathed, glancing at the door—"give Kate notice"—she raised her voice again—"we could manage our own food."

"Why not?" cried Constantia. She couldn't help smiling. The idea was so exciting. She clasped her hands. "What should we live on, Jug?"

"Oh, eggs in various forms!" said Jug, lofty again. "And, besides, there are all the cooked foods."

"But I've always heard," said Constantia, "they are considered so very expensive."

"Not if one buys them in moderation," said Josephine. But she tore herself away from this fascinating bypath and dragged Constantia after her.

"What we've got to decide now, however, is whether we really do trust Kate or not."

Constantia leaned back. Her flat little laugh flew from her lips.

"Isn't it curious, Jug," said she, "that just on this one subject I've never been able to quite make up my mind?"

11

She never had. The whole difficulty was to prove anything. How did one prove things, how could one? Suppose Kate had stood in front of her and deliberately made a face. Mightn't she very well have been in pain? Wasn't it impossible, at any rate, to ask Kate if she was making a face at her? If Kate answered "No"—and of course she would say "No"—what a position! How undignified! Then again Constantia suspected, she was almost certain that Kate went to her chest of drawers when she and Josephine were out, not to take things but to spy. Many times she had come back to find her amethyst cross in the most unlikely places, under her lace ties or on top of her evening bertha.[3] More than once she had laid a trap for Kate. She had arranged things in a special order and then called Josephine to witness.

"You see, Jug?"

"Quite, Con."

"Now we shall be able to tell."

But, oh dear, when she did go to look, she was as far off from a proof as ever! If anything was displaced, it might so very well have happened as she closed the drawer; a jolt might have done it so easily.

"You come, Jug, and decide. I really can't. It's too difficult."

But after a pause and a long glare Josephine would sigh. "Now you've put the doubt into my mind, Con, I'm sure I can't tell myself."

"Well, we can't postpone it again," said Josephine. "If we postpone it this time—"

But at that moment in the street below a barrel organ struck up. Josephine and Constantia sprang to their feet together.

"Run, Con," said Josephine. "Run quickly. There's sixpence on the—"

Then they remembered. It didn't matter. They would never have to stop the organ-grinder again. Never again would she and Constantia be told to make that monkey take his noise somewhere else. Never would sound that loud, strange bellow when father thought they were not hurrying enough. The organ-grinder might play there all day and the stick would not thump.

> *It never will thump again,*
> *It never will thump again,*

played the barrel-organ.

What was Constantia thinking? She had such a strange smile; she looked different. She couldn't be going to cry.

"Jug, Jug," said Constantia softly, pressing her hands together. "Do you know what day it is? It's Saturday. It's a week today, a whole week."

> *A week since father died,*
> *A week since father died,*

cried the barrel organ. And Josephine, too, forgot to be practical and sensible; she smiled faintly, strangely. On the Indian carpet there fell a square of sunlight, pale red; it came and went and came—and stayed, deepened—until it shone almost golden.

---

3. Detachable lace collar for low-necked dresses.

"The sun's out," said Josephine, as though it really mattered.

A perfect fountain of bubbling notes shook from the barrel organ, round, bright notes, carelessly scattered.

Constantia lifted her big, cold hands as if to catch them, and then her hands fell again. She walked over to the mantelpiece to her favorite Buddha. And the stone and gilt image, whose smile always gave her such a queer feeling, almost a pain and yet a pleasant pain, seemed today to be more than smiling. He knew something; he had a secret. "I know something that you don't know," said her Buddha. Oh, what was it, what could it be? And yet she had always felt there was . . . something.

The sunlight pressed through the windows, thieved its way in, flashed its light over the furniture and the photographs. Josephine watched it. When it came to mother's photograph, the enlargement over the piano, it lingered as though puzzled to find so little remained of mother, except the earrings shaped like tiny pagodas and a black feather boa. Why did the photographs of dead people always fade so? wondered Josephine. As soon as a person was dead their photograph died too. But, of course, this one of mother was very old. It was thirty-five years old. Josephine remembered standing on a chair and pointing out that feather boa to Constantia and telling her that it was a snake that had killed their mother in Ceylon. . . . Would everything have been different if mother hadn't died? She didn't see why. Aunt Florence had lived with them until they had left school, and they had moved three times and had their yearly holiday and . . . and there'd been changes of servants, of course.

Some little sparrows, young sparrows they sounded, chirped on the window ledge. *Yeep—eyeep—yeep.* But Josephine felt they were not sparrows, not on the window ledge. It was inside her, that queer little crying noise. *Yeep— eyeep—yeep.* Ah, what was it crying, so weak and forlorn?

If mother had lived, might they have married? But there had been nobody for them to marry. There had been father's Anglo-Indian friends before he quarreled with them. But after that she and Constantia never met a single man except clergymen. How did one meet men? Or even if they'd met them, how could they have got to know men well enough to be more than strangers? One read of people having adventures, being followed, and so on. But nobody had ever followed Constantia and her. Oh yes, there had been one year at Eastbourne[4] a mysterious man at their boarding-house who had put a note on the jug of hot water outside their bedroom door! But by the time Connie had found it the steam had made the writing too faint to read; they couldn't even make out to which of them it was addressed. And he had left next day. And that was all. The rest had been looking after father, and at the same time keeping out of father's way. But now? But now? The thieving sun touched Josephine gently. She lifted her face. She was drawn over to the window by gentle beams. . . .

Until the barrel organ stopped playing Constantia stayed before the Buddha, wondering, but not as usual, not vaguely. This time her wonder was like longing. She remembered the times she had come in here, crept out of bed in her nightgown when the moon was full, and lain on the floor with her arms outstretched, as though she was crucified. Why? The big, pale moon had made her do it. The horrible dancing figures on the carved screen had leered

---

4. Seaside resort on Sussex coast.

at her and she hadn't minded. She remembered too how, whenever they were at the seaside, she had gone off by herself and got as close to the sea as she could, and sung something, something she had made up, while she gazed all over that restless water. There had been this other life, running out, bringing things home in bags, getting things on approval, discussing them with Jug, and taking them back to get more things on approval, and arranging father's trays and trying not to annoy father. But it all seemed to have happened in a kind of tunnel. It wasn't real. It was only when she came out of the tunnel into the moonlight or by the sea or into a thunderstorm that she really felt herself. What did it mean? What was it she was always wanting? What did it all lead to? Now? Now?

She turned away from the Buddha with one of her vague gestures. She went over to where Josephine was standing. She wanted to say something to Josephine, something frightfully important, about—about the future and what . . .

"Don't you think perhaps—" she began.

But Josephine interrupted her. "I was wondering if now——" she murmured. They stopped; they waited for each either.

"Go on, Con," said Josephine.

"No, no, Jug; after you," said Constantia.

"No, say what you were going to say. You began," said Josephine.

"I . . . I'd rather hear what you were going to say first," said Constantia.

"Don't be absurd, Con."

"Really, Jug."

"Connie!"

"Oh, Jug!"

A pause. Then Constantia said faintly, "I can't say what I was going to say, Jug, because I've forgotten what it was . . . that I was going to say."

Josephine was silent for a moment. She stared at a big cloud where the sun had been. Then she replied shortly, "I've forgotten too."

1920   1922

The Garden-Party

And after all the weather was ideal. They could not have had a more perfect day for a garden-party if they had ordered it. Windless, warm, the sky without a cloud. Only the blue was veiled with a haze of light gold, as it is sometimes in early summer. The gardener had been up since dawn, mowing the lawns and sweeping them, until the grass and the dark flat rosettes where the daisy plants had been seemed to shine. As for the roses, you could not help feeling they understood that roses are the only flowers that impress people at garden-parties; the only flowers that everybody is certain of knowing. Hundreds, yes, literally hundreds, had come out in a single night; the green bushes bowed down as though they had been visited by archangels.

Breakfast was not yet over before the men came to put up the marquee.

"Where do you want the marquee put, mother?"

"My dear child, it's no use asking me. I'm determined to leave everything to you children this year. Forget I am your mother. Treat me as an honored guest."

But Meg could not possibly go and supervise the men. She had washed her hair before breakfast, and she sat drinking her coffee in a green turban, with a dark wet curl stamped on each cheek. Jose, the butterfly, always came down in a silk petticoat and a kimono jacket.

"You'll have to go, Laura; you're the artistic one."

Away Laura flew, still holding her piece of bread-and-butter. It's so delicious to have an excuse for eating out of doors, and besides, she loved having to arrange things; she always felt she could do it so much better than anybody else.

Four men in their shirt-sleeves stood grouped together on the garden path. They carried staves covered with rolls of canvas, and they had big tool-bags slung on their backs. They looked impressive. Laura wished now that she had not got the bread-and-butter, but there was nowhere to put it, and she couldn't possibly throw it away. She blushed and tried to look severe and even a little bit short-sighted as she came up to them.

"Good morning," she said, copying her mother's voice. But that sounded so fearfully affected that she was ashamed, and stammered like a little girl, "Oh—er—have you come—is it about the marquee?"

"That's right, miss," said the tallest of the men, a lanky, freckled fellow, and he shifted his tool-bag, knocked back his straw hat and smiled down at her. "That's about it."

His smile was so easy, so friendly that Laura recovered. What nice eyes he had, small, but such a dark blue! And now she looked at the others, they were smiling too. "Cheer up, we won't bite," their smile seemed to say. How very nice workmen were! And what a beautiful morning! she mustn't mention the morning; she must be businesslike. The marquee.

"Well, what about the lily-lawn? Would that do?"

And she pointed to the lily-lawn with the hand that didn't hold the bread-and-butter. They turned, they stared in the direction. A little fat chap thrust out his under-lip, and the tall fellow frowned.

"I don't fancy it," said he. "Not conspicuous enough. You see, with a thing like a marquee," and he turned to Laura in his easy way, "you want to put it somewhere where it'll give you a bang slap in the eye, if you follow me."

Laura's upbringing made her wonder for a moment whether it was quite respectful of a workman to talk to her of bangs slap in the eye. But she did quite follow him.

"A corner of the tennis-court," she suggested. "But the band's going to be in one corner."

"H'm, going to have a band, are you?" said another of the workmen. He was pale. He had a haggard look as his dark eyes scanned the tennis-court. What was he thinking?

"Only a very small band," said Laura gently. Perhaps he wouldn't mind so much if the band was quite small. But the tall fellow interrupted.

"Look here, miss, that's the place. Against those trees. Over there. That'll do fine."

Against the karakas. Then the karaka-trees would be hidden. And they were so lovely, with their broad, gleaming leaves, and their clusters of yellow fruit. They were like trees you imagined growing on a desert island, proud, solitary, lifting their leaves and fruits to the sun in a kind of silent splendor. Must they be hidden by a marquee?

They must. Already the men had shouldered their staves and were making for the place. Only the tall fellow was left. He bent down, pinched a sprig of lavender, put his thumb and forefinger to his nose and snuffed up the smell. When Laura saw that gesture she forgot all about the karakas in her wonder at him caring for things like that—caring for the smell of lavender. How many men that she knew would have done such a thing? Oh, how extraordinarily nice workmen were, she thought. Why couldn't she have workmen for friends rather than the silly boys she danced with and who came to Sunday night supper? She would get on much better with men like these.

It's all the fault, she decided, as the tall fellow drew something on the back of an envelope, something that was to be looped up or left to hang, of these absurd class distinctions. Well, for her part, she didn't feel them. Not a bit, not an atom. . . . And now there came the chock-chock of wooden hammers. Some one whistled, some one sang out, "Are you right there, matey?" "Matey!" The friendliness of it, the—the—Just to prove how happy she was, just to show the tall fellow how at home she felt, and how she despised stupid conventions, Laura took a big bite of her bread-and-butter as she stared at the little drawing. She felt just like a work-girl.

"Laura, Laura, where are you? Telephone, Laura!" a voice cried from the house.

"Coming!" Away she skimmed, over the lawn, up the path, up the steps, across the veranda, and into the porch. In the hall her father and Laurie were brushing their hats ready to go to the office.

"I say, Laura," said Laurie very fast, "you might just give a squiz at my coat before this afternoon. See if it wants pressing."

"I will," said she. Suddenly she couldn't stop herself. She ran at Laurie and gave him a small, quick squeeze. "Oh, I do love parties, don't you?" gasped Laura.

"Ra-ther," said Laurie's warm, boyish voice, and he squeezed his sister too, and gave her a gentle push. "Dash off to the telephone, old girl."

The telephone. "Yes, yes; oh yes. Kitty? Good morning, dear. Come to lunch? Do, dear. Delighted of course. It will only be a very scratch meal— just the sandwich crusts and broken meringue-shells and what's left over. Yes, isn't it a perfect morning? Your white? Oh, I certainly should. One moment— hold the line. Mother's calling." And Laura sat back. "What, mother? Can't hear."

Mrs. Sheridan's voice floated down the stairs. "Tell her to wear that sweet hat she had on last Sunday."

"Mother says you're to wear that *sweet* hat you had on last Sunday. Good. One o'clock. Bye-bye."

Laura put back the receiver, flung her arms over her head, took a deep breath, stretched and let them fall. "Huh," she sighed, and the moment after the sigh she sat up quickly. She was still, listening. All the doors in the house seemed to be open. The house was alive with soft, quick steps and running voices. The green baize door that led to the kitchen regions swung open and shut with a muffled thud. And now there came a long, chuckling absurd sound. It was the heavy piano being moved on its stiff castors. But the air! If you stopped to notice, was the air always like this? Little faint winds were playing chase, in at the tops of the windows, out at the doors. And there were two tiny spots of sun, one on the inkpot, one on a silver photograph frame, playing too. Darling little spots. Especially the one on the inkpot lid. It was quite warm. A warm little silver star. She could have kissed it.

The front door bell pealed, and there sounded the rustle of Sadie's print skirt on the stairs. A man's voice murmured; Sadie answered, careless, "I'm sure I don't know. Wait. I'll ask Mrs. Sheridan."

"What is it, Sadie?" Laura came into the hall.

"It's the florist, Miss Laura."

It was, indeed. There, just inside the door, stood a wide, shallow tray full of pots of pink lilies. No other kind. Nothing but lilies—canna lilies, big pink flowers, wide open, radiant, almost frighteningly alive on bright crimson stems.

"O-oh, Sadie!" said Laura, and the sound was like a little moan. She crouched down as if to warm herself at that blaze of lilies; she felt they were in her fingers, on her lips, growing in her breast.

"It's some mistake," she said faintly. "Nobody ever ordered so many. Sadie, go and find mother."

But at that moment Mrs. Sheridan joined them.

"It's quite right," she said calmly. "Yes, I ordered them. Aren't they lovely?" She pressed Laura's arm. "I was passing the shop yesterday, and I saw them in the window. And I suddenly thought for once in my life I shall have enough canna lilies. The garden-party will be a good excuse."

"But I thought you said you didn't mean to interfere," said Laura. Sadie had gone. The florist's man was still outside at his van. She put her arm round her mother's neck and gently, very gently, she bit her mother's ear.

"My darling child, you wouldn't like a logical mother, would you? Don't do that. Here's the man."

He carried more lilies still, another whole tray.

"Bank them up, just inside the door, on both sides of the porch, please," said Mrs. Sheridan. "Don't you agree, Laura?"

"Oh, I *do* mother."

In the drawing-room Meg, Jose and good little Hans had at last succeeded in moving the piano.

"Now, if we put this chesterfield against the wall and move everything out of the room except the chairs, don't you think?"

"Quite."

"Hans, move these tables into the smoking-room, and bring a sweeper to take these marks off the carpet and—one moment, Hans—" Jose loved giving orders to the servants, and they loved obeying her. She always made them feel they were taking part in some drama. "Tell mother and Miss Laura to come here at once."

"Very good, Miss Jose."

She turned to Meg. "I want to hear what the piano sounds like, just in case I'm asked to sing this afternoon. Let's try over 'This life is Weary.'"

Pom! Ta-ta-ta *Tee*-ta! The piano burst out so passionately that Jose's face changed. She clasped her hands. She looked mournfully and enigmatically at her mother and Laura as they came in.

> This Life is *Wee*-ary,
> A Tear—a Sigh.
> A Love that *Chan*-ges,

> This Life is *Wee*-ary,
> A Tear—a Sigh.
> A Love that *Chan*-ges,
> And then . . . Good-bye!

But at the word "Good-bye," and although the piano sounded more desperate than ever, her face broke into a brilliant, dreadfully unsympathetic smile.

"Aren't I in good voice, mummy?" she beamed.

> This Life is *Wee*-ary,
> Hope comes to Die.
> A Dream—a *Wa*-kening.

But now Sadie interrupted them. "What is it, Sadie?"

"If you please, m'm, cook says have you got the flags[1] for the sandwiches?"

"The flags for the sandwiches, Sadie?" echoed Mrs. Sheridan dreamily. And the children knew by her face that she hadn't got them. "Let me see." And she said to Sadie firmly, "Tell cook I'll let her have them in ten minutes."

Sadie went.

"Now, Laura," said her mother quickly. "Come with me into the smoking-room. I've got the names[2] somewhere on the back of an envelope. You'll have to write them out for me. Meg, go upstairs this minute and take that wet thing off your head. Jose, run and finish dressing this instant. Do you hear me, children, or shall I have to tell your father when he comes home to-night? And—and, Jose, pacify cook if you do go into the kitchen, will you? I'm terrified of her this morning."

The envelope was found at last behind the dining-room clock, though how it had got there Mrs. Sheridan could not imagine.

"One of you children must have stolen it out of my bag, because I remember vividly—cream cheese and lemon-curd. Have you done that?"

"Yes."

"Egg and—" Mrs. Sheridan held the envelope away from her. "It looks like mice. It can't be mice, can it?"

"Olive, pet," said Laura, looking over her shoulder.

"Yes, of course, olive. What a horrible combination it sounds. Egg and olive."

They were finished at last, and Laura took them off to the kitchen. She found Jose there pacifying the cook, who did not look at all terrifying.

"I have never seen such exquisite sandwiches," said Jose's rapturous voice. "How many kinds did you say there were, cook? Fifteen?"

"Fifteen, Miss Jose."

"Well, cook, I congratulate you."

Cook swept up crusts with the long sandwich knife, and smiled broadly.

"Godber's has come," announced Sadie, issuing out of the pantry. She had seen the man pass the window.

That meant the cream puffs had come. Godber's were famous for their cream puffs. Nobody ever thought of making them at home.

"Bring them in and put them on the table, my girl," ordered cook.

---

1. Little paper flags stuck in a plate of small triangular sandwiches indicating what is inside the sandwiches on each plate—an English custom adopted by the

New Zealand middle class as a sign of gentility.
2. I.e., the names of the sandwich fillings to be written on each flag.

Sadie brought them in and went back to the door. Of course Laura and Jose were far too grown-up to really care about such things. All the same, they couldn't help agreeing that the puffs looked very attractive. Very. Cook began arranging them, shaking off the extra icing sugar.

"Don't they carry one back to all one's parties?" said Laura.

"I suppose they do," said practical Jose, who never liked to be carried back. "They look beautifully light and feathery, I must say."

"Have one each, my dears," said cook in her comfortable voice. "Yer ma won't know."

Oh, impossible. Fancy cream puffs so soon after breakfast. The very idea made one shudder. All the same, two minutes later Jose and Laura were licking their fingers with that absorbed inward look that only comes from whipped cream.

"Let's go into the garden, out by the back way," suggested Laura. "I want to see how the men are getting on with the marquee. They're such awfully nice men."

But the back door was blocked by cook, Sadie, Godber's man and Hans.

Something had happened.

"Tuk-tuk-tuk," clucked cook like an agitated hen. Sadie had her hand clapped to her cheek as though she had toothache. Hans's face was screwed up in the effort to understand. Only Godber's man seemed to be enjoying himself; it was his story.

"What's the matter? What's happened?"

"There's been a horrible accident," said Cook. "A man killed."

"A man killed! Where? How? When?"

But Godber's man wasn't going to have his story snatched from under his very nose.

"Know those little cottages just below here, miss?" Know them? Of course, she knew them. "Well, there's a young chap living there, name of Scott, a carter. His horse shied at a traction-engine, corner of Hawke Street this morning, and he was thrown out on the back of his head. Killed."

"Dead!" Laura stared at Godber's man.

"Dead when they picked him up," said Godber's man with relish. "They were taking the body home as I come up here." And he said to the cook, "He's left a wife and five little ones."

"Jose, come here." Laura caught hold of her sister's sleeve and dragged her through the kitchen to the other side of the green baize door. There she paused and leaned against it. "Jose!" she said, horrified, "however are we going to stop everything?"

"Stop everything, Laura!" cried Jose in astonishment. "What do you mean?"

"Stop the garden-party, of course." Why did Jose pretend?

But Jose was still more amazed. "Stop the garden-party? My dear Laura, don't be so absurd. Of course we can't do anything of the kind. Nobody expects us to. Don't be so extravagant."

"But we can't possibly have a garden-party with a man dead just outside the front gate."

That really was extravagant, for the little cottages were in a lane to themselves at the very bottom of a steep rise that led up to the house. A broad road ran between. True, they were far too near. They were the greatest possible eyesore, and they had no right to be in that neighborhood at all. They were little mean dwellings painted a chocolate brown. In the garden patches there was nothing but cabbage stalks, sick hens and tomato cans. The very smoke coming out of their chimneys was poverty-stricken. Little rags and shreds of smoke, so unlike the great silvery plumes that uncurled from the Sheridans' chimneys. Washerwomen lived in the lane and sweeps and a cobbler, and a man whose house-front was studded all over with minute bird-cages. Children swarmed. When the Sheridans were little they were forbidden to set foot there because of the revolting language and of what they might catch. But since they were grown up, Laura and Laurie on their prowls sometimes walked through. It was disgusting and sordid. They came out with a shudder. But still one must go everywhere; one must see everything. So through they went.

"And just think of what the band would sound like to that poor woman," said Laura.

"Oh, Laura!" Jose began to be seriously annoyed. "If you're going to stop a band playing every time some one has an accident, you'll lead a very strenuous life. I'm every bit as sorry about it as you. I feel just as sympathetic." Her eyes hardened. She looked at her sister just as she used to when they were little and fighting together. "You won't bring a drunken workman back to life by being sentimental," she said softly.

"Drunk! Who said he was drunk?" Laura turned furiously on Jose. She said, just as they had used to say on those occasions, "I'm going straight up to tell mother."

"Do, dear," cooed Jose.

"Mother, can I come into your room?" Laura turned the big glass doorknob.

"Of course, child. Why, what's the matter? What's given you such a color?" And Mrs. Sheridan turned round from her dressing-table. She was trying on a new hat.

"Mother, a man's been killed," began Laura.

"Not in the garden?" interrupted her mother.

"No, no!"

"Oh, what a fright you gave me!" Mrs. Sheridan sighed with relief, and took off the big hat and held it on her knees.

"But listen, mother," said Laura. Breathless, half-choking, she told the dreadful story. "Of course, we can't have our party, can we?" she pleaded. "The band and everybody arriving. They'd hear us, mother; they're nearly neighbors!"

To Laura's astonishment her mother behaved just like Jose, it was harder to bear because she seemed amused. She refused to take Laura seriously.

"But, my dear child, use your common sense. It's only by accident we've heard of it. If some one had died there normally—and I can't understand how they keep alive in those poky little holes—we should still be having our party, shouldn't we?"

Laura had to say "yes" to that, but she felt it was all wrong. She sat down on her mother's sofa and pinched the cushion frill.

"Mother, isn't it really terribly heartless of us?" she asked.

"Darling!" Mrs. Sheridan got up and came over to her, carrying the hat. Before Laura could stop her she had popped it on. "My child!" said her mother, "the hat is yours. It's made for you. It's much too young for me. I have never seen you look such a picture. Look at yourself!" And she held up her hand-mirror.

"But, mother," Laura began again. She couldn't look at herself; she turned aside.

This time Mrs. Sheridan lost patience just as Jose had done.

"You are being very absurd, Laura," she said coldly. "People like that don't expect sacrifices from us. And it's not very sympathetic to spoil everybody's enjoyment as you're doing now."

"I don't understand," said Laura, and she walked quickly out of the room into her own bedroom. There, quite by chance, the first thing she saw was this charming girl in the mirror, in her black hat trimmed with gold daisies, and a long black velvet ribbon. Never had she imagined she could look like that. Is mother right? she thought. And now she hoped her mother was right. Am I being extravagant? Perhaps it was extravagant. Just for a moment she had another glimpse of that poor woman and those little children, and the body being carried into the house. But it all seemed blurred, unreal, like a picture in the newspaper. I'll remember it again after the party's over, she decided. And somehow that seemed quite the best plan. . . .

Lunch was over by half-past one. By half-past two they were all ready for the fray. The green-coated band had arrived and was established in a corner of the tennis-court.

"My dear!" trilled Kitty Maitland, "aren't they too like frogs for words? You ought to have arranged them round the pond with the conductor in the middle on a leaf."

Laurie arrived and hailed them on his way to dress. At the sight of him Laura remembered the accident again. She wanted to tell him. If Laurie agreed with the others, then it was bound to be all right. And she followed him into the hall.

"Laurie!"

"Hallo!" He was half-way upstairs, but when he turned round and saw Laura he suddenly puffed out his cheeks and goggled his eyes at her. "My word, Laura; you do look stunning," said Laurie. "What an absolutely topping hat!"

Laura said faintly "Is it?" and smiled up at Laurie, and didn't tell him after all.

Soon after that people began coming in streams. The band struck up; the hired waiters ran from the house to the marquee. Wherever you looked there were couples strolling, bending to the flowers, greeting, moving on over the lawn. They were like bright birds that had alighted in the Sheridans' garden for this one afternoon, on their way to—where? Ah, what happiness it is to be with people who all are happy, to press hands, press cheeks, smile into eyes.

"Darling Laura, how well you look!"

"What a becoming hat, child!"

"Laura, you look quite Spanish. I've never seen you look so striking."

And Laura, glowing, answered softly, "Have you had tea? Won't you have an ice? The passion-fruit ices really are rather special." She ran to her father and begged him. "Daddy darling, can't the band have something to drink?"

And the perfect afternoon slowly ripened, slowly faded, slowly its petals closed.

"Never a more delightful garden-party . . ." "The greatest success . . ." "Quite the most . . ."

Laura helped her mother with the good-byes. They stood side by side in the porch till it was all over.

"All over, all over, thank heaven," said Mrs. Sheridan. "Round up the others, Laura. Let's go and have some fresh coffee. I'm exhausted. Yes, it's been very successful. But oh, these parties, these parties! Why will you children insist on giving parties!" And they all of them sat down in the deserted marquee.

"Have a sandwich, daddy dear. I wrote the flag."

"Thanks." Mr. Sheridan took a bite and the sandwich was gone. He took another. "I suppose you didn't hear of a beastly accident that happened to-day?" he said.

"My dear," said Mrs. Sheridan, holding up her hand, "we did. It nearly ruined the party. Laura insisted we should put it off."

"Oh, mother!" Laura didn't want to be teased about it.

"It was a horrible affair all the same," said Mr. Sheridan. "The chap was married too. Lived just below in the lane, and leaves a wife and half a dozen kiddies, so they say."

An awkward little silence fell. Mrs. Sheridan fidgeted with her cup. Really, it was very tactless of father . . .

Suddenly she looked up. There on the table were all those sandwiches, cakes, puffs, all uneaten, all going to be wasted. She had one of her brilliant ideas.

"I know," she said. "Let's make up a basket. Let's send that poor creature some of this perfectly good food. At any rate, it will be the greatest treat for the children. Don't you agree? And she's sure to have neighbors calling in and so on. What a point to have it all ready prepared. Laura!" She jumped up. "Get me the big basket out of the stairs cupboard."

"But, mother, do you really think it's a good idea?" said Laura.

Again, how curious, she seemed to be different from them all. To take scraps from their party. Would the poor woman really like that?

"Of course! What's the matter with you to-day? An hour or two ago you were insisting on us being sympathetic, and now—"

Oh, well! Laura ran for the basket. It was filled, it was heaped by her mother.

"Take it yourself, darling," said she. "Run down just as you are. No, wait, take the arum lilies too. People of that class are so impressed by arum lilies."

"The stems will ruin her lace frock," said practical Jose.

So they would. Just in time. "Only the basket, then. And, Laura!"—her mother followed her out of the marquee—"don't on any account—"

"What, mother?"

No, better not put such ideas into the child's head! "Nothing! Run along."

It was just growing dusky as Laura shut their garden gates. A big dog ran by like a shadow. The road gleamed white, and down below in the hollow the little cottages were in deep shade. How quiet it seemed after the afternoon. Here she was going down the hill to somewhere where a man lay dead, and she couldn't realize it. Why couldn't she? She stopped a minute. And it seemed to her that kisses, voices, tinkling spoons, laughter, the smell of crushed grass were somehow inside her. She had no room for anything else.

How strange! She looked up at the pale sky, and all she thought was, "Yes, it was the most successful party."

Now the broad road was crossed. The lane began, smoky and dark. Women in shawls and men's tweed caps hurried by. Men hung over the palings; the children played in the doorways. A low hum came from the mean little cottages. In some of them there was a flicker of light, and a shadow, crab-like, moved across the window. Laura bent her head and hurried on. She wished now she had put on a coat. How her frock shone! And the big hat with the velvet streamer—if only it was another hat! Were the people looking at her? They must be. It was a mistake to have come; she knew all along it was a mistake. Should she go back even now?

No, too late. This was the house. It must be. A dark knot of people stood outside. Beside the gate an old, old woman with a crutch sat in a chair, watching. She had her feet on a newspaper. The voices stopped as Laura drew near. The group parted. It was as though she was expected, as though they had known she was coming here.

Laura was terribly nervous. Tossing the velvet ribbon over her shoulder, she said to a woman standing by, "Is this Mrs. Scott's house?" and the woman, smiling queerly, said, "It is, my lass."

Oh, to be away from this! She actually said, "Help me, God," as she walked up the tiny path and knocked. To be away from those staring eyes, or to be covered up in anything, one of those women's shawls even. I'll just leave the basket and go, she decided. I shan't even wait for it to be emptied.

Then the door opened. A little woman in black showed in the gloom.

Laura said, "Are you Mrs. Scott?" But to her horror the woman answered, "Walk in please, miss," and she was shut in the passage.

"No," said Laura, "I don't want to come in. I only want to leave this basket. Mother sent—"

The little woman in the gloomy passage seemed not to have heard her. "Step this way, please, miss," she said in an oily voice, and Laura followed her.

She found herself in a wretched little low kitchen, lighted by a smoky lamp. There was a woman sitting before the fire.

"Em," said the little creature who had let her in. "Em! It's a young lady." She turned to Laura. She said meaningly, "I'm 'er sister, Miss. You'll excuse 'er, won't you?"

"Oh, but of course!" said Laura. "Please, please don't disturb her. I—I only want to leave—"

But at that moment the woman at the fire turned round. Her face, puffed up, red, with swollen eyes and swollen lips, looked terrible. She seemed as though she couldn't understand why Laura was there. What did it mean? Why was this stranger standing in the kitchen with a basket? What was it all about? And the poor face puckered up again.

"All right, my dear," said the other. "I'll thenk the young lady."

And again she began, "You'll excuse her, miss, I'm sure," and her face, swollen too, tried an oily smile.

Laura only wanted to get out, to get away. She was back in the passage. The door opened. She walked straight through into the bedroom, where the dead man was lying.

"You'd like a look at 'im, wouldn't you?" said Em's sister, and she brushed
past Laura over to the bed. "Don't be afraid, my lass—" and now her voice
sounded fond and sly, and fondly she drew down the sheet—" 'e looks a picture. There's nothing to show. Come along, my dear."

Laura came.

There lay a young man, fast asleep—sleeping so soundly, so deeply, that he
was far, far away from them both. Oh, so remote, so peaceful. He was dreaming. Never wake him up again. His head was sunk in the pillow, his eyes were
closed; they were blind under the closed eyelids. He was given up to his
dream. What did garden-parties and baskets and lace frocks matter to him?
He was far from all those things. He was wonderful, beautiful. While they
were laughing and while the band was playing, this marvel had come to the
lane. Happy . . . happy. . . . All is well, said that sleeping face. This is just as it
should be. I am content.

But all the same you had to cry, and she couldn't go out of the room without
saying something to him. Laura gave a loud childish sob.

"Forgive my hat," she said.

And this time she didn't wait for Em's sister. She found her way out of the
door, down the path, past all those dark people. At the corner of the lane she
met Laurie.

He stepped out of the shadow. "Is that you, Laura?"

"Yes."

"Mother was getting anxious. Was it all right?"

"Yes, quite. Oh, Laurie!" She took his arm, she pressed up against him.

"I say, you're not crying, are you?" asked her brother.

Laura shook her head. She was.

Laurie put his arm round her shoulder. "Don't cry," he said in his warm,
loving voice. "Was it awful?"

"No," sobbed Laura. "It was simply marvellous. But, Laurie—" She
stopped, she looked at her brother. "Isn't life," she stammered, "isn't life—"
But what life was she couldn't explain. No matter. He quite understood.

"*Isn't* it, darling?" said Laurie.

1921   1922

SAMUEL BECKETT
1906–1989

1937:   Moved to Paris.
1952:   *Waiting for Godot.*
1969:   Nobel Prize.

Samuel Beckett, born near Dublin, took a degree at Trinity College (Dublin's
Protestant university) but then went abroad and settled for good in Paris in 1937, at
first teaching in French *lycées* and serving occasionally as James Joyce's secretary,
translator, and critical defender—but mostly writing. From the mid-1940s, he generally wrote in French as a first tongue and then sometimes translated his French

into an eloquent, Irish-tinged English. Shortly after the war, he published three interrelated novels: *Molloy, Malone Dies,* and *The Unnamable.* They may well be thought his masterpiece some day, but Beckett's first major public recognition came as a result of a somber, static, and hilarious stage-vaudeville titled *Waiting for Godot.* The play is simplicity itself. Vladimir and Estragon, a pair of derelicts, are waiting in a bleak place for Godot, who tantalizes them by promising to come but never doing so. They talk, they complain, they try to kill time; the play ends with them still waiting. It is a play without plot or intrigue, which uses brilliantly the idea of nothing happening on stage, the vacancy experienced when something is expected but never found. It is a despairing and funny play. In 1958, *Endgame,* even more despairing and just as funny, repeated the success of *Godot,* and despite predictions that each grotesque, hilarious work would be his last, Beckett continued into old age vigorously active in fiction, in drama for stage and radio, in mime, and in film. In 1969 he received the Nobel Prize for literature.

His work is always stripped, severe, grotesquely comic, and haunted by the theme of nonexistence. He seeks to represent the mind purified down to its last bitter, almost unbearably pure negation—and kept alive simply by the force of that negation. From René Descartes, the seventeenth-century French thinker, and his follower Arnold Geulincx, Beckett took over premises regarding the separation of body and mind that led him to represent, almost uniformly throughout his work, mind under the compulsion of questioning itself. Fastened to a dying animal, as Yeats said, the mind of a Beckett character seeks constantly to reassure itself of its own existence by developing a brilliant, sterile dialectic of its own. The old scarecrows and crones that animate what a clever undergraduate once called Beckett's "crucifictions" live in a disgusting world and are themselves disintegrating. They all have stories to tell, and as long as they can keep talking, can keep some sort of empty verbal game going, they need not despair of their being. But any sort of comfort or security beyond the absolute minimum eludes them. They take no action, they preach no doctrine, they know nothing save their own ignorance, they are kicked and cuffed by society, they stink, they sulk, they snarl at their own disgusting condition. And yet in some dark way, they represent humankind, "without the courage to end or the strength to go on"—as the narrator of *The End* describes himself. Whether clinging to hopelessness as their one hope or to love on the edge of the grave, they bear witness, as more comfortable folk could not, to the essential holiness of existence.

Endgame[1]

For Roger Blin

Characters

NAGG
NELL
HAMM
CLOV

Bare interior.
Gray light.
Left and right back, high up, two small windows, curtains drawn.
Front right, a door. Hanging near door, its face to wall, a picture.

---

1. Translated by the author.

Front left, touching each other, covered with an old sheet, two ashbins. Center, in an armchair on castors, covered with an old sheet, HAMM. *Motionless by the door, his eyes fixed on* HAMM, CLOV. *Very red face. Brief tableau.*

[CLOV *goes and stands under window left. Stiff, staggering walk. He looks up at window left. He turns and looks at window right. He goes and stands under window right. He looks up at window right. He turns and looks at window left. He goes out, comes back immediately with a small step-ladder, carries it over and sets it down under window left, gets up on it, draws back curtain. He gets down, takes six steps (for example) towards window right, goes back for ladder, carries it over and sets it down under window right, gets up on it, draws back curtain. He gets down, takes three steps towards window left, goes back for ladder, carries it over and sets it down under window left, gets up on it, looks out of window. Brief laugh. He gets down, takes one step towards window right, goes back for ladder, carries it over and sets it down under window right, gets up on it, looks out of window. Brief laugh. He gets down, goes with ladder towards ashbins, halts, turns, carries back ladder and sets it down under window right, goes to ashbins, removes sheet covering them, folds it over his arm. He raises one lid, stoops and looks into bin. Brief laugh. He closes lid. Same with other bin. He goes to* HAMM, *removes sheet covering him, folds it over his arm. In a dressing-gown, a stiff toque*[2] *on his head, a large blood-stained handkerchief over his face, a whistle hanging from his neck, a rug over his knees, thick socks on his feet,* HAMM *seems to be asleep.* CLOV *looks him over. Brief laugh. He goes to door, halts, turns towards auditorium.*]

CLOV: [*Fixed gaze, tonelessly.*] Finished, it's finished,[3] nearly finished, it must be nearly finished. [*Pause.*] Grain upon grain, one by one, and one day, suddenly, there's a heap, a little heap, the impossible heap. [*Pause.*] I can't be punished any more. [*Pause.*] I'll go now to my kitchen, ten feet by ten feet by ten feet, and wait for him to whistle me. [*Pause.*] Nice dimensions, nice proportions, I'll lean on the table, and look at the wall, and wait for him to whistle me.

[*He remains a moment motionless, then goes out. He comes back immediately, goes to window right, takes up the ladder and carries it out. Pause.* HAMM *stirs. He yawns under the handkerchief. He removes the handkerchief from his face. Very red face. Black glasses.*]

HAMM: Me—[*he yawns*]—to play.[4] [*He holds the handkerchief spread out before him.*] Old Stancher![5] [*He takes off his glasses, wipes his eyes, his face, the glasses, puts them on again, folds the handkerchief and puts it back neatly in the breast-pocket of his dressing-gown. He clears his throat, joins the tips of his fingers.*] Can there be misery—[*he yawns*]—

2. A kind of small hat, cap, or bonnet, without a projecting brim or with a small, rolled brim.
3. Compare Christ's last words on the Cross: "It is finished" (St. John 19.30).
4. The "endgame" is the last stage of a game of chess.

Here, Hamm acknowledges that it is his turn to make a move.
5. The handkerchief "stanches" blood and is thus an old "stancher."

loftier than mine? No doubt. Formerly. But now? [*Pause.*] My father?
[*Pause.*] My mother? [*Pause.*] My . . . dog? [*Pause.*] Oh I am willing to
believe they suffer as much as such creatures can suffer. But does that
mean their sufferings equal mine? No doubt. [*Pause.*] No, all is a—[*he
yawns*] —bsolute, [*proudly*] the bigger a man is the fuller he is. [*Pause.
Gloomily.*] And the emptier. [*He sniffs.*] Clov! [*Pause.*] No, alone.
[*Pause.*] What dreams! Those forests! [*Pause.*] Enough, it's time it
ended, in the shelter too. [*Pause.*] And yet I hesitate, I hesitate to . . . to
end. Yes, there it is, it's time it ended and yet I hesitate to—[*he
yawns*]—to end. [*Yawns.*] God, I'm tired, I'd be better off in bed. [*He
whistles. Enter* CLOV *immediately. He halts beside the chair.*] You pol-
lute the air! [*Pause.*] Get me ready, I'm going to bed.
CLOV: I've just got you up.
HAMM: And what of it?
CLOV: I can't be getting you up and putting you to bed every five minutes,
    I have things to do. [*Pause.*]
HAMM: Did you ever see my eyes?
CLOV: No.
HAMM: Did you never have the curiosity, while I was sleeping, to take off
    my glasses and look at my eyes?
CLOV: Pulling back the lids? [*Pause.*] No.
HAMM: One of these days I'll show them to you. [*Pause.*] It seems they've
    gone all white. [*Pause.*] What time is it?
CLOV: The same as usual.
HAMM: [*Gesture towards window right.*] Have you looked?
CLOV: Yes.
HAMM: Well?
CLOV: Zero.
HAMM: It'd need to rain.
CLOV: It won't rain. [*Pause.*]
HAMM: Apart from that, how do you feel?
CLOV: I don't complain.
HAMM: You feel normal?
CLOV: [*Irritably.*] I tell you I don't complain.
HAMM: I feel a little queer. [*Pause.*] Clov!
CLOV: Yes.
HAMM: Have you not had enough?
CLOV: Yes! [*Pause.*] Of what?
HAMM: Of this . . . this . . . thing.
CLOV: I always had. [*Pause.*] Not you?
HAMM: [*Gloomily.*] Then there's no reason for it to change.
CLOV: It may end. [*Pause.*] All life long the same questions, the same
    answers.
HAMM: Get me ready. [CLOV *does not move.*] Go and get the sheet. [CLOV
    does not move.] Clov!
CLOV: Yes.
HAMM: I'll give you nothing more to eat.
CLOV: Then we'll die.

HAMM: I'll give you just enough to keep you from dying. You'll be hungry all the time.

CLOV: Then we won't die. [*Pause.*] I'll go and get the sheet. [*He goes towards the door.*]

HAMM: No! [CLOV *halts.*] I'll give you one biscuit per day. [*Pause.*] One and a half. [*Pause.*] Why do you stay with me?

CLOV: Why do you keep me?

HAMM: There's no one else.

CLOV: There's nowhere else. [*Pause.*]

HAMM: You're leaving me all the same.

CLOV: I'm trying.

HAMM: You don't love me.

CLOV: No.

HAMM: You loved me once.

CLOV: Once!

HAMM: I've made you suffer too much. [*Pause.*] Haven't I?

CLOV: It's not that.

HAMM: [*Shocked.*] I haven't made you suffer too much?

CLOV: Yes!

HAMM: [*Relieved.*] Ah you gave me a fright! [*Pause. Coldly.*] Forgive me. [*Pause. Louder.*] I said, Forgive me.

CLOV: I heard you. [*Pause.*] Have you bled?

HAMM: Less. [*Pause.*] Is it not time for my pain-killer?

CLOV: No. [*Pause.*]

HAMM: How are your eyes?

CLOV: Bad.

HAMM: How are your legs?

CLOV: BAD.

HAMM: But you can move.

CLOV: Yes.

HAMM: [*Violently.*] Then move! [CLOV *goes to back wall, leans against it with his forehead and hands.*] Where are you?

CLOV: Here.

HAMM: Come back! [CLOV *returns to his place beside the chair.*] Where are you?

CLOV: Here.

HAMM: Why don't you kill me?

CLOV: I don't know the combination of the cupboard. [*Pause.*]

HAMM: Go and get two bicycle-wheels.

CLOV: There are no more bicycle-wheels.

HAMM: What have you done with your bicycle?

CLOV: I never had a bicycle.

HAMM: The thing is impossible.

CLOV: When there were still bicycles I wept to have one. I crawled at your feet. You told me to go to hell. Now there are none.

HAMM: And your rounds? When you inspected my paupers. Always on foot?

CLOV: Sometimes on horse. [*The lid of one of the bins lifts and the hands of* NAGG *appear, gripping the rim. Then his head emerges. Nightcap. Very white face.* NAGG *yawns, then listens.*] I'll leave you, I have things to do.

HAMM: In your kitchen?

CLOV: Yes.

HAMM: Outside of here it's death. [*Pause.*] All right, be off. [*Exit* CLOV. *Pause.*] We're getting on.

NAGG: Me Pap![6]

HAMM: Accursed progenitor!

NAGG: Me pap!

HAMM: The old folks at home! No decency left! Guzzle, guzzle, that's all they think of. [*He whistles. Enter* CLOV. *He halts beside the chair.*] Well! I thought you were leaving me.

CLOV: Oh not just yet, not just yet.

NAGG: Me pap!

HAMM: Give him his pap.

CLOV: There's no more pap.

HAMM: [*To* NAGG.] Do you hear that? There's no more pap. You'll never get any more pap.

NAGG: I want me pap!

HAMM: Give him a biscuit. [*Exit* CLOV.] Accursed fornicator! How are your stumps?

NAGG: Never mind me stumps.

[*Enter* CLOV *with biscuit.*]

CLOV: I'm back again, with the biscuit. [*He gives biscuit to* NAGG *who fingers it, sniffs it.*]

NAGG: [*Plaintively.*] What is it?

CLOV: Spratt's medium.[7]

NAGG: [*As before.*] It's hard! I can't!

HAMM: Bottle him!

[CLOV *pushes* NAGG *back into the bin, closes the lid.*]

CLOV: [*Returning to his place beside the chair.*] If age but knew![8]

HAMM: Sit on him!

CLOV: I can't sit.

HAMM: True. And I can't stand.

CLOV: So it is.

HAMM: Every man his speciality. [*Pause.*] No phone calls? [*Pause.*] Don't we laugh?

CLOV: [*After reflection.*] I don't feel like it.

HAMM: [*After reflection.*] Nor I. [*Pause.*] Clov!

CLOV: Yes.

HAMM: Nature has forgotten us.

CLOV: There's no more nature.

---

6. Soft, pulpy, or mashed-up food; mush.
7. A popular kind of cookie.
8. Variation of Henri Estienne's epigram "Si jeunesse savait; si vieillesse pouvait" (If youth knew; if age could).

HAMM: No more nature! You exaggerate.

CLOV: In the vicinity.

HAMM: But we breathe, we change! We lose our hair, our teeth! Our bloom! Our ideals!

CLOV: Then she hasn't forgotten us.

HAMM: But you say there is none.

CLOV: [*Sadly.*] No one that ever lived ever thought so crooked as we.

HAMM: We do what we can.

CLOV: We shouldn't. [*Pause.*]

HAMM: You're a bit of all right, aren't you?[9]

CLOV: A smithereen. [*Pause.*]

HAMM: This is slow work. [*Pause.*] Is it not time for my pain-killer?

CLOV: No. [*Pause.*] I'll leave you, I have things to do.

HAMM: In your kitchen?

CLOV: Yes.

HAMM: What, I'd like to know.

CLOV: I look at the wall.

HAMM: The wall! And what do you see on your wall? Mene, mene?[1] Naked bodies?

CLOV: I see my light dying.

HAMM: Your light dying! Listen to that! Well, it can die just as well here, *your* light. Take a look at me and then come back and tell me what you think of *your* light. [*Pause.*]

CLOV: You shouldn't speak to me like that. [*Pause.*]

HAMM: [*Coldly.*] Forgive me. [*Pause. Louder.*] I said, Forgive me.

CLOV: I heard you.

　　[*The lid of* NAGG*'s bin lifts. His hands appear, gripping the rim. Then his head emerges. In his mouth the biscuit. He listens.*]

HAMM: Did your seeds come up?

CLOV: No.

HAMM: Did you scratch round them to see if they had sprouted?

CLOV: They haven't sprouted.

HAMM: Perhaps it's still too early.

CLOV: If they were going to sprout they would have sprouted. [*Violently.*] They'll never sprout!

　　[*Pause.* NAGG *takes biscuit in his hand.*]

HAMM: This is not much fun. [*Pause.*] But that's always the way at the end of the day, isn't it, Clov?

CLOV: Always.

HAMM: It's the end of the day like any other day, isn't it, Clov?

CLOV: Looks like it. [*Pause.*]

HAMM: [*Anguished.*] What's happening, what's happening?

CLOV: Something is taking its course. [*Pause.*]

HAMM: All right, be off. [*He leans back in his chair, remains motionless.*

---

9. A slang expression meaning either "You're good-looking" or "You're pretty good." "Smithereen": small fragment or atom.
1. During a feast given by King Belshazzar of Babylon, a hand was seen to move across a wall, writing "Mene, mene, tekel, upharsin"—"Thou art weighed in the balances and found wanting," a prophecy of doom for the king. (Daniel 5.25–28)

CLOV *does not move, heaves a great groaning sigh.* HAMM *sits up.*] I thought I told you to be off.

CLOV: I'm trying. [*He goes to door, halts.*] Ever since I was whelped.

[*Exit* CLOV.]

HAMM: We're getting on.

[*He leans back in his chair, remains motionless.* NAGG *knocks on the lid of the other bin. Pause. He knocks harder. The lid lifts and the hands of* NELL *appear, gripping the rim. Then her head emerges. Lace cap. Very white face.*]

NELL: What is it, my pet? [*Pause.*] Time for love?

NAGG: Were you asleep?

NELL: Oh no!

NAGG: Kiss me.

NELL: We can't.

NAGG: Try.

[*Their heads strain towards each other, fail to meet, fall apart again.*]

NELL: Why this farce, day after day? [*Pause.*]

NAGG: I've lost me tooth.

NELL: When?

NAGG: I had it yesterday.

NELL: [*Elegiac.*] Ah yesterday!

[*They turn painfully towards each other.*]

NAGG: Can you see me?

NELL: Hardly. And you?

NAGG: What?

NELL: Can you see me?

NAGG: Hardly.

NELL: So much the better, so much the better.

NAGG: Don't say that. [*Pause.*] Our sight has failed.

NELL: Yes.

[*Pause. They turn away from each other.*]

NAGG: Can you hear me?

NELL: Yes. And you?

NAGG: Yes. [*Pause.*] Our hearing hasn't failed.

NELL: Our what?

NAGG: Our hearing.

NELL: No. [*Pause.*] Have you anything else to say to me?

NAGG: Do you remember—

NELL: No.

NAGG: When we crashed on our tandem[2] and lost our shanks.

[*They laugh heartily.*]

NELL: It was in the Ardennes.[3]

[*They laugh less heartily.*]

NAGG: On the road to Sedan. [*They laugh still less heartily.*] Are you cold?

NELL: Yes, perished. And you?

---

2. A bicycle for two riders, usually one in front of the other.

3. A district of picturesque wooded ravines and barren flat tops in northern France where some of the fierce battles of both world wars took place. "Sedan": A town in the Ardennes, once the center of the wool industry.

NAGG: [*Pause.*] I'm freezing. [*Pause.*] Do you want to go in?

NELL: Yes.

NAGG: Then go in. [NELL *does not move.*] Why don't you go in?

NELL: I don't know. [*Pause.*]

NAGG: Has he changed your sawdust?

NELL: It isn't sawdust. [*Pause. Wearily.*] Can you not be a little accurate, Nagg?

NAGG: Your sand then. It's not important.

NELL: It is important. [*Pause.*]

NAGG: It was sawdust once.

NELL: Once!

NAGG: And now it's sand. [*Pause.*] From the shore. [*Pause. Impatiently.*] Now it's sand he fetches from the shore.

NELL: Now it's sand.

NAGG: Has he changed yours?

NELL: No.

NAGG: Nor mine. [*Pause.*] I won't have it! [*Pause. Holding up the biscuit.*] Do you want a bit?

NELL: No. [*Pause.*] Of what?

NAGG: Biscuit. I've kept you half. [*He looks at the biscuit. Proudly.*] Three quarters. For you. Here. [*He proffers the biscuit.*] No? [*Pause.*] Do you not feel well?

HAMM: [*Wearily.*] Quiet, quiet, you're keeping me awake. [*Pause.*] Talk softer. [*Pause.*] If I could sleep I might make love. I'd go into the woods. My eyes would see ... the sky, the earth. I'd run, run, they wouldn't catch me. [*Pause.*] Nature! [*Pause.*] There's something dripping in my head. [*Pause.*] A heart, a heart in my head. [*Pause.*]

NAGG: [*Soft.*] Do you hear him? A heart in his head! [*He chuckles cautiously.*]

NELL: One mustn't laugh at those things, Nagg. Why must you always laugh at them?

NAGG: Not so loud!

NELL: [*Without lowering her voice.*] Nothing is funnier than unhappiness, I grant you that. But—

NAGG: [*Shocked.*] Oh!

NELL: Yes, yes, it's the most comical thing in the world. And we laugh, we laugh, with a will, in the beginning. But it's always the same thing. Yes, it's like the funny story we have heard too often, we still find it funny, but we don't laugh any more. [*Pause.*] Have you anything else to say to me?

NAGG: No.

NELL: Are you quite sure? [*Pause.*] Then I'll leave you.

NAGG: Do you not want your biscuit? [*Pause.*] I'll keep it for you. [*Pause.*] I thought you were going to leave me.

NELL: I am going to leave you.

NAGG: Could you give me a scratch before you go?

NELL: No. [*Pause.*] Where?

NAGG: In the back.

NELL: No. [*Pause.*] Rub yourself against the rim.

NAGG: It's lower down. In the hollow.

NELL: What hollow?

NAGG: The hollow! [*Pause.*] Could you not? [*Pause.*] Yesterday you scratched me there.

NELL: [*Elegiac.*] Ah yesterday!

NAGG: Could you not? [*Pause.*] Would you like me to scratch you? [*Pause.*] Are you crying again?

NELL: I was trying. [*Pause.*]

HAMM: Perhaps it's a little vein. [*Pause.*]

NAGG: What was that he said?

NELL: Perhaps it's a little vein.

NAGG: What does that mean? [*Pause.*] That means nothing. [*Pause.*] Will I tell you the story of the tailor?

NELL: No. [*Pause.*] What for?

NAGG: To cheer you up.

NELL: It's not funny.

NAGG: It always made you laugh. [*Pause.*] The first time I thought you'd die.

NELL: It was on Lake Como.[4] [*Pause.*] One April afternoon. [*Pause.*] Can you believe it?

NAGG: What?

NELL: That we once went out rowing on Lake Como. [*Pause.*] One April afternoon.

NAGG: We had got engaged the day before.

NELL: Engaged!

NAGG: You were in such fits that we capsized. By rights we should have been drowned.

NELL: It was because I felt happy.

NAGG: [*Indignant.*] It was not, it was not, it was my story and nothing else. Happy! Don't you laugh at it still? Every time I tell it. Happy!

NELL: It was deep, deep. And you could see down to the bottom. So white. So clean.

NAGG: Let me tell it again. [*Raconteur's voice.*] An Englishman, needing a pair of striped trousers in a hurry for the New Year festivities, goes to his tailor who takes his measurements. [*Tailor's voice.*] "That's the lot, come back in four days, I'll have it ready." Good. Four days later. [*Tailor's voice.*] "So sorry, come back in a week, I've made a mess of the seat." Good, that's all right, a neat seat can be very ticklish. A week later. [*Tailor's voice.*] "Frightfully sorry, come back in ten days. I've made a hash of the crotch." Good, can't be helped, a snug crotch is always a teaser. Ten days later. [*Tailor's voice.*] "Dreadfully sorry, come back in a fortnight, I've made a balls of the fly." Good, at a pinch, a smart fly is a stiff proposition. [*Pause. Normal voice.*] I never told it worse. [*Pause. Gloomy.*] I tell this story worse and worse. [*Pause. Raconteur's voice.*] Well, to make it short, the bluebells are blowing and he ballockses[5] the

---

4. A large lake in a beautiful mountainous area of northern Italy.

5. Makes a mess or "botch" of something (vulgar slang derived from "ballock," a testicle).

buttonholes. [*Customer's voice.*] "God damn you to hell, Sir, no, it's indecent, there are limits! In six days, do you hear me, six days, God made the world. Yes Sir, no less Sir, the WORLD! And you are not bloody well capable of making me a pair of trousers in three months!" [*Tailor's voice, scandalized.*] "But my dear Sir, my dear Sir, look—[*disdainful gesture, disgustedly*]—at the world—[*pause*] and look—[*loving gesture, proudly*] —at my TROUSERS!"

> [*Pause. He looks at* NELL *who has remained impassive, her eyes unseeing, breaks into a high forced laugh, cuts it short, pokes his head towards* NELL, *launches his laugh again.*]

HAMM: Silence!

> [NAGG *starts, cuts short his laugh.*]

NELL: You could see down to the bottom.

HAMM: [*Exasperated.*] Have you not finished? Will you never finish? [*With sudden fury.*] Will this never finish? [NAGG *disappears into his bin, closes the lid behind him.* NELL *does not move. Frenziedly.*] My kingdom for a nightman![6] [*He whistles. Enter* CLOV.] Clear away this muck! Chuck it in the sea!

> [CLOV *goes to bins, halts.*]

NELL: So white.

HAMM: What? What's she blathering about?

> [CLOV *stoops, takes* NELL*'s hand, feels her pulse.*]

NELL: [*To* CLOV.] Desert!

> [CLOV *lets go her hand, pushes her back in the bin, closes the lid.*]

CLOV: [*Returning to his place beside the chair*] She has no pulse.

HAMM: What was she drivelling about?

CLOV: She told me to go away, into the desert.

HAMM: Damn busybody! Is that all?

CLOV: No.

HAMM: What else?

CLOV: I didn't understand.

HAMM: Have you bottled her?

CLOV: Yes.

HAMM: Are they both bottled?

CLOV: Yes.

HAMM: Screw down the lids. [CLOV *goes towards door.*] Time enough. [CLOV *halts.*] My anger subsides, I'd like to pee.

CLOV: [*With alacrity.*] I'll go and get the catheter. [*He goes towards door.*]

HAMM: Time enough. [CLOV *halts.*] Give me my pain-killer.

CLOV: It's too soon. [*Pause.*] It's too soon on top of your tonic, it wouldn't act.

HAMM: In the morning they brace you up and in the evening they calm you down. Unless it's the other way round. [*Pause.*] That old doctor, he's dead naturally?

CLOV: He wasn't old.

---

6. This line echoes the cry of the defeated King Richard III, "A horse! a horse! My kingdom for a horse!" in Shakespeare's *Richard III* (5.4.7).

HAMM: But he's dead?

CLOV: Naturally. [*Pause.*] *You* ask *me* that? [*Pause.*]

HAMM: Take me for a little turn. [CLOV *goes behind the chair and pushes it forward.*] Not too fast! [CLOV *pushes chair.*] Right round the world! [CLOV *pushes chair.*] Hug the walls, then back to the center again. [CLOV *pushes chair.*] I was right in the center, wasn't I?

CLOV: [*Pushing*] Yes.

HAMM: We'd need a proper wheel-chair. With big wheels. Bicycle wheels! [*Pause.*] Are you hugging?

CLOV: [*Pushing.*] Yes.

HAMM: [*Groping for wall.*] It's a lie! Why do you lie to me?

CLOV: [*Bearing closer to wall.*] There! There!

HAMM: Stop! [CLOV *stops chair close to back wall.* HAMM *lays his hand against wall.*] Old wall! [*Pause.*] Beyond is the . . . other hell. [*Pause. Violently.*] Closer! Closer! Up against!

CLOV: Take away your hand. [HAMM *withdraws his hand.* CLOV *rams chair against wall.*] There!

   [HAMM *leans towards wall, applies his ear to it.*]

HAMM: Do you hear? [*He strikes the wall with his knuckles.*] Do you hear? Hollow bricks! [*He strikes again.*] All that's hollow! [*Pause. He straightens up. Violently.*] That's enough. Back!

CLOV: We haven't done the round.

HAMM: Back to my place! [CLOV *pushes chair back to center.*] Is that my place?

CLOV: Yes, that's your place.

HAMM: Am I right in the center?

CLOV: I'll measure it.

HAMM: More or less! More or less!

CLOV: [*Moving chair slightly.*] There!

HAMM: I'm more or less in the center?

CLOV: I'd say so.

HAMM: You'd say so! Put me right in the center!

CLOV: I'll go and get the tape.

HAMM: Roughly! Roughly! [CLOV *moves chair slightly.*] Bang in the center!

CLOV: There! [*Pause.*]

HAMM: I feel a little too far to the left. [CLOV *moves chair slightly.*] Now I feel a little too far to the right. [CLOV *moves chair slightly.*] I feel a little too far forward. [CLOV *moves chair slightly.*] Now I feel a little too far back. [CLOV *moves chair slightly.*] Don't stay there, [*i.e., behind the chair*] you give me the shivers.

   [CLOV *returns to his place beside the chair.*]

CLOV: If I could kill him I'd die happy. [*Pause.*]

HAMM: What's the weather like?

CLOV: As usual.

HAMM: Look at the earth.

CLOV: I've looked.

HAMM: With the glass?

CLOV: No need of the glass.

HAMM: Look at it with the glass.

CLOV: I'll go and get the glass.

[*Exit* CLOV.]

HAMM: No need of the glass!

[*Enter* CLOV *with telescope.*]

CLOV: I'm back again, with the glass. [*He goes to window right, looks up at it.*] I need the steps.

HAMM: Why? Have you shrunk? [*Exit* CLOV *with telescope.*] I don't like that, I don't like that.

[*Enter* CLOV *with ladder, but without telescope.*]

CLOV: I'm back again, with the steps. [*He sets down ladder under window right, gets up on it, realizes he has not the telescope, gets down.*] I need the glass. [*He goes towards door.*]

HAMM: [*Violently.*] But you have the glass!

CLOV: [*Halting, violently.*] No, I haven't the glass!

[*Exit* CLOV.]

HAMM: This is deadly.

[*Enter* CLOV *with telescope. He goes towards ladder.*]

CLOV: Things are livening up. [*He gets up on ladder, raises the telescope, lets it fall.*] I did it on purpose. [*He gets down, picks up the telescope, turns it on auditorium.*] I see . . . a multitude . . . in transports . . . of joy.[7] [*Pause.*] That's what I call a magnifier. [*He lowers the telescope, turns towards* HAMM.] Well? Don't we laugh?

HAMM: [*After reflection.*] I don't.

CLOV: [*After reflection.*] Nor I. [*He gets up on ladder, turns the telescope on the without.*] Let's see. [*He looks, moving the telescope.*] Zero . . . [*he looks*] . . . zero . . . [*he looks*] . . . and zero.

HAMM: Nothing stirs. All is—

CLOV: Zer—

HAMM: [*Violently.*] Wait till you're spoke to! [*Normal voice.*] All is . . . all is . . . all is what? [*Violently.*] All is what?

CLOV: What all is? In a word? Is that what you want to know? Just a moment. [*He turns the telescope on the without, looks, lowers the telescope, turns towards Hamm.*] Corpsed. [*Pause.*] Well? Content?

HAMM: Look at the sea.

CLOV: It's the same.

HAMM: Look at the ocean!

[CLOV *gets down, takes a few steps towards window left, goes back for ladder, carries it over and sets it down under window left, gets up on it, turns the telescope on the without, looks at length. He starts, lowers the telescope, examines it, turns it again on the without.*]

CLOV: Never seen anything like that!

HAMM: [*Anxious.*] What? A sail? A fin? Smoke?

CLOV: [*Looking.*] The light is sunk.

HAMM: [*Relieved.*] Pah! We all knew that.

CLOV: [*Looking.*] There was a bit left.

---

7. An ironic misquotation of Revelations 7.9–12: "After this I beheld, and, lo, a great multitude, which [. . .] cried with a loud voice [. . .] ."

HAMM: The base.

CLOV: [*Looking.*] Yes.

HAMM: And now?

CLOV: [*Looking.*] All gone.

HAMM: No gulls?

CLOV: [*Looking.*] Gulls!

HAMM: And the horizon? Nothing on the horizon?

CLOV: [*Lowering the telescope, turning towards* HAMM, *exasperated.*] What in God's name could there be on the horizon? [*Pause.*]

HAMM: The waves, how are the waves?

CLOV: The waves? [*He turns the telescope on the waves.*] Lead.

HAMM: And the sun?

CLOV: [*Looking.*] Zero.

HAMM: But it should be sinking. Look again.

CLOV: [*Looking.*] Damn the sun.

HAMM: Is it night already then?

CLOV: [*Looking.*] No.

HAMM: Then what is it?

CLOV: [*Looking.*] Gray. [*Lowering the telescope, turning towards* HAMM, *louder.*] Gray! [*Pause. Still louder.*] GRRAY! [*Pause. He gets down, approaches* HAMM *from behind, whispers in his ear.*]

HAMM: [*Starting.*] Gray! Did I hear you say gray?

CLOV: Light black. From pole to pole.

HAMM: You exaggerate. [*Pause.*] Don't stay there, you give me the shivers. [CLOV *returns to his place beside the chair.*]

CLOV: Why this farce, day after day?

HAMM: Routine. One never knows. [*Pause.*] Last night I saw inside my breast. There was a big sore.

CLOV: Pah! You saw your heart.

HAMM: No, it was living. [*Pause. Anguished.*] Clov!

CLOV: Yes.

HAMM: What's happening?

CLOV: Something is taking its course. [*Pause.*]

HAMM: Clov!

CLOV: [*Impatiently.*] What is it?

HAMM: We're not beginning to . . . to . . . mean something?

CLOV: Mean something! You and I, mean something! [*Brief laugh.*] Ah that's a good one!

HAMM: I wonder. [*Pause.*] Imagine if a rational being came back to earth, wouldn't he be liable to get ideas into his head if he observed us long enough. [*Voice of rational being.*] Ah, good, now I see what it is, yes, now I understand what they're at! [CLOV *starts, drops the telescope and begins to scratch his belly with both hands. Normal voice.*] And without going so far as that, we ourselves . . . [*with emotion*] . . . we ourselves . . . at certain moments . . . [*Vehemently.*] To think perhaps it won't all have been for nothing!

CLOV: [*Anguished, scratching himself.*] I have a flea!

HAMM: A flea! Are there still fleas?

CLOV: On me there's one. [*Scratching.*] Unless it's a crablouse.

HAMM: [*Very perturbed.*] But humanity might start from there all over again! Catch him, for the love of God!

CLOV: I'll go and get the powder.

　　[*Exit* CLOV.]

HAMM: A flea! This is awful! What a day!

　　[*Enter* CLOV *with a sprinkling-tin.*]

CLOV: I'm back again, with the insecticide.

HAMM: Let him have it!

　　[CLOV *loosens the top of his trousers, pulls it forward and shakes powder into the aperture. He stoops, looks, waits, starts, frenziedly shakes more powder, stoops, looks, waits.*]

CLOV: The bastard!

HAMM: Did you get him?

CLOV: Looks like it. [*He drops the tin and adjusts his trousers.*] Unless he's laying doggo.

HAMM: Laying! Lying you mean. Unless he's *lying* doggo.

CLOV: Ah? One says lying? One doesn't say laying?

HAMM: Use your head, can't you. If he was laying we'd be bitched.

CLOV: Ah. [*Pause.*] What about that pee?

HAMM: I'm having it.

CLOV: Ah that's the spirit, that's the spirit! [*Pause.*]

HAMM: [*With ardour.*] Let's go from here, the two of us! South! You can make a raft and the currents will carry us away, far away, to other . . . mammals!

CLOV: God forbid!

HAMM: Alone, I'll embark alone! Get working on that raft immediately. Tomorrow I'll be gone for ever.

CLOV: [*Hastening towards door.*] I'll start straight away.

HAMM: Wait! [CLOV *halts.*] Will there be sharks, do you think?

CLOV: Sharks? I don't know. If there are there will be. [*He goes towards door.*]

HAMM: Wait! [CLOV *halts.*] Is it not yet time for my pain-killer?

CLOV: [*Violently.*] No! [*He goes towards door.*]

HAMM: Wait! [CLOV *halts.*] How are your eyes?

CLOV: Bad.

HAMM: But you can see.

CLOV: All I want.

HAMM: How are your legs?

CLOV: Bad.

HAMM: But you can walk.

CLOV: I come . . . and go.

HAMM: In my house. [*Pause. With prophetic relish.*] One day you'll be blind, like me. You'll be sitting there, a speck in the void, in the dark, for ever, like me. [*Pause.*] One day you'll say to yourself, I'm tired, I'll sit down, and you'll go and sit down. Then you'll say, I'm hungry, I'll get up and get something to eat. But you won't get up. You'll say, I shouldn't have sat down, but since I have I'll sit on a little longer, then

I'll get up and get something to eat. But you won't get up and you won't get anything to eat. [*Pause.*] You'll look at the wall awhile, then you'll say, I'll close my eyes, perhaps have a little sleep, after that I'll feel better, and you'll close them. And when you open them again there'll be no wall any more. [*Pause.*] Infinite emptiness will be all around you, all the resurrected dead of all the ages wouldn't fill it, and there you'll be like a little bit of grit in the middle of the steppe. [*Pause.*] Yes, one day you'll know what it is, you'll be like me, except that you won't have anyone with you, because you won't have had pity on anyone and because there won't be anyone left to have pity on. [*Pause.*]

CLOV: It's not certain. [*Pause.*] And there's one thing you forget.

HAMM: Ah?

CLOV: I can't sit down.

HAMM: [*Impatiently.*] Well you'll lie down then, what the hell! Or you'll come to a standstill, simply stop and stand still, the way you are now. One day you'll say, I'm tired, I'll stop. What does the attitude matter? [*Pause.*]

CLOV: So you all want me to leave you.

HAMM: Naturally.

CLOV: Then I'll leave you.

HAMM: You can't leave us.

CLOV: Then I won't leave you. [*Pause.*]

HAMM: Why don't you finish us? [*Pause.*] I'll tell you the combination of the cupboard if you promise to finish me.

CLOV: I couldn't finish you.

HAMM: Then you won't finish me. [*Pause.*]

CLOV: I'll leave you, I have things to do.

HAMM: Do you remember when you came here?

CLOV: No. Too small, you told me.

HAMM: Do you remember your father?

CLOV: [*Wearily.*] Same answer. [*Pause.*] You've asked me these questions millions of times.

HAMM: I love the old questions. [*With fervor.*] Ah the old questions, the old answers, there's nothing like them! [*Pause.*] It was I was a father to you.

CLOV: Yes. [*He looks at* HAMM *fixedly.*] You were that to me.

HAMM: My house a home for you.

CLOV: Yes. [*He looks about him.*] This was that for me.

HAMM: [*Proudly.*] But for me, [*gesture towards himself*] no father. But for Hamm, [*gesture towards surroundings*] no home. [*Pause.*]

CLOV: I'll leave you.

HAMM: Did you ever think of one thing?

CLOV: Never.

HAMM: That here we're down in a hole. [*Pause.*] But beyond the hills? Eh? Perhaps it's still green. Eh? [*Pause.*] Flora! Pomona! [*Ecstatically.*] Ceres![8] [*Pause.*] Perhaps you won't need to go very far.

---

8. A Roman goddess of fertility, especially associated with cereal crops and other growing things.

CLOV: I can't go very far. [*Pause.*] I'll leave you.

HAMM: Is my dog ready?

CLOV: He lacks a leg.

HAMM: Is he silky?

CLOV: He's a kind of Pomeranian.

HAMM: Go and get him.

CLOV: He lacks a leg.

HAMM: Go and get him! [*Exit* CLOV.] We're getting on.

    [*Enter* CLOV *holding by one of its three legs a black toy dog.*]

CLOV: Your dogs are here. [*He hands the dog to* HAMM *who feels it, fondles it.*]

HAMM: He's white, isn't he?

CLOV: Nearly.

HAMM: What do you mean, nearly? Is he white or isn't he?

CLOV: He isn't. [*Pause.*]

HAMM: You've forgotten the sex.

CLOV: [*Vexed.*] But he isn't finished. The sex goes on at the end. [*Pause.*]

HAMM: You haven't put on his ribbon.

CLOV: [*Angrily.*] But he isn't finished, I tell you! First you finish your dog and then you put on his ribbon! [*Pause.*]

HAMM: Can he stand?

CLOV: I don't know.

HAMM: Try. [*He hands the dog to* CLOV *who places it on the ground.*] Well?

CLOV: Wait! [*He squats down and tries to get the dog to stand on its three legs, fails, lets it go. The dog falls on its side.*]

HAMM: [*Impatiently.*] Well?

CLOV: He's standing.

HAMM: [*Groping for the dog.*] Where? Where is he?

    [CLOV *holds up the dog in a standing position.*]

CLOV: There. [*He takes* HAMM'*s hand and guides it towards the dog's head.*]

HAMM: [*His hand on the dog's head.*] Is he gazing at me?

CLOV: Yes.

HAMM: [*Proudly.*] As if he were asking me to take him for a walk?

CLOV: If you like.

HAMM: [*As before.*] Or as if he were begging me for a bone. [*He withdraws his hand.*] Leave him like that, standing there imploring me.

    [CLOV *straightens up. The dog falls on its side.*]

CLOV: I'll leave you.

HAMM: Have you had your visions?

CLOV: Less.

HAMM: Is Mother Pegg's light on?

CLOV: Light! How could anyone's light be on?

HAMM: Extinguished!

CLOV: Naturally it's extinguished. If it's not on it's extinguished.

HAMM: No, I mean Mother Pegg.

CLOV: But naturally she's extinguished! [*Pause.*] What's the matter with you today?

HAMM: I'm taking my course. [*Pause.*] Is she buried?

CLOV: Buried! Who would have buried her?

HAMM: You.

CLOV: Me! Haven't I enough to do without burying people?

HAMM: But you'll bury me.

CLOV: No I won't bury you. [*Pause.*]

HAMM: She was bonny once, like a flower of the field. [*With reminiscent leer.*] And a great one for the men!

CLOV: We too were bonny—once. It's a rare thing not to have been bonny—once. [*Pause.*]

HAMM: Go and get the gaff.

[CLOV *goes to door, halts.*]

CLOV: Do this, do that, and I do it. I never refuse. Why?

HAMM: You're not able to.

CLOV: Soon I won't do it any more.

HAMM: You won't be able to any more. [*Exit* CLOV.] Ah the creatures, the creatures, everything has to be explained to them.

[*Enter* CLOV *with gaff.*]

CLOV: Here's your gaff. Stick it up. [*He gives the gaff to* HAMM *who, wielding it like a puntpole, tries to move his chair.*]

HAMM: Did I move?

CLOV: No.

[HAMM *throws down the gaff.*]

HAMM: Go and get the oilcan.

CLOV: What for?

HAMM: To oil the castors.

CLOV: I oiled them yesterday.

HAMM: Yesterday! What does that mean? Yesterday!

CLOV: [*Violently.*] That means that bloody awful day, long ago, before this bloody awful day. I use the words you taught me. If they don't mean anything any more, teach me others. Or let me be silent. [*Pause.*]

HAMM: I once knew a madman who thought the end of the world had come. He was a painter—and engraver. I had a great fondness for him. I used to go and see him, in the asylum. I'd take him by the hand and drag him to the window. Look! There! All that rising corn! And there! Look! The sails of the herring fleet! All that loveliness! [*Pause.*] He'd snatch away his hand and go back into his corner. Appalled. All he had seen was ashes. [*Pause.*] He alone had been spared. [*Pause.*] Forgotten. [*Pause.*] It appears the case is . . . was not so . . . so unusual.

CLOV: A madman! When was that?

HAMM: Oh way back, way back, you weren't in the land of the living.

CLOV: God be with the days!

[*Pause.* HAMM *raises his toque.*]

HAMM: I had a great fondness for him. [*Pause. He puts on his toque again.*] He was a painter—and engraver.

CLOV: There are so many terrible things.

HAMM: No, no, there are not so many now. [*Pause.*] Clov!

CLOV: Yes.

HAMM: Do you not think this has gone on long enough?

CLOV: Yes! [*Pause.*] What?

HAMM: This . . . this . . . thing.

CLOV: I've always thought so. [*Pause.*] You not?

HAMM: [*Gloomily.*] Then it's a day like any other day.

CLOV: As long as it lasts. [*Pause.*] All life long the same inanities.

HAMM: I can't leave you.

CLOV: I know. And you can't follow me. [*Pause.*]

HAMM: If you leave me how shall I know?

CLOV: [*Briskly.*] Well you simply whistle me and if I don't come running it means I've left you. [*Pause.*]

HAMM: You won't come and kiss me goodbye?

CLOV: Oh I shouldn't think so. [*Pause.*]

HAMM: But you might be merely dead in your kitchen.

CLOV: The result would be the same.

HAMM: Yes, but how would I know, if you were merely dead in your kitchen?

CLOV: Well . . . sooner or later I'd start to stink.

HAMM: You stink already. The whole place stinks of corpses.

CLOV: The whole universe.

HAMM: [*Angrily.*] To hell with the universe. [*Pause.*] Think of something.

CLOV: What?

HAMM: An idea, have an idea. [*Angrily.*] A bright idea!

CLOV: Ah good. [*He starts pacing to and fro, his eyes fixed on the ground, his hands behind his back. He halts.*] The pains in my legs! It's unbelievable! Soon I won't be able to think any more.

HAMM: You won't be able to leave me. [CLOV *resumes his pacing.*] What are you doing?

CLOV: Having an idea. [*He paces.*] Ah! [*He halts.*]

HAMM: What a brain! [*Pause.*] Well?

CLOV: Wait! [*He meditates. Not very convinced.*] Yes . . . [*Pause. More convinced.*] Yes! [*He raises his head.*] I have it! I set the alarm. [*Pause.*]

HAMM: This is perhaps not one of my bright days, but frankly—

CLOV: You whistle me. I don't come. The alarm rings. I'm gone. It doesn't ring. I'm dead. [*Pause.*]

HAMM: Is it working? [*Pause. Impatiently.*] The alarm, is it working?

CLOV: Why wouldn't it be working?

HAMM: Because it's worked too much.

CLOV: But it's hardly worked at all.

HAMM: [*Angrily.*] Then because it's worked too little!

CLOV: I'll go and see. [*Exit* CLOV. *Brief ring of alarm off. Enter* CLOV *with alarm-clock. He holds it against* HAMM*'s ear and releases alarm. They listen to it ringing to the end. Pause.*] Fit to wake the dead! Did you hear it?

HAMM: Vaguely.

CLOV: The end is terrific!

HAMM: I prefer the middle. [*Pause.*] Is it not time for my pain-killer?

CLOV: No! [*He goes to door, turns.*] I'll leave you.

HAMM: It's time for my story. Do you want to listen to my story.
CLOV: No.
HAMM: Ask my father if he wants to listen to my story.
   [CLOV *goes to bins, raises the lid of* NAGG*'s, stoops, looks into it. Pause. He straightens up.*]
CLOV: He's asleep.
HAMM: Wake him.
   [CLOV *stoops, wakes* NAGG *with the alarm. Unintelligible words.* CLOV *straightens up.*]
CLOV: He doesn't want to listen to your story.
HAMM: I'll give him a bon-bon.
   [CLOV *stoops. As before.*]
CLOV: He wants a sugar-plum.
HAMM: He'll get a sugar-plum.
   [CLOV *stoops. As before.*]
CLOV: It's a deal. [*He goes towards door.* NAGG*'s hands appear, gripping the rim. Then the head emerges.* CLOV *reaches door, turns.*] Do you believe in the life to come?
HAMM: Mine was always that. [*Exit* CLOV.] Got him that time!
NAGG: I'm listening.
HAMM: Scoundrel! Why did you engender me?
NAGG: I didn't know.
HAMM: What? What didn't you know?
NAGG: That it'd be you. [*Pause.*] You'll give me a sugar-plum?
HAMM: After the audition.
NAGG: You swear?
HAMM: Yes.
NAGG: On what?
HAMM: My honor.
   [*Pause. They laugh heartily.*]
NAGG: Two.
HAMM: One.
NAGG: One for me and one for—
HAMM: One! Silence! [*Pause.*] Where was I? [*Pause. Gloomily.*] It's finished, we're finished. [*Pause.*] Nearly finished. [*Pause.*] There'll be no more speech. [*Pause.*] Something dripping in my head, ever since the fontanelles. [*Stifled hilarity of* NAGG.] Splash, splash, always on the same spot. [*Pause.*] Perhaps it's a little vein. [*Pause.*] A little artery. [*Pause. More animated.*] Enough of that, it's story time, where was I? [*Pause. Narrative tone.*] The man came crawling towards me, on his belly. Pale, wonderfully pale and thin, he seemed on the point of—[*Pause. Normal tone.*] No, I've done that bit. [*Pause. Narrative tone.*] I calmly filled my pipe—the meerschaum, lit it with ... let us say a vesta,[9] drew a few puffs. Aah! [*Pause.*] Well, what is it *you* want? [*Pause.*] It was an extraordinarily bitter day, I remember, zero by the thermometer. But considering it was Christmas Eve there was nothing ... extra-ordinary about

9. Short wooden or wax match.

that. Seasonable weather, for once in a way. [*Pause.*] Well, what ill wind blows you my way? He raised his face to me, black with mingled dirt and tears. [*Pause. Normal tone.*] That should do it. [*Narrative tone.*] No, no, don't look at me, don't look at me. He dropped his eyes and mumbled something, apologies I presume. [*Pause.*] I'm a busy man, you know, the final touches, before the festivities, you know what it is. [*Pause. Forcibly.*] Come on now, what is the object of this invasion? [*Pause.*] It was a glorious bright day, I remember, fifty by the heliometer,[1] but already the sun was sinking down into the . . . down among the dead. [*Normal tone.*] Nicely put, that. [*Narrative tone.*] Come on now, come on, present your petition and let me resume my labors. [*Pause. Normal tone.*] There's English for you. Ah well . . . [*Narrative tone.*] It was then he took the plunge. It's my little one, he said. Tsstss, a little one, that's bad. My little boy, he said, as if the sex mattered. Where did he come from? He named the hole. A good half-day, on horse. What are you insinuating? That the place is still inhabited? No no, not a soul, except himself and the child—assuming he existed. Good. I enquired about the situation at Kov, beyond the gulf. Not a sinner. Good. And you expect me to believe you have left your little one back there, all alone, and alive into the bargain? Come now! [*Pause.*] It was a howling wild day, I remember, a hundred by the anemometer.[2] The wind was tearing up the dead pines and sweeping them . . . away. [*Pause. Normal tone.*] A bit feeble, that. [*Narrative tone.*] Come on, man, speak up, what is you want from me, I have to put up my holly. [*Pause.*] Well to make it short it finally transpired that what he wanted from me was . . . bread for his brat? Bread? But I have no bread, it doesn't agree with me. Good. Then perhaps a little corn? [*Pause. Normal tone.*] That should do it. [*Narrative tone.*] Corn, yes, I have corn, it's true, in my granaries. But use your head. I give you some corn, a pound, a pound and a half, you bring it back to your child and you make him—if he's still alive— a nice pot of porridge, [NAGG *reacts.*] a nice pot and a half of porridge, full of nourishment. Good. The colors come back into his little cheeks—perhaps. And then? [*Pause.*] I lost patience. [*Violently.*] Use your head, can't you, use your head, you're on earth, there's no cure for that! [*Pause.*] It was an exceedingly dry day, I remember, zero by the hygrometer.[3] Ideal weather, for my lumbago. [*Pause. Violently.*] But what in God's name do you imagine? That the earth will awake in spring? That the rivers and seas will run with fish again? That there's manna in heaven still for imbeciles like you? [*Pause.*] Gradually I cooled down, sufficiently at least to ask him how long he had taken on the way. Three whole days. Good. In what condition he had left the child. Deep in sleep. [*Forcibly.*] But deep in what sleep, deep in what sleep already? [*Pause.*] Well to make it short I finally offered to take him into my service. He had touched a chord. And then I imagined

---

1. From the Greek word for the sun. A device for measuring the diameter of the sun, later the angular distance between stars and, here, the strength of sunlight.
2. From the Greek word for wind. A device for measuring the force of the wind.
3. From the Greek word for moist. A device for measuring moisture or humidity.

already that I wasn't much longer for this world. [*He laughs. Pause.*] Well? [*Pause.*] Well? Here if you were careful you might die a nice natural death, in peace and comfort. [*Pause.*] Well? [*Pause.*] In the end he asked me would I consent to take in the child as well—if he were still alive. [*Pause.*] It was the moment I was waiting for. [*Pause.*] Would I consent to take in the child . . . [*Pause.*] I can see him still, down on his knees, his hands flat on the ground, glaring at me with his mad eyes, in defiance of my wishes. [*Pause. Normal tone.*] I'll soon have finished with this story. [*Pause.*] Unless I bring in other characters. [*Pause.*] But where would I find them? [*Pause.*] Where would I look for them? [*Pause. He whistles. Enter* CLOV.] Let us pray to God.

NAGG: Me sugar-plum!

CLOV: There's a rat in the kitchen!

HAMM: A rat! Are there still rats?

CLOV: In the kitchen there's one.

HAMM: And you haven't exterminated him?

CLOV: Half. You disturbed us.

HAMM: He can't get away?

CLOV: No.

HAMM: You'll finish him later. Let us pray to God.

CLOV: Again!

NAGG: Me sugar-plum!

HAMM: God first! [*Pause.*] Are you right?

CLOV: [*Resigned.*] Off we go.

HAMM: [*To* NAGG.] And you?

NAGG: [*Clasping his hands, closing his eyes, in a gabble.*] Our Father which art—[4]

HAMM: Silence! In silence! Where are your manners? [*Pause.*] Off we go. [*Attitudes of prayer. Silence. Abandoning his attitude, discouraged.*] Well?

CLOV: [*Abandoning his attitude.*] What a hope! And you?

HAMM: Sweet damn all! [*To* NAGG.] And you?

NAGG: Wait! [*Pause. Abandoning his attitude.*] Nothing doing!

HAMM: The bastard! He doesn't exist!

CLOV: Not yet.

NAGG: Me sugar-plum!

HAMM: There are no more sugar-plums! [*Pause.*]

NAGG: It's natural. After all I'm your father. It's true if it hadn't been me it would have been someone else. But that's no excuse. [*Pause.*] Turkish Delight,[5] for example, which no longer exists, we all know that, there is nothing in the world I love more. And one day I'll ask you for some, in return for a kindness, and you'll promise it to me. One must live with the times. [*Pause.*] Whom did you call when you were a tiny boy, and were frightened, in the dark? Your mother? No. Me. We let you cry. Then we moved you out of earshot, so that we might sleep in peace.

---

4. Opening words of the (Christian) Lord's prayer.
5. Gelatinous Middle Eastern sweetmeat usually fla-   vored with rose or lemon oil.

[*Pause.*] I was asleep, as happy as a king, and you woke me up to have me listen to you. It wasn't indispensable, you didn't really need to have me listen to you. [*Pause.*] I hope the day will come when you'll really need to have me listen to you, and need to hear my voice, any voice. [*Pause.*] Yes, I hope I'll live till then, to hear you calling me like when you were a tiny boy, and were frightened, in the dark, and I was your only hope. [*Pause.* NAGG *knocks on lid of* NELL's *bin. Pause.*] Nell! [*Pause. He knocks louder. Pause. Louder.*] Nell! [*Pause.* NAGG *sinks back into his bin, closes the lid behind him. Pause.*]

HAMM: Our revels now are ended.[6] [*He gropes for the dog.*] The dog's gone.

CLOV: He's not a real dog, he can't go.

HAMM: [*Groping.*] He's not there.

CLOV: He's lain down.

HAMM: Give him up to me. [CLOV *picks up the dog and gives it to* HAMM. HAMM *holds it in his arms. Pause.* HAMM *throws away the dog.*] Dirty brute! [CLOV *begins to pick up the objects lying on the ground.*] What are you doing?

CLOV: Putting things in order. [*He straightens up. Fervently.*] I'm going to clear everything away! [*He starts picking up again.*]

HAMM: Order!

CLOV: [*Straightening up.*] I love order. It's my dream. A world where all would be silent and still and each thing in its last place, under the last dust. [*He starts picking up again.*]

HAMM: [*Exasperated.*] What in God's name do you think you are doing?

CLOV: [*Straightening up.*] I'm doing my best to create a little order.

HAMM: Drop it!

   [CLOV *drops the objects he has picked up.*]

CLOV: After all, there or elsewhere. [*He goes towards door.*]

HAMM: [*Irritably.*] What's wrong with your feet?

CLOV: My feet?

HAMM: Tramp! Tramp!

CLOV: I must have put on my boots.

HAMM: Your slippers were hurting you? [*Pause.*]

CLOV: I'll leave you.

HAMM: No!

CLOV: What is there to keep me here?

HAMM: The dialogue. [*Pause.*] I've got on with my story. [*Pause.*] I've got on with it well. [*Pause. Irritably.*] Ask me where I've got to.

CLOV: Oh, by the way, your story?

HAMM: [*Surprised.*] What story?

CLOV: The one you've been telling yourself all your days.

HAMM: Ah you mean my chronicle?

CLOV: That's the one. [*Pause.*]

HAMM: [*Angrily.*] Keep going, can't you, keep going!

6. Quotation from Shakespeare's *The Tempest*, in which Prospero announces the end of the entertainment enacted by spirits (4.1.148).

CLOV: You've got on with it, I hope.

HAMM: [*Modestly.*] Oh not very far, not very far. [*He sighs.*] There are days like that, one isn't inspired. [*Pause.*] Nothing you can do about it, just wait for it to come. [*Pause.*] No forcing, no forcing, it's fatal. [*Pause.*] I've got on with it a little all the same. [*Pause.*] Technique, you know. [*Pause. Irritably.*] I say I've got on with it a little all the same.

CLOV: [*Admiringly.*] Well I never! In spite of everything you were able to get on with it!

HAMM: [*Modestly.*] Oh not very far, you know, not very far, but nevertheless, better than nothing.

CLOV: Better than nothing! Is it possible?

HAMM: I'll tell you how it goes. He comes crawling on his belly—

CLOV: Who?

HAMM: What?

CLOV: Who do you mean, he?

HAMM: Who do I mean! Yet another.

CLOV: Ah him! I wasn't sure.

HAMM: Crawling on his belly, whining for bread for his brat. He's offered a job as gardener. Before—[CLOV *bursts out laughing.*] What is there so funny about that?

CLOV: A job as gardener!

HAMM: Is that what tickles you?

CLOV: It must be that.

HAMM: It wouldn't be the bread?

CLOV: Or the brat. [*Pause.*]

HAMM: The whole thing is comical, I grant you that. What about having a good guffaw the two of us together?

CLOV: [*After reflection.*] I couldn't guffaw again today.

HAMM: [*After reflection.*] Nor I. [*Pause.*] I continue then. Before accepting with gratitude he asks if he may have his little boy with him.

CLOV: What age?

HAMM: Oh tiny.

CLOV: He would have climbed the trees.

HAMM: All the little odd jobs.

CLOV: And then he would have grown up.

HAMM: Very likely. [*Pause.*]

CLOV: Keep going, can't you, keep going!

HAMM: That's all. I stopped there. [*Pause.*]

CLOV: Do you see how it goes on.

HAMM: More or less.

CLOV: Will it not soon be the end?

HAMM: I'm afraid it will.

CLOV: Pah! You'll make up another.

HAMM: I don't know. [*Pause.*] I feel rather drained. [*Pause.*] The prolonged creative effort. [*Pause.*] If I could drag myself down to the sea! I'd make a pillow of sand for my head and the tide would come.

CLOV: There's no more tide. [*Pause.*]

HAMM: Go and see is she dead.

[CLOV *goes to bins, raises the lid of* NELL'*s, stoops, looks into it. Pause.*]

CLOV: Looks like it.

[*He closes the lid, straightens up.* HAMM *raises his toque. Pause. He puts it on again.*]

HAMM: [*With his hand to his toque.*] And Nagg?

[CLOV *raises lid of* NAGG'*s bin, stoops, looks into it. Pause.*]

CLOV: Doesn't look like it. [*He closes the lid, straightens up.*]

HAMM: [*Letting go his toque.*] What's he doing? [CLOV *raises lid of* NAGG'*s bin, stoops, looks into it. Pause.*]

CLOV: He's crying. [*He closes lid, straightens up.*]

HAMM: Then he's living. [*Pause.*] Did you ever have an instant of happiness?

CLOV: Not to my knowledge. [*Pause.*]

HAMM: Bring me under the window. [CLOV *goes towards chair.*] I want to feel the light on my face. [CLOV *pushes chair.*] Do you remember, in the beginning, when you took me for a turn? You used to hold the chair too high. At every step you nearly tipped me out. [*With senile quaver.*] Ah great fun, we had, the two of us, great fun. [*Gloomily.*] And then we got into the way of it. [CLOV *stops the chair under window right.*] There already? [*Pause. He tilts back his head.*] Is it light?

CLOV: It isn't dark.

HAMM: [*Angrily.*] I'm asking you is it light.

CLOV: Yes. [*Pause.*]

HAMM: The curtain isn't closed?

CLOV: No.

HAMM: What window is it?

CLOV: The earth.

HAMM: I knew it! [*Angrily.*] But there's no light there! The other! [CLOV *stops the chair under window left.* HAMM *tilts back his head.*] That's what I call light! [*Pause.*] Feels like a ray of sunshine. [*Pause.*] No?

CLOV: No.

HAMM: It isn't a ray of sunshine I feel on my face?

CLOV: No. [*Pause.*]

HAMM: Am I very white? [*Pause. Angrily.*] I'm asking you am I very white!

CLOV: Not more so than usual. [*Pause.*]

HAMM: Open the window.

CLOV: What for?

HAMM: I want to hear the sea.

CLOV: You wouldn't hear it.

HAMM: Even if you opened the window?

CLOV: No.

HAMM: Then it's not worth while opening it?

CLOV: No.

HAMM: [*Violently.*] Then open it! [CLOV *gets up on the ladder, opens the window. Pause.*] Have you opened it?

CLOV: Yes. [*Pause.*]

HAMM: You swear you've opened it?

CLOV: Yes. [*Pause.*]

HAMM: Well. . . ! [*Pause.*] It must be very calm. [*Pause. Violently.*] I'm asking you is it very calm!

CLOV: Yes.

HAMM: It's because there are no more navigators. [*Pause.*] You haven't much conversation all of a sudden. Do you not feel well?

CLOV: I'm cold.

HAMM: What month are we? [*Pause.*] Close the window, we're going back. [CLOV *closes the window, gets down, pushes the chair back to its place, remains standing behind it, head bowed.*] Don't stay there, you give me the shivers! [CLOV *returns to his place beside the chair.*] Father! [*Pause. Louder.*] Father! [*Pause.*] Go and see did he hear me.
  [CLOV *goes to* NAGG's *bin, raises the lid, stoops. Unintelligible words.* CLOV *straightens up.*]

CLOV: Yes.

HAMM: Both times?
  [CLOV *stoops. As before.*]

CLOV: Once only.

HAMM: The first time or the second?
  [CLOV *stoops. As before.*]

CLOV: He doesn't know.

HAMM: It must have been the second.

CLOV: We'll never know. [*He closes lid.*]

HAMM: Is he still crying?

CLOV: No.

HAMM: The dead go fast. [*Pause.*] What's he doing?

CLOV: Sucking his biscuit.

HAMM: Life goes on. [CLOV *returns to his place beside the chair.*] Give me a rug. I'm freezing.

CLOV: There are no more rugs. [*Pause.*]

HAMM: Kiss me. [*Pause.*] Will you not kiss me?

CLOV: No.

HAMM: On the forehead.

CLOV: I won't kiss you anywhere. [*Pause.*]

HAMM: [*Holding out his hand.*] Give me your hand at least. [*Pause.*] Will you not give me your hand?

CLOV: I won't touch you. [*Pause.*]

HAMM: Give me the dog. [CLOV *looks round for the dog.*] No!

CLOV: Do you not want your dog?

HAMM: No.

CLOV: Then I'll leave you.

HAMM: [*Head bowed, absently.*] That's right.
  [CLOV *goes to door, turns.*]

CLOV: If I don't kill that rat he'll die.

HAMM: [*As before.*] That's right. [*Exit* CLOV. *Pause.*] Me to play. [*He takes out his handkerchief, unfolds it, holds it spread out before him.*] We're getting on. [*Pause.*] You weep, and weep, for nothing, so as not to laugh, and little by little . . . you begin to grieve. [*He folds the handkerchief, puts it back in his pocket, raises his head.*] All those I might have helped. [*Pause.*] Helped! [*Pause.*] Saved. [*Pause.*] Saved! [*Pause.*] The place was crawling with them! [*Pause. Violently.*] Use your head, can't you, use your head, you're on earth, there's no cure for that! [*Pause.*] Get out of here and love one another! Lick your neighbor as yourself![7] [*Pause. Calmer.*] When it wasn't bread they wanted it was crumpets. [*Pause. Violently.*] Out of my sight and back to your petting parties! [*Pause.*] All that, all that! [*Pause.*] Not even a real dog! [*Calmer.*] The end is in the beginning and yet you go on. [*Pause.*] Perhaps I could go on with my story, end it and begin another. [*Pause.*] Perhaps I could throw myself out on the floor. [*He pushes himself painfully off his seat, falls back again.*] Dig my nails into the cracks and drag myself forward with my fingers. [*Pause.*] It will be the end and there I'll be, wondering what can have brought it on and wondering what can have ... [*he hesitates*] ... why it was so long coming. [*Pause.*] There I'll be, in the old shelter, alone against the silence and ... [*he hesitates*] ... the stillness. If I can hold my peace, and sit quiet, it will be all over with sound, and motion, all over and done with. [*Pause.*] I'll have called my father and I'll have called my ... [*he hesitates*] ... my son. And even twice, or three times, in case they shouldn't have heard me, the first time, or the second. [*Pause.*] I'll say to myself, He'll come back. [*Pause.*] And then? [*Pause.*] And then? [*Pause.*] He couldn't, he has gone too far. [*Pause.*] And then? [*Pause. Very agitated.*] All kinds of fantasies! That I'm being watched! A rat! Steps! Breath held and then ... [*He breathes out.*] Then babble, babble, words, like the solitary child who turns himself into children, two, three, so as to be together, and whisper together, in the dark. [*Pause.*] Moment upon moment, pattering down, like the millet grains of ... [*he hesitates*] ... that old Greek,[8] and all life long you wait for that to mount up to a life. [*Pause. He opens his mouth to continue, renounces.*] Ah let's get it over! [*He whistles. Enter* CLOV *with alarm-clock. He halts beside the chair.*] What? Neither gone nor dead?

CLOV: In spirit only.
HAMM: Which?
CLOV: Both.
HAMM: Gone from me you'd be dead.
CLOV: And vice versa.
HAMM: Outside of here it's death! [*Pause.*] And the rat?
CLOV: He's got away.
HAMM: He can't go far. [*Pause. Anxious.*] Eh?
CLOV: He doesn't need to go far. [*Pause.*]
HAMM: Is it not time for my pain-killer?
CLOV: Yes.
HAMM: Ah! At last! Give it to me! Quick! [*Pause.*]

---

7. Parodic echo of Jesus' words to his disciples: "Thou shalt love thy neighbor as thyself" (Matthew 19.19 and elsewhere).
8. "If a grain of millet falling makes no sound, how can a bushel of grains make any sound?" Aristotle, *Physics*, 5.250a.19. Typical example of *reductio ad absurdem* paradox of Zeno of Elea, a 5th-century-B.C. Greek philosopher.

CLOV: There's no more pain-killer. [*Pause.*]

HAMM: [*Appalled.*] Good. . . ! [*Pause.*] No more pain-killer!

CLOV: No more pain-killer. You'll never get any more pain-killer. [*Pause.*]

HAMM: But the little round box. It was full!

CLOV: Yes. But now it's empty.

    [*Pause.* CLOV *starts to move about the room. He is looking for a place to put down the alarm-clock.*]

HAMM: [*Soft.*] What'll I do? [*Pause. In a scream.*] What'll I do? [CLOV *sees the picture, takes it down, stands it on the floor with its face to the wall, hangs up the alarm-clock in its place.*] What are you doing?

CLOV: Winding up.

HAMM: Look at the earth.

CLOV: Again!

HAMM: Since it's calling to you.

CLOV: Is your throat sore? [*Pause.*] Would you like a lozenge? [*Pause.*] No. [*Pause.*] Pity. [*He goes, humming, towards window right, halts before it, looks up at it.*]

HAMM: Don't sing.

CLOV: [*Turning towards* HAMM.] One hasn't the right to sing any more?

HAMM: No.

CLOV: Then how can it end?

HAMM: You want it to end?

CLOV: I want to sing.

HAMM: I can't prevent you.

    [*Pause.* CLOV *turns towards window right.*]

CLOV: What did I do with that steps? [*He looks around for ladder.*] You didn't see that steps? [*He sees it.*] Ah, about time. [*He goes towards window left.*] Sometimes I wonder if I'm in my right mind. Then it passes over and I'm as lucid as before. [*He gets up on ladder, looks out of window.*] Christ, she's under water! [*He looks.*] How can that be? [*He pokes forward his head, his hand above his eyes.*] It hasn't rained. [*He wipes the pane, looks. Pause.*] Ah what a fool I am! I'm on the wrong side! [*He gets down, takes a few steps towards window right.*] Under water! [*He goes back for ladder.*] What a fool I am! [*He carries ladder towards window right.*] Sometimes I wonder if I'm in my right senses. Then it passes off and I'm as intelligent as ever. [*He sets down ladder under window right, gets up on it, looks out of window. He turns towards* HAMM.] Any particular sector you fancy? Or merely the whole thing?

HAMM: Whole thing.

CLOV: The general effect? Just a moment. [*He looks out of window. Pause.*]

HAMM: Clov.

CLOV: [*Absorbed.*] Mmm.

HAMM: Do you know what it is?

CLOV: [*As before.*] Mmm.

HAMM: I was never there. [*Pause.*] Clov!

CLOV: [*Turning towards* HAMM, *exasperated.*] What is it?

HAMM: I was never there.

CLOV: Lucky for you. [*He looks out of window.*]

HAMM: Absent, always. It all happened without me. I don't know what's happened. [*Pause.*] Do you know what's happened? [*Pause.*] Clov!

CLOV: [*Turning towards* HAMM, *exasperated.*] Do you want me to look at this muckheap, yes or no?

HAMM: Answer me first.

CLOV: What?

HAMM: Do you know what's happened?

CLOV: When? Where?

HAMM: [*Violently.*] When! What's happened? Use your head, can't you! What has happened?

CLOV: What for Christ's sake does it matter? [*He looks out of window.*]

HAMM: I don't know.

[*Pause.* CLOV *turns towards* HAMM.]

CLOV: [*Harshly.*] When old Mother Pegg asked you for oil for her lamp and you told her to get out to hell, you knew what was happening then, no? [*Pause.*] You know what she died of, Mother Pegg? Of darkness.

HAMM: [*Feebly.*] I hadn't any.

CLOV: [*As before.*] Yes, you had. [*Pause.*]

HAMM: Have you the glass?

CLOV: No, it's clear enough as it is.

HAMM: Go and get it.

[*Pause.* CLOV *casts up his eyes, brandishes his fists. He loses balance, clutches on to the ladder. He starts to get down, halts.*]

CLOV: There's one thing I'll never understand. [*He gets down.*] Why I always obey you. Can you explain that to me?

HAMM: No. . . . Perhaps it's compassion. [*Pause.*] A kind of great compassion. [*Pause.*] Oh you won't find it easy, you won't find it easy.

[*Pause.* CLOV *begins to move about the room in search of the telescope.*]

CLOV: I'm tired of our goings on, very tired. [*He searches.*] You're not sitting on it? [*He moves the chair, looks at the place where it stood, resumes his search.*]

HAMM: [*Anguished.*] Don't leave me there! [*Angrily* CLOV *restores the chair to its place.*] Am I right in the center?

CLOV: You'd need a microscope to find this—[*He sees the telescope.*] Ah, about time. [*He picks up the telescope, gets up on the ladder, turns the telescope on the without.*]

HAMM: Give me the dog.

CLOV: [*Looking.*] Quiet!

HAMM: [*Angrily.*] Give me the dog!

[CLOV *drops the telescope, clasps his hands to his head. Pause. He gets down precipitately, looks for the dog, sees it, picks it up, hastens towards* HAMM *and strikes him violently on the head with the dog.*]

CLOV: There's your dog for you!

[*The dog falls to the ground. Pause.*]

HAMM: He hit me!

CLOV: You drive me mad, I'm mad!

HAMM: If you must hit me, hit me with the axe. [*Pause.*] Or with the gaff, hit me with the gaff. Not with the dog. With the gaff. Or with the axe.

[CLOV *picks up the dog and gives it to* HAMM *who takes it in his arms.*]

CLOV: [*Imploringly.*] Let's stop playing!

HAMM: Never! [*Pause.*] Put me in my coffin.

CLOV: There are no more coffins.

HAMM: Then let it end! [CLOV *goes towards ladder.*] With a bang! [CLOV *gets up on ladder, gets down again, looks for telescope, sees it, picks it up, gets up ladder, raises telescope.*] Of darkness! And me? Did anyone ever have pity on me?

CLOV: [*Lowering the telescope, turning towards* HAMM.] What? [*Pause.*] Is it me you're referring to?

HAMM: [*Angrily.*] An aside, ape! Did you never hear an aside before? [*Pause.*] I'm warming up for my last soliloquy.

CLOV: I warn you. I'm going to look at this filth since it's an order. But it's the last time. [*He turns the telescope on the without.*] Let's see. [*He moves the telescope.*] Nothing . . . nothing . . . good . . . good . . . nothing . . . goo—[*He starts, lowers the telescope, examines it, turns it again on the without. Pause.*] Bad luck to it!

HAMM: More complications! [CLOV *gets down.*] Not an underplot, I trust.

[CLOV *moves ladder nearer window, gets up on it, turns telescope on the without.*]

CLOV: [*Dismayed.*] Looks like a small boy!

HAMM: [*Sarcastic.*] A small . . . boy!

CLOV: I'll go and see. [*He gets down, drops the telescope, goes towards door, turns.*] I'll take the gaff. [*He looks for the gaff, sees it, picks it up, hastens towards door.*]

HAMM: No! [CLOV *halts.*]

CLOV: No? A potential procreator?

HAMM: If he exists he'll die there or he'll come here. And if he doesn't . . . [*Pause.*]

CLOV: You don't believe me? You think I'm inventing? [*Pause.*]

HAMM: It's the end, Clov, we've come to the end. I don't need you any more. [*Pause.*]

CLOV: Lucky for you. [*He goes towards door.*]

HAMM: Leave me the gaff.

[CLOV *gives him the gaff, goes towards door, halts, looks at alarm-clock, takes it down, looks round for a better place to put it, goes to bins, puts it on lid of* NAGG's *bin. Pause.*]

CLOV: I'll leave you. [*He goes towards door.*]

HAMM: Before you go . . . [CLOV *halts near door.*] . . . say something.

CLOV: There is nothing to say.

HAMM: A few words . . . to ponder . . . in my heart.

CLOV: Your heart!

HAMM: Yes. [*Pause. Forcibly.*] Yes! [*Pause.*] With the rest, in the end, the

shadows, the murmurs, all the trouble, to end up with. [*Pause.*] Clov.
. . . He never spoke to me. Then, in the end, before he went, without
my having asked him, he spoke to me. He said . . .

CLOV: [*Despairingly.*] Ah. . . !

HAMM: Something . . . from your heart.

CLOV: My heart!

HAMM: A few words . . . from your heart. [*Pause.*]

CLOV: [*Fixed gaze, tonelessly, towards auditorium.*] They said to me,
That's love, yes, yes, not a doubt, now you see how—

HAMM: Articulate!

CLOV: [*As before.*] How easy it is. They said to me, That's friendship, yes,
yes, no question, you've found it. They said to me, Here's the place,
stop, raise your head and look at all that beauty. That order! They said
to me. Come now, you're not a brute beast, think upon these things
and you'll see how all becomes clear. And simple! They said to me,
What skilled attention they get, all these dying of their wounds.

HAMM: Enough!

CLOV: [*As before.*] I say to myself—sometimes, Clov, you must learn to
suffer better than that if you want them to weary of punishing you—one
day. I say to myself—sometimes, Clov, you must be there better than
that if you want them to let you go—one day. But I feel too old, and
too far, to form new habits. Good, it'll never end, I'll never go. [*Pause.*]
Then one day, suddenly, it ends, it changes, I don't understand, it dies,
or it's me, I don't understand, that either. I ask the words that remain—
sleeping, waking, morning, evening. They have nothing to say. [*Pause.*]
I open the door of the cell and go. I am so bowed I only see my feet, if
I open my eyes, and between my legs a little trail of black dust. I say to
myself that the earth is extinguished, though I never saw it lit. [*Pause.*]
It's easy going. [*Pause.*] When I fall I'll weep for happiness. [*Pause. He
goes towards door.*]

HAMM: Clov! [CLOV *halts, without turning.*] Nothing. [CLOV *moves on.*]
Clov!

       [CLOV *halts, without turning.*]

CLOV: This is what we call making an exit.

HAMM: I'm obliged to you, Clov. For your services.

CLOV: [*Turning, sharply.*] Ah pardon, it's I am obliged to you.

HAMM: It's we are obliged to each other. [*Pause.* CLOV *goes towards door.*]
One thing more. [CLOV *halts.*] A last favor. [*Exit* CLOV.] Cover me with
the sheet. [*Long pause.*] No? Good. [*Pause.*] Me to play. [*Pause. Wearily.*] Old endgame lost of old, play and lose and have done with losing.
[*Pause. More animated.*] Let me see. [*Pause.*] Ah yes! [*He tries to move
the chair, using the gaff as before. Enter* CLOV, *dressed for the road.
Panama hat, tweed coat, raincoat over his arm, umbrella, bag. He halts
by the door and stands there, impassive and motionless, his eyes fixed
on* HAMM, *till the end.* HAMM *gives up.*] Good. [*Pause.*] Discard. [*He
throws away the gaff, makes to throw away the dog, thinks better of it.*]
Take it easy. [*Pause.*] And now? [*Pause.*] Raise hat. [*He raises his
toque.*] Peace to our . . . arses. [*Pause.*] And put on again. [*He puts on*

his toque.] Deuce. [*Pause. He takes off his glasses.*] Wipe. [*He takes out his handkerchief and, without unfolding it, wipes his glasses.*] And put on again. [*He puts on his glasses, puts back the handkerchief in his pocket.*] We're coming. A few more squirms like that and I'll call. [*Pause.*] A little poetry. [*Pause.*] You prayed—[*Pause. He corrects himself.*] You CRIED for night; it comes—[*Pause. He corrects himself.*] It FALLS: now cry in darkness. [*He repeats, chanting.*] You cried for night; it falls: now cry in darkness.[9] [*Pause.*] Nicely put, that. [*Pause.*] And now? [*Pause.*] Moments for nothing, now as always, time was never and time is over, reckoning closed and story ended. [*Pause. Narrative tone.*] If he could have his child with him. . . . [*Pause.*] It was the moment I was waiting for. [*Pause.*] You don't want to abandon him? You want him to bloom while you are withering? Be there to solace your last million last moments? [*Pause.*] He doesn't realize, all he knows is hunger, and cold, and death to crown it all. But you! You ought to know what the earth is like, nowadays. Oh I put him before his respon-sibilities! [*Pause. Normal tone.*] Well, there we are, there I am, that's enough. [*He raises the whistle to his lips, hesitates, drops it. Pause.*] Yes, truly! [*He whistles. Pause. Louder. Pause.*] Good. [*Pause.*] Father! [*Pause. Louder.*] Father! [*Pause.*] Good. [*Pause.*] We're coming. [*Pause.*] And to end up with? [*Pause.*] Discard. [*He throws away the dog. He tears the whistle from his neck.*] With my compliments. [*He throws whistle towards auditorium. Pause. He sniffs. Soft.*] Clov! [*Long pause.*] No? Good. [*He takes out the handkerchief.*] Since that's the way we're playing it . . . [*he unfolds handkerchief*] . . . let's play it that way . . . [*he unfolds*] . . . and speak no more about it . . . [*he finishes unfolding*] . . . speak no more. [*He holds handkerchief spread out before him.*] Old stancher! [*Pause.*] You . . . remain.

[*Pause. He covers his face with handkerchief, lowers his arms to arm-rests, remains motionless.*]

[*Brief tableau.*]

Curtain

9. Paraphrase of a line from Baudelaire's poem "Meditation": "You were calling for evening; it falls; here it is."

W. H. AUDEN

1907–1973

Wystan Hugh Auden was born in York and educated at Gresham's School, Holt, Norfolk, and Christ Church, Oxford. After leaving Oxford he taught school from 1930 to 1935 and later worked for a government film unit. His sympathies in the 1930s were with the Left, like those of most intellectuals of his age, and he went to Spain during the Civil War, intending to serve as an ambulance driver on the left-wing Republican side. He found himself to his surprise, however, so disturbed by the sight of the many Roman Catholic churches gutted and looted by the Republicans that he returned to England without fulfilling his ambition. He traveled in Iceland and China before coming to America in 1939; in 1946 he became an American citizen. He taught at a number of American colleges and was professor of poetry at Oxford from 1956 to 1960.

Auden was the most active of the group of young English poets who, in the late 1920s and early 1930s, saw themselves bringing new techniques and attitudes to English poetry. Stephen Spender (1909–) and Cecil Day Lewis (1904–1972) were at the time the most prominent of the other members of the new school, which soon afterward fell apart, each poet going his own separate way. Like all his generation, Auden learned poetic wit and irony from T. S. Eliot, and he also learned metrical and verbal techniques from Gerard Manley Hopkins and from Wilfred Owen. His English studies at Oxford familiarized him with the rhythms and long alliterative line of Anglo-Saxon poetry as well as with the rapid and rollicking short lines (a sort of inspired doggerel) of the poet John Skelton (ca. 1460–1529); both influenced his own versification. He learned, too, from the songs of the English music hall and, later, from American blues singers.

The depression that upset America in 1929 hit England soon afterward, and Auden and his contemporaries looked out at an England of industrial stagnation and mass unemployment, seeing not the metaphorical Waste Land of Eliot but a more literal Waste Land of poverty and "depressed areas." His early poetry is much concerned with a diagnosis of the ills of his country. This diagnosis, conducted in a verse that combined deliberate irreverence and sometimes even clowning with a cunning verbal craftsmanship, drew on both Freud and Marx to show England now as a nation of neurotic invalids who must learn to "throw away their rugs" and now as the victim of an antiquated economic system. The liveliness and nervous force of this early poetry of Auden's made a great impression, even though an uncertainty about his audience led him to introduce purely private symbols, intelligible only to a few friends, in some of his poems.

Gradually, Auden learned to clarify his imagery and control his desire to shock, and he produced, in the years around 1940, some poems (such as *Lullaby*) of finely disciplined movement, pellucid clarity, and deep yet unsentimental feeling. At the same time he was developing a more complex view of the world, moving from his earlier diagnosis of modern ills in terms of Freud and Marx to a more religious view of personal responsibility and traditional value without, however, abandoning the ideas and terms he had learned from modern psychology. But he never lost his ear for popular speech or his ability to combine elements from popular art with an extreme technical formality. He was always the experimenter, particularly in ways of bringing together high artifice and a colloquial tone.

Some of Auden's most exciting work is found in his early volumes, *Poems* (1930) and *On This Island* (1937). *Another Time* (1940) shows greater control and less violence. Of his later volumes, *Nones* (1951) shows most clearly his characteristic ways of combining or alternating the grave and the flippant. For the first part of his career—the English and the early American phase—Auden was very much the poet of his times, first of the Depression and then of the Age of the Refugee. In the poems of this period he preferred to confront modern problems directly rather than to filter them, as Eliot did, through symbolic situations. The poems of the last phase of his career, notably those in *About the House* (1967) and *City without Walls* (1970), are increasingly personal in tone and combine an apparent air of offhand informality with remarkable technical skill in versification. Auden grew increasingly hostile to the modern world and skeptical of all remedies offered for modern ills: he took refuge in love and friendship, particularly the love and friendship he shared with Chester Kallmann; emotions grounded in an ever deepening but rarely obtrusive religious feeling. In the last year of his life he returned to England to live in Oxford, feeling the need to be part of a university community as a protection against loneliness. An uneven poet, a poet who in the opinion of some critics never quite fulfilled the enormous promise of his early work, Auden is nevertheless now generally recognized as one of the masters of twentieth-century English poetry, a thoughtful, seriously playful (if one may put it in this paradoxical way) poet whom more than one critic has compared with Dryden in his combination of lively intelligence and immense craftsmanship.

Petition

Sir, no man's enemy, forgiving all
But will his negative inversion, be prodigal:
Send to us power and light, a sovereign touch[1]
Curing the intolerable neural itch,
The exhaustion of weaning, the liar's quinsy,[2]   5
And the distortions of ingrown virginity.
Prohibit sharply the rehearsed response
And gradually correct the coward's stance;
Cover in time with beams those in retreat
That, spotted, they turn though the reverse were great;   10
Publish each healer that in city lives
Or country houses at the end of drives;
Harrow the house of the dead; look shining at
New styles of architecture, a change of heart.

October 1929   1930

On This Island

Look, stranger, on this island now
The leaping light for your delight discovers,
Stand stable here
And silent be,
That through the channels of the ear   5
May wander like a river
The swaying sound of the sea.

Here at the small field's ending pause
When the chalk wall falls to the foam and its tall ledges
Oppose the pluck   10
And knock of the tide,
And the shingle scrambles after the suck-
-ing surf,
And the gull lodges
A moment on its sheer side.   15

Far off like floating seeds the ships
Diverge on urgent voluntary errands,
And the full view
Indeed may enter

1. The king's touch was often regarded as miraculous cure for disease (cf. "sovereign" as an adjective, meaning "the best").
2. Tonsillitis.

And move in memory as now these clouds do,   20
   That pass the harbour mirror
   And all the summer through the water saunter.
1935   1936

Spain 1937[1]

Yesterday all the past. The language of size
Spreading to China along the trade routes; the diffusion
         Of the counting-frame and the cromlech;[2]
Yesterday the shadow-reckoning in the sunny climates.

Yesterday the assessment of insurance by cards,   5
The divination of water; yesterday the invention
         Of cart-wheels and clocks, the taming of
Horses; yesterday the bustling world of the navigators.

Yesterday the abolition of fairies and giants;
The fortress like a motionless eagle eyeing the valley,   10
         The chapel built in the forest;
Yesterday the carving of angels and of frightening gargoyles;

The trial of heretics among the columns of stone;
Yesterday the theological feuds in the taverns
         And the miraculous cure at the fountain;   15
Yesterday the Sabbath of Witches.[3] But to-day the struggle.

Yesterday the installation of dynamos and turbines;
The construction of railways in the colonial desert;
         Yesterday the classic lecture
On the origin of Mankind. But to-day the struggle.   20

Yesterday the belief in the absolute value of Greek;
The fall of the curtain upon the death of a hero;
         Yesterday the prayer to the sunset,
And the adoration of madmen. But to-day the struggle.

As the poet whispers, startled among the pines   25
Or, where the loose waterfall sings, compact, or upright
         On the crag by the leaning tower:
"O my vision. O send me the luck of the sailor."

And the investigator peers through his instruments
At the inhuman provinces, the virile bacillus   30
         Or enormous Jupiter finished:
"But the lives of my friends. I inquire, I inquire."

1. Written when the Spanish Civil War was raging. The rebellion by General Franco's right-wing army against the left-wing Spanish government, which broke out in 1936 and provoked full-scale civil war, was viewed by British liberal intellectuals at the time as a testing struggle between fascism and democracy. The poem first appeared separately in 1937, the proceeds of its sale going to "Medical Aid for Spain." This is Auden's revised version of 1940.
2. Ancient stone circle.
3. Convocation of witches in parody of Christian service.

And the poor in their fireless lodgings dropping the sheets
Of the evening paper: "Our day is our loss. O show us
                    History the operator, the   35
Organizer, Time the refreshing river."

And the nations combine each cry, invoking the life
That shapes the individual belly and orders
                    The private nocturnal terror:
"Did you not found once the city state of the sponge,   40

"Raise the vast military empires of the shark
And the tiger, establish the robin's plucky canton?[4]
                    Intervene. O descend as a dove or
A furious papa or a mild engineer: but descend."

And the life, if it answers at all, replies from the heart   45
And the eyes and the lungs, from the shops and squares of the city:
                    "O no, I am not the Mover,
Not to-day, not to you. To you I'm the

"Yes-man, the bar-companion, the easily-duped:
I am whatever you do; I am your vow to be   50
                    Good, your humorous story;
I am your business voice; I am your marriage.

"What's your proposal? To build the Just City? I will.
I agree. Or is it the suicide pact, the romantic
                    Death? Very well, I accept, for   55
I am your choice, your decision: yes, I am Spain."

Many have heard it on remote peninsulas,
On sleepy plains, in the aberrant fishermen's islands,
                    In the corrupt heart of the city;
Have heard and migrated like gulls or the seeds of a flower.   60

They clung like burrs to the long expresses that lurch
Through the unjust lands, through the night, through the alpine tunnel;
                    They floated over the oceans;
They walked the passes: they came to present their lives.

On that arid square, that fragment nipped off from hot   65
Africa, soldered so crudely to inventive Europe,
                    On that tableland scored by rivers,
Our fever's menancing shapes are precise and alive.

To-morrow, perhaps, the future: the research on fatigue
And the movements of packers; the gradual exploring of all the   70
                    Octaves of radiation;
To-morrow the enlarging of consciousness by diet and breathing.

4. District.

To-morrow the rediscovery of romantic love;
The photographing of ravens; all the fun under
          Liberty's masterful shadow;   75
To-morrow the hour of the pageant-master and the musician.

To-morrow for the young the poets exploding like bombs,
The walks by the lake, the winter of perfect communion;
          To-morrow the bicycle races
Through the suburbs on summer evenings: but to-day the struggle.   80

To-day the inevitable increase in the chances of death;
The conscious acceptance of guilt in the fact of murder;
          To-day the expending of powers
On the flat ephemeral pamphlet and the boring meeting.

To-day the makeshift consolations; the shared cigarette;   85
The cards in the candle-lit barn and the scraping concert,
          The masculine jokes; to-day the
Fumbled and unsatisfactory embrace before hurting.

The stars are dead; the animals will not look:
We are left alone with our day, and the time is short and   90
          History to the defeated
May say Alas but cannot help or pardon.
1937   1937, 1940

Musée des Beaux Arts[1]

About suffering they were never wrong,
The Old Masters: how well they understood
Its human position; how it takes place
While someone else is eating or opening a window or just walking dully along;
How, when the aged are reverently, passionately waiting   5
For the miraculous birth, there always must be
Children who did not specially want it to happen, skating
On a pond at the edge of the wood:
They never forgot
That even the dreadful martyrdom must run its course   10
Anyhow in a corner, some untidy spot
Where the dogs go on with their doggy life and the torturer's horse
Scratches its innocent behind on a tree.

In Brueghel's Icarus,[2] for instance: how everything turns away
Quite leisurely from the disaster; the ploughman may   15
Have heard the splash, the forsaken cry,
But for him it was not an important failure; the sun shone

---

1. "Museum of Fine Arts." The reference is to the Museum of Fine Arts in Brussels, which contains Brueghel's Icarus.
2. Icarus was the son of Daedalus, the cunning craftsman of ancient legend. Together they flew on artificial wings fastened to their shoulders with wax, but Icarus ventured too near the sun, which melted the wax, and so he fell and perished. The painting of the fall of Icarus is by the Flemish painter Pieter Brueghel (ca. 1520–1569): Icarus' legs are disappearing into the sea in one corner of the picture, the rest of which has nothing to do with him.

As it had to on the white legs disappearing into the green
Water; and the expensive delicate ship that must have seen
Something amazing, a boy falling out of the sky,   20
Had somewhere to get to and sailed calmly on.

December 1938   1940

Lullaby

Lay your sleeping head, my love,
Human on my faithless arm;
Time and fevers burn away
Individual beauty from
Thoughtful children, and the grave   5
Proves the child ephemeral:
But in my arms till break of day
Let the living creature lie,
Mortal, guilty, but to me
The entirely beautiful.   10

Soul and body have no bounds:
To lovers as they lie upon
Her tolerant enchanted slope
In their ordinary swoon,
Grave the vision Venus sends   15
Of supernatural sympathy,
Universal love and hope;
While an abstract insight wakes
Among the glaciers and the rocks
The hermit's carnal ecstasy.   20

Certainty, fidelity
On the stroke of midnight pass
Like vibrations of a bell,
And fashionable madmen raise
Their pedantic boring cry: 25
Every farthing[1] of the cost,
All the dreaded cards foretell,
Shall be paid, but from this night
Not a whisper, not a thought,
Not a kiss nor look be lost.   30

Beauty, midnight, vision dies:
Let the winds of dawn that blow
Softly round your dreaming head
Such a day of sweetness show
Eye and knocking heart may bless,   35
Find the mortal world enough;
Noons of dryness see you fed

---

1. At one time the smallest and least valuable British coin.

By the involuntary powers,
Nights of insult let you pass
Watched by every human love.   40

In Memory of W. B. Yeats

(*d. Jan. 1939*)

1

He disappeared in the dead of winter:
The brooks were frozen, the airports almost deserted,
And snow disfigured the public statues;
The mercury sank in the mouth of the dying day.
What instruments we have agree   5
The day of his death was a dark cold day.

Far from his illness
The wolves ran on through the evergreen forests,
The peasant river was untempted by the fashionable quays;
By mourning tongues   10
The death of the poet was kept from his poems.

But for him it was his last afternoon as himself,
An afternoon of nurses and rumours;
The provinces of his body revolted,
The squares of his mind were empty,   15
Silence invaded the suburbs,
The current of his feeling failed: he became his admirers.

Now he is scattered among a hundred cities
And wholly given over to unfamiliar affections;
To find his happiness in another kind of wood[1]   20
And be punished under a foreign code of conscience.
The words of a dead man
Are modified in the guts of the living.

But in the importance and noise of to-morrow
When the brokers are roaring like beasts on the floor of the Bourse,[2]   25
And the poor have the sufferings to which they are fairly accustomed,
And each in the cell of himself is almost convinced of his freedom,
A few thousand will think of this day
As one thinks of a day when one did something slightly unusual.
What instruments we have agree   30
The day of his death was a dark cold day.

---

1. Cf. Dante's *Inferno* 1.1–3 (translated): "In the mid-   wood where the straight way was lost."
dle of the journey of our life I came to myself in a dark   2. Stock exchange.

2

You were silly like us: your gift survived it all:
The parish of rich women, physical decay,
Yourself. Mad Ireland hurt you into poetry.
Now Ireland has her madness and her weather still,   35
For poetry makes nothing happen: it survives
In the valley of its making where executives
Would never want to tamper, flows on south
From ranches of isolation and the busy griefs,
Raw towns that we believe and die in; it survives,   40
A way of happening, a mouth.

3

Earth, receive an honoured guest:
William Yeats is laid to rest.
Let the Irish vessel lie
Emptied of its poetry.[3]   45

In the nightmare of the dark
All the dogs of Europe bark,
And the living nations wait,
Each sequestered in its hate;

Intellectual disgrace   50
Stares from every human face,
And the seas of pity lie
Locked and frozen in each eye.

Follow, poet, follow right
To the bottom of the night,   55
With your unconstraining voice
Still persuade us to rejoice;

With the farming of a verse
Make a vineyard of the curse,
Sing of human unsuccess   60
In a rapture of distress;

In the deserts of the heart
Let the healing fountain start,
In the prison of his days
Teach the free man how to praise.   65

February 1939   1940, 1966

---

3. Three stanzas that originally followed this were omitted in the 1966 edition of Auden's *Collected Shorter Poems* and thereafter: "Time that is intolerant / Of the brave and innocent, / And indifferent in a week / To a beautiful physique, / / Worships language and forgives / Everyone by whom it lives; / Pardons cowardice, conceit, / Lays its honours at their feet. / / Time that with this strange excuse / Pardoned Kipling and his views, / And will pardon Paul Claudel, / Pardons him for writing well." Kipling's views were imperialistic and jingoistic; Paul Claudel (1868–1955), French poet, dramatist, and diplomat, was an extreme right-winger in his political ideas. Yeats's own politics were at times antidemocratic and appeared to favor dictatorship.

Their Lonely Betters

As I listened from a beach-chair in the shade
To all the noises that my garden made,
It seemed to me only that words
Should be withheld from vegetables and birds.

A robin with no Christian name ran through   5
The Robin-Anthem which was all it knew,
And rustling flowers for some third party waited
To say which pairs, if any, should get mated.

Not one of them was capable of lying,
There was not one which knew that it was dying   10
Or could have with a rhythm or a rhyme
Assumed responsibility for time.

Let them leave language to their lonely betters
Who count some days and long for certain letters;
We, too, make noises when we laugh or weep,   15
Words are for those with promises to keep.

1950   1951

In Praise of Limestone[1]

If it form the one landscape that we the inconstant ones
    Are consistently homesick for, this is chiefly
Because it dissolves in water. Mark these rounded slopes
    With their surface fragrance of thyme and, beneath,
A secret system of caves and conduits; hear the springs   5
    That spurt out everywhere with a chuckle
Each filling a private pool for its fish and carving
    Its own little ravine whose cliffs entertain
The butterfly and the lizard; examine this region
    Of short distances and definite places: 10
What could be more like Mother or a fitter background
    For her son, for the flirtatious male who lounges
Against a rock in the sunlight, never doubting
    That for all his faults he is loved; whose works are but
Extensions of his power to charm? From weathered outcrop   15
    To hill-top temple, from appearing waters to
Conspicuous fountains, from a wild to a formal vineyard,
    Are ingenious but short steps that a child's wish
To receive more attention than his brothers, whether
    By pleasing or teasing, can easily take.   20

---

1. Inspired by Auden's travels in Italy. As Auden wrote to Elizabeth Mayer: "I hadn't realised till I came how like Italy is to my 'Mutterland', the Pennines. Am in fact starting on a poem, 'In Praise of Limestone', the theme of which is that that rock creates the only truly human landscape." The Pennines is the name both of an alpine range in northern Italy and of a range of hills in northern England, Auden's "motherland."

Watch, then, the band of rivals as they climb up and down
    Their steep stone gennels[2] in twos and threes, at times
Arm in arm, but never, thank God, in step; or engaged
    On the shady side of a square at midday in
Voluble discourse, knowing each other too well to think   25
    There are any important secrets, unable
To conceive a god whose temper-tantrums are moral
    And not to be pacified by a clever line
Or a good lay: for, accustomed to a stone that responds,
    They have never had to veil their faces in awe   30
Of a crater whose blazing fury could not be fixed;
    Adjusted to the local needs of valleys
Where everything can be touched or reached by walking,
    Their eyes have never looked into infinite space
Through the lattice-work of a nomad's comb;[3] born lucky,   35
    Their legs have never encountered the fungi
And insects of the jungle, the monstrous forms and lives
    With which we have nothing, we like to hope, in common.
So, when one of them goes to the bad, the way his mind works
    Remains comprehensible: to become a pimp   40
Or deal in fake jewelry or ruin a fine tenor voice
    For effects that bring down the house, could happen to all
But the best and the worst of us . . .
                                        That is why, I suppose,
    The best and worst never stayed here long but sought
Immoderate soils where the beauty was not so external,   45
    The light less public and the meaning of life
Something more than a mad camp. "Come!" cried the granite wastes,
    "How evasive is your humour, how accidental
Your kindest kiss, how permanent is death." (Saints-to-be
    Slipped away sighing.) "Come!" purred the clays and gravels.   50
"On our plains there is room for armies to drill; rivers
    Wait to be tamed and slaves to construct you a tomb
In the grand manner: soft as the earth is mankind and both
    Need to be altered." (Intendant Caesars[4] rose and
Left, slamming the door.) But the really reckless were fetched   55
    By an older colder voice, the oceanic whisper:
"I am the solitude that asks and promises nothing;
    That is how I shall set you free. There is no love;
There are only the various envies, all of them sad."

They were right, my dear, all those voices were right   60
And still are; this land is not the sweet home that it looks,
    Nor its peace the historical calm of a site
Where something was settled once and for all: A backward
    And dilapidated province, connected
To the big busy world by a tunnel, with a certain   65

Seedy appeal, is that all it is now? Not quite:
It has a worldly duty which in spite of itself
   It does not neglect, but calls into question
All the Great Powers assume; it disturbs our rights. The poet,
   Admired for his earnest habit of calling   70
The sun the sun, his mind Puzzle, is made uneasy
   By these marble statues which so obviously doubt
His antimythological myth; and these gamins,[5]
   Pursuing the scientist down the tiled colonnade
With such lively offers, rebuke his concern for Nature's   75
   Remotest aspects: I, too, am reproached, for what
And how much you know. Not to lose time, not to get caught,
   Not to be left behind, not, please! to resemble
The beasts who repeat themselves, or a thing like water
   Or stone whose conduct can be predicted, these   80
Are our Common Prayer, whose greatest comfort is music
   Which can be made anywhere, is invisible,
And does not smell. In so far as we have to look forward
   To death as a fact, no doubt we are right: But if
Sins can be forgiven, if bodies rise from the dead,   85
   These modifications of matter into
Innocent athletes and gesticulating fountains,
   Made solely for pleasure, make a further point:
The blessed will not care what angle they are regarded from,
   Having nothing to hide. Dear, I know nothing of   90
Either, but when I try to imagine a faultless love
   Or the life to come, what I hear is the murmur
Of underground streams, what I see is a limestone landscape.
May 1948   1948, 1951

The Shield of Achilles[1]

   She looked over his shoulder
      For vines and olive trees,
   Marble well-governed cities
      And ships upon untamed seas,
   But there on the shining metal   5
      His hands had put instead
   An artificial wilderness
      And a sky like lead.

A plain without a feature, bare and brown,
   No blade of grass, no sign of neighborhood,   10
Nothing to eat and nowhere to sit down,
   Yet, congregated on its blankness, stood
      An unintelligible multitude,

5. Urchins.

1. In books 16 and 17 of Homer's *Iliad*, Achilles, the chief Greek hero in the war against Troy, lends his armor to his friend Patroclus and loses it when Patroclus is killed by the Trojan hero Hector. While Achilles is mourning for his friend, his mother, the goddess Thetis, goes to Mt. Olympus to beg He-phaestos, god of fire, to forge new armor for Achilles. The splendid shield that Hephaestos then makes him is described in book 18 of the *Iliad* (lines 478–608). On it he depicts the heavens, the sea, and the earth represented by many scenes such as a city at peace and a city at war.

A million eyes, a million boots in line,
Without expression, waiting for a sign.   15

Out of the air a voice without a face
    Proved by statistics that some cause was just
In tones as dry and level as the place:
    No one was cheered and nothing was discussed;
    Column by column in a cloud of dust   20
They marched away enduring a belief
Whose logic brought them, somewhere else, to grief.

                She looked over his shoulder
                    For ritual pieties,
                White flower-garlanded heifers,   25
                    Libation and sacrifice,[2]
                But there on the shining metal
                    Where the altar should have been,
                She saw by his flickering forge-light
                    Quite another scene.   30

Barbed wire enclosed an arbitrary spot
    Where bored officials lounged (one cracked a joke)
And sentries sweated for the day was hot:
    A crowd of ordinary decent folk
    Watched from without and neither moved nor spoke   35
As three pale figures were led forth and bound
To three posts driven upright in the ground.

The mass and majesty of this world, all
    That carries weight and always weighs the same
Lay in the hands of others; they were small   40
    And could not hope for help and no help came:
    What their foes liked to do was done, their shame
Was all the worst could wish; they lost their pride
And died as men before their bodies died.

                She looked over his shoulder   45
                    For athletes at their games,
                Men and women in a dance
                    Moving their sweet limbs
                    Quick, quick, to music,
                But there on the shining shield   50
                    His hands had set no dancing-floor
                    But a weed-choked field.

A ragged urchin, aimless and alone,
    Loitered about that vacancy; a bird
Flew up to safety from his well-aimed stone: 55
    That girls are raped, that two boys knife a third,

---

2. Cf. Keats, *Ode on a Grecian Urn*, lines 31–34: "Who are these coming to the sacrifice? / To what green altar, O mysterious priest, / Lead'st thou that heifer lowing at the skies, / And all her silken flanks with garlands drest?"

Were axioms to him, who'd never heard
Of any world where promises were kept,
Or one could weep because another wept.

The thin-lipped armorer,   60
Hephaestos, hobbled away,
Thetis of the shining breasts
Cried out in dismay
At what the god had wrought
    To please her son, the strong   65
Iron-hearted man-slaying Achilles
Who would not live long.

1952   1955

DYLAN THOMAS
1914–1953

Dylan Thomas was born in Swansea, Wales, and educated at Swansea Grammar
School. After working for a time as a newspaper reporter, he was "discovered" as a
poet in 1933 through a poetry contest in a popular newspaper. The following year
his *Eighteen Poems* caused considerable excitement because of the strange violence of their imagery and their powerfully suggestive obscurity. It looked as
though a new kind of strength and romantic picturesqueness had been restored to
English poetry after the deliberately muted tones of T. S. Eliot and his followers.
Thomas did not, however, turn out to be the founder of a neo-Romantic movement, though some early critics took him to be so. As his poetry became better
known, and after he had clarified the somewhat clotted imagery of his early style
in his later volumes—*The Map of Love* (1939), *Deaths and Entrances* (1946),
Collected Poems (1953)—it became clear that he was a master craftsman, and not
the shouting rhapsodist that some had taken him to be. His images were most
carefully ordered in a patterned sequence, and his major theme was the unity of
all life, the continuing *process* of life and death and new life that linked the generations to each other. Thomas saw the workings of biology as a magical transformation producing unity out of diversity, and again and again in his poetry he sought
a poetic ritual to celebrate this unity ("The force that through the green fuse drives
the flower / Drives my green age"). He saw men and women locked in a round of
identities—with the beginning of growth also the first movement toward death,
the beginning of love leading to procreation, new growth, and so in turn to death
again and to life again, and because of this view he comforted himself with the
unity of humankind and nature, of past and present, of life and death, and so
"refused to mourn the death of a child." In his best poems the closely woven
imagery (deriving from the Bible, Welsh folklore and preaching, and Freud) is
organized to present aspects of this theme. His more open-worked poems of reminiscence and autobiographical emotion, such as *Poem in October*, communicate
more immediately to the reader through their fine lyrical feeling and compelling
use of simple natural images. His autobiographical work *Portrait of the Artist as a
Young Dog* and his radio play *Under Milk Wood* reveal a vividness of observation
and a combination of violence and tenderness in expression that show he could
handle prose as excitingly as verse.

Thomas was a brilliant talker (when he felt like it), a considerable drinker, a reckless and impulsive man whose short life was packed with emotional ups and downs. His poetry readings in the United States between 1950 and 1953 were enormous successes, in spite of his sometimes reckless antics. He died suddenly in New York, in November 1953, of what was diagnosed as "an insult to the brain," precipitated by alcohol. He acted the wild bohemian poet as that role had not been played since the 1890s; some thought this behavior wonderful, though others deplored it. He was a brilliant reader of his own and others' poems, and many people who do not normally read poetry were drawn to Thomas's by the magic of his own reading. After his premature death a reaction set in: some critics declared that he had been overrated as a poet because of the sensational role he had played in life. But a balanced view is now possible; it is clear that at his best he was an original poet of great power and beauty.

The Force That Through the Green Fuse Drives the Flower

The force that through the green fuse drives the flower
Drives my green age; that blasts the roots of trees
Is my destroyer.
And I am dumb to tell the crooked rose
My youth is bent by the same wintry fever.   5

The force that drives the water through the rocks
Drives my red blood; that dries the mouthing streams
Turns mine to wax.
And I am dumb to mouth unto my veins
How at the mountain spring the same mouth sucks.   10

The hand that whirls the water in the pool[1]
Stirs the quicksand; that ropes the blowing wind
Hauls my shroud sail.
And I am dumb to tell the hanging man
How of my clay is made the hangman's lime.[2]   15

The lips of time leech to the fountain head;
Love drips and gathers, but the fallen blood
Shall calm her sores.
And I am dumb to tell a weather's wind
How time has ticked a heaven round the stars.   20

And I am dumb to tell the lover's tomb
How at my sheet goes the same crooked worm.

                                                                        1933

After the Funeral

(In Memory of Ann Jones)[1]

After the funeral, mule praises, brays,
Windshake of sailshaped ears, muffle-toed tap

1. The hand of the angel who troubles the water of the pool Bethesda, thus rendering it curative, in John 5.1–4.
2. Quicklime was sometimes poured into the graves of victims of the public hangmen to accelerate decompo-

sition.
1. Ann Jones was Thomas's aunt; she lived at a farmhouse called Fern Hill in the Welsh landscape described in *Poem in October* and *Fern Hill*.

Tap happily of one peg in the thick
Grave's foot, blinds down the lids, the teeth in black,
The spittled eyes, the salt ponds in the sleeves,   5
Morning smack of the spade that wakes up sleep,
Shakes a desolate boy who slits his throat
In the dark of the coffin and sheds dry leaves,
That breaks one bone to light with a judgment clout,
After the feast of tear-stuffed time and thistles   10
In a room with a stuffed fox and a stale fern,
I stand, for this memorial's sake, alone
In the snivelling hours with dead, humped Ann
Whose hooded, fountain heart once fell in puddles
Round the parched worlds of Wales and drowned each sun   15
(Though this for her is a monstrous image blindly
Magnified out of praise; her death was a still drop;
She would not have me sinking in the holy
Flood of her heart's fame; she would lie dumb and deep
And need no druid[2] of her broken body).   20
But I, Ann's bard on a raised hearth, call all
The seas to service that her wood-tongued virtue
Babble like a bellbuoy over the hymning heads,
Bow down the walls of the ferned and foxy woods
That her love sing and swing through a brown chapel,   25
Bless her bent spirit with four, crossing birds.
Her flesh was meek as milk, but this skyward statue
With the wild breast and blessed and giant skull
Is carved from her in a room with a wet window
In a fiercely mourning house in a crooked year.   30
I know her scrubbed and sour humble hands
Lie with religion in their cramp, her threadbare
Whisper in a damp word, her wits drilled hollow,
Her fist of a face died clenched on a round pain;
And sculptured Ann is seventy years of stone.   35
These cloud-sopped, marble hands, this monumental
Argument of the hewn voice, gesture and psalm,
Storm me forever over her grave until
The stuffed lung of the fox twitch and cry Love
And the strutting fern lay seeds on the black sill.   40

                                                    1938, 1939

There Was a Saviour

There was a saviour
Rarer than radium,
Commoner than water, crueller than truth;
Children kept from the sun
Assembled at his tongue   5
To hear the golden note turn in a groove,
Prisoners of wishes locked their eyes
In the jails and studies of his keyless smiles.

---

2. Priest of the ancient Celtic pagans (ancestors of the modern Welsh).

The voice of children says
From a lost wilderness   10
There was calm to be done in his safe unrest,
When hindering man hurt
Man, animal, or bird
We hid our fears in that murdering breath,
Silence, silence to do, when earth grew loud,   15
In lairs and asylums of the tremendous shout.

There was glory to hear
In the churches of his tears,
Under his downy arm you sighed as he struck,
O you who could not cry   20
On to the ground when a man died
Put a tear for joy in the unearthly flood
And laid your cheek against a cloud-formed shell:
Now in the dark there is only yourself and myself.

Two proud, blacked brothers cry,   25
Winter-locked side by side,
To this inhospitable hollow year,
O we who could not stir
One lean sigh when we heard
Greed on man beating near and fire neighbour   30
But wailed and nested in the sky-blue wall
Now break a giant tear for the little known fall,

For the drooping of homes
-          That did not nurse our bones,
Brave deaths of only ones but never found,   35
Now see, alone in us,
Our own true strangers' dust
Ride through the doors of our unentered house.
Exiled in us we arouse the soft,
Unclenched, armless, silk and rough love that breaks all rocks.   40

                                                              1940

The Hunchback in the Park

The hunchback in the park
A solitary mister
Propped between trees and water
From the opening of the garden lock
That lets the trees and water enter   5
Until the Sunday sombre bell at dark

Eating bread from a newspaper
Drinking water from the chained cup
That the children filled with gravel
In the fountain basin where I sailed my ship   10

Slept at night in a dog kennel
But nobody chained him up.

Like the park birds he came early
Like the water he sat down
And Mister they called Hey mister   15
The truant boys from the town
Running when he had heard them clearly
On out of sound

Past lake and rockery
Laughing when he shook his paper   20
Hunchbacked in mockery
Through the loud zoo of the willow groves
Dodging the park keeper
With his stick that picked up leaves.

And the old dog sleeper   25
Alone between nurses and swans
While the boys among willows
Made the tigers jump out of their eyes
To roar on the rockery stones
And the groves were blue with sailors   30

Made all day until bell time
A woman figure without fault
Straight as a young elm
Straight and tall from his crooked bones
That she might stand in the night   35
After the locks and chains

All night in the unmade park
After the railings and shrubberies
The birds the grass the trees the lake
And the wild boys innocent as strawberries   40
Had followed the hunchback
To his kennel in the dark.

                                                        1941

Poem in October

It was my thirtieth year to heaven
Woke to my hearing from harbour and neighbour wood
And the mussel pooled and the heron
            Priested shore
        The morning beckon   5
With water praying and call of seagull and rook
And the knock of sailing boats on the net webbed wall
        Myself to set foot
            That second
In the still sleeping town and set forth.   10

My birthday began with the water-
Birds and the birds of the winged trees flying my name
      Above the farms and the white horses
             And I rose
           In rainy autumn 15
And walked abroad in a shower of all my days.
High tide and the heron dived when I took the road
      Over the border
          And the gates
Of the town closed as the town awoke. 20

      A springful of larks in a rolling
Cloud and the roadside bushes brimming with whistling
      Blackbirds and the sun of October
           Summery
         On the hill's shoulder, 25
Here were fond climates and sweet singers suddenly
Come in the morning where I wandered and listened
      To the rain wringing
         Wind blow cold
In the wood faraway under me. 30

      Pale rain over the dwindling harbour
And over the sea wet church the size of a snail
      With its horns through mist and the castle
         Brown as owls
        But all the gardens 35
Of spring and summer were blooming in the tall tales
Beyond the border and under the lark full cloud.
      There could I marvel
        My birthday
Away but the weather turned around. 40

      It turned away from the blithe country
And down the other air and the blue altered sky
      Streamed again a wonder of summer
         With apples
        Pears and red currants 45
And I saw in the turning so clearly a child's
Forgotten mornings when he walked with his mother
      Through the parables
        Of sun light
And the legends of the green chapels 50

      And the twice told fields of infancy
That his tears burned my cheeks and his heart moved in mine.
      These were the woods the river and sea
        Where a boy
        In the listening 55
Summertime of the dead whispered the truth of his joy
To the trees and the stones and the fish in the tide.
      And the mystery

Sang alive
Still in the water and singingbirds.   60

And there could I marvel my birthday
Away but the weather turned around. And the true
Joy of the long dead child sang burning
In the sun.
It was my thirtieth   65
Year to heaven stood there then in the summer noon
Though the town below lay leaved with October blood.
O may my heart's truth
Still be sung
On this high hill in a year's turning.   70

1945, 1946

Do Not Go Gentle into That Good Night

Do not go gentle into that good night,
Old age should burn and rave at close of day;
Rage, rage against the dying of the light.

Though wise men at their end know dark is right,
Because their words had forked no lightning they   5
Do not go gentle into that good night.

Good men, the last wave by, crying how bright
Their frail deeds might have danced in a green bay,
Rage, rage against the dying of the light.

Wild men who caught and sang the sun in flight,   10
And learn, too late, they grieved it on its way,
Do not go gentle into that good night.

Grave men, near death, who see with blinding sight
Blind eyes could blaze like meteors and be gay,
Rage, rage against the dying of the light.   15

And you, my father, there on the sad height,
Curse, bless, me now with your fierce tears, I pray.
Do not go gentle into that good night.
Rage, rage against the dying of the light.

1951, 1952

Poems in Process

In all ages, some poets have claimed that their poems were not willed but were inspired, whether by a muse, by divine visitation, or by sudden emergence from the author's subconscious mind. But as the poet Richard Aldington has remarked, "genius is not enough; one must also work." The working manuscripts of the greatest writers show that, however involuntary the origin of a poem, vision was usually followed by laborious revision before the work achieved the seeming inevitability of its final form.

Milton is the first major English author for whom we possess drafts of poems indubitably written in his own hand; the excerpt from his manuscript of *Lycidas* shows the extent to which he worked over and expanded his initial attempt. We have increasing numbers of manuscripts written in the eighteenth century, such as those reproduced below from Pope and Johnson. In the early nineteenth century the working drafts of poets began to be widely preserved, and so remain abundantly available.

The examples from major poets that are transcribed here represent various stages in the composition of a poem, and a variety of procedures by individual poets. In all these examples we look on as poets, no matter how rapidly they achieve a result they are willing to let stand, carry on their inevitably tentative efforts to meet the multiple requirements of meaning, syntax, meter, sound pattern, and the constraints imposed by a chosen stanza. And because these are all very good poets, the seeming conflict between the necessities of significance and form results not in the distortion but in the perfecting of the poetic statement.

Our transcriptions from the poets' drafts attempt to reproduce, as accurately as the change from script to print will allow, the appearance of the original manuscript page. A poet's first attempt at a line or phrase is reproduced in larger type, the emendations in smaller type. The line numbers in the headings that identify an excerpt are those of the final form of the complete poem, as reprinted in this anthology, above. The marginal numbers beside the extract from *The Vanity of Human Wishes* are Johnson's own additions.

SELECTED BIBLIOGRAPHY

Autograph Poetry in the English Language, 2 vols., 1973, compiled by P. J. Croft, reproduces and transcribes one or more pages of manuscript in the poet's own hand, from the 14th century to the present time. Volume 1 includes Blake and Burns; volume 2 includes many of the other poets represented in this volume of *The Norton Anthology of English Literature*, from Wordsworth to Dylan Thomas. Books that discuss the process of composition and revision, with examples from the manuscripts and printed versions of poems, are Charles D. Abbott, ed., *Poets at Work*, 1948; Phyllis Bartlett, *Poems in Process*, 1951; A. F. Scott, *The Poet's Craft*, 1957; George Bornstein, *Poetic Remaking: The Art of Browning, Yeats, and Pound*, 1988. In *Word for* *Word: A Study of Authors' Alterations*, 1965, Wallace Hildick analyzes the composition of prose fiction as well as poems; a shorter version, *Word for Word: The Rewriting of Fiction*, 1965, discusses the revision of novels by George Eliot, Samuel Butler, Hardy, Lawrence, James, and Woolf. Byron's "Don Juan," ed. T. G. Steffan and W. W. Pratt, 4 vols., 1957, transcribes the manuscript drafts; the Cornell Wordsworth, in process, reproduces, transcribes, and discusses various versions of Wordsworth's poems from the first manuscript drafts to the final publication in his lifetime, and the Cornell Yeats, also in process, does the same for Yeats. For facsimiles and transcripts of Keats's poems, see *John Keats: Poetry Manuscripts at Har-*

vard, ed. Jack Stillinger, 1990. Jon Stallworthy, *Between the Lines: Yeats's Poetry in the Making*, 1963, reproduces and analyzes the sequential drafts of a number of Yeats's major poems. Valerie Eliot has edited T. S. Eliot's *The Waste Land: A Facsimile and Transcript of the Original Drafts* *Including the Annotations of Ezra Pound*, 1971, while Dame Helen Gardner has transcribed and analyzed the manuscript drafts of Eliot's *Four Quartets* in *The Composition of Four Quartets*, 1978.

JOHN MILTON
From Lycidas[1]

[*Lines* 1–14][2]

yet once more O ye laurells and once more
ye myrtl's browne wth Ivie never sere
I come to pluck yor berries harsh and crude
~~before the mellowing yeare~~ and wth forc't fingers rude
~~and crop yor young~~ shatter yor leaves before ye mellowing yeare
bitter constraint, and sad occasion deare

compells me to disturbe yor season due
tor ~~young~~ Lycidas is dead, dead ere his prime
young Lycidas and hath not left his peere
who would ^not sing for Lycidas he well knew
himselfe to sing & build the loftie rime
he must not flote upon his watrie beare
unwept, and welter to the parching wind
without the meed of some melodious teare

[*Lines* 56–63]

ay mee I fondly dreame
~~had yee~~ bin there, ~~for~~ what could that have don?
~~what could the golden hayrd Calliope~~
for her inchaunting son
~~when shee beheld   (the gods farre sighted bee)~~
~~his goarie scalpe rowle downe the Thracian lee~~

whome universal nature
might lament
~~and heaven and hel deplore~~
~~when his divine head downe~~
the streame was sent
downe the Swift Hebrus to the
Lesbian shore.

[THE THIRD AND FOLLOWING LINES ARE REWRITTEN ON A SEPARATE PAGE]

~~what could the muse her selfe that Orpheus bore~~
the muse her selfe for her inchanting son
~~for her inchanting son~~
whome universal nature ~~might~~ did lament
when by the rout that made the hideous roare
gorie his ~~divine~~ gorie visage down the streame was sent
downe the swift Hebrus to ye Lesbian shoare.

1. Transcribed from a manuscript of fifty pages in the library of Trinity College, Cambridge. Among the poems written in Milton's own hand are *Lycidas*, *Comus*, seven sonnets, and several other short poems. The manuscript has been photographically reproduced, with printed transcriptions, by W. Aldis Wright, *Facsimile* *of the Manuscript of Milton's Minor Poems* (Cambridge, England, 1899).
2. This draft is written on a separate page of the manuscript, which also contains drafts of the passages, "What could the muse her selfe" and "Bring the rathe primrose," transcribed below.

[*Lines* 132–153]

Returne Alpheus the dred voice is past
 that shrunk thy streams, returne Sicilian Muse
 and call the vales and bid them hither cast
 thire bells, and flowrets of a thousand hues
 yee vallies low where the mild wispers use

 of shades, and wanton winds, and goshing brooks   ✳

                ✳ sparely
 on whose fresh lap the swart starre spárely looks   ~~faintly~~

✳ ~~bring~~ hither all yoᵘ quaint enamel'd eyes   ✳ throw
 that on the greene terfe suck the honied showrs
 and purple all the ground wᵗʰ vernal flowrs
          —— Bring the rathe &c.³
 to strew the laureat herse where Lycid' lies
 for so to interpose a little ease
    ✳ fraile
 let our ~~sad~~ thoughts dally wᵗʰ false surmise   ✳ fraile

[LINES 142–150 ARE DRAFTED ON A SEPARATE PAGE, AS FOLLOWS]

Bring the rathe primrose that unwedded dies
~~collu~~ colouring the pale cheeke of uninjoyd love
and that sad floure that strove
to write his owne woes on the vermeil graine

next adde Narcissus yᵗ still weeps in vaine
the woodbine and yᵉ pansie freak't wᵗʰ jet
the glowing violet
the cowslip wan that hangs his pensive head
and every bud that sorrows liverie weares
       with
let Daffadillies fill thire cups teares
bid Amaranthus all his beautie shed
to strew the laureat herse &c.

Bring the rathe primrose that forsaken dies
the tufted crowtoe and pale Gessamin
      yᵉ
the white pinke, and pansie freakt wᵗʰ jet
the glowing violet
     the well-attired woodbine
the muske rose and ~~the garish columbine~~
wᵗʰ cowslips wan that hang the pensive head
     ✳ weare ✳   weares
and every flower that sad escutcheon ~~beares~~ imbroidrie ~~beares~~

&
2 ~~let~~ daffadillies fill thire cups wᵗʰ teares
1 bid Amaranthus all his beauties shed
 to strew &c.

3. I.e., Milton plans to insert here the passage that follows, lines 142–150.

ALEXANDER POPE

From An Essay on Man[1]

[*From the First Manuscript*]

        we ourselves
1. Learn ~~then thyself,~~ not God presume to scan,
     But
    ~~And~~ know, the Study of Mankind is <u>Man</u>.
    Plac'd on this <u>Isthmus</u> of a Middle State,
    A Being <u>darkly wise</u>, & <u>rudely great</u>.
    With too much <u>knowledge</u> for the <u>Sceptic</u> side,
    And too much <u>Weakness</u> for a <u>Stoic's</u> Pride,
    He hangs between, uncertain where to rest;
    Whether to deem himself a <u>God</u> or <u>Beast</u>;
    Whether his <u>Mind</u> or <u>Body</u> to prefer,
    Born but to <u>die</u>, & reas'ning but to <u>err</u>;
                 his
    Alike in <u>Ignorance</u>, (~~that~~ Reason such)
    ~~Who~~   ~~who thinks~~
    Whether he thinks too <u>little</u> or too <u>much</u>:
    Chaos of <u>Thought</u> & <u>Passion</u>, all confus'd,
    Still by <u>himself</u> abus'd & dis-abus'd:
    Created half to <u>rise</u>, & half to <u>fall</u>;
    Great <u>Lord</u> of all things, yet a <u>prey</u> to all;
    Sole <u>Judge</u> of <u>Truth</u>, in endless <u>Error</u> hurl'd;
    The <u>Glory</u>, <u>Jest</u>, and <u>Riddle</u> of the World.

[*From the Second Manuscript*][2]

~~Incipit I~~   Know
~~Incipit III~~   ~~Learn~~ we ourselves, not God presume to scan,
The only Science   Convinc'd,
    ~~But know~~, the Study of Mankind is <u>Man</u>;
    ⟦Plac'd on this Isthmus of a Middle State,
    A Being darkly wise, and rudely great;
    With too much Knowledge for the Sceptic side,
         With
    ~~And~~ too much Weakness for a Stoic's Pride,
           in doubt to act or
    He hangs between, ~~uncertain where to~~ rest,
                   Part of
    Whether *To* deem himself a͜God or Beast;
       In doubt
    Whether his Mind, or Body to prefer.
    ~~This born~~   ~~that~~
    Born but to die, and reas'ning but to err;
    Alike in Ignorance, his Reason such,
    Whether he thinks   or too much.
    ~~Who thinks~~ too little, ~~or who thinks too much.~~

---

1. Two of Pope's holograph manuscripts of *An Essay on Man* have survived. The earlier one is at the Pierpont Morgan Library in New York. The second one, at the Houghton Library, Harvard, was evidently intended as a fair copy for printing; but Pope, who was an inveterate reviser, introduced some last-minute changes. The passage transcribed here from each of these manuscripts is Pope's famed description of man's "middle state" in the great chain of being; in the published ver-sion, it opens Epistle 2, lines 1–18.

2. In this version of the manuscript, Pope inserted some marginal glosses. In the right-hand margin (next to the line beginning "Learn we ourselves . . ."), he wrote, "Of Man, as an Individual," while next to the line beginning "Plac'd on this Isthmus . . . ," he wrote, "His Middle Nature." And in the left-hand margin, a little below the line beginning "With too much Knowledge . . . ," he wrote, "His Powers, and Imperfections."

Chaos of Thought and Passion, all confus'd,
Still by himself abus'd and dis-abus'd:
Created half to rise, and half to fall;
Great Lord of all things, yet a prey to all;
Sole Judge of Truth, in endless error hurl'd;
The Glory, Jest, and Riddle of the World!

SAMUEL JOHNSON

Johnson told Boswell in 1766 that when composing verses "I have generally had them in my mind, perhaps fifty at a time, walking up and down in my room; and then I have written them down, and often, from laziness, have written only half lines. . . . I remember I wrote a hundred lines of *The Vanity of Human Wishes* in a day." When the first manuscript draft of this poem turned up in the 1940s among Boswell's papers at Malahide Castle, it supported Johnson's account, for it had been written and corrected in haste, with only sparse punctuation; also, the second half of each line had been filled out, obviously from memory, at some time after the writing of the first half, in a darker ink. In the transcriptions from this manuscript (which is in the collection of Mary Hyde, Somerville, New Jersey), the half-lines and emendations that Johnson added to his initial draft are printed in boldface type.

The draft was written on the right-hand pages of a small homemade pocket book; some words in the added half-line, impinging on the right margin of the page, had to be completed above or below the line. The two added lines, "See Nations slowly wise . . . the tardy Bust," were written on the blank left-hand page, at the place where they were to be inserted. The numeration of every tenth line was added by Johnson in the manuscript, and incorporates these two additional lines.

Johnson published the poem in 1749 and revised it for a second publication in 1755, when it achieved the final form printed in the selections from Johnson, above. It was in 1755 that Johnson introduced his most famous emendation when, after his disillusionment with Lord Chesterfield as literary patron, he substituted in line 162 the word "patron" for "garret": "Toil, envy, want, the patron, and the jail."

From The Vanity of Human Wishes

[*Lines 135–164*]

When first the College Rolls **receive his nam**e
The young Enthusiast **quits his ease for fame**

Quick fires his breast
~~Each act betrays~~ **the fever of renown**
Caught from **the strong Contagion of the Gown**
On Isis banks he waves, from noise **withdrawn**
140 In sober state th'imaginary Lawn
O'er Bodley's Dome **his future Labours spread**
And Bacon's Mansion **trembles o'er his head.**
Are these thy views, **proceed illustrious Youth**

And Virtue guard **thee to the throne of Trut**^h
Yet should th~~y fate~~ Soul indulge the gen'rous
                                 Heat
Till Captive Science **yields her last Retreat**
Should Reason **guide thee with her brightest Ray**
And pour on misty Doubt **resistless day**
Should no false kindness **lure to loose delight**
150 Nor Praise relax, nor **difficulty fright**
Should tempting Novelty **thy cell refrain**
                               vain
And Sloth's bland opiates **shed their fumes in**
sShould Beuty blunt **on fops her fatal dart**
Nor claim the **triumph of a letter'd heart**
~~S Nor~~ Should no Disease **thy torpid veins invade**
Nor Melancholys Spectres **haunt thy Shade**
         hope
Yet ~~dream~~ not Life **from Grief or Danger free,**
Nor think the doom of **Man revers'd for thee**
   Deign   passing   to
~~Turn~~ on the world ~~awhile~~ turn thine eyes
160 And pause ˄awhile from Learning to be wise
There mark what **ill the Scholar's life assail**
                 the
Toil envy Want ~~a~~ Garret and the Jayl
      Dreams
If ~~Hope~~ yet flatter **once again attend**
Hear Lydiats life **and Galileo's End.**

See Nations slowly wise, and meanly just,
To buried merit raise the tardy Bust.

THOMAS GRAY

There are three manuscript versions of the *Elegy* in Gray's handwriting. The one reproduced here in part is the earliest of these, preserved at Eton College, England; Gray entitled it "Stanzas wrote in a Country Church-Yard."

It is evident that Gray originally intended to conclude his poem at the end of the fifth stanza transcribed below. At some later time he bracketed off the last four stanzas, introduced a transitional stanza that incorporated the last two lines of the original conclusion, and then went on to write a new and much enlarged conclusion to the poem, which includes the closing "Epitaph." A comparison with the final version of the *Elegy*, above, will show that the author deleted some of these added stanzas, and also made a number of verbal changes, in his published texts of the poem.

From Elegy Written in a Country Churchyard

[*Lines* 69–128]

The struggleing⸍ Pangs of conscious Truth to hide,
To quench the Blushes of ingenuous Shame,
      crown
And at the Shrine of Luxury & Pride
  With   by
~~Burn~~ Incense hallowd in the Muse's Flame.
           kindled at

The thoughtless World to Majesty may bow
Exalt the brave, & idolize Success
But more to Innocence their Safety owe
Than Power & Genius e'er conspired to bless

And thou, who mindful of the unhonour'd Dead
                    eir
Dost in these notes thy artless Tale relate
By Night & lonely Contemplation led
To linger in the gloomy Walks of Fate

Hark how the sacred Calm, that broods around
Bids ev'ry fierce tumultuous Passion cease
In still small Accents whisp'ring from the Ground
A grateful Earnest of eternal Peace

No more with Reason & thyself at Strife
Give anxious Cares & endless Wishes room
But thro' the cool sequester'd Vale of Life
Pursue the silent Tenour of thy Doom.

Far from the madding Crowd's ignoble Strife;
Their sober Wishes never knew to stray:
Along the cool sequester'd Vale of Life
                  noiseless
They kept the silent Tenour of their Way.

Yet even these Bones from Insult to protect
Some frail Memorial still erected nigh
        With
In uncouth Rhime, & shapeless Sculpture deckt
Implores the passing Tribute of a Sigh.

Their Name, their Years, spelt by th' unletter'd Muse
The Place of Fame, & Epitaph supply,
And many a holy Text around she strews
That teach the rustic Moralist to die.

For who to dumb Forgetfulness a Prey
This pleasing anxious Being e'er resign'd;
Left the warm Precincts of the chearful Day,
Nor cast one longing lingring Look behind?

On some fond Breast the parting Soul relies,
Some pious Drops the closing Eye requires:
Even from the Tomb the Voice of Nature cries,
And buried Ashes glow with social Fires
    For Thee, who mindful &c: as above.[1]

If chance that e'er some pensive Spirit more,
By sympathetic Musings here delay'd,

---

1. I.e., Gray indicates that the second bracketed stanza, above, is to be inserted here, except that the opening
"And thou" is to be altered to "For Thee."

With vain, tho' kind, Enquiry shall explore
Thy once-loved Haunt, this long-deserted Shade.

Haply some hoary-headed Swain shall say,[2]
Oft have we seen him at the Peep of Dawn
With hasty Footsteps brush the Dews away
On the high Brow of yonder hanging Lawn
Him have we seen the Green-wood Side along,
While o'er the Heath we hied, our Labours done,
Oft as the Woodlark piped her farewell Song
With whistful Eyes pursue the setting Sun.
              spreading   nodding
Oft at the Foot of yonder hoary Beech
That wreathes its old fantastic Roots so high
His listless Length at Noontide would he stretch,
And pore upon the Brook that babbles by.
     With Gestures quaint now smileing as in Scorn,
           wayward fancies   ~~loved~~ would he
     Mutt'ring his fond Conceits he ~~wont to~~ rove:
         drooping,
     Now woeful wan, ~~he droop'd~~, as one forlorn
     Or crazed with Care, or cross'd in hopeless Love.
        One Morn we miss'd him on th' accustom'd Hill,
        Along the   near
        By the Heath ~~side,~~ & at his fav'rite Tree.
        Another came, nor yet beside the Rill,
                by
        Nor up the Lawn, nor at the Wood was he.
  ~~There scatter'd oft, the earliest~~
        The next with Dirges meet in sad Array
           by
        Slow thro the Church-way Path we saw him born
        Approach & read, for thou can'st read the Lay
        Graved carved   yon
        Wrote on the Stone beneath that ancient Thorn
                        Year
        There scatter'd oft the earliest of y^e ~~Spring~~
                 showers of
        By Hands unseen are frequent Vi'lets found
        Redbreast
        The Robin loves to build & warble there,
        And little Footsteps lightly print the Ground.

Here rests his Head upon the Lap of Earth[3]
A Youth to Fortune & to Fame unknown
Fair Science frown'd not on his humble Birth
And Melancholy mark'd him for her own

Large was his Bounty & his Heart sincere;
Heaven did a Recompence as largely send.
He gave to Mis'ry all he had, a Tear.
He gain'd from Heav'n, 'twas all he wish'd, a Friend

---

2. At this point in the manuscript Gray ceases to leave
a space between the stanzas. The first edition of 1751,
at Gray's request, was printed without such spaces. They
were, however, inserted in later editions printed during

Gray's lifetime.
3. These last three stanzas (which Gray in the first edition of 1751 labeled "The Epitaph") are written in the
right-hand margin, with the page turned crosswise.

No farther seek his Merits to disclose,
      think
Nor seek to draw them from their dread Abode
(His Frailties there in trembling Hope repose)
The Bosom of his Father & his God.

WILLIAM BLAKE
The Tyger[1]

[First Draft]

The Tyger

1   Tyger Tyger burning bright
In the forests of the night
What immortal hand or eye
~~Dare~~ **Could** frame thy fearful symmetry

      Burnt in
2   ~~In what~~ distant deeps or skies
~~The cruel~~ ~~Burnt the~~ fire of thine eyes
On what wings dare he aspire
What the hand dare sieze the fire

3   And what shoulder & what art
Could twist the sinews of thy heart
And when thy heart began to beat
What dread hand & what dread feet

    ~~Could fetch it from the furnace deep~~
    ~~And in thy horrid ribs dare steep~~
    ~~In the well of sanguine woe~~
    ~~In what clay & what mould~~
    ~~Were thy eyes of fury rolld~~

    ~~Where~~   ~~where~~
4   ~~What~~ the hammer ~~what~~ the chain
In what furnace was thy brain
              dread grasp
What the anvil what ~~the arm~~ ~~arm~~ ~~grasp~~ ~~clasp~~
Dare ~~Could~~ its deadly terrors ~~clasp~~ ~~grasp~~ clasp

6   Tyger Tyger burning bright
In the forests of the night
What immortal hand & eye
       frame
Dare ~~form~~ thy fearful symmetry

---

1. These drafts have been taken from a notebook used by William Blake, called the Rossetti MS because it was once owned by Dante Gabriel Rossetti, the Victorian poet and painter; David V. Erdman's edition of *The Notebook of William Blake* (1973) contains a photographic facsimile. The stanza and line numbers were written by Blake in the manuscript.

[*Trial Stanzas*]

Burnt in distant deeps or skies
The cruel fire of thine eye,
Could heart descend or wings aspire
What the hand dare sieze the fire

dare he ~~smile~~ laugh —
5 5̷ And ~~did he laugh~~ his work to see
ankle
~~What the shoulder what the knee~~
Dare
4 ~~Did~~ he who made the lamb make thee
1 When the stars threw down their spears
2 And waterd heaven with their tears

[*Second Full Draft*]

Tyger Tyger burning bright
In the forests of the night
What Immortal hand & eye
Dare frame thy fearful symmetry

And what shoulder & what art
Could twist the sinews of thy heart
And when thy heart began to beat
What dread hand & what dread feet

When the stars threw down their spears
And waterd heaven with their tears
Did he smile his work to see
Did he who made the lamb make thee

Tyger Tyger burning bright
In the forests of the night
What immortal hand & eye
Dare frame thy fearful symmetry

[*Final Version,* 1794][2]

The Tyger

Tyger Tyger, burning bright,
In the forests of the night;
What immortal hand or eye,
Could frame thy fearful symmetry?

In what distant deeps or skies
Burnt the fire of thine eyes!
On what wings dare he aspire?
What the hand, dare sieze the fire?

2. As published in *Songs of Experience*.

And what shoulder, & what art,
Could twist the sinews of thy heart?
And when thy heart began to beat,
What dread hand? & what dread feet?

What the hammer? what the chain,
In what furnace was thy brain?
What the anvil? what dread grasp,
Dare its deadly terrors clasp?

When the stars threw down their spears
And water'd heaven with their tears:
Did he smile his work to see?
Did he who made the Lamb make thee?

Tyger, Tyger burning bright,
In the forests of the night:
What immortal hand or eye,
Dare frame thy fearful symmetry?

WILLIAM WORDSWORTH
She dwelt among the untrodden ways

[*Version in a Letter to Coleridge,
December 1798 or January 1799*][1]

My hope was one, from cities far
    Nursed on a lonesome heath:
Her lips were red as roses are,
    Her hair a woodbine wreath.

She lived among the untrodden ways
    Beside the springs of Dove,
A maid whom there were none to praise,
    And very few to love;

A violet by a mossy stone
    Half-hidden from the eye!
Fair as a star when only one
    Is shining in the sky!

And she was graceful as the broom
    That flowers by Carron's side;[2]
But slow distemper checked her bloom,
    And on the Heath she died.

---

1. Printed in Ernest de Selincourt's *Early Letters of William and Dorothy Wordsworth* (1935). By deleting two stanzas, and making a few verbal changes, Wordsworth achieved the terse published form of his great

dirge.
2. The Carron is a river in northwestern Scotland. "Broom" (preceding line) is a shrub with long slender branches and yellow flowers.

Long time before her head lay low
  Dead to the world was she:
But now she's in her grave, and Oh!
  The difference to me!

[*Final Version*, 1800][3]

Song

She dwelt among th' untrodden ways
  Beside the springs of Dove,
A Maid whom there were none to praise
  And very few to love.

A Violet by a mossy stone
  Half-hidden from the Eye!
—Fair, as a star when only one
  Is shining in the sky!

She *liv'd* unknown, and few could know
  When Lucy ceas'd to be;
But she is in her Grave, and Oh!
  The difference to me.

GEORGE GORDON, LORD BYRON
From Don Juan[1]

[*First Draft: Canto 3, Stanza 9*]

~~Life is a play and men~~
All tragedies are finished by a death,
All Comedies are ended by a marriage,
~~For Life can go no further~~
~~These two form the last gasp of Passion's breath~~
~~All further is a blank—I won't disparage~~
~~That holy state—but certainly beneath~~
~~The Sun—of human things~~
~~These two are levellers, and human breath~~
~~So~~ ~~These point the epigram of human breath;~~
~~Or any~~ The future states of both are left to faith,
~~Though Life and love I like not to disparage~~
~~The~~ For authors ~~think~~ description might disparage
                    fear

~~Tis strange that poets never try to wreathe~~ [*sic?*]
~~With eith~~ ~~Tis strange that poets of the Catholic faith~~
~~Neer go beyond~~ ~~and~~ ~~but seem to dread miscarriage~~
~~So dramas close with death or settlement for life~~
~~Veiling~~ ~~Leaving the future states of Love and Life~~
~~The paradise beyond like that of life~~
~~And neer describing either~~
~~To more conjecture of a devil~~ ~~and~~ ~~or wife~~

3. As published in the second edition of *Lyrical Bal-lads*.

1. Reproduced from transcripts made of Byron's manuscripts in T. G. Steffan and W. W. Pratt, *Byron's "Don Juan"* (1957). The stanzas were published by Bryon in their emended form.

~~And don't say much of paradise or wife~~
The worlds to come of both—~~&~~ or fall beneath,
And ~~all~~ ~~both the worlds would blame them for miscarriage~~
And then both worlds would punish their miscarriage—
~~So leaving both with priest & prayerbook ready~~
So leaving ~~Clerg both a~~ each their Priest and prayerbook ready,
They say no more of death or of the Lady.

[*First Draft: Canto 14, Stanza 95*]

      quote   seldom
Alas! ~~I speak by~~ Experience—~~never~~ yet
~~I had a paramour—and I've had many—~~
              ~~some small~~
~~To whom I did not cause a deep~~ regret—
~~Whom I had not some reason to regret~~
~~For Whom—I did not feel myself~~ a Zany—
Alas! by all experience, seldom yet
(I merely quote what I have heard from many)
Had lovers not some reason to regret
The passion which made Solomon a Zany.
~~I also had a wife~~—not to forget—
I've also seen some wives—not to forget—
The marriage state—the best or worst of any—
     were   paragons
Who ~~was~~ the very ~~paragon~~ of wives,
Yet made the misery of ~~both our~~ lives.
            ~~many~~
            ~~several~~
            ~~of~~ at least two

PERCY BYSSHE SHELLEY

The three stages of this poem labeled "First Draft" are scattered through one of Shelley's notebooks, now in the Huntington Library, San Marino, California; these drafts have been transcribed and analyzed by Bennett Weaver, "Shelley Works Out the Rhythm of *A Lament*," *PMLA* 47 (1932): 570–76. They show Shelley working with fragmentary words and phrases, and simultaneously with a wordless pattern of pulses that marked out the meter of the single lines and the shape of the lyric stanzas. Shelley left this draft unfinished.

Apparently at some later time, Shelley returned to the poem and wrote what is here called the "Second Draft"; from this he then made, on a second page, a revised fair copy that provided the text that Mary Shelley published in 1824, after the poet's death. These two manuscript pages are now in the Bodleian Library, Oxford; the first page is photographically reproduced and discussed by John Carter and John Sparrow, "Shelley, Swinburne, and Housman," *Times Literary Supplement* Nov. 21, 1968, pp. 1318–19.

O World, O Life, O Time

[*First Draft, Stage 1*]

Ah time, oh night, oh day
~~Ni nal ni na, na ni~~

~~Ni na ni na, ni na~~
Oh life O death, O time
   Time a di
~~Never Time~~
Ah time, a time O-time
  ~~Time!~~

[First Draft, Stage 2]

Oh time, oh night oh day
~~O day oh night, alas~~
  ~~O~~ Death time night ~~oh~~
Oh, Time
Oh time o night oh day

[First Draft, Stage 3]

Na na, na na ná na
Nă nă na na na—nă nă
  Nă nă nă nă nă nā
Na na nă nă nâ ă na

Na na na—nă nă—na na
  Na na na na—na na na na na
Na na na na na.
   Na na
Na na na na na
   Na na
Na na na na na ˘ na!

Oh time, oh night, o day
       alas
  O day ~~serenest,~~ o day
  O day alas the day
That thou shouldst sleep when we awake to say

O time time—o death—o day
      for
  O day, o death life is far from thee
  O thou wert never free
For death is now with thee
~~And life is far from~~
O death, o day for life is far from thee

[Second Draft][1]

Out of the day & night   I am
A joy has taken flight   despair

---

1. Shelley apparently wrote the first stanza of this draft low down on the page, and ran out of space after crowding in the third line of the second stanza; he then, in a lighter ink, wrote a revised form of the whole of the second stanza at the top of the page. In this revision, he left a space after "summer" in line 3, indicat-ing that he planned an insertion that would fill out the four-foot meter of this line, and so make it match the five feet in the corresponding line of the first stanza.

In the upper right-hand corner of this manuscript page Shelley wrote "I am despair"—seemingly to express his bleak mood at the time he wrote the poem.

Fresh spring & summer   & winter hoar
Fill my faint heart with grief, but with
          delight
   No more—o never more!

~~Wo~~
  O World, o life, o time
  ~~Will ye~~ On whose last steps I climb
Trembling at those which I have trod[2] before
When will return the glory of yr prime
  No more   Oh never more

   Out of the day & night
   A joy has taken flight—
     autumn
~~From~~ Green spring, & ~~summer gra~~[3] & winter hoar

[FAIR COPY]

O World   o Life   o Time
On whose last steps I climb
Trembling at that where I had stood before
 When will return the glory of yr prime?
  No more, o never more

     2
  Out of the day & night
  A joy has taken flight
Fresh spring & summer   [4] & winter hoar
Move my faint heart with grief but with delight
  No more, o, never more

JOHN KEATS
From The Eve of St. Agnes[1]

[*Stanza 26*]

But soon his heart revives—her prayers said
She ~~lays aside her neck~~   pearled
    strips her hair of all its ∧ wreathes pearl
~~Unclasps her bosom jewels~~
~~And twist it in one knot upon her head~~

For this draft and information, and for the transcript of the fair copy that follows, the editors are indebted to Donald H. Reiman of The Pforzheimer Library.

2. Shelley at first wrote "trod," then overwrote that with "stood." In the following line, Shelley at first wrote "yr," then overwrote "thy."

3. Not clearly legible; it is either "gra" or "gre." A difference in the ink from the rest of the line indicates that Shelley, having left a blank space, later started to fill it in, but thought better of it and crossed out the fragmentary insertion.

4. This fair copy of the second draft retains, and even enlarges, the blank space, indicating that Shelley still hasn't made up his mind what to insert after the word "summer." We may speculate, by reference to the frag-

mentary version of this stanza in the second draft, that he had in mind as possibilities either an adjective, "gray" or "green," or else the noun "autumn." Mary Shelley closed up this space when she published the poem in 1824, with the result that editors, following her version, have until very recently printed this line as though Shelley had intended it to be one metric foot shorter than the corresponding line of stanza 1.

1. Transcribed from what is probably the best known of all manuscripts, that which contains Keats's first draft of all but the first seven stanzas of *The Eve of St. Agnes*; it is now in the Houghton Library, Harvard University. Keats's published version of the poem, above, contains some further changes in wording.

But soon his heart revives—her praying done, ~~soon~~
Of all its wreathed pearl she strips her hair
Unclasps her warmed jewels one by one
Loosens ~~the boddice from her~~ *her bursting*
~~her Boddice lace string~~
~~her Boddice; and her bosom bar~~
her

[HERE KEATS BEGINS A NEW SHEET]

Loosens ~~her fragrant boddice and doth bare~~
~~Her~~

26

Anon
~~But soon~~ his heart revives—her praying done,
Of all its wreathe'd pearl her hair she ~~strips~~ *frees:*
Unclasps her warmed jewels one by one
Loosens her fragrant boddice: ~~and down slips~~ *by degrees* ~~to her knees~~
Her sweet attire ~~falls light creeps down by~~
creeps rusteling to her knees
Half hidden like a ~~Syren of the Sea~~ *Mermaid* *in sea weed*
~~And more melodious~~
She stands awhile in ∧ thought; and sees *dreaming*
In fancy fair Saint Agnes ~~in~~ her bed *on*
But dares not look behind or all the charm is ~~fl~~ dead

[*Stanza* 30]

But
~~And still she slept:~~
And still she slept an azure-lidded sleep
In blanched linen, smooth and lavender'd
While he from frorth the closet brough a heap
Of candied ~~sweets sweets, with~~ ~~fruits~~
apple Quince and plumb and gourd
With jellies soother than the ~~dairy~~ curd *creamed*
And lucent syrups ~~smooth~~ with ciannamon *tinct*
~~And sugar'd dates from that oer Euphrates fard~~
Manna and daites in ~~Bragtine transferrd~~ ~~in Brigantine transferred~~
~~And Manna wild and Bragantine~~ ~~and manna wild transferrd~~
~~In Brigantine from Fez~~ *sugar'd dates transferred*
From fez—and spiced danties every one
From ~~wealthy~~ Samarchand to cedard lebanon ~~glutted~~
silken

argosy

GERARD MANLEY HOPKINS
Thou art indeed just, Lord[1]

*Justus quidem tu es, Domine, si disputem tecum; verumtamen justa
loquar ad te: quare via impiorum prosperatur?* etc.—Jer. xii 1.

March 17 1889

Lord, if I
Thou art indeed just, ~~were I to~~ contend
      sir,   plead
With thee; but, ~~Lord,~~ so what I ~~speak~~ is just.

Why do sinners' ways prosper? and why must

Disappointment all I endeavour end?
Wert thou my enemy, O thou my friend,
How wouldst thou worse, I wonder, than thou dost
          O the sots and   of
Defeat, thwart me? ~~Ah! sots, revellers,~~ thralls ~~to~~ lust
Do in   that
In spare hours ~~do~~ more thrive than I ~~who~~ spend,
     great   See,
Sir, ~~my~~ life on thy cause. ~~Look,~~ banks and brakes
Now, leavèd   lacèd they are
~~Leavèd~~ how thick! ~~broidered all~~ again
          look
With fretty chervil, ~~now,~~ and fresh wind shakes
Them; birds build—but not I build; no, but strain,
Time's eunuch, and not breed one work that wakes.
Mine, O   send my
~~Then send,~~ thou lord of life, ~~these~~ roots ~~their~~ rain.

WILLIAM BUTLER YEATS

Yeats usually composed very slowly and with painful effort. He tells us in
his *Autobiography* that "five or six lines in two or three laborious hours were
a day's work, and I longed for somebody to interrupt me." His manuscripts
show the slow evolution of his best poems, which sometimes began with a
prose sketch, were then versified, and underwent numerous revisions. In
many instances, even after the poems had been published, Yeats continued
to revise them, sometimes drastically, in later printings.

1. From a manuscript in the Bodleian Library, Oxford University; it is a clean copy, made after earlier drafts, which Hopkins goes on to revise further. Differences in the ink show that the emendation "lacèd they are" (line 10) was made during the first writing, but that the other verbal changes were made later. The interlinear markings are Hopkins's metrical indicators; he explains their significance in the "Author's Preface," included in *Poems of Gerard Manley Hopkins* (1970), ed. W. H. Gardner and N. H. MacKenzie.

The epigraph is from the Vulgate translation of Jeremiah 12.1; a literal translation of the Latin is "Thou art indeed just, Lord, [even] if I plead with Thee; nevertheless I will speak what is just to Thee: Why does the way of the wicked prosper? etc."

Leda and the Swan[1]

[*First Version*]

Annunciation

Now can the swooping Godhead have his will
Yet hovers, though her helpless thighs are pressed
By the webbed toes; and that all powerful bill
Has suddenly bowed her face upon his breast.
How can those terrified vague fingers push
The feathered glory from her loosening thighs?
All the stretched body's laid on that white rush
            strange
And feels the ~~strong~~ heart beating where it lies
A shudder in the loins engenders there
The broken wall, the burning roof and tower
And Agamemnon dead. . . .
                    Being so caught up
Did nothing pass before her in the air?
Did she put on his knowledge with his power
Before the indifferent beak could let her drop
                    Sept 18 1923

         swooping
The ~~trembl~~ godhead is half hovering still,
     climbs
Yet ~~climbs~~ upon her trembling body pressed
    webbed
By the toes; & ~~through~~ that all powerful bill
        ~~thrown~~ bowed
Has suddenly ~~bowed~~ her face upon his breast.
How can those terrified vague fingers push
The feathered glory from her loosening thighs
             laid
All the stretched body ~~leans~~ on that white rush
          or
~~Her falling body thrown on the white~~ white rush
Can feel etc
or Her body can but lean on the white rush

     But mounts until her trembling thighs are pressed[2]
  ~~B~~
By the webbed toes; & that all powerful bill
Has suddenly bowed her head on his breast

---

1. From Yeats's manuscript *Journal*, Sections 248 and 250. This *Journal*, including facsimiles and transcriptions of the drafts of *Leda and the Swan*, has been published in W. B. Yeats, *Memoirs*, ed. Denis Donoghue (Macmillan, London, 1972).
    The first version, entitled *Annunciation*, seems to be a clean copy of earlier drafts; Yeats went on to revise it further, especially the opening octave. Neither of the other two complete drafts, each of which Yeats labeled "Final Version," was in fact final. Yeats himself crossed out the first draft. The second, although Yeats published it in 1924, was subjected to further revision be-

fore he published the poem in *The Tower* (1928), in the final form reprinted in the selections from Yeats, above.
    Yeats's handwriting is hasty and very difficult to decipher. The readings of some words, in the manuscripts both of this poem and of *After Long Silence*, below, are uncertain.
2. This passage is written across the blank page opposite the first version; Yeats drew a line indicating that it was to replace the revised lines 2–4, which he had written below the first version.

Final Version

Can hold

Annunciation

The swooping godhead is half hovering still
But mounts, until her trembling thighs are pressed
By the webbed toes, & that all powerful bill
~~Has hung~~ her helpless body
~~Has suddenly bowed her head~~ upon his breast.
How can those terrified vague fingers push
The feathered glory from her loosening thighs?
~~How~~ now its body leans on
~~With her body laid on the white rush~~
all the stretched body laid on the white rush
and ~~Can~~ feel the strange heart beating where it lies?
A shudder in the loins engenders there
The broken wall, the burning roof & tower
And Agamemnon dead . . .

Being mastered so
~~Being so caught up~~
So
~~And~~ mastered by the brute blood of the air
Being mastered so
~~Did nothing pass before her in the air?~~
Did she put on his knowledge with his power
Before the indifferent beak could let her drop.

WBY. Sept 18 1923

swoop
A ~~rush~~ upon great wings & hovering still
~~He sinks until~~
~~He has sunk on her down, & her hair~~
~~The great bird sinks, till~~
The bird descends, & her frail ~~thigh~~ thighs are pressed
By the webbed toes, & that all

that
Now ~~all~~ her body's laid on that white rush[3]
~~All the stretched body, laid on that white rush~~
~~Now that whole~~
Now that her body on the white rush
Can fee

Final Version

Leda & the Swan

A rush, a sudden wheel and
~~A swoop upon great wings &~~ hovering still
            sinks down   bare frail
stet The bird ~~descends~~ & her ~~frail,~~ thighs are pressed
By the ~~toes~~ webbed toes, & that all powerful bill
                laid
Has ~~driven~~ her helpless face upon his breast.
How can those terrified vague fingers push
The feathered glory from her loosening thighs?

3. Written on the blank page across from the complete version, with an arrow indicating that it was a revision of the seventh line.

                     s laid

All the stretched body ~~laid~~ on that white rush
And ~~feel~~ feels the strange heart beating where it lies.
A shudder in the loins engenders there
The broken wall, the burning roof & tower
And Agamemnon dead.
                Being so caught up
So mastered by the ~~br~~ brute blood of the air
Did she put on his knowledge with his power
Before the indifferent beak could let her drop.

After Long Silence[4]

[Draft 1]

Subject

Your hair is white
My hair is white
Come let us talk of love
What other theme do we know
When we were young
We were in love with one another
~~A O~~ And therefore ignorant

[Draft 2]

Those
~~Your~~ other lover s being dead & gone /

                              friendly light
                              hair is white
             ~~on love descant~~   descant
Upon the ~~sole theme~~ supreme theme of art &   song
Wherein there's theme so fitting for the aged.   ;young
We loved each other & were ignorant

[Draft 3]

~~Th~~

Once more I have kissed your hand & it is right—
All other lovers being estranged or dead
The heavy curtain drawn the candle light
Waging a doubtful battle with the shade

4. The drafts of *After Long Silence* are interspersed with other materials on seven pages of a manuscript book, begun in 1928, which includes a number of additional poems that were published in *The Winding Stair and Other Poems* (1933). It begins, like many of Yeats's poems, with a prose sketch, and is labeled simply "Subject." It then passes through a tentative versified stage (Draft 2) in which Yeats sets down four complete lines and a set of possible rhyme words; is subjected to various drafts and revisions; and concludes with the final text that Yeats published in 1933. Yeats did not add the title *After Long Silence* until he wrote out a fair copy for his typist at some time after August 14, 1931.
     David R. Clark, "After 'Silence,' The 'Supreme Theme': Eight Lines of Yeats," includes photocopies and transcripts of the drafts of this poem, together with a discussion of its biographical occasion and its interpretation (in *Myth and Reality in Irish Literature*, ed. Joseph Ronsley [Waterloo, Canada, 1977], pp. 149–73).

We call our wisdom up upon our wisdom & descant ~~discant~~
~~Upon the supreme theme of art & song~~
Decrepitude increases wisdom—young
We loved each other & were ignorant ignor   ignorant

[Draft 4]

Un
~~The~~friendly lamplight hidden by its shade
~~And shutters clapped upon the deepening night—~~
~~The candle hidden by its friendly shade~~
Those curtains drawn upon the deepening night—

                                s
~~The curtain drawn on the unfriendly night~~
That we descant & yet again descant
                    supreme theme
Upon the ~~supreme theme~~ of ~~art & song~~   art & song—
Bodily decrepitude is wisdom—young

[Final MS Version]

Speech after long silence; ~~it is right—~~
                                            or
All other lovers being estranged ~~&~~ dead,
                                            hid
Unfriendly lamp-light ~~hid~~ under its shade,
                                upon
The curtain's drawn ~~upon~~ unfriendly night—
That we descant & yet again descant
Upon the supreme theme of art & song/.
Bodily decrepitude is wisdom /, young
We loved each other & were ignorant

                                                                Nov
                                                            ~~Oct~~ 1929

D. H. LAWRENCE
The Piano[1]

Somewhere beneath that piano's superb sleek black
Must hide my mother's piano, little and brown, with
the back

---

1. Transcribed from a notebook in which Lawrence at first entered various academic assignments while he was a student at the University College of Nottingham, 1906–8, but then used to write drafts of some of his early poems. These were probably composed in the period from 1906 to 1910. The text reproduced here was revised and published with the title *Piano* in Lawrence's *New Poems*, 1918. A comparison of this draft with *Piano*, reprinted above, will show that Lawrence eliminated the first and fourth stanzas (as well as the last two lines of the third stanza); revised the remaining three stanzas, sometimes radically; and most surpris-ingly, reversed his original conclusion. As Lawrence himself explained his revisions of some of his early poems, they "had to be altered, where sometimes the hand of commonplace youth had been laid on the mouth of the demon. It is not for technique that these poems are altered: it is to say the real say."

For transcriptions and discussions of this and other poems in Lawrence's early notebook, see Vivian de Sola Pinto, "D.H. Lawrence: Letter-Writer and Craftsman in Verse," in *Renaissance and Modern Studies* 1 (1957): 5–34.

stood close to
That ~~was against~~ the wall, and the front's faded silk, both torn
And the keys with little hollows, that my mother's fingers
   had worn.

Softly, in the shadows, a woman is singing to me
Quietly, through the years I have crept back to see
A child sitting under the piano, in the boom of the
  shaking ~~tingling~~ strings
Pressing the little poised feet of the mother who smiles
   as she sings

The full throated woman has chosen a winning, living[2]
    song
And surely the heart that is in me must belong
To the old Sunday evenings, when darkness wandered
    outside
And hymns gleamed on our warm lips, as we watched
    mother's fingers glide

     is
Or ~~is~~ this my sister at home in the old front room
Singing love's first surprised gladness, alone in
    the gloom.
She will start when she sees me, and blushing,
    spread out her hands
To cover my mouth's raillery, till I'm bound in
    heart-spun
  her shame's ~~pleading~~ bands.

A woman is singing me a wild Hungarian
    air
And her arms, and her bosom and the whole
   of her soul is bare
And the great black piano is clamouring as my
   mother's never could clamour
  my mother's [ ]3 tunes are
And ~~the tunes of the past is~~ devoured of this music's
   ravaging glamour.

---

2. A conjectural reading; the word is not clearly legible. 3. An undecipherable word is crossed out here.

Selected Bibliographies

SUGGESTED GENERAL READINGS

**Histories of England and
of English Literature**

George Macaulay Trevelyan's *History of England*, rev. 1945, is an excellent survey in one volume; for detailed studies of single periods, see *The Oxford History of England*, 15 vols., 1934ff., by a variety of historians. Designed especially as a survey of history for students of literature is Robert M. Adams, *The Land and Literature of England: A Historical Account*, 1983. For single books in the comprehensive twelve-volume *Oxford History of English Literature*, ed. F. P. Wilson and Bonamy Dobrée, 1945ff., see the listings below for each period of English literature. *The New Pelican Guide to English Literature*, ed. Boris Ford, 1982–, is available in a sequence of paperbacks. Useful one-volume histories are Hardin Craig et al., *A History of English Literature*, 1950; Albert C. Baugh et al., *A Literary History of England*, rev. 1967; and (less densely factual, and more a running literary appreciation) David Daiches, *A Critical History of English Literature*, 2 vols., rev. 1970. *Annals of English Literature, 1475–1950*, rev. 1961, lists important publications year by year, together with the significant literary events in each year. Ellen Moers, *Literary Women*, 1976, is a history of the circumstances, interinfluences, and distinctive features of literature written by women; in addition, the editorial materials in Sandra M. Gilbert and Susan Gubar, *The Norton Anthology of Literature by Women*, 1985, constitute a concise history and set of biographies of women authors since the Middle Ages.

Drama

Allardyce Nicoll, *British Drama*, rev. 1962, and *A History of English Drama, 1660–1900*, 6 vols., rev. 1952–59; Richard Courtney, *Outline History of British Drama*, 1982. For the history of the physical theater from the Middle Ages to the early 20th century, see Richard Leacroft, *The Development of the English Playhouse*, 1973.

The Novel

The most detailed, although somewhat pedestrian, history is Ernest A. Baker's *History of the English Novel*, 10 vols., 1924–39. Among the short histories are Walter A. Raleigh, *The English Novel*, rev. 1911, which stops at Walter Scott; and, more up-

to-date, Arnold Kettle, *An Introduction to the English Novel*, 2 vols., 1951–53; Walter Allen, *The English Novel*, 1954; Ian Watt, *The Rise of the Novel*, 1957; and Lionel Stevenson, *The English Novel*, 1960. On the early development of the novel, see Michael McKeon, *The Origins of the English Novel, 1600–1740*, 1987, and J. Paul Hunter, *Before Novels: The Cultural Contexts of Eighteenth-Century English Fiction*, 1990. On women novelists and readers, see Nancy Armstrong, *Desire and Domestic Fiction: A Political History of the Novel*, 1987.

Poetry

W. J. Courthope, *A History of English Poetry*, 6 vols., 1895–1910, and H. J. C. Grierson and J. C. Smith, *A Critical History of English Poetry*, rev. 1947. In addition, Douglas Bush's two books, *Mythology and the Renaissance Tradition in English Poetry*, 1932, and *Mythology and the Romantic Tradition in English Poetry*, 1937, constitute an excellent account, from their special perspective, of English poetry from the 16th century through T. S. Eliot; see also Bush's *English Poetry: The Main Currents from Chaucer to the Present*, rev. 1965. Ranging from the Middle Ages through the 18th century is E. M. W. Tillyard, *The English Epic and Its Background*, 1954.

Helpful treatments and surveys of English meter, rhyme, and stanza forms are R. M. Alden, *English Verse*, 1903; Paul Fussell, Jr., *Poetic Meter and Poetic Form*, rev. 1979; Donald Wesling, *The Chances of Rhyme: Device and Modernity*, 1980; Charles O. Hartman, *Free Verse: An Essay in Prosody*, 1983; and John Hollander, *Vision and Resonance: Two Senses of Poetic Form*, rev. 1985.

Literary Criticism

The first volume of the *Cambridge History of Literary Criticism* has been published—*Classical Criticism*, ed. G. A. Kennedy, 1989. See also M. H. Abrams, *The Mirror and the Lamp: Romantic Theory and the Critical Tradition*, 1953; William K. Wimsatt and Cleanth Brooks, *Literary Criticism: A Short History*, 1957; George Watson, *The Literary Critics*, 1962; René Wellek, *A History of Modern Criticism: 1750–1950*, 1955– (seven of the projected eight volumes have been published); and Frank Lentricchia, *After the New Criticism*, 1980.

The following is a selection of books in literary criticism that have been notably influential in shaping modern approaches to English literature and literary forms: Percy Lubbock, *The Craft of Fiction*, 1926; Maud Bodkin, *Archetypal Patterns in Poetry*, 1934; Henry James, *The Art of the Novel: Critical Prefaces*, 1934; I. A. Richards, *Principles of Literary Criticism*, rev. 1934, and *Practical Criticism*, 1930; Edmund Wilson, *Axel's Castle: A Study in the Imaginative Literature of 1870–1930*, 1936, and *The Wound and the Bow*, 1941; F. R. Leavis, *Revaluation*, 1936, and *The Great Tradition* (i.e., in the novel), 1948; C. S. Lewis, *The Allegory of Love*, rev. 1938; Cleanth Brooks, *The Well-Wrought Urn*, 1947; Francis Fergusson, *The Idea of a Theater*, 1949; Lionel Trilling, *The Liberal Imagination*, 1950, and *The Opposing Self*, 1955; T. S. Eliot, *Selected Essays*, 3rd ed., 1951, and *On Poetry and Poets*, 1957; Erich Auerbach, *Mimesis: The Representation of Reality in Western Literature*, 1953; Ronald Crane, *The Languages of Criticism and the Structure of Poetry*, 1953, *The Idea of the Humanities*, 2 vols., 1967, and, as editor, *Critics and Criticism, Ancient and Modern*, 1952; William Empson, *Seven Types of Ambiguity*, 3rd ed., 1953; William K. Wimsatt, *The Verbal Icon*, 1954; Northrop Frye, *Anatomy of Criticism*, 1957; Wayne C. Booth, *The Rhetoric of Fiction*, 1961, and *A Rhetoric of Irony*, 1974; W. J. Bate, *The Burden of the Past and the English Poet*, 1970; Harold Bloom, *The Anxiety of Influence*, 1973; Paul de Man, *Allegories of Reading*, 1979; and Stephen J. Greenblatt, *Learning to Curse: Essays in Early Modern Culture*, 1990.

René Wellek and Austin Warren, *Theory of Literature*, rev. 1970, is a useful introduction to the variety of scholarly and critical approaches to literature up to the time of its publication. Convenient introductions to structuralist, deconstructive, and other recent theories are Jonathan Culler, *Structuralist Poetics*, 1975, and *On Deconstruction*, 1982; and John McGowan, *Postmodernism and Its Critics*, 1991. Anthologies representing these recent theories are David Lodge, ed., *Modern Criticism and Theory*, 1988; Robert Con Davis and Ronald Schlieffer, eds., *Contemporary Literary Criticism*, rev. 1989; and H. Aram Veeser, ed., *The New Historicism*, 1989. Among recent collections of feminist criticism are Elaine Showalter, ed., *The New Feminist Criticism*, 1985; and Robyn R. Warhol and Diane Price Herndl, eds., *Feminisms: An Anthology of Literary Theory and Criticism*, 1991.

Reference Works

The New Cambridge Bibliography of English Literature, ed. George Watson, 1969–77, lists all the books of the major and many minor British authors, together with a large selection from biographical, scholarly, and critical works written about these authors. Literary biographies and critical books published since that time can be found in the *MLA International Bibliography*; for separate periods of English literature, see listings below. F. W. Bateson, ed., *A Guide to English Literature*, rev. 1976, is a selected list of editions, as well as scholarly and critical treatments, of important English writers; for poetry only, see A. E. Dyson, ed., *English Poetry: Select Bibliographical Guides*, 1971. *Poetry Explication*, ed. Joseph M. Kuntz, rev. 1962, lists close analyses of English poems, old and recent; and I.F. Bell and Donald Baird, *The English Novel, 1578–1956*, 1958, provides a useful list of 20th-century criticisms of fiction. Further bibliographical aids are described in Arthur G. Kennedy, *A Concise Bibliography for Students of English*, rev. 1972; Richard D. Altick and Andrew Wright, *Selective Bibliography for the Study of English and American Literature*, rev. 1979; and James L. Harner, *Literary Research Guide*, rev. 1989.

For compact biographies of English authors, see the multivolume *Dictionary of National Biography*, ed. Leslie Stephen and Sidney Lee, 1885–1900, with supplements that carry the work to 1980; condensed biographies will be found in the *Concise Dictionary of National Biography*, 2 parts (1920, 1988). Handy reference books of authors, works, and various literary terms and allusions are *The Oxford Companion to the Theatre*, Phyllis Hartnoll, rev. 1967; *Princeton Encyclopedia of Poetry and Poetics*, ed. Alex Preminger and others, rev. 1979; and *The Oxford Companion to English Literature*, ed. Margaret Drabble, rev. 1985. Low-priced handbooks that define and illustrate literary concepts and terms are W. F. Thrall and Addison Hibbard, *A Handbook to Literature*, ed. C. Hugh Holman, rev. 1980; M. H. Abrams, *A Glossary of Literary Terms*, rev. 1992. On Greek and Roman background, see G. M. Kirkwood, *A Short Guide to Classical Mythology*, 1959; *The Oxford Classical Dictionary*, rev. 1970; and *The Oxford Companion to Classical Literature*, ed. M. C. Howatson, rev. 1989.

Intellectual History

Students interested in intellectual history as a background for English literature will profit from Basil Willey, *The Seventeenth Century Background*, 1934, *The Eighteenth Century Background*, 1940, and *Nineteenth Century Studies*, 1949; Arthur T. Lovejoy, *The Great Chain of Being*, 1936, and *Essays in the History of Ideas*, 1948; Marjorie Nicolson, *The Breaking of the Circle*, 1950, *Science and Imagination*, 1956, and *Mountain Gloom and Mountain Glory*, 1959; and M. H. Abrams, *Natural Supernaturalism: Tradition and Revolution in Romantic Literature*, 1971.

THE MIDDLE AGES

Scholarship during this era may be conveniently divided between the Old and Middle English periods. A reference book for the whole era is the *Dictionary of the Middle Ages* by Joseph Strayer et al., 1982–.

The Old English Period

The reader who wishes to acquire historical background for the literature of the period will profit greatly from Dorothy Whitelock's concise study, *The Beginnings of English Society*, 1952. The most detailed history is F. M. Stenton's authoritative *Anglo-Saxon England*, 3rd ed., 1971. Also highly informative are P. Hunter Blair's *An Introduction to Anglo-Saxon England*, 1956, and *Roman Britain and Early England, 55 B.C.–A.D. 871*, 1963. The classic study of the culture of the primitive Germanic peoples is H. M. Chadwick's *The Heroic Age*, 1912. For those who wish to sample basic historical documents of the period, there are available the translations by G. N. Garmonsway of *The Anglo-Saxon Chronicle*, 1953, and by L. Sherley-Price of Bede's *Ecclesiastical History*, published under the title *A History of the English Church and People*, rev. R.E. Latham, 1968.

All the surviving poetry in Old English is contained in the six volumes edited by G. P. Krapp and E. V. K. Dobbie, *The Anglo-Saxon Poetic Records*, 1931–53, but the absence of glossaries makes this edition difficult for nonspecialists. Excellent texts of the shorter poems translated in this anthology are contained in J. C. Pope's *Seven Old English Poems*, 1966. The standard text of *Beowulf and the Fight of Finnsburg* is F. Klaeber's 3rd ed., 1950; C. L. Wrenn's edition, *Beowulf, with the Finnsburg Fragment*, rev. W. F. Bolton, 1973, is very useful; H. D. Chickering, Jr., has made a dual-language edition with extensive commentary. Modern English translations of many of the Old English poems have been published under various titles by C. W. Kennedy and Michael Alexander. The senior editor's translation is the text included in *Beowulf*, A Norton Critical Edition, ed. Joseph F. Tuso, 1975.

Good critical discussion of Old English literature will be found in volume 1 of the *Cambridge History of English Literature*; in Kemp Malone's section of *A Literary History of England*, ed. A. C. Baugh, rev. 1967; in S. B. Greenfield's and D. G. Calder's *A New Critical History of Old English Literature*, 1986, Greenfield's *The Interpretation of Old English Poems*, 1972, and his *Hero and Exile: The Art of Old English Poetry*, 1989; in C. L. Wrenn, *A Study of Old English Literature*, 1966; and in D. A. Pearsall, *Old and Middle English Poetry*, 1977. Important critical articles have been collected by J. B. Bessinger and S. J. Kahrl, *Essential Articles for the Study of Old English Poetry*, 1968, and Martin Stevens and Jerome Mandel,

Old English Literature, 1968. Helen Damico and A. H. Olsen have compiled a collection on a special topic, *New Readings on Women in Old English Literature*, 1990. General introductions designed primarily for students are T. A. Shippey, *Old English Verse*, 1972, B. C. Raw, *The Art and Background of Old English Poetry*, 1978, and Michael Alexander, *Old English Literature*, 1983.

The best critical essay on *Beowulf* remains J. R. R. Tolkien's Gollancz lecture, *Beowulf, the Monsters, and the Critics*, 1937 (see Fry and Fulk, below). The most exhaustive scholarly discussion is R. W. Chambers's *Beowulf: An Introduction to the Study of the Poem*, 3rd ed., with a supplement by C. L. Wrenn, 1959. Works by Dorothy Whitelock, *The Audience of Beowulf*, 1958; A. C. Brodeur, *The Art of Beowulf*, 1959; Kenneth Sisam, *The Structure of Beowulf*, 1965; and E. B. Irving, *A Reading of Beowulf*, 1968, *Introduction to Beowulf*, 1969, and *Rereading Beowulf*, 1990, mingle fine general criticism with some highly specialized discussion. George Clark's Twayne Series *Beowulf*, 1990, is an excellent introduction to the poem. Useful collections of essays on *Beowulf*, including Tolkien's lecture, have been made by D. K. Fry, *The Beowulf Poet*, 1968, and R. D. Fulk, *Interpretations of Beowulf*, 1991.

The Middle English Period

Good and fairly compact accounts of the history of England between the Norman Conquest and the end of the Middle Ages are contained in the two volumes by Christopher Brooke, *From Alfred to Henry III, 871–1272*, 1961, and George Holmes, *The Later Middle Ages, 1272–1485*, 1962; see also May McKisack, *The Fourteenth Century, 1307–99*, 1959, and D. M. Stenton, *English Society in the Early Middle Ages (1066–1307)*, 1951, and A. R. Myers, *England in the Late Middle Ages*, 1952. Interesting illustrations of life in the Middle Ages, especially in the later centuries, will be found in three books by G. G. Coulton: *Chaucer and His England*, 1908, *The Medieval Scene*, 1930, *Medieval Panorama*, 1938; in Eileen Power's *Medieval People*, 1924; in Edith Rickert's *Chaucer's World*, 1948; in volume 1 of G. M. Trevelyan's *Illustrated English Social History*, *Chaucer's England and the Early Tudors*, 1949; see also the picture books listed under Chaucer below. The spirit of the 15th and late 14th centuries is brilliantly discussed by J. Huizinga, *The Waning of the Middle Ages*, 1924. F. R. H. Du Boulay gives an interpretation of the age that complements and qualifies Huizinga in *An Age of Ambition*, 1970.

For general discussions of Middle English literature including Chaucer, see volume 2 of the *Cambridge History of English Literature*, A. C. Baugh's section of *A Literary History of England*, edited by Baugh, rev. 1967, D. A. Pearsall, *Old and Middle*

English Poetry, 1977, J. A. Burrow, *Middle English Literature and Its Background*, 1982; *Medieval Literature: Chaucer and the Alliterative Tradition* (vol. 1 of the *New Pelican Guide to English Literature*), ed. Boris Ford, 1982; and D. S. Brewer, *English Gothic Literature*, 1983. W. P. Ker's *English Literature: Medieval*, 1912, is still provocative. D. M. Zesmer's *Guide to English Literature from Beowulf through Chaucer and Medieval Drama*, 1961, is a most useful survey; C. S. Lewis, *The Discarded Image*, 1964, is very popular; W. L. Renwick and H. Orton, *The Beginnings of English Literature to Skelton*, 3rd ed., 1966, is a good survey with bibliographical notes; also useful is H. S. Bennett, *Chaucer and the Fifteenth Century*, 1947; J. A. W. Bennett and Douglas Gray's *Middle English Literature*, 1986, goes up to 1400, excluding Chaucer. Edward Vasta's collection of essays by various scholars, *Middle English Survey: Critical Essays*, 1965, will offer stimulation to students of *Piers Plowman*, *Sir Gawain and the Green Knight*, the drama, and the ballads. J. A. Burrow, *Ricardian Poetry: Chaucer, Gower, Langland and the Gawain Poet*, 1971, is extremely interesting on the authors in his title and their period. Chapters 6–10 of Erich Auerbach's *Mimesis: The Representation of Reality in Western Literature*, trans. by W. R.

Trask, 1953, while dealing with none of the works included in this anthology, shed much light on the spirit of medieval literature. For the Middle English language, see Helge Kökeritz's *A Guide to Chaucer's Pronunciation*, 1954; Samuel Moore's *Historical Outlines of English Sounds and Inflections*, rev. A.H. Marckwardt, 1951; John W. Clark's *Early English*, 1957, 1967; and David Burnley's *A Guide to Chaucer's Language*, 1983.

For general discussion of non-Chaucerian Middle English literature, see R. M. Wilson, *Early Middle English Literature*, 1939, and E. K. Chambers, *English Literature at the Close of the Middle Ages*, 1954, which between them thoroughly cover the beginning and the end of the period. George Kane's *Middle English Literature*, 1951, has good chapters on the romances, the religious lyrics, and *Piers Plowman*. A. C. Spearing's *Medieval Dream-Poetry*, 1976, is a fine treatment of the genre. A broad sampling of non-Chaucerian literature in translation is offered by *Medieval English Verse*, ed. R. S. Loomis and R. Willard, 1948.

The standard bibliography is *A Manual of the Writings in Middle English, 1050–1500*, six vols., 1967–80, ed. J. B. Severs, A. E. Hartung, et al., which is based on and supersedes the *Manual* of J. E. Wells, 1916, with 9 supplements through 1945.

THE SIXTEENTH CENTURY

Some general books on the history of the period are J. B. Black, *The Reign of Elizabeth, 1558–1603*, 2nd ed., 1959; G. R. Elton, *England Under the Tudors*, 1955, and *Reform and Reformation: England, 1509–1559*, 1977; Conrad Russell, *The Crisis of Parliaments: English History, 1509–1660*, 1971; and John Guy, *Tudor England*, 1988. Political theory in the period is surveyed in Quentin Skinner, *The Foundations of Modern Political Thought*, 2 vols., 1978. Exploration and military history are treated in G. Mattingly, *The Armada*, 1959; and J. A. Williamson, *The Age of Drake*, 4th ed., 1960. For church history and religion, see William Haller, *The Rise of Puritanism*, 1938; P. Collinson, *The Elizabethan Puritan Movement*, 1967, rpt. 1990; and Horton Davies, *Worship and Theology in England from Cranmer to Hooker, 1534–1603*, 1970.

Important works for social and economic history are R. H. Tawney, *Religion and the Rise of Capitalism*, 1926; Louis B. Wright, *Middle Class Culture in Elizabethan England*, 1935, rpt. 1965; Lawrence Stone, *The Crisis of the Aristocracy, 1558–1641*, 1965, and *The Family, Sex, and Marriage in England, 1500–1800*, 1977; Keith Thomas, *Religion and the Decline of Magic*, 1971; Keith Wrightson, *English Society 1580–1680*, 1982; and Susan Dwyer Amussen, *An Ordered Society: Gender and Class in Early Modern England*, 1988. For an illuminating contemporary

perspective on the period see Muriel St. Clare Byrne, ed., *The Lisle Letters*, 1981.

Patronage and courtiership, with special reference to literature, are analyzed in David Javitch, *Poetry and Courtliness in Renaissance England*, 1976; Guy Fitch Lytle and Stephen Orgel, eds., *Patronage in the Renaissance*, 1981; and Frank Whigham, *Ambition and Privilege: The Social Tropes of Elizabethan Courtesy Theory*, 1984. On publishing and the book trade, see H. S. Bennett, *English Books and Readers, 1475–1557*, 1952, and *English Books and Readers, 1558–1603*, 1965; and Elizabeth L. Eisenstein, *The Printing Press as an Agent of Change*, 2 vols., 1979.

Several classic studies define the Renaissance in terms of humanism, imitation of the ancients, and individual achievement: Jacob Burckhardt, *The Civilization of the Renaissance*, 1878, rev. 1944; E. M. W. Tillyard, *The Elizabethan World Picture*, 1943; Douglas Bush, *The Renaissance and English Humanism*, 1939; Ernst Cassirer et al., eds., *The Renaissance Philosophy of Man*, 1948; Erwin Panofsky, *Renaissance and Renascences in Western Art*, 2 vols., 1960; and Paul O. Kristeller, *Renaissance Thought*, 2 vols., 1961, 1965. Revisionist analyses by new historicist and cultural materialist critics focus on the interaction of institutions, ideology, and the conditions of cultural production in the social construction of persons and literary texts. Some seminal studies are Stephen Greenblatt,

Renaissance Self-Fashioning, 1980; Stephen Greenblatt, ed., Representing the English Renaissance, 1988; Richard Helgerson, Self-Crowned Laureates: Spenser, Jonson, Milton and the Literary System, 1983; and Peter Stallybrass and Allon White, The Politics and Poetics of Transgression, 1986. (Others on the theater and on Shakespeare are noted in appropriate sections.)

Renaissance science, old and new, is discussed in A. Wolf, A History of Science, Technology, and Philosophy in the 16th and 17th Centuries, 1959; and Wayne Shumaker, The Occult Sciences in the Renaissance, 1972. Education is the subject of T. W. Baldwin, William Shakespere's Small Latine and Lesse Greeke, 2 vols., 1944; and Kenneth Charlton, Education in Renaissance England, 1965. On logic and rhetoric see W. S. Howell, Logic and Rhetoric in England, 1500–1700, 1956; Sister Miriam Joseph, Rhetoric in Shakespeare's Time, 1962; Frances Yates, The Art of Memory, 1966; and Victoria Kahn, Rhetoric and Skepticism in the Renaissance, 1985.

Some books on Renaissance art and architecture are Marcus Whiffin, An Introduction to Elizabethan and Jacobean Architecture, 1952; J. Buxton, Elizabethan Taste, 1963; Roy Strong, The English Icon: Elizabethan and Jacobean Portraiture, 1969, and The Cult of Elizabeth: Elizabethan Portraiture and Pageantry, 1977; Mark Girouard, Life in the English Country House, 1978; John King, Tudor Royal Iconography: Literature and Art in an Age of Religious Crisis, 1989; Lucy Gent, Picture and Poetry, 1560–1620, 1981; and Norman K. Farmer, Poets and the Visual Arts in Renaissance England, 1984. Renaissance iconology and emblem books often illuminate literary imagery; important studies are Erwin Panofsky, Studies in Iconology, 1939; Rosemary Freeman, English Emblem Books, 1948; Jean Seznec, The Survival of the Pagan Gods, trans. B. F. Sessions, 1963. The iconoclasm controversy is treated by John Phillips, The Reformation of Images: Destruction of Art in England, 1535–1660, 1971; and Ernest B. Gilman, Iconoclasm and Poetry in the English Reformation, 1986.

For Tudor music and musicians in relation to poetry see M. C. Boyd, Elizabethan Music and Music Criticism, 1940; E. H. Fellowes, English Madrigal Verse, rev. 1967; John Stevens, Music and Poetry in the Early Tudor Court, 1961, rpt. 1979; David Price, Patrons and Musicians of the English Renaissance, 1981; and Winifred Maynard, Elizabethan Lyric Poetry and Its Music, 1986. John Hollander studies music as symbol in The Untuning of the Sky: Ideas of Music in English Poetry, 1500–1700, 1961; and Paula Johnson analyzes structural affinities of the two art forms in Form and Transformation in Music and Poetry of the English Renaissance, 1975.

Useful anthologies of Elizabethan literary criticism are G. G. Smith, Elizabethan Critical Essays, 2 vols., 1904; and O. B. Hardison, Jr., English Literary Criticism: The Renaissance, 1963. Important studies of Renaissance literary theory and criticism include Rosamond Tuve, Elizabethan and Metaphysical Imagery, 1947; Baxter Hathaway, Marvels and Commonplaces: Renaissance Literary Criticism, 1968; Don C. Allen, Mysteriously Meant: the Rediscovery of Pagan Symbolism and Allegorical Interpretation in the Renaissance, 1970; S. K. Heninger, Touches of Sweet Harmony: Pythagorean Cosmology and Renaissance Poetics, 1974; Margaret W. Ferguson, Trials of Desire: Renaissance Defenses of Poetry, 1983; and Arthur Kinney, Humanist Poetics, 1986.

On the vernacular versions of the Bible, see David Daiches, The King James Version of the English Bible, 1968; and A. C. Partridge, English Biblical Translation, 1973. John E. Booty has edited the 1559 Book of Common Prayer, 1976, with a useful introduction.

Some distinguished historical and critical accounts of Renaissance literature include Hallett Smith, Elizabethan Poetry: A Study in Conventions, Meaning, and Expression, 1952, rpt. 1968; C. S. Lewis, English Literature in the Sixteenth Century, Excluding Drama, 1954; Douglas Bush, Mythology and the Renaissance Tradition in English Poetry, rev. 1963; Rosalie Colie, The Resources of Kind: Genre-Theory in the Renaissance, 1973; Thomas M. Greene, The Light in Troy: Imitation and Discovery in Renaissance Poetry, 1982; John King, English Reformation Literature: The Tudor Origins of the Protestant Tradition, 1982; and David Norbrook, Poetry and Politics in the English Renaissance, 1984. Important studies of particular Renaissance genres and kinds include J. W. Lever, The Elizabethan Love Sonnet, 1956; Alvin Kernan, The Cankered Muse: Satire of the English Renaissance, 1959; Lily B. Campbell, Divine Poetry and Drama in Sixteenth-Century England, 1959; Douglas L. Peterson, The English Lyric from Wyatt to Donne, 1966; Patricia Parker, Inescapable Romance, 1979; Anne Ferry, The "Inward" Language: Sonnets of Wyatt, Sidney, Shakespeare, and Donne, 1983; Janel Mueller, The Native Tongue and the Word: Developments in English Prose Style, 1380–1580, 1984; and Annabel Patterson, Pastoral and Ideology: Virgil to Valéry, 1987.

Important studies of stage history, audiences, and the development of dramatic forms include E. K. Chambers, The Elizabethan Stage, 4 vols., 1923; Allardyce Nicoll, British Drama, rev. 1962; Revels History of Drama in English, 8 vols., 1978–83; Muriel D. Bradbrook, A History of Elizabethan Drama, 6 vols., 1935–76, esp. Themes and Conventions of Elizabethan Tragedy, 1935, and The Growth and Structure of Elizabethan Comedy, 1955; F. T. Bowers, Elizabethan Revenge Tragedy, 1578–1642, 1940; Madeleine Doran, Endeavors of Art, 1954; Glynne Wickham, Early English Stages, 1300–1660, 3 vols., 1959–81; Richard Leacroft,

The Development of the English Playhouse, 1973; David Bevington, *From "Mankind" to Marlowe*, 1962; and Andrew Gurr, *Playgoing in Shakespeare's London*, 1987. Some important studies of drama in relation to contemporary politics and ideology are David Bevington, *Tudor Drama and Politics*, 1968; Robert Weiman, *Shakespeare and the Popular Tradition in the Theater*, 1967, rpt. 1987; Jonathan Dollimore, *Radical Tragedy. Religion, Ideology and Power in the Drama of Shakespeare and his Contemporaries*, 1984; Catherine Belsey, *The Subject of Tragedy: Identity and Difference in Renaissance Drama*, 1985; and Steven Mullaney, *The Place of the Stage*, 1988.

Currently, an important area of investigation in Renaissance studies involves gender issues and women's writing. For the situation of women in Renaissance England see Joan Kelly-Gadol, "Did Women Have a Renaissance?" in *Becoming Visible: Women in European History*, ed. R. Bridenthal and C. Koonz, 1977; Ian Maclean, *The Renaissance Notion of Women*, 1980; Patricia H. Labalme, ed., *Beyond Their Sex: Learned Women of the European Past*, 1980; Retha M. Warnicke, *Women of the English Renaissance and Reforma-*

tion, 1983; Linda Woodbridge, *Women and the English Renaissance: Literature and the Nature of Womankind, 1540–1640*, 1984; Margaret Ferguson et al., eds., *Rewriting the Renaissance: The Discourses of Sexual Difference in Early Modern Europe*, 1986; Elaine Beilin, *Redeeming Eve: Women Writers of the English Renaissance*, 1987; and Anne M. Haselkorn and Betty S. Travitsky, eds., *The Renaissance Englishwoman in Print: Counterbalancing the Canon*, 1990. A useful anthology is Betty Travitsky, ed., *The Paradise of Women: Writings by Englishwomen of the Renaissance*, 1981.

There are many useful collections of critical essays, including Maynard Mack and George Lord, *Poetic Traditions of the English Renaissance*, 1982; Patricia Parker and David Quint, eds., *Literary Theory/Renaissance Texts*, 1986; and Heather Dubrow and Richard Strier, eds., *The Historical Renaissance*, 1988. The Goldentree bibliography for the period, John L. Lievsay, *The Sixteenth Century: Skelton Through Hooker*, 1968, is a handy, basic reference. The journal *Studies in English Literature* contains an annual review of scholarship in the period.

THE EARLY SEVENTEENTH CENTURY

Many studies conjoin the 16th and early 17th centuries, often as "the English Renaissance." As a rule, such studies are listed in the first section of the bibliography for the 16th century. On an ongoing basis, the journal *English Literary Renaissance (ELR)* commissions overviews of recent studies of individual 16th- and 17th-century writers. These are invaluable aids to the serious student. Our listings include all that had appeared by the time this volume went to press; but the series continues, and overviews are replaced by updated ones every so often.

The best single-volume general history of England in the 17th century is by Christopher Hill, *The Century of Revolution*, 1961. Differing views of the same events are offered by the durable work of G. M. Trevelyan, *England Under the Stuarts*, 21st ed., 1949; Godfrey Davies, *The Early Stuarts*, 2nd ed., 1949; Barry Coward, *The Stuart Age*, 1980; and by J. S. Morrill, *Seventeenth-Century Britain*, 1980. A useful collection of studies of various facets of 17th-century society and culture has been edited by C. A. Patrides and Raymond Waddington, under the title of *The Age of Milton: Backgrounds to Seventeenth-Century Literature*, 1980. A close account of the crucial English rebellion and civil war will be found in two volumes by C. V. Wedgwood, *The King's Peace, 1637–1641*, 1955, and *The King's War, 1641–1647*, 1958. The "revisionist" point of view, in which the civil war was not a revolution but an accidental consequence of

politicians' incompetence, is represented by Anthony Fletcher, *The Outbreak of the English Civil War*, 1981; Conrad Russell, *The Causes of the English Civil War*, 1990; and J. S. Morrill's 17th-century history (above).

Seventeenth-century English history comes perilously close to being a self-contained subject; before getting absorbed into it, students should frame their pictures by finding out in a broad way what was happening at the same time on the European continent. Among many books serving this end are two wide-ranging but not overwhelming volumes both published in 1971: *A Modern History of Europe* by Eugen Weber, and the *Norton History of Modern Europe* under the general editorship of Felix Gilbert.

A very influential essay on the Protestant ethic and the spirit of capitalism by the German sociologist Max Weber was published in 1904 and 1905; after major modifications, its main idea was incorporated in a most eloquent book by R. H. Tawney, *Religion and the Rise of Capitalism*, 1926. The thesis that Protestant ideas, notably the doctrine of the religious calling or vocation, were engines in the hands of an aspiring capitalist class has been much disputed, with H. R. Trevor-Roper leading the attack. In the course of the controversy, many points were scored on both sides; but most recent historians have been concerned less with "interpretations" of the 17th century as a whole than with exploring limited districts, actions, or spots of time.

Specialized historical studies of interest to the literary student are to be found on every hand. Two volumes by Elizabeth Eisenstein on *The Printing Press as an Agent of Change*, 1979, are particularly relevant to the literature of the 16th and 17th centuries; while a still larger view is taken by Peter Laslett in *The World We Have Lost*, 3rd ed., 1984. To imagine life in a pre-industrial society is hard for a modern reader; Laslett's book helps. See also Keith Wrightson, *English Society, 1580–1680*, 1982; Lawrence Stone's massive study of *The Family, Sex, and Marriage in England, 1500–1800*, 1977; and David Underdown, *Revel, Riot, and Rebellion: Popular Politics and Culture in England, 1603–1660*, 1985. Michael Walzer, *The Revolution of the Saints*, 1965, examines Puritanism and its political consequences, and Christopher Hill's *The World Turned Upside Down*, 1972, studies the radical fringe in the English revolution.

Studying the development of a scientific point of view in the early 17th century is an important project, but an enormous and complicated one, because the new approach had to disentangle itself not only from the conventional assumptions of the age but from lingering presences of astrology, alchemy, cabalistic lore, hermetic teachings, natural magic, and the superstitions of witchcraft. The image of a universe bound together by strains of occult sympathy and moral analogy had been inherited from the Middle Ages, and was widely accepted at the start of the century; the scheme is described, perhaps too simply, in E. M. W. Tillyard's concise and very influential study, *The Elizabethan World Picture*, 1943; useful complications can be introduced by referring to C. S. Lewis's brilliantly polemic *The Discarded Image*, 1964; and a collection of relevant documents is assembled in James Winny's *The Frame of Order*, 1957. In his extremely influential *The Order of Things* (1970), Michel Foucault argued that the differences between 16th- and 17th-century thought (not just in science) should be understood as an "epistemic shift"—a fundamental change in the organization of knowledge. In *The Temple of the Mind*, 1969, John R. Mulder emphasized the extent to which school curricula, academic practices, and elementary catechisms shaped the thinking of the early 17th century, leaving many marks on the poetry of Milton, Herbert, and Donne. The beginnings of the Royal Society of London for Improving Natural Knowledge have been many times studied, as by Margery Purver, in *The Royal Society: Concept and Creation*, 1967, and, most recently, by Michael Hunter, in *Establishing the New Science*, 1989. Hans Blumenberg's *The Genesis of the Copernican World*, 1987, massively studies the intellectual preconditions and consequences of the heliocentric theory.

But the conventional wisdom of the age was entwined with more mysterious and sometimes superstitious strains of thought, conveniently designated occult. These are deep and murky waters, best approached through a somewhat skeptical survey like Wayne Shumaker's *The Occult Sciences in the Renaissance*, 1972. Frances Yates and her colleague at the Warburg Institute, David P. Walker, explored many of the complexities of hermetic thought, she in a brilliant and sometimes questioned series of books, the first of which was *Giordano Bruno*, 1964, he in a study of *Spiritual and Demonic Magic*, 1958. A useful and hardheaded study by Keith Thomas on *Religion and the Decline of Magic*, 1971, may provide congenial entry into the vast areas surveyed by the eight volumes of Lynn Thorndike's *History of Magic and Experimental Science*, 1923–58. From the philosophical point of view, E. A. Burtt's *Metaphysical Foundations of Modern Physical Science*, rev. 1932, is still reliable and informative; while an important sidelight is contributed by Christopher Hill in *Intellectual Origins of the English Revolution*, 1965. Perhaps the most direct way to approach this protean subject of emergent science is through the lives and works of individual scientists: Gilbert (magnetism), Napier and Wallis (mathematics), Bacon (theory), Harvey (physiology), and of course Newton, the universal genius.

General literary histories of the age include Douglas Bush, *English Literature in the Earlier Seventeenth Century*, rev. 1962, which is vol. 5 of the *Oxford History of English Literature*; also a shorter, less bibliographical introduction by C. V. Wedgwood, *Seventeenth-Century English Literature*, 1950. But the great variety of 17th-century literature does not lend itself so well to formal history as to assemblages of essays clustering around a theme or themes. An older but still informative collection is L. C. Knights, *Explorations*, 1946; more recent is Rosemond Tuve, *Essays: Spenser, Herbert, Milton*, 1970. Above all, the 17th-century essays of T. S. Eliot, which wrought a palpable revolution in modern thinking, not only about the 17th century but about poetry as such, merit thoughtful reading; they are not hard to pick out of his *Selected Essays*.

Rosemond Tuve in *Elizabethan and Metaphysical Imagery*, 1947, and Ruth Wallerstein in *Studies in Seventeenth Century Poetic*, 1950, probed the relation between critical theory and poetic practice. An elderly but unreplaced collection includes major critical documents of the age: J. E. Spingarn, *Critical Essays of the Seventeenth Century*, 1908–9 (reissued 1957); Edward Tayler edited a one-volume collection, *Literary Criticism of the Seventeenth Century*, 1967.

Other useful collections of texts include George Saintsbury's three fat volumes of the *Minor Poets of the Caroline Period*, 1905–21, and David Wooten, ed., *Divine Right and Democracy: An Anthology of Political Writing in Stuart England*, 1986. A large selection of Elizabethan and Jacobean plays has been made available at moderate price, and with competently edited texts, in three series: The New Mermaids, The Revels Plays, and Regents Renaissance Drama.

In 1937, a pioneering work of L. C. Knights, *Drama and Society in the Age of Jonson*, linked the literature of the early 17th century to the social stresses of the age. Recent "New Historicist" works engage in a similar enterprise, focusing especially on power relations. These include Jonathan Goldberg, *James I and the Politics of Literature*, 1983; Richard Helgerson, *Self-Crowned Laureates: Spenser, Jonson, Milton, and the Literary System*, 1983; David Norbrook, *Poetry and Politics in the English Renaissance*, 1984; Annabel Patterson, *Censorship and Interpretation: The Conditions of Writing and Reading in Early Modern England*, 1984; Leah Marcus, *The Politics of Mirth: Jonson, Herrick, Milton, Marvell, and the Defense of Our Holiday Pastimes*, 1986; Michael Wilding, *Dragons Teeth: Literature in the English Revolution*, 1987 (on Milton, Marvell, and Browne); Lois Potter, *Secret Rites and Secret Writing: Royalist Literature, 1641–1660*, 1989; and a collection of studies edited by Thomas Healy and Jonathan Sawday, *Literature and the English Civil War*, 1990.

Under the title *The Weaker Vessel*, 1984, Antonia Fraser has studied in fascinating detail the position of women in 17th-century England. Three recent books treating female writers in the period are Elaine Hobby, *Virtue of Necessity: English Women's Writing 1646–1688*, 1988; Tina Krontikis, *Oppositional Voices: Women as Writers and Translators of Literature in the English Renaissance*, 1992; and Barbara K. Lewalski, *Writing Women in Jacobean England*, 1993. Anthologies of writing by women in (or including) the 17th century have been edited by Betty Travitsky, *The Paradise of Women*, 1981; Angeline Goreau, *The Whole Duty of a Woman*, 1985; Moira Ferguson, *First Feminists: British Women Writers, 1578–1799*, 1985; Kathleen Henderson and Barbara McManus, *Half Humankind: Contexts and Texts of the Controversy about Women in England, 1540–1640*, 1985; Germaine Greer et al., *Kissing the Rod: An Anthology of Seventeenth-Century Women's Verse*, 1988; and Elspeth Graham et al., *Her Own Life: Autobiographical Writings by Seventeenth-Century Englishwomen*, 1989. Several of these include extensive commentary. An annotated bibliography by Hilda Smith and Susan Cardinale, *Women and the Literature of the Seventeenth Century*, 1990, gives a brief account of all the works by or about women listed in Donald Wing's *Short-Title Catalogue* of English books published between 1641 and 1700. Sara Jayne Steen reviews "Recent Studies in Women Writers of the Seventeenth Century, 1604–1674," *ELR* 24 (1994): 243–274—the latest in an ongoing series of articles.

A spate of books on the Metaphysical poets appeared during the 1930s, of which the best are those by George Williamson, 1930, Joan Bennett and J. B. Leishman, both 1934, and Helen C. White, 1936. Louis L. Martz, in *The Poetry of Meditation*, 1954, discussed a traditional mode of thought as it influenced the Metaphysicals, illustrated it with an anthology, *The Meditative Poem*, 1963, and continued the same line of investigation in *The Paradise Within*, 1964. Two other influential studies from the 1960s are Robert Ellrodt, *L'inspiration personnelle et l'esprit du temps chez les poètes métaphysiques anglais*, 1960, and A. Alvarez, *The School of Donne*, 1961. Joseph H. Summers treated both the Metaphysicals and the Cavaliers in *The Heirs of Donne and Jonson*, 1970. Earl Miner wrote on *The Metaphysical Mode from Donne to Cowley*, 1969—and went on to study *The Cavalier Mode from Jonson to Cotton*, 1971, and *The Restoration Mode from Milton to Dryden*, 1974. Barbara K. Lewalski explored the relation between theology and poetry in *Protestant Poetics and the Seventeenth-Century Religious Lyric*, 1979. Recently, most works grouping 17th-century poets have (like the New Historicist works listed above) employed rubrics other than "Metaphysicals" and "Cavaliers."

Continental perspectives on English authors of the 17th century are supplied by two important books by Mario Praz: *Studies in Seventeenth-Century Imagery*, 1939, and *The Flaming Heart*, 1958. Marjorie Nicolson's *The Breaking of the Circle*, 2nd ed., 1960, deals with the impact of developing scientific thought, largely on Donne, as her earlier *Newton Demands the Muse*, 1946, carries the same theme into the later century. Joseph A. Mazzeo's *Renaissance and Revolution: Backgrounds to Seventeenth-Century English Literature*, rev. 1967, provides an excellent introduction to the major currents of Renaissance intellectual history, with chapters on humanism, Machiavelli, Castiglione, Bacon, Hobbes, and the idea of progress. Harry Levin studied a single, but often central, theme in *The Myth of the Golden Age in the Renaissance*, 1969; his book could well be read in conjunction with that of A. Bartlett Giamatti on *The Earthly Paradise and the Renaissance Epic*, 1969. Rosalie Colie studied, in *Paradoxia Epidemica*, 1966, Renaissance applications of a single literary device; and the student of classic myth in 17th-century poetry will find Douglas Bush's *Mythology and the Renaissance Tradition in English Poetry*, rev. 1963, an indispensable guide.

Until 1969, *Studies in Philology* published an annual bibliography of Renaissance and 17th-century studies; after that date, the appropriate section of the MLA bibliography should be consulted. *Studies in English Literature* annually surveys new books in the area; as noted above, *English Literary Renaissance* regularly summarizes recent studies of individual writers.

THE RESTORATION AND THE EIGHTEENTH CENTURY

In recent decades, historians have placed less emphasis on stories about the ruling classes and their political conflicts and more on the economic and social forces that shape the lives of ordinary people. A good example of this approach is *The Peoples of the British Isles: A New History*, 3 vols., 1992; volume 2, by T. W. Heyck, covers the period from 1688 to 1870. A fuller account is provided by J. R. Jones, *Country and Court; England, 1658–1714*, 1978; W. A. Speck, *Stability and Strife: England, 1714–1760*, 1977; and Ian Christie, *Wars and Revolutions: Britain, 1760–1815*, 1982. J. H. Plumb, *England in the Eighteenth Century*, 1950, describes the structure of society, and Roy Porter, *English Society in the Eighteenth Century*, rev. 1990, is a mine of information. The life and manners of the age are surveyed by A. S. Turberville, ed., *Johnson's England*, 2 vols., 1933; Dorothy Marshall's *English People in the Eighteenth Century*, 1956; and R. B. Schwartz's *Daily Life in Johnson's England*, 1983. *The Birth of a Consumer Society*, 1982, by Neil McKendrick, John Brewer, and J. H. Plumb, traces the rise of modern commercialization in the 18th century. Useful guides to the historical and cultural contexts of literature include A. R. Humphreys's *The Augustan World*, 1954; Donald Greene's *The Age of Exuberance*, 1970; Pat Rogers, ed., *The Eighteenth Century*, 1978; and James Sambrook's *The Eighteenth Century, 1700–1789*, 1986.

On the intellectual background of the period, Sir Leslie Stephen's *History of English Thought in the Eighteenth Century*, 2 vols., 1876, remains valuable; so do A. O. Lovejoy's *The Great Chain of Being*, 1942, and *Essays in the History of Ideas*, 1948. Basil Willey's *The Eighteenth Century Background*, 1940, studies ideas about nature and Keith Thomas's *Man and the Natural World*, 1983, shows the development of a modern sensibility between 1500 and 1800. Gordon Rupp's *Religion in England, 1688–1791*, 1986, is dependable. Volumes 4 to 6 of F. C. Coplestone's *History of Philosophy*, 1960, deal with the period from Descartes to Kant; Peter Gay's *The Enlightenment: An Interpretation*, 2 vols., 1969, forcefully defends the philosophers of the Age of Reason. Paul Hazard's *The European Mind, 1680–1715*, 1953, and *European Thought in the Eighteenth Century*, 1954, trans. from French by J. L. May, are readable surveys of intellectual movements on the Continent as well as in England. J. W. Johnson's *The Formation of English Neo-Classical Thought*, 1967, and J. M. Levine's *The Battle of the Books: History and Literature in the Augustan Age*, 1991, study the ways that writers came to terms with the past. Burton Feldman's and R. D. Richardson's *The Rise of Modern Mythology 1680–1860*, 1972, and Gerald Newman's *The Rise of English Nationalism*, 1987,

deal with important new directions of thought. Valuable studies of the influence of scientific ideas include R. F. Jones's *Ancients and Moderns*, 1936; Marjorie Nicolson's *Newton Demands the Muse*, 1946, and *Science and the Imagination*, 1956; and W. P. Jones's *The Rhetoric of Science*, 1966. Myra Reynolds's *The Learned Lady in England, 1650–1760*, 1920, still useful, should be supplemented by Sylvia Myers's *The Bluestocking Circle*, 1990. Martin Price's *To the Palace of Wisdom: Studies in Order and Energy from Dryden to Blake*, 1964, Paul Fussell's *The Rhetorical World of Augustan Humanism*, 1965, W. J. Bate's *The Burden of the Past and the English Poet*, 1970, Jean Hagstrum's *Sex and Sensibility: Ideal and Erotic Love from Milton to Mozart*, 1980, John Sitter's *Literary Loneliness in Mid-Eighteenth-Century England*, 1982, and D. L. Patey's *Probability and Literary Form*, 1984, are all thoughtful and stimulating studies that relate ideas to literary art.

Good surveys of the literature of the age include George Sherburn's "The Restoration and Eighteenth Century," in A. C. Baugh, ed., *A Literary History of England*, rev. 1967; and Roger Lonsdale, ed., *Dryden to Johnson*, rev. 1987, vol. 4 of the Sphere History of Literature. Far more detailed are three volumes of the *Oxford History of English Literature*: James Sutherland's *English Literature of the Late Seventeenth Century*, 1969; Bonamy Dobrée's *English Literature in the Early Eighteenth Century, 1700–1740*, 1959; and John Butt's and Geoffrey Carnall's *English Literature in the Mid-Eighteenth Century*, 1979. On women writers they need to be supplemented by Janet Todd's *A Dictionary of British and American Women Writers, 1660–1800*, 1985.

Among books that deal with a single literary mode, James Sutherland's *A Preface to Eighteenth-Century Poetry*, 1948, is a deft introduction, and Eric Rothstein's *Restoration and Eighteenth-Century Poetry, 1660–1800*, 1981, is a fresh, informative survey. Other useful studies include Ian Jack's *Augustan Satire*, 1952; Earl Miner's *The Restoration Mode from Milton to Dryden*, 1974; Rachel Trickett's *The Honest Muse*, 1974; Margaret Doody's *The Daring Muse*, 1985; and P. W. K. Stone's *The Art of Poetry, 1750–1820*, 1967. Anne Williams's *Prophetic Strain*, 1984, and Richard Feingold's *Moralized Song*, 1989, both stress the lyricism of 18th-century poems. Two anthologies edited by Roger Lonsdale, *The New Oxford Book of Eighteenth Century Verse*, 1984, and *Eighteenth-Century Women Poets*, 1989, have sparked an interest in neglected poems about daily life, and Joyce Fullard has edited *Eighteenth-Century Women Poets 1660–1800*, 1990.

On drama, a good introduction is R. W. Bevis's *English Drama: Restoration and Eighteenth Cen-*

tury, 1660–1789, 1988. Fuller accounts appear in Allardyce Nicoll's A History of Restoration Drama 1660–1700, A History of Early Eighteenth-Century Drama, 1700–1750, and A History of Late Eighteenth-Century Drama, 1750–1800, rev. 1952; and The Revels History of Drama in English, Vol. 5, 1660–1750, 1976, and Vol. 6, 1750–1880, 1975. An invaluable store of detailed information is The London Stage, 1660–1800, 11 vols., 1960–68, the critical introductions of which have been gathered in five paperback books. Five of the most important plays of the period, together with critical commentary and background material on theaters, staging, and audience, are edited by Scott McMillin in a Norton Critical Edition, Restoration and Eighteenth-Century Comedy, 1973. Two collections, Earl Miner, ed., Restoration Dramatists, 1966, and John Loftis, ed., Restoration Drama, 1966, provide essays in criticism by various writers; Loftis has also analyzed Comedy and Society from Congreve to Fielding, 1959. Walter Graham has surveyed English Literary Periodicals, 1930. Letter writing was an important 18th-century genre, discussed by Howard Anderson, P. B. Daghlian, and Irvin Ehrenpreis, eds., The Familiar Letter in the Eighteenth Century, 1966, and Bruce Redford's The Converse of the Pen, 1987. D. A. Stauffer's English Biography before 1700, 1930, and The Art of Biography in Eighteenth-Century England, 2 vols., 1941, are standard surveys; William H. Epstein's Recognizing Biography, 1987, is a challenging theoretical study. Bunyan figures prominently in two books on autobiography, John N. Morris's Versions of the Self, 1966, and Felicity Nussbaum's The Autobiographical Subject, 1989. Patricia Spacks's Imagining a Self, 1976, discusses conceptions of personal identity in 18th-century autobiographies and novels. The novel is treated in detail by E. A. Baker's The History of the English Novel, vols. 3–5, 1930–34. A. D. McKillop's The Early Masters of English Fiction, 1956, and Clive Probyn's English Fiction of the Eighteenth Century, 1700–1789, 1987, are good introductions to major novelists. Ian Watt's The Rise of the Novel, 1957, is an influential study of Defoe, Richardson, and Fielding; it should be supplemented by Jane Spencer, The Rise of the Woman Novelist, 1986, and J. Paul Hunter, Before Novels, 1990. Interesting recent studies of special aspects of fiction include Lennard Davis's Factual Fictions, 1983, Leopold Damrosch's God's Plot and Man's Stories, 1985, Terry Castle's Masquerade and Civilization, 1986, and Nancy Armstrong's Desire and Domestic Fiction, 1989.

There is currently no standard work on 18th-century criticism, despite many specialized studies. J. E. Spingarn's Critical Essays of the Seventeenth Century, vols. 2 and 3, 1908 (the preface is still useful), and Scott Elledge's Eighteenth-Century Critical Essays, 2 vols., 1961, are valuable collections. R. S. Crane's account of "Neo-Classical Criticism," in J. T. Shipley, ed., A Dictionary of World Literature, 1943, has not been surpassed. A survey of major critical movements is provided by James Engell, Forming the Critical Mind: Dryden to Coleridge, 1989. René Wellek's A History of Modern Criticism 1750–1950, vol. 1, 1955, and W. K. Wimsatt's and Cleanth Brooks's Literary Criticism: A Short History, 1957, review important issues of theory and aesthetics. Raymond Williams's Keywords: A Vocabulary of Culture and Society, 1983, examines the changing meanings of critical terms. A feminist perspective is offered by Marilyn Williamson's Raising Their Voices: British Women Writers, 1650–1750, 1990. The issues explored by Samuel H. Monk's classic study, The Sublime, 1935, have been taken up by many later critics, among them David Morris, The Religious Sublime, 1972, and Steven Knapp, Personification and the Sublime, 1985. The theory of satire has also been a perennial source of interest, most recently in John Sitter's Arguments of Augustan Wit, 1991. Though primarily concerned with Romantic theory, M. H. Abrams's The Mirror and the Lamp, 1953, delves deeply into 18th-century critical ideas.

The relation of literature to other arts has been the subject of many instructive studies. Jean Hagstrum's The Sister Arts, 1958, compares paintings with poems; John Dixon Hunt's The Figure in the Landscape, 1977, deals with poetry, painting, and gardening; and Richard Wendorf's The Elements of Life, 1990, compares biography with portrait-painting. Lawrence Lipking discusses the first histories of the arts in The Ordering of the Arts in Eighteenth-Century England, 1970; Ronald Paulson's Breaking and Remaking, 1989, explores aesthetic practice from 1700 to 1820; and Murray Roston analyzes Changing Perspectives in Literature and the Visual Arts 1650–1820, 1990. B. Sprague Allen's Tides of English Taste 1619–1800, 2 vols., 1937, on architecture, gardening, and decoration, and Sir Kenneth Clark's The Gothic Revival, 2nd ed., 1950, on architecture, chronicle significant changes in style.

Good collections of criticism have been edited by James L. Clifford, Eighteenth-Century English Literature: Modern Essays in Criticism, 1959, and Leopold Damrosch, Modern Essays on Eighteenth-Century Literature, 1988. Essays that explore new theoretical approaches are collected by Felicity Nussbaum and Laura Brown, The New Eighteenth Century, 1987. Studies in English Literature devotes its summer issue to the Restoration and the 18th century and includes an article reviewing important work published in the preceding year. Finally, for elaborate bibliographies and reviews of 18th-century studies, the student may consult the bibliography of English literature, 1660–1800, that has appeared annually since 1926 in Philological Quarterly and, since 1976, in yearly volumes, The Eighteenth Century: A Current Bibliography.

THE ROMANTIC PERIOD

Bibliographies

The most convenient starting point is to consult the surveys by Frank Jordan and others in *The English Romantic Poets, a Review of Research and Criticism*, rev. 1985, on Blake, Wordsworth, Coleridge, Byron, Shelley, and Keats; and Carolyn W. Houtchens and Lawrence H. Houtchens, *The English Romantic Poets and Essayists*, rev. 1966, on Blake, the lesser poets, and the major essayists. Annual bibliographies of publications about these writers are to be found in *ELH*, 1937–49; *Philological Quarterly*, 1950–64; *English Language Notes*, 1965–79; and *The Romantic Movement: A Selective and Critical Bibliography*, ed. David V. Erdman, 1980–.

Political and Social Background

Succinct treatments of the political and social events in this period are the relevant chapters of G. M. Trevelyan's *British History of the Nineteenth Century*, 2nd ed., 1937, and *English Social History*, 1942. More detailed histories are Elie Halévy, *England in 1815*, rev. 1949, and *The Liberal Awakening, 1815–1830*, rev. 1949; J. Steven Watson, *The Reign of George III, 1760–1815*, 1960; Asa Briggs, *The Making of Modern England: 1783–1867*, 1959; and Marilyn Butler, *Romantics, Rebels, and Reactionaries: English Literature and Its Background, 1760–1830*, 1982. Gilbert Slater, *The Growth of Modern England*, 1932, deals especially with the industrial revolution. For English literary relations to the French Revolution, see Howard Mumford Jones, *Revolution and Romanticism*, 1974, and Ronald Paulson, *Representations of Revolution (1789–1820)*, 1983.

Intellectual Background

Illuminating analyses of important intellectual movements will be found in A. O. Lovejoy's *The Great Chain of Being*, 1936, chapters 9 and 10, and *Essays in the History of Ideas*, 1948. Other particularly useful works on intellectual history are Basil Willey, *The Eighteenth Century Background*, 1940, and *Nineteenth Century Studies: Coleridge to Matthew Arnold*, 1949; Hoxie Neale Fairchild, *Religious Trends in English Poetry*, of which vol. 3 (1949) deals with 1780–1830; H. W. Piper, *The Active Universe: Pantheism and the Concept of Imagination in the English Romantic Poets*, 1962; Carl Woodring's survey of *Politics in English Romantic Poetry*, 1970; James Engell, *The Creative Imagination: Enlightenment to Romanticism*, 1981; and Marilyn Gaull, *English Romanticism: The Human Context*, 1988. On Romantic literature in its social matrix, see the relevant chapters in Raymond Williams, *Culture and Society, 1780–1950*, 1960; and on the relations between literature and art, Karl Kroeber, *British Romantic Art*, 1986. In *Romanticism: Points of View*, rev. 1970, Robert F. Gleckner and Gerald E. Enscoe reprint major

essays on the defining features of "Romanticism"; see also the essays in *Romanticism Reconsidered*, ed. Northrop Frye, 1963, and *Romanticism: Vistas, Instances, Continuities*, ed. David Thorburn and Geoffrey Hartman, 1973.

Literary History and Criticism

Among the histories of Romantic literature are Oliver Elton, *A Survey of English Literature, 1780–1830*, 2 vols., 1928; W. L. Renwick's rather inadequate *English Literature, 1789–1815*, 1963; Ian Jack's *English Literature, 1815–1832*, 1963; and J. R. de J. Jackson's *Poetry of the Romantic Period*, 1980. Mario Praz's *The Romantic Agony*, 2nd ed., 1951, treats Satansim, sadism, vampirism, and others of the more exotic literary interests of the time; G. R. Thompson has edited *The Gothic Imagination: Essays in Dark Romanticism*, 1974; and Peter Thorslev's *The Byronic Hero*, 1962, discusses solitary or alienated hero in other writers, as well as Byron; see also Frank Kermode's *Romantic Image*, 1957, on the concept of the poet at odds with society, from the Romantic period to Yeats. Douglas Bush's *Mythology and the Romantic Tradition in English Poetry*, 1937, is so broad in its range that it constitutes an excellent survey of Romantic poetry in general. The older negative appraisal of the Romantic achievement by the neohumanist Irving Babbitt, in *Rousseau and Romanticism*, 1919, and *On Being Creative and Other Essays*, 1932, has been taken up and expanded by Edward E. Bostetter in *The Romantic Ventriloquists*, 1963. G. Wilson Knight, *The Starlit Dome*, 1941, is an influential early example of the approach to Romantic poets by the analysis of characteristic patterns of imagery. Harold Bloom, *The Visionary Company*, rev. 1971, which relates these poets to the prophetic tradition of Spenser and Milton, includes brief and stimulating commentaries on each of the important poems; Bloom's *The Ringers in the Tower*, 1971, consists of influential essays on both 19th- and 20th-century "Romantic" writers. David Perkins treats *The Quest for Permanence* in Wordsworth, Shelley, and Keats, 1959; and Northrop Frye presents an archetypal overview in *A Study of English Romanticism*, 1968. In *Natural Supernaturalism: Tradition and Revolution in Romantic Literature*, 1971, and more recently in *The Correspondent Breeze: Essays on English Romanticism*, 1984, M. H. Abrams deals with persistent themes, concepts, and designs in English and German Romantic literature, and stresses their relation both to the biblical tradition and to the intellectual ambiance of a revolutionary age. Other recent books to be noted are Michael G. Cooke, *The Romantic Will*, 1976; Thomas Weiskel, *The Romantic Sublime: Studies in the Structure and Psychology of Transcendence*, 1976; Morse Peckham, *Romanticism and Behavior*,

1976; Anne K. Mellor, *English Romantic Irony*, 1980; Thomas McFarland, *Romanticism and the Forms of Ruin: Wordsworth, Coleridge, and Modalities of Fragmentation*, 1981; and Jerome J. McGann, *The Romantic Ideology*, 1983. On women writers of the period, see Sandra M. Gilbert and Susan Gubar, *The Madwoman in the Attic: The Woman Writer and the Nineteenth-Century Literary Imagination*, 1979; Mary Poovey, *The Proper Lady and the Woman Writer: Ideology as Style in the Works of Mary Wollstonecraft, Mary Shelley, and Jane Austen*, 1984; and Margaret Homans, *Bearing the Word: Language and Female Experience in Nineteenth-Century Women's Writing*, 1986. *English Romantic Poets: Modern Essays and Criticism*, ed. M. H. Abrams, 1975, is a collection of broadly representative essays by major contemporary critics; *Romanticism and Consciousness: Essays in Criticism*, ed. Harold Bloom, 1970, focuses on some leading topics in Romantic literature. See also the essays in Frederick W. Hilles and Harold Bloom, eds., *From Sensibility to Romanticism*, 1965. For critical opinions of the poets during their own lifetime, see Donald A. Reiman's *The Romantics Reviewed: Contemporary Reviews of British Romantic Writers*, 9 vols., 1972.

Following are studies of various forms of Romantic literature. On literary criticism: M. H. Abrams, *The Mirror and the Lamp: Romantic Theory and the Critical Tradition*, 1953; René Wellek, *A History of Modern Criticism: 1750–1950*, vol. 2, *The Romantic Age*, 1955. On poetic genres: Stuart Curran, *Poetic Form and British Romanticism*, 1986. On the fragment: Marjorie Levinson, *The Romantic Fragment Poem*, 1986. On narrative poetry: Karl Kroeber, *Romantic Narrative Art*, 1960, and Brian Wilkie, *Romantic Poets and Epic Tradition*, 1965. On the novel: Ernest A. Baker, *The History of the English Novel*, vol. 6, 1961; Montague Summers, *The Gothic Quest: A History of the Gothic Novel*, 1938; and Robert Kiely, *The Romantic Novel in England*, 1972. On drama: Allardyce Nicoll, *History of Early Nineteenth-Century Drama*, 1800–50, 2 vols., rev. 1955. On the essay: William F. Bryan and Ronald S. Crane, Introduction, *The English Familiar Essay*, 1916; Marie H. Law, *The English Familiar Essay in the Early Nineteenth Century*, 1934. See also Annette Wheeler Cafarelli, *Prose in the Age of Poets: Romanticism and Biographical Narrative from Johnson to De Quincey*, 1990.

THE VICTORIAN AGE

Studies of the Victorian age and its point of view include Richard D. Altick, *Victorian People and Ideas: A Companion for the Modern Reader of Victorian Literature*, 1973; Patrick Brantlinger, *Rule of Darkness: British Literature and Imperialism, 1830–1914*, 1988; Asa Briggs, *The Age of Improvement*, 1962; W. L. Burn, *The Age of Equipoise: A Study of the Mid-Victorian Generation*, 1964; Jerome Buckley, *The Victorian Temper*, 1951; David Cannadine, *The Decline and Fall of the British Aristocracy*, 1990; A. Dwight Culler, *The Victorian Mirror of History*, 1986; Walter E. Houghton, *The Victorian Frame of Mind, 1830–1870*, 1957; *Victorian Britain: An Encyclopedia*, ed. Sally Mitchell; Richard L. Stein, *Victoria's Year: English Literature and Culture, 1837–38*, 1988; F. M. L. Thompson, *The Rise of Respectable Society: A Social History of Victorian Britain, 1830–1900*, 1988; and G. M. Young, *Victorian England: Portrait of an Age*, 1936 (republished in 1977 with 215 pages of explanatory notes by George Kitson Clark). Young's essay is a brilliant synthesis, but it can be incomprehensible to readers who are not yet adequately familiar with the history of the age. Such readers should consult David Thomson's *England in the Nineteenth Century*, 1950, or Derek Beales, *From Castlereagh to Gladstone: 1815–1885*, 1970.

Studies of special aspects of the age include Richard Altick, *The English Common Reader*, 1957; Asa Briggs, *Victorian Things*, 1989; Jerome

Buckley, *The Triumph of Time*, 1966; Peter Gay, *The Bourgeois Experience: From Victoria to Freud*, 2 vols., 1984–86; Mark Girouard, *The Return to Camelot*, 1981; Bruce Haley, *The Healthy Body and Victorian Culture*, 1978; Steven Marcus, *The Other Victorians: A Study of Sexuality and Pornography in Mid-Nineteenth-Century England*, 1964; Herbert Sussman, *Victorians and the Machine*, 1968; E. P. Thompson, *The Making of the English Working Class*, 1963; Frank M. Turner, *The Greek Heritage in Victorian Britain*, 1981; *The Victorian City*, ed. H. J. Dyos and Michael Wolff, 2 vols., 1973; Jeffrey Weeks, *Sex, Politics and Society: The Regulation of Sexuality Since 1800*, 1981; and Michael Wheeler, *Death and the Future Life in Victorian Literature and Theology*, 1991. For pictures and paintings of the Victorian scene, see Jeremy Maas, *Victorian Painters*, 1969. Also revealing are the illustrations for Henry Mayhew's *London Labour and London Poor*, originally published 1851, reprinted 1967, and Gustav Doré's *London: A Pilgrimage*, originally published 1872 and reprinted 1970. *Nature and the Victorian Imagination*, ed. U. C. Knoepflmacher and G. B. Tennyson, 1977, and *Victorian Types, Victorian Shadows: Biblical Typology in Victorian Literature, Art, and Thought*, George Landow, 1980, feature valuable treatments of literature and the visual arts.

Studies of Victorian literature include Harold Bloom, *The Ringers in the Tower*, 1971; William E. Buckler, *The Victorian Imagination*, 1980;

Douglas Bush, *Mythology and the Romantic Tradition*, 1937; Raymond Chapman, *The Sense of the Past in Victorian Literature*, 1986; Carol T. Christ, *The Finer Optic: The Aesthetic of Particularity in Victorian Poetry*, 1975, and *Victorian and Modern Poetics*, 1984; Peter Allan Dale, *The Victorian Critic and the Idea of History*, 1977; Oliver Elton, *A Survey of English Literature*, 1920, vols. 3 and 4; Avrom Fleischman, *Figures of Autobiography: The Language of Self in Victorian and Modern England*, 1983; Pauline Fletcher, *Gardens and Grim Ravines . . . Landscape in Victorian Poetry*, 1983; George Ford, *Keats and the Victorians*, 1944; E. D. H. Johnson, *The Alien Vision of Victorian Poetry*, 1952; Robert Langbaum, *The Poetry of Experience*, 1957; Dorothy Mermin, *The Audience in the Poem*, 1983; J. Hillis Miller, *The Disappearance of God: Five Nineteenth-Century Writers*, 1963; John R. Reed, *Victorian Conventions*, 1975; W. David Shaw, *The Lucid Veil: Poetic Truth in the Victorian Age*, 1987; René Wellek, *A History of Modern Criticism*, vol. 4, 1965. Helpful collections of critical essays have been compiled by Robert Preyer in his *Victorian Literature: Selected Essays*, 1965; Isabel Armstrong, *The Major Victorian Poets: Reconsiderations*, 1969; and by Michael Timko in *Victorian Poetry*, Spring 1978. Especially noteworthy is *The Art of Victorian Prose*, ed. George Levine and William Madden, 1968.

For the status of women in Victorian life and literature, see Nina Auerbach, *Woman and the Demon*, 1982, and *Romantic Imprisonment*, 1985; Sandra Gilbert and Susan Gubar, *The Madwoman in the Attic*, 1979; Elizabeth Helsinger, Robin Lauterbach Sheets, and William Veeder, *The Woman Question*, 3 vols., 1980; Margaret Homans, *Bearing the Word: Language and Female Experience in Nineteenth-Century Women's Writing*, 1986; Ellen Moers, *Literary Women*, 1976; Elaine Showalter, *A Literature of Their Own*, 1977; and Martha Vicinus, ed., *Suffer and Be Still*, 1972, *A Widening Sphere*, 1977, and *Ever Yours, Florence Nightingale, Selected Letters* (with Bea Nergaard), 1989.

For classified or annotated lists of other books and articles, see *The Victorian Poets: A Guide to Research*, ed. F. E. Faverty, rev. 1968; *Victorian Fiction: A Guide to Research*, ed. Lionel Stevenson, 1964; *Victorian Fiction: A Second Guide to Research*, ed. George H. Ford, 1978; and *Victorian Prose: A Guide to Research*, ed. David J. DeLaura, 1973.

For developments in prose fiction during the period, see Lionel Stevenson, *The English Novel: A Panorama*, 1960, and for introductions to individual novelists, see *Victorian Novelists before 1885*, ed. Ira Nadel and William Fredeman, *Dictionary of Literary Biography*, vol. 21, 1983. For special critical issues, see Peter Brooks, *Reading for the Plot: Design and Intention in Narrative*, 1984; Peter Garrett, *The Victorian Multiplot Novel*, 1980; Roger B. Henkle, *Comedy and Culture*, 1980; George Levine, *The Realistic Imagination*, 1981; J. Hillis Miller, *The Form of Victorian Fiction*, 1968; Robert M. Polhemus, *Erotic Faith*, 1990; and Donald Stone, *The Romantic Impulse in Victorian Fiction*, 1980.

THE TWENTIETH CENTURY

Vol. 4 of *The New Cambridge Bibliography of English Literature*, ed. I. R. Willison, 1972, deals with the period 1900–50 and gives a full list of critical and scholarly works about the authors of the period produced up to 1970. Current bibliographies also appear in the periodical *Twentieth-Century Literature*.

The following critical works deal with general aspects of modern English Literature: *The Present Age in British Literature*, David Daiches, 1958; *The Novel and the Modern World*, David Daiches, 2nd ed., 1960; *The Modern Poets, A Critical Introduction*, 1960, and *The New Modern Poetry*, 1967, both M. L. Rosenthal; *The Modern Poetic Sequence: The Genius of Modern Poetry*, Rosenthal and Sally M. Gall, 1983; *The New Poetic*, C. K. Stead, 1964; *The Modern Tradition: Backgrounds of Modern Literature*, ed. Richard Ellmann and Charles Feidelson, 1965; *The Struggle of the Modern*, Stephen Spender, 1963; *The Idea of the Modern*, Irving Howe, 1968; *Twentieth-Century English Literature*, Harry Blamires, rev. 1985; and *The Short Story: Henry James to Elizabeth Bowen*, John Bayley, 1988. *Eight Modern Writers*, J. I. M. Stewart (*Oxford History of English Literature*, vol. 12), 1963, includes valuable chapters on Hardy, Shaw, Conrad, Kipling, Yeats, Joyce, and Lawrence, and a comprehensive bibliography. *British Poetry since 1960: A Critical Survey*, ed. Michael Schmidt and Grevel Lindop, 1972, contains, in an appendix, a list of nearly 250 living British poets and their works and a list of forty-two anthologies of modern British poetry; and British poets are well represented, with biographical and critical notes and bibliographies, in *The Norton Anthology of Modern Poetry*, ed. Richard Ellmann and Robert O'Clair, 2nd ed., 1988. *Anglo-Irish Literature: A Review of Research*, ed. Richard J. Finneran, 1976, contains bibliographies of modern British and Anglo-Irish writers up to its date of publication. The first three chapters of *Image and Experience: Studies in a Literary Revolution*, Graham Hough, 1960, attempt to put the whole modern movement in perspective. *Modernism 1890–1930*, ed. Malcolm Bradbury and James McFarlane, 1976, includes a valuable bibliography and an excellent range of essays on modernist movements in Britain and abroad.

The social and political background is well covered in *The Great War and Modern Memory*, Paul Fussell, 1975; *The Long Week-End: A Social History of Great Britain, 1918–1939*, Robert Graves and Alan Hodge, 1940; *The Baldwin Age*, ed. John Raymond, 1960; *The Thirties*, Julian Symons, rev. 1975; *The Auden Generation: Literature and Poli-*

tics in *England in the 1930s* and *A War Imagined: The First World War and British Culture*, both Samuel Hynes, 1976 and 1990; *British Writers of the Thirties*, Valentine Cunningham, 1988; *The Social Context of Modern English Literature*, Malcolm Bradbury, 1971; and *The Twentieth-Century Mind: History, Ideas, and Literature in Britain*, ed. C. B. Cox and A. E. Dyson, 1972: vol. 1, 1900–1918, vol. 2, 1918–1945, vol. 3, 1945–1965, all of which include useful bibliographies.

Matthew Arnold

The Works, 1903, is an incomplete collection of Arnold's writings; it must be supplemented by later editions such as the elaborately annotated *Poems of Arnold*, ed. Miriam Allott, 1979, and *The Letters of Arnold to . . . Clough*, ed. H. F. Lowry, 1932. A complete collection of Arnold's letters has been projected with Cecil Lang as editor. R. H. Super has produced an authoritative edition of *The Complete Prose Works*, 11 vols., 1960–77. For a study of those prose works, see William Robbins's *The Ethical Idealism of Matthew Arnold*, 1959, and Joseph Carroll's *The Cultural Theory of Matthew Arnold*, 1982.

The most satisfactory biography is Park Honan's *Matthew Arnold: A Life*, 1981. Lionel Trilling's excellent *Matthew Arnold*, 1949, remains a standard critical and biographical study, but see also Dwight Culler's *Imaginative Reason*, 1966, and G. Robert Stange's *The Poet as Humanist*, 1967. For two centenary assessments, see Stefan Collini, *Arnold*, 1988, and David G. Riede, *Matthew Arnold and the Betrayal of Language*, 1988. Two investigations of Arnold's literary and intellectual background are Leon Gottfried, *Matthew Arnold and the Romantics*, 1983, and Ruth apRoberts, *Arnold and God*, 1983. See also Kenneth Allott, *Matthew Arnold*, 1975, and the selection of essays edited by Harold Bloom, *Matthew Arnold*, 1987.

W. H. Auden

W. H. Auden: Collected Poems, ed. Edward Mendelson, 1976, contains all the poems that the author wished to preserve, in the texts that received his final approval. *The English Auden, Poems, Essays and Dramatic Writings, 1927–1939*, ed. Edward Mendelson, 1977, reprints in their original versions all the poems Auden published in book form during the 1930s, together with some previously unpublished and uncollected poems and a selection of Auden's early prose writings. Mendelson has also edited *Plays and Other Dramatic Writings by W. H. Auden, 1928–1938*, 1989. *The Dyer's Hand and Other Essays*, 1968, brings together a selection of his stimulating literary-critical articles, lectures, and reviews. *Forewords and Afterwords*, 1973, is a

comparable collection. Auden edited a number of anthologies, including (with Norman Pearson) *Poets of the English Language*, 5 vols., 1950; (with Noah Greenberg and Charles Kallman) *An Elizabethan Songbook*, 1955; and *The Elder Edda: A Selection*, 1969. The best critical studies are *Auden: An Introductory Essay*, Richard Hoggart, 1951; *The Making of the Auden Canon*, J. W. Beach, 1957; *The Poetry of W. H. Auden*, M. K. Spears, 1963; *Auden's Poetry*, Justin Replogle, 1969; *Early Auden*, Edward Mendelson, 1981; *Auden: A Carnival of Intellect*, Edward Callan, 1983; and *W. H. Auden*, Stan Smith, 1985. *A Reader's Guide to W. H. Auden*, John Fuller, 1970, provides a commentary on Auden's poetry and drama in chronological order; while *The Auden Generation: Literature and Politics in England in the 1930s*, Samuel Hynes, 1976, is an illuminating study of Auden and his contemporaries in their historical context. The most comprehensive biography is *W. H. Auden: A Biography*, Humphrey Carpenter, 1981.

Samuel Beckett

The standard bibliography, *Samuel Beckett: His Works and His Critics*, ed. Raymond Federman and John Fletcher, 1970, deals with the criticism only through 1966. Deirdre Bair's *Samuel Beckett: A Biography*, 1978, is a very useful but problematical study. Good introductions to the works are *Samuel Beckett: A Critical Study*, 1961, and *Reader's Guide to Samuel Beckett*, 1973, both by Hugh Kenner, and *The Last Sonata of the Dead*, Michael Robinson, 1966. Beckett's philosophical and religious ideas are well presented in *The Shape of Chaos*, David T. Hesla, 1971, and *Samuel Beckett*, Declan Kiberd, 1988, which also examines his work's political implications; and *Beckett/Beckett*, Vivian Mercier, 1977, shows that the Paris flowering grew from Dublin soil. Colin Duckworth's English introduction to his edition of *En attendant Godot*, 1966, is the classic essay on the classic play *Waiting for Godot*. *The Complete Dramatic Works* was published in 1986. There is a Beckett Archive at the University of Reading; a twice-yearly *Journal of Beckett Studies* began publication in 1976.

William Blake

The beautifully printed *The Complete Writings of William Blake*, ed. Geoffrey Keynes, 1957, has now been replaced as the scholar's edition by *The Poetry and Prose of William Blake*, ed. David Erdman and Harold Bloom, rev. 1982, which includes painstaking textual notes and brief commentaries on many of the poems. Another complete version of *William Blake's Writings*, with copious illustrations, has been edited in 2 vols. by G. E. Bentley, Jr., 1978. Erdman has also prepared a modernized text of all Blake's verse, with copious explanatory notes by W. H. Stevenson, *The Poems of William Blake* (Longman-Norton Annotated English Poets), 1971; a useful annotated selection of *Blake's Poetry and Designs* has been edited by Mary Lynn Johnson and John E. Grant, 1979. There is a *Life of William Blake* by Mona Wilson, 1927, rev. 1948, and Raymond Lister's *William Blake: An Introduction to the Man and His Work*, 1968; but the first full account, Alexander Gilchrist's *The Life of William Blake*, which appeared in 1863, has been a source book for all later biographers and is available (edited and supplemented by Ruthven Todd) in Everyman's Library, 1945.

The modern era of the scholarly explication of Blake symbolism was begun by S. Foster Damon's *William Blake: His Philosophy and Symbols*, 1924; the same scholar has also published a helpful *Blake Dictionary: The Ideas and Symbols of William Blake*, 1965. Of more recent books some of the most useful are Northrop Frye's classic analysis of Blake's moral allegory, *Fearful Symmetry*, 1947; Mark Schorer's study of Blake's characteristic union of political, moral, and religious radicalism, *William Blake: The Politics of Vision*, 1946; David V. Erdman's investigation of the relation of Blake's poetry to the historical events of his time, *Blake: Prophet against Empire*, rev. 1969; Peter Fisher's exposition of Blake's thought, *The Valley of Vision*, 1961; Harold Bloom's commentaries on the individual poems, *Blake's Apocalypse: A Study in Poetic Argument*, 1963; Thomas R. Frosch's *The Awakening of Albion: The Renovation of the Body in the Poetry of William Blake*, 1973; J. A. Wittreich's *Angel of Apocalypse: Blake's Idea of Milton*, 1975; and W. J. T. Mitchell, *Blake's Composite Art: A Study of the Illuminated Poetry*, 1978.

Modern critical essays are collected in *Blake*, ed. Northrop Frye, 1966, and in *Blake's Visionary Forms Dramatic*, ed. D. V. Erdman and J. E. Grant, 1970. H. M. Margoliouth's *William Blake*, 1951, and Martin K. Nurmi's *William Blake*, 1976, are useful general introductions to the man and his work. Studies emphasizing the shorter poems are Hazard Adams, *William Blake: A Reading of the Shorter Poems*, 1963; Robert F. Gleckner, *The Piper and the Bard*, 1959; E. D. Hirsch, Jr., *Innocence and Experience: An Introduction to Blake*, 1964; and Brian Wilkie, *Blake's Thel and Oothoon*,

1990. *Blake's Sublime Allegory*, ed. Stuart Curran and Joseph Anthony Wittreich, Jr., 1973, includes essays by diverse scholars on the major prophecies, *The Four Zoas, Milton*, and *Jerusalem*. A *Concordance to the Writings of William Blake*, ed. David V. Erdman, 1967, is an important aid in elucidating his symbolism. On Blake's graphic work see David Bindman, *Blake as an Artist*, 1977; Robert N. Essick, *William Blake, Printmaker*, 1980; and Morris Eaves, *William Blake's Theory of Art*, 1982. There is a large and growing list of books that reproduce (some of them in color) Blake's etched poems, drawings, and engravings; especially useful are *The Illuminated Blake*, ed. David V. Erdman, 1974, of which the subtitle describes the contents: "All of William Blake's Illuminated Works with a Plate-by-Plate Commentary," and Erdman's reproduction, with transcripts and commentary, of *The Notebooks of William Blake*, rev. 1977. The Blake Trust has issued a splendid series of color reproductions of a number of Blake's illuminated works, in expensive limited editions, printed by the Trianon Press. *The Blake Bibliography*, ed. G. E. Bentley, Jr., and Martin K. Nurmi, 1964, is supplemented by Bentley's *Blake Records*, 1969, and his *Blake Books*, 1977.

Elizabeth Barrett Browning

The standard *Complete Works* were edited by Charlotte Porter and Helen Clarke, 6 vols., 1900. Cora Kaplan's edition of *Aurora Leigh and Other Poems*, 1978, is a useful selection. Of a projected forty-volume collection, *The Brownings' Correspondence*, ed. Philip Kelley and Ronald Hudson (1984–), eight volumes have been published. The best critical biography is Dorothy Mermin's *Elizabeth Barrett Browning: The Origins of a New Poetry*, 1989. See also Angela Leighton, *Elizabeth Barrett Browning*, 1986. Interesting recent discussions of Barrett Browning can be found in Ellen Moers, *Literary Women*, 1976; Sandra Gilbert and Susan Gubar, *The Madwoman in the Attic*, 1979; Deirdre David, *Intellectual Women and Victorian Patriarchy*, 1987; and Helen Cooper, *Elizabeth Barrett Browning, Woman and Artist*, 1988.

Robert Browning

A standard edition is *The Complete Works of Robert Browning, with Variant Readings and Annotations*, ed. Roma A. King, Jr., et al., 9 vols., 1969–89. Four volumes of a projected seven-volume annotated edition of the poetry only, *The Poetical Works of Robert Browning*, have appeared, edited by Ian Jack and Margaret Smith, 1983–88. A convenient two-volume collection of the poems edited by John Pettigrew and Thomas J. Collins was published in 1981. For the Brownings' correspondence, see entry under **Elizabeth Barrett Browning**. The standard biography is *The Book, the Ring, and the Poet*, William Irvine and Park Honan, 1974. W. C. DeVane's *A Browning Handbook*, rev. 1955, is a model compilation of factual data concerning each of Browning's poems: sources, composition, and reputation. Further information is supplied by Norman B. Crowell, *A Reader's Guide to Robert Browning*, 1972, which also offers simplified summaries of critical discussions for twenty-three monologues.

The critical assessments in G. K. Chesterton's *Robert Browning*, 1903, are colorfully expressed and often shrewd. Robert Langbaum's *The Poetry of Experience* relates Browning's monologues to some of the main developments in modern literature. See also Roma A. King, Jr., *The Bow and the Lyre*, 1957; W. O. Raymond, *The Infinite Moment*, 1965; Donald Hair, *Browning's Experiments with Genre*, 1972; Ian Jack, *Browning's Major Poetry*, 1973; Herbert Tucker, *Browning's Beginnings*, 1980; and Loy Martin, *Browning's Dramatic Monologues and the Post-Romantic Subject*, 1985. Useful collections of essays include *The Browning Critics*, ed. Boyd Litzinger and K. L. Knickerbocker, 1965; *Robert Browning: A Collection of Critical Essays*, ed. Philip Drew, 1966; *Browning: The Critical Heritage*, ed. Boyd Litzinger and Donald Smalley, 1970; *Robert Browning*, ed. Isabel Armstrong, 1974; and *Robert Browning: A Collection of Critical Essays*, ed. Harold Bloom and Adrienne Munich, 1979.

George Gordon, Lord Byron

The Works of Lord Byron, 1898–1904, contains 7 vols. of *Poetry*, ed. Ernest Hartley Coleridge, and 6 vols. of *Letters and Journals*, ed. Rowland E. Prothero; the latter has now been replaced by Leslie A. Marchand's edition of *Byron's Letters and Journals*, 12 vols., 1973–82 (see also Marchand's one-volume *Selected Letters and Journals*, 1982); the poetry volumes are being superseded by Jerome J. McGann's edition, *The Complete Poetical Works*, 6 vols. to date, 1980–. Ernest J. Lovell, Jr.'s *His Very Self and Voice*, 1954, is a compilation of Byron's conversations, and *Byron: A Self-Portrait*, ed. Peter Quennell, 2 vols., 1950, reprints selected letters and some of his diaries.

The standard biography, a circumstantial and objective narrative, is Leslie A. Marchand's *Byron: A Biography*, 3 vols., 1957; a one-volume condensation is *Byron: A Portrait*, 1970. A very readable short life is Peter Quennell, *Byron*, 1934. Among the many recent books on Byron as poet are G. Wilson Knight's symbolic interpretations and praises of Byron, *The Burning Oracle*, 1939, and *Lord Byron: Christian Virtues*, 1954; E. J. Lovell, Jr., *Byron: The Record of a Quest*, 1950; Paul West, *Byron and the Spoiler's Art*, 1960; Andrew Rutherford, *Byron*, 1961; L. A. Marchand, *Byron's Poetry: A Critical Introduction*, 1965; and Jerome J. McGann, *Fiery Dust: Byron's Poetic Development*, 1968. Bernard Blackstone's *Byron: A Survey*, 1975, is a readable, though somewhat idiosyncratic, introduction to the writer; and Charles Robinson, *Byron and Shelley: The Snake and the Eagle*

Wreathed in Fight, 1975, discusses the relations and interinfluences of these two poets. *Byron*, ed. Paul West, 1963, is a collection of 20th-century essays in criticism.

An edition of *Don Juan* that incorporates the changes Byron made in his manuscripts is *Byron's "Don Juan*," ed. T. G. Steffan and W. W. Pratt, 4 vols., 1957; the first volume, by Steffan, is an extended commentary on the poem. Other discussions of Byron's masterpiece are P. G. Trueblood, *The Flowering of Byron's Genius: Studies in Byron's "Don Juan*," 1945; E. F. Boyd, *Byron's "Don Juan": A Critical Study*, 1945; George M. Ridenour, *The Style of "Don Juan*," 1960; Jerome J. McGann, "*Don Juan*" *in Context*, 1976; and E. E. Bostetter's collection of *Twentieth Century Interpretations of "Don Juan*," 1969.

Geoffrey Chaucer

The standard edition of Chaucer's writing is *The Riverside Chaucer*, 3rd ed., 1987, ed. L. D. Benson et al., based on F. N. Robinson's edition. The senior editor's anthology of Chaucer's poetry, 2nd ed., 1975, from which are taken the selections printed here, is helpful to the nonspecialist, as are A. C. Baugh's *Chaucer's Major Poetry*, 1963, and John H. Fisher's *The Complete Poetry and Prose of Geoffrey Chaucer*, 2nd ed., 1989. Vivid presentations of Chaucer in the background of 14th-century England are found in Marchette Chute's *Geoffrey Chaucer of England*, 1946, and D. S. Brewer's *Chaucer and His World*, 1978, which is beautifully illustrated. Pictorial companions to Chaucer's works, especially the *Canterbury Tales*, include R. S. Loomis, *A Mirror of Chaucer's World*, 1965, Maurice Hussey, *Chaucer's World*, 1967, Ian Serraillier, *Chaucer and His World*, 1968, and Roger Hart, *English Life in Chaucer's Day*, 1973. The raw material for Chaucer's biography is contained in *Chaucer Life-Records*, ed. M. M. Crow and C. C. Olson, 1966. D. R. Howard's *Chaucer: His Life, His Works, His World*, 1987, contains extensive background and interpretation; a new biography by D. A. Pearsall is forthcoming. For succinct accounts of the sources and literary background of Chaucer's works, see R. D. French's *A Chaucer Handbook*, 2nd ed., 1947; reproductions of many of the known sources of the *Canterbury Tales* are contained in *Sources and Analogues of Chaucer's Canterbury Tales*, ed. W. F. Bryan and Germaine Dempster, 1941, 1958. Useful literary materials are collected in R. P. Miller's *Chaucer: Sources and Backgrounds*, 1977. Muriel Bowden, *A Commentary on the General Prologue to the Canterbury Tales*, 1948, provides a wealth of background information on the individual Canterbury pilgrims; see also J. M. Manly's *Some New Light on Chaucer*, 1926, and Jill Mann's *Chaucer and Medieval Estates Satire*, 1973. Various aspects of Chaucer's work are treated by a number of scholars in *Chaucer and*

Chaucerians, ed. D. S. Brewer, 1966; *Geoffrey Chaucer (Writers and Their Background),* ed. D. S. Brewer, 1974; *Companion to Chaucer Studies,* ed. Beryl Rowland, rev. 1979; and *The Cambridge Chaucer Companion,* ed. Piero Boitani and Jill Mann. For literary criticism on both the *Canterbury Tales* and other works by Chaucer, the following contain stimulating discussions: D. S. Brewer, *Chaucer,* 3rd ed., 1973; R. B. Burlin, *Chaucerian Fiction,* 1977; G. K. Chesterton, *Chaucer,* 1932; Nevill Coghill, *The Poet Chaucer,* 1949, and *Geoffrey Chaucer,* 1956; W. C. Curry, *Chaucer and the Medieval Sciences,* rev. 1960; Alfred David, *The Strumpet Muse,* 1976; E. T. Donaldson, *Speaking of Chaucer,* 1970, 1983; Peter Elbow, *Oppositions in Chaucer,* 1975; Maurice Hussey, A. C. Spearing, and James Winny, *An Introduction to Chaucer,* 1965; S. S. Hussey, *Chaucer: An Introduction,* 1971; George Kane, *Chaucer,* 1984; P. M. Kean, *Chaucer and the Making of English Poetry,* 2 vols., 1972; G. L. Kittredge, *Chaucer and His Poetry,* 1915; John Lawlor, *Chaucer,* 1968; J. L. Lowes, *Geoffrey Chaucer and the Development of His Genius,* 1934; Charles Muscatine, *Chaucer and the French Tradition,* 1957; H. R. Patch, *On Rereading Chaucer,* 1939; R. O Payne, *The Key of Remembrance,* 1963; Raymond Preston, *Chaucer,* 1952; R. K. Root, *The Poetry of Chaucer,* 2nd ed., 1972; T. W. Ross, *Chaucer's Bawdy,* 1972. Criticism that deals mainly with the *Canterbury Tales* and with earlier commentary on it includes C. D. Benson, *Chaucer's Drama of Style: Poetic Variety and Contrast in the Canterbury Tales,* 1986; Helen Cooper, *The Structure of the Canterbury Tales,* 1983, and *The Canterbury Tales* (Oxford Guides to Chaucer), 1989; D. R. Howard, *The Idea of the Canterbury Tales,* 1976; Traugott Lawler, *The One and the Many in the Canterbury Tales,* 1980; H. M. Leicester, *The Disenchanted Self: Representing the Subject in The Canterbury Tales,* 1990; D. A. Pearsall, *The Canterbury Tales,* 1985; P. G. Ruggiers, *The Art of the Canterbury Tales,* 1965. D. W. Robertson's *A Preface to Chaucer,* 1962, is a most learned, stimulating, and controversial introduction to the reading of Chaucer in the light of medieval aesthetic doctrines. V. A. Kolve's *Chaucer and the Imagery of Narrative,* 1984, relates the first five of the *Canterbury Tales* to medieval art. Several recent books stress the importance of oral delivery, performance, and storytelling in the *Canterbury Tales:* Betsy Bowden, *Chaucer Aloud,* 1987; J. M. Ganim, *Chaucerian Theatricality,* 1990; L. M. Koff, *Chaucer and the Art of Storytelling,* 1988; and Carl Lindahl, *Earnest Games: Folkloric Patterns in the Canterbury Tales,* 1987. The following studies relate Chaucer's works to their social and historical background: Peter Brown and Andrew Butcher, *The Age of Saturn: Literature and History in the Canterbury Tales,* 1991; Peggy Knapp, *Chaucer and the Social Contest,* 1990; Lee Patterson, *Chaucer and the Subject of History,* 1991;

and Paul Strohm, *Social Chaucer,* 1989. A pioneer feminist study of Chaucer is Carolyn Dinshaw's *Chaucer's Sexual Poetics,* 1989. The following are collections of critical essays by various writers: *Discussions of the Canterbury Tales,* ed. C. J. Owen, 1961; *Chaucer Criticism: The Canterbury Tales,* ed. R. J. Schoeck and J. Taylor, 1960; *Chaucer: Modern Essays in Criticism,* ed. E. C. Wagenknecht, 1959; *Geoffrey Chaucer: A Critical Anthology,* 1969, ed. J. A. Burrow; and *Geoffrey Chaucer* (Contemporary Studies in Literature), ed. G. D. Economou, 1975. See also the prefatory remarks on Chaucer's poems in the *Riverside Chaucer* and the commentary in E. T. Donaldson's anthology.

Perhaps the most reliable glossary is that edited by Norman Davis et al., 1979. The standard bibliographies are E. P. Hammond, *Chaucer: A Bibliographical Manual,* 1908; D. D. Griffith, *Bibliography of Chaucer,* 1955; W. R. Crawford, *1954–63,* 1967; L. Y. Baird, *1964–73,* 1977; and L. Y. Baird-Lange and H. Schnutgen, *1974–85,* 1988. Two very useful annotated bibliographies are by Mark Allen and J. H. Fisher, *The Essential Chaucer,* 1987; and John Leyerle and Anne Quick, *Chaucer: A Bibliographical Introduction,* 1986. See also Caroline Spurgeon's *Five Hundred Years of Chaucer Criticism and Allusion, 1357–1900,* 1925.

Samuel Taylor Coleridge

The Complete Works, ed. W. G. T. Shedd, 7 vols., 1853, though far from complete, is the most inclusive collection of Coleridge's works; it will be superseded by the collected edition of Coleridge's writings now in progress under the general editorship of Kathleen Coburn, 1969–. The edition of the *Complete Poetical Works* is by E. H. Coleridge, 2 vols., 1912; a one-volume edition of the *Poetical Works* by the same editor is available in Oxford Standard Authors. The most fully annotated edition of *Biographia Literaria* is that by James Engell and W. Jackson Bate, 2 vols., 1983; a useful cheap reprint of the critical classic was edited by George Watson, rev. 1965. Thomas Middleton Raysor has edited the fragmentary remains of *Coleridge's Shakespearean Criticism,* 2 vols., 1930, and *Coleridge's Miscellaneous Criticism,* 1936. The definitive edition of Coleridge's *Collected Letters* is edited by E. L. Griggs, 6 vols., 1956–71; see also *Selected Letters,* ed. H. J. Jackson, 1987. The first four volumes of Coleridge's extraordinary *Notebooks* are available, meticulously edited by Kathleen Coburn, 1957–.

Richard Holmes's *Coleridge: Early Visions,* 1989, is the first of two volumes of a new biography. There are good short studies of the life and works by Walter Jackson Bate, *Coleridge,* 1968, and, with emphasis on the philosophical and religious writings, by Basil Willey, *Samuel Taylor Coleridge,* 1972. H. M. Margoliouth has described the most fruitful literary association on record in his *Wordsworth and Coleridge, 1795–1834*, 1953; a more sophisticated study is Paul Magnuson's *Coleridge and Wordsworth: A Lyrical Dialogue*, 1988. The best older critique of Coleridge as poet is by Humphry House, *Coleridge*, 1953; for more modern analysis, see *The Poetic Voices of Coleridge*, by Max F. Schulz, 1963. John Beer has explored *Coleridge the Visionary*, 1959; Reeve Parker has written a revealing study of the "conversation poems" in *Coleridge's Meditative Art*, 1975; and M. H. Abrams, *The Correspondent Breeze*, 1984, includes several essays on Coleridge's poetry. *The Road to Xanadu*, by J. L. Lowes, 1927, rev. 1930, which investigates the sources and composition of *The Ancient Mariner* and *Kubla Khan*, has achieved the status of a critical classic. Discussion of Coleridge as critic will be found in M. H. Abrams, *The Mirror and the Lamp*, 1953; René Wellek, *A History of Modern Criticism, 1750–1950*, vol. 2, 1955; Richard Harter Fogle, *The Idea of Coleridge's Criticism*, 1962; and J. A. Appleyard, *Coleridge's Philosophy of Literature*, 1965. Norman Fruman, *Coleridge, the Damaged Archangel*, 1971, collects all the charges and evidence concerning Coleridge's "plagiarism." Among the excellent studies of Coleridge's philosophical, theological, and moral interests and achievements are Richard Haven, *Patterns of Consciousness*, 1969; Thomas McFarland's important and wide-ranging study of *Coleridge and the Pantheist Tradition*, 1969; Owen Barfield, *What Coleridge Thought*, 1971; and Lawrence S. Lockridge, *Coleridge the Moralist*, 1977. On opium and Coleridge's poetry, see M. H. Abrams, *The Milk of Paradise*, rev. 1970; Elisabeth Schneider, *Coleridge, Opium and Kubla Khan*, 1953; and Alethea Hayter, *Opium and the Romantic Imagination*, 1968. On his developing reputation see *Coleridge: The Critical Heritage*, ed. J. R. de J. Jackson, 1970. Modern essays in criticism have been collected by Kathleen Coburn, *Coleridge*, 1967, and by John Beer, *Coleridge's Variety*, 1974.

William Collins

The *Works* of Collins, which amount only to one slim volume, have been well edited by Richard Wendorf and Charles Ryskamp, 1979. Lonsdale's edition (see **Gray**) has copious notes. P. L. Carver's *The Life of a Poet*, 1967, is the fullest biography. Wendorf's *William Collins and Eighteenth-Century English Poetry*, 1981, is a fine critical study.

Joseph Conrad

Standard is *The Uniform Edition of the Works of Joseph Conrad*, 22 vols., 1923–38, reprinted in 1946–55 as *The Collected Edition of the Works of Joseph Conrad*. When completed, the Cambridge University Press's variorum edition will be the standard edition. Many of the novels are available with useful critical essays in individual paperbound editions; among the best are the Norton Critical Edi-

tions of *Heart of Darkness*, ed. Robert Kimbrough, 3rd ed., 1987; *Lord Jim*, ed. Thomas C. Moser, 1968; and *The Nigger of the "Narcissus,"* ed. Robert Kimbrough, 1979.

Conrad in the Nineteenth Century, 1981, by Ian Watt, is a monumental work, although it only goes up to 1900. Two perceptive critical studies are *Conrad the Novelist*, Albert J. Guerard, 1958, and Daniel R. Schwarz's *Conrad: "Almayer's Folly" Through "Under Western Eyes,"* 1980. *The Portable Conrad*, ed. Morton D. Zabel, 1947, contains a good selection with a helpful introduction. Notable essays are that on *Lord Jim* in *The English Novel: Form and Function*, Dorothy Van Ghent, 1953, and the introduction to the Modern Library edition of *Nostromo*, ed. Robert Penn Warren, 1951. Schwarz's *Conrad: The Later Fiction*, 1982, presents a more positive view of Conrad's later work than Thomas Moser's excellent *Joseph Conrad, Achievement and Decline*, 1957. Important studies of the political novels are *The Political Novels of Joseph Conrad*, Eloise Knapp Hay, rev. 1981; *Paradise of Snakes*, Claire Rosenfield, 1967; and *Conrad's Politics: Community and Anarchy in the Fiction of Joseph Conrad*, Avrom Fleishman, 1967. The best recent critical studies include *Language and Being: Joseph Conrad and the Literature of Personality*, Peter J. Glassman, 1976; *Conrad's Later Novels*, Garry Geddes, 1980; *A Preface to Conrad*, Cedric Watts, 1982; *Lord Jim*, John Batchelor, 1988; *Culture and Irony: Studies in Joseph Conrad's Major Novels*, Anthony Winner, 1988; and *Joseph Conrad and the Modern Temper*, Daphna Erdinast-Vulcan, 1991. Zdzislaw Najder's *Joseph Conrad: A Chronicle*, 1983, is now the standard biography. The first four volumes of the letters have recently appeared, *The Collected Letters of Joseph Conrad*, ed. Frederick R. Karl and Laurence Davies, 1983–90. Until this edition is completed *Joseph Conrad: Life and Letters*, ed. G. Jean-Aubry, 2 vols., 1927, will remain the standard if very incomplete edition. This should be supplemented by *Letters from Joseph Conrad*, ed. Edward Garnett, 1928, and *Joseph Conrad's Letters to R. B. Cunninghame Graham*, ed. C. T. Watts, 1969.

William Cowper

Poems, 1748–1782 have been expertly edited by John D. Baird and Charles Ryskamp, 1980; a second volume is forthcoming. A convenient edition in one volume is H. S. Milford's, 1934. James King and Ryskamp have edited Cowper's *Letters and Prose Writings*, 5 vols., 1979–86, and one volume of *Selected Letters*, 1989. King's *William Cowper: A Biography*, 1986, is the best full life; Ryskamp's fine *William Cowper of the Inner Temple, Esq.*, 1959, ends in 1768. Useful critical studies include Norman Nicholson's *William Cowper*, 1951, Morris Golden's *In Search of Stability: The Poetry of*

William Cowper, 1960, Vincent Newey's *Cowper's Poetry*, 1982, and Martin Priestman's *Cowper's Task*, 1983.

John Donne

For nearly fifty years the standard edition of Donne's poems was that in two volumes edited by Sir Herbert J. C. Grierson, 1912. In 1952 Dame Helen Gardner re-edited *The Divine Poems*, rev. 1978, and in 1965 a volume containing *The Elegies and The Songs and Sonnets*. In 1967, W. Milgate added to this series *The Satires, Epigrams and Verse Letters*, and in 1978 *The Epithalamions, Anniversaries and Epicedes*. These new editions alter the text of some poems in some particulars on the basis of new manuscript evidence, and offer to redate many of them. It is by no means clear that the text is always improved by the new readings, or that the new datings will stand up. Under the editorship of G. R. Potter and Evelyn Simpson, an edition of Donne's *Sermons* has been issued in 10 vols., 1953–62. Among several handy editions of the poetry, we note *The Songs and Sonets*, ed. Theodore Redpath, 1956, rev. 1983; *John Donne's Poetry*, ed. A. L. Clements for Norton Critical Editions, 1966, rev. 1992; and two editions of *The Complete English Poems*: ed. A. J. Smith, 1971, and ed. C. A. Patrides, 1985. The Oxford Authors edition, by John Carey, 1990, includes the complete poems and a selection of the prose.

The first biography of Donne was Izaak Walton's; recent ones are R. C. Bald's *John Donne: A Life*, 1970, which the author regrettably did not live to finish, John Carey's *John Donne: Life, Mind and Art*, 1981, and George Parfitt's *John Donne: A Literary Life*, 1989.

Pierre Legouis's pioneering *Donne the Craftsman*, 1928, paved the way for close studies by J. B. Leishman, 1951, Clay Hunt, 1954, Arnold Stein, 1962, Wilbur Sanders, 1971, and Murray Roston, 1974. There is a New Historicist study by Arthur Marotti, *John Donne, Coterie Poet*, and a knotty poststructuralist account by Thomas Docherty, *John Donne, Undone*, both 1986. Terry Sherwood has studied Donne's thought in *Fulfilling the Circle*, 1984. Hardly any of Donne's poems has not been the subject of several articles at least; but Cleanth Brooks's *The Well Wrought Urn*, 1947, contains in its discussion of *The Canonization* one of the most influential poetic explications of modern criticism. Joan Webber studied Donne's prose style in *Contrary Music*, 1963. Collections of critical essays by several hands have been assembled by Helen Gardner and Frank Kermode, both 1962, by A. J. Smith, 1972, and by Arthur Marotti, 1994. A. J. Smith edited *John Donne: The Critical Heritage*, 1975.

The standard bibliography of Donne, first published by Geoffrey Keynes in 1914, went into its 4th edition in 1973; and there are annotated bibliographies of modern criticism by John R. Roberts—one for the period 1912–67, published 1973, and another for 1968–78, published 1982. For a general guide to the study of Donne, see Robert H. Ray, *A John Donne Companion*, 1990.

Michael Drayton

The standard edition is by J. W. Hebel, 5 vols., 1931–41; a useful selected edition is by John Buxton, 1953. The standard biography is B. H. Newdigate, *Michael Drayton and his Circle*, 1941. Critical studies include J. A. Berthelot, *Michael Drayton*, 1967; R. F. Hardin, *Michael Drayton and the Passing of Elizabethan England*, 1973; and Jean R. Brink, *Michael Drayton Revisited*, 1990.

John Dryden

James A. Winn's *John Dryden and His World*, 1987, is the best biography. G. R. Noyes's edition of the *Poetical Works*, 2nd ed., 1950, includes a good biographical sketch; and Samuel Johnson's *Life of Dryden* is still worth reading. A fine scholarly edition of the *Works* has been appearing at intervals since 1956, under the general editorship first of E. N. Hooker, then H. T. Swedenberg, and lately Alan Roper; it had reached sixteen volumes by 1989. Keith Walker has edited a useful selected *Works*, 1987. The poems have been edited by James Kinsley, 4 vols., 1958; and the essays by W. P. Ker, 2 vols., 1900, and George Watson, 2 vols., 1962.

Mark Van Doren's *John Dryden: A Study of His Poetry*, 1920, remains valuable for its fresh critical responses, as do T. S. Eliot's brief studies, *Homage to John Dryden*, 1924, and *John Dryden the Poet, the Dramatist, and the Critic*, 1932. Important modern criticism includes Arthur Hoffman's *John Dryden's Imagery*, 1962, Alan Roper's *Dryden's Poetic Kingdoms*, 1965, and Earl Miner's *Dryden's Poetry*, 1967. David Hopkins's *John Dryden*, 1986, is a good introduction. Steven Zwicker has studied *Politics and Language in Dryden's Poetry*, 1984. The standard work on Dryden's philosophical and religious ideas is Philip Harth's *Contexts of Dryden's Thought*, 1968. Robert Hume analyzes *Dryden's Criticism*, 1970; Edward Pechter, *Dryden's Classical Theory of Literature*, 1975; and John C. Aden brings together *The Critical Opinions of John Dryden, A Dictionary*, 1963, under convenient headings.

T. S. Eliot

The fullest one-volume collections of Eliot's poetry are *Collected Poems, 1909–1963*, 1963, and *The Complete Poems and Plays* (including *Poems Written in Early Youth*), 1969. Some critical essays are in *Selected Essays*, 3rd ed., 1972; *On Poetry and Poets*, 1957; and *Selected Prose of T. S. Eliot*, ed. Frank Kermode, 1975. *T. S. Eliot, The Waste Land: A Facsimile and Transcript of the Original Drafts including the Annotations of Ezra Pound*, ed. Valerie Eliot, 1971, is an indispensable tool for study of *The Waste Land*. T. S. Eliot, *The Waste Land*, by Helen Williams, 2nd rev. ed., 1973, is a critical study of the poem taking full account of the new material made available in Valerie Eliot's edition. T. S. Eliot, *Poems in the Making*, Gertrude Patterson, 1971, also makes use of the rediscovered Eliot manuscripts of *The Waste Land* but ranges widely throughout Eliot's work. *The Composition of Four Quartets*, Helen Gardner, 1978, describes the growth of the poem from the drafts and includes new information on its sources.

Among the many books on Eliot, *The Achievement of T. S. Eliot*, F. O. Matthiessen, rev. 1947, has the enthusiasm of a pioneer work; *T. S. Eliot: A Study of His Writings by Various Hands*, ed. B. Rajan, 1947, and *T. S. Eliot, a Selected Critique*, ed. Leonard Unger, 1948, bring together a variety of critical essays including some helpful explications of *The Waste Land*, and *Four Quartets*; *The Art of T. S. Eliot*, Helen Gardner, is a perceptive critical study of his poetry; *T. S. Eliot, the Design of His Poetry*, Elizabeth Drew, 1950, is a systematic chronological survey and explanation; *A Reader's Guide to T. S. Eliot*, George Williamson, 1953, is thorough and informative in its explanation of obscurities and references; and *T. S. Eliot's Poetry and Plays*, Grover Smith, Jr., 1956, goes through the poems and plays in an exhaustive and even exhausting manner. The best short critical books on Eliot are *T. S. Eliot*, Northrop Frye, 1963, and *T. S. Eliot*, Bernard Bergonzi, 1972. *The Poetics of Impersonality*, Maud Ellmann, 1988, *and T. S. Eliot and Prejudice*, Christopher Ricks, 1989, are more specialized studies. In the absence of a full-scale biography, one is the more grateful for *The Letters of T. S. Eliot*, ed. Valerie Eliot, 1988; *T. S. Eliot*, Peter Ackroyd, 1984; *T. S. Eliot: The Man and His Work*, a collection of memoirs, ed. Allen Tate, 1967; *Notes on Some Figures behind T. S. Eliot*, Herbert Howarth, 1965; *Eliot's Early Years*, 1977, and *Eliot's New Life*, 1988, both Lyndall Gordon, and *T. S. Eliot: A Study in Character and Style*, Ronald Bush, 1984. *T. S. Eliot: A Bibliography*, ed. Donald Gallup, rev. 1969, lists the extensive criticism on Eliot through 1967.

Queen Elizabeth I

There is no complete edition of Queen Elizabeth's writings. Leicester Bradner, ed., *The Poems of Queen Elizabeth I*, 1964, prints several of her poems and verse translations. Her several partial translations have found editors: Petrarch's *Triumph of Eternity* by Ruth Hughey, the *Arundel Harington Manuscript*, 2 vols., 1960; Boethius, Plutarch, and Horace's "De Arte Poetica" by Caroline Pemberton, 1889, rpt. 1973; Queen Marguerite of Navarre's poem *The Mirror of the Sinful Soul* (in prose translation) by P. W. Ames, 1897. Adam Fox and J. P. Hodges edited and translated Elizabeth's Latin prayers, 1970. The most inclusive edition of

her letters is by G. B. Harrison, 1935; and G. P. Riche, Jr., prints twenty-one of her speeches in *The Public Speaking of Queen Elizabeth: Selections from her Official Addresses*, 1951, rpt. 1966. The standard biography remains J. E. Neale, *Queen Elizabeth I*, 1934, rpt. 1967. Maria Perry has a documentary biography, *The Word of a Prince: The Life of Elizabeth I from contemporary documents*, 1990. The queen's significance as political and cultural presence is treated by Frances Yates, *Astraea: The Imperial Theme*, 1975; Marie Axton, *The Queen's Two Bodies: Drama and the Elizabethan Succession*, 1977; and Phillippa Berry, *Of Chastity and Power: Elizabethan Literature and the Unmarried Queen*, 1989. ELR 14 (1984): 409–425, surveys recent studies of Elizabeth and other Tudor women writers.

Thomas Gray

The poems of Gray, Collins, and Goldsmith have been edited, with informative notes, by Roger Lonsdale, 1969. The standard edition of Gray's *Works* remains that of Edmund Gosse, 4 vols., rev. 1902–6; of the *Correspondence*, that of Paget Toynbee and Leonard Whibley, 3 vols., 1935; of the poems, that of H. W. Starr and J. R. Hendrickson, 1966. R. W. Ketton-Cremer's *Thomas Gray*, 1955, is the best biography. The best critical study is unfortunately in French: Roger Martin's *Essai sur Gray*, 1934; more specialized is W. P. Jones's *Thomas Gray, Scholar*, 1937. James Downey and Ben Jones have edited a collection of essays on Gray, *Fearful Joy*, 1974. *From Sensibility to Romanticism*, ed. F. W. Hilles and Harold Bloom, 1965, includes studies of the *Elegy* by Ian Jack, B. H. Bronson, and Frank Brady.

Thomas Hardy

Hardy published over a dozen volumes of poetry in his lifetime; *The Collected Poems* were issued in one volume in 1932; and *The Complete Poetical Works of Thomas Hardy*, ed. Samuel Hynes, in three volumes in 1982–85. There are several collected editions of Hardy's complete work, notably the Wessex Edition, 21 vols., 1912–14, and the Mellstock Edition, 37 vols., 1919–20. Many of the novels are in paperbound editions; among the most notable are the Norton Critical Editions of *Jude the Obscure*, ed. Norman Page, 1978; *The Mayor of Casterbridge*, ed. James K. Robinson, 1977; *The Return of the Native*, ed. James Gindin, 1969; and *Tess of the D'Urbervilles*, ed. Scott Elledge, 3rd ed., 1990.

The best biographies are *Young Thomas Hardy*, 1975, *Thomas Hardy's Later Years*, 1978, both by Robert Gittings, and *Thomas Hardy: A Biography*, Michael Millgate, 1982. Millgate and R. Purdy have edited *The Collected Letters of Thomas Hardy*, 7 vols., 1978–1988. Millgate has also edited *Selected Letters*, 1990, and Harold Orel has edited *Thomas Hardy's Personal Writings: Prefaces, Literary Opinions, Reminiscences*, 1990. The Hardy

Centennial Number of *The Southern Review*, 1940, was influential in shaping Hardy's critical reputation: the special Hardy issues of *Agenda*, 1970, and *Victorian Poetry*, 1979, are notable. *Hardy: A Collection of Critical Essays*, ed. Albert Guerard, 1963, treats both the prose and the poetry, as do *Thomas Hardy: Distance and Desire*, J. Hillis Miller, 1970; *Thomas Hardy: The Poetic Structure*, Jean R. Brooks, 1971; *An Essay on Hardy*, John Bayley, 1978; *Thomas Hardy After Fifty Years*, ed. Lance St. John Butler, 1977; and *Thomas Hardy: The Writer and His Background*, ed. Norman Page, 1980, which contains a useful bibliography. *The Great Web: The Form of Hardy's Major Fiction*, Ian Gregor, 1974, and *Critical Approaches to the Fiction of Thomas Hardy*, ed. Dale Kramer, 1979, provide good discussions of Hardy's novels. *The Pattern of Hardy's Poetry*, Samuel Hynes, 1956, remains sound and useful; *Thomas Hardy and British Poetry*, Donald Davie, 1973, is worth consulting. *The Poetry of Thomas Hardy*, ed. Patricia Clements and Juliet Grindle, 1980; *The Poetry of Thomas Hardy: A Study in Art and Ideas*, William Earl Buckler, 1983; and *Hardy's Metres and Victorian Prosody*, Dennis Taylor, 1988, contain good recent criticism of the poetry; and *The Poetry of Thomas Hardy*, J. O. Bailey, 1970, and *A Commentary on the Poems of Thomas Hardy*, F. B. Pinion, 1976, are helpful on individual poems.

George Herbert

The excellent Oxford edition of the *Works* is by F. E. Hutchinson, rev. 1945; C. A. Patrides produced a compact edition of *The English Poems*, 1974. A series of books on Herbert began appearing in the 1950s, among which may be mentioned Rosemond Tuve's *A Reading of George Herbert*, 1952—like all her work, learned and acute. Margaret Bottrall's introductory appreciation, *George Herbert*, appeared in the same year, 1954, as J. H. Summers's seminal *George Herbert: His Religion and Art*. More recent studies, which have been appearing at an accelerating rate, include those of Arnold Stein, 1968; Helen Vendler, 1975; Stanley Fish, 1978 (along with a chapter in his *Self-Consuming Artifacts*, 1972); Heather Asals, 1981; Barbara Harman, 1982; Richard Strier, 1983; Chana Bloch and Gene Veith, Jr., both 1985; Stanley Stewart, 1986; Richard Todd, 1986; Marion Singleton, 1987; Terry Sherwood, 1989. Michael Schoenfeldt, 1991; Christopher Hodgkins, 1993; and Howard Toliver, 1993. Amy M. Charles's *Life of George Herbert*, 1977, is fuller than any previous biography. John R. Roberts has edited *Essential Articles for the Study of George Herbert's Poetry*, 1979, and prepared an annotated bibliography of modern (1905–84) criticism of Herbert, 1988. C. A. Patrides has edited *George Herbert: The Critical Heritage*, 1983. Recent studies: *ELR* 18 (1988): 460–475.

Robert Herrick

The Oxford English Texts edition is the *Poetical Works*, ed. L. C. Martin, 1956; from it, Martin derived his Oxford Standard Authors edition (unannotated), 1965. J. Max Patrick has also produced an edition of the *Complete Poetry*, 1963. There are introductions to Herrick's life and works by John Press, 1961; Roger B. Rollin, 1966, rev. ed., 1992; and G. W. Scott, 1974. Two critical studies appeared in 1974: Robert Deming, *Ceremony and Art*; A. Leigh Deneef, *This Poetick Liturgie*. Ann Baynes Coiro published *Robert Herrick's "Hesperides" and the Epigram Book Tradition* in 1988. See also Leah S. Marcus, *The Politics of Mirth* (in the first section of this bibliography). A volume of essays, ed. Roger B. Rollin and J. Max Patrick, was published in 1978. Elizabeth H. Hageman produced *Robert Herrick: A Reference Guide* in 1983. Recent studies: *ELR* 3 (1973): 462–471.

Gerard Manley Hopkins

Robert Bridges edited the first (posthumous) edition of Hopkins's poems in 1918, which has been the nucleus of all subsequent editions. The most recent is *The Poetical Works of Gerard Manley Hopkins*, ed. Norman H. MacKenzie, 1990. In addition to the poems, Hopkins's letters and parts of his notebooks have been published: *The Letters of Gerard Manley Hopkins to Robert Bridges* and *The Correspondence of G. M. Hopkins and Richard Watson Dixon*, ed. C. C. Abbot, 2 vols., 1935; *Further Letters of Gerard Manley Hopkins*, ed. C. C. Abbott, 1938, rev. 1956; *The Journals and Papers of Gerard Manley Hopkins*, ed. Humphry House and Graham Storey, 1969; and *The Sermons and Devotional Writings of Gerard Manley Hopkins*, ed. Christopher Devlin, 1959. A helpful introduction to these works is Norman H. MacKenzie, *A Reader's Guide to Gerard Manley Hopkins*, 1981.

The only biography covering the poet's whole career is *Gerard Manley Hopkins: A Life*, by Eleanor Ruggles, 1944, but *Gerard Manley Hopkins: Priest and Poet*, by John Pick, 2nd ed., 1966, is also recommended. Some useful critical studies are W. H. Gardner, *G. M. Hopkins: A Study of Poetic Idiosyncrasy in Relation to Poetic Tradition*, 2 vols., 1944, 1949; Paul L. Mariani, *A Commentary on the Complete Poems of Gerard Manley Hopkins*, 1970; Alison Sulloway, *Gerard Manley Hopkins and the Victorian Temper*, 1972; Daniel Harris, *Inspirations Unbidden: The "Terrible Sonnets" of Gerard Manley Hopkins*, 1982; and Walter J. Ong, *Hopkins, the Self, and God*, 1986. Two good collections of critical essays are *Hopkins*, ed. Geoffrey Hartmann, 1966, and *Hopkins Among the Poets: Studies in Modern Responses to Gerard Manley Hopkins*, ed. Richard F. Giles, 1985.

Samuel Johnson

Others among Johnson's friends besides Boswell wrote of him: notably, Hester Lynch Thrale Piozzi, whose *Anecdotes* (1786) have been edited, along with William Shaw's *Anecdotes*, by Arthur Sherbo, 1974; Sir John Hawkins, whose *Life* (1787) has been edited and abridged by Bertram H. Davis, 1961; and Fanny Burney (Mme D'Arblay), from whose diary C. B. Tinker extracted the Johnsonian passages in *Dr. Johnson and Fanny Burney*, 1911. James L. Clifford's *Young Sam Johnson*, 1955, and *Dictionary Johnson*, 1979, are well-informed studies of the early and middle years that supplement Boswell's rather sketchy account of Johnson's life before their meeting in 1763. There are fine modern biographies by John Wain, 1975, W. J. Bate, 1977, and Robert DeMaria, Jr., 1993.

The best collected edition of Johnson's *Works* appeared as long ago as 1825. It is being replaced by an excellent scholarly edition, published by Yale, that has been coming out irregularly since 1958. The poems have been edited by D. N. Smith and E. L. McAdam, 2nd ed. rev. by J. D. Fleeman, 1974. G. B. Hill's editions of *Johnsonian Miscellanies*, 2 vols., 1897, and *The Lives of the Poets*, 3 vols., 1905, are still worth consulting for their fine notes. The first three volumes of Bruce Redford's superb edition of the *Letters* appeared in five volumes, 1992–1994.

E. L. McAdam's *Johnson and Boswell: A Survey of their Writings*, 1969, and Donald J. Greene's *Samuel Johnson*, rev. 1989, are brief useful guides. Among general introductions to Johnson's work, W. J. Bate's *The Achievement of Samuel Johnson*, 1955, is inspiring, and Paul Fussell's *Samuel Johnson and the Life of Writing*, 1971, is lively. Good specialized studies include W. K. Wimsatt's *The Prose Style of Samuel Johnson*, 1941; D. J. Greene's *The Politics of Samuel Johnson*, 2nd ed., 1990; Carey McIntosh's *The Choice of Life: Samuel Johnson and the World of Fiction*, 1973; and Charles E. Pierce's *The Religious Life of Samuel Johnson*, 1982. Aspects of Johnson's criticism are treated in Jean Hagstrum's *Samuel Johnson's Literary Criticism*, 1952; Leopold Damrosch's *The Uses of Johnson's Criticism*, 1976; and G. F. Parker's *Johnson's Shakespeare*, 1989. Joseph E. Brown has collected *The Critical Opinions of Samuel Johnson*, 1926. Good recent books on the *Dictionary* are Robert DeMaria's *Johnson's Dictionary and the Language of Learning*, 1986, and Allen Reddick's *The Making of Johnson's Dictionary, 1746–1773*, 1990. Alvin Kernan's *Printing Technology, Letters & Samuel Johnson*, 1987, argues provocatively that Johnson was a creature of print. The valuable survey and bibliography of critical studies by J. L. Clifford and D. J. Greene, rev. 1970, has been updated through 1985 by Greene and J. A. Vance, 1987.

Ben Jonson

"Monumental" is the word for the edition of Jonson's works by C. H. Herford and Percy and Evelyn Simpson, published by the Clarendon Press in 11 vols., 1925–52. This edition is meticulous in reproducing the old spellings and recording the variants; typographically it is a constant delight. The Yale edition of Ben Jonson provides a good modernized and annotated version of the major plays (one play to a volume); so does the paperback series known as The New Mermaids. Handy editions of the verse are those of W. B. Hunter, *The Complete Poetry of Ben Jonson*, 1963, and George Parfitt, 1975. The Oxford Authors edition, by Ian Donaldson, 1985, includes the poems and the major prose, as well as *Volpone* and *The Alchemist*. Stephen Orgel has edited the *Complete Masques*, 1969. There is an edition of *Timber* by Ralph Walker, 1953.

A popular introduction to Jonson's life and works is that of J. B. Bamborough, 1970. There are also two recent biographies, by Rosalind Miles, 1986, and David Riggs, 1989. Jonson's role in the consolidation of the idea of the author is studied by Richard Helgerson, in *Self-Crowned Laureates*, 1983, by Timothy Murray, in *Theatrical Legitimation: Allegories of Genius in Seventeenth-Century England and France*, 1987, and by George E. Rowe, in *Distinguishing Jonson*, 1988. Useful studies of the plays include those of E. B. Partridge, *The Broken Compass*, 1958; G. B. Jackson, *Vision and Judgment in Ben Jonson's Drama*, 1968; Ian Donaldson, *The World Upside Down*, 1970; Alexander Leggatt, *Ben Jonson, His Vision and His Art*, 1981; and Robert N. Watson, *Ben Jonson's Parodic Strategy*, 1987. G. B. Johnston, 1945, Wesley Trimpi, 1962, Richard S. Peterson, 1981, Sara J. van den Berg, 1987, and Robert C. Evans, 1989, have written accounts of Jonson's poetry. There are also chapters on the poems in Jongsook Lee, *Ben Johnson's Poesis*, 1989, and Robert Wittenberg, *Ben Jonson and Self-Love*, 1990. On the masques, see Stephen Orgel, *The Jonsonian Masque*, 1965. Students may also want to consult *Inigo Jones: The Theatre of the Stuart Court*, by Orgel and Roy Strong, 1973, for the particular delight of the drawings and designs. Walter D. Lehrman, Delores J. Sarafinski, and Elizabeth Savage published *The Plays of Ben Jonson: A Reference Guide* in 1980, and David C. Judkins published a guide called *The Nondramatic Works* in 1982. D. H. Craig edited *Ben Jonson: The Critical Heritage* in 1990. D. Heyward Brock, *A Ben Jonson Companion*, 1983, is a kind of Jonson encyclopedia, complete with bibliography.

See also *Lyric Poets of the Early Seventeenth Century*.

James Joyce

The Viking Critical Editions of *Dubliners*, ed. R. Scholes and A. W. Litz, 1969, and *A Portrait of the Artist as a Young Man*, ed. C. Anderson, 1968, offer reliable texts and valuable supplementary materials. Hans Walter Gabler's *Ulysses: A Critical and Synoptic Edition*, 3 vols., 1984, is more authoritative than all previous editions, but there is as yet no textually reliable edition of *Finnegans Wake*. *The Portable James Joyce*, ed. H. Levin, 1968, is a useful collection, and Stuart Gilbert and Richard Ellmann have edited *The Letters of James Joyce* in 3 vols., 1957–66.

Good general accounts of Joyce's work will be found in *James Joyce*, A. W. Litz, rev. 1972; *James Joyce*, A. Goldman, 1968; *James Joyce*, Bernard Benstock, 1986; *James Joyce and Sexuality*, Richard Brown, 1986; *James Joyce*, ed. Derek Attridge, 1990; and *Reauthorizing Joyce*, Vicki Mahaffey, 1990. Two useful critical works on *Dubliners* are *Twentieth-Century Interpretations of Dubliners: A Collection of Critical Essays*, ed. P. K. Garrett, 1968, and *James Joyce's Dubliners: Critical Essays*, ed. Clive Hart, 1969. The most helpful of many critical studies of *Ulysses* are *The Book as World: James Joyce's Ulysses*, Marilyn French, 1976; *Ulysses*, Hugh Kenner, 1980; *James Joyce: The Citizen and the Artist*, C. H. Peake, 1976; *James Joyce's Ulysses: Critical Essays*, ed. Clive Hart and David Hayman, 1974; *The Odyssey of Style in Ulysses*, Karen Lawrence, 1981; *Allusions in Ulysses*, Weldon Thornton, 1973; *Notes for Joyce: An Annotation of James Joyce's Ulysses*, Don Gifford and Robert Seidman, 1974; *The Classical Temper: A Study of James Joyce's Ulysses*, S. L. Goldberg, 1961; and *Joyce and Shakespeare*, William Schutte, 1957. *Surface and Symbol*, Robert M. Adams, 1963, studies the raw material of actual Dublin life in *Ulysses*. Illuminating books on *Finnegans Wake* include *The Books at the Wake*, J. S. Atherton, 1974; *A Third Census of Finnegans Wake*, Adaline Glasheen, 1976; *Structure and Motif in Finnegans Wake*, Clive Hart, 1962; *The Sigla of Finnegans Wake*, 1976, and *Annotations to Finnegans Wake*, 1980, both Roland McHugh.

James Joyce, Richard Ellmann, 2nd ed., 1982, is the standard biography; his *Ulysses on the Liffey*, 1973, and *The Consciousness of Joyce*, 1977, are also highly recommended.

John Keats
The standard edition of the poetry is Jack Stillinger's *The Poems of John Keats*, 1978. Miriam Allott's *The Poems of John Keats*, 1970, is copiously annotated. Hyder E. Rollins's *The Letters of John Keats*, 2 vols., 1958, provides exact texts based on the manuscripts.

The best biography is W. J. Bate's notable study of the poet's life, writings, and place in the English poetic tradition, *John Keats*, 1963. Shorter critical biographies are Douglas Bush, *John Keats*, 1966; Robert Gittings, *John Keats*, 1968; and Aileen Ward, *John Keats: The Making of a Poet*, rev. 1986. Among the many critical writings on the poet, the following are especially useful: C. D. Thorpe, *The Mind of John Keats*, 1926 (on Keats's thought); M. R. Ridley, *Keats' Craftsmanship*, 1933 (based on the revisions in Keats's manuscripts); R. H.

Fogle, *The Imagery of Keats and Shelley*, 1949 (a study of Keats's diction and figurative language); Earl Wasserman, *The Finer Tone*, 1953 (a close and sometimes oversubtle analysis of the major poems); E. C. Pettet, *On the Poetry of Keats*, 1957; Walter Evert, *Aesthetic and Myth in the Poetry of Keats*, 1965; Morris Dickstein, *Keats and His Poetry*, 1971; Jack Stillinger, *The Hoodwinking of Madeline and Other Essays on Keats's Poems*, 1971; Stuart Sperry, *Keats the Poet*, 1973; Christopher Ricks's lively and wide-ranging study of *Keats and Embarrassment*, 1974; Robert M. Ryan's analysis of Keats's personal creed, *Keats: The Religious Sense*, 1976; Ronald A. Sharp, *Keats, Skepticism, and the Religion of Beauty*, 1979; Wolf Z. Hirst, *John Keats*, 1981; Helen Vendler, *The Odes of John Keats*, 1983; Leon Waldoff, *Keats and the Silent Work of Imagination*, 1985; and Susan J. Wolfson, *The Questioning Presence: Wordsworth, Keats, and the Interrogative Mode in Romantic Poetry*, 1986. For other commentary on the odes see Jack Wright Rhodes, *Keats's Major Odes: An Annotated Bibliography of the Criticism*, 1984. For the poet's 19th-century reputation see *Keats: The Critical Heritage*, ed., G. M. Matthews, 1971. For useful collections of critical essays, see *Keats*, ed. W. J. Bate, 1971, and *Critical Essays on John Keats*, ed. Hermione de Almeida, 1990.

Aemilia Lanyer
Susanne Woods has edited *The Poems of Aemilia Lanyer: Salve Deus Rex Judaeorum*, 1993. Critical studies include Barbara K. Lewalski, "Imagining Female Community: Aemilia Lanyer's Poems," in *Writing Women in Jacobean England*, 1994; and Janel Mueller, "The Feminine Poetics of Aemilia Lanyer's 'Salve Deus Rex Judaeorum,' " in L. Keller and C. Miller, eds., *Feminist Measures: Soundings in Poetry and Theory*, 1993.

D. H. Lawrence
The definitive Cambridge Edition, in progress under the editorship of James T. Boulton, has to date issued several meticulously edited texts of the fiction and six volumes of a complete *Letters*. The poetry is collected in *The Complete Poems*, edited by V. de Sola Pinto and W. Roberts, 3rd ed., 1972, and much important prose in *Phoenix*, 1936, and *Phoenix II*, 1968. Most of Lawrence is available in Penguin paperback texts.

Biographical information can be found in *D. H. Lawrence: A Composite Biography*, Edward Nehls, 3 vols, 1957–59; *The Priest of Love*, Harry T. Moore, 1974; and *D. H. Lawrence: A Biography*, Jeffrey Myers, 1990.

Pioneering critical studies include *The Love Ethic of D. H. Lawrence*, Mark Spilka, 1955; *D. H. Lawrence: Novelist*, F. R. Leavis, 1956; *The Dark Sun*, Graham Hough, 1957; *The Deed of Life: The Novels and Tales of D. H. Lawrence*, Julian Moynahan, 1963; *The Forked Flame*, H. M. Daleski, 1965; and *Double Measure*, George Ford, 1965.

Among valuable recent analyses are *Acts of Attention: The Poems of D. H. Lawrence*, Sandra Gilbert, 1972; *The Mysteries of Identity*, Robert Langbaum, 1977; *Beyond Egotism*, Robert Kiely, 1980; *D. H. Lawrence and Feminism*, Hilary Simpson, 1982; *The World of Lawrence: A Passionate Appreciation*, Evelyn J. Hinz and John T. Tennissen, 1985; *D. H. Lawrence: Life into Art*, Keith Sagar, 1985; *D. H. Lawrence and Tradition*, ed. Jeffrey Myers, 1985; *The Short Fiction of D. H. Lawrence*, Janice Hubbard Harris, 1985; *The Spirit of D. H. Lawrence*, ed. Gamini Salgado and G. K. Das, 1988; *D. H. Lawrence: New Studies*, ed. Colin Milton, 1988; *A Study of the Poems of D. H. Lawrence: Thinking in Poetry*, M. J. Lockwood, 1988; and *The Challenge of D. H. Lawrence*, ed. Michael Squires and Keith Cushman, 1990. *D. H. Lawrence: A Centenary Consideration*, ed. P. Balbert and P. Marcus, 1985, is an attempt to assess Lawrence's current stature, and *D. H. Lawrence: A Guide to Research*, Thomas Jackson Rice, 1983, is an essential research tool.

Richard Lovelace

C. H. Wilkinson edited the *Poems*, 1925 (reissued in a different format, 1930 and 1953). Commentary can be found in M. Weidhorn, *Richard Lovelace*, 1970, and Earl Miner, *The Cavalier Mode from Jonson to Cotton*, 1971. Leah Marcus compares Lovelace with Marvell in chapter 7 of *The Politics of Mirth*, 1986. Recent studies: ELR 7 (1977): 248–252.

See also **Lyric Poets of the Early Seventeenth Century.**

Lyric Poets of the Early Seventeenth Century

Much basic work on the prose of the early 17th century was done by Morris Croll in a series of articles on Ciceronian and anti-Ciceronian styles in the later Renaissance: these were collected posthumously in a volume titled *Style, Rhetoric, and Rhythm*, 1966. R. F. Jones in *Ancients and Moderns*, 1936, urged the importance of the new science and the Royal Society in the development of a plain style. But there were other considerations, such as the need for Puritan preachers, pamphleteers, and propagandists to make themselves understood in the great war of words brilliantly described by William Haller in his *Rise of Puritanism*, 1938.

For the early century, George Williamson's *The Senecan Amble*, 1951, deals with an important variety of plain prose. For the later century, D. J. Milburn, *The Age of Wit*, 1966, and G. R. Cragg, *From Puritanism to the Age of Reason*, 1950, may be useful. The prose of Puritan radicals is treated in Christopher Hill's *The World Turned Upside Down*, 1972, and is the subject of Nigel Smith's *Perfection Proclaimed: Language and Literature in English Radical Religion*, 1989. Paul Salzman surveys *English Prose Fiction, 1558–1700*, 1985. In

The Eloquent "I," 1968, Joan Webber explores the manifestations of acute self-consciousness in eight prose writers of the period. An influential book is Stanley Fish, *Self-Consuming Artifacts: The Experience of Seventeenth-Century Literature*, 1972.

From plays, masques, songbooks, manuscripts, and broadsides, several pleasant and accessible anthologies of early 17th-century lyrics have been assembled by Norman Ault, 1928, 1950; by R. G. Howarth, 1931; and by H. J. C. Grierson with Geoffrey Bullough, 1934. The admirable series of Oxford English Texts includes the poems of many of our poets; these have generally been the preferred texts referred to in the individual author-bibliographies. For women poets, see the anthologies listed in the first section of this bibliography.

Criticism and commentary on 17th-century verse abounds. Much of this is listed in the first section of this bibliography, or under individual poets; other important studies include Rosemary Freeman, *English Emblem Books*, 1948; Odette de Mourgues, *Metaphysical, Baroque, and Précieux Poetry*, 1953; Earl Wasserman, *The Subtler Language*, 1959; George Williamson, *Seventeenth Century Contexts*, 1961, rev. 1969; F. J. Warnke, *European Metaphysical Poetry*, 1961; Lowry Nelson, Jr., *Baroque Lyric Poetry*, 1961; John Hollander, *The Untuning of the Sky: Ideas of Music in English Poetry, 1500–1700*, 1961; H. M. Richmond, *The School of Love*, 1964; W. B. Piper, *The Heroic Couplet*, 1969; Jerome Mazzaro, *Transformations in the English Renaissance Lyric*, 1970; Joseph Summers, *The Heirs of Donne and Jonson*, 1970; and Earl Miner's three books on 17th-century poetic modes (see the first section). There is also a collection of studies edited by Claude J. Summers and Ted-Larry Petworth, *Classic and Cavalier: Essays on Jonson and the Sons of Ben*, 1982. Several important studies are reprinted in a Norton Critical Edition, *Ben Jonson and the Cavalier Poets*, ed. Hugh Maclean, 1975.

Sir Thomas Malory

The Winchester manuscript of Malory's *Morte Darthur*, with full commentary and valuable discussion, is given in Eugène Vinaver's *The Works of Sir Thomas Malory*, 3 vols., 2nd ed., 1967; the one-volume edition, 2nd ed., Oxford, 1970, contains the text only. The Caxton version is most readily available in *Caxton's Malory*, ed. J. W. Spisak, 1983. Vinaver's *Malory*, 1929, surveys Malory's life and career. Felicity Riddy's *Sir Thomas Malory*, 1987, and Terence McCarthy's *An Introduction to Malory: Reading the Morte Darthur*, 1991, are helpful guides to the uninitiated. A number of critical problems in Malory's work, especially its unity, are discussed in three collections of essays by various scholars: *Essays on Malory*, ed. J. A. W. Bennett, 1963, *Malory's Originality*, ed. by R. M. Lumiansky, 1964, and *Studies in Malory*, ed. J. W.

Spisak, 1985. Two excellent studies of the work are those by L. D. Benson, *Malory's Morte Darthur*, 1976, and Mark Lambert, *Malory: Style and Vision in Le Morte Darthur*, 1975.

A most valuable summary of the Arthurian literary background is R. S. Loomis's *The Development of Arthurian Romance*, 1963.

Katherine Mansfield

There is a convenient complete one-volume edition of Katherine Mansfield's stories, *The Short Stories of Katherine Mansfield*, 1937. Her *Journal* was edited by Middleton Murry in 1954; *The Critical Writings of Katherine Mansfield*, by Clare Hanson, 1987; *Poems of Katherine Mansfield*, by Vincent O'Sullivan, 1988; and *The Collected Letters of Katherine Mansfield*, by O'Sullivan and Margaret Scott, 1984. The best biographies are *The Life of Katherine Mansfield*, Anthony Alpers, 2nd ed., 1979, and *Katherine Mansfield: A Secret Life*, Claire Tomalin, 1987.

Critical studies include *The Fiction of Katherine Mansfield*, Marvin Magalener, 1971; *Katherine Mansfield*, Clare Hanson and Andrew Gurr, 1981; *Katherine Mansfield and Her Confessional Stories*, C. A. Hankin, 1983; and *Katherine Mansfield*, Kate Fullbrook, 1986.

Christopher Marlowe

Fredson Bowers has edited the *Complete Works*, 2 vols., 1973, rev. 1981; R. H. Case has a modern-spelling edition, 6 vols., 1930–33, rpt. 1966; of Roma Gill's projected three-volume edition, the first two volumes appeared in 1987. W. W. Greg edited parallel texts of the two versions of *Dr. Faustus* in 1950; and Roma Gill edited the A text (our copy text for *Faustus*) in 1989. Stephen Orgel edited *The Complete Poems and Translations of Christopher Marlowe*, 1971. For Marlowe's biography see John Bakeless, *The Tragicall History of Christopher Marlowe*, 2 vols., 1942; Mark Eccles, *Christopher Marlowe in London*, 1934, rpt. 1967; and A. W. Rowse, *Christopher Marlowe: A Biography*, 1981. Valuable critical studies include Harry Levin, *The Overreacher*, 1952; W. L. Godshalk, *The Marlovian World Picture*, 1974; Millar McLure, ed., *Marlowe: The Critical Heritage*, 1979; Clifford Leech, *Christopher Marlowe: Poet for the Stage*, 1986; Simon Shepherd, *Marlowe and the Politics of Elizabethan Theatre*, 1986; *Christopher Marlowe*, in "Modern Critical Views," ed. Harold Bloom, 1986; and C. L. Barber, *Creating Elizabethan Tragedy: the Theater of Marlowe and Kyd*, 1988. For *Hero and Leander*, Louis L. Martz's facsimile of the first edition, 1972, has an important introduction. On the genre, see William Keach, *Elizabeth Erotic Narratives*, 1977; and Clark Hulse, *Metamorphic Verse: The Elizabethan Minor Epic*, 1981. "Recent Studies in Marlowe" are surveyed in *ELR* 7 (1977): 382–399 and 18 (1988): 329–342.

Andrew Marvell

The tercentenary of Marvell's birth in 1921 produced a volume of essays in tribute to a then-neglected author, among them a highly influential piece by T. S. Eliot. Since then the tide of critical commentary has risen to a flood. The standard edition is the two-volume *Poems and Letters*, ed. H. M. Margoliouth, 1927, 1952, and a 3rd ed., revised by Pierre Legouis and E. E. Duncan-Jones, 1971. The Oxford Authors edition by Frank Kermode and Keith Walker, 1990, includes most of the poetry and some of the prose. There are also handy editions of the *Complete Poetry* by George de F. Lord, 1968, and Elizabeth Story Donno, 1972. Good general introductions are those of M. C. Bradbrook and M. G. Lloyd Thomas (1940; corrected reprint, 1962) and Pierre Legouis (rev. 1968); or see John Dixon Hunt's profusely illustrated *Andrew Marvell: His Life and Writings*, 1978. In *Studies in Seventeenth-Century Poetic*, 1950, Ruth Wallerstein treated Marvell as a serious metaphysician. H. E. Toliver, *Marvell's Ironic Vision*, 1965, and J. B. Leishman, *The Art of Marvell's Poetry*, 1966, were literary in their interests. The pastoral poetry was studied by Patrick Cullen in *Spenser, Marvell, and Renaissance Pastoral*, as well as by Donald Friedman in *Marvell's Pastoral Art*, both 1970. Two general studies appeared in the same year under the titles *My Echoing Song*, by Rosalie Colie, and *The Resolved Soul*, by Anne Berthoff. Other studies of Marvell's poetry are Annabel M. Patterson, *Marvell and the Civic Crown*, 1978, Warren L. Chernaik, *The Poet's Time*, 1983, Robert Wilcher, *Andrew Marvell*, 1985, and Christine Rees, *The Judgment of Marvell*, 1989. Two books focus on Marvell's intricate political attitudes: John Wallace, *Destiny His Choice*, 1968, and the four studies in *The Political Identity of Andrew Marvell*, ed. Conal Condren and A. D. Cousins, 1990. In *The Unfortunate Fall: Theodicy and the Moral Imagination of Andrew Marvell*, 1983, John Klause views the poet's ironic detachment in a light that is not altogether flattering. Marvell is also treated in Leah Marcus, *The Politics of Mirth*, 1986. Collections of critical essays on Marvell include those edited by C. A. Patrides, 1978, R. L. Brett, 1979, Arthur Pollard, 1980, and Harold Bloom, 1989. E. S. Donno edited *Andrew Marvell: The Critical Heritage*, 1978; Dan S. Collins published *Andrew Marvell: A Reference Guide*, 1981. Recent studies: *ELR* 22 (1992): 273–295.

Middle English Lyrics

The best selections of Middle English lyrics are *Early English Lyrics*, ed. E. K. Chambers and F. Sidgwick, 1921; *Medieval English Lyrics: A Critical Anthology*, ed. R. T. Davies, 1963; *Middle English Lyrics*, A Norton Critical Edition, ed. M. S. Luria and R. L. Hoffman, 1974; *The Oxford Book of Medieval English Verse*, ed. Celia and

2618 SELECTED BIBLIOGRAPHIES

Kenneth Sisam, 1970; *English Lyrics before 1500,* ed. Theodore Silverstein, 1971. For criticism see A. K. Moore, *The Secular Lyric in Middle English,* 1951, Kane's chapter in *Middle English Literature,* Stephen Manning, *Wisdom and Number,* 1962, and Rosemary Woolf, *The English Religious Lyric in the Middle Ages,* 1968.

John Milton

The Columbia Milton, in eighteen volumes including an invaluable two-volume index, is the only edition of the complete poetry and prose. More often cited nowadays are the Yale edition of the *Prose Works,* 1953–82, and the edition of the *Poems* by John Carey and Alastair Fowler, 1968. For most purposes, students will find the single volume of Merritt Hughes's edition of the *Complete Poems and Major Prose,* 1957, sufficient. Douglas Bush's edition of the *Complete Poetical Works,* 1965, offers a reliable text and judicious, moderate annotation. Two notable student editions of *Paradise Lost* are Scott Elledge's for the Norton Critical Editions, rev. 1993, and Christopher Ricks's Penguin edition, 1968, which also includes the sequel, *Paradise Regained.* There is a four-volume facsimile of the original editions of the poetry, edited by Harris Fletcher, 1943–48. A multivolume commentary on the poetry began appearing in 1970.

The standard biography is W. R. Parker's two-volume survey, 1968. Douglas Bush's *John Milton,* 1964, is a brief introductory account of the life and works; A. N. Wilson's biography, 1983, attempts the difficult feat of reclaiming Milton for the English upper-middle class. Christopher Hill has written a masterful account of *Milton and the English Revolution,* 1977. Milton is psychoanalyzed by William Kerrigan, in *The Sacred Complex: On the Psychogenesis of "Paradise Lost,"* 1983. In the five volumes of *The Life Records of John Milton,* 1949–58, Joseph M. French collected many primary materials for Milton's biography.

General guidebooks to Milton include Marjorie Nicolson's *John Milton: A Reader's Guide to His Poetry,* 1963, Lois Potter's *Preface to Milton,* 1971, and now *The Cambridge Companion to Milton,* 1989, ed. Dennis Danielson. There is also a huge *Milton Encyclopedia,* under the general editorship of William B. Hunter, Jr., in nine volumes, 1978–83. Different positions in the lively feminist debate on Milton are taken in three works that appeared in 1987: Joseph Wittreich, *Feminist Milton;* James Turner, *One Flesh: Paradisal Marriage and Sexual Relations in the Age of Milton;* and Mary Nyquist, "The Genesis of Gendered Subjectivity in the Divorce Tracts and in *Paradise Lost,*" in *Re-membering Milton,* an important collection of essays by diverse hands edited by Nyquist and Margaret Ferguson. Cultural materialist views of Milton are found in Andrew Milner, *John Milton and the English Revolution,* 1981, in Christopher Kendrick,

Milton: A Study in Ideology and Form, 1986. Milton is also viewed in the light of current preoccupations in Herman Rapaport, *Milton and the Postmodern,* 1983, Marshall Grossman, *"Authors to Themselves": Milton and the Revelation of History,* 1987, Catherine Belsey, *John Milton: Language, Gender, Power,* 1988, and Michael Lieb, *Milton and the Culture of Violence,* 1994.

A lively, amazingly durable introduction to Milton's masterpiece is C. S. Lewis's *Preface to Paradise Lost,* 1942, a response to the attacks on Milton by F. R. Leavis (1933; rep. in *Revaluation,* 1936) and T. S. Eliot (1936; later modified in a lecture of 1947: both pieces are found in *Milton: Two Studies,* 1968). Lewis's defense, which hardly acknowledges Milton's Puritanism, is as one-sided as the attacks, but is stimulating nonetheless. Its biases were counterbalanced by such influential subsequent studies as those of A. J. A. Waldock, 1947; Joseph Summers, 1962; and Helen Gardner, 1965. Milton's God is a traditional stumbling block for readers of *Paradise Lost;* William Empson's tough, tightly argued book on the subject (rev. 1965) puts the case for the prosecution very strongly. Another such focal book is Stanley Fish's *Surprised by Sin,* 1967, which invites readers to inspect and criticize their own responses to the developing action of *Paradise Lost.* Other influential books on *Paraside Lost* have been those of Isabel MacCaffrey, 1959; Balachandra Rajan, 1962; Anne Ferry, 1963; Northrop Frye, 1965; John M. Steadman, 1967; William Kerrigan and Thomas Wheeler, both 1974; G. K. Hunter and Robert Crossman, both 1980; Michael Lieb, 1981; Dennis Danielson, 1982; Maureen Quilligan, 1983; Barbara K. Lewalski and Paul Stevens, both 1985; Charles Martindale, 1986; and Regina Schwartz, 1988. On *Paradise Lost* and the allegorical tradition, see Mindele A. Treip, *Allegorical Poetics and the Epic: The Renaissance Tradition,* 1994. A highly acclaimed account of Milton and America is Keith Stavely's *Puritan Legacies: "Paradise Lost" and the New England Tradition, 1630–1890,* 1987.

Different approaches to Milton can also be sampled in collections of critical essays edited by A. E. Barker, 1965, Louis Martz, 1966, A. P. Fiore, 1967, R. D. Emma and J. T. Shawcross, 1967, C. A. Patrides, 1968, Alan Rudrum, 1968, B. Rajan, 1969, Thomas Kranidas, 1969, and Harold Bloom, 1986; and there's an impressive collection of *Critical Essays on Milton from ELH,* also 1969, as well as the collection noted above, *Re-membering Milton.* Collections on Milton's prose have been edited by Michael Lieb and J. T. Shawcross, 1974, and by David Loewenstein and James G. Turner, 1990. In the same year, Loewenstein published a book on the prose and the major poems: *Milton and the Drama of History.* There are also collections on *Lycidas,* including those of C. A. Patrides (1961, rev. 1983) and Scott Elledge (1966). These might lead the student toward J. R.

Knott's study of pastoralism in *Paradise Lost: Milton's Pastoral Vision*, 1971. On aspects of Milton's style, one may consult F. T. Prince, *The Italian Element in Milton's Verse*, 1954; Theodore Banks, *Milton's Imagery*, 1950; Christopher Ricks, *Milton's Grand Style*, 1963; and Rosemond Tuve's characteristically incisive little book titled *Images and Themes in Five Poems by Milton*, 1957. An interest in theology might lead one through Maurice Kelley's *This Great Argument*, 1941, to Malcolm M. Ross, *Poetry and Dogma*, 1954, and to recent books on the subject by Georgia Christopher, 1982, Hugh MacCallum, 1986, and William Myers, 1987. Mary Ann Radzinowicz, *Toward Samson Agonistes: The Growth of Milton's Mind*, 1978, and Louis Martz, *Poet of Exile*, 1980, chart Milton's poetic development. Milton's epics are approached from an unusual angle in a big book by Roland M. Frye, *Milton's Imagery and the Visual Arts*, 1978.

A very welcome recent guide through the morass of studies is provided by C. A. Patrides, *An Annotated Critical Bibliography of John Milton*, 1987.

Lady Mary Wortley Montagu
The standard modern biography is Robert Halsband's *The Life of Lady Mary Wortley Montagu*, 1956. Halsband has also edited *The Complete Letters*, 3 vols., 1965–67; *Selected Letters*, 1970; and with Isobel Grundy, *Essays and Poems and Simplicity, a Comedy*, 1977.

Mystery Plays
E. K. Chambers's classic *The Medieval Stage*, 1905, remains a mine of information, though its views about the evolution of medieval drama are no longer accepted. A new understanding and appreciation of medieval drama begins with O. B. Hardison's *Christian Rite and Christian Drama in the Middle Ages*, 1965, and, for the mysteries, with V. A. Kolve's *The Play Called Corpus Christie*, 1966. Rosemary Woolf's *The English Mystery Plays*, 1972, makes detailed comparisons among the extant plays. Individual cycles are studied by Peter Travis in *Dramatic Design in the Chester Cycle*, 1982, and by Martin Stevens in *Four Middle English Mystery Cycles: Textual, Contextual, and Critical Interpretations*, 1987. G. M. Gibson fills in the social and religious background in *The Theater of Devotion: East Anglian Drama and Society in the Late Middle Ages*, 1989. Good selections of Middle English plays are presented by A. C. Cawley, *Everyman and Medieval Miracle Plays*, 1960, by D. M. Bevington, *Medieval Drama*, 1975, and by Peter Happé, *The English Mystery Plays*, 1975. Cawley's *The Wakefield Pageants in the Towneley Cycle*, 1958, has a discussion of the work of the "Wakefield Master" whose hand is seen in the *Second Shepherds' Play*. A collection of critical essays has been made by Jerome Taylor and A. H. Nelson in *Medieval English Drama*, 1972. *Approaches to Teaching Medieval Drama*, ed. Richard Emmer-

son, 1990, contains essays by many hands and comprises a nontechnical survey of current opinion. For commentary on *Everyman*, see the introduction to A.C. Cawley's 1961 edition and Robert Potter's comprehensive *The English Morality Play: Origins, History, and Influence of a Dramatic Tradition*, 1975.

Thomas Nashe
The standard edition, 5 vols., is by R. W. McKerrow, rev. F. P. Wilson, 1958; there are selected editions by Stanley Wells, 1965, and J. B. Steane, 1972. Useful critical studies include G. R. Hibbard, *Thomas Nashe, A Critical Introduction*, 1962; Jonathan V. Crewe, *Unredeemed Rhetoric: Thomas Nashe and the Scandal of Authorship*, 1982; and Lorna Hutson, *Thomas Nashe in Context*, 1989. *ELR* 11 (1981): 344–350 has a review of recent studies.

Alexander Pope
There is no really complete edition of Pope's works. Although defective in many respects, the Victorian edition by Whitwell Elwin and J. W. Courthope, 10 vols., 1871–89, must still be consulted (with caution). The excellent Twickenham Edition of the poems, 11 vols., 1939–67, a co-operative undertaking by several scholars (under John Butt), includes valuable introductory and critical materials and notes. A convenient selection in a single volume, with selected notes, omits the translations of Homer. *The Prose Works* have been edited in 2 vols., by Norman Ault, 1936, and Rosemary Cowler, 1986.

Maynard Mack's *Alexander Pope: A Life*, 1986, is a full and sympathetic biography. George Sherburn's *Early Career of Alexander Pope*, 1934, and Mack's *The Garden and the City*, 1969, on Pope's later career, are valuable studies. Howard Erskine-Hill has described *The Social Milieu of Alexander Pope*, 1975, and Valerie Rumbold, *Women's Place in Pope's World*, 1989. Sherburn's edition of the *Correspondence*, 5 vols., 1956, is standard. R. H. Griffith, *Alexander Pope: A Bibliography*, 2 vols., 1962, is a detailed list of Pope's writings.

A good critical introduction to the poems is Geoffrey Tillotson's *On the Poetry of Pope*, 2nd ed., 1950; and Tillotson's *Pope and Human Nature*, 1958, throws light on a difficult subject. David B. Morris's *Alexander Pope: The Genius of Sense*, 1984, offers fine criticism of individual poems. Reuben A. Brower's *Alexander Pope: The Poetry of Allusion*, 1959, is an enlightening study of Pope's lifelong habit of adapting phrases, images, and ideas from earlier poets, especially those of classical antiquity. Much information is gathered up in Robert W. Rogers's *The Major Satires of Alexander Pope*, 1955. Austin Warren's *Alexander Pope as Critic and Humanist*, 1929, is dated but still useful. Aubrey Williams has analyzed Pope's *Dunciad*, 1955, and John Sitter, *The Poetry of Pope's Dunciad*, 1971. Several essays on Pope are included in Maynard Mack's *Collected in Himself*, 1982. Mack has also edited *Essential Articles for the Study of Alexander Pope*, 1964, and with James Winn, *Pope: Recent Essays*, 1980; and *The Enduring Legacy*, ed. G. S. Rousseau and Pat Rogers, 1988, collects new essays on Pope.

Popular Ballads

The great ballad collection is that of F. J. Child, *The English and Scottish Popular Ballads*, 1882, more available in the somewhat abridged edition by H. C. Sargent and G. L. Kittredge, 1904. Selections will be found in *The Faber Book of Ballads*, ed. M. J. C. Hodgart, 1965, and *The Oxford Book of Ballads*, ed. James Kinsley, 1969. For general discussion, see F. B. Gummere, *The Popular Ballads*, 1907; G. H. Gerould, *The Ballad of Tradition*, 1932; W. J. Entwistle, *European Balladry*, 1939; M. J. C. Hodgart, *The Ballads*, 1950; and David Buchan, *The Ballad and the Folk*, 1972.

Matthew Prior

The complete critical edition of Prior is *Literary Works*, ed. H. B. Wright and M. K. Spears, 2 vols., 1971. The older and less complete edition in two volumes by A. R. Waller, 1905, 1907, is useful. F. M. Rippy's *Matthew Prior*, 1986, is a good brief survey. The best biography is Charles K. Eves's *Matthew Prior, Poet and Diplomatist*, 1939.

Sir Walter Ralegh

The collected edition is by William Oldys and Thomas Birch, 8 vols., 1829, rpt. 1968; the standard edition of the poems is by A. M. C. Latham, rev. 1950; a useful edition is Gerard Hammond, ed., *Selected Writings*, 1984. The best biography is Willard Wallace, *Sir Walter Ralegh*, 1959. Noteworthy studies include David B. Quinn, *Ralegh and the British Empire*, 1947, rpt. 1962; E. A. Strathmann, *Sir Walter Ralegh, A Study in Elizabethan Skepticism*, 1951; Philip Edwards, *Sir Walter Ralegh*, 1953, rpt. 1976; F. J. Levy in *Tudor Historical Thought*, 1967; and Stephen Greenblatt, *Sir Walter Ralegh*, 1973. A review of recent studies is in *ELR* 15 (1985): 225–244.

Christina Rossetti

The standard variorum edition is *The Complete Poems of Christina Rossetti*, ed. R. W. Crump, 3 vols., 1979–90. Virginia Woolf's *Second Common Reader*, 1932, contains an essay on the poet. Dolores Rosenblum's *Christina Rossetti: The Poetry of Endurance*, 1986, and Antony H. Harrison's *Christina Rossetti in Context*, 1988, are good book-length studies of the poetry.

William Shakespeare

Some important editions of the plays are the Variorum (S. B. Hemingway, ed., *1 Henry IV*, 1936, with a supplement by G. B. Evans, 1956; H. H. Furness, ed., *King Lear*, 1880); the New Arden (A. R. Humphries, ed., *1 Henry IV*, 1960; Kenneth Muir, ed., *King Lear*, rev. 1972); David Bevington, ed., *1 Henry IV*, 1987; G. B. Evans, ed., *The*

Riverside Shakespeare, 1974; and the Oxford Shakespeare, edited by Stanley Wells and Gary Taylor, 1986. Major studies treating *1 Henry IV* are E. M. W. Tillyard, *Shakespeare's History Plays*, 1944; Irving Ribner, *The English History Play in the Age of Shakespeare*, rev. 1965; Robert Ornstein, *A Kingdom for a Stage: The Achievement of Shakespeare's History Plays*, 1972; Phyllis Rackin, *Stages of History: Shakespeare's English Chronicles*, 1990; and Scott McMillin, *Shakespeare in Performance: 1 Henry IV*, 1991. Classic studies treating *King Lear* are A. C. Bradley, *Shakespearean Tragedy*, 1904; Robert Heilman, *This Great Stage: Irony and Structure in King Lear*, 1963; and W. R. Elton, *King Lear and the Gods*, 1966. Shakespeare's plays have invited analyses from new historicist, cultural materialist, feminist, psychoanalytic, and other perspectives. Some important studies and essay collections are Murray M. Schwartz and Coppelia Kahn, eds., *Representing Shakespeare: New Psychoanalytic Essays*, 1980; Lisa Jardine, *Still Harping on Daughters: Women and Drama in the Age of Shakespeare*, 1983; Jonathan Dollimore and Alan Sinfield, eds., *Political Shakespeare: New Essays in Cultural Materialism*, 1985; John Drakakis, ed., *Alternative Shakespeares*, 1985; Patricia Parker and Geoffrey Hartman, eds., *Shakespeare and the Question of Theory*, 1985; Jean Howard and M. O'Connor, eds., *Shakespeare Reproduced*, 1987; and Stephen Greenblatt, *Shakespearean Negotiations*, 1988.

Hyder Rollins's Variorum edition of the sonnets, 2 vols., 1944, summarizes many commentaries and problems; Stephen Booth's edition, 1977, presents a facsimile of the first edition and a modernized text on facing pages, with elaborate commentary; there are many paperback editions. Noteworthy criticism of the sonnets and poems include Stephen Booth, *An Essay on Shakespeare's Sonnets*, 1969; Rosalie Colie, *Shakespeare's Living Art*, 1974 (also essays on several plays); Hallett Smith, *The Tension of the Lyre: Poetry in Shakespeare's Sonnets*, 1981; Joel Fineman, *The Perjured Eye: The Invention of Poetic Subjectivity in the Sonnets*, 1986; and Heather Dubrow, *Captive Victors: Shakespeare's Narrative Poems and Sonnets*, 1987.

The life and works are treated by E. K. Chambers, *William Shakespeare: A Study of Facts and Problems*, 2 vols., 1930. S. Schoenbaum's important biographical research is recorded in *William Shakespeare: A Documentary Life*, 1975, and *A Compact Documentary Life*, 1977. Some useful aids to scholarship are Geoffrey Bullough, *Narrative and Dramatic Sources of Shakespeare*, 8 vols., 1957–75; and Kenneth Muir and S. Schoenbaum, eds., *A New Companion to Shakespeare Studies*, 1971, rpt. 1976.

Bernard Shaw

The Collected Works of Bernard Shaw, in the Ayot St. Lawrence Edition, 30 vols., appeared in 1930ff.

Collected Plays with their Prefaces, 7 vols., 1975, contains the finally revised text of all the published plays, together with historical data and miscellaneous Shavian pronouncements on each play. Many of the plays are also available in inexpensive reprints; note especially *Bernard Shaw's Plays*, a Norton Critical Edition, ed. Warren Sylvester Smith, 1970. Selections of his prose include *Bernard Shaw, Selected Prose*, ed. Diarmuid Russell, 1952; *Plays and Players* (drama criticism), ed. A. C. Ward, 1952; *The Nondramatic Literary Criticism of Bernard Shaw*, ed. Stanley Weintraub, 1972; *Shaw on Music*, ed. Eric Bentley, 1955; and *Bernard Shaw on Language*, ed. Abraham Tauber, 1963.

A still useful critical study is Eric Bentley's *Bernard Shaw: A Reconsideration*, 1947. *Shaw the Dramatist*, Louis Crompton, 1969, examines twelve major plays from the standpoint of their social, historical, and philosophical backgrounds. *Bernard Shaw and the Art of Destroying Ideals*, Charles A. Carpenter, 1969, studies Shaw's thought in relation to his evolving ideas of dramatic structure, while Edmund Wilson's essay "Shaw at Eighty," in *The Triple Thinkers*, 1952, is a stimulating discussion of Shaw as thinker and playwright. *G. B. S. 90: Aspects of Shaw's Life and Works*, ed. S. Winsten, 1946, contains recollections of Shaw's contemporaries together with essays by a variety of writers. Also useful is *G. B. Shaw, A Collection of Critical Essays*, ed. R. J. Kaufmann, 1965.

The standard biography is *Bernard Shaw*, Michael Holroyd, 3 vols., 1988–91. Also of interest is *George Bernard Shaw: His Life and Personality*, Hesketh Pearson, 1963. The *Collected Letters of Bernard Shaw*, ed. Dan H. Laurence, 4 vols., 1965–88, contains 3,000 of a postulated 100,000 that he wrote.

Percy Bysshe Shelley

The nearest to a complete collection of Shelley's writings is *The Complete Works*, ed. Roger Ingpen and Walter E. Peck, 10 vols., 1926–30. The most widely used single-volume edition of the poems has been that in the Oxford Standard Authors, ed. Thomas Hutchinson and rev. G. M. Matthews, 1970. *Shelley's Prose* was collected by David Lee Clark in 1954; and *The Letters* were edited by Frederick L. Jones in 2 vols., 1964. Because of the erratic way in which Shelley's poems and essays were published, all the collected editions are faulty; Shelley's writings are now in the process of being revised and reprinted by a number of editors. Neville Rogers's edition of *The Complete Poetical Works*, of which two volumes are in print, 1972–, has been severely criticized by scholars. The best texts are those in *The Lyrics of Shelley*, edited and sensitively interpreted by Judith Chernaik, 1972; and in the large selection of *Shelley's Poetry and Prose*, A Norton Critical Edition, ed. Donald H.

Reiman and Sharon B. Powers, 1977, which also includes a collection of critical essays on Shelley.

The classic life is Newman Ivey White's *Shelley*, 2 vols., 1940, which is also available in a condensed single volume, *Portrait of Shelley*, 1945. Richard Holmes's *Shelley: The Pursuit*, 1974, is not so detailed as White's biography, but provides a vivid sense of Shelley as a human being. Kenneth Neill Cameron, in *The Young Shelley*, 1950, and in the sequel, *Shelley: The Golden Years*, 1974, emphasizes the development of Shelley's radical social and political thinking. C. E. Pulos, *The Deep Truth: A Study of Shelley's Scepticism*, 1954, a valuable corrective of standard views of Shelley, emphasizes the philosophic skepticism at the center of his idealism.

Shelley's Major Poetry, by Carlos Baker, 1948, provides useful analyses of the longer poems that stress their ideational content; Carl H. Grabo, in *A Newton among Poets*, 1930, and Desmond King-Hele, in *Shelley: His Thought and Work*, 1960, deal with Shelley's conversion of scientific knowledge into poetic images. *The Imagery of Keats and Shelley*, by Richard H. Fogle, 1949, is an analysis of the stylistic qualities of Shelley's poetry.

As early as 1900, W. B. Yeats, in "The Philosophy of Shelley's Poetry" (reprinted in *Essays*, 1924), dealt with Shelley as one of the great symbolist poets. More recent treatments of Shelley's symbolic imagery are Peter Butter, *Shelley's Idols of the Cave*, 1954, and Harold Bloom's innovative study, *Shelley's Mythmaking*, 1959, which puts Shelley in the line of visionary poets whose imaginative processes were instinctively mythopoetic. Earl Wasserman's *Shelley: A Critical Reading*, 1971, replaces his earlier treatments of Shelley; it is a massive series of close readings of Shelley's most important poems and essays. Other useful critiques are Milton Wilson, *Shelley's Later Poetry*, 1959; R. G. Woodman, *The Apocalyptic Tradition in the Poetry of Shelley*, 1964; Stuart Curran's fine study of *Shelley's Annus Mirabilis: The Maturing of an Epic Vision*, 1975; Timothy Webb, *Shelley: A Voice Not Understood*, 1977; William Keach, *Shelley's Style*, 1984; Stuart M. Sperry, *Shelley's Major Verse: The Narrative and Dramatic Poetry*, 1988; Stephen C. Behrendt, *Shelley and His Audiences*, 1989; and Donald Reiman, *Percy Bysshe Shelley*, rev. 1990. Charles Robinson discusses the personal and poetic relations of *Byron and Shelley: The Snake and the Eagle Wreathed in Fight*, 1975. *Shelley*, ed. George M. Ridenour, 1965, is an anthology of modern critical essays.

Sir Philip Sidney

The standard edition of Sidney's poetry is by William Ringler, 1962. Jean Robertson edited the *Old Arcadia*, 1973; Victor Stretkowicz edited the *New Arcadia*, 1987. *The Defense of Poesy* is included in the *Miscellaneous Prose* edited by K. Duncan-Jones and J. Van Dorsten, 1973; there are individual editions by J . Van Dorsten, 1966; Lewis Soens, 1970; and in several anthologies. Maurice Evans edited *The Countess of Pembroke's Arcadia* (the 1593 composite version) in 1977. The earliest biography was by Fulke Greville, 1652. Modern studies of the life and works are John Buxton, *Sir Philip Sidney and the English Renaissance*, 1954, rpt. 1964; A. C. Hamilton, *Sir Philip Sidney: A Study of His Life and Works*, 1977; and James M. Osborn, *Young Philip Sidney*, 1972. Some important critical studies include Walter R. Davis and Richard Lanham, *Sidney's Arcadia*, 1965; David Kalstone, *Sidney's Poetry: Contexts and Interpretations*, 1965; Neil L. Rudenstine, *Sidney's Poetic Development*, 1967; Jon S. Lawry, *Sidney's Two Arcadias: Pattern and Proceeding*, 1972; Andrew Weiner, *Sir Philip Sidney and the Poetics of Protestantism*, 1978; and Richard C. McCoy, *Sir Philip Sidney: Rebellion in Arcadia*, 1979. Also, Stephen Greenblatt, "Murdering Peasants: Status, Genre, and the Representation of Rebellion," in *Representations* 1 (1983): 1–29; and Roland Greene in *Post-Petrarchism*, 1991. ELR 2 (1972): 148–164 and 8 (1978): 212–233 provide a review of recent studies.

Sir Gawain and the Green Knight

The standard Middle English text of the poem is that of J. R. R. Tolkien and E. V. Gordon, 1925 (rev. Norman Davis, 1967). Perhaps easier to use are the editions by R. A. Waldron, 1970, rev. for *The Poems of the Pearl Manuscript*, 1978, and J. A. Burrow, 1972. Good discussion of various aspects of the poem appear in Marie Borroff's *Sir Gawain and the Green Knight: A Stylistic and Metrical Study*, 1962; L. D. Benson, *Art and Tradition in Sir Gawain and the Green Knight*, 1965 (especially good on the sources); and J. A. Burrow, *A Reading of Sir Gawain and the Green Knight*, 1965. Interesting chapters on the poem are contributed by A.C. Spearing in *Criticism and Medieval Poetry*, 2nd ed., 1972, and *The Gawain Poet*, 1971, and D. R. Howard in *The Three Temptations: Medieval Man in Search of the World*, 1966. There are three collections of critical essays on the poet: R. J. Blanch's *Sir Gawain and Pearl*, 1966; Denton Fox's *Twentieth-Century Interpretations of Sir Gawain and the Green Knight*, 1968; and D. R. Howard and C. K. Zacher's *Critical Studies of Sir Gawain and the Green Knight*, 1968.

Edmund Spenser

Edwin A. Greenlaw et al. have edited a ten-volume Variorum edition, *The Works of Edmund Spenser*, 1932–49. Important editions of *The Faerie Queene* are by A. C. Hamilton, 1977, and Thomas P. Roche, 1978; William A. Oram et al. have edited *The Shorter Poems of Edmund Spenser*, 1989. The chief biography is *The Life of Edmund Spenser* by Alexander Judson, 1945. Important critical studies include C. S. Lewis, *The Allegory of Love*, 1936; Graham Hough, *A Preface to "The Fa-*

erie Queene," 1962; Thomas P. Roche, Jr., *The Kindly Flame* (on books 3 and 4) 1964; Paul J. Alpers, *The Poetry of The Faerie Queene*, 1967; Isabel MacCaffrey, *Spenser's Allegory: The Anatomy of Imagination*, 1975; James Nohrnberg, *The Analogy of the Faerie Queene*, 1976; Michael O'Connell, *Mirror and Veil: The Historical Dimension of Spenser's Faerie Queene*, 1977; Jonathan Goldberg, *Endlesse Worke: Spenser and the Structure of Discourse*, 1981; John Guillory, *Poetic Authority: Spenser, Milton, and Literary History*, 1983: and John N. King, *Spenser's Poetry and the Reformation Tradition*, 1990. An invaluable scholarly aid is A. C. Hamilton et al., eds., *The Spenser Encyclopedia*, 1990. A guide to recent work is Waldo F. McNeir and Foster Provost, *Edmund Spenser: An Annotated Bibliography*, 1975.

Henry Howard, Earl of Surrey

The complete edition is by F. M. Padelford, 1928, rpt. 1966; Emrys Jones's edition, 1964, has a sound introductory essay on style, themes, and influences. *Tottel's Miscellany* is edited by Hyder E. Rollins, rev. 1965. E. R. Casady's biography, 1938, and W. R. Sessions's study of life and works, 1986, bear the same title, *Henry Howard, Earl of Surrey*. Noteworthy critical studies are Walter R. Davis, "Contexts in Surrey's Poetry," ELR 4 (1974): 40–55; and the chapter in Susanne Woods, *Natural Emphasis: English Versification from Chaucer to Dryden*, 1984. Reviews of recent studies are in ELR 2 (1971): 188–191 and 19 (1989): 389–401.

Jonathan Swift

Irvin Ehrenpreis's standard, comprehensive biography, *Swift: The Man, His Works, and the Age*, consists of three volumes: *Mr. Swift and His Contemporaries*, 1962, *Dr. Swift*, 1967, and *Dean Swift*, 1983. J. A. Downie's *Jonathan Swift, Political Writer*, 1984, and David Nokes's *Jonathan Swift, A Hypocrite Reversed*, 1985, are good introductions to the life and writings. Louis A. Landa's *Swift and the Church of Ireland*, 1954, is a valuable special study.

The standard edition of the poems is by Sir Harold Williams, 2 vols., 1937, rev., 1958. Pat Rogers's edition of Swift's *Complete Poems*, 1983, is reliable and less expensive. Herbert Davis has edited the prose works in fourteen volumes, 1939–68. Swift's *Correspondence* was edited by Williams, 5 vols., 1963–65. Other distinguished editions include Davis's *The Drapier's Letters*, 1935; Williams's *Journal to Stella*, 1948; A. C. Guthkelch and D. Nichol Smith, *A Tale of a Tub*, 2nd ed., 1958; and Frank H. Ellis, *A Discourse of the Contests and Dissentions between the Nobles and the Commons in Athens and Rome*, 1967. For the Norton Critical Editions series, Robert Greenberg has edited *Gulliver's Travels*, rev. 1971, and with W. B. Piper, *The Writings of Jonathan Swift*, 1973.

Among the abundant critical studies, the student should find especially helpful Ricardo Quintana's

The Mind and Art of Jonathan Swift, 1936, and *Swift: An Introduction*, 1955. Arthur Case's *Four Essays on Gulliver's Travels*, Herbert Davis's *Jonathan Swift: Essays on his Satire and Other Studies*, 1964, and C. J. Rawson's *Gulliver and the Gentle Reader*, 1973, are all useful. After long neglect, Swift's poems have attracted a wealth of recent criticism; some of the best has been collected by David Vieth, *Essential Articles for the study of Jonathan Swift's Poetry*, 1984. Three books by Robert C. Elliott, *The Power of Satire*, 1960, *The Shape of Utopia*, 1970, and *The Literary Persona*, 1982, contain interesting chapters on Swift; so do Edward Said's *The World, the Text, and the Critic*, 1983, and Carol Houlihan Flynn's *The Body in Swift and Defoe*, 1990. Two good collections of essays are *Jonathan Swift: A Critical Anthology*, ed. Denis Donoghue, 1971, and *The Character of Swift's Satire*, ed. C. J. Rawson, 1983.

Alfred, Lord Tennyson

Tennyson's *Works* were edited by his son Hallam, Lord Tennyson, in 9 vols., 1907–8. The *Poems* in one volume were edited by Christopher Ricks in 1969 and extensively revised in three volumes in 1988. Norton Critical Editions of Tennyson's work are *Tennyson's Poetry*, ed. Robert W. Hill, Jr., 1972, and *In Memoriam*, ed. Robert H. Ross, 1974. *In Memoriam* has been edited by Susan Shatto and Marian Shaw, 1982. Two volumes of *The Letters of Alfred, Lord Tennyson*, to 1870, were edited by Cecil Y. Lang and Edgar F. Shannon, 1981–87. Hallam Tennyson's *Alfred, Lord Tennyson: A Memoir*, 2 vols., 1897, is a mine of anecdotes and valuable information. *The Tennyson Archive*, ed. Christopher Ricks and Aidan Day, 23 vols., 1987–89, is a monumental production concerning the manuscripts. The standard biography is Robert Martin, *Tennyson*, 1980. Sir Harold Nicolson's *Tennyson*, 1923, a critical study more than a biography, gives a lively but distorted assessment of Tennyson's achievement. A number of critical studies have successively corrected Nicolson's oversights and have variously demonstrated that Tennyson is one of the finest of poets. These include Jerome H. Buckley's *Tennyson: The Growth of a Poet*, 1961; Christopher Ricks's *Tennyson*, 1972; F. E. L. Priestley's *Language and Structure in Tennyson's Poetry*, 1973; James R. Kincaid's *Tennyson's Major Poems: The Comic and Ironic Patterns*, 1975; W. David Shaw's *Tennyson's Style*, 1976; and, most especially to be recommended, *The Poetry of Tennyson* by A. Dwight Culler, 1977. See also Alan Sinfield's *Alfred Tennyson*, 1986, and Herbert F. Tucker, *Tennyson and the Doom of Romanticism*, 1988.

Some of the most interesting discussions are in introductory essays to Tennyson's poems by T. S. Eliot, 1936; W. H. Auden, 1944; H. Marshall McLuhan, 1956; Jerome Buckley, 1958; and George MacBeth, 1971. Also useful are A Com-mentary on Tennyson's "In Memoriam," by A. C. Bradley, 1901; *The Alien Vision of Victorian Poetry*, by E. D. H. Johnson, 1952; and *Critical Essays on the Poetry of Tennyson*, ed. John Kilham, 1960. Book-length studies of the *Idylls* have been published by Clyde de L. Ryals, 1967, John R. Reed, 1969, and John D. Rosenberg, 1973. A collection of critical essays on *In Memoriam* was edited by John Dixon Hunt, 1970.

Dylan Thomas

The Poems of Dylan Thomas, rev. 1974, is the fullest collection of Thomas's poetry. He also wrote the autobiographical prose *Portrait of the Artist as a Young Dog*, 1940; *Adventures in the Skin Trade*, 1955; a radio play, *Under Milk Wood*, 1954, which has proved a great popular success; and *Quite Early One Morning*, 1954, a collection of stories, essays, and minor pieces. Paul Ferris edited *The Collected Letters of Dylan Thomas* in 1985, and *The Notebooks of Dylan Thomas* were edited by Ralph N. Maud in 1967. Maud's *Entrances to Dylan Thomas's Poetry*, 1963, and *The Craft and Art of Dylan Thomas*, William T. Moynahan, 1966, are good introductions to the workings of the poet's mind; *The Poetry of Dylan Thomas*, Elder Olsen, 1954, is a helpful if somewhat oversystematized discussion of his poetry; and *Dylan Thomas: The Poet and His Critics*, R. B. Kershner, 1976, is an evaluation of Thomas criticism with a useful bibliography; and John Ackerman has compiled *A Dylan Thomas Companion*, 1991. *The Life of Dylan Thomas*, Constantine Fitzgibbon, 1965, and *Dylan Thomas: A Biography*, Paul Ferris, 1977, are good biographies, while *The Days of Dylan Thomas*, Bill Read, 1964, supplements a straightforward narrative with many photographs.

Anne Finch, Countess of Winchilsea

Myra Reynolds added a long biographical introduction to her valuable edition of the *Poems*, 1903. Katharine M. Rogers has edited *Selected Poems*, 1979. A better edition is needed, for these omit many manuscript poems. Ann Messenger's "Publishing without Perishing: Lady Winchilsea's *Miscellany Poems* of 1713," *Restoration* 5 (1981): 27–37, compares published with unpublished poems. Ruth Salvaggio's *Enlightened Absence: Neoclassical Configurations of the Feminine*, 1988, includes a section on Finch. The most recent study is Barbara McGovern's *Anne Finch and Her Poetry: A Critical Biography*, 1992.

Virginia Woolf

The ten novels, *A Room of One's Own*, and *Three Guineas* are all available in paperback. *The Complete Shorter Fiction* has been edited by Susan Dick, 1985, and *The Essays* by Andrew McNeillie, 3 vols., 1986–88. *The Diary of Virginia Woolf*, 5 vols., ed. Anne Olivier Bell and Andrew McNeillie, 1977–84, and *The Letters of Virginia Woolf*, 6 vols., ed. Nigel Nicolson and Joanne Trautmann,

1975–80, provide commentary on Woolf's life and work. For her early development, see *A Passionate Apprentice: The Early Journals, 1897–1909*, ed. Mitchell A. Leaska, 1990.

Perceptive critical studies include *Virginia Woolf*, David Daiches, rev. 1963; *Virginia Woolf: Her Art as a Novelist*, Joan Bennett, 2nd ed., 1964; *Feminism and Art: A Study of Virginia Woolf*, Herbert Marder, 1968; *The Novels of Virginia Woolf*, M. Leaska, 1977; *Virginia Woolf: A Critical Reading*, Avrom Fleishman, 1975; *New Feminist Essays on Virginia Woolf*, ed. Jane Marcus, 1981; *Virginia Woolf: New Critical Essays*, ed. Patricia Clements and Isobel Grundy, 1983; *Virginia Woolf and the Real World*, Alex Zwerdling, 1986; and *Virginia Woolf: Feminist Destinations*, Rachel Bowlby, 1988.

Virginia Woolf, Quentin Bell, 2 vols., 1972, offers the fullest and most balanced account of her life; *Woman of Letters: A Life of Virginia Woolf*, Phyllis Rose, 1978, focuses on her feminism; and *Virginia Woolf: A Writer's Life*, Lyndall Gordon, 1984, shows Woolf's creative use of her own experience. *Virginia Woolf: The Impact of Childhood Sexual Abuse on Her Life and Work*, Louise A. De-Salvo, 1989, offers a revised picture of Woolf's childhood and its effect on her writing. *Moments of Being*, ed. Jeanne Schulkind, 1976, contains entertaining autobiographical fragments, as well as a helpful introduction. Of interest also are Leonard Woolf's five volumes of autobiography, *Sowing*, 1960; *Growing*, 1961; *Beginning Again*, 1964; *Downhill All the Way*, 1967; *The Journey Not the Arrival Matters*, 1975; and *Letters of Leonard Woolf*, ed. Frederic Spotts, 1989. See also *Bloomsbury*, Quentin Bell, 1968, and *The Bloomsbury Group*, ed. S. P. Rosenbaum, 1975.

William Wordsworth
Ernest de Selincourt has edited *The Poetical Works* (with Helen Darbishire), 5 vols., 1940–49; the variorum edition of *The Prelude*, with the texts of 1805 and 1850 on facing pages (rev. Helen Darbishire, 1959); and *The Letters of William and Dorothy Wordsworth*, 6 vols., 1935–39 (now being revised by C. L. Shaver and others, 1967–); a one-volume *New Selection* of the letters has been edited by Alan G. Hill, 1984. Newly edited texts of the 1805 and 1850 *Preludes* on facing pages, together with the "Two-Part *Prelude*" of 1799, various manuscript fragments of *The Prelude*, and a selection of recent critical essays on the poem, are available in *The Prelude: 1799, 1805, 1850*, A Norton Critical Edition, ed. Jonathan Wordsworth, M. H. Abrams, and Stephen Gill, 1979. Wordsworth's poems in one volume were edited for Oxford Standard Authors by Thomas Hutchinson and revised by Ernest de Selincourt, 1950. A new series, the Cornell Wordsworth, 1975–, prints texts of the poems, together with variant readings from the manuscripts (which are reproduced and transcribed) through

the final printings in Wordsworth's lifetime. W. J. B. Owen and Jane Worthington Smyser have edited *The Prose Works*, 3 vols., 1974, and there is a *Selected Prose*, ed. John O. Hayden, 1988. Owen has also printed from his edition a convenient collection of *Wordsworth's Literary Criticism*, 1974.

The standard biography is now Stephen Gill's *William Wordsworth: A Life*, 1989, superseding Mary Moorman's *William Wordsworth*, vol. 1, rev. 1968, and vol. 2, 1965. Edith Batho, *The Later Wordsworth*, 1933, and W. L. Sperry, *Wordsworth's Anti-Climax*, 1935, are studies of the poet after 1805. Mark L. Reed's scrupulous work dating precisely Wordsworth's poems, manuscripts, and the events of his daily life, has reached two volumes, *Wordsworth: The Chronology of the Early Years*, 1967, and *The Chronology of the Middle Years*, 1975.

Walter Raleigh's *Wordsworth*, 1903, Helen Darbishire's *The Poet Wordsworth*, 1950, and Carl Woodring's *Wordsworth*, 1965, are useful introductions to Wordsworth's poetry. Parul D. Sheats has written a fine study of the early poems, *The Making of Wordsworth's Poetry, 1785–1798*, 1973. Modern interest in *Lyrical Ballads* is shown in Stephen M. Parrish, *The Art of the "Lyrical Ballads,"* 1973; Mary Jacobus, *Tradition and Experiment in Wordsworth's "Lyrical Ballads," 1798*, 1976; John E. Jordan, *Why the "Lyrical Ballads"?* 1976; and Don H. Bialostosky, *Making Tales*, 1984. *The Mind of a Poet*, by Raymond D. Havens, 2 vols., 1941, is a detailed study of *The Prelude*; Herbert Lindenberger, *On Wordsworth's "Prelude,"* 1963, is a lively exploration; Richard J. Onorato, *The Character of the Poet: Wordsworth in "The Prelude,"* 1971, applies psychoanalytic concepts to the poem. Various aspects of Wordsworth's thought are discussed in Basil Willey, *The Eighteenth Century Background*, 1940; N. P. Stallknecht, *Strange Seas of Thought*, 2nd ed., 1958; James A. W. Heffernan, *Wordsworth's Theory of Poetry: The Transforming Imagination*, 1969; and Geoffrey Durrant, *Wordsworth and the Great System*, 1970. Prominent among critical studies of Wordsworth's poetry are John Jones, *The Egotistical Sublime*, 1954; David Ferry, *The Limits of Mortality*, 1959; David Perkins, *Wordswworth and the Poetry of Sincerity*, 1964; Geoffrey Hartman's impressive study of *Wordsworth's Poetry, 1787–1814*, 1964; James H. Averill, *Wordsworth and the Poetry of Human Suffering*, 1980; Kenneth R. Johnston, *Wordsworth and "The Recluse,"* 1984; Susan J. Wolfson, *The Questioning Presence: Wordsworth, Keats, and the Interrogative Mode in Romantic Poetry*, 1986; Nicholas Roe, *Wordsworth and Coleridge: The Radical Years*, 1988; and Paul Magnuson, *Coleridge and Wordsworth: A Lyrical Dialogue*, 1988. The range and diversity of critical studies are represented in *Wordsworth: A Collection of Critical Essays*, ed. M. H. Abrams, 1972, and, more recently, in *The Age of William Wordsworth: Critical Essays on the Romantic Tradition*, ed. Kenneth R. Johnston and Gene W. Ruoff, 1987.

Lady Mary Wroth
Josephine A. Roberts has edited Wroth's *Poems*, 1983, 2nd ed., 1993, and is preparing an edition of *Urania*; meanwhile, there is an edition of book 1 of *Urania*, with a modernized text, in *An Anthology of Seventeenth-Century Fiction*, ed. Paul Salzman, 1991. Studies of Wroth's works include those of Salzman, in *English Prose Fiction, 1558–1700*, 1985, Dale Spender, in *Mothers of the Novel*, 1986, Elaine Beilin, in *Redeeming Eve*, 1987, Maureen Quilligan, in *Unfolded Tales: Essays on Renaissance Romance*, ed. George M. Logan and Gordon Teskey, 1989. Tina Krontikis, in *Oppositional Voices: Women as Writers and Translators of Literature in the English Renaissance*, 1992, and Barbara K. Lewalski, in *Writing Women in Jacobean England*, 1993. See also Gary Waller, *The Sidney Family Romance: Mary Wroth, William Herbert, and the Early Modern Construction of Gender*, 1993. Essays on *Urania, Pamphilia to Amphilanthus*, and Wroth's pastoral drama *Love's Victory* are included in *The Renaissance Englishwoman in Print*, ed. Anne Haselkorn and Betty Travitsky, 1990. Recent studies: *ELR* 24 (1994): 257–259.

Sir Thomas Wyatt
The most useful edition is by Kenneth Muir and Patricia Thomson, *Collected Poems*, 1969; others are by Richard C. Harrier, 1975; J. Daalder, 1975; and R. A. Rebholz, 1978. *Tottel's Miscellany* is edited by Hyder E. Rollins, rev. 1965. Letters and life records are included in Kenneth Muir's biography, 1963; Patricia Thomson treats both life and works in *Sir Thomas Wyatt and his Background*, 1965. Critical studies include E. M. W. Tillyard, *The Poetry of Sir Thomas Wyatt*, rpt. 1949; Raymond Southall, *The Courtly Maker*, 1964; Elizabeth W. Pomeroy, *The Elizabethan Miscellanies: Their Development and Conventions*, 1973; Patricia Thomson, *Wyatt: The Critical Heritage*, 1974; and Stephen Foley, *Sir Thomas Wyatt*, 1990. Reviews of recent studies are in *ELR* 1 (1971): 178–188 and 19 (1989): 226–246.

William Butler Yeats
In addition to poems and verse plays, Yeats published essays, stories, and autobiographical writings, and produced editions of William Blake (with Edwin Ellis) and of some poems of Spenser. He also edited *The Oxford Book of Modern Verse*, 1936. The major editions of his poems and plays are *The Variorum Edition of the Poems*, ed. Peter Allt and Russell K. Alspach, 1957, corrected 3rd printing, 1966, and *The Variorum Edition of the Plays*, ed. Russell K. Alspach, 1966, corrected 2nd printing, 1966. *The Poems of W. B. Yeats*, ed. Richard J. Finneran, 1983, attempts to provide more accurate texts than those of the *Variorum*, with extensive annotation; and *Selected Poems and Two Plays of William Butler Yeats*, ed. M. L. Rosenthal, rev. 1966, is the best of several paperback selections. The fullest and most representative selection of the voluminous correspondence is *The Letters of W. B. Yeats*, ed. Allan Wade, 1954. This will be superseded by a multivolume edition, of which the first volume has appeared: *The Collected Letters of W. B. Yeats*, ed. John Kelley, 1986. Yeats's mystical work *A Vision* was first published in 1925; a much-revised edition appeared in 1937. His autobiographical writings are combined in *The Autobiography of W. B. Yeats*, 1938ff. Neither the first draft of Yeats's *Autobiography* nor his *Journals* were published until 1972, when Denis Donoghue edited them under the title *Memoirs. Mythologies*, 1959, contains the bulk of Yeats's prose fiction; *Essays and Introductions*, 1961, the most important of his critical prose; and *Explorations*, 1962, miscellaneous prose pieces not readily available elsewhere. John P. Frayne has edited *Uncollected Prose by W. B. Yeats*, 2 vols., 1970 and 1975, and William H. O'Donnell, *W. B. Yeats: Prefaces and Introductions*, 1988.

The critical literature on Yeats is more extensive than that on any other 20th-century poet, and the best guide to this is "W. B. Yeats" in *Anglo-Irish Literature: A Review of Research*, ed. Richard J. Finneran, 1976. *W. B. Yeats: A Critical Introduction*, Balachandra Rajan, 2nd ed., 1969, is the most satisfactory of many short introductory studies, though less substantial than *The Identity of Yeats*, Richard Ellmann, 2nd ed., 1964, and *The Lonely Tower: Studies in the Poetry of W. B. Yeats*, T. R. Henn, 2nd ed., 1965, the best general accounts of Yeats's work. *The Permanence of Yeats*, ed. James Hall and Martin Steinmann, 1950; *Yeats: A Collection of Critical Essays*, ed. John Unterecker, 1963; *In Excited Reverie*, ed. A. N. Jeffares and K. G. W. Cross, 1965; and *Critical Essays on W. B. Yeats*, ed. Richard Finneran, 1987, are four of several useful collections of critical essays. The most helpful commentaries are *A New Commentary on the Poems of W. B. Yeats*, 1984, and *A Commentary on The Collected Plays of W. B. Yeats*, 1975, both A. N. Jeffares. Three specialist critical studies of important areas of Yeats's work are *W. B. Yeats Self Critic: A Study of His Early Verse*, Thomas Parkinson, 1951, reprinted 1971 with *The Later Poetry* and a new foreword; *Between the Lines: W. B. Yeats's Poetry in the Making*, Jon Stallworthy, 1963, corrected 2nd imp., 1965; and *Swan and Shadow: Yeats's Dialogue with History*, Thomas R. Whitaker, 1964.

The first authorized biography was *W. B. Yeats, 1865–1939*, Joseph Hone, 2nd ed., 1962, and the most recent is *W. B. Yeats: A New Biography*, A. N. Jeffares, 1989. The best critical biography is *Yeats: The Man and the Masks*, Richard Ellmann, 1948; and *Yeats*, Frank Tuohy, 1976, supplements a straightforward narrative with many excellent illustrations.

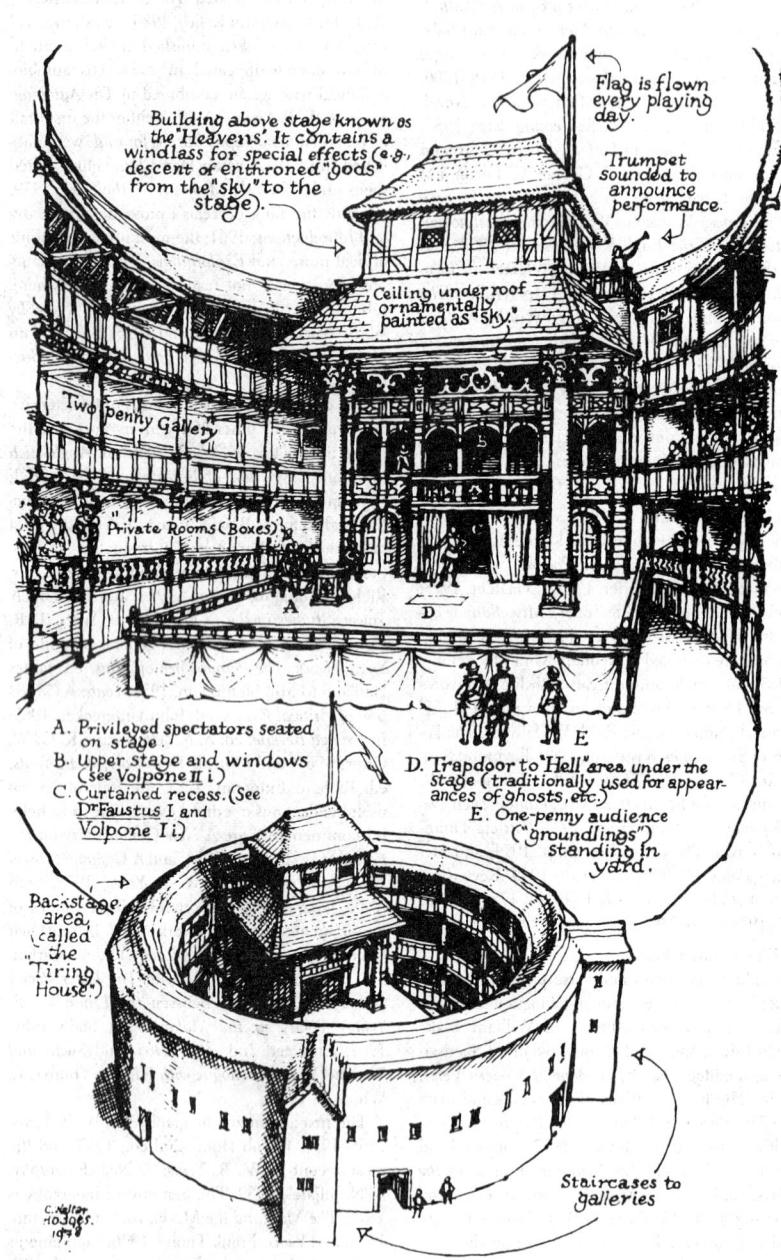

Building above stage known as the "Heavens". It contains a windlass for special effects (e.g. descent of enthroned "gods" from the "sky" to the stage).

Flag is flown every playing day.

Trumpet sounded to announce performance.

Ceiling under roof ornamentally painted as "sky".

Two penny Gallery

"Private Rooms (Boxes)

A. Privileged spectators seated on stage.
B. Upper stage and windows (see Volpone II i)
C. Curtained recess. (See Dr Faustus I and Volpone I i)

D. Trapdoor to "Hell" area under the stage (traditionally used for appearances of ghosts, etc.)
E. One-penny audience ("groundlings") standing in yard.

Backstage area, called the "Tiring House.")

Staircases to galleries

C. Walter Hodges 1948

2626

Ptolemy was a Roman astronomer of Greek descent, born in Egypt during the second century A.D.; after his death, for nearly fifteen hundred years his account of the design of the universe was accepted as standard. During that long period, the basic pattern underwent many detailed modifications and was fitted out with many astrological and pseudo-scientific trappings. But in essence Ptolemy's followers agreed in portraying the earth as the center of the universe, with the sun, planets, and fixed stars set in transparent spheres orbiting around it. In this scheme of things, as modified for Christian usage, Hell was usually placed under the earth's surface at the center of the cosmic globe, while Heaven, the abode of the blessed spirits, was in the outermost, uppermost circle, the empyrean. But in 1543 the Polish astronomer Copernicus proposed an alternative hypothesis—that the earth rotates around the sun, not vice versa; and despite theological opposition, observations with the new telescope and careful mathematical calculations insured ultimate acceptance of his view.

The map of the Ptolemaic universe represented here is a simplified version of a diagram in Peter Apian's *Cosmography* (1584). In such a diagram, the Firmament is the sphere that contained the fixed stars; the Crystalline Sphere, which contained no heavenly bodies, is a late innovation, included to explain certain anomalies in the observed movement of the heavenly bodies; and the Prime Mover is the sphere

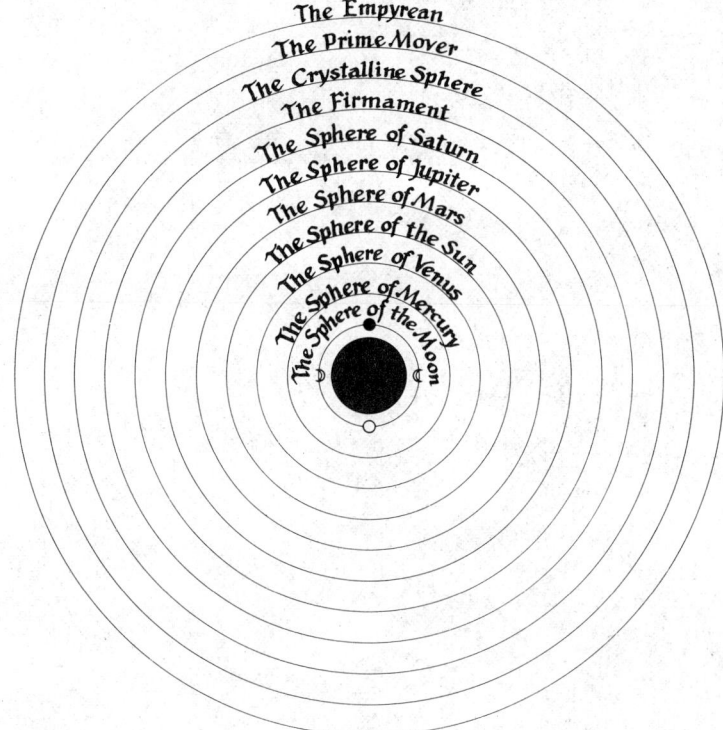

that, itself put into motion by God, imparts rotation around the earth to all the other spheres.

Milton, writing in the mid-seventeenth century, made use of two universes. The Copernican universe, though he alludes to it, was too large, formless, and unfamiliar to serve as the setting for the war between Heaven and Hell in *Paradise Lost*. He therefore adopted as his setting the Ptolemaic cosmos, but placed Heaven well outside this smaller earth-centered universe, Hell far beneath it, and assigned the vast middle space to Chaos.

British Money

Since 1971, British money has been calculated on the decimal system, with 100 pence to the pound; the pound has fluctuated from a bit more than 2 American dollars to virtual parity—whatever dollars may be worth. Before 1971, the pound consisted of 20 shillings, each containing 12 pence, thus 240 pence to the pound. In paper money the change has not been great; 5- and 10-pound notes constitute the mass of the bills under both the old and the new systems; nowadays, in addition, 20- and 50-pound notes have been added. But in the smaller coinage the change has been considerable and the simplification remarkable. Most notable is abolition of the shilling, which goes into retirement now with the mark (worth in its day two-thirds of a pound or 13 shillings 4 pence) and the angel (once worth 10 shillings but replaced by the 10-shilling note, now in its turn abolished). The guinea, an oddity of the old currency, amounted to a pound and a shilling; though it has not been minted since 1813, a very few quality items or prestige awards (like horse races) may still be quoted in guineas. Colloquially, a pound used to be a quid, a shilling a bob, sixpence a tanner, a penny, half-penny, or farthing a copper. The common signs were £ for pound, s. for shilling, d. for a penny (from Latin *denarius*). A sum would normally be written £2.19.3, i.e., 2 pounds, 19 shillings, 3 pence. That is Bloom's budget for June 16, 1904. In new currency, it would be about £2.96d.

Old	New
1 pound note	1 pound note
10 shilling (half-pound) note	50 pence
5 shilling (crown)	
2 ½ shilling (half crown)	
2 shilling (florin)	10 pence
1 shilling	5 pence
6 pence	
2 ½ pence	1 penny
2 pence	
1 penny	½ penny
½ penny	
¼ penny (farthing)	

What the pound was worth at any point in history is never easy to state. In the first part of the twentieth century, 1 pound equaled about 5 American dollars; but those dollars bought three or four times what 1990 dollars would. The value of the pound might be definable in terms of the goods and services it would purchase; but these too vary radically with special circumstances, wars, harvests, and the like. In a loose way, it's clear that money used to be worth much more than it is now. A Saxon penny was the biggest coin in general circulation; four of them would buy a

sheep. Peasants before the Black Death of the fourteenth century made 2 or 3
pence a day—an annual income of £3 or £4. At the modern ratio that would be
only $5 or so per annum. However incredibly low their standard of living, however
much they supplemented their cash income with produce from their own fields,
that figure is impossible: the pound must have been worth much more than it is
now, perhaps by a factor of several hundred. Hugh Latimer reports that in his day
(the early 1500s) it was a common saying, "Oh, he's a rich man, he's worth £500."
Probably he means, not fabulously, just comfortably rich; still, it's clear that the
pound was a solid sum of money, equal perhaps to 400 or 500 American dollars of
the modern era.

In Jonson's *Alchemist*, Subtle tells Face that as an honest servant he had been a
mere "livery-three-pound thrum"— that is, he had his uniform, food, and lodging,
plus £3 a year. By cheating on household expenses, he had built up over the years
"a pretty stock, some twenty marks," about £13. Of course, the comic point of all
this is the miserable sums involved in the lives of such squalid rascals. Forty pounds
a year in independent income (generally rents) was the minimum requirement for
a justice of the peace; it was also the sum fixed by King James at which a man
could be forced to accept knighthood. It marked the threshold of gentry, and we
must multiply it by 150 or 200 to get an equivalent in modern dollars. In 1661 that
good bourgeois Samuel Pepys, just after he began working for the navy, calculated
his worth at a modest £650; five years later, he was worth more than £6,000 and
his annual income was about £3,000—cause for complacency. Of course, he was
working for most of this income. Pepys was a rising official and would become a
very important one; but he never achieved a title or even knighthood because the
smell of commerce had never been washed from his money by possession of land.

On a far humbler level, Joseph Andrews (in Fielding's novel, published 1742)
worked as a footman in the house of Lady Booby for £8 a year; but he got his room,
board, and livery in addition, plus the occasional tip. Among the comfortable
classes again, Mr. Bennet of Jane Austen's *Pride and Prejudice* (1813) enjoyed an
income of £2,000 a year (but he had a family of five non-earning females to support, and the income ceased at his death). Mr. Bingley had £4,000 per year of his
own, Mr. Darcy close to £10,000; and this raises us close to the rarefied atmosphere
of the aristocracy. In his deepest degradation David Copperfield (of Dickens' 1850
novel) worked in the warehouse of Murdstone & Grinby for 6 or 7 shillings a week
(£15 to £18 a year). Mr. Murdstone paid extra for his lodging and laundry, but
even so the boy was bitterly impoverished, though he had only himself to feed.
When his father died, his mother was thought to be pretty well taken care of with
£105 a year, a little less than £9 per month. Only a few years later, Dorothea
Brooke of *Middlemarch* (1872) is more than easy with £700 per year of her own; if
she marries and has a son, he may inherit from her uncle as much as £3,000 per
year in addition. That is high plutocracy for the folk of Tipton parish; one may
estimate that Miss Brooke's pound is now worth between 20 and 50 American
dollars of 1990 vintage. (But we must recall that *Middlemarch*, though published
in 1872, is actually set about forty years earlier; over the interval, money had lost
a good deal of its value.) When Lady Bracknell, in Wilde's comedy *The Importance
of Being Earnest* (1895), questions Jack Worthing's financial status, she is pleased
if not impressed that he has seven or eight thousand (pounds) a year. But Lady
Bracknell is not only a snob, she is the parody of a snob. Jack has a country house
with about fifteen hundred acres attached to it, but it yields no income worth
talking about, and he also has a town house, but it is on the unfashionable side of
Belgrave Square. At the other end of the scale, when John Davidson wrote of the
horrors of being a clerk with a family at thirty bob a week, that stipend wouldn't
work out to much better than $1,500 to $3,000 of modern money. We see what
he means.

Across the centuries, it is evident that money diminished in value; it is equally apparent that in every era there's been a gap between the poor and the rich. What money was worth depended heavily on which of those classes you belonged to. It also depended on where you lived. London was always very expensive, and in the provinces (as is traditional everywhere) a small income went further. Finally, the value of money depended on the current rate of taxation. In the days of the Dane-geld (ancestor of the modern income tax), nobody was rich except the Danes. Pitt introduced the modern income tax in 1798 as a war measure, Peel in 1842 made it a routine part of government financing; and it is one reason why an income of £10,000, though it was glorious aristocratic luxury for Mr. Fitzwilliam Darcy and his Elizabeth, and was a respectable or a bit better income for Jack Worthing and his bride, represents nowadays little more than a standard of ignoble decency. For in addition to being heavily taxed, the pound's value in terms of marks, francs, yen, and the like, is sadly reduced.

Adapted from *The Land and Literature of England: A Historical Account*, Robert M. Adams (New York: Norton, 1983).

The British Baronage

The English monarchy is in principle hereditary, though at times during the middle ages the rules were subject to dispute. As a general thing, authority passes from father to elder son, to daughters in order of seniority if there is no son, to a brother if there are no children, and in default of direct descendants to collateral lines (cousins, nephews, nieces) in order of closeness. There have been breaks in the order of succession (1066, 1399, 1688), but so far as possible the usurpers always tried to paper over the break with a legitimate, i.e., a hereditary claim. When a queen succeeds to the throne and takes a husband, he does not become king unless he is in the line of blood succession; rather, he is named prince consort, as Albert was to Victoria—or on the other hand he may not, as Philip is not consort to Queen Elizabeth II. He may father kings, but is not one himself.

The original Saxon nobles were the king's thanes, ealdormen, or earls, who in return for booty, gifts, or landed estates provided the king with military service and counsel. William the Conqueror, arriving from France, where feudalism was fully developed, added largely to this group. Archbishops and bishops, abbots and priors, who frequently held their land from the king though they might hold their office from the pope, served as counselors and very often in secular offices as well, as royal administrators. In addition, as the king distributed the lands of his new kingdom, he also distributed dignities to men who became known collectively as "the baronage." "Baron" in its root meaning signifies simply "man," and barons were the king's men. As the title was common, a distinction was early made between greater and lesser barons, the former gradually assuming loftier and more impressive titles. The king, no longer duke of Normandy, created the first English duke in 1337. "Marquess," or "marquis," was created in 1385, and "viscount" in 1440 (the former pronounced "markwis," the latter "vyekount"); though it's the oldest title of all, an "earl" now comes, in order of dignity and precedence, between a marquess and a viscount; and the old term "baron" now designates a rank just below viscount. "Baronets," the title created in 1611, are marginal nobility, who sit in the House of Commons, not the Lords.

Kings and queens are addressed as "Your Majesty," princes and princesses as "Your Highness," the other hereditary nobility as "My Lord" or "Your Lordship." When a commoner is created a peer (always by the monarch), he may select his own title; thus Disraeli became earl of Beaconsfield after the town near which his house stood; Clement Attlee, prime minister from 1945 to 1951, became simply Earl Attlee. Byron was the sixth baron of that line, by birth; Tennyson was created first Baron Tennyson. Peerages (other than the recently created Life Peerages) descend by primogeniture; they are given to a man with right of succession, they are not incidental to tenure of land—though when a man is given a peerage, he is sometimes given a pension or an estate to sustain the dignity. The children, even of a duke, are commoners unless they are specifically granted some other title or inherit their father's title from him. (On the intricacies of proper address to such personages, it is advisable to consult—as the British often do themselves—*Debrett's Correct Form*, a handbook.) A peerage can be forfeited by act of attainder, as for example when a lord is convicted of treason; and, when forfeited, or lapsed for lack of a successor, can be bestowed on another family. Thus Robert Cecil was made in 1605 first earl of Salisbury in the third creation, the first creation dating from 1149, the second from 1337, the title having been in abeyance since 1539.

Scottish peers sat in the Parliament of Scotland, as English peers did in the

| The king and queen | (These are all of the royal line.) |
| Prince and princess | |

Duke and duchess	(These may or may not be of the
Marquess and marchioness	royal line, but are ordinarily
Earl and countess	remote from the succession.)
Viscount and viscountess	
Baron and baroness	
Baronet and lady	

Parliament of England, till at the Act of Union (1707) Scots peers were granted sixteen seats in the English House of Lords, to be filled by election. Similarly, Irish peers, when the Irish Parliament was abolished in 1801, were granted the right to elect twenty-eight of their number to the House of Lords in Westminister. (Now that the Republic of Ireland, or in Gaelic, Eire, is a separate nation, of course, this no longer applies.) For a genealogical guide through the tangled thickets of the aristocracy, see the classic compilation of Sir John Burke, known for brevity's sake as *Burke's Peerage*. The same author's *Landed Gentry* is popularly known in county society as "the stud book."

Below the hereditary peerage the chief title of honor is knight. Knighthood is not hereditary; it is generally a reward for services rendered. Though the word itself comes from Anglo-Saxon *cniht*, there seems to be some doubt whether knighthood amounted to much before the arrival of the Normans. The feudal system required military service as a condition of land tenure, and a man who came to serve his king at the head of an army of tenants required a title of authority and badges of identity—hence the title of knighthood and the coat of arms. During the Crusades, when men were far removed from their land (or had even sold it in order to go on crusade), more elaborate forms of fealty sprang up that soon expanded into the orders of knighthood. The Templars, Hospitallers, Knights of the Teutonic Order, Knights of Malta, and Knights of the Golden Fleece were but a few of these companionships; not all of them were available at all times in England.

Gradually, with the rise of centralized government and the decline of feudal tenures, military knighthood became obsolete, and the rank largely honorific— sometimes it even degenerated into a scheme of the royal government for making money. For hundreds of years after its establishment in the fourteenth century, the Order of the Garter was the only English order of knighthood, an exclusive courtly companionship. Then, during the late seventeenth, the eighteenth, and the nine-teenth centuries, a number of additional orders were created—the Thistle, Saint Patrick, the Bath, Saint Michael and Saint George, plus a number of special Victo-rian and Indian orders. They retain the terminology, ceremony, and dignity of knighthood, but the military implications are all vestigial.

A knight (Sir John Black) is addressed, using his first name, as "Sir John"; his wife, using the last name, is "Lady Black"—unless she is the daughter of an earl or nobleman of higher rank, when she will be "Lady Arabella." The female equiva-lent of a knight bears the title of "Dame." The Order of Merit, instituted by Edward VII, is an exclusive and very honorable order. The Distinguished Service Order and the Victoria Cross—DSO and VC—are high awards for military hero-ism, the VC the very highest. The OBE (Order of the British Empire) is awarded for services to the empire, either at home or abroad, by persons of either gender. It is but one of many special medals awarded for outstanding accomplishment in one form or another.

Adapted from *The Land and Literature of England: A Historical Account*, Robert M. Adams (New York: Norton, 1983).

The Royal Lines of England and Great Britain

England

SAXONS AND DANES

Egbert, king of Wessex	802–839
Ethelwulf, son of Egbert	839–858
Ethelbald, son of Ethelwulf	858–860
Ethelbert, second son of Ethelwulf	860–866
Ethelred I, third son of Ethelwulf	866–871
Alfred the Great, fourth son of Ethelwulf	871–899
Edward the Elder, son of Alfred	899–924
Athelstan the Glorious, son of Edward	924–940
Edmund I, third son of Edward	940–946
Edred, fourth son of Edward	946–955
Edwy the Fair, son of Edmund	955–959
Edgar the Peaceful, second son of Edmund	959–975
Edward the Martyr, son of Edgar	975–978
Ethelred II, the Unready, second son of Edgar	978–1016
Edmund II, Ironside, son of Ethelred II	1016–1016
Canute the Dane	1016–1035
Harold I, Harefoot, natural son of Canute	1035–1040
Hardecanute, son of Canute	1040–1042
Edward the Confessor, son of Ethelred II	1042–1066
Harold II, brother-in-law of Edward	1066–1066 (died in battle)

HOUSE OF NORMANDY

William I the Conqueror	1066–1087
William II, Rufus, third son of William I	1087–1100
Henry I, Beauclerc, youngest son of William I	1100–1135

HOUSE OF BLOIS

Stephen, son of Adela, daughter of William I	1135–1154

HOUSE OF PLANTAGENET

Henry II, son of Geoffrey Plantagenet by Matilda, daughter of Henry I	1154–1189
Richard I, Coeur de Lion, son of Henry II	1189–1199
John Lackland, son of Henry II	1199–1216
Henry III, son of John	1216–1272
Edward I, Longshanks, son of Henry III	1272–1307
Edward II, son of Edward I	1307–1327
Edward III of Windsor, son of Edward II	1327–1377
Richard II, grandson of Edward III	1377–1399

HOUSE OF LANCASTER

Henry IV, son of John of Gaunt, son of Edward III	1399–1413
Henry V, Prince Hal, son of Henry IV	1413–1422
Henry VI, son of Henry V	1422–1461 (deposed)

HOUSE OF YORK

Edward IV, great-great-grandson of Edward III	1461–1483
Edward V, son of Edward IV	1483–1483
Richard III, Crookback	1483–1485

HOUSE OF TUDOR

Henry VII, married daughter of Edward IV	1485–1509
Henry VIII, son of Henry VII	1509–1547
Edward VI, son of Henry VIII	1547–1553
Mary I, "Bloody," daughter of Henry VIII	1553–1558
Elizabeth I, daughter of Henry VIII	1558–1603

HOUSE OF STUART

James I (James VI of Scotland)	1603–1625
Charles I, son of James I	1625–1649 (executed)

COMMONWEALTH & PROTECTORATE

Council of State	1649–1653
Oliver Cromwell, Lord Protector	1653–1658
Richard Cromwell, son of Oliver	1658–1659 (resigned)

HOUSE OF STUART (RESTORED)

Charles II, son of Charles I	1660–1685
James II, second son of Charles I	1685–1688 (abdicated)

(INTERREGNUM, 11 DECEMBER 1688 TO 13 FEBRUARY 1689)

William III of Orange, by Mary, daughter of Charles I	1685–1701
and Mary II, daughter of James II	–1694
Anne, second daughter of James II	1702–1714

Great Britain

HOUSE OF HANOVER

George I, son of Elector of Hanover and Sophia, granddaughter of James I	1714–1727
George II, son of George I	1727–1760

George III, grandson of George II	1760–1820
George IV, son of George III	1820–1830
William IV, third son of George III	1830–1837
Victoria, daughter of Edward, fourth son of George III	1837–1901

HOUSE OF SAXE-COBURG AND GOTHA

Edward VII, son of Victoria	1901–1910

HOUSE OF WINDSOR (NAME ADOPTED 17 JULY 1917)

George V, second son of Edward VII	1910–1936
Edward VIII, eldest son of George V	1936–1936 (abdicated)
George VI, second son of George V	1936–1952
Elizabeth II, daughter of George VI	1952–

Religious Sects in England

Religious distinctions and denominations are important in British social history, hence deeply woven into the nation's literature. The numerous (over three hundred) British churches and sects divide along a scale from high to low, depending on the amount of authority they give to the church or the amount of liberty they concede to the individual conscience. At one end of the scale is the Roman Catholic church, asserting papal infallibility, universal jurisdiction, and the supreme importance of hierarchy as guide and intercessor. For political and social reasons, Catholicism struck deep roots in Ireland but in England was the object of prolonged, bitter hatred on the part of Protestants from the Reformation through the nineteenth century. The Established English (Anglican) Episcopal church has been the official national church since the sixteenth century; it enjoys the support (once direct and exclusive, now indirect and peripheral) of the national government. Its creed is defined by Thirty-Nine Articles, but these are intentionally vague, so there are numerous ways of adhering to the Church of England. Roughly and intermittently, the chief classes of Anglicans have been known as High Church (with its highest portion calling itself Anglo-Catholic); Broad Church, or Latitudinarian (when they get so broad that they admit anyone believing in God, they may be known as Deists, or some may leave the church altogether and be known as Unitarians); and Low Church, whose adherents may stay in the English church and yet come close to shaking hands with Presbyterians or Methodists. These various groups may be arranged, from the High down to the Low Church, in direct relation to the amount of ritual each prefers and in the degree of authority conceded to the upper clergy—and in inverse relation to the importance ascribed to a saving faith directly infused by God into an individual conscience.

All English Protestants who decline to subscribe to the English established church are classed as Dissenters or Nonconformists; for a time in the sixteenth and seventeenth centuries, they were also known as Puritans. (Nowadays, though Puritanism has less distinct theological meaning, it marks a distinct character type; because of his passionate emphasis on individual conscience and moral economy, George Bernard Shaw was a prototypical Puritan.) The Presbyterians model their church government on that established by John Calvin in the Swiss city of Geneva. It has no bishops, and therefore is more democratic for the clergy; but it gains energy by associating lay elders with clergymen in matters of social discipline and tends to be strict with the ungodly. From its first reformation the Scottish Kirk was fixed on the Presbyterian model. During the civil wars of the seventeenth century, a great many sects sprang up on the left wing of the Presbyterians, most of them touched by Calvinism but some rebelling against it; a few of these still survive. The Independents became our modern Congregationalists; the Quakers are still Quakers, as Baptists are still Baptists, though multiply divided. But many of the sects flourished and perished within the space of a few years. Among these now vanished groups were the Shakers (though a few groups still exist in America), the Seekers, the Ranters, the Anabaptists, the Muggletonians, the Fifth Monarchy Men, the Family of Love, the Sweet Singers of Israel, and many others, forgotten by all except scholars. During the eighteenth and nineteenth centuries, new sects arose, supplanting old ones; the Methodists, under John and Charles Wesley, became numerous and important, taking root particularly in Wales. (The three "subject" nationalities, Ireland, Scotland, and Wales, thus turned three different ways to avoid the Anglican church.) With the passage of time a small number of Swedenborgians sprang up, followers of the Swedish mystic Emanuel Swedenborg—to be followed by the Plymouth Brethren, Christian Scientists, Jehovah's Witnesses, and countless other nineteenth-century groups. All these sects constantly grow, shrink, split, and occasionally disappear as they succeed or fail in attracting new converts.

Within the various churches and sects, independent of them all but amazingly persistent, there has always survived a stream of esoteric or hermetic thought—a belief in occult powers, and sometimes in magic also, exemplified by the pseudo-sciences of astrology and alchemy but taking many other forms as well. From the mythical Egyptian seer Hermes Trismegistus through Paracelsus, Cornelius Agrippa, Giordano Bruno, Jakob Boehme, the society of Rosicrucians, and a hundred other shadowy figures, the line can be traced to William Blake and William Butler Yeats, who both in their different ways brought hermetic Protestantism close to its ultimate goal, a mystic church of a single consciousness, poised within its mind-elaborated cosmos.

Poetic Forms and
Literary Terminology

RHYTHM AND METER

Verse is generally distinguished from prose as a more compressed and more regularly rhythmic form of statement. This approximate truth underlines the importance of **meter** in poetry, as the means by which rhythm is measured and described.

In the classical languages, meter was established on a **quantitative** basis, by the regular alternation of long and short syllables (that is, syllables classified according to the time taken to pronounce them). Outside of a few experiments (and the songs of Thomas Campion), this system has never proved congenial to English, which distinguishes, instead, between **stressed** and **unstressed**, or accented and unaccented syllables. Two varieties of accented stress may be distinguished. On the one hand, there is the natural stress pattern of words themselves; *sỳllable* is accented on the first syllable, *deplòrable* on the second, and so on. Then there is the sort of stress that indicates rhetorical emphasis. If the sentence "You went to Greece?" is given a pronounced accent on the last word, it implies "Greece (of all places)?" If the accent falls on the first word, it implies "you (of all people)?" The meter of poetry—that is, its rhythm—is ordinarily built up out of a regular recurrence of accents, whether established as **word accents** or **rhetorical accents;** once started in the reader's mind, it has (like all rhythm) a persistent effect of its own.

The unit that is repeated to give steady rhythm to a poem is called a **poetic foot;** in English it usually consists of accented and unaccented syllables in one of five fairly simple patterns:

The **iambic foot** (or **iamb**) consists of an unstressed followed by a stressed syllable, as in *unìte, repeàt,* or *insìst.* Most English verse falls naturally into the iambic pattern.

The **trochaic foot** (**trochee**) inverts this order; it is a stressed followed by an unstressed syllable—for example, *ùnit, rèaper,* or *ìnstant.*

The **anapestic foot** (**anapest**) consists of two unstressed syllables followed by a stressed syllable, as in *intercède, disarrànged,* or *Cameròon.*

The **dactylic foot** (**dactyl**) consists of a stressed syllable followed by two unstressed syllables, as in *Wàshington, Ècuador,* or *àpplejack.*

The **spondaic foot** (**spondee**) consists of two successive stressed syllables, as in *heartbreak, headline,* or *Kashmir.*

In all the examples above, word accent and the quality of the metrical foot coincide exactly. But the metrical foot may well consist of several words, or, on the other hand, one word may well consist of several metrical feet. *Phòtolithògraphy* consists of two excellent dactyls in a single word; *dàrk and with spòts on it,* though it consists of six words rather than one, is also two dactyls—not quite such good ones. When we read a piece of poetry with the intention of discovering its underlying metrical pattern, we are said to scan it—that is, we go through it line by line, indicating by conventional signs which are the accented and which the unaccented syllables within the feet (the ictus generally designates accented, the morǎ unaccented syllables). We also count the number of feet in each line, or, formally, **verse** (from Latin *versus*, which means one "row" of metrical feet). Verse lengths are conventionally described in terms derived from the Greek:

    Monometer: one foot (of rare occurrence)
    Dimeter: two feet (also rare)
    Trimeter: three feet
    Tetrameter: four feet
    Pentameter: five feet
    Hexameter: six feet (six iambic feet make an **Alexandrine**)
    Heptameter: seven feet (also rare)

Samuel Johnson's little parody of simpleminded poets would thus be scanned this way:

> Ĭ pùt m̆y hàt ŭpòn m̆y hèad
> Ănd wàlked ĭntò the Strànd,
> Ănd thère Ĭ mèt ănŏthĕr màn
> Whŏse hàt wăs ìn hĭs hànd.

The poem is iambic in rhythm, alternating tetrameter and trimeter in verse length. The fact that it scans so nicely is, however, no proof that it is good poetry. Quite the contrary. Many of poetry's most subtle effects are achieved by establishing an underlying rhythm and then varying it by means of a whole series of devices, some dramatic and expressive, others designed simply to lend variety and interest to the verse. A well-known sonnet of Shakespeare's *(116)* begins,

> Let me not to the marriage of true minds
> Admit impediments. Love is not love
> Which alters when it alteration finds,
> Or bends with the remover to remove.

It is perfectly possible, if one crushes all one's sensitivities, to read the first line of this poem as mechanical iambic pentameter:

> Lĕt mè nŏt tò thĕ màrriăge ŏf trŭe mìnds.

But of course nobody ever reads it that way, except to make a point; read with normal English accent and some sense of what it is saying, the line would probably form a pattern something like this:

> Lèt mĕ nŏt tŏ thĕ màrriăge ŏf trùe mìnds,

which is neither pentameter nor in any way iambic. The second line is a little more iambic, but, read for expression, falls just as far short of pentameter:

> Ădmìt ĭmpèdĭmeńts. Lòve ĭs nŏt lòve.

Only in the third and fourth lines of the sonnet do we get verses that read as well as scan like five iambic feet.

    The fact is that perfectly regular metrical verse is easy to write and dull to read. Among the devices in common use for varying too regular a pattern are, for instance, the insertion of a trochaic foot among iambics, especially at the opening of a line, where the soft first syllable of the iambic foot often needs stiffening (see line 1 of the sonnet above); the more or less free addition of extra unaccented syllables; and the use of **caesura**, or strong grammatical pause within a line (conventionally indicated, in scanning, by the sign ‖). The second line of the sonnet above is a good example of caesura:

Admit impediments. || Love is not love.

The strength of the caesura, and its placing in the line, may be varied to produce striking variations of effect. More broadly, the whole relation between the poem's sound- and rhythm-patterns and its pattern as a sequence of assertions (phrases, clauses, sentences) may be manipulated by the poet. Sometimes the statements fit neatly within the lines, so that each line ends with a strong mark of punctuation; they are then known as **end-stopped lines.** Sometimes the sense flows over the ends of the lines, creating **run-on lines;** this process is also known, from the French, as **enjambment** (literally, "straddling").

End-stopped lines (Marlowe, *Hero and Leander,* lines 45–48):

> So lovely fair was Hero, Venus' nun,
> As Nature wept, thinking she was undone,
> Because she took more from her than she left
> And of such wondrous beauty her bereft.

Run-on lines (Keats, *Endymion* 1.89–93):

> Full in the middle of this pleasantness
> There stood a marble altar, with a tress
> Of flowers budded newly; and the dew
> Had taken fairy fantasies to strew
> Daisies upon the sacred sward, . . .

Following the example of such poets as Blake, Rimbaud, and Whitman, many poets of the twentieth century have undertaken to write what is called **free verse**— that is, verse which has neither a fixed metrical foot nor (consequently) a fixed number of feet in its lines, but which depends for its rhythm on a pattern of cadences, or the rise and fall of the voice in utterance. All freedom in art is of course relative; free verse, with its special aptitude for metrical variety and nervous, colloquial phrasing—its total responsiveness, in other words, to its subject matter—has so successfully established itself that it is now widely recognized as a new and rather demanding form of artistic discipline.

SENSE AND SOUND

The very words of which poetic lines—whether free or traditional—are composed cause them to have different sounds and produce different effects. Polysyllables, being pronounced fast, often cause a line to move swiftly; monosyllables, especially when heavy and requiring distinct accents, may cause it to move heavily, as in Milton's famous line (*Paradise Lost* 2.621):

> Rocks, caves, lakes, fens, bogs, dens, and shades of death.

Poetic assertions are often dramatized and reinforced by means of **alliteration**— that is, the use of several nearby words or stressed syllables beginning with the same consonant. When Shakespeare writes (*Sonnet 64*),

> Ruin hath taught me thus to ruminate
> That Time will come and take my love away,

the rich, round, vague echoes of the first line contrast most effectively with the sharp anxiety and directness of the alliterative *t*'s in the second. When Dryden starts *Absalom and Achitophel* with that wicked couplet,

> In pious times, ere priestcraft did begin,
> Before polygamy was made a sin,

the satiric undercutting is strongly reinforced by the triple alliteration that links "*pious*" with "*priestcraft*" and "*polygamy*."

Assonance, or repetition of the same or similar vowel sounds within a passage (usually in accented syllables), also serves to enrich it, as in two lines from Keats's *Ode on Melancholy:*

> For shade to shade will come too drowsily,
> And drown the wakeful anguish of the soul.

It is clear that the round, hollow tones of "drowsily," repeated in "drown" and darkening to the full *o*-sound of "soul," have much to do with the effect of the passage. A related device is **consonance,** or the repetition of a pattern of consonants with changes in the intervening vowels—for example: *linger, longer, languor; rider, reader, raider, ruder.*

Direct verbal imitation of natural sounds (known as **onomatopoeia**) has been much attempted, from Virgil's galloping horse—

> *Quadrupedante putrem sonitu quatit ungula campum—*

to Tennyson's account, in *The Princess,* of

> The moan of doves in immemorial elms,
> And murmuring of innumerable bees.

Often ingeniously exploited as a side effect, onomatopoeia is essentially a trick, with about the same value in poetry as it has in music.

RHYME AND STANZA

Rhyme consists of a repetition of accented sounds in words, usually those falling at the end of verse lines. If the rhyme sound is the very last syllable of the line (*rebound, sound*), the rhyme is called **masculine;** if the accented syllable is followed by an unaccented syllable (*hounding, bounding*), the rhyme is called **feminine.** Rhymes amounting to three or more syllables, like forced rhymes, generally have a comic effect in English, and have been freely used for this purpose, e.g., by Byron (*intellectual, henpecked-you-all*). Rhymes occurring within a single line are called **internal;** for instance, the Mother Goose rhyme "Mary, Mary, quite contrary," or from Coleridge's *Ancient Mariner* ("We were the first that ever burst / Into that silent sea"). **Eye rhymes** are words used as rhymes that look alike but actually sound different (for example, *alone, done; remove, love*); **off rhymes** (sometimes called **partial, imperfect,** or **slant rhymes**) are occasionally the result of pressing exigencies or lack of skill, but are also, at times, used deliberately by modern poets for special effects. For instance, a poem by Wilfred Owen (*Strange Meeting*) contains such "rhymes" as *years / yours* or *tigress / progress.* Owen called these pairings "pararhymes"; they are varieties of assonance.

Blank verse is unrhymed iambic pentameter; until the recent advent of free verse, it was the only unrhymed measure to achieve general popularity in English. Though first used by the earl of Surrey in translating Virgil's *Aeneid*, blank verse was during the sixteenth century employed primarily in plays; *Paradise Lost* was one of the first nondramatic poems in English to use it. But Milton's authority and his success were so great that during the eighteenth and nineteenth centuries blank verse came to be used for a great variety of discursive, descriptive, and philosophical poems—besides remaining the standard metrical form for epics. Thomson's *Seasons*, Cowper's *Task*, Wordsworth's *Prelude*, and Tennyson's *Idylls of the King* were all written in blank verse.

A **stanza** is a recurring unit of a poem, consisting of a number of verses. Certain poems (for example, Dryden's *Alexander's Feast*) have stanzas comprising a variable number of verses, of varying lengths. Others are more regular, hence easier to describe.

The simplest form of stanza is the **couplet**; it is two lines rhyming together. A single couplet considered in isolation is sometimes called a **distich**; when it expresses a complete thought, ending with a terminal mark of punctuation, it is called a **closed couplet.** The development of very regular end-stopped couplets in the mid-seventeenth century, their use in so-called heroic tragedies, and their consequent acquisition of the name **heroic couplets** are described in the introduction to The Early Seventeenth Century (p. 571). The heroic couplet was the principal form of English neoclassical style.

Another traditional and challenging form of couplet is the **tetrameter, or four-beat couplet.** All rhymed couplets are hard to manage without monotony; and since, in addition, a four-beat line is hard to divide by caesura without splitting it into two tick-tock dimeters, tetrameter couplets have posed a perpetual challenge to poets, and still provide an admirable finger-exercise for aspiring versifiers. A model of tetrameter couplets managed with marvelous variety, complexity, and expressiveness is Marvell's *To His Coy Mistress*:

> Thou by the Indian Ganges' side
> Shouldst rubies find; I by the tide
> Of Humber would complain. I would
> Love you ten years before the Flood,
> And you should, if you please, refuse
> Till the conversion of the Jews.

English has not done much with rhymes grouped in threes, but has borrowed from Italian the form known as **terza rima,** in which Dante composed his *Divine Comedy*. This form consists of linked groups of three rhymes according to the following pattern: *aba bcb cdc ded,* etc. Shelley's *Ode to the West Wind* is composed in stanzas of *terza rima,* the poem as a whole ending with a couplet.

Quatrains are stanzas of four lines; the lines usually rhyme alternately, *abab,* or in the second and fourth lines, *abcb.* When they alternate tetrameter and trimeter lines, as in Johnson's little poem about men in hats (above), or as in *Sir Patrick Spens,* they are called **ballad stanza.** Dryden's *Annus Mirabilis* and Gray's *Elegy Written in a Country Churchyard* are in **heroic quatrains**; these rhyme alternately, and employ five-stress iambic verse throughout. Tennyson used for *In Memoriam* a tetrameter quatrain rhymed *abba,* and FitzGerald translated *The Rubáiyát of Omar Khayyám* into a pentameter quatrain rhymed *aaba;* but these forms have not been very generally adopted.

Chaucer's *Troilus and Criseide* is the premier example in English of **rhyme royal,** a seven-line iambic pentameter stanza consisting essentially of a quatrain dovetailed onto two couplets, according to the rhyme scheme *ababbcc* (the fourth line serves both as the final line of the quatrain and as the first line of the first couplet). Closely akin to rhyme royal, but differentiated by an extra *a*-rhyme between the two *b*-rhymes, is **ottava rima,** that is, an eight-line stanza rhyming *abababcc.* As its name suggests, ottava rima is of Italian origin; it was first used in English by Wyatt. Its final couplet, being less prepared for than in rhyme royal, and usually set off as a separate verbal unit, has a special witty snap to it, for which Byron found good use in *Don Juan.*

The longest and most intricate stanza generally used for narrative purposes in English is that devised by Edmund Spenser for *The Faerie Queene.* The **Spenser-**

ian stanza has nine lines rhyming *ababbcbcc*; the first eight lines are pentameter, the last line an Alexandrine. Slow-moving, intricate of pattern, and demanding in its rhyme scheme (the *b*-sound recurs four times, the *c*-sound three), the Spenserian stanza has nonetheless appealed widely to poets seeking a rich and complicated metrical form. Keats's *Eve of St. Agnes* and Shelley's *Adonais* are brilliantly successful nineteenth-century examples of its use.

The **sonnet,** originally a stanza of Italian origin that has developed into an independent lyric form, is usually defined nowadays as fourteen lines of iambic pentameter. None of the elements in this definition is absolute and in earlier centuries there were sonnets in hexameters (the first of Sidney's *Astrophil and Stella*), and sonnets of as many as twenty lines (Milton's *On the New Forcers of Conscience*). Most, however, approximate the definition. The different varieties—Petrarchan, Shakespearean, and Spenserian—are described in the introduction to The Sixteenth-Century (p. 253). Most Elizabethan sonnets dealt with courtly love; and some poets, like Sidney, Spenser, and Shakespeare, imitated Petrarch in grouping together their sonnets dealing with a particular lady or situation. A neutral word for these gatherings is **sonnet sequences;** the extent to which they tell a sequential story, and the extent to which such stories are autobiographical, vary greatly. Since Elizabethan times, the sonnet has been applied to a wide range of subject matters—religious, political, satiric, moral, and philosophic.

In blank verse or irregularly rhymed verse, where stanzaic divisions do not exist or are indistinct, the poetry sometimes falls into **verse paragraphs,** which are in effect divisions of sense like prose paragraphs. This division can be clearly seen in Milton's *Lycidas* and *Paradise Lost*. An intermediate form, clearly stanzaic but with stanzas of varying patterns of line-length and rhyme, is illustrated by Spenser's *Epithalamion*; in this instance, the division into stanzas is reinforced by **a refrain,** which is simply a line repeated at the end of each stanza. Ballads also customarily have refrains; for example, the refrain of *Lord Randall* is

> mother, make my bed soon,
> For I'm weary wi' hunting, and fain wald lie down.

FIGURATIVE LANGUAGE

The act of bringing words together into rich and vigorous poetic lines is complex and demanding, chiefly because so many variables require control. There is the "thought" of the lines, their verbal texture, their emotional resonance, the developing perspective of the reader—all these to be managed at once. One of the poet's chief resources toward this end is figurative language. Here, as in matters of meter, one may distinguish a great variety of devices, some of which we use in everyday speech without special awareness of their names and natures. When we say someone eats "like a horse" or "like a bird," we are using a **simile,** that is, a comparison marked out by a specific word of likening—"like" or "as." When we omit the word of comparison but imply a likeness—as in the sentence "That hog has guzzled all the champagne"—we are making use of **metaphor.** The **epic simile,** frequent in epic poetry, is an extended simile in which the thing compared is described as an object in its own right, beyond its point of likeness with the main subject. Milton starts to compare Satan to Leviathan, but concludes his simile with the story of a sailor who moored his ship by mistake, one night, to a whale (*Paradise Lost* 1.200–208). Metaphors and similes have been complexly but usefully distinguished according to their special effects; they may be, for instance, violent, comic, degrading, decorative, or ennobling.

When we speak of "forty head of cattle" or ask someone to "lend a hand" with a job, we are using **synecdoche,** a figure that substitutes the part for the whole. When we speak of a statement coming "from the White House," or a man much interested in "the turf," we are using **metonymy,** or the substitution of one term for another with which it is closely associated. **Antithesis** is a device for placing opposing ideas in grammatical parallel, as, for example, in the following passage from Pope's *Rape of the Lock* (5.25–30), where there are more examples of antithesis than there are lines:

> But since, alas! frail beauty must decay,
> Curled or uncurled, since locks will turn to gray;
> Since painted, or not painted, all shall fade,
> And she who scorns a man must die a maid;
> What then remains but well our power to use,
> And keep good humor still whate'er we lose?

Irony is a verbal device that implies an attitude quite different from (and often opposite to) that which is literally expressed. When Eliot writes, in *Whispers of Immortality*, that "Grishkin is nice," the adjective is carefully chosen to let an ironic grimace of distaste appear. And when Donne "proves," in *The Canonization*, that he and his mistress are going to found a new religion of love, he seems to be inviting us to take a subtly ironic attitude toward religion as well as love.

Because it is easy to see through, **hyperbole**, or willful exaggeration, is a favorite device of irony—which is not to say that it may not be "serious" as well. When she hears that a young man is "dying for love" of her, a sensible girl does not accept this statement literally, but it may convey a serious meaning to her nonetheless. The **pun**, or play on words (known to the learned, sometimes, as **paronomasia**), may also be serious or comic in intent; witness, for example, the famous series of puns in Donne's *Hymn to God the Father*. **Oxymoron** is a figure of flat contradiction—for instance, Milton's famous description of hell as containing "darkness visible" (*Paradise Lost* 1.63). A **paradox** is a statement that seems absurd but turns out to have rational meaning after all, usually in some unexpected sense; Donne speaks of fear being great courage and high valor (*Satire* 3, line 16), and turns out to mean that fear of God is greater courage than any earthly bravery. A **conceit** is a far-fetched and ingenious comparison. Writing in the fourteenth century, the Italian poet Petrarch popularized a great number of conceits handy for use in love poetry, and readily adapted by his English imitators. Wyatt, for example, is using **Petrarchan conceits** when he compares love to a warrior, or the lover's state to that of a storm-tossed ship; and a hundred other sonneteers developed the themes of the lady's stony heart, incendiary glances, and so forth. On the other hand, the **metaphysical conceit** was a more intellectualized, many-leveled comparison, giving a strong sense of the poet's ingenuity in overcoming obstacles—for instance, Donne's comparison of separated lovers to the legs of a compass (*A Valediction: Forbidding Mourning*) or Herbert's comparison of devotion to a pulley, in the poem of that name.

Images are often described as "mental pictures"; it is more accurate to say that they are verbal representations of something capable of being visualized; some readers form such mental pictures, and respond to them, more than others. Images not only convey what things look like, but direct us, by their pattern of associated and involved feelings, in our reactions to what is being represented. Indeed, there may be such a weight of meaning or feeling behind the image that the verbal picture itself becomes transparent and its "meaning" becomes primary. Abstract ideas can get attached to specific images—water, snake, bird, sun, worm, lion, whatever—in a multitude of ways, of which the reader need sometimes only be reminded. Of course the poet can also be arbitrary about it, letting the reader know simply that Redcrosse "stands for" Holiness and Archimago "stands for" Hypocrisy. If that's as far as it goes, we have a primitive variety of **allegory** (see below). But the relation between the tenor of the image (its abstract meaning) and the vehicle (the concrete picture) can be much more indefinite and insubstantial.

If the poet mentions a peacock, he may or may not intend his reader to think of immortality, because the unfolding of the peacock's tail and the opening of its "eyes" have traditionally suggested the rebirth of the soul after death. If that is the way the image works, then it is a **symbol**. Or again, the poet who mentions a fish may well intend the reader to think of Christ. This isn't because of any similarity between the fish and Christ; the identification depends on a mildly esoteric bit of information, that the Greek word for fish, *ichthys*, forms an anagram of the Greek words for "Jesus Christ, Son of God, Savior." When the connection between tenor and vehicle is arbitrary, or involves the elements of a puzzle, the image may be referred to as an **emblem**. In the sixteenth and seventeenth centuries, emblems often took the form of puzzling little drawings, the meaning of which was explained in appended verses: for an example see the emblem prefixed to Richard Crashaw's poem *To the Countess of Denbigh*.

  Personification is the attribution of human qualities to an inanimate object (for example, the Sea) or an abstract concept (Freedom); a special variety of it is called (in a term of John Ruskin's invention) the **pathetic fallacy**. When we speak of leaves "dancing" or a lake "smiling," we attribute human traits to nonhuman objects. Ruskin thought this was false and therefore "morbid"; modern criticism tends to view the practice as artistically and morally neutral. A more formal and abstract variety of personification is **allegory,** in which a narrative (such as *Pilgrim's Progress*) is constructed by representing general concepts (Faithfulness, Sin, Despair) as persons. A **fable** (like *The Nun's Priest's Tale*) represents beasts behaving like humans; a **parable** is a brief story, or simply an observation, with strong moral application; and an **exemplum** is a story told to illustrate a point in a sermon. A special series of devices, nearly obsolete today, used to be available to poets who could count on readers trained in the classics. These were the devices of **classical epithet** and **allusion**. In their simplest form, the classic myths used to provide a repertoire of agreeable stage properties, and a convenient shorthand for expressing emotional attitudes. Picturesque creatures like centaurs, satyrs, and sphinxes, heroes and heroines like Hector and Helen, and the whole pantheon of Olympic deities could be used to make ready reference to a great many aspects of human nature. One does not have to explain the problems of a man who is "cleaning the Augean stables"; if he is afflicted with an "Achilles' heel," or is assailing "Hydra-headed difficulties," his state is clear. These epithets, or descriptive phrases, making reference to mythological stories, suggest in a phrase situations that would normally require cumbersome explanations. Conceivably other mythologies might have served the same end in analogous ways. But because they could be taken for granted as the common possession of all educated readers, the classic myths entered into English literature as early as Chaucer and are only now passing away as a viable system of allusions. In poets like Spenser and Milton, classical allusion becomes a kind of enormously learned game, in which the poet seeks to make his points as indirectly as possible. For instance, Spenser writes in the *Epithalamion,* lines 328–329:

> Lyke as when Jove with fayre Alcmena lay,
> When he begot the great Tirynthian groome.

The mere mention of Alcmena in the first line suggests, to the knowing reader, Hercules; Spenser's problem in the second line is to find a way of referring to him that is neither redundant nor heavy-handed. "Tirynthian" reminds us of his long connection with the city of Tiryns, stretching our minds (as it were) across his whole career; and "groome" compresses references to a man-child, a servant, and a bridegroom, all of which apply to different aspects of Hercules' history. Thus, far from simply avoiding redundancy, Spenser has enriched the whole texture of his verse, thought, and feeling by his gift for precise classical epithet.

Within the broad periods it is customary to group in **schools** writers who show common stylistic traits or thematic concerns. Whether they considered themselves a group doesn't much matter. None of the **Romantic poets** knew they were being romantic, although Hazlitt, Shelley, and other writers of the time recognized shared features that they called "the spirit of the age." The followers of Spenser are known as **Spenserians;** they knew they liked Spenser, but didn't realize that made them a group. **Cavalier** poets are set decisively apart from **Metaphysical** poets, though pretty surely none of the two-dozen-odd men involved knew that was what they were. And so with the **Gothic novelists,** and the so-called **Graveyard School** of the eighteenth century, so with the modern surrealists. These schools are generally grouped, defined, and named by scholars and critics after the event. Use of a common form or subject matter constitutes a more superficial similarity than use of a common style, common techniques, or common philosophical backgrounds. But literary history, being nothing if not pragmatic, makes use of all sorts of common denominators.

Intellectual affinities have led some writers to be classified under the names of the philosophical schools of Greece and Rome. These are chiefly the **Epicureans,** who specify that the aim of life and the source of value is pleasure; the **Stoics,** who emphasize stern virtue and the dignified endurance of what cannot be avoided; and the **Skeptics,** who doubt that anything can be known for sure. These categories are useful as capsule descriptions, but they aren't very tidy, as they overlap one another and cut across other categories. Dryden is an author strongly tinged with skepticism, but many of his poems suggest an unabashed epicureanism. *The Vanity of Human Wishes*, by Samuel Johnson, is the classic poem in English of stoic philosophy, but it also expresses a particularly strong coloring of Christian humanism (see the introduction to The Restoration and the Eighteenth Century, p. 819).

Plato and **Aristotle,** as they summarized contrasting attitudes toward existence, are often used to define the outlook of writers. Both were prolific writers of enormous range and complexity, but in literary contexts their names most often define attitudes toward reality. Aristotle tended to find reality, not exclusively but primarily, in concrete and particular substances, which he brilliantly categorized and generalized. Plato tended to place reality in abstract ideal forms, of which the concrete things we experience in daily life are but partial and shadowy manifestations. During the Middle Ages, many Dominican friars, of whom St. Thomas Aquinas is best known, tended to be **Aristotelian** in their assumptions and in the structure of their logic; St. Bonaventura, among the Franciscans, was more strongly tinged with a **Platonism** that he derived largely from Saint Augustine. During the Renaissance Spenser, and during the Romantic period Shelley, were **Platonists** or **Neoplatonists.** (A Neoplatonist is a Platonist diluted with other world-views—perhaps Pythagorean mysticism, perhaps Christian theology, perhaps Aristotelian thought itself. In a narrower sense, the term is applied to philosophers writing in the tradition of Plotinus [3rd century A.D.], who held that all things in the world, spiritual and material, "emanate," or flow out, from the "Absolute," or the "One"—the single source of all truth, goodness, and beauty.) **Aristotelianism,** as it is more commonsensical, had faded by Spenser's time to the common teaching of the schools, and by Shelley's time to the practical, pragmatic materialism of everyday life.

The following section groups together various sets of frequently used and closely related literary terms in an effort to discriminate and define them.

Allegory, Symbol, Emblem, Type. Allegory is an extended metaphorical narrative in which a figure (say, Spenser's Redcrosse Knight) stands for a specific quality (Holiness). A **symbol** may have several different meanings, which typically grow out of its relation to other symbols, as in the twenty-odd poems of Yeats that allude to the rose. An **emblem,** in the sixteenth and seventeenth centuries, was an enigmatic picture with a motto and an explanatory verse attached. In modern usage, an emblem is a visible object representing an abstract quality, as a dove is the emblem of peace. A **type** is a historical figure who prefigures another and later figure, as (in some Christian interpretations) Moses in liberating the children of Israel was thought to prefigure Christ in freeing men from Satan.

Baroque and **Mannerist** are terms imported into literary study from the history of art, and applied by analogy. Michelangelo is a **baroque** artist; he holds great masses in powerful dynamic tension, his style is heavily ornamented and restless. In these respects he is sometimes compared to Milton. El Greco is a **mannerist,** whose gaunt and distorted figures often seem to be laboring under great spiritual stress, whose light seems to be focused in spots against a dark background. He has been compared to Donne. Analogies of this sort are occasionally suggestive, but they must be carefully handled to avoid degenerating into parallels that are forced and nominal rather than substantial.

Bathos. See **Pathos, Bathos, and the Sublime.**

Burlesque and **Mock Heroic** differ in that the former makes its subject mean and absurd by directly cutting it down, the latter makes its subject ludicrous by inflating it. In Pope's mock-heroic *Dunciad,* the figure of Dulness (Colley Cibber) is given inappropriately heroic dimensions; in Butler's burlesque *Hudibras,* the knightly hero is characterized by low and vulgar attributes, and persistently engages in inappropriately low behavior. Burlesque contributed to the development of the English novel; and during the nineteenth century, when formal drama tended to be stagy and melodramatic, a vigorous burlesque stage flourished in England, making fun of the classics. See **Imitation and Parody.**

Catastrophe and **Catharsis.** The **catastrophe** is the conclusion of a play; the word means "down-turning," and death may be the catastrophe of one play, as marriage is of another. **Catharsis** is the purging (of fear, pity, or perhaps guilt) that Aristotle thought the special effect of tragedy.

Chiasmus and **Zeugma.** **Chiasmus** is an inversion of the word order in two parallel phrases: "Strong without rage, without o'erflowing full." **Zeugma** is the use of a single verb or adjective to control two nouns: "Albert lost his shirt and his temper."

Classic and **Neoclassic.** See **Gothic, Classic, Neoclassic.**

Convention and **Tradition. Conventions** are agreed-upon artistic procedures peculiar to an art form. None of Shakespeare's contemporaries spoke blank verse in everyday life, but characters in his plays do, and the audience accepts it—as the audience at an opera accepts that characters will sing arias to express their feelings, something that few of us do in everyday life. A **tradition** is a particular way of viewing or representing things; it generally includes a great many conventions. Often thought of as a dead weight to be overcome by "originality," tradition (since an important essay by T. S. Eliot) is now more often recognized as an active energy, working to enrich an art form that makes knowing use of it by playing variations on it.

Didactic poetry teaches a lesson, generally practical. The eighteenth century, for example, produced didactic poetry on the wool trade, field sports, health practices, and the sexuality of plants.

Dramatic irony and **Dramatic monologue** are quite different devices. In **dramatic irony** a stage character says something that has one meaning for him and for the onstage person he is addressing, but quite another for the audience. The **dramatic monologue** is a poetic form associated with Robert Browning and discussed in the introduction to that poet's work (pp. 1976–82); it presents a character as revealed unintentionally by his own words.

Eclogue. See **Pastorals.**

Emblem. See **Allegory, Symbol, Emblem, Type.**

Epigram, Epigraph, Epitaph. An **epigram** is a short, witty statement in verse or prose. "Italy is a geographical expression," said Count Metternich. An **epigraph** is an apposite quotation placed at the beginning of a book or a section of it. An **epitaph** is a brief statement about one deceased, written originally on that person's tombstone.

Eulogy and **Elegy.** The **eulogy** is a work of praise, in prose or poetry, for a person either very distinguished or recently dead; in its usual modern sense, an **elegy** is a poem of lamentation for the dead. In Greek and Latin poetry, elegies were poems written in alternating pentameters and hexameters, called elegiac meter. They could deal with a broad variety of topics, and English elegies also tended to be discursive poems on meditative themes. Donne, following his Roman predecessors, wrote some elegies that are jocose, even bawdy.

Euphemism and **Euphuism. Euphemism,** or "fine speech," is a verbal device for avoiding an unpleasant concept or expression, as when, instead of saying a person "died," we say he "passed away." Euphues was the hero of a prose romance (published 1579–80) by John Lyly; his adventures are recounted in a mannered style full of puns, alliteration, and antithetical "points." Under the name of **Euphuism** this courtly style enjoyed a brief vogue.

Fancy and **Imagination.** The distinction between these two mental powers greatly exercised the early Romantic poets. **Fancy** (a word directly derived by contraction from "fantasy") was defined by Coleridge as essentially the power of combining several known properties into new combinations; **imagination,** on the other hand, was the faculty of using those known properties to create a whole that is entirely new.

Folios, Quartos, etc., are terms used to specify the size of book pages. To make a **folio,** a sheet of paper (14″ x 20″ or larger) is folded just once (producing thereby four pages); **quartos** are folded twice (producing eight pages). Shakespeare's plays were first printed in quartos (often in several different editions), but when they were collected together, in 1623, they appeared as the First Folio.

Genre, Decorum. A **genre** is an established literary form, such as stage comedy, the picaresque novel, the epic, the sonnet. Being of a certain genre predisposes a work to represent certain characters and events and to seek certain effects. Its success in achieving these effects and avoiding incongruous ones can thus be judged; and this is one sort of **decorum** (fittingness), the decorum of genre. Satire was once considered a low, popular form, for which only low, popular language was decorous (fitting). There are also decorums of character, of occasion, of rhetorical mode, etc.

Gothic, Classic, Neoclassic. Gothic and **Classic** distinguish styles and tendencies in art and literature. **Gothic** implies vital, primitive, but irregular work, with the qualities of the barbarian North. **Classic** implies lucid, rational, and idealized work, as in the sunlit southern civilizations of Greece and Rome. For Pope and his contemporaries, "Gothic" was generally a term of contempt; for Ruskin, in the nineteenth century, it was a term of highest praise. "Gothic" novels, written in the period of transition between these two attitudes, and taking full advantage of dark medieval settings, were shockers and thrillers of the late eighteenth and early nineteenth centuries. **Neoclassicism** describes work that, while keeping one eye on a classical original, modifies it to comment on modern conditions: a literary example is Samuel Johnson's *Vanity of Human Wishes,* based on Juvenal's *Tenth Satire.*

Heroic poems, Heroic couplets. Because they concentrate on the figure of a typical hero (Achilles, Aeneas), epic poems were frequently called **"heroic."** Trying to transfer epic grandeur to the stage, playwrights of the Restoration period generally achieved only grandiosity; but the stately couplets in which they made their characters speak became known as **heroic couplets.**

Humor. See **Wit and Humor.**

Humors and **Temperaments** are psychological terms used by Renaissance writers. The four basic humors of every constitution were the **choleric** (bile), the **sanguine** (blood), the **phlegmatic** (phlegm), and the **melancholy** (black bile). A person's **temperament** was determined by the mixture of these humors, the way in which they were "tempered." When a particular humor predominated, it pushed the character in that direction: choler = anger; sanguine = geniality; phlegm = cold torpor; and melancholy = gloomy self-absorption.

Imagination. See **Fancy** and **Imagination.**

Imitation and **Parody** are devices by which a literary work assumes an attitude toward its own predecessor. **Imitation** involves not simply copying, but transposing the different features of the earlier work into modern particulars, while retaining the same pattern and the same approximate tonal level. **Parody** generally lowers the level of its original; it is a device of ridicule, though sometimes of self-ridicule. When Joyce parodies ancient Irish legend (as in the "Cyclops" chapter of *Ulysses*), there is no separating ridicule of the past from contempt for the present. See also **Burlesque.**

Irony, Sarcasm. **Irony** and **sarcasm**, though both are ways of saying one thing and meaning another, go about the job differently. **Sarcasm** is broader and more deliberate in its reversal of meanings; **irony** may be, and in literature generally is, very fine. The patriarch Job is bitterly **sarcastic** when he replies to his comforters (12.2), "No doubt but ye are the people, and wisdom shall die with you." On the other hand, Jane Austen, in the first sentence of *Pride and Prejudice*, overstates her case just enough to make it drily **ironic** when she writes, "It is a truth universally acknowledged, that a single man in possession of a good fortune, must be in want of a wife."

Legend. See **Myth and Legend.**

Logic. See **Rhetoric and Logic.**

Myth and **Legend** are stories that incorporate themselves into the instinctual thinking of humanity. **Myths** are narratives that purport to account, in supernatural terms, for why the world is as it is, why people act as they do. Myths often spring up to explain rituals, the original meanings of which have been forgotten; or they may be folk tales based on popular nightmares or fantasies. An ordinary or even inferior tale may take on mythic dimensions—witness Mary Wollstonecraft Shelley's *Frankenstein* or the wooden volumes of Horatio Alger, Jr. A **legend** is any old and popularly repeated story; the word usually implies, in addition, that the story is false. But a proper myth hardly pretends to be historically true—it is a flowering of the mind into narrative. Three great bodies of mythical material are the Celtic, the Norse or Germanic, and the classical fables. A body of associated myths is **a mythology;** a student and collector of myths is **a mythographer.**

Naturalism. See **Realism** and **Naturalism.**

Neo-Classic. See **Gothic, Classic, Neoclassic.**

Novel. See **Romance, Novel.**

Pastorals (from the Latin word for "shepherd," *pastor*) are poems set in idealized, often artificial, rural surroundings. They are sometimes called **eclogues.** Though low on the social scale and limited in his interests, the shepherd can be made to comment indirectly on large social issues. Virgil's shepherds regularly do so, and John Gay, by transferring his scene (in *The Beggar's Opera*) from the rural fields to Newgate prison, was able to make his whores and highwaymen reflect sardonically on the national politics of his day. Alice, the heroine of *Alice in Wonderland*, has been seen, very perceptively, as a pastoral figure. Clearly, the concept is highly adaptable. **Pastoral elegies** (like *Lycidas* by Milton, *Adonais* by Shelley, and *Thyrsis* by Matthew Arnold) have been particulary successful, perhaps because a somber theme adds weight to a basically artificial form.

Pathos, Bathos, and the Sublime. Pathos is the feeling of sympathy—pity or sorrow particularly—aroused by a literary work; the word comes from the Greek term for "suffering." **Bathos,** a comic parallel from the Greek word for "deep," describes the anticlimax that comes when an author, striving for elevation, trips and falls on his face. The idea of loftiness as the most desirable of literary qualities goes back to the late-classical rhetorician Longinus, who wrote a treatise *On the Sublime.* An early publication by Edmund Burke distinguishes the **sublime** (with its mixture of pain and danger) from the merely beautiful.

Poetic diction, Poetic license, Poetic justice. Poetic diction, mostly obsolete today, was a variety of artificial, "elevated" language. The "finny tribe" who inhabit the "briny deep" exemplify it. **Poetic license** is a loose phrase for absurdities or impossibilities supposed to be the privilege of imaginative writers. **Poetic justice** is the dubious principle that the end of a literary work should distribute rewards and punishments to the characters in proportion to their virtue or vice.

Quarto. See **Folios, Quartos.**

Realism and **Naturalism** are terms used to describe fiction that aims at minute fidelity to actual existence. **Realism** connotes an attempt to give the illusion of ordinary life, in which unexceptional people undergo everyday experiences. **Naturalism** is associated with the example of Émile Zola and the thesis that a novel should present a "slice of life," a cross-section of actual existence; the emphasis is usually on the instinctual nature of human beings, especially the sexual and acquisitive instincts. This type flourished during the late nineteenth and early twentieth centuries. Harold Biffen, a character in George Gissing's novel *New Grub Street,* is devoting his life to a work of "absolute realism in the sphere of the ignobly decent"—and this can epitomize realism. A work of naturalism, on the other hand, might be said to devote itself to the ignobly indecent.

Rhetoric and Logic. During the Renaissance, **rhetoric,** which is the art of persuading an audience, assumed fresh importance by contrast with the **logic** traditionally used by scholastic philosophers. Cicero particularly exemplified the "open hand" of rhetoric as opposed to the "closed fist" of Aristotelian logic. Though mostly fought out in terms of Latin style, the controversy over the relative merits and importance of rhetoric and logic had its effect on an evolving ideal of English prose. Sidney's *Defense of Poesy* and Milton's *Areopagitica* are both structured along the lines of a classical oration. During the Renaissance, "figures of rhetoric," often culled from textbooks and anthologies, comprised the substance of many schoolboy themes, and then carried over into mature works of literary art, such as (most spectacularly) the euphuistic romances of John Lyly: see **Euphemism, Euphuism.**

Romance, Novel. Medieval **romances** are narratives of adventure, following a hero through the successive episodes of a quest toward a chosen or appointed goal. **Novels** are more or less realistic studies of social relationships, more tightly structured than romances, less given to the fabulous, and dealing generally with the middle strata of society. But these distinctions were far from airtight to begin with, and with the years have grown steadily vaguer. Is Kafka's *The Castle* a novel or a romance? It is always called the former, it looks much more like the latter, and it is actually more like an extended parable.

Sarcasm. See **Irony, Sarcasm.**

Satire comes from the Latin word for medley, *satura;* the impression that it has to do with the word "satyr" is a popular delusion. Under **satire** are included all the many literary ways for diminishing a subject by making it laughable or contemptible. For a discussion of the backgrounds of English satire, see the introduction to Donne's *Satire 3* (p. 606).

Sensibility, as used in literary discussion, does not mean "sensitivity," but the entire complex of thoughts, feelings, and suppositions characteristic of an individual or an age. T. S. Eliot, borrowing the concept from Rémy de Gourmont, said the seventeenth century did not have, as people have had since, a sensibility divided between the world of rational thought and that of feeling. But this idea has not proved very applicable to studies of particular authors or periods.

Style in a minimal sense is the way anyone uses language; thus each of us possesses (for better or worse) an individual style. In the better sense of language endowed with point and force, language of special distinction that accomplishes its ends swiftly and clearly, it has been described by Swift as "proper words in proper places"—a definition on which there is no improving.

Sublime. See **Pathos, Bathos, and the Sublime.**

Symbol. See **Allegory, Symbol, Emblem, Type.**

Tradition. See **Convention and Tradition.**

Type. See **Allegory, Symbol, Emblem, Type.**

Wit and Humor. Wit is one of those words too useful ever to be exactly defined. As employed during the seventeenth and eighteenth centuries, it might mean general intelligence or the ability to say something funny, wisdom or ability, prudence, fantasy, vivacity of speech, quickness of repartee, a good command of sexual innuendo, and many other things including the current meaning of a verbal thrust or dig. **Humor** is a gentler, less intellectual quality; it is tinged with the feeling of "good humor," which is geniality.

Zeugma. See **Chiasmus** and **Zeugma.**

Rossetti, Christina: reprinted by permission from *The Complete Poems of Christina Rossetti, Volume III*, edited by R. W. Crump. Copyright © 1990 by Louisiana State University.

Shaw, Bernard: "Mrs. Warren's Profession," copyright © 1898, 1913, 1926, 1930, 1933, 1941 George Bernard Shaw, copyright © 1957, The Public Trustee as Executor of the Estate of George Bernard Shaw, © 1970 The Trustees of the British Museum, The Governors and Guardians of the National Gallery of Ireland and Royal Academy of Dramatic Art. Reprinted by permission of The Society of Authors on behalf of The Estate of Bernard Shaw.

Shelley, Percy: selections are reprinted from *Shelley's Poetry and Prose*, a Norton Critical Edition, selected and edited by Donald H. Reiman and Sharon B. Powers, with the permission of W. W. Norton & Company, Inc. Copyright © 1977 by W. W. Norton & Company, Inc.

Sidney, Sir Philip: from *The Poems of Sir Philip Sidney*, edited by William Ringler, Jr. (1962): © Oxford University Press, 1962. Used by permission of Oxford University Press.

Thomas, Dylan: from *Collected Poems*, published by J. M. Dent & Sons Ltd., reprinted by permission of David Higham Associates Ltd. From *Poems of Dylan Thomas*, copyright 1938, 1939, 1943 by New Directions Publishing Corporation, 1945 by Trustees for the copyrights of Dylan Thomas, 1952 by Dylan Thomas. "Poem in October" was first published in *Poetry* magazine. Reprinted by permission of New Directions Publishing Corporation.

Woolf, Virginia: excerpt from "A Sketch of the Past" in *Moments of Being* by Virginia Woolf, edited with Notes by Jeanne Schulkind, copyright © 1976 by Quentin Bell and Angelica Garnett, reprinted by permission of Harcourt Brace & Company. "The Legacy," "The Mark on the Wall," and "The Searchlight" from *A Haunted House and Other Short Stories* by Virginia Woolf, copyright 1944 and renewed 1972 by Harcourt Brace & Company, reprinted by permission of the publisher. "Professions for Women" in *The Death of the Moth and Other Essays* by Virginia Woolf, copyright 1942 by Harcourt Brace & Company and renewed 1970 by Marjorie T. Parsons, Executrix, reprinted by permission of the publisher. "Modern Fiction" from *The Common Reader* by Virginia Woolf, copyright 1925 by Harcourt Brace & Company and renewed 1953 by Leonard Woolf, reprinted by permission of the publisher. Excerpt from *A Room of One's Own* by Virginia Woolf, copyright 1929 by Harcourt Brace & Company and renewed 1957 by Leonard Woolf, reprinted by permission of Harcourt Brace & Company. "Modern Fiction" from *The Common Reader* by Virginia Woolf, published by The Hogarth Press; "A Sketch of the Past" from *Moments of Being* and "Professions for Women" from *The Death of the Moth and Other Essays*, published by The Hogarth Press; reprinted by permission of The Executors of the Virginia Woolf Estate and the Random Century Group.

Wordsworth, William: reprinted from William Wordsworth: *"The Ruined Cottage" and The Pedlar."* Edited by James Butler. Copyright © 1978 by Cornell University. Used by permission of the publisher, Cornell University Press. Reprinted from William Wordsworth: *The Fourteen-Book "Prelude."* Edited by W. J. B. Owen. Copyright © 1985 by Cornell University. Used by permission of the publisher, Cornell University Press.

Wroth, Lady Mary: reprinted by permission of Louisiana State University Press from *The Poems of Lady Mary Wroth*, edited by Josephine A. Roberts. Copyright © 1983 by Louisiana State University Press.

Yeats, W. B.: "Easter 1916," "The Second Coming," and "A Prayer for My Daughter" reprinted with permission of Simon & Schuster, Inc. from *The Poems of W. B. Yeats: A*

Index